2019
Key Business Directory
Volume 1

2019 Canadian Key Business Directory

Répertoire des principales entreprises Canadiennes 2019

Volume 1

This directory is the property of Mergent Inc.
Ce répertoire est la propriété de Mergent Inc.
Mergent Inc.
444 Madison Ave, Suite 1710
New York, NY 10022

Copyright © 2019

All rights reserved.
Tous droits réservés.

No part of this publication may be reproduced, stored in a
retrieval system, or transmitted, in any form or by any
means, electronic, mechanical, photocopying, recording, or
otherwise, without the written permission of the publisher   .

La reproduction, le stockage dans un système d'extraction
ou la communication d'un extrait quelconque de cette
publication par quelque procédé que ce soit, tant
électronique que mécanique, par photocopie,
enregistrement ou autres, sont interdits sans l'autorisation
écrite de l'éditeur.

ISBN 978-1-64141-257-5
Printed in the U.S.A.

Disclaimer

Any purchaser, reader or user of this directory assumes all responsibility for actions taken as a result of information provided herein. Any purchaser, reader or user agrees that D&B, its employees, subsidiaries and partners hold no liability for the interpretations derived from this directory and any subsequent actions taken as a result of that interpretation including, but not limited to, advertising, direct mailing, telemarketing and business decisions.

Démenti

N'importe quel acheteur, lecteur ou utilisateur de ce répertoire assume toute la responsabilité des mesures prises en raison des informations fournies ci-inclus. N'importe quel acheteur, lecteur ou utilisateur sont en accord que D&B, ses employés, les subsidiaires et les associés ne tiennent aucune responsabilité pour les traductions dérives de ce répertoire et d'aucune mesure subséquent pris en raison de cette interprétation.

Notice concerning use for compilation or dissemination to third parties

Subscribers to D&B Canada publications are not authorized, even on occasion, to use any D&B publication to: compile mailing lists, marketing aids, and other types of data, for sales or otherwise to a third party. Any subscriber doing so will be in direct violation of the contractual agreement under which the Directory is provided to the subscriber. D&B Canada does not permit or acquiesce in such uses of its publications. Any subscriber or other person who does not understand any aspect of this policy, please contact: D&B's Corporate Marketing and Public Affairs office at 1.800.INFO.DNB (1.800.463.6362).

Avis concernant l'utilisation aux fins de dissémination à une tierce partie

Les souscripteurs aux publications de D&B ne sont pas autorisés à utiliser, même occasionnellement, ces publications pour compiler des listes d'adresses, des supports à la commercialisation et d'autres types d'informations, et à les vendre, sinon les offrir à une tierce partie. Tout souscripteur qui agit ainsi est en violation de l'entente contractuelle sous laquelle le répertoire est fourni au souscripteur. D&B ne permet pas et n'accepte pas que ses publications soient utilisées pour les fins précitées. Tout souscripteur ou autre personne qui s'engage dans des actions non autorisées ou qui les encourage doit s'attendre à subir des conséquences d'ordre juridique et financier. Aucun amendement ou renonciation à l'entente n'engage les parties, à moins d'être exprimés par écrit et signés par un fondé de pouvoir de D&B Canada et par le souscripteur. Au cas où un souscripteur, ou toute autre personne, aurait des doutes quant à l'une des dispositions de cette politique, veuillez communiquer avec le Service de commercialisation et des affaires publiques de D&B Canada au 1.800.INFO.DNB (1.800.463.6362).

What's Inside?
Le contenu

Volume 1
Employee Stats, Statistical and County Counts

Section I **Geographic Index**

An alphabetical listing of businesses by geographic location.
Business information listed includes all details outlined above.

Inscriptions par région géographique

Une liste des entreprises dans l'ordre alphabétique par région géographique.
Chaque inscription comporte tous les éléments ci-dessus

Volume 2
Section II **Line of Business Index SIC Codes**

A numerical listing of businesses by SIC Code.
Business information listed includes all details outlined above.
An SIC Code table is available at the end of this section.

Inscriptions par domaine d'exploitation Codes C.I.S.

Une liste des entreprises dans l'ordre numérique par code C.I.S.
Chaque inscription comporte tous les éléments ci-dessus.
Un tableau des codes C.I.S. figure à la fin de cette section.

Section III **Alphabetic Listing**

An alphabetical listing of businesses.
Business information listed includes:
Legal business name and address; reference to parent company; number of employees; sales
volume; space occupied; headquarters, branch, single location indicator; primary line of business
(SIC code) and description; D-U-N-S ® Number; officers and management contact names on file.

Source d'information centrale inscriptions dans l'ordre alphabétique

Une liste des entreprises dans l'ordre alphabétique.
Chaque inscription comporte les renseignements suivants :
Raison sociale juridique de l'entreprise et son adresse, une référence à la compagnie mère, la taille
du personnel, le chiffre d'affaires, la surface occupée, un indicateur siège social, succursale,
emplacement unique, le domaine d'exploitation principal (code C.I.S.) et une description, le numéro
D-U-N-S®, les personnes-ressources au sein des membres du bureau de direction et de la direction
disponibles.

Key Business Terms Used by D&B

Branch: A secondary location of a company reporting to a headquarters or subsidiary . Branches carry the same primary name as their headquarters and can only report to a headquarters of subsidiary establishment.

Division: A separate operating unit of a corporation with a division name, performing a specific-activity .

Headquarters: An establishment that has a branch or branches operating under the same legal name.

Parent: A business establishment that controls another company through ownership of all or a majority of its shares.

Single Location: A business establishment with no branches reporting to it. A single location may be a parent or subsidiary.

Subsidiary: A corporation which is more than 50% owned by another company . Subsidiary companies are formed for several purposes. The subsidiary may conduct business totally dif ferent from that of the parent company , or may be at a different location.

D-U-N-S® Number: The D-U-N-S® Number is proprietary to D&B and helps to distinguish a business and identify it as a unique establishment. Assigned and maintained by D&B, these computer generated numbers provide common identification standards for most business establishments.

Trade Name: A trade name is used by a business for advertising and buying purposes. This should not be confused with a branch or division name. A trade name does not have to be registered.

Glossaire des mots clés de D&B

Compagnie mère : Une compagnie qui contrôle une autre compagnie grâce à la possession de toutes ou d'une tranche majoritaire des actions de cette compagnie.

Division : Une unité particulière d'une compagnie avec sa dénomination et ses propres actvités. Une division peut comporter des membres du bureau de direction mais n'a pas de capital et n'est pas constituée en compagnie.

Emplacement unique : Un établissement commercial qui n'exploite pas de succursale. Un emplacement unique peut être une compagnie mère et, ou, un filiale.

Filiale : Une compagnie dont plus de 50 % des actions sont détenues par une autre compagnie. Une filiale peut être constituée pour diverses raisons. Les activités d'une filiale peuvent être totalement différentes de celles de la compagnie mère, et elle peut être exploitée d'un emplacement différent.

Numéros D-U-N-S® : Les numéros D-U-N-S® servent à l'identification de chaque établissement unique. Affectés et mis à jour par D&B, ces numéros d'identification informatisés s'avèrent la norme en matière d'identification des établissements commerciaux.

Profil commercial (appellation commerciale) : Une dénomination utilisée par une entreprise aux fins de publicité et, ou, d'achat. À ne pas confondre avec une dénomination de succursale ou de division. Un profil commercial peut être enregistré ou non.

Siège social : Une entreprise qui exploite une ou des succursales sous la même raison sociale reconnue.

Succursale : Un emplacement secondaire d'une compagnie relevant du siège social ou d'une filiale. Une succursale est exploitée sous la même raison sociale principale que le siège social et relève exclusivement du siège social ou d'une filiale.

How to Use a D&B Canadian Directory Listing

The D&B Canadian Directories together contain more than 140,000 business listings and close to 500,000 contact names. The types of businesses reported on varies between directories.

The Canadian Key Business Directory

This directory contains listings of Canadian businesses with one or more of the following: $5 million in sales, 50 employees at a single or headquarters location, or 250 employees total. Public and private schools are excluded.

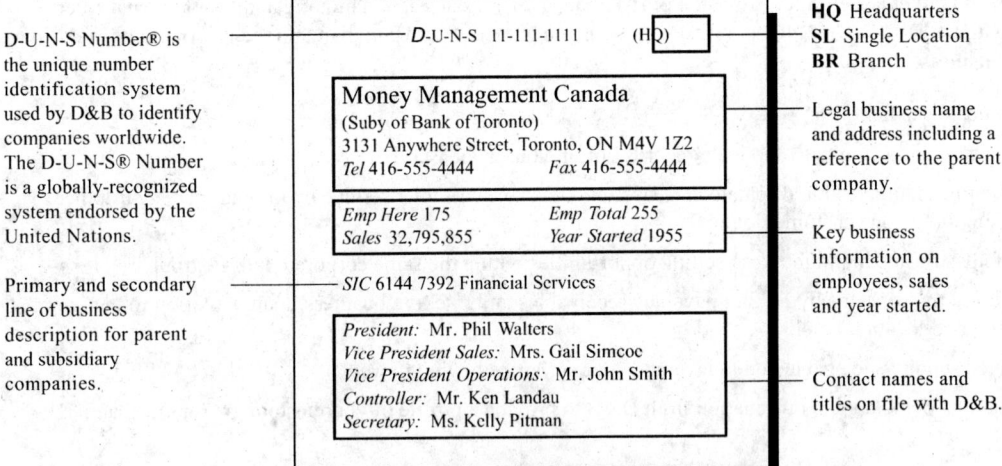

D-U-N-S Number® is the unique number identification system used by D&B to identify companies worldwide. The D-U-N-S® Number is a globally-recognized system endorsed by the United Nations.

Primary and secondary line of business description for parent and subsidiary companies.

HQ Headquarters
SL Single Location
BR Branch

Legal business name and address including a reference to the parent company.

Key business information on employees, sales and year started.

Contact names and titles on file with D&B.

Utilisation des inscriptions dans les répertoires canadiens de D&B

Au total, les répertoires commerciaux canadiens de D&B comportent plus de 140 000 inscriptions d'entreprises et près de 500 000 de personnes-ressources. Les types d'entreprises répertoriées varient d'un répertoire à l'autre.

Le Répertoire des principales entreprises canadiennes

Ce répertoire comporte les inscriptions des entreprises canadiennes qui répondent à un ou plus des critères suivants : chiffre d'affaires de 5 millions de dollars, personnel de 50 au siège social ou à un emplacement unique, ou de 250 au total. Les maisons d'enseignement publiques et privées ne sont pas répertoriées.

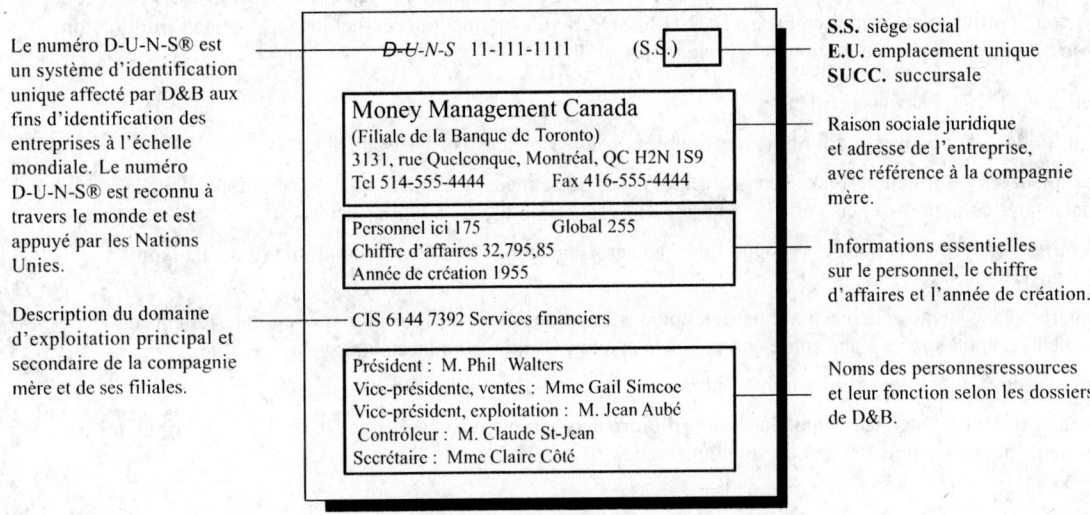

Le numéro D-U-N-S® est un système d'identification unique affecté par D&B aux fins d'identification des entreprises à l'échelle mondiale. Le numéro D-U-N-S® est reconnu à travers le monde et est appuyé par les Nations Unies.

Description du domaine d'exploitation principal et secondaire de la compagnie mère et de ses filiales.

S.S. siège social
E.U. emplacement unique
SUCC. succursale

Raison sociale juridique et adresse de l'entreprise, avec référence à la compagnie mère.

Informations essentielles sur le personnel, le chiffre d'affaires et l'année de création.

Noms des personnesressources et leur fonction selon les dossiers de D&B.

V

D&B D-U-N-S® Number

In today's global economy, D&B's Data Universal Numbering System, the D&B D-U-N-S® Number , has become the standard for keeping track of more than 97 million businesses and their corporate relationships worldwide. D-U-N-S® Numbers are unique nine-digit identification sequences that act as the nuts and bolts of D&B' s database. They provide a secure identification for individual business entities while linking corporate family structures. Used by the world's most influential standards-setting or ganizations, the D-U-N-S® Number is recognized, recommended or required by more than 50 global associations including the United Nations, the U.S. Federal Government and the European Community.

D&B is the global market leader in the provision of risk management, sales and marketing and supply management information. With the D-U-N-S® Number , D&B can help you gain access to and maintain the information you need to manage your business.

D-U-N-S® Numbers can help you:

• Consolidate, cleanse and eliminate duplicate records within your databases

• Streamline the information held in disparate databases and improve customer service by linking related customer accounts to support a "one customer" view

• Identify risk exposure and highlight cross-selling opportunities within the same corporate family group

• Integrate your internal systems by linking payables/receivables and tracking business documentation to the business entity and location level

• Link interrelated suppliers to enable you to leverage your corporate buying power

• Integrate additional demographic information from D&B to provide a profile of your customers, suppliers and prospects

Le numéro D-U-N-S® D&B

Dans l'économie à l'échelle mondiale d'aujourd'hui, le Système de numérotage universel de données D&B, le numéro D-U-N-S® D&B, est devenu la norme d'identification de plus de 97 millions d'entreprises et de leurs affiliations corporatives à travers le monde. Les numéros D-U-N-S® D&B sont un numéro d'identification unique à neuf chiffres et ils constituent l'élément d'association primordial dans la base de données D&B. Ils permettent l'identification de chaque entreprise et l'association d'entreprises qui sont membres d'une même famille corporative. Utilisés par les organismes mondiaux les plus influents en matière d'établissement de normes, ils sont reconnus, recommandés ou requis par plus de 50 associations mondiales, y compris l'organisation des Nations Unies, le Gouvernement fédéral des É.-U. et la Communauté européenne.

D&B est le premier fournisseur mondial d'information en matière de gestion du risque, de vente, de marketing et de gestion de l'approvisionnement. Le numéro D-U-N-S® D&B vous permet l'accès à et le stockage de l'information dont vous avez besoin pour la gestion de votre entreprise.

Les numéros D-U-N-S® vous permettent :

• De consolider , de nettoyer et d'éliminer les doubles de dossiers dans vos bases de données

• De rationaliser l'information stockée dans diverses bases de données et d'améliorer le service à la clientèle en associant des comptes de clients affiliés pour répondre aux besoins du "client principal"

• D'identifier le niveau du risque et les opportunités de croisement de clientèle au sein d'un groupe de familles corporatives

• D'intégrer vos systèmes internes par l'association des fonctions comptes fournisseurs / comptes clients et de documents commerciaux, à une entité commerciale et au niveau de l'emplacement

• D'associer des fournisseurs affiliés afin d'optimiser le pouvoir d'achat de votre entreprise

• D'intégrer des renseignements supplémentaires d'ordre démographique obtenus de D&B afin d'établir un profil de vos clients actuels et potentiels et de vos fournisseurs

Put the D-U-N-S® Number at the Core of Your Sales and Marketing, Risk Management and Supply Management Operations

- Within enterprise wide solutions, the D-U-N-S® Number ensures accurate data—giving you confidence in the quality of the information you use to manage your business.

- In database marketing applications, D-U-N-S® Numbering allows customers to use D&B's demographic information to profile their best customers and create a model using their characteristics to identify which business are their warmest prospects.

- In risk management, the D-U-N-S® Number can link customer files to respective parent companies to provide a view of your total credit exposure within a single corporate family. This insight into customers' corporate structures means that credit limits can be managed intelligently and collections efforts prioritized.

- The D-U-N-S® Number helps ensure receivables management efforts are carefully managed and properly targeted by pinpointing customer locations and identifying important corporate relationships.

- In supply management, the D-U-N-S® Number enables a better understanding of your supplier base by helping identify duplicate records and providing linkage information on supplier family trees. This understanding allows you to leverage your purchasing power, cut costs out of the purchasing process and reduce the number of redundant suppliers worldwide.

- For companies with an e-commerce strategy, the D-U-N-S® Number can be used as a means of identifying suppliers, trading partners and customers. Companies wishing to be recognized as a credible supplier of online services can use their D-U-N-S® Number as a means of identification allowing potential customers to verify their business credentials before starting a trading relationship.

Intégrez le numéro D-U-N-S® au sein de vos activités de vente et de marketing, de gestion du risque et de gestion de l'approvisionnement

- Peu importe les solutions utilisées au sein de votre entreprise, le numéro D-U-N-S® assure l'exactitude des données - vous pouvez ainsi avoir confiance à la qualité de l'information que vous utilisez dans la gestion de votre entreprise.

- Pour les applications base de données de marketing, le numéro D-U-N-S® permet aux clients d'utiliser l'information d'ordre démographique de D&B afin d'établir un profil de leurs meilleurs clients, et de créer un modèle en se fondant sur leurs caractéristiques pour identifier les entreprises qui s'avèrent les meilleurs clients potentiels.

- En matière de gestion du risque, le numéro D-U-N-S® permet d'associer des dossiers de clients à leur compagnie mère respective afin d'obtenir une vue d'ensemble du risque relatif à toute une famille corporative. Cette vue d'ensemble d'une structure corporative permet une gestion intelligente des plafonds de crédit et l'établissement d'un ordre de priorité en ce qui a trait aux mesures de recouvrement.

- Le numéro D-U-N-S® aide à assurer que la gestion des comptes clients est bien planifiée et bien orientée, par l'identification des emplacements des clients et des liens corporatifs importants.

- En matière de gestion de l'approvisionnement, le numéro D-U-N-S® vous permet de bien connaître votre base de fournisseurs en vous permettant d'identifier les dossiers en double et les liens du réseau filiales de vos fournisseurs. Ainsi, vous êtes en mesure d'optimiser votre pouvoir d'achat, de diminuer vos coûts d'approvisionnement et de réduire le surnombre de fournisseurs à l'échelle internationale.

- En matière de commerce électronique, le numéro D-U-N-S® s'avère une façon d'identifier les fournisseurs, les partenaires d'affaires et les clients. Les entreprises qui souhaitent être reconnues comme un fournisseur fiable de services en ligne, peuvent utiliser leur numéro D-U-N-S® à titre d'élément d'identification ce qui permet aux clients potentiels de vérifier leur situation commerciale avant d'amorcer une relation d'affaires.

How is a D-U-N-S® Number Assigned?

The D-U-N-S® Number is solely maintained by D&B. When a business is first entered into the D&B business information database we assign each location that has its own unique, separate and distinct operation, its own D-U-N-S® Number. For more information call 1.800.INFO.DNB (1.800.463.6362) or visit www.dnb.ca.

Comment un numéro D-U-N-S® est-il affecté?

Seule D&B affecte un numéro D-U-N-S®. Lors de l'intégration d'une entreprise à la base de données commerciale D&B, nous affectons un numéro D-U-N-S® unique à chacun des emplacements avec des activités particulières, indépendantes et distinctes. Pour plus de renseignements, veuillez composer 1.800.INFO.DNB (1.800.463.6362) ou visiter www.dnb.ca/fr.

D&B Ensures Data Accuracy with our Trademarked DUNSRight™ Quality Process

The DUNSRight™ Quality Process is D&B's quality assurance program to ensure data quality Our five quality drivers:

- *Global Data Collection* brings together data from a variety of worldwide sources
- *Entity Matching* is a patented process that produces a single, accurate picture of each business and our next generation of matching technology will help you find more businesses in our database
- *D-U-N-S® Numbers,* unique to each business, are a means of identifying and tracking every activity of a business
- *Corporate Linkage* exposes risk by showing related businesses such as subsidiaries and parent companies
- *Predictive Indicators* use statistical analysis to indicate how companies may perform in the future

L'exactitude des données D&B est assurée par notre processus de qualité breveté DUNSRight™

Le processus de qualité DUNSRight™ est le programme d'assurance de la qualité des données D&B. Voici nos cinq moteurs de la qualité :

- *Collecte de données internationales* auprès de nombreuses sources à travers le monde
- *Assortiment d'entités,* un processus breveté qui donne une image précise de chaque entreprise, notre prochaine génération de technologies vous permettra d'avoir accès à davantage d'entreprises dans notre base de donnée
- *Numéros D-U-N-S®,* un numéro unique affecté à chaque entreprise aux fins d'identification et de suivi de toutes les activités d'une entreprise
- *Association de sociétés,* signale le risque en précisant les entreprises affiliées telles les filiales et les compagnies mères
- *Indicateurs de prévision,* fondés sur une analyste statistique, ils indiquent comment une entreprise est susceptible de se comporter ultérieurement

COMPANY	SALES ($)	RANK	EMPLOYEES HERE	PRIMARY SIC CODE
ONTARIO TEACHERS' PENSION PLAN BOARD 5650 Yonge St Suite 300, North York, ON M2M 4H5, *Tel* (416) 228-5900	140,086,544,065	1	800	6371
WIPRO SOLUTIONS CANADA LIMITED (*Suby of* **WIPRO LIMITED**) 10040 104 St Nw Suite 100, Edmonton, AB T5J 0Z2, *Tel* (780) 420-7875	123,049,935,404	2	0	8742
LOBLAWS INC (*Suby of* **LOBLAW COMPANIES LIMITED**) 1 Presidents Choice Cir, Brampton, ON L6Y 5S5, *Tel* (905) 459-2500	97,473,376,000	3	2,300	5141
HCL AXON TECHNOLOGIES INC (*Suby of* **HCL TECHNOLOGIES LIMITED**) 77 City Centre Dr, Mississauga, ON L5B 1M5, *Tel* (905) 603-4381	60,381,717,825	4	0	7372
HOOPP INVESTMENT MANAGEMENT LIMITED 1 York St Suite 1900, Toronto, ON M5J 0B6, *Tel* (416) 369-9212	55,124,658,243	5	150	6371
ALIMENTATION COUCHE-TARD INC 4204 Boul Industriel, Montreal, QC H7L 0E3, *Tel* (450) 662-3272	51,394,400,000	6	200	5411
CINRAM INTERNATIONAL INCOME FUND 2255 Markham Rd, Scarborough, ON M1B 2W3, *Tel* (416) 298-8190	49,261,288,480	7	8,300	6722
DESJARDINS HOLDING FINANCIER INC (*Suby of* **FEDERATION DES CAISSES DESJARDINS DU QUEBEC**) 1 Rue Complexe Desjardins S 40e Etage, Montreal, QC H5B 1J1, *Tel* (418) 838-7870	48,671,296,520	8	100	6411
WORKERS COMPENSATION BOARD OF PRINCE EDWARD ISLAND (*Suby of* **PROVINCE OF PEI**) 14 Weymouth St, Charlottetown, PE C1A 4Y1, *Tel* (902) 368-5680	45,693,372,872	9	0	6331
BROOKFIELD ASSET MANAGEMENT INC 181 Bay St Suite 300, Toronto, ON M5J 2T3, *Tel* (416) 363-9491	43,038,208,642	10	200	6512
MAGNA INTERNATIONAL INC 337 Magna Dr, Aurora, ON L4G 7K1, *Tel* (905) 726-2462	40,827,000,000	11	300	3714
MANUFACTURERS LIFE INSURANCE COMPANY, THE (*Suby of* **MANULIFE FINANCIAL CORPORATION**) 200 Bloor St E Suite 1, Toronto, ON M4W 1E5, *Tel* (416) 926-3000	38,465,424,000	12	1,500	6311
GEORGE WESTON LIMITED 22 St Clair Ave E Suite 1901, Toronto, ON M4T 2S7, *Tel* (416) 922-2500	36,819,497,936	13	120	5141
NEWPORT PARTNERS HOLDINGS LP 469 King St W, Toronto, ON M5V 3M4, *Tel* (416) 867-7555	36,714,258,250	14	1	6722
POWER CORPORATION DU CANADA 751 Rue Du Square-Victoria, Montreal, QC H2Y 2J3, *Tel* (514) 286-7400	36,463,189,996	15	100	6211
POWER FINANCIAL CORPORATION (*Suby of* **POWER CORPORATION DU CANADA**) 751 Rue Du Square-Victoria, Montreal, QC H2Y 2J3, *Tel* (514) 286-7400	35,649,746,550	16	1,000	6712
EDWARD D. JONES & CO. CANADA HOLDING CO., INC (*Suby of* **JONES FINANCIAL COMPANIES, L.L.L.P.**) 90 Burnhamthorpe Rd W Suite 902, Mississauga, ON L5B 3C3, *Tel* (905) 306-8600	35,578,450,000	17	1,600	6211
LOBLAW COMPANIES LIMITED 1 Presidents Choice Cir, Brampton, ON L6Y 5S5, *Tel* (905) 459-2500	35,398,056,686	18	80	5411
ENBRIDGE INC 425 1 St Sw Suite 200, Calgary, AB T2P 3L8, *Tel* (403) 231-3900	35,159,254,556	19	234	4612
SOBEYS CAPITAL INCORPORATED (*Suby of* **EMPIRE COMPANY LIMITED**) 115 King St, Stellarton, NS B0K 0A2, *Tel* (902) 752-8371	32,968,936,000	20	200	5141
CANADA PENSION PLAN INVESTMENT BOARD (*Suby of* **GOVERNMENT OF CANADA**) 1 Queen St E, Toronto, ON M5C 2W5, *Tel* (416) 868-4075	31,785,674,965	21	0	6719
SUNCOR ENERGY INC 6 Ave Sw Suite 150, Calgary, AB T2P 3Y7, *Tel* (403) 296-8000	29,555,364,572	22	621	2911
MANULIFE FINANCIAL CORPORATION 200 Bloor St E, Toronto, ON M4W 1E5, *Tel* (416) 926-3000	29,544,751,144	23	1,000	6411
CANADIAN TEST CASE 167 5770 Hurontario St, Mississauga, ON L5R 3G5, *Tel*	28,788,247,200	24	6	7389
GREAT-WEST LIFECO INC (*Suby of* **POWER CORPORATION DU CANADA**) 100 Osborne St N, Winnipeg, MB R3C 1V3, *Tel* (204) 946-1190	28,552,961,700	25	0	6311
RIFCO INC 4909 49 St Suite 702, Red Deer, AB T4N 1V1, *Tel* (403) 314-1288	27,639,878,398	26	0	6141
IMPERIAL OIL LIMITED 505 Quarry Park Blvd Se, Calgary, AB T2C 5N1, *Tel* (800) 567-3776	26,608,622,098	27	700	2911
CANADIAN TEST CASE 177 CORP 6750 Century Ave Suite 305, Mississauga, ON L5N 2V8, *Tel* (905) 812-5920	26,557,153,480	28	500	5812
CANADIAN TEST CASE 185 6750 Century Ave Suite 300, Mississauga, ON L5N 0B7, *Tel* (905) 812-5920	25,186,611,516	29	300	3714
ONEX CORPORATION 161 Bay St, Toronto, ON M5J 2S1, *Tel* (416) 362-7711	23,785,000,000	30	0	6282
ENMAX CORPORATION (*Suby of* **CITY OF CALGARY, THE**) 141 50 Ave Se Suite 2708, Calgary, AB T2G 4S7, *Tel* (403) 514-3000	23,480,805,690	31	330	4911
TORONTO-DOMINION BANK, THE 55 King St W, Toronto, ON M5K 1A2, *Tel* (416) 982-5722	22,804,055,000	32	5,000	6021
ENBRIDGE PIPELINES INC (*Suby of* **ENBRIDGE INC**) 425 1 St Sw Suite 200, Calgary, AB T2P 3L8, *Tel* (403) 231-3900	22,248,241,400	33	100	4612
SUN LIFE ASSURANCE COMPANY OF CANADA (*Suby of* **SUN LIFE FINANCIAL INC**) 1 York St, Toronto, ON M5J 0B6, *Tel* (416) 979-9966	22,240,880,324	34	970	6311
BANK OF NOVA SCOTIA, THE 44 King St W Scotia Plaza, Toronto, ON M5H 1H1, *Tel* (416) 866-6161	22,224,313,700	35	1,100	6733
DESJARDINS GROUPE D'ASSURANCES GENERALES INC (*Suby of* **FEDERATION DES CAISSES DESJARDINS DU QUEBEC**) 6300 Boul Guillaume-Couture, Levis, QC G6V 6P9, *Tel* (418) 835-4850	21,751,394,632	36	1,500	6411
ROYAL BANK OF CANADA				

COMPANY	SALES ($)	RANK	EMPLOYEES HERE	PRIMARY SIC CODE
200 Bay St, Toronto, ON M5J 2J5, *Tel* (416) 974-3940	21,462,640,000	37	500	6021
SUN LIFE FINANCIAL INC				
1 York St, Toronto, ON M5J 0B6, *Tel* (416) 979-9966	20,466,479,694	38	1,000	6411
WOODBRIDGE COMPANY LIMITED, THE (*Suby of* **THOMSON COMPANY INC, THE**)				
65 Queen St W Suite 2400, Toronto, ON M5H 2M8, *Tel* (416) 364-8700	20,102,995,000	39	70	6712
MCCAIN FOODS GROUP INC				
8800 Main St, Florenceville-Bristol, NB E7L 1B2, *Tel* (506) 392-5541	19,495,400,000	40	5	2037
SOBEYS INC (*Suby of* **EMPIRE COMPANY LIMITED**)				
115 King St, Shelburne, NS B0T 1W0, *Tel* (902) 752-8371	19,163,076,970	41	500	5411
PATTISON, JIM GROUP INC				
1067 Cordova St W Suite 1800, Vancouver, BC V6C 1C7, *Tel* (604) 688-6764	19,049,316,000	42	0	5511
SGS CANADA INC				
5825 Explorer Dr, Mississauga, ON L4W 5P6, *Tel* (905) 364-3757	18,367,380,000	43	100	8734
CARGILL LIMITED (*Suby of* **CARGILL, INCORPORATED**)				
240 Graham Ave Suite 300, Winnipeg, MB R3C 0J7, *Tel* (204) 947-0141	18,315,770,000	44	200	5153
PROVIGO DISTRIBUTION INC (*Suby of* **LOBLAW COMPANIES LIMITED**)				
400 Av Sainte-Croix, Saint-Laurent, QC H4N 3L4, *Tel* (514) 383-3000	17,917,900,000	45	800	5141
BANK OF MONTREAL				
119 Rue Saint-Jacques, Montreal, QC H2Y 1L6, *Tel* (514) 877-7373	17,792,580,876	46	3,000	6021
BCE INC				
1 Carrefour Alexander-Graham-Bell Bureau A-8-1, Verdun, QC H3E 3B3, *Tel* (888) 932-6666	17,791,137,736	47	375	4899
FAIRFAX FINANCIAL HOLDINGS LIMITED				
95 Wellington St W Suite 800, Toronto, ON M5J 2N7, *Tel* (416) 367-4941	17,757,700,000	48	44	6282
EMPIRE COMPANY LIMITED				
115 King St, Stellarton, NS B0K 1S0, *Tel* (902) 752-8371	17,501,984,953	49	30	5149
REDBERRY FRANCHISING CORP (*Suby of* **RESTAURANT BRANDS INTERNATIONAL INC**)				
401 The West Mall Suite 700, Etobicoke, ON M9C 5J4, *Tel* (416) 626-6464	17,387,745,000	50	55	6794
HUSKY ENERGY INC				
707 8 Ave Sw, Calgary, AB T2P 1H5, *Tel* (403) 298-6111	16,616,837,738	51	100	1382
GREAT-WEST LIFE ASSURANCE COMPANY, THE (*Suby of* **POWER CORPORATION DU CANADA**)				
100 Osborne St N, Winnipeg, MB R3C 1V3, *Tel* (204) 946-1190	16,336,933,200	52	2,775	6324
COMPAGNIE DE TELEPHONE BELL DU CANADA OU BELL CANADA, LA (*Suby of* **BCE INC**)				
1 Carref Alexander-Graham-Bell Tower A-7-1, Verdun, QC H3E 3B3, *Tel* (514) 786-8424	16,325,747,200	53	368	4899
BOMBARDIER INC				
800 Boul Rene-Levesque O 29e Etage, Montreal, QC H3B 1Y8, *Tel* (514) 861-9481	16,236,000,000	54	4,500	3743
CENOVUS ENERGY INC				
500 Centre St Se, Calgary, AB T2P 0M5, *Tel* (403) 766-2000	16,215,043,678	55	1,386	1382
CANADIAN NATURAL RESOURCES LIMITED				
855 2 St Sw Suite 2100, Calgary, AB T2P 4J8, *Tel* (403) 517-6700	15,940,610,754	56	1,000	1311
LONDON INSURANCE GROUP INC (*Suby of* **POWER CORPORATION DU CANADA**)				
255 Dufferin Ave Suite 540, London, ON N6A 4K1, *Tel* (519) 432-5281	15,920,411,600	57	2,600	6311
SHELL CANADA LIMITED (*Suby of* **ROYAL DUTCH SHELL PLC**)				
400 4 Ave Sw, Calgary, AB T2P 0J4, *Tel* (403) 691-3111	14,836,656,000	58	1,600	1311
HANOVER AND DISTRICT HOSPITAL				
90 7th Ave Suite 1, Hanover, ON N4N 1N1, *Tel* (519) 364-2340	13,946,996,136	59	200	8062
CANADIAN IMPERIAL BANK OF COMMERCE				
199 Bay St Commerce Crt W, Toronto, ON M5L 1A2, *Tel* (416) 980-3096	13,774,054,232	60	3,000	6021
AGRIUM INC (*Suby of* **NUTRIEN LTD**)				
13131 Lake Fraser Dr Se, Calgary, AB T2J 7E8, *Tel* (403) 225-7000	13,766,000,000	61	335	2873
AIR CANADA				
7373 Boul De La Cote-Vertu Bureau 1290, Saint-Laurent, QC H4S 1Z3, *Tel* (514) 393-3333	13,695,112,630	62	1,000	4512
WAL-MART CANADA CORP (*Suby of* **WALMART INC.**)				
1940 Argentia Rd, Mississauga, ON L5N 1P9, *Tel* (905) 821-2111	13,689,720,000	63	1,000	5311
HEWLETT PACKARD ENTERPRISE CANADA CO (*Suby of* **HEWLETT PACKARD ENTERPRISE COMPANY**)				
5150 Spectrum Way Suite 400, Mississauga, ON L4W 5G2, *Tel* (905) 206-4725	12,244,920,000	64	60,000	8731
PANAGO PIZZA INC				
33149 Mill Lake Rd, Abbotsford, BC V2S 2A4, *Tel* (604) 859-6621	12,171,421,500	65	60	6794
DESJARDINS SECURITE FINANCIERE, COMPAGNIE D'ASSURANCE VIE (*Suby of* **FEDERATION DES CAISSES DESJARDINS DU QUEBEC**)				
200 Rue Des Commandeurs, Levis, QC G6V 6R2, *Tel* (418) 838-7800	11,520,394,488	66	1,950	6311
ROGERS COMMUNICATIONS INC				
333 Bloor St E, Toronto, ON M4W 1G9, *Tel* (416) 935-7777	11,444,307,792	67	5,000	4899
MOLSON COORS CANADA INC (*Suby of* **MOLSON COORS BREWING COMPANY**)				
33 Carlingview Dr, Etobicoke, ON M9W 5E4, *Tel* (416) 679-1786	11,002,800,000	68	100	2082
PARKLAND FUEL CORPORATION				
333 96 Ave Ne Suite 6302, Calgary, AB T3K 0S3, *Tel* (403) 567-2500	10,948,509,084	69	450	2873
COMPAGNIE DES CHEMINS DE FER NATIONAUX DU CANADA				
935 Rue De La Gauchetiere 16e Etage O, Montreal, QC H3B 2M9, *Tel* (514) 399-5430	10,856,778,742	70	1,000	4011
TELUS CORPORATION				
510 West Georgia St Fl 8, Vancouver, BC V6B 0M3, *Tel* (604) 697-8044	10,685,447,690	71	500	4899
CANADIAN TIRE CORPORATION, LIMITED				
2180 Yonge St, Toronto, ON M4S 2B9, *Tel* (416) 480-3000	10,657,928,587	72	50	5531
THOMSON COMPANY INC, THE				
65 Queen St W Suite 2400, Toronto, ON M5H 2M8, *Tel* (416) 364-8700	10,657,570,000	73	4	2731

COMPANY	SALES ($)	RANK	EMPLOYEES HERE	PRIMARY SIC CODE
CANADA LIFE ASSURANCE COMPANY, THE (*Suby of* **POWER CORPORATION DU CANADA**)				
330 University Ave Suite 2, Toronto, ON M5G 1R8, *Tel* (416) 597-1440	10,575,372,546	74	50	6311
TRANSCANADA PIPELINES LIMITED (*Suby of* **TC ENERGY CORPORATION**)				
450 1 St Sw, Calgary, AB T2P 5H1, *Tel* (403) 920-2000	10,536,982,173	75	0	4922
METRO INC				
11011 Boul Maurice-Duplessis, Montreal, QC H1C 1V6, *Tel* (514) 643-1000	10,504,943,371	76	250	5141
TC ENERGY CORPORATION				
450 1 St Sw, Calgary, AB T2P 5H1, *Tel* (403) 920-2000	10,370,077,258	77	0	4922
COSTCO WHOLESALE CANADA LTD (*Suby of* **COSTCO WHOLESALE CORPORATION**)				
415 West Hunt Club Rd, Nepean, ON K2E 1C5, *Tel* (613) 221-2010	10,081,850,000	78	190	5099
RIO TINTO ALCAN INC (*Suby of* **RIO TINTO PLC**)				
1190 Av Des Canadiens-De-Montreal Bureau 400, Montreal, QC H3B 0E3, *Tel* (514) 848-8000	9,772,176,000	79	600	3334
CO-OPERATORS GROUP LIMITED, THE				
130 Macdonell St, Guelph, ON N1H 2Z6, *Tel* (519) 824-4400	9,759,532,856	80	500	6331
MCCAIN FOODS LIMITED (*Suby of* **MCCAIN FOODS GROUP INC**)				
439 King St W Suite 500, Toronto, ON M5V 1K4, *Tel* (416) 955-1700	9,747,700,000	81	1,100	2037
FIRST CHOICE HAIRCUTTERS LTD (*Suby of* **REGIS CORPORATION**)				
6400 Millcreek Dr, Mississauga, ON L5N 3E7, *Tel* (905) 858-8100	9,737,137,200	82	20	6794
FEDERATION DES CAISSES DESJARDINS DU QUEBEC				
100 Rue Des Commandeurs, Levis, QC G6V 7N5, *Tel* (418) 835-8444	9,691,568,435	83	1,060	6062
TRENTON DISTRIBUTORS LIMITED				
75 Huff Ave, Trenton, ON K8V 0H3, *Tel* (613) 392-3875	9,597,883,322	84	27	5063
TECK RESOURCES LIMITED				
550 Burrard St Suite 3300, Vancouver, BC V6C 0B3, *Tel* (604) 699-4000	9,524,793,528	85	5,000	1021
WORKPLACE SAFETY & INSURANCE BOARD, THE				
200 Front St W Suite 101, Toronto, ON M5V 3J1, *Tel* (416) 344-1000	9,381,289,520	86	2,500	6331
SYNCRUDE CANADA LTD (*Suby of* **SUNCOR ENERGY INC**)				
9911 Macdonald Ave Suite 200, Fort Mcmurray, AB T9H 1S7, *Tel* (780) 790-5911	9,272,910,000	87	3,000	1311
SAPUTO INC (*Suby of* **JOLINA CAPITAL INC**)				
6869 Boul Metropolitain E, Saint-Leonard, QC H1P 1X8, *Tel* (514) 328-6662	9,188,003,138	88	135	2022
TELUS COMMUNICATIONS INC (*Suby of* **TELUS CORPORATION**)				
510 West Georgia St 7th Fl, Vancouver, BC V6B 0M3, *Tel* (888) 493-2007	9,032,688,000	89	1,800	4899
CERTAS HOME AND AUTO INSURANCE COMPANY (*Suby of* **FEDERATION DES CAISSES DESJARDINS DU QUEBEC**)				
6300 Boul Guillaume-Couture, Levis, QC G6V 6P9, *Tel* (418) 835-4900	9,017,597,600	90	1,900	6411
NUTRIEN LTD				
122 1st Ave S Suite 500, Saskatoon, SK S7K 7G3, *Tel* (306) 933-8500	8,892,900,000	91	250	2873
ACCOR MANAGEMENT CANADA INC				
155 Wellington St W Suite 3300, Toronto, ON M5V 0C3, *Tel* (416) 874-2600	8,891,083,200	92	200	6531
ASIG CANADA LTD				
8501 Mississauga Rd Suite 302, Brampton, ON L6Y 5G8, *Tel* (905) 497-4114	8,867,047,500	93	0	5172
CGI INC				
1350 Boul Rene-Levesque O Suite 25e, Montreal, QC H3G 1T4, *Tel* (514) 841-3200	8,808,624,126	94	1,200	7371
BAUSCH HEALTH COMPANIES INC				
2150 Boul Saint-Elzear O, Sainte-Rose, QC H7L 4A8, *Tel* (514) 744-6792	8,380,000,000	95	150	2834
GROUPE JEAN COUTU (PJC) INC, LE (*Suby of* **METRO INC**)				
245 Rue Jean-Coutu, Varennes, QC J3X 0E1, *Tel* (450) 646-9760	8,296,050,816	96	1,350	5122
INTACT FINANCIAL CORPORATION				
700 University Ave Suite 1500, Toronto, ON M5G 0A1, *Tel* (416) 341-1464	8,025,267,772	97	3,000	6331
WESTON FOODS (CANADA) INC (*Suby of* **GEORGE WESTON LIMITED**)				
1425 The Queensway, Etobicoke, ON M8Z 1T3, *Tel* (416) 252-7323	7,993,114,000	98	0	2051
COMPAGNIE D'ASSURANCES GENERALES TD (*Suby of* **TORONTO-DOMINION BANK, THE**)				
50 Boul Cremazie O Bureau 1200, Montreal, QC H2P 1B6, *Tel* (514) 382-6060	7,913,192,504	99	1	6311
CBRE LIMITEE (*Suby of* **CBRE LIMITED PARTNERSHIP**)				
145 King St W Suite 1100, Toronto, ON M5H 1J8, *Tel* (416) 362-2244	7,858,190,000	100	1,800	8748
RONA INC (*Suby of* **LOWE'S COMPANIES, INC.**)				
220 Ch Du Tremblay, Boucherville, QC J4B 8H7, *Tel* (514) 599-5900	7,820,748,000	101	1,000	5072
CROWN INVESTMENTS CORPORATION OF SASKATCHEWAN (*Suby of* **GOVERNMENT OF SASKATCHEWAN**)				
2400 College Ave Suite 400, Regina, SK S4P 1C8, *Tel* (306) 787-6851	7,818,844,800	102	60	4911
INTACT INSURANCE COMPANY (*Suby of* **INTACT FINANCIAL CORPORATION**)				
700 University Ave Suite 1500, Toronto, ON M5G 0A1, *Tel* (416) 341-1464	7,693,084,800	103	200	6331
GROUPE SNC-LAVALIN INC				
455 Boul Rene-Levesque O Bureau 202, Montreal, QC H2Z 1Z3, *Tel* (514) 393-1000	7,644,705,117	104	50	8711
WE CARE HEALTH SERVICES INC				
3300 Bloor St W Suite 900, Etobicoke, ON M8X 2X2, *Tel* (416) 922-7601	7,594,967,016	105	48	6794
NORTHBRIDGE FINANCIAL CORPORATION (*Suby of* **FAIRFAX FINANCIAL HOLDINGS LIMITED**)				
105 Adelaide St W Suite 700, Toronto, ON M5H 1P9, *Tel* (416) 350-4400	7,593,766,400	106	0	6411
MACKENZIE FINANCIAL CORPORATION (*Suby of* **POWER CORPORATION DU CANADA**)				
180 Queen St W Suite 1600, Toronto, ON M5V 3K1, *Tel* (800) 387-0614	7,588,002,500	107	1,100	6722
RBC DOMINION SECURITIES INC (*Suby of* **ROYAL BANK OF CANADA**)				
200 Bay St, Toronto, ON M5J 2W7, *Tel* (416) 842-2000	7,542,631,400	108	1,000	6282
METRO RICHELIEU INC (*Suby of* **METRO INC**)				
11011 Boul Maurice-Duplessis, Montreal, QC H1C 1V6, *Tel* (514) 643-1000	7,525,518,000	109	450	5141
BARRICK GOLD CORPORATION				

COMPANY	SALES ($)	RANK	EMPLOYEES HERE	PRIMARY SIC CODE
161 Bay St Suite 3700, Toronto, ON M5J 2S1, *Tel* (416) 861-9911	7,243,000,000	110	1,000	1041
HUDSON'S BAY COMPANY				
8925 Torbram Rd, Brampton, ON L6T 4G1, *Tel* (905) 792-4400	7,054,530,528	111	600	5311
ST. JOSEPH'S HEALTH SYSTEM				
50 Charlton Ave E, Hamilton, ON L8N 4A6, *Tel* (905) 522-4941	7,049,144,900	112	2,000	8699
MAGNA SEATING INC (*Suby of* **MAGNA INTERNATIONAL INC**)				
337 Magna Dr, Aurora, ON L4G 7K1, *Tel* (905) 726-2462	7,009,485,000	113	100	3714
AMER SPORTS CANADA INC				
2220 Dollarton Hwy Unit 110, North Vancouver, BC V7H 1A8, *Tel* (604) 960-3001	6,966,906,000	114	1,000	5091
HUSKY OIL OPERATIONS LIMITED (*Suby of* **HUSKY ENERGY INC**)				
707 8 Ave Sw, Calgary, AB T2P 1H5, *Tel* (403) 298-6111	6,861,953,400	115	1,500	1311
WORKERS' COMPENSATION BOARD OF BRITISH COLUMBIA				
6951 Westminster Hwy, Richmond, BC V7C 1C6, *Tel* (604) 231-8888	6,838,297,600	116	2,000	6331
WORKSAFEBC				
6951 Westminster Hwy Suite 600, Richmond, BC V7C 1C6, *Tel* (604) 231-8888	6,838,297,600	117	0	6331
CRAWFORD & COMPANY (CANADA) INC (*Suby of* **CRAWFORD & COMPANY**)				
539 Riverbend Dr, Kitchener, ON N2K 3S3, *Tel* (519) 578-5540	6,644,545,600	118	120	6411
CELESTICA INC (*Suby of* **ONEX CORPORATION**)				
844 Don Mills Rd, Toronto, ON M3C 1V7, *Tel* (416) 448-5800	6,633,200,000	119	100	3589
CANADA POST CORPORATION (*Suby of* **GOVERNMENT OF CANADA**)				
2701 Riverside Dr, Ottawa, ON K1A 1L5, *Tel* (613) 734-8440	6,444,881,802	120	2,500	4311
COMMISSION DES NORMES, DE L'EQUITE, DE LA SANTE ET DE LA SECURITE DU TRAVAIL, LA				
524 Rue Bourdages Bureau 370, Quebec, QC G1K 7E2, *Tel* (877) 639-0744	6,410,904,000	121	1,000	6331
FORTIS INC				
5 Springdale St Suite 1100, St. John'S, NL A1E 0E4, *Tel* (709) 737-2800	6,360,475,780	122	13	4911
CAPITALE ASSUREUR DE L'ADMINISTRATION PUBLIQUE INC, LA (*Suby of* **CAPITALE MUTUELLE DE L'ADMINISTRATION PUBLIQUE, LA**)				
625 Rue Jacques-Parizeau, Quebec, QC G1R 2G5, *Tel* (418) 644-4106	6,280,548,952	123	400	6311
FUNDEX INVESTMENTS INC (*Suby of* **INDUSTRIELLE ALLIANCE, ASSURANCE ET SERVICES FINANCIERS INC**)				
400 Applewood Cres, Concord, ON L4K 0C3, *Tel* (905) 305-1651	6,261,807,200	124	0	6211
WORLEY CANADA SERVICES LTD				
8500 Macleod Trail Se, Calgary, AB T2H 2N1, *Tel* (403) 258-8000	6,255,865,000	125	35,000	8711
LOWE'S HOLDING CANADA, ULC (*Suby of* **LOWE'S COMPANIES, INC.**)				
5150 Spectrum Way Suite 200, Mississauga, ON L4W 5G2, *Tel* (905) 219-1000	6,214,018,509	126	0	6712
AON CANADA INC (*Suby of* **AON PLC**)				
20 Bay St Suite 2400, Toronto, ON M5J 2N8, *Tel* (416) 868-5500	6,169,935,200	127	396	6411
GROUPE WSP GLOBAL INC (*Suby of* **AST TRUST COMPANY (CANADA)**)				
1600 Boul Rene-Levesque O Bureau 16, Montreal, QC H3H 1P9, *Tel* (514) 340-0046	5,995,146,426	128	7,900	8741
PCL EMPLOYEES HOLDINGS LTD				
9915 56 Ave Nw, Edmonton, AB T6E 5L7, *Tel* (780) 733-5000	5,987,037,420	129	0	6712
INDUSTRIELLE ALLIANCE, ASSURANCE ET SERVICES FINANCIERS INC				
1080 Grande Allee O, Quebec, QC G1S 1C7, *Tel* (418) 684-5000	5,950,342,598	130	700	6311
ENCANA CORPORATION				
500 Centre St Se, Calgary, AB T2G 1A6, *Tel* (403) 645-2000	5,939,000,000	131	1,133	1382
BMO NESBITT BURNS INC				
100 King St W Unit 1, Toronto, ON M5X 2A1, *Tel* (416) 643-1778	5,938,754,874	132	800	6211
INVESTORS GROUP INC (*Suby of* **POWER CORPORATION DU CANADA**)				
447 Portage Ave, Winnipeg, MB R3C 3B6, *Tel* (204) 943-0361	5,836,925,000	133	500	6722
LINAMAR CORPORATION				
287 Speedvale Ave W, Guelph, ON N1H 1C5, *Tel* (519) 836-7550	5,777,178,455	134	11,736	3714
OMERS PRIVATE EQUITY INC (*Suby of* **OMERS ADMINISTRATION CORPORATION**)				
100 Adelaide St W Suite 900, Toronto, ON M5H 0E2, *Tel* (416) 864-3200	5,692,552,000	135	0	6282
SOBEYS WEST INC (*Suby of* **EMPIRE COMPANY LIMITED**)				
1020 64 Ave Ne, Calgary, AB T2E 7V8, *Tel* (403) 730-3500	5,581,456,000	136	600	5411
PEMBINA PIPELINE CORPORATION				
585 8 Ave Sw Unit 4000, Calgary, AB T2P 1G1, *Tel* (403) 231-7500	5,572,807,802	137	370	4612
CANADIAN PACIFIC RAILWAY LIMITED				
7550 Ogden Dale Rd Se, Calgary, AB T2C 4X9, *Tel* (888) 333-6370	5,546,274,232	138	500	4011
THOMSON REUTERS CORPORATION (*Suby of* **THOMSON COMPANY INC, THE**)				
333 Bay St, Toronto, ON M5H 2R2, *Tel* (416) 687-7500	5,501,000,000	139	3,400	7299
GOLDCORP CANADA LTD (*Suby of* **NEWMONT GOLDCORP CORPORATION**)				
666 Burrard St Suite 3400, Vancouver, BC V6C 2X8, *Tel* (604) 696-3000	5,491,362,700	140	40	1041
AECOM ENERGY SERVICES LTD (*Suby of* **AECOM**)				
6025 11 St Se Suite 240, Calgary, AB T2H 2Z2, *Tel* (403) 218-7100	5,459,710,000	141	40	1389
RESTAURANT BRANDS INTERNATIONAL INC				
130 King St W Suite 300, Toronto, ON M5X 1E1, *Tel* (905) 339-5724	5,357,000,000	142	100	5812
BANQUE NATIONALE DU CANADA				
600 Rue De La Gauchetiere O Bureau 4e, Montreal, QC H3B 4L3, *Tel* (514) 394-4385	5,334,573,312	143	5,000	6021
FINNING INTERNATIONAL INC				
565 Great Northern Way Suite 300, Vancouver, BC V5T 0H8, *Tel* (604) 331-4816	5,303,681,592	144	897	5084
OLYMEL S.E.C.				
2200 Av Pratte Bureau 400, Saint-Hyacinthe, QC J2S 4B6, *Tel* (450) 771-0400	5,260,346,305	145	100	2011
STATE FARM INSURANCE				
333 First Commerce Dr, Aurora, ON L4G 8A4, *Tel* (905) 750-4100	5,220,714,400	146	0	6411

COMPANY	SALES ($)	RANK	EMPLOYEES HERE	PRIMARY SIC CODE
COMPUTERSHARE TRUST COMPANY OF CANADA (*Suby of* **COMPUTERSHARE LIMITED**) 100 University Ave Suite 800, Toronto, ON M5J 2Y1, *Tel* (416) 263-9200	5,198,604,400	147	400	6733
GIBSON ENERGY INC 440 2 Ave Sw Suite 1700, Calgary, AB T2P 5E9, *Tel* (403) 206-4000	5,190,412,814	148	100	1389
4256344 CANADA INC (*Suby of* **MANULIFE FINANCIAL CORPORATION**) 1245 Rue Sherbrooke O Bureau 2100, Montreal, QC H3G 1G3, *Tel* (877) 499-9555	5,128,723,200	149	2,400	6311
SNC-LAVALIN INC (*Suby of* **GROUPE SNC-LAVALIN INC**) 455 Boul Rene-Levesque O, Montreal, QC H2Z 1Z3, *Tel* (514) 393-1000	5,125,406,000	150	3,000	8711
DOMTAR CORPORATION 395 Boul De Maisonneuve O Bureau 200, Montreal, QC H3A 1L6, *Tel* (514) 848-5555	5,098,000,000	151	400	2611
TFORCE HOLDINGS INC (*Suby of* **TFI INTERNATIONAL INC**) 8801 Rte Transcanadienne Bureau 500, Saint-Laurent, QC H4S 1Z6, *Tel* (514) 331-4000	5,080,940,609	152	3	6719
COOP FEDEREE, LA 9001 Boul De L'Acadie Bureau 200, Montreal, QC H4N 3H7, *Tel* (514) 858-2222	5,062,373,662	153	1,000	5191
HOME DEPOT OF CANADA INC (*Suby of* **THE HOME DEPOT INC**) 1 Concorde Gate Suite 900, North York, ON M3C 4H9, *Tel* (416) 609-0852	5,058,900,000	154	110	5251
LIQUOR CONTROL BOARD OF ONTARIO, THE (*Suby of* **GOVERNMENT OF ONTARIO**) 55 Lake Shore Blvd E Suite 876, Toronto, ON M5E 1A4, *Tel* (416) 365-5900	4,970,710,095	155	100	5921
EMERA INCORPORATED 1223 Lower Water St, Halifax, NS B3J 3S8, *Tel* (902) 450-0507	4,945,857,448	156	20	4911
PUROLATOR HOLDINGS LTD (*Suby of* **GOVERNMENT OF CANADA**) 5995 Avebury Rd Suite 100, Mississauga, ON L5R 3T8, *Tel* (905) 712-1251	4,942,975,000	157	1,300	4731
GESTION LABERGE INC 6245 Boul Wilfrid-Hamel, L'Ancienne-Lorette, QC G2E 5W2, *Tel* (418) 667-1313	4,751,617,000	158	75	6712
B.C.A.A. HOLDINGS LTD 4567 Canada Way, Burnaby, BC V5G 4T1, *Tel* (604) 268-5000	4,746,104,000	159	275	6411
MARSH CANADA LIMITED (*Suby of* **MARSH & MCLENNAN COMPANIES, INC.**) 120 Bremner Blvd Suite 800, Toronto, ON M5J 0A8, *Tel* (416) 868-2600	4,746,104,000	160	500	6411
WESTLAND INSURANCE GROUP LTD 2121 160 St Suite 200, Surrey, BC V3Z 9N6, *Tel* (604) 543-7788	4,746,104,000	161	200	6411
INSURANCE CORPORATION OF BRITISH COLUMBIA (*Suby of* **GOVERNMENT OF THE PROVINCE OF BRITISH COLUMBIA**) 151 Esplanade W, North Vancouver, BC V7M 3H9, *Tel* (604) 661-2800	4,705,051,859	162	1,500	6331
TERRAVEST INCOME FUND 4901 Bruce Rd, Vegreville, AB T9C 1C3, *Tel* (780) 632-7774	4,669,540,000	163	800	6722
HYDRO ONE LIMITED 483 Bay St 8th Fl South Tower, Toronto, ON M5G 2P5, *Tel* (416) 345-5000	4,662,327,300	164	20	4911
HYDRO ONE INC (*Suby of* **HYDRO ONE LIMITED**) 483 Bay St Suite 1000, Toronto, ON M5G 2P5, *Tel* (416) 345-5000	4,659,337,719	165	3,000	4911
WEST FRASER TIMBER CO. LTD 858 Beatty St Suite 501, Vancouver, BC V6B 1C1, *Tel* (604) 895-2700	4,638,068,036	166	295	5031
FUTURE ELECTRONICS (CDA) LTD (*Suby of* **INVESTISSEMENTS ALONIM INC, LES**) 237 Boul Hymus, Pointe-Claire, QC H9R 5C7, *Tel* (514) 694-7710	4,637,914,271	167	1,500	5065
WASTE CONNECTIONS, INC 610 Applewood Cres, Vaughan, ON L4K 0C3, *Tel* (905) 532-7510	4,630,488,000	168	80	4953
METRO ONTARIO INC (*Suby of* **METRO INC**) 5559 Dundas St W, Etobicoke, ON M9B 1B9, *Tel* (416) 239-7171	4,619,136,000	169	500	5411
AGROPUR COOPERATIVE 4600 Rue Armand-Frappier, Saint-Hubert, QC J3Z 1G5, *Tel* (450) 878-2333	4,572,975,989	170	150	5143
POWER WORKERS UNION 244 Eglinton Ave E, Toronto, ON M4P 1K2, *Tel* (416) 481-4491	4,556,832,000	171	40	8631
PUROLATOR INC (*Suby of* **GOVERNMENT OF CANADA**) 5995 Avebury Rd, Mississauga, ON L5R 3P9, *Tel* (905) 712-1084	4,547,537,000	172	350	4731
FIDELITY INVESTMENTS CANADA ULC (*Suby of* **FMR LLC**) 483 Bay St Suite 200, Toronto, ON M5G 2N7, *Tel* (416) 307-5200	4,541,127,650	173	600	6722
IBM CANADA LIMITED (*Suby of* **INTERNATIONAL BUSINESS MACHINES CORPORATION**) 3600 Steeles Ave E, Markham, ON L3R 9Z7, *Tel* (905) 316-5000	4,494,032,000	174	4,000	3571
POTASH CORPORATION OF SASKATCHEWAN INC (*Suby of* **NUTRIEN LTD**) 122 1st Ave S Suite 500, Saskatoon, SK S7K 7G3, *Tel* (306) 933-8500	4,456,000,000	175	350	1474
CONOCOPHILLIPS CANADA RESOURCES CORP (*Suby of* **CONOCOPHILLIPS**) 401 9 Ave Sw Suite 1600, Calgary, AB T2P 3C5, *Tel* (403) 233-4000	4,450,996,800	176	1,500	1311
CAPITAL DESJARDINS INC (*Suby of* **FEDERATION DES CAISSES DESJARDINS DU QUEBEC**) 100 Av Des Commendeurs, Levis, QC G6V 7N5, *Tel* (418) 835-8444	4,417,899,585	177	25	6722
AXA ASSURANCES INC 2020 Boul Robert-Bourassa Bureau 100, Montreal, QC H3A 2A5, *Tel* (514) 282-1914	4,273,936,000	178	400	6311
ECONOMICAL MUTUAL INSURANCE COMPANY 111 Westmount Rd S, Waterloo, ON N2L 2L6, *Tel* (519) 570-8200	4,273,936,000	179	500	6331
SCDA (2015) INC (*Suby of* **MANULIFE FINANCIAL CORPORATION**) 1245 Rue Sherbrooke O Bureau 2100, Montreal, QC H3G 1G3, *Tel* (514) 499-8855	4,273,936,000	180	1,600	6311
CENTRE INTEGRE UNIVERSITAIRE DE SANTE ET DE SERVICES SOCIAUX DE L'ESTRIE 375 Rue Argyll, Sherbrooke, QC J1J 3H5, *Tel* (819) 780-2222	4,213,998,000	181	50	8621
ENERGIE VALERO INC (*Suby of* **VALERO ENERGY CORPORATION**) 1801 Av Mcgill College Bureau 1300, Montreal, QC H3A 2N4, *Tel* (514) 982-8200	4,137,955,500	182	425	5172

LIONS GATE ENTERTAINMENT CORP

COMPANY	SALES ($)	RANK	EMPLOYEES HERE	PRIMARY SIC CODE
250 Howe St Fl 20, Vancouver, BC V6C 3R8, *Tel* (877) 848-3866	4,129,100,000	183	0	7812
BP CANADA ENERGY COMPANY (*Suby of* **BP P.L.C.**)				
240 4 Ave Sw, Calgary, AB T2P 4H4, *Tel* (403) 233-1313	4,080,080,400	184	2,100	1311
ONTARIO POWER GENERATION INC (*Suby of* **GOVERNMENT OF ONTARIO**)				
700 University Ave, Toronto, ON M5G 1X6, *Tel* (416) 592-2555	4,041,174,366	185	800	4911
FIRST QUANTUM MINERALS LTD				
543 Granville St 14th Fl, Vancouver, BC V6C 1X8, *Tel* (604) 688-6577	3,966,000,000	186	9	1021
BRITISH COLUMBIA HYDRO AND POWER AUTHORITY (*Suby of* **GOVERNMENT OF THE PROVINCE OF BRITISH COLUMBIA**)				
333 Dunsmuir St, Vancouver, BC V6B 5R3, *Tel* (604) 224-9376	3,957,525,591	187	350	4911
METHANEX CORPORATION				
200 Burrard St Suite 1800, Vancouver, BC V6C 3M1, *Tel* (604) 661-2600	3,931,847,000	188	810	2869
BRP INC				
726 Rue Saint-Joseph, Valcourt, QC J0E 2L0, *Tel* (450) 532-2211	3,916,505,075	189	13	5012
CCL INDUSTRIES INC				
111 Gordon Baker Rd Suite 801, Toronto, ON M2H 3R1, *Tel* (416) 756-8500	3,912,943,473	190	1,200	2672
SHAW COMMUNICATIONS INC				
630 3 Ave Sw Suite 900, Calgary, AB T2P 4L4, *Tel* (403) 750-4500	3,895,938,522	191	200	4813
TFI INTERNATIONAL INC				
8801 Rte Transcanadienne Bureau 500, Saint-Laurent, QC H4S 1Z6, *Tel* (514) 331-4113	3,883,914,231	192	1,800	4213
ROYAL BANK HOLDING INC (*Suby of* **ROYAL BANK OF CANADA**)				
200 Bay St 9th Floor, Toronto, ON M5J 2J5, *Tel* (416) 974-7493	3,864,925,000	193	0	6211
SASKATCHEWAN GOVERNMENT INSURANCE (*Suby of* **GOVERNMENT OF SASKATCHEWAN**)				
2260 11th Ave Suite 18, Regina, SK S4P 0J9, *Tel* (306) 751-1200	3,846,542,400	194	1,000	6331
FORD MOTOR COMPANY OF CANADA, LIMITED (*Suby of* **FORD MOTOR COMPANY**)				
1 Canadian Rd, Oakville, ON L6J 5E4, *Tel* (905) 845-2511	3,839,220,000	195	424	3711
CANFOR CORPORATION				
1700 75th Ave W Suite 100, Vancouver, BC V6P 6G2, *Tel* (604) 661-5241	3,824,169,729	196	0	2421
JOLINA CAPITAL INC				
8000 Boul Langelier Bureau 200, Saint-Leonard, QC H1P 3K2, *Tel* (514) 328-3541	3,785,576,713	197	1	6712
CORPORATION DE SECURITE GARDA WORLD (*Suby of* **GW INTERMEDIATE HOLDCO CORPORATION**)				
1390 Rue Barre, Montreal, QC H3C 5X9, *Tel* (514) 281-2811	3,771,411,322	198	1,000	7381
MARK'S WORK WEARHOUSE LTD (*Suby of* **CANADIAN TIRE CORPORATION, LIMITED**)				
1035 64 Ave Se Suite 30, Calgary, AB T2H 2J7, *Tel* (403) 255-9220	3,768,898,500	199	382	5136
RESOLUTE FOREST PRODUCTS INC				
111 Boul Robert-Bourassa Bureau 5000, Montreal, QC H3C 2M1, *Tel* (514) 875-2160	3,756,000,000	200	0	2621
CANADIAN SOLAR INC				
545 Speedvale Ave W, Guelph, ON N1K 1E6, *Tel* (519) 837-1881	3,744,512,000	201	10	3312
CENOVUS FCCL LTD (*Suby of* **CENOVUS ENERGY INC**)				
500 Centre St Se Suite 766, Calgary, AB T2G 1A6, *Tel* (403) 766-2000	3,709,164,000	202	0	1311
PETROKAZAKHSTAN INC (*Suby of* **CHINA NATIONAL PETROLEUM CORPORATION**)				
140 4 Ave Sw Suite 1460, Calgary, AB T2P 3N3, *Tel* (403) 221-8435	3,709,164,000	203	0	1311
ATCO LTD				
5302 Forand St Sw, Calgary, AB T3E 8B4, *Tel* (403) 292-7500	3,705,602,576	204	160	4911
DESJARDINS SOCIETE FINANCIERE INC (*Suby of* **FEDERATION DES CAISSES DESJARDINS DU QUEBEC**)				
1 Complexe Desjardins, Montreal, QC H5B 1J1, *Tel* (418) 838-7870	3,681,772,157	205	1	6712
MEDAVIE INC				
644 Main St, Moncton, NB E1C 1E2, *Tel* (506) 853-1811	3,632,845,600	206	700	6321
WESTERN FINANCIAL GROUP INC				
1010 24 St Se, High River, AB T1V 2A7, *Tel* (403) 652-2663	3,632,845,600	207	119	6311
WESTJET AIRLINES LTD				
22 Aerial Pl Ne, Calgary, AB T2E 3J1, *Tel* (888) 937-8538	3,588,447,009	208	175	4512
CIBC WORLD MARKETS INC (*Suby of* **CANADIAN IMPERIAL BANK OF COMMERCE**)				
161 Bay St, Toronto, ON M5J 2S1, *Tel* (416) 594-7000	3,557,845,000	209	50	6211
TD SECURITIES INC (*Suby of* **TORONTO-DOMINION BANK, THE**)				
66 Wellington St W, Toronto, ON M5K 1A2, *Tel* (416) 307-8500	3,557,845,000	210	1,600	6211
CASCADES INC				
404 Boul Marie-Victorin, Kingsey Falls, QC J0A 1B0, *Tel* (819) 363-5100	3,524,416,198	211	100	2621
FCA CANADA INC (*Suby of* **FIAT CHRYSLER AUTOMOBILES N.V.**)				
1 Riverside Dr W, Windsor, ON N9A 5K3, *Tel* (519) 973-2000	3,492,526,800	212	500	3711
GRAHAM INCOME TRUST				
10840 27 St Se, Calgary, AB T2Z 3R6, *Tel* (403) 570-5000	3,491,960,000	213	5,000	1541
GROUPE DE SECURITE GARDA INC, LE (*Suby of* **GW INTERMEDIATE HOLDCO CORPORATION**)				
1390 Rue Barre, Montreal, QC H3C 5X9, *Tel* (514) 281-2811	3,480,974,210	214	700	7381
VALE CANADA LIMITED (*Suby of* **VALE S/A**)				
200 Bay St Suite 1500 Royal Bank Plz, Toronto, ON M5J 2K2, *Tel* (416) 361-7511	3,456,363,410	215	200	1629
GLENCORE CANADA CORPORATION (*Suby of* **GLENCORE PLC**)				
100 King St W Suite 6900, Toronto, ON M5X 2A1, *Tel* (416) 775-1200	3,452,949,000	216	350	1021
BRUCE POWER L.P.				
177 Tie Rd Municipal Kincardine Rr 2, Tiverton, ON N0G 2T0, *Tel* (519) 361-2673	3,425,999,200	217	0	4911
PRICE INDUSTRIES LIMITED				
638 Raleigh St, Winnipeg, MB R2K 3Z9, *Tel* (204) 669-4220	3,405,234,000	218	700	3496
FIDUCIE DESJARDINS INC (*Suby of* **FEDERATION DES CAISSES DESJARDINS DU QUEBEC**)				
1 Complexe Desjardins Tour S, Montreal, QC H5B 1E4, *Tel* (514) 286-9441	3,402,722,880	219	700	6733

COMPANY	SALES ($)	RANK	EMPLOYEES HERE	PRIMARY SIC CODE
RBC LIFE INSURANCE COMPANY (Suby of ROYAL BANK OF CANADA) 6880 Financial Dr Suite 1000, Mississauga, ON L5N 8E8, Tel (905) 816-2746	3,397,779,120	220	400	6311
KEYERA CORP 144 4 Ave Sw Suite 200, Calgary, AB T2P 3N4, Tel (403) 205-8300	3,385,085,390	221	250	1389
BELL ALIANT REGIONAL COMMUNICATIONS, LIMITED PARTNERSHIP 1505 Barrington St, Halifax, NS B3J 3K5, Tel (888) 214-7896	3,345,440,000	222	50	4899
CANADIAN UTILITIES LIMITED (Suby of ATCO LTD) 5302 Forand St, Calgary, AB T3E 8B4, Tel (403) 292-7500	3,318,212,454	223	0	4924
LAFARGE CANADA INC (Suby of LAFARGEHOLCIM LTD) 6509 Airport Rd, Mississauga, ON L4V 1S7, Tel (905) 738-7070	3,299,265,900	224	30	2891
BOARDWALK REAL ESTATE INVESTMENT TRUST 1501 1 St Sw Suite 200, Calgary, AB T2R 0W1, Tel (403) 531-9255	3,294,799,232	225	18	6531
LULULEMON ATHLETICA CANADA INC 1818 Cornwall Ave Suite 400, Vancouver, BC V6J 1C7, Tel (604) 732-6124	3,288,319,000	226	800	2339
ROYAL & SUN ALLIANCE INSURANCE COMPANY OF CANADA (Suby of RSA INSURANCE GROUP PLC) 18 York St Suite 800, Toronto, ON M5J 2T8, Tel (416) 366-7511	3,269,561,040	227	400	6331
FOUR SEASONS HOLDINGS INC (Suby of CASCADE INVESTMENT, L.L.C.) 1165 Leslie St, North York, ON M3C 2K8, Tel (416) 449-1750	3,252,712,000	228	100	7011
STANTEC INC 10220 103 Ave Nw Suite 400, Edmonton, AB T5J 0K4, Tel (780) 917-7000	3,247,557,348	229	1,535	8711
ALTAGAS LTD 355 4 Ave Sw Suite 1700, Calgary, AB T2P 0J1, Tel (403) 691-7575	3,227,012,783	230	14	1311
SYSCO CANADA, INC (Suby of SYSCO CORPORATION) 21 Four Seasons Pl Suite 400, Etobicoke, ON M9B 6J8, Tel (416) 234-2666	3,225,222,000	231	115	5141
KINROSS GOLD CORPORATION 25 York St 17th Fl, Toronto, ON M5J 2V5, Tel (416) 365-5123	3,212,600,000	232	3,927	1081
GROUPE PROMUTUEL FEDERATION DE SOCIETE MUTUELLES D'ASSURANCES GENERALES 2000 Boul Lebourgneuf Bureau 400, Quebec, QC G2K 0B6, Tel (418) 840-1313	3,205,452,000	233	200	6311
NORTHBRIDGE GENERAL INSURANCE CORPORATION (Suby of FAIRFAX FINANCIAL HOLDINGS LIMITED) 105 Adelaide St W 4th Fl, Toronto, ON M5H 1P9, Tel (416) 350-4400	3,205,452,000	234	0	6331
QUEBECOR INC (Suby of PLACEMENTS PELADEAU INC, LES) 612 Rue Saint-Jacques Bureau 700, Montreal, QC H3C 4M8, Tel (514) 380-1999	3,169,624,462	235	166	6712
RUSSEL METALS INC 6600 Financial Dr, Mississauga, ON L5N 7J6, Tel (905) 819-7777	3,157,494,830	236	150	5051
INVESTISSEMENTS ALONIM INC, LES 237 Boul Hymus, Pointe-Claire, QC H9R 5C7, Tel (514) 694-7710	3,147,032,490	237	1	6712
RICHARDSON INTERNATIONAL LIMITED (Suby of RICHARDSON, JAMES & SONS, LIMITED) 1 Lombard Pl Suite 2800, Winnipeg, MB R3B 0X3, Tel (204) 934-5961	3,113,680,900	238	400	5153
WINNIPEG REGIONAL HEALTH AUTHORITY, THE 650 Main St 4th Fl, Winnipeg, MB R3B 1E2, Tel (204) 926-7000	3,110,240,000	239	245	8062
LOBLAWS SUPERMARKETS LIMITED (Suby of LOBLAW COMPANIES LIMITED) 1 Presidents Choice Cir, Brampton, ON L6Y 5S5, Tel (905) 459-2500	3,079,424,000	240	300	5411
PCL CONSTRUCTION GROUP INC (Suby of PCL EMPLOYEES HOLDINGS LTD) 9915 56 Ave Nw Suite 1, Edmonton, AB T6E 5L7, Tel (780) 733-5000	3,072,924,800	241	0	1541
CONSTELLATION SOFTWARE INC 20 Adelaide St E Suite 1200, Toronto, ON M5C 2T6, Tel (416) 861-2279	3,060,100,000	242	10	7371
CANADA BROKERLINK INC (Suby of INTACT FINANCIAL CORPORATION) 1400 1 St Sw Suite 200, Calgary, AB T2R 0V8, Tel (403) 290-1541	2,990,045,520	243	45	6411
AECON CONSTRUCTION GROUP INC (Suby of AECON GROUP INC) 20 Carlson Crt Suite 800, Toronto, ON M9W 7K6, Tel (416) 293-7004	2,984,229,016	244	250	1541
NEXEN HOLDINGS (USA) INC (Suby of CHINA NATIONAL OFFSHORE OIL CORP.) 801 7 Ave Sw Suite 200, Calgary, AB T2P 3P7, Tel (403) 234-6700	2,969,185,782	245	0	1311
SHELL CANADA PRODUCTS 400 4 Ave Sw, Calgary, AB T2P 0J4, Tel (403) 691-3111	2,955,682,500	246	0	5172
FORTISBC HOLDINGS INC (Suby of FORTIS INC) 1111 Georgia St W Suite 1000, Vancouver, BC V6E 4M3, Tel (604) 443-6525	2,940,938,562	247	200	4923
PEPSI BOTTLING GROUP (CANADA), ULC, THE (Suby of PBG INVESTMENT (LUXEMBOURG) SARL) 5205 Satellite Dr, Mississauga, ON L4W 5J7, Tel (905) 212-7377	2,924,310,000	248	257	2086
GILDAN ACTIVEWEAR INC 600 Boul De Maisonneuve O 33eme Etage, Montreal, QC H3A 3J2, Tel (514) 735-2023	2,908,565,000	249	125	2259
GENERAL MOTORS OF CANADA COMPANY (Suby of GENERAL MOTORS COMPANY) 1908 Colonel Sam Dr, Oshawa, ON L1H 8P7, Tel (905) 644-5000	2,908,500,000	250	450	3711
ENBRIDGE ENERGY DISTRIBUTION INC (Suby of ENBRIDGE INC) 500 Consumers Rd, North York, ON M2J 1P8, Tel (416) 492-5000	2,905,227,988	251	400	4924
SNC-LAVALIN CONSTRUCTION INC (Suby of GROUPE SNC-LAVALIN INC) 455 Boul Rene-Levesque O Bureau 202, Montreal, QC H2Z 1Z3, Tel (514) 393-1000	2,901,120,368	252	4,154	1542
ENBRIDGE PIPELINES (NW) INC (Suby of ENBRIDGE INC) 425 1 St Sw Suite 3000, Calgary, AB T2P 3L8, Tel	2,889,382,000	253	160	4612
JUST ENERGY GROUP INC 6345 Dixie Rd Suite 400, Mississauga, ON L5T 2E6, Tel (905) 670-4440	2,886,804,119	254	0	4911
IRVING, J. D. LIMITED 300 Union St Suite 5, Saint John, NB E2L 4Z2, Tel (506) 632-7777	2,885,550,000	255	1,200	2421
FRASER HEALTH AUTHORITY (Suby of GOVERNMENT OF THE PROVINCE OF BRITISH COLUMBIA) 13450 102 Ave Suite 400, Surrey, BC V3T 0H1, Tel (604) 587-4600	2,880,229,035	256	12,000	8062

COMPANY	SALES ($)	RANK	EMPLOYEES HERE	PRIMARY SIC CODE
FAIRMONT HOTELS & RESORTS INC (Suby of ACCOR) 155 Wellington St W Suite 3300, Toronto, ON M5V 0C3, Tel (416) 874-2600	2,870,040,000	257	200	7011
TD WATERHOUSE CANADA INC (Suby of TORONTO-DOMINION BANK, THE) 77 Bloor St W Suite 3, Toronto, ON M5S 1M2, Tel (416) 982-7686	2,846,276,000	258	1,200	6211
GENERAL ELECTRIC CANADA COMPANY (Suby of GENERAL ELECTRIC COMPANY) 1919 Minnesota Crt, Mississauga, ON L5N 0C9, Tel (905) 858-5100	2,829,150,000	259	500	3625
COCA-COLA CANADA BOTTLING LIMITED 335 King St E, Toronto, ON M5A 1L1, Tel (416) 424-6000	2,826,833,000	260	0	2086
COLLIERS INTERNATIONAL GROUP INC 1140 Bay St Suite 4000, Toronto, ON M5S 2B4, Tel (416) 960-9500	2,825,427,000	261	5,860	6531
OPEN TEXT CORPORATION 275 Frank Tompa Dr, Waterloo, ON N2L 0A1, Tel (519) 888-7111	2,815,241,000	262	500	7372
SSQ SOCIETE D'ASSURANCE-VIE INC (Suby of FONDS DE SOLIDARITE DES TRAVAILLEURS DU QUEBEC (F.T.Q.)) 2525 Boul Laurier, Quebec, QC G1V 4Z6, Tel (418) 651-7000	2,805,838,984	263	650	6311
PCL CONSTRUCTORS CANADA INC (Suby of PCL EMPLOYEES HOLDINGS LTD) 2201 Bristol Cir Suite 500, Oakville, ON L6H 0J8, Tel (905) 276-7600	2,793,568,000	264	500	1542
UNIVERSITE DU QUEBEC 475 Rue Du Parvis, Quebec, QC G1K 9H7, Tel (418) 657-3551	2,790,325,098	265	135	8221
STANTEC CONSULTING LTD (Suby of STANTEC INC) 10220 103 Ave Nw Suite 400, Edmonton, AB T5J 0K4, Tel (780) 917-7000	2,777,575,790	266	1,400	8711
MARTINREA INTERNATIONAL INC 3210 Langstaff Rd, Vaughan, ON L4K 5B2, Tel (416) 749-0314	2,776,851,816	267	100	3499
CHU DE QUEBEC - UNIVERSITE LAVAL 11 Cote Du Palais, Quebec, QC G1R 2J6, Tel (418) 525-4444	2,755,107,000	268	0	8733
RICHARDSON, JAMES & SONS, LIMITED 3000 One Lombard Pl, Winnipeg, MB R3B 0Y1, Tel (204) 953-7970	2,747,365,500	269	20	5153
G4S SECURE SOLUTIONS (CANADA) LTD (Suby of G4S PLC) 703 Evans Ave Unit 103, Etobicoke, ON M9C 5E9, Tel (416) 620-0762	2,745,729,000	270	50	7381
COUCHE-TARD INC (Suby of ALIMENTATION COUCHE-TARD INC) 4204 Boul Industriel, Montreal, QC H7L 0E3, Tel (450) 662-6632	2,738,483,488	271	50	5541
DOLLARAMA L.P. 5805 Av Royalmount, Mont-Royal, QC H4P 0A1, Tel (514) 737-1006	2,737,944,000	272	245	5331
COCA-COLA REFRESHMENTS CANADA COMPANY (Suby of THE COCA-COLA COMPANY) 335 King St E, Toronto, ON M5A 1L1, Tel (416) 424-6000	2,729,356,000	273	383	2086
SCOTIA CAPITAL INC (Suby of BANK OF NOVA SCOTIA, THE) 40 King St W, Toronto, ON M5H 3Y2, Tel (416) 863-7411	2,703,962,200	274	500	6211
HYDRO ONE NETWORKS INC (Suby of HYDRO ONE LIMITED) 483 Bay St Suite 1000, Toronto, ON M5G 2P5, Tel (416) 345-5000	2,697,060,158	275	500	4911
CANADA LIFE FINANCIAL CORPORATION (Suby of POWER CORPORATION DU CANADA) 330 University Ave, Toronto, ON M5G 1R7, Tel (416) 597-1440	2,697,051,000	276	20	6351
GREAT PACIFIC INDUSTRIES INC (Suby of PATTISON, JIM GROUP INC) 19855 92a Ave, Langley, BC V1M 3B6, Tel (604) 888-1213	2,694,496,000	277	200	5411
WESTCOAST ENERGY INC (Suby of ENBRIDGE INC) 425 1 St Sw Suite 2600, Calgary, AB T2P 3L8, Tel (403) 699-1999	2,669,306,139	278	0	4924
TOROMONT INDUSTRIES LTD 3131 Highway 7 Suite A, Concord, ON L4K 5E1, Tel (416) 667-5511	2,656,568,320	279	850	5082
APOTEX INC 150 Signet Dr, Toronto, ON M9L 1T9, Tel (416) 401-7328	2,652,752,000	280	1,000	2834
MAPLE LEAF FOODS INC 6985 Financial Dr, Mississauga, ON L5N 0A1, Tel (905) 285-5000	2,649,959,945	281	665	2011
TORONTO HYDRO CORPORATION (Suby of CORPORATION OF THE CITY OF TORONTO) 14 Carlton St Suite 6, Toronto, ON M5B 1K5, Tel (416) 542-8000	2,632,660,815	282	370	4911
INDUSTRIES DOREL INC, LES 1255 Av Greene Bureau 300, Westmount, QC H3Z 2A4, Tel (514) 934-3034	2,619,513,000	283	30	2512
SCM INSURANCE SERVICES INC 5083 Windermere Blvd Sw Suite 101, Edmonton, AB T6W 0J5, Tel (780) 430-9012	2,610,357,200	284	50	6411
ROTISSERIES ST-HUBERT LTEE, LES (Suby of RECIPE UNLIMITED CORPORATION) 2500 Boul Daniel-Johnson Bureau 700, Cote Saint-Luc, QC H7T 2P6, Tel (450) 435-0674	2,608,161,750	285	135	6794
MELOCHE MONNEX INC (Suby of TORONTO-DOMINION BANK, THE) 50 Boul Cremazie O Bureau 1200, Montreal, QC H2P 1B6, Tel (514) 382-6060	2,596,575,936	286	700	6712
STAPLES CANADA ULC (Suby of SYCAMORE PARTNERS MANAGEMENT, L.P.) 6 Staples Ave, Richmond Hill, ON L4B 4W3, Tel (905) 737-1147	2,569,518,000	287	350	5943
SF INSURANCE PLACEMENT CORPORATION OF CANADA (Suby of STATE FARM MUTUAL AUTOMOBILE INSURANCE COMPANY) 333 First Commerce Dr, Aurora, ON L4G 8A4, Tel (905) 750-4100	2,564,361,600	288	30	6331
DOLLARAMA INC 5805 Av Royalmount, Mont-Royal, QC H4P 0A1, Tel (514) 737-1006	2,542,285,263	289	12,764	5999
ICT CANADA MARKETING INC (Suby of SYKES ENTERPRISES INCORPORATED) 400 Main St Suite 2004, Saint John, NB E2K 4N5, Tel (506) 653-9050	2,541,850,400	290	2	7389
NFI GROUP INC 711 Kernaghan Ave, Winnipeg, MB R2C 3T4, Tel (204) 224-1251	2,519,021,000	291	1,019	3711
CRESCENT POINT ENERGY CORP 585 8 Ave Sw Suite 2000, Calgary, AB T2P 1G1, Tel (403) 693-0020	2,517,277,691	292	604	1311

COMPANY	SALES ($)	RANK	EMPLOYEES HERE	PRIMARY SIC CODE
MOLSON BREWERIES OF CANADA LIMITED (*Suby of* **MOLSON COORS BREWING COMPANY**) 33 Carlingview Dr, Etobicoke, ON M9W 5E4, *Tel* (416) 679-1786	2,512,599,000	293	2,500	5181
MOLSON INC (*Suby of* **MOLSON COORS BREWING COMPANY**) 1555 Rue Notre-Dame E, Montreal, QC H2L 2R5, *Tel* (514) 521-1786	2,512,599,000	294	0	5181
BELL ALIANT REGIONAL COMMUNICATIONS INC (*Suby of* **BCE INC**) 1 Brunswick Pl Suite 1800, Saint John, NB E2K 1B5, *Tel* (800) 665-6000	2,509,080,000	295	100	4899
AECON GROUP INC 20 Carlson Crt Suite 800, Etobicoke, ON M9W 7K6, *Tel* (416) 297-2600	2,476,181,740	296	200	1541
IGM FINANCIAL INC (*Suby of* **POWER CORPORATION DU CANADA**) 447 Portage Ave, Winnipeg, MB R3C 3B6, *Tel* (204) 943-0361	2,463,127,223	297	0	6211
PCL CONSTRUCTORS INC (*Suby of* **PCL EMPLOYEES HOLDINGS LTD**) 9915 56 Ave Nw Suite 1, Edmonton, AB T6E 5L7, *Tel* (780) 733-5000	2,444,372,000	298	0	1541
SECURITAS CANADA LIMITED (*Suby of* **SECURITAS AB**) 400-235 Yorkland Blvd, North York, ON M2J 4Y8, *Tel* (416) 774-2500	2,440,648,000	299	45	7381
SEVEN GENERATIONS ENERGY LTD 525 8 Ave Sw Unit 4400, Calgary, AB T2P 1G1, *Tel* (403) 718-0700	2,437,373,740	300	179	1311
ARCELORMITTAL DOFASCO G.P. (*Suby of* **ARCELORMITTAL**) 1330 Burlington St E, Hamilton, ON L8N 3J5, *Tel* (905) 548-7200	2,432,310,000	301	5,000	3479
HOME HARDWARE STORES LIMITED 34 Henry St, St Jacobs, ON N0B 2N0, *Tel* (519) 664-2252	2,424,608,819	302	1,420	5211
NORBORD INC 1 Toronto St Suite 600, Toronto, ON M5C 2W4, *Tel* (416) 365-0705	2,424,000,000	303	100	2435
GOVERNING COUNCIL OF THE UNIVERSITY OF TORONTO, THE 27 King'S College Cir, Toronto, ON M5S 1A1, *Tel* (416) 978-2196	2,414,595,312	304	9,000	8221
UNITED PARCEL SERVICE CANADA LTD (*Suby of* **UNITED PARCEL SERVICE, INC.**) 1930 Derry Rd E, Mississauga, ON L5S 1E2, *Tel* (800) 742-5877	2,396,953,000	305	100	4212
BRITISH COLUMBIA LOTTERY CORPORATION (*Suby of* **GOVERNMENT OF THE PROVINCE OF BRITISH COLUMBIA**) 74 Seymour St W, Kamloops, BC V2C 1E2, *Tel* (250) 828-5500	2,393,147,467	306	800	7993
AUTOCANADA INC 15511 123 Ave Nw Unit 200, Edmonton, AB T5V 0C3, *Tel* (866) 938-0561	2,388,613,378	307	3,500	5511
HUB INTERNATIONAL CANADA WEST ULC (*Suby of* **HELLMAN & FRIEDMAN LLC**) 8346 Noble Rd, Chilliwack, BC V2P 6R5, *Tel* (604) 703-7070	2,373,052,000	308	40	6411
YOUNG MEN'S CHRISTIAN ASSOCIATION OF EDMONTON, THE 10211 105 St Nw, Edmonton, AB T5J 1E3, *Tel* (780) 429-9622	2,359,305,640	309	400	8699
TOYOTA MOTOR MANUFACTURING CANADA INC (*Suby of* **TOYOTA MOTOR CORPORATION**) 1055 Fountain St N, Cambridge, ON N3H 4R7, *Tel* (519) 653-1111	2,326,800,000	310	0	3711
WAWANESA MUTUAL INSURANCE COMPANY, THE 191 Broadway Suite 900, Winnipeg, MB R3C 3P1, *Tel* (204) 985-3923	2,324,108,821	311	217	6331
CNOOC PETROLEUM NORTH AMERICA ULC (*Suby of* **CHINA NATIONAL OFFSHORE OIL CORP.**) 500 Centre St Se Suite 2300, Calgary, AB T2G 1A6, *Tel* (403) 699-4000	2,322,560,634	312	300	1382
TRANSAT A.T. INC 300 Rue Leo-Pariseau Bureau 600, Montreal, QC H2X 4C2, *Tel* (514) 987-1616	2,311,314,723	313	120	6712
CENTRE DE SANTE ET DE SERVICES SOCIAUX DE LAVAL (*Suby of* **GOUVERNEMENT DE LA PROVINCE DE QUEBEC**) 1755 Boul Rene-Laennec, Cote Saint-Luc, QC H7M 3L9, *Tel* (450) 668-1010	2,308,699,584	314	2,815	8099
ALTAGAS NORTHWEST PROCESSING LIMITED PARTNERSHIP 55 4 Ave Sw Suite 1700, Calgary, AB T2P 0J1, *Tel* (403) 691-7196	2,303,908,000	315	300	4924
PREMIUM BRANDS HOLDINGS CORPORATION 10991 Shellbridge Way Unit 100, Richmond, BC V6X 3C6, *Tel* (604) 656-3100	2,293,865,032	316	0	2099
COTT CORPORATION 6525 Viscount Rd, Mississauga, ON L4V 1H6, *Tel* (905) 672-1900	2,269,700,000	317	2,446	2086
KRAFT HEINZ CANADA ULC (*Suby of* **THE KRAFT HEINZ COMPANY**) 95 Moatfield Dr Suite 316, North York, ON M3B 3L6, *Tel* (416) 441-5000	2,269,264,560	318	350	2043
CAE INC 8585 Ch De La Cote-De-Liesse, Saint-Laurent, QC H4T 1G6, *Tel* (514) 341-6780	2,252,722,450	319	250	3699
MINES AGNICO EAGLE LIMITEE 10200 Rte De Preissac, Rouyn-Noranda, QC J0Y 1C0, *Tel* (819) 759-3644	2,242,604,000	320	9,188	1241
PARRISH & HEIMBECKER, LIMITED 201 Portage Ave Suite 1400, Winnipeg, MB R3B 3K6, *Tel* (204) 956-2030	2,241,850,248	321	25	5153
PROVINCIAL HEALTH SERVICES AUTHORITY 1380 Burrard St Suite 700, Vancouver, BC V6Z 2H3, *Tel* (604) 675-7400	2,229,120,000	322	100	8099
FGL SPORTS LTD (*Suby of* **CANADIAN TIRE CORPORATION, LIMITED**) 824 41 Ave Ne, Calgary, AB T2E 3R3, *Tel* (403) 717-1400	2,228,139,180	323	450	5941
SECURE ENERGY SERVICES INC 205 5 Ave Sw Suite 3600, Calgary, AB T2P 2V7, *Tel* (403) 984-6100	2,226,888,994	324	300	1389
ZEHRMART INC (*Suby of* **LOBLAW COMPANIES LIMITED**) 1 Presidents Choice Cir, Brampton, ON L6Y 5S5, *Tel* (905) 459-2500	2,213,336,000	325	150	5411
SAPUTO PRODUITS LAITIERS CANADA S.E.N.C. 6869 Boul Metropolitain, Montreal, QC H1P 1X8, *Tel* (514) 328-6662	2,201,518,045	326	150	2022
GROUPE DESSAU INC 1200 Boul Saint-Martin O Bureau 300, Montreal, QC H7S 2E4, *Tel* (514) 281-1010	2,193,054,000	327	500	6712
SHATO HOLDINGS LTD 4088 Cambie St Suite 300, Vancouver, BC V5Z 2X8, *Tel* (604) 874-5533	2,193,054,000	328	2,500	6712

COMPANY	SALES ($)	RANK	EMPLOYEES HERE	PRIMARY SIC CODE
TRILOGY RETAIL ENTERPRISES L.P 161 Bay St Suite 4900, Toronto, ON M5J 2S1, *Tel* (416) 943-4110	2,193,054,000	329	6,000	6712
AGNICO EAGLE MINES LIMITED 145 King St E Suite 400, Toronto, ON M5C 2Y7, *Tel* (416) 947-1212	2,191,221,000	330	100	1041
HATCH LTD (*Suby of* **HATCHCOS HOLDINGS LTD**) 2800 Speakman Dr, Mississauga, ON L5K 2R7, *Tel* (905) 855-7600	2,168,441,000	331	500	8711
BROOKFIELD RESIDENTIAL PROPERTIES INC (*Suby of* **BROOKFIELD OFFICE PROPERTIES INC**) 4906 Richard Rd Sw, Calgary, AB T3E 6L1, *Tel* (403) 231-8900	2,162,350,000	332	20	6553
CENTRE INTEGRE UNIVERSITAIRE SANTE ET SERVICES SOCIAUX DU CENTRE-SUD-DE-L'ILE-DE-MONTREAL 155 Boul Saint-Joseph E, Montreal, QC H2T 1H4, *Tel* (514) 593-2044	2,161,560,000	333	50	8011
ALBERTA MOTOR ASSOCIATION 10310a G A Macdonald Ave Nw, Edmonton, AB T6J 6R7, *Tel* (780) 430-5555	2,157,901,500	334	310	8699
PATHEON INC (*Suby of* **THERMO FISHER SCIENTIFIC INC.**) 2100 Syntex Crt, Mississauga, ON L5N 7K9, *Tel* (905) 821-4001	2,155,361,000	335	900	2834
ROYAL GROUP, INC (*Suby of* **WESTLAKE CHEMICAL CORPORATION**) 10 Roybridge Gate Suite 201, Woodbridge, ON L4H 3M8, *Tel* (905) 264-1660	2,149,308,000	336	3,500	3089
FEDERAL EXPRESS CANADA CORPORATION (*Suby of* **FEDEX CORPORATION**) 5985 Explorer Dr, Mississauga, ON L4W 5K6, *Tel* (800) 463-3339	2,142,126,000	337	250	4512
DESJARDINS ASSURANCES GENERALES INC (*Suby of* **FEDERATION DES CAISSES DESJARDINS DU QUEBEC**) 6300 Boul De La Rive-Sud, Levis, QC G6V 6P9, *Tel* (418) 835-4850	2,136,968,000	338	625	6331
DOMINION OF CANADA GENERAL INSURANCE COMPANY, THE (*Suby of* **THE TRAVELERS COMPANIES INC**) 165 University Ave Suite 101, Toronto, ON M5H 3B9, *Tel* (416) 362-7231	2,136,968,000	339	200	6331
SUN LIFE DU CANADA, COMPAGNIE D'ASSURANCE-VIE 1155 Rue Metcalfe Bureau 1410, Montreal, QC H3B 2V9, *Tel* (514) 393-8820	2,136,968,000	340	1,000	6311
TORONTO DISTRICT SCHOOL BOARD 5050 Yonge St 5th Fl, North York, ON M2N 5N8, *Tel* (416) 397-3000	2,123,032,343	341	200	8211
ATLANTIC WHOLESALERS LTD (*Suby of* **LOBLAW COMPANIES LIMITED**) 3711 Joseph Howe Dr, Halifax, NS B3L 4H8, *Tel* (902) 468-8866	2,117,104,000	342	71	5411
BROOKFIELD INFRASTRUCTURE PARTNERS L.P. 181 Bay St Suite 300, Toronto, ON M5J 2T3, *Tel* (416) 363-9491	2,115,000,000	343	0	8711
EVERTRUST DEVELOPMENT GROUP CANADA INC 3100 Steeles Ave E Suite 302, Markham, ON L3R 8T3, *Tel* (647) 501-2345	2,095,176,000	344	3,000	1542
D+H LIMITED PARTNERSHIP (*Suby of* **VISTA EQUITY PARTNERS MANAGEMENT, LLC**) 120 Bremner Blvd 30th Fl, Toronto, ON M5J 0A8, *Tel* (416) 696-7700	2,087,059,500	345	500	6211
SUPERCLUB VIDEOTRON LTEE, LE (*Suby of* **QUEBECOR MEDIA INC**) 4545 Rue Frontenac Bureau 101, Montreal, QC H2H 2R7, *Tel* (514) 259-6000	2,086,529,400	346	60	6794
CATALYST PULP AND PAPER SALES INC (*Suby of* **CAPITAL ASSETS HOLDINGS (L) BERHAD**) 3600 Lysander Lane 2nd Fl, Richmond, BC V7B 1C3, *Tel* (604) 247-4400	2,085,900,000	347	3,000	5099
CUNNINGHAM LINDSEY CANADA LIMITED (*Suby of* **FAIRFAX FINANCIAL HOLDINGS LIMITED**) 46 Jackson St E, Hamilton, ON L8N 1L1, *Tel* (905) 528-1481	2,083,539,656	348	20	6411
GESTION D'INVESTISSEMENT 2300 INC (*Suby of* **GESTION TREE ROOTS INC**) 2300 Rue Emile-Belanger, Saint-Laurent, QC H4R 3J4, *Tel* (514) 747-2536	2,071,705,012	349	2	6712
MEG ENERGY CORP 3 Ave Sw Suite 600 25th Fl, Calgary, AB T2P 0G5, *Tel* (403) 770-0446	2,071,668,368	350	537	1311
SUPERIOR PLUS CORP 200 Wellington St W Suite 401, Toronto, ON M5V 3C7, *Tel* (416) 345-8050	2,067,116,723	351	0	2819
H.B. GROUP INSURANCE MANAGEMENT LTD (*Suby of* **CO-OPERATORS GROUP LIMITED, THE**) 5600 Cancross Crt Suite A, Mississauga, ON L5R 3E9, *Tel* (905) 507-6156	2,064,555,240	352	325	6411
SECURITE NATIONALE COMPAGNIE D'ASSURANCE (*Suby of* **TORONTO-DOMINION BANK, THE**) 50 Boul Cremazie O Bureau 1200, Montreal, QC H2P 1B6, *Tel* (514) 382-6060	2,061,105,251	353	1,500	6712
SECURITE KOLOSSAL INC (*Suby of* **GW INTERMEDIATE HOLDCO CORPORATION**) 1390 Rue Barre, Montreal, QC H3C 1N4, *Tel* (514) 253-4021	2,060,457,097	354	50	5065
CANADA BREAD COMPANY, LIMITED (*Suby of* **GRUPO BIMBO, S.A.B. DE C.V.**) 10 Four Seasons Pl Suite 1200, Etobicoke, ON M9B 6H7, *Tel* (416) 622-2040	2,059,201,625	355	200	2051
CU INC (*Suby of* **ATCO LTD**) 5302 Forand St Sw 4th Fl, Calgary, AB T3E 8B4, *Tel* (403) 292-7500	2,057,410,602	356	28	4931
BROOKFIELD RENEWABLE PARTNERS L.P. 181 Bay St Suite 300, Toronto, ON M5J 2T3, *Tel* (416) 363-9491	2,056,627,125	357	12	4911
GROUPE RESTAURANTS IMVESCOR INC (*Suby of* **GROUPE D'ALIMENTATION MTY INC**) 8150 Rte Transcanadienne Bureau 310, Montreal, QC H4S 1M5, *Tel* (514) 341-5544	2,037,843,714	358	30	6794
XEROX CANADA INC (*Suby of* **XEROX CORPORATION**) 20 York Mills Rd 5th Flr, North York, ON M2P 2C2, *Tel* (416) 229-3769	2,034,337,600	359	400	5044
STARS GROUP INC, THE 200 Bay St Suite 3205, Toronto, ON M5J 2J3, *Tel* (437) 371-5742	2,029,238,000	360	351	3944
SASKATCHEWAN POWER CORPORATION (*Suby of* **GOVERNMENT OF SASKATCHEWAN**) 2025 Victoria Ave, Regina, SK S4P 0S1, *Tel* (306) 566-2121	2,026,071,522	361	600	4911
PLAINS MIDSTREAM CANADA ULC (*Suby of* **PLAINS GP HOLDINGS, L.P.**) 607 8 Ave Sw Suite 1400, Calgary, AB T2P 0A7, *Tel* (403) 298-2100	2,022,567,400	362	570	4612
BOMBARDIER PRODUITS RECREATIFS INC (*Suby of* **BRP INC**) 726 Rue Saint-Joseph, Valcourt, QC J0E 2L0, *Tel* (450) 532-2211	2,019,662,400	363	100	3799
ENERGIR INC (*Suby of* **NOVERCO INC**) 1717 Rue Du Havre, Montreal, QC H2K 2X3, *Tel* (514) 598-3444	2,018,274,851	364	300	4924
IMPERIAL OIL RESOURCES LIMITED (*Suby of* **IMPERIAL OIL LIMITED**) 237 4 Ave Sw, Calgary, AB T2P 0H6, *Tel* (800) 567-3776	2,018,037,000	365	1,500	1382

COMPANY	SALES ($)	RANK	EMPLOYEES HERE	PRIMARY SIC CODE
TRANSPORT TFI 21, S.E.C. 8801 Rte Transcanadienne Bureau 500, Saint-Laurent, QC H4S 1Z6, *Tel* (514) 856-7500	2,013,788,000	366	50	5021
REPSOL OIL & GAS CANADA INC (*Suby of* **REPSOL SA.**) 888 3 St Sw Suite 2000, Calgary, AB T2P 5C5, *Tel*	2,013,541,048	367	50	1382
CO-OPERATORS GENERAL INSURANCE COMPANY 130 Macdonell St, Guelph, ON N1H 2Z6, *Tel* (519) 824-4400	2,007,265,873	368	500	6411
SHRED-IT JV LP (*Suby of* **STERICYCLE, INC.**) 2794 South Sheridan Way, Oakville, ON L6J 7T4, *Tel* (888) 750-6450	2,006,724,000	369	1	7389
CAPRICMW INSURANCE SERVICES LTD 1500 Hardy St Suite 100, Kelowna, BC V1Y 8H2, *Tel* (250) 860-2426	1,993,363,680	370	150	6411
CPPIB EQUITY INVESTMENTS INC 1 Queen St E Suite 2500, Toronto, ON M5C 2W5, *Tel* (416) 868-4075	1,992,393,200	371	0	6211
SEARS CANADA INC 290 Yonge St Suite 700, Toronto, ON M5B 2C3, *Tel*	1,991,921,263	372	2,900	5311
GUNGNIR RESOURCES INC 1688 152 St Suite 404, Surrey, BC V4A 4N2, *Tel* (604) 683-0484	1,988,828,317	373	4	1041
COMPAGNIE D'ASSURANCE BELAIR INC, LA (*Suby of* **INTACT FINANCIAL CORPORATION**) 7101 Rue Jean-Talon E Bureau 300, Anjou, QC H1M 3T6, *Tel* (514) 270-1700	1,987,380,240	374	450	6331
INTER PIPELINE LTD 215 2 St Sw Suite 3200, Calgary, AB T2P 1M4, *Tel* (403) 290-6000	1,965,682,676	375	263	1382
CONSUMERS' CO-OPERATIVE REFINERIES LIMITED (*Suby of* **FEDERATED CO-OPERATIVES LIMITED**) 580 Park St, Regina, SK S4N 5A9, *Tel* (306) 719-4353	1,960,188,750	376	1,150	2911
ATCO GAS AND PIPELINES LTD (*Suby of* **ATCO LTD**) 909 11 Ave Sw Suite 1200, Calgary, AB T2R 1L7, *Tel* (403) 245-7060	1,958,321,800	377	400	4923
GERDAU AMERISTEEL CORPORATION (*Suby of* **METALURGICA GERDAU S/A.**) 1 Gerdau Crt, Whitby, ON L1N 7G8, *Tel* (905) 668-8811	1,954,435,200	378	500	3312
GROUPHEALTH BENEFIT SOLUTIONS 2626 Croydon Dr Suite 200, Surrey, BC V3Z 0S8, *Tel* (604) 542-4100	1,950,648,744	379	411	6411
PEPSICO CANADA ULC (*Suby of* **PEPSICO, INC.**) 5550 Explorer Dr, Mississauga, ON L4W 0C3, *Tel* (289) 374-5000	1,949,540,000	380	80	2096
AMEC FOSTER WHEELER INC (*Suby of* **JOHN WOOD GROUP P.L.C.**) 2020 Winston Park Dr Suite 700, Oakville, ON L6H 6X7, *Tel* (905) 829-5400	1,937,197,700	381	535	6719
CENTRE UNIVERSITAIRE DE SANTE MCGILL 1001 Boul Decarie, Montreal, QC H4A 3J1, *Tel* (514) 934-1934	1,936,901,960	382	17,437	8062
FIRSTSERVICE CORPORATION 1140 Bay St Suite 4000, Toronto, ON M5S 2B4, *Tel* (416) 960-9500	1,931,473,000	383	500	6519
VANCOUVER ISLAND HEALTH AUTHORITY (*Suby of* **GOVERNMENT OF THE PROVINCE OF BRITISH COLUMBIA**) 1952 Bay St, Victoria, BC V8R 1J8, *Tel* (250) 519-7700	1,931,050,400	384	500	8011
GDI SERVICES (CANADA) LP (*Suby of* **GDI SERVICES AUX IMMEUBLES INC**) 60 Worcester Rd, Etobicoke, ON M9W 5X2, *Tel* (416) 736-1144	1,929,420,000	385	50	7349
COGECO INC (*Suby of* **GESTION AUDEM INC**) 5 Place Ville-Marie Bureau 1700, Montreal, QC H3B 0B3, *Tel* (514) 764-4700	1,929,147,523	386	497	4832
AVIVA CANADA INC (*Suby of* **GENERAL ACCIDENT PLC**) 10 Aviva Way Suite 100, Markham, ON L6G 0G1, *Tel* (416) 288-1800	1,927,074,700	387	1,250	6411
CAPITAL D'AMERIQUE CDPQ INC (*Suby of* **GOUVERNEMENT DE LA PROVINCE DE QUEBEC**) 1000 Place Jean-Paul-Riopelle Bureau 12e, Montreal, QC H2Z 2B3, *Tel* (514) 842-3261	1,923,271,200	388	900	6371
MELOCHE MONNEX FINANCIAL SERVICES INC (*Suby of* **TORONTO-DOMINION BANK, THE**) 101 Mcnabb St, Markham, ON L3R 4H8, *Tel* (416) 484-1112	1,917,426,016	389	200	6411
WOODBRIDGE FOAM CORPORATION 4240 Sherwoodtowne Blvd Suite 300, Mississauga, ON L4Z 2G6, *Tel* (905) 896-3626	1,910,496,000	390	200	3086
INVESTISSEMENTS ALT2 INC 73 Rue Queen, Sherbrooke, QC J1M 0C9, *Tel* (819) 566-8833	1,898,441,600	391	400	6411
WEST FRASER MILLS LTD (*Suby of* **WEST FRASER TIMBER CO. LTD**) 858 Beatty St Suite 501, Vancouver, BC V6B 1C1, *Tel* (604) 895-2700	1,893,052,000	392	42	2421
EMERSON ELECTRIC CANADA LIMITED (*Suby of* **EMERSON ELECTRIC CO.**) 66 Leek Cres 2nd Fl, Richmond Hill, ON L4B 1H1, *Tel* (905) 762-1010	1,888,703,985	393	3,000	5063
PCL INDUSTRIAL CONSTRUCTORS INC (*Suby of* **PCL EMPLOYEES HOLDINGS LTD**) 9915 56 Ave Nw, Edmonton, AB T6E 5L7, *Tel* (780) 733-5500	1,885,658,400	394	100	1541
SHAW CABLESYSTEMS G.P. (*Suby of* **SHAW COMMUNICATIONS INC**) 630 3 Ave Sw, Calgary, AB T2P 4L4, *Tel* (403) 750-4500	1,873,446,400	395	5,600	4841
AGF INVESTMENTS INC (*Suby of* **AGF MANAGEMENT LIMITED**) 66 Wellington St W Suite 3100, Toronto, ON M5K 1E9, *Tel* (416) 367-1900	1,867,816,000	396	0	6722
IKO ENTERPRISES LTD (*Suby of* **GOLDIS ENTERPRISES, INC.**) 1600 42 Ave Se, Calgary, AB T2G 5B5, *Tel* (403) 265-6022	1,864,095,900	397	0	6719
DEVON CANADA CORPORATION (*Suby of* **DEVON ENERGY CORPORATION**) 400 3 Ave Sw Suite 100, Calgary, AB T2P 4H2, *Tel* (403) 232-7100	1,854,582,000	398	200	1311
EXXONMOBIL CANADA LTD (*Suby of* **EXXON MOBIL CORPORATION**) 237 4 Ave Sw Suite 3000, Calgary, AB T2P 4X7, *Tel* (403) 232-5300	1,854,582,000	399	500	1311
PARKLAND INDUSTRIES LIMITED PARTNERSHIP 4919 59 St Suite 236, Red Deer, AB T4N 6C9, *Tel* (403) 343-1515	1,842,912,500	400	100	2911
COGECO COMMUNICATIONS INC (*Suby of* **GESTION AUDEM INC**) 5 Place Ville-Marie Bureau 1700, Montreal, QC H3B 0B3, *Tel* (514) 874-2600	1,842,025,688	401	400	4841
ALLSTREAM BUSINESS INC (*Suby of* **ZAYO GROUP HOLDINGS, INC.**) 5160 Orbitor Dr, Mississauga, ON L4W 5H2, *Tel* (888) 288-2273	1,839,992,000	402	2,000	4899

COMPANY	SALES ($)	RANK	EMPLOYEES HERE	PRIMARY SIC CODE
GRAND FOREST HOLDINGS INCORPORATED (*Suby of* **IRVING, J. D. LIMITED**)				
300 Union St, Saint John, NB E2L 4Z2, *Tel* (506) 635-6666	1,838,185,000	403	15	2611
TERVITA CORPORATION				
140 10 Ave Se Suite 1600, Calgary, AB T2G 0R1, *Tel* (855) 837-8482	1,824,717,933	404	800	8748
UBC PROPERTIES INVESTMENTS LTD (*Suby of* **UNIVERSITY OF BRITISH COLUMBIA, THE**)				
3313 Shrum Lane Unit 200, Vancouver, BC V6S 0C8, *Tel* (604) 731-3103	1,818,003,067	405	30	6553
UNIVERSITY OF BRITISH COLUMBIA, THE				
2329 West Mall, Vancouver, BC V6T 1Z4, *Tel* (604) 822-2211	1,818,003,067	406	10,000	8221
SAMUEL, SON & CO., LIMITED				
2360 Dixie Rd, Mississauga, ON L4Y 1Z7, *Tel* (905) 279-5460	1,802,690,388	407	400	6712
YAMANA GOLD INC				
200 Bay St Royal Bank Plaza North Tower Ste 2200, Toronto, ON M5J 2J3, *Tel* (416) 815-0220	1,798,500,000	408	40	1041
CAMSO INC (*Suby of* **COMPAGNIE GENERALE DES ETABLISSEMENTS MICHELIN**)				
2633 Rue Macpherson, Magog, QC J1X 0E6, *Tel* (819) 868-1500	1,791,090,000	409	75	3011
PRATT & WHITNEY CANADA CIE (*Suby of* **PRATT AERO LIMITED PARTNERSHIP**)				
1000 Boul Marie-Victorin, Longueuil, QC J4G 1A1, *Tel* (450) 677-9411	1,783,568,950	410	5,000	3519
PCL CONSTRUCTION HOLDINGS LTD (*Suby of* **PCL EMPLOYEES HOLDINGS LTD**)				
9915 56 Ave Nw, Edmonton, AB T6E 5L7, *Tel* (780) 733-5000	1,781,636,148	411	1	6159
CANADA IMPERIAL OIL LIMITED (*Suby of* **IMPERIAL OIL LIMITED**)				
237 4 Ave Sw Suite 2480, Calgary, AB T2P 0H6, *Tel* (800) 567-3776	1,773,409,500	412	150	5172
MANITOBA HYDRO-ELECTRIC BOARD, THE (*Suby of* **PROVINCE OF MANITOBA**)				
360 Portage Ave Suite 6, Winnipeg, MB R3C 0G8, *Tel* (204) 360-3311	1,771,333,343	413	750	4911
MONDELEZ CANADA INC (*Suby of* **MONDELEZ INTERNATIONAL, INC.**)				
3300 Bloor St W Suite 1801, Etobicoke, ON M8X 2X2, *Tel*	1,754,586,000	414	3,200	2032
UNI-SELECT INC				
170 Boul Industriel, Boucherville, QC J4B 2X3, *Tel* (450) 641-2440	1,751,965,000	415	100	5013
ABITIBIBOWATER CANADA INC (*Suby of* **RESOLUTE FOREST PRODUCTS INC**)				
111 Rue Duke Bureau 5000, Montreal, QC H3C 2M1, *Tel* (514) 875-2160	1,735,071,223	416	4	6712
LUNDIN MINING CORPORATION				
150 King St W Suite 1500, Toronto, ON M5H 1J9, *Tel* (416) 342-5560	1,725,589,000	417	0	1021
VENTRA GROUP CO (*Suby of* **FLEX-N-GATE LLC**)				
538 Blanchard Pk, Tecumseh, ON N8N 2L9, *Tel* (519) 727-3931	1,721,832,000	418	900	3714
WSP CANADA GROUP LIMITED (*Suby of* **AST TRUST COMPANY (CANADA)**)				
100 Commerce Valley Dr W, Thornhill, ON L3T 0A1, *Tel* (905) 882-1100	1,715,039,700	419	0	8711
CALFRAC WELL SERVICES LTD				
411 8 Ave Sw, Calgary, AB T2P 1E3, *Tel* (866) 770-3722	1,710,601,063	420	100	1389
PARMALAT HOLDINGS LIMITED				
405 The West Mall 10th Floor, Etobicoke, ON M9C 5J1, *Tel* (416) 626-1973	1,710,000,000	421	3,000	2026
CANACCORD GENUITY CORP (*Suby of* **CANACCORD GENUITY GROUP INC**)				
609 Granville St Suite 2200, Vancouver, BC V7Y 1H2, *Tel* (604) 643-7300	1,707,765,600	422	500	6211
NESTLE CANADA INC (*Suby of* **NESTLE S.A.**)				
25 Sheppard Ave W Suite 1700, North York, ON M2N 6S6, *Tel* (416) 512-9000	1,705,847,500	423	300	2095
TRANSALTA CORPORATION				
110 12 Ave Sw, Calgary, AB T2R 0G7, *Tel* (403) 267-7110	1,704,971,398	424	400	4911
CI FINANCIAL CORP				
2 Queen St E, Toronto, ON M5C 3G7, *Tel* (416) 364-1145	1,695,392,779	425	500	6282
LOWE'S COMPANIES CANADA, ULC (*Suby of* **LOWE'S COMPANIES, INC.**)				
5150 Spectrum Way, Mississauga, ON L4W 5G2, *Tel* (905) 219-1000	1,686,300,000	426	150	5211
ENSIGN DRILLING INC (*Suby of* **ENSIGN ENERGY SERVICES INC**)				
400 5 Ave Sw Suite 1000, Calgary, AB T2P 0L6, *Tel* (403) 262-1361	1,681,697,500	427	75	1381
TELE-MOBILE COMPANY				
200 Consilium Pl Suite 1600, Scarborough, ON M1H 3J3, *Tel* (800) 308-5992	1,672,720,000	428	500	4899
ROINS FINANCIAL SERVICES LIMITED (*Suby of* **RSA INSURANCE GROUP PLC**)				
18 York St Suite 410, Toronto, ON M5J 2T8, *Tel* (416) 366-7511	1,666,115,400	429	9	6331
GLOBAL EXCEL MANAGEMENT INC				
73 Rue Queen, Sherbrooke, QC J1M 0C9, *Tel* (819) 566-8833	1,661,136,400	430	0	6411
INTERFOR CORPORATION				
1055 Dunsmuir St Suite 3500, Vancouver, BC V7X 1H7, *Tel* (604) 689-6800	1,657,640,816	431	30	2421
UNILEVER CANADA INC (*Suby of* **UNILEVER PLC**)				
160 Bloor St E Suite 1400, Toronto, ON M4W 3R2, *Tel* (416) 415-3000	1,657,109,000	432	200	2099
CENTRE INTEGRE DE SANTE ET DE SERVICES SOCIAUX DU BAS-SAINT-LAURENT				
355 Boul Saint-Germain, Rimouski, QC G5L 3N2, *Tel* (418) 724-3000	1,656,544,000	433	200	8399
PAPIER DOMTAR (CANADA) INC (*Suby of* **DOMTAR LUXEMBOURG INVESTMENTS SARL**)				
395 Boul De Maisonneuve O Bureau 200, Montreal, QC H3A 1L6, *Tel* (514) 848-5555	1,655,101,774	434	30	2611
UNIVERSITY HEALTH NETWORK				
200 Elizabeth St, Toronto, ON M5G 2C4, *Tel* (416) 340-3111	1,650,250,111	435	3,500	8062
ALGONQUIN POWER & UTILITIES CORP				
354 Davis Rd, Oakville, ON L6J 2X1, *Tel* (905) 465-4500	1,647,387,000	436	0	6712
DOMTAR INC (*Suby of* **DOMTAR LUXEMBOURG INVESTMENTS SARL**)				
395 Boul De Maisonneuve O Bureau 200, Montreal, QC H3A 1L6, *Tel* (514) 848-5555	1,643,705,027	437	500	2611
GOVERNORS OF ST FRANCIS XAVIER UNIVERSITY				
1 West St, Antigonish, NS B2G 2W5, *Tel* (902) 863-3300	1,643,301,000	438	0	8221
J.V. DRIVER CORPORATION INC				
1205 5 St, Nisku, AB T9E 7L6, *Tel* (780) 980-5837	1,640,575,000	439	5	1629

COMPANY	SALES ($)	RANK	EMPLOYEES HERE	PRIMARY SIC CODE
CONOCOPHILLIPS WESTERN CANADA PARTNERSHIP (*Suby of* **CONOCOPHILLIPS**) 401 9 Ave Sw Suite 1600, Calgary, AB T2P 3C5, *Tel* (403) 233-4000	1,637,913,000	440	2,500	1382
SANJEL CANADA LTD 505 2 St Sw Suite 200, Calgary, AB T2P 1N8, *Tel* (403) 269-1420	1,637,913,000	441	200	1389
SPIN MASTER CORP 225 King St W Suite 200, Toronto, ON M5V 3M2, *Tel* (416) 364-6002	1,631,537,000	442	0	6712
MAXAR TECHNOLOGIES LTD (*Suby of* **MAXAR TECHNOLOGIES INC.**) 200 Burrard St Suite 1570, Vancouver, BC V6C 3L6, *Tel* (604) 974-5275	1,631,200,000	443	20	7371
TRANSCONTINENTAL INC 1 Place Ville-Marie Bureau 3240, Montreal, QC H3B 0G1, *Tel* (514) 954-4000	1,620,147,610	444	269	6712
STELLA-JONES INC 3100 Boul De La Cote-Vertu Bureau 300, Saint-Laurent, QC H4R 2J8, *Tel* (514) 934-8666	1,610,127,531	445	5	2491
MOLSON CANADA 2005 (*Suby of* **MOLSON COORS BREWING COMPANY**) 33 Carlingview Dr Suite 2005, Etobicoke, ON M9W 5E4, *Tel* (416) 679-1786	1,608,370,500	446	250	2082
INTERIOR HEALTH AUTHORITY 505 Doyle Ave, Kelowna, BC V1Y 0C5, *Tel* (250) 862-4200	1,607,176,339	447	6,000	8062
WSP CANADA INC (*Suby of* **AST TRUST COMPANY (CANADA)**) 1600 Boul Rene-Levesque O 16e Etage, Montreal, QC H3H 1P9, *Tel* (514) 340-0046	1,604,219,001	448	800	6712
CAPITALE ASSURANCES GENERALES INC, LA (*Suby of* **LA CAPITALE PARTICIPATIONS INC**) 625 Rue Jacques-Parizeau, Quebec, QC G1R 2G5, *Tel* (418) 781-1618	1,602,726,000	449	250	6321
SHAWCOR LTD 25 Bethridge Rd, Etobicoke, ON M9W 1M7, *Tel* (416) 743-7111	1,602,684,162	450	78	3533
TOURMALINE OIL CORP 250 6 Ave Sw Unit 3700, Calgary, AB T2P 3H7, *Tel* (403) 266-5992	1,595,288,443	451	0	1382
SOUTH COAST BRITISH COLUMBIA TRANSPORTATION AUTHORITY 287 Nelson'S Crt Suite 400, New Westminster, BC V3L 0E7, *Tel* (778) 375-7500	1,591,971,957	452	245	4111
CHICAGO, CENTRAL & PACIFIC RAILROAD COMPANY (*Suby of* **COMPAGNIE DES CHEMINS DE FER NATIONAUX DU CANADA**) 935 Rue De La Gauchetiere O, Montreal, QC H3B 2M9, *Tel* (514) 399-4536	1,588,993,694	453	3,218	4011
ILLINOIS CENTRAL RAILROAD COMPANY (*Suby of* **COMPAGNIE DES CHEMINS DE FER NATIONAUX DU CANADA**) 935 Rue De La Gauchetiere O Bureau 11, Montreal, QC H3B 2M9, *Tel* (514) 399-4536	1,588,993,694	454	3,218	4011
CAMECO CORPORATION 2121 11th St W, Saskatoon, SK S7M 1J3, *Tel* (306) 956-6200	1,585,692,387	455	400	1094
IRVING OIL LIMITED 10 Sydney St, Saint John, NB E2L 5E6, *Tel* (506) 202-2000	1,584,904,750	456	500	2911
METROLINX 97 Front St W Suite 200, Toronto, ON M5J 1E6, *Tel* (416) 874-5900	1,580,105,600	457	1,500	4011
DELOITTE LLP 8 Adelaide St W Suite 200, Toronto, ON M5H 0A9, *Tel* (416) 601-6150	1,578,406,000	458	90	8721
ENCON GROUP INC (*Suby of* **MARSH & MCLENNAN COMPANIES, INC.**) 1400 Blair Pl Suite 50, Gloucester, ON K1J 9B8, *Tel* (613) 786-2000	1,566,214,320	459	0	6411
CENTRE HOSPITALIER UNIVERSITAIRE DE QUEBEC 11 Cote Du Palais, Quebec, QC G1R 2J6, *Tel* (418) 525-4444	1,555,120,000	460	1,500	8062
JAZZ AVIATION LP 3 Spectacle Lake Dr Suite 100, Dartmouth, NS B3B 1W8, *Tel* (902) 873-5000	1,555,024,800	461	650	4512
IMPRIMERIES TRANSCONTINENTAL 2005 S.E.N.C. 1 Place Ville-Marie Bureau 3240, Montreal, QC H3B 0G1, *Tel* (514) 954-4000	1,550,192,000	462	100	2752
ABC TECHNOLOGIES INC (*Suby of* **CERBERUS CAPITAL MANAGEMENT, L.P.**) 2 Norelco Dr, North York, ON M9L 2X6, *Tel* (416) 246-1782	1,528,396,800	463	150	3089
ENERGIR, S.E.C. 1717 Rue Du Havre, Montreal, QC H2K 2X3, *Tel* (514) 598-3444	1,522,883,188	464	917	4924
BRICK LTD, THE (*Suby of* **LEON'S FURNITURE LIMITED**) 16930 114 Ave Nw, Edmonton, AB T5M 3S2, *Tel* (780) 930-6000	1,520,207,100	465	0	5712
NOVA SCOTIA POWER INCORPORATED (*Suby of* **EMERA INCORPORATED**) 1223 Lower Water St, Halifax, NS B3J 3S8, *Tel* (902) 428-6221	1,513,324,800	466	600	4911
NORTH WEST COMPANY INC, THE 77 Main St, Winnipeg, MB R3C 1A3, *Tel* (204) 943-0881	1,503,838,464	467	500	5311
CATALYST PAPER CORPORATION (*Suby of* **CAPITAL ASSETS HOLDINGS (L) BERHAD**) 3600 Lysander Lane Suite 200 Fl 2, Richmond, BC V7B 1C3, *Tel* (604) 247-4400	1,497,068,268	468	133	2621
WINNERS MERCHANTS INTERNATIONAL L.P. (*Suby of* **THE TJX COMPANIES INC**) 60 Standish Crt, Mississauga, ON L5R 0G1, *Tel* (905) 405-8000	1,497,060,000	469	600	5651
HSBC BANK CANADA (*Suby of* **HSBC HOLDINGS PLC**) 885 Georgia St W, Vancouver, BC V6C 3G1, *Tel* (604) 685-1000	1,496,441,070	470	300	6021
ABC BENEFITS CORPORATION 10009 108 St Nw, Edmonton, AB T5J 3C5, *Tel* (780) 498-8000	1,495,877,600	471	650	6321
BLACK & MCDONALD LIMITED (*Suby of* **BLACK & MCDONALD GROUP LIMITED**) 2 Bloor St E Suite 2100, Toronto, ON M4W 1A8, *Tel* (416) 920-5100	1,489,664,000	472	12	1711
3522997 CANADA INC 180 Montee De Liesse, Saint-Laurent, QC H4T 1N7, *Tel* (450) 455-3963	1,486,625,672	473	4,000	6712
OMERS ADMINISTRATION CORPORATION 100 Adelaide St W Suite 900, Toronto, ON M5H 0E2, *Tel* (416) 369-2400	1,482,895,769	474	500	6371
HUDBAY MINERALS INC 25 York St Suite 800, Toronto, ON M5J 2V5, *Tel* (416) 362-8181	1,472,366,000	475	1,455	1081

COMPANY	SALES ($)	RANK	EMPLOYEES HERE	PRIMARY SIC CODE
NORDIA INC (*Suby of* **PLATINUM EQUITY, LLC**) 3020 Av Jacques-Bureau 2e Etage, Montreal, QC H7P 6G2, *Tel* (514) 415-7088	1,471,597,600	476	35	7389
LABATT BREWING COMPANY LIMITED (*Suby of* **ANHEUSER-BUSCH INBEV**) 207 Queens Quay W Suite 299, Toronto, ON M5J 1A7, *Tel* (416) 361-5050	1,462,155,000	477	20	2082
SQI HOLDINGS II INC (*Suby of* **EMPIRE COMPANY LIMITED**) 115 King St, Stellarton, NS B0K 0A2, *Tel* (902) 752-8371	1,462,036,000	478	4,000	6712
I.M.P. GROUP LIMITED (*Suby of* **I.M.P. GROUP INTERNATIONAL INCORPORATED**) 2651 Joseph Howe Dr Suite 400, Halifax, NS B3L 4T1, *Tel* (902) 453-2400	1,459,819,200	479	90	4581
CAPITALE MUTUELLE DE L'ADMINISTRATION PUBLIQUE, LA 625 Rue Jacques-Parizeau, Quebec, QC G1R 2G5, *Tel* (418) 644-4229	1,458,736,674	480	11	6311
MERCER INTERNATIONAL INC 700 Pender St W Suite 1120, Vancouver, BC V6C 1G8, *Tel* (604) 684-1099	1,457,718,000	481	17	2611
HONDA CANADA INC (*Suby of* **HONDA MOTOR CO., LTD.**) 180 Honda Blvd Suite 200, Markham, ON L6C 0H9, *Tel* (905) 888-8110	1,454,250,000	482	600	3711
CANADIAN NUCLEAR LABORATORIES LTD (*Suby of* **GOVERNMENT OF CANADA**) 286 Plant Rd, Chalk River, ON K0J 1J0, *Tel* (613) 584-3311	1,445,096,250	483	3,000	2819
MCGILL UNIVERSITY HEALTH CENTRE 1650 Av Cedar, Montreal, QC H3G 1A4, *Tel* (514) 934-1934	1,444,040,000	484	200	8062
EPCOR UTILITIES INC (*Suby of* **CITY OF EDMONTON**) 10423 101 St Nw Suite 2000, Edmonton, AB T5H 0E8, *Tel* (780) 412-3414	1,439,349,170	485	1,500	4941
WILLIAMS OPERATING CORPORATION Hwy 17, Marathon, ON P0T 2E0, *Tel* (807) 238-1100	1,432,529,400	486	600	1041
GESTION ALCOA CANADA CIE (*Suby of* **ALUMINERIE LAURALCO SARL**) 1 Place Ville-Marie Bureau 2310, Montreal, QC H3B 3M5, *Tel* (514) 904-5030	1,425,109,000	487	0	3334
ESSOR ASSURANCES PLACEMENTS CONSEILS INC (*Suby of* **GROUPE FINANCIER ESSOR INC**) 1100 Boul Robert-Bourassa, Montreal, QC H3B 3A5, *Tel* (514) 878-9373	1,423,831,200	488	10	6411
SSQ SOCIETE D'ASSURANCES GENERALES INC (*Suby of* **FONDS DE SOLIDARITE DES TRAVAILLEURS DU QUEBEC (F.T.Q.)**) 2515 Boul Laurier, Quebec, QC G1V 2L2, *Tel* (819) 538-4610	1,423,831,200	489	300	6411
BANK OF MONTREAL HOLDING INC (*Suby of* **BANK OF MONTREAL**) 100 King St W 21st Floor, Toronto, ON M5X 1A1, *Tel* (416) 359-5003	1,423,138,000	490	0	6211
RBC DOMINION SECURITIES LIMITED (*Suby of* **ROYAL BANK OF CANADA**) 200 Bay St 9th Floor, Toronto, ON M5J 2J5, *Tel* (416) 842-4088	1,423,138,000	491	0	6211
GOVERNORS OF THE UNIVERSITY OF ALBERTA, THE (*Suby of* **GOVERNMENT OF THE PROVINCE OF ALBERTA**) 116 St & 85 Ave, Edmonton, AB T6G 2R3, *Tel* (780) 492-3111	1,421,916,337	492	14,000	8221
COLLIERS MACAULAY NICOLLS INC (*Suby of* **COLLIERS INTERNATIONAL GROUP INC**) 200 Granville St Unit 19, Vancouver, BC V6C 1S4, *Tel* (604) 681-4111	1,419,868,800	493	100	6531
PAGES JAUNES SOLUTIONS NUMERIQUES ET MEDIAS LIMITEE (*Suby of* **PAGES JAUNES LIMITEE**) 16 Place Du Commerce, Verdun, QC H3E 2A5, *Tel* (514) 934-2611	1,415,121,120	494	50	4899
BOYD GROUP INCOME FUND 1745 Ellice Ave, Winnipeg, MB R3H 1A6, *Tel* (204) 895-1244	1,413,566,845	495	0	7532
MAPLE LODGE FARMS LTD (*Suby of* **MAPLE LODGE HOLDING CORPORATION**) 8301 Winston Churchill Blvd, Brampton, ON L6Y 0A2, *Tel* (905) 455-8340	1,413,416,500	496	1,900	2015
CHC HELICOPTER HOLDING S.A.R.L. (*Suby of* **FRC FOUNDERS CORPORATION**) 4740 Agar Dr, Richmond, BC V7B 1A3, *Tel* (604) 276-7500	1,408,725,528	497	45	4522
COSTCO CANADA HOLDINGS INC (*Suby of* **COSTCO WHOLESALE CORPORATION**) 415 West Hunt Club Rd, Nepean, ON K2E 1C5, *Tel* (613) 221-2000	1,408,555,500	498	200	6712
LOCKERBIE & HOLE INC (*Suby of* **AECON GROUP INC**) 14940 121a Ave Nw, Edmonton, AB T5V 1A3, *Tel*	1,403,767,920	499	50	1541
CANCER CARE ONTARIO 620 University Ave Suite 1500, Toronto, ON M5G 2L7, *Tel* (416) 971-9800	1,398,278,757	500	0	8733
TOLKO INDUSTRIES LTD (*Suby of* **AMERICAN INDUSTRIAL ACQUISITION CORPORATION**) 3000 28 St, Vernon, BC V1T 1W1, *Tel* (250) 545-4411	1,391,950,000	501	180	2421
MAGRIS RESOURCES INC 333 Bay St Suite 1101, Toronto, ON M5H 2R2, *Tel* (416) 901-9877	1,391,019,600	502	0	6799
EMPIRE LIFE INSURANCE COMPANY, THE (*Suby of* **E-L FINANCIAL CORPORATION LIMITED**) 259 King St E, Kingston, ON K7L 3A8, *Tel* (613) 548-1881	1,389,029,200	503	450	6311
BRIDGESTONE CANADA INC (*Suby of* **BRIDGESTONE CORPORATION**) 5770 Hurontario St Suite 400, Mississauga, ON L5R 3G5, *Tel* (877) 468-6270	1,383,462,000	504	2,100	5014
GROUPE VOLVO CANADA INC (*Suby of* **AB VOLVO**) 1000 Boul Industriel Bureau 1160, Saint-Eustache, QC J7R 5A5, *Tel* (450) 472-6410	1,383,462,000	505	950	5012
PIVOT TECHNOLOGY SOLUTIONS INC 55 Renfrew Dr Suite 200, Markham, ON L3R 8H3, *Tel* (416) 360-4777	1,373,630,000	506	0	8731
FRONTERA ENERGY CORPORATION 333 Bay St Suite 1100, Toronto, ON M5H 2R2, *Tel* (416) 362-7735	1,371,706,000	507	30	1381
MAGNA POWERTRAIN INC (*Suby of* **MAGNA INTERNATIONAL INC**) 50 Casmir Crt, Concord, ON L4K 4J5, *Tel* (905) 532-2100	1,366,995,000	508	25	3714
FORTISBC PACIFIC HOLDINGS INC (*Suby of* **FORTIS INC**) 1975 Springfield Rd Suite 100, Kelowna, BC V1Y 7V7, *Tel* (250) 469-8000	1,359,748,000	509	0	4911
AGT FOOD AND INGREDIENTS INC 6200 E Primrose Green Dr, Regina, SK S4V 3L7, *Tel* (306) 525-4490	1,359,557,453	510	50	0723
BRICK WAREHOUSE LP, THE 16930 114 Ave Nw, Edmonton, AB T5M 3S2, *Tel* (780) 930-6000	1,359,327,971	511	100	6712
SIEMENS CANADA LIMITED (*Suby of* **SIEMENS AG**)				

COMPANY	SALES ($)	RANK	EMPLOYEES HERE	PRIMARY SIC CODE
1577 North Service Rd E, Oakville, ON L6H 0H6, *Tel* (905) 465-8000	1,357,992,000	512	300	3625
BLACK & MCDONALD GROUP LIMITED				
2 Bloor St E Suite 2100, Toronto, ON M4W 1A8, *Tel* (416) 920-5100	1,354,240,000	513	0	1711
INDEPENDENT ORDER OF FORESTERS, THE				
789 Don Mills Rd Suite 1200, North York, ON M3C 1T9, *Tel* (416) 429-3000	1,353,082,894	514	700	6311
FIRST LION HOLDINGS INC				
2001 Av Mcgill College Bureau 2200, Montreal, QC H3A 1G1, *Tel* (514) 843-3632	1,352,639,640	515	0	6411
ENVIROSYSTEMS INCORPORATED (*Suby of* **REVOLUTION ENVIRONMENTAL SOLUTIONS LP**)				
11 Brown Ave, Dartmouth, NS B3B 1Z7, *Tel* (902) 481-8008	1,352,027,625	516	100	2992
SASKATCHEWAN TELECOMMUNICATIONS HOLDING CORPORATION (*Suby of* **GOVERNMENT OF SASKATCHEWAN**)				
2121 Saskatchewan Dr, Regina, SK S4P 3Y2, *Tel* (800) 992-9912	1,348,546,864	517	200	4899
CONSEILLERS EN GESTION ET INFORMATIQUE CGI INC (*Suby of* **CGI INC**)				
1350 Boul Rene-Levesque O 15e Etage, Montreal, QC H3G 1T4, *Tel* (514) 841-3200	1,340,321,503	518	500	6712
CHEVRON CANADA LIMITED (*Suby of* **CHEVRON CORPORATION**)				
1050 Pender St W Suite 1200, Vancouver, BC V6E 3T4, *Tel* (604) 668-5300	1,340,300,000	519	350	2911
CORUS ENTERTAINMENT INC				
25 Dockside Dr, Toronto, ON M5A 0B5, *Tel* (416) 479-7000	1,339,883,643	520	200	4832
PUNA OPERATIONS INC				
1055 Dunsmuir St, Vancouver, BC V7X 1G4, *Tel* (604) 689-3846	1,339,414,989	521	0	1031
TELUS COMMUNICATIONS COMPANY (*Suby of* **TELUS CORPORATION**)				
3777 Kingsway Suite 501, Burnaby, BC V5H 3Z7, *Tel* (604) 432-2151	1,338,176,000	522	4,000	4899
RGIS CANADA ULC (*Suby of* **THE BLACKSTONE GROUP L P**)				
2560 Matheson Blvd E Suite 224, Mississauga, ON L4W 4Y9, *Tel* (905) 206-1107	1,337,816,000	523	100	7389
MAC'S CONVENIENCE STORES INC (*Suby of* **ALIMENTATION COUCHE-TARD INC**)				
305 Milner Ave Suite 400, Toronto, ON M1B 0A5, *Tel* (416) 291-4441	1,337,031,922	524	110	6712
NOVA GAS TRANSMISSION LTD (*Suby of* **TC ENERGY CORPORATION**)				
450 1 St Sw, Calgary, AB T2P 5H1, *Tel* (403) 920-2000	1,335,338,880	525	0	4923
TDL GROUP CORP, THE (*Suby of* **RESTAURANT BRANDS INTERNATIONAL INC**)				
130 King St Suite 300, Toronto, ON M5X 1E1, *Tel* (905) 845-6511	1,334,078,400	526	450	6794
CEDA INTERNATIONAL CORPORATION (*Suby of* **OMERS ADMINISTRATION CORPORATION**)				
11012 Macleod Trail Se Suite 625, Calgary, AB T2J 6A5, *Tel* (403) 253-3233	1,333,935,000	527	0	2819
EXPORT DEVELOPMENT CANADA (*Suby of* **GOVERNMENT OF CANADA**)				
150 Slater St, Ottawa, ON K1A 1K3, *Tel* (613) 598-2500	1,333,579,935	528	1,000	6111
NOVA SCOTIA HEALTH AUTHORITY (*Suby of* **NOVA SCOTIA, PROVINCE OF**)				
1276 South Park St Suite 1278, Halifax, NS B3H 2Y9, *Tel* (902) 473-5117	1,332,960,000	529	200	8062
ENBRIDGE INCOME FUND (*Suby of* **ENBRIDGE INC**)				
425 1 St Sw Suite 3000, Calgary, AB T2P 3L8, *Tel* (403) 767-3642	1,327,051,008	530	269	4922
ROYAL CANADIAN MINT (*Suby of* **GOVERNMENT OF CANADA**)				
320 Sussex Dr, Ottawa, ON K1A 0G8, *Tel* (613) 993-8990	1,325,093,867	531	400	5094
ASIAN MINERAL RESOURCES LIMITED				
120 Adelaide St W Suite 2500, Toronto, ON M5H 1T1, *Tel* (416) 360-3412	1,317,927,048	532	552	1061
ALBERTA ELECTRIC SYSTEM OPERATOR				
330 5 Ave Sw Suite 2500, Calgary, AB T2P 0L4, *Tel* (403) 539-2450	1,316,642,065	533	170	4911
NBF INC (*Suby of* **FINANCIERE BANQUE NATIONALE INC**)				
130 King St W Suite 3000, Toronto, ON M5X 1J9, *Tel* (416) 869-3707	1,313,308,125	534	225	6722
BRITISH COLUMBIA AUTOMOBILE ASSOCIATION				
4567 Canada Way, Burnaby, BC V5G 4T1, *Tel* (604) 268-5500	1,294,740,900	535	350	8699
DELOITTE MANAGEMENT SERVICES LP				
121 King St W Suite 300, Toronto, ON M5H 3T9, *Tel* (416) 775-2364	1,293,971,000	536	7,000	8721
ENERFLEX LTD				
1331 Macleod Trl Se Suite 904, Calgary, AB T2G 0K3, *Tel* (403) 387-6377	1,291,254,668	537	50	3563
LONDON DRUGS LIMITED (*Suby of* **H.Y. LOUIE CO. LIMITED**)				
12251 Horseshoe Way, Richmond, BC V7A 4X5, *Tel* (604) 272-7400	1,284,759,000	538	350	5912
SOCIETE DES ALCOOLS DU QUEBEC (*Suby of* **GOUVERNEMENT DE LA PROVINCE DE QUEBEC**)				
7500 Rue Tellier, Montreal, QC H1N 3W5, *Tel* (514) 254-6000	1,284,759,000	539	100	5921
FIRST CANADIAN TITLE COMPANY LIMITED (*Suby of* **FIRST AMERICAN FINANCIAL CORPORATION**)				
2235 Sheridan Garden Dr Suite 745, Oakville, ON L6J 7Y5, *Tel* (905) 287-1000	1,282,180,800	540	300	6361
SUN GRO HORTICULTURE CANADA LTD (*Suby of* **SUN GRO HORTICULTURE DISTRIBUTION INC.**)				
52130 Range Rd, Seba Beach, AB T0E 2B0, *Tel* (780) 797-3019	1,282,103,900	541	100	5159
SOVEREIGN GENERAL INSURANCE COMPANY, THE (*Suby of* **CO-OPERATORS GENERAL INSURANCE COMPANY**)				
6700 Macleod Trail Se Unit 140, Calgary, AB T2H 0L3, *Tel* (403) 298-4200	1,281,448,080	542	75	6411
LIVINGSTON INTERNATIONAL INC				
405 The West Mall Suite 400, Etobicoke, ON M9C 5K7, *Tel* (416) 626-2800	1,265,401,600	543	300	4731
ENTREPRISES MTY TIKI MING INC, LES (*Suby of* **GROUPE D'ALIMENTATION MTY INC**)				
8210 Rte Transcanadienne, Saint-Laurent, QC H4S 1M5, *Tel* (514) 336-8885	1,262,350,287	544	120	6794
ATCO ELECTRIC LTD (*Suby of* **ATCO LTD**)				
10035 105 St Nw, Edmonton, AB T5J 2V6, *Tel* (780) 420-7310	1,261,104,000	545	400	4911
SUNOPTA INC				
2233 Argentia Rd Suite 401, Mississauga, ON L5N 2X7, *Tel* (905) 821-9669	1,260,852,000	546	100	5149
STELCO INC (*Suby of* **BEDROCK INDUSTRIES**)				
386 Wilcox St, Hamilton, ON L8L 8K5, *Tel* (905) 528-2511	1,254,346,677	547	0	3312
7-ELEVEN CANADA, INC (*Suby of* **SEVEN & I HOLDINGS CO., LTD.**)				

COMPANY	SALES ($)	RANK	EMPLOYEES HERE	PRIMARY SIC CODE
13450 102 Ave Suite 2400, Surrey, BC V3T 0C3, *Tel* (604) 586-0711	1,251,016,000	548	120	5411
TECK COAL LIMITED (*Suby of* **TECK RESOURCES LIMITED**)				
205 9 Ave Se Suite 1000, Calgary, AB T2G 0R3, *Tel* (403) 767-8500	1,247,071,800	549	150	1221
DH CORPORATION (*Suby of* **VISTA EQUITY PARTNERS MANAGEMENT, LLC**)				
120 Bremner Blvd 30 Floor, Toronto, ON M5J 0A8, *Tel* (416) 696-7700	1,242,497,831	550	0	7371
WOLSELEY CANADA INC (*Suby of* **FERGUSON PLC**)				
880 Laurentian Dr Suite 1, Burlington, ON L7N 3V6, *Tel* (905) 335-7373	1,242,118,800	551	200	5074
NORTON ROSE FULBRIGHT CANADA LLP (*Suby of* **NORTON ROSE FULBRIGHT LLP**)				
400 3 Ave Sw Suite 3700, Calgary, AB T2P 4H2, *Tel* (403) 267-8222	1,235,256,000	552	300	8111
CRIUS ENERGY TRUST				
100 King St W Suite 3400, Toronto, ON M5X 1A4, *Tel* (416) 644-1753	1,235,112,000	553	8	4924
KRUGER INC				
3285 Ch De Bedford, Montreal, QC H3S 1G5, *Tel* (514) 343-3100	1,231,399,821	554	120	6712
EXTENDICARE (CANADA) INC (*Suby of* **EXTENDICARE INC**)				
3000 Steeles Ave E Suite 700, Markham, ON L3R 9W2, *Tel* (905) 470-1400	1,229,868,000	555	120	8051
ATB FINANCIAL (*Suby of* **GOVERNMENT OF THE PROVINCE OF ALBERTA**)				
10020 100 St Nw Suite 2100, Edmonton, AB T5J 0N3, *Tel* (780) 408-7000	1,227,656,561	556	200	6036
B2GOLD CORP				
595 Burrard St Suite 3100, Vancouver, BC V7X 1L7, *Tel* (604) 681-8371	1,225,061,000	557	400	1041
CINEPLEX INC				
1303 Yonge St Suite 300, Toronto, ON M4T 2Y9, *Tel* (416) 323-6600	1,224,200,546	558	300	7822
ALGOMA STEEL INC				
105 West St, Sault Ste. Marie, ON P6A 7B4, *Tel* (705) 945-2351	1,221,522,000	559	3,000	3312
FGF BRANDS INC				
1295 Ormont Dr, Toronto, ON M9L 2W6, *Tel* (905) 761-3333	1,218,462,500	560	125	2051
RIGHT AT HOME REALTY INC				
300 West Beaver Creek Rd Suite 202, Richmond Hill, ON L4B 3B1, *Tel* (905) 695-7888	1,217,030,400	561	3,600	6531
GIANT TIGER STORES LIMITED				
2480 Walkley Rd, Ottawa, ON K1G 6A9, *Tel* (613) 521-8222	1,216,864,000	562	350	5311
MDA SYSTEMS HOLDINGS LTD (*Suby of* **MAXAR TECHNOLOGIES INC.**)				
13800 Commerce Pkwy, Richmond, BC V6V 2J3, *Tel* (604) 278-3411	1,216,752,000	563	4,800	8748
TAQA NORTH LTD (*Suby of* **TAQA INTERNATIONAL HOLDINGS COOPERATIEF U.A.**)				
308 4 Ave Sw Suite 2100, Calgary, AB T2P 0H7, *Tel* (403) 724-5000	1,212,896,628	564	0	1311
HAMILTON HEALTH SCIENCES CORPORATION				
100 King St W Suite 2300, Hamilton, ON L8P 1A2, *Tel* (905) 521-2100	1,212,884,075	565	300	8062
CHEMTRADE LOGISTICS INCOME FUND				
155 Gordon Baker Rd Suite 300, North York, ON M2H 3N5, *Tel* (416) 496-5856	1,209,738,992	566	550	2819
INDUSTRIES LASSONDE INC (*Suby of* **3346625 CANADA INC**)				
755 Rue Principale, Rougemont, QC J0L 1M0, *Tel* (450) 469-4926	1,208,411,556	567	10	6712
PRICEWATERHOUSECOOPERS LLP				
18 York St Suite 2600, Toronto, ON M5J 0B2, *Tel* (416) 863-1133	1,201,544,500	568	2,200	8721
ALECTRA UTILITIES CORPORATION (*Suby of* **ALECTRA INC**)				
55 John St N, Hamilton, ON L8R 3M8, *Tel* (905) 522-9200	1,201,411,744	569	345	4911
NOVA CHEMICALS CORPORATION (*Suby of* **GOVERNMENT OF ABU DHABI**)				
1000 7 Ave Sw Suite 1000, Calgary, AB T2P 5L5, *Tel* (403) 750-3600	1,200,541,500	570	50	2821
CITI CARDS CANADA INC (*Suby of* **CITIGROUP INC.**)				
5900 Hurontario St, Mississauga, ON L5R 0B8, *Tel* (905) 285-7500	1,196,532,000	571	3,000	6153
ARIZONA SILVER EXPLORATION INC				
750 West Pender St Suite 804, Vancouver, BC V6C 2T7, *Tel* (604) 833-4278	1,193,774,500	572	500	1041
VERITIV CANADA, INC (*Suby of* **VERITIV CORPORATION**)				
4300 Rue Hickmore, Saint-Laurent, QC H4T 1K2, *Tel* (514) 367-3111	1,192,646,992	573	69	5111
ARTERRA WINES CANADA, INC (*Suby of* **ONTARIO TEACHERS' PENSION PLAN BOARD**)				
441 Courtneypark Dr E, Mississauga, ON L5T 2V3, *Tel* (905) 564-6900	1,188,244,630	574	150	2084
BFL CANADA INSURANCE SERVICES INC (*Suby of* **FIRST LION HOLDINGS INC**)				
1177 Hastings St W Suite 200, Vancouver, BC V6E 2K3, *Tel* (604) 669-9600	1,186,526,000	575	100	6411
BMO LIFE ASSURANCE COMPANY				
60 Yonge St, Toronto, ON M5E 1H5, *Tel* (416) 596-3900	1,186,526,000	576	230	6411
HOOPER-HOLMES CANADA LIMITED				
1059 Mcnicoll Ave, Scarborough, ON M1W 3W6, *Tel* (416) 493-2800	1,186,526,000	577	100	6411
HUESTIS INSURANCE GROUP				
11 Lloyd St, Saint John, NB E2M 4N4, *Tel* (506) 635-1515	1,181,779,896	578	10	6411
PUBLIC GUARDIAN AND TRUSTEE OF BRITISH COLUMBIA				
808 Hastings St W Suite 700, Vancouver, BC V6C 3L3, *Tel* (604) 660-4444	1,181,501,000	579	0	6733
OLD STEELCO INC (*Suby of* **ESSAR STEEL INDIA LIMITED**)				
105 West St, Sault Ste. Marie, ON P6A 7B4, *Tel* (705) 945-2351	1,180,804,600	580	2,300	3312
IKEA CANADA LIMITED PARTNERSHIP (*Suby of* **QINGDAO HONGYISEN CONSTRUCTION ENGINEERING SERVICE CO., LTD.**)				
1065 Plains Rd E, Burlington, ON L7T 4K1, *Tel* (905) 637-9440	1,180,427,478	581	569	5712
TURQUOISE HILL RESOURCES LTD				
200 Granville St Suite 354, Vancouver, BC V6C 1S4, *Tel* (604) 688-5755	1,180,022,000	582	0	1081
YMCA OF NIAGARA				
25 Ymca Dr, St Catharines, ON L2N 7P9, *Tel* (905) 646-9622	1,179,652,820	583	250	8699
NORTHLAND POWER INC				
30 St Clair Ave W 12 Fl, Toronto, ON M4V 3A1, *Tel* (416) 962-6262	1,179,293,616	584	300	4911

COMPANY	SALES ($)	RANK	EMPLOYEES HERE	PRIMARY SIC CODE
KAL TIRE LTD 1540 Kalamalka Lake Rd, Vernon, BC V1T 6V2, *Tel* (250) 542-2366	1,178,248,470	585	300	5014
AECOM PRODUCTION SERVICES LTD (*Suby of* **AECOM**) 6025 11 St Se Unit 240, Calgary, AB T2H 2Z2, *Tel* (403) 386-1000	1,177,188,250	586	100	1389
IKO INDUSTRIES LTD (*Suby of* **GOLDIS ENTERPRISES, INC.**) 80 Stafford Dr, Brampton, ON L6W 1L4, *Tel* (905) 457-2880	1,172,762,500	587	200	2952
NORTH ATLANTIC REFINING LIMITED (*Suby of* **SILVERPEAK STRATEGIC PARTNERS LP**) 29 Pippy Pl, St. John'S, NL A1B 3X2, *Tel* (709) 463-8811	1,172,762,500	588	600	2911
SUNCOR ENERGY PRODUCTS INC (*Suby of* **SUNCOR ENERGY INC**) 2489 North Sheridan Way, Mississauga, ON L5K 1A8, *Tel* (905) 804-4500	1,172,762,500	589	200	2911
SUNCOR ENERGY PRODUCTS PARTNERSHIP (*Suby of* **SUNCOR ENERGY INC**) 150 6 Ave Sw, Calgary, AB T2P 3Y7, *Tel* (403) 296-8000	1,172,762,500	590	200	2911
VIDEOTRON LTEE (*Suby of* **QUEBECOR MEDIA INC**) 612 Rue Saint-Jacques Bureau 700, Montreal, QC H3C 4M8, *Tel* (514) 281-1232	1,170,904,000	591	150	4841
RITCHIE BROS. AUCTIONEERS INCORPORATED 9500 Glenlyon Pky, Burnaby, BC V5J 0C6, *Tel* (778) 331-5500	1,170,026,000	592	350	7389
PRECISION DRILLING CORPORATION 525 8 Ave Sw Suite 800, Calgary, AB T2P 1G1, *Tel* (403) 716-4500	1,168,378,463	593	200	1381
ROGERS INSURANCE LTD 1331 Macleod Trl Se Suite 800, Calgary, AB T2G 0K3, *Tel* (403) 296-2400	1,167,541,584	594	130	6411
GESTION D'ACTIFS CIBC INC (*Suby of* **CANADIAN IMPERIAL BANK OF COMMERCE**) 1000 Rue De La Gauchetiere O Bureau 3100, Montreal, QC H3B 4W5, *Tel* (514) 875-7040	1,167,385,000	595	0	6726
MANULIFE SECURITIES INVESTMENT SERVICES INC (*Suby of* **MANULIFE FINANCIAL CORPORATION**) 1235 North Service Rd W Suite 500, Oakville, ON L6M 2W2, *Tel* (905) 469-2100	1,167,385,000	596	0	6722
WATEROUS ENERGY FUND 301 8 Ave Sw Suite 600, Calgary, AB T2P 1C5, *Tel* (403) 930-6048	1,167,385,000	597	0	6722
1032451 B.C. LTD (*Suby of* **QUEBECOR MEDIA INC**) 333 King St E Unit 1, Toronto, ON M5A 0E1, *Tel* (416) 947-2222	1,162,644,000	598	30	2711
PHILIPS ELECTRONICS LTD (*Suby of* **KONINKLIJKE PHILIPS N.V.**) 281 Hillmount Rd, Markham, ON L6C 2S3, *Tel* (905) 201-4100	1,160,494,000	599	300	5064
REXEL CANADA ELECTRICAL INC (*Suby of* **REXEL**) 5600 Keaton Cres, Mississauga, ON L5R 3G3, *Tel* (905) 712-4004	1,160,494,000	600	181	5063
BANK OF CANADA (*Suby of* **GOVERNMENT OF CANADA**) 234 Wellington St, Ottawa, ON K1A 0G9, *Tel* (613) 782-8111	1,159,154,222	601	1,111	6011
VERMILION ENERGY INC 520 3rd Ave Sw Suite 3500, Calgary, AB T2P 0R3, *Tel* (403) 269-4884	1,156,825,747	602	225	1382
WHITECAP RESOURCES INC 525 8 Ave Sw Unit 3800, Calgary, AB T2P 1G1, *Tel* (403) 817-2209	1,156,332,222	603	250	6719
AIR LIQUIDE CANADA INC 1250 Boul Rene-Levesque O Bureau 1700, Montreal, QC H3B 5E6, *Tel* (514) 933-0303	1,156,077,000	604	200	2813
TAIGA BUILDING PRODUCTS LTD 4710 Kingsway Suite 800, Burnaby, BC V5H 4M2, *Tel* (604) 438-1471	1,155,005,825	605	80	5031
LONGO BROTHERS FRUIT MARKETS INC 8800 Huntington Rd, Woodbridge, ON L4H 3M6, *Tel* (905) 264-4100	1,154,784,000	606	125	5411
BODY SHOP CANADA LIMITED, THE (*Suby of* **NATURA COSMETICOS S/A**) 1 Yorkdale Rd Suite 510, North York, ON M6A 3A1, *Tel* (416) 782-2948	1,154,546,268	607	35	6794
LORDCO PARTS LTD 22866 Dewdney Trunk Rd, Maple Ridge, BC V2X 3K6, *Tel* (604) 467-1581	1,154,504,000	608	1	5531
WEYERHAEUSER COMPANY LIMITED (*Suby of* **WEYERHAEUSER COMPANY**) 1140 Pender St W Suite 440, Vancouver, BC V6E 4G1, *Tel* (604) 661-8000	1,154,220,000	609	200	2421
KEYERA PARTNERSHIP 144 4 Ave Sw 2nd Fl Suite 600, Calgary, AB T2P 3N4, *Tel* (403) 205-8414	1,151,954,000	610	20	4925
ATI TECHNOLOGIES ULC (*Suby of* **ADVANCED MICRO DEVICES, INC.**) 1 Commerce Valley Dr E, Markham, ON L3T 7X6, *Tel* (905) 882-2600	1,151,595,700	611	0	3577
MILLER MAINTENANCE LIMITED 2064 Kennedy Rd, Scarborough, ON M1T 3V1, *Tel* (416) 332-1360	1,148,402,500	612	3,500	1611
ASSANTE CAPITAL MANAGEMENT LTD (*Suby of* **ASSANTE WEALTH MANAGEMENT (CANADA) LTD**) 2 Queen St E Suite 1900, Toronto, ON M5C 3G7, *Tel* (416) 348-9994	1,147,049,228	613	2	6211
CANADIAN FISHING COMPANY LIMITED, THE (*Suby of* **PATTISON, JIM GROUP INC**) 301 Waterfront Rd E, Vancouver, BC V6A 0B3, *Tel* (604) 681-0211	1,146,745,600	614	60	5146
GFL ENVIRONMENTAL INC 100 New Park Pl Suite 500, Vaughan, ON L4K 0H9, *Tel* (905) 326-0101	1,140,027,000	615	50	4953
JARDINE LLOYD THOMPSON CANADA INC (*Suby of* **JARDINE LLOYD THOMPSON GROUP LTD**) 1111 Georgia St W Suite 1600, Vancouver, BC V6E 4G2, *Tel* (604) 682-4211	1,139,064,960	616	85	6411
VITERRA INC (*Suby of* **GLENCORE PLC**) 2625 Victoria Ave, Regina, SK S4T 1Z8, *Tel* (306) 569-4411	1,137,630,770	617	300	4221
DOMINION DIAMOND CORPORATION (*Suby of* **WASHINGTON CORPORATIONS**) 4920 52 St Unit 900, Yellowknife, NT X1A 3T1, *Tel* (867) 669-6100	1,134,034,300	618	1	5094
CENTERRA GOLD INC 1 University Ave Suite 1500, Toronto, ON M5J 2P1, *Tel* (416) 204-1953	1,129,336,000	619	50	1081
UNIVERSITE DE MONTREAL 2900 Boul Edouard-Montpetit, Montreal, QC H3T 1J4, *Tel* (514) 343-6111	1,128,104,000	620	400	8221
RICOH CANADA INC (*Suby of* **RICOH COMPANY,LTD.**) 5560 Explorer Dr Suite 100, Mississauga, ON L4W 5M3, *Tel* (905) 795-9659	1,124,239,200	621	200	5044

COMPANY	SALES ($)	RANK	EMPLOYEES HERE	PRIMARY SIC CODE
WAJAX CORPORATION 3280 Wharton Way, Mississauga, ON L4X 2C5, *Tel* (905) 212-3300	1,123,201,649	622	0	5084
NEW BRUNSWICK POWER CORPORATION (*Suby of* **PROVINCE OF NEW BRUNSWICK**) 515 King St, Fredericton, NB E3B 1E7, *Tel* (506) 458-4444	1,118,401,075	623	0	4911
SOCIETE DE TRANSPORT DE MONTREAL 800 Rue De La Gauchetiere O Bureau 8420, Montreal, QC H5A 1J6, *Tel* (514) 786-4636	1,117,325,951	624	700	4111
MILLER PAVING LIMITED (*Suby of* **MILLER GROUP INC**) 505 Miller Ave, Markham, ON L6G 1B2, *Tel* (905) 475-6660	1,115,591,000	625	400	1611
HUB INTERNATIONAL HKMB LIMITED (*Suby of* **HELLMAN & FRIEDMAN LLC**) 595 Bay St Suite 900, Toronto, ON M5G 2E3, *Tel* (416) 597-0008	1,115,334,440	626	235	6411
RAYONIER A.M. CANADA INDUSTRIES INC (*Suby of* **RAYONIER A.M. GLOBAL HOLDINGS LUXEMBOURG SCS**) 4 Place Ville-Marie Bureau 100, Montreal, QC H3B 2E7, *Tel* (514) 871-0137	1,113,560,000	627	33	2421
CHARTWELL MASTER CARE LP 100 Milverton Dr Suite 700, Mississauga, ON L5R 4H1, *Tel* (905) 501-9219	1,113,484,000	628	0	8322
IAMGOLD CORPORATION 401 Bay St Suite 3200, Toronto, ON M5H 2Y4, *Tel* (416) 360-4710	1,111,000,000	629	55	1041
CENTRE HOSPITALIER DE L'UNIVERSITE DE MONTREAL 850 Rue Saint-Denis, Montreal, QC H2X 0A9, *Tel* (514) 890-8000	1,110,800,000	630	8,000	8062
I.M.P. GROUP INTERNATIONAL INCORPORATED 2651 Joseph Howe Dr, Halifax, NS B3L 4T1, *Tel* (902) 453-2400	1,110,732,000	631	75	4581
BELL MTS INC (*Suby of* **BCE INC**) 333 Main St, Winnipeg, MB R3C 4E2, *Tel* (204) 225-5687	1,107,860,728	632	1	4841
KIMBERLY-CLARK INC (*Suby of* **KIMBERLY-CLARK CORPORATION**) 50 Burnhamthorpe Rd W Suite 1402, Mississauga, ON L5B 3C2, *Tel* (905) 277-6500	1,102,911,000	633	80	2676
RAYONIER A.M. CANADA ENTERPRISES INC (*Suby of* **RAYONIER A.M. GLOBAL HOLDINGS LUXEMBOURG SCS**) 4 Place Ville-Marie Bureau 100, Montreal, QC H3B 2E7, *Tel* (514) 871-0137	1,102,911,000	634	0	2611
CHORUS AVIATION INC 3 Spectacle Lake Dr, Dartmouth, NS B3B 1W8, *Tel* (902) 873-5000	1,100,153,074	635	0	4512
GROUPE POMERLEAU INC 521 6e Av N, Saint-Georges, QC G5Y 0H1, *Tel* (418) 228-6688	1,096,527,000	636	1	6712
PTW ENERGY SERVICES LTD 355 4 Ave Sw Suite 600 Calgary Place Ii, Calgary, AB T2P 0J1, *Tel* (403) 956-8600	1,096,527,000	637	4	6712
SCHLUMBERGER CANADA LIMITED 125 9 Ave Se Suite 200, Calgary, AB T2G 0P6, *Tel* (403) 509-4000	1,091,942,000	638	200	1389
RBC INSURANCE COMPANY OF CANADA (*Suby of* **ROYAL BANK OF CANADA**) 6880 Financial Dr Suite 200, Mississauga, ON L5N 7Y5, *Tel* (905) 949-3663	1,091,603,920	639	120	6411
CARLTON CARDS LIMITED (*Suby of* **CLAYTON, DUBILIER & RICE, INC.**) 1820 Matheson Blvd Unit B1, Mississauga, ON L4W 0B3, *Tel* (905) 219-6410	1,088,792,900	640	60	5112
MARYNA (PRIVATE) LIMITED 9926 Keele St Unit 5444, Vaughan, ON L6A 3Y4, *Tel*	1,083,470,000	641	2,000	6726
ACKLANDS - GRAINGER INC (*Suby of* **W.W. GRAINGER, INC.**) 123 Commerce Valley Dr E Suite 700, Thornhill, ON L3T 7W8, *Tel* (905) 731-5516	1,077,883,300	642	350	5085
WASTE MANAGEMENT OF CANADA CORPORATION (*Suby of* **WASTE MANAGEMENT, INC.**) 219 Labrador Dr Suite 100, Waterloo, ON N2K 4M8, *Tel* (519) 886-3974	1,074,882,600	643	30	4953
GOODYEAR CANADA INC (*Suby of* **THE GOODYEAR TIRE & RUBBER COMPANY**) 450 Kipling Ave, Etobicoke, ON M8Z 5E1, *Tel* (416) 201-4300	1,074,654,000	644	200	3011
GREATER TORONTO AIRPORTS AUTHORITY 3111 Convair Dr, Mississauga, ON L5P 1B2, *Tel* (416) 776-3000	1,073,552,308	645	0	4581
ERICSSON CANADA INC (*Suby of* **TELEFON AB LM ERICSSON**) 8275 Rte Transcanadienne, Saint-Laurent, QC H4S 0B6, *Tel* (514) 738-8300	1,073,456,950	646	200	5065
SHOPIFY INC 150 Elgin St 8th Floor, Ottawa, ON K2P 1L4, *Tel* (613) 241-2828	1,073,229,000	647	1,800	7374
HUSKY INJECTION MOLDING SYSTEMS LTD 500 Queen St S, Bolton, ON L7E 5S5, *Tel* (905) 951-5000	1,073,134,424	648	500	6712
CUMIS GROUP LIMITED, THE 151 North Service Rd, Burlington, ON L7R 4C2, *Tel* (800) 263-9120	1,068,484,000	649	300	6311
EQUITABLE LIFE INSURANCE COMPANY OF CANADA, THE 1 Westmount Rd N, Waterloo, ON N2J 4C7, *Tel* (519) 886-5210	1,068,484,000	650	425	6311
IVARI CANADA ULC (*Suby of* **WILTON RE LTD**) 5000 Yonge St Unit 500, North York, ON M2N 7J8, *Tel* (416) 883-5000	1,068,484,000	651	500	6311
TARKETT INC (*Suby of* **SOCIETE INVESTISSEMENT DECONINCK**) 1001 Rue Yamaska E, Farnham, QC J2N 1J7, *Tel* (450) 293-3173	1,067,148,000	652	230	2851
NOVA CHEMICALS (CANADA) LTD (*Suby of* **GOVERNMENT OF ABU DHABI**) 1000 7 Ave Sw Suite 1000, Calgary, AB T2P 5L5, *Tel* (403) 750-3600	1,064,918,000	653	100	2869
MITEL NETWORKS CORPORATION 350 Legget Dr, Kanata, ON K2K 2W7, *Tel* (613) 592-2122	1,059,100,000	654	200	3661
CASH STORE FINANCIAL SERVICES INC, THE 15511 123 Ave Nw, Edmonton, AB T5V 0C3, *Tel* (780) 408-5110	1,057,340,000	655	0	6141
TORONTO HYDRO-ELECTRIC SYSTEM LIMITED (*Suby of* **CORPORATION OF THE CITY OF TORONTO**) 14 Carlton St, Toronto, ON M5B 1K5, *Tel* (416) 542-3100	1,053,804,700	656	170	4911
ARC RESOURCES LTD 308 4 Ave Sw Suite 1200, Calgary, AB T2P 0H7, *Tel* (403) 503-8600	1,053,382,729	657	250	1381
GROUPE INTERTAPE POLYMER INC, LE 9999 Boul Cavendish Bureau 200, Saint-Laurent, QC H4M 2X5, *Tel* (514) 731-7591	1,053,019,000	658	150	2672

COMPANY	SALES ($)	RANK	EMPLOYEES HERE	PRIMARY SIC CODE
HIGH LINER FOODS INCORPORATED				
100 Battery Pt, Lunenburg, NS B0J 2C0, *Tel* (902) 634-8811	1,048,531,000	659	250	2092
EBC INC				
1095 Rue Valets, L'Ancienne-Lorette, QC G2E 4M7, *Tel* (418) 872-0600	1,047,588,000	660	500	1541
QUINN CONTRACTING LTD				
27123 1 Hwy, Blackfalds, AB T0M 0J0, *Tel* (403) 885-4788	1,047,588,000	661	50	1541
BIRD CONSTRUCTION INC				
5700 Explorer Dr Suite 400, Mississauga, ON L4W 0C6, *Tel* (905) 602-4122	1,047,533,214	662	500	1542
ENERPLUS CORPORATION				
333 7 Ave Sw Suite 3000, Calgary, AB T2P 2Z1, *Tel* (403) 298-2200	1,046,914,603	663	400	1311
UNIVERSITY OF OTTAWA				
75 Laurier Ave E, Ottawa, ON K1N 6N5, *Tel* (613) 562-5700	1,045,737,000	664	0	8221
1716871 ONTARIO INC				
1460 Stone Church Rd E, Hamilton, ON L8W 3V3, *Tel* (905) 388-2264	1,043,264,700	665	45	6794
BROOKFIELD PROPERTY PARTNERS L.P.				
181 Bay St Suite 300, Toronto, ON M5J 2T3, *Tel* (416) 363-9491	1,043,264,700	666	300	6798
EMCO CORPORATION (*Suby of* **HAJOCA CORPORATION**)				
2124 Oxford St E, London, ON N5V 0B7, *Tel* (519) 453-9600	1,042,459,704	667	45	5074
CANFOR PULP PRODUCTS INC (*Suby of* **CANFOR CORPORATION**)				
1700 75th Ave W Unit 230, Vancouver, BC V6P 6G2, *Tel* (604) 661-5241	1,041,859,579	668	6	2621
VALEURS MOBILIERES DESJARDINS INC (*Suby of* **FEDERATION DES CAISSES DESJARDINS DU QUEBEC**)				
1170 Rue Peel Bureau 300, Montreal, QC H3B 0A9, *Tel* (514) 987-1749	1,041,737,016	669	200	6211
SYMCOR INC				
1 Robert Speck Pky Suite 400, Mississauga, ON L4Z 4E7, *Tel* (905) 273-1000	1,039,440,000	670	600	7374
GROUPE CANAM INC (*Suby of* **CANAM LUX PARENT COMPANY SARL**)				
11505 1re Av Bureau 500, Saint-Georges, QC G5Y 7H5, *Tel* (418) 228-8031	1,038,353,139	671	100	3441
A&W REVENUE ROYALTIES INCOME FUND				
171 Esplanade W Suite 300, North Vancouver, BC V7M 3K9, *Tel* (604) 988-2141	1,033,289,994	672	18,000	6722
NAV CANADA				
77 Metcalfe St, Ottawa, ON K1P 5L6, *Tel* (613) 563-5588	1,030,245,111	673	700	4899
BREWERS RETAIL INC				
5900 Explorer Dr, Mississauga, ON L4W 5L2, *Tel* (905) 361-1005	1,027,807,200	674	150	5921
POMERLEAU INC (*Suby of* **GROUPE POMERLEAU INC**)				
521 6e Av N, Saint-Georges, QC G5Y 0H1, *Tel* (418) 228-6688	1,027,565,073	675	125	1542
CHEMTRADE LOGISTICS INC (*Suby of* **CHEMTRADE LOGISTICS INCOME FUND**)				
155 Gordon Baker Rd Unit 300, North York, ON M2H 3N5, *Tel* (416) 496-5856	1,026,231,238	676	125	2819
COMPASS GROUP CANADA LTD (*Suby of* **COMPASS GROUP PLC**)				
1 Prologis Blvd Suite 400, Mississauga, ON L5W 0G2, *Tel* (905) 795-5100	1,026,058,000	677	150	5812
PERSONNELLE, COMPAGNIE D'ASSURANCES, LA (*Suby of* **FEDERATION DES CAISSES DESJARDINS DU QUEBEC**)				
3 Robert Speck Pky Suite 550, Mississauga, ON L4Z 3Z9, *Tel* (905) 306-5252	1,025,744,640	678	355	6331
CERVUS EQUIPMENT CORPORATION				
333 96 Ave Ne Suite 5201, Calgary, AB T3K 0S3, *Tel* (403) 567-0339	1,023,465,750	679	150	5084
NABORS DRILLING CANADA LIMITED				
500 4 Ave Sw Suite 2800, Calgary, AB T2P 2V6, *Tel* (403) 263-6777	1,022,603,683	680	0	1381
EXCEL INSURANCE AGENCY INC				
80 Acadia Ave Suite 205, Markham, ON L3R 9V1, *Tel* (905) 470-8222	1,020,412,360	681	215	6411
STELCO HOLDINGS INC (*Suby of* **BEDROCK INDUSTRIES**)				
386 Wilcox St, Hamilton, ON L8L 8K5, *Tel* (905) 528-2511	1,020,087,054	682	0	6712
CALGARY BOARD OF EDUCATION				
1221 8 St Sw, Calgary, AB T2R 0L4, *Tel* (403) 817-4000	1,012,138,044	683	200	8211
NEWFOUNDLAND & LABRADOR HYDRO (*Suby of* **PROVINCE OF NEWFOUNDLAND & LABRADOR**)				
500 Columbus Dr, St. John'S, NL A1B 4K7, *Tel* (709) 737-1400	1,008,883,200	684	300	4911
FONDATION DE L'HOPITAL GENERAL JUIF SIR MORTIMER B. DAVIS				
3755 Ch De La Cote-Sainte-Catherine Bureau A104, Montreal, QC H3T 1E2, *Tel* (514) 340-8251	1,008,214,092	685	4,869	8399
EURO SUN MINING INC				
65 Queen St W Suite 800, Toronto, ON M5H 2M5, *Tel* (416) 368-7744	1,007,545,678	686	0	1041
FONDATION DE L'UNIVERSITE DU QUEBEC EN OUTAOUAIS				
283 Boul Alexandre-Tache Bureau F-0239, Gatineau, QC J8X 3X7, *Tel* (819) 595-3900	1,006,297,776	687	6,736	8221
GUESS? CANADA CORPORATION (*Suby of* **GUESS? EUROPE, B.V.**)				
8275 19e Av, Montreal, QC H1Z 4K2, *Tel* (514) 593-4107	1,005,039,600	688	58	5136
BELL MEDIA INC (*Suby of* **BCE INC**)				
299 Queen St W, Toronto, ON M5V 2Z5, *Tel* (416) 591-5757	1,003,632,000	689	1,200	4833
ERB INTERNATIONAL INC				
290 Hamilton Rd, New Hamburg, ON N3A 1A2, *Tel* (519) 662-2710	1,003,362,000	690	0	7389
MMCC SOLUTIONS CANADA COMPANY (*Suby of* **TELEPERFORMANCE SE**)				
75 Eglinton Ave E, Toronto, ON M4P 3A4, *Tel* (416) 922-3519	1,003,362,000	691	500	7389
PEACE HILLS GENERAL INSURANCE COMPANY (*Suby of* **SAMSON CREE NATION**)				
10709 Jasper Ave Nw Suite 300, Edmonton, AB T5J 3N3, *Tel* (780) 424-3986	996,681,840	692	130	6411
CI INVESTMENTS INC (*Suby of* **CI FINANCIAL CORP**)				
1 Queen St E Suite 2000, Toronto, ON M5C 3W5, *Tel* (416) 364-1145	996,196,600	693	0	6282
MERCER (CANADA) LIMITED (*Suby of* **MARSH & MCLENNAN COMPANIES, INC.**)				
120 Bremner Blvd Suite 800, Toronto, ON M5J 0A8, *Tel* (416) 868-2000	994,619,200	694	600	6411
RBC GENERAL INSURANCE COMPANY (*Suby of* **ROYAL BANK OF CANADA**)				

COMPANY	SALES ($)	RANK	EMPLOYEES HERE	PRIMARY SIC CODE
6880 Financial Dr Suite 200, Mississauga, ON L5N 7Y5, Tel (905) 816-5400	993,690,120	695	410	6331
SOCIETE DE PORTEFEUILLE ET D'ACQUISITION BANQUE NATIONAL INC (Suby of BANQUE NATIONALE DU CANADA)				
600 Rue De La Gauchetiere O Bureau 11e, Montreal, QC H3B 4L2, Tel (514) 394-4385	992,722,444	696	500	6712
SONEPAR CANADA INC (Suby of SOCIETE DE NEGOCE ET DE PARTICIPATION)				
250 Chrysler Dr Unit 4, Brampton, ON L6S 6B6, Tel (905) 696-2838	986,419,900	697	150	5063
ENERCARE INC				
7400 Birchmount Rd, Markham, ON L3R 5V4, Tel (416) 649-1900	985,751,958	698	9	6712
PEACE RIVER HYDRO PARTNERS CONSTRUCTION LTD				
7007 269 Rd, Fort St. John, BC V1J 4M7, Tel (250) 263-9920	984,345,000	699	3,000	1629
UNITED FARMERS OF ALBERTA CO-OPERATIVE LIMITED				
4838 Richard Rd Sw Suite 700, Calgary, AB T3E 6L1, Tel (403) 570-4500	984,191,607	700	300	5172
HALLIBURTON GROUP CANADA INC (Suby of HALLIBURTON COMPANY)				
645 7 Ave Sw Suite 1600, Calgary, AB T2P 4G8, Tel (403) 231-9300	982,747,800	701	200	1389
JOHNSTON, MEIER INSURANCE AGENCIES LTD				
22367 Dewdney Trunk Rd, Maple Ridge, BC V2X 3J4, Tel (604) 467-4184	982,443,528	702	35	6411
PF RESOLU CANADA INC (Suby of RESOLUTE FOREST PRODUCTS INC)				
111 Boul Robert-Bourassa Unite 5000, Montreal, QC H3C 2M1, Tel (514) 875-2160	979,984,431	703	150	0831
CANWEL BUILDING MATERIALS GROUP LTD				
1055 Georgia St W Suite 1100, Vancouver, BC V6E 0B6, Tel (604) 432-1400	978,933,322	704	135	5039
PPG CANADA INC (Suby of PPG INDUSTRIES, INC.)				
8200 Keele St, Concord, ON L4K 2A5, Tel (905) 669-1020	978,219,000	705	50	2851
DYNACARE-GAMMA LABORATORY PARTNERSHIP (Suby of LABORATORY CORPORATION OF AMERICA HOLDINGS)				
115 Midair Crt, Brampton, ON L6T 5M3, Tel (905) 790-3515	977,913,000	706	700	8071
LIFELABS LP				
1290 Ellesmere Rd, Scarborough, ON M1P 2X9, Tel (416) 291-1464	977,913,000	707	600	8071
ELLISDON CORPORATION (Suby of ELLISDON HOLDINGS INC)				
2045 Oxford St E, London, ON N5V 2Z7, Tel (519) 455-6770	977,748,800	708	0	1542
AON PARIZEAU INC (Suby of AON PLC)				
700 Rue De La Gauchetiere O Bureau 1700, Montreal, QC H3B 0A4, Tel (514) 842-5000	977,697,424	709	200	6411
SMS EQUIPMENT INC (Suby of SUMITOMO CORPORATION)				
11285 274 St, Acheson, AB T7X 6P9, Tel (780) 454-0101	975,460,000	710	200	5082
GENERAL MILLS CANADA CORPORATION (Suby of GENERAL MILLS, INC.)				
5825 Explorer Dr, Mississauga, ON L4W 5P6, Tel (905) 212-4000	974,770,000	711	1,000	2041
PBL INSURANCE LIMITED (Suby of NFP INTERMEDIATE HOLDINGS B CORP.)				
150 Ouellette Pl Suite 100, Windsor, ON N8X 1L9, Tel (519) 254-1633	972,951,320	712	30	6411
POSTMEDIA NETWORK INC (Suby of POSTMEDIA NETWORK CANADA CORP)				
365 Bloor St E Suite 1601, Toronto, ON M4W 3L4, Tel (416) 383-2300	968,870,000	713	200	2711
CES ENERGY SOLUTIONS CORP				
332 6 Ave Sw Suite 1400, Calgary, AB T2P 0B2, Tel (403) 269-2800	963,586,305	714	115	1382
2104225 ONTARIO LTD (Suby of GEORGE WESTON LIMITED)				
1425 The Queensway, Etobicoke, ON M8Z 1T3, Tel (416) 252-7323	962,585,375	715	200	2051
T & T SUPERMARKET INC (Suby of LOBLAW COMPANIES LIMITED)				
21500 Gordon Way, Richmond, BC V6W 1J8, Tel (604) 276-9889	962,320,000	716	500	5411
AXA INSURANCE (CANADA) (Suby of AXA ASSURANCES INC)				
5700 Yonge St Suite 1400, North York, ON M2M 4K2, Tel (416) 218-4175	961,635,600	717	200	6331
DON MICHAEL HOLDINGS INC				
1400 Castlefield Ave Suite 2, Toronto, ON M6B 4N4, Tel (416) 781-3574	959,286,000	718	350	3143
UNIVERSITY OF WESTERN ONTARIO, THE				
1151 Richmond St Suite 2, London, ON N6A 5B8, Tel (519) 661-2111	958,199,021	719	3,000	8221
MULLEN GROUP LTD				
31 Southridge Dr Suite 121a, Okotoks, AB T1S 2N3, Tel (403) 995-5200	955,813,485	720	45	1389
4093879 CANADA LTD				
1771 Inkster Blvd, Winnipeg, MB R2X 1R3, Tel (204) 982-5783	950,323,400	721	2,600	6712
AZGA INSURANCE AGENCY CANADA LTD (Suby of ALLIANZ SE)				
4273 King St E, Kitchener, ON N2P 2E9, Tel (519) 742-2800	949,220,800	722	200	6411
NORTHBRIDGE INDEMNITY INSURANCE CORPORATION (Suby of FAIRFAX FINANCIAL HOLDINGS LIMITED)				
595 Burrard St Suite 1500, Vancouver, BC V7X 1G4, Tel (604) 683-5511	949,220,800	723	178	6411
ZURICH INSURANCE COMPANY LTD (Suby of ZURICH INSURANCE GROUP AG)				
100 King St W Suite 5500, Toronto, ON M5X 2A1, Tel (416) 586-3000	949,220,800	724	50	6411
ATS AUTOMATION TOOLING SYSTEMS INC				
730 Fountain St Suite 2b, Cambridge, ON N3H 4R7, Tel (519) 653-6500	947,897,920	725	100	3569
CAPITAL POWER CORPORATION				
10423 101 St Nw Suite 1200, Edmonton, AB T5H 0E9, Tel (780) 392-5100	946,869,398	726	350	4911
SASKATCHEWAN CROP INSURANCE CORPORATION (Suby of GOVERNMENT OF SASKATCHEWAN)				
484 Prince William Dr, Melville, SK S0A 2P0, Tel (306) 728-7200	946,676,824	727	121	6331
MASTRONARDI PRODUCE LIMITED				
2100 Road 4 E, Kingsville, ON N9Y 2E5, Tel (519) 326-3218	946,065,120	728	460	5148
FORTISBC ENERGY INC (Suby of FORTIS INC)				
16705 Fraser Hwy, Surrey, BC V4N 0E8, Tel (604) 576-7000	939,388,923	729	300	4923
QUEEN'S UNIVERSITY AT KINGSTON				
99 University Ave, Kingston, ON K7L 3N5, Tel (613) 533-2000	938,300,502	730	6,534	8221

EVRAZ INC. NA CANADA (Suby of EVRAZ PLC)

COMPANY	SALES ($)	RANK	EMPLOYEES HERE	PRIMARY SIC CODE
100 Armour Rd, Regina, SK S4P 3C7, *Tel* (306) 924-7700	936,500,200	731	1,000	3312
AGRICULTURE FINANCIAL SERVICES CORPORATION (*Suby of* **GOVERNMENT OF THE PROVINCE OF ALBERTA**)				
5718 56 Ave, Lacombe, AB T4L 1B1, *Tel* (403) 782-8200	933,659,377	732	300	6159
ESIT CANADA ENTERPRISE SERVICES CO (*Suby of* **DXC TECHNOLOGY COMPANY**)				
1969 Upper Water St, Halifax, NS B3J 3R7, *Tel* (902) 000-0000	933,460,500	733	885	5734
AON REED STENHOUSE INC (*Suby of* **AON PLC**)				
20 Bay St Suite 2400, Toronto, ON M5J 2N8, *Tel* (416) 868-5500	932,455,500	734	314	6411
NORANDA INCOME FUND				
100 King St W Suite 6900, Toronto, ON M5X 2A1, *Tel* (416) 775-1500	931,298,000	735	0	6722
KMC MINING CORPORATION				
28712 114 Ave, Acheson, AB T7X 6E6, *Tel* (780) 454-0664	927,291,000	736	500	1311
GREAT CANADIAN GAMING CORPORATION				
95 Schooner St, Coquitlam, BC V3K 7A8, *Tel* (604) 303-1000	925,642,542	737	9,350	7999
WORKERS' COMPENSATION BOARD ALBERTA (*Suby of* **GOVERNMENT OF THE PROVINCE OF ALBERTA**)				
9912 107 St Nw, Edmonton, AB T5K 1G5, *Tel* (780) 498-3999	924,934,475	738	500	6331
KPMG LLP				
333 Bay St Suite 4600, Toronto, ON M5H 2S5, *Tel* (416) 777-8500	924,265,000	739	150	8721
FOUNTAIN TIRE LTD				
1006 103a St Sw Suite 103, Edmonton, AB T6W 2P6, *Tel* (780) 464-3700	923,603,200	740	200	5531
KATZ GROUP INC				
10104 103 Ave Nw Suite 1702, Edmonton, AB T5J 0H8, *Tel* (780) 990-0505	922,456,962	741	2	5912
ADESA AUCTIONS CANADA CORPORATION (*Suby of* **KAR AUCTION SERVICES, INC.**)				
55 Auction Lane 2nd Floor, Brampton, ON L6T 5P4, *Tel* (905) 790-7653	922,308,000	742	35	5012
NORTH WEST COMPANY LP, THE				
77 Main St, Winnipeg, MB R3C 1A3, *Tel* (204) 943-0881	921,813,698	743	391	6712
HIGHLANDS FUEL DELIVERY G.P.				
201 Crown St, Saint John, NB E2L 5E5, *Tel* (506) 202-2000	921,563,200	744	150	4924
WOLSELEY HOLDINGS CANADA INC (*Suby of* **FERGUSON PLC**)				
880 Laurentian Dr Suite 1, Burlington, ON L7N 3V6, *Tel* (905) 335-7373	917,793,099	745	8	6712
GESTION AUDEM INC				
5 Place Ville-Marie Bureau 915, Montreal, QC H3B 2G2, *Tel* (514) 874-2600	917,772,024	746	5	4833
ALCOA CANADA CIE (*Suby of* **ALUMINERIE LAURALCO SARL**)				
1 Place Ville-Marie Bureau 2310, Montreal, QC H3B 3M5, *Tel* (514) 904-5030	916,955,848	747	100	3334
RICHARDSON MILLING LIMITED (*Suby of* **RICHARDSON, JAMES & SONS, LIMITED**)				
1 Can-Oat Dr, Portage La Prairie, MB R1N 3W1, *Tel* (204) 857-9700	915,788,500	748	500	5153
RICHARDSON PIONEER LIMITED (*Suby of* **RICHARDSON, JAMES & SONS, LIMITED**)				
1 Lombard Pl Suite 2700, Winnipeg, MB R3B 0X8, *Tel* (204) 934-5961	915,788,500	749	100	5153
SHRED-IT INTERNATIONAL ULC (*Suby of* **STERICYCLE, INC.**)				
1383 North Service Rd E, Oakville, ON L6H 1A7, *Tel* (905) 829-2794	915,243,000	750	700	7389
EXCHANGE INCOME CORPORATION				
1067 Sherwin Rd, Winnipeg, MB R3H 0T8, *Tel* (204) 982-1857	912,293,882	751	17	8249
GROUPE COLABOR INC				
1620 Boul De Montarville, Boucherville, QC J4B 8P4, *Tel* (450) 449-4911	911,933,025	752	10	5141
KRUGER PRODUCTS L.P. (*Suby of* **KRUGER INC**)				
1900 Minnesota Crt Suite 200, Mississauga, ON L5N 5R5, *Tel* (905) 812-6900	908,207,137	753	100	2621
ELLISDON HOLDINGS INC				
2045 Oxford St E, London, ON N5V 2Z7, *Tel* (519) 455-6770	907,909,600	754	0	1542
ROYAL INSTITUTE FOR ADVANCEMENT OF LEARNING MCGILL				
845 Sherbrooke Street West, Montreal, QC H3A 0G4, *Tel* (514) 398-8120	907,318,348	755	500	8221
WESTERN FOREST PRODUCTS INC				
800-1055 Georgia St W, Vancouver, BC V6E 0B6, *Tel* (604) 648-4500	907,220,663	756	40	2611
OTTAWA HOSPITAL, THE				
1053 Carling Ave, Ottawa, ON K1Y 4E9, *Tel* (613) 798-5555	905,085,755	757	2,000	8062
BLACKBERRY LIMITED				
2200 University Ave E, Waterloo, ON N2K 0A7, *Tel* (519) 888-7465	904,000,000	758	500	7371
RECIPE UNLIMITED CORPORATION				
199 Four Valley Dr, Concord, ON L4K 0B8, *Tel* (905) 760-2244	903,606,033	759	250	5812
HYDRO OTTAWA HOLDING INC (*Suby of* **CITY OF OTTAWA**)				
3025 Albion Rd N, Ottawa, ON K1V 9V9, *Tel* (613) 738-5499	902,137,726	760	0	4911
TORONTO CATHOLIC DISTRICT SCHOOL BOARD				
80 Sheppard Ave E, North York, ON M2N 6E8, *Tel* (416) 222-8282	901,710,547	761	302	8211
CHUBB INSURANCE COMPANY OF CANADA (*Suby of* **CHUBB LIMITED**)				
199 Bay St Suite 2500, Toronto, ON M5L 1E2, *Tel* (416) 863-0550	897,526,560	762	250	6331
EGR INC (*Suby of* **GROUPE FINANCIER ESSOR INC**)				
1100 Boul Robert-Bourassa 6e Etage, Montreal, QC H3B 3A5, *Tel* (514) 370-4800	897,013,656	763	20	6411
REGIONAL HEALTH AUTHORITY NB (*Suby of* **PROVINCE OF NEW BRUNSWICK**)				
180 Woodbridge St, Fredericton, NB E3B 4R3, *Tel* (506) 623-5500	893,794,100	764	1,000	8062
RIOCAN MANAGEMENT INC				
2300 Yonge St Suite 500, Toronto, ON M4P 1E4, *Tel* (800) 465-2733	893,684,792	765	0	6531
COMMISSION SCOLAIRE DE LAVAL				
955 Boul Saint-Martin O Bureau 144, Cote Saint-Luc, QC H7S 1M5, *Tel* (450) 662-7000	892,071,000	766	40	8211
H&R REAL ESTATE INVESTMENT TRUST				
3625 Dufferin St Suite 500, North York, ON M3K 1Z2, *Tel* (416) 635-7520	891,950,973	767	7	6798

COMPANY	SALES ($)	RANK	EMPLOYEES HERE	PRIMARY SIC CODE
CORPORATION MORGUARD 55 City Centre Dr Suite 800, Mississauga, ON L5B 1M3, *Tel* (905) 281-3800	890,866,887	768	350	6531
WINPAK LTD 100 Saulteaux Cres, Winnipeg, MB R3J 3T3, *Tel* (204) 889-1015	889,641,000	769	601	3081
COLAS CANADA INC (*Suby of* **BOUYGUES**) 4950 Yonge St Suite 2400, Toronto, ON M2N 6K1, *Tel* (416) 293-5443	889,519,765	770	25	1611
3M CANADA COMPANY (*Suby of* **3M COMPANY**) 300 Tartan Dr, London, ON N5V 4M9, *Tel* (519) 451-2500	889,290,000	771	1,200	2891
DOW CHEMICAL CANADA ULC (*Suby of* **DOW INC.**) 215 2 St Sw Suite 2400, Calgary, AB T2P 1M4, *Tel* (403) 267-3500	889,290,000	772	25	2899
PIONEER HI-BRED LIMITED (*Suby of* **DUPONT DE NEMOURS, INC.**) 1919 Minnesota Crt, Mississauga, ON L5N 0C9, *Tel* (905) 821-3300	889,290,000	773	300	2824
HATCHCOS HOLDINGS LTD 2800 Speakman Dr, Mississauga, ON L5K 2R7, *Tel* (905) 855-7600	887,089,500	774	2,100	8711
EDMONTON SCHOOL DISTRICT NO. 7 1 Kingsway Nw, Edmonton, AB T5H 4G9, *Tel* (780) 429-8000	885,038,806	775	500	8211
SUNNYBROOK HEALTH SCIENCES CENTRE 2075 Bayview Ave, Toronto, ON M4N 3M5, *Tel* (416) 480-6100	882,520,338	776	7,000	8062
ATLANTIC PACKAGING PRODUCTS LTD 111 Progress Ave, Scarborough, ON M1P 2Y9, *Tel* (416) 298-8101	882,328,800	777	200	2679
COGIR APARTMENTS REAL ESTATE INVESTMENT TRUST 7250 Boul Taschereau Bureau 200, Brossard, QC J4W 1M9, *Tel* (450) 672-5090	878,966,400	778	2,100	6531
SMS CONSTRUCTION AND MINING SYSTEMS INC (*Suby of* **SUMITOMO CORPORATION**) 53113 Range Road 263a, Acheson, AB T7X 5A5, *Tel* (780) 948-2200	877,914,000	779	106	5082
ENSIGN ENERGY SERVICES INC 400 5 Ave Sw Suite 1000, Calgary, AB T2P 0L6, *Tel* (403) 262-1361	876,636,554	780	450	1381
DESSAU INC (*Suby of* **GROUPE DESSAU INC**) 1200 Boul Saint-Martin O Bureau 300, Montreal, QC H7S 2E4, *Tel* (514) 281-1010	876,578,200	781	150	8742
CONNOR CLARK & LUNN PRIVATE CAPITAL LTD 130 King St W Unit 1400, Toronto, ON M5X 2A2, *Tel* (416) 214-6325	875,538,750	782	50	6722
IDL PROJECTS INC 1088 Great St, Prince George, BC V2N 2K8, *Tel* (250) 649-0561	872,990,000	783	1,250	1542
MAGNA EXTERIORS INC (*Suby of* **MAGNA INTERNATIONAL INC**) 50 Casmir Crt, Concord, ON L4K 4J5, *Tel* (905) 669-2888	872,550,000	784	1,000	3714
CHOICE PROPERTIES REAL ESTATE INVESTMENT TRUST 175 Bloor St E Suite 1400n, Toronto, ON M4W 3R8, *Tel* (416) 324-7840	870,508,058	785	1	6798
RIOCAN REAL ESTATE INVESTMENT TRUST 2300 Yonge St Suite 500, Toronto, ON M4P 1E4, *Tel* (416) 866-3033	870,181,316	786	100	6798
WASTE CONNECTIONS OF CANADA INC (*Suby of* **WASTE CONNECTIONS, INC**) 610 Applewood Cres, Concord, ON L4K 0E3, *Tel* (905) 532-7510	869,677,740	787	70	4953
WINDSOR BUILDING SUPPLIES LTD 20039 96 Ave, Langley, BC V1M 3C6, *Tel* (604) 455-9663	869,387,250	788	45	6794
H.Y. LOUIE CO. LIMITED 2821 Production Way, Burnaby, BC V5A 3G7, *Tel* (604) 421-4242	866,088,000	789	100	5411
NORTHLAND PROPERTIES CORPORATION 1755 Broadway W Suite 310, Vancouver, BC V6J 4S5, *Tel* (604) 730-6610	861,012,000	790	60	7011
BOULANGERIE VACHON INC (*Suby of* **GRUPO BIMBO, S.A.B. DE C.V.**) 8770 Boul Langelier Bureau 230, Saint-Leonard, QC H1P 3C6, *Tel* (514) 326-5084	860,059,200	791	50	5149
HARDWOODS DISTRIBUTION INC 9440 202 St Unit 306, Langley, BC V1M 4A6, *Tel* (604) 881-1988	859,890,081	792	0	5031
EXTENDICARE INC 3000 Steeles Ave E Suite 103, Markham, ON L3R 4T9, *Tel* (905) 470-4000	859,733,600	793	50	8051
LONDON HEALTH SCIENCES CENTRE 800 Commissioners Rd E, London, ON N6A 5W9, *Tel* (519) 685-8500	857,946,895	794	4,000	8062
ATLANTIC LOTTERY CORPORATION INC 922 Main St, Moncton, NB E1C 8W6, *Tel* (506) 867-5800	854,510,956	795	320	7999
GRAYMONT LIMITED 10991 Shellbridge Way Suite 200, Richmond, BC V6X 3C6, *Tel* (604) 207-4292	854,442,000	796	7	5032
PORTAGE LA PRAIRIE MUTUAL INSURANCE CO, THE 749 Saskatchewan Ave E, Portage La Prairie, MB R1N 0L3, *Tel* (204) 857-3415	854,298,720	797	82	6411
INTERNATIONAL FINANCIAL DATA SERVICES (CANADA) LIMITED 30 Adelaide St E Suite 1, Toronto, ON M5C 3G9, *Tel* (416) 506-8000	853,882,800	798	600	6289
SOURCE (BELL) ELECTRONICS INC, THE (*Suby of* **BCE INC**) 279 Bayview Dr, Barrie, ON L4M 4W5, *Tel* (705) 728-2262	853,449,600	799	372	5731
CELESTICA INTERNATIONAL INC (*Suby of* **ONEX CORPORATION**) 844 Don Mills Rd, North York, ON M3C 1V7, *Tel* (416) 448-5800	848,745,000	800	0	3679
MCMASTER UNIVERSITY 1280 Main St W Gh209, Hamilton, ON L8S 4L8, *Tel* (905) 525-9140	848,003,126	801	0	8221
DALHOUSIE UNIVERSITY 6299 South St, Halifax, NS B3H 4J1, *Tel* (902) 494-2211	846,078,000	802	0	8221
FARM CREDIT CANADA (*Suby of* **GOVERNMENT OF CANADA**) 1800 Hamilton St, Regina, SK S4P 4L3, *Tel* (306) 780-8100	845,872,000	803	700	6159
BAYTEX ENERGY CORP 520 3 Ave Sw Suite 2800, Calgary, AB T2P 0R3, *Tel* (587) 952-3000	845,371,670	804	147	1311

COMPANY	SALES ($)	RANK	EMPLOYEES HERE	PRIMARY SIC CODE
PROCTER & GAMBLE INC (*Suby of* **THE PROCTER & GAMBLE COMPANY**) 4711 Yonge St, North York, ON M2N 6K8, *Tel* (416) 730-4711	844,825,500	805	700	2841
BRACKNELL CORPORATION 195 The West Mall Ste 302, Toronto, ON M9C 5K1, *Tel*	843,661,000	806	7,000	1711
CRH CANADA GROUP INC (*Suby of* **CRH PUBLIC LIMITED COMPANY**) 2300 Steeles Ave W Suite 400, Concord, ON L4K 5X6, *Tel* (905) 532-3000	842,631,000	807	120	3531
ENMAX ENERGY CORPORATION (*Suby of* **CITY OF CALGARY, THE**) 141 50 Ave Se Suite 2708, Calgary, AB T2G 4S7, *Tel* (403) 514-3000	840,736,000	808	990	4911
REXEL AMERIQUE DU NORD INC (*Suby of* **REXEL**) 505 Rue Locke Bureau 202, Saint-Laurent, QC H4T 1X7, *Tel* (514) 332-5331	840,670,700	809	3	6712
CORIX INFRASTRUCTURE INC 1188 Georgia St W Suite 1160, Vancouver, BC V6E 4A2, *Tel* (604) 697-6700	839,574,173	810	120	6712
ELLISDON CONSTRUCTION LTD (*Suby of* **ELLISDON HOLDINGS INC**) 2045 Oxford St E, London, ON N5V 2Z7, *Tel* (519) 455-6770	838,070,400	811	120	1541
GRAHAM GROUP LTD 10840 27 St Se, Calgary, AB T2Z 3R6, *Tel* (403) 570-5000	838,070,400	812	75	1542
MUNICIPAL ENTERPRISES LIMITED 927 Rocky Lake Dr, Bedford, NS B4A 2T3, *Tel* (902) 835-3381	837,687,500	813	250	2951
GENUINE CANADIAN CORP, THE (*Suby of* **CARTER'S, INC.**) 1 Prologis Blvd, Mississauga, ON L5W 0G2, *Tel* (519) 624-6574	837,533,000	814	75	5137
GDI SERVICES AUX IMMEUBLES INC 695 90e Av, Lasalle, QC H8R 3A4, *Tel* (514) 368-1504	836,563,283	815	6	7349
PAREX RESOURCES INC 2700 Eighth Ave Pl West Tower 585 8 Ave Sw, Calgary, AB T2P 1G1, *Tel* (403) 265-4800	832,988,000	816	6	1382
CANADIAN BLOOD SERVICES 1800 Alta Vista Dr, Ottawa, ON K1G 4J5, *Tel* (613) 739-2300	830,976,351	817	400	8099
VERSACOLD INTERNATIONAL CORPORATION 2115 Commissioner St Suite 1, Vancouver, BC V5L 1A6, *Tel* (604) 255-4656	829,714,500	818	3	4222
DOMINION DIAMOND EKATI ULC (*Suby of* **WASHINGTON CORPORATIONS**) 4920 52 St Suite 900, Yellowknife, NT X1A 3A3, *Tel* (867) 669-9292	826,218,000	819	50	1499
XEROX CANADA LTD (*Suby of* **XEROX CORPORATION**) 20 York Mills Rd Suite 500, North York, ON M2P 2C2, *Tel* (416) 733-6501	825,916,500	820	350	5999
INDIGO BOOKS & MUSIC INC 620 King St W, Toronto, ON M5V 1M6, *Tel* (416) 364-4499	824,980,780	821	200	5942
HONEYWELL LIMITED (*Suby of* **HONEYWELL INTERNATIONAL INC.**) 3333 Unity Dr, Mississauga, ON L5L 3S6, *Tel* (905) 608-6000	823,110,000	822	100	3822
JOHNSON & JOHNSON INC (*Suby of* **JOHNSON & JOHNSON**) 88 Mcnabb St, Markham, ON L3R 5L2, *Tel* (905) 968-2000	823,110,000	823	350	3842
WORLEYCORD LP (*Suby of* **WORLEYPARSONS LIMITED**) 8500 Macleod Trail Se Suite 400, Calgary, AB T2H 2N1, *Tel* (780) 465-5516	820,287,500	824	1,500	1629
REPSOL CANADA ENERGY PARTNERSHIP (*Suby of* **REPSOL SA.**) 888 3 St Sw Suite 2000, Calgary, AB T2P 5C5, *Tel* (403) 237-1234	818,956,500	825	200	1382
E-L FINANCIAL CORPORATION LIMITED 165 University Ave 10th Fl, Toronto, ON M5H 3B8, *Tel* (416) 947-2578	816,242,359	826	8	6282
COMPAGNIE AMERICAINE DE FER & METAUX INC, LA 9100 Boul Henri-Bourassa E, Montreal-Est, QC H1E 2S4, *Tel* (514) 494-2000	814,348,000	827	450	3341
INDUSTRIELLE ALLIANCE, ASSURANCE AUTO ET HABITATION INC (*Suby of* **INDUSTRIELLE ALLIANCE, ASSURANCE ET SERVICES FINANCIERS INC**) 925 Grande Allee O Bureau 230, Quebec, QC G1S 1C1, *Tel* (418) 650-4600	812,047,840	828	0	6331
ZAYO CANADA INC (*Suby of* **ZAYO GROUP HOLDINGS, INC.**) 200 Wellington St W Suite 800, Toronto, ON M5V 3C7, *Tel* (416) 363-4444	811,603,744	829	120	4899
JAKKS PACIFIC (CANADA), INC (*Suby of* **JAKKS PACIFIC, INC.**) 125 Edgeware Rd Suite 15, Brampton, ON L6Y 0P5, *Tel* (905) 452-6279	810,060,000	830	12	3944
COMMISSION SCOLAIRE DE MONTREAL 3737 Rue Sherbrooke E, Montreal, QC H1X 3B3, *Tel* (514) 596-6000	809,009,278	831	367	8211
WOOD CANADA LIMITED (*Suby of* **JOHN WOOD GROUP P.L.C.**) 2020 Winston Park Dr Suite 700, Oakville, ON L6H 6X7, *Tel* (905) 829-5400	807,861,600	832	450	8741
HUB INTERNATIONAL INSURANCE BROKERS (*Suby of* **HELLMAN & FRIEDMAN LLC**) 4350 Still Creek Dr Suite 400, Burnaby, BC V5C 0G5, *Tel* (604) 293-1481	806,837,680	833	170	6411
WESTERN FINANCIAL GROUP (NETWORK) INC (*Suby of* **WESTERN FINANCIAL GROUP INC**) 1010 24 St Se, High River, AB T1V 2A7, *Tel* (403) 652-2663	806,837,680	834	5	6411
BANQUE LAURENTIENNE DU CANADA 1360 Boul Rene-Levesque O Bureau 600, Montreal, QC H3G 0E5, *Tel* (514) 284-4500	805,875,627	835	500	6712
PPG ARCHITECTURAL COATINGS CANADA INC (*Suby of* **PPG INDUSTRIES, INC.**) 500 - 1550 Rue Ampere, Boucherville, QC J4B 7L4, *Tel* (450) 655-3121	805,696,740	836	150	2851
JAFFSONS HOLDINGS LTD 100 Park Royal S Suite 300, West Vancouver, BC V7T 1A2, *Tel* (604) 925-2700	804,119,800	837	2,200	6719
AECON INDUSTRIAL WESTERN INC (*Suby of* **AECON GROUP INC**) 14940 121a Ave Nw, Edmonton, AB T5V 1A3, *Tel* (780) 452-1250	803,150,800	838	1,150	1542
PITNEY BOWES OF CANADA LTD (*Suby of* **PITNEY BOWES INC.**) 5500 Explorer Dr Suite 1, Mississauga, ON L4W 5C7, *Tel* (905) 219-3000	803,028,000	839	200	5044
LOGISTICS IN MOTION INC 500 Bayly St E, Ajax, ON L1Z 0B2, *Tel* (905) 427-5880	800,270,400	840	1,200	4731

RIGHT AT HOME REALTY, INC

COMPANY	SALES ($)	RANK	EMPLOYEES HERE	PRIMARY SIC CODE
895 Don Mills Rd Suite 202, North York, ON M3C 1W3, *Tel* (416) 391-3232	800,270,400	841	1,200	4731
ROGERS COMMUNICATIONS CANADA INC (*Suby of* **ROGERS COMMUNICATIONS INC**)				
333 Bloor St E 9th Fl, Toronto, ON M4W 1G9, *Tel* (416) 935-7777	799,652,000	842	5	4841
UNIVERSITY OF SASKATCHEWAN				
105 Administration Pl Suite E, Saskatoon, SK S7N 5A2, *Tel* (306) 966-4343	797,685,137	843	1,100	8221
ALPA LUMBER INC				
7630 Airport Rd, Mississauga, ON L4T 4G6, *Tel* (905) 612-1222	797,479,200	844	14	5031
ROCKY MOUNTAIN DEALERSHIPS INC				
3345 8 St Se Suite 301, Calgary, AB T2G 3A4, *Tel* (403) 265-7364	796,831,915	845	40	5082
VISION 7 INTERNATIONAL INC				
300 Rue Saint-Paul Bureau 300, Quebec, QC G1K 7R1, *Tel* (418) 647-2727	794,616,566	846	0	6712
VISION 7 COMMUNICATIONS INC (*Suby of* **VISION 7 INTERNATIONAL INC**)				
300 Rue Saint-Paul Bureau 300, Quebec, QC G1K 7R1, *Tel* (418) 647-2727	794,251,057	847	27	6712
INTRAWEST ULC (*Suby of* **HAWK HOLDING COMPANY, LLC**)				
375 Water St Suite 710, Vancouver, BC V6B 5C6, *Tel* (604) 695-8200	794,044,400	848	75	7011
WHEATON PRECIOUS METALS CORP				
1021 Hastings St W Suite 3500, Vancouver, BC V6E 0C3, *Tel* (604) 684-9648	794,012,000	849	0	1044
DUFFERIN-PEEL CATHOLIC DISTRICT SCHOOL BOARD				
40 Matheson Blvd W, Mississauga, ON L5R 1C5, *Tel* (905) 890-1221	792,952,000	850	100	8211
CREATION TECHNOLOGIES INC				
8999 Fraserton Crt, Burnaby, BC V5J 5H8, *Tel* (604) 430-4336	792,162,000	851	0	3679
TRILLIUM HEALTH PARTNERS				
100 Queensway W, Mississauga, ON L5B 1B8, *Tel* (905) 848-7580	790,016,724	852	1,290	8062
PAN AMERICAN SILVER CORP				
625 Howe St Suite 1440, Vancouver, BC V6C 2T6, *Tel* (604) 684-1175	784,495,000	853	4,500	1044
MERCEDES-BENZ CANADA INC (*Suby of* **DAIMLER AG**)				
98 Vanderhoof Ave, Toronto, ON M4G 4C9, *Tel* (416) 425-3550	783,961,800	854	289	5012
BOWATER PRODUITS FORESTIERS DU CANADA ULC				
1155 Metcalfe Rue Bureau 800, Montreal, QC H3B 5H2, *Tel*	783,949,000	855	4,280	2621
UNIVERSITY OF MANITOBA,THE (*Suby of* **PROVINCE OF MANITOBA**)				
727 Mcdermot Ave Suite 408, Winnipeg, MB R3E 3P5, *Tel* (204) 474-9668	783,778,930	856	300	8221
GROUPE AGF INC				
2270 Rue Garneau, Longueuil, QC J4G 1E7, *Tel* (450) 442-9494	783,276,000	857	0	7353
JONES DESLAURIERS INSURANCE MANAGEMENT INC				
2375 Skymark Ave, Mississauga, ON L4W 4Y6, *Tel* (416) 259-4625	783,107,160	858	145	6411
SAVANNA ENERGY SERVICES CORP (*Suby of* **TOTAL ENERGY SERVICES INC**)				
311 6 Ave Sw Suite 800, Calgary, AB T2P 3H2, *Tel* (403) 503-9990	782,376,443	859	84	1381
HERSHEY CANADA INC (*Suby of* **HERSHEY COMPANY**)				
5750 Explorer Dr Suite 400, Mississauga, ON L4W 0A9, *Tel* (905) 602-9200	779,816,000	860	140	2064
TEKNION CORPORATION (*Suby of* **GLOBAL UPHOLSTERY CO LIMITED**)				
1150 Flint Rd, North York, ON M3J 2J5, *Tel* (416) 661-1577	779,327,500	861	1,000	2522
NORTHERN HEALTH AUTHORITY				
299 Victoria St Suite 600, Prince George, BC V2L 5B8, *Tel* (250) 565-2649	777,560,000	862	10	8062
BANQUE DE DEVELOPPEMENT DU CANADA (*Suby of* **GOVERNMENT OF CANADA**)				
5 Place Ville-Marie Bureau 400, Montreal, QC H3B 5E7, *Tel* (514) 283-5904	777,423,156	863	750	6141
MNP LLP				
330 5 Ave Sw Suite 2000, Calgary, AB T2P 0L4, *Tel* (403) 444-0150	776,382,600	864	500	8721
INNVEST REAL ESTATE INVESTMENT TRUST				
200 Bay St Suite 3205, Toronto, ON M5J 2J1, *Tel* (416) 607-7100	774,910,800	865	1,500	7011
QUINCAILLERIE RICHELIEU LTEE				
7900 Boul Henri-Bourassa O Bureau 200, Saint-Laurent, QC H4S 1V4, *Tel* (514) 336-4144	772,861,694	866	200	5072
CALGARY CO-OPERATIVE ASSOCIATION LIMITED				
151 86 Ave Se Unit 110, Calgary, AB T2H 3A5, *Tel* (403) 219-6025	769,856,000	867	150	5411
PREMIER TECH LTEE (*Suby of* **GESTION BELANGER, BERNARD LTEE**)				
1 Av Premier Bureau 101, Riviere-Du-Loup, QC G5R 6C1, *Tel* (418) 867-8883	768,303,000	868	150	6712
CANADIAN ENERGY SERVICES INC (*Suby of* **CES ENERGY SOLUTIONS CORP**)				
700 4 Ave Sw Suite 1400, Calgary, AB T2P 3J4, *Tel* (403) 269-2800	764,359,400	869	1,400	1381
FONDS SOCIAL DES EMPLOYES DE LA CAISSE DE DEPOT ET PLACEMENT DU QUEBEC				
1000 Place Jean-Paul-Riopelle Bureau A12, Montreal, QC H2Z 2B3, *Tel* (514) 842-3261	764,164,450	870	800	6399
WESTERN INVENTORY SERVICE LTD (*Suby of* **ARES CAPITAL CORPORATION**)				
3770 Nashua Dr Suite 5, Mississauga, ON L4V 1M5, *Tel* (905) 677-1947	762,702,500	871	50	7389
IMPRIMERIES TRANSCONTINENTAL INC (*Suby of* **TRANSCONTINENTAL INC**)				
1 Place Ville-Marie Unite 3240, Montreal, QC H3B 3Y2, *Tel* (514) 954-4000	762,113,142	872	160	2752
1127770 B.C. LTD				
777 Broadway W, Vancouver, BC V5Z 4J7, *Tel*	761,009,648	873	1,398	5047
FORBES BROS. LTD				
1290 91 St Sw Suite 200, Edmonton, AB T6X 0P2, *Tel* (780) 960-1950	756,662,400	874	150	4911
PRAXAIR CANADA INC (*Suby of* **LINDE PUBLIC LIMITED COMPANY**)				
1 City Centre Dr Suite 1200, Mississauga, ON L5B 1M2, *Tel* (905) 803-1600	755,896,500	875	320	2813
ARBOR MEMORIAL SERVICES INC				
2 Jane St Suite 101, Toronto, ON M6S 4W8, *Tel* (416) 763-3230	754,882,855	876	135	6553
EECOL HOLDINGS LTD				
63 Sunpark Dr Se, Calgary, AB T2X 3V4, *Tel* (403) 571-8400	754,321,100	877	4	5063

COMPANY	SALES ($)	RANK	EMPLOYEES HERE	PRIMARY SIC CODE
SOPREMA INC (*Suby of* **HOLDING SOPREMA**) 1688 Rue Jean-Berchmans-Michaud, Drummondville, QC J2C 8E9, *Tel* (819) 478-8163	753,918,750	878	100	2952
CALERES CANADA, INC (*Suby of* **CALERES, INC.**) 1857 Rogers Rd, Perth, ON K7H 1P7, *Tel* (613) 267-0348	753,779,700	879	35	5139
GOLDER ASSOCIATES CORPORATION 6925 Century Ave Suite 100, Mississauga, ON L5N 7K2, *Tel* (905) 567-4444	752,669,929	880	0	8711
PATTISON, JIM INDUSTRIES LTD (*Suby of* **PATTISON, JIM GROUP INC**) 1067 Cordova St W Suite 1800, Vancouver, BC V6C 1C7, *Tel* (604) 688-6764	750,427,600	881	30	5511
GAP (CANADA) INC (*Suby of* **THE GAP INC**) 60 Bloor St W Suite 1501, Toronto, ON M4W 3B8, *Tel* (416) 921-2225	748,530,000	882	65	5651
AIG INSURANCE COMPANY OF CANADA (*Suby of* **AMERICAN INTERNATIONAL GROUP, INC.**) 145 Wellington St W Suite 1400, Toronto, ON M5J 1H8, *Tel* (416) 596-3000	747,938,800	883	0	6331
BFL CANADA INSURANCE SERVICES INC 1167 Kensington Cres Nw Suite 200, Calgary, AB T2N 1X7, *Tel* (403) 451-4132	747,938,800	884	350	6311
MANULIFE CANADA LTD (*Suby of* **MANULIFE FINANCIAL CORPORATION**) 500 King St N, Kitchener, ON N2J 4Z6, *Tel* (519) 747-7000	747,938,800	885	255	6311
KIRKLAND LAKE GOLD LTD 200 Bay St Suite 3120, Toronto, ON M5J 2J1, *Tel* (416) 840-7884	747,495,000	886	18	1041
UNIVERSITE MCGILL 845 Rue Sherbrooke O Bureau 310, Montreal, QC H3A 0G4, *Tel* (514) 398-4455	746,955,000	887	100	8221
DIRECT ENERGY MARKETING LIMITED (*Suby of* **CENTRICA PLC**) 525 8 Ave Sw Unit 1200, Calgary, AB T2P 1G1, *Tel* (403) 776-2000	741,832,800	888	300	1311
UAP INC (*Suby of* **GENUINE PARTS COMPANY**) 7025 Rue Ontario E, Montreal, QC H1N 2B3, *Tel* (514) 251-6565	739,468,600	889	350	5013
CALIAN LTD (*Suby of* **CALIAN GROUP LTD**) 4-770 Palladium Dr, Ottawa, ON K2V 1C8, *Tel* (613) 599-8600	735,996,800	890	100	4899
SMTC NOVA SCOTIA COMPANY (*Suby of* **SMTC CORPORATION**) 7050 Woodbine Ave Suite 300, Markham, ON L3R 4G8, *Tel* (905) 479-1810	735,579,000	891	2,600	3672
COMPAGNIE DE PAPIERS WHITE BIRCH CANADA (*Suby of* **WHITE BIRCH LUXEMBOURG HOLDING SARL**) 10 Boul Des Capucins, Quebec, QC G1J 0G9, *Tel* (418) 525-2500	735,274,000	892	50	2621
RIO TINTO FER ET TITANE INC (*Suby of* **RIO TINTO PLC**) 1625 Rte Marie-Victorin, Sorel-Tracy, QC J3R 1M6, *Tel* (450) 746-3000	732,913,200	893	0	3399
MAGELLAN AEROSPACE CORPORATION 3160 Derry Rd E, Mississauga, ON L4T 1A9, *Tel* (905) 677-1889	732,897,383	894	0	6712
STUART OLSON INC 4820 Richard Rd Sw Suite 600, Calgary, AB T3E 6L1, *Tel* (403) 685-7777	732,635,838	895	350	1541
PATERSON GLOBALFOODS INC 333 Main St 22nd Fl, Winnipeg, MB R3C 4E2, *Tel* (204) 956-2090	732,630,800	896	100	5153
599681 SASKATCHEWAN LTD (*Suby of* **BRANDT INDUSTRIES CANADA LTD**) Hwy 1 E, Regina, SK S4P 3R8, *Tel* (306) 791-7777	731,595,000	897	1	5084
HOLDING BELL MOBILITE INC (*Suby of* **BCE INC**) 1 Carref Alexander-Graham-Bell Bureau A-7, Verdun, QC H3E 3B3, *Tel* (514) 420-7700	731,110,400	898	2	4899
CAMPBELL COMPANY OF CANADA (*Suby of* **CAMPBELL SOUP COMPANY**) 60 Birmingham St, Etobicoke, ON M8V 2B8, *Tel* (416) 251-1131	731,077,500	899	700	2032
CLEARWATER SEAFOODS LIMITED PARTNERSHIP (*Suby of* **THORNVALE HOLDINGS LIMITED**) 757 Bedford Hwy, Bedford, NS B4A 3Z7, *Tel* (902) 443-0550	731,077,500	900	0	2092
SUPRALIMENT S.E.C. 2200 Av Pratte Bureau 400, Saint-Hyacinthe, QC J2S 4B6, *Tel* (450) 771-0400	731,077,500	901	150	2011
ARMOUR TRANSPORTATION SYSTEMS INC 689 Edinburgh Dr, Moncton, NB E1E 2L4, *Tel* (506) 857-0205	731,018,000	902	500	6712
NOVERCO INC 1000 Place Jean-Paul-Riopelle Bureau A12, Montreal, QC H2Z 2B3, *Tel* (514) 847-2126	731,018,000	903	0	6712
QUALICO DEVELOPMENTS CANADA LTD (*Suby of* **QUALICO GROUP LTD**) 1 Dr. David Friesen Dr, Winnipeg, MB R3X 0G8, *Tel* (204) 233-2451	731,018,000	904	200	6712
SOARING PHOENIX INC 15 Boul Du Cure-Labelle, Sainte-Therese, QC J7E 2X1, *Tel* (450) 435-6541	731,018,000	905	1	6712
TEKNION HOLDINGS (CANADA) INC (*Suby of* **GLOBAL UPHOLSTERY CO LIMITED**) 1150 Flint Rd, North York, ON M3J 2J5, *Tel* (416) 661-1577	731,018,000	906	0	6712
TELUS COMMUNICATIONS (QUEBEC) INC (*Suby of* **TELUS CORPORATION**) 6 Rue Jules-A.-Brillant Bureau 20602, Rimouski, QC G5L 1W8, *Tel* (418) 723-2271	731,018,000	907	100	6712
GROUPE BMR INC (*Suby of* **GESTION BMR INC**) 1501 Rue Ampere Bureau 200, Boucherville, QC J4B 5Z5, *Tel* (450) 655-2441	730,487,040	908	70	5039
SITQ NATIONAL INC (*Suby of* **GOUVERNEMENT DE LA PROVINCE DE QUEBEC**) 1001 Rue Du Square-Victoria Bureau C 200, Montreal, QC H2Z 2B1, *Tel* (514) 287-1852	730,285,290	909	210	6798
CANERECTOR INC 1 Sparks Ave, North York, ON M2H 2W1, *Tel* (416) 225-6240	729,693,000	910	6	3443
MARTINREA AUTOMOTIVE INC (*Suby of* **MARTINREA INTERNATIONAL INC**) 3210 Langstaff Rd, Vaughan, ON L4K 5B2, *Tel* (289) 982-3000	729,693,000	911	400	3499
STACKPOLE INTERNATIONAL ULC (*Suby of* **JOHNSON ELECTRIC HOLDINGS LIMITED**) 1325 Cormorant Rd Fl 2, Ancaster, ON L9G 4V5, *Tel* (905) 304-9455	727,125,000	912	50	3714
TELESAT CANADA (*Suby of* **RED ISLE PRIVATE INVESTMENTS INC**) 160 Elgin St Suite 2100, Ottawa, ON K2P 2P7, *Tel* (613) 748-0123	726,602,054	913	87	4841
SASKENERGY INCORPORATED (*Suby of* **GOVERNMENT OF SASKATCHEWAN**) 1777 Victoria Ave Suite 1000, Regina, SK S4P 4K5, *Tel* (306) 777-9225	725,965,680	914	400	4923

COMPANY	SALES ($)	RANK	EMPLOYEES HERE	PRIMARY SIC CODE
HOSPITAL FOR SICK CHILDREN, THE				
555 University Ave, Toronto, ON M5G 1X8, *Tel* (416) 813-1500	725,662,823	915	6,700	8069
OCEANAGOLD CORPORATION				
777 Hornby Street Suite 1910, Vancouver, BC V6Z 1S4, *Tel* (604) 235-3360	724,413,000	916	950	1081
NORBORD INDUSTRIES INC (*Suby of* **NORBORD INC**)				
1 Toronto St Unit 600, Toronto, ON M5C 2W4, *Tel* (416) 365-0705	723,814,000	917	100	2431
BMO INVESTMENTS INC (*Suby of* **BANK OF MONTREAL**)				
100 King St W 43rd Floor, Toronto, ON M5X 1A1, *Tel* (416) 359-5003	723,778,700	918	0	6722
ARAMARK CANADA LTD. (*Suby of* **ARAMARK**)				
811 Islington Ave, Etobicoke, ON M8Z 5W8, *Tel* (416) 255-1331	722,904,500	919	200	5812
MILLER GROUP INC				
505 Miller Ave, Markham, ON L6G 1B2, *Tel* (905) 475-6660	721,853,000	920	150	1611
DHL EXPRESS (CANADA) LTD (*Suby of* **DEUTSCHE POST AG**)				
18 Parkshore Dr, Brampton, ON L6T 0G7, *Tel* (905) 861-3400	719,971,000	921	150	4212
ASSINIBOINE PARK CONSERVANCY INC				
55 Pavilion Cres, Winnipeg, MB R3P 2N6, *Tel* (204) 927-6002	719,300,500	922	500	8699
BEACON COMMUNITY SERVICES				
9860 Third St, Sidney, BC V8L 4R2, *Tel* (250) 658-6407	719,300,500	923	0	8699
3958230 CANADA INC				
600 Boul De Maisonneuve O Bureau 2200, Montreal, QC H3A 3J2, *Tel* (450) 646-9760	718,590,694	924	1,966	6712
PRIMMUM INSURANCE COMPANY (*Suby of* **TORONTO-DOMINION BANK, THE**)				
50 Boul Cremazie O Bureau 1200, Montreal, QC H2P 1B6, *Tel* (514) 382-6060	718,021,248	925	260	6331
BURNBRAE FARMS LIMITED				
3356 County Road 27, Lyn, ON K0E 1M0, *Tel* (613) 345-5651	716,716,000	926	800	5144
BRITISH COLUMBIA FERRY SERVICES INC (*Suby of* **B.C. FERRY AUTHORITY, THE**)				
1321 Blanshard St Suite 500, Victoria, BC V8W 0B7, *Tel* (250) 381-1401	715,631,813	927	600	4482
TELECON INC (*Suby of* **CAPITAL REGIONAL ET COOPERATIF DESJARDINS**)				
7450 Rue Du Mile End, Montreal, QC H2R 2Z6, *Tel* (514) 644-2333	715,301,113	928	1,200	6712
ULTRACUTS LTD				
167 St Mary'S Rd, Winnipeg, MB R2H 1J1, *Tel* (204) 231-0110	712,897,545	929	200	6794
TEKNION LIMITED (*Suby of* **GLOBAL UPHOLSTERY CO LIMITED**)				
1150 Flint Rd, North York, ON M3J 2J5, *Tel* (416) 661-1577	712,528,000	930	1,400	2522
FIRST CANADIAN INSURANCE CORPORATION (*Suby of* **FIRSTCAN MANAGEMENT INC**)				
320 Sioux Rd Suite 110, Sherwood Park, AB T8A 3X6, *Tel* (780) 410-9182	711,915,600	931	0	6411
TARPON ENERGY SERVICES LTD (*Suby of* **PTW ENERGY SERVICES LTD**)				
7020 81 St Se, Calgary, AB T2C 5B8, *Tel* (403) 234-8647	709,762,300	932	250	1389
MENZIES AVIATION FUELING CANADA LIMITED				
10 Carlson Ct Unit 301, Etobicoke, ON M9W 6A2, *Tel* (647) 798-3890	709,363,800	933	17	5172
GESTION TREE ROOTS INC				
2300 Rue Emile-Belanger, Saint-Laurent, QC H4R 3J4, *Tel* (514) 747-2536	709,356,930	934	6	5661
GROUPE ALDO INC, LE (*Suby of* **GESTION TREE ROOTS INC**)				
2300 Rue Emile-Belanger, Saint-Laurent, QC H4R 3J4, *Tel* (514) 747-2536	706,861,830	935	750	5661
AG GROWTH INTERNATIONAL INC				
198 Commerce Dr, Winnipeg, MB R3P 0Z6, *Tel* (204) 489-1855	706,296,342	936	100	3496
SANOFI-AVENTIS CANADA INC (*Suby of* **SANOFI**)				
2905 Place Louis-R.-Renaud, Cote Saint-Luc, QC H7V 0A3, *Tel* (514) 331-9220	701,795,700	937	1,700	5122
KELSEY'S RESTAURANTS INC (*Suby of* **RECIPE UNLIMITED CORPORATION**)				
199 Four Valley Dr, Concord, ON L4K 0B8, *Tel* (905) 760-2244	699,585,000	938	40	5812
CONNORS BROS. CLOVER LEAF SEAFOODS COMPANY (*Suby of* **CLOVER LEAF HOLDINGS COMPANY**)				
80 Tiverton Crt Suite 600, Markham, ON L3R 0G4, *Tel* (905) 474-0608	698,798,100	939	5	5146
HOOD PACKAGING CORPORATION (*Suby of* **HOOD FLEXIBLE PACKAGING CORPORATION**)				
2380 Mcdowell Rd, Burlington, ON L7R 4A1, *Tel* (905) 637-5611	698,510,300	940	25	2674
KBR INDUSTRIAL CANADA CO. (*Suby of* **KELLOGG BROWN & ROOT HOLDING B.V.**)				
1302 10 St Nisku, Edmonton, AB T9E 8K2, *Tel* (780) 468-1341	698,392,000	941	998	1541
MOTOR COACH INDUSTRIES LIMITED (*Suby of* **NFI GROUP INC**)				
1475 Clarence Ave, Winnipeg, MB R3T 1T5, *Tel* (204) 284-5360	698,040,000	942	1,500	3711
ALTA GENETICS INC (*Suby of* **KOEPON HOLDING B.V.**)				
263090 Rge Rd 11, Rocky View County, AB T4B 2T3, *Tel* (403) 226-0666	695,999,260	943	280	5159
CANADIAN FOREST PRODUCTS LTD (*Suby of* **CANFOR CORPORATION**)				
1700 75th Ave W Unit 100, Vancouver, BC V6P 6G2, *Tel* (604) 661-5241	695,975,000	944	120	2421
TOLKO FOREST PRODUCTS LTD (*Suby of* **TIMBER INVESTMENTS LTD**)				
3000 28 St, Vernon, BC V1T 9W9, *Tel* (250) 545-4411	695,975,000	945	2,500	2421
SERVICES DE CAFE VAN HOUTTE INC (*Suby of* **KEURIG DR PEPPER INC.**)				
3700 Rue Jean-Rivard, Montreal, QC H1Z 4K3, *Tel* (514) 593-7711	695,957,600	946	1	5046
CARILLION CANADA INC (*Suby of* **CARILLION GB LIMITED**)				
7077 Keele St, Concord, ON L4K 0B6, *Tel* (905) 532-5200	695,603,800	947	0	1611
SCOULAR CANADA LTD (*Suby of* **THE SCOULAR COMPANY**)				
10201 Southport Rd Sw Suite 1110, Calgary, AB T2W 4X9, *Tel* (403) 720-9050	695,509,800	948	20	6799
ENTERTAINMENT ONE GP LIMITED (*Suby of* **4384768 CANADA INC**)				
70 Driver Rd Unit 1, Brampton, ON L6T 5V2, *Tel* (905) 624-7337	695,300,000	949	300	5099
REITMANS (CANADA) LIMITEE				
250 Rue Sauve O, Montreal, QC H3L 1Z2, *Tel* (514) 384-1140	694,481,512	950	0	5621
REVERA INC (*Suby of* **GOVERNMENT OF CANADA**)				
5015 Spectrum Way Suite 600, Mississauga, ON L4W 0E4, *Tel* (289) 360-1252	694,055,508	951	100	8051

COMPANY	SALES ($)	RANK	EMPLOYEES HERE	PRIMARY SIC CODE
OTTAWA-CARLETON DISTRICT SCHOOL BOARD 133 Greenbank Rd, Nepean, ON K2H 6L3, *Tel* (613) 721-1820	693,833,000	952	350	8211
WATERLOO REGION DISTRICT SCHOOL BOARD 51 Ardelt Ave, Kitchener, ON N2C 2R5, *Tel* (519) 570-0300	693,833,000	953	200	8211
ARCELORMITTAL PRODUITS LONGS CANADA S.E.N.C. 4000 Rte Des Acieries, Contrecoeur, QC J0L 1C0, *Tel* (450) 587-8600	692,195,800	954	50	3312
CANADIAN DEPOSITORY FOR SECURITIES LIMITED, THE 85 Richmond St W, Toronto, ON M5H 2C9, *Tel* (416) 365-8400	690,221,930	955	385	6289
AECOM CANADA LTD (*Suby of* **AECOM**) 3292 Production Way, Burnaby, BC V5A 4R4, *Tel* (604) 444-6400	689,958,500	956	100	8711
3592898 CANADA INC 1706 Ch Pink Bureau F, Gatineau, QC J9J 3N7, *Tel* (819) 771-3969	689,655,354	957	7	1752
PETRO-CANADA LUBRICANTS INC (*Suby of* **HOLLYFRONTIER CORPORATION**) 2310 Lakeshore Rd W, Mississauga, ON L5J 1K2, *Tel* (866) 335-3369	689,265,159	958	83	5172
APOTEX PHARMACEUTICAL HOLDINGS INC 150 Signet Dr, North York, ON M9L 1T9, *Tel* (416) 749-9300	689,262,000	959	1	8731
TOYS 'R' US (CANADA) LTD (*Suby of* **FAIRFAX FINANCIAL HOLDINGS LIMITED**) 2777 Langstaff Rd, Concord, ON L4K 4M5, *Tel* (905) 660-2000	688,447,287	960	192	5945
FAIRSTONE FINANCIERE INC 630 Boul Rene-Levesque O Bureau 1400, Montreal, QC H3B 1S6, *Tel* (800) 995-2274	687,271,000	961	50	6141
CIBC MELLON TRUST COMPANY 1 York St Suite 900, Toronto, ON M5J 0B6, *Tel* (416) 643-5000	685,952,516	962	400	6211
ATOMIC ENERGY OF CANADA LIMITED (*Suby of* **GOVERNMENT OF CANADA**) 286 Plant Rd Stn 508a, Chalk River, ON K0J 1J0, *Tel* (613) 584-3311	684,882,574	963	1,500	4911
CENTRE INTEGRE DE SANTE ET DE SERVICES SOCIAUX DES LAURENTIDES 290 Rue De Montigny, Saint-Jerome, QC J7Z 5T3, *Tel* (450) 432-2777	684,745,200	964	100	8011
PROVIDENCE HEALTHCARE 3276 St Clair Ave E, Scarborough, ON M1L 1W1, *Tel* (416) 285-3666	683,100,922	965	1,150	8069
TRICAN WELL SERVICE LTD 645 7 Ave Sw Suite 2900, Calgary, AB T2P 4G8, *Tel* (403) 266-0202	682,740,596	966	200	6712
ATRIUM INNOVATIONS INC (*Suby of* **NESTLE S.A.**) 3500 Boul De Maisonneuve O Bureau 2405, Westmount, QC H3Z 3C1, *Tel* (514) 205-6240	682,339,000	967	100	2023
DARE FOODS LIMITED 25 Cherry Blossom Rd, Cambridge, ON N3H 4R7, *Tel* (519) 893-5500	682,339,000	968	550	2051
DIAGEO CANADA INC (*Suby of* **DIAGEO PLC**) 401 The West Mall Suite 800, Toronto, ON M9C 5P8, *Tel* (416) 626-2000	682,339,000	969	70	2085
EXCELDOR COOPERATIVE 5700 Rue J.-B.-Michaud Suite 500, Levis, QC G6V 0B1, *Tel* (418) 830-5600	682,339,000	970	850	2015
NILSSON BROS. INC (*Suby of* **400369 ALBERTA LTD**) 101 Riel Dr Suite 100, St. Albert, AB T8N 3X4, *Tel* (780) 477-2233	682,339,000	971	25	2011
PARAMOUNT RESOURCES LTD 421-7th Ave Sw Suite 2800, Calgary, AB T2P 4K9, *Tel* (403) 290-3600	679,480,000	972	349	1311
ELLISDON CONSTRUCTION SERVICES INC (*Suby of* **ELLISDON HOLDINGS INC**) 2045 Oxford St E, London, ON N5V 2Z7, *Tel* (519) 455-6770	677,440,240	973	0	1542
BOSTON PIZZA INTERNATIONAL INC 10760 Shellbridge Way Unit 100, Richmond, BC V6X 3H1, *Tel* (604) 270-1108	674,644,506	974	59	6794
PRINCESS AUTO LTD 475 Panet Rd, Winnipeg, MB R2C 2Z1, *Tel* (204) 667-4630	674,520,000	975	300	5251
MESSER CANADA INC 5860 Chedworth Way, Mississauga, ON L5R 0A2, *Tel* (905) 501-1700	672,212,000	976	150	5169
SAFETY-KLEEN CANADA INC (*Suby of* **CLEAN HARBORS, INC.**) 300 Woolwich St S, Breslau, ON N0B 1M0, *Tel* (519) 648-2291	670,150,000	977	100	2992
CANACCORD GENUITY GROUP INC 609 Granville St Van Unit 2200, Vancouver, BC V7Y 1H2, *Tel* (604) 643-7300	669,518,331	978	345	6211
FIDO SOLUTIONS INC (*Suby of* **ROGERS COMMUNICATIONS INC**) 800 Rue De La Gauchetiere O Bureau 4000, Montreal, QC H5A 1K3, *Tel* (514) 937-2121	669,088,000	979	300	4899
ARTSMARKETING SERVICES INC 260 King St E Suite 500, Toronto, ON M5A 4L5, *Tel* (416) 941-9000	668,908,000	980	20	7389
JOHNSON CONTROLS NOVA SCOTIA U.L.C. (*Suby of* **JOHNSON CONTROLS INTERNATIONAL PUBLIC LIMITED COMPANY**) 56 Leek Cres, Richmond Hill, ON L4B 1H1, *Tel* (866) 468-1484	667,995,000	981	200	2531
VIDEOTRON SERVICE INFORMATIQUE LTEE 300 Av Viger E Bureau 6, Montreal, QC H2X 3W4, *Tel* (514) 281-1232	667,388,000	982	4,000	7374
GARDEWINE GROUP INC (*Suby of* **MULLEN GROUP LTD**) 60 Eagle Dr, Winnipeg, MB R2R 1V5, *Tel* (204) 633-5795	666,892,000	983	50	4731
CANADIAN NORTHERN SHIELD INSURANCE COMPANY (*Suby of* **RSA INSURANCE GROUP PLC**) 555 Hastings St W Unit 1900, Vancouver, BC V6B 4N6, *Tel* (604) 662-2900	664,454,560	984	89	6411
WESTLAND INSURANCE LIMITED PARTNERSHIP 2121 160 St Unit 200, Surrey, BC V3Z 9N6, *Tel* (604) 543-7788	664,454,560	985	35	6411
COMPAGNIE D'ASSURANCE SONNET (*Suby of* **ECONOMICAL MUTUAL INSURANCE COMPANY**) 5 Place Ville-Marie Bureau 1400, Montreal, QC H3B 0A8, *Tel* (514) 875-5790	662,460,080	986	210	6331
ELEMENT FLEET MANAGEMENT CORP 161 Bay St Suite 3600, Toronto, ON M5J 2S1, *Tel* (416) 386-1067	662,216,501	987	100	8742
LEISUREWORLD SENIOR CARE LP				

COMPANY	SALES ($)	RANK	EMPLOYEES HERE	PRIMARY SIC CODE
302 Town Centre Blvd Suite 200, Markham, ON L3R 0E8, *Tel* (905) 477-4006	661,312,800	988	0	8741
THAMES VALLEY DISTRICT SCHOOL BOARD				
1250 Dundas St, London, ON N5W 5P2, *Tel* (519) 452-2000	659,125,527	989	250	8211
CHARTWELL RETIREMENT RESIDENCES				
100 Milverton Dr Suite 700, Mississauga, ON L5R 4H1, *Tel* (905) 501-9219	657,012,131	990	4,701	6719
EUROVIA QUEBEC CONSTRUCTION INC (*Suby of* **VINCI**)				
1550 Rue Ampere Bureau 200, Boucherville, QC J4B 7L4, *Tel* (450) 641-8000	656,230,000	991	150	1611
CARA HOLDINGS LIMITED				
21 Bedford Rd Suite 200, Toronto, ON M5R 2J9, *Tel* (905) 760-2244	654,718,282	992	4	5812
FRANCO-NEVADA CORPORATION				
199 Bay St Suite 2000, Toronto, ON M5L 1G9, *Tel* (416) 306-6300	653,200,000	993	0	1041
ALAMOS GOLD INC				
181 Bay St Suite 3910, Toronto, ON M5J 2T3, *Tel* (416) 368-9932	651,800,000	994	0	1041
REVOLUTION ENVIRONMENTAL SOLUTIONS LP				
1100 Burloak Dr Suite 500, Burlington, ON L7L 6B2, *Tel* (800) 263-8602	651,444,000	995	25	4959
TERRAPURE ENVIRONMENTAL LTD (*Suby of* **REVOLUTION ENVIRONMENTAL SOLUTIONS LP**)				
1100 Burloak Dr Suite 500, Burlington, ON L7L 6B2, *Tel* (800) 263-8602	651,444,000	996	0	4959
DURHAM DISTRICT SCHOOL BOARD				
400 Taunton Rd E, Whitby, ON L1R 2K6, *Tel* (905) 686-2711	650,878,987	997	250	8211
TATA CONSULTANCY SERVICES CANADA INC (*Suby of* **TATA CONSULTANCY SERVICES LIMITED**)				
400 University Ave 25th Fl, Toronto, ON M5G 1S5, *Tel* (647) 790-7200	649,860,000	998	3,000	7379
PETRONAS ENERGY CANADA LTD (*Suby of* **GOVERNMENT OF MALAYSIA**)				
215 2 St Sw Suite 1600, Calgary, AB T2P 1M4, *Tel* (403) 216-2510	649,103,700	999	0	1311
FLIGHT CENTRE TRAVEL GROUP (CANADA) INC (*Suby of* **FLIGHT CENTRE TRAVEL GROUP LIMITED**)				
980 Howe St Suite 700, Vancouver, BC V6Z 0C8, *Tel* (604) 682-5202	646,541,130	1000	300	4724

COMPANY	EMPLOYEES HERE	RANK	SALES ($)	PRIMARY SIC CODE
LOKI MANAGEMENT SYSTEMS INC (*Suby of* **ZEROCHAOS, LLC**) 13351 Commerce Pky Suite 1258, Richmond, BC V6V 2X7, *Tel* (604) 249-5050	210,000	1	0	7371
HEWLETT PACKARD ENTERPRISE CANADA CO (*Suby of* **HEWLETT PACKARD ENTERPRISE COMPANY**) 5150 Spectrum Way Suite 400, Mississauga, ON L4W 5G2, *Tel* (905) 206-4725	60,000	2	12,244,920,000	8731
WORLEY CANADA SERVICES LTD 8500 Macleod Trail Se, Calgary, AB T2H 2N1, *Tel* (403) 258-8000	35,000	3	6,255,865,000	8711
TELUS COMMUNICATIONS INC (*Suby of* **TELUS CORPORATION**) 3777 Kingsway, Burnaby, BC V5H 3Z7, *Tel* (604) 432-5010	25,000	4	0	4899
COMPAGNIE DES CHEMINS DE FER NATIONAUX DU CANADA (*Suby of* **COMPAGNIE DES CHEMINS DE FER NATIONAUX DU CANADA**) 277 Front St W, Toronto, ON M5V 2X4, *Tel* (888) 888-5909	21,967	5	0	4111
A&W REVENUE ROYALTIES INCOME FUND 171 Esplanade W Suite 300, North Vancouver, BC V7M 3K9, *Tel* (604) 988-2141	18,000	6	1,033,289,994	6722
CENTRE JEUNESSE DE LA MAURICIE ET DU CENTRE-DU-QUEBEC, LE (*Suby of* **CENTRE JEUNESSE DE LA MAURICIE ET DU CENTRE-DU-QUEBEC, LE**) 1455 Boul Du Carmel, Trois-Rivieres, QC G8Z 3R7, *Tel* (819) 378-5481	18,000	7	0	8322
CENTRE UNIVERSITAIRE DE SANTE MCGILL 1001 Boul Decarie, Montreal, QC H4A 3J1, *Tel* (514) 934-1934	17,437	8	1,936,901,960	8062
PENSKE TRUCK LEASING CANADA INC (*Suby of* **PENSKE TRUCK LEASING CO., L.P.**) 2500 Boul Pitfield, Saint-Laurent, QC H4S 1Z7, *Tel* (514) 333-4080	15,000	9	0	7513
GOVERNORS OF THE UNIVERSITY OF ALBERTA, THE (*Suby of* **GOVERNMENT OF THE PROVINCE OF ALBERTA**) 116 St & 85 Ave, Edmonton, AB T6G 2R3, *Tel* (780) 492-3111	14,000	10	1,421,916,337	8221
DOLLARAMA INC 5805 Av Royalmount, Mont-Royal, QC H4P 0A1, *Tel* (514) 737-1006	12,764	11	2,542,285,263	5999
FRASER HEALTH AUTHORITY (*Suby of* **GOVERNMENT OF THE PROVINCE OF BRITISH COLUMBIA**) 13450 102 Ave Suite 400, Surrey, BC V3T 0H1, *Tel* (604) 587-4600	12,000	12	2,880,229,035	8062
OTTAWA HOSPITAL, THE (*Suby of* **OTTAWA HOSPITAL, THE**) 1053 Carling Ave Suite 119, Ottawa, ON K1Y 4E9, *Tel* (613) 722-7000	12,000	13	0	8062
LINAMAR CORPORATION 287 Speedvale Ave W, Guelph, ON N1H 1C5, *Tel* (519) 836-7550	11,736	14	5,777,178,455	3714
UNIVERSITY OF BRITISH COLUMBIA, THE 2329 West Mall, Vancouver, BC V6T 1Z4, *Tel* (604) 822-2211	10,000	15	1,818,003,067	8221
GREAT CANADIAN GAMING CORPORATION 95 Schooner St, Coquitlam, BC V3K 7A8, *Tel* (604) 303-1000	9,350	16	925,642,542	7999
MINES AGNICO EAGLE LIMITEE 10200 Rte De Preissac, Rouyn-Noranda, QC J0Y 1C0, *Tel* (819) 759-3644	9,188	17	2,242,604,000	1241
GOVERNING COUNCIL OF THE UNIVERSITY OF TORONTO, THE 27 King'S College Cir, Toronto, ON M5S 1A1, *Tel* (416) 978-2196	9,000	18	2,414,595,312	8221
CENTRE HOSPITALIER UNIVERSITAIRE DE QUEBEC (*Suby of* **CENTRE HOSPITALIER UNIVERSITAIRE DE QUE-BEC**) 10 Rue De L'Espinay Bureau 520, Quebec, QC G1L 3L5, *Tel* (418) 525-4444	8,964	19	0	8062
CINRAM INTERNATIONAL INCOME FUND 2255 Markham Rd, Scarborough, ON M1B 2W3, *Tel* (416) 298-8190	8,300	20	49,261,288,480	6722
CENTRE HOSPITALIER DE L'UNIVERSITE DE MONTREAL 850 Rue Saint-Denis, Montreal, QC H2X 0A9, *Tel* (514) 890-8000	8,000	21	1,110,800,000	8062
ENTERRA HOLDINGS LTD 6925 Century Ave Suite 100, Mississauga, ON L5N 7K2, *Tel* (905) 567-4444	8,000	22	607,602,100	7363
GROUPE WSP GLOBAL INC (*Suby of* **AST TRUST COMPANY (CANADA)**) 1600 Boul Rene-Levesque O Bureau 16, Montreal, QC H3H 1P9, *Tel* (514) 340-0046	7,900	23	5,995,146,426	8741
BRACKNELL CORPORATION 195 The West Mall Ste 302, Toronto, ON M9C 5K1, *Tel*	7,000	24	843,661,000	1711
CORREIA ENTERPRISES LTD 375 Nairn Ave, Winnipeg, MB R2L 0W8, *Tel* (204) 668-4420	7,000	25	223,776,000	7349
DELOITTE MANAGEMENT SERVICES LP 121 King St W Suite 300, Toronto, ON M5H 3T9, *Tel* (416) 775-2364	7,000	26	1,293,971,000	8721
SUNNYBROOK HEALTH SCIENCES CENTRE 2075 Bayview Ave, Toronto, ON M4N 3M5, *Tel* (416) 480-6100	7,000	27	882,520,338	8062
FONDATION DE L'UNIVERSITE DU QUEBEC EN OUTAOUAIS 283 Boul Alexandre-Tache Bureau F-0239, Gatineau, QC J8X 3X7, *Tel* (819) 595-3900	6,736	28	1,006,297,776	8221
HOSPITAL FOR SICK CHILDREN, THE 555 University Ave, Toronto, ON M5G 1X8, *Tel* (416) 813-1500	6,700	29	725,662,823	8069
QUEEN'S UNIVERSITY AT KINGSTON 99 University Ave, Kingston, ON K7L 3N5, *Tel* (613) 533-2000	6,534	30	938,300,502	8221
INTERIOR HEALTH AUTHORITY 505 Doyle Ave, Kelowna, BC V1Y 0C5, *Tel* (250) 862-4200	6,000	31	1,607,176,339	8062
TRILOGY RETAIL ENTERPRISES L.P 161 Bay St Suite 4900, Toronto, ON M5J 2S1, *Tel* (416) 943-4110	6,000	32	2,193,054,000	6712
COLLIERS INTERNATIONAL GROUP INC 1140 Bay St Suite 4000, Toronto, ON M5S 2B4, *Tel* (416) 960-9500	5,860	33	2,825,427,000	6531
SHAW CABLESYSTEMS G.P. (*Suby of* **SHAW COMMUNICATIONS INC**) 630 3 Ave Sw, Calgary, AB T2P 4L4, *Tel* (403) 750-4500	5,600	34	1,873,446,400	4841
GENIVAR INC Edifice Northern 1600 Rene-Levesque Blvd W, Montreal, QC H3H 1P9, *Tel* (514) 340-0046	5,500	35	641,324,463	8711
SIR ROYALTY INCOME FUND				

COMPANY	EMPLOYEES HERE	RANK	SALES ($)	PRIMARY SIC CODE
5360 South Service Rd Suite 200, Burlington, ON L7L 5L1, *Tel* (905) 681-2997	5,500	36	8,710,424	6726
ARCELORMITTAL DOFASCO G.P. (*Suby of* **ARCELORMITTAL**)				
1330 Burlington St E, Hamilton, ON L8N 3J5, *Tel* (905) 548-7200	5,000	37	2,432,310,000	3479
BANQUE NATIONALE DU CANADA				
600 Rue De La Gauchetiere O Bureau 4e, Montreal, QC H3B 4L3, *Tel* (514) 394-4385	5,000	38	5,334,573,312	6021
BOMBARDIER INC (*Suby of* **BOMBARDIER INC**)				
123 Garratt Blvd, North York, ON M3K 1Y5, *Tel* (416) 633-7310	5,000	39	0	3721
EASTERN REGIONAL INTEGRATED HEALTH AUTHORITY (*Suby of* **EASTERN REGIONAL INTEGRATED HEALTH AUTHORITY**)				
154 Lemarchant Rd, St. John'S, NL A1C 5B8, *Tel* (709) 777-6300	5,000	40	0	8062
FCA CANADA INC (*Suby of* **FIAT CHRYSLER AUTOMOBILES N.V.**)				
2199 Chrysler Ctr, Windsor, ON N9A 4H6, *Tel* (519) 973-2000	5,000	41	0	3711
GRAHAM INCOME TRUST				
10840 27 St Se, Calgary, AB T2Z 3R6, *Tel* (403) 570-5000	5,000	42	3,491,960,000	1541
GROUPE DE SECURITE GARDA INC, LE (*Suby of* **GW INTERMEDIATE HOLDCO CORPORATION**)				
1160 Rue Valets, L'Ancienne-Lorette, QC G2E 5Y9, *Tel* (418) 627-0088	5,000	43	0	7381
JACOBS INDUSTRIAL SERVICES (*Suby of* **JACOBS ENGINEERING GROUP INC.**)				
1104 70 Ave Nw, Edmonton, AB T6P 1P5, *Tel* (780) 468-2533	5,000	44	159,840,000	7349
MONITOR COMPANY CANADA (*Suby of* **DELOITTE LLP**)				
8 Adelaide St W Ste 20, Toronto, ON M5H 0A9, *Tel* (416) 408-4800	5,000	45	0	8741
PRATT & WHITNEY CANADA CIE (*Suby of* **PRATT AERO LIMITED PARTNERSHIP**)				
1000 Boul Marie-Victorin, Longueuil, QC J4G 1A1, *Tel* (450) 677-9411	5,000	46	1,783,568,950	3519
ROGERS COMMUNICATIONS INC				
333 Bloor St E, Toronto, ON M4W 1G9, *Tel* (416) 935-7777	5,000	47	11,444,307,792	4899
TECK RESOURCES LIMITED				
550 Burrard St Suite 3300, Vancouver, BC V6C 0B3, *Tel* (604) 699-4000	5,000	48	9,524,793,528	1021
TORONTO-DOMINION BANK, THE				
55 King St W, Toronto, ON M5K 1A2, *Tel* (416) 982-5722	5,000	49	22,804,055,000	6021
YORK UNIVERSITY				
4700 Keele St, North York, ON M3J 1P3, *Tel* (416) 736-2100	5,000	50	917,260	8221
CONCENTRIX TECHNOLOGIES SERVICES (CANADA) LIMITED (*Suby of* **SYNNEX CORPORATION**)				
1189 Colonel Sam Dr, Oshawa, ON L1H 8W8, *Tel* (416) 380-3800	4,900	51	392,681,985	4899
FONDATION DE L'HOPITAL GENERAL JUIF SIR MORTIMER B. DAVIS				
3755 Ch De La Cote-Sainte-Catherine Bureau A104, Montreal, QC H3T 1E2, *Tel* (514) 340-8251	4,869	52	1,008,214,092	8399
CANADIAN TEST CASE 168 INC.				
1450 Rue Cunard, Cote Saint-Luc, QC H7S 2B7, *Tel*	4,800	53	0	3714
MDA SYSTEMS HOLDINGS LTD (*Suby of* **MAXAR TECHNOLOGIES INC.**)				
13800 Commerce Pkwy, Richmond, BC V6V 2J3, *Tel* (604) 278-3411	4,800	54	1,216,752,000	8748
CHARTWELL RETIREMENT RESIDENCES				
100 Milverton Dr Suite 700, Mississauga, ON L5R 4H1, *Tel* (905) 501-9219	4,701	55	657,012,131	6719
BOMBARDIER INC				
800 Boul Rene-Levesque O 29e Etage, Montreal, QC H3B 1Y8, *Tel* (514) 861-9481	4,500	56	16,236,000,000	3743
PAN AMERICAN SILVER CORP				
625 Howe St Suite 1440, Vancouver, BC V6C 2T6, *Tel* (604) 684-1175	4,500	57	784,495,000	1044
VANCOUVER ISLAND HEALTH AUTHORITY (*Suby of* **GOVERNMENT OF THE PROVINCE OF BRITISH COLUMBIA**)				
3045 Gibbins Rd, Duncan, BC V9L 1E5, *Tel* (250) 737-2030	4,500	58	0	8011
BOWATER PRODUITS FORESTIERS DU CANADA ULC				
1155 Metcalfe Rue Bureau 800, Montreal, QC H3B 5H2, *Tel*	4,280	59	783,949,000	2621
SNC-LAVALIN CONSTRUCTION INC (*Suby of* **GROUPE SNC-LAVALIN INC**)				
455 Boul Rene-Levesque O Bureau 202, Montreal, QC H2Z 1Z3, *Tel* (514) 393-1000	4,154	60	2,901,120,368	1542
CALGARY BOARD OF EDUCATION (*Suby of* **CALGARY BOARD OF EDUCATION**)				
47 Fyffe Rd Se, Calgary, AB T2H 1B9, *Tel* (403) 777-6420	4,030	61	0	8211
3522997 CANADA INC				
180 Montee De Liesse, Saint-Laurent, QC H4T 1N7, *Tel* (450) 455-3963	4,000	62	1,486,625,672	6712
APOTEX INC				
200 Barmac Dr, North York, ON M9L 2Z7, *Tel* (800) 268-4623	4,000	63	0	2834
CENTRE HOSPITALIER UNIVERSITAIRE SAINTE-JUSTINE				
3175 Ch De La Cote-Sainte-Catherine, Montreal, QC H3T 1C5, *Tel* (514) 345-4931	4,000	64	499,860,000	8069
CITY OF OTTAWA (*Suby of* **CITY OF OTTAWA**)				
1500 St. Laurent Blvd, Ottawa, ON K1G 0Z8, *Tel* (613) 741-6440	4,000	65	0	4111
COMPAGNIE DE TELEPHONE BELL DU CANADA OU BELL CANADA, LA (*Suby of* **BCE INC**)				
1 Carref Alexander-Graham-Bell, Verdun, QC H3E 3B3, *Tel*	4,000	66	0	4899
FONDATION UNIVERSITE DU QUEBEC (*Suby of* **UNIVERSITE DU QUEBEC**)				
405 Rue Sainte-Catherine E, Montreal, QC H2L 2C4, *Tel*	4,000	67	0	8221
GENERAL MOTORS OF CANADA COMPANY (*Suby of* **GENERAL MOTORS COMPANY**)				
461 Park Rd S, Oshawa, ON L1J 8R3, *Tel* (905) 845-5456	4,000	68	0	3711
GMRI CANADA, INC				
790 Burnhamthorpe Rd W, Mississauga, ON L5C 4G3, *Tel* (905) 848-8477	4,000	69	186,556,000	5812
HALTON DISTRICT SCHOOL BOARD				
2050 Guelph Line, Burlington, ON L7P 5A8, *Tel* (905) 335-3663	4,000	70	415,308,610	8211
IBM CANADA LIMITED (*Suby of* **INTERNATIONAL BUSINESS MACHINES CORPORATION**)				
3600 Steeles Ave E, Markham, ON L3R 9Z7, *Tel* (905) 316-5000	4,000	71	4,494,032,000	3571
KINGSTON HEALTH SCIENCES CENTRE				
76 Stuart St, Kingston, ON K7L 2V7, *Tel* (613) 549-6666	4,000	72	444,320,000	8062

COMPANY	EMPLOYEES HERE	RANK	SALES ($)	PRIMARY SIC CODE
LONDON HEALTH SCIENCES CENTRE 800 Commissioners Rd E, London, ON N6A 5W9, *Tel* (519) 685-8500	4,000	73	857,946,895	8062
SQI HOLDINGS II INC (*Suby of* **EMPIRE COMPANY LIMITED**) 115 King St, Stellarton, NS B0K 0A2, *Tel* (902) 752-8371	4,000	74	1,462,036,000	6712
TELUS COMMUNICATIONS COMPANY (*Suby of* **TELUS CORPORATION**) 3777 Kingsway Suite 501, Burnaby, BC V5H 3Z7, *Tel* (604) 432-2151	4,000	75	1,338,176,000	4899
UNITED BROTHERHOOD OF CARPENTERS JOINERS AMERICA LOCAL 83 (*Suby of* **UNITED BROTHERHOOD OF CARPENTERS JOINERS AMERICA LOCAL 83**) 222 Rowntree Dairy Rd Suite 598, Woodbridge, ON L4L 9T2, *Tel* (416) 749-0675	4,000	76	0	8631
UNIVERSITE LAVAL (*Suby of* **UNIVERSITE LAVAL**) 1030 Av Des Sciences Humaines, Quebec, QC G1V 0A6, *Tel* (418) 656-2131	4,000	77	0	8221
VIDEOTRON SERVICE INFORMATIQUE LTEE 300 Av Viger E Bureau 6, Montreal, QC H2X 3W4, *Tel* (514) 281-1232	4,000	78	667,388,000	7374
KINROSS GOLD CORPORATION 25 York St 17th Fl, Toronto, ON M5J 2V5, *Tel* (416) 365-5123	3,927	79	3,212,600,000	1081
HEALTH SCIENCES NORTH 41 Ramsey Lake Rd, Sudbury, ON P3E 5J1, *Tel* (705) 523-7100	3,800	80	351,944,981	8062
BRUCE POWER L.P. (*Suby of* **BRUCE POWER L.P.**) 700 University Ave Suite 200, Toronto, ON M5G 1X6, *Tel* (519) 361-2673	3,700	81	0	4911
CANADIAN CORPS OF COMMISSIONAIRES (OTTAWA DIVISION) 24 Colonnade Rd N, Nepean, ON K2E 7J6, *Tel* (613) 228-0715	3,600	82	94,500,000	7381
ONTARIO POWER GENERATION INC (*Suby of* **GOVERNMENT OF ONTARIO**) 1675 Montgomery Park Rd, Pickering, ON L1V 2R5, *Tel* (905) 839-1151	3,600	83	0	4911
RIGHT AT HOME REALTY INC 300 West Beaver Creek Rd Suite 202, Richmond Hill, ON L4B 3B1, *Tel* (905) 695-7888	3,600	84	1,217,030,400	6531
AIR CANADA PILOTS ASSOCIATION (*Suby of* **AIR CANADA PILOTS ASSOCIATION**) 2000 Wellington Ave Suite 124a, Winnipeg, MB R3H 1C1, *Tel* (204) 779-0736	3,500	85	0	8641
AUTOCANADA INC 15511 123 Ave Nw Unit 200, Edmonton, AB T5V 0C3, *Tel* (866) 938-0561	3,500	86	2,388,613,378	5511
CANADA POST CORPORATION (*Suby of* **GOVERNMENT OF CANADA**) 555 Rue Mcarthur Bureau 1506, Saint-Laurent, QC H4T 1T4, *Tel* (514) 345-4571	3,500	87	0	4311
IZAAK WALTON KILLAM HEALTH CENTRE, THE (*Suby of* **NOVA SCOTIA, PROVINCE OF**) 5980 University Ave, Halifax, NS B3K 6R8, *Tel* (902) 470-8888	3,500	88	223,441,330	8069
MILLER MAINTENANCE LIMITED 2064 Kennedy Rd, Scarborough, ON M1T 3V1, *Tel* (416) 332-1360	3,500	89	1,148,402,500	1611
ROYAL GROUP, INC (*Suby of* **WESTLAKE CHEMICAL CORPORATION**) 10 Roybridge Gate Suite 201, Woodbridge, ON L4H 3M8, *Tel* (905) 264-1660	3,500	90	2,149,308,000	3089
SECURITE KOLOSSAL INC (*Suby of* **GW INTERMEDIATE HOLDCO CORPORATION**) 325 Rue Du Marais Bureau 220, Quebec, QC G1M 3R3, *Tel* (418) 683-1713	3,500	91	0	7381
SOCIETE DES CASINOS DU QUEBEC INC, LA (*Suby of* **GOUVERNEMENT DE LA PROVINCE DE QUEBEC**) 1 Av Du Casino, Montreal, QC H3C 4W7, *Tel* (514) 392-2756	3,500	92	0	7999
UNIVERSITE DU QUEBEC (*Suby of* **UNIVERSITE DU QUEBEC**) 1440 Rue Saint-Denis, Montreal, QC H3C 3P8, *Tel* (514) 987-3092	3,500	93	0	8221
UNIVERSITY HEALTH NETWORK 200 Elizabeth St, Toronto, ON M5G 2C4, *Tel* (416) 340-3111	3,500	94	1,650,250,111	8062
CASINO RAMA INC 5899 Rama Rd, Rama, ON L3V 6H6, *Tel* (705) 329-3325	3,400	95	294,780,000	7999
THOMSON REUTERS CORPORATION (*Suby of* **THOMSON COMPANY INC, THE**) 333 Bay St, Toronto, ON M5H 2R2, *Tel* (416) 687-7500	3,400	96	5,501,000,000	7299
ATLATSA RESOURCES CORPORATION 666 Burrard St Suite 1700, Vancouver, BC V6C 2X8, *Tel* (604) 631-1300	3,390	97	91,297,896	1081
CHICAGO, CENTRAL & PACIFIC RAILROAD COMPANY (*Suby of* **COMPAGNIE DES CHEMINS DE FER NATIONAUX DU CANADA**) 935 Rue De La Gauchetiere O, Montreal, QC H3B 2M9, *Tel* (514) 399-4536	3,218	98	1,588,993,694	4011
ILLINOIS CENTRAL RAILROAD COMPANY (*Suby of* **COMPAGNIE DES CHEMINS DE FER NATIONAUX DU CANADA**) 935 Rue De La Gauchetiere O Bureau 11, Montreal, QC H3B 2M9, *Tel* (514) 399-4536	3,218	99	1,588,993,694	4011
IZAAK WALTON KILLAM HEALTH CENTRE, THE (*Suby of* **NOVA SCOTIA, PROVINCE OF**) Gd, Halifax, NS B3K 6R8, *Tel* (902) 470-6682	3,200	100	0	8731
MONDELEZ CANADA INC (*Suby of* **MONDELEZ INTERNATIONAL, INC.**) 3300 Bloor St W Suite 1801, Etobicoke, ON M8X 2X2, *Tel*	3,200	101	1,754,586,000	2032
UNIVERSITE DE SHERBROOKE 2500 Boul De L'Universite, Sherbrooke, QC J1K 2R1, *Tel* (819) 821-7000	3,100	102	534,439,270	8221
MEMORIAL UNIVERSITY OF NEWFOUNDLAND 208 Elizabeth Ave, St. John'S, NL A1C 5S7, *Tel* (709) 637-6298	3,080	103	492,521,545	8221
BLACK GOLD REGIONAL DIVISION #18 (*Suby of* **BLACK GOLD REGIONAL DIVISION #18**) 105 Athabasca Ave, Devon, AB T9G 1A4, *Tel* (780) 987-3709	3,025	104	0	8211
ALGOMA STEEL INC 105 West St, Sault Ste. Marie, ON P6A 7B4, *Tel* (705) 945-2351	3,000	105	1,221,522,000	3312
BANK OF MONTREAL 119 Rue Saint-Jacques, Montreal, QC H2Y 1L6, *Tel* (514) 877-7373	3,000	106	17,792,580,876	6021
BMO NESBITT BURNS INC (*Suby of* **BMO NESBITT BURNS INC**) 1 First Canadian Pl 21st Fl, Toronto, ON M5X 1H3, *Tel* (416) 359-4000	3,000	107	0	6211
CANADA POST CORPORATION (*Suby of* **GOVERNMENT OF CANADA**)				

COMPANY	EMPLOYEES HERE	RANK	SALES ($)	PRIMARY SIC CODE
2701 Riverside Dr, Ottawa, ON K1A 0B1, *Tel* (613) 734-8440	3,000	108	0	4311
CANADA POST CORPORATION (*Suby of* GOVERNMENT OF CANADA)				
2701 Riverside Dr, Ottawa, ON K1A 1M2, *Tel* (613) 734-8440	3,000	109	0	4311
CANADIAN BROADCASTING CORPORATION (*Suby of* GOVERNMENT OF CANADA)				
205 Wellington St W Rm 4e301 B, Toronto, ON M5V 3G7, *Tel* (416) 205-5807	3,000	110	0	4833
CANADIAN BROADCASTING CORPORATION (*Suby of* GOVERNMENT OF CANADA)				
1400 Boul Rene-Levesque E, Montreal, QC H2L 2M2, *Tel* (514) 597-6000	3,000	111	0	4833
CANADIAN BROADCASTING CORPORATION (*Suby of* GOVERNMENT OF CANADA)				
250 Front St W, Toronto, ON M5V 3G5, *Tel* (416) 205-3311	3,000	112	0	4832
CANADIAN IMPERIAL BANK OF COMMERCE				
199 Bay St Commerce Crt W, Toronto, ON M5L 1A2, *Tel* (416) 980-3096	3,000	113	13,774,054,232	6021
CANADIAN NUCLEAR LABORATORIES LTD (*Suby of* GOVERNMENT OF CANADA)				
286 Plant Rd, Chalk River, ON K0J 1J0, *Tel* (613) 584-3311	3,000	114	1,445,096,250	2819
CASINO NIAGARA LIMITED (*Suby of* CASINO NIAGARA LIMITED)				
5705 Falls Ave, Niagara Falls, ON L2G 3K6, *Tel* (905) 374-3598	3,000	115	0	7999
CATALYST PULP AND PAPER SALES INC (*Suby of* CAPITAL ASSETS HOLDINGS (L) BERHAD)				
3600 Lysander Lane 2nd Fl, Richmond, BC V7B 1C3, *Tel* (604) 247-4400	3,000	116	2,085,900,000	5099
CENTRE DE SANTE ET DE SERVICES SOCIAUX DE QUEBEC-NORD (*Suby of* GOUVERNEMENT DE LA PROVINCE DE QUEBEC)				
190 76e Rue E, Quebec, QC G1H 7K4, *Tel* (418) 628-6808	3,000	117	0	8011
CENTRE HOSPITALIER UNIVERSITAIRE DE QUEBEC (*Suby of* CENTRE HOSPITALIER UNIVERSITAIRE DE QUEBEC)				
775 Rue Saint-Viateur Unite 130a, Quebec, QC G2L 2Z3, *Tel*	3,000	118	0	8062
CITI CARDS CANADA INC (*Suby of* CITIGROUP INC.)				
5900 Hurontario St, Mississauga, ON L5R 0B8, *Tel* (905) 285-7500	3,000	119	1,196,532,000	6153
EMERSON ELECTRIC CANADA LIMITED (*Suby of* EMERSON ELECTRIC CO.)				
66 Leek Cres 2nd Fl, Richmond Hill, ON L4B 1H1, *Tel* (905) 762-1010	3,000	120	1,888,703,985	5063
ERNST & YOUNG LLP (*Suby of* ERNST & YOUNG LLP)				
100 Adelaide St W Suite 3100, Toronto, ON M5H 0B3, *Tel* (416) 864-1234	3,000	121	610,014,900	8721
EVERTRUST DEVELOPMENT GROUP CANADA INC				
3100 Steeles Ave E Suite 302, Markham, ON L3R 8T3, *Tel* (647) 501-2345	3,000	122	2,095,176,000	1542
GREAT-WEST LIFE ASSURANCE COMPANY, THE (*Suby of* POWER CORPORATION DU CANADA)				
60 Osborne St N, Winnipeg, MB R3C 1V3, *Tel* (204) 946-8100	3,000	123	0	6311
HYDRO ONE INC (*Suby of* HYDRO ONE LIMITED)				
483 Bay St Suite 1000, Toronto, ON M5G 2P5, *Tel* (416) 345-5000	3,000	124	4,659,337,719	4911
INTACT FINANCIAL CORPORATION				
700 University Ave Suite 1500, Toronto, ON M5G 0A1, *Tel* (416) 341-1464	3,000	125	8,025,267,772	6331
MCGILL UNIVERSITY HEALTH CENTRE (*Suby of* MCGILL UNIVERSITY HEALTH CENTRE)				
687 Av Des Pins O Bureau 1408, Montreal, QC H3A 1A1, *Tel* (514) 934-1934	3,000	126	0	8062
PARMALAT HOLDINGS LIMITED				
405 The West Mall 10th Floor, Etobicoke, ON M9C 5J1, *Tel* (416) 626-1973	3,000	127	1,710,000,000	2026
PEACE RIVER HYDRO PARTNERS CONSTRUCTION LTD				
7007 269 Rd, Fort St. John, BC V1J 4M7, *Tel* (250) 263-9920	3,000	128	984,345,000	1629
PROVINCIAL HEALTH SERVICES AUTHORITY (*Suby of* PROVINCIAL HEALTH SERVICES AUTHORITY)				
600 10th Ave W, Vancouver, BC V5Z 4E6, *Tel* (604) 675-8251	3,000	129	0	8069
ROGERS COMMUNICATIONS CANADA INC (*Suby of* ROGERS COMMUNICATIONS INC)				
1 Mount Pleasant Rd Suite 115, Toronto, ON M4Y 2Y5, *Tel* (416) 764-2000	3,000	130	0	6712
SINAI HEALTH SYSTEM				
600 University Ave, Toronto, ON M5G 1X5, *Tel* (416) 596-4200	3,000	131	457,417,339	8062
SNC-LAVALIN INC (*Suby of* GROUPE SNC-LAVALIN INC)				
455 Boul Rene-Levesque O, Montreal, QC H2Z 1Z3, *Tel* (514) 393-1000	3,000	132	5,125,406,000	8711
ST. BONIFACE GENERAL HOSPITAL				
409 Tache Ave, Winnipeg, MB R2H 2A6, *Tel* (204) 233-8563	3,000	133	329,438,597	8062
SYNCRUDE CANADA LTD (*Suby of* SUNCOR ENERGY INC)				
9911 Macdonald Ave Suite 200, Fort Mcmurray, AB T9H 1S7, *Tel* (780) 790-5911	3,000	134	9,272,910,000	1311
TATA CONSULTANCY SERVICES CANADA INC (*Suby of* TATA CONSULTANCY SERVICES LIMITED)				
400 University Ave 25th Fl, Toronto, ON M5G 1S5, *Tel* (647) 790-7200	3,000	135	649,860,000	7379
UNIVERSITY OF GUELPH				
50 Stone Rd E, Guelph, ON N1G 2W1, *Tel* (519) 824-4120	3,000	136	630,799,140	8221
UNIVERSITY OF WESTERN ONTARIO, THE				
1151 Richmond St Suite 2, London, ON N6A 5B8, *Tel* (519) 661-2111	3,000	137	958,199,021	8221
WINDSOR CASINO LIMITED (*Suby of* HAMLET HOLDING, LLC)				
377 Riverside Dr E, Windsor, ON N9A 7H7, *Tel* (519) 258-7878	3,000	138	287,004,000	7011
CLEARSTREAM ENERGY SERVICES INC				
311 6 Ave Sw Suite 415, Calgary, AB T2P 3H2, *Tel* (587) 318-0997	2,900	139	286,814,246	8741
SEARS CANADA INC				
290 Yonge St Suite 700, Toronto, ON M5B 2C3, *Tel*	2,900	140	1,991,921,263	5311
CENTRE DE SANTE ET DE SERVICES SOCIAUX DE LAVAL (*Suby of* GOUVERNEMENT DE LA PROVINCE DE QUEBEC)				
1755 Boul Rene-Laennec, Cote Saint-Luc, QC H7M 3L9, *Tel* (450) 668-1010	2,815	141	2,308,699,584	8099
PARMALAT DAIRY & BAKERY INC				
405 The West Mall 10th Fl, Etobicoke, ON M9C 5J1, *Tel*	2,800	142	0	2026
PROVIDENCE HEALTH CARE SOCIETY				
1081 Burrard St, Vancouver, BC V6Z 1Y6, *Tel* (604) 682-2344	2,800	143	588,724,000	8062

COMPANY	EMPLOYEES HERE	RANK	SALES ($)	PRIMARY SIC CODE
GREAT-WEST LIFE ASSURANCE COMPANY, THE (*Suby of* **POWER CORPORATION DU CANADA**) 100 Osborne St N, Winnipeg, MB R3C 1V3, *Tel* (204) 946-1190	2,775	144	16,336,933,200	6324
CHIGNECTO CENTRAL REGIONAL SCHOOL BOARD 60 Lorne St, Truro, NS B2N 3K3, *Tel* (902) 897-8900	2,717	145	156,793,650	8211
QUINTERRA PROPERTY MAINTENANCE INC (*Suby of* **QUINTERRA PROPERTY MAINTENANCE INC**) 1681 Chestnut St Suite 400, Vancouver, BC V6J 4M6, *Tel* (604) 689-1800	2,700	146	0	7349
UNIVERSITY OF REGINA 3737 Wascana Pky, Regina, SK S4S 0A2, *Tel* (306) 584-1255	2,680	147	193,607,522	8221
LABRADOR IRON ORE ROYALTY CORPORATION 40 King St W, Toronto, ON M5W 2X6, *Tel* (416) 863-7133	2,620	148	99,216,599	6211
4093879 CANADA LTD 1771 Inkster Blvd, Winnipeg, MB R2X 1R3, *Tel* (204) 982-5783	2,600	149	950,323,400	6712
GENERAL MOTORS OF CANADA COMPANY (*Suby of* **GENERAL MOTORS COMPANY**) 300 Ingersoll St, Ingersoll, ON N5C 3J7, *Tel* (519) 485-6400	2,600	150	0	3711
LONDON INSURANCE GROUP INC (*Suby of* **POWER CORPORATION DU CANADA**) 255 Dufferin Ave Suite 540, London, ON N6A 4K1, *Tel* (519) 432-5281	2,600	151	15,920,411,600	6311
SMTC NOVA SCOTIA COMPANY (*Suby of* **SMTC CORPORATION**) 7050 Woodbine Ave Suite 300, Markham, ON L3R 4G8, *Tel* (905) 479-1810	2,600	152	735,579,000	3672
CIRQUE DU SOLEIL INC (*Suby of* **CIRQUE DU SOLEIL CANADA INC**) Cirque Du Soleil, Montreal, QC H1Z 4M6, *Tel* (514) 722-2324	2,560	153	346,800,000	7999
SAINT MARY'S UNIVERSITY 923 Robie St Suite 210, Halifax, NS B3H 3C3, *Tel* (902) 420-5400	2,530	154	112,320,955	8221
BANTREL CO. (*Suby of* **BECHTEL GROUP, INC.**) 1201 Glenmore Trail Sw Suite 1061, Calgary, AB T2V 4Y8, *Tel* (403) 290-5000	2,525	155	571,679,900	8711
CANADA POST CORPORATION (*Suby of* **GOVERNMENT OF CANADA**) 2701 Riverside Dr, Ottawa, ON K1A 1L5, *Tel* (613) 734-8440	2,500	156	6,444,881,802	4311
CENTRE DE SANTE ET DE SERVICES SOCIAUX - INSTITUT UNIVERSITAIRE DE GERIATRIE DE SHERBROOKE 375 Rue Argyll, Sherbrooke, QC J1J 3H5, *Tel* (819) 780-2222	2,500	157	557,280,000	8099
COMPAGNIE DES CHEMINS DE FER NATIONAUX DU CANADA (*Suby of* **COMPAGNIE DES CHEMINS DE FER NATIONAUX DU CANADA**) 11703 127 Ave Nw, Edmonton, AB T5E 0C9, *Tel* (780) 472-3486	2,500	158	0	4011
CONOCOPHILLIPS WESTERN CANADA PARTNERSHIP (*Suby of* **CONOCOPHILLIPS**) 401 9 Ave Sw Suite 1600, Calgary, AB T2P 3C5, *Tel* (403) 233-4000	2,500	159	1,637,913,000	1382
MOLSON BREWERIES OF CANADA LIMITED (*Suby of* **MOLSON COORS BREWING COMPANY**) 33 Carlingview Dr, Etobicoke, ON M9W 5E4, *Tel* (416) 679-1786	2,500	160	2,512,599,000	5181
SHATO HOLDINGS LTD 4088 Cambie St Suite 300, Vancouver, BC V5Z 2X8, *Tel* (604) 874-5533	2,500	161	2,193,054,000	6712
SIMON FRASER UNIVERSITY 8888 University Dr Suite 1200, Burnaby, BC V5A 1S6, *Tel* (778) 782-3111	2,500	162	524,279,654	8221
SUN LIFE ASSURANCE COMPANY OF CANADA (*Suby of* **SUN LIFE FINANCIAL INC**) 1155 Rue Metcalfe Bureau 20, Montreal, QC H3B 2V9, *Tel* (514) 866-6411	2,500	163	0	6311
TOLKO FOREST PRODUCTS LTD (*Suby of* **TIMBER INVESTMENTS LTD**) 3000 28 St, Vernon, BC V1T 9W9, *Tel* (250) 545-4411	2,500	164	695,975,000	2421
WILLIAM OSLER HEALTH SYSTEM 2100 Bovaird Dr E, Brampton, ON L6R 3J7, *Tel* (905) 494-2120	2,500	165	460,982,000	8062
WORKPLACE SAFETY & INSURANCE BOARD, THE 200 Front St W Suite 101, Toronto, ON M5V 3J1, *Tel* (416) 344-1000	2,500	166	9,381,289,520	6331
ROOTS CORPORATION 1400 Castlefield Ave Suite 2, Toronto, ON M6B 4N4, *Tel* (416) 781-3574	2,450	167	261,653,243	3143
COTT CORPORATION 6525 Viscount Rd, Mississauga, ON L4V 1H6, *Tel* (905) 672-1900	2,446	168	2,269,700,000	2086
4256344 CANADA INC (*Suby of* **MANULIFE FINANCIAL CORPORATION**) 1245 Rue Sherbrooke O Bureau 2100, Montreal, QC H3G 1G3, *Tel* (877) 499-9555	2,400	169	5,128,723,200	6311
BDO CANADA & ASSOCIATES LTD 36 Toronto St Suite 600, Toronto, ON M5C 2C5, *Tel* (416) 369-3100	2,400	170	498,444,000	8721
CANADIAN TEST CASE 192 (*Suby of* **CANADIAN TEST CASE 192**) 1110 Centre St Ne Suite 204, Calgary, AB T2E 2R2, *Tel* (403) 276-5546	2,400	171	0	3714
JBS CANADA INC (*Suby of* **TYSON FOODS, INC.**) Gd Stn Main, Brooks, AB T1R 1E4, *Tel* (403) 362-3457	2,400	172	0	2011
LOBLAWS INC (*Suby of* **LOBLAW COMPANIES LIMITED**) 1 Presidents Choice Cir, Brampton, ON L6Y 5S5, *Tel* (905) 459-2500	2,300	173	97,473,376,000	5141
OLD STEELCO INC (*Suby of* **ESSAR STEEL INDIA LIMITED**) 105 West St, Sault Ste. Marie, ON P6A 7B4, *Tel* (705) 945-2351	2,300	174	1,180,804,600	3312
SUNCOR ENERGY INC (*Suby of* **SUNCOR ENERGY INC**) 512 Snow Eagle Dr, Fort Mcmurray, AB T9H 0B6, *Tel* (780) 790-1999	2,300	175	0	1311
CENTRE DE SANTE ET DE SERVICES SOCIAUX DE CHICOUTIMI (*Suby of* **GOUVERNEMENT DE LA PROVINCE DE QUEBEC**) 305 Rue Saint-Vallier, Chicoutimi, QC G7H 5H6, *Tel* (418) 541-1046	2,200	176	608,662,400	8011
HYDRO-QUEBEC (*Suby of* **GOUVERNEMENT DE LA PROVINCE DE QUEBEC**) 2625 Boul Lebourgneuf Bureau 14, Quebec, QC G2C 1P1, *Tel* (888) 385-7252	2,200	177	0	4911
JAFFSONS HOLDINGS LTD 100 Park Royal S Suite 300, West Vancouver, BC V7T 1A2, *Tel* (604) 925-2700	2,200	178	804,119,800	6719
PRICEWATERHOUSECOOPERS LLP 18 York St Suite 2600, Toronto, ON M5J 0B2, *Tel* (416) 863-1133	2,200	179	1,201,544,500	8721

COMPANY	EMPLOYEES HERE	RANK	SALES ($)	PRIMARY SIC CODE
MAPLE LEAF FOODS INC (*Suby of* **MAPLE LEAF FOODS INC**) 6355 Richmond Ave E, Brandon, MB R7A 7M5, *Tel* (204) 571-2500	2,186	180	0	2011
WASTE MANAGEMENT OF CANADA CORPORATION (*Suby of* **WASTE MANAGEMENT, INC.**) 117 Wentworth Crt, Brampton, ON L6T 5L4, *Tel* (905) 595-3360	2,185	181	0	4953
MCMASTER UNIVERSITY (*Suby of* **MCMASTER UNIVERSITY**) Gd, Hamilton, ON L8N 3Z5, *Tel* (905) 521-2100	2,182	182	0	8221
BP CANADA ENERGY COMPANY (*Suby of* **BP P.L.C.**) 240 4 Ave Sw, Calgary, AB T2P 4H4, *Tel* (403) 233-1313	2,100	183	4,080,080,400	1311
BRIDGESTONE CANADA INC (*Suby of* **BRIDGESTONE CORPORATION**) 5770 Hurontario St Suite 400, Mississauga, ON L5R 3G5, *Tel* (877) 468-6270	2,100	184	1,383,462,000	5014
COGIR APARTMENTS REAL ESTATE INVESTMENT TRUST 7250 Boul Taschereau Bureau 200, Brossard, QC J4W 1M9, *Tel* (450) 672-5090	2,100	185	878,966,400	6531
EDMONTON NORTHLANDS (*Suby of* **EDMONTON NORTHLANDS**) 7424 118 Ave Nw, Edmonton, AB T5B 4M9, *Tel* (780) 471-7210	2,100	186	0	7922
HATCHCOS HOLDINGS LTD 2800 Speakman Dr, Mississauga, ON L5K 2R7, *Tel* (905) 855-7600	2,100	187	887,089,500	8711
GRAN COLOMBIA GOLD CORP 401 Bay St Suite 2400, Toronto, ON M5H 2Y4, *Tel* (416) 360-4653	2,098	188	268,525,000	1081
ARJO CANADA INC (*Suby of* **ARJOHUNTLEIGH MAGOG INC**) 90 Matheson Blvd W Suite 350, Mississauga, ON L5R 3R3, *Tel* (905) 238-7880	2,015	189	73,946,860	5047
CANADIAN CORPS OF COMMISSIONAIRES NATIONAL OFFICE, THE (*Suby of* **CANADIAN CORPS OF COMMISSIONAIRES NATIONAL OFFICE, THE**) 24 Colonnade Rd N, Nepean, ON K2E 7J6, *Tel*	2,002	190	0	7381
ALLSTREAM BUSINESS INC (*Suby of* **ZAYO GROUP HOLDINGS, INC.**) 5160 Orbitor Dr, Mississauga, ON L4W 5H2, *Tel* (888) 288-2273	2,000	191	1,839,992,000	4899
AMEX CANADA INC (*Suby of* **AMERICAN EXPRESS COMPANY**) 2225 Sheppard Ave E, North York, ON M2J 5C2, *Tel* (905) 474-8000	2,000	192	583,845,000	6099
B. GINGRAS ENTERPRISES LTD 4505 101 St Nw, Edmonton, AB T6E 5C6, *Tel* (780) 435-3355	2,000	193	63,936,000	7349
BEE-CLEAN BUILDING MAINTENANCE INCORPORATED 4505 101 St Nw, Edmonton, AB T6E 5C6, *Tel* (780) 435-3355	2,000	194	223,776,000	7349
BELL MEDIA INC (*Suby of* **BCE INC**) 9 Channel Nine Crt, Scarborough, ON M1S 4B5, *Tel* (416) 332-5000	2,000	195	0	4833
BELL MOBILITE INC (*Suby of* **BCE INC**) 200 Boul Bouchard Bureau 500, Dorval, QC H9S 5X5, *Tel* (514) 333-3336	2,000	196	0	5999
CANADIAN NATURAL RESOURCES LIMITED (*Suby of* **CANADIAN NATURAL RESOURCES LIMITED**) 324 8 Ave Sw Suite 1800, Calgary, AB T2P 2Z2, *Tel* (403) 517-6700	2,000	197	0	1311
CARGILL LIMITED (*Suby of* **CARGILL, INCORPORATED**) 472 Avenue & Hwy Suite 2a, High River, AB T1V 1P4, *Tel* (403) 652-4688	2,000	198	0	2011
CDSL CANADA LIMITED (*Suby of* **CGI INC**) 2480 Meadowvale Blvd Suite 100, Mississauga, ON L5N 8M6, *Tel* (905) 858-7100	2,000	199	0	7379
CENTRE HOSPITALIER DE L'UNIVERSITE DE MONTREAL (*Suby of* **CENTRE HOSPITALIER DE L'UNIVERSITE DE MONTREAL**) 1560 Rue Sherbrooke E, Montreal, QC H2L 4M1, *Tel* (800) 224-7737	2,000	200	0	8062
CHILDREN'S & WOMEN'S HEALTH CENTRE OF BRITISH COLUMBIA BRANCH (*Suby of* **PROVINCIAL HEALTH SERVICES AUTHORITY**) 4500 Oak St, Vancouver, BC V6H 3N1, *Tel* (604) 875-2424	2,000	201	433,212,000	8069
GENERAL DYNAMICS LAND SYSTEMS - CANADA CORPORATION (*Suby of* **GENERAL DYNAMICS CORPORATION**) 1991 Oxford St E Bldg 15, London, ON N5V 2Z7, *Tel* (519) 964-5900	2,000	202	639,870,000	3711
GENERAL MOTORS OF CANADA COMPANY (*Suby of* **GENERAL MOTORS COMPANY**) 570 Glendale Ave, St Catharines, ON L2R 7B3, *Tel* (905) 641-6424	2,000	203	0	3465
GOUVERNEMENT DE LA PROVINCE DE QUEBEC (*Suby of* **GOUVERNEMENT DE LA PROVINCE DE QUEBEC**) 116 Boul Lionel-Emond, Gatineau, QC J8Y 1W7, *Tel*	2,000	204	0	8062
GREAT-WEST LIFE ASSURANCE COMPANY, THE (*Suby of* **POWER CORPORATION DU CANADA**) 190 Simcoe St, Toronto, ON M5T 3M3, *Tel* (416) 597-1440	2,000	205		6311
HONDA CANADA INC (*Suby of* **HONDA MOTOR CO., LTD.**) 4700 Tottenham Rd, Alliston, ON L9R 1A2, *Tel* (705) 435-5561	2,000	206	0	3711
INLAND PACIFIC RESOURCES INC (*Suby of* **CORIX INFRASTRUCTURE INC**) 1188 Georgia St W Suite 1160, Vancouver, BC V6E 4A2, *Tel* (604) 697-6700	2,000	207	0	1623
INSTITUT DE CARDIOLOGIE DE MONTREAL 5000 Rue Belanger, Montreal, QC H1T 1C8, *Tel* (514) 376-3330	2,000	208	222,160,000	8069
LAKEHEAD UNIVERSITY (*Suby of* **LAKEHEAD UNIVERSITY**) 955 Oliver Rd Suite 2008, Thunder Bay, ON P7B 5E1, *Tel* (807) 343-8500	2,000	209	0	8221
MARYNA (PRIVATE) LIMITED 9926 Keele St Unit 5444, Vaughan, ON L6A 3Y4, *Tel*	2,000	210	1,083,470,000	6726
MCGILL UNIVERSITY HEALTH CENTRE (*Suby of* **MCGILL UNIVERSITY HEALTH CENTRE**) 2300 Rue Tupper Bureau F372, Montreal, QC H3H 1P3, *Tel* (514) 412-4307	2,000	211	0	8069
MCGILL UNIVERSITY HEALTH CENTRE (*Suby of* **MCGILL UNIVERSITY HEALTH CENTRE**) 3801 Rue University Bureau 548, Montreal, QC H3A 2B4, *Tel* (514) 398-6644	2,000	212	0	8062
NOVA SCOTIA COMMUNITY COLLEGE (*Suby of* **NOVA SCOTIA, PROVINCE OF**) 5685 Leeds St, Halifax, NS B3K 2T3, *Tel* (902) 491-3387	2,000	213	0	8221
NOVA SCOTIA HEALTH AUTHORITY (*Suby of* **NOVA SCOTIA, PROVINCE OF**) 1278 Tower Rd, Halifax, NS B3H 2Y9, *Tel* (902) 473-1787	2,000	214	0	8062

COMPANY	EMPLOYEES HERE	RANK	SALES ($)	PRIMARY SIC CODE
OTTAWA HOSPITAL, THE 1053 Carling Ave, Ottawa, ON K1Y 4E9, *Tel* (613) 798-5555	2,000	215	905,085,755	8062
PLASTIQUES IPL INC 1000 Sherbrooke W St Suite 700, Montreal, QC H3A 3G4, *Tel* (438) 320-6188	2,000	216	573,148,800	3089
PRAIRIE NORTH REGIONAL HEALTH AUTHORITY 1092 107th St, North Battleford, SK S9A 1Z1, *Tel* (306) 446-6600	2,000	217	3,766,859	8062
PROVINCE OF PEI (*Suby of* **PROVINCE OF PEI**) 60 Riverside Dr, Charlottetown, PE C1A 8T5, *Tel* (902) 894-2111	2,000	218	0	8062
RIO TINTO ALCAN INC (*Suby of* **RIO TINTO PLC**) 1 Smelter Site Rd, Kitimat, BC V8C 2H2, *Tel* (250) 639-8000	2,000	219	0	3334
SITA INFORMATION NETWORKING COMPUTING CANADA INC 777 Walker'S Line, Burlington, ON L7N 2G1, *Tel* (905) 681-6200	2,000	220	288,364,000	7371
ST. JOSEPH'S HEALTH SYSTEM 50 Charlton Ave E, Hamilton, ON L8N 4A6, *Tel* (905) 522-4941	2,000	221	7,049,144,900	8699
STATION MONT TREMBLANT INC (*Suby of* **HAWK HOLDING COMPANY, LLC**) 1000 Ch Des Voyageurs, Mont-Tremblant, QC J8E 1T1, *Tel* (819) 681-3000	2,000	222	191,336,000	7011
STATION MONT-TREMBLANT SOCIETE EN COMMANDITE 1000 Ch Des Voyageurs, Mont-Tremblant, QC J8E 1T1, *Tel* (819) 681-2000	2,000	223	191,336,000	7011
TORONTO EAST HEALTH NETWORK 825 Coxwell Ave, Toronto, ON M4C 3E7, *Tel* (416) 461-8272	2,000	224	333,240,000	8062
UNIFOR (*Suby of* **UNIFOR**) 1111 Homer Watson Blvd, Kitchener, ON N2C 2P7, *Tel*	2,000	225	0	8631
UNIVERSITE LAVAL (*Suby of* **UNIVERSITE LAVAL**) 1065 Av De La Medecine Pavillon Adrien-Pouliot, Quebec, QC G1V 0A6, *Tel* (418) 656-3474	2,000	226	0	8221
WORKERS' COMPENSATION BOARD OF BRITISH COLUMBIA 6951 Westminster Hwy, Richmond, BC V7C 1C6, *Tel* (604) 231-8888	2,000	227	6,838,297,600	6331
YORK UNIVERSITY (*Suby of* **YORK UNIVERSITY**) 4700 Keele St Rm 428, North York, ON M3J 1P3, *Tel* (416) 736-5113	2,000	228	0	8221
3958230 CANADA INC 600 Boul De Maisonneuve O Bureau 2200, Montreal, QC H3A 3J2, *Tel* (450) 646-9760	1,966	229	718,590,694	6712
DESJARDINS SECURITE FINANCIERE, COMPAGNIE D'ASSURANCE VIE (*Suby of* **FEDERATION DES CAISSES DESJARDINS DU QUEBEC**) 200 Rue Des Commandeurs, Levis, QC G6V 6R2, *Tel* (418) 838-7800	1,950	230	11,520,394,488	6311
CERTAS HOME AND AUTO INSURANCE COMPANY (*Suby of* **FEDERATION DES CAISSES DESJARDINS DU QUEBEC**) 6300 Boul Guillaume-Couture, Levis, QC G6V 6P9, *Tel* (418) 835-4900	1,900	231	9,017,597,600	6411
FLUOR CANADA LTD (*Suby of* **FLUOR CORPORATION**) 55 Sunpark Plaza Se, Calgary, AB T2X 3R4, *Tel* (403) 537-4000	1,900	232	473,114,400	8711
GRAND RIVER HOSPITAL CORPORATION 835 King St W, Kitchener, ON N2G 1G3, *Tel* (519) 742-3611	1,900	233	289,807,720	8062
MAPLE LODGE FARMS LTD (*Suby of* **MAPLE LODGE HOLDING CORPORATION**) 8301 Winston Churchill Blvd, Brampton, ON L6Y 0A2, *Tel* (905) 455-8340	1,900	234	1,413,416,500	2015
GOVERNING COUNCIL OF THE UNIVERSITY OF TORONTO, THE (*Suby of* **GOVERNING COUNCIL OF THE UNIVERSITY OF TORONTO, THE**) 100 St. George St, Toronto, ON M5S 3G3, *Tel* (416) 978-3383	1,806	235	0	8221
BOMBARDIER INC (*Suby of* **BOMBARDIER INC**) 200 Ch De La Cote-Vertu Bureau 1110, Dorval, QC H4S 2A3, *Tel* (514) 420-4000	1,800	236	0	3721
CANADIAN CORPS OF COMMISSIONAIRES (NORTHERN ALBERTA) 10633 124 St Nw Suite 101, Edmonton, AB T5N 1S5, *Tel* (780) 451-1974	1,800	237	47,250,000	7381
CBRE LIMITEE (*Suby of* **CBRE LIMITED PARTNERSHIP**) 145 King St W Suite 1100, Toronto, ON M5H 1J8, *Tel* (416) 362-2244	1,800	238	7,858,190,000	8748
FRASER HEALTH AUTHORITY (*Suby of* **GOVERNMENT OF THE PROVINCE OF BRITISH COLUMBIA**) 3935 Kincaid St, Burnaby, BC V5G 2X6, *Tel* (604) 434-3992	1,800	239	0	8062
LINAMAR HOLDINGS INC. (*Suby of* **LINAMAR CORPORATION**) 287 Speedvale Ave W, Guelph, ON N1H 1C5, *Tel* (519) 836-7550	1,800	240	523,530,000	3714
SAINT ELIZABETH HEALTH CARE 90 Allstate Pky Suite 300, Markham, ON L3R 6H3, *Tel* (905) 940-9655	1,800	241	176,412,300	8082
SHOPIFY INC 150 Elgin St 8th Floor, Ottawa, ON K2P 1L4, *Tel* (613) 241-2828	1,800	242	1,073,229,000	7374
TELUS COMMUNICATIONS INC (*Suby of* **TELUS CORPORATION**) 510 West Georgia St 7th Fl, Vancouver, BC V6B 0M3, *Tel* (888) 493-2007	1,800	243	9,032,688,000	4899
TFI INTERNATIONAL INC 8801 Rte Transcanadienne Bureau 500, Saint-Laurent, QC H4S 1Z6, *Tel* (514) 331-4113	1,800	244	3,883,914,231	4213
WESTERN REGIONAL INTEGRATED HEALTH AUTHORITY, THE 1 Brookfield Ave, Corner Brook, NL A2H 6J7, *Tel* (709) 637-5000	1,800	245	333,240,000	8062
BRITISH COLUMBIA MENTAL HEALTH SOCIETY (*Suby of* **PROVINCIAL HEALTH SERVICES AUTHORITY**) 2601 Lougheed Hwy, Coquitlam, BC V3C 4J2, *Tel* (604) 524-7000	1,700	246	0	8063
CONOCOPHILLIPS WESTERN CANADA PARTNERSHIP (*Suby of* **CONOCOPHILLIPS**) 401 9th Ave Sw, Calgary, AB T2P 2H7, *Tel* (403) 233-4000	1,700	247	0	1311
PACIFIC NATIONAL EXHIBITION 2901 Hastings St E, Vancouver, BC V5K 5J1, *Tel* (604) 253-2311	1,700	248	147,390,000	7999
PRAXAIR CANADA INC (*Suby of* **LINDE PUBLIC LIMITED COMPANY**) 834 51st St E Suite 5, Saskatoon, SK S7K 5C7, *Tel* (306) 242-3325	1,700	249	0	2813
SANOFI-AVENTIS CANADA INC (*Suby of* **SANOFI**)				

COMPANY	EMPLOYEES HERE	RANK	SALES ($)	PRIMARY SIC CODE
2905 Place Louis-R.-Renaud, Cote Saint-Luc, QC H7V 0A3, *Tel* (514) 331-9220	1,700	250	701,795,700	5122
SEASPAN ULC (*Suby of* **WASHINGTON CANADIAN LTD**)				
10 Pemberton Ave, North Vancouver, BC V7P 2R1, *Tel* (604) 988-3111	1,700	251	548,433,900	4492
BESRA GOLD INC				
10 King St E Suite 500, Toronto, ON M5C 1C3, *Tel* (416) 572-2525	1,681	252	429,956,094	1081
THOMPSON RIVERS UNIVERSITY				
805 Tru Way, Kamloops, BC V2C 0C8, *Tel* (250) 828-5000	1,676	253	137,217,057	8221
CANADIAN CORPS OF COMMISSIONAIRES (SOUTHERN ALBERTA)				
1107 53 Ave Ne, Calgary, AB T2E 6X9, *Tel* (403) 244-4664	1,650	254	48,267,879	7381
MOHAWK COLLEGE OF APPLIED ARTS AND TECHNOLOGY, THE (*Suby of* **MOHAWK COLLEGE OF APPLIED ARTS AND TECHNOLOGY, THE**)				
135 Fennell Ave W, Hamilton, ON L9C 0E5, *Tel* (905) 575-1212	1,650	255	0	8222
LUNDIN GOLD INC				
885 Georgia St W Suite 2000, Vancouver, BC V6C 3E8, *Tel* (604) 689-7842	1,645	256	420,748,230	1041
GCT CANADA LIMITED PARTNERSHIP (*Suby of* **GCT GLOBAL CONTAINER TERMINALS INC**)				
1285 Franklin St, Vancouver, BC V6A 1J9, *Tel* (604) 267-5200	1,614	257	560,640,654	4491
CENTRE DE SANTE ET DE SERVICES SOCIAUX DU SUD-OUEST-VERDUN (*Suby of* **GOUVERNEMENT DE LA PROVINCE DE QUEBEC**)				
4000 Boul Lasalle, Verdun, QC H4G 2A3, *Tel* (514) 362-1000	1,600	258	0	8062
CP ENERGY MARKETING INC (*Suby of* **CITY OF EDMONTON**)				
505 2 St Sw Suite 84, Calgary, AB T2P 1N8, *Tel* (403) 717-4600	1,600	259	285,982,400	8711
EDWARD D. JONES & CO. CANADA HOLDING CO., INC (*Suby of* **JONES FINANCIAL COMPANIES, L.L.L.P.**)				
90 Burnhamthorpe Rd W Suite 902, Mississauga, ON L5B 3C3, *Tel* (905) 306-8600	1,600	260	35,578,450,000	6211
MARKHAM STOUFFVILLE HOSPITAL				
381 Church St, Markham, ON L3P 7P3, *Tel* (905) 472-7000	1,600	261	188,836,000	8062
MAXSYS STAFFING & CONSULTING INC				
173 Dalhousie St Suite A, Ottawa, ON K1N 7C7, *Tel* (613) 562-9943	1,600	262	405,584,000	8748
NORTH YORK GENERAL HOSPITAL				
4001 Leslie St, North York, ON M2K 1E1, *Tel* (416) 756-6000	1,600	263	306,546,093	8062
SCDA (2015) INC (*Suby of* **MANULIFE FINANCIAL CORPORATION**)				
1245 Rue Sherbrooke O Bureau 2100, Montreal, QC H3G 1G3, *Tel* (514) 499-8855	1,600	264	4,273,936,000	6311
SHELL CANADA LIMITED (*Suby of* **ROYAL DUTCH SHELL PLC**)				
400 4 Ave Sw, Calgary, AB T2P 0J4, *Tel* (403) 691-3111	1,600	265	14,836,656,000	1311
TD SECURITIES INC (*Suby of* **TORONTO-DOMINION BANK, THE**)				
66 Wellington St W, Toronto, ON M5K 1A2, *Tel* (416) 307-8500	1,600	266	3,557,845,000	6211
UBISOFT DIVERTISSEMENTS INC (*Suby of* **UBISOFT ENTERTAINMENT**)				
5505 Boul Saint-Laurent Bureau 5000, Montreal, QC H2T 1S6, *Tel* (514) 490-2000	1,600	267	553,719,000	7371
UNIVERSITY OF NEW BRUNSWICK				
3 Bailey Dr, Fredericton, NB E3B 5A3, *Tel* (506) 453-4666	1,600	268	373,477,500	8221
ERICSSON CANADA INC (*Suby of* **TELEFON AB LM ERICSSON**)				
8400 Boul Decarie, Mont-Royal, QC H4P 2N2, *Tel* (514) 345-7900	1,550	269	0	5065
CARGILL LIMITED (*Suby of* **CARGILL, INCORPORATED**)				
781 York Rd, Guelph, ON N1E 6N1, *Tel* (519) 823-5200	1,540	270	0	2011
STANTEC INC				
10220 103 Ave Nw Suite 400, Edmonton, AB T5J 0K4, *Tel* (780) 917-7000	1,535	271	3,247,557,348	8711
ATOMIC ENERGY OF CANADA LIMITED (*Suby of* **GOVERNMENT OF CANADA**)				
286 Plant Rd Stn 508a, Chalk River, ON K0J 1J0, *Tel* (613) 584-3311	1,500	272	684,882,574	4911
BANTREL CO. (*Suby of* **BECHTEL GROUP, INC.**)				
600-1201 Glenmore Trail Sw, Calgary, AB T2V 4Y8, *Tel* (403) 290-5000	1,500	273	0	8711
BENTLEYS OF LONDON SLACKS LTD				
1309 Mountain Ave, Winnipeg, MB R2X 2Y1, *Tel* (204) 786-6081	1,500	274	205,011,000	2339
CANADIAN NATIONAL EXHIBITION ASSOCIATION				
210 Princes Blvd, Toronto, ON M6K 3C3, *Tel* (416) 263-3600	1,500	275	112,867,500	7996
CENTRE FOR ADDICTION AND MENTAL HEALTH				
1001 Queen St W Suite 301, Toronto, ON M6J 1H4, *Tel* (416) 535-8501	1,500	276	285,778,061	8093
CENTRE HOSPITALIER UNIVERSITAIRE DE QUEBEC				
11 Cote Du Palais, Quebec, QC G1R 2J6, *Tel* (418) 525-4444	1,500	277	1,555,120,000	8062
COMPAGNIE MINIERE IOC INC (*Suby of* **RIO TINTO PLC**)				
2 Avalon Dr, Labrador City, NL A2V 2Y6, *Tel* (709) 944-8400	1,500	278	0	1011
CONCORD CONCRETE GROUP INC				
125 Edilcan Dr, Concord, ON L4K 3S6, *Tel* (905) 738-7979	1,500	279	308,559,000	4213
CONOCOPHILLIPS CANADA RESOURCES CORP (*Suby of* **CONOCOPHILLIPS**)				
401 9 Ave Sw Suite 1600, Calgary, AB T2P 3C5, *Tel* (403) 233-4000	1,500	280	4,450,996,800	1311
CORRPRO CANADA, INC (*Suby of* **AEGION CORPORATION**)				
8607 101 St, Fort St. John, BC V1J 5K4, *Tel* (250) 787-9100	1,500	281	0	8711
DENTSU AEGIS NETWORK ENTERPRISE SOLUTIONS INC				
1 University Ave 10fl, Toronto, ON M5J 2P1, *Tel* (416) 473-6287	1,500	282	300,556,500	7311
DESJARDINS GROUPE D'ASSURANCES GENERALES INC (*Suby of* **FEDERATION DES CAISSES DESJARDINS DU QUEBEC**)				
6300 Boul Guillaume-Couture, Levis, QC G6V 6P9, *Tel* (418) 835-4850	1,500	283	21,751,394,632	6411
EPCOR UTILITIES INC (*Suby of* **CITY OF EDMONTON**)				
10423 101 St Nw Suite 2000, Edmonton, AB T5H 0E8, *Tel* (780) 412-3414	1,500	284	1,439,349,170	4941
ERB GROUP OF COMPANIES, THE				
290 Hamilton Rd, New Hamburg, ON N3A 1A2, *Tel* (519) 662-2710	1,500	285	308,559,000	4213

COMPANY	EMPLOYEES HERE	RANK	SALES ($)	PRIMARY SIC CODE
FUTURE ELECTRONICS (CDA) LTD (*Suby of* **INVESTISSEMENTS ALONIM INC, LES**) 237 Boul Hymus, Pointe-Claire, QC H9R 5C7, *Tel* (514) 694-7710	1,500	286	4,637,914,271	5065
GENERAL DYNAMICS LAND SYSTEMS - CANADA CORPORATION (*Suby of* **GENERAL DYNAMICS CORPORA-TION**) 1941 Robertson Rd, Nepean, ON K2H 5B7, *Tel* (613) 596-7000	1,500	287	0	3711
GRANT MACEWAN UNIVERSITY 10700 104 Ave Nw, Edmonton, AB T5J 4S2, *Tel* (780) 497-5168	1,500	288	394,836,400	8221
HOPITAL SANTA CABRINI 5655 Rue Saint-Zotique E, Montreal, QC H1T 1P7, *Tel* (514) 252-1535	1,500	289	166,620,000	8062
HUDBAY MINERALS INC (*Suby of* **HUDBAY MINERALS INC**) Gd, Flin Flon, MB R8A 1N9, *Tel* (204) 687-2385	1,500	290	0	1021
HUSKY OIL OPERATIONS LIMITED (*Suby of* **HUSKY ENERGY INC**) 707 8 Ave Sw, Calgary, AB T2P 1H5, *Tel* (403) 298-6111	1,500	291	6,861,953,400	1311
IBM CANADA LIMITED (*Suby of* **INTERNATIONAL BUSINESS MACHINES CORPORATION**) 23 Boul De L'Aeroport, Bromont, QC J2L 1A3, *Tel* (450) 534-6000	1,500	292	0	3674
IMPERIAL OIL RESOURCES LIMITED (*Suby of* **IMPERIAL OIL LIMITED**) 237 4 Ave Sw, Calgary, AB T2P 0H6, *Tel* (800) 567-3776	1,500	293	2,018,037,000	1382
INNVEST REAL ESTATE INVESTMENT TRUST 200 Bay St Suite 3205, Toronto, ON M5J 2J1, *Tel* (416) 607-7100	1,500	294	774,910,800	7011
INSURANCE CORPORATION OF BRITISH COLUMBIA (*Suby of* **GOVERNMENT OF THE PROVINCE OF BRITISH COLUMBIA**) 151 Esplanade W, North Vancouver, BC V7M 3H9, *Tel* (604) 661-2800	1,500	295	4,705,051,859	6331
LOBLAWS SUPERMARKETS LIMITED (*Suby of* **LOBLAW COMPANIES LIMITED**) 1460 Merivale Rd, Nepean, ON K2E 5P2, *Tel* (613) 226-6001	1,500	296	0	5411
MANUFACTURERS LIFE INSURANCE COMPANY, THE (*Suby of* **MANULIFE FINANCIAL CORPORATION**) 200 Bloor St E Suite 1, Toronto, ON M4W 1E5, *Tel* (416) 926-3000	1,500	297	38,465,424,000	6311
METROLINX 97 Front St W Suite 200, Toronto, ON M5J 1E6, *Tel* (416) 874-5900	1,500	298	1,580,105,600	4011
MORGAN CONSTRUCTION AND ENVIRONMENTAL LTD 17303 102 Ave Nw, Edmonton, AB T5S 1J8, *Tel* (780) 733-9100	1,500	299	492,172,500	1623
MOTOR COACH INDUSTRIES LIMITED (*Suby of* **NFI GROUP INC**) 1475 Clarence Ave, Winnipeg, MB R3T 1T5, *Tel* (204) 284-5360	1,500	300	698,040,000	3711
MUNICIPAL CONTRACTING LIMITED (*Suby of* **MUNICIPAL ENTERPRISES LIMITED**) 927 Rocky Lake Dr, Waverley, NS B2R 1S1, *Tel* (902) 835-3381	1,500	301	0	1611
NIAGARA 21ST GROUP INC (*Suby of* **NIAGARA 21ST GROUP INC**) 6740 Fallsview Blvd, Niagara Falls, ON L2G 3W6, *Tel* (905) 357-7300	1,500	302	0	7011
OLIVER & BONACINI HOSPITALITY INC 2323 Yonge St Suite 303, Toronto, ON M4P 2C9, *Tel* (416) 485-8047	1,500	303	69,958,500	5812
PIC GROUP HOLDINGS LIMITED, THE 111 Simcoe St N, Oshawa, ON L1G 4S4, *Tel* (905) 743-4600	1,500	304	548,263,500	6712
PUROLATOR INC (*Suby of* **GOVERNMENT OF CANADA**) 62 Vulcan St, Etobicoke, ON M9W 1L2, *Tel* (416) 241-4496	1,500	305	0	4731
RODFAM HOLDINGS LIMITED 2575 Airport Rd, Windsor, ON N8W 1Z4, *Tel* (519) 969-3350	1,500	306	548,263,500	6712
SAIPEM CANADA INC (*Suby of* **SAIPEM SPA**) 530 8 Ave Sw Suite 2100, Calgary, AB T2P 3S8, *Tel* (403) 441-2793	1,500	307	492,172,500	1629
SECURITAS CANADA LIMITED (*Suby of* **SECURITAS AB**) 1980 Rue Sherbrooke O Bureau 300, Montreal, QC H3H 1E8, *Tel* (514) 935-2533	1,500	308	0	7381
SECURITE NATIONALE COMPAGNIE D'ASSURANCE (*Suby of* **TORONTO-DOMINION BANK, THE**) 50 Boul Cremazie O Bureau 1200, Montreal, QC H2P 1B6, *Tel* (514) 382-6060	1,500	309	2,061,105,251	6712
SPERIDIAN TECHNOLOGIES CANADA INC 357 Bay St Suite 402, Toronto, ON M5H 2T7, *Tel* (416) 613-1621	1,500	310	219,910,449	7371
ST AMANT INC 440 River Rd, Winnipeg, MB R2M 3Z9, *Tel* (204) 256-4301	1,500	311	102,489,000	8059
ST. JOSEPH'S HEALTH CARE, LONDON (*Suby of* **ST. JOSEPH'S HEALTH CARE, LONDON**) 268 Grosvenor St, London, ON N6A 4V2, *Tel* (519) 646-6100	1,500	312	0	8093
ST. JOSEPH'S HEALTH CARE, LONDON 268 Grosvenor St, London, ON N6A 4V2, *Tel* (519) 646-6100	1,500	313	352,779,616	8361
TECK METALS LTD (*Suby of* **TECK RESOURCES LIMITED**) 25 Aldridge Ave, Trail, BC V1R 4L8, *Tel* (250) 364-4222	1,500	314	0	1081
TRANSX LTD (*Suby of* **COMPAGNIE DES CHEMINS DE FER NATIONAUX DU CANADA**) 2595 Inkster Blvd, Winnipeg, MB R3C 2E6, *Tel* (204) 632-6694	1,500	315	460,952,500	4213
TREE ISLAND STEEL LTD 3933 Boundary Rd, Richmond, BC V6V 1T8, *Tel* (604) 524-3744	1,500	316	178,385,949	3496
TRICAN WELL SERVICE LTD (*Suby of* **TRICAN WELL SERVICE LTD**) 11979 40 St Se Unit 418, Calgary, AB T2Z 4M3, *Tel* (403) 723-3688	1,500	317	0	1389
VANCOUVER ISLAND UNIVERSITY 90 Fifth St, Nanaimo, BC V9R 1N1, *Tel* (250) 753-3245	1,500	318	298,782,000	8221
VITALITE HEALTH NETWORK 330 Av Universite, Moncton, NB E1C 2Z3, *Tel* (506) 862-4000	1,500	319	277,700,000	8062
VIVA MEDIA PACKAGING (CANADA) LTD 1663 Neilson Rd Suite 13, Scarborough, ON M1X 1T1, *Tel* (416) 321-0622	1,500	320	358,218,000	3089
WINNIPEG REGIONAL HEALTH AUTHORITY, THE (*Suby of* **WINNIPEG REGIONAL HEALTH AUTHORITY, THE**) 820 Sherbrook St Suite 543, Winnipeg, MB R3A 1R9, *Tel* (204) 774-6511	1,500	321	0	8062

COMPANY	EMPLOYEES HERE	RANK	SALES ($)	PRIMARY SIC CODE
WORLEYCORD LP (*Suby of* **WORLEYPARSONS LIMITED**) 8500 Macleod Trail Se Suite 400, Calgary, AB T2H 2N1, *Tel* (780) 465-5516	1,500	322	820,287,500	1629
CSSS PIERRE-DE SAUREL 400 Av De L'Hotel-Dieu, Sorel-Tracy, QC J3P 1N5, *Tel* (450) 746-6000	1,480	323	164,398,400	8062
HUDBAY MINERALS INC 25 York St Suite 800, Toronto, ON M5J 2V5, *Tel* (416) 362-8181	1,455	324	1,472,366,000	1081
MOUNT ALLISON UNIVERSITY 65 York St, Sackville, NB E4L 1E4, *Tel* (506) 364-2269	1,435	325	214,376,085	8221
URGENCES-SANTE 6700 Rue Jarry E, Montreal, QC H1P 0A4, *Tel* (514) 723-5600	1,426	326	93,853,709	4119
HOME HARDWARE STORES LIMITED 34 Henry St, St Jacobs, ON N0B 2N0, *Tel* (519) 664-2252	1,420	327	2,424,608,819	5211
3836185 CANADA INC 2850 Av Jacques-Bureau, Laval, QC H7P 0B7, *Tel* (450) 688-6264	1,400	328	511,712,600	6712
CANADIAN ENERGY SERVICES INC (*Suby of* **CES ENERGY SOLUTIONS CORP**) 700 4 Ave Sw Suite 1400, Calgary, AB T2P 3J4, *Tel* (403) 269-2800	1,400	329	764,359,400	1381
CENTRE HOSPITALIER REGIONAL DE TROIS-RIVIERES 1991 Boul Du Carmel, Trois-Rivieres, QC G8Z 3R9, *Tel* (819) 697-3333	1,400	330	155,512,000	8069
CHC HELICOPTERS CANADA INC 4740 Agar Dr, Richmond, BC V7B 1A3, *Tel* (604) 276-7500	1,400	331	373,769,200	4522
GRAND TRUNK WESTERN RAILROAD INCORPORATED (*Suby of* **COMPAGNIE DES CHEMINS DE FER NATIONAUX DU CANADA**) 935 Rue De La Gauchetiere O Bureau 14, Montreal, QC H3B 2M9, *Tel* (514) 399-4536	1,400	332	553,613,200	4731
HUMBER RIVER HOSPITAL 1235 Wilson Ave, Toronto, ON M3M 0B2, *Tel* (416) 242-1000	1,400	333	333,240,000	8062
QUINTE HEALTHCARE CORPORATION 265 Dundas St E, Belleville, ON K8N 5A9, *Tel* (613) 969-7400	1,400	334	194,390,000	8062
ROLLS-ROYCE CANADA LIMITEE (*Suby of* **ROLLS-ROYCE HOLDINGS PLC**) 9500 Ch De La Cote-De-Liesse, Lachine, QC H8T 1A2, *Tel* (514) 631-3541	1,400	335	476,028,000	4581
SEVEN OAKS GENERAL HOSPITAL 2300 Mcphillips St, Winnipeg, MB R2V 3M3, *Tel* (204) 632-7133	1,400	336	155,512,000	8062
STANTEC CONSULTING LTD (*Suby of* **STANTEC INC**) 10220 103 Ave Nw Suite 400, Edmonton, AB T5J 0K4, *Tel* (780) 917-7000	1,400	337	2,777,575,790	8711
TEKNION LIMITED (*Suby of* **GLOBAL UPHOLSTERY CO LIMITED**) 1150 Flint Rd, North York, ON M3J 2J5, *Tel* (416) 661-1577	1,400	338	712,528,000	2522
VALE CANADA LIMITED (*Suby of* **VALE S/A**) 1 Plant Rd, Thompson, MB R8N 1P3, *Tel* (204) 778-2211	1,400	339	0	1061
1127770 B.C. LTD 777 Broadway W, Vancouver, BC V5Z 4J7, *Tel*	1,398	340	761,009,648	5047
CENOVUS ENERGY INC 500 Centre St Se, Calgary, AB T2P 0M5, *Tel* (403) 766-2000	1,386	341	16,215,043,678	1382
JOSEPH BRANT HOSPITAL 1245 Lakeshore Rd, Burlington, ON L7S 0A2, *Tel* (905) 632-3730	1,380	342	10,846,667	8062
GROUPE JEAN COUTU (PJC) INC, LE (*Suby of* **METRO INC**) 245 Rue Jean-Coutu, Varennes, QC J3X 0E1, *Tel* (450) 646-9760	1,350	343	8,296,050,816	5122
HAMILTON HEALTH SCIENCES CORPORATION (*Suby of* **HAMILTON HEALTH SCIENCES CORPORATION**) 711 Concession St Suite 201, Hamilton, ON L8V 1C3, *Tel* (905) 389-4411	1,345	344		8062
BLACKCOMB SKIING ENTERPRISES LIMITED PARTNERSHIP 4545 Blackcomb Way, Whistler, BC V8E 0X9, *Tel* (604) 932-3141	1,300	345	124,368,400	7011
BRIDGESTONE CANADA INC (*Suby of* **BRIDGESTONE CORPORATION**) 1200 Boul Firestone, Joliette, QC J6E 2W5, *Tel* (450) 756-1061	1,300	346	0	3011
CENTRE DE SANTE ET DE SERVICES SOCIAUX DE LA VIEILLE-CAPITALE 50 Rue Saint-Joseph E, Quebec, QC G1K 3A5, *Tel* (418) 529-2572	1,300	347	0	8322
GENERAL ELECTRIC CANADA COMPANY (*Suby of* **GENERAL ELECTRIC COMPANY**) 107 Park St N Suite 2, Peterborough, ON K9J 7B5, *Tel* (705) 748-8486	1,300	348	0	3625
GOUVERNEMENT DE LA PROVINCE DE QUEBEC (*Suby of* **GOUVERNEMENT DE LA PROVINCE DE QUEBEC**) 525 Boul Wilfrid-Hamel, Quebec, QC G1M 2S8, *Tel* (418) 649-3700	1,300	349	0	8093
HUDSON'S BAY COMPANY (*Suby of* **HUDSON'S BAY COMPANY**) 674 Granville St Suite 9999, Vancouver, BC V6C 1Z6, *Tel* (604) 681-6211	1,300	350	0	5311
KITCHEN CRAFT OF CANADA (*Suby of* **FORTUNE BRANDS HOME & SECURITY, INC.**) 1180 Springfield Rd, Winnipeg, MB R2C 2Z2, *Tel* (204) 224-3211	1,300	351	626,377,500	2434
MAGNA INTERNATIONAL INC (*Suby of* **MAGNA INTERNATIONAL INC**) 65 Independence Pl, Guelph, ON N1K 1H8, *Tel* (519) 763-6042	1,300	352	0	3714
MOSAIC CANADA ULC (*Suby of* **THE MOSAIC COMPANY**) 3 Kalium Rd, Belle Plaine, SK S0G 0G0, *Tel* (306) 345-8067	1,300	353	0	1474
ONTARIO SHORES CENTRE FOR MENTAL HEALTH SCIENCES 700 Gordon St, Whitby, ON L1N 5S9, *Tel* (905) 668-5881	1,300	354	103,855,700	8063
OTTAWA HOSPITAL, THE (*Suby of* **OTTAWA HOSPITAL, THE**) 725 Parkdale Ave, Ottawa, ON K1Y 4E9, *Tel* (613) 761-4395	1,300	355	0	8733
PUROLATOR HOLDINGS LTD (*Suby of* **GOVERNMENT OF CANADA**) 5995 Avebury Rd Suite 100, Mississauga, ON L5R 3T8, *Tel* (905) 712-1251	1,300	356	4,942,975,000	4731
ROYAL YORK OPERATIONS LP (*Suby of* **KINGSETT CAPITAL INC**) 100 Front St W, Toronto, ON M5J 1E3, *Tel* (416) 368-2511	1,300	357	115,989,606	7011

COMPANY	EMPLOYEES HERE	RANK	SALES ($)	PRIMARY SIC CODE
SYNDICAT DES PROFESSIONNELLES EN SOINS DU CENTRE DE SANTE ET SERVICES SOCIAUX DU COEUR DE (*Suby of* **GOUVERNEMENT DE LA PROVINCE DE QUEBEC**) 1385 Rue Jean-Talon E, Montreal, QC H2E 1S6, *Tel* (514) 495-6767	1,300	358	222,160,000	8062
UNITED ASSOCIATION OF JOURNEYMEN AND APPRENTICES OF THE PLUMBING AND PIPEFITTING INDUSTRY (*Suby of* **UNITED ASSOCIATION OF JOURNEYMEN AND APPRENTICES OF THE PLUMBING AND PIPEFITTING INDUSTRY**) 1151 Confederation St, Sarnia, ON N7S 3Y5, *Tel* (519) 337-6261	1,300	359	0	8611
UNIVERSITE DU QUEBEC (*Suby of* **UNIVERSITE DU QUEBEC**) 3351 Boul Des Forges, Trois-Rivieres, QC G8Z 4M3, *Tel* (819) 376-5011	1,300	360	0	8221
WINDSOR REGIONAL HOSPITAL 1995 Lens Ave, Windsor, ON N8W 1L9, *Tel* (519) 254-5577	1,300	361	244,376,000	8062
SAULT AREA HOSPITAL 750 Great Northern Rd Suite 1, Sault Ste. Marie, ON P6B 0A8, *Tel* (705) 759-3434	1,292	362	144,404,000	8062
GENERAL MOTORS OF CANADA COMPANY (*Suby of* **GENERAL MOTORS COMPANY**) 1550 Kildare Rd, Windsor, ON N8W 2W4, *Tel* (519) 255-4161	1,290	363	0	3714
TRILLIUM HEALTH PARTNERS 100 Queensway W, Mississauga, ON L5B 1B8, *Tel* (905) 848-7580	1,290	364	790,016,724	8062
AVIVA CANADA INC (*Suby of* **GENERAL ACCIDENT PLC**) 10 Aviva Way Suite 100, Markham, ON L6G 0G1, *Tel* (416) 288-1800	1,250	365	1,927,074,700	6411
CANADIAN WESTERN BANK 10303 Jasper Ave Nw Suite 3000, Edmonton, AB T5J 3N6, *Tel* (780) 423-8888	1,250	366	586,516,520	6021
IDL PROJECTS INC 1088 Great St, Prince George, BC V2N 2K8, *Tel* (250) 649-0561	1,250	367	872,990,000	1542
MBNA CANADA BANK (*Suby of* **TORONTO-DOMINION BANK, THE**) 1600 James Naismith Dr Suite 800, Gloucester, ON K1B 5N8, *Tel* (613) 907-4800	1,250	368	337,500,014	6021
TECK HIGHLAND VALLEY COPPER PARTNERSHIP (*Suby of* **TECK RESOURCES LIMITED**) Hwy 97c Highland Valley Copper Minesite, Logan Lake, BC V0K 1W0, *Tel* (250) 523-2443	1,250	369	319,717,500	1021
UNITED STEELWORKERS OF AMERICA (*Suby of* **UNITED STEELWORKERS**) 1 Diamond St, Trenton, NS B0K 1X0, *Tel*	1,201	370	0	8631
3M CANADA COMPANY (*Suby of* **3M COMPANY**) 300 Tartan Dr, London, ON N5V 4M9, *Tel* (519) 451-2500	1,200	371	889,290,000	2891
989116 ONTARIO LIMITED 503 Centennial Rd N, Scarborough, ON M1C 2A5, *Tel* (416) 208-5441	1,200	372	0	5112
BEAUWARD SHOPPING CENTRES LTD (*Suby of* **BEAUWARD SHOPPING CENTRES LTD**) 3200 Boul Laframboise Bureau 1009, Saint-Hyacinthe, QC J2S 4Z5, *Tel* (450) 773-8282	1,200	373	0	6512
BELL MEDIA INC (*Suby of* **BCE INC**) 299 Queen St W, Toronto, ON M5V 2Z5, *Tel* (416) 591-5757	1,200	374	1,003,632,000	4833
BOMBARDIER INC (*Suby of* **BOMBARDIER INC**) 9501 Av Ryan, Dorval, QC H9P 1A2, *Tel* (514) 855-5000	1,200	375	0	8711
BREWERS' DISTRIBUTOR LTD (*Suby of* **BREWERS' DISTRIBUTOR LTD**) 1711 Kingsway Ave, Port Coquitlam, BC V3C 0B6, *Tel* (604) 927-4055	1,200	376	0	5181
CCL INDUSTRIES INC 111 Gordon Baker Rd Suite 801, Toronto, ON M2H 3R1, *Tel* (416) 756-8500	1,200	377	3,912,943,473	2672
CGI INC 1350 Boul Rene-Levesque O Suite 25e, Montreal, QC H3G 1T4, *Tel* (514) 841-3200	1,200	378	8,808,624,126	7371
CHALLENGER MOTOR FREIGHT INC (*Suby of* **CHALLENGER INVESTMENTS II INC**) 300 Maple Grove Rd, Cambridge, ON N3E 1B7, *Tel* (519) 653-6226	1,200	379	168,141,160	4213
CLOSING THE GAP HEALTHCARE GROUP INC 2810 Matheson Blvd E Suite 100, Mississauga, ON L4W 4X7, *Tel* (905) 306-0202	1,200	380	81,991,200	8059
COCA-COLA CANADA BOTTLING LIMITED (*Suby of* **COCA-COLA CANADA BOTTLING LIMITED**) 15 Westcreek Blvd, Brampton, ON L6T 5T4, *Tel* (905) 874-7202	1,200	381	0	2086
CONSEILLERS EN GESTION ET INFORMATIQUE CGI INC (*Suby of* **CGI INC**) 410 Boul Charest E Bureau 700, Quebec, QC G1K 8G3, *Tel* (418) 623-0101	1,200	382	0	7379
CRH CANADA GROUP INC (*Suby of* **CRH PUBLIC LIMITED COMPANY**) 435 Rue Jean-Neveu, Longueuil, QC J4G 2P9, *Tel* (450) 651-1117	1,200	383	0	3241
DE HAVILLAND AIRCRAFT OF CANADA LIMITED (*Suby of* **LONGVIEW AVIATION CAPITAL CORP**) 123 Garratt Blvd, Toronto, ON M3K 1Y5, *Tel* (416) 633-7310	1,200	384	349,020,000	3721
GATE GOURMET CANADA INC (*Suby of* **RRJ MANAGEMENT (HK) LIMITED**) 2498 Britannia Rd E, Mississauga, ON L4W 2P7, *Tel* (905) 405-4100	1,200	385	56,386,551	5812
GEORGE BROWN COLLEGE OF APPLIED ARTS AND TECHNOLOGY, THE 160 Kendal Ave Suite 126a, Toronto, ON M5T 2T9, *Tel* (416) 415-5000	1,200	386	222,884,200	8221
GLOBALIVE COMMUNICATIONS CORP 48 Yonge St Suite 1200, Toronto, ON M5E 1G6, *Tel* (416) 640-1088	1,200	387	274,166,400	4899
GOUVERNEMENT DE LA PROVINCE DE QUEBEC (*Suby of* **GOUVERNEMENT DE LA PROVINCE DE QUEBEC**) 3510 Rue Cambronne, Quebec, QC G1E 7H2, *Tel* (418) 661-3700	1,200	388	0	8399
GOWLING WLG (CANADA) LLP 160 Elgin St Suite 2600, Ottawa, ON K1P 1C3, *Tel* (613) 233-1781	1,200	389	247,051,200	8111
HUDSON'S BAY COMPANY (*Suby of* **HUDSON'S BAY COMPANY**) 176 Yonge St, Toronto, ON M5C 2L7, *Tel* (416) 861-6251	1,200	390	0	5311
IFG - INTERNATIONAL FINANCIAL GROUP (US) LTD 100 King St W Suite 910, Toronto, ON M5X 1B1, *Tel* (416) 645-2434	1,200	391	91,140,315	7361
IRVING, J. D. LIMITED 300 Union St Suite 5, Saint John, NB E2L 4Z2, *Tel* (506) 632-7777	1,200	392	2,885,550,000	2421
JOHNSTON EQUIPMENT ENGINEERED				

COMPANY	EMPLOYEES HERE	RANK	SALES ($)	PRIMARY SIC CODE
5990 Avebury Rd, Mississauga, ON L5R 3R2, *Tel* (905) 712-6000	1,200	393	349,020,000	3743
LOGISTICS IN MOTION INC				
500 Bayly St E, Ajax, ON L1Z 0B2, *Tel* (905) 427-5880	1,200	394	800,270,400	4731
MAGNA INTERNATIONAL INC (*Suby of* **MAGNA INTERNATIONAL INC**)				
1 Cosma Crt, St Thomas, ON N5P 4J5, *Tel* (519) 633-8400	1,200	395	0	3714
MICHELIN AMERIQUE DU NORD (CANADA) INC (*Suby of* **COMPAGNIE GENERALE DES ETABLISSEMENTS MICHELIN**)				
866 Randolph Rd, Waterville, NS B0P 1V0, *Tel* (902) 535-3675	1,200	396	0	3089
NORTHWEST PROTECTION SERVICES LTD				
1951 Eglinton Ave W Unit 201, Toronto, ON M6E 2J7, *Tel* (416) 787-1448	1,200	397	31,500,000	7381
OLYMEL S.E.C. (*Suby of* **OLYMEL S.E.C.**)				
568 Ch De L'Ecore S, Vallee-Jonction, QC G0S 3J0, *Tel* (418) 253-5437	1,200	398	0	2011
RIGHT AT HOME REALTY, INC				
895 Don Mills Rd Suite 202, North York, ON M3C 1W3, *Tel* (416) 391-3232	1,200	399	800,270,400	4731
SNC-LAVALIN INC (*Suby of* **GROUPE SNC-LAVALIN INC**)				
605 5 Ave Sw Suite 1400, Calgary, AB T2P 3H5, *Tel* (403) 294-2100	1,200	400	0	8711
STANDARD AERO LIMITED (*Suby of* **STANDARDAERO AVIATION HOLDINGS, INC.**)				
33 Allen Dyne Rd, Winnipeg, MB R3H 1A1, *Tel* (204) 775-9711	1,200	401	493,328,000	7538
STELCO INC (*Suby of* **BEDROCK INDUSTRIES**)				
2330 Haldimand Rd 3, Nanticoke, ON N0A 1L0, *Tel* (519) 587-4541	1,200	402		3312
SYNDICAT DES INSPECTEURS ET DES REPARTITEURS DU RESEAU DE TRANSPORT DE LA CAPITALE (FISA)				
720 Rue Des Rocailles, Quebec, QC G2J 1A5, *Tel* (418) 627-2351	1,200	403	67,456,800	4111
TD WATERHOUSE CANADA INC (*Suby of* **TORONTO-DOMINION BANK, THE**)				
77 Bloor St W Suite 3, Toronto, ON M5S 1M2, *Tel* (416) 982-7686	1,200	404	2,846,276,000	6211
TELECON INC (*Suby of* **CAPITAL REGIONAL ET COOPERATIF DESJARDINS**)				
7450 Rue Du Mile End, Montreal, QC H2R 2Z6, *Tel* (514) 644-2333	1,200	405	715,301,113	6712
TRIPLE DELTA HOLDINGS INC				
6205 Airport Rd Suite 500, Mississauga, ON L4V 1E1, *Tel* (905) 677-5480	1,200	406	438,610,800	6712
UNIVERSITY OF SASKATCHEWAN (*Suby of* **UNIVERSITY OF SASKATCHEWAN**)				
107 Wiggins Rd Suite B103, Saskatoon, SK S7N 5E5, *Tel* (306) 966-6135	1,200	407	0	8221
VALEURS MOBILIERES DESJARDINS INC (*Suby of* **FEDERATION DES CAISSES DESJARDINS DU QUEBEC**)				
2 Complexe Desjardins Tour E 15 +Tage, Montreal, QC H5B 1J2, *Tel* (514) 286-3180	1,200	408	0	6211
VICTORIA GENERAL HOSPITAL				
2340 Pembina Hwy, Winnipeg, MB R3T 2E8, *Tel* (204) 269-3570	1,200	409	133,296,000	8062
WAYPOINT CENTRE FOR MENTAL HEALTH CARE				
500 Church St, Penetanguishene, ON L9M 1G3, *Tel* (705) 549-3181	1,200	410	95,866,800	8063
WORLEYPARSONSCORD LP (*Suby of* **WORLEYPARSONS LIMITED**)				
5008 86 St Nw Suite 120, Edmonton, AB T6E 5S2, *Tel* (780) 440-5300	1,200	411	0	8711
MIGAO CORPORATION				
200 University Ave Suite300, Toronto, ON M5H 4H1, *Tel* (416) 869-1108	1,196	412	377,255,345	1474
COMPASS GROUP CANADA LTD (*Suby of* **COMPASS GROUP PLC**)				
285 Mcnaughton Ave E, Chatham, ON N7L 2G7, *Tel* (519) 358-7111	1,184	413		5812
PALLISER FURNITURE UPHOLSTERY HOLDINGS LTD (*Suby of* **PALLISER FURNITURE HOLDINGS LTD**)				
70 Lexington Pk, Winnipeg, MB R2G 4H2, *Tel* (204) 988-5600	1,175	414	0	2512
BELL EXPRESSVU INC (*Suby of* **BCE INC**)				
100 Wynford Dr Suite 300, North York, ON M3C 4B4, *Tel* (416) 383-6600	1,170	415	508,506,880	4841
CANADIAN TEST CASE 110				
5770 Hurontario St, Mississauga, ON L5R 3G5, *Tel*	1,170	416	0	3949
AECON INDUSTRIAL WESTERN INC (*Suby of* **AECON GROUP INC**)				
14940 121a Ave Nw, Edmonton, AB T5V 1A3, *Tel* (780) 452-1250	1,150	417	803,150,800	1542
CONSUMERS' CO-OPERATIVE REFINERIES LIMITED (*Suby of* **FEDERATED CO-OPERATIVES LIMITED**)				
580 Park St, Regina, SK S4N 5A9, *Tel* (306) 719-4353	1,150	418	1,960,188,750	2911
PROVIDENCE HEALTHCARE				
3276 St Clair Ave E, Scarborough, ON M1L 1W1, *Tel* (416) 285-3666	1,150	419	683,100,922	8069
ENCANA CORPORATION				
500 Centre St Se, Calgary, AB T2G 1A6, *Tel* (403) 645-2000	1,133	420	5,939,000,000	1382
TORONTO STAR NEWSPAPERS LIMITED (*Suby of* **TORSTAR CORPORATION**)				
1 Yonge St Suite 400, Toronto, ON M5E 1E6, *Tel* (416) 869-4000	1,122	421	304,225,180	2711
HALLMARK HOUSEKEEPING SERVICES INC				
34 Racine Rd, Etobicoke, ON M9W 2Z3, *Tel* (416) 748-0330	1,120	422	76,723,200	7349
BANK OF CANADA (*Suby of* **GOVERNMENT OF CANADA**)				
234 Wellington St, Ottawa, ON K1A 0G9, *Tel* (613) 782-8111	1,111	423	1,159,154,222	6011
SMTC CORPORATION				
7050 Woodbine Ave Suite 300, Markham, ON L3R 4G8, *Tel* (905) 479-1810	1,110	424	216,131,000	3672
BANK OF NOVA SCOTIA, THE				
44 King St W Scotia Plaza, Toronto, ON M5H 1H1, *Tel* (416) 866-6161	1,100	425	22,224,313,700	6733
BOMBARDIER INC (*Suby of* **BOMBARDIER INC**)				
1800 Boul Marcel-Laurin, Saint-Laurent, QC H4R 1K2, *Tel* (514) 855-5000	1,100	426	0	3812
CITIGROUP GLOBAL MARKETS CANADA INC (*Suby of* **CITIGROUP INC.**)				
2920 Matheson Blvd E, Mississauga, ON L4W 5R6, *Tel* (905) 624-9889	1,100	427	0	6722
CIVEO CANADA LIMITED PARTNERSHIP (*Suby of* **CIVEO CORPORATION**)				
3790 98 St Nw, Edmonton, AB T6E 6B4, *Tel* (780) 463-8872	1,100	428	457,621,500	7389
CONCORDIA HOSPITAL				
1095 Concordia Ave, Winnipeg, MB R2K 3S8, *Tel* (204) 667-1560	1,100	429	122,188,000	8062

COMPANY	EMPLOYEES HERE	RANK	SALES ($)	PRIMARY SIC CODE
MACKENZIE FINANCIAL CORPORATION (*Suby of* **POWER CORPORATION DU CANADA**) 180 Queen St W Suite 1600, Toronto, ON M5V 3K1, *Tel* (800) 387-0614	1,100	430	7,588,002,500	6722
MCCAIN FOODS LIMITED (*Suby of* **MCCAIN FOODS GROUP INC**) 439 King St W Suite 500, Toronto, ON M5V 1K4, *Tel* (416) 955-1700	1,100	431	9,747,700,000	2037
MEGA BRANDS INC 4505 Rue Hickmore, Saint-Laurent, QC H4T 1K4, *Tel* (514) 333-5555	1,100	432	75,810,200	3944
MONERIS SOLUTIONS CORPORATION 3300 Bloor St W 10th Flr, Etobicoke, ON M8X 2X2, *Tel* (416) 734-1000	1,100	433	396,605,300	7389
NAMIBIA CRITICAL METALS INC 1550 Bedford Hwy Suite 802, Bedford, NS B4A 1E6, *Tel* (902) 835-8760	1,100	434	281,351,400	1081
QUALITY FOODS LTD (*Suby of* **PATTISON, JIM GROUP INC**) 1581 Alberni Hwy, Errington, BC V0R 1V0, *Tel* (250) 248-4004	1,100	435	211,710,400	5411
SANOFI PASTEUR LIMITED (*Suby of* **SANOFI**) 1755 Steeles Ave W, North York, ON M2R 3T4, *Tel* (416) 667-2700	1,100	436	364,753,400	2836
STREAM INTERNATIONAL CANADA ULC (*Suby of* **SYNNEX CORPORATION**) 7955 Evans Rd, Chilliwack, BC V2R 5R7, *Tel* (604) 702-5100	1,100	437	0	7389
TRANSCOM WORLDWIDE (NORTH AMERICA) INC 300 Bunting Rd 4, St Catharines, ON L2M 3Y3, *Tel* (905) 323-3939	1,100	438	251,319,200	4899
UNIVERSITY OF SASKATCHEWAN 105 Administration Pl Suite E, Saskatoon, SK S7N 5A2, *Tel* (306) 966-4343	1,100	439	797,685,137	8221
SCHERING-PLOUGH CANADA INC (*Suby of* **MERCK & CO., INC.**) 16750 Rte Transcanadienne, Kirkland, QC H9H 4M7, *Tel* (514) 426-7300	1,078	440	364,753,400	2834
LABATT BREWING COMPANY LIMITED (*Suby of* **ANHEUSER-BUSCH INBEV**) 50 Av Labatt Bureau 42, Lasalle, QC H8R 3E7, *Tel* (514) 366-5050	1,070	441	0	2082
LABORATOIRES CHARLES RIVER MONTREAL ULC (*Suby of* **CHARLES RIVER ULC**) 22022 Aut Felix-Leclerc, Senneville, QC H9X 3R3, *Tel* (514) 630-8200	1,063	442	240,612,678	8731
FEDERATION DES CAISSES DESJARDINS DU QUEBEC 100 Rue Des Commandeurs, Levis, QC G6V 7N5, *Tel* (418) 835-8444	1,060	443	9,691,568,435	6062
TECK COAL LIMITED (*Suby of* **TECK RESOURCES LIMITED**) Gd, Sparwood, BC V0B 2G0, *Tel* (250) 425-8325	1,060	444	0	1221
VANCOUVER COMMUNITY COLLEGE (*Suby of* **VANCOUVER COMMUNITY COLLEGE**) 250 Pender St W Suite 358, Vancouver, BC V6B 1S9, *Tel* (604) 443-8484	1,050	445	0	8221
CORPORATION SAVARIA 4350 Desste Chomedey (A-13) O, Saint-Laurent, QC H7R 6E9, *Tel* (450) 681-5655	1,035	446	216,842,947	3999
SEMAFO INC 100 Boul Alexis-Nihon Bureau 700, Saint-Laurent, QC H4M 2P3, *Tel* (514) 744-4408	1,034	447	296,679,000	1081
NFI GROUP INC 711 Kernaghan Ave, Winnipeg, MB R2C 3T4, *Tel* (204) 224-1251	1,019	448	2,519,021,000	3711
FRONTIER SCHOOL DIVISION (*Suby of* **FRONTIER SCHOOL DIVISION**) 1 Rossville Rd, Norway House, MB R0B 1B0, *Tel* (204) 359-4100	1,005	449	0	8211
BROOKFIELD CAPITAL PARTNERS II L.P. 181 Bay St Suite 300, Toronto, ON M5J 2T3, *Tel* (416) 363-9491	1,002	450	159,175,716	3088
PT HEALTHCARE SOLUTIONS CORP 70 Frid St Unit 2, Hamilton, ON L8P 4M4, *Tel* (877) 734-9887	1,001	451	89,351,262	8049
RITCHIE BROS. FINANCIAL SERVICES LTD (*Suby of* **RITCHIE BROS. AUCTIONEERS INCORPORATED**) 9500 Glenlyon Pky, Burnaby, BC V5J 0C6, *Tel* (778) 331-5500	1,001	452	186,692,506	8742
ACUREN GROUP INC (*Suby of* **ROCKWOOD SERVICE CORPORATION**) 7450 18 St Nw, Edmonton, AB T6P 1N8, *Tel* (780) 440-2131	1,000	453	224,490,200	8734
AIR CANADA 7373 Boul De La Cote-Vertu Bureau 1290, Saint-Laurent, QC H4S 1Z3, *Tel* (514) 393-3333	1,000	454	13,695,112,630	4512
ALGONQUIN COLLEGE OF APPLIED ARTS AND TECHNOLOGY 1385 Woodroffe Ave, Nepean, ON K2G 1V8, *Tel* (613) 727-4723	1,000	455	260,558,353	8222
ALUMINERIE DE BECANCOUR INC 5555 Rue Pierre-Thibault Bureau 217, Becancour, QC G9H 2T7, *Tel* (819) 294-6101	1,000	456	243,231,000	3463
AMER SPORTS CANADA INC 2220 Dollarton Hwy Unit 110, North Vancouver, BC V7H 1A8, *Tel* (604) 960-3001	1,000	457	6,966,906,000	5091
APOTEX INC 150 Signet Dr, Toronto, ON M9L 1T9, *Tel* (416) 401-7328	1,000	458	2,652,752,000	2834
ARCELORMITTAL EXPLOITATION MINIERE CANADA S.E.N.C. 1010 Rue De Serigny, Longueuil, QC J4K 5G7, *Tel* (418) 766-2000	1,000	459	255,774,000	1011
ASSOCIATION DES POMPIERS DE MONTREAL INC 2655 Place Chasse 2e Etage, Montreal, QC H1Y 2C3, *Tel* (514) 527-9691	1,000	460	284,802,000	8631
ASTALDI CANADA INC (*Suby of* **FIN.AST. SRL**) 358 Hamilton River Rd, Happy Valley-Goose Bay, NL A0P 1C0, *Tel* (709) 896-4470	1,000	461	0	1541
ATLIFIC INC 4960 Clifton Hill, Niagara Falls, ON L2G 3N4, *Tel* (905) 358-3293	1,000	462	0	7011
ATTRACTION IMAGES PRODUCTIONS INC 5455 Av De Gaspe Bureau 804, Montreal, QC H2T 3B3, *Tel* (514) 285-7001	1,000	463	149,813,000	7922
BARRICK GOLD CORPORATION 161 Bay St Suite 3700, Toronto, ON M5J 2S1, *Tel* (416) 861-9911	1,000	464	7,243,000,000	1041
BELL HELICOPTER TEXTRON CANADA LIMITEE (*Suby of* **TEXTRON INC.**) 12800 Rue De L'Avenir, Mirabel, QC J7J 1R4, *Tel* (450) 971-6500	1,000	465	290,850,000	3721
CANAC IMMOBILIER INC (*Suby of* **GESTION LABERGE INC**) 947 Av Royale, Quebec, QC G1E 1Z9, *Tel* (418) 667-1729	1,000	466	0	5039

COMPANY	EMPLOYEES HERE	RANK	SALES ($)	PRIMARY SIC CODE
CANADA IMPERIAL OIL LIMITED (*Suby of* **IMPERIAL OIL LIMITED**) 602 Christina St S, Sarnia, ON N7T 7M5, *Tel* (519) 339-2000	1,000	467	0	5172
CANADIAN CORPS OF COMMISSIONAIRES NATIONAL OFFICE, THE (*Suby of* **CANADIAN CORPS OF COMMIS-SIONAIRES NATIONAL OFFICE, THE**) 928 Cloverdale Ave, Victoria, BC V8X 2T3, *Tel* (250) 727-7755	1,000	468	0	7381
CANADIAN NATURAL RESOURCES LIMITED 855 2 St Sw Suite 2100, Calgary, AB T2P 4J8, *Tel* (403) 517-6700	1,000	469	15,940,610,754	1311
CANADIAN TEST CASE 174 5770 Hurontario St, Mississauga, ON L5R 3G5, *Tel*	1,000	470	19,124,700	6021
CANADIAN TIRE SERVICES LIMITED (*Suby of* **CANADIAN TIRE CORPORATION, LIMITED**) 1000 East Main St, Welland, ON L3B 3Z3, *Tel* (905) 735-3131	1,000	471	0	6153
CAPE BRETON DISTRICT HEALTH AUTHORITY (*Suby of* **NOVA SCOTIA, PROVINCE OF**) 1482 George St, Sydney, NS B1P 1P3, *Tel* (902) 567-8000	1,000	472	269,487,797	8062
CENTRE DE SANTE ET SERVICES SOCIAUX DE MONTMAGNY - L'ISLET (*Suby of* **GOUVERNEMENT DE LA PROVINCE DE QUEBEC**) 10 Rue Alphonse, Saint-Fabien-De-Panet, QC G0R 2J0, *Tel* (418) 249-2572	1,000	473	0	8062
CENTRE FOR ADDICTION AND MENTAL HEALTH (*Suby of* **CENTRE FOR ADDICTION AND MENTAL HEALTH**) 175 Brentcliffe Rd, Toronto, ON M4G 0C5, *Tel* (416) 425-3930	1,000	474	0	8093
CENTRE HOSPITALIER DE L'UNIVERSITE DE MONTREAL (*Suby of* **CENTRE HOSPITALIER DE L'UNIVERSITE DE MONTREAL**) 1058 Rue Saint-Denis, Montreal, QC H2X 3J4, *Tel* (514) 890-8000	1,000	475	0	8062
COGECO CONNEXION INC (*Suby of* **GESTION AUDEM INC**) 5 Place Ville-Marie Bureau 1700, Montreal, QC H3B 0B3, *Tel* (514) 764-4700	1,000	476	334,544,000	4841
COLLEGE AHUNTSIC 9155 Rue Saint Hubert, Montreal, QC H2M 1Y8, *Tel* (514) 389-5921	1,000	477	149,391,000	8221
COMMISSION DES NORMES, DE L'EQUITE, DE LA SANTE ET DE LA SECURITE DU TRAVAIL, LA 524 Rue Bourdages Bureau 370, Quebec, QC G1K 7E2, *Tel* (877) 639-0744	1,000	478	6,410,904,000	6331
COMPAGNIE DES CHEMINS DE FER NATIONAUX DU CANADA 935 Rue De La Gauchetiere 16e Etage O, Montreal, QC H3B 2M9, *Tel* (514) 399-5430	1,000	479	10,856,778,742	4011
COMPAGNIE DES CHEMINS DE FER NATIONAUX DU CANADA (*Suby of* **COMPAGNIE DES CHEMINS DE FER NATIONAUX DU CANADA**) 1 Administration Rd, Vaughan, ON L4K 1B9, *Tel* (905) 669-3128	1,000	480	0	4011
COMPAGNIE GE AVIATION CANADA, LA (*Suby of* **GENERAL ELECTRIC COMPANY**) 2 Boul De L'Aeroport, Bromont, QC J2L 1S6, *Tel* (450) 534-0917	1,000	481	197,131,000	8711
CONSEIL SCOLAIRE CATHOLIQUE DE DISTRICT DES GRANDES RIVIERES, LE (*Suby of* **CONSEIL SCOLAIRE CATHOLIQUE DE DISTRICT DES GRANDES RIVIERES, LE**) 75 Queen St, Kapuskasing, ON P5N 1H5, *Tel* (705) 335-6091	1,000	482	0	8211
COOP FEDEREE, LA 9001 Boul De L'Acadie Bureau 200, Montreal, QC H4N 3H7, *Tel* (514) 858-2222	1,000	483	5,062,373,662	5191
CORPORATION DE L'ECOLE POLYTECHNIQUE DE MONTREAL 2900 Boul Edouard-Montpetit, Montreal, QC H3T 1J4, *Tel* (514) 340-4711	1,000	484	141,013,000	8221
CORPORATION DE SECURITE GARDA WORLD (*Suby of* **GW INTERMEDIATE HOLDCO CORPORATION**) 1390 Rue Barre, Montreal, QC H3C 5X9, *Tel* (514) 281-2811	1,000	485	3,771,411,322	7381
ELECTROLUX CANADA CORP (*Suby of* **AB ELECTROLUX**) 802 Boul De L'Ange-Gardien, L'Assomption, QC J5W 1T6, *Tel* (450) 589-5701	1,000	486	0	3634
EMPIRE INVESTIGATIONS AND PROTECTION SERVICES INC 940 Brock Rd Unit 4, Pickering, ON L1W 2A1, *Tel* (905) 426-3909	1,000	487	26,250,000	7381
ENBRIDGE COMMERCIAL SERVICES INC (*Suby of* **ENBRIDGE INC**) 500 Consumers Rd, North York, ON M2J 1P8, *Tel* (416) 492-5000	1,000	488	0	8741
EVRAZ INC. NA CANADA (*Suby of* **EVRAZ PLC**) 100 Armour Rd, Regina, SK S4P 3C7, *Tel* (306) 924-7700	1,000	489	936,500,200	3312
EXPORT DEVELOPMENT CANADA (*Suby of* **GOVERNMENT OF CANADA**) 150 Slater St, Ottawa, ON K1A 1K3, *Tel* (613) 598-2500	1,000	490	1,333,579,935	6111
FORD MOTOR COMPANY OF CANADA, LIMITED (*Suby of* **FORD MOTOR COMPANY**) 3223 Lauzon Pky, Windsor, ON N9A 6X3, *Tel* (519) 944-8784	1,000	491	0	5521
FORD MOTOR COMPANY OF CANADA, LIMITED (*Suby of* **FORD MOTOR COMPANY**) 7654 Tecumseh Rd E, Windsor, ON N8T 1E9, *Tel* (519) 944-8564	1,000	492	0	3714
FORD MOTOR COMPANY OF CANADA, LIMITED (*Suby of* **FORD MOTOR COMPANY**) 2900 Trenton St, Windsor, ON N9A 7B2, *Tel* (519) 257-2000	1,000	493	0	3322
FORTISALBERTA INC (*Suby of* **FORTIS INC**) 320 17 Ave Sw, Calgary, AB T2S 2V1, *Tel* (403) 514-4000	1,000	494	470,047,026	4911
FRASER HEALTH AUTHORITY (*Suby of* **GOVERNMENT OF THE PROVINCE OF BRITISH COLUMBIA**) 11666 Laity St, Maple Ridge, BC V2X 5A3, *Tel* (604) 463-4111	1,000	495	0	8062
GAY LEA FOODS CO-OPERATIVE LIMITED (*Suby of* **GAY LEA FOODS CO-OPERATIVE LIMITED**) 20 Morley St, Hamilton, ON L8H 3R7, *Tel* (905) 544-6281	1,000	496	0	2021
GENERAL ELECTRIC CANADA COMPANY (*Suby of* **GENERAL ELECTRIC COMPANY**) 2 Boul De L'Aeroport, Bromont, QC J2L 1S6, *Tel* (450) 534-0917	1,000	497	0	3625
GENERAL MILLS CANADA CORPORATION (*Suby of* **GENERAL MILLS, INC.**) 5825 Explorer Dr, Mississauga, ON L4W 5P6, *Tel* (905) 212-4000	1,000	498	974,770,000	2041
GO BEE INDUSTRIES INC 1-334 A Hatt St, Dundas, ON L9H 2H9, *Tel* (289) 238-8829	1,000	499	200,371,000	7319
HATCH LTD (*Suby of* **HATCHCOS HOLDINGS LTD**) 4342 Queen St Suite 500, Niagara Falls, ON L2E 7J7, *Tel* (905) 374-5200	1,000	500	0	8711
IBM CANADA LIMITED (*Suby of* **INTERNATIONAL BUSINESS MACHINES CORPORATION**)				

COMPANY	EMPLOYEES HERE	RANK	SALES ($)	PRIMARY SIC CODE
10044 108 St Nw Suite 401, Edmonton, AB T5J 3S7, Tel (780) 642-4100	1,000	501	0	3571
ID BIOMEDICAL CORPORATION OF QUEBEC (*Suby of* **GLAXOSMITHKLINE PLC**)				
2323 Boul Du Parc-Technologique, Quebec, QC G1P 4R8, Tel (450) 978-4599	1,000	502	344,631,000	8731
INSTITUT UNIVERSITAIRE EN SANTE MENTALE DOUGLAS				
6875 Boul Lasalle, Verdun, QC H4H 1R3, Tel (514) 761-6131	1,000	503	111,080,000	8062
KRAFT HEINZ CANADA ULC (*Suby of* **THE KRAFT HEINZ COMPANY**)				
8600 Ch Devonshire, Mont-Royal, QC H4P 2K9, Tel (514) 343-3300	1,000	504	0	2022
LAKEHEAD UNIVERSITY				
955 Oliver Rd, Thunder Bay, ON P7B 5E1, Tel (807) 343-8110	1,000	505	133,703,717	8221
MAGNA EXTERIORS INC (*Suby of* **MAGNA INTERNATIONAL INC**)				
50 Casmir Crt, Concord, ON L4K 4J5, Tel (905) 669-2888	1,000	506	872,550,000	3714
MANULIFE FINANCIAL CORPORATION				
200 Bloor St E, Toronto, ON M4W 1E5, Tel (416) 926-3000	1,000	507	29,544,751,144	6411
MAPLE LODGE HOLDING CORPORATION				
8301 Winston Churchill Blvd, Brampton, ON L6Y 0A2, Tel (905) 455-8340	1,000	508	475,161,700	6712
MILLER WASTE SYSTEMS INC				
8050 Woodbine Ave, Markham, ON L3R 2N8, Tel (905) 475-6356	1,000	509	318,910,000	4953
MOLSON CANADA 2005 (*Suby of* **MOLSON COORS BREWING COMPANY**)				
1 Carlingview Dr, Etobicoke, ON M9W 5E5, Tel (416) 675-1786	1,000	510	0	2082
MT SERVICES LIMITED PARTNERSHIP				
66 Wellington St W Rd Suite 5300, Toronto, ON M5K 1E6, Tel (416) 601-8200	1,000	511	110,882,000	8111
NATIONAL STEEL CAR LIMITED				
600 Kenilworth Ave N, Hamilton, ON L8N 3J4, Tel (905) 544-3311	1,000	512	290,850,000	3743
NEWLY WEDS FOODS CO. (*Suby of* **NEWLY WEDS FOODS, INC.**)				
1381 Rue Ampere, Boucherville, QC J4B 5Z5, Tel (450) 641-2200	1,000	513	0	2099
NORTEL NETWORKS LIMITED (*Suby of* **NORTEL NETWORKS LIMITED**)				
250 Sidney St, Belleville, ON K8P 3Z3, Tel	1,000	514	0	4899
NOVA PETROCHEMICALS LTD (*Suby of* **GOVERNMENT OF ABU DHABI**)				
1000 7 Ave Sw, Calgary, AB T2P 5L5, Tel (403) 750-3600	1,000	515	256,101,000	6712
PF RESOLU CANADA INC (*Suby of* **RESOLUTE FOREST PRODUCTS INC**)				
2001 Neebing Ave, Thunder Bay, ON P7E 6S3, Tel (807) 475-2400	1,000	516	0	2621
POWER FINANCIAL CORPORATION (*Suby of* **POWER CORPORATION DU CANADA**)				
751 Rue Du Square-Victoria, Montreal, QC H2Y 2J3, Tel (514) 286-7400	1,000	517	35,649,746,550	6712
PROPAK SYSTEMS LTD (*Suby of* **MCPIKE INVESTMENTS LTD**)				
440 East Lake Rd Ne, Airdrie, AB T4A 2J8, Tel (403) 912-7000	1,000	518	308,964,700	3533
PROVIDENCE HEALTH CARE SOCIETY (*Suby of* **PROVIDENCE HEALTH CARE SOCIETY**)				
3080 Prince Edward St, Vancouver, BC V5T 3N4, Tel (604) 877-8302	1,000	519	0	8062
RBC DOMINION SECURITIES INC (*Suby of* **ROYAL BANK OF CANADA**)				
200 Bay St, Toronto, ON M5J 2W7, Tel (416) 842-2000	1,000	520	7,542,631,400	6282
REGIONAL HEALTH AUTHORITY NB (*Suby of* **PROVINCE OF NEW BRUNSWICK**)				
180 Woodbridge St, Fredericton, NB E3B 4R3, Tel (506) 623-5500	1,000	521	893,794,100	8062
REVOLUTION LANDFILL LP				
1100 Burloak Dr, Burlington, ON L7L 6B2, Tel (905) 315-6304	1,000	522	444,645,000	2844
RIO TINTO ALCAN INC (*Suby of* **RIO TINTO PLC**)				
3000 Rue Des Pins O, Alma, QC G8B 5W2, Tel (418) 480-6000	1,000	523		3399
ROGERS COMMUNICATIONS CANADA INC (*Suby of* **ROGERS COMMUNICATIONS INC**)				
333 Bloor St E Fl 8, Toronto, ON M4W 1G9, Tel (800) 485-9745	1,000	524	334,544,000	4813
RONA INC (*Suby of* **LOWE'S COMPANIES, INC.**)				
220 Ch Du Tremblay, Boucherville, QC J4B 8H7, Tel (514) 599-5900	1,000	525	7,820,748,000	5072
SASKATCHEWAN GOVERNMENT INSURANCE (*Suby of* **GOVERNMENT OF SASKATCHEWAN**)				
2260 11th Ave Suite 18, Regina, SK S4P 0J9, Tel (306) 751-1200	1,000	526	3,846,542,400	6331
SERVICES FINANCIERS NCO, INC (*Suby of* **GATESTONE & CO. INC**)				
75 Rue De Port-Royal E Bureau 240, Montreal, QC H3L 3T1, Tel (514) 385-4444	1,000	527	601,113,000	7322
SLEEP COUNTRY CANADA INC (*Suby of* **SLEEP COUNTRY CANADA HOLDINGS INC**)				
805 Boyd St Suite 100, New Westminster, BC V3M 5X2, Tel (604) 515-9711	1,000	528	0	5712
SOCIETE EN COMMANDITE AIRBUS CANADA				
13100 Boul Henri-Fabre E, Mirabel, QC J7N 3C6, Tel (514) 855-7110	1,000	529	290,850,000	3721
SPECIALTY CARE INC (*Suby of* **SPECIALTY CARE INC**)				
10260 Kennedy Rd, Brampton, ON L6Z 4N7, Tel (905) 495-4695	1,000	530	0	8059
SUN LIFE DU CANADA, COMPAGNIE D'ASSURANCE-VIE				
1155 Rue Metcalfe Bureau 1410, Montreal, QC H3B 2V9, Tel (514) 393-8820	1,000	531	2,136,968,000	6311
SUN LIFE FINANCIAL INC				
1 York St, Toronto, ON M5J 0B6, Tel (416) 979-9966	1,000	532	20,466,479,694	6411
TARGETED MICROWAVE SOLUTIONS INC				
1066 Hastings St W Suite 2300, Vancouver, BC V6E 3X2, Tel (778) 995-5833	1,000	533	227,289,000	3822
TECHNOLOGIES METAFORE INC				
9393 Boul Louis-H.-Lafontaine, Anjou, QC H1J 1Z1, Tel (514) 354-3810	1,000	534	184,573,000	7371
TEKNION CORPORATION (*Suby of* **GLOBAL UPHOLSTERY CO LIMITED**)				
1150 Flint Rd, North York, ON M3J 2J5, Tel (416) 661-1577	1,000	535	779,327,500	2522
TEMBEC INC (*Suby of* **RAYONIER A.M. GLOBAL HOLDINGS LUXEMBOURG SCS**)				
1 Government Rd W, Kapuskasing, ON P5N 2X8, Tel (705) 337-9784	1,000	536	0	2621
TORONTO REHABILITATION INSTITUTE (*Suby of* **UNIVERSITY HEALTH NETWORK**)				
550 University Ave, Toronto, ON M5G 2A2, Tel (416) 597-3422	1,000	537	136,391,400	8093

COMPANY	EMPLOYEES HERE	RANK	SALES ($)	PRIMARY SIC CODE
UNIVERSITE CONCORDIA 1455 Boul De Maisonneuve O, Montreal, QC H3G 1M8, *Tel* (514) 848-2424	1,000	538	373,477,500	8221
UNIVERSITY OF OTTAWA (*Suby of* **UNIVERSITY OF OTTAWA**) 451 Smyth Rd Suite Rgn, Ottawa, ON K1H 8M5, *Tel* (613) 562-5800	1,000	539	0	8221
VEOLIA ES CANADA SERVICES INDUSTRIELS INC (*Suby of* **VEOLIA ENVIRONNEMENT**) 7950 Av Pion, Saint-Hyacinthe, QC J2R 1R9, *Tel* (450) 796-6060	1,000	540	0	4953
WAL-MART CANADA CORP (*Suby of* **WALMART INC.**) 1940 Argentia Rd, Mississauga, ON L5N 1P9, *Tel* (905) 821-2111	1,000	541	13,689,720,000	5311
WILLIAM OSLER HEALTH SYSTEM (*Suby of* **WILLIAM OSLER HEALTH SYSTEM**) 101 Humber College Blvd, Etobicoke, ON M9V 1R8, *Tel* (416) 494-2120	1,000	542	0	8062
WOOD CANADA LIMITED (*Suby of* **JOHN WOOD GROUP P.L.C.**) 801 6 Ave Sw Suite 900, Calgary, AB T2P 3W3, *Tel* (403) 298-4170	1,000	543	0	8711
WOODBINE ENTERTAINMENT GROUP 555 Rexdale Blvd, Toronto, ON M9W 5L2, *Tel* (416) 675-7223	1,000	544	222,795,900	7948
YMCA OF HAMILTON/BURLINGTON/BRANTFORD 79 James St S, Hamilton, ON L8P 2Z1, *Tel* (905) 529-7102	1,000	545	36,493,511	7997
KBR INDUSTRIAL CANADA CO. (*Suby of* **KELLOGG BROWN & ROOT HOLDING B.V.**) 1302 10 St Nisku, Edmonton, AB T9E 8K2, *Tel* (780) 468-1341	998	546	698,392,000	1541
JACK VICTOR LIMITED 1250 Rue Saint-Alexandre Bureau 100, Montreal, QC H3B 3H6, *Tel* (514) 866-4891	997	547	265,335,000	2311
ENMAX ENERGY CORPORATION (*Suby of* **CITY OF CALGARY, THE**) 141 50 Ave Se Suite 2708, Calgary, AB T2G 4S7, *Tel* (403) 514-3000	990	548	840,736,000	4911
ROMAN CATHOLIC ARCHDIOCESE OF VANCOUVER, THE 4885 Saint John Paul Ii Way, Vancouver, BC V5Z 0G3, *Tel* (604) 683-0281	986	549	104,123,000	8661
SUN LIFE ASSURANCE COMPANY OF CANADA (*Suby of* **SUN LIFE FINANCIAL INC**) 1 York St, Toronto, ON M5J 0B6, *Tel* (416) 979-9966	970	550	22,240,880,324	6311
ACCEO SOLUTIONS INC (*Suby of* **CONSTELLATION SOFTWARE INC**) 7710 Boul Wilfrid-Hamel, Quebec, QC G2G 2J5, *Tel* (418) 877-0088	960	551	0	7372
151210 CANADA INC 245 Rue Jean-Coutu, Varennes, QC J3X 0E1, *Tel* (450) 646-9760	955	552	349,061,095	6712
BISON TRANSPORT INC (*Suby of* **JANPHER INVESTMENTS INC**) 1001 Sherwin Rd, Winnipeg, MB R3H 0T8, *Tel* (204) 833-0000	950	553	313,447,700	4213
BROSE CANADA INC (*Suby of* **BROSE FAHRZEUGTEILE GMBH & CO. KG, COBURG**) 1500 Max Brose Dr, London, ON N6N 1P7, *Tel* (519) 644-5200	950	554	268,769,250	3679
COM DEV INTERNATIONAL LTD (*Suby of* **HONEYWELL INTERNATIONAL INC.**) 155 Sheldon Dr, Cambridge, ON N1R 7H6, *Tel* (519) 622-2300	950	555	341,195,490	3669
DOMTAR INC (*Suby of* **DOMTAR LUXEMBOURG INVESTMENTS SARL**) 609 12e Rang, Val-Joli, QC J1S 0H1, *Tel* (819) 845-2771	950	556	0	2621
GROUPE VOLVO CANADA INC (*Suby of* **AB VOLVO**) 1000 Boul Industriel Bureau 1160, Saint-Eustache, QC J7R 5A5, *Tel* (450) 472-6410	950	557	1,383,462,000	5012
IMPERIAL OIL LIMITED Po Box 3004 Stn Main, Sarnia, ON N7T 7M5, *Tel* (519) 339-4015	950	558	256,743,200	2911
NIAGARA HEALTH SYSTEM (*Suby of* **NIAGARA HEALTH SYSTEM**) 5546 Portage Rd, Niagara Falls, ON L2G 5X8, *Tel* (905) 378-4647	950	559	0	8062
OCEANAGOLD CORPORATION 777 Hornby Street Suite 1910, Vancouver, BC V6Z 1S4, *Tel* (604) 235-3360	950	560	724,413,000	1081
SOEURS DE LA CHARITE D'OTTAWA, LES (*Suby of* **SOEURS DE LA CHARITE D'OTTAWA, LES**) 43 Bruyere St, Ottawa, ON K1N 5C8, *Tel* (613) 562-0050	950	561	0	8661
ST. THOMAS-ELGIN GENERAL HOSPITAL, THE 189 Elm St, St Thomas, ON N5R 5C4, *Tel* (519) 631-2030	950	562	65,219,627	8062
9130-1168 QUEBEC INC (*Suby of* **FONDS DE PLACEMENT IMMOBILIER COMINAR**) 298 Boul Armand-Theriault Bureau 2, Riviere-Du-Loup, QC G5R 4C2, *Tel* (418) 862-7848	926	563	0	6512
ENERGIR, S.E.C. 1717 Rue Du Havre, Montreal, QC H2K 2X3, *Tel* (514) 598-3444	917	564	1,522,883,188	4924
STREAM INTERNATIONAL CANADA ULC (*Suby of* **SYNNEX CORPORATION**) 95 Union St, Glace Bay, NS B1A 2P6, *Tel* (902) 842-3800	909	565	0	7389
HYDRO ALUMINIUM CANADA INC (*Suby of* **NORSK HYDRO ASA**) 2000 Av Mcgill College Bureau 2310, Montreal, QC H3A 3H3, *Tel* (514) 840-9110	902	566	0	3334
2168587 ONTARIO LTD (*Suby of* **2168587 ONTARIO LTD**) 50 Marmora St, North York, ON M9M 2X5, *Tel* (416) 661-7744	900	567	0	2053
2224855 ONTARIO INC 5450 Explorer Dr Unit 300, Mississauga, ON L4W 5M1, *Tel* (416) 649-3939	900	568	328,958,100	6712
4659555 MANITOBA LTD 328 King St Suite A, Winnipeg, MB R3B 3H4, *Tel* (204) 989-5820	900	569	67,224,600	7361
APOTEX INC 50 Steinway Blvd Suite 3, Etobicoke, ON M9W 6Y3, *Tel* (416) 675-0338	900	570	0	2834
BAYER INC (*Suby of* **BAYER AG**) 1265 Vidal St S, Sarnia, ON N7T 7M2, *Tel* (519) 337-8251	900	571	0	2822
BWXT CANADA LTD (*Suby of* **BWX TECHNOLOGIES, INC.**) 581 Coronation Blvd, Cambridge, ON N1R 3E9, *Tel* (519) 621-2130	900	572	604,589,355	3621
CAPITAL D'AMERIQUE CDPQ INC (*Suby of* **GOUVERNEMENT DE LA PROVINCE DE QUEBEC**) 1000 Place Jean-Paul-Riopelle Bureau 12e, Montreal, QC H2Z 2B3, *Tel* (514) 842-3261	900	573	1,923,271,200	6371
CARGILL LIMITED (*Suby of* **CARGILL, INCORPORATED**) 10 Cuddy Blvd, London, ON N5V 5E3, *Tel* (519) 453-4996	900	574	0	2015

COMPANY	EMPLOYEES HERE	RANK	SALES ($)	PRIMARY SIC CODE
CARGOJET AIRWAYS LTD (*Suby of* **CARGOJET HOLDINGS LIMITED PARTNERSHIP**) 2281 North Sheridan Way, Mississauga, ON L5K 2S3, *Tel* (905) 501-7373	900	575	299,993,343	4512
CORPORATION DE SECURITE GARDA CANADA (*Suby of* **GW INTERMEDIATE HOLDCO CORPORATION**) 10250 101 St Nw Suite 1010, Edmonton, AB T5J 3P4, *Tel* (780) 425-5000	900	576	0	7381
COUTTS, WILLIAM E. COMPANY, LIMITED (*Suby of* **HALLMARK CARDS, INCORPORATED**) 3762 14th Ave Unit 100, Markham, ON L3R 0G7, *Tel* (416) 492-1300	900	577	348,793,200	2771
CROSS, DR G B MEMORIAL HOSPITAL (*Suby of* **EASTERN REGIONAL INTEGRATED HEALTH AUTHORITY**) 67 Manitoba Dr, Clarenville, NL A5A 1K3, *Tel* (709) 466-3411	900	578	99,972,000	8062
DAY & ROSS DEDICATED LOGISTICS 6711 Mississauga Rd Suite 410, Mississauga, ON L5N 2W3, *Tel* (905) 285-2355	900	579	185,135,400	4212
DESJARDINS GROUPE D'ASSURANCES GENERALES INC (*Suby of* **FEDERATION DES CAISSES DESJARDINS DU QUEBEC**) 5070 Dixie Rd, Mississauga, ON L4W 1C9, *Tel* (905) 366-4430	900	580	0	6411
FONDATION DU CENTRE DE SANTE ET DE SERVICES SOCIAUX DE MANICOUAGAN (*Suby of* **GOUVERNEMENT DE LA PROVINCE DE QUEBEC**) 635 Boul Jolliet, Baie-Comeau, QC G5C 1P1, *Tel* (418) 589-3701	900	581	0	8062
GLAXOSMITHKLINE INC (*Suby of* **GLAXOSMITHKLINE PLC**) 7333 Mississauga Rd, Mississauga, ON L5N 6L4, *Tel* (905) 819-3000	900	582	596,869,200	2834
GOUVERNEMENT DE LA PROVINCE DE QUEBEC (*Suby of* **GOUVERNEMENT DE LA PROVINCE DE QUEBEC**) 50 Rue Saint-Patrice E, Magog, QC J1X 3X3, *Tel* (819) 843-2572	900	583	0	8062
INDUSTRIES SPECTRA PREMIUM INC, LES 1421 Rue Ampere, Boucherville, QC J4B 5Z5, *Tel* (450) 641-3090	900	584	462,138,900	3433
INTACT INSURANCE COMPANY (*Suby of* **INTACT FINANCIAL CORPORATION**) 321 6 Ave Sw Suite 1200, Calgary, AB T2P 3H3, *Tel* (403) 269-7961	900	585	0	6331
KIK HOLDCO COMPANY INC (*Suby of* **KIK CUSTOM PRODUCTS INC**) 2000 Kipling Ave, Etobicoke, ON M9W 4J6, *Tel* (416) 743-6255	900	586	0	2842
KNOLL NORTH AMERICA CORP (*Suby of* **KNOLL, INC.**) 1000 Arrow Rd, North York, ON M9M 2Y7, *Tel* (416) 741-5453	900	587	222,665,000	2521
MARMEN INC (*Suby of* **GESTION MARMEN INC**) 557 Rue Des Erables, Trois-Rivieres, QC G8T 8Y8, *Tel* (819) 379-0453	900	588	0	3545
MOSAIC ESTERHAZY HOLDINGS ULC (*Suby of* **THE MOSAIC COMPANY**) Hwy 80 E, Esterhazy, SK S0A 0X0, *Tel* (306) 745-4200	900	589	328,958,100	6712
MOSAIC POTASH ESTERHAZY LIMITED PARTNERSHIP (*Suby of* **THE MOSAIC COMPANY**) 80 Plant Hwy, Esterhazy, SK S0A 0X0, *Tel* (306) 745-4400	900	590	371,798,100	1474
NIAGARA HEALTH SYSTEM 1200 Fourth Ave, St Catharines, ON L2S 0A9, *Tel* (905) 378-4647	900	591	533,184,000	8062
PAGES JAUNES LIMITEE 1751 Rue Richardson Bureau 2300, Montreal, QC H3K 1G6, *Tel* (514) 934-2611	900	592	437,572,684	2741
PATHEON INC (*Suby of* **THERMO FISHER SCIENTIFIC INC.**) 2100 Syntex Crt, Mississauga, ON L5N 7K9, *Tel* (905) 821-4001	900	593	2,155,361,000	2834
PETER KIEWIT INFRASTRUCTURE CO. (*Suby of* **PETER KIEWIT SONS', INC.**) 9500 100 St Se, Calgary, AB T3S 0A2, *Tel*	900	594	0	1611
PROCTER & GAMBLE INC (*Suby of* **THE PROCTER & GAMBLE COMPANY**) 1475 California Ave, Brockville, ON K6V 6K4, *Tel* (613) 342-9592	900	595	0	2841
PWC MANAGEMENT SERVICES LP (*Suby of* **PRICEWATERHOUSECOOPERS LLP**) 10190 152a St 3 Fl, Surrey, BC V3R 1J7, *Tel* (604) 806-7000	900	596	0	8721
REGIONAL HEALTH AUTHORITY A (*Suby of* **REGIONAL HEALTH AUTHORITY A**) 1750 Sunset Dr, Bathurst, NB E2A 4L7, *Tel* (506) 544-3000	900	597	0	8062
RELIGIOUS HOSPITALLERS OF SAINT JOSEPH OF THE HOTEL DIEU OF KINGSTON (*Suby of* **RELIGIOUS HOSPITALLERS OF SAINT JOSEPH OF THE HOTEL DIEU OF KINGSTON**) 166 Brock St, Kingston, ON K7L 5G2, *Tel* (613) 549-2680	900	598	0	8069
RESEAU DE TRANSPORT DE LONGUEUIL 1150 Boul Marie-Victorin, Longueuil, QC J4G 2M4, *Tel* (450) 442-8600	900	599	0	4111
REVOLUTION ENVIRONMENTAL SOLUTIONS ACQUISITION GP INC 1100 Burloak Dr Unit 500, Burlington, ON L7L 6B2, *Tel* (800) 263-8602	900	600	287,019,000	4953
SAINE MARKETING INC 2222 Boul Rene-Levesque O Bureau 220, Montreal, QC H3H 1R6, *Tel* (514) 931-8233	900	601	197,948,700	8732
SOBEYS CAPITAL INCORPORATED (*Suby of* **EMPIRE COMPANY LIMITED**) 12910 156 St Nw, Edmonton, AB T5V 1E9, *Tel* (780) 447-1440	900	602	0	5141
ST JOSEPH'S GENERAL HOSPITAL 2137 Comox Ave, Comox, BC V9M 1P2, *Tel* (250) 339-1451	900	603	122,188,000	8062
VENTRA GROUP CO (*Suby of* **FLEX-N-GATE LLC**) 538 Blanchard Pk, Tecumseh, ON N8N 2L9, *Tel* (519) 727-3931	900	604	1,721,832,000	3714
VIDEON CABLESYSTEMS INC (*Suby of* **SHAW COMMUNICATIONS INC**) 630 3 Ave Sw Suite 900, Calgary, AB T2P 4L4, *Tel* (403) 750-4500	900	605	206,538,688	4841
WALMART CANADA LOGISTICS ULC (*Suby of* **WALMART INC.**) 3400 39 Ave Ne, Calgary, AB T1Y 7J4, *Tel* (403) 250-3648	900	606	0	4225
WEST PARK HEALTHCARE CENTRE 82 Buttonwood Ave Suite 1121, Toronto, ON M6M 2J5, *Tel* (416) 243-3600	900	607	99,972,000	8069
WSP CANADA INC (*Suby of* **AST TRUST COMPANY (CANADA)**) 3450 Boul Gene-H.-Kruger Bureau 300, Trois-Rivieres, QC G9A 4M3, *Tel* (819) 375-1292	900	608	0	8711
FINNING INTERNATIONAL INC 565 Great Northern Way Suite 300, Vancouver, BC V5T 0H8, *Tel* (604) 331-4816	897	609	5,303,681,592	5084
KRAFT HEINZ CANADA ULC (*Suby of* **THE KRAFT HEINZ COMPANY**)				

COMPANY	EMPLOYEES HERE	RANK	SALES ($)	PRIMARY SIC CODE
2150 Lake Shore Blvd W, Etobicoke, ON M8V 1A3, Tel (416) 506-6000	895	610	0	2051
MEDICAL FACILITIES CORPORATION				
45 St Clair Ave W Suite 200, Toronto, ON M4V 1K9, Tel (416) 848-7380	889	611	431,602,000	8062
ESIT CANADA ENTERPRISE SERVICES CO (*Suby of* **DXC TECHNOLOGY COMPANY**)				
1969 Upper Water St, Halifax, NS B3J 3R7, Tel (902) 000-0000	885	612	933,460,500	5734
ALLIANCE ATLANTIS COMMUNICATIONS INC				
121 Bloor St E Suite 1500, Toronto, ON M4W 3M5, Tel (416) 967-1174	871	613	202,346,035	4899
BAAGWATING COMMUNITY ASSOCIATION (*Suby of* **MISSISSAUGAS OF SCUGOG ISLAND FIRST NATION**)				
22521 Island Rd, Port Perry, ON L9L 1B6, Tel (905) 985-3337	850	614	73,695,000	7999
DOMTAR INC (*Suby of* **DOMTAR LUXEMBOURG INVESTMENTS SARL**)				
609 Rang 12, Windsor, QC J1S 2L9, Tel (800) 263-8366	850	615	0	2611
EXCELDOR COOPERATIVE				
5700 Rue J.-B.-Michaud Suite 500, Levis, QC G6V 0B1, Tel (418) 830-5600	850	616	682,339,000	2015
GLOBE AND MAIL INC, THE (*Suby of* **THOMSON COMPANY INC, THE**)				
351 King St E Suite 1600, Toronto, ON M5A 0N1, Tel (416) 585-5000	850	617	500,785,150	5192
GREY BRUCE HEALTH SERVICES				
1800 8th St E, Owen Sound, ON N4K 6M9, Tel (519) 376-2121	850	618	152,834,880	8062
KIK HOLDCO COMPANY INC (*Suby of* **KIK CUSTOM PRODUCTS INC**)				
101 Macintosh Blvd, Concord, ON L4K 4R5, Tel (905) 660-0444	850	619	365,509,000	6719
KUNTZ ELECTROPLATING INC				
851 Wilson Ave, Kitchener, ON N2C 1J1, Tel (519) 893-7680	850	620	206,746,350	3471
NOVA CHEMICALS (CANADA) LTD (*Suby of* **GOVERNMENT OF ABU DHABI**)				
Gd, Red Deer, AB T4N 5E6, Tel (403) 314-8611	850	621	0	2821
RIVERVIEW HEALTH CENTRE INC				
1 Morley Ave, Winnipeg, MB R3L 2P4, Tel (204) 478-6203	850	622	44,723,978	8051
ROCKY MOUNTAIN DEALERSHIPS INC (*Suby of* **ROCKY MOUNTAIN DEALERSHIPS INC**)				
260180 Writing Creek Cres, Rocky View County, AB T4A 0M9, Tel (403) 513-7000	850	623	0	5082
SHERIDAN COLLEGE INSTITUTE OF TECHNOLOGY AND ADVANCED LEARNING				
1430 Trafalgar Rd, Oakville, ON L6H 2L1, Tel (905) 845-9430	850	624	89,207,100	8222
TBM SERVICE GROUP INC				
2450 Dunwin Dr Unit 6, Mississauga, ON L5L 1J9, Tel (905) 608-8989	850	625	27,172,800	7349
TOROMONT INDUSTRIES LTD				
3131 Highway 7 Suite A, Concord, ON L4K 5E1, Tel (416) 667-5511	850	626	2,656,568,320	5082
TOROMONT INDUSTRIES LTD (*Suby of* **TOROMONT INDUSTRIES LTD**)				
65 Villiers St, Toronto, ON M5A 3S1, Tel (416) 465-7581	850	627	0	3585
CRYSTAL INFOSOFT				
186 Frederick St, Toronto, ON M5A 4L4, Tel	849	628	122,410,518	7371
PETAQUILLA MINERALS LTD				
777 Hornby St Suite 1230, Vancouver, BC V6Z 1S4, Tel	840	629	428,165,676	1041
CAMBRIAN COLLEGE OF APPLIED ARTS & TECHNOLOGY, THE				
1400 Barrydowne Rd, Sudbury, ON P3A 3V8, Tel (705) 566-8101	830	630	84,251,150	8222
PF CONSUMER HEALTHCARE CANADA ULC (*Suby of* **C.P. PHARMACEUTICALS INTERNATIONAL C.V.**)				
1025 Boul Marcel-Laurin, Saint-Laurent, QC H4R 1J6, Tel (514) 695-0500	829	631	274,891,426	2834
PHX ENERGY SERVICES CORP				
250 2 St Sw Suite 1400, Calgary, AB T2P 0C1, Tel (403) 543-4466	828	632	240,420,989	1381
CRYSTAL CLAIRE COSMETICS INC (*Suby of* **CRYSTAL GROUP HOLDINGS INC.**)				
165 Milner Ave, Scarborough, ON M1S 4G7, Tel (416) 421-1882	827	633	367,721,415	2844
HYDRO-QUEBEC (*Suby of* **GOUVERNEMENT DE LA PROVINCE DE QUEBEC**)				
140 Boul Cremazie O, Montreal, QC H2P 1C3, Tel (514) 858-8000	821	634	0	8731
METHANEX CORPORATION				
200 Burrard St Suite 1800, Vancouver, BC V6C 3M1, Tel (604) 661-2600	810	635	3,931,847,000	2869
CONESTOGA MEAT PACKERS LTD				
313 Menno St, Breslau, ON N0B 1M0, Tel (519) 648-2506	807	636	628,559,932	5147
UNIVERSITY OF WINNIPEG, THE				
515 Portage Ave, Winnipeg, MB R3B 2E9, Tel (204) 786-7811	805	637	99,658,393	8221
2095527 ONTARIO LIMITED				
6740 Fallsview Blvd, Niagara Falls, ON L2G 3W6, Tel (905) 356-3600	800	638	76,534,400	7011
ACCOR MANAGEMENT CANADA INC (*Suby of* **ACCOR MANAGEMENT CANADA INC**)				
900 Boul Rene-Levesque O, Montreal, QC H3B 4A5, Tel (514) 861-3511	800	639	0	7011
ACIER GENDRON LTEE				
2270 Rue Garneau, Longueuil, QC J4G 1E7, Tel (450) 442-9494	800	640	477,963,200	5051
ARMOUR TRANSPORT INC (*Suby of* **ARMOUR TRANSPORTATION SYSTEMS INC**)				
689 Edinburgh Dr, Moncton, NB E1E 2L4, Tel (506) 857-0205	800	641	295,009,600	4213
ASTRAZENECA CANADA INC (*Suby of* **ASTRAZENECA PLC**)				
1004 Middlegate Rd Suite 5000, Mississauga, ON L4Y 1M4, Tel (905) 277-7111	800	642	497,391,000	2834
BELL ALIANT REGIONAL COMMUNICATIONS INC (*Suby of* **BCE INC**)				
Gd, Saint John, NB E2L 4K2, Tel (506) 658-7169	800	643	0	4899
BELL MEDIA INC (*Suby of* **BCE INC**)				
444 Front St W, Toronto, ON M5V 2S9, Tel (416) 585-5000	800	644	0	5192
BMO NESBITT BURNS INC				
100 King St W Unit 1, Toronto, ON M5X 2A1, Tel (416) 643-1778	800	645	5,938,754,874	6211
BOMBARDIER INC (*Suby of* **BOMBARDIER INC**)				
1101 Rue Parent, Saint-Bruno, QC J3V 6E6, Tel (450) 441-2020	800	646	0	4111

COMPANY	EMPLOYEES HERE	RANK	SALES ($)	PRIMARY SIC CODE
BRITISH COLUMBIA LOTTERY CORPORATION (*Suby of* **GOVERNMENT OF THE PROVINCE OF BRITISH COLUMBIA**) 74 Seymour St W, Kamloops, BC V2C 1E2, *Tel* (250) 828-5500	800	647	2,393,147,467	7993
BROCK UNIVERSITY 1812 Sir Isaac Brock Way, St Catharines, ON L2S 3A1, *Tel* (905) 688-5550	800	648	194,208,300	8221
BURNBRAE FARMS LIMITED 3356 County Road 27, Lyn, ON K0E 1M0, *Tel* (613) 345-5651	800	649	716,716,000	5144
CANADA LIFE ASSURANCE COMPANY, THE (*Suby of* **POWER CORPORATION DU CANADA**) 1901 Scarth St Suite 414, Regina, SK S4P 4L4, *Tel* (306) 751-6000	800	650	0	6311
CANADIAN STANDARDS ASSOCIATION 178 Rexdale Blvd, Etobicoke, ON M9W 1R3, *Tel* (416) 747-4000	800	651	253,613,986	8734
CARGILL LIMITED (*Suby of* **CARGILL, INCORPORATED**) 71 Rexdale Blvd, Etobicoke, ON M9W 1P1, *Tel*	800	652	0	2011
CENTRE DE SANTE ET DE SERVICE SOCIAUX LES ESKERS DE L'ABITIBI 632 1re Rue O, Amos, QC J9T 2N2, *Tel* (819) 732-3271	800	653	0	8062
CHOEUR DU CEGEP DE SHERBROOKE 475 Rue Du Cegep, Sherbrooke, QC J1E 4K1, *Tel* (819) 564-6350	800	654	119,512,800	8221
CMC ELECTRONIQUE INC (*Suby of* **TRANSDIGM GROUP INCORPORATED**) 600 Boul Dr.-Frederik-Philips, Saint-Laurent, QC H4M 2S9, *Tel* (514) 748-3148	800	655	197,131,000	8711
COLLEGE D'ENSEIGNEMENT GENERAL ET PROFESSIONNEL JOHN ABBOTT 21275 Rue Lakeshore, Sainte-Anne-De-Bellevue, QC H9X 3L9, *Tel* (514) 457-6610	800	656	119,512,800	8221
COLLEGE OF NEW CALEDONIA, THE 3330 22nd Ave, Prince George, BC V2N 1P8, *Tel* (250) 562-2131	800	657	46,674,291	8221
CONSEIL CRI DE LA SANTE ET DES SERVICES SOCIAUX DE LA BAIE JAMES Gd, Chisasibi, QC J0M 1E0, *Tel* (819) 855-9001	800	658	159,237,482	8062
DISTRICT SCOLAIRE FRANCOPHONE SUD 425 Rue Champlain, Dieppe, NB E1A 1P2, *Tel* (506) 856-3333	800	659	79,295,200	8211
DOMTAR INC (*Suby of* **DOMTAR LUXEMBOURG INVESTMENTS SARL**) 1 Station Rd, Espanola, ON P5E 1R6, *Tel* (705) 869-2020	800	660	0	2611
EDGEWATER MANAGEMENT INC 750 Pacific Blvd Suite 311, Vancouver, BC V6B 5E7, *Tel* (604) 687-3343	800	661	76,534,400	7011
ERNST & YOUNG LLP (*Suby of* **ERNST & YOUNG LLP**) 90 Rue De Maisonneuve, Quebec, QC G1R 2C3, *Tel* (514) 875-6060	800	662	0	8721
FAIRMONT HOTELS & RESORTS INC (*Suby of* **ACCOR**) 405 Spray Ave, Banff, AB T1L 1J4, *Tel* (403) 762-6860	800	663	0	7011
FAIRMONT HOTELS & RESORTS INC (*Suby of* **ACCOR**) 111 Lake Louise Dr, Lake Louise, AB T0L 1E0, *Tel* (403) 522-3511	800	664	0	7011
FEDERATION DES CAISSES DESJARDINS DU QUEBEC (*Suby of* **FEDERATION DES CAISSES DESJARDINS DU QUEBEC**) 3155 Boul De L'Assomption, Montreal, QC H1N 3S8, *Tel* (514) 253-7300	800	665	0	4899
FIRST WEST CREDIT UNION (*Suby of* **FIRST WEST CREDIT UNION**) 9240 Young Rd, Chilliwack, BC V2P 4R2, *Tel* (604) 539-7300	800	666	0	6062
FONDS SOCIAL DES EMPLOYES DE LA CAISSE DE DEPOT ET PLACEMENT DU QUEBEC 1000 Place Jean-Paul-Riopelle Bureau A12, Montreal, QC H2Z 2B3, *Tel* (514) 842-3261	800	667	764,164,450	6399
G4S SECURE SOLUTIONS (CANADA) LTD (*Suby of* **G4S PLC**) 2 Lansing Sq Suite 204, North York, ON M2J 4P8, *Tel* (416) 490-8329	800	668	0	7381
GCIC LTD 1 Adelaide St E Suite 2800, Toronto, ON M5C 2V9, *Tel* (416) 350-3250	800	669	430,049,270	6159
GLS LOGISTICS SYSTEMS CANADA LTD (*Suby of* **ROYAL MAIL PLC**) 10755 Ch Cote-De-Liesse, Dorval, QC H9P 1A7, *Tel* (888) 463-4266	800	670	0	4212
GOODFOOD MARKET CORP 4600 Rue Hickmore, Saint-Laurent, QC H4T 1K2, *Tel* (514) 730-9530	800	671	53,585,072	8322
GOVERNORS OF THE UNIVERSITY OF CALGARY, THE 2500 University Dr Nw, Calgary, AB T2N 1N4, *Tel* (403) 220-5110	800	672	0	7389
GROUPE PAGES JAUNES CORP (*Suby of* **PAGES JAUNES LIMITEE**) 16 Place Du Commerce, Verdun, QC H3E 2A5, *Tel* (514) 934-2000	800	673	319,860,800	4899
GROUPE TVA INC (*Suby of* **QUEBECOR MEDIA INC**) 1475 Rue Alexandre-Deseve, Montreal, QC H2L 2V4, *Tel* (514) 526-9251	800	674	0	1799
HAMMOND POWER SOLUTIONS INC 595 Southgate Dr, Guelph, ON N1G 3W6, *Tel* (519) 822-2441	800	675	238,106,192	3612
HUMBER COLLEGE INSTITUTE OF TECHNOLOGY AND ADVANCE LEARNING, THE 205 Humber College Blvd, Etobicoke, ON M9W 5L7, *Tel* (416) 675-3111	800	676	346,648,446	8222
HUMBER RIVER HOSPITAL (*Suby of* **HUMBER RIVER HOSPITAL**) 2111 Finch Ave W, Toronto, ON M3N 1N1, *Tel* (416) 744-2500	800	677	0	8062
HUSKY OIL OPERATIONS LIMITED (*Suby of* **HUSKY ENERGY INC**) 5650 52 St, Lloydminster, AB T9V 0R7, *Tel*	800	678	0	1311
HYDRO-QUEBEC (*Suby of* **GOUVERNEMENT DE LA PROVINCE DE QUEBEC**) Gd, Alma, QC G8B 5V5, *Tel* (418) 668-1400	800	679	0	4911
INGRAM MICRO INC (*Suby of* **HNA TECHNOLOGY CO., LTD.**) 55 Standish Crt Suite 1, Mississauga, ON L5R 4A1, *Tel* (905) 755-5000	800	680	535,352,000	5045
INTRIA ITEMS INC (*Suby of* **CANADIAN IMPERIAL BANK OF COMMERCE**) 8301 Rue Elmslie, Lasalle, QC H8N 3H9, *Tel* (514) 368-5222	800	681	0	7374
JACOBS CANADA INC (*Suby of* **JACOBS ENGINEERING GROUP INC.**) 205 Quarry Park Blvd Se, Calgary, AB T2C 3E7, *Tel* (403) 258-6411	800	682	177,417,900	8711

COMPANY	EMPLOYEES HERE	RANK	SALES ($)	PRIMARY SIC CODE
KIRKLAND LAKE GOLD LTD (*Suby of* **KIRKLAND LAKE GOLD LTD**)				
1350 Government Rd W, Kirkland Lake, ON P2N 3J1, *Tel* (705) 567-5208	800	683	0	1081
KPMG LLP (*Suby of* **KPMG LLP**)				
777 Dunsmuir St Suite 900, Vancouver, BC V7Y 1K3, *Tel* (604) 691-3000	800	684	0	8721
L3 TECHNOLOGIES MAS INC (*Suby of* **L3HARRIS TECHNOLOGIES, INC.**)				
10000 Rue Helen-Bristol, Mirabel, QC J7N 1H3, *Tel* (450) 476-4000	800	685	89,696,000	7699
LEDCOR INDUSTRIES INC (*Suby of* **280818 ALBERTA LTD**)				
1067 Cordova St W Suite 1200, Vancouver, BC V6C 1C7, *Tel* (604) 681-7500	800	686	262,492,000	1611
LETHBRIDGE COLLEGE				
3000 College Dr S, Lethbridge, AB T1K 1L6, *Tel* (403) 320-3200	800	687	123,898,750	8222
LULULEMON ATHLETICA CANADA INC				
1818 Cornwall Ave Suite 400, Vancouver, BC V6J 1C7, *Tel* (604) 732-6124	800	688	3,288,319,000	2339
MAIBEC INC (*Suby of* **MAIBEC INC**)				
24 6e Rang Bureau 6, Saint-Pamphile, QC G0R 3X0, *Tel* (418) 356-3331	800	689	0	2421
MANUFACTURERS LIFE INSURANCE COMPANY, THE (*Suby of* **MANULIFE FINANCIAL CORPORATION**)				
2000 Rue Mansfield Unite 300, Montreal, QC H3A 2Z4, *Tel* (514) 288-6268	800	690	0	6311
MATRIX LOGISTICS SERVICES LIMITED (*Suby of* **MATRIX LOGISTICS SERVICES LIMITED**)				
2675 Steeles Ave W, Brampton, ON L6Y 5X3, *Tel* (905) 451-6792	800	691	0	4225
MCCARTHY TETRAULT LLP				
66 Wellington St W Suite 5300, Toronto, ON M5K 1E6, *Tel* (416) 362-1812	800	692	308,814,000	8111
MORNEAU SHEPELL LTD (*Suby of* **MORNEAU SHEPELL INC**)				
895 Don Mills Rd, North York, ON M3C 1W3, *Tel* (416) 445-2700	800	693	518,712,100	8999
MOSAIC SALES SOLUTIONS CANADA OPERATING CO. (*Suby of* **MACQUARIE GROUP LIMITED**)				
2700 Matheson Blvd E Unit 101, Mississauga, ON L4W 4V9, *Tel* (905) 238-8058	800	694	126,220,000	8743
NIAGARA HEALTH SYSTEM (*Suby of* **NIAGARA HEALTH SYSTEM**)				
142 Queenston St, St Catharines, ON L2R 2Z7, *Tel* (905) 684-7271	800	695	0	8062
NORDION (CANADA) INC (*Suby of* **NORDION (CANADA) INC**)				
3680 Gilmore Way, Burnaby, BC V5G 4V8, *Tel* (604) 431-5005	800	696	0	8071
NORTHBRIDGE INDEMNITY INSURANCE CORPORATION (*Suby of* **FAIRFAX FINANCIAL HOLDINGS LIMITED**)				
105 Adelaide St W Unit 700, Toronto, ON M5H 1P9, *Tel* (855) 620-6262	800	697	0	6411
OCI HOLDINGS INC (*Suby of* **OCI HOLDINGS INC**)				
20 Hope St, Souris, PE C0A 2B0, *Tel* (902) 687-1245	800	698	0	5146
ONTARIO POWER GENERATION INC (*Suby of* **GOVERNMENT OF ONTARIO**)				
700 University Ave, Toronto, ON M5G 1X6, *Tel* (416) 592-2555	800	699	4,041,174,366	4911
ONTARIO TEACHERS' PENSION PLAN BOARD				
5650 Yonge St Suite 300, North York, ON M2M 4H5, *Tel* (416) 228-5900	800	700	140,086,544,065	6371
PACCAR OF CANADA LTD (*Suby of* **PACCAR INC**)				
10 Rue Sicard, Sainte-Therese, QC J7E 4K9, *Tel* (450) 435-6171	800	701	0	3711
PROVIDENCE CARE CENTRE				
340 Union St, Kingston, ON K7L 5A2, *Tel* (613) 548-7222	800	702	122,986,800	8051
PROVIGO DISTRIBUTION INC (*Suby of* **LOBLAW COMPANIES LIMITED**)				
400 Av Sainte-Croix, Saint-Laurent, QC H4N 3L4, *Tel* (514) 383-3000	800	703	17,917,900,000	5141
RAYONIER A.M. CANADA G.P. (*Suby of* **RAYONIER A.M. CANADA G.P.**)				
10 Ch Gatineau, Temiscaming, QC J0Z 3R0, *Tel* (819) 627-4387	800	704	0	2611
RESTIGOUCHE HEALTH AUTHORITY				
189 Lily Lake Rd, Campbellton, NB E3N 3H3, *Tel* (506) 789-5000	800	705	135,739,760	8062
RIO TINTO ALCAN INC (*Suby of* **RIO TINTO PLC**)				
5000 Rte Du Petit Parc, La Baie, QC G7B 4G9, *Tel* (418) 697-9600	800	706	0	3334
ROSS MEMORIAL HOSPITAL, THE				
10 Angeline St N, Lindsay, ON K9V 4M8, *Tel* (705) 324-6111	800	707	88,864,000	8062
SCHOOL DISTRICT NO. 44 (NORTH VANCOUVER)				
2121 Lonsdale Ave, North Vancouver, BC V7M 2K6, *Tel* (604) 903-3444	800	708	196,255,620	8211
SERVICES OR LP/SEC				
1 Place Ville-Marie Unite 2500, Montreal, QC H3B 1R1, *Tel* (514) 847-4747	800	709	99,820,800	8741
SOBEYS CAPITAL INCORPORATED (*Suby of* **EMPIRE COMPANY LIMITED**)				
11281 Boul Albert-Hudon, Montreal-Nord, QC H1G 3J5, *Tel* (514) 324-1010	800	710	0	5141
STAFF OF THE NON-PUBLIC FUNDS, CANADIAN FORCES				
101 Colonel By Dr, Ottawa, ON K1A 0K2, *Tel* (613) 995-8509	800	711	165,654,400	8399
STANTEC CONSULTING LTD (*Suby of* **STANTEC INC**)				
1060 Boul Robert-Bourassa Unite 600, Montreal, QC H3B 4V3, *Tel* (514) 281-1033	800	712	0	8711
SUPRALIMENT S.E.C. (*Suby of* **SUPRALIMENT S.E.C.**)				
25 125 Rte E, Saint-Esprit, QC J0K 2L0, *Tel* (450) 839-7258	800	713	0	2011
SYMCOR INC (*Suby of* **SYMCOR INC**)				
8 Prince Andrew Pl, North York, ON M3C 2H4, *Tel* (905) 273-1000	800	714	0	8741
TERRAVEST INCOME FUND				
4901 Bruce Rd, Vegreville, AB T9C 1C3, *Tel* (780) 632-7774	800	715	4,669,540,000	6722
TERVITA CORPORATION				
140 10 Ave Se Suite 1600, Calgary, AB T2G 0R1, *Tel* (855) 837-8482	800	716	1,824,717,933	8748
UNION OF NATIONAL DEFENCE EMPLOYEES				
17 Princess Mary, Kingston, ON K7K 7B4, *Tel*	800	717	0	8631
WALMART CANADA LOGISTICS ULC (*Suby of* **WALMART INC.**)				
6800 Maritz Dr, Mississauga, ON L5W 1W2, *Tel* (905) 670-9966	800	718	575,976,800	4225
WELLS FARGO FINANCIAL RETAIL SERVICES COMPANY OF CANADA (*Suby of* **WELLS FARGO & COMPANY**)				
55 Standish Crt Suite 300, Mississauga, ON L5R 4B2, *Tel*	800	719	180,984,800	7322

COMPANY	EMPLOYEES HERE	RANK	SALES ($)	PRIMARY SIC CODE
WILFRID LAURIER UNIVERSITY				
75 University Ave W, Waterloo, ON N2L 3C5, *Tel* (519) 884-1970	800	720	257,957,995	8221
WINNERS MERCHANTS INTERNATIONAL L.P. (*Suby of* **THE TJX COMPANIES INC**)				
3185 American Dr, Mississauga, ON L4V 1B8, *Tel* (905) 672-2228	800	721	0	5651
WSP CANADA INC (*Suby of* **AST TRUST COMPANY (CANADA)**)				
1600 Boul Rene-Levesque O 16e Etage, Montreal, QC H3H 1P9, *Tel* (514) 340-0046	800	722	1,604,219,001	6712
CAPILANO UNIVERSITY (*Suby of* **GOVERNMENT OF THE PROVINCE OF BRITISH COLUMBIA**)				
2055 Purcell Way Suite 284, North Vancouver, BC V7J 3H5, *Tel* (604) 986-1911	797	723	31,559,191	8221
GENERAL DYNAMICS PRODUITS DE DEFENSE ET SYSTEMES TACTIQUES-CANADA INC (*Suby of* **GENERAL DYNAMICS CORPORATION**)				
5 Montee Des Arsenaux, Repentigny, QC J5Z 2P4, *Tel* (450) 581-3080	790	724	243,231,000	3483
ST. JOSEPH'S HEALTH CARE, LONDON (*Suby of* **ST. JOSEPH'S HEALTH CARE, LONDON**)				
850 Highbury Ave N, London, ON N5Y 1A4, *Tel* (519) 455-5110	786	725	0	8093
ALLIED INTERNATIONAL CREDIT CORP (*Suby of* **BILL GOSLING OUTSOURCING HOLDING CORP**)				
16635 Yonge St Suite 26, Newmarket, ON L3X 1V6, *Tel* (905) 470-8181	775	726	28,846,155	4899
SOCIETE DES CASINOS DU QUEBEC INC, LA (*Suby of* **GOUVERNEMENT DE LA PROVINCE DE QUEBEC**)				
500 Rue Sherbrooke O Bureau 1500, Montreal, QC H3A 3C6, *Tel* (514) 282-8000	769	727	464,625,300	7999
ALIMENTS MULTIBAR INC, LES (*Suby of* **NELLSON NUTRACEUTICAL, LLC**)				
9000 Boul Des Sciences, Anjou, QC H1J 3A9, *Tel* (514) 355-1151	765	728	548,287,740	5142
9219-1568 QUEBEC INC				
7777 Boul Decarie Bureau 300, Montreal, QC H4P 2H2, *Tel* (514) 359-3555	750	729	108,136,500	7371
AAA CANADA INC				
780 Av Brewster Bureau 03-200, Montreal, QC H4C 2K1, *Tel* (514) 733-6655	750	730	238,014,000	4581
ALMA MATER SOCIETY OF QUEEN'S UNIVERSITY INCORPORATED				
99 University Ave, Kingston, ON K7L 3N5, *Tel* (613) 533-2725	750	731	144,732,000	8742
ALUMINERIE ALOUETTE INC				
400 Ch De La Pointe-Noire, Sept-Iles, QC G4R 5M9, *Tel* (418) 964-7000	750	732	136,041,000	3334
BANQUE DE DEVELOPPEMENT DU CANADA (*Suby of* **GOVERNMENT OF CANADA**)				
5 Place Ville-Marie Bureau 400, Montreal, QC H3B 5E7, *Tel* (514) 283-5904	750	733	777,423,156	6141
BLUE TREE HOTELS INVESTMENT (CANADA), LTD (*Suby of* **BLUE TREE HOTELS INVESTMENT (CANADA), LTD**)				
Westin Harbour Castle, Toronto, ON M5J 1A6, *Tel* (416) 869-1600	750	734	0	7011
BOARD OF GOVERNOR'S OF RED RIVER COLLEGE, THE (*Suby of* **PROVINCE OF MANITOBA**)				
2055 Notre Dame Ave, Winnipeg, MB R3H 0J9, *Tel* (204) 632-3960	750	735	161,368	8222
CAMBRIA FABSHOP-TORONTO INC				
41 Simpson Rd, Bolton, ON L7E 2R6, *Tel* (905) 951-1011	750	736	166,998,750	2541
CANADIAN TEST CASE 101 LTD				
5770 Hurontario St, Mississauga, ON L5R 3G5, *Tel*	750	737	0	2899
CIBC SECURITIES INC (*Suby of* **CANADIAN IMPERIAL BANK OF COMMERCE**)				
200 King St W Suite 700, Toronto, ON M5H 4A8, *Tel* (416) 980-2211	750	738	412,494,750	6722
COMPAGNIE DES CHEMINS DE FER NATIONAUX DU CANADA (*Suby of* **COMPAGNIE DES CHEMINS DE FER NATIONAUX DU CANADA**)				
1108 Industrial Way, Prince George, BC V2N 5S1, *Tel* (250) 561-4190	750	739	0	4111
COMPAGNIE MEXX CANADA (*Suby of* **EROGLU GIYIM SANAYI TICARET ANONIM SIRKETI**)				
905 Rue Hodge, Saint-Laurent, QC H4N 2B3, *Tel* (514) 383-5555	750	740	628,149,750	5137
CORPORATION INTERNATIONALE MASONITE				
1501 Av Mcgill College Suite 26e, Montreal, QC H3A 3N9, *Tel* (514) 841-6400	750	741	208,792,500	2431
DELTA HOTELS LIMITED (*Suby of* **GOVERNMENT OF THE PROVINCE OF BRITISH COLUMBIA**)				
77 King St W Suite 2300, Toronto, ON M5K 2A1, *Tel*	750	742	311,940,000	8741
DIRECT ACTION IN SUPPORT OF COMMUNITY HOMES INCORPORATED				
117 Victor Lewis Dr Unit 1, Winnipeg, MB R3P 1J6, *Tel* (204) 987-1550	750	743	48,211,500	8361
EXCELDOR COOPERATIVE				
5700 Rue J.-B.-Michaud Bureau 500, Levis, QC G6V 0B1, *Tel* (418) 830-5600	750	744	259,267,500	2015
GLS LOGISTICS SYSTEMS CANADA LTD (*Suby of* **ROYAL MAIL PLC**)				
10500 Av Ryan, Dorval, QC H9P 2T7, *Tel* (514) 636-8033	750	745	593,157,000	4731
GROUPE ALDO INC, LE (*Suby of* **GESTION TREE ROOTS INC**)				
2300 Rue Emile-Belanger, Saint-Laurent, QC H4R 3J4, *Tel* (514) 747-2536	750	746	706,861,830	5661
HR OTTAWA, L.P.				
4837 Albion Rd, Gloucester, ON K1X 1A3, *Tel* (613) 822-8668	750	747	71,751,000	7011
HYDRO-QUEBEC (*Suby of* **GOUVERNEMENT DE LA PROVINCE DE QUEBEC**)				
1800 Boul Lionel-Boulet, Varennes, QC J3X 1P7, *Tel* (450) 925-2008	750	748	0	8731
INSTITUT DE RECHERCHE DU CENTRE UNIVERSITAIRE DE SANTE MCGILL, L'				
2155 Rue Guy Bureau 500, Montreal, QC H3H 2R9, *Tel* (514) 934-8354	750	749	244,478,250	8071
KPH TURCOT, UN PARTENARIAT S.E.N.C				
4333 Boul De La Grande-Allee, Boisbriand, QC J7H 1M7, *Tel* (450) 435-5756	750	750	139,879,500	8742
KPMG LLP (*Suby of* **KPMG LLP**)				
600 Boul De Maisonneuve O Unite1500, Montreal, QC H3A 0A3, *Tel* (514) 840-2100	750	751	0	8721
LEGAL AID ONTARIO				
Legal Aid Ontario, Toronto, ON M5G 2H1, *Tel* (416) 979-1446	750	752	154,407,000	8111
MANITOBA HYDRO-ELECTRIC BOARD, THE (*Suby of* **PROVINCE OF MANITOBA**)				
360 Portage Ave Suite 6, Winnipeg, MB R3C 0G8, *Tel* (204) 360-3311	750	753	1,771,333,343	4911
MANULIFE CANADA LTD (*Suby of* **MANULIFE FINANCIAL CORPORATION**)				
2000 Rue Mansfield Unite 200, Montreal, QC H3A 2Z4, *Tel* (514) 845-1612	750	754	0	8742
MELCO CAPITAL INC				
1000 Montee Des Pionniers Bureau 212, Terrebonne, QC J6V 1S8, *Tel* (514) 564-7600	750	755	56,962,697	7361

COMPANY	EMPLOYEES HERE	RANK	SALES ($)	PRIMARY SIC CODE
PERSONNEL UNIQUE CANADA INC (*Suby of* **GROUPE MANUCAM INC**) 455 Boul Fenelon Bureau 210, Dorval, QC H9S 5T8, *Tel* (514) 633-6220	750	756	84,152,250	8741
POSTMEDIA NETWORK INC (*Suby of* **POSTMEDIA NETWORK CANADA CORP**) 215 16 St Se, Calgary, AB T2E 7P5, *Tel* (403) 235-7168	750	757	0	2711
PRICEWATERHOUSECOOPERS LLP (*Suby of* **PRICEWATERHOUSECOOPERS LLP**) 1250 Boul Rene-Levesque O Bureau 2800, Montreal, QC H3B 4W8, *Tel* (514) 866-8409	750	758	0	8721
RG PROPERTIES LTD 1177 Hastings St W Suite 2088, Vancouver, BC V6E 2K3, *Tel* (604) 688-8999	750	759	167,544,900	6553
RIVER CREE RESORT LIMITED PARTNERSHIP 300 E Lapotac Blvd, Enoch, AB T7X 3Y3, *Tel* (780) 484-2121	750	760	71,751,000	7011
SAFRAN CABIN CANADA CO. (*Suby of* **SAFRAN**) 18107 Rte Transcanadienne, Kirkland, QC H9J 3K1, *Tel* (514) 697-5555	750	761	147,848,250	8711
SECURITAS TRANSPORT AVIATION SECURITY LTD (*Suby of* **SECURITAS AB**) 100 Av De L'Aeroport Unite 17, Rouyn-Noranda, QC J9Y 0G1, *Tel* (819) 764-3507	750	762	228,810,750	7389
SLEEMAN BREWING & MALTING COMPANY LTD, THE (*Suby of* **SAPPORO HOLDINGS LIMITED**) 551 Clair Rd W, Guelph, ON N1L 1E9, *Tel* (519) 822-1834	750	763	365,538,750	2082
SUN GRO HORTICULTURE CANADA LTD Gd, Elma, MB R0E 0Z0, *Tel* (204) 426-2121	750	764	309,831,750	1499
SWISSPORT CANADA INC (*Suby of* **SWISSPORT CANADA INC**) Gd, Richmond, BC V7B 1Y4, *Tel* (604) 303-4550	750	765	0	4581
UNIVERSITY OF OTTAWA HEART INSTITUTE 40 Ruskin St, Ottawa, ON K1Y 4W7, *Tel* (613) 696-7000	750	766	121,446,906	8731
VUTEQ CANADA INC (*Suby of* **VUTEQ CORPORATION**) 920 Keyes Dr, Woodstock, ON N4V 1C2, *Tel* (519) 421-0011	750	767	218,045,200	3089
GREGG DISTRIBUTORS CO LTD 3611 76 Ave Nw, Edmonton, AB T6B 2S8, *Tel* (780) 450-2233	744	768	153,045,264	4225
GOUVERNEMENT DE LA PROVINCE DE QUEBEC (*Suby of* **GOUVERNEMENT DE LA PROVINCE DE QUEBEC**) 7843 Rue Des Santolines, Quebec, QC G1G 0G3, *Tel* (418) 683-2511	741	769	0	8361
VEONEER CANADA, INC (*Suby of* **VEONEER, INC.**) 7455 Birchmount Rd, Markham, ON L3R 5C2, *Tel* (905) 475-4150	740	770	209,357,100	3679
SHERIDAN COLLEGE INSTITUTE OF TECHNOLOGY AND ADVANCED LEARNING (*Suby of* **SHERIDAN COLLEGE INSTITUTE OF TECHNOLOGY AND ADVANCED LEARNING**) 4180 Duke Of York Blvd, Mississauga, ON L5B 0G5, *Tel* (905) 845-9430	737	771	0	8222
CIBC MELLON GLOBAL SECURITIES SERVICES COMPANY 1 York St Suite 500, Toronto, ON M5J 0B6, *Tel* (416) 643-5000	734	772	203,878,674	6091
WATERVILLE TG INC (*Suby of* **TOYODA GOSEI CO., LTD.**) 10 Rue Du Depot, Waterville, QC J0B 3H0, *Tel* (819) 837-2421	728	773	504,227,430	2891
MENU FOODS INCOME FUND (*Suby of* **SIMMONS PET FOOD ON, INC**) 8 Falconer Dr Unit 1, Mississauga, ON L5N 1B1, *Tel* (905) 826-3870	721	774	396,544,953	6722
MDA SYSTEMS LTD (*Suby of* **MAXAR TECHNOLOGIES INC.**) 57 Auriga Dr Unit 201, Nepean, ON K2E 8B2, *Tel* (613) 727-1087	718	775	0	7373
BELL ALIANT REGIONAL COMMUNICATIONS INC (*Suby of* **BCE INC**) 1505 Barrington St Suite 1102, Halifax, NS B3J 3K5, *Tel* (902) 487-4609	711	776	0	4899
PF CONSUMER HEALTHCARE CANADA ULC (*Suby of* **PFIZER INC.**) 55 Standish Crt Suite 450, Mississauga, ON L5R 4B2, *Tel* (905) 507-7000	710	777	235,431,740	2834
GROUPE GAUDREAULT INC, LE 1500 Rue Raymond-Gaudreault, Repentigny, QC J5Y 4E3, *Tel* (450) 585-1210	705	778	257,683,845	6712
ADP CANADA CO (*Suby of* **AUTOMATIC DATA PROCESSING, INC.**) 3250 Bloor St W 6th Fl Suite 1600, Etobicoke, ON M8X 2X9, *Tel* (416) 207-2900	700	779	369,706,000	8721
AGF MANAGEMENT LIMITED (*Suby of* **AGF MANAGEMENT LIMITED**) 66 Wellington St W Fl 31, Toronto, ON M5K 1E9, *Tel* (800) 268-8583	700	780	0	6282
ALCOA CANADA CIE (*Suby of* **ALUMINERIE LAURALCO SARL**) 100 Rte Maritime, Baie-Comeau, QC G4Z 2L6, *Tel* (418) 296-3311	700	781	0	3354
ALTALINK MANAGEMENT LTD (*Suby of* **BERKSHIRE HATHAWAY INC.**) 2611 3 Ave Se, Calgary, AB T2A 7W7, *Tel* (403) 267-3400	700	782	588,515,200	4911
ARCELORMITTAL PRODUITS LONGS CANADA S.E.N.C. (*Suby of* **ARCELORMITTAL PRODUITS LONGS CANADA S.E.N.C.**) 3900 Rte Des Acieries, Contrecoeur, QC J0L 1C0, *Tel* (450) 587-8600	700	783	0	3312
AVON CANADA INC (*Suby of* **CERBERUS CAPITAL MANAGEMENT, L.P.**) 10 Purdue Crt W, Lethbridge, AB T1K 4R8, *Tel*	700	784	0	2844
BARRY GROUP INC (*Suby of* **BARRY GROUP INC**) 1 Masonic Terrace, Clarenville, NL A5A 1N2, *Tel* (709) 466-7186	700	785	0	2092
BBA INC (*Suby of* **GROUPE BBA INC**) 10 Carlson Crt Suite 420, Etobicoke, ON M9W 6L2, *Tel* (416) 585-2115	700	786	0	8711
BEST BUY CANADA LTD (*Suby of* **BEST BUY CO., INC.**) 9200 Airport Rd, Brampton, ON L6S 6G6, *Tel* (905) 494-7000	700	787	0	5065
BLAKE, CASSELS & GRAYDON LLP 199 Bay St Suite 4000, Toronto, ON M5L 1A9, *Tel* (416) 863-2400	700	788	205,876,000	8111
BLOUNT CANADA LTD (*Suby of* **AMERICAN SECURITIES LLC**) 505 Edinburgh Rd N, Guelph, ON N1H 6L4, *Tel* (519) 822-6870	700	789	196,613,900	3568
CAMPBELL COMPANY OF CANADA (*Suby of* **CAMPBELL SOUP COMPANY**) 60 Birmingham St, Etobicoke, ON M8V 2B8, *Tel* (416) 251-1131	700	790	731,077,500	2032
CANADA BREAD COMPANY, LIMITED (*Suby of* **GRUPO BIMBO, S.A.B. DE C.V.**) 3455 Av Francis-Hughes, Sainte-Rose, QC H7L 5A5, *Tel* (450) 669-2222	700	791	0	5461

COMPANY	EMPLOYEES HERE	RANK	SALES ($)	PRIMARY SIC CODE
CARGILL LIMITED (*Suby of* **CARGILL, INCORPORATED**) 7901 Rue Samuel-Hatt, Chambly, QC J3L 6V7, *Tel* (450) 447-4600	700	792	0	5153
CELESTICA INTERNATIONAL LP (*Suby of* **ONEX CORPORATION**) 844 Don Mills Rd, Toronto, ON M3C 1V7, *Tel* (416) 448-2559	700	793	567,244,575	3672
CELESTICA INTERNATIONAL LP (*Suby of* **ONEX CORPORATION**) 213 Harry Walker Pky S, Newmarket, ON L3Y 8T3, *Tel* (416) 448-2559	700	794	0	3672
CENTRE HOSPITALIER ET CENTRE DE READAPTATION ANTOINE-LABELLE 1525 Rue L'Annonciation N, Riviere-Rouge, QC J0T 1T0, *Tel* (819) 275-2411	700	795	0	8062
CML HEALTHCARE INC 60 Courtneypark Dr W Unit 1, Mississauga, ON L5W 0B3, *Tel* (905) 565-0043	700	796	353,457,560	8071
COM DEV LTD (*Suby of* **HONEYWELL INTERNATIONAL INC.**) 155 Sheldon Dr, Cambridge, ON N1R 7H6, *Tel* (519) 622-2300	700	797	206,527,950	3669
COMPAGNIE MINIERE IOC INC (*Suby of* **RIO TINTO PLC**) 1 Rue Retty, Sept-Iles, QC G4R 3C7, *Tel* (418) 968-7400	700	798	0	1011
COMPUTER SCIENCES CANADA INC (*Suby of* **DXC TECHNOLOGY COMPANY**) 1360 Boul Rene-Levesque O Bureau 300, Montreal, QC H3G 2W7, *Tel*	700	799	0	7379
CONCENTRIX TECHNOLOGIES SERVICES (CANADA) LIMITED (*Suby of* **SYNNEX CORPORATION**) 720 Coverdale Rd, Riverview, NB E1B 3L8, *Tel* (506) 860-5900	700	800	0	4899
CONFEDERATION COLLEGE OF APPLIED ARTS AND TECHNOLOGY, THE 1450 Nakina Dr, Thunder Bay, ON P7C 4W1, *Tel* (807) 475-6110	700	801	54,263,958	8222
CONNORS BROS. CLOVER LEAF SEAFOODS COMPANY (*Suby of* **CLOVER LEAF HOLDINGS COMPANY**) 180 Brunswick St, Blacks Harbour, NB E5H 1G6, *Tel* (506) 456-3391	700	802	0	5146
DISTRICT SCOLAIRE FRANCOPHONE NORD-EST 3376 Rue Principale, Tracadie-Sheila, NB E1X 1A4, *Tel* (506) 394-3400	700	803	69,383,300	8211
DYNACARE-GAMMA LABORATORY PARTNERSHIP (*Suby of* **LABORATORY CORPORATION OF AMERICA HOLDINGS**) 115 Midair Crt, Brampton, ON L6T 5M3, *Tel* (905) 790-3515	700	804	977,913,000	8071
ERNST & YOUNG LLP (*Suby of* **ERNST & YOUNG LLP**) 1 Place Ville-Marie Bureau 1900, Montreal, QC H3B 1X9, *Tel* (514) 875-6060	700	805	0	8721
FAIRMONT HOTELS & RESORTS INC (*Suby of* **ACCOR**) 900 Boul Rene-Levesque O, Montreal, QC H3B 4A5, *Tel* (514) 861-3511	700	806	0	7011
FARM CREDIT CANADA (*Suby of* **GOVERNMENT OF CANADA**) 1800 Hamilton St, Regina, SK S4P 4L3, *Tel* (306) 780-8100	700	807	845,872,000	6159
FIDUCIE DESJARDINS INC (*Suby of* **FEDERATION DES CAISSES DESJARDINS DU QUEBEC**) 1 Complexe Desjardins Tour S, Montreal, QC H5B 1E4, *Tel* (514) 286-9441	700	808	3,402,722,880	6733
FINANCIERE BANQUE NATIONALE INC 5e Etage 1155, Rue Metcalfe, Montreal, QC H3B 2V6, *Tel* (514) 879-2222	700	809	572,515,922	6021
FORD MOTOR COMPANY OF CANADA, LIMITED (*Suby of* **FORD MOTOR COMPANY**) 6500 Cantelon Dr, Windsor, ON N8T 0A6, *Tel* (519) 251-4401	700	810	0	3711
GEM HEALTH CARE GROUP LIMITED (*Suby of* **GEM HEALTH CARE GROUP LIMITED**) 15 Shoreham Lane Suite 101, Halifax, NS B3P 2R3, *Tel* (902) 429-6227	700	811	0	6712
GESTION CANADADIRECT INC 743 Av Renaud, Dorval, QC H9P 2N1, *Tel* (514) 422-8557	700	812	153,960,100	8732
GOVERNMENT OF THE PROVINCE OF ALBERTA (*Suby of* **GOVERNMENT OF THE PROVINCE OF ALBERTA**) 5718 56 Ave, Lacombe, AB T4L 1B1, *Tel* (403) 782-8309	700	813	0	6159
GROUPE CANAM INC (*Suby of* **CANAM LUX PARENT COMPANY SARL**) 115 Boul Canam N, Saint-Gedeon-De-Beauce, QC G0M 1T0, *Tel* (418) 582-3331	700	814	0	3441
GROUPE DE SECURITE GARDA INC, LE (*Suby of* **GW INTERMEDIATE HOLDCO CORPORATION**) 1390 Rue Barre, Montreal, QC H3C 5X9, *Tel* (514) 281-2811	700	815	3,480,974,210	7381
HERSHEY CANADA INC (*Suby of* **HERSHEY COMPANY**) 375 Pleasant St, Dartmouth, NS B2Y 4N4, *Tel*	700	816	0	2064
HOPITAL GENERAL DE HAWKESBURY & DISTRICT GENERAL HOSPITAL INC 1111 Ghislain St, Hawkesbury, ON K6A 3G5, *Tel* (613) 632-1111	700	817	77,756,000	8062
HUMBERVIEW GROUP LTD 2500 Bloor St W, Toronto, ON M6S 1R7, *Tel*	700	818	404,076,400	5511
I.M.P. GROUP LIMITED (*Suby of* **I.M.P. GROUP INTERNATIONAL INCORPORATED**) 10225 Av Ryan, Dorval, QC H9P 1A2, *Tel* (514) 636-7070	700	819	0	4581
IMPERIAL OIL LIMITED 505 Quarry Park Blvd Se, Calgary, AB T2C 5N1, *Tel* (800) 567-3776	700	820	26,608,622,098	2911
INDEPENDENT ORDER OF FORESTERS, THE 789 Don Mills Rd Suite 1200, North York, ON M3C 1T9, *Tel* (416) 429-3000	700	821	1,353,082,894	6311
INDUSTRIELLE ALLIANCE, ASSURANCE ET SERVICES FINANCIERS INC 1080 Grande Allee O, Quebec, QC G1S 1C7, *Tel* (418) 684-5000	700	822	5,950,342,598	6311
J&A CLEANING SOLUTIONS LTD 785 Arrow Rd, North York, ON M9M 2L4, *Tel* (416) 242-4151	700	823	22,377,600	7349
L'INDUSTRIELLE-ALLIANCE SERVICES IMMOBILIERS INC (*Suby of* **INDUSTRIELLE ALLIANCE, ASSURANCE ET SERVICES FINANCIERS INC**) 3810 Rue De Marly, Quebec, QC G1X 4B1, *Tel* (418) 651-7308	700	824	94,973,900	6513
LITENS AUTOMOTIVE PARTNERSHIP 730 Rowntree Dairy Rd, Woodbridge, ON L4L 5T7, *Tel* (905) 856-0200	700	825	364,846,500	3429
MAGELLAN AEROSPACE LIMITED (*Suby of* **MAGELLAN AEROSPACE CORPORATION**) 660 Berry St, Winnipeg, MB R3H 0S5, *Tel* (204) 775-8331	700	826	0	3728
MANITOBA PUBLIC INSURANCE CORPORATION, THE (*Suby of* **PROVINCE OF MANITOBA**) 234 Donald St Suite 912, Winnipeg, MB R3C 4A4, *Tel* (204) 985-7000	700	827	268,217,500	8743

COMPANY	EMPLOYEES HERE	RANK	SALES ($)	PRIMARY SIC CODE
MAPLE LEAF FOODS INC (*Suby of* **MAPLE LEAF FOODS INC**)				
100 Ethel Ave, Toronto, ON M6N 4Z7, *Tel* (416) 767-5151	700	828	0	2015
MAPLE TERRAZZO MARBLE & TILE INCORPORATED (*Suby of* **MAPLE TERRAZZO MARBLE & TILE INCORPORATED**)				
200 Edgeley Blvd Unit 9, Concord, ON L4K 3Y8, *Tel* (905) 760-1776	700	829	0	8631
MCMASTER STUDENTS UNION INCORPORATED				
1280 Main St W Rm 1, Hamilton, ON L8S 4K1, *Tel* (905) 525-9140	700	830	199,361,400	8631
MEDAVIE INC				
644 Main St, Moncton, NB E1C 1E2, *Tel* (506) 853-1811	700	831	3,632,845,600	6321
MELOCHE MONNEX INC (*Suby of* **TORONTO-DOMINION BANK, THE**)				
50 Boul Cremazie O Bureau 1200, Montreal, QC H2P 1B6, *Tel* (514) 382-6060	700	832	2,596,575,936	6712
METROLINX (*Suby of* **METROLINX**)				
200 Steeprock Dr, North York, ON M3J 2T4, *Tel*	700	833		4011
MONTREAL GATEWAY TERMINALS PARTNERSHIP				
305 Rue Curatteau, Montreal, QC H1L 6R6, *Tel* (514) 257-3040	700	834	243,152,700	4491
MULTI-MARQUES INC (*Suby of* **GRUPO BIMBO, S.A.B. DE C.V.**)				
3443 Av Francis-Hughes Bureau 1, Sainte-Dorothee, QC H7L 5A6, *Tel* (450) 629-9444	700	835	0	5149
NAV CANADA				
77 Metcalfe St, Ottawa, ON K1P 5L6, *Tel* (613) 563-5588	700	836	1,030,245,111	4899
NEMO PRODUCTIONS - CAN, INC				
8035 Glenwood Dr, Burnaby, BC V3N 5C8, *Tel*	700	837	62,787,200	7829
NTT DATA CANADA, INC (*Suby of* **NIPPON TELEGRAPH AND TELEPHONE CORPORATION**)				
2000 Barrington St Suite 300, Halifax, NS B3J 3K1, *Tel* (902) 422-6036	700	838	216,620,000	7379
OLYMEL S.E.C. (*Suby of* **OLYMEL S.E.C.**)				
25 Rte 125 E, Saint-Esprit, QC J0K 2L0, *Tel* (450) 839-7258	700	839	0	2011
OLYMEL S.E.C. (*Suby of* **OLYMEL S.E.C.**)				
125 Rue Saint-Isidore, Saint-Esprit, QC J0K 2L0, *Tel* (450) 839-7258	700	840	0	2011
OSLER, HOSKIN & HARCOURT LLP				
100 King St W Suite 4600 First Canadian Place, Toronto, ON M5X 1B8, *Tel* (416) 362-2111	700	841	226,463,600	8111
PARK PLACE SENIORS LIVING INC (*Suby of* **PARK PLACE SENIORS LIVING**)				
13525 Hilton Rd, Surrey, BC V3R 5J3, *Tel* (604) 588-3424	700	842	47,828,200	8051
PBC HEALTH BENEFITS SOCIETY				
4250 Canada Way, Burnaby, BC V5G 4W6, *Tel* (604) 419-2200	700	843	289,753,407	6321
PEARSON CANADA INC (*Suby of* **PEARSON PLC**)				
195 Harry Walker Pky N Suite A, Newmarket, ON L3Y 7B3, *Tel* (905) 853-7888	700	844	0	2731
PEPSICO CANADA ULC (*Suby of* **PEPSICO, INC.**)				
14 Hunter St E, Peterborough, ON K9J 7B2, *Tel* (705) 743-6330	700	845	0	2043
PLACEMENTS JEAN BEAUDRY INC, LES				
12305 Boul Metropolitain E, Pointe-Aux-Trembles, QC H1B 5R3, *Tel* (514) 640-4440	700	846	255,856,300	6712
PRICE INDUSTRIES LIMITED				
638 Raleigh St, Winnipeg, MB R2K 3Z9, *Tel* (204) 669-4220	700	847	3,405,234,000	3496
PRICEWATERHOUSECOOPERS LLP (*Suby of* **PRICEWATERHOUSECOOPERS LLP**)				
2640 Boul Laurier Bureau 1700, Quebec, QC G1V 5C2, *Tel* (418) 522-7001	700	848	0	8721
PROCTER & GAMBLE INC (*Suby of* **THE PROCTER & GAMBLE COMPANY**)				
4711 Yonge St, North York, ON M2N 6K8, *Tel* (416) 730-4711	700	849	844,825,500	2841
PROVIGO DISTRIBUTION INC (*Suby of* **LOBLAW COMPANIES LIMITED**)				
180 Ch Du Tremblay, Boucherville, QC J4B 7W3, *Tel* (450) 449-8000	700	850	0	5148
QUANTUM MURRAY-NWDD PARTNERSHIP				
3600 Viking Way Suite 100, Richmond, BC V6V 1N6, *Tel* (604) 270-7388	700	851	228,005,400	4959
SCOTIA MORTGAGE AUTHORITY (*Suby of* **BANK OF NOVA SCOTIA, THE**)				
79 Wellington St W Suite 3400, Toronto, ON M5K 1K7, *Tel* (416) 350-7400	700	852	370,069,000	6162
SERVICES DE FORAGE ORBIT GARANT INC (*Suby of* **FORAGE ORBIT GARANT INC**)				
3200 Boul Jean-Jacques-Cossette, Val-D'Or, QC J9P 6Y6, *Tel* (819) 824-2707	700	853	92,992,125	1081
SERVICES FINANCIERS NCO, INC (*Suby of* **GATESTONE & CO. INC**)				
33 Sinclair Blvd Unit 4, Brantford, ON N3S 7X6, *Tel* (519) 750-6000	700	854	0	7322
SHERRITT INTERNATIONAL CORPORATION				
22 Adelaide St W Suite 4220, Toronto, ON M5H 4E3, *Tel* (416) 924-4551	700	855	115,913,796	1081
SHRED-IT INTERNATIONAL ULC (*Suby of* **STERICYCLE, INC.**)				
1383 North Service Rd E, Oakville, ON L6H 1A7, *Tel* (905) 829-2794	700	856	915,243,000	7389
SOCIETE D'HYPOTHEQUE DE LA BANQUE ROYALE (*Suby of* **ROYAL BANK OF CANADA**)				
1 Place Ville-Marie, Montreal, QC H3C 3A9, *Tel* (514) 874-7222	700	857	279,190,800	6162
SOCIETE DE TRANSPORT DE MONTREAL				
800 Rue De La Gauchetiere O Bureau 8420, Montreal, QC H5A 1J6, *Tel* (514) 786-4636	700	858	1,117,325,951	4111
SUNCOR ENERGY INC (*Suby of* **SUNCOR ENERGY INC**)				
2489 North Sheridan Way, Mississauga, ON L5K 1A8, *Tel* (905) 804-4500	700	859	0	1389
SUNHILLS MINING LIMITED PARTNERSHIP (*Suby of* **TRANSALTA CORPORATION**)				
4419 B Sundance Rd, Seba Beach, AB T0E 2B0, *Tel* (780) 731-5300	700	860	335,750,100	1221
TELE-MOBILE COMPANY (*Suby of* **TELE-MOBILE COMPANY**)				
8851 Rte Transcanadienne Bureau 1, Saint-Laurent, QC H4S 1Z6, *Tel* (514) 832-2000	700	861	0	4899
TIMMINS AND DISTRICT HOSPITAL				
700 Ross Ave E Suite 1559, Timmins, ON P4N 8P2, *Tel* (705) 267-2131	700	862	68,422,959	8062
TRQSS, INC (*Suby of* **TOKAI RIKA CO., LTD.**)				
255 Patillo Rd, Tecumseh, ON N8N 2L9, *Tel* (519) 973-7400	700	863	238,801,500	2399
UNIFOR (*Suby of* **UNIFOR**)				

COMPANY	EMPLOYEES HERE	RANKSALES ($)	PRIMARY SIC CODE
15 Westcreek Blvd Suite 1, Brampton, ON L6T 5T4, *Tel* (905) 874-4026	700	864	0	8631
UNIVERSITY OF PRINCE EDWARD ISLAND			
550 University Ave, Charlottetown, PE C1A 4P3, *Tel* (902) 628-4353	700	865	102,357,449	8221
VECIMA NETWORKS INC (*Suby of* **VECIMA NETWORKS INC**)			
150 Cardinal Pl, Saskatoon, SK S7L 6H7, *Tel* (306) 955-7075	700	866	0	8731
WARREN GIBSON LIMITED			
206 Church St S, Alliston, ON L9R 2B7, *Tel* (705) 435-4342	700	867	143,994,200	4213
WELLINGTON CATHOLIC DISTRICT SCHOOL BOARD			
200 Clair Rd W, Guelph, ON N1L 1G1, *Tel* (519) 822-8502	700	868	0	8211
WORLEYPARSONSCORD LP (*Suby of* **WORLEYPARSONS LIMITED**)			
9405 50 St Nw Suite 101, Edmonton, AB T6B 2T4, *Tel* (780) 440-8100	700	869	0	8711
SUPERIOR TRUSS CO LTD (*Suby of* **4834772 MANITOBA LTD**)			
165 Industrial Rd, Oak Bluff, MB R4G 0A5, *Tel* (204) 888-7663	690	870	0	2439
CENTRE DE SANTE ET DE SERVICES SOCIAUX DE DORVAL-LACHINE-LASALLE			
650 16e Av, Lasalle, QC H8P 2S3, *Tel* (514) 637-2351	685	871	0	8062
BADGER DAYLIGHTING LTD			
919 11th Ave Sw Suite 400, Calgary, AB T2R 1P3, *Tel* (403) 264-8500	682	872	466,567,811	1389
SPCRC HOLDINGS INC			
850 Mont?E De Liesse, Saint-Laurent, QC H4T 1P4, *Tel* (514) 341-3550	681	873	248,911,629	6712
BONNY'S TAXI LTD			
5759 Sidley St, Burnaby, BC V5J 5E6, *Tel* (604) 435-8233	680	874	38,225,520	4121
UNIVERSITY OF ONTARIO INSTITUTE OF TECHNOLOGY			
2000 Simcoe St N, Oshawa, ON L1G 0C5, *Tel* (905) 721-8668	680	875	139,424,564	8221
BROCK CANADA FIELD SERVICES LTD			
3735 8 St Unit 200, Nisku, AB T9E 8J8, *Tel* (780) 465-9016	670	876	142,291,920	1799
ST. JOSEPH'S HEALTH CARE, LONDON (*Suby of* **ST. JOSEPH'S HEALTH CARE, LONDON**)			
Gd, St Thomas, ON N5P 3T4, *Tel* (519) 631-8510	667	877	0	8093
FIRST NATIONAL FINANCIAL LP			
100 University Ave Suite 1200, Toronto, ON M5J 1V6, *Tel* (416) 593-1100	665	878	466,783,645	6162
MAPLE LEAF FOODS INC			
6985 Financial Dr, Mississauga, ON L5N 0A1, *Tel* (905) 285-5000	665	879	2,649,959,945	2011
KRUGER PRODUCTS L.P. (*Suby of* **KRUGER INC**)			
100 1e Av, Crabtree, QC J0K 1B0, *Tel* (450) 754-2855	662	880	0	2676
RAYTHEON CANADA LIMITED (*Suby of* **RAYTHEON COMPANY**)			
450 Leitz Rd Suite 2, Midland, ON L4R 5B8, *Tel* (705) 526-5401	662	881	0	3827
HOLT, RENFREW & CIE, LIMITEE			
737 Dunsmuir St, Vancouver, BC V6C 1N5, *Tel* (604) 681-3121	660	882	0	5621
ASCENDANT RESOURCES INC			
79 Wellington St W Suite 2100, Toronto, ON M5K 1H1, *Tel* (647) 796-0066	659	883	85,618,000	1081
4520556 CANADA INC			
180 Montee De Liesse, Saint-Laurent, QC H4T 1N7, *Tel* (514) 904-1216	650	884	20,779,200	7349
ABBOTT POINT OF CARE CANADA LIMITED			
185 Corkstown Rd, Nepean, ON K2H 8V4, *Tel* (613) 688-5949	650	885	178,340,500	3841
ABC BENEFITS CORPORATION			
10009 108 St Nw, Edmonton, AB T5J 3C5, *Tel* (780) 498-8000	650	886	1,495,877,600	6321
AGNICO EAGLE MINES LIMITED (*Suby of* **AGNICO EAGLE MINES LIMITED**)			
10200 Rte De Preissac, Rouyn-Noranda, QC J0Y 1C0, *Tel* (819) 759-3700	650	887	0	1041
AGROPUR COOPERATIVE (*Suby of* **AGROPUR COOPERATIVE**)			
510 Rue Principale, Granby, QC J2G 2X2, *Tel* (450) 375-1991	650	888	0	2022
ALUMA SYSTEMS INC (*Suby of* **BRAND INDUSTRIAL SERVICES, INC.**)			
Gd Lcd Main, Fort Mcmurray, AB T9H 3E2, *Tel* (780) 790-4852	650	889	0	1799
AON REED STENHOUSE INC (*Suby of* **AON PLC**)			
700 De La Gauchetiere O Bureau 1800, Montreal, QC H3B 0A4, *Tel* (514) 842-5000	650	890	0	6411
ATTRIDGE TRANSPORTATION INCORPORATED (*Suby of* **ATTRIDGE TRANSPORTATION INCORPORATED**)			
27 Mill St S, Waterdown, ON L0R 2H0, *Tel* (905) 690-2632	650	891	0	4141
BOMBARDIER TRANSPORTATION CANADA INC (*Suby of* **BOMBARDIER INC**)			
1001 Montreal St, Thunder Bay, ON P7C 4V6, *Tel* (807) 475-2810	650	892	0	3743
CANADIAN CORPS OF COMMISSIONAIRES NATIONAL OFFICE, THE (*Suby of* **CANADIAN CORPS OF COMMISSIONAIRES NATIONAL OFFICE, THE**)			
595 Howe St Suite 801, Vancouver, BC V6C 2T5, *Tel* (604) 646-3330	650	893	0	7381
CEGEP DE TROIS-RIVIERES			
3500 Rue De Courval, Trois-Rivieres, QC G8Z 1T2, *Tel* (819) 376-1721	650	894	74,339,250	8222
CENTRE DE PROTECTION ET DE READAPTATION DE LA COTE-NORD			
835 Boul Jolliet, Baie-Comeau, QC G5C 1P5, *Tel* (418) 589-9927	650	895	0	8361
CENTRE HOSPITALIER UNIVERSITAIRE DE SHERBROOKE (*Suby of* **CENTRE INTEGRE UNIVERSITAIRE DE SANTE ET DE SERVICES SOCIAUX DE L'ESTRIE**)			
3001 12e Av N, Sherbrooke, QC J1H 5N4, *Tel* (819) 346-1110	650	896	152,172,150	8621
CENTRES JEUNESSE DE LANAUDIERE, LES			
1170 Rue Ladouceur, Joliette, QC J6E 3W7, *Tel* (450) 759-0755	650	897	0	8641
CITE COLLEGIALE, LA			
801 Aviation Pky, Ottawa, ON K1K 4R3, *Tel* (613) 742-2483	650	898	20,146,500	8222
EECOL ELECTRIC ULC			
63 Sunpark Dr Se, Calgary, AB T2X 3V4, *Tel*	650	899	0	5063
GEORGIAN BAY GENERAL HOSPITAL			

COMPANY	EMPLOYEES HERE	RANK	SALES ($)	PRIMARY SIC CODE
1112 St Andrews Dr, Midland, ON L4R 4P4, *Tel* (705) 526-1300	650	900	72,202,000	8062
JAZZ AVIATION LP				
3 Spectacle Lake Dr Suite 100, Dartmouth, NS B3B 1W8, *Tel* (902) 873-5000	650	901	1,555,024,800	4512
MCCANN WORLDGROUP CANADA INC (*Suby of* **THE INTERPUBLIC GROUP OF COMPANIES INC**)				
200 Wellington St W Suite 1300, Toronto, ON M5V 0N6, *Tel* (416) 594-6000	650	902	239,182,300	7311
NCR CANADA CORP (*Suby of* **NCR CORPORATION**)				
580 Weber St E, Kitchener, ON N2H 1G8, *Tel*	650	903	0	3578
O.E.M. REMANUFACTURING COMPANY INC (*Suby of* **FINNING INTERNATIONAL INC**)				
13315 156 St Nw, Edmonton, AB T5V 1V2, *Tel* (780) 468-6220	650	904	58,302,400	7538
PHARMASCIENCE INC (*Suby of* **JODDES LIMITEE**)				
6111 Av Royalmount Bureau 100, Montreal, QC H4P 2T4, *Tel* (514) 340-1114	650	905	497,391,000	2834
RECIPE UNLIMITED CORPORATION (*Suby of* **RECIPE UNLIMITED CORPORATION**)				
1185 Rue Rodolphe-Page Bureau 1, Dorval, QC H4Y 1H3, *Tel* (514) 636-5824	650	906	0	5812
RIO TINTO ALCAN INC (*Suby of* **RIO TINTO PLC**)				
1954 Rue Davis, Jonquiere, QC G7S 3B6, *Tel*	650	907	0	4911
ROCKWELL AUTOMATION CANADA CONTROL SYSTEMS (*Suby of* **ROCKWELL AUTOMATION, INC.**)				
135 Dundas St, Cambridge, ON N1R 5N9, *Tel* (519) 623-1810	650	908	339,498,000	3625
SAFWAY SERVICES CANADA, ULC (*Suby of* **BRAND INDUSTRIAL SERVICES, INC.**)				
1005 Memorial Dr Unit 3, Fort Mcmurray, AB T9K 0K4, *Tel* (780) 791-6473	650	909	0	1799
SIR SANDFORD FLEMING COLLEGE OF APPLIED ARTS AND TECHNOLOGY				
599 Brealey Dr, Peterborough, ON K9J 7B1, *Tel* (705) 749-5530	650	910	99,119,000	8222
SSQ SOCIETE D'ASSURANCE-VIE INC (*Suby of* **FONDS DE SOLIDARITE DES TRAVAILLEURS DU QUEBEC (F.T.Q.)**)				
2525 Boul Laurier, Quebec, QC G1V 4Z6, *Tel* (418) 651-7000	650	911	2,805,838,984	6311
STRATFORD SHAKESPEAREAN FESTIVAL OF CANADA, THE				
55 Queen St, Stratford, ON N5A 4M9, *Tel* (519) 271-4040	650	912	97,378,450	7922
SYNDICAT CANADIEN DES COMMUNICATIONS DE L'ENERGIE ET DU PAPIER				
8290 Boul Metropolitain E, Anjou, QC H1K 1A2, *Tel* (514) 259-7237	650	913	0	8631
UNIVERSITE DU QUEBEC (*Suby of* **UNIVERSITE DU QUEBEC**)				
300 Allee Des Ursulines, Rimouski, QC G5L 3A1, *Tel* (418) 723-1986	650	914	0	8221
WEYERHAEUSER COMPANY LIMITED (*Suby of* **WEYERHAEUSER COMPANY**)				
Gd Stn Main, Grande Prairie, AB T8V 3A9, *Tel* (780) 539-8500	650	915	0	5031
POSTMEDIA NETWORK INC (*Suby of* **POSTMEDIA NETWORK CANADA CORP**)				
10006 101 St Nw, Edmonton, AB T5J 0S1, *Tel* (780) 429-5100	648	916	0	2711
CANCERCARE MANITOBA FOUNDATION INC (*Suby of* **PROVINCE OF MANITOBA**)				
675 Mcdermot Ave Suite 1160, Winnipeg, MB R3E 0V9, *Tel* (204) 787-4143	647	917	133,315,996	8069
OKANAGAN COLLEGE				
1000 K.L.O. Rd, Kelowna, BC V1Y 4X8, *Tel* (250) 762-5445	647	918	88,658,810	8221
TRAFFIC TECH INC (*Suby of* **2809664 CANADA INC**)				
16711 Rte Transcanadienne, Kirkland, QC H9H 3L1, *Tel* (514) 343-0044	645	919	365,780,150	4731
EXFO INC				
400 Av Godin, Quebec, QC G1M 2K2, *Tel* (418) 683-0211	640	920	269,546,000	3827
SNC-LAVALIN INC (*Suby of* **GROUPE SNC-LAVALIN INC**)				
195 The West Mall, Etobicoke, ON M9C 5K1, *Tel* (416) 252-5315	640	921	0	8711
SYKES ASSISTANCE SERVICES CORPORATION (*Suby of* **SYKES ENTERPRISES INCORPORATED**)				
248 Pall Mall St, London, ON N6A 5P6, *Tel* (519) 434-3221	640	922	125,574,400	7549
KRAFT HEINZ CANADA ULC (*Suby of* **THE KRAFT HEINZ COMPANY**)				
3055 Rue Viau Bureau 4, Montreal, QC H1V 3J5, *Tel* (514) 259-6921	636	923	0	2051
UNIVERSITE DE MONCTON				
18 Av Antonine-Maillet, Moncton, NB E1A 3E9, *Tel* (506) 858-4000	636	924	113,797,491	8221
DU MAURIER LTEE				
3711 Rue Saint-Antoine O, Montreal, QC H4C 3P6, *Tel* (514) 932-6161	635	925	116,460,905	2111
F&P MFG INC (*Suby of* **F-TECH INC.**)				
1 Nolan Rd, Tottenham, ON L0G 1W0, *Tel* (905) 936-3435	630	926	557,897,648	3714
BRISTOL AEROSPACE LIMITED (*Suby of* **MAGELLAN AEROSPACE CORPORATION**)				
660 Berry St, Winnipeg, MB R3H 0S5, *Tel* (204) 775-8331	625	927	181,781,250	3728
CAMPBELL COMPANY OF CANADA (*Suby of* **CAMPBELL SOUP COMPANY**)				
1400 Mitchell Rd S, Listowel, ON N4W 3G7, *Tel*	625	928	0	5142
DENSO MANUFACTURING CANADA, INC (*Suby of* **DENSO CORPORATION**)				
900 Southgate Dr, Guelph, ON N1L 1K1, *Tel* (519) 837-6600	625	929	288,221,250	5013
DESJARDINS ASSURANCES GENERALES INC (*Suby of* **FEDERATION DES CAISSES DESJARDINS DU QUEBEC**)				
6300 Boul De La Rive-Sud, Levis, QC G6V 6P9, *Tel* (418) 835-4850	625	930	2,136,968,000	6331
SUNCOR ENERGY INC				
6 Ave Sw Suite 150, Calgary, AB T2P 3Y7, *Tel* (403) 296-8000	621	931	29,555,364,572	2911
BLACK BOND BOOKS LTD (*Suby of* **BLACK BOND BOOKS LTD**)				
32555 London Ave Suite 344, Mission, BC V2V 6M7, *Tel* (604) 814-2650	619	932	0	5942
SUPRALIMENT S.E.C. (*Suby of* **SUPRALIMENT S.E.C.**)				
183 Rte Du President-Kennedy, Saint-Henri-De-Levis, QC G0R 3E0, *Tel* (418) 882-2282	617	933	0	2011
4233964 CANADA INC				
2575 Boul Pitfield, Saint-Laurent, QC H4S 1T2, *Tel* (514) 383-4442	614	934	76,599,570	5621
UNIVERSITY OF THE FRASER VALLEY				
33844 King Rd, Abbotsford, BC V2S 7M8, *Tel* (604) 504-7441	614	935	97,831,407	8221
CRESCENT POINT ENERGY CORP				
585 8 Ave Sw Suite 2000, Calgary, AB T2P 1G1, *Tel* (403) 693-0020	604	936	2,517,277,691	1311

COMPANY	EMPLOYEES HERE	RANK	SALES ($)	PRIMARY SIC CODE
BOAT ROCKER RIGHTS INC 595 Adelaide St E, Toronto, ON M5A 1N8, *Tel* (416) 591-0065	602	937	86,797,564	7371
TETRA TECH QE INC (*Suby of* **TETRA TECH, INC.**) 5100 Rue Sherbrooke E Bureau 900, Montreal, QC H1V 3R9, *Tel* (514) 257-0707	602	938	61,241,117	8711
WINPAK LTD 100 Saulteaux Cres, Winnipeg, MB R3J 3T3, *Tel* (204) 889-1015	601	939	889,641,000	3081
137077 CANADA INC 203 Rochester St, Ottawa, ON K1R 7M5, *Tel* (613) 232-1579	600	940	44,816,400	7361
407 INTERNATIONAL INC (*Suby of* **FERROVIAL SA**) 6300 Steeles Ave W, Woodbridge, ON L4H 1J1, *Tel* (905) 265-4070	600	941	0	4785
AINSWORTH ENGINEERED CANADA LIMITED PARTNERSHIP (*Suby of* **NORBORD INC**) 1055 Dunsmuir St Suite 3194, Vancouver, BC V7X 1L3, *Tel* (604) 661-3200	600	942	145,938,600	3491
AIR CANADA (*Suby of* **AIR CANADA**) 355 Portage Ave Suite 3850, Winnipeg, MB R3B 0J6, *Tel* (204) 941-2684	600	943	0	4512
AIR INUIT LTEE (*Suby of* **SOCIETE MAKIVIK**) 6005 Boul De La Cote-Vertu, Saint-Laurent, QC H4S 0B1, *Tel* (514) 905-9445	600	944	193,584,720	4512
AKITA DRILLING LTD (*Suby of* **AKITA DRILLING LTD**) 2302 8 St, Nisku, AB T9E 7Z2, *Tel* (780) 955-6700	600	945	0	1381
ASPECT RETAIL LOGISTICS INC 1400 Church St, Pickering, ON L1W 4C1, *Tel* (905) 428-9947	600	946	123,423,600	4225
BAKERY DELUXE COMPANY 50 Marmora St, North York, ON M9M 2X5, *Tel* (416) 746-1010	600	947	292,431,000	2051
BELL MOBILITE INC (*Suby of* **BCE INC**) 1 Carrefour Alexander-Graham-Bell Bureau A-7, Verdun, QC H3E 3B3, *Tel* (514) 870-6550	600	948	548,332,800	4899
BLEUETS SAUVAGES DU QUEBEC INC, LES (*Suby of* **USINE DE CONGELATION DE ST-BRUNO INC**) 698 Rue Melancon Bureau 160, Saint-Bruno-Lac-Saint-Jean, QC G0W 2L0, *Tel* (418) 343-2410	600	949	430,029,600	5142
BLUEWATER HEALTH 89 Norman St, Sarnia, ON N7T 6S3, *Tel* (519) 464-4400	600	950	137,468,576	8062
BORDEN LADNER GERVAIS LLP 22 Adelaide St W Suite 3400, Toronto, ON M5H 4E3, *Tel* (416) 367-6000	600	951	370,576,800	8111
BOULANGERIE VACHON INC (*Suby of* **GRUPO BIMBO, S.A.B. DE C.V.**) 380 Rue Notre-Dame N, Sainte-Marie, QC G6E 2K7, *Tel* (418) 387-5421	600	952	0	5149
BRITISH COLUMBIA FERRY SERVICES INC (*Suby of* **B.C. FERRY AUTHORITY, THE**) 1321 Blanshard St Suite 500, Victoria, BC V8W 0B7, *Tel* (250) 381-1401	600	953	715,631,813	4482
CAN-AM PEPPER COMPANY LTD (*Suby of* **2131876 ONTARIO LIMITED**) 52999 John Wise Line, Aylmer, ON N5H 2R5, *Tel* (519) 773-3250	600	954	112,721,400	0161
CANADIAN TEST CASE 44 5770 Hurontario St, Mississauga, ON L5R 3G5, *Tel*	600	955	0	7389
CANPAR TRANSPORT L.P. (*Suby of* **CANPAR TRANSPORT L.P.**) 205 New Toronto St, Etobicoke, ON M8V 0A1, *Tel* (416) 869-1332	600	956	0	4213
CARILLION CONSTRUCTION INC 7077 Keele St, Concord, ON L4K 0B6, *Tel* (905) 532-5200	600	957	67,321,800	8741
CELESTICA INTERNATIONAL LP (*Suby of* **ONEX CORPORATION**) 3333 Unity Dr Suite A, Mississauga, ON L5L 3S6, *Tel* (416) 448-2559	600	958	0	3812
CENTRE DE SANTE ET DE SERVICES SOCIAUX DE LA VALLEE-DE-LA-BATISCAN 90 Rang Riviere Veillette, Sainte-Genevieve-De-Batiscan, QC G0X 2R0, *Tel* (418) 362-2727	600	959	0	8399
CENTRE DE SANTE ET DE SERVICES SOCIAUX DE LAVAL (*Suby of* **GOUVERNEMENT DE LA PROVINCE DE QUEBEC**) 800 Boul Chomedey Bureau 200, Montreal-Ouest, QC H7V 3Y4, *Tel* (450) 682-2952	600	960	0	8399
CHRISTIE DIGITAL SYSTEMS CANADA INC (*Suby of* **USHIO INC.**) 809 Wellington St N, Kitchener, ON N2G 4Y7, *Tel* (519) 744-8005	600	961	197,546,400	3861
CITIBANK CANADA (*Suby of* **CITIGROUP INC.**) 123 Front St W Suite 1900, Toronto, ON M5J 2M3, *Tel* (416) 947-5500	600	962	427,072,500	6021
COMMUNITY LIVING ESSEX COUNTY (*Suby of* **COMMUNITY LIVING ESSEX COUNTY**) 13158 Tecumseh Rd E, Windsor, ON N8N 3T6, *Tel* (519) 979-0057	600	963	0	8322
COMPAGNIE DES CHEMINS DE FER NATIONAUX DU CANADA (*Suby of* **COMPAGNIE DES CHEMINS DE FER NATIONAUX DU CANADA**) Gd, Concord, ON L4K 1B9, *Tel* (905) 669-3302	600	964	0	4011
CONFEDERATION DES SYNDICATS NATIONAUX (C.S.N.) 1601 Av De Lorimier, Montreal, QC H2K 4M5, *Tel* (514) 529-4993	600	965	0	8631
CONSULTANTS AECOM INC (*Suby of* **AECOM**) 85 Rue Sainte-Catherine O, Montreal, QC H2X 3P4, *Tel* (514) 287-8500	600	966	197,131,000	8711
DP WORLD (CANADA) INC (*Suby of* **DP WORLD PLC**) 777 Centennial Rd, Vancouver, BC V6A 1A3, *Tel* (604) 255-5151	600	967	208,416,600	4491
ELEMENT MATERIALS TECHNOLOGY CANADA INC (*Suby of* **ELEMENTS, INC.**) 2395 Speakman Dr Suite 583, Mississauga, ON L5K 1B3, *Tel* (905) 822-4111	600	968	607,462,300	8734
FAIRMONT HOTELS & RESORTS INC (*Suby of* **ACCOR**) 4599 Chateau Blvd, Whistler, BC V8E 0Z5, *Tel* (604) 938-8000	600	969	0	7011
FAIRMONT HOTELS & RESORTS INC (*Suby of* **ACCOR**) 181 Rue Richelieu Bureau 200, La Malbaie, QC G5A 1X7, *Tel* (418) 665-3703	600	970	0	7011
FIDELITY INVESTMENTS CANADA ULC (*Suby of* **FMR LLC**) 483 Bay St Suite 200, Toronto, ON M5G 2N7, *Tel* (416) 307-5200	600	971	4,541,127,650	6722
FRONTENAC HOTEL GP INC (*Suby of* **FRONTENAC HOTEL GP INC**) 1 Rue Des Carrieres, Quebec, QC G1R 5J5, *Tel* (418) 692-3861	600	972	0	7011

COMPANY	EMPLOYEES HERE	RANK	SALES ($)	PRIMARY SIC CODE
FUJITSU CONSEIL (CANADA) INC (*Suby of* **FUJITSU CONSULTING (CANADA) HOLDINGS, INC.**)				
2960 Boul Laurier Bureau 400, Quebec, QC G1V 4S1, *Tel*	600	973	0	7379
GATEWAY CASINOS & ENTERTAINMENT INC (*Suby of* **GATEWAY CASINOS & ENTERTAINMENT INC**)				
350 Gifford St Suite 1, New Westminster, BC V3M 7A3, *Tel* (604) 777-2946	600	974	0	7011
GDI SERVICES (CANADA) LP (*Suby of* **GDI SERVICES AUX IMMEUBLES INC**)				
931 Leathorne St Unit E, London, ON N5Z 3M7, *Tel* (519) 681-3330	600	975	0	7349
GIBRALTAR MINES LTD (*Suby of* **TASEKO MINES LIMITED**)				
1040 Georgia St W, Vancouver, BC V6E 4H1, *Tel* (778) 373-4533	600	976	166,253,100	1081
GOODLAW SERVICES INC				
250 Yonge St Suite 2400, Toronto, ON M5B 2L7, *Tel* (416) 979-2211	600	977	66,529,200	8111
GOODMANS LLP				
333 Bay St Suite 3400, Toronto, ON M5H 2S7, *Tel* (416) 979-2211	600	978	129,701,880	8111
GOUVERNEMENT DE LA PROVINCE DE QUEBEC (*Suby of* **GOUVERNEMENT DE LA PROVINCE DE QUEBEC**)				
475 Boul De Maisonneuve E, Montreal, QC H2L 5C4, *Tel* (514) 873-1100	600	979	0	8231
GOVERNMENT OF THE PROVINCE OF ALBERTA (*Suby of* **GOVERNMENT OF THE PROVINCE OF ALBERTA**)				
9820 106 St Nw Suite 534, Edmonton, AB T5K 2J6, *Tel* (780) 427-3076	600	980	0	6289
GRAND ERIE DISTRICT SCHOOL BOARD				
349 Erie Ave, Brantford, ON N3S 2H7, *Tel* (519) 756-6301	600	981	266,828,348	8211
GROUPE ADONIS INC (*Suby of* **METRO INC**)				
2001 Rue Sauve O, Montreal, QC H4N 3L6, *Tel* (514) 382-8606	600	982	0	5411
HAMILTON STREET RAILWAY COMPANY, THE (*Suby of* **CITY OF HAMILTON, THE**)				
2200 Upper James St, Mount Hope, ON L0R 1W0, *Tel* (905) 528-4200	600	983	33,728,400	4111
HANFENG EVERGREEN INC				
2 St Clair Ave W Suite 610, Toronto, ON M4V 1L5, *Tel*	600	984	353,495,400	5191
HANON SYSTEMS EFP CANADA LTD (*Suby of* **HAHN & CO. AUTO HOLDINGS CO., LTD.**)				
800 Tesma Way, Concord, ON L4K 5C2, *Tel* (905) 303-1689	600	985	174,510,000	3714
HATCH CORPORATION (*Suby of* **HATCH CORPORATION**)				
5 Place Ville-Marie Bureau 1400, Montreal, QC H3B 2G2, *Tel* (514) 861-0583	600	986	0	8711
HATCH LTD (*Suby of* **HATCHCOS HOLDINGS LTD**)				
5 Place Ville-Marie Bureau 1400, Montreal, QC H3B 2G2, *Tel* (514) 861-0583	600	987	0	8711
HEADWATERS HEALTH CARE CENTRE				
100 Rolling Hills Dr, Orangeville, ON L9W 4X9, *Tel* (519) 941-2410	600	988	50,635,572	8062
HEMA-QUEBEC				
4045 Boul De La Cote-Vertu, Saint-Laurent, QC H4R 2W7, *Tel* (514) 832-5000	600	989	266,156,928	8099
HONDA CANADA INC (*Suby of* **HONDA MOTOR CO., LTD.**)				
180 Honda Blvd Suite 200, Markham, ON L6C 0H9, *Tel* (905) 888-8110	600	990	1,454,250,000	3711
HORSESHOE RESORT CORPORATION				
1101 Horseshoe Valley Rd W, Barrie, ON L4M 4Y8, *Tel* (705) 835-2790	600	991	57,400,800	7011
HUDSON'S BAY COMPANY				
8925 Torbram Rd, Brampton, ON L6T 4G1, *Tel* (905) 792-4400	600	992	7,054,530,528	5311
HUDSON'S BAY COMPANY (*Suby of* **HUDSON'S BAY COMPANY**)				
2 Bloor St E Suite 52, Toronto, ON M4W 3H7, *Tel* (416) 972-3313	600	993	0	5311
HYDRO-QUEBEC (*Suby of* **GOUVERNEMENT DE LA PROVINCE DE QUEBEC**)				
5050 Boul Des Gradins Bureau 200, Quebec, QC G2J 1P8, *Tel* (418) 624-2811	600	994	0	8631
HYLIFE FOODS LP (*Suby of* **HYLIFE LTD**)				
623 Main St E, Neepawa, MB R0J 1H0, *Tel* (204) 476-3393	600	995	292,431,000	2011
ICT CANADA MARKETING INC (*Suby of* **SYKES ENTERPRISES INCORPORATED**)				
720 Coverdale Rd Unit 9, Riverview, NB E1B 3L8, *Tel*	600	996	0	7389
IMPERIAL TOBACCO COMPAGNIE LIMITEE (*Suby of* **IMPERIAL TOBACCO CANADA LIMITEE**)				
107 Woodlawn Rd W, Guelph, ON N1H 1B4, *Tel*	600	997	0	2111
IMPRIMERIES TRANSCONTINENTAL 2005 S.E.N.C. (*Suby of* **IMPRIMERIES TRANSCONTINENTAL 2005 S.E.N.C.**)				
2049 20th St E, Owen Sound, ON N4K 5R2, *Tel* (519) 376-8330	600	998	0	2732
IMPRIMERIES TRANSCONTINENTAL INC (*Suby of* **TRANSCONTINENTAL INC**)				
275 Wellington St E, Aurora, ON L4G 6J9, *Tel* (905) 841-4400	600	999	0	2752
IMPRIMERIES TRANSCONTINENTAL INC (*Suby of* **TRANSCONTINENTAL INC**)				
1590 20th St E, Owen Sound, ON N4K 5R2, *Tel* (519) 371-5171	600	1000	0	2752

SIC	DESCRIPTION	0-19	20-49	50-99	100-OVER	TOTAL	PRIMARY SIC ONLY
0111	Wheat	0	0	1	0	1	1
0119	Cash grains, nec	0	2	5	0	7	2
0134	Irish potatoes	1	1	1	0	3	1
0139	Field crops, except cash grain	1	0	2	0	3	0
0161	Vegetables and melons	4	4	1	3	12	4
0171	Berry crops	1	2	1	1	5	1
0172	Grapes	0	0	1	0	1	1
0181	Ornamental nursery products	3	6	10	3	22	7
0182	Food crops grown under cover	5	11	16	17	49	44
0191	General farms, primarily crop	8	32	21	15	76	73
0211	Beef cattle feedlots	0	1	0	1	2	0
0212	Beef cattle, except feedlots	0	0	3	0	3	0
0213	Hogs	1	2	5	0	8	1
0241	Dairy farms	1	6	0	0	7	4
0251	Broiler, fryer, and roaster chickens	0	0	2	0	2	0
0252	Chicken eggs	0	0	0	1	1	0
0254	Poultry hatcheries	0	0	1	1	2	1
0259	Poultry and eggs, nec	2	5	1	2	10	3
0271	Fur-bearing animals and rabbits	0	1	0	0	1	1
0273	Animal aquaculture	0	3	2	0	5	5
0279	Animal specialties, nec	1	1	0	2	4	2
0291	General farms, primarily animals	3	11	11	4	29	9
0711	Soil preparation services	2	1	1	2	6	1
0721	Crop planting and protection	1	2	0	0	3	0
0722	Crop harvesting	1	0	0	0	1	0
0723	Crop preparation services for market	9	2	6	4	21	5
0742	Veterinary services, specialties	0	1	0	0	1	1
0751	Livestock services, except veterinary	1	0	0	0	1	0
0762	Farm management services	1	1	0	0	2	0
0781	Landscape counseling and planning	2	2	1	8	13	0
0782	Lawn and garden services	0	2	1	2	5	1
0783	Ornamental shrub and tree services	0	0	1	0	1	0
0811	Timber tracts	1	0	0	0	1	0
0831	Forest products	3	0	1	1	5	1
0851	Forestry services	5	4	15	13	37	33
0912	Finfish	0	0	0	1	1	0
0913	Shellfish	0	0	0	1	1	0
0921	Fish hatcheries and preserves	0	0	1	0	1	0
1011	Iron ores	0	1	0	0	1	1
1021	Copper ores	4	2	3	5	14	3
1031	Lead and zinc ores	2	0	3	0	5	2
1041	Gold ores	32	8	7	17	64	57
1044	Silver ores	3	1	3	1	8	2
1061	Ferroalloy ores, except vanadium	4	1	0	2	7	4
1081	Metal mining services	38	7	14	27	86	67
1094	Uranium-radium-vanadium ores	0	1	0	1	2	1
1221	Bituminous coal and lignite-surface mining	0	0	1	12	13	10
1241	Coal mining services	0	0	0	1	1	1
1311	Crude petroleum and natural gas	10	3	5	12	30	20
1321	Natural gas liquids	0	1	1	2	4	0
1381	Drilling oil and gas wells	14	5	16	9	44	35
1382	Oil and gas exploration services	35	17	15	28	95	73
1389	Oil and gas field services, nec	48	36	64	63	211	176
1422	Crushed and broken limestone	1	1	1	4	7	6
1423	Crushed and broken granite	0	1	0	0	1	1
1429	Crushed and broken stone, nec	0	0	1	0	1	0
1442	Construction sand and gravel	2	0	4	2	8	2
1446	Industrial sand	0	0	1	0	1	0
1479	Chemical and fertilizer mining	0	0	0	1	1	0
1481	NonMetallic mineral services	8	3	5	9	25	16
1499	Miscellaneous nonMetallic minerals, except fuels	7	4	7	8	26	22
1521	Single-family housing construction	47	112	63	43	265	170
1522	Residential construction, nec	25	37	21	17	100	15
1531	Operative builders	4	4	5	2	15	6
1541	Industrial buildings and warehouses	44	98	62	55	259	68
1542	Nonresidential construction, nec	88	278	120	64	550	437
1611	Highway and street construction	25	16	47	29	117	33
1622	Bridge, tunnel, and elevated highway construction	17	8	17	23	65	32
1623	Water, sewer, and utility lines	34	28	88	72	222	168
1629	Heavy construction, nec	31	22	61	61	175	108
1711	Plumbing, heating, air-conditioning	24	10	36	28	98	30
1721	Painting and paper hanging	5	2	5	1	13	11
1731	Electrical work	25	17	29	36	107	33
1741	Masonry and other stonework	1	1	3	4	9	2
1742	Plastering, drywall, and insulation	7	3	2	2	14	4
1743	Terrazzo, tile, marble and mossaic work	0	0	2	0	2	0
1751	Carpentry work	8	4	8	9	29	2
1752	Floor laying and floor work, nec	7	7	3	5	22	11
1761	Roofing, siding, and sheetMetal work	8	5	18	16	47	36

SIC	DESCRIPTION	0-19	20-49	50-99	100-OVER	TOTAL	PRIMARY SIC ONLY
1771	Concrete work	6	7	11	4	28	7
1781	Water well drilling	2	0	1	1	4	2
1791	Structural steel erection	14	6	14	12	46	9
1793	Glass and glazing work	1	2	1	1	5	0
1794	Excavation work	11	6	20	19	56	17
1795	Wrecking and demolition work	5	2	2	5	14	8
1796	Installing building equipment	4	10	15	14	43	29
1799	Special trade contractors, nec	27	25	26	24	102	19
2011	Meat packing plants	10	5	21	50	86	74
2013	Sausages and other prepared meats	4	4	9	6	23	6
2015	Poultry slaughtering and processing	2	1	1	13	17	9
2021	Creamery butter	0	2	0	5	7	0
2022	Cheese; natural and processed	5	1	7	21	34	26
2023	Dry, condensed and evaporated dairy products	3	2	1	9	15	3
2024	Ice cream and frozen deserts	1	2	4	3	10	3
2026	Fluid milk	1	2	1	6	10	4
2032	Canned specialties	6	4	7	8	25	21
2033	Canned fruits and specialties	6	5	2	8	21	9
2034	Dried and dehydrated fruits, vegetables and soup mixes	1	0	5	0	6	2
2035	Pickles, sauces, and salad dressings	1	1	3	6	11	1
2037	Frozen fruits and vegetables	1	0	0	1	2	0
2038	Frozen specialties, nec	4	4	6	7	21	17
2041	Flour and other grain mill products	0	3	1	2	6	4
2043	Cereal breakfast foods	1	1	4	7	13	10
2044	Rice milling	1	0	0	0	1	0
2045	Prepared flour mixes and doughs	0	1	0	4	5	0
2047	Dog and cat food	0	0	0	3	3	0
2048	Prepared feeds, nec	5	3	3	3	14	4
2051	Bread, cake, and related products	3	7	6	6	22	9
2052	Cookies and crackers	1	0	3	0	4	1
2053	Frozen bakery products, except bread	3	2	3	7	15	11
2061	Raw cane sugar	0	0	0	1	1	1
2064	Candy and other confectionery products	5	5	3	14	27	21
2066	Chocolate and cocoa products	1	0	1	1	3	2
2067	Chewing gum	0	0	0	1	1	1
2068	Salted and roasted nuts and seeds	0	0	1	0	1	0
2076	Vegetable oil mills, nec	1	0	0	1	2	0
2077	Animal and marine fats and oils	0	0	0	2	2	3
2079	Edible fats and oils	0	1	1	7	9	4
2082	Malt beverages	8	3	6	13	30	28
2084	Wines, brandy, and brandy spirits	0	1	0	2	3	2
2086	Bottled and canned soft drinks	2	1	0	1	4	4
2087	Flavoring extracts and syrups, nec	2	3	3	4	12	4
2091	Canned and cured fish and seafoods	6	2	8	14	30	28
2092	Fresh or frozen packaged fish	5	2	4	9	20	13
2095	Roasted coffee	1	1	0	4	6	0
2096	Potato chips and similar snacks	1	0	1	7	9	7
2097	Manufactured ice	0	1	1	0	2	1
2098	Macaroni and spaghetti	3	0	2	4	9	0
2099	Food preparations, nec	12	11	23	35	81	58
2111	Cigarettes	0	0	0	3	3	3
2131	Chewing and smoking tobacco	0	0	1	0	1	1
2211	Broadwoven fabric mills, cotton	4	2	0	4	10	6
2221	Broadwoven fabric mills, manmade	1	1	2	3	7	3
2231	Broadwoven fabric mills, wool	0	0	0	1	1	1
2241	Narrow fabric mills	0	2	1	3	6	4
2252	Hosiery, nec	0	0	1	0	1	0
2253	Knit outerwear mills	0	0	1	1	2	1
2257	Weft knit fabric mills	1	0	2	0	3	2
2258	Lace and warp knit fabric mills	0	0	1	1	2	0
2259	Knitting mills, nec	0	0	0	1	1	1
2273	Carpets and rugs	0	0	0	1	1	0
2295	Coated fabrics, not rubberized	1	0	1	3	5	1
2297	Nonwoven fabrics	1	0	0	0	1	0
2299	Textile goods, nec	4	1	4	2	11	7
2311	Men's and boy's suits and coats	3	2	2	4	11	9
2321	Men's and boy's furnishings	0	0	1	1	2	1
2322	Men's and boy's underwear and nightwear	2	0	0	1	3	0
2325	Men's and boys' trousers and slacks	4	0	0	2	6	2
2326	Men's and boy's work clothing	2	0	1	0	3	1
2329	Men's and boy's clothing, nec	3	3	4	6	16	3
2331	Women's and misses' blouses and shirts	2	1	1	0	4	2
2335	Women's, junior's, and misses' dresses	2	1	0	0	3	0
2337	Women's and misses' suits and coats	3	4	1	1	9	1
2339	Women's and misses' outerwear, nec	4	6	2	7	19	4
2341	Women's and children's underwear	1	1	1	0	3	0
2342	Bras, girdles, and allied garments	0	2	0	0	2	1
2369	Girl's and children's outerwear, nec	2	0	0	0	2	0
2381	Fabric dress and work gloves	0	0	0	1	1	1

SIC	DESCRIPTION	0-19	20-49	50-99	100-OVER	TOTAL	PRIMARY SIC ONLY
2385	Waterproof outerwear	1	0	0	0	1	0
2386	Leather and sheep-lined clothing	2	0	0	1	3	0
2387	Apparel belts	1	0	0	0	1	0
2389	Apparel and accessories, nec	1	0	0	0	1	0
2391	Curtains and draperies	0	1	0	0	1	0
2392	Household furnishings, nec	3	6	1	1	11	2
2393	Textile bags	1	0	1	1	3	0
2394	Canvas and related products	1	2	0	1	4	0
2395	Pleating and stitching	0	2	0	0	2	0
2399	Fabricated textile products, nec	2	0	4	5	11	8
2411	Logging	4	2	3	6	15	5
2421	Sawmills and planing mills, general	21	6	13	24	64	26
2426	Hardwood dimension and flooring mills	2	1	2	6	11	5
2429	Special product sawmills, nec	0	1	0	0	1	0
2431	Millwork	24	8	15	36	83	43
2434	Wood kitchen cabinets	1	4	3	6	14	4
2435	Hardwood veneer and plywood	5	0	2	5	12	7
2436	Softwood veneer and plywood	0	0	0	2	2	1
2439	Structural wood members, nec	10	7	4	15	36	21
2441	Nailed wood boxes and shook	0	1	0	0	1	0
2448	Wood pallets and skids	1	2	0	2	5	1
2449	Wood containers, nec	2	1	0	0	3	0
2451	Mobile homes	1	0	0	1	2	1
2452	Prefabricated wood buildings	7	1	6	15	29	20
2491	Wood preserving	1	0	3	5	9	5
2493	Reconstituted wood products	2	1	0	1	4	0
2499	Wood products, nec	4	3	2	7	16	4
2511	Wood household furniture	4	2	3	8	17	10
2512	Upholstered household furniture	0	2	0	3	5	5
2514	Metal household furniture	2	0	1	0	3	0
2515	Mattresses and bedsprings	0	0	2	1	3	2
2519	Household furniture, nec	0	1	0	2	3	0
2521	Wood office furniture	1	0	0	5	6	2
2522	Office furniture, except wood	1	0	1	3	5	4
2531	Public building and related furniture	4	0	1	2	7	3
2541	Wood partitions and fixtures	8	1	11	14	34	23
2542	Partitions and fixtures, except wood	6	0	3	3	12	3
2591	Drapery hardware and window blinds and shades	1	1	1	1	4	0
2599	Furniture and fixtures, nec	2	0	4	6	12	9
2611	Pulp mills	10	2	4	16	32	23
2621	Paper mills	21	2	3	29	55	38
2631	Paperboard mills	6	2	4	17	29	14
2652	Setup paperboard boxes	0	0	0	1	1	1
2653	Corrugated and solid fiber boxes	0	2	2	17	21	12
2655	Fiber cans, drums, and similar products	2	0	4	0	6	3
2657	Folding paperboard boxes	1	0	2	5	8	4
2671	Paper; coated and laminated packaging	4	0	2	10	16	12
2672	Paper; coated and laminated, nec	1	1	8	6	16	14
2673	Bags: plastic, laminated, and coated	6	8	17	14	45	33
2674	Bags: uncoated paper and multiwall	3	2	1	8	14	10
2675	Die-cut paper and board	1	0	0	1	2	2
2676	Sanitary paper products	0	0	1	5	6	5
2677	Envelopes	0	0	0	1	1	1
2679	Converted paper products, nec	3	1	2	21	27	11
2711	Newspapers	9	4	14	36	63	58
2721	Periodicals	1	1	1	2	5	0
2731	Book publishing	2	4	1	8	15	8
2732	Book printing	0	1	1	1	3	1
2741	Miscellaneous publishing	3	1	5	4	13	7
2752	Commercial printing, lithographic	11	1	16	36	64	59
2754	Commercial printing, gravure	0	0	0	1	1	1
2759	Commercial printing, nec	4	2	10	12	28	8
2761	Manifold business forms	0	0	1	1	2	1
2782	Blankbooks and looseleaf binders	0	0	1	1	2	1
2789	Bookbinding and related work	0	1	1	1	3	0
2791	Typesetting	0	0	1	0	1	0
2796	Platemaking services	0	0	1	0	1	0
2812	Alkalies and chlorine	0	0	0	1	1	0
2813	Industrial gases	1	0	0	0	1	0
2816	Inorganic pigments	3	3	2	0	8	8
2819	Industrial inorganic chemicals, nec	7	2	8	5	22	7
2821	Plastics materials and resins	2	1	5	7	15	4
2822	Synthetic rubber	1	0	0	5	6	3
2833	Medicinals and botanicals	5	1	6	6	18	16
2834	Pharmaceutical preparations	21	13	21	55	110	99
2835	Diagnostic substances	0	0	2	0	2	0
2836	Biological products, except diagnostic	3	1	1	3	8	6
2841	Soap and other detergents	3	0	2	3	8	2
2842	Polishes and sanitation goods	5	8	7	9	29	21

SIC	DESCRIPTION	0-19	20-49	50-99	100-OVER	TOTAL	PRIMARY SIC ONLY
2844	Toilet preparations	4	1	6	9	20	5
2851	Paints and allied products	3	2	6	4	15	6
2865	Cyclic crudes and intermediates	0	1	2	3	6	2
2869	Industrial organic chemicals, nec	5	6	8	9	28	17
2873	Nitrogenous fertilizers	0	1	0	1	2	1
2874	Phosphatic fertilizers	3	2	3	2	10	8
2875	Fertilizers, mixing only	3	2	1	0	6	1
2879	Agricultural chemicals, nec	4	4	2	2	12	5
2891	Adhesives and sealants	3	1	2	3	9	4
2892	Explosives	2	0	0	1	3	1
2893	Printing ink	1	0	0	0	1	0
2895	Carbon black	0	0	0	1	1	1
2899	Chemical preparations, nec	7	6	6	7	26	6
2911	Petroleum refining	9	3	7	13	32	23
2951	Asphalt paving mixtures and blocks	1	1	1	3	6	0
2952	Asphalt felts and coatings	1	1	0	2	4	2
2992	Lubricating oils and greases	3	1	1	2	7	2
3011	Tires and inner tubes	0	0	0	4	4	1
3021	Rubber and plastics footwear	0	0	0	1	1	0
3052	Rubber and plastics hose and beltings	1	1	0	0	2	0
3053	Gaskets; packing and sealing devices	1	1	1	1	4	0
3061	Mechanical rubber goods	0	1	0	1	2	0
3069	Fabricated rubber products, nec	9	3	11	16	39	30
3081	Unsupported plastics film and sheet	7	2	10	16	35	29
3083	Laminated plastics plate and sheet	1	1	2	7	11	7
3084	Plastics pipe	0	0	0	4	4	2
3085	Plastics bottles	1	1	1	1	4	3
3086	Plastics foam products	3	1	10	15	29	22
3087	Custom compound purchased resins	1	0	0	1	2	2
3088	Plastics plumbing fixtures	2	1	0	5	8	5
3089	Plastics products, nec	51	10	77	115	253	200
3111	Leather tanning and finishing	1	0	0	0	1	0
3142	House slippers	0	0	1	0	1	0
3143	Men's footwear, except athletic	1	1	3	2	7	5
3144	Women's footwear, except athletic	2	1	3	2	8	2
3149	Footwear, except rubber, nec	0	0	2	0	2	0
3161	Luggage	0	0	3	2	5	3
3171	Women's handbags and purses	0	0	0	1	1	0
3172	Personal leather goods, nec	0	1	0	1	2	0
3199	Leather goods, nec	2	0	0	0	2	2
3211	Flat glass	3	3	5	7	18	13
3221	Glass containers	1	1	1	1	4	2
3229	Pressed and blown glass, nec	0	1	0	0	1	0
3231	Products of purchased glass	6	3	3	8	20	7
3241	Cement, hydraulic	0	0	0	1	1	0
3251	Brick and structural clay tile	3	1	1	2	7	1
3253	Ceramic wall and floor tile	1	0	0	0	1	1
3261	Vitreous plumbing fixtures	0	0	1	0	1	0
3263	Semivitreous table and kitchenware	1	0	0	0	1	0
3271	Concrete block and brick	4	0	2	0	6	2
3272	Concrete products, nec	8	4	4	1	17	7
3273	Ready-mixed concrete	8	2	5	8	23	9
3274	Lime	1	2	0	1	4	1
3275	Gypsum products	0	2	1	1	4	2
3281	Cut stone and stone products	9	5	6	3	23	16
3291	Abrasive products	1	0	1	0	2	1
3295	Minerals, ground or treated	2	0	0	3	5	1
3296	Mineral wool	1	2	0	0	3	2
3297	Nonclay refractories	0	1	0	0	1	0
3299	NonMetallic mineral products,	1	2	1	1	5	2
3312	Blast furnaces and steel mills	9	1	8	9	27	6
3313	ElectroMetallurgical products	0	0	0	1	1	0
3315	Steel wire and related products	1	0	1	1	3	1
3317	Steel pipe and tubes	0	0	2	1	3	1
3321	Gray and ductile iron foundries	1	1	1	0	3	1
3322	Malleable iron foundries	0	0	1	1	2	1
3324	Steel investment foundries	0	0	0	2	2	1
3325	Steel foundries, nec	1	1	0	1	3	2
3334	Primary aluminum	1	0	0	2	3	3
3339	Primary nonferrous Metals, nec	2	0	2	1	5	3
3341	Secondary nonferrous Metals	0	0	1	2	3	1
3351	Copper rolling and drawing	0	0	0	2	2	2
3353	Aluminum sheet, plate, and foil	0	0	0	1	1	0
3354	Aluminum extruded products	1	0	1	1	3	2
3355	Aluminum rolling and drawing, nec	1	0	0	1	2	1
3357	Nonferrous wiredrawing and insulating	0	0	2	2	4	2
3364	Nonferrous die-castings except aluminum	1	1	0	2	4	1
3365	Aluminum foundries	2	0	1	1	4	2
3366	Copper foundries	0	0	2	0	2	0

SIC	DESCRIPTION	0-19	20-49	50-99	100-OVER	TOTAL	PRIMARY SIC ONLY
3369	Nonferrous foundries, nec	1	0	2	1	4	2
3398	Metal heat treating	2	2	3	3	10	6
3399	Primary Metal products	7	0	7	3	17	12
3411	Metal cans	0	0	0	1	1	1
3412	Metal barrels, drums, and pails	3	0	0	0	3	1
3423	Hand and edge tools, nec	1	0	2	2	5	1
3425	Saw blades and handsaws	0	0	1	0	1	0
3429	Hardware, nec	6	3	3	7	19	3
3431	Metal sanitary ware	1	0	1	3	5	5
3432	Plumbing fixture fittings and trim	1	0	0	0	1	0
3433	Heating equipment, except electric	5	2	5	8	20	19
3441	Fabricated structural Metal	16	5	49	19	89	71
3442	Metal doors, sash, and trim	23	5	21	29	78	51
3443	Fabricated plate work (boiler shop)	9	1	7	8	25	10
3444	Sheet Metalwork	8	5	6	4	23	6
3446	Architectural Metalwork	5	1	3	2	11	4
3448	Prefabricated Metal buildings and components	3	2	0	2	7	1
3449	Miscellaneous Metalwork	4	1	2	2	9	2
3452	Bolts, nuts, rivets, and washers	1	1	1	1	4	0
3462	Iron and steel forgings	4	1	6	1	12	8
3463	Nonferrous forgings	0	0	1	2	3	2
3465	Automotive stampings	6	0	4	23	33	27
3469	Metal stampings, nec	7	3	3	14	27	10
3471	Plating and polishing	2	0	2	2	6	2
3479	Metal coating and allied services	3	2	5	6	16	8
3484	Small arms	0	0	0	1	1	1
3491	Industrial valves	2	2	0	1	5	1
3492	Fluid power valves and hose fittings	0	1	1	3	5	2
3493	Steel springs, except wire	0	0	1	4	5	3
3494	Valves and pipe fittings, nec	3	2	3	8	16	7
3495	Wire springs	0	0	1	2	3	1
3496	Miscellaneous fabricated wire products	3	1	8	13	25	18
3497	Metal foil and leaf	0	1	0	1	2	0
3498	Fabricated pipe and fittings	4	1	0	2	7	4
3499	Fabricated Metal products, nec	6	4	16	15	41	20
3511	Turbines and turbine generator sets	1	0	1	0	2	0
3519	Internal combustion engines, nec	1	0	0	5	6	4
3523	Farm machinery and equipment	7	0	3	6	16	5
3524	Lawn and garden equipment	0	0	0	3	3	1
3531	Construction machinery	11	0	12	17	40	30
3532	Mining machinery	6	3	14	8	31	19
3533	Oil and gas field machinery	8	6	6	6	26	10
3534	Elevators and moving stairways	2	0	0	3	5	3
3535	Conveyors and conveying equipment	1	0	1	4	6	2
3536	Hoists, cranes, and monorails	1	0	3	1	5	0
3537	Industrial trucks and tractors	2	0	2	1	5	1
3541	Machine tools, Metal cutting type	6	1	10	3	20	16
3542	Machine tools, Metal forming type	1	3	4	0	8	1
3544	Special dies, tools, jigs, and fixtures	13	2	25	22	62	42
3545	Machine tool accessories	5	1	4	5	15	4
3546	Power-driven handtools	1	0	0	0	1	1
3547	Rolling mill machinery	0	1	0	0	1	0
3548	Welding apparatus	2	0	2	0	4	3
3549	Metalworking machinery, nec	0	1	1	4	6	4
3553	Woodworking machinery	0	0	1	2	3	3
3554	Paper industries machinery	1	0	1	2	4	2
3555	Printing trades machinery	1	0	1	0	2	0
3556	Food products machinery	2	0	4	2	8	1
3559	Special industry machinery, nec	1	1	3	7	12	7
3561	Pumps and pumping equipment	6	2	3	6	17	11
3562	Ball and roller bearings	0	0	1	0	1	0
3563	Air and gas compressors	2	0	1	0	5	1
3564	Blowers and fans	6	1	11	8	26	16
3565	Packaging machinery	1	2	2	4	9	3
3566	Speed changers, drives, and gears	0	0	2	2	4	4
3567	Industrial furnaces and ovens	3	1	1	2	7	4
3568	Power transmission equipment, nec	4	1	1	2	8	0
3569	General industrial machinery, nec	13	5	20	20	58	25
3571	Electronic computers	1	1	1	1	4	2
3577	Computer peripheral equipment, nec	1	0	0	2	3	1
3578	Calculating and accounting equipment	0	0	0	1	1	1
3579	Office machines, nec	0	0	1	1	2	0
3581	Automatic vending machines	0	0	1	0	1	0
3585	Refrigeration and heating equipment	6	5	5	5	21	5
3589	Service industry machinery, nec	5	3	8	5	21	8
3592	Carburetors, pistons, piston rings and valves	0	0	1	1	2	1
3593	Fluid power cylinders and actuators	1	3	1	1	6	4
3594	Fluid power pumps and motors	1	0	0	0	1	0
3596	Scales and balances, except laboratory	0	0	1	0	1	0

SIC	DESCRIPTION	0-19	20-49	50-99	100-OVER	TOTAL	PRIMARY SIC ONLY
3599	Industrial machinery, nec	12	7	14	18	51	10
3612	Transformers, except electric	1	1	1	4	7	5
3613	Switchgear and switchboard apparatus	5	0	6	3	14	7
3621	Motors and generators	4	3	6	13	26	17
3625	Relays and industrial controls	6	2	5	8	21	7
3629	Electrical industrial apparatus, nec	0	0	2	1	3	0
3631	Household cooking equipment	2	0	1	2	5	3
3634	Electric housewares and fans	5	0	1	2	8	3
3635	Household vacuum cleaners	0	1	0	0	1	0
3639	Household appliances, nec	2	0	0	0	2	2
3641	Electric lamps	1	0	0	1	2	1
3643	Current-carrying wiring devices	0	2	1	1	4	1
3644	Noncurrent-carrying wiring devices	1	0	2	0	3	1
3645	Residential lighting fixtures	2	1	0	3	6	2
3646	Commercial lighting fixtures	3	1	1	3	8	1
3648	Lighting equipment, nec	1	1	1	3	6	2
3651	Household audio and video equipment	4	0	9	1	14	12
3652	Prerecorded records and tapes	0	0	0	1	1	0
3661	Telephone and telegraph apparatus	2	1	2	9	14	5
3663	Radio and t.v. communications equipment	11	2	5	11	29	19
3669	Communications equipment, nec	10	2	11	19	42	30
3671	Electron tubes	0	0	1	0	1	0
3672	Printed circuit boards	1	0	0	10	11	9
3674	Semiconductors and related devices	7	1	6	10	24	18
3675	Electronic capacitors	1	0	0	0	1	0
3676	Electronic resistors	1	0	0	0	1	0
3677	Electronic coils and transformers	0	0	3	0	3	2
3679	Electronic components, nec	8	2	9	30	49	34
3694	Engine electrical equipment	1	1	2	2	6	1
3695	Magnetic and optical recording media	0	0	1	0	1	0
3699	Electrical equipment and supplies, nec	12	5	15	17	49	35
3711	Motor vehicles and car bodies	1	0	3	8	12	8
3713	Truck and bus bodies	9	2	10	9	30	25
3714	Motor vehicle parts and accessories	18	7	19	50	94	79
3715	Truck trailers	4	1	8	8	21	20
3716	Motor homes	0	0	1	1	2	1
3721	Aircraft	0	0	0	9	9	8
3724	Aircraft engines and engine parts	1	0	0	3	4	1
3728	Aircraft parts and equipment, nec	13	3	14	19	49	40
3731	Shipbuilding and repairing	1	1	3	5	10	5
3732	Boatbuilding and repairing	0	1	5	8	14	12
3743	Railroad equipment	1	0	0	1	2	1
3751	Motorcycles, bicycles and parts	3	0	1	0	4	2
3761	Guided missiles and space vehicles	0	0	0	1	1	0
3764	Space propulsion units and parts	0	0	0	1	1	0
3769	Space vehicle equipment, nec	0	0	0	2	2	1
3792	Travel trailers and campers	1	0	2	1	4	1
3795	Tanks and tank components	1	0	0	2	3	2
3799	Transportation equipment, nec	1	0	0	6	7	4
3812	Search and navigation equipment	11	4	8	11	34	20
3821	Laboratory apparatus and furniture	7	0	9	6	22	13
3822	Environmental controls	2	0	1	2	5	1
3823	Process control instruments	5	2	1	7	15	1
3824	Fluid meters and counting devices	0	1	2	0	3	1
3825	Instruments to measure electricity	5	1	0	3	9	1
3826	Analytical instruments	2	0	2	0	4	4
3827	Optical instruments and lenses	1	5	2	8	16	10
3829	Measuring and controlling devices, nec	10	12	8	3	33	24
3841	Surgical and medical instruments	6	1	1	8	16	6
3842	Surgical appliances and supplies	11	10	14	17	52	38
3843	Dental equipment and supplies	3	1	0	1	5	3
3844	X-ray apparatus and tubes	0	0	1	3	4	2
3845	Electromedical equipment	1	1	5	3	10	7
3851	Ophthalmic goods	4	1	2	2	9	7
3861	Photographic equipment and supplies	3	2	5	3	13	13
3873	Watches, clocks, watchcases, and parts	0	1	1	0	2	0
3911	Jewelry, precious Metal	2	1	0	0	3	0
3914	Silverware and plated ware	0	1	0	0	1	0
3931	Musical instruments	0	1	0	0	1	1
3942	Dolls and stuffed toys	0	0	0	1	1	0
3944	Games, toys, and children's vehicles	0	0	0	4	4	3
3949	Sporting and athletic goods, nec	16	8	16	11	51	42
3953	Marking devices	0	0	0	1	1	1
3955	Carbon paper and inked ribbons	1	0	0	0	1	1
3961	Costume jewelry	0	2	1	0	3	1
3965	Fasteners, buttons, needles, and pins	1	0	0	0	1	1
3991	Brooms and brushes	1	0	0	0	1	0
3993	Signs and advertising specialties	5	12	29	9	55	46
3996	Hard surface floor coverings, nec	2	0	0	0	2	1

SIC	DESCRIPTION	0-19	20-49	50-99	100-OVER	TOTAL	PRIMARY SIC ONLY
3999	Manufacturing industries, nec	5	6	13	14	38	27
4011	Railroads, line-haul operating	3	2	3	16	24	20
4013	Switching and terminal services	0	1	1	1	3	2
4111	Local and suburban transit	2	1	5	14	22	14
4119	Local passenger transportation, nec	1	1	2	3	7	4
4131	Intercity and rural bus transportation	1	0	2	4	7	3
4141	Local bus charter service	0	0	0	2	2	0
4142	Bus charter service, except local	0	2	5	7	14	7
4151	School buses	2	0	3	10	15	9
4173	Bus terminal and service facilities	0	0	1	2	3	2
4212	Local trucking, without storage	57	52	65	119	293	53
4213	Trucking, except local	81	52	120	200	453	365
4214	Local trucking with storage	3	3	9	7	22	5
4215	Courier services, except by air	0	0	0	1	1	1
4221	Farm product warehousing and storage	4	2	2	1	9	0
4222	Refrigerated warehousing and storage	4	4	3	4	15	7
4225	General warehousing and storage	25	30	27	46	128	51
4226	Special warehousing and storage, nec	10	3	3	3	19	11
4231	Trucking terminal facilities	2	1	1	1	5	2
4311	U.s. postal service	1	0	0	5	6	4
4412	Deep sea foreign transportation of freight	0	0	1	2	3	3
4424	Deep sea domestic transportation of freight	2	0	1	4	7	5
4432	Freight transportation on the great lakes	1	0	0	0	1	1
4449	Water transportation of freight	2	1	0	0	3	2
4482	Ferries	2	0	0	0	2	0
4489	Water passenger transportation	0	0	1	0	1	1
4491	Marine cargo handling	1	2	4	2	9	3
4492	Towing and tugboat service	3	0	1	2	6	4
4493	Marinas	0	1	1	3	5	0
4499	Water transportation services,	0	1	3	2	6	1
4512	Air transportation, scheduled	5	4	5	10	24	13
4513	Air courier services	1	0	1	2	4	3
4522	Air transportation, nonscheduled	10	13	10	14	47	35
4581	Airports, flying fields, and services	5	9	11	13	38	19
4612	Crude petroleum pipelines	0	0	0	7	7	4
4619	Pipelines, nec	0	1	1	2	4	1
4724	Travel agencies	22	84	20	13	139	127
4725	Tour operators	10	32	11	11	64	54
4729	Passenger transportation arrangement	0	3	3	2	8	5
4731	Freight transportation arrangement	51	121	67	75	314	270
4783	Packing and crating	2	1	1	2	6	1
4785	Inspection and fixed facilities	3	5	1	5	14	12
4789	Transportation services, nec	0	2	1	3	6	2
4812	Radiotelephone communication	4	1	2	3	10	3
4813	Telephone communication, except radio	11	3	16	42	72	46
4822	Telegraph and other communications	0	0	0	1	1	0
4832	Radio broadcasting stations	9	2	15	11	37	35
4833	Television broadcasting stations	3	1	7	21	32	23
4841	Cable and other pay television services	5	1	4	13	23	19
4899	Communication services, nec	33	20	54	95	202	164
4911	Electric services	35	18	20	45	118	103
4922	Natural gas transmission	18	4	2	7	31	25
4923	Gas transmission and distribution	4	1	1	7	13	5
4924	Natural gas distribution	27	5	5	9	46	40
4925	Gas production and/or distribution	1	0	1	0	2	0
4931	Electric and other services combined	1	0	0	2	3	1
4932	Gas and other services combined	1	0	0	1	2	1
4941	Water supply	3	2	1	2	8	1
4953	Refuse systems	39	49	45	37	170	135
4959	Sanitary services, nec	5	2	6	9	22	3
4971	Irrigation systems	0	1	0	1	2	0
5012	Automobiles and other motor vehicles	14	27	20	14	75	62
5013	Motor vehicle supplies and new parts	23	25	18	21	87	22
5014	Tires and tubes	9	33	16	16	74	68
5015	Motor vehicle parts, used	0	1	1	0	2	1
5021	Furniture	9	9	4	3	25	9
5023	Homefurnishings	39	69	19	10	137	102
5031	Lumber, plywood, and millwork	53	71	37	32	193	143
5032	Brick, stone, and related material	28	44	24	16	112	87
5033	Roofing, siding, and insulation	11	9	4	4	28	23
5039	Construction materials, nec	43	64	42	28	177	122
5043	Photographic equipment and supplies	2	0	3	2	7	3
5044	Office equipment	5	6	4	4	19	5
5045	Computers, peripherals, and software	18	11	11	17	57	22
5046	Commercial equipment, nec	5	9	7	3	24	5
5047	Medical and hospital equipment	22	60	34	31	147	116
5048	Ophthalmic goods	0	3	1	0	4	3
5049	Professional equipment, nec	21	30	10	11	72	55
5051	Metals service centers and offices	144	69	28	26	267	235

SIC	DESCRIPTION	0-19	20-49	50-99	100-OVER	TOTAL	PRIMARY SIC ONLY
5052	Coal and other minerals and ores	3	0	2	0	5	0
5063	Electrical apparatus and equipment	51	86	33	41	211	153
5064	Electrical appliances, television and radio	12	18	7	9	46	35
5065	Electronic parts and equipment, nec	32	32	19	20	103	40
5072	Hardware	18	25	18	11	72	20
5074	Plumbing and heating equipment and supplies (hydronics)	30	50	14	19	113	72
5075	Warm air heating and air conditioning	21	44	11	10	86	51
5078	Refrigeration equipment and supplies	8	15	8	2	33	15
5082	Construction and mining machinery	26	44	19	12	101	73
5083	Farm and garden machinery	48	71	17	13	149	116
5084	Industrial machinery and equipment	89	145	102	59	395	254
5085	Industrial supplies	71	152	65	35	323	257
5087	Service establishment equipment	18	33	17	7	75	46
5088	Transportation equipment and supplies	4	5	1	5	15	5
5091	Sporting and recreation goods	13	14	9	10	46	15
5092	Toys and hobby goods and supplies	1	10	3	5	19	2
5093	Scrap and waste materials	25	42	6	6	79	73
5094	Jewelry and precious stones	7	28	3	1	39	34
5099	Durable goods, nec	37	58	28	22	145	90
5111	Printing and writing paper	3	1	0	6	10	2
5112	Stationery and office supplies	0	6	1	3	10	3
5113	Industrial and personal service paper	18	23	19	8	68	44
5122	Drugs, proprietaries, and sundries	25	18	10	27	80	25
5131	Piece goods and notions	6	4	2	1	13	6
5136	Men's and boy's clothing	14	24	13	12	63	14
5137	Women's and children's clothing	26	78	31	20	155	122
5139	Footwear	4	8	3	1	16	5
5141	Groceries, general line	55	103	35	50	243	190
5142	Packaged frozen goods	23	38	23	28	112	57
5143	Dairy products, except dried or canned	10	36	11	14	71	39
5144	Poultry and poultry products	13	19	13	10	55	46
5145	Confectionery	8	11	7	9	35	4
5146	Fish and seafoods	9	7	7	7	30	10
5147	Meats and meat products	31	53	22	27	133	94
5148	Fresh fruits and vegetables	41	87	35	19	182	165
5149	Groceries and related products, nec	62	69	40	40	211	128
5153	Grain and field beans	54	16	8	8	86	75
5154	Livestock	1	4	1	0	6	2
5159	Farm-product raw materials, nec	11	8	6	6	31	23
5162	Plastics materials and basic shapes	12	18	4	4	38	26
5169	Chemicals and allied products, nec	61	68	31	16	176	134
5171	Petroleum bulk stations and terminals	48	27	11	7	93	70
5172	Petroleum products, nec	126	48	19	20	213	181
5181	Beer and ale	1	2	1	3	7	2
5182	Wine and distilled beverages	3	3	1	0	7	2
5191	Farm supplies	73	60	27	14	174	120
5192	Books, periodicals, and newspapers	13	20	10	14	57	52
5193	Flowers and florists supplies	14	38	13	5	70	62
5194	Tobacco and tobacco products	5	4	4	5	18	7
5198	Paints, varnishes, and supplies	5	2	1	1	9	1
5199	Nondurable goods, nec	32	93	39	25	189	127
5211	Lumber and other building materials	64	66	68	65	263	106
5231	Paint, glass, and wallpaper stores	6	3	1	0	10	0
5251	Hardware stores	25	37	38	34	134	23
5261	Retail nurseries and garden stores	22	34	14	13	83	29
5311	Department stores	8	3	23	98	132	123
5331	Variety stores	2	0	1	1	4	1
5399	Miscellaneous general merchandise	15	14	21	29	79	42
5411	Grocery stores	61	268	332	216	877	799
5421	Meat and fish markets	6	10	11	4	31	2
5431	Fruit and vegetable markets	4	6	15	10	35	20
5441	Candy, nut, and confectionery stores	3	2	0	5	10	0
5451	Dairy products stores	2	4	2	0	8	0
5461	Retail bakeries	5	8	17	8	38	4
5499	Miscellaneous food stores	13	6	8	6	33	21
5511	New and used car dealers	26	45	39	18	128	104
5521	Used car dealers	3	0	4	2	9	2
5531	Auto and home supply stores	20	35	36	32	123	9
5541	Gasoline service stations	32	24	22	13	91	6
5551	Boat dealers	0	3	0	2	5	0
5561	Recreational vehicle dealers	4	5	1	0	10	4
5571	Motorcycle dealers	8	42	3	2	55	48
5599	Automotive dealers, nec	5	11	0	1	17	1
5611	Men's and boys' clothing stores	6	4	3	9	22	6
5621	Women's clothing stores	5	5	3	9	22	13
5632	Women's accessory and specialty stores	11	7	5	14	37	3
5641	Children's and infants' wear stores	1	2	2	0	5	2
5651	Family clothing stores	24	5	20	19	68	47
5661	Shoe stores	19	11	8	3	41	25

SIC	DESCRIPTION	0-19	20-49	50-99	100-OVER	TOTAL	PRIMARY SIC ONLY
5699	Miscellaneous apparel and accessory stores	7	2	4	7	20	1
5712	Furniture stores	12	10	5	8	35	13
5713	Floor covering stores	8	4	2	1	15	3
5714	Drapery and upholstery stores	1	1	0	0	2	0
5719	Miscellaneous homefurnishings	19	13	12	8	52	10
5722	Household appliance stores	6	10	3	2	21	1
5731	Radio, television, and electronic stores	4	0	4	3	11	2
5734	Computer and software stores	8	11	13	10	42	23
5735	Record and prerecorded tape stores	1	0	2	1	4	1
5736	Musical instrument stores	0	0	1	1	2	1
5812	Eating places	81	35	341	392	849	581
5813	Drinking places	8	2	46	60	116	7
5912	Drug stores and proprietary stores	3	3	15	25	46	27
5921	Liquor stores	6	9	13	12	40	5
5932	Used merchandise stores	3	1	2	0	6	2
5941	Sporting goods and bicycle shops	12	13	22	19	66	31
5942	Book stores	2	4	3	9	18	2
5943	Stationery stores	2	4	4	8	18	6
5944	Jewelry stores	1	2	0	1	4	3
5945	Hobby, toy, and game shops	3	1	4	2	10	3
5946	Camera and photographic supply stores	0	1	1	5	7	2
5947	Gift, novelty, and souvenir shop	17	12	15	20	64	27
5948	Luggage and leather goods stores	2	2	1	1	6	2
5949	Sewing, needlework, and piece goods	1	0	1	0	2	0
5961	Catalog and mail-order houses	6	19	11	6	42	32
5962	Merchandising machine operators	3	0	1	3	7	1
5963	Direct selling establishments	6	23	5	6	40	35
5983	Fuel oil dealers	14	6	1	2	23	3
5984	Liquefied petroleum gas dealers	5	5	2	4	16	4
5989	Fuel dealers, nec	1	0	0	0	1	0
5992	Florists	3	20	11	8	42	24
5993	Tobacco stores and stands	0	0	2	6	11	0
5994	News dealers and newsstands	1	0	1	4	6	1
5995	Optical goods stores	11	10	2	3	26	23
5999	Miscellaneous retail stores, nec	81	114	55	48	298	157
6021	National commercial banks	6	3	9	22	40	33
6036	Savings institutions, except federal	0	1	0	0	1	0
6062	State credit unions	4	9	10	12	35	35
6091	Nondeposit trust facilities	0	0	1	0	1	0
6099	Functions related to deposit banking	4	1	0	1	6	1
6111	Federal and federally sponsored credit agencies	4	1	1	1	7	5
6141	Personal credit institutions	2	1	3	5	11	8
6153	Short-term business credit institutions, except agricultural	1	1	3	3	8	4
6159	Miscellaneous business credit institutions	14	14	7	13	48	40
6162	Mortgage bankers and loan correspondents	0	3	3	7	13	4
6163	Loan brokers	1	1	2	2	6	2
6211	Security brokers and dealers	19	15	8	17	59	45
6221	Commodity contracts brokers, dealers	0	1	0	1	2	1
6282	Investment advice	33	45	11	20	109	87
6289	Security and commodity service	1	5	2	10	18	18
6311	Life insurance	7	5	2	20	34	20
6321	Accident and health insurance	4	0	1	10	15	4
6324	Hospital and medical service plans	1	0	0	3	4	3
6331	Fire, marine, and casualty insurance	7	8	4	23	42	31
6351	Surety insurance	4	3	2	10	19	5
6361	Title insurance	0	0	1	0	1	1
6371	Pension, health, and welfare funds	2	0	1	5	8	1
6399	Insurance carriers, nec	0	0	0	1	1	1
6411	Insurance agents, brokers, and service	21	21	12	43	97	65
6512	Nonresidential building operators	53	37	19	38	147	84
6513	Apartment building operators	36	27	36	52	151	106
6514	Dwelling operators, except apartments	3	3	2	4	12	0
6515	Mobile home site operators	0	0	1	0	1	0
6519	Real property lessors, nec	5	5	5	7	22	7
6531	Real estate agents and managers	117	200	161	133	611	565
6552	Subdividers and developers, nec	11	5	3	6	25	10
6553	Cemetery subdividers and developers	30	14	25	24	93	37
6712	Bank holding companies	501	128	119	220	968	505
6719	Holding companies, nec	52	23	17	33	125	84
6722	Management investment, open-end	16	9	4	19	48	32
6726	Investment offices, nec	17	5	1	3	26	16
6733	Trusts, nec	1	2	1	3	7	2
6792	Oil royalty traders	1	0	1	0	2	1
6794	Patent owners and lessors	21	13	13	28	75	11
6798	Real estate investment trusts	5	1	0	3	9	6
6799	Investors, nec	24	13	7	7	51	45
7011	Hotels and motels	60	17	106	293	476	432
7021	Rooming and boarding houses	0	1	0	0	1	0
7032	Sporting and recreational camps	1	0	0	3	4	0

SIC	DESCRIPTION	0-19	20-49	50-99	100-OVER	TOTAL	PRIMARY SIC ONLY
7033	Trailer parks and campsites	1	0	1	5	7	0
7041	Membership-basis organization hotels	1	1	0	1	3	1
7211	Power laundries, family and commercial	1	0	0	1	2	0
7212	Garment pressing and cleaners' agents	1	0	0	0	1	1
7213	Linen supply	1	0	0	1	2	2
7215	Coin-operated laundries and cleaning	1	0	0	1	2	1
7216	Drycleaning plants, except rugs	0	0	0	1	1	0
7217	Carpet and upholstery cleaning	0	3	1	5	9	0
7218	Industrial launderers	2	1	3	1	7	1
7219	Laundry and garment services, nec	0	0	0	3	3	3
7231	Beauty shops	1	0	1	1	3	0
7261	Funeral service and crematories	1	0	0	1	2	1
7291	Tax return preparation services	0	1	5	6	12	2
7299	Miscellaneous personal service	3	7	10	29	49	8
7311	Advertising agencies	12	10	35	35	92	71
7312	Outdoor advertising services	0	1	0	0	1	1
7313	Radio, television, publisher representatives	0	1	1	0	2	0
7319	Advertising, nec	3	2	2	4	11	4
7322	Adjustment and collection services	2	1	1	2	6	3
7323	Credit reporting services	1	1	1	2	5	1
7331	Direct mail advertising services	2	2	0	2	6	1
7334	Photocopying and duplicating services	2	0	0	1	3	0
7335	Commercial photography	0	0	0	1	1	1
7336	Commercial art and graphic design	3	0	6	6	15	8
7338	Secretarial and court reporting	1	0	0	2	3	0
7342	Disinfecting and pest control services	0	1	0	1	2	0
7349	Building maintenance services, nec	12	12	32	102	158	129
7352	Medical equipment rental	1	0	2	0	3	0
7353	Heavy construction equipment rental	9	19	10	12	50	10
7359	Equipment rental and leasing, nec	17	28	16	14	75	6
7361	Employment agencies	5	9	11	18	43	19
7363	Help supply services	8	10	11	25	54	34
7371	Custom computer programming services	66	16	102	112	296	217
7372	Prepackaged software	25	8	54	35	122	87
7373	Computer integrated systems design	10	8	8	12	38	20
7374	Data processing and preparation	8	2	19	26	55	34
7375	Information retrieval services	3	0	2	1	6	2
7376	Computer facilities management	1	0	1	5	7	6
7377	Computer rental and leasing	0	1	0	1	2	0
7378	Computer maintenance and repair	7	2	7	2	18	1
7379	Computer related services, nec	10	5	13	28	56	9
7381	Detective and armored car services	4	3	6	32	45	34
7382	Security systems services	2	3	4	3	12	3
7383	News syndicates	1	0	0	0	1	1
7384	Photofinish laboratories	0	0	1	2	4	1
7389	Business services, nec	52	53	38	88	231	71
7513	Truck rental and leasing, no drivers	8	7	4	4	23	2
7514	Passenger car rental	8	6	5	5	24	20
7515	Passenger car leasing	5	9	16	8	38	13
7519	Utility trailer rental	3	2	3	3	11	5
7521	Automobile parking	0	1	0	4	5	4
7532	Top and body repair and paint shops	4	6	10	7	27	3
7534	Tire retreading and repair shops	1	2	0	2	5	5
7537	Automotive transmission repair shops	0	1	1	0	2	0
7538	General automotive repair shops	30	39	44	26	139	5
7539	Automotive repair shops, nec	6	5	5	1	17	1
7542	Carwashes	3	1	3	2	9	5
7549	Automotive services, nec	6	2	5	2	15	4
7622	Radio and television repair	1	1	1	2	5	0
7623	Refrigeration service and repair	2	2	2	1	7	2
7629	Electrical repair shops	8	14	12	8	42	13
7631	Watch, clock, and jewelry repair	0	0	0	1	1	0
7641	Reupholstery and furniture repair	0	1	1	0	2	0
7692	Welding repair	3	4	7	8	22	2
7694	Armature rewinding shops	2	2	1	0	5	2
7699	Repair services, nec	63	100	59	39	261	52
7812	Motion picture and video production	2	2	2	3	9	2
7819	Services allied to motion pictures	0	2	2	7	11	8
7832	Motion picture theaters, except drive-in	1	1	2	0	4	0
7833	Drive-in motion picture theaters	0	0	0	1	1	1
7841	Video tape rental	3	0	2	0	5	0
7911	Dance studios, schools, and halls	0	0	1	1	2	0
7922	Theatrical producers and services	10	0	10	17	37	27
7929	Entertainers and entertainment groups	1	0	1	2	4	1
7933	Bowling centers	2	1	0	0	3	0
7941	Sports clubs, managers, and promoters	0	0	0	2	2	1
7948	Racing, including track operation	0	0	1	5	6	3
7991	Physical fitness facilities	1	1	5	16	23	5
7992	Public golf courses	7	1	6	11	25	3

SIC	DESCRIPTION	0-19	20-49	50-99	100-OVER	TOTAL	PRIMARY SIC ONLY
7993	Coin-operated amusement devices	1	0	2	5	8	0
7996	Amusement parks	2	0	0	3	5	1
7997	Membership sports and recreation clubs	1	0	6	4	11	3
7999	Amusement and recreation, nec	13	12	23	38	86	28
8011	Offices and clinics of medical doctors	14	6	14	24	58	48
8021	Offices and clinics of dentists	1	0	0	0	1	0
8042	Offices and clinics of optometrists	2	1	0	0	3	0
8049	Offices of health practitioner	2	5	1	9	17	16
8051	Skilled nursing care facilities	12	1	87	265	365	333
8052	Intermediate care facilities	0	0	2	6	8	8
8059	Nursing and personal care, nec	0	0	6	23	29	21
8062	General medical and surgical hospitals	29	3	19	166	217	215
8063	Psychiatric hospitals	0	0	0	4	4	2
8069	Specialty hospitals, except psychiatric	1	2	0	16	19	10
8071	Medical laboratories	2	1	1	10	14	5
8082	Home health care services	0	0	1	1	2	0
8092	Kidney dialysis centers	0	0	0	1	1	0
8093	Specialty outpatient clinics, nec	3	0	4	12	19	4
8099	Health and allied services, nec	2	1	0	0	3	1
8111	Legal services	17	9	49	112	187	179
8211	Elementary and secondary schools	60	40	261	370	731	723
8221	Colleges and universities	23	2	17	109	151	147
8222	Junior colleges	6	1	6	24	37	35
8231	Libraries	0	0	4	3	7	6
8243	Data processing schools	0	0	2	1	3	0
8249	Vocational schools, nec	0	0	0	3	3	2
8299	Schools and educational services, nec	4	1	6	11	22	6
8322	Individual and family services	13	8	25	67	113	97
8331	Job training and related services	3	0	6	6	15	5
8351	Child day care services	0	1	5	9	15	0
8361	Residential care	4	0	12	50	66	48
8399	Social services, nec	5	0	5	13	29	8
8412	Museums and art galleries	3	0	5	14	22	16
8611	Business associations	1	3	5	4	13	7
8621	Professional organizations	22	21	45	34	122	115
8631	Labor organizations	20	49	14	20	103	103
8641	Civic and social associations	7	4	19	22	52	47
8651	Political organizations	0	0	1	0	1	0
8661	Religious organizations	21	10	28	40	99	98
8699	Membership organizations, nec	2	1	2	10	15	6
8711	Engineering services	79	37	96	195	407	293
8712	Architectural services	9	5	22	29	65	53
8713	Surveying services	8	4	15	17	44	32
8721	Accounting, auditing, and bookkeeping	5	10	29	79	123	107
8731	Commercial physical research	35	10	30	68	143	86
8732	Commercial nonphysical research	17	17	33	50	117	91
8733	Noncommercial research organizations	7	9	14	16	46	34
8734	Testing laboratories	3	7	2	6	18	6
8741	Management services	108	108	107	155	478	305
8742	Management consulting services	58	53	78	113	302	175
8743	Public relations services	10	19	26	21	76	48
8748	Business consulting, nec	57	68	78	100	303	193
8811	Private households	1	0	0	0	1	1
8999	Services, nec	12	35	14	21	82	64
9121	Legislative bodies	0	0	1	1	2	0
9311	Finance, taxation, and monetary policy	0	0	1	0	1	0
9431	Administration of public health programs	0	0	0	2	2	0
9441	Administration of social and manpower programs	0	0	0	1	1	0
	TOTALS	7,142	7,024	7,631	10,277	32,074	20,514

This Page left intentionally blank

NUMBER OF BUSINESSES BY COUNTY

ALBERTA

Alberta 1

BRITISH COLUMBIA

Alberni - Clayoquot 26

Bulkley - Nechako 32

Capital 325

Cariboo 52

Central Fraser-Val 165

Central Kootenay 34

Central Okanagan 165

Columbia - Shuswap 29

Comox - Strathcona 73

Cowichan Valley 47

East Kootenay 55

Fraser-Fort George 105

Greater Vancouver 3,577

Kitimat - Stikine 21

Kootenay Boundary 18

Mount Waddington 9

Nanaimo 106

North Okanagan 20

Okanagn-Similkameen 57

Peace River - Laird 85

Powell River 9

Skeena-Qn-Charlotte 15

Squamish - Lillooet 43

Stikine Region 2

Sunshine Coast 15

Thompson - Nicola 106

NEW BRUNSWICK

Charlotte 25

NOVA SCOTIA

ONTARIO

PRINCE EDWARD ISLAND

QUEBEC

2019 Canadian Key Business Directory
Répertoire des principales entreprises Canadiennes 2019

Section I

Geographic Index

Inscriptions par
région géographique

Acadia Valley, AB T0J

D-U-N-S 25-206-0587   (HQ)
I.W. KUHN CONSTRUCTION LTD
208 Railway Ave E, Acadia Valley, AB, T0J 0A0
(403) 972-3740
Sales 12,044,200
SIC 1629 Heavy construction, nec
Jarrod Kuhn
Lorraine Kuhn

Acheson, AB T7X

D-U-N-S 25-670-6193   (HQ)
689803 ALBERTA LTD
CONTINENTAL CARTAGE
25245 111 Ave, Acheson, AB, T7X 6C8
(780) 452-9414
Emp Here 40   *Sales* 15,961,113
SIC 4213 Trucking, except local
John Assman
Rodney Boychuk
Lawrence Michael Cantera

D-U-N-S 24-802-3769   (SL)
ADLER FIRESTOPPING LTD
53016 Hwy 60 Unit 23, Acheson, AB, T7X 5A7
(780) 962-9495
Emp Here 55   *Sales* 24,707,045
SIC 7389 Business services, nec
Karla Williams

D-U-N-S 20-212-7622   (BR)
AP INFRASTRUCTURE SOLUTIONS LP
(*Suby of* TREVLUC HOLDINGS LTD)
26229 Twp Rd 531a, Acheson, AB, T7X 5A4
(780) 444-1560
Emp Here 76
SIC 3272 Concrete products, nec
Ken Bannister

D-U-N-S 24-642-3321   (SL)
ARROW-WEST EQUIPMENT LTD
53016 Hwy 60 Unit 109, Acheson, AB, T7X 5A7
(780) 962-4490
Emp Here 25   *Sales* 11,875,650
SIC 5082 Construction and mining machinery
Len Chalupa
Bill Briggs

D-U-N-S 24-413-4123   (SL)
BEAVER PLASTICS LTD
11581 272 St, Acheson, AB, T7X 6E9
(780) 962-4433
Emp Here 70   *Sales* 17,236,494
SIC 3089 Plastics products, nec
Todd Mccarthy
Bryon Mccarthy

D-U-N-S 24-333-8329   (HQ)
BRI-CHEM CORP
27075 Acheson Rd, Acheson, AB, T7X 6B1
(780) 962-9490
Emp Here 10   *Sales* 91,047,796
SIC 2899 Chemical preparations, nec
Don Caron
Jason Theiss
Eric Sauze
Brian Campbell
Albert Sharp

D-U-N-S 24-004-2622   (HQ)
CANADIAN LYNDEN TRANSPORT LTD
LYNDEN TRANSPORT
(*Suby of* LYNDEN INCORPORATED)
27340 Acheson Rd, Acheson, AB, T7X 6B1
(780) 960-9444
Emp Here 57   *Sales* 12,342,360
SIC 4213 Trucking, except local
Jim Jansen

Dan Rychlik

D-U-N-S 20-203-9165   (HQ)
CANADIAN ROAD BUILDERS INC
LAFRENTZ ROAD MARKING
(*Suby of* BOUYGUES)
26120 Acheson Rd, Acheson, AB, T7X 6B3
(780) 962-7800
Emp Here 200   *Sales* 65,623,000
SIC 1611 Highway and street construction
Curtis Prosko
Louis R Gabanna
Jacques Michel
Gustavus J. Hope

D-U-N-S 25-976-9503   (HQ)
CONTINENTAL CARTAGE INC
26215 Twp Rd 531a Unit 412, Acheson, AB, T7X 5A4
(780) 452-9414
Emp Here 58   *Sales* 12,959,478
SIC 4213 Trucking, except local
John Assman
Lawrence Cantera

D-U-N-S 24-784-3969   (SL)
DIAMONDGEAR INDUSTRIAL MANUFAC-TURING LTD
DIAMONDGEAR
26229 Twp Rd 531a Suite 206, Acheson, AB, T7X 5A4
(780) 451-3912
Emp Here 36   *Sales* 16,098,264
SIC 5063 Electrical apparatus and equipment
Jeffrey Sheckger

D-U-N-S 20-267-0209   (SL)
DIRECT HORIZONTAL DRILLING INC
26308 Twp Rd 531a Suite 3, Acheson, AB, T7X 5A3
(780) 960-6037
Emp Here 50   *Sales* 15,985,250
SIC 1381 Drilling oil and gas wells
Lon Briscoe
Neil Brown

D-U-N-S 20-118-7213   (SL)
DOUBLE STAR DRILLING (1998) LTD
25180 117 Ave, Acheson, AB, T7X 6C2
(780) 484-4276
Emp Here 100   *Sales* 24,748,300
SIC 1771 Concrete work
Ian Hunt
Jule Price
Chad Bruce
Nick Baldwin

D-U-N-S 25-099-8978   (BR)
DRIVE PRODUCTS INC
(*Suby of* DRIVE PRODUCTS INC)
26230 Twp Rd 531a Unit 111, Acheson, AB, T7X 5A4
(780) 960-6826
Emp Here 100
SIC 5084 Industrial machinery and equipment
Blaine Bilyk

D-U-N-S 24-357-3255   (HQ)
ENTREC CORPORATION
28712 114 Ave, Acheson, AB, T7X 6E6
(780) 962-1600
Emp Here 120   *Sales* 131,260,055
SIC 7389 Business services, nec
John M Stevens
Glen Fleming
Whitney Irwin
Gavin Mcleod
Jesse Taylor
Jason Vandenberg
Rod F. Marlin
Joe Brennan
Don Goodwill
Chuck Sanders

D-U-N-S 25-370-0074   (SL)
ENX INC
53016 Hwy 60 Unit 703, Acheson, AB, T7X 5A7

(780) 962-7993
Emp Here 20   *Sales* 10,006,500
SIC 5169 Chemicals and allied products, nec
Paul Johnson
Brenda Johnson
Paul Balchen

D-U-N-S 25-095-6526   (HQ)
FRAC SHACK INC
25901 114 Ave Unit 136, Acheson, AB, T7X 6E2
(780) 948-9898
Emp Here 40   *Sales* 67,267,900
SIC 1389 Oil and gas field services, nec
Todd Van Vlient
Lance Holmstrom

D-U-N-S 24-382-4104   (SL)
FRAC SHACK INTERNATIONAL INC
(*Suby of* FRAC SHACK INC)
25901 114 Ave Unit 136, Acheson, AB, T7X 6E2
(780) 948-9898
Emp Here 60   *Sales* 40,360,740
SIC 1389 Oil and gas field services, nec
Todd Van Vlient
Lance Holmstrom

D-U-N-S 20-808-7932   (SL)
G.S. HOLDINGS COMPANY LTD
GS CONSTRUCTION
27060 Acheson Rd, Acheson, AB, T7X 6B1
(780) 962-3544
Emp Here 75   *Sales* 18,933,150
SIC 1623 Water, sewer, and utility lines
Terran Sandwith

D-U-N-S 20-182-1068   (SL)
GANOTEC WEST ULC
(*Suby of* PETER KIEWIT SONS', INC.)
26230 Twp Rd 531a Unit 131, Acheson, AB, T7X 5A4
(780) 960-7450
Emp Here 200   *Sales* 139,678,400
SIC 1541 Industrial buildings and warehouses
Creg Ratcliffe

D-U-N-S 25-386-7162   (SL)
GENICS INC
27717 Acheson Rd, Acheson, AB, T7X 6B1

Emp Here 75   *Sales* 8,536,396
SIC 2491 Wood preserving
Calvin Wall
Wesley Wall

D-U-N-S 24-397-1207   (SL)
HAYWORTH EQUIPMENT SALES INC
26180 114 Ave, Acheson, AB, T7X 6R1
(780) 962-9100
Emp Here 30   *Sales* 14,942,340
SIC 5511 New and used car dealers
Doreen Schmidek
Gary Schmidek

D-U-N-S 20-072-7001   (BR)
INTEGRATED DISTRIBUTION SYSTEMS LIMITED PARTNERSHIP
WAJAX EQUIPMENT
(*Suby of* WAJAX CORPORATION)
26313 Twp Rd 531a, Acheson, AB, T7X 5A3
(780) 487-6700
Emp Here 100
SIC 5084 Industrial machinery and equipment
Rob Stasiw

D-U-N-S 25-417-9906   (SL)
IRONTECH RIG REPAIR & MANUFACTUR-ING INC
53016 Hwy 60 Unit 11, Acheson, AB, T7X 5A7
(780) 960-4881
Emp Here 40   *Sales* 12,788,200
SIC 1389 Oil and gas field services, nec
Shane Twa

D-U-N-S 24-398-8391   (SL)
JEN-COL CONSTRUCTION LTD.
(*Suby of* JODOIN HOLDINGS INC)
9620 266 St Suite 100, Acheson, AB, T7X 6H6

(780) 963-6523
Emp Here 80   *Sales* 45,627,040
SIC 1542 Nonresidential construction, nec
Cory Jodoin

D-U-N-S 20-082-8002   (HQ)
KICHTON CONTRACTING LTD
25296 117 Ave, Acheson, AB, T7X 6C2
(780) 447-1882
Sales 11,008,400
SIC 1794 Excavation work
Fred Kichton

D-U-N-S 25-416-4668   (SL)
KINSEY ENTERPRISES INC
CDN POWER PAC ELECTRICAL MECHANI-CAL, DIV OF
26650 116 Ave, Acheson, AB, T7X 6H2
(780) 452-0467
Emp Here 150   *Sales* 32,674,350
SIC 1731 Electrical work
Harold Kinsey
Elsie Kinsey

D-U-N-S 20-249-9067   (SL)
KMC MINING CORPORATION
KMC MINING
28712 114 Ave, Acheson, AB, T7X 6E6
(780) 454-0664
Emp Here 500   *Sales* 927,291,000
SIC 1311 Crude petroleum and natural gas
Craig Dirk
Allan Flemming
Daniel Klemke

D-U-N-S 20-593-7568   (HQ)
MANITOULIN TRANSPORTATION
NORTHWEST TRANSPORT
53114 Rge Rd 262 Unit 402, Acheson, AB, T7X 5A1
(780) 490-1112
Emp Here 80   *Sales* 41,141,200
SIC 4213 Trucking, except local
Peter Graham

D-U-N-S 24-255-2144   (HQ)
MYSHAK CRANE AND RIGGING LTD
(*Suby of* MYSHAK EQUIPMENT LTD)
53016 Hwy 60 Suite 42b, Acheson, AB, T7X 5A7
(780) 960-9790
Emp Here 50   *Sales* 73,579,880
SIC 7389 Business services, nec
Corey Mitchell

D-U-N-S 25-328-5191   (SL)
MYSHAK SALES & RENTALS LTD
28527 Acheson Rd, Acheson, AB, T7X 6A8
(780) 960-9255
Emp Here 100   *Sales* 38,213,900
SIC 7359 Equipment rental and leasing, nec
James Myshak
Michael Myshak
Robert Gerrard

D-U-N-S 20-357-9172   (SL)
NCSG ACQUISITION LTD
53016 Hwy 60 Unit 817, Acheson, AB, T7X 5A7
(780) 960-6300
Emp Here 49   *Sales* 11,500,104
SIC 8732 Commercial nonphysical research
Ted Redmond

D-U-N-S 20-302-0029   (HQ)
NCSG CRANE & HEAVY HAUL SERVICES LTD
(*Suby of* NCSG HOLDINGS CANADA LTD)
28765 Acheson Rd, Acheson, AB, T7X 6A8
(780) 960-6300
Emp Here 40   *Sales* 66,629,600
SIC 7353 Heavy construction equipment rental
Andrew Fraser
Heather Maccallum
Darin Coutu

D-U-N-S 25-497-0718   (SL)
NCSG CRANE & HEAVY HAUL TRANS

TECH INC
(*Suby of* NCSG HOLDINGS CANADA LTD)
28765 Acheson Rd, Acheson, AB, T7X 6A8
(780) 960-6300
Emp Here 150   *Sales* 30,855,900
SIC 4212 Local trucking, without storage
Ted Redmond
Dan Duffy
George Rogers
Glenn Dales
Terry Colban

D-U-N-S 20-385-2947   (HQ)
NCSG HOLDINGS CANADA LTD
28765 Acheson Rd, Acheson, AB, T7X 6A8
(780) 960-6300
Sales 27,335,000
SIC 6712 Bank holding companies
Darin Coutu

D-U-N-S 25-262-2790   (SL)
NELSON ENVIRONMENTAL REMEDIATION LTD
30541 100 Ave, Acheson, AB, T7X 6L8
(780) 960-3660
Emp Here 40   *Sales* 10,285,240
SIC 4959 Sanitary services, nec
Darryl Nelson
Warren Nelson
Donald Badger

D-U-N-S 20-109-0243   (SL)
NORAMA ENTERPRISES INC
(*Suby of* NORAMA INC)
53016 Hwy 60 Suite 2, Acheson, AB, T7X 5A7
(780) 960-7171
Emp Here 50   *Sales* 12,622,100
SIC 1611 Highway and street construction
Martin Gouin
Yvon J Gouin

D-U-N-S 20-692-2457   (HQ)
NORTH AMERICAN CONSTRUCTION GROUP LTD
100 Ave Acheson Suite 27287, Acheson, AB, T7X 6H8
(780) 960-7171
Sales 310,868,064
SIC 1629 Heavy construction, nec
Martin Ferron
Joe Lambert
Jason Veenstra
Barry Palmer
Robert J. Butler
Jordan A. Slator
David G. Kallay
Ronald A. Mcintosh
William C. Oehmig
Bryan Pinney

D-U-N-S 20-896-8438   (HQ)
NORTH AMERICAN CONSTRUCTION GROUP LTD
(*Suby of* NORTH AMERICAN CONSTRUCTION GROUP LTD)
27287 100 Ave, Acheson, AB, T7X 6H8
(780) 960-7171
Emp Here 160   *Sales* 227,430,600
SIC 1629 Heavy construction, nec
Martin Ferron

D-U-N-S 25-415-9536   (HQ)
NORTH AMERICAN CONSTRUCTION MANAGEMENT LTD
(*Suby of* NORTH AMERICAN CONSTRUCTION GROUP LTD)
26550 Acheson Rd, Acheson, AB, T7X 6B2
(780) 960-7171
Emp Here 150   *Sales* 222,697,021
SIC 1629 Heavy construction, nec
Martin Ferron
Joe Lambert
Barry Palmer
Rob Butler
Ron Mcintosh
William Oehmig
Bryan Pinney

Thomas Stan
Jay Thorton
John Pollesel

D-U-N-S 20-558-9158   (SL)
NORTHWELL OILFIELD HAULING (09) INC
26318 Township Rd 531a Unit 3, Acheson, AB, T7X 5A3
(780) 960-4900
Emp Here 50   *Sales* 10,506,550
SIC 1389 Oil and gas field services, nec
Neil Brown

D-U-N-S 25-093-3848   (HQ)
OLDCASTLE BUILDING PRODUCTS CANADA, INC
EXPOCRETE
(*Suby of* CRH PUBLIC LIMITED COMPANY)
28234 Acheson Rd, Acheson, AB, T7X 6A9
(780) 962-4010
Emp Here 100   *Sales* 142,407,000
SIC 5039 Construction materials, nec
Jay Frederickson
John Heffernan
Bruce Dick

D-U-N-S 20-969-5498   (SL)
PARADOX ACCESS SOLUTIONS INC
11246 261 St, Acheson, AB, T7X 6C7
(587) 461-1500
Emp Here 100   *Sales* 25,244,200
SIC 1611 Highway and street construction
Marc Breault

D-U-N-S 24-008-6426   (HQ)
PIPEWORX LTD
(*Suby of* PLH GROUP, INC.)
11122 255 St, Acheson, AB, T7X 6C9
(780) 960-2730
Emp Here 20   *Sales* 12,622,100
SIC 1623 Water, sewer, and utility lines
Kelly Gillam
Jason Ortt
Shane Cyrenne
Chad Johannsen

D-U-N-S 24-417-5936   (HQ)
POWELL CANADA INC
(*Suby of* POWELL INDUSTRIES, INC.)
10960 274 St, Acheson, AB, T7X 6P7
(780) 948-3300
Emp Here 325   *Sales* 94,203,600
SIC 1731 Electrical work
Michael Lucas
Peter Didaskalos
Milburn Honeycutt
Don Madison

D-U-N-S 24-091-6817   (SL)
RAYWALT CONSTRUCTION CO. LTD
10374 276 St, Acheson, AB, T7X 6A5
(780) 962-0030
Emp Here 45   *Sales* 10,839,780
SIC 1623 Water, sewer, and utility lines
Ron Johnson
Mark Zutz
Tom Allison

D-U-N-S 24-701-9458   (HQ)
RELIABLE TUBE (EDMONTON) LTD
26936 Acheson Rd, Acheson, AB, T7X 6B2
(780) 962-0130
Emp Here 15   *Sales* 13,415,220
SIC 5051 Metals service centers and offices
Darlene Whittaker

D-U-N-S 20-259-5906   (SL)
ROTERRA PILING LTD
25420 114 Ave, Acheson, AB, T7X 6M4
(780) 948-8556
Emp Here 50   *Sales* 15,943,450
SIC 1521 Single-family housing construction
Gene Axani

D-U-N-S 25-703-3311   (SL)
RYSEN BOBCAT SERVICES LIMITED
107-26230 Township Rd 531a, Acheson, AB, T7X 5A4

(780) 470-2085
Emp Here 40   *Sales* 11,340,960
SIC 1611 Highway and street construction
Sean Turpin

D-U-N-S 20-734-1108   (HQ)
SMS CONSTRUCTION AND MINING SYSTEMS INC
SMS RENTS
(*Suby of* SUMITOMO CORPORATION)
53113 Range Road 263a, Acheson, AB, T7X 5A5
(780) 948-2200
Emp Here 106   *Sales* 877,914,000
SIC 5082 Construction and mining machinery

D-U-N-S 20-059-4302   (HQ)
SMS EQUIPMENT INC
(*Suby of* SUMITOMO CORPORATION)
11285 274 St, Acheson, AB, T7X 6P9
(780) 454-0101
Emp Here 200   *Sales* 975,460,000
SIC 5082 Construction and mining machinery
Michael Granger
Sundeep Bhangoo
Joe Noonan

D-U-N-S 24-826-1013   (HQ)
SUPREME GROUP INC
(*Suby of* LEDER INVESTMENTS LTD)
28169 96 Ave, Acheson, AB, T7X 6J7
(780) 483-3278
Sales 438,610,800
SIC 6712 Bank holding companies
John Leder
Sally Leder

D-U-N-S 20-810-1998   (HQ)
SUPREME STEEL LP
SUPREME STEEL BRIDGE, DIV OF
(*Suby of* LEDER INVESTMENTS LTD)
28169 96 Ave, Acheson, AB, T7X 6J7
(780) 483-3278
Emp Here 260   *Sales* 158,100,150
SIC 3441 Fabricated structural Metal
John Leder
Sally Leder
Dean Arnal

D-U-N-S 20-044-1256   (HQ)
TSI INSULATION LTD
27392 Ellis Rd, Acheson, AB, T7X 6N3
(780) 484-1344
Emp Here 65   *Sales* 17,397,380
SIC 5211 Lumber and other building materials
Tom Tysiakiewicz
Roman Dyjak

D-U-N-S 25-539-1583   (SL)
VISION R.V. CORPORATION
26301a Twp Rd 531a, Acheson, AB, T7X 5A3
(780) 962-0012
Emp Here 30   *Sales* 14,942,340
SIC 5571 Motorcycle dealers
Gary Kelemen

D-U-N-S 24-716-7729   (HQ)
WESTERN STAR TRUCKS (NORTH) LTD
26229 Township Road 531a, Acheson, AB, T7X 5A4
(780) 453-3452
Emp Here 75   *Sales* 61,669,440
SIC 5511 New and used car dealers
Barry Robinson
Scott Robinson
David Robinson
Jim Sand

D-U-N-S 24-395-4559   (HQ)
WESTQUIP DIESEL SALES (ALTA) LTD
11162 261 St, Acheson, AB, T7X 6C7
(780) 960-5560
Emp Here 22   *Sales* 12,350,676
SIC 5084 Industrial machinery and equipment
Eugene W Dumont

D-U-N-S 25-679-9321   (HQ)
WESTVAC INDUSTRIAL LTD
26609 111 Ave, Acheson, AB, T7X 6E1

(780) 962-1218
Emp Here 23   *Sales* 16,625,910
SIC 5084 Industrial machinery and equipment
Gary Vermeulen
Charlotte Vermeulen

D-U-N-S 20-142-3826   (SL)
WILLIAMS SCOTSMAN OF CANADA INC
WILLSCOT
9529 266 St, Acheson, AB, T7X 6H9
(780) 638-9210
Emp Here 49   *Sales* 12,399,891
SIC 5271 Mobile home dealers
Jefferson Lavender

Acme, AB T0M

D-U-N-S 24-840-5334   (SL)
HIGHWAY 21 FEEDERS LTD
Gd, Acme, AB, T0M 0A0
(403) 546-2278
Emp Here 40   *Sales* 15,420,760
SIC 0211 Beef cattle feedlots
Ed Miller
Linda Miller

Airdrie, AB T4A

D-U-N-S 25-193-4923   (BR)
ADESA AUCTIONS CANADA CORPORATION
ADESA CALGARY
(*Suby of* KAR AUCTION SERVICES, INC.)
1621 Veterans Blvd Nw, Airdrie, AB, T4A 2G7
(403) 912-4400
Emp Here 200
SIC 5012 Automobiles and other motor vehicles
Jim Busby

D-U-N-S 24-646-3343   (SL)
AIRDRIE MOTORS (1986) LTD
AIRDRIE PONTIAC BUICK GMC
149 East Lake Cres Ne, Airdrie, AB, T4A 2H7
(403) 948-6912
Emp Here 30   *Sales* 14,942,340
SIC 5531 Auto and home supply stores
Lynden Heron

D-U-N-S 24-298-3476   (SL)
CAM CLARK FORD SALES LTD
925 Veterans Blvd Nw Bay 1, Airdrie, AB, T4A 2G6
(403) 948-6660
Emp Here 300   *Sales* 173,175,600
SIC 5511 New and used car dealers
Cameron Clark
Kevin Clark
Chris Clark
Kim Robert Clark
Irving Veno
Wendy Dickman
Anita Cob

D-U-N-S 20-012-3843   (SL)
CAPSTONE BLOWOUT RECOVERY, CAPSTONE ABANDONMENTS
32 East Lake Cir Ne, Airdrie, AB, T4A 2K1
(403) 437-8587
Emp Here 47   *Sales* 15,026,135
SIC 1389 Oil and gas field services, nec

D-U-N-S 24-518-0864   (BR)
CHAMCO INDUSTRIES LTD
(*Suby of* CHAMCO INDUSTRIES LTD)
553 Kingsview Way Se Suite 110, Airdrie, AB, T4A 0C9
(403) 945-8134
Emp Here 75
SIC 5084 Industrial machinery and equipment
Tiffany Stone

▲ Public Company   ■ Public Company Family Member   **HQ** Headquarters   **BR** Branch   **SL** Single Location

D-U-N-S 24-389-5021   (BR)
COSTCO WHOLESALE CANADA LTD
(*Suby of* COSTCO WHOLESALE CORPO-
RATION)
1003 Hamilton Blvd Ne, Airdrie, AB, T4A 0G2
(403) 945-4267
Emp Here 100
SIC 4731 Freight transportation arrangement
Robert Dennis

D-U-N-S 25-341-8677   (BR)
EATON INDUSTRIES (CANADA) COMPANY
EATON
(*Suby of* EATON CORPORATION PUBLIC
LIMITED COMPANY)
403 East Lake Blvd Ne, Airdrie, AB, T4A 2G1
(403) 948-7955
Emp Here 200
SIC 3679 Electronic components, nec
Andrew Carrothers

D-U-N-S 20-548-2347   (HQ)
FIELD OF DREAMS RV LTD
FIELD OF RV DREAMS
45 Kingsview Rd Se, Airdrie, AB, T4A 0A8
(403) 249-2123
Emp Here 1   *Sales* 25,171,200
SIC 5561 Recreational vehicle dealers
Bruce Urban

D-U-N-S 20-076-0163   (SL)
GN CORPORATIONS INC
2873 Kingsview Blvd Se, Airdrie, AB, T4A 0E1
(403) 948-6464
Emp Here 105   *Sales* 23,310,105
SIC 3533 Oil and gas field machinery
John M Plesa
Nikola Plesa

D-U-N-S 24-334-5696   (SL)
INTEGRAL ENERGY SERVICES LTD
2890 Kingsview Blvd Se Unit 101, Airdrie, AB,
T4A 0E1
(403) 912-1261
Emp Here 275   *Sales* 64,764,975
SIC 1731 Electrical work
Alan Rozak
Derek Polsfut
Roland Polsfut

D-U-N-S 25-187-7163   (BR)
LOBLAWS INC
EXTRA FOODS 9009
(*Suby of* LOBLAW COMPANIES LIMITED)
1050 Yankee Valley Blvd Se, Airdrie, AB, T4A
2E4
(403) 912-3800
Emp Here 116
SIC 5411 Grocery stores
Rob Middleditch

D-U-N-S 25-236-5358   (HQ)
MCPIKE INVESTMENTS LTD
440 East Lake Rd Ne, Airdrie, AB, T4A 2J8
(403) 912-7200
Sales 308,964,700
SIC 3533 Oil and gas field machinery
Roderick Mcpike
Wendy Mcpike

D-U-N-S 20-598-3729   (SL)
NORTH HILL MOTORS (1975) LTD
AIRDRIE CHRYSLER DODGE JEEP
139 East Lake Cres Ne, Airdrie, AB, T4A 2H7
(403) 948-2600
Emp Here 70   *Sales* 44,049,600
SIC 5511 New and used car dealers
Larry Mccook
Zia Khan
Bradley Styner
Jolayne Leger

D-U-N-S 20-310-0276   (BR)
OLD DUTCH FOODS LTD
CONDILLO FOODS, DIV OF
(*Suby of* OLD DUTCH FOODS LTD)
215 East Lake Blvd Ne, Airdrie, AB, T4A 2G1

(403) 948-3339
Emp Here 180
SIC 2096 Potato chips and similar snacks
Derek Walker

D-U-N-S 20-989-4823   (HQ)
PROPAK SYSTEMS LTD
PROPAK COMPRESSION
(*Suby of* MCPIKE INVESTMENTS LTD)
440 East Lake Rd Ne, Airdrie, AB, T4A 2J8
(403) 912-7000
Emp Here 1,000   *Sales* 308,964,700
SIC 3533 Oil and gas field machinery
Roderick A Mcpike
Andrew Mcpike

D-U-N-S 24-076-4360   (BR)
**RADIOLOGY CONSULTANTS ASSOCI-
ATED**
(*Suby of* RADIOLOGY CONSULTANTS AS-
SOCIATED)
110 Mayfair Close Se, Airdrie, AB, T4A 1T6
(403) 777-3040
Emp Here 300
SIC 8748 Business consulting, nec
Les Ree

D-U-N-S 25-504-8399   (HQ)
**TECHMATION ELECTRIC & CONTROLS
LTD**
117 Kingsview Rd Se, Airdrie, AB, T4A 0A8
(403) 243-0990
Emp Here 120   *Sales* 152,367,560
SIC 5084 Industrial machinery and equipment
Derek Polsfut
Glenn Rideout
Ronald Polsfut
Victor Witzke
Rod Mcquaig

D-U-N-S 24-311-0801   (SL)
THORLAKSON FEEDYARDS INC
NATURE'S CALL, DIV OF
Gd Stn Main, Airdrie, AB, T4A 0H4
(403) 948-5434
Emp Here 40   *Sales* 29,700,800
SIC 5191 Farm supplies
Ben Thorlakson

D-U-N-S 25-506-5369   (HQ)
TRANSCANADA TURBINES LTD
TCT
998 Hamilton Blvd Ne, Airdrie, AB, T4A 0K8
(403) 420-4200
Emp Here 94   *Sales* 34,619,040
SIC 7699 Repair services, nec
Daniel Simonelli
Eddy Stitt
Alex Pourbaix
Gary Stephen

D-U-N-S 24-673-5567   (HQ)
UNITED SAFETY LTD
104 East Lake Rd Ne, Airdrie, AB, T4A 2J8
(403) 912-3690
Emp Here 60   *Sales* 100,901,850
SIC 1389 Oil and gas field services, nec
Lee Whittaker
Daryl Helmer
Elie Daher
Randy Becker
Douglas Heeley
Yulonde Trahan
Shayne Mccallum

D-U-N-S 25-327-5846   (HQ)
WESTERN RV COUNTRY LTD
61 East Lake Ramp Ne, Airdrie, AB, T4A 2K4
(403) 912-2634
Emp Here 1   *Sales* 22,413,510
SIC 5561 Recreational vehicle dealers
Bruce Norman Urban
Cindy Mamie Urban

D-U-N-S 25-168-8644   (HQ)
WILLIAMS SCOTSMAN OF CANADA, INC
(*Suby of* WILLSCOT CORPORATION)
19 East Lake Ave, Airdrie, AB, T4A 2G9

(403) 241-5357
Emp Here 3   *Sales* 16,431,400
SIC 7519 Utility trailer rental
Alec Mcdonald
Ed Beesbrook

Airdrie, AB T4B

D-U-N-S 25-616-4070   (BR)
BETHANY CARE SOCIETY
BETHANY AIRDRIE
(*Suby of* BETHANY CARE SOCIETY)
1736 1 Ave Nw Suite 725, Airdrie, AB, T4B
2C4
(403) 948-6022
Emp Here 125
SIC 8051 Skilled nursing care facilities
Jim Moore

D-U-N-S 24-361-7169   (BR)
HOME DEPOT OF CANADA INC
HOME DEPOT
(*Suby of* THE HOME DEPOT INC)
2925 Main St Se, Airdrie, AB, T4B 3G5
(403) 945-3865
Emp Here 100
SIC 5251 Hardware stores
John Mundin

D-U-N-S 24-702-6602   (SL)
MELROSE DRUGS LTD
PHARMASAVE #338
209 Centre Ave Sw Unit 100, Airdrie, AB, T4B
3L8
(403) 948-0010
Emp Here 50   *Sales* 12,647,700
SIC 5912 Drug stores and proprietary stores

D-U-N-S 20-515-7006   (SL)
MILLER FAMILY SALES AND SERVICE LTD
CANADIAN TIRE
202 Veterans Blvd Ne Suite 300, Airdrie, AB,
T4B 3P2
(403) 948-3993
Emp Here 65   *Sales* 23,673,975
SIC 5014 Tires and tubes
Peter Miller

D-U-N-S 24-155-7743   (HQ)
**ROCKY VIEW SCHOOL DIVISION NO. 41,
THE**
2651 Chinook Winds Dr Sw, Airdrie, AB, T4B
0B4
(403) 945-4000
Emp Here 100   *Sales* 168,502,300
SIC 8211 Elementary and secondary schools
Darryl Couture

D-U-N-S 20-703-8576   (BR)
ROL-LAND FARMS MUSHROOMS INC
(*Suby of* ROL-LAND FARMS MUSHROOMS
INC)
Gd, Airdrie, AB, T4B 2A2
(403) 946-4395
Emp Here 110
SIC 0161 Vegetables and melons
Ralph Hazelwood

D-U-N-S 24-317-5317   (BR)
WAL-MART CANADA CORP
(*Suby of* WALMART INC.)
2881 Main St Se Suite 1050, Airdrie, AB, T4B
3G5
(403) 945-1295
Emp Here 200
SIC 5311 Department stores
Trent Pennock

Alberta Beach, AB T0E

D-U-N-S 24-004-7878   (SL)
ECKO MARINE LTD
ACCURATE ARCHERY

4200 47 St, Alberta Beach, AB, T0E 0A1
(780) 924-3250
Emp Here 25   *Sales* 12,451,950
SIC 5599 Automotive dealers, nec
Steven Eckert

Alder Flats, AB T0C

D-U-N-S 20-908-7410   (SL)
LAODAS-WAY HEALING LTD
Gd, Alder Flats, AB, T0C 0A0
(780) 621-0765
Emp Here 16   *Sales* 11,880,320
SIC 5199 Nondurable goods, nec

Aldersyde, AB T0L

D-U-N-S 20-952-4680   (SL)
MULLEN TRUCKING CORP
(*Suby of* MT-NU OPERATING COMPANY
INC)
80079 Maple Leaf Rd E Unit 100, Aldersyde,
AB, T0L 0A0
(403) 652-8888
Emp Here 150   *Sales* 30,855,900
SIC 4213 Trucking, except local
Murray Mullen

Alix, AB T0C

D-U-N-S 24-880-7711   (SL)
RAHR MALTING CANADA LTD
(*Suby of* RAHR MALTING CO.)
Hwy 12 E, Alix, AB, T0C 0B0
(403) 747-2777
Emp Here 40   *Sales* 13,827,600
SIC 2083 Malt
Robert Sutton
Gary Lee
Robert Michelitti

Alliance, AB T0B

D-U-N-S 24-949-8411   (SL)
HUTTERIAN BRETHREN OF SOUTH BEND
SOUTH BEND COLONY
1539 12 West Of 4th, Alliance, AB, T0B 0A0
(780) 879-2170
Emp Here 56   *Sales* 14,689,304
SIC 0119 Cash grains, nec
John R. Hofer
Samuel Mandel
Joseph G. Kleinsasser

Altario, AB T0C

D-U-N-S 24-299-2808   (SL)
330558 ALBERTA LTD
CLARK CONSTRUCTION
Gd, Altario, AB, T0C 0E0
(403) 552-2477
Emp Here 50   *Sales* 14,176,200
SIC 1611 Highway and street construction
Kevin Clark
Roxanne Clark

Anzac, AB T0P

D-U-N-S 24-348-8835   (SL)

CENTERFIRE CONTRACTING LTD
236 Stony Mountain Rd Suite 106, Anzac, AB, T0P 1J0
(780) 334-2277
Emp Here 50   *Sales* 15,985,250
SIC 1389 Oil and gas field services, nec
Michael Cheecham
Doug Snow
Levi Snow
Neil Cheecham

Ardmore, AB T0A

D-U-N-S 20-280-2141   (BR)
ROCKWELL SERVICING INC
ENSIGN ROCKWELL SERVICING
(*Suby of* ENSIGN ENERGY SERVICES INC)
440 Hwy 28, Ardmore, AB, T0A 0B0
(780) 826-6464
Emp Here 150
SIC 1389 Oil and gas field services, nec
Kevin Rudell

Ardrossan, AB T8E

D-U-N-S 20-785-8015   (BR)
ELK ISLAND PUBLIC SCHOOLS REGIONAL DIVISION NO. 14
ARDROSSAN JUNIOR SENIOR HIGH
(*Suby of* ELK ISLAND PUBLIC SCHOOLS REGIONAL DIVISION NO. 14)
53129 Range Road 222, Ardrossan, AB, T8E 2M8
(780) 922-2228
Emp Here 75
SIC 8211 Elementary and secondary schools
Dan Vanderburgh

D-U-N-S 20-346-6164   (SL)
SIGNATURE MUSHROOMS LTD
52557 Range Road 215, Ardrossan, AB, T8E 2H6
(780) 922-2535
Emp Here 45   *Sales* 15,411,015
SIC 0191 General farms, primarily crop
Terry Uppal

Ardrossan, AB T8G

D-U-N-S 24-243-0879   (HQ)
CANADA PUMP AND POWER (CPP) CORPORATION
53113 Range Road 211, Ardrossan, AB, T8G 2C5
(780) 922-1178
Emp Here 16   *Sales* 47,502,600
SIC 5084 Industrial machinery and equipment
Jeremy Leonard

Athabasca, AB T9S

D-U-N-S 20-016-0187   (HQ)
ASPEN VIEW PUBLIC SCHOOL DIVISION NO. 78
3600 48 Ave Suite 19, Athabasca, AB, T9S 1M8
(780) 675-7080
Emp Here 15   *Sales* 34,055,413
SIC 8211 Elementary and secondary schools
Mark Andrew Francis
Dennis Macneil
Amber Oko
Paul Ponich
Trevor Yeaman
Lewis Semashkewich

Elohne Chizawsky
Donna Cherniwchan
Patricia Pedersen
Mark Andrew Francis

D-U-N-S 24-001-6576   (HQ)
ATHABASCA UNIVERSITY
1 University Dr, Athabasca, AB, T9S 3A3
(780) 675-6100
Emp Here 490   *Sales* 164,985,210
SIC 8221 Colleges and universities
Barry Walker
Frits Pannekoek
Margaret Haughey
Cindy Ives
Estelle Lo
Murray Walford

D-U-N-S 24-786-8953   (HQ)
GREATER NORTH FOUNDATION
PLEASANT VALLEY LODGE
5210 47 Ave, Athabasca, AB, T9S 1K5
(780) 675-9660
Emp Here 15   *Sales* 10,160,066
SIC 6513 Apartment building operators
Lorraine Gislason
Frank Crawford
Andy Thompson
Cindy Kilborn
Jean Golonka
Derrick Kruk
Wilfred Casavant
Roger Hall
Colleen Powell

D-U-N-S 24-418-4359   (SL)
LESAGE, L.T. HOLDINGS LTD
CANADIAN TIRE
2913 48 Ave, Athabasca, AB, T9S 0A4
(780) 675-3019
Emp Here 49   *Sales* 24,405,822
SIC 5531 Auto and home supply stores
Leonard Lesage

D-U-N-S 24-786-1839   (SL)
PIPE QUEST PROJECTS LTD
Gd Stn Main, Athabasca, AB, T9S 1A2
(780) 689-9568
Emp Here 49   *Sales* 11,803,316
SIC 1623 Water, sewer, and utility lines
Jamie Morrison

Balzac, AB T4B

D-U-N-S 25-679-1609   (HQ)
TIMBER INVESTMENT HOLDINGS INC
262029 Balzac Blvd, Balzac, AB, T4B 2T3
(403) 226-8617
Emp Here 115   *Sales* 44,245,100
SIC 2439 Structural wood members, nec
Glenn German
Jaspal Bhandal

Banff, AB T1L

D-U-N-S 20-048-3175   (SL)
567945 ALBERTA LTD
HENRY'S ELECTRIC
116 Eagle Cres, Banff, AB, T1L 1A3
(403) 762-3287
Emp Here 52   *Sales* 11,327,108
SIC 1731 Electrical work
John Padgett
Phil Garber

D-U-N-S 20-720-2743   (BR)
ALBERTA HEALTH SERVICES
MINERAL SPRINGS HOSPITAL
(*Suby of* GOVERNMENT OF THE PROVINCE OF ALBERTA)
305 Lynx St, Banff, AB, T1L 1H7

(403) 762-2222
Emp Here 200
SIC 8062 General medical and surgical hospitals
Cindy Mulherin

D-U-N-S 24-319-3666   (HQ)
BANFF CARIBOU PROPERTIES LTD
BANFF LODGING COMPANY
229 Bear St Suite 300, Banff, AB, T1L 1H8
(403) 762-2642
Sales 47,834,000
SIC 7011 Hotels and motels
Gordon Lozeman

D-U-N-S 25-389-4109   (HQ)
BREWSTER INC
PACKAGE TOURS, A DIV OF
(*Suby of* VIAD CORP)
100 Gopher St, Banff, AB, T1L 1J3
(403) 762-6700
Emp Here 175   *Sales* 88,973,550
SIC 4725 Tour operators
David G Morrison
Terry Holt
James Fraser
Andrew Whittick

D-U-N-S 25-994-8065   (BR)
BREWSTER INC
MOUNT ROYAL HOTEL
(*Suby of* VIAD CORP)
Gd Stn Main, Banff, AB, T1L 1H1
(403) 762-3331
Emp Here 75
SIC 7011 Hotels and motels
William Rheaume

D-U-N-S 24-440-1188   (HQ)
CANADIAN CO CO TOURS, INC
220 Bear St Suite 306, Banff, AB, T1L 1A2
(403) 762-5600
Emp Here 48   *Sales* 53,351,360
SIC 4725 Tour operators
Shintaro Wakatsuki

D-U-N-S 20-440-9049   (HQ)
CANADIAN MOUNTAIN HOLIDAYS LIMITED PARTNERSHIP
CMH HELI-SKIING & HIKING
(*Suby of* HAWK HOLDING COMPANY, LLC)
217 Bear St, Banff, AB, T1L 1J6
(403) 762-7100
Emp Here 45   *Sales* 43,050,600
SIC 7011 Hotels and motels
Walter Bruns
Rob Rohn

D-U-N-S 24-674-8230   (BR)
FAIRMONT HOTELS & RESORTS INC
FAIRMONT BANFF SPRINGS, THE
(*Suby of* ACCOR)
405 Spray Ave, Banff, AB, T1L 1J4
(403) 762-6860
Emp Here 800
SIC 7011 Hotels and motels
Francisco Gomez

D-U-N-S 24-016-5860   (SL)
FUJI STARLIGHT EXPRESS CO., LTD
BANFF PARK LODGE
(*Suby of* FUJI PROJECT, K.K.)
222 Lynx St, Banff, AB, T1L 1K5
(403) 762-4433
Emp Here 155   *Sales* 14,828,540
SIC 7011 Hotels and motels
Frank Denouden
Ernie Kitzul
Yoichi Horiguchi
Roy Kusano
Douglas Foster
Steven Steven
Christian Mckay

D-U-N-S 24-417-5204   (HQ)
NATURE'S COIN GROUP LTD
TASAR'S
225a Bear St, Banff, AB, T1L 1B4

(403) 762-3018
Emp Here 20   *Sales* 13,438,040
SIC 5944 Jewelry stores
Ashok Arora
Saroj Arora
Prakash Arora

Barons, AB T0L

D-U-N-S 24-441-8828   (SL)
KEHO LAKE COLONY
Gd, Barons, AB, T0L 0G0
(403) 757-2330
Emp Here 100   *Sales* 10,928,900
SIC 0751 Livestock services, except veterinary
Johnny Hofer
Sam A Wurz
Ben Wurz
Daniel Wurz
Andrew Hofer
Samuel E Wurz

D-U-N-S 20-827-7152   (SL)
LITTLE BOW GAS CO-OP LTD
108 Main St, Barons, AB, T0L 0G0
(403) 757-3888
Emp Here 5   *Sales* 15,529,285
SIC 4924 Natural gas distribution
Alan Fraser
Henry Konynenbelt
Sheldon Albrecht
Arnold Odegard
Les Grasman

Barrhead, AB T7N

D-U-N-S 24-346-0107   (SL)
BARRCANA HOMES INC
59504 Range Rd 32, Barrhead, AB, T7N 1A4
(780) 305-0505
Emp Here 206   *Sales* 39,628,220
SIC 2452 Prefabricated wood buildings
John Bennett
Richard B. Hajduk
Albert Vanleeuwen
Randy Fries

D-U-N-S 24-328-2829   (SL)
BLUE HERON SUPPORT SERVICES ASSOCIATION
Gd Stn Main, Barrhead, AB, T7N 1B8
(780) 674-4944
Emp Here 170   *Sales* 10,927,940
SIC 8361 Residential care
Ralph Helder

D-U-N-S 20-949-8117   (BR)
FRESON MARKET LTD
MEDICINE SHOPPE PHARMACY
(*Suby of* ALTAMART INVESTMENTS (1993) LTD)
5020 49 Ave, Barrhead, AB, T7N 1G4
(780) 674-3784
Emp Here 80
SIC 5912 Drug stores and proprietary stores
Aron Coupts

D-U-N-S 25-269-5945   (BR)
PEMBINA HILLS REGIONAL DIVISION 7
BARRHEAD COMPOSITE HIGH SCHOOL
(*Suby of* PEMBINA HILLS REGIONAL DIVISION 7)
5307 53 Ave, Barrhead, AB, T7N 1P2
(780) 674-8521
Emp Here 85
SIC 8211 Elementary and secondary schools
Steven Kaplan

D-U-N-S 25-327-5952   (HQ)
PEMBINA HILLS REGIONAL DIVISION 7
5310 49 St, Barrhead, AB, T7N 1P3

---

(780) 674-8500
Emp Here 100   *Sales* 69,383,300
SIC 8211 Elementary and secondary schools
Jennifer Tuininga
Tracy Meunier

D-U-N-S 24-396-5279   (BR)
POLLARD BANKNOTE INCOME FUND
(Suby of POLLARD BANKNOTE INCOME
FUND)
6203 46 St, Barrhead, AB, T7N 1A1
(780) 674-4750
Emp Here 80
SIC 7999 Amusement and recreation, nec
Shelley Carlson

D-U-N-S 25-386-0928   (BR)
POLLARD EQUITIES LIMITED
POLLARD BANKNOTE
(Suby of POLLARD EQUITIES LIMITED)
Gd Stn Main, Barrhead, AB, T7N 1B8
(780) 674-4750
Emp Here 77
SIC 2759 Commercial printing, nec
Shelley Carlson

D-U-N-S 24-026-7096   (SL)
RICHARDSON MILLING LIMITED
(Suby of RICHARDSON, JAMES & SONS,
LIMITED)
Po Box 4615 Stn Main, Barrhead, AB, T7N
1A5
(780) 674-4669
Emp Here 30   *Sales* 10,370,700
SIC 2043 Cereal breakfast foods
Anthony Hiscock

D-U-N-S 20-073-4580   (SL)
STEPHANI MOTORS LTD
(Suby of 305357 ALBERTA LTD)
4811 53 St, Barrhead, AB, T7N 1G2
(780) 674-2211
Emp Here 30   *Sales* 14,942,340
SIC 5511 New and used car dealers
Ernest Stephani
Shawn Stephani

Bashaw, AB T0B

D-U-N-S 24-319-0043   (SL)
SUMMIT COMPLETIONS LTD
4912 50th St, Bashaw, AB, T0B 0H0

Emp Here 45   *Sales* 14,386,725
SIC 1389 Oil and gas field services, nec
Snadra Selbee

Bassano, AB T0J

D-U-N-S 20-724-6179   (SL)
ESSO SERVICE STATION
EMMI'S ESSO
The Transcanada Hwy 1 Service Rd, Bassano,
AB, T0J 0B0
(403) 641-3916
Emp Here 22   *Sales* 10,957,716
SIC 5541 Gasoline service stations
Larry Schaffer
Dorothy Schaffer

D-U-N-S 24-961-5014   (HQ)
FAIRVILLE FARMING CO LTD
FAIRVILLE COLONY
Gd, Bassano, AB, T0J 0B0
(403) 641-2404
Sales 11,831,750
SIC 0191 General farms, primarily crop
Joseph Wipf
Andrew P Wipf
George Waldner
Jacob Waldner
Jake Waldner

Paul J Wipf
Peter J Waldner
Peter P Waldner

Beaumont, AB T4X

D-U-N-S 20-860-6926   (SL)
1162095 ALBERTA LTD
BEAUMONT HUSKY
5204 50 St, Beaumont, AB, T4X 1E5
(780) 929-6466
Emp Here 22   *Sales* 10,957,716
SIC 5541 Gasoline service stations
Steve Kadetz

D-U-N-S 20-374-7501   (SL)
BEAR SCARE LTD
5905 44 Ave, Beaumont, AB, T4X 0J1
(780) 717-0139
Emp Here 50   *Sales* 10,619,850
SIC 8748 Business consulting, nec
Daniel Legrandeur
Laurel Legrandeur

D-U-N-S 20-709-7861   (BR)
BLACK GOLD REGIONAL DIVISION #18
*ECOLE SECONDAIRE BEAUMONT HIGH
SCHOOL*
(Suby of BLACK GOLD REGIONAL DIVISION
#18)
5417 43 Ave, Beaumont, AB, T4X 1K1
(780) 929-6282
Emp Here 80
SIC 8211 Elementary and secondary schools
John Mair

D-U-N-S 24-025-5526   (SL)
LIQUOR SOURCE CORPORATION
*LIQUOR SOURCE RETAIL LIQUOR OUT-
LETS*
4916 50 Ave, Beaumont, AB, T4X 1J9
(780) 851-7336
Emp Here 46   *Sales* 10,943,446
SIC 8742 Management consulting services
Richard Langkamp
Adrien Perrault

D-U-N-S 20-138-8761   (BR)
SOBEYS CAPITAL INCORPORATED
BEAUMONT SOBEYS
(Suby of EMPIRE COMPANY LIMITED)
5700 50 St, Beaumont, AB, T4X 1M8
(780) 929-2749
Emp Here 150
SIC 5411 Grocery stores
Brett Schilling

Beaverlodge, AB T0H

D-U-N-S 20-073-5728   (HQ)
FOSTER'S SEED AND FEED LTD
1120 8th Ave W, Beaverlodge, AB, T0H 0C0
(780) 354-2107
Emp Here 22   *Sales* 16,335,440
SIC 5191 Farm supplies
Norman Foster

D-U-N-S 24-346-5437   (BR)
**GOVERNMENT OF THE PROVINCE OF AL-
BERTA**
BEAVERLODGE MUNICIPAL HOSPITAL
(Suby of GOVERNMENT OF THE
PROVINCE OF ALBERTA)
Gd, Beaverlodge, AB, T0H 0C0
(780) 354-2136
Emp Here 150
SIC 8062 General medical and surgical hospi-
tals
Janet Wallace

D-U-N-S 24-808-4535   (SL)

NEXT GENERATION REFORESTATION LTD
Gd, Beaverlodge, AB, T0H 0C0
(780) 532-2220
Emp Here 200   *Sales* 27,351,800
SIC 0851 Forestry services
Gordon Sheepwash
Catherine Newhook

D-U-N-S 20-809-6909   (SL)
TARTAN SALES (1973) LTD
TARTAN FORD
202 10 St, Beaverlodge, AB, T0H 0C0

Emp Here 22   *Sales* 10,957,716
SIC 5511 New and used car dealers
Allen E Gaudin
A Esdale Gaudin
Merrilee Gaudin

D-U-N-S 24-982-6603   (SL)
WALKER'S GROCERY LTD
IGA
(Suby of 424488 ALBERTA LTD)
1040 First Ave, Beaverlodge, AB, T0H 0C0
(780) 354-2092
Emp Here 41   *Sales* 11,240,232
SIC 5411 Grocery stores
Jerry Walker
Ken Walker

Beiseker, AB T0M

D-U-N-S 24-272-6073   (SL)
**HUTTERIAN BRETHRAN CHURCH OF
BEISEKER**
BEISEKER COLONY
Gd, Beiseker, AB, T0M 0G0
(403) 947-2181
Emp Here 94   *Sales* 10,126,338
SIC 8661 Religious organizations
Samuel Stahl

D-U-N-S 20-799-3440   (SL)
KOCA AB SERVICES LTD
HI-WAY SALES AND SERVICE
610 Hwy 9, Beiseker, AB, T0M 0G0
(403) 947-0006
Emp Here 30   *Sales* 14,942,340
SIC 5541 Gasoline service stations
Richard Lim

D-U-N-S 24-494-7917   (SL)
SAND HILLS COLONY
*HUTTERIAN BRETHREN CHURCH OF
SANDHILL*
Gd, Beiseker, AB, T0M 0G0
(403) 947-2042
Emp Here 61   *Sales* 17,902,097
SIC 5499 Miscellaneous food stores
Andrew Wurz
Mike C Wurz
Samuel Wurz

Bittern Lake, AB T0C

D-U-N-S 24-004-8793   (SL)
ACE MANUFACTURING METALS LTD
(Suby of ACE-2 HOLDINGS LTD)
Gd, Bittern Lake, AB, T0C 0L0
(780) 352-7145
Emp Here 85   *Sales* 16,187,570
SIC 3644 Noncurrent-carrying wiring devices
John Harold Parfett
Corinne Parfett

Black Diamond, AB T0L

D-U-N-S 24-732-2381   (SL)

OILFIELDS GENERAL HOSPITAL
717 Government Rd, Black Diamond, AB, T0L
0H0
(403) 933-2222
Emp Here 130   *Sales* 14,440,400
SIC 8062 General medical and surgical hospitals
Dave Shorten

Blackfalds, AB T0C

D-U-N-S 25-115-2716   (SL)
CONTROL TECHNOLOGY INC
4305 South St, Blackfalds, AB, T0C 0B0
(403) 885-2677
Emp Here 42   *Sales* 13,427,610
SIC 1389 Oil and gas field services, nec
Sylvia Eastcott
Linda Eastcott
James Evans

Blackfalds, AB T0M

D-U-N-S 20-175-9037   (SL)
CENTRAL ALBERTA GREENHOUSES LTD
Gd, Blackfalds, AB, T0M 0J0
(403) 885-4606
Emp Here 110   *Sales* 64,807,490
SIC 5193 Flowers and florists supplies
Harold Good
Gladys Good
Kevin Wesenberg

D-U-N-S 24-673-5179   (SL)
CENTRAL CITY ASPHALT LTD
(Suby of SETTERS, J.T. & SONS CON-
STRUCTION LTD)
39327 Range Rd, Blackfalds, AB, T0M 0J0
(403) 346-5050
Emp Here 60   *Sales* 15,146,520
SIC 1611 Highway and street construction
Wayne Mclachlan
Graham Mclachlan

D-U-N-S 20-116-2604   (HQ)
COAST TO COAST HELICOPTERS INC
27312 Township Rd 394 Unit 237, Blackfalds,
AB, T0M 0J0
(403) 885-5220
Sales 15,224,180
SIC 4522 Air transportation, nonscheduled
Frederic Allard
Benoit Allard
Roxanne Allard

D-U-N-S 24-387-5403   (SL)
FORCE COPPS PILING INC
(Suby of SITE ENERGY SERVICES LTD)
27312 - 213 Twp 394, Blackfalds, AB, T0M 0J0
(403) 341-0030
Emp Here 130   *Sales* 42,654,950
SIC 1629 Heavy construction, nec
Dallas T. Lenius
Dean Hall
John S. Runge

D-U-N-S 20-770-3401   (HQ)
LEE SPECIALTIES INC
(Suby of QUINN'S PRODUCTION SERVICES
INC)
27312-68 Twp Rd 394, Blackfalds, AB, T0M
0J0
(403) 346-4487
Sales 15,540,070
SIC 3533 Oil and gas field machinery
Douglas Quinn
Chris Oddy
Kyle Baranyk
Dale Kaufmann
Cliff Wahlstrom

▲ Public Company   ■ Public Company Family Member   **HQ** Headquarters   **BR** Branch   **SL** Single Location

D-U-N-S 20-117-9921   (HQ)
MUSTANG HELICOPTERS INC
(*Suby of* COAST TO COAST HELICOPTERS INC)
237-27312 Township Rd 394, Blackfalds, AB, T0M 0J0
(403) 885-5220
Sales 32,037,360
SIC 4512 Air transportation, scheduled
Frederic Allard
Francis Maltais
Pierre Marcoux

D-U-N-S 25-507-4072   (SL)
PRO-LINE MANUFACTURING LTD
27323 Township Rd 394 Lot 48, Blackfalds, AB, T0M 0J0
(403) 885-2527
Emp Here 31   *Sales* 14,725,806
SIC 5084 Industrial machinery and equipment
Sid Doornbos
Karen Doorncos

D-U-N-S 20-635-9655   (HQ)
QUINN CONTRACTING LTD
27123 1 Hwy, Blackfalds, AB, T0M 0J0
(403) 885-4788
Emp Here 50   *Sales* 1,047,588,000
SIC 1541 Industrial buildings and warehouses
Michael Kulchisky
Dick Dornstauder

D-U-N-S 24-862-9797   (BR)
TECHNIPFMC PLC
(*Suby of* TECHNIPFMC PLC)
253 Township Rd 394 Suite 27312, Blackfalds, AB, T0M 0J0
(780) 926-2108
Emp Here 210
SIC 1389 Oil and gas field services, nec
Adam Karras

Blairmore, AB T0K

D-U-N-S 24-346-1910   (BR)
ALBERTA HEALTH SERVICES
CROWSNEST PASS HEALTH CENTRE
(*Suby of* GOVERNMENT OF THE PROVINCE OF ALBERTA)
2001 107 St, Blairmore, AB, T0K 0E0
(403) 562-5011
Emp Here 160
SIC 8062 General medical and surgical hospitals
Joan Koinberg

Blue Ridge, AB T0E

D-U-N-S 25-533-7180   (BR)
WEST FRASER MILLS LTD
RANGER BOARD
(*Suby of* WEST FRASER TIMBER CO. LTD)
Gd, Blue Ridge, AB, T0E 0B0
(780) 648-6333
Emp Here 120
SIC 2421 Sawmills and planing mills, general
Lynn Marr

Bonnyville, AB T9N

D-U-N-S 20-117-6174   (HQ)
294557 ALBERTA LTD
Gd Stn Main, Bonnyville, AB, T9N 2J6
(780) 826-3278
Sales 62,928,000
SIC 5511 New and used car dealers
Greg Ducharme

D-U-N-S 24-386-9877   (HQ)
A.J.M. MECHANICAL SERVICES LTD
5610 54 Ave, Bonnyville, AB, T9N 2N3
(780) 826-4412
Emp Here 1   *Sales* 24,054,800
SIC 6712 Bank holding companies
Allan Olszowka

D-U-N-S 24-585-6091   (HQ)
B.& R. ECKEL'S TRANSPORT LTD
5514b 50 Ave, Bonnyville, AB, T9N 2K8
(780) 826-3889
Emp Here 100   *Sales* 50,595,220
SIC 1389 Oil and gas field services, nec
Victor Ringuette
Greta Ringuette
Roxanne Ringuette
Lorne Ringuette

D-U-N-S 25-387-4994   (SL)
B.F.L. ENERGY SERVICES LTD
(*Suby of* A.J.M. MECHANICAL SERVICES LTD)
5610 54 Ave, Bonnyville, AB, T9N 2N3

Emp Here 88
SIC 3441 Fabricated structural Metal
Allan Olszowka

D-U-N-S 24-701-8682   (SL)
BONNYVILLE DODGE LTD
5605 50 Ave, Bonnyville, AB, T9N 2L1
(780) 826-2999
Emp Here 32   *Sales* 15,938,496
SIC 5511 New and used car dealers
Cory Welsh
Marlene Plaquin

D-U-N-S 20-919-4864   (SL)
BONNYVILLE REGIONAL FIRE AUTHORITY
4407 50 Ave, Bonnyville, AB, T9N 2H3
(780) 826-4755
Emp Here 35   *Sales* 15,722,665
SIC 7389 Business services, nec
Brian Macevoy

D-U-N-S 20-437-3989   (SL)
BONNYVILLE WELDING LTD
Pt Of Ne 14-616 W 4th, Bonnyville, AB, T9N 2J3
(780) 826-3847
Emp Here 125   *Sales* 31,555,250
SIC 1623 Water, sewer, and utility lines
Mike Dechaine

D-U-N-S 25-195-3600   (BR)
CANADIAN NATURAL RESOURCES LIMITED
(*Suby of* CANADIAN NATURAL RESOURCES LIMITED)
Gd Stn Main, Bonnyville, AB, T9N 2J6
(780) 826-8110
Emp Here 293
SIC 1311 Crude petroleum and natural gas
Terry Tillotson

D-U-N-S 20-048-3142   (HQ)
COUGAR FUELS LTD
5602 54 Ave, Bonnyville, AB, T9N 2N3
(780) 826-3043
Emp Here 20   *Sales* 18,760,200
SIC 5983 Fuel oil dealers
Gerald Martin
Vernon Martin

D-U-N-S 20-969-5626   (HQ)
DOVE CENTRE
DOVE CENTRE SOCIETY
6201 52 Ave, Bonnyville, AB, T9N 2L7
(780) 826-2552
Emp Here 24   *Sales* 13,476,570
SIC 7389 Business services, nec
Roger Ouellette

D-U-N-S 20-073-8540   (HQ)
DUCHARME MOTORS LTD
(*Suby of* 294557 ALBERTA LTD)

5714 50 Ave, Bonnyville, AB, T9N 2K8
(780) 826-3278
Sales 62,928,000
SIC 5511 New and used car dealers
Greg Ducharme

D-U-N-S 20-526-0396   (BR)
ENCANA CORPORATION
(*Suby of* ENCANA CORPORATION)
Gd Stn Main, Bonnyville, AB, T9N 2J6

Emp Here 106
SIC 1381 Drilling oil and gas wells
Don Rae

D-U-N-S 20-321-9993   (BR)
ENTREC CORPORATION
(*Suby of* ENTREC CORPORATION)
6708 50 Ave, Bonnyville, AB, T9N 0B7
(780) 826-4565
Emp Here 150
SIC 4213 Trucking, except local
Maurice Kisslel

D-U-N-S 20-322-0009   (BR)
ENTREC CORPORATION
(*Suby of* ENTREC CORPORATION)
4902 66 St, Bonnyville, AB, T9N 2R5
(780) 826-4565
Emp Here 100
SIC 4213 Trucking, except local
John Stevens

D-U-N-S 24-987-4673   (BR)
HSE INTEGRATED LTD
HSE FIRE SERVICES
(*Suby of* DXP ENTERPRISES, INC.)
5503 50 Ave, Bonnyville, AB, T9N 2K9
(780) 826-5300
Emp Here 100
SIC 8748 Business consulting, nec
Chris Calcon

D-U-N-S 20-810-4273   (SL)
JELSCHEN FOODS LTD
SOBEY'S
4501 50 Ave, Bonnyville, AB, T9N 2N5
(780) 826-2048
Emp Here 105   *Sales* 30,815,085
SIC 5411 Grocery stores
Monica Jelschen
Fred Jelschen

D-U-N-S 24-584-6084   (SL)
JMB CRUSHING SYSTEMS ULC
QUANTUM WINCH
660 Range Rd 455 1 Mile N And 1 Mile E, Bonnyville, AB, T9N 2H4
(780) 826-1774
Emp Here 80   *Sales* 16,456,480
SIC 4212 Local trucking, without storage
Jeffrey Buck
Andy Baldridge
Erik Tolzman
Blake Araki
Andrew Trevoy
Andy Savin

D-U-N-S 25-011-7041   (HQ)
LAKELAND ROMAN CATHOLIC SEPARATE SCHOOL DISTRICT NO. 150
4810 41 St, Bonnyville, AB, T9N 2R2
(780) 826-3764
Emp Here 100   *Sales* 24,779,750
SIC 8211 Elementary and secondary schools
Joe Arruda

D-U-N-S 25-011-7108   (HQ)
NORTHERN LIGHTS SCHOOL DIVISION NO. 69
6005 50 Ave, Bonnyville, AB, T9N 2L4
(780) 826-3145
Emp Here 20   *Sales* 69,383,300
SIC 8211 Elementary and secondary schools
Rick Tusson
Paula Elock
Arlene Hrynyk

D-U-N-S 24-395-6588   (SL)
REDA ENTERPRISES LTD
Gd Stn Main, Bonnyville, AB, T9N 2J6
(780) 826-2737
Emp Here 25   *Sales* 11,179,350
SIC 5032 Brick, stone, and related material
Edward Marchildon
Danielle Marchildon

D-U-N-S 25-692-7724   (SL)
SILVER CONCRETE LTD
4901 50 Ave, Bonnyville, AB, T9N 2J2
(780) 826-5797
Emp Here 75   *Sales* 18,463,950
SIC 1799 Special trade contractors, nec
Larry Palsat

D-U-N-S 24-365-4584   (SL)
SURE-FLOW OILFIELD SERVICES INC
50 Ave Bay Suite 5506, Bonnyville, AB, T9N 2K8
(780) 826-6864
Emp Here 250   *Sales* 168,169,750
SIC 1389 Oil and gas field services, nec
Stephen Jessome

D-U-N-S 24-773-0422   (BR)
TARPON ENERGY SERVICES LTD
TARPON ENERGY SERVICES
(*Suby of* PTW ENERGY SERVICES LTD)
5001 55 Ave, Bonnyville, AB, T9N 0A7
(780) 826-7570
Emp Here 80
SIC 1389 Oil and gas field services, nec
Braden Stolz

D-U-N-S 24-067-5652   (SL)
TERCIER MOTORS LTD
6413 50 Ave, Bonnyville, AB, T9N 2L9
(780) 826-3301
Emp Here 31   *Sales* 15,440,418
SIC 5511 New and used car dealers
Edward Tercier
Lorraine Tercier

D-U-N-S 25-314-6666   (BR)
WEATHERFORD CANADA LTD
(*Suby of* WEATHERFORD INTERNATIONAL PUBLIC LIMITED COMPANY)
4816 56 Ave, Bonnyville, AB, T9N 2N8
(780) 826-7878
Emp Here 100
SIC 3533 Oil and gas field machinery
Wendy Wilson

Bow Island, AB T0K

D-U-N-S 20-018-7623   (SL)
CONESTOGA PIPER AND SUPPLY CANADA CORP
1010 1st Ave E, Bow Island, AB, T0K 0G0
(403) 545-2935
Emp Here 49   *Sales* 15,665,545
SIC 1389 Oil and gas field services, nec
Louis Russo

D-U-N-S 25-621-4172   (SL)
SHAMROCK HUTTERIAN BRETHREN
SHAMROCK COLONY
Gd, Bow Island, AB, T0K 0G0
(403) 545-6190
Emp Here 80   *Sales* 14,446,000
SIC 8661 Religious organizations
Paul Mandel

Bowden, AB T0M

D-U-N-S 20-073-8979   (SL)
ALBERTA NURSERIES & SEEDS LTD
Gd, Bowden, AB, T0M 0K0

Emp Here 30   *Sales* 22,275,600

SIC 5191 Farm supplies
Cody James Berggren
Chris Edward Berggren
Edward C. Berggren

Boyle, AB T0A

D-U-N-S 24-809-6802   (HQ)
ALBERTA-PACIFIC FOREST INDUSTRIES INC
AL-PAC
(*Suby of* HOKUETSU CORPORATION)
P.O. Box 8000, Boyle, AB, T0A 0M0
(780) 525-8000
Emp Here 400   *Sales* 318,047,350
SIC 2611 Pulp mills
Osamu Terao
Dale Bencharsky

D-U-N-S 20-822-9240   (SL)
TRI-GEN CONSTRUCTION LTD
Gd, Boyle, AB, T0A 0M0
(780) 689-3831
Emp Here 40   *Sales* 12,754,760
SIC 1521 Single-family housing construction
Allen Szmyrko

Brant, AB T0L

D-U-N-S 24-042-5850   (SL)
HUTTERIAN BRETHREN OF BRANT, THE
BRANT COLONY
Gd, Brant, AB, T0L 0L0
(403) 684-3649
Emp Here 49   *Sales* 10,492,360
SIC 0191 General farms, primarily crop
Andrew J Gross
John D Entz
Tom J Mandel
David D Entz
Jonathan J Wurz
John J Wurz

Brooks, AB T0J

D-U-N-S 20-827-8226   (SL)
EASTERN IRRIGATION DISTRICT
550 Industrial Rd W, Brooks, AB, T0J 2A0
(403) 362-1400
Emp Here 73   *Sales* 41,251,935
SIC 4971 Irrigation systems
Ivan Friesen
Robert Chrumka
Allen Nielsen
Carl Chomistek
Neil Johnson
James Culligan
Floyd George
Ross Owen

Brooks, AB T1R

D-U-N-S 24-782-2385   (SL)
ACHIEVING EXCELLENCE
120 3 St W, Brooks, AB, T1R 0S3
(403) 362-6661
Emp Here 49   *Sales* 11,698,750
SIC 8611 Business associations
Patricia Whyte

D-U-N-S 20-016-4841   (HQ)
AGCOM PETROLEUM SALES LTD
600 Industrial Rd, Brooks, AB, T1R 1B6
(403) 362-5700
Emp Here 9   *Sales* 37,716,030

SIC 5171 Petroleum bulk stations and terminals
Harold Exner

D-U-N-S 25-135-7463   (BR)
ALBERTA HEALTH SERVICES
BROOKS HEALTH CENTRE
(*Suby of* GOVERNMENT OF THE PROVINCE OF ALBERTA)
440 3 St E Suite 300, Brooks, AB, T1R 0X8
(403) 501-3232
Emp Here 300
SIC 8062 General medical and surgical hospitals
Sandy Halldorson

D-U-N-S 20-910-1976   (SL)
ARC LINE CONSTRUCTION LTD
Gd Stn Main, Brooks, AB, T1R 1E4
(403) 362-4315
Emp Here 45   *Sales* 10,839,780
SIC 1623 Water, sewer, and utility lines
Joe Bandura

D-U-N-S 24-157-7733   (SL)
BROOKS ASPHALT AND AGGREGATE LTD
(*Suby of* SMITH GROUP HOLDINGS LTD)
Po Box 686 Stn Main, Brooks, AB, T1R 1B6
(403) 362-5597
Emp Here 65   *Sales* 16,408,730
SIC 1611 Highway and street construction
Byron Smith

D-U-N-S 20-743-9613   (HQ)
BROOKS INDUSTRIAL METALS LTD
221 7th St E, Brooks, AB, T1R 1B3
(403) 362-3544
Sales 10,506,104
SIC 5999 Miscellaneous retail stores, nec
John Duenk

D-U-N-S 20-689-2338   (HQ)
CASCADE PROCESS CONTROLS LTD
420 Aquaduct Dr, Brooks, AB, T1R 1C8
(403) 362-4722
Sales 15,248,030
SIC 1731 Electrical work
Kelly Maxwell

D-U-N-S 25-207-1758   (HQ)
CHINOOK CREDIT UNION LTD
99 2 St W, Brooks, AB, T1R 1B9
(403) 362-4233
Emp Here 61   *Sales* 18,788,110
SIC 6062 State credit unions
Tom Mossing
Maurice Landry
Doug Erlandson
Herb Tanigami
Tait White

D-U-N-S 25-971-8674   (SL)
DIABETES ASSOCIATION (BROOKS & DISTRICT)
215 3 St W, Brooks, AB, T1R 0S3

Emp Here 36   *Sales* 14,306,904
SIC 8699 Membership organizations, nec
Arlene Currie

D-U-N-S 20-829-6632   (BR)
ENCANA CORPORATION
(*Suby of* ENCANA CORPORATION)
2249 College Dr E, Brooks, AB, T1R 1G5
(403) 793-4400
Emp Here 180
SIC 1311 Crude petroleum and natural gas
Brenda Shepard

D-U-N-S 25-219-9716   (HQ)
EXCALIBUR DRILLING LTD
490 Canal St, Brooks, AB, T1R 1C8
(403) 793-2092
Emp Here 40   *Sales* 14,386,725
SIC 1381 Drilling oil and gas wells
Denis Hemsing
Wayne Sinclair

D-U-N-S 24-354-4264   (BR)
FLINT FLUID HAUL SERVICES LTD
(*Suby of* AECOM)
10 Industrial Rd, Brooks, AB, T1R 1B5
(403) 793-8384
Emp Here 80
SIC 4212 Local trucking, without storage
Larry Nowaczyk

D-U-N-S 24-440-7110   (BR)
FRESON MARKET LTD
IGA
(*Suby of* ALTAMART INVESTMENTS (1993) LTD)
330 Fairview Ave W, Brooks, AB, T1R 1K7

Emp Here 120
SIC 5411 Grocery stores
Vince Wlad

D-U-N-S 25-011-7140   (HQ)
GRASSLANDS REGIONAL DIVISION 6
GRASSLANDS PUBLIC SCHOOLS
745 2 Ave E Suite 1, Brooks, AB, T1R 1L2
(403) 793-6700
Emp Here 35   *Sales* 49,559,500
SIC 8211 Elementary and secondary schools
Lee Ann Woods
Karen Bartsch

D-U-N-S 24-675-1481   (SL)
HARWOOD FORD SALES LTD
1303 Sutherland Dr E, Brooks, AB, T1R 1C8
(403) 362-6900
Emp Here 30   *Sales* 14,942,340
SIC 5511 New and used car dealers
Gregory (Greg) Harty
David Woodcock

D-U-N-S 20-002-8889   (BR)
JBS CANADA INC
LAKESIDE PACKERS
(*Suby of* TYSON FOODS, INC.)
Gd Stn Main, Brooks, AB, T1R 1E4
(403) 362-3457
Emp Here 2,400
SIC 2011 Meat packing plants
Jack Wols

D-U-N-S 25-135-7703   (SL)
LEAGUE PROJECTS LTD
311 9th St E Bay 3, Brooks, AB, T1R 1C8
(403) 793-2648
Emp Here 130   *Sales* 87,448,270
SIC 1389 Oil and gas field services, nec
Duane Kuninchak
Blaine Brigley
Kelly Shaw
Brent Sieben
Kent Stogre
Kyle Jahraus

D-U-N-S 24-393-7021   (HQ)
LOGAN INDUSTRIES LTD
SHELL-RYN MACHINING, DIV OF
6 Boswell Cres, Brooks, AB, T1R 8B8
(403) 362-3736
Sales 87,448,270
SIC 1389 Oil and gas field services, nec
Clint Mason
Blake Mulvey
Tim Hadland
Diane Declercq
Dan Endersby
Lourens Geldenhuys

D-U-N-S 25-963-7981   (BR)
LONKAR SERVICES LTD
LONKAR SERVICES
Boswell Cr Suite 5, Brooks, AB, T1R 1C2
(403) 362-5300
Emp Here 100
SIC 1389 Oil and gas field services, nec
Carl Young

D-U-N-S 24-014-5946   (SL)
MARTIN CHRYSLER LTD

879 3 St W, Brooks, AB, T1R 1L5
(403) 362-3354
Emp Here 35   *Sales* 17,432,730
SIC 5511 New and used car dealers
James Lauber
Randy Lauber

D-U-N-S 20-200-0688   (BR)
NABORS DRILLING CANADA LIMITED
NABORS PRODUCTION SERVICES, DIV OF
(*Suby of* NABORS DRILLING CANADA LIMITED)
Gd Stn Main, Brooks, AB, T1R 1E4

Emp Here 112
SIC 1389 Oil and gas field services, nec
Pat Childs

D-U-N-S 20-646-3648   (BR)
SCHLUMBERGER CANADA LIMITED
419 Aquaduct Dr, Brooks, AB, T1R 1C5
(403) 362-3437
Emp Here 100
SIC 1389 Oil and gas field services, nec
Sean Gouch

D-U-N-S 24-767-3254   (HQ)
SMITH GROUP HOLDINGS LTD
143040 Twp Rd 191, Brooks, AB, T1R 1B6
(403) 362-4071
Emp Here 20   *Sales* 73,101,800
SIC 6712 Bank holding companies
Richard Smith
Byron Smith
Elwood Smith
Leighton Smith

D-U-N-S 25-271-0629   (BR)
SOBEYS WEST INC
SAFEWAY
(*Suby of* EMPIRE COMPANY LIMITED)
550 Cassils Rd W Suite 100, Brooks, AB, T1R 0W3
(403) 362-6851
Emp Here 85
SIC 5411 Grocery stores
Randy Elkin

D-U-N-S 20-703-0466   (BR)
TECHNIPFMC PLC
(*Suby of* TECHNIPFMC PLC)
380 Well St, Brooks, AB, T1R 1C2
(403) 363-0028
Emp Here 100
SIC 1381 Drilling oil and gas wells
David Hemsing

D-U-N-S 20-916-2317   (BR)
WAL-MART CANADA CORP
WALMART
(*Suby of* WALMART INC.)
917 3 St W Suite 3658, Brooks, AB, T1R 1L5
(403) 793-2111
Emp Here 100
SIC 5199 Nondurable goods, nec
Kent Bond

D-U-N-S 24-372-6457   (HQ)
WAV INSPECTION LTD
710 1 Ave E, Brooks, AB, T1R 1E4
(403) 362-2008
Sales 11,974,230
SIC 7389 Business services, nec
Wayde Maxwell
Brian Purves

Bruderheim, AB T0E

D-U-N-S 25-315-3159   (HQ)
WEST-CAN SEAL COATING INC
WESTERN ASPHALT PRODUCTS
55501 Rr 203, Bruderheim, AB, T0E 0S0
(780) 796-3437
Sales 50,488,400
SIC 1611 Highway and street construction

Dean Arnill
Matthew Arnill
Paul Arnill

Burdett, AB T0K

D-U-N-S 25-084-0212   (SL)
SONNY NAKASHIMA FARMS LTD
Gd, Burdett, AB, T0K 0J0
(403) 655-2270
Emp Here 41   *Sales* 14,041,147
SIC 0139 Field crops, except cash grain

Cadogan, AB T0B

D-U-N-S 20-786-5408   (SL)
CADOGAN HALL
Gd, Cadogan, AB, T0B 0T0
(780) 753-2963
Emp Here 49   *Sales* 13,937,413
SIC 6512 Nonresidential building operators
Danielle Cunningham

Calgary, AB P1X

D-U-N-S 24-318-9516   (BR)
BISON TRANSPORT INC
(*Suby of* JANPHER INVESTMENTS INC)
234090 Wrangler Rd, Calgary, AB, P1X 0K2
(403) 444-0555
Emp Here 250
SIC 4731 Freight transportation arrangement
Trevor Fridfinnson

Calgary, AB T1X

D-U-N-S 20-826-0083   (SL)
GOLIATH TRACTOR SERVICE LTD
10 Wrangler Place S.E. Suite 4, Calgary, AB, T1X 0L7
(403) 203-7352
Emp Here 100   *Sales* 14,819,200
SIC 4213 Trucking, except local
Murray Carson
Norman Myers
Victor Lawson

Calgary, AB T1Y

D-U-N-S 24-339-1302   (SL)
1294711 ALBERTA LTD
CITY FISH
3515 27 St Ne Suite 8, Calgary, AB, T1Y 5E4
(403) 250-8222
Emp Here 20   *Sales* 10,702,480
SIC 5146 Fish and seafoods
Nelson Leung
David Yip

D-U-N-S 20-322-7678   (SL)
1588545 ALBERTA LTD
SECURE PROTECTION SERVICES
3825 34 St Ne Suite 113b, Calgary, AB, T1Y 6Z8
(403) 272-3032
Emp Here 40   *Sales* 17,886,960
SIC 5065 Electronic parts and equipment, nec
Jennifer Slimmon

D-U-N-S 25-539-1351   (SL)
620205 ALBERTA LIMITED
GRAHAM AUCTIONS

4321 84 St Ne, Calgary, AB, T1Y 7H3
(403) 777-9393
Emp Here 35   *Sales* 15,522,150
SIC 7389 Business services, nec
Larry Graham
David Lyons

D-U-N-S 25-104-4723   (HQ)
ALBERTA GLASS COMPANY INC
2820 37 Ave Ne, Calgary, AB, T1Y 5T3
(403) 219-7466
Sales 24,618,600
SIC 1793 Glass and glazing work
Paul Heyens
George Kennedy

D-U-N-S 25-011-7736   (BR)
CALGARY BOARD OF EDUCATION
LESTER B. PEARSON SENIOR HIGH SCHOOL
(*Suby of* CALGARY BOARD OF EDUCATION)
3020 52 St Ne, Calgary, AB, T1Y 5P4
(403) 280-6565
Emp Here 81
SIC 8211 Elementary and secondary schools
Greg Weir

D-U-N-S 24-597-9620   (SL)
CALGARY DISTRICT PIPE TRADES HEALTH & WELFARE AND PENSION PLANS
2635 37 Ave Ne Suite 110, Calgary, AB, T1Y 5Z6
(403) 250-3534
Emp Here 10   *Sales* 10,348,810
SIC 6371 Pension, health, and welfare funds
Terry Crawley

D-U-N-S 24-962-9288   (SL)
CARLISLE DEVELOPMENTS INC
2891 Sunridge Way Ne Unit 230, Calgary, AB, T1Y 7K7
(403) 571-8400
Emp Here 35   *Sales* 11,160,415
SIC 1521 Single-family housing construction
Randy Klapstein
Brian Scoddard

D-U-N-S 24-749-2163   (SL)
CARLISLE GROUP
2891 Sunridge Way Ne Unit 230, Calgary, AB, T1Y 7K7
(403) 571-8400
Emp Here 49   *Sales* 13,881,357
SIC 8741 Management services
Ryan Stoddard

D-U-N-S 24-417-2938   (BR)
CAVALIER ENTERPRISES LTD
SHERATON CAVALIER HOTEL CALGARY
(*Suby of* ALFOUR VENTURES INC)
2620 32 Ave Ne, Calgary, AB, T1Y 6B8
(403) 291-0107
Emp Here 250
SIC 7011 Hotels and motels
Curtis Fernets

D-U-N-S 24-765-0653   (SL)
CENTINEL SECURITY
3132 26 St Ne Unit 335, Calgary, AB, T1Y 6Z1
(403) 237-8485
Emp Here 49   *Sales* 19,388,222
SIC 7381 Detective and armored car services
Jhovani Medrano

D-U-N-S 20-302-5791   (BR)
CERIDIAN CANADA LTD
(*Suby of* FOUNDATION HOLDINGS, INC.)
2618 Hopewell Pl Ne Suite 310, Calgary, AB, T1Y 7J7
(403) 262-6035
Emp Here 80
SIC 8721 Accounting, auditing, and bookkeeping
Kelly Janz

D-U-N-S 20-164-0526   (SL)

CITY WIRELESS
2150 29 St Ne Suite 10, Calgary, AB, T1Y 7G4

Emp Here 60   *Sales* 11,426,520
SIC 3651 Household audio and video equipment
John Evans

D-U-N-S 24-928-7616   (HQ)
CORAL CANADA WIDE LTD
VICTORIA REFRIGERATION
2150 29 St Ne Unit 30, Calgary, AB, T1Y 7G4
(403) 571-9200
Emp Here 20   *Sales* 38,731,264
SIC 1711 Plumbing, heating, air-conditioning
Kevin Stuckert
Allan Turner
Boyd Harris
Mark Maveal

D-U-N-S 25-287-5372   (BR)
COSTCO WHOLESALE CANADA LTD
COSTCO
(*Suby of* COSTCO WHOLESALE CORPORATION)
2853 32 St Ne, Calgary, AB, T1Y 6T7
(403) 299-1610
Emp Here 350
SIC 5099 Durable goods, nec
John Glassford

D-U-N-S 24-749-5658   (HQ)
CRUISE CANADA INC
(*Suby of* CRUISE AMERICA, INC.)
2980 26 St Ne, Calgary, AB, T1Y 6R7
(403) 291-4963
Emp Here 12   *Sales* 31,513,790
SIC 7519 Utility trailer rental
Robert Smalley
James Downs
Garth Mcalister

D-U-N-S 24-069-2942   (SL)
DET NORSKE VERITAS CANADA LTD
DET NORSKE VERITAS
(*Suby of* STIFTELSEN DET NORSKE VERITAS)
2618 Hopewell Pl Ne Suite 150, Calgary, AB, T1Y 7J7
(403) 250-9041
Emp Here 57   *Sales* 10,630,842
SIC 8742 Management consulting services
Jake Abes

D-U-N-S 20-715-8648   (BR)
EFW RADIOLOGY
(*Suby of* EFW RADIOLOGY)
2851 Sunridge Blvd Ne Suite 130, Calgary, AB, T1Y 0B7
(403) 541-1200
Emp Here 200
SIC 8071 Medical laboratories

D-U-N-S 24-598-1204   (SL)
ELAN CONSTRUCTION LIMITED
(*Suby of* ELAN INVESTMENTS LIMITED)
3639 27 St Ne Suite 100, Calgary, AB, T1Y 5E4
(403) 291-1165
Emp Here 70   *Sales* 39,923,660
SIC 1542 Nonresidential construction, nec
Todd Poulsen
Trevor R. Poulsen

D-U-N-S 20-513-2579   (SL)
ELECTROMEC INC
4300 26 St Ne Suite 125, Calgary, AB, T1Y 7H7

Emp Here 120   *Sales* 22,853,040
SIC 3679 Electronic components, nec
Harold Kunik
Mike Lie
Don Francis

D-U-N-S 20-804-1009   (SL)
EMERGENCY MEDICAL SERVICES
CALGARY E M S

3705 35 St Ne Suite 100, Calgary, AB, T1Y 6C2
(403) 955-9550
Emp Here 100   *Sales* 5,487,200
SIC 4119 Local passenger transportation, nec
Pat Weigel

D-U-N-S 20-826-3368   (BR)
EXTENDICARE (CANADA) INC
PARAMED HOME HEALTH CARE
(*Suby of* EXTENDICARE INC)
2611 37 Ave Ne Unit 7, Calgary, AB, T1Y 5V7
(403) 228-3877
Emp Here 140
SIC 8051 Skilled nursing care facilities
Denise Miller Sly

D-U-N-S 20-129-2471   (HQ)
FIELD AVIATION COMPANY INC
(*Suby of* FIELD AEROSPACE, INC.)
4300 26 St Ne Unit 125, Calgary, AB, T1Y 7H7
(403) 516-8200
Emp Here 85   *Sales* 55,217,760
SIC 1799 Special trade contractors, nec
John Mactaggart
Christina Friesen

D-U-N-S 20-299-5882   (SL)
FIELD AVIATION WEST LTD
4300 26 St Ne Unit 125, Calgary, AB, T1Y 7H7
(403) 516-8200
Emp Here 90   *Sales* 20,145,870
SIC 3728 Aircraft parts and equipment, nec
John Mactaggart

D-U-N-S 25-533-5507   (SL)
GAS ALBERTA INC
2618 Hopewell Place Ne Suite 350, Calgary, AB, T1Y 7J7
(403) 509-2600
Emp Here 10   *Sales* 60,156,671
SIC 4924 Natural gas distribution
David Symon
Harvey Yoder
Denis Dubrule
James Grose
Malcolm Davidson
Allen Dietz
William Neufeld
Leonard Spratt
Jack Goodall

D-U-N-S 20-185-0323   (SL)
HAMPTON POWER SYSTEMS LTD
3415 29 St Ne Suite 200, Calgary, AB, T1Y 5W4

Emp Here 25   *Sales* 11,179,350
SIC 5063 Electrical apparatus and equipment
James Mcquaker
Don Macdonald

D-U-N-S 20-440-0071   (SL)
HI-HOG FARM & RANCH EQUIPMENT LTD
8447 23 Ave Ne, Calgary, AB, T1Y 7G9
(403) 280-8300
Emp Here 70   *Sales* 51,976,400
SIC 5191 Farm supplies
Albert Kneeshaw
Brenda Goldstrom

D-U-N-S 20-698-6429   (BR)
HUDSON'S BAY COMPANY
HOME OUTFITTERS
(*Suby of* HUDSON'S BAY COMPANY)
3333 Sunridge Way Ne, Calgary, AB, T1Y 7H5

Emp Here 100
SIC 5311 Department stores
Elke Snowden

D-U-N-S 25-485-8004   (BR)
HUDSON'S BAY COMPANY
BAY, THE
(*Suby of* HUDSON'S BAY COMPANY)
2525 36 St Ne, Calgary, AB, T1Y 5T4
(403) 261-0759
Emp Here 130

SIC 5311 Department stores
Bette-Anne Jones

D-U-N-S 20-300-4994 (BR)
INDIGO BOOKS & MUSIC INC
CHAPTERS
(*Suby of* INDIGO BOOKS & MUSIC INC)
2555 32 St Ne Suite 500, Calgary, AB, T1Y 7J6
(403) 250-9171
Emp Here 202
SIC 5942 Book stores
Heather Reisman

D-U-N-S 20-151-2217 (HQ)
JOY GLOBAL (CANADA) LTD
(*Suby of* KOMATSU LTD.)
90-2150 29 St Ne, Calgary, AB, T1Y 7G4
(403) 730-9851
Emp Here 38   *Sales* 35,952,256
SIC 3532 Mining machinery
Mark Hardwick
Allan Mcgowan
Michael Barchard
Jim Ficzere

D-U-N-S 20-825-1561 (BR)
KLOHN CRIPPEN BERGER LTD
IEG CONSULTANTS
(*Suby of* KLOHN CRIPPEN BERGER HOLD-INGS LTD)
2618 Hopewell Pl Ne Suite 500, Calgary, AB, T1Y 7J7
(403) 274-3424
Emp Here 90
SIC 8711 Engineering services
Brian Rogers

D-U-N-S 24-415-6048 (HQ)
LEGACY KITCHEN DESIGN GROUP INC
2980 Sunridge Way Ne, Calgary, AB, T1Y 7H9
(403) 291-6868
Emp Here 100   *Sales* 66,167,320
SIC 5021 Furniture
John Buller
Chris Eden
Steven Buller
Russell Dyck

D-U-N-S 25-270-1446 (BR)
LOBLAWS INC
REAL CANADIAN SUPERSTORE
(*Suby of* LOBLAW COMPANIES LIMITED)
3575 20 Ave Ne, Calgary, AB, T1Y 6R3
(403) 280-8222
Emp Here 400
SIC 5411 Grocery stores
Matthew Walkey

D-U-N-S 25-273-1690 (BR)
LONDON DRUGS LIMITED
(*Suby of* H.Y. LOUIE CO. LIMITED)
3545 32 Ave Ne, Calgary, AB, T1Y 6M6
(403) 571-4931
Emp Here 100
SIC 5912 Drug stores and proprietary stores
Colin Campbell

D-U-N-S 25-091-4699 (BR)
LOWE'S COMPANIES CANADA, ULC
(*Suby of* LOWE'S COMPANIES, INC.)
2909 Sunridge Way Ne, Calgary, AB, T1Y 7K7
(403) 277-0044
Emp Here 130
SIC 5211 Lumber and other building materials
Mike Lindsay

D-U-N-S 25-596-0734 (BR)
MATRIX LOGISTICS SERVICES LIMITED
(*Suby of* MATRIX LOGISTICS SERVICES LIMITED)
2525 29 St Ne, Calgary, AB, T1Y 7B5
(403) 291-9292
Emp Here 180
SIC 4225 General warehousing and storage
Jacques Menard

D-U-N-S 25-538-4133 (HQ)

MEMORY EXPRESS INC
3333 34 Ave Ne, Calgary, AB, T1Y 6H2
(403) 398-4533
Sales 79,477,494
SIC 5734 Computer and software stores
Minh Ngo
Hien Ngo
Ut Ngo
Chieu Ngo
Ngoc Ly
Sienai Hoa

D-U-N-S 24-440-9793 (HQ)
MENNONITE MUTUAL INSURANCE CO. (ALBERTA) LTD
MMI
2946 32 St Ne Suite 300, Calgary, AB, T1Y 6J7
(403) 275-6996
Emp Here 13   *Sales* 16,558,096
SIC 6331 Fire, marine, and casualty insurance
Kenneth Ritchie

D-U-N-S 24-904-9362 (SL)
MENTOR ENGINEERING INC
2175 29 St Ne Suite 10, Calgary, AB, T1Y 7H8
(403) 777-3760
Emp Here 119   *Sales* 22,662,598
SIC 3669 Communications equipment, nec
Gordon Howell
Wolfgang Stichling
Stephen Hickle

D-U-N-S 20-077-0568 (HQ)
MIDWEST SURVEYS INC
2827 Sunridge Blvd Ne, Calgary, AB, T1Y 6G1
(403) 244-7471
Emp Here 159   *Sales* 25,575,287
SIC 8713 Surveying services
Kevin Swabey
Scott Boulanger
Gillian Cox
Steven Drew
Matthew Ward
Craig White

D-U-N-S 24-442-5153 (SL)
MYSTIQUE MECHANICAL LTD
3605 29 St Ne Suite 300, Calgary, AB, T1Y 5W4
Emp Here 80   *Sales* 18,645,200
SIC 1711 Plumbing, heating, air-conditioning
Ted Rohling
Darren Parkinson

D-U-N-S 25-388-6832 (SL)
NET SAFETY MONITORING INC
(*Suby of* EMERSON ELECTRIC CO.)
2721 Hopewell Pl Ne, Calgary, AB, T1Y 7J7
(403) 219-0688
Emp Here 55   *Sales* 12,500,895
SIC 3829 Measuring and controlling devices, nec
Marlene Coffey
Kenneth Coffey

D-U-N-S 20-116-1812 (BR)
NOVA CHEMICALS CORPORATION
(*Suby of* GOVERNMENT OF ABU DHABI)
3620 32 St Ne, Calgary, AB, T1Y 6G7
(403) 291-8444
Emp Here 80
SIC 2822 Synthetic rubber
Charles Russell

D-U-N-S 24-012-7787 (HQ)
O'ROURKE ENGINEERING LTD
2711 39 Ave Ne, Calgary, AB, T1Y 4T8
(403) 261-4991
Sales 11,437,270
SIC 8711 Engineering services
Jim O'rourke

D-U-N-S 25-316-4107 (BR)
PASLEY, MAX ENTERPRISES LIMITED
MCDONALD'S RESTAURANTS 13861

1920 68 St, Calgary, AB, T1Y 6Y7
(403) 280-6388
Emp Here 90
SIC 5812 Eating places
Jessica Deraans

D-U-N-S 20-315-9397 (SL)
PFB CORPORATION
2891 Sunridge Way Ne Suite 300, Calgary, AB, T1Y 7K7
(403) 569-4300
Emp Here 366   *Sales* 97,298,601
SIC 3086 Plastics foam products
C. Alan Smith
Robert Graham
James Banner
David Carr
Bruce M. Carruthers
Donald J. Douglas
Frank B. Baker
Gordon G. Tallman
John K. Read
Vanessa H. Rennie

D-U-N-S 20-316-6793 (SL)
PINEHILL MANAGEMENT CORP
CHEESECAKE CAFE, THE
2121 36 St Ne, Calgary, AB, T1Y 5S3

Emp Here 100   *Sales* 4,551,900
SIC 5812 Eating places
Lorne Bicknell

D-U-N-S 20-714-4338 (HQ)
PLASTI-FAB LTD
300-2891 Sunridge Way Ne, Calgary, AB, T1Y 7K7
(403) 569-4300
Emp Here 25   *Sales* 133,393,500
SIC 2821 Plastics materials and resins
Robert Graham
David Carr
Mirko Papuga

D-U-N-S 20-180-8669 (SL)
PLATINUM MOTOR CARS INC
PLATINUM MITSUBISHI
2720 Barlow Trail Ne, Calgary, AB, T1Y 1A1
(403) 276-4878
Emp Here 35   *Sales* 17,432,730
SIC 5521 Used car dealers
Bently Maitland

D-U-N-S 20-770-1686 (BR)
REHOBOTH A CHRISTIAN ASSOCIATION FOR THE MENTALLY HANDICAPPED OF ALBERTA
3505 29 St Ne Suite 106, Calgary, AB, T1Y 5W4
(403) 250-7333
Emp Here 100
SIC 8331 Job training and related services
Shelley Gagnon

D-U-N-S 20-005-1410 (BR)
RONA INC
RONA HOME & GARDEN
(*Suby of* LOWE'S COMPANIES, INC.)
2665 32 St Ne, Calgary, AB, T1Y 6Z7
(403) 219-5800
Emp Here 175
SIC 5211 Lumber and other building materials
Rich Howard

D-U-N-S 24-325-9335 (SL)
RX FRASER LTD
SHOPPERS DRUG MART
2525 36 St Ne Suite 135, Calgary, AB, T1Y 5T4
(403) 280-6667
Emp Here 60   *Sales* 14,659,680
SIC 5912 Drug stores and proprietary stores
Lori Fraser

D-U-N-S 24-007-1493 (SL)
SENTINEL PROTECTION SERVICES LTD
3132 26 St Ne Suite 335, Calgary, AB, T1Y 6Z1

(403) 237-8485
Emp Here 65   *Sales* 25,719,070
SIC 7381 Detective and armored car services
Jhovany Medrano
Christina Wen
Naren Gandhi

D-U-N-S 20-133-9467 (SL)
SIGNATURE INTERPRETIVE & TRANSLA-TIVE SERVICES LTD
4608 26 Ave Ne, Calgary, AB, T1Y 2R8
(403) 590-6382
Emp Here 51   *Sales* 22,910,169
SIC 7389 Business services, nec
Zakie Hage

D-U-N-S 25-271-0702 (BR)
SOBEYS WEST INC
SAFEWAY, DIV OF
(*Suby of* EMPIRE COMPANY LIMITED)
3550 32 Ave Ne Suite 286, Calgary, AB, T1Y 6J2
(403) 291-2035
Emp Here 190
SIC 5411 Grocery stores
Roger Broberg

D-U-N-S 20-078-0997 (HQ)
SOUTHERN MUSIC LTD
SML ENTERTAINMENT
3605 32 St Ne, Calgary, AB, T1Y 5Y9
(403) 291-1666
Emp Here 40   *Sales* 23,320,360
SIC 7359 Equipment rental and leasing, nec
Anthony Fisher
Otto Fisher
Dean Fisher

D-U-N-S 24-345-5128 (SL)
STAMPEDE TOYOTA & LEASING LTD
STAMPEDE TOYOTA
2508 24 Ave Ne, Calgary, AB, T1Y 6R8
(403) 291-2111
Emp Here 86   *Sales* 54,118,080
SIC 5511 New and used car dealers
Glen Rumpel

D-U-N-S 24-423-3172 (SL)
STANG'S AUTOMOTIVE ENTERPRISES INC
SUNRIDGE MAZDA
3003 32 Ave Ne, Calgary, AB, T1Y 6J1
(403) 291-7060
Emp Here 40   *Sales* 19,923,120
SIC 5511 New and used car dealers
Gord Stang

D-U-N-S 24-082-6359 (SL)
STATE FARM INSURANCE COMPANIES
2611 37 Ave Ne Suite 3, Calgary, AB, T1Y 5V7
(403) 291-1283
Emp Here 20   *Sales* 11,598,480
SIC 6411 Insurance agents, brokers, and service
Rod Lunau

D-U-N-S 20-772-4415 (SL)
STERLING TRUCKS OF CALGARY LTD
(*Suby of* UNIVERSAL FORD LINCOLN SALES LTD)
2800 Barlow Trail Ne Suite 291, Calgary, AB, T1Y 1A2
(866) 792-1443
Emp Here 25   *Sales* 15,732,000
SIC 5511 New and used car dealers
Dale Schotanus

D-U-N-S 20-827-8440 (SL)
SUNRIDGE NISSAN LTD
SUNRIDGE NISSAN
(*Suby of* AUTOPLUS RESOURCES LTD)
3131 32 Ave Ne, Calgary, AB, T1Y 6J1
(403) 291-2626
Emp Here 40   *Sales* 25,171,200
SIC 5511 New and used car dealers
Jaymal Ruparell

D-U-N-S 25-146-4921 (SL)

TURNKEY SOLUTIONS INC
4300 26 St Ne Bay Suite 105, Calgary, AB,
T1Y 7H7

Emp Here 140
SIC 3679 Electronic components, nec

D-U-N-S 25-399-3638   (HQ)
UNIFIED VALVE GROUP LTD
(Suby of VALTROL EQUIPMENT LIMITED)
3815 32 St Ne, Calgary, AB, T1Y 7C1
(403) 215-7800
Emp Here 16   Sales 14,424,600
SIC 7699 Repair services, nec
 Keith Levoir
 David Terry

D-U-N-S 20-078-5293   (HQ)
UNIVERSAL FORD LINCOLN SALES LTD
2800 Barlow Trail Ne, Calgary, AB, T1Y 1A2
(403) 291-2850
Emp Here 120   Sales 106,977,600
SIC 5511 New and used car dealers
 Dale Schotanus
 Darin Schotanus
 Scott Schotanus

D-U-N-S 20-176-3880   (BR)
VALUE VILLAGE STORES, INC
SAVERS
(Suby of SAVERS, INC.)
3405 34 St Ne, Calgary, AB, T1Y 6T6
(403) 291-3323
Emp Here 85
SIC 5399 Miscellaneous general merchandise
 Mike Dooley

D-U-N-S 20-447-9406   (HQ)
VARIPERM (CANADA) LIMITED
(Suby of NURCO HOLDINGS LTD.)
3424 26 St Ne Suite 10, Calgary, AB, T1Y 4T7
(403) 250-7263
Emp Here 30   Sales 23,751,300
SIC 5082 Construction and mining machinery
 James Nurcombe
 Ken Kornylo

D-U-N-S 20-008-3835   (BR)
WALMART CANADA LOGISTICS ULC
EXCEL
(Suby of WALMART INC.)
3400 39 Ave Ne, Calgary, AB, T1Y 7J4
(403) 250-3648
Emp Here 900
SIC 4225 General warehousing and storage

D-U-N-S 24-840-4055   (HQ)
YIKES ENTERPRISES LTD
TIM HORTONS
3508 32 Ave Ne Unit 500, Calgary, AB, T1Y
6J2
(403) 291-2925
Emp Here 40   Sales 32,282,470
SIC 5461 Retail bakeries
 Cindy Anderson
 Cody Gosling

Calgary, AB T2A

D-U-N-S 24-786-7112   (SL)
502386 ALBERTA LTD
T & T HONDA
888 Meridian Rd Ne, Calgary, AB, T2A 2N8
(403) 291-1444
Emp Here 92   Sales 57,893,760
SIC 5511 New and used car dealers
 Imtihaz Manji

D-U-N-S 25-511-1122   (SL)
614568 ALBERTA LTD
1100 Meridian Rd Ne, Calgary, AB, T2A 2N9
(403) 571-3077
Emp Here 43   Sales 53,488,800
SIC 5511 New and used car dealers

 Charles E. English

D-U-N-S 25-325-6499   (SL)
AGRISTAR INC
720 28 St Ne Suite 208, Calgary, AB, T2A 6R3
(403) 873-5177
Emp Here 50   Sales 41,778,850
SIC 5148 Fresh fruits and vegetables
 Frank Gatto
 Lori Ell

D-U-N-S 24-517-4123   (SL)
ALBERTA JANITORIAL LTD
(Suby of 104901 CANADA INC)
2520 Centre Ave Ne, Calgary, AB, T2A 2L2
(403) 272-7801
Emp Here 100   Sales 3,196,800
SIC 7349 Building maintenance services, nec
 Bonnie Watson
 Bruce Watson

D-U-N-S 25-440-6028   (HQ)
ALEXANDRA COMMUNITY HEALTH CEN-TRE
ALEX COMMUNITY HEALTH CENTRE, THE
2840 2 Ave Se Unit 101, Calgary, AB, T2A 7X9
(403) 266-2622
Emp Here 200   Sales 47,551,750
SIC 8011 Offices and clinics of medical doc-tors
 Shelley Heartwell

D-U-N-S 20-812-3278   (SL)
ALTALINK MANAGEMENT LTD
(Suby of BERKSHIRE HATHAWAY INC.)
2611 3 Ave Se, Calgary, AB, T2A 7W7
(403) 267-3400
Emp Here 700   Sales 588,515,200
SIC 4911 Electric services
 Scott Thon
 Dennis Frehlich
 David Koch
 David Tuer
 Douglas Mitchell
 Robert Turgeon
 Patricia Nelson
 Gregory Abel
 David R. Collyer
 Patrick Goodman

D-U-N-S 20-113-1864   (HQ)
ALTALINK, L.P.
(Suby of BERKSHIRE HATHAWAY INC.)
2611 3 Ave Se, Calgary, AB, T2A 7W7
(403) 267-3400
Emp Here 1   Sales 623,388,971
SIC 4911 Electric services
 Scott Thon
 David Tuer
 Gary Hart
 David Koch
 Zora Lazic
 Johanne Picard-Thompson
 Linda Shea
 Ed Rihn
 Hejdi Carlsen
 Robert Turgeon

D-U-N-S 20-254-7977   (BR)
AUTOPRO AUTOMATION CONSULTANTS LTD
(Suby of AUTOPRO AUTOMATION CONSUL-TANTS LTD)
525 28 St Se Suite 360, Calgary, AB, T2A 6W9
(403) 569-6480
Emp Here 100
SIC 8711 Engineering services
 Kenneth Sim

D-U-N-S 20-988-4543   (HQ)
BASSANO FARMS LTD
BASSANO GROWERS
923 28 St Ne, Calgary, AB, T2A 7X1
(403) 273-4557
Emp Here 30   Sales 62,668,275
SIC 5148 Fresh fruits and vegetables
 Kazumasa Yamashiro

 Julie Hironaka

D-U-N-S 24-042-5264   (HQ)
BEHR PROCESS CANADA LTD
BEHR CANADA
(Suby of MASCO CORPORATION)
2750 Centre Ave Ne, Calgary, AB, T2A 2L3
(403) 273-0226
Sales 25,988,200
SIC 5198 Paints, varnishes, and supplies
 Kevin Jaffe
 John V Croul
 Gregory Szott
 Jeffrey Filley
 John Sznewajs

D-U-N-S 20-824-4749   (BR)
BRINK'S CANADA LIMITED
BRINK'S
(Suby of THE BRINK'S COMPANY)
640 28 St Ne Unit 8, Calgary, AB, T2A 6R3
(403) 272-2259
Emp Here 160
SIC 7381 Detective and armored car services
 Peter Roberts

D-U-N-S 24-599-6103   (HQ)
BW TECHNOLOGIES LTD
ADI-QC
(Suby of HONEYWELL INTERNATIONAL INC.)
2840 2 Ave Se, Calgary, AB, T2A 7X9
(403) 248-9226
Emp Here 30   Sales 131,697,600
SIC 3829 Measuring and controlling devices, nec
 Deborah Van Damme
 Thomas Larkins
 Manish Shanbhag
 John Tus

D-U-N-S 20-573-1201   (SL)
C. HEAD LIMITED
CANADIAN TIRE ASSOCIATE STORE
3516 8 Ave Ne Suite 326, Calgary, AB, T2A 6K5
(403) 248-6400
Emp Here 120   Sales 32,118,240
SIC 5251 Hardware stores

D-U-N-S 20-713-1421   (BR)
CALGARY BOARD OF EDUCATION
FOREST LAWN HIGH SCHOOL
(Suby of CALGARY BOARD OF EDUCA-TION)
1304 44 St Se, Calgary, AB, T2A 1M8
(403) 272-6665
Emp Here 110
SIC 8211 Elementary and secondary schools
 Robert Straub

D-U-N-S 25-622-0666   (BR)
CALGARY CO-OPERATIVE ASSOCIATION LIMITED
FOREST LAWN CALGARY CO-OP, DIV
(Suby of CALGARY CO-OPERATIVE ASSO-CIATION LIMITED)
3330 17 Ave Se Suite 5, Calgary, AB, T2A 0P9
(403) 299-4461
Emp Here 250
SIC 5411 Grocery stores

D-U-N-S 25-287-4227   (SL)
CALGARY PLAZA HOTEL LTD
COAST PLAZA HOTEL
1316 33 St Ne, Calgary, AB, T2A 6B6
(403) 248-8888
Emp Here 200   Sales 18,538,000
SIC 7011 Hotels and motels
 Amir K Virani
 Richard Russell

D-U-N-S 20-831-9855   (HQ)
CALGARY VALVE & FITTING INC
3202 12 Ave Ne, Calgary, AB, T2A 6N8
(403) 243-5646
Emp Here 25   Sales 17,575,962

SIC 5085 Industrial supplies
 Jim Crozier

D-U-N-S 20-690-7870   (HQ)
CANADIAN LOCATORS INC
525 28 St Se Suite 201, Calgary, AB, T2A 6W9
(403) 263-6310
Sales 37,301,200
SIC 8742 Management consulting services
 Dimitris Agouridis
 Karima Kara

D-U-N-S 24-131-7895   (HQ)
CARDTRONICS CANADA HOLDINGS INC
DC PAYMENTS PHYSICAL
(Suby of CARDTRONICS PLC)
1420 28 St Ne Suite 6, Calgary, AB, T2A 7W6
(403) 207-1500
Sales 213,318,130
SIC 6099 Functions related to deposit banking
 James Abou-Arrage
 Steven Rathgaber
 Edward West

D-U-N-S 24-098-8514   (HQ)
CARDTRONICS CANADA OPERATIONS INC
(Suby of CARDTRONICS PLC)
1420 28 St Ne Suite 6, Calgary, AB, T2A 7W6
(403) 207-1500
Emp Here 100   Sales 12,477,600
SIC 8741 Management services
 Jeffrey J Smith

D-U-N-S 20-991-0132   (HQ)
CHECKER CABS LTD
CHECKER COURIER
316 Meridian Rd Se, Calgary, AB, T2A 1X2
(403) 299-9999
Emp Here 90   Sales 22,627,660
SIC 4212 Local trucking, without storage
 Margaret Enders

D-U-N-S 20-766-7452   (SL)
CMP - CLASSIC AUTOMOTIVE LTD
1313 36 St Ne, Calgary, AB, T2A 6P9
(403) 207-1002
Emp Here 200   Sales 90,039,400
SIC 7538 General automotive repair shops
 Rick Romeril

D-U-N-S 20-292-8065   (HQ)
CMP AUTOMOTIVE INC
(Suby of AUTOPLUS RESOURCES LTD)
1313 36 St Ne, Calgary, AB, T2A 6P9
(403) 207-1000
Sales 85,537,430
SIC 7538 General automotive repair shops
 Richard Romeril

D-U-N-S 24-089-4634   (HQ)
COFFEE CONNECTION LTD, THE
EVEREST ENTERPRISES INTERNATIONAL
401 33 St Ne Unit 3, Calgary, AB, T2A 7R3
(403) 269-5977
Emp Here 35   Sales 24,257,826
SIC 7389 Business services, nec
 William Gunning
 Delores Gunning

D-U-N-S 20-027-3289   (SL)
COMPUGEN SYSTEMS LTD
1440 28 St Ne Suite 3, Calgary, AB, T2A 7W6
(403) 571-4400
Emp Here 125   Sales 31,579,000
SIC 7373 Computer integrated systems de-sign
 Harry Zarek

D-U-N-S 20-719-4288   (SL)
DIRECT CASH (LNET)
1420 28 St Ne Suite 6, Calgary, AB, T2A 7W6
(403) 207-1500
Emp Here 80   Sales 15,792,000
SIC 6099 Functions related to deposit banking
 Jeff Smith

D-U-N-S 24-359-9292   (BR)

DNOW CANADA ULC
NATIONAL OILWELL VARCO
(Suby of NOW INC.)
1616 Meridian Rd Ne, Calgary, AB, T2A 2P1
(403) 569-2222
Emp Here 100
SIC 3533 Oil and gas field machinery
Kelly Lamont

D-U-N-S 20-827-3821   (SL)
EASTSIDE DODGE CHRYSLER LTD
815 36 St Ne, Calgary, AB, T2A 4W3
(403) 273-4313
Emp Here 110   *Sales* 69,220,800
SIC 5511 New and used car dealers
James D Mcmanes

D-U-N-S 20-233-9292   (SL)
EASTSIDE FAMILY CENTRE
495 36 St Ne Suite 255, Calgary, AB, T2A 6K3
(403) 299-9696
Emp Here 30   *Sales* 11,922,420
SIC 8699 Membership organizations, nec
Ryan Clements

D-U-N-S 25-170-6701   (SL)
ELECTRIC FOODS INC
A & W RESTAURANT
3663 12 Ave Ne, Calgary, AB, T2A 7T1
(403) 248-7640
Emp Here 200   *Sales* 9,103,800
SIC 5812 Eating places

D-U-N-S 20-549-0803   (SL)
ENGINEERED POWER GP LTD
3103 14 Ave Ne Suite 20, Calgary, AB, T2A 7N6
(403) 235-2584
Emp Here 70   *Sales* 13,330,940
SIC 3692 Primary batteries, dry and wet
Rick Marshall

D-U-N-S 20-369-5742   (SL)
ENGINEERED POWER LIMITED PARTNERSHIP
3103 14 Ave Ne Unit 20, Calgary, AB, T2A 7N6
(403) 235-2584
Emp Here 150   *Sales* 28,897,152
SIC 3692 Primary batteries, dry and wet
Stephen Rue

D-U-N-S 24-121-1077   (HQ)
FABRICLAND PACIFIC LIMITED
FABRICLAND
495 36 St Ne Suite 104, Calgary, AB, T2A 6K3
(855) 554-4840
Emp Here 20   *Sales* 91,768,500
SIC 5949 Sewing, needlework, and piece goods
Mel Kotler
Ron Kimel

D-U-N-S 20-850-4902   (HQ)
FARM BUSINESS CONSULTANTS LTD
3015 5 Ave Ne Suite 150, Calgary, AB, T2A 6T8
(403) 735-6105
Sales 18,716,400
SIC 8741 Management services
J Gary Ibbotson
Steven Ibbotson

D-U-N-S 24-840-5466   (BR)
FEDERATED CO-OPERATIVES LIMITED
(Suby of FEDERATED CO-OPERATIVES LIMITED)
2626 10 Ave Ne, Calgary, AB, T2A 2M3
(403) 531-6665
Emp Here 300
SIC 5141 Groceries, general line
Manovich Barry

D-U-N-S 24-495-4988   (HQ)
FIFTH AVENUE AUTO HAUS LTD
1120 Meridian Rd Ne, Calgary, AB, T2A 2N9
(403) 273-2500
Sales 25,171,200

SIC 5511 New and used car dealers
Bill Shostak

D-U-N-S 20-145-8424   (SL)
FOREST LAWN SOBEYS
FOREST IGA
5115 17 Ave Se, Calgary, AB, T2A 0V8
(403) 273-9339
Emp Here 120   *Sales* 35,217,240
SIC 5411 Grocery stores
Carlo Primiani

D-U-N-S 20-920-5066   (BR)
G&K SERVICES CANADA INC
(Suby of CINTAS CORPORATION)
2925 10 Ave Ne Suite 7, Calgary, AB, T2A 5L4
(403) 272-4256
Emp Here 100
SIC 7219 Laundry and garment services, nec
Kristin Moor

D-U-N-S 24-914-4838   (SL)
GLC CONTROLS INC
3300 14 Ave Ne Suite 2, Calgary, AB, T2A 6J4

Emp Here 30   *Sales* 13,640,848
SIC 5063 Electrical apparatus and equipment
Luke Beaudry

D-U-N-S 24-905-5633   (BR)
GOLDER ASSOCIATES LTD
(Suby of GOLDER ASSOCIATES CORPORATION)
2535 3 Ave Se Suite 102, Calgary, AB, T2A 7W5
(403) 299-5600
Emp Here 550
SIC 8748 Business consulting, nec
Louise Menard

D-U-N-S 20-077-7571   (HQ)
GREEN DROP LTD
1230 Meridian Rd Ne, Calgary, AB, T2A 2N9
(403) 273-9845
Emp Here 7   *Sales* 15,621,155
SIC 2874 Phosphatic fertilizers
John Robinson
Jackie Jensen

D-U-N-S 25-011-1044   (BR)
HOME DEPOT OF CANADA INC
HOME DEPOT
(Suby of THE HOME DEPOT INC)
343 36 St Ne, Calgary, AB, T2A 7S9
(403) 248-3040
Emp Here 250
SIC 5251 Hardware stores
Mark Beatty

D-U-N-S 24-773-3087   (SL)
KASCO CONSTRUCTION ALTA LTD
2770 3 Ave Ne Suite 117, Calgary, AB, T2A 2L5

Emp Here 70   *Sales* 17,670,940
SIC 1611 Highway and street construction
Karen Mccourt

D-U-N-S 24-169-0150   (SL)
KORPACH CONSULTING LTD
611 Malvern Dr Ne, Calgary, AB, T2A 5G8
(403) 219-7481
Emp Here 49   *Sales* 10,407,453
SIC 8748 Business consulting, nec
Caroline Korpach
Dave Korpach

D-U-N-S 25-414-3621   (HQ)
MODULEX AMERICAS INC
3200 14 Ave Ne Suite 1, Calgary, AB, T2A 6J4
(403) 272-0597
Emp Here 10   *Sales* 19,568,160
SIC 3993 Signs and advertising specialties
Gordon Milne

D-U-N-S 20-643-7290   (SL)
MONUMENT COMMUNITY ECONOMIC DEVELOPMENT SOCIETY

2936 Radcliffe Dr Se Suite 16, Calgary, AB, T2A 6M8
(403) 272-9323
Emp Here 37   *Sales* 14,704,318
SIC 8699 Membership organizations, nec
Walter Hossli

D-U-N-S 20-855-8879   (HQ)
PROSPECT HUMAN SERVICES SOCIETY
PROSPECT CALGARY
915 33 St Ne, Calgary, AB, T2A 6T2
(403) 273-2822
Emp Here 75   *Sales* 29,319,360
SIC 5912 Drug stores and proprietary stores
Melanie Mitra
Debbie Spaudiling

D-U-N-S 25-521-6335   (BR)
RED LOBSTER HOSPITALITY LLC
RED LOBSTER RESTAURANTS
312 35 St Ne, Calgary, AB, T2A 6S7
(403) 248-8111
Emp Here 120
SIC 5812 Eating places
Timothy Meilkle

D-U-N-S 24-438-7189   (SL)
REGAL AUCTIONS LTD
2600 7 Ave Ne, Calgary, AB, T2A 2L8
(403) 250-1995
Emp Here 30   *Sales* 13,304,700
SIC 7389 Business services, nec
Ron Henchell
Don Rhodes

D-U-N-S 24-702-0522   (SL)
REMEDY ENERGY SERVICES INC
720 28 St Ne Unit 255, Calgary, AB, T2A 6R3
(403) 272-0703
Emp Here 50   *Sales* 15,985,250
SIC 1389 Oil and gas field services, nec
Bob Dyck
Richard Hawker

D-U-N-S 20-298-8986   (SL)
RGO PRODUCTS LTD
229 33 St Ne Suite 100, Calgary, AB, T2A 4Y6
(403) 569-4400
Emp Here 250   *Sales* 143,842,000
SIC 5021 Furniture
Cathy Orr
Ross Glen
Jake Gebert
Sarah Chin

D-U-N-S 20-345-3535   (HQ)
ROKE TECHNOLOGIES LTD
1220 28 St Ne Unit 100, Calgary, AB, T2A 6A2
(403) 247-3480
Sales 12,788,200
SIC 1389 Oil and gas field services, nec
Hermann Kramer

D-U-N-S 24-344-6833   (SL)
SMARTPRACTICE CANADA ULC
(Suby of TUNILLA)
720 28th Street Ne, Ste 210, Calgary, AB, T2A 6R3
(403) 450-9997
Emp Here 10   *Sales* 11,053,450
SIC 5122 Drugs, proprietaries, and sundries
Curtis Hamann
Dan Nahom
Susan Nawrocki

D-U-N-S 25-271-0439   (BR)
SOBEYS WEST INC
(Suby of EMPIRE COMPANY LIMITED)
399 36 St Ne, Calgary, AB, T2A 7R4
(403) 248-0848
Emp Here 150
SIC 5411 Grocery stores
Darcy Cook

D-U-N-S 20-078-1250   (HQ)
SPARTAN CONTROLS LTD
STERLING VALVE AUTOMATION DIV OF
305 27 St Se, Calgary, AB, T2A 7V2

(403) 207-0797
Emp Here 250   *Sales* 312,147,200
SIC 5084 Industrial machinery and equipment
Michael Begin
Donald Cawley
David Connolly
Robert Mcalpine
Richard Anderson

D-U-N-S 20-698-4747   (BR)
STANTEC ARCHITECTURE LTD
(Suby of STANTEC INC)
325 25 St Se Suite 200, Calgary, AB, T2A 7H8
(403) 716-8000
Emp Here 203
SIC 8711 Engineering services
Russ Wlad

D-U-N-S 20-300-7182   (BR)
STANTEC GEOMATICS LTD
(Suby of STANTEC INC)
325 25 St Se Suite 200, Calgary, AB, T2A 7H8
(403) 716-8000
Emp Here 181
SIC 8713 Surveying services
Christina Han

D-U-N-S 20-065-8958   (SL)
STOUGHTON FIRE PROTECTION LTD
620 Moraine Rd Ne, Calgary, AB, T2A 2P3
(403) 291-0291
Emp Here 65   *Sales* 29,199,235
SIC 7389 Business services, nec
Kellar Stoughton

D-U-N-S 20-744-1846   (SL)
SUMWA TRADING CO. LTD
2710 5 Ave Ne, Calgary, AB, T2A 4V4
(403) 230-8823
Emp Here 30   *Sales* 20,904,300
SIC 6799 Investors, nec
Ivy Chen

D-U-N-S 25-497-1807   (HQ)
SUPPORTED LIFESTYLES LTD
495 36 St Ne Suite 210, Calgary, AB, T2A 6K3
(403) 207-5115
Sales 19,198,000
SIC 8322 Individual and family services
George Gentlemen
Luannne Smith

D-U-N-S 20-306-6167   (SL)
SURECALL CONTACT CENTERS LTD
PDL CALL CENTRES
3030 3 Ave Ne Suite 240, Calgary, AB, T2A 6T7
(403) 291-5400
Emp Here 195   *Sales* 44,552,040
SIC 4899 Communication services, nec
Desiree Bombenon
Mark Bombenon
Christine Harle

D-U-N-S 20-940-4024   (BR)
T & T SUPERMARKET INC
(Suby of LOBLAW COMPANIES LIMITED)
999 36 St Ne Suite 800, Calgary, AB, T2A 7X6
(403) 569-6888
Emp Here 200
SIC 5411 Grocery stores
Kin Ng

D-U-N-S 24-299-5942   (HQ)
TEMPCO DRILLING COMPANY INC
720 28 St Ne Suite 114, Calgary, AB, T2A 6R3
(403) 259-5533
Emp Here 52   *Sales* 17,583,775
SIC 1381 Drilling oil and gas wells
Thomas James Cascadden
Ken D Weller

D-U-N-S 24-798-4169   (SL)
TORA WESTERN CANADA LTD
GIANT TIGER
4710 17 Ave Se Suite G2, Calgary, AB, T2A 0V1
(403) 207-5200
Emp Here 30   *Sales* 14,949,660

▲ Public Company   ■ Public Company Family Member   **HQ** Headquarters   **BR** Branch   **SL** Single Location

SIC 5137 Women's and children's clothing
Paul Pryce

D-U-N-S 25-218-9857   (BR)
WAL-MART CANADA CORP
WALMART
(*Suby of* WALMART INC.)
3800 Memorial Dr Ne Suite 1100, Calgary, AB,
T2A 2K2
(403) 235-2352
Emp Here 200
SIC 5311 Department stores
Tim Braund

D-U-N-S 20-358-9338   (SL)
WARRIOR RIG TECHNOLOGIES LIMITED
1515 28 St Ne, Calgary, AB, T2A 3T1
(403) 291-6444
Emp Here 79   *Sales* 17,538,079
SIC 3533 Oil and gas field machinery
Darrell Mcgarth

D-U-N-S 24-013-9449   (SL)
WARRIOR RIG TECHNOLOGIES LIMITED
1515 28 St Ne, Calgary, AB, T2A 3T1
(403) 291-6444
Emp Here 56   *Sales* 26,601,456
SIC 5084 Industrial machinery and equipment
Tom Whalen
Mike Moellenbeck
Gustavo Lis

D-U-N-S 24-442-5674   (SL)
WATT CONSULTING GROUP LTD
3016 5 Ave Ne Suite 310, Calgary, AB, T2A
6K4
(403) 273-9001
Emp Here 75   *Sales* 13,196,850
SIC 8711 Engineering services
David A Watt
Nicholas Finn
Thomas Medlicott
Grant Mcdonald
Egbert-Jan Van Weelderen
Michael Richards
Michael Szarmes
Bruce Nelligan
Colette Hyde

D-U-N-S 20-034-9368   (SL)
WESTERN IMPACT SALES & MARKETING INC
3223 5 Ave Ne Unit 309, Calgary, AB, T2A 6E9
(403) 272-3065
Emp Here 21   *Sales* 17,547,117
SIC 5141 Groceries, general line
Robert (Bob) Martin
Jason Martin
Jamie Martin

D-U-N-S 24-160-3612   (BR)
WESTERN INVENTORY SERVICE LTD
WIS INTERNATIONAL
(*Suby of* ARES CAPITAL CORPORATION)
720 28 St Ne Suite 128, Calgary, AB, T2A 6R3
(403) 272-3850
Emp Here 80
SIC 7389 Business services, nec
Jennie Keating

D-U-N-S 25-217-3455   (HQ)
YORK ELECTRONICS (2010) LTD
1430 28 St Ne Unit 8, Calgary, AB, T2A 7W6
(403) 207-0202
Emp Here 20   *Sales* 11,179,350
SIC 5065 Electronic parts and equipment, nec
York Forrington
Dale Lohmer

D-U-N-S 24-864-0687   (SL)
ZONE DIRECT MWD SERVICES LTD
EZMWD
15-2916 5 Ave Ne, Calgary, AB, T2A 6K4
(403) 457-0133
Emp Here 50   *Sales* 15,985,250
SIC 1381 Drilling oil and gas wells
Igor Todorovic

David Villemaire

Calgary, AB T2B

D-U-N-S 24-089-4337   (HQ)
ALGGIN METAL INDUSTRIES LTD
4540 46 Ave Se, Calgary, AB, T2B 3N7
(403) 252-0132
Emp Here 73   *Sales* 17,287,650
SIC 3444 Sheet Metalwork
Gary Bianchini
Allan Bianchini

D-U-N-S 20-990-7781   (SL)
ANTHRATECH WESTERN INC
AWI
4450 46 Ave Se, Calgary, AB, T2B 3N7
(403) 255-7377
Emp Here 25   *Sales* 11,179,350
SIC 5074 Plumbing and heating equipment
and supplies (hydronics)
David Hambley
Philip Hambley

D-U-N-S 20-267-6813   (BR)
AP INFRASTRUCTURE SOLUTIONS LP
(*Suby of* TREVLUC HOLDINGS LTD)
4300 50 Ave Se Suite 217, Calgary, AB, T2B
2T7
(403) 248-3171
Emp Here 150
SIC 3272 Concrete products, nec

D-U-N-S 24-929-0289   (HQ)
BETHANY CARE SOCIETY
2915 26 Ave Se Unit 100, Calgary, AB, T2B
2W6
(403) 210-4600
Emp Here 50   *Sales* 92,150,400
SIC 8322 Individual and family services
Jennifer Mccue
Alasdair Smith
R Greer Black

D-U-N-S 24-440-0412   (SL)
BIRCHWOOD FURNITURE CO INC
4770 46 Ave Se, Calgary, AB, T2B 3T7
(403) 252-5111
Emp Here 70   *Sales* 10,802,540
SIC 2512 Upholstered household furniture
Bryan Frischbutter

D-U-N-S 24-495-4152   (HQ)
BRITE-LITE INC
BRITE-LITE CALGARY
2880 45 Ave Se Unit 252, Calgary, AB, T2B
3M1
(403) 720-6877
Emp Here 25   *Sales* 20,122,830
SIC 5063 Electrical apparatus and equipment
Barry Kirshenblatt
Brian Roach

D-U-N-S 24-246-5594   (SL)
CANADIAN TRUCKSTOPS LTD
CALGARY FUEL STOP
2515 50 Ave Se, Calgary, AB, T2B 3R8
(403) 236-2515
Emp Here 40   *Sales* 19,923,120
SIC 5541 Gasoline service stations
Elias Ade

D-U-N-S 24-674-6531   (HQ)
CANEDA TRANSPORT LTD
(*Suby of* MULLEN GROUP LTD)
4330 46 Ave Se, Calgary, AB, T2B 3N7
(403) 236-7900
Emp Here 55   *Sales* 14,399,420
SIC 4213 Trucking, except local
Heather Mathiesen

D-U-N-S 25-107-9695   (HQ)
CTR REFRIGERATION AND FOOD STORE EQUIPMENT LTD
4840 52 St Se, Calgary, AB, T2B 3R2

(403) 444-2877
Emp Here 20   *Sales* 11,653,250
SIC 1711 Plumbing, heating, air-conditioning
Cal Ashby
William Hammond
Robert Schmuck

D-U-N-S 20-075-4604   (BR)
CUMMINS WESTERN CANADA LIMITED PARTNERSHIP
(*Suby of* CUMMINS WESTERN CANADA
LIMITED PARTNERSHIP)
4887 35 St Se, Calgary, AB, T2B 3H6
(403) 569-1122
Emp Here 100
SIC 5084 Industrial machinery and equipment
Kent Henry

D-U-N-S 24-598-5361   (HQ)
EDO INTERNATIONAL FOOD INC
EDO JAPAN
4838 32 St Se, Calgary, AB, T2B 2S6
(403) 215-8800
Sales 77,433,300
SIC 6794 Patent owners and lessors

D-U-N-S 24-552-3014   (HQ)
ENGENIUM CHEMICALS CORP
4333 46 Ave Se, Calgary, AB, T2B 3N5
(403) 279-8545
Sales 23,512,272
SIC 2911 Petroleum refining
Greg Martin
Peter Stevens
Vlad Baron

D-U-N-S 24-526-7427   (SL)
EVASION STREET ENERGY LTD
3412 33a Ave Se, Calgary, AB, T2B 0K4

Emp Here 6   *Sales* 18,635,142
SIC 4925 Gas production and/or distribution

D-U-N-S 20-345-4194   (SL)
FBM CANADA GSD, INC
(*Suby of* FOUNDATION BUILDING MATERI-
ALS, INC.)
5155 48 Ave Se, Calgary, AB, T2B 3S8
(403) 255-8157
Emp Here 45   *Sales* 20,122,830
SIC 5039 Construction materials, nec
Reg Lillico

D-U-N-S 25-527-9192   (BR)
FEDERATED CO-OPERATIVES LIMITED
FOOD WAREHOUSE
(*Suby of* FEDERATED CO-OPERATIVES
LIMITED)
3333 52 St Se, Calgary, AB, T2B 1N3
(403) 531-6600
Emp Here 130
SIC 5141 Groceries, general line
Peter Kreis

D-U-N-S 24-850-9452   (HQ)
GAS DRIVE GLOBAL LP
(*Suby of* ENERFLEX LTD)
4700 47 St Se, Calgary, AB, T2B 3R1
(403) 387-6300
Emp Here 10   *Sales* 13,592,100
SIC 7699 Repair services, nec
Bradley Beebe

D-U-N-S 24-525-3054   (SL)
GE ENERGY OILFIELD TECHNOLGY CANADA INC
2880 45 Ave Se Suite 432, Calgary, AB, T2B
3M1

Emp Here 35   *Sales* 16,625,910
SIC 5084 Industrial machinery and equipment
Jim Junker

D-U-N-S 24-808-7249   (BR)
HARRIS STEEL ULC
HARRIS REBAR
(*Suby of* NUCOR CORPORATION)
3208 52 St Se, Calgary, AB, T2B 1N2

(403) 272-8801
Emp Here 130
SIC 3441 Fabricated structural Metal
Jack Vanier

D-U-N-S 24-347-7676   (HQ)
HERBALIFE OF CANADA LTD
(*Suby of* HERBALIFE NUTRITION LTD.)
4550 25 St Se Suite 120, Calgary, AB, T2B
3P1
(403) 204-2264
Sales 56,372,595
SIC 5122 Drugs, proprietaries, and sundries
Dominique Schroeder

D-U-N-S 24-732-6804   (HQ)
IGLOO ERECTORS LTD
3468 46 Ave Se, Calgary, AB, T2B 3J2
(403) 253-1121
Emp Here 75   *Sales* 15,090,313
SIC 1761 Roofing, siding, and sheetMetal
work
Dennis Hayden

D-U-N-S 24-298-2775   (SL)
KEYSTONE EXCAVATING LTD
4860 35 St Se, Calgary, AB, T2B 3M6
(403) 274-5452
Emp Here 130   *Sales* 32,004,180
SIC 1794 Excavation work
Ken Elias
James Elias
Les Elias

D-U-N-S 25-315-3357   (HQ)
KROWN PRODUCE INC
KROWN IMPORTS
4923 47 St Se, Calgary, AB, T2B 3S5

Emp Here 125   *Sales* 107,507,400
SIC 5148 Fresh fruits and vegetables
David Dube
Sui Ma
Ian Buckwold
Leslie Dube

D-U-N-S 25-998-7378   (SL)
MCMILLAN-MCGEE CORP
4895 35b St Se, Calgary, AB, T2B 3M9
(403) 569-5100
Emp Here 20   *Sales* 10,119,044
SIC 8711 Engineering services
Bruce Mcgee
Brent Winder

D-U-N-S 24-368-7477   (HQ)
NEW WEST FREIGHTLINER INC
3444 44 Ave Se, Calgary, AB, T2B 3J9
(403) 569-4800
Emp Here 60   *Sales* 47,196,000
SIC 5511 New and used car dealers
Greg Stahl

D-U-N-S 20-337-9052   (HQ)
NORTHPOINT TECHNICAL SERVICES ULC
4920 43 St Se, Calgary, AB, T2B 3N3
(403) 279-2211
Emp Here 25   *Sales* 10,185,800
SIC 7694 Armature rewinding shops
Paul Crawford
Brad Wellicome

D-U-N-S 20-187-4067   (HQ)
NOV ENERFLOW ULC
*NOV COILED TUBING PRESSURE PUMP-
ING CANADA*
(*Suby of* NATIONAL OILWELL VARCO, INC.)
4800 27 St Se, Calgary, AB, T2B 3M4
(403) 279-9696
Sales 112,350,800
SIC 3533 Oil and gas field machinery
John Gatlin
Mark Williamson
Larry Lindholm
Glen Arnelien

D-U-N-S 24-960-9751   (SL)
PEDDIE ROOFING & WATERPROOFING

LTD
3352 46 Ave Se, Calgary, AB, T2B 3J2
(403) 273-7000
Emp Here 65   *Sales* 14,158,885
SIC 1761 Roofing, siding, and sheetMetal work
David Peddie

D-U-N-S 20-732-6617   (BR)
PEPSICO CANADA ULC
FRITO LAY CANADA
(*Suby of* PEPSICO, INC.)
2867 45 Ave Se, Calgary, AB, T2B 3L8
(403) 571-9530
Emp Here 170
SIC 2096 Potato chips and similar snacks
Aaron White

D-U-N-S 24-853-1758   (SL)
REGGIN TECHNICAL SERVICES LTD
4550 35 St Se, Calgary, AB, T2B 3S4
(403) 287-2540
Emp Here 80   *Sales* 18,645,200
SIC 1711 Plumbing, heating, air-conditioning
Eugene Gamble
Steven Richards

D-U-N-S 24-368-5943   (SL)
REV ENGINEERING LTD
3236 50 Ave Se, Calgary, AB, T2B 3A3
(403) 287-0156
Emp Here 70   *Sales* 13,462,960
SIC 7629 Electrical repair shops
Ray Bartman
Roland Davidson
Jason Molstad
Shawn Oldenburger
Dean Petig

D-U-N-S 20-295-8179   (HQ)
SAEXPLORATION HOLDINGS INC
4860 25 St Se, Calgary, AB, T2B 3M2
(403) 776-1950
Sales 255,856,300
SIC 6712 Bank holding companies
Forest Burkholder
Jeff Mackie

D-U-N-S 24-760-7828   (HQ)
SLICED FC LTD
(*Suby of* STAR INVESTMENT CORP)
4936 52 St Se, Calgary, AB, T2B 3R2
(403) 508-6868
Emp Here 95   *Sales* 22,607,650
SIC 0723 Crop preparation services for market
Greg Kennedy
Glenn Baty

D-U-N-S 24-786-2428   (SL)
VAIL, MIKE TRUCKING LTD
4531 32 St Se, Calgary, AB, T2B 3P8
(403) 272-5487
Emp Here 125   *Sales* 25,713,250
SIC 4212 Local trucking, without storage
Mike Vail
Susan Vail

D-U-N-S 24-385-4325   (HQ)
VARISYSTEMS CORP
5304 Hubalta Rd Se, Calgary, AB, T2B 1T6
(403) 272-0318
Sales 19,044,200
SIC 3679 Electronic components, nec
Kevin Dancey

D-U-N-S 25-978-6358   (HQ)
WARD TIRES, INC
WOODTIRE CRAFT
3307 48 Ave Se, Calgary, AB, T2B 2Y8
(403) 273-0202
Emp Here 20   *Sales* 15,732,000
SIC 5531 Auto and home supply stores
Darren Lyons

D-U-N-S 24-272-7378   (BR)
WASTE MANAGEMENT OF CANADA COR-

PORATION
(*Suby of* WASTE MANAGEMENT, INC.)
4668 25 St Se, Calgary, AB, T2B 3M2

Emp Here 112
SIC 4953 Refuse systems
John Hooper

D-U-N-S 25-115-9851   (SL)
X-ACT TECHNOLOGIES LTD
4447 46 Ave Se Suite 151, Calgary, AB, T2B 3N6
(403) 291-9175
Emp Here 118   *Sales* 22,666,030
SIC 3496 Miscellaneous fabricated wire products
Eric Amos

Calgary, AB T2C

D-U-N-S 24-423-4501   (SL)
1238902 ALBERTA CORP
(*Suby of* SKION GMBH)
200 Rivercrest Dr Se Suite 160, Calgary, AB, T2C 2X5
(403) 203-4747
Emp Here 120   *Sales* 39,373,800
SIC 1629 Heavy construction, nec
Wally Hunter
Bill Jones
Khalil Maalouf
Kevin Slough
Nancy Laird
Stephan Wessel

D-U-N-S 20-334-4051   (HQ)
1942675 ALBERTA LTD
GREAT WESTERN CONTAINERS
7905 46 St Se, Calgary, AB, T2C 2Y6
(403) 279-2090
Emp Here 10   *Sales* 60,807,750
SIC 3412 Metal barrels, drums, and pails
Nils Bodtker

D-U-N-S 25-268-2901   (BR)
3618358 CANADA INC
ATS
(*Suby of* 3618358 CANADA INC)
2680 61 Ave Se, Calgary, AB, T2C 4V2
(403) 279-5208
Emp Here 80
SIC 4212 Local trucking, without storage
Kevin Wobschall

D-U-N-S 25-520-8514   (SL)
698004 ALBERTA LTD
SOBEYS RIVERBEND
8338 18 St Se Suite 100, Calgary, AB, T2C 4E4
(403) 279-9070
Emp Here 120   *Sales* 20,868,600
SIC 0742 Veterinary services, specialties
Ray Busby

D-U-N-S 20-336-9504   (BR)
ABB INC
PROCESS AUTOMATION OIL, GAS & PETROCHEMICAL
(*Suby of* ABB LTD)
2 Smed Lane Se Suite 110, Calgary, AB, T2C 4T5
(403) 806-1700
Emp Here 135
SIC 5063 Electrical apparatus and equipment
Joonas Eronen

D-U-N-S 20-120-4125   (HQ)
ACCULOGIX DISTRIBUTION SERVICES
4747 68 Ave Se, Calgary, AB, T2C 4Z4
(403) 236-1555
Emp Here 150   *Sales* 188,932,500
SIC 8742 Management consulting services
Brent Wright

D-U-N-S 20-123-1789   (HQ)

ACCURATE SCREEN LTD
7571 57 St Se, Calgary, AB, T2C 5M2
(403) 723-0323
Sales 22,358,700
SIC 5051 Metals service centers and offices
Todd Bigelow

D-U-N-S 25-741-6529   (BR)
AECOM PRODUCTION SERVICES LTD
FLINT ENERGY SERVICES
(*Suby of* AECOM)
9727 40 St Se, Calgary, AB, T2C 2P4
(403) 236-5611
Emp Here 100
SIC 3494 Valves and pipe fittings, nec
Brian Smith

D-U-N-S 20-075-0826   (BR)
AIR LIQUIDE CANADA INC
3004 54 Ave Se, Calgary, AB, T2C 0A7
(403) 310-9353
Emp Here 75
SIC 5169 Chemicals and allied products, nec
Greg Berry

D-U-N-S 20-380-2525   (SL)
ALBERTA CONSTRUCTION GROUP CORP
6565 40 St Se Unit 11, Calgary, AB, T2C 2J9
(587) 349-3000
Emp Here 60   *Sales* 34,220,280
SIC 1542 Nonresidential construction, nec
John Schmidt
Robert Munro

D-U-N-S 24-854-6517   (HQ)
ALBI CORP
4770 110 Ave Se, Calgary, AB, T2C 2T8
(403) 236-4032
Emp Here 30   *Sales* 20,320,650
SIC 1521 Single-family housing construction
Thomas (Tom) Mauro
Allan Klassen

D-U-N-S 24-522-0178   (SL)
ALLIED CONTRACTORS INC.
7003 30 St Se Bay 26, Calgary, AB, T2C 1N6
(403) 243-3311
Emp Here 67   *Sales* 10,879,527
SIC 1742 Plastering, drywall, and insulation
Gabriel Ouellette
Justin Pierre Blain
Sebastien Couture

D-U-N-S 20-058-8650   (BR)
ALSTOM CANADA INC
ALSTOM TRANSPORT, DIV OF
(*Suby of* GE RENEWABLE HOLDING B.V.)
7550 Ogden Dale Rd Se Suite 200, Calgary, AB, T2C 4X9

Emp Here 400
SIC 4789 Transportation services, nec

D-U-N-S 24-750-3738   (SL)
ALTA PROCESSING CO
7030 Ogden Dale Pl Se, Calgary, AB, T2C 2A3
(403) 279-4441
Emp Here 49   *Sales* 11,017,895
SIC 2077 Animal and marine fats and oils
Mark Conway

D-U-N-S 20-636-1370   (SL)
AMBASSADOR SALES (SOUTHERN) LTD
EQUAL DOOR INDUSTRIES
4110 76 Ave Se, Calgary, AB, T2C 2J2
(403) 720-2012
Emp Here 40   *Sales* 10,122,360
SIC 5211 Lumber and other building materials
Les Walkeden
Richard Walkeden

D-U-N-S 24-827-9650   (BR)
AP INFRASTRUCTURE SOLUTIONS LP
ARMTEC
(*Suby of* TREVLUC HOLDINGS LTD)
8916 48 St Se, Calgary, AB, T2C 2P9

(403) 204-8500
Emp Here 100
SIC 3312 Blast furnaces and steel mills
Kevin Quinn

D-U-N-S 20-757-3825   (HQ)
APEL EXTRUSIONS LIMITED
(*Suby of* ANVIL HOLDINGS LTD)
7929 30 St Se, Calgary, AB, T2C 1H7
(403) 279-3321
Emp Here 108   *Sales* 19,952,680
SIC 3354 Aluminum extruded products
Michael Flynn
Gerald Price
Joe Cyr

D-U-N-S 24-928-9612   (HQ)
ARLYN ENTERPRISES LTD
BOSS LUBRICANTS
6303 30 St Se Unit 112, Calgary, AB, T2C 1R4
(403) 279-2223
Emp Here 30   *Sales* 100,576,080
SIC 5172 Petroleum products, nec
Murray Flegel
Jarrett Flegel
William K. Dickson

D-U-N-S 20-074-4878   (SL)
ARPI'S INDUSTRIES LTD
6815 40 St Se, Calgary, AB, T2C 2W7
(403) 236-2444
Emp Here 364   *Sales* 98,588,672
SIC 1711 Plumbing, heating, air-conditioning
Julie Berdin
Barry Cousins

D-U-N-S 24-159-6782   (SL)
ARTISTIC STAIRS LTD
3504 80 Ave Se, Calgary, AB, T2C 1J3
(403) 279-5898
Emp Here 90   *Sales* 14,027,670
SIC 2431 Millwork
Bill Langen
Cecil Hoffman

D-U-N-S 25-218-7604   (BR)
ASSOCIATED MATERIALS CANADA LIMITED
GENTEK BUILDING PRODUCTS
(*Suby of* ASSOCIATED MATERIALS GROUP, INC.)
4069 112 Ave Se Suite 7, Calgary, AB, T2C 0J4
(403) 640-0906
Emp Here 150
SIC 3444 Sheet Metalwork
Don Wren

D-U-N-S 25-832-3120   (BR)
BAKER HUGHES CANADA COMPANY
BJ PIPELINE INSPECTION SERVICES
(*Suby of* GENERAL ELECTRIC COMPANY)
4839 90 Ave Se Suite Frnt, Calgary, AB, T2C 2S8
(403) 531-5300
Emp Here 120
SIC 1389 Oil and gas field services, nec
Dale Kakoschke

D-U-N-S 24-853-1501   (SL)
BARTIN PIPE & PILING SUPPLY LTD.
6835 Glenmore Trail Se, Calgary, AB, T2C 2S2
(403) 279-7473
Emp Here 10   *Sales* 10,003,390
SIC 5051 Metals service centers and offices
Harold Browne
Randy Grayson

D-U-N-S 25-977-8959   (HQ)
BAYER CROPSCIENCE INC
(*Suby of* BAYER AG)
160 Quarry Park Blvd Se Suite 200, Calgary, AB, T2C 3G3
(403) 723-7400
Sales 111,161,250
SIC 2879 Agricultural chemicals, nec
Paula Moore

Kamel Beliazi
Christian Lauterbach
James Blome

D-U-N-S 24-859-9388 (HQ)
**BIDELL EQUIPMENT LIMITED PARTNER-
SHIP**
6900 112 Ave Se, Calgary, AB, T2C 4Z1
(403) 235-5877
Sales 31,080,140
SIC 3563 Air and gas compressors
Sean Ulmer
Mat Clark

D-U-N-S 20-277-9971 (SL)
BIG BRANDS INC
5329 72 Ave Se, Calgary, AB, T2C 4X6
(587) 470-5810
Emp Here 25   *Sales* 27,633,625
SIC 5122 Drugs, proprietaries, and sundries
George Muzaic

D-U-N-S 20-193-7401 (HQ)
BIG ROCK BREWERY INC
5555 76 Ave Se Suite 1, Calgary, AB, T2C 4L8
(403) 720-3239
Emp Here 100   *Sales* 36,955,956
SIC 2082 Malt beverages
Wayne Arsenault
Paul Gautreau
Paul Howden
Scott Matheson
Susanne Fox
Brad Goddard
Don Sewell
Michael G. Kohut
Kathleen Mcnally-Leitch
Robert G. Peters

D-U-N-S 24-375-4202 (HQ)
BODTKER GROUP OF COMPANIES LTD
7905 46 St Se, Calgary, AB, T2C 2Y6
(403) 279-2191
Emp Here 9   *Sales* 91,377,250
SIC 6712 Bank holding companies
Nils Bodtker

D-U-N-S 20-958-7687 (SL)
BOLDER GRAPHICS INCORPORATED
10 Smed Lane Se Unit 110, Calgary, AB, T2C
4T5
(403) 259-0054
Emp Here 70   *Sales* 14,820,680
SIC 7336 Commercial art and graphic design
Kevin Mccoy

D-U-N-S 24-320-1157 (SL)
BOLT OFFSITE LTD
7007 84 St Se, Calgary, AB, T2C 4T6
(403) 921-5318
Emp Here 50   *Sales* 15,943,450
SIC 1521 Single-family housing construction
Daniel Fernandez
Shawn Decoste

D-U-N-S 25-265-5055 (SL)
BRAZZO CONTRACTORS (CALGARY) LTD
A S M INDUSTRIES
2624 54 Ave Se Unit 1, Calgary, AB, T2C 1R5
(403) 279-1983
Emp Here 110   *Sales* 25,637,150
SIC 1711 Plumbing, heating, air-conditioning
Raymond Gertz
David Neilsen

D-U-N-S 20-337-9045 (HQ)
BRIDGE 8 INVESTMENTS INC
7805 46 St Se, Calgary, AB, T2C 2Y5
(403) 236-0305
Emp Here 2   *Sales* 27,335,000
SIC 6712 Bank holding companies
Kirk Hudson
Kyle Hudson

D-U-N-S 24-388-9438 (HQ)
BRIGHTPATH EARLY LEARNING INC
200 Rivercrest Dr Se Suite 201, Calgary, AB,
T2C 2X5

(403) 705-0362
Sales 51,190,091
SIC 8299 Schools and educational services,
nec
Mary Ann Curran
Dale Kearns
Jane Todd
Samaya Khattak
Mary Mutchler
Carol Caddoo
Marnie Falkiner
Eva Kanovich

D-U-N-S 25-180-8986 (SL)
BRONZART CASTING LTD
4315 64 Ave Se Suite 1, Calgary, AB, T2C 2C8
(403) 279-6584
Emp Here 15   *Sales* 15,005,085
SIC 5051 Metals service centers and offices
Vaughn Stewart

D-U-N-S 24-426-4821 (BR)
BUY-LOW FOODS LTD
(Suby of PATTISON, JIM GROUP INC*)*
7100 44 St Se, Calgary, AB, T2C 2V7
(403) 236-6300
Emp Here 100
SIC 5411 Grocery stores
Larry Chmielewski

D-U-N-S 25-218-3256 (SL)
CALGARY AGGREGATE RECYCLING LTD
6020 94 Ave Se, Calgary, AB, T2C 3Z3
(403) 279-8330
Emp Here 35   *Sales* 10,539,970
SIC 4953 Refuse systems
John Dorchak
Vete Dorchak

D-U-N-S 24-273-0646 (SL)
**CALGARY HUMANE SOCIETY FOR PRE-
VENTION OF CRUELTY TO ANIMALS**
S P C A
4455 110 Ave Se, Calgary, AB, T2C 2T7
(403) 205-4455
Emp Here 65   *Sales* 46,098,780
SIC 8699 Membership organizations, nec
Nancy Golding
Heather Gnenz
Greg Kelly
Ramona Ernst

D-U-N-S 20-057-7588 (SL)
CALHEX INDUSTRIES LTD
9515 48 St Se, Calgary, AB, T2C 2R1
(403) 225-4395
Emp Here 58   *Sales* 11,140,930
SIC 3443 Fabricated plate work (boiler shop)
Martin Sojka
Darren Kladnik

D-U-N-S 20-990-1628 (HQ)
CAM DISTRIBUTORS LTD
CAM INDUSTRIAL
7095 64 St Se Unit 20, Calgary, AB, T2C 5C3
(403) 720-0076
Emp Here 10   *Sales* 16,625,910
SIC 5085 Industrial supplies
Parker Foord
Peter Brar
Neil Hussey
Jimmy Foord
Charlotte Foord

D-U-N-S 25-416-7216 (BR)
CANADA BREAD COMPANY, LIMITED
CANADA BREAD FROZEN BAKERY
(Suby of GRUPO BIMBO, S.A.B. DE C.V.*)*
4320 80 Ave Se, Calgary, AB, T2C 4N6
(403) 203-1675
Emp Here 165
SIC 2051 Bread, cake, and related products
Grant Bistritz

D-U-N-S 20-012-3230 (BR)
**CANADA CARTAGE SYSTEM LIMITED
PARTNERSHIP**
CANADA CARTAGE

(Suby of CANADA CARTAGE SYSTEM LIM-
ITED PARTNERSHIP*)*
4700 102 Ave Se, Calgary, AB, T2C 2X8
(403) 296-0290
Emp Here 250
SIC 4213 Trucking, except local

D-U-N-S 24-139-2278 (BR)
CANADIAN INTERMODAL SERVICES LTD
CONTAINER WEST
5402 44 St Se, Calgary, AB, T2C 4M8
(403) 920-0577
Emp Here 100   *Sales* 714,124
SIC 5085 Industrial supplies
Dean Olund

D-U-N-S 20-019-8369 (HQ)
CANADIAN PACIFIC RAILWAY LIMITED
7550 Ogden Dale Rd Se, Calgary, AB, T2C
4X9
(888) 333-6370
Emp Here 500   *Sales* 5,546,274,232
SIC 4011 Railroads, line-haul operating
Keith Creel
Robert Johnson
Nadeem Velani
Tony Marquis
Scott Macdonald
Mark Redd
Laird Pitz
John Brooks
Jeffrey Ellis
Michael Redeker

D-U-N-S 24-765-0786 (SL)
CANRIG DRILLING TECHNOLOGY LTD
(Suby of NABORS INDUSTRIES LTD.*)*
5250 94 Ave Se, Calgary, AB, T2C 3Z3
(403) 279-3466
Emp Here 501   *Sales* 273,531,471
SIC 1389 Oil and gas field services, nec
Chris Papouras

D-U-N-S 25-330-3101 (HQ)
CAPITAL PAPER RECYCLING LTD
10595 50 St Se, Calgary, AB, T2C 3E3
(403) 543-3322
Emp Here 30   *Sales* 22,358,700
SIC 5044 Office equipment
Sean Burns
Douglas Houser

D-U-N-S 20-827-6907 (HQ)
CARDEL CONSTRUCTION LTD
180 Quarry Park Blvd Se, Calgary, AB, T2C
3G3
(403) 258-1511
Sales 13,077,650
SIC 6712 Bank holding companies
Ryan Ockey
Neil Kuntz

D-U-N-S 24-764-8335 (HQ)
CARDEL HOMES LIMITED PARTNERSHIP
(Suby of CARDEL CONSTRUCTION LTD*)*
180 Quarry Park Blvd Se Suite 200, Calgary,
AB, T2C 3G3
(403) 258-1511
Sales 13,276,158
SIC 1521 Single-family housing construction
Ryan Ockey

D-U-N-S 24-853-3275 (BR)
CARPENTER CANADA CO
(Suby of CARPENTER CO.*)*
5800 36 St Se, Calgary, AB, T2C 2A9
(403) 279-2466
Emp Here 100
SIC 3089 Plastics products, nec
Max Ten Pow

D-U-N-S 25-147-2452 (SL)
CATALYST LLP
200 Quarry Park Blvd Se Suite 250, Calgary,
AB, T2C 5E3
(403) 296-0082
Emp Here 60   *Sales* 12,461,100

SIC 8721 Accounting, auditing, and book-
keeping
Brock Cairns
Gerald Coakwell
Cameron Crawford
David Laycaft
Timothy Coakwell
Carl Scholz
Paige Shaw
Christopher Alexander
Terri Holowath

D-U-N-S 25-194-5721 (HQ)
CDN ENERGY AND POWER CORP
(Suby of DSD HOLDINGS INC*)*
10550 42 St Se Suite 107, Calgary, AB, T2C
5C7
(403) 236-0333
Emp Here 14   *Sales* 47,768,195
SIC 5063 Electrical apparatus and equipment
Shawn Sauer
Dean Smurthwaite
Andrew Maclennan

D-U-N-S 20-699-6857 (HQ)
CEMATRIX CORPORATION
5440 53 St Se, Calgary, AB, T2C 4B6
(403) 219-0484
Emp Here 5   *Sales* 13,312,814
SIC 3272 Concrete products, nec
Jeffrey Kendrick
Steve Bent
James Chong
Robert Benson
Steve Bjornson
Rick Breen
Dan Koyich
Minaz Lalani

D-U-N-S 24-088-7265 (HQ)
CH2M HILL ENERGY CANADA LTD
VECO CANADA
(Suby of JACOBS ENGINEERING GROUP
INC.*)*
205 Quarry Park Blvd Se, Calgary, AB, T2C
3E7
(403) 407-6000
Sales 25,349,000
SIC 8748 Business consulting, nec
Thomas G. Searle

D-U-N-S 25-680-7009 (SL)
CHIEF HAULING CONTRACTORS INC
(Suby of GIBSON ENERGY INC*)*
5654 55 St Se, Calgary, AB, T2C 3G9
(403) 215-4312
Emp Here 75   *Sales* 15,427,950
SIC 4212 Local trucking, without storage
Eugene Millet

D-U-N-S 24-899-2794 (SL)
CICHLID WHOLESALE LTD
7503 35 St Se Unit 25, Calgary, AB, T2C 1V3
(403) 720-8355
Emp Here 30   *Sales* 22,275,600
SIC 5199 Nondurable goods, nec
Paul Godden

D-U-N-S 24-731-0477 (HQ)
**CITY WIDE TOWING AND RECOVERY SER-
VICE LTD**
BIG I TOWING
10885 84 St Se, Calgary, AB, T2C 5A6
(403) 798-0876
Emp Here 36   *Sales* 28,330,000
SIC 7549 Automotive services, nec
Jack Richards
Wendy Voelk
Patricia A. Richards

D-U-N-S 25-677-5115 (HQ)
COLUMBIA INDUSTRIES LTD
7150 112 Ave Se, Calgary, AB, T2C 4Z1
(403) 236-3420
Emp Here 4   *Sales* 12,311,365
SIC 3728 Aircraft parts and equipment, nec
Michael Monaghan

Sean Monaghan

D-U-N-S 20-554-5424   (SL)
COMPRESSCO CANADA INC
(*Suby of* TETRA TECHNOLOGIES, INC.)
5050 76 Ave Se, Calgary, AB, T2C 2X2
(403) 279-5866
Emp Here 23   *Sales* 10,925,598
SIC 5084 Industrial machinery and equipment
Michael Sparks

D-U-N-S 20-521-9132   (BR)
CONSOLIDATED FASTFRATE INC
FASTFRATE
11440 54 St Se, Calgary, AB, T2C 4Y6
(403) 264-1687
Emp Here 75
SIC 4731 Freight transportation arrangement
Kevin Hankinson

D-U-N-S 24-732-2738   (SL)
CONSTANT FIRE PROTECTION SYSTEMS LTD
5442 56 Ave Se, Calgary, AB, T2C 4M6
(403) 279-7973
Emp Here 38   *Sales* 16,852,620
SIC 7389 Business services, nec
Jim Anderson
Raymond Anderson

D-U-N-S 25-105-2031   (SL)
CONTROL INNOVATIONS INC
11222 42 St Se, Calgary, AB, T2C 0J9
(403) 720-0277
Emp Here 64   *Sales* 20,461,120
SIC 1389 Oil and gas field services, nec
Douglas Keller

D-U-N-S 25-367-8635   (HQ)
CORDY OILFIELD SERVICES INC
5366 55 St Se, Calgary, AB, T2C 3G9
(403) 262-7667
Sales 11,982,560
SIC 1382 Oil and gas exploration services
Darrick J. Evong
David E. Mullen
Timothy H. Urquhart
Michael Smith
Rick Manhas
Stuart King
Luke Caplette

D-U-N-S 25-416-5723   (SL)
CRATEX INDUSTRIES (CALGARY) LTD
3347 57 Ave Se, Calgary, AB, T2C 0B2
(403) 203-0880
Emp Here 37   *Sales* 19,238,779
SIC 4783 Packing and crating
Ron Holdinga
Terry Hennessey

D-U-N-S 24-299-9266   (BR)
CROWN METAL PACKAGING CANADA LP
(*Suby of* CROWN HOLDINGS INC.)
4455 75 Ave Se, Calgary, AB, T2C 2K8
(403) 236-0241
Emp Here 120
SIC 3411 Metal cans
Mark Petursson

D-U-N-S 24-715-5690   (HQ)
DATALOG TECHNOLOGY INC
10707 50 St Se, Calgary, AB, T2C 3E5
(403) 243-2024
Emp Here 296   *Sales* 163,791,300
SIC 1389 Oil and gas field services, nec
Peter Huff
Ian Underdown

D-U-N-S 25-485-8178   (BR)
DAVIDSON ENMAN LUMBER LIMITED
TRUSS DIVISION
(*Suby of* DAVIDSON ENMAN LUMBER LIMITED)
9515 44 St Se, Calgary, AB, T2C 2P7
(403) 279-5525
Emp Here 100

SIC 2439 Structural wood members, nec
Lyle Englund

D-U-N-S 25-519-5463   (BR)
DIRECT LIMITED PARTNERSHIP
DIRECT TRANSPORT
(*Suby of* DIRECT LIMITED PARTNERSHIP)
5555 69 Ave Se Suite 121, Calgary, AB, T2C 4Y7
(403) 296-0291
Emp Here 100
SIC 4212 Local trucking, without storage
Hrysak Tom

D-U-N-S 25-372-0551   (HQ)
DIRTT ENVIRONMENTAL SOLUTIONS LTD
7303 30 St Se, Calgary, AB, T2C 1N6
(403) 723-5000
Emp Here 345   *Sales* 231,794,265
SIC 2522 Office furniture, except wood
Kevin O'meara
Mark Greffen
Joseph Zirkman
Krista Pell
Kingsley Koch
Geoff Gosling
Geoffrey Krause
Jeffrey A. Calkins

D-U-N-S 24-334-3493   (HQ)
DOKA CANADA LTD./LTEE
(*Suby of* UMDASCH GROUP AG)
5404 36 St Se, Calgary, AB, T2C 1P1
(403) 243-6629
Emp Here 30   *Sales* 33,538,050
SIC 5039 Construction materials, nec
Gunnar Falke

D-U-N-S 25-167-7647   (HQ)
DOUBLE R BUILDING PRODUCTS LTD
DOUBLE R TRUSS AND FLOOR
8209 30 St Se, Calgary, AB, T2C 1H7
(403) 236-8322
Emp Here 40   *Sales* 29,066,310
SIC 5039 Construction materials, nec
Ronald Desnoyers
Ron Tillapaugh

D-U-N-S 20-278-3098   (SL)
DRECO ENERGY SERVICES ULC
(*Suby of* NATIONAL OILWELL VARCO, INC.)
6771 84 St Se, Calgary, AB, T2C 4T6
(403) 319-2333
Emp Here 60   *Sales* 13,320,060
SIC 3533 Oil and gas field machinery
Albert Roy

D-U-N-S 24-983-8434   (SL)
DRILLING FLUIDS TREATMENT SYSTEMS INC
7530 114 Ave Se, Calgary, AB, T2C 4T3
(403) 279-0123
Emp Here 27   *Sales* 12,825,702
SIC 5085 Industrial supplies
Edward A Kutryk

D-U-N-S 25-681-0466   (SL)
DURWEST CONSTRUCTION SYSTEMS (ALBERTA) LTD
10665 46 St Se, Calgary, AB, T2C 5C2
(403) 253-7385
Emp Here 43   *Sales* 10,881,537
SIC 5211 Lumber and other building materials
David Cook

D-U-N-S 25-365-3687   (HQ)
DYNAMIC AIR SHELTERS LTD
(*Suby of* DYNAMIC SHELTERS INC)
200 Rivercrest Dr Se Suite 170, Calgary, AB, T2C 2X5
(403) 203-9311
Emp Here 70   *Sales* 31,694,025
SIC 3448 Prefabricated Metal buildings and components
Harold Warner
Terry French

D-U-N-S 20-351-0206   (HQ)

DYNAMIC CONCRETE PUMPING INC
10720 48 St Se, Calgary, AB, T2C 3E1
(403) 236-9511
Emp Here 77   *Sales* 37,617,456
SIC 1771 Concrete work
Joseph Delahay
Trevor Mooney
Pamela Manthey

D-U-N-S 24-346-5820   (SL)
DYNAMIC FURNITURE CORP
(*Suby of* REGENCY FURNITURE CORP)
5300 61 Ave Se, Calgary, AB, T2C 4N1
(403) 236-3220
Emp Here 200   *Sales* 30,864,400
SIC 2511 Wood household furniture
Dean Mohamed Sunderji

D-U-N-S 20-286-3015   (SL)
DYNASTY FURNITURE MANUFACTURING INC
(*Suby of* DYNASTY REAL PROPERTIES INC)
3344 54 Ave Se, Calgary, AB, T2C 0A8
(403) 279-2958
Emp Here 110   *Sales* 16,975,420
SIC 2512 Upholstered household furniture
Zaherali Sunderji
Faizel Sunderji
Rosmin Sunderji

D-U-N-S 24-054-1615   (HQ)
DYNO NOBEL CANADA INC
(*Suby of* INCITEC PIVOT LIMITED)
48 Quarry Park Blvd Se Suite 210, Calgary, AB, T2C 5P2
(403) 726-7500
Emp Here 25   *Sales* 222,322,500
SIC 2892 Explosives
Yves Tremblay
David Mcconnach

D-U-N-S 25-947-4521   (SL)
EAST LAKE HUSKY MARKET TRUCK STOP
5225 106 Ave Se, Calgary, AB, T2C 5N2
(403) 236-5225
Emp Here 23   *Sales* 11,455,794
SIC 5541 Gasoline service stations
Musard Hassin

D-U-N-S 25-266-4735   (BR)
EECOL ELECTRIC CORP
(*Suby of* WESCO INTERNATIONAL, INC.)
11004 48 St Se, Calgary, AB, T2C 3E1
(403) 243-5594
Emp Here 100
SIC 5063 Electrical apparatus and equipment
Cliff Gehlert

D-U-N-S 20-769-0736   (HQ)
ELJAY IRRIGATION LTD
3700 78 Ave Se Suite 3, Calgary, AB, T2C 2L8
(403) 279-2425
Emp Here 7   *Sales* 13,300,728
SIC 5083 Farm and garden machinery

D-U-N-S 24-014-0541   (HQ)
ELRUS INC
ELRUS AGGREGATE SYSTEMS
4409 Glenmore Trail Se, Calgary, AB, T2C 2R8
(403) 279-7741
Emp Here 80   *Sales* 64,971,885
SIC 1411 Dimension stone
Carollyne Coulson
Corae Russell

D-U-N-S 24-309-6034   (BR)
EMERSON ELECTRIC CANADA LIMITED
EMERSON PROCESS MANAGEMENT
(*Suby of* EMERSON ELECTRIC CO.)
110 Quarry Park Blvd Se Suite 200, Calgary, AB, T2C 3G3
(403) 258-6200
Emp Here 100
SIC 5063 Electrical apparatus and equipment

Dave Taylor

D-U-N-S 20-106-7639   (BR)
EMERSON ELECTRIC CANADA LIMITED
EMERSON PROCESS MANAGEMENT, DIV OF
(*Suby of* EMERSON ELECTRIC CO.)
110 Quarry Park Blvd Se Suite 200, Calgary, AB, T2C 3G3
(403) 258-6200
Emp Here 200
SIC 8711 Engineering services
Dave Taylor

D-U-N-S 24-677-7994   (BR)
ENMAX CORPORATION
(*Suby of* CITY OF CALGARY, THE)
8820 52 St Se Suite 1940, Calgary, AB, T2C 4E7
(403) 514-3700
Emp Here 300
SIC 4911 Electric services
Jack Li

D-U-N-S 20-075-7631   (HQ)
ESKIMO REFRIGERATION LTD
4705 61 Ave Se, Calgary, AB, T2C 4W1
(403) 279-8091
Emp Here 20   *Sales* 17,886,960
SIC 5078 Refrigeration equipment and supplies
Larry Fleming
Robbie Fleming
Arthena Fleming

D-U-N-S 24-387-0271   (BR)
EVRAZ INC. NA CANADA
EVRAZ NORTH AMERICA
(*Suby of* EVRAZ PLC)
7201 Ogden Dale Rd Se, Calgary, AB, T2C 2A4
(403) 279-3351
Emp Here 500
SIC 3312 Blast furnaces and steel mills
Sam Hadi

D-U-N-S 24-805-8591   (HQ)
EXCHANGER INDUSTRIES LIMITED
(*Suby of* COOPERATIE NOVA ARGENT U.A.)
5811 46 St Se Suite 200, Calgary, AB, T2C 4Y5
(403) 236-0166
Emp Here 130   *Sales* 27,852,325
SIC 3443 Fabricated plate work (boiler shop)
Mark El-Baroudi
John Michelin
Gavin Exon
David Neufeld

D-U-N-S 20-120-3077   (HQ)
FEDEX SUPPLY CHAIN DISTRIBUTION SYSTEM OF CANADA, INC
SYSTEME DE DISTRIBUTION DE LA CHAINE D'APPROVISIONNEMENT FEDEX DU CANADA
(*Suby of* FEDEX CORPORATION)
6336 114 Ave Se, Calgary, AB, T2C 4T9
(800) 463-3339
Emp Here 20   *Sales* 197,719,000
SIC 4731 Freight transportation arrangement
Arthur F. Smuck Iii
Bradley R. Peacock
Michael K. Fox
Edward C. Klank Iii

D-U-N-S 20-075-8548   (HQ)
FISH CREEK EXCAVATING LTD
7515 84 St Se, Calgary, AB, T2C 4Y1
(403) 248-8222
Emp Here 10   *Sales* 13,540,230
SIC 1794 Excavation work
John Armstrong
Blaine Shae
Vadim Barabash

D-U-N-S 25-684-8862   (BR)
FJORDS PROCESSING CANADA INC
KVAERNER PROCESS SYSTEMS, DIV OF

(*Suby of* NATIONAL OILWELL VARCO, INC.)
115 Quarry Park Rd Se Suite 110, Calgary, AB, T2C 5G9
(403) 640-4230
Emp Here 100
SIC 3823 Process control instruments
Christine Zoller

D-U-N-S 24-205-1071   (SL)
FLAIR ENTERPRISES INC
3916 72 Ave Se, Calgary, AB, T2C 2E2
(403) 219-1006
Emp Here 50   *Sales* 21,222,844
SIC 5021 Furniture
Kamaljeet Minhas
Bill Minhas

D-U-N-S 25-505-4926   (SL)
FLAIR FLEXIBLE PACKAGING (CANADA) CORPORATION
4100 72 Ave Se, Calgary, AB, T2C 2C1
(403) 207-3226
Emp Here 96   *Sales* 71,281,920
SIC 5199 Nondurable goods, nec
Young So

D-U-N-S 24-016-7072   (HQ)
FLEET BRAKE PARTS & SERVICE LTD
7707 54 St Se, Calgary, AB, T2C 4R7
(403) 476-9011
Emp Here 60   *Sales* 29,599,680
SIC 7538 General automotive repair shops
John Bzeta

D-U-N-S 24-156-1778   (SL)
FLO-SKID MANUFACTURING INC
6725 86 Ave Se, Calgary, AB, T2C 2S4
(403) 279-6602
Emp Here 24   *Sales* 11,400,624
SIC 5084 Industrial machinery and equipment
Frank Kaplan

D-U-N-S 20-113-9511   (HQ)
FMI LOGISTICS INC
7151 44 St Se Unit 111, Calgary, AB, T2C 4E8
(866) 723-6660
Emp Here 1   *Sales* 18,198,845
SIC 4731 Freight transportation arrangement
Darryl Stanier

D-U-N-S 24-767-8733   (SL)
FOCUS AUTO DESIGN INC
6159 40 St Se, Calgary, AB, T2C 2B1
(403) 255-4711
Emp Here 25   *Sales* 12,451,950
SIC 5511 New and used car dealers
Frederick Phillips

D-U-N-S 25-217-9346   (SL)
G K D INDUSTRIES LTD
7939 54 St Se, Calgary, AB, T2C 4R7
(403) 279-8087
Emp Here 40   *Sales* 19,001,040
SIC 5084 Industrial machinery and equipment
George Plesa
Elvira Plesa
Brad Narfason

D-U-N-S 20-829-1567   (HQ)
GENTHERM GLOBAL POWER TECHNOLOGIES INC
(*Suby of* GENTHERM INCORPORATED)
7875 57 St Se Unit 16, Calgary, AB, T2C 5K7
(403) 236-5556
Emp Here 85   *Sales* 26,661,880
SIC 3629 Electrical industrial apparatus, nec
James Bolen
Garry Forbes
Collin Newman

D-U-N-S 20-303-4129   (HQ)
GIENOW CANADA INC
PLY GEM
7140 40 St Se, Calgary, AB, T2C 2B6
(403) 203-8200
Emp Here 500   *Sales* 113,604,165
SIC 2431 Millwork

Ron Cauchi

D-U-N-S 25-389-2079   (SL)
GLENMORE INN HOLDINGS LTD
GLENMORE INN
(*Suby of* RESMAN HOLDINGS LTD)
2720 Glenmore Trail Se, Calgary, AB, T2C 2E6
(403) 279-8611
Emp Here 130   *Sales* 12,436,840
SIC 7011 Hotels and motels
David Taylor

D-U-N-S 20-560-2290   (SL)
GOLDRAY INDUSTRIES LTD
GOLDRAY GLASS
4605 52 Ave Se, Calgary, AB, T2C 4N7
(403) 236-1333
Emp Here 91   *Sales* 16,308,929
SIC 3211 Flat glass
Cathie Saroka
Michael Saroka
Theresa Kosek
Ted Jones

D-U-N-S 20-357-8620   (SL)
GRAINSCONNECT CANADA OPERATIONS INC
GRAINSCONNECT CANADA
48 Quarry Park Blvd Se Suite 260, Calgary, AB, T2C 5P2
(403) 879-2727
Emp Here 17   *Sales* 20,576,749
SIC 5153 Grain and field beans
Warren Stow

D-U-N-S 24-156-9107   (SL)
GRAND WEST ELECTRIC LTD
2408 91 Ave Se, Calgary, AB, T2C 5H2
(403) 291-2688
Emp Here 75   *Sales* 31,142,175
SIC 4931 Electric and other services combined
Anthony Dallazanna
Gabe Rosati

D-U-N-S 20-646-0511   (HQ)
H & R TRANSPORT LIMITED
4540 54 Ave Se, Calgary, AB, T2C 2Y8
(403) 720-8344
Emp Here 100   *Sales* 237,262,800
SIC 4731 Freight transportation arrangement
Al Foder
D'arcy Foder
David Westwood
Mark Foder
Ross Sten

D-U-N-S 24-016-5753   (SL)
HAYLEY INDUSTRIAL ELECTRONICS LTD
7071 112 Ave Se, Calgary, AB, T2C 5A5
(403) 259-5575
Emp Here 62   *Sales* 13,764,062
SIC 3569 General industrial machinery, nec
Noel Hayley
Darrell Hayley
Gloria Hayley

D-U-N-S 20-639-2107   (SL)
HEAVY INDUSTRIES THEMING CORPORATION
HEAVY INDUSTRIES
(*Suby of* FLYNN CANADA LTD)
9192 52 St Se, Calgary, AB, T2C 5A9
(403) 252-6603
Emp Here 65   *Sales* 16,002,090
SIC 1799 Special trade contractors, nec
Ryan Bessant
Renato Giordani

D-U-N-S 25-213-9204   (SL)
HMT CANADA LTD
RANGER INSPECTION
11051 50 St Se Unit 130, Calgary, AB, T2C 3E5
(403) 252-4487
Emp Here 30   *Sales* 13,304,700

SIC 7389 Business services, nec
Alex Ronanow

D-U-N-S 24-336-4101   (BR)
HOOD PACKAGING CORPORATION
(*Suby of* HOOD FLEXIBLE PACKAGING CORPORATION)
5615 44 St Se, Calgary, AB, T2C 1V2
(403) 279-4000
Emp Here 125
SIC 2674 Bags: uncoated paper and multiwall
Greg Shepherd

D-U-N-S 25-536-9738   (SL)
HOOVER MECHANICAL PLUMBING & HEATING LTD
3640 61 Ave Se Suite 1, Calgary, AB, T2C 2J3
(403) 217-5655
Emp Here 225   *Sales* 60,940,800
SIC 1711 Plumbing, heating, air-conditioning
Robert Purcell

D-U-N-S 24-673-7779   (HQ)
I-XL MASONRY SUPPLIES LTD
(*Suby of* I-XL LTD)
4900 102 Ave Se, Calgary, AB, T2C 2X8
(403) 243-6031
Emp Here 1   *Sales* 28,171,962
SIC 5032 Brick, stone, and related material
Malcolm Sissons
Clayton Sissons

D-U-N-S 25-183-3745   (SL)
ICE WESTERN SALES LTD
ICE WESTERN (BC) SALES
9765 54 St Se, Calgary, AB, T2C 5J6
(403) 252-5577
Emp Here 100   *Sales* 47,502,600
SIC 5084 Industrial machinery and equipment
James Clancy

D-U-N-S 20-271-9217   (SL)
ICONIC POWER SYSTEMS INC
11090 48 St Se, Calgary, AB, T2C 3E1
(403) 910-3823
Emp Here 60   *Sales* 13,069,740
SIC 1731 Electrical work
Scott Ebner
Jay Bruchet
Bev Stewart

D-U-N-S 20-167-4926   (HQ)
IMPERIAL OIL LIMITED
AIRWORLD
505 Quarry Park Blvd Se, Calgary, AB, T2C 5N1
(800) 567-3776
Emp Here 700   *Sales* 26,608,622,098
SIC 2911 Petroleum refining
Rich M. Kruger
John Whelan
Daniel (Dan) Lyons
Theresa Redburn
Peter M. Dinnick
Glenn Peterson
David Cornhill
Krystyna Hoeg
Miranda Hubbs
Jack M. Mintz

D-U-N-S 20-879-7139   (SL)
IMS INNOVATIVE MANUFACTURING SOURCE INC
3855 64 Ave Se Suite 3, Calgary, AB, T2C 2V5
(403) 279-7702
Emp Here 90   *Sales* 11,264,970
SIC 3679 Electronic components, nec
Dave Elhard

D-U-N-S 25-105-1710   (HQ)
INA INTERNATIONAL LTD
(*Suby of* CANADIAN TIRE CORPORATION, LIMITED)
110250 Quarry Park Blvd Se, Calgary, AB, T2C 3E7
(403) 717-1400
Emp Here 30   *Sales* 31,232,520

SIC 5091 Sporting and recreation goods
Robert Sartor
Richard Burnet

D-U-N-S 24-346-7433   (BR)
INDEPENDENT COUNSELLING ENTERPRISES INC
4888 72 Ave Se Suite 200e, Calgary, AB, T2C 3Z2
(403) 219-0503
Emp Here 150
SIC 8322 Individual and family services
Deanna Rachkewich

D-U-N-S 20-439-7426   (HQ)
JACOBS CANADA INC
(*Suby of* JACOBS ENGINEERING GROUP INC.)
205 Quarry Park Blvd Se, Calgary, AB, T2C 3E7
(403) 258-6411
Emp Here 800   *Sales* 177,417,900
SIC 8711 Engineering services
Steven J. Demetriou
Graig Landry
Brian Thurgood

D-U-N-S 24-674-0344   (HQ)
JACOBS INDUSTRIAL SERVICES ULC
(*Suby of* JACOBS ENGINEERING GROUP INC.)
205 Quarry Park Blvd Se Suite 200, Calgary, AB, T2C 3E7
(403) 258-6899
Emp Here 25   *Sales* 159,840,000
SIC 7349 Building maintenance services, nec
Earl J Mitchell
N.L.H. Frederiksen
Rejean J Thibeault

D-U-N-S 25-766-5083   (HQ)
JADE STONE LTD
6429 79 Ave Se, Calgary, AB, T2C 5P1
(403) 287-0398
Emp Here 13   *Sales* 11,671,750
SIC 3281 Cut stone and stone products
Tony Tang
Fu Deng

D-U-N-S 20-550-3654   (HQ)
JEPSON PETROLEUM (ALBERTA) LTD
PETRO CANADA
5215 61 Ave Se, Calgary, AB, T2C 3Y6
(403) 215-1449
Emp Here 25   *Sales* 44,002,035
SIC 5172 Petroleum products, nec
Dave Jepson
Chris Jepson
Deborah Jepson
Debra Jepson

D-U-N-S 20-352-4082   (SL)
KAL TIRE ALBERTA LTD
KAL TIRE
5375 68 Ave Se, Calgary, AB, T2C 5A7
(403) 236-7171
Emp Here 60   *Sales* 37,756,800
SIC 5531 Auto and home supply stores
Kent Peedie

D-U-N-S 24-300-8794   (SL)
KEVCO PIPELINES LTD
5050 54 Ave Se, Calgary, AB, T2C 2Y8
(403) 279-5050
Emp Here 50   *Sales* 12,044,200
SIC 1623 Water, sewer, and utility lines

D-U-N-S 24-042-9589   (SL)
KIDCO CONSTRUCTION LTD
4949 76 Ave Se, Calgary, AB, T2C 3C6
(403) 730-2029
Emp Here 175   *Sales* 44,177,350
SIC 1629 Heavy construction, nec
Ryan Erickson
Jay Masciangelo
Kyle Thomson
D-U-N-S 24-068-0710   (BR)

KINDERSLEY TRANSPORT LTD
(*Suby of EKS HOLDINGS LTD*)
5515 98 Ave Se, Calgary, AB, T2C 4L1
(403) 279-8721
Emp Here 100
SIC 4213 Trucking, except local
Danny Todd

   D-U-N-S 20-076-6509   (HQ)
KRISTIAN ELECTRIC LTD
4215 64 Ave Se, Calgary, AB, T2C 2C8
(403) 292-9111
Emp Here 25   *Sales* 10,578,040
SIC 7699 Repair services, nec
Kevin Gjertsen
Randi Thompson
Bertha Gjertsen
Dean Gjertsen
Wayne Gjertsen
Chad Gjertsen

   D-U-N-S 24-806-8967   (HQ)
KUDU INDUSTRIES INC
9112 40 St Se, Calgary, AB, T2C 2P3
(403) 279-5838
Emp Here 45   *Sales* 56,576,680
SIC 5084 Industrial machinery and equipment
Robert Mills
Ray Mills

   D-U-N-S 25-193-5151   (HQ)
LIGHT SPEED LOGISTICS INC
5720 84 Ave Se, Calgary, AB, T2C 4T6
(403) 208-5441
Emp Here 150   *Sales* 47,939,060
SIC 4213 Trucking, except local
Gurpreet Randhawa
Ashish Gill
Hira Randhawa

   D-U-N-S 24-204-9083   (BR)
LOBLAWS INC
WESTERN GROCERS
(*Suby of LOBLAW COMPANIES LIMITED*)
6810 40 St Se, Calgary, AB, T2C 2A5
(905) 459-2500
Emp Here 200
SIC 5411 Grocery stores
Robert Howell

   D-U-N-S 20-441-2449   (HQ)
MANTEI'S TRANSPORT LTD
(*Suby of SEABOARD LIQUID CARRIERS LIMITED*)
8715 44 St Se, Calgary, AB, T2C 2P5
(403) 531-1600
Emp Here 60   *Sales* 20,570,600
SIC 4212 Local trucking, without storage
Joseph Shannon
Mark Shannon

   D-U-N-S 25-505-7010   (SL)
MARYN INTERNATIONAL SALES LTD
POWER UP
4216 54 Ave Se Suite 8, Calgary, AB, T2C 2E3
(403) 252-2239
Emp Here 15   *Sales* 15,492,120
SIC 5172 Petroleum products, nec
Mark Bishop

   D-U-N-S 20-322-4840   (HQ)
MCILVEEN LUMBER INDUSTRIES (ALTA.)(2012) LTD
MCILVEEN LUMBER
(*Suby of GILLFOR DISTRIBUTION INC*)
9440 48 St Se, Calgary, AB, T2C 2R2
(403) 273-5333
Emp Here 19   *Sales* 10,732,176
SIC 5031 Lumber, plywood, and millwork
Gary Gill
Bob Dosanjh

   D-U-N-S 24-378-7152   (HQ)
MENTAL HEALTH COMMISSION OF CANADA
110 Quarry Park Blvd Se Suite 320, Calgary, AB, T2C 3G3

(403) 255-5808
Emp Here 1   *Sales* 24,822,420
SIC 8699 Membership organizations, nec
Chuck Bruce
Louise Bradley
Kellie Garrett
Lynne Mcvey
Carole Shankaruk

   D-U-N-S 24-330-0931   (BR)
METRIE CANADA LTD
SAUDER MOULDINGS CALGARY
(*Suby of ELSWOOD INVESTMENT CORPORATION*)
5367 50 St Se, Calgary, AB, T2C 3W1
(403) 543-3260
Emp Here 100
SIC 2431 Millwork
Sascha Chirzynski

   D-U-N-S 24-674-7869   (HQ)
MID WESTERN MACHINE WORKS (1987) INC
7815 46 St Se, Calgary, AB, T2C 2Y5
(403) 279-0727
Emp Here 30   *Sales* 50,450,925
SIC 1389 Oil and gas field services, nec
Roger Davis
Patrick Budgell

   D-U-N-S 24-320-9827   (SL)
MMR CANADA LIMITED
(*Suby of MMR GROUP, INC.*)
11083 48 St Se, Calgary, AB, T2C 1G8
(403) 720-9000
Emp Here 150   *Sales* 35,326,350
SIC 1731 Electrical work
John Courville
John Dobson
James Rutland
Thomas Welborn

   D-U-N-S 20-077-1020   (HQ)
MODERN TOOL LTD
11488 70 St Se, Calgary, AB, T2C 4Y3
(403) 236-1150
Emp Here 22   *Sales* 12,497,170
SIC 5084 Industrial machinery and equipment
George Senecal
Lila Senecal

   D-U-N-S 24-731-5252   (HQ)
MORRISON CONSTRUCTION (1983) LTD
MORRISON HOMES
11158 42 St Se, Calgary, AB, T2C 0J9
(403) 279-7600
Sales 23,030,070
SIC 1521 Single-family housing construction
David Gladney
Al Morrison

   D-U-N-S 24-517-8710   (SL)
NARDEI FABRICATORS LTD
8915 44 St Se, Calgary, AB, T2C 2P5
(403) 279-3301
Emp Here 60   *Sales* 10,141,500
SIC 3498 Fabricated pipe and fittings
Brian Kargus

   D-U-N-S 24-905-7217   (HQ)
NATCO CANADA, LTD
9423 Shepard Rd Se, Calgary, AB, T2C 4R6
(403) 203-2119
Emp Here 100   *Sales* 49,862,355
SIC 3443 Fabricated plate work (boiler shop)
James Crittall
Ryan Chase
Haimie Ledergerber
Michael J Mayer

   D-U-N-S 25-538-2822   (HQ)
NATIONAL PROCESS EQUIPMENT INC
NATPRO
(*Suby of DXP ENTERPRISES, INC.*)
5409 74 Ave Se, Calgary, AB, T2C 3C9
(403) 724-4300
Emp Here 1   *Sales* 33,744,152
SIC 3561 Pumps and pumping equipment

Frank Killoran
David Harvey
Murray Brown

   D-U-N-S 20-346-3559   (HQ)
NEWSCO INTERNATIONAL ENERGY SERVICES INC
4855 102 Ave Se Suite 11, Calgary, AB, T2C 2X7
(403) 243-2331
Sales 15,985,250
SIC 1381 Drilling oil and gas wells
Steve Mravunac

   D-U-N-S 20-177-3939   (BR)
NOV ENERFLOW ULC
NOV HYDRA RIG
(*Suby of NOV ENERFLOW ULC*)
4910 80 Ave Se, Calgary, AB, T2C 2X3
(403) 569-2222
Emp Here 150
SIC 1389 Oil and gas field services, nec
Skinner Andrew

   D-U-N-S 24-379-7565   (BR)
NOV ENERFLOW ULC
NOV ENERFLOW
(*Suby of NATIONAL OILWELL VARCO, INC.*)
8625 68 St Se, Calgary, AB, T2C 2R6
(403) 695-3189
Emp Here 80
SIC 3533 Oil and gas field machinery
Jim Turner

   D-U-N-S 20-311-6025   (SL)
OAK CREEK DEVELOPMENTS
3816 64 Ave Se, Calgary, AB, T2C 2B4
(403) 279-2904
Emp Here 49   *Sales* 24,405,822
SIC 5599 Automotive dealers, nec
Barrie Carpenter

   D-U-N-S 20-744-1643   (HQ)
OAKCREEK GOLF & TURF LP
3816 64 Ave Se, Calgary, AB, T2C 2B4
(403) 279-2907
Emp Here 61   *Sales* 52,054,200
SIC 5091 Sporting and recreation goods
Barrie Carpenter
Patrick Nolan

   D-U-N-S 20-077-3430   (BR)
OLD DUTCH FOODS LTD
(*Suby of OLD DUTCH FOODS LTD*)
3103 54 Ave Se, Calgary, AB, T2C 0A9
(403) 279-2771
Emp Here 230
SIC 2096 Potato chips and similar snacks
Scott Kelemen

   D-U-N-S 20-440-3679   (HQ)
OLIVIER'S CANDIES LTD
(*Suby of BLACKSTONE CREEK INVESTMENTS LIMITED*)
2828 54 Ave Se Bay Ctr, Calgary, AB, T2C 0A7
(403) 266-6028
Emp Here 36   *Sales* 30,080,772
SIC 5149 Groceries and related products, nec
Wally Marcolin

   D-U-N-S 24-493-7280   (SL)
PALMER, JACKIE DISTRIBUTORS LTD
6957 48 St Se, Calgary, AB, T2C 5A4

Emp Here 18   *Sales* 13,365,360
SIC 5192 Books, periodicals, and newspapers
Jackie Palmer
George Palmer

   D-U-N-S 20-048-8331   (BR)
PEPSI BOTTLING GROUP (CANADA), ULC, THE
PEPSICO BEVERAGES CANADA
(*Suby of PBG INVESTMENT (LUXEMBOURG) SARL*)
4815 78 Ave Se, Calgary, AB, T2C 2Y9

(403) 279-1500
Emp Here 200
SIC 2086 Bottled and canned soft drinks
Kurtis Mccartney

   D-U-N-S 24-459-6391   (HQ)
PIPE & PILING SUPPLIES (WESTERN) LTD
(*Suby of PLACEMENTS MIKE DYM LTEE, LES*)
5515 40 St Se, Calgary, AB, T2C 2A8
(403) 236-1332
Sales 13,415,220
SIC 5051 Metals service centers and offices
Jack Dym
Freida Dym
Jeff Wagman

   D-U-N-S 20-178-7871   (SL)
PLANET FOODS INC
4040e 80 Ave Se, Calgary, AB, T2C 2J7
(403) 281-7911
Emp Here 25   *Sales* 20,889,425
SIC 5149 Groceries and related products, nec
Antonio Franko
John Stiles
Clay Gillies

   D-U-N-S 24-598-0966   (HQ)
POLAR MOBILITY RESEARCH LTD
7860 62 St Se, Calgary, AB, T2C 5K2
(403) 279-3633
Emp Here 12   *Sales* 18,781,308
SIC 5075 Warm air heating and air conditioning
Jeff Schmode

   D-U-N-S 24-016-3105   (HQ)
PRAIRIE HYDRAULIC EQUIPMENT LTD
7824 56 St Se, Calgary, AB, T2C 4S9
(403) 279-2070
Sales 11,875,650
SIC 5084 Industrial machinery and equipment
Earl Farmer

   D-U-N-S 25-386-3005   (HQ)
PRIME FASTENERS LTD
5940 30 St Se Suite 6, Calgary, AB, T2C 1X8
(403) 279-1043
Emp Here 20   *Sales* 24,594,570
SIC 5072 Hardware
Brian Gingera
David Scheidt

   D-U-N-S 20-829-8372   (SL)
PROFESSIONAL EXCAVATORS LTD
10919 84 St Se, Calgary, AB, T2C 5A6
(403) 236-5686
Emp Here 60   *Sales* 14,771,160
SIC 1794 Excavation work
Richard Wolkowski

   D-U-N-S 24-700-0610   (SL)
PROMAC INDUSTRIES LIMITED PARTNERSHIP
7150 112 Ave Se, Calgary, AB, T2C 4Z1
(403) 279-8333
Emp Here 40   *Sales* 19,001,040
SIC 5084 Industrial machinery and equipment
Sean Monaghan

   D-U-N-S 24-358-3114   (BR)
PRONGHORN CONTROLS LTD
(*Suby of PRONGHORN CONTROLS LTD*)
4919 72 Ave Se Unit 101, Calgary, AB, T2C 3H3
(403) 720-2526
Emp Here 125
SIC 5084 Industrial machinery and equipment
Kevin Fisher

   D-U-N-S 25-990-5701   (HQ)
PRONGHORN CONTROLS LTD
4919 72 Ave Se Suite 101, Calgary, AB, T2C 3H3
(403) 720-2526
Emp Here 25   *Sales* 49,332,800
SIC 7629 Electrical repair shops
Yves Tremblay

▲ Public Company   ■ Public Company Family Member   **HQ** Headquarters   **BR** Branch   **SL** Single Location

Dean Toly
Jason Boyd
Lyn Luciani
Colin Parks
Troy Madson

D-U-N-S 24-962-7654 (HQ)
PROPHIT MANAGEMENT LTD
4540 54 Ave Se Unit 200, Calgary, AB, T2C 2Y8
(403) 640-0200
Sales 27,433,200
SIC 8741 Management services
Cliff Francisn
Steffen Holdt
Marco Holdt

D-U-N-S 24-805-0952 (BR)
PRUDENTIAL STEEL ULC
(*Suby of* ROCCA & PARTNERS STICHTING ADMINISTRATIEKANTOOR AANDELEN SAN FAUSTIN)
8919 Barlow Trail Se, Calgary, AB, T2C 2N7
(403) 279-4401
Emp Here 400
SIC 3312 Blast furnaces and steel mills
Dianluca Greco

D-U-N-S 24-346-2041 (HQ)
RBS BULK SYSTEMS INC
(*Suby of* REIMER CONSOLIDATED CORP)
9910 48 St Se, Calgary, AB, T2C 2R2
(403) 248-1530
Emp Here 50 *Sales* 34,970,020
SIC 4213 Trucking, except local
Brian Murray
Donald S Reimer
Anne Reimer

D-U-N-S 20-690-9447 (SL)
REED ATWOOD BUILDERS INC
5716 35 St Se, Calgary, AB, T2C 2G3

Emp Here 30 *Sales* 14,121,930
SIC 1542 Nonresidential construction, nec
Marlin Slemp
Russell Petterson

D-U-N-S 25-265-7408 (HQ)
RITE-WAY FENCING (2000) INC
7710 40 St Se, Calgary, AB, T2C 3S4
(403) 243-8733
Emp Here 35 *Sales* 24,618,600
SIC 1799 Special trade contractors, nec
Scott Ruzesky

D-U-N-S 20-353-0220 (SL)
ROBERTSON BULK SALES CALGARY LTD
6811 52 St Se, Calgary, AB, T2C 4J5
(403) 531-5700
Emp Here 15 *Sales* 15,492,120
SIC 5172 Petroleum products, nec
Mark Hyderman

D-U-N-S 20-374-9064 (SL)
ROUGHRIDER CIVIL INFRASTRUCTURE LTD
7003 30 St Se Bay 16, Calgary, AB, T2C 1N6
(403) 243-1666
Emp Here 50 *Sales* 14,176,200
SIC 1611 Highway and street construction
David Secord
Laura Secord

D-U-N-S 24-314-7969 (BR)
RUSSEL METALS INC
(*Suby of* RUSSEL METALS INC)
5724 40 St Se, Calgary, AB, T2C 2A1
(403) 279-6600
Emp Here 100
SIC 3312 Blast furnaces and steel mills
Mike Goodrow

D-U-N-S 24-224-7075 (HQ)
S MALIK INVESTMENTS LTD
PETRO CANADA
8338 18 St Se Suite 432, Calgary, AB, T2C 4E4

(403) 236-2776
Emp Here 5 *Sales* 24,903,900
SIC 5541 Gasoline service stations
Sabiha Malik

D-U-N-S 24-554-4374 (SL)
SABRE INSTRUMENT SERVICES LTD
4460 54 Ave Se, Calgary, AB, T2C 3A8
(403) 258-0566
Emp Here 80 *Sales* 19,694,880
SIC 1796 Installing building equipment
Keith Mclennan

D-U-N-S 20-321-4635 (BR)
SANJEL CANADA LTD
SANJEL ENERGY SERVICES
10774 42 St Se, Calgary, AB, T2C 0L5
(403) 215-4420
Emp Here 350
SIC 1389 Oil and gas field services, nec

D-U-N-S 25-414-9263 (SL)
SAPUNJIS ENTERPRISES INC
7520 114 Ave Se, Calgary, AB, T2C 4T3
(403) 216-5150
Emp Here 18 *Sales* 18,006,102
SIC 5051 Metals service centers and offices
David Sapunjis

D-U-N-S 25-150-3371 (BR)
SCHLUMBERGER CANADA LIMITED
8087 54 St Se, Calgary, AB, T2C 4R7
(403) 509-4300
Emp Here 130
SIC 1389 Oil and gas field services, nec
Bryce Stanley

D-U-N-S 20-903-9130 (HQ)
SCHNEIDER ELECTRIC SOFTWARE CANADA INC
SCHNEIDER ELECTRIC CANADA
(*Suby of* SCHNEIDER ELECTRIC SE)
49 Quarry Park Blvd Se Suite 100, Calgary, AB, T2C 5H9
(403) 253-8848
Emp Here 455 *Sales* 111,666,665
SIC 7371 Custom computer programming services
David Jardine
Cameron Demcoe
Tom Dilworth

D-U-N-S 20-030-4869 (SL)
SERVA GROUP (CANADA) ULC
(*Suby of* AIP, LLC)
7345 110 Ave Se, Calgary, AB, T2C 3B8
(403) 269-7847
Emp Here 42 *Sales* 24,988,376
SIC 3533 Oil and gas field machinery
Ray Baker

D-U-N-S 20-749-1523 (SL)
SHANAHAN'S BUILDING SPECIALTIES LIMITED
SHANAHAN'S INDUSTRIES
2808 58 Ave Se Suite 2, Calgary, AB, T2C 0B3
(403) 279-2782
Emp Here 35 *Sales* 62,659,080
SIC 5039 Construction materials, nec
William Mey
Gerrit Mey
Gerald Mey
Robert Cyr

D-U-N-S 24-535-3834 (HQ)
SHANAHAN'S LIMITED PARTNERSHIP
SHANAHAN'S MANUFACTURING
(*Suby of* SHANAHAN'S LIMITED PARTNERSHIP)
2731 57 Ave Se Suite 1, Calgary, AB, T2C 0B2
(403) 279-2890
Sales 43,781,580
SIC 3499 Fabricated Metal products, nec
Gerrit Mey
Bill Mey
Gerald Mey
Bradley Gaukel
Robert Cyr

D-U-N-S 20-599-3967 (HQ)
SIMARK CONTROLS LTD
10509 46 St Se, Calgary, AB, T2C 5C2
(403) 236-0580
Emp Here 29 *Sales* 19,001,040
SIC 5084 Industrial machinery and equipment
Mark Wheeler
Naresh Shankardass
Perry Jamart
George Rouault

D-U-N-S 25-673-1902 (BR)
SOBEYS CAPITAL INCORPORATED
SOBEY'S WEST, DIV OF
(*Suby of* EMPIRE COMPANY LIMITED)
7704 30 St Se, Calgary, AB, T2C 1M8

Emp Here 260
SIC 5141 Groceries, general line
Ryan Eifler

D-U-N-S 25-271-1056 (BR)
SOBEYS WEST INC
SAFEWAY
(*Suby of* EMPIRE COMPANY LIMITED)
7740 18 St Se, Calgary, AB, T2C 2N5
(403) 236-0559
Emp Here 80
SIC 5411 Grocery stores
Polutnick Heather

D-U-N-S 25-483-9491 (BR)
SOBEYS WEST INC
LUCERNE FOODS
(*Suby of* EMPIRE COMPANY LIMITED)
3440 56 Ave Se, Calgary, AB, T2C 2C3
(403) 279-2555
Emp Here 550
SIC 2011 Meat packing plants
Stephen Enfoen

D-U-N-S 20-294-6091 (SL)
SOUTHAMPTON INDUSTRIAL MANUFACTURING INC
SOUTHAMPTON TRAIN INDUSTRIAL
5605 48 St Se, Calgary, AB, T2C 4X8
(403) 930-9299
Emp Here 56 *Sales* 10,756,760
SIC 3494 Valves and pipe fittings, nec
Stephen Zakreski
Todd Storey

D-U-N-S 24-376-1835 (HQ)
SOUTHAMPTON-TRANE AIR CONDITIONING (CALGARY) INC
SOUTHAMPTON-TRANE
10905 48 St Se Suite 157, Calgary, AB, T2C 1G8
(403) 301-0090
Sales 11,155,344
SIC 5722 Household appliance stores
Steven Michael Zakreski

D-U-N-S 24-981-1670 (SL)
SPECIALTY LAMINATE MANUFACTURING LTD
2624 54 Ave Se Bay Suite B, Calgary, AB, T2C 1R5
(403) 273-3800
Emp Here 90 *Sales* 14,027,670
SIC 2493 Reconstituted wood products
Victor Nikolic
Robert Tutty
Linda Nikolic

D-U-N-S 25-329-5851 (SL)
SPROUSE FIRE & SAFETY (1996) CORP
5329 72 Ave Se, Calgary, AB, T2C 4X6
(403) 265-3891
Emp Here 32 *Sales* 15,200,832
SIC 5087 Service establishment equipment
Larry Holling
Randy Repas

D-U-N-S 20-166-1841 (SL)
SPROUSE FIRE SAFETY LTD
5329 72 Ave Se Ste 38, Calgary, AB, T2C 4X6

Emp Here 52 *Sales* 23,359,388
SIC 7389 Business services, nec
Rick Mooers

D-U-N-S 25-204-8327 (SL)
STAR ALUMINUM RAILING SYSTEMS INC
STAR SYSTEM
3511 64 Ave Se Unit 1, Calgary, AB, T2C 1N3
(403) 640-7878
Emp Here 13 *Sales* 13,004,407
SIC 5051 Metals service centers and offices
Sergio Zen
Paul Zen

D-U-N-S 20-826-3137 (HQ)
STARTEC REFRIGERATION SERVICES LTD
(*Suby of* CAWTHORN INVESTMENTS LTD)
9423 Shepard Rd Se, Calgary, AB, T2C 4R6
(403) 295-5855
Emp Here 50 *Sales* 17,760,080
SIC 3563 Air and gas compressors
Joel Cawthorn
Kristi Cawthorn
Kurt Schaerer

D-U-N-S 24-984-0034 (SL)
STERLING WESTERN STAR TRUCKS ALBERTA LTD
9115 52 St Se, Calgary, AB, T2C 2R4
(403) 720-3400
Emp Here 102 *Sales* 64,186,560
SIC 5511 New and used car dealers
Kelly Clark
Anne Clark

D-U-N-S 24-339-0171 (SL)
STEWART & STEVENSON CANADA INC
(*Suby of* KIRBY CORPORATION)
3111 Shepard Pl Se Suite 403, Calgary, AB, T2C 4P1
(403) 215-5300
Emp Here 220 *Sales* 61,792,940
SIC 3533 Oil and gas field machinery
Jason Clark
Robert Hargrave

D-U-N-S 24-329-5255 (HQ)
STIMLINE SERVICES INC
(*Suby of* STIMLINE AS)
7475 51 St Se, Calgary, AB, T2C 4L6
(403) 720-0874
Sales 17,316,078
SIC 3533 Oil and gas field machinery
Tom Fedog

D-U-N-S 25-062-1828 (SL)
SUMMIT SALON SERVICES INC
10905 48 St Se Suite 105, Calgary, AB, T2C 1G8
(403) 252-6201
Emp Here 65 *Sales* 30,876,690
SIC 5087 Service establishment equipment
David Mcmahon
Michael Mcmahon

D-U-N-S 20-441-0047 (SL)
SUPREME WINDOWS (CALGARY) INC
4705 102 Ave Se, Calgary, AB, T2C 2X7
(403) 279-2797
Emp Here 90 *Sales* 18,170,730
SIC 3089 Plastics products, nec
Ann Mackenna Huber
Dennis Huber
Gerard Huber

D-U-N-S 20-188-6350 (BR)
SYSCO CANADA, INC
SYSCO FOOD SERVICES OF CALGARY
(*Suby of* SYSCO CORPORATION)
4639 72 Ave Se, Calgary, AB, T2C 4H7
(403) 720-1300
Emp Here 350
SIC 5141 Groceries, general line
Randy White

D-U-N-S 24-854-6574 (HQ)

▲ Public Company ■ Public Company Family Member **HQ** Headquarters **BR** Branch **SL** Single Location

SYSTECH INSTRUMENTATION INC
3-4351 104 Ave Se, Calgary, AB, T2C 5C6
(403) 291-3535
Emp Here 11   *Sales* 11,875,650
SIC 5084 Industrial machinery and equipment
Darrell Mohn
Neale German
Arlene Round
Harvey Prang

D-U-N-S 25-412-8028   (HQ)
TARPON ENERGY SERVICES LTD
(*Suby of* PTW ENERGY SERVICES LTD)
7020 81 St Se, Calgary, AB, T2C 5B8
(403) 234-8647
Emp Here 250   *Sales* 709,762,300
SIC 1389 Oil and gas field services, nec
Greg Young
Dean Tingley

D-U-N-S 24-929-6005   (SL)
TARPON ENERGY SERVICES(PROCESS SYSTEMS)LTD
7020 81 St Se, Calgary, AB, T2C 5B8
(403) 234-8647
Emp Here 50   *Sales* 23,751,300
SIC 5084 Industrial machinery and equipment
Wade Fleury

D-U-N-S 25-408-6028   (BR)
TDL GROUP CORP, THE
TIM HORTON REGIONAL OFFICE
(*Suby of* RESTAURANT BRANDS INTERNATIONAL INC)
7460 51 St Se, Calgary, AB, T2C 4B4
(403) 203-7400
Emp Here 100
SIC 5812 Eating places
Doug Anthony

D-U-N-S 20-013-4349   (SL)
TEKNION (ALBERTA) LTD
TEKNION SOLUTIONS WOODWORK
(*Suby of* GLOBAL UPHOLSTERY CO LIMITED)
6403 48 St Se Suite 60, Calgary, AB, T2C 3J7
(403) 264-4210
Emp Here 80   *Sales* 12,345,760
SIC 2521 Wood office furniture
David Feldberg
Myron Heppner

D-U-N-S 20-530-5597   (SL)
TERVITA DRILLING AND CORING SERVICES LTD
(*Suby of* TERVITA CORPORATION)
9919 Shepard Rd Se, Calgary, AB, T2C 3C5
(855) 837-8482
Emp Here 240   *Sales* 61,385,760
SIC 1081 Metal mining services
Garry Wegleitner

D-U-N-S 20-058-8254   (BR)
TETRA TECH CANADA INC
(*Suby of* TETRA TECH, INC.)
200 Rivercrest Dr Se Suite 115, Calgary, AB, T2C 2X5
(403) 203-3355
Emp Here 100
SIC 8711 Engineering services
Paul Evans

D-U-N-S 25-505-5121   (HQ)
THOMAS FRESH INC
5470 76 Ave Se, Calgary, AB, T2C 4S3
(403) 236-8234
Emp Here 50   *Sales* 65,937,872
SIC 5148 Fresh fruits and vegetables
Roy Hinchey
Laurie Wagner
Harry Meyers
Mark Landa
Calvin Popff

D-U-N-S 20-268-0075   (BR)
THYSSENKRUPP ELEVATOR (CANADA) LIMITED

THYSSENKRUPP ELEVATORS
(*Suby of* THYSSENKRUPP AG)
2419 52 Ave Se Unit 5, Calgary, AB, T2C 4X7
(403) 259-4183
Emp Here 80
SIC 7699 Repair services, nec
Blaine Coupal

D-U-N-S 20-558-1957   (HQ)
TIW WESTERN INC
(*Suby of* CANERECTOR INC)
7770 44 St Se, Calgary, AB, T2C 2L5
(403) 279-8310
Emp Here 61   *Sales* 16,678,244
SIC 3433 Heating equipment, except electric
Cecil Hawkins
Bill Nickel
Amanda Hawkins
Chad Goll

D-U-N-S 20-743-7922   (SL)
TOP NOTCH CONSTRUCTION LTD
5415 56 Ave Se, Calgary, AB, T2C 3X6

Emp Here 191   *Sales* 47,021,526
SIC 1794 Excavation work
John N. Craig
Shannon Dayment
Cindy Hilton

D-U-N-S 24-087-7290   (SL)
TOPMADE ENTERPRISES LTD
7177 40 St Se, Calgary, AB, T2C 2H7
(403) 236-7557
Emp Here 40   *Sales* 33,423,080
SIC 5141 Groceries, general line
Hayden Wong
Quincy Wong

D-U-N-S 20-581-2626   (SL)
TOSHIBA BUSINESS SYSTEMS
TOSHIBA BUSINESS SOLUTIONS
5329 72 Ave Se Unit 62, Calgary, AB, T2C 4X6
(403) 273-5200
Emp Here 30   *Sales* 13,304,700
SIC 7389 Business services, nec
Ryan Stethanson

D-U-N-S 24-308-4329   (BR)
TOTAL ENERGY SERVICES INC
BIDELL GAS COMPRESSION
(*Suby of* TOTAL ENERGY SERVICES INC)
6900 112 Ave Se, Calgary, AB, T2C 4Z1
(403) 235-5877
Emp Here 100
SIC 1382 Oil and gas exploration services
Sean Ulmer

D-U-N-S 24-802-5970   (SL)
TRANS-OCEANIC HUMAN RESOURCES INC
5515 40 St Se, Calgary, AB, T2C 2A8

Emp Here 50   *Sales* 12,047,777
SIC 7361 Employment agencies
Jack Dym

D-U-N-S 20-383-3264   (BR)
TRANSOURCE FREIGHTWAYS LTD
TRANSOURCE FREIGHTWAYS
(*Suby of* TRANSOURCE FREIGHTWAYS LTD)
19-6991 48 St Se, Calgary, AB, T2C 5A4
(403) 726-4366
Emp Here 100
SIC 4213 Trucking, except local

D-U-N-S 20-639-2024   (SL)
TRIANGLE STEEL LTD
2915 54 Ave Se, Calgary, AB, T2C 0A9
(403) 279-2622
Emp Here 70   *Sales* 16,340,450
SIC 3312 Blast furnaces and steel mills
Philip Sommerville

D-U-N-S 24-827-4354   (SL)
TRIQUEST NONDESTRUCTIVE TESTING

CORP
TRIQUEST NDT
7425 107 Ave Se, Calgary, AB, T2C 5N6
(403) 263-2216
Emp Here 45   *Sales* 10,561,320
SIC 8734 Testing laboratories
Michael Chevrier

D-U-N-S 24-117-7294   (HQ)
TROJAN INDUSTRIES INC
TITAN FOUNDRY
4900 54 Ave Se, Calgary, AB, T2C 2Y8
(403) 269-6525
Emp Here 19   *Sales* 16,545,438
SIC 5051 Metals service centers and offices
David Gooding
John Dane

D-U-N-S 25-329-1751   (BR)
TROPHY FOODS INC
(*Suby of* TROPHY FOODS INC)
6210 44 St Se, Calgary, AB, T2C 4L3
(403) 571-6887
Emp Here 100
SIC 5149 Groceries and related products, nec
Dianne Mcgillis

D-U-N-S 25-195-7486   (SL)
TRUEMAN DISTRIBUTION LTD
6280 76 Ave Se Unit 10, Calgary, AB, T2C 5N5
(403) 236-3008
Emp Here 30   *Sales* 25,067,310
SIC 5149 Groceries and related products, nec
Paul Trueman

D-U-N-S 25-106-0497   (SL)
TSE STEEL LTD
4436 90 Ave Se, Calgary, AB, T2C 2S7
(403) 279-6060
Emp Here 50   *Sales* 10,141,500
SIC 3441 Fabricated structural Metal
Troy Branch

D-U-N-S 24-732-0443   (SL)
ULTRA-LITE OVERHEAD DOORS LTD
ULTRA-LITE DOORS
7307 40 St Se, Calgary, AB, T2C 2K4
(403) 280-2000
Emp Here 60   *Sales* 11,752,155
SIC 5031 Lumber, plywood, and millwork
Alven Abrahamson
Dan Ptycia

D-U-N-S 25-330-4398   (BR)
UNIFIRST CANADA LTD
(*Suby of* UNIFIRST CORPORATION)
5728 35 St Se, Calgary, AB, T2C 2G3
(403) 279-2800
Emp Here 90
SIC 7213 Linen supply
Don Beakin

D-U-N-S 25-413-8563   (SL)
UNIQUE SCAFFOLD INC
4750 104 Ave Se, Calgary, AB, T2C 2H3
(403) 203-3422
Emp Here 70   *Sales* 17,233,020
SIC 1799 Special trade contractors, nec
Jason Procyk
William Procyk

D-U-N-S 24-673-0584   (BR)
VERSACOLD GROUP LIMITED PARTNERSHIP
5600 76 Ave Se, Calgary, AB, T2C 4N4
(403) 216-5600
Emp Here 125
SIC 4222 Refrigerated warehousing and storage
Mike Agnew

D-U-N-S 24-155-8295   (BR)
WEST COAST REDUCTION LTD
ALBERTA PROCESSING
(*Suby of* RUFUS HOLDINGS LTD)
7030 Ogden Dale Pl Se, Calgary, AB, T2C 2A3

(403) 279-4441
Emp Here 80
SIC 2077 Animal and marine fats and oils
Geoff Smolkin

D-U-N-S 20-017-3958   (SL)
WESTBRIDGE PET CONTAINERS LIMITED
3838e 80 Ave Se, Calgary, AB, T2C 2J7
(403) 248-1513
Emp Here 51   *Sales* 10,296,747
SIC 3089 Plastics products, nec
David Birkby
Harry Logan
Murray Haines

D-U-N-S 20-824-5167   (BR)
WESTCAN BULK TRANSPORT LTD
(*Suby of* THE KENAN ADVANTAGE GROUP INC)
3780 76 Ave Se, Calgary, AB, T2C 1J8
(403) 279-5505
Emp Here 143
SIC 4131 Intercity and rural bus transportation
Howard August

D-U-N-S 25-217-7316   (SL)
WESTECH BUILDING PRODUCTS ULC
(*Suby of* WESTLAKE CHEMICAL CORPORATION)
5201 64 Ave Se, Calgary, AB, T2C 4Z9
(403) 279-4497
Emp Here 180   *Sales* 28,594,440
SIC 3089 Plastics products, nec

D-U-N-S 20-598-4701   (HQ)
WESTERN MATERIALS HANDLING & EQUIPMENT LTD
(*Suby of* BRIDGE 8 INVESTMENTS INC)
7805 46 St Se, Calgary, AB, T2C 2Y5
(403) 236-0305
Emp Here 10   *Sales* 21,095,976
SIC 5084 Industrial machinery and equipment
Kirk Hudson
Lloyd Cunningham
Edith Hudson
Janet Fitzgerald

D-U-N-S 24-807-1961   (BR)
WESTFAIR DRUGS LTD
(*Suby of* LOBLAW COMPANIES LIMITED)
3916 72 Ave Se, Calgary, AB, T2C 2E2
(403) 279-1600
Emp Here 120
SIC 5199 Nondurable goods, nec
Diane Rusk

D-U-N-S 25-206-3177   (HQ)
WESTPOWER EQUIPMENT LTD
4451 54 Ave Se, Calgary, AB, T2C 2A2
(403) 720-3300
Sales 38,002,080
SIC 5084 Industrial machinery and equipment
Dave Goddard
Don Liddell

D-U-N-S 25-617-2537   (HQ)
WESTROW FOOD BROKERS INC
WESTROW FOOD GROUP
2880 Glenmore Trail Se Suite 115, Calgary, AB, T2C 2E7
(403) 720-0703
Emp Here 11   *Sales* 19,218,271
SIC 5141 Groceries, general line
Brad Shackman
Don Macsorley
Tony Milina
John Madonia

D-U-N-S 24-230-8882   (HQ)
WHOLESOME HARVEST BAKING LTD
4320 80 Ave Se, Calgary, AB, T2C 4N6
(403) 203-1675
Emp Here 100   *Sales* 146,215,500
SIC 2051 Bread, cake, and related products
Joseph Mccarthy
Lynn Langrock
Geraldine Wright

D-U-N-S 25-261-9515   (SL)
WORX ENVIRONMENTAL PRODUCTS OF CANADA INC
2305 52 Ave Se Unit 10, Calgary, AB, T2C 4X7
(403) 538-0203
Emp Here 25   *Sales* 18,258,625
SIC 5169 Chemicals and allied products, nec
Jack Neufeld
Sergio Abarca

D-U-N-S 24-079-4268   (SL)
YOKOGAWA CANADA INC
(*Suby of* YOKOGAWA ELECTRIC CORPORATION)
11133 40 St Se Suite 4, Calgary, AB, T2C 2Z4
(403) 258-2681
Emp Here 50   *Sales* 11,714,400
SIC 8742 Management consulting services
Ian Verhappen

Calgary, AB T2E

D-U-N-S 24-157-2379   (BR)
1032451 B.C. LTD
CALGARY SUN, THE
(*Suby of* QUEBECOR MEDIA INC)
2615 12 St Ne Suite 1, Calgary, AB, T2E 7W9
(403) 250-4192
Emp Here 250
SIC 2711 Newspapers
Gordon Norrie

D-U-N-S 25-416-5970   (HQ)
489425 ALBERTA LTD
NORTH AMERICAN GREENHOUSE SUPPLIES
1204 Edmonton Trail Ne Unit 1, Calgary, AB, T2E 3K5
(403) 276-5156
Emp Here 1   *Sales* 22,275,600
SIC 5191 Farm supplies
Mark Sutherland
Carol Desroches

D-U-N-S 20-297-3462   (SL)
550338 ALBERTA LIMITED
SERVICE MASTER OF CALGARY JMS
3530 11a St Ne Suite 1, Calgary, AB, T2E 6M7
(403) 250-7878
Emp Here 200   *Sales* 6,393,600
SIC 7349 Building maintenance services, nec

D-U-N-S 25-206-4019   (SL)
574852 ALBERTA LIMITED
LINA'S ITALIAN MARKET
2202 Centre St Ne, Calgary, AB, T2E 2T5
(403) 277-9166
Emp Here 41   *Sales* 11,240,232
SIC 5411 Grocery stores
Lina Castle
Marino Santarelli

D-U-N-S 24-366-9962   (SL)
771922 ALBERTA INC
NORTH HILL MAZDA
1211 Centre St Nw, Calgary, AB, T2E 2R3
(403) 930-0610
Emp Here 43   *Sales* 21,417,354
SIC 5511 New and used car dealers
Asheet Ruparell
Dilip Chakraborty

D-U-N-S 24-808-3800   (SL)
800743 ALBERTA LTD
BINGO PAPER COMPANY, THE
(*Suby of* CANUCK AMUSEMENTS AND MERCHANDISING LTD)
1225 34 Ave Ne, Calgary, AB, T2E 6N4
(403) 291-4239
Emp Here 36   *Sales* 11,740,896
SIC 3944 Games, toys, and children's vehicles
Douglas Earle
Daniel Earle

D-U-N-S 20-293-4360   (SL)
967210 ALBERTA LTD
EASTSIDE KIA
2256 23 St Ne, Calgary, AB, T2E 8N3
(403) 250-2502
Emp Here 50   *Sales* 24,903,900
SIC 5511 New and used car dealers
James Mcmanes
Michael Mcmanes
Kelly Temple

D-U-N-S 25-681-3247   (SL)
ABCO MAINTENANCE SYSTEMS INC
260 20 Ave Ne, Calgary, AB, T2E 1P9
(403) 293-5752
Emp Here 105   *Sales* 3,356,640
SIC 7349 Building maintenance services, nec
Buta Rehill

D-U-N-S 25-106-4812   (HQ)
ADVANCED ORTHOMOLECULAR RESEARCH INC
AOR
3900 12 St Ne, Calgary, AB, T2E 8H9
(403) 250-9997
Sales 66,320,700
SIC 5122 Drugs, proprietaries, and sundries
Dallas Thorsteinson

D-U-N-S 24-207-5690   (BR)
AERO AVIATION INC
(*Suby of* AERO AVIATION INC)
393 Palmer Rd Ne Suite 59, Calgary, AB, T2E 7G4
(403) 250-3663
Emp Here 80
SIC 4581 Airports, flying fields, and services
Don Pott

D-U-N-S 24-343-7639   (HQ)
AERO AVIATION INC
2139 Pegasus Way Ne Suite 13, Calgary, AB, T2E 8T2
(403) 250-7553
Emp Here 10   *Sales* 26,697,800
SIC 4581 Airports, flying fields, and services
Adrian Cruse
Donald Pott

D-U-N-S 24-160-5914   (HQ)
AGAT LABORATORIES LTD
AGAT
2905 12 St Ne, Calgary, AB, T2E 7J2
(403) 736-2000
Emp Here 130   *Sales* 275,704,800
SIC 8731 Commercial physical research
John Desanti
Allan Kostanuick

D-U-N-S 24-098-5247   (BR)
AGAT LABORATORIES LTD
CORE GEOLOGY BUILDING
3801 21 St Ne, Calgary, AB, T2E 6T5
(403) 216-2077
Emp Here 160
SIC 8734 Testing laboratories
John Desanti

D-U-N-S 25-535-9234   (BR)
AGRIFOODS INTERNATIONAL COOPERATIVE LTD
DAIRYWORLD FOODS
(*Suby of* AGRIFOODS INTERNATIONAL COOPERATIVE LTD)
4215 12 St Ne, Calgary, AB, T2E 4P9
(403) 571-6400
Emp Here 350
SIC 2026 Fluid milk
Jack Kitteringham

D-U-N-S 24-525-6651   (SL)
AIR PARTNERS CORP
TAKE FLIGHT
(*Suby of* NR HOLDINGS INC)
263 Aero Way Ne, Calgary, AB, T2E 6K2
(403) 275-3930
Emp Here 75   *Sales* 9,358,200

SIC 8741 Management services
Vishal Saini
Gene Rodman
Wade Brummet

D-U-N-S 20-106-8447   (HQ)
AIRPORT TERMINAL SERVICES CANADIAN COMPANY
(*Suby of* AIRPORT TERMINAL SERVICES INC)
8075 22 St Ne, Calgary, AB, T2E 7Z6
(403) 291-0965
Emp Here 25   *Sales* 266,978,000
SIC 4581 Airports, flying fields, and services
Richard Hawes
Sally Leible
John Tucker

D-U-N-S 20-305-4569   (HQ)
AIRSPRINT INC
1910 Mccall Landng Ne, Calgary, AB, T2E 9B5
(403) 730-2344
Emp Here 60   *Sales* 27,765,712
SIC 4522 Air transportation, nonscheduled
Judson T. Macor
Michael N. Knapp
James A. Elian
Ted P. Sheldon
Scott Wenz
Phillip J. Dewsnap

D-U-N-S 20-831-1605   (HQ)
ALBERTA BEVERAGE CONTAINER RECYCLING CORPORATION
ABCRC
901 57 Ave Ne, Calgary, AB, T2E 8X9
(403) 264-0170
Emp Here 81   *Sales* 51,344,510
SIC 4953 Refuse systems
Guy West
Colin Carter
Jim Brent
Lori Koebel
Mike Battista

D-U-N-S 24-043-3714   (SL)
ALBERTA COMPUTER CABLE INC
ACC CABLES
1816 25 Ave Ne, Calgary, AB, T2E 7K1
(403) 291-5560
Emp Here 65   *Sales* 29,066,310
SIC 5065 Electronic parts and equipment, nec
Robert Kirkby
Louise Nesterenko

D-U-N-S 24-442-7514   (HQ)
ALTAVERO HAIRCARE LTD
FIRST CHOICE HAIR CUTTERS
1144 29 Ave Ne Suite 110w, Calgary, AB, T2E 7P1
(403) 266-4595
Emp Here 9   *Sales* 21,356,400
SIC 7231 Beauty shops
Laverne Mcgregor

D-U-N-S 20-631-6242   (SL)
ALYKHAN VELJI DESIGNS INC
217 4 St Ne, Calgary, AB, T2E 3S1
(403) 617-2406
Emp Here 34   *Sales* 15,273,446
SIC 7389 Business services, nec

D-U-N-S 20-985-2701   (SL)
AMBYINT INC
1440 Aviation Pk Ne Suite 119, Calgary, AB, T2E 7E2
(800) 205-1311
Emp Here 32   *Sales* 15,200,832
SIC 5084 Industrial machinery and equipment
Nav Dhunay

D-U-N-S 20-895-2887   (SL)
AMELCO ELECTRIC (CALGARY) LTD
2230 22 St Ne, Calgary, AB, T2E 8B7
(403) 250-1270
Emp Here 130   *Sales* 28,317,770
SIC 1731 Electrical work

Ivan Houde

D-U-N-S 25-452-7385   (SL)
APEX REALTY EXECUTIVES
1212 31 Ave Ne Suite 105, Calgary, AB, T2E 7S8
(403) 250-5803
Emp Here 55   *Sales* 23,038,895
SIC 6531 Real estate agents and managers
Maurice Roy

D-U-N-S 24-013-4114   (HQ)
ARCTEC ALLOYS LIMITED
4304 10 St Ne, Calgary, AB, T2E 6K3
(403) 250-9355
Emp Here 15   *Sales* 19,001,040
SIC 5085 Industrial supplies
Joseph N Trenke
Gudrun Trenke
Ron Middleton
Ove Olesen

D-U-N-S 20-285-1572   (SL)
ARTE GROUP INC
ARTE STRUCTURES
4300 5 St Ne, Calgary, AB, T2E 7C3
(403) 640-4559
Emp Here 100   *Sales* 42,273,700
SIC 1541 Industrial buildings and warehouses
Boaz Shilmover
David Shilmover

D-U-N-S 20-300-0786   (SL)
ASPEN FAMILY AND COMMUNITY NETWORK SOCIETY
2609 15 St Ne Suite 200, Calgary, AB, T2E 8Y4
(403) 219-3477
Emp Here 120   *Sales* 8,442,122
SIC 8699 Membership organizations, nec
Shirley Purves
Henry Kutarna
Michael Kurtz
Alisa Sorochan
Louise Morrin
Stephen Burns
Benjamin Kis
Rosanna Manaloto

D-U-N-S 20-201-6015   (BR)
ATCO GAS AND PIPELINES LTD
(*Suby of* ATCO LTD)
4415 12 St Ne, Calgary, AB, T2E 4R1
(403) 245-7857
Emp Here 80
SIC 4923 Gas transmission and distribution
Ray St Denis

D-U-N-S 20-537-9332   (HQ)
ATLAS TRAILER COACH PRODUCTS LTD
(*Suby of* CRYSTAL INVESTMENTS INC)
2530 21 St Ne, Calgary, AB, T2E 7L3
(403) 291-1225
Emp Here 12   *Sales* 13,111,740
SIC 5013 Motor vehicle supplies and new parts

D-U-N-S 24-316-1870   (SL)
ATTABOTICS INC
7944 10 St Ne, Calgary, AB, T2E 8W1
(403) 909-8230
Emp Here 60   *Sales* 14,057,280
SIC 8742 Management consulting services
Scott Gravelle
Jacques Lapointe
Robert Cowley
Tony Woolf
Eli Aviv
Shawn Needham
Jen Aubin

D-U-N-S 24-880-6093   (SL)
AUGUST ELECTRONICS INC
1810 Centre Ave Ne, Calgary, AB, T2E 0A6
(403) 273-3131
Emp Here 75   *Sales* 14,283,150
SIC 3699 Electrical equipment and supplies,

nec
John T. Francis
Peter Wilson

D-U-N-S 25-415-5948 (HQ)
AUTOTEMP INC
3419 12 St Ne Suite 3, Calgary, AB, T2E 6S6
(403) 250-7837
Emp Here 7   *Sales* 11,332,000
SIC 7539 Automotive repair shops, nec
Paul Bruce

D-U-N-S 24-376-8731 (SL)
AVMAX AIRCRAFT LEASING INC
(*Suby of* SUNWARD INTELLIGENT EQUIP-
MENT CO., LTD.)
380 Mctavish Rd Ne Suite 3, Calgary, AB, T2E
7G5
(403) 735-3299
Emp Here 450   *Sales* 219,478,500
SIC 5088 Transportation equipment and sup-
plies
John Binder
Richard Giacomuzzi

D-U-N-S 20-120-4562 (BR)
AVMAX GROUP INC
WESTERN AVIONICS
(*Suby of* SUNWARD INTELLIGENT EQUIP-
MENT CO., LTD.)
275 Palmer Rd Ne, Calgary, AB, T2E 7G4
(403) 250-2644
Emp Here 80
SIC 7622 Radio and television repair
Vince Scott

D-U-N-S 24-685-4066 (BR)
AVMAX GROUP INC
MAINTENANCE, DIV OF
(*Suby of* SUNWARD INTELLIGENT EQUIP-
MENT CO., LTD.)
380 Mctavish Rd Ne, Calgary, AB, T2E 7G5
(403) 735-3299
Emp Here 80
SIC 4581 Airports, flying fields, and services
Al Young

D-U-N-S 25-385-5498 (HQ)
AVMAX GROUP INC
MAINTENANCE DIV OF
(*Suby of* SUNWARD INTELLIGENT EQUIP-
MENT CO., LTD.)
2055 Pegasus Rd Ne, Calgary, AB, T2E 8C3
(403) 291-2464
Emp Here 200   *Sales* 87,271,800
SIC 4581 Airports, flying fields, and services
John Binder
Don Parkin
Russ Binder
Zhihong Xia
Jian Wang

D-U-N-S 24-364-8248 (HQ)
BAILEY HELICOPTERS LTD
600 Palmer Rd Ne, Calgary, AB, T2E 7R3
(403) 219-2770
Sales 16,237,700
SIC 4522 Air transportation, nonscheduled
Dan Wuthrich
Randy Gee

D-U-N-S 24-809-5713 (HQ)
BELLARE INDUSTRIAL COATINGS INC
636 36 Ave Ne, Calgary, AB, T2E 2L7
(403) 295-9676
Emp Here 1   *Sales* 18,563,000
SIC 5198 Paints, varnishes, and supplies
Kenneth Quantz

D-U-N-S 24-737-2084 (HQ)
BENEVITY, INC
611 Meredith Rd Ne Unit 700, Calgary, AB,
T2E 2W5
(403) 237-7875
Sales 51,680,440
SIC 7371 Custom computer programming ser-
vices

Bryan De Lottinville
David Panenter
Robert Egpurdy

D-U-N-S 20-831-1589 (SL)
BOW CITY DELIVERY (1989) LTD
BOW CITY
1423 45 Ave Ne Bay Ctr, Calgary, AB, T2E
2P3
(403) 250-5329
Emp Here 76   *Sales* 34,140,644
SIC 7389 Business services, nec
Carl Hollick

D-U-N-S 24-982-1182 (SL)
BOWNESS BAKERY (ALBERTA) INC
4280 23 St Ne Suite 1, Calgary, AB, T2E 6X7
(403) 250-9760
Emp Here 70   *Sales* 24,198,300
SIC 2051 Bread, cake, and related products
Shams Habib

D-U-N-S 20-068-9961 (SL)
BRAVO REALTY LIMITED
2116 27 Ave Ne Suite 122, Calgary, AB, T2E
7A6
(403) 818-2020
Emp Here 100   *Sales* 27,490,345
SIC 6531 Real estate agents and managers
James Lam

D-U-N-S 20-514-0572 (BR)
BUREAU VERITAS CANADA (2019) INC
*MAXXAM ANALYTICS INTERNATIONAL
CORPORATION*
(*Suby of* BUREAU VERITAS)
2021 41 Ave Ne, Calgary, AB, T2E 6P2
(403) 291-3077
Emp Here 150
SIC 8734 Testing laboratories
Scott Cantwell

D-U-N-S 20-830-9971 (SL)
BYBLOS BAKERY LTD
2479 23 St Ne, Calgary, AB, T2E 8J8
(403) 250-3711
Emp Here 100   *Sales* 34,569,000
SIC 2051 Bread, cake, and related products
George Daklala
Elias Daklala
Sleiman Daklala

D-U-N-S 20-733-1948 (SL)
**C H R CENTRAL PRODUCTION PHAR-
MACY**
1119 55 Ave Ne, Calgary, AB, T2E 6W1

Emp Here 65   *Sales* 17,982,900
SIC 2834 Pharmaceutical preparations

D-U-N-S 24-156-3402 (SL)
C L CONSULTANTS LIMITED
DRILLTEL SYSTEMS
(*Suby of* CONTINENTAL LABORATORIES
(1985) LTD)
3601 21 St Ne Suite A, Calgary, AB, T2E 6T5
(403) 250-3982
Emp Here 28   *Sales* 11,888,996
SIC 8999 Services, nec
Deno Adams
James Pennington
Donald Tetz

D-U-N-S 24-554-8805 (HQ)
C.H. ROBINSON PROJECT LOGISTICS LTD
(*Suby of* C.H. ROBINSON WORLDWIDE,
INC.)
6715 8 St Ne Suite 102, Calgary, AB, T2E 7H7
(403) 295-1505
Emp Here 29   *Sales* 43,347,980
SIC 4731 Freight transportation arrangement
Frank Guzman

D-U-N-S 20-327-8585 (BR)
CABELA'S RETAIL CANADA INC
CABELA'S
(*Suby of* BASS PRO GROUP, LLC)
851 64 Ave Ne, Calgary, AB, T2E 3B8

(403) 910-0200
Emp Here 150
SIC 5941 Sporting goods and bicycle shops

D-U-N-S 24-396-4538 (SL)
CALALTA SUPPLY LTD
3800 19 St Ne Unit 8, Calgary, AB, T2E 6V2
(403) 250-3195
Emp Here 24   *Sales* 10,732,176
SIC 5063 Electrical apparatus and equipment
Loren Gilbert Calalta

D-U-N-S 24-929-0255 (HQ)
CALGARY AIRPORT AUTHORITY, THE
CALGARY INTERNATIONAL AIRPORT
2000 Airport Rd Ne, Calgary, AB, T2E 6W5
(403) 735-1200
Sales 288,479,301
SIC 4581 Airports, flying fields, and services
Garth F Atkinson
Douglas Mitchell
Frank J Jakowski
R.J. (Bob) Schmitt
Bernie Humphries
Stephan Poirier

D-U-N-S 20-650-4065 (BR)
**CALGARY CO-OPERATIVE ASSOCIATION
LIMITED**
CALGARY CO-OP
(*Suby of* CALGARY CO-OPERATIVE ASSO-
CIATION LIMITED)
540 16 Ave Ne, Calgary, AB, T2E 1K4
(403) 299-4276
Emp Here 100
SIC 5411 Grocery stores
Deane Collinson

D-U-N-S 20-828-6849 (SL)
**CALGARY ELKS LODGE #4 SOCIETY OF
THE B.P.O.E. OF CANADA**
CALGARY ELKS LODGE & GOLF CLUB
2502 6 St Ne, Calgary, AB, T2E 3Z3
(403) 250-7391
Emp Here 125   *Sales* 9,818,125
SIC 7992 Public golf courses
Shawn Lavoie

D-U-N-S 20-373-6103 (SL)
CALGARY H MOTORS LP
CALGARY HYUNDAI
(*Suby of* AUTOCANADA INC)
1920 23 St Ne, Calgary, AB, T2E 8N3
(403) 250-9990
Emp Here 65   *Sales* 40,903,200
SIC 5511 New and used car dealers

D-U-N-S 24-299-0059 (SL)
CALGARY HANDI-BUS ASSOCIATION
231 37 Ave Ne, Calgary, AB, T2E 8J2
(403) 276-8028
Emp Here 240   *Sales* 18,430,080
SIC 8322 Individual and family services
George Penny
Brent Kirkby
Robert Mcclinton
Jim Brown

D-U-N-S 24-119-2897 (SL)
**CALGARY REAL ESTATE BOARD CO-
OPERATIVE LIMITED**
300 Manning Rd Ne, Calgary, AB, T2E 8K4
(403) 263-4940
Emp Here 68   *Sales* 16,235,000
SIC 8611 Business associations
Ron Esch
Marilyn R Jones
Diane Payne
Don Dickson
Kevin Clark
Howie Attfield
Ron Stanners
Terry Banks
Ed Jensen
Jim English

D-U-N-S 24-714-6798 (SL)
CALGARY SCIENCE CENTRE SOCIETY

TELUS SPARK
220 St Georges Dr Ne, Calgary, AB, T2E 5T2
(403) 817-6800
Emp Here 75   *Sales* 6,852,675
SIC 8412 Museums and art galleries
Jennifer Martin

D-U-N-S 20-641-1279 (SL)
CALGARY SCOPE SOCIETY
219 18 St Se, Calgary, AB, T2E 6J5
(403) 509-0200
Emp Here 250   *Sales* 19,198,000
SIC 8322 Individual and family services
Bob Gentals

D-U-N-S 20-769-0025 (SL)
CALGARY ZOOLOGICAL SOCIETY, THE
CALGARY ZOO
1300 Zoo Rd Ne, Calgary, AB, T2E 7V6
(403) 232-9300
Emp Here 150   *Sales* 14,242,950
SIC 7999 Amusement and recreation, nec
Clement Lanthier
Gary Durbeniuk
Allan Pedden

D-U-N-S 20-128-7427 (HQ)
CAMERON FLOW SYSTEMS LTD
7944 10 St Ne, Calgary, AB, T2E 8W1
(403) 291-4814
Emp Here 52   *Sales* 36,366,240
SIC 3825 Instruments to measure electricity
Warren Jale
William C Lemmer

D-U-N-S 20-107-6549 (BR)
**CANADIAN CONTRACT CLEANING SPE-
CIALISTS, INC**
(*Suby of* HARVEST PARTNERS, LP)
1420 40 Ave Ne Suite 3, Calgary, AB, T2E 6L1
(403) 259-5560
Emp Here 250
SIC 7349 Building maintenance services, nec
Duy Nguyen

D-U-N-S 20-830-0202 (SL)
**CANADIAN CORPS OF COMMISSION-
AIRES (SOUTHERN ALBERTA)**
1107 53 Ave Ne, Calgary, AB, T2E 6X9
(403) 244-4664
Emp Here 1,650   *Sales* 48,267,879
SIC 7381 Detective and armored car services
John Fletcher
Steve Gagnon
Barbara Mikus

D-U-N-S 20-012-9521 (HQ)
CANADIAN NORTH INC
(*Suby of* INUVIALUIT REGIONAL CORPO-
RATION)
150 Palmer Rd Ne, Calgary, AB, T2E 7R3
(780) 890-8600
Emp Here 76   *Sales* 338,890,366
SIC 4729 Passenger transportation arrange-
ment
Steve Hankirk
Lorraine Bonner
Don Maclellan
John Hankirk
Gerry Roy
Wayne Gordon
Patrick Gruben
Cathy Munro
Wilf Wilcox
James Kinney

D-U-N-S 24-677-8000 (BR)
CANADIAN NORTH INC
(*Suby of* INUVIALUIT REGIONAL CORPO-
RATION)
580 Palmer Rd Ne Suite 200, Calgary, AB,
T2E 7R3
(403) 503-2310
Emp Here 150
SIC 4512 Air transportation, scheduled
Lisa Hicks

D-U-N-S 24-315-8842 (BR)
CANADIAN TEST CASE 192
BAKE INC
(*Suby of* CANADIAN TEST CASE 192)
1110 Centre St Ne Suite 204, Calgary, AB, T2E 2R2
(403) 276-5546
Emp Here 2,400
SIC 3714 Motor vehicle parts and accessories

D-U-N-S 24-417-2847 (BR)
CANPAR TRANSPORT L.P.
CANPAR CARRIER
(*Suby of* CANPAR TRANSPORT L.P.)
707 Barlow Trail Se Unit D, Calgary, AB, T2E 8C2
(800) 387-9335
Emp Here 75
SIC 7389 Business services, nec
Tom Parker

D-U-N-S 25-325-8974 (SL)
CARDIOLOGY PLUS (CALGARY) INC
CARDIOLOGY PLUS
803 1 Ave Ne Suite 306, Calgary, AB, T2E 7C5
(403) 571-8600
Emp Here 45 *Sales* 10,561,320
SIC 8734 Testing laboratories
Jim Stone

D-U-N-S 24-962-0675 (SL)
CAVALIER LAND LTD
DIVESTCO INC, DIV OF
1223 31 Ave Ne Suite 100, Calgary, AB, T2E 7W1
(403) 264-5188
Emp Here 40 *Sales* 16,774,200
SIC 6712 Bank holding companies
Steve Sinclair-Smith

D-U-N-S 24-961-2805 (HQ)
CAWTHORN INVESTMENTS LTD
6700 9 St Ne, Calgary, AB, T2E 8K6
(403) 295-5855
Sales 21,868,000
SIC 6712 Bank holding companies
Joseph Cawthorn

D-U-N-S 20-389-7483 (HQ)
CENTRE STREET CHURCH
3900 2 St Ne, Calgary, AB, T2E 9C1
(403) 293-3900
Sales 18,627,067
SIC 8661 Religious organizations
Teresa Davidson
Michelle Bonnier
Brian Hennig
Angie Redecopp
Edwin Beaman
Geogy Joseph
Melanie Nelson
Wendell Klassen

D-U-N-S 20-556-0233 (HQ)
CHIEF MEDICAL SUPPLIES LTD
411 19 St Se, Calgary, AB, T2E 6J7
(403) 207-6034
Sales 17,893,323
SIC 2834 Pharmaceutical preparations
Paul Tulan
Ramesh Singh

D-U-N-S 24-700-4278 (HQ)
CINNAROLL BAKERIES LIMITED
CINNZEO DIV
(*Suby of* SKIDMORE DEVELOPMENT GROUP LTD)
2140 Pegasus Rd Ne, Calgary, AB, T2E 8G8
(403) 255-4556
Emp Here 100 *Sales* 44,021,550
SIC 5461 Retail bakeries
Brad Turner

D-U-N-S 24-599-2144 (HQ)
CLASSIC KITCHENS & CABINETS LIMITED
1122 40 Ave Ne, Calgary, AB, T2E 5T8
(403) 250-9470
Emp Here 130 *Sales* 26,931,800

SIC 2434 Wood kitchen cabinets
Yusufali Esmail
Salim Kanji

D-U-N-S 20-646-2517 (SL)
CLOVER LEAF CHEESE LTD
CLOVER LEAF CHEESE
(*Suby of* HOFFCO MANAGEMENT LTD)
1201 45 Ave Ne, Calgary, AB, T2E 2P2
(403) 250-3780
Emp Here 65 *Sales* 54,312,505
SIC 5143 Dairy products, except dried or canned
Robert W. Brinkerhoff Jr
Brad Lake
Laurie Lautenslager

D-U-N-S 25-455-9669 (BR)
COCA-COLA CANADA BOTTLING LIMITED
COCA-COLA BOTTLING COMPANY
(*Suby of* COCA-COLA CANADA BOTTLING LIMITED)
3851 23 St Ne, Calgary, AB, T2E 6T2
(403) 291-3111
Emp Here 400
SIC 2086 Bottled and canned soft drinks
Trevor Lamb

D-U-N-S 20-255-3038 (SL)
COCOCO CHOCOLATIERS INC
CHOCOLATERIE BERBARD CALLEBAUT
2320 2 Ave Se, Calgary, AB, T2E 6J9
(403) 265-5777
Emp Here 150 *Sales* 51,853,500
SIC 2066 Chocolate and cocoa products
Kristi Mehr

D-U-N-S 20-946-9980 (HQ)
COLE INTERNATIONAL INC
(*Suby of* NOMA BROKERAGE LIMITED)
1111 49 Ave Ne, Calgary, AB, T2E 8V2
(403) 262-2771
Emp Here 95 *Sales* 197,719,000
SIC 4731 Freight transportation arrangement
Donald Lucky
Kyle Johnston
David Bosse

D-U-N-S 24-733-4634 (SL)
COLUMBIA COLLEGE CORP
COLUMBIA COLLEGE
802 Manning Rd Ne, Calgary, AB, T2E 7N8
(403) 235-9300
Emp Here 110 *Sales* 13,214,190
SIC 8299 Schools and educational services, nec
Thomas (Tom) Snell
Nola M Snell

D-U-N-S 20-398-2108 (SL)
CONCORDE BAGGAGE SERVICES INC
CONCORDE AIRPORT SERVICES
2000 Airport Rd Ne, Calgary, AB, T2E 6W5
(403) 735-5317
Emp Here 537 *Sales* 17,166,816
SIC 7349 Building maintenance services, nec
Anthony Mak
Philip Tsang

D-U-N-S 20-991-4191 (HQ)
CONTINENTAL LABORATORIES (1985) LTD
3601 21 St Ne Unit A, Calgary, AB, T2E 6T5
(403) 250-3982
Sales 34,979,308
SIC 1389 Oil and gas field services, nec

D-U-N-S 25-218-3066 (HQ)
CORE LABORATORIES CANADA LTD
SAYBOLT, DIV OF
(*Suby of* CORE LABORATORIES N.V.)
2810 12 St Ne, Calgary, AB, T2E 7P7
(403) 250-4000
Emp Here 25 *Sales* 115,098,120
SIC 8734 Testing laboratories
Stephen Lee
Brian Tofselmire

D-U-N-S 24-244-9978 (BR)
CORE LABORATORIES CANADA LTD
(*Suby of* CORE LABORATORIES N.V.)
2810 12 St Ne, Calgary, AB, T2E 7P7
(403) 250-4000
Emp Here 100
SIC 8734 Testing laboratories
Rochard Thom

D-U-N-S 20-294-7461 (HQ)
CORRIDOR COMMUNICATIONS, INC
CCI WIRELESS
465 Aviation Rd Ne Suite 137, Calgary, AB, T2E 7H8
(888) 240-2224
Sales 22,847,200
SIC 4813 Telephone communication, except radio
Jordan Young
Adam Lamont
Dareld Cholak
James Cooper
Jack Eccles
Joe Kutanzi
Bert Paulssen
Wayne Slenders
Rick Thorne
Gary Turner

D-U-N-S 25-450-0077 (BR)
CORUS MEDIA HOLDINGS INC
GLOBAL TELEVISION
(*Suby of* SHAW COMMUNICATIONS INC)
222 23 St Ne, Calgary, AB, T2E 7N2
(403) 235-7777
Emp Here 210
SIC 4833 Television broadcasting stations
Ron Ball

D-U-N-S 20-599-3025 (SL)
CUSTOM ELECTRIC LTD
1725 27 Ave Ne, Calgary, AB, T2E 7E1
(403) 736-0205
Emp Here 250 *Sales* 58,877,250
SIC 1731 Electrical work
Brian Phels
Richard Sleurant
Gord Dandy

D-U-N-S 20-522-2644 (HQ)
CYBA STEVENS MANAGEMENT GROUP INC
5735 7 St Ne Suite 100, Calgary, AB, T2E 8V3
(403) 291-3288
Emp Here 25 *Sales* 62,668,275
SIC 5141 Groceries, general line
Boyd Stevens
John Lemoine

D-U-N-S 25-534-6959 (HQ)
DE BEERS CANADA INC
SNAP LAKE PROJECT
(*Suby of* DE BEERS GROUP SERVICES (PTY) LTD)
1601 Airport Rd Ne Suite 300, Calgary, AB, T2E 6Z8
(403) 930-0991
Sales 103,277,250
SIC 1499 Miscellaneous nonMetallic minerals, except fuels
Kim Truter
Brad Baylis
Erik Madsen
Eric Ingle

D-U-N-S 24-156-7650 (BR)
DELTA HOTELS LIMITED
DELTA CALGARY AIRPORT HOTEL
(*Suby of* GOVERNMENT OF THE PROVINCE OF BRITISH COLUMBIA)
2001 Airport Rd Ne, Calgary, AB, T2E 6Z8
(403) 291-2600
Emp Here 240
SIC 8741 Management services
David Bird

D-U-N-S 24-318-6496 (BR)

DIVESTCO INC
1223 31 Ave Ne, Calgary, AB, T2E 7W1
(403) 237-9170
Emp Here 120 *Sales* 322,580
SIC 7371 Custom computer programming services
Peter Zyla

D-U-N-S 20-771-4937 (SL)
DOMINION PROTECTION SERVICES LTD
1935 32 Ave Ne Suite 124, Calgary, AB, T2E 3R1
(403) 717-1732
Emp Here 25 *Sales* 11,179,350
SIC 5065 Electronic parts and equipment, nec
Zahir Ismail

D-U-N-S 24-015-9772 (HQ)
EAGLE COPTERS LTD
EAGLE WORLDWIDE FLEET MANAGEMENT
823 Mctavish Rd Ne, Calgary, AB, T2E 7G9
(403) 250-7370
Sales 20,154,690
SIC 6159 Miscellaneous business credit institutions
Barry Kohler
Melvin O'reilly
Zita Mulligan

D-U-N-S 25-359-4568 (SL)
EAGLE COPTERS MAINTENANCE LTD
(*Suby of* EAGLE COPTERS LTD)
823 Mctavish Rd Ne, Calgary, AB, T2E 7G9
(403) 250-7370
Emp Here 100 *Sales* 26,697,800
SIC 4581 Airports, flying fields, and services
Michael P. O'reilly

D-U-N-S 20-195-9207 (BR)
EARL'S RESTAURANTS CARRELL LTD
EARL'S
(*Suby of* EARL'S RESTAURANTS CARRELL LTD)
3030 23 St Ne, Calgary, AB, T2E 8R7
(403) 291-6700
Emp Here 80
SIC 5812 Eating places
Lauren Bar

D-U-N-S 20-345-6157 (SL)
ECHO SEISMIC LTD
(*Suby of* MATCO INVESTMENTS LTD)
4500 8a St Ne, Calgary, AB, T2E 4J7
(403) 216-0999
Emp Here 15 *Sales* 15,867,144
SIC 1382 Oil and gas exploration services
Richard Haviak
Ronald Mathison
Bruce Moyes
Dan Mcarthur

D-U-N-S 24-300-0346 (SL)
ELECTRICAL WHOLESALERS (CALGARY) LTD
1323 36 Ave Ne, Calgary, AB, T2E 6T6
(403) 250-7060
Emp Here 38 *Sales* 16,992,612
SIC 5063 Electrical apparatus and equipment
Rudy Van Es
Dorothy Van Es

D-U-N-S 20-369-0610 (HQ)
ENERGY SAFETY CANADA
5055 11 St Ne, Calgary, AB, T2E 8N4
(403) 516-8000
Emp Here 1 *Sales* 30,418,800
SIC 8748 Business consulting, nec
John Rhind

D-U-N-S 24-119-8662 (SL)
ENGEL'S BAKERIES LTD
4709 14 St Ne Unit 6, Calgary, AB, T2E 6S4
(403) 250-9560
Emp Here 70 *Sales* 15,739,850
SIC 2051 Bread, cake, and related products
Mithoo Gillani

Firoz Hirji

D-U-N-S 25-416-0021   (SL)
ENMAX POWER SERVICES CORP
(*Suby of* CITY OF CALGARY, THE)
239 Mayland Pl Ne, Calgary, AB, T2E 7Z8
(403) 514-3000
Emp Here 493   *Sales* 414,482,848
SIC 4911 Electric services
 Gary Holden
 Paul Dawson
 Robert Hawkesworth
 Dale Hodges
 Francis Leong
 H Tompson Macdonald

D-U-N-S 25-620-9867   (BR)
ENTERPRISE RENT-A-CAR CANADA COM-PANY
(*Suby of* THE CRAWFORD GROUP INC)
2335 78 Ave Ne, Calgary, AB, T2E 7L2
(403) 250-1395
Emp Here 200
SIC 7514 Passenger car rental
 Angus Watson

D-U-N-S 20-639-2230   (HQ)
EVANS CONSOLES CORPORATION
1616 27 Ave Ne, Calgary, AB, T2E 8W4
(403) 291-4444
Sales 28,549,570
SIC 2521 Wood office furniture
 Greg Smith
 William C Burkett

D-U-N-S 24-981-0037   (HQ)
EXECUTIVE FLIGHT CENTRE FUEL SER-VICES LTD
EXECUTIVE FLIGHT CENTRE
680 Palmer Rd Ne Suite 200, Calgary, AB, T2E 7R3
(403) 291-2825
Emp Here 24   *Sales* 153,695,490
SIC 5172 Petroleum products, nec
 Kenneth Lett
 Dean Buckland

D-U-N-S 24-341-0615   (BR)
FEDERAL EXPRESS CANADA CORPORA-TION
FEDEX SHIP CENTRE
(*Suby of* FEDEX CORPORATION)
24 Aero Dr Ne, Calgary, AB, T2E 8Z9
(800) 463-3339
Emp Here 250
SIC 7389 Business services, nec

D-U-N-S 24-857-1544   (HQ)
FGL SPORTS LTD
ATMOSPHERE
(*Suby of* CANADIAN TIRE CORPORATION, LIMITED)
824 41 Ave Ne, Calgary, AB, T2E 3R3
(403) 717-1400
Emp Here 450   *Sales* 2,228,139,180
SIC 5941 Sporting goods and bicycle shops
 John Chimienti
 Eleni Damianakis
 Richard Burnet
 Duncan Fulton
 Kristi Lalach

D-U-N-S 24-948-2340   (HQ)
FIBRECLEAN SUPPLIES LTD
3750 19 St Ne Suite 101, Calgary, AB, T2E 6V2
(403) 291-3991
Emp Here 7   *Sales* 11,400,624
SIC 5087 Service establishment equipment
 Timothy Hendrix

D-U-N-S 24-616-0746   (SL)
FILTEX VACUUMS OF CANADA
3103 Centre St Nw, Calgary, AB, T2E 2X3
(403) 277-5511
Emp Here 30   *Sales* 14,250,780
SIC 5087 Service establishment equipment

Moe Hamadiya

D-U-N-S 20-183-6538   (HQ)
FLYHT AEROSPACE SOLUTIONS LTD
1144 29 Ave Ne Suite 300e, Calgary, AB, T2E 7P1
(403) 250-9956
Sales 10,302,997
SIC 3812 Search and navigation equipment
 Thomas R. Schmutz
 Bill Tempany
 Doug Marlin
 Jeffrey Rex
 Derek Taylor
 Mike Brown
 Barry Eccleston
 Nina Jonsson
 Jack Olcott
 Mark Rosenker

D-U-N-S 24-320-8365   (HQ)
FOREMOST INDUSTRIES LP
1225 64 Ave Ne, Calgary, AB, T2E 8P9
(403) 295-5800
Emp Here 100   *Sales* 84,263,100
SIC 3531 Construction machinery
 Kevin Johnson
 Mike Mccarthy

D-U-N-S 25-957-0836   (BR)
G4S CASH SOLUTIONS (CANADA) LTD
(*Suby of* G4S PLC)
5040 Skyline Way Ne, Calgary, AB, T2E 6V1
(403) 974-8350
Emp Here 100
SIC 7381 Detective and armored car services
 Johnathan Whale

D-U-N-S 25-990-1247   (SL)
GARROD FOOD BROKERS LTD
CONCORD NATIONAL (PRAIRIE DIVISION)
7777 10 St Ne Suite 120, Calgary, AB, T2E 8X2
(403) 291-2818
Emp Here 43   *Sales* 35,929,811
SIC 5141 Groceries, general line
 Tim Moore
 Robert Schwartz
 Blaine Petkau

D-U-N-S 25-449-9965   (BR)
GENERAL DYNAMICS LAND SYSTEMS - CANADA CORPORATION
(*Suby of* GENERAL DYNAMICS CORPORA-TION)
1020 68 Ave Ne, Calgary, AB, T2E 8P2
(403) 295-6700
Emp Here 503
SIC 7371 Custom computer programming ser-vices
 David Ibbetson

D-U-N-S 20-695-0938   (SL)
GENESIS BUILDERS GROUP INC
(*Suby of* GENESIS LAND DEVELOPMENT CORP)
7315 8 St Ne, Calgary, AB, T2E 8A2
(403) 265-9237
Emp Here 50   *Sales* 13,547,100
SIC 1521 Single-family housing construction
 Stephen Griggs

D-U-N-S 25-205-3517   (HQ)
GENESIS LAND DEVELOPMENT CORP
7315 8 St Ne, Calgary, AB, T2E 8A2
(403) 266-0746
Emp Here 12   *Sales* 118,252,534
SIC 6553 Cemetery subdividers and develop-ers
 Stephen J. Griggs
 Bruce Rudichuk
 Parveshindera Sidhu
 Arnie Stefaniuk
 Brian Whitwell
 Wayne King
 Yazdi Bharucha
 Michael Brodsky

Mark W. Mitchell
Loudon Owen

D-U-N-S 24-017-0761   (BR)
GRAND & TOY LIMITED
WAREHOUSE DISTRIBUTION CENTRE
(*Suby of* OFFICE DEPOT, INC.)
37 Aero Dr Ne, Calgary, AB, T2E 8Z9
(866) 391-8111
Emp Here 160
SIC 5021 Furniture
 Martin Lapointe

D-U-N-S 20-599-3868   (HQ)
GRAYMONT WESTERN CANADA INC
(*Suby of* GRAYMONT LIMITED)
3025 12 St Ne Suite 190, Calgary, AB, T2E 7J2
(403) 250-9100
Emp Here 14   *Sales* 25,449,098
SIC 3274 Lime
 William Dodge
 Peter Darbeyshyre
 Stuart Wolfe
 John Jordan
 Anthony Graham
 Allan Laird
 Dorothy Mills

D-U-N-S 20-076-1302   (HQ)
GREAT WEST ITALIAN IMPORTERS LTD
SCARPONE'S
5130 Skyline Way Ne, Calgary, AB, T2E 6V1
(403) 275-8222
Sales 25,067,310
SIC 5141 Groceries, general line
 Alberto Iamartino
 Christina Iamartino

D-U-N-S 20-831-6331   (SL)
H. T. DRYWALL (CLG) LTD
908 53 Ave Ne Suite F, Calgary, AB, T2E 6N9
(403) 295-8404
Emp Here 70   *Sales* 11,366,670
SIC 1742 Plastering, drywall, and insulation
 Dennis Raffan
 Kathleen Raffan

D-U-N-S 24-415-7087   (SL)
HARLEY-DAVIDSON OF SOUTHERN AL-BERTA INC
CALGARY HARLEY-DAVIDSON
2245 Pegasus Rd Ne, Calgary, AB, T2E 8C3
(403) 250-3141
Emp Here 45   *Sales* 22,413,510
SIC 5571 Motorcycle dealers
 James Wild

D-U-N-S 24-621-1457   (SL)
HERITAGE SURFACE SOLUTIONS
6815 8 St Ne Suite 165, Calgary, AB, T2E 7H7
(403) 291-2804
Emp Here 22   *Sales* 14,936,306
SIC 6211 Security brokers and dealers
 Wally Tomie

D-U-N-S 20-706-9209   (BR)
HOST INTERNATIONAL OF CANADA, LTD
(*Suby of* EDIZIONE SRL)
2000 Airport Rd Ne Suite 160, Calgary, AB, T2E 6W5
(403) 503-2214
Emp Here 80
SIC 5812 Eating places

D-U-N-S 25-678-5163   (HQ)
HUNTING ENERGY SERVICES (CANADA) LTD
(*Suby of* HUNTING PLC)
5550 Skyline Way Ne, Calgary, AB, T2E 7Z7
(403) 543-4477
Emp Here 100   *Sales* 134,535,800
SIC 1389 Oil and gas field services, nec
 Dennis Proctor
 Elmer Campbell

D-U-N-S 20-179-9942   (BR)
HUNTING ENERGY SERVICES (CANADA)

LTD
HUNTING THREADTECH
(*Suby of* HUNTING PLC)
5550 Skyline Way Ne, Calgary, AB, T2E 7Z7
(403) 543-4477
Emp Here 200
SIC 5541 Gasoline service stations
 Chris Wallace

D-U-N-S 20-082-9179   (BR)
IBI GROUP
(*Suby of* IBI GROUP)
611 Meredith Rd Ne Suite 500, Calgary, AB, T2E 2W5
(403) 270-5600
Emp Here 100
SIC 8712 Architectural services
 Elvin Karpovich

D-U-N-S 24-088-9720   (SL)
INDO CANADIAN CENTRE
826 Edmonton Trail Ne, Calgary, AB, T2E 3J6
(403) 277-1459
Emp Here 27   *Sales* 18,813,870
SIC 6732 Trusts: educational, religious, etc.
 Cd Lad

D-U-N-S 20-639-2651   (SL)
INNOVATIVE GLOBAL SOLUTIONS INC
320 19 St Se, Calgary, AB, T2E 6J6
(403) 204-1198
Emp Here 32   *Sales* 15,946,304
SIC 5136 Men's and boy's clothing
 Clif Burnette

D-U-N-S 25-388-2310   (HQ)
INSTABOX (ALBERTA) INC
1139 40 Ave Ne, Calgary, AB, T2E 6M9
(403) 250-9217
Emp Here 55   *Sales* 15,970,976
SIC 2653 Corrugated and solid fiber boxes
 Greg Mace

D-U-N-S 20-798-0637   (SL)
INSTIMAX CORPORATION
IETICKETS
901 Centre St Nw Unit 303, Calgary, AB, T2E 2P6
(403) 398-8911
Emp Here 100   *Sales* 16,402,700
SIC 2759 Commercial printing, nec
 Henry Vi

D-U-N-S 20-016-6937   (HQ)
ITN INTERNATIONAL CORP
ITN LOGISTICS
2915 21 St Ne Suite 201, Calgary, AB, T2E 7T1
(403) 219-8440
Emp Here 1   *Sales* 14,039,109
SIC 4731 Freight transportation arrangement
 Paul Lobas

D-U-N-S 20-365-8757   (BR)
JWP PUBLISHING LIMITED PARTNERSHIP
JUNE WARREN PUBLISHING
(*Suby of* GLACIER MEDIA INC)
816 55 Ave Ne 2nd Fl, Calgary, AB, T2E 6Y4
(403) 265-3700
Emp Here 100
SIC 2721 Periodicals
 Bill Witelaw

D-U-N-S 20-801-4543   (SL)
K N CUSTOMS BROKERS
KUEHNE + NAGEO
2415 Pegasus Rd Ne Unit 210, Calgary, AB, T2E 8C3
(403) 250-3075
Emp Here 30   *Sales* 15,599,010
SIC 4731 Freight transportation arrangement
 Amerik Hair

D-U-N-S 24-299-9571   (SL)
KANE, BRIAN INSURANCE AGENCIES LTD
BKI RISK MANAGEMENT
(*Suby of* TREDD INSURANCE BROKERS LTD)

6815 8 St Ne Suite 120, Calgary, AB, T2E 7H7
(403) 276-8766
Emp Here 20   *Sales* 11,598,480
SIC 6411 Insurance agents, brokers, and service
Brian Kane
Tim D Kane

D-U-N-S 24-338-1733   (SL)
KELSON CANADA INC
2431 37 Ave Ne Suite 430, Calgary, AB, T2E 6Y7
(403) 296-1500
Emp Here 50   *Sales* 13,297,600
SIC 6712 Bank holding companies
Don Walters
Neal Cody
Jesse Gardner
Gerald Diener
Jeffrey Kirshner

D-U-N-S 24-332-4662   (HQ)
KENN BOREK AIR LTD
KBAL
(*Suby of* BOREK CONSTRUCTION LTD)
290 Mctavish Rd Ne Suite 4, Calgary, AB, T2E 7G5
(403) 291-3300
Emp Here 200   *Sales* 126,940,800
SIC 4522 Air transportation, nonscheduled
Rosella Borek
Chris Vipond
John Harmer

D-U-N-S 20-391-5640   (SL)
LBCO CONTRACTING LTD
623 35 Ave Ne, Calgary, AB, T2E 2L2
(403) 277-9555
Emp Here 45   *Sales* 10,839,780
SIC 1629 Heavy construction, nec
Fernando Nogueira

D-U-N-S 24-786-2444   (SL)
LEAR CONSTRUCTION SERVICES INC
(*Suby of* CHRYBR CONSULTING SERVICES LTD)
4200 10 St Ne, Calgary, AB, T2E 6K3
(403) 250-3818
Emp Here 50   *Sales* 28,516,900
SIC 1542 Nonresidential construction, nec
Phil Bazant

D-U-N-S 20-766-7924   (HQ)
LEMMER SPRAY SYSTEMS LTD
4624 12 St Ne, Calgary, AB, T2E 4R4
(403) 250-7735
Emp Here 15   *Sales* 11,875,650
SIC 5084 Industrial machinery and equipment
Christian Lemmer
Thomas Lemmer
Michael Lemmer

D-U-N-S 20-051-8517   (BR)
LOBLAW COMPANIES LIMITED
WESTFAIR FOODS
(*Suby of* LOBLAW COMPANIES LIMITED)
3225 12 St Ne, Calgary, AB, T2E 7S9
(403) 291-7700
Emp Here 200
SIC 5411 Grocery stores
Gordon Chem

D-U-N-S 20-595-5847   (BR)
LOBLAWS INC
REAL CANADIAN WHOLESALE CLUB
(*Suby of* LOBLAW COMPANIES LIMITED)
2928 23 St Ne, Calgary, AB, T2E 8R7
(403) 291-2810
Emp Here 100
SIC 5141 Groceries, general line
Bharat Desai

D-U-N-S 20-599-0328   (SL)
LUX WINDOWS AND GLASS LTD
LUX WINDOWS
6875 9 St Ne, Calgary, AB, T2E 8R9
(403) 276-7770
Emp Here 130   *Sales* 25,008,100

SIC 2431 Millwork
John Petrillo
Tony Ambrogiano

D-U-N-S 24-700-9509   (BR)
MARTIN-BROWER OF CANADA CO
(*Suby of* REYES HOLDINGS, L.L.C.)
4242 21 St Ne, Calgary, AB, T2E 9A6
(403) 255-3278
Emp Here 80
SIC 5141 Groceries, general line

D-U-N-S 25-188-1181   (SL)
MEDICAL MERCY CANADA SOCIETY
1216 34 Ave Ne Suite 6, Calgary, AB, T2E 6L9
(403) 717-0933
Emp Here 100   *Sales* 15,634,600
SIC 8099 Health and allied services, nec
Stanley Odut
Joanne Newedul
Linda Lynch-Staunton
Sonia Brennan

D-U-N-S 20-350-7462   (SL)
MENZIES AVIATION (CANADA) LTD
(*Suby of* JOHN MENZIES PLC)
175 Aero Way Ne Unit 130, Calgary, AB, T2E 6K2
(403) 250-2033
Emp Here 100   *Sales* 7,527,200
SIC 4111 Local and suburban transit
Daniel Smith

D-U-N-S 24-767-3924   (SL)
METROMEDIA MARKETING LTD
5774 10 St Ne, Calgary, AB, T2E 8W7
(403) 291-3912
Emp Here 25   *Sales* 18,563,000
SIC 5199 Nondurable goods, nec
Nicholas Thompson
Laura Thompson
David Thompson

D-U-N-S 24-000-9550   (SL)
MOORE'S INDUSTRIAL SERVICE LTD
3333 23 St Ne, Calgary, AB, T2E 6V8
(403) 219-7160
Emp Here 147   *Sales* 13,185,312
SIC 7699 Repair services, nec
Robert Newman
Bill Cheyne

D-U-N-S 24-929-7052   (HQ)
MRO ELECTRONIC SUPPLY LTD
2240 Pegasus Rd Ne, Calgary, AB, T2E 8G8
(403) 291-0501
Emp Here 22   *Sales* 10,261,783
SIC 5065 Electronic parts and equipment, nec
Kevin Stiles
Stephen Shepherd
Sandra Stiles
Mark Stiles
Phillip Stiles

D-U-N-S 24-978-7763   (HQ)
MRS. WILLMAN'S BAKING LIMITED
(*Suby of* BEAUMONT SELECT CORPORATIONS INC)
4826 11 St Ne Unit 4, Calgary, AB, T2E 2W7

Emp Here 100
SIC 2051 Bread, cake, and related products
Winston Ho Fatt

D-U-N-S 25-099-3359   (SL)
MRT ENTERPRISES INC
FAMILY FOODS
817 19 St Ne Suite 109, Calgary, AB, T2E 4X5
(403) 216-8800
Emp Here 55   *Sales* 16,141,235
SIC 5411 Grocery stores
Tony Peters
Mitch Peters
Randy Friesan

D-U-N-S 25-013-8195   (HQ)
NORTH WEST GEOMATICS LTD
NORTH WEST GROUP

(*Suby of* HEXAGON AB)
245 Aero Way Ne, Calgary, AB, T2E 6K2
(403) 295-0694
Sales 34,783,216
SIC 7389 Business services, nec
John F.A. Welter
Juergen Dold
Shaju Kariath
Hongquan Li

D-U-N-S 25-360-9143   (BR)
NOVA CHEMICALS (CANADA) LTD
NOVA CHEMICALS RESEARCH CENTER
(*Suby of* GOVERNMENT OF ABU DHABI)
2928 16 St Ne, Calgary, AB, T2E 7K7

Emp Here 150
SIC 2869 Industrial organic chemicals, nec
Daryll Harrison

D-U-N-S 25-314-1352   (SL)
NOVATEL WIRELESS TECHNOLOGIES LTD
(*Suby of* INSEEGO CORP.)
6715 8 St Ne Suite 200, Calgary, AB, T2E 7H7

Emp Here 70   *Sales* 15,993,040
SIC 4899 Communication services, nec
Peter Leparulo
Gayle Gartner

D-U-N-S 20-690-3788   (SL)
NT SERVICES LIMITED
PAYSAFE GROUP
215 16 St Se 3rd Fl, Calgary, AB, T2E 7P5
(403) 769-3600
Emp Here 400   *Sales* 93,415,200
SIC 6099 Functions related to deposit banking
Enman Ma
Tim Tomanik

D-U-N-S 20-117-4120   (HQ)
OIL LIFT TECHNOLOGY INC
(*Suby of* APERGY CORPORATION)
950 64 Ave Ne, Calgary, AB, T2E 8S8
(403) 291-5300
Emp Here 43   *Sales* 11,544,052
SIC 3533 Oil and gas field machinery
Vern Arthur Hult
Dianne Crockett

D-U-N-S 24-880-1763   (SL)
OPTIMA MANUFACTURING INC
(*Suby of* 470570 ALBERTA INC)
2480 Pegasus Rd Ne, Calgary, AB, T2E 8G8
(403) 291-2007
Emp Here 49   *Sales* 10,878,049
SIC 3599 Industrial machinery, nec
Duane Hertzer
Joseph Trotta

D-U-N-S 25-359-4006   (BR)
P.R. DEVELOPMENTS LTD
EXECUTIVE ROYAL INN
2828 23 St Ne, Calgary, AB, T2E 8T4
(403) 291-2003
Emp Here 110
SIC 7011 Hotels and motels
Dave Korpach

D-U-N-S 25-323-3428   (HQ)
PACEKIDS SOCIETY FOR CHILDREN WITH SPECIAL NEEDS
808 55 Ave Ne, Calgary, AB, T2E 6Y4
(403) 234-7876
Emp Here 123   *Sales* 11,365,216
SIC 8322 Individual and family services
R. Alex Reed
John Pieri
Kelly Ross
Rocky Mix
Brittney Labranche
Henry Chow
Hugh Erickson
Leanne Hullick-Reyes
Tina Lee

D-U-N-S 20-617-4328   (HQ)

PACIFIC WESTERN TRANSPORTATION LTD
SAFELY HOME
1857 Centre Ave Se, Calgary, AB, T2E 6L3
(403) 248-4300
Sales 89,942,400
SIC 4111 Local and suburban transit
Michael Colborne
Rick Colborne
Lynne Brennan
Catherine Vogelgesang
Dan Finley
Garry Clermont
Trevor Webb
Mark Hannah
Stephen Evans
Thomas Schmidt

D-U-N-S 24-807-0591   (HQ)
PARTS CANADA DEVELOPMENT CO.
(*Suby of* LEMANS CORPORATION)
2916 21 St Ne, Calgary, AB, T2E 6Z2
(403) 250-6611
Sales 78,396,180
SIC 5013 Motor vehicle supplies and new parts
James Danyluk

D-U-N-S 25-452-2089   (BR)
PCL CONSTRUCTION MANAGEMENT INC
(*Suby of* PCL EMPLOYEES HOLDINGS LTD)
2882 11 St Ne, Calgary, AB, T2E 7S7
(403) 250-4800
Emp Here 145
SIC 8741 Management services
Blain Maciborsky

D-U-N-S 24-441-0015   (SL)
PDL MOBILITY LIMITED
(*Suby of* BOMBENON, MARC ENTERPRISES LTD)
2420 42 Ave Ne, Calgary, AB, T2E 7T6
(403) 291-5400
Emp Here 100
SIC 5999 Miscellaneous retail stores, nec
Marc Bombenon

D-U-N-S 20-353-2072   (SL)
PERATON CANADA CORP
(*Suby of* VERITAS CAPITAL FUND MANAGEMENT, L.L.C.)
6732 8 St Ne, Calgary, AB, T2E 8M4
(403) 295-4770
Emp Here 90   *Sales* 30,324,080
SIC 7699 Repair services, nec
Jeremy Wensinger
Jim Gillespie

D-U-N-S 24-809-8006   (SL)
PERMA INSURANCE CONTINENTAL INC
PERMA INSURANCE ANGENCY
901 Centre St Nw Suite 200, Calgary, AB, T2E 2P6
(403) 230-0808
Emp Here 25   *Sales* 14,498,100
SIC 6411 Insurance agents, brokers, and service
Raymond Kan

D-U-N-S 20-077-4727   (SL)
PETERS' DRIVE INN
219 16 Ave Ne, Calgary, AB, T2E 1J9
(403) 277-2747
Emp Here 80   *Sales* 3,641,520
SIC 5812 Eating places
Joanne Rowe

D-U-N-S 24-345-9351   (SL)
PISCES EXOTICA PET EMPORIUM LTD
PISCES PET EMPORIUM
4921 Skyline Way Ne, Calgary, AB, T2E 4G5
(403) 274-3314
Emp Here 40   *Sales* 13,024,000
SIC 5999 Miscellaneous retail stores, nec
Peter Hoeper
Ave Hoeper

D-U-N-S 20-077-5336   (SL)
POCKAR MASONRY LTD
4632 5 St Ne, Calgary, AB, T2E 7C3
(403) 276-5591
Emp Here 65   *Sales* 10,554,765
SIC 1741 Masonry and other stonework
Malcolm Holbrook
Mirko Pockar
Emil Pockar

D-U-N-S 25-997-2693   (SL)
POINTE OF VIEW MARKETING & MANAGE-MENT INC
1121 Centre St Nw Suite 500, Calgary, AB,
T2E 7K6
(403) 571-8400
Emp Here 140   *Sales* 66,743,880
SIC 1531 Operative builders
Randy Klapstien

D-U-N-S 24-159-7723   (BR)
POSTMEDIA NETWORK INC
CALGARY HERALD, THE
(*Suby of* POSTMEDIA NETWORK CANADA CORP)
215 16 St Se, Calgary, AB, T2E 7P5
(403) 235-7168
Emp Here 750
SIC 2711 Newspapers
Malcolm Kirk

D-U-N-S 20-823-5296   (HQ)
PRIMARY ENGINEERING AND CON-STRUCTION CORPORATION
207 39 Ave Ne, Calgary, AB, T2E 7E3
(403) 873-0400
Sales 14,956,430
SIC 8711 Engineering services
Kevin Jones
Dave Peterson

D-U-N-S 20-299-2199   (BR)
PUROLATOR INC
(*Suby of* GOVERNMENT OF CANADA)
30 Aero Dr Ne, Calgary, AB, T2E 8Z9
(403) 516-6200
Emp Here 250
SIC 4731 Freight transportation arrangement
Clint Caron

D-U-N-S 20-718-6110   (BR)
RAYTHEON CANADA LIMITED
SERVICE & SUPPORT DIVISION
(*Suby of* RAYTHEON COMPANY)
919 72 Ave Ne, Calgary, AB, T2E 8N9
(403) 295-6900
Emp Here 80
SIC 3812 Search and navigation equipment
Terry Manion

D-U-N-S 24-081-8604   (SL)
RAZOR SHARP MAGNETICS INC
RAZO
314 11 Ave Ne, Calgary, AB, T2E 0Z1

Emp Here 40   *Sales* 13,243,048
SIC 5999 Miscellaneous retail stores, nec
Maxine Power

D-U-N-S 20-176-4847   (BR)
REMAI HOLDINGS LTD
ROYAL INN NORTH CALGARY
2828 23 St Ne, Calgary, AB, T2E 8T4
(403) 291-2003
Emp Here 125
SIC 7011 Hotels and motels
Michael Sieger

D-U-N-S 25-136-9914   (SL)
RESIDENTIAL ELECTRICAL CONTRAC-TOR CORPORATION, THE
TRECC ELECTRIC
2616 16 St Ne Suite 4, Calgary, AB, T2E 7J8
(403) 735-6120
Emp Here 95   *Sales* 20,693,755
SIC 1731 Electrical work
William Crippin

Susan Crippin

D-U-N-S 20-322-0025   (HQ)
RIDGELINE CANADA INC
3016 19 St Ne Suite 101, Calgary, AB, T2E 6Y9
(403) 806-2380
Emp Here 15   *Sales* 11,714,400
SIC 8748 Business consulting, nec
Tyler Heathcote
Brad Shybunka
Jason Flatla

D-U-N-S 20-705-7626   (HQ)
RISING EDGE TECHNOLOGIES LTD
2620 22 St Ne, Calgary, AB, T2E 7L9
(403) 202-8751
Emp Here 20   *Sales* 55,217,760
SIC 1796 Installing building equipment
Nick Maher

D-U-N-S 20-012-7749   (HQ)
SAFETY BOSS INC
17-2135 32 Ave Ne, Calgary, AB, T2E 6Z3
(403) 261-5075
Emp Here 9   *Sales* 43,051,456
SIC 1389 Oil and gas field services, nec
Michael Miller
Mark Brown
Heidi Lasante
Mike Martel
Monty Mason
Tyler Farmer
Corey Dool
Sonia Rehal

D-U-N-S 20-369-9814   (SL)
SALERS ASSOCIATION OF CANADA
5160 Skyline Way Ne, Calgary, AB, T2E 6V1
(403) 264-5850
Emp Here 49   *Sales* 11,451,055
SIC 8621 Professional organizations
Gar Williams

D-U-N-S 20-077-9155   (SL)
SCHMIDT, WM. MECHANICAL CONTRAC-TORS LTD
4603 13 St Ne Suite D, Calgary, AB, T2E 6M3
(403) 250-1157
Emp Here 100   *Sales* 23,306,500
SIC 1711 Plumbing, heating, air-conditioning
William Schmidt
Erna Schmidt

D-U-N-S 20-036-2585   (SL)
SCRAPBOOK, EH WHOLESALE LTD
5421 11 St Ne Unit 109, Calgary, AB, T2E 6M4
(403) 229-1058
Emp Here 80   *Sales* 40,292,640
SIC 5112 Stationery and office supplies
Leslie Lee
Murray Lee

D-U-N-S 24-859-4785   (BR)
SHANE HOLDINGS LTD
(*Suby of* SHANE HOLDINGS LTD)
5661 7 St Ne, Calgary, AB, T2E 8V3
(403) 536-2200
Emp Here 77
SIC 1521 Single-family housing construction

D-U-N-S 25-539-5352   (HQ)
SHANE HOLDINGS LTD
5661 7 St Ne, Calgary, AB, T2E 8V3
(403) 536-2200
Emp Here 1   *Sales* 20,320,650
SIC 1521 Single-family housing construction
Shane Wenzel

D-U-N-S 24-158-2840   (SL)
SHANE HOMES LIMITED
(*Suby of* SHANE HOLDINGS LTD)
5661 7 St Ne, Calgary, AB, T2E 8V3
(403) 536-2200
Emp Here 75   *Sales* 20,320,650
SIC 1521 Single-family housing construction
Calvin Wenzel
Edith Wenzel

Shane Wenzel
Gerry Dyck

D-U-N-S 25-290-8132   (HQ)
SHAW CABLESYSTEMS LIMITED
(*Suby of* SHAW COMMUNICATIONS INC)
2400 32 Ave Ne, Calgary, AB, T2E 9A7
(403) 750-4500
Emp Here 100   *Sales* 228,472,000
SIC 4833 Television broadcasting stations
James Shaw Sr
Jim Shaw Jr
Margot Micallef

D-U-N-S 24-906-1110   (HQ)
SHOCK TRAUMA AIR RESCUE SERVICE
STARS AIR AMBULANCE SERVICE
1441 Aviation Pk Ne Unit 570, Calgary, AB, T2E 8M7
(403) 295-1811
Emp Here 206   *Sales* 27,541,303
SIC 4522 Air transportation, nonscheduled
Andrea Robertson
Greg Powell
Jeff Quick

D-U-N-S 24-360-1437   (HQ)
SHOEMAKER DRYWALL SUPPLIES LTD
(*Suby of* GMS INC.)
7012 8 St Ne, Calgary, AB, T2E 8L8
(403) 291-1013
Emp Here 50   *Sales* 24,357,150
SIC 1742 Plastering, drywall, and insulation
Ryan Shoemaker
Scott Friesen

D-U-N-S 25-614-6994   (BR)
SIEMENS CANADA LIMITED
FIRE SAFETY DIVISION
(*Suby of* SIEMENS AG)
1930 Maynard Rd Se Unit 24, Calgary, AB, T2E 6J8
(403) 259-3404
Emp Here 100
SIC 7382 Security systems services
Rick Mckay

D-U-N-S 24-702-4870   (BR)
SIEMENS CANADA LIMITED
LANDIS, DIV OF
(*Suby of* SIEMENS AG)
1930 Maynard Rd Se Unit 24, Calgary, AB, T2E 6J8
(403) 259-3404
Emp Here 102
SIC 1711 Plumbing, heating, air-conditioning
Dean Mazera

D-U-N-S 20-213-4529   (BR)
SIEMENS CANADA LIMITED
(*Suby of* SIEMENS AG)
1930 Maynard Rd Se Unit 24, Calgary, AB, T2E 6J8
(403) 259-3404
Emp Here 240
SIC 3679 Electronic components, nec
Keith Triginier

D-U-N-S 25-538-0990   (SL)
SILVERBIRCH NO. 4 OPERATIONS LIM-ITED PARTNERSHIP
RADISSON HOTEL CALGARY AIRPORT
2120 16 Ave Ne, Calgary, AB, T2E 1L4
(403) 291-4666
Emp Here 130   *Sales* 12,049,700
SIC 7011 Hotels and motels
Richard Boustead

D-U-N-S 24-030-3367   (BR)
SKYSERVICE BUSINESS AVIATION INC
(*Suby of* SKYSERVICE INVESTMENTS INC)
575 Palmer Rd Ne, Calgary, AB, T2E 7G4
(403) 592-3700
Emp Here 80
SIC 7363 Help supply services
Alastair Cook

D-U-N-S 20-109-8852   (HQ)

SOBEYS WEST INC
SAFEWAY
(*Suby of* EMPIRE COMPANY LIMITED)
1020 64 Ave Ne, Calgary, AB, T2E 7V8
(403) 730-3500
Emp Here 600   *Sales* 5,581,456,000
SIC 5411 Grocery stores
Marc Poulin
Clinton Keay
Karin Mccaskill
Francois Vimard
Jane Mcdow

D-U-N-S 25-015-0885   (BR)
SOBEYS WEST INC
CANADA SAFEWAY 263
(*Suby of* EMPIRE COMPANY LIMITED)
1818 Centre St Ne Suite 20, Calgary, AB, T2E 2S6
(403) 276-3328
Emp Here 150
SIC 5411 Grocery stores
Roger Staines

D-U-N-S 25-919-5667   (HQ)
STAR CHOICE TELEVISION NETWORK IN-CORPORATED
STAR CHOICE BUSINESS TELEVISION
(*Suby of* SHAW COMMUNICATIONS INC)
2924 11 St Ne, Calgary, AB, T2E 7L7
(403) 538-4672
Emp Here 200   *Sales* 228,472,000
SIC 4841 Cable and other pay television ser-vices
Peter Bissonnette
Brad Shaw

D-U-N-S 25-679-9404   (SL)
STARS AVIATION CANADA INC
(*Suby of* SHOCK TRAUMA AIR RESCUE SERVICE)
1441 Aviation Pk Ne, Calgary, AB, T2E 8M7
(403) 295-1811
Emp Here 150   *Sales* 40,046,700
SIC 4522 Air transportation, nonscheduled
Gregory Powell

D-U-N-S 20-840-6061   (SL)
STARTEC REFRIGERATION & COMPRES-SION
7664 10 St Ne Suite 11, Calgary, AB, T2E 8W1
(403) 347-1131
Emp Here 49   *Sales* 10,825,766
SIC 1711 Plumbing, heating, air-conditioning
Goel Cawthorn
Kristy Zadderey

D-U-N-S 20-694-1515   (HQ)
STILES' CLOTHIERS INC
UNDERGROUND CLOTHING
1435 40 Ave Ne Unit 4, Calgary, AB, T2E 8N6
(403) 230-8515
Emp Here 7   *Sales* 13,454,700
SIC 5651 Family clothing stores
John Stiles

D-U-N-S 20-234-0936   (SL)
STRIDE MANAGEMENT CORP
3950 12 St Ne, Calgary, AB, T2E 8H9
(403) 508-7313
Emp Here 124   *Sales* 28,330,528
SIC 4899 Communication services, nec
Robert Wallace

D-U-N-S 20-302-3747   (BR)
SWISSPORT CANADA INC
(*Suby of* SWISSPORT CANADA INC)
1601 Airport Rd Ne Suite 810, Calgary, AB, T2E 6Z8
(403) 221-1660
Emp Here 150
SIC 4581 Airports, flying fields, and services
Rodney Stinn

D-U-N-S 20-733-7853   (HQ)
TBM HOLDCO LTD
1601 Airport Rd Ne Suite 705, Calgary, AB,

T2E 6Z8
(800) 663-3342
Sales 10,122,360
SIC 5211 Lumber and other building materials
Bernie Owens

D-U-N-S 24-422-6283   (SL)
TEKTELIC COMMUNICATIONS INC
7657 10 St Ne, Calgary, AB, T2E 8X2
(403) 338-6900
Emp Here 55   *Sales* 10,163,890
SIC 4899 Communication services, nec
Roman Nemish
David Tholl

D-U-N-S 25-519-7246   (HQ)
THERMON CANADA INC
THERMON HEAT TRACING
(*Suby of* THERMON GROUP HOLDINGS, INC.)
1806 Centre Ave Ne, Calgary, AB, T2E 0A6
(403) 273-5558
Emp Here 92   *Sales* 87,037,050
SIC 5063 Electrical apparatus and equipment
Bruce Thames
Candace Peterson
David Buntin
Eric Reitler
Rene Van Der Salm
Jim Pribble
Mark Roberts
Jay Peterson

D-U-N-S 24-300-5303   (SL)
THIBEAULT MASONRY LTD
1815 27 Ave Ne Suite 7, Calgary, AB, T2E 7E1

Emp Here 200   *Sales* 32,476,200
SIC 1741 Masonry and other stonework
Darrel Mcdaniel

D-U-N-S 20-552-8362   (HQ)
THOMAS GROUP INC
1115 55 Ave Ne, Calgary, AB, T2E 6W1
(403) 275-3666
Emp Here 120   *Sales* 24,357,150
SIC 1742 Plastering, drywall, and insulation
Erhardt Tutto
Bob Martineau

D-U-N-S 20-348-7256   (SL)
TIM HORTONS
1185 49 Ave Ne, Calgary, AB, T2E 8V2
(403) 730-0556
Emp Here 40   *Sales* 10,966,080
SIC 5461 Retail bakeries
Tia Hamielec
Reynal Reyes

D-U-N-S 24-860-8874   (HQ)
TIM-BR MARTS LTD
(*Suby of* TBM HOLDCO LTD)
1601 Airport Rd Ne Suite 705, Calgary, AB, T2E 6Z8
(403) 717-1990
Emp Here 25   *Sales* 15,722,665
SIC 7389 Business services, nec
John Steen
Randy Martin
Don Dyk

D-U-N-S 24-271-8088   (HQ)
TIMBERTOWN BUILDING CENTRE LTD
TRC TIMBER REALISATION COMPANY, A DIV OF
3440 12 St Ne Suite G, Calgary, AB, T2E 6N1

(403) 291-1317
Emp Here 40   *Sales* 40,147,800
SIC 5211 Lumber and other building materials
Matthew Stayner
Dick Karperien

D-U-N-S 24-161-2357   (HQ)
TRADEX SUPPLY LTD
BARBEQUES GALORE & WOOD FIRE-PLACES, DIV OF
3505 Edmonton Trail Ne, Calgary, AB, T2E 3N9
(403) 250-7842
Emp Here 12   *Sales* 20,821,680
SIC 5099 Durable goods, nec
Ross Mikkelsen
Andrea Kingwell
Micheal Mikkelsen

D-U-N-S 20-910-2651   (BR)
TYCO INTEGRATED FIRE & SECURITY CANADA, INC
SIMPLEXGRINNELL
(*Suby of* JOHNSON CONTROLS INTERNATIONAL PUBLIC LIMITED COMPANY)
615 18 St Se, Calgary, AB, T2E 3L9
(403) 569-4606
Emp Here 150
SIC 1731 Electrical work
Misty Gibson

D-U-N-S 25-418-0417   (BR)
UNITED PARCEL SERVICE CANADA LTD
UPS
(*Suby of* UNITED PARCEL SERVICE, INC.)
3650 12 St Ne Suite D, Calgary, AB, T2E 6N1

Emp Here 200
SIC 4731 Freight transportation arrangement

D-U-N-S 24-042-6338   (HQ)
UNIVERSAL REHABILITATION SERVICE AGENCY
URSA
808 Manning Rd Ne, Calgary, AB, T2E 7N8
(403) 272-7722
Sales 12,856,400
SIC 8361 Residential care
Douglas Hauser
Beverly Maclachlan

D-U-N-S 20-000-4355   (SL)
US CUSTOMS & BORDER PROTECTION
2016d Airport Road Ne Unit 172a, Calgary, AB, T2E 3B9
(403) 221-1641
Emp Here 28   *Sales* 14,559,076
SIC 4731 Freight transportation arrangement

D-U-N-S 24-517-8397   (SL)
V I P GARMENTS OF CANADA LTD
V I P GARMENTS
1339 40 Ave Ne Suite 11, Calgary, AB, T2E 8N6

Emp Here 26   *Sales* 12,956,372
SIC 5137 Women's and children's clothing
Dorothy Allred
Jeff Allred
Ken Allred

D-U-N-S 25-993-0865   (SL)
VERICO CML CANADIAN MORTGAGE LENDER INC
CML CANADIAN MORTGAGE LENDER
2316 6 St Ne, Calgary, AB, T2E 3Z1
(866) 265-7988
Emp Here 36   *Sales* 24,441,228
SIC 6211 Security brokers and dealers
Pierre Delesalle
Garth Lyon

D-U-N-S 20-735-0591   (BR)
VERITIV CANADA, INC
INTER-CITY PAPERS INTERNATIONAL
(*Suby of* VERITIV CORPORATION)
6040 11 St Ne, Calgary, AB, T2E 9B1

(403) 250-5416
Emp Here 115
SIC 5111 Printing and writing paper
Deborah Noulty

D-U-N-S 20-177-0034   (SL)
VIVANT GROUP INC, THE
1820 30 Ave Ne Suite 3, Calgary, AB, T2E 7M5
(403) 974-0370
Emp Here 30   *Sales* 12,580,650
SIC 6712 Bank holding companies
Randy Shima

D-U-N-S 25-218-9899   (BR)
WAL-MART CANADA CORP
(*Suby of* WALMART INC.)
1110 57 Ave Ne Suite 3013, Calgary, AB, T2E 9B7
(403) 730-0990
Emp Here 250
SIC 5311 Department stores
Gerald Gill

D-U-N-S 20-337-6611   (SL)
WAYFINDER CORP
(*Suby of* ARC FINANCIAL MANAGEMENT INC)
4311 12 St Ne Suite 305, Calgary, AB, T2E 4P9

Emp Here 35   *Sales* 11,189,675
SIC 1389 Oil and gas field services, nec
Chad Bremner
Shane Hooker
Darren K Mitchell
Michael Burnyeat

D-U-N-S 24-086-4561   (HQ)
WEATHERFORD LABORATORIES (CANADA) LTD
1620 27 Ave Ne, Calgary, AB, T2E 8W4
(403) 736-3500
Emp Here 10   *Sales* 20,677,860
SIC 8731 Commercial physical research
Douglas Bennion
Tony Ma
Brent Thomas
Donald Frame

D-U-N-S 24-298-0456   (SL)
WEST AIR SHEET METAL LTD
1238 45 Ave Ne, Calgary, AB, T2E 2P1
(403) 250-7518
Emp Here 80   *Sales* 17,426,320
SIC 1761 Roofing, siding, and sheetMetal work
Santino Volponi
Ersilia Volponi

D-U-N-S 20-549-3294   (SL)
WESTCOR CONSTRUCTION LTD
2420 39 Ave Ne, Calgary, AB, T2E 6X1
(403) 663-8677
Emp Here 24   *Sales* 11,297,544
SIC 1542 Nonresidential construction, nec
Robert Robinson
Brad Hammond
Val Stordy
Andrew Morgan

D-U-N-S 24-732-9436   (SL)
WESTERN POLYMERS CORP
1003 55 Ave Ne Suite A, Calgary, AB, T2E 6W1
(403) 295-7194
Emp Here 24   *Sales* 11,400,624
SIC 5085 Industrial supplies
Allan S. Huehn
Jean Bundschuh
Ralph Gallup

D-U-N-S 25-289-2591   (HQ)
WESTJET AIRLINES LTD
WESTJET
22 Aerial Pl Ne, Calgary, AB, T2E 3J1
(888) 937-8538
Emp Here 175   *Sales* 3,588,447,009

SIC 4512 Air transportation, scheduled
Edward Sims
Steven Greenway
Craig Maccubbin
Charles Duncan
Barbara Munroe
Mark Porter
Harry Taylor
Jeffrey Martin
Arved Von Zur Muehlen
Clive Beddoe

D-U-N-S 24-826-7317   (HQ)
WESTRON PUMPS & COMPRESSORS LTD
3600 21 St Ne Unit 3, Calgary, AB, T2E 6V6
(403) 291-6777
Emp Here 10   *Sales* 11,544,052
SIC 3561 Pumps and pumping equipment
Ronald Sigurdson
Stefan Sigurdson

D-U-N-S 20-829-0452   (HQ)
WINGENBACK INC
707 Barlow Trail Se, Calgary, AB, T2E 8C2
(403) 221-8120
Emp Here 55   *Sales* 32,259,420
SIC 3299 NonMetallic mineral products,
Wayne Wingenbach
Dennis Wingenbach
Bill Vander Doelen
Barry Emo
Paul Partlo
Chris Cote

D-U-N-S 25-386-0753   (BR)
WORKERS' COMPENSATION BOARD ALBERTA
(*Suby of* GOVERNMENT OF THE PROVINCE OF ALBERTA)
4311 12 St Ne Suite 150, Calgary, AB, T2E 4P9
(403) 517-6000
Emp Here 150
SIC 6331 Fire, marine, and casualty insurance
Dennis Cornish

D-U-N-S 20-767-7352   (HQ)
WYCLIFFE BIBLE TRANSLATORS OF CANADA INC
WYCLIFFE CANADA
4316 10 St Ne, Calgary, AB, T2E 6K3
(403) 250-5411
Emp Here 70   *Sales* 143,388,070
SIC 7389 Business services, nec
Roy Eyre
Jannice Moore
Don Buhler

D-U-N-S 24-390-4070   (HQ)
XACT DOWNHOLE TELEMETRY INC
906 55 Ave Ne, Calgary, AB, T2E 6Y4
(403) 568-6010
Sales 10,230,560
SIC 1389 Oil and gas field services, nec
Issam Dairanieh
Michael Reeves
Jason Roe
James Saretsky
Paul Camwell
Martha Mantikoski

D-U-N-S 24-885-7356   (SL)
ZUBAR HOLDINGS LTD
919 Drury Ave Ne, Calgary, AB, T2E 0M3
(403) 813-1914
Emp Here 41   *Sales* 17,193,555
SIC 6712 Bank holding companies
Barr Jim

Calgary, AB T2G

D-U-N-S 24-346-9389   (SL)
1184892 ALBERTA LTD
RUTH'S CHRIS STEAK HOUSE

▲ Public Company   ■ Public Company Family Member   **HQ** Headquarters   **BR** Branch   **SL** Single Location

115 9 Ave Se Suite 294, Calgary, AB, T2G 0P5
(403) 246-3636
Emp Here 100   *Sales* 4,551,900
SIC 5812 Eating places
Marcelle Kuenxler

D-U-N-S 24-423-3156   (SL)
1253207 ALBERTA LTD
MEDICHAIR CALGARY
4040 Blackfoot Trail Se Suite 120, Calgary,
AB, T2G 4E6
(403) 252-5366
Emp Here 35   *Sales* 16,625,910
SIC 5084 Industrial machinery and equipment
Byron Mclellan

D-U-N-S 20-341-8777   (SL)
1840807 ALBERTA LTD
STONY MOUNTAIN WASTE MANAGEMENT
1208 3 St Se Unit 11, Calgary, AB, T2G 2S9
(403) 460-1401
Emp Here 90   *Sales* 13,337,280
SIC 4212 Local trucking, without storage
Shawn Daschuk
Jim Macpherson

D-U-N-S 25-081-1635   (SL)
320114 ALBERTA INC
VISION (2000) TRAVEL GROUP-ALBERTA
328 Centre St Se Suite 202, Calgary, AB, T2G
4X6
(403) 777-0777
Emp Here 36   *Sales* 18,718,812
SIC 4724 Travel agencies
Anthony Tonkinson
Michael Broadhurst
Doug Boyd
Rick Goebel

D-U-N-S 24-731-6755   (SL)
376599 ALBERTA INC
BACK ALLEY, THE
4630 Macleod Trail Sw, Calgary, AB, T2G 5E8
(403) 287-2500
Emp Here 90   *Sales* 3,858,570
SIC 5813 Drinking places

D-U-N-S 25-102-4766   (HQ)
700635 ALBERTA LTD
CALGARY FASTENERS AND TOOLS
1288 42 Ave Se Unit 1, Calgary, AB, T2G 5P1
(403) 287-5340
Sales 41,002,500
SIC 6712 Bank holding companies
Gerry Miller
Ronald Hal

D-U-N-S 25-536-2097   (BR)
ABB INC
(*Suby of* ABB LTD)
4411 6 St Se Unit 110, Calgary, AB, T2G 4E8
(403) 253-0271
Emp Here 90
SIC 8711 Engineering services
Michael Telmosse

D-U-N-S 24-347-8765   (HQ)
ACCU-FLO METER SERVICE LTD
JOHN D. ELECTRIC
4024 7 St Se, Calgary, AB, T2G 2Y8
(403) 243-1425
Emp Here 10   *Sales* 14,250,780
SIC 5084 Industrial machinery and equipment
Steve Mayer
Ross Lemire
Ryan Pribyl

D-U-N-S 25-581-0517   (BR)
ADM AGRI-INDUSTRIES COMPANY
ADM MILLING DIV OF
(*Suby of* ARCHER-DANIELS-MIDLAND
COMPANY)
4002 Bonnybrook Rd Se, Calgary, AB, T2G
4M9
(403) 267-5600
Emp Here 85
SIC 2045 Prepared flour mixes and doughs

Gord Smith

D-U-N-S 24-297-9870   (SL)
ADRICO MACHINE WORKS LTD
1165j 44 Ave Se, Calgary, AB, T2G 4X4
(403) 243-7930
Emp Here 60   *Sales* 13,320,060
SIC 3599 Industrial machinery, nec
Ivan Polancec

D-U-N-S 25-229-4947   (HQ)
AIRTEX MANUFACTURING PARTNERSHIP
ENGINEERED AIR, DIV
(*Suby of* RESMAN HOLDINGS LTD)
1401 Hastings Cres Se Suite 1421, Calgary,
AB, T2G 4C8
(403) 287-2590
Emp Here 60   *Sales* 170,261,700
SIC 3433 Heating equipment, except electric
David Taylor

D-U-N-S 20-082-6407   (SL)
AKINAI CANADA INC
ACI TECTNOLOGY
2600 Portland St Se Suite 1010, Calgary, AB,
T2G 4M6
(403) 280-6482
Emp Here 50   *Sales* 22,617,657
SIC 5044 Office equipment
Ross Tyrell
Leslie Cole

D-U-N-S 20-108-5792   (SL)
ALBERTA DISTILLERS LIMITED
(*Suby of* KOTOBUKI REALTY CO., LTD.)
1521 34 Ave Se, Calgary, AB, T2G 1V9
(403) 265-2541
Emp Here 120   *Sales* 41,482,800
SIC 2085 Distilled and blended liquors
Michael Donohoe
Jeff Conder
Jim Rogerson

D-U-N-S 25-539-4850   (HQ)
APLIN, DAVID & ASSOCIATES INC
APLIN, DAVID GROUP
(*Suby of* PINELLAS ENTERPRISES INC)
140 10 Ave Se Ste 500, Calgary, AB, T2G 0R1
(403) 261-9000
Emp Here 150   *Sales* 31,371,480
SIC 7361 Employment agencies
David Aplin
Grace Elizabeth Aplin

D-U-N-S 24-343-8736   (HQ)
**AUDIO VISUAL SYSTEMS INTEGRATION
INC**
SHARP'S AUDIO VISUAL
(*Suby of* AVI-SPL HOLDINGS, INC.)
3636 7 St Se, Calgary, AB, T2G 2Y8
(403) 255-4123
Emp Here 50   *Sales* 55,061,100
SIC 5999 Miscellaneous retail stores, nec
Jeff Faber
Tim St.Louis
Andrew Searby

D-U-N-S 24-805-6504   (HQ)
AUTOPLUS RESOURCES LTD
KAIZEN AUTOMOTIVE GROUP
4620 Blackfoot Trail Se, Calgary, AB, T2G 4G2
(403) 243-6200
Sales 634,977,200
SIC 5511 New and used car dealers
Richard Romeril

D-U-N-S 24-129-2445   (SL)
BLACKFOOT MOTORCYCLE LTD
BLACKFOOT MOTOSPORTS
6 Highfield Cir Se, Calgary, AB, T2G 5N5
(403) 243-2636
Emp Here 80   *Sales* 50,342,400
SIC 5571 Motorcycle dealers
Patrick Chambers
Douglas Macrae
Jason Mitchell

D-U-N-S 24-358-1415   (SL)

BLACKLINE SAFETY CORP
803 24 Ave Se Unit 100, Calgary, AB, T2G
1P5
(403) 451-0327
Emp Here 175   *Sales* 13,726,322
SIC 3663 Radio and t.v. communications
equipment
Cody Slater
Barry Moore
Sean Stinson
Bernadette Geronazzo
Kevin Meyers
Shane Grennan
Brendon Cook
Michael Hayduk
John Finbow
Robert J. Herdman

D-U-N-S 24-483-5815   (SL)
BLUE CIRCLE INSURANCE LTD
BLUECIRCLE INSURANCE BROKERS
3402 8 St Se Unit 200, Calgary, AB, T2G 5S7
(403) 770-4949
Emp Here 26   *Sales* 15,078,024
SIC 6411 Insurance agents, brokers, and ser-
vice
Gerry Baert
Terry Bradley
Dirk Bruggencate

D-U-N-S 20-057-0302   (HQ)
**BOARD OF GOVERNERS OF BOW VALLEY
COLLEGE, THE**
BOW VALLEY COLLEGE
345 6 Ave Se, Calgary, AB, T2G 4V1
(403) 410-1400
Emp Here 350   *Sales* 76,006,007
SIC 8221 Colleges and universities
Sharon Carry
David Collyer
Anna Kae Todd
Gayle Burnett
David J. Mitchell
Catherine Koch

D-U-N-S 20-743-7062   (HQ)
BOLT SUPPLY HOUSE LTD, THE
(*Suby of* LAWSON PRODUCTS, INC.)
3909 Manchester Rd Se Unit C, Calgary, AB,
T2G 4A1
(403) 245-2818
Emp Here 10   *Sales* 47,502,600
SIC 5085 Industrial supplies
Kurt Mario
Brett Wilson
Wiley Auch
Jeff Mccaig

D-U-N-S 25-902-9549   (SL)
**BRAND ENERGY SOLUTION (CANADA)
LTD**
601 34 Ave Se, Calgary, AB, T2G 1V2
(403) 243-0283
Emp Here 49   *Sales* 10,028,977
SIC 3644 Noncurrent-carrying wiring devices
Rick Lofstrom

D-U-N-S 20-281-5791   (HQ)
BRUDERHEIM ENERGY TERMINAL LTD
(*Suby of* CENOVUS ENERGY INC)
500 Centre St Se Suite 2600, Calgary, AB,
T2G 1A6
(403) 766-2000
Emp Here 5   *Sales* 40,168,975
SIC 5169 Chemicals and allied products, nec
Kent Avery
Robert Pease

D-U-N-S 24-158-8623   (HQ)
BUL RIVER MINERAL CORPORATION
4723 1 St Sw Suite 350, Calgary, AB, T2G 4Y8

Emp Here 8   *Sales* 13,539,230
SIC 1081 Metal mining services
Ross Stanfield

D-U-N-S 25-314-9488   (SL)

**BUSY BEE EXPRESS LINES INCORPO-
RATED**
4127 16 St Se, Calgary, AB, T2G 3R9
(403) 233-2353
Emp Here 31   *Sales* 12,147,080
SIC 4731 Freight transportation arrangement

D-U-N-S 24-351-1750   (HQ)
BW TECHNOLOGIES PARTNERSHIP
BW TECHNOLOGIES BY HONEYWELL
4411 6 St Se Suite 110, Calgary, AB, T2G 4E8
(403) 248-9226
Sales 11,364,450
SIC 3829 Measuring and controlling devices,
nec
Darius Adamczyk

D-U-N-S 20-831-7891   (HQ)
C B ENGINEERING LTD
(*Suby of* CBENG GROUP LTD)
5040 12a St Se, Calgary, AB, T2G 5K9
(403) 259-6220
Emp Here 35   *Sales* 21,376,170
SIC 5084 Industrial machinery and equipment
Sevy Nazarene
Heather Bowyer

D-U-N-S 20-558-9190   (SL)
**C.R.A. COLLATERAL RECOVERY & AD-
MINISTRATION INC**
1289 Highfield Cres Se Unit 109, Calgary, AB,
T2G 5M2
(403) 240-3450
Emp Here 50   *Sales* 19,783,900
SIC 7381 Detective and armored car services
Wayne T Naylor
Lillian Gauthier
Christopher E Burden
James M Voice

D-U-N-S 20-566-1684   (SL)
CALCON MANAGEMENT, L.P.
700 Centre St Se, Calgary, AB, T2G 5P6
(403) 537-4426
Emp Here 375   *Sales* 42,563,447
SIC 8741 Management services
Ross Salmon

D-U-N-S 24-300-6251   (SL)
**CALGARY CENTRE FOR PERFORMING
ARTS**
ARTS COMMONS
205 8 Ave Se Suite 1205, Calgary, AB, T2G
0K9
(403) 294-7455
Emp Here 175   *Sales* 26,217,275
SIC 7929 Entertainers and entertainment
groups
Johann Zietsman

D-U-N-S 24-089-2125   (SL)
CALGARY CHAMBER OF COMMERCE
237 8 Ave Se Suite 600, Calgary, AB, T2G
5C3
(403) 750-0400
Emp Here 50   *Sales* 11,937,500
SIC 8611 Business associations
Adam Legge
Rob Hawley
Michael Andriescu

D-U-N-S 25-498-8405   (SL)
**CALGARY CONVENTION CENTRE AU-
THORITY**
CALGARY TELUS CONVENTION CENTRE
120 9 Ave Se, Calgary, AB, T2G 0P3
(403) 261-8500
Emp Here 100   *Sales* 66,890,800
SIC 7389 Business services, nec
Clark Grue
Dave Bronconnier
Robert Fraser
Stephanie C. Ho
Dale Hodges
Chris Hopfner
Brad Krizan
Jack Reed

Margaret M. Walsh
Laurel Wood

D-U-N-S 25-673-3502   (SL)
CALGARY COUNSELLING CENTRE
105 12 Ave Se Suite 100, Calgary, AB, T2G
1A1
(403) 265-4980
Emp Here 87   *Sales* 5,952,714
SIC 8322 Individual and family services
Robbie Babins-Wagner

D-U-N-S 25-059-8133   (SL)
**CALGARY DROP-IN & REHAB CENTRE
SOCIETY**
1 Dermot Baldwin Way Se, Calgary, AB, T2G
0P8
(403) 266-3600
Emp Here 138   *Sales* 28,575,384
SIC 8399 Social services, nec
Sandra Clarkson

D-U-N-S 20-768-1735   (HQ)
**CALGARY EXHIBITION AND STAMPEDE
LIMITED**
CALGARY STAMPEDE
1410 Olympic Way Se, Calgary, AB, T2G 2W1
(403) 261-0101
Emp Here 1   *Sales* 164,730,000
SIC 7999 Amusement and recreation, nec
Vern Kimball
Warren Connell
Paul Harrison
Paul Rosenberg
Susan Garnett

D-U-N-S 24-119-7060   (HQ)
CALGARY FASTENERS & TOOLS LTD
(*Suby of* 700635 ALBERTA LTD)
1288 42 Ave Se Unit 1, Calgary, AB, T2G 5P1
(403) 287-5340
Emp Here 65   *Sales* 73,159,500
SIC 5085 Industrial supplies
Ronald Hall

D-U-N-S 24-272-7444   (HQ)
**CALGARY FLAMES LIMITED PARTNER-
SHIP**
CALGARY FLAMES HOCKEY CLUB
555 Saddledome Rise Se, Calgary, AB, T2G
2W1
(403) 777-2177
Sales 103,146,250
SIC 7941 Sports clubs, managers, and pro-
moters
Kenneth King

D-U-N-S 20-645-8411   (SL)
CALGARY HOMELESS FOUNDATION
615 Macleod Trail Se Suite 1500, Calgary, AB,
T2G 4T8
(403) 237-6456
Emp Here 40   *Sales* 15,896,560
SIC 8699 Membership organizations, nec
Diana Krecsy

D-U-N-S 20-040-8933   (SL)
**CALGARY IMMIGRANT WOMEN'S ASSO-
CIATION**
CIWA
138 4 Ave Se Suite 200, Calgary, AB, T2G 4Z6
(403) 517-8830
Emp Here 120   *Sales* 24,848,160
SIC 8399 Social services, nec
Edna Sutherland

D-U-N-S 24-310-3863   (SL)
CALGARY METAL RECYCLING INC
3415 Ogden Rd Se, Calgary, AB, T2G 4N4
(403) 262-4542
Emp Here 60   *Sales* 31,232,520
SIC 5093 Scrap and waste materials
Gabriel Davis
Mark Clarke

D-U-N-S 20-867-4650   (BR)
CALGARY PARKING AUTHORITY
CALGARY IMPOUND

(*Suby of* CITY OF CALGARY, THE)
400 39 Ave Se, Calgary, AB, T2G 5P8
(403) 537-7100
Emp Here 200
SIC 7521 Automobile parking
Mindy Jensen

D-U-N-S 24-159-9984   (HQ)
CALGARY PUBLIC LIBRARY
(*Suby of* CITY OF CALGARY, THE)
800 3 St Se, Calgary, AB, T2G 2E7
(403) 260-2712
Emp Here 150   *Sales* 53,226,600
SIC 8231 Libraries
Jamie Niessen

D-U-N-S 24-039-8698   (SL)
CALGARY SCIENTIFIC INC
1210 20 Ave Se Suite 208, Calgary, AB, T2G
1M8
(403) 270-7159
Emp Here 62   *Sales* 10,993,282
SIC 7374 Data processing and preparation
Byron Osing

D-U-N-S 20-398-2900   (SL)
**CALGARY YOUNG WOMEN'S CHRISTIAN
ASSOCIATION**
YWCA CALGARY
1715 17 Ave Se, Calgary, AB, T2G 5J1
(403) 262-0498
Emp Here 300   *Sales* 62,120,400
SIC 8399 Social services, nec
Tom Ney

D-U-N-S 25-479-9158   (HQ)
**CALGARY YOUNG WOMEN'S CHRISTIAN
ASSOCIATION, THE**
YWCA OF CALGARY
320 5 Ave Se, Calgary, AB, T2G 0E5
(403) 263-1550
Sales 17,147,370
SIC 8322 Individual and family services
Sue Tomney
Anna Nelson
Jan Damery
Heather Morley
Kate Thompson
Lara Murphy
Elaine Young
Shannon Young
Amie Blanchette
Sharon Carry

D-U-N-S 20-115-0518   (SL)
CALTRAX INC
1805 30 Ave Se, Calgary, AB, T2G 4X8
(403) 234-0585
Emp Here 50   *Sales* 25,998,350
SIC 4789 Transportation services, nec
Jeff Robson

D-U-N-S 20-161-1274   (HQ)
CANADA MALTING CO. LIMITED
(*Suby of* GRAINCORP LIMITED)
3316 Bonnybrook Rd Se, Calgary, AB, T2G
4M9
(403) 571-7000
Emp Here 1   *Sales* 90,653,610
SIC 2083 Malt
Armand Parisien
Bruce French
Robert Chappell
Dale Paul
Carlo Ricci
Rich Joy
Jay Hamachek
Bob Mcwilliam
Ryan Dodd
Matthew Letki

D-U-N-S 24-380-9949   (BR)
**CANADIAN LINEN AND UNIFORM SER-
VICE CO**
(*Suby of* ARAMARK)
4525 Manilla Rd Se, Calgary, AB, T2G 4B6

(403) 243-8080
Emp Here 165
SIC 7213 Linen supply
Rick Archibald

D-U-N-S 24-674-0724   (SL)
CANTERBURY ROOFING LTD
3810 16 St Se, Calgary, AB, T2G 3R7
(403) 234-8582
Emp Here 60   *Sales* 13,069,740
SIC 1761 Roofing, siding, and sheetMetal
work
Al Smith
Nancy Smith

D-U-N-S 25-415-0527   (SL)
CAON SERVICES INC
1143 42 Ave Se, Calgary, AB, T2G 1Z3
(403) 279-6641
Emp Here 66   *Sales* 15,382,290
SIC 1711 Plumbing, heating, air-conditioning
Vern Cornwell
Wendy Cornwell
Daniel Bates
Tony Pogue
Jody Koszak

D-U-N-S 24-374-3155   (SL)
CARBON CONSTRUCTORS INC
3915 8 St Se, Calgary, AB, T2G 3A5
(403) 203-4900
Emp Here 50   *Sales* 23,536,550
SIC 1542 Nonresidential construction, nec
Terry Androsoff

D-U-N-S 24-517-4537   (HQ)
CEB INVESTMENTS INC
250 42 Ave Se, Calgary, AB, T2G 1Y4
(403) 265-4155
Emp Here 80   *Sales* 84,783,240
SIC 1731 Electrical work
Bernie Mccaffery
Jan Mccaffery

D-U-N-S 24-319-5497   (HQ)
CENOVUS FCCL LTD
CENOVUS ENERGY
(*Suby of* CENOVUS ENERGY INC)
500 Centre St Se Suite 766, Calgary, AB, T2G
1A6
(403) 766-2000
Sales 3,709,164,000
SIC 1311 Crude petroleum and natural gas
Brian Ferguson
John Brannan
Harbir Chhina
Robert Pease
Ivor Ruste
Kerry Dyte
Judy Fairburn
Sheila Mcintosh
Donald Swystun
Hayward Walls

D-U-N-S 20-522-7143   (SL)
CENTAUR IMPORT MOTORS (1977) LTD
CENTAUR SUBARU
3819 Macleod Trail Sw, Calgary, AB, T2G 2R3
(403) 287-2544
Emp Here 23   *Sales* 11,455,794
SIC 5511 New and used car dealers
Bruce Williams
Patricia Williams

D-U-N-S 25-236-6778   (HQ)
CENTENNIAL 89 CORP
4412 Manilla Rd Se Suite 1, Calgary, AB, T2G
4B7
(403) 214-0044
Emp Here 3   *Sales* 314,363,325
SIC 2011 Meat packing plants
Ronald Kovitz
J R (Robert) Kalef
Nasir Vasanji

D-U-N-S 24-342-5621   (HQ)
CENTENNIAL FOODSERVICE
(*Suby of* PREMIUM BRANDS HOLDINGS

CORPORATION)
4412 Manilla Rd Se Suite 1, Calgary, AB, T2G
4B7
(403) 214-0044
Emp Here 30   *Sales* 340,440,100
SIC 5142 Packaged frozen goods
David Carriere

D-U-N-S 25-191-0915   (HQ)
CENTRAL AIR EQUIPMENT LTD
1322 Hastings Cres Se, Calgary, AB, T2G 4C9
(403) 243-8003
Emp Here 29   *Sales* 11,752,155
SIC 5084 Industrial machinery and equipment
Ronald Fry

D-U-N-S 24-853-2707   (HQ)
**CENTRAL AUTO PARTS DISTRIBUTORS
LTD**
(*Suby of* SCRIVENS GROUP INC)
34 Highfield Cir Se, Calgary, AB, T2G 5N5
(403) 259-8655
Sales 46,115,400
SIC 5013 Motor vehicle supplies and new
parts
Darrell Scrivens
Daniel Scrivens
Janice Scrivens
Gail Scrivens
Lauren White

D-U-N-S 25-682-6066   (SL)
**CH2M HILL CONSTRUCTION CANADA,
LTD**
(*Suby of* JACOBS ENGINEERING GROUP
INC.)
1100 1 St Se Suite 1400, Calgary, AB, T2G
1B1
(403) 232-9800
Emp Here 35   *Sales* 14,795,795
SIC 1541 Industrial buildings and warehouses
Danny Daoust
Rene Massinone
George Lemmon
Ralph Mckee

D-U-N-S 24-274-9604   (SL)
CHALMERS INVESTMENT CORP LTD
STAGE WEST THEATRE RESTAURANT
(*Suby of* MAYFIELD INVESTMENTS LTD)
727 42 Ave Se, Calgary, AB, T2G 1Y8
(403) 243-6642
Emp Here 100   *Sales* 4,551,900
SIC 5812 Eating places
Gary Tse

D-U-N-S 25-360-9309   (BR)
CINTAS CANADA LIMITED
SALLY FOURMY & ASSOCIATES
(*Suby of* CINTAS CORPORATION)
1235 23 Ave Se, Calgary, AB, T2G 5S5

Emp Here 120
SIC 7218 Industrial launderers
Scott Farmer

D-U-N-S 20-515-0456   (BR)
CITY OF CALGARY, THE
*COMMUNITY & NEIGHBOURHOOD SER-
VICES*
(*Suby of* CITY OF CALGARY, THE)
315 10 Ave Se Suite 101, Calgary, AB, T2G
0W2
(403) 268-5153
Emp Here 200
SIC 8399 Social services, nec
Chris Branch

D-U-N-S 20-076-4934   (HQ)
**CNOOC PETROLEUM NORTH AMERICA
ULC**
(*Suby of* CHINA NATIONAL OFFSHORE OIL
CORP.)
500 Centre St Se Suite 2300, Calgary, AB,
T2G 1A6
(403) 699-4000
Emp Here 300   *Sales* 2,322,560,634

▲ Public Company   ■ Public Company Family Member   **HQ** Headquarters   **BR** Branch   **SL** Single Location

SIC 1382 Oil and gas exploration services
Kevin Reinhart
Jim Arnold
Ron Bailey
Alan O'brien
Peter Addy
Pierre Alvarez
Patrick Mcveigh
Alistair Mooney
Quinn Wilson
Archie Kennedy

D-U-N-S 25-415-1673   (SL)
CONCEPT ELECTRIC LTD
CONCEPT GROUP
(*Suby of* BOW-ALTA ELECTRIC LTD)
1260 Highfield Cres Se, Calgary, AB, T2G
5M3
(403) 287-8777
Emp Here 560   *Sales* 131,885,040
SIC 1731 Electrical work
David Kinley
Shirley Schmold

D-U-N-S 25-229-6967   (SL)
CONSITE CONSTRUCTION LTD
1802 17 Ave Se, Calgary, AB, T2G 1K4
(403) 265-0700
Emp Here 60   *Sales* 14,848,980
SIC 1771 Concrete work
Slade Stephenson
Dean Bottolfs
Kenneth Welter

D-U-N-S 20-599-8263   (HQ)
CONTEMPORARY OFFICE INTERIORS LTD
COI
2206 Portland St Se, Calgary, AB, T2G 4M6
(403) 265-1133
Emp Here 44   *Sales* 25,442,800
SIC 5021 Furniture
Rory Ellis
Scott Ellis
Brad Woolner
Cal Mcinnis
Michael Draycott

D-U-N-S 24-766-0152   (SL)
**CONTINENTAL ELECTRICAL MOTOR SER-
VICES LTD**
CONTINENTAL GROUP
4015 8 St Se Suite 201, Calgary, AB, T2G 3A5
(403) 236-9428
Emp Here 110   *Sales* 21,156,080
SIC 7694 Armature rewinding shops
Scott Pyett

D-U-N-S 25-682-9797   (HQ)
CORIL HOLDINGS LTD
1100 1 St Se Suite 600, Calgary, AB, T2G 1B1
(403) 231-7700
Emp Here 20   *Sales* 402,059,900
SIC 6719 Holding companies, nec
Kevin Beingessner
Ronald N. Mannix
John Taylor
Kenneth Wilson
Don Walker
Brenda Bruce
Fathia Durai
Paul V. Wilson
Robert B. Michaleski
Thomas D'aquino

D-U-N-S 20-050-3758   (HQ)
**CRITICAL CONTROL ENERGY SERVICES
CORP**
140 10 Ave Se Suite 800, Calgary, AB, T2G
0R1
(403) 705-7500
Emp Here 70   *Sales* 20,369,443
SIC 7371 Custom computer programming ser-
vices
Alykhan Mamdani
George Watson
Dennis Nerland
Gary Bentham

Kevin Lo
Nizar Jaffer Somji

D-U-N-S 20-075-5171   (HQ)
DAVIDSON ENMAN LUMBER LIMITED
*DAVIDSON ENMAN LUMBER TRUSS, DIV
OF*
452 42 Ave Se, Calgary, AB, T2G 1Y5
(403) 243-2566
Emp Here 15   *Sales* 20,073,900
SIC 5211 Lumber and other building materials
Greg Davidson
D.W. Davidson

D-U-N-S 24-013-8297   (SL)
DAWSCO COFFEE SERVICE LTD
DAWSON'S OFFICE COFFEE SERVICES
4325 1 St Se, Calgary, AB, T2G 2L2
(403) 250-7494
Emp Here 40   *Sales* 17,739,600
SIC 7389 Business services, nec
Scott Dawson
Ernie Graveline

D-U-N-S 24-158-9217   (BR)
DELTA HOTELS LIMITED
DELTA BOW VALLEY HOTEL
(*Suby of* GOVERNMENT OF THE
PROVINCE OF BRITISH COLUMBIA)
209 4 Ave Se, Calgary, AB, T2G 0C6
(403) 266-1980
Emp Here 260
SIC 8741 Management services
James Tingley

D-U-N-S 25-676-8094   (SL)
DIACO INTERNATIONAL INC
3620 Blackburn Rd Se, Calgary, AB, T2G 4A5
(403) 287-4494
Emp Here 25   *Sales* 11,179,350
SIC 5039 Construction materials, nec
Frank Babienko
Sam (Shan) Liu

D-U-N-S 20-831-0201   (HQ)
DIALOG
134 11 Ave Se Suite 300, Calgary, AB, T2G
0X5
(403) 541-5501
Emp Here 200   *Sales* 116,701,552
SIC 8712 Architectural services
Robert Adamson
James Goodwin
Gerald Carson
Robert Swart
Lynn Webster
Adrian Lao
Mark Wallace
Doug Carlyle
Antonio Gomez-Palacio
David Cerny

D-U-N-S 24-327-5125   (HQ)
DOLEMO DEVELOPMENT CORPORATION
(*Suby of* BULOVA DEVELOPMENTS INC)
128 2 Ave Se Unit 200, Calgary, AB, T2G 5J5
(403) 699-8830
Emp Here 15   *Sales* 54,670,000
SIC 6719 Holding companies, nec
Martin Dolemo

D-U-N-S 20-703-1621   (HQ)
EDON PROPERTIES INC
EDON MANAGEMENT
1441 Hastings Cres Se, Calgary, AB, T2G 4C8
(403) 245-1941
Sales 13,442,268
SIC 8741 Management services
Edward Lazdowski

D-U-N-S 24-324-1564   (HQ)
**ELECTRONIC RECYCLING ASSOCIATION
OF ALBERTA, THE**
1301 34 Ave Se, Calgary, AB, T2G 1V8
(403) 262-4488
Emp Here 30   *Sales* 17,540,050
SIC 4953 Refuse systems

Bojan Paduh
Joanna Trebon
Paul Kloepfer
David Maxwell

D-U-N-S 24-347-6611   (SL)
ELITE FLEET COURIER LTD
3615 Manchester Rd Se, Calgary, AB, T2G
3Z7
(403) 263-1247
Emp Here 150
SIC 7389 Business services, nec
Nash Virji

D-U-N-S 20-564-5034   (HQ)
ENABIL SOLUTIONS LTD
438 11 Ave Se Suite 500, Calgary, AB, T2G
0Y4
(403) 398-1600
Emp Here 80   *Sales* 26,999,050
SIC 8721 Accounting, auditing, and book-
keeping
Murray Korth
James Korth
Mike Little

D-U-N-S 20-075-1980   (HQ)
ENCANA CORPORATION
500 Centre St Se, Calgary, AB, T2G 1A6
(403) 645-2000
Emp Here 1,133   *Sales* 5,939,000,000
SIC 1382 Oil and gas exploration services
Douglas Suttles
Joanne Alexander
Corey Code
David Hill
Michael Mcallister
Mike Williams
Renee Zemljak
Clayton Woitas
Peter Dea
Fred Fowler

D-U-N-S 20-553-7041   (HQ)
ENCORE CORING & DRILLING INC
1345 Highfield Cres Se, Calgary, AB, T2G 5N2
(403) 287-0123
Sales 136,492,750
SIC 1381 Drilling oil and gas wells
Tom Connors

D-U-N-S 25-505-6921   (HQ)
ENERFLEX LTD
ENERFLEX SERVICE
1331 Macleod Trl Se Suite 904, Calgary, AB,
T2G 0K3
(403) 387-6377
Emp Here 50   *Sales* 1,291,254,668
SIC 3563 Air and gas compressors
J. Blair Goertzen
D. James Harbilas
Marc Rossiter
Stephen Savidant
Robert Boswell
W. Byron Dunn
Maureen Cormier Jackson
H. Stanley Marshall
Kevin Reinhart
Michael Weill

D-U-N-S 25-505-1583   (HQ)
ENMAX CORPORATION
(*Suby of* CITY OF CALGARY, THE)
141 50 Ave Se Suite 2708, Calgary, AB, T2G
4S7
(403) 514-3000
Emp Here 330   *Sales* 23,480,805,690
SIC 4911 Electric services
Gianna Manes
David Halford
Robert Hemstock
Dale Mcmaster
James Mckee
Dave Rehn
Lonnie Enns
Erin Kurchina
Tamera Van Brunt

Diana Stephenson

D-U-N-S 25-101-0807   (HQ)
ENMAX ENERGY CORPORATION
(*Suby of* CITY OF CALGARY, THE)
141 50 Ave Se Suite 2708, Calgary, AB, T2G
4S7
(403) 514-3000
Emp Here 990   *Sales* 840,736,000
SIC 4911 Electric services
Gerry Holden
Dwayne Dubois
H. Thompson Macdonald
Michael Harris
Robert Hawkesworth
Donald Lenz
Francis Leong
F. Gordon Lowe
Ian Macgregor
Greg Melchin

D-U-N-S 25-173-2525   (SL)
ENMAX ENERGY MARKETING INC
(*Suby of* CITY OF CALGARY, THE)
141 50 Ave Se, Calgary, AB, T2G 4S7
(403) 514-3000
Emp Here 25   *Sales* 16,996,850
SIC 4911 Electric services
Ken Willis
Bob Hawkesworth
Francis Leong
Paul Dawson
George Cornish

D-U-N-S 25-521-1385   (BR)
**ENTERPRISE RENT-A-CAR CANADA COM-
PANY**
NATIONAL CAR RENTAL
(*Suby of* THE CRAWFORD GROUP INC)
114 5 Ave Se, Calgary, AB, T2G 0E2
(403) 264-0424
Emp Here 75
SIC 7514 Passenger car rental
Angus Watson

D-U-N-S 25-537-0504   (HQ)
F & D SCENE CHANGES LTD
GREAT LAKES SCENIC STUDIOS
803 24 Ave Se Suite 2b, Calgary, AB, T2G 1P5
(403) 233-7633
Emp Here 1   *Sales* 39,136,320
SIC 3999 Manufacturing industries, nec
Leyton Morris
Dave Stevens

D-U-N-S 20-273-5515   (SL)
FALCO ELECTRICAL SYSTEMS LTD
3606 Manchester Rd Se, Calgary, AB, T2G
3Z5
(403) 287-7632
Emp Here 92   *Sales* 11,432,055
SIC 1731 Electrical work
Miles Gillham

D-U-N-S 20-521-9595   (HQ)
FOOTHILLS CREAMERY LTD
(*Suby of* WESTERN INVESTMENT COM-
PANY OF CANADA LIMITED, THE)
2825 Bonnybrook Rd Se, Calgary, AB, T2G
4N1
(403) 263-7725
Emp Here 52   *Sales* 33,210,964
SIC 2021 Creamery butter
Don Bayreck

D-U-N-S 20-364-5895   (HQ)
**FORT CALGARY PRESERVATION SOCI-
ETY**
750 9 Ave Se, Calgary, AB, T2G 5E1
(403) 290-1875
Emp Here 40   *Sales* 15,896,560
SIC 8699 Membership organizations, nec
Linda Mclean

D-U-N-S 20-364-9330   (SL)
FRATELLO GROUP INC
FRATELLO ANALOG CAFE
4021 9 St Se, Calgary, AB, T2G 3C7

(403) 265-2112
Emp Here 50   *Sales* 11,242,750
SIC 2095 Roasted coffee
Russell Prefontaine
Christopher Prefontaine

D-U-N-S 20-315-5168   (SL)
G F LTD
GENERAL FASTENERS
2270 Portland St Se, Calgary, AB, T2G 4M6
(403) 287-7111
Emp Here 40   *Sales* 13,024,000
SIC 5999 Miscellaneous retail stores, nec
Doug Martin

D-U-N-S 24-245-5546   (BR)
GATEWAY MECHANICAL SERVICES INC
4001 16a St Se, Calgary, AB, T2G 3T5
(403) 265-0010
Emp Here 100
SIC 1711 Plumbing, heating, air-conditioning
Jim Mortwedt

D-U-N-S 20-174-7388   (BR)
GDI SERVICES (CANADA) LP
(*Suby of* GDI SERVICES AUX IMMEUBLES INC)
437 36 Ave Se, Calgary, AB, T2G 1W5
(403) 232-8402
Emp Here 350
SIC 7349 Building maintenance services, nec
Fred Edwards

· *D-U-N-S* 24-906-9964   (SL)
GEOPHYSICAL EXPLORATION & DEVELOPMENT CORPORATION
GEDCO
125 9 Ave Se Unit 200, Calgary, AB, T2G 0P6
(403) 262-5780
Emp Here 30   *Sales* 12,738,210
SIC 8999 Services, nec
Andreas Cordsen
John W. Peirce

D-U-N-S 24-495-2917   (SL)
GIBBS GAGE ARCHITECTS
350-140 10 Ave Se, Calgary, AB, T2G 0R1
(403) 233-2000
Emp Here 110   *Sales* 19,661,290
SIC 8712 Architectural services
Wade Gibbs
Douglas Gage
Richard Lewis
Vincent Dods
Stephen Mahler

D-U-N-S 20-832-0788   (SL)
GLENBOW-ALBERTA INSTITUTE
GLENBOW MUSEUM
130 9 Ave Se, Calgary, AB, T2G 0P3
(403) 268-4100
Emp Here 115   *Sales* 10,507,435
SIC 8412 Museums and art galleries
Donna Livingstone

D-U-N-S 24-991-2242   (HQ)
GLOBAL RAYMAC SURVEYS INC
4000 4 St Se Suite 312, Calgary, AB, T2G 2W3
(403) 283-5455
Emp Here 148   *Sales* 26,810,850
SIC 8713 Surveying services
Jason Thistle
Luke Dixon
Jason Thistle

D-U-N-S 25-409-3743   (SL)
GRAF CANADA LTD
2308 Portland St Se, Calgary, AB, T2G 4M6
(403) 287-8585
Emp Here 70   *Sales* 22,829,520
SIC 3949 Sporting and athletic goods, nec
John Pagotto

D-U-N-S 24-598-7888   (HQ)
GRAND-PRIX AUTOMOTIVE DISTRIBUTORS INC
4313 Manhattan Rd Se, Calgary, AB, T2G 4B1

(403) 243-5622
Sales 15,732,000
SIC 5511 New and used car dealers
Scott Hutchinson

D-U-N-S 25-518-4046   (SL)
HARDCASTLE DESIGNS LTD
1316 9 Ave Se Suite 200, Calgary, AB, T2G 0T3
(403) 250-7733
Emp Here 24   *Sales* 10,643,760
SIC 7389 Business services, nec
Kevin Berry

D-U-N-S 24-673-6789   (HQ)
HBI - HERITAGE BUSINESS INTERIORS INC
2600 Portland St Se Suite 2050, Calgary, AB, T2G 4M6
(403) 252-2888
Sales 16,268,210
SIC 5712 Furniture stores
Michael (Mike) Taylor
Malcolm Taylor
Cynthia Taylor

D-U-N-S 24-344-0104   (SL)
HENINGER TOYOTA
3640 Macleod Trail Se, Calgary, AB, T2G 2P9
(403) 243-8000
Emp Here 96   *Sales* 60,410,880
SIC 5511 New and used car dealers
Brian Heninger
Dave Stewart

D-U-N-S 24-417-6272   (SL)
HITACHI ID SYSTEMS HOLDING, INC
(*Suby of* HITACHI, LTD.)
1401 1 St Se Suite 500, Calgary, AB, T2G 2J3
(403) 233-0740
Emp Here 140   *Sales* 20,185,480
SIC 7371 Custom computer programming services
Gedion Shoham

D-U-N-S 25-325-7505   (HQ)
HITACHI ID SYSTEMS, INC
(*Suby of* HITACHI, LTD.)
1401 1 St Se Suite 500, Calgary, AB, T2G 2J3
(403) 233-0740
Sales 20,185,480
SIC 7371 Custom computer programming services
Gideon Shoham
Idan Shoham
John Mansfield
Steve Carbone
David Karas

D-U-N-S 24-853-9199   (HQ)
HUMPTY'S RESTAURANTS INTERNATIONAL INC
HUMPTY'S CLASSIC CAFES
2505 Macleod Trail Sw, Calgary, AB, T2G 5J4
(403) 269-4675
Emp Here 11   *Sales* 469,469,115
SIC 6794 Patent owners and lessors
Donald Koenig
Janice Koenig
Albert Jakubec
Carolyn Messier
A.D. (Bert) Messier

D-U-N-S 24-319-3310   (SL)
ICON STONE & TILE INC
521 36 Ave Se, Calgary, AB, T2G 1W5
(403) 532-3383
Emp Here 35   *Sales* 15,651,090
SIC 5032 Brick, stone, and related material
Jean St-Onge
Raphael Soligo
Jaques Lambert

D-U-N-S 25-359-7827   (HQ)
IHS ENERGY (CANADA) LTD
IHS
(*Suby of* IHS MARKIT LTD)
1331 Macleod Trail Suite 200, Calgary, AB,

T2G 0K3
(403) 532-8175
Emp Here 100
SIC 8741 Management services
Chris Jones
Vinod Kothari
Stephen Green
Michael Mccrory

D-U-N-S 24-682-1123   (HQ)
IKO ENTERPRISES LTD
(*Suby of* GOLDIS ENTERPRISES, INC.)
1600 42 Ave Se, Calgary, AB, T2G 5B5
(403) 265-6022
Sales 1,864,095,900
SIC 6719 Holding companies, nec
Saul Koschitzky
David Koschitzky
David Laven

D-U-N-S 20-337-1922   (HQ)
INNOVA GLOBAL LTD
(*Suby of* TRIWEST CAPITAL PARTNERS INC)
4000 4 St Se Suite 222, Calgary, AB, T2G 2W3
(403) 292-7804
Emp Here 130   *Sales* 13,881,660
SIC 1541 Industrial buildings and warehouses
Harry Wong

D-U-N-S 24-377-0109   (SL)
ISTOCKPHOTO L.P.
ISTOCKPHOTO
1240 20 Ave Se Suite 200, Calgary, AB, T2G 1M8
(403) 265-3062
Emp Here 130   *Sales* 13,881,660
SIC 7299 Miscellaneous personal service
Kjelti Kellough
John J Lapham, Iii
Jodi Colligan

D-U-N-S 24-368-5786   (SL)
ISTOCKPHOTO ULC
(*Suby of* GETTY IMAGES LUXEMBOURG SARL)
1240 20 Ave Se Suite 200, Calgary, AB, T2G 1M8
(403) 265-3062
Emp Here 130
SIC 7299 Miscellaneous personal service
Kjelti Kellough
John J. Lapham Iii

D-U-N-S 24-014-2778   (HQ)
J & L SUPPLY CO. LTD
4511 Manitoba Rd Se, Calgary, AB, T2G 4B9
(403) 287-3300
Emp Here 35   *Sales* 23,751,300
SIC 5082 Construction and mining machinery
Ronald Shon Carey

D-U-N-S 20-832-2172   (SL)
JAMES ELECTRIC MOTOR SERVICES LTD
(*Suby of* FERGUSON PLC)
4020 8 St Se, Calgary, AB, T2G 3A7
(403) 252-5477
Emp Here 60   *Sales* 29,263,800
SIC 5084 Industrial machinery and equipment
Douglas Rick James
Ron M

D-U-N-S 25-538-3697   (HQ)
JBW PIPE & SUPPLY LTD
FRONTIER PLUMBING & HEATING SUPPLY, DIV OF
1320 Highfield Cres Se, Calgary, AB, T2G 5M3
(403) 259-6671
Emp Here 15   *Sales* 11,179,350
SIC 5074 Plumbing and heating equipment and supplies (hydronics)
Wayne Walker
Brian Findlay
Martin Deschenes
Jacques Deschenes

D-U-N-S 20-076-5493   (SL)
KANE'S MOTOR CYCLE SHOP LTD
KANE'S HARLEY-DAVIDSON
914 11 St Se, Calgary, AB, T2G 3E8
(403) 262-5462
Emp Here 33   *Sales* 16,436,574
SIC 5571 Motorcycle dealers
Mick Cawthorn

D-U-N-S 24-767-3320   (SL)
KBM COMMERCIAL FLOOR COVERINGS INC
1260 26 Ave Se, Calgary, AB, T2G 5S2
(403) 274-5292
Emp Here 165   *Sales* 38,858,985
SIC 1752 Floor laying and floor work, nec
Mike Kulyk
Beverley Ann Kulyk
Barbara Bauer
Kevin Kulyk
Michael Kulyk

D-U-N-S 20-521-3671   (HQ)
KELLER EQUIPMENT SUPPLY LTD
1228 26 Ave Se, Calgary, AB, T2G 5S2
(403) 243-8666
Emp Here 10   *Sales* 31,430,025
SIC 5172 Petroleum products, nec
Paul Mckay
Drew Keller
Carole Paterson
Bob Mcgregor
Gino Porco

D-U-N-S 20-441-1698   (SL)
LABBE-LEECH INTERIORS LTD
2600 Portland St Se Suite 2020, Calgary, AB, T2G 4M6
(403) 252-9991
Emp Here 150   *Sales* 31,856,400
SIC 1799 Special trade contractors, nec
William Jordanov

D-U-N-S 25-993-3018   (SL)
LIGHTHOUSE CAMP SERVICES LTD
LIGHTHOUSE LOGISTICS, A DIV OF
(*Suby of* ICEGATE HOLDINGS INC.)
714 1 St Se Unit 300, Calgary, AB, T2G 2G8
(403) 265-5190
Emp Here 150   *Sales* 13,903,500
SIC 7011 Hotels and motels
Dario Berloni

D-U-N-S 20-176-2965   (BR)
LILYDALE INC
LILYDALE POULTRY
(*Suby of* SOFINA FOODS INC)
2126 Hurst Rd Se, Calgary, AB, T2G 4M5
(403) 265-9010
Emp Here 375
SIC 2015 Poultry slaughtering and processing
Robin Jean

D-U-N-S 24-441-1161   (SL)
LINDSAY PARK SPORTS SOCIETY
TALISMAN CENTRE
2225 Macleod Trail Se, Calgary, AB, T2G 5B6
(403) 233-8393
Emp Here 180   *Sales* 14,138,100
SIC 7991 Physical fitness facilities
Garth Glover
Alec Milne
Jon Truswell

D-U-N-S 25-063-1520   (SL)
LUCIANO'S RESTAURANT GROUP
316 3 St Se, Calgary, AB, T2G 2S4

Emp Here 340
SIC 5812 Eating places

D-U-N-S 25-096-9029   (BR)
LUXURY HOTELS INTERNATIONAL OF CANADA ULC
LUXURY HOTELS INTERNATIONAL OF CANADA, ULC
(*Suby of* MARRIOTT INTERNATIONAL, INC.)

110 9 Ave Se, Calgary, AB, T2G 5A6
(403) 266-7331
Emp Here 300
SIC 7011 Hotels and motels
Joseph Clohessy

D-U-N-S 25-676-5389   (HQ)
MAINSTREET EQUITY CORP
305 10 Ave Se, Calgary, AB, T2G 0W2
(403) 215-6060
Emp Here 250   *Sales* 83,447,616
SIC 6513 Apartment building operators
Bob Dhillon
Sheena Keslick
Johnny Lam
Trina Cui
John Irwin
Joe Amantea
Rich Grimaldi
K.V. Dhillon
Ron Anderson

D-U-N-S 20-324-7499   (SL)
MANATOKAN OILFIELD SERVICES INC
237 8 Ave Se Suite 222, Calgary, AB, T2G
5C3
(403) 718-9842
Emp Here 100   *Sales* 31,970,500
SIC 1389 Oil and gas field services, nec
Fabian Walsh
Mona Doyle
Allan Mytrash

D-U-N-S 20-510-9973   (BR)
MCELHANNEY LAND SURVEYS LTD
*MCELHANNEY GEOMATICS ENGINEERING
LTD*
(*Suby of* MCELHANNEY LAND SURVEYS
LTD)
100-402 11 Ave Se, Calgary, AB, T2G 0Y4
(403) 245-4711
Emp Here 80
SIC 8713 Surveying services
Bernie Mckenna

D-U-N-S 24-731-6219   (SL)
MINI DIG CORP
2222 Alyth Pl Se, Calgary, AB, T2G 3K9
(403) 274-0090
Emp Here 60   *Sales* 14,771,160
SIC 1795 Wrecking and demolition work
David Neiley
Kenneth Haggert
Kevin Haggart

D-U-N-S 24-714-9628   (HQ)
MODERN BEAUTY SUPPLIES INC
415 Manitou Rd Se, Calgary, AB, T2G 4C2
(403) 259-4442
Emp Here 33   *Sales* 73,159,500
SIC 5087 Service establishment equipment
Mike Jomaa
Fay Jomaa
Helen Beally
Amer Jomaa
Jamal Jomaa
Medina Jomaa

D-U-N-S 20-083-5569   (HQ)
NORTHERN HARDWARE LTD
ORIENCE INTEGRATION, DIV OF
549 Cleveland Cres Se, Calgary, AB, T2G 4R8
(403) 243-5401
Emp Here 1   *Sales* 27,724,788
SIC 5072 Hardware
Brian Dumonceaux
Phil Grant
Robert Shearer

D-U-N-S 24-676-6385   (HQ)
**NORTHRIDGE ENERGY DEVELOPMENT
GROUP INC**
1509 Centre St Sw Suite 500, Calgary, AB,
T2G 2E6

Emp Here 20   *Sales* 11,714,400
SIC 8742 Management consulting services

Jon Harrison
Jon Ouellette
Lance Fugate

D-U-N-S 24-766-2976   (SL)
NORWEST CORPORATION
(*Suby of* NORWEST CORPORATION)
411 1 St Se Suite 2700, Calgary, AB, T2G 4Y5
(403) 237-7763
Emp Here 200   *Sales* 50,698,000
SIC 8748 Business consulting, nec
Donovan Symonds
Joe Aiello
Geoff Jordan
Steve Cameron
Craig Acott
Andrew Scrymgeour

D-U-N-S 24-439-3435   (SL)
NUT MAN COMPANY INC, THE
4112 8 St Se, Calgary, AB, T2G 3A7
(403) 287-1983
Emp Here 39   *Sales* 10,691,928
SIC 5441 Candy, nut, and confectionery
stores
James Ross Miller
Allan Jonas
Patricia Miller
Christine Jonas

D-U-N-S 25-972-3989   (SL)
NUUN DIGITAL INC
(*Suby of* NUUN & CO INC)
1206 20 Ave Se, Calgary, AB, T2G 1M8
(403) 907-0997
Emp Here 89   *Sales* 4,596,966
SIC 7371 Custom computer programming ser-
vices
Feras Nasser

D-U-N-S 24-494-9004   (SL)
O'DELL ELECTRIC LTD
3827 15a St Se, Calgary, AB, T2G 3N7
(403) 266-2935
Emp Here 130   *Sales* 11,476,321
SIC 1731 Electrical work
Randy O'dell
Drew Woolsey

D-U-N-S 25-533-1563   (HQ)
OLYMPIA FINANCIAL GROUP INC
125 9 Ave Se Suite 2300, Calgary, AB, T2G
0P6
(403) 261-0900
Sales 37,927,525
SIC 6091 Nondeposit trust facilities
Rick Skauge
Gerhard Barnard
Ryan Mckenna
Craig Skauge
Jonathan Bahnuik
Gerard Janssen
Brian Newman
Tony Lanzl
Diana Wolfe
Dennis Nerland

D-U-N-S 25-686-6161   (HQ)
OLYMPIA TRUST COMPANY
(*Suby of* OLYMPIA FINANCIAL GROUP INC)
125 9 Ave Se Suite 2300, Calgary, AB, T2G
0P6
(403) 261-0900
Sales 14,805,000
SIC 6091 Nondeposit trust facilities
Rick Skauge
Charles Chebry
Robin Fry
Randy Gregory
Lori Ryan
Brenda J. Eprile

D-U-N-S 20-286-1191   (SL)
OLYMPIC INTEGRATED SERVICES INC
(*Suby of* OLYMPIC INTERNATIONAL AGEN-
CIES LTD)
2226 Portland St Se, Calgary, AB, T2G 4M6

(587) 955-9977
Emp Here 46   *Sales* 20,570,004
SIC 5075 Warm air heating and air condition-
ing
Michael Mahannah

D-U-N-S 24-766-2448   (SL)
ORION MANAGEMENT INC
4015 1 St Se Unit 3a, Calgary, AB, T2G 4X7
(403) 243-8292
Emp Here 35   *Sales* 11,449,445
SIC 6531 Real estate agents and managers
John Wagenaar
Clarence Wagenaar

D-U-N-S 24-156-4913   (SL)
PARMX CHEESE CO. LTD
4117 16a St Se, Calgary, AB, T2G 3T7
(403) 237-0707
Emp Here 20   *Sales* 10,702,480
SIC 5143 Dairy products, except dried or
canned
Theresa Aiello
Frank Luigi Aiello
Paul Maurice Aiello

D-U-N-S 20-549-8491   (HQ)
PET PLANET LTD
600 Manitou Rd Se, Calgary, AB, T2G 4C5
(403) 777-4664
Emp Here 4   *Sales* 13,024,000
SIC 5999 Miscellaneous retail stores, nec
Laura Leah English
Joan Bauer

D-U-N-S 24-388-2805   (HQ)
PPI SOLUTIONS INC
FM GROUP OF COMPANIES
340 50 Ave Se Suite 1340, Calgary, AB, T2G
2B1
(403) 243-6163
Sales 92,332,950
SIC 6311 Life insurance
Bruce Tetz

D-U-N-S 24-346-1324   (HQ)
PRAIRIE LUBE LTD
MR LUBE
5040 12a St Se Unit B, Calgary, AB, T2G 5K9
(403) 243-7800
Emp Here 7   *Sales* 76,533,490
SIC 7549 Automotive services, nec
Marvin Guenter
James Guenter

D-U-N-S 20-441-0229   (HQ)
PRAIRIE VIEW HOLDINGS LTD
BUDGET RENT-A-CAR OF CALGARY
(*Suby of* SM2 HOLDINGS LTD)
140 6 Ave Se, Calgary, AB, T2G 0G2
(403) 232-4725
Sales 63,027,580
SIC 7514 Passenger car rental
Mohamed Ali
Mithoo Gillani
Shiraz Ali

D-U-N-S 24-786-6957   (SL)
PRESTIGE LANDSCAPE GROUP
105-1212 34 Ave Se, Calgary, AB, T2G 1V7
(403) 280-5400
Emp Here 90   *Sales* 9,836,010
SIC 0781 Landscape counseling and planning
Mike Haberl

D-U-N-S 24-850-0212   (SL)
PRO-LINE BUILDING MATERIALS LTD
4910 Builders Rd Se, Calgary, AB, T2G 4C6
(403) 262-1008
Emp Here 50   *Sales* 12,044,200
SIC 1623 Water, sewer, and utility lines
Ron Roller
Evan Swifan

D-U-N-S 24-894-9240   (SL)
PRODUCTIVE SPACE INC
3632 Burnsland Rd Se, Calgary, AB, T2G 3Z2

Emp Here 30   *Sales* 13,304,700
SIC 7389 Business services, nec
David Fehr

D-U-N-S 24-013-2902   (SL)
**PROFESSIONAL GARDENER CO. LTD,
THE**
915 23 Ave Se, Calgary, AB, T2G 1P1
(403) 263-4200
Emp Here 25   *Sales* 11,768,275
SIC 1542 Nonresidential construction, nec
Hans R. Johansen
Gordon F. Dixon

D-U-N-S 25-518-4624   (SL)
**PROGRESSIVE ALTERNATIVES SOCIETY
OF CALGARY**
4014 Macleod Trail Se Suite 211, Calgary, AB,
T2G 2R7
(403) 262-8515
Emp Here 90   *Sales* 12,011,310
SIC 8399 Social services, nec
Bill Forman

D-U-N-S 25-990-6113   (SL)
PROMARK UTILITY LOCATORS INC
4538 Manilla Rd Se, Calgary, AB, T2G 4B7
(403) 243-1993
Emp Here 75   *Sales* 31,142,175
SIC 4931 Electric and other services com-
bined
Harris Toth

D-U-N-S 20-283-5468   (SL)
RADIOWORLD CENTRAL INC
GPS CENTRAL
(*Suby of* NORHAM RADIO INC)
711 48 Ave Se Unit 8, Calgary, AB, T2G 4X2
(587) 317-2000
Emp Here 16   *Sales* 10,503,424
SIC 5961 Catalog and mail-order houses
Angelo Meffe
George Valentine
Gregory Kulin

D-U-N-S 20-270-1413   (SL)
RANGER TIRE INC
4020 9 St Se Unit 2, Calgary, AB, T2G 3C4
(403) 723-0777
Emp Here 14   *Sales* 23,504,310
SIC 5014 Tires and tubes
Paul Blomfield
Steven Selleran

D-U-N-S 24-880-3652   (HQ)
RENAISSANCE WINE MERCHANTS LTD
RENAISSANCE WINE & SPIRITS
3303 8 St Se, Calgary, AB, T2G 3A4
(403) 296-0170
Emp Here 9   *Sales* 14,109,984
SIC 5182 Wine and distilled beverages
Mark Ferrier

D-U-N-S 24-272-6610   (HQ)
**ROCKY CROSS CONSTRUCTION (CAL-
GARY) LIMITED**
444 42 Ave Se Suite 4, Calgary, AB, T2G 1Y4

Emp Here 40   *Sales* 17,725,392
SIC 1799 Special trade contractors, nec
Rodger Cumberland

D-U-N-S 24-355-2200   (HQ)
ROCKY MOUNTAIN DEALERSHIPS INC
ROCKY MOUNTAIN EQUIPMENT
3345 8 St Se Suite 301, Calgary, AB, T2G 3A4
(403) 265-7364
Emp Here 40   *Sales* 796,831,915
SIC 5082 Construction and mining machinery
Garrett Ganden
Jim Wood
Jerald Palmer Jr
Matthew Campbell
Derek Stimson
Robert Mackay
Scott Tannas
William Dejong

Cameron Crawford
Robert Herdman

D-U-N-S 24-301-2796   (HQ)
ROGERS INSURANCE LTD
1331 Macleod Trl Se Suite 800, Calgary, AB,
T2G 0K3
(403) 296-2400
Emp Here 130   *Sales* 1,167,541,584
SIC 6411 Insurance agents, brokers, and service
Peter Rogers
Lee Rogers
Bruce Rabik
Karyn Fair
Austen Lillies
Rosetta Bilodeau
Sara Smith
Lena Tityk
Lindsay Mather

D-U-N-S 25-096-2623   (SL)
SAEXPLORATION (CANADA) LTD
(*Suby of* SAEXPLORATION HOLDINGS INC)
3333 8 St Se Suite 300, Calgary, AB, T2G 3A4
(403) 776-1950
Emp Here 30   *Sales* 20,180,370
SIC 1382 Oil and gas exploration services
Brian Beatty
Jeff Hastings
Eric Rosenfeld
David Sgro
Gary Dalton
Gregory Monahan

D-U-N-S 20-441-2738   (HQ)
SCHLUMBERGER CANADA LIMITED
WESTERNGECO CANADA
125 9 Ave Se Suite 200, Calgary, AB, T2G 0P6
(403) 509-4000
Emp Here 200   *Sales* 1,091,942,000
SIC 1389 Oil and gas field services, nec
Mark O'byrne
Celine B.Gerson

D-U-N-S 24-086-7689   (SL)
SCOTT SPRINGFIELD MFG. INC
(*Suby of* OLYMPIC INTERNATIONAL AGENCIES LTD)
2234 Portland St Se, Calgary, AB, T2G 4M6
(403) 236-1212
Emp Here 150   *Sales* 28,812,750
SIC 3433 Heating equipment, except electric
Michael Mahannah

D-U-N-S 25-687-5725   (BR)
SOBEYS WEST INC
MCDONALD CONSOLIDATED
(*Suby of* EMPIRE COMPANY LIMITED)
203 42 Ave Se, Calgary, AB, T2G 1Y3
(403) 287-4048
Emp Here 130
SIC 4225 General warehousing and storage
Philip Beatty

D-U-N-S 20-278-3189   (SL)
SOURCE ENERGY SERVICES CANADA LP GP LTD
438 11 Ave Se Unit 500, Calgary, AB, T2G 0Y4
(403) 262-1312
Emp Here 475   *Sales* 259,336,225
SIC 1389 Oil and gas field services, nec
Brad Thomson
Joe Jackson
Derren Newell
Scott Melbourn
Stew Hanlon
Jim Mcmahon
Jeff Belford
Mick Macbean
Ken Seitz
Carrie Lonardelli

D-U-N-S 20-357-9396   (HQ)
SOURCE ENERGY SERVICES LTD
438 11 Ave Se Suite 500, Calgary, AB, T2G

0Y4
(403) 262-1312
Sales 314,632,799
SIC 3532 Mining machinery
Brad Thomson
Cody Church
Joe Jackson
Derren Newell
Scott Melbourn
Jeff Belford
James (Jim) Mcmahon
Neil Cameron
Marshall Mcrae
Stew Hanlon

D-U-N-S 24-598-2004   (HQ)
SOUTHLAND TRANSPORTATION LTD
(*Suby of* PACIFIC WESTERN TRANSPORTATION LTD)
823 Highfield Ave Se, Calgary, AB, T2G 4C7
(403) 287-1395
Emp Here 100   *Sales* 137,973,576
SIC 4151 School buses
Michael Colborne
Thomas Jezersek

D-U-N-S 24-518-4262   (SL)
SPOLETINI/PALUMBO INC
SPOLUMBO'S FINE FOOD & DELI
1308 9 Ave Se, Calgary, AB, T2G 0T3
(403) 537-1161
Emp Here 53   *Sales* 15,554,281
SIC 5411 Grocery stores
Tom Spoletini
Tony Spoletini
Mike Palumbo

D-U-N-S 20-078-0229   (BR)
SSH BEDDING CANADA CO
SSH BEDDING CANADA CO.
(*Suby of* SSH BEDDING CANADA CO)
3636 11a St Se, Calgary, AB, T2G 3H3
(403) 287-0600
Emp Here 120
SIC 2394 Canvas and related products
Alok Sarkar

D-U-N-S 24-330-7464   (BR)
STAR BUILDING MATERIALS (ALBERTA) LTD
STAR BUILDING MATERIALS
(*Suby of* QUALICO GROUP LTD)
2345 Alyth Rd Se, Calgary, AB, T2G 5T8
(403) 720-0010
Emp Here 100
SIC 5211 Lumber and other building materials
Rich Tunnicliffe

D-U-N-S 24-417-2821   (HQ)
STEINBOCK DEVELOPMENT CORPORATION LTD
PARK N JET
(*Suby of* SM2 HOLDINGS LTD)
140 6 Ave Se, Calgary, AB, T2G 0G2
(403) 232-4725
Emp Here 45   *Sales* 18,981,100
SIC 7521 Automobile parking
Mohamed Ali
Shiraz Ali

D-U-N-S 25-105-3617   (SL)
SUBNET SOLUTIONS INC
916 42 Ave Se Unit 110, Calgary, AB, T2G 1Z2
(403) 270-8885
Emp Here 68   *Sales* 14,541,868
SIC 7372 Prepackaged software
Ameen Hamdon
Jocelyn Hamdon
Anthony Eshpeter
Travis Jaffrey

D-U-N-S 20-512-4261   (HQ)
TECK COAL LIMITED
(*Suby of* TECK RESOURCES LIMITED)
205 9 Ave Se Suite 1000, Calgary, AB, T2G 0R3

(403) 767-8500
Emp Here 150   *Sales* 1,247,071,800
SIC 1221 Bituminous coal and lignite-surface mining
Donald R. Lindsay
Ronald A. Millos
Dean C. Windsor
Andrew A. Stonkus

D-U-N-S 24-948-6002   (HQ)
TERVITA CORPORATION
140 10 Ave Se Suite 1600, Calgary, AB, T2G 0R1
(855) 837-8482
Emp Here 800   *Sales* 1,824,717,933
SIC 8748 Business consulting, nec
John Cooper
Rob Dawson
Grant Billing
Kevin Walbridge
Doug Ramsay
Cameron Kramer
Jay Thornton
Allen Hagerman
Susan Riddell Rose

D-U-N-S 20-826-7518   (SL)
TOURISM CALGARY-CALGARY CONVENTION & VISITORS BUREAU
238 11 Ave Se Suite 200, Calgary, AB, T2G 0X8
(403) 263-8510
Emp Here 40   *Sales* 17,968,760
SIC 7389 Business services, nec
Randy Williams
Aldon Wells
Peter Wallis
Kurby Court
Mark Willson
George Brookman
Daniel Pigeon
Adam Pekarsky
Maureen Payne
Larry Ryder

D-U-N-S 20-522-9458   (SL)
TOYOTA DEALERS ADVERTISING ASSOCIATION
411 11 Ave Se, Calgary, AB, T2G 0Y5
(403) 237-2388
Emp Here 37   *Sales* 18,428,886
SIC 5521 Used car dealers
Marie Langille

D-U-N-S 24-853-3788   (SL)
TRIPLE THREE TRADING LTD
908 34 Ave Se, Calgary, AB, T2G 1V3
(403) 240-2540
Emp Here 45   *Sales* 10,504,575
SIC 2673 Bags: plastic, laminated, and coated
Ben Ng
Meng Ng
Kit Lai

D-U-N-S 20-191-6983   (BR)
TYCO INTEGRATED FIRE & SECURITY CANADA, INC
SIMPLEX GRINNELL
(*Suby of* JOHNSON CONTROLS INTERNATIONAL PUBLIC LIMITED COMPANY)
431 Manitou Rd Se, Calgary, AB, T2G 4C2
(403) 287-3202
Emp Here 120
SIC 7389 Business services, nec
Bruce Ellis

D-U-N-S 20-829-2599   (HQ)
UNICOM GRAPHICS LIMITED
4501 Manitoba Rd Se, Calgary, AB, T2G 4B9
(403) 287-2020
Sales 16,402,700
SIC 2752 Commercial printing, lithographic
Gerald Parcells
Dick Reuser
Bruce Fraser
Donald Mcleod

D-U-N-S 24-930-0617   (SL)
UPSIDE ENGINEERING LTD
409 10 Ave Se, Calgary, AB, T2G 0W3
(403) 290-4650
Emp Here 120   *Sales* 21,448,680
SIC 8711 Engineering services
Rod Evans
Donna Evans

D-U-N-S 24-701-1547   (HQ)
VANTAGE FOODS INC
(*Suby of* WESTAR FOODS LTD)
4000 4 St Se Suite 225, Calgary, AB, T2G 2W3
(403) 215-2820
Emp Here 6   *Sales* 243,692,500
SIC 2011 Meat packing plants
Gary Haley
Leonal Kilgore
Rob Dettlinger
Yemi Ogunrinola
Jim Good
Sheilah Lee Restall
Don Finstad
Alan Cook
Yves Moser
Jon Tucker

D-U-N-S 24-342-3998   (SL)
VAP HOLDINGS L.P.
(*Suby of* GMP CAPITAL INC)
4211 13a St Se, Calgary, AB, T2G 3J6
(403) 299-0844
Emp Here 300
SIC 2011 Meat packing plants
Anthony Speteri

D-U-N-S 24-015-8519   (SL)
VIKING INSTALLATIONS (CALGARY) LTD
4020 4 St Se, Calgary, AB, T2G 2W3
(403) 273-7716
Emp Here 110   *Sales* 25,637,150
SIC 1711 Plumbing, heating, air-conditioning
Ross Sinclaire

D-U-N-S 24-715-1228   (SL)
VISTA PROJECTS LIMITED
4000 4 St Se Suite 330, Calgary, AB, T2G 2W3
(403) 255-3455
Emp Here 200   *Sales* 35,747,800
SIC 8711 Engineering services
Bashar Hussein
Brian Jewer
Patrick Reilly
Richard Campbell
Alex Campbell
Ian Urich
Nick Campbell
Tyler Elchuk
Warren Strickland

D-U-N-S 20-830-5961   (HQ)
VYEFIELD ENTERPRISES LTD
SR PACKAGING, DIV OF
3815 16 St Se, Calgary, AB, T2G 4W5
(403) 290-1838
Emp Here 10   *Sales* 14,789,372
SIC 5144 Poultry and poultry products
Hessel Kielstra
Herman Kielstra
Edward Kielstra
Larry Kielstra

D-U-N-S 20-723-7525   (HQ)
WEST CANADIAN DIGITAL IMAGING INC
1601 9 Ave Se Suite 200, Calgary, AB, T2G 0H4
(403) 245-2555
Emp Here 200   *Sales* 32,805,400
SIC 2752 Commercial printing, lithographic
Sid Nieuwdort
George Brookman

D-U-N-S 24-673-6953   (HQ)
WEST CANADIAN INDUSTRIES GROUP LTD

ORANGE DOOR DIRECT
1601 9 Ave Se Suite 200, Calgary, AB, T2G 0H4
(403) 245-2555
Emp Here 145   *Sales* 60,111,300
SIC 7336 Commercial art and graphic design
 George Brookman
 Irene Price

D-U-N-S 20-076-8430   (BR)
WESTROCK COMPANY OF CANADA CORP
(Suby of WESTROCK COMPANY*)*
1115 34 Ave Se, Calgary, AB, T2G 1V5
(403) 214-5200
Emp Here 200
SIC 2653 Corrugated and solid fiber boxes
 Jeff Craig

D-U-N-S 20-831-4823   (SL)
WOOD GROUP ASSET INTEGRITY SOLU-TIONS, INC
(Suby of JOHN WOOD GROUP P.L.C.*)*
4242 7 St Se Suite 118, Calgary, AB, T2G 2Y8
(403) 245-5666
Emp Here 65   *Sales* 11,618,035
SIC 8711 Engineering services
 Russell Barss
 Max Slipek
 Marjorie Knight

D-U-N-S 25-519-7741   (SL)
WORK COMP TECH LTD
1401 1 St Se Suite 200, Calgary, AB, T2G 2J3
(403) 294-0501
Emp Here 14   *Sales* 10,156,146
SIC 6331 Fire, marine, and casualty insurance
 Karl Elias

D-U-N-S 20-796-8640   (BR)
YOUNG WOMEN'S CHRISTIAN ASSOCIA-TION OF CANADA, THE
YWCA SHERIFF KING HOME
(Suby of YOUNG WOMEN'S CHRISTIAN AS-SOCIATION OF CANADA, THE*)*
2003 16 St Se, Calgary, AB, T2G 5B7
(403) 266-0707
Emp Here 100
SIC 8322 Individual and family services
 Gary Gibbens

D-U-N-S 20-825-6248   (SL)
ZAZULA PROCESS EQUIPMENT LTD
4609 Manitoba Rd Se, Calgary, AB, T2G 4B9
(403) 244-0751
Emp Here 25   *Sales* 11,875,650
SIC 5084 Industrial machinery and equipment
 Stanley J Zazula
 Aurora Zazula

Calgary, AB T2H

D-U-N-S 20-891-0153   (SL)
1004907 ALBERTA LTD
LEXUS OF CALGARY
22 Heritage Meadows Rd Se, Calgary, AB, T2H 3C1
(403) 250-4930
Emp Here 45   *Sales* 22,413,510
SIC 5511 New and used car dealers
 Glen Rumpel

D-U-N-S 20-401-4620   (SL)
1768652 ALBERTA LTD
TOWER CLEANERS
402 53 Ave Se, Calgary, AB, T2H 0N4
(403) 262-3791
Emp Here 120   *Sales* 12,813,840
SIC 7216 Drycleaning plants, except rugs
 Tony Stephen
 Elizabeth Stephen
 Rajesh Manan

D-U-N-S 20-521-7698   (SL)
28 AUGUSTA FUND LTD

SMUGGLER'S INN
6920 Macleod Trail Se, Calgary, AB, T2H 0L3
(403) 259-3119
Emp Here 140   *Sales* 6,372,660
SIC 5812 Eating places
 Frank Krowicki

D-U-N-S 25-054-8765   (SL)
504147 ALBERTA LTD
CALGARY BMW
34 Heritage Meadows Rd Se, Calgary, AB, T2H 3C1
(403) 253-0338
Emp Here 120   *Sales* 75,513,600
SIC 5511 New and used car dealers
 Ram Dilawri
 Tony Dilawri

D-U-N-S 25-290-8629   (HQ)
668824 ALBERTA LTD
VISIONS ELECTRONICS
6009 1a St Sw Suite 1, Calgary, AB, T2H 0G5
(403) 255-2270
Emp Here 30   *Sales* 133,351,500
SIC 5731 Radio, television, and electronic stores
 Rick Stewart

D-U-N-S 20-393-9850   (SL)
7648243 CANADA LIMITED
SERVPRO OF CALGARY SOUTH
5730 Burbank Rd Se, Calgary, AB, T2H 1Z4
(403) 255-0202
Emp Here 52   *Sales* 12,801,672
SIC 1799 Special trade contractors, nec
 Fred Edwards
 Rick Templeman

D-U-N-S 20-979-3186   (SL)
975002 ALBERTA INC
MINI CALGARY
161 Glendeer Cir Se, Calgary, AB, T2H 2S8
(403) 275-6464
Emp Here 70   *Sales* 44,049,600
SIC 5521 Used car dealers
 Terry Switzer

D-U-N-S 20-777-9765   (SL)
998699 ALBERTA LTD
HYATT MITSUBISHI
168 Glendeer Cir Se, Calgary, AB, T2H 2V4
(403) 253-6800
Emp Here 25   *Sales* 12,451,950
SIC 5511 New and used car dealers
 Barry Jordan

D-U-N-S 20-824-9862   (SL)
A-1 AUTO BODY LTD
5304 1a St Se, Calgary, AB, T2H 1J2
(403) 253-7867
Emp Here 100   *Sales* 28,330,000
SIC 7532 Top and body repair and paint shops
 Gary Miller

D-U-N-S 20-108-9906   (BR)
ADP CANADA CO
ADP
(Suby of AUTOMATIC DATA PROCESSING, INC.*)*
6025 11 St Se Suite 100, Calgary, AB, T2H 2Z2
(888) 901-7402
Emp Here 80
SIC 8721 Accounting, auditing, and book-keeping
 Pam Stewart

D-U-N-S 25-452-7369   (SL)
ADVANTAGE MANAGEMENT INC
REREALTY PROFESSIONALS
6020 1a St Sw Suite 10, Calgary, AB, T2H 0G3
(403) 259-4141
Emp Here 125   *Sales* 52,361,125
SIC 6531 Real estate agents and managers
 Douglas Koop

D-U-N-S 20-278-3713   (BR)

AECOM CANADA LTD
(Suby of AECOM*)*
6807 Railway St Se Suite 200, Calgary, AB, T2H 2V6
(403) 270-9200
Emp Here 175
SIC 8711 Engineering services

D-U-N-S 25-538-7953   (HQ)
AECOM ENERGY SERVICES LTD
URS FLINT
(Suby of AECOM*)*
6025 11 St Se Suite 240, Calgary, AB, T2H 2Z2
(403) 218-7100
Emp Here 40   *Sales* 5,459,710,000
SIC 1389 Oil and gas field services, nec
 William J. Lingard
 Bryce Satter
 Sean Fitzgerald
 Brad Mcfarlane
 Paul Boechler
 Deon Walsh
 Glen Greenshields
 Joel Jarding
 Neil Wotton
 Steve Russom

D-U-N-S 20-064-7332   (HQ)
AECOM FACILITY CONSTRUCTION LTD
(Suby of AECOM*)*
1209 59 Ave Se Suite 205, Calgary, AB, T2H 2P6
(403) 218-7113
Emp Here 200   *Sales* 131,246,000
SIC 1623 Water, sewer, and utility lines
 Brian Butlin

D-U-N-S 24-334-1588   (SL)
AECOM MAINTENANCE SERVICES LTD
FT SERVICES
6025 11 St Se Suite 240, Calgary, AB, T2H 2Z2
(403) 265-9033
Emp Here 250   *Sales* 31,194,000
SIC 8741 Management services
 Andy Brookes

D-U-N-S 24-158-0968   (HQ)
AECOM PRODUCTION SERVICES LTD
(Suby of AECOM*)*
6025 11 St Se Unit 240, Calgary, AB, T2H 2Z2
(403) 386-1000
Emp Here 100   *Sales* 1,177,188,250
SIC 1389 Oil and gas field services, nec
 Bill Linguard
 Terry Freeman

D-U-N-S 25-384-7180   (SL)
ALLIED PROJECTS LTD
7017 Farrell Rd Se, Calgary, AB, T2H 0T3
(403) 543-4530
Emp Here 120   *Sales* 26,139,480
SIC 1731 Electrical work
 Michael J. Brunner

D-U-N-S 24-674-8099   (SL)
ARROWHEAD SPRING WATER LTD
5730 Burbank Rd Se, Calgary, AB, T2H 1Z4

Emp Here 45   *Sales* 12,544,331
SIC 5499 Miscellaneous food stores
 Dan Demaere

D-U-N-S 20-832-1190   (HQ)
ASSOCIATE VETERINARY CLINIC (1981) LTD
7140 12 St Se, Calgary, AB, T2H 2Y4
(403) 541-0815
Emp Here 25   *Sales* 34,781,000
SIC 0742 Veterinary services, specialties
 Alun Cooksley
 Andrew Vanniekerk

D-U-N-S 24-495-6397   (BR)
BAGOS BUN BAKERY LTD
SONS BAKERY
(Suby of BAGOS BUN BAKERY LTD*)*

303 58 Ave Se Suite 3, Calgary, AB, T2H 0P3
(403) 252-3660
Emp Here 100
SIC 2051 Bread, cake, and related products
 Peter Mclaughlin

D-U-N-S 24-325-9343   (SL)
BERTOLIN, S. PHARMACY LTD
SHOPPERS DRUG MART
6455 Macleod Trail S Unit Y003, Calgary, AB, T2H 0K4
(403) 253-2424
Emp Here 70   *Sales* 17,102,960
SIC 5912 Drug stores and proprietary stores
 Susan Bertolin

D-U-N-S 24-554-2436   (BR)
BEST BUY CANADA LTD
FUTURE SHOP
(Suby of BEST BUY CO., INC.*)*
6909 Macleod Trail Sw, Calgary, AB, T2H 0L6

Emp Here 100
SIC 5734 Computer and software stores
 Bob Neilson

D-U-N-S 24-346-3056   (HQ)
BIG 4 MOTORS LTD
BIG 4 DODGE JEEP
7330 Macleod Trail Se, Calgary, AB, T2H 0L9
(403) 252-6671
Sales 47,196,000
SIC 5511 New and used car dealers
 Rob Coleman

D-U-N-S 20-744-1718   (SL)
BLACKFOOT MOTOR INN LTD
BLACKFOOT INN
5940 Blackfoot Trail Se, Calgary, AB, T2H 2B5
(403) 252-2253
Emp Here 200   *Sales* 18,538,000
SIC 7011 Hotels and motels
 Glen Bogdan
 Scott Warner
 Philip Libin
 Maurice Paperny
 Mark Zivot
 Ralph Gurevitch

D-U-N-S 24-290-6688   (SL)
BMP MECHANICAL LTD
6420 6a St Se Suite 110, Calgary, AB, T2H 2B7
(403) 816-4409
Emp Here 200   *Sales* 46,613,000
SIC 1711 Plumbing, heating, air-conditioning
 Brad Shalagan

D-U-N-S 24-808-4774   (SL)
BONDAR'S FINE FURNITURE LTD
6999 11 St Se Bay Suite 110, Calgary, AB, T2H 2S1
(403) 253-8200
Emp Here 60   *Sales* 13,944,180
SIC 5712 Furniture stores
 Stewart Bondar

D-U-N-S 24-554-7062   (HQ)
BOUVRY EXPORTS CALGARY LTD
222 58 Ave Sw Suite 312, Calgary, AB, T2H 2S3
(403) 253-0717
Emp Here 4   *Sales* 51,853,500
SIC 2011 Meat packing plants
 Claude Bouvry
 Alain Bouvry

D-U-N-S 20-521-0529   (SL)
BRASSO NISSAN LTD
195 Glendeer Cir Se, Calgary, AB, T2H 2S8
(403) 253-5555
Emp Here 75   *Sales* 47,196,000
SIC 5511 New and used car dealers
 Einar Brasso

D-U-N-S 20-232-3189   (SL)
BRAZILIAN CANADIAN COFFEE ALBERTA INC

BRAZILIAN COFFEE CALGARY
6812 6 St Se Bay Suite J, Calgary, AB, T2H 2K4

Emp Here 33   *Sales* 27,574,041
SIC 5141 Groceries, general line
Roger Kramer
Robert Hason

D-U-N-S 20-521-8878   (HQ)
BURNCO ROCK PRODUCTS LTD
155 Glendeer Cir Se Suite 200, Calgary, AB, T2H 2S8
(403) 255-2600
Emp Here 60   *Sales* 204,552,000
SIC 3273 Ready-mixed concrete
Scott Burns
Mike Powell

D-U-N-S 25-946-2240   (SL)
C.O.M. RESOURCES LTD
6223 2 St Se Suite 165, Calgary, AB, T2H 1J5
(403) 299-9400
Emp Here 80   *Sales* 14,076,640
SIC 8711 Engineering services
John Edwards

D-U-N-S 20-591-1493   (BR)
CALGARY BOARD OF EDUCATION
LE ROI DANIELS ELEMENTARY SCHOOL
(*Suby of* CALGARY BOARD OF EDUCA-TION)
47 Fyffe Rd Se, Calgary, AB, T2H 1B9
(403) 777-6420
Emp Here 4,030
SIC 8211 Elementary and secondary schools
Daren Patterson

D-U-N-S 25-269-4369   (BR)
CALGARY BOARD OF EDUCATION
LORD BEAVERBROOK SENIOR HIGH SCHOOL
(*Suby of* CALGARY BOARD OF EDUCA-TION)
9019 Fairmount Dr Se, Calgary, AB, T2H 0Z4
(403) 259-5585
Emp Here 150
SIC 8211 Elementary and secondary schools
Diane Yee

D-U-N-S 20-343-5755   (SL)
CALGARY C MOTORS LP
COURTESY CHRYSLER DODGE JEEP RAM
(*Suby of* AUTOCANADA INC)
125 Glendeer Cir Se Suite 200, Calgary, AB, T2H 2S8
(403) 255-8111
Emp Here 150   *Sales* 94,392,000
SIC 5511 New and used car dealers
Kris Laughton

D-U-N-S 20-074-9372   (HQ)
CALGARY CO-OPERATIVE ASSOCIATION LIMITED
CALGARY CO-OP
151 86 Ave Se Unit 110, Calgary, AB, T2H 3A5
(403) 219-6025
Emp Here 150   *Sales* 769,856,000
SIC 5411 Grocery stores
Patricia Mcleod
Lori Ell
Lisa Wise
Ken Keelor
Paul Harrison
Jeff Ambrose
Danielle Bussieres
Doug Newstead
Damon Tanzola
Bart Willmore

D-U-N-S 20-076-4520   (SL)
CALGARY ITALIAN BAKERY LTD
5310 5 St Se, Calgary, AB, T2H 1L2
(403) 255-3515
Emp Here 85   *Sales* 29,383,650
SIC 2051 Bread, cake, and related products
Luigi Bontorin
Louis Jr Bontorin

David Bontorin

D-U-N-S 20-079-1133   (SL)
CALGARY M VEHICLES GP INC
COURTESY MITSUBISHI
(*Suby of* AUTOCANADA INC)
168 Glendeer Circle Se, Calgary, AB, T2H 2V4
(403) 253-6800
Emp Here 65   *Sales* 40,903,200
SIC 5511 New and used car dealers

D-U-N-S 24-734-2009   (HQ)
CALGARY STOCKYARDS LTD
THE ELECTRONIC AUCTION MARKET
5925 12 St Se Rm 200, Calgary, AB, T2H 2M3
(403) 234-7429
Emp Here 25   *Sales* 58,707,680
SIC 5154 Livestock
Don Danard
Will Irvine

D-U-N-S 20-074-8796   (HQ)
CANA CONSTRUCTION CO. LTD
(*Suby of* CHIMO CONSTRUCTION LTD)
5720 4 St Se Suite 100, Calgary, AB, T2H 1K7
(403) 255-5521
Sales 87,299,000
SIC 1542 Nonresidential construction, nec
John D. Simpson

D-U-N-S 24-417-3266   (SL)
CANA HIGH VOLTAGE LTD
(*Suby of* CHIMO CONSTRUCTION LTD)
5720 4 St Se Unit 100, Calgary, AB, T2H 1K7
(403) 247-3121
Emp Here 145   *Sales* 25,917,155
SIC 8711 Engineering services
Norbert Klatt
David Bissett

D-U-N-S 24-042-8854   (HQ)
CANA LIMITED
(*Suby of* CHIMO CONSTRUCTION LTD)
5720 4 St Se Suite 100, Calgary, AB, T2H 1K7
(403) 255-5521
Sales 38,474,000
SIC 2421 Sawmills and planing mills, general
John Simpson
Dwayne Dubois

D-U-N-S 24-702-3526   (SL)
CANA PROJECT MANAGEMENT LTD
(*Suby of* CHIMO CONSTRUCTION LTD)
5720 4 St Se Unit 100, Calgary, AB, T2H 1K7
(403) 255-5521
Emp Here 50   *Sales* 13,716,600
SIC 8741 Management services
John Simpson
Roger Boseher

D-U-N-S 20-342-0518   (SL)
CANA SERVICES LTD
(*Suby of* CHIMO CONSTRUCTION LTD)
5720 4 St Se Suite 100, Calgary, AB, T2H 1K7
(403) 255-5521
Emp Here 100
SIC 8741 Management services
John Simpson

D-U-N-S 20-074-2617   (SL)
CANA UTILITIES LTD
(*Suby of* CHIMO CONSTRUCTION LTD)
5720 4 St Se Unit 100, Calgary, AB, T2H 1K7
(403) 255-5521
Emp Here 100   *Sales* 25,244,200
SIC 1623 Water, sewer, and utility lines
John Simpson

D-U-N-S 24-418-0522   (SL)
CANADIAN PARAMEDICAL SERVICES INC
7053 Farrell Rd Se Suite 5, Calgary, AB, T2H 0T3
(403) 259-8399
Emp Here 46   *Sales* 16,616,902
SIC 8049 Offices of health practitioner
Allan Hudye
Drew Parker

D-U-N-S 20-440-5583   (SL)
CARRIAGE HOUSE MOTOR INN LTD
CARRIAGE HOUSE INN
9030 Macleod Trail Se, Calgary, AB, T2H 0M4
(403) 253-1101
Emp Here 200   *Sales* 18,538,000
SIC 7011 Hotels and motels
Alvin Libin
Maurice Paperny

D-U-N-S 24-156-5290   (BR)
CASCADES CANADA ULC
NORAMPAC-CALGARY, DIV OF
(*Suby of* CASCADES INC)
416 58 Ave Se, Calgary, AB, T2H 0P4
(403) 531-3800
Emp Here 160
SIC 2653 Corrugated and solid fiber boxes
Anton Stein

D-U-N-S 25-990-8721   (HQ)
CATHEDRAL ENERGY SERVICES LTD
6030 3 St Se, Calgary, AB, T2H 1K2
(403) 265-2560
Emp Here 35   *Sales* 121,923,270
SIC 1381 Drilling oil and gas wells
P. Scott Macfarlane
Randy Pustanyk
Ian Brown
Rod Maxwell
Scott Sarjeant
Jay Zammit
Dale E. Tremblay
Michael Hill

D-U-N-S 24-442-9619   (SL)
CEDARGLEN GROUP INC, THE
CEDARGLEN HOMES
550 71 Ave Se Suite 140, Calgary, AB, T2H 0S6
(403) 255-2000
Emp Here 75   *Sales* 20,320,650
SIC 1521 Single-family housing construction
Scott Haggins
Bruce Hall

D-U-N-S 24-314-3257   (HQ)
CELERO SOLUTIONS INC
8500 Macleod Trail Se Suite 350n, Calgary, AB, T2H 2N1
(403) 258-5900
Emp Here 100   *Sales* 57,892,800
SIC 8742 Management consulting services
Bob Rezcka
Catherine Boynton
Garth Manness
Glenn Friesen
Glenn Stang
Ian Burns
Keith Nixon

D-U-N-S 24-300-8372   (SL)
CENTCOM CONSTRUCTION LTD
7220 Fisher St Se Suite 310, Calgary, AB, T2H 2H8
(403) 252-5571
Emp Here 30   *Sales* 14,121,930
SIC 1542 Nonresidential construction, nec
Christopher Craig
Nick Unrau
David Jonasson
Edward S Jonasson

D-U-N-S 24-088-5371   (SL)
CENTRE FOR AFFORDABLE WATER AND SANITATION TECHNOLOGY (CAWST)
6020 2 St Se Unit B12, Calgary, AB, T2H 2L8
(403) 243-3285
Emp Here 48   *Sales* 10,887,984
SIC 8399 Social services, nec
Camille Dow Baker

D-U-N-S 25-328-6074   (SL)
CHARIOT CARRIERS INC
5760 9 St Se Unit 105, Calgary, AB, T2H 1Z9
(403) 640-0822
Emp Here 180   *Sales* 125,154,000

SIC 5091 Sporting and recreation goods
Dan Britton
Chris Britton

D-U-N-S 24-318-8104   (SL)
CIMARRON PROJECTS LTD
6025 11 St Se Suite 300, Calgary, AB, T2H 2Z2
(403) 252-3436
Emp Here 150   *Sales* 26,810,850
SIC 8711 Engineering services
Ken Colvin

D-U-N-S 24-035-3560   (HQ)
CLAROCITY CORPORATION
6940 Fisher Rd Se Suite 200, Calgary, AB, T2H 0W3
(403) 984-9246
Emp Here 8   *Sales* 10,381,070
SIC 7374 Data processing and preparation
Shane Copeland
Tom Signorello
Dave Guebert
Jim Boyle
Willem Galle
Walter Andri
Robert Gloer
Nick Tillema

D-U-N-S 24-157-0357   (HQ)
COMMUNITY NATURAL FOODS LTD
6120 1a St Sw, Calgary, AB, T2H 0G3
(403) 252-0011
Emp Here 60   *Sales* 39,455,120
SIC 5499 Miscellaneous food stores
Garry Wilkes
Michael Collens

D-U-N-S 24-313-5279   (BR)
COMMUNITY NATURAL FOODS LTD
(*Suby of* COMMUNITY NATURAL FOODS LTD)
202 61 Ave Sw, Calgary, AB, T2H 0B4
(403) 930-6363
Emp Here 80
SIC 5411 Grocery stores
Liam Muzichuk

D-U-N-S 20-133-1787   (SL)
COMPUTER TRENDS CANADA
5738 Burbank Cres Se, Calgary, AB, T2H 1Z6

Emp Here 1   *Sales* 30,801,450
SIC 5311 Department stores
Christopher Steele

D-U-N-S 20-142-2578   (HQ)
CONVERGINT TECHNOLOGIES LTD
(*Suby of* CONVERGINT TECHNOLOGIES LLC)
6020 11 St Se Suite 2, Calgary, AB, T2H 2L7
(403) 291-3241
Sales 29,134,457
SIC 8711 Engineering services
Dan Moceri
Tony Wang
Ken Lochiatto
Jim Boutwell
Mike Mathes
Sean Flint
Tony Varco
Barry Yatzor
Alan Bergschneider
Leslie Evans

D-U-N-S 25-287-5299   (BR)
COSTCO WHOLESALE CANADA LTD
COSTCO
(*Suby of* COSTCO WHOLESALE CORPO-RATION)
99 Heritage Gate Se, Calgary, AB, T2H 3A7
(403) 313-7650
Emp Here 300
SIC 5099 Durable goods, nec
Heather Downey

D-U-N-S 20-074-9331   (HQ)

COURTESY CHRYSLER DODGE (1987) LTD
(*Suby of* R.P. TAYLOR HOLDINGS LTD)
125 Glendeer Cir Se, Calgary, AB, T2H 2S8
(403) 255-8111
Sales 57,893,760
SIC 5511 New and used car dealers
Richard Taylor
Gail Jones

    D-U-N-S 20-737-6034   (SL)
COURTESY CHRYSLER DODGE JEEP
125 Glendeer Cir Se, Calgary, AB, T2H 2S8
(403) 255-9100
Emp Here 200   *Sales* 127,313,653
SIC 5511 New and used car dealers
Gerald Panasiphuk

    D-U-N-S 20-831-8253   (HQ)
CREDIT UNION CENTRAL ALBERTA LIMITED
ALBERTA CENTRAL
8500 Macleod Trail Se Suite 350n, Calgary, AB, T2H 2N1
(403) 258-5900
Sales 38,942,628
SIC 6062 State credit unions
Ian Burns

    D-U-N-S 24-998-0285   (SL)
D.C.M. MECHANICAL LTD
6335 10 St Se Suite 6, Calgary, AB, T2H 2Z9
(403) 255-9161
Emp Here 80   *Sales* 18,645,200
SIC 1711 Plumbing, heating, air-conditioning
Daniel C. Mchugh

    D-U-N-S 20-075-5635   (SL)
DEVITT & FORAND CONTRACTORS INC
5716 Burbank Cres Se, Calgary, AB, T2H 1Z6
(403) 255-8565
Emp Here 45   *Sales* 21,182,895
SIC 1542 Nonresidential construction, nec
Alphonse Brunette

    D-U-N-S 20-113-5139   (SL)
DMX MUSIC CANADA INC
DMX MUSIC
(*Suby of* MOOD MEDIA ENTERTAINMENT LTD)
7260 12 St Se Suite 120, Calgary, AB, T2H 2S5
(403) 640-8525
Emp Here 32   *Sales* 14,375,008
SIC 7389 Business services, nec
Brad Trumble
John D. Cullen
Paul D. Stone

    D-U-N-S 20-128-8631   (HQ)
EAGLE CANADA, INC
(*Suby of* DAWSON GEOPHYSICAL COMPANY)
6806 Railway St Se, Calgary, AB, T2H 3A8
(403) 781-1192
Emp Here 35   *Sales* 67,267,900
SIC 1382 Oil and gas exploration services
Robert Wood

    D-U-N-S 24-906-8693   (SL)
EMPIRE KITCHEN & BATH LTD
(*Suby of* AKITA INTERNATIONAL LTD)
5539 1 St Se, Calgary, AB, T2H 1H9
(403) 252-2458
Emp Here 40   *Sales* 10,706,080
SIC 5211 Lumber and other building materials
Kevin Mullen

    D-U-N-S 20-910-1489   (HQ)
ENERSUL INC
7210 Blackfoot Trail Se, Calgary, AB, T2H 1M5
(403) 253-5969
Sales 45,443,360
SIC 2819 Industrial inorganic chemicals, nec
Jeffrey Anderson
Marc Proulx

    D-U-N-S 24-807-5251   (HQ)
ENERSUL LIMITED PARTNERSHIP

ENERSUL
7210 Blackfoot Trail Se, Calgary, AB, T2H 1M5
(403) 253-5969
Emp Here 86   *Sales* 80,721,480
SIC 1389 Oil and gas field services, nec
Marc Proulx

    D-U-N-S 24-381-4386   (SL)
FABUTAN CORPORATION
5925 3 St Se, Calgary, AB, T2H 1K3
(403) 640-2100
Emp Here 40   *Sales* 27,872,400
SIC 6794 Patent owners and lessors
Douglas Mcnabb

    D-U-N-S 25-416-8594   (HQ)
FFCA CHARTER SCHOOL SOCIETY
7000 Railway St Se, Calgary, AB, T2H 3A8
(403) 520-3206
Emp Here 35   *Sales* 16,850,230
SIC 8211 Elementary and secondary schools
Jay Pritchard
Bill Mcgregor
Rita Morgan

    D-U-N-S 24-905-4552   (SL)
FIRST IMPRESSIONS SPORTSWEAR & CRESTING INC
6130 4 St Se Unit 7, Calgary, AB, T2H 2B6
(403) 258-3212
Emp Here 30   *Sales* 13,476,570
SIC 7389 Business services, nec
Garth Brookwell

    D-U-N-S 24-674-2324   (SL)
FLAG WORKS INC
FLAGWORKSGROUP
5622 Burleigh Cres Se Unit 1-4, Calgary, AB, T2H 1Z8
(403) 265-5595
Emp Here 30   *Sales* 14,949,660
SIC 5131 Piece goods and notions
Arlene Flock
Shayne Morgan
Marion Hurley

    D-U-N-S 20-382-5245   (SL)
FOOTHILLS INDUSTRIAL PRODUCTS
15-6143 4 St Se, Calgary, AB, T2H 2H9
(403) 255-3250
Emp Here 5   *Sales* 15,529,285
SIC 4925 Gas production and/or distribution

    D-U-N-S 25-329-6784   (HQ)
GALVANIC APPLIED SCIENCES INC
7000 Fisher Rd Se, Calgary, AB, T2H 0W3
(403) 252-8470
Emp Here 50   *Sales* 15,910,230
SIC 3825 Instruments to measure electricity
S. Grant Reeves
Peter C. Bourgeois
Gerrard Abraham
Walter Chayka
Robert Johnston

    D-U-N-S 25-595-5668   (BR)
GAP (CANADA) INC
GAP
(*Suby of* THE GAP INC)
6455 Macleod Trail Sw Suite 151, Calgary, AB, T2H 0K3
(403) 640-1305
Emp Here 150
SIC 5651 Family clothing stores
Glenn Murphy

    D-U-N-S 25-650-6007   (BR)
GAP (CANADA) INC
GAP
(*Suby of* THE GAP INC)
6455 Macleod Trail Sw Suite 210, Calgary, AB, T2H 0K8
(403) 640-1303
Emp Here 75
SIC 5651 Family clothing stores
Cathy Jackson

    D-U-N-S 25-680-4253   (HQ)

GINGER BEEF EXPRESS LTD
(*Suby of* GINGER BEEF CORPORATION)
5521 3 St Se, Calgary, AB, T2H 1K1
(403) 272-8088
Emp Here 5   *Sales* 11,242,750
SIC 2032 Canned specialties
Stanley Leung
Ted Yan

    D-U-N-S 20-234-3195   (HQ)
GLASSMASTERS AUTOGLASS LTD
6221 Centre St Sw, Calgary, AB, T2H 0C7
(403) 692-0934
Emp Here 10   *Sales* 11,179,350
SIC 5031 Lumber, plywood, and millwork
Miles Palmer

    D-U-N-S 25-313-8739   (SL)
GREAT EVENTS CATERING INC
7207 Fairmount Dr Se, Calgary, AB, T2H 0X6
(403) 256-7150
Emp Here 250   *Sales* 11,659,750
SIC 5812 Eating places
Ulrich Kuenz
Monika Kuenz

    D-U-N-S 25-386-6552   (HQ)
GREAT WEST KENWORTH LTD
5909 6 St Se, Calgary, AB, T2H 1L8
(403) 253-7555
Emp Here 95   *Sales* 122,709,600
SIC 5511 New and used car dealers
John Jeffrey (Jeff) Storwick
Paul Storwick

    D-U-N-S 24-339-8778   (BR)
GREGG DISTRIBUTORS LIMITED PARTNERSHIP
(*Suby of* GREGG DISTRIBUTORS LIMITED PARTNERSHIP)
5755 11 St Se, Calgary, AB, T2H 1M7
(403) 253-6463
Emp Here 110
SIC 5085 Industrial supplies
Perry Mccormack

    D-U-N-S 24-099-3217   (BR)
GROUPE DE SECURITE GARDA INC, LE
(*Suby of* GROUPE DE SECURITE GARDA INC, LE)
8989 Macleod Trail Sw Suite 118, Calgary, AB, T2H 0M2
(403) 517-5899
Emp Here 510
SIC 7381 Detective and armored car services
Michael Brown

    D-U-N-S 24-552-7478   (SL)
HI-TECH BEAUTY SUPPLIES LTD
5718 Burbank Cres Se, Calgary, AB, T2H 1Z6
(403) 253-3113
Emp Here 25   *Sales* 11,875,650
SIC 5087 Service establishment equipment
Mike Khalil

    D-U-N-S 24-087-6628   (HQ)
HOME-RAIL (CALGARY) LTD
5520 4 St Se, Calgary, AB, T2H 1K7
(403) 202-5493
Sales 10,003,390
SIC 5051 Metals service centers and offices
Cheryll Fawcett
Leanne Joncas

    D-U-N-S 24-119-2012   (SL)
HOMES BY AVI (CALGARY) INC
(*Suby of* SILVER DAWN HOLDINGS LTD)
245 Forge Rd Se, Calgary, AB, T2H 0S9
(403) 536-7000
Emp Here 220   *Sales* 102,030,720
SIC 1521 Single-family housing construction
Pavel Amir
Rachel Amir
Sharron Ungar
Alice Mateyko
Darren Soltes
Einat Soltes

Vered Amir
Lamont Kendall

    D-U-N-S 24-379-0131   (HQ)
HOMES BY AVI (CANADA) INC
RENOVATIONS BY AVI
(*Suby of* SILVER DAWN HOLDINGS LTD)
245 Forge Rd Se, Calgary, AB, T2H 0S9
(403) 536-7000
Emp Here 150   *Sales* 17,939,200
SIC 7514 Passenger car rental
Avi Amir
Rachel Amir
Vered Amir
Einat Soltes
Charron Ungar

    D-U-N-S 25-616-6828   (BR)
HUDSON'S BAY COMPANY
BAY, THE
(*Suby of* HUDSON'S BAY COMPANY)
6455 Macleod Trail Sw, Calgary, AB, T2H 0K8
(403) 255-6121
Emp Here 250
SIC 5311 Department stores
Fred Amen

    D-U-N-S 24-731-3174   (HQ)
HYATT AUTO SALES & LEASING INC
HYATT GROUP
161 Glendeer Cir Se, Calgary, AB, T2H 2S8
(403) 252-8833
Sales 49,083,840
SIC 5511 New and used car dealers

    D-U-N-S 24-674-0732   (BR)
IMPRIMERIES TRANSCONTINENTAL INC
TRANSCONTINENTAL PRINTING INC
(*Suby of* TRANSCONTINENTAL INC)
5516 5 St Se, Calgary, AB, T2H 1L3
(403) 258-3788
Emp Here 420
SIC 2752 Commercial printing, lithographic
Tim Smith

    D-U-N-S 20-304-0258   (HQ)
IMT STANDEN'S LIMITED PARTNERSHIP
(*Suby of* IMT CORPORATION)
1222 58 Ave Se, Calgary, AB, T2H 2E9
(403) 258-7800
Emp Here 475   *Sales* 121,615,500
SIC 3493 Steel springs, except wire
Mel Svendson
Dean Davenport
Paul Takalo

    D-U-N-S 24-071-2203   (HQ)
INSIGHTS LEARNING & DEVELOPMENT LTD
5824 2 St Sw Suite 302, Calgary, AB, T2H 0H2
(403) 233-7263
Emp Here 5   *Sales* 11,714,400
SIC 8748 Business consulting, nec
Andrew Lothian

    D-U-N-S 25-133-8349   (SL)
INTEGRAL PROPERTY SERVICES LTD
343 Forge Rd Se Suite 9, Calgary, AB, T2H 0S9
(403) 296-2206
Emp Here 200   *Sales* 6,393,600
SIC 7349 Building maintenance services, nec
Scott Drews

    D-U-N-S 25-518-6934   (BR)
JBS CANADA INC
XL FOODS
(*Suby of* TYSON FOODS, INC.)
5101 11 St Se, Calgary, AB, T2H 1M7

Emp Here 160
SIC 2011 Meat packing plants
Kevin Grimshire

    D-U-N-S 20-127-1134   (SL)
JCB INDUSTRIAL INC
6031 4 St Se, Calgary, AB, T2H 2A5

(587) 349-1071
Emp Here 43   *Sales* 10,585,998
SIC 1796 Installing building equipment

D-U-N-S 24-041-4693   (SL)
KANAS HOLDINGS CORPORATION
KANAS
5312 3 St Se, Calgary, AB, T2H 1J8
(403) 283-2566
Emp Here 20   *Sales* 20,006,780
SIC 5051 Metals service centers and offices
 Rob Sipka

D-U-N-S 25-521-7044   (BR)
KEG RESTAURANTS LTD
KEG STEAKHOUSE & BAR, THE
(*Suby of* RECIPE UNLIMITED CORPORA-
TION)
7104 Macleod Trail Se, Calgary, AB, T2H 0L3
(403) 253-2534
Emp Here 103
SIC 5812 Eating places
 Piraux Chuck

D-U-N-S 20-555-6918   (HQ)
**KVAERNER PROCESS SYSTEMS CANADA
INC**
1209 59 Ave Se Suite 100, Calgary, AB, T2H
2P6
(403) 640-4230
Emp Here 60   *Sales* 20,570,600
SIC 4213 Trucking, except local
 Stewart Mulvey
 Stjern Egil
 Harold Kongelf
 Odd Olsen

D-U-N-S 20-027-4228   (SL)
L'ARCHE ASSOCIATION OF CALGARY
307 57 Ave Sw, Calgary, AB, T2H 2T6
(403) 571-0155
Emp Here 45   *Sales* 17,883,630
SIC 8699 Membership organizations, nec
 Peggy Loescher

D-U-N-S 20-580-5773   (SL)
LINEAR LOGISTICS LTD
7015 Macleod Trail Sw Unit 603, Calgary, AB,
T2H 2K6
(587) 353-5454
Emp Here 14   *Sales* 11,289,550
SIC 4213 Trucking, except local
 Dean Duffin
 Andrew Wheatley

D-U-N-S 24-345-9161   (HQ)
LONE STAR INC
LONE STAR MERCEDES-BENZ
10 Heritage Meadows Rd Se, Calgary, AB,
T2H 3C1
(403) 253-1333
Emp Here 1   *Sales* 78,660,000
SIC 5511 New and used car dealers
 Fleming Wong
 Wayne Desrosiers
 David Choi

D-U-N-S 24-879-5072   (HQ)
LPI COMMUNICATIONS GROUP INC
LPI GROUP
253 62 Ave Se Suite 101, Calgary, AB, T2H
0R5
(403) 735-0655
Emp Here 40   *Sales* 11,714,400
SIC 8743 Public relations services
 Craig Lindsay
 Stean Smith
 Darryl Smith
 Ray Smith

D-U-N-S 24-359-9250   (HQ)
MACLEAN HOLDINGS LTD
7220 Fisher St Se, Calgary, AB, T2H 2H8
(403) 640-7400
Sales 16,998,000
SIC 7538 General automotive repair shops
 Gerry Wood

D-U-N-S 20-076-8414   (SL)

MACLIN MOTORS LIMITED
MACLIN FORD
135 Glendeer Cir Se, Calgary, AB, T2H 2S8
(403) 252-0101
Emp Here 62   *Sales* 39,015,360
SIC 5511 New and used car dealers
 Shelley Mccullough

D-U-N-S 24-012-5070   (HQ)
MARK'S WORK WEARHOUSE LTD
L'EQUIPEUR
(*Suby of* CANADIAN TIRE CORPORATION,
LIMITED)
1035 64 Ave Se Suite 30, Calgary, AB, T2H
2J7
(403) 255-9220
Emp Here 382   *Sales* 3,768,898,500
SIC 5136 Men's and boy's clothing
 Stephen Wetmore
 Michael Strachan
 Karen Bentley
 Eleni Damianakis
 Candace Maclean
 Debbie Champion
 Harry Taylor

D-U-N-S 20-816-2011   (SL)
**MASTER MECHANICAL PLUMBING &
HEATING LTD**
6025 12 St Se Suite 19, Calgary, AB, T2H 2K1
(403) 243-5880
Emp Here 50   *Sales* 11,046,700
SIC 1711 Plumbing, heating, air-conditioning
 Deana Hubert

D-U-N-S 24-158-3319   (HQ)
MAVERICK LAND CONSULTANTS LTD
(*Suby of* HMA LAND SERVICES LTD.)
6940 Fisher Rd Se Suite 310, Calgary, AB,
T2H 0W3
(403) 243-7833
Emp Here 29   *Sales* 12,788,200
SIC 1389 Oil and gas field services, nec
 Brent Davidson

D-U-N-S 20-824-6074   (HQ)
MCCRUM'S DIRECT SALES LTD
MCCRUM'S OFFICE FURNISHINGS
(*Suby of* MCCRUM'S GROUP INC)
5310 1 St Sw, Calgary, AB, T2H 0C8
(403) 259-4939
Sales 23,240,300
SIC 5712 Furniture stores
 Ryan Mcmillan
 Bob Malone
 Norm Asuchak

D-U-N-S 20-439-5917   (SL)
MCKAY PONTIAC BUICK (1979) LTD
MCKAY PONTIAC BUICK GMC
7711 Macleod Trail Sw, Calgary, AB, T2H 0M1
(403) 243-0109
Emp Here 70   *Sales* 44,049,600
SIC 5511 New and used car dealers
 Bob Mckay
 Shauna Thomson

D-U-N-S 20-260-0644   (BR)
**MCMAN YOUTH, FAMILY AND COMMUNITY
SERVICES ASSOCIATION**
(*Suby of* MCMAN YOUTH, FAMILY AND
COMMUNITY SERVICES ASSOCIATION)
6712 Fisher St Se Unit 80, Calgary, AB, T2H
2A7
(403) 508-7742
Emp Here 75
SIC 8641 Civic and social associations
 Paula Telfer

D-U-N-S 24-382-0714   (HQ)
MEI MILLER ENTERPRISES INC
7523 Flint Rd Se, Calgary, AB, T2H 1G3

Sales 24,226,326
SIC 5085 Industrial supplies
 Mike Miller

D-U-N-S 20-139-7226   (SL)

MERLIN PLASTICS ALBERTA INC
616 58 Ave Se, Calgary, AB, T2H 0P8
(403) 259-6637
Emp Here 40   *Sales* 10,285,240
SIC 4953 Refuse systems
 Tony Moucachen
 Joyce Kneeland

D-U-N-S 20-826-0794   (HQ)
METROPOLITAN CALGARY FOUNDATION
MCF HOUSING FOR SENIORS
7015 Macleod Trail Sw Suite 804, Calgary, AB,
T2H 2K6
(403) 276-5541
Emp Here 12   *Sales* 16,070,500
SIC 8361 Residential care
 Lauren Ingalls

D-U-N-S 20-232-4104   (BR)
MORRISON HERSHFIELD LIMITED
(*Suby of* MORRISON HERSHFIELD GROUP
INC)
6807 Railway St Se Suite 300, Calgary, AB,
T2H 2V6
(403) 246-4500
Emp Here 100
SIC 8711 Engineering services
 Dwayne Johnston

D-U-N-S 20-075-6638   (HQ)
MR IMAGING CORP
CANADA DIAGNOSTICS CENTRES
5920 1a St Sw Unit 301, Calgary, AB, T2H
0G3
(403) 253-4666
Emp Here 30   *Sales* 41,238,720
SIC 8099 Health and allied services, nec
 Lorne Paperny
 Leanne Brinton
 Gayle Burnett
 Robert Davies

D-U-N-S 24-588-7310   (HQ)
NEC CANADA, INC.
(*Suby of* NEC CORPORATION)
7260 12 St Se Unit 110, Calgary, AB, T2H 2S5
(403) 640-6400
Emp Here 13   *Sales* 17,886,960
SIC 5065 Electronic parts and equipment, nec
 Sophie Veilleux

D-U-N-S 20-292-7687   (SL)
**NEW AGE MARKETING & BRAND MAN-
AGEMENT INC**
7210h 5 St Se, Calgary, AB, T2H 2L9
(403) 212-1055
Emp Here 25   *Sales* 20,889,425
SIC 5149 Groceries and related products, nec
 Frank Gallucci
 Marco Blouin
 Kenneth Kwong
 Alexander Fossella

D-U-N-S 24-367-8161   (HQ)
NEWSWEST INC
5716 Burbank Rd Se, Calgary, AB, T2H 1Z4
(403) 253-8856
Emp Here 50   *Sales* 117,831,800
SIC 5192 Books, periodicals, and newspapers
 Daniel Shapiro
 David Whelan
 Robert Campbell

D-U-N-S 20-276-4825   (BR)
NORDSTROM CANADA RETAIL, INC
NORDSTROM CHINOOK CENTRE
(*Suby of* NORDSTROM, INC.)
6455 Macleod Trail Sw, Calgary, AB, T2H 0K8
(780) 291-2000
Emp Here 80
SIC 5311 Department stores
 Alysia Wheeler

D-U-N-S 20-994-3906   (BR)
**NORTHLAND PROPERTIES CORPORA-
TION**
*SANDMAN HOTEL & SUITES CALGARY
SOUTH*

(*Suby of* NORTHLAND PROPERTIES COR-
PORATION)
8001 11 St Se, Calgary, AB, T2H 0B8
(403) 252-7263
Emp Here 80
SIC 7011 Hotels and motels
 Bill Gaglardi

D-U-N-S 20-123-0930   (HQ)
**NORTHVIEW APARTMENT REAL ESTATE
INVESTMENT TRUST**
6131 6 St Se Suite 200, Calgary, AB, T2H 1L9
(403) 531-0720
Emp Here 50   *Sales* 275,924,869
SIC 6722 Management investment, open-end
 Todd Cook
 Richard Anda
 Lizaine Wheeler
 Bo Rasmussen
 Travis Beatty
 Leslie Veiner
 Scott Thon
 Daniel Drimmer
 Kevin Grayston
 Dennis Hoffman

D-U-N-S 20-077-3018   (HQ)
NORWESCO INDUSTRIES (1983) LTD
6908 6 St Se Bay Suite L, Calgary, AB, T2H
2K4
(403) 258-3883
Emp Here 42   *Sales* 31,339,080
SIC 3492 Fluid power valves and hose fittings
 Rodney Milton
 Nordert Shuh
 Steve Froder
 Dirk Visser
 Grace Schoorl
 Murray Brunt
 Pat Boyko

D-U-N-S 20-252-0920   (HQ)
NPR LIMITED PARTNERSHIP
NORTHVIEW APARTMENT REIT
6131 6 St Se Suite 200, Calgary, AB, T2H 1L9
(403) 531-0720
Sales 202,838,400
SIC 6531 Real estate agents and managers
 Todd Cook
 Leslie Veiner
 Travis Beatty

D-U-N-S 20-267-9986   (BR)
OTIS CANADA, INC
OTIS ELEVATORS
(*Suby of* UNITED TECHNOLOGIES CORPO-
RATION)
777 64 Ave Se Suite 7, Calgary, AB, T2H 2C3
(403) 244-1040
Emp Here 170
SIC 7699 Repair services, nec
 Darren Riley

D-U-N-S 25-533-4278   (SL)
OUTLAWS GROUP INC
OUTLAWS NIGHTCLUB
7400 Macleod Trail Se Suite 24, Calgary, AB,
T2H 0L9
(403) 255-4646
Emp Here 100   *Sales* 4,551,900
SIC 5813 Drinking places
 Trevor Tomanik

D-U-N-S 24-000-4791   (BR)
PALADIN TECHNOLOGIES INC
PALADIN SECURITY
(*Suby of* PALADIN TECHNOLOGIES INC)
6455 Macleod Trail Sw Unit 701, Calgary, AB,
T2H 0K9
(403) 508-1888
Emp Here 100
SIC 7381 Detective and armored car services
 Jason Begin

D-U-N-S 24-086-8596   (SL)
PASON SYSTEMS CORP
(*Suby of* PASON SYSTEMS INC)

6130 3 St Se, Calgary, AB, T2H 1K4
(403) 301-3400
Emp Here 180   *Sales* 34,279,560
SIC 3699 Electrical equipment and supplies, nec
James Hill
Harold Allsopp

D-U-N-S 25-388-6444   (HQ)
PASON SYSTEMS INC
6130 3 St Se, Calgary, AB, T2H 1K4
(403) 301-3400
Sales 232,277,146
SIC 1389 Oil and gas field services, nec
Marcel Kessler
Kevin Boston
Russell Smith
Kevin Lo
Lars Olesen
Ryan Van Beurden
Bryce Mclean
Jon Faber
James Hill
James Howe

D-U-N-S 20-232-4047   (SL)
PERFORMANCE DRIVER SERVICES INC
5925 12 St Se Suite 220, Calgary, AB, T2H 2M3

Emp Here 94   *Sales* 14,604,874
SIC 7361 Employment agencies
Rob Harrison

D-U-N-S 24-495-4173   (SL)
PORSCHE CENTRE CALGARY
5512 Macleod Trail Sw, Calgary, AB, T2H 0J5
(403) 243-8101
Emp Here 40   *Sales* 19,923,120
SIC 5511 New and used car dealers
Craig Stostrak

D-U-N-S 24-157-0217   (SL)
PRECISION MOTORS LTD
PRECISION HYUNDAI
130 Glendeer Cir Se, Calgary, AB, T2H 2V4
(403) 243-8344
Emp Here 30   *Sales* 14,942,340
SIC 5511 New and used car dealers
John W Robinson

D-U-N-S 20-522-0762   (SL)
QUALICO DEVELOPMENTS CALGARY LTD
(*Suby of* QUALICO GROUP LTD)
5709 2 St Se Suite 200, Calgary, AB, T2H 2W4
(403) 253-3311
Emp Here 400   *Sales* 185,510,400
SIC 1521 Single-family housing construction
Richard Hendry

D-U-N-S 25-677-2229   (HQ)
QUALICO DEVELOPMENTS WEST LTD
(*Suby of* QUALICO GROUP LTD)
5716 1 St Se Unit 100, Calgary, AB, T2H 1H8
(403) 253-3311
Sales 12,653,760
SIC 6553 Cemetery subdividers and developers
E. Ruth Hastings
Brian Hastings

D-U-N-S 25-590-0730   (SL)
QUORUM INFORMATION SYSTEMS INC
(*Suby of* QUORUM INFORMATION TECHNOLOGIES INC)
7500 Macleod Trail Se Suite 200, Calgary, AB, T2H 0L9
(403) 777-0036
Emp Here 95
SIC 7371 Custom computer programming services
Maury Marks

D-U-N-S 20-105-2441   (HQ)
QUORUM INFORMATION TECHNOLOGIES INC
7500 Macleod Trail Se Suite 200, Calgary, AB,

T2H 0L9
(403) 777-0036
Emp Here 45   *Sales* 12,463,709
SIC 7371 Custom computer programming services
Maury Marks
Mark Allen
Dan Ichelson
Michael Podovilnikoff
Rick Johnston
Mick Podovilnikoff
Joe Campbell
John Carmichael
Scot Eisenfelder
Jon Hook

D-U-N-S 25-206-9240   (HQ)
RAWLCO CAPITAL LTD
6807 Railway St Se Suite 140, Calgary, AB, T2H 2V6
(403) 451-9893
Emp Here 1   *Sales* 14,783,840
SIC 4832 Radio broadcasting stations
Gordon Rawlinson

D-U-N-S 25-452-2527   (BR)
RED LOBSTER HOSPITALITY LLC
RED LOBSTER RESTAURANTS
6100 Macleod Trail Sw Suite 100, Calgary, AB, T2H 0K5
(403) 252-8818
Emp Here 100
SIC 5812 Eating places

D-U-N-S 25-261-6560   (HQ)
REGAL BUILDING MATERIALS LTD
7131 6 St Se Suite D, Calgary, AB, T2H 2M8
(403) 253-2010
Sales 18,735,640
SIC 5211 Lumber and other building materials
Roger Cundy
Barry Hanna
Bonnie Dolan
Howard Zerr

D-U-N-S 24-583-3509   (SL)
RESMAN MANAGEMENT LIMITED
1209 59 Ave Se Suite 245, Calgary, AB, T2H 2P6
(403) 259-8826
Emp Here 49   *Sales* 13,881,357
SIC 8741 Management services
Ed Lazewoski

D-U-N-S 24-494-7867   (SL)
RINAX SYSTEMS LTD
RINAX COMPUTER SYSTEMS
5542 1a St Sw, Calgary, AB, T2H 0E7
(403) 243-4074
Emp Here 25   *Sales* 11,179,350
SIC 5045 Computers, peripherals, and software
Gregory Ford

D-U-N-S 20-897-9849   (HQ)
ROBYN'S TRANSPORTATION & DISTRIBUTION SERVICES LTD
6404 Burbank Rd Se, Calgary, AB, T2H 2C2
(403) 292-9260
Emp Here 131
SIC 4213 Trucking, except local
David Donaldson
Robyn Jackson

D-U-N-S 20-440-2903   (HQ)
ROLLING MIX MANAGEMENT LTD
ROLLING MIX CONCRETE
7209 Railway St Se, Calgary, AB, T2H 2V6
(403) 253-6426
Sales 16,340,450
SIC 3273 Ready-mixed concrete
Guido Distefano
Tony Distefano
Rick Distefano

D-U-N-S 25-217-5906   (HQ)
ROOFMART ALBERTA INC
6125 11 St Se Suite 250, Calgary, AB, T2H

2L6
(403) 233-8030
Emp Here 10   *Sales* 26,830,440
SIC 5033 Roofing, siding, and insulation
Robert Foley

D-U-N-S 25-621-2002   (HQ)
ROOFMART PACIFIC LTD
6125 11 St Se Suite 250, Calgary, AB, T2H 2L6
(403) 233-8030
Emp Here 1   *Sales* 12,968,046
SIC 5033 Roofing, siding, and insulation
Bob Foley

D-U-N-S 20-841-8194   (HQ)
ROOFMART WESTERN LTD
6125 11 St Se Suite 250, Calgary, AB, T2H 2L6
(403) 233-8030
Emp Here 1   *Sales* 11,179,350
SIC 5033 Roofing, siding, and insulation
David Lavin
A D Mcintosh
Morris Schumacker
Robert Foley

D-U-N-S 20-522-3480   (SL)
RUSSELL FOOD EQUIPMENT (CALGARY) LIMITED
5707 4 St Se, Calgary, AB, T2H 1K8
(403) 253-1383
Emp Here 25   *Sales* 11,179,350
SIC 5046 Commercial equipment, nec
Donald K Russell
David Russell

D-U-N-S 24-439-3104   (SL)
SCOT YOUNG (WESTERN) LIMITED
413 Forge Rd Se, Calgary, AB, T2H 0S9
(403) 259-2293
Emp Here 200   *Sales* 6,393,600
SIC 7349 Building maintenance services, nec
Robert Young
Agnes Young
Karen Meek

D-U-N-S 24-438-5316   (SL)
SEISLAND SURVEYS LTD
7235 Flint Rd Se, Calgary, AB, T2H 1G2
(403) 255-2770
Emp Here 75   *Sales* 13,196,850
SIC 8713 Surveying services
Garvin Geck

D-U-N-S 24-519-0723   (HQ)
SERENA FASHIONS (ALBERTA) LTD
BELLISSIMA
6737 Fairmount Dr Se Suite 60, Calgary, AB, T2H 0X6
(403) 255-1551
Emp Here 16   *Sales* 19,015,976
SIC 5621 Women's clothing stores
Viviana Shaneman
River Kwei
Serena Kwei
Roger Shaneman

D-U-N-S 24-785-3435   (HQ)
SHAMROCK FLOORING ACCESSORIES LTD
7510 5 St Se Unit D, Calgary, AB, T2H 2L9
(403) 253-5330
Emp Here 12   *Sales* 14,756,824
SIC 5023 Homefurnishings
Grant Medhurst
Randy Duchanan
Trudy Duchanan

D-U-N-S 25-519-5505   (HQ)
SHAWN & ASSOCIATES MANAGEMENT LTD
EDON MANAGEMENT
(*Suby of* EDON PROPERTIES INC)
1209 59 Ave Se Suite 100, Calgary, AB, T2H 2P6
(403) 255-5017
Sales 18,716,400

SIC 8741 Management services
Edward (Ed) Lazdowski

D-U-N-S 20-232-5689   (SL)
SHOOTING EDGE INC, THE
SHOOTING EDGE
510 77 Ave Se Suite 4, Calgary, AB, T2H 1C3
(403) 720-4867
Emp Here 56   *Sales* 13,682,368
SIC 5941 Sporting goods and bicycle shops
James (Jr) Cox

D-U-N-S 24-673-4438   (SL)
SILVERHILL MOTORS LTD
SILVERHILL ACURA
(*Suby of* CARTRADAN HOLDINGS LTD)
5728 Macleod Trail Sw, Calgary, AB, T2H 0J6
(403) 253-6060
Emp Here 65   *Sales* 40,903,200
SIC 5511 New and used car dealers
Marilyn Sheftel
Kent R. Alfaro

D-U-N-S 24-723-7212   (SL)
SMART DESIGN & DEVELOPMENT
7130 Fisher Rd Se Suite 10, Calgary, AB, T2H 0W3

Emp Here 35   *Sales* 11,160,415
SIC 1521 Single-family housing construction
Ron Patrick

D-U-N-S 20-116-9245   (SL)
SOUTH ALBERTA RIBS (2002) LTD
TONY ROMA'S
6712 Macleod Trail Se, Calgary, AB, T2H 0L3
(403) 301-7427
Emp Here 95   *Sales* 4,072,935
SIC 5812 Eating places
Henri Cynamon
Abe Goldstein

D-U-N-S 25-124-6773   (SL)
SOUTHLAND CANADA STORE
6015 4 St Se, Calgary, AB, T2H 2A5
(403) 253-6218
Emp Here 49   *Sales* 13,433,448
SIC 5411 Grocery stores
Matthew Ajan

D-U-N-S 24-122-8303   (SL)
SOVEREIGN GENERAL INSURANCE COMPANY, THE
6700 Macleod Trail Se Suite 140, Calgary, AB, T2H 0L3

Emp Here 65   *Sales* 151,494,563
SIC 6331 Fire, marine, and casualty insurance

D-U-N-S 24-342-7510   (HQ)
SOVEREIGN GENERAL INSURANCE COMPANY, THE
(*Suby of* CO-OPERATORS GENERAL INSURANCE COMPANY)
6700 Macleod Trail Se Unit 140, Calgary, AB, T2H 0L3
(403) 298-4200
Emp Here 75   *Sales* 1,281,448,080
SIC 6411 Insurance agents, brokers, and service
Rob Wesseling
Rod F. Bresciani
Herb Cline

D-U-N-S 25-389-3275   (SL)
STANDEN'S MANAGEMENT INC
1222 58 Ave Se, Calgary, AB, T2H 2E9
(403) 258-7800
Emp Here 501   *Sales* 145,715,850
SIC 3714 Motor vehicle parts and accessories
Melvin Svendsen
Gerald C Lockey

D-U-N-S 24-702-8673   (HQ)
STERLING HOMES LTD
PACESETTER HOMES
(*Suby of* QUALICO GROUP LTD)
5709 2 St Se Suite 200, Calgary, AB, T2H

2W4
(403) 253-7476
Sales 27,094,200
SIC 1522 Residential construction, nec
 Bill Bobyk

D-U-N-S 25-776-9844   (BR)
SUNCO DRYWALL LTD
7835 Flint Rd Se, Calgary, AB, T2H 1G3
(403) 250-9701
Emp Here 80
SIC 1742 Plastering, drywall, and insulation
 Chad Bigham

D-U-N-S 20-825-1892   (HQ)
SWIMCO AQUATIC SUPPLIES LTD
SWIMCO FOR SWIMWEAR
6403 Burbank Rd Se Suite 1, Calgary, AB,
T2H 2E1
(403) 259-6113
Emp Here 45   *Sales* 31,188,750
SIC 5699 Miscellaneous apparel and acces-
sory stores
 Lori Bacon
 Steve Forseth
 David Bacon

D-U-N-S 24-680-5795   (HQ)
TARGET EMISSION SERVICES INC
1235 64 Ave Se Suite 12 B, Calgary, AB, T2H
2J7
(403) 225-8755
Sales 127,425,600
SIC 1799 Special trade contractors, nec
 Terrance Trefiak
 Dan Bulat

D-U-N-S 25-406-4785   (HQ)
THURBER ENGINEERING LTD
7330 Fisher St Se Suite 180, Calgary, AB, T2H
2H8
(403) 253-9217
Emp Here 100   *Sales* 35,569,061
SIC 8741 Engineering services
 P.K. Chattergi
 Stephen Bean

D-U-N-S 20-771-6908   (SL)
TIM HORTONS
5a Heritage Gate Se, Calgary, AB, T2H 3A7
(403) 692-6629
Emp Here 60   *Sales* 17,608,620
SIC 5461 Retail bakeries
 James Kowbel

D-U-N-S 20-343-2075   (HQ)
TORNADO GLOBAL HYDROVACS LTD
7015 Macleod Trail Sw Suite 510, Calgary, AB,
T2H 2K6
(403) 204-6363
Emp Here 6   *Sales* 23,332,729
SIC 3531 Construction machinery
 William Rollins
 George Tai
 Connie Ping
 K. Guy Nelson
 James Chui
 Darrick Evong

D-U-N-S 20-377-0099   (SL)
TRAIL APPLIANCES HOLDINGS LTD
TRAIL APPLIANCES
6880 11 St Se, Calgary, AB, T2H 2T9
(403) 253-5442
Emp Here 495   *Sales* 132,017,985
SIC 5722 Household appliance stores
 Paul Broderick
 Gerry Muth

D-U-N-S 20-354-5892   (BR)
TRAIL APPLIANCES LTD
(*Suby of* TRAIL APPLIANCES LTD)
6880 11 St Se, Calgary, AB, T2H 2T9
(403) 253-5442
Emp Here 375
SIC 5722 Household appliance stores
 John Broderick Iii

D-U-N-S 20-397-4092   (HQ)
TRAIL APPLIANCES LTD
6880 11 St Se, Calgary, AB, T2H 2T9
(403) 253-5442
Emp Here 1   *Sales* 132,017,985
SIC 5722 Household appliance stores
 Paul Broderick Jr

D-U-N-S 24-309-8089   (HQ)
TRIPLE FLIP INC
6120 11 St Se Unit 7, Calgary, AB, T2H 2L7
(403) 769-3547
Emp Here 125   *Sales* 22,424,500
SIC 5621 Women's clothing stores
 Linda Maslechko

D-U-N-S 25-372-3043   (SL)
**TROTTER & MORTON FACILITY SERVICES
INC**
(*Suby of* TROTTER AND MORTON LIMITED)
5711 1 St Se, Calgary, AB, T2H 1H9
(403) 255-7535
Emp Here 50   *Sales* 11,653,250
SIC 1711 Plumbing, heating, air-conditioning
 Mike Ryan
 Mike Watson

D-U-N-S 24-854-4520   (HQ)
**TROTTER AND MORTON BUILDING TECH-
NOLOGIES INC**
(*Suby of* TROTTER AND MORTON LIMITED)
5711 1 St Se, Calgary, AB, T2H 1H9
(403) 255-7535
Emp Here 345   *Sales* 338,560,000
SIC 1711 Plumbing, heating, air-conditioning
 Jim Baskerville

D-U-N-S 20-078-4742   (HQ)
TROTTER AND MORTON LIMITED
5711 1 St Se, Calgary, AB, T2H 1H9
(403) 255-7535
Emp Here 40   *Sales* 129,033,450
SIC 8741 Management services
 Michael Watson
 Steven Salt
 John Paul Ryan
 Jane Ryan
 Dave Ryan

D-U-N-S 24-346-1618   (SL)
TRUE NORTH AUTOMATION INC
TRUE NORTH SOLUTIONS
7180 11 St Se, Calgary, AB, T2H 2S9
(403) 984-2000
Emp Here 71   *Sales* 16,634,448
SIC 8742 Management consulting services
 Blair Hanel
 Gordon Gibson

D-U-N-S 24-337-9992   (BR)
**TYCO INTEGRATED FIRE & SECURITY
CANADA, INC**
SIMPLEXGRINNELL
(*Suby of* JOHNSON CONTROLS INTERNA-
TIONAL PUBLIC LIMITED COMPANY)
401 Forge Rd Se, Calgary, AB, T2H 0S9

Emp Here 150
SIC 8748 Business consulting, nec

D-U-N-S 24-000-4452   (BR)
UAP INC
NAPA AUTOPARTS DIV OF
(*Suby of* GENUINE PARTS COMPANY)
5530 3 St Se Suite 489, Calgary, AB, T2H 1J9
(403) 212-4600
Emp Here 80
SIC 5013 Motor vehicle supplies and new
parts
 Steve Wurastic

D-U-N-S 24-967-6404   (HQ)
UNIFIED SYSTEMS GROUP INC
1235 64 Ave Se Unit 4a, Calgary, AB, T2H 2J7
(403) 240-2280
Emp Here 13   *Sales* 21,347,242
SIC 1731 Electrical work

 Edward Taaffe
 Glenn Boyd
 George Tamminen
 Kevin Briscoe
 Sean Pridmore

D-U-N-S 24-598-0685   (SL)
**UNITECH ELECTRICAL CONTRACTING
INC**
700 58 Ave Se Suite 11, Calgary, AB, T2H 2E2
(403) 255-2277
Emp Here 120   *Sales* 26,139,480
SIC 1731 Electrical work
 Keith Brooke
 Charles Pollhaus

D-U-N-S 24-715-6490   (HQ)
UNITED LIBRARY SERVICES INC
7140 Fairmount Dr Se, Calgary, AB, T2H 0X4
(403) 252-4426
Emp Here 1   *Sales* 59,401,600
SIC 5192 Books, periodicals, and newspapers
 Maurice Paperny
 Daniel Shapiro
 Robert Campbell
 Lorne Paperny

D-U-N-S 20-378-0697   (SL)
VIIZ COMMUNICATIONS CANADA INC
(*Suby of* WIMACTEL CANADA INC)
6420 6a St Se Unit 200, Calgary, AB, T2H 2B7
(403) 476-9400
Emp Here 100   *Sales* 22,847,200
SIC 4899 Communication services, nec
 James Mackenzie
 John Wilson
 Trevor Oseen
 Gail Strickland

D-U-N-S 20-075-5668   (HQ)
VOLKER STEVIN CONTRACTING LTD
(*Suby of* KONINKLIJKE VOLKERWESSELS
N.V.)
7175 12 St Se Suite 7175, Calgary, AB, T2H
2S6
(403) 571-5800
Sales 229,680,500
SIC 1611 Highway and street construction
 Kern Briscoe
 Fred Desjarlais
 Mike Festa
 Greg Hooper
 Jase Vanover

D-U-N-S 20-463-8709   (SL)
**WALKERS OWN PRODUCE INTERNA-
TIONAL INC**
THE MARKET ON MACLEOD
7711 Macleod Trail Sw, Calgary, AB, T2H 0M1
(587) 583-8050
Emp Here 48   *Sales* 13,159,296
SIC 5431 Fruit and vegetable markets

D-U-N-S 20-120-7649   (HQ)
**WEICHERT   WORKFORCE   MOBILITY
CANADA ULC**
(*Suby of* WEICHERT WORKFORCE MOBIL-
ITY HOLDINGS INC)
6700 Macleod Trail Se Suite 210, Calgary, AB,
T2H 0L3
(888) 588-6664
Sales 15,722,665
SIC 7389 Business services, nec
 Debbie Allan

D-U-N-S 25-313-8804   (HQ)
WENZEL DOWNHOLE TOOLS LTD
(*Suby of* BASIN HOLDINGS LLC)
5920 Macleod Trail Sw Suite 504, Calgary, AB,
T2H 0K2
(403) 205-6696
Emp Here 5   *Sales* 30,896,470
SIC 3533 Oil and gas field machinery
 Jonathan Thiele
 Cindy Hart
 Rick Doiron
 Rishi Gurjar

 Jennifer Camwell
 Dirk Von Kittliz
 Don Ormstrup

D-U-N-S 20-278-0722   (SL)
WEST OILFIELD HOLDINGS LTD
5940 Macleod Trail Sw Unit 202, Calgary, AB,
T2H 2G4
(403) 452-0844
Emp Here 49   *Sales* 10,296,419
SIC 1389 Oil and gas field services, nec
 James Dyack

D-U-N-S 24-906-0930   (SL)
WESTCAL INSULATION LTD
7005 Fairmount Dr Se Unit 4165, Calgary, AB,
T2H 0J1
(403) 242-1357
Emp Here 60   *Sales* 13,983,900
SIC 1711 Plumbing, heating, air-conditioning
 Sasha Cesto

D-U-N-S 25-195-0622   (SL)
**WESTCO   INTERNATIONAL   DEVELOP-
MENT CORP**
7245 12 St Se, Calgary, AB, T2H 2S6

Emp Here 90
SIC 6712 Bank holding companies

D-U-N-S 20-635-9085   (HQ)
WESTECH INDUSTRIAL LTD
(*Suby of* LAPP MANAGEMENT SERVICES
LTD)
5636 Burbank Cres Se, Calgary, AB, T2H 1Z6
(403) 252-8803
Emp Here 36   *Sales* 28,501,560
SIC 5084 Industrial machinery and equipment
 Jason Lapp
 Russ Lapp
 Jeff Scott

D-U-N-S 24-327-8814   (SL)
WORLEY CANADA SERVICES LTD
8500 Macleod Trail Se, Calgary, AB, T2H 2N1
(403) 258-8000
Emp Here 35,000   *Sales* 6,255,865,000
SIC 8711 Engineering services
 Andrew Wood

D-U-N-S 20-379-8715   (HQ)
WORLEYCORD LP
(*Suby of* WORLEYPARSONS LIMITED)
8500 Macleod Trail Se Suite 400, Calgary, AB,
T2H 2N1
(780) 465-5516
Emp Here 1,500   *Sales* 820,287,500
SIC 1629 Heavy construction, nec
 Brad Van De Veen

Calgary, AB T2J

D-U-N-S 25-329-9903   (SL)
504148 ALBERTA INC
CALGARY HONDA
11700 Lake Fraser Dr Se, Calgary, AB, T2J
7J5
(403) 253-6531
Emp Here 60   *Sales* 37,756,800
SIC 5511 New and used car dealers
 Tony L Dilawri

D-U-N-S 24-323-0575   (SL)
870892 ALBERTA LTD
ARTEC CONSTRUCTION
11435 Wilkes Rd Se, Calgary, AB, T2J 2E5
(403) 452-3122
Emp Here 35   *Sales* 11,666,655
SIC 1541 Industrial buildings and warehouses
 Marvin Boyko

D-U-N-S 24-809-9087   (HQ)
A-WIN INSURANCE LTD
(*Suby of* ROGERS INSURANCE LTD)
10325 Bonaventure Dr Se Suite 100, Calgary,

AB, T2J 7E4
(403) 278-1050
Emp Here 5   *Sales* 32,226,280
SIC 6411 Insurance agents, brokers, and service
Debi Walker
Kimberly Toller
Pamela Woodhurst
Mayanne Campbell

D-U-N-S 25-325-2621   (SL)
ADVANTAGE FORD SALES LTD
12800 Macleod Trail Se, Calgary, AB, T2J 7E5
(403) 225-3636
Emp Here 63   *Sales* 39,644,640
SIC 5511 New and used car dealers
Gerry Wood

D-U-N-S 24-956-8056   (HQ)
AGRIUM INC
CROP PRODUCTION SERVICES (CPS)
(Suby of NUTRIEN LTD)
13131 Lake Fraser Dr Se, Calgary, AB, T2J 7E8
(403) 225-7000
Emp Here 335   *Sales* 13,766,000,000
SIC 2873 Nitrogenous fertilizers

D-U-N-S 24-241-5136   (HQ)
ALPINE INSURANCE & FINANCIAL INC
8820 Blackfoot Trail Se Suite 123, Calgary, AB, T2J 3J1
(403) 270-8822
Emp Here 20   *Sales* 38,162,700
SIC 6411 Insurance agents, brokers, and service
Cam Clay
Kenneth Hughes

D-U-N-S 20-146-1196   (SL)
CALGARY CO-OP HOME HEALTH CARE LIMITED
COMFORT SHOP, THE
9309 Macleod Trail Sw Suite 3, Calgary, AB, T2J 0P6
(403) 252-2266
Emp Here 50   *Sales* 24,916,100
SIC 5137 Women's and children's clothing
Linda Keeley

D-U-N-S 25-316-1145   (BR)
CALGARY CO-OPERATIVE ASSOCIATION LIMITED
CALGARY CO-OP
(Suby of CALGARY CO-OPERATIVE ASSOCIATION LIMITED)
1221 Canyon Meadows Dr Se Suite 95, Calgary, AB, T2J 6G2
(403) 299-4350
Emp Here 320
SIC 5411 Grocery stores
Ian Perkins

D-U-N-S 25-330-0438   (SL)
CANYON CREEK TOYOTA INC
370 Canyon Meadows Dr Se, Calgary, AB, T2J 7C6
(403) 278-6066
Emp Here 62   *Sales* 39,015,360
SIC 5511 New and used car dealers
Peter Mckeen
Jack Carter

D-U-N-S 25-386-9317   (HQ)
CEDA INTERNATIONAL CORPORATION
(Suby of OMERS ADMINISTRATION CORPORATION)
11012 Macleod Trail Se Suite 625, Calgary, AB, T2J 6A5
(403) 253-3233
Sales 1,333,935,000
SIC 2819 Industrial inorganic chemicals, nec
Kevin Fleury
Chad Thompson
Pat Cantner
Spencer Fried
Troy Tangedal

Paula Breeze
Gary Belcher
David Churchill

D-U-N-S 24-518-3389   (SL)
CENTRON CONSTRUCTION LIMITED
8826 Blackfoot Trail Se Unit 104, Calgary, AB, T2J 3J1
(403) 252-1120
Emp Here 40   *Sales* 18,829,240
SIC 1542 Nonresidential construction, nec
Robert Harris

D-U-N-S 20-251-2034   (SL)
CENTRON GROUP OF COMPANIES INC
CENTRON EAGLE RIDGE
8826 Blackfoot Trail Se Suite 104, Calgary, AB, T2J 3J1
(403) 252-1120
Emp Here 42   *Sales* 19,770,702
SIC 1542 Nonresidential construction, nec
Robert Harris

D-U-N-S 25-980-3620   (BR)
CRATE AND BARREL CANADA INC
(Suby of KG ATLAS VERMOGENSVERWALTUNGSGESELLSCHAFT & CO.)
100 Anderson Rd Se Suite 273, Calgary, AB, T2J 3V1
(403) 278-7020
Emp Here 80
SIC 5712 Furniture stores
Eric Glafrud

D-U-N-S 24-272-2155   (SL)
DAND AUTO PARTS LIMITED
CANADIAN TIRE STORE 313
9940 Macleod Trail Se Suite 3, Calgary, AB, T2J 3K9
(403) 278-4040
Emp Here 142   *Sales* 29,158,706
SIC 5311 Department stores
Joseph Dand

D-U-N-S 25-622-1888   (BR)
EARL'S RESTAURANTS LTD
EARL WILLOW PARK
(Suby of EARL'S RESTAURANTS LTD)
10640 Macleod Trail Se, Calgary, AB, T2J 0P8
(403) 278-7860
Emp Here 75
SIC 5812 Eating places
Reilly Whitman

D-U-N-S 24-439-1462   (SL)
FAMILY LEISURE CENTRE ASSOCIATION OF SOUTHEAST CALGARY, THE
FAMILY LEISURE CENTRE
11150 Bonaventure Dr Se, Calgary, AB, T2J 6R9
(403) 278-7542
Emp Here 170   *Sales* 14,739,000
SIC 7999 Amusement and recreation, nec
Don Burdeyney
Mike Mikkelson
Jan De Bruyn
Alan Gomes
Dorraine Neal

D-U-N-S 20-522-5345   (SL)
HOSPITALITY INNS LTD
DELTA CALGARY SOUTH
135 Southland Dr Se, Calgary, AB, T2J 5X5
(403) 278-5050
Emp Here 195   *Sales* 18,074,550
SIC 7011 Hotels and motels
Keith Bryant
Marc Rheume

D-U-N-S 20-989-4708   (BR)
HUDSON'S BAY COMPANY
THE BAY SOUTH CENTRE
(Suby of HUDSON'S BAY COMPANY)
100 Anderson Rd Se, Calgary, AB, T2J 3V1
(403) 278-9520
Emp Here 170
SIC 5311 Department stores
Anita Hertz

D-U-N-S 24-271-4186   (SL)
KOOPMAN RESOURCES, INC
UNIWORLD APPAREL INDUSTRIES
10919 Willowglen Pl Se, Calgary, AB, T2J 1R8
(403) 271-4564
Emp Here 100   *Sales* 31,970,500
SIC 1311 Crude petroleum and natural gas

D-U-N-S 24-646-5942   (BR)
LAFARGE CANADA INC
LAFARGE AGGREGATES AND CONCRETE
(Suby of LAFARGEHOLCIM LTD)
10511 15 St Se, Calgary, AB, T2J 7H7
(403) 292-1555
Emp Here 200
SIC 1442 Construction sand and gravel
Bob Spence

D-U-N-S 25-505-8489   (SL)
LLAP HOLDINGS LTD
DEER POINT SOBEYS
14939 Deer Ridge Dr Se, Calgary, AB, T2J 7C4
(403) 278-2626
Emp Here 90   *Sales* 26,412,930
SIC 5411 Grocery stores
Anthony Kearney

D-U-N-S 20-609-3143   (SL)
REMAX FIRST REALTY
9625 Macleod Trail Sw, Calgary, AB, T2J 0P6
(403) 938-4848
Emp Here 97   *Sales* 40,632,233
SIC 6531 Real estate agents and managers
John Riseborough

D-U-N-S 24-014-9476   (SL)
REMAX REAL ESTATE CALGARY SOUTH LTD
RE/MAX FIRST
8820 Blackfoot Trail Se Suite 115, Calgary, AB, T2J 3J1
(403) 278-2900
Emp Here 90   *Sales* 24,458,040
SIC 6531 Real estate agents and managers
Richard Campos

D-U-N-S 20-302-3101   (SL)
SEVENTH LEVEL MANAGEMENT LTD
KELLER WILLIAMS REALTY SOUTH
11012 Macleod Trail Se Suite 600, Calgary, AB, T2J 6A5
(403) 837-1195
Emp Here 110   *Sales* 46,077,790
SIC 6531 Real estate agents and managers
Wayne Henuset

D-U-N-S 25-271-0744   (BR)
SOBEYS WEST INC
SAFEWAY SOUTHCENTRE
(Suby of EMPIRE COMPANY LIMITED)
11011 Bonaventure Dr Se, Calgary, AB, T2J 6S1
(403) 278-5225
Emp Here 120
SIC 5912 Drug stores and proprietary stores
Randy Alison

D-U-N-S 25-271-0637   (BR)
SOBEYS WEST INC
(Suby of EMPIRE COMPANY LIMITED)
9737 Macleod Trail Sw, Calgary, AB, T2J 0P6
(403) 252-8199
Emp Here 138
SIC 5411 Grocery stores
Greg Mix

D-U-N-S 25-271-0678   (BR)
SOBEYS WEST INC
SAFEWAY BONAVISTA SHOPPING PLAZA
(Suby of EMPIRE COMPANY LIMITED)
1755 Lake Bonavista Dr Se Suite 1, Calgary, AB, T2J 0N3
(403) 271-1616
Emp Here 80
SIC 5411 Grocery stores
Heather Polutnik

D-U-N-S 24-158-2030   (SL)
SOUTHGATE CHEVROLET BUICK GMC LTD
13103 Lake Fraser Dr Se, Calgary, AB, T2J 3H5
(403) 256-4960
Emp Here 86   *Sales* 54,118,080
SIC 5511 New and used car dealers
Linder Armitage
Harry Brugmans

D-U-N-S 20-598-6169   (SL)
SOUTHSIDE MOTORS LTD
KRAMER MAZDA
11888 Macleod Trail Se, Calgary, AB, T2J 7J2
(403) 252-4327
Emp Here 40   *Sales* 19,923,120
SIC 5511 New and used car dealers
Deepak Ruparell
Vinay Ruperall

D-U-N-S 24-701-4822   (SL)
STANLEY PARK INVESTMENTS LTD
HOLIDAY INN EXPRESS HOTEL & SUITES
12025 Lake Fraser Dr Se, Calgary, AB, T2J 7G5
(403) 225-3000
Emp Here 75   *Sales* 7,117,425
SIC 7011 Hotels and motels
Salim Dhanji

D-U-N-S 20-991-5008   (SL)
TOWER CHRYSLER PLYMOUTH LTD
10901 Macleod Trail Sw, Calgary, AB, T2J 4L3
(403) 278-2020
Emp Here 100   *Sales* 62,928,000
SIC 5511 New and used car dealers
Edward Rewucki
Agnes Rewucki

D-U-N-S 20-120-1433   (SL)
TWR C MOTORS LP
TOWER CHRYSLER DODGE JEEP RAM
(Suby of AUTOCANADA INC)
10901 Macleod Trail Sw, Calgary, AB, T2J 4L3
(403) 225-6193
Emp Here 65   *Sales* 40,903,200
SIC 5511 New and used car dealers
Brent Johnson

D-U-N-S 25-218-9816   (BR)
WAL-MART CANADA CORP
(Suby of WALMART INC.)
9650 Macleod Trail Se, Calgary, AB, T2J 0P7
(403) 258-3988
Emp Here 300
SIC 5311 Department stores
Mark Schaffel

D-U-N-S 20-082-8775   (BR)
WE CARE HOME HEALTH SERVICES
10325 Bonaventure Dr Se Suite 100, Calgary, AB, T2J 7E4
(403) 225-1222
Emp Here 300
SIC 8059 Nursing and personal care, nec
Wes Campbell

Calgary, AB T2K

D-U-N-S 24-043-5032   (SL)
ACTIVE MARBLE & TILE LTD
GRANITE WORX
5355 8 St Ne, Calgary, AB, T2K 5R9
(403) 274-2111
Emp Here 70   *Sales* 18,735,640
SIC 5211 Lumber and other building materials
Frank Golemme
Natalie Golemme

D-U-N-S 24-066-5125   (SL)
BENSON, GARRY W ENTERPRISES LTD
CANADIAN TIRE
40 Hunterhorn Dr Ne, Calgary, AB, T2K 6H2

Emp Here 125
SIC 5531 Auto and home supply stores

D-U-N-S 25-485-8384   (BR)
CALGARY BOARD OF EDUCATION
JOHN G DIEFENBAKER HIGH SCHOOL
(*Suby of* CALGARY BOARD OF EDUCA-
TION)
6620 4 St Nw, Calgary, AB, T2K 1C2
(403) 274-2240
Emp Here 90
SIC 8211 Elementary and secondary schools
 Bob Tink

D-U-N-S 25-681-4757   (HQ)
CAREY MANAGEMENT INC
5445 8 St Ne, Calgary, AB, T2K 5R9
(403) 275-7360
Emp Here 200   *Sales* 192,257,734
SIC 6712 Bank holding companies
 Frank Carey
 David Blom
 Pat Carey
 Jackie Bellrose
 David Morgan
 Ron Funk

D-U-N-S 20-852-8575   (SL)
CHINESE ACADEMY FOUNDATION, THE
THE CHINESE ACADEMY
6600 4 St Nw, Calgary, AB, T2K 1C2
(403) 777-7663
Emp Here 118   *Sales* 16,007,880
SIC 8299 Schools and educational services,
nec
 Alice Chow
 Elaine Chan

D-U-N-S 24-347-5030   (HQ)
EMS CANADA, INC
K & D OILFIELD SERVICES
(*Suby of* ENERGY MAINTENANCE SER-
VICES GROUP I, INC.)
5010 4 St Ne Suite 207, Calgary, AB, T2K 5X8
(403) 508-2111
Emp Here 7   *Sales* 15,985,250
SIC 1389 Oil and gas field services, nec
 Harvey Schneitzer
 Alfred Bruce

D-U-N-S 20-187-6178   (SL)
INTERNATIONAL VISION ORGANIZATION
44 Coleridge Cres Nw, Calgary, AB, T2K 1X9

Emp Here 150   *Sales* 16,662,000
SIC 8062 General medical and surgical hospi-
tals
 Peter Huang

D-U-N-S 24-359-1208   (BR)
LOBLAWS INC
REAL CANADIAN SUPERSTORE
(*Suby of* LOBLAW COMPANIES LIMITED)
7020 4 St Nw, Calgary, AB, T2K 1C4
(403) 516-8519
Emp Here 100
SIC 5411 Grocery stores
 Dave Brown

D-U-N-S 24-906-3348   (HQ)
MANTEI HOLDINGS LTD
5935 6 St Ne, Calgary, AB, T2K 5R5
(403) 295-0028
Emp Here 43   *Sales* 14,985,600
SIC 2431 Millwork
 Carey Mantei

D-U-N-S 24-118-7111   (SL)
MARMOT CONSTRUCTION LTD
636 Beaver Dam Rd Ne, Calgary, AB, T2K
4W6
(403) 730-8711
Emp Here 160   *Sales* 39,597,280
SIC 1771 Concrete work
 W R Todd Gardiner
 Helen Hincks

D-U-N-S 20-636-2436   (SL)
NICK'S WOODCRAFT INDUSTRIES LTD
112 Skyline Cres Ne, Calgary, AB, T2K 5X7
(403) 275-6432
Emp Here 39   *Sales* 16,354,845
SIC 6712 Bank holding companies
 Nick Lobello
 Anna-Lisa Lobello
 Guy Lobello

D-U-N-S 25-316-4214   (BR)
PASLEY, MAX ENTERPRISES LIMITED
MCDONALD'S RESTAURANTS
6820 4 St Nw, Calgary, AB, T2K 1C2
(403) 295-1004
Emp Here 81
SIC 5812 Eating places
 Randall Agharsingh

D-U-N-S 24-419-9076   (SL)
PINKWOOD LTD
5929 6 St Ne, Calgary, AB, T2K 5R5
(403) 279-3700
Emp Here 60   *Sales* 11,542,200
SIC 2499 Wood products, nec
 Richard Dettbarn
 Brad Parsons
 Allen Jian
 Chunks Chunkouh

D-U-N-S 25-364-9370   (BR)
SOBEYS WEST INC
THORNCLIFFE SAFEWAY
(*Suby of* EMPIRE COMPANY LIMITED)
5607 4 St Nw, Calgary, AB, T2K 1B3
(403) 730-5080
Emp Here 100
SIC 5411 Grocery stores
 Jamie Oliver

D-U-N-S 20-296-5760   (BR)
SOBEYS WEST INC
SAFEWAY
(*Suby of* EMPIRE COMPANY LIMITED)
215 42 Ave Nw, Calgary, AB, T2K 0H3
(403) 730-3500
Emp Here 87
SIC 4225 General warehousing and storage
 Kevin Baines

D-U-N-S 24-732-3363   (HQ)
SUNDOG DISTRIBUTING INC
SUNDOG EYEWARE
83 Skyline Cres Ne, Calgary, AB, T2K 5X2
(403) 516-6600
Sales 15,616,260
SIC 5099 Durable goods, nec
 William Hoogstraten
 Rod Hoogstraten

D-U-N-S 25-979-8411   (SL)
T.F. LYNN AND ASSOCIATES INC
*ADVANTAGE LOSS PREVENTION SER-
VICES (ALPS)*
5512 4 St Nw Suite 224, Calgary, AB, T2K 1A9
(403) 215-6880
Emp Here 30   *Sales* 13,415,220
SIC 5065 Electronic parts and equipment, nec
 Timothy Lynn
 J L Lynn
 Teresa Lynn
 Paul Lynn

D-U-N-S 25-205-5579   (SL)
**VARSITY CHRYSLER JEEP DODGE RAM
LTD**
VARSITY CHRYSLER JEEP DODGE
665 Goddard Ave Ne, Calgary, AB, T2K 6K1
(403) 730-4000
Emp Here 122   *Sales* 76,772,160
SIC 5511 New and used car dealers
 Gordon Moors
 James Mcmanes

D-U-N-S 25-417-2307   (SL)
**VARSITY PLYMOUTH CHRYSLER (1994)
LTD**

AUTOMAXX AUTOMOTIVE SALES, DIV OF
4914 6 St Ne, Calgary, AB, T2K 4W5
(403) 250-5541
Emp Here 28   *Sales* 13,946,184
SIC 5521 Used car dealers
 Gordon Moors
 James Mcmanes

D-U-N-S 20-078-6218   (HQ)
WALLACE & CAREY INC
(*Suby of* CAREY MANAGEMENT INC)
5445 8 St Ne, Calgary, AB, T2K 5R9
(403) 275-7360
Emp Here 200   *Sales* 441,869,250
SIC 5194 Tobacco and tobacco products
 Patrick Carey

Calgary, AB T2L

D-U-N-S 25-386-6347   (SL)
588388 ALBERTA LTD
NORTHLAND VOLKSWAGEN
4849 Northland Dr Nw, Calgary, AB, T2L 2K3
(403) 286-4849
Emp Here 50   *Sales* 24,903,900
SIC 5511 New and used car dealers
 Perry Itzcovitch

D-U-N-S 20-519-3266   (BR)
CALGARY BOARD OF EDUCATION
SIR WINSTON CHURCHILL HIGH SCHOOL
(*Suby of* CALGARY BOARD OF EDUCA-
TION)
5220 Northland Dr Nw, Calgary, AB, T2L 2J6
(403) 289-9241
Emp Here 140
SIC 8211 Elementary and secondary schools
 Arvin Rajan

D-U-N-S 25-316-1426   (BR)
**CALGARY CO-OPERATIVE ASSOCIATION
LIMITED**
BRENTWOOD CO-OP
(*Suby of* CALGARY CO-OPERATIVE ASSO-
CIATION LIMITED)
4122 Brentwood Rd Nw Suite 4, Calgary, AB,
T2L 1K8
(403) 299-4301
Emp Here 100
SIC 5411 Grocery stores
 Jim Derraugh

D-U-N-S 20-580-7923   (BR)
**CALGARY ROMAN CATHOLIC SEPARATE
SCHOOL DISTRICT #1**
SAINT FRANCIS HIGH SCHOOL (10-12)
(*Suby of* CALGARY ROMAN CATHOLIC
SEPARATE SCHOOL DISTRICT #1)
877 Northmount Dr Nw, Calgary, AB, T2L 0A3
(403) 500-2026
Emp Here 150
SIC 8211 Elementary and secondary schools
 John Mcfarland

D-U-N-S 25-459-4711   (SL)
CALGARY V MOTORS LP
NORTHLAND VOLKSWAGEN
(*Suby of* AUTOCANADA INC)
4849 Northland Dr Nw, Calgary, AB, T2L 2K3
(403) 286-4849
Emp Here 65   *Sales* 40,903,200
SIC 5511 New and used car dealers

D-U-N-S 24-298-5935   (HQ)
COMPUTER MODELLING GROUP LTD
CMG
3710 33 St Nw, Calgary, AB, T2L 2M1
(403) 531-1300
Emp Here 45   *Sales* 56,601,698
SIC 7371 Custom computer programming ser-
vices
 Ryan Schneider
 John Zaozirny
 Long Nghiem

 Anjani Kumar
 Sandra Balic
 Judith Athaide
 Ken Dedeluk
 Christopher Fong
 Patrick Jamieson
 Peter Kinash

D-U-N-S 20-648-7576   (BR)
DOUBLE ARROW VENTURES LTD
KILKENNY IRISH PUB
(*Suby of* DOUBLE ARROW VENTURES LTD)
3630 Brentwood Rd Nw Suite 500, Calgary,
AB, T2L 1K8
(403) 284-4404
Emp Here 75
SIC 5812 Eating places
 Sandy Olthuis

D-U-N-S 20-064-9023   (SL)
MEGAFORTUNE INTERNATIONAL INC
3500 Varsity Dr Nw Unit 1608, Calgary, AB,
T2L 1Y3
(403) 261-8881
Emp Here 30   *Sales* 20,904,300
SIC 6798 Real estate investment trusts
 Jason Poon

D-U-N-S 24-810-0679   (SL)
NORWEST REAL ESTATE LTD
SUTTON GROUP
3604 52 Ave Nw Suite 114, Calgary, AB, T2L
1V9
(403) 282-7770
Emp Here 110   *Sales* 46,077,790
SIC 6531 Real estate agents and managers
 Chris Bolt

D-U-N-S 20-551-4149   (HQ)
RS TECHNOLOGIES INC
RS COMPOSITE UTILITY POLES
3553 31 St Nw, Calgary, AB, T2L 2K7
(403) 219-8000
Emp Here 4   *Sales* 14,867,260
SIC 2499 Wood products, nec
 Howard Elliott
 David Werklund
 Joel Tennison
 Joel Tennison
 Domenic Varacalli
 Tracy Mcdonald

D-U-N-S 24-379-7524   (HQ)
SMART TECHNOLOGIES INC
(*Suby of* HON HAI PRECISION INDUSTRY
CO., LTD.)
3636 Research Rd Nw, Calgary, AB, T2L 1Y1
(403) 245-0333
Emp Here 50   *Sales* 367,789,500
SIC 3674 Semiconductors and related devices
 Neil Gaydon
 Debra Milimaka Miles
 Nicholas Svensson
 Jeff Lowe
 Michael Mueller
 Robert Hagerty
 Greg Hughes
 Ian Mckinnon

D-U-N-S 24-807-4098   (HQ)
SMART TECHNOLOGIES ULC
(*Suby of* HON HAI PRECISION INDUSTRY
CO., LTD.)
3636 Research Rd Nw, Calgary, AB, T2L 1Y1
(403) 245-0333
Emp Here 600   *Sales* 367,789,500
SIC 3674 Semiconductors and related devices
 Neil Gaydon
 David A Martin
 Nancy Knowlton
 Thomas F Hodson

D-U-N-S 25-271-0900   (BR)
SOBEYS WEST INC
BRENTWOOD SAFEWAY
(*Suby of* EMPIRE COMPANY LIMITED)
3636 Brentwood Rd Nw, Calgary, AB, T2L 1K8

(403) 289-1424
Emp Here 100
SIC 5411 Grocery stores
  Trent Aush

D-U-N-S 24-107-3472   (BR)
SOBEYS WEST INC
SAFEWAY
(*Suby of* EMPIRE COMPANY LIMITED)
3636 Morley Tr Nw, Calgary, AB, T2L 1K8
(403) 289-9890
Emp Here 100
SIC 5411 Grocery stores
  Steven Burd

D-U-N-S 20-201-6189   (SL)
W MODE INC
3553 31 St Nw Suite 201, Calgary, AB, T2L
2K7
(403) 260-8690
Emp Here 80   *Sales* 17,306,224
SIC 7372 Prepackaged software
  Robert Woodward
  Duane Sharman
  Dennis Woronuk

D-U-N-S 25-218-9931   (BR)
WAL-MART CANADA CORP
(*Suby of* WALMART INC.)
5005 Northland Drive Nw, Calgary, AB, T2L
2K1
(403) 247-8585
Emp Here 320
SIC 5311 Department stores
  Pennock Trent

D-U-N-S 20-922-7136   (SL)
WESTPOINT MANAGEMENT INC
MAXWELL CAPITAL REALTY
3604 52 Ave Nw Suite 114, Calgary, AB, T2L
1V9
(403) 282-7770
Emp Here 49   *Sales* 16,029,223
SIC 6531 Real estate agents and managers
  Jason Watson

D-U-N-S 20-136-3491   (BR)
**WINNERS MERCHANTS INTERNATIONAL
L.P.**
WINNERS
(*Suby of* THE TJX COMPANIES INC)
5111 Northland Dr Nw Suite 200, Calgary, AB,
T2L 2J8
(403) 247-8100
Emp Here 90
SIC 5651 Family clothing stores
  Linda Swanberg

Calgary, AB T2M

D-U-N-S 24-168-6760   (SL)
1046809 ALBERTA INC
LIQUOR BOX
2112 Crowchild Trail Nw, Calgary, AB, T2M
3Y7
(403) 338-1268
Emp Here 45   *Sales* 13,460,850
SIC 5921 Liquor stores
  Amar Wedhwani

D-U-N-S 25-521-6053   (SL)
ALLIANCE REAL ESTATE CALGARY LTD
2003 14 St Nw Suite 107, Calgary, AB, T2M
3N4
(403) 270-7676
Emp Here 40   *Sales* 13,085,080
SIC 6531 Real estate agents and managers
  Jan Neyrinck

D-U-N-S 20-522-1760   (BR)
CALGARY BOARD OF EDUCATION
WILLIAM ABERHART SCHOOL
(*Suby of* CALGARY BOARD OF EDUCA-
TION)
3009 Morley Trail Nw, Calgary, AB, T2M 4G9

(403) 289-2551
Emp Here 110
SIC 8211 Elementary and secondary schools
  Jacques Ferguson

D-U-N-S 20-266-7569   (BR)
CALGARY BOARD OF EDUCATION
CRESCENT HEIGHTS HIGH SCHOOL
(*Suby of* CALGARY BOARD OF EDUCA-
TION)
1019 1 St Nw, Calgary, AB, T2M 2S2
(403) 276-5521
Emp Here 120
SIC 8211 Elementary and secondary schools
  Jackie Chapman-Brown

D-U-N-S 20-233-3089   (SL)
CAPITOL HILL COMMUNITY ASSOCIATION
1531 21 Ave Nw, Calgary, AB, T2M 1L9
(403) 289-0859
Emp Here 45   *Sales* 10,207,485
SIC 8399 Social services, nec
  Fred Baker

D-U-N-S 25-522-1624   (BR)
EARL'S RESTAURANTS LTD
EARL'S
(*Suby of* EARL'S RESTAURANTS LTD)
1110 16 Ave Nw, Calgary, AB, T2M 0K8
(403) 289-2566
Emp Here 100
SIC 5812 Eating places
  Jordan Morgan

D-U-N-S 20-698-6221   (BR)
HOME DEPOT OF CANADA INC
(*Suby of* THE HOME DEPOT INC)
1818 16 Ave Nw, Calgary, AB, T2M 0L8
(403) 284-7931
Emp Here 200
SIC 5251 Hardware stores
  Cam Sadler

D-U-N-S 20-772-9737   (SL)
NUCOR SYSTEMS INC
LUSH LAWN IRRIGATION
918 16 Ave Nw Suite 349, Calgary, AB, T2M
0K3
(403) 236-2824
Emp Here 30   *Sales* 14,250,780
SIC 5083 Farm and garden machinery
  Marvin Smith

D-U-N-S 20-537-1581   (SL)
RE/MAX CENTRAL
2411 4 St Nw Suite 206, Calgary, AB, T2M
2Z8
(403) 241-8199
Emp Here 49   *Sales* 41,554,940
SIC 6411 Insurance agents, brokers, and service
  Ian Cooper

D-U-N-S 20-188-7093   (BR)
ROYAL HOST INC
BEST WESTERN VILLAGE PARK INN
(*Suby of* HOLLOWAY LODGING CORPORA-
TION)
1804 Crowchild Trail Nw, Calgary, AB, T2M
3Y7
(403) 289-0241
Emp Here 120
SIC 7011 Hotels and motels
  Jason Clark

D-U-N-S 25-483-6448   (BR)
SODEXO CANADA LTD
(*Suby of* SODEXO)
1301 16 Ave Nw, Calgary, AB, T2M 0L4
(403) 284-8536
Emp Here 120
SIC 7349 Building maintenance services, nec
  Robert Gehlen

D-U-N-S 24-553-7030   (SL)
STADIUM NISSAN INC
2420 Crowchild Trail Nw, Calgary, AB, T2M
4N5

(403) 284-4611
Emp Here 60   *Sales* 37,756,800
SIC 5511 New and used car dealers
  Peter Mckeen
  Lawrence Bates
  Gregory Bates
  Carol Clark

D-U-N-S 24-716-8149   (SL)
SUNNY HOLDINGS LIMITED
ARBY'S
1140 16 Ave Nw, Calgary, AB, T2M 0K8

Emp Here 120   *Sales* 5,462,280
SIC 5812 Eating places
  Sunny Tang

D-U-N-S 20-336-6013   (SL)
TECH INCENTIVES INC
1816 Crowchild Trail Nw Unit 700, Calgary,
AB, T2M 3Y7
(403) 713-1050
Emp Here 49   *Sales* 10,582,494
SIC 8748 Business consulting, nec
  Omar Odibat

D-U-N-S 20-871-2534   (SL)
VILLAGE MALL DELICATESSEN LTD
1921 20 Ave Nw, Calgary, AB, T2M 1H6
(403) 282-6600
Emp Here 2   *Sales* 20,967,750
SIC 6712 Bank holding companies
  Stan Kundert
  Marianne Kundert

Calgary, AB T2N

D-U-N-S 24-393-2188   (HQ)
1249413 ALBERTA LTD
INTERSPORT NORTH HILL
1632 14 Ave Nw Suite 1774, Calgary, AB, T2N
1M7
(403) 289-4441
Emp Here 1   *Sales* 20,767,880
SIC 5941 Sporting goods and bicycle shops
  Basil Bark
  Mike Yarrow

D-U-N-S 24-850-1314   (SL)
APEX LIMITED PARTNERSHIP
1710 14 Ave Nw Suite 300, Calgary, AB, T2N
4Y6
(403) 210-3473
Emp Here 160   *Sales* 43,350,720
SIC 1521 Single-family housing construction
  Frank Boyd
  Evelyn Fulton
  Greg Lefebre
  Mark Schuparski
  David Bissett

D-U-N-S 25-622-0138   (BR)
BETHANY CARE SOCIETY
BETHANY CARE CENTRE CALGARY
(*Suby of* BETHANY CARE SOCIETY)
916 18a St Nw Suite 3085, Calgary, AB, T2N
1C6
(403) 284-0161
Emp Here 500
SIC 8051 Skilled nursing care facilities
  Dana Penner

D-U-N-S 24-850-4768   (SL)
BFL CANADA INSURANCE SERVICES INC
1167 Kensington Cres Nw Suite 200, Calgary,
AB, T2N 1X7
(403) 451-4132
Emp Here 350   *Sales* 747,938,800
SIC 6311 Life insurance
  Barry Lorenzette

D-U-N-S 25-593-9803   (HQ)
**CALGARY ALTERNATIVE SUPPORT SER-
VICES INC**
1240 Kensington Rd Nw Suite 408, Calgary,

AB, T2N 3P7
(403) 283-0611
Emp Here 33   *Sales* 13,054,640
SIC 8322 Individual and family services
  Steven Law

D-U-N-S 20-713-1058   (BR)
CALGARY BOARD OF EDUCATION
QUEEN ELIZABETH HIGH SCHOOL
(*Suby of* CALGARY BOARD OF EDUCA-
TION)
512 18 St Nw, Calgary, AB, T2N 2G5
(403) 777-6380
Emp Here 75
SIC 8211 Elementary and secondary schools
  Steve Young

D-U-N-S 20-830-2141   (BR)
**CANADIAN BROADCASTING CORPORA-
TION**
CBC/CBRT/CBR
(*Suby of* GOVERNMENT OF CANADA)
1724 Westmount Blvd Nw, Calgary, AB, T2N
3G7
(403) 521-6000
Emp Here 160
SIC 4832 Radio broadcasting stations
  Don Orchard

D-U-N-S 25-518-9474   (BR)
EXTENDICARE (CANADA) INC
EXTENDICARE HILLCREST
(*Suby of* EXTENDICARE INC)
1512 8 Ave Nw, Calgary, AB, T2N 1C1
(403) 289-0236
Emp Here 120
SIC 8051 Skilled nursing care facilities
  Betty Dyck

D-U-N-S 20-766-3915   (HQ)
**GOVERNORS OF THE UNIVERSITY OF
CALGARY, THE**
BIOGEOSCIENCE INSTITUTE
2500 University Dr Nw, Calgary, AB, T2N 1N4
(403) 220-5110
Emp Here 800
SIC 7389 Business services, nec
  Elizabeth Cannon
  Jonathan Gebert
  Elisabbeth Osler
  John R Perraton
  Meghan King

D-U-N-S 25-371-4687   (BR)
**GOVERNORS OF THE UNIVERSITY OF
CALGARY, THE**
FACULTY OF MEDECINE
(*Suby of* GOVERNORS OF THE UNIVER-
SITY OF CALGARY, THE)
3330 Hospital Dr Nw Suite 3330, Calgary, AB,
T2N 4N1

Emp Here 100
SIC 8733 Noncommercial research organiza-
tions
  Marta Cyperling

D-U-N-S 24-982-2586   (HQ)
HEARING LOSS CLINIC INC, THE
1632 14 Ave Nw Suite 251, Calgary, AB, T2N
1M7
(403) 289-3290
Emp Here 12   *Sales* 16,280,000
SIC 5999 Miscellaneous retail stores, nec
  Connie Sakundiak

D-U-N-S 24-345-7041   (BR)
KEG RESTAURANTS LTD
KEG STEAKHOUSE & BAR, THE
(*Suby of* RECIPE UNLIMITED CORPORA-
TION)
1923 Uxbridge Dr Nw, Calgary, AB, T2N 2V2
(403) 282-0020
Emp Here 90
SIC 5812 Eating places
  Kristy Blake

D-U-N-S 25-506-3844   (SL)

NEUFELD, C. M. PHARMACY LTD
SHOPPERS DRUG MART
1632 14 Ave Nw Unit 1790, Calgary, AB, T2N
1M7
(403) 289-6761
Emp Here 50   *Sales* 12,647,700
SIC 5912 Drug stores and proprietary stores
 Carol Neufeld

        D-U-N-S 24-771-4277   (SL)
PROCON SYSTEMS INC
1403 29 St Nw, Calgary, AB, T2N 2T9
(780) 499-7088
Emp Here 45   *Sales* 21,735,691
SIC 5084 Industrial machinery and equipment
 Steve Siebold

        D-U-N-S 25-090-6112   (SL)
PROVINCIAL LAB FOR PUBLIC HEALTH
3030 Hospital Dr Nw, Calgary, AB, T2N 4W4
(403) 944-1200
Emp Here 75   *Sales* 5,853,600
SIC 8071 Medical laboratories
 Kit Johnson

        D-U-N-S 24-007-7789   (SL)
SERVANTAGE SERVICES INC
(*Suby of* SERVANTAGE SERVICES CORP)
4 Parkdale Cres Nw, Calgary, AB, T2N 3T8
(403) 263-8170
Emp Here 140   *Sales* 4,475,520
SIC 7349 Building maintenance services, nec
 Craig Peterson
 John Peterson

        D-U-N-S 25-271-0934   (BR)
SOBEYS WEST INC
SAFEWAY
(*Suby of* EMPIRE COMPANY LIMITED)
410 10 St Nw, Calgary, AB, T2N 1V9
(403) 270-3054
Emp Here 110
SIC 5411 Grocery stores
 Teresa Kruigers

        D-U-N-S 25-138-3634   (BR)
SOBEYS WEST INC
SAFEWAY
(*Suby of* EMPIRE COMPANY LIMITED)
1632 14 Ave Nw Unit 1846, Calgary, AB, T2N
1M7
(403) 210-0002
Emp Here 150
SIC 5411 Grocery stores
 Hoa Ly

        D-U-N-S 24-099-4082   (SL)
STREAM OIL & GAS LTD
609 14 St Nw Suite 300, Calgary, AB, T2N 2A1
(403) 531-2358
Emp Here 460   *Sales* 309,432,340
SIC 1382 Oil and gas exploration services
 Sotirios Kapotas
 Georgios-Antonios Mortakis-Martakis
 Robert Hall

        D-U-N-S 20-324-9664   (HQ)
UNIGLOBE BEACON TRAVEL LTD
1400 Kensington Rd Nw Suite 200, Calgary,
AB, T2N 3P9
(877) 596-6860
Emp Here 55   *Sales* 34,317,822
SIC 4724 Travel agencies
 David Kruschell
 Richard Gardner
 Anthony Johnston

        D-U-N-S 24-767-2827   (HQ)
VENTURE COMMUNICATIONS LTD
2540 Kensington Rd Nw, Calgary, AB, T2N
3S3
(403) 265-4659
Emp Here 1   *Sales* 13,762,060
SIC 7311 Advertising agencies
 Arlene Dickinson

        D-U-N-S 20-375-0765   (SL)
WOOD HOMES FOUNDATION

WOODS HOMES
805 37 St Nw, Calgary, AB, T2N 4N8
(403) 270-1718
Emp Here 350   *Sales* 26,877,200
SIC 8322 Individual and family services
 Jane Matheson

        D-U-N-S 20-832-1885   (HQ)
WOOD'S HOMES SOCIETY
805 37 St Nw, Calgary, AB, T2N 4N8
(403) 220-0349
Emp Here 35   *Sales* 26,303,000
SIC 8641 Civic and social associations
 Jane Matheson
 Scott Doupe
 Peggy Rodway
 John Stankiewicz
 Heather Heasman
 Kim Hubick
 Dave Johnson
 Brian Rayner
 Frank Rosar
 David Olson

Calgary, AB T2P

        D-U-N-S 25-506-5526   (SL)
1334130 ALBERTA LTD
SEITEL
(*Suby of* PULSE SEISMIC INC)
550 6 Ave Sw Suite 1000, Calgary, AB, T2P
0S2
(403) 515-2800
Emp Here 50   *Sales* 15,985,250
SIC 1382 Oil and gas exploration services
 Randy Sides
 Jude Affonso
 Marcia Kendrick

        D-U-N-S 24-320-1578   (SL)
1986114 ALBERTA INC
605 5 Ave Sw Suite 3200, Calgary, AB, T2P
3H5
(403) 269-4400
Emp Here 300   *Sales* 201,803,700
SIC 1311 Crude petroleum and natural gas
 Hao Wang
 Wentao Yang

        D-U-N-S 20-922-5197   (SL)
320114 ALBERTA INC
VISION 2000 TRAVEL GROUP
400 4 Ave Sw Suite 230, Calgary, AB, T2P 0J4

Emp Here 45   *Sales* 23,398,515
SIC 4724 Travel agencies
 Anthony Ponkinson

        D-U-N-S 24-013-9241   (HQ)
3ES INNOVATION INC
AUCERNA
250 2 St Sw Suite 800, Calgary, AB, T2P 0C1
(403) 270-3270
Emp Here 150   *Sales* 59,986,225
SIC 7371 Custom computer programming services
 Wayne Sim
 Sandy Moreland
 Salvador Clave
 Steven Guevarra

        D-U-N-S 20-376-6279   (HQ)
4513380 CANADA INC
450 1 St Sw Suite 2500, Calgary, AB, T2P 5H1

Sales 365,509,000
SIC 6712 Bank holding companies
 Laurie Woodruff
 Michael Drai

        D-U-N-S 25-313-9927   (HQ)
701671 ALBERTA LTD
(*Suby of* TC ENERGY CORPORATION)
450 1 St Sw, Calgary, AB, T2P 5H1

(403) 920-2000
Emp Here 1   *Sales* 10,393,100
SIC 4911 Electric services
 Harold Kvisle

        D-U-N-S 20-039-2335   (SL)
744648 ALBERTA LTD
OMNICOM LANGUAGE SERVICES
840 6 Ave Sw Suite 100, Calgary, AB, T2P
3E5
(403) 265-6936
Emp Here 40   *Sales* 17,739,600
SIC 7389 Business services, nec
 Ian Huntley

        D-U-N-S 25-987-0616   (SL)
817936 ALBERTA LTD
CEILI'S IRISH PUB & RESTAURANT
513 8 Ave Sw Suite 126, Calgary, AB, T2P
1G1
(403) 508-9999
Emp Here 100   *Sales* 4,287,300
SIC 5812 Eating places
 Paul Vickers
 Mike Joseph

        D-U-N-S 24-318-6280   (HQ)
ACCESS PIPELINE INC
(*Suby of* WOLF MIDSTREAM INC)
520 3 Ave Sw Suite 1500, Calgary, AB, T2P
0R3
(403) 264-6514
Emp Here 60   *Sales* 50,304,492
SIC 4619 Pipelines, nec
 Kent Reardon
 Bill Mccaffrey
 Don Moe
 Keith Fardy
 Robert Dutton

        D-U-N-S 24-099-2581   (BR)
ACCOR SERVICES CANADA INC
(*Suby of* ACCOR)
133 9 Ave Sw, Calgary, AB, T2P 2M3
(403) 262-1234
Emp Here 300
SIC 7011 Hotels and motels
 Brigitte Fritz

        D-U-N-S 24-375-8310   (SL)
ACERO ENGINEERING INC
600 6 Ave Sw Suite 900, Calgary, AB, T2P
0S5
(403) 237-7388
Emp Here 60   *Sales* 10,557,480
SIC 8711 Engineering services
 Mark Kuppe
 Rola Bittar

        D-U-N-S 25-387-8979   (SL)
ACUMEN CAPITAL FINANCE PARTNERS LIMITED
ACUMEN CAPITAL PARTNERS
404 6 Ave Sw Unit 700, Calgary, AB, T2P 0R9
(403) 571-0300
Emp Here 31   *Sales* 16,467,417
SIC 6211 Security brokers and dealers
 Brian Parker

        D-U-N-S 25-417-9161   (SL)
ADVANCE DRILLING LTD
100 4 Ave Sw Suite 706, Calgary, AB, T2P
3N2

Emp Here 60   *Sales* 13,069,740
SIC 1781 Water well drilling
 Paul K. Cheung
 Scott Mackenzie

        D-U-N-S 20-181-2844   (HQ)
ADVANTAGE OIL & GAS LTD
440 2 Ave Sw Suite 2200, Calgary, AB, T2P
5E9
(403) 718-8000
Sales 185,089,087
SIC 1382 Oil and gas exploration services
 Andy J. Mah
 Craig Blackwood
 Michael Belenkie

 Neil Bokenfohr
 David Sterna
 Jay P. Reid
 Ronald A. Mcintosh
 Stephen E. Balog
 Grant B. Fagerheim
 Paul G. Haggis

        D-U-N-S 24-247-1048   (SL)
AECO GAS STORAGE PARTNERSHIP
NISKA GAS STORAGE
607 8 Ave Sw Suite 400, Calgary, AB, T2P
0A7
(403) 513-8600
Emp Here 100   *Sales* 182,976,600
SIC 4922 Natural gas transmission
 Simon Dupere

        D-U-N-S 20-271-7492   (HQ)
AIR LIQUIDE GLOBAL E&C SOLUTIONS CANADA INC
140 4 Ave Sw Suite 550, Calgary, AB, T2P
3N3
(403) 774-4300
Sales 10,006,500
SIC 5169 Chemicals and allied products, nec
 Cameron Mason

        D-U-N-S 20-301-4295   (SL)
AIR LIQUIDE GLOBAL E&C SOLUTIONS CANADA LP
1404 Ave Sw Suite 550, Calgary, AB, T2P 3N3
(403) 774-4300
Emp Here 50   *Sales* 36,517,250
SIC 5169 Chemicals and allied products, nec
 Cameron Mason

        D-U-N-S 24-948-8552   (HQ)
AKITA DRILLING LTD
333 7 Ave Sw Unit 1000, Calgary, AB, T2P
2Z1
(403) 292-7979
Emp Here 14   *Sales* 89,729,711
SIC 1382 Oil and gas exploration services
 Karl Ruud
 Darcy Reynolds
 Raymond Coleman
 Fred Hensel
 Colin A. Dease
 Craig Kushner
 Loraine Charlton
 Linda Southern-Heathcott
 Harish K Mohan
 Dale Richardson

        D-U-N-S 20-185-1867   (SL)
ALBERTA ELECTRIC SYSTEM OPERATOR
AESO
330 5 Ave Sw Suite 2500, Calgary, AB, T2P
0L4
(403) 539-2450
Emp Here 170   *Sales* 1,316,642,065
SIC 4911 Electric services
 David Erickson
 Todd Fior
 Wayne St. Amour
 Bill Burch
 Ron George
 Nancy Laird

        D-U-N-S 24-702-1421   (SL)
ALBERTA TUBULAR PRODUCTS LTD
500 4 Ave Sw Suite 1100, Calgary, AB, T2P
2V6
(403) 264-2136
Emp Here 30   *Sales* 13,415,220
SIC 5051 Metals service centers and offices
 Bruce J Stuart
 Steve Sutton
 Bill Thomas

        D-U-N-S 25-685-0595   (SL)
ALLIANCE PIPELINE LIMITED PARTNERSHIP
605 5 Ave Sw Suite 800, Calgary, AB, T2P
3H5
(403) 266-4464
Emp Here 391   *Sales* 439,691,993

SIC 4922 Natural gas transmission
Terrance Kutryk
Keith Palmer
William Christensen
Derek Riphagen
Daniel Sutherland
Jim Walsh

D-U-N-S 25-384-6620   (HQ)
ALLIANCE PIPELINE LTD
605 5 Ave Sw Suite 800, Calgary, AB, T2P
3H5
(403) 266-4464
Emp Here 45   *Sales* 39,271,050
SIC 8741 Management services
Terrance Kutryk
Keith Palmer
William Christensen

D-U-N-S 24-679-0856   (SL)
ALTACORP CAPITAL INC
585 8 Ave Sw Unit 410, Calgary, AB, T2P 1G1
(403) 539-8600
Emp Here 20   *Sales* 13,578,460
SIC 6282 Investment advice
Jon Horsman
Paul Sarachman
Michael Kehler
Dave Mowat
Ian Wild
Lynn Tsutsumi

D-U-N-S 20-285-5573   (SL)
ALTAGAS EXTRACTION AND TRANSMISSION LIMITED PARTNERSHIP
(*Suby of* ALTAGAS LTD)
355 4 Ave Sw Unit 1700, Calgary, AB, T2P 0J1
(403) 691-7575
Emp Here 350   *Sales* 403,183,900
SIC 4923 Gas transmission and distribution
David Harris

D-U-N-S 20-392-4576   (SL)
ALTAGAS LPG LIMITED PARTNERSHIP
355 4 Ave Sw Suite 1700, Calgary, AB, T2P 0J1
(403) 691-7196
Emp Here 5   *Sales* 15,529,285
SIC 4924 Natural gas distribution
David Harris

D-U-N-S 20-693-3090   (HQ)
ALTAGAS LTD
355 4 Ave Sw Suite 1700, Calgary, AB, T2P 0J1
(403) 691-7575
Emp Here 14   *Sales* 3,227,012,783
SIC 1311 Crude petroleum and natural gas
Randy Crawford
D. James Harbilas
Brad Grant
Tim Watson
Randy Toone
Fred Dalena
Corine Bushfield
David W. Cornhill
Catherine Best
Victoria Calvert

D-U-N-S 20-371-6295   (HQ)
ALTAGAS NORTHWEST PROCESSING LIMITED PARTNERSHIP
55 4 Ave Sw Suite 1700, Calgary, AB, T2P 0J1
(403) 691-7196
Emp Here 300   *Sales* 2,303,908,000
SIC 4924 Natural gas distribution
David Harris

D-U-N-S 24-014-2161   (HQ)
ALTEX ENERGY LTD
700 9 Ave Sw Suite 1100, Calgary, AB, T2P 3V4
(403) 508-7525
Emp Here 24   *Sales* 15,985,250
SIC 1389 Oil and gas field services, nec
John Zahary
Greg Molaro

Aaron Bishop
Randy Meyer
Jeff Van Steenburgen
Scott Pearl

D-U-N-S 24-380-6283   (HQ)
ALTURA ENERGY INC
640 5 Ave Sw Suite 2500, Calgary, AB, T2P 3G4
(403) 984-5197
Sales 12,771,744
SIC 1382 Oil and gas exploration services
David Burghardt
Tavis Carlson
Jeff Mazurak
Robert Pinckston
Travis Stephenson
Craig Stayura
John Mcaleer
Darren Gee
Brian Lavergne
Robert Maitland

D-U-N-S 24-311-1148   (HQ)
ALTUS ENERGY SERVICES LTD
222 3 Ave Sw Suite 740, Calgary, AB, T2P 0B4

Emp Here 200   *Sales* 240,227,240
SIC 1389 Oil and gas field services, nec
Christopher Haslam
Frederick Moore
Norman S. Denoon
Darren K. Glover

D-U-N-S 20-296-4854   (SL)
ALVOPETRO ENERGY LTD
525 8 Ave Sw Suite 1700, Calgary, AB, T2P 1G1
(587) 794-4224
Emp Here 42   *Sales* 77,892,444
SIC 1311 Crude petroleum and natural gas
Corey C Ruttan
Andrea Hatzinikolas
Alison Howard
Firoz Talakshi
Geir Ytreland
Kenneth R Mckinnon
Roderick L Fraser

D-U-N-S 24-441-4876   (SL)
AMEC BDR LIMITED
(*Suby of* JOHN WOOD GROUP P.L.C.)
401 9 Ave Sw Suite 1300, Calgary, AB, T2P 3C5
(403) 283-0060
Emp Here 100   *Sales* 17,873,900
SIC 8711 Engineering services
Ken Damberger
Samir Brikho

D-U-N-S 25-096-4772   (BR)
AMEC FOSTER WHEELER INC
AMEC ENGINEERING
(*Suby of* JOHN WOOD GROUP P.L.C.)
801 6 Ave Sw Suite 900, Calgary, AB, T2P 3W3
(403) 298-4170
Emp Here 500
SIC 6712 Bank holding companies
Doug Annable

D-U-N-S 24-424-0078   (SL)
ANTHEM RIVERFRONT LAND LIMITED PARTNERSHIP
104 2 St Sw, Calgary, AB, T2P 0C7
(403) 536-8802
Emp Here 325   *Sales* 60,502,325
SIC 6553 Cemetery subdividers and developers
Eric Carlson

D-U-N-S 20-824-4830   (BR)
AON REED STENHOUSE INC
(*Suby of* AON PLC)
600 3 Ave Sw Suite 1800, Calgary, AB, T2P 0G5

(403) 267-7010
Emp Here 150
SIC 6411 Insurance agents, brokers, and service
Michael Bagby

D-U-N-S 25-168-0294   (SL)
AOT ENERGY CANADA INC
(*Suby of* TRANSCOR ASTRA GROUP)
520 3 Ave Sw Suite 3120, Calgary, AB, T2P 0R3
(403) 770-2700
Emp Here 10   *Sales* 12,572,010
SIC 5172 Petroleum products, nec
Kumar Mendis
Kerry Tychonick

D-U-N-S 20-558-2070   (SL)
AOT ENERGY CANADA NATURAL GAS INC
(*Suby of* TRANSCOR ASTRA GROUP)
520 3 Ave Sw Unit 3120, Calgary, AB, T2P 0R3
(403) 770-2700
Emp Here 10   *Sales* 12,572,010
SIC 5172 Petroleum products, nec
Kerry Tychonick
Kumar Mendis
Martin Fasser
Brian Porich

D-U-N-S 25-977-3059   (HQ)
APEX DISTRIBUTION INC
APEX
(*Suby of* RUSSEL METALS INC)
407 2 St Sw Suite 550, Calgary, AB, T2P 2Y3
(403) 268-7333
Emp Here 25   *Sales* 101,447,840
SIC 5084 Industrial machinery and equipment
Ken Wallewein
Ryan Mahony
Bill Ouwejan
Vanessa Reay

D-U-N-S 25-387-5702   (HQ)
ARC RESOURCES LTD
308 4 Ave Sw Suite 1200, Calgary, AB, T2P 0H7
(403) 503-8600
Emp Here 250   *Sales* 1,053,382,729
SIC 1381 Drilling oil and gas wells
Myron M. Stadnyk
P. Van R Dafoe
Terry Anderson
Bevin Wirzba
Chris Baldwin
Ryan Berrett
Kristen Bibby
Sean Calder
Lara Conrad
Armin Jahangiri

D-U-N-S 20-920-9944   (SL)
ARCHEAN ENERGY LTD
GRIZZLY RESOURCES
(*Suby of* EAGLE RESOURCES LTD)
324 8 Ave Sw Suite 1000, Calgary, AB, T2P 2Z2
(403) 237-9600
Emp Here 25   *Sales* 12,451,950
SIC 5541 Gasoline service stations
Larry Parks
Gerry Quinn

D-U-N-S 20-365-3613   (SL)
ARCIS SEISMIC SOLUTIONS CORP
(*Suby of* TGS NOPEC GEOPHYSICAL COMPANY ASA)
250 5 St Sw Suite 2100, Calgary, AB, T2P 0R4
(403) 781-1700
Emp Here 75   *Sales* 50,450,925
SIC 1382 Oil and gas exploration services
John Ropchan
Graziella Kirtland Grech

D-U-N-S 20-334-2451   (HQ)
ARGO SALES INC
717 7 Ave Sw Suite 1300, Calgary, AB, T2P 0Z3

(403) 265-6633
Sales 19,208,500
SIC 3443 Fabricated plate work (boiler shop)
William Hlynsky

D-U-N-S 20-034-5432   (HQ)
ASPEN PROPERTIES LTD
150 9 Ave Sw Unit 1510, Calgary, AB, T2P 3H9
(403) 216-2660
Sales 33,511,120
SIC 6531 Real estate agents and managers
R. Scott Hutcheson

D-U-N-S 25-235-7132   (HQ)
ATCO MIDSTREAM LTD
(*Suby of* ATCO LTD)
240 4 Ave Sw Suite 900, Calgary, AB, T2P 4H4
(403) 513-3700
Emp Here 74   *Sales* 34,270,800
SIC 4899 Communication services, nec
Nancy C Southern
Marie Yan
Rob Harper
Arnold Macburnie

D-U-N-S 24-322-4016   (HQ)
ATHABASCA OIL CORPORATION
215 9 Ave Sw Suite 1200, Calgary, AB, T2P 1K3
(403) 237-8227
Emp Here 129   *Sales* 602,614,522
SIC 5172 Petroleum products, nec
Rob Broen
Kevin Smith
Karla Ingoldsby
Dave Stewart
Angela Avery
Matt Taylor
Kim Anderson
Ronald Eckhardt
Bryan Begley
Anne Downey

D-U-N-S 20-464-4962   (SL)
AUSENCO ENGINEERING CANADA INC
401 9 Ave Sw Ste 1430, Calgary, AB, T2P 3C5
(403) 705-4100
Emp Here 100   *Sales* 31,970,500
SIC 1382 Oil and gas exploration services
Zimi Meka

D-U-N-S 20-369-1485   (SL)
AVALANT INTERNATIONAL LTD
315 8 Ave Sw, Calgary, AB, T2P 4K1

Emp Here 6   *Sales* 18,635,142
SIC 4925 Gas production and/or distribution

D-U-N-S 24-318-0515   (HQ)
AVEDA TRANSPORTATION AND ENERGY SERVICES INC
ABILITY HAULING DIV OF
(*Suby of* DASEKE, INC.)
435 4 Ave Sw Suite 300, Calgary, AB, T2P 3A8
(403) 264-4950
Emp Here 40   *Sales* 156,392,978
SIC 1389 Oil and gas field services, nec
Ronnie Witherspoon
Bharat Mahajan
Les Ovelson
David P. Werklund
Stefan Erasmus
Doug Mccartney
Paul Shelley
Larry Heidt

D-U-N-S 20-059-8915   (SL)
AVENIR TRADING CORP
808 1 St Sw Suite 300, Calgary, AB, T2P 1M9
(403) 237-9949
Emp Here 4   *Sales* 12,423,428
SIC 4924 Natural gas distribution
William Gallacher

D-U-N-S 20-824-6306   (BR)

AVIVA INSURANCE COMPANY OF CANADA
C G U INSURANCE
(*Suby of* GENERAL ACCIDENT PLC)
140 4 Ave Sw Suite 2400, Calgary, AB, T2P 3W4
(403) 750-0600
Emp Here 100
SIC 6331 Fire, marine, and casualty insurance
Terry Lineker

D-U-N-S 25-326-1267   (HQ)
BAKER HUGHES CANADA COMPANY
BAKER ATLAS
(*Suby of* GENERAL ELECTRIC COMPANY)
401 9 Ave Sw Suite 1000, Calgary, AB, T2P 3C5
(403) 537-3400
Emp Here 200   *Sales* 536,503,000
SIC 5084 Industrial machinery and equipment
Lorenzo Simonelli
Neil Saunders
Maria Claudia Borras
Jen Hartsock
Brian Worrell
Harry Elsinga
Derek Mathieson

D-U-N-S 25-516-3156   (BR)
BAKER HUGHES CANADA COMPANY
BAKER OIL TOOLS
(*Suby of* GENERAL ELECTRIC COMPANY)
401 9 Ave Sw Suite 1300, Calgary, AB, T2P 3C5

Emp Here 100
SIC 5169 Chemicals and allied products, nec
Jim Vanhoozen

D-U-N-S 20-130-8926   (HQ)
BAKER HUGHES INC
(*Suby of* GENERAL ELECTRIC COMPANY)
401 9 Ave Sw Suite 1000, Calgary, AB, T2P 3C5
(403) 537-3400
Sales 84,263,100
SIC 3533 Oil and gas field machinery
Mike Davis

D-U-N-S 25-204-6073   (SL)
BANKERS PETROLEUM LTD
(*Suby of* GEO-JADE PETROLEUM CORPORATION)
3700-888 3 St Sw, Calgary, AB, T2P 5C5
(403) 513-2699
Emp Here 230   *Sales* 125,573,330
SIC 1382 Oil and gas exploration services
Douglas Urch
Suneel Gupta
Bayne Assmus
Robert Carss
Mark Hodgson
Craig Nardone
Richard Pawluk

D-U-N-S 25-518-9219   (BR)
BANQUE NATIONALE DU CANADA
WELLINGTON WEST
(*Suby of* BANQUE NATIONALE DU CANADA)
450 1 St Sw Suite 2800, Calgary, AB, T2P 5H1
(403) 266-1116
Emp Here 80
SIC 8741 Management services
Elodie Darde

D-U-N-S 25-518-5274   (BR)
BANQUE NATIONALE DU CANADA
(*Suby of* BANQUE NATIONALE DU CANADA)
407 8 Ave Sw Suite 1000, Calgary, AB, T2P 1E5
(403) 294-4917
Emp Here 85
SIC 6021 National commercial banks
Louise Vachon

D-U-N-S 24-702-0712   (SL)

BAYCOR INDUSTRIES LTD
404 6 Ave Sw Suite 300, Calgary, AB, T2P 0R9
(403) 294-0600
Emp Here 200   *Sales* 187,835,400
SIC 6211 Security brokers and dealers
Kevin R Baker

D-U-N-S 24-984-4952   (HQ)
BAYTEX ENERGY CORP
520 3 Ave Sw Suite 2800, Calgary, AB, T2P 0R3
(587) 952-3000
Emp Here 147   *Sales* 845,371,670
SIC 1311 Crude petroleum and natural gas
Edward Lafehr
Rodney D. Gray
Jason Jaskela
Brian Ector
Kendall Arthur
Jonathan Grimwood
Chad Kalmakoff
Scott Lovett
Chad Lundberg
Scott Rideout

D-U-N-S 24-553-7410   (BR)
BDO CANADA LLP
(*Suby of* BDO CANADA LLP)
903 8 Ave Sw Suite 620, Calgary, AB, T2P 0P7
(403) 266-5608
Emp Here 80
SIC 8721 Accounting, auditing, and bookkeeping
Patrick Kramer

D-U-N-S 20-318-5202   (SL)
BEARSTONE ENVIRONMENTAL SOLUTIONS INC
435 4 Ave Sw Suite 500, Calgary, AB, T2P 3A8
(403) 984-9798
Emp Here 50   *Sales* 15,057,100
SIC 4959 Sanitary services, nec
Gerry Kerkhoff

D-U-N-S 24-849-4721   (SL)
BEDFORD BIOFUELS INC
510 5 St Sw Suite 1500, Calgary, AB, T2P 3S2
(403) 648-6100
Emp Here 50   *Sales* 10,798,463
SIC 8748 Business consulting, nec
David Mcclure

D-U-N-S 24-391-0846   (HQ)
BELLATRIX EXPLORATION LTD
800 5 Ave Sw Unit 1920, Calgary, AB, T2P 3T6
(403) 266-8670
Sales 155,352,536
SIC 1381 Drilling oil and gas wells
Brent Eshleman
Steve Toth
Maxwell Lof
Charles Kraus
Garrett Ulmer
Murray Todd
Murray Cobbe
Keith Macdonald
Keith Turnbull
John Cuthbertson

D-U-N-S 20-829-0015   (HQ)
BENNETT JONES LLP
855 2 St Sw Suite 4500, Calgary, AB, T2P 4K7
(403) 298-3100
Emp Here 180   *Sales* 205,876,000
SIC 8111 Legal services
Hugh Mackinnon
Stephen W. Bowman
Enzo J. Barichello

D-U-N-S 24-316-5706   (SL)
BEYOND ENERGY & TRADE INC
205 5 Ave Sw Suite 1870, Calgary, AB, T2P 2V7

(403) 531-2699
Emp Here 4   *Sales* 12,423,428
SIC 4924 Natural gas distribution
Darcy White

D-U-N-S 20-336-3080   (HQ)
BEYOND ENERGY SERVICES & TECHNOLOGY CORP
444 5 Ave Sw, Calgary, AB, T2P 2T8
(403) 506-1514
Sales 47,087,530
SIC 1381 Drilling oil and gas wells
Jason Lock
Keri Lock
Mike Macpherson
Eric Legge

D-U-N-S 20-302-5551   (SL)
BIALIK, DON & ASSOCIATES
255 5 Ave Sw Suite 3100, Calgary, AB, T2P 3G6
(403) 515-6900
Emp Here 185   *Sales* 31,385,836
SIC 7379 Computer related services, nec
Don Bialik

D-U-N-S 20-700-2457   (HQ)
BIRCHCLIFF ENERGY LTD
600 3rd Ave Sw Suite 1000, Calgary, AB, T2P 0G5
(403) 261-6401
Emp Here 150   *Sales* 479,397,929
SIC 1382 Oil and gas exploration services
A. Jeffery Tonken
Bruno P. Geremia
David Humphreys
Myles R. Bosman
Christopher Carlsen
James W Surbey
Dennis Dawson
Debbie Gerlach
Stacey Mcdonald

D-U-N-S 24-494-8501   (SL)
BISSETT RESOURCE CONSULTANTS LTD
839 5 Ave Sw Suite 250, Calgary, AB, T2P 3C8
(403) 263-0073
Emp Here 50   *Sales* 15,985,250
SIC 1389 Oil and gas field services, nec
Richard Bissett
Chris Bissett
Russell Brown

D-U-N-S 20-364-1238   (SL)
BJ SERVICES HOLDINGS CANADA ULC
215 9 Ave Sw Unit 800, Calgary, AB, T2P 1K3
(587) 324-2058
Emp Here 400   *Sales* 269,071,600
SIC 1382 Oil and gas exploration services
Warren Zemlak

D-U-N-S 24-391-5456   (HQ)
BLACK DIAMOND GROUP LIMITED
BLACK DIAMOND CAMPS
440 2 Ave Sw Suite 1000, Calgary, AB, T2P 5E9
(403) 206-4747
Emp Here 100   *Sales* 125,792,623
SIC 7353 Heavy construction equipment rental
Trevor Haynes
Tory Labrie
Troy Cleland
Mike Ridley
Patrick Melanson
Robert Wagemakers
Robert Herdman
Barbara Kelley
Edward H. Kernaghan
David Olsson

D-U-N-S 24-187-3368   (HQ)
BLACK DIAMOND LIMITED PARTNERSHIP
BLACK DIAMOND CAMPS, DIV OF
440 2 Ave Sw Suite 1000, Calgary, AB, T2P 5E9

(403) 206-4747
Emp Here 50   *Sales* 65,273,000
SIC 7359 Equipment rental and leasing, nec
Trevor Haynes
Paul Wright
Patrick Melanson
Toby Labrie
Steve Langmaid

D-U-N-S 24-309-4831   (HQ)
BLACKPEARL RESOURCES INC
(*Suby of* INTERNATIONAL PETROLEUM CORPORATION)
215 9 Ave Sw Unit 900, Calgary, AB, T2P 1K3
(403) 215-8313
Emp Here 28   *Sales* 14,386,725
SIC 1382 Oil and gas exploration services
Chris Hogue
Ed Sobel
Christophe Nerguararian
Jeffrey Fountain

D-U-N-S 24-854-4363   (BR)
BLAKE, CASSELS & GRAYDON LLP
(*Suby of* BLAKE, CASSELS & GRAYDON LLP)
855 2 St Sw Suite 3500, Calgary, AB, T2P 4J8
(403) 260-9600
Emp Here 220
SIC 8111 Legal services
Ken Mills

D-U-N-S 24-992-1979   (BR)
BMO NESBITT BURNS INC
NESBITT BURNS
(*Suby of* BMO NESBITT BURNS INC)
525 8 Ave Sw Suite 3200, Calgary, AB, T2P 1G1
(403) 261-9550
Emp Here 100
SIC 6211 Security brokers and dealers

D-U-N-S 20-194-0082   (HQ)
BONAVISTA ENERGY CORPORATION
525 8 Ave Sw Suite 1500, Calgary, AB, T2P 1G1
(403) 213-4300
Sales 390,397,513
SIC 1311 Crude petroleum and natural gas
Jason E. Skehar
Bruce W. Jensen
Dean M. Kobelka
Rochelle L. Estep
Colin J. Ranger
Lynda J. Robinson
Scott W. Shimek
Keith A. Macphail
Ian S. Brown
David P. Carey

D-U-N-S 25-171-1560   (BR)
BORDEN LADNER GERVAIS LLP
BLG
(*Suby of* BORDEN LADNER GERVAIS LLP)
520 3 Ave Sw Suite 1900, Calgary, AB, T2P 0R3
(403) 232-9500
Emp Here 160
SIC 8111 Legal services
Doug Mitchell

D-U-N-S 20-295-2560   (SL)
BOW RIVER ENERGY LTD
321 6 Ave Sw Suite 500, Calgary, AB, T2P 3H3
(403) 475-4100
Emp Here 60   *Sales* 40,360,740
SIC 1382 Oil and gas exploration services
Henry A. Cohen
Daniel G. Belot
Josh Caswell
Robert Dumaine
Randy Eresman
Edward Bogle
Ralph Scurfield

D-U-N-S 20-077-3919   (HQ)
BP CANADA ENERGY COMPANY

▲ Public Company   ■ Public Company Family Member   **HQ** Headquarters   **BR** Branch   **SL** Single Location

(*Suby of* BP P.L.C.)
240 4 Ave Sw, Calgary, AB, T2P 4H4
(403) 233-1313
Emp Here 2,100 *Sales* 4,080,080,400
SIC 1311 Crude petroleum and natural gas
  Anne Drinkwater
  Gerald K. Maxwell
  Delwyn Robostan
  Stephen Willis
  Jeffrey Tanner
  David Campbell
  Tyler A Rimbey
  Elizabeth Matheson
  Mark Manser
  Macsen Jay Nuttall

D-U-N-S 24-879-9413 (SL)
BP CANADA ENERGY MARKETING CORP
(*Suby of* BP P.L.C.)
240 4 Ave Sw, Calgary, AB, T2P 4H4
(403) 233-1313
Emp Here 10 *Sales* 12,572,010
SIC 5172 Petroleum products, nec
  Brian Frank

D-U-N-S 20-041-8228 (SL)
BRIDGEWATER BANK
(*Suby of* ALBERTA MOTOR ASSOCIATION)
926 5 Ave Sw Suite 150, Calgary, AB, T2P 0N7
(866) 243-4301
Emp Here 100 *Sales* 20,144,700
SIC 6021 National commercial banks
  Peter O'neill
  Gord Follett
  Mary Jayne Crocker
  Dave Sanders
  Glenn Halliday
  Todd Poberznick

D-U-N-S 25-519-8442 (HQ)
BROMWICH & SMITH INC
1000 9 Ave Sw Suite 201, Calgary, AB, T2P 2Y6
(855) 884-9243
Emp Here 1 *Sales* 10,626,759
SIC 8111 Legal services
  David L Smith
  Shawn Stack
  Loren Starno

D-U-N-S 24-227-7684 (HQ)
BROWN & ASSOCIATES PLANNING GROUP LTD
215 9 Ave Sw Suite 600, Calgary, AB, T2P 1K3
(403) 269-4733
Emp Here 20 *Sales* 11,714,400
SIC 8748 Business consulting, nec
  Greg Brown
  Darrell Grant
  Ronald Wrigley
  Kathy Oberg
  Ken Venner
  Nathan Petherick
  Pam Macinnis
  Vern Hart

D-U-N-S 20-766-2792 (SL)
BSL PROPERTY GROUP INC
RANCHMAN'S
335 8 Ave Sw, Calgary, AB, T2P 1C9
(403) 253-1100
Emp Here 80 *Sales* 11,855,360
SIC 4213 Trucking, except local
  Kevin Baker

D-U-N-S 20-354-6239 (SL)
BURSTALL NGL STORAGE L.P.
222 3 Ave Sw Suite 900, Calgary, AB, T2P 0B4
(403) 296-0140
Emp Here 5 *Sales* 15,529,285
SIC 4922 Natural gas transmission
  Don Althoff

D-U-N-S 25-990-1353 (HQ)

CALFRAC WELL SERVICES LTD
411 8 Ave Sw, Calgary, AB, T2P 1E3
(866) 770-3722
Emp Here 100 *Sales* 1,710,601,063
SIC 1389 Oil and gas field services, nec
  Fernando Aguilar
  Ronald Mathison
  Douglas Ramsay
  Gregory Fletcher
  James Blair
  Kevin Baker
  Lorne Gartner
  Michael Olinek
  Lindsay Link

D-U-N-S 24-417-0072 (HQ)
CALGARY FOREIGN EXCHANGE LTD
CALFOREX
255 5 Ave Suite 480, Calgary, AB, T2P 3G6
(403) 290-0400
Emp Here 20 *Sales* 25,689,180
SIC 6099 Functions related to deposit banking
  Toni Treutler
  Tracy Mccaig
  Oswald Treutler

D-U-N-S 20-830-7371 (SL)
CALGARY PETROLEUM CLUB
319 5 Ave Sw, Calgary, AB, T2P 0L5
(403) 269-7981
Emp Here 130 *Sales* 17,096,950
SIC 8641 Civic and social associations
  Sippi Chhina

D-U-N-S 25-217-5856 (SL)
CALGARY RAMADA DOWNTOWN LIMITED PARTNERSHIP
RAMADA HOTEL
708 8 Ave Sw, Calgary, AB, T2P 1H2
(403) 263-7600
Emp Here 100 *Sales* 9,489,900
SIC 7011 Hotels and motels
  Mahesh Hathiramani

D-U-N-S 20-988-4998 (HQ)
CALGARY ROMAN CATHOLIC SEPARATE SCHOOL DISTRICT #1
CALGARY CATHOLIC SCHOOL DISTRICT
1000 5 Ave Sw Suite 1, Calgary, AB, T2P 4T9
(403) 500-2000
Emp Here 100 *Sales* 396,476,000
SIC 8211 Elementary and secondary schools
  Lucy Miller
  John Deausy

D-U-N-S 24-340-4899 (SL)
CALGARY TOWER FACILITIES LTD
(*Suby of* ASPEN PROPERTIES LTD)
101 9 Ave Sw, Calgary, AB, T2P 1J9
(403) 266-7171
Emp Here 100 *Sales* 4,551,900
SIC 5812 Eating places
  Don Dempson

D-U-N-S 20-829-3498 (HQ)
CALGARY YOUNG MEN'S CHRISTIAN ASSOCIATION, THE
Y M C A CALGARY
101 3 St Sw, Calgary, AB, T2P 4G6
(403) 269-6701
Emp Here 50 *Sales* 25,985,122
SIC 8399 Social services, nec
  Shannon Doram
  Kelly Smith
  James K Grayd
  Robert Savin
  Catherine Angus
  Michael Crape
  Randy Green
  W. Clarke Hunter
  Sue Lee
  Fauzia Lalani

D-U-N-S 20-388-1839 (SL)
CAMPUS ENERGY PARTNERS LP
355 4 Ave Sw Suite 1700, Calgary, AB, T2P 0J1

(403) 691-7575
Emp Here 75 *Sales* 245,192,220
SIC 4922 Natural gas transmission
  Jeremy Baines

D-U-N-S 25-456-0311 (BR)
CANACCORD GENUITY CORP
(*Suby of* CANACCORD GENUITY GROUP INC)
450 1 St Sw Suite 2200, Calgary, AB, T2P 5H1
(403) 508-3800
Emp Here 80
SIC 6211 Security brokers and dealers
  John Kenny

D-U-N-S 24-869-1958 (HQ)
CANACOL ENERGY LTD
585 8 Ave Sw Suite 2650, Calgary, AB, T2P 1G1
(403) 561-1648
Sales 222,413,000
SIC 1311 Crude petroleum and natural gas
  Charle Gamba
  Jason Bednar
  Ravi Sharma
  Mark Teare
  Luis Baena
  Anthony Zaidi
  Diego Carvajal
  Nicolas Acuna
  Tracy Whitmore
  Michael Hibberd

D-U-N-S 24-809-5770 (HQ)
CANADA IMPERIAL OIL LIMITED
(*Suby of* IMPERIAL OIL LIMITED)
237 4 Ave Sw Suite 2480, Calgary, AB, T2P 0H6
(800) 567-3776
Emp Here 150 *Sales* 1,773,409,500
SIC 5172 Petroleum products, nec
  Keith W Malverin

D-U-N-S 24-929-7953 (HQ)
CANADIAN ASSOCIATION OF PETROLEUM PRODUCERS
CAPP
350 7 Ave Sw Suite 2100, Calgary, AB, T2P 3N9
(403) 267-1100
Sales 12,930,750
SIC 8611 Business associations
  Dave Collyer
  Greg Stringham
  David Pryce
  Brian Maynard
  Nick Schultz

D-U-N-S 20-388-2142 (BR)
CANADIAN BLOOD SERVICES
(*Suby of* CANADIAN BLOOD SERVICES)
200 Barclay Parade Sw Unit 10, Calgary, AB, T2P 4R5

Emp Here 100
SIC 8099 Health and allied services, nec
  Jennifer Biemans

D-U-N-S 24-929-8894 (SL)
CANADIAN COASTAL RESOURCES LTD
202 6 Ave Sw Suite 900, Calgary, AB, T2P 2R9

Emp Here 90 *Sales* 28,773,450
SIC 1311 Crude petroleum and natural gas
  Gregg Scott

D-U-N-S 20-283-4859 (SL)
CANADIAN ENERGY SERVICES INC
(*Suby of* CES ENERGY SOLUTIONS CORP)
700 4 Ave Sw Suite 1400, Calgary, AB, T2P 3J4
(403) 269-2800
Emp Here 1,400 *Sales* 764,359,400
SIC 1381 Drilling oil and gas wells
  Thomas Simons
  Kyle D. Kitagawa
  James M. Pasieka

  Craig Nieboer
  Burton J. Ahrens
  Stella Cosby

D-U-N-S 24-340-5292 (BR)
CANADIAN NATURAL RESOURCES LIMITED
(*Suby of* CANADIAN NATURAL RESOURCES LIMITED)
324 8 Ave Sw Suite 1800, Calgary, AB, T2P 2Z2
(403) 517-6700
Emp Here 2,000
SIC 1311 Crude petroleum and natural gas
  Steve Brown

D-U-N-S 20-913-7967 (HQ)
CANADIAN NATURAL RESOURCES LIMITED
855 2 St Sw Suite 2100, Calgary, AB, T2P 4J8
(403) 517-6700
Emp Here 1,000 *Sales* 15,940,610,754
SIC 1311 Crude petroleum and natural gas
  N. Murray Edwards
  Tim Mckay
  Betty Yee
  Paul Mendes
  Trevor J. Cassidy
  Pamela A. Mcintyre
  Jay E. Froc
  Robin Zabek
  Ken Stagg
  Bill Peterson

D-U-N-S 20-524-9852 (SL)
CANADIAN TUBULARS (1997) LTD
825 8 Ave Sw Suite 4100, Calgary, AB, T2P 2T4
(403) 266-2218
Emp Here 14 *Sales* 14,004,746
SIC 5051 Metals service centers and offices
  Brian Huffman

D-U-N-S 20-702-5730 (HQ)
CANEXUS CHEMICALS CANADA LTD
144 4 Ave Sw Unit 2100, Calgary, AB, T2P 3N4
(403) 571-7300
Sales 302,495,400
SIC 5169 Chemicals and allied products, nec
  Gary Kubera

D-U-N-S 20-382-8934 (SL)
CANGAS SOLUTIONS INC
555 4 Ave Sw Suite 1250, Calgary, AB, T2P 3E7
(403) 930-0123
Emp Here 5 *Sales* 15,529,285
SIC 4924 Natural gas distribution

D-U-N-S 20-381-1109 (SL)
CANOE EIT INCOME FUND
421 7 Ave Sw Suite 2750, Calgary, AB, T2P 4K9
(403) 571-5554
Emp Here 6 *Sales* 35,021,550
SIC 6726 Investment offices, nec
  Jodi Peake
  Robert J. Taylor
  David Rain
  Darcy Hulston
  Rafi G. Tahmazian
  Renata Colic

D-U-N-S 25-529-2005 (HQ)
CANORO RESOURCES LTD
717 7 Ave Sw Suite 700, Calgary, AB, T2P 0Z3
(403) 543-5747
Emp Here 10 *Sales* 56,505,036
SIC 1311 Crude petroleum and natural gas
  Leslie Kondratoff
  D Nolan Blades
  Jeff Clarke
  Harley L Winger
  Douglas R Martin
  John Boyd

D-U-N-S 20-995-3157 (SL)

CANTAK CORPORATION
(*Suby of* MITSUBISHI CORPORATION)
355 4 Ave Sw Suite 1050, Calgary, AB, T2P
0J1
(403) 269-5536
Emp Here 25   *Sales* 11,179,350
SIC 5051 Metals service centers and offices
Chad Kozak
Matt Stewart
Hiroshi Kawaishi
Scott Gerla
Scott Haderer

D-U-N-S 25-091-9441   (HQ)
CANWEST PROPANE PARTNERSHIP
(*Suby of* SUPERIOR PLUS CORP)
440 2 Ave Sw Suite 1700, Calgary, AB, T2P
5E9
(403) 206-4000
Emp Here 20   *Sales* 115,592,010
SIC 5084 Industrial machinery and equipment
A. Stewart Hanlon

D-U-N-S 20-699-7558   (HQ)
CANYON SERVICES GROUP INC
(*Suby of* TRICAN WELL SERVICE LTD)
645 7 Ave Sw Suite 2900, Calgary, AB, T2P
4G8
(403) 266-0202
Emp Here 200   *Sales* 177,193,794
SIC 1389 Oil and gas field services, nec
Brad Fedora
Barry Obrien
Todd Thue
Chuck Vozniak
Quentin Walker
Robert Skilnick
Todd Den Engelsen
David Westlund
Garnet Olson
Gord Haycraft

D-U-N-S 25-681-0367   (HQ)
CANYON TECHNICAL SERVICES LTD
(*Suby of* TRICAN WELL SERVICE LTD)
255 5 Ave Sw Suite 2900, Calgary, AB, T2P
3G6
(403) 355-2300
Sales 124,445,615
SIC 1389 Oil and gas field services, nec
Bradley J Fedora

D-U-N-S 20-315-3713   (SL)
CARDINAL ENERGY LTD
400 3 Ave Sw Suite 600, Calgary, AB, T2P
4H2
(403) 234-8681
Emp Here 124   *Sales* 229,968,168
SIC 1311 Crude petroleum and natural gas
M. Scott Ratushny
Robert Wollmann
Connie Shevkenek
Laurence Broos
Scott Ratushny
John A. Brussa
David D. Johnson
Gregory Tisdale
Stephanie Sterling
Shawn Van Spankeren

D-U-N-S 24-323-9600   (BR)
CBRE LIMITEE
CBRE LIMITED
(*Suby of* CBRE LIMITED PARTNERSHIP)
530 8 Ave Sw Suite 500, Calgary, AB, T2P
3S8
(403) 536-1290
Emp Here 100
SIC 6531 Real estate agents and managers
Linda Chapman

D-U-N-S 20-183-0226   (SL)
CELTIC EXPLORATION ULC
505 3 St Sw Suite 500, Calgary, AB, T2P 3E6
(403) 201-5340
Emp Here 47   *Sales* 15,200,166
SIC 1382 Oil and gas exploration services

David Wilson
Robert Dales
Eldon Mcintyre
Neil Sinclair
Douglas Macarthur
Patrick Miles
Douglas Enrico
Alan Franks
Sadiq Lalani
William Guinan

D-U-N-S 24-387-5593   (HQ)
CENOVUS ENERGY INC
500 Centre St Se, Calgary, AB, T2P 0M5
(403) 766-2000
Emp Here 1,386   *Sales* 16,215,043,678
SIC 1382 Oil and gas exploration services
Alex Pourbaix
Jonathan Mckenzie
Keith Chiasson
Harbir Chhina
Al Reid
Drew Zieglgansberger
Sarah Walters
Kam Sandhar
Patrick Daniel
Susan Dabarno

D-U-N-S 24-025-2416   (SL)
CENTRILIFT A BAKER HUGHES COMPANY
CENTRILIFT, A DIVISION OF
401 9 Ave Sw Suite 1000, Calgary, AB, T2P
3C5
(403) 537-3400
Emp Here 138   *Sales* 63,639,252
SIC 5013 Motor vehicle supplies and new
parts
Chris Mackie

D-U-N-S 24-014-0462   (HQ)
CEQUENCE ENERGY LTD
215-9th Ave Sw Suite 1400, Calgary, AB, T2P
1K3
(403) 229-3050
Sales 47,172,139
SIC 1382 Oil and gas exploration services
Todd Brown
Allan Mowbray
David Robinson
Christopher Soby
Don Archibald
Peter Bannister
Brian Felesky
Howard Crone
Dan O'neil
Erin Thompson

D-U-N-S 24-312-4380   (HQ)
CES ENERGY SOLUTIONS CORP
AES DRILLING FLUIDS
332 6 Ave Sw Suite 1400, Calgary, AB, T2P
0B2
(403) 269-2800
Emp Here 115   *Sales* 963,586,305
SIC 1382 Oil and gas exploration services
Thomas J Simons
James Pasieka
Richard Baxter
Vern Disney
Craig F. Nieboer
Kyle D. Kitagawa
Burton Joel Ahrens
Colin Boyer
Rodney L. Carpenter
Stella Cosby

D-U-N-S 25-388-9091   (HQ)
CFR CHEMICALS INC
525 8 Ave Sw Suite 1920, Calgary, AB, T2P
1G1
(587) 320-1097
Emp Here 5   *Sales* 29,944,145
SIC 5169 Chemicals and allied products, nec
Brian Mckay
Kim Ludtke
Srecko Zizakovic
David Arbuthnot

Steve Nerland

D-U-N-S 25-094-3925   (SL)
CHARLES TAYLOR CONSULTING SER-VICES (CANADA) INC
CHARLES TAYLOR ADJUSTING
(*Suby of* CHARLES TAYLOR ADJUSTING
LIMITED)
321 6 Ave Sw Suite 910, Calgary, AB, T2P
3H3
(403) 266-3336
Emp Here 50   *Sales* 42,403,000
SIC 6411 Insurance agents, brokers, and ser-vice
Gordon Moore
Dallas Hirshey

D-U-N-S 24-320-1900   (SL)
CHARTERED PROFESSIONAL ACCOUN-TANTS OF ALBERTA
CPA ALBERTA
444 7 Ave Sw Suite 800, Calgary, AB, T2P
0X8
(403) 299-1300
Emp Here 120   *Sales* 28,093,320
SIC 8621 Professional organizations
Curtis Palichuk
Rachel Miller

D-U-N-S 20-693-9295   (HQ)
CHEMTRADE ELECTROCHEM INC
(*Suby of* CHEMTRADE LOGISTICS INCOME
FUND)
144 4 Ave Sw Suite 2100, Calgary, AB, T2P
3N4

Emp Here 2   *Sales* 188,084,835
SIC 2812 Alkalies and chlorine
Doug Wonnacott
Dean Beacon
Brian Bourgeois
Ross Wonnick
Grant Van Shaik
Nancy Houston
David Collyer
Stephanie Felesky
Douglas Hayhurst
Arthur Korpach

D-U-N-S 24-962-8132   (SL)
CHEVRON RESOURCES LTD
(*Suby of* CHEVRON CORPORATION)
500 5 Ave Sw Suite 700, Calgary, AB, T2P 0L7
(403) 234-5000
Emp Here 250
SIC 1311 Crude petroleum and natural gas
Wayne Scott

D-U-N-S 20-193-6528   (HQ)
CHINOOK ENERGY INC
222 3rd Av Sw Suite 1610, Calgary, AB, T2P
0B4
(403) 261-6883
Emp Here 18   *Sales* 19,670,473
SIC 1382 Oil and gas exploration services
Walter Vrataric
Jason Dranchuk
Darrel Zacharias
Chad Lerner
Fred Davidson
Tim Halpen
P. Grant Wierzba
Robert J. Herdman
Jill Angevine
Robert Iverach

D-U-N-S 20-075-2798   (HQ)
CHURGIN, ARNOLD SHOES LIMITED
227 8 Ave Sw, Calgary, AB, T2P 1B7
(403) 262-3366
Emp Here 22   *Sales* 11,660,740
SIC 5661 Shoe stores
Geta Churgin
Craig Churgin

D-U-N-S 20-456-6511   (SL)
CISTEK SOLUTIONS INC.

Suite 1000 605 5 Ave Sw, Calgary, AB, T2P
3H5
(403) 264-0018
Emp Here 5   *Sales* 15,529,285
SIC 4922 Natural gas transmission
Marty Francis

D-U-N-S 25-952-9584   (HQ)
**CLEAN HARBORS SURFACE RENTALS
PARTNERSHIP**
(*Suby of* CLEAN HARBORS, INC.)
222 3 Ave Sw Suite 900, Calgary, AB, T2P
0B4
(403) 543-7325
Emp Here 100   *Sales* 436,776,800
SIC 1389 Oil and gas field services, nec
Curtis Whitteron
Monty Balderston

D-U-N-S 25-191-6755   (HQ)
CLEARSTREAM ENERGY SERVICES INC
311 6 Ave Sw Suite 415, Calgary, AB, T2P
3H2
(587) 318-0997
Emp Here 2,900   *Sales* 286,814,246
SIC 8741 Management services
Yves Paletta
Herb Thomas
Randy Watt
Neil Wotton
Barry Card
Angela Thompson
Renee Linssen
Deloris Hetherington
Sean Mcmaster
Dean Macdonald

D-U-N-S 20-635-6102   (SL)
CMN CALGARY INC
335 8 Ave Sw Suite 1000, Calgary, AB, T2P
1C9
(403) 266-5544
Emp Here 70   *Sales* 19,022,920
SIC 6531 Real estate agents and managers
Randy Fennessey
Richard Schwann
Carrie Stokes

D-U-N-S 25-261-1082   (HQ)
CNOOC MARKETING CANADA
801 7 Ave Sw Suite 1700, Calgary, AB, T2P
3P7
(403) 699-4000
Sales 101,981,100
SIC 4911 Electric services
Robert Black

D-U-N-S 20-699-0884   (SL)
CNR (ECHO) RESOURCES INC
(*Suby of* CANADIAN NATURAL RE-SOURCES LIMITED)
855 2 St Sw Suite 2500, Calgary, AB, T2P 4J8

Emp Here 25   *Sales* 16,816,975
SIC 1311 Crude petroleum and natural gas
Allan P. Markin
Steve W Laut
John G Langille
N Murray Edwards
Bruce E Mcgrath

D-U-N-S 25-677-4852   (HQ)
COAST ENERGY CANADA INC
530 8 Ave Sw Suite 920, Calgary, AB, T2P
3S8
(403) 508-6700
Emp Here 1   *Sales* 31,058,570
SIC 4924 Natural gas distribution
Dorothy Griffiths
Keith Baxter
Daniel Newell

D-U-N-S 20-175-4715   (SL)
COGNERA
530 8 Ave Sw Suite 920, Calgary, AB, T2P
3S8
(403) 218-2010
Emp Here 53   *Sales* 14,539,596

SIC 8741 Management services
Randy Brookes

D-U-N-S 20-347-2766   (BR)
COLLIERS MACAULAY NICOLLS INC
(*Suby of* COLLIERS INTERNATIONAL GROUP INC)
335 8 Ave Sw 900 Royal Bank Bldg, Calgary, AB, T2P 1C9
(403) 265-9180
Emp Here 140
SIC 6531 Real estate agents and managers
Randy Fennessey

D-U-N-S 24-424-5622   (HQ)
CONA RESOURCES LTD
(*Suby of* WATEROUS ENERGY FUND)
421 7 Ave Sw Suite 1900, Calgary, AB, T2P 4K9
(403) 930-3000
Emp Here 7   *Sales* 54,051,200
SIC 2911 Petroleum refining
Robert Morgan
Nolan Lerner
Michael Makinson
Wendy Mullane
Adam Waterous
Henry Hager
Andrew Kim

D-U-N-S 24-949-0855   (SL)
CONDOMINIUM FIRST MANAGEMENT SERVICES LTD
840 7 Ave Sw Suite 600, Calgary, AB, T2P 3G2
(403) 299-1810
Emp Here 42   *Sales* 13,739,334
SIC 6531 Real estate agents and managers
Don Davies
Robert Davies
Doug Davies

D-U-N-S 24-523-4302   (HQ)
CONDOR PETROLEUM INC
2400 144 4 Ave Sw, Calgary, AB, T2P 3N4
(403) 201-9694
Emp Here 10   *Sales* 12,118,260
SIC 1382 Oil and gas exploration services
Don Streu
Sandy Quilty
Blair Anderson
William Hatcher
Sean Roosen
Edward Bogle
Dennis Balderston
Walter Dawson
Stefan Kaltenbach
Werner Zoellner

D-U-N-S 24-363-7563   (SL)
CONESTOGA PIPE & SUPPLY CANADA CORPORATION
736 8 Ave Sw Suite 430, Calgary, AB, T2P 1H4
(403) 444-5554
Emp Here 25   *Sales* 11,179,350
SIC 5051 Metals service centers and offices
Wayne Caldwell
Louis Russo
Dennis Carmichael

D-U-N-S 20-628-8164   (SL)
CONFORM WORKS INC
Gd Lcd 1, Calgary, AB, T2P 2G8
(403) 243-2250
Emp Here 170   *Sales* 71,865,290
SIC 1541 Industrial buildings and warehouses
Bradley Rasmussen

D-U-N-S 20-016-0351   (HQ)
CONNACHER OIL AND GAS LIMITED
640 5 Ave Sw Suite 1040, Calgary, AB, T2P 3G4
(403) 538-6201
Sales 129,104,771
SIC 1382 Oil and gas exploration services
Merle Johnson

Jeff Beeston
Suzanne Loov
Gene Davis
Douglas Dreisinger
Jason Hammerman
Daryl H. Gilbert
Scott Pearl
Evgeny Vasilyev

D-U-N-S 20-160-6118   (HQ)
CONOCOPHILLIPS CANADA RESOURCES CORP
CONOCOPHILLIPS
(*Suby of* CONOCOPHILLIPS)
401 9 Ave Sw Suite 1600, Calgary, AB, T2P 3C5
(403) 233-4000
Emp Here 1,500   *Sales* 4,450,996,800
SIC 1311 Crude petroleum and natural gas
Ken H Lueers
Angela R Avery

D-U-N-S 20-051-8707   (HQ)
CONOCOPHILLIPS WESTERN CANADA PARTNERSHIP
CONOCOPHILLIPS CANADA
(*Suby of* CONOCOPHILLIPS)
401 9 Ave Sw Suite 1600, Calgary, AB, T2P 3C5
(403) 233-4000
Emp Here 2,500   *Sales* 1,637,913,000
SIC 1382 Oil and gas exploration services
Brent Smolik

D-U-N-S 20-245-9454   (BR)
CONOCOPHILLIPS WESTERN CANADA PARTNERSHIP
CONOCOPHILLIPS CANADA RESOURCES
(*Suby of* CONOCOPHILLIPS)
401 9th Ave Sw, Calgary, AB, T2P 2H7
(403) 233-4000
Emp Here 1,700
SIC 1311 Crude petroleum and natural gas

D-U-N-S 24-317-2843   (HQ)
CONTINENTAL ALLOYS & SERVICES INC
(*Suby of* RELIANCE STEEL & ALUMINUM CO.)
1440-530 8 Ave Sw, Calgary, AB, T2P 3S8
(403) 216-5150
Emp Here 20   *Sales* 11,875,650
SIC 5084 Industrial machinery and equipment
David Sapungis

D-U-N-S 20-038-9570   (SL)
CORUS AUDIO & ADVERTISING SERVICES LTD
CORUS ENTERTAINMENT
(*Suby of* CORUS ENTERTAINMENT INC)
630 3 Ave Sw Suite 501, Calgary, AB, T2P 4L4
(403) 716-6500
Emp Here 60   *Sales* 13,708,320
SIC 4832 Radio broadcasting stations
Tyler Alton

D-U-N-S 20-010-2387   (SL)
CP ENERGY MARKETING INC
(*Suby of* CITY OF EDMONTON)
505 2 St Sw Suite 84, Calgary, AB, T2P 1N8
(403) 717-4600
Emp Here 1,600   *Sales* 285,982,400
SIC 8711 Engineering services
Stuart Anthony Lee
Brian Tellef Vaasjo

D-U-N-S 24-382-6232   (HQ)
CRESCENT POINT ENERGY CORP
585 8 Ave Sw Suite 2000, Calgary, AB, T2P 1G1
(403) 693-0020
Emp Here 604   *Sales* 2,517,277,691
SIC 1311 Crude petroleum and natural gas
Craig Bryksa
Ryan Gritzfeldt
Ken Lamont
Brad Borggard
Mark Eade

Scott Tuttle
Robert F. Heinemann
Peter Bannister
Laura A. Cillis
John Dielwart

D-U-N-S 20-568-1104   (HQ)
CREW ENERGY INC
250 5 St Sw Suite 800, Calgary, AB, T2P 0R4
(403) 266-2088
Emp Here 63   *Sales* 144,657,396
SIC 1311 Crude petroleum and natural gas
Dale O. Shwed
John G. Leach
Jamie L. Bowman
Kurtis Fischer
Paul Dever
Kevin G. Evers
Mark Miller
James Taylor
John A. Brussa
Jeffery E. Errico

D-U-N-S 25-404-4696   (SL)
CROSSALTA GAS STORAGE & SERVICES LTD
(*Suby of* TC ENERGY CORPORATION)
700 2 St Sw Suite 1600, Calgary, AB, T2P 2W1
(403) 298-3575
Emp Here 12   *Sales* 13,866,780
SIC 4922 Natural gas transmission
Kevin Olsen

D-U-N-S 20-201-7815   (HQ)
CROWN CAPITAL PARTNERS INC
888 3 St Sw Fl 10, Calgary, AB, T2P 5C5
(403) 775-2554
Emp Here 5   *Sales* 24,764,160
SIC 8741 Management services
Christopher A. Johnson
Brent G. Hughes
Tim Oldfield
Michael Overvelde
Paul Budovitch
Daniella Gan
Adam Jenkins
Marnie Miglioranza
Alan Rowe
Robert Gillis

D-U-N-S 24-766-3409   (HQ)
CROWN POINT ENERGY INC
Gd, Calgary, AB, T2P 0T8
(403) 232-1150
Emp Here 5   *Sales* 38,722,121
SIC 1382 Oil and gas exploration services
Brian J. Moss
Marisa Tormakh
Gordon Kettleson
Keith Turnbull
Pablo Bernardo Peralta
Gabriel Dario Obrador

D-U-N-S 20-283-0139   (SL)
CSV MIDSTREAM SOLUTIONS CORP
355 4 Ave Sw Suite 700, Calgary, AB, T2P 0J1
(587) 316-6900
Emp Here 11   *Sales* 34,164,427
SIC 4923 Gas transmission and distribution
Daniel Clarke
Ian Wesch
Oliver Wagner
David Sevalrud
Randy Toone
David Boone
Richard Bower
Greg Beard
Rakesh Wilson
Wilson Handler

D-U-N-S 20-562-2546   (HQ)
CWC ENERGY SERVICES CORP
CWC
205 5 Ave Sw Suite 610, Calgary, AB, T2P 2V7

(403) 264-2177
Emp Here 20   *Sales* 109,744,362
SIC 1382 Oil and gas exploration services
Duncan Au
Paul Donohue
Darwin Mcintyre
Bob Apps
Mike Dubois
Stuart King
Jim Reid
Gary Bentham
Wade Mcgowan
Daryl Austin

D-U-N-S 20-934-9062   (BR)
DAVIS LLP
DLA PIPER
(*Suby of* DAVIS LLP)
250 2 St Sw Suite 1000, Calgary, AB, T2P 0C1
(403) 296-4470
Emp Here 100
SIC 8111 Legal services
Robert Calvert

D-U-N-S 20-341-1967   (BR)
DELOITTE LLP
(*Suby of* DELOITTE LLP)
850 2 St Sw Suite 700, Calgary, AB, T2P 0R8
(403) 267-1700
Emp Here 500
SIC 8721 Accounting, auditing, and bookkeeping
Frank Vettesse

D-U-N-S 20-051-3690   (HQ)
DELPHI ENERGY CORP
333 7 Ave Sw Suite 2300, Calgary, AB, T2P 2Z1
(403) 265-6171
Sales 96,470,754
SIC 1382 Oil and gas exploration services
David J. Reid
John Behr
Rod Hume
Hugo Batteke
Michael Galvin
Glenn A. Hamilton
Peter T. Harrison
Robert A. Lehodey
David J. Sandmeyer
Lamont C. Tolley

D-U-N-S 20-040-9113   (BR)
DENTONS CANADA LLP
(*Suby of* DENTONS CANADA LLP)
850 2 St Sw Suite 1500, Calgary, AB, T2P 0R8
(403) 268-7000
Emp Here 343
SIC 8111 Legal services
Don Leitch

D-U-N-S 24-347-4053   (HQ)
DEVON CANADA CORPORATION
(*Suby of* DEVON ENERGY CORPORATION)
400 3 Ave Sw Suite 100, Calgary, AB, T2P 4H2
(403) 232-7100
Emp Here 200   *Sales* 1,854,582,000
SIC 1311 Crude petroleum and natural gas
J. Larry Nichols
John Richels
Rob Dutton
Thomas Mitchell
Murray Brown
Jeffrey Ritenour
Chris R. Seasons

D-U-N-S 24-703-0505   (HQ)
DIRECT ENERGY MARKETING LIMITED
DIRECT ENERGY ESSENTIAL HOME SERVICES, DIV OF
(*Suby of* CENTRICA PLC)
525 8 Ave Sw Unit 1200, Calgary, AB, T2P 1G1
(403) 776-2000
Emp Here 300   *Sales* 741,832,800
SIC 1311 Crude petroleum and natural gas

Christopher P A Weston
Janice Thomson
Adele Malo
Kumud Kalia
James Spence

D-U-N-S 25-313-9307   (BR)
DIRECT ENERGY MARKETING LIMITED
JUST DIRECT ENERGY
(*Suby of* CENTRICA PLC)
111 5 Ave Sw Suite 1000, Calgary, AB, T2P
3Y6
(403) 266-6393
Emp Here 300
SIC 1311 Crude petroleum and natural gas
Topp Lori

D-U-N-S 24-678-3067   (SL)
DIRECT ENERGY PARTNERSHIP
(*Suby of* CENTRICA PLC)
525 8 Ave Sw Suite 501, Calgary, AB, T2P
1G1
(403) 261-9810
Emp Here 100   *Sales* 21,782,900
SIC 1731 Electrical work
John Schultz

D-U-N-S 24-682-2154   (SL)
DISABILITY CONCEPTS INC
DIVISION OF HAMILTON AND PARTNERS
736 6 Ave Sw Suite 1500, Calgary, AB, T2P
3T7
(403) 262-2080
Emp Here 26   *Sales* 15,078,024
SIC 6411 Insurance agents, brokers, and service
Kelly Little
Ian Sarrer

D-U-N-S 20-075-9306   (HQ)
DNOW CANADA ULC
DISTRIBUTION NOW
(*Suby of* NOW INC.)
401 9 Ave Sw Suite 845, Calgary, AB, T2P
3C5
(403) 531-5600
Emp Here 40   *Sales* 165,828,200
SIC 5084 Industrial machinery and equipment
Michael West
Robert Mcclinton
Derren Newell
Michael Hogan
John Kennedy
Kjell-Erik Oestdahl
Bradley Thompson
Keith Turnbull

D-U-N-S 20-831-1068   (BR)
DOMINION OF CANADA GENERAL INSURANCE COMPANY, THE
(*Suby of* THE TRAVELERS COMPANIES
INC)
777 8 Ave Sw Suite 1700, Calgary, AB, T2P
3R5
(403) 231-6600
Emp Here 100
SIC 6411 Insurance agents, brokers, and service
Randy Siver

D-U-N-S 24-868-5901   (HQ)
DOW AGROSCIENCES CANADA INC.
DAS
(*Suby of* CORTEVA, INC.)
215 2 St Sw Suite 2400, Calgary, AB, T2P
1M4
(403) 735-8800
Emp Here 55   *Sales* 42,603,150
SIC 2879 Agricultural chemicals, nec
Jim Wispinski

D-U-N-S 24-391-7064   (HQ)
DOW CANADA HOLDING LP
(*Suby of* DOW INC.)
450 1 St Sw Suite 2100, Calgary, AB, T2P 5H1
(403) 267-3500
Sales 182,754,500
SIC 6712 Bank holding companies

Mark Bradley

D-U-N-S 20-148-9580   (HQ)
DOW CHEMICAL CANADA ULC
(*Suby of* DOW INC.)
215 2 St Sw Suite 2400, Calgary, AB, T2P
1M4
(403) 267-3500
Emp Here 25   *Sales* 889,290,000
SIC 2899 Chemical preparations, nec
Mark A Bradley
Joe Deutscher
Don Fysh
Jeff J Johnston

D-U-N-S 24-523-0821   (SL)
DYNASTY POWER INC
638 6 Ave Sw Unit 200, Calgary, AB, T2P 0S4
(403) 613-6882
Emp Here 25   *Sales* 12,991,375
SIC 4911 Electric services
Allan Cho
Gaurav Sharma
Jason Brown

D-U-N-S 24-906-9337   (HQ)
E.O.S. PIPELINE & FACILITIES INCORPORATED
736 6 Ave Sw Suite 1205, Calgary, AB, T2P
3T7
(403) 232-8446
Emp Here 25   *Sales* 25,244,200
SIC 1623 Water, sewer, and utility lines
Dean Peterson

D-U-N-S 24-737-3082   (SL)
EAGLE ENERGY INC
EAGLE ENERGY TRUST
500 4 Ave Sw Suite 2710, Calgary, AB, T2P
2V6
(403) 531-1575
Emp Here 43   *Sales* 28,259,010
SIC 6726 Investment offices, nec
Wayne Wisniewski
Glen Glass
Brenda Galonski
Jo-Anne M. Bund
Richard W. Clark
Warren Steckley
Bruce Gibson
F. Wayne Mcwhorter
John Melton

D-U-N-S 24-161-0179   (BR)
ECONOMICAL MUTUAL INSURANCE COMPANY
ECONOMICAL INSURANCE GROUP
(*Suby of* ECONOMICAL MUTUAL INSURANCE COMPANY)
801 6 Ave Sw Suite 2700, Calgary, AB, T2P
3W2
(403) 265-8590
Emp Here 100
SIC 6331 Fire, marine, and casualty insurance
James Setch

D-U-N-S 24-495-8765   (HQ)
ELBOW RIVER MARKETING LTD
(*Suby of* PARKLAND FUEL CORPORATION)
335 8 Ave Sw Suite 810, Calgary, AB, T2P
1C9
(403) 232-6868
Sales 47,773,638
SIC 5172 Petroleum products, nec
Ed Malcolm
Arie Prins
Todd Greiner
Todd Mazzei
Mark Anderson
Bill Niquidet
Ian Williams

D-U-N-S 24-858-5791   (HQ)
ELEMENT TECHNICAL SERVICES INC
810-530 8 Ave Sw, Calgary, AB, T2P 3S8
(403) 930-0246
Emp Here 1   *Sales* 269,071,600
SIC 1389 Oil and gas field services, nec

Jason Nikish
Ryan Birnie
Brendan Nelson

D-U-N-S 20-695-8642   (SL)
EMBER RESOURCES INC
(*Suby of* BROOKFIELD ASSET MANAGEMENT INC)
400 3 Ave Sw Suite 800, Calgary, AB, T2P
4H2
(403) 270-0803
Emp Here 31   *Sales* 20,853,049
SIC 1382 Oil and gas exploration services
Douglas A. Dafoe
Bruce C. Ryan
Steven Gell
Quinton Rafuse
Kenneth Ronaghan
Thomas Zuorro
Jim Reid
Dean Schultz
Deborah Close
Glenn Hamilton

D-U-N-S 24-906-3751   (HQ)
ENBRIDGE INC
425 1 St Sw Suite 200, Calgary, AB, T2P 3L8
(403) 231-3900
Emp Here 234   *Sales* 35,159,254,556
SIC 4612 Crude petroleum pipelines
Al Monaco
Cynthia Hansen
Guy Jarvis
Byron Neiles
Bob Rooney
John K. Whelen
William T. Yardley
Vern Yu
Matthew Akman
Allen Capps

D-U-N-S 20-191-4905   (HQ)
ENBRIDGE INCOME FUND
(*Suby of* ENBRIDGE INC)
425 1 St Sw Suite 3000, Calgary, AB, T2P 3L8
(403) 767-3642
Emp Here 269   *Sales* 1,327,051,008
SIC 4922 Natural gas transmission
Ernest Roberts
Richard Bird
Laura Cillis
Brian Frank
George Lewis
Bruce Waterman
John Whelen

D-U-N-S 25-499-5368   (HQ)
ENBRIDGE PIPELINES (ATHABASCA) INC
(*Suby of* ENBRIDGE INC)
425 1 St Sw Suite 3000, Calgary, AB, T2P 3L8
(780) 392-4179
Sales 28,889,125
SIC 4922 Natural gas transmission
J Richard Bird
Derek Truswell

D-U-N-S 25-679-5980   (HQ)
ENBRIDGE PIPELINES (NW) INC
(*Suby of* ENBRIDGE INC)
425 1 St Sw Suite 3000, Calgary, AB, T2P 3L8

Emp Here 160   *Sales* 2,889,382,000
SIC 4612 Crude petroleum pipelines
Brian F. Macneill

D-U-N-S 25-977-3732   (SL)
ENBRIDGE PIPELINES (WOODLAND) INC
(*Suby of* ENBRIDGE INC)
425 1 St Sw Suite 3000, Calgary, AB, T2P 3L8
(780) 392-4179
Emp Here 4   *Sales* 12,423,428
SIC 4922 Natural gas transmission
Jarvis D Guy
D T Robottom
John Whelen
Leon A Zupan

D-U-N-S 20-167-6467   (HQ)
ENBRIDGE PIPELINES INC
(*Suby of* ENBRIDGE INC)
425 1 St Sw Suite 200, Calgary, AB, T2P 3L8
(403) 231-3900
Emp Here 100   *Sales* 22,248,241,400
SIC 4612 Crude petroleum pipelines
Al Monaco
Cynthia Hansen
Guy Jarvis
Byron Neiles
Karen Radford
Bob Rooney
John Whelen
Vern Yu
William Yardley
Gregory Ebel

D-U-N-S 20-120-9454   (HQ)
ENERCORP SAND SOLUTIONS INC
(*Suby of* ENERCORP SAND SOLUTIONS
PARTNERSHIP)
815 8 Ave Sw Suite 510, Calgary, AB, T2P
3P2
(403) 217-1332
Emp Here 10   *Sales* 40,360,740
SIC 1389 Oil and gas field services, nec
Justin Morin
James Pung
Jesse Permann
Christina Meineke
Eric Omenson
Bruce Mckenna
Alan Snow
Gerardo Smith
Rory Nagge
Gareth Young

D-U-N-S 25-977-5653   (HQ)
ENERCORP SAND SOLUTIONS PARTNERSHIP
520 3 Ave Sw Unit 530, Calgary, AB, T2P 0R3
(403) 217-1332
Sales 41,033,419
SIC 1382 Oil and gas exploration services
Justin Morin

D-U-N-S 25-415-2408   (HQ)
ENERPLUS CORPORATION
333 7 Ave Sw Suite 3000, Calgary, AB, T2P
2Z1
(403) 298-2200
Emp Here 400   *Sales* 1,046,914,603
SIC 1311 Crude petroleum and natural gas
Ian Dundas
Raymond Daniels
Jodine Jenson Labrie
Shaina Morihira
Nathan Fisher
Daniel Fitzgerald
John Hoffman
Garth R. Doll
David Mccoy
Elliott Pew

D-U-N-S 24-598-8464   (HQ)
ENERPLUS GLOBAL ENERGY MANAGEMENT CO
(*Suby of* ENERPLUS CORPORATION)
333 7 Ave Sw Suite 3000, Calgary, AB, T2P
2Z1
(403) 298-2200
Emp Here 200   *Sales* 43,671,600
SIC 8741 Management services
Gordon Kerr
Robert J Waters
Wayne T Foch

D-U-N-S 20-305-2360   (SL)
ENERVEST DIVERSIFIED MANAGEMENT INC
700 9 Ave Sw Suite 2800, Calgary, AB, T2P
3V4
(403) 571-5550
Emp Here 30   *Sales* 12,580,650
SIC 6719 Holding companies, nec
Nevin Markwart

D-U-N-S 24-131-1062   (SL)
ENERVEST MANAGEMENT LTD
CAMILLE FINANCIAL
350 7 Ave Sw Suite 3900, Calgary, AB, T2P 3N9
(403) 571-5550
Emp Here 49   *Sales* 35,939,148
SIC 6722 Management investment, open-end
Nevin Markwart

D-U-N-S 20-524-7773   (HQ)
ENHANCED PETROLEUM SERVICES PARTNERSHIP
ENHANCED DRILL SYSTEMS, DIV OF
400 5 Ave Sw Unit 900, Calgary, AB, T2P 0L6
(403) 262-1361
Sales 53,814,320
SIC 1381 Drilling oil and gas wells
Jason Hager

D-U-N-S 24-807-6390   (HQ)
ENSIGN DRILLING INC
(*Suby of* ENSIGN ENERGY SERVICES INC)
400 5 Ave Sw Suite 1000, Calgary, AB, T2P 0L6
(403) 262-1361
Emp Here 75   *Sales* 1,681,697,500
SIC 1381 Drilling oil and gas wells
Robert Geddes
Selby Porter

D-U-N-S 24-733-4204   (HQ)
ENSIGN ENERGY SERVICES INC
400 5 Ave Sw Suite 1000, Calgary, AB, T2P 0L6
(403) 262-1361
Emp Here 450   *Sales* 876,636,554
SIC 1381 Drilling oil and gas wells
N. Murray Edwards
Robert Geddes
Mike Gray
Tom Connors
James Howe
Len Kangas
Cary Moomjian, Jr
John Schroeder
Gail Surkan
Barth Whitham

D-U-N-S 25-682-9656   (SL)
ENSIGN SERVICING PARTNERSHIP
400 5 Ave Sw Suite 900, Calgary, AB, T2P 0L6
(403) 262-1361
Emp Here 150   *Sales* 100,901,850
SIC 1381 Drilling oil and gas wells
Glenn Dagenais

D-U-N-S 20-016-5038   (SL)
ENTERO CORPORATION
ENTERO VISION
1040 7 Ave Sw Suite 500, Calgary, AB, T2P 3G9
(403) 261-1820
Emp Here 60   *Sales* 10,638,660
SIC 7371 Custom computer programming services
Steve Remmington
Mike Lake

D-U-N-S 24-736-2218   (HQ)
ENTUITIVE CORPORATION
150 9 Ave Sw Suite 1610, Calgary, AB, T2P 3H9
(403) 879-1270
Emp Here 35   *Sales* 26,810,850
SIC 8711 Engineering services
Barry Charnish
Sameer Dhargalkar

D-U-N-S 24-360-4779   (HQ)
EQUINOR CANADA LTD
(*Suby of* EQUINOR ASA)
308 4 Ave Sw Suite 3600, Calgary, AB, T2P 0H7
(403) 234-0123
Emp Here 119   *Sales* 120,409,541
SIC 1381 Drilling oil and gas wells
Nina Koch

Lorne Cannon
Tor Kjollesdal
Kurt Middleton

D-U-N-S 25-677-1486   (HQ)
EQUINOX ENGINEERING LTD
940 6 Ave Sw Unit 400, Calgary, AB, T2P 3T1
(587) 390-1000
Sales 31,815,542
SIC 8711 Engineering services
Dean Lubarsky

D-U-N-S 24-439-7568   (BR)
ERNST & YOUNG LLP
(*Suby of* ERNST & YOUNG LLP)
215 2 St Sw Suite 2200, Calgary, AB, T2P 1M4
(403) 290-4100
Emp Here 200
SIC 8721 Accounting, auditing, and bookkeeping
Barry Monroe

D-U-N-S 20-057-0294   (HQ)
ESI ENERGY SERVICES INC
727 7 Ave Sw Suite 500, Calgary, AB, T2P 0Z5
(403) 262-9344
Sales 11,035,691
SIC 4911 Electric services
Robert Dunstan
Ted Rigaux

D-U-N-S 24-125-1771   (BR)
ESIT CANADA ENTERPRISE SERVICES CO
ESIT CANADA ENTERPRISE SERVICES CO
(*Suby of* DXC TECHNOLOGY COMPANY)
240 4 Ave Sw Suite 500, Calgary, AB, T2P 4H4
(403) 508-4500
Emp Here 350
SIC 7379 Computer related services, nec
Ross Manning

D-U-N-S 24-424-9426   (HQ)
ESSENTIAL ENERGY SERVICES LTD
ESSENTIAL WELL SERVICE
250 2 St Sw Unit 1100, Calgary, AB, T2P 0C1
(403) 263-6778
Emp Here 350   *Sales* 143,959,021
SIC 1389 Oil and gas field services, nec
Garnet K. Amundson
Eldon Heck
Karen Perasalo
Jeff Newman
James A. Banister
Robert T. German
Nicholas G. Kirton
Michael J. Black
Robert Michaleski

D-U-N-S 20-119-7188   (SL)
EXXONMOBIL CANADA ENERGY
237 4 Ave Sw, Calgary, AB, T2P 0H6
(403) 260-7910
Emp Here 400   *Sales* 218,388,400
SIC 1382 Oil and gas exploration services
Tim Cutt

D-U-N-S 20-077-0873   (HQ)
EXXONMOBIL CANADA LTD
EMC
(*Suby of* EXXON MOBIL CORPORATION)
237 4 Ave Sw Suite 3000, Calgary, AB, T2P 4X7
(403) 232-5300
Emp Here 500   *Sales* 1,854,582,000
SIC 1311 Crude petroleum and natural gas
Jerry Anderson
Michael Morin
Wayne Kubasek

D-U-N-S 25-228-6927   (SL)
EXXONMOBIL CANADA PROPERTIES
(*Suby of* EXXON MOBIL CORPORATION)
237 4 Ave Sw Suite 4063, Calgary, AB, T2P 0H6
(403) 260-7910
Emp Here 500   *Sales* 272,985,500

SIC 1382 Oil and gas exploration services
Jeff Woodbury
Randy Gillis

D-U-N-S 20-635-2890   (BR)
FAIRMONT HOTELS & RESORTS INC
FAIRMONT PALLISER, THE
(*Suby of* ACCOR)
133 9 Ave Sw, Calgary, AB, T2P 2M3
(403) 262-1234
Emp Here 375
SIC 7011 Hotels and motels
Brigitte Fritz

D-U-N-S 25-063-1421   (BR)
FAIRMONT HOTELS & RESORTS INC
SHERATON SUITES CALGARY EAU CLAIRE
(*Suby of* ACCOR)
255 Barclay Parade Sw, Calgary, AB, T2P 5C2
(403) 266-7200
Emp Here 400
SIC 7011 Hotels and motels
Ross Meredith

D-U-N-S 24-103-8632   (BR)
FAIRMONT HOTELS & RESORTS INC
PALLISER, THE
(*Suby of* ACCOR)
133 9 Ave Sw, Calgary, AB, T2P 2M3
(403) 262-1234
Emp Here 300
SIC 7011 Hotels and motels
Brigitta Fritz

D-U-N-S 20-180-9212   (HQ)
FERUS INC
(*Suby of* THE ENERGY & MINERALS GROUP FUND III LP)
401 9 Ave Sw Suite 1220, Calgary, AB, T2P 3C5
(403) 517-8777
Emp Here 50   *Sales* 287,988,500
SIC 4925 Gas production and/or distribution
Richard Brown
Sean Lalani
Ronald Porter
John Raymond
Jeff Ball
Jeff Rawls
Robert Rooney
Henry Sykes

D-U-N-S 20-268-3108   (SL)
FERUS NATURAL GAS FUELS INC
401 9 Ave Sw Suite 1220, Calgary, AB, T2P 3C5
(403) 517-8777
Emp Here 20   *Sales* 62,117,140
SIC 4925 Gas production and/or distribution
Dick Brown
Chad Porter
Paul Evans
Rick Miller

D-U-N-S 20-007-9767   (BR)
FIELD LLP
(*Suby of* FIELD LLP)
444 7 Ave Sw Suite 400, Calgary, AB, T2P 0X8
(403) 260-8500
Emp Here 80
SIC 8111 Legal services
Larry Butler

D-U-N-S 20-838-2494   (BR)
FIREMASTER OILFIELD SERVICES INC
(*Suby of* FIREMASTER OILFIELD SERVICES INC)
441 5 Ave Sw Suite 570, Calgary, AB, T2P 2V1
(403) 266-1811
Emp Here 150
SIC 1389 Oil and gas field services, nec
Bryce Hume

D-U-N-S 24-981-2439   (SL)
FIRSTENERGY CAPITAL CORP

311 6 Ave Sw Suite 1100, Calgary, AB, T2P 3H2
(403) 262-0600
Emp Here 90   *Sales* 84,525,930
SIC 6211 Security brokers and dealers
Jim Davidson
Chandra Henry
Ruby Wallis

D-U-N-S 20-286-7826   (SL)
FIRSTSERVICE RESIDENTIAL ALBERTA LTD
(*Suby of* FIRSTSERVICE CORPORATION)
840 7 Ave Sw Suite 1100, Calgary, AB, T2P 3G2
(403) 299-1810
Emp Here 150   *Sales* 20,351,550
SIC 6519 Real property lessors, nec
Glenne Manlig
Roger Davies
David Porter
Andrea Alexander

D-U-N-S 24-350-8426   (HQ)
FJORDS PROCESSING CANADA INC
(*Suby of* NATIONAL OILWELL VARCO, INC.)
237 4 Ave Sw Unit 2200, Calgary, AB, T2P 4K3
(403) 640-4230
Sales 11,509,380
SIC 1389 Oil and gas field services, nec
Janet Green
Harald Gulaker
Per Harald Kongelf
Michael Hambly
Craig Weinstock
Glen Arnelien

D-U-N-S 20-285-7470   (SL)
FOOTHILLS PIPE LINES (SOUTH B.C.) LTD
112 4 Ave Sw Suite 300, Calgary, AB, T2P 0H3
(403) 920-2000
Emp Here 45   *Sales* 139,763,565
SIC 4922 Natural gas transmission
Anthony Palmer
Karl Johannson

D-U-N-S 20-989-5556   (HQ)
FOOTHILLS PIPE LINES LTD
(*Suby of* TC ENERGY CORPORATION)
450 1 St Sw, Calgary, AB, T2P 5H1
(403) 920-2000
Emp Here 44   *Sales* 52,000,425
SIC 4922 Natural gas transmission
Dennis Mcconaghy
Anthony Palmer
David Kohlenberg
Karl Johannson

D-U-N-S 25-700-6929   (SL)
FRACTION ENERGY SERVICES LTD
(*Suby of* TRICAN WELL SERVICE LTD)
255 5 Ave Sw Unit 2900, Calgary, AB, T2P 3G6
(403) 385-4300
Emp Here 150   *Sales* 100,901,850
SIC 1389 Oil and gas field services, nec
Brad Fedora

D-U-N-S 25-528-9084   (HQ)
FREEHOLD ROYALTIES LTD
144 4 Ave Sw Suite 400, Calgary, AB, T2P 3N4
(403) 221-0802
Emp Here 10   *Sales* 109,577,579
SIC 6792 Oil royalty traders
Thomas Mullane
Alan Withey
Robert Lamond
David M. Spyker
Michael J. Stone
Marvin F. Romanow
Gary R. Bugeaud
Peter T Harrison
J. Douglas Kay
Arthur N. Korpach

D-U-N-S 20-316-0028   (SL)
FREEHOLD ROYALTIES PARTNERSHIP
(*Suby of* FREEHOLD ROYALTIES LTD)
144 4 Ave Sw Suite 400, Calgary, AB, T2P
3N4
(403) 221-0802
Emp Here 80   *Sales* 21,620,480
SIC 2911 Petroleum refining
 Tom Mullane

D-U-N-S 25-292-0731   (BR)
FUJITSU CONSEIL (CANADA) INC
FUJITSU CONSULTING
(*Suby of* FUJITSU CONSULTING (CANADA)
HOLDINGS, INC.)
606 4 St Sw Suite 1500, Calgary, AB, T2P 1T1
(403) 265-6001
Emp Here 110
SIC 7379 Computer related services, nec
 Harris Shawn

D-U-N-S 25-991-6328   (SL)
G & L SLOTCO OILFIELD SERVICES LTD
700 4 Ave Sw Suite 1110, Calgary, AB, T2P
3J4
(403) 261-1717
Emp Here 2   *Sales* 11,525,100
SIC 3443 Fabricated plate work (boiler shop)
 Perry Parker
 Troy Ducharme

D-U-N-S 20-365-4686   (SL)
GAIN ENERGY LTD
520 3 Ave Sw 30th Fl, Calgary, AB, T2P 0R3
(403) 294-1336
Emp Here 40   *Sales* 12,788,200
SIC 1382 Oil and gas exploration services
 Jennifer Holmes
 John Ruffolo
 Paul Manias
 Peter Josephson
 Olivia Aylon

D-U-N-S 24-419-3335   (SL)
GATEWAY TUBULARS LTD
144 4 Ave Sw Suite 2800, Calgary, AB, T2P
3N4
(403) 457-2288
Emp Here 15   *Sales* 15,005,085
SIC 5051 Metals service centers and offices
 Fred Moore
 Brent Quinton
 Randy Beekhuizen
 Doug Ripley

D-U-N-S 24-525-9341   (HQ)
GEAR ENERGY LTD
240 4th Ave Sw Suite 2600, Calgary, AB, T2P
4H4
(403) 538-8435
Emp Here 4   *Sales* 73,125,003
SIC 1382 Oil and gas exploration services
 Ingram B Gillmore
 David Hwang
 Jason Kaluski
 Yvan Chretien
 Bryan Dozzi
 Dustin Ressler
 Don T. Gray
 Raymond P. Cej
 Harry English
 Kevin Olson

D-U-N-S 24-334-8088   (SL)
GEMINI ENGINEERING LIMITED
GENSOLUTIONS
839 5 Ave Sw Suite 400, Calgary, AB, T2P
3C8
(403) 255-2916
Emp Here 120   *Sales* 21,448,680
SIC 8711 Engineering services
 Carl Johnson
 Marlene Quiring
 Robert Brookwell

D-U-N-S 20-507-3856   (HQ)
GEMINI FIELD SOLUTIONS LTD
KINETIC PROJECTS

839 5 Ave Sw Suite 400, Calgary, AB, T2P
3C8
(403) 255-2006
Sales 25,244,200
SIC 1629 Heavy construction, nec
 Carl Johnson

D-U-N-S 24-599-0957   (HQ)
GEOLOGIC SYSTEMS LTD
401 9 Ave Sw Suite 1500, Calgary, AB, T2P
3C5
(403) 262-1992
Sales 20,185,480
SIC 7371 Custom computer programming services
 Joe Harris
 David Hood
 Denise Harris
 Sean Udell

D-U-N-S 24-737-3256   (HQ)
GIBSON ENERGY INC
440 2 Ave Sw Suite 1700, Calgary, AB, T2P
5E9
(403) 206-4000
Emp Here 100   *Sales* 5,190,412,814
SIC 1389 Oil and gas field services, nec
 Steve Spaulding
 Sean Brown
 Sean Wilson
 Michael Lindsay
 James M. Estey
 Douglas P. Bloom
 James J. Cleary
 John L. Festival
 Marshall L. Mcrae
 Mary Ellen Peters

D-U-N-S 20-076-0288   (HQ)
GIBSON ENERGY ULC
(*Suby of* GIBSON ENERGY INC)
440 2 Ave Sw Suite 1700, Calgary, AB, T2P
5E9
(403) 206-4000
Emp Here 300   *Sales* 4,779,867
SIC 5172 Petroleum products, nec
 Stewart Hanlon
 Rodney J. Bantle
 Donald A. Fowlis
 Richard M. Wise

D-U-N-S 24-786-5165   (SL)
GLJ PETROLEUM CONSULTANTS LTD
400 3 Ave Sw Suite 4100, Calgary, AB, T2P
4H2
(403) 266-9500
Emp Here 100   *Sales* 67,267,900
SIC 1389 Oil and gas field services, nec
 Harry Jung
 Dana Laustsen
 Jim Willmon
 Keith Braaten
 Doug Sutton

D-U-N-S 25-538-8860   (SL)
GLOBAL PETROLEUM MARKETING INC
600 6 Ave Sw Suite 600, Calgary, AB, T2P
0S5
(403) 237-7828
Emp Here 10   *Sales* 11,555,650
SIC 4924 Natural gas distribution
 Gordon Weicker
 Alec Avramenko

D-U-N-S 20-114-4453   (BR)
GOWLING WLG (CANADA) LLP
GOWLINGS
(*Suby of* GOWLING WLG (CANADA) LLP)
421 7 Ave Sw Unit 1600, Calgary, AB, T2P
4K9
(403) 298-1000
Emp Here 213
SIC 8111 Legal services
 Andrew Oppenheim

D-U-N-S 20-697-0506   (HQ)
GRAN TIERRA ENERGY INC
520 3rd Ave Sw Suite 900, Calgary, AB, T2P

0R3
(403) 265-3221
Emp Here 94   *Sales* 613,431,000
SIC 1382 Oil and gas exploration services
 Gary S. Guidry
 Ed Caldwell
 Jim Evans
 Alan Johnson
 Glen Mah
 Rodger Trimble
 Lawrence West
 Susan Mawdsley
 Ryan Ellson
 Robert Hodgins

D-U-N-S 24-313-0379   (HQ)
GRAND POWER LOGISTICS GROUP INC
505 6 St Sw Suite 2806, Calgary, AB, T2P 1X5
(403) 237-8211
Emp Here 1   *Sales* 51,775,150
SIC 4731 Freight transportation arrangement

D-U-N-S 20-536-5880   (HQ)
GRANDE CACHE COAL CORPORATION
800 5 Ave Sw Suite 1610, Calgary, AB, T2P
3T6
(403) 543-7070
Emp Here 20   *Sales* 248,455,074
SIC 1221 Bituminous coal and lignite-surface mining
 Ian J. Bootle
 Robert G. Brawn
 Barry T. Davies
 Donald J. Douglas
 John R. Morgan
 Nicholas G. Kirton

D-U-N-S 20-259-2515   (SL)
GRANITE OIL CORP
308 4 Ave Sw Suite 3230, Calgary, AB, T2P
0H7
(587) 349-9113
Emp Here 10   *Sales* 30,632,384
SIC 1311 Crude petroleum and natural gas
 Michael Kabanuk
 Tyler Klatt
 Gail Hannon
 Brendan Carrigy
 Martin Cheyne
 Kevin Andrus
 Bradley Porter
 Henry Hamm
 Kathy Turgeon

D-U-N-S 24-380-6309   (SL)
GRANITE OIL CORP
308 4 Ave Sw Suite 3230, Calgary, AB, T2P
0H7

Emp Here 25   *Sales* 32,879,642
SIC 1081 Metal mining services
 Michael Kabanuk
 Devon Griffiths
 Jack Smith

D-U-N-S 20-114-4107   (HQ)
GRANT CORPORATION
540 5 Ave Sw Suite 1850, Calgary, AB, T2P
0M2
(403) 663-0050
Sales 84,757,554
SIC 1389 Oil and gas field services, nec
 Grant Stevens

D-U-N-S 20-114-9445   (HQ)
GRANT PRODUCTION TESTING SERVICES LTD
(*Suby of* GRANT CORPORATION)
505 8 Ave Sw Suite 200, Calgary, AB, T2P
1G2
(403) 663-0050
Emp Here 9   *Sales* 84,757,554
SIC 1389 Oil and gas field services, nec
 Grant Stevens

D-U-N-S 20-374-7543   (SL)
GREAT LAKES PIPELINE CANADA LTD
450 1 St Sw, Calgary, AB, T2P 5H1

(403) 920-6852
Emp Here 50   *Sales* 157,904,687
SIC 4922 Natural gas transmission
 Christine Johnston
 Tracy Robinson

D-U-N-S 24-320-1230   (SL)
GREENFIRE OIL AND GAS LTD
444 5 Ave Sw Suite 1650, Calgary, AB, T2P
2T8
(403) 681-7377
Emp Here 42   *Sales* 13,427,610
SIC 1382 Oil and gas exploration services
 Robert Logan
 Albert Luong
 Albert Stark
 Allan Bezanson
 Rick Pawluk
 William Roach
 David Werklund

D-U-N-S 24-849-6999   (HQ)
GRIFFITHS ENERGY INTERNATIONAL INC
555 4 Ave Sw Suite 2100, Calgary, AB, T2P
3E7
(403) 724-7200
Sales 15,026,135
SIC 1382 Oil and gas exploration services
 Gary Guidry
 Roger Thomas
 Trevor Peters
 Dean Tucker

D-U-N-S 24-677-9115   (SL)
GRIZZLY OIL SANDS ULC
(*Suby of* GRIZZLY HOLDINGS INC)
605 5 Ave Sw Suite 2700, Calgary, AB, T2P
3H5
(403) 930-6400
Emp Here 45   *Sales* 14,386,725
SIC 1311 Crude petroleum and natural gas
 John Pears
 Mike Liddell
 Antony Lundy

D-U-N-S 25-978-7760   (HQ)
GUEST-TEK INTERACTIVE ENTERTAINMENT LTD
(*Suby of* 1456537 ALBERTA LTD)
777 8 Ave Sw Suite 600, Calgary, AB, T2P
3R5
(403) 509-1010
Emp Here 322   *Sales* 124,450,368
SIC 4813 Telephone communication, except radio
 Arnon Levy
 Kelly Blake
 Jim Glasspoole
 Greg Lindsay
 Stephen Verhoeff
 Tadashi Ishihara
 Naohiro Sato
 Masuo Yoshimoto

D-U-N-S 20-769-9133   (HQ)
H & R BLOCK CANADA, INC
CASH BACK
(*Suby of* H&R BLOCK, INC.)
700 2 St Sw Suite 2600, Calgary, AB, T2P
2W2
(403) 254-8689
Emp Here 55   *Sales* 89,696,000
SIC 7291 Tax return preparation services
 Henry Bloch
 Richard Bloch

D-U-N-S 25-681-1258   (HQ)
HALLIBURTON GROUP CANADA INC
HALLIBURTON ENERGY SERVICES DIVISION
(*Suby of* HALLIBURTON COMPANY)
645 7 Ave Sw Suite 1600, Calgary, AB, T2P
4G8
(403) 231-9300
Emp Here 200   *Sales* 982,747,800
SIC 1383 Oil and gas field services, nec
 David Lesar

D-U-N-S 24-347-0069   (HQ)
HALLMARK TUBULARS LTD
HALLMARK TECHNICAL SERVICES DIV OF
(*Suby of* MARUBENI-ITOCHU STEEL INC.)
308 4 Ave Sw Suite 400, Calgary, AB, T2P
0H7
(403) 266-3807
Emp Here 45   *Sales* 83,643,560
SIC 5051 Metals service centers and offices
Henry Ewert
Greg Northcott
Shawn Baumgardner
Russ Strilchuk
Dean Kueber

D-U-N-S 24-410-6089   (SL)
HAMILTON AND PARTNERS
734 7 Ave Sw Suite 1100, Calgary, AB, T2P
3P8
(403) 262-2080
Emp Here 27   *Sales* 27,941,787
SIC 6311 Life insurance
Darol Hamilton

D-U-N-S 20-258-3852   (SL)
HAMMERHEAD RESOURCES INC
CIOC
525 8 Ave Sw Suite 2700, Calgary, AB, T2P
1G1
(403) 930-0560
Emp Here 50   *Sales* 10,506,550
SIC 1381 Drilling oil and gas wells
Scott Sobie
Scott Sobie
David Anderson

D-U-N-S 20-561-5003   (HQ)
HARMATTAN GAS PROCESSING LIMITED
PARTNERSHIP
355 4 Ave Sw Suite 1700, Calgary, AB, T2P
0J1
(403) 691-7575
Emp Here 18   *Sales* 47,087,530
SIC 1389 Oil and gas field services, nec
Bob Pritchard

D-U-N-S 20-181-7959   (HQ)
HARVEST OPERATIONS CORP
(*Suby of* GOVERNMENT OF THE REPUBLIC
OF KOREA)
700 2 St Sw Suite 1500, Calgary, AB, T2P
2W1
(403) 265-1178
Emp Here 250   *Sales* 223,447,640
SIC 1311 Crude petroleum and natural gas
Byeongil Kim
Cheolwoong Choi
Mark Tysowski
Jinha Woo

D-U-N-S 24-006-7459   (SL)
HIGH ARCTIC ENERGY SERVICES INC
CONCORD ENERGY WELL SERVICES
700 2nd St Sw Suite 500, Calgary, AB, T2P
2W1
(403) 508-7836
Emp Here 500   *Sales* 164,686,865
SIC 1381 Drilling oil and gas wells
Cameron Bailey
Michael Binnion
Donald Pack
Simon Batcup
Steven Vasey
Daniel Bordessa
Joseph Oliver
Ember Shmitt
James Hodgson

D-U-N-S 24-157-7816   (BR)
HOLT, RENFREW & CIE, LIMITEE
HOLT RENFREW
8 Ave Sw Unit 510, Calgary, AB, T2P 4H9
(403) 269-7341
Emp Here 120
SIC 5651 Family clothing stores
Deb Kerr

D-U-N-S 24-423-8809   (HQ)

HORIZON NORTH CAMP & CATERING
PARTNERSHIP
HORIZON NORTH CAMPS & CATERING,
DIV OF
(*Suby of* HORIZON NORTH LOGISTICS INC)
240 4 Ave Sw Suite 900, Calgary, AB, T2P
4H4
(403) 517-4654
Emp Here 25   *Sales* 13,991,700
SIC 5812 Eating places
Robert German

D-U-N-S 24-316-2174   (HQ)
HORIZON NORTH LOGISTICS INC
HORIZON NORTH CAMPS & CATERING
240 4 Ave Sw Suite 900, Calgary, AB, T2P
4H4
(403) 517-4654
Emp Here 200   *Sales* 298,877,923
SIC 4731 Freight transportation arrangement
Rod W. Graham
Scott Matson
J.P. (Joe) Kiss
Mark Becker
Marci Laurence
Kevin D. Nabholz
Russell A. Newmark
Dale E. Tremblay
Bradley P.D. Fedora
Ann I Rooney

D-U-N-S 20-373-3357   (SL)
HORIZON NORTH MODULAR MANUFAC-
TURING INC
(*Suby of* HORIZON NORTH LOGISTICS INC)
240 4 Ave Sw Suite 900, Calgary, AB, T2P
4H4
(403) 517-4654
Emp Here 400   *Sales* 111,356,000
SIC 2452 Prefabricated wood buildings
Rod Graham
Joseph Kiss
Scott Matson

D-U-N-S 24-619-5320   (SL)
HORIZON NORTH POWER SYTEMS
HORIZON NORTH CAMP & CATERING
PARTNERSHIP, DIV OF
(*Suby of* HORIZON NORTH LOGISTICS INC)
900-240 4 Ave Sw, Calgary, AB, T2P 4H4
(780) 955-2992
Emp Here 100   *Sales* 44,717,400
SIC 5063 Electrical apparatus and equipment
Robert German

D-U-N-S 20-052-4986   (HQ)
HSE INTEGRATED LTD
HSE FIRE SERVICES
(*Suby of* DXP ENTERPRISES, INC.)
630 6 Ave Sw Suite 1000, Calgary, AB, T2P
0S8
(403) 266-1833
Emp Here 60   *Sales* 165,935,700
SIC 8748 Business consulting, nec
Marty Jordens
Dwyne Cichon
Tim White
Umair Hussain
Sarah Hermary

D-U-N-S 20-076-3720   (BR)
HUDSON'S BAY COMPANY
BAY, THE
(*Suby of* HUDSON'S BAY COMPANY)
200 8 Ave Sw, Calgary, AB, T2P 1B5
(403) 262-0345
Emp Here 450
SIC 5311 Department stores
John Briale

D-U-N-S 24-879-7060   (SL)
HUSKY (U.S.A.), INC
(*Suby of* HUSKY ENERGY INC)
707 8 Ave Sw, Calgary, AB, T2P 1H5
(403) 298-6111
Emp Here 201   *Sales* 73,467,309
SIC 6712 Bank holding companies

John Chin Sung Lau

D-U-N-S 25-106-4861   (HQ)
HUSKY ENERGY INC
707 8 Ave Sw, Calgary, AB, T2P 1H5
(403) 298-6111
Emp Here 100   *Sales* 16,616,837,738
SIC 1382 Oil and gas exploration services
Robert J. Peabody
Jeffrey E. Rinker
Trevor Pritchard
David A. Gardner
Andrew Dahlin
Janet Annesley
Bradley H. Allison
Gerald F. Alexander
James Girgulis
Nancy F. Foster

D-U-N-S 20-700-1772   (SL)
HUSKY ENERGY INTERNATIONAL SUL-
PHUR CORPORATION
(*Suby of* HUSKY ENERGY INC)
707 8 Ave Sw, Calgary, AB, T2P 1H5
(403) 298-6111
Emp Here 120   *Sales* 80,721,480
SIC 1311 Crude petroleum and natural gas
John Lau

D-U-N-S 24-949-6076   (SL)
HUSKY GAS MARKETING INC
(*Suby of* HUSKY ENERGY INC)
707 8 Ave Sw, Calgary, AB, T2P 1H5

Emp Here 200   *Sales* 365,953,200
SIC 4923 Gas transmission and distribution
John Lau

D-U-N-S 20-699-0520   (SL)
HUSKY OIL LIMITED
HUSKY OIL MARKETING CO
(*Suby of* HUSKY ENERGY INC)
707 8 Ave Sw, Calgary, AB, T2P 1H5
(403) 298-6111
Emp Here 100   *Sales* 67,267,900
SIC 1311 Crude petroleum and natural gas
Robert J. Peabody
Jonathan M. Mckenzie

D-U-N-S 20-767-3393   (HQ)
HUSKY OIL OPERATIONS LIMITED
(*Suby of* HUSKY ENERGY INC)
707 8 Ave Sw, Calgary, AB, T2P 1H5
(403) 298-6111
Emp Here 1,500   *Sales* 6,861,953,400
SIC 1311 Crude petroleum and natural gas
Asim Ghosh
Alister Cowan

D-U-N-S 20-913-4944   (BR)
IBM CANADA LIMITED
(*Suby of* INTERNATIONAL BUSINESS MA-
CHINES CORPORATION)
639 5 Ave Sw Suite 2100, Calgary, AB, T2P
0M9

Emp Here 110
SIC 7371 Custom computer programming ser-
vices
Peter Huggard

D-U-N-S 24-982-1380   (SL)
ICE NGX CANADA INC
NGX
(*Suby of* INTERCONTINENTAL EXCHANGE,
INC.)
300 5 Ave Sw Suite 1000, Calgary, AB, T2P
3C4
(403) 974-1700
Emp Here 50   *Sales* 51,622,200
SIC 6799 Investors, nec
Peter Krenkel

D-U-N-S 25-100-9445   (SL)
ICOM PRODUCTIONS INC
140 8 Ave Sw Suite 400, Calgary, AB, T2P
1B3

(403) 539-9276
Emp Here 50   *Sales* 10,619,850
SIC 8748 Business consulting, nec
Gregory Surbey

D-U-N-S 24-025-4867   (SL)
IKKUMA RESOURCES CORP
(*Suby of* PIERIDAE ENERGY LIMITED)
605 5 Ave Sw Suite 2700, Calgary, AB, T2P
3H5
(403) 261-5900
Emp Here 44   *Sales* 29,597,876
SIC 1382 Oil and gas exploration services
Tim De Freitas
John Van De Pol
Yvonne Mcleod
Greg Feltham
Rich Rowe
Robert Dales
William Guinan
Charle Gamba
Michael Kohut
David Anderson

D-U-N-S 20-276-6036   (SL)
ILF CONSULTANTS INC
833 4 Ave Sw Suite 600, Calgary, AB, T2P 3T5
(587) 288-2600
Emp Here 63   *Sales* 11,085,354
SIC 8711 Engineering services
Andrew Mather
Patrizia Banducci

D-U-N-S 24-043-4886   (HQ)
IMMIGRANT SERVICES CALGARY SOCI-
ETY
IMMIGRANT LANGUAGE & VOCATIONAL
ASSESSMENT & REFERAL CENTRE
910 7 Ave Sw Suite 1200, Calgary, AB, T2P
3N8
(403) 265-1120
Sales 10,674,088
SIC 8322 Individual and family services
Krystyna Biel
Michelle Johnson
Shirley Philips
Anita Remartinez
Raymond Cheung
Nishi Thusoo
Paul Avender
Haritha Devulapally
Ada Adeleke-Kelani
Lisa Clarke

D-U-N-S 24-016-4582   (HQ)
IMPERIAL OIL RESOURCES LIMITED
(*Suby of* IMPERIAL OIL LIMITED)
237 4 Ave Sw, Calgary, AB, T2P 0H6
(800) 567-3776
Emp Here 1,500   *Sales* 2,018,037,000
SIC 1382 Oil and gas exploration services
Rich Kruger
Daniel Lyons
Peter Dinnick
Glenn Peterson

D-U-N-S 20-383-3249   (SL)
INDEPENDENT SYSTEM OPERATOR
2500-330 5 Ave Sw, Calgary, AB, T2P 0L4
(403) 539-2450
Emp Here 600   *Sales* 504,441,600
SIC 4911 Electric services

D-U-N-S 24-857-0751   (BR)
INFOSYS LIMITED
(*Suby of* INFOSYS LIMITED)
888 3 St Sw Suite 1000, Calgary, AB, T2P 5C5
(403) 444-6896
Emp Here 90
SIC 7379 Computer related services, nec
Jeff Glen

D-U-N-S 25-756-7227   (SL)
INPLAY OIL CORP
640 5 Ave Sw Suite 920, Calgary, AB, T2P
3G4
(587) 955-9570
Emp Here 31   *Sales* 51,861,758

SIC 1311 Crude petroleum and natural gas
Douglas J. Bartole
Gordon Reese
Kevin Yakiwchuk
Thane Jensen
Donald Cowie
Craig Golinowski
Dennis L. Nerland
Stephen C. Nikiforuk
Dale O. Shwed
Stephen Yuzpe

D-U-N-S 20-552-0609　(BR)
INTACT INSURANCE COMPANY
SURETY, DIV OF
(*Suby of* INTACT FINANCIAL CORPORA-
TION)
321 6 Ave Sw Suite 1200, Calgary, AB, T2P
3H3
(403) 269-7961
Emp Here 900
SIC 6331 Fire, marine, and casualty insurance
Lisa Dickie

D-U-N-S 25-092-2262　(SL)
**INTEGRATED SUSTAINABILITY CONSUL-
TANTS LTD**
INTEGRATED SUSTAINABILITY
1600-400 3 Ave Sw, Calgary, AB, T2P 4H2

Emp Here 48　*Sales* 10,195,056
SIC 8748 Business consulting, nec
Stuart Torr

D-U-N-S 25-539-1773　(HQ)
INTER PIPELINE LTD
215 2 St Sw Suite 3200, Calgary, AB, T2P
1M4
(403) 290-6000
Emp Here 263　*Sales* 1,965,682,676
SIC 1382 Oil and gas exploration services
Christian P. Bayle
James J. Madro
Jeremy A. Roberge
Jeffrey D. Marchant
David Chappell
Anita Dusevic Oliva
Spil Kousinioris
Cory W. Neufeld
Bernard Perron
Richard Sawyer

D-U-N-S 20-373-0788　(SL)
INTER PIPELINE US MARKETING LTD
(*Suby of* INTER PIPELINE LTD)
215 2nd St Sw Suite 3200, Calgary, AB, T2P
1M4
(403) 538-9015
Emp Here 8　*Sales* 10,057,608
SIC 5172 Petroleum products, nec
David Chapel

D-U-N-S 24-876-4888　(HQ)
**INTERNATIONAL COMMODITIES EXPORT
COMPANY OF CANADA LIMITED**
ICEC CANADA
(*Suby of* H.J. BAKER & BRO., LLC)
606 4 St Sw Suite 1020, Calgary, AB, T2P 1T1
(403) 264-8954
Sales 44,551,200
SIC 5191 Farm supplies
Don G Roberts
Jeremy Sheppe

D-U-N-S 24-320-4614　(SL)
ISH EQUIPMENT LTD
700 4 Ave Sw Unit 310, Calgary, AB, T2P 3J4

Emp Here 100　*Sales* 27,794,742
SIC 6712 Bank holding companies
John Anhang
Adir Koschitzky
Yedidia Koschitzky
Shel Laven

D-U-N-S 20-697-2049　(SL)
ITHACA ENERGY INC

333 7 Ave Sw Suite 1600, Calgary, AB, T2P
2Z1
(403) 234-3338
Emp Here 366　*Sales* 143,691,000
SIC 1382 Oil and gas exploration services
Leslie James Thomas
Graham Forbes
Roy Buchan
Richard Smith
Brad Hurtubise
Ron Brenneman
Jay Zammit
Alec Carstairs
Josef Asaf Bartfeld
Yosef Abu

D-U-N-S 24-011-9305　(HQ)
J R & S HOLDINGS LTD
SIGNALTA
605 5 Ave Sw Suite 1000, Calgary, AB, T2P
3H5
(403) 265-5091
Sales 18,542,890
SIC 1311 Crude petroleum and natural gas
Robert Chad

D-U-N-S 24-701-6199　(HQ)
JAPAN CANADA OIL SANDS LIMITED
JACOS
(*Suby of* JAPAN PETROLEUM EXPLO-
RATION CO.,LTD.)
639 5 Ave Sw Suite 2300, Calgary, AB, T2P
0M9
(403) 264-9046
Emp Here 120　*Sales* 31,016,790
SIC 8731 Commercial physical research
Toshi Hirata
Yukio Kishigami

D-U-N-S 25-205-9498　(HQ)
JENNINGS CAPITAL INC
308 4 Ave Sw Suite 2700, Calgary, AB, T2P
0H7
(403) 292-0970
Emp Here 27　*Sales* 77,951,691
SIC 6211 Security brokers and dealers
Robert G. Jennings
David Lawson
Larry Farrell
Daryl Hodges
Peter Taylor

D-U-N-S 20-138-6609　(SL)
JOEY TOMATO'S (EAU CLAIRE) INC
JOEY'S
208 Barclay Parade Sw, Calgary, AB, T2P 4R4
(403) 263-6336
Emp Here 100　*Sales* 4,551,900
SIC 5812 Eating places
Jeffrey Fuller

D-U-N-S 20-766-9144　(HQ)
JOMAX DRILLING (1988) LTD
355 4 Ave Sw Suite 2020, Calgary, AB, T2P
0J1
(403) 265-5312
Emp Here 5　*Sales* 168,169,750
SIC 1381 Drilling oil and gas wells
Brian Levang
Tom Levang

D-U-N-S 25-538-5205　(HQ)
JURA ENERGY CORPORATION
150-6th Ave Sw Suite 5100, Calgary, AB, T2P
3Y7
(403) 266-6364
Sales 11,902,697
SIC 1382 Oil and gas exploration services
Nadeem Farooq
Arif Siddiq
Timothy Elliott
Stephen Smith
Stephen C. Akerfeldt
Frank Turner
Syed Hasan Akbar Kazmi

D-U-N-S 25-972-4847　(SL)
KARVE ENERGY INC

205 5 Ave Sw Suite 1700, Calgary, AB, T2P
2V7
(403) 809-5896
Emp Here 5　*Sales* 56,997,952
SIC 1382 Oil and gas exploration services
Bob Chaisson
Derek Kreba
Ken Mcneill
Shane Helwer
Justin Crawford
Cliff Brown
Silas Ehlers
Don Engle
James Lough
Howard Crone

D-U-N-S 20-137-0827　(BR)
**KASIAN ARCHITECTURE INTERIOR DE-
SIGN AND PLANNING LTD**
(*Suby of* KASIAN ARCHITECTURE INTE-
RIOR DESIGN AND PLANNING LTD)
1011 9 Ave Sw, Calgary, AB, T2P 1L3
(403) 265-2440
Emp Here 100
SIC 8712 Architectural services
Oliver San Agustin

D-U-N-S 20-320-1462　(HQ)
KATALYST DATA MANAGEMENT LP
540 5 Ave Sw Suite 1490, Calgary, AB, T2P
0M2
(403) 294-5274
Emp Here 50　*Sales* 70,631,295
SIC 1382 Oil and gas exploration services
Seymour Epstein
Oded Levi
Steve Darnell
Neil Baker
Debbie L Garbutt

D-U-N-S 20-304-4409　(SL)
KEANE COMPLETIONS CN CORP
435 4 Ave Sw Suite 380, Calgary, AB, T2P
2S6
(587) 390-0863
Emp Here 50　*Sales* 15,985,250
SIC 1381 Drilling oil and gas wells
Vince Kozak
Greg Powell

D-U-N-S 20-321-5744　(HQ)
KELT EXPLORATION LTD
311 Sixth Ave Sw Suite 300, Calgary, AB, T2P
3H2
(403) 294-0154
Emp Here 14　*Sales* 20,200,927
SIC 1382 Oil and gas exploration services
David J. Wilson
Patrick Miles
Douglas J. Errico
Sadiq H. Lalani
David A. Gillis
Alan G. Franks
Carol Van Brunschot
Bruce D. Gigg
Douglas O. Macarthur
William C. Guinan

D-U-N-S 24-040-3746　(SL)
KEY SEISMIC SOLUTIONS LTD
205 5 Ave Sw Suite 700, Calgary, AB, T2P
2V7
(403) 232-6557
Emp Here 37　*Sales* 15,710,459
SIC 8999 Services, nec
Darren Olson
Keith Wilkinson
Blaine Frehlich
Bernard Law
William Smithwick

D-U-N-S 25-096-3352　(HQ)
KEYERA CORP
144 4 Ave Sw Suite 200, Calgary, AB, T2P
3N4
(403) 205-8300
Emp Here 250　*Sales* 3,385,085,390

SIC 1389 Oil and gas field services, nec
David G. Smith
Steven B. Kroeker
Bradley W. Lock
Dean Setoguchi
Graham Balzun
Jarrod Beztilny
Mike Freeman
Rick Koshman
Dion Kostiuk
Eileen Marikar

D-U-N-S 24-326-4376　(HQ)
KEYERA ENERGY LTD
(*Suby of* KEYERA CORP)
144 4 Ave Sw Suite 600, Calgary, AB, T2P
3N4
(403) 205-8300
Emp Here 5　*Sales* 31,058,570
SIC 4922 Natural gas transmission
David G Smith
Jim V Bertram

D-U-N-S 24-680-2438　(HQ)
KEYERA PARTNERSHIP
144 4 Ave Sw 2nd Fl Suite 600, Calgary, AB,
T2P 3N4
(403) 205-8414
Emp Here 20　*Sales* 1,151,954,000
SIC 4925 Gas production and/or distribution
David G. Smith
Eileen Marikar
Janet P. Woodruff
Charlene Ripley
Thomas C. O'connor
Michael J. Norris
Donald J. Nelson
Gianna Manes
Jim V. Bertram
Steven B. Kroeker

D-U-N-S 20-393-8574　(HQ)
KILLICK AEROSPACE HOLDING INC.
855 2 St Sw Suite 3500, Calgary, AB, T2P 4J8

Sales 10,462,120
SIC 6712 Bank holding companies
Mark Dobbin

D-U-N-S 24-271-6991　(BR)
KPMG LLP
(*Suby of* KPMG LLP)
205 5 Avenue Sw Suite 3100, Calgary, AB,
T2P 4B9
(403) 691-8000
Emp Here 350
SIC 8721 Accounting, auditing, and book-
keeping
Keith Turnbull

D-U-N-S 24-827-4388　(SL)
**LAPRAIRIE WORKS OILFIELDS SERVICES
INC**
505 2 St Sw Suite 702, Calgary, AB, T2P 1N8
(403) 767-9942
Emp Here 70　*Sales* 47,087,530
SIC 1389 Oil and gas field services, nec
Scott Laprairie
Carl Laprairie
Jim Feragen
Reagan Laprairie
Roachelle Laprairie
Kelly Mcmanus
Cliff Laprairie

D-U-N-S 24-188-7509　(SL)
LARICINA ENERGY LTD
(*Suby of* CANADIAN NATURAL RE-
SOURCES LIMITED)
425 1 St Sw Suite 800, Calgary, AB, T2P 3L8
(403) 750-0810
Emp Here 181　*Sales* 121,754,899
SIC 1311 Crude petroleum and natural gas
Diane Koenig
Noralee Bradley
Jennifer Kennedy
Gary Mihaichuk

Paul Shopiro
Kazim Tahir-Kheli

D-U-N-S 24-826-3746   (SL)
LAUREN ENGINEERS & CONSTRUCTORS, ULC
LAUREN CONCISE
(*Suby of* THE LAUREN CORPORATION)
736 6 Ave Sw Unit 800, Calgary, AB, T2P 3T7
(403) 237-7160
Emp Here 100   *Sales* 17,873,900
SIC 8711 Engineering services
Rod Phipps

D-U-N-S 20-514-6827   (SL)
LD ENERGY CANADA LP
350 7 Ave Sw, Calgary, AB, T2P 3N9
(403) 410-1199
Emp Here 10   *Sales* 12,103,970
SIC 5153 Grain and field beans
David Delainey

D-U-N-S 24-854-8521   (SL)
LEEDE JONES GABLE INC.
421 7 Ave Sw Suite 3415, Calgary, AB, T2P 4K9
(403) 531-6800
Emp Here 125   *Sales* 177,892,250
SIC 6211 Security brokers and dealers
Robert Harrison
Gordon Medland
Gordon Medland
Victor Toboika
Brian Bergen
William Cummins
James Dale
Randy Butchard
Charles Laddish
Richard Carter

D-U-N-S 24-313-3357   (HQ)
LEGACY OIL + GAS INC
525 8 Ave Sw Suite 4400, Calgary, AB, T2P 1G1
(403) 206-5035
Emp Here 70   *Sales* 598,733,101
SIC 1382 Oil and gas exploration services
Trent Yanko
Matthew Janisch
Curt Labelle
Dale Mennis
Bill Wee
Curt Ziemer
Mark Franko
Randal Brockway
Jim Bertram
Jim Nieuwenburg

D-U-N-S 20-283-5625   (SL)
LEUCROTTA EXPLORATION INC
639 5 Ave Sw Suite 700, Calgary, AB, T2P 0M9
(403) 705-4525
Emp Here 12   *Sales* 242,629,029
SIC 1382 Oil and gas exploration services
Robert Zakresky
Rick Sereda
Terry Trudeau
Nolan Chicoine
Helmut Eckert
Peter Cochrane
John Brussa
Donald Cowie
Daryl Gilbert
Kelvin Johnston

D-U-N-S 25-915-1145   (HQ)
LITHION POWER GROUP LTD
333 7 Ave Sw Unit 970, Calgary, AB, T2P 2Z1
(587) 349-5468
Emp Here 5   *Sales* 48,283,570
SIC 2819 Industrial inorganic chemicals, nec
Tyler Armstrong
David Bookbinder
Art Kopach
Mitch Putnam
Arthur Robinson

Robert Russel
Corey Ruttan
Craig Wong

D-U-N-S 20-368-8718   (SL)
LMB AUTOMOBILE INC
BMW MINI LAVAL
520 3 Ave Sw Suite 1900, Calgary, AB, T2P 0R3

Emp Here 230   *Sales* 135,000,956
SIC 5511 New and used car dealers
Steve Landry

D-U-N-S 20-016-3967   (HQ)
LOGAN COMPLETION SYSTEMS INC
(*Suby of* LOGAN INDUSTRIES INTERNATIONAL CORPORATION)
635 8 Ave Sw Suite 850, Calgary, AB, T2P 3M3
(403) 930-6810
Emp Here 14   *Sales* 13,427,610
SIC 1389 Oil and gas field services, nec
Mike Reed

D-U-N-S 24-805-1182   (SL)
LONE PINE RESOURCES INC
640 5 Ave Sw Suite 1100, Calgary, AB, T2P 3G4
(403) 292-8000
Emp Here 9   *Sales* 29,575,200
SIC 1382 Oil and gas exploration services
Tim Granger
Robert Guy
Mimi Lai
Patrick Mcdonald
David Fitzpatrick
Rob Wonnacott
Terence Flynn
Will Matthews
Ajay Sabherwal

D-U-N-S 24-366-9152   (HQ)
LONG RUN EXPLORATION LTD
600 3 Ave Sw Unit 600, Calgary, AB, T2P 0G5
(403) 261-6012
Sales 234,413,628
SIC 1382 Oil and gas exploration services
William Andrew
Dale Miller
Corine Bushfield
Dale Orton
Devin Sundstrom
Jana King
Jason Fleury
John Brussa
Edward Chwyl
Jeffrey Errico

D-U-N-S 25-993-2259   (HQ)
LONG VIEW SYSTEMS CORPORATION
250 2 St Sw Suite 2100, Calgary, AB, T2P 0C1
(403) 515-6900
Emp Here 500   *Sales* 166,847,000
SIC 7379 Computer related services, nec
Don Bialik
Gord Mawhinney
Dan Sottile
Glen Hawker

D-U-N-S 24-673-4545   (HQ)
M-I DRILLING FLUIDS CANADA, INC
M-I SWACO, DIV OF
700 2 St Sw Suite 500, Calgary, AB, T2P 2W1
(403) 290-5300
Emp Here 50   *Sales* 191,089,850
SIC 1389 Oil and gas field services, nec
Robert Tilley
Andrew Fisher
James Webster
Wayne Burgess

D-U-N-S 24-086-9925   (SL)
MACKIMMIE MATTHEWS
401 9 Ave Sw Suite 700, Calgary, AB, T2P 3C5

Emp Here 160   *Sales* 17,741,120

SIC 8111 Legal services
Gordon Griffiths
J.H. Selby
D.S. Mackimmie
J.P. Carleton
R.J. Engbloom
C.G. Mack
J.R. Houghton
L.C. Fontaine
B.E. Leroy
D.I. Holm

D-U-N-S 24-358-1068   (HQ)
MADALENA ENERGY INC
333 7 Ave Sw, Calgary, AB, T2P 2Z1
(403) 264-1915
Emp Here 10   *Sales* 30,887,000
SIC 1311 Crude petroleum and natural gas
Jose David Penafiel
Ezequiel Martinez Ariet
Alejandro Penafiel
Gus Halas
Ruben Etcheverry
Ralph Gillcrist
Barry Larson
Leonardo Madcur
Eric Mark
Alejandro Augusto Penafiel

D-U-N-S 20-108-1432   (HQ)
MANCAL CORPORATION
530 8 Ave Sw Suite 1600, Calgary, AB, T2P 3S8
(403) 231-7580
Sales 86,344,245
SIC 6733 Trusts, nec
Robert A.M. Young
Lorne Gordon
Stephen Letwin
Frederick Mannix
Margaret-Jean Mannix
Michael Walker

D-U-N-S 20-894-8690   (SL)
MANPOWER PROFESSIONAL INC
MANPOWER SERVICES
734 7 Ave Sw Suite 120, Calgary, AB, T2P 3P8
(403) 269-6936
Emp Here 65   *Sales* 10,099,115
SIC 7361 Employment agencies
Randy Upright
Shameer Tharani

D-U-N-S 20-296-1665   (SL)
MANUS INC
350 7 Ave Sw Suite 1400, Calgary, AB, T2P 3N9
(403) 299-9600
Emp Here 53   *Sales* 12,417,264
SIC 8742 Management consulting services
Dennis Nerland

D-U-N-S 20-152-8812   (SL)
MARATHON OIL CANADA CORPORATION
(*Suby of* MARATHON OIL CORPORATION)
440 2 Ave Sw Suite 2400, Calgary, AB, T2P 5E9
(403) 233-1700
Emp Here 40   *Sales* 12,788,200
SIC 1382 Oil and gas exploration services
Joanne Alexander
Richard Horstman
Tony Kraljic
Craig Ritchie

D-U-N-S 24-521-3244   (SL)
MARLER MINI MART (CAMROSE) LTD
MARLER MINI MART GROUP
350 7 Ave Sw Suite 2900, Calgary, AB, T2P 3N9

Emp Here 38   *Sales* 10,417,776
SIC 5411 Grocery stores

D-U-N-S 24-419-3442   (HQ)
MARQUEE ENERGY LTD
(*Suby of* PRAIRIE PROVIDENT RE-

SOURCES INC)
500 4 Ave Sw Suite 1700, Calgary, AB, T2P 2V6
(403) 384-0000
Emp Here 11   *Sales* 11,189,675
SIC 1382 Oil and gas exploration services
William Roach
Adam Jenkins
Dave Washenfelder
Howard Bolinger
Rob Lemermeyer
Sam Yip
Adrian Goodisman
Stephen Griggs
Paul Moase
Leonard Sokolow

D-U-N-S 20-829-6855   (BR)
MARSH CANADA LIMITED
(*Suby of* MARSH & MCLENNAN COMPANIES, INC.)
222 3 Ave Sw Suite 1100, Calgary, AB, T2P 0B4
(403) 290-7900
Emp Here 200
SIC 6411 Insurance agents, brokers, and service
Tom Blenkhorn

D-U-N-S 20-350-7223   (HQ)
MASTEC CANADA INC
(*Suby of* MASTEC, INC.)
333 7 Ave Sw Unit 2000, Calgary, AB, T2P 2Z1
(403) 770-7365
Emp Here 20   *Sales* 12,682,110
SIC 1541 Industrial buildings and warehouses
Trevor Mitzel
Sherry Macdonald
Ryan Resch
Brad Gooding

D-U-N-S 25-386-5372   (SL)
MATRIX GEOSERVICES LTD
808 4 Ave Sw Suite 600, Calgary, AB, T2P 3E8
(403) 294-0707
Emp Here 110   *Sales* 18,353,170
SIC 7374 Data processing and preparation
Mark Harrison
Ying Cheung
Lain Eng

D-U-N-S 25-206-5545   (HQ)
MAXIM POWER CORP
715 5 Ave Sw Suite 1210, Calgary, AB, T2P 2X6
(403) 263-3021
Sales 14,967,966
SIC 4911 Electric services
M. Bruce Chernoff
Michael (Mike) Mayder
W. Brett Wilson
Robert (Bob) Emmott
Rob Watson
Kyle Mitton
Kim Karran
Wiley Auch
Johann Polz
Brad Wall

D-U-N-S 24-786-2345   (BR)
MCCARTHY TETRAULT LLP
(*Suby of* MCCARTHY TETRAULT LLP)
421 7 Ave Sw Suite 4000, Calgary, AB, T2P 4K9
(403) 260-3500
Emp Here 200
SIC 8111 Legal services
Greg Turnbull

D-U-N-S 25-205-9910   (SL)
MCDANIEL GROUP HOLDING CORPORATION, THE
255 5 Ave Sw Suite 2200, Calgary, AB, T2P 3G6
(403) 262-5506
Emp Here 64   *Sales* 17,557,248

SIC 8741 Management services
Mike Seth

D-U-N-S 20-119-7469 (SL)
MEG ENERGY CORP
3 Ave Sw Suite 600 25th Fl, Calgary, AB, T2P
0G5
(403) 770-0446
Emp Here 537 *Sales* 2,071,668,368
SIC 1311 Crude petroleum and natural gas
,Derek Evans
Grant Borbridge
Aidan Mills
Eric L. Toews
Chi-Tak Yee
Jeffrey J. Mccaig
Grant Billing
Ian Bruce
Harvey Doerr
Judy Fairburn

D-U-N-S 25-416-4544 (BR)
MERCER (CANADA) LIMITED
(*Suby of* MARSH & MCLENNAN COMPA-
NIES, INC.)
222 3 Ave Sw Suite 1200, Calgary, AB, T2P
0B4
(403) 269-4945
Emp Here 110
SIC 8999 Services, nec
Daniel Audet

D-U-N-S 20-440-1822 (SL)
METRO FORD SALES LTD
1111 9 Ave Sw, Calgary, AB, T2P 1L3
(403) 263-4530
Emp Here 100 *Sales* 62,928,000
SIC 5511 New and used car dealers
Reg Pattermore

D-U-N-S 24-174-8982 (BR)
MICROSOFT CANADA INC
(*Suby of* MICROSOFT CORPORATION)
500 4 Ave Sw Suite 1900, Calgary, AB, T2P
2V6
(403) 296-6500
Emp Here 250
SIC 7371 Custom computer programming ser-
vices
Sonia Skortz

D-U-N-S 20-390-9346 (SL)
**MIDSTREAM ENERGY PARTNERS (USA),
LLC**
205 5 Ave Sw Suite 3900, Calgary, AB, T2P
2V7
(403) 296-1660
Emp Here 120 *Sales* 141,872,760
SIC 5172 Petroleum products, nec
Stanley Owerko

D-U-N-S 24-734-1787 (HQ)
MIDSTREAM LPG PARTNERSHIP
(*Suby of* PETROGAS ENERGY CORP)
205 5 Ave Sw Suite 3900, Calgary, AB, T2P
2V7
(403) 266-1985
Sales 15,086,412
SIC 5172 Petroleum products, nec
Steve Spaulding

D-U-N-S 20-297-3082 (BR)
MILLER THOMSON LLP
MILTON MANAGEMENT
(*Suby of* MILLER THOMSON LLP)
700 9 Ave Sw Suite 3000, Calgary, AB, T2P
3V4
(403) 298-2400
Emp Here 100
SIC 8111 Legal services
Stephanie Thompson

D-U-N-S 20-549-9192 (HQ)
MILNER POWER INC
(*Suby of* MAXIM POWER CORP)
715 5 Ave Sw Suite 1220, Calgary, AB, T2P
2X6
(403) 750-9300
Sales 40,729,910

SIC 4911 Electric services
John Bobenic
Victor Dusik

D-U-N-S 20-267-7225 (SL)
MILNER POWER LIMITED PARTNERHSIP
(*Suby of* MAXIM POWER CORP)
715 5 Ave Sw Suite 1210, Calgary, AB, T2P
2X6
(403) 263-3021
Emp Here 50 *Sales* 31,330,700
SIC 4911 Electric services
John Bobenic
James Pollock

D-U-N-S 25-385-5738 (HQ)
MINDORO RESOURCES LTD
639 5 Ave Sw Suite 1250, Calgary, AB, T2P
0M9
(780) 413-8187
Sales 102,309,600
SIC 1081 Metal mining services
Mary Anne Antazo
Federico Zarate Jr.
Edsel Abrasaldo
Arturo De Los Santos
Geocel D Olanday

D-U-N-S 20-759-4300 (HQ)
MNP LLP
330 5 Ave Sw Suite 2000, Calgary, AB, T2P
0L4
(403) 444-0150
Emp Here 500 *Sales* 776,382,600
SIC 8721 Accounting, auditing, and book-
keeping
Jason Tuffs
Kelly Bernakevitch
Jeremy Cole
Sean Wallace
Darren Turchansky
Laurel Wood

D-U-N-S 24-667-4506 (SL)
MONTAGE TECHNOLOGIES INC
Gd Lcd 1, Calgary, AB, T2P 2G8
(403) 263-4089
Emp Here 49 *Sales* 13,881,357
SIC 8741 Management services
Daryl Thachuk

D-U-N-S 25-091-9458 (HQ)
MOOSE JAW REFINERY ULC
(*Suby of* GIBSON ENERGY INC)
440 2 Ave Sw Suite 1700, Calgary, AB, T2P
5E9
(403) 206-4000
Sales 33,985,224
SIC 5032 Brick, stone, and related material
A. Stewart Hanlon

D-U-N-S 20-305-9923 (SL)
MORTGAGE 1 CORPORATION
700 4 Ave Sw Suite 1700, Calgary, AB, T2P
3J4

Emp Here 68 *Sales* 15,282,592
SIC 6163 Loan brokers
Michael Savage
Daryn Broers

D-U-N-S 20-397-9422 (HQ)
MRC GLOBAL (CANADA) LTD
(*Suby of* MRC GLOBAL INC.)
255 5 Ave Sw Suite 910, Calgary, AB, T2P
3G6
(403) 233-7166
Emp Here 5 *Sales* 22,200,100
SIC 3519 Internal combustion engines, nec
Andrew Lane
James Braun
Daniel Churay
Grant Bates
John Bowhay
Tod Moss
Robert Stein
Karl Witt

D-U-N-S 25-686-8720 (SL)
MUNICIPAL TANK LINES LIMITED
TRIMAC
800 5 Ave Sw Suite 1700, Calgary, AB, T2P
3T6
(403) 298-5100
Emp Here 300 *Sales* 61,711,800
SIC 4213 Trucking, except local
Jeff Mccaig

D-U-N-S 20-077-1749 (HQ)
MURPHY OIL COMPANY LTD
(*Suby of* MURPHY OIL CORPORATION)
520 3 Ave Sw Suite 4000, Calgary, AB, T2P
0R3
(403) 294-8000
Emp Here 78 *Sales* 587,902,494
SIC 1311 Crude petroleum and natural gas
Stephen Crosby
George Dembroski
Richard Matthews
Claiborne Deming
Steven Cosse
Bill Stobaugh

D-U-N-S 24-356-8347 (HQ)
NABORS DRILLING CANADA LIMITED
ABANDONRITE ENVIRO SERVICES
500 4 Ave Sw Suite 2800, Calgary, AB, T2P
2V6
(403) 263-6777
Sales 1,022,603,683
SIC 1381 Drilling oil and gas wells
Anthony Petrello
William Restrepo
Mark Andrews
John Yearwood
Tanya Beder
James Crane
John Kotts
Michael Linn
Dag Skattum
Martin Whitman

D-U-N-S 25-047-9438 (HQ)
NAL RESOURCES LIMITED
(*Suby of* MANULIFE FINANCIAL CORPORA-
TION)
550 6 Ave Sw Suite 600, Calgary, AB, T2P
0S2
(403) 294-3600
Sales 12,572,010
SIC 5171 Petroleum bulk stations and termi-
nals
Kevin Stashin
Keith Steeves
Darcy Reding
Shelley Leggitt
Paul Kunkel
Cory Bergh
John Kanik
Angele Mullins
Kevin J.E. Adolphe
Donald P. Driscoll

D-U-N-S 24-808-7769 (HQ)
NAL RESOURCES MANAGEMENT LIMITED
(*Suby of* MANULIFE FINANCIAL CORPORA-
TION)
550 6 Ave Sw Suite 600, Calgary, AB, T2P
0S2
(403) 294-3600
Emp Here 220 *Sales* 28,050,750
SIC 8741 Management services
Kevin Stashin
Jeffrey Smith
William J Eeuwes
Brian Lemke
Donald Driscoll

D-U-N-S 20-377-4070 (HQ)
NALCO CANADA ULC
*NALCO CHAMPION, AN ECOLAB COM-
PANY*
(*Suby of* ECOLAB LUX & CO HOLDINGS
SCA)
815 8 Ave Sw Suite 1400, Calgary, AB, T2P

3P2
(403) 234-7881
Sales 134,442,400
SIC 5169 Chemicals and allied products, nec
Christophe Beck
Scott Kirkland
Joseph Ross Rae

D-U-N-S 24-849-9902 (HQ)
NCS MULTISTAGE INC
MONGOOSE
(*Suby of* NCS MULTISTAGE HOLDINGS,
INC.)
333 7 Ave Sw Suite 700, Calgary, AB, T2P 2Z1
(403) 984-7674
Emp Here 41 *Sales* 43,051,456
SIC 1389 Oil and gas field services, nec
Robert Nipper
Marty Stromquist
Don Battenfelder
Dustin Ellis
Mike Mckown
Richard Finney
Shawn Leggett
Roger Dwyer
Kevin Trautner
Don Getzlaf

D-U-N-S 20-286-7503 (SL)
NEW WAVE ENERGY SERVICES LTD
(*Suby of* NEW WAVE ENERGY SERVICES
GROUP LTD)
140 4 Ave Sw Suite 1955, Calgary, AB, T2P
3N3
(403) 453-2925
Emp Here 55 *Sales* 36,997,345
SIC 1389 Oil and gas field services, nec
Liam Balfour
Mark Hopper

D-U-N-S 25-235-6555 (HQ)
NEW WEST ENERGY SERVICES INC
435 4 Ave Sw Suite 500, Calgary, AB, T2P
3A8
(403) 984-9798
Sales 15,386,447
SIC 1389 Oil and gas field services, nec
Gerry E. Kerkhoff
Erinn B. Broshko
James Devitt
Wade Smith
William A. Rand
Robert F. Chase
Ralph T. Strother
Timothy A. Young
Pardeep Sibia

D-U-N-S 25-532-8221 (SL)
NEWPARK CANADA INC
*NEWPARK MAT & INTEGRATED SERVICES,
DIV OF*
(*Suby of* NEWPARK RESOURCES INC.)
635 6 Ave Sw Suite 300, Calgary, AB, T2P 0T5
(403) 266-7383
Emp Here 50 *Sales* 15,985,250
SIC 1381 Drilling oil and gas wells
Paul Howes
Neil Mckenzie

D-U-N-S 24-359-2404 (SL)
**NEWPARK CANADA INVESTMENTS LIM-
ITED PARTNERSHIP**
635 6 Ave Sw Suite 300, Calgary, AB, T2P 0T5
(403) 266-7383
Emp Here 55 *Sales* 14,385,415
SIC 6712 Bank holding companies
Bruce Smith

D-U-N-S 25-290-8298 (HQ)
NEXEN HOLDINGS (USA) INC
(*Suby of* CHINA NATIONAL OFFSHORE OIL
CORP.)
801 7 Ave Sw Suite 200, Calgary, AB, T2P
3P7
(403) 234-6700
Sales 2,969,185,782
SIC 1311 Crude petroleum and natural gas

Charles W. Fisher
Douglas B. Otten
Marvin F Romanow

D-U-N-S 25-290-8371   (SL)
NEXEN PETROLEUM INTERNATIONAL LTD
(*Suby of* CHINA NATIONAL OFFSHORE OIL CORP.)
801 7 Ave Sw Suite 2900, Calgary, AB, T2P 3P7
(403) 234-6700
Emp Here 111   *Sales* 205,858,602
SIC 1311 Crude petroleum and natural gas
Edward W Bogle
Patricia L Horsfall
Harry D Wasden
John Patterson
Laurence Murphy

D-U-N-S 24-785-7477   (HQ)
NGL SUPPLY CO. LTD
435 4 Ave Sw Suite 550, Calgary, AB, T2P 3A8
(403) 265-1977
Emp Here 9   *Sales* 26,401,221
SIC 5172 Petroleum products, nec
Andrew Edwards

D-U-N-S 24-734-0409   (HQ)
NIKO RESOURCES LTD
800 6 Ave Sw Suite 510, Calgary, AB, T2P 3G3
(403) 262-1020
Emp Here 90   *Sales* 28,773,450
SIC 1311 Crude petroleum and natural gas
William T. Hornaday
Douglas Cole
Glen R, Valk
Larry Fisher
Chris H. Rudge
Alan Knowles
Glenn Carley
Scott Brandt

D-U-N-S 25-230-9570   (HQ)
NINE ENERGY CANADA INC
INTEGRATED PRODUCTION SERVICES
(*Suby of* NINE ENERGY SERVICE, INC.)
840 7 Ave Sw Suite 1840, Calgary, AB, T2P 3G2
(403) 266-0908
Emp Here 30   *Sales* 163,791,300
SIC 1389 Oil and gas field services, nec
John Geddes
Robert Duval
Dennis Hassel
Michael Taton
Nicholas Drake

D-U-N-S 25-260-5860   (HQ)
NORALTA TECHNOLOGIES INC
808 4 Ave Sw Unit 100, Calgary, AB, T2P 3E8
(403) 269-4237
Emp Here 42   *Sales* 20,931,834
SIC 7629 Electrical repair shops
Cameron Zarowny
Shelley Zarowny

D-U-N-S 20-011-9514   (HQ)
NORREP CAPITAL MANAGEMENT LTD
(*Suby of* NORREP INVESTMENT MANAGEMENT GROUP INC)
333 7 Ave Sw Suite 1850, Calgary, AB, T2P 2Z1
(403) 531-2650
Emp Here 25   *Sales* 10,973,280
SIC 8741 Management services
Alexander Sasso

D-U-N-S 24-850-2937   (HQ)
NORTH WEST REDWATER PARTNERSHIP
140 4 Ave Sw Suite 2800, Calgary, AB, T2P 3N3
(403) 398-0900
Sales 336,750,375
SIC 2911 Petroleum refining
Chris Covert

D-U-N-S 20-904-6143   (SL)
NORTHERN BLIZZARD
440 2 Ave Sw, Calgary, AB, T2P 5E9
(403) 930-3000
Emp Here 29   *Sales* 20,207,490
SIC 6792 Oil royalty traders

D-U-N-S 20-389-0780   (SL)
NORTHRIVER MIDSTREAM INC
425 1 St Sw Suite 2200, Calgary, AB, T2P 3L8
(403) 699-1955
Emp Here 5   *Sales* 15,529,285
SIC 4923 Gas transmission and distribution
Bob Bissett
Brian Baker
Paul Hawksworth
Mark Murski

D-U-N-S 24-439-6966   (HQ)
NORTHSTAR DRILLSTEM TESTERS INC
440 2 Ave Sw Unit 750, Calgary, AB, T2P 5E9
(403) 265-8987
Sales 53,814,320
SIC 1389 Oil and gas field services, nec
Keith Marshall
Neil Marshall

D-U-N-S 24-850-9072   (HQ)
NORTON ROSE FULBRIGHT CANADA LLP
(*Suby of* NORTON ROSE FULBRIGHT LLP)
400 3 Ave Sw Suite 3700, Calgary, AB, T2P 4H2
(403) 267-8222
Emp Here 300   *Sales* 1,235,256,000
SIC 8111 Legal services
Jim Coleman
Marcus Archer
Aldo Argento
Bill Armstrong
Michael Bolitho
Rick Borden
Aaron Bowler
Everett Bunnell
John Carleton
Ray Chartier

D-U-N-S 24-702-4201   (HQ)
NOVA CHEMICALS (CANADA) LTD
(*Suby of* GOVERNMENT OF ABU DHABI)
1000 7 Ave Sw Suite 1000, Calgary, AB, T2P 5L5
(403) 750-3600
Emp Here 100   *Sales* 1,064,918,000
SIC 2869 Industrial organic chemicals, nec
Todd Karran
Julie Beck
John Thayer
Naushad Jamani
Arnel Santos
Ronald E.J. Kemle
Grant Thomson

D-U-N-S 25-678-0123   (HQ)
NOVA CHEMICALS CORPORATION
(*Suby of* GOVERNMENT OF ABU DHABI)
1000 7 Ave Sw Suite 1000, Calgary, AB, T2P 5L5
(403) 750-3600
Emp Here 50   *Sales* 1,200,541,500
SIC 2821 Plastics materials and resins
Todd Karran
Julie Beck
Naushad Jamani
Arnel Santos
John Thayer
Suhail Al Mazrouei
Musabbeh Al Kaabi
Abdulaziz Alhajri
Mark Garrett
Stephen Soules

D-U-N-S 25-678-0156   (HQ)
NOVA GAS TRANSMISSION LTD
ALBERTA SYSTEM, THE
(*Suby of* TC ENERGY CORPORATION)
450 1 St Sw, Calgary, AB, T2P 5H1

(403) 920-2000
Sales 1,335,338,880
SIC 4923 Gas transmission and distribution
Ronald Turner
Donald Marchand
Russell Girling
Albrecht Bellstedt

D-U-N-S 24-894-7624   (SL)
NOVA PETROCHEMICALS LTD
(*Suby of* GOVERNMENT OF ABU DHABI)
1000 7 Ave Sw, Calgary, AB, T2P 5L5
(403) 750-3600
Emp Here 1,000   *Sales* 256,101,000
SIC 6712 Bank holding companies

D-U-N-S 20-835-5789   (SL)
NOVUS ENERGY INC.
(*Suby of* YANCHANG PETROLEUM INTERNATIONAL LIMITED)
700 4 Ave Sw Unit 1700, Calgary, AB, T2P 3J4
(403) 263-4310
Emp Here 22   *Sales* 14,798,938
SIC 1382 Oil and gas exploration services
Hugh Ross
Julian Din
Harry L. Knutson
Al J. Kroontje
A Bruce Macdonald
Michael Halvorson
Larry C Mah

D-U-N-S 20-189-8199   (HQ)
NUVISTA ENERGY LTD
525 8 Ave Sw Suite 2500, Calgary, AB, T2P 1G1
(403) 538-8500
Sales 409,053,645
SIC 1382 Oil and gas exploration services
Jonathan Wright
Ross Andreachuk
Kevin Asman
Mike Lawford
Chris Mcdavid
Ryan Paulgaard
Joshua Truba
Keith Macphail
Ronald Eckhardt
Pentti Karkkainen

D-U-N-S 24-157-7774   (HQ)
OBSIDIAN ENERGY LTD
PENN WEST ENERGY TRUST
207 9 Ave Sw Suite 200, Calgary, AB, T2P 1K3
(403) 777-2500
Emp Here 50   *Sales* 336,597,288
SIC 1311 Crude petroleum and natural gas
Michael J. Faust
Aaron Smith
Andrew Sweerts
David Hendry
Gordon Ritchie
Raymond D. Crossley
William A. Friley
Maureen Cormier Jackson
Edward H. Kernaghan
Stephen Loukas

D-U-N-S 25-092-1991   (HQ)
OCULUS TRANSPORT LTD.
444 5 Ave Sw Suite 650, Calgary, AB, T2P 2T8
(403) 262-0006
Emp Here 3   *Sales* 28,798,840
SIC 4213 Trucking, except local
Rick Peterson

D-U-N-S 24-204-3821   (HQ)
OGI GROUP CORPORATION
888 3 St Sw Unit 1000, Calgary, AB, T2P 5C5
(403) 233-7777
Emp Here 10   *Sales* 67,267,900
SIC 1382 Oil and gas exploration services
Amer Gabouri
Ali Algebori
Donald Currie

D-U-N-S 24-583-5327   (HQ)

OPSMOBIL INC
815 8 Ave Sw Suite 1200, Calgary, AB, T2P 3P2
(877) 926-5558
Emp Here 300   *Sales* 201,803,700
SIC 1389 Oil and gas field services, nec
Harold Neil Narfason

D-U-N-S 20-296-2668   (HQ)
ORYX PETROLEUM CORPORATION LIMITED
350 7 Ave Sw Suite 3400, Calgary, AB, T2P 3N9
(403) 261-5350
Emp Here 10   *Sales* 97,642,000
SIC 1381 Drilling oil and gas wells
Vance Querio
Jean Claude Gandur
Kevin Mcphee
Scott Lewis
Peter Newman
Bradford Camp
Peter Janele

D-U-N-S 25-196-0100   (BR)
OSLER, HOSKIN & HARCOURT LLP
(*Suby of* OSLER, HOSKIN & HARCOURT LLP)
450 1 St Sw Suite 2500, Calgary, AB, T2P 5H1
(403) 260-7000
Emp Here 130
SIC 8111 Legal services
Joann Kolodychuk

D-U-N-S 20-694-6464   (SL)
P2 ENERGY SOLUTIONS ALBERTA ULC
(*Suby of* P2 ACQUISITION, LLC)
639 5 Ave Sw Suite 2100, Calgary, AB, T2P 0M9
(403) 774-1000
Emp Here 120   *Sales* 17,301,840
SIC 7371 Custom computer programming services
Bruce Macdonald
Michael Danielewicz
Sherry Sturko

D-U-N-S 20-052-8284   (HQ)
PACIFIC TUBULARS LTD
734 7 Ave Sw Suite 600, Calgary, AB, T2P 3P8
(403) 269-7600
Sales 33,773,730
SIC 5051 Metals service centers and offices
Richard Shields
Bruce Thompson
Mike Ferrey
Chris Thompson
Carol Desjardins

D-U-N-S 20-143-9507   (HQ)
PACKERS PLUS ENERGY SERVICES INC
205 5 Ave Sw Suite 2200, Calgary, AB, T2P 2V7
(403) 263-7587
Emp Here 15   *Sales* 47,087,530
SIC 1382 Oil and gas exploration services
Daniel Themig
Peter Krabben
Ken Paltzat

D-U-N-S 24-135-0151   (HQ)
PACRIM PIPES (CANADA) ULC
(*Suby of* PACRIM PIPES LLC)
505 4 Ave Sw Suite 1610, Calgary, AB, T2P 0J8
(403) 234-8228
Emp Here 2   *Sales* 13,004,407
SIC 5051 Metals service centers and offices
Owen Sun
Sandra Leung

D-U-N-S 24-343-9218   (HQ)
PAINTED PONY ENERGY LTD
PAINTED PONY
520 3rd Ave Sw Suite 1200, Calgary, AB, T2P 0R3

▲ Public Company   ■ Public Company Family Member   **HQ** Headquarters   **BR** Branch   **SL** Single Location

(403) 475-0440
Emp Here 15   *Sales* 301,745,065
SIC 1311 Crude petroleum and natural gas
Patrick R. Ward
Edwin (Ted) S. Hanbury
L. Barry Mcnamara
Tonya L. Fleming
Stuart W. Jaggard
Richard (Rick) W. Kessy
Glenn R. Carley
Kevin D. Angus
Paul Beitel
Joan E. Dunne

D-U-N-S 20-702-5037   (HQ)
PAN ORIENT ENERGY CORP
505 3rd St Sw Suite 1505, Calgary, AB, T2P
3E6
(403) 294-1770
Emp Here 6   *Sales* 296,733,120
SIC 1311 Crude petroleum and natural gas
Jeff Chisholm
Bill Ostlund
Gerald Macey
Michael Hibberd
Cameron Taylor
Richard M Alexander

D-U-N-S 25-676-9878   (HQ)
PARAMOUNT RESOURCES (ACL) LTD
(*Suby of* PARAMOUNT RESOURCES LTD)
421 7 Ave Sw Suite 2800, Calgary, AB, T2P
4K9
(403) 261-1200
Emp Here 200   *Sales* 305,743,760
SIC 1382 Oil and gas exploration services
J.H.T. (Jim) Riddell
Rob Spitzer
Obie O'brien
B.K. (Bernie) Lee
Al Buron

D-U-N-S 20-741-5170   (HQ)
PARAMOUNT RESOURCES (TEC) LTD
(*Suby of* PARAMOUNT RESOURCES LTD)
332 6 Ave Sw Suite 1400, Calgary, AB, T2P
0B2
(403) 290-2900
Sales 134,958,585
SIC 1311 Crude petroleum and natural gas
James H. T. Riddell
Clayton H Riddell
John Williams
Gail Yester
Michael Kohut
Wilfred Gobert
Mick Dilger
Keith Macleod
Robert Macdonald
E Mitchell Shier

D-U-N-S 24-119-7748   (HQ)
PARAMOUNT RESOURCES LTD
421-7th Ave Sw Suite 2800, Calgary, AB, T2P
4K9
(403) 290-3600
Emp Here 349   *Sales* 679,480,000
SIC 1311 Crude petroleum and natural gas
James Riddell
Clayton Riddell
D. Blake Reid
John Williams
Rodrigo Sousa
Bernard Lee
Garth Stotts
Joerg Wittenberg
Paul Kinvig
Phil Tahmazian

D-U-N-S 24-397-2655   (HQ)
PAREX RESOURCES INC
2700 Eighth Ave Pl West Tower 585 8 Ave Sw,
Calgary, AB, T2P 1G1
(403) 265-4800
Emp Here 6   *Sales* 832,988,000
SIC 1382 Oil and gas exploration services
David Taylor

Mike Kruchten
Stuart Davie
Ryan W. Fowler
Kenneth Pinsky
Eric Furlan
Wayne K. Foo
Curtis Bartlett
Robert Engbloom
Ron Miller

D-U-N-S 20-302-7037   (HQ)
**PARKBRIDGE LIFESTYLE COMMUNITIES
INC**
(*Suby of* GOVERNMENT OF THE
PROVINCE OF BRITISH COLUMBIA)
500 4 Ave Sw Suite 1500, Calgary, AB, T2P
2V6
(403) 215-2100
Emp Here 25   *Sales* 292,407,200
SIC 6719 Holding companies, nec
Andrew Blair
Joseph F. Killi
Walter Borthwick
Ian Cockwell
James Hankins
Gary Perron
David Richards
Ken Cullen

D-U-N-S 20-990-3744   (BR)
PARLEE MCLAWS LLP
(*Suby of* PARLEE MCLAWS LLP)
421 7 Ave Sw Unit 3300, Calgary, AB, T2P
4K9
(403) 294-7000
Emp Here 150
SIC 8111 Legal services

D-U-N-S 25-168-4221   (HQ)
PATTERSON-UTI DRILLING CO. CANADA
(*Suby of* PATTERSON-UTI ENERGY, INC.)
734 7 Ave Sw Suite 720, Calgary, AB, T2P
3P8
(403) 269-2858
Emp Here 35   *Sales* 15,985,250
SIC 1381 Drilling oil and gas wells
Cloyce Talbott
John Brown
John Vollmer
Douglas Wall

D-U-N-S 25-415-7118   (SL)
PEAK ENERGY SERVICES LTD
222 3 Ave Sw Suite 900, Calgary, AB, T2P
0B4
(403) 543-7325
Emp Here 263   *Sales* 153,192,169
SIC 1389 Oil and gas field services, nec

D-U-N-S 24-858-3259   (SL)
PEMBINA NGL CORPORATION
(*Suby of* PEMBINA PIPELINE CORPORA-
TION)
525 8 Ave Sw Suite 3800, Calgary, AB, T2P
1G1
(403) 231-7500
Emp Here 249   *Sales* 286,836,546
SIC 4922 Natural gas transmission
Bob Michaleski
Brent Heagy

D-U-N-S 24-806-4461   (SL)
PEMBINA PIPELINE
(*Suby of* PEMBINA PIPELINE CORPORA-
TION)
585 8 Ave Sw Unit 4000, Calgary, AB, T2P
1G1
(403) 231-7500
Emp Here 150   *Sales* 59,886,300
SIC 4619 Pipelines, nec
Michael Dilger
Scott Burrows

D-U-N-S 24-701-8146   (HQ)
PEMBINA PIPELINE CORPORATION
585 8 Ave Sw Unit 4000, Calgary, AB, T2P
1G1

(403) 231-7500
Emp Here 370   *Sales* 5,572,807,802
SIC 4612 Crude petroleum pipelines
Michael (Mick) Dilger
Scott Burrows
Paul Murphy
Stuart (Stu) Taylor
Harry Andersen
Jaret Sprott
Jason Wiun
Randall J. Findlay
Anne-Marie Ainsworth
Doug Arnell

D-U-N-S 24-868-4375   (HQ)
PENGROWTH ENERGY CORPORATION
222 3 Ave Sw Suite 2100, Calgary, AB, T2P
0B4
(403) 233-0224
Emp Here 10   *Sales* 404,902,278
SIC 1311 Crude petroleum and natural gas
Peter D. Sametz
Douglas Bowles
Dave Granger
Chris Webster
Randy Steele
Kelvin B. Johnston
Wayne K. Foo
James D. Mcfarland
A. Terence Poole
Jamie Sokalsky

D-U-N-S 24-520-2382   (BR)
PEO CANADA LTD
DIVERSIFIED PAYROLL SOLUTIONS
(*Suby of* PEO CANADA LTD)
805 5 Ave Sw Suite 100, Calgary, AB, T2P
0N6
(403) 237-5577
Emp Here 100
SIC 8721 Accounting, auditing, and book-
keeping
Randy Ward

D-U-N-S 24-087-9452   (HQ)
PEO CANADA LTD
805 5 Ave Sw Suite 100, Calgary, AB, T2P
0N6
(403) 237-5577
Sales 10,083,690
SIC 7361 Employment agencies
Randy Ward

D-U-N-S 24-039-4259   (SL)
PEOPLE PLACE, THE
805 5 Ave Sw, Calgary, AB, T2P 0N6
(403) 705-2353
Emp Here 49   *Sales* 11,611,530
SIC 7361 Employment agencies
Randy Ward

D-U-N-S 25-399-5567   (SL)
PERFORMANCE WELL SERVICING LTD
604 8 Ave Sw Suite 510, Calgary, AB, T2P
1G4

Emp Here 60   *Sales* 19,182,300
SIC 1389 Oil and gas field services, nec
Scott Darling

D-U-N-S 24-424-9400   (HQ)
PERPETUAL ENERGY INC
605 5 Ave Sw Suite 3200, Calgary, AB, T2P
3H5
(403) 269-4400
Emp Here 11   *Sales* 142,802,814
SIC 1311 Crude petroleum and natural gas
Susan L. Riddell Rose
W. Mark Schweitzer
Linda L. Mckean
Jeffrey R. Green
Marcello M. Rapini
Ryan A. Shay
Robert A. Maitland
Geoffrey C. Merritt
Donald J. Nelson
Howard R. Ward

D-U-N-S 24-348-8140   (SL)
PERSTA RESOURCES INC
888 3 St Sw Suite 3600, Calgary, AB, T2P 5C5
(403) 355-6623
Emp Here 20   *Sales* 12,459,552
SIC 1382 Oil and gas exploration services
Le Bo
Pingzai (Dave) Wang
Binyou Dai
Lei Song
Richard D Orman
Bryan D. Pinney
Peter D. Robertson
Yuan Jing
Richard D. Orman

D-U-N-S 20-828-1279   (HQ)
PETERS & CO. LIMITED
308 4 Ave Sw Suite 2300, Calgary, AB, T2P
0H7
(403) 261-4850
Emp Here 75   *Sales* 72,316,629
SIC 6211 Security brokers and dealers
Ian Bruce
Michael J Tims
Christopher S Potter
Andrew V Boland
Mitchell Molloy
Ronald Wigham
Holly Benson

D-U-N-S 25-291-3046   (SL)
PETROCAPITA INCOME TRUST
717 7 Ave Sw Suite 1400, Calgary, AB, T2P
0Z3
(587) 393-3450
Emp Here 65   *Sales* 22,379,350
SIC 1382 Oil and gas exploration services
Richard Mellis
Greg Marr
Ben Van Rootselaar

D-U-N-S 20-326-0203   (HQ)
PETROCHINA CANADA LTD
707 5 St Sw Suite 2700, Calgary, AB, T2P 1V8
(403) 265-6635
Sales 134,535,800
SIC 1382 Oil and gas exploration services
Jilin Fu
Bob Shepherd
Qiang Luo
Judy Mah
Junhong Wei

D-U-N-S 20-282-8182   (SL)
**PETROCHINA INTERNATIONAL (CANADA)
TRADING LTD**
111 5 Ave Sw Suite 1800, Calgary, AB, T2P
3Y6
(587) 233-1200
Emp Here 150   *Sales* 274,464,900
SIC 4924 Natural gas distribution
Shaolin Li
Jie Wang

D-U-N-S 24-675-0798   (HQ)
PETROGAS ENERGY CORP
205 5 Ave Sw Suite 3900, Calgary, AB, T2P
2V7
(403) 266-1985
Emp Here 60   *Sales* 342,859,170
SIC 5172 Petroleum products, nec
Stanley Owerko
Nigel Richardson
Derek Robertson

D-U-N-S 24-701-5563   (HQ)
PETROKAZAKHSTAN INC
(*Suby of* CHINA NATIONAL PETROLEUM
CORPORATION)
140 4 Ave Sw Suite 1460, Calgary, AB, T2P
3N3
(403) 221-8435
Sales 3,709,164,000
SIC 1311 Crude petroleum and natural gas
Yuxiang Wei
Gang Liu

▲ Public Company   ■ Public Company Family Member   **HQ** Headquarters   **BR** Branch   **SL** Single Location

Douglas Bryce
Yaming Cao
Yaozhong Lu
Elinore Richardson

D-U-N-S 25-505-2490 (HQ)
PETRONAS ENERGY CANADA LTD
(*Suby of* GOVERNMENT OF MALAYSIA)
215 2 St Sw Suite 1600, Calgary, AB, T2P
1M4
(403) 216-2510
Sales 649,103,700
SIC 1311 Crude petroleum and natural gas
Michael Culbert
Mark Fitzgerald
John Brussa
Howard Crone
Gary Perron
Donald Archibald
Fred Coles

D-U-N-S 24-859-9115 (HQ)
PETRONOVA INC
144 4 Ave Sw Suite 1600, Calgary, AB, T2P
3N4
(403) 398-2152
Sales 12,788,200
SIC 1311 Crude petroleum and natural gas
Antonio Jose Vincentelli
Stelvio Di Cecco
Jose Paz
Eugenio Ochoa

D-U-N-S 20-123-1011 (SL)
PETROSHALE INC
421 7th Ave Sw Suite 3230, Calgary, AB, T2P
4K9
(403) 266-1717
Emp Here 11 *Sales* 27,328,461
SIC 1381 Drilling oil and gas wells
M. Bruce Chernoff
Mike Wood
Tony Izzo
Dominic Pallone
David Rain
Brett Herman
Jacob Roorda
Ken Mccagherty
Brooks M. Shughart

D-U-N-S 24-272-8830 (SL)
PETROTAL CORP
421 7th Ave Sw Suite 4000, Calgary, AB, T2P
4K9
(403) 813-4237
Emp Here 41 *Sales* 13,107,905
SIC 1382 Oil and gas exploration services
John Rapach
Christine Shinnie
Tracy Lessard
Jacob Ulrich
Gavin Wilson
Eleanor Barker
Mark Mccomiskey

D-U-N-S 24-327-8087 (HQ)
PETROWEST CORPORATION
407 2 St Sw Suite 800, Calgary, AB, T2P 2Y3
(403) 237-0881
Emp Here 24 *Sales* 110,119,087
SIC 4213 Trucking, except local
Jim Moffatt
Bernie Reed
Gerry Romanzin
Garry Wetsch
Roy Larson
Rick Quigley

D-U-N-S 24-841-5254 (SL)
PETRUS RESOURCES LTD
240 4 Ave Sw Suite 2400, Calgary, AB, T2P
4H4
(403) 984-4014
Emp Here 22 *Sales* 61,190,961
SIC 1382 Oil and gas exploration services
Neil Korchinski
Cheree Stephenson

Brett Booth
Marcus Schlegel
Ross Keilly
Don Gray
Patrick Arnell
Donald Cormack
Stephen White

D-U-N-S 25-677-8903 (SL)
**PEYTO EXPLORATION & DEVELOPMENT
CORP**
600 3 Ave Sw Suite 300, Calgary, AB, T2P
0G5
(403) 261-6081
Emp Here 50 *Sales* 380,677,887
SIC 1311 Crude petroleum and natural gas
Darren Gee
Donald Gray
Tim Louie
Jean-Paul 'jp' Lachance
David Thomas
Kathy Turgeon
Brian Davis
Greg Fletcher
Michael Macbean
John Rossall

D-U-N-S 24-702-7097 (HQ)
PHOENIX TECHNOLOGY SERVICES INC
250 2 St Sw Suite 1400, Calgary, AB, T2P 0C1
(403) 543-4466
Emp Here 25 *Sales* 134,535,800
SIC 1381 Drilling oil and gas wells
John Hooks
Michael Buker
Dan Blanchard
Cameron Ritchie
Jeff Lawson

D-U-N-S 20-315-7102 (SL)
PHOENIX TECHNOLOGY SERVICES LP
250 2 St Sw Suite 1400, Calgary, AB, T2P 0C1
(403) 543-4466
Emp Here 50 *Sales* 16,170,390
SIC 1381 Drilling oil and gas wells
Michael Buker
John Hooks

D-U-N-S 20-954-7848 (SL)
PHX ENERGY SERVICES CORP
250 2 St Sw Suite 1400, Calgary, AB, T2P 0C1
(403) 543-4466
Emp Here 828 *Sales* 240,420,989
SIC 1381 Drilling oil and gas wells
John Hooks
Mike Buker
Cameron Ritchie
Craig Brown
Jeff Shafer
Dan Blanchard
Myron A. Tetreault
Randy M. Charron
Judith J Athaide
Lawrence (Larry) Hibbard

D-U-N-S 24-358-4757 (HQ)
PLAINS MIDSTREAM CANADA ULC
(*Suby of* PLAINS GP HOLDINGS, L.P.)
607 8 Ave Sw Suite 1400, Calgary, AB, T2P
0A7
(403) 298-2100
Emp Here 570 *Sales* 2,022,567,400
SIC 4612 Crude petroleum pipelines
Jason Balasch
Tyler Rimbey
Sandi Wingert
Brad Deets
Scott Sill
Louis Caron
Don Lacey
Neil Lyons

D-U-N-S 20-734-8785 (SL)
**POLYGON INTERNATIONAL TECHNOL-
OGY INC**
400 5 Ave Sw Suite 300, Calgary, AB, T2P 0L6

(403) 984-2759
Emp Here 47 *Sales* 22,326,222
SIC 5085 Industrial supplies
Gong Steven Li
Xizhen Wu

D-U-N-S 25-313-6543 (HQ)
**PRAIRIE PROVIDENT RESOURCES
CANADA LTD**
640 5 Ave Sw Suite 1100, Calgary, AB, T2P
3G4
(403) 292-8000
Sales 43,724,135
SIC 1311 Crude petroleum and natural gas
Tim S. Granger
Mimi Lai
Robert Guy
Patrick Mcdonald
David Fitzpatrick
Terence Flynn
Derek Petrie
Ajay Sabherwal
Rob Wonnacott

D-U-N-S 25-972-7196 (HQ)
PRAIRIE PROVIDENT RESOURCES INC
640 5 Ave Sw Suite 1100, Calgary, AB, T2P
3G4
(403) 292-8000
Sales 64,303,728
SIC 1382 Oil and gas exploration services
Tim S. Granger
Patrick R. Mcdonald
Brad Likuski
Tony Van Winkoop
Gjoa Taylor
Mimi M. Lai
Terence Flynn
Derek Petrie
Ajay Sabherwal
William Roach

D-U-N-S 20-775-4953 (SL)
PRAIRIESKY ROYALTY LTD
350 7th Ave Sw Suite 1700, Calgary, AB, T2P
3N9
(587) 293-4000
Emp Here 60 *Sales* 207,568,328
SIC 1382 Oil and gas exploration services
Andrew Phillips
Pamela Kazeil
Cameron Proctor
James Estey
Sheldon Steeves
Grant Zawalsky
Margaret Mckenzie
Myron Stadnyk
P. Jane Gavan

D-U-N-S 20-077-5641 (HQ)
PRECISION DRILLING CORPORATION
PRECISION DRILLING, DIV OF
525 8 Ave Sw Suite 800, Calgary, AB, T2P
1G1
(403) 716-4500
Emp Here 200 *Sales* 1,168,378,463
SIC 1381 Drilling oil and gas wells
Kevin A. Neveu
Steven Krablin
Carey Ford
Darren Ruhr
Veronica Foley
Michael Culbert
William Donovan
Brian Gibson
Allen R. Haggerman
Susan M. Mackenzie

D-U-N-S 24-684-5502 (SL)
PRECISION LIMITED PARTNERSHIP
SMOKY OILFIELD RENTALS
150 6 Ave Sw Suite 4200, Calgary, AB, T2P
3Y7
(403) 781-5555
Emp Here 50 *Sales* 15,985,250
SIC 1389 Oil and gas field services, nec
Douglas Strong

D-U-N-S 20-827-7975 (SL)
PREMSTEEL FABRICATORS INC
Gd Lcd 1, Calgary, AB, T2P 2G8
(403) 720-6907
Emp Here 50 *Sales* 10,141,500
SIC 3441 Fabricated structural Metal
Daniel Pacitti
Lesley Pacitti

D-U-N-S 25-344-6199 (SL)
PROCALL MARKETING INC
100 4 Ave Sw Unit 200, Calgary, AB, T2P 3N2
(403) 265-4014
Emp Here 50 *Sales* 22,174,500
SIC 7389 Business services, nec
Trent Dickson

D-U-N-S 24-996-9122 (SL)
PROGAS ENTERPRISES LIMITED
(*Suby of* BP P.L.C.)
240 4 Ave Sw Suite 2400, Calgary, AB, T2P
4H4
(403) 233-1301
Emp Here 7 *Sales* 21,740,999
SIC 4924 Natural gas distribution
Del Robostan

D-U-N-S 25-206-6782 (SL)
PROGAS USA INC
(*Suby of* BP P.L.C.)
240 4 Ave Sw Suite 2400, Calgary, AB, T2P
4H4
(403) 233-1301
Emp Here 19 *Sales* 21,955,735
SIC 4923 Gas transmission and distribution
Ken Macdonald
Kevin Olsen

D-U-N-S 20-304-2288 (HQ)
PTW ENERGY SERVICES LTD
355 4 Ave Sw Suite 600 Calgary Place Ii, Cal-
gary, AB, T2P 0J1
(403) 956-8600
Emp Here 4 *Sales* 1,096,527,000
SIC 6712 Bank holding companies
Don Basnett

D-U-N-S 25-206-7582 (HQ)
Q'MAX SOLUTIONS INC
585 8 Ave Sw Suite 1210, Calgary, AB, T2P
1G1
(403) 269-2242
Emp Here 40 *Sales* 245,686,950
SIC 1389 Oil and gas field services, nec
Paul Meek
Anthony Davis
William Hans
Bob Hans
Ed Fercho

D-U-N-S 25-152-4237 (SL)
QUESTERRE ENERGY CORPORATION
801 6 Ave Sw Suite 1650, Calgary, AB, T2P
3W2
(403) 777-1185
Emp Here 10 *Sales* 24,993,865
SIC 1382 Oil and gas exploration services
Michael Binnion
Bjorn Inge Tonnessen
John Brodylo
Peter Coldham
Rick Tityk
Earl Hickok
Alain Sans Cartier
Hans Jacob Holden
Dennis Sykora
Jason D'silva

D-U-N-S 20-310-9074 (HQ)
QUESTFIRE ENERGY CORP
350 7 Ave Sw Suite 1100, Calgary, AB, T2P
3N9
(403) 263-6688
Sales 20,022,975
SIC 1381 Drilling oil and gas wells
Richard H. Dahl
John Ramescu
Bruce K. Shepard

Alfred J. Laudel
Ronald Williams
Darren Kisser
Graham Norris
Neil I. Dell
Roger O. Macleod

D-U-N-S 25-521-3217   (BR)
RAYMOND JAMES LTD
(*Suby of* RAYMOND JAMES FINANCIAL, INC.)
525 8 Ave Sw Suite 161, Calgary, AB, T2P 1G1
(403) 221-0333
Emp Here 80
SIC 6211 Security brokers and dealers
Mike Irwin

D-U-N-S 20-358-0626   (SL)
RAZOR ENERGY CORP
500 5 Ave Sw Suite 800, Calgary, AB, T2P 3L5
(403) 262-0242
Emp Here 18   *Sales* 93,169,978
SIC 1311 Crude petroleum and natural gas
Doug Bailey
Frank Muller
Marc Bergevin
Lisa Mueller
Devin Sundstrom
Stephen Sych
Kevin Braun
Sanjib (Sony) Gill
Shahin (Sonny) Mottahed
Vick Saxon

D-U-N-S 24-308-7819   (SL)
RBC DEXIA INVESTORS SERVICES
335 8 Ave Sw, Calgary, AB, T2P 1C9
(403) 292-3978
Emp Here 32   *Sales* 16,998,624
SIC 6211 Security brokers and dealers
Lori Warner

D-U-N-S 24-204-6667   (HQ)
RECON PETROTECHNOLOGIES LTD
RECON
510 5 St Sw Unit 410, Calgary, AB, T2P 3S2
(403) 517-3266
Emp Here 30   *Sales* 15,985,250
SIC 1389 Oil and gas field services, nec
Michael Boyle

D-U-N-S 24-394-9828   (HQ)
REDLINE DRAFTING INC
1000 7 Ave Sw Suite 600, Calgary, AB, T2P 5L5
(403) 452-3810
Sales 18,587,800
SIC 6712 Bank holding companies
Som Khousakom

D-U-N-S 24-008-6459   (HQ)
REFORM ENERGY SERVICES CORP
808 4 Ave Sw Suite 500, Calgary, AB, T2P 3E8
(403) 262-2181
Emp Here 1   *Sales* 15,665,545
SIC 1381 Drilling oil and gas wells
Brent Tiedemann Tiedemann
Jamon Ludwar

D-U-N-S 25-676-7559   (SL)
REPLICON INC
(*Suby of* REPLICON SOFTWARE INC.)
910 7 Ave Sw Suite 800, Calgary, AB, T2P 3N8
(403) 262-6519
Emp Here 500   *Sales* 92,286,500
SIC 7371 Custom computer programming services
Raj Narayanaswamy
Lakshmi Raj
Jason Green
Suresh Kuppahally
Peter Kinash
Maggie Deptuck

D-U-N-S 20-548-0218   (HQ)

REPSOL CANADA ENERGY PARTNERSHIP
(*Suby of* REPSOL SA.)
888 3 St Sw Suite 2000, Calgary, AB, T2P 5C5
(403) 237-1234
Emp Here 200   *Sales* 818,956,500
SIC 1382 Oil and gas exploration services
Jill Terakita-Jones

D-U-N-S 24-906-3835   (HQ)
REPSOL OIL & GAS CANADA INC
(*Suby of* REPSOL SA.)
888 3 St Sw Suite 2000, Calgary, AB, T2P 5C5

Emp Here 50   *Sales* 2,013,541,048
SIC 1382 Oil and gas exploration services
Luis Cabra Duenas
David Charlton
John Rossall
Albrecht W.A. Bellstedt
F. Javier Sanz Cedron
Thomas W. Ebbern
Josu Jon Imaz San Miguel
Miguel Klingenberg Calvo
Michael T. Waites

D-U-N-S 20-822-5149   (BR)
RICHARDSON GMP LIMITED
(*Suby of* RICHARDSON GMP LIMITED)
525 8 Ave Sw Suite 4700, Calgary, AB, T2P 1G1
(403) 355-7735
Emp Here 100
SIC 8742 Management consulting services
Grant Mutch

D-U-N-S 20-355-0942   (HQ)
RIDGEBACK RESOURCES INC
(*Suby of* APOLLO GLOBAL MANAGEMENT, LLC)
525 8 Ave Sw Unit 2800, Calgary, AB, T2P 1G1
(403) 268-7800
Emp Here 5   *Sales* 254,630,025
SIC 1382 Oil and gas exploration services
J. Paul Charron
David Broshko
Paul Masse
Cory Dean
Thomas Emerson
Sean Kinoshita
David Sakal
Jeffrey Wallace

D-U-N-S 24-752-6259   (SL)
RIEGER
808 4 Ave Sw Suite 600, Calgary, AB, T2P 3E8
(403) 537-7642
Emp Here 49   *Sales* 41,554,940
SIC 6411 Insurance agents, brokers, and service
Larry Rhode

D-U-N-S 24-417-1237   (HQ)
RIFE RESOURCES LTD
(*Suby of* COMPAGNIE DES CHEMINS DE FER NATIONAUX DU CANADA)
144 4 Ave Sw Suite 400, Calgary, AB, T2P 3N4
(403) 221-0800
Sales 67,267,900
SIC 1311 Crude petroleum and natural gas
Thomas J. Mullane
Peter T. Harrison
Russell J. Hiscock
David Sandmeyer
William Ingram

D-U-N-S 20-601-0191   (HQ)
ROCKWELL SERVICING INC
(*Suby of* ENSIGN ENERGY SERVICES INC)
400 5 Ave Sw Suite 1000, Calgary, AB, T2P 0L6
(403) 265-6361
Sales 336,339,500
SIC 1389 Oil and gas field services, nec

Glenn Dagenais
Robert Geddes
Bryan Toth

D-U-N-S 20-036-3906   (BR)
ROGERS MEDIA INC
JACK FM
(*Suby of* ROGERS COMMUNICATIONS INC)
535 7 Ave Sw, Calgary, AB, T2P 0Y4
(403) 250-9797
Emp Here 120
SIC 4832 Radio broadcasting stations
Gayle Zarbatany

D-U-N-S 20-178-1288   (HQ)
ROHDE & LIESENFELD CANADA INC
ROLIPROJECTS
144 4 Ave Sw Suite 1600, Calgary, AB, T2P 3N4
(403) 514-6907
Emp Here 11   *Sales* 15,669,540
SIC 4731 Freight transportation arrangement
Jan L. Beringer
Michael Rasmussen
Gregory Smith

D-U-N-S 24-156-0424   (HQ)
RPS CANADA LIMITED
555 4 Ave Sw Suite 700, Calgary, AB, T2P 3E7
(403) 691-9717
Sales 29,244,360
SIC 8999 Services, nec
Peter Mulholland

D-U-N-S 24-358-3817   (SL)
RPS ENERGY CANADA LTD
(*Suby of* R P S GROUP PLC)
800 5 Ave Sw Suite 1400, Calgary, AB, T2P 3T6
(403) 265-7226
Emp Here 100   *Sales* 17,873,900
SIC 8711 Engineering services
Peter Mulholland
John Willams
Gary Young

D-U-N-S 25-191-0709   (SL)
RYAN ENERGY TECHNOLOGIES
500 4 Ave Sw Suite 2800, Calgary, AB, T2P 2V6
(403) 263-6777
Emp Here 160   *Sales* 107,628,640
SIC 1381 Drilling oil and gas wells
Richard Ryan

D-U-N-S 25-179-5704   (HQ)
S.I. SYSTEMS LTD
401 9 Ave Sw Suite 309, Calgary, AB, T2P 3C5
(403) 263-1200
Emp Here 25   *Sales* 13,716,600
SIC 8741 Management services
Larry Fichtner
Derek Bullen
Ken Krawic
Chandra Ramasamy
Jennifer Foster
Ed Malysa
Jane Hein
Brian Mckenzie

D-U-N-S 24-419-1230   (HQ)
S.I. SYSTEMS PARTNERSHIP
401 9 Ave Sw Suite 309, Calgary, AB, T2P 3C5
(403) 286-1200
Emp Here 21   *Sales* 15,597,000
SIC 8741 Management services
Derek Bullen
Ed Malysa
Jane Hein
Brian Mckenzie

D-U-N-S 24-325-6786   (HQ)
SABRE WELL SERVICING INC
SWS
435 4 Ave Sw Suite 380, Calgary, AB, T2P

3A8
(403) 237-0309
Emp Here 10   *Sales* 12,788,200
SIC 1389 Oil and gas field services, nec
Imran Malik
Dave Southerland

D-U-N-S 24-714-0473   (SL)
SAGE-LINK LTD
700 4 Ave Sw Suite 1180, Calgary, AB, T2P 3J4
(403) 457-1590
Emp Here 90   *Sales* 28,773,450
SIC 1389 Oil and gas field services, nec
Roy White

D-U-N-S 24-041-3182   (SL)
SAIPEM CANADA INC
SAIPEM CONSTRUCTION CANADA
(*Suby of* SAIPEM SPA)
530 8 Ave Sw Suite 2100, Calgary, AB, T2P 3S8
(403) 441-2793
Emp Here 1,500   *Sales* 492,172,500
SIC 1629 Heavy construction, nec
Paolo Parisi

D-U-N-S 24-700-3098   (HQ)
SANJEL CANADA LTD
505 2 St Sw Suite 200, Calgary, AB, T2P 1N8
(403) 269-1420
Emp Here 200   *Sales* 1,637,913,000
SIC 1389 Oil and gas field services, nec
Shane Hooker
Murray Bickley
Leonard Cornez
Darcy Kardash
Jeff Spence
Melanie Nahayowski
Sam Okasha

D-U-N-S 20-344-7081   (SL)
SANLING ENERGY LTD
250 2 St Sw Suite 1700, Calgary, AB, T2P 0C1
(403) 303-8500
Emp Here 50   *Sales* 10,506,550
SIC 1311 Crude petroleum and natural gas
Jeremy Song

D-U-N-S 25-149-1403   (HQ)
SAVANNA ENERGY SERVICES CORP
(*Suby of* TOTAL ENERGY SERVICES INC)
311 6 Ave Sw Suite 800, Calgary, AB, T2P 3H2
(403) 503-9990
Emp Here 84   *Sales* 782,376,443
SIC 1381 Drilling oil and gas wells
Ken Mullen
Rick Torriero
John Cooper
George Chow
Darcy Draudson
Dwayne Lamontagne
Rachel Moore
Lori Connell
James Saunders
Allen Brooks

D-U-N-S 24-385-7609   (HQ)
SAVANNA WELL SERVICING INC
(*Suby of* TOTAL ENERGY SERVICES INC)
311 6 Ave Sw Suite 800, Calgary, AB, T2P 3H2
(403) 503-0650
Sales 27,494,630
SIC 1389 Oil and gas field services, nec
George K Chow
Kenneth B Mullen

D-U-N-S 24-425-6751   (SL)
SB NAVITAS TUBULAR INC
435 4 Ave Sw Suite 480, Calgary, AB, T2P 3A8
(403) 984-9548
Emp Here 20   *Sales* 20,006,780
SIC 5051 Metals service centers and offices
Mark Hopkins
Shane Jones

D-U-N-S 24-929-8290   (BR)
SCOTIA CAPITAL INC
SCOTIA MCLEOD
(*Suby of* BANK OF NOVA SCOTIA, THE)
119 6 Ave Sw Suite 300, Calgary, AB, T2P
0P8
(403) 298-4000
Emp Here 100
SIC 6211 Security brokers and dealers
Brad Whyte

D-U-N-S 24-353-5965   (HQ)
SCOTIA WATEROUS INC
(*Suby of* WATEROUS INTERNATIONAL (IRE-
LAND) LIMITED)
225 6 Ave Sw Ste 1700, Calgary, AB, T2P 1M2
(403) 410-9947
Sales 56,350,620
SIC 6211 Security brokers and dealers
Adam Waterous
David Potter

D-U-N-S 24-928-7160   (HQ)
SCOTT LAND & LEASE LTD
202 6 Ave Sw Suite 900, Calgary, AB, T2P
2R9
(403) 261-1000
Emp Here 100   *Sales* 187,835,400
SIC 6211 Security brokers and dealers
Gregg Scott
Lona Gabora

D-U-N-S 24-374-3734   (HQ)
SDX ENERGY INC
520 3 Ave Sw Suite 1900, Calgary, AB, T2P
0R3
(403) 457-5035
Sales 39,166,000
SIC 1382 Oil and gas exploration services
Paul Welch
Mark Reid
Michael Doyle
David Mitchell
David Richards
Michael Raynes

D-U-N-S 24-348-3406   (HQ)
SECURE ENERGY SERVICES INC
205 5 Ave Sw Suite 3600, Calgary, AB, T2P
2V7
(403) 984-6100
Emp Here 300   *Sales* 2,226,888,994
SIC 1389 Oil and gas field services, nec
Rene Amirault
Allen Gransch
Chad Magus
Daniel Steinke
Dave Engel
Corey Higham
George Wadsworth
David Mattinson
Brian Mcgurk
Mike Mikuska

D-U-N-S 20-018-5835   (BR)
SECURE ENERGY SERVICES INC
DRILLING SERVICES DIVISION
(*Suby of* SECURE ENERGY SERVICES INC)
205 5 Ave Sw Suite 3600, Calgary, AB, T2P
2V7
(403) 264-1588
Emp Here 100
SIC 1389 Oil and gas field services, nec

D-U-N-S 20-381-9669   (HQ)
SEMCAMS MIDSTREAM ULC
SEMCAMS
520 3 Ave Suite 700, Calgary, AB, T2P 0R3
(403) 536-3000
Emp Here 75   *Sales* 207,468,980
SIC 1389 Oil and gas field services, nec
David Williams
David Goose
Christopher Dutcher
Leanne Campbell
Jody Klotz

D-U-N-S 24-618-0157   (SL)

SEMINOLE CANADA GAS CO
350 7 Ave Sw Suite 2200, Calgary, AB, T2P
3N9

Emp Here 10   *Sales* 12,572,010
SIC 5172 Petroleum products, nec

D-U-N-S 24-371-4453   (SL)
SEVEN GENERATIONS ENERGY LTD
525 8 Ave Sw Unit 4400, Calgary, AB, T2P
1G1
(403) 718-0700
Emp Here 179   *Sales* 2,437,373,740
SIC 1311 Crude petroleum and natural gas
Marty Proctor
Derek Aylesworth
David Holt
Kyle Brunner
Chris Feltin
Randall Hnatuik
Barry Hucik
Kevin Johnston
Jordan Johnsen
Brian Newmarch

D-U-N-S 20-803-8851   (SL)
SHANGHAI ENERGY CORPORATION
605 5 Ave Sw Unit 700, Calgary, AB, T2P 3H5
(587) 393-3600
Emp Here 55   *Sales* 36,997,345
SIC 1311 Crude petroleum and natural gas
Anthony Kuehne
Tian Bo Weng
Zhen Huang
Thomas Lee

D-U-N-S 25-414-3415   (HQ)
SHAW CABLESYSTEMS G.P.
(*Suby of* SHAW COMMUNICATIONS INC)
630 3 Ave Sw, Calgary, AB, T2P 4L4
(403) 750-4500
Emp Here 5,600   *Sales* 1,873,446,400
SIC 4841 Cable and other pay television ser-
vices
J R Shaw
Peter Bissonnette
Michael D'avella
Ken C. C. Stien
James F Dinning

D-U-N-S 20-636-5447   (HQ)
SHAW COMMUNICATIONS INC
SHAW CABLE
630 3 Ave Sw Suite 900, Calgary, AB, T2P 4L4
(403) 750-4500
Emp Here 200   *Sales* 3,895,938,522
SIC 4813 Telephone communication, except
radio
Bradley Shaw
Jr Shaw
Jay Mehr
Trevor English
Zoran Stakic
Peter Johnson
Janice Davis
Dan Markou
Peter Bissonnette
Adrian Burns

D-U-N-S 20-175-2268   (HQ)
SHELL CANADA LIMITED
(*Suby of* ROYAL DUTCH SHELL PLC)
400 4 Ave Sw, Calgary, AB, T2P 0J4
(403) 691-3111
Emp Here 1,600   *Sales* 14,836,656,000
SIC 1311 Crude petroleum and natural gas
Michael Crothers
Jason Anderson
Gordon Mccue
Zoe Baldwin
Jason Anderson
Andrea Brecka
Gordon Mccue
Philippe Gauthier

D-U-N-S 24-312-1949   (HQ)
SHELL CANADA PRODUCTS

400 4 Ave Sw, Calgary, AB, T2P 0J4
(403) 691-3111
Sales 2,955,682,500
SIC 5172 Petroleum products, nec
Michael Crothers
Jason Anderson
Zoe Baldwin
Andrea Brecka
Jason Anderson

D-U-N-S 25-357-5609   (HQ)
**SHELL ENERGY NORTH AMERICA
(CANADA) INC**
(*Suby of* ROYAL DUTCH SHELL PLC)
400 4 Ave Sw Suite 212, Calgary, AB, T2P 0J4
(403) 216-3600
Emp Here 100   *Sales* 252,220,800
SIC 4911 Electric services
Arnold Macburnie
James Chunn
Nick Dimarzo
Drew Harris

D-U-N-S 20-565-4093   (SL)
SHELL GLOBAL SOLUTIONS CANADA INC
(*Suby of* ROYAL DUTCH SHELL PLC)
400 4 Ave Sw, Calgary, AB, T2P 0J4
(403) 691-3540
Emp Here 90   *Sales* 60,499,080
SIC 5169 Chemicals and allied products, nec
Andy C Kinmonth
M. Fran Keeth
Mark Anderson

D-U-N-S 24-676-9728   (HQ)
**SHERRITT INTERNATIONAL OIL AND GAS
LIMITED**
(*Suby of* SHERRITT INTERNATIONAL COR-
PORATION)
425 1 St Sw Suite 2000, Calgary, AB, T2P 3L8
(403) 260-2900
Sales 40,360,740
SIC 1382 Oil and gas exploration services
Twyla Thompson

D-U-N-S 20-827-0918   (HQ)
SIGNALTA RESOURCES LIMITED
(*Suby of* J R & S HOLDINGS LTD)
840 6 Ave Sw Suite 700, Calgary, AB, T2P
3E5
(403) 265-5091
Sales 39,015,382
SIC 1311 Crude petroleum and natural gas
Howard Sorenson
Robert Chad
Gordon Bradford
B James Mccashin

D-U-N-S 25-365-8637   (SL)
**SINOCANADA PETROLEUM CORPORA-
TION**
444 7 Ave Sw Unit 800, Calgary, AB, T2P 0X8

Emp Here 100   *Sales* 125,720,100
SIC 5172 Petroleum products, nec
Pngfei Yin

D-U-N-S 24-124-5179   (HQ)
SINOPEC DAYLIGHT ENERGY LTD
SINOPEC CANADA
(*Suby of* CHINA PETROCHEMICAL GROUP
CO., LTD.)
112 4 Ave Sw Suite 2700, Calgary, AB, T2P
0H3
(403) 266-6900
Sales 525,564,120
SIC 2911 Petroleum refining
Brian Tuffs
Feng Zhiqiang
Hansheng Mou
Derek Mccoubrey
Lydia Li
Jim Broughton
Zeng Fanli
Deng Hanshen
Michael Laffin
Howard Balloch

D-U-N-S 25-522-3505   (SL)
SIZELAND EVANS INTERIOR DESIGN INC
441 5 Ave Sw Suite 700, Calgary, AB, T2P
2V1

Emp Here 40   *Sales* 17,739,600
SIC 7389 Business services, nec
Patricia Evans

D-U-N-S 20-120-1675   (SL)
SNC-LAVALIN ATP INC
(*Suby of* GROUPE SNC-LAVALIN INC)
640 5 Ave Sw Unit 300, Calgary, AB, T2P 3G4
(403) 539-4550
Emp Here 260   *Sales* 51,254,060
SIC 8711 Engineering services
Neil Bruce
Kevin G. Lynch
James Cullens
Sylvain Girard
Hartland J.A Paterson
Erik J. Ryan
Chantal Sorel
Jacques Bougie
Isabelle Courville
Catherine J. Hughes

D-U-N-S 20-188-2532   (BR)
SNC-LAVALIN INC
*HYDROCARBONS AND CHEMICALS DIVI-
SION*
(*Suby of* GROUPE SNC-LAVALIN INC)
605 5 Ave Sw Suite 1400, Calgary, AB, T2P
3H5
(403) 294-2100
Emp Here 1,200
SIC 8711 Engineering services
Jean Beaudoin

D-U-N-S 24-391-3717   (BR)
SNC-LAVALIN INTERNATIONAL INC
(*Suby of* GROUPE SNC-LAVALIN INC)
605 5 Ave Sw Suite 1400, Calgary, AB, T2P
3H5
(403) 294-2100
Emp Here 500
SIC 8711 Engineering services
Jean Beaudion

D-U-N-S 20-344-2637   (SL)
SOCAR TRADING (CANADA) LTD
118 8 Ave Sw Unit 200, Calgary, AB, T2P 1B3
(587) 956-1100
Emp Here 10   *Sales* 12,572,010
SIC 5172 Petroleum products, nec
Simon Kaufmann
Andrew Machalshi

D-U-N-S 25-998-7097   (HQ)
SOLIUM CAPITAL INC
(*Suby of* MORGAN STANLEY)
600 3 Ave Sw Suite 1500, Calgary, AB, T2P
0G5
(403) 515-3910
Emp Here 35   *Sales* 401,952,200
SIC 6211 Security brokers and dealers
Marcos Lopez
Cameron Hall
Gary Levine
Lance Titchkosky
Janice Webster
Michael Broadfoot
Tom Muir
Shawn Abbott
Laura Cillis
Brian Craig

D-U-N-S 24-715-7055   (SL)
SONORO ENERGY LTD
520 5 Ave Sw Suite 900, Calgary, AB, T2P
3R7
(403) 262-3252
Emp Here 100   *Sales* 31,970,500
SIC 1382 Oil and gas exploration services
Chris Atkinson
Richard Wadsworth
David Winter

Dean Callaway
Bill Marpe Marpe

D-U-N-S 24-351-4960   (HQ)
SPECTRA ENERGY EMPRESS L.P.
(*Suby of* ENBRIDGE INC)
425 1 St Sw Suite 2600, Calgary, AB, T2P 3L8
(403) 699-1999
Emp Here 20   *Sales* 21,994,300
SIC 8732 Commercial nonphysical research
Peter Hoy

D-U-N-S 24-324-7223   (HQ)
SPECTRA ENERGY MIDSTREAM CORPO-RATION
(*Suby of* ENBRIDGE INC)
425 1 St Sw Suite 2200, Calgary, AB, T2P 3L8
(403) 699-1900
Sales 53,814,320
SIC 1389 Oil and gas field services, nec
Douglas J Haughey
Bruce E Pydee
Duane Rae

D-U-N-S 20-766-6850   (HQ)
SPROULE ASSOCIATES LIMITED
140 4 Ave Sw Unit 900, Calgary, AB, T2P 3N3
(403) 294-5500
Emp Here 80   *Sales* 20,376,246
SIC 8711 Engineering services
Cam Six

D-U-N-S 24-374-4088   (HQ)
SPROULE HOLDINGS LIMITED
140 4 Ave Sw Suite 900, Calgary, AB, T2P 3N3
(403) 294-5500
Sales 21,448,680
SIC 8711 Engineering services
Keith Macleod

D-U-N-S 24-339-2367   (SL)
SPROULE INTERNATIONAL LIMITED
(*Suby of* SPROULE HOLDINGS LIMITED)
140 4 Ave Sw Suite 900, Calgary, AB, T2P 3N3
(403) 294-5500
Emp Here 102   *Sales* 18,231,378
SIC 8711 Engineering services
R Keith Macleod

D-U-N-S 24-421-2846   (SL)
STAMPEDE DRILLING INC
250 6 Ave Sw 22nd Flr, Calgary, AB, T2P 3H7
(403) 984-5042
Emp Here 15   *Sales* 15,823,863
SIC 7353 Heavy construction equipment rental
Lyle Whitmarsh
Terry Kulper
Bill Devins

D-U-N-S 20-645-4068   (SL)
STAMPEDE PONTIAC BUICK (1988) LTD
STAMPEDE PONTIAC BUICK GMC
1110 9 Ave Sw, Calgary, AB, T2P 1M1

Emp Here 99   *Sales* 62,298,720
SIC 5511 New and used car dealers
David Bridarolli
Mike Collinson

D-U-N-S 25-513-3357   (SL)
STANDARD LAND COMPANY INC
734 7 Ave Sw Suite 1400, Calgary, AB, T2P 3P8
(403) 269-3931
Emp Here 81   *Sales* 22,220,892
SIC 8741 Management services
Winston Gaskin

D-U-N-S 25-988-0359   (BR)
STARWOOD CANADA ULC
WESTIN CALGARY, THE
(*Suby of* MARRIOTT INTERNATIONAL, INC.)
320 4 Ave Sw, Calgary, AB, T2P 2S6
(403) 266-1611
Emp Here 500

SIC 7011 Hotels and motels
Brian Gillett

D-U-N-S 24-804-6935   (HQ)
STEP ENERGY SERVICES LTD
205 5 Ave Sw Suite 1200, Calgary, AB, T2P 2V7
(403) 457-1772
Sales 592,656,094
SIC 1731 Electrical work
Regan Davis
Steve Glanville
Mike Burvill
Bailey Epp
Todd Rainville
David Johnson
Lori Mcleod-Hill
Rory Thompson
Brock Duhon
Shane Persad

D-U-N-S 24-524-9938   (HQ)
STORM RESOURCES LTD
215 2 St Sw Suite 600, Calgary, AB, T2P 1M4
(403) 817-6145
Sales 165,365,547
SIC 1382 Oil and gas exploration services
Brian Lavergne
Jamie P. Conboy
H. Darren Evans
Bret A. Kimpton
Emily Wignes
Michael J. Hearn
Stuart G. Clark
Matthew J. Brister
John A. Brussa
Mark A. Butler

D-U-N-S 24-025-1871   (HQ)
STRAD INC
440 2 Ave Sw Suite 1200, Calgary, AB, T2P 5E9
(403) 232-6900
Emp Here 20   *Sales* 90,913,108
SIC 7353 Heavy construction equipment rental
Andy Pernal
Shane Hopkie
Michael Donovan
Michael J. (Mick) Mcnulty
Tom Alford
Craig Hruska
Lyle Wood
Jack H. Nodwell
Kristi Cawthorn
Lee Matheson

D-U-N-S 25-116-2517   (HQ)
STRATEGIC OIL & GAS LTD
645 7 Ave Sw Suite 1100, Calgary, AB, T2P 4G8
(403) 767-9000
Emp Here 10   *Sales* 26,638,218
SIC 1382 Oil and gas exploration services
Tony Berthelet
Amanda Reitenbach
Aaron Thompson
Thomas Claugus
John W. Harkins
Rodger Hawkins
Jim Riddell
D. Richard Skeith
Michael Graham
Michael Watzky

D-U-N-S 20-189-9049   (HQ)
STRATEGIC REALTY MANAGEMENT CORP
STRATEGIC GROUP
630 8 Ave Sw Suite 400, Calgary, AB, T2P 1G6
(403) 770-2300
Emp Here 200   *Sales* 101,419,200
SIC 6531 Real estate agents and managers
Riaz Mamdani
Ken Toews
Elise Bacon

Randy Ferguson
Graham Garner

D-U-N-S 24-553-0100   (HQ)
STREAM-FLO RESOURCES LTD
202 6 Ave Sw Suite 400, Calgary, AB, T2P 2R9
(403) 269-5531
Emp Here 5   *Sales* 38,378,445
SIC 6712 Bank holding companies
Mark Mcneill
Duncan Mcneill
Doug Jarvin
Abbey Raikles
Len Lambert

D-U-N-S 24-324-2794   (HQ)
STRIKE GROUP INC
505 3 St Sw Suite 1300, Calgary, AB, T2P 3E6
(403) 232-8448
Emp Here 10   *Sales* 436,776,800
SIC 1389 Oil and gas field services, nec
Stephen Smith
Debbie Brittner
Tyler Pawsey
Michael M Tumback
Glen Greenshields

D-U-N-S 20-334-0256   (HQ)
STRIKE GROUP LIMITED PARTNERSHIP
(*Suby of* STRIKE HOLDINGS LIMITED PART-NERSHIP)
505 3 St Sw Suite 1300, Calgary, AB, T2P 3E6
(403) 232-8448
Emp Here 10   *Sales* 218,388,400
SIC 1389 Oil and gas field services, nec
Stephen Smith
Michael Tumback
Tyler Pawsey
Debbie Brittner

D-U-N-S 20-116-3136   (HQ)
SUMITOMO CANADA LIMITED
(*Suby of* SUMITOMO CORPORATION)
350 7 Ave Sw Suite 2400, Calgary, AB, T2P 3N9
(403) 264-7021
Emp Here 6   *Sales* 13,415,220
SIC 5051 Metals service centers and offices
Yasushi Tago
Brian Lambert
Pierre Lemire

D-U-N-S 24-180-4681   (HQ)
SUNCOR ENERGY INC
PETRO CANADA
6 Ave Sw Suite 150, Calgary, AB, T2P 3Y7
(403) 296-8000
Emp Here 621   *Sales* 29,555,364,572
SIC 2911 Petroleum refining
Mark Little
Eric Axford
Alister Cowan
Paul Gardner
Mike Macsween
Steve Reynish
Kris Smith
Arlene Strom
Bruno Francoeur
Michael Wilson

D-U-N-S 25-678-8639   (HQ)
SUNCOR ENERGY MARKETING INC
CHEMICALS MARKETING DIVISION
(*Suby of* SUNCOR ENERGY INC)
150 6 Ave Sw, Calgary, AB, T2P 3Y7
(403) 296-8000
Sales 125,720,100
SIC 5172 Petroleum products, nec
Jay Thornton

D-U-N-S 24-365-3818   (SL)
SUNCOR ENERGY OIL SANDS LIMITED PARTNERSHIP
(*Suby of* SUNCOR ENERGY INC)
150 6 Ave Sw Unit 2, Calgary, AB, T2P 3Y7

(403) 296-8000
Emp Here 100   *Sales* 67,267,900
SIC 1311 Crude petroleum and natural gas
Richard George
Janice B. Odegaard

D-U-N-S 24-524-7171   (HQ)
SUNCOR ENERGY PRODUCTS PARTNER-SHIP
(*Suby of* SUNCOR ENERGY INC)
150 6 Ave Sw, Calgary, AB, T2P 3Y7
(403) 296-8000
Emp Here 200   *Sales* 1,172,762,500
SIC 2911 Petroleum refining
Steve Williams
Jonathan Mckenzie

D-U-N-S 24-354-2540   (HQ)
SUNSHINE OILSANDS LTD
903 8 Ave Sw Unit 1020, Calgary, AB, T2P 0P7
(403) 984-1450
Emp Here 10   *Sales* 28,055,081
SIC 1311 Crude petroleum and natural gas
Kwok Ping Sun
Pui Yun Ho
Michael J. Hibberd
Linna Liu
Xijuan Jiang
Raymond Fong
Joanne Yan
(Yi) David He

D-U-N-S 24-726-9983   (SL)
SUPERIOR PROPANE INC.
425 1 St Sw Suite 1400, Calgary, AB, T2P 3L8

Emp Here 6   *Sales* 18,635,142
SIC 4924 Natural gas distribution

D-U-N-S 25-991-7664   (HQ)
SURGE ENERGY INC
635 8 Ave Sw Suite 2100, Calgary, AB, T2P 3M3
(403) 930-1010
Sales 230,877,690
SIC 1382 Oil and gas exploration services
Paul Colborne
James Pasieka
Jared Ducs
Margaret Elekes
Jim Stannard
Robert Leach
Keith Macdonald
Murray Smith
Dan O'neil
Daryl Gilbert

D-U-N-S 20-270-3492   (SL)
SURGE GENERAL PARTNERSHIP
(*Suby of* SURGE ENERGY INC)
635 8 Ave Sw Suite 2100, Calgary, AB, T2P 3M3
(403) 930-1010
Emp Here 95
SIC 1382 Oil and gas exploration services
Paul Colborne

D-U-N-S 25-372-8448   (BR)
SYMANTEC (CANADA) CORPORATION
(*Suby of* SYMANTEC CORPORATION)
100 4 Ave Sw Suite 1000, Calgary, AB, T2P 3N2

Emp Here 100
SIC 4813 Telephone communication, except radio

D-U-N-S 20-852-5837   (BR)
SYNCRUDE CANADA LTD
(*Suby of* SUNCOR ENERGY INC)
525 3 Ave Sw Suite 525, Calgary, AB, T2P 0G4
(403) 385-2400
Emp Here 200
SIC 1311 Crude petroleum and natural gas

D-U-N-S 20-351-9574   (SL)

TAIL RISK SYSTEMS SOLUTIONS LTD
202 6 Ave Sw Suite 1110, Calgary, AB, T2P
2R9
(587) 352-5071
Emp Here 33   *Sales* 24,380,525
SIC 5169 Chemicals and allied products, nec
  Michael Yurkovich
  Hani Tabesh
  Lane Mathes

D-U-N-S 24-420-6384   (HQ)
TAMARACK VALLEY ENERGY LTD
425 1st St Sw Suite 600, Calgary, AB, T2P 3L8
(403) 263-4440
Emp Here 14   *Sales* 279,552,387
SIC 1311 Crude petroleum and natural gas
  Brian Schmidt
  Scott Reimond
  Ken Cruikshank
  Ronald Hozjan
  Kevin Screen
  Dave Christensen
  June-Marie Innes
  Floyd Price
  Jeffrey Boyce
  Noralee Bradley

D-U-N-S 24-340-8312   (HQ)
TAQA NORTH LTD
(*Suby of* TAQA INTERNATIONAL HOLDINGS
COOPERATIEF U.A.)
308 4 Ave Sw Suite 2100, Calgary, AB, T2P
0H7
(403) 724-5000
Sales 1,212,896,628
SIC 1311 Crude petroleum and natural gas
  Edward Lafehr
  Joel Corteau
  Todd Mcrae
  Vincent Pellegrino
  Jay Lance Petersen
  Erick Reyna
  Graeme Lindsay
  Doreen Brown
  David Cook
  Frederic Lesage

D-U-N-S 24-324-0616   (HQ)
TARTAN CANADA CORPORATION
(*Suby of* STUART OLSON INC)
401 9th Ave Sw Suite 960, Calgary, AB, T2P
2H7
(780) 455-3804
Emp Here 50   *Sales* 191,089,850
SIC 1389 Oil and gas field services, nec
  Doug Lautermilch
  Randy Boomhour
  Joe Bandura
  Randy Vandervoort
  Jason Beaman
  Mike Martin
  David Eisler
  Murray Peterson
  Pat Breen

D-U-N-S 20-117-7057   (HQ)
TC ENERGY CORPORATION
450 1 St Sw, Calgary, AB, T2P 5H1
(403) 920-2000
Sales 10,370,077,258
SIC 4922 Natural gas transmission
  Russell K. Girling
  Karl Johannson
  Stanley G. Chapman, Iii
  Paul Miller
  Donald R. Marchand
  Wendy Hanrahan
  Francois Poirier
  Tracy Robinson
  Kristine Delkus
  Siim A. Vanaselja

D-U-N-S 20-178-4944   (SL)
TD ENERGY TRADING INC
421 7 Ave Sw Suite 36, Calgary, AB, T2P 4K9
(403) 299-8572
Emp Here 30   *Sales* 34,666,950

SIC 4924 Natural gas distribution
  Mark Faicloth
  Richard Merer
  Christopher D Dyrda
  Michael French
  William Furlong
  John Krill
  Drew E Macintyre

D-U-N-S 24-997-5947   (SL)
TEKNICA OVERSEAS LTD
350 7 Ave Sw Suite 2700, Calgary, AB, T2P
3N9

Emp Here 74   *Sales* 31,420,918
SIC 8999 Services, nec
  Mickey S Abougoush

D-U-N-S 20-717-0932   (HQ)
**TENARIS GLOBAL SERVICES (CANADA)
INC**
(*Suby of* ROCCA & PARTNERS STICHT-
ING ADMINISTRATIEKANTOOR AANDELEN
SAN FAUSTIN)
530 8 Ave Sw Suite 400, Calgary, AB, T2P
3S8
(403) 767-0100
Emp Here 74   *Sales* 19,045,740
SIC 3312 Blast furnaces and steel mills
  Paola Rocca
  Darren Flack
  Edgaros Caprera

D-U-N-S 24-618-0843   (SL)
TERASEN PIPELINES PETROLEUM
300 5 Ave Sw Suite 2700, Calgary, AB, T2P
5J2
(403) 514-6400
Emp Here 4   *Sales* 12,423,428
SIC 4923 Gas transmission and distribution
  John Fingarson

D-U-N-S 24-395-8493   (HQ)
TERRACON GEOTECHNIQUE LTD
800-734 7 Ave Sw, Calgary, AB, T2P 3P8
(403) 266-1150
Sales 107,628,640
SIC 1389 Oil and gas field services, nec
  Lee Nichols
  Emmett Horne
  Sarah List
  Victoria Mabilog
  Margaret (Peggy) Smith
  Amant Prasad
  Vassil Valchev
  Ian Cotton

D-U-N-S 25-505-7028   (SL)
TIDAL ENERGY MARKETING INC
(*Suby of* ENBRIDGE INC)
237 4 Ave Sw Suite 2000, Calgary, AB, T2P
4K3
(403) 205-7770
Emp Here 26   *Sales* 32,687,226
SIC 5172 Petroleum products, nec
  Leigh Cruess
  James Lagadin
  Leigh Cruess
  Vernon Yu
  Colin Gruending

D-U-N-S 20-260-8402   (HQ)
**TIDEWATER MIDSTREAM AND INFRAS-
TRUCTURE LTD**
222 3 Ave Sw Suite 900, Calgary, AB, T2P
0B4
(587) 475-0210
Sales 245,844,898
SIC 4922 Natural gas transmission
  Joel A. Macleod
  Tobias J. Mckenna
  David Barva
  Jarvis A. Williams
  Jeff T. Ketch
  Reed Mcdonnell
  Brent Booth
  Joel K. Vorra

  Doug Fraser
  Stephen Holyoake

D-U-N-S 24-683-7558   (SL)
TORC OIL & GAS LTD
525 8 Ave Sw Suite 1800, Calgary, AB, T2P
1G1
(403) 930-4120
Emp Here 98   *Sales* 338,162,011
SIC 1381 Drilling oil and gas wells
  Brett Herman
  Jason Zabinsky
  Sandy Brown
  Shane Manchester
  Jeremy Wallis
  Marvin Tang
  Mike Wihak
  David D. Johnson
  John Brussa
  Mary-Jo Case

D-U-N-S 20-643-4388   (SL)
TORODE RESIDENTIAL LTD
209 8 Ave Sw Suite 301, Calgary, AB, T2P
1B8
(403) 355-6000
Emp Here 45   *Sales* 12,986,235
SIC 1522 Residential construction, nec
  John Torode

D-U-N-S 20-305-3392   (HQ)
**TOSCANA ENERGY INCOME CORPORA-
TION**
207 9 Ave Sw Suite 900, Calgary, AB, T2P
1K3
(403) 410-6790
Sales 13,040,844
SIC 1311 Crude petroleum and natural gas
  Joseph Durante
  Stan Smith
  Brian Krausert
  Anand Ramnath
  Lew Hayes
  Donald Copeland
  John Festival

D-U-N-S 20-583-2061   (SL)
TOTAL E&P CANADA LTD
(*Suby of* TOTAL SA)
240 4 Ave Sw Suite 2900, Calgary, AB, T2P
4H4
(403) 571-7599
Emp Here 231   *Sales* 428,408,442
SIC 1311 Crude petroleum and natural gas
  Jean-Michel Gires
  Gary Houston

D-U-N-S 24-797-6608   (HQ)
TOTAL ENERGY SERVICES INC
311 6 Ave Sw Suite 800, Calgary, AB, T2P
3H2
(403) 216-3939
Emp Here 50   *Sales* 645,758,107
SIC 1382 Oil and gas exploration services
  Daniel Halyk
  Gerry Crawford
  Cam Danyluk
  Yuliya Gorbach
  William Kosich
  Brad Macson
  Bruce Pachkowski
  George Chow
  Glenn Dagenais
  Greg Melchin

D-U-N-S 24-300-3308   (HQ)
TOUCHSTONE EXPLORATION INC
350 7th Ave Sw Unit 4100, Calgary, AB, T2P
3N9
(403) 750-4400
Sales 65,516,520
SIC 1381 Drilling oil and gas wells
  Paul R. Baay
  Scott Budau
  James Shipka
  John D. Wright
  Kenneth R. Mckinnon

  Harrie Vredenburg
  Thomas Valentine
  Peter Nicol
  Stanley Smith

D-U-N-S 24-381-3578   (HQ)
TOURMALINE OIL CORP
250 6 Ave Sw Unit 3700, Calgary, AB, T2P
3H7
(403) 266-5992
Sales 1,595,288,443
SIC 1382 Oil and gas exploration services
  Michael Rose
  Brian Robinson
  Ronald Hill
  Drew Tumbach
  Allan Bush
  Earl Mckinnon
  W. Scott Kirker
  Jill Angevine
  William Armstrong
  Lee Baker

D-U-N-S 24-439-0985   (BR)
TOWERS WATSON CANADA INC
(*Suby of* WILLIS TOWERS WATSON PUBLIC
LIMITED COMPANY)
111 5 Ave Sw Suite 1600, Calgary, AB, T2P
3Y6
(403) 261-1400
Emp Here 90
SIC 8741 Management services
  Anne Dowdall

D-U-N-S 24-809-6026   (SL)
TOYO ENGINEERING CANADA LTD
(*Suby of* TOYO ENGINEERING CORPORA-
TION)
727 7 Ave Sw Suite 1400, Calgary, AB, T2P
0Z5
(403) 266-4400
Emp Here 313   *Sales* 61,702,003
SIC 8711 Engineering services
  Taro Takahashi
  Roberto Rodriguez
  Al Waahlsarom
  Raul Alvarez
  Juan Cascillo
  Akira Shigeta
  Toni Wiebe
  Sandra Wiebe

D-U-N-S 20-694-1622   (SL)
**TRAFIGURA CANADA GENERAL PART-
NERSHIP**
400 3 Ave Sw Suite 3450, Calgary, AB, T2P
4H2
(403) 294-0400
Emp Here 20   *Sales* 13,578,460
SIC 6211 Security brokers and dealers
  Ian Singer

D-U-N-S 20-116-6493   (HQ)
TRANS MOUNTAIN CANADA INC
(*Suby of* KINDER MORGAN INC)
300 5 Ave Sw Suite 2700, Calgary, AB, T2P
5J2
(403) 514-6400
Emp Here 125   *Sales* 361,172,750
SIC 4612 Crude petroleum pipelines
  Ian Anderson
  David Safari
  Mike Bangle
  Michael Davies
  Paul Huddleston
  Maureen Neufeldt
  Norm Rinne
  Scott Stoness

D-U-N-S 20-343-5276   (SL)
TRANSALTA RENEWABLES INC
110 12th Ave Sw, Calgary, AB, T2P 2M1
(403) 267-2520
Emp Here 10   *Sales* 313,854,228
SIC 4911 Electric services
  Brett M. Gellner
  John Kousinioris

Aron Willis
Scott Jeffers
Brent Ward
Todd J. Stack
Kathryn B. Mcquade
Paul Taylor
David W. Drinkwater
Allen R. Hagerman

D-U-N-S 24-905-2259   (HQ)
TRANSCANADA PIPELINE USA LTD
(*Suby of* TC ENERGY CORPORATION)
450 1 St Sw, Calgary, AB, T2P 5H1
(403) 920-2000
Emp Here 7   *Sales* 95,823,832
SIC 5541 Gasoline service stations
Lee G Hobbs
Jon A Dobson
Sean M Brett
William C Taylor
Sean D Mcmaster
Michael E Hachey
Catharine Davis

D-U-N-S 20-177-2480   (HQ)
TRANSCANADA PIPELINES LIMITED
(*Suby of* TC ENERGY CORPORATION)
450 1 St Sw, Calgary, AB, T2P 5H1
(403) 920-2000
Sales 10,536,982,173
SIC 4922 Natural gas transmission
Russell K. Girling
Wendy L. Hanrahan
Donald Marchand
Dennis J. Mcconaghy
Sean Mcmaster
Donald M Wishart
Donald J. Degrandis
Sean M. Brett
Joel E. Hunter
G. Glenn Menuz

D-U-N-S 25-677-9844   (HQ)
TRANSCANADA PIPELINES SERVICES LTD
(*Suby of* TC ENERGY CORPORATION)
450 1 St Sw, Calgary, AB, T2P 5H1
(403) 920-2000
Emp Here 1   *Sales* 84,084,875
SIC 1389 Oil and gas field services, nec
Harold Kvisle

D-U-N-S 20-798-0947   (HQ)
TRANSGLOBE ENERGY CORPORATION
250 5th St Sw Suite 2300, Calgary, AB, T2P 0R4
(403) 264-9888
Emp Here 12   *Sales* 176,797,000
SIC 1382 Oil and gas exploration services
Randall C. Neely
Ross G. Clarkson
Geoffrey Probert
Edward Ok
Lloyd W. Herrick
Susan Mackenzie
David Cook
Steven Sinclair
Edward D. Lafehr
Carol Bell

D-U-N-S 25-417-3966   (HQ)
TRICAN WELL SERVICE LTD
645 7 Ave Sw Suite 2900, Calgary, AB, T2P 4G8
(403) 266-0202
Emp Here 200   *Sales* 682,740,596
SIC 6712 Bank holding companies
Dale Dusterhoft
Michael Baldwin
Robert J. Cox
Dawn Sweany
David Westlund
Chika Onwuekwe
Shaun Kelly
Robert Skilnick
Murray L. Cobbe

G. Allen Brooks

D-U-N-S 20-116-4865   (SL)
TRIDENT EXPLORATION CORP
(*Suby of* TRIDENT RESOURCES CORP)
3100-888 3 St Sw, Calgary, AB, T2P 5C5
(403) 770-0333
Emp Here 70   *Sales* 47,087,530
SIC 1382 Oil and gas exploration services
Alan Withey
Mark Smith
Jean-Pierre Buyze
David Dean
Ken Young
Darren O'brien
Eugene Davis
Marc Dworsky
Daryl Gilbert
Julie Klaff

D-U-N-S 24-424-0516   (HQ)
TRIDENT RESOURCES CORP
888 3 St Sw Suite 3100, Calgary, AB, T2P 5C5
(403) 770-0333
Emp Here 70   *Sales* 47,087,530
SIC 1382 Oil and gas exploration services
Todd Dillabough
Colin Michael Finn
Tracey Bell
Alan Witney
Harry Quarls
Harrison Bubrosky
John Forsgren
Daryl Gilbert
Stuart Wagner
Timothy Bernlohr

D-U-N-S 25-408-9394   (SL)
TRIMAC TRANSPORTATION MANAGEMENT LTD
800 5 Ave Sw Unit 2100, Calgary, AB, T2P 3T6
(403) 298-5100
Emp Here 175
SIC 6712 Bank holding companies

D-U-N-S 25-389-0529   (HQ)
TRINIDAD DRILLING LTD
400 5th Ave Suite 1000, Calgary, AB, T2P 0L6
(403) 262-1361
Emp Here 60   *Sales* 393,003,815
SIC 1381 Drilling oil and gas wells
Robert H. Geddes
Michael Gray
Gary Casswell
James B. Howe
Len O. Kangas
John G. Schroeder

D-U-N-S 24-169-3808   (SL)
TRINITY CAPITAL GP LTD
205 5 Ave Sw Suite 3030, Calgary, AB, T2P 2V7
(403) 266-1985
Emp Here 55   *Sales* 69,146,055
SIC 5172 Petroleum products, nec
Stan Owerko

D-U-N-S 24-701-7288   (HQ)
TUCKER WIRELINE SERVICES CANADA INC
(*Suby of* STEP ENERGY SERVICES LTD)
444 5 Ave Sw Suite 900, Calgary, AB, T2P 2T8
(403) 264-7040
Emp Here 37   *Sales* 121,754,899
SIC 1389 Oil and gas field services, nec
Dave Jaellett
Wayne Tucker
Shawn Tucker

D-U-N-S 25-228-7974   (SL)
TUSK ENERGY INC
700 4 Ave Sw Suite 1950, Calgary, AB, T2P 3J4

Emp Here 23   *Sales* 37,735,445
SIC 1311 Crude petroleum and natural gas

D-U-N-S 20-037-7732   (SL)
TVI PACIFIC INC
505 2 St Sw Suite 806, Calgary, AB, T2P 1N8
(403) 265-4356
Emp Here 201   *Sales* 51,410,574
SIC 1081 Metal mining services
Clifford M. James
Patrick Hanna
Luis Santos Jr
Robert Armstrong
Brian Cramm
Jan Horejsi
David Moscovitz

D-U-N-S 24-806-6149   (SL)
UNIVERSAL GEOSYSTEMS
910 7 Ave Sw Suite 1015, Calgary, AB, T2P 3N8
(403) 262-1336
Emp Here 40   *Sales* 12,788,200
SIC 1382 Oil and gas exploration services
Greg Doggs

D-U-N-S 20-557-6809   (SL)
VALEURA ENERGY INC
202 6 Ave Sw Suite 1200, Calgary, AB, T2P 2R9
(403) 237-7102
Emp Here 10   *Sales* 10,775,662
SIC 1382 Oil and gas exploration services
Sean Guest
Tim Marchant
Gord Begg
Rob Sadownyk
Stephanie Stimpson
Russell Hiscock
Jim Mcfarland
Ron Royal
Kimberley Wood
Steve Bjornson

D-U-N-S 25-150-3405   (HQ)
VALUE CREATION INC
635 8 Ave Sw Unit 1100, Calgary, AB, T2P 3M3
(403) 539-4500
Emp Here 15   *Sales* 15,985,250
SIC 1382 Oil and gas exploration services
Columba Yeung
Ian Chan
Bovornrat Darakananda
R Scott Jolliffe
John Lacey

D-U-N-S 20-488-3591   (SL)
VECTOR ENERGY INC
855 2 St Sw Suite 1760, Calgary, AB, T2P 4J7
(403) 265-9500
Emp Here 5   *Sales* 15,529,285
SIC 4924 Natural gas distribution
Jack Kaston

D-U-N-S 20-260-2488   (SL)
VERESEN MIDSTREAM LIMITED PARTNERSHIP
222 3 Ave Sw Suite 900, Calgary, AB, T2P 0B4
(403) 296-0140
Emp Here 9   *Sales* 27,952,713
SIC 4922 Natural gas transmission
Chris Rusch

D-U-N-S 20-306-7660   (HQ)
VERMILION ENERGY INC
520 3rd Ave Sw Suite 3500, Calgary, AB, T2P 0R3
(403) 269-4884
Emp Here 225   *Sales* 1,156,825,747
SIC 1382 Oil and gas exploration services
Anthony J. Marino
Dion Hatcher
Jenson Tan
Lars Glemser
Terry Hergott
Mona Jasinski
Michael Kaluza
Robert J. Engbloom

Bryce Kremnica
Timothy R. Morris

D-U-N-S 20-009-9810   (HQ)
VIDEON CABLESYSTEMS INC
D&D CABLE VISION
(*Suby of* SHAW COMMUNICATIONS INC)
630 3 Ave Sw Suite 900, Calgary, AB, T2P 4L4
(403) 750-4500
Emp Here 900   *Sales* 206,538,688
SIC 4841 Cable and other pay television services
Peter Bissonnette

D-U-N-S 25-290-9965   (HQ)
WALTON INTERNATIONAL GROUP INC
215 2 St Sw Suite 2500, Calgary, AB, T2P 1M4
(403) 265-4255
Sales 365,509,000
SIC 6719 Holding companies, nec
William K. Doherty
Terry Kent
Leslie Fryers
John Plastiras
David Baukol

D-U-N-S 20-372-6042   (HQ)
WATEROUS ENERGY FUND
301 8 Ave Sw Suite 600, Calgary, AB, T2P 1C5
(403) 930-6048
Sales 1,167,385,000
SIC 6722 Management investment, open-end
Adam Waterous
Andrew Kim
Sara Pettigrew
David Roosth

D-U-N-S 24-715-5133   (HQ)
WERKLUND CAPITAL CORPORATION
400 3 Ave Sw Suite 4500, Calgary, AB, T2P 4H2
(403) 231-6545
Sales 168,169,750
SIC 1389 Oil and gas field services, nec
David Werklund

D-U-N-S 20-349-1824   (HQ)
WEST LAKE ENERGY CORP
600 3 Ave Sw Suite 700, Calgary, AB, T2P 0G5
(403) 215-2045
Sales 57,177,715
SIC 1382 Oil and gas exploration services
David Middleton
Alan Steele

D-U-N-S 20-117-2186   (HQ)
WESTCOAST ENERGY INC
ENBRIDGE
(*Suby of* ENBRIDGE INC)
425 1 St Sw Suite 2600, Calgary, AB, T2P 3L8
(403) 699-1999
Sales 2,669,306,139
SIC 4924 Natural gas distribution
Douglas Bloom
Bruce Pydee
Bohdan Bodnar
Duane Rae
John Patrick Reddy

D-U-N-S 20-731-8309   (HQ)
WESTERN ENERGY SERVICES CORP
HORIZON DRILLING
215 9th Ave Sw Suite 1700, Calgary, AB, T2P 1K3
(403) 984-5916
Emp Here 80   *Sales* 179,222,894
SIC 1389 Oil and gas field services, nec
Alex R.N. Macausland
David G. Trann
Peter J. Balkwill
Jeffrey Bowers
Darcy D. Reinboldt
Rick M. Harrison
Dan Lundstrom
Ronald Mathison

▲ Public Company   ■ Public Company Family Member   **HQ** Headquarters   **BR** Branch   **SL** Single Location

Donald Copeland
Lorne Gartner

D-U-N-S 24-360-1791   (HQ)
WESTERNZAGROS RESOURCES ULC
255 5 Ave Sw Suite 1000, Calgary, AB, T2P 3G6
(403) 693-7001
Emp Here 34   *Sales* 14,434,000
SIC 1382 Oil and gas exploration services
Simon Hatfield
Tony Kraljic
Lance Berg
George Pinckney
Lianne Tysowski
Bruce Garland
Grant Harms
Greg Stevenson
David J. Boone
John Frangos

D-U-N-S 25-977-2697   (SL)
WESTMOUNT MORTGAGE CORPORATION
605 5 Ave Sw Suite 2300, Calgary, AB, T2P 3H5
(403) 269-1027
Emp Here 100   *Sales* 22,474,400
SIC 6162 Mortgage bankers and loan correspondents
Patrick J Doherty

D-U-N-S 24-388-6053   (SL)
WHITECAP RESOURCES INC
525 8 Ave Sw Unit 3800, Calgary, AB, T2P 1G1
(403) 817-2209
Emp Here 250   *Sales* 1,156,332,222
SIC 6719 Holding companies, nec
Grant Fagerheim
Joel M. Armstrong
Daniel J. Christensen
Darin R. Dunlop
Thanh C. Kang
Gary Lesback
David M. Mombourquette
Jeffrey Zdunich B.
Kenneth S. Sickland
Heather J. Culbert

D-U-N-S 25-505-9248   (SL)
WILD GOOSE STORAGE INC. & DESIGN
607 8 Ave Sw Suite 400, Calgary, AB, T2P 0A7
(403) 513-8616
Emp Here 100   *Sales* 115,556,500
SIC 4922 Natural gas transmission
Bill Shea
Rick Staples
Kris Yadav

D-U-N-S 25-219-3719   (BR)
WOOD CANADA LIMITED
(*Suby of* JOHN WOOD GROUP P.L.C.)
801 6 Ave Sw Suite 900, Calgary, AB, T2P 3W3
(403) 298-4170
Emp Here 1,000
SIC 8711 Engineering services
Thomas Grell

D-U-N-S 24-598-8360   (BR)
WORLD WIDE CUSTOMS BROKERS LTD
(*Suby of* KINETSU WORLD EXPRESS, INC.)
Gd Lcd 1, Calgary, AB, T2P 2G8
(403) 538-3199
Emp Here 150
SIC 4731 Freight transportation arrangement
Tim Pearce

D-U-N-S 24-851-3215   (BR)
WSP CANADA INC
GENIVAR
(*Suby of* AST TRUST COMPANY (CANADA))
112 4 Ave Sw Suite 1000, Calgary, AB, T2P 0H3
(403) 266-2800
Emp Here 78

SIC 1382 Oil and gas exploration services
Rick Giammarino

D-U-N-S 24-324-7405   (BR)
WSP CANADA INC
(*Suby of* AST TRUST COMPANY (CANADA))
717 7 Ave Sw Suite 1800, Calgary, AB, T2P 0Z3
(403) 263-8200
Emp Here 100
SIC 8713 Surveying services
Jim Macleod

D-U-N-S 20-693-8883   (HQ)
XTREME DRILLING CORP
(*Suby of* AKITA DRILLING LTD)
333 7th Ave Sw Suite 1000, Calgary, AB, T2P 2Z1
(403) 292-7979
Emp Here 10   *Sales* 48,587,326
SIC 1381 Drilling oil and gas wells
Matthew S. Porter
Douglas A. Dafoe
John Wray
Martin Ramirez
Randolph M. Charron
Colin Burnett
David W. Wehlmann
James B. Renfroe
Jack William Franklin

D-U-N-S 24-828-6551   (SL)
YANGARRA RESOURCES LTD
715 5 Ave Sw Suite 1530, Calgary, AB, T2P 2X6
(403) 262-9558
Emp Here 19   *Sales* 92,164,734
SIC 1311 Crude petroleum and natural gas
James Evaskevich
Lorne Simpson
Randall Faminow
Gurdeep Gill
Trish Olynyk
James Glessing
Gordon Bowerman
Neil Mackenzie
Ted Morton
Robert Weir

D-U-N-S 20-897-5441   (HQ)
ZEDCOR ENERGY INC
330 5 Ave Sw Suite 2400, Calgary, AB, T2P 0L4
(403) 930-5430
Sales 13,230,396
SIC 1389 Oil and gas field services, nec
Dean Swanberg
Todd Ziniuk
James Leganchuk
Todd Dean
Colin Chorney
Kim Cotter
Ian Mckinnon
Andy Purves
Dean Shillington
Brian Mcgill

D-U-N-S 24-277-0130   (SL)
ZEDCOR ENERGY SERVICES CORP
500 4 Ave Sw Unit 3000, Calgary, AB, T2P 2V6
(403) 930-5430
Emp Here 14   *Sales* 11,466,969
SIC 7353 Heavy construction equipment rental
Dean Swanberg
Todd Ziniuk
Colin Chorney
Todd Dean
Kim Cotter
James Leganchuk
Ian Mckinnon
Andy Purves
Dean Shillington
Brian Mcgill

Calgary, AB T2R

D-U-N-S 24-680-2644   (SL)
1504953 ALBERTA LTD
HOTEL ARTS
(*Suby of* 1140021 ALBERTA LTD)
119 12 Ave Sw, Calgary, AB, T2R 0G8
(403) 206-9565
Emp Here 80   *Sales* 7,415,200
SIC 7011 Hotels and motels
Gerald Albert
Adrian Munro
David Munro

D-U-N-S 24-352-2989   (HQ)
4211596 CANADA INC
PPI FINANCIAL GROUP
326 11 Ave Sw Suite 500, Calgary, AB, T2R 0C5
(403) 262-8868
Emp Here 10   *Sales* 42,403,000
SIC 6411 Insurance agents, brokers, and service
James A Burton

D-U-N-S 25-533-1209   (SL)
702856 ALBERTA LTD
CONTINENTAL IMAGING PRODUCTS
940a 11 Ave Sw, Calgary, AB, T2R 0E7
(403) 262-7224
Emp Here 43   *Sales* 19,228,482
SIC 5044 Office equipment
Stephen Goodwin

D-U-N-S 20-013-2319   (HQ)
ALBERTA POWER (2000) LTD
(*Suby of* ATCO LTD)
919 11 Ave Sw Suite 400, Calgary, AB, T2R 1P3
(403) 209-6900
Sales 210,184,000
SIC 4911 Electric services
Nancy Southern
Richard H Walthall
William Britton
Karen M. Watson
Basil French
Ronald Southern

D-U-N-S 24-213-1410   (HQ)
ALTER NRG CORP
227 11 Ave Sw Suite 460, Calgary, AB, T2R 1R9
(403) 806-3875
Sales 21,248,995
SIC 8731 Commercial physical research
Walter Howard
Richard Fish
Danny Hay

D-U-N-S 25-095-1717   (SL)
ARCURVE INC
902 11 Ave Sw Suite 300, Calgary, AB, T2R 0E7
(403) 242-4361
Emp Here 50   *Sales* 10,692,550
SIC 7372 Prepackaged software
Jay Gohill
Michael Mcgovern
Stuart O'connor
Mike Bauer

D-U-N-S 25-172-4423   (SL)
ATCO ENERGY SOLUTIONS LTD
ATCO WATER, DIV OF
(*Suby of* ATCO LTD)
909 11 Ave Sw Suite 800, Calgary, AB, T2R 1L7
(403) 292-7500
Emp Here 100   *Sales* 67,987,400
SIC 4911 Electric services
Nancy Southern
Ronald D Southern

D-U-N-S 24-906-7059   (HQ)
ATCO FRONTEC LTD

RESOLUTE BAY HOTEL, DIV
(*Suby of* ATCO LTD)
909 11 Ave Sw Suite 300, Calgary, AB, T2R 1L7
(403) 245-7757
Emp Here 10   *Sales* 95,668,000
SIC 7011 Hotels and motels
Ronald Southern
Nancy C Southern

D-U-N-S 24-334-3253   (BR)
ATCO GAS AND PIPELINES LTD
ATCO GAS
(*Suby of* ATCO LTD)
1040 11 Ave Sw, Calgary, AB, T2R 0G3
(403) 245-7551
Emp Here 100
SIC 4923 Gas transmission and distribution
Brian Brown

D-U-N-S 20-075-1055   (HQ)
ATCO GAS AND PIPELINES LTD
ATCO GAS, DIV OF
(*Suby of* ATCO LTD)
909 11 Ave Sw Suite 1200, Calgary, AB, T2R 1L7
(403) 245-7060
Emp Here 400   *Sales* 1,958,321,800
SIC 4923 Gas transmission and distribution
Patrick J House
J A Campbell
Ronald D Southern
Craighton O Twa
Basil K French
William L Britton
Nancy C Southern

D-U-N-S 20-269-4519   (HQ)
ATCO POWER (2010) LTD
919 11 Ave Sw Suite 400, Calgary, AB, T2R 1P3
(403) 209-6900
Sales 18,798,420
SIC 4911 Electric services
Nancy C. Southern
James W. Simpson
Ronald D. Southern
Charles W. Wilson
Brian Bale
Siegfried W. Kiefer

D-U-N-S 25-172-4175   (HQ)
ATCO POWER CANADA LTD
(*Suby of* ATCO LTD)
919 11 Ave Sw Suite 400, Calgary, AB, T2R 1P3
(403) 209-6900
Sales 62,661,400
SIC 4911 Electric services
Rick Brouwer

D-U-N-S 25-414-2979   (HQ)
AXIA NETMEDIA CORPORATION
AXIA FIBRENET
(*Suby of* BCE INC)
220 12 Ave Sw Suite 110, Calgary, AB, T2R 0E9
(403) 538-4000
Emp Here 134   *Sales* 47,884,982
SIC 4813 Telephone communication, except radio
Arthur R. Price
Alan Hartslief
Robert Price
Mark Blake
Cameron Barrett
Dean Tremaine
Lindsay Skabar
Erin Basarsky
John K Read
Kent C. Jespersen

D-U-N-S 20-014-8182   (SL)
AXIA SUPERNET LTD
(*Suby of* BCE INC)
220 12 Ave Sw Suite 110, Calgary, AB, T2R 0E9

(403) 538-4000
Emp Here 106   *Sales* 24,218,032
SIC 4813 Telephone communication, except radio
Murray Sigler
Arthur Price

D-U-N-S 24-131-2250   (HQ)
BADGER DAYLIGHTING LTD
BENKO SEWER SERVICES
919 11th Ave Sw Suite 400, Calgary, AB, T2R 1P3
(403) 264-8500
Emp Here 682   *Sales* 466,567,811
SIC 1389 Oil and gas field services, nec
Paul Vanderberg
Darren Yaworsky
Tracey Wallace
Tim Reiber
Jay Bachman
Elizabeth Peterson
Kevin Carnahan
Mike Tunney
Wade Wilson
John Kelly

D-U-N-S 24-803-9450   (SL)
BLUEARTH RENEWABLES INC
214 11 Ave Sw Suite 400, Calgary, AB, T2R 0K1
(403) 668-1575
Emp Here 100   *Sales* 67,987,400
SIC 4911 Electric services
Grant Arnold
Kathy Bolton
Kelly Matheson-King
Jamey Fitzgibbon
Nick Boyd

D-U-N-S 24-997-2902   (HQ)
BOARDWALK REAL ESTATE INVESTMENT TRUST
BOARDWALK RENTAL COMMUNITIES
1501 1 St Sw Suite 200, Calgary, AB, T2R 0W1
(403) 531-9255
Emp Here 18   *Sales* 3,294,799,232
SIC 6531 Real estate agents and managers
Sam Kolias
Roberto Geremia
Jeff Klaus
Bhavnesh Jairam
James Ha
Leonora Davida
Jonathan Brimmell
Helen Mix
Kelly Mahajan
Van Kolias

D-U-N-S 24-101-4112   (HQ)
BOARDWALK REIT LIMITED PARTNERSHIP
BOARDWALK RENTAL COMMUNITIES
1501 1 St Sw Suite 200, Calgary, AB, T2R 0W1
(403) 531-9255
Emp Here 300   *Sales* 62,818,451
SIC 6513 Apartment building operators
Jody Derkach
William Wong

D-U-N-S 25-538-7904   (HQ)
BONTERRA ENERGY CORP
1015 4 St Sw Suite 901, Calgary, AB, T2R 1J4
(403) 262-5307
Sales 170,566,127
SIC 1311 Crude petroleum and natural gas
George F. Fink
Brad Curtis
Robb Thompson
Gary J. Drummond
Randy M Jarock
Rodger A. Tourigny
Aidan M. Walsh
Dan Reuter
Adrian Neumann

D-U-N-S 20-825-8418   (HQ)

CALGARY BOARD OF EDUCATION
1221 8 St Sw, Calgary, AB, T2R 0L4
(403) 817-4000
Emp Here 200   *Sales* 1,012,138,044
SIC 8211 Elementary and secondary schools
David Stevenson
Brad Grundy

D-U-N-S 24-011-9623   (BR)
CALGARY CATHOLIC IMMIGRATION SOCIETY
(*Suby of* CALGARY CATHOLIC IMMIGRATION SOCIETY)
1111 11 Ave Sw Unit 111, Calgary, AB, T2R 0G5
(403) 262-2006
Emp Here 240
SIC 8322 Individual and family services
Fariborz Virjandian

D-U-N-S 25-021-4756   (HQ)
CALGARY CATHOLIC IMMIGRATION SOCIETY
CCIS
1111 11 Ave Sw Suite 103, Calgary, AB, T2R 0G5
(403) 262-5692
Emp Here 40   *Sales* 18,430,080
SIC 8322 Individual and family services
Herman Van Reekum
Farivorz Birjandian

D-U-N-S 25-136-0947   (HQ)
CALGARY URBAN PROJECT SOCIETY
CUPS
1001 10 Ave Sw, Calgary, AB, T2R 0B7
(403) 221-8780
Emp Here 150   *Sales* 10,752,734
SIC 8093 Specialty outpatient clinics, nec
Carlene Donnelly
Dean Schroeder
Robert Perry
Darryn Werth
Cheryl Lemieux

D-U-N-S 25-325-9097   (HQ)
CALTECH GROUP LTD
1011 1 St Sw Suite 520, Calgary, AB, T2R 1J2
(403) 263-8055
Emp Here 115   *Sales* 25,023,460
SIC 8713 Surveying services
Harvey Goosens

D-U-N-S 24-209-2919   (SL)
CALTEST ENERGY SERVICES LTD
602 12 Ave Sw Suite 610, Calgary, AB, T2R 1J3

Emp Here 10   *Sales* 31,058,570
SIC 4925 Gas production and/or distribution
Christine Hart
Gregg Timms
Quynh Vo
Charlene Wing
Michael Smith

D-U-N-S 20-828-5296   (HQ)
CAN-AM GEOMATICS CORP
340 12 Ave Sw Suite 900, Calgary, AB, T2R 1L5
(403) 269-8887
Emp Here 70   *Sales* 26,810,850
SIC 8713 Surveying services
Donald Tomkinson
John Wallace
Garth Hopfe
Reg Butler
Roger Ross
Monte Wilson
Chris Goldring
Blaine Benson
David Thomas
Keith Mcnaughton

D-U-N-S 25-387-9324   (HQ)
CANADA BROKERLINK INC
(*Suby of* INTACT FINANCIAL CORPORA-

TION)
1400 1 St Sw Suite 200, Calgary, AB, T2R 0V8
(403) 290-1541
Emp Here 45   *Sales* 2,990,045,520
SIC 6411 Insurance agents, brokers, and service
Peter Weightman
Thomas Reid

D-U-N-S 24-806-8074   (HQ)
CANADIAN HYDRO DEVELOPERS, INC
(*Suby of* TRANSALTA CORPORATION)
110 12 Ave Sw, Calgary, AB, T2R 0G7
(403) 267-7110
Emp Here 3   *Sales* 67,987,400
SIC 4911 Electric services
Maryse St Laurent
Ted Stickland
Brett Gellner

D-U-N-S 25-094-2257   (SL)
CATHOLIC FAMILY SERVICE OF CALGARY, THE
707 10 Ave Sw Suite 250, Calgary, AB, T2R 0B3
(403) 233-2360
Emp Here 80   *Sales* 5,473,760
SIC 8322 Individual and family services
David Gregory (Greg) Campbell

D-U-N-S 24-677-0288   (BR)
CBI LIMITED
CBI HEALTH CENTRE
(*Suby of* CBI LIMITED)
1400 1 St Sw Suite 500, Calgary, AB, T2R 0V8
(403) 232-8770
Emp Here 100
SIC 8049 Offices of health practitioner

D-U-N-S 25-680-1499   (SL)
CREATIVE AVENUES INC
211 10 Ave Sw, Calgary, AB, T2R 0A4
(403) 292-0360
Emp Here 25   *Sales* 11,087,250
SIC 7389 Business services, nec
Richard Gilman

D-U-N-S 20-767-2767   (SL)
EMERALD MANAGEMENT & REALTY LTD
1036 10 Ave Sw, Calgary, AB, T2R 1M4
(403) 237-8600
Emp Here 91   *Sales* 22,117,459
SIC 6514 Dwelling operators, except apartments
Gary Kaechele

D-U-N-S 24-855-0584   (SL)
ENVIRO-TECH SURVEYS LTD
1020 14 Ave Sw, Calgary, AB, T2R 0P1
(403) 345-2901
Emp Here 100   *Sales* 31,970,500
SIC 1382 Oil and gas exploration services
Robert Nelson
Debbie Brackenbury

D-U-N-S 20-357-7317   (SL)
EPFC CORP
999 8 St Sw Suite 555, Calgary, AB, T2R 1J5
(403) 541-9400
Emp Here 120   *Sales* 23,050,200
SIC 3498 Fabricated pipe and fittings
Michael Esfarjani
Stephen Weiderick
Jeff Schoenhals

D-U-N-S 25-229-5274   (HQ)
FACTOR GAS LIQUIDS INC
611 10 Ave Sw Suite 180, Calgary, AB, T2R 0B2
(403) 266-8778
Emp Here 6   *Sales* 13,866,780
SIC 4925 Gas production and/or distribution
Barry Vosburg
Russ Duffee
Kathryn Poole
Robb Fransoo
Tony Torti

Shayne Rodrigues

D-U-N-S 20-826-5939   (SL)
GODFREY-MORROW INSURANCE & FINANCIAL SERVICES LTD
1003 11 Ave Sw, Calgary, AB, T2R 0G2
(403) 244-4945
Emp Here 35   *Sales* 20,297,340
SIC 6411 Insurance agents, brokers, and service
Hugh Mctavish

D-U-N-S 20-565-5892   (HQ)
GROUNDSWELL GROUP INC
214 11 Ave Sw Suite 200, Calgary, AB, T2R 0K1
(403) 262-2041
Emp Here 160   *Sales* 45,473,760
SIC 7373 Computer integrated systems design
Darren Sartison
Morgan Arndt
Ivaylo Guenov
Adrian Hull
Marianne Divjak
Dan Mccleary
Jose Herrera
Darren Sartison

D-U-N-S 24-826-2862   (SL)
HELCIM INC
1300 8 St Sw Suite 403, Calgary, AB, T2R 1B2
(403) 291-1172
Emp Here 25   *Sales* 16,973,075
SIC 6211 Security brokers and dealers
Nicolas Beique

D-U-N-S 24-350-2171   (BR)
HITACHI SOLUTIONS CANADA, LTD
(*Suby of* HITACHI, LTD.)
550 11 Ave Sw Suite 1000, Calgary, AB, T2R 1M7
(866) 231-4332
Emp Here 100
SIC 7372 Prepackaged software
Evan Hu

D-U-N-S 24-118-9448   (SL)
HUDSON & CO
625 11 Ave Sw Suite 300, Calgary, AB, T2R 0E1
(403) 265-4357
Emp Here 49   *Sales* 10,245,165
SIC 8721 Accounting, auditing, and bookkeeping
Blaine Hudson
Bruce Hudson
Harland Sundal
Douglas Holland
Dave Pilkington
G. Max Webe
Robert Price

D-U-N-S 24-039-3053   (SL)
IODE BARGAIN SHOP
OFFBEAT OUTFITTERS I O D E SHOP
1320 1 St Sw, Calgary, AB, T2R 0V7
(403) 266-6855
Emp Here 49   *Sales* 19,473,286
SIC 8699 Membership organizations, nec
Shirley Whitehouse

D-U-N-S 24-339-2235   (SL)
JOURNEY ENERGY INC
517 10 Ave Sw Suite 700, Calgary, AB, T2R 0A8
(403) 294-1635
Emp Here 83   *Sales* 71,836,229
SIC 1382 Oil and gas exploration services
Alex G. Verge
Brett R. Boklaschuk
Terry J. Moore
Anthony V. Polini
Gerald N. Gilewicz
Howard Crone
Dana B. Laustsen
Ryan A. Shay

Glenn A. Hamilton

D-U-N-S 24-598-2652   (SL)
LAKE LOUISE SKI AREA LTD, THE
1333 8 St Sw Suite 908, Calgary, AB, T2R
1M6
(403) 244-4449
Emp Here 600   *Sales* 57,400,800
SIC 7011 Hotels and motels
  Charles Lock
  Derek Kwaskey
  Louise Lock
  Norbert Mazenod

D-U-N-S 24-522-2518   (SL)
LANCO WELL SERVICES LTD
525 11 Ave Sw Suite 201, Calgary, AB, T2R
0C9

Emp Here 150   *Sales* 100,901,850
SIC 1389 Oil and gas field services, nec
  Peter Landry
  Curtis Landry

D-U-N-S 20-524-7922   (HQ)
LANDSOLUTIONS LP
601 10 Ave Sw Suite 200, Calgary, AB, T2R
0B2
(403) 290-0008
Emp Here 1   *Sales* 15,936,210
SIC 6211 Security brokers and dealers
  Ronald Vermeulen

D-U-N-S 24-119-6518   (HQ)
LAW SOCIETY OF ALBERTA
ALBERTA LAWYERS INSURANCE ASSOCI-
ATION, THE
919 11 Ave Sw Suite 500, Calgary, AB, T2R
1P3
(403) 229-4700
Emp Here 1   *Sales* 14,490,900
SIC 8621 Professional organizations
  Don Thompson
  Bill Wakefield

D-U-N-S 20-435-4435   (HQ)
LOUIS DREYFUS COMPANY CANADA ULC
(*Suby of* LOUIS DREYFUS HOLDING B.V.)
525 11 Ave Sw Suite 500, Calgary, AB, T2R
0C9
(403) 205-3322
Emp Here 25   *Sales* 311,368,090
SIC 5153 Grain and field beans
  Brant Randles
  Ian Mcintosh
  Federico Cerisoli
  Andrea Maserati

D-U-N-S 24-390-8196   (HQ)
LOUIS DREYFUS COMPANY YORKTON
TRADING LP
LDM FOODS
(*Suby of* LOUIS DREYFUS HOLDING B.V.)
525 11 Ave Sw Suite 500, Calgary, AB, T2R
0C9
(403) 205-3322
Sales 14,676,920
SIC 5153 Grain and field beans
  Brent Randles

D-U-N-S 20-968-5879   (SL)
M PRIVATE RESIDENCES INC
322 11 Ave Sw Suite 205, Calgary, AB, T2R
0C5
(403) 264-0993
Emp Here 16   *Sales* 11,148,960
SIC 6799 Investors, nec
  Paul Poscente
  Jim Hilsenteger
  Ken Maclean
  Donald Nelson
  Wilfred Gobert
  Brian Anderson
  Susan Desbarats
  Lyle Edwards
  Robert Maitland
  David Schaus

D-U-N-S 20-881-9347   (SL)
MARSHALL ANDERSON TOURS LTD
ANDERSON VACATIONS
(*Suby of* 1209545 ALBERTA LTD)
1117 1 St Sw Suite 303, Calgary, AB, T2R 0T9
(780) 417-2642
Emp Here 22   *Sales* 11,439,274
SIC 4724 Travel agencies
  Jai Mukerii

D-U-N-S 25-681-1969   (HQ)
MATRIX SOLUTIONS INC
214 11 Ave Sw Suite 600, Calgary, AB, T2R
0K1
(403) 237-0606
Emp Here 300   *Sales* 126,745,000
SIC 8748 Business consulting, nec

D-U-N-S 20-296-5745   (SL)
MAWER GLOBAL SMALL CAP FUND LTD
517 10 Ave Sw Suite 600, Calgary, AB, T2R
0A8
(403) 267-1988
Emp Here 40   *Sales* 33,494,570
SIC 6722 Management investment, open-end
  Jamie Hyndman

D-U-N-S 24-127-3999   (HQ)
MAWER INVESTMENT MANAGEMENT LTD
600-517 10 Ave Sw, Calgary, AB, T2R 0A8
(403) 262-4673
Sales 24,833,310
SIC 6722 Management investment, open-end
  Gerald Cooper-Key
  William Maclachlan
  Martin Ferguson
  Darrell Anderson

D-U-N-S 20-015-4511   (SL)
MCLEAN & PARTNERS WEALTH MANAGE-
MENT LTD
801 10 Ave Sw, Calgary, AB, T2R 0B4
(403) 234-0005
Emp Here 28   *Sales* 19,009,844
SIC 6282 Investment advice
  Brent Mclean
  Kevin Dehod

D-U-N-S 20-232-9871   (SL)
MILLENIA RESOURCE CONSULTING
628 11 Ave Sw Suite 200, Calgary, AB, T2R
0E2
(403) 571-0510
Emp Here 70   *Sales* 12,317,060
SIC 8711 Engineering services
  Jeffery Scott
  Tim Olsen
  Ric Ewasiuk

D-U-N-S 24-118-4217   (BR)
MOUNTAIN EQUIPMENT CO-OPERATIVE
(*Suby of* MOUNTAIN EQUIPMENT CO-
OPERATIVE)
830 10 Ave Sw, Calgary, AB, T2R 0A9
(403) 269-2420
Emp Here 80
SIC 5941 Sporting goods and bicycle shops
  Peter Tucker

D-U-N-S 24-336-6635   (SL)
MULLEN OILFIELD SERVICES LP
333 11 Ave Sw Suite 600, Calgary, AB, T2R
1L9
(403) 213-4715
Emp Here 4   *Sales* 15,985,250
SIC 1389 Oil and gas field services, nec
  Bruce Mullen

D-U-N-S 24-593-6195   (SL)
NORFOLK MOBILITY BENEFITS INC
999 8 St Sw Suite 300, Calgary, AB, T2R 1N7
(403) 232-8545
Emp Here 96   *Sales* 177,279,264
SIC 6321 Accident and health insurance
  Richard Albert

D-U-N-S 24-441-4082   (HQ)
PILLAR RESOURCE SERVICES INC

PILLAR FABRICATORS, DIV OF
550 11 Ave Sw, Calgary, AB, T2R 1M7
(403) 266-7070
Sales 136,492,750
SIC 1389 Oil and gas field services, nec
  Joseph Samaska
  Robert Unrau
  Dean Samaska
  Rob Milner
  Dan Hayes
  Devin Scherger

D-U-N-S 24-081-7754   (HQ)
PINE CLIFF ENERGY LTD
1015 4 St Sw Suite 850, Calgary, AB, T2R 1J4
(403) 269-2289
Sales 75,857,960
SIC 1381 Drilling oil and gas wells
  Philip Hodge
  Christopher Lee
  Heather Isidoro
  Alan Macdonald
  Terry Mcneil
  Cheryne Lowe
  George Fink
  William Rice
  Randy Jarock
  Phil Hodge

D-U-N-S 20-644-2670   (HQ)
PLATINUM EQUITIES INC
906 12 Ave Sw Suite 910, Calgary, AB, T2R
1K7
(403) 228-4799
Emp Here 1   *Sales* 15,329,820
SIC 6799 Investors, nec
  Philip Pincus

D-U-N-S 24-317-8428   (HQ)
POLYCORE TUBULAR LININGS CORPO-
RATION
(*Suby of* CONESTOGA SUPPLY CORPORA-
TION)
1011 1 St Sw Suite 510, Calgary, AB, T2R 1J2
(403) 444-5554
Emp Here 18   *Sales* 10,141,500
SIC 3443 Fabricated plate work (boiler shop)
  Louis Russo
  Dennis Carmichael

D-U-N-S 20-337-1955   (SL)
PROCEED SOLUTIONS INC
906 12 Ave Sw Suite 600, Calgary, AB, T2R
1K7
(403) 685-8390
Emp Here 65   *Sales* 15,228,720
SIC 8748 Business consulting, nec
  Robin Reese

D-U-N-S 25-506-8645   (HQ)
PURE TECHNOLOGIES LTD
705 11 Ave Sw Suite 300, Calgary, AB, T2R
0E3
(403) 266-6794
Emp Here 5   *Sales* 85,113,909
SIC 7371 Custom computer programming ser-
vices
  Mark Holley
  Muthu Chandrasekaran
  Michael Higgins
  Michael Wrigglesworth
  Robert Budianto

D-U-N-S 20-719-8610   (SL)
RANGELAND ENGINEERING LTD
1520 4 St Sw Suite 1000, Calgary, AB, T2R
1H5
(403) 265-5130
Emp Here 14   *Sales* 26,810,850
SIC 8711 Engineering services
  Ronald Daye
  Diane Yuill
  Ian Alcorn
  Ryan Beamin

D-U-N-S 24-667-4514   (HQ)
REDROCK CAMPS INC

322 11 Avenue Sw Ste 302, Calgary, AB, T2R
0C5
(403) 264-7610
Sales 77,332,740
SIC 2411 Logging
  Troy Ferguson

D-U-N-S 20-830-7876   (BR)
ROYAL & SUN ALLIANCE INSURANCE
COMPANY OF CANADA
RSA GROUP
(*Suby of* RSA INSURANCE GROUP PLC)
326 11 Ave Sw Suite 300, Calgary, AB, T2R
0C5
(403) 233-6000
Emp Here 260
SIC 6331 Fire, marine, and casualty insurance
  Irene B'ianchi

D-U-N-S 20-029-7625   (BR)
SCHLUMBERGER CANADA LIMITED
SCHLUMBERGER INFORMATION SOLU-
TIONS
322 11 Ave Sw Suite 600, Calgary, AB, T2R
0C5

Emp Here 150
SIC 1389 Oil and gas field services, nec
  Russ Sagert

D-U-N-S 24-016-2842   (HQ)
SIMMONS EDECO INC
1414 8 St Sw Suite 500, Calgary, AB, T2R 1J6
(403) 244-5340
Emp Here 11   *Sales* 24,660,906
SIC 1381 Drilling oil and gas wells
  Victor Redekop
  David Crowshaw
  Jay Simmons
  Christopher Reimchen
  Ronald Packard

D-U-N-S 25-079-8485   (BR)
SOBEYS WEST INC
CANADA SAFEWAY
(*Suby of* EMPIRE COMPANY LIMITED)
813 11 Ave Sw, Calgary, AB, T2R 0E6
(403) 264-1375
Emp Here 250
SIC 5411 Grocery stores
  Bill Forgay

D-U-N-S 24-810-7943   (SL)
STOODLEY BRIAN
1014 12 Ave Sw Unit A, Calgary, AB, T2R 0J6
(403) 262-9402
Emp Here 4   *Sales* 12,423,428
SIC 4925 Gas production and/or distribution
  Brian Stoodley

D-U-N-S 24-299-2162   (HQ)
SUNSHINE VILLAGE CORPORATION
BANFF/LAKE LOUISE CENTRE RESERVA-
TIONS
1037 11 Ave Sw, Calgary, AB, T2R 0G1
(403) 705-4000
Sales 71,751,000
SIC 7011 Hotels and motels
  Ralph D. Scurfield
  Sergei S. Scurfield

D-U-N-S 20-990-0026   (SL)
TOMKINSON, D.N. INVESTMENTS LTD
340 12 Ave Sw Suite 900, Calgary, AB, T2R
1L5
(403) 269-8887
Emp Here 150   *Sales* 26,810,850
SIC 8713 Surveying services
  Donald Tomkinson

D-U-N-S 24-895-0677   (HQ)
TRANSALTA CORPORATION
110 12 Ave Sw, Calgary, AB, T2R 0G7
(403) 267-7110
Emp Here 400   *Sales* 1,704,971,398
SIC 4911 Electric services
  Dawn L. Farrell
  Wayne Collins

▲ Public Company   ■ Public Company Family Member   **HQ** Headquarters   **BR** Branch   **SL** Single Location

Aron Willis
Scott Jeffers
Brent Ward
Dawn De Lima
Todd Stack
Gordon D. Giffin
John P. Dielwart
Yakout Mansour

D-U-N-S 25-532-6795 (SL)
TRANSALTA ENERGY MARKETING CORP
(Suby of TRANSALTA CORPORATION)
110 12 Ave Sw, Calgary, AB, T2R 0G7
(403) 267-7987
Emp Here 160   *Sales* 35,190,880
SIC 8732 Commercial nonphysical research
Stephen Snyder

D-U-N-S 25-682-9763 (HQ)
TRANSALTA GENERATION PARTNERSHIP
TA COGEN
110 12 Ave Sw, Calgary, AB, T2R 0G7
(403) 267-7110
Sales 37,861,365
SIC 4931 Electric and other services combined
Ian A. Bourne

D-U-N-S 25-533-5697 (HQ)
TREELINE WELL SERVICES INC
333 11 Ave Sw Suite 750, Calgary, AB, T2R 1L9
(403) 266-2868
Emp Here 10   *Sales* 100,901,850
SIC 1381 Drilling oil and gas wells
G. Ben Docktor
Dan Bryson
Terry Andresen

D-U-N-S 24-997-9550 (HQ)
TRICO DEVELOPMENTS CORPORATION
TRICO HOMES
1005 11 Ave Sw, Calgary, AB, T2R 0G1
(403) 287-9300
Sales 32,513,040
SIC 1521 Single-family housing construction
Wayne Chiu
Tom Chisholm
Georg Paffrath
Eleanor Chiu

D-U-N-S 25-154-8772 (SL)
TRICO HOMES INC
(Suby of TRICO DEVELOPMENTS CORPORATION)
1005 11 Ave Sw, Calgary, AB, T2R 0G1
(403) 287-9300
Emp Here 120   *Sales* 22,339,320
SIC 6553 Cemetery subdividers and developers
Tom Chisholm
Wayne Chiu

D-U-N-S 25-999-7351 (SL)
VITAL BENEFITS INCORPORATED
(Suby of ARTHUR J. GALLAGHER & CO.)
224 11 Ave Sw Suite 301, Calgary, AB, T2R 0C3
(403) 209-3817
Emp Here 14   *Sales* 25,853,226
SIC 6311 Life insurance
Melanie Jeannotte
Laura Barkley

D-U-N-S 24-327-5265 (SL)
VOIS INC
628 12 Ave Sw Unit 201, Calgary, AB, T2R 0H6
(403) 775-2000
Emp Here 100   *Sales* 18,479,800
SIC 4899 Communication services, nec
Priya Mitra
Harpreet Randhawa

D-U-N-S 24-915-5490 (BR)
WAWANESA LIFE INSURANCE COMPANY, THE
WAWANESA MUTUAL INSURANCE COMPANY
(Suby of WAWANESA MUTUAL INSURANCE COMPANY, THE)
708 11 Ave Sw Suite 600, Calgary, AB, T2R 0E4
(403) 536-9258
Emp Here 150
SIC 6311 Life insurance
Louise Stewart

D-U-N-S 25-207-5320 (BR)
WAWANESA MUTUAL INSURANCE COMPANY, THE
(Suby of WAWANESA MUTUAL INSURANCE COMPANY, THE)
708 11 Ave Sw Suite 600, Calgary, AB, T2R 0E4
(403) 266-8600
Emp Here 140
SIC 6331 Fire, marine, and casualty insurance

D-U-N-S 24-393-2485 (BR)
WORLEYPARSONSCORD LP
(Suby of WORLEYPARSONS LIMITED)
540 12 Ave Sw, Calgary, AB, T2R 0H4

Emp Here 300
SIC 8711 Engineering services
Neil Gornall

D-U-N-S 24-715-3034 (SL)
ZEDI CANADA INC
(Suby of ZEDI INC)
902 11 Ave Sw, Calgary, AB, T2R 0E7
(403) 444-1100
Emp Here 135   *Sales* 65,843,550
SIC 5084 Industrial machinery and equipment
Mathew Heffernan
Keith Smith
Robert W. Gordon

D-U-N-S 25-386-1561 (HQ)
ZEDI INC
GLOBALEYE
902 11 Ave Sw, Calgary, AB, T2R 0E7
(403) 444-1100
Emp Here 100   *Sales* 30,380,661
SIC 1731 Electrical work
Matthew Heffernan
Ilario (Larry) Spagnolo
Christine Barr
Grant Exner
Clement Gaudet

D-U-N-S 20-107-6234 (SL)
ZENAR GROUP INC, THE
1508 8 St Sw Suite 203, Calgary, AB, T2R 1R6
(403) 261-1566
Emp Here 19   *Sales* 10,167,356
SIC 5141 Groceries, general line
Jamie Sharpe

Calgary, AB T2S

D-U-N-S 20-285-7405 (HQ)
1391130 ALBERTA LTD
CRL SYNERGY
333 24 Ave Sw Suite 300, Calgary, AB, T2S 3E6
(403) 861-1556
Sales 18,867,198
SIC 7389 Business services, nec
Regan Perron

D-U-N-S 25-218-8289 (SL)
599515 ALBERTA LTD
MELROSE CAFE & BAR
730 17 Ave Sw, Calgary, AB, T2S 0B7
(403) 228-3566
Emp Here 83   *Sales* 3,778,077
SIC 5813 Drinking places
Kent Leong
Wayne Leong
Gene Loeng

D-U-N-S 24-375-4079 (SL)
ALARIS ROYALTY CORP
333 24th Ave Sw Suite 250, Calgary, AB, T2S 3E6
(403) 228-0873
Emp Here 10   *Sales* 75,870,090
SIC 6159 Miscellaneous business credit institutions
Stephen W. King
Darren Driscoll
Mike Ervin
Gregg Delcourt
Curtis Krawetz
Amanda Frazer
Liz Mccarthy
Devin Timberlake
Shawn Ostrow
Dan Maceachern

D-U-N-S 20-810-1865 (HQ)
ALBERTA BALLET COMPANY, THE
141 18 Ave Sw, Calgary, AB, T2S 0B8
(403) 228-4430
Emp Here 51   *Sales* 11,741,816
SIC 7922 Theatrical producers and services
Chris George
Larry Clausen
George Goldhoff
Frank Molnar
Chandra Henry
Kevin Krausert
Ron Bryant
John Masters

D-U-N-S 20-036-2171 (BR)
ALTUS GEOMATICS LIMITED PARTNERSHIP
ALTUS GROUP
(Suby of ALTUS GROUP LIMITED)
2020 4th St Sw Unit 310, Calgary, AB, T2S 1W3
(403) 508-7770
Emp Here 85
SIC 8713 Surveying services
Angelo Bartolini

D-U-N-S 20-646-3374 (HQ)
AURUM CERAMIC DENTAL LABORATORIES LTD
(Suby of TGM HOLDINGS LTD)
115 17 Ave Sw, Calgary, AB, T2S 0A1
(403) 228-5120
Emp Here 15   *Sales* 109,652,700
SIC 6712 Bank holding companies
Hans Maier
Diane Maier

D-U-N-S 20-713-1439 (BR)
CALGARY BOARD OF EDUCATION
WESTERN CANADA HIGH SCHOOL
(Suby of CALGARY BOARD OF EDUCATION)
641 17 Ave Sw, Calgary, AB, T2S 0B5
(403) 228-5363
Emp Here 125
SIC 8211 Elementary and secondary schools
Martin Poirier

D-U-N-S 25-600-4276 (BR)
CALGARY ROMAN CATHOLIC SEPARATE SCHOOL DISTRICT #1
ST. MARY'S SENIOR HIGH SCHOOL
(Suby of CALGARY ROMAN CATHOLIC SEPARATE SCHOOL DISTRICT #1)
111 18 Ave Sw Suite 1, Calgary, AB, T2S 0B8
(403) 500-2024
Emp Here 85
SIC 8211 Elementary and secondary schools
Frank Durante

D-U-N-S 24-599-1575 (HQ)
CANADIAN ROCKY MOUNTAIN RESORTS LTD
BUFFALO MOUNTAIN LODGE
332 17 Ave Sw, Calgary, AB, T2S 0A8
(403) 233-8066
Emp Here 8   *Sales* 33,483,800

SIC 7011 Hotels and motels
Patrick O'connor

D-U-N-S 20-825-1546 (SL)
CERUM DENTAL SUPPLIES LTD
115 17 Ave Sw, Calgary, AB, T2S 0A1
(403) 228-5199
Emp Here 30   *Sales* 13,415,220
SIC 5047 Medical and hospital equipment
Hans Maier
Peter Seidel
Doug Patrick
Richard Charlebois

D-U-N-S 25-011-2265 (HQ)
CLASSIC DENTAL LABORATORIES LTD
(Suby of TGM HOLDINGS LTD)
115 17 Ave Sw, Calgary, AB, T2S 0A1
(403) 228-5120
Sales 45,635,940
SIC 8072 Dental laboratories
Hans Maier

D-U-N-S 25-236-2629 (HQ)
COCHRANE GROUP INC
320 23 Ave Sw Suite 104, Calgary, AB, T2S 0J2
(403) 262-3638
Emp Here 20   *Sales* 49,282,750
SIC 8711 Engineering services
Trevor Cochrane

D-U-N-S 24-977-2489 (SL)
CUSTOM TRAVEL SOLUTIONS INC
2424 4 St Sw Suite 800, Calgary, AB, T2S 2T4
(403) 272-1000
Emp Here 74   *Sales* 38,477,558
SIC 4724 Travel agencies
Elizabeth Gardner
Vaughan Tyne

D-U-N-S 24-068-4261 (BR)
EARL'S RESTAURANTS LTD
PIN PALACE
(Suby of EARL'S RESTAURANTS LTD)
2401 4 St Sw, Calgary, AB, T2S 1X5
(403) 228-4141
Emp Here 100
SIC 5812 Eating places
Rielly Whitman

D-U-N-S 20-232-3510 (BR)
ENTERPRISE UNIVERSAL INC
BOW RIVER PROPERTY MANAGEMENT & LEASING
(Suby of ENTERPRISE UNIVERSAL INC)
2210 2 St Sw Unit B250, Calgary, AB, T2S 3C3
(403) 228-4431
Emp Here 100
SIC 6519 Real property lessors, nec
Kithsiri Lihinikaduwa

D-U-N-S 25-100-9007 (HQ)
FORTISALBERTA INC
(Suby of FORTIS INC)
320 17 Ave Sw, Calgary, AB, T2S 2V1
(403) 514-4000
Emp Here 1,000   *Sales* 470,047,026
SIC 4911 Electric services
Michael Mosher
Cam Aplin
Todd Dettling
Curtis Eck
Janine Sullivan
Rob Tisdale
Heather Speers
Roger Thomas
Susan Mackenzie
Bill Giebelhaus

D-U-N-S 20-338-4805 (HQ)
FOUNDERS ADVANTAGE CAPITAL CORP
2207 4th St Sw Suite 400, Calgary, AB, T2S 1X1
(403) 455-9660
Emp Here 12   *Sales* 64,954,161
SIC 6211 Security brokers and dealers

Stephen Reid
Amar S. Leekha
Harpreet Padda
Melanie Litoski
James Bell
J.R. Kingsley Ward
Peter Mcrae
Anthony Lacavera
Ron Gratton
Gary Mauris

D-U-N-S 24-524-0382   (HQ)
FYI EYE CARE SERVICES AND PRODUCTS INC
FYI DOCTORS
2424 4 St Sw Suite 300, Calgary, AB, T2S 2T4
(403) 234-2020
Emp Here 18   *Sales* 204,552,000
SIC 3229 Pressed and blown glass, nec
Alan Ulsifer
Tim Degelman
John Mastronardi
Michael Ross
Craig Meckelborg
Arlene Dickinson
Bruce Bowser
Dino Trevisani
Winston Koo
Joanne Nemeroff

D-U-N-S 25-679-6061   (HQ)
GENOIL INC
1811 4 St Sw Suite 218, Calgary, AB, T2S 1W2
(587) 400-0249
Emp Here 8   *Sales* 15,665,545
SIC 1382 Oil and gas exploration services
David K. Lifschultz
Bruce Abbott
Conan Taylor
Bengt Koch
Timothy Bojar
Haiming Lai

D-U-N-S 24-766-6324   (HQ)
GLENCOE CLUB, THE
636 29 Ave Sw, Calgary, AB, T2S 0P1
(403) 214-0032
Sales 33,860,250
SIC 7997 Membership sports and recreation clubs
Daryl Moir
Greg Lundmark

D-U-N-S 20-590-3334   (SL)
HOPEWELL CAPITAL CORPORATION
2020 4 St Sw Suite 410, Calgary, AB, T2S 1W3
(403) 232-8821
Emp Here 80   *Sales* 21,675,360
SIC 1522 Residential construction, nec
Sanders Lee

D-U-N-S 20-286-7859   (SL)
HOPEWELL RESIDENTIAL MANAGEMENT LP
2020 4 St Sw Suite 410, Calgary, AB, T2S 1W3
(403) 232-8821
Emp Here 300   *Sales* 101,419,200
SIC 6531 Real estate agents and managers
Paul Taylor

D-U-N-S 25-372-8844   (HQ)
IONA HOLDINGS CORPORATION
CATHOLIC PASTORAL CENTRE
120 17 Ave Sw, Calgary, AB, T2S 2T2
(403) 218-5500
Emp Here 20   *Sales* 15,499,146
SIC 8699 Membership organizations, nec
Michael Chan

D-U-N-S 24-033-2655   (SL)
MERCATO INTERNATIONAL LTD
2224 4 St Sw, Calgary, AB, T2S 1W9
(403) 263-5535
Emp Here 80   *Sales* 3,641,520

SIC 5812 Eating places
Dom Cariciollo

D-U-N-S 24-736-8454   (HQ)
MOSAIC CAPITAL CORPORATION
2424 4 St Sw Suite 400, Calgary, AB, T2S 2T4
(403) 218-6500
Emp Here 100   *Sales* 301,056,708
SIC 6719 Holding companies, nec
Mark Gardhouse
John Mackay
Cam Deller
Monty Balderston
William H. Smith
Harold Kunik
Gary Bentham
George Flemming

D-U-N-S 24-984-1487   (SL)
RAREMETHOD INTERACTIVE STUDIOS INC
RARE METHOD
1812 4 St Sw Suite 601, Calgary, AB, T2S 1W1

Emp Here 75   *Sales* 14,092,956
SIC 4899 Communication services, nec
Roger Jewett

D-U-N-S 20-599-5343   (HQ)
SMITTY'S CANADA INC
(*Suby of* W. CHAN INVESTMENTS LTD)
501 18 Ave Sw Suite 600, Calgary, AB, T2S 0C7
(403) 229-3838
Emp Here 15   *Sales* 13,991,700
SIC 5812 Eating places
Steven Fee
Eric Metzler

D-U-N-S 25-271-0868   (BR)
SOBEYS WEST INC
SAFEWAY
(*Suby of* EMPIRE COMPANY LIMITED)
524 Elbow Dr Sw, Calgary, AB, T2S 2H6
(403) 228-6141
Emp Here 100
SIC 5411 Grocery stores
Pickering Jill

D-U-N-S 25-450-4186   (HQ)
SPACE MAINTAINERS LAB CANADA LTD
115 17 Ave Sw, Calgary, AB, T2S 0A1
(403) 228-7001
Emp Here 1   *Sales* 55,415,070
SIC 8072 Dental laboratories
Doug Patrick

D-U-N-S 24-495-0366   (HQ)
STITTCO ENERGY LIMITED
255 17 Ave Sw Unit 303, Calgary, AB, T2S 2T8
(403) 228-5815
Emp Here 5   *Sales* 21,105,225
SIC 5984 Liquefied petroleum gas dealers
Gale S Stitt
Glen C Mullback

D-U-N-S 24-855-1988   (HQ)
TGM HOLDINGS LTD
115 17 Ave Sw, Calgary, AB, T2S 0A1
(403) 228-5120
Emp Here 2   *Sales* 65,194,200
SIC 8072 Dental laboratories
Hans Maier

D-U-N-S 24-854-1930   (HQ)
W. CHAN INVESTMENTS LTD
501 18 Ave Sw Suite 600, Calgary, AB, T2S 0C7
(403) 229-3838
Emp Here 12   *Sales* 83,777,800
SIC 6531 Real estate agents and managers
Walter Chan
Christopher Chan

D-U-N-S 20-639-1539   (SL)
WAX PARTNERSHIP INCORPORATED

333 24 Ave Sw Suite 320, Calgary, AB, T2S 3E6
(403) 262-9323
Emp Here 26   *Sales* 11,530,740
SIC 7389 Business services, nec
Daniel Wright

Calgary, AB T2T

D-U-N-S 24-923-5268   (SL)
BCC HOLDINGS INC
1912 13 St Sw, Calgary, AB, T2T 3P6
(403) 617-0806
Emp Here 80   *Sales* 20,924,240
SIC 6712 Bank holding companies

D-U-N-S 20-437-4387   (SL)
CALGARY SILVER LININGS FOUNDATION
2009 33 Ave Sw Suite 2, Calgary, AB, T2T 1Z5
(403) 536-4025
Emp Here 150   *Sales* 16,662,000
SIC 8062 General medical and surgical hospitals

D-U-N-S 20-016-8693   (SL)
CANADIAN GAS & ELECTRIC INC
(*Suby of* TRANSALTA CORPORATION)
1324 17 Ave Sw Suite 500, Calgary, AB, T2T 5S8
(403) 269-9379
Emp Here 120
SIC 4911 Electric services
Kent Brown
Ross Keating
John Keating

D-U-N-S 24-646-4952   (SL)
CENTURY 21 BAMBER REALTY LTD
1612 17 Ave Sw, Calgary, AB, T2T 0E3
(403) 875-4653
Emp Here 120   *Sales* 50,266,680
SIC 6531 Real estate agents and managers
George Bamber

D-U-N-S 24-013-1391   (HQ)
DYCK INSURANCE SERVICE LTD
DYCK INSURANCE
24 St Sw, Calgary, AB, T2T 5H9
(403) 246-4600
Emp Here 28   *Sales* 27,137,920
SIC 6411 Insurance agents, brokers, and service
Denis Dyck Sr
Marilyn Dyck

D-U-N-S 24-246-4399   (SL)
M30 RETAIL SERVICES INC
(*Suby of* MSI HOLDING COMPANY, INC.)
332 20 St W Unit 415, Calgary, AB, T2T 6S1
(403) 313-9105
Emp Here 100   *Sales* 18,650,600
SIC 8742 Management consulting services
Richard Labbe
R Christopher Malcolm
Jon Johnstone
Michael Sills

D-U-N-S 20-456-5076   (SL)
MADE BY MARCUS LTD
1013 17 Ave Sw Suite 121, Calgary, AB, T2T 0A7
(403) 452-1692
Emp Here 37   *Sales* 10,858,649
SIC 5451 Dairy products stores

D-U-N-S 20-052-2121   (HQ)
RESORTS OF THE CANADIAN ROCKIES INC
TRICKLE CREEK MARRIOTT
1505 17 Ave Sw, Calgary, AB, T2T 0E2
(403) 254-7669
Emp Here 40   *Sales* 86,700,000
SIC 7999 Amusement and recreation, nec
Murray Edwards

John Shea
Larry G. Moeller
Rick Dyjak
Paul Bates

D-U-N-S 20-078-1375   (SL)
SPORTSMAN LIMITED, THE
SKI CELLAR SNOWBOARD
1442 17 Ave Sw, Calgary, AB, T2T 0C8
(403) 245-4311
Emp Here 90   *Sales* 21,989,520
SIC 5941 Sporting goods and bicycle shops
Jean Hunt
Peter Lane
Donald Maher
Brian Anderson
Daniel Russell
Edward Rahal
Betty Conklin

D-U-N-S 20-767-0670   (SL)
TOOLE PEET & CO LIMITED
TOOLE PEET INSURANCE
(*Suby of* TOOLE PEET HOLDINGS LIMITED)
1135 17 Ave Sw, Calgary, AB, T2T 0B6
(403) 245-4366
Emp Here 75   *Sales* 31,416,675
SIC 6531 Real estate agents and managers
Laurence Toole

D-U-N-S 20-744-1999   (HQ)
WALLS ALIVE LTD
(*Suby of* 623203 ALBERTA LTD)
1328 17 Ave Sw, Calgary, AB, T2T 0C3
(403) 244-8931
Emp Here 12   *Sales* 11,137,800
SIC 5198 Paints, varnishes, and supplies
Greg Stebbe

Calgary, AB T2V

D-U-N-S 24-518-2886   (SL)
ALBERTA BUILDING CONTRACTORS LTD
WEST COUNTRY NURSERY & LANDSCAPE CENTRE
9232 Horton Rd Sw, Calgary, AB, T2V 2X4
(403) 888-1960
Emp Here 50   *Sales* 37,126,000
SIC 5193 Flowers and florists supplies
Helmut Barwich
Anne Marie Barwich

D-U-N-S 24-753-7538   (BR)
BANTREL CO.
(*Suby of* BECHTEL GROUP, INC.)
600-1201 Glenmore Trail Sw, Calgary, AB, T2V 4Y8
(403) 290-5000
Emp Here 1,500
SIC 8711 Engineering services
Darrel Donly

D-U-N-S 24-441-2425   (HQ)
BANTREL CO.
(*Suby of* BECHTEL GROUP, INC.)
1201 Glenmore Trail Sw Suite 1061, Calgary, AB, T2V 4Y8
(403) 290-5000
Emp Here 2,525   *Sales* 571,679,900
SIC 8711 Engineering services
Darrel Donly
Kenneth L Baron
Douglas S Barth
Mike Gordon
Gerald Mulvany
Dan Michaud

D-U-N-S 24-961-8117   (HQ)
BOW VALLEY INSURANCE SERVICES (1992) LTD
9805 Horton Rd Sw, Calgary, AB, T2V 2X5
(403) 297-9400
Emp Here 42   *Sales* 41,554,940
SIC 6411 Insurance agents, brokers, and ser-

vice
Kirit Gohill

D-U-N-S 25-130-7435   (BR)
CALGARY BOARD OF EDUCATION
HENRY WISE WOOD HIGH SCHOOL
(*Suby of* CALGARY BOARD OF EDUCA-
TION)
910 75 Ave Sw, Calgary, AB, T2V 0S6
(403) 253-2261
Emp Here 130
SIC 8211 Elementary and secondary schools
Jim Scott

D-U-N-S 25-121-0795   (BR)
**CALGARY ROMAN CATHOLIC SEPARATE
SCHOOL DISTRICT #1**
BISHOP GRANDIN SENIOR HIGH SCHOOL
(*Suby of* CALGARY ROMAN CATHOLIC
SEPARATE SCHOOL DISTRICT #1)
111 Haddon Rd Sw, Calgary, AB, T2V 2Y2
(403) 500-2047
Emp Here 110
SIC 8211 Elementary and secondary schools
John Mcdonald

D-U-N-S 20-209-3659   (BR)
**CALGARY YOUNG MEN'S CHRISTIAN AS-
SOCIATION**
YMCA HERITAGE
(*Suby of* CALGARY YOUNG MEN'S CHRIS-
TIAN ASSOCIATION, THE)
11 Haddon Rd Sw, Calgary, AB, T2V 2X8

Emp Here 120
SIC 8399 Social services, nec
Joann Hook

D-U-N-S 20-161-0255   (SL)
CAMP B B-RIBACK
1607 90 Ave Sw, Calgary, AB, T2V 4V7

Emp Here 107   *Sales* 9,917,830
SIC 7032 Sporting and recreational camps
Max Lipsman

D-U-N-S 20-052-4838   (HQ)
CANADA BROKERLINK (ONTARIO) INC
(*Suby of* INTACT FINANCIAL CORPORA-
TION)
1201 Glenmore Trail Sw Suite 100, Calgary,
AB, T2V 4Y8
(403) 209-6300
Emp Here 32   *Sales* 166,296,780
SIC 6411 Insurance agents, brokers, and ser-
vice
Guy Desjardins
Roger Randall
Tom Reid

D-U-N-S 25-388-8325   (SL)
CITY COIN VENDING SERVICES LTD
9212 Horton Rd Sw Unit J, Calgary, AB, T2V
2X4
(403) 253-0324
Emp Here 30   *Sales* 19,693,920
SIC 5962 Merchandising machine operators
Jay Hamilton
Evelyn Hamilton

D-U-N-S 20-831-4138   (SL)
HERITAGE PARK SOCIETY
HERITAGE PARK HISTORICAL VILLAGE
1900 Heritage Dr Sw, Calgary, AB, T2V 2X3
(403) 268-8526
Emp Here 75   *Sales* 7,864,500
SIC 8412 Museums and art galleries
Wayne Chodzicki
Robert Tilden
Wendy Best
Martin Booth
Jim Brown
Susan Church
Wayne Dwyer
Jeannette Kirchner
Kim Sarjeant
Joe Doolan

D-U-N-S 25-218-4403   (HQ)
LUNDGREN & YOUNG INSURANCE LTD
9705 Horton Rd Sw Suite 200c, Calgary, AB,
T2V 2X5
(403) 253-1980
Sales 18,657,320
SIC 6411 Insurance agents, brokers, and ser-
vice
Jack Lundgren
Tom Young
Valerie Young

D-U-N-S 24-343-9676   (SL)
NOSE CREEK FOREST PRODUCTS CORP
184 Malibou Rd Sw, Calgary, AB, T2V 1X9

Emp Here 65   *Sales* 10,131,095
SIC 2431 Millwork
Donald Plewes

D-U-N-S 24-805-4574   (SL)
OPUS CORPORATION
5119 Elbow Dr Sw Unit 500, Calgary, AB, T2V
1H2
(403) 209-5555
Emp Here 30   *Sales* 14,121,930
SIC 1542 Nonresidential construction, nec
Hannes Kovac

D-U-N-S 25-206-9018   (HQ)
PROCON SYSTEMS (2013) INC
9504 Horton Rd Sw, Calgary, AB, T2V 2X4
(403) 255-2921
Emp Here 10   *Sales* 14,725,806
SIC 5084 Industrial machinery and equipment
Ronald Schuhknecht
Robert Knowles
Dean Smith
Jeffrey Walters
Robert Watts
Murray Sherwin
Brad Emes
Ryan Burek
Martin Robichaud

D-U-N-S 24-058-4599   (HQ)
**RADIOLOGY CONSULTANTS ASSOCI-
ATED**
RCA DIAGNOSTICS
6707 Elbow Dr Sw Suite 120, Calgary, AB,
T2V 0E3
(403) 777-3007
Emp Here 14   *Sales* 43,231,200
SIC 8011 Offices and clinics of medical doc-
tors
John Jackson
Kenneth Sato
Robert T Diamond
Frank H Brandschwei
Steve Kolodinsky
Michael M Welsh
Brian Yacyshyn
Corinne Dyke

D-U-N-S 25-321-4217   (BR)
REVERA INC
RENOIR RETIREMENT RESIDENCE
(*Suby of* GOVERNMENT OF CANADA)
9229 16 St Sw, Calgary, AB, T2V 5H3
(403) 255-2105
Emp Here 160
SIC 8361 Residential care
Lynne Majander

D-U-N-S 25-389-2830   (SL)
SAM HOLDINGS LTD
1623 96 Ave Sw, Calgary, AB, T2V 5E5
(403) 266-1985
Emp Here 17   *Sales* 17,557,736
SIC 5172 Petroleum products, nec
Stan Owerko
Margaret Owerko

D-U-N-S 25-271-0512   (BR)
SOBEYS WEST INC
SAFEWAY
(*Suby of* EMPIRE COMPANY LIMITED)

1600 90 Ave Sw, Calgary, AB, T2V 5A8
(403) 255-2755
Emp Here 140
SIC 5411 Grocery stores
Roy Mcfadyen

D-U-N-S 20-989-8170   (SL)
TRAVOIS HOLDINGS LTD
GLAMORGAN CARE CENTRE
8240 Collicutt St Sw, Calgary, AB, T2V 2X1
(403) 252-4445
Emp Here 260   *Sales* 17,764,760
SIC 8051 Skilled nursing care facilities
Joel Bond

D-U-N-S 25-051-7323   (SL)
VESPUCCI HOLDINGS INC
8244 Elbow Dr Sw, Calgary, AB, T2V 1K4
(403) 252-9558
Emp Here 40   *Sales* 16,774,200
SIC 6712 Bank holding companies
Brent Rawlinson
Dianne Rawlinson

D-U-N-S 25-522-5799   (BR)
**VICTORIAN ORDER OF NURSES FOR
CANADA**
VON CALGARY DISTRICT
(*Suby of* VICTORIAN ORDER OF NURSES
FOR CANADA)
9705 Horton Rd Sw Suite 100, Calgary, AB,
T2V 2X5
(403) 640-4765
Emp Here 150
SIC 8082 Home health care services
Jackie Saber

Calgary, AB T2W

D-U-N-S 24-777-4214   (BR)
ALBERTA HEALTH SERVICES
DAVID THOMPSON HEALTH REGION
(*Suby of* GOVERNMENT OF THE
PROVINCE OF ALBERTA)
10101 Southport Rd Sw, Calgary, AB, T2W
3N2
(403) 943-1111
Emp Here 300
SIC 8011 Offices and clinics of medical doc-
tors
Duncan Campbell

D-U-N-S 24-442-6730   (HQ)
BAYMAG INC
(*Suby of* ALEXANDER-TUTSEK-STIFTUNG)
10655 Southport Rd Sw Suite 800, Calgary,
AB, T2W 4Y1
(403) 271-9400
Emp Here 20   *Sales* 29,728,160
SIC 1459 Clay and related minerals, nec
Hagen Schultes
Ronald Moore
Denis Malig

D-U-N-S 20-590-7897   (BR)
CALGARY BOARD OF EDUCATION
WILLIAM ROPER HULL SCHOOL
(*Suby of* CALGARY BOARD OF EDUCA-
TION)
2266 Woodpark Ave Sw, Calgary, AB, T2W
2Z8
(403) 251-8022
Emp Here 80
SIC 8211 Elementary and secondary schools
Catherine Forbes

D-U-N-S 20-070-1832   (HQ)
CAREWEST
CAREWEST ROYAL PARK
(*Suby of* GOVERNMENT OF THE
PROVINCE OF ALBERTA)
10301 Southport Lane Sw, Calgary, AB, T2W
1S7
(403) 943-8140
Emp Here 50   *Sales* 116,154,200

SIC 8059 Nursing and personal care, nec
Dale Forbes

D-U-N-S 24-553-7451   (HQ)
CIRCA ENTERPRISES INC
CIRCA TELECOM, DIV OF
10333 Southport Rd Sw Suite 535, Calgary,
AB, T2W 3X6
(403) 258-2011
Emp Here 50   *Sales* 22,698,332
SIC 3643 Current-carrying wiring devices
Grant Reeves
Cory Tamagi
Peter C. Bourgeois
Robert Bruce Johnston
M. Sweatt
Warren J. White

D-U-N-S 20-551-7386   (SL)
DREAM RIDGE HOMES CORP
232 Woodpark Bay Sw, Calgary, AB, T2W 6H2
(403) 616-3542
Emp Here 40   *Sales* 12,754,760
SIC 1521 Single-family housing construction
Joel Semmens

D-U-N-S 20-938-3798   (HQ)
DYNAMIC SHELTERS INC
10333 Southport Rd Sw Suite 523, Calgary,
AB, T2W 3X6
(403) 203-9311
Sales 12,485,525
SIC 3448 Prefabricated Metal buildings and
components
Harold Warner
Terry French

D-U-N-S 24-523-9715   (SL)
HENUSET PIPELINE CONSTRUCTION INC
13024 Canso Pl Sw, Calgary, AB, T2W 3A8
(403) 252-5386
Emp Here 49   *Sales* 11,803,316
SIC 1623 Water, sewer, and utility lines
Arthur Henuset

D-U-N-S 24-949-2810   (SL)
HERITAGE HILL INSURANCE LTD
ANTHONY CLARK INSURANCE
10333 Southport Rd Sw Suite 355, Calgary,
AB, T2W 3X6

Emp Here 60   *Sales* 50,883,600
SIC 6411 Insurance agents, brokers, and ser-
vice
Tony Consalvo

D-U-N-S 20-829-2326   (HQ)
HULL SERVICES
HULL CHILD & FAMILY SERVICES
2266 Woodpark Ave Sw, Calgary, AB, T2W
2Z8
(403) 251-8000
Emp Here 350   *Sales* 25,116,394
SIC 8399 Social services, nec
Harold Chornoboy
Kerry Dyte
Michael Freeborn
Victor Kroeger
John Poetker
Chethan Lakshman
Sarine Mustapha
Stuart O'connor
John Sparks
Doug Mackenzie

D-U-N-S 25-045-3243   (SL)
JEMCO VENTURES INC
*EXPEDIA CRUISE SHIP CENTRE FISH
CREEK*
11440 Braeside Dr Sw Suite 25, Calgary, AB,
T2W 3N4
(403) 278-7447
Emp Here 30   *Sales* 15,599,010
SIC 4724 Travel agencies
John Mcintyre

D-U-N-S 24-101-8543   (HQ)
KIEWIT CONSTRUCTION SERVICES ULC

(*Suby of* PETER KIEWIT SONS', INC.)
10333 Southport Rd Sw Suite 200, Calgary, AB, T2W 3X6
(403) 693-8701
Sales 12,682,110
SIC 1541 Industrial buildings and warehouses
Dan Levert
Michael Piechoski
Michael Norton
Stephen Thomas
Douglas Patterson
David Claggett

D-U-N-S 24-982-1828   (BR)
LOBLAWS INC
REAL CANADIAN SUPERSTORE
(*Suby of* LOBLAW COMPANIES LIMITED)
10505 Southport Rd Sw Suite 1, Calgary, AB, T2W 3N2
(403) 225-6207
Emp Here 300
SIC 5411 Grocery stores
Rod Hill

D-U-N-S 25-386-8962   (HQ)
SCOULAR CANADA LTD
(*Suby of* THE SCOULAR COMPANY)
10201 Southport Rd Sw Suite 1110, Calgary, AB, T2W 4X9
(403) 720-9050
Emp Here 20   *Sales* 695,509,800
SIC 6799 Investors, nec
David Faith
Roger Barber
John Heck

D-U-N-S 25-271-0355   (BR)
SOBEYS WEST INC
SAFEWAY
(*Suby of* EMPIRE COMPANY LIMITED)
2525 Woodview Dr Sw, Calgary, AB, T2W 4N4
(403) 238-1400
Emp Here 110
SIC 5411 Grocery stores
Tommy Au

D-U-N-S 20-813-9217   (SL)
UPA CONSTRUCTION GROUP LIMITED PARTNERSHIP
10655 Southport Rd Sw Suite 700, Calgary, AB, T2W 4Y1
(403) 262-4440
Emp Here 50   *Sales* 13,547,100
SIC 1522 Residential construction, nec
Richard Allen
Linda Bailey

Calgary, AB T2X

D-U-N-S 24-014-0210   (SL)
ADVANTAGE DISTRIBUTORS LTD
SPRUCE MEADOWS
18011 Spruce Meadows Way Sw, Calgary, AB, T2X 4B7
(403) 974-4200
Emp Here 80   *Sales* 6,970,240
SIC 7941 Sports clubs, managers, and promoters
Ronald Southern

D-U-N-S 20-554-8576   (BR)
AECOM CANADA LTD
(*Suby of* AECOM)
340 Midpark Way Se Suite 300, Calgary, AB, T2X 1P1
(403) 270-9200
Emp Here 200
SIC 8711 Engineering services
Eric Aretz

D-U-N-S 24-853-5866   (HQ)
AGRITEAM CANADA CONSULTING LTD
14707 Bannister Rd Se Unit 200, Calgary, AB, T2X 1Z2

(403) 253-5298
Emp Here 55   *Sales* 17,744,300
SIC 8748 Business consulting, nec
Robert B. Francis
Alex Schumacher
Gayle Turner

D-U-N-S 20-376-7384   (HQ)
EECOL ELECTRIC CORP
(*Suby of* WESCO INTERNATIONAL, INC.)
63 Sunpark Dr Se, Calgary, AB, T2X 3V4
(403) 253-1952
Emp Here 1   *Sales* 290,123,500
SIC 5063 Electrical apparatus and equipment
Brian Begg
Nelson Squires
Mi Yuan
Domenic Macioce Iii

D-U-N-S 24-298-7600   (SL)
EECOL ELECTRIC ULC
63 Sunpark Dr Se, Calgary, AB, T2X 3V4

Emp Here 650
SIC 5063 Electrical apparatus and equipment

D-U-N-S 25-192-9469   (HQ)
EECOL HOLDINGS LTD
63 Sunpark Dr Se, Calgary, AB, T2X 3V4
(403) 571-8400
Emp Here 4   *Sales* 754,321,100
SIC 5063 Electrical apparatus and equipment
Thomas Crist
Darren Buium
Karleen Gobeil
Marion Sinneave

D-U-N-S 24-352-4266   (SL)
EPSILON ENERGY LTD
14505 Bannister Rd Se Suite 300, Calgary, AB, T2X 3J3

Emp Here 20   *Sales* 29,684,205
SIC 1311 Crude petroleum and natural gas
Michael Raleigh
Paul Atwood
Shannon Lemke
B. Lane Bond
Henry Clanton
John Lovoi
Matthew Dougherty
Ryan Roebuck
Jacob Roorda
Tracy Stephens

D-U-N-S 20-410-7734   (HQ)
FLUOR CANADA LTD
(*Suby of* FLUOR CORPORATION)
55 Sunpark Plaza Se, Calgary, AB, T2X 3R4
(403) 537-4000
Emp Here 1,900   *Sales* 473,114,400
SIC 8711 Engineering services
James Brittain
Peter Hatcher

D-U-N-S 24-808-2687   (SL)
FLUOR CONSTRUCTORS CANADA LTD
(*Suby of* FLUOR CORPORATION)
60 Sunpark Dr Se, Calgary, AB, T2X 3Y2
(403) 537-4600
Emp Here 200   *Sales* 139,678,400
SIC 1541 Industrial buildings and warehouses

D-U-N-S 24-959-9754   (SL)
GENSTAR DEVELOPMENT COMPANY
280 Midpark Way Se Suite 100, Calgary, AB, T2X 2B5
(403) 256-4000
Emp Here 10   *Sales* 12,044,200
SIC 1629 Heavy construction, nec

D-U-N-S 20-299-1493   (SL)
INNOVATIVE PIPELINE CROSSINGS INC
(*Suby of* BOTHAR GROUP PTY LTD)
340 Midpark Way Se Suite 300, Calgary, AB, T2X 1P1
(403) 455-0380
Emp Here 15   *Sales* 26,533,570

SIC 1623 Water, sewer, and utility lines
Gregg Biggs

D-U-N-S 24-438-6231   (HQ)
LANSDOWNE EQUITY VENTURES LTD
295 Midpark Way Se Suite 350, Calgary, AB, T2X 2A8
(403) 254-6440
Sales 20,501,250
SIC 6719 Holding companies, nec
Brian Sidorsky
Gail Sidorsky

D-U-N-S 24-674-6374   (HQ)
MCLEOD & COMPANY LLP
MKRT MANAGEMENT
14505 Bannister Rd Se Suite 300, Calgary, AB, T2X 3J3
(403) 225-6400
Emp Here 85   *Sales* 11,088,200
SIC 8111 Legal services
Ross Kaplan
Bill Walker
Robin Lokhorst
Theresa Carswell
Neil Hutton
Darren Fach
Rick Breen
Brent Cooper
Barry Steinfeld
Jane (Deb) Poppock

D-U-N-S 20-090-4159   (SL)
PASUTTO'S HOTELS (1984) LTD
GARDEN TERRACE LOUNGE
400 Midpark Way Se, Calgary, AB, T2X 3S4
(403) 514-0099
Emp Here 240   *Sales* 22,960,320
SIC 7011 Hotels and motels
Allan Pasutto

D-U-N-S 20-582-6324   (SL)
REID CROWTHER & PARTNERS LIMITED
EARTH TECH REID CROWTHER
340 Midpark Way Se Suite 300, Calgary, AB, T2X 1P1

Emp Here 130   *Sales* 26,521,403
SIC 8711 Engineering services

D-U-N-S 25-976-0890   (BR)
RENFREW EDUCATIONAL SERVICES SOCIETY
75 Sunpark Dr Se, Calgary, AB, T2X 3V4
(403) 291-5038
Emp Here 400
SIC 8211 Elementary and secondary schools
Lynne Martel

D-U-N-S 20-275-7852   (HQ)
SOUTH CALGARY PRIMARY CARE NETWORK, THE
SCPCN
1800 194 Ave Se Suite 4000, Calgary, AB, T2X 0R3
(403) 256-3222
Sales 16,064,600
SIC 8011 Offices and clinics of medical doctors
Oliver Schmid

D-U-N-S 20-379-1830   (SL)
SPRUCE MEADOWS LTD
18011 Spruce Meadows Way Sw, Calgary, AB, T2X 4B7
(403) 974-4200
Emp Here 145   *Sales* 12,092,275
SIC 7941 Sports clubs, managers, and promoters
Linda Heathcott

D-U-N-S 20-030-1401   (SL)
ST MARY'S UNIVERSITY
14500 Bannister Rd Se 4th Fl, Calgary, AB, T2X 1Z4
(403) 531-9130
Emp Here 150   *Sales* 22,408,650
SIC 8221 Colleges and universities

Gerry Turcotte
Gregory Mcintomny
Tara Hyland-Russell
Bob Hann
Therese Takacs

D-U-N-S 20-719-5129   (SL)
STEWART, JAMIE D MCLEOD & COMPANY LLP LAWYERS
14505 Bannister Rd Se, Calgary, AB, T2X 3J3
(403) 225-6412
Emp Here 75   *Sales* 11,745,096
SIC 8111 Legal services
Ross Paplan

Calgary, AB T2Y

D-U-N-S 20-933-6374   (SL)
668977 ALBERTA INC
BOSTON PIZZA
235 Shawville Blvd Se, Calgary, AB, T2Y 3H9
(403) 256-6999
Emp Here 80   *Sales* 3,641,520
SIC 5812 Eating places
Ted Tomanik

D-U-N-S 20-549-5661   (SL)
969642 ALBERTA LIMITED
FISH CREEK NISSAN
14750 5 St Sw, Calgary, AB, T2Y 2E7
(403) 256-4788
Emp Here 35   *Sales* 17,432,730
SIC 5511 New and used car dealers
Steve Itzcovitch

D-U-N-S 20-643-1764   (BR)
BEST BUY CANADA LTD
FUTURE SHOP
(*Suby of* BEST BUY CO., INC.)
350 Shawville Blvd Se Unit 110, Calgary, AB, T2Y 3S4
(403) 509-9120
Emp Here 100
SIC 5734 Computer and software stores

D-U-N-S 24-345-5982   (BR)
CALGARY YOUNG MEN'S CHRISTIAN ASSOCIATION, THE
CALGARY YOUNG MEN'S CHRISTIAN ASSOCIATION
(*Suby of* CALGARY YOUNG MEN'S CHRISTIAN ASSOCIATION, THE)
333 Shawville Blvd Se Suite 400, Calgary, AB, T2Y 4H3
(403) 256-5533
Emp Here 220
SIC 8322 Individual and family services
Joann Hook

D-U-N-S 20-053-9370   (SL)
CANADIAN TIRE
250 Shawville Way Se, Calgary, AB, T2Y 3J1
(403) 201-2002
Emp Here 30   *Sales* 10,926,450
SIC 5014 Tires and tubes

D-U-N-S 24-441-4025   (HQ)
CAROLINA HOMES INC
230 Eversyde Blvd Sw Suite 2101, Calgary, AB, T2Y 0J4
(403) 256-5544
Emp Here 26   *Sales* 10,203,808
SIC 1521 Single-family housing construction
Paul Unger
Stan Unger

D-U-N-S 24-882-9319   (SL)
HLADY, RONALD H. AUTO SALES LTD
CANADIAN TIRE SHAWNESSY
250 Shawville Way Se, Calgary, AB, T2Y 3J1

Emp Here 140   *Sales* 88,099,200
SIC 5531 Auto and home supply stores
Ronald H. Hlady

D-U-N-S 20-003-3921   (BR)
HOME DEPOT OF CANADA INC
HOME DEPOT
(*Suby of* THE HOME DEPOT INC)
390 Shawville Blvd Se, Calgary, AB, T2Y 3S4
(403) 201-5611
Emp Here 250
SIC 5251 Hardware stores
  Ralph Aktug

D-U-N-S 25-087-6943   (BR)
LOBLAWS INC
REAL CANADIAN SUPERSTORE
(*Suby of* LOBLAW COMPANIES LIMITED)
15915 Macleod Trail Se Unit 100, Calgary, AB,
T2Y 3R9
(403) 254-3637
Emp Here 250
SIC 5411 Grocery stores
  Jared Laidley

D-U-N-S 20-813-0588   (SL)
PHOENIX GRILL LTD, THE
16061 Macleod Trail Se Suite 335, Calgary,
AB, T2Y 3S5
(403) 509-9111
Emp Here 80   *Sales* 3,641,520
SIC 5812 Eating places
  Daryl Achen

D-U-N-S 24-018-9683   (BR)
SOBEYS CAPITAL INCORPORATED
SOBEYS
(*Suby of* EMPIRE COMPANY LIMITED)
150 Millrise Blvd Sw Unit 3109, Calgary, AB,
T2Y 5G7
(403) 873-5085
Emp Here 100
SIC 5411 Grocery stores
  Bell Allen

D-U-N-S 20-806-2294   (BR)
SOBEYS CAPITAL INCORPORATED
SOBEYS STORE 1117
(*Suby of* EMPIRE COMPANY LIMITED)
2335 162 Ave Sw Suite 100, Calgary, AB, T2Y
4S6
(403) 873-0101
Emp Here 100
SIC 5411 Grocery stores
  Kevin Kam

D-U-N-S 24-523-0615   (BR)
SYMPHONY SENIOR LIVING INC
(*Suby of* SYMPHONY SENIOR LIVING INC)
2220 162 Ave Sw Suite 210, Calgary, AB, T2Y
5E3
(403) 201-3555
Emp Here 100
SIC 8361 Residential care
  Mario Stamm

D-U-N-S 20-748-8367   (BR)
TRIPLE A LIVING COMMUNITIES INC
MILLRISE PLACE
(*Suby of* PR SENIORS HOUSING MANAGE-
MENT LTD)
14911 5 St Sw Suite 115, Calgary, AB, T2Y
5B9
(403) 410-9155
Emp Here 80
SIC 8059 Nursing and personal care, nec
  Carol Marcial

D-U-N-S 25-498-2820   (BR)
WAL-MART CANADA CORP
(*Suby of* WALMART INC.)
310 Shawville Blvd Se Suite 100, Calgary, AB,
T2Y 3S4
(403) 201-5415
Emp Here 200
SIC 5311 Department stores
  Serry Callahan

Calgary, AB T2Z

D-U-N-S 20-836-0979   (SL)
ALPHA BETTER LANDSCAPING LTD
11800 40 St Se, Calgary, AB, T2Z 4T1
(403) 248-3559
Emp Here 100   *Sales* 10,928,900
SIC 0782 Lawn and garden services
  Phil Paxton

D-U-N-S 20-703-8063   (SL)
BABLAKE LTD
11800 40 St Se, Calgary, AB, T2Z 4T1
(403) 248-3559
Emp Here 100   *Sales* 26,155,300
SIC 6712 Bank holding companies
  Phil Paxton
  Barry Paxton

D-U-N-S 20-030-6848   (SL)
BEATTIE HOMES LTD
3165 114 Ave Se, Calgary, AB, T2Z 3X2

Emp Here 77   *Sales* 21,213,417
SIC 1521 Single-family housing construction
  William Beattie

D-U-N-S 20-067-5523   (SL)
**BISHOP, DONALD H. PROFESSIONAL
CORPORATION**
BISHOP & ASSOCIATES
11410 27 St Se Unit 6, Calgary, AB, T2Z 3R6
(403) 974-3937
Emp Here 60   *Sales* 10,212,300
SIC 8042 Offices and clinics of optometrists
  Don Bishop

D-U-N-S 20-744-0124   (HQ)
BOUTIQUE OF LEATHERS LTD, THE
OPEN ROAD
12012 44 St Se, Calgary, AB, T2Z 4A2
(403) 259-2726
Emp Here 12   *Sales* 28,097,720
SIC 5948 Luggage and leather goods stores
  Barry Lammle

D-U-N-S 20-074-3243   (HQ)
BREWERS' DISTRIBUTOR LTD
B D L
11500 29 St Se Suite 101, Calgary, AB, T2Z
3W9
(800) 661-2337
Emp Here 75   *Sales* 129,066,700
SIC 4225 General warehousing and storage
  Garry Clermont
  Neil Sweeney
  Mike Ross
  Greg D'Abignon
  Charles Oliver
  Daren Hawrish
  John Aiken
  Linda Thomas
  Trent Carroll

D-U-N-S 25-314-0735   (HQ)
BREWS SUPPLY LTD
12203 40 St Se, Calgary, AB, T2Z 4E6
(403) 243-1144
Emp Here 33   *Sales* 25,488,918
SIC 5063 Electrical apparatus and equipment
  Dale Berstad
  Kevin Howell

D-U-N-S 20-599-5889   (HQ)
CALGARY PETERBILT LTD
11550 44 St Se, Calgary, AB, T2Z 4A2
(403) 235-2550
Sales 57,644,250
SIC 5012 Automobiles and other motor vehicles

D-U-N-S 24-786-4150   (SL)
CANXPRESS LTD
(*Suby of* COMPAGNIE DES CHEMINS DE
FER NATIONAUX DU CANADA)
11400 27 St Se, Calgary, AB, T2Z 3R6
(403) 236-9088
Emp Here 150   *Sales* 30,855,900

SIC 4213 Trucking, except local
  Paul Tolaini

D-U-N-S 24-016-9763   (SL)
CANYON PLUMBING & HEATING LTD
3185 114 Ave Se, Calgary, AB, T2Z 3X2
(403) 258-1505
Emp Here 168   *Sales* 39,154,920
SIC 1711 Plumbing, heating, air-conditioning
  Jason Chupik
  Mark Chupik

D-U-N-S 20-304-9978   (SL)
CHINOOK INFRASTRUCTURE
3131 114 Ave Se Suite 100, Calgary, AB, T2Z
3X2
(403) 355-1655
Emp Here 90   *Sales* 25,517,160
SIC 1611 Highway and street construction
  Jaine Martin Cereno

D-U-N-S 24-032-4306   (SL)
DEERFOOT INN & CASINO INC
(*Suby of* GAMEHOST INC)
11500 35 St Se Suite 1000, Calgary, AB, T2Z
3W4
(403) 236-7529
Emp Here 400   *Sales* 38,267,200
SIC 7011 Hotels and motels
  Noel Marcelo
  Raffy Pampolina

D-U-N-S 25-217-6664   (SL)
**DURA-LITE HEAT TRANSFER PRODUCTS
LTD**
12012 44 St Se, Calgary, AB, T2Z 4A2
(403) 259-2691
Emp Here 100   *Sales* 22,384,300
SIC 3714 Motor vehicle parts and accessories
  Reginald Sissons
  Kelly Sissons

D-U-N-S 20-109-0508   (SL)
FRESH DIRECT FOODS LTD
11505 35 St Se Unit 103, Calgary, AB, T2Z
4B1
(403) 508-6868
Emp Here 60   *Sales* 13,491,300
SIC 2099 Food preparations, nec
  Ronald Lemiski
  Yvonne Lemiski

D-U-N-S 20-075-1584   (SL)
GLENMAC CORPORATION LTD
CARTER, JACK CHEVROLET CADILLAC
11555 29 St Se, Calgary, AB, T2Z 0N4
(403) 258-6300
Emp Here 90   *Sales* 56,635,200
SIC 5511 New and used car dealers
  Jack Carter
  Peter Mckeen
  David Deeth

D-U-N-S 24-552-6959   (HQ)
**GRAHAM CONSTRUCTION AND ENGI-
NEERING INC**
GRACOM MASONRY, DIV OF
(*Suby of* GRAHAM GROUP LTD)
10840 27 St Se, Calgary, AB, T2Z 3R6
(403) 570-5000
Emp Here 90   *Sales* 114,067,600
SIC 1542 Nonresidential construction, nec
  Grant Beck
  Cecil Dawe
  Tim Heavenor
  Andy Trewick

D-U-N-S 20-249-3524   (SL)
**GRAHAM CONSTRUCTION AND ENGI-
NEERING LP**
10840 27 St Se, Calgary, AB, T2Z 3R6
(403) 570-5000
Emp Here 150   *Sales* 85,550,700
SIC 1542 Nonresidential construction, nec
  Tom Baxtee
  William Flaig
  Dous Bespalko

D-U-N-S 25-217-9825   (HQ)
GRAHAM GROUP LTD
AECOM-GRAHAM JOINT VENTURE
10840 27 St Se, Calgary, AB, T2Z 3R6
(403) 570-5000
Emp Here 75   *Sales* 838,070,400
SIC 1542 Nonresidential construction, nec
  Grant Beck
  Jeff Schippmann
  Tim Johnson
  Tony Clark
  Tim Heavenor

D-U-N-S 20-397-5250   (SL)
GRAHAM INCOME TRUST
GRAHAM CONSTRUCTION
10840 27 St Se, Calgary, AB, T2Z 3R6
(403) 570-5000
Emp Here 5,000   *Sales* 3,491,960,000
SIC 1541 Industrial buildings and warehouses
  Grant Beck
  Andy Trewick
  Tim Heavenor
  Tony Clark
  Jeff Schippmann
  Colin Aitken
  Cecil Dawe
  John Connolly
  Ian Dickinson

D-U-N-S 20-954-6808   (SL)
GREG SAARI MERCHANDISING LTD
CANADIAN TIRE
4155 126 Ave Se, Calgary, AB, T2Z 0A1
(403) 257-4729
Emp Here 80   *Sales* 21,412,160
SIC 5251 Hardware stores

D-U-N-S 24-271-1943   (SL)
GUNNAR MANUFACTURING INC
GUNNAR OFFICE FURNISHINGS
3200 118 Ave Se, Calgary, AB, T2Z 3X1
(403) 236-1828
Emp Here 100   *Sales* 23,240,300
SIC 5712 Furniture stores
  Ron Quigley
  Judy Quigley

D-U-N-S 20-976-6021   (HQ)
HIGHWOOD DISTILLERS LTD
4948 126 Ave Se Unit 23, Calgary, AB, T2Z
0A9
(403) 216-2440
Emp Here 17   *Sales* 14,697,900
SIC 5182 Wine and distilled beverages
  William Miller
  Barry W Wilde
  Glen Hopkins
  Gerald A Berkhold
  J C Anderson
  H. Douglas Hunter
  Ronald L Graham

D-U-N-S 24-000-3041   (BR)
HOME DEPOT OF CANADA INC
(*Suby of* THE HOME DEPOT INC)
5125 126 Ave Se, Calgary, AB, T2Z 0B2
(403) 257-8756
Emp Here 130
SIC 5251 Hardware stores
  David Poliquin

D-U-N-S 20-115-3223   (SL)
HOME SOLUTIONS CORPORATION
HOME SOLUTIONS
11550 40 St Se, Calgary, AB, T2Z 4V6
(403) 216-0000
Emp Here 60   *Sales* 14,771,160
SIC 1799 Special trade contractors, nec
  Soren Nielsen
  Wendy Mcallister

D-U-N-S 24-418-8277   (HQ)
INFOSAT COMMUNICATIONS LP
(*Suby of* RED ISLE PRIVATE INVESTMENTS
INC)
3130 114 Ave Se, Calgary, AB, T2Z 3V6

(403) 543-8188
Sales 15,203,916
SIC 5063 Electrical apparatus and equipment
Gary Grainger
Krista Ramlu
Mike Colberg

D-U-N-S 24-271-7841   (HQ)
JAYMAN BUILT LTD
JAYMAN BUILDER
3132 118 Ave Se Suite 200, Calgary, AB, T2Z 3X1
(403) 258-3772
Emp Here 200   *Sales* 139,132,800
SIC 1521 Single-family housing construction
Jay Westman
Scott Weiler
Aasit Amin
Stephanie Myers
Larry Noer
Chris Jones
Wallace Chow

D-U-N-S 24-494-1415   (SL)
JOHNSON, S.E. MANAGEMENT LTD
4330 122 Ave Se, Calgary, AB, T2Z 0A6
(403) 291-9600
Emp Here 110   *Sales* 25,637,150
SIC 1711 Plumbing, heating, air-conditioning
Bruce Thorlakson

D-U-N-S 24-439-8780   (HQ)
LAMMLE'S WESTERN WEAR LTD
12012 44 St Se, Calgary, AB, T2Z 4A2
(403) 255-0272
Emp Here 40   *Sales* 31,188,750
SIC 5699 Miscellaneous apparel and accessory stores
Barry Lammle

D-U-N-S 20-051-1967   (BR)
LENNOX INDUSTRIES (CANADA) LTD
CLASSIC FIREPLACE DISTRIBUTORS & CENTRAL AIR HEATING & AIR CONDITIONING
(*Suby of* LENNOX INTERNATIONAL INC.)
11500 35 St Se Suite 8002, Calgary, AB, T2Z 3W4
(403) 279-4448
Emp Here 75
SIC 5023 Homefurnishings
Wayne Maskewich

D-U-N-S 20-844-8816   (SL)
MATRIX LABOUR LEASING LTD
11420 27 St Se Suite 204, Calgary, AB, T2Z 3R6
(403) 201-9520
Emp Here 100   *Sales* 15,537,100
SIC 7361 Employment agencies
Shannon Warren

D-U-N-S 24-339-1278   (HQ)
MEQUIPCO LTD
5126 126 Ave Se Unit 101, Calgary, AB, T2Z 0H2
(403) 259-8333
Emp Here 2   *Sales* 43,704,000
SIC 3589 Service industry machinery, nec
Bradley Hussack
David Stephens
Devlin Wing
Daniel Landry

D-U-N-S 20-984-8428   (SL)
MULTIWOOD INC
MULTIWOOD
(*Suby of* 347458 ALBERTA LTD)
11580 40 St Se, Calgary, AB, T2Z 4V6
(403) 279-7789
Emp Here 115   *Sales* 26,726,345
SIC 5712 Furniture stores
Sid De Graaf

D-U-N-S 25-453-5792   (SL)
PANOPTIC AUTOMATION SOLUTIONS INC
3320 114 Ave Se, Calgary, AB, T2Z 3V6
(587) 315-1450
Emp Here 25   *Sales* 16,411,600

SIC 5962 Merchandising machine operators
Barry Becker

D-U-N-S 24-346-5338   (BR)
REVERA INC
MCKENZIE TOWN CARE CENTRE
(*Suby of* GOVERNMENT OF CANADA)
80 Promenade Way Se, Calgary, AB, T2Z 4G4
(403) 508-9808
Emp Here 150
SIC 8051 Skilled nursing care facilities
Bev Drever

D-U-N-S 20-161-7748   (BR)
SOBEYS CAPITAL INCORPORATED
SOBEYS MCKENZIE TOWNE MARKET
(*Suby of* EMPIRE COMPANY LIMITED)
20 Mckenzie Towne Ave Se, Calgary, AB, T2Z 3S7
(403) 257-4343
Emp Here 150
SIC 5411 Grocery stores
Dawn Racette

D-U-N-S 20-337-3949   (SL)
SOUTH TRAIL CHRYSLER LTD
6103 130 Ave Se, Calgary, AB, T2Z 5E1
(587) 349-7272
Emp Here 80   *Sales* 50,342,400
SIC 5521 Used car dealers
Michael Mcmanes

D-U-N-S 24-320-4411   (SL)
STAMPEDE ELECTRIC INC
4300 118 Ave Se, Calgary, AB, T2Z 4A4
(587) 327-2777
Emp Here 70   *Sales* 15,248,030
SIC 1731 Electrical work
Walter Kemble
Barry Toovey

D-U-N-S 20-335-3565   (SL)
STRATUS ELECTRICAL & INSTRUMENTATION LTD
12204 40 St Se Unit 12, Calgary, AB, T2Z 4K6
(403) 775-7599
Emp Here 130   *Sales* 25,002,640
SIC 7629 Electrical repair shops
Robert Brown
David Smith

D-U-N-S 20-864-6203   (SL)
TIM HORTONS
11488 24 St Se Suite 400, Calgary, AB, T2Z 4C9
(403) 236-3749
Emp Here 50   *Sales* 13,707,600
SIC 5461 Retail bakeries
Scott Milsap

D-U-N-S 24-022-2740   (BR)
TRICAN WELL SERVICE LTD
CALGARY R&D CENTRE
(*Suby of* TRICAN WELL SERVICE LTD)
11979 40 St Se Unit 418, Calgary, AB, T2Z 4M3
(403) 723-3688
Emp Here 1,500
SIC 1389 Oil and gas field services, nec
Marlin Balaux

D-U-N-S 24-325-8303   (HQ)
TUNDRA PROCESS SOLUTIONS LTD
(*Suby of* MEI MILLER ENTERPRISES INC)
3200 118 Ave Se, Calgary, AB, T2Z 3X1
(403) 255-5222
Emp Here 80   *Sales* 76,573,610
SIC 5085 Industrial supplies
Mike Miller
Dan Peet
Blaine Barnes
Ashley Allers
Peter Mcaleer
Iggy Domagaiski

D-U-N-S 24-357-7892   (SL)
W.O.H.A HOLDINGS LIMITED
11505 35 St Se Suite 111, Calgary, AB, T2Z

4B1
(403) 250-5722
Emp Here 4   *Sales* 32,953,700
SIC 8748 Business consulting, nec
John Holland
Donald Pinchin
Don Jakul
Steve Wilk

D-U-N-S 25-328-0887   (SL)
WHISSELL CONTRACTING LTD
WHISSELL ENGINEERING
2500 107 Ave Se Suite 200, Calgary, AB, T2Z 3R7
(403) 236-2200
Emp Here 280   *Sales* 91,872,200
SIC 1623 Water, sewer, and utility lines
Brian Whissell

D-U-N-S 20-964-6475   (SL)
WOOD AUTOMOTIVE GROUP
11580 24 St Se, Calgary, AB, T2Z 3K1
(403) 640-8494
Emp Here 30   *Sales* 14,942,340
SIC 5531 Auto and home supply stores
Gerry Wood
Dick Lau

D-U-N-S 24-442-2598   (HQ)
WOODRIDGE FORD LINCOLN LTD
11580 24 St Se, Calgary, AB, T2Z 3K1
(403) 253-2211
Emp Here 130   *Sales* 94,392,000
SIC 5511 New and used car dealers
Gerry Wood

Calgary, AB T3A

D-U-N-S 24-039-1941   (BR)
BBW INTERNATIONAL INC
75 Edgevalley Cir Nw, Calgary, AB, T3A 4Y9

Emp Here 200
SIC 7389 Business services, nec

D-U-N-S 24-419-6213   (SL)
DAVENPORT SALES & AUTO SERVICE LTD
CANADIAN TIRE
5404 Dalton Dr Nw Suite 299, Calgary, AB, T3A 2C3
(403) 288-1100
Emp Here 120   *Sales* 75,513,600
SIC 5531 Auto and home supply stores
David Davenport

D-U-N-S 25-682-0226   (BR)
EARL'S RESTAURANTS LTD
(*Suby of* EARL'S RESTAURANTS LTD)
5005 Dalhousie Dr Nw Suite 605, Calgary, AB, T3A 5R8
(403) 247-1143
Emp Here 100
SIC 5812 Eating places
Nick Blodtky

D-U-N-S 25-622-2555   (BR)
GAP (CANADA) INC
GAP
(*Suby of* THE GAP INC)
3625 Shaganappi Trail Nw, Calgary, AB, T3A 0E2
(403) 288-5188
Emp Here 85
SIC 5651 Family clothing stores
Melissa Boutilier

D-U-N-S 24-598-2033   (SL)
GOTREKKERS INC
4625 Varsity Dr Nw Suite 305, Calgary, AB, T3A 0Z9
(403) 289-6938
Emp Here 29   *Sales* 11,175,440
SIC 4725 Tour operators
Martin Shutt

D-U-N-S 24-611-2796   (SL)
HAMPTONS GOLF COURSE LTD
69 Hamptons Dr Nw, Calgary, AB, T3A 5H7
(403) 239-8088
Emp Here 150   *Sales* 14,242,950
SIC 7999 Amusement and recreation, nec
Barry Ehlert
Gordon Courage

D-U-N-S 20-635-8079   (BR)
HUDSON'S BAY COMPANY
(*Suby of* HUDSON'S BAY COMPANY)
3625 Shaganappi Trail Nw, Calgary, AB, T3A 0E2
(403) 286-1220
Emp Here 280
SIC 5311 Department stores
Larry Henry

D-U-N-S 24-494-1886   (SL)
I CARE SERVICE LTD
GIMBLE EYE CENTER, THE
4935 40 Ave Nw Suite 450, Calgary, AB, T3A 2N1
(403) 286-3022
Emp Here 100   *Sales* 18,534,000
SIC 8011 Offices and clinics of medical doctors
Howard Gimbel
Judy Gimbel

D-U-N-S 25-205-0604   (HQ)
INTERNATIONAL FITNESS HOLDINGS INC
WORLD HEALTH CLUB
7222 Edgemont Blvd Nw, Calgary, AB, T3A 2X7
(403) 278-2499
Emp Here 10   *Sales* 15,551,910
SIC 7991 Physical fitness facilities
Rob Leach
Brian Hoban
Dave Wakefield

D-U-N-S 20-722-4648   (SL)
KANJEE ENTERPRISES LTD
SHOPPERS DRUG MART
3625 Shaganappi Trail Nw Suite 356, Calgary, AB, T3A 0E2
(403) 288-0111
Emp Here 60   *Sales* 14,659,680
SIC 5912 Drug stores and proprietary stores
Amyn Kanjee

D-U-N-S 25-270-1487   (BR)
LOBLAWS INC
REAL CANADIAN SUPERSTORE
(*Suby of* LOBLAW COMPANIES LIMITED)
5251 Country Hills Blvd Nw Suite 1575, Calgary, AB, T3A 5H8
(403) 241-4027
Emp Here 300
SIC 5411 Grocery stores
Derren Paterson

D-U-N-S 25-629-2913   (BR)
MOXIE'S RESTAURANTS, LIMITED PARTNERSHIP
3625 Shaganappi Trail Nw, Calgary, AB, T3A 0E2
(403) 288-2663
Emp Here 130
SIC 5812 Eating places
Cody Carignan

D-U-N-S 20-647-3899   (SL)
REAL ESTATE INVESTMENT TRUST
EDGEMONT RETIREMENT RESIDENCE
80 Edenwold Dr Nw, Calgary, AB, T3A 5R9
(403) 241-8990
Emp Here 49   *Sales* 11,412,639
SIC 6513 Apartment building operators
Andries Fliergans

D-U-N-S 24-554-7351   (HQ)
REMAX REAL ESTATE 'MOUNTAIN VIEW' LTD
4625 Varsity Dr Nw Suite 222, Calgary, AB, T3A 0Z9

▲ Public Company   ■ Public Company Family Member   **HQ** Headquarters   **BR** Branch   **SL** Single Location

(403) 651-4400
Emp Here 2   *Sales* 39,794,455
SIC 6531 Real estate agents and managers
  Lowell Martens

D-U-N-S 20-991-5115   (SL)
SHAGANAPPI MOTORS (1976) LTD
SHAGANAPPI GM
4720 Crowchild Trail Nw, Calgary, AB, T3A
2N2
(403) 288-0444
Emp Here 125   *Sales* 78,660,000
SIC 5511 New and used car dealers
  Gary Sartorio

D-U-N-S 25-118-7571   (SL)
SUNORA FOODS INC
SUNERA
4616 Valiant Dr Nw Suite 205, Calgary, AB,
T3A 0X9
(403) 247-8300
Emp Here 12   *Sales* 11,004,117
SIC 2079 Edible fats and oils
  Stephen Bank
  Ali Chatur
  James Lawson
  Alan Chan
  Eric Dahlberg

Calgary, AB T3B

D-U-N-S 25-231-5791   (SL)
425579 ALBERTA LTD
ECONO-CHEM
130 Bowness Ctr Nw, Calgary, AB, T3B 5M5
(403) 242-1020
Emp Here 20   *Sales* 10,006,500
SIC 5169 Chemicals and allied products, nec
  Ragan Niepel
  Paolo Rigoni

D-U-N-S 25-366-0161   (SL)
**ALBERTA CHILDREN'S HOSPITAL FOUN-
DATION**
2888 Shaganappi Trail Nw, Calgary, AB, T3B
6A8
(403) 955-8818
Emp Here 30   *Sales* 26,972,680
SIC 8699 Membership organizations, nec
  Saifa Koonar
  Tacy Gerlitz
  Joanne Weninger
  Belinda Lamb
  Liz Ballendine
  Christine Hardy
  Patty Bambrick
  Justine Clay
  Jan Golightly
  Karen Radford

D-U-N-S 25-408-9964   (HQ)
ALPINE CANADA ALPIN
CANADIAN ALPINE SKI TEAM, DIV OF
151 Canada Olympic Rd Sw Suite 302, Cal-
gary, AB, T3B 6B7
(403) 777-3200
Emp Here 1   *Sales* 19,870,700
SIC 8699 Membership organizations, nec
  Mark Rubinstein

D-U-N-S 20-074-7467   (SL)
BOW CYCLE & MOTOR CO LTD
8525 Bowfort Rd Nw, Calgary, AB, T3B 2V2
(403) 288-5421
Emp Here 35   *Sales* 17,432,730
SIC 5511 New and used car dealers
  Todd Starchuck

D-U-N-S 25-097-6180   (SL)
BOW CYCLE & SPORTS LTD
6501 Bowness Rd Nw, Calgary, AB, T3B 0E8
(403) 288-5422
Emp Here 70   *Sales* 17,102,960
SIC 5941 Sporting goods and bicycle shops
  John Franzky

Darrell Elliott
Kurt Christensen
Kevin Senior
Dave Leung

D-U-N-S 20-768-7427   (HQ)
**BRENDA STRAFFORD FOUNDATION LTD,
THE**
BOW VIEW MANOR
4628 Montgomery Blvd Nw, Calgary, AB, T3B
0K7
(403) 288-1780
Sales 11,615,420
SIC 8051 Skilled nursing care facilities
  Barrie Strafford

D-U-N-S 25-485-7998   (BR)
CALGARY BOARD OF EDUCATION
BOWNESS HIGH SCHOOL
(*Suby of* CALGARY BOARD OF EDUCA-
TION)
4627 77 St Nw, Calgary, AB, T3B 2N6
(403) 286-5092
Emp Here 85
SIC 8211 Elementary and secondary schools
  Jana Macdonald

D-U-N-S 20-813-1305   (SL)
CALGARY GYMNASTICS CENTRE
179 Canada Olympic Rd Sw, Calgary, AB, T3B
5R5
(403) 242-1171
Emp Here 80   *Sales* 7,684,219
SIC 7999 Amusement and recreation, nec
  Bonnie Semeschuk

D-U-N-S 24-554-8243   (HQ)
**CALGARY OLYMPIC DEVELOPMENT AS-
SOCIATION**
WINSPORT CANADA
88 Canada Olympic Rd Sw, Calgary, AB, T3B
5R5
(403) 247-5452
Sales 10,404,000
SIC 7999 Amusement and recreation, nec
  Guy Huntingford
  John Langille
  Catriona Lemay-Doan
  Colin Macdonald
  Trevor Nakka
  Rob Paradis
  Gordon Ritchie
  Jane Savidant
  Shelley Shea
  Stephen Sibold

D-U-N-S 25-505-3068   (HQ)
ENTERPRISE UNIVERSAL INC
4411 16 Ave Nw, Calgary, AB, T3B 0M3
(403) 209-4780
Sales 13,252,260
SIC 6512 Nonresidential building operators
  Peter Huang
  Ian Huang

D-U-N-S 20-890-1900   (HQ)
HOCKEY CANADA
151 Canada Olympic Rd Sw Suite 201, Cal-
gary, AB, T3B 6B7
(403) 777-3636
Emp Here 10   *Sales* 63,829,080
SIC 8699 Membership organizations, nec
  Scott Smith

D-U-N-S 20-346-1285   (SL)
INN AT THE PARK INC
FOUR POINTS HOTEL SUITES
8220 Bowridge Cres Nw, Calgary, AB, T3B
2V1
(403) 288-4441
Emp Here 80   *Sales* 7,591,920
SIC 7011 Hotels and motels
  Ed Bhanji
  Rahim Lakhoo

D-U-N-S 20-130-8900   (SL)
LODGE AT VALLEY RIDGE, THE
THE DIVERSICARE CANADA

11479 Valley Ridge Dr Nw Suite 332, Calgary,
AB, T3B 5V5
(403) 286-4414
Emp Here 100   *Sales* 9,489,900
SIC 7041 Membership-basis organization ho-
tels
  Ruth Langdon

D-U-N-S 25-098-9985   (BR)
REVERA INC
*RETIREMENT RESIDENCES REAL ESTATE
INVESTMENT TRUST*
(*Suby of* GOVERNMENT OF CANADA)
5927 Bowness Rd Nw, Calgary, AB, T3B 0C7
(403) 288-2373
Emp Here 200
SIC 8051 Skilled nursing care facilities
  Kathy Clark

D-U-N-S 25-992-8281   (HQ)
SURGICAL CENTRES INC
3125 Bowwood Dr Nw, Calgary, AB, T3B 2E7
(403) 640-1188
Emp Here 20   *Sales* 11,245,220
SIC 8011 Offices and clinics of medical doc-
tors
  G. Mohamed Nanji
  Fatima Fazal
  Terry J. Stewart

D-U-N-S 20-082-9211   (BR)
WOOD'S HOMES SOCIETY
WOOD'S HOMES BOWNESS TREATMENT
(*Suby of* WOOD'S HOMES SOCIETY)
9400 48 Ave Nw, Calgary, AB, T3B 2B2
(403) 247-6751
Emp Here 100
SIC 8361 Residential care
  Jane Matheson

Calgary, AB T3C

D-U-N-S 20-057-1409   (SL)
4359241 MANITOBA INC
JUBILATIONS DINNER THEATRE
1002 37 St Sw, Calgary, AB, T3C 1S1
(403) 249-7799
Emp Here 200   *Sales* 9,103,800
SIC 5812 Eating places
  Doug Stephen
  Dale Colbran

D-U-N-S 20-217-8781   (HQ)
587577 ALBERTA LIMITED
HYATT AUTO GALLERY
909 15 St Sw, Calgary, AB, T3C 1E5
(403) 232-6400
Emp Here 22   *Sales* 10,957,716
SIC 5511 New and used car dealers
  Mike Edgar

D-U-N-S 24-495-6207   (SL)
CALHOME PROPERTIES LTD
CALGARY HOUSING COMPANY
(*Suby of* CITY OF CALGARY, THE)
820 Pine Pl Sw, Calgary, AB, T3C 3N1
(403) 217-7933
Emp Here 100   *Sales* 13,567,700
SIC 6514 Dwelling operators, except apart-
ments
  Dale Stamm

D-U-N-S 20-786-6562   (BR)
COMMUNITY NATURAL FOODS LTD
(*Suby of* COMMUNITY NATURAL FOODS
LTD)
1304 10 Ave Sw, Calgary, AB, T3C 0J2
(403) 930-6363
Emp Here 200
SIC 5499 Miscellaneous food stores
  Robin Pritchard

D-U-N-S 24-035-4980   (BR)
DATA COMMUNICATIONS MANAGEMENT

CORP
SUNDOG PRINTING, DIV OF
(*Suby of* DATA COMMUNICATIONS MAN-
AGEMENT CORP)
1311 9 Ave Sw Suite 300, Calgary, AB, T3C
0H9
(403) 272-7440
Emp Here 225
SIC 2759 Commercial printing, nec
  Todd Schmautz

D-U-N-S 24-676-6815   (SL)
DECO WINDSHIELD REPAIR INC
1602 42 St Sw, Calgary, AB, T3C 1Z5
(403) 829-6289
Emp Here 96   *Sales* 27,196,800
SIC 7536 Automotive glass replacement
shops
  Matt Horne

D-U-N-S 24-906-8156   (SL)
EXPLORATION DATA SYSTEMS INC
M J SYSTEMS
2410 10 Ave Sw, Calgary, AB, T3C 0K6
(403) 249-8931
Emp Here 45   *Sales* 14,386,725
SIC 1389 Oil and gas field services, nec
  Peter J Weston
  Robert R Hamilton
  Jack Wahl

D-U-N-S 24-552-6587   (BR)
EXTENDICARE INC
EXTENDICARE CEDARS VILLA
(*Suby of* EXTENDICARE INC)
3330 8 Ave Sw, Calgary, AB, T3C 0E7
(403) 249-8915
Emp Here 220
SIC 8051 Skilled nursing care facilities
  Lori Young

D-U-N-S 25-313-9281   (HQ)
**GREYHOUND CANADA TRANSPORTA-
TION ULC**
FIRSTGROUP AMERICA
(*Suby of* FIRSTGROUP PLC)
877 Greyhound Way Sw, Calgary, AB, T3C
3V8
(403) 218-3000
Emp Here 350   *Sales* 151,777,800
SIC 4131 Intercity and rural bus transportation
  Dave Leach
  Karim Lalani
  Stuart Kendrick

D-U-N-S 24-441-3126   (SL)
**GSL CHEVROLET OLDSMOBILE CADIL-
LAC (1986) LIMITED**
GSL CHEV CITY
1720 Bow Trail Sw, Calgary, AB, T3C 2E4
(403) 781-1519
Emp Here 135   *Sales* 84,952,800
SIC 5511 New and used car dealers
  Robert Wolfe
  Brydon Mcleod
  Donald Rivard

D-U-N-S 20-076-1567   (HQ)
**GUNTHER'S BUILDING SUPPLIES LIM-
ITED**
2100 10 Ave Sw, Calgary, AB, T3C 0K5
(403) 245-3311
Emp Here 2   *Sales* 10,483,875
SIC 6712 Bank holding companies
  Peter R. Kockerbeck
  Conrad Kockerbeck

D-U-N-S 24-118-8598   (SL)
KARO GROUP INC
1817 10 Ave Sw, Calgary, AB, T3C 0K2
(403) 266-4094
Emp Here 42   *Sales* 18,626,580
SIC 7389 Business services, nec
  Christopher Bedford
  Michael Dangelmaier
  Alex Berenyi
  Joe Strasser

D-U-N-S 24-070-4325   (HQ)
KIDZINC SCHOOL AGE CARE SOCIETY OF ALBERTA
4411 10 Ave Sw, Calgary, AB, T3C 0L9
(403) 240-2059
Emp Here 15   *Sales* 11,922,420
SIC 8699 Membership organizations, nec
Michael Leong-Machielse

D-U-N-S 24-187-4317   (HQ)
MAXWELL WESTVIEW REALTY
STRAIGHT AWAY MANAGEMENT
1200 37 St Sw Suite 41, Calgary, AB, T3C 1S2
(403) 256-6015
Emp Here 1   *Sales* 25,133,340
SIC 6531 Real estate agents and managers
Alex Dabisza

D-U-N-S 24-016-3212   (HQ)
PIONEER ENVIRO GROUP LTD
PIONEER LAND & ENVIROMENTAL SERVICES
1711 10 Ave Sw Suite 200, Calgary, AB, T3C 0K1
(403) 229-3969
Emp Here 45   *Sales* 40,205,990
SIC 6712 Bank holding companies
Terry Stevenson
Lorne Smeland

D-U-N-S 20-077-6870   (SL)
RENFREW CHRYSLER INC.
RENFREW CHRYSLER JEEP
(*Suby of* RENFREW NATIONAL LEASING LTD)
1920 Pumphouse Rd Sw, Calgary, AB, T3C 3N4
(403) 266-1920
Emp Here 130   *Sales* 81,806,400
SIC 5511 New and used car dealers
Mike Tarp

D-U-N-S 20-114-8223   (HQ)
RENFREW NATIONAL LEASING LTD
1920 Pumphouse Rd Sw, Calgary, AB, T3C 3N4
(403) 266-1920
Sales 81,806,400
SIC 5511 New and used car dealers
Mike Tarp

D-U-N-S 20-828-2392   (HQ)
SANEAL CAMERA SUPPLIES LTD
SANEAL CAMERA
1402 11 Ave Sw, Calgary, AB, T3C 0M8
(403) 228-1865
Emp Here 20   *Sales* 14,659,680
SIC 5946 Camera and photographic supply stores
Neal Arya
Sandeep Arya

D-U-N-S 20-078-1219   (HQ)
SPALDING HARDWARE LTD
SPALDING HARDWARE SYSTEMS
1616 10 Ave Sw, Calgary, AB, T3C 0J5
(403) 244-5531
Emp Here 21   *Sales* 22,358,700
SIC 5072 Hardware
John W Manes
Ed Toy

D-U-N-S 24-388-4405   (SL)
SPALDING HARDWARE SYSTEMS INC
1616 10 Ave Sw, Calgary, AB, T3C 0J5
(403) 244-5531
Emp Here 40   *Sales* 17,886,960
SIC 5072 Hardware
John Manes
Edwin Toy

D-U-N-S 25-218-9774   (BR)
WAL-MART CANADA CORP
(*Suby of* WALMART INC.)
1212 37 St Sw Suite 3009, Calgary, AB, T3C 1S3
(403) 242-2205
Emp Here 250

SIC 5311 Department stores
Gile Gerald

Calgary, AB T3E

D-U-N-S 20-114-1830   (HQ)
923416 ALBERTA LTD
GLENMORE AUDI
25 Richard Way Sw, Calgary, AB, T3E 7M8
(403) 568-2834
Sales 16,389,675
SIC 5012 Automobiles and other motor vehicles
Douglas Shostak
Lori Shostak

D-U-N-S 20-829-7176   (BR)
ALBERTA MOTOR ASSOCIATION
A M A
(*Suby of* ALBERTA MOTOR ASSOCIATION)
4700 17 Ave Sw, Calgary, AB, T3E 0E3
(403) 240-5300
Emp Here 180
SIC 4724 Travel agencies
Art Price

D-U-N-S 20-074-5065   (HQ)
ATCO LTD
ATCO GROUP
5302 Forand St Sw, Calgary, AB, T3E 8B4
(403) 292-7500
Emp Here 160   *Sales* 3,705,602,576
SIC 4911 Electric services
Nancy C Southern
Siegfried W. Kiefer
Dennis Dechamplain
M. George Constantinescu
George J. Lidgett
Wayne K. Stensby
Adam Beattie
Jim Landon
Linda A. Southern-Heathcott
Robert T Booth

D-U-N-S 24-383-3345   (HQ)
ATCO STRUCTURES & LOGISTICS LTD
(*Suby of* ATCO LTD)
115 Peacekeepers Dr, Calgary, AB, T3E 7X4
(403) 662-8500
Emp Here 200   *Sales* 54,957,300
SIC 1742 Plastering, drywall, and insulation
Steve Lockwood

D-U-N-S 20-335-2489   (SL)
ATCO TWO RIVERS LODGING CONSTRUCTION LIMITED PARTNERSHIP
(*Suby of* ATCO LTD)
4838 Richard Rd Sw Suite 300, Calgary, AB, T3E 6L1
(403) 662-8500
Emp Here 100   *Sales* 42,273,700
SIC 1541 Industrial buildings and warehouses
Stephen Lockwood

D-U-N-S 24-805-6496   (HQ)
BROOKFIELD RESIDENTIAL PROPERTIES INC
(*Suby of* BROOKFIELD OFFICE PROPERTIES INC)
4906 Richard Rd Sw, Calgary, AB, T3E 6L1
(403) 231-8900
Emp Here 20   *Sales* 2,162,350,000
SIC 6553 Cemetery subdividers and developers
Alan Norris
Adrian Foley
Shane Pearson
Thomas Lui
Trent Edwards
Peter Nesbitt
Don Merlo
Warren Krug

D-U-N-S 25-011-2141   (BR)

CALGARY BOARD OF EDUCATION
CENTRAL MEMORIAL HIGH SCHOOL
(*Suby of* CALGARY BOARD OF EDUCATION)
5111 21 St Sw, Calgary, AB, T3E 1R9
(403) 243-8880
Emp Here 150
SIC 8211 Elementary and secondary schools
Nancy Lisi

D-U-N-S 25-269-4443   (BR)
CALGARY BOARD OF EDUCATION
LORD SHAUGHNESSY HIGH SCHOOL
(*Suby of* CALGARY BOARD OF EDUCATION)
2336 53 Ave Sw, Calgary, AB, T3E 1L2
(403) 243-4500
Emp Here 75
SIC 8211 Elementary and secondary schools
Adams Brad

D-U-N-S 20-012-3433   (BR)
CALGARY BOARD OF EDUCATION
CHINOOK LEARNING SERVICES
(*Suby of* CALGARY BOARD OF EDUCATION)
2519 Richmond Rd Sw Suite 168, Calgary, AB, T3E 4M2
(403) 777-7200
Emp Here 100
SIC 8221 Colleges and universities
Mary Ellen Dewar

D-U-N-S 25-269-4542   (BR)
CALGARY ROMAN CATHOLIC SEPARATE SCHOOL DISTRICT #1
BISHOP CARROLL HIGH SCHOOL
(*Suby of* CALGARY ROMAN CATHOLIC SEPARATE SCHOOL DISTRICT #1)
4624 Richard Rd Sw, Calgary, AB, T3E 6L1
(403) 500-2056
Emp Here 125
SIC 8211 Elementary and secondary schools
Neil O'flaherty

D-U-N-S 20-081-1792   (HQ)
CANADIAN UTILITIES LIMITED
(*Suby of* ATCO LTD)
5302 Forand St, Calgary, AB, T3E 8B4
(403) 292-7500
Sales 3,318,212,454
SIC 4924 Natural gas distribution
Siegfried Kiefer
Dennis Dechamplain
M. George Constantinescu
Brenda J. Black
Lillian L. Brewster
G. Dale Friesen
Deanna M. Girard
Robert C. Neumann
Katie Patrick
Alan M. Skiffington

D-U-N-S 20-190-8287   (HQ)
CANTELON ENTERPRISES INC
MIDAS
2529 17 Ave Sw, Calgary, AB, T3E 0A2
(403) 246-1176
Emp Here 4   *Sales* 12,580,650
SIC 6712 Bank holding companies
Harold R Cantelon
Bonnie Cantelon

D-U-N-S 20-827-4464   (HQ)
CANUCK AMUSEMENTS AND MERCHANDISING LTD
3911 37 St Sw, Calgary, AB, T3E 6L6
(403) 249-6641
Emp Here 18   *Sales* 10,410,840
SIC 5092 Toys and hobby goods and supplies
Julie Earle
Douglas Earle

D-U-N-S 24-673-9663   (SL)
CENTURION MECHANICAL LTD
2509 Dieppe Ave Sw Unit 301, Calgary, AB, T3E 7J9

(403) 452-6761
Emp Here 50   *Sales* 11,046,700
SIC 1711 Plumbing, heating, air-conditioning
Anthony Kelly
Anne Marie Patmore

D-U-N-S 20-304-4990   (SL)
CLOSE TO HOME
CLOSER TO HOME COMMUNITY SERVICE
3507 17 Ave Sw Suite A, Calgary, AB, T3E 0B6
(403) 543-0550
Emp Here 45   *Sales* 17,883,630
SIC 8699 Membership organizations, nec
Karen Olivier

D-U-N-S 24-667-4423   (SL)
COMPLYWORKS LTD
4838 Richard Rd Sw Suite 600, Calgary, AB, T3E 6L1
(403) 219-4792
Emp Here 49   *Sales* 11,657,149
SIC 8742 Management consulting services
Cal Fairbanks
David Bischoff
Darcy Mcfeetors

D-U-N-S 25-098-3442   (HQ)
CU INC
(*Suby of* ATCO LTD)
5302 Forand St Sw 4th Fl, Calgary, AB, T3E 8B4
(403) 292-7500
Emp Here 28   *Sales* 2,057,410,602
SIC 4931 Electric and other services combined
Nancy Southern
Siegfried Kiefer
Patrick Tait
Alan Skiffington
Anthony Maher
Robert Neumann
G. Dale Friesen
Lillian Brewster
Brenda Black
Katie Patrick

D-U-N-S 24-465-4674   (SL)
GLENDALE GLENDALE MEADOWS COMMUNITY ASSOCIATION
2405 Glenmount Dr Sw, Calgary, AB, T3E 4C1
(403) 242-2110
Emp Here 45   *Sales* 10,743,750
SIC 8611 Business associations
George Hopkins

D-U-N-S 24-016-2941   (SL)
GRIFA, BLAISE LTD
CANADIAN TIRE
5200 Richmond Rd Sw Suite 302, Calgary, AB, T3E 6M9
(403) 246-1961
Emp Here 85   *Sales* 53,488,800
SIC 5531 Auto and home supply stores
Terry Mckinnon

D-U-N-S 20-439-9513   (SL)
HALFORD & VALENTINE (1991) LTD
VALENTINE VOLVO
11 Richard Way Sw, Calgary, AB, T3E 7M8
(403) 217-1722
Emp Here 45   *Sales* 22,413,510
SIC 5511 New and used car dealers
Ted Valentine
Paul Valentine
Shirley Valentine

D-U-N-S 20-105-6681   (HQ)
IBERDROLA CANADA ENERGY SERVICES LTD
(*Suby of* IBERDROLA, SOCIEDAD ANONIMA)
5 Richard Way Sw Suite 208, Calgary, AB, T3E 7M8
(403) 206-3160
Sales 62,117,140
SIC 4922 Natural gas transmission
Mark Tumbach

Matt Morrow
Ralph Currey

D-U-N-S 25-522-7803 (HQ)
IMAGINE WIRELESS INC
ROGERS AT & T
4550 17 Ave Sw Unit 28, Calgary, AB, T3E
7B9
(403) 974-3150
Emp Here 18 *Sales* 13,024,000
SIC 5999 Miscellaneous retail stores, nec
Bruce Giesinger
Chris Churchill

D-U-N-S 25-315-8943 (BR)
**INVESTORS GROUP FINANCIAL SER-
VICES INC**
(*Suby of* POWER CORPORATION DU
CANADA)
37 Richard Way Sw Unit 100, Calgary, AB,
T3E 7M8
(403) 253-4840
Emp Here 130
SIC 8742 Management consulting services
Girish Agrawal

D-U-N-S 24-880-7182 (SL)
K L S CONTRACTING LTD
7 Glenbrook Pl Sw Suite 206, Calgary, AB,
T3E 6W4
(403) 240-3030
Emp Here 60 *Sales* 14,771,160
SIC 1794 Excavation work
Doug Renton

D-U-N-S 25-273-0981 (BR)
LONDON DRUGS LIMITED
(*Suby of* H.Y. LOUIE CO. LIMITED)
5255 Richmond Rd Sw Suite 300, Calgary,
AB, T3E 7C4
(403) 571-4932
Emp Here 100
SIC 5912 Drug stores and proprietary stores
Colleen Lancaster

D-U-N-S 20-369-7149 (SL)
MAGNA INSURANCE CORP
MAGNA INSURANCE GROUP
5 Richard Way Sw Unit 104, Calgary, AB, T3E
7M8
(403) 930-0466
Emp Here 200 *Sales* 369,548,400
SIC 6411 Insurance agents, brokers, and ser-
vice
Chris Sikorski
Brian Jardine
Ed Sikorski
Jim Royer

D-U-N-S 20-767-3708 (HQ)
MOUNT ROYAL UNIVERSITY
4825 Mount Royal Gate Sw, Calgary, AB, T3E
6K6
(403) 440-6111
Emp Here 560 *Sales* 176,877,706
SIC 8222 Junior colleges
David Marshall
Jeffrey Goldberg
Duane Anderson
Steve Fitterer
Paul Rossmann
Bryan Pinney
Jim Campbell
Eleanor Chiu
David Clemis
Daryl Fridhandler

D-U-N-S 20-279-0531 (HQ)
PACIFIC WINE & SPIRITS INC
2505 17 Ave Sw Unit 208, Calgary, AB, T3E
7V3
(403) 226-0214
Sales 12,934,152
SIC 5182 Wine and distilled beverages
Linda Robinson
John Alcook
William Bowlen

D-U-N-S 24-345-5078 (SL)
SARCEE MOTORS LTD
HONDA WEST
55 Glenbrook Pl Sw, Calgary, AB, T3E 6W4
(403) 249-9166
Emp Here 85 *Sales* 53,488,800
SIC 5511 New and used car dealers
Christopher L. Simpkins

D-U-N-S 20-539-7607 (HQ)
STUART OLSON BUILDINGS LTD
(*Suby of* STUART OLSON INC)
4954 Richard Rd Sw Suite 400, Calgary, AB,
T3E 6L1
(403) 520-2767
Emp Here 10 *Sales* 213,336,960
SIC 1522 Residential construction, nec
Don Pearson
James Houck
Daryl Sands

D-U-N-S 24-522-2773 (HQ)
STUART OLSON CONSTRUCTION LTD
(*Suby of* STUART OLSON INC)
4820 Richard Rd Sw Suite 600, Calgary, AB,
T3E 6L1
(403) 520-2767
Sales 139,132,800
SIC 1522 Residential construction, nec
Norm Rokosh
Alf Stowkowy
Don Goedbloed
Ian T Morris
Dave Smith

D-U-N-S 24-767-3635 (HQ)
STUART OLSON INC
4820 Richard Rd Sw Suite 600, Calgary, AB,
T3E 6L1
(403) 685-7777
Emp Here 350 *Sales* 732,635,838
SIC 1541 Industrial buildings and warehouses
David Lemay
Daryl Sands
Joette Decore
Paul Polson
Bob Myles
Richard Ballantyne
Albrecht Bellstedt
Chad Danard
Rod Graham
Wendy Hanrahan

D-U-N-S 20-830-3776 (SL)
**STUDENTS ASSOCIATION OF MOUNT
ROYAL COLLEGE**
4825 Mount Royal Gate Sw, Calgary, AB, T3E
6K6
(403) 440-6077
Emp Here 45 *Sales* 12,317,805
SIC 8651 Political organizations
James Wood
Mark Sullis
Brad Needham
Erin Macdoanld

D-U-N-S 25-386-2080 (HQ)
SYLOGIST LTD
BELLAMY SOFTWARE
5 Richard Way Sw Suite 102, Calgary, AB,
T3E 7M8
(403) 266-4808
Emp Here 15 *Sales* 29,236,472
SIC 7372 Prepackaged software
James D Wilson
David O.C. Elder
Xavier Shorter
Andre Drouillard
Donna Smiley
Ronald Cherkas
C. Elliott
Taylor Gray

D-U-N-S 20-640-4696 (HQ)
**THIRD ACADEMY INTERNATIONAL LTD,
THE**
THIRD ACADEMY , THE

2452 Battleford Ave Sw, Calgary, AB, T3E 7K9
(403) 288-5335
Emp Here 75
SIC 8211 Elementary and secondary schools
Lal Mattu

D-U-N-S 20-700-8850 (HQ)
**THYSSENKRUPP INDUSTRIAL SOLU-
TIONS (CANADA) INC**
(*Suby of* THYSSENKRUPP AG)
4838 Richard Rd Sw Suite 400, Calgary, AB,
T3E 6L1
(403) 245-2866
Sales 19,661,290
SIC 8711 Engineering services
Nejo Kuljic
Robert Poffenroth
Ramsis Shenata

D-U-N-S 20-078-5111 (HQ)
**UNITED FARMERS OF ALBERTA CO-
OPERATIVE LIMITED**
UFA
4838 Richard Rd Sw Suite 700, Calgary, AB,
T3E 6L1
(403) 570-4500
Emp Here 300 *Sales* 984,191,607
SIC 5172 Petroleum products, nec
Carol Kitchen
Kevin Hoppins
James Bettcher
Harvey Hagman
Rick Hansen
Jim Laverick
Harold Haugen
Tim Nakaska
Mic Thiessen
Cindy Bjorklund

D-U-N-S 20-035-0184 (SL)
**WESTMOUNT CHARTER SCHOOL SOCI-
ETY**
2519 Richmond Rd Sw, Calgary, AB, T3E 4M2
(403) 217-0426
Emp Here 100 *Sales* 9,282,600
SIC 8211 Elementary and secondary schools
Megan O'hara

D-U-N-S 24-298-4698 (BR)
XEROX CANADA LTD
(*Suby of* XEROX CORPORATION)
37 Richard Way Sw Suite 200, Calgary, AB,
T3E 7M8
(403) 260-8800
Emp Here 75
SIC 5044 Office equipment
Brad Stanghetta

D-U-N-S 25-741-7733 (BR)
Z69115 ALBERTA LTD
ROYAL LEPAGE FOOTHILLS
(*Suby of* Z69115 ALBERTA LTD)
37 Richard Way Sw Suite 200, Calgary, AB,
T3E 7M8

Emp Here 90
SIC 6531 Real estate agents and managers
Ted Zaharko

Calgary, AB T3G

D-U-N-S 24-338-6336 (HQ)
586307 ALBERTA LTD
CROWFOOT LIQUOR STORE
7422 Crowfoot Rd Nw Unit 201, Calgary, AB,
T3G 3N7
(403) 296-2200
Emp Here 40 *Sales* 14,956,500
SIC 5921 Liquor stores
Terry Richardson

D-U-N-S 25-776-9729 (SL)
724053 ALBERTA LIMITED
NORTHWEST ACURA
125 Crowfoot Way Nw, Calgary, AB, T3G 2R2

(403) 239-6677
Emp Here 48 *Sales* 23,907,744
SIC 5511 New and used car dealers
Scott Wright

D-U-N-S 24-848-5992 (SL)
**ABSOLUTE COMPLETION TECHNOLO-
GIES LTD**
302-600 Crowfoot Cres Nw, Calgary, AB, T3G
0B4
(403) 266-5027
Emp Here 84 *Sales* 14,780,472
SIC 8711 Engineering services
Julian Haskell
John Jack Debeau
Thane Russell

D-U-N-S 25-194-6588 (HQ)
ABSOLUTE ENERGY LTD
600 Crowfoot Cres Nw Suite 302, Calgary, AB,
T3G 0B4
(403) 509-4000
Emp Here 10 *Sales* 27,335,000
SIC 6712 Bank holding companies
Thane Russell

D-U-N-S 25-943-7739 (HQ)
AMARANTH WHOLE FOODS MARKET INC
AMARANTH HEALTH AND WELLNESS
7 Arbour Lake Dr Nw, Calgary, AB, T3G 5G8
(403) 547-6333
Emp Here 40 *Sales* 13,206,465
SIC 5499 Miscellaneous food stores
Kenneth Klatt

D-U-N-S 24-440-2038 (BR)
**ASSOCIATED ENGINEERING ALBERTA
LTD**
(*Suby of* ASHCO SHAREHOLDERS INC)
600 Crowfoot Cres Nw Suite 400, Calgary, AB,
T3G 0B4
(403) 262-4500
Emp Here 90
SIC 8711 Engineering services
Alan Craven

D-U-N-S 25-316-1061 (BR)
**CALGARY CO-OPERATIVE ASSOCIATION
LIMITED**
CALGARY CO-OP
(*Suby of* CALGARY CO-OPERATIVE ASSO-
CIATION LIMITED)
35 Crowfoot Way Nw, Calgary, AB, T3G 2L4
(403) 216-4500
Emp Here 320
SIC 5411 Grocery stores
Jim Hurst

D-U-N-S 25-677-7426 (BR)
**CALGARY YOUNG MEN'S CHRISTIAN AS-
SOCIATION, THE**
*CALGARY YOUNG MEN'S CHRISTIAN AS-
SOCIATION*
(*Suby of* CALGARY YOUNG MEN'S CHRIS-
TIAN ASSOCIATION, THE)
8100 John Laurie Blvd Nw, Calgary, AB, T3G
3S3
(403) 547-6576
Emp Here 250
SIC 8399 Social services, nec
Susan Moorman

D-U-N-S 25-289-9356 (SL)
CANYON CREEK SOUP COMPANY LTD
(*Suby of* CANYON CREEK FOOD COMPANY
LTD)
60 Crowfoot Cres Nw Suite 204, Calgary, AB,
T3G 3J9

Emp Here 35 *Sales* 12,099,150
SIC 2032 Canned specialties
Terrance Alty
Brian Halina

D-U-N-S 24-879-3879 (SL)
CROWFOOT DODGE CHRYSLER INC
CROWFOOT DODGE
20 Crowfoot Rise Nw, Calgary, AB, T3G 3S7

(403) 241-0300
Emp Here 83   *Sales* 52,230,240
SIC 5511 New and used car dealers
Vicki Appleby

D-U-N-S 20-373-6111   (SL)
CROWFOOT H MOTORS LP
CROWFOOT HYUNDAI
(Suby of AUTOCANADA INC)
710 Crowfoot Crescent Nw, Calgary, AB, T3G
4S3
(403) 252-8833
Emp Here 65   *Sales* 40,903,200
SIC 5511 New and used car dealers

D-U-N-S 20-236-6071   (SL)
CROWFOOT IMAGE AUTO BODY LTD
141 Crowfoot Way Nw Unit 25, Calgary, AB,
T3G 4B7
(403) 547-4932
Emp Here 30   *Sales* 14,942,340
SIC 5511 New and used car dealers
Dave Fox

D-U-N-S 25-195-6496   (HQ)
DUFFIN FAMILY HOLDINGS LTD
CROWFOOT FORD
9 Crowfoot Cir Nw, Calgary, AB, T3G 3J8
(403) 239-1115
Emp Here 70   *Sales* 24,601,500
SIC 6712 Bank holding companies
Francis Duffin
Carrolle-Lynne Duffin

D-U-N-S 20-518-8985   (SL)
**DUGGAN, PAT REAL ESTATE SERVICES
LTD**
FIRST PLACE REALTY
156 Citadel Close Nw, Calgary, AB, T3G 4A6
(403) 547-8401
Emp Here 45   *Sales* 12,229,020
SIC 6531 Real estate agents and managers
Pat Duggan

D-U-N-S 25-648-3132   (HQ)
ELIZABETHS BAKERY LTD
TIM HORTONS
79 Crowfoot Way Nw, Calgary, AB, T3G 2R2
(403) 239-2583
Emp Here 80   *Sales* 3,778,077
SIC 5812 Eating places
Wes Jantz

D-U-N-S 20-282-7697   (SL)
EURO-TECH CONSTRUCTION INC
855 Arbour Lake Rd Nw, Calgary, AB, T3G
5J2
(403) 457-1277
Emp Here 35   *Sales* 16,475,585
SIC 1542 Nonresidential construction, nec
Chad Kuczaj

D-U-N-S 24-549-1290   (SL)
GANGSTER ENTERPRISES LTD
600 Crowfoot Cres Nw Suite 230, Calgary,
T3G 0B4
(403) 241-9494
Emp Here 80   *Sales* 11,855,360
SIC 4212 Local trucking, without storage
Rolf Reule

D-U-N-S 20-334-1677   (SL)
JOEY CROWFOOT
50 Crowfoot Way Nw, Calgary, AB, T3G 4C8
(403) 547-5639
Emp Here 160   *Sales* 7,283,040
SIC 5812 Eating places
Brian Dillon

D-U-N-S 24-573-2297   (SL)
KRUGER INDUSTRIES INC
28 Crowfoot Terrace Nw, Calgary, AB, T3G
5W2
(403) 276-6900
Emp Here 43   *Sales* 10,881,537
SIC 5211 Lumber and other building materials

D-U-N-S 20-388-0286   (SL)
OPEN CALL CENTRE INC

OCC
600 Crowfoot Cres Nw Suite 340, Calgary, AB,
T3G 0B4
(888) 582-4515
Emp Here 128   *Sales* 29,244,416
SIC 4899 Communication services, nec
Ross Cordoviz

D-U-N-S 20-305-0935   (SL)
ROBERT THIRSK HIGH SCHOOL
8777 Nose Hill Dr Nw, Calgary, AB, T3G 5T3
(403) 817-3400
Emp Here 95   *Sales* 8,818,470
SIC 8211 Elementary and secondary schools
Matt Christison

D-U-N-S 24-586-1484   (SL)
VEA GROUP INC, THE
150 Crowfoot Cres Nw Suite 105, Calgary, AB,
T3G 3T2
(403) 547-7727
Emp Here 40   *Sales* 11,157,837
SIC 8741 Management services
Madeleine Ficaccio

D-U-N-S 20-916-2341   (BR)
WAL-MART CANADA CORP
(Suby of WALMART INC.)
8888 Country Hills Blvd Nw Suite 200, Cal-
gary, AB, T3G 5T4
(403) 567-1502
Emp Here 375
SIC 5311 Department stores
Steven Redmond

Calgary, AB T3H

D-U-N-S 20-830-9401   (HQ)
**ALBERTA NEW HOME WARRANTY PRO-
GRAM, THE**
30 Springborough Blvd Sw Suite 301, Calgary,
AB, T3H 0N9
(403) 253-3636
Emp Here 47   *Sales* 67,947,990
SIC 6351 Surety insurance
Schuyler Wensel
John Kozole
Tom Skomorowski

D-U-N-S 20-011-5769   (SL)
AMBROSE UNIVERSITY COLLEGE
AMBROSE
150 Ambrose Cir Sw, Calgary, AB, T3H 0L5
(403) 410-2000
Emp Here 120   *Sales* 17,926,920
SIC 8221 Colleges and universities
Gordon Smith
Jo-Ann Badley
Roland K Laing
David Hearn
Ian Fitzpatrick
Christopher Perumalla
Jay Pullen
Lawrence Stalder
Calvin Buss
Kenneth Tsang

D-U-N-S 25-522-4933   (HQ)
ANGLES SALON INC
ANGLES HAIR DESIGN
555 Strathcona Blvd Sw Suite 420, Calgary,
AB, T3H 2Z9
(403) 242-6057
Emp Here 2   *Sales* 21,356,400
SIC 7231 Beauty shops
Lawrence Rizzuto
Dominic Rizzuto

D-U-N-S 20-046-1106   (BR)
BELL MEDIA INC
CTV TELEVISION
(Suby of BCE INC)
80 Patina Rise Sw, Calgary, AB, T3H 2W4

(403) 240-5600
Emp Here 130
SIC 4833 Television broadcasting stations
Donabon Fuessel

D-U-N-S 24-033-6938   (SL)
BLUSH LANE ORGANIC PRODUCE LTD
10 Aspen Stone Blvd Sw Suite 3000, Calgary,
AB, T3H 0K3
(403) 210-1247
Emp Here 40   *Sales* 33,423,080
SIC 5148 Fresh fruits and vegetables
Robert Horricks

D-U-N-S 25-485-8160   (SL)
**CALGARY FRENCH & INTERNATIONAL
SCHOOL SOCIETY, THE**
CFIS LANGUAGE SCHOOLS
700 77 St Sw, Calgary, AB, T3H 5R1
(403) 240-1500
Emp Here 80   *Sales* 12,834,080
SIC 8299 Schools and educational services,
nec
Dave Jackson

D-U-N-S 20-650-3349   (BR)
CAREWEST
(Suby of GOVERNMENT OF THE
PROVINCE OF ALBERTA)
6363 Simcoe Rd Sw, Calgary, AB, T3H 4M3
(403) 240-7950
Emp Here 88
SIC 8051 Skilled nursing care facilities
Daria Armstrong

D-U-N-S 20-304-2601   (HQ)
EQUICAPITA INCOME TRUST
8561 8a Ave Sw Suite 2210, Calgary, AB, T3H
0V5
(587) 887-1538
Emp Here 5   *Sales* 26,560,350
SIC 6211 Security brokers and dealers
Stephen Johnston
Thomas Syvret
Michael Cook
Greg Tooth

D-U-N-S 25-792-1312   (BR)
LOBLAWS INC
REAL CANADIAN SUPERSTORE
(Suby of LOBLAW COMPANIES LIMITED)
5858 Signal Hill Ctr Sw Suite 1577, Calgary,
AB, T3H 3P8
(403) 686-8035
Emp Here 200
SIC 5141 Groceries, general line
Dave Reid

D-U-N-S 25-316-4180   (BR)
PASLEY, MAX ENTERPRISES LIMITED
MCDONALD'S RESTAURANTS
100 Stewart Green Sw Unit 100, Calgary, AB,
T3H 3C8
(403) 246-1577
Emp Here 75
SIC 5812 Eating places
Adrian Santos

D-U-N-S 25-616-6943   (HQ)
STATESMAN CORPORATION
ADVANCED MEDICAL GROUP
(Suby of STATESMAN GROUP OF COMPA-
NIES LTD, THE)
7370 Sierra Morena Blvd Sw, Calgary, AB,
T3H 4H9
(403) 256-4151
Sales 85,622,680
SIC 1522 Residential construction, nec
M Garth Mann
Morgan Tingle
Kevin Ingalls

D-U-N-S 24-203-4382   (HQ)
**STATESMAN GROUP OF COMPANIES LTD,
THE**
7370 Sierra Morena Blvd Sw Suite 200, Calgary, AB, T3H 4H9

(403) 256-4151
Sales 19,314,650
SIC 1531 Operative builders
Garth Mann
Jeff Mann
Kevin Ingalls

D-U-N-S 25-107-6105   (SL)
WEBBER ACADEMY FOUNDATION
1515 93 St Sw, Calgary, AB, T3H 4A8
(403) 277-4700
Emp Here 100   *Sales* 9,282,600
SIC 8211 Elementary and secondary schools
Neil Webber

D-U-N-S 25-294-0473   (BR)
**WINNERS MERCHANTS INTERNATIONAL
L.P.**
WINNERS
(Suby of THE TJX COMPANIES INC)
5498 Signal Hill Ctr Sw, Calgary, AB, T3H 3P8
(403) 246-4999
Emp Here 100
SIC 5651 Family clothing stores
Jason Baird

Calgary, AB T3J

D-U-N-S 20-770-9887   (SL)
1009931 ALBERTA LTD
COUNTRY HILLS TOYOTA
20 Freeport Landng Ne, Calgary, AB, T3J 5H6
(403) 290-1111
Emp Here 154   *Sales* 96,909,120
SIC 5511 New and used car dealers
Naushad Jiwani

D-U-N-S 20-159-8200   (SL)
CAN WEST PROJECTS INC
85 Freeport Blvd Ne Suite 202, Calgary, AB,
T3J 4X8

Emp Here 105   *Sales* 26,506,410
SIC 1623 Water, sewer, and utility lines
Gord Brons
Wes Andrews

D-U-N-S 24-360-1932   (HQ)
CGG SERVICES (CANADA) INC
3675 63 Ave Ne, Calgary, AB, T3J 5K1
(403) 291-1434
Sales 92,286,500
SIC 7371 Custom computer programming ser-
vices
Michael Scott
Kent Milani
Susan Stewart

D-U-N-S 24-442-0881   (SL)
**DIAMOND FIREPLACE DISTRIBUTORS
LTD**
10221 15 St Ne Suite 4, Calgary, AB, T3J 0T1
(403) 273-0000
Emp Here 25   *Sales* 10,669,918
SIC 5023 Homefurnishings
Gary Greves
Richard Fankhanel
Kent Greves

D-U-N-S 25-996-0706   (SL)
DYNAMIC SOURCE MANUFACTURING INC
DSM
2765 48 Ave Ne Unit 117, Calgary, AB, T3J
5M9
(403) 516-1888
Emp Here 125   *Sales* 23,805,250
SIC 3679 Electronic components, nec
Duane Macauley
Sherman Cunningham

D-U-N-S 25-676-6064   (HQ)
IMARKETING SOLUTIONS GROUP INC
3710 Westwinds Dr Ne Unit 24, Calgary, AB,
T3J 5H3

---

(403) 531-6157
Emp Here 500   *Sales* 414,136,000
SIC 8399 Social services, nec
  Andrew Langhorne
  David Winograd
  Michael Davis
  Upkar Arora
  Jim Ambrose
  Michael Neuman
  Michael Platz
  Richard Reid

      D-U-N-S 24-327-2213   (SL)
KANJI RX DRUG LTD
SHOPPERS DRUG MART
600 Saddletowne Cir Ne Suite 101, Calgary,
AB, T3J 5M1
(403) 568-7143
Emp Here 50   *Sales* 12,647,700
SIC 5912 Drug stores and proprietary stores
  Yasmin Kanji

      D-U-N-S 25-363-1295   (BR)
LOBLAWS INC
REAL CANADIAN SUPERSTORE
(*Suby of* LOBLAW COMPANIES LIMITED)
3633 Westwinds Dr Ne Unit 100, Calgary, AB,
T3J 5K3
(403) 590-3347
Emp Here 100
SIC 5411 Grocery stores
  Robert Bjordalen

      D-U-N-S 24-128-8146   (SL)
MATRIX MOTORSPORTS
20 Freeport Landng Ne, Calgary, AB, T3J 5H6
(403) 265-5000
Emp Here 210   *Sales* 33,360,180
SIC 3089 Plastics products, nec
  Jim Jiwani

      D-U-N-S 25-992-9938   (BR)
MITCHELL GROUP ALBERTA INC
*COURTYARD BY MARRIOTT CALGARY
AIRPORT*
2500 48 Ave Ne, Calgary, AB, T3J 4V8
(403) 238-1000
Emp Here 100
SIC 7011 Hotels and motels
  Richard Main

      D-U-N-S 20-798-5255   (BR)
**MOXIE'S RESTAURANTS, LIMITED PART-
NERSHIP**
MOXIE'S CLASSIC GRILL
25 Hopewell Way Ne, Calgary, AB, T3J 4V7
(403) 291-4636
Emp Here 100
SIC 5812 Eating places
  Gord Gtant

      D-U-N-S 25-316-4099   (BR)
PASLEY, MAX ENTERPRISES LIMITED
MCDONALD'S
5219 Falsbridge Dr Ne, Calgary, AB, T3J 3C1
(403) 293-4052
Emp Here 90
SIC 5812 Eating places
  Augusto Villanueva

      D-U-N-S 20-582-5404   (SL)
**ROCKY CROSS CONSTRUCTION (NORTH)
LTD**
1610 104 Ave Ne Unit 145, Calgary, AB, T3J
0T5
(403) 252-2550
Emp Here 58   *Sales* 14,354,014
SIC 1771 Concrete work
  Alan Welton
  Marjt Welton

      D-U-N-S 20-058-9658   (BR)
SAPUTO INC
SAPUTO FOOD
(*Suby of* JOLINA CAPITAL INC)
5434 44 St Ne, Calgary, AB, T3J 3Z3
(403) 568-3800
Emp Here 175

SIC 4222 Refrigerated warehousing and storage
  James Gary

      D-U-N-S 25-146-5019   (HQ)
SHARK CLUBS OF CANADA INC
SHARK CLUB QUESNEL
31 Hopewell Way Ne, Calgary, AB, T3J 4V7
(403) 543-2600
Emp Here 3   *Sales* 11,659,750
SIC 5812 Eating places
  R Thomas Gaglardi

      D-U-N-S 24-309-0516   (BR)
SYMCOR INC
(*Suby of* SYMCOR INC)
3663 63 Ave Ne, Calgary, AB, T3J 0G6
(905) 273-1000
Emp Here 270
SIC 7389 Business services, nec

      D-U-N-S 24-394-6212   (SL)
**TELEMETRIX DOWNHOLE TECHNOLO-
GIES INC**
85 Freeport Blvd Be Bay 102, Calgary, AB,
T3J 4X8
(403) 243-2331
Emp Here 49   *Sales* 10,296,419
SIC 1381 Drilling oil and gas wells
  Terry Cennon

Calgary, AB T3K

      D-U-N-S 24-960-9277   (SL)
1 UP INSURANCE INC
36 Panatella Link Nw, AB, T3K 0T6
(403) 910-2442
Emp Here 30   *Sales* 25,441,800
SIC 6411 Insurance agents, brokers, and service
  Kelly Markevich Vanderheyden

      D-U-N-S 25-186-6166   (SL)
B.B. INVESTMENTS INC
BOSTON PIZZA 111
388 Country Hills Blvd Ne Suite 600, Calgary,
AB, T3K 5J6
(403) 226-7171
Emp Here 75   *Sales* 3,413,925
SIC 5812 Eating places
  Dennis Bailey

      D-U-N-S 20-164-0005   (SL)
BEAUMARK PROTECTION SERVICES
20 Country Hills Mews Nw, Calgary, AB, T3K
4S4
(403) 803-1567
Emp Here 30   *Sales* 11,870,340
SIC 7381 Detective and armored car services
  Mark Mitchell

      D-U-N-S 20-552-2357   (SL)
**BEDDINGTON HEIGHTS COMMUNITY AS-
SOCIATION**
375 Bermuda Dr Nw, Calgary, AB, T3K 2J5
(403) 295-8837
Emp Here 27   *Sales* 10,730,178
SIC 8699 Membership organizations, nec
  Michelle Toombs

      D-U-N-S 20-650-3091   (BR)
BETHANY CARE SOCIETY
BETHANY HARVEST HILLS
(*Suby of* BETHANY CARE SOCIETY)
19 Harvest Gold Manor Ne, Calgary, AB, T3K
4Y1
(403) 226-8200
Emp Here 100
SIC 8051 Skilled nursing care facilities
  Nadine Buchart

      D-U-N-S 25-169-9666   (SL)
CALDWELL, C. MARK ENTERPRISE LTD
CANADIAN TIRE
388 Country Hills Blvd Ne Unit 200, Calgary,

AB, T3K 5J6
(403) 226-9550
Emp Here 90   *Sales* 24,088,680
SIC 5251 Hardware stores
  Mark Caldwell
  Christina Caldwell

      D-U-N-S 20-342-5970   (SL)
CERVUS AG EQUIPMENT LP
(*Suby of* CERVUS EQUIPMENT CORPORA-
TION)
333 96 Ave Ne Suite 5201, Calgary, AB, T3K
0S3
(403) 567-0339
Emp Here 100   *Sales* 13,675,900
SIC 0851 Forestry services
  Graham Drake

      D-U-N-S 20-650-6862   (SL)
CERVUS CONTRACTORS EQUIPMENT LTD
JCB EDMONTON
(*Suby of* CERVUS LP)
333 96 Ave Ne Suite 5201, Calgary, AB, T3K
0S3
(877) 567-0339
Emp Here 50   *Sales* 23,751,300
SIC 5082 Construction and mining machinery
  Peter Lacey

      D-U-N-S 25-105-8509   (HQ)
CERVUS CORPORATION
120 Country Hills Landng Nw Suite 205, Cal-
gary, AB, T3K 5P3
(403) 567-0339
Emp Here 5   *Sales* 52,998,805
SIC 6712 Bank holding companies
  Peter Lacey
  Graham Drake
  Gregg Johnson
  Howard Bolinger
  Mike Kohut

      D-U-N-S 20-700-7563   (HQ)
CERVUS EQUIPMENT CORP
333 96 Ave Ne Unit 5201, Calgary, AB, T3K
0S3
(403) 567-0339
Emp Here 4   *Sales* 47,502,600
SIC 5082 Construction and mining machinery
  Peter Lacey

      D-U-N-S 24-828-1685   (HQ)
CERVUS EQUIPMENT CORPORATION
333 96 Ave Ne Suite 5201, Calgary, AB, T3K
0S3
(403) 567-0339
Emp Here 150   *Sales* 1,023,465,750
SIC 5084 Industrial machinery and equipment
  Angela Lekatsas
  Adam Lowther
  Stella Cosby
  Fred Hnatiw
  Cal Johnson
  Peter Lacey
  Larry Benke
  Don Bell
  Steven Collicutt
  Dan Sobic

      D-U-N-S 24-310-5686   (HQ)
CERVUS LP
333 96 Ave Ne Suite 5201, Calgary, AB, T3K
0S3
(403) 275-2215
Emp Here 10   *Sales* 73,414,800
SIC 5999 Miscellaneous retail stores, nec
  Peter Lacey

      D-U-N-S 20-911-0068   (SL)
FRIENDLY TELECOM INC
CALGARY TELECOM
44 Berkshire Crt Nw, Calgary, AB, T3K 1Z5
(403) 243-6688
Emp Here 111   *Sales* 25,360,392
SIC 4899 Communication services, nec
  Brian Jerome

      D-U-N-S 24-369-9910   (SL)

HARMONY LOGISTICS CANADA INC
(*Suby of* DEUTSCHE POST AG)
1724 115 Ave Ne, Calgary, AB, T3K 0P9
(403) 537-8996
Emp Here 150   *Sales* 100,033,800
SIC 4731 Freight transportation arrangement
  Jim Gehr

      D-U-N-S 25-169-9781   (BR)
HOME DEPOT OF CANADA INC
HOME DEPOT
(*Suby of* THE HOME DEPOT INC)
388 Country Hills Blvd Ne Unit 100, Calgary,
AB, T3K 5J6
(403) 226-7500
Emp Here 200
SIC 5251 Hardware stores
  Danielle Schule

      D-U-N-S 24-389-2804   (HQ)
INOVA SYSTEMS CORPORATION
(*Suby of* CHINA NATIONAL PETROLEUM
CORPORATION)
1769 120 Ave Ne, Calgary, AB, T3K 0S5
(403) 537-2100
Sales 19,657,438
SIC 3829 Measuring and controlling devices,
nec
  Glenn Hauer
  Keith Witt
  Tim Hladik

      D-U-N-S 24-013-1086   (HQ)
INTERGRAPH CANADA LTD
(*Suby of* HEXAGON AB)
10921 14 St Ne, Calgary, AB, T3K 2L5
(877) 569-5500
Emp Here 71   *Sales* 81,373,504
SIC 5045 Computers, peripherals, and soft-
ware
  Halsey Wise
  Gerhard Sallinger
  Douglas Morrison
  Peter Thomson
  David Vance Lucas
  R Reid French Jr

      D-U-N-S 25-206-2419   (HQ)
MATRIX VIDEO COMMUNICATIONS CORP
1626 115 Ave Ne Unit 103, Calgary, AB, T3K
2E4
(403) 640-4490
Emp Here 21   *Sales* 21,017,178
SIC 5065 Electronic parts and equipment, nec
  Glenn Burgess
  David Campbell
  Shelly Burgess

      D-U-N-S 24-493-8072   (HQ)
MICRO-WATT CONTROL DEVICES LTD
MICRO-WATT
11141 15 St Ne, Calgary, AB, T3K 0Z5
(403) 250-1594
Emp Here 40   *Sales* 23,751,300
SIC 5084 Industrial machinery and equipment
  Marlene Coffey
  Kenneth Coffey

      D-U-N-S 25-535-1017   (SL)
MICROHARD SYSTEMS INC
150 Country Hills Landng Nw Suite 101, Cal-
gary, AB, T3K 5P3
(403) 248-0028
Emp Here 50   *Sales* 10,233,650
SIC 3669 Communications equipment, nec
  Hany Shenouda

      D-U-N-S 20-900-6555   (SL)
NOTRE DAME HIGH SCHOOL
11900 Country Village Link Ne, Calgary, AB,
T3K 6E4
(403) 500-2109
Emp Here 85   *Sales* 9,156,795
SIC 8661 Religious organizations
  Luc Marmelic

      D-U-N-S 24-066-2007   (HQ)

NOVATEL INC
ADVANCE
(*Suby of* HEXAGON AB)
10921 14 St Ne, Calgary, AB, T3K 2L5
(403) 295-4500
Sales 92,737,060
SIC 3812 Search and navigation equipment
Michael Ritter

D-U-N-S 25-538-3556   (HQ)
NUFARM AGRICULTURE INC
(*Suby of* NUFARM LIMITED)
333 96 Ave Ne Suite 5101, Calgary, AB, T3K
0S3
(403) 692-2500
Sales 24,141,785
SIC 2879 Agricultural chemicals, nec
Brendan Deck
Grant Deveson
Greg Hunt
Lachlan Mckinnon

D-U-N-S 20-112-3440   (HQ)
PARKLAND FUEL CORPORATION
333 96 Ave Ne Suite 6302, Calgary, AB, T3K
0S3
(403) 567-2500
Emp Here 450   *Sales* 10,948,509,084
SIC 2873 Nitrogenous fertilizers
Robert (Bob) Espey
Michael S.H. Mcmillan
C. Peter Kilty
Ian White
Ryan Krogmeier
Christy Elliott
Darren Smart
Ian White
Jim Pantelidis
John Bechtold

D-U-N-S 25-372-2656   (SL)
SUMMIT CARE CORPORATION LTD
NEWPORT HARBOUR CARE CENTRE
10 Country Village Cove Ne, Calgary, AB, T3K
6B4
(403) 567-0461
Emp Here 200   *Sales* 13,713,200
SIC 8051 Skilled nursing care facilities
Joel Bond

Calgary, AB T3L

D-U-N-S 24-361-7193   (BR)
HOME DEPOT OF CANADA INC
HOME DEPOT
(*Suby of* THE HOME DEPOT INC)
5019 Nose Hill Dr Nw, Calgary, AB, T3L 0A2
(403) 241-4060
Emp Here 100
SIC 5251 Hardware stores

D-U-N-S 20-647-3907   (BR)
REVERA INC
SCENIC ACRES RETIREMENT RESIDENCE
(*Suby of* GOVERNMENT OF CANADA)
150 Scotia Landng Nw, Calgary, AB, T3L 2K1
(403) 208-0338
Emp Here 100
SIC 8322 Individual and family services
Sander Duncan

D-U-N-S 20-806-2310   (BR)
SOBEYS CAPITAL INCORPORATED
SOBEYS
(*Suby of* EMPIRE COMPANY LIMITED)
11300 Tuscany Blvd Nw Suite 2020, Calgary,
AB, T3L 2V7
(403) 375-0595
Emp Here 100
SIC 5411 Grocery stores
Maxine Mitchell

Calgary, AB T3M

D-U-N-S 20-284-8719   (BR)
**ALL SENIORS CARE LIVING CENTRES
LTD**
*AUBURN HEIGHTS RETIREMENT RESI-
DENCE*
(*Suby of* ALL SENIORS CARE HOLDINGS
INC)
21 Auburn Bay St Se Suite 428, Calgary, AB,
T3M 2A9
(403) 234-9695
Emp Here 90
SIC 6513 Apartment building operators
Dorothy Britten

D-U-N-S 25-686-3374   (SL)
**COMPUTER UPGRADING SPECIALISTS
LTD**
232 Mahogany Terr Se, Calgary, AB, T3M 0T5
(403) 271-3800
Emp Here 50   *Sales* 10,590,200
SIC 7373 Computer integrated systems de-
sign
Jonathan Redekop

D-U-N-S 25-415-2564   (HQ)
EFW RADIOLOGY
3883 Front St Se Suite 312, Calgary, AB, T3M
2J6
(403) 541-1200
Emp Here 5   *Sales* 31,384,155
SIC 8011 Offices and clinics of medical doctors
David Wiseman

Calgary, AB T3N

D-U-N-S 25-370-1304   (HQ)
ELITE INTERNATIONAL FOODS INC
10725 25 St Ne Bay 124 Bldg B, Calgary, AB,
T3N 0A4
(403) 291-0660
Sales 25,067,310
SIC 5149 Groceries and related products, nec
Adrian Feddema
Brian Boychuk

D-U-N-S 24-786-4796   (HQ)
WORLD WIDE CUSTOMS BROKERS LTD
(*Suby of* KINTETSU WORLD EXPRESS,
INC.)
10710 25 St Ne Unit 133, Calgary, AB, T3N
0A1
(403) 291-2543
Emp Here 14   *Sales* 20,798,680
SIC 4731 Freight transportation arrangement
Des Gouveia
Wendy Edwards
Frank Fujita

Calgary, AB T3P

D-U-N-S 25-109-3563   (HQ)
MJS MECHANICAL LTD
2401 144 Ave Ne, Calgary, AB, T3P 0T3
(403) 250-1355
Sales 11,046,700
SIC 1711 Plumbing, heating, air-conditioning
Bradley Diggens

Calgary, AB T3R

D-U-N-S 24-731-5757   (SL)
CHARLESGLEN LTD
CHARLESGLEN TOYOTA
7687 110 Ave Nw Suite 7687, Calgary, AB,

T3R 1R8
(403) 241-0888
Emp Here 90   *Sales* 56,635,200
SIC 5511 New and used car dealers
Glen Rumpel
Glen Richardson

D-U-N-S 24-308-3586   (BR)
COSTCO WHOLESALE CANADA LTD
(*Suby of* COSTCO WHOLESALE CORPO-
RATION)
11588 Sarcee Trail Nw Suite 543, Calgary, AB,
T3R 0A1
(403) 516-3700
Emp Here 280
SIC 5099 Durable goods, nec
Rick Firth

D-U-N-S 24-101-5259   (BR)
HOME DEPOT OF CANADA INC
HOME DEPOT
(*Suby of* THE HOME DEPOT INC)
11320 Sarcee Trail Nw, Calgary, AB, T3R 0A1
(403) 374-3866
Emp Here 100
SIC 5211 Lumber and other building materials
Cheryl Gathercole

D-U-N-S 24-419-6254   (SL)
LINCIA CORPORATION
CANADIAN TIRE
11940 Sarcee Trail Nw, Calgary, AB, T3R 0A1
(403) 295-0200
Emp Here 40   *Sales* 19,923,120
SIC 5531 Auto and home supply stores
Chris Pustowka

D-U-N-S 24-968-3731   (HQ)
MAVERICK OILFIELD SERVICES LTD
15 Royal Vista Pl Nw Unit 320, Calgary, AB,
T3R 0P3
(403) 234-8822
Emp Here 35   *Sales* 19,182,300
SIC 1389 Oil and gas field services, nec
Michael Schnell
Chris Challis
Kevin Fawns

D-U-N-S 20-026-5024   (SL)
MECHANOVA INC
2501 Bearspaw Summit Pl, Calgary, AB, T3R
1B5

Emp Here 4   *Sales* 12,423,428
SIC 4922 Natural gas transmission

D-U-N-S 24-850-0139   (SL)
PINNACLE WEALTH BROKERS INC
15 Royal Vista Pl Nw Suite 250, Calgary, AB,
T3R 0P3
(855) 628-4286
Emp Here 156   *Sales* 146,511,612
SIC 6211 Security brokers and dealers
Darvin Zurfluh

D-U-N-S 25-831-4934   (SL)
ROYAL OAK LEXUS
7677 112 Ave Nw, Calgary, AB, T3R 1R8
(403) 261-9977
Emp Here 40   *Sales* 19,923,120
SIC 5511 New and used car dealers
Todd Richardson

Calgary, AB T3S

D-U-N-S 24-578-5170   (BR)
ABB INC
(*Suby of* ABB LTD)
9800 Endeavor Dr Se, Calgary, AB, T3S 0A1
(403) 252-7551
Emp Here 150
SIC 3621 Motors and generators
Vaughn Bend

D-U-N-S 24-674-6291   (HQ)

ARBORCARE TREE SERVICE LTD
10100 114 Ave Se, Calgary, AB, T3S 0A5
(403) 273-6378
Emp Here 65   *Sales* 19,999,075
SIC 0783 Ornamental shrub and tree services
Jim Fisher

D-U-N-S 20-110-2183   (HQ)
CHAMCO INDUSTRIES LTD
8900 Venture Ave Se, Calgary, AB, T3S 0A2
(403) 777-1200
Emp Here 60   *Sales* 65,843,550
SIC 5084 Industrial machinery and equipment
Malcolm Cox
Brian Blann
Don Carscadden
Norrey Von Sturmer
George St Clair
Grant Burton

D-U-N-S 25-763-2737   (SL)
ELITE FORMWORK INC
9935 Enterprise Way Se, Calgary, AB, T3S
0A1
(403) 236-7751
Emp Here 65   *Sales* 17,397,380
SIC 5211 Lumber and other building materials
Bill Kerridge
Moira K Jensen
Catherine E.C. Distefano

D-U-N-S 20-317-6776   (SL)
GIUSTI GROUP LIMITED PARTNERSHIP
GIUSTI GROUP
4 Industry Way Se, Calgary, AB, T3S 0A2
(403) 203-0492
Emp Here 100   *Sales* 47,674,200
SIC 1531 Operative builders
Joe Giusti

D-U-N-S 24-346-5924   (SL)
HCM CONTRACTORS INC
9777 Enterprise Way Se, Calgary, AB, T3S
0A1
(403) 248-4884
Emp Here 60   *Sales* 14,771,160
SIC 1794 Excavation work
Craig Rowe
Ron Amos
Brandon Baczkowski

D-U-N-S 24-715-7506   (HQ)
HTH HEATECH INC
61 Industry Way Se, Calgary, AB, T3S 0A2
(403) 279-1990
Emp Here 1   *Sales* 11,626,524
SIC 5074 Plumbing and heating equipment
and supplies (hydronics)
Robert Fitz
Henry Jakl
Greg Pachal

D-U-N-S 25-098-9480   (SL)
NORTH STAR CONTRACTING INC
64 Technology Way Se, Calgary, AB, T3S 0B9
(403) 228-3421
Emp Here 170   *Sales* 42,915,140
SIC 1623 Water, sewer, and utility lines
Steve Skiba

D-U-N-S 25-850-2819   (BR)
PETER KIEWIT INFRASTRUCTURE CO.
(*Suby of* PETER KIEWIT SONS', INC.)
9500 100 St Se, Calgary, AB, T3S 0A2

Emp Here 900
SIC 1611 Highway and street construction

D-U-N-S 20-350-4279   (HQ)
QUANTA TELECOM CANADA LTD
9595 Enterprise Way Se, Calgary, AB, T3S
0A1
(587) 620-0201
Emp Here 1   *Sales* 98,434,500
SIC 1623 Water, sewer, and utility lines
Adam Budzinski
Ken Spangler

▲ Public Company   ■ Public Company Family Member   **HQ** Headquarters   **BR** Branch   **SL** Single Location

Charissa Wangsawidya
David Morettin
Trevor Newington

D-U-N-S 24-308-1366   (SL)
TOTRAN TRANSPORTATION SERVICES LTD
9350 Venture Ave Se, Calgary, AB, T3S 0A2
(403) 723-0025
Emp Here 70   *Sales* 14,399,420
SIC 4213 Trucking, except local
Paul Bamber
Robert Miller
Rosemary Marr
Brad Haaek

D-U-N-S 20-766-8971   (HQ)
TRANS AM PIPING PRODUCTS LTD
(*Suby of* MIRLEVEL SA)
9335 Endeavor Dr Se, Calgary, AB, T3S 0A1
(403) 236-0601
Emp Here 22   *Sales* 25,221,174
SIC 5085 Industrial supplies
Rod Lipman
Dolores Denault

Calgary, AB T3Z

D-U-N-S 20-512-1986   (SL)
BRADON CONSTRUCTION LTD
250031 Mountain View Trail, Calgary, AB, T3Z 3S3
(403) 229-4022
Emp Here 50   *Sales* 15,943,450
SIC 1521 Single-family housing construction
Brad Prather

D-U-N-S 20-181-4337   (HQ)
ICS GROUP INC
250081 Mountain View Trail, Calgary, AB, T3Z 3S3
(403) 247-4440
Emp Here 25   *Sales* 11,387,747
SIC 5722 Household appliance stores
William Henderson
Rick Gamracy
Ken Kachur
Steven Loeppky

D-U-N-S 25-167-3372   (SL)
JERTYNE INTERIOR SERVICES LTD
60 Commercial Dr, Calgary, AB, T3Z 2A7
(403) 219-1046
Emp Here 62   *Sales* 10,067,622
SIC 1742 Plastering, drywall, and insulation
Robert Legault
Lori Legault

D-U-N-S 25-217-7803   (SL)
PETER THE PLANTMAN INC
250010 Mountain View Trail, Calgary, AB, T3Z 3S3
(403) 270-8451
Emp Here 40   *Sales* 13,698,680
SIC 0181 Ornamental nursery products
Peter Hughes

D-U-N-S 20-365-2235   (SL)
ZOMONGO.TV CORP
229 Avro Lane, Calgary, AB, T3Z 3S5
(403) 870-4951
Emp Here 12   *Sales* 36,788,551
SIC 7311 Advertising agencies
Jeremy Ostrowski
Jocelyne Hughes-Ostrowski

Calgary, AB T4B

D-U-N-S 24-373-1226   (SL)
CALGARY ENERGY CENTRE NO. 2 INC
(*Suby of* CITY OF CALGARY, THE)
14417 68 St Ne, Calgary, AB, T4B 2T4

(403) 567-5135
Emp Here 20   *Sales* 12,532,280
SIC 4911 Electric services
Benjamin Abedine

Camrose, AB T4V

D-U-N-S 20-397-2492   (SL)
2122256 ALBERTA LTD
HEAVY METAL EQUIPMENT & RENTALS
4613 41 St, Camrose, AB, T4V 2Y8
(780) 991-9997
Emp Here 300   *Sales* 99,944,400
SIC 7353 Heavy construction equipment rental
Jesse Van Der Werf
Callen Nowicki

D-U-N-S 24-378-2989   (HQ)
BATTLE RIVER IMPLEMENTS LTD
4717 38 St, Camrose, AB, T4V 3W9
(780) 672-4463
Emp Here 50   *Sales* 20,523,552
SIC 5999 Miscellaneous retail stores, nec
Terry Hamilton
Jack Helm

D-U-N-S 25-325-2829   (HQ)
BATTLE RIVER REGIONAL DIVISION 31
5402 48a Ave, Camrose, AB, T4V 0L3
(780) 672-6131
Emp Here 30   *Sales* 63,815,538
SIC 8211 Elementary and secondary schools
Rita Marler
Laurie Skori
Lorrie Sitler
Tracey Boast Radley
Susan Chromik
Norm Erickson
Rebecca Heiberg
Kendall Severson

D-U-N-S 25-969-9809   (SL)
CAMROSE ASSOCIATION FOR COMMU-NITY LIVING
4604 57 St, Camrose, AB, T4V 2E7
(780) 672-0257
Emp Here 125   *Sales* 8,035,250
SIC 8361 Residential care
Karin Naslund
Harold Criggar

D-U-N-S 25-313-5974   (SL)
CAMROSE CHRYSLER LTD
3511 48 Ave, Camrose, AB, T4V 0K9
(780) 672-2476
Emp Here 30   *Sales* 14,942,340
SIC 5511 New and used car dealers
Mike Rodin

D-U-N-S 24-002-7011   (SL)
CAMROSE REGIONAL EXHIBITION AND AGRICULTURAL SOCIETY
4250 Exhibition Dr, Camrose, AB, T4V 4Z8
(780) 672-3640
Emp Here 40   *Sales* 17,968,760
SIC 7389 Business services, nec
Thomas Gerling
Bill Anderson
Chuck Erma

D-U-N-S 20-718-3562   (SL)
CAMROSE SOBEYS CORP
4820 66 St, Camrose, AB, T4V 4P6
(780) 672-5969
Emp Here 80   *Sales* 23,478,160
SIC 5411 Grocery stores
Alain Paquette

D-U-N-S 24-317-2785   (HQ)
CANADIAN NATIONAL STEEL CORPORA-TION
OSM TUBULAR CAMROSE
(*Suby of* EVRAZ PLC)
5302 39 St, Camrose, AB, T4V 2N8

(780) 672-3116
Sales 27,208,200
SIC 3312 Blast furnaces and steel mills
Mike Rehwinkel
Michael Howard

D-U-N-S 24-715-5534   (SL)
CENTRAL AGENCIES INC
4870 51 St, Camrose, AB, T4V 1S1
(780) 679-2170
Emp Here 30   *Sales* 17,397,720
SIC 6411 Insurance agents, brokers, and service
Norman Mayer
Betty Mayer

D-U-N-S 24-827-3927   (HQ)
CROP MANAGEMENT NETWORK INC
4232 41 St Suite 110, Camrose, AB, T4V 4E5
(587) 322-2767
Sales 29,700,800
SIC 5191 Farm supplies
James Mitchell

D-U-N-S 20-969-5373   (SL)
DUTCHMEN EQUIPMENT LTD
4613 41 St, Camrose, AB, T4V 2Y8
(780) 672-7946
Emp Here 249   *Sales* 22,334,304
SIC 7699 Repair services, nec
Jesse Van Der Werf
John Van Der Werf

D-U-N-S 24-001-3136   (SL)
HAUSER, R BUILDING MATERIALS LTD
HAUSER HOME HARDWARE BUILDING CENTRE
6809 48 Ave, Camrose, AB, T4V 4W1
(780) 672-8818
Emp Here 69   *Sales* 18,467,988
SIC 5211 Lumber and other building materials
Robert (Rob) Hauser

D-U-N-S 20-079-0178   (HQ)
HI-WAY 13 TRANSPORT LTD
4621 39 St, Camrose, AB, T4V 0Z4
(780) 672-1695
Emp Here 1   *Sales* 20,570,600
SIC 4212 Local trucking, without storage
Frederick A O'riordan Jr
Robert O'riordan
Kerry O'riordan
Micheal O'riordan

D-U-N-S 20-896-0674   (HQ)
HUTTERIAN BRETHREN CHURCH OF CAMROSE
Gd Lcd Main, Camrose, AB, T4V 1X1
(780) 672-1553
Emp Here 4   *Sales* 11,349,407
SIC 8661 Religious organizations
Paul Tschetter
John Tschetter

D-U-N-S 20-745-7854   (SL)
LAMB FORD SALES LTD
3771 48 Ave, Camrose, AB, T4V 3T4
(780) 672-2411
Emp Here 35   *Sales* 17,432,730
SIC 5511 New and used car dealers
Cliff Denham
Brenda Denham
John Denham
Brian Denham

D-U-N-S 24-393-3731   (SL)
MCCLELLAN WHEATON CHEVROLET LTD
MCCLELLAN WHEATON CHEVROLET BUICK GMS
3850 48 Ave, Camrose, AB, T4V 3Z8
(780) 672-2355
Emp Here 40   *Sales* 19,923,120
SIC 5511 New and used car dealers
William Mcclellan

D-U-N-S 24-686-0154   (BR)
MERIDIAN MANUFACTURING INC
(*Suby of* TREVLUC HOLDINGS LTD)

4232 38 St, Camrose, AB, T4V 4B2
(780) 672-4516
Emp Here 170
SIC 3545 Machine tool accessories
Jeff Kenzie

D-U-N-S 24-004-3893   (SL)
NORSEMEN INN CAMROSE CORPORA-TION
6505 48 Ave, Camrose, AB, T4V 3K3
(780) 672-9171
Emp Here 85   *Sales* 8,066,415
SIC 7011 Hotels and motels
Paula Cramer
Sean Willms

D-U-N-S 24-205-7490   (SL)
NU EDGE CONSTRUCTION LTD
3815a 47 Ave, Camrose, AB, T4V 4S4
(780) 679-7825
Emp Here 8   *Sales* 12,548,800
SIC 1623 Water, sewer, and utility lines
Wayne Bowman

D-U-N-S 24-520-6982   (HQ)
ROSS AGRI-SUPPLIES (CAMROSE) INC
3838 47 Ave, Camrose, AB, T4V 3W8
(780) 672-2529
Emp Here 12   *Sales* 12,901,693
SIC 5171 Petroleum bulk stations and terminals
Roderick Ross
Sheilagh Ross

D-U-N-S 24-206-5964   (BR)
SOBEYS WEST INC
SAFEWAY
(*Suby of* EMPIRE COMPANY LIMITED)
6800 48 Ave Suite 200, Camrose, AB, T4V 4T1
(780) 672-1211
Emp Here 75
SIC 5411 Grocery stores
Tim Burrell

D-U-N-S 25-625-8484   (SL)
ST MARY'S HOSPITAL CAMROSE
4607 53 St, Camrose, AB, T4V 1Y5
(780) 679-6100
Emp Here 249   *Sales* 27,658,920
SIC 8062 General medical and surgical hospitals
John Kelly

D-U-N-S 20-870-0554   (SL)
TITAN LUMBER CORP
4615 39 St, Camrose, AB, T4V 0Z4
(780) 608-1236
Emp Here 10   *Sales* 10,195,213
SIC 5211 Lumber and other building materials
Cary Cruickshank

D-U-N-S 20-736-1739   (BR)
WAL-MART CANADA CORP
(*Suby of* WALMART INC.)
6800 48 Ave Unit 400, Camrose, AB, T4V 4T1
(780) 608-1211
Emp Here 200
SIC 5311 Department stores
Jim Mckay

Canmore, AB T1W

D-U-N-S 20-547-2132   (BR)
ALBERTA HEALTH SERVICES
CANMORE GENERAL HOSPITAL
(*Suby of* GOVERNMENT OF THE PROVINCE OF ALBERTA)
1100 Hospital Pl, Canmore, AB, T1W 1N2
(403) 678-3769
Emp Here 250
SIC 6324 Hospital and medical service plans
Barbara Shellian

D-U-N-S 24-016-2446   (HQ)

CAN-BOW MOTORS LTD
707 Railway Ave, Canmore, AB, T1W 1P2
(403) 678-4222
Sales 14,444,262
SIC 5511 New and used car dealers
Kenneth Pauls
Gaye Pauls

D-U-N-S 24-980-3243   (SL)
CANADIAN TIRE
1110 Gateway Ave, Canmore, AB, T1W 0J1
(403) 678-3295
Emp Here 30   *Sales* 10,926,450
SIC 5014 Tires and tubes
Martha Billes

D-U-N-S 20-807-5718   (SL)
GRAND CANADIAN RESORTS INC
91 Three Sisters Dr, Canmore, AB, T1W 3A1
(403) 678-0018
Emp Here 80   *Sales* 7,679,849
SIC 7011 Hotels and motels
Chi Fang Kim
John Third

D-U-N-S 24-415-9661   (SL)
PIONEER MEATS LTD
VALBELLA MEATS
104 Elk Run Blvd, Canmore, AB, T1W 1L1
(403) 678-4109
Emp Here 20   *Sales* 10,702,480
SIC 5147 Meats and meat products
Walter Von Rotz
Leonie Von Rotz

D-U-N-S 20-515-6339   (SL)
WILD BILL'S SALOON INC
WILD BILLS
737 Main St, Canmore, AB, T1W 2B2
(403) 762-0333
Emp Here 90   *Sales* 4,165,612
SIC 5812 Eating places
Jeff Whitefield

Carbon, AB T0M

D-U-N-S 24-733-0459   (SL)
BERTRAM DRILLING CORP
347 Caradoc Ave, Carbon, AB, T0M 0L0
(403) 572-3591
Emp Here 15   *Sales* 31,372,000
SIC 1382 Oil and gas exploration services
Brian Bertram
Darrell Bertram

D-U-N-S 25-608-6414   (SL)
BRITESTONE HUTTERIAN BRETHREN
Gd, Carbon, AB, T0M 0L0
(403) 572-3046
Emp Here 100   *Sales* 16,902,500
SIC 0119 Cash grains, nec
Michael Mandel

Cardston, AB T0K

D-U-N-S 24-439-4359   (SL)
HUTTERIAN BRETHREN CHURCH OF EAST CARDSTON (1977)
EAST CARDSTON COLONY
Po Box 2520, Cardston, AB, T0K 0K0
(403) 653-2451
Emp Here 84   *Sales* 22,033,956
SIC 0191 General farms, primarily crop
David J Hofer
Gideon A Hofer

D-U-N-S 25-122-4536   (SL)
TALL TIMBER LTD
Gd, Cardston, AB, T0K 0K0

Emp Here 35   *Sales* 17,725,927

SIC 5541 Gasoline service stations
Lester Tailfeathers

D-U-N-S 20-711-3338   (BR)
WESTWIND SCHOOL DIVISION #74
CARDSTON ELEMENTARY SCHOOL
730 4th Ave W, Cardston, AB, T0K 0K0
(403) 653-4955
Emp Here 100
SIC 8211 Elementary and secondary schools
Mark Bennett

Caroline, AB T0M

D-U-N-S 25-686-7177   (BR)
SHELL CANADA LIMITED
(*Suby of* ROYAL DUTCH SHELL PLC)
Gd, Caroline, AB, T0M 0M0
(403) 722-7000
Emp Here 130
SIC 1389 Oil and gas field services, nec
Dave Hamilton

Castor, AB T0C

D-U-N-S 20-770-3518   (SL)
893278 ALBERTA LTD
O K TIRE
5501 50 Ave, Castor, AB, T0C 0X0
(403) 882-4040
Emp Here 100   *Sales* 28,330,000
SIC 7538 General automotive repair shops
Patrick Kelly
Christine Kelly

D-U-N-S 24-494-6810   (SL)
HUTTERIAN BRETHREN CHURCH OF CASTOR
CASTOR COLONY
Gd, Castor, AB, T0C 0X0
(403) 882-3305
Emp Here 122   *Sales* 12,703,006
SIC 8661 Religious organizations
Peter Weldner
David Weldner

D-U-N-S 20-082-7124   (BR)
PARAMOUNT RESOURCES (ACL) LTD
(*Suby of* PARAMOUNT RESOURCES LTD)
5018 50 Ave, Castor, AB, T0C 0X0
(403) 882-3751
Emp Here 150
SIC 1311 Crude petroleum and natural gas

Cayley, AB T0L

D-U-N-S 24-748-1745   (SL)
MACMILLAN HUTTERIAN BRETHREN
658 32 St Sw, Cayley, AB, T0L 0P0
(403) 395-2221
Emp Here 100   *Sales* 10,557,246
SIC 8661 Religious organizations
Tobias Waldner

Champion, AB T0L

D-U-N-S 24-554-5736   (SL)
HUTTERIAN BRETHREN CHURCH OF THE LITTLE BOW
Gd, Champion, AB, T0L 0R0
(403) 897-3838
Emp Here 117   *Sales* 12,182,391
SIC 8661 Religious organizations
Edward Hofer
Joseph Hofer

Paul Hofer
John Hofer
Mike Hofer
Dan Hofer

Chard, AB T0P

D-U-N-S 20-301-5433   (SL)
DENE SKY SITE SERVICES LTD
351 Richard St, Chard, AB, T0P 1G0
(780) 559-2202
Emp Here 50   *Sales* 12,044,200
SIC 1629 Heavy construction, nec
Sherri Herman
Kelly Herman

D-U-N-S 20-525-3920   (SL)
T.J.'S OILFIELD CONTRACTING LTD
Gd, Chard, AB, T0P 1G0

Emp Here 100   *Sales* 31,970,500
SIC 1389 Oil and gas field services, nec
Jaime L. Janvier

Chauvin, AB T0B

D-U-N-S 24-274-5420   (SL)
BENOIT OILFIELD CONSTRUCTION (1997) LTD
(*Suby of* BENOIT OILFIELD CONSTRUCTION LTD)
302 Rupert St, Chauvin, AB, T0B 0V0
(780) 858-3794
Emp Here 50   *Sales* 12,622,100
SIC 1623 Water, sewer, and utility lines
Calvin Winterholt
Daniel Delemont

D-U-N-S 25-679-6368   (HQ)
BENOIT OILFIELD CONSTRUCTION LTD
302 Rupert St, Chauvin, AB, T0B 0V0
(780) 858-3794
Sales 30,293,040
SIC 1623 Water, sewer, and utility lines
Calvin Winterholt
Dan Delemont

D-U-N-S 20-380-5416   (SL)
STEEL VIEW ENERGY & INDUSTRIAL SERVICES LTD
222 Main St, Chauvin, AB, T0B 0V0
(780) 858-3820
Emp Here 52   *Sales* 16,624,660
SIC 1389 Oil and gas field services, nec
Rodney Stang

Chestermere, AB T1X

D-U-N-S 24-363-3844   (BR)
SOBEYS WEST INC
CHESTERMERE SAFEWAY
(*Suby of* EMPIRE COMPANY LIMITED)
135 Chestermere Station Way Unit 100, Chestermere, AB, T1X 1V2
(403) 410-9700
Emp Here 165
SIC 5411 Grocery stores
David Duckworth

D-U-N-S 24-502-5528   (BR)
TDL GROUP CORP, THE
TIM HORTONS
(*Suby of* RESTAURANT BRANDS INTERNATIONAL INC)
120 John Morris Way Suite 300, Chestermere, AB, T1X 1V3
(403) 248-0000
Emp Here 90

SIC 5812 Eating places
Valerie Bruce

Clairmont, AB T8X

D-U-N-S 20-327-7413   (SL)
1673594 ALBERTA LTD
PEACE FUEL DISTRIBUTORS
10702 79 Ave, Clairmont, AB, T8X 5G9
(780) 538-2445
Emp Here 40   *Sales* 50,288,040
SIC 5172 Petroleum products, nec
Ryan Hale

D-U-N-S 20-297-2548   (BR)
AECOM PRODUCTION SERVICES LTD
(*Suby of* AECOM)
10414 84 Ave, Clairmont, AB, T8X 5B2
(780) 539-0069
Emp Here 100
SIC 1731 Electrical work
Ford Randy

D-U-N-S 24-850-2986   (SL)
AUREUS ENERGY SERVICES INC
9510 78 Ave, Clairmont, AB, T8X 0M2
(780) 567-3009
Emp Here 200   *Sales* 37,905,100
SIC 3567 Industrial furnaces and ovens
Jason Tocheniuk

D-U-N-S 24-425-9110   (BR)
CANYON TECHNICAL SERVICES LTD
(*Suby of* TRICAN WELL SERVICE LTD)
9102 102 St Suite 55, Clairmont, AB, T8X 5G8
(780) 357-2250
Emp Here 150
SIC 1389 Oil and gas field services, nec
Dennis Morin

D-U-N-S 24-025-0519   (SL)
EVERGREEN ENERGY LTD
9416 69 Ave, Clairmont, AB, T8X 5B3
(780) 538-3680
Emp Here 140   *Sales* 45,936,100
SIC 1623 Water, sewer, and utility lines
Steve Davie
Jason Van Nieuwkerk
Don Robertson
Shawn Mowet
Brian Pahl

D-U-N-S 20-718-6391   (SL)
FABCOR 2001 INC
(*Suby of* MASTEC, INC.)
10202 74 Ave, Clairmont, AB, T8X 5A7
(780) 532-3350
Emp Here 50   *Sales* 12,622,100
SIC 1623 Water, sewer, and utility lines
Robert Shipway

D-U-N-S 20-086-0807   (BR)
FINNING INTERNATIONAL INC
FINNING CANADA
(*Suby of* FINNING INTERNATIONAL INC)
7601 99 St, Clairmont, AB, T8X 5B1
(780) 831-2600
Emp Here 100
SIC 5082 Construction and mining machinery
Brad Dean

D-U-N-S 25-014-1009   (BR)
HALLIBURTON GROUP CANADA INC
(*Suby of* HALLIBURTON COMPANY)
10202 70 Ave Suite 780, Clairmont, AB, T8X 5A7
(780) 513-8888
Emp Here 500
SIC 1389 Oil and gas field services, nec
Shawn Curry

D-U-N-S 20-979-3517   (HQ)
IPAC SERVICES CORPORATION
8701 102 St, Clairmont, AB, T8X 5G8

▲ Public Company   ■ Public Company Family Member   **HQ** Headquarters   **BR** Branch   **SL** Single Location

(780) 532-7350
Emp Here 100   *Sales* 114,840,250
SIC 1623 Water, sewer, and utility lines
Ron Ward
Derrick Mysko

D-U-N-S 20-248-9373   (SL)
LEADER ENERGY SERVICES LTD
7001 96 St, Clairmont, AB, T8X 5B3
(780) 402-9876
Emp Here 49   *Sales* 15,665,545
SIC 1389 Oil and gas field services, nec
Robert Olivers

D-U-N-S 20-003-6036   (HQ)
NORTHERN MAT & BRIDGE LIMITED PART-NERSHIP
NORTHERN MAT & BRIDGE
8001 99 St, Clairmont, AB, T8X 5B1
(780) 538-4135
Emp Here 20   *Sales* 39,977,760
SIC 7353 Heavy construction equipment rental
Darren Francis
Scott Henderson
Scott Vyse
Collin Wood
Carson Kowal
Shane Stewart
Richard Cotter

D-U-N-S 24-343-1413   (BR)
SCHLUMBERGER CANADA LIMITED
9602 72 Ave, Clairmont, AB, T8X 5B3
(780) 830-4501
Emp Here 200
SIC 1389 Oil and gas field services, nec
John Styre

D-U-N-S 20-720-2859   (SL)
STRATUS PIPELINES LTD
10828 99 St Suite 3, Clairmont, AB, T8X 5B4
(780) 897-0605
Emp Here 80   *Sales* 20,195,360
SIC 1623 Water, sewer, and utility lines
Randy Galbreath
Miles Estabroke

D-U-N-S 20-096-7768   (HQ)
TRANS PEACE CONSTRUCTION (1987) LTD
9626 69 Ave, Clairmont, AB, T8X 5A1
(780) 539-6855
Emp Here 40   *Sales* 15,146,520
SIC 1629 Heavy construction, nec
Paul Dagesse
Greg Haugen

D-U-N-S 20-130-3836   (BR)
TRICAN WELL SERVICE LTD
TRICAN PARTNESHIP
(*Suby of* TRICAN WELL SERVICE LTD)
9701 99 St, Clairmont, AB, T8X 5A8
(780) 567-5200
Emp Here 250
SIC 1389 Oil and gas field services, nec
Rod Sisk

D-U-N-S 24-206-3324   (BR)
WEATHERFORD CANADA LTD
WEATHER WIRELINE
(*Suby of* WEATHERFORD INTERNATIONAL PUBLIC LIMITED COMPANY)
8001 102 St, Clairmont, AB, T8X 5A7
(780) 539-6400
Emp Here 120
SIC 3533 Oil and gas field machinery
Mitch Bacon

Claresholm, AB T0L

D-U-N-S 24-518-8867   (HQ)
WATT & STEWART COMMODITIES INC
4134 3 St E, Claresholm, AB, T0L 0T0

---

(403) 625-4436
Sales 15,567,840
SIC 4213 Trucking, except local
Neil Watt
John Stewart

Cleardale, AB T0H

D-U-N-S 20-694-8460   (SL)
HUTTERIAN BRETHREN CHURCH OF CLEARDALE
CLEARDALE COLONY
Gd, Cleardale, AB, T0H 3Y0
(780) 685-2870
Emp Here 70   *Sales* 12,640,250
SIC 8661 Religious organizations
Eli Stahl

Coaldale, AB T1M

D-U-N-S 20-989-6760   (SL)
BETHEL WINDOWS & DOORS LTD
1504 12 St, Coaldale, AB, T1M 1M3
(403) 345-4401
Emp Here 50   *Sales* 12,652,950
SIC 5211 Lumber and other building materials
Gerald Van Seters

D-U-N-S 20-830-9393   (HQ)
INTERCONTINENTAL TRUCK BODY LTD
I.T.B.
1806 11 St, Coaldale, AB, T1M 1N1
(403) 345-4427
Sales 30,218,805
SIC 3713 Truck and bus bodies
Jacob Van Seters Jr
Arie Van Seters
Harold Vriend
Casey Van Seters

D-U-N-S 25-681-2330   (SL)
NEWCO GRAIN LTD
Gd, Coaldale, AB, T1M 1K8
(403) 345-3335
Emp Here 17   *Sales* 20,576,749
SIC 5153 Grain and field beans

D-U-N-S 25-289-1254   (SL)
ROCK LAKE HUTTERIAN BRETHREN
ROCK LAKE COLONY
Gd Stn Main, Coaldale, AB, T1M 1K8
(403) 345-3892
Emp Here 115   *Sales* 19,437,875
SIC 0191 General farms, primarily crop
Eli Entz

Coalhurst, AB T0L

D-U-N-S 25-682-5654   (SL)
HEADWATER EQUIPMENT SALES LTD
HEADWATER EQUIPMENT
592041 River Ridge Rd Unit 2, Coalhurst, AB, T0L 0V0
(403) 327-3681
Emp Here 30   *Sales* 14,250,780
SIC 5084 Industrial machinery and equipment
Michael E. Stringer
Matthew Stringer

Cochrane, AB T4C

D-U-N-S 24-598-9066   (SL)
641100 ALBERTA LTD
COCHRANE DODGE CHRYSLER JEEP
544 Railway St W, Cochrane, AB, T4C 2E2

---

(403) 932-4072
Emp Here 38   *Sales* 18,926,964
SIC 5511 New and used car dealers
Glen Rumpel
Alex Baum

D-U-N-S 24-159-2427   (SL)
ALL SPAN BUILDING SYSTEMS LTD
424 Griffin Rd W, Cochrane, AB, T4C 2E1
(403) 932-7878
Emp Here 144   *Sales* 27,701,280
SIC 2439 Structural wood members, nec
Bert Lehmann

D-U-N-S 25-703-4996   (SL)
AQUATECH CANADIAN WATER SERVICES INC.
Bay 5 41070 Cook Rd, Cochrane, AB, T4C 1A1
(403) 932-4507
Emp Here 49   *Sales* 14,564,858
SIC 4941 Water supply
Rodney R Schlachter
Jean Pierre Azzopardi

D-U-N-S 25-522-9056   (BR)
BETHANY CARE SOCIETY
(*Suby of* BETHANY CARE SOCIETY)
32 Quigley Dr Unit 1000, Cochrane, AB, T4C 1X9
(403) 932-6422
Emp Here 150
SIC 8051 Skilled nursing care facilities
Jennifer Simon

D-U-N-S 20-303-4301   (BR)
CLEARSTREAM ENERGY SERVICES LIM-ITED PARTNERSHIP
INDUSTRIAL SERVICES - SOUTH REGION
(*Suby of* CLEARSTREAM ENERGY SER-VICES INC)
141 2 Ave E, Cochrane, AB, T4C 2B9
(403) 932-9565
Emp Here 160
SIC 1389 Oil and gas field services, nec
Chuck Lyons

D-U-N-S 20-291-4438   (SL)
COCHRANE MOTOR PRODUCTS LTD
COCHRANE DODGE
6 River Heights Dr, Cochrane, AB, T4C 0N8
(403) 932-4072
Emp Here 45   *Sales* 22,413,510
SIC 5511 New and used car dealers
Rob Pfiefer

D-U-N-S 20-720-2578   (SL)
COCHRANE/EMPRESS V PARTNERSHIP
(*Suby of* INTER PIPELINE LTD)
262145 Range Road 43, Cochrane, AB, T4C 2J8
(403) 932-8555
Emp Here 50   *Sales* 13,477,450
SIC 4619 Pipelines, nec
David W Fesyk

D-U-N-S 25-099-8630   (SL)
GARMIN CANADA INC
DYNASTREAM INNOVATIONS
(*Suby of* GARMIN LTD.)
30 Bow St Common Unit 124, Cochrane, AB, T4C 2N1
(403) 932-9292
Emp Here 78   *Sales* 17,920,812
SIC 8731 Commercial physical research
James Rooney
Andrew Skarsgard

D-U-N-S 25-173-7565   (SL)
HATCH, ROBERT RETAIL INC
CANADIAN TIRE #493
320 5 Ave W, Cochrane, AB, T4C 2E3
(403) 851-0894
Emp Here 52   *Sales* 32,722,560
SIC 5531 Auto and home supply stores
Robert Hatch

D-U-N-S 24-200-3968   (SL)
HEATHERGLENEAGLES GOLF COMPANY

LTD
PLAY GOLF CALGARY
100 Gleneagles Dr, Cochrane, AB, T4C 1P5
(403) 932-1100
Emp Here 400   *Sales* 30,098,000
SIC 7992 Public golf courses
Scott Atkinson
Slade King

D-U-N-S 25-591-3738   (SL)
LINKS OF GLENEAGLES GOLF CORPO-RATION LTD, THE
100 Gleneagles Dr, Cochrane, AB, T4C 1P5
(403) 932-1100
Emp Here 100   *Sales* 7,639,700
SIC 7992 Public golf courses
Scott Atkinson
Slade King

D-U-N-S 20-078-2980   (BR)
SOUTHLAND TRANSPORTATION LTD
(*Suby of* PACIFIC WESTERN TRANSPORTA-TION LTD)
216 Griffin Rd E, Cochrane, AB, T4C 2B9
(403) 932-7100
Emp Here 100
SIC 4151 School buses
Faye Rosling

D-U-N-S 20-079-1333   (SL)
SPRAY LAKE SAWMILLS (1980) LTD
305 Griffin Rd W, Cochrane, AB, T4C 2C4
(403) 932-2234
Emp Here 200   *Sales* 38,474,000
SIC 2491 Wood preserving
Barry Mjolsness

D-U-N-S 24-418-8830   (SL)
WEALTHTERRA CAPITAL MANAGEMENT INC
105 1st St W Suite 104, Cochrane, AB, T4C 1A4
(403) 981-1156
Emp Here 22   *Sales* 14,936,306
SIC 6211 Security brokers and dealers
Nadine Wellwood
Jason Brown

Cold Lake, AB T9M

D-U-N-S 24-392-9692   (SL)
320364 ALBERTA LTD
LAKELAND INN
5411 55 St, Cold Lake, AB, T9M 1R6
(780) 594-3311
Emp Here 100   *Sales* 29,347,700
SIC 5411 Grocery stores
Georges Brosseau
Andries Debeer

D-U-N-S 24-275-3259   (HQ)
370071 ALBERTA LTD
BUMPER TO BUMPER
5609 55 St, Cold Lake, AB, T9M 1R6
(780) 594-4666
Emp Here 12   *Sales* 17,482,320
SIC 5013 Motor vehicle supplies and new parts
Jason Fournier

D-U-N-S 24-034-2480   (BR)
AECOM ENERGY SERVICES LTD
AECOM ENERGY SERVICES LTD
(*Suby of* AECOM)
Hwy 55 W, Cold Lake, AB, T9M 1P7
(780) 639-6034
Emp Here 150
SIC 1799 Special trade contractors, nec
Thomas Lance

D-U-N-S 20-375-0302   (SL)
FEDERATION CONSTRUCTION SERVICES INC
43220 Township Rd 634, Cold Lake, AB, T9M

1N1
(780) 639-0073
Emp Here 50   *Sales* 16,666,650
SIC 1541 Industrial buildings and warehouses
Dave Brown
Robert Cadieux
Michael Patry

D-U-N-S 20-652-6555   (SL)
LAKELAND FETAL ALCOHOL SPECTRUM DISORDER SOCIETY
LAKELAND CENTRE F A S D
4823 50 Ave, Cold Lake, AB, T9M 1Y2
(780) 594-9905
Emp Here 29   *Sales* 20,567,148
SIC 8699 Membership organizations, nec
Coleen Manary
Carmen Bull
Stephanie Oleksyn
Lee Phillip
Michelle Dargis
Bob Wilson
Lorne Kaban
Sandy Kingdon
Audrey Mcfarlane

D-U-N-S 24-598-1282   (SL)
M.P.S. WELDING INC
Gd, Cold Lake, AB, T9M 1P3

Emp Here 215   *Sales* 45,660,840
SIC 1799 Special trade contractors, nec
Nathan Turchyn
Matt Brown
Tyrel Turchyn
Sean Quigg

D-U-N-S 24-034-4122   (BR)
SOBEYS CAPITAL INCORPORATED
COLD LAKE FOODS
(*Suby of* EMPIRE COMPANY LIMITED)
6403 51 St, Cold Lake, AB, T9M 1C8
(780) 594-3335
Emp Here 120
SIC 5411 Grocery stores
Rod Andriachuk

D-U-N-S 20-918-2471   (BR)
WAL-MART CANADA CORP
(*Suby of* WALMART INC.)
4702 43 Ave Suite 3640, Cold Lake, AB, T9M 1M9
(780) 840-2340
Emp Here 120
SIC 5311 Department stores
Elf White

Conklin, AB T0P

D-U-N-S 24-349-3405   (SL)
KINGDOM CATS LTD
108 Christina Lake Dr, Conklin, AB, T0P 1H1
(780) 715-4356
Emp Here 40   *Sales* 18,829,240
SIC 1542 Nonresidential construction, nec
Jason King

Coronation, AB T0C

D-U-N-S 25-681-6034   (HQ)
M & N CONSTRUCTION LTD
(*Suby of* API GROUP INC.)
4511 Victoria Ave, Coronation, AB, T0C 1C0
(403) 578-2016
Sales 52,498,400
SIC 1623 Water, sewer, and utility lines
Archie Merchant
Darcey Hewitt
Bryan Tellier

Cremona, AB T0M

D-U-N-S 25-236-2298   (HQ)
DALZIEL ENTERPRISES LTD
3439 Hwy 580, Cremona, AB, T0M 0R0
(403) 337-3264
Emp Here 4   *Sales* 14,850,400
SIC 5191 Farm supplies
Gilbert Dalziel
Barbara Dalziel

Crooked Creek, AB T0H

D-U-N-S 25-084-9619   (SL)
RIDGE VALLEY COLONY LTD
Gd, Crooked Creek, AB, T0H 0Y0
(780) 957-2607
Emp Here 80   *Sales* 10,940,720
SIC 0291 General farms, primarily animals
Ike Walter

Crossfield, AB T0M

D-U-N-S 24-420-2458   (SL)
DEMON OILFIELD SERVICES INC
812 Laut Ave, Crossfield, AB, T0M 0S0
(403) 946-4800
Emp Here 90   *Sales* 28,773,450
SIC 1389 Oil and gas field services, nec
Cory Finley
Robin Finley

D-U-N-S 24-914-5579   (SL)
FAIRVIEW COLONY
Gd, Crossfield, AB, T0M 0S0
(403) 946-4524
Emp Here 30   *Sales* 10,274,010
SIC 0119 Cash grains, nec
Peter Holfer

D-U-N-S 20-867-4767   (HQ)
GREYWOLF PRODUCTION SYSTEMS INC
(*Suby of* TETRA TECHNOLOGIES, INC.)
805 Laut Ave, Crossfield, AB, T0M 0S0
(403) 946-4445
Sales 28,773,450
SIC 1389 Oil and gas field services, nec
Mark Stormoen
J.P. Trottier

D-U-N-S 24-893-6333   (BR)
HIGHLINE MUSHROOMS WEST LIMITED
HIGHLINE MUSHROOMS
(*Suby of* HIGHLINE MUSHROOMS WEST LIMITED)
281090 Service Rd, Crossfield, AB, T0M 0S0
(403) 464-4396
Emp Here 100
SIC 0182 Food crops grown under cover

D-U-N-S 20-200-1587   (SL)
KOWAL CONSTRUCTION ALTA. LTD
601 Mccool St, Crossfield, AB, T0M 0S0
(403) 946-4450
Emp Here 150   *Sales* 36,927,900
SIC 1794 Excavation work
Carter Kowal

D-U-N-S 20-115-3892   (HQ)
MAXFIELD INC
(*Suby of* TERRAVEST INDUSTRIES INC)
1026 Western Dr, Crossfield, AB, T0M 0S0
(403) 946-5678
Emp Here 112   *Sales* 56,175,400
SIC 3533 Oil and gas field machinery
Mitch Debelser
Andy Robert
Cedric Schwartz
Logan Leys

Elmo Lim
Steve Hemphill

D-U-N-S 20-772-7129   (SL)
MODUS STRUCTURES INC
34 Mccool Cres, Crossfield, AB, T0M 0S0
(403) 274-2422
Emp Here 120   *Sales* 23,050,200
SIC 3448 Prefabricated Metal buildings and components
John Verhagen
Maurizio Simonelli
Joe Dotto
Mark Cole
Cal Harvey
Chris Denis
James Nicholson
Tom Payne

D-U-N-S 24-777-5757   (SL)
NEUDORF COLONY EQUIPMENT CO LTD
Gd, Crossfield, AB, T0M 0S0
(403) 946-4801
Emp Here 40   *Sales* 13,698,680
SIC 0191 General farms, primarily crop

D-U-N-S 24-119-4992   (SL)
PALLISER LUMBER SALES LTD
(*Suby of* BRINK FOREST PRODUCTS LTD)
16 Mccool Cres, Crossfield, AB, T0M 0S0
(403) 946-5494
Emp Here 180
SIC 2421 Sawmills and planing mills, general
Howie Kroon
Bob Murphy
Patrick Carley

D-U-N-S 24-854-8067   (BR)
PLASTI-FAB LTD
(*Suby of* PLASTI-FAB LTD)
802 Mccool St, Crossfield, AB, T0M 0S0
(403) 946-4576
Emp Here 100
SIC 2821 Plastics materials and resins
Thomas Edward Green

Cypress County, AB T1A

D-U-N-S 20-378-1807   (SL)
MURRAY LAKE COLONY FARMING CO. LTD
6517 Township Rd 110, Cypress County, AB, T1A 7N3
(587) 824-2004
Emp Here 25   *Sales* 15,669,540
SIC 0191 General farms, primarily crop
Richard Hoser

Cypress County, AB T1B

D-U-N-S 20-565-0745   (SL)
STEEP ROCK LTD
11524 Range Road 52 Unit 1, Cypress County, AB, T1B 0K7
(403) 529-9668
Emp Here 24   *Sales* 10,732,176
SIC 5032 Brick, stone, and related material
Douglas Bauman

Daysland, AB T0B

D-U-N-S 25-236-3569   (BR)
ALBERTA HEALTH SERVICES
DAYSLAND HEALTH CENTRE
(*Suby of* GOVERNMENT OF THE PROVINCE OF ALBERTA)
5920 51 Ave, Daysland, AB, T0B 1A0

(780) 374-3746
Emp Here 100
SIC 8062 General medical and surgical hospitals
Mariann Wolbeck

De Winton, AB T0L

D-U-N-S 24-363-9064   (SL)
ARTISTIC STUCCO LTD
Gd, De Winton, AB, T0L 0X0
(403) 888-7412
Emp Here 24   *Sales* 11,297,544
SIC 1542 Nonresidential construction, nec
Mario Rusnac
Cameilia Rusnac

D-U-N-S 24-344-2431   (SL)
HAMER TREE SERVICES LTD
SASKATOON FARM, THE
Gd, De Winton, AB, T0L 0X0
(403) 938-6245
Emp Here 40   *Sales* 13,024,000
SIC 5992 Florists
Paul Hamer
Karen Hamer

D-U-N-S 24-675-2257   (SL)
MULDOWNEY HOLDINGS LTD
Gd, De Winton, AB, T0L 0X0
(403) 253-0399
Emp Here 200   *Sales* 97,546,000
SIC 5084 Industrial machinery and equipment
Celia Muldowney
Gerard Muldowney

D-U-N-S 25-507-3538   (SL)
WESTECH INTERIORS LTD
21 Pinehurst Rr 3, De Winton, AB, T0L 0X0
(403) 630-6768
Emp Here 40   *Sales* 17,739,600
SIC 7389 Business services, nec
Greg Newhouse
Sharra Newhouse

Delburne, AB T0M

D-U-N-S 25-846-5066   (SL)
GRAEME'S AUTO SERVICE
Po Box 115, Delburne, AB, T0M 0V0
(403) 318-6088
Emp Here 36   *Sales* 22,654,080
SIC 5541 Gasoline service stations

Devon, AB T9G

D-U-N-S 25-135-6028   (BR)
BLACK GOLD REGIONAL DIVISION #18
JOHN MALAND HIGH SCHOOL
(*Suby of* BLACK GOLD REGIONAL DIVISION #18)
105 Athabasca Ave, Devon, AB, T9G 1A4
(780) 987-3709
Emp Here 3,025
SIC 8211 Elementary and secondary schools
Darren Caldwell

D-U-N-S 20-044-6167   (SL)
DEVON CHRYSLER DODGE JEEP RAM LTD
7 Saskatchewan Ave W, Devon, AB, T9G 1B2
(888) 342-9117
Emp Here 38   *Sales* 23,912,640
SIC 5511 New and used car dealers

D-U-N-S 25-555-2148   (SL)
PURE ENERGY REIKI
16 Wild Hay Dr, Devon, AB, T9G 1S4

---

(780) 405-7606
Emp Here 5   *Sales* 15,529,285
SIC 4924 Natural gas distribution

Didsbury, AB T0M

D-U-N-S 24-451-0835   (BR)
ACCREDITED SUPPORTS TO THE COMMUNITY
(*Suby of* ACCREDITED SUPPORTS TO THE COMMUNITY)
1709 15th Ave, Didsbury, AB, T0M 0W0
(403) 335-8671
Emp Here 100
SIC 8322 Individual and family services
Kathy Williams

D-U-N-S 25-194-3619   (BR)
ALBERTA HEALTH SERVICES
DIDSBURY DISTRICT HEALTH SERVICES
(*Suby of* GOVERNMENT OF THE PROVINCE OF ALBERTA)
1210 20e Ave, Didsbury, AB, T0M 0W0
(403) 335-9393
Emp Here 250
SIC 8062 General medical and surgical hospitals
Leone Regner

D-U-N-S 25-230-2302   (SL)
CHRISTOPHER'S WELDING LTD
CWL
Gd, Didsbury, AB, T0M 0W0

Emp Here 60   *Sales* 19,182,300
SIC 1389 Oil and gas field services, nec
Christopher Overwater
William Shaw

D-U-N-S 24-647-0835   (HQ)
MOUNTAIN VIEW SENIORS HOUSING
1100a 20 Ave, Didsbury, AB, T0M 0W0
(403) 335-8404
Emp Here 1   *Sales* 10,927,940
SIC 8361 Residential care
Alvin Melton
Ernie Ryckman

D-U-N-S 20-090-8031   (SL)
TARA OILFIELD SERVICES LTD
1805 19 St, Didsbury, AB, T0M 0W0
(403) 335-9158
Emp Here 50   *Sales* 10,506,550
SIC 1389 Oil and gas field services, nec
Marty Sheridan

Drayton Valley, AB T7A

D-U-N-S 20-114-6144   (SL)
BAILEY'S WELDING & CONSTRUCTION INC
6205 56 Ave, Drayton Valley, AB, T7A 1S5
(780) 542-3578
Emp Here 55   *Sales* 13,540,230
SIC 1799 Special trade contractors, nec
Dennis Bailey
Rhonda Bailey

D-U-N-S 20-364-2210   (BR)
BELLATRIX EXPLORATION LTD
(*Suby of* BELLATRIX EXPLORATION LTD)
5516 Industrial Rd, Drayton Valley, AB, T7A 1R1
(403) 266-8670
Emp Here 85
SIC 1381 Drilling oil and gas wells
Allan Winters

D-U-N-S 24-553-4318   (SL)
BOB DALE OILFIELD CONSTRUCTION LTD
DEAN SEELY BOBDALE
5309 56th Ave, Drayton Valley, AB, T7A 1S7

(780) 542-4834
Emp Here 250   *Sales* 82,028,750
SIC 1629 Heavy construction, nec
Dale Maconochie
Beverly Maconochie

D-U-N-S 24-065-3451   (HQ)
BRANDETTE WELL SERVICING LTD
3202 63 St, Drayton Valley, AB, T7A 1R6
(780) 542-3404
Sales 31,970,500
SIC 1389 Oil and gas field services, nec
Brian Winder
Claudette Winder

D-U-N-S 24-103-9424   (BR)
CONOCOPHILLIPS WESTERN CANADA PARTNERSHIP
BURLINGTON RESOURCES
(*Suby of* CONOCOPHILLIPS)
Gd Stn Main, Drayton Valley, AB, T7A 1T1

Emp Here 80
SIC 1311 Crude petroleum and natural gas
Mark Novak

D-U-N-S 24-671-7904   (SL)
CROSSROADS REGIONAL HEALTH AUTHORITY
DRAYTON VALLEY HOSPTIAL HEALTH CENTRE
4550 Madsen Ave, Drayton Valley, AB, T7A 1N8
(780) 542-5321
Emp Here 250   *Sales* 27,770,000
SIC 8062 General medical and surgical hospitals
Malcolm Maxwell

D-U-N-S 20-838-3328   (SL)
DIAL OILFIELD SERVICES 2006 LTD
5136 54 St, Drayton Valley, AB, T7A 1S2
(780) 542-5879
Emp Here 86   *Sales* 27,494,630
SIC 1389 Oil and gas field services, nec
Len Thesen
Valerie Thesen

D-U-N-S 24-520-3281   (SL)
DOCKTOR OILFIELD TRANSPORT CORP
6225 54 Ave, Drayton Valley, AB, T7A 1S8

Emp Here 35   *Sales* 11,377,872
SIC 1389 Oil and gas field services, nec
James Chaput

D-U-N-S 24-068-1288   (SL)
DRAYTON VALLEY FORD SALES LTD
5214 Power Centre Blvd, Drayton Valley, AB, T7A 0A5
(780) 542-4438
Emp Here 44   *Sales* 21,915,432
SIC 5511 New and used car dealers
Robert Leasack

D-U-N-S 24-129-2635   (SL)
HAYDUK PICKER SERVICE LTD
Gd, Drayton Valley, AB, T7A 1T1
(780) 542-3217
Emp Here 50   *Sales* 10,506,550
SIC 1389 Oil and gas field services, nec
Kevin Hayduk

D-U-N-S 20-282-1315   (HQ)
KANDREA INSULATION (1995) LIMITED
5604b 58 Ave, Drayton Valley, AB, T7A 0B1
(780) 542-6847
Emp Here 44   *Sales* 16,238,100
SIC 1742 Plastering, drywall, and insulation
Jason Vogel
Sadek El Choufi
Chris Martel
Gilles Wandler
Michael Ceniza
Jason Mcmullen
Dylan James
Glen Mitchell

D-U-N-S 20-918-5276   (SL)
KELLY, JIM BUILDING MATERIALS LTD
DRAYTON VALLEY HOME HARDWARE
4221 50 St, Drayton Valley, AB, T7A 1S1
(780) 542-4044
Emp Here 60   *Sales* 16,059,120
SIC 5251 Hardware stores
James Kelly

D-U-N-S 24-732-3124   (SL)
NELSON BROS. OILFIELD SERVICES 1997 LTD
(*Suby of* NELSON BROS. OILFIELD SERVICES LTD)
5399 Jubilee Ave, Drayton Valley, AB, T7A 1R9
(780) 542-5777
Emp Here 35   *Sales* 11,189,675
SIC 1389 Oil and gas field services, nec
Donald Nelson
Garry Nelson

D-U-N-S 20-087-7368   (HQ)
NELSON BROS. OILFIELD SERVICES LTD
5399 Jubilee Ave, Drayton Valley, AB, T7A 1R9
(780) 542-5777
Sales 11,189,675
SIC 1389 Oil and gas field services, nec
Donald Nelson

D-U-N-S 24-238-2732   (SL)
NEWFORCE ENERGY SERVICES LTD
5710 - 57 Ave, Drayton Valley, AB, T7A 1S7
(780) 514-7882
Emp Here 60   *Sales* 15,146,520
SIC 1623 Water, sewer, and utility lines
Darren Nelson

D-U-N-S 24-227-5555   (BR)
NUVISTA ENERGY LTD
(*Suby of* NUVISTA ENERGY LTD)
5219 53 Ave, Drayton Valley, AB, T7A 1R9

Emp Here 150
SIC 1389 Oil and gas field services, nec
Chris Mcdavid

D-U-N-S 25-679-4900   (SL)
PRAIRIE MOUNTAIN OILFIELD CONSTRUCTION INC
4002 62 St, Drayton Valley, AB, T7A 1S1
(780) 542-3995
Emp Here 100   *Sales* 31,970,500
SIC 1389 Oil and gas field services, nec
James Pollock
Clinton Coyne

D-U-N-S 25-992-9388   (SL)
STETSON MOTORS (2000) LTD
2451 50th St, Drayton Valley, AB, T7A 1S4
(780) 542-5391
Emp Here 30   *Sales* 14,942,340
SIC 5511 New and used car dealers
Scott Swendseid
Cole Swendseid

D-U-N-S 24-319-1074   (BR)
WAL-MART CANADA CORP
WALMART
(*Suby of* WALMART INC.)
5217 Power Centre Blvd, Drayton Valley, AB, T7A 0A5
(780) 514-3207
Emp Here 120
SIC 5311 Department stores
Tina Bough

D-U-N-S 25-684-2733   (BR)
WEYERHAEUSER COMPANY LIMITED
(*Suby of* WEYERHAEUSER COMPANY)
Gd Stn Main, Drayton Valley, AB, T7A 1T1
(780) 542-8000
Emp Here 500
SIC 2493 Reconstituted wood products
Jeff Fickett

D-U-N-S 24-816-0264   (SL)

WILLOWS CONSTRUCTION (2001) LTD
WILLOWS NATURAL RESOURCE GROUP
6305 54 Ave, Drayton Valley, AB, T7A 1R0
(780) 621-0447
Emp Here 50   *Sales* 12,309,300
SIC 1794 Excavation work
Robert L Willows

Drumheller, AB T0J

D-U-N-S 24-980-2992   (SL)
DRUMHELLER AND REGION TRANSITION SOCIETY
D.A.R.T.S.
105 3rd Ave E, Drumheller, AB, T0J 0Y0
(403) 823-6690
Emp Here 80   *Sales* 5,473,760
SIC 8322 Individual and family services
Lorelei Martin
Patsy Stokalko
Colleen Pennington

D-U-N-S 20-080-1850   (SL)
DRUMHELLER CO-OP LTD
555 Hwy 10 E, Drumheller, AB, T0J 0Y0
(403) 823-5555
Emp Here 95   *Sales* 27,725,066
SIC 5411 Grocery stores
Brent Walker
David Kosolofski
Eric Poettcker
Barry Fullerton

D-U-N-S 20-635-9713   (HQ)
HI-WAY 9 EXPRESS LTD
(*Suby of* MULLEN GROUP LTD)
711 Elgin Close, Drumheller, AB, T0J 0Y0
(403) 823-4242
Emp Here 35   *Sales* 55,314,300
SIC 4212 Local trucking, without storage
Reg Trentham
Joe Hearn
Virginia Rathberger
Jerry Allen
Graham Mcdonald

D-U-N-S 24-125-2019   (HQ)
SMH MANAGEMENT INC
CANALTA HOTELS
545 Hwy 10 E, Drumheller, AB, T0J 0Y0
(403) 823-2030
Emp Here 40   *Sales* 10,973,280
SIC 8741 Management services
Sharlene Christianson

D-U-N-S 24-552-3774   (SL)
VERDANT VALLEY FARMING CO LTD
Gd, Drumheller, AB, T0J 0Y0
(403) 823-4388
Emp Here 64   *Sales* 21,917,888
SIC 0191 General farms, primarily crop
Benjamin Wipf
John Wipf

D-U-N-S 24-647-4902   (BR)
W. RALSTON (CANADA) INC
(*Suby of* INTEPLAST GROUP CORPORATION)
1100 Railway Ave S, Drumheller, AB, T0J 0Y0
(403) 823-3468
Emp Here 75
SIC 3089 Plastics products, nec
Michael Conley

D-U-N-S 24-319-6917   (BR)
WAL-MART CANADA CORP
WALMART
(*Suby of* WALMART INC.)
1801 South Railway Ave, Drumheller, AB, T0J 0Y2
(403) 820-7744
Emp Here 120
SIC 5311 Department stores
Dexter Heide

D-U-N-S 20-990-6338   (SL)
WESTERN CHEVROLET PONTIAC BUICK GMC LTD
906 Hwy 9 S, Drumheller, AB, T0J 0Y0
(403) 823-3371
Emp Here 32   *Sales* 15,938,496
SIC 5511 New and used car dealers
Hellar Pylypiw
Glen Riger

Duchess, AB T0J

D-U-N-S 24-344-3686   (SL)
SPRINGSIDE HUTTERIAN BRETHREN LTD
Gd, Duchess, AB, T0J 0Z0
(403) 378-4734
Emp Here 107   *Sales* 13,351,032
SIC 8741 Management services
David P. Wipf
Elias Wipf
Peter P. Hofer Jr

Dunmore, AB T0J

D-U-N-S 24-068-4907   (SL)
EAGLE BUTTE CROSSING (TEMPO)
7 3rd Ave E; Dunmore, AB, T0J 1A1
(403) 526-6552
Emp Here 25   *Sales* 12,451,950
SIC 5541 Gasoline service stations
Jamie White

Dunmore, AB T1B

D-U-N-S 20-119-3799   (SL)
LMT ENTERPRISES LTD
2235 2 Ave, Dunmore, AB, T1B 0K3
(403) 527-1562
Emp Here 60   *Sales* 15,146,520
SIC 1629 Heavy construction, nec
Terrance Meier
Darcy Meier

D-U-N-S 24-490-4681   (SL)
MEDICINE HAT HARLEY-DAVIDSON
1923 2 Ave, Dunmore, AB, T1B 0K3
(403) 527-9235
Emp Here 30   *Sales* 18,878,400
SIC 5571 Motorcycle dealers
Ivan Karsten

D-U-N-S 24-673-8389   (SL)
WEDDINGSTAR INC
2032 Bullshead Rd, Dunmore, AB, T1B 0K9
(403) 529-1110
Emp Here 107   *Sales* 22,275,600
SIC 5199 Nondurable goods, nec
Richard Brink
Helle Bertram Brink

Eckville, AB T0M

D-U-N-S 20-080-3567   (SL)
SKOCDOPOLE CONSTRUCTION LTD
ALUMINIUM PIPE SYSTEMS
Gd, Eckville, AB, T0M 0X0
(403) 746-5744
Emp Here 50   *Sales* 12,044,200
SIC 1623 Water, sewer, and utility lines
Clifford Skocdopole

Edberg, AB T0B

D-U-N-S 20-267-2791   (SL)
SIEMENS CONSTRUCTION INC
Gd, Edberg, AB, T0B 1J0
(780) 877-2478
Emp Here 30   *Sales* 14,285,489
SIC 1542 Nonresidential construction, nec
Vernon Siemens

D-U-N-S 20-118-5639   (SL)
SIEMENS, VERNON CONSTRUCTION INC
Gd, Edberg, AB, T0B 1J0
(780) 877-2478
Emp Here 30   *Sales* 14,121,930
SIC 1542 Nonresidential construction, nec
Vernon Siemens
Rhonda Siemens

Edmonton, AB T5A

D-U-N-S 25-272-6302   (BR)
ALBERTA HEALTH SERVICES
NORTHEAST COMMUNITY HEALTH CENTRE
(*Suby of* GOVERNMENT OF THE PROVINCE OF ALBERTA)
14007 50 St Nw, Edmonton, AB, T5A 5E4
(780) 342-4000
Emp Here 229
SIC 8062 General medical and surgical hospitals
Heather Dursling

D-U-N-S 20-101-1962   (HQ)
BARTLE & GIBSON CO LTD
13475 Fort Rd Nw, Edmonton, AB, T5A 1C6
(780) 472-2850
Emp Here 100   *Sales* 174,816,720
SIC 5074 Plumbing and heating equipment and supplies (hydronics)
Robert Whitty
Martin Lower

D-U-N-S 25-269-8675   (SL)
BATEMAN FOODS (1995) LTD
13504 Victoria Trail Nw, Edmonton, AB, T5A 5C9
(780) 432-1535
Emp Here 200   *Sales* 58,695,400
SIC 5411 Grocery stores
Michael Bateman
Deanne Bateman

D-U-N-S 20-081-2014   (HQ)
CAPITAL PACKERS HOLDINGS INC
12907 57 St Nw, Edmonton, AB, T5A 0E7
(780) 476-1391
Sales 32,802,000
SIC 6719 Holding companies, nec
Brent Komarnicki

D-U-N-S 25-105-3534   (SL)
CAPITAL PACKERS INC
(*Suby of* CAPITAL PACKERS HOLDINGS INC)
12907 57 St Nw, Edmonton, AB, T5A 0E7
(780) 476-1391
Emp Here 120   *Sales* 41,482,800
SIC 2011 Meat packing plants
Brent Komarnicki

D-U-N-S 24-331-4101   (SL)
CROZIER, DONNA & JOHN LIMITED
CANADIAN TIRE STORE
13211 Fort Rd Nw, Edmonton, AB, T5A 1C3
(780) 473-2394
Emp Here 120   *Sales* 75,513,600
SIC 5531 Auto and home supply stores
John Crozier
Donna Crozier

D-U-N-S 25-206-2476   (SL)
EARL'S RESTAURANT (CLAREVIEW) LTD
13330 50 St Nw, Edmonton, AB, T5A 4Z8

(780) 473-9008
Emp Here 150   *Sales* 6,827,850
SIC 5812 Eating places
Leroy E. Fuller
J. Cameron Allard

D-U-N-S 24-978-5338   (BR)
HOME DEPOT OF CANADA INC
HOME DEPOT
(*Suby of* THE HOME DEPOT INC)
13304 50 St Nw, Edmonton, AB, T5A 4Z8
(780) 478-7133
Emp Here 120
SIC 5251 Hardware stores
Mike Wiley

D-U-N-S 24-394-1770   (SL)
LONDONDERRY DODGE CHRYSLER JEEP LTD
13333 Fort Rd Nw, Edmonton, AB, T5A 1C3
(780) 665-4851
Emp Here 190   *Sales* 119,563,200
SIC 5511 New and used car dealers
Robert Harms

D-U-N-S 25-260-0564   (SL)
NORTH-ED (1994) LTD
TIM HORTONS
12996 50 St Nw, Edmonton, AB, T5A 4L2
(780) 457-0221
Emp Here 170   *Sales* 7,738,230
SIC 5812 Eating places
Dale Reinke
Janet Reinke

D-U-N-S 20-810-3908   (BR)
REVERA LONG TERM CARE INC
MILLER CROSSING CARE CENTRE
(*Suby of* GOVERNMENT OF CANADA)
14251 50 St Nw, Edmonton, AB, T5A 5J4
(780) 478-9212
Emp Here 170
SIC 8051 Skilled nursing care facilities
Kelly Roberts

D-U-N-S 25-271-0801   (BR)
SOBEYS WEST INC
SAFEWAY
(*Suby of* EMPIRE COMPANY LIMITED)
500 Manning Cross Nw, Edmonton, AB, T5A 5A1
(780) 475-2896
Emp Here 210
SIC 5411 Grocery stores
Wes Mayes

Edmonton, AB T5B

D-U-N-S 24-281-2592   (HQ)
AXE MUSIC INC
11931 Wayne Gretzky Drive Northbound Nw, Edmonton, AB, T5B 1Y4
(780) 471-2001
Emp Here 70   *Sales* 23,240,300
SIC 5736 Musical instrument stores
Brian Holowaychuk
Darrell Holowaychuk

D-U-N-S 20-069-0985   (HQ)
BEN CALF ROBE SOCIETY OF EDMONTON
12046 77 St Nw, Edmonton, AB, T5B 2G7
(780) 477-6648
Emp Here 75   *Sales* 5,815,870
SIC 8322 Individual and family services
Patricia Dallaire

D-U-N-S 20-899-8468   (HQ)
CONCORDIA UNIVERSITY COLLEGE OF ALBERTA
CONCORDIA UNIVERSITY OF EDMONTON
(*Suby of* LUTHERAN CHURCH-CANADA)
7128 Ada Blvd Nw, Edmonton, AB, T5B 4E4
(780) 479-8481
Emp Here 300   *Sales* 49,354,550
SIC 8221 Colleges and universities

Gerald Krispin
Richard Willie
Richard Currie
Martin Mueller
Mark Damielson
Ken Eifert
Merv Fingas
Al Gerdung
Joel Haberstock
Mark Hennig

D-U-N-S 24-360-4811   (BR)
EDMONTON NORTHLANDS
NORTHLANDS SPECTRUM
(*Suby of* EDMONTON NORTHLANDS)
7410 Borden Park Rd Nw, Edmonton, AB, T5B 0H8
(780) 471-8174
Emp Here 400
SIC 7999 Amusement and recreation, nec
Chris Roberts

D-U-N-S 24-318-6751   (BR)
EDMONTON NORTHLANDS
REXALL PLACE
(*Suby of* EDMONTON NORTHLANDS)
7424 118 Ave Nw, Edmonton, AB, T5B 4M9
(780) 471-7210
Emp Here 2,100
SIC 7922 Theatrical producers and services
Sherilee Fosum

D-U-N-S 25-262-9647   (SL)
EDMONTON NORTHSTARS ATHLETIC CLUB
7308 112 Ave Nw, Edmonton, AB, T5B 0E3
(780) 471-0010
Emp Here 30   *Sales* 21,276,360
SIC 8699 Membership organizations, nec
Rick Mcadie
Shayne Mcara
Laurie Mcara
Kim Green
Kevin Jennings

D-U-N-S 20-081-8904   (HQ)
EDMONTON TRANSFER LTD
SOKIL TRANSPORTATION SERVICES
8830 126 Ave Nw, Edmonton, AB, T5B 1G9
(780) 477-1111
Emp Here 145   *Sales* 41,141,200
SIC 4213 Trucking, except local
William Sokil
Robert Sokil
Gregory Sokil
Russell Sokil

D-U-N-S 24-396-9128   (SL)
FABKO FOOD LTD
(*Suby of* 400369 ALBERTA LTD)
8715 126 Ave Nw, Edmonton, AB, T5B 1G8

Emp Here 35   *Sales* 10,271,695
SIC 5421 Meat and fish markets
Frank Bassili
Kathren Bassili

D-U-N-S 20-028-8954   (SL)
HABITAT FOR HUMANITY EDMONTON SOCIETY
8210 Yellowhead Trail Nw, Edmonton, AB, T5B 1G5
(780) 479-3566
Emp Here 40   *Sales* 10,837,680
SIC 1521 Single-family housing construction
Alfred Nikolai

D-U-N-S 20-869-6208   (SL)
HALFORD HIDE TRADING CO. LTD
8629 126 Ave Nw, Edmonton, AB, T5B 1G8
(780) 474-4989
Emp Here 10   *Sales* 12,244,157
SIC 5159 Farm-product raw materials, nec
Steven Unrau

D-U-N-S 20-807-5093   (SL)
HARLEY DAVIDSON MOTORCYCLES OF EDMONTON (1980) LTD

7420 Yellowhead Trail Nw, Edmonton, AB, T5B
1G3
(780) 451-7857
Emp Here 30   *Sales* 14,942,340
SIC 5571 Motorcycle dealers
Kenneth Kent
Alma Kent

D-U-N-S 24-139-9521   (HQ)
LIFT BOSS INC
LIFT BOSS MATERIAL HANDLING GROUP
7912 Yellowhead Trail Nw, Edmonton, AB, T5B
1G3
(780) 474-9900
Emp Here 26   *Sales* 18,526,014
SIC 5084 Industrial machinery and equipment
Andre Gagnon
Dale Beatty
Marc Tougas

D-U-N-S 20-276-9899   (BR)
**PREMIUM BRANDS HOLDINGS CORPO-
RATION**
QUALITY FAST FOOD
(*Suby of* PREMIUM BRANDS HOLDINGS
CORPORATION)
12251 William Short Rd Nw, Edmonton, AB,
T5B 2B7
(780) 474-5201
Emp Here 100
SIC 2099 Food preparations, nec
Kevin Kelly

D-U-N-S 20-066-5037   (SL)
PROTEGRA INC
12031 76 St Nw, Edmonton, AB, T5B 2C9

Emp Here 182   *Sales* 22,709,232
SIC 8741 Management services
Norbert Frank

D-U-N-S 25-993-0303   (HQ)
R.T.A. HOLDINGS LTD
RBL WAREHOUSE DISTRIBUTORS
12029 75 St Nw, Edmonton, AB, T5B 0X3
(780) 436-9949
Sales 14,932,815
SIC 5013 Motor vehicle supplies and new
parts
Doug Ripley
Eric Nitschman

D-U-N-S 20-084-4124   (HQ)
SOKIL EXPRESS LINES LTD
8830 126 Ave Nw, Edmonton, AB, T5B 1G9
(780) 479-1955
Emp Here 50   *Sales* 37,027,080
SIC 4213 Trucking, except local
William Sokil
Russell Sokil

Edmonton, AB T5C

D-U-N-S 24-702-9820   (SL)
394045 ALBERTA LTD
J & D FOOD SERVICES
8007 127 Ave Nw, Edmonton, AB, T5C 1R9
(780) 473-6567
Emp Here 65   *Sales* 54,312,505
SIC 5141 Groceries, general line
Linda Lee
Wendy Wong
Ck Chan

D-U-N-S 24-333-3593   (BR)
ARMY & NAVY DEPT. STORE LIMITED
ARMY & NAVY DEPT. STORE NO.12
(*Suby of* ARMY & NAVY DEPT. STORE LIM-
ITED)
100 Londonderry Mall Unit A, Edmonton, AB,
T5C 3C8

Emp Here 75
SIC 5399 Miscellaneous general merchandise
Russell Kennedy

D-U-N-S 20-651-6390   (BR)
EDMONTON SCHOOL DISTRICT NO. 7
M.E. LAZERTE SCHOOL
(*Suby of* EDMONTON SCHOOL DISTRICT
NO. 7)
6804 144 Ave Nw, Edmonton, AB, T5C 3C7
(780) 408-9800
Emp Here 138
SIC 8211 Elementary and secondary schools
Kim Backs

D-U-N-S 25-110-0012   (BR)
HUDSON'S BAY COMPANY
BAY, THE
(*Suby of* HUDSON'S BAY COMPANY)
1 Londonderry Mall Nw Unit 86, Edmonton,
AB, T5C 3C8
(780) 478-2931
Emp Here 132
SIC 5311 Department stores
Roger Blum

D-U-N-S 24-582-3489   (HQ)
**ST MICHAEL'S EXTENDED CARE CENTRE
SOCIETY**
ST. MICHAEL'S HEALTH GROUP
7404 139 Ave Nw, Edmonton, AB, T5C 3H7
(780) 473-5621
Emp Here 374   *Sales* 25,622,250
SIC 8051 Skilled nursing care facilities
Stan Fisher
Wendy King

D-U-N-S 20-974-4130   (HQ)
**ST MICHAEL'S LONG TERM CARE CEN-
TRE**
ST MICHAEL'S HEALTH GROUP
(*Suby of* ST MICHAEL'S EXTENDED CARE
CENTRE SOCIETY)
7404 139 Ave Nw, Edmonton, AB, T5C 3H7
(780) 473-5621
Sales 23,914,100
SIC 8051 Skilled nursing care facilities
John Kopeck

Edmonton, AB T5E

D-U-N-S 20-210-1866   (HQ)
963618 ALBERTA LTD
PETRO CANADA
13205 97 St Nw, Edmonton, AB, T5E 4C7
(780) 478-7833
Emp Here 5   *Sales* 24,903,900
SIC 5541 Gasoline service stations
Tanya Leverington

D-U-N-S 20-573-2329   (BR)
**COMPAGNIE DES CHEMINS DE FER NA-
TIONAUX DU CANADA**
CANADIAN NATIONAL RAILWAY
(*Suby of* COMPAGNIE DES CHEMINS DE
FER NATIONAUX DU CANADA)
10229 127 Ave Nw, Edmonton, AB, T5E 0B9
(780) 472-3452
Emp Here 300
SIC 4011 Railroads, line-haul operating
Lyle Peterson

D-U-N-S 20-573-2964   (BR)
**COMPAGNIE DES CHEMINS DE FER NA-
TIONAUX DU CANADA**
(*Suby of* COMPAGNIE DES CHEMINS DE
FER NATIONAUX DU CANADA)
11703 127 Ave Nw, Edmonton, AB, T5E 0C9
(780) 472-3486
Emp Here 2,500
SIC 4011 Railroads, line-haul operating

D-U-N-S 24-354-3951   (HQ)
DEALERSHIP INVESTMENTS LIMITED
13145 97 St Nw, Edmonton, AB, T5E 4C4
(780) 476-6221
Sales 37,756,800
SIC 5511 New and used car dealers

Fred W Gibson

D-U-N-S 25-269-7040   (SL)
EDMONTON CATHOLIC SCHOOLS
*ARCHBISHOP O'LEARY CATHOLIC HIGH
SCHOOL*
8760 132 Ave Nw, Edmonton, AB, T5E 0X8
(780) 476-6251
Emp Here 135   *Sales* 13,381,065
SIC 8211 Elementary and secondary schools
Alan Jenkins
Art Uganec

D-U-N-S 20-551-2655   (SL)
EL BASIL GROUP INC
SPASATION SALON & DAY SPA
13026 97 St Nw Suite 203, Edmonton, AB,
T5E 4C6
(780) 406-7272
Emp Here 180   *Sales* 14,138,100
SIC 7991 Physical fitness facilities
Hussein Rahal

D-U-N-S 25-388-5669   (SL)
KENTWOOD FORD SALES INC
13344 97 St Nw, Edmonton, AB, T5E 4C9
(780) 476-8600
Emp Here 120   *Sales* 75,513,600
SIC 5511 New and used car dealers
Michael Priestner

D-U-N-S 20-436-9177   (HQ)
KINGSWAY MOTORS (1982) LTD
KINGSWAY TOYOTA
12820 97 St Nw, Edmonton, AB, T5E 4C3
(780) 478-8300
Emp Here 57   *Sales* 53,488,800
SIC 5511 New and used car dealers
Daniel Ens
Herbert Anton
Kyle Richard
Paul Stocks
Bill Jensen

D-U-N-S 24-014-4357   (SL)
KIPNESS CENTRE FOR VETERANS INC
CAPITAL CARE
4470 Mccrae Ave Nw, Edmonton, AB, T5E
6M8
(780) 442-5700
Emp Here 140   *Sales* 20,003,060
SIC 8641 Civic and social associations
Betty Kolewaski

D-U-N-S 20-437-1025   (SL)
**NORTHGATE CHEVROLET BUICK GMC
LIMITED PARTNERSHIP**
13215 97 St Nw, Edmonton, AB, T5E 4C7
(780) 476-3371
Emp Here 90   *Sales* 56,635,200
SIC 5511 New and used car dealers
Don Humphreys
Bob Humphreys

D-U-N-S 20-084-4942   (SL)
STEDELBAUER CHEVROLET INC
(*Suby of* DEALERSHIP INVESTMENTS LIM-
ITED)
13145 97 St Nw, Edmonton, AB, T5E 4C4
(780) 476-6221
Emp Here 60   *Sales* 37,756,800
SIC 5511 New and used car dealers
Frederick W. Gibson
Ronald W. Gibson

D-U-N-S 24-854-0890   (SL)
VENTA CARE CENTRE LTD
13525 102 St Nw, Edmonton, AB, T5E 4K3
(780) 476-6633
Emp Here 100   *Sales* 6,873,300
SIC 8051 Skilled nursing care facilities
Peter Birzgalis
Ausma Birzgalis
John Birzgalis

D-U-N-S 25-408-9279   (SL)
ZANE HOLDINGS LTD
ALBERTA HONDA

9525 127 Ave Nw, Edmonton, AB, T5E 6M7
(780) 474-7921
Emp Here 65   *Sales* 18,414,500
SIC 7538 General automotive repair shops
Bart Yachimec

Edmonton, AB T5G

D-U-N-S 24-523-7730   (HQ)
301776 ALBERTA LTD
HEALTH CARE & REHAB SPECIALTY
10611 Kingsway Nw Suite 114, Edmonton,
AB, T5G 3C8
(780) 424-6094
Sales 22,358,700
SIC 5047 Medical and hospital equipment
Murray Mack

D-U-N-S 24-642-9021   (HQ)
ADTEL INC
11630 Kingsway Nw, Edmonton, AB, T5G 0X5
(780) 424-7777
Sales 13,476,570
SIC 7389 Business services, nec
Gerald Gerling

D-U-N-S 20-086-6952   (HQ)
BUCHANAN, GORDON ENTERPRISES LTD
BUCHANAN LUMBER DIV OF
34 Airport Rd Nw, Edmonton, AB, T5G 0W7
(780) 424-2202
Emp Here 2   *Sales* 34,049,490
SIC 2421 Sawmills and planing mills, general
Gordon Buchanan
Greg Buchanan

D-U-N-S 20-746-2128   (SL)
**CHATEAU LOUIS HOTEL & CONFERENCE
CENTRE LTD**
CHATEAU LOUIS
11727 Kingsway Nw, Edmonton, AB, T5G 3A1
(780) 452-7770
Emp Here 150   *Sales* 13,903,500
SIC 7011 Hotels and motels
Julian Koziak
Donald Koziak
Neil Koziak
Kathy Grey
Basil Koziak

D-U-N-S 24-480-7400   (SL)
**CHIP REIT NO 16 OPERATIONS LIMITED
PARTNERSHIP**
RAMADA HOTEL & CONFERENCE CENTER
11830 Kingsway Nw Suite 906, Edmonton,
AB, T5G 0X5
(780) 454-9521
Emp Here 200   *Sales* 18,538,000
SIC 7011 Hotels and motels
Kevin Grayston
Ed Pitoniak

D-U-N-S 25-513-3811   (SL)
CITITEL INC
(*Suby of* MOBILCAST CORPORATION)
11830 114 Ave Nw Suite 202, Edmonton, AB,
T5G 0E1
(780) 489-1212
Emp Here 30   *Sales* 13,476,570
SIC 7389 Business services, nec
Joseph Kantor
Donna Martell

D-U-N-S 25-269-5747   (SL)
DAVENPORT SALES & AUTO SERVICE LTD
CANADIAN TIRE ASSOCIATE STORE
11839 Kingsway Nw, Edmonton, AB, T5G 3J7
(780) 413-8473
Emp Here 100   *Sales* 62,928,000
SIC 5531 Auto and home supply stores
David Davenport
Jacqueline Davenport

D-U-N-S 20-360-2458   (SL)

EDMONTON INVESTORS GROUP LTD
EDMONTON OILERS OFFICES
11230 110 St Nw, Edmonton, AB, T5G 3H7
(780) 414-4000
Emp Here 80   *Sales* 6,970,240
SIC 7941 Sports clubs, managers, and promoters
Patrick Laforge
Kevin Lowe
Darryl Boessenkool
Stew Macdonald

        D-U-N-S 20-970-2471   (SL)
EDMONTON PETROLEUM CLUB
11110 108 St Nw Suite 1, Edmonton, AB, T5G 2T2
(780) 474-3411
Emp Here 75   *Sales* 18,113,625
SIC 8621 Professional organizations
David Wright
Wayne Mcarthur

        D-U-N-S 20-698-6460   (BR)
HUDSON'S BAY COMPANY
(*Suby of* HUDSON'S BAY COMPANY)
650 Kingsway Garden Mall Nw, Edmonton, AB, T5G 3E6
(780) 479-7100
Emp Here 100
SIC 5311 Department stores
Dave Reid

        D-U-N-S 20-016-3314   (HQ)
INSPECTIONS GROUP INC, THE
12010 111 Ave Nw, Edmonton, AB, T5G 0E6
(780) 454-5048
Emp Here 60   *Sales* 26,953,140
SIC 7389 Business services, nec
John Kasper
Randy Peterson

        D-U-N-S 20-198-4940   (BR)
LAVTOR HOLDINGS (ALBERTA) LTD
SMITTY'S FAMILY RESTAURANT
(*Suby of* LAVTOR HOLDINGS (ALBERTA) LTD)
1 Kingsway Garden Mall Nw Suite 555, Edmonton, AB, T5G 3A6
(780) 479-1313
Emp Here 120
SIC 5812 Eating places
Douglas Bisset

        D-U-N-S 20-197-3968   (BR)
MCG RESTAURANTS LTD
MOXIE'S CLASSIC GRILL RESTAURANTS
(*Suby of* MCG RESTAURANTS LTD)
10628 Kingsway Nw, Edmonton, AB, T5G 0W8
(780) 944-0232
Emp Here 100
SIC 5812 Eating places
Ian Jones

        D-U-N-S 20-809-8772   (HQ)
METIS EDUCATION FOUNDATION OF THE METIS NATION OF ALBERTA ASSOCIATION, THE
11738 Kingsway Nw Suite 100, Edmonton, AB, T5G 0X5
(780) 455-2200
Emp Here 40   *Sales* 39,009,250
SIC 8651 Political organizations
Audrey Poitras
Trevor Gladuee
Lorne Gladue
Irene Collins

        D-U-N-S 24-330-3125   (SL)
MGN CONSTRUCTORS INC
11760 109 St Nw Unit W306, Edmonton, AB, T5G 2T8
(780) 471-4840
Emp Here 35   *Sales* 11,666,655
SIC 1541 Industrial buildings and warehouses
Dennis Lawrence

        D-U-N-S 25-499-1060   (HQ)

MOBILE INSURANCE SERVICE LTD
11356 119 St Nw Unit 201, Edmonton, AB, T5G 2X4
(780) 477-8838
Emp Here 20   *Sales* 18,657,320
SIC 6411 Insurance agents, brokers, and service
Joe Tinelli

        D-U-N-S 24-025-4172   (SL)
N.S.M. AUTO LTD
NORTH SIDE MITSUBISHI
9670 125a Ave Nw Suite Side, Edmonton, AB, T5G 3E5
(780) 479-5700
Emp Here 50   *Sales* 24,903,900
SIC 5511 New and used car dealers
Darien Bannink

        D-U-N-S 20-242-3062   (SL)
NITE TOURS INTERNATIONAL
SANDCASTLE TOURS
67 Airport Rd Nw, Edmonton, AB, T5G 0W6

Emp Here 25   *Sales* 12,999,175
SIC 4725 Tour operators
Darin Feth

        D-U-N-S 24-395-2751   (HQ)
NORTHERN ALBERTA INSTITUTE OF TECHNOLOGY
NAIT
11762 106 St Nw Unit 108, Edmonton, AB, T5G 3H2
(780) 471-6248
Emp Here 5   *Sales* 287,146,291
SIC 8222 Junior colleges
Glenn Feltham
James Cumming
James Block
Berry Calder
George Andrews
Diane Brickner
Kerry Brown
Jeff Fitzner
Allan Mah
Keith Meagher

        D-U-N-S 20-718-2259   (BR)
NORTHERN ALBERTA INSTITUTE OF TECHNOLOGY
NAIT
(*Suby of* NORTHERN ALBERTA INSTITUTE OF TECHNOLOGY)
10504 Princess Elizabeth Ave Nw, Edmonton, AB, T5G 3K4
(780) 471-6248
Emp Here 500
SIC 8222 Junior colleges
Jean Knutson

        D-U-N-S 24-854-8208   (SL)
PEMCO CONSTRUCTION LTD
50 Airport Rd Nw, Edmonton, AB, T5G 0W7
(780) 414-5410
Emp Here 24   *Sales* 11,968,177
SIC 8742 Management consulting services
Milan Fischgrund
Josef Lapes

        D-U-N-S 25-149-8994   (SL)
RGO OFFICE PRODUCTS EDMONTON LTD
11624 120 St Nw, Edmonton, AB, T5G 2Y2
(780) 413-6600
Emp Here 50   *Sales* 10,880,650
SIC 5943 Stationery stores
Kenneth Barry

        D-U-N-S 20-178-5867   (HQ)
WESTERN HOG EXCHANGE
10319 Princess Elizabeth Ave Nw, Edmonton, AB, T5G 0Y5
(780) 474-8292
Emp Here 10   *Sales* 15,735,161
SIC 5154 Livestock
Mack Rennie

        Edmonton, AB T5H

        D-U-N-S 24-584-4220   (HQ)
340107 ALBERTA LTD
SORRENTINO'S BISTRO BAR
10665 109 St Nw, Edmonton, AB, T5H 3B5
(780) 474-6466
Emp Here 25   *Sales* 13,991,700
SIC 5812 Eating places
Carmelo Rago
Maria Saccomanno

        D-U-N-S 20-014-0429   (HQ)
595028 ALBERTA LTD
DOTS
11825 105 Ave Nw, Edmonton, AB, T5H 0L9
(780) 421-7361
Emp Here 20   *Sales* 13,454,700
SIC 5621 Women's clothing stores
April Glowicki

        D-U-N-S 24-864-0203   (HQ)
902776 N.W.T. LIMITED
FROBISHER INN
10835 120 St Nw, Edmonton, AB, T5H 3P9
(780) 452-4333
Emp Here 5   *Sales* 10,290,500
SIC 7011 Hotels and motels
Douglas Cox

        D-U-N-S 24-320-4449   (BR)
ALBERTA HEALTH SERVICES
ROYAL ALEXANDRA HOSPITAL
(*Suby of* GOVERNMENT OF THE PROVINCE OF ALBERTA)
10240 Kingsway Nw, Edmonton, AB, T5H 3V9
(780) 735-4111
Emp Here 100
SIC 8062 General medical and surgical hospitals

        D-U-N-S 20-084-8224   (HQ)
ALBERTS RESTAURANTS LTD
ALBERTS FAMILY RESTAURANT
10550 115 St Nw, Edmonton, AB, T5H 3K6
(780) 429-1259
Sales 13,292,115
SIC 5812 Eating places
Henry Cynamon
Moshe Felber
Abe Goldstein

        D-U-N-S 24-398-7104   (HQ)
BOYS & GIRLS CLUBS OF EDMONTON, THE
9425 109a Ave Nw, Edmonton, AB, T5H 1G1
(780) 424-8181
Emp Here 30   *Sales* 15,742,360
SIC 8322 Individual and family services
Ross Tyson
Carol Johnson
Guy Smith

        D-U-N-S 20-081-1636   (BR)
CANADIAN LINEN AND UNIFORM SERVICE CO
CANADIAN DOORMAT AND MOP SERVICES
(*Suby of* ARAMARK)
8631 Stadium Rd Nw, Edmonton, AB, T5H 3W9
(780) 665-3905
Emp Here 115
SIC 7213 Linen supply

        D-U-N-S 24-854-5535   (HQ)
CANADIAN URBAN LIMITED
10572-105 St Nw, Edmonton, AB, T5H 2W7
(780) 424-7722
Emp Here 62   *Sales* 15,228,720
SIC 8742 Management consulting services
David Lopatka
Jay Hamilton

        D-U-N-S 24-384-2213   (HQ)
CAPITAL POWER CORPORATION

10423 101 St Nw Suite 1200, Edmonton, AB, T5H 0E9
(780) 392-5100
Emp Here 350   *Sales* 946,869,398
SIC 4911 Electric services
Brian Vaasjo
Kate Chisholm
Darcy Trufyn
Jacquie Pylypiuk
Bryan Deneve
Mark Zimmerman
Donald Lowry
Albrecht Bellstedt
Doyle Beneby
Jill Gardiner

        D-U-N-S 20-919-1670   (BR)
CATHOLIC SOCIAL SERVICES
(*Suby of* CATHOLIC SOCIAL SERVICES)
10709 105 St Nw, Edmonton, AB, T5H 2X3
(780) 424-3545
Emp Here 80
SIC 8399 Social services, nec
Buddy Winder

        D-U-N-S 20-888-7757   (SL)
CHIMO YOUTH RETREAT CENTRE
10585 111 St Nw Suite 103, Edmonton, AB, T5H 3E8
(780) 420-0324
Emp Here 80   *Sales* 5,473,760
SIC 8322 Individual and family services
Frank Wingrove

        D-U-N-S 24-582-7019   (HQ)
CONSTRUCTION & GENERAL WORKERS UNION LOCAL NO. 92
THE LABORS INTERNATIONAL UNION OF NORTH AMERICA
(*Suby of* LABORERS INTERNATIONAL UNION OF NORTH AMERICA)
10319 106 Ave Nw Suite 104, Edmonton, AB, T5H 0P4
(780) 426-6630
Emp Here 19   *Sales* 10,170,108
SIC 8631 Labor organizations
Patrick Mcgill
Larry Sandham

        D-U-N-S 25-100-7753   (SL)
CP ENERGY MARKETING L.P.
EPCOR CANADA
(*Suby of* CAPITAL POWER CORPORATION)
2000-10423 101 St Nw, Edmonton, AB, T5H 0E8
(403) 717-4600
Emp Here 200
SIC 4911 Electric services
Donald Lowry

        D-U-N-S 25-400-1589   (BR)
EDMONTON CATHOLIC SEPARATE SCHOOL DISTRICT NO.7
ST. JOSEPH HIGH SCHOOL AND ASCENSION COLLEGIATE
(*Suby of* EDMONTON CATHOLIC SEPARATE SCHOOL DISTRICT NO.7)
10830 109 St Nw, Edmonton, AB, T5H 3C1
(780) 426-2010
Emp Here 100
SIC 8211 Elementary and secondary schools
Hugh Macdonald

        D-U-N-S 20-029-0232   (HQ)
EDMONTON CITY CENTRE CHURCH CORPORATION
KIDS IN THE HALL BISTRO
9321 Jasper Ave Nw, Edmonton, AB, T5H 3T7
(780) 424-1201
Emp Here 200   *Sales* 10,027,385
SIC 5812 Eating places
Kristin Morra
Ross Lizzote

        D-U-N-S 24-135-7784   (SL)
EDMONTON DENTAL SUPPLIES LTD
INTER PRO DENTAL LAB
10578 109 St Nw, Edmonton, AB, T5H 3B2

(780) 429-2567
Emp Here 40   *Sales* 17,886,960
SIC 5047 Medical and hospital equipment
 Kim Starko

D-U-N-S 20-808-7890   (HQ)
EDMONTON SCHOOL DISTRICT NO. 7
EDMONTON PUBLIC SCHOOL BOARD
1 Kingsway Nw, Edmonton, AB, T5H 4G9
(780) 429-8000
Emp Here 500   *Sales* 885,038,806
SIC 8211 Elementary and secondary schools
 Michelle Draper
 Bridget Stirling
 Todd Burnstad

D-U-N-S 24-353-7771   (HQ)
EPCOR DISTRIBUTION & TRANSMISSION INC
(*Suby of* CITY OF EDMONTON)
10423 101 St Nw Suite 2000, Edmonton, AB, T5H 0E8
(780) 412-3414
Emp Here 45   *Sales* 626,348,320
SIC 4911 Electric services
 Hugh John Bolton
 James Edward Clarke Carter
 Alexander Mackay
 Steven Emmanuel Matyas
 Allister John Mcphearson
 Douglas Harding Mitchell
 Robert Lawrence Philips
 Laurence Pollock
 Helen Katrina Sinclair
 Wesley Robert Twiss

D-U-N-S 25-389-1311   (HQ)
EPCOR UTILITIES INC
(*Suby of* CITY OF EDMONTON)
10423 101 St Nw Suite 2000, Edmonton, AB, T5H 0E8
(780) 412-3414
Emp Here 1,500   *Sales* 1,439,349,170
SIC 4941 Water supply
 Stuart Lee
 Guy Bridgeman
 Jennifer Addison
 John Elford
 Frank Mannarino
 Amanda Rosychuk
 Stephen Stanley
 Hugh Bolton
 Sheila Weatherill
 Richard Cruickshank

D-U-N-S 20-515-2254   (HQ)
EPCOR WATER SERVICES INC
(*Suby of* CITY OF EDMONTON)
10423 101 St Nw Suite 2000, Edmonton, AB, T5H 0E8
(780) 412-3850
Sales 61,420,100
SIC 4971 Irrigation systems
 Stuart Lee
 John Patterson
 Tony Scozzafava
 Guy Bridgeman
 Jennifer Addison

D-U-N-S 20-896-0344   (HQ)
EXCEL RESOURCES SOCIETY
27 DOLLAR BUSINESS CARD CO
10814 106 Ave Nw Suite 300, Edmonton, AB, T5H 4E1
(780) 455-2601
Emp Here 25   *Sales* 82,827,200
SIC 8399 Social services, nec
 Sharon Read
 Scott Kashuba
 Gary Rentz

D-U-N-S 24-333-4120   (BR)
GOVERNING COUNCIL OF THE SALVA-TION ARMY IN CANADA, THE
GOVERNING COUNCIL OF THE SALVATION ARMY IN CANADA,
(*Suby of* GOVERNING COUNCIL OF THE SALVATION ARMY IN CANADA, THE)

9611 102 Ave Nw, Edmonton, AB, T5H 0E5
(780) 429-4274
Emp Here 80
SIC 8322 Individual and family services
 Mark Stanley

D-U-N-S 24-394-6985   (HQ)
HOPE MISSION SOCIETY
9908 106 Ave Nw, Edmonton, AB, T5H 0N6
(780) 422-2018
Emp Here 1   *Sales* 41,413,600
SIC 8399 Social services, nec
 Bruce Reith

D-U-N-S 20-082-6220   (HQ)
ITALIAN CENTRE SHOP SOUTH LTD
10878 95 St Nw, Edmonton, AB, T5H 2E4
(780) 424-4869
Emp Here 89   *Sales* 55,467,153
SIC 5411 Grocery stores
 Teresa Spinelli

D-U-N-S 24-003-7788   (HQ)
K.R.S. TECHNICAL SERVICES LIMITED
COLOURS ART
10660 105 St Nw, Edmonton, AB, T5H 2W9
(780) 426-7820
Emp Here 5   *Sales* 13,077,650
SIC 6712 Bank holding companies
 Keith Harcus
 Susan Harcus
 Kenneth Harcus

D-U-N-S 24-983-5471   (HQ)
KINNIKINNICK FOODS INC
10940 120 St Nw, Edmonton, AB, T5H 3P7
(780) 732-7527
Emp Here 125   *Sales* 46,956,320
SIC 5461 Retail bakeries
 Jerry Bigam

D-U-N-S 20-083-2012   (HQ)
MCBAIN CAMERA LTD
(*Suby of* MCB HOLDINGS LTD)
10805 107 Ave Nw, Edmonton, AB, T5H 0W9
(780) 420-0404
Emp Here 30   *Sales* 21,989,520
SIC 5946 Camera and photographic supply stores
 Allen Ross Mcbain
 Neil Mcbain

D-U-N-S 20-852-5290   (SL)
MCCALLUM PRINTING GROUP INC
BURKE MEDIA
11755 108 Ave Nw, Edmonton, AB, T5H 1B8
(780) 455-8885
Emp Here 90   *Sales* 12,184,740
SIC 2759 Commercial printing, nec
 Darren Pohl
 Sandy Maclellan
 Reginald Stanton

D-U-N-S 25-231-7326   (HQ)
MDS INVESTMENTS LTD
10914 120 St Nw, Edmonton, AB, T5H 3P7
(780) 452-3110
Emp Here 1   *Sales* 69,006,600
SIC 5075 Warm air heating and air condition-ing
 Daniel Sorochan

D-U-N-S 25-385-9300   (HQ)
MEDICAL IMAGING CONSULTANTS
11010 101 St Nw Suite 203, Edmonton, AB, T5H 4B9
(780) 426-1121
Emp Here 80   *Sales* 66,572,450
SIC 8011 Offices and clinics of medical doc-tors
 Ron Van Vliet

D-U-N-S 24-894-9166   (SL)
PURVIS HOLDINGS LTD
WATERLOO FORD
11420 107 Ave Nw, Edmonton, AB, T5H 0Y5
(780) 423-4330
Emp Here 150   *Sales* 41,002,500

SIC 6712 Bank holding companies
 Randall Purvis
 Janey Purvis-Ross
 Jeanne Purvis

D-U-N-S 20-084-3753   (HQ)
SINCLAIR SUPPLY LTD
(*Suby of* MDS INVESTMENTS LTD)
10914 120 St Nw, Edmonton, AB, T5H 3P7
(780) 452-3110
Emp Here 65   *Sales* 69,006,600
SIC 5075 Warm air heating and air condition-ing
 Paul K. Lachambre

D-U-N-S 20-084-4249   (HQ)
SOPER'S SUPPLY LTD
(*Suby of* WAYMOR HOLDINGS LTD)
10519 114 St Nw, Edmonton, AB, T5H 3J6
(780) 423-4066
Emp Here 15   *Sales* 12,520,872
SIC 5063 Electrical apparatus and equipment
 James Moroz
 Ileen Moroz

D-U-N-S 20-083-1766   (SL)
SUM IT CORPORATION
EDEN TEXTILES
(*Suby of* SUMM IT CORPORATION)
10934 120 St Nw, Edmonton, AB, T5H 3P7
(780) 452-7200
Emp Here 50   *Sales* 24,916,100
SIC 5131 Piece goods and notions
 Steven Rice
 Mike Wilson

D-U-N-S 25-359-3990   (HQ)
TECHNICARE IMAGING LTD
TECHNICARE
10924 119 St Nw, Edmonton, AB, T5H 3P5
(780) 424-7161
Emp Here 27   *Sales* 19,783,900
SIC 7384 Photofinish laboratories
 Tom Harmon

D-U-N-S 24-321-2532   (SL)
TRAVEL ALBERTA IN-PROVINCE
10949 120 St Nw, Edmonton, AB, T5H 3R2

Emp Here 30   *Sales* 15,599,010
SIC 4724 Travel agencies
 Jim Vincent

D-U-N-S 24-339-8083   (SL)
VISTEK WEST CALGARY INC
(*Suby of* VISTEK LTD)
10569 109 St Nw, Edmonton, AB, T5H 3B1
(780) 484-0333
Emp Here 42   *Sales* 10,261,776
SIC 5946 Camera and photographic supply stores
 Garry Soon

Edmonton, AB T5J

D-U-N-S 24-135-0375   (SL)
1067863 ALBERTA LTD
COLLINS BARRELL CHARTER ACCOUN-TANTS
10250 101 St Nw Suite 1550, Edmonton, AB, T5J 3P4
(780) 428-1522
Emp Here 23   *Sales* 15,615,229
SIC 6211 Security brokers and dealers
 Samuel Young

D-U-N-S 25-147-6545   (SL)
3761258 CANADA INC
(*Suby of* SCIQUEST PARENT, LLC)
10180 101 St Nw Suite 310, Edmonton, AB, T5J 3S4
(780) 702-1432
Emp Here 130   *Sales* 21,690,110
SIC 7372 Prepackaged software
 Ashif Mawji

D-U-N-S 25-507-6515   (HQ)
416818 ALBERTA LTD
DESIGN GROUP STAFFING
10012 Jasper Ave Nw, Edmonton, AB, T5J 1R2
(780) 428-1505
Emp Here 95   *Sales* 85,550,700
SIC 1542 Nonresidential construction, nec
 Michael Duff

D-U-N-S 25-486-3301   (HQ)
683060 ALBERTA LTD
COOKIES BY GEORGE
8 Edmonton City Centre Nw, Edmonton, AB, T5J 2Y7
(780) 477-6853
Sales 17,608,620
SIC 5461 Retail bakeries
 Judah Busheikin

D-U-N-S 20-384-5123   (SL)
8056323 CANADA INC
CSG INDUSTRIES
10665 Jasper Ave Nw Suite 900, Edmonton, AB, T5J 3S9
(587) 206-8611
Emp Here 53   *Sales* 14,539,596
SIC 8741 Management services
 Robby Soodhar

D-U-N-S 20-554-7958   (BR)
955 BAY STREET HOSPITALITY INC
SUTTON PLACE GRANDE LIMITED
(*Suby of* NORTHLAND PROPERTIES COR-PORATION)
10235 101 St Nw, Edmonton, AB, T5J 3E8
(780) 428-7111
Emp Here 150
SIC 7011 Hotels and motels
 John Sandor

D-U-N-S 24-086-8323   (HQ)
ABC BENEFITS CORPORATION
ALBERTA BLUE CROSS
10009 108 St Nw, Edmonton, AB, T5J 3C5
(780) 498-8000
Emp Here 650   *Sales* 1,495,877,600
SIC 6321 Accident and health insurance
 Ray Pisani
 Dianne Balon
 Dominique Gregoire

D-U-N-S 24-949-7926   (HQ)
ADVANIS INC
10123 99 St Nw Suite 1600, Edmonton, AB, T5J 3H1
(780) 944-9212
Sales 12,477,600
SIC 8741 Management services
 Michael Williams

D-U-N-S 24-014-5974   (BR)
ALBERTA DISTANCE LEARNING CENTRE
(*Suby of* PEMBINA HILLS REGIONAL DIVI-SION 7)
10055 106 St Nw Suite 300, Edmonton, AB, T5J 2Y2
(780) 452-4655
Emp Here 100
SIC 8211 Elementary and secondary schools
 Ralf Helder

D-U-N-S 20-898-9897   (HQ)
ALBERTA EASTER SEALS SOCIETY
ALBERTA EASTER SEALS MCQUEEN RES-IDENCE
10025 106 St Nw Suite 1408, Edmonton, AB, T5J 1G4
(780) 429-0137
Emp Here 1   *Sales* 13,909,490
SIC 8699 Membership organizations, nec
 Susan Law
 Tammy Bergen

D-U-N-S 24-358-1704   (HQ)
ALBERTA HEALTH SERVICES
(*Suby of* GOVERNMENT OF THE PROVINCE OF ALBERTA)

▲ Public Company   ■ Public Company Family Member   **HQ** Headquarters   **BR** Branch   **SL** Single Location

10030 107 St Nw Suite 9, Edmonton, AB, T5J 3E4
(403) 944-5705
Emp Here 250   *Sales* 10,898,990
SIC 8011 Offices and clinics of medical doctors
Verna Yiu
Deb Rhodes
Kathryn Todd
Brenda Huband
Colleen Turner
David Mador
Deb Gordon
Francois Belanger
Mauro Chies
Sean Chilton

D-U-N-S 25-265-5980   (HQ)
ALBERTA INSURANCE COUNCIL
10104 103 Ave Nw Suite 600, Edmonton, AB, T5J 0H8
(780) 421-4148
Emp Here 10   *Sales* 36,466,580
SIC 6411 Insurance agents, brokers, and service
Larry Lutz
Mel Niebrugge
Doug Macrae

D-U-N-S 24-397-3943   (SL)
ALBERTA INVESTMENT MANAGEMENT CORPORATION
AIMCO
10830 Jasper Ave Nw Suite 1100, Edmonton, AB, T5J 2B3
(780) 392-3600
Emp Here 49   *Sales* 346,778,656
SIC 6719 Holding companies, nec
Kevin Uebelein
Jackie Sheppard
Peter Pontikes
Sandra Lau
Robin Heard
Michael Baker
Ben Hawkins
Peter Teti
Steve Stewart
Jon Reay

D-U-N-S 24-968-9159   (SL)
ANDERSON, RHONDA MPA KPMG LLP LAWYER
10175 101 St Nw Unit 2200, Edmonton, AB, T5J 0H3
(780) 429-7300
Emp Here 150   *Sales* 16,632,300
SIC 8111 Legal services
Robert Borrelli
Karina Guy
Deborah Macpherson
John Stelter
Michael Capus
David Magdalinski
Roblyn Eeson
Gibson Turley

D-U-N-S 25-305-0371   (BR)
AON REED STENHOUSE INC
(*Suby of* AON PLC)
10025 102a Ave Nw Suite 900, Edmonton, AB, T5J 0Y2
(780) 423-9801
Emp Here 85
SIC 6411 Insurance agents, brokers, and service
David Angus

D-U-N-S 25-681-6349   (HQ)
ARC BUSINESS SOLUTIONS INC
10088 102 Ave Nw Suite 2507, Edmonton, AB, T5J 2Z1
(780) 702-5022
Emp Here 50   *Sales* 10,678,208
SIC 7379 Computer related services, nec
Graham Murray
Wes Heard
Jacob Koshy

Darwin Perrier

D-U-N-S 24-391-4223   (HQ)
ASSOCIATED ENGINEERING ALBERTA LTD
(*Suby of* ASHCO SHAREHOLDERS INC)
9888 Jasper Ave Nw Suite 500, Edmonton, AB, T5J 5C6
(780) 451-7666
Emp Here 75   *Sales* 29,491,935
SIC 8711 Engineering services
Gary T Hussey
Herb R Kuehne
R.H. Karius
Alistar Black

D-U-N-S 24-391-4124   (HQ)
ASSOCIATED ENGINEERING GROUP LTD
(*Suby of* ASHCO SHAREHOLDERS INC)
9888 Jasper Ave Nw Suite 500, Edmonton, AB, T5J 5C6
(780) 451-7666
Sales 50,071,274
SIC 8711 Engineering services
Alistair Black
Vincent Borch
Wayne J Delbeke
Kerry Rudd
Margaret Smolcic

D-U-N-S 24-068-5396   (HQ)
ASSOCIATION OF PROFESSIONAL ENGINEERS AND GEOSCIENTISTS OF ALBERTA, THE
APEGA
10060 Jasper Ave Nw Suite 1500, Edmonton, AB, T5J 4A2
(780) 426-3990
Emp Here 50   *Sales* 24,259,264
SIC 8621 Professional organizations
Jay Nagendran
Jason Schembri

D-U-N-S 24-785-7725   (HQ)
ATB FINANCIAL
(*Suby of* GOVERNMENT OF THE PROVINCE OF ALBERTA)
10020 100 St Nw Suite 2100, Edmonton, AB, T5J 0N3
(780) 408-7000
Emp Here 200   *Sales* 1,227,656,561
SIC 6036 Savings institutions, except federal
Curtis Stange
Sheldon Dyck
Rob Bennett
Peggy Garrity
Wellington Holbrook
Ian Wild
Stuart Mckeller
Omar Rehman
Jim Mckillop
Bob Mann

D-U-N-S 20-637-0934   (HQ)
ATCO ELECTRIC LTD
(*Suby of* ATCO LTD)
10035 105 St Nw, Edmonton, AB, T5J 2V6
(780) 420-7310
Emp Here 400   *Sales* 1,261,104,000
SIC 4911 Electric services
Nancy Southern
Loraine Charlton
James Simpson
Siegfried Kiefer
Dennis Dechamplain

D-U-N-S 20-359-5074   (SL)
ATCO TECHNOLOGY MANAGEMENT LTD
(*Suby of* ATCO LTD)
10035 105 St, Edmonton, AB, T5J 2V6
(403) 292-7500
Emp Here 30   *Sales* 18,798,420
SIC 4911 Electric services
Nancy C. Southern
Clinton G. Warkentin
Brian R. Bale

D-U-N-S 24-274-3128   (BR)
AVIVA INSURANCE COMPANY OF CANADA
AVIVA CANADA
(*Suby of* GENERAL ACCIDENT PLC)
10250 101 St Nw Suite 1700, Edmonton, AB, T5J 3P4
(780) 428-1822
Emp Here 100
SIC 6331 Fire, marine, and casualty insurance
Sheri Hall

D-U-N-S 20-651-6259   (BR)
BEST BUY CANADA LTD
FUTURE SHOP
(*Suby of* BEST BUY CO., INC.)
10304 109 St Nw, Edmonton, AB, T5J 1M3
(780) 498-5505
Emp Here 100
SIC 5731 Radio, television, and electronic stores

D-U-N-S 24-841-1472   (HQ)
BISHOP & MCKENZIE LLP
10180 101 St Suite 2300, Edmonton, AB, T5J 1V3
(780) 426-5550
Emp Here 80   *Sales* 11,088,200
SIC 8111 Legal services
Ross Kneteman

D-U-N-S 24-643-2694   (SL)
BLUE TREE HOTELS GP ULC
WESTIN EDMONTON, THE
10135 100 St Nw, Edmonton, AB, T5J 0N7
(780) 426-3636
Emp Here 300   *Sales* 28,700,400
SIC 7011 Hotels and motels
Roula Haskett
Dan Desantis

D-U-N-S 24-982-4830   (SL)
BRENNEIS MARKET GARDENS INC
Gd Stn Main, Edmonton, AB, T5J 2G8
(780) 473-7733
Emp Here 45   *Sales* 12,336,840
SIC 5431 Fruit and vegetable markets
Sharon Stepanick
Glen Stepanick

D-U-N-S 20-268-8842   (SL)
BRIDGE GAP CHATEAU INC
CHATEAU LACOMBE HOTEL
10111 Bellamy Hill Nw, Edmonton, AB, T5J 1N7
(780) 428-6611
Emp Here 150   *Sales* 13,903,500
SIC 7011 Hotels and motels
Mike Mrdjenovich

D-U-N-S 24-583-2043   (HQ)
BROWNLEE LLP
10155 102 St Nw Suite 2200, Edmonton, AB, T5J 4G8
(780) 497-4800
Emp Here 40   *Sales* 13,084,076
SIC 8111 Legal services
David M. Pick
Jill L.A. Sheward
Barry A. Sjolie
Rodd C. Thorkelsson
Michael S. Solowan
Paul V. Stocco
Jillian L. Swainson
Roger I. Swainson
Shad A. Chapman
Joe F. Chivers

D-U-N-S 20-897-6944   (SL)
BRYAN & COMPANY LLP
10180 101 St Nw Suite 2600, Edmonton, AB, T5J 3Y2
(780) 423-5730
Emp Here 90   *Sales* 13,860,990
SIC 8111 Legal services
Lawrence W Olesen

D-U-N-S 20-349-6760   (HQ)

CANADA ICI CAPITAL CORPORATION
10180 101 St Nw Suite 3540, Edmonton, AB, T5J 3S4
(780) 990-1144
Emp Here 60   *Sales* 17,915,280
SIC 6163 Loan brokers
Dale Klein

D-U-N-S 24-700-0982   (BR)
CANADIAN BROADCASTING CORPORATION
RADIO CANADA
(*Suby of* GOVERNMENT OF CANADA)
123 Edmonton City Centre Nw, Edmonton, AB, T5J 2Y8
(780) 468-7777
Emp Here 130
SIC 4833 Television broadcasting stations
Rodney Lamarre

D-U-N-S 25-090-8241   (BR)
CANADIAN UTILITIES LIMITED
ATCO ITEK
(*Suby of* ATCO LTD)
10035 105 St Nw, Edmonton, AB, T5J 1C8
(780) 420-7209
Emp Here 400
SIC 4911 Electric services
Denis Ellard

D-U-N-S 24-394-4014   (HQ)
CANADIAN WESTERN BANK
10303 Jasper Ave Nw Suite 3000, Edmonton, AB, T5J 3N6
(780) 423-8888
Emp Here 1,250   *Sales* 586,516,520
SIC 6021 National commercial banks
Christopher Fowler
Robert L. Phillips
Carolyn Graham
Kelly Blackett
Niall P. Boles
Vladimir Ahmad
Albrecht W.A. Bellstedt
Andrew J. Bibby
Linda M.O. Hohol
Robert A. Manning

D-U-N-S 24-003-8984   (HQ)
CANAPEN INVESTMENTS LTD
CANAPEN GROUP F COMPANIES, THE
(*Suby of* COMPAGNIE DES CHEMINS DE FER NATIONAUX DU CANADA)
10020 101a Ave Nw Suite 800, Edmonton, AB, T5J 3G2
(780) 428-0511
Emp Here 50   *Sales* 16,565,325
SIC 6512 Nonresidential building operators
Russell Hiscock
Mark Beard
Clifton Isings

D-U-N-S 24-387-9934   (SL)
CAPITAL POWER (K3) LIMITED PARTNERSHIP
(*Suby of* CAPITAL POWER CORPORATION)
10065 Jasper Ave Nw, Edmonton, AB, T5J 3B1
(780) 392-5305
Emp Here 100
SIC 5063 Electrical apparatus and equipment
Donald Lowry

D-U-N-S 20-302-2751   (SL)
CASTLE ROCK RESEARCH CORPORATION
10180 101 St Nw Suite 2410, Edmonton, AB, T5J 3S4
(780) 448-9619
Emp Here 61   *Sales* 10,005,647
SIC 2731 Book publishing
Gautam Rao
Ugendra Prasad

D-U-N-S 20-346-3526   (HQ)
CELANESE CANADA ULC
4405 101 Ave, Edmonton, AB, T5J 2K1

(780) 468-0800
Sales 56,804,200
SIC 2821 Plastics materials and resins
  Roger Page

D-U-N-S 24-838-9850   (SL)
CHATEAU LACOMBE HOTEL LTD
CROWNE PLAZA CHATEAU LACOMBE
(*Suby of* ALLIED HOLDINGS LTD)
10111 Bellamy Hill Nw, Edmonton, AB, T5J
1N7
(780) 428-6611
Emp Here 225   *Sales* 21,525,300
SIC 7011 Hotels and motels
  Anthony Eng
  John Ellen

D-U-N-S 24-810-5249   (SL)
CHOICE OFFICE PERSONNEL LTD
10025 102a Ave Nw Suite 1102, Edmonton,
AB, T5J 2Z2
(780) 424-6816
Emp Here 250   *Sales* 18,673,500
SIC 7363 Help supply services
  Colleen Reid

D-U-N-S 20-580-9796   (BR)
CIBC WORLD MARKETS INC
CIBC WOOD GUNDY
(*Suby of* CANADIAN IMPERIAL BANK OF
COMMERCE)
10180 101 St Nw Suite 1800, Edmonton, AB,
T5J 3S4
(780) 429-8900
Emp Here 140
SIC 6211 Security brokers and dealers
  Fred Patton

D-U-N-S 20-183-0424   (BR)
COAST HOTELS LIMITED
COAST EDMONTON PLAZA HOTEL
(*Suby of* OKABE CO., LTD.)
10155 105 St Nw, Edmonton, AB, T5J 1E2
(780) 423-4811
Emp Here 125
SIC 7011 Hotels and motels
  Kelly Mccauley

D-U-N-S 24-399-6626   (SL)
**COLLEGE OF PHYSICIANS & SURGEONS
OF ALBERTA**
10020 100 St Nw Suite 2700, Edmonton, AB,
T5J 0N3
(780) 423-4764
Emp Here 70   *Sales* 11,245,220
SIC 8011 Offices and clinics of medical doc-
tors
  James Bell
  Randall Sargent
  Linda Spencer

D-U-N-S 25-977-6334   (BR)
**COMPAGNIE DE TELEPHONE BELL DU
CANADA OU BELL CANADA, LA**
(*Suby of* BCE INC)
10104 103 Ave Nw Suite 2800, Edmonton, AB,
T5J 0H8
(780) 409-6800
Emp Here 100
SIC 4899 Communication services, nec
  Robert Lai

D-U-N-S 24-928-7509   (BR)
**CONSEILLERS EN GESTION ET INFORMA-
TIQUE CGI INC**
CGI
(*Suby of* CGI INC)
10303 Jasper Ave Nw Suite 800, Edmonton,
AB, T5J 3N6
(780) 409-2200
Emp Here 350
SIC 7379 Computer related services, nec
  Bill Clark

D-U-N-S 20-539-6864   (BR)
CONSOLIDATED FASTRATE INC
7725 101 St, Edmonton, AB, T5J 2M1
(780) 439-0061
Emp Here 100

SIC 4731 Freight transportation arrangement
  William Shupenia

D-U-N-S 24-132-0915   (BR)
CORONADO CONTRACTING CORP
Th Po Box 17 Stn Main, Edmonton, AB, T5J
2G9
(780) 449-1654
Emp Here 95
SIC 1611 Highway and street construction

D-U-N-S 20-059-7438   (BR)
**CORPORATION DE SECURITE GARDA
CANADA**
*GARDA CANADA SECURITY CORPORA-
TION*
(*Suby of* GW INTERMEDIATE HOLDCO
CORPORATION)
10250 101 St Nw Suite 1010, Edmonton, AB,
T5J 3P4
(780) 425-5000
Emp Here 900
SIC 7381 Detective and armored car services
  Debbie Rogers

D-U-N-S 24-399-0983   (SL)
**CREDIT UNION DEPOSIT GUARANTEE
CORPORATION**
(*Suby of* GOVERNMENT OF THE
PROVINCE OF ALBERTA)
10104 103 Ave Nw Suite 2000, Edmonton, AB,
T5J 0H8
(780) 428-6680
Emp Here 37   *Sales* 68,326,383
SIC 6399 Insurance carriers, nec
  Paul A. Kennett
  Ken Motiuk

D-U-N-S 24-318-6686   (BR)
**CRITICAL CONTROL ENERGY SERVICES
CORP**
(*Suby of* CRITICAL CONTROL ENERGY
SERVICES CORP)
10130 103 St Nw Suite 1500, Edmonton, AB,
T5J 3N9
(780) 423-3100
Emp Here 100
SIC 7371 Custom computer programming ser-
vices
  Doris Choi

D-U-N-S 24-332-5131   (SL)
CW EDMONTON INC
CUSHMAN & WAKEFIELD
10088 102 Ave Nw Unit 2700, Edmonton, AB,
T5J 2Z1
(780) 420-1177
Emp Here 50   *Sales* 16,356,350
SIC 6531 Real estate agents and managers
  Gary Killips
  Neil Calhoun
  John Macdonald
  Mark Mccann

D-U-N-S 25-359-6324   (BR)
DELOITTE LLP
(*Suby of* DELOITTE LLP)
10180 101 St Nw Suite 2000, Edmonton, AB,
T5J 4E4
(780) 421-3611
Emp Here 210
SIC 8721 Accounting, auditing, and book-
keeping
  Gordon Smith

D-U-N-S 25-012-1829   (BR)
DELTA HOTELS LIMITED
DELTA EDMONTON CENTRE SUITE HOTEL
(*Suby of* GOVERNMENT OF THE
PROVINCE OF BRITISH COLUMBIA)
10222 102 St Nw, Edmonton, AB, T5J 4C5
(780) 429-3900
Emp Here 124
SIC 8741 Management services
  Brian Spiegl

D-U-N-S 24-880-6739   (BR)
DENTONS CANADA LLP

(*Suby of* DENTONS CANADA LLP)
10180 101 St Nw Suite 2900, Edmonton, AB,
T5J 3V5
(780) 423-7100
Emp Here 200
SIC 8111 Legal services
  Dennis Picco

D-U-N-S 24-090-0472   (HQ)
DESIGN GROUP STAFFING INC
DESIGN GROUP STAFFING
(*Suby of* 416818 ALBERTA LTD)
10012 Jasper Ave Nw, Edmonton, AB, T5J
1R2
(780) 448-5850
Emp Here 80   *Sales* 23,902,080
SIC 7361 Employment agencies
  Michael Duff
  Stephane Frechette
  Kathleen Doyle-Linden

D-U-N-S 24-498-0694   (BR)
DIALOG
(*Suby of* DIALOG)
10237 104 St Nw Suite 100, Edmonton, AB,
T5J 1B1
(780) 429-1580
Emp Here 80
SIC 8712 Architectural services
  Doug Mcconnell

D-U-N-S 25-326-7736   (HQ)
DIRK ENTERPRISES LTD
10235 101 St Nw Suite 800, Edmonton, AB,
T5J 3G1
(780) 944-9994
Emp Here 1   *Sales* 54,670,000
SIC 6712 Bank holding companies
  Dianne Kipnes

D-U-N-S 24-367-4368   (BR)
DIVERSIFIED TRANSPORTATION LTD
RED ARROW EXPRESS, DIV OF
(*Suby of* PACIFIC WESTERN TRANSPORTA-
TION LTD)
10014 104 St Nw Unit 20, Edmonton, AB, T5J
0Z1
(780) 425-0820
Emp Here 100
SIC 4142 Bus charter service, except local
  John Stepovy

D-U-N-S 24-808-8890   (HQ)
DUNCAN CRAIG LLP
10060 Jasper Ave Nw Suite 2800, Edmonton,
AB, T5J 3V9
(780) 428-6036
Emp Here 80   *Sales* 9,979,380
SIC 8111 Legal services
  Darren Bieganek
  Douglas P. Gahn
  Brewster H.P. Kwan

D-U-N-S 25-012-9095   (HQ)
DYNALIFEDX
*DYNALIFEDX DIAGNOSTIC LABORATORY
SERVICE*
10150 102 St Nw Suite 200, Edmonton, AB,
T5J 5E2
(780) 451-3702
Emp Here 500   *Sales* 391,165,200
SIC 8071 Medical laboratories
  Jason Pincock
  Martha Krauze

D-U-N-S 20-808-6843   (SL)
EDMONTON CITY CENTRE
10025 102a Ave Nw Suite 1700, Edmonton,
AB, T5J 2Z2
(780) 426-8444
Emp Here 45   *Sales* 12,982,455
SIC 6512 Nonresidential building operators
  Frank Robinson

D-U-N-S 24-962-2200   (SL)
**EDMONTON CONCERT HALL FOUNDA-
TION**
WINSPEAR CENTRE FOR MUSIC

9720 102 Ave Nw, Edmonton, AB, T5J 4B2
(780) 429-1992
Emp Here 100   *Sales* 13,345,900
SIC 8399 Social services, nec
  Elaine Calder
  Gary Clark
  Mark Gunderson
  Travis Huckell
  Doug Noble
  Catrin Owen
  Eddie Bayens
  Mary Johnson
  Edith Stacey
  Jennifer Weingardt

D-U-N-S 20-561-9328   (BR)
**EDMONTON ECONOMIC DEVELOPMENT
CORPORATION**
SHAW CONFERENCE CENTRE
(*Suby of* CITY OF EDMONTON)
9797 Jasper Ave Nw, Edmonton, AB, T5J 1N9
(780) 421-9797
Emp Here 400
SIC 7389 Business services, nec
  Ron Gilbertson

D-U-N-S 24-390-9520   (HQ)
**EDMONTON ECONOMIC DEVELOPMENT
CORPORATION**
SHAW CONFERENCE CENTRE
(*Suby of* CITY OF EDMONTON)
9990 Jasper Ave Nw 3rd Fl, Edmonton, AB,
T5J 1P7
(780) 424-9191
Emp Here 75   *Sales* 274,572,900
SIC 7389 Business services, nec
  Brad Ferguson
  Corinne Ferguson
  Angela Fong
  John Babic
  Brian Baker
  Douglas Cox
  Jason Ding
  Joseph Doucet
  Sharilee Fossum
  Kris Hildebrand

D-U-N-S 24-326-7684   (SL)
EDMONTON HOUSE REALTY LTD
10205 100 Ave Nw Suite 3400, Edmonton, AB,
T5J 4B5
(780) 420-4040
Emp Here 50   *Sales* 19,904,329
SIC 6798 Real estate investment trusts
  Marc De La Bruyere
  Alastair Mactaggart

D-U-N-S 20-327-7546   (BR)
EDMONTON PUBLIC LIBRARY
ENTERPRISE SQUARE
(*Suby of* EDMONTON PUBLIC LIBRARY)
7 Sir Winston Churchill Sq Nw, Edmonton, AB,
T5J 2V4
(780) 496-7000
Emp Here 80
SIC 8231 Libraries
  Richard Thornley

D-U-N-S 24-384-6164   (HQ)
EDMONTON PUBLIC LIBRARY
7 Sir Winston Churchill Sq Nw Suite 5, Edmon-
ton, AB, T5J 2V4
(780) 496-7050
Emp Here 50   *Sales* 47,557,800
SIC 8231 Libraries
  Pilar Martinez
  Gastone Monai

D-U-N-S 24-556-4153   (SL)
EDON MANAGEMENT
SEVENTH STREET PLAZA
10030 107 St Nw, Edmonton, AB, T5J 3E4
(780) 428-1742
Emp Here 49   *Sales* 13,937,413
SIC 6512 Nonresidential building operators
  Peter Vaters

D-U-N-S 25-194-5358   (SL)
ENBRIDGE OPERATIONAL SERVICES INC
(*Suby of* ENBRIDGE INC)
10201 Jasper Ave Nw, Edmonton, AB, T5J 3N7
(780) 420-8850
Emp Here 30   *Sales* 34,666,950
SIC 4923 Gas transmission and distribution
Greg Sevick

D-U-N-S 25-152-4781   (SL)
EPCOR POWER DEVELOPMENT CORPORATION
(*Suby of* CITY OF EDMONTON)
10065 Jasper Ave Nw, Edmonton, AB, T5J 3B1
(780) 412-3191
Emp Here 230   *Sales* 133,456,810
SIC 5063 Electrical apparatus and equipment
Don Lowry
Mark Wiltzen

D-U-N-S 20-998-8315   (SL)
EWASIUK RICK W QC
10180 101 St Nw Suite 3200, Edmonton, AB, T5J 3W8
(780) 497-3384
Emp Here 70   *Sales* 10,780,770
SIC 8111 Legal services
Rick Ewasiuk

D-U-N-S 24-097-8879   (BR)
FAIRMONT HOTELS & RESORTS INC
FAIRMONT HOTEL MACDONALD, THE
(*Suby of* ACCOR)
10065 100 St Nw, Edmonton, AB, T5J 0N6
(780) 424-5181
Emp Here 200
SIC 7011 Hotels and motels
Garrett Turta

D-U-N-S 25-329-3328   (HQ)
FAMILY VISION CARE LTD
VISION MED
10088 102 Ave Nw Suite 1805, Edmonton, AB, T5J 2Z1
(780) 423-2128
Emp Here 7   *Sales* 20,767,880
SIC 5995 Optical goods stores
Michael Melynchuck
Jeff Marsh

D-U-N-S 25-683-5182   (SL)
FAS BENEFIT ADMINISTRATORS LTD
10154 108 St Nw, Edmonton, AB, T5J 1L3
(780) 452-5161
Emp Here 42   *Sales* 30,804,984
SIC 6726 Investment offices, nec
Deb Petryk

D-U-N-S 24-416-2897   (HQ)
FIELD LLP
FIELD LAW
10175 101 St Nw Suite 2500, Edmonton, AB, T5J 0H3
(780) 423-3003
Emp Here 70   *Sales* 47,351,480
SIC 8111 Legal services
Robert Teskey
James Casey
Jean Van Der Lee

D-U-N-S 20-058-0111   (HQ)
FIRMA FOREIGN EXCHANGE CORPORATION
FIRMA FX
10205 101 St Nw Suite 400, Edmonton, AB, T5J 2P4
(780) 426-4946
Emp Here 100   *Sales* 52,546,050
SIC 6099 Functions related to deposit banking
Micheal Oshry
David Dominy
Michael Zvonkovic
Alex Eadie
Brad Clark
Nigel Hobson

D-U-N-S 24-065-7155   (BR)
FUJITSU CONSEIL (CANADA) INC
FUJITSU CONSULTING
(*Suby of* FUJITSU CONSULTING (CANADA) HOLDINGS, INC.)
10020 101a Ave Nw Suite 1500, Edmonton, AB, T5J 3G2
(780) 423-2070
Emp Here 200
SIC 7376 Computer facilities management
Llyod Rehman

D-U-N-S 20-179-6310   (SL)
GE FANUC AUTOMATION CANADA COMPANY
10235 101 St Nw, Edmonton, AB, T5J 3E9
(780) 420-2000
Emp Here 100   *Sales* 21,385,100
SIC 7372 Prepackaged software
Sandra Cox

D-U-N-S 20-810-6062   (HQ)
GRANT MACEWAN UNIVERSITY
10700 104 Ave Nw, Edmonton, AB, T5J 4S2
(780) 497-5168
Emp Here 1,500   *Sales* 394,836,400
SIC 8221 Colleges and universities
David Atkinson
John Corlett
Cathryn Heslep
Michelle Plouffe
Brent Quinton

D-U-N-S 24-703-0091   (BR)
GRANT THORNTON LLP
(*Suby of* GRANT THORNTON LLP)
10060 Jasper Ave Nw Suite 1701, Edmonton, AB, T5J 3R8
(780) 422-7114
Emp Here 120
SIC 8721 Accounting, auditing, and bookkeeping
Al Mondor

D-U-N-S 24-002-4208   (BR)
GREAT-WEST LIFE ASSURANCE COMPANY, THE
(*Suby of* POWER CORPORATION DU CANADA)
10110 104 St Nw Suite 202, Edmonton, AB, T5J 4R5
(780) 917-7800
Emp Here 80
SIC 6321 Accident and health insurance
Cindy Savoie

D-U-N-S 25-217-5773   (SL)
HAEMONETICS CANADA LTD
5 D INFORMATION MANAGEMENT
(*Suby of* HAEMONETICS CORPORATION)
10025 102a Ave Nw Suite 500, Edmonton, AB, T5J 2Z2
(780) 425-6560
Emp Here 150   *Sales* 21,627,300
SIC 7371 Custom computer programming services
Tom Britton

D-U-N-S 25-329-7360   (SL)
HEALY FORD SALES LIMITED
HEALY FORD
10616 103 Ave Nw, Edmonton, AB, T5J 0J2

Emp Here 87   *Sales* 54,747,360
SIC 5511 New and used car dealers
Mark Hicks

D-U-N-S 20-084-3787   (HQ)
HENRY SINGER FASHION GROUP LTD
HENRY SINGER
(*Suby of* HENRY SINGER LTD.)
10180 101 St Nw Suite 165, Edmonton, AB, T5J 3S4
(780) 420-0909
Emp Here 12   *Sales* 11,660,740
SIC 5611 Men's and boys' clothing stores
Fred Singer

Jordan Singer

D-U-N-S 20-185-1958   (HQ)
HENRY SINGER LTD.
10180 101 St Nw Suite 160, Edmonton, AB, T5J 3S4
(780) 420-0909
Emp Here 12   *Sales* 45,688,625
SIC 6712 Bank holding companies
Fred Singer

D-U-N-S 20-082-4811   (BR)
HOLT, RENFREW & CIE, LIMITEE
HOLT RENFREW
10180 101 St Nw, Edmonton, AB, T5J 3S4
(780) 425-5300
Emp Here 95
SIC 5611 Men's and boys' clothing stores
Rob Mendoza

D-U-N-S 20-357-6533   (BR)
HONEYWELL LIMITED
HONEYWELL ADVANCED SOLUTIONS
(*Suby of* HONEYWELL INTERNATIONAL INC.)
10405 Jasper Ave Nw Suite 1800, Edmonton, AB, T5J 3N4
(780) 448-1010
Emp Here 100
SIC 7371 Custom computer programming services
Michael Brown

D-U-N-S 24-003-6459   (BR)
IBI GROUP
(*Suby of* IBI GROUP)
10830 Jasper Ave Nw Suite 300, Edmonton, AB, T5J 2B3
(780) 428-4000
Emp Here 130
SIC 8712 Architectural services
Peter Moore

D-U-N-S 25-989-6629   (BR)
IBM CANADA LIMITED
(*Suby of* INTERNATIONAL BUSINESS MACHINES CORPORATION)
10044 108 St Nw Suite 401, Edmonton, AB, T5J 3S7
(780) 642-4100
Emp Here 1,000
SIC 3571 Electronic computers
Mikkelson Bill

D-U-N-S 24-283-4752   (BR)
IMPERIAL PARKING CANADA CORPORATION
IMPARK
(*Suby of* GATES GROUP CAPITAL PARTNERS, LLC)
10239 107 St Nw, Edmonton, AB, T5J 1K1
(780) 420-1976
Emp Here 110
SIC 7521 Automobile parking
David Wellendorf

D-U-N-S 24-280-7956   (SL)
INSTITUTE OF CHARTERED ACCOUNTANTS OF ALBERTA
CHARTERED PROFESSIONAL ACCOUNTANTS OF ALBERTA
10088 102 Ave Nw Unit 1900 Td Tower, Edmonton, AB, T5J 2Z1
(780) 424-7391
Emp Here 53   *Sales* 12,800,295
SIC 8621 Professional organizations
Jane Halford

D-U-N-S 20-651-6481   (BR)
INVESTORS GROUP FINANCIAL SERVICES INC
(*Suby of* POWER CORPORATION DU CANADA)
10060 Jasper Ave Nw Suite 2400, Edmonton, AB, T5J 3R8
(780) 448-1988
Emp Here 100
SIC 8741 Management services

Nathan Giesbrecht

D-U-N-S 20-050-8294   (HQ)
KATZ GROUP INC
10104 103 Ave Nw Suite 1702, Edmonton, AB, T5J 0H8
(780) 990-0505
Emp Here 2   *Sales* 922,456,962
SIC 5912 Drug stores and proprietary stores
Daryl Katz
Frank Scorpiniti
Sharon Driscoll

D-U-N-S 24-125-2522   (SL)
KINGSTON ROSS PASNAK LLP
9888 Jasper Ave Nw Suite 1500, Edmonton, AB, T5J 5C6
(780) 424-3000
Emp Here 91   *Sales* 19,026,735
SIC 8721 Accounting, auditing, and bookkeeping
Bob Wilson

D-U-N-S 24-671-2376   (BR)
KPMG INC
(*Suby of* KPMG INC)
10125 102 St Nw, Edmonton, AB, T5J 3V8
(780) 429-7300
Emp Here 250
SIC 8721 Accounting, auditing, and bookkeeping
Ivor Ruste

D-U-N-S 25-301-5556   (BR)
KPMG LLP
K P M G MANAGEMENT CONSULTING
(*Suby of* KPMG LLP)
2200-10175 101 St Nw, Edmonton, AB, T5J 3V8
(780) 429-7300
Emp Here 200
SIC 8721 Accounting, auditing, and bookkeeping
Ivor Ruste

D-U-N-S 24-807-4866   (HQ)
LEGAL AID SOCIETY OF ALBERTA
10320 102 Ave Nw Suite 300, Edmonton, AB, T5J 4A1
(780) 427-7575
Emp Here 15   *Sales* 22,176,400
SIC 8111 Legal services
Nancy Brown Medwid
Olga Dobrowney
Wanda Fish

D-U-N-S 24-906-4619   (HQ)
MACLAB ENTERPRISES CORPORATION
MIDWEST PROPERTY MANAGEMENT
10205 100 Ave Nw Suite 3400, Edmonton, AB, T5J 4B5
(780) 420-4000
Emp Here 40   *Sales* 37,989,560
SIC 6513 Apartment building operators
J. Gregory Greenough
Sandy Mactaggart
Alastair Mactaggart
Marc De Labruyere
Bruce Bentley

D-U-N-S 24-394-2018   (HQ)
MANPOWER SERVICES (ALBERTA) LTD
MANPOWER SERVICES
10201 Jasper Ave Nw Suite 102, Edmonton, AB, T5J 3N7
(780) 420-0110
Emp Here 35   *Sales* 13,983,390
SIC 7363 Help supply services
Audrey Luft
Randy Upright

D-U-N-S 24-961-1153   (HQ)
MARTECH MARKETING LIMITED
10060 Jasper Ave Nw Suite 1701, Edmonton, AB, T5J 3R8
(780) 454-2006
Emp Here 13   *Sales* 11,155,347
SIC 6221 Commodity contracts brokers, deal-

ers
Marvin Verlage
Ray Verlage

D-U-N-S 25-101-7109   (HQ)
MATRIKON INC
MATRIKON INTERNATIONAL
(*Suby of* HONEYWELL INTERNATIONAL INC.)
10405 Jasper Ave Nw Suite 1800, Edmonton, AB, T5J 3N4
(780) 448-1010
Emp Here 250   *Sales* 100,592,285
SIC 7371 Custom computer programming services
Hugh J Bolton
C Kent Jespersen
Robert L Moore
Michael B Percy
Janice G Rennie
Eric Rosenfeld

D-U-N-S 20-810-0263   (HQ)
MAYFIELD INVESTMENTS LTD
MEDICINE HAT LODGE HOTEL
10010 106 St Nw Suite 1005, Edmonton, AB, T5J 3L8
(780) 424-2921
Emp Here 50   *Sales* 18,538,000
SIC 7011 Hotels and motels
Howard Pechet

D-U-N-S 20-637-3680   (HQ)
MELCOR DEVELOPMENTS LTD
10310 Jasper Ave Nw Suite 900, Edmonton, AB, T5J 1Y8
(780) 423-6931
Emp Here 37   *Sales* 202,742,250
SIC 6553 Cemetery subdividers and developers
Darin Rayburn
Timothy C. Melton
Gordon J. Clanachan
Ross A. Grieve
Kathleen M. Melton
Eric P. Newell
Catherine M. Roozen
Andrew J. Melton
Allan E. Scott
Ralph B. Young

D-U-N-S 20-299-8761   (SL)
MELCOR REAL ESTATE INVESTMENT TRUST
10310 Jasper Ave Suite 900, Edmonton, AB, T5J 1Y8
(780) 423-6931
Emp Here 8   *Sales* 202,742,250
SIC 6722 Management investment, open-end
Darin Rayburn
Timothy C. Melton
Gordon J. Clanachan
Eric P. Newell
Allan E. Scott
Ralph B. Young
Ross A. Grieve
Catherine M. Roozen
Naomi Stefura

D-U-N-S 25-451-1751   (BR)
MELOCHE MONNEX FINANCIAL SERVICES INC
MELOCHE MONNEX ASSURANCE ET SERVICES FINANCIERS INC
(*Suby of* TORONTO-DOMINION BANK, THE)
10115 100a St Nw Suite 600, Edmonton, AB, T5J 2W2
(780) 429-1112
Emp Here 200
SIC 6411 Insurance agents, brokers, and service
Daniel Chris

D-U-N-S 20-810-1691   (HQ)
METROPOLITAN CREDIT ADJUSTERS LTD
METCREDIT
10310 Jasper Ave Nw Suite 400, Edmonton,

AB, T5J 2W4
(780) 423-2231
Emp Here 60   *Sales* 27,050,085
SIC 7322 Adjustment and collection services
Brian Summerfelt

D-U-N-S 20-561-9419   (BR)
MILLER THOMSON LLP
(*Suby of* MILLER THOMSON LLP)
10155 102 St Nw Suite 2700, Edmonton, AB, T5J 4G8
(780) 429-1751
Emp Here 150
SIC 8111 Legal services
Sandra Hawes

D-U-N-S 20-304-1900   (BR)
MNP LLP
(*Suby of* MNP LLP)
10235 101 St Nw Suite 1600, Edmonton, AB, T5J 3G1
(780) 451-4406
Emp Here 225
SIC 8721 Accounting, auditing, and bookkeeping

D-U-N-S 20-287-0234   (SL)
MURSKA MANAGEMENT (1969) LTD
10180 101 St Nw Suite 3200, Edmonton, AB, T5J 3W8
(780) 425-9510
Emp Here 50   *Sales* 13,716,600
SIC 8741 Management services
William Barclay
D Lucky
T Mavko
Jeremy Taitinger
M Mccabe
C Mccreary
S Mcnaughtan
Atul Omkar
Kelsey Becker Brookes
Nick Parker

D-U-N-S 25-272-3416   (HQ)
NORQUEST COLLEGE FOUNDATION, THE
10215 108 St Nw, Edmonton, AB, T5J 1L6
(780) 644-6300
Emp Here 400   *Sales* 67,225,950
SIC 8221 Colleges and universities
Wayne Shillington

D-U-N-S 20-388-3157   (SL)
OILERSNATION.COM LTD
10020 100 St Nw, Edmonton, AB, T5J 0N3
(780) 909-2445
Emp Here 95   *Sales* 8,277,160
SIC 7941 Sports clubs, managers, and promoters
Jay Downton

D-U-N-S 20-341-7936   (SL)
ONE PROPERTIES CORPORATION
(*Suby of* ONE PROPERTIES HOLDINGS CORP)
10111 104 Ave Nw Suite 2500, Edmonton, AB, T5J 0J4
(780) 423-5525
Emp Here 63   *Sales* 26,390,007
SIC 6531 Real estate agents and managers
Darren Durstling

D-U-N-S 24-025-3851   (SL)
OXFORD SEMINARS
162221-10405 Jasper Ave Nw, Edmonton, AB, T5J 3N4
(780) 428-8700
Emp Here 50   *Sales* 11,684,750
SIC 8621 Professional organizations
Sandra Tavares

D-U-N-S 20-896-4411   (HQ)
PARLEE MCLAWS LLP
10175 101 St Nw, Edmonton, AB, T5J 0H3
(780) 423-8500
Sales 19,404,350
SIC 8111 Legal services
Michael D Macdonald

James F. Mcginnis
Robert P James
Terry Cockrall
David Finlay
William R. Pieschel
Gordon M. Adams
Lindsay J. Holmes
Richard B. Mask
Bruce A. Lawrence

D-U-N-S 24-331-8565   (HQ)
PEACE HILLS GENERAL INSURANCE COMPANY
PEACE HILLS INSURANCE
(*Suby of* SAMSON CREE NATION)
10709 Jasper Ave Nw Suite 300, Edmonton, AB, T5J 3N3
(780) 424-3986
Emp Here 130   *Sales* 996,681,840
SIC 6411 Insurance agents, brokers, and service
Kathy Boychuk
Marvin Yellowbird

D-U-N-S 24-273-6171   (HQ)
PEACE HILLS TRUST COMPANY
10011 109 St Nw 10th Fl, Edmonton, AB, T5J 3S8
(780) 421-1606
Emp Here 28   *Sales* 19,338,912
SIC 6021 National commercial banks
David Boisvert
Robert Louie
Stewart Paul
Thomas Amgwerd
Dawn Madahbee Leach
Larron Northwest
Chris Hopfner
Robert Rollingson
Darcy Bear
Katherine Swampy

D-U-N-S 20-205-4586   (BR)
PERSONNEL DEPARTMENT LTD, THE
(*Suby of* PERSONNEL DEPARTMENT LTD, THE)
10665 Jasper Ave Nw Suite 850, Edmonton, AB, T5J 3S9
(780) 421-1811
Emp Here 275
SIC 7361 Employment agencies
Lynda Higgs

D-U-N-S 25-217-4016   (SL)
PETROLEUM TANK MANAGEMENT ASSOCIATION OF ALBERTA
PTMAA
10303 Jasper Ave Nw Suite 980, Edmonton, AB, T5J 3N6
(780) 425-8265
Emp Here 5   *Sales* 15,529,285
SIC 4922 Natural gas transmission
Mark Tse
Donald Edgecombe

D-U-N-S 25-064-4341   (BR)
POSTMEDIA NETWORK INC
EDMONTON JOURNAL, THE
(*Suby of* POSTMEDIA NETWORK CANADA CORP)
10006 101 St Nw, Edmonton, AB, T5J 0S1
(780) 429-5100
Emp Here 648
SIC 2711 Newspapers
John Mcdonald Iii

D-U-N-S 25-995-4311   (BR)
PRICEWATERHOUSECOOPERS LLP
(*Suby of* PRICEWATERHOUSECOOPERS LLP)
10088 102 Ave Nw Suite 1501, Edmonton, AB, T5J 3N5
(780) 441-6700
Emp Here 200
SIC 8721 Accounting, auditing, and bookkeeping
Barry James

D-U-N-S 20-195-4232   (BR)
REVERA INC
CHURCHILL RETIREMENT COMMUNITY, THE
(*Suby of* GOVERNMENT OF CANADA)
10015 103 Ave Nw Suite 1208, Edmonton, AB, T5J 0H1
(780) 420-1222
Emp Here 80
SIC 8361 Residential care
Brian King

D-U-N-S 24-274-4167   (SL)
REYNOLDS MIRTH RICHARDS & FARMER LLP
10180 101 St Nw Suite 3200, Edmonton, AB, T5J 3W8
(780) 425-9510
Emp Here 75   *Sales* 11,550,825
SIC 8111 Legal services
Emmanuel Mirth
Allan Farmer

D-U-N-S 20-809-9432   (SL)
ROYAL GLENORA CLUB
ROYAL GLENORA PRO SHOP
11160 River Valley Rd, Edmonton, AB, T5J 2G7
(780) 482-2371
Emp Here 130   *Sales* 10,210,850
SIC 7997 Membership sports and recreation clubs
Dustin Mcavoy

D-U-N-S 20-895-5567   (SL)
ROYAL MAYFAIR GOLF CLUB LTD
9450 Groat Rd Nw, Edmonton, AB, T5J 2G8
(780) 432-0066
Emp Here 160   *Sales* 12,567,200
SIC 7997 Membership sports and recreation clubs
Mathew Thomas

D-U-N-S 24-346-8928   (SL)
RUTH'S CHRIS STEAK HOUSE EDMONTON
10103 100 St Nw, Edmonton, AB, T5J 0N8
(780) 990-0123
Emp Here 90   *Sales* 4,096,710
SIC 5812 Eating places
Brian Collins

D-U-N-S 20-720-0387   (HQ)
SAWRIDGE ENTERPRISES LTD
SAWRIDGE INN & CONFERENCE CENTRE JASPER
10104 103 Ave Nw Unit 1910, Edmonton, AB, T5J 0H8
(780) 428-3330
Sales 47,834,000
SIC 7011 Hotels and motels
Bertha L'hirondelle-Twin
Walter Felix Twin

D-U-N-S 20-720-7184   (BR)
SCOTIA CAPITAL INC
SCOTIA MCLEOD
(*Suby of* BANK OF NOVA SCOTIA, THE)
10104 103 Ave Nw Suite 2000, Edmonton, AB, T5J 0H8
(780) 497-3200
Emp Here 75
SIC 6211 Security brokers and dealers
Corey Johnson

D-U-N-S 24-701-7155   (HQ)
SENTINEL SELF-STORAGE CORPORATION
SENTINEL BUSINESS CENTRE (DIV OF)
10123 99 St Nw Suite 1970, Edmonton, AB, T5J 3H1
(780) 424-8945
Emp Here 7   *Sales* 20,570,600
SIC 4225 General warehousing and storage
William H Bowes Sr
William E Bowes Jr
Orest Gauk
John D.R. Watson

D-U-N-S 24-961-0171   (BR)
SIERRA SYSTEMS GROUP INC
(*Suby* of NIPPON TELEGRAPH AND TELE-
PHONE CORPORATION)
10104 103 Ave Nw Unit 1300, Edmonton, AB,
T5J 0H8
(780) 424-0852
Emp Here 81
SIC 7379 Computer related services, nec
Wendy Hoffmann

D-U-N-S 24-125-8164   (BR)
SNC-LAVALIN INC
(*Suby* of GROUPE SNC-LAVALIN INC)
10235 101 St Nw Suite 608, Edmonton, AB,
T5J 3G1
(780) 426-1000
Emp Here 250
SIC 8711 Engineering services
Donald Mcleod

D-U-N-S 25-341-7679   (BR)
SOBEYS WEST INC
(*Suby* of EMPIRE COMPANY LIMITED)
1858230 82nd Ave, Edmonton, AB, T5J 2K2
(780) 469-9452
Emp Here 150
SIC 5411 Grocery stores
Chris Wilkes

D-U-N-S 24-734-1696   (HQ)
SORRELL FINANCIAL INC
10111 104 Ave Nw Unit 2600, Edmonton, AB,
T5J 0J4
(780) 424-1424
Emp Here 19   *Sales* 25,441,800
SIC 6411 Insurance agents, brokers, and ser-
vice
Peter Sorrell
Paola Zanuttini
Noah Jones
Wayne Lasher
David Beavis
Salvatore Corea
Ross Langford

D-U-N-S 20-192-0019   (HQ)
STANTEC ARCHITECTURE LTD
(*Suby* of STANTEC INC)
10220 103 Ave Nw Suite 400, Edmonton, AB,
T5J 0K4
(780) 917-7000
Emp Here 60   *Sales* 124,192,530
SIC 8712 Architectural services
Gord Johnston
Bruce Raber
Stanis Ir Smith
Robert J Gomes
Alan Hartley

D-U-N-S 20-699-7707   (HQ)
**STANTEC CONSULTING INTERNATIONAL
LTD**
(*Suby* of STANTEC INC)
10220 103 Ave Nw Suite 400, Edmonton, AB,
T5J 0K4
(780) 917-7000
Emp Here 250   *Sales* 302,596,085
SIC 8711 Engineering services
Gord Johnston
Daniel J Lefaivre
Paul J.D. Alpern
John R. Adams
Jennifer Al Addison

D-U-N-S 25-415-9825   (HQ)
STANTEC CONSULTING LTD
(*Suby* of STANTEC INC)
10220 103 Ave Nw Suite 400, Edmonton, AB,
T5J 0K4
(780) 917-7000
Emp Here 1,400   *Sales* 2,777,575,790
SIC 8711 Engineering services
Gord Johnston
Daniel J. Lefaivre
Richard K. Allen
Tino Dimanno

Scott Murray
Steve Fleck
Leonard Castro

D-U-N-S 20-320-1769   (HQ)
STANTEC GEOMATICS LTD
(*Suby* of STANTEC INC)
10220 103 Ave Nw Suite 400, Edmonton, AB,
T5J 0K4
(780) 917-7000
Emp Here 100   *Sales* 274,364,365
SIC 8713 Surveying services
Gord Johnston

D-U-N-S 24-642-2307   (HQ)
STANTEC INC
10220 103 Ave Nw Suite 400, Edmonton, AB,
T5J 0K4
(780) 917-7000
Emp Here 1,535   *Sales* 3,247,557,348
SIC 8711 Engineering services
Gord Johnston
Aram H. Keith
Dan Lefaivre
Tino Dimanno
Scott Murray
Steve Fleck
Leonard Castro
Kirk Morrison
Bob Seagar
Marshall Davert

D-U-N-S 25-361-1933   (BR)
SUNCOR ENERGY INC
EDMONTON REFINERY
(*Suby* of SUNCOR ENERGY INC)
Gd Stn Main, Edmonton, AB, T5J 2G8
(780) 410-5610
Emp Here 350
SIC 2911 Petroleum refining
Tom Day

D-U-N-S 25-315-5287   (BR)
TORONTO-DOMINION BANK, THE
TD BANK
(*Suby* of TORONTO-DOMINION BANK, THE)
10004 Jasper Ave Nw Suite 500, Edmonton,
AB, T5J 1R3
(780) 448-8251
Emp Here 300
SIC 6021 National commercial banks
Dale Safinuk

D-U-N-S 20-076-5100   (SL)
TRI-CORP CANADA INVESTMENTS INC
203 Tri-Corp Centre, Edmonton, AB, T5J 1V8
(780) 496-9607
Emp Here 22   *Sales* 14,936,306
SIC 6211 Security brokers and dealers
Neil Lymer

D-U-N-S 24-671-2707   (HQ)
UNIGLOBE GEO TRAVEL LTD
GEO EVERYTHING FOR TRAVEL
10237 109 St Nw, Edmonton, AB, T5J 1N2
(780) 424-8310
Emp Here 60   *Sales* 18,479,800
SIC 4899 Communication services, nec
William Hsu

D-U-N-S 24-345-7558   (BR)
UNIVERSITY OF LETHBRIDGE, THE
(*Suby* of UNIVERSITY OF LETHBRIDGE,
THE)
10707 100 Ave Nw Suite 1100, Edmonton, AB,
T5J 3M1

Emp Here 100
SIC 8221 Colleges and universities
Robert Turner

D-U-N-S 20-308-5956   (SL)
WHOLESALE STONE INDUSTRIES INC
WSI MANUFACTURING
10180 101 St Nw Suite 3400, Edmonton, AB,
T5J 3S4
(587) 523-1127
Emp Here 93   *Sales* 21,709,455

SIC 3281 Cut stone and stone products
Jenna Jones

D-U-N-S 20-980-0577   (SL)
WINDSPEAR CENTRE
9720 102 Ave Nw, Edmonton, AB, T5J 4B2
(780) 401-2520
Emp Here 49   *Sales* 19,473,286
SIC 8699 Membership organizations, nec
Ann Marie Tetrov

D-U-N-S 20-299-9533   (HQ)
WIPRO SOLUTIONS CANADA LIMITED
(*Suby* of WIPRO LIMITED)
10040 104 St Nw Suite 100, Edmonton, AB,
T5J 0Z2
(780) 420-7875
Sales 123,049,935,404
SIC 8742 Management consulting services
Abidali Z. Neemuchwala
Azim H Premji

D-U-N-S 20-070-4299   (HQ)
WITTEN LLP
10303 Jasper Ave Nw Suite 2500, Edmonton,
AB, T5J 3N6
(780) 428-0501
Emp Here 26   *Sales* 11,088,200
SIC 8111 Legal services
David Margolus

D-U-N-S 25-505-5543   (BR)
XEROX CANADA INC
(*Suby* of XEROX CORPORATION)
10180 101 St Nw Suite 1350, Edmonton, AB,
T5J 3S4
(780) 493-7800
Emp Here 100
SIC 5044 Office equipment
Brad Stanghetta

D-U-N-S 20-355-2414   (HQ)
YMCA OF NORTHERN ALBERTA
YMCA TRANSITIONAL HOUSING
10030 102a Ave Nw Suite 300, Edmonton, AB,
T5J 0G5
(780) 421-9622
Emp Here 1   *Sales* 15,896,560
SIC 8699 Membership organizations, nec
Franco Savoia

D-U-N-S 24-773-1982   (SL)
YMCA OF WOOD BUFFALO
10030 102a Ave Nw Suite 300, Edmonton, AB,
T5J 0G5
(780) 423-9609
Emp Here 49   *Sales* 19,473,286
SIC 8699 Membership organizations, nec
Marguerite Arsenault

D-U-N-S 24-280-6123   (HQ)
**YOUNG MEN'S CHRISTIAN ASSOCIATION
OF EDMONTON, THE**
YMCA OF NORTHERN ALBERTA
10211 105 St Nw, Edmonton, AB, T5J 1E3
(780) 429-9622
Emp Here 400   *Sales* 2,359,305,640
SIC 8699 Membership organizations, nec
Nick Parkinson

D-U-N-S 25-269-6083   (BR)
**YOUNG WOMEN'S CHRISTIAN ASSOCIA-
TION OF CANADA, THE**
(*Suby* of YOUNG WOMEN'S CHRISTIAN AS-
SOCIATION OF CANADA, THE)
10080 Jasper Ave Nw Suite 400, Edmonton,
AB, T5J 1V9
(780) 423-9922
Emp Here 150
SIC 8399 Social services, nec
Freda Badry

Edmonton, AB T5K

D-U-N-S 20-974-4726   (BR)

ALBERTA HEALTH SERVICES
CHARITAS HEALTH GROUP
(*Suby* of GOVERNMENT OF THE
PROVINCE OF ALBERTA)
11111 Jasper Ave Nw, Edmonton, AB, T5K
0L4
(780) 482-8111
Emp Here 100
SIC 8011 Offices and clinics of medical doc-
tors
Mollie Cole

D-U-N-S 24-347-9578   (BR)
ALBERTA HEALTH SERVICES
EDMONTON MENTAL HEALTH CLINIC
(*Suby* of GOVERNMENT OF THE
PROVINCE OF ALBERTA)
9942 108 St Nw, Edmonton, AB, T5K 2J5
(780) 342-7700
Emp Here 300
SIC 8062 General medical and surgical hospi-
tals
Mark Snaterse

D-U-N-S 20-069-1728   (SL)
**BANISTER RESEARCH & CONSULTING
INC**
11223 99 Ave Nw, Edmonton, AB, T5K 0G9
(780) 451-4444
Emp Here 49   *Sales* 11,500,104
SIC 8732 Commercial nonphysical research
Linda Banister

D-U-N-S 25-313-5453   (HQ)
CAPITAL CARE GROUP INC
(*Suby* of GOVERNMENT OF THE
PROVINCE OF ALBERTA)
9925 109 St Nw Suite 500, Edmonton, AB,
T5K 2J8
(780) 448-2400
Sales 177,647,600
SIC 8051 Skilled nursing care facilities
Neil Wilkinson
Karen Polowick
Susan Paul

D-U-N-S 20-438-7732   (HQ)
CAPITAL MANAGEMENT LTD
PINE CREEK CANADA PARTNERSHIP
9747 104 St Nw Suite 1604, Edmonton, AB,
T5K 0Y6
(780) 428-6511
Sales 11,588,790
SIC 1531 Operative builders
Bruce Sembaliuk
Julie Trache
Violet Hitchon

D-U-N-S 20-896-3587   (SL)
**CAPITAL REGION HOUSING CORPORA-
TION**
(*Suby* of GOVERNMENT OF THE
PROVINCE OF ALBERTA)
10232 112 St Nw, Edmonton, AB, T5K 1M4
(780) 408-3301
Emp Here 49   *Sales* 41,888,900
SIC 6531 Real estate agents and managers
Doug Topping
Gregory Bounds

D-U-N-S 24-904-7929   (SL)
CONSOLIDATED MONITORING LTD
9707 110 St Nw Suite 404, Edmonton, AB,
T5K 2L9
(780) 488-3777
Emp Here 30   *Sales* 11,870,340
SIC 7381 Detective and armored car services
Edward Pringle

D-U-N-S 20-648-2445   (BR)
**CRITICAL CONTROL ENERGY SERVICES
CORP**
(*Suby* of CRITICAL CONTROL ENERGY
SERVICES CORP)
10045 111 St Nw, Edmonton, AB, T5K 2M5
(780) 423-3100
Emp Here 100
SIC 8742 Management consulting services

▲ Public Company   ■ Public Company Family Member   **HQ** Headquarters   **BR** Branch   **SL** Single Location

Willis Groshong

D-U-N-S 20-081-6684   (HQ)
DISPENSARIES WHOLESALE (1991) LIM-ITED
10326 112 St Nw, Edmonton, AB, T5K 1N2
(780) 426-1664
Sales 38,687,075
SIC 5122 Drugs, proprietaries, and sundries
Michael A Stanley
Darren Berlin

D-U-N-S 24-643-3619   (BR)
EARL'S RESTAURANTS LTD
EARL'S TIN PALACE RESTAURANT
(*Suby of* EARL'S RESTAURANTS LTD)
11830 Jasper Ave Nw, Edmonton, AB, T5K 0N7
(780) 488-6582
Emp Here 140
SIC 5812 Eating places
Robert Aoki

D-U-N-S 20-808-1919   (HQ)
EDMONTON CATHOLIC SEPARATE SCHOOL DISTRICT NO.7
EDMONTON CATHOLIC SCHOOLS
106 St Nw Suite Suite 9807, Edmonton, AB, T5K 1C2
(780) 441-6000
Emp Here 120   *Sales* 391,196,024
SIC 8211 Elementary and secondary schools
Barry Devlin

D-U-N-S 20-081-8623   (SL)
EDMONTON MOTORS LIMITED
11445 Jasper Ave Nw, Edmonton, AB, T5K 0M6
(780) 482-7809
Emp Here 95   *Sales* 59,781,600
SIC 5511 New and used car dealers
Robert Wolfe
Brydon Mcleod

D-U-N-S 24-227-7494   (BR)
GOVERNMENT OF THE PROVINCE OF AL-BERTA
ALBERTA TREASURY BOARD
(*Suby of* GOVERNMENT OF THE PROVINCE OF ALBERTA)
9820 106 St Nw Suite 534, Edmonton, AB, T5K 2J6
(780) 427-3076
Emp Here 600
SIC 6289 Security and commodity service
Robin Campbell

D-U-N-S 24-077-8600   (BR)
HOPE MISSION SOCIETY
(*Suby of* HOPE MISSION SOCIETY)
10336 114 St Nw, Edmonton, AB, T5K 1S3
(780) 453-3877
Emp Here 180
SIC 8399 Social services, nec
Steve Berg

D-U-N-S 25-991-7995   (HQ)
HUMFORD MANAGEMENT INC
10050 112 St Nw Suite 300, Edmonton, AB, T5K 2J1
(780) 426-4960
Emp Here 31   *Sales* 12,229,020
SIC 6531 Real estate agents and managers
David J Judge
Kathleen Neilson
Pat Perpeluk

D-U-N-S 20-249-7140   (SL)
INDEPENDENT ADVOCACY INC
10050 112 St Nw Suite 201, Edmonton, AB, T5K 2J1
(780) 452-9616
Emp Here 130   *Sales* 17,349,670
SIC 8399 Social services, nec
Christine Topping

D-U-N-S 25-326-5417   (BR)
JOEY TOMATO'S KITCHENS INC
JOEY TOMATO'S RESTAURANT

(*Suby of* JOEY TOMATO'S)
11228 Jasper Ave Nw, Edmonton, AB, T5K 2V2
(780) 420-1996
Emp Here 166
SIC 5812 Eating places

D-U-N-S 24-325-9442   (SL)
KELLY, MARIA ENTERPRISES INC
SHOPPERS DRUG MART
11408 Jasper Ave Nw, Edmonton, AB, T5K 0M1
(780) 482-1011
Emp Here 45   *Sales* 11,382,930
SIC 5912 Drug stores and proprietary stores
Maria Kelly

D-U-N-S 25-413-5460   (HQ)
MCBRIDE CAREER GROUP INC
10045 111 St Nw Suite 910, Edmonton, AB, T5K 2M5
(780) 448-1380
Emp Here 30   *Sales* 17,282,916
SIC 8741 Management services
Shirley Mcbride
Noel Mcbride

D-U-N-S 20-083-4141   (HQ)
MURRAY HILL DEVELOPMENTS LTD
9833 110 St Nw, Edmonton, AB, T5K 2P5
(780) 488-0287
Emp Here 6   *Sales* 23,038,895
SIC 6531 Real estate agents and managers
Eric Wiedman
Betty Lou Sully

D-U-N-S 24-894-4597   (HQ)
PC CORP INC
9947 109 St Nw, Edmonton, AB, T5K 1H6
(780) 428-3000
Emp Here 1   *Sales* 20,122,830
SIC 5045 Computers, peripherals, and software
Isabel Bernete
Eldon Morrison

D-U-N-S 20-897-6225   (HQ)
PRINCETON DEVELOPMENTS LTD
9915 108 St Nw Suite 1400, Edmonton, AB, T5K 2G8
(780) 423-7775
Emp Here 10   *Sales* 12,653,760
SIC 6553 Cemetery subdividers and developers
John Ferguson
Raymond Hawrelak
Peter Lougheed

D-U-N-S 25-271-0413   (BR)
SOBEYS WEST INC
OLIVER SAFEWAY
(*Suby of* EMPIRE COMPANY LIMITED)
11410 104 Ave Nw, Edmonton, AB, T5K 2S5
(780) 424-0666
Emp Here 175
SIC 5411 Grocery stores
Dan Kolba

D-U-N-S 24-065-7346   (HQ)
UNITED NURSES OF ALBERTA
11150 Jasper Ave Nw Suite 700, Edmonton, AB, T5K 0C7
(780) 425-1025
Sales 12,800,295
SIC 8621 Professional organizations
Heather Smith

D-U-N-S 20-895-4685   (HQ)
WORKERS' COMPENSATION BOARD AL-BERTA
WCB ALBERTA
(*Suby of* GOVERNMENT OF THE PROVINCE OF ALBERTA)
9912 107 St Nw, Edmonton, AB, T5K 1G5
(780) 498-3999
Emp Here 500   *Sales* 924,934,475
SIC 6331 Fire, marine, and casualty insurance
Trevor Alexander

D-U-N-S 20-281-5726   (BR)
WSP CANADA INC
(*Suby of* AST TRUST COMPANY (CANADA))
9925 109 St Nw Suite 1000, Edmonton, AB, T5K 2J8
(780) 466-6555
Emp Here 100
SIC 8713 Surveying services

Edmonton, AB T5L

D-U-N-S 20-251-4550   (SL)
1471899 ALBERTA LTD
WOODWOORK & PUB INTERIORS
13040 148 St, Edmonton, AB, T5L 2H8
(780) 460-2399
Emp Here 28   *Sales* 13,180,468
SIC 1542 Nonresidential construction, nec
Cory Brightwell

D-U-N-S 20-736-1531   (SL)
293967 ALBERTA LTD
TIM HORTONS
13080 St Albert Trail Nw, Edmonton, AB, T5L 4Y6
(780) 482-5696
Emp Here 218   *Sales* 10,167,302
SIC 5812 Eating places
Arthtur Jenkins
Chad Jenkins
Joan Jenkins
Steven Crumb

D-U-N-S 24-523-6971   (HQ)
312407 ALBERTA LTD
SUNRISE BAKERY
14728 119 Ave Nw, Edmonton, AB, T5L 2P2
(780) 454-5797
Sales 31,112,100
SIC 2051 Bread, cake, and related products
Gary Huising
Eric Haak
Hank Renzenbrink
Anthony Bron

D-U-N-S 24-851-8003   (HQ)
324007 ALBERTA LTD
NILSSON BROS. LIVESTOCK EXCHANGE
(*Suby of* 400369 ALBERTA LTD)
13220 St Albert Trail Nw Suite 303, Edmonton, AB, T5L 4W1
(780) 477-2233
Emp Here 30   *Sales* 294,319,520
SIC 7389 Business services, nec
Lee William Nilsson
William T Grieve
Brian Lynn Nilsson
Patrick Bieleny

D-U-N-S 24-312-1832   (HQ)
944128 ALBERTA LTD
14440 Yellowhead Trail Nw, Edmonton, AB, T5L 3C5
(780) 413-0900
Sales 17,767,750
SIC 6712 Bank holding companies
Guy Bouvier

D-U-N-S 24-213-6575   (SL)
961945 ALBERTA LTD
SERVICEMASTER
12240 142 St Nw, Edmonton, AB, T5L 2G9
(780) 443-4338
Emp Here 110   *Sales* 27,080,460
SIC 1799 Special trade contractors, nec
Grant Miller

D-U-N-S 24-357-0285   (HQ)
965591 ALBERTA LTD
14721 123 Ave Nw, Edmonton, AB, T5L 2Y6
(780) 455-3000
Sales 15,683,688
SIC 1731 Electrical work
Kelly Mccarthy

D-U-N-S 24-204-8978   (BR)
ACKLANDS - GRAINGER INC
WESTWARD TOOLS & EQUIPMENT, DIV OF
(*Suby of* W.W. GRAINGER, INC.)
14360 123 Ave Nw, Edmonton, AB, T5L 2Y3

Emp Here 75
SIC 5085 Industrial supplies
Glenn Wallace

D-U-N-S 20-373-1802   (BR)
AGROPUR COOPERATIVE
EDMONTON ICE CREAM
(*Suby of* AGROPUR COOPERATIVE)
13944 Yellowhead Trail Nw, Edmonton, AB, T5L 3C2
(780) 488-2214
Emp Here 75
SIC 2024 Ice cream and frozen deserts
Chris Hestbak

D-U-N-S 20-574-6720   (HQ)
ALSCO CANADA CORPORATION
ALSCO UNIFORM & LINEN SERVICES
(*Suby of* ALSCO LTD.)
14630 123 Ave Nw, Edmonton, AB, T5L 2Y4
(780) 452-5955
Emp Here 10   *Sales* 71,756,800
SIC 7213 Linen supply
William Miller
Robert C Steiner
Steven Larson
James Hyland

D-U-N-S 24-326-4822   (BR)
ALSCO CANADA CORPORATION
(*Suby of* ALSCO INC.)
14710 123 Ave Nw, Edmonton, AB, T5L 2Y4
(780) 454-9641
Emp Here 100
SIC 7211 Power laundries, family and commercial
Dave Rothenbusch

D-U-N-S 25-680-9542   (SL)
ALTA PRO ELECTRIC LTD
13415 149 St Nw, Edmonton, AB, T5L 2T3
(780) 444-6510
Emp Here 83   *Sales* 18,079,807
SIC 1731 Electrical work
Hubert De Bruin
Jeanette De Bruin

D-U-N-S 24-888-2784   (SL)
AQUA INSURAQUA INSURANCE
13220 St Albert Trail Nw Suite 302, Edmonton, AB, T5L 4W1
(780) 448-0100
Emp Here 40   *Sales* 33,922,400
SIC 6411 Insurance agents, brokers, and service
Saleem Dhalla

D-U-N-S 24-325-4153   (SL)
ARPI'S NORTH INC
14445 123 Ave Nw, Edmonton, AB, T5L 2Y1
(780) 452-2096
Emp Here 203   *Sales* 54,982,144
SIC 1711 Plumbing, heating, air-conditioning
Donald Grundy
Todd Grundy
Lisa An
Greg Hensch
Roger Buksa
Liz Fursiewicz

D-U-N-S 24-509-3716   (HQ)
ARROW ENGINEERING INC
13167 146 St Nw Suite 202, Edmonton, AB, T5L 4S8
(780) 801-6100
Sales 12,493,018
SIC 8711 Engineering services
Greg Burghardt
Paul Burdett

D-U-N-S 20-808-1737   (SL)
BARCOL DOOR LTD

▲ Public Company   ■ Public Company Family Member   **HQ** Headquarters   **BR** Branch   **SL** Single Location

BARCOL DOORS & WINDOWS
(*Suby of* MIHALCHEON HOLDINGS LTD)
14820 Yellowhead Trail Nw, Edmonton, AB, T5L 3C5
(780) 452-7140
Emp Here 80   *Sales* 21,412,160
SIC 5211 Lumber and other building materials
Nick Ellis

D-U-N-S 20-080-9200   (SL)
BLANCHETT NEON LIMITED
12850 St Albert Trail Nw, Edmonton, AB, T5L 4H6
(780) 453-2441
Emp Here 46   *Sales* 10,065,904
SIC 3993 Signs and advertising specialties
Keith Blanchett
Daryl Blanchett
Verna Blanchett

D-U-N-S 20-898-4294   (BR)
BRINK'S CANADA LIMITED
(*Suby of* THE BRINK'S COMPANY)
14680 134 Ave Nw, Edmonton, AB, T5L 4T4
(780) 453-5057
Emp Here 120
SIC 7381 Detective and armored car services
Ronald Lock

D-U-N-S 24-003-1633   (HQ)
CALMONT LEASING LTD
CALMONT TRUCK RENTAL & LEASING
14610 Yellowhead Trail Nw, Edmonton, AB, T5L 3C5
(780) 454-0491
Emp Here 50   *Sales* 24,217,920
SIC 7513 Truck rental and leasing, no drivers
Lawrence Publowski

D-U-N-S 24-393-9295   (SL)
CAMPBELL SCIENTIFIC (CANADA) CORP
14532 131 Ave Nw, Edmonton, AB, T5L 4X4
(780) 454-2505
Emp Here 63   *Sales* 17,126,046
SIC 7629 Electrical repair shops
Brian Day
Carl De Leeuw
Glenn Bosch

D-U-N-S 20-969-9933   (HQ)
CAN-CELL INDUSTRIES INC
(*Suby of* TIEM HOLDINGS INC)
14735 124 Ave Nw, Edmonton, AB, T5L 3B2
(780) 447-1255
Emp Here 60   *Sales* 23,372,160
SIC 2621 Paper mills
Harold Tiemstra
Karl Tiemstra
Warren Tiemstra
Waltraut Tiemstra

D-U-N-S 25-506-4289   (SL)
CANADIAN MDF PRODUCTS COMPANY
(*Suby of* PACIFIC MDF PRODUCTS INCORPORATED)
14810 131 Ave Nw Suite 2, Edmonton, AB, T5L 4Y3
(780) 452-5406
Emp Here 60   *Sales* 16,059,120
SIC 5211 Lumber and other building materials
Douglas Hanzlick

D-U-N-S 24-808-8957   (SL)
CANUS CONSTRUCTION INC
13030 146 St Nw, Edmonton, AB, T5L 2H7

Emp Here 30   *Sales* 14,121,930
SIC 1542 Nonresidential construction, nec
Rudy Hahn
Carolyn Hahn

D-U-N-S 24-767-3627   (HQ)
CAPITAL PRINTING & FORMS INC
CAPITAL PRINTING & FORMS INK
14133 128a Ave Nw, Edmonton, AB, T5L 4P5
(780) 453-5039
Emp Here 51   *Sales* 27,701,190
SIC 5112 Stationery and office supplies

Brian Harding
Ernest Deadmarsh
Dwayne Richard

D-U-N-S 20-896-2282   (HQ)
CHRYSALIS: AN ALBERTA SOCIETY FOR CITIZENS WITH DISABILITIES
CHRYSALIS
13325 St Albert Trail Nw, Edmonton, AB, T5L 4R3
(780) 454-9656
Emp Here 110   *Sales* 7,963,395
SIC 8331 Job training and related services
Lorri Martin
Leona Colijn
Kristen Read
Ray Gosselin
Shafyn Manji
Colleen Foster
Christopher Kumar
Andrew Lamb
Matt Mandrusiak
Russell Bird

D-U-N-S 20-580-4912   (BR)
COMPAGNIE DES CHEMINS DE FER NATIONAUX DU CANADA
C N RAIL
(*Suby of* COMPAGNIE DES CHEMINS DE FER NATIONAUX DU CANADA)
12103 127 Ave Nw, Edmonton, AB, T5L 4X7
(780) 472-3261
Emp Here 190
SIC 4011 Railroads, line-haul operating
Robert Emod

D-U-N-S 24-103-9135   (BR)
COMPAGNIE DES CHEMINS DE FER NATIONAUX DU CANADA
(*Suby of* COMPAGNIE DES CHEMINS DE FER NATIONAUX DU CANADA)
12646 124 St Nw, Edmonton, AB, T5L 0N9
(780) 472-3078
Emp Here 100
SIC 4111 Local and suburban transit
Kevin Clifford

D-U-N-S 24-854-9339   (SL)
CRUST CRAFT INC
13211 146 St Nw, Edmonton, AB, T5L 4S8
(780) 466-1333
Emp Here 70   *Sales* 20,543,390
SIC 5461 Retail bakeries
Paul Flesher
Lyle Huston
Bruce Flesher

D-U-N-S 20-081-6213   (SL)
DELTON CABINET MFG LTD
14135 128 Ave Nw, Edmonton, AB, T5L 3H3
(780) 413-2260
Emp Here 50   *Sales* 12,652,950
SIC 5211 Lumber and other building materials
Jeff Balchin

D-U-N-S 24-702-9515   (HQ)
DENILLE INDUSTRIES LTD
AUBURN RENTALS
(*Suby of* 944128 ALBERTA LTD)
14440 Yellowhead Trail Nw, Edmonton, AB, T5L 3C5
(780) 413-0900
Emp Here 62   *Sales* 29,262,805
SIC 7519 Utility trailer rental
Guy Bouvier

D-U-N-S 24-283-7268   (HQ)
DONG-PHUONG ORIENTAL MARKET LTD
CDN CERTIFIED IMPORTERS, DIV OF
14810 131 Ave Nw, Edmonton, AB, T5L 4Y3
(780) 447-2883
Sales 29,347,700
SIC 5411 Grocery stores
Ba Tan Nguyen
Diep Nguyen

D-U-N-S 20-081-5694   (HQ)
DSL LTD

(*Suby of* SUMM IT CORPORATION)
14520 128 Ave Nw, Edmonton, AB, T5L 3H6
(780) 452-7580
Emp Here 50   *Sales* 35,773,920
SIC 5078 Refrigeration equipment and supplies
Brian Tiedemann
Michael Wilson
Steven Rice
Steven Barwick

D-U-N-S 24-850-9726   (SL)
ECCO TRANSPORT SERVICES LTD
12841 141 St Nw, Edmonton, AB, T5L 4N1
(780) 454-4495
Emp Here 40   *Sales* 15,414,400
SIC 4731 Freight transportation arrangement
Graham Newton

D-U-N-S 20-117-9947   (HQ)
ELITE SPORTSWEAR & AWARDS LTD
(*Suby of* ALBERTA TROPHY HOLDINGS LTD)
14703 118 Ave Nw, Edmonton, AB, T5L 2M7
(780) 454-9775
Emp Here 100   *Sales* 27,609,064
SIC 5999 Miscellaneous retail stores, nec
Drew Schamehorn
Harvey Bishop
Bryan Thomas

D-U-N-S 20-081-9431   (HQ)
ENDURA MANUFACTURING COMPANY LIMITED
12425 149 St Nw, Edmonton, AB, T5L 2J6
(780) 451-4242
Emp Here 50   *Sales* 19,881,470
SIC 2851 Paints and allied products
Curtis Lee

D-U-N-S 25-170-1132   (SL)
EPCOR TECHNOLOGIES INC
(*Suby of* CITY OF EDMONTON)
13410 St Albert Trail Nw, Edmonton, AB, T5L 4P2
(780) 412-3414
Emp Here 400   *Sales* 77,190,400
SIC 8742 Management consulting services
John Patterson
Bruce Dick
Guy Bridgeman
David Steven

D-U-N-S 20-141-1449   (HQ)
ETELLIGENT SOLUTIONS INC
11820 121 St Nw, Edmonton, AB, T5L 5H5
(780) 452-3033
Emp Here 20   *Sales* 15,109,740
SIC 5112 Stationery and office supplies
Don Prefontaine
Scott Mchale

D-U-N-S 24-702-0688   (HQ)
FORMATIONS INC
12220 142 St Nw, Edmonton, AB, T5L 2G9
(780) 451-6400
Emp Here 9   *Sales* 33,538,050
SIC 5039 Construction materials, nec
Mark Hill
Tyler Hill
Glen Hodgins

D-U-N-S 20-537-9811   (HQ)
GATEWAY MECHANICAL SERVICES INC
SATELITE MECHANICAL SERVICES
14605 118 Ave Nw, Edmonton, AB, T5L 2M7
(780) 426-6055
Emp Here 60   *Sales* 94,796,800
SIC 1711 Plumbing, heating, air-conditioning
Jackson Ohe
Mark Ohe

D-U-N-S 24-088-4932   (SL)
GEM CABINETS LTD
(*Suby of* WOODSCO LTD)
14019 128 Ave Nw, Edmonton, AB, T5L 3H3
(780) 454-8652
Emp Here 75   *Sales* 20,073,900

SIC 5211 Lumber and other building materials
Donald R. Woods
Leona Woods

D-U-N-S 24-840-0889   (HQ)
GENESIS INTEGRATION INC
(*Suby of* 965591 ALBERTA LTD)
14721 123 Ave Nw, Edmonton, AB, T5L 2Y6
(780) 455-3000
Emp Here 30   *Sales* 15,683,688
SIC 1731 Electrical work
Kelly Mccarthy
Gabriel Gely

D-U-N-S 20-082-2963   (HQ)
GREER, W.E. LIMITED
14704 119 Ave Nw, Edmonton, AB, T5L 2P1
(780) 451-1516
Emp Here 22   *Sales* 21,910,350
SIC 5169 Chemicals and allied products, nec
John Greer
Norman Turtle
Marjorie Bakewell

D-U-N-S 24-232-1359   (HQ)
H & W PRODUCE CORPORATION
H & W PRODUCE
12510 132 Ave Nw, Edmonton, AB, T5L 3P9
(780) 451-3700
Emp Here 35   *Sales* 20,543,390
SIC 5431 Fruit and vegetable markets
Richard Harrison

D-U-N-S 24-079-0600   (HQ)
HELIX ADVANCED COMMUNICATIONS & INFRASTRUCTURE, INC
WESTCAN WIRELESS
12540 129 St Nw, Edmonton, AB, T5L 4R4
(780) 451-2357
Emp Here 45   *Sales* 17,102,960
SIC 5999 Miscellaneous retail stores, nec
Rudy Dyck
Robin Thurston
Kevin Dyck

D-U-N-S 20-746-1583   (SL)
HERITAGE FROZEN FOODS LTD
CHEEMO
14615 124 Ave Nw, Edmonton, AB, T5L 3B2
(780) 454-7383
Emp Here 62   *Sales* 21,432,780
SIC 2099 Food preparations, nec
Joseph Makowecki
Walter Makowecki
Eileen Makowecki

D-U-N-S 25-688-2143   (BR)
HOME DEPOT OF CANADA INC
HOME DEPOT, THE
(*Suby of* THE HOME DEPOT INC)
13360 137 Ave Nw, Edmonton, AB, T5L 5C9
(780) 472-4201
Emp Here 200
SIC 1521 Single-family housing construction
Patty Oneill

D-U-N-S 25-418-1191   (SL)
ICON INDUSTRIAL CONTRACTORS LTD
12849 141 St Nw, Edmonton, AB, T5L 4N1
(780) 455-2299
Emp Here 65   *Sales* 15,149,225
SIC 1711 Plumbing, heating, air-conditioning
David Darichuk

D-U-N-S 24-351-6510   (HQ)
INOVATA FOODS CORP
(*Suby of* PASTA MILL LTD, THE)
12803 149 St Nw, Edmonton, AB, T5L 2J7
(780) 454-8665
Emp Here 70   *Sales* 121,846,250
SIC 2099 Food preparations, nec
Steve Parsons
Jason Yohemas
James Stevens

D-U-N-S 24-810-2824   (SL)
K-RITE CONSTRUCTION LTD
12849 148 St Nw, Edmonton, AB, T5L 2H9

(780) 452-6291
Emp Here 50   *Sales* 23,536,550
SIC 1542 Nonresidential construction, nec
Jim Kratchkowski

D-U-N-S 20-866-3638   (SL)
KEG STEAKHOUSE AND BAR
SKYVIEW KEG
13960 137 Ave Nw, Edmonton, AB, T5L 5H1
(780) 472-0707
Emp Here 100   *Sales* 4,551,900
SIC 5812 Eating places
Owen Abrams

D-U-N-S 24-096-6333   (SL)
KIA MOTORS LP
NORTH EDMONTON KIA
(*Suby of* AUTOCANADA INC)
13634 St Albert Trail Nw, Edmonton, AB, T5L
4P3
(780) 509-1550
Emp Here 65   *Sales* 40,903,200
SIC 5511 New and used car dealers
Caddarao Bonifacio

D-U-N-S 24-392-3224   (BR)
LOBLAWS INC
SUPERSTORE
(*Suby of* LOBLAW COMPANIES LIMITED)
12350 137 Ave Nw, Edmonton, AB, T5L 4X6
(780) 406-3768
Emp Here 300
SIC 5411 Grocery stores
Lori Razzolini

D-U-N-S 20-083-0925   (SL)
MADSEN'S CUSTOM CABINETS (1983) LTD
14504 123 Ave Nw, Edmonton, AB, T5L 2Y3
(780) 454-6790
Emp Here 80   *Sales* 12,469,040
SIC 2431 Millwork
Kent Madsen

D-U-N-S 25-013-8344   (HQ)
MCELHANNEY LAND SURVEYS LTD
14315 118 Ave Nw Suite 138, Edmonton, AB,
T5L 4S6
(780) 451-3420
Sales 53,621,700
SIC 8713 Surveying services
O'brian Blackall
Pamela Montgomery
Bernard J Mckenna
Bruce Winton

D-U-N-S 20-583-9058   (SL)
METALSMITH ACCESSORIES
Po Box 3391 Stn D, Edmonton, AB, T5L 4J2
(780) 454-0736
Emp Here 168   *Sales* 83,718,096
SIC 5137 Women's and children's clothing

D-U-N-S 24-643-7339   (HQ)
MILLTECH MILLWORK LTD
12410 142 St Nw, Edmonton, AB, T5L 4K2
(780) 455-6655
Emp Here 70   *Sales* 18,735,640
SIC 5211 Lumber and other building materials
Keith Waldbillig
Mike Millard
Nathan Schmidt

D-U-N-S 20-083-4026   (HQ)
MTE LOGISTIX EDMONTON INC
14627 128 Ave Nw, Edmonton, AB, T5L 3H3
(780) 944-9009
Sales 30,855,900
SIC 4225 General warehousing and storage
Dennis Nolin
Michael Haas
Gloria Morhun

D-U-N-S 20-063-7551   (HQ)
NELSON LUMBER COMPANY LTD
INTERCOAST TRUSS, DIV OF
12727 St Albert Trail Nw, Edmonton, AB, T5L
4H5
(780) 452-9151
Emp Here 100   *Sales* 112,420,000

SIC 5211 Lumber and other building materials
Jason Pehl
Dennis Patterson
Brian Holterhus
Robert Adria

D-U-N-S 20-539-3937   (SL)
NORTHGATE INDUSTRIES LTD
12345 121 St Nw, Edmonton, AB, T5L 4Y7
(780) 448-9222
Emp Here 160   *Sales* 30,779,200
SIC 2452 Prefabricated wood buildings
Sid Braaksma
Nellie Braaksma

D-U-N-S 24-583-3280   (SL)
NORTHSTAR MOTORS LTD
NORTHSTAR HYUNDAI
13634 St Albert Trail Nw, Edmonton, AB, T5L
4P3
(780) 478-7669
Emp Here 24   *Sales* 11,953,872
SIC 5511 New and used car dealers
Kari Ericksen

D-U-N-S 20-288-2564   (SL)
NOVA BUILDERS INC
14020 128 Ave Nw Unit 200, Edmonton, AB,
T5L 4M8
(780) 702-6682
Emp Here 100   *Sales* 20,388,300
SIC 6552 Subdividers and developers, nec
Mike Mrdjenovich

D-U-N-S 24-281-8276   (HQ)
PAGE, CHRIS AND ASSOCIATES LTD
14435 124 Ave Nw, Edmonton, AB, T5L 3B2
(780) 451-4373
Emp Here 34   *Sales* 50,288,040
SIC 5172 Petroleum products, nec
Christopher Page

D-U-N-S 24-982-4962   (SL)
PEARL VILLA HOMES LTD
14315 118 Ave Nw Suite 140, Edmonton, AB,
T5L 4S6
(780) 499-2337
Emp Here 100   *Sales* 6,456,000
SIC 8059 Nursing and personal care, nec
Nazli Qureshi
Bashir Qureshi

D-U-N-S 24-733-1044   (SL)
QZINA SPECIALTY FOODS INC
12547 129 St Nw, Edmonton, AB, T5L 1H7
(780) 447-4499
Emp Here 34   *Sales* 28,409,618
SIC 5149 Groceries and related products, nec
Richard Foley
Rex Ciavola
Jessie Wood
Tony Canino
Birger Andersen

D-U-N-S 25-387-9894   (HQ)
ROTEX SUPPLY INC
14360 123 Ave Nw, Edmonton, AB, T5L 2Y3
(780) 465-0637
Sales 13,300,728
SIC 5085 Industrial supplies
Alan Ditschun

D-U-N-S 24-004-1707   (SL)
ROYER DEVELOPMENTS 2015 LTD.
14635 134 Ave Nw, Edmonton, AB, T5L 4S9
(780) 454-9677
Emp Here 100   *Sales* 24,618,600
SIC 1794 Excavation work
Albert J Royer

D-U-N-S 25-064-6189   (SL)
SATURN SAAB ISUZU OF EDMONTON
14803 137 Ave Nw, Edmonton, AB, T5L 2L5
(780) 484-4455
Emp Here 30   *Sales* 14,942,340
SIC 5511 New and used car dealers
Roy Evans

D-U-N-S 24-671-7946   (HQ)

SCANDINAVIAN BUILDING SERVICES LTD
14238 134 Ave Nw, Edmonton, AB, T5L 5V8
(780) 477-3311
Emp Here 98   *Sales* 4,020,900
SIC 7349 Building maintenance services, nec
Terry Hay
Wilda Hay

D-U-N-S 20-069-1983   (SL)
SCANDINAVIAN HERITAGE SOCIETY OF EDMONTON
12336 St Albert Trail Nw, Edmonton, AB, T5L
4G8
(780) 451-3868
Emp Here 30   *Sales* 11,922,420
SIC 8699 Membership organizations, nec
Linnea Lodge

D-U-N-S 20-536-7332   (HQ)
SCHEFFER ANDREW LTD
12204 145 St Nw, Edmonton, AB, T5L 4V7
(780) 732-7800
Sales 12,317,060
SIC 8711 Engineering services
Rien Scheffer

D-U-N-S 25-453-8978   (BR)
SCHNEIDER ELECTRIC CANADA INC
SCHNEIDER ELECTRIC
(*Suby of* SCHNEIDER ELECTRIC SE)
12825 144 St Nw, Edmonton, AB, T5L 4N7
(780) 453-3561
Emp Here 86
SIC 5063 Electrical apparatus and equipment
Thatem Khalil

D-U-N-S 24-949-2153   (SL)
SHAMROCK BUILDING SERVICES LTD
12673 125 St Nw, Edmonton, AB, T5L 0T6
(780) 472-7351
Emp Here 40   *Sales* 12,754,760
SIC 1521 Single-family housing construction
Brendan Brady

D-U-N-S 24-063-5925   (BR)
SHEPHERD'S CARE FOUNDATION
SHEPHERD'S CARE FOUNDATION KENS-INGTON VILLAGE
(*Suby of* SHEPHERD'S CARE FOUNDA-TION)
12603 135 Ave Nw, Edmonton, AB, T5L 5B2
(780) 447-3840
Emp Here 200
SIC 8322 Individual and family services
Vera St Jean

D-U-N-S 24-888-5076   (SL)
SLAVE LAKE EQUITIES INC
13920 Yellowhead Trail Nw Suite 1000, Ed-monton, AB, T5L 3C2
(780) 702-6682
Emp Here 95   *Sales* 19,368,885
SIC 6553 Cemetery subdividers and develop-ers
Mike Mrejenovich

D-U-N-S 24-887-9327   (BR)
SOBEYS CAPITAL INCORPORATED
(*Suby of* EMPIRE COMPANY LIMITED)
13140 St Albert Trail Nw, Edmonton, AB, T5L
4P6
(780) 486-4800
Emp Here 100
SIC 5411 Grocery stores
Peppi Ruvo

D-U-N-S 24-392-3059   (BR)
SOBEYS WEST INC
SAFEWAY
(*Suby of* EMPIRE COMPANY LIMITED)
12950 137 Ave Nw, Edmonton, AB, T5L 4Y8
(780) 377-2402
Emp Here 120
SIC 5411 Grocery stores
Cheryl Dimos

D-U-N-S 20-084-4967   (HQ)
STEEL - CRAFT DOOR PRODUCTS LTD

(*Suby of* MIHALCHEON HOLDINGS LTD)
13504 St Albert Trail Nw, Edmonton, AB, T5L
4P4
(780) 453-3761
Emp Here 200   *Sales* 72,969,300
SIC 3442 Metal doors, sash, and trim
Kimberly Mihalcheon

D-U-N-S 24-854-5048   (SL)
SUNAC WOODWORK INC
13030 146 St Nw, Edmonton, AB, T5L 2H7

Emp Here 80   *Sales* 35,773,920
SIC 5031 Lumber, plywood, and millwork
Rudy Hahn

D-U-N-S 20-082-6345   (SL)
SUNRISE BAKERY LTD
(*Suby of* 312407 ALBERTA LTD)
14728 119 Ave Nw, Edmonton, AB, T5L 2P2
(780) 454-5797
Emp Here 60   *Sales* 20,741,400
SIC 2051 Bread, cake, and related products
Gary Huising
Eric Haak
Hank Renzenbrink

D-U-N-S 24-124-8876   (SL)
SUPERIOR PROPANE INC
14820 123 Ave Nw, Edmonton, AB, T5L 2Y3
(780) 732-3636
Emp Here 26   *Sales* 12,194,130
SIC 5984 Liquefied petroleum gas dealers
Peter Poshpar

D-U-N-S 20-705-7956   (HQ)
SUPERIOR SAFETY CODES INC
14613 134 Ave Nw, Edmonton, AB, T5L 4S9
(780) 489-4777
Emp Here 48   *Sales* 22,460,950
SIC 7389 Business services, nec
Terry Booth

D-U-N-S 20-617-3924   (SL)
TELSCO SECURITY SYSTEMS INC
TELSCO ALARM
12750 127 St Nw, Edmonton, AB, T5L 1A5
(780) 424-6971
Emp Here 50   *Sales* 22,358,700
SIC 5065 Electronic parts and equipment, nec
William Lazaruk
Joan Lazaruk
Shawn Lazaruk
Tina Lazaruk

D-U-N-S 24-713-5317   (SL)
TIRECRAFT WESTERN CANADA LTD
(*Suby of* ATD CORPORATION)
14404 128 Ave Nw, Edmonton, AB, T5L 3H6
(780) 509-1664
Emp Here 100   *Sales* 62,928,000
SIC 5531 Auto and home supply stores
Robert Labossiere

D-U-N-S 20-065-5699   (BR)
TRANSPORT TFI 7 S.E.C
CANADIAN FREIGHTWAYS
(*Suby of* TRANSPORT TFI 7 S.E.C)
14520 130 Ave Nw, Edmonton, AB, T5L 3M6
(780) 482-9483
Emp Here 150
SIC 4731 Freight transportation arrangement
Rendel Elock

D-U-N-S 24-700-7412   (HQ)
WAYNE BUILDING PRODUCTS LTD
12603 123 St Nw, Edmonton, AB, T5L 0H9
(780) 455-8929
Emp Here 24   *Sales* 13,415,220
SIC 5039 Construction materials, nec
Kevin Dale
Dennis Dale

D-U-N-S 20-590-4068   (HQ)
WESTCAN WIRELESS
(*Suby of* HELIX ADVANCED COMMUNICA-TIONS & INFRASTRUCTURE, INC)
12540 129 St Nw, Edmonton, AB, T5L 4R4

(780) 451-2355
Emp Here 68   *Sales* 18,734,704
SIC 4899 Communication services, nec
  Rudy Dyck
  Wayne Mclean
  Craig Baker

Edmonton, AB T5M

D-U-N-S 20-458-1920   (SL)
1496803 ALBERTA INC
HIBCO CONSTRUCTION
15849 116 Ave Nw, Edmonton, AB, T5M 3W1
(780) 463-7787
Emp Here 45   *Sales* 10,705,545
SIC 8742 Management consulting services
  Hani Barzagar

D-U-N-S 20-352-5076   (HQ)
564967 ALBERTA LTD
11703 160 St Nw, Edmonton, AB, T5M 3Z3
(780) 451-0060
Sales 24,054,800
SIC 6712 Bank holding companies
  John Storey

D-U-N-S 24-143-7917   (SL)
792259 ALBERTA LTD
NELRO SERVICES
15377 117 Ave Nw, Edmonton, AB, T5M 3X4
(780) 454-4838
Emp Here 30   *Sales* 12,580,650
SIC 6712 Bank holding companies
  Nelson Caron

D-U-N-S 24-335-4185   (BR)
ACKLANDS - GRAINGER INC
AGI
(*Suby of* W.W. GRAINGER, INC.)
11708 167 St Nw, Edmonton, AB, T5M 3Z2
(780) 453-0300
Emp Here 300
SIC 5085 Industrial supplies
  Henry Buckley

D-U-N-S 20-111-5433   (HQ)
AGRIFOODS INTERNATIONAL COOPERA-TIVE LTD
11671 160 St Nw, Edmonton, AB, T5M 3Z3
(780) 962-5787
Emp Here 25   *Sales* 22,101,973
SIC 4212 Local trucking, without storage
  Myron Glatt
  Ben Brandsema

D-U-N-S 20-080-5737   (HQ)
ALLDRITT DEVELOPMENT LIMITED
SHAMROCK PROPERTY MANAGEMENT
14310 111 Ave Nw Suite 305, Edmonton, AB, T5M 3Z7
(780) 453-5631
Emp Here 60   *Sales* 14,356,615
SIC 6512 Nonresidential building operators
  Stanley H Alldritt

D-U-N-S 20-052-5421   (BR)
ALLDRITT DEVELOPMENT LIMITED
JETCO MECHANICAL
15035 114 Ave Nw, Edmonton, AB, T5M 2Z1
(780) 451-2732
Emp Here 120
SIC 1711 Plumbing, heating, air-conditioning
  John Mcmurdo

D-U-N-S 20-809-1231   (SL)
ALLWEST FURNISHINGS LTD
14325 112 Ave Nw, Edmonton, AB, T5M 2V3
(780) 452-8212
Emp Here 60   *Sales* 30,531,360
SIC 5021 Furniture
  Clayton Shaw
  Pat Johnston
  Roberta Van Wyk
  David Law

D-U-N-S 24-395-0318   (HQ)
ASHLEY CARPETS LTD
ASHLEY FINE FLOORS
14340 111 Ave Nw, Edmonton, AB, T5M 2P4
(780) 454-9503
Sales 13,944,180
SIC 5713 Floor covering stores
  Robert Heslip

D-U-N-S 25-090-6245   (SL)
AYRE & OXFORD INC
13455 114 Ave Nw Unit 203, Edmonton, AB, T5M 2E2
(780) 448-4984
Emp Here 42   *Sales* 13,739,334
SIC 6531 Real estate agents and managers
  John Ayre
  Donald Oxford

D-U-N-S 24-245-2789   (SL)
B SQUARED AIRSOFT LTD
14574 116 Ave Nw, Edmonton, AB, T5M 3E9
(780) 884-8292
Emp Here 23   *Sales* 11,972,466
SIC 5099 Durable goods, nec

D-U-N-S 20-720-1005   (HQ)
BINDER CONSTRUCTION LIMITED
11635 160 St Nw, Edmonton, AB, T5M 3Z3
(780) 452-2740
Sales 11,768,275
SIC 1542 Nonresidential construction, nec
  Duncan Binder
  Colin Binder

D-U-N-S 20-567-0024   (HQ)
BRICK LTD, THE
(*Suby of* LEON'S FURNITURE LIMITED)
16930 114 Ave Nw, Edmonton, AB, T5M 3S2
(780) 930-6000
Sales 1,520,207,100
SIC 5712 Furniture stores
  Dave Freeman
  Greg Nakonechny
  Ken Grondin
  Terry Leon
  Dominic Scarangella
  Ed Leon
  John Cooney

D-U-N-S 20-720-9172   (HQ)
BRICK WAREHOUSE LP, THE
BRICK
16930 114 Ave Nw, Edmonton, AB, T5M 3S2
(780) 930-6000
Emp Here 100   *Sales* 1,359,327,971
SIC 6712 Bank holding companies
  Crystal Haining
  David Green

D-U-N-S 24-582-2994   (HQ)
BUFFALO PARCEL COURIER SERVICE LTD
BUFFALO AIR EXPRESS
11310 153 St Nw, Edmonton, AB, T5M 1X6
(780) 455-9283
Sales 11,974,230
SIC 7389 Business services, nec
  Joseph Mcbryan
  Sharon Mcbryan

D-U-N-S 24-004-2705   (HQ)
C.A. FISCHER LUMBER CO. LTD
WESTLOCK BUILDINGS SUPPLIES, A DIV OF
16210 114 Ave Nw Suite 200, Edmonton, AB, T5M 2Z5
(780) 453-1994
Emp Here 5   *Sales* 22,750,420
SIC 5211 Lumber and other building materials
  Charles Fischer
  Kenneth Mccourt
  Gary Klassen
  Ron Jakimchuk

D-U-N-S 20-808-2024   (BR)
CANEM SYSTEMS LTD
(*Suby of* STUART OLSON INC)

11320 151 St Nw, Edmonton, AB, T5M 4A9
(780) 454-0381
Emp Here 140
SIC 1731 Electrical work
  Peter Rasmussen

D-U-N-S 24-618-5172   (SL)
CANTEGA TECHNOLOGIES INC
11603 165 St Nw, Edmonton, AB, T5M 3Z1
(780) 448-9700
Emp Here 50   *Sales* 10,233,650
SIC 3699 Electrical equipment and supplies, nec
  Brent Stankowski
  Marty Niles

D-U-N-S 20-969-8380   (SL)
COLLEGE AND ASSOCIATION OF REGIS-TERED NURSES OF ALBERTA
11620 168 St Nw, Edmonton, AB, T5M 4A6
(780) 451-0043
Emp Here 50   *Sales* 11,684,750
SIC 8621 Professional organizations
  Mary-Anne Robinson

D-U-N-S 20-081-4507   (HQ)
CORMODE & DICKSON CONSTRUCTION (1983) LTD
(*Suby of* ELZEN HOLDINGS LTD)
11450 160 St Nw Unit 200, Edmonton, AB, T5M 3Y7
(780) 701-9300
Emp Here 50   *Sales* 22,827,798
SIC 1541 Industrial buildings and warehouses
  Berend Elzen

D-U-N-S 25-385-4566   (SL)
CTS EQUIPMENT TRANSPORT LTD
CLIFF TOWING
11480 156 St Nw, Edmonton, AB, T5M 3N2
(780) 451-3900
Emp Here 95   *Sales* 26,913,500
SIC 7549 Automotive services, nec
  Phil Strong

D-U-N-S 20-100-7577   (SL)
D.M. EXPRESS
11616 145 St Nw, Edmonton, AB, T5M 1V8
(780) 454-1188
Emp Here 27   *Sales* 11,974,230
SIC 7389 Business services, nec
  Douglas Mochinski
  Dianne Mochinski

D-U-N-S 24-834-2508   (SL)
DUCHESS BAKE SHOP LTD
DUCHESS ATELIER
10718 124 St, Edmonton, AB, T5M 0H1
(780) 488-4999
Emp Here 60   *Sales* 17,608,620
SIC 5461 Retail bakeries
  Jacob Pelletier
  Garner Beggs
  Giselle Courteau

D-U-N-S 20-135-8798   (HQ)
DYAND MECHANICAL SYSTEMS INC
WOOD & ENERGY STORE
14840 115 Ave Nw, Edmonton, AB, T5M 3C1
(780) 452-5800
Emp Here 126   *Sales* 31,762,640
SIC 5999 Miscellaneous retail stores, nec
  Art Dyck

D-U-N-S 20-081-8060   (HQ)
ECCO HEATING PRODUCTS LTD
ECCO SUPPLY
14310 111 Ave Nw Suite 300, Edmonton, AB, T5M 3Z7
(780) 452-7350
Emp Here 24   *Sales* 144,159,768
SIC 3433 Heating equipment, except electric
  Stanley H. Alldritt
  Shaine Nobert

D-U-N-S 20-594-5694   (SL)
EDMONTON COIN VENDING (1970) LTD
11690 147 St Nw, Edmonton, AB, T5M 1W2

(780) 452-2727
Emp Here 25   *Sales* 16,411,600
SIC 5962 Merchandising machine operators
  Abe Goldstein
  Henri Cynamon
  Gerald Mcgregor

D-U-N-S 24-441-9214   (HQ)
EDMONTON FASTENERS & TOOLS LTD
16409 111 Ave Nw, Edmonton, AB, T5M 2S2
(780) 484-3113
Emp Here 35   *Sales* 28,501,560
SIC 5085 Industrial supplies
  Mark Elliott

D-U-N-S 20-895-1491   (HQ)
EDMONTON GEAR CENTRE LTD
GEAR CENTRE, THE
14811 116 Ave Nw, Edmonton, AB, T5M 3E8
(780) 452-6933
Emp Here 25   *Sales* 124,511,580
SIC 5013 Motor vehicle supplies and new parts
  Robert Gibson

D-U-N-S 20-810-5056   (SL)
EDMONTON REAL ESTATE BOARD CO-OPERATIVE LISTING BUREAU LIMITED
REALTORS ASSOCIATION OF EDMONTON
14220 112 Ave Nw, Edmonton, AB, T5M 2T8
(780) 451-6666
Emp Here 50   *Sales* 12,930,750
SIC 8611 Business associations
  Michael Thompson
  James Mabey
  Darcy Torhjelm
  Lindsay Carlson
  John Carle
  Michael Brodrick
  Brad Woodward
  Kathy Schmidt
  Tom Shearer

D-U-N-S 24-394-4196   (SL)
EDMONTON SPACE & SCIENCE FOUNDA-TION
TELUS WORLD OF SCIENCE-EDMONTON
11211 142 St Nw, Edmonton, AB, T5M 4A1
(780) 452-9100
Emp Here 130   *Sales* 13,631,800
SIC 8412 Museums and art galleries
  Scott Henderson

D-U-N-S 25-363-6997   (HQ)
ELZEN HOLDINGS LTD
11450 160 St Nw Suite 200, Edmonton, AB, T5M 3Y7
(780) 453-6944
Sales 22,827,798
SIC 1541 Industrial buildings and warehouses
  Ben Elzen
  Michael Deacon

D-U-N-S 24-327-7282   (HQ)
FIRST TRUCK CENTRE INC
(*Suby of* FIRST INDUSTRIES CORPORA-TION)
11313 170 St Nw, Edmonton, AB, T5M 3P5
(780) 413-8800
Sales 125,856,000
SIC 5511 New and used car dealers
  David Leeworthy

D-U-N-S 24-274-4050   (BR)
GDI SERVICES (CANADA) LP
(*Suby of* GDI SERVICES AUX IMMEUBLES INC)
14588 116 Ave Nw, Edmonton, AB, T5M 3E9
(780) 428-9508
Emp Here 250
SIC 7349 Building maintenance services, nec
  Hayley Lillico

D-U-N-S 25-013-7072   (SL)
GETTING READY FOR INCLUSION TODAY (THE GRIT PROGRAM) SOCIETY OF ED-MONTON
GRIT PROGRAM, THE

14930 114 Ave Nw, Edmonton, AB, T5M 4G4
(780) 454-9910
Emp Here 75   *Sales* 4,580,175
SIC 8351 Child day care services
 Barbara Reid

D-U-N-S 25-325-7372   (HQ)
GIBSON, R. W. CONSULTING SERVICES LTD
PAT'S DRIVELINE, DIV OF
14713 116 Ave Nw, Edmonton, AB, T5M 3E8
(780) 452-8800
Sales 524,103,404
SIC 8741 Management services
 Robert W Gibson

D-U-N-S 20-082-2252   (SL)
GLENORA LUMBER & BUILDING SUPPLIES LTD
14505 116 Ave Nw, Edmonton, AB, T5M 3E8
(780) 453-5691
Emp Here 25   *Sales* 11,179,350
SIC 5031 Lumber, plywood, and millwork
 Barbara Galbraith

D-U-N-S 20-895-3216   (HQ)
GOLDEN FLOORING ACCESSORIES PS LTD
(*Suby of* FASCO FLOORING ACCESSORIES SYSTEM CORP)
11662 154 St Nw, Edmonton, AB, T5M 3N8
(780) 451-4222
Emp Here 5   *Sales* 10,224,830
SIC 5169 Chemicals and allied products, nec
 Leon Simon

D-U-N-S 24-064-5622   (BR)
GRAND & TOY LIMITED
(*Suby of* OFFICE DEPOT, INC.)
11522 168 St Nw, Edmonton, AB, T5M 3T9
(866) 391-8111
Emp Here 80
SIC 5112 Stationery and office supplies
 Brian Kirdeikis

D-U-N-S 24-308-1598   (HQ)
GRIMSHAW TRUCKING LP
(*Suby of* MULLEN GROUP LTD)
11510 151 St Nw, Edmonton, AB, T5M 3N6
(780) 414-2850
Emp Here 20   *Sales* 20,570,600
SIC 4212 Local trucking, without storage
 Joe Bogach
 Gary Leddy
 Tom Hanna
 Curtis Timmer
 Craig Schmit

D-U-N-S 24-803-5474   (BR)
HOME DEPOT OF CANADA INC
HOME DEPOT
(*Suby of* THE HOME DEPOT INC)
1 Westmount Shopping Ctr Nw Suite 604, Edmonton, AB, T5M 3L7
(780) 732-9225
Emp Here 80
SIC 5251 Hardware stores
 Will Levirs

D-U-N-S 25-451-1520   (BR)
HUNTER DOUGLAS CANADA HOLDINGS INC
15508 114 Ave Nw, Edmonton, AB, T5M 3S8
(800) 265-1363
Emp Here 150
SIC 2591 Drapery hardware and window blinds and shades
 Noel Bartholomew

D-U-N-S 25-677-3123   (SL)
INSURANCE BANK
LUNDGREN & YOUNG
16403 111 Ave Nw, Edmonton, AB, T5M 2S2
(780) 439-2265
Emp Here 18   *Sales* 10,438,632
SIC 6411 Insurance agents, brokers, and service
 Adrienne Healey

D-U-N-S 24-855-8756   (SL)
JETCO MECHANICAL LIMITED
15035 114 Ave Nw, Edmonton, AB, T5M 2Z1
(780) 451-2732
Emp Here 100   *Sales* 44,717,400
SIC 5074 Plumbing and heating equipment and supplies (hydronics)
 Gary Key

D-U-N-S 20-639-5688   (SL)
KASTNER AUCTIONS LTD
11205 149 St Nw, Edmonton, AB, T5M 1W6
(780) 447-0596
Emp Here 31   *Sales* 13,748,190
SIC 7389 Business services, nec
 David (Dave) Mclachlan
 Sean Kastner

D-U-N-S 20-921-5289   (SL)
KEETHILLS AGGREGATE CO LTD
11428 168 St Nw Suite 100, Edmonton, AB, T5M 3T9

Emp Here 60   *Sales* 26,830,440
SIC 5032 Brick, stone, and related material
 John Whissell

D-U-N-S 20-746-2367   (HQ)
KELLER CONSTRUCTION LTD
11430 160 St Nw, Edmonton, AB, T5M 3Y7
(780) 484-1010
Emp Here 45   *Sales* 42,775,350
SIC 1542 Nonresidential construction, nec
 John Cameron
 Christine Marchuk

D-U-N-S 20-101-8095   (BR)
LOBLAWS INC
REAL CANADIAN SUPERSTORE
(*Suby of* LOBLAW COMPANIES LIMITED)
14740 111 Ave Nw, Edmonton, AB, T5M 2P5
(780) 452-5411
Emp Here 150
SIC 5141 Groceries, general line
 Tyrone Barceski

D-U-N-S 24-391-8307   (SL)
M.A.P WATER AND SEWER SERVICES LTD
14303 116 Ave Nw, Edmonton, AB, T5M 4G2
(780) 453-6996
Emp Here 85   *Sales* 21,457,570
SIC 1623 Water, sewer, and utility lines
 Nick Matera
 Tony Matera

D-U-N-S 25-106-7484   (HQ)
MAINLINE EQUIPMENT LTD
14535 114 Ave Nw, Edmonton, AB, T5M 2Y8
(780) 453-3695
Emp Here 21   *Sales* 15,675,858
SIC 5084 Industrial machinery and equipment
 Chris Treasure

D-U-N-S 24-393-4049   (HQ)
MCMAN YOUTH, FAMILY AND COMMUNITY SERVICES ASSOCIATION
MCMAN SUPPORTED INDEPENDENT LIVING
11016 127 St Nw, Edmonton, AB, T5M 0T2
(780) 482-4461
Sales 61,433,600
SIC 8322 Individual and family services
 Danica Frazer
 John Meston
 Rick Newcombe
 Luba Rusyn

D-U-N-S 20-775-5620   (SL)
MHK INSURANCE INC
12316 107 Ave Nw, Edmonton, AB, T5M 1Z1
(780) 454-9363
Emp Here 40   *Sales* 23,196,960
SIC 6411 Insurance agents, brokers, and service
 Jefffrey Homynyk
 Dale Faulkner

D-U-N-S 25-539-0015   (HQ)

MILLAR WESTERN FOREST PRODUCTS LTD
SPRUCELAND MILLWORKS
(*Suby of* MILLAR, HUGH FAMILY HOLDINGS INC)
16640 111 Ave Nw, Edmonton, AB, T5M 2S5
(780) 486-8200
Sales 199,994,528
SIC 2611 Pulp mills
 J. Craig Armstrong
 David Anderson
 Brian Mcconkey
 H. Mackenzie Millar
 Andrew Bursky
 Timothy Fazio
 Jacob Hudson

D-U-N-S 24-333-0099   (HQ)
MILLAR WESTERN INDUSTRIES LTD
MILLAR WESTERN FOREST PRODUCT
(*Suby of* MILLAR, HUGH FAMILY HOLDINGS INC)
16640 111 Ave Nw, Edmonton, AB, T5M 2S5
(780) 486-8200
Emp Here 5   *Sales* 56,804,200
SIC 2819 Industrial inorganic chemicals, nec
 Craig Armstrong
 H Mackenzie Millar

D-U-N-S 24-984-3236   (HQ)
MILLAR, HUGH FAMILY HOLDINGS INC
16640 111 Ave Nw, Edmonton, AB, T5M 2S5
(780) 486-8200
Emp Here 2   *Sales* 20,952,686
SIC 1611 Highway and street construction
 Jim Millar
 Mackenzie H Millar

D-U-N-S 20-083-4232   (SL)
MUTUAL PROPANE LIMITED
16203 114 Ave Nw, Edmonton, AB, T5M 2Z3
(780) 451-4454
Emp Here 38   *Sales* 17,822,190
SIC 5984 Liquefied petroleum gas dealers
 Darren Smith
 Stanley J Chevraux
 Robert Suder
 Gary Bertrand
 Corry Osland
 Mitchelle Rasmussan

D-U-N-S 24-301-2114   (SL)
MUTUAL TANKS LTD
16203 114 Ave Nw, Edmonton, AB, T5M 2Z3
(780) 451-4454
Emp Here 40   *Sales* 19,075,724
SIC 5984 Liquefied petroleum gas dealers
 Darren Smith

D-U-N-S 24-984-1776   (HQ)
NATION-WIDE HOME SERVICES CORP
(*Suby of* MANNAMARK HOLDINGS INC)
11228 142 St Nw, Edmonton, AB, T5M 1T9
(780) 454-1937
Sales 21,594,650
SIC 6712 Bank holding companies

D-U-N-S 24-805-7080   (HQ)
NATIONAL CONCRETE ACCESSORIES CANADA INC
(*Suby of* COOPERATIE NOVA ARGENT U.A.)
14760 116 Ave Nw, Edmonton, AB, T5M 3G1
(780) 451-1212
Emp Here 95   *Sales* 113,925,600
SIC 5032 Brick, stone, and related material
 Mike Hardman
 Dan Walda
 Marvin Ramsay
 Andrew Boulanger

D-U-N-S 20-345-4160   (SL)
NIS NORTHERN INDUSTRIAL SALES LTD
11440 163 St Nw, Edmonton, AB, T5M 3T3
(780) 454-2682
Emp Here 92   *Sales* 43,702,392
SIC 5085 Industrial supplies
 Timothy Mcdonald

 Braden Green
 Glenn Watt

D-U-N-S 24-716-3470   (HQ)
NORSEMAN GROUP LTD
14545 115 Ave Nw, Edmonton, AB, T5M 3B8
(780) 451-6939
Emp Here 15   *Sales* 99,500,625
SIC 2394 Canvas and related products
 Al Bryant
 Ronald Bryant
 Terry Bryant

D-U-N-S 20-083-6013   (HQ)
NORSEMAN INC
NORSEMAN STRUCTURES
(*Suby of* NORSEMAN GROUP LTD)
14545 115 Ave Nw, Edmonton, AB, T5M 3B8
(780) 451-6828
Emp Here 100   *Sales* 74,331,600
SIC 1791 Structural steel erection
 Ronald Bryant
 Terry Bryant

D-U-N-S 20-083-6385   (HQ)
O'HANLON PAVING LTD
16511 116 Ave Nw, Edmonton, AB, T5M 3V1
(780) 434-8555
Sales 15,146,520
SIC 1611 Highway and street construction
 Ronald Fath
 Thomas Fath
 Mary Fath

D-U-N-S 24-227-5113   (HQ)
PAT'S DRIVE LINE SPECIALTY & MACHINE EDMONTON LTD
14715 116 Ave Nw, Edmonton, AB, T5M 3E8
(780) 453-5105
Emp Here 1   *Sales* 22,384,300
SIC 3714 Motor vehicle parts and accessories
 Robert Gibson

D-U-N-S 24-984-2956   (SL)
RESCOM INC
IMPORTANT AND MECHANT SMALLER PROJECT
(*Suby of* SUTHERLAND DEVELOPMENT GROUP LTD)
12704 110 Ave Nw, Edmonton, AB, T5M 2L7
(780) 454-6500
Emp Here 80   *Sales* 9,982,080
SIC 8741 Management services
 John Donald Agnew
 Anne Agnew
 Reg Kinal

D-U-N-S 24-379-5551   (HQ)
ROCKY MOUNTAIN LIQUOR INC
11478 149 St, Edmonton, AB, T5M 1W7
(780) 483-8183
Emp Here 45   *Sales* 34,174,484
SIC 5921 Liquor stores
 Peter Byrne
 Allyson Byrne
 Sarah Stelmack
 Frank Coleman
 Robert Normandeau

D-U-N-S 24-522-8911   (HQ)
ROMADOR ENTERPRISES LTD
INTERNATIONAL BEAUTY SERVICES
11348 142 St Nw, Edmonton, AB, T5M 1T9
(780) 454-3388
Sales 46,077,522
SIC 5087 Service establishment equipment
 Leigh Tait
 Graham Kenny

D-U-N-S 24-523-7318   (HQ)
S.I.F. SUPERIOR INDUSTRIAL FRICTIONS LTD
11570 154 St Nw, Edmonton, AB, T5M 3N8
(780) 451-6894
Emp Here 60   *Sales* 16,788,225
SIC 3714 Motor vehicle parts and accessories
 Cordell Allers
 Don Shultz

Manfred Glombick
Adelhardt Glombick

D-U-N-S 20-703-9160   (BR)
SAPUTO PRODUITS LAITIERS CANADA S.E.N.C.
(Suby of SAPUTO PRODUITS LAITIERS CANADA S.E.N.C.)
16110 116 Ave Nw, Edmonton, AB, T5M 3V4
(514) 328-3366
Emp Here 370
SIC 5141 Groceries, general line
Chuck Frederic

D-U-N-S 24-331-2782   (BR)
SEALY CANADA LTD
(Suby of TEMPUR SEALY INTERNATIONAL, INC.)
14550 112 Ave Nw, Edmonton, AB, T5M 2T9
(780) 452-3070
Emp Here 100
SIC 2515 Mattresses and bedsprings
Paul Ralph

D-U-N-S 25-453-9141   (BR)
SLH TRANSPORT INC
SLH TRANSPORT
(Suby of HOLDING CANADIAN AMERICAN TRANSPORTATION C.A.T. INC)
14525 112 Ave Nw, Edmonton, AB, T5M 2V5
(780) 451-7543
Emp Here 80
SIC 4212 Local trucking, without storage
Murray Parr

D-U-N-S 20-059-4385   (BR)
SMS EQUIPMENT INC
CONECO EQUIPMENT
(Suby of SUMITOMO CORPORATION)
16116 111 Ave Nw, Edmonton, AB, T5M 2S1
(780) 451-2630
Emp Here 160
SIC 5082 Construction and mining machinery
Bart Boos

D-U-N-S 25-185-8239   (BR)
SOBEYS WEST INC
CANADA SAFEWAY #838
(Suby of EMPIRE COMPANY LIMITED)
601 Westmount Shopping Center, Edmonton, AB, T5M 3L7
(780) 451-1860
Emp Here 155
SIC 5411 Grocery stores
Mark Schuck

D-U-N-S 24-585-4054   (SL)
SPAR CONSTRUCTION (EDMONTON) LTD
14415 114 Ave Nw, Edmonton, AB, T5M 2Y8
(780) 453-3555
Emp Here 50   *Sales* 15,943,450
SIC 1521 Single-family housing construction
Colin Campbell
Ken Lakhram
Mark Comeau
Rick Woodcock

D-U-N-S 24-066-2551   (SL)
ST ANDREWS HOUSING LIMITED
ST ANDREWS CENTRE
12720 111 Ave Nw Suite 345, Edmonton, AB, T5M 3X3
(780) 452-4444
Emp Here 60   *Sales* 13,252,260
SIC 6513 Apartment building operators
Paula Boissonnault

D-U-N-S 24-983-2577   (HQ)
STORDOR INVESTMENTS LTD
OVERHEAD DOOR COMPANY OF EDMONTON
(Suby of 564967 ALBERTA LTD)
11703 160 St Nw, Edmonton, AB, T5M 3Z3
(780) 451-0060
Sales 22,750,420
SIC 5211 Lumber and other building materials
John Rodney Storey

D-U-N-S 25-643-4593   (SL)
STREAMLINE FIRE PROTECTION LTD
15695 116 Ave Nw, Edmonton, AB, T5M 3W1
(780) 436-6911
Emp Here 24   *Sales* 10,020,144
SIC 7382 Security systems services
Michelle Namchuk

D-U-N-S 24-378-5842   (SL)
TRANS GLOBAL LIFE INSURANCE COMPANY
(Suby of BRICK WAREHOUSE LP, THE)
16930 114 Ave Nw Suite 275, Edmonton, AB, T5M 3S2
(780) 930-6000
Emp Here 10   *Sales* 18,466,590
SIC 6311 Life insurance
David Freeman
Gregory Nakonechny
Gary G. Campbell
Domenic Ieraci
Dominic Scarangella
Frank Gagliano
James Caldwell
Mary Ann Leon

D-U-N-S 24-786-9027   (HQ)
UNICON CONCRETE SPECIALTIES LTD
11740 156 St Nw, Edmonton, AB, T5M 3T5
(780) 455-3737
Emp Here 34   *Sales* 12,044,340
SIC 5211 Lumber and other building materials
Brett Desroches

D-U-N-S 25-064-5298   (BR)
UNITED PARCEL SERVICE CANADA LTD
UPS
(Suby of UNITED PARCEL SERVICE, INC.)
11204 151 St Nw, Edmonton, AB, T5M 4A9
(800) 742-5877
Emp Here 80
SIC 7389 Business services, nec
Mike Jarrett

D-U-N-S 25-158-6210   (SL)
VESTATE (CANADA) LTD
VESTATE MOULDING
16602 114 Ave Nw, Edmonton, AB, T5M 3R8
(780) 433-1695
Emp Here 26   *Sales* 13,230,256
SIC 5023 Homefurnishings
Wei Wong
Eng Yong
Ding Yim
Teck Tang

D-U-N-S 24-984-2378   (SL)
VISIONCORP INTERNATIONAL INC
16715 113 Ave Nw, Edmonton, AB, T5M 2X2
(780) 489-2012
Emp Here 43   *Sales* 22,383,306
SIC 5099 Durable goods, nec
Brad Margolis
Mike Cooke
Nancy Prokopuk
Ted Allsopp

D-U-N-S 20-895-3000   (HQ)
WAYMARC INDUSTRIES LTD
16304 117 Ave Nw, Edmonton, AB, T5M 3W2
(780) 453-2358
Emp Here 32   *Sales* 27,724,788
SIC 5046 Commercial equipment, nec
Jamie Pernisie
Steve Atkinson
Robert Knibbs

D-U-N-S 20-896-4866   (HQ)
WESCLEAN EQUIPMENT & CLEANING SUPPLIES LTD
(Suby of BUNZL PUBLIC LIMITED COMPANY)
11450 149 St Nw, Edmonton, AB, T5M 1W7
(780) 451-1533
Emp Here 54   *Sales* 85,352,750
SIC 5087 Service establishment equipment
Reid Toreson

William Shepherd

D-U-N-S 20-790-6244   (BR)
WINNIFRED STEWART ASSOCIATION FOR THE MENTALLY HANDICAPPED
WORK OPPORTUNITIES
(Suby of WINNIFRED STEWART ASSOCIATION FOR THE MENTALLY HANDICAPPED)
11130 131 St Nw, Edmonton, AB, T5M 1C1
(780) 453-6707
Emp Here 150
SIC 8322 Individual and family services
Larry Smook

Edmonton, AB T5N

D-U-N-S 20-594-1768   (HQ)
AIRSPRAY (1967) LTD
(Suby of HAMILTON AVIATION LTD)
10141 122 St Nw, Edmonton, AB, T5N 1L7
(780) 453-1737
Emp Here 3   *Sales* 10,940,720
SIC 0851 Forestry services
Paul Lane
Kirk Carleton
Tanya Gray

D-U-N-S 20-896-6945   (HQ)
ALBERTA TEACHERS' ASSOCIATION, THE
11010 142 St Nw, Edmonton, AB, T5N 2R1
(780) 447-9400
Emp Here 114   *Sales* 42,720,300
SIC 8631 Labor organizations
Greg Jeffery
Jenny Regal
Jason Schilling
Dennis Theobald
Janice Sledz

D-U-N-S 24-400-4743   (SL)
ALBERTA TEACHERS' RETIREMENT FUND BOARD
ATRF
11010 142 St Nw Suite 600, Edmonton, AB, T5N 2R1
(780) 451-4166
Emp Here 37   *Sales* 45,710,466
SIC 6371 Pension, health, and welfare funds
Emilian Groch
Randy Round
Michael E. Griffiths
James Fleming
Lowell Epp
Greg Meeker
Sharon L. Vogrinetz
Gene Williams

D-U-N-S 24-766-6837   (SL)
CANADIAN CORPS OF COMMISSIONAIRES (NORTHERN ALBERTA)
NORTHERN ALBERTA DIVISION
10633 124 St Nw Suite 101, Edmonton, AB, T5N 1S5
(780) 451-1974
Emp Here 1,800   *Sales* 47,250,000
SIC 7381 Detective and armored car services
John D Slater
Jennifer Daly

D-U-N-S 20-014-7598   (HQ)
COMPUTRONIX CORPORATION
(Suby of H.W.L. FAMILY ENTERPRISES INC)
10216 124 St Nw Suite 200, Edmonton, AB, T5N 4A3
(780) 454-3700
Emp Here 2   *Sales* 12,976,380
SIC 7371 Custom computer programming services
Harmen Leusink
James Den Otter

D-U-N-S 24-356-3132   (HQ)
DRAYDEN INSURANCE LTD
10310 124 St Nw Suite 100, Edmonton, AB,

T5N 1R2
(780) 482-6300
Sales 569,532,480
SIC 6411 Insurance agents, brokers, and service
Glenn Baron
Loreen Belovich
Armand Nielsen
Pearl Nielsen
Brian Nielsen

D-U-N-S 20-713-9325   (HQ)
ELVES SPECIAL NEEDS SOCIETY
ELVES CHILD DEVELOPMENT CENTER
10825 142 St Nw, Edmonton, AB, T5N 3Y7
(780) 454-5310
Sales 19,823,800
SIC 8211 Elementary and secondary schools
Barbara Tymchak-Olafson

D-U-N-S 25-266-0568   (HQ)
GREATER EDMONTON FOUNDATION
14220 109 Ave Nw, Edmonton, AB, T5N 4B3
(780) 482-6561
Sales 18,156,000
SIC 8361 Residential care
Karen Lynch
Catherine Cheng
Nomagugu Baleni
Bernadette Bolton
Jacquie Eales
Francine Gregory
Craig Henderson
Jack Little
James Murphy, Q.C.

D-U-N-S 20-934-9591   (BR)
JOHNSON INC
(Suby of RSA INSURANCE GROUP PLC)
12220 Stony Plain Rd Nw Suite 301, Edmonton, AB, T5N 3Y4
Emp Here 100
SIC 6331 Fire, marine, and casualty insurance
Ken Bennett

D-U-N-S 20-117-5101   (HQ)
LIGHTFORM CANADA INC
10545 124 St Nw, Edmonton, AB, T5N 1R8
(780) 413-9898
Sales 13,415,220
SIC 5063 Electrical apparatus and equipment
Richard Assaly

D-U-N-S 20-895-7993   (HQ)
LLOYD SADD INSURANCE BROKERS LTD
10240 124 St Nw Unit 700, Edmonton, AB, T5N 3W6
(780) 483-4544
Sales 147,819,360
SIC 6411 Insurance agents, brokers, and service

D-U-N-S 24-853-5072   (HQ)
MCLENNAN ROSS LLP
12220 Stony Plain Rd Nw Suite 600, Edmonton, AB, T5N 3Y4
(780) 482-9200
Emp Here 1   *Sales* 13,305,840
SIC 8111 Legal services
Roderick A Mclennan
David J R Ross

D-U-N-S 20-070-2673   (SL)
NET-LINX AMERICAS, INC
12431 Stony Plain Rd Nw Suite 200, Edmonton, AB, T5N 3N3
Emp Here 200   *Sales* 33,357,147
SIC 2741 Miscellaneous publishing
Holm Hallbauer

Edmonton, AB T5P

D-U-N-S 20-969-1906   (HQ)

ALBERTA UNION OF PROVINCIAL EM-PLOYEES, THE
AUPE.
10451 170 St Nw Suite 200, Edmonton, AB, T5P 4S7
(780) 930-3300
Emp Here 60   *Sales* 41,296,290
SIC 8631 Labor organizations
Guy Smith
Mike Dempsey
Bonnie Gostola
Carrie-Lynn Rusznak
Glen Scott
Susan Slade
Karen Weiers
Jason Heistad

D-U-N-S 20-515-5984   (BR)
GOLDER ASSOCIATES LTD
(*Suby of* GOLDER ASSOCIATES CORPORATION)
16820 107 Ave Nw, Edmonton, AB, T5P 4C3
(780) 483-3499
Emp Here 126
SIC 8711 Engineering services
Kurtis Saker

D-U-N-S 25-065-1460   (BR)
GRANT MACEWAN UNIVERSITY
HAAR, JOHN L. THEATRE
(*Suby of* GRANT MACEWAN UNIVERSITY)
10045 156 St Nw Rm 402, Edmonton, AB, T5P 2P7
(780) 497-4310
Emp Here 250
SIC 8299 Schools and educational services, nec
Dianne Westwood

D-U-N-S 20-050-6918   (SL)
INSURANCE GUYS INC, THE
16612 109 Ave Nw, Edmonton, AB, T5P 1C2
(780) 448-2298
Emp Here 25   *Sales* 14,498,100
SIC 6411 Insurance agents, brokers, and service
Karen Hoslin

D-U-N-S 24-149-6517   (SL)
INTEGRATED FINANCIAL GROUP INC
INDUSTRIAL ALLIANCE PACIFIC LIFE INSURANCE
10220 156 St Nw Suite 200, Edmonton, AB, T5P 2R1
(780) 454-6505
Emp Here 50   *Sales* 28,996,200
SIC 6411 Insurance agents, brokers, and service
Brad Liem

D-U-N-S 24-327-3836   (BR)
LONDON DRUGS LIMITED
(*Suby of* H.Y. LOUIE CO. LIMITED)
14951 Stony Plain Rd Nw, Edmonton, AB, T5P 4W1
(780) 944-4522
Emp Here 100
SIC 5912 Drug stores and proprietary stores
Charlene Schindel

D-U-N-S 25-207-0008   (SL)
MCL POWER INC
(*Suby of* SUDDEN VALLEY HOLDINGS LTD)
16821 107 Ave Nw, Edmonton, AB, T5P 0Y8
(780) 440-8775
Emp Here 75   *Sales* 16,337,175
SIC 1731 Electrical work
Les Rattai

D-U-N-S 24-385-8763   (HQ)
MEDICENTRES CANADA INC
10458 Mayfield Rd Nw Suite 204, Edmonton, AB, T5P 4P4
(780) 483-7115
Emp Here 25   *Sales* 57,062,100
SIC 8011 Offices and clinics of medical doctors
John Reddington

Andrew Johnston

D-U-N-S 24-064-4831   (HQ)
MICHENER-ALLEN AUCTIONEERING LTD
Hwy 16 A, Edmonton, AB, T5P 4V8
(780) 470-5584
Emp Here 40   *Sales* 26,953,140
SIC 7389 Business services, nec
Ethel Michener
Wade Michener
Ian Michener
Vance Michener

D-U-N-S 24-420-3795   (SL)
PARK LIGHTING AND FURNITURE LTD
10353 170 St Nw, Edmonton, AB, T5P 4V4
(780) 434-9600
Emp Here 70   *Sales* 16,268,210
SIC 5719 Miscellaneous homefurnishings
Victor Johannesen

D-U-N-S 24-086-9818   (SL)
WESTVIEW INN LTD
CONTINENTAL INN
16625 Stony Plain Rd Nw, Edmonton, AB, T5P 4A8
(780) 484-7751
Emp Here 100   *Sales* 9,269,000
SIC 7011 Hotels and motels
Michael Gales
Shirley Werstiuk
Daniel Beniuk
Anne Bilinske
Robert Broada
Peter Kule
Catherine Mazepa
Victor Pysyk
David Trofimuk
Ben Starkman

D-U-N-S 24-282-4118   (HQ)
WESTWORLD COMPUTERS LTD
10333 170 St Nw, Edmonton, AB, T5P 4V4
(780) 454-5190
Emp Here 23   *Sales* 11,652,072
SIC 4899 Communication services, nec
Carl Harr
Gail Frances Harr
Tracy Ricard

Edmonton, AB T5R

D-U-N-S 20-080-4474   (SL)
ADVANCE FOODS LTD
VALLEYVIEW IGA
9106 142 St Nw, Edmonton, AB, T5R 0M7
(780) 483-1525
Emp Here 70   *Sales* 20,543,390
SIC 5411 Grocery stores
Andrew Taschuk
Peter Taschuk
Gerrie Taschuk
Lena Taschuk

D-U-N-S 20-897-6258   (SL)
CANTERBURY FOUNDATION
8403 142 St Nw Suite 125, Edmonton, AB, T5R 4L3
(780) 483-5361
Emp Here 155   *Sales* 9,963,710
SIC 8361 Residential care
Tom Collier

D-U-N-S 25-091-1534   (BR)
CAPITAL CARE GROUP INC
CAPITAL CARE LYNNWOOD
(*Suby of* GOVERNMENT OF THE PROVINCE OF ALBERTA)
8740 165 St Nw Suite 438, Edmonton, AB, T5R 2R8
(780) 341-2300
Emp Here 500
SIC 8059 Nursing and personal care, nec
Francine Drisner

D-U-N-S 20-027-3899   (BR)
EDMONTON CATHOLIC SEPARATE SCHOOL DISTRICT NO.7
ST. FRANCIS XAVIER HIGH SCHOOL
(*Suby of* EDMONTON CATHOLIC SEPARATE SCHOOL DISTRICT NO.7)
9250 163 St Nw, Edmonton, AB, T5R 0A7
(780) 489-2571
Emp Here 95
SIC 8211 Elementary and secondary schools
Dan Donnelly

D-U-N-S 25-013-8435   (HQ)
INSIGHT MEDICAL HOLDINGS LTD
MEADOWLARK DIAGNOSTIC IMAGING
200 Meadowlark Shopping Ctr Nw, Edmonton, AB, T5R 5W9
(780) 489-8430
Emp Here 40   *Sales* 71,713,620
SIC 8071 Medical laboratories
Ralph Carter
R Ross Mcewen
Randolph Pawluk
Eric Joseph Preville
David Shamchuk
Thomas C Spiers
Joanne Swersky
Carl Torbiak
Christine Huber
Timothy Black

D-U-N-S 25-045-4451   (SL)
INSIGHT MEDICAL IMAGING
200 Meadowlark Shopping Ctr Nw, Edmonton, AB, T5R 5W9
(780) 489-3391
Emp Here 200   *Sales* 38,041,400
SIC 8011 Offices and clinics of medical doctors
Thomas C. Spiers

D-U-N-S 25-321-4530   (BR)
REVERA INC
CENTRAL PARK LODGES
(*Suby of* GOVERNMENT OF CANADA)
8903 168 St Nw, Edmonton, AB, T5R 2V6
(780) 489-4931
Emp Here 100
SIC 8051 Skilled nursing care facilities
Margaret Plaizier

D-U-N-S 24-733-5326   (HQ)
RISKTECH INSURANCE SERVICES INC
300-14727 87 Ave Nw, Edmonton, AB, T5R 4E5
(780) 732-7129
Emp Here 8   *Sales* 593,263,000
SIC 6411 Insurance agents, brokers, and service
Douglas Morrow

D-U-N-S 20-593-7592   (HQ)
VANAN FOODS LIMITED
SPRUCE GROVE I G A
9106 142 St Nw, Edmonton, AB, T5R 0M7
(780) 483-1525
Emp Here 25   *Sales* 41,086,780
SIC 5411 Grocery stores
Andy Taschuk
Waine Van De Ligt
Gerrie Taschuk
Wendy Van De Ligt

Edmonton, AB T5S

D-U-N-S 24-701-8450   (SL)
1583647 ALBERTA LTD
GO HONDA
10220 184 St Nw, Edmonton, AB, T5S 0B9
(780) 483-4024
Emp Here 70   *Sales* 44,049,600
SIC 5511 New and used car dealers
Peter Yachimec
Linda Yachimec

D-U-N-S 24-950-1206   (HQ)
518162 ALBERTA INC
CROSSROADS C & I DISTRIBUTORS
11104 180 St Nw, Edmonton, AB, T5S 2X5
(780) 452-7410
Emp Here 110   *Sales* 74,051,640
SIC 5033 Roofing, siding, and insulation
Martin Bates
Shawn Tilson
Skip Eaman
Gerald Hodder
John Stoski
Terry Monette
Tom Angotti

D-U-N-S 20-256-1614   (HQ)
569398 ALBERTA LTD
BOLT SECURITY SYSTEMS
17311 103 Ave Nw Unit 100, Edmonton, AB, T5S 1J4
(780) 454-5864
Sales 11,179,350
SIC 5065 Electronic parts and equipment, nec
Robert Gylytiuk
Brian Gylytiuk
Gary Gylytiuk

D-U-N-S 20-075-1779   (SL)
648781 ALBERTA LTD
LA-Z-BOY FURNITURE GALLERIES
17109 109 Ave Nw, Edmonton, AB, T5S 2H8
(780) 481-7800
Emp Here 48   *Sales* 11,056,320
SIC 5712 Furniture stores
Mohammad Moussa

D-U-N-S 25-506-1814   (SL)
767405 ALBERTA LTD
MAYFIELD TOYOTA
10220 170 St Nw, Edmonton, AB, T5S 1N9
(780) 420-1111
Emp Here 150   *Sales* 94,392,000
SIC 5511 New and used car dealers
Naushad Jiwani

D-U-N-S 25-149-2229   (SL)
864475 ALBERTA LTD
KIA WEST EDMONTON
10151 179 St Nw, Edmonton, AB, T5S 1P9
(780) 444-8645
Emp Here 40   *Sales* 19,923,120
SIC 5511 New and used car dealers
Larry Ricci
Gary Kelemen

D-U-N-S 20-191-8997   (SL)
965515 ALBERTA LTD
WEST SIDE MITSUBISHI
17920 100 Ave Nw Suite Side, Edmonton, AB, T5S 2T6
(780) 481-0924
Emp Here 35   *Sales* 17,432,730
SIC 5511 New and used car dealers
Bart Yachimec
Daryl Lord

D-U-N-S 20-335-5578   (SL)
970426 ALBERTA LTD
BUMPER TO BUMPER
11754 170 St Nw, Edmonton, AB, T5S 1J7
(780) 452-0220
Emp Here 35   *Sales* 17,432,730
SIC 5531 Auto and home supply stores
Gord Olitch

D-U-N-S 24-400-4768   (HQ)
ACRODEX INC
PCM CANADA
(*Suby of* PCM, INC.)
11420 170 St Nw, Edmonton, AB, T5S 1L7
(780) 426-4444
Emp Here 250   *Sales* 122,449,200
SIC 8731 Commercial physical research
Karim Amarshi
Barkat Chatur
Nazir Javer
Yasmin Jivraj

Jaferali Surmawala
Salma Rajwani
Nash Marani
Nadir Jivraj
Al-Karim Chatur
Salim Chatur

D-U-N-S 25-146-0572   (HQ)
ACUITY HOLDINGS, INC
ZEP MANUFACTURING COMPANY OF CANADA
(*Suby of* NM Z PARENT INC.)
11627 178 St Nw, Edmonton, AB, T5S 1N6
(780) 453-5800
Emp Here 68   *Sales* 138,729,240
SIC 2844 Toilet preparations
Ralph Puertas
Al-Karim Hamir
Andre Quennedille

D-U-N-S 20-539-5700   (BR)
AECOM CANADA LTD
SWAN HILLS TREATMENT CENTER
(*Suby of* AECOM)
17203 103 Ave Nw, Edmonton, AB, T5S 1J4
(780) 488-2121
Emp Here 80
SIC 8711 Engineering services
Radeana Elakey

D-U-N-S 24-773-2501   (SL)
AGS INTERNATIONAL
17942 105 Ave Nw Suite 200, Edmonton, AB, T5S 2H5
(780) 455-0199
Emp Here 49   *Sales* 11,673,194
SIC 8748 Business consulting, nec
Corey Froese

D-U-N-S 20-010-6925   (HQ)
ALBERTA HIGHWAY SERVICES LTD
(*Suby of* BOUYGUES)
11010 178 St Nw Suite 200, Edmonton, AB, T5S 1R7
(780) 701-8668
Emp Here 12   *Sales* 37,866,300
SIC 1611 Highway and street construction
Jacques Michel

D-U-N-S 24-312-9645   (HQ)
ALCANNA INC
LIQUOR DEPOT
17220 Stony Plain Rd Suite 101, Edmonton, AB, T5S 1K6
(780) 944-9994
Emp Here 80   *Sales* 499,536,909
SIC 5921 Liquor stores
James Burns
John Barnett
Marcie Kiziak
Denis Ryan
Karen Prentice
Peter Lynch
Darren Karasiuk
David Gordey
Paul Reid

D-U-N-S 20-106-0956   (HQ)
ALCOR FACILITIES MANAGEMENT INC
10470 176 St Nw Suite 206, Edmonton, AB, T5S 1L3
(780) 483-1213
Emp Here 10   *Sales* 24,955,200
SIC 8741 Management services
Allan Burry
Randy Koroluk
Michael Crawford

D-U-N-S 20-044-1140   (SL)
ALIGN-TECH INDUSTRIES INC
18114 107 Ave Nw, Edmonton, AB, T5S 1K5
(780) 448-7303
Emp Here 30   *Sales* 12,580,650
SIC 6712 Bank holding companies
Jack Siemens

D-U-N-S 25-235-1895   (HQ)
ALL WEATHER WINDOWS LTD

(*Suby of* CAPE-MAN HOLDINGS LTD)
18550 118a Ave Nw, Edmonton, AB, T5S 2K7
(780) 468-2989
Emp Here 425   *Sales* 170,261,700
SIC 3442 Metal doors, sash, and trim
Gord Wiebe
Roger Hutlet
Richard Scott

D-U-N-S 20-050-2818   (SL)
ALLIANCE BUILDING MAINTENANCE LTD
18823 111 Ave Nw, Edmonton, AB, T5S 2X4
(780) 447-2574
Emp Here 105   *Sales* 3,356,640
SIC 7349 Building maintenance services, nec
Brendan Connolly
Frank Byrne

D-U-N-S 24-668-3770   (HQ)
ALLSTAR CONSTRUCTION LTD
11130 199 St, Edmonton, AB, T5S 2C6
(780) 452-6330
Sales 24,245,780
SIC 8742 Management consulting services
Sergei Ewachniuk
Jodi Martins

D-U-N-S 20-080-5919   (SL)
ALPINE HEATING LTD
10333 174 St Nw, Edmonton, AB, T5S 1H1
(780) 469-0491
Emp Here 50   *Sales* 11,653,250
SIC 1711 Plumbing, heating, air-conditioning
Jack Strause
Sherry Strause

D-U-N-S 24-356-3173   (HQ)
ALTUS GEOMATICS LIMITED PARTNERSHIP
ALTUS GROUP
(*Suby of* ALTUS GROUP LIMITED)
17327 106a Ave Nw, Edmonton, AB, T5S 1M7
(780) 481-3399
Emp Here 10   *Sales* 42,897,360
SIC 8713 Surveying services
Mitch Attinger

D-U-N-S 25-677-7202   (SL)
ALZAC HOLDINGS LTD
PRIME TIME COURIER
18011 105 Ave Nw, Edmonton, AB, T5S 2E1
(780) 447-4303
Emp Here 25   *Sales* 11,087,250
SIC 7389 Business services, nec
Wade Antosh

D-U-N-S 24-584-2885   (SL)
ANDREWS, DENNY FORD SALES INC
18208 Stony Plain Rd Nw, Edmonton, AB, T5S 1A7
(780) 489-9999
Emp Here 180   *Sales* 113,270,400
SIC 5511 New and used car dealers
Dennis Lee Andrews

D-U-N-S 24-470-6730   (SL)
APX HOSPITALITY MANAGEMENT INC
18335 105 Ave Nw Suite 101, Edmonton, AB, T5S 2K9
(780) 484-1515
Emp Here 100   *Sales* 9,489,900
SIC 7011 Hotels and motels
Jonn Pow

D-U-N-S 20-358-2783   (SL)
AQUACLEAR FILTRATION
10518 180 St Nw Unit 101, Edmonton, AB, T5S 2P1
(780) 809-3146
Emp Here 25   *Sales* 11,179,350
SIC 5074 Plumbing and heating equipment and supplies (hydronics)
Jason Billey

D-U-N-S 20-643-6383   (SL)
ARMOUR-CLAD CONTRACTING INC
18035 114 Ave Nw, Edmonton, AB, T5S 1T8

Emp Here 25   *Sales* 11,768,275

SIC 1542 Nonresidential construction, nec
Ken Fraser
Martin Mclean

D-U-N-S 20-086-1516   (HQ)
ARMTEC INC
ARMTEC CANADA CULVERT
(*Suby of* TREVLUC HOLDINGS LTD)
10423 178 St Nw Unit 201, Edmonton, AB, T5S 1R5
(780) 487-3404
Emp Here 6   *Sales* 10,141,500
SIC 3498 Fabricated pipe and fittings
Gary Edwards
Kevin Edwards

D-U-N-S 20-437-8905   (HQ)
ARROW WELDING & INDUSTRIAL SUPPLIES INC
17811 107 Ave Nw, Edmonton, AB, T5S 1R8
(780) 483-2050
Sales 18,050,988
SIC 5084 Industrial machinery and equipment
Thomas Lloyd
Robert Elliot
Greg Berry
Luc Doyon

D-U-N-S 20-080-6263   (SL)
ATKIN, MICHAEL HOLDINGS INC
ANGLO CANADIAN MOTORS
17415 103 Ave Nw, Edmonton, AB, T5S 1J4
(780) 486-5100
Emp Here 24   *Sales* 11,953,872
SIC 5511 New and used car dealers
Michael Atkin

D-U-N-S 20-248-0344   (SL)
ATS ANDLAUER TRANSPORTATION SERVICES INC
11264 186 St Nw, Edmonton, AB, T5S 2W2
(780) 440-4005
Emp Here 40   *Sales* 15,414,400
SIC 4731 Freight transportation arrangement
Blair Scott

D-U-N-S 24-733-1754   (SL)
BAVARIA AUTOHAUS (1997) LTD
BAVARIA BMW
18925 Stony Plain Rd Nw, Edmonton, AB, T5S 2Y4
(780) 484-0000
Emp Here 72   *Sales* 45,308,160
SIC 5511 New and used car dealers
Hans Maier
Klaus Maier

D-U-N-S 20-555-8955   (BR)
BELFOR (CANADA) INC
BELFOR RESTORATION SERVICES
(*Suby of* BELFOR HOLDINGS INC.)
17408 116 Ave Nw, Edmonton, AB, T5S 2X2
(780) 455-5566
Emp Here 105
SIC 1799 Special trade contractors, nec
Sandie Ernst

D-U-N-S 25-685-3284   (BR)
BELL MEDIA INC
CFRN TV
(*Suby of* BCE INC)
18520 Stony Plain Rd Nw Suite 100, Edmonton, AB, T5S 1A8
(780) 486-2800
Emp Here 100
SIC 4833 Television broadcasting stations
Lloyd Lewis

D-U-N-S 25-106-8854   (BR)
BRANDT TRACTOR LTD
(*Suby of* BRANDT INDUSTRIES CANADA LTD)
10630 176 St Nw, Edmonton, AB, T5S 1M2
(780) 484-6613
Emp Here 120
SIC 5084 Industrial machinery and equipment
Greg Davidson

D-U-N-S 25-986-2399   (SL)
BRITISH FINE CARS LTD
JAGUAR LAND ROVER EDMONTON
17007-111 Ave, Edmonton, AB, T5S 0J5
(780) 484-1818
Emp Here 22   *Sales* 10,957,716
SIC 5511 New and used car dealers
Philip Neufeld

D-U-N-S 24-765-8776   (HQ)
CALMONT TRUCK CENTRE LTD
VOLVO TRUCK CENTRE-EDMONTON
(*Suby of* CALMONT LEASING LTD)
11403 174 St Nw, Edmonton, AB, T5S 2P4
(780) 451-2680
Sales 43,420,320
SIC 5511 New and used car dealers

D-U-N-S 20-369-8118   (SL)
CANADIAN CLAIMS SERVICES INC
17958 106 Ave, Edmonton, AB, T5S 1V4
(780) 443-1185
Emp Here 21   *Sales* 12,178,404
SIC 6411 Insurance agents, brokers, and service
David Riddell
Richard Lawrence

D-U-N-S 20-852-5308   (BR)
CANADIAN LOCATORS INC
18215 114 Ave Nw Unit 101, Edmonton, AB, T5S 2P6
(780) 487-7553
Emp Here 75
SIC 1623 Water, sewer, and utility lines
Mel Holman

D-U-N-S 24-354-2185   (SL)
CAPITAL ENGINEERING
17187 114 Ave Nw Suite 101, Edmonton, AB, T5S 2N5
(780) 488-2504
Emp Here 70   *Sales* 12,317,060
SIC 8711 Engineering services
Rodney Derworiz
Scott Martin
Paul Dean

D-U-N-S 24-374-0763   (SL)
CARDONE INDUSTRIES ULC
(*Suby of* CARDONE INDUSTRIES, INC.)
17803 111 Ave Nw, Edmonton, AB, T5S 2X3
(780) 444-5033
Emp Here 50   *Sales* 18,210,750
SIC 5013 Motor vehicle supplies and new parts
Morgan Lutz

D-U-N-S 20-051-1892   (HQ)
CASH STORE INC, THE
(*Suby of* CASH STORE FINANCIAL SERVICES INC, THE)
17631 103 Ave Nw, Edmonton, AB, T5S 1N8
(780) 408-5110
Emp Here 100   *Sales* 422,936,000
SIC 6141 Personal credit institutions
Gordon Reykdal

D-U-N-S 25-840-4628   (SL)
CCI INC
17816 118 Ave Nw, Edmonton, AB, T5S 2W3
(780) 784-1990
Emp Here 49   *Sales* 10,378,396
SIC 7373 Computer integrated systems design
Brent Goerz

D-U-N-S 24-524-5431   (HQ)
CCS ADJUSTERS INC
CANADIAN CLAIMS SERVICES-VANCOUVER
10120 175 St Nw, Edmonton, AB, T5S 1L1
(780) 443-1185
Emp Here 5   *Sales* 11,598,480
SIC 6411 Insurance agents, brokers, and service
David Riddell
Jason Harris

Richard Lawrence

D-U-N-S 24-553-3104   (HQ)
CCS CONTRACTING LTD
18039 114 Ave Nw, Edmonton, AB, T5S 1T8
(780) 481-1776
Emp Here 45   *Sales* 43,565,800
SIC 1761 Roofing, siding, and sheetMetal
work
Martin Mclean

D-U-N-S 20-920-5140   (SL)
CIVEO STRUCTURES INC
(Suby of CIVEO CORPORATION)
21216 113 Ave Nw, Edmonton, AB, T5S 1Y6
(780) 447-2333
Emp Here 250   *Sales* 115,944,000
SIC 1521 Single-family housing construction
David Gowans

D-U-N-S 24-314-9031   (SL)
CKB CONSTRUCTION (2004) LTD
10828 209 St Nw, Edmonton, AB, T5S 1Z9
(780) 453-6611
Emp Here 75   *Sales* 18,463,950
SIC 1794 Excavation work
Clifford Pannebaker
Lindsay Pannebaker

D-U-N-S 25-987-4923   (SL)
COMFORT FURNITURE GALLERIES
LA-Z-BOY GALLERIES
17109 109 Ave Nw, Edmonton, AB, T5S 2H8
(780) 481-7800
Emp Here 60   *Sales* 13,944,180
SIC 5712 Furniture stores
Mohammed Moussa

D-U-N-S 20-119-3021   (BR)
COMPAGNIE KATOEN NATIE CANADA
KATOEN NATIE EDMONTON
(Suby of KATOEN NATIE GROUP SA)
18210 109 Ave Nw, Edmonton, AB, T5S 2K2
(780) 489-9040
Emp Here 100
SIC 4225 General warehousing and storage
Bruno Rubbens

D-U-N-S 24-807-4445   (HQ)
CONSOLIDATED GYPSUM SUPPLY LTD
11660 170 St Nw, Edmonton, AB, T5S 1J7
(780) 452-7786
Emp Here 55   *Sales* 85,444,200
SIC 5039 Construction materials, nec
Hans Sturm
Larry Farmer
David Archutick

D-U-N-S 25-265-6061   (BR)
CORPORATION MCKESSON CANADA, LA
*(Suby of MCKESSON FINANCIAL HOLD-
INGS II UNLIMITED COMPANY)*
10931 177 St Nw, Edmonton, AB, T5S 1P6
(780) 486-8700
Emp Here 150
SIC 5122 Drugs, proprietaries, and sundries
Marc Essensa

D-U-N-S 20-538-1270   (HQ)
CORRPRO CANADA, INC
(Suby of AEGION CORPORATION)
10848 214 St Nw, Edmonton, AB, T5S 2A7
(780) 447-4565
Emp Here 150   *Sales* 68,995,850
SIC 8711 Engineering services
Charles Goreon
Dave Bittner
Kent Bartholomew
Bo Botteicher
Jennifer Koenig
Rhoda Banks

D-U-N-S 25-316-9346   (HQ)
COVENTRY HOMES INC
17615 111 Ave Nw, Edmonton, AB, T5S 0A1
(780) 453-5100
Sales 10,203,808
SIC 1521 Single-family housing construction

Henri Rodier
Diane Bush
Darren Hart

D-U-N-S 25-266-7969   (SL)
COWBOYS COUNTRY SALOON LTD
10102 180 St Nw, Edmonton, AB, T5S 1N4

Emp Here 120   *Sales* 5,462,280
SIC 5813 Drinking places
Paul Vickers
Shiraz Karmali

D-U-N-S 20-145-3651   (HQ)
CRANE CARRIER (CANADA) LIMITED
CANADA POWERTRAIN, DIV OF
11523 186 St Nw, Edmonton, AB, T5S 2W6
(780) 443-2493
Emp Here 20   *Sales* 31,322,490
SIC 5013 Motor vehicle supplies and new
parts
Mark Ristow
Mary Ann Spiegel
Roland Martel

D-U-N-S 20-512-7389   (BR)
**CUMMINS WESTERN CANADA LIMITED
PARTNERSHIP**
*(Suby of CUMMINS WESTERN CANADA
LIMITED PARTNERSHIP)*
11751 181 St Nw, Edmonton, AB, T5S 2K5
(780) 455-2151
Emp Here 100
SIC 5084 Industrial machinery and equipment

D-U-N-S 20-849-3002   (SL)
DAYS INN & SUITES WEST EDMONTON
10010 179a St Nw, Edmonton, AB, T5S 2T1
(780) 444-4440
Emp Here 100   *Sales* 9,489,900
SIC 7011 Hotels and motels
Dave Turna

D-U-N-S 25-206-1478   (HQ)
DAYTONA CAPITAL CORPORATION
DAYTONA HOMES
*(Suby of HUTCHINSON ACQUISITIONS
CORP)*
11504 170 St Nw Suite 101, Edmonton, AB,
T5S 1J7
(780) 452-2288
Emp Here 35   *Sales* 13,547,100
SIC 1522 Residential construction, nec
Ralph G Hutchinson
Glen Jarbeau

D-U-N-S 20-737-8485   (SL)
DEVONIAN MOTOR INCORPORATION
SUBARU CITY
17708 111 Ave Nw, Edmonton, AB, T5S 0A2
(780) 484-7733
Emp Here 75   *Sales* 21,247,500
SIC 7538 General automotive repair shops
Cameron Mcpherson
Mike Duff

D-U-N-S 20-609-6948   (BR)
DHL EXPRESS (CANADA) LTD
(Suby of DEUTSCHE POST AG)
10918 184 St Nw, Edmonton, AB, T5S 2N9
(855) 345-7447
Emp Here 200
SIC 7389 Business services, nec
Will Nault

D-U-N-S 24-332-7434   (HQ)
DIAMOND INTERNATIONAL TRUCKS LTD
*SOUTHSIDE INTERNATIONAL TRUCKS,
DIV OF*
(Suby of SCOMAC HOLDINGS INC)
17020 118 Ave Nw, Edmonton, AB, T5S 1S4
(780) 454-1541
Emp Here 75   *Sales* 62,928,000
SIC 5511 New and used car dealers
Don Macadam
Scott Thresher

D-U-N-S 25-216-3605   (HQ)

DIX PERFORMANCE NORTH LTD
(Suby of J.B.'S AUTOMOTIVE CENTRE LTD)
11670 170 St Nw, Edmonton, AB, T5S 1J7
(780) 465-9266
Emp Here 5   *Sales* 10,926,450
SIC 5013 Motor vehicle supplies and new
parts
James Bell
Barbara Bell
Shawn Landsman

D-U-N-S 20-898-1050   (SL)
DONMAR CAR SALES LTD
SUNDANCE MAZDA
17990 102 Ave Nw, Edmonton, AB, T5S 1M9
(780) 454-0422
Emp Here 30   *Sales* 14,942,340
SIC 5511 New and used car dealers
Jeffrey C Reid
Brian Poluk

D-U-N-S 24-004-4560   (HQ)
DRIVING FORCE INC, THE
DRIVING FORCE
17631 103 Ave Nw, Edmonton, AB, T5S 1N8
(780) 483-9559
Emp Here 60   *Sales* 44,049,600
SIC 5511 New and used car dealers
Mark Nolin
Ayman Ammoura
Steve Carlstrom
Tammy Hamilton
Montana Currie
Mark Dobko
Craig Strachan
Greg Tilley

D-U-N-S 24-810-4721   (HQ)
DURABUILT WINDOWS & DOORS INC
10920 178 St Nw, Edmonton, AB, T5S 1R7
(780) 455-0440
Emp Here 250   *Sales* 109,453,950
SIC 3442 Metal doors, sash, and trim
Harry Sunner

D-U-N-S 20-869-7396   (SL)
DURAGUARD WHOLESALE FENCE LTD
10624 214 St Nw, Edmonton, AB, T5S 2A5
(780) 447-5465
Emp Here 35   *Sales* 15,651,090
SIC 5031 Lumber, plywood, and millwork
Jay Champigny

D-U-N-S 24-807-3660   (SL)
DYNALINE INDUSTRIES INC
18070 109 Ave Nw, Edmonton, AB, T5S 2K2
(780) 453-3964
Emp Here 25   *Sales* 11,875,650
SIC 5085 Industrial supplies
Alfred Otto

D-U-N-S 20-259-1939   (SL)
EARTHWISE CONSTRUCTION LTD
20104 107 Ave Nw, Edmonton, AB, T5S 1W9
(780) 413-4235
Emp Here 49   *Sales* 13,892,676
SIC 1611 Highway and street construction
Ryan Dory
Tom Dasko
Ryan Brown

D-U-N-S 25-399-5468   (SL)
EARTHWISE CONTRACTING LTD
20104 107 Ave Nw, Edmonton, AB, T5S 1W9
(780) 413-4235
Emp Here 45   *Sales* 12,758,580
SIC 1611 Highway and street construction

D-U-N-S 24-786-8441   (SL)
**ECO ENVIRONMENT PRODUCTS (1989)
LTD**
ECO MEDICAL EQUIPMENT, DIV OF
18303 107 Ave Nw Suite 1989, Edmonton, AB,
T5S 1K4
(780) 483-6232
Emp Here 30   *Sales* 13,415,220
SIC 5047 Medical and hospital equipment
Michael Costanzo

Gordon Hollman
Bill Congdon

D-U-N-S 24-520-8228   (HQ)
EDGEWOOD MATTING LTD
18120 109 Ave Nw, Edmonton, AB, T5S 2K2
(780) 466-2084
Emp Here 1   *Sales* 10,685,976
SIC 5023 Homefurnishings
Terry Rosenau
Brett Whittington
Rob Unrau

D-U-N-S 24-810-8063   (SL)
EDMONTON HORTICULTURAL SOCIETY
10746 178 St Nw, Edmonton, AB, T5S 1J3
(780) 456-3324
Emp Here 200   *Sales* 34,781,000
SIC 0781 Landscape counseling and planning
Maggie Easton

D-U-N-S 24-330-9317   (HQ)
EDMONTON KENWORTH LTD
*EDMONTON KENWORTH PACLEASE, DIV
OF*
17335 118 Ave Nw, Edmonton, AB, T5S 2P5
(780) 453-3431
Emp Here 50   *Sales* 161,433,600
SIC 5511 New and used car dealers
Gary King
Michael King
Collin Ferguson

D-U-N-S 20-123-2225   (SL)
**ENVIROCLEAN BUILDING MAINTENANCE
LTD**
17233 109 Ave Nw Suite 101, Edmonton, AB,
T5S 1H7
(780) 489-0500
Emp Here 80   *Sales* 3,216,720
SIC 7349 Building maintenance services, nec
Calvin Parks

D-U-N-S 20-273-5155   (SL)
EQUBE GAMING LIMITED
10493 184 St Nw Suite 100, Edmonton, AB,
T5S 2L1
(780) 414-8890
Emp Here 169   *Sales* 5,418,088
SIC 7371 Custom computer programming ser-
vices
John Purcell
Stephen O'donovan
Sandi Johnston
Andrew Janko
Donald Sutherland
Douglas Osrow
Mitch Debelser

D-U-N-S 20-270-4342   (BR)
**EVER GREEN ECOLOGICAL SERVICES
INC**
*(Suby of EVER GREEN ECOLOGICAL SER-
VICES INC)*
20204 113 Ave Nw, Edmonton, AB, T5S 0G3
(780) 239-9419
Emp Here 80
SIC 4953 Refuse systems
Ron Rose

D-U-N-S 25-262-0232   (SL)
FIREBALL EQUIPMENT LTD
17509 109a Ave Nw, Edmonton, AB, T5S 2W4
(780) 944-4818
Emp Here 45   *Sales* 21,376,170
SIC 5084 Industrial machinery and equipment
Joe Murphy

D-U-N-S 24-669-2396   (BR)
FORD CREDIT CANADA LIMITED
(Suby of FORD MOTOR COMPANY)
10335 172 St Nw Suite 300, Edmonton, AB,
T5S 1K9

Emp Here 75
SIC 8742 Management consulting services

D-U-N-S 24-067-8714   (BR)

FORD MOTOR COMPANY OF CANADA, LIMITED
FORD PARTS DISTRIBUTION CENTER
(*Suby of* FORD MOTOR COMPANY)
11604 181 St Nw, Edmonton, AB, T5S 1M6
(780) 454-9621
Emp Here 150
SIC 5013 Motor vehicle supplies and new parts
Jim Hartford

D-U-N-S 24-090-4060   (HQ)
FOSTER PARK BROKERS INC
17704 103 Ave Nw Suite 200, Edmonton, AB, T5S 1J9
(780) 489-4961
Emp Here 25   *Sales* 101,625,810
SIC 6411 Insurance agents, brokers, and service
Mark Wiens
Andre Charrois
Steve Whitehouse

D-U-N-S 20-075-9595   (HQ)
FULLER AUSTIN INC
(*Suby of* STUART OLSON INC)
11604 186 St Nw, Edmonton, AB, T5S 0C4
(780) 452-1701
Emp Here 25   *Sales* 84,950,400
SIC 1799 Special trade contractors, nec
Ron Richards
Perry Pugh

D-U-N-S 20-594-4390   (BR)
GENERAL MOTORS OF CANADA COMPANY
GM CANADA EDMONTON PDC 21
(*Suby of* GENERAL MOTORS COMPANY)
17707 118 Ave Nw, Edmonton, AB, T5S 1P7
(780) 451-7000
Emp Here 75
SIC 5531 Auto and home supply stores
Nicholas Batchelor

D-U-N-S 24-950-8099   (HQ)
GO AUTO CORPORATION
10220 184 St Nw, Edmonton, AB, T5S 0B9
(780) 701-9999
Sales 15,732,000
SIC 5511 New and used car dealers
Mike Priestner
Grant Ericksen
Tom Wilson
Jared Priestner
Dave Doerksen
Latha Thomas-Back
Jason Smith
Jimmy Pietrarca
Dan Rideout
Ashley Roy

D-U-N-S 20-894-8653   (SL)
GOLDEN ARROW SCHOOLBUSES LTD
20204 111 Ave Nw, Edmonton, AB, T5S 2G6
(780) 447-1538
Emp Here 130   *Sales* 9,785,360
SIC 4151 School buses
Sigmund Bartel
Arlene Bartel

D-U-N-S 20-522-2289   (SL)
GREAT WEST CHRYSLER INC
17817 Stony Plain Rd Nw, Edmonton, AB, T5S 1B4
(780) 483-5337
Emp Here 110   *Sales* 69,220,800
SIC 5511 New and used car dealers
Bart Yachimec

D-U-N-S 25-497-2862   (HQ)
HANSON RESTAURANTS (TB) INC
TACO BELL OF CANADA
10114 175 St Nw, Edmonton, AB, T5S 1L1
(780) 484-2896
Emp Here 6   *Sales* 18,655,600
SIC 5812 Eating places
William (Bill) Hanson

D-U-N-S 25-190-0887   (SL)
HELIX IT INC
18211 105 Ave Nw Unit 101, Edmonton, AB, T5S 2L5
(780) 454-3549
Emp Here 40   *Sales* 16,984,280
SIC 8999 Services, nec
Doug Hudson

D-U-N-S 20-916-2994   (SL)
HERBLENS MOTORS INC
LEXUS OF EDMONTON
11204 170 St Nw, Edmonton, AB, T5S 2X1
(780) 466-8300
Emp Here 70   *Sales* 44,049,600
SIC 5511 New and used car dealers
Herbert Anton

D-U-N-S 20-082-5354   (HQ)
HUGHES PETROLEUM LTD
10330 178 St Nw, Edmonton, AB, T5S 1J2
(780) 444-4040
Sales 20,181,600
SIC 7542 Carwashes
Brian R Hughes

D-U-N-S 25-325-7620   (SL)
IGL CANADA (WESTERN) LTD
17515 106a Ave Nw, Edmonton, AB, T5S 1M7
(780) 489-3245
Emp Here 200   *Sales* 50,488,400
SIC 1623 Water, sewer, and utility lines
Wayne Lyons
Larry Semeniuk

D-U-N-S 20-086-5954   (HQ)
IGLOO BUILDING SUPPLIES GROUP LTD
PERFORMANCE DRYWALL
21421 111 Ave Nw, Edmonton, AB, T5S 1Y1
(780) 451-0600
Emp Here 240   *Sales* 70,054,920
SIC 5039 Construction materials, nec
Barry Stewart
Barbara Doiron
Simon King

D-U-N-S 20-316-7395   (SL)
IGLOO MANUFACTURING LTD
21421 111 Ave Nw, Edmonton, AB, T5S 1Y1
(780) 451-0600
Emp Here 150   *Sales* 85,444,200
SIC 5039 Construction materials, nec
Barry Stuart

D-U-N-S 24-862-5282   (BR)
INTEGRATED DISTRIBUTION SYSTEMS LIMITED PARTNERSHIP
WAJAX EQUIPMENT
(*Suby of* WAJAX CORPORATION)
17604 105 Ave Nw, Edmonton, AB, T5S 1G4
(780) 483-6641
Emp Here 80
SIC 5084 Industrial machinery and equipment
Ryan Cooley

D-U-N-S 24-002-3440   (HQ)
INTERNATIONAL UNION OF OPERATING ENGINEERS LOCAL 955
17603 114 Ave Nw, Edmonton, AB, T5S 2R9
(780) 483-8955
Emp Here 1   *Sales* 11,734,740
SIC 8631 Labor organizations
Bruce Moffatt

D-U-N-S 20-082-6253   (HQ)
J.B.'S AUTOMOTIVE CENTRE LTD
J.B.'S POWER CENTRE
11670 170 St Nw Suite 80, Edmonton, AB, T5S 1J7
(780) 435-3681
Emp Here 20   *Sales* 24,903,900
SIC 5511 New and used car dealers
Jim Bell

D-U-N-S 24-815-3913   (SL)
JOE MARTIN & SONS LTD
18335 105 Ave Nw Unit 201, Edmonton, AB, T5S 2K9

(780) 455-0550
Emp Here 15   *Sales* 15,492,120
SIC 5172 Petroleum products, nec
Bryan Martin

D-U-N-S 20-898-9061   (SL)
K-JAY ELECTRIC LTD
10752 178 St Nw, Edmonton, AB, T5S 1J3
(780) 484-1721
Emp Here 70   *Sales* 15,248,030
SIC 1731 Electrical work
John Bakker

D-U-N-S 20-538-2799   (HQ)
KANE VETERINARY SUPPLIES LTD
WALCO CANADA ANIMAL HEALTH
(*Suby of* PATTERSON COMPANIES, INC.)
11204 186 St Nw, Edmonton, AB, T5S 2W2
(780) 453-1516
Emp Here 68   *Sales* 52,464,496
SIC 5047 Medical and hospital equipment
Damian Olthoff
Stephen Olsson
Jon Kuehl
Jeff Hyde
Steve Olson
Mark Panganiban

D-U-N-S 25-260-6256   (HQ)
KASH VENTURES LTD
310 DUMP
11403 199 St Nw, Edmonton, AB, T5S 2C6
(780) 428-3867
Emp Here 30   *Sales* 17,999,170
SIC 4953 Refuse systems
Greg Kirkwood
Sam Soliman

D-U-N-S 20-969-7515   (HQ)
LAVTOR HOLDINGS (ALBERTA) LTD
SMITTY'S FAMILY RESTAURANT
17865 106a Ave Nw Unit 101, Edmonton, AB, T5S 1V8
(780) 483-7545
Emp Here 10   *Sales* 18,655,600
SIC 5812 Eating places
Arthur Hauser
Daniel G. Miller

D-U-N-S 24-205-1352   (HQ)
LEASE LINK CANADA CORP
17220 Stony Plain Rd Nw Suite 201a, Edmonton, AB, T5S 1K6
(780) 414-0616
Emp Here 25   *Sales* 16,123,752
SIC 6159 Miscellaneous business credit institutions
James Jang
Steve Passant
Penny Thome
Darren Brooks

D-U-N-S 24-732-6085   (HQ)
LEIBEL INSURANCE GROUP CORP
17415 102 Ave Nw Suite 102, Edmonton, AB, T5S 1J8
(780) 484-8880
Emp Here 20   *Sales* 20,353,440
SIC 6411 Insurance agents, brokers, and service
Jerry Leibel
Chad Leibel

D-U-N-S 20-012-4076   (HQ)
LITTLE POTATO COMPANY LTD, THE
11749 180 St Nw, Edmonton, AB, T5S 2H6
(780) 414-6075
Sales 75,971,896
SIC 5148 Fresh fruits and vegetables
Angela Santiago
Jacob Van Der Schaaf

D-U-N-S 25-270-1453   (BR)
LOBLAWS INC
REAL CANADIAN SUPERSTORE 1573
(*Suby of* LOBLAW COMPANIES LIMITED)
17303 Stony Plain Rd Nw Suite 1573, Edmonton, AB, T5S 1B5

(780) 486-8452
Emp Here 320
SIC 5141 Groceries, general line
Aileen Jones

D-U-N-S 20-518-5668   (SL)
LOGI-TEC MANAGEMENT LIMITED PARTNERSHIP
18110 118 Ave Nw, Edmonton, AB, T5S 2G2
(780) 452-6225
Emp Here 49   *Sales* 24,405,822
SIC 5511 New and used car dealers
Jason Langner

D-U-N-S 20-305-3780   (BR)
LOWE'S COMPANIES CANADA, ULC
(*Suby of* LOWE'S COMPANIES, INC.)
10225 186 St Nw, Edmonton, AB, T5S 0G5
(780) 486-2508
Emp Here 145
SIC 5211 Lumber and other building materials
Kevin Graham

D-U-N-S 20-522-8526   (SL)
MARSH PRIVATE CLIENT SERVICES
17420 Stony Plain Rd Nw Suite 100, Edmonton, AB, T5S 1K6

Emp Here 25   *Sales* 21,558,084
SIC 6411 Insurance agents, brokers, and service
Chuck Hoffmann

D-U-N-S 25-387-2857   (SL)
MEANEY, B. CONSULTING LTD
21110 108 Ave Nw, Edmonton, AB, T5S 1X4

Emp Here 150   *Sales* 18,716,400
SIC 8741 Management services
Brian Meaney
Kathleen Meaney

D-U-N-S 24-323-4296   (SL)
MECHET CHARITIES LIMITED
18216 102 Ave Nw Suite 200, Edmonton, AB, T5S 1S7
(780) 442-3640
Emp Here 49   *Sales* 15,416,968
SIC 8699 Membership organizations, nec
Jason Morran

D-U-N-S 25-168-8784   (HQ)
METALSMITHS MASTER ARCHITECTS OF JEWELRY INC
MTL GROUP
17410 107 Ave Nw, Edmonton, AB, T5S 1E9
(780) 454-0736
Emp Here 10   *Sales* 55,061,100
SIC 5944 Jewelry stores
Peter Konidas
Elias Konidas

D-U-N-S 20-896-8693   (HQ)
MID-ARCTIC TRANSPORTATION CO. LTD
MATCO TRANSPORTATION SYSTEMS
18151 107 Ave Nw, Edmonton, AB, T5S 1K4
(780) 484-8800
Emp Here 30   *Sales* 31,267,312
SIC 4213 Trucking, except local
Myles Macleod
Gordon Smith

D-U-N-S 24-178-7576   (SL)
MIDWEST FABRICATORS LTD
18073 107 Ave Nw Suite 235, Edmonton, AB, T5S 1K3
(780) 447-0747
Emp Here 60   *Sales* 11,525,100
SIC 3499 Fabricated Metal products, nec
Pat Morrow

D-U-N-S 24-680-6025   (HQ)
MMD SALES LTD
MARTIN MOTOR SPORTS SOUTH
17104 118 Ave Nw, Edmonton, AB, T5S 2L7
(780) 452-2790
Emp Here 345   *Sales* 219,478,500
SIC 5083 Farm and garden machinery
Merrill Martin

Gilbert Greenwood

D-U-N-S 20-192-7857   (BR)
MOORE CANADA CORPORATION
R.R. DONNELLEY
(*Suby of* R. R. DONNELLEY & SONS COMPANY)
18330 102 Ave Nw, Edmonton, AB, T5S 2J9
(780) 452-5592
Emp Here 250
SIC 2761 Manifold business forms
Alister Nicoll

D-U-N-S 20-821-8532   (SL)
MORGAN CONSTRUCTION AND ENVIRON-MENTAL LTD
17303 102 Ave Nw, Edmonton, AB, T5S 1J8
(780) 733-9100
Emp Here 1,500   *Sales* 492,172,500
SIC 1623 Water, sewer, and utility lines
Peter Kiss

D-U-N-S 24-671-5007   (SL)
MORRIS, DAVID FINE CARS LTD
17407 111 Ave Nw, Edmonton, AB, T5S 0A1
(780) 484-9000
Emp Here 58   *Sales* 36,498,240
SIC 5511 New and used car dealers
David Morris
John Mcbean

D-U-N-S 20-555-9623   (BR)
MTE LOGISTIX EDMONTON INC
BDL
11250 189 St Nw, Edmonton, AB, T5S 2V6
(780) 944-9009
Emp Here 150
SIC 4225 General warehousing and storage
Tom Turner

D-U-N-S 24-330-9606   (SL)
NASON CONTRACTING GROUP LTD
(*Suby of* BIRD CONSTRUCTION INC)
18304 105 Ave Nw Suite 205, Edmonton, AB, T5S 0C6
(780) 460-7142
Emp Here 60   *Sales* 25,364,220
SIC 1541 Industrial buildings and warehouses
Darrell Stang
Murray Nason
Bob Andrusiw
Taylor Green
David Jenkins

D-U-N-S 24-400-0865   (SL)
NOBLE ACCEPTANCE LTD
NOBLE HOMES
21216 113 Ave Nw, Edmonton, AB, T5S 1Y6

Emp Here 100
SIC 3448 Prefabricated Metal buildings and components

D-U-N-S 20-775-8459   (SL)
NORDEN VOLKSWAGEN LIMITED
NORDEN AUTOHAUS
17820 Stony Plain Rd Nw, Edmonton, AB, T5S 1A4
(780) 426-3000
Emp Here 70   *Sales* 44,049,600
SIC 5511 New and used car dealers
Grant Ericksen
Tom Wilson

D-U-N-S 24-674-5582   (HQ)
NORTRUX INC
18110 118 Ave Nw, Edmonton, AB, T5S 2G2
(780) 452-6225
Emp Here 65   *Sales* 92,230,800
SIC 5012 Automobiles and other motor vehicles
Art Langner
Jason Langner
Dan Robinson
Andy Tarrant

D-U-N-S 20-083-6468   (BR)
OLD DUTCH FOODS LTD

(*Suby of* OLD DUTCH FOODS LTD)
18027 114 Ave Nw, Edmonton, AB, T5S 1T8
(780) 453-2341
Emp Here 75
SIC 4225 General warehousing and storage
William Carew

D-U-N-S 20-594-3798   (HQ)
PAINE, J. R. & ASSOCIATES LTD
(*Suby of* PAINE, J R HOLDINGS LTD)
17505 106 Ave Nw, Edmonton, AB, T5S 1E7
(780) 489-0700
Emp Here 60   *Sales* 22,032,800
SIC 8734 Testing laboratories
Roman Stefaniw

D-U-N-S 20-305-1917   (SL)
PALS GEOMATICS CORP
10704 176 St Nw, Edmonton, AB, T5S 1G7
(780) 455-3177
Emp Here 140   *Sales* 25,023,460
SIC 8713 Surveying services
Blake Shewthuk
Lawrence Pals
Peter Jackson

D-U-N-S 25-261-6784   (HQ)
PARIS JEWELLERS LTD
PARIS JEWELLERS CANADA
18913 111 Ave Nw, Edmonton, AB, T5S 2X4
(780) 930-1418
Emp Here 5   *Sales* 15,881,320
SIC 5944 Jewelry stores
De Trung Vo
Thu Vo

D-U-N-S 24-786-2915   (BR)
PEPSI BOTTLING GROUP (CANADA), ULC, THE
PEPSI BOTTLING GROUP
(*Suby of* PBG INVESTMENT (LUXEMBOURG) SARL)
11315 182 St Nw, Edmonton, AB, T5S 1R3
(780) 930-7700
Emp Here 200
SIC 2086 Bottled and canned soft drinks

D-U-N-S 24-853-8084   (SL)
PERMASTEEL PROJECTS LTD
PERMASTEEL
17430 103 Ave Nw, Edmonton, AB, T5S 2K8
(780) 452-7281
Emp Here 25   *Sales* 14,258,450
SIC 1542 Nonresidential construction, nec
Norman S Elliott
David Dunn
Steven Elliott

D-U-N-S 20-112-9475   (HQ)
PETER KIEWIT INFRASTRUCTURE CO.
(*Suby of* PETER KIEWIT SONS', INC.)
11211 Winterburn Rd Nw, Edmonton, AB, T5S 2B2
(780) 447-3509
Emp Here 85   *Sales* 229,680,500
SIC 1611 Highway and street construction
Louis Chapdelaine
Bruce E Grewcock
Michael F Norton
Gregory D Dixon
Michael J Whetstine
Dan H Levert
Michael J Piechoski
Frank J Margitan
John W Neal

D-U-N-S 20-825-3513   (SL)
PETROCOM CONSTRUCTION LTD
17505 109a Ave Nw, Edmonton, AB, T5S 2W4
(780) 481-5181
Emp Here 50   *Sales* 23,536,550
SIC 1542 Nonresidential construction, nec
Gerrit Dehaan

D-U-N-S 20-538-7855   (HQ)
PF CUSTOM COUNTERTOPS LTD
10417 174 St Nw, Edmonton, AB, T5S 1H1

(780) 484-0831
Emp Here 74   *Sales* 13,271,692
SIC 2541 Wood partitions and fixtures
John Holzapfel
Edward Holzapfel

D-U-N-S 20-692-2309   (HQ)
PLATINUM INVESTMENTS LTD
HILTON GARDEN INN
17610 Stony Plain Rd Nw, Edmonton, AB, T5S 1A2
(780) 443-2233
Emp Here 100   *Sales* 38,267,200
SIC 7011 Hotels and motels
Ali Meghji

D-U-N-S 24-394-6662   (SL)
PLUTO INVESTMENTS LTD
WEST END NISSAN
10152 179 St Nw, Edmonton, AB, T5S 1S1
(780) 486-1780
Emp Here 60   *Sales* 37,756,800
SIC 5511 New and used car dealers
Bart Yachimec
Peter Yachimec

D-U-N-S 20-657-1106   (HQ)
PRECISION GEOMATICS INC
17403 105 Ave Nw, Edmonton, AB, T5S 2G8
(780) 470-4000
Emp Here 15   *Sales* 11,613,228
SIC 8713 Surveying services
Roy Devlin
Darren Eklund

D-U-N-S 20-251-7157   (SL)
PROFAB ENERGY SERVICES INC
17303 102 Ave Nw Suite 200, Edmonton, AB, T5S 1J8
(780) 236-2450
Emp Here 80   *Sales* 12,050,912
SIC 1541 Industrial buildings and warehouses
Jeffrey Houghton

D-U-N-S 24-313-8737   (SL)
PROWEST SHIPPING & PACKAGING LTD
21635 115 Ave Nw, Edmonton, AB, T5S 2N6
(780) 455-5026
Emp Here 35   *Sales* 15,522,150
SIC 7389 Business services, nec
Chad Goforth
Derrick Smolski
Kim Smolski
Natalia Goforth

D-U-N-S 24-978-3465   (SL)
PUGWASH HOLDINGS LTD
INDEPENDENT JEWELLERS
11248 170 St Nw, Edmonton, AB, T5S 2X1
(780) 484-6342
Emp Here 50   *Sales* 12,216,400
SIC 5944 Jewelry stores
Gerry Gilroy

D-U-N-S 20-184-8533   (BR)
QSI INTERIORS LTD
(*Suby of* QSI INTERIORS LTD)
10240 180 St Nw, Edmonton, AB, T5S 1E2
(780) 489-4462
Emp Here 100
SIC 1742 Plastering, drywall, and insulation
Dean Vereschagin

D-U-N-S 24-810-0513   (SL)
RAM MANUFACTURING LTD
TRUS(T)LIFT
10203 184 St Nw, Edmonton, AB, T5S 2J4
(780) 484-4776
Emp Here 60   *Sales* 28,501,560
SIC 5084 Industrial machinery and equipment
Richard Meunier
Sandra Smart

D-U-N-S 20-954-8010   (HQ)
RAPTOR MINING PRODUCTS INC
RAPTOR WEAR PARTS
18131 Ave Nw Suite 118, Edmonton, AB, T5S 1M8

(780) 444-1284
Emp Here 3   *Sales* 119,493,850
SIC 5082 Construction and mining machinery
Craig Harder
Paul Weber
Grant Seshul

D-U-N-S 24-265-8086   (HQ)
RAYDON RENTALS LTD
CAT RENTAL STORE, THE
(*Suby of* FINNING INTERNATIONAL INC)
10235 180 St Nw, Edmonton, AB, T5S 1C1
(780) 989-1301
Emp Here 30   *Sales* 104,436,800
SIC 7353 Heavy construction equipment rental
Harry Hoyer
Joel Harrod
Miles Hunt
Steven Mandziuk
David Parker

D-U-N-S 25-453-8705   (BR)
RED LOBSTER HOSPITALITY LLC
OLIVE GARDEN
10121 171 St Nw, Edmonton, AB, T5S 1S6
(780) 484-0700
Emp Here 110
SIC 5812 Eating places
Bill Rees

D-U-N-S 20-003-7492   (BR)
RED LOBSTER HOSPITALITY LLC
RED LOBSTER RESTAURANTS
10111 171 St Nw, Edmonton, AB, T5S 1S6
(780) 484-0660
Emp Here 110
SIC 5812 Eating places
Laura Tiamzon

D-U-N-S 24-395-1183   (HQ)
REID-BUILT HOMES LTD
(*Suby of* REID-WORLD WIDE CORPORATION)
18140 107 Ave Nw, Edmonton, AB, T5S 1K5
(780) 486-3666
Sales 22,217,244
SIC 1521 Single-family housing construction
Emilie Reid

D-U-N-S 24-981-2546   (HQ)
REID-WORLD WIDE CORPORATION
18140 107 Ave Nw Suite 200, Edmonton, AB, T5S 1K5
(780) 451-7778
Emp Here 100
SIC 6552 Subdividers and developers, nec
Arthur Reid
Shane Parker

D-U-N-S 20-050-3873   (SL)
RIDGE DEVELOPMENT CORPORATION
17307 106 Ave Nw, Edmonton, AB, T5S 1E7
(780) 483-7077
Emp Here 40   *Sales* 11,543,320
SIC 1522 Residential construction, nec
John Barath

D-U-N-S 20-512-4006   (SL)
RIVER CITY ELECTRIC LTD
11323 174 St Nw, Edmonton, AB, T5S 0B7
(780) 484-6676
Emp Here 90   *Sales* 19,604,610
SIC 1731 Electrical work
Frank Krupka
Peter Rasmussen
Fred Rivett

D-U-N-S 24-322-8066   (SL)
RMR BONDING LTD
SADD, LLOYD
17413 107 Ave Nw, Edmonton, AB, T5S 1E5
(780) 465-4422
Emp Here 45   *Sales* 20,214,855
SIC 7389 Business services, nec
Marshall Sadd

D-U-N-S 25-454-4554   (SL)

ROLLING MIX CONCRETE (EDMONTON) LTD
22235 115 Ave Nw, Edmonton, AB, T5S 2N6
(780) 434-3736
Emp Here 80　*Sales* 18,674,800
SIC 3273 Ready-mixed concrete
Antonio Distefano
Ricardo Distefano

D-U-N-S 24-840-2836　(SL)
ROYAL WEST EDMONTON INN LTD
STEELS CAFE & GRILL
10010 178 St Nw, Edmonton, AB, T5S 1T3
(780) 484-6000
Emp Here 75　*Sales* 7,117,425
SIC 7011 Hotels and motels
Darrell Pearson

D-U-N-S 20-070-2350　(BR)
RRGB RESTAURANTS CANADA INC
RED ROBIN RESTAURANT
(*Suby of* RRGB RESTAURANTS CANADA INC)
10010 171 St Nw, Edmonton, AB, T5S 1S3
(780) 484-6735
Emp Here 75
SIC 5812 Eating places
Jason Vissei

D-U-N-S 24-806-8082　(BR)
RTL- ROBINSON ENTERPRISES LTD
(*Suby of* RTL- ROBINSON ENTERPRISES LTD)
10821 209 St Nw, Edmonton, AB, T5S 1Z7
(780) 447-4900
Emp Here 75
SIC 4213 Trucking, except local
Rick Robinson

D-U-N-S 24-328-0013　(SL)
SCHENDEL MECHANICAL CONTRACTING LTD
20310 107 Ave Nw, Edmonton, AB, T5S 1W9
(780) 447-3400
Emp Here 90　*Sales* 20,975,850
SIC 1711 Plumbing, heating, air-conditioning
Oscar Schendel
Bruno Schendel

D-U-N-S 25-539-4314　(SL)
SCORPIO MASONRY (NORTHERN) INC
SCORPIO STONE
20203 113 Ave Nw, Edmonton, AB, T5S 2W1
(780) 447-1682
Emp Here 80　*Sales* 12,990,480
SIC 1741 Masonry and other stonework
Mirko Ambrozic
Michelle Steele
Chris Ambrozic

D-U-N-S 24-063-4121　(SL)
SERV-ALL MECHANICAL SERVICES LTD
18120 107 Ave Nw, Edmonton, AB, T5S 1K5
(780) 484-6681
Emp Here 48　*Sales* 10,604,832
SIC 1711 Plumbing, heating, air-conditioning
Victor P Bogdanski
Wesley Bogdanski

D-U-N-S 20-585-2549　(BR)
SHAW CABLESYSTEMS G.P.
(*Suby of* SHAW COMMUNICATIONS INC)
10450 178 St Nw, Edmonton, AB, T5S 1S2
(780) 490-3555
Emp Here 600
SIC 4841 Cable and other pay television services

D-U-N-S 25-271-5586　(BR)
SHAW COMMUNICATIONS INC
SHAW CABLE
(*Suby of* SHAW COMMUNICATIONS INC)
10450 178 St Nw, Edmonton, AB, T5S 1S2
(780) 490-3555
Emp Here 500
SIC 4841 Cable and other pay television services
Steve Baker

D-U-N-S 24-353-5411　(HQ)
SIRVA CANADA LP
10403 172 St Nw Suite 310, Edmonton, AB, T5S 1K9
(780) 443-6800
Emp Here 45　*Sales* 11,930,948
SIC 4214 Local trucking with storage
Thomas Oberdorf
Wes W Lucas
Andrew P Coolidge

D-U-N-S 25-139-1470　(SL)
SIS STRATEGIC INFORMATION SYSTEMS INC
11432 Winterburn Rd Nw, Edmonton, AB, T5S 2Y3
(780) 701-4050
Emp Here 24　*Sales* 10,732,176
SIC 5045 Computers, peripherals, and software
Lyndon Lobo
Bruce Burman

D-U-N-S 20-047-7722　(BR)
SONEPAR CANADA INC
TEXCAN, DIV OF
(*Suby of* SOCIETE DE NEGOCE ET DE PARTICIPATION)
11330 189 St Nw, Edmonton, AB, T5S 2V6
(780) 944-9331
Emp Here 150
SIC 5063 Electrical apparatus and equipment
Mark Alexander

D-U-N-S 24-367-3444　(SL)
SONEX CONSTRUCTION GROUP LTD
21110 108 Ave Nw, Edmonton, AB, T5S 1X4
(780) 447-4409
Emp Here 100
SIC 1629 Heavy construction, nec
Brian Meaney

D-U-N-S 24-031-2152　(BR)
SPEEDY CREEK (2011) LTD
(*Suby of* SPEEDY CREEK (2011) LTD)
17724 102 Ave Nw, Edmonton, AB, T5S 1H5

Emp Here 600
SIC 5812 Eating places
Gerry Inglis

D-U-N-S 24-583-7257　(SL)
SPINDLE FACTORY LTD, THE
11319 199 St Nw, Edmonton, AB, T5S 2C6
(780) 453-5973
Emp Here 70　*Sales* 10,910,410
SIC 2431 Millwork
Colleen Halliday
Larry Halliday

D-U-N-S 20-898-3114　(HQ)
STAHL PETERBILT INC
STAHL PETERBILT PACLEASE
18020 118 Ave Nw, Edmonton, AB, T5S 2G2
(780) 483-6666
Emp Here 134　*Sales* 100,684,800
SIC 5511 New and used car dealers
Edward Stahl
Eddy Stahl
Paige Stahl

D-U-N-S 24-971-1263　(BR)
STOCK TRANSPORTATION LTD
(*Suby of* NATIONAL EXPRESS GROUP PLC)
11454 Winterburn Rd Nw, Edmonton, AB, T5S 2Y3
(780) 451-9536
Emp Here 100
SIC 4151 School buses
Chris Paquette

D-U-N-S 24-841-4369　(SL)
STREAMLINE CONSTRUCTION CO. LTD
11030 205 St Nw, Edmonton, AB, T5S 1Z4
(780) 447-4518
Emp Here 60　*Sales* 15,146,520
SIC 1623 Water, sewer, and utility lines
Ken Allen

Matt Baniak

D-U-N-S 25-334-9005　(HQ)
TECO-WESTINGHOUSE MOTORS (CANADA) INC
(*Suby of* TECO ELECTRIC & MACHINERY CO., LTD.)
18060 109 Ave Nw, Edmonton, AB, T5S 2K2
(780) 444-8933
Emp Here 22　*Sales* 20,122,830
SIC 5063 Electrical apparatus and equipment
Cheng-Hsiung Tang
Li Chang
Fang Sheng Sun
Sophia Chiu
Sheng Chyuan Lin

D-U-N-S 24-065-5969　(HQ)
TELFORD INVESTMENTS LTD
SUPER LOVE BOUTIQUE
(*Suby of* 275719 ALBERTA LTD)
17551 108 Ave Nw, Edmonton, AB, T5S 1G2
(780) 489-9562
Emp Here 16　*Sales* 21,989,520
SIC 5947 Gift, novelty, and souvenir shop
Gwen Telford

D-U-N-S 20-084-6996　(HQ)
TIME BUSINESS MACHINES LTD
17620 107 Ave Nw, Edmonton, AB, T5S 1G8
(780) 483-3040
Emp Here 31　*Sales* 10,994,760
SIC 5999 Miscellaneous retail stores, nec
Gregory Bird

D-U-N-S 24-362-9719　(HQ)
TIRECRAFT EDMONTON TRUCK CENTRE INC
TIRECRAFT
17803 118 Ave Nw, Edmonton, AB, T5S 1L6
(780) 452-4481
Emp Here 1　*Sales* 19,923,120
SIC 5531 Auto and home supply stores
Patrick Gurasek

D-U-N-S 25-414-3506　(SL)
TRACER CANADA COMPANY
(*Suby of* TRACER INDUSTRIES, INC.)
11004 174 St Nw, Edmonton, AB, T5S 2P3
(780) 455-8111
Emp Here 22　*Sales* 14,798,938
SIC 1389 Oil and gas field services, nec
Rosella Truly
David Megna
James Redmond
James Flittner
Jeff Megna

D-U-N-S 25-414-3548　(HQ)
TRACER INDUSTRIES CANADA LIMITED
(*Suby of* TRACER INDUSTRIES, INC.)
11004 174 St Nw, Edmonton, AB, T5S 2P3
(780) 455-8111
Sales 15,985,250
SIC 1389 Oil and gas field services, nec
Brendan Drews

D-U-N-S 20-776-3335　(BR)
TYCO INTEGRATED FIRE & SECURITY CANADA, INC
SIMPLEXGRINNELL, A DIV
(*Suby of* JOHNSON CONTROLS INTERNATIONAL PUBLIC LIMITED COMPANY)
17402 116 Ave Nw, Edmonton, AB, T5S 2X2
(780) 452-5280
Emp Here 170
SIC 7389 Business services, nec
Barry Poposs

D-U-N-S 20-981-5880　(BR)
UNI-SELECT EASTERN INC
UNI SELECT PRAIRIES DIV
(*Suby of* UNI-SELECT INC)
11754 170 St Nw, Edmonton, AB, T5S 1J7
(780) 452-2440
Emp Here 100
SIC 5013 Motor vehicle supplies and new parts

Brad Freysteinson

D-U-N-S 24-002-0495　(HQ)
UNIPAC PACKAGING PRODUCTS LTD
11133 184 St Nw, Edmonton, AB, T5S 2L6
(780) 466-3121
Emp Here 13　*Sales* 11,739,080
SIC 5411 Grocery stores
Lyle Mcdermid

D-U-N-S 25-207-0842　(HQ)
UNLIMITED POTENTIAL COMMUNITY SERVICES SOCIETY
10403 172 St Nw Suite 145, Edmonton, AB, T5S 1K9
(780) 440-0708
Sales 25,341,360
SIC 8322 Individual and family services
Darcy Petrovic

D-U-N-S 25-978-1011　(SL)
VISIONWALL CORPORATION
17915 118 Ave Nw, Edmonton, AB, T5S 1L6
(780) 451-4000
Emp Here 80　*Sales* 21,412,160
SIC 5211 Lumber and other building materials
Gregory Clarahan
Jan M Alston
Franz J Albrecht
Peter Schaub

D-U-N-S 24-003-0783　(HQ)
VULCAN ELECTRICAL LTD
18225 107 Ave Nw, Edmonton, AB, T5S 1K4
(780) 483-0036
Emp Here 15　*Sales* 26,139,480
SIC 1731 Electrical work
Dennis Gehl
Brendan Gehl

D-U-N-S 25-219-0293　(BR)
WAL-MART CANADA CORP
(*Suby of* WALMART INC.)
18521 Stony Plain Rd Nw Suite 3027, Edmonton, AB, T5S 2V9
(780) 487-8626
Emp Here 350
SIC 5311 Department stores
Odegard Mike

D-U-N-S 20-811-2722　(BR)
WESCO DISTRIBUTION CANADA LP
(*Suby of* WESCO INTERNATIONAL, INC.)
18207 111 Ave Nw, Edmonton, AB, T5S 2P2
(780) 452-7920
Emp Here 80
SIC 5063 Electrical apparatus and equipment
Tyler Medori

D-U-N-S 24-394-2133　(SL)
WESTERN DRUG DISTRIBUTION CENTER LIMITED
17611 109a Ave Nw, Edmonton, AB, T5S 2W4
(780) 413-2508
Emp Here 53　*Sales* 23,700,222
SIC 5047 Medical and hospital equipment
Gregory Hall
Kerry Heise
Lloyd Abbey

D-U-N-S 20-015-4396　(HQ)
WESTERN PONTIAC BUICK GMC (1999) LTD
18325 Stony Plain Rd Nw, Edmonton, AB, T5S 1C6
(780) 486-3333
Sales 49,713,120
SIC 5511 New and used car dealers
Robert Wolfe

D-U-N-S 20-065-5731　(SL)
WESTERN PONTIAC GMC 1999 LTD
18325 Stony Plain Rd, Edmonton, AB, T5S 1C6
(780) 486-3333
Sales 11,788,940
SIC 5511 New and used car dealers
Peter Heppner

▲ Public Company　■ Public Company Family Member　**HQ** Headquarters　**BR** Branch　**SL** Single Location

D-U-N-S 20-212-9024   (SL)
WESTERN STERLING TRUCKS LTD
OK TIRE
18353 118 Ave Nw, Edmonton, AB, T5S 1M8
(780) 481-7400
Emp Here 42   *Sales* 20,919,276
SIC 5511 New and used car dealers
Kenneth Zender

D-U-N-S 20-898-9012   (SL)
WESTGATE CHEVROLET LTD
CHEVY FARM
(*Suby of* TWING HOLDINGS LTD)
10145 178 St Nw, Edmonton, AB, T5S 1E4
(780) 483-3320
Emp Here 90   *Sales* 56,635,200
SIC 5511 New and used car dealers
Gary Relling

D-U-N-S 20-184-3773   (SL)
XENALI INC
XENALI CORPORATE FURNISHINGS
11430 170 St Nw, Edmonton, AB, T5S 1L7
(780) 487-6669
Emp Here 30   *Sales* 15,265,680
SIC 5021 Furniture
Nash Marani

D-U-N-S 25-064-6171   (SL)
ZACH & KAYLYN ENTERPRISES INC
WEST SIDE ACURA
17707 111 Ave Nw, Edmonton, AB, T5S 0A1
(780) 484-5444
Emp Here 45   *Sales* 22,413,510
SIC 5511 New and used car dealers
Bart Yachimec

Edmonton, AB T5T

D-U-N-S 25-068-9106   (BR)
ALBERTS RESTAURANTS LTD
TONY ROMA'S
(*Suby of* ALBERTS RESTAURANTS LTD)
1640 Burlington Ave, Edmonton, AB, T5T 3J7
(780) 444-3105
Emp Here 105
SIC 5812 Eating places
Siderson Mark

D-U-N-S 25-064-6452   (BR)
CHIRO FOODS LIMITED
OUTBACK STEAKHOUSE
(*Suby of* CHIRO FOODS LIMITED)
17118 90 Ave Nw, Edmonton, AB, T5T 4C8
(780) 438-8848
Emp Here 75
SIC 5812 Eating places
Brent Murton

D-U-N-S 24-394-4352   (BR)
CINEPLEX ODEON CORPORATION
SCOTIABANK THEATRE WEST EDMONTON MALL
(*Suby of* CINEPLEX INC)
8882 170 St Nw Suite 3030, Edmonton, AB, T5T 4M2
(780) 444-2400
Emp Here 154
SIC 7832 Motion picture theaters, except drive-in
Jess Simmons

D-U-N-S 24-273-8722   (SL)
ECHO CYCLE LTD
21220 100 Ave Nw, Edmonton, AB, T5T 5X8
(780) 447-3246
Emp Here 25   *Sales* 12,451,950
SIC 5571 Motorcycle dealers
Paul Goldbeck
Jolene Goldbeck
David Boire

D-U-N-S 25-832-2429   (SL)
FEIST ENTERPRISES LTD
CANADIAN TIRE

9909 178 St Nw Suite 288, Edmonton, AB, T5T 6H6
(780) 444-1816
Emp Here 140   *Sales* 50,990,100
SIC 5014 Tires and tubes
Gerry Feist
Carol Feist

D-U-N-S 25-678-9389   (HQ)
HANSON RESTAURANTS INC
APPLEBEE'S NEIGHBOURHOOD GRILL & BAR
9768 170 St Nw Suite 284, Edmonton, AB, T5T 5L4
(780) 484-2896
Emp Here 5   *Sales* 51,302,900
SIC 5812 Eating places
William Hanson
Katherine Hanson

D-U-N-S 25-514-3166   (BR)
HOME DEPOT OF CANADA INC
HOME DEPOT
(*Suby of* THE HOME DEPOT INC)
17404 99 Ave Nw, Edmonton, AB, T5T 5L5
(780) 484-5100
Emp Here 220
SIC 5251 Hardware stores
Al Windsor

D-U-N-S 24-398-4564   (BR)
HUDSON'S BAY COMPANY
BAY, THE
(*Suby of* HUDSON'S BAY COMPANY)
8882 170 St Nw Suite 1001, Edmonton, AB, T5T 3J7
(780) 444-1550
Emp Here 150
SIC 5311 Department stores
Shirley Ford

D-U-N-S 20-317-7048   (SL)
KEG RESTAURANTS LTD
9960 170 St Nw, Edmonton, AB, T5T 6G7
(780) 414-1114
Emp Here 100   *Sales* 4,551,900
SIC 5812 Eating places
Patti Prostebby

D-U-N-S 25-454-4877   (SL)
LOWES PHARMACY LIMITED
SHOPPERS DRUG MART
6655 178 St Nw Unit 610, Edmonton, AB, T5T 4J5
(780) 487-1013
Emp Here 40   *Sales* 10,118,160
SIC 5912 Drug stores and proprietary stores
William Lowe

D-U-N-S 24-809-2504   (BR)
NEWCAP INC
NEWCAP RADIO ALBERTA
(*Suby of* GROUPE STINGRAY INC)
2394 West Edmonton Mall, Edmonton, AB, T5T 4M2
(780) 432-3165
Emp Here 110
SIC 4832 Radio broadcasting stations
Randy Lemay

D-U-N-S 24-366-0557   (BR)
NEWCAP INC
BIG EARL RADIO
(*Suby of* GROUPE STINGRAY INC)
8882 170 St Nw Suite 2394, Edmonton, AB, T5T 4M2
(780) 451-8097
Emp Here 75
SIC 4832 Radio broadcasting stations
Randy Lemay

D-U-N-S 20-197-6623   (SL)
OLD SPAGHETTI FACTORY (EDMONTON) LTD
OLD SPAGHETTI FACTORY, THE
8882 170 St Nw Suite 1632, Edmonton, AB, T5T 4M2
(780) 444-2181
Emp Here 100   *Sales* 4,551,900

SIC 5812 Eating places
Bruce Mcbride

D-U-N-S 24-556-0375   (SL)
SALMEER ENTERPRISES
17046 90 Ave Nw, Edmonton, AB, T5T 1L6
(780) 486-6466
Emp Here 5   *Sales* 15,529,285
SIC 4925 Gas production and/or distribution
Zuli Karmali

D-U-N-S 25-533-9632   (BR)
SOBEYS WEST INC
SAFEWAY
(*Suby of* EMPIRE COMPANY LIMITED)
6655 178 St Nw Suite 600, Edmonton, AB, T5T 4J5
(780) 481-7646
Emp Here 200
SIC 5411 Grocery stores
Jim Weideger

D-U-N-S 25-362-7756   (BR)
T & T SUPERMARKET INC
(*Suby of* LOBLAW COMPANIES LIMITED)
8882 170 St Nw Suite 2580, Edmonton, AB, T5T 4M2
(780) 483-6638
Emp Here 80
SIC 5411 Grocery stores
Sung Amen

D-U-N-S 25-361-7542   (SL)
TRIPLE FIVE CORPORATION INC
8882 170 St Nw Suite 3000, Edmonton, AB, T5T 4M2
(780) 444-8100
Emp Here 60   *Sales* 15,693,180
SIC 6712 Bank holding companies
Eskander Ghermezian
Nader Ghermezian

D-U-N-S 25-217-8165   (HQ)
WEM HOLDINGS INC
WEST EDMONTON MALL
8882 170 St Nw Suite 3000, Edmonton, AB, T5T 4M2
(780) 444-5200
Emp Here 2   *Sales* 365,509,000
SIC 6712 Bank holding companies
Eskandar Ghermezian
Nader Ghermezian

D-U-N-S 24-395-7347   (HQ)
WEST EDMONTON MALL PROPERTY INC
(*Suby of* WEM HOLDINGS INC)
8882 170 St Nw Suite 3000, Edmonton, AB, T5T 4M2
(780) 444-5200
Sales 135,677,000
SIC 6512 Nonresidential building operators
Eskandar Ghermezian
Nader Ghermezian
Danielle Woo

D-U-N-S 25-453-8457   (BR)
YOUNG MEN'S CHRISTIAN ASSOCIATION OF EDMONTON, THE
YOUNG MENS' CHRISTIAN ASSOCIATION FOUNDATION OF ED
(*Suby of* YOUNG MEN'S CHRISTIAN ASSOCIATION OF EDMONTON, THE)
7121 178 St Nw, Edmonton, AB, T5T 5T9
(780) 930-2311
Emp Here 125
SIC 8699 Membership organizations, nec
Joleen Schmitt

Edmonton, AB T5V

D-U-N-S 25-231-6609   (HQ)
605494 ALBERTA LTD
INK QUEST
15462 131 Ave Nw, Edmonton, AB, T5V 0A1

(780) 454-4321
Emp Here 7   *Sales* 12,087,792
SIC 5112 Stationery and office supplies
Ali Sachedina
Anisha Sachedina

D-U-N-S 25-369-7148   (SL)
ABALONE CONSTRUCTION (WESTERN) INC
15531 131 Ave Nw, Edmonton, AB, T5V 0A4
(780) 451-3681
Emp Here 50   *Sales* 12,044,200
SIC 1629 Heavy construction, nec
Terry Chalupa

D-U-N-S 25-194-1472   (SL)
AECON INDUSTRIAL WESTERN INC
(*Suby of* AECON GROUP INC)
14940 121a Ave Nw, Edmonton, AB, T5V 1A3
(780) 452-1250
Emp Here 1,150   *Sales* 803,150,800
SIC 1542 Nonresidential construction, nec
James Hole
Gordon Panas
Darcy Trufyn
Reid Drury
Steve Mulherin
Tom Sabourin

D-U-N-S 25-236-1803   (SL)
ALASKAN TECHNOLOGIES CORP
11810 152 St Nw, Edmonton, AB, T5V 1E3
(780) 447-2660
Emp Here 50   *Sales* 11,046,700
SIC 1711 Plumbing, heating, air-conditioning
Chris Rypkema
Dave Terriff

D-U-N-S 20-639-5696   (SL)
ALBERTA ENVIRONMENTAL RUBBER PRODUCTS INC
13520 170 St Nw, Edmonton, AB, T5V 1M7
(780) 447-1994
Emp Here 51   *Sales* 13,113,681
SIC 4953 Refuse systems
Allan Swerling

D-U-N-S 20-044-3088   (HQ)
ALBERTA REGL COUNCIL CARPENTERS CORP
15210 123 Ave Nw Suite 176, Edmonton, AB, T5V 0A3
(780) 474-8599
Emp Here 1   *Sales* 19,557,900
SIC 8631 Labor organizations
Martyn Piper

D-U-N-S 20-616-6357   (HQ)
ALBERTA WILBERT SALES LTD
(*Suby of* TRAUB, L. HOLDINGS LTD)
16910 129 Ave Nw Suite 1, Edmonton, AB, T5V 1L1
(780) 447-2222
Sales 26,830,440
SIC 5032 Brick, stone, and related material
Leonard L Traub

D-U-N-S 24-068-1098   (SL)
ANTLER EXPRESS LTD
16389 130 Ave Nw, Edmonton, AB, T5V 1K5
(780) 447-1639
Emp Here 25   *Sales* 11,087,250
SIC 7389 Business services, nec
Gerald (Gerry) Graf

D-U-N-S 24-389-2895   (HQ)
AUTOCANADA INC
15511 123 Ave Nw Unit 200, Edmonton, AB, T5V 0C3
(866) 938-0561
Emp Here 3,500   *Sales* 2,388,613,378
SIC 5511 New and used car dealers
Steven Landry
Michael Rawluk
Erin Oor
Christopher Burrows
Gordon Barefoot
Dennis Desrosiers

Barry James
Maryann Keller
Paul W. Antony

D-U-N-S 24-997-4221   (HQ)
BCOM COMPUTER CENTRE INC
15051 118 Ave Nw, Edmonton, AB, T5V 1H9
(780) 481-8855
Sales 23,240,300
SIC 5734 Computer and software stores
Terry Lee

D-U-N-S 20-071-1088   (BR)
CANADA BREAD COMPANY, LIMITED
(*Suby of* GRUPO BIMBO, S.A.B. DE C.V.)
12151 160 St Nw, Edmonton, AB, T5V 1M4
(780) 451-4663
Emp Here 200
SIC 2051 Bread, cake, and related products
Linda Walker

D-U-N-S 20-179-4976   (HQ)
CASH STORE FINANCIAL SERVICES INC, THE
15511 123 Ave Nw, Edmonton, AB, T5V 0C3
(780) 408-5110
Sales 1,057,340,000
SIC 6141 Personal credit institutions
Gordon Reykdal
Geordie Williams
S.W. (Bill) Johnson
Michael Thompson
Edward C. Mcclelland
William Dunn
J. Albert Mondor
Robert J.S. Gibson
Ron Chicoyne
Michael M. Shaw

D-U-N-S 24-000-7849   (SL)
CENTRAL CARRIERS (EDMONTON) LTD
13008 163 St Nw, Edmonton, AB, T5V 1L6
(780) 447-1610
Emp Here 51   *Sales* 10,491,006
SIC 4231 Trucking terminal facilities
Edgar Klak
William Zacharko
Oscar Klak
Melvin Hickey
Rod Kornberger
Phillip Topilka
David Evasiuk
Jack Mcdermott

D-U-N-S 20-776-1685   (SL)
CHOWN ELECTRICAL CONTRACTORS LTD
12230 163 St Nw, Edmonton, AB, T5V 1S2
(780) 447-4525
Emp Here 50   *Sales* 10,891,450
SIC 1731 Electrical work
Leslie J Chown

D-U-N-S 25-620-4710   (BR)
CHRISTIAN LABOUR ASSOCIATION OF CANADA
(*Suby of* CHRISTIAN LABOUR ASSOCIATION OF CANADA)
14920 118 Ave Nw, Edmonton, AB, T5V 1B8
(780) 454-6181
Emp Here 75
SIC 8611 Business associations
Dick Heinen

D-U-N-S 20-776-2246   (HQ)
CITY LUMBER CORPORATION
CITY LUMBER & MILLWORK
15711 128 Ave Nw, Edmonton, AB, T5V 1K4
(780) 447-1344
Sales 11,179,350
SIC 5039 Construction materials, nec
Robert Rosen
Stephanie Berry

D-U-N-S 24-784-3027   (BR)
CLEARTECH INDUSTRIES INC
(*Suby of* J.W. YUEL HOLDINGS LTD)
12720 Inland Way Nw, Edmonton, AB, T5V

1K2
(800) 387-7503
Emp Here 125
SIC 2819 Industrial inorganic chemicals, nec
Pero Stopic

D-U-N-S 25-417-5433   (SL)
COMPUVISION SYSTEMS INC
15511 123 Ave Nw Suite 101, Edmonton, AB, T5V 0C3
(587) 525-7600
Emp Here 150   *Sales* 25,027,050
SIC 7379 Computer related services, nec
Ryan Vestby
Paul Thorsteinson

D-U-N-S 24-350-8335   (BR)
COSTCO WHOLESALE CANADA LTD
COSTCO
(*Suby of* COSTCO WHOLESALE CORPORATION)
12450 149 St Nw Suite 154, Edmonton, AB, T5V 1G9
(780) 453-8470
Emp Here 330
SIC 5099 Durable goods, nec
Adam Bains

D-U-N-S 20-538-2260   (HQ)
CREATIVE DOOR SERVICES LTD
(*Suby of* SANWA HOLDINGS CORPORATION)
14904 135 Ave Nw, Edmonton, AB, T5V 1R9
(780) 483-1789
Emp Here 363   *Sales* 117,754,500
SIC 1751 Carpentry work
David Fraser

D-U-N-S 25-148-5991   (HQ)
DANDY OIL PRODUCTS LTD
WEST END PETRO PASS
15630 118 Ave Nw, Edmonton, AB, T5V 1C4
(780) 452-1104
Emp Here 10   *Sales* 44,002,035
SIC 5172 Petroleum products, nec
Danny Lipinski
Vandy Lipinski

D-U-N-S 24-328-7596   (SL)
EBERHARDT FOODS LTD
12165 154 St Nw, Edmonton, AB, T5V 1J3
(780) 454-8331
Emp Here 29   *Sales* 24,231,733
SIC 5141 Groceries, general line
Theodore Eberhardt
Jeffrey Eberhardt

D-U-N-S 24-394-4923   (SL)
EDMONTON HUMANE SOCIETY FOR THE PREVENTION OF CRUELTY TO ANIMALS
13620 163 St Nw, Edmonton, AB, T5V 0B2
(780) 471-1774
Emp Here 100   *Sales* 70,921,200
SIC 8699 Membership organizations, nec
Stephanie Mcdonald

D-U-N-S 20-742-6623   (SL)
EDMONTON KUBOTA LTD
15550 128 Ave Nw, Edmonton, AB, T5V 1S7
(780) 443-3800
Emp Here 20   *Sales* 10,000,000
SIC 5083 Farm and garden machinery
Ryan Oswald

D-U-N-S 20-385-5957   (SL)
EDMONTON POTATO GROWERS COOPERATIVE INC
12220 170 St Nw, Edmonton, AB, T5V 1L7
(780) 447-1860
Emp Here 24   *Sales* 20,053,848
SIC 5148 Fresh fruits and vegetables
Wayne Groot
Jake Hoogland
Klaas Bakker
Russ Van Boom
Gordon Visser
John Haarfma
Don Keltie

Tyler Buba
Tony Kirkland
Ron Prins

D-U-N-S 24-273-6007   (SL)
ENVIRONMENTAL DYNAMICS LTD
11810 152 St Nw, Edmonton, AB, T5V 1E3
(780) 421-0686
Emp Here 54   *Sales* 12,585,510
SIC 1711 Plumbing, heating, air-conditioning
Aaron Chetek

D-U-N-S 25-368-2181   (BR)
FEDERATED CO-OPERATIVES LIMITED
TGP
(*Suby of* FEDERATED CO-OPERATIVES LIMITED)
13232 170 St Nw, Edmonton, AB, T5V 1M7
(780) 447-5700
Emp Here 100
SIC 5141 Groceries, general line
Cliff Cook

D-U-N-S 24-396-9078   (HQ)
FISHIN' HOLE (1982) LTD, THE
FISHIN' HOLE
11829 154 St Nw, Edmonton, AB, T5V 1G6
(780) 469-6630
Emp Here 16   *Sales* 18,080,272
SIC 5941 Sporting goods and bicycle shops
David Johnston
Darrell Johnston
Mark Cram

D-U-N-S 20-898-2926   (SL)
GLENDALE GOLF & COUNTRY CLUB LTD
12410 199 St Nw, Edmonton, AB, T5V 1T8
(780) 447-3529
Emp Here 90   *Sales* 7,069,050
SIC 7997 Membership sports and recreation clubs
Mary Lemessurier
Garry Ollis
Jim Filewich

D-U-N-S 24-642-6811   (HQ)
GREGG DISTRIBUTORS LIMITED PARTNERSHIP
16215 118 Ave Nw, Edmonton, AB, T5V 1C7
(780) 447-3447
Emp Here 300   *Sales* 322,807,800
SIC 5013 Motor vehicle supplies and new parts
Gary Gregg

D-U-N-S 25-388-9836   (SL)
GROUPEX SYSTEMS CANADA INC
GROUPEX SERVICE EDM (GPX)
15102 128 Ave Nw, Edmonton, AB, T5V 1A8
(780) 454-3366
Emp Here 38   *Sales* 16,852,620
SIC 7389 Business services, nec
Douglas Needham
David Harris

D-U-N-S 20-044-2150   (HQ)
HEXION CANADA INC
(*Suby of* HEXION HOLDINGS LLC)
12621 156 St Nw, Edmonton, AB, T5V 1E1
(780) 447-1270
Emp Here 103   *Sales* 51,123,780
SIC 2821 Plastics materials and resins
William H. Carter
Ellen German Berndt
Dan Gouthro
George F. Knight

D-U-N-S 20-691-5097   (HQ)
IMPERIAL DISTRIBUTORS CANADA INC
(*Suby of* AP MARTIN PHARMACEUTICAL SUPPLIES LTD)
16504 121a Ave Nw, Edmonton, AB, T5V 1J9
(780) 484-2287
Sales 14,544,747
SIC 5122 Drugs, proprietaries, and sundries
Paul Fu
Ruby Hari
Andrew Yu

D-U-N-S 24-281-7310   (HQ)
INTERTEK INSPECTION SERVICES, LTD
INTERTEK
(*Suby of* INTERTEK GROUP PLC)
14920 135 Ave Nw, Edmonton, AB, T5V 1R9
(780) 482-5911
Emp Here 15   *Sales* 12,578,132
SIC 7389 Business services, nec
David Corbett
Joe Keating
William Tiffin
Mark Vise
Gregg Timann
Mark Fernandes

D-U-N-S 20-032-0993   (SL)
JIMSAR BUSINESS SERVICES INC
CAPITAL INSURANCE BROKER
13141 156 St Nw, Edmonton, AB, T5V 1V2
(780) 476-1600
Emp Here 15   *Sales* 10,881,585
SIC 6331 Fire, marine, and casualty insurance
Jack Rao

D-U-N-S 20-561-4642   (HQ)
K-BRO LINEN INC
14903 137 Ave Nw, Edmonton, AB, T5V 1R9
(780) 453-5218
Emp Here 6   *Sales* 181,591,204
SIC 7212 Garment pressing and cleaners' agents
Linda Mccurdy
Sean Curtis
Kristie Plaquin
Ross Smith
Matthew Hills
Steven Matyas
Michael Percy

D-U-N-S 20-861-0019   (BR)
K-BRO LINEN SYSTEMS INC
(*Suby of* K-BRO LINEN INC)
15253 121a Ave Nw, Edmonton, AB, T5V 1N1
(780) 451-3131
Emp Here 400
SIC 7219 Laundry and garment services, nec
Jim Crawford

D-U-N-S 25-256-7771   (HQ)
K-BRO LINEN SYSTEMS INC
(*Suby of* K-BRO LINEN INC)
14903 137 Ave Nw, Edmonton, AB, T5V 1R9
(780) 453-6855
Emp Here 9   *Sales* 133,629,054
SIC 7218 Industrial launderers
Linda Mccurdy
Ross Smith
Sean Curtis
Matthew Hills
Steven Matyas
Michael Percy
Kristie Plaquin

D-U-N-S 24-375-8278   (HQ)
LEHIGH HANSON MATERIALS LIMITED
LEHIGH CEMENT
(*Suby of* HEIDELBERGCEMENT AG)
12640 Inland Way Nw, Edmonton, AB, T5V 1K2
(780) 420-2500
Emp Here 150   *Sales* 434,673,000
SIC 3241 Cement, hydraulic
Christopher Ward
David Blackley
Alexander Car
Shawn Mcmillan
Carol Lowry
Jonathan Morrish
David Blackley
Lorenz Naeger

D-U-N-S 25-234-3769   (HQ)
LOCKERBIE & HOLE CONTRACTING LIMITED
(*Suby of* AECON GROUP INC)
14940 121a Ave Nw, Edmonton, AB, T5V 1A3

(780) 452-1250
Emp Here 40   *Sales* 135,424,000
SIC 1711 Plumbing, heating, air-conditioning
Jeff Pigott

D-U-N-S 25-195-3451   (HQ)
LOCKERBIE & HOLE INC
(*Suby of* AECON GROUP INC)
14940 121a Ave Nw, Edmonton, AB, T5V 1A3

Emp Here 50   *Sales* 1,403,767,920
SIC 1541 Industrial buildings and warehouses
Gordon Panas
James Hole
Steve Mulherin
Robert Noramand
William Grace
John Thompson

D-U-N-S 24-583-0153   (SL)
MAGAL MANUFACTURING LTD
14940 121a Ave Nw, Edmonton, AB, T5V 1A3
(780) 452-1250
Emp Here 75   *Sales* 31,705,275
SIC 1541 Industrial buildings and warehouses
Harold Barson
James D Hole

D-U-N-S 24-627-8055   (HQ)
MCCAFFERY GROUP INC
12160 160 St Nw, Edmonton, AB, T5V 1H5
(780) 452-8375
Emp Here 50   *Sales* 19,062,960
SIC 3088 Plastics plumbing fixtures
Neil Macdonald
Mary Mccaffery

D-U-N-S 24-068-5024   (HQ)
MCKILLICAN CANADIAN INC
(*Suby of* MCKILLICAN INTERNATIONAL, INC)
16420 118 Ave Nw, Edmonton, AB, T5V 1C8
(780) 453-3841
Emp Here 24   *Sales* 40,245,660
SIC 5039 Construction materials, nec
Gary Mckillican
Lynn Mckillican

D-U-N-S 25-192-5814   (HQ)
MCKILLICAN INTERNATIONAL, INC
16420 118 Ave Nw, Edmonton, AB, T5V 1C8
(780) 453-3841
Emp Here 2   *Sales* 113,925,600
SIC 5039 Construction materials, nec
Gary Mckillican
Jamie Barnes
Kevin Slabaugh
Lynn Mckillican

D-U-N-S 25-388-4357   (SL)
MILRON METAL FABRICATORS INC
12145 156 St Nw, Edmonton, AB, T5V 1N4
(780) 451-3258
Emp Here 45   *Sales* 21,376,170
SIC 5084 Industrial machinery and equipment
Curt Thompson
Ron Hodgson

D-U-N-S 24-065-0010   (HQ)
NATIVE COUNSELLING SERVICES OF ALBERTA
14904 121a Ave Nw, Edmonton, AB, T5V 1A3
(780) 451-4002
Emp Here 19   *Sales* 13,899,352
SIC 8322 Individual and family services
Allen Benson
Patti Laboucane-Benson
Claire Carefoot
Karen Erickson
Robyn Scott
Ian Thompson

D-U-N-S 25-230-6287   (SL)
NORFAB MFG. (1993) INC
16425 130 Ave Nw, Edmonton, AB, T5V 1K5
(780) 447-5454
Emp Here 54   *Sales* 10,372,590
SIC 3441 Fabricated structural Metal

Gregory Van Halst
Rhonda Moynes

D-U-N-S 20-734-5302   (BR)
NORTHERN ALBERTA INSTITUTE OF TECHNOLOGY
(*Suby of* NORTHERN ALBERTA INSTITUTE OF TECHNOLOGY)
12204 149 St Nw, Edmonton, AB, T5V 1A2
(780) 378-7200
Emp Here 100
SIC 8222 Junior colleges

D-U-N-S 25-370-5115   (SL)
O.E.M. REMANUFACTURING COMPANY INC
(*Suby of* FINNING INTERNATIONAL INC)
13315 156 St Nw, Edmonton, AB, T5V 1V2
(780) 468-6220
Emp Here 650   *Sales* 58,302,400
SIC 7538 General automotive repair shops
Chris Goodwin

D-U-N-S 20-083-8142   (HQ)
PETRIN MECHANICAL LTD
12180 152 St Nw, Edmonton, AB, T5V 1S1
(780) 451-4943
Sales 12,194,192
SIC 1711 Plumbing, heating, air-conditioning
Normand D Petrin
Marcel M Petrin
Kevin Sprague

D-U-N-S 24-331-2493   (HQ)
PHOENIX FENCE CORP
12816 156 St Nw, Edmonton, AB, T5V 1E9
(780) 447-1919
Sales 24,305,992
SIC 3315 Steel wire and related products
Dale Zaps
Collin Rowe
Simon Koch
Dan Jacques

D-U-N-S 24-393-0380   (HQ)
POLYTUBES 2009 INC
16221 123 Ave Nw, Edmonton, AB, T5V 1N9
(780) 453-2211
Emp Here 125   *Sales* 19,857,250
SIC 3084 Plastics pipe
Mike Lecavalier

D-U-N-S 20-118-8955   (SL)
POLYTUBES INC
(*Suby of* MCCAFFERY GROUP INC)
12160 160 St Nw, Edmonton, AB, T5V 1H5
(780) 453-2211
Emp Here 120   *Sales* 19,062,960
SIC 3088 Plastics plumbing fixtures
Robert D Miller
Neil Macdonald
Barb Brochu
Mary Mccaffery

D-U-N-S 20-776-3400   (SL)
PRAIRIE METAL INDUSTRIES INC
16420 130 Ave Nw, Edmonton, AB, T5V 1J8
(780) 447-1400
Emp Here 100   *Sales* 23,306,500
SIC 1711 Plumbing, heating, air-conditioning
Gary Ewoniak

D-U-N-S 24-283-3705   (SL)
PRICE STEEL LTD
13500 156 St Nw, Edmonton, AB, T5V 1L3
(780) 447-9999
Emp Here 50   *Sales* 22,358,700
SIC 5051 Metals service centers and offices
Asher Pertman
Alan Swerling
Wayne Pertman

D-U-N-S 25-064-4077   (BR)
PURE CANADIAN GAMING CORP
CASINOYELLOWHEAD
12464 153rd St, Edmonton, AB, T5V 3C5
(780) 424-9467
Emp Here 300

SIC 7999 Amusement and recreation, nec
Peter Wong

D-U-N-S 20-013-8464   (BR)
SIKA CANADA INC
(*Suby of* SIKA AG)
16910 129 Ave Nw Suite 1, Edmonton, AB, T5V 1L1
(780) 453-3060
Emp Here 200
SIC 2891 Adhesives and sealants
Gary Fisher

D-U-N-S 24-035-6985   (SL)
SKYVIEW ELECTRIC INC
12850 149 St Nw, Edmonton, AB, T5V 1A4

Emp Here 85   *Sales* 18,515,465
SIC 1731 Electrical work
Ken Perry

D-U-N-S 24-972-0038   (BR)
SOBEYS CAPITAL INCORPORATED
SOBEYS
(*Suby of* EMPIRE COMPANY LIMITED)
12910 156 St Nw, Edmonton, AB, T5V 1E9
(780) 447-1440
Emp Here 900
SIC 5141 Groceries, general line
Kevin Lynch

D-U-N-S 20-795-8633   (SL)
STANDARD GENERAL ASPHALT PLANT INC
12230 170 St Nw, Edmonton, AB, T5V 1L7
(780) 447-1666
Emp Here 100   *Sales* 23,343,500
SIC 2951 Asphalt paving mixtures and blocks
Robert Wilson

D-U-N-S 20-354-3848   (HQ)
TETRA TECH CANADA INC
(*Suby of* TETRA TECH, INC.)
14940 123 Ave Nw, Edmonton, AB, T5V 1B4
(780) 451-2121
Emp Here 500   *Sales* 625,586,500
SIC 8711 Engineering services
William R Brownlie
Robert J Sumsion
Richard A Lemmon

D-U-N-S 20-593-8897   (HQ)
THERMO KING WESTERN INC
15825 118 Ave Nw, Edmonton, AB, T5V 1B7
(780) 447-1578
Sales 17,907,440
SIC 3713 Truck and bus bodies
John Yewchuk
Tim Yewchuk
Rachelle Beger

D-U-N-S 24-642-6076   (HQ)
UNIVERSAL GEOMATICS SOLUTIONS CORP.
15111 123 Ave Nw, Edmonton, AB, T5V 1J7
(780) 454-3030
Emp Here 30   *Sales* 26,810,850
SIC 8713 Surveying services
Greg Boggs
Brian Ross
Linda Playfair
Gordis Blackmer
Andrew Miles
Steve Keddy

D-U-N-S 20-968-9819   (SL)
WAIWARD CONSTRUCTION MANAGEMENT INC
13015 163 St Nw, Edmonton, AB, T5V 1M5
(780) 447-1308
Emp Here 150   *Sales* 37,866,300
SIC 1623 Water, sewer, and utility lines
Donald Oborowsky
Dennis Degner

D-U-N-S 24-369-2725   (HQ)
WATER BLAST MANUFACTURING LP
HOTSY CLEANING SYSTEMS

(*Suby of* EXCHANGE INCOME CORPORATION)
16712 118 Ave Nw, Edmonton, AB, T5V 1P7
(780) 451-4521
Emp Here 40   *Sales* 15,636,992
SIC 5999 Miscellaneous retail stores, nec
Raymond Moher
Darrell Johnston

D-U-N-S 24-854-3712   (HQ)
WELDCO-BEALES MFG. ALBERTA LTD
WELDCO COMPANIES
12155 154 St Nw, Edmonton, AB, T5V 1J3
(780) 454-5244
Emp Here 200   *Sales* 98,306,950
SIC 3531 Construction machinery
Doug Schindel

D-U-N-S 24-583-6986   (SL)
WEST EDMONTON TRUCKLAND LTD
16806 118 Ave Nw, Edmonton, AB, T5V 1M8
(780) 452-3532
Emp Here 60   *Sales* 37,756,800
SIC 5541 Gasoline service stations
Robert Yeung
Tak-Fai Shum
Steve Tong
Dick Wong

D-U-N-S 24-396-4657   (SL)
XTOWN MOTORS LP
CROSSTOWN CHRYSLER DODGE JEEP RAM
(*Suby of* AUTOCANADA INC)
15520 123 Ave Nw, Edmonton, AB, T5V 1K8
(780) 488-4881
Emp Here 175   *Sales* 110,124,000
SIC 5511 New and used car dealers
Patrick Priestner
Dan Wincentaylo

D-U-N-S 20-775-7253   (SL)
YELLOWHEAD MOTOR INN LTD
YELLOWHEAD MOTOR INN
15004 Yellowhead Trail Nw, Edmonton, AB, T5V 1A1
(780) 447-2400
Emp Here 75   *Sales* 7,117,425
SIC 7011 Hotels and motels
Nizar Somji
Salima Mawani
Amin Rawj

D-U-N-S 24-124-8280   (BR)
YRC FREIGHT CANADA COMPANY
YRC REIMER
(*Suby of* YRC WORLDWIDE INC.)
16060 128 Ave Nw, Edmonton, AB, T5V 1B6
(780) 447-2434
Emp Here 200
SIC 4213 Trucking, except local
M Murdoch

Edmonton, AB T5W

D-U-N-S 20-210-0314   (SL)
ACI MANAGEMENT GROUP INC
12531 60 St Nw, Edmonton, AB, T5W 5J5
(780) 476-3098
Emp Here 35   *Sales* 14,847,418
SIC 6712 Bank holding companies
Andrew Wolthuis

D-U-N-S 20-745-1709   (SL)
BEVERLY CREST MOTOR INN LTD
3414 118 Ave Nw, Edmonton, AB, T5W 0Z4
(780) 474-0456
Emp Here 120   *Sales* 11,122,800
SIC 7011 Hotels and motels
Ernie Mekechuk
Eugene Demkiw
Mike Kawulych
Norm Lesyk
Victor Ewanko

Peter Kule
Rose Melenka
George Melenka

D-U-N-S 20-811-1443   (SL)
HIGHLANDS GOLF CLUB
6603 Ada Blvd Nw, Edmonton, AB, T5W 4N5
(780) 474-4211
Emp Here 100   *Sales* 7,854,500
SIC 7997 Membership sports and recreation clubs
Ted Smith

D-U-N-S 24-325-9459   (SL)
LAM, MICHELLE PHARMACY LTD
SHOPPERS DRUG MART
3812 118 Ave Nw Suite 318, Edmonton, AB, T5W 5C7
(780) 474-2424
Emp Here 50   *Sales* 12,647,700
SIC 5912 Drug stores and proprietary stores
Michelle Lam

D-U-N-S 25-271-0256   (BR)
SOBEYS WEST INC
(*Suby of* EMPIRE COMPANY LIMITED)
3004 118 Ave Nw, Edmonton, AB, T5W 4W3
(780) 477-6923
Emp Here 82
SIC 5411 Grocery stores
Jason Johnston

Edmonton, AB T5X

D-U-N-S 24-997-1946   (SL)
REALTY EXECUTIVE SYNERGY INC
15341 97 St Nw, Edmonton, AB, T5X 5V3
(780) 699-7347
Emp Here 40   *Sales* 13,085,080
SIC 6531 Real estate agents and managers
Richard Audy

D-U-N-S 20-806-2344   (BR)
SOBEYS CAPITAL INCORPORATED
SOBEYS STORE 3132
(*Suby of* EMPIRE COMPANY LIMITED)
15367 Castle Downs Rd Nw, Edmonton, AB, T5X 6C3
(780) 472-0100
Emp Here 160
SIC 5411 Grocery stores
Thomas Pugh

D-U-N-S 20-545-7588   (SL)
SOBEYS WESTERN CELLARS
SOBEYS ESPIRIT WINE AND COLD BEER
15353 Castle Downs Rd Nw, Edmonton, AB, T5X 6C3
(780) 473-7800
Emp Here 25   *Sales* 14,697,900
SIC 5182 Wine and distilled beverages
Darsy Platz

D-U-N-S 20-346-3828   (SL)
TIM HORTONS
9902 153 Ave Nw, Edmonton, AB, T5X 6A4
(780) 448-9722
Emp Here 42   *Sales* 11,514,384
SIC 5461 Retail bakeries
Elizabeth Haley

Edmonton, AB T5Y

D-U-N-S 24-345-0264   (BR)
ALBERTA HEALTH SERVICES
ALBERTA HOSPITAL EDMONTON
(*Suby of* GOVERNMENT OF THE PROVINCE OF ALBERTA)
17480 Fort Rd Nw Suite 175, Edmonton, AB, T5Y 6A8
(780) 342-5555
Emp Here 400

SIC 8063 Psychiatric hospitals
Sharon Heinrich

D-U-N-S 24-013-0802   (SL)
INNOVATIVE INTERIOR SYSTEMS
2050 227 Ave Ne, Edmonton, AB, T5Y 6H5
(780) 414-0637
Emp Here 50   *Sales* 22,174,500
SIC 7389 Business services, nec
Richard Fournier

D-U-N-S 25-504-9900   (SL)
NORTH COUNTRY LIVESTOCK LTD
24040 17 St Ne, Edmonton, AB, T5Y 6J6
(780) 478-2333
Emp Here 10   *Sales* 12,103,970
SIC 5154 Livestock
Ken Danard

D-U-N-S 25-370-3623   (BR)
NORTH WEST COMPANY LP, THE
GIANT TIGER
(*Suby of* NORTH WEST COMPANY LP, THE)
14097 Victoria Trail Nw, Edmonton, AB, T5Y 2B6
(780) 472-7780
Emp Here 82
SIC 5411 Grocery stores
Pierre Marchand

D-U-N-S 20-198-0930   (BR)
RRGB RESTAURANTS CANADA INC
(*Suby of* RRGB RESTAURANTS CANADA INC)
4950 137 Ave Nw, Edmonton, AB, T5Y 2V4
(780) 456-8700
Emp Here 100
SIC 5812 Eating places
Jeff Frewin

D-U-N-S 24-715-5018   (BR)
SOBEYS CAPITAL INCORPORATED
SOBEYS HOLLICK KENYON
(*Suby of* EMPIRE COMPANY LIMITED)
5119 167 Ave Nw, Edmonton, AB, T5Y 0L2
(780) 478-4740
Emp Here 150
SIC 5411 Grocery stores
Evan Sillier

D-U-N-S 25-219-0053   (BR)
WAL-MART CANADA CORP
WAL-MART NORTHEAST
(*Suby of* WALMART INC.)
13703 40 St Nw Suite 3028, Edmonton, AB, T5Y 3B5
(780) 476-4460
Emp Here 300
SIC 5311 Department stores
Gord Weirn

Edmonton, AB T5Z

D-U-N-S 24-671-9124   (SL)
HOLOWAYCHUK, L.B. PHARMACY LTD
SHOPPERS DRUG MART
16504 95 St Nw Suite 375, Edmonton, AB, T5Z 3L7
(780) 456-5557
Emp Here 50   *Sales* 12,647,700
SIC 5912 Drug stores and proprietary stores
Lavonne Holowaychuk

D-U-N-S 20-178-9349   (SL)
MACKINTOSH, K.J. SALES LTD
CANADIAN TIRE
9603 162 Ave Nw Suite 397, Edmonton, AB, T5Z 3T6
(780) 495-9696
Emp Here 65   *Sales* 40,903,200
SIC 5531 Auto and home supply stores
Kirk James Mackintosh
Mary Kathryn Mackintosh

D-U-N-S 25-271-1080   (BR)

SOBEYS WEST INC
SAFEWAY
(*Suby of* EMPIRE COMPANY LIMITED)
8720 156 Ave Nw, Edmonton, AB, T5Z 3B4
(780) 486-0584
Emp Here 120
SIC 5411 Grocery stores
Jack Lowe

Edmonton, AB T6A

D-U-N-S 24-356-9634   (HQ)
AT FILMS INC
RPC BPI AGRICULTURE
(*Suby of* RPC GROUP LIMITED)
4605 101a Ave Nw, Edmonton, AB, T6A 0L3
(780) 450-7760
Sales 16,887,624
SIC 1742 Plastering, drywall, and insulation
Calvin Mazurenko

D-U-N-S 24-392-2077   (HQ)
CHALLENGER GEOMATICS LTD
CHALLENGER ENGINEERING
9945 50 St Nw Suite 200, Edmonton, AB, T6A 0L4
(780) 424-5511
Sales 30,385,630
SIC 8713 Surveying services
Dave Thomson
Tim Harding
Al Zaver

D-U-N-S 20-251-1465   (BR)
EPCOR WATER SERVICES INC
(*Suby of* CITY OF EDMONTON)
10977 50 St Nw, Edmonton, AB, T6A 2E9
(780) 969-8496
Emp Here 160
SIC 1629 Heavy construction, nec
Simon Thomas

D-U-N-S 24-527-4258   (SL)
FEDERATION-ALBERTA GAS COOPS
9945 50 St Nw Suite 400, Edmonton, AB, T6A 0L4
(780) 469-3200
Emp Here 4   *Sales* 12,423,428
SIC 4924 Natural gas distribution
Mike Heck

D-U-N-S 20-810-8845   (SL)
HARDISTY NURSING HOME INC
6420 101 Ave Nw, Edmonton, AB, T6A 0H5
(780) 466-9267
Emp Here 200   *Sales* 13,713,200
SIC 8051 Skilled nursing care facilities
Hubert Hoffman

D-U-N-S 20-897-3081   (SL)
JUBILEE LODGE NURSING HOME LTD
10333 76 St Nw, Edmonton, AB, T6A 3A8
(780) 469-4456
Emp Here 150   *Sales* 10,284,900
SIC 8051 Skilled nursing care facilities
Blaine Turner

D-U-N-S 24-732-0906   (SL)
M & V ENTERPRISES LTD
BOSTON PIZZA CAPILANO
5515 101 Ave Nw, Edmonton, AB, T6A 3Z7
(780) 465-0771
Emp Here 110   *Sales* 5,007,090
SIC 5812 Eating places
Dale Nisbet
Dean Nisbet
Imran Usman

D-U-N-S 24-171-3437   (SL)
STROUD AGENCIES LTD
STROUD AGENCIES INSURANCE BROKERS
9945 50 St Nw Unit 304, Edmonton, AB, T6A 0L4

(780) 426-2400
Emp Here 15   *Sales* 10,881,585
SIC 6311 Life insurance
Fred Stroud
Cheryl Stroud

D-U-N-S 24-316-9096   (BR)
WAL-MART CANADA CORP
WALMART
(*Suby of* WALMART INC.)
5004 98 Ave Nw Suite 1, Edmonton, AB, T6A 0A1
(780) 466-2002
Emp Here 100
SIC 5311 Department stores
Glen Guysborough

Edmonton, AB T6B

D-U-N-S 25-370-2161   (BR)
1032451 B.C. LTD
EDMONTON SUN, THE
(*Suby of* QUEBECOR MEDIA INC)
9300 47 St Nw, Edmonton, AB, T6B 2P6
(780) 468-0506
Emp Here 100
SIC 2711 Newspapers
Mark Pragaer

D-U-N-S 24-328-4536   (BR)
1032451 B.C. LTD
EDMONTON SUN
(*Suby of* QUEBECOR MEDIA INC)
4990 92 Ave Nw Suite 350, Edmonton, AB, T6B 3A1
(780) 468-0100
Emp Here 400
SIC 2711 Newspapers
John Caputo

D-U-N-S 24-135-0797   (SL)
227835 ALBERTA LTD
9211 48 St Nw, Edmonton, AB, T6B 2R9
(780) 465-9321
Emp Here 50   *Sales* 12,044,200
SIC 1623 Water, sewer, and utility lines
Keith Walsh

D-U-N-S 20-085-0287   (HQ)
316291 ALBERTA LTD
WESTERN ARCHRIB
4315 92 Ave Nw, Edmonton, AB, T6B 3M7
(780) 465-9771
Emp Here 70   *Sales* 23,084,400
SIC 2439 Structural wood members, nec
Kent Fargey
Joan Fargey

D-U-N-S 24-854-2078   (HQ)
401919 ALBERTA LTD
COLLINS INDUSTRIES
3740 73 Ave Nw, Edmonton, AB, T6B 2Z2
(780) 440-1414
Emp Here 1   *Sales* 17,863,905
SIC 3441 Fabricated structural Metal
Paul Collins

D-U-N-S 24-840-4709   (SL)
464161 ALBERTA LTD
HOLIDAY INN CONVENTION CENTRE
4520 76 Ave Nw, Edmonton, AB, T6B 0A5
(780) 468-5400
Emp Here 75   *Sales* 7,117,425
SIC 7011 Hotels and motels
Karima Suleman
Sadrudin Suleman

D-U-N-S 25-679-8539   (SL)
595140 ALBERTA LTD
5219 47 St Nw, Edmonton, AB, T6B 3N4
(780) 444-7766
Emp Here 120   *Sales* 32,802,000
SIC 6712 Bank holding companies
Ronald Brown
Shirley Rae

▲ Public Company   ■ Public Company Family Member   **HQ** Headquarters   **BR** Branch   **SL** Single Location

D-U-N-S 20-188-6871   (HQ)
619249 ALBERTA LTD
4143 78 Ave Nw, Edmonton, AB, T6B 2N3
(780) 469-7799
Sales 19,028,940
SIC 7623 Refrigeration service and repair
Jean-Louis Cloutier
Vivian Cloutier

D-U-N-S 25-388-5800   (HQ)
620126 ALBERTA LTD
CROWN STAR FOODS-EDMONTON
6803 72 Ave Nw, Edmonton, AB, T6B 3A5
(780) 465-3499
Emp Here 17   *Sales* 20,889,425
SIC 5145 Confectionery
Haiderali Walji

D-U-N-S 25-417-3925   (SL)
669021 ALBERTA LTD
NORWEST CONSTRUCTION, DIV OF
5104 55 Ave Nw, Edmonton, AB, T6B 3C6
(780) 865-4183
Emp Here 50   *Sales* 12,652,950
SIC 5211 Lumber and other building materials
Don Roberts

D-U-N-S 20-617-0284   (SL)
A & H STEEL LTD
4710 82 Ave Nw, Edmonton, AB, T6B 0E4
(780) 465-6425
Emp Here 70   *Sales* 13,445,950
SIC 3441 Fabricated structural Metal
Craig Kotun
Craig Kotun
Olga Chebuk

D-U-N-S 20-104-5130   (BR)
ABSOLUTE ENERGY SOLUTIONS INC
ABSOULUTE COMPLETION TECHNOLO-GIES
(*Suby of* ABSOLUTE ENERGY LTD)
5710 36 St Nw, Edmonton, AB, T6B 3T2
(780) 440-9058
Emp Here 100
SIC 3545 Machine tool accessories
Phil Mcdullococh

D-U-N-S 20-374-6011   (SL)
ACADEMY CONSTRUCTION & MAINTE-NANCE LIMITED PARTNERSHIP
(*Suby of* HILLCORE GROUP HOLDINGS LTD)
4066 78 Ave Nw, Edmonton, AB, T6B 3M8
(780) 395-4914
Emp Here 100
SIC 3498 Fabricated pipe and fittings
Dustin Medori
Garrett Wenckowski

D-U-N-S 20-354-4916   (SL)
ACADEMY CONSTRUCTION & MAINTE-NANCE LTD
(*Suby of* HILLCORE GROUP HOLDINGS LTD)
4066 78 Ave Nw, Edmonton, AB, T6B 3M8
(780) 466-6360
Emp Here 100   *Sales* 19,208,500
SIC 3498 Fabricated pipe and fittings
Duane Nelson
Ryan Bourke
Garry Brown

D-U-N-S 20-374-5997   (HQ)
ACADEMY FABRICATORS GROUP LIM-ITED PARTNERSHIP
(*Suby of* HILLCORE GROUP HOLDINGS LTD)
4066-78 Ave, Edmonton, AB, T6B 3M8
(780) 395-4914
Sales 284,627,600
SIC 6211 Security brokers and dealers
Jean-Marc Bougie

D-U-N-S 24-004-2630   (SL)
ALBERTA PETROLEUM INDUSTRIES LTD
API
6607 59 St Nw, Edmonton, AB, T6B 3P8

(780) 436-9693
Emp Here 22   *Sales* 10,450,572
SIC 5082 Construction and mining machinery
Scott Delbridge
Shelley Delbridge

D-U-N-S 24-773-1081   (SL)
ALBERTA SAFETY COUNCIL, THE
4831 93 Ave Nw, Edmonton, AB, T6B 3A2
(780) 462-7300
Emp Here 49   *Sales* 11,480,112
SIC 8748 Business consulting, nec
Laurie Billings

D-U-N-S 25-145-6109   (SL)
ALIYA'S FOODS LIMITED
CHEF BOMBAY
6364 Roper Rd Nw, Edmonton, AB, T6B 3P9
(780) 467-4600
Emp Here 180   *Sales* 24,456,896
SIC 2038 Frozen specialties, nec
Noorudin Jiwani
Anis Jiwani

D-U-N-S 20-346-7717   (SL)
ALL 4 WATER CORP
7115 Girard Rd Nw, Edmonton, AB, T6B 2C5

Emp Here 50   *Sales* 11,242,750
SIC 2086 Bottled and canned soft drinks
Ron Hoyda
Murray Toews
Justin Hoyda

D-U-N-S 20-015-9080   (SL)
ALTEX INDUSTRIES INC
ALTEX FIELD SERVICES
6831 42 St Nw, Edmonton, AB, T6B 2X1
(780) 468-6862
Emp Here 180   *Sales* 34,575,300
SIC 3443 Fabricated plate work (boiler shop)
Durwill Dennis
Tim Carlson
Stephen Hutchison
Michael Myshak

D-U-N-S 24-786-0414   (HQ)
AQUA AIR SYSTEMS LTD
8703 50 St Nw, Edmonton, AB, T6B 1E7
(780) 465-8011
Emp Here 19   *Sales* 13,721,856
SIC 5075 Warm air heating and air condition-ing
James Delaney
Andrew Gauthier

D-U-N-S 24-851-0351   (BR)
ATCO GAS AND PIPELINES LTD
ATCO GAS
(*Suby of* ATCO LTD)
5623 82 Ave Nw, Edmonton, AB, T6B 0E8
(780) 733-2552
Emp Here 200
SIC 0721 Crop planting and protection
Barry Russ

D-U-N-S 20-513-9095   (BR)
BAKER HUGHES CANADA COMPANY
PROCESS & PIPELINE SEVICES, DIV OF
(*Suby of* GENERAL ELECTRIC COMPANY)
9010 34 St Nw, Edmonton, AB, T6B 2V1
(780) 465-9495
Emp Here 75
SIC 1389 Oil and gas field services, nec
Gordon Bradbury

D-U-N-S 25-328-1992   (BR)
BANTREL CO.
(*Suby of* BECHTEL GROUP, INC.)
4999 98 Ave Nw Unit 401, Edmonton, AB, T6B 2X3
(780) 462-5600
Emp Here 150
SIC 8711 Engineering services
Peter Churchill

D-U-N-S 25-532-1788   (SL)
BHD TUBULAR LIMITED

6903 72 Ave Nw, Edmonton, AB, T6B 3A5
(780) 434-6824
Emp Here 13   *Sales* 13,004,407
SIC 5051 Metals service centers and offices
Ken Hesse
Larry Hesse
Brian Beattie

D-U-N-S 20-327-9831   (BR)
BLACK CAT WEAR PARTS LTD
(*Suby of* TONUX INC)
5720 59 St Nw, Edmonton, AB, T6B 3L4
(780) 465-6666
Emp Here 150
SIC 3531 Construction machinery
Terry Mckay

D-U-N-S 24-396-5621   (HQ)
BLACK CAT WEAR PARTS LTD
(*Suby of* TONUX INC)
5604 59 St Nw, Edmonton, AB, T6B 3C3
(780) 465-6666
Emp Here 210   *Sales* 98,306,950
SIC 3531 Construction machinery
James Buxton
Richard Buxton
Henry Ruis
David Holubitsky
Felicia Brooks

D-U-N-S 24-332-0587   (HQ)
BOB DALE GLOVES & IMPORTS LTD
4504 82 Ave Nw, Edmonton, AB, T6B 2S4
(780) 469-2100
Emp Here 14   *Sales* 12,458,050
SIC 5136 Men's and boy's clothing
Denis Dale
Steve Chan
Paul Hazlett

D-U-N-S 20-539-5809   (SL)
BRANDON PETROLEUM SALES LTD
BRANDON PETROLEUM
3515 76 Ave Nw, Edmonton, AB, T6B 2S8
(780) 413-1826
Emp Here 20   *Sales* 20,656,160
SIC 5171 Petroleum bulk stations and termi-nals
Norman Bohl
Mark Hyderman

D-U-N-S 24-393-9050   (SL)
BUFFALO INSPECTION SERVICES (2005) INC
3867 Roper Rd Nw, Edmonton, AB, T6B 3S5
(780) 486-7344
Emp Here 100   *Sales* 22,032,800
SIC 8734 Testing laboratories
Bari Walsh

D-U-N-S 24-731-1632   (BR)
BUREAU VERITAS CANADA (2019) INC
MAXXAM ANALYTICS
(*Suby of* BUREAU VERITAS)
6744 50 St Nw, Edmonton, AB, T6B 3M9
(780) 378-8500
Emp Here 100
SIC 8734 Testing laboratories
Bernie Brassard

D-U-N-S 24-026-3199   (SL)
CANADIAN CONDOMINIUM MANAGE-MENT CORP
9440 49 St Nw Suite 230, Edmonton, AB, T6B 2M9
(780) 485-0505
Emp Here 30   *Sales* 11,588,790
SIC 1531 Operative builders
Rod Osborne

D-U-N-S 20-637-3102   (HQ)
CANTERBURY FOOD SERVICE (ALTA) LTD
CANTERBURY COFFEE
(*Suby of* CANTERBURY COFFEE CORPO-RATION)
4803 93 Ave Nw, Edmonton, AB, T6B 3A2
(780) 468-6363
Sales 23,396,156

SIC 5149 Groceries and related products, nec
Murray Dunlop
Ed Andrews
Eric Lightheart

D-U-N-S 20-799-2038   (SL)
CAREFREE COACH & RV LTD
4510 51 Ave Nw, Edmonton, AB, T6B 2W2
(780) 438-2008
Emp Here 45   *Sales* 28,317,600
SIC 5561 Recreational vehicle dealers
Elmer Lastiwka
Phil Turgeon
Darcy Turgeon
Laura Lastiwka

D-U-N-S 20-360-1406   (SL)
CAREFREE RV LTD
4510 51 Ave Nw, Edmonton, AB, T6B 2W2
(780) 438-2008
Emp Here 30   *Sales* 14,942,340
SIC 5521 Used car dealers
Elmer Lastiwka

D-U-N-S 24-391-7882   (HQ)
CASH CANADA FINANCIAL CENTERS LTD
8170 50 St Nw Suite 325, Edmonton, AB, T6B 1E6
(780) 424-1080
Emp Here 20   *Sales* 11,237,200
SIC 6163 Loan brokers
Tim Latimer

D-U-N-S 25-218-7935   (HQ)
CB PARTNERS CORPORATION
CLARK BUILDERS
4703 52 Ave Nw, Edmonton, AB, T6B 3R6
(780) 395-3300
Emp Here 140   *Sales* 488,874,400
SIC 1542 Nonresidential construction, nec
Paul Verhesen
Lars Leitner
Adrienne Lynn
Pete Simpson

D-U-N-S 24-438-8559   (HQ)
CEDA FIELD SERVICES LP
CEDA
(*Suby of* OMERS ADMINISTRATION COR-PORATION)
6005 72a Ave Nw, Edmonton, AB, T6B 2J1
(780) 377-4306
Emp Here 13   *Sales* 62,787,200
SIC 7699 Repair services, nec
Roger Hearn
Jan Campbell

D-U-N-S 20-272-7210   (SL)
CLEARSTREAM TRANSPORTATION SER-VICES LP
(*Suby of* CLEARSTREAM ENERGY SER-VICES INC)
7809 34 St Nw, Edmonton, AB, T6B 2V5
(780) 410-1960
Emp Here 100   *Sales* 67,267,900
SIC 1389 Oil and gas field services, nec
Bruce Powell

D-U-N-S 24-391-7952   (SL)
COLLINS INDUSTRIES LTD
(*Suby of* 401919 ALBERTA LTD)
3740 73 Ave Nw, Edmonton, AB, T6B 2Z2
(780) 440-1796
Emp Here 92   *Sales* 17,671,820
SIC 3441 Fabricated structural Metal
Ryan Collins
Kim Collins
Jason Collins
Kerry Collins

D-U-N-S 25-085-7505   (SL)
CONTINENTAL CHAIN & RIGGING LTD
7011 Girard Rd Nw, Edmonton, AB, T6B 2C4
(780) 437-2701
Emp Here 50   *Sales* 10,141,500
SIC 3462 Iron and steel forgings
Ian Mcclurg
Leanne Brouwer

Trevor Lindstrom

D-U-N-S 20-617-3627   (HQ)
COWAN GRAPHICS INC
COWAN IMAGING GROUP
4864 93 Ave Nw, Edmonton, AB, T6B 2P8
(780) 577-5700
Emp Here 85   *Sales* 18,042,970
SIC 2759 Commercial printing, nec
Blaine Macmillan
Kevin Macmillan
Muriel Jensen

D-U-N-S 24-320-1759   (SL)
CRATEX INDUSTRIES LTD
4735 82 Ave Nw, Edmonton, AB, T6B 0E5
(780) 468-4769
Emp Here 80   *Sales* 41,597,360
SIC 4783 Packing and crating
Myles Macleod
Gordon Smith

D-U-N-S 20-081-5645   (HQ)
DAAM GALVANIZING CO. LTD
DAAM GALVANIZING - EDMONTON
9390 48 St Nw, Edmonton, AB, T6B 2R3
(780) 468-6868
Emp Here 70   *Sales* 11,524,275
SIC 3479 Metal coating and allied services
Darcy Pretula
Dale Butterworth
Pat Lauriks

D-U-N-S 24-716-6242   (HQ)
DAWSON WALLACE CONSTRUCTION LTD
4611 Eleniak Rd Nw, Edmonton, AB, T6B 2N1
(780) 466-8700
Emp Here 75   *Sales* 57,033,800
SIC 1542 Nonresidential construction, nec
Peter Dawson
Wayne Wallace

D-U-N-S 24-397-1728   (HQ)
DELNOR CONSTRUCTION LTD
3609 74 Ave Nw, Edmonton, AB, T6B 2T7
(780) 469-1304
Sales 108,364,220
SIC 1542 Nonresidential construction, nec
Ed Cyrankiewicz
John Vandenberg

D-U-N-S 20-915-1435   (BR)
DNOW CANADA ULC
NATIONAL OILWELL VARCO
(Suby of NOW INC.)
7127 56 Ave Nw, Edmonton, AB, T6B 3L2
(780) 465-0999
Emp Here 97
SIC 3533 Oil and gas field machinery
Charlie Chrenek

D-U-N-S 25-993-0613   (SL)
DOUBLE G MECHANICAL LTD
8170 50 St Nw Unit 430, Edmonton, AB, T6B
1E6

Emp Here 49   *Sales* 10,825,766
SIC 1711 Plumbing, heating, air-conditioning
Chantale Leblanc

D-U-N-S 24-281-8557   (HQ)
DRADER MANUFACTURING INDUSTRIES LTD
5750 50 St Nw, Edmonton, AB, T6B 2Z8
(780) 440-2231
Emp Here 105   *Sales* 23,828,700
SIC 3089 Plastics products, nec
Gordon Mctavish
Ronald W Swane
Nicholas Pich
Shirley Ann Carson
Maynard Vollan

D-U-N-S 20-030-7861   (SL)
DUNRITE EXPRESS & HOTSHOT INC
9435 47 St Nw, Edmonton, AB, T6B 2R7
(780) 463-8880
Emp Here 40   *Sales* 17,739,600

SIC 7389 Business services, nec
Peter Sledz

D-U-N-S 25-686-1519   (SL)
DYNAENERGETICS CANADA HOLDINGS INC
5911 56 Ave Nw, Edmonton, AB, T6B 3E2
(780) 490-0939
Emp Here 33   *Sales* 10,550,265
SIC 1389 Oil and gas field services, nec
Ian Brooker
Rolf Rospek
Richard Santa

D-U-N-S 20-838-1249   (HQ)
DYNAENERGETICS CANADA INC
(Suby of DMC GLOBAL INC.)
5911 56 Ave Nw, Edmonton, AB, T6B 3E2
(780) 490-0939
Emp Here 27   *Sales* 10,550,265
SIC 1389 Oil and gas field services, nec
Ian Brooker
Rolf Rospek
Richard Santa

D-U-N-S 20-154-8117   (BR)
EDMONTON CATHOLIC SEPARATE SCHOOL DISTRICT NO.7
AUSTIN O'BRIEN CATHOLIC HIGH SCHOOL
(Suby of EDMONTON CATHOLIC SEPARATE SCHOOL DISTRICT NO.7)
6110 95 Ave Nw, Edmonton, AB, T6B 1A5
(780) 466-3161
Emp Here 80
SIC 8211 Elementary and secondary schools
David Warawa

D-U-N-S 24-010-0250   (HQ)
EVER GREEN ECOLOGICAL SERVICES INC
6105 76 Ave Nw, Edmonton, AB, T6B 0A7
(780) 417-2282
Sales 12,856,550
SIC 4953 Refuse systems
Lorenzo Donini
Tamara Brown

D-U-N-S 24-948-9915   (SL)
FIRE PROTECTION INC
6748 59 St Nw, Edmonton, AB, T6B 3N6
(780) 469-1454
Emp Here 40   *Sales* 17,968,760
SIC 7389 Business services, nec

D-U-N-S 20-065-7091   (SL)
FIRST GENERAL SERVICES (EDMONTON) INC
7311 77 Ave Nw, Edmonton, AB, T6B 0B7
(780) 463-4040
Emp Here 25   *Sales* 25,872,025
SIC 6321 Accident and health insurance
Bob Bunker

D-U-N-S 20-337-8906   (HQ)
FLEXITALLIC CANADA LTD
(Suby of THE FLEXITALLIC GROUP)
4340 78 Ave Nw, Edmonton, AB, T6B 3J5
(780) 466-5050
Emp Here 155   *Sales* 25,417,280
SIC 3053 Gaskets; packing and sealing devices
Jon Stokes
Ken Berry
Gerry Maters

D-U-N-S 24-854-8513   (HQ)
FMC TECHNOLOGIES COMPANY
(Suby of TECHNIPFMC PLC)
6703 68 Ave Nw, Edmonton, AB, T6B 3E3
(780) 468-9231
Emp Here 50   *Sales* 40,377,210
SIC 5084 Industrial machinery and equipment
John T. Gremp
Jay A. Nutt
Douglas J. Pferdehirt
Maryann T. Seaman

D-U-N-S 20-878-5084   (HQ)

GENERAL RECYCLING INDUSTRIES LTD
4120 84 Ave Nw, Edmonton, AB, T6B 3H3
(780) 461-5555
Sales 52,054,200
SIC 5093 Scrap and waste materials
Wayne Pertman
Kevin Swerling

D-U-N-S 20-898-8659   (SL)
GENERAL SCRAP IRON & METALS LTD
4120 84 Ave Nw, Edmonton, AB, T6B 3H3
(780) 452-5865
Emp Here 30   *Sales* 15,616,260
SIC 5093 Scrap and waste materials
Wayne Pertman

D-U-N-S 24-809-8634   (HQ)
GOODKEY SHOW SERVICES LTD
5506-48 St Nw, Edmonton, AB, T6B 2Z1
(780) 426-2211
Emp Here 12   *Sales* 15,722,665
SIC 7389 Business services, nec
Calvin Goodkey
Rodella Goodkey

D-U-N-S 25-677-2534   (SL)
GREEN LINE HOSE & FITTINGS (ALBERTA) LTD
(Suby of GREEN LINE SALES LTD)
7003 Roper Rd Nw, Edmonton, AB, T6B 3K3
(780) 465-5216
Emp Here 64   *Sales* 17,129,728
SIC 5251 Hardware stores
Michael Blackmore

D-U-N-S 24-128-6884   (SL)
GREGG DISTRIBUTORS CO LTD
GREGG DISTRIBUTORS
3611 76 Ave Nw, Edmonton, AB, T6B 2S8
(780) 450-2233
Emp Here 744   *Sales* 153,045,264
SIC 4225 General warehousing and storage
Gary Gregg

D-U-N-S 20-538-3912   (HQ)
GRENCO INDUSTRIES LTD
3710 78 Ave Nw, Edmonton, AB, T6B 3E5
(780) 468-2000
Emp Here 30   *Sales* 12,210,055
SIC 3533 Oil and gas field machinery
Eduard Grenke
Arthur Grenke

D-U-N-S 25-475-1647   (HQ)
HARSCO CANADA CORPORATION
PATENT CONSTRUCTION SYSTEMS CANADA
(Suby of HARSCO CORPORATION)
7030 51 Ave Nw, Edmonton, AB, T6B 2P4
(780) 468-3292
Emp Here 20   *Sales* 14,771,160
SIC 1799 Special trade contractors, nec
Martin Hayward

D-U-N-S 24-584-8403   (HQ)
HI-KALIBRE EQUIPMENT LIMITED
7321 68 Ave Nw, Edmonton, AB, T6B 3T6
(780) 435-1111
Emp Here 155   *Sales* 17,287,650
SIC 3491 Industrial valves
Patrick Rabby
Tod Hohl
Derek Duncombe
Lee Makelki

D-U-N-S 24-983-9226   (HQ)
INTERNATIONAL ASPHALT LEASING INC
6105 76 Ave Nw, Edmonton, AB, T6B 0A7
(780) 469-7304
Sales 13,077,650
SIC 6712 Bank holding companies
Brian Sehn

D-U-N-S 25-315-6699   (BR)
IPEX INC
IPEX MANAGEMENT
(Suby of ALIAXIS)
4225 92 Ave Nw, Edmonton, AB, T6B 3M7

(780) 415-5300
Emp Here 300
SIC 3089 Plastics products, nec
Gean Doyon

D-U-N-S 25-536-0596   (SL)
JET LABEL AND PACKAGING LTD
JET LABEL
9445 49 St Nw, Edmonton, AB, T6B 2L8
(780) 440-5135
Emp Here 70   *Sales* 13,633,760
SIC 2679 Converted paper products, nec
Darrell Friesen
Rod Froment
Steve Smith
Neil Mcdonald

D-U-N-S 24-887-2637   (SL)
JET POWER AND CONTROLS SYSTEMS LTD
7730 34 St Nw, Edmonton, AB, T6B 3J6
(780) 485-1438
Emp Here 49   *Sales* 10,028,977
SIC 3621 Motors and generators
Devon Sandford
David Sadnford
Brock Stewart

D-U-N-S 20-143-0878   (SL)
KENTUCKY BLUE GRASS LTD
LAWN MAINTANCE/LANDSCAPING
6107 34 St Nw, Edmonton, AB, T6B 2V6
(780) 415-5201
Emp Here 50   *Sales* 17,123,350
SIC 0181 Ornamental nursery products
Gary Schmidt

D-U-N-S 24-090-8004   (SL)
KING'S UNIVERSITY COLLEGE, THE
9125 50 St Nw, Edmonton, AB, T6B 2H3
(780) 465-3500
Emp Here 200   *Sales* 29,878,200
SIC 8221 Colleges and universities
J. Harry Fernhout
Irene Vanderkloet
John Kamphof

D-U-N-S 20-085-7514   (HQ)
LAIRD ELECTRIC INC
(Suby of STUART OLSON INC)
6707 59 St Nw, Edmonton, AB, T6B 3P8
(780) 450-9636
Emp Here 25   *Sales* 94,203,600
SIC 1731 Electrical work
Robert Myles
Warren Stein
Daryl Sands
Randy Morgan

D-U-N-S 25-168-5970   (HQ)
LANDTRAN LOGISTICS INC
4819 90a Ave Nw, Edmonton, AB, T6B 2Y3
(780) 486-8607
Emp Here 10   *Sales* 30,855,900
SIC 4213 Trucking, except local
John Assman
Rob Stasiw
Lawrence Centera
Kelly Kopinsky
Les Gray
Gord Froest

D-U-N-S 24-839-1559   (HQ)
LANDTRAN SYSTEMS INC
9011 50 St Nw, Edmonton, AB, T6B 2Y2
(780) 468-4300
Emp Here 20   *Sales* 129,066,700
SIC 4212 Local trucking, without storage
John Assman
James Maxwell

D-U-N-S 24-685-7556   (HQ)
LEDCOR CONTRACTORS LTD
(Suby of 280818 ALBERTA LTD)
7008 Roper Rd Nw, Edmonton, AB, T6B 3H2
(780) 395-5400
Sales 25,244,200
SIC 1611 Highway and street construction

Tom Lassu
Rodney Neys
Ronald Stevenson

D-U-N-S 24-716-3108   (SL)
LEHMANN PLUMBING LTD
3645 73 Ave Nw, Edmonton, AB, T6B 2T8
(780) 465-4434
Emp Here 64   *Sales* 14,916,160
SIC 1711 Plumbing, heating, air-conditioning
Richard Lehmann
Marietta Lehmann

D-U-N-S 20-328-9194   (HQ)
LIFTING SOLUTIONS INC
3710 78 Ave Nw, Edmonton, AB, T6B 3E5
(780) 784-7725
Emp Here 50   *Sales* 22,358,700
SIC 5051 Metals service centers and offices
David Labonte
Greg Kauffman
Douglas Freel
Bill Slavin

D-U-N-S 20-082-9943   (SL)
LISTER INDUSTRIES LTD
7410 68 Ave Nw, Edmonton, AB, T6B 0A1
(780) 468-2040
Emp Here 40   *Sales* 12,788,200
SIC 1389 Oil and gas field services, nec
Peter Ellmann
Jane Ellmann

D-U-N-S 24-372-4890   (SL)
LJ WELDING AUTOMATION LTD
4747 76 Ave Nw, Edmonton, AB, T6B 0A3
(780) 466-6658
Emp Here 67   *Sales* 12,021,743
SIC 3544 Special dies, tools, jigs, and fixtures
Adam Carpenter
Ryan Holt

D-U-N-S 25-013-8070   (SL)
M & D DRAFTING LTD
3604 76 Ave Nw, Edmonton, AB, T6B 2N8
(780) 465-1520
Emp Here 75   *Sales* 33,691,425
SIC 7389 Business services, nec
Terry Devine

D-U-N-S 20-104-8589   (HQ)
MACCOSHAM INC
7220 68 Ave Nw, Edmonton, AB, T6B 0A1
(780) 448-1910
Emp Here 2   *Sales* 30,855,900
SIC 4225 General warehousing and storage
Jay Lilage
Bob Van Norman

D-U-N-S 24-274-7467   (SL)
MAPLE LEAF METALS (A PARTNERSHIP)
4510 68 Ave Nw, Edmonton, AB, T6B 2P3
(780) 468-3951
Emp Here 70   *Sales* 33,251,820
SIC 5085 Industrial supplies
Don Hruba

D-U-N-S 24-907-0848   (HQ)
MASTER FLO VALVE INC.
(*Suby of* STREAM-FLO RESOURCES LTD)
4611 74 Ave Nw, Edmonton, AB, T6B 2H5
(780) 468-4433
Emp Here 180   *Sales* 49,862,355
SIC 3494 Valves and pipe fittings, nec
Mark Mcneill
Len Lambert
Larry Walton

D-U-N-S 24-858-9686   (HQ)
MAVIRO CATALYST CANADA INC
7805 34 St Nw, Edmonton, AB, T6B 2V5
(780) 430-9696
Emp Here 150   *Sales* 15,685,740
SIC 7363 Help supply services
Brian Fitzmaurice

D-U-N-S 24-820-7891   (SL)
MAXX NORTH AMERICA SERVICES LTD

5311 72a Ave Nw, Edmonton, AB, T6B 2J1
(780) 482-4144
Emp Here 150   *Sales* 37,866,300
SIC 1623 Water, sewer, and utility lines
Bob Chorney

D-U-N-S 24-086-9172   (HQ)
MCCOY GLOBAL INC
9910 39th Ave Nw Suite 201, Edmonton, AB,
T6B 3H2
(780) 453-8451
Emp Here 9   *Sales* 37,204,614
SIC 5013 Motor vehicle supplies and new
parts
James Rakievich
Bing Deng
Suzanne Langier
Christopher Seaver
Dale Tremblay
Terry D. Freeman
Carmen Loberg

D-U-N-S 20-691-1245   (SL)
METALOGIC INSPECTION SERVICES INC
7211 68 Ave Nw, Edmonton, AB, T6B 3T6
(780) 469-6161
Emp Here 50   *Sales* 22,460,950
SIC 7389 Business services, nec
Robert Simmons
Paul Brum
Allan Cleiren

D-U-N-S 20-047-9652   (SL)
MFP RESOURCES CORP
5920 76 Ave Nw, Edmonton, AB, T6B 0A6
(780) 465-9668
Emp Here 25   *Sales* 31,430,025
SIC 5172 Petroleum products, nec
Warren Stevenson

D-U-N-S 24-283-5064   (SL)
**MID-CITY CONSTRUCTION MANAGEMENT
INC**
7103 42 St Nw, Edmonton, AB, T6B 2T1
(780) 463-0385
Emp Here 80   *Sales* 19,694,880
SIC 1794 Excavation work
Rod Stawnychy
Marian Stawnychy
Daniel Stawnychy

D-U-N-S 24-582-3083   (SL)
MOGO ELECTRICAL SERVICES LTD
5663 70 St Nw, Edmonton, AB, T6B 3P6
(780) 438-3440
Emp Here 75   *Sales* 16,337,175
SIC 1731 Electrical work
Marilyn Bohn
Gordon Bohn
Lloyd Klatt

D-U-N-S 20-355-2260   (HQ)
MOLY-COP ALTASTEEL LTD
ALTA STEEL
9401 34 St Nw, Edmonton, AB, T6B 2X6
(780) 468-1133
Sales 162,869,600
SIC 3312 Blast furnaces and steel mills
Jon Hobbs

D-U-N-S 25-703-5571   (SL)
MRC CANADA ULC
4103 53 Ave Nw Suite 726, Edmonton, AB,
T6B 3R5
(780) 466-0328
Emp Here 35   *Sales* 16,625,910
SIC 5085 Industrial supplies
Shane Olsen

D-U-N-S 20-013-0602   (SL)
MURRAY'S TRUCKING INC
6211 76 Ave Nw, Edmonton, AB, T6B 0A7
(780) 439-2222
Emp Here 112   *Sales* 23,039,072
SIC 4213 Trucking, except local
Gerard Murray
Chantal Geoffrioin

D-U-N-S 20-379-3281   (SL)
MYE CANADA INC
7115 Girard Rd Nw, Edmonton, AB, T6B 2C5
(780) 486-6663
Emp Here 40   *Sales* 13,093,760
SIC 2899 Chemical preparations, nec
Hassin Mraiche

D-U-N-S 25-329-6743   (SL)
NORDIC MECHANICAL SERVICES LTD
(*Suby of* 619249 ALBERTA LTD)
4143 78 Ave Nw, Edmonton, AB, T6B 2N3
(780) 469-7799
Emp Here 50   *Sales* 13,592,100
SIC 7623 Refrigeration service and repair
John Cloutier
Sandra Doyle

D-U-N-S 24-356-3918   (SL)
NORQUEST INDUSTRIES INC
3911 74 Ave Nw, Edmonton, AB, T6B 2Z7
(780) 434-3322
Emp Here 65   *Sales* 14,430,065
SIC 3599 Industrial machinery, nec
Douglas Hayward
Rose Spence

D-U-N-S 20-083-5593   (HQ)
NORTHERN INDUSTRIAL CARRIERS LTD
NIC
(*Suby of* 321485 ALBERTA LTD)
7823 34 St Nw, Edmonton, AB, T6B 2V5
(780) 465-0341
Emp Here 30   *Sales* 44,251,440
SIC 4213 Trucking, except local
Simon Sochatsky

D-U-N-S 24-026-4718   (SL)
ONEC CONSTRUCTION INC
3811 78 Ave Nw, Edmonton, AB, T6B 3N8
(780) 440-0400
Emp Here 130   *Sales* 18,023,952
SIC 7363 Help supply services
Denis Wiart
Ken Blake
Ian Park
David Kwok
Jerome Radawetz
Richard Holley
Shaun Jones

D-U-N-S 20-010-9515   (HQ)
ONEC ENGINEERING INC
3821 78 Ave Nw, Edmonton, AB, T6B 3N8
(780) 485-5375
Sales 10,557,480
SIC 8711 Engineering services

D-U-N-S 24-989-4556   (SL)
ORGANIC BOX LTD
5712 59 St Nw, Edmonton, AB, T6B 3L4
(780) 469-1900
Emp Here 49   *Sales* 13,433,448
SIC 5431 Fruit and vegetable markets
Danny Turner

D-U-N-S 20-141-8410   (SL)
**ORION BUILDING MAINTENANCE (OBM)
LTD**
5503 76 Ave Nw, Edmonton, AB, T6B 0A7
(780) 440-0136
Emp Here 45   *Sales* 14,652,000
SIC 5999 Miscellaneous retail stores, nec
Cara Schafer

D-U-N-S 25-115-4423   (BR)
PILLAR RESOURCE SERVICES INC
PILLAR OILFIELD PROJECTS
(*Suby of* PILLAR RESOURCE SERVICES
INC)
4155 84 Ave Nw, Edmonton, AB, T6B 2Z3
(780) 440-2212
Emp Here 100
SIC 1629 Heavy construction, nec
Frank Neufeld

D-U-N-S 20-438-4135   (HQ)
PRECISION GIANT SYSTEMS INC

PRECISION SCALE
(*Suby of* PRECISION INVESTMENT GROUP
INC)
7217 Girard Rd Nw, Edmonton, AB, T6B 2C5
(780) 463-0026
Emp Here 15   *Sales* 11,179,350
SIC 5046 Commercial equipment, nec
Jerry Gunn
Tony Vu

D-U-N-S 24-608-8272   (HQ)
PRO-TECH VALVE SALES INC
5880 56 Ave Nw, Edmonton, AB, T6B 3E4
(780) 466-4405
Emp Here 33   *Sales* 17,100,936
SIC 5085 Industrial supplies
Dave Embury
Greg O'brien
Steve Twellman

D-U-N-S 20-775-5232   (SL)
PROLINE PIPE EQUIPMENT INC
(*Suby of* PROLINE RESOURCES INC)
7141 67 St Nw, Edmonton, AB, T6B 3L7
(780) 465-6161
Emp Here 40   *Sales* 17,968,760
SIC 7389 Business services, nec
Raymond Smitke
Clifford Anderson

D-U-N-S 24-367-4582   (HQ)
PROLINE RESOURCES INC
PROLINE PIPE EQUIPMENT
7141 67 St Nw, Edmonton, AB, T6B 3L7
(780) 465-6161
Sales 13,077,650
SIC 6712 Bank holding companies
Raymond Smitke
Clifford Anderson

D-U-N-S 24-006-4159   (SL)
PROTOTECH SERVICES LTD
6916 68 Ave Nw, Edmonton, AB, T6B 3C5
(780) 433-2133
Emp Here 24   *Sales* 11,400,624
SIC 5084 Industrial machinery and equipment
Myron Johnson

D-U-N-S 20-730-9753   (SL)
PROVINCIAL ELECTRICAL SERVICES INC
7429 72a Ave Nw, Edmonton, AB, T6B 1Z3
(780) 490-1183
Emp Here 60   *Sales* 13,069,740
SIC 1731 Electrical work
Terry Emmerson

D-U-N-S 24-337-7673   (SL)
QUALITY HVAC PRODUCTS LTD
3904 53 Ave Nw, Edmonton, AB, T6B 3N7
(780) 643-3215
Emp Here 42   *Sales* 18,781,308
SIC 5075 Warm air heating and air condition-
ing
Steven Weiss
Marty Bruin
Herman Bruin
Robert Weiss

D-U-N-S 24-701-8773   (HQ)
RTD QUALITY SERVICES INC
APPLUS RTD
(*Suby of* APPLUS SERVICES SA.)
5504 36 St Nw, Edmonton, AB, T6B 3P3
(780) 440-6600
Emp Here 40   *Sales* 76,270,250
SIC 7389 Business services, nec
Denis Fourny
Marcel Blinde
Rob Van Doorn

D-U-N-S 24-394-6399   (SL)
RUNNERS LIGHT HAULING (2006) LTD
4320 82 Ave Nw, Edmonton, AB, T6B 2S4
(780) 465-5311
Emp Here 25   *Sales* 11,087,250
SIC 7389 Business services, nec
Jeff Lemaistre

D-U-N-S 20-898-7040   (HQ)
SHIPPERS SUPPLY INC
(*Suby of* CNG CANADA HOLDING INC.)
5219 47 St Nw, Edmonton, AB, T6B 3N4
(780) 444-7777
Emp Here 120   *Sales* 167,506,600
SIC 5113 Industrial and personal service paper
 Ronald Brown
 Jerry Wertypora
 Miles Kern
 Jerry Pierce

D-U-N-S 25-453-9117   (BR)
SIEMENS CANADA LIMITED
(*Suby of* SIEMENS AG)
6652 50 St Nw, Edmonton, AB, T6B 2N7
(780) 450-6762
Emp Here 200
SIC 8742 Management consulting services
 Rob Ailleo

D-U-N-S 25-678-9280   (SL)
SOLOMON COATINGS LTD
6382 50 St Nw, Edmonton, AB, T6B 2N7
(780) 413-4545
Emp Here 67   *Sales* 18,981,100
SIC 7532 Top and body repair and paint shops
 Thomas Wright

D-U-N-S 20-979-9258   (HQ)
SPACES INC
CDI SPACES
9319 47 St Nw, Edmonton, AB, T6B 2R7
(587) 855-6684
Emp Here 66   *Sales* 19,546,240
SIC 5999 Miscellaneous retail stores, nec
 Kelvin Devenish

D-U-N-S 20-084-5345   (SL)
STOGRYN SALES LTD
6808 82 Ave Nw, Edmonton, AB, T6B 0E7
(780) 465-6408
Emp Here 32   *Sales* 15,200,832
SIC 5087 Service establishment equipment
 Glen Stogryn

D-U-N-S 20-440-3455   (HQ)
STREAM-FLO INDUSTRIES LTD
(*Suby of* STREAM-FLO RESOURCES LTD)
4505 74 Ave Nw, Edmonton, AB, T6B 2H5
(780) 468-6789
Emp Here 300   *Sales* 337,052,400
SIC 3533 Oil and gas field machinery
 Duncan Mcneill
 Mark Mcneill
 Tony Lam
 Len Lambert
 Abbey Raikles
 Doug Jarvin

D-U-N-S 20-084-2388   (SL)
SUN DISTRIBUTION
4990 92 Ave Nw, Edmonton, AB, T6B 3A1

Emp Here 75   *Sales* 12,302,025
SIC 2711 Newspapers
 Craig Martin

D-U-N-S 25-992-8125   (SL)
SUNRAY MANUFACTURING INC
SUN RAY SPAS
7509 72a St Nw, Edmonton, AB, T6B 1Z3
(780) 440-1595
Emp Here 36   *Sales* 11,721,600
SIC 5999 Miscellaneous retail stores, nec
 Bradley Roberts

D-U-N-S 20-690-5676   (SL)
SYSTEM ONE MFG INC
4420 76 Ave Nw, Edmonton, AB, T6B 0A5
(780) 485-6006
Emp Here 58   *Sales* 12,982,894
SIC 3713 Truck and bus bodies
 Ryan Kaczur
 Tim Morrison
 Andre Mccuticheon
 Colette Morrison

Patricia Morrison
Tanya Kackaczur

D-U-N-S 20-910-1364   (SL)
TARPON CONSTRUCTION MANAGEMENT LTD
(*Suby of* PTW ENERGY SERVICES LTD)
3944 53 Ave Nw, Edmonton, AB, T6B 3N7
(780) 468-6333
Emp Here 170   *Sales* 40,036,530
SIC 1731 Electrical work
 Murray Leimert

D-U-N-S 24-396-6603   (HQ)
THERMO DESIGN INSULATION LTD
3520 56 Ave Nw, Edmonton, AB, T6B 3S7
(780) 468-2077
Emp Here 60   *Sales* 29,228,580
SIC 1742 Plastering, drywall, and insulation
 Renny Rantucci
 Joyce Mah

D-U-N-S 25-677-8655   (BR)
THERMON CANADA INC
THERMON HEAT TRACING SERVICES
(*Suby of* THERMON GROUP HOLDINGS, INC.)
5607 67 St Nw, Edmonton, AB, T6B 3H5
(780) 437-6326
Emp Here 200
SIC 5075 Warm air heating and air conditioning
 Brian Mclennan

D-U-N-S 20-139-8786   (HQ)
THERMON HEATING SYSTEMS, INC
(*Suby of* THERMON GROUP HOLDINGS, INC.)
5918 Roper Rd Nw, Edmonton, AB, T6B 3E1
(780) 466-3178
Emp Here 125   *Sales* 73,212,531
SIC 3443 Fabricated plate work (boiler shop)
 Harold Roozen
 Bernard Moore
 Chris Donnelly

D-U-N-S 20-331-4687   (HQ)
TS LP
TITAN SUPPLY
5135 67 Ave Nw, Edmonton, AB, T6B 2R8
(780) 481-1122
Emp Here 1   *Sales* 15,669,540
SIC 5084 Industrial machinery and equipment
 Terry Komick
 Randy Knapp

D-U-N-S 20-081-2782   (HQ)
VALLEN CANADA INC
VALLEN
(*Suby of* SOCIETE DE NEGOCE ET DE PARTICIPATION)
4810 92 Ave Nw, Edmonton, AB, T6B 2X4
(780) 468-3366
Emp Here 150   *Sales* 292,638,000
SIC 5085 Industrial supplies
 Guy Mersereau
 Paul Trudel
 Francois Poncet
 Marie-Christine Coisne
 Olivier Verley
 Franck Bruel
 Philippe De Moustier
 Francois Anquetil

D-U-N-S 24-525-6776   (BR)
VARCO CANADA ULC
(*Suby of* NATIONAL OILWELL VARCO, INC.)
7127 56 Ave Nw, Edmonton, AB, T6B 3L2
(780) 665-0200
Emp Here 100
SIC 7353 Heavy construction equipment rental
 James Monroe

D-U-N-S 20-703-5390   (HQ)
VECTOR ELECTRIC AND CONTROLS
VECTOR GROUP, THE

5344 36 St Nw, Edmonton, AB, T6B 3P3
(780) 469-7900
Sales 21,782,900
SIC 1731 Electrical work
 Gino Moscardelli
 Douglas Maclean
 David Nielsen

D-U-N-S 24-269-3596   (HQ)
VELOCITY EXPRESS CANADA LTD
4424 55 Ave Nw, Edmonton, AB, T6B 3S2
(780) 465-3777
Sales 104,349,648
SIC 7389 Business services, nec
 David Van Dusen
 Greg Mcmanus

D-U-N-S 20-084-8992   (SL)
VET'S SHEET METAL LTD
VETS GROUP
6111 56 Ave Nw, Edmonton, AB, T6B 3E2
(780) 434-7476
Emp Here 200   *Sales* 46,613,000
SIC 1711 Plumbing, heating, air-conditioning
 Sean Rayner

D-U-N-S 20-084-9263   (HQ)
VOICE CONSTRUCTION LTD
7545 52 St Nw, Edmonton, AB, T6B 2G2
(780) 469-1351
Emp Here 75   *Sales* 139,448,875
SIC 1629 Heavy construction, nec
 Howard Ratti
 Michael Hrynchuk
 Garnet Clark
 Douglas Annable
 Edmund Carpenter
 Robert Rutledge
 Samuel Spanglet

D-U-N-S 20-114-4867   (SL)
VOLANT PRODUCTS INC
4110 56 Ave Nw, Edmonton, AB, T6B 3R8
(780) 490-5185
Emp Here 175   *Sales* 38,850,175
SIC 3533 Oil and gas field machinery
 William Roggensack
 Daniel Shute

D-U-N-S 20-637-1122   (SL)
WAIWARD INDUSTRIAL LIMITED PARTNERSHIP
(*Suby of* HILLCORE GROUP HOLDINGS LTD)
10030 34 St Nw, Edmonton, AB, T6B 2Y5
(780) 469-1258
Emp Here 500   *Sales* 83,391,220
SIC 3499 Fabricated Metal products, nec
 Andy Brooks

D-U-N-S 24-000-5611   (SL)
WEISS-JOHNSON SHEET METAL LTD
5803 Roper Rd Nw, Edmonton, AB, T6B 3L6
(780) 463-3096
Emp Here 65   *Sales* 14,158,885
SIC 1731 Electrical work
 Donald Johnson
 Dennis Johnson
 Mark Johnson

D-U-N-S 24-394-2013   (HQ)
WHITEMUD GROUP LTD
8170 50 St Nw Suite 300, Edmonton, AB, T6B 1E6
(780) 701-3295
Emp Here 12   *Sales* 63,712,800
SIC 1791 Structural steel erection
 Edward Cote
 Pat Cote

D-U-N-S 24-425-7213   (HQ)
WHITEMUD IRONWORKS GROUP INC
(*Suby of* WHITEMUD GROUP LTD)
8170 50 St Nw Suite 300, Edmonton, AB, T6B 1E6
(780) 701-3295
Emp Here 12   *Sales* 63,712,800
SIC 1791 Structural steel erection

Edward Cote
Pat Cote

D-U-N-S 25-068-5642   (HQ)
WILKENING, HARV TRANSPORT LTD
WILKENING TRANSPORT
4205 76 Ave Nw, Edmonton, AB, T6B 2H7
(780) 466-9155
Emp Here 110   *Sales* 30,855,900
SIC 4213 Trucking, except local
 Lily-Ann Siemens

D-U-N-S 25-505-5964   (SL)
WINDSHIELD SURGEONS LTD
ARNOLD WINDSHIELD DISTRIBUTORS
5203 82 Ave Nw, Edmonton, AB, T6B 2J6
(780) 466-9166
Emp Here 50   *Sales* 10,131,450
SIC 7536 Automotive glass replacement shops
 Russell Lang
 Cynthia Lang

D-U-N-S 25-265-9511   (BR)
WOOD CANADA LIMITED
AMEC ENVIRONMENT & INFRASTRACTURE, DIV OF
(*Suby of* JOHN WOOD GROUP P.L.C.)
5681 70 St Nw, Edmonton, AB, T6B 3P6
(780) 436-2152
Emp Here 150
SIC 8711 Engineering services
 Dennis Krochak

D-U-N-S 25-261-7246   (BR)
WORLEYPARSONSCORD LP
COSYN TECHNOLOGY
(*Suby of* WORLEYPARSONS LIMITED)
9405 50 St Nw Suite 101, Edmonton, AB, T6B 2T4
(780) 440-8100
Emp Here 700
SIC 8711 Engineering services
 Geoff Rackete

D-U-N-S 20-693-0658   (SL)
ZP HOLDINGS INC
EDMONTON BMW MINI EDMONTON
7450 Roper Rd Nw, Edmonton, AB, T6B 3L9
(780) 490-5269
Emp Here 28   *Sales* 13,946,184
SIC 5511 New and used car dealers
 Bart Yachimac

Edmonton, AB T6C

D-U-N-S 20-047-7714   (HQ)
CONSEIL SCOLAIRE CENTRE-NORD
8627 91 St Nw Suite 322, Edmonton, AB, T6C 3N1
(780) 468-5250
Emp Here 100   *Sales* 29,735,700
SIC 8211 Elementary and secondary schools
 Rober Lessard
 Josee Devaney
 Georges Veilleux

D-U-N-S 25-361-7005   (HQ)
CRI CANADA INC
(*Suby of* AEGON N.V.)
8925 82 Ave Nw Suite 207, Edmonton, AB, T6C 0Z2
(780) 469-3808
Emp Here 1   *Sales* 15,034,250
SIC 6712 Bank holding companies
 Paul Latchford

D-U-N-S 20-141-2892   (BR)
EDMONTON SCHOOL DISTRICT NO. 7
METRO CONTINUING EDUCATION
(*Suby of* EDMONTON SCHOOL DISTRICT NO. 7)
7835 76 Ave Nw, Edmonton, AB, T6C 2N1
(780) 428-1111
Emp Here 100

SIC 8211 Elementary and secondary schools
Dave Jones

D-U-N-S 25-012-9640   (BR)
EXTENDICARE (CANADA) INC
EXTENDICARE HOLYROOD
(*Suby of* EXTENDICARE INC)
8008 95 Ave Nw, Edmonton, AB, T6C 2T1
(780) 469-1307
Emp Here 100
SIC 8051 Skilled nursing care facilities
Kelly Short

D-U-N-S 20-637-4654   (SL)
FREEDOM FORD SALES LIMITED
7505 75 St Nw, Edmonton, AB, T6C 4H8
(780) 465-9411
Emp Here 115   *Sales* 72,367,200
SIC 5511 New and used car dealers
Robert G Bentley

D-U-N-S 20-897-6068   (HQ)
GOOD SAMARITAN SOCIETY, THE (A LUTHERAN SOCIAL SERVICE ORGANIZATION)
GOOD SAMARITAN SOCIETY
8861 75 St Nw, Edmonton, AB, T6C 4G8
(780) 431-3600
Emp Here 100   *Sales* 366,564,000
SIC 8069 Specialty hospitals, except psychiatric
Carla Gregor
Roy Wilson
Bill Chestnutt
Hans Lung

D-U-N-S 24-523-0925   (HQ)
KRAWFORD CONSTRUCTION INC
8055 Argyll Rd Nw, Edmonton, AB, T6C 4A9
(780) 436-4381
Sales 11,768,275
SIC 1542 Nonresidential construction, nec
Terry Tanasiuk
Colleen Kerfoot

D-U-N-S 20-775-8160   (HQ)
PURE CANADIAN GAMING CORP
CASINO ABS
7055 Argyll Rd Nw, Edmonton, AB, T6C 4A5
(780) 465-5377
Emp Here 100   *Sales* 95,370,000
SIC 7999 Amusement and recreation, nec
George Goldhoff
Lucy Papp
Mark Mactadish
Michael Lay
Evan Hershberg

D-U-N-S 20-515-9184   (BR)
SOBEYS WEST INC
BONNIE DOON SAFEWAY
(*Suby of* EMPIRE COMPANY LIMITED)
8330 82 Ave Nw, Edmonton, AB, T6C 0Y6
(780) 469-9464
Emp Here 160
SIC 5411 Grocery stores
Chris Wilts

D-U-N-S 24-228-4144   (SL)
ST THOMAS CENTRE DE SANTE
ST THOMAS HEALTH CENTER
8411 91 St Nw Suite 234, Edmonton, AB, T6C 1Z9
(780) 450-2987
Emp Here 110   *Sales* 6,517,170
SIC 8361 Residential care
Paula Rozenski

D-U-N-S 20-822-0256   (SL)
SURECAN CONSTRUCTION LTD
7707 71 Ave Nw, Edmonton, AB, T6C 0A9
(780) 469-3162
Emp Here 50   *Sales* 15,943,450
SIC 1521 Single-family housing construction
Richard Stephen

Edmonton, AB T6E

D-U-N-S 25-454-3374   (HQ)
470858 ALBERTA LTD
LUBE CITY
5674 75 St Nw, Edmonton, AB, T6E 5X6
(780) 485-9905
Emp Here 65   *Sales* 21,247,500
SIC 7549 Automotive services, nec
Wayne Kallis

D-U-N-S 20-772-6212   (SL)
483696 ALBERTA LTD
FIFE N'DEKEL
7921 Coronet Rd Nw, Edmonton, AB, T6E 4N7

Emp Here 90   *Sales* 4,096,710
SIC 5812 Eating places
Ann Liske

D-U-N-S 25-360-8723   (BR)
511670 ALBERTA LTD
CORAM CONSTRUCTION
4220 98 St Nw Suite 201, Edmonton, AB, T6E 6A1
(780) 466-1262
Emp Here 400
SIC 1542 Nonresidential construction, nec
Paul Rivington

D-U-N-S 20-154-0460   (HQ)
675122 ALBERTA LTD
LAST CALL GROUP
4207 98 St Nw Suite 102, Edmonton, AB, T6E 5R7

Sales 21,012,208
SIC 5921 Liquor stores
Doug Muhossand
Karen Nagy

D-U-N-S 20-803-6520   (SL)
967530 ALBERTA LTD
SOUTHVIEW ACURA
9820 34 Ave Nw, Edmonton, AB, T6E 6L1
(780) 989-8888
Emp Here 40   *Sales* 19,923,120
SIC 5511 New and used car dealers
Dave King

D-U-N-S 25-359-9542   (SL)
974307 ALBERTA LTD
9850 41 Ave Nw, Edmonton, AB, T6E 5L6
(780) 414-0980
Emp Here 36   *Sales* 15,096,780
SIC 6712 Bank holding companies
Donald Muth

D-U-N-S 20-640-0207   (SL)
979094 ALBERTA LTD
SOUTHSIDE MITSUBISHI
9605 34 Ave Nw, Edmonton, AB, T6E 5W8
(780) 465-5252
Emp Here 40   *Sales* 19,923,120
SIC 5511 New and used car dealers
Kevin Robertson

D-U-N-S 24-766-6829   (HQ)
ACCESS INSURANCE GROUP LTD
4435 99 St Nw, Edmonton, AB, T6E 5B6
(780) 435-2400
Emp Here 1   *Sales* 30,530,160
SIC 6411 Insurance agents, brokers, and service
James Sklarchuk
Brad Sklarchuk
Karen Sklarchuk
Chad Hudson

D-U-N-S 20-021-7870   (SL)
ACOUSTICAL CEILING & BUILDING MAINTENANCE LTD
ACOUSTICAL & TOTAL CLEANING SERVICES
7940 Coronet Rd Nw, Edmonton, AB, T6E 4N8

(780) 496-9035
Emp Here 140   *Sales* 4,475,520
SIC 7349 Building maintenance services, nec
Boris Sukalsky
Ted Abbott

D-U-N-S 20-580-0456   (BR)
AIR LIQUIDE CANADA INC
10020 56 Ave Nw, Edmonton, AB, T6E 5Z2
(780) 434-2060
Emp Here 115
SIC 2813 Industrial gases
Tim Thaneuf

D-U-N-S 20-080-4631   (BR)
AKHURST MACHINERY LIMITED
(*Suby of* AKHURST HOLDINGS LIMITED)
9615 63 Ave Nw, Edmonton, AB, T6E 0G2
(780) 435-3936
Emp Here 153
SIC 5084 Industrial machinery and equipment
Bill Cameron

D-U-N-S 20-300-7161   (BR)
ALBERTA MOTOR ASSOCIATION
A M A
(*Suby of* ALBERTA MOTOR ASSOCIATION)
9520 42 Ave Nw, Edmonton, AB, T6E 5Y4
(780) 989-6230
Emp Here 400
SIC 8699 Membership organizations, nec
Corine Gylytiuk

D-U-N-S 24-583-0906   (SL)
ALBERTA SPECIAL EVENT EQUIPMENT RENTALS & SALES LTD
SPECIAL EVENT RENTALS
6010 99 St Nw, Edmonton, AB, T6E 3P2
(780) 435-2211
Emp Here 60   *Sales* 11,481,240
SIC 7359 Equipment rental and leasing, nec
Neil Goodkey

D-U-N-S 20-743-7740   (HQ)
ALCO GAS & OIL PRODUCTION EQUIPMENT LTD
(*Suby of* ALCO INDUSTRIAL INC)
5203 75 St Nw, Edmonton, AB, T6E 5S5
(780) 465-9061
Emp Here 122   *Sales* 27,750,125
SIC 3533 Oil and gas field machinery
David Higgins
Robert Taubner

D-U-N-S 20-720-2094   (HQ)
APOLLO MACHINE & WELDING LTD
APOLLO MACHINE
4141 93 St Nw, Edmonton, AB, T6E 5Y3
(780) 463-3060
Emp Here 181   *Sales* 42,846,193
SIC 3533 Oil and gas field machinery
Wayne Norton
Lawrence Zarb

D-U-N-S 24-584-9476   (HQ)
ARAMARK REMOTE WORKPLACE SERVICES LTD
(*Suby of* ARAMARK)
9647 45 Ave Nw, Edmonton, AB, T6E 5Z8
(780) 437-5665
Emp Here 40   *Sales* 13,991,700
SIC 5812 Eating places
John Dampf

D-U-N-S 20-080-6586   (HQ)
ARGUS MACHINE CO. LTD
5820 97 St Nw, Edmonton, AB, T6E 3J1
(780) 434-9451
Emp Here 100   *Sales* 34,575,300
SIC 3494 Valves and pipe fittings, nec

D-U-N-S 24-981-9889   (HQ)
ATI TELECOM INTERNATIONAL, COMPANY
ALTA TELECOM
4336 97 St Nw, Edmonton, AB, T6E 5R9
(780) 424-9100
Emp Here 10   *Sales* 183,999,200

SIC 4899 Communication services, nec
Ronald Newitt
William Elsey

D-U-N-S 20-898-2421   (SL)
B J ELECTRIC SUPPLIES LTD
4143 97 St Nw, Edmonton, AB, T6E 6E9
(780) 461-2334
Emp Here 26   *Sales* 11,626,524
SIC 5063 Electrical apparatus and equipment
Kenneth Decoursey
Michael Thompson

D-U-N-S 24-221-8733   (SL)
B. GINGRAS ENTERPRISES LTD
BEE CLEAN
4505 101 St Nw, Edmonton, AB, T6E 5C6
(780) 435-3355
Emp Here 2,000   *Sales* 63,936,000
SIC 7349 Building maintenance services, nec
Brian Gingras

D-U-N-S 20-080-8350   (SL)
BEE BELL HEALTH BAKERY INC
10416 80 Ave Nw, Edmonton, AB, T6E 5T7

Emp Here 80   *Sales* 23,478,160
SIC 5461 Retail bakeries
Gary Huising

D-U-N-S 24-715-4446   (HQ)
BEE-CLEAN BUILDING MAINTENANCE INCORPORATED
BEE-CLEAN
4505 101 St Nw, Edmonton, AB, T6E 5C6
(780) 435-3355
Emp Here 2,000   *Sales* 223,776,000
SIC 7349 Building maintenance services, nec
Joe Correia
Brian Gingras
Dennis Correia

D-U-N-S 24-002-8902   (HQ)
BELOW THE BELT LTD
FERN AND FEATHER
5611 86 St Nw, Edmonton, AB, T6E 6H7
(780) 469-5301
Emp Here 30   *Sales* 37,905,100
SIC 5611 Men's and boys' clothing stores
Janet Payne

D-U-N-S 25-215-4745   (HQ)
BELOW THE BELT STORE (VANCOUVER) LTD
BELOW THE BELT
5611 86 St Nw, Edmonton, AB, T6E 6H7
(780) 469-5301
Emp Here 15   *Sales* 17,939,600
SIC 5611 Men's and boys' clothing stores
Cathy Lepore
Alex Payne
Janet Payne

D-U-N-S 20-256-2778   (HQ)
BERETTA PROTECTIVE SERVICES INTERNATIONAL INC
9404 58 Ave Nw, Edmonton, AB, T6E 0B6
(780) 481-6348
Sales 19,783,900
SIC 7381 Detective and armored car services
James Senecal
Barry Sharkey
Pierrette Chretien
Russell Luke

D-U-N-S 25-169-2125   (SL)
BFI CONSTRUCTORS LTD
8404 Mcintyre Rd Nw, Edmonton, AB, T6E 6V3
(780) 485-2703
Emp Here 50   *Sales* 16,946,963
SIC 1541 Industrial buildings and warehouses
Ronald Mondor

D-U-N-S 24-790-2229   (SL)
BILGEN, BERK INSURANCE LTD
(*Suby of* HELLMAN & FRIEDMAN LLC)
8925 51 Ave Nw Suite 311, Edmonton, AB,

▲ Public Company   ■ Public Company Family Member   **HQ** Headquarters   **BR** Branch   **SL** Single Location

T6E 5J3
(780) 822-6042
Emp Here 20   *Sales* 11,598,480
SIC 6411 Insurance agents, brokers, and service
Berk Bilgen

D-U-N-S 25-106-0208   (SL)
BIOPAK LIMITED
7824 51 Ave Nw, Edmonton, AB, T6E 6W2

Emp Here 80   *Sales* 27,655,200
SIC 2023 Dry, condensed and evaporated dairy products
Bret Smith

D-U-N-S 24-033-1186   (SL)
BLACK SUN RISING INC
10548 82 Ave Nw Suite G, Edmonton, AB, T6E 2A4

Emp Here 45   *Sales* 21,376,170
SIC 5082 Construction and mining machinery
Tim Biscope

D-U-N-S 24-714-6475   (HQ)
BLU'S CLOTHING LTD
BLU'S WOMENS WEAR
4719 101 St Nw, Edmonton, AB, T6E 5C6
(780) 437-3991
Emp Here 15   *Sales* 10,763,760
SIC 5621 Women's clothing stores
John Leavitt
Jennifer Leavitt

D-U-N-S 20-081-0018   (SL)
BRAYER, L. A. INDUSTRIES LTD
3811 93 St Nw, Edmonton, AB, T6E 5K5
(780) 462-4812
Emp Here 100   *Sales* 23,306,500
SIC 1711 Plumbing, heating, air-conditioning
Dean Brayer

D-U-N-S 20-115-9931   (HQ)
BRELCOR HOLDINGS LTD
EDMONTON NUT & BOLT
8635 63 Ave Nw, Edmonton, AB, T6E 0E8
(780) 465-1466
Emp Here 45   *Sales* 20,122,830
SIC 5072 Hardware
Bryce Misener

D-U-N-S 24-426-1769   (SL)
BROCK CANADA MANAGEMENT CORPORATION
(Suby of BROCK CANADA INC)
8925 62 Ave Nw, Edmonton, AB, T6E 5L2
(780) 465-9016
Emp Here 50   *Sales* 13,716,600
SIC 8741 Management services
Willi Hamm

D-U-N-S 24-675-0046   (SL)
BRYTEX BUILDING SYSTEMS INC
(Suby of 589076 ALBERTA LTD)
5610 97 St Nw, Edmonton, AB, T6E 3J1
(780) 437-7970
Emp Here 60   *Sales* 11,525,100
SIC 3448 Prefabricated Metal buildings and components
Allan Stix
Darrell Stix
Paul Stix

D-U-N-S 20-081-0505   (HQ)
BUDGET RENT-A-CAR OF EDMONTON LTD
4612 95 St Nw, Edmonton, AB, T6E 5Z6
(780) 448-2060
Emp Here 30   *Sales* 90,039,400
SIC 7514 Passenger car rental
Lionel Groberman
Gary Hill
Gordon Reynen

D-U-N-S 24-715-4487   (HQ)
BUSY-BEE SANITARY SUPPLIES INC
4004 97 St Nw Unit 24, Edmonton, AB, T6E 6N1

(780) 462-0075
Emp Here 13   *Sales* 16,625,910
SIC 5087 Service establishment equipment
Jeffrey Malott
James Malott

D-U-N-S 20-081-0935   (SL)
C.W. CARRY LTD
5815 75 St Nw, Edmonton, AB, T6E 0T3
(780) 465-0381
Emp Here 75   *Sales* 44,809,050
SIC 5051 Metals service centers and offices
Roger Carry

D-U-N-S 24-642-6407   (HQ)
CAN ALTA BINDERY CORP
8445 Davies Rd Nw, Edmonton, AB, T6E 4N3
(780) 466-9973
Emp Here 47   *Sales* 12,216,400
SIC 5943 Stationery stores
Brian Ceminchuk

D-U-N-S 24-810-5181   (SL)
CAN-DER CONSTRUCTION LTD
5410 97 St Nw, Edmonton, AB, T6E 5C1
(780) 436-2980
Emp Here 75   *Sales* 20,320,650
SIC 1522 Residential construction, nec
Peter Dirksen
Greg Christenson

D-U-N-S 20-182-7933   (HQ)
CARFINCO INCOME FUND
(Suby of BANCO SANTANDER SA)
4245 97 St Nw Suite 300, Edmonton, AB, T6E 5Y7
(780) 413-7549
Sales 525,323,250
SIC 6722 Management investment, open-end
Tracy Graf
Troy Graf
David Rosenkrantz
David Prussky
Maurice Kagan
Simon Serruya
J. Daryl Maclellan
Brent Channell

D-U-N-S 20-081-2287   (HQ)
CARLSON BODY SHOP SUPPLY LTD
5308 97 St Nw, Edmonton, AB, T6E 5W5
(780) 438-0808
Emp Here 20   *Sales* 18,210,750
SIC 5013 Motor vehicle supplies and new parts
Sumio (Chris) Kikuchi
Robert (Rob) Neale
Brian Tod
Gordon Milford

D-U-N-S 24-328-3033   (HQ)
CATHOLIC SOCIAL SERVICES
CATHOLIC CHARITIES
8815 99 St Nw, Edmonton, AB, T6E 3V3
(780) 432-1137
Emp Here 61   *Sales* 96,423,000
SIC 8361 Residential care
Christopher Leung
Tracy Tanasichuk

D-U-N-S 20-594-5926   (SL)
CAVAN CONTRACTORS LTD
3722 91 St Nw, Edmonton, AB, T6E 5M3
(780) 462-5311
Emp Here 25   *Sales* 11,768,275
SIC 1542 Nonresidential construction, nec
Cal Phare
Jack Jones
Chuck Long

D-U-N-S 20-203-9017   (SL)
CENTRE FOR AUTISM SERVICES ALBERTA
4752 99 St Nw, Edmonton, AB, T6E 5H5
(780) 488-6600
Emp Here 130   *Sales* 187,018,130
SIC 8699 Membership organizations, nec
Deborah Allard Usunier

D-U-N-S 24-399-0298   (HQ)
CESSCO FABRICATION & ENGINEERING LIMITED
(Suby of CANERECTOR INC)
7310 99 St Nw, Edmonton, AB, T6E 3R8
(780) 433-9531
Emp Here 100   *Sales* 19,784,755
SIC 3499 Fabricated Metal products, nec
Dave Hummel
Amanda Hawkins

D-U-N-S 20-316-5522   (SL)
CHEVROLET TRUCKS LTD
10727 82 Ave Nw, Edmonton, AB, T6E 2B1
(780) 439-0071
Emp Here 100   *Sales* 62,928,000
SIC 5511 New and used car dealers
Don Wheaton Sr

D-U-N-S 20-377-5515   (HQ)
CIVEO CANADA LIMITED PARTNERSHIP
(Suby of CIVEO CORPORATION)
3790 98 St Nw, Edmonton, AB, T6E 6B4
(780) 463-8872
Emp Here 1,100   *Sales* 457,621,500
SIC 7389 Business services, nec
Bradley Dodson

D-U-N-S 20-255-4853   (SL)
CIVEO CORPORATION
3790 98 St Nw, Edmonton, AB, T6E 6B4
(780) 463-8872
Emp Here 1   *Sales* 382,276,000
SIC 7021 Rooming and boarding houses
Bradley J. Dodson
Richard A. Navarre
Frank C. Steininger
Allan D. Schoening
Peter Mccann
C Ronald Blankenship
Ronald J. Gilbertson
Martin A. Lambert

D-U-N-S 24-715-9569   (HQ)
COLOR COMPASS CORPORATION
5308 97 St Nw, Edmonton, AB, T6E 5W5
(780) 438-0808
Sales 73,101,800
SIC 6712 Bank holding companies
Sumio Kikuchi
Rob Neale
Roy Hodgins
Gord Milford

D-U-N-S 20-081-3889   (HQ)
COMMERCIAL BEARING SERVICE (1966) LTD.
(Suby of GENUINE PARTS COMPANY)
4203 95 St Nw Suite 1966, Edmonton, AB, T6E 5R6
(780) 432-1611
Emp Here 125   *Sales* 121,932,500
SIC 5085 Industrial supplies
Jim Barker

D-U-N-S 25-681-4930   (HQ)
COMMERCIAL SOLUTIONS INC
COMMERCIAL BEARING SERVICE
(Suby of GENUINE PARTS COMPANY)
4203 95 St Nw, Edmonton, AB, T6E 5R6
(780) 432-1611
Emp Here 45   *Sales* 119,493,850
SIC 5085 Industrial supplies
Dermot Strong

D-U-N-S 24-850-8140   (SL)
COMPRESSOR PRODUCTS INTERNATIONAL CANADA INC
CPI SERVICE
(Suby of ENPRO INDUSTRIES, INC.)
6308 Davies Rd Nw, Edmonton, AB, T6E 4M9
(780) 468-5145
Emp Here 50   *Sales* 13,592,100
SIC 7699 Repair services, nec
Tony Gioffredi

D-U-N-S 20-718-4578   (HQ)
CORIX CONTROL SOLUTIONS LIMITED

PARTNERSHIP
(Suby of CORIX INFRASTRUCTURE INC)
8803 58 Ave Nw, Edmonton, AB, T6E 5X1
(780) 468-6950
Emp Here 40   *Sales* 51,796,283
SIC 1389 Oil and gas field services, nec
Brett Hodson
Randy Helgren
Dennis Dodo

D-U-N-S 25-288-8144   (SL)
CRANESMART SYSTEMS INC
4908 97 St Nw, Edmonton, AB, T6E 5S1
(780) 437-2986
Emp Here 60   *Sales* 28,501,560
SIC 5084 Industrial machinery and equipment
Tom Bilodeau

D-U-N-S 24-091-1834   (SL)
CREATIVE CONCEPTS D.V.R. INC
4404 94 St Nw, Edmonton, AB, T6E 6T7
(780) 438-3044
Emp Here 26   *Sales* 19,305,520
SIC 5199 Nondurable goods, nec
Peter Kmech
Pete Kmech
Alice Kmech

D-U-N-S 25-260-0820   (HQ)
CUSTOM ENERGIZED AIR LTD
9555 62 Ave Nw, Edmonton, AB, T6E 0E1
(780) 465-2247
Emp Here 20   *Sales* 11,400,624
SIC 5082 Construction and mining machinery
Rod Kuffler
John Northcott
Brad Simpson
Al Kovacs

D-U-N-S 24-064-1670   (HQ)
CVS CONTROLS LTD
3900 101 St Nw, Edmonton, AB, T6E 0A5
(780) 437-3055
Emp Here 65   *Sales* 21,129,350
SIC 3491 Industrial valves
Lyle Kurtz
Marie Kurtz

D-U-N-S 24-421-1582   (SL)
CWP CONSTRUCTORS LTD
8702 48 Ave Nw Suite 210, Edmonton, AB, T6E 5L1
(780) 757-5834
Emp Here 60   *Sales* 16,256,520
SIC 1521 Single-family housing construction
Mark Witholt

D-U-N-S 20-127-0425   (SL)
CXD MAINTENANCE SERVICE LTD
6276 92 St Nw, Edmonton, AB, T6E 3A7
(780) 391-1565
Emp Here 39   *Sales* 11,048,700
SIC 7539 Automotive repair shops, nec

D-U-N-S 20-413-8346   (SL)
CYCLE WORKS MOTORSPORTS LTD
5688 75 St Nw, Edmonton, AB, T6E 5X6
(780) 440-3200
Emp Here 30   *Sales* 14,942,340
SIC 5599 Automotive dealers, nec
Jim Roth

D-U-N-S 20-118-8583   (SL)
DACRO INDUSTRIES INC
9325 51 Ave Nw, Edmonton, AB, T6E 4W8
(780) 434-8900
Emp Here 80   *Sales* 19,001,325
SIC 3443 Fabricated plate work (boiler shop)
Marvin Kossowan

D-U-N-S 20-698-8102   (HQ)
DALMAC ENERGY INC
4934 89 St Nw, Edmonton, AB, T6E 5K1
(780) 988-8510
Emp Here 11   *Sales* 13,270,528
SIC 1382 Oil and gas exploration services
John Ivan Babic
Tim Sturko

Steven M Babic
Shawn T Szydlowski
Derek Callfas
David E. Olson

D-U-N-S 24-290-8478   (SL)
DALMAC OILFIELD SERVICES INC
(*Suby of* DALMAC ENERGY INC)
4934 89 St Nw, Edmonton, AB, T6E 5K1
(780) 988-8510
Emp Here 220   *Sales* 120,113,620
SIC 1389 Oil and gas field services, nec
John Babic

D-U-N-S 20-081-6742   (HQ)
DIVERSIFIED TRANSPORTATION LTD
RED ARROW EXPRESS, DIV OF
(*Suby of* PACIFIC WESTERN TRANSPORTA-
TION LTD)
8351 Mcintyre Rd Nw, Edmonton, AB, T6E
5J7
(780) 468-6771
Emp Here 100   *Sales* 22,485,600
SIC 4142 Bus charter service, except local
Bob Colborne
William Hamilton
Rick Colborne
Michael Colborne

D-U-N-S 24-809-8253   (HQ)
**DIVERSITY TECHNOLOGIES CORPORA-
TION**
CANAMARAUNITED, DIV OF
8750 53 Ave Nw, Edmonton, AB, T6E 5G2
(780) 440-4923
Emp Here 60   *Sales* 100,831,800
SIC 5169 Chemicals and allied products, nec
Dirk Lepoole

D-U-N-S 25-955-9508   (BR)
DNOW CANADA ULC
NATIONAL-OILWELL VARCO
(*Suby of* NOW INC.)
6415 75 St Nw, Edmonton, AB, T6E 0T3

Emp Here 200
SIC 3533 Oil and gas field machinery
Dale Chereinski

D-U-N-S 20-913-1163   (BR)
DNOW CANADA ULC
DOWNHOLE TOOLS
(*Suby of* NOW INC.)
3550 93 St Nw, Edmonton, AB, T6E 5N3
(780) 465-9500
Emp Here 300
SIC 3533 Oil and gas field machinery
Garren Hayes

D-U-N-S 20-057-6820   (HQ)
DOMINO MACHINE INC
4040 98 St Nw, Edmonton, AB, T6E 3L3
(780) 809-1787
Sales 19,208,500
SIC 3499 Fabricated Metal products, nec
Dietmar Sedens
Werner Harder

D-U-N-S 24-280-6990   (HQ)
DONALCO WESTERN INC
8218 Mcintyre Rd Nw, Edmonton, AB, T6E
5C4
(780) 448-1660
Sales 14,771,160
SIC 1799 Special trade contractors, nec
Gerry Somers
Reg Fidgeon

D-U-N-S 20-248-0547   (HQ)
DRECO INTERNATIONAL HOLDINGS ULC
DRECO
(*Suby of* NATIONAL OILWELL VARCO, INC.)
6415 75 St Nw, Edmonton, AB, T6E 0T3
(780) 944-3800
Sales 140,438,500
SIC 3533 Oil and gas field machinery
Roman Konowalec

D-U-N-S 24-701-6595   (HQ)
DRESSER-RAND CANADA, ULC
(*Suby of* SIEMENS AG)
9330 45 Ave Nw, Edmonton, AB, T6E 6S1
(780) 436-0604
Emp Here 45   *Sales* 31,826,742
SIC 5085 Industrial supplies
Derek Hosking

D-U-N-S 20-203-8738   (SL)
ECONOFAST SHIPPING SYSTEMS INC
9742 54 Ave Nw, Edmonton, AB, T6E 0A9
(780) 461-0578
Emp Here 25   *Sales* 12,999,175
SIC 4731 Freight transportation arrangement
Kevin Ripplinger

D-U-N-S 24-853-3671   (SL)
**EDMONTON EXCHANGER & MANUFAC-
TURING LTD**
*EDMONTON EXCHANGER GROUP OF
COMPANIES*
(*Suby of* GUSSE HOLDINGS LIMITED)
5545 89 St Nw, Edmonton, AB, T6E 5W9
(780) 468-6722
Emp Here 188   *Sales* 34,100,944
SIC 3312 Blast furnaces and steel mills
Henry Gusse
Larry Gusse

D-U-N-S 20-895-1723   (SL)
**EDMONTON EXCHANGER & REFINERY
SERVICES LTD**
(*Suby of* GUSSE HOLDINGS LIMITED)
5545 89 St Nw, Edmonton, AB, T6E 5W9
(780) 468-6722
Emp Here 70   *Sales* 13,462,960
SIC 7699 Repair services, nec
Henry Gusse
Larry Gusse
Barbara Zerbin

D-U-N-S 24-392-1103   (HQ)
EDMONTON RUNNING ROOM LTD
EAT & RUN, DIV
9750 47 Ave Nw, Edmonton, AB, T6E 5P3
(780) 439-3099
Emp Here 75
SIC 5661 Shoe stores
John Stanton
Beverley Stanton

D-U-N-S 25-454-5205   (BR)
EDMONTON SCHOOL DISTRICT NO. 7
STRATHCONA SCHOOL
(*Suby of* EDMONTON SCHOOL DISTRICT
NO. 7)
10450 72 Ave Nw, Edmonton, AB, T6E 0Z6
(780) 439-3957
Emp Here 84
SIC 8211 Elementary and secondary schools
Hans Van Ginhoven

D-U-N-S 25-683-0126   (SL)
EDMONTON STEEL PLATE LTD
(*Suby of* GUSSE HOLDINGS LIMITED)
5545 89 St Nw, Edmonton, AB, T6E 5W9
(780) 468-6722
Emp Here 130   *Sales* 77,669,020
SIC 5051 Metals service centers and offices
Larry Gusse
Adelle Gusse

D-U-N-S 20-081-8946   (HQ)
EDMONTON VALVE & FITTING INC
4503 93 St Nw, Edmonton, AB, T6E 5S9
(780) 437-0640
Sales 23,751,300
SIC 5085 Industrial supplies
Keith Johns

D-U-N-S 20-081-9100   (HQ)
ELECTRIC MOTOR SERVICE LIMITED
8835 60 Ave Nw, Edmonton, AB, T6E 6L9
(780) 496-9300
Emp Here 50   *Sales* 11,539,680
SIC 7694 Armature rewinding shops
Robert Knickle

David Ash
Jacqueline Knickle

D-U-N-S 25-192-4080   (BR)
EMERSON ELECTRIC CANADA LIMITED
EMERSON PROCESS MANAGEMENT
(*Suby of* EMERSON ELECTRIC CO.)
4112 91a St Nw, Edmonton, AB, T6E 5V2
(780) 450-3600
Emp Here 150
SIC 3533 Oil and gas field machinery
Reid Bill

D-U-N-S 20-127-8558   (SL)
**EMPLOYEE BENEFIT FUNDS ADMINIS-
TRATION LTD**
4224 93 St Nw Suite 200, Edmonton, AB, T6E
5P5
(780) 465-2882
Emp Here 15   *Sales* 10,881,585
SIC 6371 Pension, health, and welfare funds
Paulette Szabo

D-U-N-S 24-733-0053   (HQ)
ENERCON PRODUCTS LTD
(*Suby of* BEACON ROOFING SUPPLY, INC.)
9610 54 Ave Nw, Edmonton, AB, T6E 5V1
(780) 437-7003
Emp Here 15   *Sales* 29,620,656
SIC 5033 Roofing, siding, and insulation
Stephen Ewanchuk
Kevin Mcintosh
Irene Mciver
Michael (Mike) Witzke
Alec Mciver
Douglas G. Macphail
Justin P. Rumpel
Michael (Don) Peccusch
Ernest (Ernie) Ewanchuk
Lawrence Dale Sexauer

D-U-N-S 24-390-9884   (HQ)
ENNIS, J. FABRICS LTD
VISION FABRICS
6111 91 St Nw, Edmonton, AB, T6E 6V6
(780) 474-5414
Emp Here 75   *Sales* 146,568,275
SIC 5131 Piece goods and notions
James Ennis
Lois Ennis
Sandy Slator
Les Bellan
Brian Trendel

D-U-N-S 20-636-8771   (HQ)
FACTOR FORMS WEST LTD
8411 Mcintyre Rd Nw, Edmonton, AB, T6E
6G3
(780) 468-1111
Emp Here 90   *Sales* 86,265,899
SIC 5112 Stationery and office supplies
Greg Drechsler

D-U-N-S 25-148-6056   (SL)
**FILLMORE CONSTRUCTION MANAGE-
MENT INC**
(*Suby of* FILLMORE HOLDINGS INC)
9114 34a Ave Nw, Edmonton, AB, T6E 5P4
(780) 430-0005
Emp Here 160   *Sales* 62,670,796
SIC 1542 Nonresidential construction, nec
Chris Fillmore
Jeff Fillmore
Terry Fillmore
Brent Fillmore

D-U-N-S 24-357-3602   (HQ)
FOURQUEST ENERGY INC
9304 39 Ave Nw, Edmonton, AB, T6E 5T9
(780) 485-0690
Emp Here 41   *Sales* 15,985,250
SIC 1389 Oil and gas field services, nec
Nik Grgic
Dave Wilson
Karl Gannon
Zoran Bajic

D-U-N-S 24-000-2089   (SL)

FRANK HENRY EQUIPMENT (1987) LTD
9810 60 Ave Nw, Edmonton, AB, T6E 0C5
(780) 434-8778
Emp Here 35   *Sales* 16,625,910
SIC 5084 Industrial machinery and equipment
Joan Snyder
Dave Cole
Nancy Snyder
Mark Debogorski

D-U-N-S 25-205-8458   (BR)
G4S SECURE SOLUTIONS (CANADA) LTD
(*Suby of* G4S PLC)
9618 42 Ave Nw Suite 100, Edmonton, AB,
T6E 5Y4
(780) 423-4444
Emp Here 150
SIC 7381 Detective and armored car services
David Price

D-U-N-S 20-281-1998   (HQ)
GE OIL & GAS CANADA INC
(*Suby of* GENERAL ELECTRIC COMPANY)
3575 97 St Nw, Edmonton, AB, T6E 5S7
(780) 450-1031
Sales 15,985,250
SIC 1389 Oil and gas field services, nec
H. Lawrence Culp, Jr

D-U-N-S 24-497-7625   (HQ)
GENERAL BODY & EQUIPMENT LTD
8124 Davies Rd Nw, Edmonton, AB, T6E 4N2
(780) 468-5359
Emp Here 43   *Sales* 22,384,300
SIC 3713 Truck and bus bodies
Wolfgang Kaminski
Gerald Marcoux
Cam Barnfather

D-U-N-S 20-896-6218   (HQ)
**GOODWILL INDUSTRIES OF ALBERTA
(REGISTERED SOCIETY)**
GOODWILL REHAB. SERVICE
8761 51 Ave Nw, Edmonton, AB, T6E 5H1
(780) 944-1414
Emp Here 70   *Sales* 21,264,400
SIC 8331 Job training and related services
Larry Brownoff
Drew Thomson
Dorothy Chan
Liliana Levesconte
Mirande Alexandre
Onita Blankenfeldt
Bikram Daulay
Jennifer Fowler
Stefan Kreptul
Adrianna Laszlo

D-U-N-S 24-978-6617   (BR)
GRAHAM GROUP LTD
GRAHAM INDUSTRIAL SERVICES AT J V
(*Suby of* GRAHAM GROUP LTD)
8404 Mcintyre Rd Nw, Edmonton, AB, T6E
6V3
(780) 430-9600
Emp Here 130
SIC 1541 Industrial buildings and warehouses
Pecil Dawe

D-U-N-S 24-128-5100   (SL)
GREAT NORTH EQUIPMENT INC
8743 50 Ave Nw, Edmonton, AB, T6E 5H4
(780) 461-7400
Emp Here 50   *Sales* 14,608,450
SIC 7353 Heavy construction equipment
rental
Stephen Forberg
David Wootton
Brent Forberg

D-U-N-S 25-115-9752   (SL)
GREAT WEST DRUGS (SOUTHGATE) LTD
REXALL LONG TERM CARE PHARMACY
4484 97 St Nw, Edmonton, AB, T6E 5R9
(780) 496-9366
Emp Here 40   *Sales* 10,118,160
SIC 5912 Drug stores and proprietary stores

Darrell Katz

D-U-N-S 24-090-9226   (HQ)
GRIMES WELL SERVICING LTD
4526 97 St Nw, Edmonton, AB, T6E 5N9
(780) 437-7871
Emp Here 4   *Sales* 19,182,300
SIC 1381 Drilling oil and gas wells
Gary Grimes
Beverley Grimes

D-U-N-S 20-852-5365   (SL)
HI SIGNS THE FATH GROUP LTD
9570 58 Ave Nw, Edmonton, AB, T6E 0B6
(780) 468-6181
Emp Here 50   *Sales* 10,941,200
SIC 3993 Signs and advertising specialties
Dave Kelloway

D-U-N-S 24-841-1670   (HQ)
HI-TECH SEALS INC
9211 41 Ave Nw, Edmonton, AB, T6E 6R5
(780) 438-6055
Emp Here 59   *Sales* 40,377,210
SIC 5085 Industrial supplies
James Bond
Tony Boken

D-U-N-S 25-679-7606   (HQ)
HOME HEALTH CARE SOLUTIONS INC
HEALTHCARE SOLUTIONS
5405 99 St Nw, Edmonton, AB, T6E 3N8
(780) 434-3131
Emp Here 25   *Sales* 14,309,568
SIC 5047 Medical and hospital equipment
Brian Scherba

D-U-N-S 25-106-5314   (SL)
IDEAL CONTRACT SERVICES LTD
9825 45 Ave Nw, Edmonton, AB, T6E 5C8
(780) 463-2424
Emp Here 150   *Sales* 63,410,550
SIC 1541 Industrial buildings and warehouses
Ron Normandin

D-U-N-S 20-082-5735   (HQ)
IMPORT TOOL CORPORATION LTD
10340 71 Ave Nw, Edmonton, AB, T6E 0W8
(780) 434-3464
Emp Here 40   *Sales* 34,141,100
SIC 5084 Industrial machinery and equipment
Robert K. Macleod
Peter J. Aiello
Michael Nobrega
Mike Edmonds
Jim Knee
Kyle Mowbray
Randy Parker

D-U-N-S 20-637-2781   (HQ)
IRISNDT CORP
(*Suby of* IRISNDT INSPECTION & ENGI-
NEERING INC)
5311 86 St Nw, Edmonton, AB, T6E 5T8
(780) 437-2022
Emp Here 90   *Sales* 81,632,800
SIC 8734 Testing laboratories
James Sheard

D-U-N-S 20-015-8157   (HQ)
IS2 WORKFORCE SOLUTIONS INC
8023 Roper Rd Nw, Edmonton, AB, T6E 6S4
(780) 420-9999
Emp Here 1   *Sales* 10,426,680
SIC 7361 Employment agencies
Barbara Dale
Eric Germain

D-U-N-S 24-331-0984   (HQ)
**ISL ENGINEERING AND LAND SERVICES
LTD**
(*Suby of* ISL HOLDINGS INC)
7909 51 Ave Nw Suite 100, Edmonton, AB,
T6E 5L9
(780) 438-9000
Emp Here 156   *Sales* 47,311,440
SIC 8711 Engineering services
Gary Mack

D-U-N-S 24-310-6866   (HQ)
ISL HOLDINGS INC
7909 51 Ave Nw, Edmonton, AB, T6E 5L9
(780) 438-9000
Emp Here 140   *Sales* 41,397,510
SIC 8711 Engineering services
Gary Mack
John Mcmanus
Edward Kolla
West Stemaugh
Randy Rosen
Peter Fairbridge
Rodney Peacock

D-U-N-S 25-272-9488   (BR)
KEG RESTAURANTS LTD
KEG STEAKHOUSE & BAR, THE
(*Suby of* RECIPE UNLIMITED CORPORA-
TION)
8020 105 St Nw, Edmonton, AB, T6E 4Z4

Emp Here 90
SIC 5812 Eating places
Gregg Kenney

D-U-N-S 24-091-4721   (SL)
KERR INTERIOR SYSTEMS LTD
9335 62 Ave Nw, Edmonton, AB, T6E 0E1
(780) 466-2800
Emp Here 80   *Sales* 9,902,503
SIC 1742 Plastering, drywall, and insulation
Darryl Wiebe
Wendell Wiebe
Barry Derkson

D-U-N-S 25-831-7601   (BR)
LABATT BREWING COMPANY LIMITED
LABATT BREWERIES WESTERN CANADA
(*Suby of* ANHEUSER-BUSCH INBEV)
10119 45 Ave Nw, Edmonton, AB, T6E 0G8
(780) 436-6060
Emp Here 170
SIC 2082 Malt beverages
Carlos Birto

D-U-N-S 24-273-6064   (SL)
LAKEWOOD CHEVROLET LTD
9150 34 Ave Nw, Edmonton, AB, T6E 5P2
(780) 462-5959
Emp Here 100   *Sales* 62,928,000
SIC 5511 New and used car dealers
Patrick Healy

D-U-N-S 24-984-0042   (SL)
LAMCORP MANAGEMENT LTD
5708 75 St Nw, Edmonton, AB, T6E 5X6
(780) 413-8388
Emp Here 35   *Sales* 14,677,425
SIC 6712 Bank holding companies
David Lam

D-U-N-S 20-106-6227   (HQ)
LEDCOR INDUSTRIAL LIMITED
(*Suby of* 280818 ALBERTA LTD)
9910 39 Ave Nw, Edmonton, AB, T6E 5H8
(780) 462-9616
Sales 42,273,700
SIC 1541 Industrial buildings and warehouses
Ron Stevenson
Don Breen
Bob Pullen

D-U-N-S 25-796-7146   (SL)
**LIQUOR DEPOT AT WINDERMERE CROSS-
ING**
10508 82 Ave Nw Unit 300, Edmonton, AB,
T6E 2A4
(780) 702-7400
Emp Here 49   *Sales* 14,657,370
SIC 5921 Liquor stores
Steven Bebis

D-U-N-S 24-983-2122   (HQ)
LIQUOR STORES GP INC
(*Suby of* ALCANNA INC)
10508 82 Ave Nw Suite 300, Edmonton, AB,
T6E 2A4

(780) 944-9994
Emp Here 9   *Sales* 24,432,800
SIC 5921 Liquor stores
Irving Kipnes
Glen Heximer
David Margolus
Rick Crook
Pat De Grace
Henry Bereznicki
John Butler
Gary Collins
Jim Dinning
Robert Green

D-U-N-S 20-719-5152   (HQ)
LIQUOR STORES LIMITED PARTNERSHIP
(*Suby of* ALCANNA INC)
10508 82 Ave Nw Suite 300, Edmonton, AB,
T6E 2A4
(780) 944-9994
Sales 367,074,000
SIC 5921 Liquor stores
Stephen Bebis

D-U-N-S 24-337-0876   (SL)
MARBLE RESTAURANTS LTD
PIZZA HUT
9054 51 Ave Nw Suite 200, Edmonton, AB,
T6E 5X4
(780) 462-5755
Emp Here 200   *Sales* 9,103,800
SIC 5812 Eating places
Shamez Jivraj
Aly Jivraj
Mohamed Jivraj

D-U-N-S 20-015-7977   (SL)
MCGREGOR CONSTRUCTION 2000 LTD
(*Suby of* QUANTA SERVICES, INC.)
9925 62 Ave Nw, Edmonton, AB, T6E 0E7
(780) 437-1340
Emp Here 110   *Sales* 36,092,650
SIC 1623 Water, sewer, and utility lines
Barkley Adams

D-U-N-S 24-808-6092   (HQ)
MID-NITE SUN TRANSPORTATION LTD
5805 98 St Nw, Edmonton, AB, T6E 3L4
(780) 431-2877
Emp Here 5   *Sales* 60,845,730
SIC 4213 Trucking, except local
Carl Rosenau
William Rosenau
Lyle Rosenau
Rodney Rosenau
Timothy Rosenau
Valerie Stevenson

D-U-N-S 20-788-5133   (SL)
**MIKE PRIESTNER AUTOMOTIVE GROUP
LTD**
SOUTHTOWN HYUNDAI
3603 99 St Nw Suite 780, Edmonton, AB, T6E
6K6
(780) 450-1021
Emp Here 40   *Sales* 19,923,120
SIC 5511 New and used car dealers
Mike Priestner

D-U-N-S 25-098-1297   (SL)
MUTH ELECTRICAL MANAGEMENT INC
MUTH ENERGY MANAGEMENT
9850 41 Ave Nw, Edmonton, AB, T6E 5L6
(780) 414-0980
Emp Here 100   *Sales* 21,782,900
SIC 1731 Electrical work
Donald Muth
Doreen Muth

D-U-N-S 20-559-5585   (SL)
NILEX CONSTRUCTION INC
(*Suby of* NILEX INC)
9304 39 Ave Nw, Edmonton, AB, T6E 5T9
(780) 463-9535
Emp Here 48   *Sales* 11,816,928
SIC 1799 Special trade contractors, nec
Ian Wilson

D-U-N-S 20-350-6654   (SL)
NORTHSHORE SUDBURY LTD
OTR WHEEL ENGINEERING CANADA
8113 Coronet Rd Nw, Edmonton, AB, T6E
4N7
(780) 455-5177
Emp Here 83   *Sales* 16,045,228
SIC 3714 Motor vehicle parts and accessories
Fred Taylor
Claude St Louis

D-U-N-S 24-553-3237   (HQ)
P.B.E. DISTRIBUTORS INC
5308 97 St Nw, Edmonton, AB, T6E 5W5
(780) 438-0303
Emp Here 14   *Sales* 18,210,750
SIC 5013 Motor vehicle supplies and new
parts
Robert Neale
Gord Milford
Ray Hodgins

D-U-N-S 24-523-7433   (HQ)
PCL CONSTRUCTION GROUP INC
(*Suby of* PCL EMPLOYEES HOLDINGS LTD)
9915 56 Ave Nw Suite 1, Edmonton, AB, T6E
5L7
(780) 733-5000
Sales 3,072,924,800
SIC 1541 Industrial buildings and warehouses
Dave Filipchuk
Paul Douglas
Ross Grieve
Gordon Stephenson
Gordon Panas
Mike Wieninger

D-U-N-S 24-001-5024   (HQ)
PCL CONSTRUCTION HOLDINGS LTD
(*Suby of* PCL EMPLOYEES HOLDINGS LTD)
9915 56 Ave Nw, Edmonton, AB, T6E 5L7
(780) 733-5000
Emp Here 1   *Sales* 1,781,636,148
SIC 6159 Miscellaneous business credit insti-
tutions
Paul Douglas
Ross Grieve
Gordon Stephenson
Gordon Panas
Gordon Maron
Peter Beaupre
David Filipchuk
Michael Kehoe
Peter Stalenhoef
Shaun Yancey

D-U-N-S 24-982-4780   (HQ)
PCL CONSTRUCTION MANAGEMENT INC
(*Suby of* PCL EMPLOYEES HOLDINGS LTD)
5400 99 St Nw, Edmonton, AB, T6E 3P4
(780) 733-6000
Emp Here 200   *Sales* 62,388,000
SIC 8741 Management services
Alan Kuysters
Robert Holmberg

D-U-N-S 24-399-2328   (HQ)
PCL CONSTRUCTION RESOURCES INC
(*Suby of* PCL EMPLOYEES HOLDINGS LTD)
5410 99 St Nw, Edmonton, AB, T6E 3P4
(780) 733-5400
Emp Here 30   *Sales* 11,197,050
SIC 6159 Miscellaneous business credit insti-
tutions
Dave Filipchuk
Jim Barry
Gordon Stephenson
Gordon Panas
Mike Wieninger

D-U-N-S 20-647-5415   (SL)
PCL CONSTRUCTORS EASTERN INC
(*Suby of* PCL EMPLOYEES HOLDINGS LTD)
9915 56 Ave Nw, Edmonton, AB, T6E 5L7

Emp Here 50   *Sales* 13,547,100
SIC 1521 Single-family housing construction

James Dougan
Rob Holmberg

D-U-N-S 24-982-4822   (HQ)
PCL CONSTRUCTORS INC
(*Suby of* PCL EMPLOYEES HOLDINGS LTD)
9915 56 Ave Nw Suite 1, Edmonton, AB, T6E
5L7
(780) 733-5000
Sales 2,444,372,000
SIC 1541 Industrial buildings and warehouses
 Paul Douglas
 Gordon Stephenson
 Ross Grieve

D-U-N-S 24-982-4707   (SL)
PCL CONSTRUCTORS NORTHERN INC
(*Suby of* PCL EMPLOYEES HOLDINGS LTD)
9915 56 Ave Nw Suite 1, Edmonton, AB, T6E
5L7
(780) 733-5000
Emp Here 400   *Sales* 279,356,800
SIC 1542 Nonresidential construction, nec
 Roger Dootson
 Dave Filipchuck

D-U-N-S 24-522-2591   (HQ)
PCL EMPLOYEES HOLDINGS LTD
9915 56 Ave Nw, Edmonton, AB, T6E 5L7
(780) 733-5000
Sales 5,987,037,420
SIC 6712 Bank holding companies
 Paul Douglas
 Ross Grieve
 Steve Richards
 Gordon Panas

D-U-N-S 24-642-7017   (HQ)
PCL INDUSTRIAL CONSTRUCTORS INC
(*Suby of* PCL EMPLOYEES HOLDINGS LTD)
9915 56 Ave Nw, Edmonton, AB, T6E 5L7
(780) 733-5500
Emp Here 100   *Sales* 1,885,658,400
SIC 1541 Industrial buildings and warehouses
 Gary Truhn

D-U-N-S 25-168-2506   (HQ)
PII (CANADA) LIMITED
GE OIL & GAS
(*Suby of* GENERAL ELECTRIC COMPANY)
3575 97 St Nw, Edmonton, AB, T6E 5S7
(780) 450-1031
Emp Here 5   *Sales* 77,593,328
SIC 7389 Business services, nec
 Daryl Ronsky
 Robert Vilyus
 Thomas Hirst

D-U-N-S 20-539-0438   (SL)
PLAINSMAN MFG. INC
8305 Mcintyre Rd Nw, Edmonton, AB, T6E
5J7
(780) 496-9800
Emp Here 53   *Sales* 11,766,053
SIC 3533 Oil and gas field machinery
 Mike Kittlitz

D-U-N-S 20-338-0238   (SL)
POWER EXPRESS INC
4182 93 St Nw, Edmonton, AB, T6E 5P5
(780) 461-4000
Emp Here 30   *Sales* 13,304,700
SIC 7389 Business services, nec
 Lawrence Zdrill

D-U-N-S 25-679-1211   (SL)
PRAIRIE NORTH CONST. LTD
4936 87 St Nw Suite 280, Edmonton, AB, T6E
5W3
(780) 463-3363
Emp Here 75   *Sales* 18,933,150
SIC 1611 Highway and street construction
 F Craig Robertson
 D Alvin Spray

D-U-N-S 20-083-9082   (HQ)
PRICE, GORDON MUSIC LTD
MOTHERS MUSIC

10828 82 Ave Nw, Edmonton, AB, T6E 2B3
(780) 439-0007
Emp Here 21   *Sales* 12,549,762
SIC 5736 Musical instrument stores
 Warren Price

D-U-N-S 24-522-1072   (HQ)
PRINTWORKS LTD
3850 98 St Nw, Edmonton, AB, T6E 3L2
(780) 452-8921
Emp Here 108   *Sales* 18,042,970
SIC 2752 Commercial printing, lithographic
 Darryl Smith
 Raymond Smith

D-U-N-S 24-895-2103   (SL)
PRIORITY MECHANICAL LTD
9259 35 Ave Nw, Edmonton, AB, T6E 5Y1
(780) 435-3636
Emp Here 100   *Sales* 23,306,500
SIC 1711 Plumbing, heating, air-conditioning
 Jody Mcneill
 Brian Olafson

D-U-N-S 24-353-4729   (HQ)
PROFESSIONAL GROUP INC, THE
PROFESSIONAL REALTY GROUP
9920 63 Ave Nw Suite 130, Edmonton, AB,
T6E 0G9
(780) 439-9818
Emp Here 49   *Sales* 23,876,673
SIC 6531 Real estate agents and managers
 Russ Robideau

D-U-N-S 24-981-4112   (SL)
PROFESSIONAL GROUP INC, THE
*PROFESSIONAL REALTY GROUP, THE DIV
OF*
9222 51 Ave Nw, Edmonton, AB, T6E 5L8
(780) 439-9818
Emp Here 68   *Sales* 18,479,408
SIC 6531 Real estate agents and managers
 Russel Robideau
 Helen D Robideau

D-U-N-S 24-063-5474   (SL)
RAE ENGINEERING & INSPECTION LTD
4810 93 St Nw, Edmonton, AB, T6E 5M4
(780) 469-2401
Emp Here 75   *Sales* 33,691,425
SIC 7389 Business services, nec
 Izak Roux
 Al Keeler

D-U-N-S 24-330-0605   (HQ)
RE/MAX REAL ESTATE (EDMONTON) LTD
4245 97 St Nw Suite 102, Edmonton, AB, T6E
5Y7
(780) 434-2323
Emp Here 4   *Sales* 67,612,800
SIC 6531 Real estate agents and managers
 Bill Briggs

D-U-N-S 20-084-0684   (HQ)
RICE ENGINEERING & OPERATING LTD
9333 41 Ave Nw, Edmonton, AB, T6E 6R5
(780) 469-1356
Emp Here 50   *Sales* 10,205,564
SIC 8711 Engineering services
 Terry W Kunyk
 Ramtin Nouzari

D-U-N-S 25-454-4547   (SL)
ROHIT DEVELOPMENTS LTD
9636 51 Ave Nw, Edmonton, AB, T6E 6A5
(780) 436-9015
Emp Here 84
SIC 1522 Residential construction, nec
 Radhe Gupta

D-U-N-S 20-296-2403   (BR)
ROSENAU TRANSPORT LTD
(*Suby of* MID-NITE SUN TRANSPORTATION
LTD)
5805 98 St Nw, Edmonton, AB, T6E 3L4
(780) 431-2065
Emp Here 100
SIC 4213 Trucking, except local

Chad Arb

D-U-N-S 25-218-1425   (HQ)
RUNNING ROOM CANADA INC
RUNNING ROOM, THE
(*Suby of* EDMONTON RUNNING ROOM LTD)
9750 47 Ave Nw Suite 60, Edmonton, AB, T6E
5P3
(780) 439-3099
Emp Here 75   *Sales* 99,804,000
SIC 5661 Shoe stores
 John Stanton
 Mike O'dell
 Jason Stanton
 John Stanton Jr.
 Roger Dang

D-U-N-S 24-905-1137   (BR)
RUSSEL METALS INC
(*Suby of* RUSSEL METALS INC)
7016 99 St Nw, Edmonton, AB, T6E 3R3

Emp Here 90
SIC 5051 Metals service centers and offices
 Bruce Robb

D-U-N-S 25-326-0442   (BR)
SCHLUMBERGER CANADA LIMITED
5003 93 St Nw, Edmonton, AB, T6E 5S9
(780) 434-3476
Emp Here 120
SIC 3533 Oil and gas field machinery
 Cam Smith

D-U-N-S 25-107-6048   (SL)
SCONA ELECTRIC INC
10003 69 Ave Nw, Edmonton, AB, T6E 0T1
(780) 433-4247
Emp Here 28   *Sales* 17,545,192
SIC 4911 Electric services
 Valter Schmidt
 Terrence Folk

D-U-N-S 24-137-6511   (HQ)
SEGUE SYSTEMS INC
4504 101 St Nw, Edmonton, AB, T6E 5G9
(780) 442-2340
Emp Here 20   *Sales* 20,122,830
SIC 5044 Office equipment
 Brian Clark

D-U-N-S 24-585-5671   (HQ)
SELECT COMMUNICATIONS INC
SELECT CALL CENTRE
10368 82 Ave Nw Suite 201, Edmonton, AB,
T6E 1Z8
(780) 917-5400
Sales 24,707,045
SIC 7389 Business services, nec
 Leslie Bidewell
 Sandra Bidewell

D-U-N-S 24-806-3893   (SL)
SEQUITER INC
LAWDEPOT
9644 54 Ave Nw Unit 209, Edmonton, AB, T6E
5V1
(780) 437-2410
Emp Here 65   *Sales* 11,525,215
SIC 7371 Custom computer programming ser-
vices
 Kenneth Sawyer

D-U-N-S 24-391-7721   (SL)
SILVACOM LTD
3912 91 St Nw, Edmonton, AB, T6E 5K7
(780) 462-3238
Emp Here 75   *Sales* 20,574,900
SIC 8741 Management services
 Thomas Grabowski
 Robert Morton

D-U-N-S 25-385-0648   (HQ)
SIMMAX CORP
8750 58 Ave Nw, Edmonton, AB, T6E 6G6
(780) 437-9315
Emp Here 3   *Sales* 21,782,900
SIC 1731 Electrical work

Daryl Kruper

D-U-N-S 25-140-1634   (SL)
SIMPLY BOSS INC
REGENT INDUSTRIES
4529 97 St Nw, Edmonton, AB, T6E 5Y8

Emp Here 25   *Sales* 11,179,350
SIC 5063 Electrical apparatus and equipment
 Richard Boissonneault
 Henry Houle

D-U-N-S 20-115-9563   (HQ)
SIMSON MAXWELL
(*Suby of* SIMMAX CORP)
8750 58 Ave Nw, Edmonton, AB, T6E 6G6
(780) 434-6431
Emp Here 40   *Sales* 63,892,630
SIC 5084 Industrial machinery and equipment
 Daryl Kruper
 Brad Kruper

D-U-N-S 24-894-4811   (SL)
SOUTHGATE PONTIAC BUICK GMC LTD
9751 34 Ave Nw, Edmonton, AB, T6E 5X9
(855) 971-6989
Emp Here 90   *Sales* 56,635,200
SIC 5511 New and used car dealers
 James Hodgson
 Ron Hodgson

D-U-N-S 20-084-4512   (BR)
SPARTAN CONTROLS LTD
STERLING VALVE AUTOMATION, DIV. OF
(*Suby of* SPARTAN CONTROLS LTD)
8403 51 Ave Nw, Edmonton, AB, T6E 5L9
(780) 468-5463
Emp Here 200
SIC 5085 Industrial supplies
 Sandy Johnson

D-U-N-S 25-454-5072   (SL)
SPECIAL D. BAKING LTD
6003 92 St Nw, Edmonton, AB, T6E 3A5
(780) 436-9650
Emp Here 20   *Sales* 10,702,480
SIC 5149 Groceries and related products, nec
 Richard Manley

D-U-N-S 25-978-8677   (SL)
SRW TECHNOLOGIES
4521 101 St Nw, Edmonton, AB, T6E 5C6
(780) 413-4833
Emp Here 40   *Sales* 10,873,680
SIC 7692 Welding repair
 Donavan Glover

D-U-N-S 20-084-4793   (HQ)
**STAMCO SPECIALTY TOOL & MFG. CO.
(1979) LTD**
STAMCO PLASTICS
6048 97 St Nw, Edmonton, AB, T6E 3J4
(780) 436-2647
Sales 12,432,056
SIC 3599 Industrial machinery, nec
 Giuseppe Franco

D-U-N-S 20-905-7327   (SL)
**STEELE SECURITY & INVESTIGATION
SERVICE DIVISION OF UNITED PROTEC-
TIONS**
UNITED PROTECTIONS
8055 Coronet Rd Nw, Edmonton, AB, T6E
4N7

Emp Here 100   *Sales* 39,567,800
SIC 7381 Detective and armored car services
 Frederick (Freddie) Ramsoondar

D-U-N-S 20-058-7587   (BR)
SUEZ CANADA WASTE SERIVCES INC
(*Suby of* SUEZ CANADA WASTE SERIVCES
INC)
9426 51 Ave Nw Suite 307, Edmonton, AB,
T6E 5A6
(780) 391-7303
Emp Here 81
SIC 2875 Fertilizers, mixing only

Rob Rennie

D-U-N-S 24-760-3280   (HQ)
SUEZ CANADA WASTE SERIVCES INC
SWAN HILLS TREATMENT CENTRE
9426 51 Ave Nw Suite 307, Edmonton, AB,
T6E 5A6
(780) 989-5212
Emp Here 5   *Sales* 35,080,100
SIC 4953 Refuse systems
Thomas Brown
Michael Algranati
Patrick Cairo
David Clancy
Wayne Gingrich
Robert J Iacullo
Edward J Imparato

D-U-N-S 25-454-5247   (SL)
SUN TOYOTA LTD
10130 82 Ave Nw, Edmonton, AB, T6E 1Z4
(780) 433-2411
Emp Here 55   *Sales* 34,610,400
SIC 5511 New and used car dealers
Nash Padamsey

D-U-N-S 24-274-6568   (SL)
TERRITORIAL ELECTRIC LTD
8303 Roper Rd Nw, Edmonton, AB, T6E 6S4
(780) 465-7591
Emp Here 75   *Sales* 16,337,175
SIC 1731 Electrical work
Donald Daly
Didier (Dj) Coppens
Don Johnston

D-U-N-S 24-839-9024   (BR)
THURBER ENGINEERING LTD
(*Suby of* THURBER ENGINEERING LTD)
9636 51 Ave Nw Suite 200, Edmonton, AB,
T6E 6A5
(780) 438-1460
Emp Here 100
SIC 8711 Engineering services
Campbell Chow

D-U-N-S 20-287-1463   (SL)
TIER 1 ENERGY SOLUTIONS INC
453-97 St Edmonton Ab, Edmonton, AB, T6E
5Y7
(780) 476-0099
Emp Here 300   *Sales* 201,803,700
SIC 1382 Oil and gas exploration services
Kristyn Rayfield

D-U-N-S 24-064-2694   (SL)
TRAIL BUILDING SUPPLIES LTD
9450 45 Ave Nw, Edmonton, AB, T6E 5V3
(780) 463-1737
Emp Here 124   *Sales* 33,188,848
SIC 5211 Lumber and other building materials
Roger Ayotte
Wesley Alexander
Gary Fletcher

D-U-N-S 24-335-1397   (HQ)
UNIFIED ALLOYS (EDMONTON) LTD
UNIFIED ALLOYS
(*Suby of* UNIFIED ALLOYS LTD)
8835 50 Ave Nw, Edmonton, AB, T6E 5H4
(780) 468-5656
Emp Here 42   *Sales* 24,147,396
SIC 5051 Metals service centers and offices
Darren Hansen

D-U-N-S 25-094-7504   (BR)
UNIFIRST CANADA LTD
(*Suby of* UNIFIRST CORPORATION)
3691 98 St Nw, Edmonton, AB, T6E 5N2
(780) 423-0384
Emp Here 80
SIC 7213 Linen supply
Joe Eiswerth

D-U-N-S 24-080-2558   (SL)
UNION, THE
6240 99 St Nw, Edmonton, AB, T6E 6C7
(780) 702-2582
Emp Here 49   *Sales* 13,937,413

SIC 6512 Nonresidential building operators

D-U-N-S 20-084-8349   (SL)
**UNITED CYCLE & MOTOR COMPANY
(1975) LIMITED**
UNITED CYCLE SOURCE FOR SPORTS
7620 Gateway Blvd Nw, Edmonton, AB, T6E
4Z8
(780) 433-1181
Emp Here 200   *Sales* 48,865,600
SIC 5941 Sporting goods and bicycle shops
Wilfred Brooks
Iola Bots
Jason Bots

D-U-N-S 20-084-8596   (SL)
UNIVERSE MACHINE CORPORATION
UNIVERSE MACHINE & WELDING, DIV
(*Suby of* FEIGEL INVESTMENTS LTD)
5545 91 St Nw, Edmonton, AB, T6E 6K4
(780) 468-5211
Emp Here 100   *Sales* 19,208,500
SIC 3494 Valves and pipe fittings, nec
Kurt Feigel
Erna Feigel

D-U-N-S 24-065-6033   (HQ)
VALARD CONSTRUCTION LTD
(*Suby of* QUANTA SERVICES, INC.)
4209 99 St Nw Suite 308, Edmonton, AB, T6E
5V7
(780) 436-9876
Emp Here 100   *Sales* 229,680,500
SIC 1623 Water, sewer, and utility lines
Victor Budzinski
Adam Budzinski
Phillip Seeley

D-U-N-S 24-420-5522   (SL)
**WALDORF EDUCATION SOCIETY OF ED-
MONTON**
7114 98 St Nw, Edmonton, AB, T6E 3M1
(780) 466-3312
Emp Here 35   *Sales* 13,909,490
SIC 8699 Membership organizations, nec

D-U-N-S 24-805-6210   (HQ)
WAREHOUSE SERVICES INC
9815 42 Ave Nw, Edmonton, AB, T6E 0A3
(780) 437-4917
Emp Here 60   *Sales* 48,421,170
SIC 5013 Motor vehicle supplies and new
parts
Thomas Wayne Scherr
Scott Scherr
Dave Curie
Kelly Scherr
Pauline Scherr

D-U-N-S 20-811-3019   (BR)
**WAWANESA MUTUAL INSURANCE COM-
PANY, THE**
(*Suby of* WAWANESA MUTUAL INSURANCE
COMPANY, THE)
8657 51 Ave Nw Suite 100, Edmonton, AB,
T6E 6A8
(780) 469-5700
Emp Here 119
SIC 6331 Fire, marine, and casualty insurance
Neil Miller

D-U-N-S 24-089-3057   (HQ)
WAYNE'S TIRE WAREHOUSE LTD
TIRE WAREHOUSE, THE
(*Suby of* 293675 ALBERTA LTD)
4717 99 St Nw, Edmonton, AB, T6E 4Y1
(780) 437-4555
Emp Here 13   *Sales* 62,928,000
SIC 5531 Auto and home supply stores
Wayne Harris
Doug Buhler
Nettie Harris

D-U-N-S 24-065-6504   (SL)
**WILLOW SPRING CONSTRUCTION (ALTA)
LTD**
(*Suby of* ELLISDON HOLDINGS INC)
8616 51 Ave Unit 250, Edmonton, AB, T6E

6E6
(780) 438-1990
Emp Here 23   *Sales* 13,117,774
SIC 1542 Nonresidential construction, nec
Amy Mc Williams

D-U-N-S 24-396-2776   (BR)
WORLEYPARSONSCORD LP
WORLEYPARSONS EDMONTON
(*Suby of* WORLEYPARSONS LIMITED)
5008 86 St Nw Suite 120, Edmonton, AB, T6E
5S2
(780) 440-5300
Emp Here 1,200
SIC 8711 Engineering services
Jacob Kellerman

Edmonton, AB T6G

D-U-N-S 20-105-5469   (SL)
360 STEEL INC
11050 University Ave Nw, Edmonton, AB, T6G
1Y3
(780) 429-0360
Emp Here 17   *Sales* 17,005,763
SIC 5051 Metals service centers and offices
James Cameron

D-U-N-S 20-867-4395   (BR)
ARAMARK CANADA LTD.
ARAMARK MANAGED SERVICES
(*Suby of* ARAMARK)
125 University Campus Nw, Edmonton, AB,
T6G 2H6
(780) 492-5800
Emp Here 100
SIC 5812 Eating places
Susan Mundy

D-U-N-S 24-997-8446   (HQ)
BUNCHES FLOWER COMPANY
7108 109 St Nw, Edmonton, AB, T6G 1B8
(780) 447-5359
Emp Here 57   *Sales* 14,659,680
SIC 5992 Florists
Sharon Armstrong
Judith Armstrong

D-U-N-S 24-951-4183   (SL)
CAMPUS TOWER SUITE HOTEL
11145 87 Ave Nw, Edmonton, AB, T6G 0Y1
(780) 439-6060
Emp Here 30   *Sales* 13,304,700
SIC 7389 Business services, nec
Matthew Foster

D-U-N-S 20-334-3228   (BR)
EARL'S RESTAURANTS LTD
EARL'S
(*Suby of* EARL'S RESTAURANTS LTD)
8629 112 St Nw, Edmonton, AB, T6G 1K8
(780) 439-4848
Emp Here 130
SIC 5812 Eating places
Jessica Ellis

D-U-N-S 24-397-4110   (SL)
**FACULTY CLUB OF THE UNIVERSITY OF
ALBERTA EDMONTON, THE**
11435 Saskatchewan Dr Nw, Edmonton, AB,
T6G 2G9
(780) 492-4231
Emp Here 75   *Sales* 3,413,925
SIC 5812 Eating places
Brendan Robbins

D-U-N-S 20-553-7009   (BR)
**GOVERNORS OF THE UNIVERSITY OF AL-
BERTA, THE**
CAMERON LIBRARY
(*Suby of* GOVERNMENT OF THE
PROVINCE OF ALBERTA)
52 University Campus Nw, Edmonton, AB,
T6G 2J8
(780) 492-3790
Emp Here 400

SIC 8231 Libraries
Kathleen De Long

D-U-N-S 24-387-4422   (BR)
**GOVERNORS OF THE UNIVERSITY OF AL-
BERTA, THE**
FACULTY OF ARTS
(*Suby of* GOVERNMENT OF THE
PROVINCE OF ALBERTA)
5 Humanities Ctr Unit 6, Edmonton, AB, T6G
2E5
(780) 492-2787
Emp Here 100
SIC 8221 Colleges and universities
Lesley Cormack

D-U-N-S 20-317-1277   (BR)
**GOVERNORS OF THE UNIVERSITY OF AL-
BERTA, THE**
FACULTY OF LAW
(*Suby of* GOVERNMENT OF THE
PROVINCE OF ALBERTA)
111 89 Ave, Edmonton, AB, T6G 2H5
(780) 492-3111
Emp Here 100
SIC 8221 Colleges and universities
Paul Paton

D-U-N-S 20-809-5844   (HQ)
**GOVERNORS OF THE UNIVERSITY OF AL-
BERTA, THE**
RESEARCH SERVICES OFFICE
(*Suby of* GOVERNMENT OF THE
PROVINCE OF ALBERTA)
116 St & 85 Ave, Edmonton, AB, T6G 2R3
(780) 492-3111
Emp Here 14,000   *Sales* 1,421,916,337
SIC 8221 Colleges and universities
David Turpin
Steven Dew
Andrew Sharman
Gitta Kulczycki
Jacqui Tam
Brad Hamdon

D-U-N-S 20-184-8459   (BR)
**GOVERNORS OF THE UNIVERSITY OF AL-
BERTA, THE**
RESEARCH SERVICES OFFICE
(*Suby of* GOVERNMENT OF THE
PROVINCE OF ALBERTA)
8625 112 St Nw Suite 222, Edmonton, AB,
T6G 1K8
(780) 492-5787
Emp Here 100
SIC 8733 Noncommercial research organiza-
tions
Walter Dixon

D-U-N-S 25-064-9233   (BR)
**GOVERNORS OF THE UNIVERSITY OF AL-
BERTA, THE**
SCHOOL OF DENTISTRY
(*Suby of* GOVERNMENT OF THE
PROVINCE OF ALBERTA)
11405 87 Ave 5th Fl, Edmonton, AB, T6G 1C9
(780) 492-5391
Emp Here 250
SIC 8221 Colleges and universities
Paul Major

D-U-N-S 25-093-4812   (BR)
**GOVERNORS OF THE UNIVERSITY OF AL-
BERTA, THE**
*DEPARTMENT OF MATHEMATICAL & STA-
TISTICAL SCIENCES*
(*Suby of* GOVERNMENT OF THE
PROVINCE OF ALBERTA)
51 University Campus Nw Suite 632, Edmon-
ton, AB, T6G 2G1
(780) 492-3396
Emp Here 200
SIC 8221 Colleges and universities
Arturo Pianzola

D-U-N-S 25-065-4167   (BR)
GOVERNORS OF THE UNIVERSITY OF AL-

BERTA, THE
U OF A STUDENT UNION
(Suby of GOVERNMENT OF THE
PROVINCE OF ALBERTA)
8900 114 St Nw, Edmonton, AB, T6G 2V2
(780) 492-4241
Emp Here 100
SIC 8742 Management consulting services
Marina Banister

D-U-N-S 20-273-5023   (BR)
**GOVERNORS OF THE UNIVERSITY OF AL-
BERTA, THE**
EARTH & ATMOSPHERIC SCIENCES
(Suby of GOVERNMENT OF THE
PROVINCE OF ALBERTA)
26 Earth Sciences Bldg Unit 1, Edmonton, AB,
T6G 2E3
(780) 492-3265
Emp Here 89
SIC 8221 Colleges and universities
Stephen Johnston

D-U-N-S 20-913-1007   (BR)
**GOVERNORS OF THE UNIVERSITY OF AL-
BERTA, THE**
*INFORMATION SERVICES AND TECHNOL-
OGY*
(Suby of GOVERNMENT OF THE
PROVINCE OF ALBERTA)
302 General Services Bldg, Edmonton, AB,
T6G 2E1
(780) 492-9400
Emp Here 300
SIC 8221 Colleges and universities
Mike Mcgregor

D-U-N-S 20-058-8296   (BR)
MEDICAL IMAGING CONSULTANTS
(Suby of MEDICAL IMAGING CONSUL-
TANTS)
8215 112 St Nw Suite 700, Edmonton, AB,
T6G 2C8
(780) 432-1121
Emp Here 100
SIC 8011 Offices and clinics of medical doc-
tors
Ron Gulayets

D-U-N-S 25-065-2013   (HQ)
OPTIMUM HEALTH CHOICES INC
OPTIMUM HEALTH VITAMINS & MORE
7115 109 St Nw Suite 2, Edmonton, AB, T6G
1B9
(780) 432-5464
Emp Here 28   *Sales* 11,739,080
SIC 5499 Miscellaneous food stores
John Biggs

D-U-N-S 24-627-9996   (SL)
UPPER CRUST CATERERS LTD
UPPER CRUST CAFE
10909 86 Ave Nw, Edmonton, AB, T6G 0W8
(780) 758-5599
Emp Here 14   *Sales* 3,215,475
SIC 5812 Eating places
Sheila Rich
Karen Fulton

D-U-N-S 24-005-4411   (HQ)
WESTCAN TRAVEL LTD
TREK ESCAPE
8412 109 St Nw, Edmonton, AB, T6G 1E2
(780) 439-9118
Emp Here 7   *Sales* 17,678,878
SIC 4724 Travel agencies
Allan Ronneseth
Terri Ronneseth

D-U-N-S 24-367-4590   (HQ)
WESTCORP PROPERTIES INC
8215 112 St Nw Suite 200, Edmonton, AB,
T6G 2C8
(780) 431-3300
Emp Here 35   *Sales* 152,128,800
SIC 6531 Real estate agents and managers
Phillip Milroy

Edmonton, AB T6H

D-U-N-S 25-261-6412   (HQ)
392268 ALBERTA LTD
*CANADA AUTO REMARKETING SUPER-
STORE*
5305 Allard Way Nw Suite 310, Edmonton,
AB, T6H 5X8
(780) 777-7776
Emp Here 16   *Sales* 44,049,600
SIC 5561 Recreational vehicle dealers
Sami Osman

D-U-N-S 24-810-0257   (HQ)
402909 ALBERTA LTD
BIG RIG COLLISION REPAIRS
5834 Gateway Blvd Nw, Edmonton, AB, T6H
2H6
(780) 434-7471
Emp Here 14   *Sales* 14,165,000
SIC 7532 Top and body repair and paint shops
Doug Sperle
Barry Pajak
William (Bill) Ripley

D-U-N-S 24-565-1505   (SL)
753146 ALBERTA LTD
ULTRASOL INDUSTRIES
10755 69 Ave Nw, Edmonton, AB, T6H 2C9
(780) 432-6535
Emp Here 3   *Sales* 17,854,488
SIC 5963 Direct selling establishments
Grigg Kellock
Philippa Gaston-Kellock

D-U-N-S 20-065-7687   (SL)
921325 ALBERTA LTD
CENTURY 21 PLATINUM REALTY
5620 104 St Nw, Edmonton, AB, T6H 2K2
(780) 710-9112
Emp Here 55   *Sales* 14,946,580
SIC 6531 Real estate agents and managers
Barry Munro

D-U-N-S 25-505-7184   (SL)
A.M.A. INSURANCE AGENCY LTD
(Suby of ALBERTA MOTOR ASSOCIATION)
10310 39a Ave, Edmonton, AB, T6H 5X9
(780) 430-5555
Emp Here 32   *Sales* 27,137,920
SIC 6411 Insurance agents, brokers, and ser-
vice
Doug Hollands
Don Smitten
Ron Grieve

D-U-N-S 25-505-7226   (HQ)
**ALBERTA MOTOR ASSOCIATION TRAVEL
AGENCY LTD**
AMA TRAVEL
(Suby of ALBERTA MOTOR ASSOCIATION)
10310 39a Ave, Edmonton, AB, T6H 5X9
(780) 430-5555
Emp Here 50   *Sales* 150,050,700
SIC 4724 Travel agencies
Don Smitten
Doug Creighton
Michelle Chimko

D-U-N-S 25-073-4654   (SL)
**ALBERTA SCHOOL EMPLOYEE BENEFIT
PLAN, THE**
ASEBP
6104 104 St Nw Suite 301, Edmonton, AB,
T6H 2K7
(780) 438-5300
Emp Here 200   *Sales* 427,393,600
SIC 6371 Pension, health, and welfare funds
Karen Holloway

D-U-N-S 20-920-6858   (BR)
ALBERTS RESTAURANTS LTD
ALBERTS FAMILY RESTAURANT
(Suby of ALBERTS RESTAURANTS LTD)
10362 51 Ave Nw, Edmonton, AB, T6H 5X6

(780) 437-7081
Emp Here 75
SIC 5812 Eating places
Miles Jewett

D-U-N-S 24-582-6540   (HQ)
ALCO INC
(Suby of ALCO INDUSTRIAL INC)
6925 104 St Nw, Edmonton, AB, T6H 2L5
(780) 435-3502
Emp Here 60   *Sales* 98,306,950
SIC 3541 Machine tools, Metal cutting type
Robert Taubner

D-U-N-S 20-341-3245   (SL)
AUTO PARTS PLUS
10341 58 Ave Nw, Edmonton, AB, T6H 5E4
(780) 437-4917
Emp Here 80   *Sales* 29,474,664
SIC 5013 Motor vehicle supplies and new
parts
Scott Sherr

D-U-N-S 20-898-3122   (HQ)
B.G.E. SERVICE & SUPPLY LTD
FILTER SHOP, THE
5711 103a St Nw, Edmonton, AB, T6H 2J6
(780) 436-6960
Emp Here 100   *Sales* 63,404,900
SIC 5085 Industrial supplies
Roberta Macgillivray

D-U-N-S 25-262-5967   (SL)
BIOWARE CORP
(Suby of ELECTRONIC ARTS INC.)
4445 Calgary Trail Nw Suite 200, Edmonton,
AB, T6H 5R7
(780) 430-0164
Emp Here 180   *Sales* 25,952,760
SIC 7371 Custom computer programming ser-
vices
Gregory Zeschuk
Raymond Muzyka
Richard Iwaniuk

D-U-N-S 24-400-4800   (HQ)
CHIRO FOODS LIMITED
A & W RESTAURANTS
5041 Gateway Blvd Nw Unit 100, Edmonton,
AB, T6H 4R7
(780) 438-8848
Emp Here 10   *Sales* 30,315,350
SIC 5812 Eating places
Brian Goheen
Robert Rowe
Raymond Mcmurray
Norman Horne
Ronald Cooper

D-U-N-S 20-894-9750   (SL)
COLORFAST CORPORATION
6115 Gateway Blvd Nw, Edmonton, AB, T6H
2H3

Emp Here 40   *Sales* 16,700,240
SIC 7384 Photofinish laboratories
Dave Marvin
Ian Stirling

D-U-N-S 20-128-1461   (SL)
CONNECT SOCIETY
6240 113 St Nw, Edmonton, AB, T6H 3L2
(780) 454-9581
Emp Here 35   *Sales* 13,909,490
SIC 8699 Membership organizations, nec
Claire Gallant

D-U-N-S 20-048-8018   (BR)
CORUS MEDIA HOLDINGS INC
GLOBAL TELEVISION
(Suby of SHAW COMMUNICATIONS INC)
5325 Allard Way Nw, Edmonton, AB, T6H 5B8
(780) 436-1250
Emp Here 200
SIC 7822 Motion picture and tape distribution
Timothy Spelliscy

D-U-N-S 24-715-3307   (HQ)

**CRITERION CATALYSTS & TECHNOLO-
GIES CANADA, INC**
(Suby of ROYAL DUTCH SHELL PLC)
5241 Calgary Trail Nw Unit 810, Edmonton,
AB, T6H 5G8
(780) 438-4188
Emp Here 6   *Sales* 17,325,281
SIC 2819 Industrial inorganic chemicals, nec
Sheila Wong
Richard Redmond
Brian Smith

D-U-N-S 20-081-8417   (HQ)
CRYSTAL GLASS CANADA LTD
CAN-AM AUTO GLASS & SUPPLIES
6424 Gateway Blvd Nw, Edmonton, AB, T6H
2H9
(780) 652-2512
Emp Here 25   *Sales* 44,848,000
SIC 7536 Automotive glass replacement
shops
Edwin E Bean
Terry A Bean
Ingrid Bean

D-U-N-S 25-012-1803   (BR)
**DAVEY TREE EXPERT CO. OF CANADA,
LIMITED**
(Suby of THE DAVEY TREE EXPERT COM-
PANY)
5622 103a St Nw, Edmonton, AB, T6H 2J5
(780) 428-8733
Emp Here 100
SIC 0783 Ornamental shrub and tree services
Kevin Cassells

D-U-N-S 20-699-9174   (BR)
DELTA HOTELS LIMITED
*DELTA EDMONTON SOUTH HOTEL AND
CONFERENCE CENTER*
(Suby of GOVERNMENT OF THE
PROVINCE OF BRITISH COLUMBIA)
4404 Gateway Blvd Nw, Edmonton, AB, T6H
5C2
(780) 434-6415
Emp Here 200
SIC 7011 Hotels and motels
Tiina Randorg

D-U-N-S 25-507-0682   (SL)
**DELTA HOTELS NO. 2 LIMITED PARTNER-
SHIP**
DELTA EDMONTON SOUTH
4404 Gateway Blvd Nw, Edmonton, AB, T6H
5C2
(780) 434-6415
Emp Here 300   *Sales* 28,700,400
SIC 7011 Hotels and motels
Martin Stitt

D-U-N-S 24-000-3996   (SL)
DERRICK DODGE (1980) LTD
6211 104 St Nw, Edmonton, AB, T6H 2K8
(780) 435-9500
Emp Here 240   *Sales* 138,540,480
SIC 5511 New and used car dealers
Lorne Isfeld
Bryon Isfeld
Al Backman

D-U-N-S 20-774-6947   (SL)
DEVONIAN MOTOR CORPORATION
RALLY SUBARU
5220 Gateway Blvd, Edmonton, AB, T6H 4J7
(780) 462-8846
Emp Here 35   *Sales* 17,432,730
SIC 5511 New and used car dealers
Cam Mcpherson

D-U-N-S 25-617-5287   (SL)
ECHELON FINANCIAL CORP
6328 104 St Nw 2nd Flr, Edmonton, AB, T6H
2K9
(780) 989-2777
Emp Here 18   *Sales* 13,202,136
SIC 6722 Management investment, open-end
Ron Sege

D-U-N-S 25-194-1225　　(BR)
HOME DEPOT OF CANADA INC
HOME DEPOT
(Suby of THE HOME DEPOT INC)
6725 104 St Nw, Edmonton, AB, T6H 2L3
(780) 431-4743
Emp Here 200
SIC 5251 Hardware stores
　Paddy Oneill

D-U-N-S 20-616-4931　　(BR)
HUDSON'S BAY COMPANY
BAY, THE
(Suby of HUDSON'S BAY COMPANY)
150 Southgate Shopping Ctr Nw, Edmonton, AB, T6H 4M7
(780) 435-9211
Emp Here 110
SIC 5311 Department stores
　Chuck Gerhart

D-U-N-S 24-038-7154　　(HQ)
INTELLIGENT IMAGING SYSTEMS, INC
DRIVEWYZE
6325 Gateway Blvd Nw Suite 170, Edmonton, AB, T6H 5H6
(780) 461-3355
Emp Here 70　　*Sales* 44,246,070
SIC 5099 Durable goods, nec
　Brian Heath
　Fred Ko

D-U-N-S 24-804-7941　　(BR)
ITALIAN CENTRE SHOP SOUTH LTD
(Suby of ITALIAN CENTRE SHOP SOUTH LTD)
5028 104a St Nw, Edmonton, AB, T6H 6A2
(780) 989-4869
Emp Here 100
SIC 5411 Grocery stores
　Joe Antonucci

D-U-N-S 24-894-4324　　(SL)
J & S BROKERAGE LTD
J & S DISTRIBUTORS
6040 Gateway Blvd Nw, Edmonton, AB, T6H 2H6
(780) 435-5446
Emp Here 22　　*Sales* 18,382,694
SIC 5141 Groceries, general line

D-U-N-S 24-732-8008　　(SL)
KOCH FORD LINCOLN SALES LTD
(Suby of KOCH SALES LTD)
5121 Gateway Blvd Nw, Edmonton, AB, T6H 5W5
(780) 434-8411
Emp Here 100　　*Sales* 62,928,000
SIC 5511 New and used car dealers
　Murray Koch
　Wayne Chesney
　Loris Koch

D-U-N-S 24-082-1665　　(SL)
LANSDOWNE I G A
5120 122 St Nw, Edmonton, AB, T6H 3S2
(780) 436-8387
Emp Here 43　　*Sales* 11,986,805
SIC 5411 Grocery stores

D-U-N-S 24-776-3597　　(HQ)
LIBERTY SECURITY SYSTEMS INC
5640 104 St Nw, Edmonton, AB, T6H 2K2
(780) 988-7233
Emp Here 10　　*Sales* 15,936,210
SIC 6211 Security brokers and dealers
　Nathan Bladry
　Russell Keddie

D-U-N-S 24-392-3281　　(BR)
LOBLAWS INC
REAL CANADIAN SUPERSTORE, THE
(Suby of LOBLAW COMPANIES LIMITED)
4821 Calgary Trail Nw Suite 1570, Edmonton, AB, T6H 5W8
(780) 430-2797
Emp Here 400
SIC 5411 Grocery stores

Aileen Jones

D-U-N-S 25-206-1247　　(SL)
MOUNTAIN VIEW LEASING INC
4916 Whitemud Rd Nw, Edmonton, AB, T6H 5M3
(780) 462-9600
Emp Here 65　　*Sales* 10,131,095
SIC 2452 Prefabricated wood buildings
　Lyle Lakusta

D-U-N-S 25-416-7018　　(SL)
MR. SNACK (1997) INC
6551 Gateway Blvd Nw, Edmonton, AB, T6H 2J1
(780) 414-0505
Emp Here 29　　*Sales* 24,231,733
SIC 5149 Groceries and related products, nec
　Kanwaljit Sidhu

D-U-N-S 24-005-3041　　(SL)
SAWMILL RESTAURANT GROUP LTD
SAWMILL RESTAURANT & LOUNGE
4810 Calgary Trail Nw, Edmonton, AB, T6H 5H5
(780) 463-4499
Emp Here 250　　*Sales* 11,659,750
SIC 5812 Eating places
　Tom Goodchild

D-U-N-S 20-812-3286　　(SL)
SILVERBIRCH NO. 38 OPERATIONS LIMITED PARTNERSHIP
RADISSON HOTEL EDMONTON SOUTH
4440 Gateway Blvd Nw, Edmonton, AB, T6H 5C2
(780) 437-6010
Emp Here 180　　*Sales* 16,684,200
SIC 7011 Hotels and motels
　Robin Cumine

D-U-N-S 25-012-8329　　(BR)
SUNTERRA ENTERPRISES INC
SUNTERRA MARKET PLACE
5728 111 St Nw, Edmonton, AB, T6H 3G1
(780) 434-2610
Emp Here 85
SIC 5411 Grocery stores
　Eric Graff

D-U-N-S 24-349-5756　　(SL)
TOUCH CANADA BROADCASTING INC
5316 Calgary Trail Nw, Edmonton, AB, T6H 4J8
(780) 469-5200
Emp Here 65　　*Sales* 12,011,870
SIC 4832 Radio broadcasting stations
　Charles Allard

D-U-N-S 25-267-8503　　(HQ)
TRUCK OUTFITTERS INC, THE
ACCESSORY WAREHOUSE
6525 Gateway Blvd Nw, Edmonton, AB, T6H 2J1
(780) 439-2360
Emp Here 7　　*Sales* 33,351,840
SIC 5531 Auto and home supply stores
　Fred Fishburne
　Jim White

Edmonton, AB T6J

D-U-N-S 20-918-4535　　(SL)
1140456 ALBERTA LTD
RE/MAX ACCORD
2852 Calgary Trail Nw, Edmonton, AB, T6J 6V7
(780) 485-5005
Emp Here 45　　*Sales* 14,720,715
SIC 6531 Real estate agents and managers
　Jeffrey Michaud
　Arnold Hickey

D-U-N-S 25-408-6374　　(SL)
742718 ALBERTA LTD
HOLIDAY INN THE PALACE

4235 Gateway Blvd Nw, Edmonton, AB, T6J 5H2
(780) 438-1222
Emp Here 78　　*Sales* 7,402,122
SIC 7011 Hotels and motels
　Peter Sikora

D-U-N-S 24-232-2613　　(BR)
ALBERTA HEALTH SERVICES
ST JOSEPHS AUXILIARY HOSPITAL
(Suby of GOVERNMENT OF THE PROVINCE OF ALBERTA)
10707 29 Ave Nw, Edmonton, AB, T6J 6W1
(780) 430-9110
Emp Here 200
SIC 8062 General medical and surgical hospitals
　Janet Eggert

D-U-N-S 20-809-4532　　(HQ)
ALBERTA MOTOR ASSOCIATION
10310a G A Macdonald Ave Nw, Edmonton, AB, T6J 6R7
(780) 430-5555
Emp Here 310　　*Sales* 2,157,901,500
SIC 8699 Membership organizations, nec
　Don Smitten

D-U-N-S 20-808-0432　　(SL)
DERRICK GOLF AND WINTER CLUB
3500 119 St Nw, Edmonton, AB, T6J 5P5
(780) 437-1833
Emp Here 150　　*Sales* 11,286,750
SIC 7997 Membership sports and recreation clubs
　Bruce Comeau
　Darren Crocker
　Mark Comeau
　Denis Rowley
　Tom Richards
　Jan Novotny
　John Nielsen

D-U-N-S 25-013-8021　　(BR)
EDMONTON CATHOLIC SEPARATE SCHOOL DISTRICT NO.7
LOUIS ST. LAURENT SCHOOL
(Suby of EDMONTON CATHOLIC SEPARATE SCHOOL DISTRICT NO.7)
11230 43 Ave Nw, Edmonton, AB, T6J 0X8
(780) 435-3964
Emp Here 82
SIC 8211 Elementary and secondary schools
　Tim Cusack

D-U-N-S 25-082-7490　　(HQ)
EYEWEAR PLACE LTD, THE
ALLIANCE CENTER
2065 111 St Nw, Edmonton, AB, T6J 4V9
(780) 433-4888
Emp Here 20　　*Sales* 13,024,000
SIC 5995 Optical goods stores
　Rob Miller

D-U-N-S 24-628-1927　　(SL)
FINESSE HOME LIVING INC
FINESSE FURNITURE
4210 Gateway Blvd Nw, Edmonton, AB, T6J 7K1
(780) 444-7100
Emp Here 50　　*Sales* 11,517,000
SIC 5712 Furniture stores
　Jack Saroukian
　George Saroukian
　Dorothy Saroukian
　Naoum Saroukian

D-U-N-S 25-453-8697　　(BR)
RED LOBSTER HOSPITALITY LLC
OLIVE GARDEN RESTAURANT
4110 Calgary Trl Nw, Edmonton, AB, T6J 6Y6
(780) 437-3434
Emp Here 110
SIC 5812 Eating places
　Chris Illing

D-U-N-S 25-453-8812　　(BR)
RED LOBSTER HOSPITALITY LLC

RED LOBSTER RESTAURANTS
4111 Calgary Trail Nw, Edmonton, AB, T6J 6S6
(780) 436-8510
Emp Here 80
SIC 5812 Eating places
　Colin Grant

D-U-N-S 24-584-7389　　(SL)
SISTERS OF CHARITY OF PROVIDENCE OF WESTERN CANADA, THE
SISTERS OF PROVIDENCE
3005 119 St Nw, Edmonton, AB, T6J 5R5
(780) 430-9491
Emp Here 100　　*Sales* 10,772,700
SIC 8661 Religious organizations
　Gloria Keylor

D-U-N-S 20-362-3686　　(BR)
SOBEYS CAPITAL INCORPORATED
HERITAGE SOBEYS
(Suby of EMPIRE COMPANY LIMITED)
2011 111 St Nw, Edmonton, AB, T6J 4V9
(780) 435-1224
Emp Here 150
SIC 5411 Grocery stores
　Wes Dagg

D-U-N-S 20-871-3540　　(BR)
SOBEYS WEST INC
SAFEWAY
(Suby of EMPIRE COMPANY LIMITED)
2304 109 St Nw, Edmonton, AB, T6J 3S8
(780) 430-4278
Emp Here 130
SIC 5411 Grocery stores

D-U-N-S 20-002-5083　　(BR)
SPEEDY CREEK (2011) LTD
CHILIS TEXAS GRILL
(Suby of SPEEDY CREEK (2011) LTD)
10333 34 Ave Nw, Edmonton, AB, T6J 6V1

Emp Here 100
SIC 5812 Eating places
　Fritz Dave

D-U-N-S 25-269-5580　　(SL)
STEVEN K. LEE AND CO. LTD
CANADIAN TIRE SOUTHPARK
3803 Calgary Trail Nw Suite 550, Edmonton, AB, T6J 5M8
(780) 438-4921
Emp Here 130　　*Sales* 58,525,610
SIC 7538 General automotive repair shops
　Steven Lee

Edmonton, AB T6K

D-U-N-S 20-738-1802　　(HQ)
COVENANT HEALTH
3033 66 St Nw, Edmonton, AB, T6K 4B2
(780) 735-9000
Sales 333,240,000
SIC 8062 General medical and surgical hospitals
　Patrick Dumelie
　Sheli Murphy
　Mary-Ann Clarkes

D-U-N-S 25-995-2257　　(SL)
M. & P. VARLEY ENTERPRISES LTD
CANADIAN TIRE
2331 66 St Nw Unit 200, Edmonton, AB, T6K 4B4
(780) 450-1800
Emp Here 100　　*Sales* 36,421,500
SIC 5014 Tires and tubes
　Mike Varley

D-U-N-S 20-293-5458　　(SL)
OSMAN GLOBAL TRADING LTD
AT-TAIBAH HALAL
3214 82 St Nw, Edmonton, AB, T6K 3Y3

---

(780) 757-8100
Emp Here 35   *Sales* 24,388,350
SIC 6799 Investors, nec
King Osman

D-U-N-S 24-392-3208   (HQ)
SHEPHERD'S CARE FOUNDATION
MILLWOODS SHEPARD'S CARE CENTRE
6620 28 Ave Nw, Edmonton, AB, T6K 2R1
(780) 463-9810
Emp Here 200   *Sales* 44,411,900
SIC 8051 Skilled nursing care facilities
John Pray

D-U-N-S 25-271-1049   (BR)
SOBEYS WEST INC
MILLBOURNE SAFEWAY
(*Suby of* EMPIRE COMPANY LIMITED)
38 Avenue & Millwoods Rd Suite 100, Edmonton, AB, T6K 3L6
(780) 462-4424
Emp Here 90
SIC 5411 Grocery stores
Walter Yu

D-U-N-S 24-065-0796   (BR)
SOBEYS WEST INC
SAFEWAY
(*Suby of* EMPIRE COMPANY LIMITED)
2331 66 St Nw Suite 341, Edmonton, AB, T6K 4B4
(780) 450-8180
Emp Here 120
SIC 5411 Grocery stores
Norm Thom

D-U-N-S 20-084-7960   (SL)
SOUTHTOWN CHRYSLER INC
4404 66 St Nw, Edmonton, AB, T6K 4E7
(780) 490-3200
Emp Here 100   *Sales* 62,928,000
SIC 5511 New and used car dealers
Michael Priestner

Edmonton, AB T6L

D-U-N-S 25-834-9927   (SL)
DYNAMEX INDUSTRIAL SUPPLY LTD
6558 28 Ave Nw Unit 295, Edmonton, AB, T6L 6N3
(780) 904-3451
Emp Here 44   *Sales* 20,901,144
SIC 5085 Industrial supplies
Shawn Holden
Steven Klaver
Jean Donnal

D-U-N-S 25-268-3545   (SL)
GRAY HOUSE GUILD, THE
ALLEN GRAY CONTINUING CARE CENTRE
5005 28 Ave Nw, Edmonton, AB, T6L 7G1
(780) 469-2371
Emp Here 219   *Sales* 14,963,394
SIC 8051 Skilled nursing care facilities
Charlotte Mcfadden

D-U-N-S 20-802-8410   (BR)
MCDONALD'S RESTAURANTS OF CANADA LIMITED
MCDONALD'S #8449
(*Suby of* MCDONALD'S CORPORATION)
5360 23 Ave Nw, Edmonton, AB, T6L 6X2
(780) 414-8449
Emp Here 100
SIC 5812 Eating places
Abdul Tunzamali

D-U-N-S 20-976-5903   (SL)
P D G (MILLWOODS GOOD SAMARITAN)
101 Youville Drive East Nw, Edmonton, AB, T6L 7A4
(780) 485-0816
Emp Here 119   *Sales* 8,142,218
SIC 8322 Individual and family services
Tamsin Walker

D-U-N-S 20-736-9450   (BR)
SOBEYS CAPITAL INCORPORATED
(*Suby of* EMPIRE COMPANY LIMITED)
5011 23 Ave Nw, Edmonton, AB, T6L 7G5
(780) 485-6622
Emp Here 180
SIC 5411 Grocery stores
Gary Aquino

Edmonton, AB T6N

D-U-N-S 24-627-9830   (SL)
338802 ALBERTA LTD
MILLWOODS BOTTLE DEPOT
2830 Parsons Rd Nw, Edmonton, AB, T6N 1H3
(780) 944-6922
Emp Here 45   *Sales* 20,214,855
SIC 7389 Business services, nec

D-U-N-S 20-272-7509   (BR)
A.R. THOMSON GROUP
(*Suby of* A.R. THOMSON GROUP)
10030 31 Ave Nw, Edmonton, AB, T6N 1G4
(780) 450-8080
Emp Here 100
SIC 3053 Gaskets; packing and sealing devices

D-U-N-S 25-409-3685   (HQ)
ALBERTA BOILERS SAFETY ASSOCIATION (ABSA)
ABSA THE PRESSURE EQUIPMENT SAFETY AUTHORITY
9410 20 Ave Nw, Edmonton, AB, T6N 0A4
(780) 437-9100
Emp Here 60   *Sales* 40,878,929
SIC 7389 Business services, nec
Allen Mccallister
Gordon Campbell
Winnie Wong

D-U-N-S 24-396-3758   (SL)
ARMOR MACHINE & MANUFACTURING LIMITED
9962 29 Ave Nw, Edmonton, AB, T6N 1A2
(780) 465-6152
Emp Here 70   *Sales* 15,540,070
SIC 3599 Industrial machinery, nec
Conrad St Jean

D-U-N-S 20-105-2573   (HQ)
BIONEUTRA GLOBAL CORPORATION
9608 25 Ave Nw, Edmonton, AB, T6N 1J4
(780) 466-1481
Sales 28,593,417
SIC 5149 Groceries and related products, nec
Jianhua Zhu
Bill Smith
Darren John Kostiw
Lei Ling
Warren Michaels
Kent Wang
Warren M. Cabral
Timothy Lee
James Li
Jon Havelock

D-U-N-S 25-417-1069   (HQ)
C-FER TECHNOLOGIES (1999) INC
200 Karl Clark Rd Nw, Edmonton, AB, T6N 1H2
(780) 450-3300
Sales 20,279,200
SIC 8748 Business consulting, nec
Francisco Alhanati

D-U-N-S 24-068-3524   (HQ)
CHANDOS CONSTRUCTION LTD
9604 20 Ave Nw, Edmonton, AB, T6N 1G1
(780) 436-8617
Emp Here 40   *Sales* 192,057,800
SIC 1542 Nonresidential construction, nec
Tom Redl

Roger Babichuk

D-U-N-S 20-338-0811   (BR)
CINEPLEX ENTERTAINMENT LIMITED PARTNERSHIP
THE REC ROOM
(*Suby of* CINEPLEX INC)
1725 99 St Nw, Edmonton, AB, T6N 1K5
(587) 585-3760
Emp Here 300
SIC 7999 Amusement and recreation, nec
Dave Terry

D-U-N-S 20-004-3284   (BR)
CINEPLEX ODEON CORPORATION
CINEPLEX CINEMAS SOUTH EDMONTON
(*Suby of* CINEPLEX INC)
1525 99 St Nw, Edmonton, AB, T6N 1K5
(780) 436-3675
Emp Here 95
SIC 7832 Motion picture theaters, except drive-in
Jeff Simmons

D-U-N-S 20-081-3673   (BR)
COCA-COLA CANADA BOTTLING LIMITED
(*Suby of* COCA-COLA CANADA BOTTLING LIMITED)
9621 27 Ave Nw, Edmonton, AB, T6N 1E7
(780) 450-2653
Emp Here 200
SIC 2086 Bottled and canned soft drinks
Jim White

D-U-N-S 24-282-6964   (HQ)
COMPANY'S COMING PUBLISHING LIMITED
(*Suby of* PARE, JEAN HOLDINGS LTD)
2311 96 St Nw, Edmonton, AB, T6N 1G3
(780) 450-6223
Sales 11,317,863
SIC 2731 Book publishing
Grant Lovig
Jean Pare

D-U-N-S 24-330-1280   (HQ)
CSM COMPRESSOR INC
9330 27 Ave Nw, Edmonton, AB, T6N 1B2
(780) 435-5722
Emp Here 40   *Sales* 12,232,890
SIC 7699 Repair services, nec
Chris Machan

D-U-N-S 24-203-1834   (SL)
DETON'CHO / NUNA JOINT VENTURE
9839 31 Ave Nw, Edmonton, AB, T6N 1C5
(780) 434-9114
Emp Here 70   *Sales* 16,861,880
SIC 1629 Heavy construction, nec
Mervyn Hempenstall
Pam Alloway

D-U-N-S 24-684-8878   (HQ)
FEEL LIKE TALKING CONNECTIONS LTD
9848 33 Ave Nw, Edmonton, AB, T6N 1C6
(780) 465-6055
Emp Here 6   *Sales* 11,087,880
SIC 4899 Communication services, nec
Reshamdeep Mundy
Savi Kachroo

D-U-N-S 24-785-9747   (SL)
FOREVER IN DOUGH INC
BOSTON PIZZA
9804 22 Ave Nw, Edmonton, AB, T6N 1L1
(780) 463-9086
Emp Here 75   *Sales* 3,413,925
SIC 5812 Eating places
Samira Shariff

D-U-N-S 20-895-5831   (SL)
GREENOUGH, L C CONSTRUCTION LTD
2503 Parsons Rd Nw, Edmonton, AB, T6N 1B8
(780) 463-4977
Emp Here 40   *Sales* 18,829,240
SIC 1542 Nonresidential construction, nec
Gary Greenough

Donna Greenough

D-U-N-S 20-809-5117   (HQ)
HERBERS AUTO BODY REPAIR LTD
2721 Parsons Rd Nw, Edmonton, AB, T6N 1B8
(780) 469-8888
Emp Here 25   *Sales* 57,175,019
SIC 7532 Top and body repair and paint shops
Collin Herbers
Henry Herbers

D-U-N-S 25-514-3208   (BR)
HOME DEPOT OF CANADA INC
HOME DEPOT
(*Suby of* THE HOME DEPOT INC)
2020 101 St Nw, Edmonton, AB, T6N 1J2
(780) 433-6370
Emp Here 200
SIC 1522 Residential construction, nec
Fritz Jean-Louis

D-U-N-S 20-059-7826   (BR)
HUDSON'S BAY COMPANY
HOME OUTFITTERS
(*Suby of* HUDSON'S BAY COMPANY)
9738 19 Ave Nw, Edmonton, AB, T6N 1K6
(780) 414-5850
Emp Here 100
SIC 5311 Department stores
Paul Hojka

D-U-N-S 20-651-7588   (BR)
IKEA LIMITED
IKEA CANADA
(*Suby of* STICHTING INGKA FOUNDATION)
1311 102 St Nw, Edmonton, AB, T6N 1M3
(866) 866-4532
Emp Here 300
SIC 5712 Furniture stores
Russenhol Jeff

D-U-N-S 25-235-7496   (HQ)
INLAND INDUSTRIAL SUPPLY LTD
9949 29a Ave Nw, Edmonton, AB, T6N 1A9
(780) 413-0029
Emp Here 44   *Sales* 23,751,300
SIC 5085 Industrial supplies
Gordon Dixon

D-U-N-S 24-393-4762   (HQ)
INNOTECH ALBERTA INC
(*Suby of* GOVERNMENT OF THE PROVINCE OF ALBERTA)
250 Karl Clark Rd, Edmonton, AB, T6N 1E4
(780) 450-5111
Emp Here 300   *Sales* 112,245,100
SIC 8733 Noncommercial research organizations
Ross Chow

D-U-N-S 20-807-3981   (SL)
INTERNATIONAL COOLING TOWER INC
ICT
3310 93 St Nw, Edmonton, AB, T6N 1C7
(780) 469-4900
Emp Here 300   *Sales* 26,908,800
SIC 7699 Repair services, nec
Doug Baron
Min Hafso
Laurel Baron
Brent Middleton
Tary Raposo

D-U-N-S 24-333-1316   (BR)
KEG RESTAURANTS LTD
KEG STEAKHOUSE & BAR, THE
(*Suby of* RECIPE UNLIMITED CORPORATION)
1631 102 St Nw, Edmonton, AB, T6N 1M3
(780) 485-6530
Emp Here 112
SIC 5812 Eating places
Owen Abrams

D-U-N-S 25-832-1074   (BR)
KONICA MINOLTA BUSINESS SOLUTIONS (CANADA) LTD

KONICA MINOLTA
(*Suby of* KONICA MINOLTA, INC.)
9651 25 Ave Nw, Edmonton, AB, T6N 1H7
(780) 465-6232
Emp Here 95
SIC 5044 Office equipment
 Mel Kunico

D-U-N-S 20-059-8857   (BR)
LOBLAWS INC
REAL CANADIAN-SUPERSTORES
(*Suby of* LOBLAW COMPANIES LIMITED)
9711 23 Ave Nw, Edmonton, AB, T6N 1K7
(780) 490-3935
Emp Here 100
SIC 5141 Groceries, general line
 Suzanne Turner

D-U-N-S 24-983-4011   (HQ)
LOGICAN TECHNOLOGIES INC
150 Karl Clark Rd Nw, Edmonton, AB, T6N 1E2
(780) 450-4400
Emp Here 158   *Sales* 30,470,720
SIC 3679 Electronic components, nec
 Michael Melle

D-U-N-S 20-305-4119   (BR)
LOWE'S COMPANIES CANADA, ULC
(*Suby of* LOWE'S COMPANIES, INC.)
10141 13 Ave Nw, Edmonton, AB, T6N 0B6
(780) 430-1344
Emp Here 140
SIC 5211 Lumber and other building materials
 Duane Oldham

D-U-N-S 24-982-4129   (SL)
MACHAN CONSULTING SERVICES LTD
9330 27 Ave Nw, Edmonton, AB, T6N 1B2
(780) 435-5722
Emp Here 1   *Sales* 20,967,750
SIC 6712 Bank holding companies
 Tim Lillak

D-U-N-S 24-522-1080   (SL)
MICRALYNE INC
(*Suby of* FTC TECHNOLOGIES INC)
1911 94 St Nw, Edmonton, AB, T6N 1E6
(780) 431-4400
Emp Here 95   *Sales* 18,091,990
SIC 3674 Semiconductors and related devices
 John Harley
 Dan Djukich
 Stephen Bonham
 Darrell Mathison

D-U-N-S 24-014-0793   (SL)
MONTANA'S COOKHOUSE SALOON
1720 99 St Nw, Edmonton, AB, T6N 1M5
(780) 466-8520
Emp Here 90   *Sales* 4,096,710
SIC 5812 Eating places
 Alicia Parson

D-U-N-S 20-981-5422   (BR)
NEWLY WEDS FOODS CO.
NEWLY WEDS FOODS
(*Suby of* NEWLY WEDS FOODS, INC.)
9110 23 Ave Nw, Edmonton, AB, T6N 1H9
(780) 414-9500
Emp Here 120
SIC 2099 Food preparations, nec
 Julie Prokuda

D-U-N-S 20-268-0448   (SL)
NUNA CONTRACTING LTD
9839 31 Ave Nw, Edmonton, AB, T6N 1C5
(780) 434-9114
Emp Here 250   *Sales* 53,094,000
SIC 1794 Excavation work
 Mervyn Hempenstall
 Pam Alloway
 Robert Gilroy
 John Zigarlick
 Courtland Smith

D-U-N-S 24-807-9741   (HQ)
PARKLAND RESPIRATORY CARE LTD

3152 Parsons Rd Nw, Edmonton, AB, T6N 1L6
(780) 430-8999
Emp Here 14   *Sales* 18,258,625
SIC 5169 Chemicals and allied products, nec
 Margeret Tse

D-U-N-S 20-921-1338   (BR)
PUROLATOR INC
(*Suby of* GOVERNMENT OF CANADA)
3104 97 St Nw, Edmonton, AB, T6N 1K3
(780) 408-2420
Emp Here 110
SIC 7389 Business services, nec
 John Troung

D-U-N-S 25-370-7947   (BR)
RANCHO REALTY (EDMONTON) LTD
QUALICO DEVELOPMENT WEST
(*Suby of* RANCHO MANAGEMENT SERVICES CORPORATION)
3203 93 St Nw Suite 300, Edmonton, AB, T6N 0B2
(780) 463-2132
Emp Here 80
SIC 6553 Cemetery subdividers and developers
 Shane Erikson

D-U-N-S 24-364-0690   (SL)
RODA DEACO VALVE INC
(*Suby of* ROPER TECHNOLOGIES, INC.)
3230 97 St Nw, Edmonton, AB, T6N 1K4
(780) 465-4429
Emp Here 50   *Sales* 10,141,500
SIC 3491 Industrial valves
 Denise Green

D-U-N-S 20-014-0544   (BR)
SCHLUMBERGER CANADA LIMITED
DBR TECHNOLOGY CENTER DIVISION
9450 17 Ave Nw, Edmonton, AB, T6N 1M9

Emp Here 95
SIC 3821 Laboratory apparatus and furniture
 Matteo Niloletti

D-U-N-S 20-288-4979   (SL)
SDS INDUSTRIAL BUILDING SUPPLIES LTD
SHOEMAKER DRYWALL SUPPLIES
2920 101 St Nw, Edmonton, AB, T6N 1A6
(780) 224-8058
Emp Here 47   *Sales* 21,017,178
SIC 5039 Construction materials, nec
 John Langdon

D-U-N-S 20-809-5828   (HQ)
SERVUS CREDIT UNION LTD
SERVUS CREDIT UNION
151 Karl Clark Rd Nw, Edmonton, AB, T6N 1H5
(780) 496-2000
Emp Here 450   *Sales* 409,922,400
SIC 6062 State credit unions
 Garth Warner
 Taras Nohas
 Ian Glassford
 Caroline Ziober
 Dan Bruinooge
 Darcy Peelar
 Gail Stepanik-Keber
 Yves Auger

D-U-N-S 24-855-1202   (HQ)
SOMAGEN DIAGNOSTICS INC
(*Suby of* DIPLOMA PLC)
9220 25 Ave Nw, Edmonton, AB, T6N 1E1
(780) 702-9500
Sales 32,121,120
SIC 5049 Professional equipment, nec
 Thomas Brown
 Kevin Blackburn
 Craig Gardiner
 Debbie Johnson

D-U-N-S 24-809-7768   (SL)
STERLING HOMES (EDMONTON) LTD

(*Suby of* QUALICO GROUP LTD)
3203 93 St Nw, Edmonton, AB, T6N 0B2
(780) 461-8369
Emp Here 35   *Sales* 16,685,970
SIC 1531 Operative builders
 Miles Kohan

D-U-N-S 24-423-5938   (BR)
SYNCRUDE CANADA LTD
EDMONTON RESEARCH CENTRE
(*Suby of* SUNCOR ENERGY INC)
9421 17 Ave Nw, Edmonton, AB, T6N 1H4
(780) 970-6800
Emp Here 100
SIC 8731 Commercial physical research
 Gary Brennan

D-U-N-S 24-391-2185   (SL)
TEAM FORD SALES LIMITED
3304 91 St Nw, Edmonton, AB, T6N 1C1
(780) 462-8300
Emp Here 105   *Sales* 66,074,400
SIC 5511 New and used car dealers
 Mike Priestner

D-U-N-S 24-776-2938   (BR)
THOMSON, A R LTD
10030 31 Ave Nw, Edmonton, AB, T6N 1G4
(780) 450-8080
Emp Here 100
SIC 6712 Bank holding companies
 Shane Boyle

D-U-N-S 20-183-0200   (HQ)
TOPCO OILSITE PRODUCTS LTD
TOPCO MFG RECERTIFICATION CENTRE, DIV OF
9519 28 Ave Nw, Edmonton, AB, T6N 0A3
(800) 222-6448
Emp Here 25   *Sales* 53,814,320
SIC 1389 Oil and gas field services, nec
 Alan Huehn

D-U-N-S 25-218-9972   (BR)
WAL-MART CANADA CORP
(*Suby of* WALMART INC.)
1203 Parsons Rd Nw Suite 3029, Edmonton, AB, T6N 0A9
(780) 468-1755
Emp Here 365
SIC 5311 Department stores
 Gige Pucci

D-U-N-S 25-684-6114   (BR)
WENZEL DOWNHOLE TOOLS LTD
MANUFACTURING / SALES FACILITIES
(*Suby of* BASIN HOLDINGS LLC)
3115 93 St Nw, Edmonton, AB, T6N 1L7
(780) 440-4220
Emp Here 120
SIC 3533 Oil and gas field machinery
 Michael Jamieson

D-U-N-S 24-582-8199   (HQ)
WIKA INSTRUMENTS LTD
(*Suby of* WIKA ALEXANDER WIEGAND SE & CO. KG)
3103 Parsons Rd Nw, Edmonton, AB, T6N 1C8
(780) 438-6662
Emp Here 133   *Sales* 37,502,685
SIC 3823 Process control instruments
 Colin Brook
 Matt Matia

Edmonton, AB T6P

D-U-N-S 20-113-6772   (HQ)
1688150 ALBERTA LTD
PEGASUS PAPER WAREHOUSE
2004 80 Ave Nw, Edmonton, AB, T6P 1N2
(780) 462-4430
Emp Here 20   *Sales* 11,400,624
SIC 5087 Service establishment equipment
 Brian Blacklock

 Wayne Leong

D-U-N-S 24-384-9325   (HQ)
993106 ALBERTA LTD
1444 78 Ave Nw, Edmonton, AB, T6P 1L7
(780) 438-5930
Emp Here 40   *Sales* 236,454,600
SIC 5172 Petroleum products, nec
 Parker Mclean
 Kim Mclean

D-U-N-S 24-984-2345   (SL)
ACTION ELECTRICAL LTD
(*Suby of* BUNTING HOLDINGS CO LTD)
2333 91 Ave, Edmonton, AB, T6P 1L1
(780) 465-0792
Emp Here 75   *Sales* 16,337,175
SIC 1731 Electrical work
 Donald Bunting
 Grace Bunting

D-U-N-S 24-598-1329   (HQ)
ACUREN GROUP INC
(*Suby of* ROCKWOOD SERVICE CORPORATION)
7450 18 St Nw, Edmonton, AB, T6P 1N8
(780) 440-2131
Emp Here 1,000   *Sales* 224,490,200
SIC 8734 Testing laboratories
 Peter Scannell
 Fran Pimentel

D-U-N-S 24-928-3763   (HQ)
AFD PETROLEUM LTD
ALBERTA FUEL
(*Suby of* 993106 ALBERTA LTD)
1444 78 Ave Nw, Edmonton, AB, T6P 1L7
(780) 438-5930
Emp Here 32   *Sales* 70,403,256
SIC 5172 Petroleum products, nec
 Parker Mclean

D-U-N-S 24-853-0818   (SL)
ALBERTA ENVIROFUELS INC
9511 17 St Nw, Edmonton, AB, T6P 1Y3
(780) 449-7800
Emp Here 100   *Sales* 23,343,500
SIC 2911 Petroleum refining
 Dave Groenendyk

D-U-N-S 24-949-6233   (SL)
ALBERTA EXCHANGER LTD
2210 70 Ave Nw, Edmonton, AB, T6P 1N6
(780) 440-1045
Emp Here 85   *Sales* 23,106,570
SIC 7699 Repair services, nec
 Guy Kjosness
 Clare Kjosness

D-U-N-S 20-439-0926   (SL)
ALBERTA TRUSS LTD
2140 Railway St Nw, Edmonton, AB, T6P 1X3
(780) 464-5551
Emp Here 30   *Sales* 13,415,220
SIC 5031 Lumber, plywood, and millwork
 David Foreman

D-U-N-S 24-088-1631   (HQ)
ARRKANN TRAILER & SPORT CENTRE LTD
1904 80 Ave Nw, Edmonton, AB, T6P 1N2
(780) 440-4811
Sales 13,844,160
SIC 5561 Recreational vehicle dealers
 Kenneth Friedenberg

D-U-N-S 20-537-7989   (HQ)
ATS TRAFFIC - ALBERTA LTD
(*Suby of* ATS TRAFFIC-BRITISH COLUMBIA LTD)
9015 14 St Nw, Edmonton, AB, T6P 0C9
(780) 440-4114
Emp Here 75   *Sales* 32,613,600
SIC 3993 Signs and advertising specialties
 Lorne Hooper
 Laine Hooper
 Prosper Boisvert

▲ Public Company   ■ Public Company Family Member   **HQ** Headquarters   **BR** Branch   **SL** Single Location

D-U-N-S 20-262-4201   (HQ)
ATS TRAFFIC GROUP LTD
9015 14 St Nw, Edmonton, AB, T6P 0C9
(780) 440-4114
Sales 34,093,350
SIC 3812 Search and navigation equipment
Laine Hooper

D-U-N-S 24-714-9073   (HQ)
ATS TRAFFIC-BRITISH COLUMBIA LTD
7798 16 St Nw, Edmonton, AB, T6P 1L9
(780) 440-4114
Emp Here 6   *Sales* 84,874,500
SIC 3669 Communications equipment, nec
Lorne J Hooper
Van Sielhader

D-U-N-S 24-573-0002   (SL)
CANADIAN DEWATERING (2006) LTD
(*Suby of* MT-U OPERATING COMPANY INC)
8350 1 St Nw, Edmonton, AB, T6P 1X2
(780) 400-2260
Emp Here 250   *Sales* 121,932,500
SIC 5084 Industrial machinery and equipment
Clayton Kammer

D-U-N-S 24-338-1618   (HQ)
CANADIAN DEWATERING L.P.
(*Suby of* MULLEN GROUP LTD)
8350 1 St Nw, Edmonton, AB, T6P 1X2
(780) 400-2260
Emp Here 50   *Sales* 121,932,500
SIC 5084 Industrial machinery and equipment
Dale Marchand
Shaun Fielding
Mary Ellen Vandusen

D-U-N-S 24-040-2318   (SL)
CANADIAN INDUSTRIAL PARAMEDICS
CIP
8917 13 St Nw, Edmonton, AB, T6P 0C7
(780) 467-4262
Emp Here 250   *Sales* 19,198,000
SIC 8322 Individual and family services
Barry Croft

D-U-N-S 24-209-7129   (HQ)
CAPITAL INDUSTRIAL SALES & SERVICE LTD
851 77 Ave Nw, Edmonton, AB, T6P 1S9
(780) 440-4467
Emp Here 27   *Sales* 23,751,300
SIC 5084 Industrial machinery and equipment
Ronald Eade
Marie Eade

D-U-N-S 25-678-6005   (SL)
CLEARWATER FABRICATION GP INC
CLEARWATER FABRICATION
5710 17 St Nw, Edmonton, AB, T6P 1S4
(780) 464-4230
Emp Here 150   *Sales* 36,927,900
SIC 1791 Structural steel erection
Alan Clark
Chris Cloutier
Douglas Golosky

D-U-N-S 20-808-9656 ·   (SL)
CONTINENTAL ELECTRICAL MOTOR SER-VICES (NORTHERN) LTD
CONTINENTAL GROUP
8909 15 St Nw, Edmonton, AB, T6P 0B8
(780) 410-8800
Emp Here 60   *Sales* 16,310,520
SIC 7694 Armature rewinding shops
Robert Baker

D-U-N-S 24-766-3644   (HQ)
COUGAR DRILLING SOLUTIONS INC
COUGAR TOOL
7319 17 St Nw, Edmonton, AB, T6P 1P1
(780) 440-2400
Sales 23,320,360
SIC 7353 Heavy construction equipment rental
Greg Mittelsteadt
Blaine Labonte
David Case

Kent Wilkinson
Graham Goodall
Dan Marson

D-U-N-S 24-352-2310   (BR)
CWS INDUSTRIES (MFG) CORP
(*Suby of* CWS INDUSTRIES (MFG) CORP)
7622 18 St Nw, Edmonton, AB, T6P 1Y6
(780) 469-9185
Emp Here 102
SIC 3545 Machine tool accessories
Earl Hirtz

D-U-N-S 20-809-6982   (HQ)
DFI CORPORATION
DFI
(*Suby of* FREELAND HOLDINGS INC)
2404 51 Ave Nw, Edmonton, AB, T6P 0E4
(780) 466-5237
Emp Here 78   *Sales* 19,952,680
SIC 3312 Blast furnaces and steel mills
David Alexander Freeland
Barry Strauss
Sean Freeland

D-U-N-S 20-181-2364   (BR)
DNOW CANADA ULC
DISTRIBUTIONNOW
(*Suby of* NOW INC.)
2603 76 Ave Nw, Edmonton, AB, T6P 1P6
(780) 944-1000
Emp Here 100
SIC 5084 Industrial machinery and equipment
Nan Mifflin

D-U-N-S 20-082-1007   (BR)
DNOW CANADA ULC
(*Suby of* NOW INC.)
2603 76 Ave Nw, Edmonton, AB, T6P 1P6
(780) 944-1000
Emp Here 100
SIC 5084 Industrial machinery and equipment
Daryl Campbel

D-U-N-S 25-217-5617   (SL)
DYNA-FLO CONTROL VALVE SERVICES LTD
1911 66 Ave Nw, Edmonton, AB, T6P 1M5
(780) 469-4000
Emp Here 80   *Sales* 38,002,080
SIC 5085 Industrial supplies
Cam B. Robinson
Mike J. Homeniuk

D-U-N-S 20-050-6462   (HQ)
E CONSTRUCTION LTD
RUEL BROS. CONTRACTING
(*Suby of* BOUYGUES)
10130 21 St Nw, Edmonton, AB, T6P 1W7
(780) 467-7701
Sales 12,622,100
SIC 1611 Highway and street construction
D.K.(Douglas) Ellett
Dave Manchakowski
Darryl Zaharichuk

D-U-N-S 20-107-6291   (BR)
EMCO CORPORATION
(*Suby of* HAJOCA CORPORATION)
3011 101 Ave Nw, Edmonton, AB, T6P 1X7
(780) 440-7333
Emp Here 100
SIC 5074 Plumbing and heating equipment and supplies (hydronics)
Rob Tinaglai

D-U-N-S 25-389-3911   (HQ)
F I OILFIELD SERVICES CANADA ULC
(*Suby of* FRANK'S INTERNATIONAL N.V.)
2880 64 Ave Nw, Edmonton, AB, T6P 1W6
(780) 463-3333
Emp Here 35   *Sales* 84,084,875
SIC 1389 Oil and gas field services, nec
Gord Robb

D-U-N-S 24-394-8247   (SL)
FIBREWALL CANADA LTD
FIBRE DECOR

1309 77 Ave Nw, Edmonton, AB, T6P 1M8
(780) 945-0561
Emp Here 60   *Sales* 44,551,200
SIC 5198 Paints, varnishes, and supplies

D-U-N-S 20-271-7500   (SL)
GLOBAL ALLOY PIPE AND SUPPLY, INC
BRI-STEEL DISTRIBUTION
2125 64 Ave Nw, Edmonton, AB, T6P 1Z4
(780) 469-6603
Emp Here 10   *Sales* 10,003,390
SIC 5051 Metals service centers and offices
Neil Rasmussen
Rahul Shah

D-U-N-S 24-858-3663   (SL)
GOLDBAR CONTRACTORS INC
1415 90 Ave Nw Suite 100, Edmonton, AB, T6P 0C8
(780) 440-6440
Emp Here 90   *Sales* 33,284,025
SIC 1711 Plumbing, heating, air-conditioning
Eldon Campbell
David Theodore Reinholt

D-U-N-S 24-892-0022   (SL)
HAMILTON METALS CANADA, LLC
3215 76 Ave Nw, Edmonton, AB, T6P 1T4
(587) 881-3921
Emp Here 10   *Sales* 10,003,390
SIC 5051 Metals service centers and offices
James Millman

D-U-N-S 24-785-3740   (HQ)
INSITUFORM TECHNOLOGIES LIMITED
(*Suby of* AEGION CORPORATION)
7605 18 St Nw, Edmonton, AB, T6P 1N9
(780) 413-0200
Sales 28,849,200
SIC 7699 Repair services, nec
Kenneth Foster

D-U-N-S 24-533-7733   (SL)
JACOBS INDUSTRIAL SERVICES
(*Suby of* JACOBS ENGINEERING GROUP INC.)
1104 70 Ave Nw, Edmonton, AB, T6P 1P5
(780) 468-2533
Emp Here 5,000   *Sales* 159,840,000
SIC 7349 Building maintenance services, nec
Earl Mitchell

D-U-N-S 20-047-2541   (SL)
KLEWCHUK CONSTRUCTION LTD
503 69 Ave Nw, Edmonton, AB, T6P 0C2

Emp Here 48   *Sales* 15,305,712
SIC 1521 Single-family housing construction
Larry Klewchuk

D-U-N-S 24-852-6741   (SL)
KOR-ALTA CONSTRUCTION LTD
2461 76 Ave Nw, Edmonton, AB, T6P 1Y8
(780) 440-6661
Emp Here 45   *Sales* 21,182,895
SIC 1542 Nonresidential construction, nec
Ralph Corbett
Kenneth Corbett
Theodore Commandeur

D-U-N-S 24-880-1243   (SL)
LEXON PROJECTS INC
2327 91 Ave Nw, Edmonton, AB, T6P 1L1
(780) 435-7476
Emp Here 42   *Sales* 21,577,023
SIC 1542 Nonresidential construction, nec
Harold Steinbrenner
Christopher Ryan Steinbrenner

D-U-N-S 20-629-0616   (HQ)
LINK SCAFFOLD SERVICES INC
2102 102 Ave Nw, Edmonton, AB, T6P 1W3
(780) 449-6111
Emp Here 97   *Sales* 36,927,900
SIC 1799 Special trade contractors, nec
Porfirio Simoes

D-U-N-S 24-089-9666   (SL)

M & Z INDUSTRIAL SUPPLY LTD
7823 25 St Nw, Edmonton, AB, T6P 1N4
(780) 440-2737
Emp Here 46   *Sales* 18,057,672
SIC 5085 Industrial supplies
Phillip Zaboroski
Ernest Christman
Jonathan Drew Schofield
Dan Kupchenko

D-U-N-S 24-394-1127   (HQ)
MANUS ABRASIVE SYSTEMS INC
(*Suby of* MARCO GROUP INTERNATIONAL, INC.)
1040 78 Ave Nw, Edmonton, AB, T6P 1L7
(780) 468-2588
Emp Here 25   *Sales* 19,951,092
SIC 5085 Industrial supplies
Cory Maclean
Marilyn Maclean

D-U-N-S 20-070-4158   (BR)
MAPLE LEAF FOODS INC
MAPLE LEAF POULTRY
(*Suby of* MAPLE LEAF FOODS INC)
2619 91 Ave Nw, Edmonton, AB, T6P 1S3
(780) 467-6022
Emp Here 380
SIC 2015 Poultry slaughtering and processing
Ian Bellett

D-U-N-S 20-437-5380   (SL)
MASTER MECHANICAL PLUMBING & HEATING (1986) LTD
2107 87 Ave Nw, Edmonton, AB, T6P 1L5
(780) 449-1400
Emp Here 80   *Sales* 18,645,200
SIC 1711 Plumbing, heating, air-conditioning
Gary Gellhaus
Wayne Gellhaus
William S Strong

D-U-N-S 24-002-1824   (HQ)
NILEX INC
6810 8 St Nw, Edmonton, AB, T6P 0C5
(780) 463-9535
Emp Here 68   *Sales* 112,229,422
SIC 5131 Piece goods and notions
Glenn Leroux
Ed Mah

D-U-N-S 20-511-8131   (HQ)
OLD HIPPY WOOD PRODUCTS INC
2415 80 Ave Nw, Edmonton, AB, T6P 1N3
(780) 448-1163
Emp Here 25   *Sales* 12,721,400
SIC 5021 Furniture
Dean Phillips
Joanne Armstrong

D-U-N-S 20-083-6765   (HQ)
OSTREM CHEMICAL COMPANY LTD
2310 80 Ave Nw, Edmonton, AB, T6P 1N2
(780) 440-1911
Emp Here 33   *Sales* 10,236,420
SIC 2842 Polishes and sanitation goods
Roar Tungland
Marilyn Tungland

D-U-N-S 24-701-0523   (SL)
PIONEER TRUCK LINES LTD
8321 1 St Nw, Edmonton, AB, T6P 1X2
(780) 467-8880
Emp Here 120   *Sales* 80,721,480
SIC 1389 Oil and gas field services, nec
Dale Dubinsky
Miles Dubinsky

D-U-N-S 24-004-0394   (SL)
PITBULL ENERGY SERVICES INC
2424 91 Ave Nw, Edmonton, AB, T6P 1K9
(780) 757-1688
Emp Here 50   *Sales* 10,506,550
SIC 1389 Oil and gas field services, nec
Sami Hayek

D-U-N-S 20-287-2750   (SL)
POWER EXPRESS

303 69 Ave Nw, Edmonton, AB, T6P 0C2
(780) 461-4000
Emp Here 49   *Sales* 18,882,640
SIC 4731 Freight transportation arrangement
Lawrence Zdrill

D-U-N-S 20-773-9546   (HQ)
PRO-ROD INC
(*Suby of* APERGY CORPORATION)
3201 84 Ave Nw Suite 3201, Edmonton, AB,
T6P 1K1
(780) 449-7101
Sales 14,511,040
SIC 3354 Aluminum extruded products
Andre Hebert

D-U-N-S 24-423-6907   (HQ)
PROCRANE INC
STERLING CRANE DIV.
(*Suby of* BERKSHIRE HATHAWAY INC.)
2440 76 Ave Nw, Edmonton, AB, T6P 1J5
(780) 440-4434
Emp Here 140   *Sales* 221,928,200
SIC 7353 Heavy construction equipment
rental
Ben Pieyre

D-U-N-S 20-895-2440   (HQ)
PSL PARTITION SYSTEMS LTD
PARTITION SYSTEMS
1105 70 Ave Nw, Edmonton, AB, T6P 1N5
(780) 465-0001
Emp Here 45   *Sales* 10,932,359
SIC 3275 Gypsum products
Mark Lindeman
Tom Gilmore

D-U-N-S 20-636-6239   (SL)
RED CARPET TRANSPORT LTD
TOMMY'S TRANSPORT, DIV OF
6303 18 St Nw, Edmonton, AB, T6P 0B6
(780) 463-3936
Emp Here 35   *Sales* 14,677,425
SIC 6712 Bank holding companies
Tom Cutts
Ann Cutts

D-U-N-S 24-380-1821   (HQ)
RELIANCE METALS CANADA LIMITED
EARLE M. JORGENSEN (CANADA), DIV OF
(*Suby of* RELIANCE STEEL & ALUMINUM
CO.)
6925 8 St Nw, Edmonton, AB, T6P 1T9
(780) 801-4114
Emp Here 6   *Sales* 139,804,236
SIC 5051 Metals service centers and offices
David Sapunjis
David Hannah
Gregg Mollins

D-U-N-S 24-714-9123   (HQ)
RIG SHOP LIMITED, THE
1704 66 Ave Nw, Edmonton, AB, T6P 1M4
(780) 440-4202
Emp Here 50   *Sales* 15,984,072
SIC 3533 Oil and gas field machinery
James Clish

D-U-N-S 20-594-5173   (HQ)
ROSENAU TRANSPORT LTD
(*Suby of* MID-NITE SUN TRANSPORTATION
LTD)
3300 76 Ave Nw, Edmonton, AB, T6P 1J4
(780) 431-2877
Emp Here 35   *Sales* 99,565,740
SIC 4213 Trucking, except local
Ken Rosenau
Rodney Rosenau
Timothy Rosenau
Valerie Stevenson
Ken Rosenau
Patricia Young

D-U-N-S 24-242-1803   (SL)
SCORE (CANADA) LIMITED
(*Suby of* SCORE GROUP PLC)
9192 14 St Nw, Edmonton, AB, T6P 0B7

(780) 455-5273
Emp Here 60   *Sales* 40,360,740
SIC 1389 Oil and gas field services, nec
Nelson Ritchie
Robert Murdoch
Jonathan Hargreaves

D-U-N-S 25-626-4037   (BR)
SHAWCOR LTD
SHAW PIPE PROTECTION
(*Suby of* SHAWCOR LTD)
10275 21 St Nw, Edmonton, AB, T6P 1P3
(780) 467-5501
Emp Here 80
SIC 3479 Metal coating and allied services
Kelvin Wiebe

D-U-N-S 24-370-7416   (HQ)
SHERWOOD STEEL LTD
3303 84 Ave Nw, Edmonton, AB, T6P 1K1
(780) 449-6548
Emp Here 1   *Sales* 10,732,176
SIC 5051 Metals service centers and offices
Hank Kotun
Claire Kotun

D-U-N-S 25-083-8968   (HQ)
SILENT AIRE MANUFACTURING INC
7107 8 St Nw, Edmonton, AB, T6P 1T9
(780) 456-1061
Sales 112,350,800
SIC 3585 Refrigeration and heating equip-
ment
Daniel Leckelt
Lindsey Leckelt

D-U-N-S 20-354-0703   (SL)
SILENT-AIRE LIMITED PARTNERSHIP
7107 8 St Nw, Edmonton, AB, T6P 1T9
(780) 456-1061
Emp Here 400   *Sales* 112,350,800
SIC 3585 Refrigeration and heating equip-
ment
Daniel Leckelt
Lindsey Leckelt

D-U-N-S 24-283-1576   (HQ)
SOLAR TURBINES CANADA LTD
(*Suby of* CATERPILLAR INC.)
2510 84 Ave Nw, Edmonton, AB, T6P 1K3
(780) 464-8900
Emp Here 25   *Sales* 13,300,728
SIC 5084 Industrial machinery and equipment
Larry Woods
Charles J Swiniarski
Herb Zechel
Jacquiline Loaiza
Daniel Boylan
David Esbeck
Stephen A Gosselin

D-U-N-S 24-360-9851   (BR)
SUPREME STEEL LP
SUPREME STEEL BRIDGE, DIV OF
(*Suby of* LEDER INVESTMENTS LTD)
10496 21 St Nw, Edmonton, AB, T6P 1W4
(780) 467-2266
Emp Here 120
SIC 1622 Bridge, tunnel, and elevated high-
way construction
Todd Collister

D-U-N-S 25-148-2212   (HQ)
SUREWAY CONSTRUCTION LTD
9175 14 St Nw, Edmonton, AB, T6P 0C9
(780) 440-2121
Sales 213,274,750
SIC 1623 Water, sewer, and utility lines
Dennis O'rourke
Bruce Hagstrom
Marlea Sleeman

D-U-N-S 20-767-2361   (HQ)
SUREWAY EQUIPMENT LEASING LTD
9175 14 St Nw, Edmonton, AB, T6P 0C9
(780) 440-2121
Sales 17,670,940
SIC 1623 Water, sewer, and utility lines

Dennis O'rourke

D-U-N-S 24-065-6736   (HQ)
THERMO DESIGN ENGINEERING LTD
1424 70 Ave Nw, Edmonton, AB, T6P 1P5
(780) 440-6064
Emp Here 450   *Sales* 59,875,760
SIC 3569 General industrial machinery, nec
James Montgomery
Boris Grafer
Dennis Wiun
Sean Montgomery

D-U-N-S 24-313-4082   (HQ)
TOP-CO INC
RUBICON OILFIELD INTERNATIONAL
(*Suby of* RUBICON OILFIELD INTERNA-
TIONAL HOLDINGS, LLC)
7720 17 St Nw, Edmonton, AB, T6P 1S7
(780) 440-4440
Emp Here 50   *Sales* 70,219,250
SIC 3559 Special industry machinery, nec
Mike Reeves
Peter Bernard
Cory Roclawski
Margaret Dorman
Tom Holloway

D-U-N-S 20-970-1929   (HQ)
V.D.M. TRUCKING SERVICE LTD
2010 76 Ave Nw, Edmonton, AB, T6P 1J5
(780) 467-9897
Emp Here 110   *Sales* 28,798,840
SIC 4213 Trucking, except local
Vern Dubinsky
Donna Dubinsky

D-U-N-S 24-438-5191   (HQ)
**VAN LEEUWEN PIPE AND TUBE (CANADA)
INC**
(*Suby of* VAN LEEUWEN BUIZEN GROEP
B.V.)
2875 64 Ave Nw, Edmonton, AB, T6P 1R1
(780) 469-7410
Sales 12,520,872
SIC 5051 Metals service centers and offices
Vern Klein

D-U-N-S 20-010-4755   (BR)
WEATHERFORD CANADA LTD
MANUFACTURING CENTER
(*Suby of* WEATHERFORD INTERNATIONAL
PUBLIC LIMITED COMPANY)
2004 64 Ave Nw, Edmonton, AB, T6P 1Z3
(780) 465-9311
Emp Here 100
SIC 3533 Oil and gas field machinery
Dave Reed

D-U-N-S 24-467-6644   (BR)
WEATHERFORD CANADA LTD
(*Suby of* WEATHERFORD INTERNATIONAL
PUBLIC LIMITED COMPANY)
1917a 84 Ave Nw, Edmonton, AB, T6P 1K1
(780) 449-3266
Emp Here 100
SIC 3533 Oil and gas field machinery
Barry Kaminskas

D-U-N-S 20-910-1059   (SL)
WEINRICH CONTRACTING LTD
7212 8 St Nw, Edmonton, AB, T6P 1V1
(780) 487-6734
Emp Here 47   *Sales* 13,325,628
SIC 1611 Highway and street construction
Scott Weinrich

D-U-N-S 24-840-2505   (SL)
WHITEMUD IRONWORKS LIMITED
(*Suby of* WHITEMUD GROUP LTD)
7727 18 St Nw, Edmonton, AB, T6P 1N9
(780) 465-5888
Emp Here 110   *Sales* 23,361,360
SIC 1791 Structural steel erection
Pat Cote
Corey Cote
Ed Cote

D-U-N-S 20-720-6905   (SL)
**YELLOWHEAD PETROLEUM PRODUCTS
LTD**
8901 20 St Nw, Edmonton, AB, T6P 1K8
(780) 449-1171
Emp Here 12   *Sales* 12,393,696
SIC 5171 Petroleum bulk stations and termi-
nals
Bryan Bradley

Edmonton, AB T6R

D-U-N-S 25-158-3688   (HQ)
COVE PROPERTIES LTD
316-14127 23 Ave Nw, Edmonton, AB, T6R
0G4
(780) 469-2683
Emp Here 25   *Sales* 14,429,150
SIC 1522 Residential construction, nec
Grant Klapstein
Clay Hamdon
Doug Mazurek
James Weissner

D-U-N-S 20-726-8041   (SL)
**EXPEDIA CRUISE SHIP CENTRES, TER-
WILLEGAR**
14256 23 Ave Nw, Edmonton, AB, T6R 3B9
(780) 822-9283
Emp Here 25   *Sales* 12,999,175
SIC 4724 Travel agencies
Scarlet Hiller

D-U-N-S 25-234-9543   (HQ)
PETROCORP GROUP INC
14032 23 Ave Nw Suite 166, Edmonton, AB,
T6R 3L6
(780) 910-9436
Emp Here 90   *Sales* 65,348,700
SIC 1731 Electrical work
Andrew Lindzon
David Bernholtz
Hal Beauclair
Larry Patriquin
Garry Wetsch

D-U-N-S 20-139-0080   (SL)
RIVERBEND RETIREMENT RESIDENCE
103 Rabbit Hill Crt Nw, Edmonton, AB, T6R
2V3
(780) 438-2777
Emp Here 100   *Sales* 22,087,100
SIC 6513 Apartment building operators
Denisse Pratt

D-U-N-S 20-806-2369   (BR)
SOBEYS CAPITAL INCORPORATED
SOBEYS
(*Suby of* EMPIRE COMPANY LIMITED)
2430 Rabbit Hill Rd Nw, Edmonton, AB, T6R
3B5
(780) 989-1610
Emp Here 180
SIC 5411 Grocery stores
John Radostits

D-U-N-S 25-271-0215   (BR)
SOBEYS WEST INC
SAFEWAY
(*Suby of* EMPIRE COMPANY LIMITED)
576 Riverbend Sq Nw Suite 802, Edmonton,
AB, T6R 2E3
(780) 434-6124
Emp Here 150
SIC 5411 Grocery stores
Sam Bartucci

D-U-N-S 20-365-4371   (HQ)
SPEEDY CREEK (2011) LTD
CHILI'S TEXAS GRILL
514 Ronning St Nw, Edmonton, AB, T6R 1B7
(780) 486-2882
Emp Here 35   *Sales* 34,840,500
SIC 6794 Patent owners and lessors
Gerry Inglis

▲ Public Company   ■ Public Company Family Member   **HQ** Headquarters   **BR** Branch   **SL** Single Location

D-U-N-S 20-971-8894   (SL)
SUMMIT CARE CORPORATION (EDMON-TON) LTD
DEVONSHIRE CARE CENTRE
1808 Rabbit Hill Rd Nw, Edmonton, AB, T6R 3H2
(780) 665-8050
Emp Here 250   *Sales* 16,070,500
SIC 8361 Residential care
Karen Fitzgerald

Edmonton, AB T6S

D-U-N-S 24-322-3166   (HQ)
543077 ALBERTA LTD
SIL INDUSTRIAL MINERALS
305 116 Ave Nw, Edmonton, AB, T6S 1G3
(780) 440-2121
Sales 13,415,220
SIC 5032 Brick, stone, and related material
Dennis O'rourke

D-U-N-S 20-309-2242   (SL)
ENERKEM ALBERTA BIOFUELS LP
BIOCARBURANTS ENERKEM ALBERTA
(*Suby of* ENERKEM INC)
250 Aurum Rd Ne Suite 460, Edmonton, AB, T6S 1G9
(780) 473-2896
Emp Here 60   *Sales* 17,041,260
SIC 2869 Industrial organic chemicals, nec
Vincent Chornet

D-U-N-S 24-598-2363   (SL)
GEEP ALBERTA INC
(*Suby of* MG HOLDINGS INC)
250 Aurum Rd Ne Suite 700, Edmonton, AB, T6S 1G9
(780) 475-6545
Emp Here 80   *Sales* 25,512,800
SIC 4953 Refuse systems
Victor Roth

D-U-N-S 20-745-2996   (SL)
GILEAD ALBERTA ULC
(*Suby of* GILEAD SCIENCES, INC.)
1021 Hayter Rd Nw, Edmonton, AB, T6S 1A1
(780) 701-6400
Emp Here 200   *Sales* 56,804,200
SIC 2834 Pharmaceutical preparations
Daniel Oday
Jacqueline K. Barton

D-U-N-S 24-583-6713   (HQ)
HIGH LINE ELECTRICAL CONSTRUCTORS LTD
2304 119 Ave Ne Suite 200, Edmonton, AB, T6S 1B3
(780) 452-8900
Emp Here 75   *Sales* 41,387,510
SIC 1731 Electrical work
Scott Hutton
Tony Broadhurst
Chris Rauschning
Tim Ashton

D-U-N-S 24-523-3957   (HQ)
INDUSTRIAL CONSTRUCTION INVEST-MENTS INC
11850 28 St Ne, Edmonton, AB, T6S 1G6
(780) 478-4688
Sales 36,927,900
SIC 1799 Special trade contractors, nec
Jeff Granberg

D-U-N-S 25-116-7532   (HQ)
MAMMOET CANADA WESTERN LTD
12920 33 St Ne, Edmonton, AB, T6S 1H6
(780) 449-0552
Sales 32,912,960
SIC 4213 Trucking, except local
Joery Van Vlierden
Keith Guiochet
Kent Lee

D-U-N-S 20-694-0608   (HQ)
MAMMOET CRANE INC
12920 33 St Ne, Edmonton, AB, T6S 1H6
(780) 449-0552
Emp Here 119   *Sales* 32,912,960
SIC 4212 Local trucking, without storage
Tim Sittler
Herman Smit
Gijs Verdeijen

D-U-N-S 24-063-5326   (BR)
OC CANADA HOLDINGS COMPANY
OWEN CORNING
(*Suby of* OWENS CORNING)
831 Hayter Rd Nw, Edmonton, AB, T6S 1A1
(780) 472-6644
Emp Here 130
SIC 5033 Roofing, siding, and insulation

D-U-N-S 20-538-8457   (BR)
PARK DEROCHIE INC
(*Suby of* INDUSTRIAL CONSTRUCTION IN-VESTMENTS INC)
11850 28 St Ne, Edmonton, AB, T6S 1G6
(780) 478-4688
Emp Here 250
SIC 1799 Special trade contractors, nec
Jeff Granberg

D-U-N-S 20-077-4107   (HQ)
PARK DEROCHIE INC
(*Suby of* INDUSTRIAL CONSTRUCTION IN-VESTMENTS INC)
11850 28 St Ne, Edmonton, AB, T6S 1G6
(780) 478-4688
Emp Here 1   *Sales* 74,331,600
SIC 1799 Special trade contractors, nec
Michael Fownes
Mark Walker
Jeff Granberg

D-U-N-S 24-392-1301   (SL)
RUSHTON GAS & OIL EQUIPMENT (1991) LTD
2331 121 Ave Ne, Edmonton, AB, T6S 1B2
(780) 475-8801
Emp Here 35   *Sales* 16,625,910
SIC 5084 Industrial machinery and equipment
Carl Canning
Pauline Canning

D-U-N-S 25-093-4739   (BR)
SUNCOR ENERGY INC
(*Suby of* SUNCOR ENERGY INC)
801 Petroleum Way Nw, Edmonton, AB, T6S 1H5
(780) 410-5681
Emp Here 500
SIC 2911 Petroleum refining
John Prusakowski

D-U-N-S 20-807-8626   (SL)
TBG CONTRACTING LTD
12311 17 St Ne, Edmonton, AB, T6S 1A7

Emp Here 100
SIC 1442 Construction sand and gravel

D-U-N-S 20-745-3655   (HQ)
TRENDWOOD LIMITED
2431 121 Ave Ne, Edmonton, AB, T6S 1B2
(780) 472-6606
Sales 13,519,142
SIC 4731 Freight transportation arrangement
Brian Sylvester

D-U-N-S 20-440-1012   (HQ)
WESTCAN BULK TRANSPORT LTD
WESTCAN FREIGHT SYSTEMS
(*Suby of* THE KENAN ADVANTAGE GROUP INC)
12110 17 St Ne, Edmonton, AB, T6S 1A5
(780) 472-6951
Emp Here 300   *Sales* 119,847,650
SIC 4212 Local trucking, without storage
Tom Kenny
Shawn Mcmillan

D-U-N-S 20-348-4498   (BR)
WORLEYCORD LP
WORLEYPARSONSCORD LP
(*Suby of* WORLEYPARSONS LIMITED)
2455 130 Ave Ne, Edmonton, AB, T6S 0A4
(780) 440-6942
Emp Here 150
SIC 1623 Water, sewer, and utility lines
Patrick Lavin

Edmonton, AB T6T

D-U-N-S 24-325-9566   (SL)
CASPEN DRUGS LTD
SHOPPERS DRUG MART
3945 34 St Nw Suite 371, Edmonton, AB, T6T 1L5
(780) 461-6768
Emp Here 50   *Sales* 12,647,700
SIC 5912 Drug stores and proprietary stores
Huy Luong

D-U-N-S 24-361-7235   (BR)
HOME DEPOT OF CANADA INC
HOME DEPOT
(*Suby of* THE HOME DEPOT INC)
4430 17 St Nw, Edmonton, AB, T6T 0B4
(780) 577-3575
Emp Here 100
SIC 5251 Hardware stores

D-U-N-S 24-385-2451   (BR)
LOBLAWS INC
REAL CANADIAN SUPERSTORE
(*Suby of* LOBLAW COMPANIES LIMITED)
4410 17 St Nw, Edmonton, AB, T6T 0C1
(780) 450-2041
Emp Here 300
SIC 5411 Grocery stores
Nigel Chapil

D-U-N-S 20-560-2381   (SL)
RMS BUILDERS INC
150 West Railway St Nw, Edmonton, AB, T6T 1J1
(780) 414-0330
Emp Here 25   *Sales* 14,258,450
SIC 1542 Nonresidential construction, nec
Curtis Way

Edmonton, AB T6V

D-U-N-S 24-521-8870   (SL)
CITY FORD SALES LTD
14750 Mark Messier Trail Nw, Edmonton, AB, T6V 1H5
(780) 454-2000
Emp Here 100   *Sales* 62,928,000
SIC 5511 New and used car dealers
Robert J Balkan

D-U-N-S 24-671-9801   (SL)
E.B.C. HOLDINGS LTD
DAIRY QUEEN
12708 140 Ave Nw, Edmonton, AB, T6V 1K4
(780) 454-5258
Emp Here 27   *Sales* 11,322,585
SIC 6712 Bank holding companies
Marc Cardinal

D-U-N-S 20-154-2540   (SL)
GATEWAY REPAIRS TRUCK & TRAILER LTD
14203 157 Ave Nw, Edmonton, AB, T6V 0K8
(780) 451-3343
Emp Here 85   *Sales* 24,080,500
SIC 7539 Automotive repair shops, nec
Aaron Beaupre

D-U-N-S 20-082-7087   (HQ)
HIGHLAND MOVING & STORAGE LTD
THE MOVER

(*Suby of* CAMPBELL BROS. MOVERS LIM-ITED)
14490 157 Ave Nw, Edmonton, AB, T6V 0K8
(780) 453-6777
Emp Here 75   *Sales* 19,542,070
SIC 4214 Local trucking with storage
Donald Kachur

D-U-N-S 25-153-5998   (SL)
WILCO CONTRACTORS NORTHWEST INC
14420 154 Ave Nw Suite 107, Edmonton, AB, T6V 0K8
(780) 447-1199
Emp Here 180   *Sales* 33,571,080
SIC 8742 Management consulting services
Arthur Maat

Edmonton, AB T6W

D-U-N-S 24-065-6108   (SL)
BLUMENSCHEIN HOLDINGS LTD
FORT MCMURRAY IGA
11750 30 Ave Sw, Edmonton, AB, T6W 1A8

Emp Here 100   *Sales* 29,347,700
SIC 5411 Grocery stores
Steve Blumenschein
Pat Blumenschein

D-U-N-S 24-068-2690   (SL)
CO-PAR ELECTRIC LTD
1132 156 St Sw, Edmonton, AB, T6W 1A4
(780) 453-1414
Emp Here 60   *Sales* 13,069,740
SIC 1731 Electrical work
Douglas Cook
David Ramler

D-U-N-S 20-384-0454   (SL)
ELLERSLIE ROAD BAPTIST CHURCH SO-CIETY
10603 Ellerslie Rd Sw, Edmonton, AB, T6W 1A1
(780) 437-5433
Emp Here 32   *Sales* 12,717,248
SIC 8699 Membership organizations, nec
Curtis Johnston
David Mcdermott

D-U-N-S 20-139-8937   (SL)
ERICKSEN M-B LTD
MERCEDES-BENZ HERITAGE VALLEY
(*Suby of* AUTOCANADA INC)
2120 103a St Sw, Edmonton, AB, T6W 2P6
(780) 431-5100
Emp Here 65   *Sales* 40,903,200
SIC 5511 New and used car dealers
Colaco Anatol

D-U-N-S 24-733-7116   (HQ)
FOUNTAIN TIRE LTD
1006 103a St Sw Suite 103, Edmonton, AB, T6W 2P6
(780) 464-3700
Emp Here 200   *Sales* 923,603,200
SIC 5531 Auto and home supply stores
Brent Hesje
Brian Hesje
David Janzen
Pat Witiw
Nelson Tonn

D-U-N-S 20-648-7006   (SL)
GATEWAY MOTORS (EDMONTON) LTD
GATEWAY TOYOTA
2020 103a St Sw, Edmonton, AB, T6W 2P6
(780) 439-3939
Emp Here 55   *Sales* 34,610,400
SIC 5511 New and used car dealers
Neal Gratton

D-U-N-S 25-205-8771   (SL)
HERITAGE HARLEY-DAVIDSON LTD
HERITAGE HARLEY-DAVIDSON/BUELL
1616 Calgary Trail Sw, Edmonton, AB, T6W

1A1
(780) 430-7200
Emp Here 25   *Sales* 12,451,950
SIC 5571 Motorcycle dealers
Hob Murphy
Autumn Murphy

D-U-N-S 24-803-5490   (BR)
HOME DEPOT OF CANADA INC
HOME DEPOT
(*Suby of* THE HOME DEPOT INC)
6218 Currents Dr Nw, Edmonton, AB, T6W
0L8
(780) 989-7460
Emp Here 100
SIC 5251 Hardware stores
Devon Laforet

D-U-N-S 20-255-9241   (SL)
PUBLIC SERVICE PENSION PLAN
5103 Windermere Blvd Sw, Edmonton, AB,
T6W 0S9
(800) 358-0840
Emp Here 17   *Sales* 17,592,977
SIC 6371 Pension, health, and welfare funds

D-U-N-S 24-734-0474   (HQ)
SCM INSURANCE SERVICES INC
CLAIMSPRO
5083 Windermere Blvd Sw Suite 101, Edmonton, AB, T6W 0J5
(780) 430-9012
Emp Here 50   *Sales* 2,610,357,200
SIC 6411 Insurance agents, brokers, and service
Bob Fitzgerald
Ross Betteridge
Ken Hansen
Larry Shumka
Peter Watson
Ken Smee

Edmonton, AB T6X

D-U-N-S 24-822-4318   (SL)
1412873 ALBERTA LTD
VOLVO OF EDMONTON
1205 101 St Sw, Edmonton, AB, T6X 1A1
(780) 486-5100
Emp Here 30   *Sales* 14,942,340
SIC 5511 New and used car dealers
Michael Norris

D-U-N-S 25-654-4169   (SL)
1454615 ALBERTA LTD
LEXUS SOUTH POINTE
830 100 St Sw, Edmonton, AB, T6X 0S8
(780) 989-2222
Emp Here 49   *Sales* 24,405,822
SIC 5511 New and used car dealers
Naushad Jiwani

D-U-N-S 24-556-8832   (SL)
2071848 ALBERTA LTD
SOUTHGATE AUDI
1235 101 St Sw, Edmonton, AB, T6X 1A1
(780) 462-2834
Emp Here 62   *Sales* 39,015,360
SIC 5511 New and used car dealers
James Allan

D-U-N-S 20-738-8021   (SL)
ALBERTA HOTEL & LODGING ASSOCIATION
AHLA
2707 Ellwood Dr Sw, Edmonton, AB, T6X 0P7
(780) 436-6112
Emp Here 50   *Sales* 12,930,750
SIC 8611 Business associations
Dave Kaiser
Lina Venchiarutti
Doug Shandro
Matt Rowlette
Dave Korpach

Sandra Schweitzer
Tracy Douglas-Blowers
Leanne Floden
Hany Assal
Michael Mazepa

D-U-N-S 24-702-7303   (SL)
ALBERTA MILK
(*Suby of* GOVERNMENT OF THE PROVINCE OF ALBERTA)
1303 91 St Sw, Edmonton, AB, T6X 1H1
(780) 453-5942
Emp Here 14   *Sales* 444,196,814
SIC 8732 Commercial nonphysical research

D-U-N-S 24-584-5698   (SL)
ALBERTA MILK
1303 91 St Sw, Edmonton, AB, T6X 1H1
(780) 453-5942
Emp Here 24   *Sales* 556,915,412
SIC 8611 Business associations
Mike Southwood
Tom Kootstra
Stuart Boeve
Gert Schrijver
Gezinus Martens
Miranda Verhoef
Heini Hehli
Pieter Ijff
Martin Van Diemen
Conrad Van Hierden

D-U-N-S 25-229-0325   (HQ)
ALMITA PILING INC
1603 91 St Sw Suite 200, Edmonton, AB, T6X 0W8
(800) 363-4868
Emp Here 20   *Sales* 25,394,320
SIC 3312 Blast furnaces and steel mills
Jeffrey Lloyd

D-U-N-S 20-537-6684   (HQ)
AMRE SUPPLY COMPANY LIMITED
1259 91 St Sw Ste 201, Edmonton, AB, T6X 1E9
(780) 461-2929
Emp Here 26   *Sales* 38,009,790
SIC 5064 Electrical appliances, television and radio
Ronald Swane
Doug Swane
Calvin Swane

D-U-N-S 20-638-0008   (HQ)
B & B ELECTRONICS LTD
CERTIFIED RADIO SOUTH, DIV OF
4316 Savaryn Dr Sw, Edmonton, AB, T6X 1Z9
(780) 439-3901
Sales 19,754,255
SIC 5731 Radio, television, and electronic stores
Murray Cusack
Ole Jensen

D-U-N-S 24-397-3604   (SL)
BACKWOODS CONTRACTING LTD
BACKWOODS ENERGY SERVICES
(*Suby of* ALEXIS NAKOTA SIOUX NATION)
1259 91 St Sw Unit 301, Edmonton, AB, T6X 1E9
(587) 880-2937
Emp Here 150   *Sales* 100,901,850
SIC 1389 Oil and gas field services, nec
Paul Poscente
Ryan Mcquilter

D-U-N-S 24-522-9638   (SL)
CAPITAL MOTORS LTD
CAPITAL CHRYSLER JEEP DODGE RAM
1311 101 St Sw, Edmonton, AB, T6X 1A1
(780) 435-4711
Emp Here 80   *Sales* 50,342,400
SIC 5511 New and used car dealers
Brad Jinjoe

D-U-N-S 20-327-2703   (SL)
CONNECTRA TECHNOLOGIES INC
OPTIC SOLUTIONS

1803 91 St Suite 102, Edmonton, AB, T6X 0W8
(888) 731-5210
Emp Here 45   *Sales* 10,705,545
SIC 8742 Management consulting services
Arsh Saini

D-U-N-S 24-966-8658   (BR)
DATA COMMUNICATIONS MANAGEMENT CORP
DATA GROUP OF COMPANIES
(*Suby of* DATA COMMUNICATIONS MANAGEMENT CORP)
9503 12 Ave Sw, Edmonton, AB, T6X 0C3
(780) 462-9700
Emp Here 130
SIC 5112 Stationery and office supplies
Rick Barron

D-U-N-S 24-998-0020   (HQ)
EDGEN MURRAY CANADA INC
(*Suby of* EM HOLDINGS, LLC)
1253 91 St Sw Suite 302e, Edmonton, AB, T6X 1E9
(780) 440-1475
Emp Here 6   *Sales* 15,204,864
SIC 5051 Metals service centers and offices
Daniel O'leary
Greg Baker
Kevin Hoekstra

D-U-N-S 25-482-4634   (SL)
EDMONTON SCOTTISH SOCIETY
3105 101 St Sw, Edmonton, AB, T6X 1A1
(780) 988-5357
Emp Here 150   *Sales* 14,242,950
SIC 7999 Amusement and recreation, nec
Peter Dolan

D-U-N-S 20-271-7732   (SL)
ELLISDON INDUSTRIAL SERVICES INC
(*Suby of* ELLISDON HOLDINGS INC)
1430 91 St Sw Unit 101, Edmonton, AB, T6X 1M5
(780) 669-8530
Emp Here 85   *Sales* 21,457,570
SIC 1629 Heavy construction, nec
Allan Tarasuk

D-U-N-S 20-166-1220   (HQ)
ERIKS INDUSTRIAL SERVICES LP
9748 12 Ave Sw, Edmonton, AB, T6X 0J5
(780) 437-1260
Emp Here 51   *Sales* 53,650,300
SIC 5085 Industrial supplies
Simon Franken
Ryan Antoniadis
Roger Sonneville
Just In 't Velt
Eric Otto
Floris Jan Cuypers

D-U-N-S 20-293-7033   (HQ)
FORBES BROS. LTD
R.S. LINE CONTR. CO.
1290 91 St Sw Suite 200, Edmonton, AB, T6X 0P2
(780) 960-1950
Emp Here 150   *Sales* 756,662,400
SIC 4911 Electric services
Mark Forbes
Robert Forbes
Earl Forbes
Don Forsythe

D-U-N-S 20-379-8160   (SL)
FORUM CANADA ULC
9503 12 Ave Sw, Edmonton, AB, T6X 0C3
(825) 410-1200
Emp Here 50   *Sales* 10,506,550
SIC 1389 Oil and gas field services, nec
Mardy Mattson
Williams Lyle

D-U-N-S 24-859-2276   (SL)
FOUR POINTS BY SHERATON EDMONTON GATEWAY
10010 12 Ave Sw, Edmonton, AB, T6X 0P9

(780) 801-4000
Emp Here 100   *Sales* 9,489,900
SIC 7011 Hotels and motels
Farid Janmohamed

D-U-N-S 20-014-4454   (HQ)
LANDMARK HOMES (EDMONTON) INC
1103 95 St Sw Unit 301, Edmonton, AB, T6X 0P8
(780) 436-5959
Emp Here 108   *Sales* 40,641,300
SIC 1521 Single-family housing construction
Reza Nasseri
Edward Tang

D-U-N-S 24-733-4626   (SL)
MCDONALD & BYCHKOWSKI LTD
CMB INSURANCE BROKERS
1430 91 St Sw Suite 201, Edmonton, AB, T6X 1M5
(780) 424-2727
Emp Here 22   *Sales* 12,758,328
SIC 6411 Insurance agents, brokers, and service
Mark Mcdonald

D-U-N-S 24-392-9536   (SL)
MILLS NISSAN LTD
GO NISSAN
1275 101 St Sw, Edmonton, AB, T6X 1A1
(780) 463-5700
Emp Here 33   *Sales* 16,436,574
SIC 5511 New and used car dealers
Lance Mills

D-U-N-S 20-296-2788   (HQ)
NATIONAL HOME WARRANTY PROGRAMS LTD
9808 12 Ave Sw, Edmonton, AB, T6X 0J5
(780) 425-2981
Emp Here 15   *Sales* 80,302,170
SIC 6351 Surety insurance
Ken Burton
Janet Folk
Malcolm Dion

D-U-N-S 24-001-2435   (HQ)
NORDIC HOLDINGS LTD
CAN-SCAN IMPORTS
2303 91 St Sw, Edmonton, AB, T6X 1V8
(780) 437-1527
Emp Here 25   *Sales* 19,754,255
SIC 5712 Furniture stores
Jorgen Gustavsson
Bengt Johannesson

D-U-N-S 20-807-8253   (HQ)
NORTHWEST HYDRAULIC CONSULTANTS LTD
9819 12 Ave Sw, Edmonton, AB, T6X 0E3
(780) 436-5868
Emp Here 25   *Sales* 22,342,375
SIC 8711 Engineering services
Herbert Wiebe
Gerald Mutter
Michael H Okun

D-U-N-S 20-538-5735   (HQ)
NUNASTAR PROPERTIES INC
1281 91 St Sw Suite 200, Edmonton, AB, T6X 1H1
(780) 452-4333
Emp Here 10   *Sales* 24,421,860
SIC 6512 Nonresidential building operators
Douglas Cox

D-U-N-S 24-383-2743   (SL)
REVCON OILFIELD CONSTRUCTORS INCORPORATED
625 Parsons Rd Sw Suite 201, Edmonton, AB, T6X 0N9
(780) 497-8586
Emp Here 185   *Sales* 46,701,770
SIC 1623 Water, sewer, and utility lines
Dave Szatkowski

D-U-N-S 20-695-2959   (SL)
ROHIT COMMUNITIES INC
550 91 St Sw, Edmonton, AB, T6X 0V1

---

(780) 436-9015
Emp Here 150   *Sales* 23,725,800
SIC 6552 Subdividers and developers, nec
  Radhe Gupta
  Rohit Gupta
  Christopher Rypkema

  D-U-N-S 25-194-2202   (SL)
SATRANG DESIGNER WEAR INC
2956 Ellwood Dr Sw, Edmonton, AB, T6X 0A9
(780) 245-0043
Emp Here 23   *Sales* 15,098,672
SIC 5961 Catalog and mail-order houses
  James Overend

  D-U-N-S 20-193-7013   (BR)
SCHLUMBERGER CANADA LIMITED
*SCHLUMBERGER EDMONTON PRODUCT
CENTRE*
9803 12 Ave Sw, Edmonton, AB, T6X 0E3

Emp Here 100
SIC 3533 Oil and gas field machinery
  Alexander Gillard

  D-U-N-S 24-854-1880   (HQ)
STUART OLSON INDUSTRIAL INC
(*Suby of* STUART OLSON INC)
2627 Ellwood Dr Sw Suite 201, Edmonton,
AB, T6X 0P7
(780) 450-9636
Emp Here 54   *Sales* 279,356,800
SIC 1541 Industrial buildings and warehouses
  David Lemay
  Leanne Tenbrink

  D-U-N-S 24-381-5318   (HQ)
WILLBROS MINE SERVICES, L.P.
WILLBROS CANADA
(*Suby of* PRIMORIS SERVICES CORPORA-
TION)
1103 95 St Sw, Edmonton, AB, T6X 0P8
(780) 400-4200
Emp Here 2   *Sales* 147,651,750
SIC 1623 Water, sewer, and utility lines
  Brian Pratt
  David King
  Tom Mccormick
  Ken M Dodgen
  John Moreno

  D-U-N-S 20-321-0448   (SL)
**WILLBROS PSS MIDSTREAM (CANADA)
L.P.**
(*Suby of* PRIMORIS SERVICES CORPORA-
TION)
1103 95 St Sw, Edmonton, AB, T6X 0P8
(780) 400-4200
Emp Here 100   *Sales* 25,244,200
SIC 1623 Water, sewer, and utility lines
  Michael Jurcevic

  D-U-N-S 24-733-2760   (SL)
ZCL COMPOSITES INC
1420 Parsons Rd Sw, Edmonton, AB, T6X
1M5

Emp Here 573   *Sales* 147,426,084
SIC 3299 NonMetallic mineral products,

Edmonton, AB T9E

  D-U-N-S 24-859-9016   (SL)
HUDSON DUFRY - EDMONTON
(*Suby of* DUFRY AG)
Po Box 9898, Edmonton, AB, T9E 0V3
(780) 890-7263
Emp Here 100
SIC 5441 Candy, nut, and confectionery
stores
  Dave Neil

  D-U-N-S 20-576-0882   (HQ)
KBR INDUSTRIAL CANADA CO.
(*Suby of* KELLOGG BROWN & ROOT HOLD-

ING B.V.)
1302 10 St Nisku, Edmonton, AB, T9E 8K2
(780) 468-1341
Emp Here 998   *Sales* 698,392,000
SIC 1541 Industrial buildings and warehouses
  Christian Brown
  William Pohl

Edson, AB T7E

  D-U-N-S 20-109-0326   (SL)
DOUBLE C. DISTRIBUTORS LTD
PETRO-PASS CARDLOCK
6330 4 Ave, Edson, AB, T7E 1M1
(780) 723-3141
Emp Here 21   *Sales* 26,401,221
SIC 5172 Petroleum products, nec
  Cheryl Haverluck

  D-U-N-S 20-292-5066   (SL)
EDSON CHRYSLER DODGE JEEP LTD
7440 4th Ave, Edson, AB, T7E 1V8
(780) 723-9500
Emp Here 33   *Sales* 16,436,574
SIC 5511 New and used car dealers
  Kamsen Iyer
  Dwight Kennedy

  D-U-N-S 25-014-4342   (SL)
FOUNTAIN TIRE (EDSON) LTD
4619 2 Ave, Edson, AB, T7E 1C1
(780) 723-7666
Emp Here 21   *Sales* 10,459,638
SIC 5531 Auto and home supply stores
  Lorne Garner

  D-U-N-S 24-001-7749   (HQ)
**GRANDE YELLOWHEAD PUBLIC SCHOOL
DIVISION 77**
3656 1 Ave Suite 35, Edson, AB, T7E 1N9
(780) 723-4471
Emp Here 20   *Sales* 76,164,900
SIC 8211 Elementary and secondary schools
  Dean Lindquist
  Edward Letka
  John Stitzenberger
  Shirley Caputo
  Lynda Akers
  Robert Krewusk
  Hazel Shearer
  Betsy Anne Declercq

  D-U-N-S 20-776-0737   (SL)
JERRY FORD SALES LTD
5908 4 Ave, Edson, AB, T7E 1L9
(780) 723-4441
Emp Here 25   *Sales* 12,451,950
SIC 5511 New and used car dealers
  Cathy Pasychny

  D-U-N-S 24-126-8791   (SL)
**PETROCARE SERVICES LIMITED PART-
NERSHIP**
4515 2 Ave, Edson, AB, T7E 1C1
(780) 723-4237
Emp Here 200   *Sales* 50,488,400
SIC 1623 Water, sewer, and utility lines
  Robert (Bob) Palmer

  D-U-N-S 20-016-3868   (BR)
PRAIRIE MINES & ROYALTY ULC
(*Suby of* WESTMORELAND COAL COM-
PANY)
Gd, Edson, AB, T7E 1W1
(780) 794-8100
Emp Here 500
SIC 1221 Bituminous coal and lignite-surface
mining
  Tim Rolse

  D-U-N-S 24-319-5000   (BR)
WAL-MART CANADA CORP
WALMART
(*Suby of* WALMART INC.)
5750 2 Ave, Edson, AB, T7E 0A1

(780) 723-6357
Emp Here 120
SIC 5311 Department stores
  Miriam Dassouki

Elk Point, AB T0A

  D-U-N-S 20-354-1032   (SL)
**HAHN WELDING & OILFIELD SERVICES
LTD**
5205 47 St, Elk Point, AB, T0A 1A0
(780) 724-3323
Emp Here 80   *Sales* 20,195,360
SIC 1623 Water, sewer, and utility lines
  George Hahn

  D-U-N-S 24-615-3162   (BR)
K+S SEL WINDSOR LTEE
CANADIAN SALT COMPANY
(*Suby of* K+S AG)
Gd, Elk Point, AB, T0A 1A0
(780) 724-4180
Emp Here 100
SIC 1479 Chemical and fertilizer mining
  John Williams

Enoch, AB T7X

  D-U-N-S 24-320-5254   (SL)
**RIVER CREE RESORT LIMITED PARTNER-
SHIP**
RIVER CREE RESORT AND CASINO, THE
300 E Lapotac Blvd, Enoch, AB, T7X 3Y3
(780) 484-2121
Emp Here 750   *Sales* 71,751,000
SIC 7011 Hotels and motels
  Brian Lee

Etzikom, AB T0K

  D-U-N-S 24-155-6278   (SL)
COUNTY OF FORTY MILE NO 8
Gd, Etzikom, AB, T0K 0W0
(403) 666-2082
Emp Here 40   *Sales* 11,340,960
SIC 1611 Highway and street construction
  Bill Nickel

  D-U-N-S 24-063-5024   (SL)
ROSEDALE HUTTERIAN BRETHREN
ROSEDALE COLONY
Gd, Etzikom, AB, T0K 0W0
(587) 787-2456
Emp Here 40   *Sales* 10,492,360
SIC 0191 General farms, primarily crop
  George Waldner
  John J. Waldner
  David Hofer
  John G. Waldner
  Mike Hofer
  Joe Waldner

  D-U-N-S 25-339-6022   (SL)
SUNRISE HUTTERIAN BRETHREN
SUNRISE COLONY
Gd, Etzikom, AB, T0K 0W0
(403) 666-3787
Emp Here 55   *Sales* 13,941,950
SIC 8748 Business consulting, nec
  David Wurz

Exshaw, AB T0L

  D-U-N-S 20-063-4900   (BR)
**CALGARY YOUNG MEN'S CHRISTIAN AS-
SOCIATION**

Y M C A
(*Suby of* CALGARY YOUNG MEN'S CHRIS-
TIAN ASSOCIATION, THE)
Gd, Exshaw, AB, T0L 2C0
(403) 673-3858
Emp Here 200
SIC 8621 Professional organizations
  Jill Jamieson

Fairview, AB T0H

  D-U-N-S 20-153-7755   (BR)
AECOM ENERGY SERVICES LTD
(*Suby of* AECOM)
10211 98 St, Fairview, AB, T0H 1L0
(403) 218-7100
Emp Here 120
SIC 1389 Oil and gas field services, nec
  George Hill

  D-U-N-S 24-121-6535   (BR)
ALBERTA HEALTH SERVICES
FAIRVIEW HEALTH COMPLEX
(*Suby of* GOVERNMENT OF THE
PROVINCE OF ALBERTA)
10628 100th St, Fairview, AB, T0H 1L0
(780) 835-6100
Emp Here 100
SIC 8062 General medical and surgical hospi-
tals
  David Westcott

  D-U-N-S 20-897-2729   (BR)
DEVON CANADA CORPORATION
(*Suby of* DEVON ENERGY CORPORATION)
10924 92nd Ave, Fairview, AB, T0H 1L0

Emp Here 115
SIC 1382 Oil and gas exploration services
  John Richels

  D-U-N-S 25-181-8233   (SL)
**DUNVEGAN NORTH OILFIELD SERVICES
ULC**
Gd, Fairview, AB, T0H 1L0
(780) 835-3511
Emp Here 50   *Sales* 12,044,200
SIC 1623 Water, sewer, and utility lines
  Gerard Biegel

  D-U-N-S 24-850-3539   (SL)
GPRC FAIRVIEW CAMPUS
11235 98th Ave, Fairview, AB, T0H 1L0
(780) 835-6600
Emp Here 170   *Sales* 15,780,420
SIC 8211 Elementary and secondary schools
  Don Gnaeiuk

  D-U-N-S 20-809-4029   (SL)
NORTH PEACE GAS CO-OPERATIVE LTD
10908 92 Ave, Fairview, AB, T0H 1L0
(780) 835-5444
Emp Here 11   *Sales* 34,164,427
SIC 4924 Natural gas distribution
  Andy Coulas
  Ronald Heck
  Gerald Raspberry

  D-U-N-S 20-043-8682   (HQ)
ROY NORTHERN LAND SERVICE LTD
*ROY NORTHERN LAND AND EVIRONMEN-
TAL*
10912-100f, Fairview, AB, T0H 1L0
(780) 835-2682
Emp Here 37   *Sales* 17,571,600
SIC 8748 Business consulting, nec
  Doug Roy
  Rodney Peters

Falher, AB T0H

  D-U-N-S 20-085-5344   (SL)

FALHER AND DISTRICT COOPERATIVE ASSOCIATION LTD, THE
108 Main St, Falher, AB, T0H 1M0
(780) 837-2261
Emp Here 32   *Sales* 10,335,008
SIC 5411 Grocery stores
Gilles Garant
Patrick Desranlau

D-U-N-S 24-032-4785   (BR)
OBSIDIAN ENERGY LTD
GIROUXVILLE PLANT
(*Suby of* OBSIDIAN ENERGY LTD)
Gd, Falher, AB, T0H 1M0
(780) 837-2929
Emp Here 100
SIC 2911 Petroleum refining

D-U-N-S 25-316-7951   (SL)
TWILIGHT HUTTERIAN BRETHREN
TWILIGHT COLONY
Gd, Falher, AB, T0H 1M0

Emp Here 140
SIC 7389 Business services, nec
John B Wipf
Sam Entz
Paul M Wipf
Peter M Entz
Elias Wipf
Paul A Wipf
Lawrence K Entz

Foothills, AB T1S

D-U-N-S 25-701-1593   (SL)
COTTONWOOD GOLF & COUNTRY CLUB
88008 226 Ave E, Foothills, AB, T1S 4A6
(403) 938-7216
Emp Here 75   *Sales* 5,729,775
SIC 7997 Membership sports and recreation clubs
Lyle Edward

Foremost, AB T0K

D-U-N-S 24-786-1040   (SL)
STARBRITE HUTTERIAN BRETHREN
Gd, Foremost, AB, T0K 0X0
(403) 867-2299
Emp Here 22   *Sales* 18,382,694
SIC 5144 Poultry and poultry products
John R. Entz
John J.R. Entz
Sam S Entz
George J Entz
Ruben Entz

Forestburg, AB T0B

D-U-N-S 24-786-2964   (BR)
PRAIRIE MINES & ROYALTY ULC
(*Suby of* WESTMORELAND COAL COMPANY)
Gd, Forestburg, AB, T0B 1N0
(403) 884-3000
Emp Here 100
SIC 1221 Bituminous coal and lignite-surface mining
Walter Klassen

Fort Macleod, AB T0L

D-U-N-S 25-266-4321   (BR)
BOUVRY EXPORTS CALGARY LTD

(*Suby of* BOUVRY EXPORTS CALGARY LTD)
Gd, Fort Macleod, AB, T0L 0Z0
(403) 553-4431
Emp Here 110
SIC 2011 Meat packing plants
Ton Niers

D-U-N-S 25-967-1311   (BR)
EXTENDICARE (CANADA) INC
EXTENDICARE FORT MACLEOD
(*Suby of* EXTENDICARE INC)
654 29th St, Fort Macleod, AB, T0L 0Z0
(403) 553-3955
Emp Here 75
SIC 8051 Skilled nursing care facilities
Karen Pack

D-U-N-S 24-476-7955   (BR)
GOVERNMENT OF THE PROVINCE OF ALBERTA
HEALTH CARE CENTRE
(*Suby of* GOVERNMENT OF THE PROVINCE OF ALBERTA)
744 26th St, Fort Macleod, AB, T0L 0Z0
(403) 553-5300
Emp Here 150
SIC 8062 General medical and surgical hospitals

D-U-N-S 24-042-8755   (SL)
HUTTERIAN BRETHREN CHURCH OF EWELME COLONY
Gd, Fort Macleod, AB, T0L 0Z0
(403) 553-2606
Emp Here 85   *Sales* 9,156,795
SIC 8661 Religious organizations
Peter Walter
George Hofer
Darius Walter
Elias Walter
Kenneth Hofer

D-U-N-S 24-651-7549   (SL)
HUTTERIAN BRETHREN OF SPRING POINT COLONY, THE
Gd, Fort Macleod, AB, T0L 0Z0
(403) 553-2284
Emp Here 82   *Sales* 8,961,698
SIC 0762 Farm management services
Jake Walter

Fort Mcmurray, AB T9H

D-U-N-S 24-858-4349   (SL)
1172895 ALBERTA LTD
OIL CITY EXPRESS
145 Maclean Rd, Fort Mcmurray, AB, T9H 4X2
(780) 790-9292
Emp Here 23   *Sales* 10,200,270
SIC 7389 Business services, nec
Terry Lush

D-U-N-S 24-066-9234   (HQ)
ALCOR HOLDINGS LTD
ALCOR COMMERCIAL REALTY
305 Macdonald Cres Unit 1, Fort Mcmurray, AB, T9H 4B7
(780) 743-1343
Sales 11,449,445
SIC 6531 Real estate agents and managers
Allan Burry
Brian Johnson

D-U-N-S 25-947-6398   (BR)
ALUMA SYSTEMS INC
(*Suby of* BRAND INDUSTRIAL SERVICES, INC.)
Gd Lcd Main, Fort Mcmurray, AB, T9H 3E2
(780) 790-4852
Emp Here 650
SIC 1799 Special trade contractors, nec
Mick Herke

D-U-N-S 25-153-1638   (SL)
AQUA INDUSTRIAL LTD
9912 Franklin Ave Suite 205, Fort Mcmurray, AB, T9H 2K5
(780) 799-7300
Emp Here 80   *Sales* 19,694,880
SIC 1791 Structural steel erection
Gerald Gionet

D-U-N-S 25-681-2835   (SL)
ATHABASCA TRIBAL COUNCIL LTD
9206 Mccormick Dr, Fort Mcmurray, AB, T9H 1C7
(780) 791-6538
Emp Here 30   *Sales* 11,922,420
SIC 8699 Membership organizations, nec
Karla Buffalo

D-U-N-S 24-082-3430   (SL)
AURORA HELICOPTERS LTD
WOOD BUFFALO HELICOPTERS
410 Snow Eagle Dr, Fort Mcmurray, AB, T9H 0H7
(780) 743-5588
Emp Here 45   *Sales* 14,613,930
SIC 4522 Air transportation, nonscheduled
Michael Morin
Sharon Morin

D-U-N-S 20-105-5295   (SL)
BOND CONSTRUCTION INC
295 Macdonald Cres, Fort Mcmurray, AB, T9H 4B7
(780) 743-3448
Emp Here 40   *Sales* 18,829,240
SIC 1542 Nonresidential construction, nec
Gene Dobie

D-U-N-S 24-750-7051   (SL)
BOUCHIER CONTRACTING LTD
BOUCHIER GROUP
Gd Lcd Main, Fort Mcmurray, AB, T9H 3E2
(780) 828-4010
Emp Here 500   *Sales* 164,057,500
SIC 1629 Heavy construction, nec
Nicole Bourque-Boucher
David Boucher
Roland Jones

D-U-N-S 24-394-9898   (HQ)
C. B. S. CONSTRUCTION LTD
CBS
150 Mackay Cres, Fort Mcmurray, AB, T9H 4W8
(780) 743-1810
Emp Here 300   *Sales* 114,840,250
SIC 1629 Heavy construction, nec
Garry Fizzell
Jay Lines

D-U-N-S 20-334-8839   (SL)
CANADIAN TIRE ASSOCIATE STORE
1 Hospital St, Fort Mcmurray, AB, T9H 5C1
(780) 791-6400
Emp Here 120   *Sales* 75,513,600
SIC 5531 Auto and home supply stores
Matt Stern

D-U-N-S 20-065-7315   (BR)
CARMACKS ENTERPRISES LTD
CARMACKS INDUSTRIES
(*Suby of* VINCI)
Gd Lcd Main, Fort Mcmurray, AB, T9H 3E2
(780) 598-1376
Emp Here 100
SIC 1611 Highway and street construction
David Scragg

D-U-N-S 20-692-5674   (SL)
CASMAN BUILDING SOLUTIONS INC
(*Suby of* CASMAN INC)
330 Mackenzie Blvd, Fort Mcmurray, AB, T9H 4C4
(780) 791-9283
Emp Here 90   *Sales* 51,330,420
SIC 1542 Nonresidential construction, nec
Norman Castiglione

D-U-N-S 25-206-9406   (HQ)
CASMAN INC
CASMAN GROUP OF COMPANIES
330 Mackenzie Blvd, Fort Mcmurray, AB, T9H 4C4
(780) 791-9283
Emp Here 50   *Sales* 98,434,500
SIC 1611 Highway and street construction
Will Sawchyn
Norman Castiglione
Margaret Castiglione

D-U-N-S 24-584-3321   (SL)
CASMAN INDUSTRIAL CONSTRUCTION INC
(*Suby of* CASMAN INC)
330 Mackenzie Blvd, Fort Mcmurray, AB, T9H 4C4
(780) 791-9283
Emp Here 305   *Sales* 24,854,449
SIC 1629 Heavy construction, nec
Sherri Castiglione
Erik Horne
Norman Castiglione

D-U-N-S 24-804-5119   (SL)
CENTERLINE GEOMATICS LTD
Gd Lcd Main, Fort Mcmurray, AB, T9H 3E2
(780) 881-4696
Emp Here 60   *Sales* 10,557,480
SIC 8713 Surveying services
Peter Humphries
Jamie Tucker

D-U-N-S 24-025-7779   (BR)
CHEMCO ELECTRICAL CONTRACTORS LTD
(*Suby of* BALM MANAGEMENT ENTERPRISES LTD)
210 Macalpine Cres Suite 6, Fort Mcmurray, AB, T9H 4A6
(780) 714-6206
Emp Here 100
SIC 1731 Electrical work
Bryan Halina

D-U-N-S 24-516-2065   (SL)
CHINOOK FUELS LTD
160 Mackay Cres, Fort Mcmurray, AB, T9H 4W8
(780) 743-2381
Emp Here 26   *Sales* 32,687,226
SIC 5171 Petroleum bulk stations and terminals
Mark Macdonald

D-U-N-S 24-399-6915   (SL)
CHRISTINA RIVER ENTERPRISES LIMITED PARTNERSHIP
Gd Lcd Main, Fort Mcmurray, AB, T9H 3E2
(780) 334-2446
Emp Here 135   *Sales* 25,969,950
SIC 2448 Wood pallets and skids
Maxine Butt

D-U-N-S 24-378-7285   (BR)
CLEAN HARBORS ENERGY AND INDUSTRIAL SERVICES CORP
(*Suby of* CLEAN HARBORS, INC.)
26 Airport Rd, Fort Mcmurray, AB, T9H 5B4
(780) 743-0222
Emp Here 300
SIC 7349 Building maintenance services, nec
Glen Fleming

D-U-N-S 20-329-4756   (SL)
CLEARWATER ENERGY SERVICES LP
(*Suby of* CLEARSTREAM ENERGY SERVICES INC)
355 Mackenzie Blvd, Fort Mcmurray, AB, T9H 5E2
(780) 743-2171
Emp Here 25   *Sales* 10,568,425
SIC 1541 Industrial buildings and warehouses
Deanna Beeler

D-U-N-S 24-671-8621   (SL)
CONSUN CONTRACTING LTD

---

195 Macdonald Cres, Fort Mcmurray, AB, T9H 4B3
(780) 743-3163
Emp Here 120   *Sales* 30,293,040
SIC 1629 Heavy construction, nec
Ed Tatum

D-U-N-S 24-255-1526   (BR)
CORPORATION DE SECURITE GARDA CANADA
GARDA CANADA SECURITY CORPORATION
(*Suby of* GW INTERMEDIATE HOLDCO CORPORATION)
8600 Franklin Ave Suite 606, Fort Mcmurray, AB, T9H 4G8
(780) 791-7087
Emp Here 350
SIC 6289 Security and commodity service
Angela Krszwda

D-U-N-S 20-051-6230   (SL)
DEMERS CONTRACTING SERVICES LTD
DCS
240 Maclennan Cres, Fort Mcmurray, AB, T9H 4G1
(780) 799-3222
Emp Here 150   *Sales* 37,866,300
SIC 1611 Highway and street construction
Hector Demers

D-U-N-S 24-014-8101   (SL)
DIAMOND PARK BUILDERS (2004) INC
425 Gregoire Dr Suite 600, Fort Mcmurray, AB, T9H 4K7

Emp Here 50   *Sales* 23,536,550
SIC 1542 Nonresidential construction, nec
Lawrence Carr
Gordon Hoover
William Kujat
Farouk Shah

D-U-N-S 25-954-4989   (BR)
DIVERSIFIED TRANSPORTATION LTD
(*Suby of* PACIFIC WESTERN TRANSPORTATION LTD)
120 Maclennan Cres, Fort Mcmurray, AB, T9H 4E8
(780) 743-2244
Emp Here 250
SIC 4142 Bus charter service, except local
Roger Pigden

D-U-N-S 25-951-7530   (BR)
DIVERSIFIED TRANSPORTATION LTD
(*Suby of* PACIFIC WESTERN TRANSPORTATION LTD)
8030 Golosky Ave, Fort Mcmurray, AB, T9H 1V5
(780) 790-3960
Emp Here 100
SIC 4111 Local and suburban transit
Roger Pigdom

D-U-N-S 25-538-2475   (SL)
FMR MECHANICAL ELECTRICAL INC
(*Suby of* CASMAN INC)
330 Mackenzie Blvd, Fort Mcmurray, AB, T9H 4C4
(780) 791-9283
Emp Here 39   *Sales* 10,601,838
SIC 7623 Refrigeration service and repair
Ben Dutton
Norman Castiglione
Margaret Castiglione

D-U-N-S 20-252-1522   (SL)
FORT MCKAY METIS GROUP LTD
Gd Lcd Main, Fort Mcmurray, AB, T9H 3E2
(780) 828-4581
Emp Here 25   *Sales* 11,768,275
SIC 1542 Nonresidential construction, nec
Ron Quintal
John Paquette
Margie Wood
Lauretta Waquan

D-U-N-S 20-528-4370   (SL)
FORT MCKAY SERVICES LIMITED PARTNERSHIP
FORT MCKAY GROUP OF COMPANIES
Gd Lcd Main, Fort Mcmurray, AB, T9H 3E2
(780) 828-2400
Emp Here 480   *Sales* 98,738,880
SIC 4225 General warehousing and storage
Frederick Mcdonald
Rick Baker

D-U-N-S 20-552-3710   (SL)
FORT MCMURRAY PIZZA LTD
BOSTON PIZZA
10202 Macdonald Ave, Fort Mcmurray, AB, T9H 1T4
(780) 743-5056
Emp Here 100   *Sales* 4,551,900
SIC 5812 Eating places
Michael Legate

D-U-N-S 24-627-8410   (HQ)
FORT MCMURRAY PUBLIC SCHOOL DISTRICT #2833
231 Hardin St Suite 2833, Fort Mcmurray, AB, T9H 2G2
(780) 799-7900
Emp Here 50   *Sales* 54,403,500
SIC 8211 Elementary and secondary schools
Gary Stevenson
Kath Rhyason
Jeff Thompson
Glenn Doonanco
Angela Adams
Glenn Cooper
Elizabeth Enkooren

D-U-N-S 20-712-1869   (BR)
FORT MCMURRAY PUBLIC SCHOOL DISTRICT #2833
DR K A CLARK ELEMENTARY SCHOOL
(*Suby of* FORT MCMURRAY PUBLIC SCHOOL DISTRICT #2833)
8453 Franklin Ave, Fort Mcmurray, AB, T9H 2J2
(780) 743-2444
Emp Here 75
SIC 8211 Elementary and secondary schools
Merrie Mitsopoulos

D-U-N-S 24-334-5480   (BR)
GAMEHOST INC
BOOM TOWN CASINO
(*Suby of* GAMEHOST INC)
9825 Hardin St, Fort Mcmurray, AB, T9H 4G9
(780) 790-9739
Emp Here 100
SIC 7999 Amusement and recreation, nec
Gwen Coston

D-U-N-S 25-014-4672   (SL)
GENROC DRYWALL LTD
7307 Railway Ave, Fort Mcmurray, AB, T9H 1B9

Emp Here 80   *Sales* 12,990,480
SIC 1742 Plastering, drywall, and insulation
Michael (Mike) Yeoman

D-U-N-S 24-171-4971   (SL)
GENRON ENTERPRISES LTD
BOND-A-PLY ALBERTA
295 Macdonald Cres, Fort Mcmurray, AB, T9H 4B7
(780) 743-3445
Emp Here 60   *Sales* 13,069,740
SIC 1761 Roofing, siding, and sheetMetal work
Gene Dobie
Rudy Van Spronsen
Tom Van Spronsen
Andrew Thorne

D-U-N-S 20-217-8773   (SL)
GREGG DISTRIBUTORS (FORT MCMURRAY) LTD
325 Macalpine Cres, Fort Mcmurray, AB, T9H 4Y4

(780) 715-4000
Emp Here 30   *Sales* 14,250,780
SIC 5085 Industrial supplies
Kyle Tavack

D-U-N-S 24-386-9133   (HQ)
GUTHRIE INVESTMENTS LTD
9912 Manning Ave, Fort Mcmurray, AB, T9H 2B9
(780) 791-1367
Sales 135,424,000
SIC 1711 Plumbing, heating, air-conditioning
Laurie Guthrie

D-U-N-S 24-809-0185   (SL)
GUTHRIE MECHANICAL SERVICES LTD
(*Suby of* GUTHRIE INVESTMENTS LTD)
9912 Manning Ave, Fort Mcmurray, AB, T9H 2B9
(780) 791-1367
Emp Here 500   *Sales* 107,971,566
SIC 1711 Plumbing, heating, air-conditioning
Douglas Bruce
Jeffrie Shaughnessy
Steve Jani

D-U-N-S 20-359-5850   (SL)
HINES INDUSTRIAL SITE SERVICES GROUP INC
8130 Manning Ave, Fort Mcmurray, AB, T9H 1V7
(780) 790-3500
Emp Here 250   *Sales* 7,992,000
SIC 7349 Building maintenance services, nec
Corey Hines
Raymond Hines

D-U-N-S 20-887-5554   (SL)
KEYANO COLLEGE
8115 Franklin Ave, Fort Mcmurray, AB, T9H 2H7
(780) 791-4800
Emp Here 404   *Sales* 64,112,052
SIC 8221 Colleges and universities
Kevin Nagel
Catherine Koch
Therese Greenwood
Henry Hunter
Kara Flynn
Andrew Carter
Nicole Bourque-Bouchier
Brent Davis
Bryan Rabik
Doreen Cole

D-U-N-S 25-245-9789   (SL)
LN LAND DEVELOPMENT TECHNOLOGIES INC
9908 Franklin Ave Unit 4, Fort Mcmurray, AB, T9H 2K5
(780) 791-0075
Emp Here 67   *Sales* 11,789,186
SIC 8713 Surveying services
Lance Normanz

D-U-N-S 25-960-0070   (BR)
LOBLAWS INC
REAL CANADIAN SUPERSTORE
(*Suby of* LOBLAW COMPANIES LIMITED)
9 Haineault St, Fort Mcmurray, AB, T9H 1R8
(780) 790-3827
Emp Here 240
SIC 5411 Grocery stores
Anne Callaghan

D-U-N-S 24-681-9937   (BR)
MCDONALD'S RESTAURANTS OF CANADA LIMITED
MCDONALD'S
(*Suby of* MCDONALD'S CORPORATION)
450 Gregoire Dr, Fort Mcmurray, AB, T9H 3R2
(780) 791-0551
Emp Here 80
SIC 5812 Eating places
Sarah Viel

D-U-N-S 24-009-9452   (SL)
METALCARE GROUP INC

291 Macalpine Cres Unit A, Fort Mcmurray, AB, T9H 4Y4
(780) 715-1889
Emp Here 40   *Sales* 17,968,760
SIC 7389 Business services, nec
Muthu Palanisamy

D-U-N-S 20-257-6690   (SL)
METALCARE GROUP INC
400 Mackenzie Blvd Suite 201, Fort Mcmurray, AB, T9H 4C4
(780) 715-1889
Emp Here 40   *Sales* 17,739,600
SIC 7389 Business services, nec
Muthu Palanisamy

D-U-N-S 24-399-0967   (SL)
NEEGAN DEVELOPMENT CORPORATION LTD
Gd Lcd Main, Fort Mcmurray, AB, T9H 3E2
(780) 791-0654
Emp Here 65   *Sales* 16,408,730
SIC 1611 Highway and street construction
David Tuccaro
Lawrence Tuccaro

D-U-N-S 24-282-9265   (SL)
NORAL MOTORS (1983) LTD
NORAL TOYOTA
10129 Macdonald Ave, Fort Mcmurray, AB, T9H 1T2
(780) 743-5444
Emp Here 21   *Sales* 13,214,880
SIC 5511 New and used car dealers
Jeff Polovick
Gerard Levasseur
Helga Levasseur

D-U-N-S 20-325-1962   (BR)
NORALTA LODGE LTD
BUFFALO LODGE
7210 Cliff Ave Suite 7202, Fort Mcmurray, AB, T9H 1A1
(780) 791-3334
Emp Here 75   *Sales* 461,736
SIC 7041 Membership-basis organization hotels
James Maloney

D-U-N-S 24-228-5448   (SL)
NORCAN ELECTRIC INC
380 Mackenzie Blvd Suite 6b, Fort Mcmurray, AB, T9H 4C4
(780) 799-3292
Emp Here 500   *Sales* 117,754,500
SIC 1731 Electrical work
Cameron Cassels

D-U-N-S 25-950-9958   (BR)
NORTH AMERICAN CONSTRUCTION MANAGEMENT LTD
NORTH AMERICAN MINING DIVISION
(*Suby of* NORTH AMERICAN CONSTRUCTION GROUP LTD)
Gd, Fort Mcmurray, AB, T9H 3E2
(780) 791-1997
Emp Here 300
SIC 1629 Heavy construction, nec
Tom Logan

D-U-N-S 24-349-3264   (BR)
PALADIN TECHNOLOGIES INC
(*Suby of* PALADIN TECHNOLOGIES INC)
604 Signal Rd, Fort Mcmurray, AB, T9H 4Z4
(780) 743-1422
Emp Here 100
SIC 7381 Detective and armored car services
Amir Atri

D-U-N-S 25-193-4782   (SL)
PARAMOUNT PARTS INC
NAPA AUTO PARTS
36 Riedel St Suite 1, Fort Mcmurray, AB, T9H 3E1
(780) 791-3000
Emp Here 50   *Sales* 24,903,900
SIC 5531 Auto and home supply stores
Brent Usick

D-U-N-S 25-670-5989   (SL)
PEDERSON FAMILY PHARMACY LTD
SHOPPERS DRUG MART # 327
8600 Franklin Ave Suite 501, Fort Mcmurray,
AB, T9H 4G8
(780) 743-1251
Emp Here 40   *Sales* 10,118,160
SIC 5912 Drug stores and proprietary stores
Eric Pederson
Vanessa Pederson

D-U-N-S 24-004-1157   (BR)
RONA INC
RONA HOME CENTRE FORT MCMURRAY
(*Suby of* LOWE'S COMPANIES, INC.)
8408 Manning Ave, Fort Mcmurray, AB, T9H
5G2
(780) 743-4666
Emp Here 130
SIC 5251 Hardware stores
Ghazwan Wanous

D-U-N-S 24-761-9377   (BR)
SGS CANADA INC
235 Macdonald Cres, Fort Mcmurray, AB, T9H
4B5
(780) 791-6454
Emp Here 200
SIC 8734 Testing laboratories
Francisco Vaamonde

D-U-N-S 25-999-0542   (BR)
SMS EQUIPMENT INC
CONECO EQUIPMENT
(*Suby of* SUMITOMO CORPORATION)
22k Highway 63 North, Fort Mcmurray, AB,
T9H 3G2
(780) 714-5300
Emp Here 600
SIC 5082 Construction and mining machinery
Dirk Maritz

D-U-N-S 25-271-0769   (BR)
SOBEYS WEST INC
SAFEWAY
(*Suby of* EMPIRE COMPANY LIMITED)
9601 Franklin Ave, Fort Mcmurray, AB, T9H
2J8
(780) 790-1988
Emp Here 80
SIC 5411 Grocery stores
Sallah Tuer

D-U-N-S 25-271-0728   (BR)
SOBEYS WEST INC
THICKWOOD SAFEWAY
(*Suby of* EMPIRE COMPANY LIMITED)
131 Signal Rd, Fort Mcmurray, AB, T9H 4N6
(780) 791-3909
Emp Here 84
SIC 5411 Grocery stores
Dave Chizem

D-U-N-S 20-853-0977   (BR)
SUNCOR ENERGY INC
(*Suby of* SUNCOR ENERGY INC)
Gd Lcd Main, Fort Mcmurray, AB, T9H 3E2
(780) 743-6411
Emp Here 500
SIC 1311 Crude petroleum and natural gas
Mel Rampersad

D-U-N-S 24-398-3418   (BR)
SUNCOR ENERGY INC
OIL SANDS GROUP
(*Suby of* SUNCOR ENERGY INC)
512 Snow Eagle Dr, Fort Mcmurray, AB, T9H
0B6
(780) 790-1999
Emp Here 2,300
SIC 1311 Crude petroleum and natural gas
Kirk Bailey

D-U-N-S 24-034-1722   (SL)
SURMONT SAND & GRAVEL LTD
431 Mackenzie Blvd Unit 8, Fort Mcmurray,
AB, T9H 4C5

(780) 743-2533
Emp Here 60   *Sales* 16,059,120
SIC 5211 Lumber and other building materials
David Laboucane

D-U-N-S 20-084-6335   (HQ)
SYNCRUDE CANADA LTD
(*Suby of* SUNCOR ENERGY INC)
9911 Macdonald Ave Suite 200, Fort Mcmur-
ray, AB, T9H 1S7
(780) 790-5911
Emp Here 3,000   *Sales* 9,272,910,000
SIC 1311 Crude petroleum and natural gas
Doreen Cole
Pablo Borgnino
Kara Flynn
Greg Fuhr
Ray Hansen
Jerry Mcpherson
Peter Read
Christian Matte
Steve Yatauro
Bill Chase

D-U-N-S 25-153-2370   (BR)
TERRACON GEOTECHNIQUE LTD
(*Suby of* TERRACON GEOTECHNIQUE LTD)
8212 Manning Ave, Fort Mcmurray, AB, T9H
1V9
(780) 743-9343
Emp Here 220
SIC 8711 Engineering services
Andrew Taylor

D-U-N-S 24-382-1035   (SL)
TUC'S CONTRACTING LTD
(*Suby of* TUCCARO INC)
283 Macalpine Cres Suite C, Fort Mcmurray,
AB, T9H 4Y4
(780) 743-8110
Emp Here 85   *Sales* 17,485,010
SIC 4212 Local trucking, without storage
John Tuccaro

D-U-N-S 20-044-2213   (SL)
**UNIVERSAL AVIATION SERVICES CORPO-
RATION**
Gd Lcd Main, Fort Mcmurray, AB, T9H 3E2
(780) 791-9881
Emp Here 26   *Sales* 32,687,226
SIC 5172 Petroleum products, nec
Trent Obrigewitsch
Howard Heffernan
Diane Heffernan
Lee Obrigewitsch
Cathy Schulte

D-U-N-S 25-947-6711   (BR)
VOICE CONSTRUCTION LTD
(*Suby of* VOICE CONSTRUCTION LTD)
200 Macdonald Cres, Fort Mcmurray, AB, T9H
4B2
(780) 790-0981
Emp Here 500
SIC 1794 Excavation work
Mike Stenbold

D-U-N-S 25-498-2945   (BR)
WAL-MART CANADA CORP
(*Suby of* WALMART INC.)
2 Hospital St, Fort Mcmurray, AB, T9H 5E4
(780) 790-6012
Emp Here 190
SIC 5311 Department stores
Mark Noel

D-U-N-S 24-325-9293   (SL)
WAPOSE MEDICAL SERVICES INC
431 Mackenzie Blvd Suite 12, Fort Mcmurray,
AB, T9H 4C5
(780) 714-6654
Emp Here 50   *Sales* 11,848,500
SIC 7363 Help supply services
Ryan Purden

D-U-N-S 24-840-2380   (SL)
WILLIAMS CHRYSLER LTD
WILLIAMS CHRYSLER JEEP & RV CENTRE

324 Gregoire Dr, Fort Mcmurray, AB, T9H 3R2
(780) 790-9000
Emp Here 43   *Sales* 21,417,354
SIC 5511 New and used car dealers
Irvin Williams

D-U-N-S 20-918-2638   (HQ)
**WOOD BUFFALO HOUSING & DEVELOP-
MENT CORPORATION**
9915 Franklin Ave Suite 9011, Fort Mcmurray,
AB, T9H 2K4
(780) 799-4050
Emp Here 21   *Sales* 19,610,512
SIC 6531 Real estate agents and managers
Bryan Lutes
David Peters
Kim Jenkins

D-U-N-S 20-243-6981   (SL)
YMCA OF WOOD BUFFALO
221 Tundra Dr, Fort Mcmurray, AB, T9H 4Z7
(780) 790-9622
Emp Here 49   *Sales* 19,473,286
SIC 8699 Membership organizations, nec
Margaret Reid

Fort Mcmurray, AB T9K

D-U-N-S 20-742-7373   (BR)
ACUREN GROUP INC
(*Suby of* ROCKWOOD SERVICE CORPORA-
TION)
240 Taiganova Cres Unit 2, Fort Mcmurray,
AB, T9K 0T4
(780) 790-1776
Emp Here 200
SIC 8711 Engineering services
Jason Caruso

D-U-N-S 24-238-6212   (SL)
FISHER POWERLINE CONSTRUCTION LTD
230 Taiganova Cres Suite 2b, Fort Mcmurray,
AB, T9K 0T4
(780) 713-3474
Emp Here 300   *Sales* 140,109,840
SIC 1623 Water, sewer, and utility lines
Roger Fisher
Shyerene Fisher
Shawn Woon

D-U-N-S 25-153-1497   (BR)
**FORT MCMURRAY PUBLIC SCHOOL DIS-
TRICT #2833**
TIMBERLEA PUBLIC SCHOOL
(*Suby of* FORT MCMURRAY PUBLIC
SCHOOL DISTRICT #2833)
107 Brett Dr, Fort Mcmurray, AB, T9K 1V1
(780) 743-1079
Emp Here 95
SIC 8211 Elementary and secondary schools
Richard Thorne

D-U-N-S 24-715-4995   (SL)
H. WILSON INDUSTRIES (2010) LTD
(*Suby of* KONINKLIJKE VOLKERWESSELS
N.V.)
1045 Memorial Dr, Fort Mcmurray, AB, T9K
0K4
(780) 743-1881
Emp Here 140   *Sales* 37,931,880
SIC 1521 Single-family housing construction
Wes Holodniuk
Kirsten Larsen

D-U-N-S 24-853-6252   (SL)
MIDLITE CONSTRUCTION LTD
135 Boreal Ave, Fort Mcmurray, AB, T9K 0T4
(780) 714-6559
Emp Here 100   *Sales* 25,244,200
SIC 1623 Water, sewer, and utility lines
Rocky Buksa

D-U-N-S 24-851-6622   (BR)
SAFWAY SERVICES CANADA, ULC

(*Suby of* BRAND INDUSTRIAL SERVICES,
INC.)
1005 Memorial Dr Unit 3, Fort Mcmurray, AB,
T9K 0K4
(780) 791-6473
Emp Here 650
SIC 1799 Special trade contractors, nec
Chris Nash

D-U-N-S 25-056-9308   (BR)
SOBEYS CAPITAL INCORPORATED
THICKWOOD GARDEN MARKET I G A
(*Suby of* EMPIRE COMPANY LIMITED)
210 Thickwood Blvd, Fort Mcmurray, AB, T9K
1X9
(780) 743-9339
Emp Here 100
SIC 5411 Grocery stores
Ryan Sparks

D-U-N-S 20-513-7941   (SL)
STONY VALLEY CONTRACTING LTD
245 Taiganova Cres, Fort Mcmurray, AB, T9K
0T4
(780) 743-0527
Emp Here 105   *Sales* 59,810,940
SIC 5032 Brick, stone, and related material
Dan Fouts
Tara Sinanan
Wayne Woodhouse

D-U-N-S 20-164-5230   (SL)
VAULT PIPELINES LTD
142 Dickins Dr Bay 4, Fort Mcmurray, AB, T9K
1X4
(587) 537-5520
Emp Here 4   *Sales* 12,423,428
SIC 4922 Natural gas transmission
Matthew Deeprose

D-U-N-S 24-254-6815   (BR)
WILLBROS MINE SERVICES, L.P.
WILLBROS CANADA
(*Suby of* PRIMORIS SERVICES CORPORA-
TION)
1005 Memorial Dr, Fort Mcmurray, AB, T9K
0K4
(780) 743-6247
Emp Here 535
SIC 1623 Water, sewer, and utility lines
Darleen Perrier

Fort Saskatchewan, AB T8L

D-U-N-S 24-714-9933   (SL)
301726 ALBERTA LTD
BOSTON PIZZA
8751 94 St, Fort Saskatchewan, AB, T8L 4P7
(780) 998-9999
Emp Here 85   *Sales* 3,644,205
SIC 5812 Eating places
Grant Nisbet
Marilyn Nisbet

D-U-N-S 25-014-5059   (BR)
ALBERTA HEALTH SERVICES
*FORT SASKATCHEWAN COMMUNITY HOS-
PITAL*
(*Suby of* GOVERNMENT OF THE
PROVINCE OF ALBERTA)
9401 86 Ave, Fort Saskatchewan, AB, T8L
0C6
(780) 998-2256
Emp Here 120
SIC 8062 General medical and surgical hospi-
tals
Heather Dursling

D-U-N-S 24-905-0246   (SL)
CAREY INDUSTRIAL SERVICES LTD
9918a 102 St, Fort Saskatchewan, AB, T8L
2C3
(780) 998-1919
Emp Here 90   *Sales* 13,983,390
SIC 7361 Employment agencies

▲ Public Company   ■ Public Company Family Member   **HQ** Headquarters   **BR** Branch   **SL** Single Location

Lyle Carey

D-U-N-S 24-960-9967   (HQ)
DEERLAND FARM EQUIPMENT (1985) LTD
(*Suby of* STOKKE, DALE INVESTMENTS LTD)
8599 112 St, Fort Saskatchewan, AB, T8L 3V3
(780) 998-3249
Sales 16,625,910
SIC 5083 Farm and garden machinery
  Dale Stokke
  Dave Austin

D-U-N-S 20-085-8033   (BR)
DOW CHEMICAL CANADA ULC
(*Suby of* DOW INC.)
Highway 15, Fort Saskatchewan, AB, T8L 2P4
(780) 998-8000
Emp Here 500
SIC 2899 Chemical preparations, nec
  Robert Lacroix

D-U-N-S 20-287-2677   (SL)
FDS PRIME ENERGY SERVICES LTD
11870 88 Ave Unit 148, Fort Saskatchewan, AB, T8L 0K1

Emp Here 49   *Sales* 16,333,317
SIC 1541 Industrial buildings and warehouses
  Brian Fahner

D-U-N-S 24-343-4177   (BR)
HARRIS STEEL ULC
HARRIS REBAR
(*Suby of* NUCOR CORPORATION)
11215 87 Ave, Fort Saskatchewan, AB, T8L 2S3
(780) 992-0777
Emp Here 150
SIC 3499 Fabricated Metal products, nec
  Gary Kiziak

D-U-N-S 25-613-4995   (SL)
HIGH ROLLERS CUSTOM MOTOR PARTS
11091 86 Ave, Fort Saskatchewan, AB, T8L 3T7
(780) 992-3225
Emp Here 28   *Sales* 17,619,840
SIC 5571 Motorcycle dealers

D-U-N-S 20-299-8431   (SL)
INTERNATIONAL BULK SERVICES
OIL GAS DISTRIBUTION
21423 Township Road 554, Fort Saskatchewan, AB, T8L 4A4
(780) 220-9264
Emp Here 5   *Sales* 15,529,285
SIC 4924 Natural gas distribution

D-U-N-S 24-327-9965   (HQ)
J. MCEWEN'S PETROLEUMS LTD
MCEWEN'S FUELS & FERTILIZERS
11141 89 Ave, Fort Saskatchewan, AB, T8L 2S6
(780) 997-4120
Emp Here 1   *Sales* 44,551,200
SIC 5191 Farm supplies
  Chris Mcewen

D-U-N-S 24-065-8336   (BR)
MANDERLEY TURF PRODUCTS INC
MANDERLEY TURFGRASS
(*Suby of* MANDERLEY TURF PRODUCTS INC)
55403 Range Rd 222, Fort Saskatchewan, AB, T8L 2N9
(780) 998-1995
Emp Here 100
SIC 5261 Retail nurseries and garden stores
  Marco Yris

D-U-N-S 20-321-2808   (HQ)
MCEWEN'S FUELS & FERTILIZERS INC
11141 89 Ave, Fort Saskatchewan, AB, T8L 2S6
(780) 998-2058
Emp Here 17   *Sales* 18,563,000
SIC 5191 Farm supplies

Chris Mcewen

D-U-N-S 24-353-3960   (HQ)
MEGLOBAL CANADA INC
Bag 16 Hwy 15, Fort Saskatchewan, AB, T8L 2P4
(780) 992-4250
Emp Here 40   *Sales* 36,517,250
SIC 5169 Chemicals and allied products, nec
  Mohammad Rashed Jasem
  Jeff Johnston

D-U-N-S 20-373-1109   (SL)
MEGLOBAL CANADA ULC
Hwy 15 Bag 16, Fort Saskatchewan, AB, T8L 2P4
(877) 885-7237
Emp Here 45   *Sales* 14,730,480
SIC 2819 Industrial inorganic chemicals, nec
  Ramesh Ramachandran

D-U-N-S 24-522-3847   (SL)
NOYEN CONSTRUCTION LTD
8309 113 St, Fort Saskatchewan, AB, T8L 4K7
(780) 998-3974
Emp Here 50   *Sales* 14,176,200
SIC 1611 Highway and street construction
  Peter Noyen

D-U-N-S 20-644-5673   (HQ)
OERLIKON METCO (CANADA) INC
(*Suby of* OC OERLIKON CORPORATION AG, PFAFFIKON)
10108 114 St, Fort Saskatchewan, AB, T8L 4R1
(780) 992-5100
Sales 12,878,548
SIC 3399 Primary Metal products
  Gerald Deck
  Neil Marshall
  Friedrich Herold
  Marc Hamacher
  Jurg Fedier

D-U-N-S 20-979-2436   (SL)
P M L INSPECTION SERVICES LTD
11110 88 Ave Suite 2, Fort Saskatchewan, AB, T8L 3K8
(780) 992-9360
Emp Here 29   *Sales* 13,027,351
SIC 7389 Business services, nec
  Phil Larochelle

D-U-N-S 24-829-2711   (SL)
PME INC
8402 116 St, Fort Saskatchewan, AB, T8L 0G8
(780) 992-2280
Emp Here 35   *Sales* 11,666,655
SIC 1541 Industrial buildings and warehouses
  Gil Brulotte

D-U-N-S 20-969-5469   (SL)
RIVERCREST LODGE NURSING HOME LTD
RIVERCREST CARE CENTRE
10104 101 Ave, Fort Saskatchewan, AB, T8L 2A5
(780) 998-2425
Emp Here 75   *Sales* 5,154,975
SIC 8051 Skilled nursing care facilities
  Greg Ulveland
  Lee Turner
  Art Ulveland

D-U-N-S 20-116-8643   (HQ)
SAFWAY SERVICES CANADA, ULC
(*Suby of* BRAND INDUSTRIAL SERVICES, INC.)
11237 87 Ave, Fort Saskatchewan, AB, T8L 2S3
(780) 992-1929
Emp Here 23   *Sales* 13,047,858
SIC 1799 Special trade contractors, nec
  Marc J. Wilson
  F. Gerard Johns
  Robert M. Sukalich
  William Rogers

D-U-N-S 24-397-9382   (BR)
SHELL CANADA LIMITED
SCOTFORD COMPLEX
(*Suby of* ROYAL DUTCH SHELL PLC)
55522 Range Road 214, Fort Saskatchewan, AB, T8L 4A4
(780) 992-3600
Emp Here 250
SIC 2911 Petroleum refining
  Arnel Santos

D-U-N-S 25-746-4008   (BR)
SHERRITT INTERNATIONAL CORPORATION
MOA NICKLE S.A. DIV OF
(*Suby of* SHERRITT INTERNATIONAL CORPORATION)
10101 114 St, Fort Saskatchewan, AB, T8L 2T3
(780) 992-7000
Emp Here 600
SIC 3339 Primary nonferrous Metals, nec

D-U-N-S 20-832-5287   (SL)
SMITH INSURANCE SERVICE
9902 102 St, Fort Saskatchewan, AB, T8L 2C3
(780) 998-2501
Emp Here 20   *Sales* 11,598,480
SIC 6411 Insurance agents, brokers, and service
  David Coleman

D-U-N-S 20-640-1783   (BR)
SOBEYS CAPITAL INCORPORATED
SOBEYS PHARMACY
(*Suby of* EMPIRE COMPANY LIMITED)
10004 99 Ave, Fort Saskatchewan, AB, T8L 3Y1
(780) 998-5429
Emp Here 100
SIC 5411 Grocery stores
  Patricia Hawryluk

D-U-N-S 20-970-1101   (SL)
SOUTH FORT CHEVROLET LTD
10109 89 Ave, Fort Saskatchewan, AB, T8L 3V5
(780) 998-7881
Emp Here 30   *Sales* 14,942,340
SIC 5511 New and used car dealers
  Donald Schroder
  Rhonda Schroder

D-U-N-S 25-314-6971   (SL)
STAMBAUGH HOLDINGS LTD
18 Westpark Crt, Fort Saskatchewan, AB, T8L 3W9
(780) 992-1600
Emp Here 25   *Sales* 10,483,875
SIC 6712 Bank holding companies

D-U-N-S 24-316-6761   (SL)
TAURUS SITE SERVICES INC
11401 85 Ave, Fort Saskatchewan, AB, T8L 0A9
(780) 998-5001
Emp Here 100   *Sales* 25,244,200
SIC 1611 Highway and street construction
  Coruie Mitchell

D-U-N-S 24-807-1193   (SL)
VENTURES WEST TRANSPORT INC
182 Sturgeon Way, Fort Saskatchewan, AB, T8L 2N9
(780) 449-5542
Emp Here 80   *Sales* 11,855,360
SIC 4213 Trucking, except local
  Glenn Bauer

D-U-N-S 20-736-2505   (BR)
WAL-MART CANADA CORP
(*Suby of* WALMART INC.)
9551 87 Ave, Fort Saskatchewan, AB, T8L 4N3
(780) 998-3633
Emp Here 200
SIC 5311 Department stores

Paul Daniel

D-U-N-S 20-825-3299   (SL)
WILLOWRIDGE CONSTRUCTION LTD
11870 88 Ave Unit 148, Fort Saskatchewan, AB, T8L 0K1
(780) 998-9133
Emp Here 35   *Sales* 11,666,655
SIC 1541 Industrial buildings and warehouses
  Glen Gabert
  Jordan Rumohr
  Tyler Gabert

Fort Vermilion, AB T0H

D-U-N-S 20-897-6134   (HQ)
FORT VERMILION SCHOOL DIVISON NO. 52
5213 River Rd, Fort Vermilion, AB, T0H 1N0
(780) 927-3766
Emp Here 12   *Sales* 34,691,650
SIC 8211 Elementary and secondary schools
  Clark Mcaskile
  Norman Buhler

Fox Creek, AB T0H

D-U-N-S 24-520-9168   (SL)
248276 ALBERTA LTD
KODIAK OILFIELD SERVICES
100 1st St, Fox Creek, AB, T0H 1P0
(780) 622-3566
Emp Here 44   *Sales* 12,855,436
SIC 7359 Equipment rental and leasing, nec
  Larry Davidson
  Brian Davidson
  Michael Davidson

Fox Lake, AB T0H

D-U-N-S 25-000-5089   (SL)
LITTLE RED RIVER CREE NATION BOARD OF EDUCATION
Gd, Fox Lake, AB, T0H 1R0
(780) 759-3912
Emp Here 100   *Sales* 9,282,600
SIC 8211 Elementary and secondary schools
  Nelson Mason

Grande Cache, AB T0E

D-U-N-S 25-106-7633   (SL)
ASENIWUCHE DEVELOPEMENT CORPORATION
ADC
10028 99 St, Grande Cache, AB, T0E 0Y0
(780) 827-5510
Emp Here 100   *Sales* 67,267,900
SIC 1389 Oil and gas field services, nec
  David Macphee
  Billy Mcdonald
  Philomene Moberly
  Michael Moberly
  Gordon Frentz

D-U-N-S 25-371-1188   (SL)
FOOTHILLS FOREST PRODUCTS INC
Highway 40 S, Grande Cache, AB, T0E 0Y0
(780) 827-2225
Emp Here 80   *Sales* 15,389,600
SIC 2426 Hardwood dimension and flooring mills
  Mike Hayman

D-U-N-S 25-372-2466   (BR)

GRANDE CACHE COAL CORPORATION
(*Suby of* GRANDE CACHE COAL CORPO-
RATION)
Gd, Grande Cache, AB, T0E 0Y0
(780) 827-4646
Emp Here 200
SIC 1221 Bituminous coal and lignite-surface
mining
Tim Riordon

D-U-N-S 20-012-6014   (SL)
MICHEL'S SUPER A FOODS LTD
3100 Pine Plaza, Grande Cache, AB, T0E 0Y0
(780) 827-2434
Emp Here 40   *Sales* 10,966,080
SIC 5411 Grocery stores
Michel Beland
Jillian Beland

D-U-N-S 24-000-2485   (SL)
**MISTAHIA REGIONAL HEALTH AUTHOR-
ITY**
GRANDE CACHE GENERAL HOSPITAL
10200 Shand Ave, Grande Cache, AB, T0E
0Y0
(780) 827-3701
Emp Here 40   *Sales* 10,462,120
SIC 6712 Bank holding companies
Betty Daynes

D-U-N-S 25-272-5718   (BR)
WEYERHAEUSER COMPANY LIMITED
(*Suby of* WEYERHAEUSER COMPANY)
Gd, Grande Cache, AB, T0E 0Y0

Emp Here 150
SIC 2421 Sawmills and planing mills, general

Grande Prairie, AB T8V

D-U-N-S 25-014-0936   (BR)
1032451 B.C. LTD
DAILY HERALD TRIBUNE, THE
(*Suby of* QUEBECOR MEDIA INC)
10604 100 St, Grande Prairie, AB, T8V 2M5
(780) 532-1110
Emp Here 100
SIC 2711 Newspapers
Margaret Steele

D-U-N-S 20-734-0188   (HQ)
1089243 ALBERTA LTD
PROPIPE MANUFACTURING DIV OF
9625 144 Ave, Grande Prairie, AB, T8V 7V4
(780) 830-0955
Emp Here 200   *Sales* 84,263,100
SIC 3533 Oil and gas field machinery
Mike Esfarjani

D-U-N-S 24-967-9879   (HQ)
287706 ALBERTA LTD
STANFORD INN
11401 100 Ave, Grande Prairie, AB, T8V 5M6
(780) 539-5678
Emp Here 85   *Sales* 15,293,850
SIC 7011 Hotels and motels
V K Thapar
Darryl Hay
Naomi Ducklow

D-U-N-S 20-086-2555   (HQ)
4475470 CANADA INC
PAT'S AUTO BUMPER TO BUMPER
12803 100 St Suite 100, Grande Prairie, AB,
T8V 4H3
(780) 532-4488
Emp Here 33   *Sales* 13,840,170
SIC 5013 Motor vehicle supplies and new
parts
Kenton Switzer

D-U-N-S 24-879-5395   (SL)
467935 ALBERTA LTD
GRANDE PRAIRIE INN
11633 Clairmont Rd, Grande Prairie, AB, T8V

3Y4
(780) 532-5221
Emp Here 150   *Sales* 13,903,500
SIC 7011 Hotels and motels
Inayatali Sumar

D-U-N-S 24-003-5832   (SL)
530664 ALBERTA LTD
NORTHGATE HONDA
13116 100 St Suite 780, Grande Prairie, AB,
T8V 4H9
(780) 532-8010
Emp Here 34   *Sales* 16,934,652
SIC 5511 New and used car dealers
Ken Grubisich
Sheila Grubisich
Charlie Grubisich

D-U-N-S 20-299-0953   (SL)
ALL PEACE PROTECTION LTD
APP PARKING
11117 100 St Suite 202, Grande Prairie, AB,
T8V 2N2
(780) 538-1166
Emp Here 44   *Sales* 3,937,500
SIC 7381 Detective and armored car services
Ron Hyggen

D-U-N-S 20-552-9592   (HQ)
AQUATERA UTILITIES INC
11101 104 Ave, Grande Prairie, AB, T8V 8H6
(780) 532-9725
Sales 47,836,500
SIC 4953 Refuse systems
Bernd Manz
Gary Marcotte
Jim Smith
Andy Beal
Darlene Halwas
Gerry Marcotte
Abe Neufeld
Elizabeth Soria
David Urness
Catherine Connolly

D-U-N-S 25-686-7672   (BR)
ATCO ELECTRIC LTD
ATCO ELECTRIC
(*Suby of* ATCO LTD)
9717 97 Ave, Grande Prairie, AB, T8V 6L9
(780) 538-7032
Emp Here 280
SIC 4911 Electric services
Barry Goy

D-U-N-S 24-806-2580   (HQ)
BARON OILFIELD SUPPLY
(*Suby of* NORTHERN METALIC SALES
(ALTA) LTD)
9515 108 St, Grande Prairie, AB, T8V 5R7
(780) 532-5661
Emp Here 130   *Sales* 73,159,500
SIC 5084 Industrial machinery and equipment
Barry Smith
Brad Hooper
Colleen Rose

D-U-N-S 20-894-7804   (SL)
**BEAIRSTO & ASSOCIATES ENGINEERING
LTD**
10940 92 Ave, Grande Prairie, AB, T8V 6B5
(780) 532-4919
Emp Here 65   *Sales* 11,437,270
SIC 8711 Engineering services
Bruce Beairsto
Ian Ketchum
Darrin Trydal
Dennis Hussey
Frederick Beairsto

D-U-N-S 24-385-0992   (SL)
BOCCIOLETTI, J & M SALES LTD
CANADIAN TIRE GRANDE PRAIRIE
11311 99 St, Grande Prairie, AB, T8V 2H6
(780) 539-9292
Emp Here 45   *Sales* 22,413,510
SIC 5531 Auto and home supply stores

Mary Boccioletti
Jim Boccioletti

D-U-N-S 24-337-9752   (SL)
BOREAL WELL SERVICES
13701 99 St, Grande Prairie, AB, T8V 7N9
(780) 513-3400
Emp Here 48   *Sales* 15,603,939
SIC 1381 Drilling oil and gas wells
Randy Graham

D-U-N-S 24-274-0512   (SL)
BRADVIN TRAILER SALES LTD
10920 87 Ave, Grande Prairie, AB, T8V 8K4
(780) 539-6260
Emp Here 40   *Sales* 19,001,040
SIC 5084 Industrial machinery and equipment
Jim Willsey

D-U-N-S 24-367-0192   (HQ)
BROGAN SAFETY SUPPLY LTD
12002 101 Ave Suite 101, Grande Prairie, AB,
T8V 8B1
(780) 539-9004
Emp Here 60   *Sales* 52,054,200
SIC 5099 Durable goods, nec
Darryl Bodnar
Sean Doerkson's

D-U-N-S 20-189-2135   (BR)
**CANADIAN NATURAL RESOURCES LIM-
ITED**
CNRL
(*Suby of* CANADIAN NATURAL RE-
SOURCES LIMITED)
9705 97 St, Grande Prairie, AB, T8V 8B9
(780) 831-7475
Emp Here 200
SIC 1311 Crude petroleum and natural gas

D-U-N-S 24-026-2170   (SL)
CDN CONTROLS LTD
10306 118 St, Grande Prairie, AB, T8V 3X9
(780) 532-8151
Emp Here 300   *Sales* 70,652,700
SIC 1731 Electrical work
Dean Fraser
Nick Stewart
Jamie Saunders

D-U-N-S 25-524-6696   (BR)
COSTCO WHOLESALE CANADA LTD
COSTCO
(*Suby of* COSTCO WHOLESALE CORPO-
RATION)
9901 116 St Unit 102, Grande Prairie, AB, T8V
6H6
(780) 538-2911
Emp Here 200
SIC 5099 Durable goods, nec
Mike Rizzo

D-U-N-S 20-146-2723   (SL)
COVER ALL NORTH INC
Gd Lcd Main, Grande Prairie, AB, T8V 2Z7
(780) 532-0366
Emp Here 30   *Sales* 10,115,809
SIC 1541 Industrial buildings and warehouses
Mark Loos

D-U-N-S 25-762-0898   (SL)
**CTP DISTRIBUTORS CUSTOM TRUCK
PARTS INC**
CUSTOM TRUCK PARTS
13313 100 St, Grande Prairie, AB, T8V 4H4
(780) 538-2211
Emp Here 73   *Sales* 26,587,695
SIC 5013 Motor vehicle supplies and new
parts
Charles Grubisich
William Kluyt
Garth Grubisich

D-U-N-S 24-066-1694   (SL)
D & J ISLEY & SONS CONTRACTING LTD
CANADIAN WESTERN AGGREGATE
11517 89 Ave, Grande Prairie, AB, T8V 5Z2

(780) 539-7580
Emp Here 100   *Sales* 19,237,000
SIC 2411 Logging
Morgan Isley
Roy Isley

D-U-N-S 24-394-7301   (BR)
DEVON CANADA CORPORATION
(*Suby of* DEVON ENERGY CORPORATION)
9601 116 St Unit 101, Grande Prairie, AB, T8V
5W3
(403) 517-6700
Emp Here 100
SIC 1382 Oil and gas exploration services
Vern Black

D-U-N-S 24-281-1339   (HQ)
DIRHAM CONSTRUCTION LTD
DIRHAM HOMES, DIV OF
10127 121 Ave Unit 201, Grande Prairie, AB,
T8V 7V3
(780) 539-4776
Sales 11,160,415
SIC 1521 Single-family housing construction
Henry Hamm

D-U-N-S 20-086-3009   (SL)
DOUG MARSHALL MOTOR CITY LTD
(*Suby of* MARSHALL, DOUG PROPERTY IN-
VESTMENTS LTD)
11044 100 St, Grande Prairie, AB, T8V 2N1
(780) 532-9333
Emp Here 50   *Sales* 24,903,900
SIC 5511 New and used car dealers
Doug Marshall
Dawn Logan

D-U-N-S 25-014-5505   (SL)
EARLS MARKET SQUARE LTD
EARL'S RESTAURANT
9825 100 St, Grande Prairie, AB, T8V 6X3
(780) 538-3275
Emp Here 85   *Sales* 3,869,115
SIC 5812 Eating places
Laurie Mroczek

D-U-N-S 24-004-0605   (SL)
ERNIE'S FITNESS EXPERTS
11500 100 St Suite 1, Grande Prairie, AB, T8V
4C2
(780) 539-9505
Emp Here 80   *Sales* 19,546,240
SIC 5941 Sporting goods and bicycle shops
Darrell Radbourne

D-U-N-S 20-437-3179   (SL)
ERNIE'S SPORT CENTRE (1983) LTD
ERNIE'S SPORTS EXPERT
11500 100 St Unit 1, Grande Prairie, AB, T8V
4C2
(780) 539-6262
Emp Here 65   *Sales* 15,881,320
SIC 5941 Sporting goods and bicycle shops
Darrell Radbourne
Dean Radbourne

D-U-N-S 24-523-1316   (HQ)
ERNIE'S SPORTS (S3) INC
11500 100 St Unit 1, Grande Prairie, AB, T8V
4C2
(780) 539-6262
Sales 24,432,800
SIC 5941 Sporting goods and bicycle shops
Darrell Radbourne
Dan Sieben

D-U-N-S 25-329-2767   (SL)
EXPERT MOBILE COMMUNICATIONS LTD
8701 112 St, Grande Prairie, AB, T8V 6A4
(780) 539-3962
Emp Here 32   *Sales* 14,309,568
SIC 5065 Electronic parts and equipment, nec
Garry Mcgovern
Connie Mcgovern

D-U-N-S 20-271-0153   (SL)
FIRST ALERT LOCATING LTD
72022b Rd 713, Grande Prairie, AB, T8V 3A1

▲ Public Company   ■ Public Company Family Member   **HQ** Headquarters   **BR** Branch   **SL** Single Location

(780) 538-9936
Emp Here 50   *Sales* 10,506,550
SIC 1382 Oil and gas exploration services
Martin Andersen
Jamie Andersen

D-U-N-S 25-985-6151   (SL)
FISCHER, C.A. LIMBER, CO. LTD
WOODLAND HOME HARDWARE BUILDING CENTRE
(*Suby of* DIRHAM CONSTRUCTION LTD)
11105 100 Ave, Grande Prairie, AB, T8V 3J9
(780) 538-1340
Emp Here 90   *Sales* 24,088,680
SIC 5211 Lumber and other building materials
Henry Hamm

D-U-N-S 24-523-5411   (HQ)
FOUNTAIN TIRE (G.P.) LTD
FOUNTAIN TIRE
13003 100 St, Grande Prairie, AB, T8V 4H3
(780) 539-1710
Emp Here 15   ·*Sales* 28,317,600
SIC 5531 Auto and home supply stores
Kalvin Giebelhaus

D-U-N-S 25-775-1768   (BR)
FRESON MARKET LTD
IGA
(*Suby of* ALTAMART INVESTMENTS (1993) LTD)
11417 99 St, Grande Prairie, AB, T8V 2H6
(780) 532-2920
Emp Here 76
SIC 5411 Grocery stores
Cam Dowden

D-U-N-S 24-067-5561   (SL)
G & M PLUMBING & HEATING LTD
10944 96 Ave, Grande Prairie, AB, T8V 3J5
(780) 538-3222
Emp Here 40   *Sales* 10,706,080
SIC 5251 Hardware stores
Gerry Marcotte

D-U-N-S 25-314-7060   (BR)
GIBSON ENERGY ULC
(*Suby of* GIBSON ENERGY INC)
9502 42 Ave, Grande Prairie, AB, T8V 5N3
(780) 539-4427
Emp Here 100
SIC 5172 Petroleum products, nec
Darcy Rautenstrauch

D-U-N-S 24-001-2880   (HQ)
GOLD STAR TRANSPORT (1975) LTD
(*Suby of* ARROW TRANSPORTATION SYSTEMS INC)
11002 89 Ave, Grande Prairie, AB, T8V 4W4
(780) 532-0773
Emp Here 30   *Sales* 30,855,900
SIC 4213 Trucking, except local
Jack Charles
Bob Munro

D-U-N-S 20-344-6885   (SL)
GP BREWING CO. LTD
8812 111a St, Grande Prairie, AB, T8V 5L3
(780) 533-4677
Emp Here 62   *Sales* 13,941,010
SIC 2082 Malt beverages
Matthew Toni
John Neudorf
Dean Swanberg

D-U-N-S 20-802-4393   (SL)
GRAND PRAIRIE LIVESTOCK MARKET
14809 100 St, Grande Prairie, AB, T8V 7C2

Emp Here 25   *Sales* 36,692,300
SIC 5154 Livestock
Marty Gilfillan

D-U-N-S 20-369-5445   (SL)
GRANDE PRAIRIE AIRPORT COMMISSION
10610 Airport Dr Suite 220, Grande Prairie, AB, T8V 7Z5
(780) 539-5270
Emp Here 52   *Sales* 13,882,856

SIC 4581 Airports, flying fields, and services
Brian Grant

D-U-N-S 24-003-2755   (HQ)
GRANDE PRAIRIE AND DISTRICT ASSOCIATION FOR PERSONS WITH DEVELOPMENTAL DISABILITIES
SWAN INDUSTRIES, DIV OF
8702 113 St, Grande Prairie, AB, T8V 6K5
(780) 532-0236
Emp Here 20   *Sales* 13,822,560
SIC 8322 Individual and family services
Barry Buckmell
Gail Furgeson
Eda Bonetti

D-U-N-S 24-521-8227   (SL)
GRANDE PRAIRIE ASSOCIATES REALTY LTD
RE/MAX GRANDE PRAIRIE
10114 100 St, Grande Prairie, AB, T8V 2L9
(780) 538-4700
Emp Here 40   *Sales* 13,085,080
SIC 6531 Real estate agents and managers
Barry Diedrich

D-U-N-S 24-331-7302   (HQ)
GRANDE PRAIRIE CATHOLIC SCHOOL DISTRICT 28
CATHOLIC EDUCATION CENTRE
9902 101 St Suite 28, Grande Prairie, AB, T8V 2P4
(780) 532-3013
Emp Here 30   *Sales* 45,099,145
SIC 8211 Elementary and secondary schools
Karl Germann

D-U-N-S 25-269-7347   (BR)
GRANDE PRAIRIE PUBLIC SCHOOL DISTRICT #2357
CRYSTAL PARK SCHOOL
(*Suby of* GRANDE PRAIRIE PUBLIC SCHOOL DISTRICT #2357)
9351 116 Ave, Grande Prairie, AB, T8V 6L5
(780) 830-3384
Emp Here 145
SIC 8211 Elementary and secondary schools
Charlene Ungstad

D-U-N-S 20-023-9304   (BR)
GRANDE PRAIRIE PUBLIC SCHOOL DISTRICT #2357
GRANDE PRAIRIE COMPOSITE HIGH SCHOOL
(*Suby of* GRANDE PRAIRIE PUBLIC SCHOOL DISTRICT #2357)
11202 104 St Suite 2357, Grande Prairie, AB, T8V 2Z1
(780) 532-7721
Emp Here 100
SIC 8211 Elementary and secondary schools
Rick Gilson

D-U-N-S 24-766-3149   (HQ)
GRANDE PRAIRIE PUBLIC SCHOOL DISTRICT #2357
10127 120 Ave, Grande Prairie, AB, T8V 8H8
(780) 532-4491
Sales 70,724,550
SIC 8211 Elementary and secondary schools
Russell Horswill
Wade Webb
Chris Gonnet

D-U-N-S 24-003-0122   (HQ)
GRANDE PRAIRIE REGIONAL COLLEGE
GPRC
10726 106 Ave, Grande Prairie, AB, T8V 4C4
(780) 539-2911
Emp Here 48   *Sales* 42,303,900
SIC 8221 Colleges and universities
Don Gnatiuk
Michael O'connor
Dan Lemieux
Jackie Clayton
Richard Horner
Anita Luck

Pete Merlo
Tim Garner
Grant Menzies

D-U-N-S 20-797-1974   (HQ)
HAPPY TRAILS R.V. INC
15211 100 St, Grande Prairie, AB, T8V 7C2
(780) 538-2120
Sales 38,386,080
SIC 5561 Recreational vehicle dealers
Peter Teichroeb

D-U-N-S 24-767-7685   (HQ)
HI-TECH BUSINESS SYSTEMS LTD
10115 100 Ave, Grande Prairie, AB, T8V 0V4
(780) 538-4128
Sales 20,122,830
SIC 5044 Office equipment
Kevin Szakacs

D-U-N-S 20-514-9326   (BR)
HOME DEPOT OF CANADA INC
HOME DEPOT
(*Suby of* THE HOME DEPOT INC)
11222 103 Ave, Grande Prairie, AB, T8V 7H1
(780) 831-3160
Emp Here 100
SIC 5211 Lumber and other building materials
Tasha Pfleging

D-U-N-S 24-357-1093   (BR)
HORIZON NORTH LOGISTICS INC
(*Suby of* HORIZON NORTH LOGISTICS INC)
10320 140 Ave Suite 102, Grande Prairie, AB, T8V 8A4
(780) 830-5333
Emp Here 80
SIC 4731 Freight transportation arrangement
Michael Hammerschmidt

D-U-N-S 20-345-7528   (SL)
INTERNATIONAL PAPER CANADA PULP HOLDINGS ULC
(*Suby of* INTERNATIONAL PAPER COMPANY)
Gd, Grande Prairie, AB, T8V 6V4
(780) 539-8500
Emp Here 300   *Sales* 110,291,100
SIC 2611 Pulp mills
Charles Rutledge

D-U-N-S 24-009-2101   (BR)
ISOLATION EQUIPMENT SERVICES INC
(*Suby of* ISOLATION EQUIPMENT SERVICES INC)
12925 97b St, Grande Prairie, AB, T8V 6K1
(780) 402-3060
Emp Here 75
SIC 3533 Oil and gas field machinery
Gord Allard

D-U-N-S 24-436-8622   (SL)
JANDEL HOMES
9407 153 Ave, Grande Prairie, AB, T8V 0B6
(780) 402-3170
Emp Here 49   *Sales* 12,399,891
SIC 5271 Mobile home dealers
Mark Huchalk

D-U-N-S 20-008-9121   (HQ)
KATES' PHARMACY LTD
SHOPPERS DRUG MART # 213
11801 100 St Suite 137, Grande Prairie, AB, T8V 3Y2
(780) 357-9301
Emp Here 40   *Sales* 19,546,240
SIC 5912 Drug stores and proprietary stores
Sam Kates

D-U-N-S 20-594-3475   (HQ)
KEN SARGENT GMC BUICK LTD
(*Suby of* SARGENT, KEN HOLDINGS LTD)
12308 100 St, Grande Prairie, AB, T8V 4H7
(780) 532-8865
Emp Here 66   *Sales* 59,781,600
SIC 5511 New and used car dealers
Ken Sargent

D-U-N-S 25-270-1131   (BR)
LOBLAWS INC
REAL CANADIAN SUPERSTORE
(*Suby of* LOBLAW COMPANIES LIMITED)
12225 99 St Suite 1544, Grande Prairie, AB, T8V 6X9
(780) 831-3827
Emp Here 275
SIC 5411 Grocery stores
Matt Robson

D-U-N-S 25-014-5836   (SL)
MANTO, MARK BUILDING MATERIALS LTD
GRANDE PRAIRIE HOME HARDWARE
10921 100 St, Grande Prairie, AB, T8V 2M9
(780) 532-2092
Emp Here 50   *Sales* 22,358,700
SIC 5072 Hardware
Mark Manto

D-U-N-S 24-374-1506   (SL)
MEDALLION ENERGY SERVICES INC
9516 146 Ave, Grande Prairie, AB, T8V 7V9
(780) 357-2164
Emp Here 100   *Sales* 31,970,500
SIC 1389 Oil and gas field services, nec
Kristopher Glenn
Jason Moodie

D-U-N-S 20-736-1663   (SL)
MJY AUTO SALES & LEASING LTD
GRANDE PRAIRIE MAZDA
12709 100 St, Grande Prairie, AB, T8V 4H2
(780) 532-5005
Emp Here 30   *Sales* 14,942,340
SIC 5511 New and used car dealers
Lionel Robins
John Klassen
Jessy Prihar
Yad Minhas

D-U-N-S 24-332-2286   (HQ)
N.P.A. LTD
WAPITI GRAVEL SUPPLIERS, DIV OF
(*Suby of* BOUYGUES)
4201 93 Rd St, Grande Prairie, AB, T8V 6T4
(780) 532-4600
Sales 25,244,200
SIC 1611 Highway and street construction
Lorne Davies
Robert Cote
Louis Gabanna
Kathy Milliken

D-U-N-S 25-367-6951   (BR)
NABORS DRILLING CANADA LIMITED
NABORS PRODUCTION SERVICES, DIV OF
(*Suby of* NABORS DRILLING CANADA LIMITED)
Hwy 40 W, Grande Prairie, AB, T8V 3A1

Emp Here 200
SIC 1389 Oil and gas field services, nec
Ken Ebert

D-U-N-S 24-372-2720   (HQ)
NEW HORIZON CO-OPERATIVE LTD
RYCROFT CO-OP
9831 100 Ave, Grande Prairie, AB, T8V 0T7
(780) 539-6111
Emp Here 5   *Sales* 14,673,850
SIC 5411 Grocery stores
Sandy Bennion
Laurie D Gronhovd
Sharon Schneider
Maureen Pearcy
Mort Timanson
Audrey Gustafson
Ike Hartman
Derrill Skaley
Gail Briggs

D-U-N-S 24-281-8391   (HQ)
NOR-COM INVESTMENT ENTERPRISES LTD
10525 100 Ave Suite 200, Grande Prairie, AB, T8V 0V8

(780) 539-6080
Sales 10,702,480
SIC 5149 Groceries and related products, nec
Charles Grubisich

D-U-N-S 24-608-6102   (SL)
NOR-LAN CHRYSLER INC
NOR-LAN CHRYSLER DODGE JEEP
12517 100 St, Grande Prairie, AB, T8V 4H2
(780) 978-9335
Emp Here 64   Sales 40,273,920
SIC 5511 New and used car dealers
Keith Jones

D-U-N-S 25-261-4656   (BR)
NORBORD INC
(Suby of NORBORD INC)
6700 Hwy 40 S, Grande Prairie, AB, T8V 6Y9
(780) 831-2500
Emp Here 200
SIC 2493 Reconstituted wood products
Mark Cunningham

D-U-N-S 20-538-3557   (HQ)
NORTHERN METALIC SALES (ALTA) LTD
10625 West Side Dr Unit 206, Grande Prairie,
AB, T8V 8E6
(780) 513-6095
Sales 32,802,000
SIC 6719 Holding companies, nec
Hassin Ali (Alex) Side

D-U-N-S 25-192-3827   (HQ)
NORTHERN METALIC SALES (G.P.) LTD
(Suby of NORTHERN METALIC SALES
(ALTA) LTD)
9708 108 St, Grande Prairie, AB, T8V 4E2
(780) 539-9555
Emp Here 60   Sales 24,356,332
SIC 5251 Hardware stores
Al Side
Gene Bombier

D-U-N-S 25-014-5893   (HQ)
PEACE WAPITI SCHOOL DIVISION NO.76
8611a 108 St, Grande Prairie, AB, T8V 4C5
(780) 532-8133
Emp Here 40   Sales 62,448,995
SIC 8211 Elementary and secondary schools
Dana Mcintosh
Stacey Pellend
Sharilyn Anderson
Richard Lappenbush
Kim Moodie
Wendy Kelm
Dale Crane
Stefanie Clarke
Bob Knull
Joy Joachim

D-U-N-S 20-522-4814   (SL)
PIONEER LAND SERVICES LTD
10537 98 Ave Suite 201, Grande Prairie, AB,
T8V 4L1
(780) 532-7707
Emp Here 15   Sales 15,492,120
SIC 5172 Petroleum products, nec
Kirk Fowler

D-U-N-S 20-323-3879   (SL)
POINTS WEST LIVING GP INC
11460 104 Ave Suite 403, Grande Prairie, AB,
T8V 3G9
(780) 357-5700
Emp Here 200   Sales 13,713,200
SIC 8051 Skilled nursing care facilities
Robert Jaberman
Paul Melanson
Steve Klemke

D-U-N-S 24-205-0842   (HQ)
POMEROY LODGING LP
POMEROY INN & SUITES FORT ST JOHN
9820 100 Ave, Grande Prairie, AB, T8V 0T8
(780) 814-5295
Emp Here 1   Sales 47,834,000
SIC 7011 Hotels and motels
Ryan Pomeroy

Bob Pomery
Stefan Nasalki
Jackie Clayton

D-U-N-S 25-681-0524   (SL)
PRAIRIE TRUCK LTD
9916 108 St, Grande Prairie, AB, T8V 4E2
(780) 532-3541
Emp Here 30   Sales 14,942,340
SIC 5511 New and used car dealers
Dale Chornoboy
Kerry Brown

D-U-N-S 20-690-8654   (HQ)
PRAIRIECOAST EQUIPMENT INC
15102 101 St, Grande Prairie, AB, T8V 0P7
(780) 532-8402
Emp Here 5   Sales 53,650,300
SIC 5083 Farm and garden machinery
Dennis Landis
James Frame

D-U-N-S 20-282-6798   (SL)
PURNELL ENERGY SERVICES LTD
10502 123 St, Grande Prairie, AB, T8V 8B8
(587) 259-9600
Emp Here 50   Sales 25,982,750
SIC 4911 Electric services
Hayden Newey
Nathan Purnell

D-U-N-S 25-970-5101   (SL)
QUEEN ELIZABETH TWO HOSPITAL
10409 98 St, Grande Prairie, AB, T8V 2E8
(780) 538-7100
Emp Here 49   Sales 11,480,112
SIC 8742 Management consulting services
Charlotte Robb

D-U-N-S 25-184-0609   (HQ)
REES N.D.T. INSPECTION SERVICES LTD
15612 89 St, Grande Prairie, AB, T8V 2N8
(780) 539-3594
Emp Here 1   Sales 13,476,570
SIC 7389 Business services, nec
Ron Vader

D-U-N-S 20-086-2670   (HQ)
RENTCO EQUIPMENT LTD
RENTCO'S TOOL SHED
11437 97 Ave, Grande Prairie, AB, T8V 5R8
(780) 539-7860
Emp Here 37   Sales 33,314,800
SIC 7353 Heavy construction equipment
rental
George Shields

D-U-N-S 24-809-3312   (SL)
RISLEY MANUFACTURING LTD
RISLEY EQUIPMENT, DIV OF
9024 108 St, Grande Prairie, AB, T8V 4C8
(780) 532-3282
Emp Here 180   Sales 39,960,180
SIC 3531 Construction machinery
Reggald Isley
Dean Isley

D-U-N-S 25-385-6025   (SL)
ROSKA DBO INC
TOTAL ENERFLEX
9715 115 St, Grande Prairie, AB, T8V 5S4
(780) 532-8347
Emp Here 100   Sales 31,970,500
SIC 1389 Oil and gas field services, nec
Clayton Roska
Brad Welsh
Brian Furman

D-U-N-S 25-451-7709   (SL)
S & T ALLARD FOOD LTD
TIM HORTONS
10206 100 St Suite 640, Grande Prairie, AB,
T8V 3K1
(780) 532-6660
Emp Here 125   Sales 5,689,875
SIC 5812 Eating places
Serge Allard
Tracy Allard

D-U-N-S 20-273-2033   (BR)
SECURE ENERGY SERVICES INC
(Suby of SECURE ENERGY SERVICES INC)
9516 146 Ave, Grande Prairie, AB, T8V 7V9
(780) 357-5600
Emp Here 100
SIC 1389 Oil and gas field services, nec

D-U-N-S 25-182-3720   (BR)
SHARK CLUBS OF CANADA INC
SHARK CLUB
(Suby of SHARK CLUBS OF CANADA INC)
9898 99 St, Grande Prairie, AB, T8V 2H2
(780) 513-5450
Emp Here 90
SIC 5813 Drinking places
Ryan Kospuck

D-U-N-S 24-000-4176   (SL)
SHAW, K. & SONS CONTRACTING LTD
10424 96 Ave, Grande Prairie, AB, T8V 5V2
(780) 539-6960
Emp Here 30   Sales 14,121,930
SIC 1542 Nonresidential construction, nec
Ken Shaw
Len Shaw

D-U-N-S 25-271-1007   (BR)
SOBEYS WEST INC
NORTHGATE SAFEWAY
(Suby of EMPIRE COMPANY LIMITED)
9925 114 Ave, Grande Prairie, AB, T8V 4A9
(780) 532-1627
Emp Here 120
SIC 5411 Grocery stores
Mary Chailler

D-U-N-S 25-767-9279   (SL)
STREAM FLO INDUSTRIES
15501 89 Street, Grande Prairie, AB, T8V 0V7
(780) 532-1433
Emp Here 45   Sales 14,386,725
SIC 1389 Oil and gas field services, nec
Andrew Dawe

D-U-N-S 20-114-7316   (HQ)
SUREPOINT SERVICES INC
(Suby of WYNNCHURCH CAPITAL, LTD.)
11004 96 Ave, Grande Prairie, AB, T8V 3J5
(780) 832-0551
Emp Here 14   Sales 31,971,700
SIC 8734 Testing laboratories
Cordell Weber
Todd Trepanier
Andrea Trepanier

D-U-N-S 24-348-8934   (BR)
TARPON ENERGY SERVICES LTD
SYNTEX-ENERFLEX
(Suby of PTW ENERGY SERVICES LTD)
11418 91 Ave, Grande Prairie, AB, T8V 6K6
(780) 539-9696
Emp Here 120
SIC 1389 Oil and gas field services, nec
Harvey Gillet

D-U-N-S 20-372-8605   (SL)
TORQ INSTRUMENT SUPPLY INC
11436 97 Ave, Grande Prairie, AB, T8V 5Z5
(780) 532-1115
Emp Here 26   Sales 16,291,964
SIC 4911 Electric services

D-U-N-S 25-206-5453   (SL)
TURCON UNITED BUILDING SYSTEMS INC
TURCON CONSTRUCTION GROUP
99200 100 Ave Suite B, Grande Prairie, AB,
T8V 0T9
(780) 532-5533
Emp Here 25   Sales 11,768,275
SIC 1542 Nonresidential construction, nec
Clifford Turner
Michael O'connor

D-U-N-S 24-377-0430   (BR)
VALARD CONSTRUCTION LTD
(Suby of QUANTA SERVICES, INC.)
14310 97 St, Grande Prairie, AB, T8V 7B7

(780) 539-4750
Emp Here 250
SIC 1623 Water, sewer, and utility lines
Phil Seeley

D-U-N-S 24-948-4676   (SL)
VECTOR COMMUNICATIONS LTD
11213 97 Ave, Grande Prairie, AB, T8V 5N5
(780) 532-2555
Emp Here 44   Sales 14,326,400
SIC 5999 Miscellaneous retail stores, nec
Donald Crowshaw
Andrew Madsen
Stanley Crowshaw

D-U-N-S 24-978-3635   (SL)
VERTICAL BUILDING SOLUTIONS INC
64071 Hwy 43, Grande Prairie, AB, T8V 3A5
(780) 532-0366
Emp Here 25   Sales 11,700,690
SIC 1791 Structural steel erection
Mark Loos
Kevin Hrab

D-U-N-S 25-253-5443   (SL)
VIEWORX GEOPHOTO INC
8716 108 St Unit 112, Grande Prairie, AB, T8V
4C7
(780) 532-3353
Emp Here 65   Sales 27,477,905
SIC 1541 Industrial buildings and warehouses
Michael Head
Loran Swanberg
Morgan Beaupre
Jim Pollock

D-U-N-S 25-978-2944   (SL)
W.E. RENTALS 2K LTD
11489 95 Ave, Grande Prairie, AB, T8V 5P7
(780) 539-1709
Emp Here 40   Sales 11,883,317
SIC 7353 Heavy construction equipment
rental
Andy Dort

D-U-N-S 25-498-2986   (BR)
WAL-MART CANADA CORP
WALMART
(Suby of WALMART INC.)
11050 103 Ave, Grande Prairie, AB, T8V 7H1
(780) 513-3740
Emp Here 200
SIC 5311 Department stores
Corey Gillon

D-U-N-S 25-451-7808   (SL)
WAYDEX SERVICES LP
11420 96 Ave, Grande Prairie, AB, T8V 5M4
(780) 538-9101
Emp Here 60   Sales 40,360,740
SIC 1389 Oil and gas field services, nec
Dexter Mosenko
Al Longson
Floyd Bozarth

D-U-N-S 20-921-4746   (BR)
WEATHERFORD CANADA LTD
(Suby of WEATHERFORD INTERNATIONAL
PUBLIC LIMITED COMPANY)
9601 156 Ave, Grande Prairie, AB, T8V 2P3
(780) 567-6250
Emp Here 118
SIC 3533 Oil and gas field machinery
Ron Kowalyk

D-U-N-S 24-948-9741   (BR)
WEYERHAEUSER COMPANY LIMITED
(Suby of WEYERHAEUSER COMPANY)
Gd Stn Main, Grande Prairie, AB, T8V 3A9
(780) 539-8500
Emp Here 650
SIC 5031 Lumber, plywood, and millwork
Alisa Tasker

D-U-N-S 20-086-3306   (HQ)
WINDSOR MOTORS (1975) LTD
WINDSOR FORD
13105 100 St, Grande Prairie, AB, T8V 4H3

(780) 532-9153
Emp Here 1   *Sales* 69,220,800
SIC 5511 New and used car dealers
Charles Alexander Longmate

Grande Prairie, AB T8W

D-U-N-S 20-138-7706   (SL)
324126 ALBERTA LTD
10514 67 Ave Unit 401, Grande Prairie, AB,
T8W 0K8
(780) 532-7771
Emp Here 26   *Sales* 10,903,230
SIC 6712 Bank holding companies
Ian Kay

D-U-N-S 20-040-0625   (HQ)
**AUTOPRO AUTOMATION CONSULTANTS
LTD**
11039 78 Ave Suite 103, Grande Prairie, AB,
T8W 2J7
(780) 539-2450
Emp Here 20   *Sales* 43,056,042
SIC 8711 Engineering services
Mike Lane
David Nakasaka
Robert Beattie
Tom Adkins
Brad Holub
Jason Brown
Gordon Clissold

D-U-N-S 25-191-7258   (HQ)
BONNETT'S ENERGY CORP
65007 Hwy 43, Grande Prairie, AB, T8W 5E7
(403) 264-3010
Emp Here 20   *Sales* 163,791,300
SIC 1389 Oil and gas field services, nec
Murray Toews
Patrick G Powell
Wayne E Ehgoetz
David V Richards
David Ross

D-U-N-S 24-311-8598   (HQ)
BONNETT'S ENERGY SERVICES LP
BONNETT'S WIRELINE, DIV
65007 Hwy 43, Grande Prairie, AB, T8W 5E7
(780) 532-5700
Emp Here 5   *Sales* 15,985,250
SIC 1389 Oil and gas field services, nec
David Ross

D-U-N-S 20-524-6015   (SL)
CAPSTAN HAULING LTD
10903 78 Ave, Grande Prairie, AB, T8W 2L2
(780) 402-3110
Emp Here 32   *Sales* 10,230,560
SIC 1389 Oil and gas field services, nec
Richard Wells
John Smith Wells

D-U-N-S 20-293-0939   (HQ)
CONTROL TECH 2011 LTD
11001 78 Ave, Grande Prairie, AB, T8W 2J7
(780) 539-7114
Emp Here 1   *Sales* 71,115,300
SIC 8748 Business consulting, nec
Tali Hughes
Greg Kjemhus
Dustin Richarde

D-U-N-S 25-230-3581   (SL)
DIVERSE HOLDINGS LTD
9610 62 Ave, Grande Prairie, AB, T8W 2C3
(780) 539-6104
Emp Here 75   *Sales* 19,616,475
SIC 6712 Bank holding companies
Gerald Sam
Marlene Sam

D-U-N-S 20-251-4329   (HQ)
E.S. WILLIAMS & ASSOCIATES INC
10514 67 Ave Suite 306, Grande Prairie, AB,
T8W 0K8

(780) 539-4544
Emp Here 20   *Sales* 10,730,544
SIC 7379 Computer related services, nec
Graham Plett
Jon Plett

D-U-N-S 20-205-5005   (BR)
ENCANA CORPORATION
(*Suby of* ENCANA CORPORATION)
11040 78 Ave, Grande Prairie, AB, T8W 2M2
(780) 539-4422
Emp Here 350
SIC 5541 Gasoline service stations
Roger Henault

D-U-N-S 24-767-3007   (SL)
J.D.A. VENTURES LTD
JDA OILFIELD HAULING
713031 Range Road 64, Grande Prairie, AB,
T8W 5E5
(780) 532-5101
Emp Here 80   *Sales* 25,576,400
SIC 1389 Oil and gas field services, nec
Jarvis Dawson
Tony Madocag

D-U-N-S 25-766-6727   (SL)
MAYFAIR PERSONNEL (NORTHERN) LTD
MAYFAIR BUSINESS COLLEGE
11039 78 Ave Suite 102, Grande Prairie, AB,
T8W 2J7
(780) 539-5090
Emp Here 50   *Sales* 11,848,500
SIC 7361 Employment agencies
Michael Rigler
Carol Rigler

D-U-N-S 24-785-4524   (HQ)
PEACE LIBRARY SYSTEM
8301 110 St, Grande Prairie, AB, T8W 6T2
(780) 538-4656
Sales 10,395,280
SIC 5192 Books, periodicals, and newspapers
Linda Duplessis

D-U-N-S 24-319-7705   (HQ)
VERTEX
705079 Range Road 61, Grande Prairie, AB,
T8W 5A8
(780) 532-7707
Emp Here 50   *Sales* 10,619,850
SIC 8748 Business consulting, nec
Stephanie Brown

D-U-N-S 20-023-0220   (HQ)
WILLIAMS, E. S. & ASSOCIATES INC
ESWIT
10514 67 Ave Suite 306, Grande Prairie, AB,
T8W 0K8
(780) 539-4544
Emp Here 18   *Sales* 14,632,560
SIC 7379 Computer related services, nec
Graham Plett
Jonathan Plett
James Balisky

Grande Prairie, AB T8X

D-U-N-S 25-165-6153   (SL)
ARCTIC CRANE SERVICE LTD
14915 89 St, Grande Prairie, AB, T8X 0J2
(780) 814-6990
Emp Here 45   *Sales* 19,957,050
SIC 7389 Business services, nec
Rob Cloutier
Rick Carey

D-U-N-S 24-684-2657   (SL)
CORAL OILFIELD SERVICES INC
15303 94 St Suite 15303, Grande Prairie, AB,
T8X 0L2
(780) 402-9800
Emp Here 35   *Sales* 11,189,675
SIC 1389 Oil and gas field services, nec
Cory Young

D-U-N-S 20-293-7280   (SL)
D & D ENERGY SERVICES LTD
D & D WELL SERVICES
9201 163 Ave, Grande Prairie, AB, T8X 0B6
(780) 402-0383
Emp Here 70   *Sales* 10,373,440
SIC 4213 Trucking, except local
Darcy Geherman
Rudy Geherman
Dennis Geherman
Donna Geherman

D-U-N-S 24-320-1827   (SL)
GV COLONY FARMING CO. LTD
723042a Range Road 74, Grande Prairie, AB,
T8X 4L1
(780) 539-6513
Emp Here 100   *Sales* 26,230,900
SIC 0139 Field crops, except cash grain
Elias Hofer
Levi Hofer

D-U-N-S 24-327-3000   (SL)
**HUTTERIAN BRETHREN CHURCH OF
GRANDVIEW**
GRANDVIEW COLONY
723042a Range Road 74, Grande Prairie, AB,
T8X 4L1
(780) 532-6500
Emp Here 115   *Sales* 11,974,145
SIC 8661 Religious organizations
Elias Hofer
Levi Hofer

D-U-N-S 20-086-2290   (HQ)
NORTHERN BOTTLING LTD
NORTHERN BOTTLING DISTRUTORS
15415 91 St, Grande Prairie, AB, T8X 0B4
(780) 532-4222
Sales 10,118,475
SIC 2086 Bottled and canned soft drinks
Ken Orchuk

D-U-N-S 20-997-0305   (BR)
PETROWEST TRANSPORTATION LP
MURTRON HAULING, DIV OF
9201 163 Ave, Grande Prairie, AB, T8X 0B6
(780) 402-0383
Emp Here 75   *Sales* 630,393
SIC 1382 Oil and gas exploration services
Darcy Geherman

D-U-N-S 24-343-5851   (SL)
PROPIPE GROUP LTD
(*Suby of* 1089243 ALBERTA LTD)
15201 91 St, Grande Prairie, AB, T8X 0B3
(780) 830-0955
Emp Here 60   *Sales* 40,360,740
SIC 1389 Oil and gas field services, nec
Mike Esfarjani
Rob Hanrieder

Grande Prairie, AB T9E

D-U-N-S 20-317-1145   (SL)
AERO MAG 2000 (YEG) INC
4123 39 St E, Grande Prairie, AB, T9E 0V4
(780) 890-7273
Emp Here 65   *Sales* 21,109,010
SIC 4581 Airports, flying fields, and services
Mario Letin

D-U-N-S 20-084-9722   (HQ)
BBE EXPEDITING LTD
BRADEN-BURRY EXPEDITING
1759 35 Ave E, Grande Prairie, AB, T9E 0V6
(780) 890-8611
Emp Here 40   *Sales* 15,500,056
SIC 4731 Freight transportation arrangement
Heather Stewart
Rita Becker

D-U-N-S 20-059-5291   (HQ)
CANADIAN HELICOPTERS LIMITED
1000 Airport Rd Suite 4500, Grande Prairie,

AB, T9E 0V3
(780) 429-6900
Emp Here 70   *Sales* 158,676,000
SIC 4522 Air transportation, nonscheduled
Don E Wall

D-U-N-S 24-928-0090   (SL)
**EDMONTON REGIONAL AIRPORTS AU-
THORITY**
EDMONTON INTERNATIONAL AIRPORT
1000 Airport Rd Terminal 1, Grande Prairie,
AB, T9E 0V3
(780) 890-8900
Emp Here 300   *Sales* 158,212,093
SIC 4581 Airports, flying fields, and services
Naseem Bashir
Suromitra Sanatani
Joan Hertz
Naseem Bashir
Leonard Blumenthal
Mary Cameron
Murray Hales
Darrell Jones
Dale Klein
Robert Petryk

D-U-N-S 20-720-9164   (HQ)
MORNINGSTAR AIR EXPRESS INC
3759 60 Ave E, Grande Prairie, AB, T9E 0V4
(780) 453-3022
Emp Here 30   *Sales* 32,037,360
SIC 4522 Air transportation, nonscheduled
Donald A Wheaton
Bill Mcgoey

D-U-N-S 20-058-8338   (BR)
NAV CANADA
(*Suby of* NAV CANADA)
4396 34 St E, Grande Prairie, AB, T9E 0V4
(780) 890-8360
Emp Here 420
SIC 4581 Airports, flying fields, and services
Dave Mastel

D-U-N-S 20-297-7351   (SL)
NORTHERN LIGHTS AVIATION LTD
3795 56 Ave E, Grande Prairie, AB, T9E 0V4
(780) 890-1300
Emp Here 100   *Sales* 23,428,800
SIC 8748 Business consulting, nec
David Robertson

D-U-N-S 25-359-3370   (BR)
SHOCK TRAUMA AIR RESCUE SERVICE
STARS
(*Suby of* SHOCK TRAUMA AIR RESCUE
SERVICE)
1519 35 Ave E Suite 100, Grande Prairie, AB,
T9E 0V6
(780) 890-3131
Emp Here 87
SIC 4522 Air transportation, nonscheduled
Bill Werny

Grassland, AB T0A

D-U-N-S 24-418-1561   (SL)
413877 ALBERTA LTD
PETRO CANADA GRASSLAND
4703 50 Ave Unit A, Grassland, AB, T0A 1V0
(780) 525-2295
Emp Here 9   *Sales* 19,106,950
SIC 5541 Gasoline service stations
Ryan Park

D-U-N-S 20-436-9565   (SL)
DERKO'S SERVICE LTD
5008 50 Ave, Grassland, AB, T0A 1V0
(780) 525-3931
Emp Here 28   *Sales* 35,201,628
SIC 5171 Petroleum bulk stations and termi-
nals
Arnold Derko

▲ Public Company   ■ Public Company Family Member   HQ Headquarters   BR Branch   SL Single Location

Grimshaw, AB T0H

D-U-N-S 20-086-3900   (SL)
JUNCTION MOTORS LTD
5309 50 St, Grimshaw, AB, T0H 1W0
(780) 332-2886
Emp Here 22   *Sales* 10,957,716
SIC 5511 New and used car dealers
  John Clague
  Evelyn Clague

D-U-N-S 25-388-1171   (HQ)
LAPRAIRIE WORKS INC
Gd, Grimshaw, AB, T0H 1W0
(780) 332-4452
Emp Here 125   *Sales* 82,028,750
SIC 1611 Highway and street construction
  Scott Laprairie
  Jim Feragen
  Carl Laprairie
  Reagan Laprairie
  Cliff Laprairie

D-U-N-S 25-804-1284   (HQ)
NORTH PEACE HOUSING FOUNDATION
4918 49 Ave, Grimshaw, AB, T0H 1W0

Emp Here 50   *Sales* 37,187,040
SIC 6531 Real estate agents and managers
  Richard Walisser

D-U-N-S 25-192-5798   (SL)
R K R FOODS LTD
SUPER A FOODS
5023 54 Ave, Grimshaw, AB, T0H 1W0
(780) 332-4495
Emp Here 42   *Sales* 11,514,384
SIC 5411 Grocery stores
  Rick Kyca
  Jason Doris
  Brian Allen

D-U-N-S 20-616-4089   (SL)
ROCKY MOUNTAIN DEALERSHIPS INC
HOULDER FARM SUPPLY
4802 57th Ave, Grimshaw, AB, T0H 1W0
(780) 332-4691
Emp Here 30   *Sales* 14,250,780
SIC 5083 Farm and garden machinery
  Harold Houlder
  Kenneth Houlder
  Elizabeth Anne Houlder
  Edna Houlder

Hairy Hill, AB T0B

D-U-N-S 25-563-4909   (SL)
HAIRY HILL COLONY LTD
HAIRY HILL COLONY
Gd, Hairy Hill, AB, T0B 1S0
(780) 768-3770
Emp Here 62   *Sales* 16,263,158
SIC 0191 General farms, primarily crop
  Mike Hofer
  Dave Hofer

Hanna, AB T0J

D-U-N-S 24-346-5346   (BR)
ALBERTA HEALTH SERVICES
HANNA HEALTH CENTRE
(*Suby of* GOVERNMENT OF THE PROVINCE OF ALBERTA)
904 Centre St N, Hanna, AB, T0J 1P0
(403) 854-3331
Emp Here 150
SIC 8062 General medical and surgical hospitals
  Sandra Rubbelke

D-U-N-S 25-316-7142   (BR)
ATCO ELECTRIC LTD
ATCO POWER
(*Suby of* ATCO LTD)
Gd, Hanna, AB, T0J 1P0
(403) 854-5141
Emp Here 100
SIC 4911 Electric services
  Kevin Burgmeister

D-U-N-S 25-678-7383   (BR)
PRAIRIE MINES & ROYALTY ULC
(*Suby of* WESTMORELAND COAL COMPANY)
Gd, Hanna, AB, T0J 1P0
(403) 854-5200
Emp Here 100
SIC 1221 Bituminous coal and lignite-surface mining
  Clark Crippin

D-U-N-S 24-042-5504   (SL)
STEWART DRUGS HANNA (1984) LTD
PHARMASAVE 354
610 2nd Ave W, Hanna, AB, T0J 1P0
(403) 854-4154
Emp Here 50   *Sales* 13,707,600
SIC 5411 Grocery stores

Hardisty, AB T0B

D-U-N-S 25-385-4533   (SL)
GCS ENERGY SERVICES LTD
4411 49th St, Hardisty, AB, T0B 1V0
(780) 888-3845
Emp Here 192   *Sales* 48,468,864
SIC 1623 Water, sewer, and utility lines
  Greg Schmidt
  Trevor Bitzer
  Kevin Sandquist

High Level, AB T0H

D-U-N-S 25-903-0331   (SL)
CANADIAN TIRE
1 Gateway Blvd Ss 1 Suite 908, High Level, AB, T0H 1Z0
(780) 926-1908
Emp Here 30   *Sales* 14,942,340
SIC 5531 Auto and home supply stores
  Susan O Brien

D-U-N-S 24-333-0495   (HQ)
DECHANT CONSTRUCTION LTD
11004 97 St, High Level, AB, T0H 1Z0
(780) 926-4411
Sales 50,488,400
SIC 1611 Highway and street construction
  Alphonse Dechant
  Daniel Dechant
  Doug Dechant
  Wayne Dechant

D-U-N-S 25-097-7956   (SL)
FOOTNER FOREST PRODUCTS LTD
(*Suby of* NORBORD INC)
Gd, High Level, AB, T0H 1Z0
(780) 841-0008
Emp Here 180   *Sales* 34,626,600
SIC 2493 Reconstituted wood products
  Allan Ainsworth
  Peter Grant Sr

D-U-N-S 24-905-6540   (HQ)
FOUR WINDS HOTELS MANAGEMENT CORP
10302 97 St, High Level, AB, T0H 1Z0
(780) 220-1840
Emp Here 50   *Sales* 36,649,200
SIC 5921 Liquor stores
  Ronald Hoyda

  Rosemarie Hoyda

D-U-N-S 25-363-7193   (BR)
STRIKE GROUP LIMITED PARTNERSHIP
(*Suby of* STRIKE HOLDINGS LIMITED PARTNERSHIP)
10600 94 St Ss 1, High Level, AB, T0H 1Z0
(780) 926-2429
Emp Here 90
SIC 1389 Oil and gas field services, nec
  Harvey Hilhorst

D-U-N-S 20-174-5036   (BR)
TOLKO INDUSTRIES LTD
HIGH LEVEL LUMBER DIVISION
(*Suby of* AMERICAN INDUSTRIAL ACQUISITION CORPORATION)
11401 92 St Ss 1 Suite 1, High Level, AB, T0H 1Z0
(780) 926-3781
Emp Here 220
SIC 2421 Sawmills and planing mills, general
  Troy Connolly

D-U-N-S 24-273-7849   (SL)
WOLVERINE FORD SALES (2006) LTD
10102 97 St Ss 1, High Level, AB, T0H 1Z0
(780) 926-2291
Emp Here 22   *Sales* 10,957,716
SIC 5511 New and used car dealers
  Daniel Lapointe

High Prairie, AB T0G

D-U-N-S 25-686-9892   (SL)
BIG LAKES DODGE LTD
5109 41 St, High Prairie, AB, T0G 1E0
(780) 523-5007
Emp Here 21   *Sales* 10,459,638
SIC 5511 New and used car dealers
  Christopher Semple

D-U-N-S 24-385-7898   (BR)
BUCHANAN, GORDON ENTERPRISES LTD
BUCHANAN LUMBER DIV OF
(*Suby of* BUCHANAN, GORDON ENTERPRISES LTD)
1 Railway Ave, High Prairie, AB, T0G 1E0
(780) 523-4544
Emp Here 175
SIC 2421 Sawmills and planing mills, general
  Gordon Buchanan

D-U-N-S 24-702-0803   (BR)
FRESON MARKET LTD
(*Suby of* ALTAMART INVESTMENTS (1993) LTD)
5032 53rd Ave, High Prairie, AB, T0G 1E0
(780) 523-3253
Emp Here 75
SIC 5411 Grocery stores
  Matthew Lovsin

D-U-N-S 24-880-2969   (SL)
HIGH PRAIRIE & DISTRICT REGIONAL RECREATION BOARD
HIGH PRAIRIE & DISTRICT RECREATION BOARD
5209 50th St, High Prairie, AB, T0G 1E0
(780) 536-2630
Emp Here 40   *Sales* 28,368,480
SIC 8699 Membership organizations, nec
  Rick Dumont
  Crystal Sekulich
  Randy Ehman
  Kenneth Mathews
  David Vanderwell

D-U-N-S 24-327-8777   (SL)
HIGH PRAIRIE FORD SALES & SERVICE LTD
MONAHAN FORD KAWASAKI
5404 40 St, High Prairie, AB, T0G 1E0
(780) 523-4193
Emp Here 29   *Sales* 14,444,262

SIC 5511 New and used car dealers
  Lionel Robins

D-U-N-S 24-090-0217   (HQ)
HIGH PRAIRIE SCHOOL DIVISION NO 48
16532 Township Rd 744, High Prairie, AB, T0G 1E0
(780) 523-3337
Sales 38,953,362
SIC 8211 Elementary and secondary schools
  Joyce Devornek
  Laura Poloz
  Paul Burrows

D-U-N-S 25-316-8793   (BR)
TOLKO INDUSTRIES LTD
HIGH PRAIRIE DIVISION
(*Suby of* AMERICAN INDUSTRIAL ACQUISITION CORPORATION)
Hwy 2 W, High Prairie, AB, T0G 1E0
(780) 523-2101
Emp Here 178
SIC 2631 Paperboard mills
  Perry Fox

High River, AB T1V

D-U-N-S 25-080-9274   (SL)
618382 ALBERTA LTD
HIGH RIVER AUTOPLEX & RV
102 24 St Se, High River, AB, T1V 0B3
(403) 652-3171
Emp Here 30   *Sales* 14,942,340
SIC 5561 Recreational vehicle dealers
  Douglas Mclaughlin

D-U-N-S 20-890-4230   (BR)
ALBERTA HEALTH SERVICES
HIGH RIVER GENERAL HOSPITAL
(*Suby of* GOVERNMENT OF THE PROVINCE OF ALBERTA)
560 9 Ave Sw, High River, AB, T1V 1B3
(403) 652-2200
Emp Here 300
SIC 8062 General medical and surgical hospitals
  Lise Brisebois-Blouin

D-U-N-S 24-885-6093   (SL)
ARP AUTOMATION CONTROLS INC
80042 475 Ave E Unit 200, High River, AB, T1V 1M3
(403) 652-7130
Emp Here 50   *Sales* 10,233,650
SIC 3625 Relays and industrial controls
  Keith Church
  Cory Ziebart

D-U-N-S 20-107-6507   (BR)
CANADIAN CONTRACT CLEANING SPECIALISTS, INC
(*Suby of* HARVEST PARTNERS, LP)
603 10 Ave Se, High River, AB, T1V 1K2

Emp Here 102
SIC 7349 Building maintenance services, nec
  Ruben Bayona

D-U-N-S 24-734-1571   (BR)
CARGILL LIMITED
CARGILL FOODS
(*Suby of* CARGILL, INCORPORATED)
472 Avenue & Hwy Suite 2a, High River, AB, T1V 1P4
(403) 652-4688
Emp Here 2,000
SIC 2011 Meat packing plants
  Kerry Hawkins

D-U-N-S 25-362-3961   (SL)
CHRISTIANSON PIPE INC
Gd Stn Main, High River, AB, T1V 1M2
(403) 652-4336
Emp Here 10   *Sales* 10,003,390
SIC 5051 Metals service centers and offices

Brian Wilson
Reece Kosek
Gary D. Haug

D-U-N-S 25-056-5710   (SL)
COUNTRY ENTERPRISES LTD
COUNTRY CHRYSLER
1103 14 St Se, High River, AB, T1V 1L5

Emp Here 30   *Sales* 14,942,340
SIC 5511 New and used car dealers
  Gary Smith
  Scott Caron
  David Jackson

D-U-N-S 20-955-6120   (SL)
FACTORY OUTLET TRAILERS INC
80010 475 Ave, High River, AB, T1V 1M3
(403) 603-3311
Emp Here 22   *Sales* 10,957,716
SIC 5599 Automotive dealers, nec
  David Chuchmuch
  Vickie Chuchmuch

D-U-N-S 25-539-7200   (SL)
**FOOTHILLS COWBOYS ASSOCIATION,
THE**
609 Centre St Sw Unit 7, High River, AB, T1V
2C2
(403) 652-1405
Emp Here 30   *Sales* 11,922,420
SIC 8699 Membership organizations, nec
  Murray Mcgonigle
  Pat Dillman

D-U-N-S 24-347-4426   (HQ)
FOOTHILLS SCHOOL DIVISION NO. 38
120 5 Ave Se Suite 38, High River, AB, T1V
1G2
(403) 652-3001
Emp Here 24   *Sales* 84,251,150
SIC 8211 Elementary and secondary schools
  Diana Froc
  Laurie Copland

D-U-N-S 24-438-7916   (SL)
GREEN, DON HOLDINGS LTD
702 11 Ave Se, High River, AB, T1V 1P2
(403) 652-2000
Emp Here 27   *Sales* 11,322,585
SIC 6719 Holding companies, nec
  Donald Green
  Bette Green

D-U-N-S 24-442-1616   (SL)
**HIGH COUNTRY CHEVROLET BUICK GMC
LTD**
702 11 Ave Se, High River, AB, T1V 1M3
(403) 652-2000
Emp Here 25   *Sales* 12,451,950
SIC 5511 New and used car dealers
  Don Green

D-U-N-S 25-060-0475   (HQ)
HIGH RIVER FORD SALES
FOOTHILLS FORD SALES
1103 11 Ave Se, High River, AB, T1V 1P2

Emp Here 20   *Sales* 17,432,730
SIC 5511 New and used car dealers
  Paul Morrison
  Lyle Swallow

D-U-N-S 20-429-9698   (SL)
ICG PROPANE
430 8 St Sw, High River, AB, T1V 1B9

Emp Here 5   *Sales* 15,709,144
SIC 4924 Natural gas distribution

D-U-N-S 24-948-9824   (SL)
ROLLOVER PREMIUM PET FOOD LTD
FARM MEATS CANADA DIV
12 11 Ave Se, High River, AB, T1V 1E6

Emp Here 60   *Sales* 20,741,400
SIC 2047 Dog and cat food
  Wayne Skogman

Judy Harvey

D-U-N-S 24-517-3208   (HQ)
ROSEBURN RANCHES LTD
Gd Stn Main, High River, AB, T1V 1M2
(403) 652-3257
Sales 19,275,950
SIC 0211 Beef cattle feedlots
  Brian Morrison
  Peter Morrison

D-U-N-S 25-369-6462   (SL)
STEELHORSE FREIGHT SERVICES INC
82054 466 Ave, High River, AB, T1V 1P3

Emp Here 27   *Sales* 14,039,109
SIC 4731 Freight transportation arrangement
  Roderick (Rod) Vatcher
  Leanne Vatcher

D-U-N-S 20-431-3808   (SL)
STRAIGHT SHOOTER SAFETY INC
Gd, High River, AB, T1V 1M3
(403) 336-1124
Emp Here 36   *Sales* 11,721,600
SIC 5999 Miscellaneous retail stores, nec

D-U-N-S 20-069-0860   (HQ)
**WESTERN   FINANCIAL   GROUP (NET-
WORK) INC**
(*Suby of* WESTERN FINANCIAL GROUP
INC)
1010 24 St Se, High River, AB, T1V 2A7
(403) 652-2663
Emp Here 5   *Sales* 806,837,680
SIC 6411 Insurance agents, brokers, and ser-
vice
  Kenny Nicholls
  Lisa Osachoff
  Doug Bennett
  Mary Lou Charles
  Joe Sirianni
  Nancy Green
  Evan Johnston
  Jeff Goy
  Gary Timlick

D-U-N-S 25-329-5836   (HQ)
WESTERN FINANCIAL GROUP INC
1010 24 St Se, High River, AB, T1V 2A7
(403) 652-2663
Emp Here 119   *Sales* 3,632,845,600
SIC 6311 Life insurance
  Scott A. Tannas
  Kenny Nicholls
  Nancy Green

D-U-N-S 24-320-4767   (HQ)
**WESTERN INVESTMENT COMPANY OF
CANADA LIMITED, THE**
1010 24 St Se, High River, AB, T1V 2A7
(403) 701-7546
Emp Here 20   *Sales* 85,292,375
SIC 2021 Creamery butter
  Scott Tannas
  Shafeen Mawani
  Stacey Cross
  James F. Dinning
  Willard Yuill
  Robert Espey
  Kabir Jivraj
  Jennie Moushos

Hines Creek, AB T0H

D-U-N-S 20-638-0123   (SL)
DEI, CHARLES CONSTRUCTION LTD
Gd, Hines Creek, AB, T0H 2A0
(780) 494-3838
Emp Here 80   *Sales* 25,576,400
SIC 1389 Oil and gas field services, nec
  Charles Dei
  Leslie Dei

Hinton, AB T7V

D-U-N-S 20-337-8448   (HQ)
389987 ALBERTA LTD
NAPA AUTO PARTS
120 North St, Hinton, AB, T7V 1S8
(780) 865-8800
Emp Here 15   *Sales* 16,436,574
SIC 5531 Auto and home supply stores
  Gordon Ireland

D-U-N-S 20-280-0020   (HQ)
ALSTAR OILFIELD CONTRACTORS LTD
310 River Rd E, Hinton, AB, T7V 1X5
(780) 865-5938
Sales 60,541,110
SIC 1389 Oil and gas field services, nec
  Scott Fofonoff
  Gregory Recto
  Kristopher Ring
  Chris Genert
  Corey Johnson

D-U-N-S 24-394-8531   (SL)
ALTA WEST INDUSTRIES
141 Hampshire Rd, Hinton, AB, T7V 1G8
(780) 865-2930
Emp Here 80   *Sales* 38,002,080
SIC 5085 Industrial supplies
  David Zaharia
  Pamela Buttazzoni

D-U-N-S 20-322-3342   (SL)
BARROW SAFETY SERVICES INC
889 Switzer Dr, Hinton, AB, T7V 1V1
(780) 865-7763
Emp Here 52   *Sales* 12,182,976
SIC 8748 Business consulting, nec
  Glen Barrow

D-U-N-S 20-336-9314   (SL)
CANADIAN TIRE ASSOCIATE STORE
868 Carmichael Lane, Hinton, AB, T7V 1Y6
(780) 865-6198
Emp Here 35   *Sales* 17,432,730
SIC 5531 Auto and home supply stores
  Shannon Booth

D-U-N-S 20-537-6601   (SL)
CARDINAL RIVER COALS LTD
(*Suby of* TECK RESOURCES LIMITED)
Gd, Hinton, AB, T7V 1V5
(780) 692-5100
Emp Here 350
SIC 1221 Bituminous coal and lignite-surface
mining
  James Gardiner
  Ronald Millos

D-U-N-S 20-822-9778   (SL)
CLARK CONSTRUCTION
Gd Stn Main, Hinton, AB, T7V 1T9
(780) 865-5822
Emp Here 40   *Sales* 12,936,312
SIC 1389 Oil and gas field services, nec
  Kevin Clark

D-U-N-S 24-767-1647   (HQ)
EVERGREENS FOUNDATION
PARKLAND LODGE
102 Government Rd, Hinton, AB, T7V 2A6
(780) 865-5444
Emp Here 5   *Sales* 22,087,100
SIC 6513 Apartment building operators
  Gloria Kongsrud

D-U-N-S 24-025-5468   (BR)
TECK COAL LIMITED
CARDINAL RIVER OPERATIONS
(*Suby of* TECK RESOURCES LIMITED)
Gd Stn Main, Hinton, AB, T7V 1T9
(780) 692-5100
Emp Here 335
SIC 1221 Bituminous coal and lignite-surface
mining

Terrance Fredin

D-U-N-S 25-290-9569   (SL)
TIMBERLAND HOTEL CORPORATION
114 Park St, Hinton, AB, T7V 2B1
(780) 865-2231
Emp Here 40   *Sales* 11,965,200
SIC 5921 Liquor stores
  Raymond Kim

D-U-N-S 25-297-6030   (BR)
WAL-MART CANADA CORP
(*Suby of* WALMART INC.)
900 Carmichael Lane Suite 100, Hinton, AB,
T7V 1Y6
(780) 865-1421
Emp Here 110
SIC 5311 Department stores
  Kevin Evans

D-U-N-S 24-962-1749   (BR)
WEST FRASER MILLS LTD
HINTON WOOD PRODUCTS
(*Suby of* WEST FRASER TIMBER CO. LTD)
99 West River Rd, Hinton, AB, T7V 1Y7
(780) 865-8900
Emp Here 240
SIC 5211 Lumber and other building materials
  David Walgren

Hobbema, AB T0C

D-U-N-S 24-370-2516   (HQ)
**MIYO WAHKOHTOWIN COMMUNITY EDU-
CATION AUTHORITY**
*ERMINESKIN JUNIOR SENIOR HIGH COM-
MUNITY SCHOOL*
Gd, Hobbema, AB, T0C 1N0
(780) 585-2118
Emp Here 140   *Sales* 14,867,850
SIC 8211 Elementary and secondary schools
  Brian Wildcat

Hythe, AB T0H

D-U-N-S 24-888-3410   (HQ)
SOUTH PEACE DISTRIBUTORS LTD
Ab-43, Hythe, AB, T0H 2C0
(780) 356-3970
Sales 10,328,080
SIC 5172 Petroleum products, nec
  Harold Kjemhus

Innisfail, AB T4G

D-U-N-S 24-387-8670   (HQ)
1309497 ALBERTA LTD
W.A. GRAIN PULSE SOLUTIONS
4923 50 St, Innisfail, AB, T4G 1T1
(403) 227-2774
Sales 54,304,604
SIC 5153 Grain and field beans
  Christopher Chivilo

D-U-N-S 25-192-9279   (SL)
**BILTON WELDING AND MANUFACTURING
LTD**
5815 37 St, Innisfail, AB, T4G 1S8
(403) 227-7799
Emp Here 125   *Sales* 27,750,125
SIC 3533 Oil and gas field machinery
  Robert Maxwell Bilton
  Lynne De Boon

D-U-N-S 25-384-9871   (HQ)
**CHINOOKS EDGE SCHOOL DIVISION NO.
73**
4904 50 St, Innisfail, AB, T4G 1W4

---

(403) 227-7070
Emp Here 50   *Sales* 94,956,700
SIC 8211 Elementary and secondary schools

D-U-N-S 24-089-1341   (SL)
CROSSROADS GAS CO-OP LTD
36060 Range Road 282, Innisfail, AB, T4G 1T5
(403) 227-4861
Emp Here 14   *Sales* 43,481,998
SIC 4911 Natural gas distribution
Reg Olson
Herb Nisbet
Claude Trenholm
Richard Biggs
Pat Hemninger
Angus Park
Kent Knudsen
Bill Stevenett
Charles Moore
Ken Hoppins

D-U-N-S 25-408-5988   (HQ)
DENHAM HOLDINGS LTD
FOURLANE FORD
4412 50 St, Innisfail, AB, T4G 1P7
(403) 227-3311
Sales 16,774,200
SIC 6712 Bank holding companies
Len Denham
Jeff Denham

D-U-N-S 20-315-7722   (SL)
EQUS REA LTD
EQUS
5803 42 St, Innisfail, AB, T4G 1S8
(403) 227-4011
Emp Here 100   *Sales* 62,661,400
SIC 4911 Electric services
Glen Fox
Patricia Bourne

D-U-N-S 25-329-2437   (SL)
FOURLANE FORD SALES LTD
(*Suby of* DENHAM HOLDINGS LTD)
4412 50 St, Innisfail, AB, T4G 1P7
(403) 227-3311
Emp Here 40   *Sales* 19,923,120
SIC 5511 New and used car dealers
Jeff Denham
Leonard Denham

D-U-N-S 24-495-1174   (SL)
INNISFAIL MEAT PACKERS LTD
5107 47 Ave, Innisfail, AB, T4G 1P8
(403) 277-5166
Emp Here 40   *Sales* 33,423,080
SIC 5147 Meats and meat products
Ron Burndred

D-U-N-S 24-963-4817   (HQ)
JOHNS MANVILLE CANADA INC
(*Suby of* BERKSHIRE HATHAWAY INC.)
5301 42 Ave, Innisfail, AB, T4G 1A2
(403) 227-7100
Emp Here 200   *Sales* 76,707,000
SIC 3299 NonMetallic mineral products,
Jim Wilson

D-U-N-S 20-175-3873   (BR)
NESTLE CANADA INC
NESTLE PURINA PET CARE DIV OF
(*Suby of* NESTLE S.A.)
5128 54 St, Innisfail, AB, T4G 1S1
(403) 227-3777
Emp Here 80
SIC 2047 Dog and cat food
Leason Harold

D-U-N-S 20-296-5158   (SL)
NOSSACK GOURMET FOODS LTD
5804 37 St, Innisfail, AB, T4G 1S8
(403) 227-2121
Emp Here 49   *Sales* 11,017,895
SIC 2099 Food preparations, nec
Karsten Nossack

D-U-N-S 20-990-1511   (HQ)

NUTRI-DYN PRODUCTS LTD
PROFESSIONAL HEALTH PRODUCTS
4307 49 St, Innisfail, AB, T4G 1P3
(403) 227-3926
Emp Here 9   *Sales* 12,158,795
SIC 5122 Drugs, proprietaries, and sundries
Derrill Herman
Lea Herman

D-U-N-S 20-280-2591   (HQ)
NWP INDUSTRIES LP
(*Suby of* TERRAVEST INDUSTRIES INC)
4017 60 Ave, Innisfail, AB, T4G 1S9
(403) 227-4100
Emp Here 20   *Sales* 23,050,200
SIC 3443 Fabricated plate work (boiler shop)
Mitch Debelser

D-U-N-S 24-553-0498   (SL)
PALLISER CHEVROLET LTD
PALLISER RV SALES
4604 42 Ave, Innisfail, AB, T4G 1P6
(403) 227-1434
Emp Here 24   *Sales* 11,953,872
SIC 5511 New and used car dealers
Mike O'dwyer

D-U-N-S 24-003-9003   (SL)
PROMAX TRANSPORT LTD
4215 52 Street Close, Innisfail, AB, T4G 1P9
(403) 227-2852
Emp Here 40   *Sales* 15,414,400
SIC 4731 Freight transportation arrangement
Kirk Fulton
Barry Fulton

D-U-N-S 24-892-3778   (SL)
SUNSET MANSUNSET MANOR
INNISFAIL SUNSET MANOR
3312 52 Ave Suite 3402, Innisfail, AB, T4G 0C3
(403) 227-8200
Emp Here 49   *Sales* 11,412,639
SIC 6513 Apartment building operators
Jenny Jenkins

D-U-N-S 25-360-4755   (SL)
SUNTERRA MEATS LTD
4312 51 St, Innisfail, AB, T4G 1A3
(403) 442-4202
Emp Here 150   *Sales* 44,021,550
SIC 5421 Meat and fish markets
Ray Price

Innisfree, AB T0B

D-U-N-S 20-896-5558   (SL)
MINCO GAS CO-OP LTD
4907 51 St, Innisfree, AB, T0B 2G0
(780) 592-3911
Emp Here 15   *Sales* 46,587,855
SIC 4923 Gas transmission and distribution
Randy Horon

Irma, AB T0B

D-U-N-S 25-058-1550   (SL)
GRATTON COULEE AGRI PARTS LTD
Hwy 881 S, Irma, AB, T0B 2H0
(780) 754-2303
Emp Here 21   *Sales* 10,931,382
SIC 5093 Scrap and waste materials
Richard C Glover
Joseph Glover

D-U-N-S 20-970-1523   (SL)
HUTTERIAN BRETHREN CHURCH OF HOLT
HOLT COLONY
Gd, Irma, AB, T0B 2H0
(780) 754-2175
Emp Here 80   *Sales* 14,446,000

SIC 8661 Religious organizations
Jacob Tschetter

Irricana, AB T0M

D-U-N-S 24-417-3738   (SL)
HUTTERIAN BRETHREN CHURCH OF TSCHETTER
Gd, Irricana, AB, T0M 1B0
(403) 935-2362
Emp Here 67   *Sales* 12,098,525
SIC 8661 Religious organizations
Ben Hofer
Jacob Hofer

Irvine, AB T0J

D-U-N-S 24-416-8209   (SL)
HUTTERIAN BRETHREN CHURCH OF ELK-WATER
Gd, Irvine, AB, T0J 1V0
(403) 525-4256
Emp Here 65   *Sales* 17,050,085
SIC 0191 General farms, primarily crop
John B Hofer

Islay, AB T0A

D-U-N-S 20-951-0440   (SL)
LAC LA BICHE TRANSPORT LTD
66569 Rr 143, Islay, AB, T0A 2C0
(780) 623-4711
Emp Here 70   *Sales* 10,373,440
SIC 4212 Local trucking, without storage
Gerald Wowk

Jasper, AB T0E

D-U-N-S 20-645-3487   (BR)
ALBERTA HEALTH SERVICES
JASPER SETON HEALTHCARE CENTRE
(*Suby of* GOVERNMENT OF THE PROVINCE OF ALBERTA)
518 Robson St, Jasper, AB, T0E 1E0
(780) 852-3344
Emp Here 110
SIC 8062 General medical and surgical hospitals
Lorna Chisholm

D-U-N-S 25-362-6634   (BR)
FAIRMONT HOTELS & RESORTS INC
FAIRMONT JASPER PARK LODGE
(*Suby of* ACCOR)
1 Lodge Rd, Jasper, AB, T0E 1E0
(780) 852-3301
Emp Here 550
SIC 7011 Hotels and motels
Amanda Robinson

D-U-N-S 20-115-2902   (BR)
JAS DAY INVESTMENTS LTD
MOUNTAIN PARK LODGES
(*Suby of* JAS DAY INVESTMENTS LTD)
94 Geikie St, Jasper, AB, T0E 1E0
(780) 852-4431
Emp Here 75
SIC 7011 Hotels and motels
Brian Higginson

D-U-N-S 24-676-7318   (BR)
JAS DAY INVESTMENTS LTD
CHATEAU JASPER
(*Suby of* JAS DAY INVESTMENTS LTD)
96 Geikie St, Jasper, AB, T0E 1E0

(780) 852-5644
Emp Here 100
SIC 7011 Hotels and motels
Malcolm Anderson

D-U-N-S 20-392-2567   (SL)
SKI MARMOT BASIN LIMITED PARTNER-SHIP
Gd, Jasper, AB, T0E 1E0
(780) 852-3816
Emp Here 250   *Sales* 23,917,000
SIC 7011 Hotels and motels
Dave Gibson

D-U-N-S 20-380-0938   (SL)
SKI MARMOT GP CORP
SKI NAKISKA
(*Suby of* 1018465 ALBERTA LTD)
Gd, Jasper, AB, T0E 1E0
(780) 852-3816
Emp Here 100   *Sales* 9,269,000
SIC 7011 Hotels and motels
Mike Irvine
Doug Goss
John Day
Gerry Levasseur
Bruno Ritter
Ralph Scurfield

Kananaskis, AB T0L

D-U-N-S 25-952-6309   (BR)
TIM HORTON CHILDREN'S FOUNDATION, INC
TIM HORTON CHILDREN'S RANCH
(*Suby of* TIM HORTON CHILDREN'S FOUN-DATION, INC)
Gd, Kananaskis, AB, T0L 2H0
(403) 673-2494
Emp Here 75
SIC 7032 Sporting and recreational camps
Jeff Storck

Kehewin, AB T0A

D-U-N-S 24-642-1614   (HQ)
PIMEE WELL SERVICING LTD
Gd, Kehewin, AB, T0A 1C0
(780) 826-6392
Sales 15,985,250
SIC 1389 Oil and gas field services, nec
Tim Schultz
Tom Houle
Eddy Makokis
Al Lameman
Morris Monias

La Crete, AB T0H

D-U-N-S 24-063-2083   (HQ)
KNELSEN SAND & GRAVEL LTD
10005 100 St, La Crete, AB, T0H 2H0
(780) 928-3935
Emp Here 25   *Sales* 341,776,800
SIC 5032 Brick, stone, and related material
Raymond Knelsen
Ann Knelsen

D-U-N-S 24-086-6350   (SL)
LA CRETE CO-OP LIMITED
10502 100 St, La Crete, AB, T0H 2H0
(780) 928-2900
Emp Here 70   *Sales* 20,543,390
SIC 5411 Grocery stores
John R. Braun
Waldemar Schroeder
John W. Braun

D-U-N-S 24-520-8137   (SL)
LA CRETE SAWMILLS LTD
LA CRETE PELLET
Gd, La Crete, AB, T0H 2H0
(780) 928-2292
Emp Here 115   *Sales* 22,122,550
SIC 2421 Sawmills and planing mills, general
John Unger
George Friesen
David Janzen
Raymond Knelsen
Isaac Dyck
Jake Wiebe

D-U-N-S 20-898-0255   (SL)
MACKENZIE HOUSING MANAGEMENT BOARD
HEIMSTAED LODGE
9802 105 St, La Crete, AB, T0H 2H0
(780) 928-3677
Emp Here 45   *Sales* 10,480,995
SIC 6513 Apartment building operators
Wally Sthroder

D-U-N-S 24-379-6484   (HQ)
NORPINE AUTO SUPPLY (96) LTD
10533 100 St, La Crete, AB, T0H 2H0
(780) 928-3912
Emp Here 1   *Sales* 15,200,832
SIC 5084 Industrial machinery and equipment
Jacob Elias

D-U-N-S 24-284-0320   (SL)
NORTHERN LIGHTS GAS CO-OP LTD
10205 101 St, La Crete, AB, T0H 2H0
(780) 928-3881
Emp Here 16   *Sales* 49,693,712
SIC 4923 Gas transmission and distribution
Jack Eccles
William (Bill) Neufeld
Ernest Dick
David Neufeld
David Fehr
Corny F Driedger
Henry Wieler
Edward Froese

D-U-N-S 24-078-6611   (SL)
SUREWAY LOGGING LTD
Gd, La Crete, AB, T0H 2H0
(780) 539-0388
Emp Here 32   *Sales* 15,200,832
SIC 5082 Construction and mining machinery
Andrew Fehr

Lac La Biche, AB T0A

D-U-N-S 24-091-8474   (SL)
ABOUGOUCHE BROS ENTERPRISES LTD
LAC LA BICHE SOBEY'S
10114 101 St, Lac La Biche, AB, T0A 2C0
(780) 623-4234
Emp Here 55   *Sales* 16,141,235
SIC 5411 Grocery stores
Khalil Abougouche
Iche Abougouche
Willy Abougouche
Moe Abougouche

D-U-N-S 20-920-5405   (SL)
ASPEN REGIONAL HEALTH
HEALTH UNIT
9503 Beaver Hill Rd, Lac La Biche, AB, T0A 2C0
(780) 623-4472
Emp Here 49   *Sales* 11,451,055
SIC 8621 Professional organizations
Tracy Smith

D-U-N-S 20-895-7522   (SL)
CALNASH TRUCKING LTD
1 Parker Rd, Lac La Biche, AB, T0A 2C0

Emp Here 180   *Sales* 37,027,080

SIC 4213 Trucking, except local
Frank Nashim

D-U-N-S 24-281-1941   (SL)
LAC LA BICHE INN LTD
YOUNG BROTHERS
10030 101st Ave, Lac La Biche, AB, T0A 2C0
(780) 623-4427
Emp Here 100   *Sales* 9,269,000
SIC 7011 Hotels and motels
Duane Young

D-U-N-S 24-000-0067   (SL)
LAC LA BICHE SPORTING GOODS LTD
13337 101 Ave, Lac La Biche, AB, T0A 2C0
(780) 623-4145
Emp Here 23   *Sales* 11,455,794
SIC 5571 Motorcycle dealers
Ahmed Moghrabi
Omer Moghrabi

D-U-N-S 20-616-7728   (SL)
LAC LA BICHE TRANSPORT LTD
555 Tower Rd, Lac La Biche, AB, T0A 2C0
(780) 623-4711
Emp Here 80   *Sales* 11,855,360
SIC 4212 Local trucking, without storage
Gerald Wowk
Randy Wowk
Steven Wowk

D-U-N-S 25-171-2246   (HQ)
PORTAGE COLLEGE
9531 94 Ave, Lac La Biche, AB, T0A 2C0
(780) 623-5511
Emp Here 200   *Sales* 37,347,750
SIC 8221 Colleges and universities
Bill Persley
Ed Behnke
Nancy Broadbent

Lacombe, AB T4L

D-U-N-S 25-217-9759   (HQ)
AGRICULTURE FINANCIAL SERVICES CORPORATION
AFSC
(*Suby of* GOVERNMENT OF THE PROVINCE OF ALBERTA)
5718 56 Ave, Lacombe, AB, T4L 1B1
(403) 782-8200
Emp Here 300   *Sales* 933,659,377
SIC 6159 Miscellaneous business credit institutions
Steve Blakely
David Maddox
Karla Kochan
Craig Floden
Chris Dyck
Jj Campbell
Darryl Kay
Jennifer Wood
Gerald Bouma
Gordon Cove

D-U-N-S 24-301-4776   (HQ)
ALBERTA CONFERENCE OF THE SEVENTH-DAY ADVENTISTS CHURCH, THE
5816 Highway 2a, Lacombe, AB, T4L 2G5
(403) 342-5044
Emp Here 20   *Sales* 20,824,600
SIC 8661 Religious organizations
Ken Weibe
Robert Holdal

D-U-N-S 20-087-3966   (SL)
BURMAN UNIVERSITY
6730 University Dr Room A104, Lacombe, AB, T4L 2E5
(403) 782-3381
Emp Here 150   *Sales* 22,408,650
SIC 8221 Colleges and universities
Loren Agrey

Noble Donkor
Jr Ferrer
Darrell Huether
Stacy Hunter

D-U-N-S 20-090-1668   (SL)
CATONS LTD
3806 53 Ave, Lacombe, AB, T4L 0A9
(403) 786-9999
Emp Here 24   *Sales* 11,400,624
SIC 5083 Farm and garden machinery
William Caton

D-U-N-S 24-984-6911   (SL)
FARMER'S EDGE WEST INC
3413 53 Ave, Lacombe, AB, T4L 0C6
(403) 782-2204
Emp Here 33   *Sales* 11,491,487
SIC 0139 Field crops, except cash grain
Jay Bruggencate

D-U-N-S 20-969-7239   (BR)
GOVERNMENT OF THE PROVINCE OF ALBERTA
CORPORATE MANAGEMENT
(*Suby of* GOVERNMENT OF THE PROVINCE OF ALBERTA)
5718 56 Ave, Lacombe, AB, T4L 1B1
(403) 782-8309
Emp Here 700
SIC 6159 Miscellaneous business credit institutions

D-U-N-S 25-768-6923   (HQ)
LACOMBE ACTION GROUP FOR THE HANDICAPPED
ACTION GROUP
4 Iron Wolf Blvd, Lacombe, AB, T4L 2K6
(403) 782-5531
Sales 16,894,240
SIC 8322 Individual and family services
Debbie Martin

D-U-N-S 24-136-7361   (SL)
LACOMBE FORD SALES LTD
FAST LANE
5610 Highway 2a, Lacombe, AB, T4L 1A3
(403) 782-6811
Emp Here 60   *Sales* 37,756,800
SIC 5511 New and used car dealers
Darren Gagnon
Robert Leasak

D-U-N-S 24-347-1182   (HQ)
PENTAGON FARM CENTRE LTD
4950 Harrington Ridge Unit 1, Lacombe, AB, T4L 1A8
(403) 782-6873
Sales 16,280,000
SIC 5999 Miscellaneous retail stores, nec
Brian Williams

D-U-N-S 20-087-4634   (HQ)
POPOW & SONS BODY SHOP LTD
5017 49 St, Lacombe, AB, T4L 1Y2
(403) 782-6941
Emp Here 10   *Sales* 15,616,260
SIC 5093 Scrap and waste materials
Robert Popow
Leo Popow
Donna Popow
Dorothy Popow

D-U-N-S 25-139-1509   (SL)
SUN LIFE FINANCIAL AND DEPATIE FINANCIAL SERVICES INC
DEPATIE FINANCIAL SERVICES
4906 50 Ave, Lacombe, AB, T4L 1Y1
(403) 782-3555
Emp Here 49   *Sales* 11,480,112
SIC 8742 Management consulting services
Scott Depatie

D-U-N-S 20-087-4568   (SL)
WEIDNER MOTORS LIMITED
WEIDNER CHEVROLET
5640 Highway 2a, Lacombe, AB, T4L 1A3

---

(403) 782-3626
Emp Here 30   *Sales* 14,942,340
SIC 5511 New and used car dealers
David Weidner
Robert Weidner
Bill Wright

D-U-N-S 25-766-8541   (SL)
WOLF CREEK BUILDING SUPPLIES LTD
5645 Wolf Creek Dr Suite 5808, Lacombe, AB, T4L 2H8
(403) 782-1780
Emp Here 48   *Sales* 21,464,352
SIC 5031 Lumber, plywood, and millwork
Ronald Haan
John Deregt

Lacombe County, AB T4L

D-U-N-S 25-737-8711   (SL)
LACOMBE RV 2000 LTD
ROADMASTER RV, DIV OF
27211 Highway 12 Suite 96, Lacombe County, AB, T4L 0E3
(403) 782-4544
Emp Here 42   *Sales* 20,919,276
SIC 5561 Recreational vehicle dealers
Chris Epp

D-U-N-S 24-395-0750   (HQ)
SCHIPPERS CANADA LTD
27211 Highway 12 Suite 120, Lacombe County, AB, T4L 0E3
(403) 786-9911
Sales 64,237,950
SIC 5999 Miscellaneous retail stores, nec
Arian Dekker

Lake Louise, AB T0L

D-U-N-S 25-293-2587   (BR)
ATLIFIC INC
LAKE LOUISE INN
210 Village Rd, Lake Louise, AB, T0L 1E0
(403) 522-3791
Emp Here 150
SIC 7011 Hotels and motels
Gerry Vartleuk

D-U-N-S 20-305-6556   (SL)
CANADIAN ALPINE CENTRE
203 Village Rd, Lake Louise, AB, T0L 1E0
(403) 522-2200
Emp Here 30   *Sales* 13,304,700
SIC 7389 Business services, nec
Kitty Hill

D-U-N-S 24-701-0812   (BR)
FAIRMONT HOTELS & RESORTS INC
FAIRMONT CHATEAU LAKE LOUISE, THE
(*Suby of* ACCOR)
111 Lake Louise Dr, Lake Louise, AB, T0L 1E0
(403) 522-3511
Emp Here 800
SIC 7011 Hotels and motels
Gregor Resch

D-U-N-S 20-824-6017   (SL)
LAKE LOUISE LIMITED PARTNERSHIP
210 Village Rd, Lake Louise, AB, T0L 1E0
(403) 522-3791
Emp Here 110   *Sales* 21,514,396
SIC 7011 Hotels and motels
Gino Romagnoli
Richard N. Blair
Arni Thorsteinson
Sean Hunt
Lawrence W. Hoskin

D-U-N-S 24-376-9119   (SL)
LAKE LOUISE SKI AREA LTD, THE
1 Whitehorn Rd, Lake Louise, AB, T0L 1E0

---

(403) 522-3555
Emp Here 100   *Sales* 9,489,900
SIC 7011 Hotels and motels
N. Murray Edwards
Charles B. Locke
Louise Locke

D-U-N-S 20-829-6574   (BR)
RESORTS OF THE CANADIAN ROCKIES INC
LAKE LOUISE SKI AREA
(*Suby of* RESORTS OF THE CANADIAN ROCKIES INC)
1 Whait Horn Rd, Lake Louise, AB, T0L 1E0
(403) 522-3555
Emp Here 150
SIC 7999 Amusement and recreation, nec
Rick Weineo

D-U-N-S 20-087-5052   (SL)
SKI CLUB OF THE CANADIAN ROCKIES LIMITED, THE
POST HOTEL
200 Pipestone Rd, Lake Louise, AB, T0L 1E0
(403) 522-3989
Emp Here 110   *Sales* 10,195,900
SIC 7011 Hotels and motels
Andre Schwarz
George Schwarz
Fergus Wilmer
Ka-Shing Lee

Lamont, AB T0B

D-U-N-S 20-438-9704   (SL)
BEAVER CREEK CO-OP ASSN LIMITED
CO-OP
Hwy 15 & 831, Lamont, AB, T0B 2R0
(780) 895-2241
Emp Here 16   *Sales* 17,413,168
SIC 5171 Petroleum bulk stations and terminals
Kevin Andrychuk

Langdon, AB T0J

D-U-N-S 20-692-2333   (SL)
BOULDER CREEK GOLF COURSE LTD
333 Boulder Creek Dr Suite 3, Langdon, AB, T0J 1X3
(403) 936-8777
Emp Here 25   *Sales* 10,483,875
SIC 6712 Bank holding companies
Kyle Stanford

Leduc, AB T9E

D-U-N-S 24-702-5745   (BR)
1032451 B.C. LTD
REPRESENTATIVE WEBCO BOWES
(*Suby of* QUEBECOR MEDIA INC)
4504 61 Ave, Leduc, AB, T9E 3Z1
(780) 986-2271
Emp Here 80
SIC 2711 Newspapers
Neil Sutcliffe

D-U-N-S 24-065-8625   (SL)
714638 ALBERTA LTD
LEDUC TRUST
4507 61 Ave, Leduc, AB, T9E 7B5
(780) 986-0334
Emp Here 150   *Sales* 33,130,650
SIC 6519 Real property lessors, nec
Cliff Paulson
Russ Dyson
Gordon Tober
Harold Cox

D-U-N-S 20-083-8381   (HQ)
ALTAGAS UTILITIES INC
(*Suby of* ALTAGAS LTD)
5509 45 St, Leduc, AB, T9E 6T6
(780) 986-5215
Emp Here 70   *Sales* 268,975,602
SIC 4923 Gas transmission and distribution
Lorne M Heikkinen
David Cornhill
Patricia Newson
Earl Tuele
Peter Whalley

D-U-N-S 24-948-8479   (HQ)
AMECO SERVICES INC
(*Suby of* FLUOR CORPORATION)
6909 42 St Unit 101, Leduc, AB, T9E 0W1
(780) 440-6633
Emp Here 300   *Sales* 82,243,980
SIC 7353 Heavy construction equipment rental
Raylene Kajner

D-U-N-S 24-890-1634   (SL)
ARISS CONTROLS & ELECTRIC INC
6800 39 St, Leduc, AB, T9E 0Z4
(780) 986-1147
Emp Here 40   *Sales* 12,360,945
SIC 1731 Electrical work
Richard Ariss

D-U-N-S 20-112-9652   (HQ)
ASPEN CUSTOM TRAILERS
3914 81 Ave, Leduc, AB, T9E 0C3
(780) 980-1925
Emp Here 125   *Sales* 68,282,200
SIC 5088 Transportation equipment and supplies
W Murray Johnston
Naidra Johnston

D-U-N-S 24-275-2525   (BR)
BAKER HUGHES CANADA COMPANY
CENTRILIFT
(*Suby of* GENERAL ELECTRIC COMPANY)
7016 45 St, Leduc, AB, T9E 7E7
(780) 986-5559
Emp Here 100
SIC 5084 Industrial machinery and equipment
Don Senske

D-U-N-S 24-239-4565   (SL)
BAKER HUGHES CANADA COMPANY
3905 71 Ave, Leduc, AB, T9E 0R8
(780) 612-3150
Emp Here 100   *Sales* 100,901,850
SIC 1389 Oil and gas field services, nec
William Marsh
Joe Ballew

D-U-N-S 24-399-7459   (SL)
BARRY, ART FORD SALES LTD
8012 Sparrow Cres, Leduc, AB, T9E 7G1
(780) 986-1100
Emp Here 30   *Sales* 14,942,340
SIC 5511 New and used car dealers
Robert Wispinski
Neil Reid
Arthur Barry

D-U-N-S 25-594-4886   (SL)
BROMLEY FOODS LTD
SOBEYS READY TO SERVE LEDUC
5421 50 St, Leduc, AB, T9E 6Z7
(780) 986-2289
Emp Here 165   *Sales* 48,423,705
SIC 5411 Grocery stores
Graham Bromley
Karen Bromley

D-U-N-S 24-890-4471   (BR)
CLEAN HARBORS ENERGY AND INDUSTRIAL SERVICES CORP
(*Suby of* CLEAN HARBORS, INC.)
3902 77 Ave, Leduc, AB, T9E 0B6
(780) 980-1868
Emp Here 500

SIC 7349 Building maintenance services, nec
Kevin Mcgonigal

D-U-N-S 24-322-2127   (BR)
CLEAN HARBORS SURFACE RENTALS PARTNERSHIP
(*Suby of* CLEAN HARBORS, INC.)
3902 77 Ave, Leduc, AB, T9E 0B6
(780) 980-1868
Emp Here 75
SIC 1389 Oil and gas field services, nec
Kevin Emes

D-U-N-S 24-930-0575   (SL)
D K FORD SALES LTD
6559 Sparrow Dr, Leduc, AB, T9E 7L1
(780) 986-2929
Emp Here 40   *Sales* 19,923,120
SIC 5511 New and used car dealers
David Koch
Duane Koch
Richard Koch

D-U-N-S 24-334-6363   (BR)
DNOW CANADA ULC
NATIONAL OILWELL VARCO
(*Suby of* NOW INC.)
6621 45 St, Leduc, AB, T9E 7E3
(780) 980-1490
Emp Here 200
SIC 5084 Industrial machinery and equipment
Randy Baudin

D-U-N-S 24-715-2085   (BR)
EXTENDICARE (CANADA) INC
EXTENDICARE LEDUC
(*Suby of* EXTENDICARE INC)
4309 50 St, Leduc, AB, T9E 6K6
(780) 986-2245
Emp Here 75
SIC 8051 Skilled nursing care facilities
Elizabeth Sousa

D-U-N-S 24-043-4501   (SL)
FORCE INSPECTION SERVICES INC
7500a 43 St, Leduc, AB, T9E 7E8
(780) 955-2370
Emp Here 80   *Sales* 35,937,520
SIC 7389 Business services, nec
Nicholas Donohoe
Cameron Maccarthy

D-U-N-S 24-089-8841   (SL)
KUNY'S LEATHER MANUFACTURING COMPANY LTD
5901 44a St, Leduc, AB, T9E 7B8
(780) 986-1151
Emp Here 100   *Sales* 24,432,800
SIC 5948 Luggage and leather goods stores
Mike Danceinger
Brian Kuny

D-U-N-S 25-627-4408   (SL)
LAURION, S. & J. LIMITED
CANADIAN TIRE
5402 Discovery Way, Leduc, AB, T9E 8L9
(780) 986-5229
Emp Here 90   *Sales* 18,480,870
SIC 5399 Miscellaneous general merchandise
Steve Laurion
Jody Laurion

D-U-N-S 20-539-2947   (SL)
LEDUC CHRYSLER LTD
LEDUC CHRYSLER JEEP
6102 46a St, Leduc, AB, T9E 7A7
(780) 986-2051
Emp Here 50   *Sales* 24,903,900
SIC 5511 New and used car dealers
Richard Rivard
Miguel Hormazabal

D-U-N-S 20-087-6076   (SL)
LEDUC CO-OP LTD
5403 50 St, Leduc, AB, T9E 6Z7
(780) 986-3036
Emp Here 75   *Sales* 50,232,600
SIC 5541 Gasoline service stations

Rick Polasek
Peter Brauer
Randy Wetter
Cor Abma
Harvey Hoshowski
Norman Schneider
James Mcilroy
John Taekema

D-U-N-S 20-703-4732   (SL)
LEDUC TRUSS INC
4507 61 Ave, Leduc, AB, T9E 7B5
(780) 986-0334
Emp Here 108   *Sales* 20,775,960
SIC 2439 Structural wood members, nec
Russell Dyson

D-U-N-S 24-165-3708   (SL)
MAR-QUINN INDUSTRIES LTD
7115 Sparrow Dr, Leduc, AB, T9E 7L1
(780) 986-7805
Emp Here 60   *Sales* 13,320,060
SIC 3533 Oil and gas field machinery
Daryl Martin
Joan Martin

D-U-N-S 24-371-8835   (SL)
MATRIX SERVICE CANADA ULC
(*Suby of* MATRIX SERVICE COMPANY)
7105 39 St Unit 102, Leduc, AB, T9E 0R8
(780) 986-4058
Emp Here 50   *Sales* 12,309,300
SIC 1791 Structural steel erection
John Hewitt
Joseph Montalbano
Kevin Cavanah

D-U-N-S 20-515-3203   (SL)
MIXCOR HOLDINGS INC
MIXCOR AGGREGATES
6303 43 St, Leduc, AB, T9E 0G8
(780) 986-6721
Emp Here 70   *Sales* 18,308,710
SIC 6712 Bank holding companies
Terry Mix

D-U-N-S 24-715-8546   (SL)
NISKU TRUCK STOP LTD
NISKU TRUCK STOP
8020 Sparrow Dr Suite 201, Leduc, AB, T9E 7G3
(780) 986-5312
Emp Here 150   *Sales* 94,392,000
SIC 5541 Gasoline service stations
Simon Cook

D-U-N-S 20-334-9345   (SL)
NORTH WEST CRANE ENTERPRISES LTD
7015 Sparrow Dr, Leduc, AB, T9E 7L1
(780) 980-2227
Emp Here 65   *Sales* 29,199,235
SIC 7389 Business services, nec
Jon Janssen
Dave Friesen
Don Kurjata

D-U-N-S 20-025-1924   (SL)
ORIGINAL JOE'S
5411 Discovery Way Unit 101, Leduc, AB, T9E 8N4
(780) 986-6965
Emp Here 20   *Sales* 16,711,540
SIC 5149 Groceries and related products, nec

D-U-N-S 24-767-7537   (BR)
PEACE HILLS INVESTMENTS LTD
DENHAM INN & SUITES
(*Suby of* PEACE HILLS INVESTMENTS LTD)
5207 50 Ave, Leduc, AB, T9E 6V3
(780) 986-2241
Emp Here 100
SIC 7011 Hotels and motels
Perry Batke

D-U-N-S 24-090-3815   (SL)
SALEM MANOR SOCIETY, THE
SALEM MANOR NURSING HOME
4419 46 St Suite 612, Leduc, AB, T9E 6L2

▲ Public Company   ■ Public Company Family Member   **HQ** Headquarters   **BR** Branch   **SL** Single Location

(780) 986-8654
Emp Here 152   *Sales* 10,385,552
SIC 8051 Skilled nursing care facilities
 Bernie Pankonin
 Richard Garrett

D-U-N-S 24-732-2340   (SL)
SARENS CANADA INC
(*Suby of* SARENS BESTUUR)
6019 35 St, Leduc, AB, T9E 1E6
(780) 612-4400
Emp Here 200   *Sales* 35,256,465
SIC 7353 Heavy construction equipment rental
 Mike Hussey
 Ken Burke
 Ludo Sarens
 Steven Sarens
 Wim Sarens

D-U-N-S 25-271-0652   (BR)
SOBEYS WEST INC
SAFEWAY #801
(*Suby of* EMPIRE COMPANY LIMITED)
6112 50 St Suite 6112, Leduc, AB, T9E 6N7
(780) 986-0390
Emp Here 132
SIC 5411 Grocery stores
 Steve Klask

D-U-N-S 24-732-7653   (HQ)
STRATHCONA MECHANICAL LIMITED
6612 44 St, Leduc, AB, T9E 7E4
(780) 980-1122
Emp Here 60   *Sales* 14,683,095
SIC 1711 Plumbing, heating, air-conditioning
 David Christman
 Neil Touw
 Cody Christman

D-U-N-S 25-219-6357   (BR)
TUCKER WIRELINE SERVICES CANADA INC
(*Suby of* STEP ENERGY SERVICES LTD)
7123 Sparrow Dr, Leduc, AB, T9E 7L1

Emp Here 100
SIC 1389 Oil and gas field services, nec
 Dave Jellett

D-U-N-S 24-715-4490   (SL)
ULTERRA LP
7010 45 St, Leduc, AB, T9E 7E7
(780) 980-3500
Emp Here 100   *Sales* 67,267,900
SIC 1381 Drilling oil and gas wells
 Scott Mcmillan
 John Clume

D-U-N-S 20-552-3751   (SL)
UNDERHILL FOOD SERVICES LTD
MCDONALDS
6504 Sparrow Dr, Leduc, AB, T9E 6T9
(780) 986-5323
Emp Here 80   *Sales* 3,641,520
SIC 5812 Eating places
 John Underhill

D-U-N-S 20-826-0273   (HQ)
VARCO CANADA ULC
(*Suby of* NATIONAL OILWELL VARCO, INC.)
6621 45 St, Leduc, AB, T9E 7E3
(780) 986-6063
Emp Here 90   *Sales* 67,883,920
SIC 7353 Heavy construction equipment rental
 Clay Williams
 Dwight W Retting
 Daniel Molinaro
 David J Keener
 Raymond W Chang
 Vincent J Gillespie
 Glen Arnelien
 Sharon Durling

D-U-N-S 20-918-2521   (BR)
WAL-MART CANADA CORP
(*Suby of* WALMART INC.)

5302 Discovery Way, Leduc, AB, T9E 8J7
(780) 986-7574
Emp Here 150
SIC 5311 Department stores

D-U-N-S 25-990-1635   (SL)
WESTERN RV CENTRE LEDUC INC
WESTERN RV COUNTRY
7503 Sparrow Dr, Leduc, AB, T9E 0H3
(780) 986-2880
Emp Here 44   *Sales* 21,915,432
SIC 5571 Motorcycle dealers
 Bruce Norman Urban

D-U-N-S 24-817-5288   (SL)
WRANGLER RENTALS LTD
3911 Allard Ave, Leduc, AB, T9E 0R8
(780) 980-1331
Emp Here 109   *Sales* 36,313,132
SIC 7359 Equipment rental and leasing, nec
 Roderick Woolf
 Bill Mcdougall

Leduc County, AB T4X

D-U-N-S 20-273-8894   (HQ)
COMMAND FISHING AND PIPE RECOVERY LTD
24521 Township Road 510, Leduc County, AB, T4X 0T4
(780) 979-2220
Emp Here 50   *Sales* 53,814,320
SIC 1389 Oil and gas field services, nec
 Patrick Powell
 Darren Acheson
 Lee Nilsson
 Bryn Jones

Legal, AB T0G

D-U-N-S 25-236-0904   (SL)
CHAMPAGNE EDITION INC
ECO-FLEX
57425 Rge Rd 253, Legal, AB, T0G 1L0
(780) 961-3229
Emp Here 50   *Sales* 10,094,850
SIC 3069 Fabricated rubber products, nec
 Alan Champagne

D-U-N-S 20-120-7797   (SL)
RUBBER TECH. INTERNATIONAL LTD
Gd, Legal, AB, T0G 1L0
(780) 961-3229
Emp Here 100   *Sales* 75,111,980
SIC 5199 Nondurable goods, nec
 Alan Champagne

Leslieville, AB T0M

D-U-N-S 20-990-5546   (SL)
POLLITT, R. OILFIELD CONSTRUCTION LTD
Gd, Leslieville, AB, T0M 1H0
(403) 588-1230
Emp Here 180   *Sales* 45,439,560
SIC 1623 Water, sewer, and utility lines
 Darren Pollitt
 Rocky Blair

D-U-N-S 20-329-2636   (SL)
WPW INC
(*Suby of* US SHALE SOLUTIONS, INC.)
Gd, Leslieville, AB, T0M 1H0
(403) 729-3007
Emp Here 250   *Sales* 36,982,250
SIC 1623 Water, sewer, and utility lines
 Wayne Pidhirney
 Grant Fulton

Lethbridge, AB T1H

D-U-N-S 25-313-5719   (HQ)
612337 ALBERTA LTD.
SILVER AUTOMOTIVE
3042 2 Ave N, Lethbridge, AB, T1H 0C6
(403) 328-9621
Emp Here 1   *Sales* 10,198,020
SIC 5013 Motor vehicle supplies and new parts
 Ronald Fraser

D-U-N-S 25-014-6990   (HQ)
AGCOM LTD
AGCOM PETROLEUM SALES
3240 2 Ave N, Lethbridge, AB, T1H 0C6
(403) 328-9228
Emp Here 7   *Sales* 17,557,736
SIC 5172 Petroleum products, nec
 Harold Exner
 Kathryn Exner

D-U-N-S 24-679-8560   (SL)
CAMPBELL, RON G SALES LTD
CANADIAN TIRE
1240 2a Ave N Suite 2, Lethbridge, AB, T1H 0E4
(403) 320-6191
Emp Here 30   *Sales* 14,942,340
SIC 5531 Auto and home supply stores
 Ron Campbell

D-U-N-S 20-829-9586   (SL)
CHALLENGER BUILDING SUPPLIES LTD
3304 8 Ave N, Lethbridge, AB, T1H 5C9
(403) 327-8501
Emp Here 36   *Sales* 16,098,264
SIC 5039 Construction materials, nec
 Vincent Toth
 David Toth

D-U-N-S 20-087-7397   (SL)
CHARLTON & HILL LIMITED
2620 5 Ave N, Lethbridge, AB, T1H 6J6
(403) 328-2665
Emp Here 140   *Sales* 32,629,100
SIC 1711 Plumbing, heating, air-conditioning
 James Hill

D-U-N-S 20-284-9667   (SL)
CONSTELLATION BRANDS SCHENLEY ULC
BLACK VELVET DISTILLING CO, THE
(*Suby of* CONSTELLATION BRANDS, INC.)
2925 9 Ave N, Lethbridge, AB, T1H 5E3
(403) 317-2100
Emp Here 65   *Sales* 22,469,850
SIC 2085 Distilled and blended liquors
 Claude Bilodeau
 Daniel J. Mccarthy
 Judy A. Schmeling
 Keith E. Wandell
 Richard Sands
 Robert Sands
 Frederic Cumenal
 Jerry Fowden
 Barry A. Fromberg
 Robert L. Hanson

D-U-N-S 20-090-0587   (SL)
COX, G W CONSTRUCTION LTD
1210 31 St N, Lethbridge, AB, T1H 5J8
(403) 328-1346
Emp Here 65   *Sales* 16,002,090
SIC 1794 Excavation work
 Darrell Cox

D-U-N-S 20-073-4577   (SL)
D.A. BUILDING SYSTEMS LTD
2808 2 Ave N, Lethbridge, AB, T1H 0C2
(403) 328-4427
Emp Here 35   *Sales* 11,666,655
SIC 1541 Industrial buildings and warehouses
 Douglas Grenier
 Scott Grenier

D-U-N-S 25-536-9803   (HQ)
DUNLOP STERLING TRUCK CENTRE LTD
DUNLOP STERLING WESTERN STAR
4110 9 Ave N, Lethbridge, AB, T1H 6L9
(403) 317-2450
Sales 12,753,772
SIC 4212 Local trucking, without storage
 Randy Dunlop
 Gary Dunlop

D-U-N-S 20-598-8033   (SL)
ELDORADO R V SALES LTD
711 2a Ave N, Lethbridge, AB, T1H 0E1
(403) 329-3933
Emp Here 21   *Sales* 10,459,638
SIC 5561 Recreational vehicle dealers
 Bert Knopp
 Ron Hall

D-U-N-S 24-879-8142   (HQ)
ENERCON WATER TREATMENT LTD
NEOCHEM (DIV OF)
(*Suby of* DYCHEM INVESTMENTS INC)
3606 6 Ave N, Lethbridge, AB, T1H 5C4
(403) 328-9730
Sales 29,213,800
SIC 5169 Chemicals and allied products, nec

D-U-N-S 20-920-4200   (SL)
EXTERIORS BY LEROY & DARCY LTD
3404 12 Ave N, Lethbridge, AB, T1H 5V1
(403) 327-9113
Emp Here 60   *Sales* 13,069,740
SIC 1761 Roofing, siding, and sheetMetal work
 Darcy Jerome

D-U-N-S 24-357-0434   (HQ)
FORTIFIED NUTRITION LIMITED
3613 9 Ave N, Lethbridge, AB, T1H 6G8
(403) 320-0401
Emp Here 1   *Sales* 16,335,440
SIC 5191 Farm supplies
 Larry Smid

D-U-N-S 24-174-5541   (BR)
GOVERNMENT OF THE PROVINCE OF ALBERTA
SOUTHWEST ALBERTA CHILD & FAMILY SERVICES
(*Suby of* GOVERNMENT OF THE PROVINCE OF ALBERTA)
3305 18 Ave N Suite 107, Lethbridge, AB, T1H 5S1
(403) 381-5543
Emp Here 200
SIC 8322 Individual and family services
 Gord Johnston

D-U-N-S 20-744-7293   (HQ)
GREEN'S POP SHOP LTD
613 13 St N, Lethbridge, AB, T1H 2S7
(403) 329-4848
Emp Here 31   *Sales* 16,728,189
SIC 5411 Grocery stores
 David Green

D-U-N-S 24-599-5253   (SL)
HANLON AG CENTRE LTD
3005 18 Ave N, Lethbridge, AB, T1H 5V2
(403) 329-8686
Emp Here 25   *Sales* 11,875,650
SIC 5083 Farm and garden machinery
 Timothy Hanlon
 Keith Shirakawa
 Brendon Hanlon
 Michael Anderson

D-U-N-S 24-554-6684   (SL)
HAUL-ALL EQUIPMENT LTD
SURE FLAME PRODUCTS, DIV OF
4115 18 Ave N, Lethbridge, AB, T1H 5G1
(403) 328-5353
Emp Here 110   *Sales* 24,420,110
SIC 3564 Blowers and fans
 Kevin Neufeldt

D-U-N-S 24-647-8036   (SL)

K.B. HEATING & AIR CONDITIONING LTD
3569 32 Ave N, Lethbridge, AB, T1H 7C2
(403) 328-0337
Emp Here 60   *Sales* 13,983,900
SIC 1711 Plumbing, heating, air-conditioning
Keith Broadbent
Greg Broadbent
Ronna Broadbent

D-U-N-S 24-416-3812   (BR)
KAWNEER COMPANY CANADA LIMITED
(*Suby of* ARCONIC INC.)
4000 18 Ave N Suite Side, Lethbridge, AB,
T1H 5S8
(403) 320-7755
Emp Here 300
SIC 3442 Metal doors, sash, and trim
Judy Burek

D-U-N-S 20-088-0102   (SL)
**LETHBRIDGE IRON WORKS COMPANY
LIMITED**
LETH IRON
720 32 St N, Lethbridge, AB, T1H 5K5
(403) 329-4242
Emp Here 130   *Sales* 23,580,440
SIC 3321 Gray and ductile iron foundries
John R Davies
Richard Carr
Blair Lozza
Richard Dietl

D-U-N-S 20-029-7781   (BR)
LETHBRIDGE SCHOOL DISTRICT NO. 51
WINSTON CHURCHILL HIGH SCHOOL
(*Suby of* LETHBRIDGE SCHOOL DISTRICT
NO. 51)
1605 15 Ave N, Lethbridge, AB, T1H 1W4
(403) 328-4723
Emp Here 78
SIC 8211 Elementary and secondary schools
Carey Rowntree

D-U-N-S 20-336-6955   (BR)
LETHBRIDGE SCHOOL DISTRICT NO. 51
WILSON MIDDLE SCHOOL
(*Suby of* LETHBRIDGE SCHOOL DISTRICT
NO. 51)
2003 9 Ave N, Lethbridge, AB, T1H 1J3
(403) 329-3144
Emp Here 75
SIC 8211 Elementary and secondary schools
Dean Hawkins

D-U-N-S 20-038-5958   (BR)
LETHBRIDGE, CITY OF
LETHBRIDGE TRANSIT
(*Suby of* LETHBRIDGE, CITY OF)
619 4 Ave N, Lethbridge, AB, T1H 0K4
(403) 320-3885
Emp Here 120
SIC 4111 Local and suburban transit
Marge Vanrijan

D-U-N-S 20-046-0520   (SL)
LO-COST PROPANE LTD
(*Suby of* SAVE X LP GAS LTD)
3191 5 Ave N, Lethbridge, AB, T1H 0P2
(403) 380-3536
Emp Here 50   *Sales* 12,216,400
SIC 5984 Liquefied petroleum gas dealers
Ralph Bruinsma

D-U-N-S 25-507-1136   (HQ)
LOGIC HOLDINGS LTD
LOGIC LUMBER
1217 39 St N, Lethbridge, AB, T1H 6Y8
(403) 328-7755
Emp Here 2   *Sales* 20,967,750
SIC 6712 Bank holding companies
Thomas Dixon
Linda Dixon

D-U-N-S 24-495-6314   (SL)
LOGIC LUMBER (LETH.) LTD
(*Suby of* LOGIC HOLDINGS LTD)
1217 39 St N, Lethbridge, AB, T1H 6Y8

(403) 328-7755
Emp Here 50   *Sales* 13,382,600
SIC 5211 Lumber and other building materials
Thomas Dixon
Linda Dixon

D-U-N-S 24-118-0934   (BR)
MAPLE LEAF FOODS INC
MAPLE LEAF POTOTOES, DIV OF
(*Suby of* MAPLE LEAF FOODS INC)
2720 2a Ave N, Lethbridge, AB, T1H 5B4
(403) 380-9900
Emp Here 120
SIC 5148 Fresh fruits and vegetables
Lee Glein

D-U-N-S 24-161-1847   (HQ)
MEDBRIDGE INVESTMENTS LTD
OVERHEAD DOOR COMPANY
2835 12 Ave N, Lethbridge, AB, T1H 5K9
(403) 328-0922
Emp Here 25   *Sales* 33,538,050
SIC 5031 Lumber, plywood, and millwork
Don Donison

D-U-N-S 20-308-4389   (HQ)
MERIDIAN MANUFACTURING INC
(*Suby of* TREVLUC HOLDINGS LTD)
3125 24 Ave N, Lethbridge, AB, T1H 5G2
(403) 320-7070
Emp Here 150   *Sales* 252,789,300
SIC 3545 Machine tool accessories
Paul Cunningham
Russell Edwards
Victor Holodryga
Bernie Thiessen
Gary Edwards
Kevin Edwards
Edna Edwards
Glen Friesen
Mike Froese
Margaret Morgan

D-U-N-S 20-197-8397   (SL)
PEPSI BOTTLING GROUP
2400 31 St N, Lethbridge, AB, T1H 5K8
(403) 327-1310
Emp Here 20   *Sales* 10,702,480
SIC 5149 Groceries and related products, nec
Jasmine Peloquin

D-U-N-S 25-014-1405   (BR)
PEPSICO CANADA ULC
HOSTESS FRITO-LAY
(*Suby of* PEPSICO, INC.)
2200 31 St N, Lethbridge, AB, T1H 5K8
(403) 380-5775
Emp Here 250
SIC 2096 Potato chips and similar snacks
Gary Smith

D-U-N-S 25-014-9507   (BR)
PRATT & WHITNEY CANADA CIE
(*Suby of* PRATT AERO LIMITED PARTNER-
SHIP)
4045 26 Ave N, Lethbridge, AB, T1H 6G2
(403) 380-5100
Emp Here 125
SIC 3519 Internal combustion engines, nec
Christina Barnum

D-U-N-S 24-618-2468   (BR)
RICHARDSON OILSEED LIMITED
(*Suby of* RICHARDSON, JAMES & SONS,
LIMITED)
2415 2a Ave N, Lethbridge, AB, T1H 6P5
(403) 329-5500
Emp Here 150
SIC 2079 Edible fats and oils
Gary Tombsta

D-U-N-S 20-100-2594   (SL)
SAVE-X-LP GAS LTD
LOW COST PROPANE
3195 5 Ave N, Lethbridge, AB, T1H 0P2
(403) 380-3536
Emp Here 35   *Sales* 16,415,175
SIC 5984 Liquefied petroleum gas dealers

Ralph Bruinsma

D-U-N-S 20-645-5651   (SL)
SILVER AUTOMOTIVE (LETHBRIDGE) LTD
SILVER AUTOMOTIVE
(*Suby of* 612337 ALBERTA LTD.)
3042 2 Ave N, Lethbridge, AB, T1H 0C6
(403) 328-9621
Emp Here 28   *Sales* 10,198,020
SIC 5013 Motor vehicle supplies and new
parts
Ronald Fraser
Gary Winters

D-U-N-S 20-743-2274   (BR)
SOBEYS CAPITAL INCORPORATED
(*Suby of* EMPIRE COMPANY LIMITED)
327 Bluefox Blvd N, Lethbridge, AB, T1H 6T3
(403) 320-5154
Emp Here 100
SIC 5411 Grocery stores
Parrish Hanelt

D-U-N-S 25-271-0389   (BR)
SOBEYS WEST INC
PARK MEADOWS SAFEWAY
(*Suby of* EMPIRE COMPANY LIMITED)
1702 23 St N, Lethbridge, AB, T1H 5B3
(403) 320-2231
Emp Here 80
SIC 5411 Grocery stores
Jone Bain

D-U-N-S 25-143-7935   (SL)
**SOUTHERN ALBERTA COMMUNITY LIV-
ING ASSOCIATION**
SACLA
401 21a St N, Lethbridge, AB, T1H 6L6
(403) 329-1525
Emp Here 141   *Sales* 202,842,741
SIC 8699 Membership organizations, nec
Susan Manery

D-U-N-S 24-494-1134   (SL)
**SOUTHLAND INTERNATIONAL TRUCKS
LTD**
4310 9 Ave N, Lethbridge, AB, T1H 6N1
(403) 328-0808
Emp Here 45   *Sales* 22,413,510
SIC 5511 New and used car dealers
George Kirkham

D-U-N-S 24-345-9005   (HQ)
SOUTHLAND TRAILER CORP
LETHBRIDGE TRUCK EQUIPMENT, DIV OF
1405 41 St N, Lethbridge, AB, T1H 6G3
(403) 327-8212
Sales 33,576,450
SIC 3715 Truck trailers
Monty Sailer

D-U-N-S 20-991-2260   (HQ)
ST. MARY RIVER IRRIGATION DISTRICT
SMRID
1210 36 St N, Lethbridge, AB, T1H 5H8
(403) 380-6152
Emp Here 25   *Sales* 33,788,401
SIC 4971 Irrigation systems
R. James Csabay
Tom Crooks
Leron Torrie
Les Enns
Robert Dykstra
Gary Bierback
Gary Franz
John Belanger

D-U-N-S 24-495-6256   (HQ)
TIMBER-TECH TRUSS INC
1405 31 St N, Lethbridge, AB, T1H 5G8
(403) 328-5499
Emp Here 40   *Sales* 15,389,600
SIC 2439 Structural wood members, nec
Derrill Murphy
Mary Pearl Murphy
Brian Peters
Kelly Skauge

Wendy Going

D-U-N-S 25-389-2095   (SL)
TRIPLE M HOUSING LTD
BELCARRA
3501 Giffen Rd N, Lethbridge, AB, T1H 0E8
(403) 320-8588
Emp Here 275   *Sales* 52,901,750
SIC 2451 Mobile homes
Rick Weste
Cahd Danard
Norm Rokosh

D-U-N-S 24-731-2689   (SL)
VANEE FARM CENTRE INC
510 36 St N, Lethbridge, AB, T1H 5H6
(403) 327-1100
Emp Here 25   *Sales* 11,875,650
SIC 5083 Farm and garden machinery
Hank Vanee

D-U-N-S 25-685-0280   (BR)
VARSTEEL LTD
(*Suby of* VARZARI TRADING LTD)
2900 5 Ave N, Lethbridge, AB, T1H 6K3
(403) 329-0233
Emp Here 100
SIC 5051 Metals service centers and offices
Lorne Mackenzie

D-U-N-S 25-387-6270   (BR)
VOLKER STEVIN CONTRACTING LTD
VOLKER STEVIN HIGHWAY
(*Suby of* KONINKLIJKE VOLKERWESSELS
N.V.)
4004 6 Ave N, Lethbridge, AB, T1H 6W4
(403) 320-4920
Emp Here 200
SIC 1611 Highway and street construction
Dean Jetten

D-U-N-S 24-345-6758   (BR)
WAL-MART CANADA CORP
(*Suby of* WALMART INC.)
3195 26 Ave N Suite 1078, Lethbridge, AB,
T1H 5P3
(403) 380-6722
Emp Here 400
SIC 5311 Department stores

D-U-N-S 24-879-7920   (HQ)
WALTER, B & D TRUCKING LTD
WALTER'S TRUCKING
1435 31 St N, Lethbridge, AB, T1H 5G8
Emp Here 30   *Sales* 15,427,950
SIC 4213 Trucking, except local
Ben Walter

D-U-N-S 24-299-6247   (SL)
WARD BROS CONSTRUCTION LTD
3604 18 Ave N, Lethbridge, AB, T1H 5S7
(403) 328-6698
Emp Here 25   *Sales* 11,768,275
SIC 1542 Nonresidential construction, nec
Cecil Ward

D-U-N-S 24-678-9155   (HQ)
WESTERN TRACTOR COMPANY INC
3214 5 Ave N, Lethbridge, AB, T1H 0P4
(403) 327-5512
Emp Here 10   *Sales* 16,625,910
SIC 5083 Farm and garden machinery
Grant Mcgrath
Steven Dyck
Dallas Smith

D-U-N-S 20-178-0157   (HQ)
WOODHAVEN CAPITAL CORP
(*Suby of* TREVLUC HOLDINGS LTD)
3125 24 Ave N, Lethbridge, AB, T1H 5G2
(403) 320-7070
Emp Here 150
SIC 6712 Bank holding companies
Paul Cunningham

▲ Public Company   ■ Public Company Family Member   **HQ** Headquarters   **BR** Branch   **SL** Single Location

Lethbridge, AB T1J

D-U-N-S 24-906-5590 (HQ)
512844 ALBERTA LTD
(Suby of STIMSON, DEREK HOLDINGS LTD)
3939 1 Ave S, Lethbridge, AB, T1J 4P8
(403) 327-3154
Emp Here 50   Sales 43,861,080
SIC 6712 Bank holding companies
Derek Stimson
Susan Stimson-Kasun

D-U-N-S 24-372-1185 (BR)
ALBERTA HEALTH SERVICES
CHINOOK REGIONAL HOSPITAL
(Suby of GOVERNMENT OF THE
PROVINCE OF ALBERTA)
960 19 St S Suite 110, Lethbridge, AB, T1J
1W5
(403) 388-6009
Emp Here 100
SIC 8062 General medical and surgical hospitals
Carl Amrhein

D-U-N-S 20-015-7951 (SL)
ASTRO INSURANCE 1000 INC
(Suby of 764824 ALBERTA LTD)
542 7 St S Unit 100, Lethbridge, AB, T1J 2H1
(403) 320-6700
Emp Here 18   Sales 10,438,632
SIC 6411 Insurance agents, brokers, and service
Mark D Swartout
Cindy Swartout
Ed Sawicki

D-U-N-S 25-064-3053 (HQ)
AVONLEA HOMES LTD
AVONLEA MASTER BUILDER
1111 3 Ave S, Lethbridge, AB, T1J 0J5
(403) 320-1989
Emp Here 25   Sales 15,943,450
SIC 1521 Single-family housing construction
John Wickey
Steven Meszaros

D-U-N-S 24-346-8477 (SL)
BALOG AUCTION SERVICES INC
Gd, Lethbridge, AB, T1J 3Y2
(403) 320-1980
Emp Here 45   Sales 66,046,140
SIC 5154 Livestock
Robert C Balog

D-U-N-S 24-416-2889 (HQ)
BIGELOW FOWLER CLINIC
1605 9 Ave S, Lethbridge, AB, T1J 1W2
(403) 327-3121
Emp Here 45   Sales 12,173,248
SIC 8011 Offices and clinics of medical doctors
Allan Mcpherson
D.F. Meller
Christine Watke
L M Bezuidenhout
R T Garnett
P G Greidanus
A T Billett
D.R. Gibb
James Kozan

D-U-N-S 24-716-1003 (HQ)
BRIDGE CITY CHRYSLER DODGE JEEP LTD
3216 1 Ave S, Lethbridge, AB, T1J 4H2
(403) 328-3325
Emp Here 73   Sales 58,523,040
SIC 5511 New and used car dealers
Clarence Arnoldussen
Wendy Borthwick
Jonas Arnoldussen

D-U-N-S 25-098-8086 (SL)
BRIDGE COUNTY RACEWAY LTD
BCR

Gd Lcd Main, Lethbridge, AB, T1J 3Y2

Emp Here 35   Sales 14,830,550
SIC 7948 Racing, including track operation
George Mercer

D-U-N-S 24-134-0194 (BR)
CANADIAN CORPS OF COMMISSION-AIRES NATIONAL OFFICE, THE
(Suby of CANADIAN CORPS OF COMMISSIONAIRES NATIONAL OFFICE, THE)
1222 3 Ave S, Lethbridge, AB, T1J 0J9
(403) 327-1222
Emp Here 180
SIC 8621 Professional organizations
Lori Brewer

D-U-N-S 24-517-7951 (SL)
CENTRAL TRUCK EQUIPMENT INC
VANEE MOTORS
3521 1 Ave S, Lethbridge, AB, T1J 4H1
(403) 328-4189
Emp Here 21   Sales 10,459,638
SIC 5511 New and used car dealers
Jo Vanee

D-U-N-S 25-217-8397 (BR)
CHANTELLE MANAGEMENT LTD
CAVELL, EDITH CARE CENTRE
1255 5 Ave S, Lethbridge, AB, T1J 0V6
(403) 328-6631
Emp Here 120
SIC 8051 Skilled nursing care facilities
Teierle Marian

D-U-N-S 20-521-9574 (SL)
CHIP REIT NO 18 OPERATIONS LIMITED PARTNERSHIP
LETHBRIDGE LODGE HOTEL AND CON-FERENECE CENTRE
320 Scenic Dr S, Lethbridge, AB, T1J 4B4
(403) 328-1123
Emp Here 200   Sales 18,538,000
SIC 7011 Hotels and motels
Rob Alldred

D-U-N-S 20-520-9679 (SL)
COLLEGE FORD LINCOLN LTD
3975 1 Ave S, Lethbridge, AB, T1J 4P8
(403) 329-0333
Emp Here 44   Sales 21,915,432
SIC 5511 New and used car dealers
Derek Stimson
Matt Furukawa

D-U-N-S 25-312-9308 (SL)
DAV-BAR-DAL INSURANCE SERVICES LTD
SCHWARTZ RELIANCE INSURANCE & REGISTRIES
300 10 St S, Lethbridge, AB, T1J 2M6
(403) 320-1010
Emp Here 23   Sales 13,338,252
SIC 6411 Insurance agents, brokers, and service
David Howe
Dalton Howe

D-U-N-S 20-087-8312 (HQ)
DAVIS GMC BUICK LTD
AUTOS ALBERTA
(Suby of DAVIS PROPERTIES LTD)
115 Wt Hill Blvd S, Lethbridge, AB, T1J 4T6
(403) 329-4444
Emp Here 25   Sales 61,669,440
SIC 5511 New and used car dealers
John M. Davis
Michael S Davis

D-U-N-S 24-440-1881 (SL)
GALKO HOMES LTD
407 Mayor Magrath Dr S, Lethbridge, AB, T1J 3L8
(403) 329-3221
Emp Here 35   Sales 11,160,415
SIC 1521 Single-family housing construction
Chloe Galts

D-U-N-S 24-672-2623 (HQ)

GAS KING OIL CO. LTD
1604 2 Ave S, Lethbridge, AB, T1J 0G2
(403) 320-2142
Emp Here 12   Sales 62,928,000
SIC 5541 Gasoline service stations
Brent Morris

D-U-N-S 24-672-3001 (SL)
GILMAR CRANE SERVICE LTD
3216 3 Ave S, Lethbridge, AB, T1J 4H5
(403) 327-6511
Emp Here 25   Sales 11,087,250
SIC 7389 Business services, nec
Robert E. Gilmar

D-U-N-S 25-996-3502 (HQ)
GREEN PRAIRIE INTERNATIONAL INC
(Suby of CASCADE FARMS LTD)
210072 Township Rd 90b, Lethbridge, AB, T1J 5P1
(403) 327-9941
Sales 58,915,900
SIC 5191 Farm supplies
John Van Hierden

D-U-N-S 25-133-0684 (SL)
GREYSTOKE HOMES & SUPPORT SERVICES INC
701 2 Ave S, Lethbridge, AB, T1J 0C4
(403) 320-0911
Emp Here 170   Sales 11,656,220
SIC 8059 Nursing and personal care, nec
James Seaborn

D-U-N-S 25-301-2744 (BR)
HUDSON'S BAY COMPANY
BAY, THE
(Suby of HUDSON'S BAY COMPANY)
200 4 Ave S Suite 200, Lethbridge, AB, T1J 4C9
(403) 329-3131
Emp Here 100
SIC 5311 Department stores
Charity Kirton

D-U-N-S 20-243-8474 (SL)
K.O.P.S. SECURITY & INVESTIGATIONS INC
1518 3 Ave S, Lethbridge, AB, T1J 0K8
(403) 331-5677
Emp Here 25   Sales 10,437,650
SIC 7382 Security systems services
Jerry Herassemluk

D-U-N-S 20-826-0760 (HQ)
LETHBRIDGE SCHOOL DISTRICT NO. 51
433 15 St S, Lethbridge, AB, T1J 2Z4
(403) 380-5321
Emp Here 40   Sales 74,485,971
SIC 8211 Elementary and secondary schools
Barry Litun
Christine Lee
Don Lussier
Gary Bartlett
Keith Fowler
Tyler Demers
Mich Forster
Jan Foster
Lola Major
Lea Switzer

D-U-N-S 20-831-9459 (SL)
LETHBRIDGE YOUNG MEN'S CHRISTIAN ASSOCIATION, THE
YMCA OF LETHBRIDGE
74 Mauretania Rd W Unit 140, Lethbridge, AB, T1J 5L4
(403) 942-5757
Emp Here 250   Sales 359,650,250
SIC 8699 Membership organizations, nec
Jennifer Petracek-Kolb
Ross Jacobs

D-U-N-S 24-808-0251 (BR)
LONDON DRUGS LIMITED
(Suby of H.Y. LOUIE CO. LIMITED)
905 1 Ave S Suite 110, Lethbridge, AB, T1J 4M7

(403) 320-8899
Emp Here 100
SIC 5912 Drug stores and proprietary stores
Christopher Mabel

D-U-N-S 20-048-5816 (BR)
MAPLE LEAF FOODS INC
MAPLE LEAF PORK
(Suby of MAPLE LEAF FOODS INC)
4141 1 Ave S, Lethbridge, AB, T1J 4P8
(403) 328-1756
Emp Here 200
SIC 2011 Meat packing plants
Dave Wood

D-U-N-S 25-451-2429 (BR)
MNP LLP
MNP
(Suby of MNP LLP)
3425 2 Ave S Suite 1, Lethbridge, AB, T1J 4V1
(403) 380-1600
Emp Here 130
SIC 8721 Accounting, auditing, and book-keeping

D-U-N-S 25-014-1504 (BR)
MOXIE'S RESTAURANTS, LIMITED PARTNERSHIP
MOXIE'S RESTAURANT
1621 3 Ave S, Lethbridge, AB, T1J 0L1
(403) 320-1102
Emp Here 100
SIC 5812 Eating places
Mike Marcotte

D-U-N-S 25-267-6697 (HQ)
MPE ENGINEERING LTD
714 5 Ave S Suite 300, Lethbridge, AB, T1J 0V1
(403) 329-3442
Emp Here 50   Sales 20,554,985
SIC 8711 Engineering services
Ronald Hust
Randy Boras
Peter Brouwer
Daniel Parker
Douglas Mickey
Gerald Veldman
Gordon Ayers
Michael Breunig
Myles Kasun

D-U-N-S 25-316-4016 (BR)
PASLEY, MAX ENTERPRISES LIMITED
MCDONALD'S
217 3 Ave S, Lethbridge, AB, T1J 4L6
(403) 328-8844
Emp Here 86
SIC 5812 Eating places
Ivan Harris

D-U-N-S 25-965-4085 (BR)
PURE CANADIAN GAMING CORP
CASINO LETHBRIDGE
1251 3 Ave S, Lethbridge, AB, T1J 0K1
(403) 381-9467
Emp Here 275
SIC 7999 Amusement and recreation, nec
Lori Potter

D-U-N-S 24-858-2103 (BR)
ROCKY MOUNTAIN DEALERSHIPS INC
ROCKY MOUNTAIN EQUIPMENT
(Suby of ROCKY MOUNTAIN DEALERSHIPS INC)
3939 1 Ave S, Lethbridge, AB, T1J 4P8
(403) 327-3154
Emp Here 100
SIC 5082 Construction and mining machinery
Darell Steinky

D-U-N-S 25-955-8997 (SL)
ROCKY MOUNTAIN TURF CLUB INC
BULLYS SPORT & ENTERTAINMENT CENTRE
3401 Parkside Dr S, Lethbridge, AB, T1J 4R3
(403) 380-1905
Emp Here 42   Sales 17,796,660

SIC 7948 Racing, including track operation
Max Gibb

D-U-N-S 25-272-5585   (SL)
SILVER RIDGE MOTOR PRODUCTS LTD
LETHBRIDGE TOYOTA
3524 2 Ave S, Lethbridge, AB, T1J 4T9
(403) 329-6888
Emp Here 25   *Sales* 12,451,950
SIC 5511 New and used car dealers
Doug Ulmer
Ross Ulmer
Andrea Ulmer

D-U-N-S 20-088-2975   (SL)
TOLLESTRUP HOLDINGS LTD
806 2 Ave S, Lethbridge, AB, T1J 0C6
(403) 328-8196
Emp Here 50   *Sales* 12,622,100
SIC 1611 Highway and street construction
James Tollestrup

D-U-N-S 20-829-8802   (HQ)
VARSTEEL LTD
VALUE STEEL & PIPE, DIV OF
(*Suby of* VARZARI TRADING LTD)
220 4 St S Suite 330, Lethbridge, AB, T1J 4J7
(403) 320-1953
Emp Here 35   *Sales* 253,917,950
SIC 5051 Metals service centers and offices
Gerald Varzari

D-U-N-S 24-554-3038   (HQ)
VARZARI TRADING LTD
VALUE STEEL & PIPE
220 4 St S Unit 330, Lethbridge, AB, T1J 4J7
(403) 320-1953
Sales 119,490,800
SIC 5051 Metals service centers and offices
Gerald Varzari

D-U-N-S 24-915-5859   (SL)
WISE OWL FRAUD PREVENTION
135 1 Ave S, Lethbridge, AB, T1J 0A1
(403) 330-5020
Emp Here 49   *Sales* 19,388,222
SIC 7381 Detective and armored car services
Tom Mckenzie

Lethbridge, AB T1K

D-U-N-S 20-700-0790   (HQ)
1ST CHOICE SAVINGS AND CREDIT UNION LTD
45 Fairmont Blvd S, Lethbridge, AB, T1K 1T1
(403) 320-4600
Sales 13,355,457
SIC 6062 State credit unions
Jason Centes

D-U-N-S 24-011-7999   (BR)
AVON CANADA INC
(*Suby of* CERBERUS CAPITAL MANAGEMENT, L.P.)
10 Purdue Crt W, Lethbridge, AB, T1K 4R8

Emp Here 700
SIC 2844 Toilet preparations
Marilyn Marshman

D-U-N-S 25-482-9591   (BR)
COSTCO WHOLESALE CANADA LTD
COSTCO
(*Suby of* COSTCO WHOLESALE CORPORATION)
3200 Mayor Magrath Dr S, Lethbridge, AB, T1K 6Y6
(403) 320-8917
Emp Here 200
SIC 5099 Durable goods, nec
Rae Temple

D-U-N-S 24-646-8342   (SL)
D. R. PERRY PHARMACY LTD
SHOPPERS DRUG MART

2045 Mayor Magrath Dr S Unit 102, Lethbridge, AB, T1K 2S2
(403) 328-5509
Emp Here 50   *Sales* 12,647,700
SIC 5912 Drug stores and proprietary stores
Doran Perry
Shirley Perry

D-U-N-S 25-014-1330   (BR)
EXTENDICARE INC
EXTENDICARE FAIRMONT
(*Suby of* EXTENDICARE INC)
115 Fairmont Blvd S, Lethbridge, AB, T1K 5V2
(403) 320-0120
Emp Here 140
SIC 8051 Skilled nursing care facilities
Joyce Adachi

D-U-N-S 20-990-1164   (SL)
FLOORRIGHT INTERIORS LTD
3021 32 St S, Lethbridge, AB, T1K 7B1
(587) 800-0848
Emp Here 40   *Sales* 10,122,360
SIC 5211 Lumber and other building materials
Robert Moore
Darryl Moore
Virginia Moore

D-U-N-S 25-995-6324   (SL)
HARTEK HOLDINGS LTD
SOBEYS SCENIC SQUARE
2920 26 Ave S, Lethbridge, AB, T1K 7K8
(403) 320-2272
Emp Here 110   *Sales* 32,282,470
SIC 5411 Grocery stores
Dallas Harty
Katrina Harty

D-U-N-S 20-176-7154   (BR)
HOME DEPOT OF CANADA INC
HOME DEPOT
(*Suby of* THE HOME DEPOT INC)
3708 Mayor Magrath Dr S, Lethbridge, AB, T1K 7V1
(403) 331-3581
Emp Here 150
SIC 5251 Hardware stores
Jeremy Rhiel

D-U-N-S 20-552-2498   (SL)
LACHANCE, B.D. SALES LTD
CANADIAN TIRE STORE
2720 Fairway Rd S, Lethbridge, AB, T1K 7A5
(403) 394-9633
Emp Here 60   *Sales* 37,756,800
SIC 5531 Auto and home supply stores
Brian Lachance

D-U-N-S 20-766-6199   (HQ)
LETHBRIDGE COLLEGE
3000 College Dr S, Lethbridge, AB, T1K 1L6
(403) 320-3200
Emp Here 800   *Sales* 123,898,750
SIC 8222 Junior colleges
Simon Griffiths
Coreen Roth

D-U-N-S 20-826-3426   (SL)
LETHBRIDGE COUNTRY CLUB
101 Country Club Rd, Lethbridge, AB, T1K 7N9
(403) 327-6900
Emp Here 90   *Sales* 7,069,050
SIC 7997 Membership sports and recreation clubs
Brian Huculak

D-U-N-S 20-852-6280   (BR)
LETHBRIDGE FAMILY SERVICES
1410 Mayor Magrath Dr S Suite 106, Lethbridge, AB, T1K 2R3
(403) 317-4624
Emp Here 200
SIC 8361 Residential care
Deb Henry

D-U-N-S 25-992-6731   (SL)
MURRAY AUTO GROUP LETHBRIDGE LTD

MURRAY CHEVROLET CADILLAC LETHBRIDGE
2815 26 Ave S, Lethbridge, AB, T1K 7K7
(403) 328-1101
Emp Here 68   *Sales* 42,791,040
SIC 5511 New and used car dealers
Christopher Murray
Douglas Murray
Paul Murray
Dan Murray

D-U-N-S 20-767-8830   (SL)
PERLICH BROS. AUCTION MARKET LTD
MIDWAY LIVESTOCK
Gd, Lethbridge, AB, T1K 4P4
(403) 329-3101
Emp Here 25   *Sales* 11,087,250
SIC 7389 Business services, nec
John Perlich
Robert Perlich

D-U-N-S 20-645-1676   (SL)
PETERS DAIRY BAR LTD
DAIRY QUEEN
1152 Mayor Magrath Dr S, Lethbridge, AB, T1K 2P8
(403) 327-6440
Emp Here 80   *Sales* 3,429,840
SIC 5812 Eating places
Patsy Peters
Patsy Peters

D-U-N-S 20-249-7074   (SL)
PROFESSIONAL WAREHOUSE DEMONSTRATIONS
3200 Mayor Magrath Dr S, Lethbridge, AB, T1K 6Y6

Emp Here 35   *Sales* 15,701,926
SIC 7389 Business services, nec
Nadine Seely

D-U-N-S 25-020-0722   (BR)
SOBEYS WEST INC
(*Suby of* EMPIRE COMPANY LIMITED)
2750 Fairway Plaza Rd S, Lethbridge, AB, T1K 6Z3
(403) 328-0330
Emp Here 180
SIC 5411 Grocery stores
Dave Sawchuk

D-U-N-S 20-827-5701   (HQ)
UNIVERSITY OF LETHBRIDGE, THE
4401 University Dr W, Lethbridge, AB, T1K 3M4
(403) 329-2244
Sales 159,450,208
SIC 8221 Colleges and universities
William Cade
Nancy Walker
Robert Turner

D-U-N-S 25-534-0978   (BR)
VALUE VILLAGE STORES, INC
(*Suby of* SAVERS, INC.)
1708 Mayor Magrath Dr S, Lethbridge, AB, T1K 2R5
(403) 320-5358
Emp Here 76
SIC 5399 Miscellaneous general merchandise
Alysa Jeanotte

D-U-N-S 25-219-0095   (BR)
WAL-MART CANADA CORP
VISION CENTER AT WALMART
(*Suby of* WALMART INC.)
3700 Mayor Magrath Dr S Suite 3048, Lethbridge, AB, T1K 7T6
(403) 328-6277
Emp Here 150
SIC 5311 Department stores
Porter Dave

D-U-N-S 24-578-0630   (HQ)
WILBUR-ELLIS COMPANY OF CANADA LIMITED
WECO

(*Suby of* WILBUR-ELLIS HOLDINGS, INC.)
212084 Township Road 81a, Lethbridge, AB, T1K 8G6
(403) 328-3311
Emp Here 25   *Sales* 37,126,000
SIC 5191 Farm supplies
Robert Fullerton
Brent Quinton
John Thacher
David Granoff
Barrie Broughton
Michael Hunter

Linden, AB T0M

D-U-N-S 24-345-5438   (BR)
ALBERTA HEALTH SERVICES
LINDEN NURSING HOME
(*Suby of* GOVERNMENT OF THE PROVINCE OF ALBERTA)
700 Nursing Home Rd, Linden, AB, T0M 1J0
(403) 546-3966
Emp Here 80
SIC 8051 Skilled nursing care facilities
Roland Toews

D-U-N-S 20-989-6257   (SL)
CBI MANUFACTURING LTD
702 1 Ave Nw, Linden, AB, T0M 1J0
(403) 546-3851
Emp Here 85   *Sales* 19,026,655
SIC 3713 Truck and bus bodies
James Aaron Courtney
Murray Regehr
Sandra Courtney
Karen Lynn Regehr

Lloydminster, AB T9V

D-U-N-S 20-063-8161   (HQ)
AGLAND CORP
Hwy 16, Lloydminster, AB, T9V 3A2
(780) 874-4154
Emp Here 70   *Sales* 46,334,350
SIC 5083 Farm and garden machinery

D-U-N-S 25-051-0778   (SL)
BANDIT ENERGY SERVICES
500018 Rr21 & Hwy 16 West, Lloydminster, AB, T9V 3C5
(780) 875-8764
Emp Here 49   *Sales* 13,207,901
SIC 4619 Pipelines, nec
Jamie Walker

D-U-N-S 20-854-1623   (HQ)
BEA FISHER CENTRE INC, THE
3514 51 Ave, Lloydminster, AB, T9V 1C8
(780) 875-3633
Emp Here 1   *Sales* 12,286,720
SIC 8322 Individual and family services
George Zaychkowsky

D-U-N-S 25-506-4883   (SL)
BORDER CITY BUILDING CENTRE LTD
HOME HARDWARE BUILDING CENTRE
2802 50 Ave, Lloydminster, AB, T9V 2S3
(780) 875-7762
Emp Here 50   *Sales* 12,652,950
SIC 5251 Hardware stores
Richard Rurka
Donna Rurka

D-U-N-S 24-039-1487   (SL)
BOUNDARY FORD SALES LTD
2502 50 Ave, Lloydminster, AB, T9V 2S3
(780) 872-7755
Emp Here 50   *Sales* 24,903,900
SIC 5511 New and used car dealers
Warren Lux

D-U-N-S 20-616-0368   (SL)
CALROC INDUSTRIES INC
6847 66 St, Lloydminster, AB, T9V 3R7
(780) 875-8802
Emp Here 40   *Sales* 19,001,040
SIC 5082 Construction and mining machinery
Deni Echino
Ron Fehr
Allan Echino
Karl Klipper

D-U-N-S 24-310-5801   (BR)
DNOW CANADA ULC
NATIONAL OILWELL VARCO
(*Suby of* NOW INC.)
6452 66 St, Lloydminster, AB, T9V 3T6
(780) 875-5504
Emp Here 300
SIC 5084 Industrial machinery and equipment
Murray Brost

D-U-N-S 25-596-0684   (BR)
DNOW CANADA ULC
NATIONAL OILWELL VARCO
(*Suby of* NOW INC.)
Gd Rpo 10, Lloydminster, AB, T9V 2H2

Emp Here 100
SIC 5084 Industrial machinery and equipment

D-U-N-S 24-207-1764   (HQ)
EUROPUMP SYSTEMS INC
MIDFIELD
6204 44 St, Lloydminster, AB, T9V 1V9
(780) 872-7084
Emp Here 1   *Sales* 15,985,250
SIC 1389 Oil and gas field services, nec
Dave Anderson

D-U-N-S 20-013-9397   (HQ)
GRIT INDUSTRIES INC
A-FIRE BURNER SYSTEMS
(*Suby of* SAND CONTROL SYSTEMS LTD)
10-50-1-4 Airport Rd Nw, Lloydminster, AB,
T9V 3A5
(780) 875-5577
Emp Here 65   *Sales* 14,406,375
SIC 3433 Heating equipment, except electric
Wayne King
Tom Anweiler

D-U-N-S 20-120-9827   (HQ)
HANCOCK PETROLEUM INC
PETRO-CANADA ALBERTA
5904 44 St, Lloydminster, AB, T9V 1V7
(780) 875-2495
Emp Here 1   *Sales* 50,288,040
SIC 5171 Petroleum bulk stations and terminals
Jason Hancock
Laurienne Hancock

D-U-N-S 20-881-0619   (SL)
HEAVY CRUDE HAULING L.P.
6601 62 St, Lloydminster, AB, T9V 3T6
(780) 875-5358
Emp Here 95   *Sales* 19,542,070
SIC 4213 Trucking, except local
Murray Mullen

D-U-N-S 24-775-2496   (SL)
HERLE'S HOLDINGS LTD
HERLE'S TRUCK & AUTO SPECIALISTS
6214 50 Ave, Lloydminster, AB, T9V 2C9
(780) 875-3422
Emp Here 50   *Sales* 24,903,900
SIC 5541 Gasoline service stations
Robert Herle

D-U-N-S 24-803-5508   (BR)
HOME DEPOT OF CANADA INC
HOME DEPOT
(*Suby of* THE HOME DEPOT INC)
7705 44 St, Lloydminster, AB, T9V 0X9
(780) 870-9420
Emp Here 80
SIC 5251 Hardware stores

Rod Woodland

D-U-N-S 25-367-6050   (BR)
HUSKY ENERGY INC
HUSKY OIL
(*Suby of* HUSKY ENERGY INC)
5650 52 St, Lloydminster, AB, T9V 0R7
(780) 871-6571
Emp Here 100
SIC 5033 Roofing, siding, and insulation
Garold Danyluk

D-U-N-S 20-861-0076   (BR)
HUSKY OIL OPERATIONS LIMITED
(*Suby of* HUSKY ENERGY INC)
5650 52 St, Lloydminster, AB, T9V 0R7

Emp Here 800
SIC 1311 Crude petroleum and natural gas
Dabur Naqvi

D-U-N-S 20-335-0538   (SL)
KAVANAGH INVESTMENTS LTD
CANADIAN TIRE
4215 70 Ave, Lloydminster, AB, T9V 2X2
(780) 875-4410
Emp Here 80   *Sales* 50,342,400
SIC 5531 Auto and home supply stores
John Kavanagh

D-U-N-S 25-971-5043   (SL)
KAYFORE HOLDINGS LTD
KING'S HUSKY
5310 52nd St, Lloydminster, AB, T9V 3B5
(780) 875-2266
Emp Here 26   *Sales* 32,687,226
SIC 5171 Petroleum bulk stations and terminals
Darren King
Joan King

D-U-N-S 20-446-8987   (HQ)
KONDRO ELECTRIC 1980 LTD
6202 50 Ave, Lloydminster, AB, T9V 2C9
(780) 875-6226
Emp Here 50   *Sales* 14,812,372
SIC 1731 Electrical work
Willard Kondro

D-U-N-S 24-114-7776   (HQ)
LLOYDMINSTER SCHOOL DIVISION NO 99
LLOYDMINSTER PUBLIC SCHOOL DIVISION
5017 46 St Suite 99, Lloydminster, AB, T9V
1R4
(780) 875-5541
Emp Here 25   *Sales* 37,169,625
SIC 8211 Elementary and secondary schools
Matt Read
Todd Robinson

D-U-N-S 25-014-9614   (BR)
LOBLAWS INC
REAL CANADIAN SUPERSTORES
(*Suby of* LOBLAW COMPANIES LIMITED)
5031 44 St, Lloydminster, AB, T9V 0A6
(780) 871-8060
Emp Here 200
SIC 5411 Grocery stores
Tom Kelly

D-U-N-S 24-655-0198   (HQ)
PRECISION CONTRACTORS LTD
5912 50 Ave Suite 101, Lloydminster, AB, T9V
0X6
(780) 875-1962
Emp Here 65   *Sales* 30,371,975
SIC 1389 Oil and gas field services, nec
Elwin R Page

D-U-N-S 24-347-4595   (BR)
PYRAMID CORPORATION
(*Suby of* PTW ENERGY SERVICES LTD)
6304 56 St, Lloydminster, AB, T9V 3T7
(780) 875-6644
Emp Here 90
SIC 1731 Electrical work
Chris Harrower

D-U-N-S 24-949-7343   (SL)
R'OHAN RIG SERVICES LTD
Gd, Lloydminster, AB, T9V 3C1
(780) 872-7887
Emp Here 49   *Sales* 10,407,453
SIC 8748 Business consulting, nec
Graham Holmedel

D-U-N-S 24-031-7276   (SL)
R.J. HOFFMAN HOLDINGS LTD
Gd Rpo 10, Lloydminster, AB, T9V 2H2
(780) 871-0723
Emp Here 200   *Sales* 134,535,800
SIC 1389 Oil and gas field services, nec
Robert Hoffman

D-U-N-S 25-966-7418   (SL)
SILVERWOOD MOTOR PRODUCTS LTD
SILVERWOOD TOYOTA
5103 25 St, Lloydminster, AB, T9V 3G2
(780) 870-5166
Emp Here 24   *Sales* 11,953,872
SIC 5511 New and used car dealers
Daniel Ulmer
Joy Hanchar
Ross Ulmer

D-U-N-S 20-806-2385   (BR)
SOBEYS CAPITAL INCORPORATED
SOBEYS STORE 3170
(*Suby of* EMPIRE COMPANY LIMITED)
4227 75 Ave, Lloydminster, AB, T9V 2X4
(780) 871-0955
Emp Here 130
SIC 5411 Grocery stores
Kevin Rusteika

D-U-N-S 25-569-5942   (BR)
SOBEYS CAPITAL INCORPORATED
SOBEYS
(*Suby of* EMPIRE COMPANY LIMITED)
4227 75 Ave, Lloydminster, AB, T9V 2X4
(780) 875-3215
Emp Here 150
SIC 5411 Grocery stores
Kevin Rusteika

D-U-N-S 25-271-0686   (BR)
SOBEYS WEST INC
LLOYDMINSTER SAFEWAY
(*Suby of* EMPIRE COMPANY LIMITED)
5211 44 St, Lloydminster, AB, T9V 0A7
(780) 875-3448
Emp Here 75
SIC 5411 Grocery stores
Rod Woodland

D-U-N-S 20-081-3769   (SL)
SUPERIOR PROPANE INC
6210 44 St, Lloydminster, AB, T9V 1V9

Emp Here 28   *Sales* 13,132,140
SIC 5984 Liquefied petroleum gas dealers
Larry Nogue

D-U-N-S 20-864-5999   (SL)
TIM HORTONS
4301 75 Ave, Lloydminster, AB, T9V 2X4
(780) 808-2600
Emp Here 50   *Sales* 13,707,600
SIC 5461 Retail bakeries
Nicole Hartman

D-U-N-S 24-360-5651   (HQ)
TRYTON TOOL SERVICES LTD
6702 56 St, Lloydminster, AB, T9V 3T7
(780) 875-0800
Emp Here 1   *Sales* 14,430,065
SIC 3533 Oil and gas field machinery
Eldon Heck

D-U-N-S 25-679-4876   (HQ)
UNIVERSAL INDUSTRIES (FOREMOST) CORP
FOREMOST LLOYDMINSTER
5014 65 St, Lloydminster, AB, T9V 2K2
(780) 875-6161
Sales 116,994,111

SIC 3443 Fabricated plate work (boiler shop)
Pat Breen
James Grenon
Glen Swail

D-U-N-S 20-172-9303   (BR)
WAL-MART CANADA CORP
(*Suby of* WALMART INC.)
4210 70 Ave Suite 3168, Lloydminster, AB,
T9V 2X3
(780) 875-4777
Emp Here 200
SIC 5311 Department stores
Pascal Levesque

D-U-N-S 24-717-7215   (SL)
WAYSIDE MANAGEMENT LTD
BEST WESTERN WAYSIDE INN & SUITE
5411 44 St, Lloydminster, AB, T9V 0A9
(780) 875-4404
Emp Here 75   *Sales* 6,951,750
SIC 7011 Hotels and motels
Doug Jobb
Lou Warring

D-U-N-S 20-270-4057   (HQ)
WEATHERFORD ARTIFICIAL LIFT SYSTEMS CANADA LTD
BMW PRODUCTS & SERVICES
(*Suby of* WEATHERFORD INTERNATIONAL PUBLIC LIMITED COMPANY)
4206 59 Ave, Lloydminster, AB, T9V 2V4
(780) 875-2730
Emp Here 230   *Sales* 168,169,750
SIC 1389 Oil and gas field services, nec
Geoffrey Inose
Burt M Martin

D-U-N-S 20-178-7780   (BR)
WEATHERFORD CANADA LTD
NORTHERN METALIC SALES (ALTA)
(*Suby of* WEATHERFORD INTERNATIONAL PUBLIC LIMITED COMPANY)
4604 62 Ave, Lloydminster, AB, T9V 2G2
(780) 875-6123
Emp Here 100
SIC 3533 Oil and gas field machinery
Roland Moneta

D-U-N-S 20-063-7635   (SL)
WESTRIDGE PONTIAC BUICK GMC LTD
WESTRIDGE BUICK GMC
2406 50 Ave, Lloydminster, AB, T9V 2W7
(780) 875-3366
Emp Here 40   *Sales* 19,923,120
SIC 5511 New and used car dealers
Joseph Ross Ulmer
Douglas Alan Ulmer

Lomond, AB T0L

D-U-N-S 24-651-6954   (SL)
ARMADA COLONY
Gd, Lomond, AB, T0L 1G0
(403) 792-3388
Emp Here 49   *Sales* 16,780,883
SIC 0191 General farms, primarily crop
Edward Mandel
Michael Mandel

Lundbreck, AB T0K

D-U-N-S 24-373-1259   (SL)
LIVINGSTONE HUTTERIAN BRETHREN
LIVINGSTONE COLONY
Gd, Lundbreck, AB, T0K 1H0
(403) 628-2226
Emp Here 50   *Sales* 17,123,350
SIC 0191 General farms, primarily crop
Michael Walter

Ma-Me-O Beach, AB T0C

D-U-N-S 20-789-8342   (SL)
TRIPLE P POWER SERVICE LTD
Gd, Ma-Me-O Beach, AB, T0C 1X0
(780) 586-2778
Emp Here 49   *Sales* 12,001,834
SIC 1623 Water, sewer, and utility lines
 John Ng

Magrath, AB T0K

D-U-N-S 25-317-1144   (SL)
DEERFIELD HUTTERIAN BRETHERN
DEERFIELD COLONY
Gd, Magrath, AB, T0K 1J0
(403) 758-6461
Emp Here 90   *Sales* 9,836,010
SIC 0762 Farm management services
 Eli Waldner
 Edward J Wurtz

D-U-N-S 24-069-1761   (SL)
HUTTERVILLE HUTTERIAN BRETHREN
HUTTERVILLE COLONY
Gd, Magrath, AB, T0K 1J0
(403) 758-3143
Emp Here 72   *Sales* 18,886,248
SIC 0191 General farms, primarily crop
 Peter Waldner

D-U-N-S 24-518-8982   (SL)
**ROCKPORT HUTTERIAN BRETHREN COR-
PORATION**
Gd, Magrath, AB, T0K 1J0
(403) 758-3077
Emp Here 32   *Sales* 10,958,944
SIC 0191 General farms, primarily crop
 John Hofer

D-U-N-S 25-813-3581   (SL)
SUREXDIRECT.COM LTD
6 South 1st St W, Magrath, AB, T0K 1J0
(403) 388-2387
Emp Here 30   *Sales* 25,441,800
SIC 6411 Insurance agents, brokers, and ser-
vice
 Lance Miller

Manning, AB T0H

D-U-N-S 25-325-8743   (BR)
ALBERTA HEALTH SERVICES
MANNING COMMUNITY HEALTH CENTRE
(*Suby of* GOVERNMENT OF THE
PROVINCE OF ALBERTA)
600 2nd St, Manning, AB, T0H 2M0
(780) 836-3391
Emp Here 100
SIC 8062 General medical and surgical hospi-
tals
 Georgia Kelemen

D-U-N-S 24-962-8199   (HQ)
MANNING FOREST PRODUCTS LTD
(*Suby of* WEST FRASER TIMBER CO. LTD)
Gd, Manning, AB, T0H 2M0
(780) 836-3111
Sales 25,008,100
SIC 2421 Sawmills and planing mills, general
 Real Arseneault
 Steve Kaufmann
 Alphonse Dechante
 Robert Schmidt
 Florence Wanuch

Mannville, AB T0B

D-U-N-S 25-576-3062   (SL)
**HUTTERIAN BRETHREN MANNVILLE
COLONY**
Gd, Mannville, AB, T0B 2W0
(780) 763-3079
Emp Here 95   *Sales* 24,919,355
SIC 0191 General farms, primarily crop
 Peter Tschetter
 George Tschetter

Mayerthorpe, AB T0E

D-U-N-S 25-820-9626   (BR)
EXTENDICARE INC
EXTENDICARE MAYERTHORPE
(*Suby of* EXTENDICARE INC)
4706 54 St, Mayerthorpe, AB, T0E 1N0
(780) 786-2211
Emp Here 75
SIC 8051 Skilled nursing care facilities
 Patricia White

Mclennan, AB T0H

D-U-N-S 20-896-1268   (BR)
ALBERTA HEALTH SERVICES
*SACRED HEART COMMUNITY HEALTH
CENTRE*
(*Suby of* GOVERNMENT OF THE
PROVINCE OF ALBERTA)
350 3rd Ave Nw, Mclennan, AB, T0H 2L0
(780) 324-3730
Emp Here 180
SIC 8062 General medical and surgical hospi-
tals
 Larry Meardi

Medicine Hat, AB T1A

D-U-N-S 25-532-8411   (HQ)
415329 ALBERTA LTD
MARIO'S
439 5 Ave Se, Medicine Hat, AB, T1A 2P9
(403) 529-2600
Sales 10,483,875
SIC 6712 Bank holding companies
 Kevin Pudwell
 Sharon Pudwell

D-U-N-S 24-338-8381   (BR)
ARGO SALES INC
BROMLEY MECHANICAL SERVICES
(*Suby of* ARGO SALES INC)
925 23 St Sw, Medicine Hat, AB, T1A 8R1
(403) 526-3142
Emp Here 75
SIC 3443 Fabricated plate work (boiler shop)
 George Van Dermolen

D-U-N-S 25-329-1793   (SL)
BLINDS BY VERTICAN INC
549 17 St Sw, Medicine Hat, AB, T1A 7W5
(403) 527-9084
Emp Here 70   *Sales* 16,268,210
SIC 5719 Miscellaneous homefurnishings
 Andre Lemire
 Ryan Lemire
 Lenore Lemire

D-U-N-S 20-439-9877   (HQ)
BOYLAN GROUP LTD, THE
BOYLAN'S PHOTOCOPY CENTRE
540 18 St Sw, Medicine Hat, AB, T1A 8A7
(403) 526-7799
Emp Here 12   *Sales* 20,767,880
SIC 5912 Drug stores and proprietary stores

 James Boylan
 Daryl Krepps

D-U-N-S 24-298-4797   (SL)
**BREWMASTER COFFEE ENTERPRISES
(M.H.) INC**
764 7 St Se, Medicine Hat, AB, T1A 1K6
(403) 526-0791
Emp Here 24   *Sales* 20,053,848
SIC 5141 Groceries, general line
 David Camphor
 Grant Farmer

D-U-N-S 24-552-9516   (SL)
CANADIAN FERTILIZERS LIMITED
CF INDUSTRIES
(*Suby of* CF INDUSTRIES HOLDINGS, INC.)
1250 52 St Nw, Medicine Hat, AB, T1A 7R9
(403) 527-8887
Emp Here 165   *Sales* 73,366,425
SIC 2873 Nitrogenous fertilizers
 Tony Will
 Doug Barnard
 Bert Frost
 Susan L Menzel
 Dennis Kelleher

D-U-N-S 24-984-1958   (SL)
CHINOOK VILLAGE HOUSING SOCIETY
CHINOOK VILLAGE
2801 13 Ave Se, Medicine Hat, AB, T1A 3R1
(403) 526-6951
Emp Here 60   *Sales* 13,252,260
SIC 6514 Dwelling operators, except apart-
ments
 John Stokoe
 Al Widmer
 Linda Hygard

D-U-N-S 25-015-6510   (SL)
**CITY PLYMOUTH CHRYSLER (MEDICINE
HAT) LTD**
CITY CHRYSLER JEEP
982 Redcliff Dr Sw, Medicine Hat, AB, T1A
5E4
(403) 526-6944
Emp Here 32   *Sales* 15,938,496
SIC 5511 New and used car dealers
 Paul Nelson

D-U-N-S 20-797-2790   (SL)
CLASSIC CONSTRUCTION LTD
CLASSIC COMMUNITIES
671 Industrial Ave Se, Medicine Hat, AB, T1A
3L5
(403) 528-2793
Emp Here 80   *Sales* 21,675,360
SIC 1522 Residential construction, nec
 Murray Prokosch
 Gerald Pahl

D-U-N-S 25-015-6528   (SL)
**CORE(CLIENT ONGOING REHABILITA-
TION AND EQUALITY) ASSOCIATION**
412 3 St Se, Medicine Hat, AB, T1A 0H1
(403) 527-3302
Emp Here 175   *Sales* 13,438,600
SIC 8322 Individual and family services
 Jan Olechewski

D-U-N-S 24-345-4808   (HQ)
D & L CRANSTON HOLDINGS LTD
NUTTER'S BULK & NATURAL FOODS
1601 Dunmore Rd Se Suite 107, Medicine
Hat, AB, T1A 1Z8
(800) 665-5122
Emp Here 10   *Sales* 17,420,250
SIC 6794 Patent owners and lessors
 Donald Cranston
 Lynn Cranston
 Julia Cranston

D-U-N-S 25-994-3173   (BR)
G4S SECURE SOLUTIONS (CANADA) LTD
(*Suby of* G4S PLC)
525 4 St Se, Medicine Hat, AB, T1A 0K7
(403) 526-2001
Emp Here 200

SIC 7381 Detective and armored car services

D-U-N-S 24-984-3186   (SL)
HUTTERIAN BRETHREN OF WINNIFRED
WINNIFRED COLONY
Gd Lcd 1, Medicine Hat, AB, T1A 7E4

Emp Here 70   *Sales* 10,276,070
SIC 4212 Local trucking, without storage
 Amos Hofer

D-U-N-S 24-494-0672   (SL)
HYDRACO INDUSTRIES LTD
2111 9 Ave Sw, Medicine Hat, AB, T1A 8M9
(403) 528-4400
Emp Here 100   *Sales* 47,502,600
SIC 5084 Industrial machinery and equipment
 Patrick Janzer
 Michael Janzer

D-U-N-S 20-830-2497   (HQ)
I-XL LTD
525 2 St Se, Medicine Hat, AB, T1A 0C5
(403) 526-5501
Emp Here 100
SIC 3251 Brick and structural clay tile
 Clayton Sissons
 Graham Sissons
 Malcolm Sissons
 Quentin Brehmer

D-U-N-S 20-088-8980   (HQ)
I.XL INDUSTRIES LTD
(*Suby of* I-XL LTD)
612 Porcelain Ave Se, Medicine Hat, AB, T1A
8S4
(403) 526-5901
Emp Here 80   *Sales* 63,922,500
SIC 3251 Brick and structural clay tile
 Malcolm Sissons
 Clayton Sissons
 Quentin Brehmer
 Thomas Sissons
 Graham Sissons
 Paul Sissons

D-U-N-S 20-257-4356   (SL)
JOUJAN BROTHERS FLOORING INC
CASH & CARRY CARPETS
941 South Railway St Se Unit 3, Medicine Hat,
AB, T1A 2W3
(403) 528-8008
Emp Here 78   *Sales* 18,127,434
SIC 5713 Floor covering stores
 Herb Joujan
 Jana Joujan

D-U-N-S 20-088-8576   (HQ)
KOST FIRE EQUIPMENT LTD
KOST FIRE SAFETY
677 14 St Sw, Medicine Hat, AB, T1A 4V5
(403) 527-1500
Emp Here 12   *Sales* 12,372,800
SIC 5999 Miscellaneous retail stores, nec
 Robert Kost
 Audrey Kost

D-U-N-S 24-299-9514   (SL)
M J B ENTERPRISES LTD
601 17 St Sw, Medicine Hat, AB, T1A 4X6
(403) 527-3600
Emp Here 60   *Sales* 25,364,220
SIC 1541 Industrial buildings and warehouses
 Douglas Stober
 James Behrman

D-U-N-S 25-015-6551   (HQ)
**MEDICINE HAT CATHOLIC BOARD OF ED-
UCATION**
*MEDICINE HAT CATHOLIC SEPARATE RE-
GIONAL DIVISION NO.20*
1251 1 Ave Sw Suite 20, Medicine Hat, AB,
T1A 8B4
(403) 527-2292
Emp Here 100   *Sales* 34,691,650
SIC 8211 Elementary and secondary schools
 Stan Aberle
 Jody Churla

▲ Public Company   ■ Public Company Family Member   **HQ** Headquarters   **BR** Branch   **SL** Single Location

Greg Macpherson
David Leahy

D-U-N-S 24-345-7942   (SL)
**MEDICINE HAT EXHIBITION & STAMPEDE
CO LTD**
2055 21 Ave Se, Medicine Hat, AB, T1A 7N1
(403) 527-1234
Emp Here 80   *Sales* 7,596,240
SIC 7999 Amusement and recreation, nec
James Macarthur

D-U-N-S 24-089-0434   (HQ)
**MEDICINE HAT FAMILY YOUNG MEN'S
CHRISTIAN ASSOCIATION**
MEDICINE HAT FAMILY YMCA
150 Ash Ave Se, Medicine Hat, AB, T1A 3A9
(403) 529-8115
Emp Here 18   *Sales* 28,368,480
SIC 8699 Membership organizations, nec
James (Jim) Smith
Tom Coulter
Todd O'reilly
John Schwab

D-U-N-S 20-989-5002   (HQ)
MEDICINE HAT SCHOOL DISTRICT NO. 76
601 1 Ave Sw, Medicine Hat, AB, T1A 4Y7
(403) 528-6700
Emp Here 30   *Sales* 81,605,250
SIC 8211 Elementary and secondary schools
Grant Henderson
Jerry Labossiere
Gitta Hashizume
Roy Wilson
Deborah Forbes
Terry Riley
Greg Bender

D-U-N-S 25-000-5170   (BR)
MEDICINE HAT SCHOOL DISTRICT NO. 76
CRESCENT HEIGHTS HIGH SCHOOL
(*Suby of* MEDICINE HAT SCHOOL DISTRICT
NO. 76)
1201 Division Ave N, Medicine Hat, AB, T1A
5Y8
(403) 527-6641
Emp Here 90
SIC 8211 Elementary and secondary schools
Pat Grisonich

D-U-N-S 20-825-8103   (SL)
MEDICINE HAT WHOLESALE FOODS LTD
(*Suby of* PINNACLE DISTRIBUTION INC)
702 Industrial Ave Se, Medicine Hat, AB, T1A
3L8
(403) 527-4481
Emp Here 45   *Sales* 37,600,965
SIC 5141 Groceries, general line
Harry Mitzner
Janet Mitzner

D-U-N-S 24-336-5496   (BR)
MEDICINE HAT, CITY OF
*NATURAL GAS AND PETROLEUM RE-
SOURCES*
(*Suby of* MEDICINE HAT, CITY OF)
364 Kipling St Se, Medicine Hat, AB, T1A 1Y4
(403) 529-8190
Emp Here 148
SIC 4925 Gas production and/or distribution
David Tandabaker

D-U-N-S 20-389-9989   (SL)
NUTTER'S BULK & NATURAL FOODS INC
1601 Dunmore Rd Se Suite 107, Medicine
Hat, AB, T1A 1Z8
(403) 529-1664
Emp Here 3   *Sales* 21,937,356
SIC 5149 Groceries and related products, nec
Donald Cranston

D-U-N-S 25-321-4613   (BR)
REVERA INC
RIVERVIEW CARE CENTRE
(*Suby of* GOVERNMENT OF CANADA)
603 Prospect Dr Sw, Medicine Hat, AB, T1A
4C2

(403) 527-5531
Emp Here 150
SIC 8051 Skilled nursing care facilities
Dawn Smythes

D-U-N-S 20-282-2359   (SL)
RYKER OILFIELD HAULING LTD
1779 9 Ave Sw, Medicine Hat, AB, T1A 8S2
(403) 529-9090
Emp Here 50   *Sales* 10,506,550
SIC 1389 Oil and gas field services, nec
Kerwin Mondor
Ric Verhoeven

D-U-N-S 20-088-9814   (SL)
**SCOTT, S.F. MANUFACTURING CO. LIM-
ITED**
BLUE IMP PLAYGROUND EQUIPMENT
724 14 St Sw, Medicine Hat, AB, T1A 4V7
(403) 526-9170
Emp Here 55   *Sales* 17,937,480
SIC 3949 Sporting and athletic goods, nec
Donald Scott
Stuart Scott

D-U-N-S 20-092-2425   (HQ)
SOUTH COUNTRY CO-OP LIMITED
969 16 St Sw, Medicine Hat, AB, T1A 4X5
(403) 528-6600
Emp Here 24   *Sales* 379,713,590
SIC 5171 Petroleum bulk stations and termi-
nals
Norman Rubbelke
Roger Vizbar
Craig Weich
Mike Clement
Jan Bennen
Wayne Brost
Tim Heeg
Ben Janz
Richard Potter
Marcel Vandendungen

D-U-N-S 24-043-3979   (HQ)
**THOMSON SCHINDLE GREEN INSUR-
ANCE & FINANCIAL SERVICES LTD**
TSG INSURANCE
(*Suby of* INTACT FINANCIAL CORPORA-
TION)
623 4 St Se Suite 100, Medicine Hat, AB, T1A
0L1
(403) 526-3283
Emp Here 1   *Sales* 29,682,100
SIC 6411 Insurance agents, brokers, and ser-
vice
David Thomson
Kenneth Schindle
Stuart Green

D-U-N-S 24-961-7994   (SL)
WAHL CONSTRUCTION LTD
830 15 St Sw, Medicine Hat, AB, T1A 4W7
(403) 526-6235
Emp Here 45   *Sales* 14,349,105
SIC 1521 Single-family housing construction
Richard Wahl

Medicine Hat, AB T1B

D-U-N-S 20-747-1801   (SL)
1131898 ALBERTA LTD
SOUTHLAND VOLKSWAGEN
1450 Strachan Rd Se, Medicine Hat, AB, T1B
4V2
(403) 526-3633
Emp Here 30   *Sales* 14,942,340
SIC 5511 New and used car dealers
Robert Aaltonen

D-U-N-S 25-265-8315   (SL)
636066 ALBERTA LTD
SUN VALLEY HONDA
16 Strachan Crt Se, Medicine Hat, AB, T1B
4R7

(403) 526-0626
Emp Here 25   *Sales* 12,451,950
SIC 5511 New and used car dealers
Kevin Knight

D-U-N-S 25-987-1291   (SL)
783814 ALBERTA LTD
CORNERSTONE SOBEYS
1960 Strachan Rd Se, Medicine Hat, AB, T1B
4K4
(403) 504-5400
Emp Here 140   *Sales* 41,086,780
SIC 5411 Grocery stores
James Turner
Wendy Turner

D-U-N-S 20-827-6407   (SL)
976576 ALBERTA LTD
UFA
1433 30 St Sw, Medicine Hat, AB, T1B 3N4
(403) 529-9099
Emp Here 11   *Sales* 11,360,888
SIC 5172 Petroleum products, nec
Clinton Straub

D-U-N-S 24-006-8838   (HQ)
988690 ALBERTA INC
*ENTEGRA CONTROLS & ENERGY SER-
VICES*
1771 30 St Sw Suite 8, Medicine Hat, AB, T1B
3N5
(403) 529-6559
Emp Here 10   *Sales* 19,182,300
SIC 1382 Oil and gas exploration services
Cam Marshall

D-U-N-S 24-731-7548   (SL)
BIG M FORD LINCOLN LTD
1312 Trans Canada Way Se, Medicine Hat,
AB, T1B 3Z9
(403) 527-4406
Emp Here 37   *Sales* 18,428,886
SIC 5511 New and used car dealers
John Mcleod

D-U-N-S 24-225-6902   (BR)
DAVIS GMC BUICK LTD
(*Suby of* DAVIS PROPERTIES LTD)
1450 Trans Canada Way Se, Medicine Hat,
AB, T1B 4M2
(403) 527-1115
Emp Here 100
SIC 7532 Top and body repair and paint shops
Tim Davis

D-U-N-S 20-088-7800   (SL)
GARDNER MOTORS (1981) LTD
JACKSON DODGE CHRYSLER
1500 Strachan Rd Se, Medicine Hat, AB, T1B
4V2
(403) 527-2248
Emp Here 25   *Sales* 12,451,950
SIC 5511 New and used car dealers
Mickey Mcgarvie

D-U-N-S 24-346-5544   (BR)
**GOOD SAMARITAN SOCIETY, THE (A
LUTHERAN SOCIAL SERVICE ORGANIZA-
TION)**
GOOD SAMARITAN SOCIETY, THE
(*Suby of* GOOD SAMARITAN SOCIETY, THE
(A LUTHERAN SOCIAL SERVICE ORGANI-
ZATION))
550 Spruce Way Se, Medicine Hat, AB, T1B
4P1
(403) 528-5050
Emp Here 140
SIC 8699 Membership organizations, nec
Nancy Fenner

D-U-N-S 20-698-6189   (BR)
HOME DEPOT OF CANADA INC
(*Suby of* THE HOME DEPOT INC)
1851 Strachan Rd Se, Medicine Hat, AB, T1B
4V7
(403) 581-4300
Emp Here 100
SIC 5251 Hardware stores
Darrell Bennett

D-U-N-S 25-301-2629   (BR)
HUDSON'S BAY COMPANY
BAY
(*Suby of* HUDSON'S BAY COMPANY)
3292 Dunmore Rd Se Suite F7, Medicine Hat,
AB, T1B 2R4
(403) 526-7888
Emp Here 80
SIC 5311 Department stores
Harney Mike

D-U-N-S 20-743-6486   (SL)
KURT'S IRON WORKS LTD
933 19 St Sw, Medicine Hat, AB, T1B 0A2
(403) 527-2844
Emp Here 27   *Sales* 12,825,702
SIC 5084 Industrial machinery and equipment
Hardy Hilgendorf
Frank Hilgendorf

D-U-N-S 25-270-1099   (BR)
LOBLAWS INC
REAL CANADIAN SUPERSTORE 1550
(*Suby of* LOBLAW COMPANIES LIMITED)
1792 Trans Canada Way Se Suite 1550,
Medicine Hat, AB, T1B 4C6
(403) 528-5727
Emp Here 260
SIC 5411 Grocery stores
Carey Boughen

D-U-N-S 24-841-5408   (BR)
MAYFIELD INVESTMENTS LTD
MEDICINE HAT LODGE HOTEL
(*Suby of* MAYFIELD INVESTMENTS LTD)
1051 Ross Glen Dr Se, Medicine Hat, AB, T1B
3T8
(403) 502-8185
Emp Here 220
SIC 7011 Hotels and motels
Tingley Kelly

D-U-N-S 20-088-8998   (HQ)
MEDICINE HAT CO-OP LIMITED
3030 13 Ave Se Suite 100, Medicine Hat, AB,
T1B 1E3
(403) 528-6604
Emp Here 100   *Sales* 45,613,968
SIC 5411 Grocery stores
Rodger Vizbar
Methodious Rodych
Michael Jamieson

D-U-N-S 24-271-6421   (HQ)
**MID-WEST DESIGN & CONSTRUCTION
LTD**
1065 30 St Sw, Medicine Hat, AB, T1B 3N3
(403) 526-0925
Emp Here 20   *Sales* 14,258,450
SIC 1542 Nonresidential construction, nec
Fred Keck
Ron Helwer

D-U-N-S 20-334-4010   (SL)
MOXIE'S RESTAURANTS INC
3090 Dunmore Rd Se, Medicine Hat, AB, T1B
2X2
(403) 528-8628
Emp Here 85   *Sales* 3,869,115
SIC 5812 Eating places
Matthew Peterson

D-U-N-S 20-734-8058   (BR)
**MURRAY CHEVROLET OLDSMOBILE
CADILLAC LTD**
(*Suby of* MURRAY CHEVROLET OLDSMO-
BILE CADILLAC LTD)
1270 Trans Canada Way Se, Medicine Hat,
AB, T1B 1J5
(403) 527-1141
Emp Here 100
SIC 7532 Top and body repair and paint shops
Derek Keeler

D-U-N-S 20-645-3292   (HQ)
**MURRAY CHEVROLET OLDSMOBILE
CADILLAC LTD**
MURRAY CHEV OLDS CADILLAC SALES

1270 Trans Canada Way Se, Medicine Hat, AB, T1B 1J5
(403) 527-5544
Emp Here 75   *Sales* 54,747,360
SIC 5511 New and used car dealers
Paul Murray

D-U-N-S 24-929-3549   (SL)
PAD-CAR MECHANICAL LTD
3271 17 Ave Sw, Medicine Hat, AB, T1B 4B1
(403) 528-3353
Emp Here 52   *Sales* 12,119,380
SIC 1711 Plumbing, heating, air-conditioning
Tim Padfield
Randy Carvell
Dallas Heath

D-U-N-S 25-015-7088   (SL)
REMAX MEDALTA REAL ESTATE (1989) LTD
1235 Southview Dr Se Unit 109, Medicine Hat, AB, T1B 4K3
(403) 529-9393
Emp Here 35   *Sales* 11,449,445
SIC 6531 Real estate agents and managers
Bert Kleis

D-U-N-S 25-179-2925   (BR)
REVERA INC
MEADOWLANDS RETIREMENT RESIDENCE
(*Suby of* GOVERNMENT OF CANADA)
223 Park Meadows Dr Se Suite 127, Medicine Hat, AB, T1B 4K7
(403) 504-5123
Emp Here 80
SIC 6513 Apartment building operators
Joyce Turner

D-U-N-S 20-265-9954   (HQ)
ROYAL LEPAGE COMMUNITY REALTY LTD
1202 Southview Dr Se, Medicine Hat, AB, T1B 4B6
(403) 528-4222
Emp Here 55   *Sales* 29,322,230
SIC 6531 Real estate agents and managers
Bogdan (Bob) Kalista

D-U-N-S 24-805-4744   (SL)
SLEEPING BAY BUILDING CORP
MEDICINE HAT MALL
3292 Dunmore Rd Se Suite F7, Medicine Hat, AB, T1B 2R4
(403) 526-4888
Emp Here 50   *Sales* 14,424,950
SIC 6512 Nonresidential building operators
Andrew Tylman
Joseph Tenenbaum
Bob Palmer

D-U-N-S 20-140-6258   (SL)
SOUTHERN ALBERTA WEB PRINTERS
3257 Dunmore Rd Se, Medicine Hat, AB, T1B 3R2
(403) 528-5674
Emp Here 90   *Sales* 14,762,430
SIC 2759 Commercial printing, nec
Thomas Peterson

D-U-N-S 24-597-8767   (SL)
TRANSIT PAVING INC
3047 Gershaw Dr Sw, Medicine Hat, AB, T1B 3N1
(403) 526-0386
Emp Here 40   *Sales* 11,340,960
SIC 1611 Highway and street construction
Dean Dinning

D-U-N-S 25-677-2492   (SL)
VANSHAW ENTERPRISES LTD
CASINO BY VANSHAW
1051 Ross Glen Dr Se, Medicine Hat, AB, T1B 3T8
(403) 504-4584
Emp Here 100   *Sales* 7,639,700
SIC 7993 Coin-operated amusement devices
Kevin Vanderkooy
Shawn Stange

D-U-N-S 25-498-2861   (BR)
WAL-MART CANADA CORP
(*Suby of* WALMART INC.)
2051 Strachan Rd Se, Medicine Hat, AB, T1B 0G4
(403) 504-4410
Emp Here 218
SIC 5311 Department stores
Norm Henke

Medicine Hat, AB T1C

D-U-N-S 24-961-3639   (SL)
BYZ CONSTRUCTION INC
2196 Brier Park Pl Nw, Medicine Hat, AB, T1C 1S6
Emp Here 70   *Sales* 17,233,020
SIC 1794 Excavation work
Robert Zmurchyk
Karen Zmurchyk

D-U-N-S 20-830-8130   (HQ)
CANCARB LIMITED
(*Suby of* TOKAI CARBON CO., LTD.)
1702 Brier Park Cres Nw, Medicine Hat, AB, T1C 1T9
(403) 527-1121
Sales 23,289,722
SIC 2895 Carbon black
Ken Tate

D-U-N-S 24-354-4066   (BR)
COSTCO WHOLESALE CANADA LTD
COSTCO
(*Suby of* COSTCO WHOLESALE CORPORATION)
2350 Box Springs Blvd Nw Box Suite 593, Medicine Hat, AB, T1C 0C8
(403) 581-5700
Emp Here 160
SIC 5099 Durable goods, nec
Bill Foots

D-U-N-S 20-599-7562   (BR)
GOODYEAR CANADA INC
(*Suby of* THE GOODYEAR TIRE & RUBBER COMPANY)
1271 12 St Nw, Medicine Hat, AB, T1C 1W8
(403) 527-3353
Emp Here 340
SIC 3011 Tires and inner tubes
Mike Drian

D-U-N-S 20-990-4168   (BR)
HALLIBURTON GROUP CANADA INC
HALLIBURTON ENERGY SERVICES
(*Suby of* HALLIBURTON COMPANY)
2175 Brier Park Pl Nw, Medicine Hat, AB, T1C 1S7
(403) 527-8895
Emp Here 200
SIC 1389 Oil and gas field services, nec
Dave Robertson

D-U-N-S 24-376-9952   (BR)
MASTEC CANADA INC
(*Suby of* MASTEC, INC.)
1010 Brier Park Dr Nw, Medicine Hat, AB, T1C 1Z7
(403) 529-6444
Emp Here 100
SIC 1623 Water, sewer, and utility lines
Cameron Anhelher

D-U-N-S 20-352-4103   (SL)
QINETIQ GROUP CANADA INC
QINETIQ TARGET SYSTEMS
(*Suby of* QINETIQ GROUP PLC)
1735 Brier Park Rd Nw Unit 3, Medicine Hat, AB, T1C 1V5
(403) 528-8782
Emp Here 45   *Sales* 10,072,935
SIC 3728 Aircraft parts and equipment, nec
Peter Longstaff

Corrissa Dale

D-U-N-S 24-441-6921   (SL)
RODEO FORD SALES LIMITED
1788 Saamis Dr Nw, Medicine Hat, AB, T1C 1W7
(403) 529-2777
Emp Here 42   *Sales* 20,919,276
SIC 5511 New and used car dealers
A A (Leo) Lant
Richard Lant

D-U-N-S 24-840-3321   (BR)
SCHLUMBERGER CANADA LIMITED
SCHLUMBERGER WELL SERVICES
2167 Brier Park Pl Nw, Medicine Hat, AB, T1C 1S7
(403) 527-8895
Emp Here 90
SIC 1389 Oil and gas field services, nec
Layton Deroldes

D-U-N-S 20-521-8118   (SL)
STARKS PLUMBING AND HEATING LTD
STARKS PLUMBING HEATING & ELECTRICAL
4850 Box Springs Rd Nw, Medicine Hat, AB, T1C 0C8
(403) 527-2929
Emp Here 75   *Sales* 17,479,875
SIC 1711 Plumbing, heating, air-conditioning
Albert Stark
Warren Stark

Medicine Hat, AB T9E

D-U-N-S 20-081-0208   (SL)
BROCK CONSTRUCTION LTD
BROCK CANADA
3735 8 St, Medicine Hat, AB, T9E 8J8
(403) 526-8930
Emp Here 50   *Sales* 21,320,402
SIC 6719 Holding companies, nec
Keith Scruggs

Milk River, AB T0K

D-U-N-S 20-829-5592   (SL)
CHINOOK GAS CO-OP LTD
125 8 Ave Nw, Milk River, AB, T0K 1M0
(403) 647-3588
Emp Here 13   *Sales* 40,376,141
SIC 4923 Gas transmission and distribution
Scott Russell
Roy Brown
Kevin Reese
David Erickson
Conrad Galts
Ted Swanson
Joan Hughson
Marilyn Johnson
Robert Laackmann
Rylan King

Minburn, AB T0B

D-U-N-S 20-970-5094   (SL)
HUTTERIAN BRETHERN OF MIXBURN LTD
MIXBURN COLONY
Gd, Minburn, AB, T0B 3B0
(780) 628-5147
Emp Here 90   *Sales* 12,308,310
SIC 0291 General farms, primarily animals
Mark Tschetter
Paul Tschetter

Morinville, AB T8R

D-U-N-S 24-335-5497   (SL)
1019728 ALBERTA LTD
FLYNN PROJECTS
8902 95 St, Morinville, AB, T8R 1K7
(780) 939-3000
Emp Here 37   *Sales* 15,516,135
SIC 6712 Bank holding companies
Barry Flynn
Joe Tomanek

D-U-N-S 25-370-3946   (SL)
FLYNN BROS. PROJECTS INC
FLYNN BROS
8902 95 St, Morinville, AB, T8R 1K7
(780) 939-3000
Emp Here 50   *Sales* 21,136,850
SIC 1541 Industrial buildings and warehouses
Barry Flynn
Joe Tomanek
Jim Ricard
Darrin Flynn

D-U-N-S 20-894-7994   (SL)
G.B. BUSINESS ENTERPRISES LTD
RV CITY
8704 100 St, Morinville, AB, T8R 1K6
(780) 939-3666
Emp Here 75   *Sales* 47,196,000
SIC 5511 New and used car dealers
Ross Hodgins

D-U-N-S 24-323-1060   (SL)
GARNEAU MANUFACTURING INC
8806 98 St, Morinville, AB, T8R 1K7
(780) 939-2129
Emp Here 55   *Sales* 10,564,675
SIC 3499 Fabricated Metal products, nec
Richard Caron
Don Caron

D-U-N-S 20-374-8173   (HQ)
HOMELAND HOUSING
9922 103 St, Morinville, AB, T8R 1R7
(780) 939-5116
Emp Here 1   *Sales* 28,050,750
SIC 8741 Management services
Raymond Cormie
Dwayne Kalke
Jorge Mesen

D-U-N-S 25-347-1791   (SL)
MORINVILLE COLONY LTD
Gd, Morinville, AB, T8R 1A1
(780) 939-2118
Emp Here 120   *Sales* 30,418,800
SIC 8748 Business consulting, nec
John Wurtz

D-U-N-S 25-269-4435   (BR)
RADCO FOOD STORES LTD
MORINVILLE SOBEYS
10003 100 St, Morinville, AB, T8R 1R5
(780) 939-4418
Emp Here 150
SIC 5411 Grocery stores
Steve Hunter

D-U-N-S 24-400-1673   (SL)
STURGEON FOUNDATION
9922 103 St, Morinville, AB, T8R 1R7
(780) 939-5116
Emp Here 100   *Sales* 12,477,600
SIC 8741 Management services
Dennis Magnusson
Mel Smith
Susan Evans
Alex Mackenzie
Louise Baudner
Carol Tremblay
Gord Putnam
Wes Brodhead

D-U-N-S 20-896-3520   (HQ)
STURGEON SCHOOL DIVISION #24
STURGEON PUBLIC SCHOOL DIVISION

▲ Public Company   ■ Public Company Family Member   **HQ** Headquarters   **BR** Branch   **SL** Single Location

9820 104 St, Morinville, AB, T8R 1L8
(780) 939-4341
Emp Here 25   *Sales* 49,559,500
SIC 8211 Elementary and secondary schools
 Mary Lynne R Campbell

Mundare, AB T0B

D-U-N-S 24-067-9829   (HQ)
STAWNICHY'S HOLDINGS LTD
STAWNICHY'S MEAT PROCESSING
5212 50 St, Mundare, AB, T0B 3H0
(780) 764-3912
Emp Here 45   *Sales* 18,782,528
SIC 5421 Meat and fish markets
 Jeanette Stawnichy
 Cheryl Zeleny
 Colette Hennig

Nanton, AB T0L

D-U-N-S 24-346-9434   (SL)
HUTTERIAN BRETHREN OF PARKLAND, THE
PARKLAND COLONY
Gd, Nanton, AB, T0L 1R0
(403) 646-5761
Emp Here 97   *Sales* 25,443,973
SIC 0191 General farms, primarily crop
 Leonard Wipf

D-U-N-S 20-527-9123   (SL)
MOUNTAIN TOP FOODS LTD
2301 18 Ave, Nanton, AB, T0L 1R0
(403) 646-0038
Emp Here 50   *Sales* 13,707,600
SIC 5421 Meat and fish markets
 Juanita Calvert
 Jason Calvert

New Dayton, AB T0K

D-U-N-S 20-829-3720   (HQ)
NEW ROCKPORT HUTTERIAN BRETHREN
Gd, New Dayton, AB, T0K 1P0
(403) 733-2122
Sales 17,123,350
SIC 0191 General farms, primarily crop
 Michel Waldner
 Jonathan Wips
 Steve Wips
 David Waldner

Nisku, AB T9E

D-U-N-S 25-625-6389   (SL)
1484174 ALBERTA LTD
ACTION EXPRESS & HOTSHOT
1601 13 St, Nisku, AB, T9E 0Y2
(780) 454-9231
Emp Here 100   *Sales* 44,921,900
SIC 7389 Business services, nec
 Michael V Mayorchak
 Carol A Cooper

D-U-N-S 25-539-7416   (SL)
347678 ALBERTA LTD
ALTA-FAB STRUCTURES
1205 5 St, Nisku, AB, T9E 7L6
(780) 955-7733
Emp Here 300   *Sales* 109,652,700
SIC 6712 Bank holding companies
 Mark Taillefer
 Helen Taillefer
 Raymond Taillefer

D-U-N-S 24-593-2541   (SL)
5BLUE PROCESS EQUIPMENT INC
2303 8 St, Nisku, AB, T9E 7Z3
(780) 955-2040
Emp Here 54   *Sales* 20,668,851
SIC 5085 Industrial supplies
 Kelly Smith
 Peter Smith

D-U-N-S 24-028-4914   (SL)
ABRASIVE BLAST & PAINT INC
1207 16 Ave, Nisku, AB, T9E 0A8
(780) 955-3616
Emp Here 25   *Sales* 11,875,650
SIC 5085 Industrial supplies
 Lorne Fedoruk
 Paula Federuk

D-U-N-S 24-300-7879   (SL)
ACE VEGETATION CONTROL SERVICE LTD
ACE VEGETATION SERVICE
2001 8 St, Nisku, AB, T9E 7Z1
(780) 955-8980
Emp Here 55   *Sales* 13,884,310
SIC 1629 Heavy construction, nec
 Richard Law
 Ian Mcdonald

D-U-N-S 20-351-5028   (BR)
ACR FULLER GROUP
(*Suby of* ACR FULLER GROUP)
511 12 Ave, Nisku, AB, T9E 7N8
(780) 955-2802
Emp Here 100
SIC 3069 Fabricated rubber products, nec

D-U-N-S 20-294-2983   (BR)
ADESA AUCTIONS CANADA CORPORATION
ADESA EDMONTON
(*Suby of* KAR AUCTION SERVICES, INC.)
1701 9 St, Nisku, AB, T9E 8M8
(780) 955-4400
Emp Here 130
SIC 5012 Automobiles and other motor vehicles
 Richard Sawatzky

D-U-N-S 24-400-4479   (BR)
AKITA DRILLING LTD
AKITA DRILLING LTD
(*Suby of* AKITA DRILLING LTD)
2302 8 St, Nisku, AB, T9E 7Z2
(780) 955-6700
Emp Here 600
SIC 1381 Drilling oil and gas wells
 Steve Hakim

D-U-N-S 24-391-6244   (SL)
ALTA-FAB STRUCTURES LTD
1205 5 St, Nisku, AB, T9E 7L6
(780) 955-7733
Emp Here 150   *Sales* 28,855,500
SIC 2452 Prefabricated wood buildings
 Han Van Weelden
 Cameron Bowie

D-U-N-S 25-469-5554   (HQ)
BLACK GOLD REGIONAL DIVISION #18
BLACK GOLD REGIONAL SCHOOLS
1101 5 St Suite 301, Nisku, AB, T9E 7N3
(780) 955-6025
Emp Here 40   *Sales* 99,119,000
SIC 8211 Elementary and secondary schools
 Norman Yanitski
 Orville Borys
 Barb Martinson

D-U-N-S 24-385-0695   (SL)
BORETS CANADA LTD
BORETS-WEATHERFORD
(*Suby of* SULTECOR INVESTMENTS LIMITED)
2305 8 St, Nisku, AB, T9E 7Z3
(780) 955-4795
Emp Here 71   *Sales* 34,628,830
SIC 5084 Industrial machinery and equipment

Philip Fouillard
Sergey Alehkin

D-U-N-S 24-715-4516   (SL)
BROCK CANADA FIELD SERVICES LTD
3735 8 St Unit 200, Nisku, AB, T9E 8J8
(780) 465-9016
Emp Here 670   *Sales* 142,291,920
SIC 1799 Special trade contractors, nec
 Dean Dancey

D-U-N-S 24-861-1790   (HQ)
BROCK CANADA INC
3735 8 St, Nisku, AB, T9E 8J8
(780) 465-9016
Emp Here 40   *Sales* 436,776,800
SIC 1389 Oil and gas field services, nec
 Willi Hamm

D-U-N-S 20-743-8805   (HQ)
BROCK CANADA INDUSTRIAL LTD
(*Suby of* BROCK CANADA INC)
3735 8 St, Nisku, AB, T9E 8J8
(780) 465-9016
Emp Here 3   *Sales* 375,905,520
SIC 1799 Special trade contractors, nec
 Patrick F. Ross
 Mike Mcginnis

D-U-N-S 24-929-5932   (HQ)
CAMEX EQUIPMENT SALES & RENTALS INC
CAMEX
1806 2 St, Nisku, AB, T9E 0W8
(780) 955-2770
Sales 26,651,840
SIC 7353 Heavy construction equipment rental
 Andy Fraser
 Pat Boeker
 Duane Reid
 Lew Knechtel

D-U-N-S 24-939-1939   (HQ)
CARMACKS ENTERPRISES LTD
(*Suby of* VINCI)
701 25 Ave, Nisku, AB, T9E 0C1
(780) 955-5545
Emp Here 50   *Sales* 205,776,990
SIC 1611 Highway and street construction
 Keith James

D-U-N-S 20-084-4025   (HQ)
CHEMCO ELECTRICAL CONTRACTORS LTD
(*Suby of* BALM MANAGEMENT ENTERPRISES LTD)
3135 4 St, Nisku, AB, T9E 8L1
(780) 436-9570
Emp Here 120   *Sales* 588,772,500
SIC 1731 Electrical work
 Brian Halina
 Terry Milot
 Todd Halina
 Jill Halina

D-U-N-S 25-416-7679   (HQ)
CROSSING COMPANY INCORPORATED, THE
(*Suby of* RIVERSIDE RENTALS INC)
1807 8 St, Nisku, AB, T9E 7S8
(780) 955-5051
Emp Here 98   *Sales* 25,244,200
SIC 1623 Water, sewer, and utility lines
 Ryan Maclean
 Paul Martens
 William D Grace

D-U-N-S 20-268-6874   (SL)
CUSTOM VACUUM SERVICES LTD
904 29 Ave, Nisku, AB, T9E 1B7
(780) 955-9344
Emp Here 48   *Sales* 11,056,320
SIC 5722 Household appliance stores
 Randy Luck
 Trevor Snyder

D-U-N-S 24-949-5789   (BR)

D-U-N-S 24-273-9274   (HQ)
DRECO ENERGY SERVICES ULC
NATIONAL OIL WELL VARCO
(*Suby of* NATIONAL OILWELL VARCO, INC.)
506 17 Ave, Nisku, AB, T9E 7T1
(780) 955-5451
Emp Here 140
SIC 3533 Oil and gas field machinery
 Don Dostie

D-U-N-S 24-273-9274   (HQ)
DRECO ENERGY SERVICES ULC
DRECO RIG TECHNOLOGY & CONSTRUCTION
(*Suby of* NATIONAL OILWELL VARCO, INC.)
1704 5 St, Nisku, AB, T9E 8P8
(780) 944-3800
Emp Here 550   *Sales* 379,183,950
SIC 3533 Oil and gas field machinery
 Roman Konowalec
 Frederick W Phaesy
 Glen Arnelien

D-U-N-S 25-415-0410   (SL)
ENER-RIG SUPPLY INC
2104 7 St Suite 2, Nisku, AB, T9E 7Y2
(780) 955-2067
Emp Here 35   *Sales* 15,651,090
SIC 5063 Electrical apparatus and equipment
 Kevin Brown
 Bill Stroshein

D-U-N-S 24-425-9136   (BR)
FLINT TUBULAR MANAGEMENT SERVICES LTD
(*Suby of* FLINT TUBULAR MANAGEMENT SERVICES LTD)
950 30 Ave, Nisku, AB, T9E 0S2
(780) 955-3380
Emp Here 100
SIC 1389 Oil and gas field services, nec
 Georges Baker

D-U-N-S 24-848-8053   (SL)
FOSSIL EPC LTD
(*Suby of* FOSSIL GROUP LTD)
1805 8 St, Nisku, AB, T9E 7S8
(780) 449-0773
Emp Here 40   *Sales* 10,973,280
SIC 8741 Management services
 Robert Jesse Lodge

D-U-N-S 24-399-7491   (HQ)
FRANK FLAMAN SALES LTD
(*Suby of* FLAMAN, FRANK INVESTMENTS LTD)
2310 Sparrow Dr, Nisku, AB, T9E 8A2
(780) 955-3400
Emp Here 41   *Sales* 16,369,976
SIC 5999 Miscellaneous retail stores, nec
 Frank Flaman

D-U-N-S 25-367-9096   (BR)
GISBORNE INDUSTRIAL CONSTRUCTION LTD
GISBORNE FIRE PROTECTION
(*Suby of* GISBORNE HOLDINGS LTD)
1201 6 St, Nisku, AB, T9E 7P1

Emp Here 100
SIC 1541 Industrial buildings and warehouses
 Ron Spirenollo

D-U-N-S 24-732-7075   (BR)
HALLIBURTON GROUP CANADA INC
SPERRY-SUN DRILLING SERVICES
(*Suby of* HALLIBURTON COMPANY)
1400 5 St, Nisku, AB, T9E 7R6
(800) 335-6333
Emp Here 300
SIC 1389 Oil and gas field services, nec
 Ray Smith

D-U-N-S 25-977-5661   (SL)
HYDRIL CANADIAN COMPANY LIMITED PARTNERSHIP
2307 8 St, Nisku, AB, T9E 7Z3
(780) 955-2045
Emp Here 49   *Sales* 23,276,274

SIC 5084 Industrial machinery and equipment
Dale Parker

D-U-N-S 24-068-5198   (SL)
HYDUKE DRILLING SOLUTIONS INC
(Suby of HYDUKE ENERGY SERVICES INC)
2107 6 St, Nisku, AB, T9E 7X8
(780) 955-0360
Emp Here 94   Sales 18,078,832
SIC 7692 Welding repair
Gordon Mccormack
Eugene Wirsta
Boris Makowecki
Myron Yurko
Erv Lack
Michael Hill

D-U-N-S 25-329-7030   (HQ)
HYDUKE ENERGY SERVICES INC
2107 6 St, Nisku, AB, T9E 7X8
(780) 955-0360
Emp Here 50   Sales 18,317,019
SIC 1389 Oil and gas field services, nec
Patrick F. Ross
Jane Halford
Boyd Mahon
Nick Cristiano
Willi Hamm
Vahan Kololian

D-U-N-S 24-627-8873   (SL)
INTER-ALBERTA HOLDINGS CORPORA-TION
NISKU INN & CONFERENCE CENTRE
1101 4 St, Nisku, AB, T9E 7N1
(780) 955-7744
Emp Here 167   Sales 15,479,230
SIC 7011 Hotels and motels
Nizar Mawani

D-U-N-S 20-003-2089   (HQ)
IRONLINE COMPRESSION LIMITED PART-NERSHIP
(Suby of STAPLE STREET CAPITAL LLC)
700 15 Ave, Nisku, AB, T9E 7S2
(780) 955-0700
Emp Here 40   Sales 31,339,080
SIC 7699 Repair services, nec
Timothy Kelley
Aaron Chronik

D-U-N-S 24-868-2341   (HQ)
J.V. DRIVER CORPORATION INC
JV DRIVER GROUP
1205 5 St, Nisku, AB, T9E 7L6
(780) 980-5837
Emp Here 5   Sales 1,640,575,000
SIC 1629 Heavy construction, nec
Charles Sanders

D-U-N-S 24-423-2919   (SL)
J.V. DRIVER FABRICATORS INC
(Suby of J.V. DRIVER CORPORATION INC)
706 25 Ave, Nisku, AB, T9E 0G6
(780) 955-4282
Emp Here 100   Sales 18,138,800
SIC 3312 Blast furnaces and steel mills
Corey Callahan

D-U-N-S 24-324-2943   (SL)
J.V. DRIVER PROJECTS INC
(Suby of J.V. DRIVER CORPORATION INC)
1205 5 St, Nisku, AB, T9E 7L6
(780) 980-5837
Emp Here 500   Sales 349,196,000
SIC 1541 Industrial buildings and warehouses
Bill Elkington

D-U-N-S 24-425-4442   (SL)
KBR CANADA LTD
KBR INDUSTRIAL CANADA COMPANY
(Suby of KBR, INC.)
1302 10 S, Nisku, AB, T9E 8K2
(780) 468-1341
Emp Here 500   Sales 56,101,500
SIC 8741 Management services
Carl Roberts

D-U-N-S 20-023-0456   (SL)
KHEERAN INSPECTION SERVICES INC
702 23 Ave, Nisku, AB, T9E 7Y6
(780) 800-6295
Emp Here 42   Sales 18,626,580
SIC 7389 Business services, nec
Bala Vanumamalai

D-U-N-S 25-409-4246   (SL)
KSM INC
1904 4 St, Nisku, AB, T9E 7T8
(780) 955-3456
Emp Here 25   Sales 11,875,650
SIC 5084 Industrial machinery and equipment
Gerald Knoll

D-U-N-S 24-737-3298   (HQ)
LEADING MANUFACTURING GROUP HOLDINGS INC
801 25 Ave, Nisku, AB, T9E 7Z4
(780) 955-8895
Emp Here 1   Sales 13,445,950
SIC 3443 Fabricated plate work (boiler shop)
Lee Gottschlich

D-U-N-S 24-802-2449   (SL)
LEADING MANUFACTURING GROUP INC
LMG
(Suby of LEADING MANUFACTURING GROUP HOLDINGS INC)
2313 8 St, Nisku, AB, T9E 7Z3
(780) 955-8895
Emp Here 70   Sales 13,445,950
SIC 3443 Fabricated plate work (boiler shop)
Lee Gottschlich

D-U-N-S 20-209-1992   (BR)
LEDCOR INDUSTRIES INC
LEDCOR FABRICATION
(Suby of 280818 ALBERTA LTD)
3925 8 St, Nisku, AB, T9E 8M1
(780) 955-1400
Emp Here 250
SIC 1611 Highway and street construction
Laurie Draker

D-U-N-S 24-855-4151   (HQ)
LINK SUSPENSIONS OF CANADA, LIM-ITED PARTNERSHIP
(Suby of LINK MFG., LTD.)
601 18 Ave, Nisku, AB, T9E 7T7
(780) 955-2859
Emp Here 50   Sales 12,828,100
SIC 3842 Surgical appliances and supplies
Chris English

D-U-N-S 20-083-0313   (SL)
LUFKIN INDUSTRIES CANADA ULC
(Suby of GENERAL ELECTRIC COMPANY)
1107 8a St, Nisku, AB, T9E 7R3
(780) 955-7566
Emp Here 106   Sales 23,532,106
SIC 3561 Pumps and pumping equipment
Ron Hetlinger

D-U-N-S 24-731-2374   (HQ)
MAKLOC BUILDINGS INC
(Suby of MAKLOC GROUP INC)
706 17 Ave, Nisku, AB, T9E 7T1
(780) 955-2951
Emp Here 30   Sales 19,208,500
SIC 3448 Prefabricated Metal buildings and components
Enio Zanello
James Zanello
Charles Gaisson

D-U-N-S 20-189-2366   (SL)
MELLOY INDUSTRIAL SERVICES INC
(Suby of PCL EMPLOYEES HOLDINGS LTD)
2305 5 St, Nisku, AB, T9E 7X1
(780) 955-8500
Emp Here 65   Sales 14,430,065
SIC 3569 General industrial machinery, nec
John Aitken

D-U-N-S 25-367-6878   (BR)
NABORS DRILLING CANADA LIMITED

NABORS DRILLING
(Suby of NABORS DRILLING CANADA LIM-ITED)
902 20 Ave, Nisku, AB, T9E 7Z6
(780) 955-2381
Emp Here 140
SIC 1381 Drilling oil and gas wells
Dave Miller

D-U-N-S 24-340-9559   (SL)
NORTHSTAR SHARP'S FOUNDATION SPE-CIALISTS LTD
(Suby of QUANTA SERVICES, INC.)
1511 Sparrow Dr, Nisku, AB, T9E 8H9
(780) 955-2108
Emp Here 100   Sales 25,244,200
SIC 1622 Bridge, tunnel, and elevated high-way construction
Tony Evangelista
Blaine Colbert
Rob Beard
Kevin Sharp

D-U-N-S 20-083-6112   (SL)
NORWOOD FOUNDRY LIMITED
605 18 Ave, Nisku, AB, T9E 7T7
(780) 955-8844
Emp Here 80   Sales 18,674,800
SIC 3365 Aluminum foundries
Bart Dornan

D-U-N-S 24-805-0945   (HQ)
NOV ENERFLOW ULC
2201 9 St, Nisku, AB, T9E 7Z7
(780) 955-7675
Emp Here 10   Sales 168,169,750
SIC 1389 Oil and gas field services, nec
Greg Jorgenson

D-U-N-S 25-498-3414   (BR)
NOV ENERFLOW ULC
TUBOSCOPE CANADA
(Suby of NOV ENERFLOW ULC)
2201 9 St, Nisku, AB, T9E 7Z7
(780) 955-7675
Emp Here 75
SIC 1389 Oil and gas field services, nec
Greg Jorgenson

D-U-N-S 25-680-6548   (SL)
O.J. PIPELINES CANADA
RMS WELDING SYSTEMS, DIV OF
(Suby of QUANTA SERVICES, INC.)
1409 4 St, Nisku, AB, T9E 7M9
(780) 955-3900
Emp Here 200   Sales 65,623,000
SIC 1623 Water, sewer, and utility lines
David Kavanaugh

D-U-N-S 20-881-0783   (SL)
PATRIK'S WATER HAULING LTD
504 19 Ave, Nisku, AB, T9E 7W1
(780) 955-8878
Emp Here 80   Sales 11,855,360
SIC 4212 Local trucking, without storage
Patrik Ondris

D-U-N-S 25-235-5730   (HQ)
PHOENIX INDUSTRIAL MAINTENANCE LTD
PHOENIX INDUSTRIAL
903 9 Ave, Nisku, AB, T9E 1C8
(780) 428-3130
Sales 279,356,800
SIC 1541 Industrial buildings and warehouses
James Adams
Kelly Adams

D-U-N-S 24-419-9167   (SL)
PYRAMID PROCESS FABRICATORS COR-PORATION
(Suby of PTW ENERGY SERVICES LTD)
2308 8 St, Nisku, AB, T9E 7Z2
(780) 955-2708
Emp Here 50   Sales 11,671,750
SIC 3312 Blast furnaces and steel mills
Don Basnett

Keith Basnett
Garth Deacon

D-U-N-S 20-084-0221   (HQ)
RED-L DISTRIBUTORS LTD
3675 13 St, Nisku, AB, T9E 1C5
(780) 437-2630
Emp Here 60   Sales 53,650,300
SIC 5085 Industrial supplies
Guy Ludwig
Jamie Ludwig
Rick Lafrance
Jeffrey Resnick

D-U-N-S 24-773-2378   (SL)
REED HYCALOG CORING SERVICES
1507 4 St, Nisku, AB, T9E 7M9
(780) 955-8929
Emp Here 49   Sales 15,665,545
SIC 1389 Oil and gas field services, nec

D-U-N-S 24-365-8957   (SL)
RELIANCE INDUSTRIAL INVESTMENTS LTD
606 19 Ave, Nisku, AB, T9E 7W1
(780) 955-7115
Emp Here 64   Sales 16,739,392
SIC 6712 Bank holding companies
Georg Eger
Michael Sirois

D-U-N-S 20-557-5827   (HQ)
RIVERSIDE RENTALS INC
1807 8 St, Nisku, AB, T9E 7S8
(780) 955-5051
Emp Here 5   Sales 25,244,200
SIC 1623 Water, sewer, and utility lines
Ryan Maclean
Paul Martens
Robert Maclean
William D Grace

D-U-N-S 24-204-9877   (BR)
ROCKWELL SERVICING INC
ENSIGN ROCKWELL SERVICING
(Suby of ENSIGN ENERGY SERVICES INC)
2105 8 St, Nisku, AB, T9E 7Z1
(780) 955-7066
Emp Here 80
SIC 1389 Oil and gas field services, nec
Daniel Shihinski

D-U-N-S 24-354-8380   (BR)
SAMUEL, SON & CO., LIMITED
OMEGA JOIST
(Suby of SAMUEL, SON & CO., LIMITED)
1709 8 St, Nisku, AB, T9E 7S8
(780) 955-7516
Emp Here 80
SIC 5051 Metals service centers and offices
Brian Granfield

D-U-N-S 25-136-9679   (SL)
SASKATCHEWAN
2510 Sparrow Dr, Nisku, AB, T9E 8N5
(780) 955-3639
Emp Here 35   Sales 13,909,490
SIC 8699 Membership organizations, nec
Bev Ward

D-U-N-S 20-152-6725   (BR)
SCHLUMBERGER CANADA LIMITED
ARTIFICIAL LIFT
1606 8 St, Nisku, AB, T9E 7S6
(780) 955-2800
Emp Here 90
SIC 1389 Oil and gas field services, nec
Song Shang

D-U-N-S 25-533-4286   (BR)
SCHLUMBERGER CANADA LIMITED
SMITH SERVICES
406 22 Ave, Nisku, AB, T9E 7W8
(780) 979-0627
Emp Here 100
SIC 1389 Oil and gas field services, nec
Eleanor Arnold

D-U-N-S 20-117-2041   (HQ)
SHAW'S ENTERPRISES LTD
2801 5 St, Nisku, AB, T9E 0C2
(780) 955-7222
Emp Here 2   *Sales* 40,377,210
SIC 5085 Industrial supplies
Darren P Shaw

D-U-N-S 24-389-1822   (SL)
SNUBCO GROUP INC
502 23a Ave, Nisku, AB, T9E 8G2
(780) 955-3550
Emp Here 80   *Sales* 25,576,400
SIC 1389 Oil and gas field services, nec
John Taskinen

D-U-N-S 20-154-0346   (HQ)
SNUBCO PRESSURE CONTROL LTD
502 23a Ave, Nisku, AB, T9E 8G2
(780) 955-3550
Emp Here 35   *Sales* 15,985,250
SIC 1389 Oil and gas field services, nec
John Taskinen
Kar Bauer

D-U-N-S 24-966-8315   (SL)
SS RIG & VAC LTD
1801 8 St, Nisku, AB, T9E 7S8
(780) 979-9987
Emp Here 40   *Sales* 29,700,800
SIC 5199 Nondurable goods, nec
Derick Petrie
Darcy Nystrom
Michael Sirois
Robert Tyldsley

D-U-N-S 25-533-2363   (SL)
STRAD MANUFACTURING INC
(*Suby of* STRAD INC)
602 25 Ave, Nisku, AB, T9E 0G6
(780) 955-9393
Emp Here 25   *Sales* 15,665,350
SIC 4911 Electric services
Robert Grandfield
Byron Johnson
Andrew Pernal
Henry Van Der Sloot

D-U-N-S 25-978-9451   (SL)
SUPER SLINGS INC
505 11 Ave, Nisku, AB, T9E 7N5
(780) 955-7111
Emp Here 22   *Sales* 10,450,572
SIC 5085 Industrial supplies
Aaron Giesinger
Myron Ohlmann

D-U-N-S 24-322-0493   (BR)
SUREPOINT SERVICES INC
(*Suby of* WYNNCHURCH CAPITAL, LTD.)
1211 8a St, Nisku, AB, T9E 7R3
(780) 955-3939
Emp Here 100
SIC 5084 Industrial machinery and equipment
Trevor Muir

D-U-N-S 20-293-7538   (HQ)
SUREPOINT TECHNOLOGIES GROUP INC
1211 8a St, Nisku, AB, T9E 7R3
(780) 955-3939
Emp Here 25   *Sales* 44,394,240
SIC 1381 Drilling oil and gas wells
Trevor Muir
Cameron Cragg

D-U-N-S 24-928-6915   (HQ)
TIGER CALCIUM SERVICES INC
(*Suby of* TPC ADMINISTRATION INC)
603 15 Ave, Nisku, AB, T9E 7M6
(403) 955-5004
Emp Here 25   *Sales* 82,621,800
SIC 1499 Miscellaneous nonMetallic minerals, except fuels
Clark Sazwan
Brandy Deford
Richard Kolodziej
Shilo Sazwan
Rod Senst

Rob Wildeman

D-U-N-S 24-896-7817   (SL)
TITAN TUBULAR SOLUTIONS LTD
606 22 Ave, Nisku, AB, T9E 7X6
(780) 955-7002
Emp Here 10   *Sales* 10,003,390
SIC 5051 Metals service centers and offices
Leo Provencher

D-U-N-S 24-998-0186   (SL)
TRAILBLAZER R.V. CENTRE LTD
2302 Sparrow Dr, Nisku, AB, T9E 8A2
(780) 955-0300
Emp Here 30   *Sales* 14,942,340
SIC 5571 Motorcycle dealers
Keith Graham
Laura Graham
Kim Graham
Colleen Graham

D-U-N-S 20-280-2471   (BR)
TRICAN WELL SERVICE LTD
TRICAN PRODUCTION SERVICES
(*Suby of* TRICAN WELL SERVICE LTD)
2305 5a St, Nisku, AB, T9E 8G6
(780) 955-5675
Emp Here 88
SIC 1389 Oil and gas field services, nec
James Young

D-U-N-S 20-355-2625   (SL)
TUBOSCOPE VETCO CANADA ULC
TUBOSCOPE
2201 9 St, Nisku, AB, T9E 7Z7
(780) 955-7675
Emp Here 300   *Sales* 201,803,700
SIC 1389 Oil and gas field services, nec
Greg Jorgenson
Ken Skuba

D-U-N-S 24-628-5308   (SL)
TWA PANEL SYSTEMS INC
1201 4 St, Nisku, AB, T9E 7L3
(780) 955-8757
Emp Here 50   *Sales* 10,233,650
SIC 3634 Electric housewares and fans
Mark Linde

D-U-N-S 20-084-8307   (HQ)
UNION TRACTOR LTD
DELTA WAREHOUSES, DIV OF
3750 13 St, Nisku, AB, T9E 1C6
(780) 979-8500
Emp Here 100   *Sales* 28,849,200
SIC 7699 Repair services, nec
David Mcalpine
Max Yuen

D-U-N-S 20-703-9970   (BR)
WEATHERFORD CANADA LTD
(*Suby of* WEATHERFORD INTERNATIONAL PUBLIC LIMITED COMPANY)
2603 5 St, Nisku, AB, T9E 0C2
(780) 979-4500
Emp Here 110
SIC 3533 Oil and gas field machinery
Don Cappelli

D-U-N-S 24-714-7788   (HQ)
WF STEEL & CRANE LTD
(*Suby of* CAMBER CORPORATION)
705 23 Ave, Nisku, AB, T9E 7Y5
(587) 410-0625
Emp Here 84   *Sales* 40,377,210
SIC 5084 Industrial machinery and equipment
Curtis Rozendaal
Ian Olthuis
Ryan Schram

D-U-N-S 24-397-2460   (HQ)
WILLIAMS, R. B. INDUSTRIAL SUPPLY LTD
3280 10 St, Nisku, AB, T9E 1E7
(780) 955-9332
Sales 30,876,690
SIC 5085 Industrial supplies
Richard Williams
Lynn Williams

Nobleford, AB T0L

D-U-N-S 24-089-0199   (SL)
834 HUTTERIEN BRETHERN OF WHITE-LAKE
Gd, Nobleford, AB, T0L 1S0
(403) 824-3688
Emp Here 49   *Sales* 13,442,268
SIC 8741 Management services
Thomas Tschetter

D-U-N-S 24-818-2649   (BR)
AG GROWTH INTERNATIONAL INC
EDWARDS GROUP
(*Suby of* AG GROWTH INTERNATIONAL INC)
215 Barons St, Nobleford, AB, T0L 1S0
(403) 320-5585
Emp Here 100
SIC 3523 Farm machinery and equipment

D-U-N-S 20-089-3790   (SL)
NIEBOER FARM SUPPLIES (1977) LTD
233016 Hwy 519, Nobleford, AB, T0L 1S0
(403) 824-3404
Emp Here 30   *Sales* 14,250,780
SIC 5083 Farm and garden machinery
William Nieboer
Kevin Nieboer
Pearl Nieboer

D-U-N-S 25-110-0491   (SL)
OUTLOOK PORK LTD
Gd, Nobleford, AB, T0L 1S0

Emp Here 35   *Sales* 13,493,165
SIC 0213 Hogs
Peter Klok

Okotoks, AB T1S

D-U-N-S 24-299-3616   (SL)
425507 ALBERTA LTD
OKOTOKS HONDA
100 Northgate Blvd, Okotoks, AB, T1S 0H9
(403) 842-1100
Emp Here 42   *Sales* 20,919,276
SIC 5511 New and used car dealers
Rahim Premji

D-U-N-S 20-255-5780   (SL)
945575 ALBERTA LTD
BOSTON PIZZA
10 Southridge Dr, Okotoks, AB, T1S 1N1
(403) 995-0224
Emp Here 75   *Sales* 3,413,925
SIC 5812 Eating places
Trevor Tominik
Tony Grey
Ted Tominik
Bill Tominik

D-U-N-S 24-025-3232   (BR)
ALBERTA HEALTH SERVICES
OKOTOKS HEALTH AND WELLNESS CEN-TRE
(*Suby of* GOVERNMENT OF THE PROVINCE OF ALBERTA)
11 Cimarron Common, Okotoks, AB, T1S 2E9
(403) 995-2600
Emp Here 100
SIC 8093 Specialty outpatient clinics, nec
Janet Davidson

D-U-N-S 24-326-6272   (SL)
BROWN'S GENERAL STORE LTD
SHOPPERS DRUG MART
31 Southridge Dr Suite 171, Okotoks, AB, T1S 2N3
(403) 995-3798
Emp Here 40   *Sales* 10,118,160
SIC 5912 Drug stores and proprietary stores

Robert (Bob) Brown
Anita Brown

D-U-N-S 20-710-8296   (BR)
FOOTHILLS SCHOOL DIVISION NO. 38
FOOTHILLS COMPOSITE HIGH SCHOOL AND ALBERTA HIGH SCHOOL OF FINE ARTS
(*Suby of* FOOTHILLS SCHOOL DIVISION NO. 38)
229 Woodhaven Dr, Okotoks, AB, T1S 2A7
(403) 938-6116
Emp Here 80
SIC 8211 Elementary and secondary schools
Vince Hunter

D-U-N-S 24-014-3487   (SL)
GILBERT HOLDINGS LTD
SOBEYS OKOTOKS
201 Southridge Dr Unit 700, Okotoks, AB, T1S 2E1
(403) 938-3439
Emp Here 185   *Sales* 54,293,245
SIC 5411 Grocery stores
David Gilbert

D-U-N-S 24-858-9918   (HQ)
HI-PRO FEEDS LP
TROUW NUTRITION
Hwy 2a 306 Ave, Okotoks, AB, T1S 1A2
(403) 938-8350
Emp Here 150   *Sales* 78,737,373
SIC 5999 Miscellaneous retail stores, nec
Daren Kennett
Mark Knief
Jeff Dykstra

D-U-N-S 24-364-7240   (BR)
HOME DEPOT OF CANADA INC
HOME DEPOT
(*Suby of* THE HOME DEPOT INC)
101 Southbank Blvd Unit 10, Okotoks, AB, T1S 0G1
(403) 995-4710
Emp Here 150
SIC 5211 Lumber and other building materials
Rick Nelson

D-U-N-S 25-183-6615   (SL)
KORTH GROUP LTD
(*Suby of* 784700 ALBERTA LTD)
64186 393 Loop E, Okotoks, AB, T1S 0L1
(403) 938-3255
Emp Here 20   *Sales* 10,410,840
SIC 5091 Sporting and recreation goods
Terry Korth
Donna Korth

D-U-N-S 24-300-8869   (HQ)
MILLER SUPPLY LTD.
ESSO BULK AGENT
48223 338 Ave E, Okotoks, AB, T1S 1B2
(403) 995-4797
Emp Here 20   *Sales* 56,574,045
SIC 5171 Petroleum bulk stations and terminals
Robert Miller
Krista Miller

D-U-N-S 24-761-3768   (HQ)
MT-U OPERATING COMPANY INC
31 Southridge Dr Suite 121a, Okotoks, AB, T1S 2N3
(403) 995-5217
Emp Here 5   *Sales* 13,077,650
SIC 6712 Bank holding companies
Stephen Lockwood

D-U-N-S 20-831-1266   (HQ)
MULLEN GROUP LTD
MULLEN TRANSPORTATION
31 Southridge Dr Suite 121a, Okotoks, AB, T1S 2N3
(403) 995-5200
Emp Here 45   *Sales* 955,813,485
SIC 1389 Oil and gas field services, nec
Murray K. Mullen
Richard J. Maloney

Joanna K. Scott
P. Stephen Clark
Greg Bay
Stephen H. Lockwood
Christine Mcginley
David E. Mullen
Philip J. Scherman
Sonia Tibbatts

D-U-N-S 24-523-2009   (SL)
OCL GROUP INC
325 Woodgate Rd, Okotoks, AB, T1S 2A5
(403) 982-9090
Emp Here 104   *Sales* 43,592,229
SIC 1623 Water, sewer, and utility lines
Bradley Dean Maguire
Trevor Replinger
Rick Henderson
Kevin Kirchmaier
Peter Nickerson
Don Underchute

D-U-N-S 20-336-9363   (SL)
OKOTOKS LINCOLN MERCURY
OKOTOKS FORD
4 Westland Rd, Okotoks, AB, T1S 1N1
(403) 938-2255
Emp Here 30   *Sales* 14,942,340
SIC 5511 New and used car dealers
Cleone Godwin

D-U-N-S 24-805-4447   (HQ)
PICKFORD GROUP LTD, THE
1237-200 Southridge Dr, Okotoks, AB, T1S 0N8
(403) 571-0571
Emp Here 9   *Sales* 11,400,624
SIC 5084 Industrial machinery and equipment
Mel Kassian

D-U-N-S 20-806-2401   (BR)
SOBEYS CAPITAL INCORPORATED
SOBEYS STORE 1130
(*Suby of* EMPIRE COMPANY LIMITED)
201 Southridge Dr Suite 700, Okotoks, AB, T1S 2E1
(403) 995-4088
Emp Here 185
SIC 5411 Grocery stores
David Gilbert

D-U-N-S 24-363-3869   (BR)
SOBEYS WEST INC
OKOTOKS SAFEWAY
(*Suby of* EMPIRE COMPANY LIMITED)
610 Big Rock Ln, Okotoks, AB, T1S 1L2
(403) 938-9341
Emp Here 150
SIC 5411 Grocery stores
Jill Pickering

D-U-N-S 20-087-4563   (SL)
SOUTHRIDGE CHRYSLER LTD
12 Southridge Dr, Okotoks, AB, T1S 1N1
(403) 938-3636
Emp Here 30   *Sales* 14,942,340
SIC 5511 New and used car dealers
John Gotch

D-U-N-S 24-014-5912   (SL)
STRATHCONA-TWEEDSMUIR SCHOOL
STS
Gd, Okotoks, AB, T1S 1A3
(403) 938-4431
Emp Here 105   *Sales* 10,407,495
SIC 8211 Elementary and secondary schools
William Jones

D-U-N-S 25-119-4270   (SL)
TOMANICK GROUP, THE
BOSTON PIZZA OKOTOKS 149
10 Southridge Dr, Okotoks, AB, T1S 1N1
(403) 995-0224
Emp Here 75   *Sales* 3,413,925
SIC 5812 Eating places
Trevor Tomanick

D-U-N-S 20-294-9033   (SL)

XTECH EXPLOSIVE DECONTAMINATION INC
900 Village Lane Suite 14, Okotoks, AB, T1S 1Z6
(403) 938-3883
Emp Here 50   *Sales* 36,940,190
SIC 5169 Chemicals and allied products, nec
Robert Enman

Olds, AB T4H

D-U-N-S 25-417-2489   (SL)
551546 ALBERTA LTD
OLDS DODGE CHRYSLER JEEP
6207 46 St, Olds, AB, T4H 1L7
(403) 556-7332
Emp Here 27   *Sales* 13,448,106
SIC 5511 New and used car dealers
Joseph Kasawal
Daniel Wiebe

D-U-N-S 25-313-0819   (SL)
645373 ALBERTA LTD
B & M HOME HARDWARE BUILDING CENTRE
6307 46 St, Olds, AB, T4H 1L7
(403) 556-2550
Emp Here 60   *Sales* 16,059,120
SIC 5251 Hardware stores
Bruce Bieber
Mary Bieber

D-U-N-S 24-554-0752   (HQ)
ACCREDITED SUPPORTS TO THE COMMUNITY
ACCREDITED SUPPORTS
4322 50 Ave, Olds, AB, T4H 1A5
(403) 556-4110
Emp Here 92   *Sales* 6,842,200
SIC 8322 Individual and family services
Linda Maxwell
Garry Vooys

D-U-N-S 20-828-4109   (BR)
ALBERTA HEALTH SERVICES
OLDS HOSPITAL & CARE CENTRE
(*Suby of* GOVERNMENT OF THE PROVINCE OF ALBERTA)
3901 57 Ave, Olds, AB, T4H 1T4
(403) 556-3381
Emp Here 230
SIC 8062 General medical and surgical hospitals
Collin Simon

D-U-N-S 25-993-0055   (SL)
B-LINE UTILITIES LTD
5703 48 Ave, Olds, AB, T4H 1V1
(403) 556-8563
Emp Here 50   *Sales* 12,044,200
SIC 1623 Water, sewer, and utility lines
Mark Breakell

D-U-N-S 25-366-7620   (HQ)
BARR-AG LTD
5837 Imperial Dr, Olds, AB, T4H 1G6
(403) 507-8660
Sales 11,137,800
SIC 5191 Farm supplies
Barry Schmitt

D-U-N-S 25-995-6704   (SL)
DELLA SIEGA ENTERPRISES LTD
OLDS GARDENS MARKET IGA
6700 46 St Suite 300, Olds, AB, T4H 0A2
(403) 556-7384
Emp Here 80   *Sales* 23,478,160
SIC 5411 Grocery stores
Rob Della Siega

D-U-N-S 20-521-7920   (SL)
HILDEBRAND MOTORS LTD
6401 46 St, Olds, AB, T4H 1L7
(403) 556-3371
Emp Here 32   *Sales* 15,938,496

SIC 5511 New and used car dealers
Edward P Hildebrand
Marian Hildebrand

D-U-N-S 25-389-1279   (HQ)
MOUNTAIN VIEW CREDIT UNION LTD
4920 50 Ave, Olds, AB, T4H 1P5
(403) 556-3306
Sales 12,280,880
SIC 6062 State credit unions
Neil Venderzwan
Vance Van Dame

D-U-N-S 25-073-8861   (HQ)
MOUNTAIN VIEW PUBLISHING INC
OLDS ALBERTAN, THE
(*Suby of* GREAT WEST NEWSPAPERS LIMITED PARTNERSHIP)
5021 51 St, Olds, AB, T4H 1P6
(403) 556-7510
Emp Here 30   *Sales* 22,275,600
SIC 5192 Books, periodicals, and newspapers
Murray Elliott

D-U-N-S 24-298-1942   (SL)
NETOOK CONSTRUCTION LTD
Gd Stn Main, Olds, AB, T4H 1R4
(403) 556-2166
Emp Here 50   *Sales* 19,182,300
SIC 1389 Oil and gas field services, nec
John Doyle
Katherine Doyle

D-U-N-S 20-636-0091   (SL)
OLDS AUCTION MART LTD
ROSEHILL AUCTION SERVICE
(*Suby of* ROSEHILL AUCTION SERVICE LTD)
4613 54 St, Olds, AB, T4H 1E9
(403) 556-3655
Emp Here 40   *Sales* 17,968,760
SIC 7389 Business services, nec
Danny Rosehill
Jim Crawford

D-U-N-S 20-305-0547   (HQ)
PROALL INTERNATIONAL MFG. INC
5810 47 Ave, Olds, AB, T4H 1V1
(403) 335-9500
Emp Here 50   *Sales* 13,320,060
SIC 3531 Construction machinery
Larry Koop

D-U-N-S 20-988-8197   (HQ)
RICHARDSON BROS (OLDS) LIMITED
Gd, Olds, AB, T4H 1P4
(403) 556-6366
Sales 12,622,100
SIC 1611 Highway and street construction
John (Jack) Richardson
Jeanine Richardson
Lawrence Richardson
Stephen Richardson
Frank Richardson

D-U-N-S 24-014-4840   (HQ)
ROSEHILL AUCTION SERVICE LTD
4613 54 St, Olds, AB, T4H 1E9
(403) 556-3655
Sales 17,968,760
SIC 7389 Business services, nec
Daniel Rosehill
James Crawford
Greg Sanderson

D-U-N-S 20-648-4110   (BR)
SOBEYS CAPITAL INCORPORATED
SOBEYS
(*Suby of* EMPIRE COMPANY LIMITED)
6700 46 St Suite 300, Olds, AB, T4H 0A2
(403) 556-3113
Emp Here 100
SIC 5411 Grocery stores
Robert Dellasigea

D-U-N-S 20-089-4855   (HQ)
WESTVIEW CO-OPERATIVE ASSOCIATION LIMITED

OLD CO-OPERATIVE
5330 46 St, Olds, AB, T4H 1P6
(403) 556-3335
Emp Here 100   *Sales* 44,021,550
SIC 5411 Grocery stores
Rodney Perigny
Keith Norish
Wanda Blatz
Rudy Durieux
Ronald Brown

Onoway, AB T0E

D-U-N-S 20-374-6008   (SL)
ACADEMY FABRICATORS LIMITED PARTNERSHIP
ACADEMY GROUP, THE
(*Suby of* HILLCORE GROUP HOLDINGS LTD)
5208 Lac Ste Anne Tr N, Onoway, AB, T0E 1V0
(780) 967-3111
Emp Here 100   *Sales* 19,208,500
SIC 3498 Fabricated pipe and fittings
Dustin Medori
Garrett Wenckowski

D-U-N-S 24-767-8725   (SL)
MORAND INDUSTRIES LTD
5502 Lac Suite Anne, Onoway, AB, T0E 1V0
(780) 967-2500
Emp Here 40   *Sales* 29,700,800
SIC 5191 Farm supplies
Larry Morrill

Oyen, AB T0J

D-U-N-S 25-317-0765   (BR)
ALBERTA HEALTH SERVICES
BIG COUNTRY HOSPITAL
(*Suby of* GOVERNMENT OF THE PROVINCE OF ALBERTA)
312 3 St E, Oyen, AB, T0J 2J0
(403) 664-3528
Emp Here 110
SIC 8062 General medical and surgical hospitals
Dianne Swantz

Paddle Prairie, AB T0H

D-U-N-S 24-404-4645   (SL)
PADDLE PRAIRIE GAS CO-OP LTD
Gd, Paddle Prairie, AB, T0H 2W0
(780) 981-2467
Emp Here 4   *Sales* 12,423,428
SIC 4925 Gas production and/or distribution
Ken Mcgillivray

Paradise Valley, AB T0B

D-U-N-S 24-702-2783   (SL)
SUNDERLAND HOG FARMS LTD
Gd, Paradise Valley, AB, T0B 3R0
(780) 745-2214
Emp Here 15   *Sales* 18,155,955
SIC 5154 Livestock
Myron Sunderland
Dale Sunderland
Delmer Sunderland

Peace River, AB T8S

D-U-N-S 24-054-3665   (SL)
ADVANCED PARAMEDIC LTD
8703 75 St W, Peace River, AB, T8S 0A5
(780) 624-4911
Emp Here 48   *Sales* 17,339,376
SIC 8049 Offices of health practitioner
Stephen Woodburn

D-U-N-S 25-015-7708   (HQ)
**HOLY FAMILY CATHOLIC REGIONAL DIVI-
SION 37**
HOLY FAMILY CATHOLICS SCHOOLS
10307 99 St, Peace River, AB, T8S 1K1
(780) 624-3956
Emp Here 16   *Sales* 29,735,700
SIC 8211 Elementary and secondary schools
Betty Turpin

D-U-N-S 25-991-7925   (SL)
I C G PROPANE
9504 94 St, Peace River, AB, T8S 1J2

Emp Here 5   *Sales* 15,529,285
SIC 4924 Natural gas distribution

D-U-N-S 20-538-0173   (SL)
**MARSHALL AUTOMOTIVE (PEACE RIVER)
LTD**
7501 100 Ave, Peace River, AB, T8S 1M5
(780) 428-0563
Emp Here 45   *Sales* 22,673,101
SIC 5511 New and used car dealers
Marshall Eliuk
Terry Rosychuk
Denis Kruse

D-U-N-S 24-002-5247   (HQ)
NORTHLAND SCHOOL DIVISION 61
9809 77 Ave, Peace River, AB, T8S 1C9
(780) 624-2060
Emp Here 55   *Sales* 51,541,880
SIC 8211 Elementary and secondary schools
Collin Kelly
Dennis Walsh
Donna Barrett

D-U-N-S 24-002-8969   (SL)
PEACE COUNTRY CO-OP LIMITED
9714 96 Ave, Peace River, AB, T8S 1H8
(780) 624-1096
Emp Here 45   *Sales* 12,336,840
SIC 5411 Grocery stores
Mike Maciasac
Gwenda Fortin
Lance Bushie
Peter Gunning
Joan Jensen
Don Mcivor
Brian Randall
Louise Woroniuk
Rick Biggs
Roy Spychka

D-U-N-S 20-246-1013   (SL)
PEACE FUEL DISTRIBUTORS LTD
PETRO CANADA, DIV OF
7510 99 Ave, Peace River, AB, T8S 1M5
(780) 624-3003
Emp Here 15   *Sales* 15,492,120
SIC 5172 Petroleum products, nec
Ivan Cop

D-U-N-S 20-970-6118   (HQ)
PEACE RIVER SCHOOL DIVISION 10
PRSD
10018 101 St Suite 10, Peace River, AB, T8S
2A5
(780) 624-3601
Emp Here 20   *Sales* 39,647,600
SIC 8211 Elementary and secondary schools
Paul Bennett
Karen Penney
Rhonda Freeman

D-U-N-S 24-672-1237   (BR)
SHELL CANADA LIMITED
(*Suby of* ROYAL DUTCH SHELL PLC)

100 St, Peace River, AB, T8S 1V8
(780) 624-6800
Emp Here 90
SIC 1311 Crude petroleum and natural gas
Cindy Kuhl

D-U-N-S 25-734-0331   (SL)
WEAVER WELDING LTD
7501 107 Ave, Peace River, AB, T8S 1M6
(780) 618-7522
Emp Here 250   *Sales* 99,810,500
SIC 4619 Pipelines, nec
Darren Weaver

Pickardville, AB T0G

D-U-N-S 20-015-2325   (SL)
POLAR BEAR WATER GROUP (1978) LTD
1 Main St, Pickardville, AB, T0G 1W0
(780) 349-4872
Emp Here 24   *Sales* 11,400,624
SIC 5084 Industrial machinery and equipment
Christopher Link

Picture Butte, AB T0K

D-U-N-S 20-547-6877   (SL)
**PICTURE BUTTE AUCTION MARKET 2001
LTD**
Gd, Picture Butte, AB, T0K 1V0
(403) 732-4400
Emp Here 10   *Sales* 12,103,970
SIC 5154 Livestock
Eric Dunsbergen

D-U-N-S 20-354-0133   (HQ)
VAN RAAY PASKAL FARMS LTD
Gd, Picture Butte, AB, T0K 1V0
(403) 732-5641
Sales 308,042,934
SIC 0211 Beef cattle feedlots
Richard Paskal
Colleen Teresa
Cornelius Van Raay
Dwayne Beaton

Pincher Creek, AB T0K

D-U-N-S 25-273-5378   (BR)
ALBERTA HEALTH SERVICES
PINCHER CREEK HOSPITAL
(*Suby of* GOVERNMENT OF THE
PROVINCE OF ALBERTA)
1222 Bev Mclachlin Dr, Pincher Creek, AB,
T0K 1W0
(403) 627-1946
Emp Here 100
SIC 8062 General medical and surgical hospi-
tals
Jordan Koch

D-U-N-S 25-508-5532   (SL)
CASTLE MOUNTAIN RESORT INC
Gd, Pincher Creek, AB, T0K 1W0
(403) 627-5101
Emp Here 150   *Sales* 14,350,200
SIC 7011 Hotels and motels
Ross Mccarthy
Laurent Marechal
Andrew Searby
Darrel Lewko
Emile St. Amand
Jim Harker
Norma Hodgson
Dieter Gerngross
Doug Lougheed
Derrill Murphy

D-U-N-S 20-089-8252   (HQ)
**PINCHER CREEK CO-OPERATIVE ASSO-
CIATION LIMITED**
Gd, Pincher Creek, AB, T0K 1W0
(403) 627-2607
Emp Here 60   *Sales* 23,577,072
SIC 5411 Grocery stores
Ron Knight
Mary E Gambel

D-U-N-S 20-089-8468   (HQ)
RANCHERS SUPPLY INC
1165 Main St, Pincher Creek, AB, T0K 1W0
(403) 627-4451
Emp Here 30   *Sales* 28,501,560
SIC 5083 Farm and garden machinery
Merlin Lewis
Randall Marsh
Mark Hofman
Robin Lewis

D-U-N-S 24-272-6115   (BR)
SHELL CANADA LIMITED
SHELL WATERTON COMPLEX
(*Suby of* ROYAL DUTCH SHELL PLC)
Gd, Pincher Creek, AB, T0K 1W0
(403) 627-7200
Emp Here 150
SIC 1311 Crude petroleum and natural gas
Izak Van Dermerwe

D-U-N-S 24-330-0535   (BR)
WAL-MART CANADA CORP
(*Suby of* WALMART INC.)
1100 Table Mountain Rd, Pincher Creek, AB,
T0K 1W0
(403) 627-1790
Emp Here 200
SIC 5311 Department stores
Don Young

D-U-N-S 20-824-6819   (HQ)
WESTCASTLE MOTORS LTD
1100 Waterton Ave, Pincher Creek, AB, T0K
1W0
(403) 627-3223
Emp Here 26   *Sales* 13,448,106
SIC 5511 New and used car dealers
James Szakacs
Keith Foster

Plamondon, AB T0A

D-U-N-S 20-209-3592   (SL)
SAN FORESTRY LTD
9925 100 St, Plamondon, AB, T0A 2T0

Emp Here 70   *Sales* 10,910,410
SIC 2411 Logging
Nikita Kuznetsov

Ponoka, AB T4J

D-U-N-S 24-351-8326   (BR)
ALBERTA HEALTH SERVICES
PONOKA HOSPITAL & CARE CENTRE
(*Suby of* GOVERNMENT OF THE
PROVINCE OF ALBERTA)
5800 57 Ave, Ponoka, AB, T4J 1P1
(403) 783-8135
Emp Here 200
SIC 8062 General medical and surgical hospi-
tals
Susan Mackenzie

D-U-N-S 20-593-3505   (HQ)
GALLOWAY CONSTRUCTION GROUP LTD
431029 Range Rd 261, Ponoka, AB, T4J 1R4
(403) 783-2599
Emp Here 40   *Sales* 31,555,250
SIC 1623 Water, sewer, and utility lines

Wade Galloway
Lynette Galloway

D-U-N-S 20-384-2740   (SL)
GEMINI FABRICATION LTD
4100 67 St, Ponoka, AB, T4J 1J8

Emp Here 130   *Sales* 24,971,050
SIC 3499 Fabricated Metal products, nec
Andrew Farrow

D-U-N-S 25-361-0257   (BR)
GEMINI FIELD SOLUTIONS LTD
(*Suby of* GEMINI FIELD SOLUTIONS LTD)
4100 67 St, Ponoka, AB, T4J 1J8

Emp Here 140
SIC 7692 Welding repair
Dave Hummel

D-U-N-S 24-643-6919   (SL)
**HUTTERIAN BRETHREN CHURCH OF FER-
RYBANK**
FERRYBANK COLONY
Gd, Ponoka, AB, T4J 1R9
(403) 783-2259
Emp Here 70   *Sales* 12,640,250
SIC 8661 Religious organizations
Andy Gross
Johny Gross
Eddie Gross

D-U-N-S 25-741-9820   (HQ)
LEGACY FORD PONOKA
6305 42 Ave, Ponoka, AB, T4J 1J8
(403) 783-5501
Emp Here 25   *Sales* 17,432,730
SIC 5511 New and used car dealers

D-U-N-S 25-601-9704   (SL)
MORSKATE MANUFACTURING LTD
431053 Range Rd Suite 261, Ponoka, AB, T4J
1R4
(403) 783-6140
Emp Here 50   *Sales* 10,185,800
SIC 7692 Welding repair
Paul Morskate
Ben Morskate

D-U-N-S 20-267-9796   (SL)
PONOKA CHEVROLET OLDSMOBILE LTD
PONOKA CHEVROLET
6305 44 Ave, Ponoka, AB, T4J 1J8
(403) 783-4494
Emp Here 22   *Sales* 10,957,716
SIC 5511 New and used car dealers
Lyle Guthrie

D-U-N-S 20-089-9342   (SL)
PONOKA FOODS LTD
HAMILTON'S IGA
4502 50 St Unit 1, Ponoka, AB, T4J 1J5
(403) 783-4528
Emp Here 45   *Sales* 13,206,465
SIC 5411 Grocery stores
Thomas Allan Hamilton
Martha Peggy Hamilton
James Hamilton

D-U-N-S 24-733-7665   (SL)
**RE/MAX REAL ESTATE CENTRAL AL-
BERTA**
6000 48 Ave Suite 2, Ponoka, AB, T4J 1K2
(403) 783-5007
Emp Here 49   *Sales* 34,143,690
SIC 6799 Investors, nec
Dale Russell

D-U-N-S 24-905-3778   (HQ)
RIMOKA HOUSING FOUNDATION
5608 57 Ave Suite 101, Ponoka, AB, T4J 1P2
(403) 783-0128
Emp Here 1   *Sales* 31,416,675
SIC 6531 Real estate agents and managers
Dale Barr

D-U-N-S 20-775-2452   (HQ)
VOLD, JONES & VOLD AUCTION CO LTD

4410 Highway 2a, Ponoka, AB, T4J 1J8
(403) 783-5561
Sales 95,399,980
SIC 5154 Livestock
Ralph Vold
Blaire Vold

D-U-N-S 25-496-4109   (HQ)
WOLF CREEK SCHOOL DIVISION NO.72
WOLF CREEK PUBLIC SCHOOL
6000 Highway 2a, Ponoka, AB, T4J 1P6
(403) 783-5441
Emp Here 45   *Sales* 71,912,438
SIC 8211 Elementary and secondary schools
Jayson Lovell

Provost, AB T0B

D-U-N-S 24-379-1717   (SL)
1001511 ALBERTA LTD
HARD FLUSHBY
Gd, Provost, AB, T0B 3S0
(780) 753-6404
Emp Here 40   *Sales* 12,788,200
SIC 1389 Oil and gas field services, nec
Brian Varty
Chris Werenka
Darcy Varty
Wesley Ganser

D-U-N-S 20-897-0012   (BR)
ALBERTA HEALTH SERVICES
PROVOST HEALTH CENTRE
(*Suby of* GOVERNMENT OF THE
PROVINCE OF ALBERTA)
5002 54 Ave, Provost, AB, T0B 3S0
(780) 753-2291
Emp Here 100
SIC 8062 General medical and surgical hospitals
Lane Clarke

D-U-N-S 25-538-8233   (SL)
TARGET EXCAVATING INC
Gd, Provost, AB, T0B 3S0
(780) 753-3931
Emp Here 50   *Sales* 12,044,200
SIC 1623 Water, sewer, and utility lines
Harvey Booker

D-U-N-S 20-090-0165   (HQ)
WILMAR IMPLEMENT CO LTD
5803 47 Ave, Provost, AB, T0B 3S0
(780) 753-2278
Emp Here 15   *Sales* 16,150,884
SIC 5083 Farm and garden machinery
Keith Mcelhinney

Rainbow Lake, AB T0H

D-U-N-S 25-971-6314   (BR)
HUSKY OIL OPERATIONS LIMITED
(*Suby of* HUSKY ENERGY INC)
Hwy 58 W, Rainbow Lake, AB, T0H 2Y0
(780) 956-8000
Emp Here 175
SIC 1311 Crude petroleum and natural gas
Dean Lypkie

Raymond, AB T0K

D-U-N-S 25-483-4906   (BR)
**GOVERNMENT OF THE PROVINCE OF AL-
BERTA**
RAYMOND HEALTH CENTRE
(*Suby of* GOVERNMENT OF THE
PROVINCE OF ALBERTA)
150 N 400 E, Raymond, AB, T0K 2S0

(403) 752-5411
Emp Here 100
SIC 8062 General medical and surgical hospitals
Brenda Wright

D-U-N-S 20-990-2931   (SL)
HEGGIE, R. K. GRAIN LTD
Gd, Raymond, AB, T0K 2S0

Emp Here 16   *Sales* 19,366,352
SIC 5153 Grain and field beans
Ronald Heggie
Joanne Heggie

D-U-N-S 24-158-7500   (SL)
MILFORD COLONY FARMING CO. LTD
HUTTERIAN BRETHREN OF MILFORD
Gd, Raymond, AB, T0K 2S0
(403) 752-4478
Emp Here 115   *Sales* 19,437,875
SIC 0111 Wheat
Joseph Kleinsasser

D-U-N-S 20-588-3858   (BR)
WESTWIND SCHOOL DIVISION #74
RAYMOND ELEMENTARY SCHOOL
145 N 200 W, Raymond, AB, T0K 2S0
(403) 752-3004
Emp Here 75
SIC 8211 Elementary and secondary schools
Marlin Hogg

Red Deer, AB T4N

D-U-N-S 25-268-5698   (SL)
341-7777 TAXI LTD
ALBERTA GOLD TAXI
4819 48 Ave Unit 280, Red Deer, AB, T4N 3T2
(403) 341-7777
Emp Here 85   *Sales* 4,664,120
SIC 4121 Taxicabs
John Whittingham
Michelle Trithart
Guy Brousseau
Peter Braconnier

D-U-N-S 20-553-3297   (SL)
835799 ALBERTA LTD
4814 50 St Suite 300, Red Deer, AB, T4N 1X4
(403) 346-7555
Emp Here 50   *Sales* 21,210,597
SIC 6712 Bank holding companies

D-U-N-S 25-269-1241   (SL)
ABACUS DATAGRAPHICS LTD
4814 50 St Suite 300, Red Deer, AB, T4N 1X4
(403) 346-7555
Emp Here 60   *Sales* 10,557,480
SIC 8713 Surveying services
Ted Davis
Noreen Salvais

D-U-N-S 25-947-4971   (BR)
**AGRIFOODS INTERNATIONAL COOPERA-
TIVE LTD**
(*Suby of* AGRIFOODS INTERNATIONAL CO-
OPERATIVE LTD)
5410 50 Ave, Red Deer, AB, T4N 4B5

Emp Here 100
SIC 2021 Creamery butter
Alex Sawchuk

D-U-N-S 20-016-4080   (SL)
ATEK DEVELOPMENTS INC
6320 50 Ave Unit 405, Red Deer, AB, T4N 4C6
(403) 342-4885
Emp Here 100   *Sales* 57,033,800
SIC 1542 Nonresidential construction, nec
Jim Scott
Ray Keller

D-U-N-S 25-273-5394   (BR)
BOARD OF TRUSTEES OF THE RED DEER

PUBLIC SCHOOL DISTRICT NO. 104, THE
*LINDSAY THURBER COMPREHENSIVE
HIGH SCHOOL*
4204 58 St, Red Deer, AB, T4N 2L6
(403) 347-1171
Emp Here 160
SIC 8211 Elementary and secondary schools
Jim Clevette

D-U-N-S 25-948-2602   (BR)
**CANADIAN CORPS OF COMMISSION-
AIRES NATIONAL OFFICE, THE**
*CANADIAN CORPS OF COMMISSION-
AIRES*
(*Suby of* CANADIAN CORPS OF COMMIS-
SIONAIRES NATIONAL OFFICE, THE)
4807 50 Ave Suite 107, Red Deer, AB, T4N
4A5
(403) 314-4142
Emp Here 140
SIC 7381 Detective and armored car services
Eric Taylor

D-U-N-S 24-373-4733   (BR)
CANYON TECHNICAL SERVICES LTD
(*Suby of* TRICAN WELL SERVICE LTD)
28042 Hwy 11 Unit 322, Red Deer, AB, T4N
5H3

Emp Here 120
SIC 1389 Oil and gas field services, nec
Barry Obrien

D-U-N-S 24-552-8955   (HQ)
CASCADIA MOTIVATION INC
4646 Riverside Dr Suite 14a, Red Deer, AB,
T4N 6Y5
(403) 340-8687
Sales 20,798,680
SIC 4724 Travel agencies
Carl Thorsteinson
Robert Thorsteinson
Randy Thorsteinson

D-U-N-S 24-346-3002   (BR)
CATHOLIC SOCIAL SERVICES
(*Suby of* CATHOLIC SOCIAL SERVICES)
5104 48 Ave, Red Deer, AB, T4N 3T8
(403) 347-8844
Emp Here 500
SIC 8361 Residential care
Karen Murphy

D-U-N-S 25-617-8364   (HQ)
CENTRAL ALBERTA CO-OP LTD
6201 46 Ave, Red Deer, AB, T4N 6Z1
(403) 309-8913
Emp Here 10   *Sales* 14,673,850
SIC 5411 Grocery stores
Kelvin Mcgillivray
Wayne Mcallister
Rick Kemp
Garth Yeomans
Dale Hansen
Marno Hultin
Garry Devries
Garry Didrickson
Richard Lemke

D-U-N-S 20-574-5297   (SL)
**CENTRAL ALBERTA RESIDENCE SOCI-
ETY**
C A R S
5000 50 Ave Suite 300, Red Deer, AB, T4N
6C2
(403) 342-4550
Emp Here 49   *Sales* 19,473,286
SIC 8699 Membership organizations, nec
Pat Schropfer

D-U-N-S 25-417-2869   (SL)
DEAN INDUSTRIES, INC
4915 54 St 3rd Flr, Red Deer, AB, T4N 2G7

Emp Here 67   *Sales* 29,960,658
SIC 5051 Metals service centers and offices
Dean Burles
Michelle Burles

D-U-N-S 20-517-3771   (SL)
DEER PARK HOLDINGS LTD
QUALITY INN & CONFERENCE CENTRE
7150 50 Ave, Red Deer, AB, T4N 6A5
(403) 343-8800
Emp Here 150   *Sales* 13,903,500
SIC 7011 Hotels and motels
Steve Park

D-U-N-S 20-547-5853   (BR)
DJ WILL HOLDINGS LIMITED
NORTH HILL INN
(*Suby of* DJ WILL HOLDINGS LIMITED)
7150 50 Ave, Red Deer, AB, T4N 6A5
(403) 343-8800
Emp Here 100
SIC 7011 Hotels and motels
Karen Begin

D-U-N-S 24-906-5392   (BR)
DOW CHEMICAL CANADA ULC
ALBERTA OPERATIONS, PRENTISS SITE
(*Suby of* DOW INC.)
Gd, Red Deer, AB, T4N 6N1
(403) 885-7000
Emp Here 202
SIC 2899 Chemical preparations, nec
Joe Deutscher

D-U-N-S 25-068-0527   (HQ)
EXHAUST MASTERS INC
APD AUTOMOTIVE PARTS DISTRIBUTORS
Gd Stn Postal Box Ctr Box, Red Deer, AB, T4N
5E6
(403) 885-5800
Emp Here 8   *Sales* 17,482,320
SIC 5013 Motor vehicle supplies and new
parts
Kim Schumacher
Donald Schumacher

D-U-N-S 20-090-2419   (HQ)
FARGEYS PAINT & WALL COVERINGS LTD
FARGEY'S DECORATING CENTRE
3433 50 Ave, Red Deer, AB, T4N 3Y3
(403) 343-3133
Emp Here 14   *Sales* 14,850,400
SIC 5198 Paints, varnishes, and supplies
Ed Makarenko

D-U-N-S 24-196-9191   (SL)
**GO AUTO RED DEER CHRYSLER DODGE
JEEP RAM LTD**
3115 50 Ave, Red Deer, AB, T4N 3X8
(403) 352-7999
Emp Here 58   *Sales* 36,498,240
SIC 5511 New and used car dealers
Kevin Allison
Matthew Lauinger

D-U-N-S 20-555-2495   (SL)
HDQ INVESTMENTS LTD
DAIRY QUEEN
4202 50 Ave, Red Deer, AB, T4N 3Z3
(403) 346-3518
Emp Here 105   *Sales* 4,779,495
SIC 5812 Eating places
Rob Hamel
Heather Hamel

D-U-N-S 20-287-1237   (HQ)
HERITAGE FAMILY SERVICES LTD
4825 47 St Suite 300, Red Deer, AB, T4N 1R3
(403) 343-3428
Emp Here 1   *Sales* 11,518,800
SIC 8322 Individual and family services
Henry (Hank) Hubert

D-U-N-S 24-420-4603   (SL)
INEOS CANADA COMPANY
(*Suby of* INEOS AG)
Hwy 815, Red Deer, AB, T4N 6A1
(403) 314-4500
Emp Here 86   *Sales* 23,508,100
SIC 6712 Bank holding companies
Robert Learman
Barry Mackenzie
Gary Cole

▲ Public Company   ■ Public Company Family Member   **HQ** Headquarters   **BR** Branch   **SL** Single Location

D-U-N-S 20-364-3978   (SL)
INEOS CANADA PARTNERSHIP
Gd, Red Deer, AB, T4N 6A1
(403) 314-4500
Emp Here 100   *Sales* 28,402,100
SIC 2869 Industrial organic chemicals, nec
Barry Mckenzie

D-U-N-S 24-029-2131   (SL)
IP FABRICATIONS LTD
6835 52 Ave, Red Deer, AB, T4N 4L2
(403) 343-1797
Emp Here 51   *Sales* 12,555,486
SIC 1799 Special trade contractors, nec
Alex Ivaeenko

D-U-N-S 20-208-4674   (BR)
LEDCOR INDUSTRIES INC
LEDCOR ALBERTA
(*Suby of* 280818 ALBERTA LTD)
27420 Township Rd Suite 374, Red Deer, AB, T4N 5H3
(403) 309-7129
Emp Here 150
SIC 1611 Highway and street construction
Gary Mayhew

D-U-N-S 24-982-1745   (BR)
LOBLAWS INC
REAL CANADIAN SUPERSTORE
(*Suby of* LOBLAW COMPANIES LIMITED)
5016a 51 Ave, Red Deer, AB, T4N 4H5
(403) 350-3531
Emp Here 200
SIC 5411 Grocery stores
Kevin Le

D-U-N-S 24-802-8404   (BR)
MEGLOBAL CANADA INC
(*Suby of* MEGLOBAL CANADA INC)
Hwy 597 Prentiss Rd, Red Deer, AB, T4N 6N1
(403) 885-7000
Emp Here 100
SIC 5169 Chemicals and allied products, nec
Rocco Schurink

D-U-N-S 20-373-1112   (SL)
MEGLOBAL CANADA ULC
Hwy 597 & Prentiss Rd, Red Deer, AB, T4N 6N1

Emp Here 100   *Sales* 27,666,000
SIC 2819 Industrial inorganic chemicals, nec

D-U-N-S 20-920-3111   (SL)
MENTAL HEALTH SERVICES
4733 49 St, Red Deer, AB, T4N 1T6
(403) 340-5466
Emp Here 100   *Sales* 7,512,900
SIC 8093 Specialty outpatient clinics, nec
Eric Johnson

D-U-N-S 24-700-3130   (SL)
MOONEY INSURANCE AGENCY LTD
4910 45 St, Red Deer, AB, T4N 1K6

Emp Here 37   *Sales* 18,950,800
SIC 6411 Insurance agents, brokers, and service
Bryan Pobihushchy
Clayton Dexter
Larry Carr

D-U-N-S 25-400-2058   (SL)
MURRAY, DON A. HOLDINGS LTD
CANADIAN TIRE
6380 50 Ave Suite 300, Red Deer, AB, T4N 4C6
(403) 346-1497
Emp Here 75   *Sales* 15,400,725
SIC 5311 Department stores
Don Murray
Debbie Murray

D-U-N-S 20-090-3961   (SL)
NORTHWEST MOTORS (RED DEER) LIMITED
3115 50 Ave, Red Deer, AB, T4N 3X8

(403) 346-2035
Emp Here 65   *Sales* 40,903,200
SIC 5511 New and used car dealers
Graham Moore
Fred Moore
Brent Moore
Daniel T. Moore
Ruth M. Moore
Joanne K. Moore
Isabelle Moore
Laura Moore
Carla Moore

D-U-N-S 25-453-9810   (BR)
NOVA CHEMICALS (CANADA) LTD
NOVA CHEMICALS
(*Suby of* GOVERNMENT OF ABU DHABI)
Gd, Red Deer, AB, T4N 5E6
(403) 314-8611
Emp Here 850
SIC 2821 Plastics materials and resins
Terry Vanzeist

D-U-N-S 24-599-3704   (SL)
OGILVIE, BRIAN HOLDING LTD
88 Howarth St Suite 5, Red Deer, AB, T4N 6V9
(403) 342-6307
Emp Here 67   *Sales* 42,161,760
SIC 5541 Gasoline service stations
Brian Ogilvie

D-U-N-S 25-217-5500   (SL)
PARKLAND COMMUNITY LIVING AND SUPPORTS SOCIETY
PARKLAND C.L.A.S.S.
6010 45 Ave, Red Deer, AB, T4N 3M4
(403) 347-3333
Emp Here 600   *Sales* 46,075,200
SIC 8322 Individual and family services
Daniel (Dan) Verstraete

D-U-N-S 20-122-7480   (HQ)
PARKLAND INDUSTRIES LIMITED PARTNERSHIP
COLUMBIA FUELS, DIV OF
4919 59 St Suite 236, Red Deer, AB, T4N 6C9
(403) 343-1515
Emp Here 100   *Sales* 1,842,912,500
SIC 2911 Petroleum refining
Phyllis Hay

D-U-N-S 25-316-4297   (BR)
PASLEY, MAX ENTERPRISES LIMITED
MCDONALD'S RESTAURANTS 7031
7149 50 Ave, Red Deer, AB, T4N 4E4
(403) 342-2226
Emp Here 80
SIC 5812 Eating places
Jennifer Derlago

D-U-N-S 24-962-3539   (HQ)
PHONE EXPERTS COMMUNICATIONS LTD, THE
4724 60 St, Red Deer, AB, T4N 7C7
(403) 343-1122
Emp Here 60   *Sales* 27,416,640
SIC 4899 Communication services, nec
Clint Oakley
Bradley Dufresne
Ivan Becker

D-U-N-S 20-636-5322   (SL)
PRAIRIE BUS LINES LTD
(*Suby of* PACIFIC WESTERN TRANSPORTATION LTD)
5310 54 St, Red Deer, AB, T4N 6M1
(403) 342-6390
Emp Here 90   *Sales* 6,774,480
SIC 4151 School buses
Robert Colborne
William Hamilton

D-U-N-S 25-770-3488   (BR)
PRIMERICA LIFE INSURANCE COMPANY OF CANADA
PRIMERICA FINANCIAL SERVICES
(*Suby of* PRIMERICA, INC.)

5580 45 St Unit C 8, Red Deer, AB, T4N 1L1
(403) 347-2829
Emp Here 80
SIC 8741 Management services
Bernadette Lougheed

D-U-N-S 24-364-7554   (SL)
QUALITY TUBING CANADA INC
QUALITY TUBING
4610 49 Ave Suite 103, Red Deer, AB, T4N 6M5
(403) 342-1000
Emp Here 10   *Sales* 10,003,390
SIC 5051 Metals service centers and offices
Terry O'connor

D-U-N-S 20-090-4381   (HQ)
QUINN'S PRODUCTION SERVICES INC
6798 52 Ave, Red Deer, AB, T4N 4K9
(780) 499-0299
Emp Here 95   *Sales* 70,219,250
SIC 3533 Oil and gas field machinery
Doug Quinn

D-U-N-S 25-497-3076   (HQ)
RED DEER CATHOLIC REGIONAL DIVISION NO. 39
5210 61 St, Red Deer, AB, T4N 6N8
(403) 343-1055
Emp Here 20   *Sales* 81,948,136
SIC 8211 Elementary and secondary schools
Paul Mason

D-U-N-S 24-854-2854   (SL)
RED DEER CHILD CARE SOCIETY
5571 45 St Unit 2, Red Deer, AB, T4N 1L2
(403) 347-7973
Emp Here 100   *Sales* 6,106,900
SIC 8351 Child day care services
Rob Elliot
Erin Tibble
Jennifer Winters

D-U-N-S 20-090-4472   (HQ)
RED DEER CO-OP LIMITED
5118 47 Ave, Red Deer, AB, T4N 3P7
(403) 340-1766
Emp Here 75   *Sales* 117,390,800
SIC 5411 Grocery stores
Larry Parks
Jim Dick

D-U-N-S 20-990-6973   (HQ)
RED DEER COLLEGE
100 College Blvd, Red Deer, AB, T4N 5H5
(403) 342-3300
Sales 94,956,002
SIC 8222 Junior colleges
Joel Ward
Jim Brinkhurst

D-U-N-S 20-070-4091   (SL)
RED DEER LODGE LTD
4311 49 Ave, Red Deer, AB, T4N 5Y7
(403) 754-5503
Emp Here 200   *Sales* 18,538,000
SIC 7011 Hotels and motels
John Mytz

D-U-N-S 20-112-2301   (HQ)
RIFCO INC
4909 49 St Suite 702, Red Deer, AB, T4N 1V1
(403) 314-1288
Sales 27,639,878,398
SIC 6141 Personal credit institutions
Bill Graham
Warren Van Orman
Doug Decksheimer
Roger Saran
Jim Nieuwenburg
Stuart Hensman
K. Gerry Wagner
Lance Kadatz
Barry Shafran

D-U-N-S 20-337-5100   (SL)
RIFCO NATIONAL AUTO FINANCE CORPORATION

(*Suby of* RIFCO INC)
4909 49 St Suite 702, Red Deer, AB, T4N 1V1
(403) 314-1288
Emp Here 83   *Sales* 18,587,103
SIC 6141 Personal credit institutions
William Graham

D-U-N-S 24-805-5782   (HQ)
ROLL'N OILFIELD INDUSTRIES LTD
(*Suby of* ROWDAR INDUSTRIES INC)
5208 53 Ave Suite 305, Red Deer, AB, T4N 5K2
(403) 343-1710
Sales 27,335,000
SIC 6719 Holding companies, nec
Brad Rowbotham

D-U-N-S 24-647-1783   (SL)
SCOTT, GORD NISSAN INC
6863 50 Ave, Red Deer, AB, T4N 4E2
(403) 347-2258
Emp Here 25   *Sales* 12,451,950
SIC 5511 New and used car dealers
Gordon Scott

D-U-N-S 20-439-3540   (SL)
SCOTT, KIPP PONTIAC BUICK LTD
6841 50 Ave, Red Deer, AB, T4N 4E2
(403) 343-6633
Emp Here 60   *Sales* 37,756,800
SIC 5511 New and used car dealers
Griffith (Kipp) Scott
Gordon Scott

D-U-N-S 20-725-5253   (BR)
SERVUS CREDIT UNION LTD
(*Suby of* SERVUS CREDIT UNION LTD)
4901 48 St Suite 201, Red Deer, AB, T4N 6M4
(403) 342-5533
Emp Here 300
SIC 6062 State credit unions
Jenine Angell

D-U-N-S 24-086-5477   (SL)
SHUNDA CONSULTING & CONSTRUCTION MANAGEMENT LTD
SHUNDA CONSTRUCTION
6204 46 Ave, Red Deer, AB, T4N 7A2
(403) 347-6931
Emp Here 50   *Sales* 28,516,900
SIC 1542 Nonresidential construction, nec
Ben Meyer

D-U-N-S 25-271-0504   (BR)
SOBEYS WEST INC
PORT O'CALL SAFEWAY
(*Suby of* EMPIRE COMPANY LIMITED)
4408 50 Ave, Red Deer, AB, T4N 3Z6
(403) 346-1886
Emp Here 100
SIC 5411 Grocery stores

D-U-N-S 20-768-5413   (HQ)
TERROCO INDUSTRIES LTD
TERROCO OILFIELD SERVICES
Gd, Red Deer, AB, T4N 5E1
(403) 346-1171
Emp Here 100   *Sales* 100,901,850
SIC 1389 Oil and gas field services, nec
John Amundson

D-U-N-S 20-090-5289   (SL)
TRIPLE A ELECTRIC LTD
6209 46 Ave Suite 1, Red Deer, AB, T4N 6Z1
(403) 346-6156
Emp Here 75   *Sales* 16,337,175
SIC 1731 Electrical work
Malcolm Hough
Lorraine Hough
Allan S Hough

D-U-N-S 25-777-1212   (SL)
VALLEY PARK MANOR NURSING HOME
5505 60 Ave, Red Deer, AB, T4N 4W2

Emp Here 112   *Sales* 7,679,392
SIC 8051 Skilled nursing care facilities
Pam Krill

▲ Public Company   ■ Public Company Family Member   **HQ** Headquarters   **BR** Branch   **SL** Single Location

D-U-N-S 20-740-7730   (BR)
WAL-MART CANADA CORP
(Suby of WALMART INC.)
6375 50 Ave, Red Deer, AB, T4N 4C7
(403) 346-6650
Emp Here 200
SIC 5311 Department stores
Rob Martin

Red Deer, AB T4P

D-U-N-S 24-242-0730   (SL)
1076528 ALBERTA LTD
RED DEER MOTORS
6720 Johnstone Dr, Red Deer, AB, T4P 3Y2
(403) 347-7777
Emp Here 25   *Sales* 12,451,950
SIC 5521 Used car dealers
Rich Anderson

D-U-N-S 24-352-5917   (HQ)
1246607 ALBERTA LTD
8080 Edgar Industrial Cres, Red Deer, AB, T4P 3R3
(403) 347-9727
Sales 73,994,690
SIC 1381 Drilling oil and gas wells
Frank Tirpak
Patricia Tirpak
Grant Hater

D-U-N-S 25-764-2702   (SL)
406421 ALBERTA LTD
8133 Edgar Industrial Close, Red Deer, AB, T4P 3R4
(403) 340-9825
Emp Here 100   *Sales* 31,970,500
SIC 1381 Drilling oil and gas wells
Jed Wood

D-U-N-S 24-442-7910   (SL)
804652 ALBERTA LTD
RED DEER OVER DOOR
7703 Edgar Industrial Dr Suite 1, Red Deer, AB, T4P 3R2
(403) 343-1316
Emp Here 35   *Sales* 15,651,090
SIC 5031 Lumber, plywood, and millwork
Kenneth (Ken) Unger
Sandra Unger

D-U-N-S 20-273-8845   (SL)
8273537 CANADA LIMITED
SINNOTT'S YIG
3 Clearview Market Way, Red Deer, AB, T4P 0M9
(403) 342-1265
Emp Here 49   *Sales* 13,433,448
SIC 5411 Grocery stores

D-U-N-S 20-191-7767   (BR)
BAKER HUGHES CANADA COMPANY
COILED TUBING DISTRICT, DIV OF
(Suby of GENERAL ELECTRIC COMPANY)
4089 77 St, Red Deer, AB, T4P 2T3
(403) 357-1401
Emp Here 180
SIC 1389 Oil and gas field services, nec
Ken Koizumi

D-U-N-S 20-191-8773   (BR)
BAKER HUGHES CANADA COMPANY
(Suby of GENERAL ELECTRIC COMPANY)
7880 Edgar Industrial Dr, Red Deer, AB, T4P 3R2
(403) 340-3015
Emp Here 300
SIC 1389 Oil and gas field services, nec
Ralph Underwood

D-U-N-S 20-090-1445   (HQ)
BORDER PAVING LTD
6711 Golden West Ave, Red Deer, AB, T4P 1A7

(403) 343-1177
Emp Here 40   *Sales* 35,846,764
SIC 1611 Highway and street construction
Victor G. Walls
Wendolyne Walls
Tim Smith

D-U-N-S 20-090-1502   (SL)
BRUIN'S PLUMBING & HEATING LTD
7026 Johnstone Dr, Red Deer, AB, T4P 3Y6
(403) 343-6060
Emp Here 85   *Sales* 19,810,525
SIC 1711 Plumbing, heating, air-conditioning
Herman Bruin
Reyer Cor Bruin
Carol Bruin

D-U-N-S 20-208-3858   (BR)
CALFRAC WELL SERVICES LTD
(Suby of CALFRAC WELL SERVICES LTD)
7310 Edgar Industrial Dr, Red Deer, AB, T4P 3R2
(866) 772-3722
Emp Here 100
SIC 1381 Drilling oil and gas wells
Bard Larson

D-U-N-S 24-517-4073   (SL)
CAMDON CONSTRUCTION LTD
6780 76 St, Red Deer, AB, T4P 4G6
(403) 343-1233
Emp Here 30   *Sales* 14,121,930
SIC 1542 Nonresidential construction, nec
Troy Spelt

D-U-N-S 20-894-6488   (BR)
CANADIAN CONTRACT CLEANING SPECIALISTS, INC
(Suby of HARVEST PARTNERS, LP)
7550 40 Ave, Red Deer, AB, T4P 2H8
(403) 348-8440
Emp Here 75
SIC 7349 Building maintenance services, nec
Tyler Webb

D-U-N-S 24-647-0421   (HQ)
CANALTA CONTROLS LTD
(Suby of BLUE ROCK MANAGEMENT LTD)
6759 65 Ave, Red Deer, AB, T4P 1X5
(403) 342-4494
Emp Here 62   *Sales* 38,002,080
SIC 5084 Industrial machinery and equipment
Derold Clark
Michael Clark

D-U-N-S 20-086-7385   (SL)
CANTECH TUBULAR SERVICES LTD
7983 Edgar Industrial Dr Suite A, Red Deer, AB, T4P 3R2

Emp Here 52   *Sales* 23,253,048
SIC 5051 Metals service centers and offices
Darcy Ludwig
Craig Dore

D-U-N-S 24-725-3615   (SL)
CGC GYPSUM
7550 40 Ave, Red Deer, AB, T4P 2H8
(403) 277-0586
Emp Here 49   *Sales* 10,197,652
SIC 3699 Electrical equipment and supplies, nec
Tyler Webb

D-U-N-S 24-382-5689   (HQ)
COLLICUTT ENERGY SERVICES CORP
8133 Edgar Industrial Close, Red Deer, AB, T4P 3R4
(403) 309-9250
Emp Here 55   *Sales* 33,538,050
SIC 5063 Electrical apparatus and equipment
Steven Collicutt
Ryan Krutzfeldt

D-U-N-S 24-906-7117   (SL)
COMMUNICATIONS GROUP RED DEER LTD
7434 50 Ave, Red Deer, AB, T4P 1X7

(403) 347-0777
Emp Here 75   *Sales* 13,859,850
SIC 4899 Communication services, nec
Bruce Heroux
Eugene Andres

D-U-N-S 20-740-7573   (SL)
COSMOS I BOTTLE DEPOT
7428 49 Ave Suite 1, Red Deer, AB, T4P 1M2
(403) 342-2034
Emp Here 90   *Sales* 40,429,710
SIC 7389 Business services, nec
Lynda Olson

D-U-N-S 20-599-7737   (SL)
DEERMART EQUIPMENT SALES LTD
6705 Golden West Ave, Red Deer, AB, T4P 1A7
(403) 343-2238
Emp Here 42   *Sales* 13,675,200
SIC 5999 Miscellaneous retail stores, nec
John Donald
Abe Derksen
Jack Donald

D-U-N-S 20-743-9258   (HQ)
DUCKERING'S TRANSPORT LTD
7794 47 Avenue Close, Red Deer, AB, T4P 2J9
(403) 346-8855
Emp Here 25   *Sales* 13,337,280
SIC 4213 Trucking, except local
Dan Duckering
Dave Duckering
Ian Littlefair

D-U-N-S 20-731-7020   (SL)
ECHO NDE INC
53 Burnt Park Dr, Red Deer, AB, T4P 0J7
(403) 347-7042
Emp Here 60   *Sales* 19,182,300
SIC 1389 Oil and gas field services, nec
Jeffrey Leedahl

D-U-N-S 25-087-8980   (HQ)
ELECTROGAS MONITORS LTD
7961 49 Ave Suite 1, Red Deer, AB, T4P 2V5
(403) 341-6167
Emp Here 20   *Sales* 11,451,924
SIC 5099 Durable goods, nec
Lana Stenhouse
Ashley Hoffer

D-U-N-S 20-296-1707   (HQ)
EXPRO GROUP CANADA INC
8130 49 Ave Close, Red Deer, AB, T4P 2V5
(877) 340-0911
Emp Here 1   *Sales* 12,788,200
SIC 1389 Oil and gas field services, nec
Frank Oriold

D-U-N-S 25-999-2829   (BR)
EXTENDICARE INC
EXTENDICARE MICHENER HILL
(Suby of EXTENDICARE INC)
12 Michener Blvd Suite 3609, Red Deer, AB, T4P 0M1
(403) 348-0340
Emp Here 400
SIC 8051 Skilled nursing care facilities
Terry Van Bocquestal

D-U-N-S 20-776-3363   (SL)
F C C REPAIRS
7493 49 Ave Cres Suite 5, Red Deer, AB, T4P 1X6
(403) 343-0092
Emp Here 30   *Sales* 14,942,340
SIC 5541 Gasoline service stations
Dwayne Knight

D-U-N-S 20-114-3091   (HQ)
FIREMASTER OILFIELD SERVICES INC
4728 78a St Close, Red Deer, AB, T4P 2J2
(403) 342-7500
Emp Here 55   *Sales* 35,488,600
SIC 8748 Business consulting, nec
Bryce Hume
William Monkman

D-U-N-S 24-012-6813   (SL)
FREIGHTLINER OF RED DEER INC
8046 Edgar Industrial Cres, Red Deer, AB, T4P 3R3
(403) 309-8225
Emp Here 45   *Sales* 22,413,510
SIC 5511 New and used car dealers

D-U-N-S 20-052-7013   (SL)
GOLDEC HAMMS MANUFACTURING LTD
6760 65 Ave, Red Deer, AB, T4P 1A5
(403) 343-6607
Emp Here 55   *Sales* 10,564,675
SIC 3443 Fabricated plate work (boiler shop)
David Gerrard

D-U-N-S 24-300-1237   (SL)
GOODMEN ROOFING LTD
7700 76 St Close Suite 110, Red Deer, AB, T4P 4G6
(403) 343-0380
Emp Here 65   *Sales* 14,158,885
SIC 1761 Roofing, siding, and sheetMetal work
Michel Jacques

D-U-N-S 24-174-7521   (BR)
GRANT PRODUCTION TESTING SERVICES LTD
(Suby of GRANT CORPORATION)
6750 Golden West Ave, Red Deer, AB, T4P 1A8
(403) 314-0042
Emp Here 100
SIC 8748 Business consulting, nec
Dustin Money

D-U-N-S 24-971-9089   (BR)
HALLIBURTON GROUP CANADA INC
HALLIBURTON ENERGY SERVICES
(Suby of HALLIBURTON COMPANY)
8145 Edgar Industrial Close, Red Deer, AB, T4P 3R4
(800) 335-6333
Emp Here 280
SIC 1389 Oil and gas field services, nec
Chris Anderson

D-U-N-S 20-708-9504   (BR)
HI-WAY 9 EXPRESS LTD
(Suby of MULLEN GROUP LTD)
4120 78 St Cres Suite 4120, Red Deer, AB, T4P 3E3
(403) 342-4266
Emp Here 90
SIC 4212 Local trucking, without storage
Rick Johnson

D-U-N-S 24-552-3287   (HQ)
IROC ENERGY SERVICES CORP
(Suby of WESTERN ENERGY SERVICES CORP)
8113 49 Ave Close, Red Deer, AB, T4P 2V5
(403) 346-9710
Emp Here 1   *Sales* 191,089,850
SIC 1389 Oil and gas field services, nec
Thomas M Alford
Brian D Neeland
Bradley Fedora
Donald Copeland
William Austin

D-U-N-S 20-921-2401   (HQ)
ISOLATION EQUIPMENT SERVICES INC
8102 49 Ave Close Unit B, Red Deer, AB, T4P 2V5
(403) 342-0032
Emp Here 40   *Sales* 80,721,480
SIC 1389 Oil and gas field services, nec
Bruce Cherewyk
Jerry Johnson

D-U-N-S 24-810-5652   (SL)
L & R DISTRIBUTORS LTD
8120 Edgar Industrial Dr, Red Deer, AB, T4P 3R2

Emp Here 11   *Sales* 11,360,888

SIC 5171 Petroleum bulk stations and terminals
Gerald (Jerry) Derko
Arnie Derko

D-U-N-S 24-552-8765   (HQ)
LONKAR SERVICES LTD
8080 Edgar Industrial Cres, Red Deer, AB,
T4P 3R3
(403) 347-9727
Emp Here 25   *Sales* 84,084,875
SIC 1389 Oil and gas field services, nec
Frank Tirpak
Tim Albers

D-U-N-S 20-181-1028   (BR)
MCCOY GLOBAL INC
MCCOY CORPORATION
(*Suby of* MCCOY GLOBAL INC)
7911 Edgar Industrial Dr, Red Deer, AB, T4P
3R2
(780) 453-3277
Emp Here 90
SIC 3533 Oil and gas field machinery
Kelly Carlson

D-U-N-S 20-334-6064   (HQ)
MISTRAS CANADA, INC
(*Suby of* MISTRAS GROUP, INC.)
8109 Edgar Industrial Dr, Red Deer, AB, T4P
3R2
(403) 556-1350
Sales 26,953,140
SIC 7389 Business services, nec
Sotirios Vahaviolos

D-U-N-S 25-533-4062   (BR)
NABORS DRILLING CANADA LIMITED
NABORS PRODUCTION SERVICES
(*Suby of* NABORS DRILLING CANADA LIMITED)
8112 Edgar Industrial Dr, Red Deer, AB, T4P
3R2

Emp Here 125
SIC 1389 Oil and gas field services, nec
Darrell Mcintyre

D-U-N-S 24-364-3314   (SL)
NOSSACK DISTRIBUTION CENTRE
7240 Johnstone Dr Suite 100, Red Deer, AB,
T4P 3Y6
(403) 346-5006
Emp Here 55   *Sales* 19,012,950
SIC 2099 Food preparations, nec
Karsten Nossack

D-U-N-S 24-119-3218   (SL)
NOSSACK FINE MEATS LTD
7240 Johnstone Dr Suite 100, Red Deer, AB,
T4P 3Y6
(403) 346-5006
Emp Here 70   *Sales* 58,490,390
SIC 5147 Meats and meat products
Karsten Nossack
Ingrid Nossack

D-U-N-S 24-013-9225   (BR)
NOVA CHEMICALS (CANADA) LTD
(*Suby of* GOVERNMENT OF ABU DHABI)
4940 81 St Suite 6, Red Deer, AB, T4P 3V3
(403) 314-8611
Emp Here 500
SIC 2869 Industrial organic chemicals, nec
Rick Vanhemmen

D-U-N-S 20-830-5029   (HQ)
PEAVEY INDUSTRIES LIMITED
PEAVEY MART
7740 40 Ave, Red Deer, AB, T4P 2H9
(403) 346-8991
Emp Here 100   *Sales* 151,204,900
SIC 5251 Hardware stores
Richard M. Anderson
George Majkut
Kevin Higa
Andrew Logsdail

D-U-N-S 24-785-9333   (SL)

PHOENIX CONSTRUCTION INC
7887 50 Ave Suite 8, Red Deer, AB, T4P 1M8
(403) 342-2225
Emp Here 40   *Sales* 18,829,240
SIC 1542 Nonresidential construction, nec
Howard Beamish
Doug Davies
Ken Erickson

D-U-N-S 24-203-0190   (HQ)
**PREMIER INTEGRATED TECHNOLOGIES
LTD**
(*Suby of* SUPERIOR ENERGY SERVICES,
INC.)
14 Burnt Valley Ave Unit 210, Red Deer, AB,
T4P 0M5
(403) 887-1200
Sales 38,342,703
SIC 1389 Oil and gas field services, nec
Tomas (Tom) Code

D-U-N-S 20-280-4993   (SL)
PRIME BOILER SERVICES LTD
155 Queens Dr, Red Deer, AB, T4P 0R3
(403) 314-2140
Emp Here 200   *Sales* 46,613,000
SIC 1711 Plumbing, heating, air-conditioning
Eric Madsen
Jayne Madsen
Calvin Madsen

D-U-N-S 25-681-2025   (HQ)
PUMPS & PRESSURE INC
7018 Johnstone Dr, Red Deer, AB, T4P 3Y6
(403) 340-3666
Emp Here 50   *Sales* 56,088,950
SIC 5084 Industrial machinery and equipment
John Tremain
Dale Cripps
Sandra Tremain
Wes Gyori

D-U-N-S 20-352-6686   (HQ)
Q2 ARTIFICIAL LIFT SERVICES ULC
7883 Edgar Industrial Way, Red Deer, AB, T4P
3R2
(403) 343-8802
Emp Here 100   *Sales* 121,932,500
SIC 5082 Construction and mining machinery
Douglas Quinn
Colin Heidel
David St. Louis
Michael Conner

D-U-N-S 20-269-0541   (SL)
QUINN DRILLING INC
788 St Edgar Industrial Way, Red Deer, AB,
T4P 3R2
(403) 343-8802
Emp Here 150   *Sales* 37,866,300
SIC 1629 Heavy construction, nec
Douglas Quinn

D-U-N-S 20-090-4456   (SL)
RED DEER BOTTLING COMPANY LTD
RED DEER BOTTLING COCA COLA
6855 Edgar Industrial Dr, Red Deer, AB, T4P
3R2
(403) 346-2585
Emp Here 36   *Sales* 30,080,772
SIC 5149 Groceries and related products, nec
Alfio Truant
Mike Truant

D-U-N-S 24-313-4272   (HQ)
RED DEER IRONWORKS INC
RDI
(*Suby of* DOMINO MACHINE INC)
6430 Golden West Ave, Red Deer, AB, T4P
1A6
(403) 343-1141
Sales 15,540,070
SIC 3533 Oil and gas field machinery
Gregory Bertelsen

D-U-N-S 20-049-0113   (SL)
RED FLAME INDUSTRIES INC
(*Suby of* STEEL WORKS CANADA LTD)

6736 71 St, Red Deer, AB, T4P 3Y7
(403) 343-2012
Emp Here 35   *Sales* 11,189,675
SIC 1389 Oil and gas field services, nec
Jared Sayers

D-U-N-S 24-031-9942   (SL)
**REZONE WELL OIL AND GAS SERVICE
REPAIR**
8071 Edgar Industrial Dr, Red Deer, AB, T4P
3R2
(403) 342-7772
Emp Here 55   *Sales* 17,583,775
SIC 1381 Drilling oil and gas wells
Dave Malone

D-U-N-S 24-041-4586   (SL)
RICHARDSON, ALISON REALTOR
SUDDEN REALTY
47 Roth Cres, Red Deer, AB, T4P 2Y7
(403) 358-1557
Emp Here 40   *Sales* 11,053,064
SIC 6531 Real estate agents and managers
Alison Richardson

D-U-N-S 25-682-3600   (BR)
SANJEL CANADA LTD
8051 Edgar Industrial Dr, Red Deer, AB, T4P
3R2
(403) 357-1616
Emp Here 120
SIC 1389 Oil and gas field services, nec
Barry Mawer

D-U-N-S 25-453-9646   (BR)
SCHLUMBERGER CANADA LIMITED
SCHLUMBERGER WELL SERVICES
6794 65 Ave, Red Deer, AB, T4P 1A5
(403) 356-4398
Emp Here 200
SIC 1389 Oil and gas field services, nec
Darren Wolverton

D-U-N-S 24-159-4449   (HQ)
SCOTT BUILDERS INC
8105 49 Ave Close, Red Deer, AB, T4P 2V5
(403) 343-7270
Emp Here 50   *Sales* 31,705,275
SIC 1541 Industrial buildings and warehouses
Murray Cunningham
Hans Te Stroete
Terry Bolen

D-U-N-S 25-766-6107   (HQ)
SPM FLOW CONTROL LTD
(*Suby of* WEIR GROUP PLC(THE))
8060 Edgar Industrial Cres Unit A, Red Deer,
AB, T4P 3R3
(403) 341-3410
Emp Here 25   *Sales* 15,026,135
SIC 1389 Oil and gas field services, nec
Craig Ralston
Gavin Nicol

D-U-N-S 24-803-1283   (SL)
STANDARD WEST STEEL LTD
6749 65 Ave, Red Deer, AB, T4P 1X5
(403) 358-4227
Emp Here 50   *Sales* 10,141,500
SIC 3441 Fabricated structural Metal
Jeffrey Anderson

D-U-N-S 20-385-9020   (SL)
**STUART OLSON INDUSTRIAL SERVICES
LTD**
(*Suby of* STUART OLSON INC)
8024 Edgar Industrial Cres Unit 102, Red
Deer, AB, T4P 3R3
(780) 481-9600
Emp Here 200   *Sales* 23,504,310
SIC 1541 Industrial buildings and warehouses
David Lemay
Richard Stone
Bill Pohl

D-U-N-S 25-230-9893   (HQ)
STUDON ELECTRIC & CONTROLS INC
8024 Edgar Industrial Cres Unit 102, Red

Deer, AB, T4P 3R3
(403) 342-1666
Sales 57,935,214
SIC 1731 Electrical work
Douglas Rogers
Donald Sutherland
Martin Hilsenteger

D-U-N-S 24-767-0268   (SL)
TIMCON CONSTRUCTION (1988) LTD
7445 45 Ave Close Suite 100, Red Deer, AB,
T4P 4C2
(403) 347-1953
Emp Here 25   *Sales* 11,768,275
SIC 1542 Nonresidential construction, nec
Dirk Wunsch
Paul Beaumont

D-U-N-S 25-387-5157   (HQ)
WATTS PROJECTS INC
82 Queens Dr, Red Deer, AB, T4P 0R4
(403) 358-5555
Emp Here 1   *Sales* 20,798,680
SIC 4789 Transportation services, nec
Collin Watts
Wes Gyori

D-U-N-S 20-744-3581   (HQ)
WESTWARD PARTS SERVICES LTD
6517 67 St, Red Deer, AB, T4P 1A3
(403) 347-2200
Emp Here 65   *Sales* 38,002,080
SIC 5083 Farm and garden machinery
Gary Harris
Ryan Harris

Red Deer, AB T4R

D-U-N-S 24-495-3667   (SL)
307711 ALBERTA LTD
HONDA RED DEER SALES
(*Suby of* GO AUTO CORPORATION)
1824 49 Ave, Red Deer, AB, T4R 2N7
(403) 347-7700
Emp Here 60   *Sales* 37,756,800
SIC 5511 New and used car dealers
Michael Priestner

D-U-N-S 25-371-6989   (BR)
BEST BUY CANADA LTD
BEST BUY
(*Suby of* BEST BUY CO., INC.)
5001 19 St Unit 800, Red Deer, AB, T4R 3R1
(403) 314-5645
Emp Here 100
SIC 5731 Radio, television, and electronic
stores

D-U-N-S 24-986-2868   (BR)
BETHANY CARE SOCIETY
(*Suby of* BETHANY CARE SOCIETY)
99 College Cir, Red Deer, AB, T4R 0M3
(403) 357-3700
Emp Here 300
SIC 8322 Individual and family services
Val Trotter

D-U-N-S 24-806-2374   (SL)
BLACK KNIGHT INN LTD
2929 50 Ave, Red Deer, AB, T4R 1H1
(403) 343-6666
Emp Here 120   *Sales* 11,122,800
SIC 7011 Hotels and motels
Ken Mandrusiak

D-U-N-S 20-116-8254   (BR)
BLACK PRESS GROUP LTD
RED DEER ADVOCATE
(*Suby of* BLACK PRESS HOLDINGS LTD)
2950 Bremner Ave, Red Deer, AB, T4R 1M9
(403) 343-2400
Emp Here 150
SIC 2711 Newspapers
Fred Gorman

▲ Public Company   ■ Public Company Family Member   **HQ** Headquarters   **BR** Branch   **SL** Single Location

D-U-N-S 25-269-7479   (BR)
BOARD OF TRUSTEES OF THE RED DEER PUBLIC SCHOOL DISTRICT NO. 104, THE
HUNTING HILLS HIGH SCHOOL
150 Lockwood Ave, Red Deer, AB, T4R 2M4
(403) 342-6655
Emp Here 120
SIC 8211 Elementary and secondary schools
Darwin Roscoe

D-U-N-S 20-740-7581   (SL)
DANDCO ENTERPRISES LTD
CANADIAN TIRE ASSOCIATE STORE
2510 50 Ave, Red Deer, AB, T4R 1M3
(403) 342-2223
Emp Here 70   *Sales* 44,049,600
SIC 5531 Auto and home supply stores
Joe Dand

D-U-N-S 24-517-5278   (SL)
EARLS RESTAURANT (RED DEER) LTD
EARLS PLACE
2111 50 Ave, Red Deer, AB, T4R 1Z4
(403) 342-4055
Emp Here 75   *Sales* 3,413,925
SIC 5812 Eating places
William Olafson

D-U-N-S 20-105-8281   (BR)
HOME DEPOT OF CANADA INC
HOME DEPOT
(*Suby of* THE HOME DEPOT INC)
2030 50 Ave, Red Deer, AB, T4R 3A2
(403) 358-7550
Emp Here 130
SIC 5251 Hardware stores
Paul Vandenbosch

D-U-N-S 20-645-4340   (BR)
HUDSON'S BAY COMPANY
BAY, THE
(*Suby of* HUDSON'S BAY COMPANY)
4900 Molly Bannister Dr, Red Deer, AB, T4R 1N9
(403) 347-2211
Emp Here 120
SIC 5311 Department stores
Jack Hoar

D-U-N-S 24-118-7129   (HQ)
ING & MCKEE INSURANCE LTD
2830 Bremner Ave, Red Deer, AB, T4R 1M9
(403) 346-5547
Emp Here 44   *Sales* 41,554,940
SIC 6411 Insurance agents, brokers, and service
Brad Romans
Darcy Cavanaugh
Jeff Skinner

D-U-N-S 20-090-3573   (SL)
M.G.M. FORD LINCOLN SALES LTD
3010 50 Ave, Red Deer, AB, T4R 1M5
(403) 346-6621
Emp Here 64   *Sales* 40,273,920
SIC 5511 New and used car dealers
Andrew Goodacre

D-U-N-S 24-438-8112   (SL)
MACLEAN, K. T. (KEN) LIMITED
CANADIAN TIRE
2510 50 Ave, Red Deer, AB, T4R 1M3
(403) 342-2222
Emp Here 150   *Sales* 94,392,000
SIC 5531 Auto and home supply stores
Joel Dand
Deborah Macarthur

D-U-N-S 20-522-2193   (SL)
PIKE WHEATON CHEVROLET OLDSMOBILE LTD
(*Suby of* WHEATON, DON LTD)
3110 50 Ave, Red Deer, AB, T4R 1M6
(403) 343-8918
Emp Here 65   *Sales* 40,903,200
SIC 5511 New and used car dealers
Gordon Pike
Donald Wheaton

D-U-N-S 25-770-3876   (SL)
RED DEER GYMNASTIC ASSOCIATION
EXELTA GYMNASTIC
3031 30 Ave, Red Deer, AB, T4R 2Z7
(403) 342-4940
Emp Here 45   *Sales* 17,883,630
SIC 8699 Membership organizations, nec
Marjary Sutherland

D-U-N-S 20-090-4944   (SL)
SIM'S FURNITURE LIMITED
2811 Bremner Ave Unit A, Red Deer, AB, T4R 1P7
(403) 342-7467
Emp Here 45   *Sales* 10,365,300
SIC 5712 Furniture stores
Timothy Sinclair
Sherry Sinclair

D-U-N-S 24-984-2691   (SL)
SIMPSON'S SPORTS LIMITED
RED DEER REBELS
4847 19 St Suite C, Red Deer, AB, T4R 2N7
(403) 341-6000
Emp Here 33   *Sales* 13,983,090
SIC 7941 Sports clubs, managers, and promoters
Terry Simpson
Wayne Simpson

D-U-N-S 20-798-7988   (BR)
SOBEYS CAPITAL INCORPORATED
SOBEYS
(*Suby of* EMPIRE COMPANY LIMITED)
2110 50 Ave, Red Deer, AB, T4R 2K1
(403) 348-0848
Emp Here 100
SIC 5411 Grocery stores
John Battista

D-U-N-S 20-599-4890   (SL)
SOUTHSIDE PLYMOUTH CHRYSLER LTD
SOUTHSIDE DODGE CHRYSLER & R.V. CENTRE
2804 50 Ave, Red Deer, AB, T4R 1M4
(403) 346-5577
Emp Here 103   *Sales* 64,815,840
SIC 5511 New and used car dealers
Peter Swainson
Christine Wiggett
Bryan Swainson

D-U-N-S 20-990-9985   (SL)
VELLNER LEISURE PRODUCTS (1980) LTD
1890 49 Ave, Red Deer, AB, T4R 2N7
(403) 343-1464
Emp Here 35   *Sales* 17,432,730
SIC 5561 Recreational vehicle dealers
Marty Vellner

D-U-N-S 20-552-2316   (BR)
WAL-MART CANADA CORP
(*Suby of* WALMART INC.)
2010 50 Ave Suite 3194, Red Deer, AB, T4R 3A2
(403) 358-5842
Emp Here 300
SIC 5311 Department stores
Lee Myers

D-U-N-S 25-770-5848   (HQ)
WOODY'S RV WORLD LTD
1702 49 Ave, Red Deer, AB, T4R 2N7
(403) 346-1130
Emp Here 85   *Sales* 106,977,600
SIC 5561 Recreational vehicle dealers
Woody Paylor
Darren Paylor
Darva Macbeth

Red Deer, AB T4S

D-U-N-S 25-169-1358   (HQ)
FUTURE AG INC
69 Belich Cres, Red Deer, AB, T4S 2K5

(403) 343-6101
Emp Here 21   *Sales* 18,526,014
SIC 5083 Farm and garden machinery
Josef Felder
Larry Watt

Red Deer County, AB T4E

D-U-N-S 24-733-4931   (SL)
388010 ALBERTA LTD
MOE, GARY VOLKSWAGEN
142 Leva Ave, Red Deer County, AB, T4E 1B9
(403) 342-2923
Emp Here 21   *Sales* 10,459,638
SIC 5511 New and used car dealers
Gary Moe
Susan Moe

D-U-N-S 20-825-8137   (HQ)
CORVET CONSTRUCTION (1977) LTD
37565 Highway 2 Suite 107, Red Deer County, AB, T4E 1B4
(403) 340-3535
Emp Here 2   *Sales* 10,839,780
SIC 1623 Water, sewer, and utility lines
Edward Zaparniuk
Lorne Zaparniuk

D-U-N-S 25-524-6647   (BR)
COSTCO WHOLESALE CANADA LTD
COSTCO
(*Suby of* COSTCO WHOLESALE CORPORATION)
37400 Highway 2 Unit 162, Red Deer County, AB, T4E 1B9
(403) 340-3736
Emp Here 130
SIC 5099 Durable goods, nec
Daniel Parent

D-U-N-S 25-416-1284   (HQ)
DIGITEX CANADA INC
130 Leva Ave, Red Deer County, AB, T4E 1B9
(403) 309-3341
Emp Here 50   *Sales* 41,587,182
SIC 5044 Office equipment
Hugh Porter
Robert Barden
Andre Brosseau

D-U-N-S 20-049-0220   (SL)
FESTIVAL FORD SALES (1983) LTD
FESTIVAL RV
37400 Highway 2 Suite 421, Red Deer County, AB, T4E 1B9
(403) 343-3673
Emp Here 72   *Sales* 45,308,160
SIC 5511 New and used car dealers
Chuck Easy

D-U-N-S 20-698-6056   (HQ)
GAMEHOST INC
BOOMTOWN CASINO
548 Laura Ave Suite 104, Red Deer County, AB, T4E 0A5
(403) 346-4545
Emp Here 8   *Sales* 53,370,381
SIC 7011 Hotels and motels
David J. Will
Darcy J. Will
Craig Thomas M.
Elston Noren
James Mcpherson
Timothy J (Tim) Sebastian
Jerry P. Van Someren
Peter L. Miles

D-U-N-S 24-893-6630   (SL)
GILMAR CONSTRUCTION LTD.
129 Clearwill Ave, Red Deer County, AB, T4E 0A1
(403) 343-1028
Emp Here 49   *Sales* 15,624,581
SIC 1521 Single-family housing construction
Gil Marshall

D-U-N-S 25-972-5778   (SL)
GO RV & MARINE RED DEER LTD
UNCLE BEN'S
29 Petrolia Dr, Red Deer County, AB, T4E 1B3
(403) 347-5546
Emp Here 49   *Sales* 24,405,822
SIC 5571 Motorcycle dealers
Tony Fumalatis

D-U-N-S 24-370-8455   (HQ)
LONESTAR WEST INC
(*Suby of* CLEAN HARBORS, INC.)
105 Kuusamo Dr, Red Deer County, AB, T4E 2J5
(403) 887-2074
Sales 63,712,800
SIC 1796 Installing building equipment
James Horvath
Chris Anderson
Tracy Graf
Joe Maclean
Maurice Kagan
David Prussky
Kristin York
Delanie Hill

D-U-N-S 24-350-7287   (SL)
NEXUS ENERGY TECHNOLOGIES INC
175 Clearview Dr Unit 100, Red Deer County, AB, T4E 0A1
(403) 314-0607
Emp Here 52   *Sales* 24,701,352
SIC 5084 Industrial machinery and equipment
Ryan Smith
Brent Close
Stephen Mccall

D-U-N-S 24-368-6990   (HQ)
PREDATOR DRILLING INC
PREDATOR DRILLING
210 Clearskye Way, Red Deer County, AB, T4E 0A1
(403) 346-0870
Emp Here 50   *Sales* 15,985,250
SIC 1381 Drilling oil and gas wells
Shane Walper
Peter Entz
Travis Hertz
Bryan Goudie

D-U-N-S 24-493-6469   (SL)
RED DEER RV COUNTRY LTD
PARADISE RV
1 Gasoline Alley E, Red Deer County, AB, T4E 1B3
(403) 340-1132
Emp Here 35   *Sales* 17,432,730
SIC 5561 Recreational vehicle dealers
Peter Schmucker
Craig Amstead

D-U-N-S 25-183-7139   (SL)
TOYOTA CANADA
413 Lantern St, Red Deer County, AB, T4E 0A5
(403) 343-3444
Emp Here 40   *Sales* 19,923,120
SIC 5511 New and used car dealers
Anne Tran

D-U-N-S 20-090-5313   (SL)
TURPLE BROS LTD
175 Leva Ave, Red Deer County, AB, T4E 0A5
(403) 346-5238
Emp Here 30   *Sales* 14,942,340
SIC 5571 Motorcycle dealers
Glenn W Turple
Gordon Turple
Brenda Neufeld
Terry Morris

D-U-N-S 25-206-1858   (HQ)
WESTRIDGE CABINETS (1993) LTD
(*Suby of* SIGNAL HILL EQUITY PARTNERS INC)
412 Liberty Ave, Red Deer County, AB, T4E 1B9

(403) 342-6671
Emp Here 240   *Sales* 83,517,000
SIC 2434 Wood kitchen cabinets
Ron Goss

Red Deer County, AB T4G

D-U-N-S 25-678-3044   (SL)
RAINBOW COLONY FARMING CO LTD
HUTTERIAN BRETHERN CHURCH OF RAINBOW
26052 Township Road 350, Red Deer County, AB, T4G 0M4
(403) 227-6465
Emp Here 57   *Sales* 10,292,775
SIC 8661 Religious organizations
Sam Hofer
Joshua Hofer
Darius Hofer

Red Deer County, AB T4S

D-U-N-S 20-245-2038   (SL)
115419 ALBERTA LTD
28042 Hwy 11 Unit 231, Red Deer County, AB, T4S 2L4
(403) 347-6222
Emp Here 63   *Sales* 15,903,846
SIC 1629 Heavy construction, nec
Jason Weinberger

D-U-N-S 24-308-4634   (HQ)
APEX OILFIELD SERVICES (2000) INC
5402 Blindman Cres, Red Deer County, AB, T4S 2M4
(403) 314-3385
Emp Here 30   *Sales* 39,977,760
SIC 7353 Heavy construction equipment rental
Lyle Kallis
Mike Jaillet
Wade Michalenko
Peter Innes
Ian Glackin
Kenny Cheung

D-U-N-S 20-746-4202   (SL)
C.B. INVESTMENTS LTD
CINNZEO BAKERIES
28042 Hwy 11 Suite 207, Red Deer County, AB, T4S 2L4
(403) 346-2948
Emp Here 85   *Sales* 29,383,650
SIC 2051 Bread, cake, and related products
Randy Safronovich

D-U-N-S 20-256-1429   (HQ)
CHATTERS LIMITED PARTNERSHIP
271 Burnt Park Dr, Red Deer County, T4S 0K7
(403) 342-5055
Emp Here 1   *Sales* 10,678,200
SIC 7231 Beauty shops
Jason Volk

D-U-N-S 20-051-6636   (BR)
CORE LABORATORIES CANADA LTD
OWEN OIL TOOLS
(*Suby of* CORE LABORATORIES N.V.)
39139 Highway 2a Unit 5409, Red Deer County, AB, T4S 2A8
(403) 340-1017
Emp Here 150
SIC 1389 Oil and gas field services, nec
Rob Lesiuk

D-U-N-S 20-524-6320   (SL)
KING'S ENERGY SERVICES LTD
277 Burnt Park Dr, Red Deer County, AB, T4S 0K7
(403) 343-2822
Emp Here 90   *Sales* 42,752,340

SIC 5085 Industrial supplies
Jason King
Scott Fraser

D-U-N-S 20-827-5503   (HQ)
LAEBON DEVELOPMENTS LTD
LAEBON HOMES
289 Burnt Park Dr, Red Deer County, AB, T4S 2L4
(403) 346-7273
Emp Here 1   *Sales* 18,965,940
SIC 1521 Single-family housing construction
W.G. (Gord) Bontje

D-U-N-S 24-348-2069   (BR)
NINE ENERGY CANADA INC
IPS WIRELINE, DIV OF
(*Suby of* NINE ENERGY SERVICE, INC.)
37337 Burnt Lake Trail Unit 30, Red Deer County, AB, T4S 2K5
(403) 340-4218
Emp Here 160
SIC 1389 Oil and gas field services, nec
Ivan Perry

D-U-N-S 20-136-4135   (HQ)
OIL STATES ENERGY SERVICES (CANADA) INCORPORATED
28042 Highway 11 Suite 334, Red Deer County, AB, T4S 2L4
(403) 340-0716
Emp Here 35   *Sales* 13,718,466
SIC 1389 Oil and gas field services, nec
Bob Mcguire

D-U-N-S 25-083-6343   (SL)
ROAD TRAIN OILFIELD TRANSPORT LTD
39139 Highway 2a Suite 4328, Red Deer County, AB, T4S 2A8
(403) 346-5311
Emp Here 50   *Sales* 10,506,550
SIC 1389 Oil and gas field services, nec
Darryl Leyen
David Manning

D-U-N-S 24-849-9266   (SL)
ROTATING ENERGY SERVICES CA CORP
39139 Highway 2a Suite 4016, Red Deer County, AB, T4S 2A8
(403) 358-5577
Emp Here 20   *Sales* 10,393,100
SIC 4911 Electric services
John Carlson
Kim Gray
Jason Tymko

D-U-N-S 20-091-4778   (SL)
WASCHUK PIPE LINE CONSTRUCTION LTD
39015 Highway 2a Suite 127, Red Deer County, AB, T4S 2A3
(403) 346-1114
Emp Here 500   *Sales* 164,057,500
SIC 1623 Water, sewer, and utility lines
William Waschuk
Wesley Waschuk
Kevin Waschuk

Redcliff, AB T0J

D-U-N-S 24-009-7001   (BR)
AECON ENERGY SERVICES LTD
AECOM ENERGY SERVICES LTD
(*Suby of* AECOM)
1901 Highway Ave Se, Redcliff, AB, T0J 2P0

Emp Here 210
SIC 8742 Management consulting services
Ken Mccutcheon

D-U-N-S 20-829-8968   (HQ)
AECON TRANSPORTATION WEST LTD
(*Suby of* AECON GROUP INC)
590 Highway Ave Ne, Redcliff, AB, T0J 2P0

---

(403) 548-3961
Sales 88,591,050
SIC 1611 Highway and street construction
Lary Mcgregor
Rick Englot
Mick Nodwell

D-U-N-S 20-191-7809   (BR)
BAKER HUGHES CANADA COMPANY
PUMPING SERVICES, DIV OF
(*Suby of* GENERAL ELECTRIC COMPANY)
1901 Broadway Ave E, Redcliff, AB, T0J 2P0

Emp Here 250
SIC 1389 Oil and gas field services, nec
Mike Vanak

D-U-N-S 24-158-3194   (SL)
EL DORADO VEGETABLE FARMS LTD
860 Broadway Ave W, Redcliff, AB, T0J 2P0
(403) 548-6671
Emp Here 50   *Sales* 41,778,850
SIC 5148 Fresh fruits and vegetables
Curtis Huber
Morris Huber

D-U-N-S 24-806-2762   (SL)
GVN STRUCTURES INC
1611 Broadway Ave E Suite 1, Redcliff, AB, T0J 2P0
(403) 548-3100
Emp Here 35   *Sales* 11,666,655
SIC 1541 Industrial buildings and warehouses
Doug Turner

D-U-N-S 24-025-3083   (SL)
HARDROCK BITS & OILFIELD SUPPLIES LTD
CANCORD DRILLING, DIV OF
2200 South Highway Dr Se, Redcliff, AB, T0J 2P0
(403) 529-2100
Emp Here 22   *Sales* 10,450,572
SIC 5084 Industrial machinery and equipment
Tammy Meyer

D-U-N-S 20-692-1848   (SL)
IRON HORSE COILED TUBING INC
IRON HORSE ENERGY SERVICES
(*Suby of* PROSPECT CAPITAL CORPORATION)
1901 Dirkson Dr Ne, Redcliff, AB, T0J 2P0
(403) 526-4600
Emp Here 38   *Sales* 12,148,790
SIC 1389 Oil and gas field services, nec
Tom Coolen
Danny Meier
Brendon Hamilton

D-U-N-S 25-135-8495   (BR)
PATTISON, JIM BROADCAST GROUP LTD
CHAT RADIO 94.5 FM
(*Suby of* PATTISON, JIM GROUP INC)
10 Boundary Rd Se, Redcliff, AB, T0J 2P0
(403) 548-8282
Emp Here 80
SIC 4832 Radio broadcasting stations
Dave Sherwood

D-U-N-S 20-440-7373   (SL)
RED HAT CO-OPERATIVE LTD
809 Broadway Ave E, Redcliff, AB, T0J 2P0
(403) 548-6453
Emp Here 160   *Sales* 133,692,320
SIC 5148 Fresh fruits and vegetables
Gillian Digman
Lyle Aleman

D-U-N-S 20-647-6546   (BR)
SANJEL CANADA LTD
1901 Dirkson Dr Ne, Redcliff, AB, T0J 2P0

Emp Here 170
SIC 1389 Oil and gas field services, nec
Rob Young

D-U-N-S 20-037-8623   (SL)
TRANSCANADA TRUCK STOP LTD

TRUKKERS
1900 Hwy Dr S Unit 2, Redcliff, AB, T0J 2P0
(403) 548-7333
Emp Here 25   *Sales* 12,451,950
SIC 5541 Gasoline service stations
Kwan Lee

Redwater, AB T0A

D-U-N-S 20-813-9076   (SL)
TARTAN INDUSTRIAL LTD
5007 48 Ave, Redwater, AB, T0A 2W0
(780) 942-3802
Emp Here 50   *Sales* 10,506,550
SIC 1389 Oil and gas field services, nec

Rimbey, AB T0C

D-U-N-S 20-827-8242   (SL)
BUIST MOTOR PRODUCTS LTD
4230 50 Ave, Rimbey, AB, T0C 2J0
(403) 843-2244
Emp Here 25   *Sales* 12,451,950
SIC 5511 New and used car dealers
Tyman Buist

D-U-N-S 24-077-1316   (SL)
COUNTY LINE FARMS LTD
Gd, Rimbey, AB, T0C 2J0
(403) 843-6275
Emp Here 35   *Sales* 11,986,345
SIC 0191 General farms, primarily crop
Theresa Scholten

D-U-N-S 24-342-3741   (BR)
KEYERA PARTNERSHIP
RIMBEY GAS PLANT
(*Suby of* KEYERA PARTNERSHIP)
44-01 W5 03-05, Rimbey, AB, T0C 2J0
(403) 843-7100
Emp Here 77
SIC 1311 Crude petroleum and natural gas
Julie Gunderson

D-U-N-S 25-313-1551   (SL)
RIMBEY AUCTION MART (1996) LTD
4831 47 St, Rimbey, AB, T0C 2J0
(403) 843-2439
Emp Here 25   *Sales* 36,692,300
SIC 5154 Livestock
Allen Olson

D-U-N-S 20-090-6675   (SL)
RIMBEY CO-OP ASSOCIATION LTD
4625 51 St, Rimbey, AB, T0C 2J0
(403) 843-2258
Emp Here 60   *Sales* 16,449,120
SIC 5411 Grocery stores
Steffen Olsen
William Loov

Rocky Mountain House, AB T4T

D-U-N-S 24-417-5972   (SL)
381616 ALBERTA LTD
KAL TIRE
4315 44 St, Rocky Mountain House, AB, T4T 1A4
(403) 845-3633
Emp Here 21   *Sales* 10,459,638
SIC 5531 Auto and home supply stores
Darren Frizzley

D-U-N-S 20-086-1086   (HQ)
CARRINGTON-O'BRIEN FOODS LTD
SOBEYS ROCKY MOUNTAIN HOUSE
(*Suby of* 299644 ALBERTA LTD)
Gd, Rocky Mountain House, AB, T4T 1T1

---

(403) 845-2110
Emp Here 4   *Sales* 58,695,400
SIC 5411 Grocery stores
Craig Protsack
Volodymar Protsack
William H Bowes Sr
William E Bowes Jr

D-U-N-S 20-990-5736   (SL)
CHALLAND PIPELINE LTD
Hwy 11 S, Rocky Mountain House, AB, T4T 1B4
(403) 845-2469
Emp Here 200   *Sales* 50,488,400
SIC 1623 Water, sewer, and utility lines
Wade Challand
Elaine Challand
Clint Challand

D-U-N-S 24-678-3109   (SL)
CML BOSWELL HOLDINGS LTD
CANADIAN TIRE
5440 46 St, Rocky Mountain House, AB, T4T 1B3
(403) 846-0077
Emp Here 50   *Sales* 24,903,900
SIC 5531 Auto and home supply stores
Kelly Boswell

D-U-N-S 24-495-3493   (HQ)
DORAN STEWART OILFIELD SERVICES (1990) LTD
391043 752 Hwy, Rocky Mountain House, AB, T4T 1B3
(403) 845-4044
Emp Here 50   *Sales* 25,244,200
SIC 1623 Water, sewer, and utility lines
Everett Stewart
Clint Stewart

D-U-N-S 20-090-7467   (SL)
EDWARDS GARAGE LIMITED
4403 42nd Ave, Rocky Mountain House, AB, T4T 1A6
(403) 845-3328
Emp Here 55   *Sales* 34,610,400
SIC 5511 New and used car dealers
Clayton Kennedy
Brent Kennedy
Luella Kennedy
Mary Kennedy

D-U-N-S 20-635-2635   (HQ)
PIDHERNEY'S INC
Hwy 11 Range Rd 70, Rocky Mountain House, AB, T4T 1A7
(403) 845-3072
Emp Here 238   *Sales* 114,840,250
SIC 1629 Heavy construction, nec
Mervyn Pidherney
Earlyne Pidherney

D-U-N-S 20-645-5602   (SL)
RAINBOW FORD SALES INC
Hwy 11e 42 Ave, Rocky Mountain House, AB, T4T 1A9
(403) 845-3673
Emp Here 27   *Sales* 13,448,106
SIC 5511 New and used car dealers
William N Speight
Greg Gordon
Dale Speight

D-U-N-S 20-827-3896   (SL)
ROCKY GAS CO-OP LTD
4920 43 St, Rocky Mountain House, AB, T4T 1A5
(403) 845-2766
Emp Here 22   *Sales* 25,422,430
SIC 4923 Gas transmission and distribution
Mike Maki
Cinda Montgomery

D-U-N-S 25-235-3719   (SL)
ROCKY MOUNTAIN DODGE CHRYSLER JEEP LTD
4415 42nd Ave, Rocky Mountain House, AB, T4T 1B6

(403) 845-2851
Emp Here 25   *Sales* 12,451,950
SIC 5511 New and used car dealers
Kamsen Iyer
Vibishen (Ben) Iyer

D-U-N-S 24-346-2918   (SL)
ROCKY SUPPORT SERVICES SOCIETY
4940 50 Ave, Rocky Mountain House, AB, T4T 1A8
(403) 845-4080
Emp Here 80   *Sales* 10,676,720
SIC 8399 Social services, nec
Pat Ferguson

D-U-N-S 20-090-7889   (SL)
ROCKY WOOD PRESERVERS LTD
ULLINWOOD BUILDING SUPPLIES, DIV OF
Gd Stn Main, Rocky Mountain House, AB, T4T 1T1
(403) 845-2212
Emp Here 65   *Sales* 10,131,095
SIC 2421 Sawmills and planing mills, general
William Luoma
Robert Luoma
Timothy Luoma

D-U-N-S 20-806-2419   (BR)
SOBEYS CAPITAL INCORPORATED
SOBEYS STORE# 3149
(*Suby of* EMPIRE COMPANY LIMITED)
4419 52 Ave, Rocky Mountain House, AB, T4T 1A3
(403) 846-0038
Emp Here 125
SIC 5411 Grocery stores
Craig Protsack

D-U-N-S 25-809-4101   (BR)
SOBEYS CAPITAL INCORPORATED
SOBEYS ROCKY MOUNTAIN HOUSE
(*Suby of* EMPIRE COMPANY LIMITED)
5427 52 Ave, Rocky Mountain House, AB, T4T 1S9
(403) 845-3371
Emp Here 110
SIC 5411 Grocery stores
Mike Hoffarth

D-U-N-S 20-174-7248   (HQ)
TOMCO PRODUCTION SERVICES LTD
4227 46th Ave, Rocky Mountain House, AB, T4T 1A8
(403) 844-2141
Emp Here 15   *Sales* 40,360,740
SIC 1389 Oil and gas field services, nec
Rodney Tomyn
Ardith Tomyn

D-U-N-S 20-699-8648   (BR)
WEST FRASER TIMBER CO. LTD
WEST FRASER LVL
(*Suby of* WEST FRASER TIMBER CO. LTD)
Gd Stn Main, Rocky Mountain House, AB, T4T 1T1
(403) 845-5522
Emp Here 190
SIC 5031 Lumber, plywood, and millwork
Al Simcoe

D-U-N-S 20-086-5579   (HQ)
WILD ROSE SCHOOL DIVISION NO. 66
AURORA ELEMENTARY SCHOOL
4912 43 St, Rocky Mountain House, AB, T4T 1P4
(403) 845-3376
Emp Here 27   *Sales* 47,956,178
SIC 8211 Elementary and secondary schools
Brad Volkman

D-U-N-S 20-583-9124   (SL)
X-CALIBUR PIPELINE AND UTILITY LOCATION INC
X-CALIBUR GROUND DISTURBANCE SOLUTIONS
4407 45a Ave, Rocky Mountain House, AB, T4T 1T1
(403) 844-8662
Emp Here 100   *Sales* 13,337,398

SIC 1389 Oil and gas field services, nec
Jason Quintal
Lindsay Quintal

Rocky View County, AB T1X

D-U-N-S 20-547-0839   (HQ)
CLEAN HARBORS ENERGY AND INDUSTRIAL SERVICES CORP
(*Suby of* CLEAN HARBORS, INC.)
235133 Ryan Rd, Rocky View County, AB, T1X 0K1
(403) 236-9891
Emp Here 30   *Sales* 15,984,000
SIC 7349 Building maintenance services, nec
Rod Marlin
Kirk Calvert
Bert Holtby

D-U-N-S 20-181-0293   (HQ)
COMPASS ENERGY SYSTEMS LTD
COMPASS
285028 Frontier Rd, Rocky View County, AB, T1X 0V9
(403) 262-2487
Emp Here 65   *Sales* 38,417,000
SIC 3491 Industrial valves
John Forgeron
Phil Ness
Scott Douglas

D-U-N-S 24-997-7521   (SL)
CONTOUR EARTHMOVING LTD
285019 Wrangler Way, Rocky View County, AB, T1X 0K3
(403) 275-0154
Emp Here 60   *Sales* 15,146,520
SIC 1629 Heavy construction, nec
Kevin Middlemiss
Bernie Burchill

D-U-N-S 20-359-2972   (SL)
CYNTECH CONSTRUCTION LTD
(*Suby of* KELLER GROUP PLC)
235061 Wrangler Link, Rocky View County, AB, T1X 0K3
(403) 228-1767
Emp Here 25   *Sales* 11,875,650
SIC 5085 Industrial supplies
Arthur Rick

D-U-N-S 24-716-3975   (SL)
DESA HOLDINGS LTD
DESA GLASS
(*Suby of* DAGA INVESTMENTS LTD)
285079 Bluegrass Dr, Rocky View County, AB, T1X 0P5
(403) 230-5011
Emp Here 125   *Sales* 24,046,250
SIC 2431 Millwork
Daniel Barker

D-U-N-S 25-099-5768   (HQ)
DIVINE HARDWOOD FLOORING LTD
235075 Ryan Rd, Rocky View County, AB, T1X 0K3
(403) 285-2188
Emp Here 12   *Sales* 30,531,360
SIC 5023 Homefurnishings
Carlos Soares

D-U-N-S 24-791-6351   (BR)
FLYNN CANADA LTD
(*Suby of* FLYNN CANADA LTD)
285221 Kleysen Way, Rocky View County, AB, T1X 0K1
(403) 720-8155
Emp Here 100
SIC 1761 Roofing, siding, and sheetMetal work
Gary Playsted

D-U-N-S 20-556-2601   (SL)
IRON HORSE EARTHWORKS INC
235090 Wrangler Dr, Rocky View County, AB,

T1X 0K3
(403) 217-2711
Emp Here 50   *Sales* 11,008,400
SIC 1794 Excavation work
Chris Bews
Gordon Weinberger

D-U-N-S 20-323-1782   (SL)
KLS EARTHWORKS INC
240039 Frontier Cres, Rocky View County, AB, T1X 0W6
(403) 240-3030
Emp Here 140   *Sales* 34,466,040
SIC 1794 Excavation work
Travis Powell

D-U-N-S 24-160-9320   (HQ)
LUFF INDUSTRIES LTD
235010 Wrangler Rd, Rocky View County, AB, T1X 0K3
(403) 279-3555
Emp Here 86   *Sales* 156,961,193
SIC 3535 Conveyors and conveying equipment
Steven Pace
Valerie Fasoli
Matthew Fasoli

D-U-N-S 20-178-9166   (SL)
MEARS CANADA CORP
(*Suby of* QUANTA SERVICES, INC.)
235080 Ryan Rd, Rocky View County, AB, T1X 0K3
(587) 471-2344
Emp Here 60   *Sales* 15,146,520
SIC 1623 Water, sewer, and utility lines
James H Maddox
Derrick A Jensen
Tana L Pool

D-U-N-S 24-351-3392   (SL)
RIG LOGISTICS INC
10 Wrangler Pl Unit 4, Rocky View County, AB, T1X 0L7
(403) 285-1111
Emp Here 250   *Sales* 51,426,500
SIC 4212 Local trucking, without storage
Inderjit Sanga
Dalwinder Sanga

D-U-N-S 20-768-0851   (BR)
ROSENAU TRANSPORT LTD
(*Suby of* MID-NITE SUN TRANSPORTATION LTD)
234180 Wrangler Rd, Rocky View County, AB, T1X 0K2
(403) 279-4800
Emp Here 75
SIC 4212 Local trucking, without storage
Dale Hart

D-U-N-S 20-024-7344   (SL)
STREAMLINE INSPECTION LIMITED
240040 Frontier Pl Unit 5, Rocky View County, AB, T1X 0N2
(403) 454-6630
Emp Here 33   *Sales* 14,635,170
SIC 7389 Business services, nec
Michael Pfister
Brian Boulet

D-U-N-S 20-598-3208   (HQ)
SUREWAY METAL SYSTEMS LIMITED
285120 Duff Dr, Rocky View County, AB, T1X 0K1
(403) 287-2742
Sales 19,208,500
SIC 3499 Fabricated Metal products, nec
David Evans
Penny Evans
Shannon Soares

D-U-N-S 24-702-0282   (BR)
TRANSX LTD
TRANSX LOGISTICS
(*Suby of* COMPAGNIE DES CHEMINS DE FER NATIONAUX DU CANADA)
285115 61 Ave Se, Rocky View County, AB,

T1X 0K3
(403) 236-9300
Emp Here 90
SIC 4213 Trucking, except local
Jamie Burkett

D-U-N-S 24-323-5970   (SL)
TRI-LINE CARRIERS LP
235185 Ryan Rd, Rocky View County, AB,
T1X 0K1
(403) 279-7070
Emp Here 200   *Sales* 41,141,200
SIC 4213 Trucking, except local
Stan Dunford
Greg Rumble
Jamie Clark

D-U-N-S 20-048-4934   (SL)
ULS MAINTENANCE & LANDSCAPING INC
240085 Frontier Cres, Rocky View County, AB,
T1X 0W2
(403) 235-5353
Emp Here 140   *Sales* 24,346,700
SIC 0781 Landscape counseling and planning
Steven Wheatcroft
Ross Rayment

D-U-N-S 20-304-2296   (SL)
WARWICK STRUCTURES GROUP LTD
(*Suby of* PTW ENERGY SERVICES LTD)
285188a Frontier Rd, Rocky View County, AB,
T1X 0V9
(403) 695-9999
Emp Here 100   *Sales* 24,618,600
SIC 1791 Structural steel erection
Don Basnett
Rod Phillips

D-U-N-S 24-272-9408   (BR)
WASTE CONNECTIONS OF CANADA INC
BFI CANADA
(*Suby of* WASTE CONNECTIONS, INC)
285122 Bluegrass Dr, Rocky View County, AB,
T1X 0P5
(403) 236-3883
Emp Here 85
SIC 4953 Refuse systems
Harold Richardson

Rocky View County, AB T4A

D-U-N-S 24-355-7399   (HQ)
1009833 ALBERTA LTD
PETLAND
261116 Wagon Wheel Way, Rocky View
County, AB, T4A 0E3
(403) 250-8484
Emp Here 25   *Sales* 38,801,800
SIC 5999 Miscellaneous retail stores, nec
Robert Brissette
Barbara Brissette

D-U-N-S 25-687-8141   (HQ)
CANADREAM CORPORATION
CANADREAM RV RENTALS & SALES
(*Suby of* APOLLO TOURISM & LEISURE
LTD)
292154 Crosspointe Dr, Rocky View County,
AB, T4A 0V2
(403) 291-1000
Emp Here 45   *Sales* 10,942,912
SIC 7519 Utility trailer rental
Brian Gronberg
Kariann Burmaster
Blaine Nicholson
Gerald Wood
Scott Graham
Louis Trouchet

D-U-N-S 25-287-8335   (HQ)
CANADREAM INC
CANADREAM CAMPERS
(*Suby of* APOLLO TOURISM & LEISURE
LTD)
292154 Crosspointe, Rocky View County,

AB, T4A 0V2

Emp Here 47   *Sales* 81,035,460
SIC 7519 Utility trailer rental
Brian Gronberg
Kelly Shier

D-U-N-S 25-004-6471   (SL)
CLEANTEK INDUSTRIES INC
261106 Wagon Wheel Cres Suite 1, Rocky
View County, AB, T4A 0E2
(403) 567-8700
Emp Here 35   *Sales* 11,189,675
SIC 1389 Oil and gas field services, nec
Josh Curlett
Jesse Curlett
Hugues Wanlin
Aly Khan Musani
Kristine Mcphail
Dale Tremblay
James Kidd

D-U-N-S 24-747-2249   (BR)
COSTCO WHOLESALE CANADA LTD
COSTCO STORE#1076
(*Suby of* COSTCO WHOLESALE CORPO-
RATION)
293020 Crossiron Common Suite 300, Rocky
View County, AB, T4A 0J6
(403) 516-5050
Emp Here 280
SIC 5099 Durable goods, nec
Rick Huick

D-U-N-S 20-268-3942   (BR)
GORDON FOOD SERVICE CANADA LTD
GFS CALGARY
(*Suby of* GORDON FOOD SERVICE, INC.)
290212 Township Road 261, Rocky View
County, AB, T4A 0V6
(403) 235-8555
Emp Here 380
SIC 5141 Groceries, general line

D-U-N-S 24-266-6014   (SL)
HARMONY BEEF COMPANY, LTD
260036 Rge Rd 291, Rocky View County, AB,
T4A 0T8
(587) 230-2060
Emp Here 250   *Sales* 86,422,500
SIC 2011 Meat packing plants
Richard Vesta
Christopher Vesta

D-U-N-S 24-803-5037   (BR)
LOWE'S COMPANIES CANADA, ULC
(*Suby of* LOWE'S COMPANIES, INC.)
261199 Crossiron Blvd Unit 300, Rocky View
County, AB, T4A 0J6
(403) 567-7440
Emp Here 160
SIC 5211 Lumber and other building materials
Mike Lindsay

D-U-N-S 24-387-7979   (HQ)
NCSG HAULING & RIGGING LTD
(*Suby of* NCSG HOLDINGS CANADA LTD)
261106 Wagon Wheel Cres Suite 3, Rocky
View County, AB, T4A 0E2
(403) 276-9955
Sales 11,230,475
SIC 7389 Business services, nec
Jamie Mullen

D-U-N-S 24-852-2125   (SL)
PRATTS FOOD SERVICE (ALBERTA) LTD
291196 Wagon Wheel Rd Suite 403, Rocky
View County, AB, T4A 0E2
(403) 476-7728
Emp Here 25   *Sales* 20,889,425
SIC 5141 Groceries, general line
Jason Baranyk

D-U-N-S 24-890-1204   (BR)
ROCKY MOUNTAIN DEALERSHIPS INC
ROCKY MOUNTAIN EQUIPMENT
(*Suby of* ROCKY MOUNTAIN DEALERSHIPS

INC)
260180 Writing Creek Cres, Rocky View
County, AB, T4A 0M9
(403) 513-7000
Emp Here 850
SIC 5082 Construction and mining machinery
Sheldon Chamberind

D-U-N-S 24-517-4578   (HQ)
THERMAL SYSTEMS KWC LTD
261185 Wagon Wheel Way, Rocky View
County, AB, T4A 0E2
(403) 250-5507
Emp Here 400   *Sales* 77,208,400
SIC 1761 Roofing, siding, and sheetMetal
work
Trevor Kent
James Weisgerber

D-U-N-S 24-393-4754   (HQ)
**TORNADO COMBUSTION TECHNOLOGIES
INC**
(*Suby of* CANERECTOR INC)
261200 Wagon Wheel Way Suite 200, Rocky
View County, AB, T4A 0E3
(403) 244-3333
Sales 15,540,070
SIC 3533 Oil and gas field machinery
Rick Sawatzky

D-U-N-S 24-685-8729   (BR)
WALMART CANADA LOGISTICS ULC
(*Suby of* WALMART INC.)
261039 Wagon Wheel Cres, Rocky View
County, AB, T4A 0E2
(403) 295-8364
Emp Here 280
SIC 4225 General warehousing and storage
Jeff Kelly

D-U-N-S 20-743-7583   (SL)
WRD BORGER CONSTRUCTION LTD
261046 High Plains Blvd, Rocky View County,
AB, T4A 3L3
(403) 279-7235
Emp Here 200   *Sales* 50,488,400
SIC 1623 Water, sewer, and utility lines
Robert Borger
David Borger
William H Borger

Rocky View County, AB T4B

D-U-N-S 24-647-4019   (HQ)
ALTA GENETICS INC
(*Suby of* KOEPON HOLDING B.V.)
263090 Rge Rd 11, Rocky View County, AB,
T4B 2T3
(403) 226-0666
Emp Here 280   *Sales* 695,999,260
SIC 5159 Farm-product raw materials, nec
Cees Hartmans
Wijnand Pon
Hans Hannema
Paul Hunt

Rockyford, AB T0J

D-U-N-S 24-731-7779   (SL)
**HUTTERIAN BRETHEREN CHURCH OF
STAHLVILLE**
Gd, Rockyford, AB, T0J 2R0
(403) 533-2102
Emp Here 120   *Sales* 12,927,240
SIC 8661 Religious organizations
Chris Waldner Sr

Rosebud, AB T0J

D-U-N-S 25-289-1304   (SL)
**HUTTERIAN BRETHERN CHURCH OF
HILLVIEW COLONY**
HILLVIEW COLONY
Gd, Rosebud, AB, T0J 2T0
(403) 677-2360
Emp Here 91   *Sales* 9,803,157
SIC 8661 Religious organizations
Jake Hofer
Frank Hofer

Rosedale Station, AB T0J

D-U-N-S 20-065-5038   (HQ)
INLAND PLASTICS LTD
201 Centre St, Rosedale Station, AB, T0J 2V0
(403) 823-6252
Emp Here 55   *Sales* 17,084,250
SIC 2394 Canvas and related products
John W Goudy Jr
Lorna Goudy

Rosemary, AB T0J

D-U-N-S 24-105-5651   (SL)
CRITTERS & CROPS LTD
Gd, Rosemary, AB, T0J 2W0
(403) 378-4934
Emp Here 28   *Sales* 10,794,532
SIC 0291 General farms, primarily animals
Rodney Dyck

Seba Beach, AB T0E

D-U-N-S 25-337-8434   (HQ)
SUN GRO HORTICULTURE CANADA LTD
(*Suby of* SUN GRO HORTICULTURE DIS-
TRIBUTION INC.)
52130 Range Rd, Seba Beach, AB, T0E 2B0
(780) 797-3019
Emp Here 100   *Sales* 1,282,103,900
SIC 5159 Farm-product raw materials, nec
Mitchell J Weaver
Jack Edwards
John Zaplatynsky
John Mclaughlin
David E Sutin
Craig Graham

D-U-N-S 20-304-5570   (SL)
**SUNHILLS MINING LIMITED PARTNER-
SHIP**
(*Suby of* TRANSALTA CORPORATION)
4419 B Sundance Rd, Seba Beach, AB, T0E
2B0
(780) 731-5300
Emp Here 700   *Sales* 335,750,100
SIC 1221 Bituminous coal and lignite-surface
mining
Hugo Shaw
David Koch

Sedgewick, AB T0B

D-U-N-S 20-074-4829   (HQ)
**ARNETT & BURGESS OIL FIELD CON-
STRUCTION LIMITED**
(*Suby of* ARNETT & BURGESS PIPELINERS
LTD)
4510 50 St, Sedgewick, AB, T0B 4C0
(780) 384-4050
Emp Here 50   *Sales* 12,044,200
SIC 1623 Water, sewer, and utility lines

Carey Arnett
Tom Arnett

D-U-N-S 24-397-2072   (HQ)
ARNETT & BURGESS PIPELINERS LTD
4510 50 St S, Sedgewick, AB, T0B 4C0
(780) 384-4050
Sales 303,240,800
SIC 1623 Water, sewer, and utility lines
Carrey Arnett
Tom Arnett

Sherwood Park, AB T8A

D-U-N-S 25-234-3439   (SL)
310104 ALBERTA LTD
FIN'S SEAFOOD DISTRIBUTORS
(*Suby of* SYSCO CORPORATION)
278 Cree Rd, Sherwood Park, AB, T8A 4G2
(780) 449-3710
Emp Here 29   *Sales* 24,231,733
SIC 5146 Fish and seafoods
Scott Wagner

D-U-N-S 20-152-8747   (HQ)
ALBERTA CONSERVATION ASSOCIATION
ACA
9 Chippewa Rd Suite 101, Sherwood Park, AB, T8A 6J7
(780) 410-1999
Emp Here 15   *Sales* 25,861,500
SIC 8611 Business associations
Brian Bildson
Ward Mclean
Randy Collins

D-U-N-S 25-316-8744   (SL)
ARCTIC CHILLER LTD
100 Cree Rd, Sherwood Park, AB, T8A 3X8
(780) 449-0459
Emp Here 21   *Sales* 17,547,117
SIC 5149 Groceries and related products, nec
Dave Hygaard

D-U-N-S 20-317-1798   (BR)
ARROW RELOAD SYSTEMS INC
(*Suby of* ARROW TRANSPORTATION SYSTEMS INC)
53309 Range Road 232 Unit 38, Sherwood Park, AB, T8A 4V2
(780) 464-4640
Emp Here 465
SIC 4789 Transportation services, nec
Wayne Peyre

D-U-N-S 24-000-3863   (SL)
CONMAR JANITORIAL CO. LTD
50 Ridgeview Crt, Sherwood Park, AB, T8A 6B4
(780) 441-5459
Emp Here 75   *Sales* 3,066,395
SIC 7349 Building maintenance services, nec
Brendan Connolly

D-U-N-S 24-168-6224   (SL)
DATA GATHERING SERVICE INC
320 Sioux Rd Suite 110, Sherwood Park, AB, T8A 3X6
(780) 467-9575
Emp Here 49   *Sales* 90,486,291
SIC 6331 Fire, marine, and casualty insurance

D-U-N-S 25-015-9076   (BR)
ELK ISLAND PUBLIC SCHOOLS REGIONAL DIVISION NO. 14
SALISBURY COMPOSITE HIGH SCHOOL
(*Suby of* ELK ISLAND PUBLIC SCHOOLS REGIONAL DIVISION NO. 14)
20 Festival Way, Sherwood Park, AB, T8A 4Y1
(780) 467-8816
Emp Here 100
SIC 8211 Elementary and secondary schools
Todd Filipek

D-U-N-S 24-853-9058   (HQ)

FIRST CANADIAN INSURANCE CORPORATION
(*Suby of* FIRSTCAN MANAGEMENT INC)
320 Sioux Rd Suite 110, Sherwood Park, AB, T8A 3X6
(780) 410-9182
Sales 711,915,600
SIC 6411 Insurance agents, brokers, and service
Donald A Wheaton
Dean Mccurdy
W.G Wheaton
D.M Erker
S.D Laird

D-U-N-S 25-015-7898   (SL)
GARNET INSTRUMENTS LTD
286 Kaska Rd, Sherwood Park, AB, T8A 4G7
(780) 467-1010
Emp Here 45   *Sales* 21,376,170
SIC 5084 Industrial machinery and equipment
George Fraser

D-U-N-S 24-003-0270   (SL)
GREENLAND NURSERY & LANDSCAPING LTD
GREENLAND GARDEN CENTRE
23108 16 Hwy, Sherwood Park, AB, T8A 4V2
(780) 467-7557
Emp Here 120   *Sales* 33,726,000
SIC 5261 Retail nurseries and garden stores
Rodney Sirman
Wayne Chichak
Timothy Chichak
Deborah Sirman
John Chichak

D-U-N-S 24-327-2718   (SL)
HACKMAN, RICHARD B. DRUGS LTD
SHOPPERS DRUG MART
2020 Sherwood Dr Unit 600, Sherwood Park, AB, T8A 3H9
(780) 464-9788
Emp Here 50   *Sales* 12,647,700
SIC 5912 Drug stores and proprietary stores
Rick Hackman

D-U-N-S 24-392-8694   (SL)
JIM BROWN PHARMACY LTD
SHOPPERS DRUG MART NO. 333
2020 Sherwood Dr Unit 600, Sherwood Park, AB, T8A 3H9
(780) 464-9788
Emp Here 40   *Sales* 10,118,160
SIC 5912 Drug stores and proprietary stores
James Brown
Audrey Brown

D-U-N-S 20-287-4210   (SL)
KEYMAY INTERNATIONAL INC
53169 Range Road 225, Sherwood Park, AB, T8A 4T7
(780) 417-1955
Emp Here 50   *Sales* 23,751,300
SIC 5085 Industrial supplies
Don Gunn

D-U-N-S 20-295-0924   (SL)
MAN-SHIELD (ALTA) CONSTRUCTION INC
MAN-SHIELD CONSTRUCTION
201 Kaska Rd Unit 167, Sherwood Park, AB, T8A 2J6
(780) 467-2601
Emp Here 32   *Sales* 18,250,816
SIC 1542 Nonresidential construction, nec
Peter Belluz
Joseph Bova
Antonio Eismendi
Teodoro Ferraro
Antonio Ferraro
Nerino Molinari
Ted Nocita
Tony Nocita
William Sharpe

D-U-N-S 20-800-6986   (BR)
MCDONALD'S   RESTAURANTS   OF

CANADA LIMITED
MCDONALD'S
(*Suby of* MCDONALD'S CORPORATION)
950 Ordze Rd, Sherwood Park, AB, T8A 4L8
(780) 467-6490
Emp Here 75
SIC 5812 Eating places
Jackie Gourgon

D-U-N-S 20-142-7569   (SL)
MILLENNIUM INSURANCE CORPORATION
(*Suby of* FIRSTCAN MANAGEMENT INC)
340 Sioux Rd, Sherwood Park, AB, T8A 3X6
(780) 467-1500
Emp Here 60   *Sales* 110,864,520
SIC 6411 Insurance agents, brokers, and service
Aaron Perdue
Donald Wheaton
William G Wheaton
Donald A Wheaton
Denis Brown
Dennis Erker
Stephen Laird
Kim Ward

D-U-N-S 25-015-8086   (SL)
PIONEER HOUSING FOUNDATION
495 Woodbridge Way, Sherwood Park, AB, T8A 4P1

Emp Here 70   *Sales* 29,322,230
SIC 6531 Real estate agents and managers
Don Moulds
Peter Wlodarczak
Linda Osinchuk
Roxanne Carr

D-U-N-S 20-577-1731   (SL)
REALTY EXECUTIVES DEVONSHIRE
37 Athabascan Ave Suite 101, Sherwood Park, AB, T8A 4H3
(780) 464-7700
Emp Here 45   *Sales* 12,229,020
SIC 6531 Real estate agents and managers
Maurice Roy

D-U-N-S 25-516-8304   (SL)
REALTY EXECUTIVES TELOR
REALTY EXECUTIVE DEVONSHIRE
37 Athabascan Ave Suite 101, Sherwood Park, AB, T8A 4H3
(780) 464-7700
Emp Here 56   *Sales* 15,218,336
SIC 6531 Real estate agents and managers
Darren Leew

D-U-N-S 24-949-3198   (SL)
SHERWOOD CARE
2020 Brentwood Blvd, Sherwood Park, AB, T8A 0X1
(780) 467-2281
Emp Here 116   *Sales* 7,925,816
SIC 8051 Skilled nursing care facilities
Gerald Northam

D-U-N-S 20-827-5094   (SL)
SHERWOOD PARK IGA
SOBEY'S
688 Wye Rd, Sherwood Park, AB, T8A 6G3
(780) 416-7920
Emp Here 50   *Sales* 13,707,600
SIC 5411 Grocery stores
Lori Shave

D-U-N-S 25-014-9820   (BR)
SOBEYS WEST INC
(*Suby of* EMPIRE COMPANY LIMITED)
985 Fir St, Sherwood Park, AB, T8A 4N5
(780) 467-0177
Emp Here 175
SIC 5411 Grocery stores
Denis Taillefer

D-U-N-S 25-271-0330   (BR)
SOBEYS WEST INC
SHERWOOD SAFEWAY
(*Suby of* EMPIRE COMPANY LIMITED)

2020 Sherwood Dr, Sherwood Park, AB, T8A 3H9
(780) 467-3037
Emp Here 140
SIC 5411 Grocery stores
Jose Araujo

D-U-N-S 20-898-3304   (SL)
STREAMLINE MECHANICAL L.P.
STREAMLINE MECHANICAL
53113 21 Hwy, Sherwood Park, AB, T8A 4T7
(780) 467-6941
Emp Here 100   *Sales* 23,306,500
SIC 1711 Plumbing, heating, air-conditioning
Douglas Bach
Justine Bach

D-U-N-S 25-451-1173   (BR)
SUNCOR ENERGY INC
SUNCOR SOCIAL CLUB
(*Suby of* SUNCOR ENERGY INC)
241 Kaska Rd, Sherwood Park, AB, T8A 4E8
(780) 449-2100
Emp Here 100
SIC 4613 Refined petroleum pipelines
Dave Perrott

D-U-N-S 24-859-4942   (SL)
T.C. BACKHOE & DIRECTIONAL DRILLING LIMITED PARTNERSHIP
(*Suby of* ENTERPRISE GROUP, INC)
302 Cree Rd, Sherwood Park, AB, T8A 4G2
(780) 467-1367
Emp Here 50   *Sales* 12,622,100
SIC 1629 Heavy construction, nec
Leonard Jaroszuk

D-U-N-S 24-367-1026   (SL)
TAHK PROJECTS LTD
296 Kaska Rd, Sherwood Park, AB, T8A 4G7
(780) 416-7770
Emp Here 50   *Sales* 12,044,200
SIC 1623 Water, sewer, and utility lines
Ashley Godwin
Kyle Melnyk

D-U-N-S 20-358-5505   (SL)
TERRAPRO INC
53345 Range Road 232, Sherwood Park, AB, T8A 4V2
(780) 449-2091
Emp Here 50   *Sales* 15,985,250
SIC 1389 Oil and gas field services, nec
Colin Schmidt
Jeff Schellenberg
L. Evan Baergen
C. James Davis
Wade Mcgohan
Doug Mccartney
Paul Shelley

D-U-N-S 24-395-1118   (HQ)
WOWU FACTOR DESSERTS LTD
152 Cree Rd, Sherwood Park, AB, T8A 3X8
(780) 464-0303
Emp Here 35   *Sales* 20,741,400
SIC 2053 Frozen bakery products, except bread
Debbie Guess
Ron Kent
George Yakoweshyn
Robert Callow

Sherwood Park, AB T8B

D-U-N-S 24-786-8177   (SL)
BARLBOROUGH BUSINESS ENTERPRISES LTD
DAIRY QUEEN
192 Ordze Ave, Sherwood Park, AB, T8B 1M6
(780) 449-1616
Emp Here 25   *Sales* 10,483,875
SIC 6712 Bank holding companies
Greg Smith

D-U-N-S 24-702-7741   (SL)
EARL'S RESTAURANT (SHERWOOD PARK) LTD
194 Ordze Ave, Sherwood Park, AB, T8B 1M6
(780) 449-2575
Emp Here 80   *Sales* 2,037,250
SIC 5812 Eating places
Harold Mueller
Larry Stewart

D-U-N-S 25-015-7831   (HQ)
ELK ISLAND PUBLIC SCHOOLS RE-GIONAL DIVISION NO. 14
683 Wye Rd, Sherwood Park, AB, T8B 1N2
(780) 464-3477
Emp Here 160   *Sales* 152,329,800
SIC 8211 Elementary and secondary schools
Paul Dolynny
Glen Buchan
Brian Smith
Mae Adamyk
W.H. Gordon
Lynn Patterson
Lisa Brower
Bonnie Riddell
Pat Mclauchlan
Lois Byers

D-U-N-S 25-269-5549   (SL)
K RICE RETAILING INC
CANADIAN TIRE 428
169 Ordze Ave Suite 428, Sherwood Park, AB, T8B 1M6
(780) 449-1577
Emp Here 135   *Sales* 32,984,280
SIC 5941 Sporting goods and bicycle shops
Kenneth Rice

D-U-N-S 25-498-2788   (BR)
WAL-MART CANADA CORP
(*Suby of* WALMART INC.)
239 Wye Rd, Sherwood Park, AB, T8B 1N1
(780) 464-2105
Emp Here 263
SIC 5311 Department stores
Brad Acins

Sherwood Park, AB T8H

D-U-N-S 24-370-6426   (SL)
1185140 ALBERTA LTD
SHERWOOD PARK TOYOTA
31 Automall Rd, Sherwood Park, AB, T8H 0C7
(780) 410-2455
Emp Here 120   *Sales* 75,513,600
SIC 5511 New and used car dealers
Patrick Priestner
Arthur Angielski

D-U-N-S 24-420-4041   (SL)
1443803 ALBERTA LTD
SHERWOOD HONDA
30 Automall Rd, Sherwood Park, AB, T8H 2N1
(780) 417-0005
Emp Here 50   *Sales* 24,903,900
SIC 5511 New and used car dealers
Ronald Kary
Shelly Kary

D-U-N-S 25-099-9430   (HQ)
3033441 NOVA SCOTIA COMPANY
ALLIED FITTING CANADA
(*Suby of* ALLIED INTERNATIONAL SRL)
172 Turbo Dr, Sherwood Park, AB, T8H 2J6
(780) 464-7774
Emp Here 30   *Sales* 19,001,040
SIC 5085 Industrial supplies
Marc Herstein

D-U-N-S 25-360-2437   (SL)
6094376 CANADA LTD
SUBMERSIBLE CONSULTING & ENGI-NEERING
117 Pembina Rd Suite 109, Sherwood Park,

AB, T8H 0J4
(780) 467-4118
Emp Here 35   *Sales* 20,649,632
SIC 3679 Electronic components, nec
Brian Burton
Mohammad Aborrob

D-U-N-S 20-868-5339   (HQ)
A & B RAIL SERVICES LTD
FRONTLINE CIVIL MANAGEMENT
(*Suby of* UNIVERSAL RAIL SYSTEMS INC)
50 Strathmoor Dr Suite 200, Sherwood Park, AB, T8H 2B6
(780) 449-7699
Emp Here 45   *Sales* 25,244,200
SIC 1629 Heavy construction, nec
Paul H Brum
Troy Hilliker
Daniel Jacques
Neil Johansen
Paul Rowe

D-U-N-S 20-069-2668   (SL)
ALBERTA COLLEGE OF PARAMEDICS
2755 Broadmoor Blvd Unit 220, Sherwood Park, AB, T8H 2W7
(780) 449-3114
Emp Here 20   *Sales* 53,979,666
SIC 8221 Colleges and universities
Peter Helfrich
Melissa Manio
Dusty Schlitter

D-U-N-S 20-069-7865   (BR)
ALBERTA HEALTH SERVICES
STRATHCONA COUNTY HEALTH CENTER
(*Suby of* GOVERNMENT OF THE PROVINCE OF ALBERTA)
2 Brower Dr, Sherwood Park, AB, T8H 1V4
(780) 342-4600
Emp Here 150
SIC 8059 Nursing and personal care, nec
Stacy Valaire

D-U-N-S 24-320-2803   (SL)
APTIM SERVICES CANADA CORP
(*Suby of* APTIM HOLDINGS LLC)
15 Turbo Dr Unit 1, Sherwood Park, AB, T8H 2J6
(780) 467-2411
Emp Here 120   *Sales* 21,448,680
SIC 8711 Engineering services
James Brewer
Bradley Lowe
Joshua A. Decuir

D-U-N-S 20-805-0331   (SL)
AUTO-NET AUTOMOBILE SALES LTD
SHERWOOD NISSAN
10 Broadway Blvd, Sherwood Park, AB, T8H 2A2
(780) 449-5775
Emp Here 75   *Sales* 47,196,000
SIC 5511 New and used car dealers
Robert Harms
Ty Newbiggings

D-U-N-S 24-398-1842   (SL)
BELVEDERE GOLF & COUNTRY CLUB
51418 Hwy 21 S, Sherwood Park, AB, T8H 2T2
(780) 467-2025
Emp Here 80   *Sales* 6,283,600
SIC 7997 Membership sports and recreation clubs
Cameron White

D-U-N-S 24-355-3786   (BR)
BISON TRANSPORT INC
(*Suby of* JANPHER INVESTMENTS INC)
80 Liberty Rd, Sherwood Park, AB, T8H 2J6
(780) 416-7736
Emp Here 150
SIC 4213 Trucking, except local
Blair Scott

D-U-N-S 20-952-5778   (SL)
CHARTWELL COUNTRY COTTAGE RE-

TIREMENT RESIDENCE
(*Suby of* CHARTWELL MASTER CARE LP)
75 Cranford Way, Sherwood Park, AB, T8H 2B9
(780) 417-0757
Emp Here 50   *Sales* 11,645,550
SIC 6513 Apartment building operators
Gloria Kondel

D-U-N-S 24-810-1185   (SL)
CLIMATE CHANGE EMISSIONS MANAGE-MENT (CCEMC) CORPORATION
300 Palisades Way, Sherwood Park, AB, T8H 2T9
(780) 417-1920
Emp Here 30   *Sales* 13,703,230
SIC 7389 Business services, nec
Aleasa Tasker
Doug Beever
Brenda Kenny
Jim Carter
Aaron Falkenberg
Robert Mansell
Eric Newell
David Lewin

D-U-N-S 24-312-3002   (BR)
COSTCO WHOLESALE CANADA LTD
(*Suby of* COSTCO WHOLESALE CORPO-RATION)
2201 Broadmoor Blvd, Sherwood Park, AB, T8H 0A1
(780) 410-2520
Emp Here 200
SIC 5099 Durable goods, nec
Dana Herrington

D-U-N-S 20-558-9141   (HQ)
CRS CRANESYSTEMS INC
333 Strathmoor Way, Sherwood Park, AB, T8H 2K2
(780) 416-8800
Sales 15,540,070
SIC 3531 Construction machinery
Nigel Roots
Richard Semeniuk
Mark Lodge
James Caldwell

D-U-N-S 24-418-1181   (HQ)
DCM INTEGRATED SOLUTIONS INC
DCM
56 Liberty Rd, Sherwood Park, AB, T8H 2J6
(780) 464-6733
Emp Here 100   *Sales* 164,057,500
SIC 1629 Heavy construction, nec
Serge Tousignant
Robert Dowler
Stephane Tousignant
Andre Boisclair
Rejean Normandin
Richard Gadoury
Claude Thibault
Neil Macrae

D-U-N-S 20-081-8466   (HQ)
EDMONTON NORTHLANDS
NORTHLANDS PARK
2693 Broadmoor Blvd Suite 132, Sherwood Park, AB, T8H 0G1
(780) 471-7210
Emp Here 50   *Sales* 82,541,270
SIC 7999 Amusement and recreation, nec
Tim Reid
Geoffrey Oberg
Lisa Holmes
Shiva Dean
Kevin Gunderman
Burke Perry
Jennifer Wood
Gordon Wilson
Christy Morin
Roberto Noce

D-U-N-S 20-720-8646   (SL)
ESKIMO STEEL LTD
526 Streambank Ave, Sherwood Park, AB,

T8H 1N1
(780) 417-9200
Emp Here 60   *Sales* 11,525,100
SIC 3441 Fabricated structural Metal
Brian Watson
Kent Fargey

D-U-N-S 20-141-9681   (HQ)
FGG INSPECTIONS INC
140 Portage Close, Sherwood Park, AB, T8H 2W2
(780) 464-3444
Emp Here 21   *Sales* 11,230,475
SIC 7389 Business services, nec
Simon Gosselin
Ed Gulliver

D-U-N-S 20-114-7480   (SL)
FIRE TECH FIRE PROTECTION INC
FIRE TECH
2210 Premier Way Unit 170, Sherwood Park, AB, T8H 2L2
(780) 400-3473
Emp Here 30   *Sales* 13,304,700
SIC 7389 Business services, nec
William Rogers

D-U-N-S 25-328-6496   (SL)
FLINT FABRICATION AND MODULARIZA-TION LTD
(*Suby of* AECOM)
180 Strathmoor Dr, Sherwood Park, AB, T8H 2B7
(780) 416-3501
Emp Here 115
SIC 3443 Fabricated plate work (boiler shop)
Kerri Beuk
Donald Nehajowich

D-U-N-S 24-168-2512   (HQ)
HELICAL PIER SYSTEMS LTD
180 Strathmoor Dr, Sherwood Park, AB, T8H 2B7
(780) 400-3700
Emp Here 30   *Sales* 96,500,238
SIC 3312 Blast furnaces and steel mills
Lou Doiron
Bruce Weaver

D-U-N-S 20-177-5041   (BR)
HOME DEPOT OF CANADA INC
HOME DEPOT
(*Suby of* THE HOME DEPOT INC)
390 Baseline Rd Suite 200, Sherwood Park, AB, T8H 1X1
(780) 417-7875
Emp Here 150
SIC 5251 Hardware stores
Mike Macleod

D-U-N-S 24-715-3935   (HQ)
INTEGRATED PROTECTIVE COATINGS INC
(*Suby of* 897049 ALBERTA INC)
500 Streambank Ave, Sherwood Park, AB, T8H 1N1
(780) 467-3299
Emp Here 60   *Sales* 11,525,100
SIC 3479 Metal coating and allied services
Barry Giovanetto
Robert Franke

D-U-N-S 24-071-3136   (BR)
JOEY TOMATO'S KITCHENS INC
JOEY RESTAURANT
(*Suby of* JOEY TOMATO'S)
222 Baseline Rd Unit 250, Sherwood Park, AB, T8H 1S8
(780) 449-1161
Emp Here 150
SIC 5812 Eating places
Nekko Leiterman

D-U-N-S 24-330-6169   (SL)
LAZY DAYS RV CENTRE INC
ALLSTAR RV
137 Turbo Dr, Sherwood Park, AB, T8H 2J6
(780) 449-6177
Emp Here 40   *Sales* 19,923,120

SIC 5561 Recreational vehicle dealers
Bruce Urban

D-U-N-S 25-148-1800   (BR)
LOBLAWS INC
REAL CANADIAN SUPERSTORE
(*Suby of* LOBLAW COMPANIES LIMITED)
410 Baseline Rd Suite 100, Sherwood Park,
AB, T8H 2A7
(780) 417-5212
Emp Here 300
SIC 5411 Grocery stores
Dale Nelly

D-U-N-S 20-251-5714   (BR)
LOCAL PUBLIC EATERY LTD
(*Suby of* LOCAL PUBLIC EATERY LTD)
222 Baseline Rd Suite 330, Sherwood Park,
AB, T8H 1S8
(780) 417-3182
Emp Here 100
SIC 5812 Eating places
Nekko Leiterman

D-U-N-S 20-143-8525   (HQ)
MILLENNIUM EMS SOLUTIONS LTD
2257 Premier Way Unit 148, Sherwood Park,
AB, T8H 2M8
(780) 496-9048
Emp Here 140   *Sales* 40,558,400
SIC 8748 Business consulting, nec
Ian Terry
Randy Rodolph
David Williams
Terry Bachynski
Kim Goheen

D-U-N-S 20-343-6530   (HQ)
NCS FLUID HANDLING SYSTEMS INC
280 Portage Close Unit 530, Sherwood Park,
AB, T8H 2R6
(780) 910-7951
Emp Here 16   *Sales* 10,450,572
SIC 5084 Industrial machinery and equipment
Owen Gilbert
Shawn Kirwan

D-U-N-S 20-807-9947   (SL)
NORTH WEST PAVING LTD
20 Turbo Dr, Sherwood Park, AB, T8H 2J6
(780) 468-4144
Emp Here 180   *Sales* 30,448,360
SIC 1611 Highway and street construction
Kerry Hetu
Matthew Ulmer
Ross Mitchell
Douglas Buryn

D-U-N-S 20-720-5212   (SL)
NORTHERN WELD ARC LTD
141 Strathmoor Way, Sherwood Park, AB,
T8H 1Z7
(780) 467-1522
Emp Here 50   *Sales* 10,141,500
SIC 3441 Fabricated structural Metal
Gayle Holpz
Shirley Holtz

D-U-N-S 24-068-5966   (SL)
**PETERSEN PONTIAC BUICK GMC (ALTA)
INC**
SHERWOOD BUICK GMC
10 Automall Rd, Sherwood Park, AB, T8H 2N1
(587) 805-0959
Emp Here 104   *Sales* 65,445,120
SIC 5511 New and used car dealers
Al Petersen
Carmen Anton
Merv Brown
Dave Quest

D-U-N-S 25-680-4154   (SL)
**ROADKING TRAVEL CENTRE STRATH-
CONA INC**
26 Strathmoor Dr Suite 164, Sherwood Park,
AB, T8H 2B6
(780) 417-9400
Emp Here 60   *Sales* 37,756,800

SIC 5541 Gasoline service stations
Glen Hommy
Robert Dawe
Brian Falkner
Curt Vos
Erin Oor
Alan Tookey

D-U-N-S 24-767-0003   (BR)
RRGB RESTAURANTS CANADA INC
RED ROBIN
(*Suby of* RRGB RESTAURANTS CANADA
INC)
8005 Emerald Dr Suite 250, Sherwood Park,
AB, T8H 0P1
(587) 269-4401
Emp Here 76
SIC 5812 Eating places
Brian Treichel

D-U-N-S 24-809-0644   (SL)
SHERWOOD FORD
2540 Broadmoor Blvd, Sherwood Park, AB,
T8H 1B4
(780) 449-3673
Emp Here 130   *Sales* 24,245,780
SIC 8742 Management consulting services
Jimmy Jasnan
Kelly O'connel

D-U-N-S 20-718-5583   (SL)
SHERWOOD PARK AUTO SALES LTD
SHERWOOD KIA
20 Broadway Blvd, Sherwood Park, AB, T8H
2A2
(780) 449-4499
Emp Here 70   *Sales* 44,049,600
SIC 5521 Used car dealers
Mark Kostic

D-U-N-S 24-358-4161   (SL)
**SHERWOOD PARK DODGE CHRYSLER
JEEP LTD**
230 Provincial Ave, Sherwood Park, AB, T8H
0E1
(780) 410-4100
Emp Here 105   *Sales* 66,074,400
SIC 5511 New and used car dealers
Scott Held

D-U-N-S 24-330-0410   (SL)
SHERWOOD PARK VEHICLES LP
SHERWOOD PARK HYUNDAI
(*Suby of* AUTOCANADA INC)
41 Automall Rd, Sherwood Park, AB, T8H 0C7
(780) 410-2450
Emp Here 43   *Sales* 27,059,040
SIC 5511 New and used car dealers
Tom Bradshaw

D-U-N-S 24-581-7239   (HQ)
SITE ENERGY SERVICES LTD
120 Pembina Rd Suite 170, Sherwood Park,
AB, T8H 0M2
(780) 400-7483
Emp Here 10   *Sales* 15,985,250
SIC 1389 Oil and gas field services, nec
Lyle Reid
Chris Martineau
Danny Dion
Roger Didychuk
Brad Jennings
Ron Yoneda

D-U-N-S 20-645-8999   (BR)
SOBEYS CAPITAL INCORPORATED
SOBEYS
(*Suby of* EMPIRE COMPANY LIMITED)
590 Baseline Rd Unit 100, Sherwood Park,
AB, T8H 1Y4
(780) 417-0419
Emp Here 150
SIC 5411 Grocery stores
Dave Lukawenko

D-U-N-S 20-352-1112   (SL)
SPV MOTORS LP
SHERWOOD PARK VOLKSWAGEN

(*Suby of* AUTOCANADA INC)
2365 Broadmoor Blvd, Sherwood Park, AB,
T8H 1B4
(780) 400-4800
Emp Here 22   *Sales* 10,957,716
SIC 5511 New and used car dealers
Steven Landry
Christopher Burrows

D-U-N-S 24-345-6006   (BR)
STRATHCONA COUNTY
*MILLENNIUM   PLACE   STRATHCONA
COUNTY*
(*Suby of* STRATHCONA COUNTY)
2000 Premier Way, Sherwood Park, AB, T8H
2G4
(780) 416-3300
Emp Here 250
SIC 7999 Amusement and recreation, nec
Troy Fleming

D-U-N-S 24-961-7762   (SL)
TIGER MACHINING INC.
15 Turbo Dr, Sherwood Park, AB, T8H 2J6

Emp Here 37   *Sales* 10,482,100
SIC 7538 General automotive repair shops
Joe Basse
Eva Basse

D-U-N-S 20-673-8452   (SL)
TRANSCANADA PIPELINES LTD
2301 Premier Way Unit 112, Sherwood Park,
AB, T8H 2K8

Emp Here 4   *Sales* 12,423,428
SIC 4922 Natural gas transmission

D-U-N-S 24-133-6007   (HQ)
VERTEX RESOURCE GROUP LTD
2055 Premier Way Suite 161, Sherwood Park,
AB, T8H 0G2
(780) 464-3295
Emp Here 355   *Sales* 92,778,563
SIC 1522 Residential construction, nec
Terry Stephenson
Jason Clemett
Paul Blenkhorn
Deon Walsh
Sherry Bielopotocky
Michael Zvonkovic
Brian Butlin
Terry Freeman
Trent Baker
Stuart O'connor

D-U-N-S 24-349-7760   (HQ)
VERTEX RESOURCE SERVICES LTD
(*Suby of* VERTEX RESOURCE GROUP LTD)
2055 Premier Way Suite 161, Sherwood Park,
AB, T8H 0G2
(780) 464-3295
Emp Here 200   *Sales* 349,196,000
SIC 1542 Nonresidential construction, nec
Brian Butlin
Terry Stephenson
Jason Clemett

D-U-N-S 24-860-4659   (BR)
WSP CANADA INC
GENIVAR
(*Suby of* AST TRUST COMPANY (CANADA))
2693 Broadmoor Blvd Suite 132, Sherwood
Park, AB, T8H 0G1
(780) 410-6740
Emp Here 85
SIC 8711 Engineering services
Christine Mryglode

Siksika, AB T0J

D-U-N-S 25-506-3240   (HQ)
SIKSIKA BOARD OF EDUCATION
Po Box 1099, Siksika, AB, T0J 3W0

(403) 734-5400
Emp Here 1   *Sales* 12,885,470
SIC 8211 Elementary and secondary schools
Jackie Many Guns
Adrien Sr Stinson
Hector Winnipeg

Slave Lake, AB T0G

D-U-N-S 24-320-0057   (SL)
BLACK TIGER FUELS LTD
Gd, Slave Lake, AB, T0G 2A0
(780) 849-3616
Emp Here 22   *Sales* 27,658,422
SIC 5172 Petroleum products, nec
Roger Crabtree

D-U-N-S 24-672-2185   (SL)
DEUCE DISPOSAL LTD
240 Balsom Rd Ne, Slave Lake, AB, T0G 2A0
(780) 849-3334
Emp Here 40   *Sales* 12,045,680
SIC 4953 Refuse systems
John Schueller
Janine Schueller

D-U-N-S 24-391-4876   (SL)
EXACT OILFIELD DEVELOPING LTD
1412 Tamarack Rd Ne, Slave Lake, AB, T0G
2A0
(780) 849-2211
Emp Here 60   *Sales* 19,182,300
SIC 1389 Oil and gas field services, nec
Kenneth Carpenter

D-U-N-S 24-584-6530   (SL)
HEAVY EQUIPMENT REPAIR LTD
404 Balsam Rd, Slave Lake, AB, T0G 2A0
(780) 849-3768
Emp Here 50   *Sales* 10,185,800
SIC 7699 Repair services, nec
Herb Gehrling
Barbara Lynn Gehrling

D-U-N-S 24-880-7380   (HQ)
MAX FUEL DISTRIBUTORS LTD
*PETRO-CANADA   WHOLESALE   MARKET-
ING*
701 12 Ave Ne, Slave Lake, AB, T0G 2A2
(780) 849-3820
Emp Here 25   *Sales* 62,860,050
SIC 5171 Petroleum bulk stations and termi-
nals
Ingo Von Wackerbarth
Barrie Deschover

D-U-N-S 20-837-8716   (SL)
NORTHERN REFORESTATION INC
1312 Tamarack Rd Ne, Slave Lake, AB, T0G
2A0
(780) 849-1980
Emp Here 83   *Sales* 11,350,997
SIC 0851 Forestry services
Peter Dueck

D-U-N-S 25-679-7234   (SL)
S.L. FORD SALES LTD
309 1a Ave Se Ss 3, Slave Lake, AB, T0G 2A3
(780) 849-4419
Emp Here 32   *Sales* 15,938,496
SIC 5511 New and used car dealers
Douglas Babiy
Marshall Eliuk

D-U-N-S 25-983-1019   (SL)
**SLAVE LAKE CHRYSLER DODGE JEEP
RAM LTD**
SLAVE LAKE CHRYSLER
701 15 Ave Sw, Slave Lake, AB, T0G 2A4
(780) 849-5225
Emp Here 26   *Sales* 12,950,028
SIC 5511 New and used car dealers
Stefan Plouffe

D-U-N-S 24-807-0872   (HQ)
SLAVE LAKE PULP CORPORATION

▲ Public Company   ■ Public Company Family Member   **HQ** Headquarters   **BR** Branch   **SL** Single Location

(*Suby of* WEST FRASER TIMBER CO. LTD)
Gd, Slave Lake, AB, T0G 2A0
(780) 849-7777
Emp Here 100   *Sales* 19,476,800
SIC 2611 Pulp mills
Peter Rippon
Vince Parrot
Henry Ketchum Iii
Gerry Miller
Martti Solin

D-U-N-S 20-775-6388   (SL)
SPILAK TANK TRUCK SERVICE LTD
911 6 Ave Nw, Slave Lake, AB, T0G 2A1
(780) 849-2757
Emp Here 95   *Sales* 14,078,240
SIC 4212 Local trucking, without storage
Brad Spilak
Brad Spilak
Darrin Spilak
Judy Spilak

D-U-N-S 20-091-5361   (SL)
VANDERWELL CONTRACTORS (1971) LTD
695 West Mitsue Ind Rd, Slave Lake, AB, T0G
2A0
(780) 849-3824
Emp Here 160   *Sales* 30,779,200
SIC 2421 Sawmills and planing mills, general
Kenneth Vanderwell

D-U-N-S 24-019-1721   (BR)
WAL-MART CANADA CORP
WALMART
(*Suby of* WALMART INC.)
1500 Main St Sw, Slave Lake, AB, T0G 2A4
(780) 849-9579
Emp Here 120
SIC 5311 Department stores
Bart Caputo

D-U-N-S 24-522-0111   (BR)
WEST FRASER MILLS LTD
ALBERTA PLYWOOD
(*Suby of* WEST FRASER TIMBER CO. LTD)
Gd, Slave Lake, AB, T0G 2A0
(780) 849-4145
Emp Here 180
SIC 2421 Sawmills and planing mills, general
Shea Pletzer

D-U-N-S 24-391-7937   (HQ)
WHITECAP MOTORS
WHITECAP RECREATION, DIV OF
804 Main St Sw, Slave Lake, AB, T0G 2A0
(780) 849-2600
Emp Here 34   *Sales* 27,059,040
SIC 5511 New and used car dealers
Karl Gongos
Roland Eben

Smoky Lake, AB T0A

D-U-N-S 24-906-3280   (SL)
SMOKY LAKE COLONY LTD
Gd, Smoky Lake, AB, T0A 3C0
(780) 656-2372
Emp Here 40   *Sales* 10,492,360
SIC 0191 General farms, primarily crop
Andy Stahl
George R. Hoffer
Jake Stahl
Mike Stahl
Ben Stahl

Spirit River, AB T0H

D-U-N-S 24-399-4050   (SL)
CENTRAL PEACE HEALTH COMPLEX
5010 45th Ave, Spirit River, AB, T0H 3G0
(780) 864-3993
Emp Here 80   *Sales* 8,170,640

SIC 8062 General medical and surgical hospitals
Kelli Mack

Spruce Grove, AB T7X

D-U-N-S 24-767-1563   (SL)
ALBERTA SPRUCE INDUSTRIES LTD
26322 Twp Rd Suite 524, Spruce Grove, AB,
T7X 3H2
(780) 962-5118
Emp Here 30   *Sales* 13,304,700
SIC 7389 Business services, nec
Neil Miller
Roberta Miller

D-U-N-S 24-821-3113   (SL)
COPPERLINE EXCAVATING LTD
375 Saskatchewan Ave, Spruce Grove, AB,
T7X 3A1
(780) 968-3805
Emp Here 80   *Sales* 19,694,880
SIC 1796 Installing building equipment
Jamie Black

D-U-N-S 25-194-9426   (SL)
D.G.C. CONTRACTING INC
40 Diamond Ave, Spruce Grove, AB, T7X 3A8

Emp Here 42   *Sales* 10,117,128
SIC 1623 Water, sewer, and utility lines
David Crawford
Lorriane Crawford

D-U-N-S 20-809-5971   (SL)
ELITE CAMP SERVICES INC
340 Acheson Rd, Spruce Grove, AB, T7X 5A7

Emp Here 190   *Sales* 8,861,410
SIC 5812 Eating places
Ross Hudson
Paul Dougay
William Saunders

D-U-N-S 24-043-3599   (SL)
ELIZABETHAN CATERING SERVICES LTD
55 Alberta Ave, Spruce Grove, AB, T7X 4B9
(780) 962-3663
Emp Here 100   *Sales* 4,551,900
SIC 5812 Eating places
Steven Marsh

D-U-N-S 25-015-9639   (HQ)
**EVERGREEN CATHOLIC SEPARATE RE-
GIONAL DIVISION 2**
381 Grove Dr Unit 110, Spruce Grove, AB,
T7X 2Y9
(780) 962-5627
Emp Here 11   *Sales* 48,963,150
SIC 8211 Elementary and secondary schools
Ron Mckay
Ronald Mckay
Franco Maisano
Cindi Vaselenak
Micheal Paonessa

D-U-N-S 25-169-6480   (SL)
EVOLVED ENERGY SERVICES INC
Po Box 3946 Stn Main, Spruce Grove, AB,
T7X 3B2
(780) 960-2790
Emp Here 75   *Sales* 23,977,875
SIC 1389 Oil and gas field services, nec
Joe Foster
Chris Turner
Adam Jose

D-U-N-S 25-364-0486   (SL)
FREETEK CONSTRUCTION LTD
130 Yellowhead Rd, Spruce Grove, AB, T7X
3B5
(780) 960-4848
Emp Here 38   *Sales* 12,117,022
SIC 1521 Single-family housing construction
Dean Fraser

D-U-N-S 24-001-3755   (SL)
GROUP FIVE INVESTORS LTD
GROVE MOTOR INN
Gd Lcd Main, Spruce Grove, AB, T7X 3A1
(780) 962-5000
Emp Here 100   *Sales* 9,489,900
SIC 7011 Hotels and motels
Ed Kalynchuk
Dennis Kalynchuk
Wayne Kalynchuk

D-U-N-S 20-091-2996   (SL)
GROVE PONTIAC BUICK GMC LTD
Highway 16a W, Spruce Grove, AB, T7X 3B2

Emp Here 60   *Sales* 37,756,800
SIC 5511 New and used car dealers
Gerard Levasseur
Helga Levasseur
Gerard P. Levasseur

D-U-N-S 24-398-6114   (SL)
GRV C MOTORS LP
GROVE CHRYSLER DODGE JEEP RAM
(*Suby of* AUTOCANADA INC)
200 St. Matthews Ave, Spruce Grove, AB, T7X
3A6
(780) 809-9971
Emp Here 45   *Sales* 28,317,600
SIC 5511 New and used car dealers
Steven Landry

D-U-N-S 25-365-8629   (BR)
HOME DEPOT OF CANADA INC
HOME DEPOT
(*Suby of* THE HOME DEPOT INC)
168 16a Hwy, Spruce Grove, AB, T7X 3X3
(780) 960-5600
Emp Here 100
SIC 5251 Hardware stores
Jeff Tymo

D-U-N-S 25-142-0493   (BR)
LOBLAWS INC
REAL CANADIAN SUPERSTORE
(*Suby of* LOBLAW COMPANIES LIMITED)
100 Jennifer Heil Way Suite 10, Spruce Grove,
AB, T7X 4B8
(780) 960-7400
Emp Here 375
SIC 5411 Grocery stores
Cathwyn Philpotts

D-U-N-S 20-091-2988   (HQ)
MCLEOD MERCANTILE LTD
MCLEOD HOME BUILDING CENTRE
135 South Ave, Spruce Grove, AB, T7X 3A5
(780) 962-2575
Emp Here 1   *Sales* 26,765,200
SIC 5211 Lumber and other building materials
Duncan Mcleod
Wilson Mcleod
Dalene Mcleod

D-U-N-S 20-655-1355   (BR)
PARKLAND SCHOOL DIVISION NO. 70
*SPRUCE GROVE COMPOSITE HIGH
SCHOOL*
(*Suby of* PARKLAND SCHOOL DIVISION NO.
70)
1000 Calahoo Rd, Spruce Grove, AB, T7X
2T7
(780) 962-0800
Emp Here 100
SIC 8211 Elementary and secondary schools
David Pysyk

D-U-N-S 25-087-2132   (BR)
PARKLAND SCHOOL DIVISION NO. 70
ECOLE BROXTON PARK SCHOOL
(*Suby of* PARKLAND SCHOOL DIVISION NO.
70)
505 Mcleod Ave Suite 505, Spruce Grove, AB,
T7X 2Y5
(780) 962-0212
Emp Here 108
SIC 8211 Elementary and secondary schools

Randy Hetherington

D-U-N-S 24-643-8139   (SL)
SPRUCE GROVE PIZZA LTD
BOSTON PIZZA
201 Calahoo Rd, Spruce Grove, AB, T7X 1R1
(780) 962-0224
Emp Here 85   *Sales* 3,869,115
SIC 5812 Eating places
Shaila Barnes

D-U-N-S 24-808-6076   (HQ)
SUN COUNTRY HOLDINGS LTD
411 South Ave, Spruce Grove, AB, T7X 3B5
(780) 962-1030
Emp Here 2   *Sales* 213,274,750
SIC 1629 Heavy construction, nec
John Thompson
Larry Thompson

D-U-N-S 20-166-4871   (SL)
TERRATEAM EQUIPMENT RENTALS INC
110 Manitoba Crt, Spruce Grove, AB, T7X 0V5
(780) 962-9598
Emp Here 2   *Sales* 55,609,056
SIC 7353 Heavy construction equipment
rental
Dean Eastman
Dallas Eastman

D-U-N-S 20-073-4614   (HQ)
THOMPSON BROS. (CONSTR.) LTD
(*Suby of* SUN COUNTRY HOLDINGS LTD)
411 South Ave, Spruce Grove, AB, T7X 3B4
(780) 962-1030
Sales 213,274,750
SIC 1629 Heavy construction, nec
Larry Thompson

D-U-N-S 20-334-4015   (SL)
THOMPSON INFRASTRUCTURE LTD
(*Suby of* SUN COUNTRY HOLDINGS LTD)
411 South Ave, Spruce Grove, AB, T7X 3B4
(780) 962-1030
Emp Here 80   *Sales* 18,803,448
SIC 1623 Water, sewer, and utility lines
Larry Thompson
Neil Matheson
John Klassen
Glenn Fereday

D-U-N-S 24-088-0922   (HQ)
ZENCOR EQUITIES LIMITED
Hwy 16a Golden Spike Rd, Spruce Grove, AB,
T7X 2Y3
(780) 962-3000
Sales 42,791,040
SIC 5511 New and used car dealers
Kenneth Zender

D-U-N-S 24-328-4957   (SL)
ZENDER FORD SALES LTD
(*Suby of* ZENCOR EQUITIES LIMITED)
Hwy 16a Golden Spike Rd, Spruce Grove, AB,
T7X 2Y3

Emp Here 68   *Sales* 42,791,040
SIC 5511 New and used car dealers
Kenneth Zender
Codie Richard

St Paul, AB T0A

D-U-N-S 24-390-5833   (SL)
**(S.P.A.N.) ST PAUL ABILITIES NETWORK
(SOCIETY)**
*HABITAT ENTERPRISES UNLIMITED, DIV.
OF*
4637 45 Ave, St Paul, AB, T0A 3A3
(780) 645-3405
Emp Here 150   *Sales* 7,239,450
SIC 8331 Job training and related services
Tim Bear
Sam Chang

D-U-N-S 24-346-4422   (BR)
ALBERTA HEALTH SERVICES
ST THERESE HEALTH CENTRE
(*Suby of* GOVERNMENT OF THE
PROVINCE OF ALBERTA)
4713 48 Ave, St Paul, AB, T0A 3A3
(780) 645-3331
Emp Here 200
SIC 8062 General medical and surgical hospitals
Bev Belland

D-U-N-S 20-788-5083   (SL)
ATRC ENTERPRISES
ST PAUL CO-OP GAS BAR & CONVENIENCE STORE
5005 42 St Ss 2, St Paul, AB, T0A 3A2
(780) 645-3227
Emp Here 23   *Sales* 11,455,794
SIC 5541 Gasoline service stations
Kelly Mckelvie

D-U-N-S 20-368-8481   (BR)
CORNERSTONE CO-OPERATIVE
(*Suby of* CORNERSTONE CO-OPERATIVE)
5017 43 St Suite 3, St Paul, AB, T0A 3A2
(780) 645-3351
Emp Here 260
SIC 5411 Grocery stores
Graham Getz

D-U-N-S 25-121-2619   (BR)
EXTENDICARE INC
EXTENDICARE ST. PAUL
(*Suby of* EXTENDICARE INC)
4614 47 Ave, St Paul, AB, T0A 3A3
(780) 645-3375
Emp Here 120
SIC 8051 Skilled nursing care facilities
Jack Mcintyre

D-U-N-S 24-227-1463   (BR)
GOVERNMENT OF THE PROVINCE OF ALBERTA
(*Suby of* GOVERNMENT OF THE
PROVINCE OF ALBERTA)
5025 49 Ave, St Paul, AB, T0A 3A4
(780) 645-6210
Emp Here 120
SIC 8741 Management services
Alex Coffey

D-U-N-S 24-048-8358   (SL)
KOTOWICH HARDWARE LTD
*ST PAUL HOME HARDWARE BUILDING
CENTRE*
4001 50 Ave, St Paul, AB, T0A 3A2
(780) 645-3173
Emp Here 50   *Sales* 12,652,950
SIC 5211 Lumber and other building materials
Gerald Kotowich
Joanne Kotowhich

D-U-N-S 20-028-8632   (HQ)
**REGIONAL AUTHORITY OF THE EAST
CENTRAL FRANCOPHONE EDUCATION
REGION NO.3, THE**
4617 50 Ave, St Paul, AB, T0A 3A3
(780) 645-3888
Emp Here 100   *Sales* 14,867,850
SIC 8211 Elementary and secondary schools
Natalie Beland
Reginald Roy
Jannick Roy-Plante
Marc Dumont

D-U-N-S 20-091-0412   (HQ)
SMYL MOTORS LTD
SMYL RV CENTRE
5015 44 St Ss 2, St Paul, AB, T0A 3A2
(780) 645-4414
Emp Here 37   *Sales* 30,205,440
SIC 5511 New and used car dealers
Bernard Smyl
Henry Smyl
Danny Smyl

D-U-N-S 20-773-7581   (SL)

ST PAUL DODGE LTD
4014 50 Ave, St Paul, AB, T0A 3A2

Emp Here 25   *Sales* 12,451,950
SIC 5511 New and used car dealers
Len Gagne

D-U-N-S 24-331-6692   (HQ)
ST. PAUL EDUCATION REGIONAL DIVISION NO 1
4313 48 Ave Suite 1, St Paul, AB, T0A 3A3
(780) 645-3323
Emp Here 3   *Sales* 61,453,780
SIC 8211 Elementary and secondary schools
Glen Brodziak
Jean Champagne

D-U-N-S 20-029-7567   (BR)
ST. PAUL EDUCATION REGIONAL DIVISION NO 1
GLEN AVON SCHOOL
(*Suby of* ST. PAUL EDUCATION REGIONAL
DIVISION NO 1)
5201 50 Ave, St Paul, AB, T0A 3A0
(780) 645-3237
Emp Here 77
SIC 8211 Elementary and secondary schools
Kandy Songer

D-U-N-S 20-567-9066   (HQ)
XTREME OILFIELD TECHNOLOGY LTD
4905 50 Ave, St Paul, AB, T0A 3A0
(780) 645-5979
Emp Here 85   *Sales* 67,267,900
SIC 1389 Oil and gas field services, nec
Eugene Labant
Ken Siewiertoka

D-U-N-S 20-637-4621   (SL)
ZAROWNY MOTORS (ST PAUL) LTD
5508 50 Ave, St Paul, AB, T0A 3A1
(780) 645-4468
Emp Here 50   *Sales* 24,903,900
SIC 5511 New and used car dealers
David Zarowny
Daniel Zarowny

St. Albert, AB T8N

D-U-N-S 24-777-3927   (SL)
1529813 ALBERTA LTD
BOOSTER JUICE
5 Giroux Rd Suite 420, St. Albert, AB, T8N
6J8
(780) 460-7499
Emp Here 40   *Sales* 10,966,080
SIC 5499 Miscellaneous food stores
Raymond Davidson

D-U-N-S 24-497-9704   (SL)
293564 ALBERTA LTD
RIVERSIDE HONDA & SKIDOO SALES
(*Suby of* 393346 ALBERTA LTD)
15 Inglewood Dr Suite 2, St. Albert, AB, T8N
5E2
(780) 458-7227
Emp Here 45   *Sales* 28,317,600
SIC 5571 Motorcycle dealers
Arthur Perrott
Kevin Perrott

D-U-N-S 24-880-0096   (HQ)
393346 ALBERTA LTD
RIVERSIDE HONDA & SKI-DOO SALES
15 Inglewood Dr Unit 2, St. Albert, AB, T8N
5E2
(780) 458-7227
Sales 22,413,510
SIC 5571 Motorcycle dealers
Arthur Perrott
Kevin Perrott

D-U-N-S 24-606-3031   (HQ)
846840 ALBERTA LTD
PETRO CANADA

174 St Albert Trail, St. Albert, AB, T8N 0P7
(780) 418-1165
Emp Here 5   *Sales* 24,903,900
SIC 5541 Gasoline service stations
Lisa Baker

D-U-N-S 24-399-2278   (SL)
ACCESS PLUMBING & HEATING LTD
215 Carnegie Dr Unit 5, St. Albert, AB, T8N
5B1
(780) 459-5999
Emp Here 50   *Sales* 11,046,700
SIC 1711 Plumbing, heating, air-conditioning
Don Tougas

D-U-N-S 20-646-8667   (HQ)
ALLIANCE READY MIX LTD
47 Elliot St, St. Albert, AB, T8N 5S5
(780) 459-1090
Emp Here 50   *Sales* 12,652,950
SIC 5211 Lumber and other building materials
Arash Vahdaty

D-U-N-S 25-990-4803   (SL)
B-LINE TIRE & AUTO SUPPLY LTD
32 Rayborn Cres, St. Albert, AB, T8N 4B1
(780) 458-7619
Emp Here 49   *Sales* 22,864,110
SIC 5014 Tires and tubes
Michael Bolduc

D-U-N-S 24-880-0369   (SL)
BENEDICT HOLDINGS LTD
VALLEY SHELL
390 St Albert Trail, St. Albert, AB, T8N 5J9
(780) 459-5447
Emp Here 21   *Sales* 10,459,638
SIC 5541 Gasoline service stations
James Benedict
Judy Benedict

D-U-N-S 24-133-5988   (HQ)
CAPE-MAN HOLDINGS LTD
11 Estate Cres, St. Albert, AB, T8N 5X2
(780) 459-0510
Sales 170,261,700
SIC 3442 Metal doors, sash, and trim
Gord Wiebe

D-U-N-S 25-067-2466   (HQ)
CONNECT LOGISTICS SERVICES INC
50 Corriveau Ave, St. Albert, AB, T8N 3T5
(780) 458-4492
Sales 82,282,400
SIC 4226 Special warehousing and storage,
nec
Greg Foreman
Robert Edmunds

D-U-N-S 25-676-8979   (SL)
COX MECHANICAL LTD
65 Corriveau Ave, St. Albert, AB, T8N 5A3
(780) 459-2530
Emp Here 55   *Sales* 12,818,575
SIC 1711 Plumbing, heating, air-conditioning
Arthur Cox

D-U-N-S 24-927-9266   (SL)
EBS CONTRACTING INC
14 Rayborn Cres Suite 200, St. Albert, AB,
T8N 4B1
(780) 459-7110
Emp Here 30   *Sales* 12,580,650
SIC 6712 Bank holding companies
Ron Simonsmeier

D-U-N-S 24-325-9582   (SL)
ELAINE MAH PHARMACY LTD
SHOPPERS DRUG MART
140 St Albert Trail Suite 570, St. Albert, AB,
T8N 7C8
(780) 460-9222
Emp Here 65   *Sales* 15,881,320
SIC 5912 Drug stores and proprietary stores
Elaine Mah

D-U-N-S 24-018-9519   (HQ)
ENTERPRISE GROUP, INC
64 Riel Dr Suite 2, St. Albert, AB, T8N 4A4

(780) 418-4400
Emp Here 10   *Sales* 15,525,635
SIC 1629 Heavy construction, nec
Leonard D. Jaroszuk
Desmond O'kell
Warren Cabral
John Pinsent
John Campbell
Neil Darling

D-U-N-S 24-282-1189   (SL)
GRANDIN MEDICAL HOLDINGS LTD
1 St Anne St, St. Albert, AB, T8N 2E8

Emp Here 30   *Sales* 12,580,650
SIC 6712 Bank holding companies
Ken Chow
Louise Harrison

D-U-N-S 24-273-4432   (HQ)
**GREAT WEST NEWSPAPERS LIMITED
PARTNERSHIP**
340 Carleton Dr, St. Albert, AB, T8N 7L3
(780) 460-5500
Emp Here 100   *Sales* 32,805,400
SIC 2711 Newspapers
Donald W. Jamison
Ernie W Jamison
Mary Jamison
Paula Jamison

D-U-N-S 25-235-3313   (HQ)
**GREATER ST. ALBERT ROMAN CATHOLIC
SEPARATE SCHOOL DISTRICT NO. 734**
*GREATER ST. ALBERT CATHOLIC
SCHOOLS*
6 St Vital Ave, St. Albert, AB, T8N 1K2
(780) 459-7711
Emp Here 30   *Sales* 55,437,879
SIC 8211 Elementary and secondary schools
David Keohane

D-U-N-S 24-332-8812   (SL)
HODGSCO EQUITIES LTD
5 Galarneau Pl, St. Albert, AB, T8N 2Y3
(780) 458-7100
Emp Here 90   *Sales* 56,635,200
SIC 5511 New and used car dealers
Ron G Hodgeson

D-U-N-S 24-090-5521   (SL)
HOLE'S GREENHOUSES & GARDENS LTD
101 Riel Dr, St. Albert, AB, T8N 3X4
(780) 651-7355
Emp Here 50   *Sales* 16,280,000
SIC 5992 Florists
William Hole
Lois Hole
Michael Hole

D-U-N-S 24-014-3474   (BR)
HOME DEPOT OF CANADA INC
(*Suby of* THE HOME DEPOT INC)
750 St Albert Trail, St. Albert, AB, T8N 7H5
(780) 458-4026
Emp Here 100
SIC 5251 Hardware stores
Colin Dutton

D-U-N-S 25-301-2348   (BR)
HUDSON'S BAY COMPANY
(*Suby of* HUDSON'S BAY COMPANY)
375 St Albert Trail Suite 300, St. Albert, AB,
T8N 3K8
(780) 458-5800
Emp Here 110
SIC 5311 Department stores
Robert Strawson

D-U-N-S 25-414-4181   (SL)
JOHNSTON BUILDERS LTD
265 Carleton Dr Unit 201, St. Albert, AB, T8N
4J9
(780) 460-0441
Emp Here 50   *Sales* 23,536,550
SIC 1542 Nonresidential construction, nec
James Hackney

D-U-N-S 20-970-8148   (HQ)

KAEFER INTEGRATED SERVICES LTD
(*Suby of* KAEFER ISOLIERTECHNIK GMBH & CO. KG)
25 Corriveau Ave, St. Albert, AB, T8N 5A3
(780) 484-4310
Emp Here 26   *Sales* 46,722,720
SIC 1799 Special trade contractors, nec

D-U-N-S 20-034-8782   (SL)
LO-SE-CA FOUNDATION - A CHRISTIAN SOCIETY FOR PERSONS WITH DISABILITIES
215 Carnegie Dr Suite 1, St. Albert, AB, T8N 5B1
(780) 460-1400
Emp Here 100   *Sales* 6,842,200
SIC 8322 Individual and family services
 Marie Renaud

D-U-N-S 25-148-1842   (BR)
LOBLAWS INC
REAL CANADIAN SUPERSTORE
(*Suby of* LOBLAW COMPANIES LIMITED)
101 St Albert Rd Suite 1, St. Albert, AB, T8N 6L5
(780) 418-6818
Emp Here 200
SIC 5399 Miscellaneous general merchandise
 Grant Smith

D-U-N-S 25-609-2164   (BR)
LONDON DRUGS LIMITED
LONDON DRUGS
(*Suby of* H.Y. LOUIE CO. LIMITED)
19 Bellerose Dr Suite 10, St. Albert, AB, T8N 5E1
(780) 944-4548
Emp Here 90
SIC 5912 Drug stores and proprietary stores
 Carrie Vanderwell

D-U-N-S 20-328-2538   (HQ)
MCF HOLDINGS LTD
MOUNTAIN CREEK FARMS
(*Suby of* 400369 ALBERTA LTD)
101 Riel Dr Suite 100, St. Albert, AB, T8N 3X4
(780) 477-2233
Emp Here 40   *Sales* 73,384,600
SIC 5154 Livestock
 Lee Wilson Nilsson
 Dawn Andrews

D-U-N-S 24-701-7114   (HQ)
NILSSON BROS. INC
DIRECT SALES, DIV OF
(*Suby of* 400369 ALBERTA LTD)
101 Riel Dr Suite 100, St. Albert, AB, T8N 3X4
(780) 477-2233
Emp Here 25   *Sales* 682,339,000
SIC 2011 Meat packing plants
 Lee Nilsson
 Brian Nilsson
 William Grieve

D-U-N-S 25-169-3263   (SL)
ORION PLASTICS INC
35 Calder Pl, St. Albert, AB, T8N 5A6
(780) 431-2112
Emp Here 50   *Sales* 10,094,850
SIC 3089 Plastics products, nec
 Stephen Moore
 Greg Makar
 Nuno Branco

D-U-N-S 25-609-5928   (SL)
PARADISE PET CENTER LTD
580 St Albert Trail Suite 50, St. Albert, AB, T8N 6M9
(780) 459-6896
Emp Here 33   *Sales* 10,744,800
SIC 5999 Miscellaneous retail stores, nec
 Jayne Terrault

D-U-N-S 20-538-5362   (SL)
PRO-WESTERN PLASTICS LTD
30 Riel Dr, St. Albert, AB, T8N 3Z7
(780) 459-4491
Emp Here 160   *Sales* 25,417,280

SIC 3089 Plastics products, nec
 Paul Lacroix
 David Lacroix
 Real Chamberland
 Greg Karbonik
 Michael Lacroix

D-U-N-S 24-309-3189   (BR)
QUALICARE HEALTH SERVICES CORPORATION
(*Suby of* QUALICARE HEALTH SERVICES CORPORATION)
25 Erin Ridge Rd, St. Albert, AB, T8N 7K8
(780) 458-3044
Emp Here 220
SIC 8051 Skilled nursing care facilities
 Blair Holliday

D-U-N-S 20-896-5129   (SL)
RIVERSIDE SALES LTD
RIVERSIDE YAMAHA-SUZUKI
15 Inglewood Dr Suite 2, St. Albert, AB, T8N 5E2
(780) 458-7272
Emp Here 50   *Sales* 24,903,900
SIC 5571 Motorcycle dealers
 Art Perrott
 Ronald Perrott
 Marilyn Perrott

D-U-N-S 24-003-6699   (SL)
RON HODGSON CHEVROLET BUICK GMC LTD
CHEVROLET BUICK GMC
5 Galarneau Pl, St. Albert, AB, T8N 2Y3
(780) 458-7100
Emp Here 110   *Sales* 69,220,800
SIC 5511 New and used car dealers
 Jeffrey Hodgson
 Tim Filtz
 Tiffany Hodgson

D-U-N-S 24-396-7429   (SL)
ROSE BUILDING MAINTENANCE LTD
7 St Anne St Suite 223, St. Albert, AB, T8N 2X4
(780) 459-4146
Emp Here 75   *Sales* 3,015,675
SIC 7349 Building maintenance services, nec
 Sarwan Gill
 Balbir Gill

D-U-N-S 20-126-4112   (SL)
SAN RUFO HOMES LTD
35c Rayborn Cres, St. Albert, AB, T8N 4A9
(780) 470-4070
Emp Here 29   *Sales* 13,825,518
SIC 1531 Operative builders

D-U-N-S 20-191-3261   (SL)
SELECT EQUIPMENT RENTALS LTD
4 Riel Dr, St. Albert, AB, T8N 3Z7
(780) 419-6100
Emp Here 45   *Sales* 13,147,605
SIC 7353 Heavy construction equipment rental
 Richard Durocher
 Patricia Durocher

D-U-N-S 24-327-2163   (SL)
SERVUS CREDIT UNION PLACE
400 Campbell Rd, St. Albert, AB, T8N 0R8
(780) 418-6088
Emp Here 49   *Sales* 19,473,286
SIC 8699 Membership organizations, nec
 Diane Enger

D-U-N-S 20-314-7137   (SL)
SHEARWALL TRIFORCE INCORPORATED
340 Circle Dr Unit 200, St. Albert, AB, T8N 7L5
(780) 459-4777
Emp Here 25   *Sales* 11,768,275
SIC 1542 Nonresidential construction, nec
 Morris Kadylo

D-U-N-S 24-330-4065   (BR)
SOBEYS CAPITAL INCORPORATED

SOBEYS
(*Suby of* EMPIRE COMPANY LIMITED)
392 St Albert Rd, St. Albert, AB, T8N 5J9
(780) 459-5909
Emp Here 100
SIC 5411 Grocery stores
 Tony Caputo

D-U-N-S 25-271-0496   (BR)
SOBEYS WEST INC
ST ALBERT/INGLEWOOD SAFEWAY
(*Suby of* EMPIRE COMPANY LIMITED)
395 St Albert Trail, St. Albert, AB, T8N 5Z9
(780) 458-3620
Emp Here 250
SIC 5411 Grocery stores
 Louise Sharren

D-U-N-S 25-271-0538   (BR)
SOBEYS WEST INC
SAFEWAY, DIV OF
(*Suby of* EMPIRE COMPANY LIMITED)
2 Hebert Rd Suite 300, St. Albert, AB, T8N 5T8
(780) 460-9356
Emp Here 180
SIC 5411 Grocery stores
 Rob Howe

D-U-N-S 24-091-8912   (SL)
ST. ALBERT DODGE CHRYSLER LTD
184 St Albert Trail, St. Albert, AB, T8N 0P7
(780) 238-8787
Emp Here 50   *Sales* 24,903,900
SIC 5511 New and used car dealers
 Phillip Belland

D-U-N-S 24-421-1277   (BR)
ST. ALBERT PUBLIC SCHOOL DISTRICT NO. 5565
KANE, PAUL HIGH SCHOOL
(*Suby of* ST. ALBERT PUBLIC SCHOOL DISTRICT NO. 5565)
12 Cunningham Rd, St. Albert, AB, T8N 2E9
(780) 459-4405
Emp Here 85
SIC 8211 Elementary and secondary schools
 Larry Dick

D-U-N-S 20-894-7408   (HQ)
ST. ALBERT PUBLIC SCHOOL DISTRICT NO. 5565
60 Sir Winston Churchill Ave, St. Albert, AB, T8N 0G4
(780) 460-3712
Emp Here 30   *Sales* 71,556,446
SIC 8211 Elementary and secondary schools
 Barry Wowk
 Krimsen Sumners
 Michael Brenneis
 Marianne Barrett
 Cheryl Dumont
 Glenys Edwards
 Kim Armstrong
 Gerry Martins
 Sheri Wright

D-U-N-S 20-008-2647   (BR)
ST. ALBERT PUBLIC SCHOOL DISTRICT NO. 5565
BELLEROSE COMPOSITE HIGH SCHOOL
(*Suby of* ST. ALBERT PUBLIC SCHOOL DISTRICT NO. 5565)
49 Giroux Rd, St. Albert, AB, T8N 6N4
(780) 460-8490
Emp Here 90
SIC 8211 Elementary and secondary schools
 Jyoti Mangat

D-U-N-S 25-020-1910   (BR)
ST. ALBERT, CITY OF
ST ALBERT FIRE SERVICES
(*Suby of* ST. ALBERT, CITY OF)
18 Sir Winston Churchill Ave, St. Albert, AB, T8N 2W5
(780) 459-7021
Emp Here 80

SIC 7389 Business services, nec
 Tracy Young

D-U-N-S 25-995-8247   (HQ)
STANDARD GENERAL INC
(*Suby of* BOUYGUES)
250 Carleton Dr, St. Albert, AB, T8N 6W2
(780) 459-6611
Sales 72,185,300
SIC 1611 Highway and street construction
 Chris Greenwood
 Brian Creeling

D-U-N-S 20-746-2508   (SL)
STURGEON HOTEL LTD
ST. ALBERT INN & SUITES
156 St Albert Trail Suite 10, St. Albert, AB, T8N 0P5
(780) 459-5551
Emp Here 105   *Sales* 9,732,450
SIC 7011 Hotels and motels
 Michael Mazepa
 Howard Starkman
 Ed Mazepa
 Debbie Falk
 Daniel Beniuk
 David Trofimuk
 Art Gawryluk
 Clarence Holinski
 Mike Galas
 Peter Radish

D-U-N-S 25-676-6627   (SL)
SYNERGY PROJECTS LTD
SYNERGY BUILDING SOLUTIONS
110 Carleton Dr Suite 120, St. Albert, AB, T8N 3Y4
(780) 459-3344
Emp Here 60   *Sales* 34,220,280
SIC 1542 Nonresidential construction, nec
 Dennis Mozak

D-U-N-S 25-219-0210   (BR)
WAL-MART CANADA CORP
(*Suby of* WALMART INC.)
700 St Albert Trail Suite 3087, St. Albert, AB, T8N 7A5
(780) 458-1629
Emp Here 300
SIC 5311 Department stores
 Marv Deruigh

D-U-N-S 20-048-5279   (HQ)
WESTCON PRECAST INC
(*Suby of* ZENCO ALBERTA LTD)
19 Riel Dr, St. Albert, AB, T8N 3Z2
(780) 459-6695
Emp Here 20   *Sales* 11,671,750
SIC 3272 Concrete products, nec
 Zennie Andrusiw
 Jason Andrusiw
 Robin Andrusiw
 Cory Andrusiw

D-U-N-S 25-515-9220   (SL)
YOUVILLE HOME (GREY NUNS) OF ST ALBERT
YOUVILLE HOME
9 St Vital Ave, St. Albert, AB, T8N 1K1
(780) 460-6900
Emp Here 250   *Sales* 17,081,500
SIC 8059 Nursing and personal care, nec
 Ken Pickard

D-U-N-S 25-414-2797   (HQ)
ZENCO ALBERTA LTD
19 Riel Dr, St. Albert, AB, T8N 3Z2
(780) 459-6695
Emp Here 1   *Sales* 11,671,750
SIC 3272 Concrete products, nec
 Zennie Andrusiw

Stand Off, AB T0L

D-U-N-S 24-441-6616   (HQ)

BLOOD TRIBE DEPARTMENT OF HEALTH INC
Main St, Stand Off, AB, T0L 1Y0
(403) 737-3888
Emp Here 1   *Sales* 33,130,880
SIC 8399 Social services, nec
Cecilia Black Water
Derrick Fox
Lilian Crow Eared Wolf
Mike Frank
Gerri Eagle Speaker
Mike Day Chief
Lance Tail Feathers
Marcel Weasel Head
Nolan Little Bear
Annette Soup

  D-U-N-S 20-391-8383   (SL)
BLOOD TRIBE DEPARTMENT OF HEALTH INC
BLOOD TRIBE EMERGENCY SERVICES
Gd, Stand Off, AB, T0L 1Y0
(403) 737-2102
Emp Here 250   *Sales* 55,728,000
SIC 8099 Health and allied services, nec
Kevin Cowan
Derrick Fox

Standard, AB T0J

  D-U-N-S 20-192-2536   (HQ)
TWIN CREEK HUTTERIAN BRETHREN
TWIN CREEK COLONY
Gd, Standard, AB, T0J 3G0
(403) 644-2283
Sales 10,881,864
SIC 8811 Private households
Jacob Wurtz

Stavely, AB T0L

  D-U-N-S 20-037-9233   (SL)
FOOTHILLS LIVESTOCK AUCTION LTD
Gd, Stavely, AB, T0L 1Z0
(403) 549-2120
Emp Here 15   *Sales* 18,155,955
SIC 5154 Livestock
Sharon Bergervin

Stettler, AB T0C

  D-U-N-S 24-809-2025   (HQ)
ALBERTA PRAIRIE STEAM TOURS LTD
ALTA PRAIRIE RAILWAY EXCURSION
4611 47th Ave, Stettler, AB, T0C 2L0
(403) 742-2811
Sales 18,198,845
SIC 4725 Tour operators
Robert Willis
Jean Macdonald
Peter Hodgeson

  D-U-N-S 24-378-5636   (HQ)
BANNEX PARTNERSHIP
BRICK, THE
6610 50 Ave, Stettler, AB, T0C 2L2
(403) 742-4737
Emp Here 1   *Sales* 10,706,080
SIC 5211 Lumber and other building materials
Len Hoac
Cam Christianson

  D-U-N-S 24-495-0101   (SL)
CJ OILFIELD CONSTRUCTION LTD
4607 42 St, Stettler, AB, T0C 2L0
(403) 742-1102
Emp Here 53   *Sales* 22,405,061
SIC 1541 Industrial buildings and warehouses

Doug Cumberland
Grace Stewart
Al Mattie

  D-U-N-S 24-962-4354   (HQ)
COUNTY STETTLER HOUSING AUTHORITY, THE
WILLOW CREEK LODGE
620 47th Ave Suite 111, Stettler, AB, T0C 2L1
(403) 742-2953
Emp Here 1   *Sales* 19,878,390
SIC 6513 Apartment building operators
Betty Tschritter
Les Stulberg

  D-U-N-S 25-140-9306   (BR)
COUNTY STETTLER HOUSING AUTHORITY, THE
(*Suby of* COUNTY STETTLER HOUSING AUTHORITY, THE)
611 50th Ave, Stettler, AB, T0C 2L1
(403) 742-9220
Emp Here 110
SIC 6513 Apartment building operators
Carol Dyck

  D-U-N-S 20-280-0541   (SL)
DNR PRESSURE WELDING LTD
(*Suby of* QUANTA SERVICES, INC.)
39123 Range Rd 19-3, Stettler, AB, T0C 2L0
(403) 742-2859
Emp Here 55   *Sales* 13,540,230
SIC 1799 Special trade contractors, nec
Aaron Nixon
Ryan Nixon
Noel Nixon

  D-U-N-S 25-998-8194   (BR)
DYNAMIC ATTRACTIONS LTD
PETRO FIELD INDUSTRY
(*Suby of* DYNAMIC ATTRACTIONS LTD)
4102 44 Ave, Stettler, AB, T0C 2L0

Emp Here 80
SIC 3713 Truck and bus bodies
Paul Patterson

  D-U-N-S 20-829-4470   (SL)
HUTTERIAN BRETHREN OF RED WILLOW
RED WILLOW COLONY
Gd, Stettler, AB, T0C 2L0
(403) 742-3988
Emp Here 50   *Sales* 17,123,350
SIC 0119 Cash grains, nec
Jake Hofer

  D-U-N-S 25-093-1115   (HQ)
PETROFIELD INDUSTRIES INC
4102 44th Ave, Stettler, AB, T0C 2L0
(403) 883-2400
Sales 13,320,060
SIC 3533 Oil and gas field machinery
Bill Rollins

  D-U-N-S 25-770-4635   (BR)
SOBEYS CAPITAL INCORPORATED
STETTLER SOBEYS
(*Suby of* EMPIRE COMPANY LIMITED)
4607 50 St, Stettler, AB, T0C 2L0
(403) 742-5025
Emp Here 88
SIC 5411 Grocery stores
Dwayne Grover

  D-U-N-S 24-853-7979   (SL)
STETTLER AUCTION MART (1990) LTD
4305 52 Ave, Stettler, AB, T0C 2L0
(403) 742-2369
Emp Here 40   *Sales* 58,707,680
SIC 5154 Livestock
Greg Hayden
James Abel
Marilyn Abel
Karen Hayden

  D-U-N-S 20-565-3806   (SL)
STETTLER DODGE LTD
4406 44 Ave, Stettler, AB, T0C 2L0

(403) 742-3000
Emp Here 38   *Sales* 18,926,964
SIC 5511 New and used car dealers
Kelly Hicks

  D-U-N-S 25-505-4777   (SL)
STETTLER MOTORS (1998) LTD
STETTLER GM
6115 50 Ave Ss 2, Stettler, AB, T0C 2L2
(403) 742-3407
Emp Here 30   *Sales* 14,942,340
SIC 5511 New and used car dealers
Brenda Esquirol

  D-U-N-S 20-547-8840   (HQ)
STRAD COMPRESSION AND PRODUCTION SERVICES LTD
(*Suby of* STRAD INC)
Hwy 12 W, Stettler, AB, T0C 2L0
(403) 742-6900
Emp Here 36   *Sales* 25,824,990
SIC 7699 Repair services, nec
Brady Flett
Wayne Long

  D-U-N-S 24-961-5774   (SL)
TKS CONTROLS LTD
4605 41 St, Stettler, AB, T0C 2L0
(403) 740-4071
Emp Here 22   *Sales* 10,450,572
SIC 5084 Industrial machinery and equipment
Brad Syson
Brent Kranzler

  D-U-N-S 24-025-9833   (BR)
WAL-MART CANADA CORP
WALMART
(*Suby of* WALMART INC.)
4724 70th St, Stettler, AB, T0C 2L1
(403) 742-4404
Emp Here 120
SIC 5311 Department stores

  D-U-N-S 24-418-4425   (SL)
WARDELL, A & M SALES LTD
CANADIAN TIRE
6607 50 Ave, Stettler, AB, T0C 2L2
(403) 742-8319
Emp Here 30   *Sales* 14,942,340
SIC 5531 Auto and home supply stores
Adrian Wardell

Stony Plain, AB T7Z

  D-U-N-S 20-293-5193   (HQ)
1742009 ALBERTA INC
AGRITERRA EQUIPMENT
28007 Highway 16, Stony Plain, AB, T7Z 1S5
(780) 963-2251
Emp Here 27   *Sales* 32,412,146
SIC 3523 Farm machinery and equipment
Brian Taschuk
Lars Gauthier
Stan Topola
Sanjiv Kashyap

  D-U-N-S 25-681-2306   (SL)
CASTLE ROCK CONTRACTING LTD
967 Boulder Blvd Suite 101, Stony Plain, AB, T7Z 0E7
(780) 968-6828
Emp Here 30   *Sales* 14,121,930
SIC 1542 Nonresidential construction, nec
Leland Wilburn
Brenda Wilburn

  D-U-N-S 24-068-1957   (HQ)
COMPETITION CHEVROLET LTD
40 Boulder Blvd, Stony Plain, AB, T7Z 1V7
(780) 963-6121
Emp Here 1   *Sales* 44,049,600
SIC 5511 New and used car dealers
Blair Pollock

  D-U-N-S 20-086-8883   (HQ)

FRESON MARKET LTD
BARRHEAD IGA
(*Suby of* ALTAMART INVESTMENTS (1993) LTD)
4401 48 St Unit 130, Stony Plain, AB, T7Z 1N3
(780) 968-6924
Emp Here 8   *Sales* 192,464,000
SIC 5411 Grocery stores
Frank Lovsin
Mike Lovsin
Shawn Gavigan
Dan Lovsin
Douglas Lovsin
Ken Lovsin

  D-U-N-S 24-880-7927   (SL)
I HAVE A CHANCE SUPPORT SERVICES LTD
990 Boulder Blvd, Stony Plain, AB, T7Z 0E5
(780) 962-0433
Emp Here 140   *Sales* 10,518,060
SIC 8093 Specialty outpatient clinics, nec
Carol Zito
Gary Zito

  D-U-N-S 25-262-3421   (SL)
LAGRANGE MECHANICAL SERVICES LTD
970 Boulder Blvd, Stony Plain, AB, T7Z 0E6
(780) 968-1782
Emp Here 49   *Sales* 10,825,766
SIC 1711 Plumbing, heating, air-conditioning
Gwen La Grange

  D-U-N-S 20-911-0985   (BR)
NORQUEST COLLEGE FOUNDATION, THE
NORQUEST COLLEGE
(*Suby of* NORQUEST COLLEGE FOUNDATION, THE)
3201 43 Ave, Stony Plain, AB, T7Z 1L1
(780) 968-6489
Emp Here 100
SIC 8221 Colleges and universities
Glen Mc Calpin

  D-U-N-S 24-375-3907   (SL)
NORTH CENTRAL CO-OPERATIVE ASSOCIATION LTD
4917 50 Ave, Stony Plain, AB, T7Z 1W6
(780) 963-2272
Emp Here 35   *Sales* 11,303,915
SIC 5411 Grocery stores
Cancace Kline

  D-U-N-S 20-091-5056   (SL)
PARKLAND FARM EQUIPMENT (1990) LTD
34 Boulder Blvd, Stony Plain, AB, T7Z 1V7
(780) 963-7411
Emp Here 24   *Sales* 10,669,918
SIC 5999 Miscellaneous retail stores, nec
Henry George
Richard George
Stanley George
John George

  D-U-N-S 25-168-6010   (HQ)
PARKLAND SCHOOL DIVISION NO. 70
4603 48 St, Stony Plain, AB, T7Z 2A8
(780) 963-4010
Emp Here 50   *Sales* 80,881,104
SIC 8211 Elementary and secondary schools
Mary Lynne Campbell
Claire Jonsson

  D-U-N-S 20-091-5080   (HQ)
RAY AGRO & PETROLEUM LTD
18 Boulder Blvd, Stony Plain, AB, T7Z 1V7
(780) 963-2078
Sales 22,275,600
SIC 5191 Farm supplies
Elmer Ray

  D-U-N-S 24-031-2343   (SL)
SAINT JOHN'S SCHOOL OF ALBERTA
Gd, Stony Plain, AB, T7Z 1X5
(780) 701-5625
Emp Here 30   *Sales* 11,922,420
SIC 8699 Membership organizations, nec

Peter Jackson

D-U-N-S 24-733-2612   (SL)
STONY PLAIN CHRYSLER LTD
4004 51 St, Stony Plain, AB, T7Z 0A2
(780) 963-2236
Emp Here 46   *Sales* 22,911,588
SIC 5511 New and used car dealers
Wes Kulak
Dale Fellows

Strathmore, AB T1P

D-U-N-S 24-416-5767   (SL)
6842071 CANADA INC
STRATHMORE HUSKY
436 Ridge Rd Suite 1, Strathmore, AB, T1P 1B5

Emp Here 24   *Sales* 11,953,872
SIC 5541 Gasoline service stations
Christine Katterhagen

D-U-N-S 20-971-6955   (BR)
CALGARY CO-OPERATIVE ASSOCIATION LIMITED
CALGARY CO-OP
(*Suby of* CALGARY CO-OPERATIVE ASSOCIATION LIMITED)
320 2nd St, Strathmore, AB, T1P 1K1
(403) 934-3121
Emp Here 130
SIC 5411 Grocery stores
Steve Jones

D-U-N-S 20-644-2902   (SL)
CANADIAN TIRE
900 Pine Rd Suite 109, Strathmore, AB, T1P 0A2
(403) 934-9733
Emp Here 30   *Sales* 14,942,340
SIC 5531 Auto and home supply stores
Shelley Orford

D-U-N-S 24-322-7662   (HQ)
EAGLE LAKE TURF FARMS LTD
EAGLE LAKE PROFESSIONAL LANDSCAPE SUPPLY
Gd Stn Main, Strathmore, AB, T1P 1J5
(403) 934-6808
Sales 15,411,015
SIC 0181 Ornamental nursery products
Eric Heuver

D-U-N-S 20-182-2801   (HQ)
GLOBAL INTERNATIONAL INC
Gd Stn Main, Strathmore, AB, T1P 1J5
(403) 934-5046
Sales 15,209,400
SIC 8748 Business consulting, nec
Debbie Shelley

D-U-N-S 24-423-8817   (SL)
HUTTERIAN BRETHREN CHURCH OF MOUNTAINVIEW, THE
Gd Stn Main, Strathmore, AB, T1P 1J5
(403) 935-4210
Emp Here 104   *Sales* 10,828,792
SIC 8661 Religious organizations
David Tschetter
Walter Hofer
John Hofer

D-U-N-S 20-200-1579   (SL)
NAMAKA FARMS INC
Gd Stn Main, Strathmore, AB, T1P 1J5
(403) 934-6122
Emp Here 30   *Sales* 11,565,570
SIC 0212 Beef cattle, except feedlots
Edward Thiessen
Donna Thiessen
Brian Stewart

D-U-N-S 24-731-2577   (SL)
NO FRILLS

900 Pine Rd Suite 101, Strathmore, AB, T1P 0A2
(403) 934-6500
Emp Here 49   *Sales* 12,394,746
SIC 5912 Drug stores and proprietary stores
Tina Shipley

D-U-N-S 25-315-4553   (SL)
SMITH, BYRON FORD SALES INC
1040 Westridge Rd, Strathmore, AB, T1P 1H8
(403) 934-2100
Emp Here 30   *Sales* 14,942,340
SIC 5511 New and used car dealers
Byron Smith

D-U-N-S 20-827-1692   (SL)
STRATHMORE MOTOR PRODUCTS LTD
900 Westridge Rd, Strathmore, AB, T1P 1H8
(403) 934-3334
Emp Here 30   *Sales* 14,942,340
SIC 5511 New and used car dealers
Hal Lust

D-U-N-S 24-319-5158   (BR)
WAL-MART CANADA CORP
WAL-MART
(*Suby of* WALMART INC.)
200 Ranch Market, Strathmore, AB, T1P 0A8
(403) 934-9776
Emp Here 120
SIC 5311 Department stores

Sturgeon County, AB T0G

D-U-N-S 20-303-3816   (BR)
LIBERTY TIRE RECYCLING CANADA LTD
LIBERTY TIRE RECYCLING CANADA (AB)
(*Suby of* LAUREL MOUNTAIN PARTNERS LLC)
57425 Rge Rd 253, Sturgeon County, AB, T0G 1L1
(780) 961-2090
Emp Here 80
SIC 4953 Refuse systems
Terrie-Lynn Miller

Sturgeon County, AB T8L

D-U-N-S 25-409-2356   (SL)
GUARDIAN CHEMICALS INC
TRAXOL CHEMICALS
(*Suby of* SKYLINE PRODUCTS LTD)
55202 825 Hwy Suite 155, Sturgeon County, AB, T8L 5C1
(780) 998-3771
Emp Here 55   *Sales* 15,621,155
SIC 2819 Industrial inorganic chemicals, nec
Stewart Roth
Wilf Nikolaj

D-U-N-S 20-048-5290   (HQ)
HORTON CBI, LIMITED
(*Suby of* MCDERMOTT INTERNATIONAL, INC.)
55116 Hwy 825, Sturgeon County, AB, T8L 5C1
(780) 998-2800
Emp Here 40   *Sales* 24,618,600
SIC 1791 Structural steel erection
Greg Guse
Kim Tsang
Brian Sherman
Rafael Velasco
Karl Thiessen
Bridget Toms
Jonathan Cahwoon

Sturgeon County, AB T8R

D-U-N-S 20-894-9024   (HQ)
CALAHOO MEATS LTD
3 54416 Rge Rd 280, Sturgeon County, AB, T8R 1Z5
(780) 458-2136
Sales 71,024,045
SIC 5147 Meats and meat products
Ken Berube

Sturgeon County, AB T8T

D-U-N-S 20-315-9595   (SL)
CANADIAN OATS MILLING LTD
55021 Rge Rd 234a, Sturgeon County, AB, T8T 2A9
(780) 973-9102
Emp Here 35   *Sales* 51,369,220
SIC 5153 Grain and field beans
Felipe Gomez Fajardo
Luis Gomez
Arthur Ruiz

D-U-N-S 20-810-7565   (HQ)
DELTA HELICOPTERS LTD
26004 Twp Rd 544 Unit 13, Sturgeon County, AB, T8T 0B6
(780) 458-3564
Emp Here 17   *Sales* 10,392,128
SIC 4522 Air transportation, nonscheduled
Donald Stubbs
Kathy Stubbs

D-U-N-S 25-231-0396   (SL)
HELIQWEST AVIATION INC
(*Suby of* HELIQWEST INTERNATIONAL INC.)
27018 Sh 633 Unit 37, Sturgeon County, AB, T8T 0E3
(780) 458-3005
Emp Here 50   *Sales* 16,237,700
SIC 4522 Air transportation, nonscheduled
Robert Chalifoux

D-U-N-S 24-399-2716   (SL)
MILEPOST OILFIELD SERVICES LTD
MILEPOST MANUFACTURING, DIV OF
26004 Twp Rd 544 Unit 43, Sturgeon County, AB, T8T 0B6
(780) 459-1030
Emp Here 60   *Sales* 11,525,100
SIC 3443 Fabricated plate work (boiler shop)
Dwayne Bendfeld

D-U-N-S 20-329-6525   (SL)
ON-TRACK RAILWAY OPERATIONS LTD
55024 Rge Rd 234, Sturgeon County, AB, T8T 2A7
(780) 973-6003
Emp Here 65   *Sales* 17,520,685
SIC 4011 Railroads, line-haul operating
Crystal Mendiuk

D-U-N-S 25-272-6476   (SL)
WHITSON CONTRACTING LTD
51-26004 Twp Rd 544, Sturgeon County, AB, T8T 0B6
(780) 421-4292
Emp Here 30   *Sales* 15,405,827
SIC 1542 Nonresidential construction, nec
Philip Whitson
Connor Whitson
Clinton Whitson
Layne Whitson

Sturgeon County, AB T8W

D-U-N-S 24-338-1584   (HQ)
WITHERS L.P.
WITHERS TRUCKING
(*Suby of* MULLEN GROUP LTD)
3602 93 St, Sturgeon County, AB, T8W 5A8

(780) 539-5347
Emp Here 35   *Sales* 15,427,950
SIC 4213 Trucking, except local
Donna Brancati

Sundre, AB T0M

D-U-N-S 20-778-1910   (BR)
ALBERTA HEALTH SERVICES
SUNDRE HOSPITAL & CARE CENTRE
(*Suby of* GOVERNMENT OF THE PROVINCE OF ALBERTA)
709 1 St Ne, Sundre, AB, T0M 1X0
(403) 638-3033
Emp Here 100
SIC 8062 General medical and surgical hospitals
Audrey Mckenzie

D-U-N-S 24-673-1889   (SL)
SUNDRE FOREST PRODUCTS INC
(*Suby of* WEST FRASER TIMBER CO. LTD)
5541 Hwy 584 W, Sundre, AB, T0M 1X0
(403) 638-4093
Emp Here 249   *Sales* 69,319,110
SIC 2421 Sawmills and planing mills, general
Brian Balkwill
Martti Solin
Gerald J Miller
Henry H Ketcham

D-U-N-S 20-091-6302   (SL)
SUNDRE MOTORS LTD
104 Main Ave Ne, Sundre, AB, T0M 1X0

Emp Here 25   *Sales* 12,451,950
SIC 5511 New and used car dealers
Edwin Morgan

D-U-N-S 20-645-2385   (SL)
WILD'S TIMBER CONTRACTORS LTD
WILD'S HOME HARDWARE BUILDING CENTRE
Highway 584 W, Sundre, AB, T0M 1X0
(403) 638-3508
Emp Here 46   *Sales* 11,640,714
SIC 5251 Hardware stores
Les Hengen
Michele Hengen

Swan Hills, AB T0G

D-U-N-S 20-741-7515   (BR)
DEVON CANADA CORPORATION
(*Suby of* DEVON ENERGY CORPORATION)
Gd, Swan Hills, AB, T0G 2C0
(780) 333-7800
Emp Here 75
SIC 5172 Petroleum products, nec
Anthony Jackson

D-U-N-S 24-389-3083   (BR)
KMC OILFIELD MAINTENANCE LTD
(*Suby of* KMC OILFIELD MAINTENANCE LTD)
4728 Watson Cres, Swan Hills, AB, T0G 2C0
(780) 333-4300
Emp Here 100
SIC 4212 Local trucking, without storage
Kelvin Badger

D-U-N-S 25-507-2175   (BR)
PENGROWTH ENERGY CORPORATION
JUDY CREEK OPERATIONS
(*Suby of* PENGROWTH ENERGY CORPORATION)
Gd, Swan Hills, AB, T0G 2C0
(780) 333-7100
Emp Here 100
SIC 1311 Crude petroleum and natural gas
Ron Shannon

▲ Public Company   ■ Public Company Family Member   **HQ** Headquarters   **BR** Branch   **SL** Single Location

D-U-N-S 24-337-5800   (BR)
SUEZ CANADA WASTE SERIVCES INC
SWAN HILLS TREATMENT CENTRE
(*Suby of* SUEZ CANADA WASTE SERIVCES INC)
10000 Chrystina Lake Rd, Swan Hills, AB, T0G 2C0
(780) 333-4197
Emp Here 110
SIC 4953 Refuse systems
Don Freckelton

Sylvan Lake, AB T4S

D-U-N-S 25-483-9913   (SL)
BIG MOO ICE CREAM PARLOURS, THE
4603 Lakeshore Dr, Sylvan Lake, AB, T4S 1C3
(403) 887-5533
Emp Here 60   *Sales* 17,608,620
SIC 5451 Dairy products stores
Steven Pritchard
Louise Pritchard

D-U-N-S 25-678-8555   (HQ)
CANADIAN ENGINEERED WOOD PRODUCTS LTD
CEWP
1 Erickson Dr, Sylvan Lake, AB, T4S 1P5
(403) 887-6677
Emp Here 1   *Sales* 12,968,046
SIC 5031 Lumber, plywood, and millwork
Griffin Jones
Dave Lebreton
Ferg Evans

D-U-N-S 25-632-4013   (SL)
CANADIAN TIRE
62 Thevenaz Ind. Trail Unit 200, Sylvan Lake, AB, T4S 0B6
(403) 887-0581
Emp Here 30   *Sales* 14,942,340
SIC 5531 Auto and home supply stores
Michael Medline

D-U-N-S 20-922-4836   (SL)
COBB'S AG FOODS LTD
5015 50 St Suite 2, Sylvan Lake, AB, T4S 1P9

Emp Here 60   *Sales* 17,608,620
SIC 5411 Grocery stores
Donald Gummo

D-U-N-S 20-524-2436   (SL)
FALCON HOMES LTD
17 Beju Industrial Dr, Sylvan Lake, AB, T4S 2J4
(403) 887-7333
Emp Here 35   *Sales* 11,160,415
SIC 1521 Single-family housing construction
Kevin Pardy

D-U-N-S 24-072-4138   (SL)
MOUNTAIN WEST SERVICES LTD
14 Thevenaz Ind. Trail Unit 3, Sylvan Lake, AB, T4S 2J5
(403) 887-3562
Emp Here 49   *Sales* 10,296,419
SIC 1389 Oil and gas field services, nec
Jim Damini

D-U-N-S 20-300-9444   (HQ)
NEXSOURCE POWER INC
40 Industrial Dr, Sylvan Lake, AB, T4S 1P4
(403) 887-3654
Emp Here 50   *Sales* 81,584,880
SIC 4911 Electric services
Dakin Darnell
Fraser Darcy
Hamm Martin

D-U-N-S 25-384-7388   (HQ)
SPARTEK SYSTEMS INC
1 Thevenaz Ind. Trail, Sylvan Lake, AB, T4S 2J6

(403) 887-2443
Emp Here 48   *Sales* 18,183,120
SIC 3829 Measuring and controlling devices, nec
Matthew Schmidt
Curtis Warnick
Sun Gengwen

D-U-N-S 24-599-2008   (BR)
WAL-MART CANADA CORP
WALMART
(*Suby of* WALMART INC.)
3420 47 Ave, Sylvan Lake, AB, T4S 0B6
(403) 887-7590
Emp Here 150
SIC 5311 Department stores
Hans Skjonsberg

Taber, AB T1G

D-U-N-S 25-170-3526   (HQ)
BOARD OF TRUSTEES OF HORIZON SCHOOL DIVISION NO 67
HORIZON SCHOOL DIVISION NO 67
6302 56 St, Taber, AB, T1G 1Z9
(403) 223-3547
Emp Here 15   *Sales* 36,694,121
SIC 8211 Elementary and secondary schools
Wilco Tymensen
Barbara Mcdonald
Philip Johansen
Marie Logan
Bruce Francis
Jennifer Crowson
Terry Michaelis
Derek Baron
Rick Anderson
Blair Lowry

D-U-N-S 20-794-6729   (BR)
FIRSTCANADA ULC
FIRST STUDENT
(*Suby of* FIRSTGROUP PLC)
6304b 52 St, Taber, AB, T1G 1J7
(403) 223-5670
Emp Here 110
SIC 4151 School buses
Cheryl Shimbashi

D-U-N-S 25-539-3704   (HQ)
FLEXIBLE SOLUTIONS INTERNATIONAL INC
6001 54 Ave, Taber, AB, T1G 1X4
(403) 223-2995
Emp Here 3   *Sales* 17,829,518
SIC 3949 Sporting and athletic goods, nec
Daniel O'brien
Robert O'brien
John H. Bientjes

D-U-N-S 24-415-9190   (HQ)
GREAT GARB BOUTIQUE (TABER) LTD
5221 48 Ave, Taber, AB, T1G 1S8

Emp Here 7   *Sales* 16,145,640
SIC 5621 Women's clothing stores
Barbara Blanchette

D-U-N-S 25-539-3845   (BR)
LAMB WESTON CANADA ULC
CONAGRA LAMB WESTON
(*Suby of* LAMB WESTON CANADA ULC)
102017 Ridge Rd, Taber, AB, T1G 2E5
(403) 223-3088
Emp Here 225
SIC 2099 Food preparations, nec
Cindy Fauth

D-U-N-S 24-439-7527   (BR)
LANTIC INC
(*Suby of* ROGERS SUGAR INC)
5405 64 St, Taber, AB, T1G 2C4
(403) 223-3535
Emp Here 115

SIC 5149 Groceries and related products, nec
Douglas Emek

D-U-N-S 20-831-7149   (SL)
NEW-WAY IRRIGATION LTD
6003 54 Ave, Taber, AB, T1G 1X4
(403) 223-3591
Emp Here 40   *Sales* 19,001,040
SIC 5083 Farm and garden machinery
Rob Duncan

D-U-N-S 25-057-0512   (SL)
OAKLANE HUTTERIAN BRETHREN
OAKLANE COLONY
Gd Stn Main, Taber, AB, T1G 2E5
(403) 223-2950
Emp Here 57   *Sales* 14,951,613
SIC 0111 Wheat
Eli Waldener
Paul Waldener
John Kleinsser

D-U-N-S 24-014-5540   (BR)
PEPSICO CANADA ULC
HOSTESS FRITO-LAY
(*Suby of* PEPSICO, INC.)
5904 54 Ave, Taber, AB, T1G 1X3
(403) 223-3574
Emp Here 200
SIC 2096 Potato chips and similar snacks
Len Deboer

D-U-N-S 25-955-4038   (SL)
ROWLAND SEEDS INC
ROWLAND FARMS
6210 64 St, Taber, AB, T1G 1Z3
(403) 223-8164
Emp Here 45   *Sales* 15,411,015
SIC 0119 Cash grains, nec
Roy Brewin

D-U-N-S 24-011-9789   (BR)
SOBEYS WEST INC
LUCERNE FOODS, DIV OF
(*Suby of* EMPIRE COMPANY LIMITED)
4926 46 Ave, Taber, AB, T1G 2A4
(403) 223-5749
Emp Here 120
SIC 5411 Grocery stores
Rod Yokoyama

D-U-N-S 20-917-9675   (SL)
SOUTH COUNTRY AGENCIES
SWG
5300 47 Ave, Taber, AB, T1G 1R1
(403) 223-8123
Emp Here 20   *Sales* 20,697,620
SIC 6351 Surety insurance
Bart Robinson

D-U-N-S 20-091-8159   (HQ)
SUMMIT MOTORS LTD
4801 46 Ave, Taber, AB, T1G 2A4
(403) 223-3563
Sales 27,316,125
SIC 5012 Automobiles and other motor vehicles
Rick Tams

D-U-N-S 20-072-4339   (HQ)
TABER SPECIAL NEEDS SOCIETY
6005 60 Ave, Taber, AB, T1G 2C1
(403) 223-4941
Sales 42,552,720
SIC 8699 Membership organizations, nec
Krista Douglas

D-U-N-S 24-319-5018   (BR)
WAL-MART CANADA CORP
WALMART
(*Suby of* WALMART INC.)
4500 64 St Suite 1, Taber, AB, T1G 0A4
(403) 223-3458
Emp Here 101
SIC 5311 Department stores
Joshua Brown

D-U-N-S 24-827-1079   (HQ)

WELL-TECH ENERGY SERVICES INC
6006 58 St, Taber, AB, T1G 2B8
(403) 223-4244
Emp Here 60   *Sales* 10,335,823
SIC 1389 Oil and gas field services, nec
Brad Lockhart
Ken Shelstad
Jeff Lockhart
Brandon Harker

Thorsby, AB T0C

D-U-N-S 25-206-2823   (HQ)
BLUE FALLS MANUFACTURING LTD
ARCTIC SPAS
(*Suby of* SPA LOGIC INC)
4549 52 St, Thorsby, AB, T0C 2P0
(780) 789-2626
Emp Here 120   *Sales* 45,985,176
SIC 3999 Manufacturing industries, nec
Darcy Amendt
Brent Macklin
Dennis Kellner

D-U-N-S 25-976-3563   (BR)
WESTOWER COMMUNICATIONS LTD
(*Suby of* EXCHANGE INCOME CORPORATION)
4933 46th St, Thorsby, AB, T0C 2P0
(780) 789-2375
Emp Here 80
SIC 1623 Water, sewer, and utility lines
Peter Jeffrey

Three Hills, AB T0M

D-U-N-S 24-229-7872   (SL)
825209 ALBERTA LTD
BCP CONSTRUCTION
121 - 17 Ave Ne, Three Hills, AB, T0M 2A0
(403) 443-2601
Emp Here 49   *Sales* 15,624,581
SIC 1521 Single-family housing construction
Billy Coles

D-U-N-S 20-377-3536   (SL)
AQUA 7 REGIONAL WATER COMMISSION
Gd, Three Hills, AB, T0M 2A0
(403) 443-5541
Emp Here 100   *Sales* 29,724,200
SIC 4941 Water supply
Jerry Wittstock
Deanna Keiver

D-U-N-S 24-733-2075   (HQ)
KOCH FUEL PRODUCTS INC
PETRO-CANADA
1221 2nd St N, Three Hills, AB, T0M 2A0
(403) 443-5770
Emp Here 14   *Sales* 31,430,025
SIC 5171 Petroleum bulk stations and terminals
Elroy Koch
Carol Ann Koch

D-U-N-S 25-481-2183   (SL)
THREE HILLS FOOD STORES LTD
THREE HILLS IGA
119 4th Ave N, Three Hills, AB, T0M 2A0
(403) 443-5022
Emp Here 65   *Sales* 19,076,005
SIC 5411 Grocery stores
Adrien Luijkx

Tofield, AB T0B

D-U-N-S 20-166-1688   (SL)
BEAVER HILL AUCTION SERVICES LTD

▲ Public Company   ■ Public Company Family Member   **HQ** Headquarters   **BR** Branch   **SL** Single Location

Gd, Tofield, AB, T0B 4J0
(780) 662-9384
Emp Here 50   *Sales* 73,384,600
SIC 5154 Livestock
Doug Verstraete

D-U-N-S 24-089-2984   (SL)
HARE FOODS LTD
TOFIELD I G A
4902 51 Ave, Tofield, AB, T0B 4J0
(780) 662-3718
Emp Here 40   *Sales* 10,966,080
SIC 5411 Grocery stores
Dave Hare
Mieke Hare

D-U-N-S 20-531-8053   (SL)
TOFIELD HEALTH CENTER
5543 44 St, Tofield, AB, T0B 4J0
(780) 662-3263
Emp Here 200   *Sales* 20,663,179
SIC 8062 General medical and surgical hospitals
Melody Henrickson

Torrington, AB T0M

D-U-N-S 20-828-6955   (SL)
HUTTERIAN BRETHREN CHURCH OF VALLEYVIEW RANCH
VALLEYVIEW COLONY
Gd, Torrington, AB, T0M 2B0
(403) 631-2372
Emp Here 80   *Sales* 15,829,440
SIC 8661 Religious organizations
David Stahl Sr
Samuel Stahl
Jonathon Stahl

Trochu, AB T0M

D-U-N-S 24-104-8938   (SL)
LEMAY LAND & LIVESTOCK CO
Gd, Trochu, AB, T0M 2C0
(403) 442-3022
Emp Here 10   *Sales* 12,103,970
SIC 5154 Livestock
Cameron Lemay

D-U-N-S 24-011-9735   (SL)
TROCHU MEAT PROCESSORS LTD
SUNTERRA MEATS TROCHU
233 North Rd, Trochu, AB, T0M 2C0
(403) 442-4202
Emp Here 115   *Sales* 82,422,340
SIC 5142 Packaged frozen goods
Ray Price

D-U-N-S 20-092-0692   (SL)
TROCHU MOTORS LTD
102 Eckenfelder St, Trochu, AB, T0M 2C0
(403) 442-3866
Emp Here 42   *Sales* 13,675,200
SIC 5999 Miscellaneous retail stores, nec
Donald Stankievech
Richmond Meding

Tsuu T'Ina, AB T3E

D-U-N-S 24-682-6650   (SL)
SONCO GAMING LIMITED PARTNERSHIP
GREY EAGLE CASINO & BINGO
377 Grey Eagle Dr, Tsuu T'Ina, AB, T3E 3X8
(403) 385-3777
Emp Here 400   *Sales* 34,680,000
SIC 7999 Amusement and recreation, nec
Martin Brickstock
Britt Gudmundson

Turin, AB T0K

D-U-N-S 25-338-9340   (SL)
GOLDRIDGE FARMING CO. LTD
TURIN COLONY
Gd, Turin, AB, T0K 2H0
(403) 359-5111
Emp Here 48   *Sales* 16,438,416
SIC 0119 Cash grains, nec
Darius Walter
Chris Walder

Turner Valley, AB T0L

D-U-N-S 20-374-9820   (SL)
PORCHLIGHT DEVELOPMENTS LTD
414 Main St Nw, Turner Valley, AB, T0L 2A0
(403) 933-3440
Emp Here 65   *Sales* 15,228,720
SIC 8742 Management consulting services
Robert Butler
Neil Braun
James Weigel

Two Hills, AB T0B

D-U-N-S 24-236-1942   (SL)
COUNTY OF TWO HILLS NATURAL GAS
5606 51 St, Two Hills, AB, T0B 4K0
(780) 657-2800
Emp Here 7   *Sales* 21,740,999
SIC 4924 Natural gas distribution
Robert Jorverson

Valleyview, AB T0H

D-U-N-S 20-538-3680   (SL)
E & T FOODS LTD
5203 50 Ave, Valleyview, AB, T0H 3N0
(780) 524-4424
Emp Here 40   *Sales* 10,966,080
SIC 5411 Grocery stores
Edward R Chychul
Theresa Chychul

D-U-N-S 20-809-1439   (SL)
HOLLINGWORTH, A B & SON CONSTRUCTION LTD
Gd, Valleyview, AB, T0H 3N0
(780) 524-4233
Emp Here 100   *Sales* 31,970,500
SIC 1389 Oil and gas field services, nec
Richard Hollingworth
Lydia Hollingworth

D-U-N-S 20-733-8133   (SL)
REWARD OILFIELD SERVICES LTD
Se 15- 70- 22 W 5, Valleyview, AB, T0H 3N0
(780) 524-5220
Emp Here 68   *Sales* 21,739,940
SIC 1389 Oil and gas field services, nec
Mitch Caron

Vauxhall, AB T0K

D-U-N-S 25-228-8014   (SL)
PRAIRIEVIEW SEED POTATOES LTD
162035 Township Rd 125, Vauxhall, AB, T0K 2K0
(403) 654-2475
Emp Here 50   *Sales* 17,123,350
SIC 0139 Field crops, except cash grain
William Delanoy

Ann Zalik
Luke Delanoy

Vegreville, AB T9C

D-U-N-S 24-414-0963   (HQ)
BUHLER EZEE-ON, INC
(*Suby of* ROSTSELMASH, PAO)
5110 62 St, Vegreville, AB, T9C 1N6
(780) 632-2126
Emp Here 1   *Sales* 18,870,085
SIC 3523 Farm machinery and equipment
Dmitry Lyubimov
Maxim Loktionov
Leo Turko

D-U-N-S 25-628-5891   (SL)
FOOD BANK
4615 60 St, Vegreville, AB, T9C 1N4
(780) 632-6002
Emp Here 30   *Sales* 11,922,420
SIC 8699 Membership organizations, nec
Nelly Highet

D-U-N-S 24-388-9230   (SL)
MALGO, JA SALES LTD
CANADIAN TIRE
6623 16a Hwy W, Vegreville, AB, T9C 0A3

Emp Here 40   *Sales* 19,923,120
SIC 5531 Auto and home supply stores
John Malgo

D-U-N-S 20-860-6918   (BR)
PORTAGE COLLEGE
HIMSL LAW OFFICE
(*Suby of* PORTAGE COLLEGE)
5005 50 Ave, Vegreville, AB, T9C 1T1

Emp Here 250
SIC 8221 Colleges and universities
Damon Himsl

D-U-N-S 25-595-1220   (SL)
PRAIRIE FUELS
4744 51 Ave, Vegreville, AB, T9C 1S1
(780) 632-4987
Emp Here 24   *Sales* 24,787,392
SIC 5171 Petroleum bulk stations and terminals
Clifford Drever
David Drever

D-U-N-S 24-627-9699   (SL)
ST JOSEPH'S GENERAL HOSPITAL
5241 43rd St, Vegreville, AB, T9C 1R5
(780) 632-2811
Emp Here 165   *Sales* 18,328,200
SIC 8062 General medical and surgical hospitals
Eugene Rudyk
Anton Powley

D-U-N-S 20-563-1778   (SL)
TERRAVEST INCOME FUND
4901 Bruce Rd, Vegreville, AB, T9C 1C3
(780) 632-7774
Emp Here 800   *Sales* 4,669,540,000
SIC 6722 Management investment, open-end
John Maynard
Dale H. Laniuk
John B. Zaozimy
Robert L. Phillips
D. Murray Wallace
George S. Armoyan

D-U-N-S 20-305-3442   (HQ)
TERRAVEST INDUSTRIES INC
4901 Bruce Rd, Vegreville, AB, T9C 1C3
(780) 632-2040
Emp Here 50   *Sales* 153,512,199
SIC 3714 Motor vehicle parts and accessories
Charles Pellerin
Dustin Haw

Pierre Fournier
Michael Gering
Mitchell Gilbert
Blair Cook
Dale H. Lanuik
Michael Macbean

D-U-N-S 20-092-2672   (HQ)
TERRAVEST INDUSTRIES LIMITED PARTNERSHIP
R.J.V. GAS FIELD SERVICES
4901 Bruce Rd, Vegreville, AB, T9C 1C3
(780) 632-2040
Emp Here 100   *Sales* 27,750,125
SIC 3533 Oil and gas field machinery
Paul Casey
Dale Laniuk

D-U-N-S 20-895-9999   (HQ)
VANTAGE BUILDERS LTD
4723 49 Ave, Vegreville, AB, T9C 1L1
(780) 632-3422
Sales 28,516,900
SIC 1542 Nonresidential construction, nec
Hugh Ziprick
Walter Gegolick
Darren Davis

D-U-N-S 20-092-3332   (SL)
VEGREVILLE & DISTRICT CO-OP LTD
4914 51 Ave Gd, Vegreville, AB, T9C 1V5
(780) 632-2884
Emp Here 50   *Sales* 13,707,600
SIC 5411 Grocery stores

D-U-N-S 24-906-5574   (SL)
VEGREVILLE FORD SALES & SERVICE INC
6106 50 Ave, Vegreville, AB, T9C 1N6
(780) 632-2060
Emp Here 40   *Sales* 19,923,120
SIC 5511 New and used car dealers
Brian Baron

D-U-N-S 24-330-0550   (BR)
WAL-MART CANADA CORP
(*Suby of* WALMART INC.)
6809 16a Hwy W, Vegreville, AB, T9C 0A2
(780) 632-6016
Emp Here 200
SIC 5311 Department stores
Jackie Coers

Vermilion, AB T9X

D-U-N-S 25-236-3726   (BR)
ALBERTA HEALTH SERVICES
VERMILION HEALTH CARE CENTRE
(*Suby of* GOVERNMENT OF THE PROVINCE OF ALBERTA)
5720 50 Ave, Vermilion, AB, T9X 1K7
(780) 853-5305
Emp Here 180
SIC 8062 General medical and surgical hospitals
Darlene Mcquid

D-U-N-S 25-953-4048   (SL)
COLLEGE PARK MOTOR PRODUCTS LTD
4512 Railway Ave, Vermilion, AB, T9X 1E9
(780) 853-4646
Emp Here 25   *Sales* 12,451,950
SIC 5511 New and used car dealers
Ross Ulmer
Douglas Alan Ulmer
Larry Alward

D-U-N-S 20-655-2031   (SL)
EAST CENTRAL HEALTH AND PUBLIC HEATH HOMECARE AND REHABILITATION
4701 52 St Suite 11, Vermilion, AB, T9X 1J9
(780) 853-5270
Emp Here 45   *Sales* 10,516,275
SIC 8621 Professional organizations

Jo-Anne Brady

D-U-N-S 24-088-9394   (HQ)
LAKELAND COLLEGE
5707 College Dr, Vermilion, AB, T9X 1K5
(780) 853-8400
Emp Here 300   *Sales* 45,594,740
SIC 8222 Junior colleges
Alice Wainwright-Stewart

D-U-N-S 20-026-9876   (BR)
**LEADING   MANUFACTURING   GROUP
HOLDINGS INC**
(*Suby of* LEADING MANUFACTURING
GROUP HOLDINGS INC)
3801 48 Ave, Vermilion, AB, T9X 1G9
(780) 854-0004
Emp Here 100
SIC 3443 Fabricated plate work (boiler shop)
Debra Budson

D-U-N-S 20-135-6510   (SL)
MEN'S DEN, THE
4902 50 Ave, Vermilion, AB, T9X 1A4
(780) 581-0100
Emp Here 28   *Sales* 13,953,016
SIC 5136 Men's and boy's clothing

Veteran, AB T0C

D-U-N-S 24-494-4682   (SL)
**HUTTERIAN BRETHREN CHURCH OF VET-
ERAN**
VETERAN COLONY
Gd, Veteran, AB, T0C 2S0
(403) 575-2169
Emp Here 120   *Sales* 12,494,760
SIC 8661 Religious organizations
Joseph Stahl
Mike K Stahl
Martin Stahl
Chris Stahl
George Stahl

Viking, AB T0B

D-U-N-S 25-969-6961   (BR)
EXTENDICARE INC
EXTENDICARE VIKING
(*Suby of* EXTENDICARE INC)
5020 57th Ave, Viking, AB, T0B 4N0
(780) 336-4790
Emp Here 80
SIC 8051 Skilled nursing care facilities
Mary Hanson

D-U-N-S 24-064-7763   (SL)
VIKING AUCTION MARKET LTD
Gd, Viking, AB, T0B 4N0
(780) 688-2020
Emp Here 25   *Sales* 11,087,250
SIC 7389 Business services, nec
Clifford Grinde

Vulcan, AB T0L

D-U-N-S 25-060-0061   (SL)
FIRST STREET FOODS LTD
MARKET STREET VULCAN
221 2 S, Vulcan, AB, T0L 2B0
(403) 485-6955
Emp Here 50   *Sales* 13,707,600
SIC 5411 Grocery stores
Scott Mitchell

D-U-N-S 24-732-1300   (SL)
MIALTA HUTTERIAN BRETHREN
MIALTA COLONY

Gd, Vulcan, AB, T0L 2B0

Emp Here 100   *Sales* 9,282,600
SIC 8211 Elementary and secondary schools
Jacob Gross
Chris Gross
Benjamin (Ben) Mandel

Wabasca, AB T0G

D-U-N-S 25-990-3557   (SL)
A.I.M. HOLDINGS INC
AIM OILDFIELD SERVICES
2300 Pellican Dr, Wabasca, AB, T0G 2K0
(780) 891-1018
Emp Here 30   *Sales* 12,580,650
SIC 6712 Bank holding companies
Phil Brown

D-U-N-S 25-417-0715   (SL)
BVL CONSTRUCTION SERVICES INC
Gd, Wabasca, AB, T0G 2K0

Emp Here 125   *Sales* 27,750,125
SIC 3533 Oil and gas field machinery
Marcel Auger

D-U-N-S 25-532-1606   (SL)
ERIC AUGER & SONS CONTRACTING LTD
61 Maxim Rd, Wabasca, AB, T0G 2K0
(780) 891-3751
Emp Here 50   *Sales* 14,176,200
SIC 1611 Highway and street construction
Eric Auger

Wainwright, AB T9W

D-U-N-S 24-345-8804   (BR)
AECOM CANADA LTD
(*Suby of* AECOM)
1718 23rd Ave, Wainwright, AB, T9W 1T2
(780) 842-4220
Emp Here 100
SIC 7692 Welding repair
Quinn Olsen

D-U-N-S 25-496-1584   (HQ)
**BUFFALO TRAIL PUBLIC SCHOOLS RE-
GIONAL DIVISION NO. 28**
1041 10a St, Wainwright, AB, T9W 2R4
(780) 842-6144
Emp Here 30   *Sales* 62,564,025
SIC 8211 Elementary and secondary schools
Darcy Eddleston
Lanie Tarr
David Nelson
Robert Brown
Bob Allen
Faye Dunne

D-U-N-S 24-397-2916   (SL)
DAVCO WELDING LTD
DAVCO WELDING & CRANES
Gd Stn Main, Wainright, AB, T9W 1M3
(780) 842-5559
Emp Here 105   *Sales* 25,849,530
SIC 1799 Special trade contractors, nec
David Faas
Connie Faas

D-U-N-S 24-766-3628   (HQ)
**EAST CENTRAL ALBERTA CATHOLIC
SEPERATE SCHOOLS REGIONAL DIVI-
SION NO 16**
1018 1 Ave, Wainwright, AB, T9W 1G9
(780) 842-3992
Emp Here 8   *Sales* 34,691,650
SIC 8211 Elementary and secondary schools
Valery Burgargt
Jim Bradly

D-U-N-S 25-157-5387   (SL)
NORRIS FORD SALES LTD
2929 15 Ave, Wainwright, AB, T9W 0A4
(780) 842-4400
Emp Here 26   *Sales* 12,950,028
SIC 5511 New and used car dealers
Anthony Norris

D-U-N-S 20-092-6418   (HQ)
PERKINS FARMS INC
Gd Stn Main, Wainwright, AB, T9W 1M3
(780) 842-3642
Sales 33,756,916
SIC 5154 Livestock
Bryan Perkins
Sharon Perkins
Ian Perkins

D-U-N-S 24-391-9867   (SL)
WAINALTA MOTORS (1988) LTD
2110 15 Ave, Wainwright, AB, T9W 1L2
(780) 842-4255
Emp Here 23   *Sales* 11,455,794
SIC 5511 New and used car dealers
Kathy Keely

D-U-N-S 24-330-0568   (BR)
WAL-MART CANADA CORP
(*Suby of* WALMART INC.)
2901 13 Ave Suite 1062, Wainwright, AB, T9W
0A2
(780) 842-3144
Emp Here 200
SIC 5311 Department stores
Wes Woodbury

Walsh, AB T0J

D-U-N-S 20-826-0315   (SL)
**HUTTERIAN BRETHREN SPRING CREEK
COLONY**
SPRING CREEK COLONY
Gd, Walsh, AB, T0J 3L0
(403) 937-2524
Emp Here 80   *Sales* 14,446,000
SIC 8661 Religious organizations
Joseph Hofer

Wanham, AB T0H

D-U-N-S 24-044-6646   (SL)
SHADY LANE GRAIN FACILITY
Gd, Wanham, AB, T0H 3P0
(780) 694-3005
Emp Here 30   *Sales* 44,030,760
SIC 5153 Grain and field beans
Ben Tschetter

Warburg, AB T0C

D-U-N-S 25-831-8534   (BR)
PRAIRIE MINES & ROYALTY ULC
(*Suby of* WESTMORELAND COAL COM-
PANY)
Gd, Warburg, AB, T0C 2T0
(780) 848-7786
Emp Here 81
SIC 1221 Bituminous coal and lignite-surface
mining
Mike Peck

D-U-N-S 24-891-7291   (SL)
WILF BRANDT TRUCKING LTD
48176 Hwy 770, Warburg, AB, T0C 2T0
(780) 848-7668
Emp Here 58   *Sales* 13,475,257
SIC 4212 Local trucking, without storage
Wilf Brandt

Warner, AB T0K

D-U-N-S 24-271-3329   (SL)
HUTTERIAN BRETHREN
SUNNY SITE COLONY
Gd, Warner, AB, T0K 2L0
(403) 642-2407
Emp Here 95   *Sales* 9,552,060
SIC 8211 Elementary and secondary schools
Jake Wurz

D-U-N-S 24-961-4868   (SL)
HUTTERIAN BRETHREN OF MILTOW
MILTOW COLONY
Gd, Warner, AB, T0K 2L0
(403) 642-0004
Emp Here 119   *Sales* 20,113,975
SIC 0191 General farms, primarily crop
Joseph Pa Wipf
Sam P Wipf
Sam K Wipf
John Hofer
Paul Kleinsasser
John Mandel

Waskatenau, AB T0A

D-U-N-S 24-674-1177   (SL)
PEPPERS HIGHWAY SERVICE INC
PETRO CANADA
Highway 28, Waskatenau, AB, T0A 3P0
(780) 358-2644
Emp Here 30   *Sales* 14,942,340
SIC 5541 Gasoline service stations
Ernie Dombrosky
Dale Dombrosky

Wembley, AB T0H

D-U-N-S 20-811-7569   (HQ)
CERTEK HEAT MACHINES INC
11101 St Wembley St, Wembley, AB, T0H 3S0
(780) 832-3962
Sales 15,985,250
SIC 1389 Oil and gas field services, nec
Dick Bareneregt
Morgan Bareneregt

Westlock, AB T7P

D-U-N-S 24-243-3473   (SL)
10373532 CANADA LTD
10851 100 St, Westlock, AB, T7P 2R5
(780) 349-7040
Emp Here 80   *Sales* 66,846,160
SIC 5141 Groceries, general line
Trent Finney

D-U-N-S 25-762-0989   (BR)
ALBERTA HEALTH SERVICES
WESTLOCK HEALTHCARE CENTRE
(*Suby of* GOVERNMENT OF THE
PROVINCE OF ALBERTA)
10220 93 St, Westlock, AB, T7P 2G4
(780) 349-3301
Emp Here 100
SIC 8062 General medical and surgical hospi-
tals
Lorraine Oleski

D-U-N-S 20-020-5540   (SL)
CIVIC POWER SPORTS
10111 107 St, Westlock, AB, T7P 1W9
(780) 349-5277
Emp Here 49   *Sales* 10,722,376
SIC 3949 Sporting and athletic goods, nec

▲ Public Company   ■ Public Company Family Member   **HQ** Headquarters   **BR** Branch   **SL** Single Location

Ereth Horinec

D-U-N-S 20-092-7739   (SL)
CIVIC TIRE & BATTERY (WESTLOCK) LTD
KAL TIRE
10111 107 St, Westlock, AB, T7P 1W9
(780) 349-3351
Emp Here 22   *Sales* 10,957,716
SIC 5531 Auto and home supply stores
Douglas Ritter
Joyce Ritter

D-U-N-S 20-913-0975   (SL)
DAPP POWER L.P.
(*Suby of* VERDANT ENERGY LTD)
Rr 1, Westlock, AB, T7P 2N9
(780) 954-2089
Emp Here 27   *Sales* 16,918,578
SIC 4911 Electric services
Grant Noll

D-U-N-S 24-786-1289   (SL)
LAND AIR CONTRACTORS LTD
10011 106 St Suite 205, Westlock, AB, T7P 2K3

Emp Here 100   *Sales* 31,970,500
SIC 1389 Oil and gas field services, nec
Dalton Roska

D-U-N-S 24-818-9776   (SL)
PRECISION TRUCK ACCESSORIES
9024 100 St, Westlock, AB, T7P 2L4
(780) 349-3010
Emp Here 49   *Sales* 24,405,822
SIC 5531 Auto and home supply stores
Angel Kostiw

D-U-N-S 20-092-8208   (SL)
TRIPLE J LIVESTOCK LTD
9004 110a St, Westlock, AB, T7P 2N4
(780) 349-3153
Emp Here 46   *Sales* 67,513,832
SIC 5154 Livestock
Gary Jarvis

D-U-N-S 24-282-7681   (SL)
WABASH MFG. INC
9312 110a St, Westlock, AB, T7P 2M4
(780) 349-4282
Emp Here 95   *Sales* 18,248,075
SIC 3443 Fabricated plate work (boiler shop)
Ernest Hunt
Ronald Riopel

D-U-N-S 20-118-8773   (SL)
WESTLOCK TERMINALS (NGC) LTD
9921 108 St, Westlock, AB, T7P 2J1
(780) 349-7034
Emp Here 9   *Sales* 10,893,573
SIC 5153 Grain and field beans
Bill Hall
Clifford Bell
Richard Krikke
Christopher Rottier
Wayne Peyre
Alan Watt
Steven Miller
Harry Dewindt
Lonnie Brown
Johan Von Rennenkampff

Wetaskiwin, AB T9A

D-U-N-S 20-895-1673   (SL)
1133571 ALBERTA LTD
TOYOTA CITY (WETASKIWIN)
4120 56 St, Wetaskiwin, AB, T9A 1V3
(780) 352-2225
Emp Here 22   *Sales* 10,957,716
SIC 5511 New and used car dealers
Hugh Denham
Geoffrey Skakun

D-U-N-S 20-184-2726   (SL)

747395 ALBERTA LTD
Gd Lcd Main, Wetaskiwin, AB, T9A 1W7
(780) 352-6041
Emp Here 60   *Sales* 19,182,300
SIC 1389 Oil and gas field services, nec
Jack Sundberg
Travis Sundberg

D-U-N-S 20-636-9647   (SL)
BRENTRIDGE FORD SALES LTD
5604 41 Ave, Wetaskiwin, AB, T9A 3M7
(780) 352-6048
Emp Here 31   *Sales* 15,440,418
SIC 5511 New and used car dealers
Brent Denham
Brian Denham

D-U-N-S 25-560-8655   (BR)
CATHOLIC SOCIAL SERVICES
(*Suby of* CATHOLIC SOCIAL SERVICES)
5206 51 Ave, Wetaskiwin, AB, T9A 0V4
(780) 352-5535
Emp Here 200
SIC 8361 Residential care
Donlad Branfill

D-U-N-S 20-059-6120   (HQ)
COMPTON, CLARKE FINANCIAL INC
5402 56 St, Wetaskiwin, AB, T9A 2B3
(780) 352-3311
Sales 22,911,588
SIC 5511 New and used car dealers
Clark Compton

D-U-N-S 20-092-8877   (SL)
DENHAM FORD SALES LTD
5601 45 Ave, Wetaskiwin, AB, T9A 2G2
(780) 352-6043
Emp Here 45   *Sales* 22,413,510
SIC 5511 New and used car dealers
Brent Denham

D-U-N-S 24-679-8586   (SL)
DEWLING, S & C SALES LTD
CANADIAN TIRE
3851 56 St, Wetaskiwin, AB, T9A 2B1
(780) 352-7175
Emp Here 30   *Sales* 14,942,340
SIC 5531 Auto and home supply stores
Steve Dewling

D-U-N-S 24-642-7306   (SL)
DOPKO FOOD SERVICES LTD
MCDONALD'S RESTAURANTS
5517 37a Ave, Wetaskiwin, AB, T9A 3A5
(780) 986-5322
Emp Here 87   *Sales* 3,960,153
SIC 5812 Eating places
Ralph Dopko

D-U-N-S 20-939-7020   (BR)
DUNCAN CRAIG LLP
(*Suby of* DUNCAN CRAIG LLP)
4725 56 St Suite 103, Wetaskiwin, AB, T9A 3M2
(780) 352-1662
Emp Here 140
SIC 8111 Legal services
Darren Bieganek

D-U-N-S 24-567-5645   (HQ)
DYCK INSURANCE AGENCY (WETASKIWIN) LTD.
5105 47 Ave, Wetaskiwin, AB, T9A 0K4
(780) 352-9222
Sales 20,353,440
SIC 6411 Insurance agents, brokers, and service
Frank Dyck
Robert Dyck
Mark Dyck

D-U-N-S 24-064-4799   (SL)
HI LINE FARM EQUIPMENT LTD
4723 39 Ave, Wetaskiwin, AB, T9A 2J4
(780) 352-9244
Emp Here 35   *Sales* 16,625,910
SIC 5083 Farm and garden machinery

Andy Vanderburg
Carla Vanderburg

D-U-N-S 24-399-0546   (BR)
HOME HARDWARE STORES LIMITED
HOME HARDWARE DISTRIBUTION CENTRE
(*Suby of* HOME HARDWARE STORES LIMITED)
6410 36 St, Wetaskiwin, AB, T9A 3B6
(780) 352-1984
Emp Here 396
SIC 5211 Lumber and other building materials
Phil Kohlman

D-U-N-S 24-854-2011   (SL)
HUNCO HOLDINGS LTD
6010 47 St, Wetaskiwin, AB, T9A 2R3
(780) 352-6061
Emp Here 80   *Sales* 17,760,080
SIC 3523 Farm machinery and equipment
George Hunerfauth
Annabelle Dick
Karl Hunerfauth
Marlene Wyness

D-U-N-S 24-058-0253   (SL)
MANLUK INDUSTRIES (2008) INC
MANLUK GLOBAL MANUFACTURING SOLUTIONS
(*Suby of* 1418856 ALBERTA LTD)
4815 42 Ave, Wetaskiwin, AB, T9A 2P6
(780) 352-5522
Emp Here 160   *Sales* 22,540,562
SIC 3494 Valves and pipe fittings, nec
Frank Luebke
Manfred Luebke

D-U-N-S 24-066-6693   (SL)
MANLUK INDUSTRIES INC
4815 42 Ave, Wetaskiwin, AB, T9A 2P6
(780) 352-5522
Emp Here 190   *Sales* 42,180,190
SIC 3532 Mining machinery
Frank Luebke
Juergen Luebke
Manfred Luebke

D-U-N-S 24-673-7688   (HQ)
PEACE HILLS INVESTMENTS LTD
BEST WESTERN WAYSIDE INN
4103 56 St, Wetaskiwin, AB, T9A 1V2
(780) 312-7300
Sales 18,538,000
SIC 7011 Hotels and motels
Brian Denham

D-U-N-S 20-980-0593   (BR)
SOBEYS CAPITAL INCORPORATED
(*Suby of* EMPIRE COMPANY LIMITED)
4703 50 St, Wetaskiwin, AB, T9A 1J6
(780) 352-2227
Emp Here 100
SIC 5411 Grocery stores
Darren Macwilliams

D-U-N-S 24-318-3543   (SL)
SPIRIT PIPELINES LTD
Gd Lcd Main, Wetaskiwin, AB, T9A 1W7
(780) 352-7305
Emp Here 100   *Sales* 26,954,900
SIC 4619 Pipelines, nec
Ryan Hilton

D-U-N-S 20-092-8620   (HQ)
SUPREME INTERNATIONAL LIMITED
6010 47 St, Wetaskiwin, AB, T9A 2R3
(780) 352-6061
Sales 59,401,600
SIC 5191 Farm supplies
George Hunerfauth
Jeannette Guertin

D-U-N-S 25-194-4823   (SL)
WETASKIWIN CHEVROLET OLDSMOBILE (2001) LTD
4710 56 St, Wetaskiwin, AB, T9A 1V7

Emp Here 35   *Sales* 17,432,730
SIC 5511 New and used car dealers
Darrell Schwab

D-U-N-S 20-092-9933   (HQ)
WETASKIWIN CO-OPERATIVE ASSOCIATION LIMITED
COUNTRY JUNCTION DIV OF
4707 40 Ave, Wetaskiwin, AB, T9A 2B8
(780) 352-9121
Emp Here 25   *Sales* 50,816,430
SIC 2048 Prepared feeds, nec
Henrik Bruun
Ken Adair
Tim Hofstra
Boyd Hutchings
Nels Jevne
Warren Lyle
Jeff Morgan
Adri Palsma
Colleen Zimmerman

D-U-N-S 20-271-8219   (SL)
WETASKIWIN READY MIX LTD
5410 50 St, Wetaskiwin, AB, T9A 2G9
(780) 352-4301
Emp Here 60   *Sales* 14,006,100
SIC 3273 Ready-mixed concrete
Doug Markevich

D-U-N-S 20-260-1217   (BR)
WETASKIWIN REGIONAL PUBLIC SCHOOLS
WETASKIWIN COMPOSITE HIGHSCHOOL
(*Suby of* WETASKIWIN REGIONAL PUBLIC SCHOOLS)
4619 50 Ave, Wetaskiwin, AB, T9A 0R6
(780) 352-2295
Emp Here 80
SIC 8211 Elementary and secondary schools
Kris Denney

D-U-N-S 24-364-2944   (HQ)
WETASKIWIN REGIONAL PUBLIC SCHOOLS
5515 47a Ave, Wetaskiwin, AB, T9A 3S3
(780) 352-6018
Emp Here 18   *Sales* 71,861,275
SIC 8211 Elementary and secondary schools
Terry Pearson

Whitecourt, AB T7S

D-U-N-S 24-880-4148   (SL)
2125341 ALBERTA LTD
WHITE COURT IGA
4802 51 St Suite 1, Whitecourt, AB, T7S 1R9
(780) 778-5900
Emp Here 105   *Sales* 30,815,085
SIC 5411 Grocery stores
Doug Andrews

D-U-N-S 24-586-4660   (SL)
875647 ALBERTA LTD
ELITE HOLDINGS INC
Gd Stn Main, Whitecourt, AB, T7S 1S1
(780) 778-6975
Emp Here 25   *Sales* 10,483,875
SIC 6712 Bank holding companies
Earryl Mcphee

D-U-N-S 24-006-7962   (SL)
878175 ALBERTA LTD
SELECT PRODUCTION SERVICES
3365 33 St, Whitecourt, AB, T7S 0A2

Emp Here 65   *Sales* 20,780,825
SIC 1389 Oil and gas field services, nec
Jay Davie

D-U-N-S 20-286-1548   (BR)
BIG COUNTRY ENERGY SERVICES LIMITED PARTNERSHIP
3905 35 St Suite 3, Whitecourt, AB, T7S 0A2

(780) 706-2141
Emp Here 100   *Sales* 722,652
SIC 1623 Water, sewer, and utility lines
Jason Slynn

D-U-N-S 25-269-3072   (SL)
BLUE RIDGE LUMBER INC
(*Suby of* WEST FRASER TIMBER CO. LTD)
Gd Stn Main, Whitecourt, AB, T7S 1S1
(780) 648-6200
Emp Here 250   *Sales* 142,407,000
SIC 5031 Lumber, plywood, and millwork
Scott Macdougall
Henry H Ketcham Iii
Gerry Miller
Martti Solin

D-U-N-S 24-140-8355   (SL)
BOHN PETROLEUM SERVICES LTD
3449 33 St, Whitecourt, AB, T7S 1X4
(780) 778-8551
Emp Here 49   *Sales* 10,296,419
SIC 1389 Oil and gas field services, nec
Alvin Bohn

D-U-N-S 25-131-6840   (SL)
EAGLE RIVER CHRYSLER LTD
3315 Caxton St, Whitecourt, AB, T7S 1P4
(780) 778-2844
Emp Here 22   *Sales* 10,957,716
SIC 5511 New and used car dealers
Mike Stuckless
Hugh Keller

D-U-N-S 24-702-2429   (SL)
FIRST CHOICE TRUCK & CAR WASH INC
FIRST CHOICE HUSKY
3530 Kepler St, Whitecourt, AB, T7S 0B5
(780) 778-3377
Emp Here 30   *Sales* 14,942,340
SIC 5541 Gasoline service stations
Wayne Bronson

D-U-N-S 24-009-3513   (SL)
FUNKTIONAL SLEEP SOLUTIONS LTD
FUNKTIONAL LIFE SOLUTIONS
4920 51st Ave, Whitecourt, AB, T7S 1W2
(780) 778-6461
Emp Here 37   *Sales* 11,302,760
SIC 8999 Services, nec
Donald Funk

D-U-N-S 25-013-7445   (SL)
H D F INSURANCE & FINANCIAL GROUP
5111 50 Ave, Whitecourt, AB, T7S 1S8
(780) 778-8828
Emp Here 30   *Sales* 25,441,800
SIC 6411 Insurance agents, brokers, and service
Leonard Billand

D-U-N-S 20-895-8413   (SL)
KANA OILFIELD SERVICES LTD
4107 41 St, Whitecourt, AB, T7S 0A9
(780) 778-2385
Emp Here 50   *Sales* 10,506,550
SIC 1389 Oil and gas field services, nec
Norm Nolette

D-U-N-S 25-170-7873   (HQ)
LIVING WATERS CATHOLIC REGIONAL DIVISION NO.42
4204 Kepler St Unit 1, Whitecourt, AB, T7S 0A3
(780) 778-5044
Emp Here 6   *Sales* 26,762,130
SIC 8211 Elementary and secondary schools
Carol Lemay
Gemma Christie
Joanne Lanctot

D-U-N-S 20-012-3367   (HQ)
MAX FUEL DISTRIBUTORS (1998) LTD
5503 Kepler St, Whitecourt, AB, T7S 1X7
(780) 778-2346
Emp Here 8   *Sales* 14,459,312
SIC 5172 Petroleum products, nec
Ingo Von Wackerbarth

D-U-N-S 25-483-1563   (BR)
MILLAR WESTERN FOREST PRODUCTS LTD
WHITECOURT PULP DIVISION
(*Suby of* MILLAR, HUGH FAMILY HOLDINGS INC)
5501 50 Ave, Whitecourt, AB, T7S 1N9
(780) 778-2036
Emp Here 130
SIC 2611 Pulp mills
Dave Martell

D-U-N-S 24-330-5075   (BR)
MILLAR WESTERN INDUSTRIES LTD
WHITECOURT WOOD PRODUCT DIVISION
(*Suby of* MILLAR, HUGH FAMILY HOLDINGS INC)
5004 52 St, Whitecourt, AB, T7S 1N2
(780) 778-2221
Emp Here 250
SIC 2421 Sawmills and planing mills, general
Stefan Demharter

D-U-N-S 25-021-9284   (HQ)
NORTHERN GATEWAY REGIONAL DIVISION #10
NORTHERN GATEWAY PUBLIC SCHOOLS
4816 49 Ave, Whitecourt, AB, T7S 0E8
(780) 778-2800
Emp Here 15   *Sales* 59,471,400
SIC 8211 Elementary and secondary schools
Lachllan Watley

D-U-N-S 20-375-0398   (SL)
POMEROY HOTEL LIMITED
4121 Kepler St, Whitecourt, AB, T7S 0A3
(780) 778-8908
Emp Here 100   *Sales* 9,489,900
SIC 7021 Rooming and boarding houses
Dennis Brown

D-U-N-S 20-088-0271   (SL)
SCOTT SAFETY SUPPLY SERVICES LTD
3365 33 St, Whitecourt, AB, T7S 0A2
(780) 778-3389
Emp Here 50   *Sales* 16,280,000
SIC 5999 Miscellaneous retail stores, nec
Brent Stark

D-U-N-S 20-084-9441   (BR)
SEMCAMS MIDSTREAM ULC
(*Suby of* SEMCAMS MIDSTREAM ULC)
Gd, Whitecourt, AB, T7S 1S1
(780) 778-7800
Emp Here 75
SIC 1389 Oil and gas field services, nec
Randie Brown

D-U-N-S 24-380-7349   (SL)
SMYL CHEVROLET PONTIAC BUICK GMC LTD
SMYL GM
3520 Kepler St, Whitecourt, AB, T7S 1N9
(780) 778-2202
Emp Here 28   *Sales* 13,946,184
SIC 5511 New and used car dealers
Joseph Smyl
Duane Smyl
Randy Smyl
Wayne Smyl

D-U-N-S 25-207-2970   (HQ)
SPRUCELAND FORD SALES LTD
4144 Kepler St, Whitecourt, AB, T7S 0A3
(780) 778-4777
Emp Here 30   *Sales* 24,903,900
SIC 5511 New and used car dealers
Gregory Kallal

D-U-N-S 20-261-7593   (SL)
STRATTY ENTERPRISES LTD
5116 59 St, Whitecourt, AB, T7S 1X7
(780) 706-4889
Emp Here 60   *Sales* 11,481,240
SIC 7353 Heavy construction equipment rental
Patrick Stratton

William Ternan
Leanne Stratton

D-U-N-S 24-844-1136   (SL)
VENOM ENERGY
3749 30 St, Whitecourt, AB, T7S 0E4
(780) 778-2440
Emp Here 40   *Sales* 12,788,200
SIC 1389 Oil and gas field services, nec
Logan Crosslan

D-U-N-S 24-030-8408   (BR)
WAL-MART CANADA CORP
(*Suby of* WALMART INC.)
5005 Dahl Dr, Whitecourt, AB, T7S 1X6
(780) 706-3323
Emp Here 200
SIC 5311 Department stores

D-U-N-S 24-808-3420   (BR)
WEST FRASER TIMBER CO. LTD
ALBERTA NEWSPRINT
(*Suby of* WEST FRASER TIMBER CO. LTD)
9 Km W Of Whitecourt Hwy Suite 43, Whitecourt, AB, T7S 1P9
(780) 778-7000
Emp Here 200
SIC 2621 Paper mills
Mike Putzke

D-U-N-S 20-393-4633   (SL)
WHITECOURT FORD INC
4144 Kepler St, Whitecourt, AB, T7S 0A3
(780) 778-4777
Emp Here 33   *Sales* 16,436,574
SIC 5511 New and used car dealers
Brandon Schroder

Yellowhead County, AB T7E

D-U-N-S 20-383-6924   (BR)
WEST FRASER MILLS LTD
(*Suby of* WEST FRASER TIMBER CO. LTD)
53115 Hwy 47, Yellowhead County, AB, T7E 3E9
(780) 723-3977
Emp Here 200
SIC 5031 Lumber, plywood, and millwork

100 Mile House, BC V0K

D-U-N-S 24-372-3855   (SL)
100 MILE DISTRICT GENERAL HOSPITAL
SOUTH CARIBOO HEALTH CENTRE
555 Cedar Ave, 100 Mile House, BC, V0K 2E0
(250) 395-7600
Emp Here 200   *Sales* 22,216,000
SIC 8062 General medical and surgical hospitals
Angie Evans

D-U-N-S 20-333-3856   (BR)
NORBORD INC
(*Suby of* NORBORD INC)
995 Exeter Stn Rd, 100 Mile House, BC, V0K 2E0
(250) 395-6246
Emp Here 140
SIC 2435 Hardwood veneer and plywood
Rick Tagaki

D-U-N-S 20-146-6328   (SL)
SUNRISE FORD SALES LTD
872 Alpine Rd, 100 Mile House, BC, V0K 2E0
(250) 395-2414
Emp Here 30   *Sales* 14,942,340
SIC 5511 New and used car dealers
James French

D-U-N-S 20-700-0253   (BR)
WEST FRASER TIMBER CO. LTD
100 MILE LUMBER
(*Suby of* WEST FRASER TIMBER CO. LTD)
910 Exeter Rd, 100 Mile House, BC, V0K 2E0
(250) 395-8200
Emp Here 230
SIC 5031 Lumber, plywood, and millwork
Peter Andrews

108 Mile Ranch, BC V0K

D-U-N-S 20-971-0867   (SL)
TUCKER'S TRAFFIC CONTROL
5195 Odian St, 108 Mile Ranch, BC, V0K 2Z0
(250) 791-5725
Emp Here 40   *Sales* 11,686,760
SIC 7359 Equipment rental and leasing, nec
Keith Tucker

70 Mile House, BC V0K

D-U-N-S 20-165-4089   (BR)
WEST FRASER MILLS LTD
CHASM SAWMILLS
(*Suby of* WEST FRASER TIMBER CO. LTD)
1020 Chasm Rd, 70 Mile House, BC, V0K 2K0
(250) 459-2229
Emp Here 200
SIC 2421 Sawmills and planing mills, general
Jason Foote

Abbotsford, BC V2S

D-U-N-S 25-654-1533   (SL)
446784 B.C. LTD
WE CARE HOME HEALTH SERVICES
2291 West Railway St Suite B, Abbotsford, BC, V2S 2E3
(604) 864-9682
Emp Here 75   *Sales* 6,949,875
SIC 8322 Individual and family services
Kathy Phillips

D-U-N-S 24-397-6144   (SL)
A C PRODUCTS LTD

3422 Mccallum Rd, Abbotsford, BC, V2S 7W6
(604) 852-4967
Emp Here 49   *Sales* 11,270,931
SIC 3272 Concrete products, nec
Chris Leach
Keith Leach
Cliff Leach

D-U-N-S 25-606-0641   (SL)
ABBOTSFORD CHRISTIAN SCHOOL SOCIETY
35011 Old Clayburn Rd, Abbotsford, BC, V2S 7L7
(604) 755-1891
Emp Here 110   *Sales* 11,453,530
SIC 8661 Religious organizations
Lorraine Brandt

D-U-N-S 24-750-2482   (HQ)
ABBOTSFORD COMMUNITY SERVICES
2420 Montrose Ave, Abbotsford, BC, V2S 3S9
(604) 859-7681
Emp Here 10   *Sales* 11,114,817
SIC 8399 Social services, nec
Rod Santiago

D-U-N-S 24-797-3860   (SL)
ABBOTSFORD CONCRETE PRODUCTS LTD
3422 Mccallum Rd, Abbotsford, BC, V2S 7W6
(604) 852-4967
Emp Here 78   *Sales* 18,207,930
SIC 3271 Concrete block and brick
Clifford Leach
Christopher Leach

D-U-N-S 24-293-7399   (SL)
ABBOTSFORD DENTAL GROUP INC
33782 Marshall Rd, Abbotsford, BC, V2S 1L1
(604) 853-6441
Emp Here 100   *Sales* 8,952,200
SIC 8021 Offices and clinics of dentists
G Tsang

D-U-N-S 25-183-8702   (SL)
ABBOTSFORD RESTAURANTS LTD
KEG IN THE VALLEY
2142 West Railway St, Abbotsford, BC, V2S 2E2
(604) 855-9893
Emp Here 80   *Sales* 3,641,520
SIC 5812 Eating places
Stephen Tidball
Kurt Landert
Robert J Matheson
Neal Pearson

D-U-N-S 20-714-9188   (HQ)
AVENUE MACHINERY CORP
1521 Sumas Way, Abbotsford, BC, V2S 8M9
(604) 792-4111
Emp Here 35   *Sales* 26,126,430
SIC 5083 Farm and garden machinery

D-U-N-S 20-016-8891   (HQ)
BD ENGINE BRAKE INC
BD DIESEL PERFORMANCE
33541 Maclure Rd, Abbotsford, BC, V2S 7W2
(604) 853-6096
Sales 12,485,525
SIC 3465 Automotive stampings
Brian Roth
Ronald Roth

D-U-N-S 25-682-8575   (SL)
BIG RIG COLLISION AND PAINT LTD
BIG RIG HEAVY DUTY PARTS
933 Coutts Way, Abbotsford, BC, V2S 7M2
(604) 857-4915
Emp Here 46   *Sales* 13,031,800
SIC 7532 Top and body repair and paint shops
Paul Roderick Macleod
Douglas John Froese
Larry Wiebe
John Wiebe
Jake Wiebe

D-U-N-S 24-318-8260   (BR)

BLACK PRESS GROUP LTD
ABBOTSFORD NEWS, THE
(*Suby of* BLACK PRESS HOLDINGS LTD)
34375 Gladys Ave, Abbotsford, BC, V2S 2H5
(604) 853-1144
Emp Here 130
SIC 2711 Newspapers
Andrew Franklin

D-U-N-S 20-585-0217   (SL)
BLACKWOOD BUILDING CENTRE LTD
BLACKWOOD BUILDING CENTRE
33050 South Fraser Way, Abbotsford, BC, V2S 2A9
(604) 853-6471
Emp Here 40   *Sales* 10,122,360
SIC 5211 Lumber and other building materials
Abram (Abe) Konrad
Joan Brooks
Bruce Konrad

D-U-N-S 20-622-5674   (SL)
BRABER EQUIPMENT LTD
34425 Mcconnell Rd Suite 117, Abbotsford, BC, V2S 7P1
(604) 850-7770
Emp Here 35   *Sales* 16,625,910
SIC 5083 Farm and garden machinery
Nick Braber

D-U-N-S 20-981-8090   (SL)
CALAIS FARMS LTD
33418 Downes Rd, Abbotsford, BC, V2S 7T4
(604) 852-1660
Emp Here 30   *Sales* 10,274,010
SIC 0191 General farms, primarily crop
Marcus Janzen

D-U-N-S 24-657-0030   (HQ)
CAN-AM WEST CARRIERS INC
400 Riverside Rd, Abbotsford, BC, V2S 7M4
(604) 857-1375
Emp Here 398   *Sales* 73,752,400
SIC 4213 Trucking, except local
Larry Wiebe
Rod Wiebe
Brad Wiebe

D-U-N-S 25-234-4767   (SL)
CANNOR NURSERIES (1989) LTD
34261 Marshall Rd, Abbotsford, BC, V2S 1L8

Emp Here 44   *Sales* 11,134,596
SIC 5261 Retail nurseries and garden stores
Gordon Mathies
Sandy Mathies
Ellen Mathies

D-U-N-S 25-789-4246   (SL)
CENTRAL FRASER VALLEY SEARCH & RESCUE SOCIETY
C F V S A R
1594 Riverside Rd, Abbotsford, BC, V2S 8J2
(604) 852-7271
Emp Here 30   *Sales* 12,738,210
SIC 8999 Services, nec
Lee Holeczek

D-U-N-S 20-994-5930   (SL)
CHET CONSTRUCTION LTD
33759 Morey Ave Suite 1, Abbotsford, BC, V2S 2W5
(604) 859-1441
Emp Here 45   *Sales* 10,839,780
SIC 1623 Water, sewer, and utility lines
Raymond Burdeyny

D-U-N-S 20-864-4526   (HQ)
CLAYBURN INDUSTRIES LTD
CLAYBURN REFRACTORIES
33765 Pine St, Abbotsford, BC, V2S 5C1
(604) 859-5288
Sales 17,921,900
SIC 3255 Clay refractories
David Lane
Clayton Sissons
J. Donald Harris
Len Metcalfe

D-U-N-S 25-287-5695   (BR)
COSTCO WHOLESALE CANADA LTD
(*Suby of* COSTCO WHOLESALE CORPORATION)
1127 Sumas Way, Abbotsford, BC, V2S 8H2
(604) 850-3458
Emp Here 200
SIC 5099 Durable goods, nec

D-U-N-S 20-117-5309   (HQ)
CULLEN WESTERN STAR TRUCK INC
380 Riverside Rd Suite 3, Abbotsford, BC, V2S 7M4
(604) 504-5904
Sales 18,926,964
SIC 5511 New and used car dealers
R. Allan Cullen
Gerald G. Cullen
Dave Cappon
Anne M. Stewart

D-U-N-S 24-274-0608   (SL)
DOMINION CROWN MOULDING INC
34450 Vye Rd, Abbotsford, BC, V2S 7P6
(604) 852-4224
Emp Here 25   *Sales* 11,179,350
SIC 5031 Lumber, plywood, and millwork
Ramzi Astiso

D-U-N-S 20-802-8303   (BR)
EARL'S RESTAURANTS LTD
(*Suby of* EARL'S RESTAURANTS LTD)
32900 South Fraser Way Suite 1, Abbotsford, BC, V2S 5A1

Emp Here 100
SIC 5812 Eating places
Jason Koningen

D-U-N-S 20-369-1808   (SL)
ESPO BROTHERS MANAGEMENT I LTD
33780 King Rd, Abbotsford, BC, V2S 7P2
(604) 859-2220
Emp Here 50   *Sales* 11,985,728
SIC 7361 Employment agencies
Paul Esposito

D-U-N-S 24-155-3601   (SL)
EVANS ENGINE SHOP LTD
(*Suby of* WAKEFIELD-SPERLING AUTO PARTS LTD)
33406 South Fraser Way, Abbotsford, BC, V2S 2B5

Emp Here 67   *Sales* 12,885,976
SIC 7694 Armature rewinding shops
Roy Evans
James Evans

D-U-N-S 25-361-8680   (HQ)
FRASER VALLEY PACKERS HOLDINGS LTD
260 Short Rd, Abbotsford, BC, V2S 8A7
(604) 852-3525
Sales 91,377,250
SIC 6712 Bank holding companies
Arvender Randhwa
Malkit Dhesi

D-U-N-S 20-137-0678   (SL)
FRASER VALLEY PACKERS INC
(*Suby of* FRASER VALLEY PACKERS HOLDINGS LTD)
260 Short Rd, Abbotsford, BC, V2S 8A7
(604) 852-3525
Emp Here 200   *Sales* 34,781,000
SIC 0723 Crop preparation services for market
Gord Cheema
Malkit Dhesi
Arvinder Randhawa

D-U-N-S 24-072-3742   (HQ)
FRASER VALLEY REGIONAL LIBRARY DISTRICT
FRASER VALLEY REGIONAL LIBRARY
34589 Delair Rd, Abbotsford, BC, V2S 5Y1

(604) 859-7141
Emp Here 40   *Sales* 27,742,050
SIC 8231 Libraries
Scott Hargrove

D-U-N-S 20-425-2050   (HQ)
FRIESEN EQUIPMENT LTD
(*Suby of* PRAIRIECOAST EQUIPMENT INC)
339 Sumas Way, Abbotsford, BC, V2S 8E5
(604) 864-9844
Sales 21,376,170
SIC 5083 Farm and garden machinery
Dave Jelinski
Howard Jelinski
Anastasia Jelinski
Norbert Jelinski
Paul Jelinski

D-U-N-S 20-314-7467   (SL)
GREWAL FARMS INC
1088 Sumas Way, Abbotsford, BC, V2S 8H2
(604) 832-0083
Emp Here 30   *Sales* 11,565,570
SIC 0291 General farms, primarily animals
Surjit Singh Grewal

D-U-N-S 24-856-1383   (SL)
H.P. CONSTRUCTION LTD
33386 South Fraser Way Suite 202, Abbotsford, BC, V2S 2B5
(604) 850-1288
Emp Here 60   *Sales* 14,848,980
SIC 1771 Concrete work
Henry Penner

D-U-N-S 20-179-6161   (BR)
HOME DEPOT OF CANADA INC
HOME DEPOT
(*Suby of* THE HOME DEPOT INC)
1956 Vedder Way, Abbotsford, BC, V2S 8K1
(604) 851-4400
Emp Here 150
SIC 5211 Lumber and other building materials
Paul Gislason

D-U-N-S 24-072-1779   (HQ)
HOMELIFE GLENAYRE REALTY COMPANY LTD
3033 Immel St Unit 360, Abbotsford, BC, V2S 6S2
(604) 520-6829
Emp Here 1   *Sales* 54,455,570
SIC 6531 Real estate agents and managers
Walter Brown

D-U-N-S 25-301-2587   (BR)
HUDSON'S BAY COMPANY
(*Suby of* HUDSON'S BAY COMPANY)
32900 South Fraser Way Suite 2, Abbotsford, BC, V2S 5A1
(604) 853-7711
Emp Here 100
SIC 5311 Department stores
Linda Marples

D-U-N-S 20-388-3327   (SL)
IDH INVESTMENTS LTD
NOODLEBOX
2455 West Railway St, Abbotsford, BC, V2S 2E3
(604) 744-2444
Emp Here 90   *Sales* 4,096,710
SIC 5812 Eating places
Dustin May

D-U-N-S 25-386-6800   (SL)
J. FLORIS CONSTRUCTION LTD
2776 Bourquin Cres W Suite 204, Abbotsford, BC, V2S 6A4
(604) 864-6471
Emp Here 26   *Sales* 12,239,006
SIC 1542 Nonresidential construction, nec
John Floris
Catharina Floris

D-U-N-S 24-158-5900   (SL)
LITTLE OAK REALTY LTD
REMAX LITTLE OAK REALTY

2630 Bourquin Cres W Suite 9, Abbotsford, BC, V2S 5N7
(604) 309-5729
Emp Here 130   *Sales* 54,455,570
SIC 6531 Real estate agents and managers
Donald (Don) Goertz Jr
Raymond (Ray) Yenkana
David Richel

D-U-N-S 24-448-3707   (SL)
MAGNUM TRAILER AND EQUIPMENT INC
660 Riverside Rd, Abbotsford, BC, V2S 7M6
(604) 855-7544
Emp Here 110   *Sales* 24,622,730
SIC 3715 Truck trailers
Robert Willock
Edward (Ted) Willock
Donna Willock
Mary Willock

D-U-N-S 20-797-8370   (SL)
MCCLARY STOCKYARDS LIMITED
34559 Mcclary Ave, Abbotsford, BC, V2S 7N3
(604) 864-2381
Emp Here 18   *Sales* 21,787,146
SIC 5154 Livestock
Sheila Rushton
Jonathon Rushton
David Rushton

D-U-N-S 25-483-1787   (BR)
MENNONITE BENEVOLENT SOCIETY
MENNO HOME
32910 Brundige Ave Suite 257, Abbotsford, BC, V2S 1N2
(604) 853-2411
Emp Here 200
SIC 8059 Nursing and personal care, nec
Karen Baillie

D-U-N-S 25-992-3035   (BR)
MENNONITE CENTRAL COMMITTEE CANADA
MCC SUPPORTIVE CARE SERVICES
(*Suby of* MENNONITE CENTRAL COMMITTEE CANADA)
2776 Bourquin Cres W Suite 103, Abbotsford, BC, V2S 6A4
(604) 850-6608
Emp Here 350
SIC 8399 Social services, nec
Steve Thiessen

D-U-N-S 24-681-8991   (HQ)
MOUNTAIN VIEW RELOAD INC
419 Sumas Way, Abbotsford, BC, V2S 8E5

Emp Here 6   *Sales* 20,798,680
SIC 4789 Transportation services, nec
Norman Daignault
Ronald Kohlman
Erna Kohlman

D-U-N-S 20-955-9124   (SL)
MOUNTAIN VIEW SPECIALTY PRODUCTS INC
3013 Turner St, Abbotsford, BC, V2S 7T9
(604) 850-2070
Emp Here 57   *Sales* 25,488,918
SIC 5031 Lumber, plywood, and millwork
Robert Calvin Chimko

D-U-N-S 20-429-7584   (SL)
NORTH WEST RUBBER LTD
33850 Industrial Ave, Abbotsford, BC, V2S 7T9
(604) 859-2002
Emp Here 120   *Sales* 23,050,200
SIC 3496 Miscellaneous fabricated wire products
Leithton Fiesen
Roy Dehaan
Adam Hill
David Pruim
Catherine Shaw
Jody Kirchner

D-U-N-S 24-798-5146   (SL)

PACIFIC COAST FRUIT PRODUCTS LTD
34352 Industrial Way, Abbotsford, BC, V2S 7M6
(604) 850-3505
Emp Here 60   *Sales* 20,741,400
SIC 2037 Frozen fruits and vegetables
Dianne Klatt
Ellen Macintyre

D-U-N-S 24-367-3092   (HQ)
PACIFIC VETERINARY SALES LIMITED
34079 Gladys Ave, Abbotsford, BC, V2S 2E8
(604) 850-1510
Emp Here 34   *Sales* 50,134,620
SIC 5149 Groceries and related products, nec
Thomas Mcbratney
Phil Klaassen
Ken Kasdorf

D-U-N-S 25-261-4334   (SL)
PAN PACIFIC PET LIMITED
34079 Gladys Ave, Abbotsford, BC, V2S 2E8
(604) 850-1510
Emp Here 60   *Sales* 50,134,620
SIC 5149 Groceries and related products, nec
Jane Mcbratney

D-U-N-S 24-682-2506   (HQ)
PANAGO PIZZA INC
33149 Mill Lake Rd, Abbotsford, BC, V2S 2A4
(604) 859-6621
Emp Here 60   *Sales* 12,171,421,500
SIC 6794 Patent owners and lessors
Ernest Rooke
Brian Rooke
Ken Rooke

D-U-N-S 25-621-1830   (SL)
POLAR ELECTRIC INC
2236 West Railway St Unit 1, Abbotsford, BC, V2S 2E2
(604) 850-7522
Emp Here 65   *Sales* 14,158,885
SIC 1731 Electrical work
Darren Postma

D-U-N-S 24-072-7156   (SL)
QUADRA WOOD PRODUCTS LTD
SUMAS CEDAR
34371 Industrial Way, Abbotsford, BC, V2S 7M6
(604) 854-1835
Emp Here 50   *Sales* 22,358,700
SIC 5031 Lumber, plywood, and millwork
Dave Sweeney
Robert West
Brent Kean

D-U-N-S 25-086-5714   (SL)
R.D.M. MANAGEMENT COMPANY (1987) LTD
33695 South Fraser Way, Abbotsford, BC, V2S 2C1

Emp Here 72   *Sales* 19,751,904
SIC 8741 Management services
Gael Downe

D-U-N-S 20-428-2487   (HQ)
RITCHIE-SMITH FEEDS INC
SURE CROP FEEDS
(*Suby of* F.R.M. HOLDINGS LTD)
33777 Enterprise Ave, Abbotsford, BC, V2S 7T9
(604) 859-7128
Emp Here 70   *Sales* 66,284,360
SIC 2048 Prepared feeds, nec
Richard Reimer
Frederick Fleming
Kenneth Mackenzie
Kenneth Warkentin
Leanna Bailey

D-U-N-S 25-627-2386   (BR)
RRGB RESTAURANTS CANADA INC
(*Suby of* RRGB RESTAURANTS CANADA INC)
33011 South Fraser Way, Abbotsford, BC, V2S

2A6
(604) 853-8185
Emp Here 75
SIC 5812 Eating places
Neil Biggerstaff

D-U-N-S 24-639-8796   (BR)
SAPUTO INC
SAPUTO FOODS
(*Suby of* JOLINA CAPITAL INC)
1799 Riverside Rd Suite 48, Abbotsford, BC, V2S 4J8
(604) 853-2225
Emp Here 100
SIC 5143 Dairy products, except dried or canned

D-U-N-S 25-136-8460   (BR)
SCHOOL DISTRICT NO 34 (ABBOTSFORD)
YALE SECONDARY SCHOOL
34620 Old Yale Rd, Abbotsford, BC, V2S 7S6
(604) 853-0778
Emp Here 100
SIC 8211 Elementary and secondary schools
Glen Rogers

D-U-N-S 25-014-8293   (BR)
SCHOOL DISTRICT NO 34 (ABBOTSFORD)
ROBERT BATEMAN SECONDARY SCHOOL
35045 Exbury Ave, Abbotsford, BC, V2S 7L1
(604) 864-0220
Emp Here 90
SIC 8211 Elementary and secondary schools
Jinder Sarowa

D-U-N-S 20-298-8689   (SL)
TILT-TECH CONSTRUCTION LTD
34077 Gladys Ave Unit 320, Abbotsford, BC, V2S 2E8
(604) 746-5456
Emp Here 40   *Sales* 18,829,240
SIC 1542 Nonresidential construction, nec
Richard Matis

D-U-N-S 20-864-8659   (HQ)
UNIVERSITY OF THE FRASER VALLEY
UFV BOOKSTORE
33844 King Rd, Abbotsford, BC, V2S 7M8
(604) 504-7441
Emp Here 614   *Sales* 97,831,407
SIC 8221 Colleges and universities
Joannemark Maclean

D-U-N-S 25-386-1272   (HQ)
VEDDER TRANSPORT LTD
400 Riverside Rd, Abbotsford, BC, V2S 7M4
(604) 853-3341
Sales 13,633,664
SIC 4213 Trucking, except local
Larry Wiebe
Jacob Wiebe
John Wiebe

D-U-N-S 20-256-7942   (HQ)
VIBRANT HEALTH PRODUCTS INC
SILVER HILLS BAKERY
34494 Mclary Ave, Abbotsford, BC, V2S 4N8
(604) 850-5600
Sales 11,242,750
SIC 2051 Bread, cake, and related products
Stan Smith
Brad Brousson
Kathryn Smith

D-U-N-S 24-805-9370   (HQ)
VISIONS ONE HOUR OPTICAL LTD
2030 Sumas Way Unit 100, Abbotsford, BC, V2S 2C7
(604) 854-3266
Emp Here 12   *Sales* 13,637,340
SIC 3851 Ophthalmic goods
Andy Martens Sr
Andy Martens Jr
Richard Martens

D-U-N-S 20-586-0299   (HQ)
WAKEFIELD-SPERLING AUTO PARTS LTD
33406 South Fraser Way, Abbotsford, BC, V2S

2B5
(604) 853-8179
Emp Here 33   *Sales* 14,568,600
SIC 5013 Motor vehicle supplies and new parts
Jim Evans

D-U-N-S 25-296-4994   (BR)
WAL-MART CANADA CORP
(*Suby of* WALMART INC.)
1812 Vedder Way Suite 3019, Abbotsford, BC, V2S 8K1
(604) 854-3575
Emp Here 270
SIC 5311 Department stores
Tomarenski Eugene

D-U-N-S 20-703-5911   (BR)
WASTE CONNECTIONS OF CANADA INC
(*Suby of* WASTE CONNECTIONS, INC)
34321 Industrial Way, Abbotsford, BC, V2S 7M6
(604) 517-2617
Emp Here 100
SIC 4953 Refuse systems
Craig Chambers

D-U-N-S 20-610-7596   (SL)
WESTBERRY FARMS LTD
34488 Bateman Rd, Abbotsford, BC, V2S 7Y8
(604) 850-0377
Emp Here 50   *Sales* 17,123,350
SIC 0171 Berry crops
Parm Bains

Abbotsford, BC V2T

D-U-N-S 20-712-6012   (SL)
ABBOTSFORD CHRYSLER DODGE JEEP RAM LTD
30285 Automall Dr, Abbotsford, BC, V2T 5M1
(604) 857-1000
Emp Here 44   *Sales* 27,688,320
SIC 5511 New and used car dealers
Jia Ling Chiang
Viola Chiang
Donna Gibbons
Mitch Trotman

D-U-N-S 24-504-2379   (SL)
ABBOTSFORD NISSAN LTD
30180 Automall Dr, Abbotsford, BC, V2T 5M1
(604) 857-7755
Emp Here 22   *Sales* 13,844,160
SIC 5511 New and used car dealers
Robert Moon

D-U-N-S 24-009-5328   (SL)
ABBOTSFORD SECURITY SERVICES
1ST SECURE
2669 Langdon St Suite 201, Abbotsford, BC, V2T 3L3
(604) 870-4731
Emp Here 100   *Sales* 39,567,800
SIC 7381 Detective and armored car services
Sam Dhaliwal

D-U-N-S 20-355-8999   (HQ)
ABBSRY USED TIRES LTD
ABBSRY NEW & USED TIRES
31088 Peardonville Rd Unit 1, Abbotsford, BC, V2T 6K5
(604) 870-0490
Emp Here 1   *Sales* 11,455,794
SIC 5531 Auto and home supply stores
Wade Larson
Parvinder Grewal

D-U-N-S 20-512-4840   (HQ)
ADVANCED NUTRIENTS LTD
32526 George Ferguson Way Suite 102, Abbotsford, BC, V2T 4Y1
(604) 854-6793
Sales 24,709,827
SIC 2873 Nitrogenous fertilizers

Michael Straumietis
Eugene Yordanov

D-U-N-S 25-418-0789   (HQ)
APEX FOODSOURCE LTD
30530 Progressive Way, Abbotsford, BC, V2T 6W3
(604) 854-1492
Emp Here 52   *Sales* 45,956,735
SIC 5149 Groceries and related products, nec
Brian Rooke
Ken Rooke

D-U-N-S 24-348-8652   (SL)
BATH MILL INC
2637 Deacon St, Abbotsford, BC, V2T 6L4
(604) 302-2284
Emp Here 30   *Sales* 15,616,260
SIC 5099 Durable goods, nec
Surinder Bath
Aman Bath
Agit Bath

D-U-N-S 25-316-9817   (HQ)
BE PRESSURE SUPPLY INC
30585 Progressive Way, Abbotsford, BC, V2T 6W3
(604) 850-6662
Emp Here 85   *Sales* 27,750,125
SIC 3589 Service industry machinery, nec
Susan Lois Braber

D-U-N-S 24-324-2786   (SL)
BERT'S ELECTRIC (2001) LTD
2258 Peardonville Rd, Abbotsford, BC, V2T 6J8
(604) 850-8731
Emp Here 80   *Sales* 17,426,320
SIC 1731 Electrical work
Albert Heinrichs

D-U-N-S 24-683-2034   (SL)
CAMPBELL HELICOPTERS LTD
30740 Threshold Dr, Abbotsford, BC, V2T 6H5
(604) 852-1122
Emp Here 39   *Sales* 12,665,406
SIC 4522 Air transportation, nonscheduled
Bruce Campbell
Laura Siemens

D-U-N-S 24-790-5396   (SL)
CANADIAN TIRE
32513 South Fraser Way Suite 434, Abbotsford, BC, V2T 4N5
(604) 870-4134
Emp Here 30   *Sales* 14,942,340
SIC 5531 Auto and home supply stores
Chester Wionzek

D-U-N-S 20-104-3416   (SL)
CASCADE AEROSPACE INC
(*Suby of* I.M.P. GROUP INTERNATIONAL INCORPORATED)
1337 Townline Rd, Abbotsford, BC, V2T 6E1
(604) 850-7372
Emp Here 550   *Sales* 174,543,600
SIC 4581 Airports, flying fields, and services
K. Barry Marsden
David Schellenberg
Kevin Lemke
Dwayne Lucas
Stu Mcintosh
Rick Renard
Justin Carrie
David Birnie
George Doumet
Eric Harris

D-U-N-S 25-616-3635   (BR)
CITY OF ABBOTSFORD
MATSQUI RECREATION CENTRE
(*Suby of* CITY OF ABBOTSFORD)
3106 Clearbrook Rd, Abbotsford, BC, V2T 4N6
(604) 855-0500
Emp Here 100
SIC 7999 Amusement and recreation, nec
Catherine Betts

D-U-N-S 25-831-8765   (BR)
CITY OF ABBOTSFORD
ABBOTSFORD FIRE RESCUE SERVICE
(*Suby of* CITY OF ABBOTSFORD)
32270 George Ferguson Way, Abbotsford, BC, V2T 2L1
(604) 853-3566
Emp Here 200
SIC 7389 Business services, nec
Don Beer

D-U-N-S 20-094-8479   (HQ)
CLEARBROOK GRAIN & MILLING COMPANY LIMITED
(*Suby of* JAKE FRIESEN INC)
2425 Townline Rd, Abbotsford, BC, V2T 6L6
(604) 850-1108
Sales 22,469,850
SIC 2048 Prepared feeds, nec
Jake Friesen
Erna Friesen
Marvin Friesen

D-U-N-S 20-622-3471   (HQ)
COLUMBIA KITCHEN CABINETS LTD
2221 Townline Rd, Abbotsford, BC, V2T 6H1
(604) 850-3538
Emp Here 1   *Sales* 28,855,500
SIC 2434 Wood kitchen cabinets
Hans Kruger
Dave Kish

D-U-N-S 20-514-2045   (HQ)
CONAIR GROUP INC
1510 Tower St, Abbotsford, BC, V2T 6H5
(604) 855-1171
Emp Here 196   *Sales* 112,721,400
SIC 0851 Forestry services
Barry Marsden
Rick Pedersen
Ray Horton
Paul Kennelly
Brent Misura
Claude Marchand
Michael Chuahuico
Matt Bradley

D-U-N-S 25-416-4320   (SL)
DONALD E. CHARLTON LTD
IMPORT AUTO RECYCLING
2035 Queen St, Abbotsford, BC, V2T 6J3
(604) 854-6499
Emp Here 40   *Sales* 20,821,680
SIC 5093 Scrap and waste materials
Donald E Charlton

D-U-N-S 20-525-3193   (SL)
DRIVING FORCE DECKS INT'L LTD
30691 Simpson Rd, Abbotsford, BC, V2T 6C7
(604) 514-1191
Emp Here 70   *Sales* 10,373,440
SIC 4213 Trucking, except local
Carey Halovich
Cathy Halovich

D-U-N-S 20-376-9658   (SL)
EGGSOLUTIONS - VANDERPOLS INC
3911 Mt Lehman Rd, Abbotsford, BC, V2T 5W5
(604) 856-4127
Emp Here 80   *Sales* 27,291,672
SIC 5144 Poultry and poultry products
Michael Vanderpols
George Leroux
Aaron Kwinter
William Gray

D-U-N-S 20-910-0606   (SL)
ESCAPE FIRE PROTECTION LTD
30465 Progressive Way Unit 8, Abbotsford, BC, V2T 6W3
(604) 864-0376
Emp Here 26   *Sales* 11,530,740
SIC 7389 Business services, nec
Ezra Zapanta

D-U-N-S 25-108-9160   (HQ)
FLEXIFORCE CANADA INC

FLEXIFORCE
(*Suby of* ASSA ABLOY AB)
30840 Peardonville Rd, Abbotsford, BC, V2T 6K2
(604) 854-3660
Sales 26,507,730
SIC 3429 Hardware, nec
Juan Vargues
Laurel Beier
Per Hansson
Joseph Clauff

D-U-N-S 25-267-7034   (SL)
FOURTH-RITE CONSTRUCTION (1994) LTD
2609 Progressive Way Suite B, Abbotsford, BC, V2T 6H8
(604) 850-7684
Emp Here 50   *Sales* 14,429,150
SIC 1522 Residential construction, nec
Mike Kuhn
Geoff Wade

D-U-N-S 24-319-4425   (HQ)
FRASERWAY RV LIMITED PARTNERSHIP
FRASERWAY RV RENTALS
30440 South Fraser Way, Abbotsford, BC, V2T 6L4
(604) 850-1976
Emp Here 120   *Sales* 138,540,480
SIC 5561 Recreational vehicle dealers
James Epp

D-U-N-S 20-181-2232   (SL)
FUNKS FOODS LTD
2580 Clearbrook Rd, Abbotsford, BC, V2T 2Y5

Emp Here 70   *Sales* 20,888,905
SIC 5411 Grocery stores
Paul Funk

D-U-N-S 24-777-3880   (SL)
GENERAL GLASS INDUSTRIES LTD
GLASS WORLD
2146 Queen St, Abbotsford, BC, V2T 6J4
(604) 854-5757
Emp Here 60   *Sales* 14,006,100
SIC 3231 Products of purchased glass
Daryl Waddell

D-U-N-S 25-682-8641   (HQ)
GLENCO HOLDINGS LTD
2121 Peardonville Rd, Abbotsford, BC, V2T 6J7
(604) 850-1499
Emp Here 1   *Sales* 10,462,120
SIC 6712 Bank holding companies
Leslie Coughlan

D-U-N-S 20-994-9247   (SL)
GOLDEN VALLEY FOODS LTD
3841 Vanderpol Crt, Abbotsford, BC, V2T 5W5
(604) 857-0704
Emp Here 120   *Sales* 24,794,040
SIC 0252 Chicken eggs
Jennifer Akitt

D-U-N-S 20-460-2268   (SL)
HOUSE OF SHER 2018 LTD
2131 Queen St Suite 104, Abbotsford, BC, V2T 6J3
(604) 859-3030
Emp Here 21   *Sales* 17,547,117
SIC 5141 Groceries, general line
Harsharan Brar
Raman Deep Ramona Brar
Gurbachan Brar

D-U-N-S 25-679-9339   (SL)
HSS HELITECH SUPPORT SERVICES LTD
1640 Threshold Dr, Abbotsford, BC, V2T 6H5
(604) 557-9690
Emp Here 60   *Sales* 19,485,240
SIC 4581 Airports, flying fields, and services
Warren Malmberg

D-U-N-S 25-140-1006   (SL)
IMAGE PLUS

▲ Public Company   ■ Public Company Family Member   **HQ** Headquarters   **BR** Branch   **SL** Single Location

CLEARBROOK PLAZA
31935 South Fraser Way Unit 104, Abbotsford,
BC, V2T 5N7
(604) 504-7222
Emp Here 50   Sales 19,783,900
SIC 7384 Photofinish laboratories
Chan Song
Nam Song

D-U-N-S 20-873-3092   (SL)
ISFELD, LOU LINCOLN MERCURY SALES
LTD
32562 South Fraser Way, Abbotsford, BC, V2T
1X6
(604) 857-1327
Emp Here 49   Sales 24,405,822
SIC 5511 New and used car dealers
Lawrence Isfeld

D-U-N-S 25-496-1527   (HQ)
JAKE FRIESEN INC
2425 Townline Rd, Abbotsford, BC, V2T 6L6
(604) 850-1108
Sales 24,198,300
SIC 2048 Prepared feeds, nec
Jake Friesen

D-U-N-S 20-334-9084   (SL)
JBE HOME & AUTO LIMITED
CANADIAN TIRE ASSOCIATE STORE
32513 South Fraser Way Suite 434, Abbots-
ford, BC, V2T 4N5
(604) 870-4125
Emp Here 100   Sales 62,928,000
SIC 5531 Auto and home supply stores
Brad Elliott
Heather Elliott

D-U-N-S 25-500-0127   (SL)
K & R POULTRY LTD
FARM FED, DIV OF
31171 Peardonville Rd Unit 2, Abbotsford, BC,
V2T 6K6
(604) 850-5808
Emp Here 84   Sales 29,037,960
SIC 2015 Poultry slaughtering and processing

D-U-N-S 24-535-0822   (BR)
LILYDALE INC
LILYDALE FOODS
(Suby of SOFINA FOODS INC)
31894 Marshall Pl Suite 5, Abbotsford, BC,
V2T 5Z9
(604) 850-2633
Emp Here 166
SIC 2015 Poultry slaughtering and processing
John Franck

D-U-N-S 24-899-1432   (BR)
LONDON DRUGS LIMITED
(Suby of H.Y. LOUIE CO. LIMITED)
32700 South Fraser Way Suite 26, Abbotsford,
BC, V2T 4M5
(604) 852-0936
Emp Here 100
SIC 5912 Drug stores and proprietary stores
Shelly Deglan

D-U-N-S 25-088-4483   (SL)
M.D. TRANSPORT CO. LTD
1683 Mt Lehman Rd, Abbotsford, BC, V2T
6H6
(604) 850-1818
Emp Here 40   Sales 11,282,616
SIC 4213 Trucking, except local
Major Dhillon

D-U-N-S 20-995-9709   (SL)
MAGNUSON FORD SALES LTD
32562 South Fraser Way, Abbotsford, BC, V2T
1X6
(604) 853-7401
Emp Here 45   Sales 22,413,510
SIC 5511 New and used car dealers
Layne Magnuson
Layne Sr. Magnuson

D-U-N-S 20-749-6860   (SL)

MAINLAND MACHINERY LTD
(Suby of 516094 B.C. LTD)
2255 Townline Rd, Abbotsford, BC, V2T 6H1
(604) 854-4244
Emp Here 100   Sales 22,200,100
SIC 3569 General industrial machinery, nec
Paul Hiebert
David Hiebert
Henry Hiebert

D-U-N-S 24-368-3075   (SL)
MENNO TRAVEL SERVICE CANADA LTD
RAPTIM HUMANITARIAN TRAVEL
Gd, Abbotsford, BC, V2T 0A1
(604) 853-0751
Emp Here 21   Sales 10,919,307
SIC 4724 Travel agencies
Bart Kruijsen

D-U-N-S 24-292-2847   (SL)
MIERAU CONSTRUCTION LTD
30444 Great Northern Ave Suite 201, Abbots-
ford, BC, V2T 6Y6
(604) 850-3536
Emp Here 30   Sales 14,121,930
SIC 1542 Nonresidential construction, nec
Larry Mierau
Maureen Mierau

D-U-N-S 24-380-2373   (SL)
MITRUX SERVICES LTD
2160 Peardonville Rd, Abbotsford, BC, V2T
6J8
(604) 746-1008
Emp Here 130   Sales 26,741,780
SIC 4213 Trucking, except local
Jaswinder Arora

D-U-N-S 20-093-3414   (SL)
MSA FORD SALES LTD
30295 Automall Dr, Abbotsford, BC, V2T 5M1
(604) 856-9000
Emp Here 65   Sales 40,903,200
SIC 5511 New and used car dealers
Bernie Saywell
Norm Grant

D-U-N-S 20-714-7455   (SL)
MURRAY PONTIAC BUICK GMC LIMITED
PARTNERSHIP
MURRAY GM
30355 Automall Dr, Abbotsford, BC, V2T 5M1
(604) 857-0742
Emp Here 45   Sales 22,413,510
SIC 5511 New and used car dealers
Dan Murray
Ray Solberg

D-U-N-S 20-336-4823   (SL)
NATURE'S   TOUCH   FROZEN   FOODS
(WEST) INC
(Suby of NATURE'S TOUCH FROZEN
FOODS INC)
31122 South Fraser Way, Abbotsford, BC, V2T
6L5
(604) 854-1191
Emp Here 130   Sales 22,607,650
SIC 0723 Crop preparation services for mar-
ket
John Tentomas
Theo Ptokos

D-U-N-S 24-316-3875   (SL)
NEOVA TECHNOLOGIES INC
(Suby of APARTS 2 SRL)
31212 Peardonville Rd, Abbotsford, BC, V2T
6K8
(604) 504-0695
Emp Here 55   Sales 15,621,155
SIC 2899 Chemical preparations, nec
Lavi Nio

D-U-N-S 25-673-3999   (SL)
NEW WORLD TECHNOLOGIES INCORPO-
RATED
RAD TORQUE SYSTEMS
30580 Progressive Way, Abbotsford, BC, V2T
6Z2

(604) 852-0405
Emp Here 80   Sales 21,412,160
SIC 5251 Hardware stores
Daniel Provost
Lynda Provost

D-U-N-S 24-593-9611   (HQ)
OCEANS RETAIL INVESTMENTS INC
PETRO CANADA
2096 Clearbrook Rd, Abbotsford, BC, V2T
2X2
(604) 852-1950
Emp Here 5   Sales 24,903,900
SIC 5541 Gasoline service stations
Gurinder Virk
Narvinder S. Virk

D-U-N-S 20-863-6571   (SL)
PARK AVENUE ENTERPRISES LTD
HONDA WAY, THE
30360 Automall Dr, Abbotsford, BC, V2T 5M1
(604) 857-1430
Emp Here 40   Sales 19,923,120
SIC 5511 New and used car dealers
Byron Hall

D-U-N-S 25-215-8928   (SL)
PHANTOM MFG. (INT'L) LTD
PHANTOM SCREENS
30451 Simpson Rd, Abbotsford, BC, V2T 6C7

Emp Here 70   Sales 18,735,640
SIC 5211 Lumber and other building materials
Esther Dewolde
Brian Rooke
Kenneth Rooke

D-U-N-S 24-355-7241   (HQ)
PNR RAILWORKS INC
PNR
(Suby of WIND POINT PARTNERS, L.P.)
2595 Deacon St, Abbotsford, BC, V2T 6L4
(604) 850-9166
Emp Here 40   Sales 38,061,340
SIC 1629 Heavy construction, nec
Jamey Craig
Peter Pearce
Jeff Loewen
John August
Jeffrey Levey

D-U-N-S 24-154-5946   (HQ)
REIMER HARDWOODS LTD
31135 Peardonville Rd, Abbotsford, BC, V2T
6K6
(604) 850-9281
Emp Here 1   Sales 18,781,308
SIC 5031 Lumber, plywood, and millwork
Gordon Reimer
Colin Reimer
Diane Reimer

D-U-N-S 25-288-5207   (BR)
SCHOOL DISTRICT NO 34 (ABBOTSFORD)
W.J. MOUAT SECONDARY SCHOOL
32355 Mouat Dr, Abbotsford, BC, V2T 4E9
(604) 853-7191
Emp Here 120
SIC 8211 Elementary and secondary schools
Jay Pankratz

D-U-N-S 20-591-4117   (BR)
SCHOOL DISTRICT NO 34 (ABBOTSFORD)
RICK HANSEN SECONDARY SCHOOL
31150 Blueridge Dr, Abbotsford, BC, V2T 5R2
(604) 864-0011
Emp Here 80
SIC 8211 Elementary and secondary schools
David Dewit

D-U-N-S 20-278-9822   (SL)
SHEARFORCE EQUIPMENT
WEST COAST MACHINERY, DIV OF
2707 Progressive Way Suite 107, Abbotsford,
BC, V2T 0A7
(604) 855-5101
Emp Here 32   Sales 15,200,832
SIC 5082 Construction and mining machinery

Brad Dewit

D-U-N-S 24-165-1280   (SL)
STATUS ELECTRICAL CORPORATION
2669 Deacon St, Abbotsford, BC, V2T 6L4
(604) 859-1892
Emp Here 210   Sales 49,456,890
SIC 1731 Electrical work
Keith Falardeau

D-U-N-S 25-150-1201   (SL)
STRUCTURECRAFT BUILDERS INC
1929 Foy St, Abbotsford, BC, V2T 6B1
(604) 940-8889
Emp Here 25   Sales 11,768,275
SIC 1542 Nonresidential construction, nec
Gerald Epp

D-U-N-S 20-093-3505   (SL)
SUNRISE SERVICE ABBOTSFORD LTD
SUNRISE TOYOTA
30210 Automall Dr, Abbotsford, BC, V2T 5M1
(604) 857-2658
Emp Here 42   Sales 20,919,276
SIC 5511 New and used car dealers
David Yakashiro
Deanne Larsen

D-U-N-S 25-409-0012   (SL)
SUNWEST FOOD PROCESSORS LTD
31100 Wheel Ave, Abbotsford, BC, V2T 6H1
(604) 852-3760
Emp Here 35   Sales 29,245,195
SIC 5141 Groceries, general line
Peter Shoore

D-U-N-S 20-918-9091   (SL)
TABOR HOME SOCIETY
TABOR MANOR
31944 Sunrise Cres, Abbotsford, BC, V2T 1N5
(604) 859-8718
Emp Here 125   Sales 8,540,750
SIC 8059 Nursing and personal care, nec
Dan Levitt

D-U-N-S 20-371-6449   (HQ)
TNT CRANE & RIGGING CANADA INC
STAMPEDE CRANE & RIGGING
2190 Carpenter St, Abbotsford, BC, V2T 6B4
(800) 667-2215
Emp Here 64   Sales 21,153,879
SIC 7353 Heavy construction equipment
rental
Robert Fairbank
Moreno Ciapponi

D-U-N-S 24-839-6186   (SL)
TOWNE MILLWORK LTD
2690 Progressive Way Suite A, Abbotsford,
BC, V2T 6H9
(604) 850-7738
Emp Here 75   Sales 33,538,050
SIC 5031 Lumber, plywood, and millwork
Greg Hesketh
Gayle Hesketh

D-U-N-S 24-665-5885   (SL)
TRIPLE EIGHT TRANSPORT INC
2548 Clearbrook Rd 1st Fl, Abbotsford, BC,
V2T 2Y4
(604) 755-2285
Emp Here 16   Sales 24,274,781
SIC 4213 Trucking, except local
Pardeep Arora

D-U-N-S 20-995-6259   (SL)
V.I.P. SALES LTD
V.I.P. MAZDA
30270 Automall Dr, Abbotsford, BC, V2T 5M1
(604) 857-1600
Emp Here 26   Sales 12,950,028
SIC 5511 New and used car dealers
William Warkentin
Linda Warkentin

D-U-N-S 24-980-1689   (HQ)
VALLEY COUNTER TOPS LTD
30781 Simpson Rd, Abbotsford, BC, V2T 6X4

(604) 852-8125
Sales 19,134,500
SIC 6712 Bank holding companies
Abe Krahn
John Krahn
Agatha Krahn
Wes Neufeld

D-U-N-S 20-559-1568   (SL)
VITALUS NUTRITION INC
3911 Mt Lehman Rd, Abbotsford, BC, V2T 5W5
(604) 857-9080
Emp Here 70   *Sales* 24,198,300
SIC 2023 Dry, condensed and evaporated dairy products
George Leroux
Phillip Vanderpol
Doug Brown
Scott Born

D-U-N-S 24-995-8307   (SL)
WESTCAN RAIL LTD
31220 South Fraser Way, Abbotsford, BC, V2T 6L5
(604) 534-0124
Emp Here 25   *Sales* 11,875,650
SIC 5088 Transportation equipment and supplies
Peter Siemens

D-U-N-S 20-093-5369   (SL)
WESTERN HATCHERY LTD
505 Hamm St Suite 1, Abbotsford, BC, V2T 6B6
(604) 859-7168
Emp Here 38   *Sales* 14,649,722
SIC 0254 Poultry hatcheries
Clifford Pollan

Abbotsford, BC V3G

D-U-N-S 20-198-9337   (SL)
I & G BISMARKATING LTD
TIM HORTONS
2054 Whatcom Rd Suite 1, Abbotsford, BC, V3G 2K8
(604) 855-9655
Emp Here 45   *Sales* 12,336,840
SIC 5461 Retail bakeries
Ivan Nachtigal

D-U-N-S 25-898-9102   (SL)
LAMB PROPERTIES INC
RAMADA PLAZA
36035 North Parallel Rd, Abbotsford, BC, V3G 2C6
(604) 870-1050
Emp Here 200   *Sales* 18,538,000
SIC 7011 Hotels and motels
Lane Sweeting

D-U-N-S 25-146-6405   (SL)
MOUNTAIN VIEW MUSHROOMS LTD
38061 Atkinson Rd, Abbotsford, BC, V3G 2G6

Emp Here 45   *Sales* 15,411,015
SIC 0182 Food crops grown under cover
Ron De Ruiter

D-U-N-S 24-665-6446   (SL)
REMPLE DISPOSAL INC
35321 Delair Rd, Abbotsford, BC, V3G 2C8
(604) 866-9020
Emp Here 49   *Sales* 12,599,419
SIC 4953 Refuse systems

D-U-N-S 24-244-3864   (SL)
SAHOTA FARMS LTD
40990 No. 3 Rd, Abbotsford, BC, V3G 2S1
(604) 823-2341
Emp Here 20   *Sales* 10,702,480
SIC 5148 Fresh fruits and vegetables
Karn Paul Sahota

D-U-N-S 24-803-3875   (SL)

VALLEY SELECT FOODS INC
41212 No. 3 Rd, Abbotsford, BC, V3G 2S1
(604) 823-2341
Emp Here 60   *Sales* 31,135,520
SIC 0723 Crop preparation services for market
Parmpal Sahota

D-U-N-S 24-292-9297   (HQ)
VAN BELLE NURSERY INC
34825 Hallert Rd, Abbotsford, BC, V3G 1R3
(604) 853-3415
Sales 18,952,550
SIC 5193 Flowers and florists supplies
Dave Van Belle

Abbotsford, BC V4X

D-U-N-S 20-328-9459   (SL)
0962358 B.C. LTD
CANWEST INNOVATIONS
29898 Maclure Rd, Abbotsford, BC, V4X 1G5
(604) 825-5060
Emp Here 25   *Sales* 22,779,042
SIC 5065 Electronic parts and equipment, nec
Sanjeet Raiwal

D-U-N-S 25-678-8548   (SL)
4 SEASON KING MUSHROOM LTD
28345 King Rd, Abbotsford, BC, V4X 1C9
(604) 857-2790
Emp Here 80   *Sales* 20,984,720
SIC 0182 Food crops grown under cover
Pauline Tang
Vien Quach

D-U-N-S 25-107-7665   (SL)
A & P FRUIT GROWERS LTD
1794 Peardonville Rd, Abbotsford, BC, V4X 2M4
(604) 864-4900
Emp Here 150   *Sales* 51,853,500
SIC 2033 Canned fruits and specialties
Sukhminder Bath

D-U-N-S 24-897-8405   (SL)
ANSWER GARDEN PRODUCTS LTD, THE
(Suby of CONSOLIDATED ENVIROWASTE INDUSTRIES INC)
27715 Huntingdon Rd, Abbotsford, BC, V4X 1B6
(604) 856-6221
Emp Here 14   *Sales* 10,395,280
SIC 5191 Farm supplies
Douglas Halward

D-U-N-S 24-103-7220   (SL)
AVINA FRESH PRODUCE LTD
28265 58 Ave, Abbotsford, BC, V4X 2E8
(604) 856-9833
Emp Here 65   *Sales* 17,050,085
SIC 0182 Food crops grown under cover
Huu Quach

D-U-N-S 20-355-2505   (SL)
BRADNER B.C. ORGANIC FEED LTD
BRADNER FARMS
28670 58 Ave, Abbotsford, BC, V4X 2E8
(604) 835-3299
Emp Here 50   *Sales* 19,275,950
SIC 0254 Poultry hatcheries
Robert Donaldson
Patricia Donaldson

D-U-N-S 20-384-5172   (SL)
DONALDSON FAMILY - BRADNER FARMS
28670 58 Ave, Abbotsford, BC, V4X 2E8
(604) 857-1206
Emp Here 50   *Sales* 19,499,202
SIC 0212 Beef cattle, except feedlots
Robert Donaldson
Patricia Donaldson

D-U-N-S 20-843-0160   (SL)
FARMERS' FRESH MUSHROOMS INC

(Suby of ROSS LAND MUSHROOM FARM LTD)
3555 Ross Rd, Abbotsford, BC, V4X 1M6
(604) 857-5610
Emp Here 148   *Sales* 25,015,700
SIC 0182 Food crops grown under cover
Tan Khanh Truong

D-U-N-S 20-795-2284   (SL)
FRASER VALLEY STEEL & WIRE LTD
3174 Mt Lehman Rd, Abbotsford, BC, V4X 2M9
(604) 856-3391
Emp Here 27   *Sales* 14,968,940
SIC 5051 Metals service centers and offices
Walter Wiebe

D-U-N-S 24-824-4394   (SL)
GLADWIN FARMS LTD
5327 Gladwin Rd, Abbotsford, BC, V4X 1X8
(604) 859-6820
Emp Here 20   *Sales* 29,353,840
SIC 5159 Farm-product raw materials, nec
Rajinder Lally
Shubhlkhen Lally
Rajvinder Singh Lally
Raminder Singh Lally

D-U-N-S 24-995-5931   (SL)
JONKMAN EQUIPMENT LTD
28355 Fraser Hwy, Abbotsford, BC, V4X 1K9
(604) 857-2000
Emp Here 25   *Sales* 11,875,650
SIC 5083 Farm and garden machinery
David Jonkman

D-U-N-S 24-803-3503   (SL)
LALLY FARMS INC
5327 Gladwin Rd, Abbotsford, BC, V4X 1X8
(604) 859-6820
Emp Here 200   *Sales* 33,805,000
SIC 0171 Berry crops
Rajvinder Lally

D-U-N-S 20-982-1305   (SL)
MB MISSION
MULTIPLY
32040 Downes Rd Suite 300, Abbotsford, BC, V4X 1X5
(604) 859-6267
Emp Here 200   *Sales* 20,824,600
SIC 8661 Religious organizations
Randy Friesen

D-U-N-S 24-446-3337   (SL)
MENNONITE EDUCATIONAL INSTITUTE SOCIETY
MEI
4081 Clearbrook Rd, Abbotsford, BC, V4X 2M8
(604) 859-3700
Emp Here 222   *Sales* 22,004,418
SIC 8211 Elementary and secondary schools
Peter Froese
Tim Regehr
Marilyn Edwards

D-U-N-S 25-094-6910   (SL)
MEROM FARMS LTD
2244 Lefeuvre Rd, Abbotsford, BC, V4X 1C6
(604) 856-3511
Emp Here 35   *Sales* 11,986,345
SIC 0181 Ornamental nursery products
Donald Voth
Kenneth Voth

D-U-N-S 24-345-1390   (SL)
NARANG FARMS & PROCESSORS LTD
351 Bradner Rd, Abbotsford, BC, V4X 2J5
(604) 856-2020
Emp Here 43   *Sales* 14,726,081
SIC 0171 Berry crops
Gurmail (Gary) Narang
Amarjid Narang
Amrick Narang

D-U-N-S 20-124-9195   (SL)
NORDIC NURSERIES LTD

29386 Haverman Rd, Abbotsford, BC, V4X 2P3
(604) 607-7074
Emp Here 50   *Sales* 17,123,350
SIC 0181 Ornamental nursery products
Glenn Andersen

D-U-N-S 24-823-7802   (SL)
OVERLANDERS MANUFACTURING LP
(Suby of EXCHANGE INCOME CORPORATION)
30320 Fraser Hwy, Abbotsford, BC, V4X 1G1
(604) 856-6815
Emp Here 60   *Sales* 13,069,740
SIC 1761 Roofing, siding, and sheetMetal work
Randy Lowry

D-U-N-S 24-373-8796   (SL)
PANNU BROS. TRUCKING LTD
30260 Fraser Hwy, Abbotsford, BC, V4X 1G2
(604) 857-2213
Emp Here 165   *Sales* 33,941,490
SIC 4213 Trucking, except local
Satwant (Dave) Pannu
Rupinder (Roop) Pannu
Jinder Jill

D-U-N-S 20-566-5339   (HQ)
RANDHAWA FARMS LTD
33677 Hallert Rd, Abbotsford, BC, V4X 1W9
(604) 864-8896
Sales 28,734,250
SIC 0191 General farms, primarily crop
Kanwar Randhawa
Eijay Randhawa
Ajay Randhawa
Amit Randhawa

D-U-N-S 24-394-5248   (HQ)
ROSS LAND MUSHROOM FARM LTD
3555 Ross Rd, Abbotsford, BC, V4X 1M6

Sales 23,663,500
SIC 0182 Food crops grown under cover
Tan Khanh Truong

D-U-N-S 25-415-1418   (HQ)
ROSSDOWN FARMS LTD
2325 Bradner Rd, Abbotsford, BC, V4X 1E2
(604) 856-6698
Emp Here 45   *Sales* 12,308,310
SIC 0259 Poultry and eggs, nec
Dan Wiebe
Dion Wiebe
Stan Thiessen
Patrick Wiebe

D-U-N-S 20-796-6243   (SL)
VALLEY CARRIERS LTD
4491 Gladwin Rd, Abbotsford, BC, V4X 1W6
(604) 853-1075
Emp Here 100   *Sales* 20,570,600
SIC 4213 Trucking, except local
Travis Klassen
Rita Klassen
Dennis Klassen
Mervin Klassen
Reginald Klassen
Erin Klassen-Parkes

D-U-N-S 20-867-6080   (SL)
VALLEY GRAVEL SALES LTD
700 Lefeuvre Rd, Abbotsford, BC, V4X 1H7
(604) 856-4461
Emp Here 50   *Sales* 22,358,700
SIC 5032 Brick, stone, and related material
Alan Mclean
Barry Mclean

Agassiz, BC V0M

D-U-N-S 24-898-9394   (BR)
BRITCO LP
1825 Tower Dr, Agassiz, BC, V0M 1A2

---

(604) 796-2257
Emp Here 95   *Sales* 273,308
SIC 2452 Prefabricated wood buildings
Obie Erickson

D-U-N-S 24-310-6254   (SL)
ECLIPSE TRANSPORT LTD
3120 Cemetery Rd, Agassiz, BC, V0M 1A1
(604) 796-8972
Emp Here 21   *Sales* 10,040,524
SIC 4213 Trucking, except local
Ryan Yanagisawa
Marianna Braila

D-U-N-S 25-660-1170   (BR)
SEABIRD ISLAND INDIAN BAND
(*Suby of* SEABIRD ISLAND INDIAN BAND)
2895 Chowat Rd Rr 2, Agassiz, BC, V0M 1A2
(604) 796-2177
Emp Here 150
SIC 8299 Schools and educational services,
nec
Darryl Mcneil

Aiyansh, BC V0J

D-U-N-S 25-604-2672   (HQ)
SCHOOL DISTRICT NO. 92 (NISGA'A)
5002 Skateen Ave, Aiyansh, BC, V0J 1A0
(250) 633-2228
Emp Here 8   *Sales* 10,209,257
SIC 8211 Elementary and secondary schools
Peter Leeson

Aldergrove, BC V4W

D-U-N-S 24-372-6494   (SL)
**ALDERGROVE LIONS SENIORS HOUSING
SOCIETY**
JACKMAN MANOR
27477 28 Ave, Aldergrove, BC, V4W 3L9
(604) 856-4161
Emp Here 120   *Sales* 8,199,120
SIC 8051 Skilled nursing care facilities
Sheila Bridger

D-U-N-S 20-189-7944   (HQ)
ALLIANCE CONCRETE PUMPS INC
26162 30a Ave, Aldergrove, BC, V4W 2W5
(604) 607-0908
Sales 14,430,065
SIC 3561 Pumps and pumping equipment
Clayton White
Larry Koop
Robert Fritezke
Mike Enns

D-U-N-S 25-387-4671   (SL)
ALUM-TEK INDUSTRIES LTD
26221 30a Ave, Aldergrove, BC, V4W 2W6

Emp Here 70   *Sales* 13,445,950
SIC 3448 Prefabricated Metal buildings and
components
Jim Butler
Eric Peura

D-U-N-S 24-957-1415   (BR)
ASPLUNDH CANADA ULC
(*Suby of* ASPLUNDH TREE EXPERT, LLC)
26050 31b Ave, Aldergrove, BC, V4W 2Z6
(604) 856-2222
Emp Here 100
SIC 0783 Ornamental shrub and tree services
Remo Maddalozzo

D-U-N-S 20-178-4712   (SL)
CHAMP'S MUSHROOMS INC
CHAMP'S MUSHROOM'S GROUP
3151 260 St, Aldergrove, BC, V4W 2Z6
(604) 607-0789
Emp Here 66   *Sales* 17,312,394

SIC 0182 Food crops grown under cover
Duke Tran
Vien Quach
Pauline Tang
Tony Doan

D-U-N-S 25-650-9928   (BR)
CREDIT UNION CENTRAL OF CANADA
ALDERGROVE CREDIT UNION
(*Suby of* CREDIT UNION CENTRAL OF
CANADA)
2941 272 St, Aldergrove, BC, V4W 3R3
(604) 856-7724
Emp Here 85
SIC 6062 State credit unions
Shel Gould

D-U-N-S 25-500-3576   (SL)
DINESEN NURSERIES LTD
2110 272 St, Aldergrove, BC, V4W 2R1
(604) 856-2290
Emp Here 30   *Sales* 10,274,010
SIC 0181 Ornamental nursery products
Sukhmail Bassi

D-U-N-S 20-800-2493   (SL)
FRASER VALLEY REFRIGERATION LTD
(*Suby of* FRASER VALLEY HOLDINGS LTD)
26121 Fraser Hwy, Aldergrove, BC, V4W 2W8
(604) 856-8644
Emp Here 85   *Sales* 19,810,525
SIC 1711 Plumbing, heating, air-conditioning
Peter Masztalar
Ross Krafte

D-U-N-S 20-344-4252   (HQ)
**GRANDE   WEST   TRANSPORTATION
GROUP INC**
3168 262 St, Aldergrove, BC, V4W 2Z6
(604) 607-4000
Emp Here 5   *Sales* 42,857,705
SIC 3711 Motor vehicles and car bodies
William R. Trainer
Jean-Marc Landry
John Wang
John Lagourgue
Dan Buckle
Joseph Miller
Andrew Imanse
Keith T. Parker

D-U-N-S 24-337-8630   (SL)
J.B.M. ENTERPRISES
5000 256 St, Aldergrove, BC, V4W 1J4
(604) 856-1466
Emp Here 19   *Sales* 10,167,356
SIC 5148 Fresh fruits and vegetables
Athina Parson
Gregory Parson
Joseph Parson
David Parson

D-U-N-S 20-012-4746   (SL)
J.R.T. FARM LTD
2396 272 St, Aldergrove, BC, V4W 2R1
(604) 856-5552
Emp Here 70   *Sales* 18,361,630
SIC 0119 Cash grains, nec
Jaspal K Aujla
Jagjit Aujla

D-U-N-S 24-317-0656   (SL)
KLONDIKE LUBRICANTS CORPORATION
3078 275 St, Aldergrove, BC, V4W 3L4
(604) 856-5335
Emp Here 24   *Sales* 30,172,824
SIC 5172 Petroleum products, nec
Bradley Mitchell
Phil Jenner
Phil Jenner

D-U-N-S 25-616-3965   (BR)
LOBLAWS INC
EXTRA FOODS
(*Suby of* LOBLAW COMPANIES LIMITED)
3100 272 St, Aldergrove, BC, V4W 3N7

(604) 859-6501
Emp Here 100
SIC 5411 Grocery stores
Monica Truong

D-U-N-S 25-138-3035   (SL)
MAGNUM CONCRETE INC
26162 30a Ave Suite 201, Aldergrove, BC,
V4W 2W5
(604) 607-6576
Emp Here 30   *Sales* 13,415,220
SIC 5032 Brick, stone, and related material
Kelly Nichols

D-U-N-S 24-292-3407   (HQ)
MARNOR HOLDINGS LTD
3243 264 St, Aldergrove, BC, V4W 2X3
(604) 857-8853
Emp Here 3   *Sales* 12,342,360
SIC 4213 Trucking, except local
Craig Nicholson
Brian Nicholson

D-U-N-S 20-368-8783   (SL)
R.J.T. BLUEBERRY PARK INC
HONEYVIEW FARM
25990 48 Ave, Aldergrove, BC, V4W 1J2
(604) 381-4562
Emp Here 20   *Sales* 10,702,480
SIC 5142 Packaged frozen goods
Tina Chow

D-U-N-S 24-073-3816   (BR)
SCHOOL DISTRICT NO. 35 (LANGLEY)
*ALDERGROVE COMMUNITY SECONDARY
SCHOOL*
26850 29 Ave, Aldergrove, BC, V4W 3C1
(604) 856-2521
Emp Here 80
SIC 8211 Elementary and secondary schools
John Pusic

D-U-N-S 20-294-8196   (SL)
SHELTER MODULAR INC
(*Suby of* HORIZON NORTH LOGISTICS INC)
3294 262 St, Aldergrove, BC, V4W 2X2
(604) 856-1311
Emp Here 50   *Sales* 21,136,850
SIC 1541 Industrial buildings and warehouses
Harold Clifford

D-U-N-S 25-015-0117   (BR)
SOBEYS WEST INC
CANADA SAFEWAY # 165
(*Suby of* EMPIRE COMPANY LIMITED)
27566 Fraser Hwy, Aldergrove, BC, V4W 3N5
(604) 857-1351
Emp Here 100
SIC 5411 Grocery stores
Paul Harvey

D-U-N-S 20-692-5385   (HQ)
SUNSELECT PRODUCE INC
349 264 St, Aldergrove, BC, V4W 2K1
(604) 607-7655
Sales 17,050,085
SIC 0181 Ornamental nursery products
Gerhard Krahn
Louise Krahn
Edith Gubiotti

D-U-N-S 24-369-7257   (SL)
TRUONG'S ENTERPRISES LTD
40 264 St, Aldergrove, BC, V4W 2L6
(604) 856-5674
Emp Here 40   *Sales* 13,698,680
SIC 0182 Food crops grown under cover
Quan Truong
Chiraphon Truong

Anahim Lake, BC V0L

D-U-N-S 25-261-8475   (SL)
**WEST CHILCOTIN FOREST PRODUCTS
LTD**

21841 Chilcotin Hwy Suite 20, Anahim Lake,
BC, V0L 1C0

Emp Here 60   *Sales* 26,830,440
SIC 5031 Lumber, plywood, and millwork
William Kordyban Jr

Armstrong, BC V0E

D-U-N-S 24-311-5149   (SL)
AGRI TRANS SERVICES INC
2200 Kirton Ave, Armstrong, BC, V0E 1B0
(250) 546-8898
Emp Here 49   *Sales* 18,882,640
SIC 4731 Freight transportation arrangement
Randy Hawley

D-U-N-S 20-798-4019   (SL)
ARMSTRONG REGIONAL CO-OPERATIVE
SALMON ARM GAS BAR
973 Otter Lake Cross Rd, Armstrong, BC, V0E
1B6
(250) 546-9438
Emp Here 41   *Sales* 14,558,075
SIC 5541 Gasoline service stations
Jeff Payne

D-U-N-S 20-093-6086   (SL)
ARMSTRONG REGIONAL COOPERATIVE
973 Otter Lake Cross Rd, Armstrong, BC, V0E
1B6
(250) 546-9438
Emp Here 33   *Sales* 34,082,664
SIC 5171 Petroleum bulk stations and terminals
Patty Patterson

D-U-N-S 24-150-2517   (SL)
COLONIAL FARMS LTD
3830 Okanagan St, Armstrong, BC, V0E 1B0
(250) 546-3008
Emp Here 80   *Sales* 27,655,200
SIC 2015 Poultry slaughtering and processing
Dave Pollon

D-U-N-S 20-536-2614   (SL)
INTERIOR PROVINCIAL EXHIBITION, THE
*INTERIOR PROVINCIAL EXHIBITION AND
STAMPEDE*
3371 Peasant Valley Rd, Armstrong, BC, V0E
1B0
(250) 546-9406
Emp Here 33   *Sales* 13,114,662
SIC 8699 Membership organizations, nec
Shirley Fowler

D-U-N-S 25-884-9954   (SL)
JPW ROAD & BRIDGE INC
2310 Kirton Ave, Armstrong, BC, V0E 1B0
(250) 546-3765
Emp Here 100   *Sales* 25,244,200
SIC 1611 Highway and street construction
Joseph Wrobel

D-U-N-S 20-024-4726   (BR)
**NORTH OKANAGAN SHUSWAP SCHOOL
DISTRICT 83**
PLEASANT VALLEY SECONDARY SCHOOL
2365 Pleasant Valley Rd, Armstrong, BC, V0E
1B2
(250) 546-3114
Emp Here 80
SIC 8211 Elementary and secondary schools
Joe Rhodes

D-U-N-S 24-726-3064   (HQ)
RAFFAN INVESTMENTS LTD
903 Hwy 97a Rr 7, Armstrong, BC, V0E 1B7
(250) 546-9420
Sales 51,369,220
SIC 5154 Livestock
Don Raffan
Peter Raffan

D-U-N-S 25-090-0529   (SL)

RICK NICKELL TRUCKING INC
4280 Spallumcheen Dr, Armstrong, BC, V0E 1B6
(250) 546-2566
Emp Here 80   *Sales* 11,855,360
SIC 4213 Trucking, except local
Rick Nickell

D-U-N-S 24-373-6303   (HQ)
ROGERS FOODS LTD
(*Suby of* NISSHIN SEIFUN GROUP INC.)
4420 Larkin Cross Rd, Armstrong, BC, V0E 1B6
(250) 546-8744
Emp Here 70   *Sales* 44,939,700
SIC 2041 Flour and other grain mill products
Joe Girdner

D-U-N-S 20-714-0252   (SL)
SHEPHERD'S HARDWARE LIMITED
HOME HARDWARE BUILDING CENTRE
3525 Mill St, Armstrong, BC, V0E 1B0
(250) 546-3002
Emp Here 72   *Sales* 17,529,151
SIC 5211 Lumber and other building materials
Dale Melvin
Kyle Melvin
James Hudson
Brett Melvin

D-U-N-S 24-504-7378   (SL)
SNOWCAP INTERIOR FOOD SERVICES LTD
4130 Spallumcheen Dr, Armstrong, BC, V0E 1B6
(250) 546-8781
Emp Here 22   *Sales* 18,382,694
SIC 5149 Groceries and related products, nec
Duncan Macdonald
Fred Sieffert
Linda Sieffert

D-U-N-S 24-207-5682   (BR)
TOLKO INDUSTRIES LTD
(*Suby of* AMERICAN INDUSTRIAL ACQUISITION CORPORATION)
844 Otter Lake Cross Rd, Armstrong, BC, V0E 1B6
(250) 546-3171
Emp Here 550
SIC 2421 Sawmills and planing mills, general
Pat Donnelly

D-U-N-S 24-154-5375   (SL)
VALLEY AUCTION LTD
(*Suby of* RAFFAN INVESTMENTS LTD)
903 Hwy 97a, Armstrong, BC, V0E 1B7
(250) 546-9420
Emp Here 35   *Sales* 51,369,220
SIC 5154 Livestock
Don Raffan
Peter J Raffan

D-U-N-S 24-778-0364   (HQ)
VSA HIGHWAY MAINTENANCE LTD
1504 Blattner Rd, Armstrong, BC, V0E 1B0
(250) 546-8844
Emp Here 13   *Sales* 16,403,346
SIC 1611 Highway and street construction
Fred Gilowski
Bob Gilowski
David Gilowski
Ron Gilowski
Barrie Satchell

D-U-N-S 20-333-9890   (SL)
WOODTONE SPECIALTIES INC
(*Suby of* W. I. WOODTONE INDUSTRIES INC)
4175 Crozier Rd, Armstrong, BC, V0E 1B6
(250) 546-6808
Emp Here 80   *Sales* 15,389,600
SIC 2431 Millwork
Hal Hanlon
Christopher Young
Kevin Young

Arras, BC V0C

D-U-N-S 24-255-2128   (SL)
RANDON ENTERPRISES LTD
11953 241 Rd, Arras, BC, V0C 1B0
(250) 843-7394
Emp Here 30   *Sales* 11,560,800
SIC 4789 Transportation services, nec

Ashcroft, BC V0K

D-U-N-S 24-371-6743   (HQ)
SCHOOL DISTRICT #74 (GOLD TRAIL)
400 Hollis Rd, Ashcroft, BC, V0K 1A0
(250) 453-9101
Emp Here 1   *Sales* 17,841,420
SIC 8211 Elementary and secondary schools
Carmen Ranta
Valerie Adrian

Barriere, BC V0E

D-U-N-S 20-098-2205   (SL)
GILBERT SMITH FOREST PRODUCTS LTD
4411 Borthwick Ave, Barriere, BC, V0E 1E0
(250) 672-9435
Emp Here 75   *Sales* 20,073,900
SIC 5211 Lumber and other building materials
Ted Smith
Carman Smith
R R Smith
T W A Smith
Greg Smith

Bear Lake, BC V0J

D-U-N-S 24-824-3222   (BR)
CANADIAN FOREST PRODUCTS LTD
POLAR, DIV
(*Suby of* CANFOR CORPORATION)
36654 Hart Hwy, Bear Lake, BC, V0J 3G0
(250) 972-4700
Emp Here 140
SIC 2421 Sawmills and planing mills, general
Lyle Disher

Blue River, BC V0E

D-U-N-S 24-646-9381   (SL)
CARIBOO HELICOPTER SKIING (88) LTD
MIKE WIEGELE HELICOPTER SKIING
1 Harrwood Dr, Blue River, BC, V0E 1J0
(250) 673-8381
Emp Here 80   *Sales* 7,591,920
SIC 7011 Hotels and motels

Brentwood Bay, BC V8M

D-U-N-S 20-650-1178   (SL)
BRENTWOOD BAY LODGE LTD
BRENTWOOD BAY RESORT & SPA
849 Verdier Ave, Brentwood Bay, BC, V8M 1C5
(250) 544-2079
Emp Here 90   *Sales* 6,955,364
SIC 7991 Physical fitness facilities
Daniel Behune

D-U-N-S 20-804-9445   (SL)
BUTCHART GARDENS LTD, THE
800 Benvenuto Ave, Brentwood Bay, BC, V8M 1J8
(250) 652-5256
Emp Here 300   *Sales* 31,458,000
SIC 8422 Botanical and zoological gardens
Richard Taylor
Peter Klassen
Robin Clarke

D-U-N-S 24-249-7709   (SL)
EUROSA FARMS LTD
1304 Greig Ave, Brentwood Bay, BC, V8M 1J6
(250) 652-5812
Emp Here 32   *Sales* 10,958,944
SIC 0181 Ornamental nursery products
Johannes Bulk
Deborah Bulk

D-U-N-S 20-921-3060   (SL)
PACIFIC COMPANION ENTERPRISES INC
7083 Silverdale Pl, Brentwood Bay, BC, V8M 1G9

Emp Here 18   *Sales* 13,277,520
SIC 6324 Hospital and medical service plans
David Davenport
Gloria Davenport

D-U-N-S 20-015-5583   (BR)
SCHOOL DISTRICT 63 (SAANICH)
BAYSIDE MIDDLE SCHOOL
1101 Newton Pl, Brentwood Bay, BC, V8M 1G3
(250) 652-1135
Emp Here 75
SIC 8211 Elementary and secondary schools
Wendy Macdonald

D-U-N-S 20-093-8603   (SL)
TRUE VALUE FOOD CENTRE LTD
BRENTWOOD TRUE VALUE FOOD CENTRE
7108 West Saanich Rd, Brentwood Bay, BC, V8M 1P8
(250) 544-8183
Emp Here 137   *Sales* 40,206,349
SIC 5411 Grocery stores
Jerry Rainer

Bridge Lake, BC V0K

D-U-N-S 24-160-2122   (SL)
INTERLAKES VOLUNTEER FIRE DEPARTMENT
7657 Little Fort Hwy Suite 24, Bridge Lake, BC, V0K 1E0
(250) 593-4266
Emp Here 42   *Sales* 19,184,521
SIC 7389 Business services, nec
Doug Townsend

Brisco, BC V0A

D-U-N-S 20-114-9056   (SL)
RIVER BUTTE MANAGEMENT LTD
2866 Brisco Rd, Brisco, BC, V0A 1B0
(250) 346-3315
Emp Here 46   *Sales* 13,031,478
SIC 8741 Management services
Robert Mccue

Burnaby, BC V3J

D-U-N-S 20-591-2202   (BR)
BURNABY SCHOOL BOARD DISTRICT 41
BURNABY MOUNTAIN SECONDARY SCHOOL
(*Suby of* BURNABY SCHOOL BOARD DIS-
TRICT 41)
8800 Eastlake Dr, Burnaby, BC, V3J 7X5
(604) 296-6870
Emp Here 150
SIC 8211 Elementary and secondary schools
Andy Chin

D-U-N-S 25-271-6931   (BR)
SOBEYS WEST INC
SAFEWAY PHARMACY
(*Suby of* EMPIRE COMPANY LIMITED)
9855 Austin Rd, Burnaby, BC, V3J 1N4
(604) 420-8091
Emp Here 125
SIC 5411 Grocery stores
Randy Klarsnick

D-U-N-S 25-730-9633   (BR)
WAL-MART CANADA CORP
(*Suby of* WALMART INC.)
9855 Austin Rd Suite 300, Burnaby, BC, V3J 1N5
(604) 421-0661
Emp Here 325
SIC 5311 Department stores
Ariel Dizon

D-U-N-S 25-663-1367   (BR)
WHITE SPOT LIMITED
WHITE SPOT RESTAURANT
(*Suby of* SHATO HOLDINGS LTD)
4075 North Rd, Burnaby, BC, V3J 1S3
(604) 421-4620
Emp Here 75
SIC 5812 Eating places
William Warwick

Burnaby, BC V3N

D-U-N-S 20-346-0043   (HQ)
18 WHEELS LOGISTICS LTD
7185 11th Ave, Burnaby, BC, V3N 2M5
(604) 439-8938
Emp Here 5   *Sales* 12,999,175
SIC 4731 Freight transportation arrangement
Perry Wong
Adrian Wen Comm

D-U-N-S 25-415-9304   (HQ)
406106 ALBERTA INC
AM PM SERVICE
6741 Cariboo Rd Suite 101, Burnaby, BC, V3N 4A3
(604) 421-5677
Emp Here 40   *Sales* 107,070,400
SIC 5044 Office equipment
John Chan
Karen Chan
Kathy Lau
Ken Tjia

D-U-N-S 24-996-2135   (HQ)
429149 B.C. LTD
QUILTS ETC
(*Suby of* 888999 INVESTMENTS LTD)
8168 Glenwood Dr, Burnaby, BC, V3N 5E9
(604) 549-2000
Emp Here 35   *Sales* 106,681,200
SIC 5719 Miscellaneous homefurnishings
Howard Haugom
Jixin Xu

D-U-N-S 24-033-2544   (HQ)
A.B.C. HOLDINGS LTD
8081 Meadow Ave, Burnaby, BC, V3N 2V9

Sales 31,232,520
SIC 5093 Scrap and waste materials
David Yochlowitz
Harold Yochlowitz
Melvyn Yochlowitz
Helen Alco

D-U-N-S 20-108-4274   (HQ)

▲ Public Company   ■ Public Company Family Member   **HQ** Headquarters   **BR** Branch   **SL** Single Location

A.B.C. RECYCLING LTD
(*Suby of* A.B.C. HOLDINGS LTD)
8081 Meadow Ave, Burnaby, BC, V3N 2V9
(604) 522-9727
Emp Here 20   *Sales* 139,060,000
SIC 5093 Scrap and waste materials
 Harold Yochlowitz
 Melvyn Yochlowitz
 Dirk Odenwald

D-U-N-S 24-725-5516   (HQ)
A.M.P.M. SERVICE LTD
(*Suby of* 514647 B.C. LTD)
6741 Cariboo Rd Unit 101, Burnaby, BC, V3N
4A3
(604) 421-5677
Emp Here 60   *Sales* 19,232,800
SIC 7629 Electrical repair shops
 John Chan
 Ken Tjia

D-U-N-S 20-031-0754   (SL)
AGROPUR COOPERATIVE
7650 18th St, Burnaby, BC, V3N 4K3
(604) 524-4491
Emp Here 49   *Sales* 18,890,431
SIC 0241 Dairy farms
 Senthil Vijayakumar

D-U-N-S 24-566-4446   (SL)
**BRITISH COLUMBIA RAPID TRANSIT
COMPANY LTD**
SKYTRAIN
(*Suby of* SOUTH COAST BRITISH
COLUMBIA TRANSPORTATION AUTHOR-
ITY)
6800 14th Ave, Burnaby, BC, V3N 4S7
(604) 520-3641
Emp Here 580   *Sales* 32,604,120
SIC 4111 Local and suburban transit
 Haydn Acheson
 Mike Richard
 Tracy Bolognese

D-U-N-S 24-513-7273   (BR)
BURNABY SCHOOL BOARD DISTRICT 41
BYRNE CREEK SECONDARY SCHOOL
(*Suby of* BURNABY SCHOOL BOARD DIS-
TRICT 41)
7777 18th St, Burnaby, BC, V3N 5E5
(604) 296-6885
Emp Here 85
SIC 8211 Elementary and secondary schools
 David Starr

D-U-N-S 20-875-3934   (BR)
BURNABY SCHOOL BOARD DISTRICT 41
CARIBOO HILL SECONDARY SCHOOL
(*Suby of* BURNABY SCHOOL BOARD DIS-
TRICT 41)
8580 16th Ave, Burnaby, BC, V3N 1S6
(604) 296-6890
Emp Here 80
SIC 8211 Elementary and secondary schools
 Sue Montabello

D-U-N-S 24-723-9197   (HQ)
**COVANTA BURNABY RENEWABLE EN-
ERGY, INC / ENERGIE RENOUVELABLE
COVANTA BURNABY, INC**
(*Suby of* COVANTA HOLDING CORPORA-
TION)
5150 Riverbend Dr, Burnaby, BC, V3N 4V3
(604) 521-1025
Sales 18,685,305
SIC 4961 Steam and air-conditioning supply
 Anthony Orlando
 Mark Pytosh
 Timothy Simpson

D-U-N-S 25-011-9823   (SL)
DETECTEX SECURITY SERVICES CORP
8557 Government St Suite 102, Burnaby, BC,
V3N 4S9

Emp Here 30   *Sales* 11,870,340
SIC 7381 Detective and armored car services

Karen Scott

D-U-N-S 20-511-8722   (SL)
GARIBALDI GLASS INDUSTRIES INC
8183 Wiggins St, Burnaby, BC, V3N 0C4
(604) 420-4527
Emp Here 150   *Sales* 26,882,850
SIC 3231 Products of purchased glass
 Carey Mobius
 Christian Mobius
 Roger Gil

D-U-N-S 24-419-8276   (HQ)
GENERAL FUSION INC
3680 Bonneville Pl Suite 106, Burnaby, BC,
V3N 4T5
(604) 420-0920
Sales 13,785,240
SIC 8731 Commercial physical research
 Christofer Mowry
 Michel Laberge
 Bruce Colwill
 Fred Buckman
 Jacques Besnainou
 Mike Sherman
 Shahril Ibrahim
 Klaas De Boer

D-U-N-S 25-012-0631   (SL)
GEORGE DERBY CARE SOCIETY
GEORGE DERBY CENTRE
7550 Cumberland St, Burnaby, BC, V3N 3X5
(604) 521-2676
Emp Here 350   *Sales* 23,914,100
SIC 8051 Skilled nursing care facilities
 Valentine Drayton
 William James Watson
 Donald Winch
 Roger Zahar
 Doug Germaine
 Phillip Luniw
 Margaret Koster
 Edward Eberlein
 Anthony Grasset
 Larry Harrison

D-U-N-S 20-725-5519   (BR)
**GULF AND FRASER FISHERMEN'S
CREDIT UNION**
G&F FINANCIAL GROUP
(*Suby of* GULF AND FRASER FISHERMEN'S
CREDIT UNION)
7375 Kingsway, Burnaby, BC, V3N 3B5
(604) 419-8888
Emp Here 175
SIC 6062 State credit unions
 Richard Davies

D-U-N-S 25-418-9715   (HQ)
**GULF AND FRASER FISHERMEN'S
CREDIT UNION**
G&F FINANCIAL GROUP
7375 Kingsway, Burnaby, BC, V3N 3B5
(604) 517-5100
Emp Here 65   *Sales* 29,890,175
SIC 6062 State credit unions
 Jeff Shewfelt
 Juliana Yung
 Ken Mcbain
 William Kiss

D-U-N-S 25-400-4161   (HQ)
HORIZON DISTRIBUTORS LTD
TARA NATURAL
5589 Trapp Ave, Burnaby, BC, V3N 0B2
(604) 524-6610
Sales 143,343,200
SIC 5149 Groceries and related products, nec
 Ronald Francisco
 Terri Newell
 Gayle Thom
 Shannen Lohnes
 Barbara Fulgham
 Anita Pollard

D-U-N-S 24-247-3288   (HQ)
J & R HOME PRODUCTS LTD

5628 Riverbend Dr Unit 1, Burnaby, BC, V3N
0C1
(604) 525-8333
Emp Here 44   *Sales* 31,302,180
SIC 5072 Hardware
 Stuart Watson
 Rosemary Watson
 Becky Gilligan

D-U-N-S 25-099-5784   (SL)
JHL INTERNATIONAL TRADING CO. LTD
(*Suby of* 888999 INVESTMENTS LTD)
8168 Glenwood Dr, Burnaby, BC, V3N 5E9
(604) 421-5520
Emp Here 2   *Sales* 23,795,337
SIC 5023 Homefurnishings
 Jixin Xu
 Howard Haugom

D-U-N-S 24-579-5182   (HQ)
**LANCASTER MEDICAL SUPPLIES AND
PRESCRIPTIONS LTD**
6741 Cariboo Rd Unit 203, Burnaby, BC, V3N
4A3
(604) 708-8181
Emp Here 3   *Sales* 33,160,350
SIC 5122 Drugs, proprietaries, and sundries
 David Kotow

D-U-N-S 20-114-0506   (SL)
MITCHELL PRESS LIMITED
8328 Riverbend Crt, Burnaby, BC, V3N 5C9
(604) 528-9882
Emp Here 80   *Sales* 13,122,160
SIC 2752 Commercial printing, lithographic
 Howard Mitchell
 Daniel Castilloux
 David Mitchell

D-U-N-S 20-315-4919   (SL)
NEMO PRODUCTIONS - CAN, INC
8035 Glenwood Dr, Burnaby, BC, V3N 5C8

Emp Here 700   *Sales* 62,787,200
SIC 7829 Motion picture distribution services
 Arthur Evrensel
 John Martin Willhite

D-U-N-S 20-800-5926   (SL)
**NORWEGIAN OLD PEOPLE'S HOME AS-
SOCIATION**
NORMANNA REST HOME
7725 4th St, Burnaby, BC, V3N 5B6
(604) 522-5812
Emp Here 100   *Sales* 5,924,700
SIC 8361 Residential care
 Margaret Douglas-Matthews

D-U-N-S 20-359-0724   (SL)
**PACIFIC WELLFARE RESOURCE INVEST-
MENT INC**
8218 North Fraser Way, Burnaby, BC, V3N
0E9
(778) 989-6678
Emp Here 50   *Sales* 41,778,850
SIC 5149 Groceries and related products, nec
 Tony Ma

D-U-N-S 25-326-2117   (HQ)
R-FOUR CONTRACTING LTD
7185 11th Ave, Burnaby, BC, V3N 2M5
(604) 522-4402
Emp Here 1   *Sales* 18,829,240
SIC 1542 Nonresidential construction, nec
 Rick Spence

D-U-N-S 24-120-6028   (SL)
SNOW CAP ENTERPRISES LTD
5698 Trapp Ave Suite 564, Burnaby, BC, V3N
5G4
(604) 515-3202
Emp Here 130   *Sales* 38,152,010
SIC 5461 Retail bakeries
 Linda Seiffert
 Ella Seiffert

D-U-N-S 20-690-3523   (HQ)
SSI SUSTAINABLE SOLUTIONS INTERNA-

TIONAL PARTNERS
8395 Riverbend Crt, Burnaby, BC, V3N 5E7
(604) 430-2020
Sales 16,580,175
SIC 5122 Drugs, proprietaries, and sundries
 Douglas Sproule
 David Morris
 Glenn Sheargold

D-U-N-S 20-116-5107   (SL)
TRAPP AVE INDUSTRIES
6010 Trapp Ave App Ave, Burnaby, BC, V3N
2V4
(604) 526-2333
Emp Here 50   *Sales* 10,141,500
SIC 3441 Fabricated structural Metal
 Rob Third

D-U-N-S 25-256-0339   (HQ)
VALUE VILLAGE STORES, INC
SAVERS
(*Suby of* SAVERS, INC.)
7350 Edmonds St, Burnaby, BC, V3N 0G7
(604) 540-4916
Emp Here 5   *Sales* 380,270,000
SIC 5399 Miscellaneous general merchandise
 Thomas Ellison
 Rodney Van Leeuwen
 Kenneth Alterman

D-U-N-S 20-979-0372   (SL)
VINTECH DRAFTING INC
7893 Edmonds St Suite 203, Burnaby, BC,
V3N 1B9
(604) 523-6439
Emp Here 30   *Sales* 13,304,700
SIC 7389 Business services, nec
 Vincent Psang

D-U-N-S 24-227-4413   (HQ)
WESTKEY GRAPHICS LTD
8315 Riverbend Crt, Burnaby, BC, V3N 5E7
(604) 549-2350
Emp Here 112   *Sales* 25,144,569
SIC 5943 Stationery stores

Burnaby, BC V5A

D-U-N-S 24-245-9568   (SL)
A.P.T. AUTO PARTS TRADING CO. LTD
7342 Winston St Unit 10, Burnaby, BC, V5A
2H1
(604) 421-2781
Emp Here 40   *Sales* 25,171,200
SIC 5531 Auto and home supply stores
 Angela Abu-Ata
 Salim Abu-Ata
 John Abu-Ata
 Jim Abu-Ata
 Suzy Hodali

D-U-N-S 20-827-6290   (SL)
**ADVANTAGE DATASYSTEMS CORPORA-
TION**
ADVANTAGE PARTS SOULTION
8061 Lougheed Hwy Suite 110, Burnaby, BC,
V5A 1W9
(604) 415-3950
Emp Here 110   *Sales* 26,876,080
SIC 5963 Direct selling establishments
 Steve Kirstiuk

D-U-N-S 24-366-0847   (HQ)
AECOM CANADA LTD
(*Suby of* AECOM)
3292 Production Way, Burnaby, BC, V5A 4R4
(604) 444-6400
Emp Here 100   *Sales* 689,958,500
SIC 8711 Engineering services
 Michael S Burke
 Bob Ledford
 Marc Delvin
 Steve Morris

D-U-N-S 24-773-0224   (BR)

ALS CANADA LTD
ALS ENVIRONMENTAL
(*Suby of* ALS LIMITED)
8081 Lougheed Hwy Suite 100, Burnaby, BC,
V5A 1W9
(778) 370-3150
Emp Here 200
SIC 8071 Medical laboratories

D-U-N-S 20-159-3019   (HQ)
ALTROM AUTO GROUP LTD
ALTROM GROUP
(*Suby of* GENUINE PARTS COMPANY)
4242 Phillips Ave Unit C, Burnaby, BC, V5A
2X2
(604) 294-2311
Emp Here 80   *Sales* 138,346,200
SIC 5015 Motor vehicle parts, used
  Dieter Gamm
  David Powlowski
  Thomas Seidel

D-U-N-S 24-339-3969   (SL)
AMGEN BRITISH COLUMBIA INC
(*Suby of* AMGEN INC.)
7990 Enterprise St, Burnaby, BC, V5A 1V7
(604) 415-1800
Emp Here 50   *Sales* 55,267,250
SIC 5122 Drugs, proprietaries, and sundries
  Dennis Fenton
  Richard Nanula
  David Scott

D-U-N-S 20-272-2851   (SL)
BINARY STREAM SOFTWARE INC
4238 Lozells Ave Unit 201, Burnaby, BC, V5A
0C4
(604) 522-6300
Emp Here 60   *Sales* 10,638,660
SIC 7371 Custom computer programming services
  Lakvir Chahal

D-U-N-S 24-314-6052   (SL)
BOLD EVENT CREATIVE INC
7570 Conrad St, Burnaby, BC, V5A 2H7
(604) 437-7677
Emp Here 50   *Sales* 10,941,200
SIC 3999 Manufacturing industries, nec
  Brock Lumsden

D-U-N-S 25-011-1309   (BR)
BRICK WAREHOUSE LP, THE
BRICK, THE
(*Suby of* BRICK WAREHOUSE LP, THE)
3100 Production Way Suite 103, Burnaby, BC,
V5A 4R4
(604) 415-4900
Emp Here 300
SIC 5712 Furniture stores
  John Evans

D-U-N-S 25-719-2963   (SL)
BRITE BLINDS LTD
4275 Phillips Ave Suite C, Burnaby, BC, V5A
2X4
(604) 420-8820
Emp Here 75   *Sales* 17,430,225
SIC 5719 Miscellaneous homefurnishings
  David Brooks

D-U-N-S 24-514-5144   (BR)
**CANADIAN UTILITY CONSTRUCTION
CORP**
(*Suby of* QUANTA SERVICES, INC.)
7950 Venture St, Burnaby, BC, V5A 1V3

Emp Here 80
SIC 1623 Water, sewer, and utility lines
  Mike Gray

D-U-N-S 25-095-9707   (BR)
CANPAR TRANSPORT L.P.
(*Suby of* CANPAR TRANSPORT L.P.)
8399 Eastlake Dr, Burnaby, BC, V5A 4W2
(604) 421-3452
Emp Here 110
SIC 4731 Freight transportation arrangement

  Ted Donnelly

D-U-N-S 20-799-3411   (HQ)
CENTAUR PRODUCTS INC
3145 Thunderbird Cres, Burnaby, BC, V5A
3G1
(604) 357-3510
Emp Here 25   *Sales* 13,745,270
SIC 1752 Floor laying and floor work, nec
  Dave Wilson
  Leslie Wilson
  Leif Mathiesen
  Hugh Hamilton
  Gerald Demeria

D-U-N-S 25-195-5886   (BR)
COSTCO WHOLESALE CANADA LTD
(*Suby of* COSTCO WHOLESALE CORPO-
RATION)
3550 Brighton Ave Suite 51, Burnaby, BC, V5A
4W3
(604) 420-2668
Emp Here 250
SIC 5099 Durable goods, nec
  Darren Springford

D-U-N-S 20-918-8978   (HQ)
DOLPHIN DELIVERY LTD
DOLPHIN TRANSPORT
4201 Lozells Ave, Burnaby, BC, V5A 2Z4
(604) 421-1115
Emp Here 100   *Sales* 46,095,250
SIC 4212 Local trucking, without storage
  William Morris Peter

D-U-N-S 20-749-4618   (SL)
DRYCO DRYWALL SUPPLIES LTD
7027 Winston St, Burnaby, BC, V5A 2G7
(604) 253-4121
Emp Here 300   *Sales* 170,888,400
SIC 5032 Brick, stone, and related material
  Bruno Mauro
  Ken Kabush
  Vince Mauro

D-U-N-S 20-111-7736   (HQ)
GLENTEL INC
BOUTIQUE WAVE SANS FIL
8501 Commerce Crt, Burnaby, BC, V5A 4N3
(604) 415-6500
Emp Here 150   *Sales* 635,633,600
SIC 4813 Telephone communication, except
radio
  Ravi Nookala
  Erika Tse
  Damon A. Jones
  Daniel Phillips
  Harry Parmar

D-U-N-S 24-382-4286   (SL)
GOLDEN BOY FOODS GP (2007) INC
7725 Lougheed Hwy, Burnaby, BC, V5A 4V8
(778) 373-3800
Emp Here 300   *Sales* 146,215,500
SIC 2099 Food preparations, nec
  Richard Harris

D-U-N-S 24-370-4033   (HQ)
GOLDEN BOY FOODS LTD
GOLDEN BOY
(*Suby of* POST HOLDINGS, INC.)
7725 Lougheed Hwy, Burnaby, BC, V5A 4V8
(604) 433-2200
Emp Here 220   *Sales* 136,467,800
SIC 2068 Salted and roasted nuts and seeds
  Paul Henderson
  Gord Love
  Ali Rezaei
  Brian Irving

D-U-N-S 20-554-0250   (BR)
GOLDEN BOY FOODS LTD
(*Suby of* POST HOLDINGS, INC.)
3151 Lake City Way, Burnaby, BC, V5A 3A3
(604) 421-4500
Emp Here 200
SIC 4226 Special warehousing and storage,

nec
  Lobos Novak

D-U-N-S 25-710-8019   (HQ)
GOLDEN TRIM ENTERPRISES INC
8411 Lougheed Hwy, Burnaby, BC, V5A 1X3
(604) 421-3998
Emp Here 5   *Sales* 15,265,680
SIC 5023 Homefurnishings
  John Wong
  Joseph Ho

D-U-N-S 24-355-2820   (HQ)
**GREENLIGHT INNOVATION CORPORA-
TION**
3430 Brighton Ave Unit 104a, Burnaby, BC,
V5A 3H4
(604) 676-4000
Sales 12,058,414
SIC 3821 Laboratory apparatus and furniture
  Ross Bailey
  Mark Olfert
  Christian Bosio
  Greg Walsh

D-U-N-S 20-113-4061   (HQ)
H.Y. LOUIE CO. LIMITED
CASH & CARRY
2821 Production Way, Burnaby, BC, V5A 3G7
(604) 421-4242
Emp Here 100   *Sales* 866,088,000
SIC 5411 Grocery stores
  Brandt Louie
  Anthony Tang
  Randy Melnychenko
  Scott Coburn

D-U-N-S 24-797-2235   (SL)
**HAZMASTERS ENVIRONMENTAL CON-
TROLS INC**
3131 Underhill Ave, Burnaby, BC, V5A 3C8
(604) 420-0025
Emp Here 40   *Sales* 19,001,040
SIC 5084 Industrial machinery and equipment
  Randal Myers
  Thomas Bowen

D-U-N-S 25-452-9498   (SL)
HITFAR CONCEPTS LTD
2999 Underhill Ave Suite 109, Burnaby, BC,
V5A 3C2
(604) 873-8364
Emp Here 30   *Sales* 13,415,220
SIC 5065 Electronic parts and equipment, nec
  Troy Fargey

D-U-N-S 25-715-1936   (SL)
ICAN CONTRACTING LTD
ICAN TILE DISTRIBUTORS
3131 Thunderbird Cres, Burnaby, BC, V5A
3G1
(604) 299-0146
Emp Here 12   *Sales* 11,464,476
SIC 5032 Brick, stone, and related material
  Tony Baldassarre

D-U-N-S 20-181-9450   (SL)
INTERBEST HOUSEWARES INC
INTER-BEST
(*Suby of* INTERNATIONAL SOURCES LTD)
7588 Winston St, Burnaby, BC, V5A 4X5
(604) 216-3333
Emp Here 35   *Sales* 17,809,960
SIC 5023 Homefurnishings
  Johnny Fong

D-U-N-S 25-216-8927   (SL)
INTERSTYLE CERAMIC & GLASS LTD
3625 Brighton Ave, Burnaby, BC, V5A 3H5
(604) 421-7229
Emp Here 90   *Sales* 21,009,150
SIC 3231 Products of purchased glass
  Georgia Hauner
  Luca Michele Hauner
  Kim M. Hauner

D-U-N-S 24-037-0606   (SL)
J.L. & SONS TRADING COMPANY LTD

DIRECT LIQUIDATION
6990 Greenwood St, Burnaby, BC, V5A 1X8
(604) 294-2331
Emp Here 16   *Sales* 10,513,972
SIC 7389 Business services, nec
  Jeff Schwarz

D-U-N-S 25-068-8447   (BR)
JET EQUIPMENT & TOOLS LTD
(*Suby of* JET EQUIPMENT & TOOLS LTD)
3260 Production Way, Burnaby, BC, V5A 4W4
(800) 472-7686
Emp Here 90
SIC 5085 Industrial supplies
  Craig Diamond

D-U-N-S 20-333-9341   (SL)
JUBILEE TOURS & TRAVEL LTD
TRAVEL BEST BETS
3011 Underhill Ave Suite 201, Burnaby, BC,
V5A 3C2
(604) 669-6607
Emp Here 25   *Sales* 12,999,175
SIC 4724 Travel agencies
  Claire Newell

D-U-N-S 25-012-2462   (BR)
KRAFT HEINZ CANADA ULC
(*Suby of* THE KRAFT HEINZ COMPANY)
2700 Production Way Suite 450, Burnaby, BC,
V5A 4X1
(604) 420-2511
Emp Here 100
SIC 5149 Groceries and related products, nec
  Kandell Miller

D-U-N-S 24-803-1267   (SL)
LAMI GLASS PRODUCTS, LLC
HARTUNG GLASS CANADA
(*Suby of* HARTUNG GLASS INDUSTRIES,
INC.)
7344 Winston St, Burnaby, BC, V5A 2G9
(604) 420-3600
Emp Here 70   *Sales* 12,545,330
SIC 3231 Products of purchased glass
  Nick Sciola

D-U-N-S 24-135-3650   (SL)
LEWIS-GOETZ ULC
GOODALL RUBBER
3181 Thunderbird Cres, Burnaby, BC, V5A
3G1
(604) 444-4885
Emp Here 20   *Sales* 10,006,500
SIC 5169 Chemicals and allied products, nec
  Patrick Green

D-U-N-S 24-806-9981   (HQ)
MINEWORX TECHNOLOGIES LTD
MINEWORX
8331 Eastlake Dr Unit 114, Burnaby, BC, V5A
4W2
(250) 751-3661
Sales 131,315,195
SIC 1081 Metal mining services
  Greg Pendura
  Gavin Watkins
  Don Weatherbee
  Darcy Thiele
  Akiva Borenstein
  Rick Gliege
  A.J. (Pine) Pienaar
  Rick Purdy

D-U-N-S 20-275-8165   (SL)
OLSON INTERNATIONAL TRADING LTD
OLSON INTERNATIONAL
4098 Mcconnell Dr, Burnaby, BC, V5A 3Y9
(604) 420-8022
Emp Here 22   *Sales* 18,382,694
SIC 5141 Groceries, general line
  Michael Jang

D-U-N-S 24-492-5640   (SL)
PBF PITA BREAD FACTORY LTD
8000 Winston St, Burnaby, BC, V5A 2H5
(604) 528-6111
Emp Here 100   *Sales* 34,569,000

SIC 2051 Bread, cake, and related products
Fady Hayek
Sid Hayek
Ron Hayek

D-U-N-S 20-621-3571   (HQ)
PICO OF CANADA LTD
7590 Conrad St, Burnaby, BC, V5A 2H7
(604) 438-7571
Emp Here 22   Sales 16,025,460
SIC 5013 Motor vehicle supplies and new parts

D-U-N-S 24-381-4352   (HQ)
QUIKRETE CANADA HOLDINGS, LIMITED
(Suby of QUIKRETE HOLDINGS, INC.)
8535 Eastlake Dr, Burnaby, BC, V5A 4T7
(604) 444-3620
Emp Here 3   Sales 27,335,000
SIC 6712 Bank holding companies
Dennis Arbour
John O Winchester
James E Winchester
Dennis C Winchester

D-U-N-S 20-349-8709   (SL)
ROYAL CITY RECORDS NOW
NOW NEWSPAPERS
3430 Brighton Ave Suite 201a, Burnaby, BC, V5A 3H4

Emp Here 45   Sales 33,413,400
SIC 5192 Books, periodicals, and newspapers
Brad Alden

D-U-N-S 20-108-8473   (SL)
RUSSELL INDUSTRIES LTD
4062 Mcconnell Dr, Burnaby, BC, V5A 3A8
(604) 420-2440
Emp Here 24   Sales 10,732,176
SIC 5063 Electrical apparatus and equipment
Alexander Richardson
Douglas Richardson

D-U-N-S 20-213-4347   (BR)
SAPUTO PRODUITS LAITIERS CANADA S.E.N.C.
(Suby of SAPUTO PRODUITS LAITIERS CANADA S.E.N.C.)
6800 Lougheed Hwy Suite 3, Burnaby, BC, V5A 1W2
(604) 420-6611
Emp Here 500
SIC 2023 Dry, condensed and evaporated dairy products
Anton Donkers

D-U-N-S 20-994-9494   (SL)
SIMON FRASER STUDENT SOCIETY
8888 University Dr Suite 2250, Burnaby, BC, V5A 1S6
(778) 782-3111
Emp Here 82   Sales 11,716,078
SIC 8641 Civic and social associations
Kurt Belliveau
Carlos Garcia
Kate Berniaz

D-U-N-S 20-803-2946   (HQ)
SIMON FRASER UNIVERSITY
SFU
8888 University Dr Suite 1200, Burnaby, BC, V5A 1S6
(778) 782-3111
Emp Here 2,500   Sales 524,279,654
SIC 8221 Colleges and universities
Andrew Petter
Joanne Curry
Peter Keller
Martin Pochurko
Joy Johnson

D-U-N-S 20-797-8610   (HQ)
SKY-HI SCAFFOLDING LTD
(Suby of NORTHSTAR SCAFFOLD SERVICES INC)
3195 Production Way, Burnaby, BC, V5A 3H2

(604) 291-7245
Emp Here 35   Sales 17,233,020
SIC 1799 Special trade contractors, nec
Kevin Lottis
Lynn Perlstrom
James Johnson

D-U-N-S 24-867-3105   (HQ)
SMITH, M.R. LIMITED
IMPERIAL OIL
3100 Underhill Ave, Burnaby, BC, V5A 3C6
(604) 420-4331
Emp Here 22   Sales 31,430,025
SIC 5172 Petroleum products, nec
Michael Smith

D-U-N-S 24-797-3753   (SL)
SQUIRREL SYSTEMS OF CANADA, LTD
(Suby of MARIN INVESTMENTS LTD)
8585 Baxter Pl, Burnaby, BC, V5A 4V7
(604) 412-3300
Emp Here 150   Sales 21,627,300
SIC 7371 Custom computer programming services
Bob Maekett
Joseph G. Cortese
David Atkinson

D-U-N-S 25-679-1302   (SL)
STEELHEAD CONTRACTING RENOVATION LTD
4179 Mcconnell Dr, Burnaby, BC, V5A 3J7
(604) 420-9368
Emp Here 44   Sales 12,697,652
SIC 1522 Residential construction, nec
Donald Tatham
Craig Dabner

D-U-N-S 24-373-0939   (BR)
STRYKER CANADA HOLDING COMPANY
(Suby of STRYKER CORPORATION)
8329 Eastlake Dr Unit 101, Burnaby, BC, V5A 4W2
(604) 232-9861
Emp Here 80
SIC 8731 Commercial physical research

D-U-N-S 24-109-2533   (HQ)
SULZER PUMPS (CANADA) INC
4129 Lozells Ave, Burnaby, BC, V5A 2Z5
(604) 415-7800
Emp Here 100   Sales 30,858,139
SIC 3561 Pumps and pumping equipment
Bantoo Gill

D-U-N-S 20-015-4768   (HQ)
SWISS WATER DECAFFEINATED COFFEE INC
SWISS WATER
3131 Lake City Way, Burnaby, BC, V5A 3A3
(604) 420-4050
Sales 65,620,116
SIC 5149 Groceries and related products, nec
Frank Dennis
Eve Bartnik
David Rowntree
Richard Mahler
Diane Fulton
Roland Veit
Anne Saunders

D-U-N-S 20-116-4308   (HQ)
TARGET PRODUCTS LTD
QUIKRETE
(Suby of QUIKRETE HOLDINGS, INC.)
8535 Eastlake Dr, Burnaby, BC, V5A 4T7
(604) 444-3620
Emp Here 30   Sales 26,882,850
SIC 3272 Concrete products, nec
James Winchester
John Winchester
Dennis Winchester

D-U-N-S 20-572-6128   (HQ)
TCG INTERNATIONAL INC
8658 Commerce Crt, Burnaby, BC, V5A 4N6
(604) 438-1000
Emp Here 30   Sales 31,393,600

SIC 7536 Automotive glass replacement shops
Thomas E Skidmore
Allan Skidmore
Arthur Skidmore
Erica Tse

D-U-N-S 24-698-1976   (SL)
TERASEN WESTERN REGION
7815 Shellmont St, Burnaby, BC, V5A 4S9

Emp Here 5   Sales 15,529,285
SIC 4923 Gas transmission and distribution

D-U-N-S 25-160-8816   (HQ)
TERRY FOX FOUNDATION, THE
8960 University High St Suite 150, Burnaby, BC, V5A 4Y6
(604) 200-0541
Emp Here 3   Sales 35,866,071
SIC 6732 Trusts: educational, religious, etc.
Darrell Fox
Brett Fohali
Rhonda Risebrough
Victor Ling
Tim Rahilly
David Newman
Rob Shea

D-U-N-S 24-157-6818   (HQ)
TIERRA SOL CERAMIC TILE LTD
(Suby of GESCO LIMITED PARTNERSHIP)
4084 Mcconnell Crt Unit 100, Burnaby, BC, V5A 3L8
(604) 435-5400
Emp Here 30   Sales 42,722,100
SIC 5032 Brick, stone, and related material
Edward Porter

D-U-N-S 25-246-6222   (SL)
TRACTION SALES AND MARKETING INC
TRACTION ON DEMAND
2700 Production Way Suite 500, Burnaby, BC, V5A 0C2
(604) 917-0274
Emp Here 50   Sales 14,164,650
SIC 8741 Management services
Gregory Malpass

D-U-N-S 24-346-4489   (BR)
TRANSPORT TFI 7 S.E.C
CANADIAN FREIGHTWAYS
(Suby of TRANSPORT TFI 7 S.E.C)
7867 Express St, Burnaby, BC, V5A 1S7
(604) 420-2030
Emp Here 130
SIC 4213 Trucking, except local
Ed Ryan

D-U-N-S 24-940-3262   (SL)
TRENDS ELECTRONICS INTERNATIONAL INC
2999 Underhill Ave Suite 202, Burnaby, BC, V5A 3C2
(604) 988-2966
Emp Here 29   Sales 12,968,046
SIC 5065 Electronic parts and equipment, nec
Mitchell Irving
Grant Daoust

D-U-N-S 20-735-6549   (BR)
WESTKEY GRAPHICS LTD
VESTKEY GRAPHIC COMMUNICATIONS INC
(Suby of WESTKEY GRAPHICS LTD)
3212 Lake City Way, Burnaby, BC, V5A 3A4
(604) 421-7778
Emp Here 120
SIC 5734 Computer and software stores
Greg Don

D-U-N-S 25-386-2684   (SL)
WHITE HOUSE DESIGN COMPANY INC
SYMPLI
3676 Bainbridge Ave Unit 100, Burnaby, BC, V5A 2T4
(604) 451-1539
Emp Here 62   Sales 10,909,396

SIC 8712 Architectural services
Janet Stimpson
Virginia Beltjens

Burnaby, BC V5B

D-U-N-S 20-027-0010   (SL)
3DS THREE DIMENSIONAL SERVICES INC
3 D S
2829 Norland Ave, Burnaby, BC, V5B 3A9
(604) 980-2450
Emp Here 25   Sales 11,230,475
SIC 7389 Business services, nec
Ross Ireland

D-U-N-S 20-794-8704   (HQ)
ALL-CAN EXPRESS LTD
ACE COURIER SERVICES
2830 Norland Ave, Burnaby, BC, V5B 3A7
(604) 294-8631
Emp Here 3   Sales 41,141,200
SIC 4212 Local trucking, without storage
Tom Uhreniuk
Jim Mcmullin

D-U-N-S 20-993-1203   (SL)
ANDERSON WATTS LTD
6336 Darnley St, Burnaby, BC, V5B 3B1
(604) 291-7751
Emp Here 35   Sales 29,245,195
SIC 5141 Groceries, general line
John Smithson
Edward C. Anderson
Thomas K. Watts

D-U-N-S 20-797-9618   (SL)
ATLAS POWER SWEEPING LTD
2796 Norland Ave, Burnaby, BC, V5B 3A6
(604) 294-6333
Emp Here 40   Sales 12,045,680
SIC 4959 Sanitary services, nec
Mike Menzies
Paul Cloth

D-U-N-S 20-428-9987   (SL)
AUSTIN METAL LIMITED PARTNERSHIP
5414 Goring St, Burnaby, BC, V5B 3A3
(604) 291-7381
Emp Here 50   Sales 23,751,300
SIC 5084 Industrial machinery and equipment
Robert Mason
Len Mueller
Darryl Gordon
Michael Mueller
Mark Green
Eric Staniscia

D-U-N-S 20-527-5519   (SL)
BELPACIFIC EXCAVATING & SHORING LIMITED PARTNERSHIP
BEL CONTRACTING
3183 Norland Ave, Burnaby, BC, V5B 3A9
(604) 291-1255
Emp Here 300   Sales 98,434,500
SIC 1623 Water, sewer, and utility lines
Dale Beker
Sean Frost

D-U-N-S 20-225-0267   (SL)
BODY PLUS
6200 Darnley St Suite 204, Burnaby, BC, V5B 3B1

Emp Here 30   Sales 33,160,350
SIC 5122 Drugs, proprietaries, and sundries
Norm Daniels

D-U-N-S 24-881-7959   (SL)
BRENTA CONSTRUCTION INC
2810 Norland Ave, Burnaby, BC, V5B 3A6
(604) 430-5887
Emp Here 75   Sales 42,775,350
SIC 1542 Nonresidential construction, nec
Settimo Perizzolo

D-U-N-S 20-803-2763   (SL)
BROADWAY REFRIGERATION AND AIR CONDITIONING CO. LTD
2433 Holdom Ave, Burnaby, BC, V5B 5A1
(604) 255-2461
Emp Here 50   *Sales* 11,046,700
SIC 1711 Plumbing, heating, air-conditioning
Thomas James Millar
Laird O'connor

D-U-N-S 25-011-9021   (BR)
BURNABY SCHOOL BOARD DISTRICT 41
BURNABY NORTH SECONDARY SCHOOL
(*Suby of* BURNABY SCHOOL BOARD DISTRICT 41)
751 Hammarskjold Dr Rm 115, Burnaby, BC, V5B 4A1

Emp Here 200
SIC 8211 Elementary and secondary schools
Glen Archer

D-U-N-S 24-456-3938   (HQ)
CANADA GARDENWORKS LTD
GARDENWORKS
6250 Lougheed Hwy, Burnaby, BC, V5B 2Z9
(604) 299-0621
Emp Here 50   *Sales* 63,236,250
SIC 5261 Retail nurseries and garden stores
John Zaplatynsky
Roderick Senft
Bruce Meyers
Mel Rinald
Leanne Johnson

D-U-N-S 20-585-2908   (HQ)
CANLAN ICE SPORTS CORP
8-RINK ICE SPORTS CENTRE
6501 Sprott St, Burnaby, BC, V5B 3B8
(604) 291-0626
Emp Here 500   *Sales* 66,438,543
SIC 7999 Amusement and recreation, nec
Joey St-Aubin
Michael F. Gellard
Mark Faubert
Hailey Clark
Mark E. Reynolds
Ken Male
Greg Porcellato
Ivan C. Wu
W. Grant Ballantyne
Frank Barker

D-U-N-S 24-682-9105   (HQ)
CASCADE AQUA-TECH LTD
3215 Norland Ave Suite 100, Burnaby, BC, V5B 3A9
(604) 291-6101
Emp Here 30   *Sales* 37,977,940
SIC 5169 Chemicals and allied products, nec
David Metzler
Ranada Pritchard
Neil Pritchard

D-U-N-S 24-327-2452   (SL)
D'SA, MEL M. INC
SHOPPERS DRUG MART
6508 Hastings St Suite 214, Burnaby, BC, V5B 1S2
(604) 291-0638
Emp Here 48   *Sales* 12,141,792
SIC 5912 Drug stores and proprietary stores
Mel D'sa

D-U-N-S 20-794-6021   (SL)
DOWCO CONSULTANTS LTD
2433 Holdom Ave, Burnaby, BC, V5B 5A1
(604) 606-5800
Emp Here 130   *Sales* 32,004,180
SIC 1791 Structural steel erection
Hugh Dobbie Sr
Ewen Dobbie
Susan Dobbie

D-U-N-S 24-620-3095   (HQ)
INFORM BROKERAGE INC
2286 Holdom Ave, Burnaby, BC, V5B 4Y5

(604) 324-0565
Sales 25,067,310
SIC 5141 Groceries, general line
Craig James
Napoleon Veltri

D-U-N-S 20-587-9406   (SL)
JONES FOOD STORE EQUIPMENT LTD
2896 Norland Ave, Burnaby, BC, V5B 3A6
(604) 294-6321
Emp Here 50   *Sales* 22,358,700
SIC 5078 Refrigeration equipment and supplies
Barrie Jones
Darren Jones

D-U-N-S 24-321-1849   (HQ)
NUCASA MILLING COMPANY LIMITED
6150 Lougheed Hwy, Burnaby, BC, V5B 2Z9
(604) 294-3232
Emp Here 10   *Sales* 13,382,600
SIC 5211 Lumber and other building materials
David Laniado

D-U-N-S 24-899-1077   (HQ)
PACIFIC BLASTING & DEMOLITION LTD
3183 Norland Ave, Burnaby, BC, V5B 3A9
(604) 291-1255
Sales 44,623,640
SIC 1629 Heavy construction, nec
David Reynolds
Samuel Gudewill
Timothy Doucette
Ron Woolf
Vince Alvernaz
Dale Bekar

D-U-N-S 25-013-1638   (SL)
PCM POMERY CONSTRUCTION & MAINTENANCE LTD
3060 Norland Ave Suite 109, Burnaby, BC, V5B 3A6
(604) 294-6700
Emp Here 50   *Sales* 15,943,450
SIC 1521 Single-family housing construction
Bruce D Pomeroy

D-U-N-S 20-426-0111   (BR)
REXEL CANADA ELECTRICAL INC
WESTBURNE ELECTRIC SUPPLY BC
(*Suby of* REXEL)
5700 Kingsland Dr, Burnaby, BC, V5B 4W6
(604) 205-2700
Emp Here 80
SIC 5063 Electrical apparatus and equipment
Thomas Mikes

D-U-N-S 24-579-8293   (SL)
SASCO CONTRACTORS LTD
3060 Norland Ave Suite 114, Burnaby, BC, V5B 3A6
(604) 299-1640
Emp Here 100   *Sales* 21,782,900
SIC 1731 Electrical work
Craig Paquin
Brian Hirakida

Burnaby, BC V5C

D-U-N-S 20-646-7925   (SL)
3D DISTRIBUTION CANADA INC
5045 Still Creek Ave, Burnaby, BC, V5C 5V1
(604) 299-5045
Emp Here 20   *Sales* 10,826,435
SIC 5149 Groceries and related products, nec
Jake Dadam

D-U-N-S 20-108-4381   (HQ)
A. C. T. EQUIPMENT SALES LTD
4455 Alaska St, Burnaby, BC, V5C 5T3
(604) 294-6271
Emp Here 40   *Sales* 28,501,560
SIC 5085 Industrial supplies
Alfred John W Barbour
Scott Barbour

Sheryl Graham

D-U-N-S 24-446-3279   (HQ)
AAA ENTERPRISES INC
HOUSE OF KNIVES
3918 Kitchener St, Burnaby, BC, V5C 3M2
(604) 558-2250
Emp Here 5   *Sales* 10,458,135
SIC 5719 Miscellaneous homefurnishings
Andre Eng

D-U-N-S 20-797-6531   (SL)
ACTION LINE HOUSING SOCIETY
SEATON VILLA
3755 Mcgill St, Burnaby, BC, V5C 1M2
(604) 291-0607
Emp Here 85   *Sales* 5,035,995
SIC 8361 Residential care
Brian Beach
Jim Storie

D-U-N-S 20-112-3775   (SL)
ALFRED HORIE CONSTRUCTION CO. LTD
3830 1st Ave, Burnaby, BC, V5C 3W1
(604) 291-8156
Emp Here 30   *Sales* 14,121,930
SIC 1542 Nonresidential construction, nec
Stephen Paone
John Paone

D-U-N-S 25-012-2272   (SL)
ALLTECK LINE CONTRACTORS INC
(*Suby of* QUANTA SERVICES, INC.)
4333 Still Creek Dr Suite 300, Burnaby, BC, V5C 6S6
(604) 857-6600
Emp Here 50   *Sales* 73,497,760
SIC 1623 Water, sewer, and utility lines
Keith Sones
Robin Lucas
David Hill
Mike Scott
Doug Allen
Nicholas Grindstaff

D-U-N-S 20-749-5219   (HQ)
ARGUS CARRIERS LTD
3839 Myrtle St, Burnaby, BC, V5C 4G1
(604) 433-2066
Emp Here 1   *Sales* 20,570,600
SIC 4212 Local trucking, without storage
John Skeens

D-U-N-S 24-620-6791   (HQ)
ASCENT REAL ESTATE MANAGEMENT CORPORATION
2176 Willingdon Ave, Burnaby, BC, V5C 5Z9
(604) 521-7653
Emp Here 51   *Sales* 23,038,895
SIC 6531 Real estate agents and managers
Richard Dickson

D-U-N-S 24-620-8557   (HQ)
AUGUST CORPORATE PARTNERS INC
4445 Lougheed Hwy Suite 1001, Burnaby, BC, V5C 0E4
(604) 731-0441
Sales 100,568,394
SIC 6712 Bank holding companies
Bradley Johansen
Brian Elcock
Jeevan Minhas

D-U-N-S 20-864-9517   (HQ)
B A S P BUY & SELL PRESS LTD, THE
BUY & SELL PRESS
4664 Lougheed Hwy Suite 202, Burnaby, BC, V5C 5T5
(604) 540-4455
Emp Here 144   *Sales* 46,505,760
SIC 2711 Newspapers
Kirk Romero

D-U-N-S 20-696-2206   (SL)
BLUE CASTLE GAMES INC
(*Suby of* CAPCOM CO., LTD.)
4401 Still Creek Dr Unit 300, Burnaby, BC, V5C 6G9

(604) 299-5626
Emp Here 80   *Sales* 13,347,760
SIC 7372 Prepackaged software
Rob Barrett
Daniel Brady

D-U-N-S 25-219-2208   (SL)
BRITISH COLUMBIA NURSES UNION
BCNU
4060 Regent St, Burnaby, BC, V5C 6P5
(604) 433-2268
Emp Here 80   *Sales* 31,396,000
SIC 8631 Labor organizations
Anne Harvey
Debra Mcpherson
Patricia Shuttleworth

D-U-N-S 25-165-4851   (BR)
BURNABY SCHOOL BOARD DISTRICT 41
ALPHA SECONDARY SCHOOL
(*Suby of* BURNABY SCHOOL BOARD DISTRICT 41)
4600 Parker St, Burnaby, BC, V5C 3E2
(604) 296-6865
Emp Here 90
SIC 8211 Elementary and secondary schools
Paul Fester

D-U-N-S 24-422-1367   (SL)
C&S GROUP OPERATIONS LTD
2820 Ingleton Ave, Burnaby, BC, V5C 6G7
(604) 435-4431
Emp Here 40   *Sales* 17,886,960
SIC 5032 Brick, stone, and related material
Claudio Corra
Esther Chow
Sara Corra

D-U-N-S 24-372-3764   (SL)
C.T. CONTROL TEMP LTD
(*Suby of* INTERNATIONAL HYDRO MIST LTD)
4340 Dawson St, Burnaby, BC, V5C 4B6
(604) 298-2000
Emp Here 60   *Sales* 27,602,640
SIC 5078 Refrigeration equipment and supplies
John Devita
Dean Gabriele
Dino Gabriele

D-U-N-S 25-127-8248   (BR)
CACTUS RESTAURANTS LTD
CACTUS CLUB CAFE
(*Suby of* CACTUS RESTAURANTS LTD)
4219b Lougheed Hwy, Burnaby, BC, V5C 3Y6
(604) 291-6606
Emp Here 125
SIC 5812 Eating places
Margarita Cucca

D-U-N-S 20-993-3977   (SL)
CANADA WIDE MEDIA LIMITED
WESTWORLD ALBERTA
4180 Lougheed Hwy Suite 102, Burnaby, BC, V5C 6A7
(604) 299-7311
Emp Here 100   *Sales* 16,402,700
SIC 2721 Periodicals
Peter Legge
Karen Foss
Neil Soper
Heather Parker
Samantha Legge-Stollery
Millie Warren

D-U-N-S 25-415-2648   (BR)
CANADIAN LINEN AND UNIFORM SERVICE CO
QUEBEC LINGE
(*Suby of* ARAMARK)
2750 Gilmore Ave, Burnaby, BC, V5C 4T9
(778) 331-6200
Emp Here 160
SIC 7213 Linen supply
N Nairouz

D-U-N-S 24-939-0196   (HQ)

CANADIAN UTILITY CONSTRUCTION CORP
NORTHERN TRAFFIC SERVICE
(*Suby of* QUANTA SERVICES, INC.)
4333 Still Creek Dr Suite 300, Burnaby, BC, V5C 6S6
(604) 574-6640
Emp Here 100   *Sales* 67,263,575
SIC 1623 Water, sewer, and utility lines
Robin Lucas
Mike Scott
Patty Edwards
Kerry Mcdowell

    D-U-N-S 20-110-0468   (HQ)
CARTER CHEVROLET CADILLAC BUICK GMC BURNABY LTD
4550 Lougheed Hwy, Burnaby, BC, V5C 3Z5
(604) 291-6474
Emp Here 159   *Sales* 113,270,400
SIC 5511 New and used car dealers
George H Mitchell
Margaret Carter
William Mitchell

    D-U-N-S 20-109-3986   (SL)
CARTER DODGE CHRYSLER LTD
4650 Lougheed Hwy, Burnaby, BC, V5C 4A6
(604) 299-2681
Emp Here 65   *Sales* 40,903,200
SIC 5511 New and used car dealers
Joe Mitchell
Sadhu Thiara
William Mitchell
Margaret E Carter

    D-U-N-S 20-994-8603   (SL)
CARTER, HOWARD LEASE LTD
4550 Lougheed Hwy, Burnaby, BC, V5C 3Z5
(604) 291-8899
Emp Here 534   *Sales* 47,897,664
SIC 7515 Passenger car leasing

    D-U-N-S 20-803-8224   (HQ)
CBV COLLECTION SERVICES LTD
CBV COLLECTIONS
(*Suby of* YELLOW POINT EQUITY PARTNERS LIMITED PARTNERSHIP)
4664 Lougheed Hwy Unit 20, Burnaby, BC, V5C 5T5
(604) 687-4559
Emp Here 275   *Sales* 120,222,600
SIC 7322 Adjustment and collection services
Robert Richards
Bryan Waters

    D-U-N-S 24-203-1065   (HQ)
CHANNEL GATE TECHNOLOGIES INC
CYMAX CANADA
4170 Still Creek Dr Suite 310, Burnaby, BC, V5C 6C6
(604) 683-0313
Emp Here 1   *Sales* 17,102,960
SIC 5961 Catalog and mail-order houses
Arash Fasihi
David Sela

    D-U-N-S 24-787-0405   (BR)
CHEVRON CANADA LIMITED
(*Suby of* CHEVRON CORPORATION)
355 Willingdon Ave N, Burnaby, BC, V5C 1X4
(604) 257-4040
Emp Here 200
SIC 2911 Petroleum refining
Doug Hinzie

    D-U-N-S 24-376-7121   (HQ)
CHEYENNE HOLDINGS INC
3855 Henning Dr Suite 109, Burnaby, BC, V5C 6N3
(604) 291-9000
Sales 31,368,590
SIC 1542 Nonresidential construction, nec
Jim Bond

    D-U-N-S 25-087-2751   (BR)
CITY OF BURNABY
EILEEN DAILLY LEISURE POOL AND FIT-

NESS CENTRE
(*Suby of* CITY OF BURNABY)
240 Willingdon Ave, Burnaby, BC, V5C 5E9
(604) 298-7946
Emp Here 100
SIC 7999 Amusement and recreation, nec
Lorretta Wren

    D-U-N-S 24-777-3989   (SL)
CITY PROJECTS LTD
4483 Juneau St, Burnaby, BC, V5C 4C4
(604) 874-5566
Emp Here 70   *Sales* 39,923,660
SIC 1542 Nonresidential construction, nec
Moss Thomas

    D-U-N-S 25-076-6433   (HQ)
CMW INSURANCE SERVICES LTD
1901 Rosser Ave Unit 700, Burnaby, BC, V5C 6R6
(604) 294-3301
Emp Here 58   *Sales* 116,407,746
SIC 6411 Insurance agents, brokers, and service
Andrew Kemp

    D-U-N-S 20-058-9732   (BR)
COAST MOUNTAIN BUS COMPANY LTD
CMBC
(*Suby of* SOUTH COAST BRITISH COLUMBIA TRANSPORTATION AUTHORITY)
3855 Kitchener St Suite 420, Burnaby, BC, V5C 3L8
(604) 205-6111
Emp Here 350
SIC 4111 Local and suburban transit
John Dickson

    D-U-N-S 24-798-2762   (HQ)
COASTAL INSURANCE SERVICES LTD
4350 Still Creek Dr Suite 400, Burnaby, BC, V5C 0G5
(604) 269-1000
Emp Here 24   *Sales* 21,201,500
SIC 6411 Insurance agents, brokers, and service
Mike Valiquette

    D-U-N-S 20-182-2066   (HQ)
COBRA INTEGRATED SYSTEMS LTD
4427 Dawson St, Burnaby, BC, V5C 4B8
(604) 664-7671
Emp Here 10   *Sales* 33,538,050
SIC 5065 Electronic parts and equipment, nec
Scott Knutsen
Brian Sylvester

    D-U-N-S 25-749-4559   (SL)
CRI CREDIT GROUP SERVICES INC
CRI CANADA
(*Suby of* AEGON N.V.)
4185 Still Creek Dr Unit 350a, Burnaby, BC, V5C 6G9
(604) 438-7785
Emp Here 30   *Sales* 55,432,260
SIC 6411 Insurance agents, brokers, and service
Anne Bjornson

    D-U-N-S 24-068-4246   (SL)
DESTINATION AUTO ENTERPRISES INC
DESTINATION TOYOTA
4278 Lougheed Hwy, Burnaby, BC, V5C 3Y5
(604) 294-2111
Emp Here 40   *Sales* 19,923,120
SIC 5511 New and used car dealers
Azizdin Ahamed

    D-U-N-S 24-457-2095   (SL)
DESTINATION AUTO VENTURES INC
DESTINATION CHRYSLER JEEP DODGE NORTHSHORE
4278 Lougheed Hwy, Burnaby, BC, V5C 3Y5
(604) 294-2111
Emp Here 150   *Sales* 94,392,000
SIC 5511 New and used car dealers
Aziz Ahamed

    D-U-N-S 25-735-9497   (SL)
DIGITAL PAYMENT TECHNOLOGIES CORP
4260 Still Creek Dr Suite 330, Burnaby, BC, V5C 6C6
(604) 317-4055
Emp Here 57   *Sales* 12,955,473
SIC 3824 Fluid meters and counting devices
Andrew Scott
Mark Gemino
Chris Chettle
Chris Macphail
Bjorn Clason

    D-U-N-S 24-979-6046   (SL)
DORIGO SYSTEMS LTD
3885 Henning Dr, Burnaby, BC, V5C 6N5
(604) 294-4600
Emp Here 70   *Sales* 13,330,940
SIC 3679 Electronic components, nec
Mark Pillon

    D-U-N-S 25-710-0065   (BR)
EARL'S RESTAURANTS LTD
EARL'S BRIDGE PARK
(*Suby of* EARL'S RESTAURANTS LTD)
3850 Lougheed Hwy, Burnaby, BC, V5C 6N4
(604) 291-1019
Emp Here 100
SIC 5812 Eating places
Eric Holland

    D-U-N-S 20-915-1166   (SL)
ELK TRADING CO. LTD
(*Suby of* EMACHU HOLDINGS CO., LTD.)
4664 Lougheed Hwy Suite 174, Burnaby, BC, V5C 5T5
(604) 684-6688
Emp Here 3   *Sales* 16,886,865
SIC 5031 Lumber, plywood, and millwork
Soichi Ema
Satoshi Yamamoto

    D-U-N-S 20-526-3408   (SL)
EMBASSY DEVELOPMENT CORPORATION
(*Suby of* 664291 BC LTD)
2025 Willingdon Ave Suite 1300, Burnaby, BC, V5C 0J3
(604) 294-0666
Emp Here 50   *Sales* 10,194,150
SIC 6553 Cemetery subdividers and developers
Natale Bosa
Ryan Bosa
Jim Bosa

    D-U-N-S 24-254-4792   (SL)
ETRO CONSTRUCTION LIMITED
4727 Hastings St, Burnaby, BC, V5C 2K8
(604) 492-0920
Emp Here 45   *Sales* 14,349,105
SIC 1521 Single-family housing construction
Michael Maierle

    D-U-N-S 25-290-8835   (HQ)
EXECUTIVE HOTELS GENERAL PARTNERSHIP
EXECUTIVE HOTELS & RESORTS
4201 Lougheed Hwy, Burnaby, BC, V5C 3Y6
(604) 298-2010
Emp Here 200   *Sales* 38,267,200
SIC 7011 Hotels and motels
Noordin Sayani
Farida Sayani

    D-U-N-S 24-856-2894   (HQ)
FAIRDEAL IMPORT & EXPORT LTD
3855 Henning Dr Unit 116, Burnaby, BC, V5C 6N3
(604) 257-2939
Emp Here 80   *Sales* 66,826,800
SIC 5199 Nondurable goods, nec
Akbarali Bandeali
Malka Bandeali

    D-U-N-S 25-295-2262   (BR)
FEDERAL EXPRESS CANADA CORPORATION

FEDEX SHIP CENTRE
(*Suby of* FEDEX CORPORATION)
4270 Dawson St, Burnaby, BC, V5C 4B1
(800) 463-3339
Emp Here 119
SIC 7389 Business services, nec

    D-U-N-S 24-104-1735   (HQ)
FORTINET TECHNOLOGIES (CANADA) ULC
FORTIGATE
(*Suby of* FORTINET, INC.)
4190 Still Creek Dr Unit 400, Burnaby, BC, V5C 6C6
(604) 430-1297
Emp Here 180   *Sales* 31,700,930
SIC 7379 Computer related services, nec
Ken Xie
Michael Xie
Keith Jensen

    D-U-N-S 20-383-2522   (SL)
GG BROADWAY INVESTMENTS LIMITED PARTNERSHIP
GOLD'S GYM BRITISH COLUMBIA
3823 Henning Dr Unit 215, Burnaby, BC, V5C 6P3
(604) 293-0152
Emp Here 200   *Sales* 18,990,600
SIC 7999 Amusement and recreation, nec
Victor Newman

    D-U-N-S 20-104-3200   (BR)
GREAT PACIFIC INDUSTRIES INC
SAVE-ON-FOODS
(*Suby of* PATTISON, JIM GROUP INC)
4399 Lougheed Hwy Suite 996, Burnaby, BC, V5C 3Y7
(604) 298-8412
Emp Here 110
SIC 5411 Grocery stores
Cam Bates

    D-U-N-S 20-082-2864   (HQ)
GWIL INDUSTRIES INC
BIRTLEY COAL TESTING, DIV OF
(*Suby of* 629886 LEASING INC)
5337 Regent St, Burnaby, BC, V5C 4H4
(604) 291-9404
Emp Here 2   *Sales* 10,907,178
SIC 7353 Heavy construction equipment rental
Hugh Magee
Robert Magee
Brian Greer

    D-U-N-S 20-805-1540   (HQ)
HOLLAND IMPORTS INC
CHRISTMAS FOREVER
(*Suby of* CG PUNJANI INVESTMENTS LTD)
2306 Madison Ave, Burnaby, BC, V5C 4Y9
(604) 299-5741
Emp Here 60   *Sales* 59,805,720
SIC 5072 Hardware
Shamser Punjani
Nazmudin Punjani
Mohamed Punjani

    D-U-N-S 25-012-2165   (BR)
HOME DEPOT OF CANADA INC
HOME DEPOT
(*Suby of* THE HOME DEPOT INC)
3950 Henning Dr, Burnaby, BC, V5C 6M2
(604) 294-3077
Emp Here 250
SIC 5251 Hardware stores
Edward Stevenson

    D-U-N-S 24-008-4392   (HQ)
HOSKIN SCIENTIFIC LIMITED
3735 Myrtle St, Burnaby, BC, V5C 4E7
(604) 872-7894
Emp Here 30   *Sales* 22,358,700
SIC 5049 Professional equipment, nec
Rod Mckeown
Shaun Lewis

    D-U-N-S 20-321-9951   (SL)

HUB INTERNATIONAL INSURANCE BROKERS
(*Suby of* HELLMAN & FRIEDMAN LLC)
4350 Still Creek Dr Suite 400, Burnaby, BC,
V5C 0G5
(604) 293-1481
Emp Here 170   *Sales* 806,837,680
SIC 6411 Insurance agents, brokers, and service
Tina Osen

D-U-N-S 24-886-9299   (HQ)
IMMACULATE CONFECTION LTD
ROCKY MOUNTAIN CHOCOLATE FACTORY
5284 Still Creek Ave, Burnaby, BC, V5C 4E4
(604) 293-1600
Emp Here 25   *Sales* 58,695,400
SIC 5441 Candy, nut, and confectionery stores
Brian Kerzner
Tammi Kerzner

D-U-N-S 20-727-3587   (SL)
INDIANLIFE FOOD CORPORATION
3835 2nd Ave, Burnaby, BC, V5C 3W7
(604) 205-9176
Emp Here 55   *Sales* 19,012,950
SIC 2032 Canned specialties
Rakesh Raniga

D-U-N-S 25-415-8777   (HQ)
INETCO SYSTEMS LTD
4664 Lougheed Hwy Suite 295, Burnaby, BC,
V5C 5T5
(604) 451-1567
Sales 13,415,220
SIC 5045 Computers, peripherals, and software
Bijan Sanii

D-U-N-S 20-623-9063   (HQ)
INLAND KENWORTH LTD
INLAND PACLEASE
2482 Douglas Rd, Burnaby, BC, V5C 6C9
(604) 291-6021
Emp Here 60   *Sales* 536,503,000
SIC 5082 Construction and mining machinery
William Currie
Jason Wheeler
Leigh Parker
Richard Mcconnachie

D-U-N-S 20-393-5965   (SL)
INTEGRATED FINANCIAL TECHNOLOGIES INC
IFT SOLUTIONS
4180 Lougheed Hwy Unit 400, Burnaby, BC,
V5C 6A7
(844) 303-4899
Emp Here 50   *Sales* 11,714,400
SIC 8742 Management consulting services
James Case
Mark Sweeney
Roberto Cortese
Vladimir Kovacevic
Tod Chisholm

D-U-N-S 25-452-9860   (SL)
ISLAND TUG AND BARGE LTD
(*Suby of* TIDEWATER HOLDINGS, INC.)
800 Glasgow Ave, Burnaby, BC, V5C 0C9
(604) 873-4312
Emp Here 100   *Sales* 39,372,400
SIC 4492 Towing and tugboat service

D-U-N-S 24-133-6325   (SL)
KENORA ENTERPRISES LTD
4638 Hastings St, Burnaby, BC, V5C 2K5
(604) 294-0038
Emp Here 55   *Sales* 13,884,310
SIC 1623 Water, sewer, and utility lines
Kenia Strania

D-U-N-S 24-029-9917   (HQ)
KERR WOOD LEIDAL ASSOCIATES LTD
KWL
4185a Still Creek Dr Suite 200, Burnaby, BC,
V5C 6G9

(604) 294-2088
Emp Here 96   *Sales* 23,126,744
SIC 8742 Management consulting services
Michael Currie

D-U-N-S 25-215-8605   (HQ)
KITO CANADA INC
(*Suby of* KITO CORPORATION)
3815 1st Ave Suite 309, Burnaby, BC, V5C
3V6
(888) 322-5486
Emp Here 20   *Sales* 15,392,973
SIC 5084 Industrial machinery and equipment
Marc Premont
Yoshio Kito

D-U-N-S 25-318-1796   (BR)
MCDONALD'S   RESTAURANTS   OF CANADA LIMITED
MCDONALD'S 8784
(*Suby of* MCDONALD'S CORPORATION)
4805 Hastings St, Burnaby, BC, V5C 2L1
(604) 718-1015
Emp Here 80
SIC 5812 Eating places
Shannon Searle

D-U-N-S 20-861-1553   (BR)
MCDONALD'S   RESTAURANTS   OF CANADA LIMITED
MCDONALD'S
(*Suby of* MCDONALD'S CORPORATION)
4400 Still Creek Dr, Burnaby, BC, V5C 6C6
(604) 294-2181
Emp Here 85
SIC 5812 Eating places
Ailene Macdougall

D-U-N-S 24-760-7658   (BR)
MCDONALD'S   RESTAURANTS   OF CANADA LIMITED
MCDONALD'S #8341
(*Suby of* MCDONALD'S CORPORATION)
4400 Still Creek Dr, Burnaby, BC, V5C 6C6
(604) 718-1090
Emp Here 100
SIC 5812 Eating places
Mike Williams

D-U-N-S 25-721-8404   (SL)
MOBILE 1 MESSENGERS INC
3737 Napier St Suite 200, Burnaby, BC, V5C
3E4
(604) 681-4227
Emp Here 30   *Sales* 13,304,700
SIC 7389 Business services, nec
John Figliola

D-U-N-S 24-371-9853   (HQ)
MODERN HOUSEWARE IMPORTS INC
2300 Madison Ave, Burnaby, BC, V5C 4Y9
(604) 299-5132
Emp Here 28   *Sales* 22,898,520
SIC 5023 Homefurnishings
Siaz Punjani

D-U-N-S 24-625-1271   (HQ)
MUNN ENTERPRISES LTD
PETRO CANADA
1969 Willingdon Ave, Burnaby, BC, V5C 5J3
(604) 299-1124
Emp Here 5   *Sales* 24,903,900
SIC 5541 Gasoline service stations
Rajvinder Dhillon

D-U-N-S 24-976-4569   (SL)
NEW CITY SERVICES GROUP INC.
4170 Still Creek Dr Suite 200, Burnaby, BC,
V5C 6C6
(604) 473-7769
Emp Here 40   *Sales* 18,829,240
SIC 1542 Nonresidential construction, nec
George Tsamkiranis

D-U-N-S 24-715-7469   (SL)
NEW DEMOCRATIC PARTY OF B.C.
BC NDP
4180 Lougheed Hwy Unit 301, Burnaby, BC,

V5C 6A7
(604) 430-8600
Emp Here 49   *Sales* 13,412,721
SIC 8651 Political organizations
Craig Keating

D-U-N-S 20-180-1805   (HQ)
NEWWAY CONCRETE FORMING LTD
3750 1st Ave, Burnaby, BC, V5C 3V9
(604) 299-3709
Sales 24,618,600
SIC 1799 Special trade contractors, nec
Ezio Bortolussi

D-U-N-S 25-975-3270   (SL)
PACIFIC FIRST
UNIVERSAL DENTAL & PACIFIC RIM
3993 Henning Dr Unit 215, Burnaby, BC, V5C
6P7
(604) 293-1974
Emp Here 11   *Sales* 11,383,691
SIC 6321 Accident and health insurance
Douglas Anderson

D-U-N-S 25-362-8523   (SL)
PALADIN SECURITY SYSTEMS LTD
4664 Lougheed Hwy Suite 295, Burnaby, BC,
V5C 5T5
(416) 591-1745
Emp Here 50   *Sales* 22,358,700
SIC 5065 Electronic parts and equipment, nec
Fraser Cooper

D-U-N-S 24-620-8797   (SL)
PAX CONSTRUCTION LTD
4452 Juneau St, Burnaby, BC, V5C 4C8
(604) 291-8885
Emp Here 40   *Sales* 18,829,240
SIC 1542 Nonresidential construction, nec
Peter Brauer
Paul Loewen
Josephine Li

D-U-N-S 20-114-8533   (HQ)
PEERLESS ENGINEERING SALES LTD
4015 1st Ave, Burnaby, BC, V5C 3W5
(604) 659-4100
Sales 19,001,040
SIC 5084 Industrial machinery and equipment
Giuseppe (Joe) Magnolo
Jeff Magnolo
Doris Magnolo
Ron Magnolo

D-U-N-S 25-483-1902   (BR)
PETER KIEWIT INFRASTRUCTURE CO.
KIEWIT, PETER INFRASTRUCTURE
(*Suby of* PETER KIEWIT SONS', INC.)
4350 Still Creek Dr Suite 310, Burnaby, BC,
V5C 0G5
(604) 629-5419
Emp Here 80
SIC 1629 Heavy construction, nec
Trevor Wall

D-U-N-S 20-986-8137   (SL)
PRIME GRAPHIC RESOURCES LTD
STILL CREEK PRESS
3988 Still Creek Ave, Burnaby, BC, V5C 6N9
(604) 437-5800
Emp Here 70   *Sales* 11,481,890
SIC 2759 Commercial printing, nec

D-U-N-S 24-930-1425   (HQ)
PROCON MINING & TUNNELLING LTD
PROCON GROUP OF COMPANIES, THE
4664 Lougheed Hwy Unit 108, Burnaby, BC,
V5C 5T5
(604) 291-8292
Emp Here 40   *Sales* 306,928,800
SIC 1081 Metal mining services
John Mcvey
Colin Wilson
Christina Cheung

D-U-N-S 24-227-7288   (SL)
RADISYS CANADA INC
RADISYS

(*Suby of* RADISYS CORPORATION)
4190 Still Creek Dr Suite 300, Burnaby, BC,
V5C 6C6
(604) 918-6300
Emp Here 60   *Sales* 13,708,320
SIC 4899 Communication services, nec
Mike Dagenais
C. Scott Gibson
Brian Bronson
David Smith

D-U-N-S 24-457-9272   (SL)
RAICOR CONTRACTING LTD
3993 Henning Dr Unit 101, Burnaby, BC, V5C
6P7
(604) 293-7702
Emp Here 65   *Sales* 10,554,765
SIC 1742 Plastering, drywall, and insulation
Raimo Vare

D-U-N-S 25-537-6816   (HQ)
RDH BUILDING SCIENCE INC
4333 Still Creek Dr Suite 400, Burnaby, BC,
V5C 6S6
(604) 873-1181
Emp Here 86   *Sales* 28,598,240
SIC 8711 Engineering services
Dave Ricketts
Brian Hubbs
Marcus J. Dell

D-U-N-S 24-931-5417   (SL)
REGENCY AUTO ENTERPRISE INC
REGENCY TOYOTA BURNABY
4278 Lougheed Hwy, Burnaby, BC, V5C 3Y5
(604) 291-8122
Emp Here 38   *Sales* 18,926,964
SIC 5511 New and used car dealers
Amir Ahamed
Aziz Ahamed

D-U-N-S 25-705-0880   (SL)
RELIANCE INSURANCE AGENCIES LTD
4853 Hastings St Suite 100, Burnaby, BC,
V5C 2L1
(604) 255-4616
Emp Here 40   *Sales* 23,196,960
SIC 6411 Insurance agents, brokers, and service
James (Jim) Ball

D-U-N-S 24-132-9655   (SL)
ROSS MORRISON ELECTRICAL LTD
3950 1st Ave, Burnaby, BC, V5C 3W2
(604) 299-0281
Emp Here 65   *Sales* 14,158,885
SIC 1731 Electrical work
Dave Morrison
R Wayne Morrison

D-U-N-S 20-113-2680   (SL)
SANOOR INVESTMENT LTD
EXECUTIVE PLAZA VANCOUVER DOWN TOWN
4201 Lougheed Hwy, Burnaby, BC, V5C 3Y6
(604) 298-2010
Emp Here 500   *Sales* 62,388,000
SIC 8741 Management services
Noordin Sayani

D-U-N-S 25-237-4355   (SL)
SKYBOX LABS INC
4190 Lougheed Hwy Suite 200, Burnaby, BC,
V5C 6A8
(604) 558-4330
Emp Here 40   *Sales* 20,821,680
SIC 5092 Toys and hobby goods and supplies
Shyang Kong
Derek Macneil
Steve Silvester

D-U-N-S 25-364-9339   (BR)
SOBEYS WEST INC
SAFEWAY
(*Suby of* EMPIRE COMPANY LIMITED)
4440 Hastings St Suite E, Burnaby, BC, V5C
2K2

(604) 205-7497
Emp Here 175
SIC 5411 Grocery stores
Peter Lemon

D-U-N-S 20-116-1643   (HQ)
STANDARD BUILDING SUPPLIES LTD
4925 Still Creek Ave, Burnaby, BC, V5C 5V1
(604) 294-4411
Sales 40,245,660
SIC 5031 Lumber, plywood, and millwork
Bruce Kehler
Ron Haan
Darcy Doroshenko

D-U-N-S 20-995-2092   (HQ)
STORMTECH PERFORMANCE APPAREL LTD
3773 Still Creek Ave, Burnaby, BC, V5C 4E2
(866) 407-2222
Emp Here 110   *Sales* 125,629,950
SIC 5136 Men's and boy's clothing
Blake Annable
Karen Inman

D-U-N-S 24-856-5780   (SL)
SUPREME MEAT SUPPLIES LTD
1725 Macdonald Ave, Burnaby, BC, V5C 4P3
(604) 299-0541
Emp Here 30   *Sales* 25,067,310
SIC 5147 Meats and meat products
Robert Chow
Edward Ho
Ivan Chow
Wing Chow

D-U-N-S 20-511-1883   (HQ)
TRAILER WIZARDS LTD
4649 Hastings St, Burnaby, BC, V5C 2K6
(604) 320-1666
Emp Here 13   *Sales* 26,908,800
SIC 7519 Utility trailer rental
Carl P. Vanderspek
Arthur Christakos
Stanley Chan

D-U-N-S 24-335-4227   (BR)
UNFI CANADA, INC
PRO ORGANICS, DIV OF
(*Suby of* UNITED NATURAL FOODS, INC.)
4535 Still Creek Ave, Burnaby, BC, V5C 5W1
(604) 253-6549
Emp Here 75
SIC 5149 Groceries and related products, nec
Stephen Boyle

D-U-N-S 24-930-0872   (SL)
VENTANA CONSTRUCTION CORPORATION
(*Suby of* CHEYENNE HOLDINGS INC)
3875 Henning Dr Suite 100, Burnaby, BC, V5C 6N5
(604) 291-9000
Emp Here 150   *Sales* 104,758,800
SIC 1542 Nonresidential construction, nec
James Bond

D-U-N-S 24-446-4897   (HQ)
WELCO LUMBER CORP
(*Suby of* AUGUST CORPORATE PARTNERS INC)
4445 Lougheed Hwy Suite 1001, Burnaby, BC, V5C 0E4
(604) 732-1411
Emp Here 31   *Sales* 17,886,960
SIC 5031 Lumber, plywood, and millwork
Bradley Johansen
Brian Elcock
Michael Thelin

D-U-N-S 24-033-7188   (BR)
WOOD CANADA LIMITED
AMEC EARTH & ENVIRONMENTAL, DIV OF
(*Suby of* JOHN WOOD GROUP P.L.C.)
4445 Lougheed Hwy Suite 600, Burnaby, BC, V5C 0E4
(604) 294-3811
Emp Here 90

SIC 8711 Engineering services
Steve Rice

D-U-N-S 20-646-4443   (BR)
WORLEYPARSONSCORD LP
(*Suby of* WORLEYPARSONS LIMITED)
4321 Still Creek Dr Suite 600, Burnaby, BC, V5C 6S7
(604) 298-1616
Emp Here 176
SIC 8711 Engineering services
Jason Tielker

D-U-N-S 20-918-9034   (HQ)
WOTHERSPOON, DON & ASSOCIATES LTD
4634 Hastings St Suite 101, Burnaby, BC, V5C 2K5
(604) 294-3242
Emp Here 12   *Sales* 33,922,400
SIC 6411 Insurance agents, brokers, and service
Don Wotherspoon

D-U-N-S 25-216-6780   (SL)
XYNYTH MANUFACTURING CORP
(*Suby of* ABACUS MANAGEMENT INC)
3989 Henning Dr Unit 122, Burnaby, BC, V5C 6P8
(604) 473-9343
Emp Here 140   *Sales* 3,900,230
SIC 2899 Chemical preparations, nec
Kevin Wice

D-U-N-S 25-505-6483   (BR)
YRC FREIGHT CANADA COMPANY
FAST AS FLITE
(*Suby of* YRC WORLDWIDE INC.)
3985 Still Creek Ave, Burnaby, BC, V5C 4E2
(604) 433-3321
Emp Here 150
SIC 4213 Trucking, except local
Rob Coghill

Burnaby, BC V5E

D-U-N-S 20-860-8153   (SL)
D.M.S. MECHANICAL LTD
D.M.S. PLUMBING HEATING AND AIR CONDITIONING
7449 Conway Ave Unit 104, Burnaby, BC, V5E 2P7
(604) 437-8996
Emp Here 50   *Sales* 11,046,700
SIC 1711 Plumbing, heating, air-conditioning
Reno Mauro
Joe Ciulla
Josie Mauro
John Willshear

D-U-N-S 20-800-1396   (SL)
EAST & WEST ALUM CRAFT LTD
7465 Conway Ave, Burnaby, BC, V5E 2P7
(604) 438-6261
Emp Here 80   *Sales* 15,366,800
SIC 3446 Architectural Metalwork
Paul Guiseppe

D-U-N-S 20-732-1063   (BR)
ESSILOR GROUPE CANADA INC
(*Suby of* ESSILORLUXOTTICA)
7541 Conway Ave Suite 5, Burnaby, BC, V5E 2P7
(604) 437-5300
Emp Here 100
SIC 3851 Ophthalmic goods
Bryan Maspit

D-U-N-S 25-401-9763   (BR)
ESSILOR GROUPE CANADA INC
ESSILOR NETWORK IN CANADA INC
(*Suby of* ESSILORLUXOTTICA)
7541 Conway Ave Suite 5, Burnaby, BC, V5E 2P7

(604) 437-5333
Emp Here 100
SIC 5049 Professional equipment, nec
Bryan Nisbet

D-U-N-S 24-579-2379   (HQ)
GISBORNE FIRE PROTECTION ALBERTA LTD
(*Suby of* GISBORNE HOLDINGS LTD)
7476 Hedley Ave, Burnaby, BC, V5E 2P9
(604) 520-7300
Emp Here 60   *Sales* 23,306,500
SIC 1711 Plumbing, heating, air-conditioning
James Sawers
Leslie Maivs

D-U-N-S 24-767-3312   (HQ)
GISBORNE HOLDINGS LTD
GISBORNE GROUP, THE
7476 Hedley Ave, Burnaby, BC, V5E 2P9
(604) 520-7300
Emp Here 400   *Sales* 146,203,600
SIC 6719 Holding companies, nec
Rae Clarkson
Les Maivs
Ron Spironello

D-U-N-S 20-016-8073   (HQ)
GISBORNE INDUSTRIAL CONSTRUCTION LTD
(*Suby of* GISBORNE HOLDINGS LTD)
7476 Hedley Ave, Burnaby, BC, V5E 2P9
(604) 520-7300
Emp Here 45   *Sales* 209,517,600
SIC 1541 Industrial buildings and warehouses
Rae Clarkson
Les Maivs
James Sawers

D-U-N-S 24-855-8504   (SL)
KOREAN BUSINESSMEN'S COOPERATIVE ASSOCIATION
6373 Arbroath St, Burnaby, BC, V5E 1C3
(604) 431-7373
Emp Here 27   *Sales* 20,048,040
SIC 5199 Nondurable goods, nec
Andrew Kim
Hung Sik Han
Ki Seo Kim
Hyun Myung Lee
Young Ho Lee
Heung Sik Yang
Kyung Suhk Yang
Seung Man Yang
Kwang Ho Yoon

D-U-N-S 20-911-6367   (SL)
NEW VISTA SOCIETY, THE
7550 Rosewood St Suite 235, Burnaby, BC, V5E 3Z3
(604) 521-7764
Emp Here 200   *Sales* 12,856,400
SIC 8361 Residential care
Sonja Alton
Nan Blackmore
Art Kube
Gord Mcnaughton

D-U-N-S 25-412-6469   (SL)
SNAP TIGHT ALUMINUM RAILING SYSTEM INTERNATIONAL LTD
STAR SYSTEM INTERNATIONAL
7465 Conway Ave, Burnaby, BC, V5E 2P7
(604) 438-6261
Emp Here 32   *Sales* 14,309,568
SIC 5051 Metals service centers and offices
Sergio Zen
Paul Zen

D-U-N-S 20-102-1151   (HQ)
WESTERN BELTING & HOSE (1986) LTD
6468 Beresford St, Burnaby, BC, V5E 1B6
(604) 451-4133
Sales 23,751,300
SIC 5084 Industrial machinery and equipment
David Bennett
Victor Loski

Burnaby, BC V5G

D-U-N-S 25-329-0464   (HQ)
341234 B.C. LTD
MICROSERVE BUSINESS COMPUTER SERVICES
4400 Dominion Unit 280, Burnaby, BC, V5G 4G3
(604) 473-9889
Emp Here 95   *Sales* 48,000,080
SIC 7373 Computer integrated systems design
David Matthews
Heather Schaan
Mike Gazzola
Sylvian Jazob
Jim Scarrow
Charisma Maharaj

D-U-N-S 25-329-0431   (HQ)
AIC GLOBAL COMMUNICATIONS INC
3707 Wayburne Dr, Burnaby, BC, V5G 3L1
(604) 708-3899
Emp Here 80
SIC 4899 Communication services, nec
Victor Fung

D-U-N-S 20-587-3797   (HQ)
ALLIANCE MERCANTILE INC
3451 Wayburne Dr, Burnaby, BC, V5G 3L1
(604) 299-3566
Emp Here 45   *Sales* 57,193,821
SIC 5023 Homefurnishings
Douglas Bell

D-U-N-S 20-689-2221   (HQ)
ALLIED VISION TECHNOLOGIES CANADA INC
(*Suby of* TKH GROUP N.V.)
4621 Canada Way Suite 300, Burnaby, BC, V5G 4X8
(604) 875-8855
Sales 27,274,680
SIC 3861 Photographic equipment and supplies
Steve Prescesky

D-U-N-S 25-363-7284   (BR)
AMER SPORTS CANADA INC
ARC'TERYX EQUIPMENT DIV.
4250 Manor St, Burnaby, BC, V5G 1B2
(604) 454-9900
Emp Here 290
SIC 3949 Sporting and athletic goods, nec
Josie Lin

D-U-N-S 25-737-0981   (BR)
ASSOCIATED ENGINEERING GROUP LTD
ASSOCIATED ENGINEERING (BC)
(*Suby of* ASHCO SHAREHOLDERS INC)
4940 Canada Way Suite 300, Burnaby, BC, V5G 4K6
(604) 293-1411
Emp Here 140
SIC 8711 Engineering services
Martin Jopke

D-U-N-S 20-336-8238   (SL)
AVISINA PROPERTIES LTD
3787 Canada Way Unit 200, Burnaby, BC, V5G 1G5
(604) 419-6000
Emp Here 50   *Sales* 14,164,650
SIC 8741 Management services
Minaz Shajani

D-U-N-S 20-956-9086   (HQ)
B.C.A.A. HOLDINGS LTD
B.C.A.A. TRAVEL, DIV OF
4567 Canada Way, Burnaby, BC, V5G 4T1
(604) 268-5000
Emp Here 275   *Sales* 4,746,104,000
SIC 6411 Insurance agents, brokers, and service
William Bullis

▲ Public Company   ■ Public Company Family Member   **HQ** Headquarters   **BR** Branch   **SL** Single Location

Imelda Harris
Elizabeth J Gronbach
Dan Smithon
Douglas W Potentier
Brian E Minter
John Sturgess
Howard Lailey
Keith Dunn
Craig East

D-U-N-S 24-639-6535   (HQ)
BC GOVERNMENT AND SERVICE EM-PLOYEES' UNION
BCGEU
4911 Canada Way Suite 101, Burnaby, BC, V5G 3W3
(604) 291-9611
Emp Here 90   *Sales* 56,960,400
SIC 8631 Labor organizations
Darryl Walker
Judi Filion

D-U-N-S 20-702-6381   (BR)
BC GOVERNMENT AND SERVICE EM-PLOYEES' UNION
(*Suby of* BC GOVERNMENT AND SERVICE EMPLOYEES' UNION)
4925 Canada Way, Burnaby, BC, V5G 1M1
(604) 291-9611
Emp Here 100
SIC 8631 Labor organizations
Stephanie Smith

D-U-N-S 24-248-1877   (SL)
BEEDIE CONSTRUCTION CO LTD
(*Suby of* KEBET HOLDINGS LTD)
3030 Gilmore Divers, Burnaby, BC, V5G 3B4
(604) 435-3321
Emp Here 40   *Sales* 10,973,280
SIC 8741 Management services
Keith Beedie
Ryan Beedie

D-U-N-S 20-586-3319   (HQ)
BINNIE, R.F. & ASSOCIATES LTD
BINNIE
300-4940 Canada Way, Burnaby, BC, V5G 4K6
(604) 420-1721
Emp Here 11   *Sales* 50,046,920
SIC 8711 Engineering services
Michael Richardson
James Martins
Stuart Macinnes

D-U-N-S 24-839-5113   (SL)
BRIGHTER MECHANICAL LIMITED
107-4585 Canada Way, Burnaby, BC, V5G 4L6
(604) 279-0901
Emp Here 65   *Sales* 15,149,225
SIC 1711 Plumbing, heating, air-conditioning
Robert Vincent
Edward Mcdowall

D-U-N-S 20-803-9362   (HQ)
BRITISH COLUMBIA AUTOMOBILE ASSO-CIATION
BCAA INSURANCE
4567 Canada Way, Burnaby, BC, V5G 4T1
(604) 268-5500
Emp Here 350   *Sales* 1,294,740,900
SIC 8699 Membership organizations, nec
Shom Sen
Roger Barnsley
Clayton Buckingham
Brent Cuthbertson

D-U-N-S 24-566-2747   (HQ)
BRITISH COLUMBIA INSTITUTE OF TECH-NOLOGY, THE
BCIT
3700 Willingdon Ave, Burnaby, BC, V5G 3H2
(604) 434-5734
Emp Here 50   *Sales* 214,345,688
SIC 8221 Colleges and universities
Chris Golding

Tomi Eeckhout
Lorcan O'melinn
Justin Kohlman
Paul Dangerfield
Randy Friesen
Zareen Naqvi
David Pepper
Larry Vezina

D-U-N-S 25-714-8577   (SL)
BRITISH COLUMBIA LIFE AND CASUALTY COMPANY
(*Suby of* PBC HEALTH BENEFITS SOCIETY)
4250 Canada Way, Burnaby, BC, V5G 4W6
(604) 419-8000
Emp Here 60   *Sales* 74,125,080
SIC 6311 Life insurance
Robert Bucher
John Crawford
Wren Long

D-U-N-S 20-353-6701   (BR)
BSM TECHNOLOGIES LTD
(*Suby of* GEOTAB INC)
4299 Canada Way Suite 215, Burnaby, BC, V5G 1H3
(604) 434-7337
Emp Here 82
SIC 3699 Electrical equipment and supplies, nec

D-U-N-S 20-555-7890   (BR)
BUREAU VERITAS CANADA (2019) INC
MAXXAM ANALYTICS INTERNATIONAL CORPORATION
(*Suby of* BUREAU VERITAS)
4606 Canada Way, Burnaby, BC, V5G 1K5
(604) 734-7276
Emp Here 350
SIC 8734 Testing laboratories
Rob Gilbert

D-U-N-S 20-868-5651   (HQ)
BURNABY SCHOOL BOARD DISTRICT 41
ARMSTRONG ELEMENTARY SCHOOL
5325 Kincaid St, Burnaby, BC, V5G 1W2
(604) 296-6900
Emp Here 75   *Sales* 202,002,049
SIC 8211 Elementary and secondary schools
Greg Frank
Claudio Morelli

D-U-N-S 24-032-8799   (HQ)
CANADIAN AUTOMATED MANAGEMENT SYSTEMS LTD
AMS COMPUTER GROUP
(*Suby of* A. M. S. ACCOUNTING MACHINE SERVICES LTD)
3707 Wayburne Dr, Burnaby, BC, V5G 3L1
(604) 430-5677
Emp Here 16   *Sales* 11,816,352
SIC 5962 Merchandising machine operators
Bob Johnson

D-U-N-S 24-535-4949   (SL)
CANADIAN HOME BUILDERS' ASSOCIA-TION OF BRITISH COLUMBIA
CHBABC
3700 Willingdon Ave, Burnaby, BC, V5G 3H2
(604) 432-7112
Emp Here 46   *Sales* 10,749,970
SIC 8621 Professional organizations
Mj Whitemarsh
Chris Ricketts
John Barth

D-U-N-S 25-216-3076   (BR)
CANADIAN UNION OF PUBLIC EMPLOY-EES
CUPE BRITISH COLUMBIA REGIONAL OF-FICE
(*Suby of* CANADIAN UNION OF PUBLIC EM-PLOYEES)
4940 Canada Way Suite 500, Burnaby, BC, V5G 4T3
(604) 291-1940
Emp Here 80

SIC 8631 Labor organizations
Barbara Dafoe

D-U-N-S 24-643-9558   (SL)
CENTURA (VANCOUVER) LIMITED
CENTURA FLOOR & WALL FASHIONS
(*Suby of* CENTURA LIMITED)
4616 Canada Way, Burnaby, BC, V5G 1K5
(604) 298-8453
Emp Here 25   *Sales* 11,179,350
SIC 5032 Brick, stone, and related material
Brian Cowie
Peter Donath
Mike Macaulay

D-U-N-S 20-252-2751   (HQ)
CLARIUS MOBILE HEALTH CORP
3605 Gilmore Way Suite 350, Burnaby, BC, V5G 4X5
(778) 800-9975
Sales 18,183,120
SIC 3829 Measuring and controlling devices, nec
Laurent Pelissier
Donald Wright

D-U-N-S 20-180-9063   (HQ)
COASTAL RANGE SYSTEMS INC
6400 Roberts St Suite 200, Burnaby, BC, V5G 4C9
(604) 473-2100
Emp Here 41   *Sales* 22,358,700
SIC 5045 Computers, peripherals, and soft-ware
Steven Loyd
Peter Van Leeuwen
Lorne Drozdowski

D-U-N-S 20-939-1056   (HQ)
D-WAVE SYSTEMS INC
3033 Beta Ave, Burnaby, BC, V5G 4M9
(604) 630-1428
Sales 32,004,360
SIC 5734 Computer and software stores
Vern Brownell
Jeremy Hilton
William Macready
David Pires
Warren Wall
Roslynn Drewitt-Lange
Paul Lee
Alexei Andreev
Geoff Catherwood
Haig Farris

D-U-N-S 20-806-9856   (SL)
D. A. TOWNLEY & ASSOCIATES LTD
4400 Dominion St Suite 160, Burnaby, BC, V5G 4G3
(604) 299-7482
Emp Here 60   *Sales* 50,883,600
SIC 6411 Insurance agents, brokers, and ser-vice
Harvey Mason
Catherine Mcguinty
Cheri Mason

D-U-N-S 24-536-3486   (SL)
DANIA HOME SOCIETY
4279 Norland Ave, Burnaby, BC, V5G 3Z6
(604) 299-1370
Emp Here 100   *Sales* 5,924,700
SIC 8361 Residential care
Pia Petersen
Per Christensen
Anne-Sophie Christiansen
Dan Olsen
Peter Jensen
Peter Wilhelmsen
Kjeld Christensen
Aksel Jensen
Jesper Raagner
Tina Taylor

D-U-N-S 25-991-4216   (SL)
DELTA-Q TECHNOLOGIES CORP
3755 Willingdon Ave, Burnaby, BC, V5G 3H3

(604) 327-8244
Emp Here 75   *Sales* 14,283,150
SIC 3629 Electrical industrial apparatus, nec
Kenneth Fielding
Sarah Mackinnon

D-U-N-S 25-099-3268   (SL)
DOCUSYSTEMS INTEGRATIONS INC
3920 Norland Ave Suite 101, Burnaby, BC, V5G 4K7

Emp Here 24   *Sales* 10,732,176
SIC 5044 Office equipment
Ryan Peek
Owen Rogan

D-U-N-S 24-804-0011   (HQ)
DOLLAR TREE STORES CANADA, INC
(*Suby of* DOLLAR TREE, INC.)
3185 Willingdon Green Suite 206, Burnaby, BC, V5G 4P3
(604) 321-2550
Emp Here 50   *Sales* 146,829,600
SIC 5999 Miscellaneous retail stores, nec
Joseph Calvano
Gary Philbin
Bob Sasser
Kevin S Wampler

D-U-N-S 20-110-9592   (HQ)
DOUGLAS LIGHTING CONTROLS INC
3605 Gilmore Way Suite 280, Burnaby, BC, V5G 4X5
(604) 873-2797
Emp Here 40   *Sales* 11,426,520
SIC 3625 Relays and industrial controls
Michael Bolton
Patricia Bolton
Eric Spika

D-U-N-S 24-825-1589   (HQ)
ELECTRONIC ARTS (CANADA) INC
EA SPORTS
(*Suby of* ELECTRONIC ARTS INC.)
4330 Sanderson Way, Burnaby, BC, V5G 4X1
(604) 456-3600
Emp Here 20   *Sales* 184,573,000
SIC 7371 Custom computer programming ser-vices
V Paul Lee

D-U-N-S 25-100-2887   (HQ)
ENCORP PACIFIC (CANADA)
4259 Canada Way Suite 100, Burnaby, BC, V5G 4Y2
(604) 473-2400
Sales 12,916,234
SIC 4953 Refuse systems
Scott Fraser
Sandy Sigmund
Dan Wong

D-U-N-S 24-374-4851   (HQ)
EURO CERAMIC TILE DISTRIBUTORS LTD
4288 Manor St, Burnaby, BC, V5G 1B2
(604) 437-3876
Emp Here 20   *Sales* 13,415,220
SIC 5032 Brick, stone, and related material
Eugenio Aquila
Renato Aquila

D-U-N-S 20-733-6418   (BR)
EXP SERVICES INC
(*Suby of* EXP GLOBAL INC)
3001 Wayburne Dr Suite 275, Burnaby, BC, V5G 4W3
(604) 874-1245
Emp Here 80
SIC 8711 Engineering services
Vlad Stritesky

D-U-N-S 20-201-4226   (SL)
FIRST RESOLUTION MANAGEMENT COR-PORATION
4585 Canada Way Suite 320, Burnaby, BC, V5G 4L6

Emp Here 40   *Sales* 10,092,440

SIC 7322 Adjustment and collection services
Kenneth Healey
Clayton T. Rodenbush

D-U-N-S 20-646-1357   (BR)
FRASER HEALTH AUTHORITY
BURNABY HOSPITAL
(Suby of GOVERNMENT OF THE PROVINCE OF BRITISH COLUMBIA)
3935 Kincaid St, Burnaby, BC, V5G 2X6
(604) 434-3992
Emp Here 1,800
SIC 8062 General medical and surgical hospitals
Arden Krystal

D-U-N-S 24-365-1499   (HQ)
GATEWAY CASINOS & ENTERTAINMENT INC
STARLIGHT CASINO
4331 Dominion St, Burnaby, BC, V5G 1C7
(604) 412-0166
Emp Here 20   Sales 334,838,000
SIC 7011 Hotels and motels
Tony Santo
Rowen B Craigie
Benjamin W Perham
Michael D Smerdon
James D Packer
Bob Kocienski

D-U-N-S 20-374-5448   (HQ)
GATEWAY CASINOS & ENTERTAINMENT LIMITED
4331 Dominion St, Burnaby, BC, V5G 1C7
(604) 412-0166
Sales 574,008,000
SIC 7011 Hotels and motels
Anthony Santo
Bradley Bardua
Tolek Strukoff
Robert Ward
Carrie Kormos
Scott Phillips
Michael Snider

D-U-N-S 24-694-5653   (SL)
GENTLE CARE DRAPERY & CARPET CLEANERS LTD
COIT SERVICES
3755 Wayburne Dr, Burnaby, BC, V5G 3L1
(604) 296-4000
Emp Here 80   Sales 7,170,320
SIC 7217 Carpet and upholstery cleaning
Brent Pullan

D-U-N-S 20-868-0439   (HQ)
INTERNATIONAL UNION OF OPERATING ENGINEERS LOCAL 115
IUOE
4333 Ledger Ave Suite 115, Burnaby, BC, V5G 4G9
(604) 291-8831
Sales 29,840,960
SIC 8742 Management consulting services
Lionel Railton
Brian Cochrane

D-U-N-S 24-824-5474   (SL)
KEYSTONE ENVIRONMENTAL LTD
4400 Dominion St Suite 320, Burnaby, BC, V5G 4G3
(604) 430-0671
Emp Here 70   Sales 16,400,160
SIC 8748 Business consulting, nec
William R Donald
Kenneth Evans

D-U-N-S 20-271-6791   (SL)
KODAK CANADA ULC
(Suby of EASTMAN KODAK COMPANY)
4225 Kincaid St, Burnaby, BC, V5G 4P5
(604) 451-2700
Emp Here 375   Sales 102,888,750
SIC 3861 Photographic equipment and supplies
Jeff Clarke

David Bullwinkle

D-U-N-S 25-995-9690   (SL)
LRG CONSTRUCTION LTD
5655 Monarch St, Burnaby, BC, V5G 2A2
(604) 291-2135
Emp Here 30   Sales 14,121,930
SIC 1542 Nonresidential construction, nec
Louis Gil

D-U-N-S 20-699-7103   (BR)
NORDION (CANADA) INC
MDS DIAGNOSTIC SERVICES
(Suby of NORDION (CANADA) INC)
3680 Gilmore Way, Burnaby, BC, V5G 4V8
(604) 431-5005
Emp Here 800
SIC 8071 Medical laboratories

D-U-N-S 25-680-9674   (SL)
ODENZA MARKETING GROUP INC
FUN PLANET VACATIONS
4370 Dominion St Suite 600, Burnaby, BC, V5G 4L7
(604) 451-1414
Emp Here 32   Sales 16,638,944
SIC 4724 Travel agencies
Parminder Sodi Hundal
Darlene Howatson

D-U-N-S 20-648-4029   (SL)
OPERATING ENGINEERS BENEFITS & PENSION PLANS
4333 Ledger Ave Suite 402, Burnaby, BC, V5G 4G9
(604) 299-8341
Emp Here 18   Sales 10,438,632
SIC 6411 Insurance agents, brokers, and service
Lionel Railton

D-U-N-S 24-762-6489   (HQ)
OSI GEOSPATIAL INC
OSI MARITIME SYSTEMS
4585 Canada Way Suite 400, Burnaby, BC, V5G 4L6
(778) 373-4600
Sales 26,126,430
SIC 5088 Transportation equipment and supplies
Kenneth Kirkpatrick

D-U-N-S 24-536-5127   (HQ)
OSI MARITIME SYSTEMS LTD
4585 Canada Way Suite 400, Burnaby, BC, V5G 4L6
(778) 373-4600
Sales 31,820,460
SIC 3812 Search and navigation equipment
Kenneth Kirkpatrick
James Girard

D-U-N-S 24-866-8089   (HQ)
PACIFIC WESTERN BREWING COMPANY LTD
3876 Norland Ave, Burnaby, BC, V5G 4T9
(604) 421-2119
Sales 20,741,400
SIC 2082 Malt beverages
Kazuko Komatsu

D-U-N-S 20-365-3720   (HQ)
PALADIN TECHNOLOGIES INC
3001 Wayburne Dr Suite 201, Burnaby, BC, V5G 4W3
(604) 677-8700
Emp Here 5   Sales 13,151,250
SIC 7381 Detective and armored car services
Ted Reid
Ashley Cooper
Fraser Cooper

D-U-N-S 20-862-5814   (HQ)
PBC HEALTH BENEFITS SOCIETY
PACIFIC BLUE CROSS
4250 Canada Way, Burnaby, BC, V5G 4W6
(604) 419-2200
Emp Here 700   Sales 289,753,407

SIC 6321 Accident and health insurance
John Crawford
John D. Crawford
Anne Kinvig
Leza Muir
Glen Copping
Barry M. Rivelis
Heidi Worthington

D-U-N-S 20-575-8808   (BR)
PITNEY BOWES OF CANADA LTD
(Suby of PITNEY BOWES INC.)
3001 Wayburne Dr Suite 125, Burnaby, BC, V5G 4W3
(778) 328-8900
Emp Here 75
SIC 5044 Office equipment
Justine Harrison

D-U-N-S 25-366-3884   (HQ)
POLYCOM CANADA LTD
(Suby of PLANTRONICS, INC.)
3605 Gilmore Way Suite 200, Burnaby, BC, V5G 4X5
(604) 453-9400
Emp Here 55   Sales 26,830,440
SIC 5065 Electronic parts and equipment, nec
Robert Hagert

D-U-N-S 20-338-4284   (SL)
SEQUEL NATURALS ULC
VEGA
(Suby of DANONE)
3001 Wayburne Dr Unit 101, Burnaby, BC, V5G 4W3
(866) 839-8863
Emp Here 20   Sales 16,711,540
SIC 5149 Groceries and related products, nec
Brendan Brazier

D-U-N-S 20-914-8790   (HQ)
STUDENT ASSOCIATION OF THE BRITISH COLUMBIA INSTITUTE OF TECHNOLOGY
STUDENT ASSOCIATION OF THE BCIT
3700 Willingdon Ave Suite 260, Burnaby, BC, V5G 3H2
(604) 432-8847
Emp Here 50   Sales 16,141,235
SIC 5411 Grocery stores
Caroline Gagnon

D-U-N-S 25-505-5519   (HQ)
TANTALUS SYSTEMS CORP
3555 Gilmore Way Suite 200, Burnaby, BC, V5G 0B3
(604) 299-0458
Sales 15,993,040
SIC 4899 Communication services, nec
Eric Murray
John Brett
Charles Cheng
John Haylock
Dominic Geraghty
Keith Martin

D-U-N-S 20-693-6770   (HQ)
TERADICI CORPORATION
4601 Canada Way Suite 300, Burnaby, BC, V5G 4X8
(604) 451-5800
Sales 10,233,650
SIC 3674 Semiconductors and related devices
David Smith
Bob Johnson

D-U-N-S 25-092-0241   (HQ)
THEMIS SOLUTIONS INC
CLIO
4611 Canada Way Suite 300, Burnaby, BC, V5G 4X3
(604) 210-2944
Sales 10,993,282
SIC 7371 Custom computer programming services
Jack Newton
Rian Gauvreau

D-U-N-S 24-760-6478   (HQ)

TIMECO WATCH & CLOCK REPAIRS LTD
4459 Canada Way, Burnaby, BC, V5G 1J3
(604) 435-6383
Emp Here 12   Sales 17,669,730
SIC 7631 Watch, clock, and jewelry repair
Pravin Soni
Ramanlal Jogia

D-U-N-S 25-719-4605   (BR)
TRADER CORPORATION
HOMEBASE MEDIA
(Suby of APAX PARTNERS LLP)
3555 Gilmore Way 1 West, Burnaby, BC, V5G 0B3
(604) 540-4455
Emp Here 200
SIC 2721 Periodicals
Michelle Terrebonne

D-U-N-S 25-104-9230   (SL)
VISION33 CANADA INC
6400 Roberts St Suite 200, Burnaby, BC, V5G 4C9
(604) 473-2100
Emp Here 80   Sales 17,108,080
SIC 7372 Prepackaged software
Tony Whalen

D-U-N-S 20-052-8698   (SL)
XENON PHARMACEUTICALS INC
3650 Gilmore Way, Burnaby, BC, V5G 4W8
(604) 484-3300
Emp Here 81   Sales 16,530,642
SIC 8731 Commercial physical research
Ian Mortimer
Simon Primstone
Robin Sherrington
James Empfield
Mohammad Azab
Steven Gannon
Michael Hayden
Frank Holler
Gary Patou
Richard Scheller

Burnaby, BC V5H

D-U-N-S 25-902-2762   (BR)
ADP CANADA CO
ADP DEALER SERVICES
(Suby of AUTOMATIC DATA PROCESSING, INC.)
4720 Kingsway Suite 500, Burnaby, BC, V5H 4N2
(604) 431-2700
Emp Here 130
SIC 8721 Accounting, auditing, and bookkeeping
Mike Woods

D-U-N-S 25-497-3183   (HQ)
BURNABY PUBLIC LIBRARY
6100 Willingdon Ave, Burnaby, BC, V5H 4N5
(604) 436-5400
Emp Here 120   Sales 19,815,750
SIC 8231 Libraries
Sharon Freeman
Edel Toner-Rogala

D-U-N-S 20-591-2087   (BR)
BURNABY SCHOOL BOARD DISTRICT 41
CHAFFEY-BURKE ELEMENTARY SCHOOL
(Suby of BURNABY SCHOOL BOARD DISTRICT 41)
4404 Sardis St, Burnaby, BC, V5H 1K7

Emp Here 80
SIC 8211 Elementary and secondary schools
Claudio Bortolussi

D-U-N-S 25-013-0945   (BR)
BURNABY SCHOOL BOARD DISTRICT 41
ECOLE MARLBOROUGH ELEMENTARY SCHOOL

(Suby of BURNABY SCHOOL BOARD DISTRICT 41)
6060 Marlborough Ave, Burnaby, BC, V5H 3L7
(604) 296-9021
Emp Here 77
SIC 8211 Elementary and secondary schools
Shelley Parks

D-U-N-S 20-547-0912   (HQ)
CAC ENTERPRISES GROUP INC
CAC RECYCLING
4538 Kingsway Unit 619, Burnaby, BC, V5H 4T9
(604) 430-8835
Emp Here 40   *Sales* 22,358,700
SIC 5051 Metals service centers and offices
Harold H Yang
Wei Cao
Feng Yang

D-U-N-S 25-960-1763   (HQ)
CASCADE INSURANCE AGENCIES (BURNABY) INC
4683 Kingsway, Burnaby, BC, V5H 2B3

Emp Here 24   *Sales* 39,858,820
SIC 6411 Insurance agents, brokers, and service
Gary Puri
Amarjeet Puri

D-U-N-S 24-384-0423   (HQ)
CELLULAR BABY CELL PHONE ACCESSORIES SPECIALIST LTD
4710 Kingsway Unit 1028, Burnaby, BC, V5H 4M2
(604) 437-9977
Emp Here 10   *Sales* 48,865,600
SIC 5999 Miscellaneous retail stores, nec
Peter Wong

D-U-N-S 20-189-8678   (BR)
CH2M HILL CANADA LIMITED
VBC
(Suby of JACOBS ENGINEERING GROUP INC.)
4720 Kingsway Suite 2100, Burnaby, BC, V5H 4N2
(604) 684-3282
Emp Here 100
SIC 8711 Engineering services
Bill Hayes

D-U-N-S 24-345-9497   (BR)
CITY OF BURNABY
BURNABY PARKS & RECREATION
(Suby of CITY OF BURNABY)
6533 Nelson Ave, Burnaby, BC, V5H 0C2

Emp Here 200
SIC 8322 Individual and family services
Teri Sabot

D-U-N-S 24-503-9870   (HQ)
CONCORD SECURITY CORPORATION
(Suby of 417289 B.C. LTD)
4710 Kingsway Suite 925, Burnaby, BC, V5H 4M2
(604) 689-4005
Sales 21,000,000
SIC 7381 Detective and armored car services
John Henry Jr
Clare Edmundson

D-U-N-S 20-393-1741   (SL)
D-THIND DEVELOPMENT LTD
700-4211 Kingsway, Burnaby, BC, V5H 1Z6
(604) 451-7780
Emp Here 40   *Sales* 11,543,320
SIC 1522 Residential construction, nec
Dal Tit
David Lee

D-U-N-S 20-645-2489   (SL)
DIGIFACTS SYNDICATE
4720 Kingsway Suite 900, Burnaby, BC, V5H 4N2

(604) 435-4317
Emp Here 52   *Sales* 10,872,420
SIC 8721 Accounting, auditing, and bookkeeping
Don Willoughby

D-U-N-S 24-327-2353   (SL)
DZOMBETA DRUG LTD
SHOPPERS DRUG MART
4827 Kingsway Suite 2283, Burnaby, BC, V5H 4T6
(604) 433-2721
Emp Here 45   *Sales* 11,382,930
SIC 5912 Drug stores and proprietary stores
Bojana Dzombeta

D-U-N-S 20-388-3140   (SL)
EXCEL INSURANCE BROKERS (METRO VANCOUVER) INC
4720 Kingsway Unit 2600, Burnaby, BC, V5H 4N2
(604) 282-7719
Emp Here 22   *Sales* 12,758,328
SIC 6411 Insurance agents, brokers, and service
Ricardo De Guzman Jr

D-U-N-S 25-686-5171   (HQ)
FIRST CANADIAN MANAGEMENT CORP
5945 Kathleen Ave Suite 220, Burnaby, BC, V5H 4J7
(604) 689-2467
Sales 23,917,000
SIC 7011 Hotels and motels
Fayaz Manji

D-U-N-S 25-736-2053   (BR)
GAP (CANADA) INC
GAP
(Suby of THE GAP INC)
4700 Kingsway Suite 2138, Burnaby, BC, V5H 4M1
(604) 431-6559
Emp Here 75
SIC 5651 Family clothing stores
Alison Malone

D-U-N-S 25-192-3488   (SL)
GREATER VANCOUVER WATER DISTRICT
4330 Kingsway Suite 505, Burnaby, BC, V5H 4G8
(604) 432-6200
Emp Here 500   *Sales* 167,419,000
SIC 4941 Water supply
Jim Rusnak

D-U-N-S 25-327-7446   (HQ)
HEMMERA ENVIROCHEM INC
4730 Kingsway 18 Fl, Burnaby, BC, V5H 0C6
(604) 669-0424
Emp Here 100   *Sales* 43,600,280
SIC 8748 Business consulting, nec
Paul Hemsley
Shawn Cornett
Jeff Devins
Jim Stewart

D-U-N-S 25-684-1248   (SL)
HILTON VANCOUVER METROTOWN
(Suby of NIKE, INC.)
6083 Mckay Ave, Burnaby, BC, V5H 2W7
(604) 438-1200
Emp Here 156   *Sales* 14,924,208
SIC 7011 Hotels and motels
Chris Perna

D-U-N-S 25-120-1604   (SL)
HOSPITALITY CAREERS ONLINE INC
HCAREERS.COM
4789 Kingsway Suite 400, Burnaby, BC, V5H 0A3
(604) 435-8991
Emp Here 90   *Sales* 19,055,160
SIC 7311 Advertising agencies
Eden Slegr

D-U-N-S 25-301-2306   (BR)
HUDSON'S BAY COMPANY
BAY, THE

(Suby of HUDSON'S BAY COMPANY)
4850 Kingsway, Burnaby, BC, V5H 4P2
(604) 436-1196
Emp Here 200
SIC 5311 Department stores
Barry Wilson

D-U-N-S 24-040-3118   (BR)
HUDSON'S BAY COMPANY
HOME OUTFITTERS
(Suby of HUDSON'S BAY COMPANY)
4800 Kingsway Suite 118, Burnaby, BC, V5H 4J2

Emp Here 376
SIC 5719 Miscellaneous homefurnishings
Devi Sharma

D-U-N-S 25-831-1430   (SL)
I.W.A. FOREST INDUSTRY PENSION & PLAN
3777 Kingsway Suite 2100, Burnaby, BC, V5H 3Z7
(604) 433-6310
Emp Here 50   *Sales* 11,714,400
SIC 8748 Business consulting, nec
Robert Bishoff

D-U-N-S 25-014-1819   (BR)
KPMG LLP
KPMG
(Suby of KPMG LLP)
4720 Kingsway Suite 2400, Burnaby, BC, V5H 4N2
(604) 527-3600
Emp Here 150
SIC 8721 Accounting, auditing, and bookkeeping
Kyle Titte

D-U-N-S 25-082-4455   (SL)
LANGLEY FARM MARKET (1997) INC
4820 Kingsway Suite 316, Burnaby, BC, V5H 4P1
(604) 521-2883
Emp Here 19   *Sales* 10,167,356
SIC 5148 Fresh fruits and vegetables
Wayne Zhang

D-U-N-S 24-311-0509   (BR)
LONDON DRUGS LIMITED
(Suby of H.Y. LOUIE CO. LIMITED)
4970 Kingsway, Burnaby, BC, V5H 2E2
(604) 448-4806
Emp Here 100
SIC 5912 Drug stores and proprietary stores
Shock Debra

D-U-N-S 25-318-1952   (BR)
MCDONALD'S   RESTAURANTS   OF CANADA LIMITED
MCDONALD'S
(Suby of MCDONALD'S CORPORATION)
4700 Kingsway Suite 1160, Burnaby, BC, V5H 4M1
(604) 718-1005
Emp Here 95
SIC 5812 Eating places
Sarah Fussey

D-U-N-S 24-850-5187   (HQ)
MERIDIAN ONECAP CREDIT CORP
MERIDIAN ONECAP
(Suby of MERIDIAN CREDIT UNION LIMITED)
4710 Kingsway Suite 1500, Burnaby, BC, V5H 4M2
(604) 646-2247
Emp Here 25   *Sales* 16,795,575
SIC 6159 Miscellaneous business credit institutions
Joe Laleggia
Mark Cannon
Robert Murphy
Bob Mormina
Lui Spizzirri

D-U-N-S 24-069-4216   (HQ)

METRO VANCOUVER HOUSING CORPORATION
MVHC
(Suby of GREATER VANCOUVER REGIONAL DISTRICT)
4330 Kingsway Suite 505, Burnaby, BC, V5H 4G7
(604) 432-6300
Sales 27,646,674
SIC 6531 Real estate agents and managers
Gordon Nicol

D-U-N-S 24-725-6126   (HQ)
METROTOWN OPTICAL LTD
UNITED OPTICAL
6411 Nelson Ave Suite 105, Burnaby, BC, V5H 4H3

Sales 11,396,000
SIC 5995 Optical goods stores
Gary Efonoff
Denise Efonoff

D-U-N-S 20-113-9920   (SL)
MILANI PLUMBING DRAINAGE & HEATING LTD
5526 Kingsway, Burnaby, BC, V5H 2G2
(604) 453-1234
Emp Here 100   *Sales* 24,432,800
SIC 5999 Miscellaneous retail stores, nec
Vern Milani

D-U-N-S 24-778-1388   (HQ)
N R S WESTBURN REALTY LTD
COLDWELL BANKER
5489 Kingsway, Burnaby, BC, V5H 2G1
(604) 209-1225
Emp Here 1   *Sales* 62,833,350
SIC 6531 Real estate agents and managers
Paul Prade

D-U-N-S 24-151-6442   (SL)
OFFICE AND PROFESSIONAL EMPLOYEES INTERNATIONAL UNION
MOVEUP
4501 Kingsway Unit 301, Burnaby, BC, V5H 0E5
(604) 299-0378
Emp Here 40   *Sales* 15,646,320
SIC 8631 Labor organizations
David Black

D-U-N-S 24-161-4726   (HQ)
OPTIMUM WEST INSURANCE COMPANY INC
(Suby of OPTIGAM INC)
4211 Kingsway Suite 600, Burnaby, BC, V5H 1Z6
(604) 688-1541
Sales 84,946,314
SIC 6331 Fire, marine, and casualty insurance
Jean-Claude Page
Clifford Quesnel
Henri Joli-Coeur
Gilles Blondeau
Gilles Demers
Gaston Paradis
Martin Carrier

D-U-N-S 24-761-0749   (SL)
ORBIS INVESTMENTS (CANADA) LIMITED
4710 Kingsway Suite 2600, Burnaby, BC, V5H 4M2
(778) 331-3000
Emp Here 49   *Sales* 33,267,227
SIC 6282 Investment advice
Garth Rempel
Alexander Cutler
Edwin Gillespie

D-U-N-S 20-709-2631   (BR)
ROGERS COMMUNICATIONS INC
ROGERS SHARED OPERATIONS
(Suby of ROGERS COMMUNICATIONS INC)
4710 Kingsway Suite 1900, Burnaby, BC, V5H 4W4
(604) 431-1400
Emp Here 400

SIC 4899 Communication services, nec
Liza Gates

D-U-N-S 25-712-9445   (BR)
RRGB RESTAURANTS CANADA INC
(*Suby of* RRGB RESTAURANTS CANADA INC)
4640 Kingsway Suite 112, Burnaby, BC, V5H 4L9

Emp Here 95
SIC 5812 Eating places
Jessica Tremblay

D-U-N-S 25-533-9061   (HQ)
SCOTT CONSTRUCTION LTD
SCOTT CONSTRUCTION GROUP
3777 Kingsway Unit 1750, Burnaby, BC, V5H 3Z7
(604) 874-8228
Emp Here 60   *Sales* 90,790,960
SIC 1542 Nonresidential construction, nec
John Scott
Laura Suhner
Don Nishimura

D-U-N-S 24-797-8849   (BR)
SECURITAS CANADA LIMITED
(*Suby of* SECURITAS AB)
5172 Kingsway Suite 270, Burnaby, BC, V5H 2E8
(604) 454-3600
Emp Here 300
SIC 7381 Detective and armored car services
Perry Clarke

D-U-N-S 24-166-9378   (HQ)
SMG ADVISORS INC
4250 Kingsway Suite 213, Burnaby, BC, V5H 4T7
(604) 419-0455
Emp Here 1   *Sales* 14,057,280
SIC 8742 Management consulting services
Claire Mood
Jung Moon

D-U-N-S 20-337-8997   (HQ)
STANTEC LAND SURVEYING LTD.
(*Suby of* STANTEC INC)
4730 Kingsway Suite 500, Burnaby, BC, V5H 0C6
(604) 436-3014
Emp Here 197   *Sales* 46,522,916
SIC 8713 Surveying services
Gordon Johnston

D-U-N-S 25-718-5199   (BR)
T & T SUPERMARKET INC
METROTOWN STORE
(*Suby of* LOBLAW COMPANIES LIMITED)
4800 Kingsway Suite 147, Burnaby, BC, V5H 4J2
(604) 436-4881
Emp Here 150
SIC 5411 Grocery stores
Fred Hsu

D-U-N-S 20-749-1002   (HQ)
TAIGA BUILDING PRODUCTS LTD
DYNAMIC FOREST PRODUCTS, DIV OF
4710 Kingsway Suite 800, Burnaby, BC, V5H 4M2
(604) 438-1471
Emp Here 80   *Sales* 1,155,005,825
SIC 5031 Lumber, plywood, and millwork
Trent Balog
Russ Permann
Grant Sali
Mark Schneidereit-Hsu
Ian Tong
Douglas Morris
Cam White
Kooi Ong Tong
Brian Flagel
Otto-Hans Nowak

D-U-N-S 20-153-1998   (SL)
TELECOMMUNICATION WORKERS PEN-

SION PLAN
4603 Kingsway Suite 303, Burnaby, BC, V5H 4M4
(604) 430-1317
Emp Here 14   *Sales* 14,488,334
SIC 6371 Pension, health, and welfare funds
Debbie Ellis

D-U-N-S 24-325-7768   (SL)
TELUS COMMUNICATIONS COMPANY
(*Suby of* TELUS CORPORATION)
3777 Kingsway Suite 501, Burnaby, BC, V5H 3Z7
(604) 432-2151
Emp Here 4,000   *Sales* 1,338,176,000
SIC 4899 Communication services, nec
Darren Entwistle
John Gossling
R.H (Dick) Auchinleck
Lisa De Wilde
Raymond T. Chan
Stockwell Day
Mary Jo Haddad
Kathy Kinloch
William (Bill) A. Mackinnon
John Manley

D-U-N-S 20-555-8039   (BR)
TELUS COMMUNICATIONS INC
TELUS TV
(*Suby of* TELUS CORPORATION)
3777 Kingsway, Burnaby, BC, V5H 3Z7
(604) 432-5010
Emp Here 25,000
SIC 4899 Communication services, nec

D-U-N-S 24-657-5435   (SL)
UNITED FOOD & COMMERCIAL WORKERS UNION LOCAL 1518
4021 Kingsway, Burnaby, BC, V5H 1Y9
(604) 434-3101
Emp Here 46   *Sales* 17,993,268
SIC 8631 Labor organizations
Frank Pozzobon
Ivan Limpright
Sandra Hill

D-U-N-S 24-042-8552   (HQ)
VFA CANADA CORPORATION
4211 Kingsway Suite 400, Burnaby, BC, V5H 1Z6
(604) 685-3757
Emp Here 24   *Sales* 11,948,688
SIC 8748 Business consulting, nec
Susan Anson
Lynda Gabriel

D-U-N-S 20-863-4634   (SL)
WILLINGDON PARK HOSPITAL LTD
WILLINGDON CARE CENTRE
4435 Grange St, Burnaby, BC, V5H 1P4
(604) 433-2455
Emp Here 100   *Sales* 6,873,300
SIC 8051 Skilled nursing care facilities
Arnold Bennewith

D-U-N-S 24-265-5907   (SL)
YI JIA INTERNATIONAL GROUP (CANADA) LTD
4720 Kingsway Unit 2335, Burnaby, BC, V5H 4N2
(778) 379-0118
Emp Here 26   *Sales* 13,811,382
SIC 6211 Security brokers and dealers

Burnaby, BC V5J

D-U-N-S 20-091-7339   (SL)
2 SISTERS POULTRY & MEAT LTD
5791 Sidley St, Burnaby, BC, V5J 5E6
(604) 327-5526
Emp Here 40   *Sales* 33,423,080
SIC 5142 Packaged frozen goods
Buta Uppal

D-U-N-S 24-695-0307   (SL)
305466 B.C. LTD
SERVICEMASTER RESTORATION
8155 North Fraser Way Unit 100, Burnaby, BC, V5J 5M8
(604) 435-1220
Emp Here 100   *Sales* 57,033,800
SIC 1542 Nonresidential construction, nec
Warren Groom

D-U-N-S 24-957-5440   (SL)
ACOM BUILDING MAINTENANCE LTD
3871 North Fraser Way Unit 23, Burnaby, BC, V5J 5G6
(604) 436-2121
Emp Here 250   *Sales* 7,992,000
SIC 7349 Building maintenance services, nec
Soony Kohu
Sandra Kohu

D-U-N-S 24-786-9704   (HQ)
ADVANCED MOBILITY PRODUCTS LTD
8620 Glenlyon Pky Suite 101, Burnaby, BC, V5J 0B6
(604) 293-0002
Sales 15,628,800
SIC 5999 Miscellaneous retail stores, nec
David Elder
Cathy Elder

D-U-N-S 24-360-9182   (SL)
AFCC AUTOMOTIVE FUEL CELL COOPERATION CORP
AFCC
(*Suby of* DAIMLER AG)
9000 Glenlyon Pky, Burnaby, BC, V5J 5J8
(604) 415-7290
Emp Here 200   *Sales* 50,698,000
SIC 8748 Business consulting, nec
Joachim Blum
Christian Mohrdiel
Jim Boerger
Andreas Schamel
Kevin E. Layden
Thomas Lehnert
Bill Obermaier
Rolf Schurr
Tim Bovich

D-U-N-S 20-797-8339   (SL)
ALGO COMMUNICATION PRODUCTS LTD
4500 Beedie St, Burnaby, BC, V5J 5L2
(604) 438-3333
Emp Here 70   *Sales* 12,935,860
SIC 4899 Communication services, nec
Douglas Zoehner
Paul Zoehner

D-U-N-S 20-279-3238   (SL)
ALL THERM SERVICES INC
8528 Glenlyon Pky Unit 141, Burnaby, BC, V5J 0B6
(604) 559-4331
Emp Here 30   *Sales* 13,415,220
SIC 5033 Roofing, siding, and insulation
Chris Iskanian

D-U-N-S 24-032-7411   (HQ)
ALPHA TECHNOLOGIES LTD
(*Suby of* ENERSYS)
7700 Riverfront Gate, Burnaby, BC, V5J 5M4
(604) 436-5900
Emp Here 468   *Sales* 141,457,500
SIC 3669 Communications equipment, nec
Ian Kane
David Boroevich
Samuel Wong
John Kalbfleish

D-U-N-S 24-333-8741   (HQ)
ARBUTUS BIOPHARMA CORPORATION
8900 Glenlyon Pky Suite 100, Burnaby, BC, V5J 5J8
(604) 419-3200
Emp Here 20   *Sales* 10,700,000
SIC 2834 Pharmaceutical preparations
Mark J. Murray
Elizabeth Howard

David C. Hastings
Michael J. Sofia
William T. Symonds
Vivek Ramaswamy
Daniel Burgess
Herbert J. Conrad
Richard C. Henriques
Keith Manchester

D-U-N-S 20-108-8226   (SL)
ARMATURE ELECTRIC LIMITED
3811 North Fraser Way, Burnaby, BC, V5J 5J2
(604) 879-6141
Emp Here 50   *Sales* 10,891,450
SIC 1731 Electrical work
Neil Amyotte
Richard Gallant
Blair Mcewen
Erik Furstrand

D-U-N-S 20-374-8269   (SL)
ARTRON LABORATORIES INC
3938 North Fraser Way, Burnaby, BC, V5J 5H6
(604) 415-9757
Emp Here 50   *Sales* 12,828,100
SIC 3841 Surgical and medical instruments
Cenk Ozkan

D-U-N-S 20-955-3812   (SL)
AUTHENTIC WINE AND SPIRITS MERCHANTS
7432 Fraser Park Dr, Burnaby, BC, V5J 5B9
(604) 708-5022
Emp Here 29   *Sales* 17,049,564
SIC 5182 Wine and distilled beverages
Darryl Weinbren
Richard Carras

D-U-N-S 24-696-5107   (HQ)
AUTOGAS PROPANE LTD
(*Suby of* A-1 INDUSTRIAL PROPANE HOLDINGS LTD)
5605 Byrne Rd, Burnaby, BC, V5J 3J1
(604) 433-4900
Emp Here 40   *Sales* 19,546,240
SIC 5984 Liquefied petroleum gas dealers
Robert Good
Jamie Good
Bill Good

D-U-N-S 25-216-9040   (SL)
B.C. COMFORT AIR CONDITIONING LIMITED
7405 Lowland Dr, Burnaby, BC, V5J 5A8
(604) 439-3344
Emp Here 60   *Sales* 13,983,900
SIC 1711 Plumbing, heating, air-conditioning
Robert Noel
Brian Leek

D-U-N-S 24-382-4039   (HQ)
BALLARD POWER SYSTEMS INC
9000 Glenlyon Pky, Burnaby, BC, V5J 5J8
(604) 454-0900
Emp Here 443   *Sales* 96,586,000
SIC 3674 Semiconductors and related devices
Randall Macewen
Rob Campbell
Kevin Colbow
Jan Laishley
Tony Guglielmin
Sarbjot (Jyoti) Sidhu
Jim Roche
Doug Hayhurst
Ian Sutcliffe
Duy-Loan Le

D-U-N-S 24-312-0367   (SL)
BARE SPORTS CANADA LTD
HUISH OUTDOORS
3711 North Fraser Way Suite 50, Burnaby, BC, V5J 5J2
(604) 235-2630
Emp Here 90   *Sales* 14,297,220
SIC 3069 Fabricated rubber products, nec
Gerry May
Jorma Kallio

Neil Melliship

D-U-N-S 20-109-1212   (HQ)
BEAVER ELECTRICAL MACHINERY LTD
7440 Lowland Dr, Burnaby, BC, V5J 5A4
(604) 431-5000
Emp Here 45   Sales 13,742,550
SIC 7694 Armature rewinding shops
Serg Nosella
Dave Flumerfelt
Dave Nosella

D-U-N-S 24-290-1999   (HQ)
BECK, WILSON M INSURANCE SERVICES
INC
8678 Greenall Ave Suite 303, Burnaby, BC,
V5J 3M6
(604) 437-6200
Emp Here 34   Sales 37,314,640
SIC 6411 Insurance agents, brokers, and ser-
vice
Wilson Beck
David Beck
Chris Haag
Carole Scannell

D-U-N-S 24-957-3452   (HQ)
BEST BUY CANADA LTD
FUTURE SHOP
(Suby of BEST BUY CO., INC.)
8800 Glenlyon Pky, Burnaby, BC, V5J 5K3
(604) 435-8223
Emp Here 45   Sales 266,703,000
SIC 5731 Radio, television, and electronic
stores
Ron Wilson
Earl Ellis
Kamy Scarlett
Philippe Arrata
Michael Pratt
Carol A Surface
David J. Deno
Michael A. Vitelli
Elizabeth Erickson
Todd Hartman

D-U-N-S 24-154-3834   (SL)
BONNY'S TAXI LTD
QUEEN CITY TAXI & BURNABBY ELI
5759 Sidley St, Burnaby, BC, V5J 5E6
(604) 435-8233
Emp Here 680   Sales 38,225,520
SIC 4121 Taxicabs
Major Dhillon
Manjig Gosal
Bikman Parmer
Valver Gill
George Lapthorne

D-U-N-S 25-011-9070   (BR)
BURNABY SCHOOL BOARD DISTRICT 41
BURNABY SOUTH SECONDARY SCHOOL
(Suby of BURNABY SCHOOL BOARD DIS-
TRICT 41)
5455 Rumble St, Burnaby, BC, V5J 2B7
(604) 296-6880
Emp Here 250
SIC 8211 Elementary and secondary schools
Leeanne Kristnanson

D-U-N-S 25-408-6010   (SL)
C&O APPAREL INC
3788 North Fraser Way, Burnaby, BC, V5J
5G1
(604) 451-9799
Emp Here 150   Sales 20,501,100
SIC 2329 Men's and boy's clothing, nec
Simpson Ma

D-U-N-S 24-725-6100   (HQ)
CANADIAN CONSTRUCTION MATERIALS
ENGINEERING & TESTING INC
CCMET GROUP
6991 Curragh Ave, Burnaby, BC, V5J 4V6
(604) 436-9111
Sales 23,978,775
SIC 8734 Testing laboratories

Robert Gilbert

D-U-N-S 20-018-8639   (SL)
CANADIAN TIRE ASSOCIATE STORE
7200 Market Cross, Burnaby, BC, V5J 0A2
(604) 451-5888
Emp Here 30   Sales 14,942,340
SIC 5531 Auto and home supply stores
Dan Howlett

D-U-N-S 24-386-8440   (HQ)
CANDA SIX FORTUNE ENTERPRISE CO.
LTD
(Suby of LOBLAW COMPANIES LIMITED)
8138 North Fraser Way, Burnaby, BC, V5J 0E7
(604) 432-9000
Emp Here 40   Sales 33,423,080
SIC 5149 Groceries and related products, nec
Tina Lee
Cindy Lee
Robert Balcom
Sarah Davis
Grant Froese
Peter Mclaughlin
Deborah Morshead
Robert Stassen
Irene Tsui

D-U-N-S 24-212-2448   (HQ)
CANSEL SURVEY EQUIPMENT INC
CANSEL
3900 North Fraser Way, Burnaby, BC, V5J 5H6
(604) 299-5766
Emp Here 18   Sales 116,758,200
SIC 5049 Professional equipment, nec

D-U-N-S 24-312-5697   (HQ)
CANTERBURY COFFEE CORPORATION
8080 North Fraser Way Unit 1, Burnaby, BC,
V5J 0E6
(604) 431-4400
Sales 33,423,080
SIC 5149 Groceries and related products, nec
Murray Dunlop

D-U-N-S 24-957-8972   (HQ)
CANTERBURY FOOD SERVICE LTD
CANTERBURY COFFEE
(Suby of CANTERBURY COFFEE CORPO-
RATION)
8080 North Fraser Way Unit 1, Burnaby, BC,
V5J 0E6
(604) 431-4400
Sales 29,347,700
SIC 5499 Miscellaneous food stores
Murray Dunlop

D-U-N-S 24-162-5839   (HQ)
CERTIFIED GENERAL ACCOUNTANTS AS-
SOCIATION OF CANADA
CGA CANADA
4200 North Fraser Way Suite 100, Burnaby,
BC, V5J 5K7
(604) 408-6660
Emp Here 117   Sales 29,263,875
SIC 8621 Professional organizations
Tony Ducie
Terry Leblanc

D-U-N-S 20-558-2666   (SL)
CITADEL COMMERCE CORP
8610 Glenlyon Pky Unit 130, Burnaby, BC,
V5J 0B6
(604) 299-6924
Emp Here 100   Sales 16,684,700
SIC 7372 Prepackaged software
Michael Meeks
Ian Franks
Mary Betts
Colin Ramsay
Ivan Metalnikov
Patti Nakashima

D-U-N-S 20-110-3942   (HQ)
COLUMBIA MANUFACTURING CO. LTD
4575 Tillicum St, Burnaby, BC, V5J 5K9
(604) 437-3377
Emp Here 30   Sales 29,066,310

SIC 5031 Lumber, plywood, and millwork
Michael Williams

D-U-N-S 25-715-5093   (SL)
CORINTHIAN DISTRIBUTORS LTD
8118 North Fraser Way Unit 1, Burnaby, BC,
V5J 0E5
(604) 431-5058
Emp Here 18   Sales 15,040,386
SIC 5141 Groceries, general line
Edward Chua
Vincent Uy
Kenneth Co
Pacita Chua
Dorothy Uy
Myra Uy
Edward Limoanco

D-U-N-S 24-857-0236   (HQ)
CREATION TECHNOLOGIES INC
8999 Fraserton Crt, Burnaby, BC, V5J 5H8
(604) 430-4336
Sales 792,162,000
SIC 3679 Electronic components, nec
Bhawnesh Mathur
Geoffrey Reed
Rodolfo Archbold
Michael Mazan
David Samuel
Arthur Walker
Micheal Walsh

D-U-N-S 20-333-2432   (BR)
CREATION TECHNOLOGIES LP
(Suby of CREATION TECHNOLOGIES LP)
8997 Fraserton Crt Suite 102, Burnaby, BC,
V5J 5H8
(604) 430-4336
Emp Here 400
SIC 3679 Electronic components, nec

D-U-N-S 24-365-3925   (HQ)
CREATION TECHNOLOGIES LP
8999 Fraserton Crt, Burnaby, BC, V5J 5H8
(604) 430-4336
Emp Here 90   Sales 63,655,875
SIC 3679 Electronic components, nec
Bhawnesh Mathur
Geoff Reed
Michael Conway
Steve Mceuen
Annette Cosworth
Ashley Dafel
Rodolfo Archbold
Michael Mazan
David Samuel
Michael Walsh

D-U-N-S 24-457-2772   (SL)
DEER LAKE SALES & SERVICE LTD
METROTOWN MITSUBISHI
5965 Kingsway, Burnaby, BC, V5J 1H1
(604) 434-2488
Emp Here 40   Sales 19,923,120
SIC 5511 New and used car dealers
Bruce Riddell

D-U-N-S 25-414-4983   (SL)
DNA DATA NETWORKING AND ASSEM-
BLIES LTD
8057 North Fraser Way, Burnaby, BC, V5J
5M8
(604) 439-1099
Emp Here 70   Sales 13,330,940
SIC 3678 Electronic connectors
Martin T. Pashak

D-U-N-S 24-795-4949   (SL)
FEMO CONSTRUCTION LTD
8555 Greenall Ave Suite 1, Burnaby, BC, V5J
3M8
(604) 254-3999
Emp Here 200   Sales 49,496,600
SIC 1771 Concrete work
Emilio Zanna

D-U-N-S 25-449-8983   (SL)
FIRE-PRO FIRE PROTECTION LTD

FIRE-PRO
3871 North Fraser Way Suite 15, Burnaby, BC,
V5J 5G6
(604) 299-1030
Emp Here 26   Sales 11,530,740
SIC 7389 Business services, nec
Andy Howie
Donald J Davis
Dave Diachuk

D-U-N-S 24-523-1324   (SL)
FIRST CHOICE FOODS INC
8125 North Fraser Way, Burnaby, BC, V5J
5M8
(604) 515-8885
Emp Here 30   Sales 25,067,310
SIC 5149 Groceries and related products, nec
Nashir Virani
Aaleem Virani

D-U-N-S 20-619-7659   (HQ)
FLORA MANUFACTURING AND DIS-
TRIBUTING LTD
7400 Fraser Park Dr, Burnaby, BC, V5J 5B9
(604) 436-6000
Emp Here 150   Sales 62,224,200
SIC 2032 Canned specialties
Thomas Greither

D-U-N-S 20-006-6541   (BR)
GRAND & TOY LIMITED
(Suby of OFFICE DEPOT, INC.)
4560 Tillicum St, Burnaby, BC, V5J 5L4
(866) 391-8111
Emp Here 110
SIC 5943 Stationery stores
Dean Bertram

D-U-N-S 20-728-3982   (SL)
GREER CONTRACTING LTD
6955 Buller Ave, Burnaby, BC, V5J 4S1
(604) 438-3550
Emp Here 25   Sales 11,768,275
SIC 1542 Nonresidential construction, nec
Matt Stevens

D-U-N-S 20-576-1448   (HQ)
HOULE ELECTRIC LIMITED
(Suby of H.E.L. INVESTMENTS LTD)
5050 North Fraser Way, Burnaby, BC, V5J 0H1
(604) 434-2681
Emp Here 170   Sales 211,958,100
SIC 1731 Electrical work
Robert Lashin
Rois Rizzo
Rob Locke

D-U-N-S 20-298-3008   (SL)
HUDSON PLATING AND COATING CO. LTD
HUDSON POWDER COATING
3750 North Fraser Way Unit 102, Burnaby,
V5J 5E9
(604) 430-8384
Emp Here 50   Sales 10,141,500
SIC 3479 Metal coating and allied services
Bob Scott

D-U-N-S 25-175-2499   (SL)
INTERNATIONAL CROWD MANAGEMENT
INC
6881 Russell Ave, Burnaby, BC, V5J 4R8
(604) 688-0070
Emp Here 150   Sales 140,876,550
SIC 6289 Security and commodity service
Brent Pollock

D-U-N-S 24-848-8327   (SL)
INVENTYS THERMAL TECHNOLOGIES INC
INVENTYS
8528 Glenlyon Pky Unit 143, Burnaby, BC,
V5J 0B6
(604) 456-0504
Emp Here 40   Sales 11,066,400
SIC 2813 Industrial gases
Andre Boulet
Brett Henkel

D-U-N-S 24-848-0043   (SL)

KARDIUM INC
8518 Glenlyon Pky Suite 155, Burnaby, BC, V5J 0B6
(604) 248-8891
Emp Here 50   *Sales* 11,734,800
SIC 8731 Commercial physical research
Doug Goertzen
Amos Michelson
Stefan Avall

D-U-N-S 24-368-8702   (HQ)
KEY FOOD EQUIPMENT SERVICES LTD
(*Suby of* HERITAGE FOOD SERVICE GROUP, INC.)
8528 Glenlyon Pky Suite 145, Burnaby, BC, V5J 0B6
(800) 665-2655
Emp Here 50   *Sales* 33,075,640
SIC 5023 Homefurnishings
Jean Choquette
Janon Hamel

D-U-N-S 25-539-0734   (SL)
LASFAM INVESTMENTS INC
SANI-SERVICE
3751 North Fraser Way Suite 12, Burnaby, BC, V5J 5G4
(604) 327-7264
Emp Here 70   *Sales* 17,999,170
SIC 4959 Sanitary services, nec
Elliot Laskin

D-U-N-S 20-112-9678   (HQ)
LIVANOVA CANADA CORP
REGIONAL SELLING, DIVISION OF
(*Suby of* LIVANOVA PLC)
5005 North Fraser Way, Burnaby, BC, V5J 5M1
(604) 412-5650
Emp Here 50   *Sales* 82,311,000
SIC 3841 Surgical and medical instruments
Paul Parsons
Ken Aravindan
Jennifer Arnporp

D-U-N-S 25-327-7206   (HQ)
LMI TECHNOLOGIES INC
LMI
(*Suby of* TKH GROUP N.V.)
9200 Glenlyon Pky Unit 1, Burnaby, BC, V5J 5J8
(604) 636-1011
Emp Here 136   *Sales* 39,516,178
SIC 3545 Machine tool accessories
Terry Arden
Len Chamberlain
Mark Radford

D-U-N-S 20-047-1329   (SL)
LYNCH BUS LINES LTD
4687 Byrne Rd, Burnaby, BC, V5J 3H6
(604) 439-0842
Emp Here 130   *Sales* 9,785,360
SIC 4151 School buses
Thomas Lynch

D-U-N-S 20-799-8287   (SL)
MAIL-O-MATIC SERVICES LIMITED
7550 Lowland Dr, Burnaby, BC, V5J 5A4
(604) 439-9668
Emp Here 55   *Sales* 11,644,820
SIC 7331 Direct mail advertising services
Kenneth Frew
Scott Thomson

D-U-N-S 24-930-1318   (SL)
MAKE SCENTS FLOWER DISTRIBUTORS INC
WESTCAN FLOWERS
3777 Marine Way, Burnaby, BC, V5J 5A7
(604) 433-3552
Emp Here 30   *Sales* 10,714,290
SIC 5193 Flowers and florists supplies
Darin Kreps
Darcy Kreps

D-U-N-S 20-703-7040   (SL)
MARINE ROOFING & SHEET METAL LTD

4909 Byrne Rd Suite 4, Burnaby, BC, V5J 3H6
(604) 433-4322
Emp Here 200   *Sales* 43,565,800
SIC 1761 Roofing, siding, and sheetMetal work
Gary Moss

D-U-N-S 24-012-5083   (SL)
MARINE ROOFING LTD
4909 Byrne Rd Suite 4, Burnaby, BC, V5J 3H6
(604) 433-4322
Emp Here 100   *Sales* 21,782,900
SIC 1761 Roofing, siding, and sheetMetal work
Gary Moss

D-U-N-S 25-453-1080   (SL)
MEDI-TRAN SERVICES (1993) LTD
MTS LOGISTICS
7125 Curragh Ave, Burnaby, BC, V5J 4V6
(604) 872-5293
Emp Here 50   *Sales* 22,174,500
SIC 7389 Business services, nec
Bernard Kooner
Tammy Schultz

D-U-N-S 24-899-2463   (HQ)
MEDIACO THE PRESENTATION COMPANY INC
4595 Tillicum St, Burnaby, BC, V5J 5K9
(604) 871-1000
Sales 101,610,140
SIC 7359 Equipment rental and leasing, nec
Kevin Leinbach
James Brett

D-U-N-S 20-646-0545   (HQ)
MOTION INDUSTRIES (CANADA), INC
MOTION CANADA
(*Suby of* GENUINE PARTS COMPANY)
8985 Fraserwood Ct, Burnaby, BC, V5J 5E8
(604) 521-3207
Emp Here 150   *Sales* 268,251,500
SIC 5085 Industrial supplies
Dermot Strong
Brent Pope
Timothy Breen
Paul Donahue

D-U-N-S 24-368-3427   (HQ)
MOTT ELECTRIC GENERAL PARTNERSHIP
MTI
4599 Tillicum St Suite 100, Burnaby, BC, V5J 3J9
(604) 522-5757
Emp Here 30   *Sales* 58,877,250
SIC 1731 Electrical work
Dan Mott
Robert Brett
Graham Trafford

D-U-N-S 25-387-9019   (SL)
MUSTANG SURVIVAL ULC
(*Suby of* MAUI ACQUISITION CORP.)
7525 Lowland Dr, Burnaby, BC, V5J 5L1
(604) 270-8631
Emp Here 350   *Sales* 83,584,200
SIC 3069 Fabricated rubber products, nec
James (Jim) Hartt
Sean Mccarthy

D-U-N-S 24-319-2452   (SL)
NATURAL LIFE NUTRITION INC
7337 North Fraser Way Unit 108, Burnaby, BC, V5J 0G7
(604) 207-0493
Emp Here 40   *Sales* 33,423,080
SIC 5149 Groceries and related products, nec
Yoon Deok Kim

D-U-N-S 24-286-9688   (SL)
NEW B INNOVATION LIMITED
NEW B INNOVATION CANADA
8508 Glenlyon Pky Unit 168, Burnaby, BC, V5J 0B6
(604) 421-7308
Emp Here 70   *Sales* 12,629,050

SIC 8731 Commercial physical research
Benjamin Chi Yin Wai
Bing Lou Wong
Norman Fung Man Wai

D-U-N-S 24-309-8381   (SL)
NORTH WEST WHOLESALE FLORISTS LTD
8580 Greenall Ave, Burnaby, BC, V5J 3M6
(604) 430-0593
Emp Here 26   *Sales* 19,305,520
SIC 5193 Flowers and florists supplies
Timothy Funk

D-U-N-S 25-366-4528   (SL)
PACIFIC SPECIALTY BRANDS CO. ULC
7595 Lowland Dr, Burnaby, BC, V5J 5L1
(604) 430-5253
Emp Here 27   *Sales* 12,073,698
SIC 5064 Electrical appliances, television and radio
Mike Kipp
Jody Neilstorm

D-U-N-S 25-723-8477   (SL)
PATHWAY DESIGN & MANUFACTURING INC
7400 Macpherson Ave Suite 111, Burnaby, BC, V5J 5B6
(604) 603-1053
Emp Here 55   *Sales* 11,104,335
SIC 3089 Plastics products, nec
Colin Adamson

D-U-N-S 20-172-8479   (SL)
PNP PHARMACEUTICALS INC
9388 North Fraser Cres, Burnaby, BC, V5J 0E3
(604) 435-6200
Emp Here 100   *Sales* 34,569,000
SIC 2023 Dry, condensed and evaporated dairy products
Glen North
Dennis Thneah

D-U-N-S 20-115-2550   (HQ)
REFRIGERATIVE SUPPLY
8028 North Fraser Way, Burnaby, BC, V5J 0E1
(604) 435-7151
Emp Here 20   *Sales* 57,505,500
SIC 5075 Warm air heating and air conditioning
Ray Newstead
Alison Hamilton

D-U-N-S 24-421-5039   (SL)
RITCHIE BROS. AUCTIONEERS (INTERNATIONAL) LTD
(*Suby of* RITCHIE BROS. AUCTIONEERS INCORPORATED)
9500 Glenlyon Pky Suite 300, Burnaby, BC, V5J 0C6
(778) 331-5500
Emp Here 50   *Sales* 16,280,000
SIC 5999 Miscellaneous retail stores, nec
Robert Mackay
Peter Blake

D-U-N-S 24-355-0345   (HQ)
RITCHIE BROS. AUCTIONEERS INCORPORATED
RITCHIE BROS.
9500 Glenlyon Pky, Burnaby, BC, V5J 0C6
(778) 331-5500
Emp Here 350   *Sales* 1,170,026,000
SIC 7389 Business services, nec
Ravi Saligram
Karl Werner
Brian Glenn
Doug Feick
Becky Alseth
Matt Ackley
Darren Watt
Kieran Holm
Todd Wohler
Marianne Marck

D-U-N-S 20-344-8998   (SL)

RITCHIE BROS. FINANCIAL SERVICES LTD
(*Suby of* RITCHIE BROS. AUCTIONEERS INCORPORATED)
9500 Glenlyon Pky, Burnaby, BC, V5J 0C6
(778) 331-5500
Emp Here 1,001   *Sales* 186,692,506
SIC 8742 Management consulting services
Ravi Saligram

D-U-N-S 24-760-3389   (HQ)
SENSUS COMMUNICATION SOLUTIONS INC
5589 Byrne Rd Suite 124, Burnaby, BC, V5J 3J1
(604) 263-9399
Emp Here 19   *Sales* 29,066,310
SIC 5065 Electronic parts and equipment, nec
Matthew Pratt
Kenneth W. Mahon
Kevin K Mahon
Randy M Pratt

D-U-N-S 24-380-4239   (HQ)
SILLIKER JR LABORATORIES, ULC
(*Suby of* COMPAGNIE MERIEUX ALLIANCE)
3871 North Fraser Way Unit 12, Burnaby, BC, V5J 5G6
(604) 432-9311
Emp Here 50   *Sales* 11,016,400
SIC 8734 Testing laboratories
Jimmy Chang

D-U-N-S 24-681-4552   (SL)
SISU INC
(*Suby of* KKR & CO. INC.)
7635 North Fraser Way Suite 102, Burnaby, BC, V5J 0B8
(604) 420-6610
Emp Here 50   *Sales* 55,267,250
SIC 5122 Drugs, proprietaries, and sundries
John Stephen

D-U-N-S 24-246-5797   (SL)
ST MICHAEL'S CENTRE HOSPITAL SOCIETY
ST MICHAEL'S CENTRE
7451 Sussex Ave, Burnaby, BC, V5J 5C2
(604) 434-1323
Emp Here 250   *Sales* 27,770,000
SIC 8069 Specialty hospitals, except psychiatric
Barbara Spitz
Helene Elias

D-U-N-S 25-361-0521   (HQ)
STYLUS SOFAS INC
STYLUS MADE TO ORDER SOFAS
7885 Riverfront Gate, Burnaby, BC, V5J 5L6
(604) 436-4100
Emp Here 181   *Sales* 28,549,570
SIC 2512 Upholstered household furniture
Rick Ripoli
Dennis Ripoli
Derek Barichello

D-U-N-S 24-940-4708   (SL)
SUDDEN SERVICE TECHNOLOGIES CORPORATION
SUDDEN TECHNOLOGIES
7635 North Fraser Way Unit 103, Burnaby, BC, V5J 0B8
(604) 873-3910
Emp Here 35   *Sales* 15,651,090
SIC 5045 Computers, peripherals, and software
Charles Tsoi
Kenny Tsoi
Mark Rademaker
Katherine Finnegan

D-U-N-S 25-328-2354   (HQ)
SUMAS ENVIRONMENTAL SERVICES INC
SUMAS
4623 Byrne Rd, Burnaby, BC, V5J 3H6
(604) 682-6678
Emp Here 56   *Sales* 23,141,790
SIC 4953 Refuse systems

Saeed H. Javadi
Cathy Tosling

D-U-N-S 20-172-9071   (SL)
SUN PROCESSING LTD
STAR PRODUCE
7580 Lowland Dr, Burnaby, BC, V5J 5A4
(604) 688-8372
Emp Here 53   *Sales* 44,285,581
SIC 5148 Fresh fruits and vegetables
Lori Budd
David Karwacki
Laurie Karwacki

D-U-N-S 24-857-4001   (HQ)
SUNCO FOODS INC
9208 North Fraser Cres, Burnaby, BC, V5J 0E3
(604) 451-9208
Sales 41,778,850
SIC 5149 Groceries and related products, nec
Nizar Virani
Samir Virani

D-U-N-S 25-757-6611   (SL)
THAI UNITED FOOD TRADING LTD
7978 North Fraser Way Suite 2, Burnaby, BC, V5J 0C7
(604) 437-4933
Emp Here 20   *Sales* 10,702,480
SIC 5149 Groceries and related products, nec
John Keomany
Bobby Keomany
Tommy Keomany

D-U-N-S 25-141-4488   (SL)
TIME BOMB TRADING INC
8067 North Fraser Way, Burnaby, BC, V5J 5M8
(604) 251-1097
Emp Here 60   *Sales* 29,899,320
SIC 5139 Footwear
Kinny Cheung
Nicholas Louie
Garret Louie
Kinson Cheung

D-U-N-S 24-029-4447   (HQ)
TOTEM APPLIANCE & REFRIGERATION LTD
5950 Imperial St, Burnaby, BC, V5J 4M2
(604) 437-5136
Sales 11,539,680
SIC 7629 Electrical repair shops
Rod Williscroft
Terry Levangie
Patty Wilson
Frank Beer

D-U-N-S 25-202-5838   (HQ)
TR WESTCAN INC
8035 North Fraser Way, Burnaby, BC, V5J 5M8
(604) 324-5015
Emp Here 1   *Sales* 14,605,126
SIC 4214 Local trucking with storage
Brenda Naylor

D-U-N-S 25-231-3663   (HQ)
TRANSTAR SANITATION SUPPLY LTD.
3975 North Fraser Way, Burnaby, BC, V5J 5H9
(604) 439-9585
Emp Here 19   *Sales* 11,400,624
SIC 5087 Service establishment equipment
Jasbir Mand
Donville Wolfe

D-U-N-S 20-863-2067   (HQ)
UNITED FLORAL HOLDINGS INC
UFG FLORAL SUPPLIES
4085 Marine Way, Burnaby, BC, V5J 5E2
(604) 438-3535
Sales 100,336,200
SIC 7389 Business services, nec
Robert Pringle
Kevin Snider
John Kerkhoven
Aart Breugem

Alex Vander Eyk
Stan Vander Waal

D-U-N-S 24-165-5125   (SL)
UNITED FLORAL INC
(*Suby of* UNITED FLORAL HOLDINGS INC)
4085 Marine Way, Burnaby, BC, V5J 5E2
(604) 438-3535
Emp Here 25   *Sales* 18,563,000
SIC 5193 Flowers and florists supplies
Kenny Kirby
Beverly Kirby

D-U-N-S 24-856-8586   (HQ)
URBAN BARN LTD
4085 Marine Way Unit 1, Burnaby, BC, V5J 5E2
(604) 456-2200
Emp Here 35   *Sales* 106,681,200
SIC 5712 Furniture stores
Richard Bohonis
Craig Stewart
Rosemary Pritchard
Sebastien Fauteux
Peter Schneider

D-U-N-S 24-425-0648   (SL)
VANRX PHARMASYSTEMS INC
3811 North Fraser Way Suite 200, Burnaby, BC, V5J 5J2
(604) 453-8660
Emp Here 51   *Sales* 11,322,051
SIC 3559 Special industry machinery, nec
Christopher Procyshyn
Ross Gold

D-U-N-S 20-117-1329   (HQ)
WATSON, JOHN LIMITED
WATSON GLOVES
7955 North Fraser Way, Burnaby, BC, V5J 0A4
(604) 874-1105
Emp Here 101   *Sales* 108,879,290
SIC 5136 Men's and boy's clothing
Barrie Moore
Martin Moore
Michelle Moore
John Pyper

D-U-N-S 20-800-1743   (SL)
WEE-TOTE ENTERPRISES LTD
7011 Randolph Ave, Burnaby, BC, V5J 4W5
(604) 430-1411
Emp Here 35   *Sales* 15,522,150
SIC 7389 Business services, nec
Eileen Snook

D-U-N-S 24-761-8648   (SL)
ZORBA'S BAKERY & FOODS LTD
7173 Buller Ave, Burnaby, BC, V5J 4S1
(604) 439-7731
Emp Here 22   *Sales* 18,382,694
SIC 5149 Groceries and related products, nec
Susan Dendis
Christina Mellios
Cathi Stipancik

Burnaby, BC V5K

D-U-N-S 20-026-9418   (SL)
I.A.T.S.E. LOCAL 891 MOTION PICTURE STUDIO PRODUCTION TECHTIONS
I.A.T.S.E. LOCAL 891
1640 Boundary Rd Suite 891, Burnaby, BC, V5K 4V4
(604) 664-8910
Emp Here 35   *Sales* 13,690,530
SIC 8631 Labor organizations
Ken Anderson

Burnaby, BC V5M

D-U-N-S 25-169-3966   (SL)

ELITE PACIFIC REALTY INC
SUTTON CENTRE REALTY
3010 Boundary Rd, Burnaby, BC, V5M 4A1
(604) 671-5259
Emp Here 160   *Sales* 67,022,240
SIC 6531 Real estate agents and managers
Eileen Smith-Allen
Dick Coates

D-U-N-S 24-614-0511   (HQ)
LUGARO JEWELLERS LTD
3114 Boundary Rd, Burnaby, BC, V5M 4A2
(604) 454-1200
Emp Here 7   *Sales* 12,216,400
SIC 5944 Jewelry stores
Steve Agopian

Burns Lake, BC V0J

D-U-N-S 24-898-4460   (SL)
BABINE FOREST PRODUCTS LIMITED
(*Suby of* HAMPTON LUMBER MILLS, INC.)
19479 16 Hwy E Rr 3, Burns Lake, BC, V0J 1E3
(250) 692-7177
Emp Here 150   *Sales* 97,934,625
SIC 2421 Sawmills and planing mills, general
Steve Zika

D-U-N-S 25-313-6733   (SL)
DECKER LAKE FOREST PRODUCTS LTD
(*Suby of* HAMPTON LUMBER MILLS, INC.)
Gd, Burns Lake, BC, V0J 1E0
(250) 698-7304
Emp Here 100   *Sales* 19,237,000
SIC 2421 Sawmills and planing mills, general
Gordon Would
Vicki Shaylor

D-U-N-S 24-333-9624   (SL)
HAMPTON LUMBER MILLS - CANADA, LTD
(*Suby of* HAMPTON LUMBER MILLS, INC.)
Gd, Burns Lake, BC, V0J 1E0
(250) 692-7177
Emp Here 350   *Sales* 127,928,150
SIC 6712 Bank holding companies
Steve Zika

D-U-N-S 24-825-9137   (HQ)
LAKES DISTRICT MAINTENANCE INC
881 16 Hwy W, Burns Lake, BC, V0J 1E0
(250) 692-7766
Emp Here 15   *Sales* 73,825,875
SIC 1611 Highway and street construction
Wendy Benyk
Edward Williams

D-U-N-S 20-875-3280   (BR)
NORTHERN HEALTH AUTHORITY
LAKE DISTRICT HOSPITAL
(*Suby of* NORTHERN HEALTH AUTHORITY)
741 Ctr St, Burns Lake, BC, V0J 1E0
(250) 692-2400
Emp Here 200
SIC 6324 Hospital and medical service plans
Marie Hunter

Cache Creek, BC V0K

D-U-N-S 25-312-2816   (SL)
DSM INVESTMENTS INC
HUSKY TRUCK STOP
959 Trans Canada Hwy S, Cache Creek, BC, V0K 1H0
(250) 457-9312
Emp Here 30   *Sales* 14,942,340
SIC 5541 Gasoline service stations
Dennis Peters

Campbell River, BC V9H

D-U-N-S 20-798-6258   (HQ)
DISCOVERY FOODS LTD
2207 Glenmore Rd Unit 1, Campbell River, BC, V9H 1E1
(250) 923-7733
Emp Here 30   *Sales* 10,966,080
SIC 5411 Grocery stores
Wayne Nicholas
Walter Stenback

D-U-N-S 20-279-1828   (SL)
UPLAND CONTRACTING LTD
7295 Gold River Hwy, Campbell River, BC, V9H 1P1
(250) 286-1148
Emp Here 100   *Sales* 24,618,600
SIC 1794 Excavation work
George Stuart
Mark Stuart

D-U-N-S 20-794-8308   (HQ)
UPLAND EXCAVATING LTD
7295 Gold River Hwy, Campbell River, BC, V9H 1P1
(250) 286-1148
Sales 27,335,000
SIC 6712 Bank holding companies
George Stuart

Campbell River, BC V9W

D-U-N-S 24-491-9593   (SL)
ADVANCE REALTY LTD
ROYAL LEPAGE ADVANCE
972 Shoppers Row, Campbell River, BC, V9W 2C5
(250) 202-0160
Emp Here 60   *Sales* 16,305,360
SIC 6531 Real estate agents and managers
Stephen Grant

D-U-N-S 20-146-5700   (HQ)
BILL HOWICH CHRYSLER LTD
BILL HOWICH CHRYSLER JEEP
2777 Island Hwy, Campbell River, BC, V9W 2H4
(250) 287-9133
Emp Here 10   *Sales* 20,919,276
SIC 5511 New and used car dealers
Bill Howich

D-U-N-S 20-786-4583   (SL)
BROWN, BARRIE PONTIAC BUICK GMC LTD
2700 Island Hwy, Campbell River, BC, V9W 2H5

Emp Here 26   *Sales* 12,950,028
SIC 5511 New and used car dealers
Barrie Brown

D-U-N-S 25-852-7720   (HQ)
CAMPBELL RIVER AND DISTRICT ASSOCIATION FOR COMMUNITY LIVING
C.R.A.D.A.C.L.
1153 Greenwood St, Campbell River, BC, V9W 3C5
(250) 287-9731
Emp Here 190   *Sales* 44,105,484
SIC 8399 Social services, nec
Greg Hill

D-U-N-S 24-957-4963   (HQ)
CAMPBELL RIVER FISHING CO LTD
1330 Homewood Rd, Campbell River, BC, V9W 6Y5
(250) 286-0887
Sales 16,711,540
SIC 5142 Packaged frozen goods
Takao Matsunaga
Fujio Matsunaga
Osamu Matsunaga

D-U-N-S 24-761-3698   (HQ)
CERMAQ CANADA LTD
(Suby of MC OCEAN HOLDINGS LIMITED)
919 Island Hwy Unit 203, Campbell River, BC,
V9W 2C2
(250) 286-0022
Emp Here 30   *Sales* 51,654,250
SIC 0273 Animal aquaculture
David Kiemele
Peter Harper
German Campos

D-U-N-S 20-623-6507   (SL)
CHOO KIN ENTERPRISES LTD
SEYMOUR PEOPLE DRUG MART #174
984 Shoppers Row, Campbell River, BC, V9W
2C5

Emp Here 54   *Sales* 13,193,712
SIC 5912 Drug stores and proprietary stores
Victor Choo
Judith Choo

D-U-N-S 25-936-2408   (BR)
COAST HOTELS LIMITED
COAST DISCOVERY INN & MARINA
(Suby of OKABE CO., LTD.)
975 Shoppers Row, Campbell River, BC, V9W
2C4
(250) 287-9225
Emp Here 75
SIC 7011 Hotels and motels
Sukhy Bains

D-U-N-S 25-129-3809   (BR)
COMOX VALLEY REGIONAL DISTRICT
STRATHCONA GARDENS RECREATION
(Suby of COMOX VALLEY REGIONAL DIS-
TRICT)
225 Dogwood St S, Campbell River, BC, V9W
8C8
(250) 287-9234
Emp Here 88
SIC 7999 Amusement and recreation, nec
Ray Boogaards

D-U-N-S 24-135-1477   (HQ)
CR 92 HOLDINGS LTD
COASTAL MOUNTAIN FUELS
1720 Maple St, Campbell River, BC, V9W 3G2
(250) 287-4214
Emp Here 9   *Sales* 14,459,312
SIC 5172 Petroleum products, nec
Stephen Gabrysh

D-U-N-S 25-290-4586   (SL)
GRIEG SEAFOOD B.C. LTD
1180 Ironwood St Suite 106, Campbell River,
BC, V9W 5P7
(250) 286-0838
Emp Here 110   *Sales* 22,727,870
SIC 0912 Finfish
Rocky Boschman

D-U-N-S 24-804-3098   (SL)
GTA GOLF
500 Colwyn St Suite 58, Campbell River, BC,
V9W 5J2
(250) 255-8897
Emp Here 120   *Sales* 9,425,400
SIC 7997 Membership sports and recreation
clubs

D-U-N-S 24-980-3446   (HQ)
**KETZA PACIFIC CONSTRUCTION (1993)
LTD**
2990 Island Hwy, Campbell River, BC, V9W
2H5
(250) 850-2002
Sales 17,110,140
SIC 1542 Nonresidential construction, nec
Wayne Schofield
Tyler Schofield

D-U-N-S 25-148-7583   (BR)
LOBLAWS INC
REAL CANADIAN SUPERSTORE
(Suby of LOBLAW COMPANIES LIMITED)

1424 Island Hwy Suite 1524, Campbell River,
BC, V9W 8C9
(250) 830-2736
Emp Here 200
SIC 5411 Grocery stores
Gary Ogorodnik

D-U-N-S 24-207-5146   (HQ)
MARINE HARVEST NORTH AMERICA INC
1334 Island Hwy Suite 124, Campbell River,
BC, V9W 8C9
(250) 850-3276
Emp Here 3   *Sales* 201,029,950
SIC 6712 Bank holding companies
Vincent Ernest

D-U-N-S 20-094-1367   (SL)
MARSHALL, STEVE MOTORS (1996) LTD
STEVE MARSHALL FORD
2300 Island Hwy, Campbell River, BC, V9W
2G8
(250) 287-9171
Emp Here 75   *Sales* 47,196,000
SIC 5511 New and used car dealers
Steve Marshall

D-U-N-S 24-573-8695   (HQ)
MOWI CANADA WEST INC
(Suby of MARINE HARVEST NORTH AMER-
ICA INC)
1334 Island Hwy Suite 124, Campbell River,
BC, V9W 8C9
(250) 850-3276
Emp Here 50   *Sales* 113,639,350
SIC 0273 Animal aquaculture
Vincent Ernest
Chris Leighton

D-U-N-S 20-040-5210   (BR)
NORTH ISLAND COLLEGE
1685 Dogwood St S, Campbell River, BC,
V9W 8C1
(250) 923-9700
Emp Here 200
SIC 8221 Colleges and universities
Lou Dryden

D-U-N-S 20-581-4002   (HQ)
NYRSTAR MYRA FALLS LTD.
(Suby of NYRSTAR)
1 Boliden Mine St, Campbell River, BC, V9W
5E2
(250) 287-9271
Emp Here 379   *Sales* 156,981,420
SIC 1481 NonMetallic mineral services
John Galassini
Sara Smith

D-U-N-S 24-535-1663   (SL)
OCEAN PACIFIC MARINE SUPPLY LTD
1370 Island Hwy Suite 102, Campbell River,
BC, V9W 8C9
(250) 286-1011
Emp Here 30   *Sales* 14,250,780
SIC 5088 Transportation equipment and sup-
plies
Bruce Kempling

D-U-N-S 25-129-6067   (SL)
RON DITTBERNER LTD
CANADIAN TIRE
1444 Island Hwy, Campbell River, BC, V9W
8C9
(250) 286-0122
Emp Here 80   *Sales* 21,412,160
SIC 5251 Hardware stores
Ron Dittberner

D-U-N-S 24-137-2440   (SL)
ROYAL COACHMAN INN LTD, THE
84 Dogwood St, Campbell River, BC, V9W
2X7
(250) 286-0231
Emp Here 48   *Sales* 14,358,240
SIC 5921 Liquor stores
Theresa Marson
Earle Phillips

D-U-N-S 20-995-8107   (SL)
SCEPTER DRUGS LTD
SHOPPERS DRUG MART
1297 Shoppers Row Suite 209, Campbell
River, BC, V9W 2C7
(250) 286-1166
Emp Here 47   *Sales* 11,888,838
SIC 5912 Drug stores and proprietary stores
Derek Michael Obertas

D-U-N-S 25-417-4022   (SL)
SEYMOUR PACIFIC DEVELOPMENTS LTD
100 St. Ann'S Rd, Campbell River, BC, V9W
4C4
(250) 286-8045
Emp Here 150   *Sales* 40,641,300
SIC 1522 Residential construction, nec
Krisjan Daniel Mailman

D-U-N-S 24-029-7788   (SL)
TAT PROPERTIES LTD
Gd Stn A, Campbell River, BC, V9W 4Z8
(250) 287-7813
Emp Here 100   *Sales* 26,155,300
SIC 6712 Bank holding companies
Brian Armstrong

D-U-N-S 24-695-9092   (SL)
TYEE CHEVROLET BUICK GMC LTD
570 13th Ave, Campbell River, BC, V9W 4G8
(250) 287-9511
Emp Here 35   *Sales* 17,432,730
SIC 5511 New and used car dealers
Brian Mclean

D-U-N-S 25-896-1614   (SL)
UNCLE RAY'S RESTAURANT CO. LTD
MCDONALD'S RESTAURANT
1361 16th Ave, Campbell River, BC, V9W 2C9
(250) 287-2631
Emp Here 100   *Sales* 4,551,900
SIC 5812 Eating places
Jens Rolinski

D-U-N-S 20-789-5199   (SL)
**WATSON & ASH TRANSPORTATION COM-
PANY LTD**
1050 9th Ave, Campbell River, BC, V9W 4C2
(250) 287-7433
Emp Here 30   *Sales* 11,560,800
SIC 4731 Freight transportation arrangement
Leo Richards

D-U-N-S 20-191-3139   (HQ)
WAYPOINT INSURANCE SERVICES INC
PORT HARDY INSURANCENTRE
1400 Dogwood St Unit 700, Campbell River,
BC, V9W 3A6
(250) 287-9184
Emp Here 10   *Sales* 267,922,590
SIC 6411 Insurance agents, brokers, and ser-
vice
Richard Burley

Castlegar, BC V1N

D-U-N-S 25-055-2031   (SL)
526293 BC LTD
EXTRA FOODS
1502 Columbia Ave Unit 1, Castlegar, BC,
V1N 4G5
(250) 304-2470
Emp Here 52   *Sales* 15,260,804
SIC 5411 Grocery stores
Tom Zelke

D-U-N-S 24-030-2869   (SL)
**KALAWSKY PONTIAC BUICK G M C (1989)
LTD**
(Suby of KALAWSKY MANAGEMENT SER-
VICES LTD)
1700 Columbia Ave, Castlegar, BC, V1N 2W4
(250) 365-2155
Emp Here 25   *Sales* 12,451,950

SIC 5511 New and used car dealers
Neil Kalawsky
Darlene Kalawsky

D-U-N-S 20-108-0751   (SL)
KALESNIKOFF LUMBER CO. LTD
2090 3a Hwy, Castlegar, BC, V1N 4N1
(250) 399-4211
Emp Here 100   *Sales* 15,586,300
SIC 2421 Sawmills and planing mills, general
Kenneth Kalesnikoff

D-U-N-S 20-690-3531   (SL)
MERCER CELGAR PULP LTD
(Suby of MERCER INTERNATIONAL INC)
1921 Arrow Lakes Dr, Castlegar, BC, V1N 3H9
(250) 365-7211
Emp Here 420   *Sales* 154,407,540
SIC 2611 Pulp mills
Jimmy Lee
David M Gandossi

D-U-N-S 24-329-8874   (HQ)
SELKIRK COLLEGE
301 Frank Beinder Way, Castlegar, BC, V1N
4L3
(250) 365-7292
Emp Here 250   *Sales* 36,688,987
SIC 8221 Colleges and universities
Angus Graeme

D-U-N-S 20-429-3591   (HQ)
WEST ARM TRUCK LINES LTD
1077 Columbia Rd, Castlegar, BC, V1N 4K5
(250) 365-2127
Emp Here 20   *Sales* 20,570,600
SIC 4213 Trucking, except local
Jim O'connor

D-U-N-S 20-378-2875   (SL)
**ZELLSTOFF CELGAR LIMITED PARTNER-
SHIP**
(Suby of MERCER INTERNATIONAL INC)
1921 Arrow Lakes Dr, Castlegar, BC, V1N 3H9
(250) 365-7211
Emp Here 420   *Sales* 154,407,540
SIC 2611 Pulp mills
Jimmy Lee
David M Gandossi

Charlie Lake, BC V0C

D-U-N-S 25-415-3695   (HQ)
ENERGETIC SERVICES INC
13366 Tompkins Frontage Rd, Charlie Lake,
BC, V0C 1H0
(250) 785-4761
Emp Here 50   *Sales* 45,742,172
SIC 1389 Oil and gas field services, nec
Brennan Ross
Ryan Ross
William (Bill) Mcfetridge
Kent Jensen
Ingrid Jeannotte

Chase, BC V0E

D-U-N-S 20-528-7209   (SL)
ECONOSPAN STRUCTURES CORP
472 Aylmer Rd, Chase, BC, V0E 1M1
(250) 679-3400
Emp Here 50   *Sales* 10,141,500
SIC 3448 Prefabricated Metal buildings and
components
Douglas Nelson

D-U-N-S 24-724-9717   (BR)
INTERFOR CORPORATION
ADAMS LAKE LUMBER
(Suby of INTERFOR CORPORATION)
9200 Holding Rd Suite 2, Chase, BC, V0E

1M2
(250) 679-3234
Emp Here 200
SIC 2421 Sawmills and planing mills, general
Larry Price

D-U-N-S 24-029-3944   (SL)
SAFETY MART NO. 7 (2001) LTD
SAFETY MART FOODS
305 Brook Dr Unit 6, Chase, BC, V0E 1M0
(250) 679-8515
Emp Here 48   *Sales* 13,159,296
SIC 5411 Grocery stores
Brooke Kynoch
Linda Kynoch

Chemainus, BC V0R

D-U-N-S 20-574-6410   (SL)
CHEMAINUS HEALTH CARE CENTRE
9909 Esplanade St, Chemainus, BC, V0R 1K1
(250) 737-2040
Emp Here 100   *Sales* 8,183,300
SIC 8069 Specialty hospitals, except psychiatric
Wendy Carmichael

D-U-N-S 25-504-9181   (SL)
ISLAND INDEPENDENT BUYING GROUP LTD
COUNTRY GROCER
3110 Hope Pl, Chemainus, BC, V0R 1K4
(250) 246-1828
Emp Here 38   *Sales* 31,751,926
SIC 5141 Groceries, general line
Walter Martin Large
Henry Zwynenburg
Peter Cavin
Mark Wilson

D-U-N-S 20-192-7568   (SL)
ISLAND PACIFIC LOGGING LTD
3473 Smiley Rd Rr 4, Chemainus, BC, V0R 1K4
(250) 246-1414
Emp Here 200   *Sales* 38,474,000
SIC 2411 Logging
Lyle Newton

D-U-N-S 20-094-4338   (SL)
JONES MARINE GROUP LTD
9871 Esplanade St, Chemainus, BC, V0R 1K1
(250) 246-1100
Emp Here 60   *Sales* 16,172,940
SIC 4492 Towing and tugboat service
Daryl Jones

D-U-N-S 25-366-8859   (BR)
WESTERN FOREST PRODUCTS INC
CHEMAINUS SAWMILL
(*Suby of* WESTERN FOREST PRODUCTS INC)
2860 Victoria St, Chemainus, BC, V0R 1K0
(250) 246-3221
Emp Here 190
SIC 2611 Pulp mills
Mark Buckley

D-U-N-S 20-561-3768   (BR)
WESTERN FOREST PRODUCTS INC
VALUE ADDED REMAN
(*Suby of* WESTERN FOREST PRODUCTS INC)
9469 Trans Canada Hwy, Chemainus, BC, V0R 1K4
(250) 246-1566
Emp Here 75
SIC 2611 Pulp mills
David Turnbull

Chetwynd, BC V0C

D-U-N-S 20-821-0984   (SL)
DUZ CHO CONSTRUCTION LIMITED PARTNERSHIP
4821 Access Rd S, Chetwynd, BC, V0C 1J0
(250) 788-3120
Emp Here 50   *Sales* 13,477,450
SIC 4619 Pipelines, nec
Arlene Salones

D-U-N-S 24-333-3437   (BR)
PEACE VALLEY INDUSTRIES (2016) LTD
PEACE VALLEY INDUSTRIES
(*Suby of* PEACE VALLEY INDUSTRIES (2016) LTD)
4311 46th St, Chetwynd, BC, V0C 1J0
(250) 788-2922
Emp Here 206
SIC 7692 Welding repair
Robin Perish

D-U-N-S 24-066-8665   (BR)
WEST FRASER MILLS LTD
CHETWYND FOREST INDUSTRIES
(*Suby of* WEST FRASER TIMBER CO. LTD)
3598 Fraser St W, Chetwynd, BC, V0C 1J0
(250) 788-2686
Emp Here 200
SIC 2421 Sawmills and planing mills, general
Darren Brkic

D-U-N-S 20-094-5194   (SL)
WESTWARD ENTERPRISES LTD
IGA
5001 50th Ave, Chetwynd, BC, V0C 1J0
(250) 788-2422
Emp Here 40   *Sales* 10,966,080
SIC 5411 Grocery stores
Kim Stewart
Edward R Chychul

Chilliwack, BC V2P

D-U-N-S 20-803-7812   (SL)
BARNES WHEATON CHEVROLET CADILLAC LTD
46125 Olds Dr, Chilliwack, BC, V2P 0B5
(604) 792-1391
Emp Here 50   *Sales* 25,192,335
SIC 5511 New and used car dealers
Fred Meyerink
Karen Armstrong
Greg Barnes

D-U-N-S 20-718-3711   (SL)
CHILLIWACK GENERAL HOSPITAL
45600 Menholm Rd, Chilliwack, BC, V2P 1P7
(604) 795-4141
Emp Here 249   *Sales* 27,658,920
SIC 8062 General medical and surgical hospitals
Elma Pauls

D-U-N-S 20-623-7885   (SL)
CHILLIWACK TAXI LTD
45877 Hocking Ave, Chilliwack, BC, V2P 1B5
(604) 795-9111
Emp Here 85   *Sales* 4,664,120
SIC 4121 Taxicabs
Harjinder Sandhu
Omkar Hundal

D-U-N-S 20-788-7949   (SL)
DAVIS, ANN TRANSITION SOCIETY
ANN DAVIS SRVC
9046 Young Rd, Chilliwack, BC, V2P 4R6
(604) 792-2760
Emp Here 25   *Sales* 10,615,175
SIC 8999 Services, nec
Patti Macaahonic

D-U-N-S 24-394-8820   (SL)
DEVRY CUSTOM WORK LTD
49259 Castleman Rd, Chilliwack, BC, V2P 6H4

(604) 794-3874
Emp Here 100   *Sales* 26,155,300
SIC 6712 Bank holding companies
Arie Devrij
Bertha Devrij

D-U-N-S 25-635-0380   (HQ)
DEVRY GREENHOUSES (1989) LTD
DEVRY GROUP OF COMPANIES
49259 Castleman Rd, Chilliwack, BC, V2P 6H4
(604) 794-3874
Emp Here 100   *Sales* 26,765,200
SIC 5261 Retail nurseries and garden stores
Arie De Vrij
Peter De Vrij
Arnold De Vrij
Bertha De Vrij
Willeke De Vrij

D-U-N-S 25-782-1777   (BR)
EDENVALE RESTORATION SPECIALISTS LTD
8465 Harvard Pl Suite 5, Chilliwack, BC, V2P 7Z5
(604) 795-4884
Emp Here 200
SIC 1542 Nonresidential construction, nec
Debbie Emerson

D-U-N-S 24-595-1850   (SL)
FAIRFIELD PROPAGATORS LTD
10718 Bell Rd, Chilliwack, BC, V2P 6H5
(604) 792-9988
Emp Here 34   *Sales* 11,643,878
SIC 0181 Ornamental nursery products
Jan Sommer
Jane Sommer
Dianne Venhoeben

D-U-N-S 24-120-3871   (BR)
FIRST WEST CREDIT UNION
ENVISION FINANCIAL
(*Suby of* FIRST WEST CREDIT UNION)
9240 Young Rd, Chilliwack, BC, V2P 4R2
(604) 539-7300
Emp Here 800
SIC 6062 State credit unions
Ruth Mcmaccan

D-U-N-S 25-956-5273   (HQ)
FORTIN'S SUPPLY LTD
45750 Airport Rd, Chilliwack, BC, V2P 1A2
(604) 795-9739
Emp Here 22   *Sales* 10,926,450
SIC 5013 Motor vehicle supplies and new parts
Jeffrey Fortin
Shauna Fortin

D-U-N-S 25-451-4839   (BR)
FRASER HEALTH AUTHORITY
CHILLIWACK HEALTH UNIT
(*Suby of* GOVERNMENT OF THE PROVINCE OF BRITISH COLUMBIA)
45470 Menholm Rd, Chilliwack, BC, V2P 1M2
(604) 702-4900
Emp Here 150
SIC 8011 Offices and clinics of medical doctors

D-U-N-S 20-512-1817   (HQ)
FRASER VALLEY MEAT SUPPLIES LTD
45735 Alexander Ave, Chilliwack, BC, V2P 1L6
(604) 792-4723
Emp Here 25   *Sales* 10,966,080
SIC 5421 Meat and fish markets
Ken Kooyman
Jeff Kooyman

D-U-N-S 24-424-4252   (SL)
GORE BROTHERS VINTAGE HOMES INC
10805 Mcdonald Rd, Chilliwack, BC, V2P 6H5
(604) 824-1902
Emp Here 45   *Sales* 14,349,105
SIC 1521 Single-family housing construction
Tony Gore

D-U-N-S 24-327-2478   (SL)
HOANA DRUGS LTD
SHOPPERS DRUG MART
45905 Yale Rd Unit 30, Chilliwack, BC, V2P 2M6
(604) 792-7377
Emp Here 60   *Sales* 14,659,680
SIC 5912 Drug stores and proprietary stores
George Ho

D-U-N-S 20-798-3446   (HQ)
HUB INTERNATIONAL CANADA WEST ULC
HUB INTERNATIONAL BARTON INSURANCE BROKERS
(*Suby of* HELLMAN & FRIEDMAN LLC)
8346 Noble Rd, Chilliwack, BC, V2P 6R5
(604) 703-7070
Emp Here 40   *Sales* 2,373,052,000
SIC 6411 Insurance agents, brokers, and service
Chad Robertson
Mark Pyka

D-U-N-S 25-892-8407   (BR)
MCDONALD'S RESTAURANTS OF CANADA LIMITED
MCDONALD'S
(*Suby of* MCDONALD'S CORPORATION)
45816 Yale Rd, Chilliwack, BC, V2P 2N7
(604) 795-5911
Emp Here 100
SIC 5812 Eating places
Geoff Grace

D-U-N-S 20-094-5509   (SL)
MERTIN CHEVROLET CADILLAC PONTIAC BUICK GMC LTD
MERTIN G M LEASING
45930 Airport Rd, Chilliwack, BC, V2P 1A2
(604) 795-9104
Emp Here 120   *Sales* 75,513,600
SIC 5511 New and used car dealers
Harry Mertin

D-U-N-S 20-873-2375   (SL)
MERTIN HYUNDAI
45753 Yale Rd, Chilliwack, BC, V2P 2N5
(604) 702-1000
Emp Here 25   *Sales* 12,451,950
SIC 5511 New and used car dealers
Harry Mertin

D-U-N-S 24-809-8365   (SL)
MERTIN NISSAN
8287 Young Rd, Chilliwack, BC, V2P 4N8
(604) 792-8218
Emp Here 30   *Sales* 14,942,340
SIC 5511 New and used car dealers
Jason Arnold

D-U-N-S 20-992-5643   (HQ)
O'CONNOR MOTORS LTD
O'CONNOR DODGE CHRYSLER JEEP
45730 Hocking Ave, Chilliwack, BC, V2P 1B3
(604) 792-2754
Emp Here 35   *Sales* 35,868,960
SIC 5511 New and used car dealers
John O'connor
Shane O'connor
Sylvia Jardine

D-U-N-S 20-094-7489   (SL)
PIONEER BUILDING SUPPLIES LTD
PIONEER TIM-BR MART
45754 Yale Rd, Chilliwack, BC, V2P 2N4
(604) 795-7238
Emp Here 43   *Sales* 10,881,537
SIC 5211 Lumber and other building materials
John Giesbrecht
Barry Giesbrecht
Beatrice Giesbrecht
Shirley Giesbrecht
Donna Giesbrecht
Wendy Murphy
Randall Giesbrecth

▲ Public Company   ■ Public Company Family Member   **HQ** Headquarters   **BR** Branch   **SL** Single Location

D-U-N-S 24-163-5119   (HQ)
SCHOOL DISTRICT NO 33 CHILLIWACK
8430 Cessna Dr, Chilliwack, BC, V2P 7K4
(604) 792-1321
Emp Here 60   *Sales* 116,390,852
SIC 8211 Elementary and secondary schools
Walt Krahn
Silvia Dyck

D-U-N-S 25-538-7888   (BR)
SCHOOL DISTRICT NO 33 CHILLIWACK
CHILLIWACK SECONDARY SCHOOL
(*Suby of* SCHOOL DISTRICT NO 33 CHILLI-WACK)
46363 Yale Rd, Chilliwack, BC, V2P 2P8
(604) 795-7295
Emp Here 92
SIC 8211 Elementary and secondary schools
David Manuel

D-U-N-S 20-985-1885   (HQ)
TEKSMED SERVICES INC
QUICKCARE
8635 Young Rd Suite 7, Chilliwack, BC, V2P 4P3
(604) 702-3380
Emp Here 42   *Sales* 110,864,520
SIC 6411 Insurance agents, brokers, and service
Ted Shipley

D-U-N-S 20-373-3352   (BR)
TROUW NUTRITION CANADA INC
46255 Chilliwack Central Rd, Chilliwack, BC, V2P 1J7
(604) 702-4500
Emp Here 85
SIC 2048 Prepared feeds, nec
Paul Goerzen

D-U-N-S 24-646-3046   (SL)
VT VENTURES INC
VALLEY TOYOTA
8750 Young Rd, Chilliwack, BC, V2P 4P4
(604) 792-1167
Emp Here 43   *Sales* 21,417,354
SIC 5511 New and used car dealers
Ronald Gibson
Frederick Gibson
Larry Mcclure

D-U-N-S 24-042-6176   (BR)
YMCA OF GREATER VANCOUVER, THE
YOUNG MEN'S CHRISTIAN ASSOCIATION OF GREATER VANCOUVER
(*Suby of* YMCA OF GREATER VANCOUVER, THE)
45844 Hocking Ave, Chilliwack, BC, V2P 1B4
(604) 792-3371
Emp Here 75
SIC 7999 Amusement and recreation, nec
Sheri Josephson

Chilliwack, BC V2R

D-U-N-S 25-231-5197   (SL)
639809 BC LTD
RICKYS ALL DAY GRILL
45389 Luckakuck Way Unit 100, Chilliwack, BC, V2R 3V1
(604) 858-5663
Emp Here 45   *Sales* 18,870,975
SIC 6712 Bank holding companies
Robert Matzek

D-U-N-S 20-232-2256   (SL)
ATCHELITZ THREHERMEN'S ASSOCIATION
ATA
44146 Luckakuck Way, Chilliwack, BC, V2R 4A7
(604) 858-2119
Emp Here 25   *Sales* 11,230,475
SIC 7389 Business services, nec

Casey Van Den Dorple
Ronald Finnigan

D-U-N-S 20-094-5285   (HQ)
AULD PHILLIPS LTD
AULD PHILLIPS
8040 Evans Rd, Chilliwack, BC, V2R 5R8
(604) 792-8518
Emp Here 20   *Sales* 21,527,520
SIC 5621 Women's clothing stores
James D Gilbert
Stephen J Bowen

D-U-N-S 25-196-0233   (SL)
BEKAR & ASSOCIATES ENTERPRISES LIMITED
MARK'S WORK WEARHOUSE
45737 Luckakuck Way, Chilliwack, BC, V2R 4E8
(604) 858-4199
Emp Here 100   *Sales* 17,939,600
SIC 5699 Miscellaneous apparel and accessory stores
Brian Bekar
Steve Bekar
Sharon Bekar

D-U-N-S 24-446-5001   (SL)
CANEX BUILDING SUPPLIES LTD
46070 Knight Rd, Chilliwack, BC, V2R 1B7
(604) 858-8188
Emp Here 60   *Sales* 26,830,440
SIC 5039 Construction materials, nec
Bruce Kehler
Bruce Van Den Brink

D-U-N-S 20-937-0407   (SL)
COOKIES GRILL
44335 Yale Rd Suite 3a, Chilliwack, BC, V2R 4H2
(604) 792-0444
Emp Here 69   *Sales* 20,249,913
SIC 5461 Retail bakeries
Colleen Connolly

D-U-N-S 24-503-9060   (SL)
FRASER VALLEY DUCK & GOOSE LTD
(*Suby of* TWIN MAPLE PRODUCE LTD)
4540 Simmons Rd, Chilliwack, BC, V2R 4R7
(604) 823-4435
Emp Here 65   *Sales* 22,469,850
SIC 2015 Poultry slaughtering and processing
Abe Falk
Ken Falk
Ron Born

D-U-N-S 20-232-2017   (SL)
FRASER VALLEY ROOFING LTD
44687 Chalmer Pl, Chilliwack, BC, V2R 0H8
(604) 795-6620
Emp Here 70   *Sales* 15,248,030
SIC 1761 Roofing, siding, and sheetMetal work
Wesley Peters

D-U-N-S 24-724-3579   (SL)
FREEBORN MOTORS LTD
PERFORMANCE HONDA
44954 Yale Rd W, Chilliwack, BC, V2R 4H1
(604) 792-2724
Emp Here 22   *Sales* 10,957,716
SIC 5511 New and used car dealers
Marvin Jones

D-U-N-S 20-293-6555   (SL)
FRONTLINE MACHINERY LTD
43779 Progress Way, Chilliwack, BC, V2R 0E6
(604) 625-2009
Emp Here 30   *Sales* 14,529,024
SIC 5082 Construction and mining machinery
Daryl Todd
Royden Todd
Steve Todd
Dinora Swanson

D-U-N-S 24-225-5029   (SL)
GARRISON ESTATES INC
5905 Cowichan St, Chilliwack, BC, V2R 0G8

(604) 634-3508
Emp Here 40   *Sales* 12,754,760
SIC 1521 Single-family housing construction
Mark Gore

D-U-N-S 24-802-2456   (SL)
HARMONIC MACHINE INC
44365 Progress Way, Chilliwack, BC, V2R 0L1
(604) 823-4479
Emp Here 55   *Sales* 12,210,055
SIC 3599 Industrial machinery, nec
Nathan Neels

D-U-N-S 24-682-0125   (HQ)
IMW INDUSTRIES LTD
CLEAN ENERGY COMPRESSION
(*Suby of* GIREFIN SPA)
44688 South Sumas Rd Unit 610, Chilliwack, BC, V2R 5M3
(604) 795-9491
Sales 60,807,750
SIC 3491 Industrial valves
Andrew J. Littlefair
Stephen Scully
Nate Jensen
Chad M. Lindholm
Robert Vreeland
Mitchell Pratt
Tyler Henn

D-U-N-S 25-965-3863   (SL)
JOHNSTON PACKERS (1995) LTD
5828 Promontory Rd, Chilliwack, BC, V2R 4M4
(604) 858-4882
Emp Here 113   *Sales* 39,062,970
SIC 2011 Meat packing plants
Matthew Ball

D-U-N-S 25-643-0489   (HQ)
JOHNSTON PACKERS LTD
JOHNSTON BUTCHER SHOP
7339 Vedder Rd, Chilliwack, BC, V2R 4E4
(604) 824-1985
Emp Here 15   *Sales* 32,840,550
SIC 2011 Meat packing plants
Donald Ball

D-U-N-S 25-360-1298   (BR)
JOHNSTON PACKERS LTD
(*Suby of* JOHNSTON PACKERS LTD)
5828 Promontory Rd, Chilliwack, BC, V2R 4M4
(604) 858-4121
Emp Here 100
SIC 2011 Meat packing plants
Ivan Tenbos

D-U-N-S 24-640-3976   (SL)
LICKMAN TRAVEL CENTRE INC
BEST WESTERN RAINBOW COUNTRY INN
43971 Industrial Way Suite 2, Chilliwack, BC, V2R 3A4
(604) 795-3828
Emp Here 80   *Sales* 7,591,920
SIC 7011 Hotels and motels
Don Ball
Hans Bodden

D-U-N-S 20-299-1501   (SL)
MURRAY MOTORS CHILLIWACK LIMITED PARTNERSHIP
MURRAY HONDA CHILLIWACK
44954 Yale Rd W, Chilliwack, BC, V2R 4H1
(604) 792-2724
Emp Here 30   *Sales* 14,942,340
SIC 5511 New and used car dealers
Charles Van Den Braek
Darren Bosch
Deborah Francis

D-U-N-S 25-168-3389   (SL)
NADEAU, MARCEL MANAGEMENT INC
CANADIAN TIRE
7560 Vedder Rd, Chilliwack, BC, V2R 4E7
(604) 858-7230
Emp Here 80   *Sales* 50,342,400
SIC 5531 Auto and home supply stores

Marcel Nadeau

D-U-N-S 24-695-9720   (SL)
O'CONNOR RV CENTRES
O'CONNOR RV CENTRES
44430 Yale Rd, Chilliwack, BC, V2R 4H1
(604) 792-2747
Emp Here 39   *Sales* 19,425,042
SIC 5561 Recreational vehicle dealers
John O'connor
Shane O'connor

D-U-N-S 24-594-5548   (SL)
PACIFIC DAIRY CENTRE LTD
8558 Chilliwack Mountain Rd, Chilliwack, BC, V2R 3W8
(604) 852-9020
Emp Here 30   *Sales* 14,250,780
SIC 5083 Farm and garden machinery
John Bruinsma
Garry Franz

D-U-N-S 20-790-8349   (SL)
PALADIN VANCOUVER SECURITY SYSTEMS LTD
4691 Wilson Rd, Chilliwack, BC, V2R 5C4
(604) 823-2428
Emp Here 30   *Sales* 12,525,180
SIC 7382 Security systems services
Ted Reid

D-U-N-S 24-631-2933   (BR)
PRAIRIECOAST EQUIPMENT INC
(*Suby of* PRAIRIECOAST EQUIPMENT INC)
44158 Progress Way, Chilliwack, BC, V2R 0W3
(604) 792-1516
Emp Here 250
SIC 5083 Farm and garden machinery

D-U-N-S 24-867-4095   (SL)
RAINBOW GREENHOUSES INC
RAINBOW
43756 South Sumas Rd, Chilliwack, BC, V2R 4L6
(604) 858-8100
Emp Here 190   *Sales* 32,025,053
SIC 0181 Ornamental nursery products
Stanley Vander Waal
Wilma Vander Waal

D-U-N-S 20-512-0082   (SL)
SARDIS EXPLOSIVES (2000) LTD
WESTERN EXPLOSIVES
6890 Lickman Rd, Chilliwack, BC, V2R 4A9
(604) 858-6919
Emp Here 20   *Sales* 10,006,500
SIC 5169 Chemicals and allied products, nec
Bryan Kirkness

D-U-N-S 25-538-7938   (BR)
SCHOOL DISTRICT NO 33 CHILLIWACK
SARDIS SECONDARY SCHOOL
(*Suby of* SCHOOL DISTRICT NO 33 CHILLI-WACK)
45460 Stevenson Rd, Chilliwack, BC, V2R 2Z6
(604) 858-9424
Emp Here 120
SIC 8211 Elementary and secondary schools
Diego Testa

D-U-N-S 24-940-1431   (SL)
SHOKER FARMS LTD
46825 Bailey Rd, Chilliwack, BC, V2R 4S8
(604) 824-1541
Emp Here 80   *Sales* 20,984,720
SIC 0139 Field crops, except cash grain
Ajit Shoker
Manjit Shoker

D-U-N-S 20-514-3378   (BR)
STREAM INTERNATIONAL CANADA ULC
SOLECTRON GLOBAL SERVICES
(*Suby of* SYNNEX CORPORATION)
7955 Evans Rd, Chilliwack, BC, V2R 5R7
(604) 702-5100
Emp Here 1,100

SIC 7389 Business services, nec
Michael Robinson

D-U-N-S 24-374-0990   (BR)
UNIVERSITY OF THE FRASER VALLEY
UCFV
(*Suby of* UNIVERSITY OF THE FRASER VALLEY)
45190 Caen Ave, Chilliwack, BC, V2R 0N3
(604) 792-0025
Emp Here 600
SIC 8221 Colleges and universities
Jackie Snodjrass

D-U-N-S 25-452-3868   (SL)
VANCOUVER   WATER   ENTERPRISES CANADA CO., LTD
44488 South Sumas Rd Suite 125, Chilliwack, BC, V2R 5M3
(604) 824-7455
Emp Here 20   *Sales* 10,702,480
SIC 5149 Groceries and related products, nec
Ying Chun Wang
Ning Ma

D-U-N-S 20-015-2200   (BR)
VANTAGE FOODS INC
(*Suby of* WESTAR FOODS LTD)
8200 Brannick Pl, Chilliwack, BC, V2R 0E9
(604) 795-4774
Emp Here 150
SIC 2011 Meat packing plants
John Bannerman

D-U-N-S 25-416-0518   (HQ)
VISSCHER LUMBER INC
VISSCHER SPECIALTY PRODUCTS
6545 Lickman Rd, Chilliwack, BC, V2R 4A9
(604) 858-3375
Sales 39,873,960
SIC 5031 Lumber, plywood, and millwork
Peter L Visscher
Darrell Balbar
Theodore Visscher
Peter Visscher
Art Dekker
Leonard Visscher
Christopher Visscher

D-U-N-S 24-798-5880   (HQ)
W. I. WOODTONE INDUSTRIES INC
8007 Aitken Rd, Chilliwack, BC, V2R 4H5
(604) 792-3680
Sales 53,273,376
SIC 5031 Lumber, plywood, and millwork
James Young
Christopher Young
Kevin Young

D-U-N-S 25-498-2598   (BR)
WAL-MART CANADA CORP
(*Suby of* WALMART INC.)
45610 Luckakuck Way Unit 200, Chilliwack, BC, V2R 1A2
(604) 858-5100
Emp Here 150
SIC 5311 Department stores
Kerton Wendy

D-U-N-S 20-287-1211   (HQ)
WESTECK WINDOWS MFG. INC
WESTECK WINDOWS & DOORS
8104 Evans Rd, Chilliwack, BC, V2R 5R8
(604) 792-6700
Sales 29,441,720
SIC 5211 Lumber and other building materials
Casey Kerkhoff

D-U-N-S 25-416-0476   (HQ)
WESTFORM METALS INC
6435 Lickman Rd, Chilliwack, BC, V2R 4A9
(604) 858-7134
Emp Here 65   *Sales* 38,461,540
SIC 3444 Sheet Metalwork
Christopher Visscher
Art Dekker
Peter L. Visscher
Theodore Visscher

Leonard Visscher

Chilliwack, BC V4Z

D-U-N-S 24-394-9349   (SL)
INLINE NURSERIES (2010) INC
49944 Yale Rd, Chilliwack, BC, V4Z 0B3
(604) 794-7096
Emp Here 20   *Sales* 14,850,400
SIC 5193 Flowers and florists supplies
Gordon Eckhardt
Ronald Maljaars
Jeffrey Vrieselaar
Thomas Berger
Wendy Purvis

D-U-N-S 25-117-8869   (SL)
QUIK'S FARM LIMITED
8340 Prest Rd, Chilliwack, BC, V4Z 0A6
(604) 795-4651
Emp Here 40   *Sales* 13,698,680
SIC 0181 Ornamental nursery products
Harry Quik

Clearwater, BC V0E

D-U-N-S 24-162-8957   (SL)
SAFETY MART #5 (1994) LTD
SAFETY MART FOODS
74 Young Rd, Clearwater, BC, V0E 1N2
(250) 674-2213
Emp Here 50   *Sales* 13,707,600
SIC 5411 Grocery stores
Rob Sunderman
Wade Elliot
Kelvin Arndt

Cobble Hill, BC V0R

D-U-N-S 20-886-1885   (SL)
CEDARS DISCOVERY CENTRE LTD
CEDARS AT COBBLE HILL
3741 Holland Ave, Cobble Hill, BC, V0R 1L0
(250) 733-2006
Emp Here 100   *Sales* 13,204,000
SIC 8093 Specialty outpatient clinics, nec
Carson Mcpherson

D-U-N-S 20-095-0756   (HQ)
PACIFIC BUILDERS SUPPLIES
PACIFIC TRUSS
3730 Trans Canada Hwy, Cobble Hill, BC, V0R 1L7
(250) 743-5584
Emp Here 125   *Sales* 38,474,000
SIC 2452 Prefabricated wood buildings
Wayne Mckinnon
Grant Mckinnon

D-U-N-S 24-336-8367   (SL)
PACIFIC BUILDING SYSTEMS INC
TRU LINE TRUSS
3730 Trans Canada Hwy, Cobble Hill, BC, V0R 1L7
(250) 743-5584
Emp Here 75   *Sales* 31,705,275
SIC 1541 Industrial buildings and warehouses
Wayne Mckinnon
Grant Mckinnon

D-U-N-S 20-201-7435   (SL)
VENTURI-SCHULZE LTD
VENTURI-SCHULZE VINEYARDS
4235 Vineyard Rd, Cobble Hill, BC, V0R 1L5
(250) 743-5630
Emp Here 30   *Sales* 17,637,480
SIC 5182 Wine and distilled beverages
Marilyn Venturi

Coldstream, BC V1B

D-U-N-S 20-518-3218   (SL)
NORMAC EQUIPMENT SALES LTD
8409 Kalavista Dr, Coldstream, BC, V1B 1K4
(250) 542-4726
Emp Here 105   *Sales* 51,211,650
SIC 5083 Farm and garden machinery
Rob Mckay

D-U-N-S 24-787-0926   (BR)
TOLKO INDUSTRIES LTD
LAVINGTON PLANER DIVISION
(*Suby of* AMERICAN INDUSTRIAL ACQUISITION CORPORATION)
6200 Jeffers Dr, Coldstream, BC, V1B 3G4
(250) 545-4992
Emp Here 200
SIC 2421 Sawmills and planing mills, general
Pat Donnelly

Comox, BC V9M

D-U-N-S 20-428-7692   (SL)
ACE PHARMACY LTD
206 Port Augusta St, Comox, BC, V9M 3N1
(250) 339-2235
Emp Here 24   *Sales* 10,064,520
SIC 6712 Bank holding companies
Melvin Clark
Gordon Wrightman

D-U-N-S 20-956-3415   (BR)
BERWICK   RETIREMENT   COMMUNITIES LTD
(*Suby of* BERWICK RETIREMENT COMMUNITIES LTD)
1700 Comox Ave, Comox, BC, V9M 4H4
(250) 339-1690
Emp Here 80
SIC 8361 Residential care
Jackie Holt

D-U-N-S 20-374-9259   (SL)
JOHN'S YOUR INDEPENDENT GROCER
215 Port Augusta St Unit C, Comox, BC, V9M 3M9
(250) 339-7651
Emp Here 70   *Sales* 58,490,390
SIC 5141 Groceries, general line
John Gerczynsky

D-U-N-S 20-957-3047   (HQ)
ST JOSEPH'S GENERAL HOSPITAL
UPPER ISLAND GERIATRIC OUTREACH PROGRAM
2137 Comox Ave, Comox, BC, V9M 1P2
(250) 339-1451
Emp Here 900   *Sales* 122,188,000
SIC 8062 General medical and surgical hospitals
Michael Pontus

Coombs, BC V0R

D-U-N-S 20-992-9850   (SL)
BILLY GRUFF MARKETING LTD
THE OLD COUNTRY MARKET
2310 Alberni Hwy, Coombs, BC, V0R 1M0
(250) 248-6272
Emp Here 70   *Sales* 20,543,390
SIC 5411 Grocery stores
Larry Geekie

Coquitlam, BC V3B

D-U-N-S 25-714-7686   (HQ)
A.B. IMAGE OPTICS INC
AR BOYCO IMAGE OPTOMETRY
2764 Barnet Hwy Suite 101, Coquitlam, BC, V3B 1B9
(604) 942-1642
Emp Here 5   *Sales* 16,280,000
SIC 5995 Optical goods stores
Alan Boyco
Tom Bowlware

D-U-N-S 25-680-9500   (HQ)
ALUMET MFG., INC
2660 Barnet Hwy, Coquitlam, BC, V3B 1B7
(604) 464-5451
Emp Here 35   *Sales* 25,442,800
SIC 5023 Homefurnishings
Wallace H Peterson
Anne Peterson

D-U-N-S 25-496-1725   (SL)
COQUITLAM SUPERMARKETS LTD
HENDERSON SUPERMARKET
1163 Pinetree Way Suite 1056, Coquitlam, BC, V3B 8A9
(604) 552-6108
Emp Here 74   *Sales* 21,717,298
SIC 5411 Grocery stores
Allen Lai
Ping Hop Kwok

D-U-N-S 20-364-0149   (SL)
EVERGREEN WEST REALTY
2963 Glen Dr Suite 206, Coquitlam, BC, V3B 2P7
(604) 782-7327
Emp Here 45   *Sales* 12,229,020
SIC 6531 Real estate agents and managers
Roloff Veld

D-U-N-S 24-979-7440   (BR)
HUDSON'S BAY COMPANY
THE BAY
(*Suby of* HUDSON'S BAY COMPANY)
2929 Barnet Hwy Suite 100, Coquitlam, BC, V3B 5R9
(604) 468-4453
Emp Here 160
SIC 5311 Department stores
Peter Beraldin

D-U-N-S 24-624-3245   (BR)
KEG RESTAURANTS LTD
KEG STEAKHOUSE & BAR, THE
(*Suby of* RECIPE UNLIMITED CORPORATION)
2991 Lougheed Hwy Unit 130, Coquitlam, BC, V3B 6J6
(604) 464-5340
Emp Here 90
SIC 5812 Eating places
Brad Patterson

D-U-N-S 25-013-0440   (HQ)
KIRMAC   AUTOMOTIVE   COLLISION   SYSTEMS (CANADA) INC
KIRMAC CARSTAR COLLISION
2714 Barnet Hwy Suite 104, Coquitlam, BC, V3B 1B8
(604) 461-4494
Emp Here 20   *Sales* 54,023,640
SIC 7532 Top and body repair and paint shops
Ian Mcintosh
Kenneth Mcintosh

D-U-N-S 25-718-8920   (SL)
RAND AND FOWLER INSURANCE COQUITLAM LTD
2918 Glen Dr Unit 103, Coquitlam, BC, V3B 2P5
(604) 941-3212
Emp Here 30   *Sales* 17,397,720
SIC 6411 Insurance agents, brokers, and service
Steve Clements

D-U-N-S 20-713-4722   (BR)
SCHOOL DISTRICT NO. 43 (COQUITLAM)

GLENEAGLE SECONDARY SCHOOL
(*Suby of* SCHOOL DISTRICT NO. 43 (CO-QUITLAM))
1195 Lansdowne Dr, Coquitlam, BC, V3B 7Y8
(604) 464-5793
Emp Here 103
SIC 8211 Elementary and secondary schools
Ken Cober

D-U-N-S 25-094-3388   (BR)
SOBEYS WEST INC
(*Suby of* EMPIRE COMPANY LIMITED)
3051 Lougheed Hwy Suite 100, Coquitlam, BC, V3B 1C6

Emp Here 300
SIC 5411 Grocery stores
Gord Mccaullum

D-U-N-S 24-593-5903   (HQ)
STONEWATER GROUP OF FRANCHISES
MR MIKES STEAK HOUSE & BAR
2991 Lougheed Hwy Unit 32, Coquitlam, BC, V3B 6J6
(604) 529-9220
Emp Here 1   *Sales* 34,840,500
SIC 6794 Patent owners and lessors
Darren Flintoff
Kelly Ranford

D-U-N-S 24-641-6978   (SL)
SUPERIOR POULTRY PROCESSORS LTD
2784 Aberdeen Ave, Coquitlam, BC, V3B 1A3
(604) 464-0533
Emp Here 200   *Sales* 143,343,200
SIC 5144 Poultry and poultry products
Bruce Arabsky

D-U-N-S 25-718-3962   (BR)
WHITE SPOT LIMITED
(*Suby of* SHATO HOLDINGS LTD)
3025 Lougheed Hwy Suite 500, Coquitlam, BC, V3B 6S2
(604) 942-9224
Emp Here 80
SIC 5812 Eating places
Diane Taggert

Coquitlam, BC V3C

D-U-N-S 24-761-6873   (SL)
BRITISH COLUMBIA MENTAL HEALTH SO-CIETY
RIVERVIEW HOSPITAL
(*Suby of* PROVINCIAL HEALTH SERVICES AUTHORITY)
2601 Lougheed Hwy, Coquitlam, BC, V3C 4J2
(604) 524-7000
Emp Here 1,700
SIC 8063 Psychiatric hospitals
Leslie Arnold

D-U-N-S 24-505-0885   (SL)
COQUITLAM CHRYSLER DODGE JEEP LTD
COQUITLAM CHRYSLER
2960 Christmas Way, Coquitlam, BC, V3C 4E6
(604) 464-6611
Emp Here 85   *Sales* 53,488,800
SIC 5511 New and used car dealers
Anthony Polegato
Lawrence Isfeld
Allan Backman

D-U-N-S 25-021-9532   (HQ)
FORENSIC PSYCHIATRIC SERVICES COM-MISSION
(*Suby of* PROVINCIAL HEALTH SERVICES AUTHORITY)
70 Colony Farm Rd, Coquitlam, BC, V3C 5X9
(604) 524-7700
Emp Here 400   *Sales* 39,944,500
SIC 8063 Psychiatric hospitals

Leslie M Arnold

Coquitlam, BC V3E

D-U-N-S 25-662-7720   (HQ)
ABHAY ENTERPRISES LTD
PETRO-CANADA
1401 Johnson St, Coquitlam, BC, V3E 3J3
(604) 464-1347
Emp Here 5   *Sales* 24,903,900
SIC 5541 Gasoline service stations
Prabhjit Sokhi

D-U-N-S 20-101-1608   (HQ)
ALLARD CONTRACTORS LTD
1520 Pipeline Rd, Coquitlam, BC, V3E 3P6
(604) 944-2556
Emp Here 1   *Sales* 31,302,180
SIC 5032 Brick, stone, and related material
Barry Allard
Jim Allard

D-U-N-S 20-549-2114   (SL)
DATEK INDUSTRIAL TECHNOLOGIES LTD
3268 Chartwell Green, Coquitlam, BC, V3E 3M9
(604) 468-8615
Emp Here 3   *Sales* 26,615,686
SIC 5084 Industrial machinery and equipment
Yao Wang
Wei Wang

D-U-N-S 24-776-9474   (SL)
EAGLE RIDGE CHEVROLET BUICK GMC LTD
(*Suby of* GIMLI AUTO LTD)
2595 Barnet Hwy, Coquitlam, BC, V3E 1K9
(604) 464-3941
Emp Here 71   *Sales* 44,678,880
SIC 5511 New and used car dealers
Lorne Isfeld
Lori Isfeld

D-U-N-S 25-067-8851   (SL)
PLATEAU FOODS LTD
IGA
1410 Parkway Blvd Unit A, Coquitlam, BC, V3E 3J7
(604) 464-8506
Emp Here 45   *Sales* 12,336,840
SIC 5411 Grocery stores
Fin O'riordan

D-U-N-S 25-485-7055   (BR)
WESBILD HOLDINGS LTD
WESTWOOD PLATEAU GOLF & COUNTRY CLUB
3251 Plateau Blvd, Coquitlam, BC, V3E 3B8
(604) 945-4007
Emp Here 200
SIC 7997 Membership sports and recreation clubs
Cronk James

Coquitlam, BC V3H

D-U-N-S 20-574-4626   (SL)
WESTMINSTER VOLKSWAGEN LTD
2555 Barnet Hwy, Coquitlam, BC, V3H 1W4
(604) 461-5000
Emp Here 45   *Sales* 22,413,510
SIC 5511 New and used car dealers
Erich Schmidt Sr
Erich Schmidt Jr
Louis Eggers

Coquitlam, BC V3J

D-U-N-S 24-103-3914   (SL)
COMFORTING CARE LTD
657 Gatensbury St, Coquitlam, BC, V3J 5G9

Emp Here 40   *Sales* 14,449,480
SIC 8049 Offices of health practitioner
Carmen Sadden

D-U-N-S 24-683-0954   (SL)
PARKWOOD CONSTRUCTION LTD
1404 Ross Ave, Coquitlam, BC, V3J 2K1
(604) 936-2792
Emp Here 25   *Sales* 11,768,275
SIC 1542 Nonresidential construction, nec
Silvano Facchin

D-U-N-S 25-013-9425   (BR)
SCHOOL DISTRICT NO. 43 (COQUITLAM)
DR CHARLES BEST SECONDARY SCHOOL
(*Suby of* SCHOOL DISTRICT NO. 43 (CO-QUITLAM))
2525 Como Lake Ave, Coquitlam, BC, V3J 3R8
(604) 461-5581
Emp Here 85
SIC 8211 Elementary and secondary schools
Carol Coulson

D-U-N-S 24-249-9937   (BR)
SCHOOL DISTRICT NO. 43 (COQUITLAM)
CENTENNIAL SECONDARY SCHOOL
(*Suby of* SCHOOL DISTRICT NO. 43 (CO-QUITLAM))
570 Poirier St, Coquitlam, BC, V3J 6A8
(604) 939-9201
Emp Here 110
SIC 8211 Elementary and secondary schools
Robert Zambrano

D-U-N-S 25-013-9649   (HQ)
SCHOOL DISTRICT NO. 43 (COQUITLAM)
ASPENWOOD
550 Poirier St, Coquitlam, BC, V3J 6A7
(604) 939-9201
Emp Here 70   *Sales* 435,228,000
SIC 8211 Elementary and secondary schools
Tom Grant
Brian Robinson
Melissa Hyndes
Cheryl Quinton
Gail Alty
Judy Shirra
Holly Butterfield
Gerri Wallis
John Keryluk
Keith Watkins

Coquitlam, BC V3K

D-U-N-S 20-141-3808   (SL)
9391134 CANADA LTD
YOGIBO LIFESTYLE
91 Golden Dr Unit 18, Coquitlam, BC, V3K 6R2
(604) 428-9644
Emp Here 25   *Sales* 12,721,400
SIC 5021 Furniture
Yoav Dagony

D-U-N-S 24-898-9295   (HQ)
A.G. PROFESSIONAL HAIR CARE PROD-UCTS LTD
A.G. HAIR COSMETICS
14 King Edward St, Coquitlam, BC, V3K 0E7
(604) 294-8870
Emp Here 57   *Sales* 20,449,512
SIC 2844 Toilet preparations
John Davis
Charlotte Davis

D-U-N-S 20-009-8064   (HQ)
ACT II CHILD & FAMILY SERVICES SOCI-ETY
1034 Austin Ave, Coquitlam, BC, V3K 3P3

(604) 937-7776
Emp Here 9   *Sales* 10,434,318
SIC 8399 Social services, nec
Bradley Watson

D-U-N-S 20-369-1886   (SL)
AG HAIR LTD
14 King Edward St, Coquitlam, BC, V3K 0E7
(604) 294-8870
Emp Here 57   *Sales* 16,189,197
SIC 2844 Toilet preparations
John Davis

D-U-N-S 20-562-8345   (SL)
AIM HOLDING TRUST
2000 Brigantine Dr, Coquitlam, BC, V3K 7B5
(604) 525-3900
Emp Here 500
SIC 6712 Bank holding companies
Gary Peters

D-U-N-S 24-657-7324   (SL)
ALASKAN COPPER & BRASS CANADA INC
ALASKAN COPPER & BRASS COMPANY
(*Suby of* ALCO INVESTMENT COMPANY)
225 North Rd, Coquitlam, BC, V3K 3V7
(604) 937-6620
Emp Here 29   *Sales* 12,968,046
SIC 5051 Metals service centers and offices
Kari Kerr
Brian Lucarelli

D-U-N-S 24-129-7568   (BR)
AMPCO MANUFACTURERS INC
(*Suby of* AMG HOLDINGS INC)
9 Burbidge St Unit 101, Coquitlam, BC, V3K 7B2

Emp Here 120
SIC 2759 Commercial printing, nec
Ron Sun

D-U-N-S 24-030-3834   (HQ)
AMPCO MANUFACTURERS INC
AMPCO GRAFIX DIV OF
(*Suby of* AMG HOLDINGS INC)
9 Burbidge St Suite 101, Coquitlam, BC, V3K 7B2
(604) 472-3800
Emp Here 95   *Sales* 19,683,240
SIC 2759 Commercial printing, nec
Dann Konkin
Tanya Vermeulen

D-U-N-S 20-574-3354   (SL)
APOLLO SHEET METAL LTD
(*Suby of* APOLLO SHEET METAL HOLD-INGS LTD)
2095 Brigantine Dr, Coquitlam, BC, V3K 7B8
(604) 525-8299
Emp Here 80   *Sales* 18,645,200
SIC 1711 Plumbing, heating, air-conditioning
Angelo Paris
Antonio Paris
Maria Paris

D-U-N-S 25-789-4162   (SL)
ASSOCIATED LABELS & PRINTING LTD
ELLWORTH INDUSTRIES
61 Clipper St, Coquitlam, BC, V3K 6X2
(604) 525-4764
Emp Here 120   *Sales* 23,372,160
SIC 2679 Converted paper products, nec
Rusty Ashworth
Sean Ashworth
Dianne Ashworth

D-U-N-S 25-363-9603   (SL)
AVCOM SYSTEMS INC
1312 Ketch Crt Unit 101, Coquitlam, BC, V3K 6W1
(604) 944-8650
Emp Here 40   *Sales* 10,262,480
SIC 3829 Measuring and controlling devices, nec
Raymond Wood

D-U-N-S 24-209-1608 (SL)
AXIUM SOLUTIONS ULC
EXAN GROUP
(*Suby of* HENRY SCHEIN, INC.)
1963 Lougheed Hwy, Coquitlam, BC, V3K 3T8
(604) 468-6820
Emp Here 85   *Sales* 12,255,470
SIC 7371 Custom computer programming services
Ted Devries

D-U-N-S 24-790-2153 (SL)
BENCHMARK BUILDING SYSTEMS LTD
145 Schoolhouse St Suite 13, Coquitlam, BC, V3K 4X8
(604) 524-6533
Emp Here 30   *Sales* 14,121,930
SIC 1542 Nonresidential construction, nec
Dan Kitto

D-U-N-S 20-109-2699 (HQ)
BISSETT FASTENERS LIMITED
63 Fawcett Rd, Coquitlam, BC, V3K 6V2
(604) 540-0200
Emp Here 30   *Sales* 22,801,248
SIC 5085 Industrial supplies
Matthew Sauder
Irina Razoumova

D-U-N-S 24-291-6930 (HQ)
BROCK CANADA WEST LTD
(*Suby of* BROCK CANADA INC)
1650 Brigantine Dr Suite 100, Coquitlam, BC, V3K 7B5
(604) 519-6788
Emp Here 15   *Sales* 12,309,300
SIC 1799 Special trade contractors, nec
Willi Hamm

D-U-N-S 24-641-3140 (HQ)
BROTHERS COMPANY GLASS CAR CARE LTD
BROCO AUTO GLASS & UPHOLSTERY
802 Brunette Ave, Coquitlam, BC, V3K 1C4
(604) 517-0215
Emp Here 15   *Sales* 14,771,160
SIC 1793 Glass and glazing work
Fred Beck
Merle Beck

D-U-N-S 25-483-1829 (SL)
BURQUITLAM CARE SOCIETY
BURQUITLAM LIONS CARE CENTRE
560 Sydney Ave, Coquitlam, BC, V3K 6A4

Emp Here 85   *Sales* 5,828,110
SIC 8051 Skilled nursing care facilities
Werner Bernhardt
Joanne Easdown
Robert Fanzega
Lawrence Fleming
Dolores Hallson
Jon Samson
Karin Williams

D-U-N-S 20-976-8253 (SL)
CANADA SECURITY SERVICES LTD
91 Golden Dr Suite 27, Coquitlam, BC, V3K 6R2

Emp Here 30   *Sales* 12,069,985
SIC 7381 Detective and armored car services
Karen Morris

D-U-N-S 24-682-8024 (HQ)
CANSTAR CONSTRUCTION LTD
CANSTAR RESTORATIONS
78 Fawcett Rd, Coquitlam, BC, V3K 6V5
(604) 549-0099
Emp Here 80   *Sales* 25,849,530
SIC 1799 Special trade contractors, nec
Jay Dargatz

D-U-N-S 20-353-1819 (SL)
CARBONMASTERS INNOVATION LTD
CARBONMASTERS
35 Leeder St, Coquitlam, BC, V3K 3V5

(778) 684-2096
Emp Here 35   *Sales* 15,651,090
SIC 5075 Warm air heating and air conditioning
Axel Winkelmann
Timothy Brereton
Bruce Langston
Timothy Brereton
Axel Winkelmann

D-U-N-S 25-485-7386 (SL)
CARTIER HOUSE CARE CENTRE LTD
1419 Cartier Ave, Coquitlam, BC, V3K 2C6
(604) 939-4654
Emp Here 85   *Sales* 5,531,375
SIC 8361 Residential care
Altaf Jina
Jenny Jina

D-U-N-S 24-248-9342 (HQ)
CHAMBERS ELECTRICAL CORP
204 Cayer St Unit 101, Coquitlam, BC, V3K 5B1
(604) 526-5688
Sales 11,544,937
SIC 1731 Electrical work
Ronald Chambers

D-U-N-S 24-165-2254 (HQ)
CLASSIC PACKAGING CORPORATION
1580 Brigantine Dr Suite 100, Coquitlam, BC, V3K 7C1
(604) 523-6700
Emp Here 20   *Sales* 11,230,475
SIC 7389 Business services, nec
Wesley Palmer

D-U-N-S 24-034-8792 (SL)
COQUITLAM CRUISESHIPCENTERS
1021 Austin Ave, Coquitlam, BC, V3K 3N9
(604) 937-7125
Emp Here 25   *Sales* 13,217,805
SIC 4724 Travel agencies
Barbara Addy

D-U-N-S 25-003-0756 (BR)
COQUITLAM, CITY OF
PLACE DES ARTS
(*Suby of* COQUITLAM, CITY OF)
1120 Brunette Ave, Coquitlam, BC, V3K 1G2
(604) 664-1636
Emp Here 92
SIC 8299 Schools and educational services, nec
Joan Roberts

D-U-N-S 24-825-5846 (BR)
CORPORATION MCKESSON CANADA, LA
(*Suby of* MCKESSON FINANCIAL HOLDINGS II UNLIMITED COMPANY)
71 Glacier St, Coquitlam, BC, V3K 5Z1
(604) 942-7111
Emp Here 100
SIC 5122 Drugs, proprietaries, and sundries
Bryan Cuming

D-U-N-S 24-980-7561 (SL)
COST LESS EXPRESS LTD
LYKKI.COM
11 Burbidge St Suite 204, Coquitlam, BC, V3K 7B2
(604) 444-4467
Emp Here 23   *Sales* 10,285,002
SIC 5044 Office equipment
Calvin Johnson

D-U-N-S 20-001-2185 (SL)
CROISSANTS D' OLIVIER LTD, LES
12 King Edward St Unit 101, Coquitlam, BC, V3K 0E7
(778) 285-8662
Emp Here 45   *Sales* 10,118,475
SIC 2051 Bread, cake, and related products
Olivier Audibert

D-U-N-S 24-029-1281 (SL)
CROSS PACIFIC INVESTMENT GROUP INC
PEARL FEVER TEA HOUSE
62 Fawcett Rd Suite 13, Coquitlam, BC, V3K

6V5
(604) 522-8144
Emp Here 35   *Sales* 29,245,195
SIC 5141 Groceries, general line
Haojan Cho

D-U-N-S 24-566-8207 (HQ)
DARYL-EVANS MECHANICAL LTD
211 Schoolhouse St Unit 1, Coquitlam, BC, V3K 4X9
(604) 525-3523
Emp Here 1   *Sales* 17,479,875
SIC 1711 Plumbing, heating, air-conditioning
Daryl Tisseur

D-U-N-S 20-232-3460 (HQ)
DAVID OPPENHEIMER & ASSOCIATES GENERAL PARTNERSHIP
OPPENHEIMER
11 Burbidge St Suite 101, Coquitlam, BC, V3K 7B2
(604) 461-6779
Emp Here 30   *Sales* 16,902,500
SIC 0181 Ornamental nursery products
John Anderson

D-U-N-S 24-505-1099 (SL)
DEE ENTERPRISES LTD
EXTRA FOODS
455 North Rd, Coquitlam, BC, V3K 3V9
(604) 937-1205
Emp Here 80   *Sales* 23,478,160
SIC 5411 Grocery stores
Kevin Young

D-U-N-S 20-224-2488 (SL)
DELTA TEXTILES INC
61 Glacier St, Coquitlam, BC, V3K 5Z1
(604) 942-2214
Emp Here 65   *Sales* 32,390,930
SIC 5131 Piece goods and notions
Klid Meizi

D-U-N-S 20-565-1875 (SL)
DICKINSON MARINE (1997) LTD
204 Cayer St Unit 407, Coquitlam, BC, V3K 5B1
(604) 525-4444
Emp Here 30   *Sales* 13,415,220
SIC 5074 Plumbing and heating equipment and supplies (hydronics)
Don Perry

D-U-N-S 24-788-3056 (SL)
DYNAMIC RESCUE SYSTEMS INC
63a Clipper St, Coquitlam, BC, V3K 6X2
(604) 522-0228
Emp Here 50   *Sales* 15,274,000
SIC 8999 Services, nec
John Dennis
John Kenyon
Alberto Burrero
Grant Frost

D-U-N-S 25-677-5289 (HQ)
EAGLE QUEST GOLF CENTERS INC
1001 United Blvd, Coquitlam, BC, V3K 4S8
(604) 523-6400
Emp Here 6   *Sales* 14,002,900
SIC 7999 Amusement and recreation, nec
Nawaz Hirji

D-U-N-S 24-150-1899 (SL)
ELLWORTH INDUSTRIES LTD
ASSOCIATED LABELS
61 Clipper St Suite 61, Coquitlam, BC, V3K 6X2
(604) 525-4764
Emp Here 115   *Sales* 22,398,320
SIC 2672 Paper; coated and laminated, nec
Gordon Ashworth

D-U-N-S 20-748-1151 (HQ)
ENTERPRISE PAPER CO. LTD
95 Brigantine Dr, Coquitlam, BC, V3K 6Y9
(604) 522-6295
Emp Here 90   *Sales* 108,879,290
SIC 5113 Industrial and personal service pa-

per
Kenneth Plumb
Graham Wong
Patrick Mulhern

D-U-N-S 25-456-0725 (HQ)
ESCENTS BODY PRODUCTS INC
ESCENTS AROMA THERAPY
18 Fawcett Rd, Coquitlam, BC, V3K 6X9
(604) 298-9298
Emp Here 10   *Sales* 21,301,575
SIC 2841 Soap and other detergents
Jacqui Macneill

D-U-N-S 24-341-2165 (BR)
EXECUTIVE HOTELS GENERAL PARTNERSHIP
EXECUTIVE HOTELS & RESORTS
(*Suby of* EXECUTIVE HOTELS GENERAL PARTNERSHIP)
405 North Rd, Coquitlam, BC, V3K 3V9
(604) 936-9399
Emp Here 100
SIC 7011 Hotels and motels
Tasha Sheikh

D-U-N-S 25-328-2701 (HQ)
FACTORS GROUP OF NUTRITIONAL COMPANIES INC
NATURAL FACTORS
1550 United Blvd, Coquitlam, BC, V3K 6Y2
(604) 777-1757
Emp Here 400   *Sales* 331,594,000
SIC 2833 Medicinals and botanicals
Roland Jacques Gahler

D-U-N-S 24-505-1685 (SL)
FEATURE MILLWORK INC
204 Cayer St Unit 301, Coquitlam, BC, V3K 5B1
(604) 522-7951
Emp Here 40   *Sales* 10,122,360
SIC 5211 Lumber and other building materials
Rosario Greco
Ernesto Silveri

D-U-N-S 20-116-1754 (HQ)
FLEETMIND SEON SOLUTIONS INC
SEON DESIGN
3b Burbidge St Suite 111, Coquitlam, BC, V3K 7B2
(604) 941-0880
Sales 19,044,200
SIC 3699 Electrical equipment and supplies, nec
Tom Gill
David Gordon
James Bain

D-U-N-S 25-676-4846 (SL)
GFR PHARMA LTD
65 North Bend St Unit 65, Coquitlam, BC, V3K 6N9
(604) 460-8440
Emp Here 110   *Sales* 31,242,310
SIC 2833 Medicinals and botanicals
Richard Pierce
Tom Tardi
Eric Van Roon
John Stephen
Surjit Hundal
Shelley Berry

D-U-N-S 24-309-4398 (HQ)
GLASWEGIAN ENTERPRISES INC
AUDIO VIDEO UNLIMITED
1090 Lougheed Hwy Suite 214, Coquitlam, BC, V3K 6G9
(604) 522-4000
Sales 23,691,540
SIC 6794 Patent owners and lessors
Jim Orr

D-U-N-S 20-123-1755 (HQ)
GRANDVIEW BROKERAGE LIMITED
OPPENHEIMER GROUP, THE
(*Suby of* TOTAL PRODUCE PUBLIC LIMITED COMPANY)

11 Burbidge St Suite 101, Coquitlam, BC, V3K 7B2
(604) 461-6779
Emp Here 100   *Sales* 76,830,300
SIC 6712 Bank holding companies
John Anderson
Doug Grant
Nigel Fripp
Rory Byrne
Seamus Mulvenna

D-U-N-S 20-013-6724   (HQ)
GREAT CANADIAN CASINOS INC
(*Suby of* GREAT CANADIAN GAMING CORPORATION)
95 Schooner St, Coquitlam, BC, V3K 7A8
(604) 303-1000
Emp Here 10   *Sales* 346,800,000
SIC 7999 Amusement and recreation, nec
Rod Baker
Brian Egli

D-U-N-S 20-059-3544   (BR)
GREAT CANADIAN CASINOS INC
HARD ROCK CASINO
(*Suby of* GREAT CANADIAN GAMING CORPORATION)
2080 United Blvd Suite D, Coquitlam, BC, V3K 6W3
(604) 523-6888
Emp Here 250
SIC 7999 Amusement and recreation, nec
David Prupas

D-U-N-S 25-536-4614   (HQ)
GREAT CANADIAN GAMING CORPORATION
95 Schooner St, Coquitlam, BC, V3K 7A8
(604) 303-1000
Emp Here 9,350   *Sales* 925,642,542
SIC 7999 Amusement and recreation, nec
Rod N. Baker
Terrance Doyle
John Russo
Craig Demarta
Raj Mutti
Walter Soo
Chuck Keeling
Jackie Gorton
Matt Newsome
Darren Gwozd

D-U-N-S 20-867-6192   (SL)
HANAHREUM MART INC
329 North Rd Suite 100, Coquitlam, BC, V3K 3V8
(604) 939-0135
Emp Here 50   *Sales* 13,707,600
SIC 5411 Grocery stores
Kwon Byoung Li

D-U-N-S 24-957-9590   (SL)
HILLS FOODS LTD
130 Glacier St Unit 1, Coquitlam, BC, V3K 5Z6
(604) 472-1500
Emp Here 20   *Sales* 10,702,480
SIC 5149 Groceries and related products, nec
Mark Hills
Tina Hills

D-U-N-S 25-514-3216   (BR)
HOME DEPOT OF CANADA INC
HOME DEPOT
(*Suby of* THE HOME DEPOT INC)
1900 United Blvd Suite D, Coquitlam, BC, V3K 6Z1
(604) 540-6277
Emp Here 200
SIC 5251 Hardware stores
Ronda Brayshaw

D-U-N-S 24-424-8519   (SL)
HONAJI FOOD LTD
42 Fawcett Rd Unit 109, Coquitlam, BC, V3K 6X9
(604) 759-2886
Emp Here 19   *Sales* 10,167,356
SIC 5149 Groceries and related products, nec

Jie Zhang

D-U-N-S 20-797-9246   (SL)
INLET ELECTRIC LTD
169 Golden Dr Unit 2, Coquitlam, BC, V3K 6T1
(604) 464-3133
Emp Here 75   *Sales* 16,337,175
SIC 1731 Electrical work
Mario Dallazanna
Bruna Dallazanna

D-U-N-S 20-584-1831   (BR)
INSURANCE CORPORATION OF BRITISH COLUMBIA
ICBC CENTRAL ESTIMATING FACILITY
(*Suby of* GOVERNMENT OF THE PROVINCE OF BRITISH COLUMBIA)
1575 Hartley Ave, Coquitlam, BC, V3K 6Z7
(604) 777-4627
Emp Here 120
SIC 6331 Fire, marine, and casualty insurance
Tony Hamilton

D-U-N-S 20-510-4888   (HQ)
JET EQUIPMENT & TOOLS LTD
SUREWERX
49 Schooner St, Coquitlam, BC, V3K 0B3
(604) 523-8665
Emp Here 78   *Sales* 64,438,670
SIC 5084 Industrial machinery and equipment
Christopher Baby
Kevin Karr

D-U-N-S 24-948-3058   (HQ)
JOEY TOMATO'S KITCHENS INC
JOEY TOMATO'S RESTAURANT
(*Suby of* JOEY TOMATO'S)
550 Lougheed Hwy, Coquitlam, BC, V3K 3S3
(604) 939-3077
Emp Here 50   *Sales* 51,302,900
SIC 5812 Eating places
Jeff Fuller
Peter Upton
Leroy Fuller

D-U-N-S 24-135-1915   (SL)
JOHN B PUB LTD
JOHN B NEIGHBOURHOOD PUB, THE
1000 Austin Ave, Coquitlam, BC, V3K 3P1
(604) 931-5115
Emp Here 45   *Sales* 13,460,850
SIC 5921 Liquor stores
John Lepinski
Brent Lepinski

D-U-N-S 20-140-1754   (HQ)
JYSK LINEN'N FURNITURE INC
(*Suby of* JYSK HOLDING A/S)
25 King Edward St Unit 101, Coquitlam, BC, V3K 4S8
(604) 472-0769
Emp Here 100   *Sales* 165,355,860
SIC 5712 Furniture stores
Ludvik G. Kristjansson
Mohammed Mahabub

D-U-N-S 24-578-2362   (HQ)
K. M. S. TOOLS & EQUIPMENT LTD
110 Woolridge St, Coquitlam, BC, V3K 5V4
(604) 522-5599
Sales 24,088,680
SIC 5251 Hardware stores
Stanley Pridham
Kathy Pridham

D-U-N-S 24-171-1337   (SL)
LEADING EDGE FORMING LTD
137 Glacier St Unit 107, Coquitlam, BC, V3K 5Z1

Emp Here 80   *Sales* 19,694,880
SIC 1799 Special trade contractors, nec
Luigi Sepe
Zelko Ruzic

D-U-N-S 25-618-7428   (BR)
LOBLAWS INC

REAL CANADIAN-SUPERSTORES
(*Suby of* LOBLAW COMPANIES LIMITED)
1301 Lougheed Hwy, Coquitlam, BC, V3K 6P9
(604) 520-8339
Emp Here 300
SIC 5411 Grocery stores
Rob Holt

D-U-N-S 20-378-0536   (SL)
LUKANDA HOLDINGS LTD
LOUGHEED HYUNDAI
1288 Lougheed Hwy, Coquitlam, BC, V3K 6S4
(604) 523-3009
Emp Here 22   *Sales* 10,957,716
SIC 5511 New and used car dealers
Howard Chiang

D-U-N-S 20-914-8365   (SL)
MAC'S II AGENCIES LTD
1851 Brigantine Dr Unit 100, Coquitlam, BC, V3K 7B4
(604) 540-6646
Emp Here 50   *Sales* 22,358,700
SIC 5063 Electrical apparatus and equipment
Paul Gill
Kyle Embley
Wesley Oliver

D-U-N-S 24-308-6068   (SL)
MARKETWEST FOOD GROUP LIMITED PARTNERSHIP
1580 Brigantine Dr Suite 200, Coquitlam, BC, V3K 7C1
(604) 526-1788
Emp Here 30   *Sales* 25,067,310
SIC 5141 Groceries, general line
Grant Huxtable
Neil Johanson

D-U-N-S 20-188-0114   (SL)
MATCON EXCAVATION & SHORING LTD
2208 Hartley Ave, Coquitlam, BC, V3K 6X3
(604) 520-5909
Emp Here 80   *Sales* 19,694,880
SIC 1794 Excavation work
Adam Heath
Stephen Jungaro

D-U-N-S 25-085-3264   (SL)
MILLWOOD FURNITURE ENT. LTD
HOME STORE
1365 United Blvd, Coquitlam, BC, V3K 6Y3
(604) 777-1365
Emp Here 60   *Sales* 13,944,180
SIC 5712 Furniture stores
Aaron Miller
Lynn Woodward

D-U-N-S 24-844-5491   (HQ)
MOTOSEL INDUSTRIAL GROUP INC
204 Cayer St Unit 407, Coquitlam, BC, V3K 5B1
(604) 629-8733
Sales 591,136,500
SIC 5172 Petroleum products, nec
Morteza Iranpour
David Mah

D-U-N-S 20-562-8329   (HQ)
NATURAL FACTORS NUTRITIONAL PRODUCTS LTD
1550 United Blvd, Coquitlam, BC, V3K 6Y2
(604) 777-1757
Sales 55,267,250
SIC 5122 Drugs, proprietaries, and sundries
Roland Jacques Gahler

D-U-N-S 24-477-3461   (HQ)
NCS INTERNATIONAL CO
NATIONAL CABLE SPECIALIST, DIV OF
(*Suby of* GII HOLDINGS CORP)
70 Glacier St, Coquitlam, BC, V3K 5Y9
(604) 472-6980
Emp Here 25   *Sales* 92,839,520
SIC 5063 Electrical apparatus and equipment
Robert J. Bouchard
Gary Mcneil

D-U-N-S 25-505-1369   (HQ)
NII NORTHERN INTERNATIONAL INC
NORTHERN INTERNATIONAL
1 Burbidge St Suite 101, Coquitlam, BC, V3K 7B2
(604) 464-8606
Emp Here 45   *Sales* 26,830,440
SIC 5063 Electrical apparatus and equipment
Steve Gula

D-U-N-S 24-979-7697   (HQ)
OPPENHEIMER, DAVID AND COMPANY I, LLC
OPPENHEIMER GROUP, THE
(*Suby of* TOTAL PRODUCE PUBLIC LIMITED COMPANY)
11 Burbidge St Suite 101, Coquitlam, BC, V3K 7B2
(604) 461-6779
Emp Here 52   *Sales* 195,663,468
SIC 5148 Fresh fruits and vegetables
John Anderson
Nigel Fripp

D-U-N-S 24-448-2964   (SL)
P.T.I. PUNCH TOOLS INC
P.T.I.
211 Schoolhouse St Suite 11, Coquitlam, BC, V3K 4X9
(604) 521-3143
Emp Here 40   *Sales* 19,001,040
SIC 5084 Industrial machinery and equipment
James Mckinlay
Robert Farr

D-U-N-S 24-886-9877   (SL)
PACIFIC MAINLAND HOLDINGS LTD
LOUGHEED ACURA
1288 Lougheed Hwy, Coquitlam, BC, V3K 6S4
(604) 522-6140
Emp Here 34   *Sales* 16,934,652
SIC 5511 New and used car dealers
Jimmy Chiang

D-U-N-S 24-762-1303   (SL)
POINT FOUR SYSTEMS INC
16 Fawcett Rd Unit 103, Coquitlam, BC, V3K 6X9

Emp Here 22   *Sales* 10,450,572
SIC 5084 Industrial machinery and equipment
Brian Hirsch
Mohammad Mohseni

D-U-N-S 20-064-8520   (SL)
PR POMEROY RESTORATION & CONSTRUCTION LTD
2075 Brigantine Dr Unit 18, Coquitlam, BC, V3K 7B8
(604) 529-9200
Emp Here 40   *Sales* 11,543,320
SIC 1522 Residential construction, nec
Dean Pomeroy

D-U-N-S 25-882-5975   (SL)
PRAIRIE NATURALS HEALTH PRODUCTS INC
56 Fawcett Rd, Coquitlam, BC, V3K 6V5
(800) 931-4247
Emp Here 30   *Sales* 33,160,350
SIC 5122 Drugs, proprietaries, and sundries
Robert Pierce

D-U-N-S 25-384-4617   (HQ)
PRIMELINE FOOD PARTNERS LTD
PJB-PRIMELINE
1580 Brigantine Dr Suite 200, Coquitlam, BC, V3K 7C1
(604) 526-1788
Emp Here 20   *Sales* 23,396,156
SIC 5141 Groceries, general line
Grant Christopher Huxtable

D-U-N-S 20-115-2980   (HQ)
RELIABLE PARTS LTD
85 North Bend St, Coquitlam, BC, V3K 6N1
(604) 941-1355
Emp Here 54   *Sales* 37,184,480

SIC 5722 Household appliance stores
Martin Street
James Shelby Marlow

D-U-N-S 20-798-9039   (SL)
RICHFORM CONSTRUCTION SUPPLY CO LTD
35 Leeder St Unit A, Coquitlam, BC, V3K 3V5
(604) 777-9974
Emp Here 14   *Sales* 14,004,746
SIC 5051 Metals service centers and offices
Dan L. Fritz
Brad Bond

D-U-N-S 20-334-9373   (SL)
RIDGEWAY MECHANICAL LTD
925 Sherwood Ave Unit 1, Coquitlam, BC, V3K 1A9
(604) 525-0238
Emp Here 50   *Sales* 11,046,700
SIC 1711 Plumbing, heating, air-conditioning
Robert Mcneice
Jack Mcneice

D-U-N-S 20-261-5647   (SL)
RPC HISTORICAL LIMITED PARTNERSHIP
ROKSTAD
(*Suby of* CCI (B.C) LIMITED PARTNERSHIP)
80 Golden Dr, Coquitlam, BC, V3K 6T1
(604) 553-1810
Emp Here 400   *Sales* 84,950,400
SIC 1796 Installing building equipment
Aaron Rokstad
Bernard Rokstad
Emma Mercer
Darren Mcqueen

D-U-N-S 20-993-2045   (SL)
SANDY'S FURNITURE LTD
1335 United Blvd Suite D, Coquitlam, BC, V3K 6V3
(604) 520-0800
Emp Here 45   *Sales* 10,365,300
SIC 5712 Furniture stores
Alexandre (Sandy) Seney
Moe Samuel

D-U-N-S 20-044-2502   (BR)
SAYANI INVESTMENTS LTD
EXECUTIVE PLAZA
(*Suby of* SAYANI INVESTMENTS LTD)
405 North Rd, Coquitlam, BC, V3K 3V9
(604) 936-9399
Emp Here 100
SIC 7011 Hotels and motels
Pasha Shaeikh

D-U-N-S 20-956-0077   (HQ)
SCAN DESIGNS LTD
SCANDESIGNS
1400 United Blvd, Coquitlam, BC, V3K 6Y2
(604) 524-3444
Sales 11,517,000
SIC 5712 Furniture stores
Soren Kornerup
Gert Knudsen

D-U-N-S 20-917-4838   (SL)
SIMON FRASER SOCIETY FOR COMMUNITY LIVING, THE
SIMON FRASER SOCIETY, THE
218 Blue Mountain St Suite 300, Coquitlam, BC, V3K 4H2
(604) 525-9494
Emp Here 180   *Sales* 13,822,560
SIC 8322 Individual and family services
Dale Alexander
Dave Russell

D-U-N-S 20-512-1465   (SL)
SMITHRITE DISPOSAL LTD
70 Golden Dr, Coquitlam, BC, V3K 6B5
(604) 529-4030
Emp Here 50   *Sales* 15,057,100
SIC 4953 Refuse systems
Gordon Smith

D-U-N-S 25-371-0412   (SL)

SMITHRITE PORTABLE SERVICES LTD
1650 Hartley Ave, Coquitlam, BC, V3K 7A1
(604) 529-4028
Emp Here 70   *Sales* 13,394,780
SIC 7359 Equipment rental and leasing, nec
Gordon Smith

D-U-N-S 25-015-0174   (BR)
SOBEYS WEST INC
CANADA SAFEWAY 76
(*Suby of* EMPIRE COMPANY LIMITED)
1033 Austin Ave, Coquitlam, BC, V3K 3P2
(604) 939-2850
Emp Here 100
SIC 5411 Grocery stores
David Owen

D-U-N-S 20-271-7427   (HQ)
SUNBELT RENTALS OF CANADA INC
(*Suby of* ASHTEAD GROUP PUBLIC LIMITED COMPANY)
93 North Bend St Suite 838, Coquitlam, BC, V3K 6N1
(604) 291-8001
Emp Here 22   *Sales* 130,546,000
SIC 7359 Equipment rental and leasing, nec
Brendan Horgan
Chris Van Mook
Kurt Kenkel

D-U-N-S 25-262-8904   (SL)
T-BROTHERS FOOD AND TRADING LTD
88 Brigantine Dr Suite 100, Coquitlam, BC, V3K 6Z6
(604) 540-0306
Emp Here 35   *Sales* 29,245,195
SIC 5141 Groceries, general line
Terry Kim
Terry Park

D-U-N-S 24-134-8101   (SL)
THERMO KING OF BRITISH COLUMBIA INC
68 Fawcett Rd, Coquitlam, BC, V3K 6V5
(604) 526-4414
Emp Here 50   *Sales* 10,185,800
SIC 7623 Refrigeration service and repair
Stuart Kristoff
Don Watts

D-U-N-S 24-761-1049   (HQ)
TOYO PUMPS NORTH AMERICA CORP
(*Suby of* DE-VELDE INTERNATIONAL ENGINEERING CORPORATION)
1550 Brigantine Dr, Coquitlam, BC, V3K 7C1
(604) 298-1213
Sales 14,430,065
SIC 3561 Pumps and pumping equipment
Peter Van De Velde
Bob Malli

D-U-N-S 24-365-9401   (HQ)
TRICORBRAUN CANADA, INC
TRICORBRAUN
(*Suby of* TRICORBRAUN HOLDINGS, INC.)
1650 Brigantine Dr Suite 500, Coquitlam, BC, V3K 7B5
(604) 540-8166
Emp Here 15   *Sales* 15,616,260
SIC 5099 Durable goods, nec
Keith Strope
Larry West
Neil Tzinberg

D-U-N-S 20-692-3323   (HQ)
TRINITY POWER CORPORATION
TRINITY POWER RENTALS
1301 Ketch Crt Unit 8b, Coquitlam, BC, V3K 6X7
(604) 529-1134
Sales 10,393,100
SIC 4911 Electric services
Todd Johnson

D-U-N-S 25-483-6638   (HQ)
UNI-SELECT PACIFIC INC
(*Suby of* UNI-SELECT INC)
91 Glacier St, Coquitlam, BC, V3K 5Z1

(604) 472-4900
Emp Here 50   *Sales* 57,644,250
SIC 5013 Motor vehicle supplies and new parts
Henry Buckley
Eric Bussieres

D-U-N-S 20-393-9074   (SL)
VANCOUVER GOLF CLUB
771 Austin Ave, Coquitlam, BC, V3K 3N2
(604) 936-3404
Emp Here 125   *Sales* 9,818,125
SIC 7997 Membership sports and recreation clubs
Paul Batchlor
Richard Creally

D-U-N-S 25-646-8844   (SL)
VANHOUTTE COFFEE SERVICES LTD
9 Burbidge St Suite 120, Coquitlam, BC, V3K 7B2
(604) 552-5452
Emp Here 60   *Sales* 26,953,140
SIC 7389 Business services, nec
Morten Schroder

D-U-N-S 24-679-4510   (HQ)
WEATHERHAVEN GLOBAL RESOURCES LTD
2120 Hartley Ave, Coquitlam, BC, V3K 6W5
(604) 451-8900
Sales 13,382,600
SIC 5211 Lumber and other building materials
James A Allan
Raymond Castelli
Brian P Hanna
Brian D Johnson
Glen V Thorne

D-U-N-S 20-117-1667   (SL)
WELSH, FRED LTD
94 Glacier St Unit 201, Coquitlam, BC, V3K 6B2
(604) 942-0012
Emp Here 50   *Sales* 11,046,700
SIC 1711 Plumbing, heating, air-conditioning
Michael Ohlmann
Chris Welsh
Andrew Welsh

D-U-N-S 24-594-4517   (SL)
WESPAC ELECTRICAL CONTRACTORS LTD
106 Blue Mountain St, Coquitlam, BC, V3K 4G8
(604) 522-1322
Emp Here 65   *Sales* 14,158,885
SIC 1731 Electrical work
Roland Thiel
Christina Thiel

D-U-N-S 24-338-3234   (SL)
WEST AUTO SALES LTD
KIA WEST
1881 United Blvd Suite D, Coquitlam, BC, V3K 0B6
(604) 777-1292
Emp Here 50   *Sales* 24,903,900
SIC 5511 New and used car dealers
Mark Anhert

D-U-N-S 24-856-8263   (HQ)
WESTERN LOGISTICS INC
1555 Brigantine Dr, Coquitlam, BC, V3K 7C2
(604) 525-7211
Emp Here 10   *Sales* 83,361,500
SIC 4731 Freight transportation arrangement
Mary Waring
Domenic Russo

D-U-N-S 20-513-6786   (HQ)
WESTERN PACIFIC ENTERPRISES GP
1321 Ketch Crt, Coquitlam, BC, V3K 6X7
(604) 540-1321
Sales 70,652,700
SIC 1731 Electrical work
David Fettback
Ron Fettback

Mark Fettback
Hal Moore
Wayne Fettback

D-U-N-S 20-117-3903   (HQ)
WHITE & PETERS LTD
1368 United Blvd Unit 101, Coquitlam, BC, V3K 6Y2
(604) 540-6585
Emp Here 20   *Sales* 21,852,900
SIC 5013 Motor vehicle supplies and new parts
Sumio Kikuchi
Mort Hall
Rob Neale
Martin Gifford

D-U-N-S 20-117-4562   (HQ)
WILLIAMS MOVING & STORAGE (B.C.) LTD
WILLIAMS MOVING INTERNATIONAL
2401 United Blvd, Coquitlam, BC, V3K 5X9

Emp Here 75   *Sales* 55,314,300
SIC 4214 Local trucking with storage
George Williams Jr
Glenn Thomsen
Verna Williams
Ernie Klassen

D-U-N-S 25-388-1403   (HQ)
WN PHARMACEUTICALS LTD
WEBBER NATURALS
2000 Brigantine Dr, Coquitlam, BC, V3K 7B5
(778) 284-7400
Emp Here 90   *Sales* 28,402,100
SIC 2834 Pharmaceutical preparations
Robin Hobbis
Terry Boyle
Don Bird
Michael Tate

D-U-N-S 25-986-4221   (SL)
WOODY'S ON BRUNETTE
WOODY'S ON BRUNETTE PUB
935 Brunette Ave, Coquitlam, BC, V3K 1C8
(604) 526-1718
Emp Here 60   *Sales* 14,659,680
SIC 5921 Liquor stores
Arline Buchanan

Courtenay, BC V9J

D-U-N-S 24-825-2744   (SL)
MT. WASHINGTON SKI RESORT LTD
MT. WASHINGTON ALPINE RESORT
1 Strathcona Pky, Courtenay, BC, V9J 1L0
(250) 338-1386
Emp Here 200   *Sales* 18,538,000
SIC 7011 Hotels and motels
George Stewart
Brian Stamp
Ted Foster

D-U-N-S 24-072-1233   (SL)
MUCHALAT CONSTRUCTION LTD
3326 Dove Creek Rd, Courtenay, BC, V9J 1P3
(250) 338-0995
Emp Here 35   *Sales* 13,520,255
SIC 1531 Operative builders
Joseph Formosa

Courtenay, BC V9N

D-U-N-S 24-456-1999   (SL)
AUSTIN POWDER LTD
(*Suby of* DAVIS MINING & MANUFACTURING, INC.)
4919 Island Hwy N, Courtenay, BC, V9N 5Z2
(250) 334-2624
Emp Here 19   *Sales* 13,876,555
SIC 5169 Chemicals and allied products, nec

Brenda Wilson

D-U-N-S 25-538-2715   (SL)
CAMCOURT HOLDINGS LTD
THRIFTY FOODS
660 England Ave, Courtenay, BC, V9N 2N4
(250) 338-1383
Emp Here 100   *Sales* 29,347,700
SIC 5411 Grocery stores
Alex A Campbell
Josephine Campbell
Laury Haines

D-U-N-S 24-033-7139   (HQ)
COAST COUNTRY INSURANCE SERVICES LTD
COAST COUNTRY FINANCIAL
426 8th St, Courtenay, BC, V9N 1N5
(250) 334-3443
Emp Here 18   *Sales* 23,745,680
SIC 6411 Insurance agents, brokers, and service
Dale Roberts
Maureen Roberts

D-U-N-S 20-573-9717   (SL)
COMOX VALLEY DODGE CHRYSLER JEEP LTD
4847 Island Hwy N, Courtenay, BC, V9N 5Y8
(250) 338-5451
Emp Here 33   *Sales* 16,436,574
SIC 5511 New and used car dealers
Bradley Trotman

D-U-N-S 20-585-3265   (SL)
COMOX VALLEY TRANSITION SOCIETY
625 England Ave, Courtenay, BC, V9N 2N5
(250) 897-0511
Emp Here 30   *Sales* 11,922,420
SIC 8699 Membership organizations, nec
Darry Oudendag

D-U-N-S 20-797-8490   (BR)
CORPORATION OF THE CITY OF COURTENAY, THE
COURTENAY RECREATION CENTRE
(*Suby of* CORPORATION OF THE CITY OF COURTENAY, THE)
489 Old Island Hwy, Courtenay, BC, V9N 3P5
(250) 338-5371
Emp Here 80
SIC 7999 Amusement and recreation, nec
Jim Stevenson

D-U-N-S 24-448-4465   (SL)
COURTENAY LODGE LTD
BEST WESTERN THE WESTERLY HOTEL, DIV OF
1590 Cliffe Ave, Courtenay, BC, V9N 2K4
(250) 338-7741
Emp Here 75   *Sales* 7,117,425
SIC 7011 Hotels and motels
Richard Gibbons

D-U-N-S 20-388-1339   (SL)
CVH AUTO INC
COMOX VALLEY HYUNDAI
250 Old Island Hwy, Courtenay, BC, V9N 3P1
(250) 334-2441
Emp Here 27   *Sales* 13,448,106
SIC 5511 New and used car dealers
Corey Sawchuk
Amanda Conly

D-U-N-S 24-042-2266   (SL)
ECOFISH RESEARCH LTD
450 8th St Suite F, Courtenay, BC, V9N 1N5
(250) 334-3042
Emp Here 49   *Sales* 10,407,453
SIC 8748 Business consulting, nec
Adam Lewis

D-U-N-S 25-977-4607   (SL)
GABRIELLA'S KITCHEN INC
910 Fitzgerald Ave Unit 301, Courtenay, BC, V9N 2R5
(250) 334-3209
Emp Here 50   *Sales* 41,778,850

SIC 5149 Groceries and related products, nec
Margot Micallef
Vincent Micallef
Christopher Fenn

D-U-N-S 24-373-5867   (SL)
GLACIER VIEW LODGE SOCIETY
2450 Back Rd, Courtenay, BC, V9N 8B5
(250) 338-1451
Emp Here 140   *Sales* 9,565,640
SIC 8051 Skilled nursing care facilities
Micheal Pontus
Sandy Dreger
Ron Webber

D-U-N-S 25-415-7787   (SL)
HEERINGA, J.L. ENTERPRISES LTD
CANADIAN TIRE
278 Old Island Hwy, Courtenay, BC, V9N 3P1
(250) 338-6553
Emp Here 100   *Sales* 26,155,300
SIC 6712 Bank holding companies
Jacob Heeringa

D-U-N-S 20-556-2270   (BR)
HOME DEPOT OF CANADA INC
HOME DEPOT
(*Suby of* THE HOME DEPOT INC)
388 Lerwick Rd, Courtenay, BC, V9N 9E5
(250) 334-5400
Emp Here 151
SIC 5211 Lumber and other building materials
Patrick Mckenna

D-U-N-S 20-914-8782   (SL)
J D M PHARMACY LTD
SHOPPERS DRUG MART
310 8th St, Courtenay, BC, V9N 1N3
(250) 334-3134
Emp Here 50   *Sales* 12,647,700
SIC 5912 Drug stores and proprietary stores
Jeff Matell

D-U-N-S 24-696-1759   (SL)
MCLEAN, BRIAN CHEVROLET LTD
2145 Cliffe Ave, Courtenay, BC, V9N 2L5
(250) 334-3400
Emp Here 38   *Sales* 18,926,964
SIC 5511 New and used car dealers
Brian D. Mclean

D-U-N-S 20-804-7563   (SL)
MT BECHER SKI RENTALS LTD
SKI TAK HUT
267 6th St, Courtenay, BC, V9N 1L9
(250) 334-2537
Emp Here 24   *Sales* 10,064,520
SIC 6712 Bank holding companies
Art Hobson
Maudy Hobson

D-U-N-S 25-215-9868   (BR)
PR SENIORS HOUSING MANAGEMENT LTD
COMOX VALLEY SENIORS VILLAGE
(*Suby of* PR SENIORS HOUSING MANAGEMENT LTD)
4640 Headquarters Rd Suite 227, Courtenay, BC, V9N 7J3
(250) 331-1183
Emp Here 200
SIC 8322 Individual and family services
Blake Mooney

D-U-N-S 24-166-2139   (SL)
RICE AUTOMOTIVE INVESTMENTS LTD
COURTENAY TOYOTA
445 Crown Isle Blvd, Courtenay, BC, V9N 9W1
(250) 338-6761
Emp Here 35   *Sales* 17,432,730
SIC 5511 New and used car dealers
Brian Rice

D-U-N-S 20-713-6123   (BR)
SCHOOL DISTRICT NO. 71 (COMOX VALLEY)
MARK ISFELD SCHOOL
1551 Lerwick Rd, Courtenay, BC, V9N 9B5

(250) 334-2428
Emp Here 110
SIC 8211 Elementary and secondary schools
Jeff Taylor

D-U-N-S 25-326-4295   (HQ)
SILVERADO LAND CORP
CROWN ISLE RESORT & GOLF COMMUNITY
399 Clubhouse Dr, Courtenay, BC, V9N 9G3
(250) 897-0233
Emp Here 50   *Sales* 15,817,200
SIC 6553 Cemetery subdividers and developers
Richard Jackson
Ronald J Coulson
Richard Wallhouse

D-U-N-S 25-685-1528   (SL)
SOUP BONE ENTERPRISES INC
ROYAL LEPAGE IN THE COMOX VALLEY
750 Comox Rd Suite 121, Courtenay, BC, V9N 3P6
(250) 897-1300
Emp Here 49   *Sales* 20,548,395
SIC 6712 Bank holding companies
Gregg Hart

D-U-N-S 24-641-6853   (SL)
SUNWEST AUTO CENTRE LTD
401 Ryan Rd, Courtenay, BC, V9N 3R5
(250) 338-7565
Emp Here 25   *Sales* 12,451,950
SIC 5511 New and used car dealers
Barry Willis

D-U-N-S 20-867-6882   (BR)
TOWN OF COMOX, THE
COMOX VALLEY SPORTS & AQUATIC CENTRES
(*Suby of* TOWN OF COMOX, THE)
377 Lerwick Rd, Courtenay, BC, V9N 9G4
(250) 334-2527
Emp Here 80
SIC 7999 Amusement and recreation, nec
Ray Bogards

D-U-N-S 24-329-5487   (HQ)
VISTA RADIO LTD
910 Fitzgerald Ave Unit 201, Courtenay, BC, V9N 2R5
(250) 334-2421
Emp Here 30   *Sales* 100,363,200
SIC 4832 Radio broadcasting stations
Margot Micallef
Terry Coles
Barbara Fairclough
Bryan Edwards
Paul Mann
Jason Mann

D-U-N-S 20-269-5227   (HQ)
WESTVIEW FORD SALES LTD
4901 Island Hwy N, Courtenay, BC, V9N 5Y9
(250) 334-3161
Emp Here 40   *Sales* 22,413,510
SIC 5511 New and used car dealers
Neil Van Ierland

Cranbrook, BC V1C

D-U-N-S 24-891-6301   (SL)
0889541 BC LTD
SPRING HONDA
1027 Victoria Ave N, Cranbrook, BC, V1C 3Y6
(250) 489-4311
Emp Here 26   *Sales* 12,950,028
SIC 5511 New and used car dealers
David Spring

D-U-N-S 24-726-9918   (SL)
B. C. GAS UTILITY LTD.
110 Slater Rd Nw, Cranbrook, BC, V1C 5C8
(250) 426-6388
Emp Here 6   *Sales* 18,635,142

SIC 4923 Gas transmission and distribution

D-U-N-S 20-334-9092   (SL)
CANADIAN TIRE ASSOCIATE STORE
1100 Victoria Ave N, Cranbrook, BC, V1C 6G7
(250) 489-5563
Emp Here 70   *Sales* 44,049,600
SIC 5531 Auto and home supply stores
Richard Reinders

D-U-N-S 20-990-7732   (HQ)
COLLEGE OF THE ROCKIES
2700 College Way, Cranbrook, BC, V1C 5L7
(250) 489-2751
Emp Here 512   *Sales* 31,195,738
SIC 8222 Junior colleges
David Walls
Wilda Schab
Krys Sikora
Jim Abbott
Glen Campbell
David Handy
Darryl Hyde
Steen Jorgensen
Jesse Nicholas
Gloria Perry

D-U-N-S 24-784-3225   (SL)
COMMUNITY CONNECTIONS SOCIETY OF SOUTHEAST BC
209 16th Ave N, Cranbrook, BC, V1C 5S8
(250) 426-2976
Emp Here 75   *Sales* 11,652,825
SIC 7361 Employment agencies
Laura Wilson

D-U-N-S 20-915-7242   (SL)
CRANBROOK DODGE
1725 Cranbrook St N, Cranbrook, BC, V1C 3S9
(888) 697-0855
Emp Here 30   *Sales* 14,942,340
SIC 5521 Used car dealers
David Girling

D-U-N-S 25-500-6645   (SL)
CRANBROOK SOCIETY FOR COMMUNITY LIVING
CSCL
1629 Baker St Suite 100, Cranbrook, BC, V1C 1B4
(250) 426-7588
Emp Here 110   *Sales* 8,447,120
SIC 8322 Individual and family services
Diane Baher
Wayne Eberne
Micheal Adams
Brandon Arnett

D-U-N-S 24-027-5607   (SL)
DACOTA FREIGHT SERVICE LTD
1474 Theatre Rd, Cranbrook, BC, V1C 7G1
(250) 426-3808
Emp Here 30   *Sales* 11,560,800
SIC 4731 Freight transportation arrangement
Dean Uphill
Tina Uphill

D-U-N-S 20-358-1947   (SL)
FR RENTALS LTD
2495 Theatre Rd, Cranbrook, BC, V1C 7B8
(778) 517-8388
Emp Here 40   *Sales* 11,686,760
SIC 7359 Equipment rental and leasing, nec
Michael Kozinuk

D-U-N-S 20-230-4353   (SL)
FW GREEN HOME, THE
NURSES OFFICE
1700 4th St S, Cranbrook, BC, V1C 6E1
(250) 426-8016
Emp Here 100   *Sales* 6,456,000
SIC 8059 Nursing and personal care, nec
Jeff Betker

D-U-N-S 20-095-4972   (HQ)
G.G.C.S. HOLDINGS LTD
MISTER TIRE

820 Cranbrook St N, Cranbrook, BC, V1C 3R9
(250) 426-5208
Emp Here 13   *Sales* 12,451,950
SIC 5531 Auto and home supply stores
Glen Lynn
Stan Jarabek

D-U-N-S 25-533-3304   (HQ)
GOLDEN LIFE MANAGEMENT CORP
1800 Willowbrook Dr, Cranbrook, BC, V1C
7H9
(250) 489-0667
Sales 135,225,600
SIC 6531 Real estate agents and managers
Endre Lillejord

D-U-N-S 24-361-7227   (BR)
HOME DEPOT OF CANADA INC
HOME DEPOT
(*Suby of* THE HOME DEPOT INC)
2000 Mcphee Rd, Cranbrook, BC, V1C 0A3
(250) 420-4250
Emp Here 100
SIC 5251 Hardware stores
Steve Wilson

D-U-N-S 25-104-3832   (HQ)
KOKANEE FOOD SERVICES INC
MCDONALD'S RESTAURANTS
(*Suby of* KAISER, DAVID INVESTMENTS
INC)
1405 Cranbrook St N, Cranbrook, BC, V1C
3S7
(250) 426-7767
Emp Here 89   *Sales* 5,829,875
SIC 5812 Eating places
David Kaiser

D-U-N-S 25-384-3593   (HQ)
KOOTENAY MARKET LTD
2 Cranbrook St N Suite 320, Cranbrook, BC,
V1C 3P6
(250) 426-1846
Emp Here 7   *Sales* 17,608,620
SIC 5411 Grocery stores
George Wood
Sandra Debbie
Debbie Wood

D-U-N-S 25-108-7235   (BR)
**MAINROAD EAST KOOTENAY CONTRACT-
ING LTD**
258 Industrial Road F, Cranbrook, BC, V1C
6N8
(250) 417-4624
Emp Here 100
SIC 1611 Highway and street construction
Kari Koivisto

D-U-N-S 25-140-2863   (SL)
QUAD CITY BUILDING MATERIALS LTD
HOME HARDWARE BUILDING CENTRE
1901 Mcphee Rd, Cranbrook, BC, V1C 7J2
(250) 426-6288
Emp Here 50   *Sales* 12,652,950
SIC 5251 Hardware stores
Martin Torgerson
Dawn Torgerson
Ken Peterson

D-U-N-S 24-983-1272   (SL)
RICHARD REINDERS SALES LTD
CANADIAN TIRE 395
1100 Victoria Ave N Suite 395, Cranbrook, BC,
V1C 6G7
(250) 489-3300
Emp Here 60   *Sales* 37,756,800
SIC 5531 Auto and home supply stores
Richard Reinders

D-U-N-S 25-154-1512   (BR)
**SCHOOL DISTRICT NO 5 (SOUTHEAST
KOOTENAY)**
*MOUNT BAKER SENIOR SECONDARY
SCHOOL*
940 Industrial Road 1 Suite 1, Cranbrook, BC,
V1C 4C6

(250) 426-4201
Emp Here 80
SIC 8211 Elementary and secondary schools
Debra Empson

D-U-N-S 25-497-9404   (HQ)
SELKIRK BEVERAGES LTD
604 Industrial Road C, Cranbrook, BC, V1C
4Y8
(250) 426-2731
Emp Here 19   *Sales* 16,411,600
SIC 5962 Merchandising machine operators
Cecil Olson

D-U-N-S 24-442-1897   (HQ)
SELKIRK SIGNS & SERVICES LTD
421 Patterson St W, Cranbrook, BC, V1C 6T3
(250) 489-3321
Emp Here 40   *Sales* 24,460,200
SIC 3993 Signs and advertising specialties
Hans Mehrle
Barry Naddin

D-U-N-S 20-566-6162   (SL)
SEM RESORT LIMITED PARTNERSHIP
SAINT EUGENE MISSION RESORT
7777 Mission Rd, Cranbrook, BC, V1C 7E5
(250) 420-2000
Emp Here 150   *Sales* 14,350,200
SIC 7011 Hotels and motels
Monir Nasif
Dan Shilling
Sophie Pierre
Denise Lightning

D-U-N-S 25-272-0123   (BR)
SOBEYS WEST INC
SAFEWAY, DIV OF
(*Suby of* EMPIRE COMPANY LIMITED)
1200 Baker St, Cranbrook, BC, V1C 1A8
(250) 417-0221
Emp Here 130
SIC 5411 Grocery stores
Rod Mccallum

D-U-N-S 20-867-6895   (SL)
TOP CROP GARDEN FARM & PET
2101 Cranbrook St N, Cranbrook, BC, V1C
5M6
(250) 489-4555
Emp Here 70   *Sales* 18,361,630
SIC 0181 Ornamental nursery products
Greg Fisher

D-U-N-S 24-317-1829   (BR)
WAL-MART CANADA CORP
WALMART
(*Suby of* WALMART INC.)
2100 Willowbrook Dr Suite 3183, Cranbrook,
BC, V1C 7H2
(250) 489-3202
Emp Here 185
SIC 5311 Department stores
Paul Custard

Creston, BC V0B

D-U-N-S 20-230-4676   (SL)
**CRESTON PET ADOPTION & WELFARE
SOCIETY**
PAWS CRESTON
2805 Lower Wynndel Rd, Creston, BC, V0B
1G8
(250) 428-7297
Emp Here 30   *Sales* 11,922,420
SIC 8699 Membership organizations, nec
Vicki Mcdonald

D-U-N-S 25-742-2980   (SL)
CRESTON VALLEY GLEANERS SOCIETY
807 Canyon St, Creston, BC, V0B 1G3
(250) 428-4106
Emp Here 100   *Sales* 13,345,900
SIC 8399 Social services, nec
Eleanor W. Szoke

Karen Sabiston
Beth Terriff
Virginia Buck

D-U-N-S 20-393-3903   (SL)
RIVER'S END FARMS LTD
(*Suby of* A&KB VENTURES (2007) INC)
2046 Corn Creek Rd, Creston, BC, V0B 1G7
(250) 428-3905
Emp Here 40   *Sales* 10,492,360
SIC 0181 Ornamental nursery products
Andre Baley
Krista Baley

D-U-N-S 20-059-4369   (SL)
RK SCHEPERS HOLDINGS LTD
HOME HARDWARE BUILDING CENTRE
1608 Northwest Blvd, Creston, BC, V0B 1G6
(250) 428-9388
Emp Here 50   *Sales* 12,652,950
SIC 5211 Lumber and other building materials
Robert Schepers
Kimberley Schepers

Crofton, BC V0R

D-U-N-S 20-327-4774   (BR)
CATALYST PAPER CORPORATION
CROFTON MILL
(*Suby of* CAPITAL ASSETS HOLDINGS (L)
BERHAD)
8541 Hay Road N, Crofton, BC, V0R 1R0
(250) 246-6100
Emp Here 578
SIC 2621 Paper mills

Cumberland, BC V0R

D-U-N-S 24-136-8323   (BR)
**VANCOUVER ISLAND HEALTH AUTHOR-
ITY**
CUMBERLAND HEALTH CENTRE
(*Suby of* GOVERNMENT OF THE
PROVINCE OF BRITISH COLUMBIA)
2696 Windermere St, Cumberland, BC, V0R
1S0
(250) 331-8505
Emp Here 85
SIC 8011 Offices and clinics of medical doc-
tors
Donna Walsh

Dawson Creek, BC V1G

D-U-N-S 20-539-9058   (SL)
ASPOL MOTORS (1982) LTD
ASPOL FORD
1125 102 Ave, Dawson Creek, BC, V1G 2C2
(250) 782-5804
Emp Here 27   *Sales* 13,448,106
SIC 5511 New and used car dealers
Fran Schilds

D-U-N-S 20-095-7371   (HQ)
BOREK CONSTRUCTION LTD
9630 Rd 223, Dawson Creek, BC, V1G 4H8
(250) 782-5561
Emp Here 150   *Sales* 107,628,640
SIC 1389 Oil and gas field services, nec
Dean Borek
Christien Vipond

D-U-N-S 24-396-3568   (SL)
BROWNS' CHEVROLET LIMITED
12109 8 St, Dawson Creek, BC, V1G 5A5
(250) 782-9155
Emp Here 30   *Sales* 14,942,340
SIC 5511 New and used car dealers

Charlie Grubisich
June Vekved
Garth Grubisich
Kevin Kutschinski

D-U-N-S 20-538-1742   (SL)
CAPITAL MOTORS (1985) LTD
CAPITAL MOTORS
1609 Alaska Ave, Dawson Creek, BC, V1G
1Z9
(250) 782-8589
Emp Here 60   *Sales* 37,756,800
SIC 5511 New and used car dealers

D-U-N-S 20-537-5462   (HQ)
DAWSON CO-OPERATIVE UNION
DAWSON CO-OP
10200 8 St Suite 3, Dawson Creek, BC, V1G
3P8
(250) 782-2217
Emp Here 80   *Sales* 163,436,130
SIC 5171 Petroleum bulk stations and termi-
nals
Allen Watson
Reg Norman
Gordon Parslow

D-U-N-S 20-325-2502   (BR)
EPSCAN INDUSTRIES LTD
(*Suby of* EPSCAN INDUSTRIES LTD)
600 113 Ave, Dawson Creek, BC, V1G 2Y6
(250) 782-9656
Emp Here 130
SIC 1731 Electrical work
Don Stirling

D-U-N-S 24-627-7537   (SL)
GEAR-O-RAMA SUPPLY LTD
9300 Golf Course Rd, Dawson Creek, BC,
V1G 4E9
(250) 782-8126
Emp Here 25   *Sales* 12,451,950
SIC 5511 New and used car dealers
Richard Hackworth
Andreas Schurmann
Barrie Beddel

D-U-N-S 24-987-5944   (SL)
ICG PROPANE INC.
10117 17 St, Dawson Creek, BC, V1G 4C1

Emp Here 6   *Sales* 18,635,142
SIC 4924 Natural gas distribution

D-U-N-S 24-098-3551   (SL)
INLAND AUTO CENTRE LTD
11600 8 St, Dawson Creek, BC, V1G 4R7
(250) 782-5507
Emp Here 32   *Sales* 16,835,964
SIC 5511 New and used car dealers
James Inkster

D-U-N-S 20-095-8304   (HQ)
LAWRENCE MEAT PACKING CO. LTD
BUTCHER BLOCK, THE
11088 4th St, Dawson Creek, BC, V1G 4H8
(250) 782-5111
Emp Here 20   *Sales* 62,668,275
SIC 5147 Meats and meat products
Joseph Lafond
Jerry Lafond
Maurice Lafond
Irene Lafond

D-U-N-S 25-108-3515   (SL)
M.R. BAULDIC ENTERPRISES INC
CANADIAN TIRE
11628 8 St, Dawson Creek, BC, V1G 4R7
(250) 782-9552
Emp Here 45   *Sales* 22,413,510
SIC 5531 Auto and home supply stores
Mike Bauldic
Sandy Bauldic

D-U-N-S 20-898-7966   (HQ)
NORTHERN LIGHTS COLLEGE
11401 8 St, Dawson Creek, BC, V1G 4G2
(250) 782-5251
Emp Here 20   *Sales* 23,491,203

SIC 8222 Junior colleges
Bryn Kulmatycki

D-U-N-S 24-584-0140   (SL)
P.C. OILFIELD SUPPLIES LTD
501 Rolla Rd, Dawson Creek, BC, V1G 4E9
(250) 782-5134
Emp Here 50   Sales 11,500,950
SIC 3272 Concrete products, nec
Herbert Nodes
Myrna Nodes
Joe Nodes

D-U-N-S 24-068-7061   (HQ)
SCHOOL DISTRICT #59 PEACE RIVER
SOUTH
SCHOOL BUS GARAGE
11600 7 St, Dawson Creek, BC, V1G 4R8
(250) 782-2106
Emp Here 19   Sales 74,339,250
SIC 8211 Elementary and secondary schools
William Deith

D-U-N-S 24-522-2112   (SL)
SOUTH PEACE COMMUNITY RESOURCES
SOCIETY
10110 13 St, Dawson Creek, BC, V1G 3W2
(250) 782-9174
Emp Here 115   Sales 23,812,820
SIC 8399 Social services, nec
Jane Harper

D-U-N-S 24-129-8806   (BR)
WAL-MART CANADA CORP
(Suby of WALMART INC.)
600 Highway 2, Dawson Creek, BC, V1G 0A4
(250) 719-0128
Emp Here 100
SIC 5311 Department stores

Dease Lake, BC V0C

D-U-N-S 20-114-4024   (SL)
SPATSIZI REMOTE SERVICES CORPORA-
TION
(Suby of TAHLTAN NATION DEVELOPMENT
CORPORATION)
Gd, Dease Lake, BC, V0C 1L0
(250) 771-5484
Emp Here 160
SIC 5812 Eating places
Bill Adsit

D-U-N-S 24-726-1522   (HQ)
TAHLTAN NATION DEVELOPMENT COR-
PORATION
Hwy 37 N, Dease Lake, BC, V0C 1L0
(250) 771-5482
Emp Here 50   Sales 21,457,570
SIC 1611 Highway and street construction
Calvin Carlick
Norman Day
Peter Arendt
Ty Benoit
Edward Van Meirlo
Ron Burton
Hankin Asp

Delta, BC V3M

D-U-N-S 24-161-7992   (HQ)
0429746 B.C. LTD
ORIGINAL CAKERIE, THE
1345 Cliveden Ave, Delta, BC, V3M 6C7
(604) 515-4555
Emp Here 280   Sales 250,850,600
SIC 5142 Packaged frozen goods
Kent Norris

D-U-N-S 20-108-4621   (SL)
A-Z FOAM LTD

811 Cundy Ave, Delta, BC, V3M 5P6
(604) 525-1665
Emp Here 50   Sales 10,094,850
SIC 3086 Plastics foam products
Nav Gill

D-U-N-S 20-619-4219   (HQ)
ACRYLCO MFG. LTD
711 Derwent Way, Delta, BC, V3M 5P9
(604) 524-9441
Sales 16,067,590
SIC 5162 Plastics materials and basic shapes
Rafael Filosof
Robert Schwartz

D-U-N-S 25-073-8358   (SL)
ADVANCE SHEET METAL LTD
1546 Derwent Way Suite 311c, Delta, BC,
V3M 6M4
(604) 540-4955
Emp Here 48   Sales 10,604,832
SIC 1711 Plumbing, heating, air-conditioning
Terry Calam
Ron Carr

D-U-N-S 24-977-2992   (HQ)
AIRGAS CANADA INC
(Suby of L'AIR LIQUIDE SOCI-
ETE ANONYME POUR L'ETUDE ET
L'EXPLOITATION DES PROCEDES
GEORGES CLAUDE)
634 Derwent Way, Delta, BC, V3M 5P8

Emp Here 30   Sales 21,910,350
SIC 5169 Chemicals and allied products, nec
Peter Mccausland
Michael Molinini

D-U-N-S 25-216-9701   (HQ)
AKHURST HOLDINGS LIMITED
1669 Foster'S Way, Delta, BC, V3M 6S7
(604) 540-1430
Sales 38,002,080
SIC 5084 Industrial machinery and equipment
Eric Stebner
Brian James Akhurst
Bruce Akhurst

D-U-N-S 20-108-5644   (HQ)
AKHURST MACHINERY LIMITED
(Suby of AKHURST HOLDINGS LIMITED)
1669 Foster'S Way, Delta, BC, V3M 6S7
(604) 540-1430
Emp Here 35   Sales 41,457,050
SIC 5084 Industrial machinery and equipment
Eric Stebner
Brian Akhurst
Bruce Akhurst

D-U-N-S 24-613-6972   (SL)
ALMETCO BUILDING PRODUCTS LTD
620 Audley Blvd, Delta, BC, V3M 5P2

Emp Here 170   Sales 32,654,450
SIC 3442 Metal doors, sash, and trim
Dave Munro
Dennis Zentner
Mike Lefroy
Doug Paterson

D-U-N-S 20-689-7667   (SL)
AXTON INCORPORATED
441 Derwent Pl, Delta, BC, V3M 5Y9
(604) 522-2731
Emp Here 85   Sales 11,264,970
SIC 3399 Primary Metal products
George Cook
Alfred A Guenkel
John M Raie
Tom W Maloney
James Leslie Grisdale
Kevin Dodds
Tom Hamilton

D-U-N-S 20-514-0270   (HQ)
BELTERRA CORPORATION
(Suby of MARUBENI CORPORATION)

1609 Derwent Way, Delta, BC, V3M 6K8
(604) 540-0044
Emp Here 15   Sales 170,705,500
SIC 5084 Industrial machinery and equipment
Janice Stasiuk
Mike Lake
Sergio Restagno

D-U-N-S 24-837-8135   (SL)
CANADIAN VINYLTEK WINDOWS CORPO-
RATION
VINYLTEK WINDOWS
587 Ebury Pl, Delta, BC, V3M 6M8
(604) 540-0029
Emp Here 70   Sales 18,735,640
SIC 5211 Lumber and other building materials
Peter Gudewill

D-U-N-S 25-506-8728   (BR)
CATELLI FOODS CORPORATION
OLIVIERI FOODS DIV
(Suby of EBRO FOODS, SA)
1631 Derwent Way, Delta, BC, V3M 6K8
(604) 525-2278
Emp Here 80
SIC 2098 Macaroni and spaghetti
Tom Cobden

D-U-N-S 20-553-3586   (BR)
CERTAINTEED GYPSUM CANADA, INC
1070 Derwent Way, Delta, BC, V3M 5R1
(604) 527-1405
Emp Here 80   Sales 690,057
SIC 3275 Gypsum products
Lance Woodring

D-U-N-S 24-558-5575   (SL)
CHEWTERS CHOCOLATES (1992) INC
1648 Derwent Way, Delta, BC, V3M 6R9
(888) 515-7117
Emp Here 50   Sales 11,242,750
SIC 2066 Chocolate and cocoa products
Wade Pugh
Richard Foley

D-U-N-S 24-535-5201   (HQ)
CIPA LUMBER CO. LTD
DELTA PANEL, DIV OF
(Suby of ITOCHU CORPORATION)
797 Carlisle Rd, Delta, BC, V3M 5P4
(604) 523-2250
Emp Here 120   Sales 26,931,800
SIC 2436 Softwood veneer and plywood
Toshihiro Matsuki
Akihiko Yoshioka

D-U-N-S 20-731-9372   (HQ)
COMMERCIAL EQUIPMENT CORP
COMMERCIAL TRUCK EQUIPMENT
591 Chester Rd, Delta, BC, V3M 6G7
(604) 526-6126
Emp Here 10   Sales 29,451,612
SIC 5082 Construction and mining machinery
Dean Mackay
Steve Tatone

D-U-N-S 24-416-7532   (HQ)
COMMERCIAL LIGHTING PRODUCTS LTD
1535 Cliveden Ave, Delta, BC, V3M 6P7
(604) 540-4999
Emp Here 27   Sales 26,830,440
SIC 5063 Electrical apparatus and equipment
Don Paul
Phil Dovey
Gord Carson

D-U-N-S 24-310-7617   (HQ)
CRYOPAK INDUSTRIES (2007) ULC
(Suby of TCP RELIABLE INC.)
1081 Cliveden Ave Suite 110, Delta, BC, V3M
5V1
(604) 515-7977
Emp Here 45   Sales 22,728,900
SIC 3822 Environmental controls
Raj Gill

D-U-N-S 25-161-3071   (HQ)
CVC SLING SHOT TRANSPORTATION INC

1345 Derwent Way, Delta, BC, V3M 5V9
(604) 515-9462
Emp Here 23   Sales 17,678,878
SIC 4731 Freight transportation arrangement
Jas Gill
Amrik Dulla
Michael Gill

D-U-N-S 24-134-8986   (SL)
DBC MARINE SAFETY SYSTEMS LTD
SURVITEC GROUP
(Suby of SURVITEC GROUP LIMITED)
1689 Cliveden Ave, Delta, BC, V3M 6V5
(604) 278-3221
Emp Here 102   Sales 22,831,986
SIC 3732 Boatbuilding and repairing
Franck Palomba
Mark Hansen

D-U-N-S 24-291-3358   (SL)
EAB TOOL COMPANY INC
584 Ebury Pl, Delta, BC, V3M 6M8
(604) 526-4595
Emp Here 40   Sales 19,001,040
SIC 5084 Industrial machinery and equipment
Robert Forbes

D-U-N-S 24-309-7524   (SL)
ENCHANTED MEADOW ESSENTIALS INC
1480 Cliveden Ave, Delta, BC, V3M 6L9
(604) 540-2999
Emp Here 15   Sales 11,137,800
SIC 5199 Nondurable goods, nec
Richard Gaetz
Barbara Gaetz
Juliuf Setiawan
James Gaetz
David Rivard

D-U-N-S 20-279-1562   (SL)
ENGLISH BAY BATTER L.P.
904 Cliveden Ave, Delta, BC, V3M 5R5
(604) 540-0622
Emp Here 100   Sales 34,569,000
SIC 2045 Prepared flour mixes and doughs
Anthony Sigel

D-U-N-S 25-680-8270   (HQ)
ENGLISH BAY ENTERPRISES INC
904 Cliveden Ave, Delta, BC, V3M 5R5
(604) 540-0622
Sales 73,101,800
SIC 6712 Bank holding companies
Ronald John Seguin

D-U-N-S 25-192-3553   (HQ)
ENWAVE CORPORATION
1668 Derwent Way Unit 1, Delta, BC, V3M
6R9
(604) 806-6110
Emp Here 11   Sales 12,720,459
SIC 3569 General industrial machinery, nec
Brent Charleton
John Budreski
Reihaneh Noorbakhsh
Richard Mitchell
John Zhang
Gary Sandberg
Leon Fu
Stewart Ritchie
Hugh Mckinnon
Mary C. Ritchie

D-U-N-S 24-860-0269   (HQ)
FHC ENTERPRISES LTD
FIELDS STORES
766 Cliveden Pl Suite 150, Delta, BC, V3M
6C7
(604) 549-9280
Emp Here 25   Sales 53,237,800
SIC 5399 Miscellaneous general merchandise
Jason Mcdougall
Ian Officer

D-U-N-S 20-329-0890   (SL)
FROBISHER INTERNATIONAL ENTER-
PRISE LTD
OCEANMAMA SEAFOOD

787 Cliveden Pl Unit 600, Delta, BC, V3M 6C7
(604) 523-8108
Emp Here 30   *Sales* 25,067,310
SIC 5146 Fish and seafoods
 Peter Fu

D-U-N-S 25-539-1427   (HQ)
GASTALDO CONCRETE HOLDINGS LTD
482 Fraserview Pl, Delta, BC, V3M 6H4
(604) 525-3636
Sales 17,767,750
SIC 6712 Bank holding companies
 George Gastaldo
 Paolo Carraro

D-U-N-S 20-747-9163   (SL)
GASTALDO CONCRETE LTD
(*Suby of* GASTALDO CONCRETE HOLD-
INGS LTD)
482 Fraserview Pl, Delta, BC, V3M 6H4
(604) 526-6262
Emp Here 70   *Sales* 17,323,810
SIC 1771 Concrete work
 George Gastaldo
 Paolo Carraro
 Paolo Gastaldo

D-U-N-S 25-103-7537   (SL)
GASTALDO PUMP SALES LTD
482 Fraserview Pl, Delta, BC, V3M 6H4
(604) 526-6262
Emp Here 70   *Sales* 33,251,820
SIC 5084 Industrial machinery and equipment
 George Gastaldo
 Silvano Gastaldo
 Paolo Carraro
 Paolo Gastaldo

D-U-N-S 24-320-3000   (SL)
GOLDEN WEST BAKING COMPANY ULC
(*Suby of* C.H. GUENTHER & SON LLC)
1111 Derwent Way, Delta, BC, V3M 5R4
(604) 525-2491
Emp Here 50   *Sales* 14,673,850
SIC 5461 Retail bakeries
 Rene Fluri

D-U-N-S 20-267-0100   (BR)
**GREATER VANCOUVER REGIONAL DIS-
TRICT**
*ANNACIS ISLAND WASTE WATER TREAT-
MENT PLANT*
(*Suby of* GREATER VANCOUVER RE-
GIONAL DISTRICT)
1299 Derwent Way, Delta, BC, V3M 5V9
(604) 525-5681
Emp Here 92
SIC 4953 Refuse systems
 Vince Chiu

D-U-N-S 20-557-5512   (HQ)
GREEN LINE HOSE & FITTINGS LTD
(*Suby of* GREEN LINE SALES LTD)
1477 Derwent Way, Delta, BC, V3M 6N3
(604) 670-1647
Emp Here 160   *Sales* 146,319,000
SIC 5085 Industrial supplies
 Andrew Dunham

D-U-N-S 20-513-0255   (HQ)
GREEN LINE SALES LTD
1477 Derwent Way, Delta, BC, V3M 6N3
(604) 525-6800
Emp Here 35   *Sales* 97,546,000
SIC 5085 Industrial supplies
 Andrew Dunham
 Timothy Becker

D-U-N-S 20-939-8465   (SL)
GROUNDSTAR EXPRESS LTD
1260 Cliveden Ave, Delta, BC, V3M 6Y1
(604) 527-1038
Emp Here 25   *Sales* 11,087,250
SIC 7389 Business services, nec
 Roger Sidhu

D-U-N-S 24-339-7309   (SL)
GUARD RFID SOLUTIONS INC

766 Cliveden Pl Unit 140, Delta, BC, V3M 6C7
(604) 998-4018
Emp Here 30   *Sales* 13,415,220
SIC 5065 Electronic parts and equipment, nec
 Zahir Abji
 James Topham
 Gary Smith
 Norman Toms

D-U-N-S 24-979-6137   (BR)
HENRY SCHEIN CANADA, INC
(*Suby of* HENRY SCHEIN, INC.)
1619 Foster'S Way, Delta, BC, V3M 6S7
(604) 527-8888
Emp Here 120
SIC 5047 Medical and hospital equipment
 Cy Elborne

D-U-N-S 20-698-5314   (HQ)
I.C.T.C. HOLDINGS CORPORATION
H.E.R.O. PRODUCTS GROUP
720 Eaton Way, Delta, BC, V3M 6J9
(604) 522-6543
Sales 12,828,100
SIC 3821 Laboratory apparatus and furniture
 Anthony Traub
 Stephen Balmer

D-U-N-S 24-249-6024   (SL)
IBOX PACKAGING LTD
IBOX
620 Audley Blvd, Delta, BC, V3M 5P2
(604) 522-4269
Emp Here 43   *Sales* 10,037,705
SIC 2653 Corrugated and solid fiber boxes
 Peter Watson

D-U-N-S 20-586-3012   (SL)
IDEAL WELDERS LTD
(*Suby of* R. JAY MANAGEMENT LTD)
660 Caldew St, Delta, BC, V3M 5S2
(604) 525-5558
Emp Here 85   *Sales* 16,327,225
SIC 3498 Fabricated pipe and fittings
 R. James Longo
 Roy Kinders
 Jon Ballantyne

D-U-N-S 24-980-6472   (BR)
IMPRIMERIES TRANSCONTINENTAL INC
TRANSCONTINENTAL PRINTING INC
(*Suby of* TRANSCONTINENTAL INC)
725 Hampstead Close, Delta, BC, V3M 6R6
(604) 540-2333
Emp Here 200
SIC 2752 Commercial printing, lithographic
 Hans Neilsen

D-U-N-S 20-106-1970   (SL)
IND DIAGNOSTIC INC
1629 Foster'S Way, Delta, BC, V3M 6S7

Emp Here 80   *Sales* 18,183,120
SIC 3841 Surgical and medical instruments
 Shuli Wang
 Jiabei Zhu

D-U-N-S 25-357-4438   (SL)
INNOVATIVE MANUFACTURING INC
861 Derwent Way Suite 877, Delta, BC, V3M
5R4
(604) 522-2811
Emp Here 37   *Sales* 27,473,240
SIC 5198 Paints, varnishes, and supplies
 Craig Anderson
 Ivan Wirch
 Marjory Anderson

D-U-N-S 24-980-5045   (SL)
**INTERNATIONAL NEWTECH DEVELOP-
MENT INCORPORATED**
1629 Foster'S Way, Delta, BC, V3M 6S7

Emp Here 120   *Sales* 27,570,480
SIC 8731 Commercial physical research
 Jesse Zhu

D-U-N-S 20-109-2723   (HQ)

**KAMAN INDUSTRIAL TECHNOLOGIES,
LTD**
(*Suby of* KAMAN CORPORATION)
746 Chester Rd, Delta, BC, V3M 6J1
(604) 523-2356
Emp Here 10   *Sales* 16,625,910
SIC 5085 Industrial supplies
 Steven J. Smidler
 Robert D. Starr
 Roger S. Jorgensen
 Michael J. Lyon
 Carl A. Conlon
 Shawn G. Lisle
 Richard S. Smith
 Neal J. Keating

D-U-N-S 24-796-0763   (BR)
KONE INC
(*Suby of* KONE OYJ)
1488 Cliveden Ave, Delta, BC, V3M 6L9
(604) 777-5663
Emp Here 75
SIC 1799 Special trade contractors, nec
 Gurveer Gill

D-U-N-S 24-024-6694   (HQ)
LOCHER EVERS INTERNATIONAL INC
LEI
(*Suby of* LOCHER HOLDINGS LTD)
456 Humber Pl, Delta, BC, V3M 6A5
(604) 523-5100
Emp Here 75   *Sales* 126,709,480
SIC 4731 Freight transportation arrangement
 Chris Locher
 Greg Locher
 Peter Broerken

D-U-N-S 24-639-4811   (BR)
LOCHER EVERS INTERNATIONAL INC
L E I
(*Suby of* LOCHER HOLDINGS LTD)
456 Humber Pl, Delta, BC, V3M 6A5
(604) 525-0577
Emp Here 90
SIC 4225 General warehousing and storage
 Penny Robinson

D-U-N-S 20-102-8388   (HQ)
**MAGNACHARGE BATTERY CORPORA-
TION**
1279 Derwent Way Unit 1, Delta, BC, V3M
5V9
(604) 525-0391
Emp Here 20   *Sales* 19,546,240
SIC 5999 Miscellaneous retail stores, nec
 Greg Granholm
 Justin Bakhsh
 Darrell Kure
 Chris Christopher
 Ed Loftus

D-U-N-S 24-000-9501   (BR)
MARK ANTHONY GROUP INC
(*Suby of* PELECANUS HOLDINGS LTD)
465 Fraserview Pl, Delta, BC, V3M 6H4
(604) 519-5370
Emp Here 100
SIC 2084 Wines, brandy, and brandy spirits
 Anthony Von Mandl

D-U-N-S 20-509-4881   (HQ)
MASON LIFT LTD
(*Suby of* DINAT RESOURCES LTD)
1605 Cliveden Ave, Delta, BC, V3M 6P7
(604) 517-6500
Emp Here 61   *Sales* 39,977,760
SIC 7359 Equipment rental and leasing, nec
 D. George Peles
 Jennifer Peles
 Leslie Lee

D-U-N-S 20-375-0427   (HQ)
MERCURY PLASTICS OF CANADA INC
(*Suby of* MERCURY PLASTICS, INC.)
880 Cliveden Ave, Delta, BC, V3M 5R5
(604) 525-1061
Emp Here 150   *Sales* 31,771,600

SIC 3081 Unsupported plastics film and sheet
 Amber Jordan

D-U-N-S 25-216-3167   (HQ)
**METROPOLITAN HARDWOOD FLOORS,
INC**
811 Cliveden Ave, Delta, BC, V3M 5R6
(604) 395-2000
Emp Here 68   *Sales* 38,164,200
SIC 5023 Homefurnishings
 Paul Anderson
 Dave Sandover
 Brady Page
 Gordon Payseno

D-U-N-S 24-439-4763   (SL)
MOBIL SHRED INC
RECALL
(*Suby of* BRAMBLES LIMITED)
588 Annance Crt Unit 4, Delta, BC, V3M 6Y8
(604) 526-2622
Emp Here 140   *Sales* 93,647,120
SIC 7389 Business services, nec
 Al Trujillo

D-U-N-S 24-371-1033   (HQ)
NATIONAL SIGNCORP INVESTMENTS LTD
SIGNCORP
1471 Derwent Way, Delta, BC, V3M 6N2
(604) 525-4300
Emp Here 45   *Sales* 19,568,160
SIC 3993 Signs and advertising specialties
 Mike Armitage
 Charynne Armitage

D-U-N-S 24-329-9877   (SL)
NIRADIA ENTERPRISES INC
460 Fraserview Pl, Delta, BC, V3M 6H4
(604) 523-6188
Emp Here 60   *Sales* 15,693,180
SIC 6712 Bank holding companies
 Guerrino Nichele

D-U-N-S 20-136-8136   (SL)
P.E.T. PROCESSING INC
PTI
917 Cliveden Ave Unit 105, Delta, BC, V3M
5R6
(604) 522-6727
Emp Here 40   *Sales* 10,285,240
SIC 4953 Refuse systems
 Antoine Moucachen

D-U-N-S 24-446-1026   (HQ)
PACE CHEMICALS LTD
1597 Derwent Way Fl 2, Delta, BC, V3M 6K8
(604) 520-6211
Sales 18,258,625
SIC 5169 Chemicals and allied products, nec
 Wesley Martin

D-U-N-S 20-005-5619   (SL)
PACIFIC RIM CABINETS LTD
640 Belgrave Way, Delta, BC, V3M 5R7
(604) 515-7377
Emp Here 50   *Sales* 11,517,000
SIC 5712 Furniture stores
 Bill Dewinetz

D-U-N-S 20-865-2685   (SL)
PANORAMA BUILDING SYSTEMS LTD
460 Fraserview Pl, Delta, BC, V3M 6H4
(604) 522-4980
Emp Here 150   *Sales* 37,122,450
SIC 1771 Concrete work
 Gerry Nichele

D-U-N-S 25-994-5442   (BR)
**PEPSI BOTTLING GROUP (CANADA), ULC,
THE**
PEPSICO BEVERAGES CANADA
(*Suby of* PBG INVESTMENT (LUXEM-
BOURG) SARL)
747 Chester Rd, Delta, BC, V3M 6E7
(604) 520-8000
Emp Here 300
SIC 2086 Bottled and canned soft drinks
 Kurtis Mc Catney

D-U-N-S 24-995-6103   (BR)
PRAXAIR CANADA INC
(*Suby of* LINDE PUBLIC LIMITED COMPANY)
1470 Derwent Way, Delta, BC, V3M 6H9
(604) 527-0700
Emp Here 100
SIC 5169 Chemicals and allied products, nec
Randy Michael

D-U-N-S 25-978-0757   (HQ)
PRISM CONSTRUCTION LTD
(*Suby of* SPECTRUM HOLDINGS LTD)
1525 Cliveden Ave Suite 201, Delta, BC, V3M 6L2
(604) 526-3731
Sales 22,813,520
SIC 1542 Nonresidential construction, nec
Amin A Rawji

D-U-N-S 20-105-7155   (SL)
QM BEARINGS & POWER TRANSMISSION LTD
1511 Derwent Way Suite 205, Delta, BC, V3M 6N4
(604) 521-7226
Emp Here 35   *Sales* 16,625,910
SIC 5084 Industrial machinery and equipment
Cory Shaw
Justin Gu
John Sethen
Mark Flaherty
Donald Yorston

D-U-N-S 24-029-8299   (HQ)
RAMPION ENTERPRISES LTD
1555 Cliveden Ave, Delta, BC, V3M 6P7
(604) 395-8225
Emp Here 1   *Sales* 11,451,924
SIC 5091 Sporting and recreation goods
David Williams

D-U-N-S 24-867-1851   (BR)
RUSSEL METALS INC
A.J. FORSYTH, A DIVISION OF RUSSEL METALS
(*Suby of* RUSSEL METALS INC)
830 Carlisle Rd, Delta, BC, V3M 5P4
(604) 525-0544
Emp Here 100
SIC 5051 Metals service centers and offices
Gary Dyck

D-U-N-S 24-930-3660   (HQ)
S.P. RICHARDS CO. CANADA INC
(*Suby of* GENUINE PARTS COMPANY)
820 Cliveden Pl Unit 4, Delta, BC, V3M 6C7
(604) 540-0444
Sales 42,810,930
SIC 5112 Stationery and office supplies
Peter Dalglish
Warren Hastings

D-U-N-S 25-094-7132   (HQ)
SSAB SWEDISH STEEL LTD
(*Suby of* SSAB AB)
1031 Cliveden Ave, Delta, BC, V3M 5V1
(604) 526-3700
Emp Here 21   *Sales* 17,886,960
SIC 5051 Metals service centers and offices
Louis Bolen
Olof Martinsson
Peter Tang

D-U-N-S 20-586-1347   (HQ)
TAYMOR INDUSTRIES LTD
1655 Derwent Way, Delta, BC, V3M 6K8
(604) 540-9525
Emp Here 100   *Sales* 46,004,400
SIC 5072 Hardware
Nathan Zalkow
Vivian Zalkow
Nelson Nogales
Meghan Henderson
David Crystal

D-U-N-S 24-824-2372   (SL)
THORNTON STEAD ENTERPRISES INC

1223 Derwent Way, Delta, BC, V3M 5V9
(604) 524-8000
Emp Here 63   *Sales* 16,477,839
SIC 6712 Bank holding companies
Robert Thornton
Mike Mogan

D-U-N-S 20-175-1471   (HQ)
TRANSCOLD DISTRIBUTION LTD
1460 Cliveden Ave, Delta, BC, V3M 6L9
(604) 519-0600
Emp Here 45   *Sales* 41,778,850
SIC 5143 Dairy products, except dried or canned
John Coughlan
Melissa Coughlan
Curtis Wright

D-U-N-S 24-338-2004   (HQ)
TRANSOURCE FREIGHTWAYS LTD
1659 Foster'S Way, Delta, BC, V3M 6S7
(604) 525-0527
Sales 23,802,847
SIC 4213 Trucking, except local
Kal Kajla
Debbie Kajla
Randy Dulay

D-U-N-S 25-370-2245   (BR)
TYCO INTEGRATED FIRE & SECURITY CANADA, INC
SIMPLEXGRINNELL
(*Suby of* JOHNSON CONTROLS INTERNATIONAL PUBLIC LIMITED COMPANY)
1485 Lindsey Pl, Delta, BC, V3M 6V1
(604) 515-8872
Emp Here 98
SIC 7389 Business services, nec

D-U-N-S 20-793-2950   (BR)
UNITED PARCEL SERVICE CANADA LTD
UPS
(*Suby of* UNITED PARCEL SERVICE, INC.)
790 Belgrave Way, Delta, BC, V3M 5R9
(800) 742-5877
Emp Here 300
SIC 7389 Business services, nec
Dominic Porporino

D-U-N-S 25-109-5386   (SL)
V K DELIVERY & MOVING SERVICES LTD
588 Annance Crt Unit 2, Delta, BC, V3M 6Y8
(604) 540-0384
Emp Here 35   *Sales* 13,487,600
SIC 4731 Freight transportation arrangement
Ved Kaler

D-U-N-S 24-069-6146   (BR)
VERITIV CANADA, INC
(*Suby of* VERITIV CORPORATION)
1425 Derwent Way, Delta, BC, V3M 6N3
(604) 520-7500
Emp Here 150
SIC 5199 Nondurable goods, nec
Steven Arp

D-U-N-S 25-270-5272   (BR)
VERSACOLD GROUP LIMITED PARTNERSHIP
VERSACOLD LOGISTICS SERVICES
1188 Derwent Way, Delta, BC, V3M 5R1
(604) 216-6238
Emp Here 112
SIC 4222 Refrigerated warehousing and storage
Steven Smith

D-U-N-S 20-585-8962   (HQ)
VULCAN AUTOMOTIVE EQUIPMENT LTD
788 Caldew St Unit 121, Delta, BC, V3M 5S2
(604) 526-1167
Emp Here 30   *Sales* 28,317,600
SIC 5511 New and used car dealers
Thomas Alan Meikle

D-U-N-S 24-640-6581   (SL)
WALLACE & CAREY (B.C.) LTD
(*Suby of* CAREY MANAGEMENT INC)

551 Chester Rd, Delta, BC, V3M 6G7
(604) 522-9930
Emp Here 95   *Sales* 79,379,815
SIC 5141 Groceries, general line
Frank Carey

D-U-N-S 20-284-2097   (SL)
WALLACE & CAREY INC
CDC
551 Chester Rd, Delta, BC, V3M 6G7
(604) 522-9930
Emp Here 49   *Sales* 40,943,273
SIC 5148 Fresh fruits and vegetables
Frank Carey

D-U-N-S 24-979-4710   (SL)
WESTERN CONCORD MANUFACTURING (NEW WEST) LTD
880 Cliveden Ave, Delta, BC, V3M 5R5
(604) 525-1061
Emp Here 245   *Sales* 38,920,210
SIC 3086 Plastics foam products
Clive Beddoe
Linda Simpson
Lonnie Lock

D-U-N-S 24-898-3561   (HQ)
WESTERN WAFFLES CORP
(*Suby of* TREEHOUSE FOODS, INC.)
529 Annance Crt, Delta, BC, V3M 6Y7
(604) 524-2540
Sales 34,569,000
SIC 2038 Frozen specialties, nec
Gene Diakow

D-U-N-S 24-357-2836   (BR)
WEYERHAEUSER COMPANY LIMITED
ILEVEL
(*Suby of* WEYERHAEUSER COMPANY)
1272 Derwent Way, Delta, BC, V3M 5R1
(604) 526-4665
Emp Here 190
SIC 2421 Sawmills and planing mills, general
David Graham

D-U-N-S 20-862-1375   (SL)
WWL VEHICLE SERVICES CANADA LTD
(*Suby of* WALLENIUS WILHELMSEN ASA)
820 Dock Rd Unit 100, Delta, BC, V3M 6A3
(604) 521-6681
Emp Here 150   *Sales* 59,886,300
SIC 4013 Switching and terminal services
Howard Williams
Christopher Connor

Delta, BC V4C

D-U-N-S 24-309-4414   (HQ)
ATKINSON & TERRY INSURANCE BROKERS
8067 120 St Suite 120, Delta, BC, V4C 6P7
(604) 596-3350
Emp Here 30   *Sales* 616,993,520
SIC 6411 Insurance agents, brokers, and service
Brent Atkinson
Don Terry
Donald Sache

D-U-N-S 24-613-9356   (SL)
ATM FOODS LTD
EXTRA FOODS NO. 8561
8037 120 St, Delta, BC, V4C 6P7

Emp Here 125   *Sales* 36,684,625
SIC 5411 Grocery stores
Thomas Douglas

D-U-N-S 20-085-1561   (SL)
CANADA ROAD CARRIER LTD
11440 73 Ave, Delta, BC, V4C 1B7
(604) 502-0240
Emp Here 50   *Sales* 22,174,500
SIC 7389 Business services, nec

Harjainder Kandola
Davinder Kandola

D-U-N-S 20-794-4898   (BR)
CITY OF DELTA
CORPORATION OF DELTA, THE
(*Suby of* CITY OF DELTA)
7815 112 St, Delta, BC, V4C 4V9
(604) 952-3075
Emp Here 100
SIC 7999 Amusement and recreation, nec
Patrick Ansell

D-U-N-S 20-747-8645   (HQ)
DELTA CEDAR PRODUCTS LTD
10104 River Rd, Delta, BC, V4C 2R3
(604) 583-4159
Sales 111,356,000
SIC 2421 Sawmills and planing mills, general
Brian Dyck
Errol Wintemute

D-U-N-S 20-689-3716   (SL)
DELTA CEDAR SPECIALTIES LTD
SUNBURY CEDAR SALES, DIV OF
10104 River Rd, Delta, BC, V4C 2R3
(604) 589-9006
Emp Here 200   *Sales* 38,474,000
SIC 2499 Wood products, nec
Dean Garosano
Karen Morrision

D-U-N-S 20-005-5205   (BR)
DELTA SCHOOL DISTRICT NO.37
DELVIEW ADULT LEARNING CENTRE
9115 116 St, Delta, BC, V4C 5W8
(604) 594-6100
Emp Here 100
SIC 8211 Elementary and secondary schools
Brent Koot

D-U-N-S 25-013-9961   (BR)
DELTA SCHOOL DISTRICT NO.37
NORTH DELTA SENIOR SECONDARY SCHOOL
11447 82 Ave, Delta, BC, V4C 5J6
(604) 596-7471
Emp Here 86
SIC 8211 Elementary and secondary schools
Rod Allnut

D-U-N-S 20-651-7224   (BR)
FRASER HEALTH AUTHORITY
(*Suby of* GOVERNMENT OF THE PROVINCE OF BRITISH COLUMBIA)
11245 84 Ave Suite 101, Delta, BC, V4C 2L9
(604) 507-5400
Emp Here 100
SIC 8062 General medical and surgical hospitals
Carla Kraft

D-U-N-S 20-354-9345   (HQ)
GATEWAY PROPERTY MANAGEMENT CORPORATION
11950 80 Ave Suite 400, Delta, BC, V4C 1Y2
(604) 635-5000
Emp Here 2   *Sales* 16,459,920
SIC 8741 Management services
Randall Scott Ullrich
Ken Axenty

D-U-N-S 20-555-7700   (BR)
LOBLAWS INC
REAL CANADIAN SUPERSTORE
(*Suby of* LOBLAW COMPANIES LIMITED)
8195 120 St, Delta, BC, V4C 6P7
(604) 592-5218
Emp Here 322
SIC 5411 Grocery stores
Stephen Tam

D-U-N-S 25-230-8960   (SL)
ROADSTAR TRANSPORT COMPANY LTD
10064 River Rd, Delta, BC, V4C 2R3
(604) 882-7623
Emp Here 100   *Sales* 14,819,200
SIC 4212 Local trucking, without storage

Peter Confortin

D-U-N-S 24-897-8421   (HQ)
SILVER PACIFIC INVESTMENTS INC
SPI INTERNATIONAL TRANSPORTATION
7337 120 St Suite 245, Delta, BC, V4C 6P5
(604) 588-0227
Emp Here 1   *Sales* 11,439,274
SIC 4731 Freight transportation arrangement
Joe Chandler
James Taggart

D-U-N-S 24-524-1190   (SL)
SVAH TRADERS INC
11322 77 Ave, Delta, BC, V4C 1L9
(604) 897-8272
Emp Here 30   *Sales* 13,415,220
SIC 5052 Coal and other minerals and ores
Richard Singh

D-U-N-S 24-393-2543   (SL)
**TORNADO   BUILDING   MAINTENANCE
CORPORATION**
TORNADO
9453 120 St Suite 201, Delta, BC, V4C 6S2
(604) 930-6030
Emp Here 200   *Sales* 6,393,600
SIC 7349 Building maintenance services, nec
Jim Sundar

D-U-N-S 20-043-8443   (HQ)
WESTVIEW SALES LTD
7251 120 St, Delta, BC, V4C 6P5
(604) 591-7747
Emp Here 1   *Sales* 10,003,390
SIC 5051 Metals service centers and offices
Trevor Brien
Regina Brien

Delta, BC V4E

D-U-N-S 25-071-6446   (BR)
DELTA SCHOOL DISTRICT NO.37
SCAQUAM SECONDARY SCHOOL
11584 Lyon Rd, Delta, BC, V4E 2K4
(604) 946-4101
Emp Here 85
SIC 8211 Elementary and secondary schools
Gordon Collings

D-U-N-S 25-318-1598   (BR)
**MCDONALD'S   RESTAURANTS   OF
CANADA LIMITED**
MCDONALD'S 8075
(*Suby of* MCDONALD'S CORPORATION)
7005 120 St, Delta, BC, V4E 2A9
(604) 592-1330
Emp Here 85
SIC 5812 Eating places
Melissa White

D-U-N-S 25-262-6882   (SL)
NORTHCREST CARE CENTRE LTD
6771 120 St, Delta, BC, V4E 2A7
(604) 597-7878
Emp Here 75   *Sales* 5,154,975
SIC 8051 Skilled nursing care facilities
Otto Forelich
Gerd Reefschlager
David Aune

D-U-N-S 24-210-0573   (SL)
TYAM EXCAVATION & SHORING LTD
6955 120 St Suite 202, Delta, BC, V4E 2A8
(778) 593-2900
Emp Here 10   *Sales* 11,700,690
SIC 1794 Excavation work
Ranjit Dhanda

Delta, BC V4G

D-U-N-S 24-979-9719   (HQ)

112792 CANADA INC
AMJ CAMPBELL VAN LINES
9924 River Rd, Delta, BC, V4G 1B5
(604) 940-4208
Sales 14,399,420
SIC 4212 Local trucking, without storage
Tom Finlay
Kevin Brown

D-U-N-S 24-205-1089   (HQ)
21 CENTURY TRADING INC
6951 72 St Unit 110, Delta, BC, V4G 0A2
(604) 952-4565
Emp Here 16   *Sales* 25,902,887
SIC 5141 Groceries, general line
Michael Seo
Fred Lee

D-U-N-S 24-621-0512   (SL)
327494 B.C. LTD
MONTE CRISTO BAKERY
7763 Progress Way, Delta, BC, V4G 1A3
(604) 420-3511
Emp Here 140   *Sales* 100,340,240
SIC 5149 Groceries and related products, nec
Karim Nathoo

D-U-N-S 24-397-5989   (SL)
AIRBORNE ENGINES LTD
(*Suby of* M INTERNATIONAL, INC.)
7762 Progress Way, Delta, BC, V4G 1A4
(604) 244-1668
Emp Here 48   *Sales* 11,700,690
SIC 8711 Engineering services
Rob Ruck
Ming Cheung
Darcy Mcalpine
Joe Miller

D-U-N-S 20-288-6743   (SL)
ARC PROTECTION CORP
7351 Vantage Way Unit 3, Delta, BC, V4G 1C9
(604) 345-0215
Emp Here 80   *Sales* 75,134,160
SIC 6289 Security and commodity service
Scot Filer
Robert Jonatschich
Joel Pouliot
Rick Moss

D-U-N-S 20-801-3375   (HQ)
**ARPAC STORAGE SYSTEMS CORPORA-
TION**
7663 Progress Way, Delta, BC, V4G 1A2
(604) 940-4000
Emp Here 100   *Sales* 25,463,130
SIC 2542 Partitions and fixtures, except wood
Art Wuschke

D-U-N-S 20-547-2991   (SL)
ASCO AEROSPACE CANADA LTD
(*Suby of* S.R.I.F.)
8510 River Rd, Delta, BC, V4G 1B5
(604) 946-4900
Emp Here 112   *Sales* 21,513,520
SIC 3429 Hardware, nec
Trude Motmans
David Belanger
Kevin Russell

D-U-N-S 24-634-4469   (HQ)
AVCORP INDUSTRIES INC
10025 River Way, Delta, BC, V4G 1M7
(604) 582-1137
Emp Here 100   *Sales* 117,085,937
SIC 3728 Aircraft parts and equipment, nec
Amandeep Kaler
Jessica Gill
Edward Merlo
David Levi
Jaap Rosen Jacobson
Elizabeth Otis
Ken Robertson

D-U-N-S 24-850-6995   (SL)
BC STEVENS COMPANY
8188 Swenson Way, Delta, BC, V4G 1J6

(604) 634-3088
Emp Here 51   *Sales* 22,805,874
SIC 5047 Medical and hospital equipment
Rod Hilliard
Scott Baker
Mike Wheatley
Laura Bailey

D-U-N-S 24-034-3384   (HQ)
BCF INVESTMENTS INC
9829 River Rd, Delta, BC, V4G 1B4
(604) 583-3474
Sales 53,236,260
SIC 2091 Canned and cured fish and
seafoods
William Bingham
Tim Turyk

D-U-N-S 24-448-0026   (SL)
BRENCO INDUSTRIES LTD
10030 River Way, Delta, BC, V4G 1M9
(604) 584-2700
Emp Here 65   *Sales* 12,485,525
SIC 3441 Fabricated structural Metal
Steven Heim

D-U-N-S 24-866-6067   (SL)
BROCKMANN CHOCOLATE INC
7863 Progress Way, Delta, BC, V4G 1A3
(604) 946-4111
Emp Here 30   *Sales* 10,370,700
SIC 2066 Chocolate and cocoa products
Norbert Brockmann
Marianne Brockmann

D-U-N-S 24-724-8362   (SL)
BRONCO INDUSTRIES INC
7988 82 St, Delta, BC, V4G 1L8
(604) 940-8821
Emp Here 60   *Sales* 14,006,100
SIC 3211 Flat glass
Bronson Lam
Sam Chang

D-U-N-S 20-013-0180   (SL)
BUCKEYE CANADA CO.
7979 Vantage Way, Delta, BC, V4G 1A6

Emp Here 150   *Sales* 29,215,200
SIC 2621 Paper mills
Kristopher Matula
Charles Aiken
Stephen Dean
Sheila Cunningham

D-U-N-S 24-505-0281   (HQ)
C. KEAY INVESTMENTS LTD
OCEAN TRAILER
9076 River Rd, Delta, BC, V4G 1B5
(604) 940-0210
Emp Here 86   *Sales* 18,836,160
SIC 7519 Utility trailer rental
Sid Keay
Mike Keay

D-U-N-S 24-897-1947   (SL)
CANADIAN AIR-CRANE LTD
7293 Wilson Ave, Delta, BC, V4G 1E5
(604) 940-1715
Emp Here 75   *Sales* 11,689,725
SIC 2411 Logging
Ralph Torney
Dave Heyes

D-U-N-S 24-493-0954   (SL)
CANADIAN AUTOPARTS TOYOTA INC
(*Suby of* TOYOTA MOTOR CORPORATION)
7233 Progress Way, Delta, BC, V4G 1E7
(604) 946-5636
Emp Here 250   *Sales* 72,712,500
SIC 3714 Motor vehicle parts and accessories
Al Hossack

D-U-N-S 24-980-3156   (SL)
**CANADIAN   ENGINEERED   PRODUCTS
AND SALES LTD**
CANNEPP
7449 Hume Ave Suite 6, Delta, BC, V4G 1C3

(604) 940-8188
Emp Here 25   *Sales* 11,179,350
SIC 5075 Warm air heating and air condition-
ing
Nick Eaden
Mark Simpson

D-U-N-S 20-111-0731   (HQ)
CAPLAN INDUSTRIES INC
TASK TOOLS
6800 Dennett Pl, Delta, BC, V4G 1N4
(604) 946-3100
Emp Here 75   *Sales* 55,205,280
SIC 5072 Hardware
Craig Caplan
Bearl Caplan
Hilary Dore

D-U-N-S 25-930-0051   (HQ)
CASCADIA METALS LTD
(*Suby of* R & R TRADING CO. LTD)
7630 Berg Rd, Delta, BC, V4G 1G4
(604) 946-3890
Emp Here 75   *Sales* 40,245,660
SIC 5051 Metals service centers and offices
Earl William Ritchie
Florence Ritchie

D-U-N-S 24-359-9599   (HQ)
CMP GROUP LTD
(*Suby of* IRONBRIDGE EQUITY PARTNERS
II, LP)
7733 Progress Way, Delta, BC, V4G 1A3
(604) 940-2010
Sales 53,770,860
SIC 5051 Metals service centers and offices
John Mitchell
Theo Vanden Hoven
Peter Samson
Jeffrey Murphy
Walter Szwez
Daivik Doshi

D-U-N-S 20-114-0659   (HQ)
DAMCO DISTRIBUTION CANADA INC
(*Suby of* A.P. MOLLER OG HUSTRU CHAS-
TINE MC-KINNEY MOLLERS FOND TIL
ALMENE FORMAAL)
8400 River Rd, Delta, BC, V4G 1B5
(604) 940-1357
Emp Here 115   *Sales* 58,760,775
SIC 4731 Freight transportation arrangement
Nick Taro
John Crewson

D-U-N-S 24-373-9331   (SL)
DELTA AGGREGATES LTD
7469 Hume Ave, Delta, BC, V4G 1C3
(604) 940-1300
Emp Here 40   *Sales* 17,886,960
SIC 5032 Brick, stone, and related material
Gary Green
David Green
Richard Green
Dave Taylor
Bob Hobbs

D-U-N-S 20-267-8660   (SL)
DOMINION PIPE & PILING LTD
6845 Tilbury Rd, Delta, BC, V4G 0A3
(604) 946-2655
Emp Here 10   *Sales* 10,003,390
SIC 5051 Metals service centers and offices
Gerald Varzari

D-U-N-S 25-216-1328   (HQ)
EUROLINE WINDOWS INC
7620 Macdonald Rd, Delta, BC, V4G 1N2
(604) 940-8485
Emp Here 70   *Sales* 11,914,350
SIC 3089 Plastics products, nec
Isbrand Funk

D-U-N-S 20-623-8453   (HQ)
EVERGRO CANADA INC
AGRITEC
7430 Hopcott Rd Suite 1, Delta, BC, V4G 1B6

(604) 940-0290
Emp Here 50   *Sales* 66,826,800
SIC 5193 Flowers and florists supplies
David Gingrich
Bonnie Schmelke

D-U-N-S 24-824-8304   (SL)
F.A.S.T. FIRST AID & SURVIVAL TECH-NOLOGIES LIMITED
FAST
8850 River Rd, Delta, BC, V4G 1B5
(604) 940-3222
Emp Here 40   *Sales* 10,262,480
SIC 3842 Surgical appliances and supplies
Nadine Miller

D-U-N-S 20-550-1302   (SL)
FAMA INDUSTRIES CORPORATION
KARADON
(*Suby of* FAMA HOLDINGS LTD)
7480 Macdonald Rd, Delta, BC, V4G 1N2
(604) 952-0880
Emp Here 120
SIC 5031 Lumber, plywood, and millwork
Abolghassem Aghtai
Mehran Aghtai
Michael Aghtai

D-U-N-S 25-505-3357   (SL)
FIREPLACE PRODUCTS U.S., INC
(*Suby of* NIBE INDUSTRIER AB)
6988 Venture St, Delta, BC, V4G 1H4
(604) 946-5155
Emp Here 75   *Sales* 17,430,225
SIC 5719 Miscellaneous homefurnishings
Robert Little
Anthony Woodruff
Mino Padda

D-U-N-S 20-794-9611   (HQ)
FORMULA DISTRIBUTORS LTD
7205 Brown St, Delta, BC, V4G 1G5
(604) 946-0146
Emp Here 20   *Sales* 20,031,825
SIC 5014 Tires and tubes
James Macdonald
Sally Mutis

D-U-N-S 24-247-0086   (HQ)
FPI FIREPLACE PRODUCTS INTERNA-TIONAL LTD
(*Suby of* NIBE INDUSTRIER AB)
6988 Venture St, Delta, BC, V4G 1H4
(604) 946-5155
Emp Here 300   *Sales* 97,292,400
SIC 3433 Heating equipment, except electric
Robert Little
Anthony Woodruff
Tracy Zomar
Mino Padda

D-U-N-S 24-493-4196   (HQ)
FRONTIER POWER PRODUCTS LTD
7983 Progress Way, Delta, BC, V4G 1A3
(604) 946-5531
Emp Here 50   *Sales* 24,757,460
SIC 3621 Motors and generators
Larrie York
Geoff Bannoff
Randy Shore

D-U-N-S 24-456-4795   (SL)
GENFOR MACHINERY INC
8320 River Rd, Delta, BC, V4G 1B5
(604) 946-6911
Emp Here 90   *Sales* 16,148,610
SIC 3553 Woodworking machinery
Ross Chapman
Fred Chapman

D-U-N-S 20-734-8579   (SL)
GML MECHANICAL LTD
7355 72 St Suite 13, Delta, BC, V4G 1L5
(604) 940-9686
Emp Here 65   *Sales* 15,149,225
SIC 1711 Plumbing, heating, air-conditioning
Marcel Zastre

D-U-N-S 24-389-5732   (SL)
HARBOUR LINK CONTAINER SERVICES INC
7420 Hopcott Rd, Delta, BC, V4G 1B6
(604) 940-5522
Emp Here 70   *Sales* 10,373,440
SIC 4213 Trucking, except local
David Payne

D-U-N-S 24-566-3554   (SL)
HEXCEL CONSTRUCTION LTD
7119 River Rd, Delta, BC, V4G 1A9
(604) 946-8744
Emp Here 70   *Sales* 17,233,020
SIC 1794 Excavation work
Ronald Wilson

D-U-N-S 24-249-1322   (HQ)
HI-CUBE STORAGE PRODUCTS LTD
7363 Wilson Ave, Delta, BC, V4G 1E5
(604) 946-4838
Emp Here 24   *Sales* 11,179,350
SIC 5046 Commercial equipment, nec
Peter Crichton
Larry Robertson

D-U-N-S 24-293-7795   (HQ)
HILLMAR INDUSTRIES LIMITED
7371 Vantage Way, Delta, BC, V4G 1C9
(604) 946-7115
Sales 10,564,675
SIC 3499 Fabricated Metal products, nec
Ian Bourhill
Margaret Bourhill

D-U-N-S 24-327-1660   (HQ)
INTEPLAST BAGS AND FILMS CORPORA-TION
(*Suby of* INTEPLAST GROUP CORPORA-TION)
7503 Vantage Pl, Delta, BC, V4G 1A5
(604) 946-5431
Emp Here 35   *Sales* 17,529,120
SIC 2673 Bags: plastic, laminated, and coated
Joe Chen
Ben Tseng
Robert H Wang
Joseph Wang
John Ding-E Young

D-U-N-S 24-996-8231   (SL)
INTERNATIONAL DIRECT RESPONSE SERVICES LTD
IDRS - DATA PRINT MAIL
10159 Nordel Crt, Delta, BC, V4G 1J8
(604) 951-6855
Emp Here 60   *Sales* 14,659,680
SIC 5961 Catalog and mail-order houses
Wendy Mcgregor
James Rippinger
Terry Morris

D-U-N-S 20-870-4978   (SL)
ISM INDUSTRIAL STEEL & MANUFACTUR-ING INC
7690 Vantage Way, Delta, BC, V4G 1A7
(604) 940-4769
Emp Here 35   *Sales* 11,524,275
SIC 3441 Fabricated structural Metal
Mario Scarpino

D-U-N-S 24-760-8870   (HQ)
JJM CONSTRUCTION LTD
8218 River Way, Delta, BC, V4G 1C4
(604) 946-0978
Emp Here 200   *Sales* 82,028,750
SIC 1611 Highway and street construction
John James Miller
Nadine Joy Miller
Craig Peddie

D-U-N-S 20-582-7462   (HQ)
LINWOOD HOMES LTD
LINWOOD
8250 River Rd, Delta, BC, V4G 1B5
(604) 946-5421
Emp Here 55   *Sales* 19,237,000

SIC 2452 Prefabricated wood buildings
William T D Mascott
Don Jewel
Paul Cosulich

D-U-N-S 24-839-6566   (SL)
M AND J WOODCRAFTS LTD
7338 Progress Way Unit 1, Delta, BC, V4G 1L4
(604) 946-4767
Emp Here 110   *Sales* 21,160,700
SIC 2431 Millwork
Michael Williams

D-U-N-S 20-746-4269   (SL)
MADDIES NATURAL PET PRODUCTS LTD
6655 Dennett Pl, Delta, BC, V4G 1N4
(604) 946-7977
Emp Here 25   *Sales* 20,889,425
SIC 5149 Groceries and related products, nec
Dave Prevost

D-U-N-S 24-866-6620   (HQ)
MARPOLE TRANSPORT LIMITED
(*Suby of* R B R HOLDINGS INC)
7086 Brown St, Delta, BC, V4G 1G8
(604) 940-7000
Emp Here 30   *Sales* 18,924,952
SIC 4213 Trucking, except local
Bhajan (Pudge) Bawa
John Ross Grant
Suhkdave S. Lashman
Sarban Bawa

D-U-N-S 20-067-7478   (SL)
MAZZA INNOVATION LTD
7901 Progress Way, Delta, BC, V4G 1A3
(604) 337-1578
Emp Here 30   *Sales* 25,067,310
SIC 5149 Groceries and related products, nec
Benjamin Lightburn
James Pratt
Sean Hodgins
Giuseppe Mazza
Troy Rhonemus

D-U-N-S 20-150-6297   (SL)
MCRAE'S ENVIRONMENTAL SERVICES LTD
MCRAE'S SPEC LIQUID WASTE
7783 Progress Way, Delta, BC, V4G 1A3
(604) 434-8313
Emp Here 50   *Sales* 11,008,400
SIC 1794 Excavation work
Drew Clark

D-U-N-S 24-357-1895   (HQ)
MURCHIE'S TEA & COFFEE (2007) LTD
(*Suby of* BELMONT MANAGEMENT LTD)
8028 River Way, Delta, BC, V4G 1K9
(604) 231-7501
Sales 17,608,620
SIC 5499 Miscellaneous food stores
Grant Kuelbler
Kelly Robinson

D-U-N-S 24-681-9387   (HQ)
NORTH AMERICAN PIPE & STEEL LTD
NAP STEEL
(*Suby of* R & R TRADING CO. LTD)
7449 River Rd, Delta, BC, V4G 1B9
(604) 946-0916
Sales 16,545,438
SIC 5051 Metals service centers and offices
Earl Ritchie

D-U-N-S 24-031-0912   (SL)
NORTH AMERICAN TEA & COFFEE INC
(*Suby of* TREEHOUSE FOODS, INC.)
7861 82 St, Delta, BC, V4G 1L9
(604) 940-7861
Emp Here 250
SIC 5141 Groceries, general line
Gulam Jagani
Riyaz Devji

D-U-N-S 24-614-0974   (SL)
NORTH DELTA SEAFOODS LTD

7857 Huston Rd, Delta, BC, V4G 1M1
(604) 582-8268
Emp Here 100   *Sales* 83,557,700
SIC 5146 Fish and seafoods
Larry Wick
Gwendolyn Wick
Mike Wick

D-U-N-S 24-151-0643   (SL)
NORTHERN FEATHER CANADA LTD
8088 River Way, Delta, BC, V4G 1K9
(604) 940-8283
Emp Here 70   *Sales* 12,838,210
SIC 2221 Broadwoven fabric mills, manmade
Tage Nilsson

D-U-N-S 25-362-2963   (SL)
NORTHWESTERN SYSTEMS CORPORA-TION
BETTER BUILT
7601 Macdonald Rd, Delta, BC, V4G 1N3
(604) 952-0925
Emp Here 70   *Sales* 13,445,950
SIC 3499 Fabricated Metal products, nec
Christopher Ramsden
Harry Lin

D-U-N-S 24-456-6196   (SL)
OPTIMIL MACHINERY INC
EDEM STEEL DIV OF
8320 River Rd, Delta, BC, V4G 1B5
(604) 946-6911
Emp Here 90   *Sales* 19,980,090
SIC 3553 Woodworking machinery
Ross Chapman
Frederic Chapman

D-U-N-S 25-679-2383   (SL)
PACIFIC SIGN GROUP INC
KNIGHT SIGN
7462 Progress Way, Delta, BC, V4G 1E1
(604) 940-2211
Emp Here 84   *Sales* 27,395,424
SIC 3993 Signs and advertising specialties
Mitchell Taylor
Steven Mander
Bruno Kristensen
Lydia Taylor
Brodie Kristensen

D-U-N-S 24-359-7601   (HQ)
PHOENIX GLASS INC
COLUMBIA ALUMINUM PRODUCTS
(*Suby of* GROUPE ATIS INC)
8166 92 St, Delta, BC, V4G 0A4
(604) 525-2800
Sales 31,302,180
SIC 5031 Lumber, plywood, and millwork
Steve Lebedovich
Jim Lebedovich
Christopher Brind'amour
Andre Parent
Jerry Donatelli
Leland Lewis
Beth Laschinger

D-U-N-S 24-166-8532   (SL)
PREPAC MANUFACTURING LTD
6705 Dennett Pl, Delta, BC, V4G 1N4
(604) 940-2300
Emp Here 90   *Sales* 13,888,980
SIC 2541 Wood partitions and fixtures
Steve Simpson

D-U-N-S 25-849-8401   (HQ)
QUALITY MOVE MANAGEMENT INC
ALLIED INTERNATIONAL OF VANCOUVER
7979 82 St, Delta, BC, V4G 1L7
(604) 952-3650
Emp Here 30   *Sales* 38,183,615
SIC 7389 Business services, nec
Kevin St George
Scott Shaw

D-U-N-S 24-567-2274   (HQ)
R & R TRADING CO. LTD
7449 River Rd, Delta, BC, V4G 1B9

▲ Public Company   ■ Public Company Family Member   **HQ** Headquarters   **BR** Branch   **SL** Single Location

(604) 946-0916
Sales 119,490,800
SIC 5051 Metals service centers and offices
Earl Ritchie
James Ritchie
Mark Ritchie

D-U-N-S 20-802-1402   (HQ)
RADION LABORATORIES LTD
BOWERS MEDICAL SUPPLY
7198 Progress Way, Delta, BC, V4G 1J2
(604) 946-7712
Sales 29,066,310
SIC 5047 Medical and hospital equipment
Francis Bowers
Brittany Bowers
Christina Ann Bowers

D-U-N-S 24-639-7822   (SL)
RAM CONSTRUCTION INC
8369 River Way Suite 101, Delta, BC, V4G
1G2
(604) 501-5265
Emp Here 35   *Sales* 16,475,585
SIC 1542 Nonresidential construction, nec
Stephen Knoblauch

D-U-N-S 24-996-5328   (SL)
ROYAL CITY CHARTER COACH LINES LTD
8730 River Rd, Delta, BC, V4G 1B5
(604) 940-1707
Emp Here 155   *Sales* 42,369,250
SIC 6712 Bank holding companies
Sheldon Eggen
Wayne Eggen
Verna Eggen

D-U-N-S 24-856-7653   (HQ)
S.O.F. WHITE PAPER COMPANY LTD
WHITE PAPER COMPANY
9990 River Way, Delta, BC, V4G 1M9
(604) 951-3900
Emp Here 40   *Sales* 37,270,692
SIC 5111 Printing and writing paper
Michael Shein
Reginald Fitzergald

D-U-N-S 24-135-3010   (SL)
SEASIDE PAPER PRODUCTS LTD
9999 River Way, Delta, BC, V4G 1M8
(604) 930-2700
Emp Here 80   *Sales* 18,674,800
SIC 2679 Converted paper products, nec
Duncan White
Neil Piper

D-U-N-S 25-066-0784   (HQ)
SEASPAN FERRIES CORPORATION
7700 Hopcott Rd, Delta, BC, V4G 1B6
(604) 940-7228
Emp Here 1   *Sales* 26,954,900
SIC 4482 Ferries
Steve Roth
Mike Fournier

D-U-N-S 24-313-6116   (HQ)
SEI INDUSTRIES LTD
(*Suby of* SEI MANUFACTURING INC)
7400 Wilson Ave, Delta, BC, V4G 1H3
(604) 946-3131
Sales 18,595,530
SIC 0851 Forestry services

D-U-N-S 24-492-2654   (SL)
TERRA NOVA STEEL INC
7812 Progress Way, Delta, BC, V4G 1A4
(604) 946-5383
Emp Here 36   *Sales* 21,339,836
SIC 5051 Metals service centers and offices
Jerry Lozinski
Robert Gutjahr
Christopher Seggie

D-U-N-S 24-898-7950   (SL)
UNIFILLER SYSTEMS INC
7621 Macdonald Rd, Delta, BC, V4G 1N3
(604) 940-2233
Emp Here 80   *Sales* 23,478,160

SIC 5461 Retail bakeries
Kuno Kurschner
Benno Boucher
Stewart Macpherson

D-U-N-S 24-535-4659   (SL)
**UNITREND PLASTICS MANUFACTURING
LTD**
7351 Progress Pl, Delta, BC, V4G 1A1
(604) 940-8900
Emp Here 47   *Sales* 10,971,445
SIC 2673 Bags: plastic, laminated, and
coated
Barry Reber
Carlos Utegra

D-U-N-S 24-133-4606   (SL)
VALMONT WC ENGINEERING GROUP LTD
(*Suby of* VALMONT INDUSTRIES, INC.)
7984 River Rd, Delta, BC, V4G 1E3
(604) 946-1256
Emp Here 107   *Sales* 30,072,350
SIC 5211 Lumber and other building materials
Ted Brockman

D-U-N-S 20-712-7697   (SL)
VANCOUVER TOURS AND TRANSIT LTD
CHARTER BUS LINES OF BC
8730 River Rd, Delta, BC, V4G 1B5
(604) 940-1707
Emp Here 150   *Sales* 11,290,800
SIC 4142 Bus charter service, except local
Sheldon Eggen
Wayne Eggen

D-U-N-S 25-326-7744   (HQ)
VIKING CHAINS INC
7392 Progress Pl, Delta, BC, V4G 1A1
(604) 952-4146
Emp Here 22   *Sales* 11,179,350
SIC 5072 Hardware
Clifford Lane
Ronald Gillespie
Leslie Forrington

D-U-N-S 25-682-3592   (HQ)
WALLSA HOLDINGS LTD
CHOICES MARKET
8188 River Way, Delta, BC, V4G 1K5
(604) 940-8891
Sales 20,570,600
SIC 4225 General warehousing and storage
Lloyd Lockhart
Wayne Lockhart
Salim Jamal Ahmed

D-U-N-S 20-110-7034   (HQ)
WESBRIDGE STEELWORKS LIMITED
7480 Wilson Ave, Delta, BC, V4G 1H3
(604) 946-8618
Sales 13,540,230
SIC 1791 Structural steel erection
George Sze

D-U-N-S 20-799-0326   (SL)
ZODIAC HURRICANE TECHNOLOGIES INC
(*Suby of* THE CARLYLE GROUP L P)
7830 Vantage Way, Delta, BC, V4G 1A7
(604) 940-2999
Emp Here 200   *Sales* 44,768,600
SIC 3732 Boatbuilding and repairing
Jean Jacques Arignon
Sandra Kyle
Ernie Hammond

Delta, BC V4K

D-U-N-S 24-931-6829   (HQ)
BC FRESH VEGETABLES INC
4363 King St, Delta, BC, V4K 0A5
(604) 946-3139
Sales 65,028,591
SIC 5148 Fresh fruits and vegetables
Murray Driediger

Peter Guichon
Randy Sihota
Brent Kelly
Edward Mckim
Don Bernard
Pori Gerrard

D-U-N-S 24-374-3262   (HQ)
CACHE EXPLORATION INC
4770 72nd St, Delta, BC, V4K 3N3
(604) 306-5285
Emp Here 10   *Sales* 10,206,500
SIC 1041 Gold ores
Jack Bal
Sonny Janda
Chris Pennimpede
Ian Graham
Dean Pikeski

D-U-N-S 25-092-0985   (SL)
DELTA COUNTRY FARMS (BC) LTD
3752 Arthur Dr, Delta, BC, V4K 3N2
(604) 940-1881
Emp Here 200   *Sales* 143,343,200
SIC 5149 Groceries and related products, nec
Reza Bakhtiyari

D-U-N-S 24-120-6379   (SL)
DELTA PACIFIC SEAFOODS LTD
(*Suby of* PATTISON, JIM GROUP INC)
6001 60 Ave, Delta, BC, V4K 0B2
(604) 946-5160
Emp Here 50   *Sales* 17,284,500
SIC 2092 Fresh or frozen packaged fish
Don Pollard

D-U-N-S 25-019-3307   (BR)
DELTA SCHOOL DISTRICT NO.37
DELTA SECONDARY SCHOOL
4615 51 St, Delta, BC, V4K 2V8
(604) 946-4194
Emp Here 100
SIC 8211 Elementary and secondary schools
Terry Tainge

D-U-N-S 20-797-7000   (SL)
DELTA VIEW FARMS LTD
3330 41b St, Delta, BC, V4K 3N2
(604) 946-1776
Emp Here 100   *Sales* 26,230,900
SIC 0182 Food crops grown under cover
Eric Schlacht

D-U-N-S 25-752-7689   (SL)
DELTA VIEW HABILITATION CENTRE LTD
9341 Burns Dr, Delta, BC, V4K 3N3
(604) 501-6700
Emp Here 79
SIC 7389 Business services, nec
Nurjehan Devji
Salim Devji
Amin Devji
Aly Devji

D-U-N-S 20-860-8294   (SL)
**DELTA VIEW LIFE ENRICHMENT CENTRES
LTD**
9341 Burns Dr, Delta, BC, V4K 3N3
(604) 501-6700
Emp Here 100   *Sales* 6,019,800
SIC 8052 Intermediate care facilities
Amin Devji
Aly Devji
Jane Devji

D-U-N-S 20-407-4319   (SL)
DUNBAR LUMBER SUPPLY
4989 Bridge St, Delta, BC, V4K 2K3
(604) 946-7322
Emp Here 36   *Sales* 16,098,264
SIC 5031 Lumber, plywood, and millwork
Dave Atkinson

D-U-N-S 20-731-7228   (BR)
**GOVERNMENT OF THE PROVINCE OF
BRITISH COLUMBIA**
DELTA HOSPITAL
(*Suby of* GOVERNMENT OF THE

PROVINCE OF BRITISH COLUMBIA)
5800 Mountain View Blvd, Delta, BC, V4K 3V6
(604) 946-1121
Emp Here 250
SIC 8062 General medical and surgical hospitals
Lori Maclennan

D-U-N-S 24-387-2376   (SL)
GREENHOUSE GROWN FOODS INC
WINDSET FARMS
(*Suby of* WINDSET HOLDINGS 2010 LTD)
3660 41b St, Delta, BC, V4K 3N2
(604) 940-7700
Emp Here 100   *Sales* 250,173,660
SIC 0182 Food crops grown under cover
Steven Newell
John Newell
John Newell Jr
Anthony Martin

D-U-N-S 24-069-1089   (HQ)
HUSBY FOREST PRODUCTS LTD
6425 River Rd, Delta, BC, V4K 5B9
(604) 940-1234
Emp Here 20   *Sales* 28,798,840
SIC 4212 Local trucking, without storage
Dave Husby

D-U-N-S 20-112-4914   (SL)
IDEAL GEAR AND MACHINE WORKS INC
6415 River Rd, Delta, BC, V4K 5B9
(604) 952-4327
Emp Here 35   *Sales* 16,625,910
SIC 5085 Industrial supplies
William Ahnert

D-U-N-S 20-113-3287   (HQ)
LIONS GATE FISHERIES LTD
4179 River Rd W, Delta, BC, V4K 1R9
(604) 946-1361
Sales 86,005,920
SIC 5146 Fish and seafoods
Jack Waterfield
Todd W. Waterfield
Marilyn A. Waterfield
David Wei

D-U-N-S 20-057-1060   (SL)
**MILLENNIUM PACIFIC GREENHOUSES
PARTNERSHIP**
3752 Arthur Dr, Delta, BC, V4K 3N2
(604) 940-4440
Emp Here 80   *Sales* 13,522,000
SIC 0182 Food crops grown under cover
Shirvan Bakhtiyari

D-U-N-S 24-071-0574   (SL)
S.M. PRODUCTS (B.C.) LTD
3827 River Rd W, Delta, BC, V4K 3N2
(604) 946-7665
Emp Here 20   *Sales* 10,702,480
SIC 5146 Fish and seafoods
Carl Nordmann
Rob Kaczynski

D-U-N-S 20-336-6872   (BR)
SCHENKER OF CANADA LIMITED
(*Suby of* BUNDESREPUBLIK DEUTSCH-
LAND)
8181 Churchill St, Delta, BC, V4K 0C2
(604) 688-8511
Emp Here 200
SIC 4731 Freight transportation arrangement
Ian Morton

D-U-N-S 25-415-7001   (HQ)
VILLAGE FARMS INTERNATIONAL INC
VILLAGE FARMS
4700 80 St, Delta, BC, V4K 3N3
(604) 940-6012
Emp Here 10   *Sales* 150,000,000
SIC 6712 Bank holding companies
Michael A. Degiglio
Stephen C. Ruffini
Bret Wiley
Michael Bledsoe
Michael Minerva

▲ Public Company   ■ Public Company Family Member   **HQ** Headquarters   **BR** Branch   **SL** Single Location

Dirk De Jong
Paul Selina
Bill Lowe
Andrew Gigante
Jonathan Bos

D-U-N-S 25-108-3424   (SL)
WESTCOAST VEGETABLES LTD
5369 49b Ave, Delta, BC, V4K 4R7
(604) 940-4748
Emp Here 45   *Sales* 12,336,840
SIC 5431 Fruit and vegetable markets
Jane Van Marrewyk

D-U-N-S 20-699-1338   (SL)
WINDSET FARMS
3660 41b St, Delta, BC, V4K 3N2
(604) 940-7700
Emp Here 45   *Sales* 11,803,905
SIC 0182 Food crops grown under cover
Steven Newell
John Newell

D-U-N-S 20-137-0397   (SL)
WINDSET FARMS (CANADA) LTD
3660 41b St, Delta, BC, V4K 3N2
(604) 940-7700
Emp Here 50   *Sales* 17,123,350
SIC 0182 Food crops grown under cover
Steven Newell
John Jr Newell
John Perry Newell
Sylvia Newell

D-U-N-S 24-805-1372   (HQ)
WINDSET HOLDINGS 2010 LTD
WINDSET FARMS
3660 41b St, Delta, BC, V4K 3N2
(604) 940-7700
Emp Here 6   *Sales* 13,115,450
SIC 0182 Food crops grown under cover
Steven Newell
John Newell Jr
John Newell Sr
Sylvia Newell
Ron Midyett
Anthony Martin

Delta, BC V4L

D-U-N-S 20-544-4545   (SL)
653457 B.C. LTD
SHOPPERS DRUG MART
1215c 56 St Unit C, Delta, BC, V4L 2A6
(604) 943-1144
Emp Here 60   *Sales* 14,659,680
SIC 5912 Drug stores and proprietary stores
Shin Dinza

D-U-N-S 24-155-2801   (SL)
HOUWELING NURSERIES LTD
2776 64 St, Delta, BC, V4L 2N7
(604) 946-0844
Emp Here 100   *Sales* 26,230,900
SIC 0182 Food crops grown under cover
Cornelius (Casey) Houweling

D-U-N-S 20-703-2462   (BR)
JACE HOLDINGS LTD
THRIFTY FOODS
1270 56 St, Delta, BC, V4L 2A4
(604) 948-9210
Emp Here 170   *Sales* 822,456
SIC 5411 Grocery stores
Michael Saysell

D-U-N-S 24-062-1958   (HQ)
SJR FOOD SERVICES LTD
MCDONALD'S RESTAURANTS
1835 56 St Unit 44, Delta, BC, V4L 2M1
(604) 948-3630
Emp Here 80   *Sales* 3,641,520
SIC 5812 Eating places
Steve Krawchuk

D-U-N-S 25-710-2913   (SL)
UNIVERSITY SPRINKLER SYSTEMS IN-CORPORATED
UNIVERSITY SPRINKLERS
1777 56 St Unit 500, Delta, BC, V4L 0A6
(604) 421-4555
Emp Here 100   *Sales* 23,306,500
SIC 1711 Plumbing, heating, air-conditioning

D-U-N-S 24-570-6804   (SL)
WEST COAST SEEDS LTD
WEST COAST SEEDS RETAIL STORE
5344 34b Ave, Delta, BC, V4L 2P1
(604) 952-8820
Emp Here 43   *Sales* 31,928,360
SIC 5191 Farm supplies
Mary Ballon

Delta, BC V4M

D-U-N-S 25-683-3047   (SL)
DACKIR DISTRIBUTIONS
5305 12 Ave, Delta, BC, V4M 2B1
(604) 318-1235
Emp Here 116   *Sales* 68,342,444
SIC 5192 Books, periodicals, and newspapers
Juhli Derwin-Chan

D-U-N-S 20-591-3085   (BR)
DELTA SCHOOL DISTRICT NO.37
SOUTH DELTA SECONDARY SCHOOL
750 53 St, Delta, BC, V4M 3B7
(604) 943-7407
Emp Here 100
SIC 8211 Elementary and secondary schools
Ted Johnson

D-U-N-S 24-246-0202   (SL)
KINSMEN RETIREMENT CENTRE ASSOCI-ATION
5410 10 Ave, Delta, BC, V4M 3X8
(604) 943-0155
Emp Here 140   *Sales* 8,999,480
SIC 8361 Residential care
Gerald Arksey
Florence Wilson

D-U-N-S 20-575-0516   (SL)
WESTSHORE TERMINALS LTD
(*Suby of* WESTSHORE TERMINALS IN-VESTMENT CORPORATION)
1 Roberts Bank Rd, Delta, BC, V4M 4G5
(604) 946-4491
Emp Here 195   *Sales* 67,735,395
SIC 4491 Marine cargo handling
William Stinsen
Glenn Dudar
David Honsberger
Angela Morfitt
Greg Andrew

Douglas Lake, BC V0E

D-U-N-S 25-505-6830   (HQ)
DOUGLAS LAKE CATTLE COMPANY
DOUGLAS LAKE RANCH
Gd, Douglas Lake, BC, V0E 1S0
(250) 350-3344
Sales 26,860,210
SIC 0212 Beef cattle, except feedlots
Stanley Kroenke
Joseph Gardner

D-U-N-S 20-527-8323   (HQ)
DOUGLAS LAKE EQUIPMENT LIMITED PARTNERSHIP
111 Douglas Lake Rd, Douglas Lake, BC, V0E 1S0
(250) 851-2044
Emp Here 11   *Sales* 63,892,630
SIC 5083 Farm and garden machinery

Joe Gardiner

Duncan, BC V9L

D-U-N-S 20-371-8895   (SL)
1946328 ONTARIO LIMITED
VANCOUVER ISLAND MOTORSPORT CIR-CUIT
4063 Cowichan Valley Hwy, Duncan, BC, V9L 6K4
(250) 856-0122
Emp Here 27   *Sales* 11,440,710
SIC 7948 Racing, including track operation
Peter Trzewik

D-U-N-S 25-236-1027   (SL)
458890 B.C. LTD
DUNCAN WHITE SPOT
101 Trans Canada Hwy, Duncan, BC, V9L 3P8
(250) 748-5151
Emp Here 80   *Sales* 3,641,520
SIC 5812 Eating places
Martin Goliath

D-U-N-S 25-087-8311   (SL)
ADAMS 22 HOLDINGS LTD
TIM HORTONS
2628 Beverly St, Duncan, BC, V9L 5C7
(250) 709-2205
Emp Here 50   *Sales* 13,707,600
SIC 5461 Retail bakeries
Gregory Adams

D-U-N-S 20-651-8016   (SL)
BOW MEL CHRYSLER LTD
461 Trans Canada Hwy, Duncan, BC, V9L 3R7
(250) 748-8144
Emp Here 28   *Sales* 13,946,184
SIC 5511 New and used car dealers
Connie Johnston
Todd Blumel

D-U-N-S 20-011-1750   (SL)
BRIDGER, BOB ENTERPRISES INC
CANADIAN TIRE
2929 Green Rd, Duncan, BC, V9L 0C1
(250) 748-5557
Emp Here 120   *Sales* 75,513,600
SIC 5531 Auto and home supply stores
Robert B. Bridger

D-U-N-S 20-958-6832   (SL)
COMMUNITY FARM STORE LTD, THE
DUNCAN GARAGE CAFE & BAKERY
330 Duncan St Suite 101, Duncan, BC, V9L 3W4
(250) 748-6223
Emp Here 38   *Sales* 31,751,926
SIC 5149 Groceries and related products, nec
Nicolette Genier
Susan Minette

D-U-N-S 25-936-3596   (SL)
COWICHAN VALLEY INDEPENDENT LIV-ING RESOURCES CENTRE SOCIETY
COWICHAN INDEPENDENT LIVING
121 First St Unit 103, Duncan, BC, V9L 1R1
(250) 746-3930
Emp Here 26   *Sales* 10,332,764
SIC 8699 Membership organizations, nec
Colin Owen-Slood

D-U-N-S 24-773-1271   (SL)
CRAIG STREET BREWING COMPANY
25 Craig St, Duncan, BC, V9L 1V7
(250) 737-2337
Emp Here 49   *Sales* 11,017,895
SIC 2082 Malt beverages
Lance Steward

D-U-N-S 20-995-9345   (SL)
DISCOVERY MOTORS LTD
DISCOVERY HONDA
6466 Bell Mckinnon Rd, Duncan, BC, V9L 6C1

(250) 748-5814
Emp Here 36   *Sales* 22,654,080
SIC 5511 New and used car dealers
Pieter Baljet
John Horgan
Rosemary Horgan

D-U-N-S 20-096-0599   (SL)
DUNCAN AUTO PARTS (1983) LTD
DUNCAN AUTO PARTS
5829 Duncan St, Duncan, BC, V9L 3W7
(250) 746-5431
Emp Here 30   *Sales* 18,878,400
SIC 5531 Auto and home supply stores
John Dallaway
Richard Cooper
Margo Young

D-U-N-S 20-586-5231   (SL)
EVANS, KEN FORD SALES LTD
439 Trans Canada Hwy, Duncan, BC, V9L 3R7
(250) 748-5555
Emp Here 40   *Sales* 19,923,120
SIC 5511 New and used car dealers
Victor Scudder

D-U-N-S 25-119-7075   (HQ)
G.M. PACE ENTERPRISES INC
4801 Trans Canada Hwy Suite 3, Duncan, BC, V9L 6L3
(250) 246-4448
Emp Here 4   *Sales* 19,923,120
SIC 5541 Gasoline service stations
Mervin Gordon Pace

D-U-N-S 20-998-9008   (SL)
GREEN ISLAND G AUTO LTD
ISLAND GM
(*Suby of* AUTOCANADA INC)
6300 Trans Canada Hwy, Duncan, BC, V9L 0C1
(250) 746-7131
Emp Here 70   *Sales* 44,049,600
SIC 5511 New and used car dealers
Peter Baljet

D-U-N-S 20-781-0602   (SL)
HANCO MANAGEMENT LTD
HALE AND PARTNERS
372 Coronation Ave, Duncan, BC, V9L 2T3
(250) 748-3761
Emp Here 28   *Sales* 11,741,940
SIC 6712 Bank holding companies
Cindy Wilson

D-U-N-S 24-989-6007   (SL)
HARMONY HEALTH CARE
2753 Charlotte Rd Suite 2a, Duncan, BC, V9L 5J2
(250) 701-9990
Emp Here 49   *Sales* 11,451,055
SIC 8621 Professional organizations
John Mc

D-U-N-S 24-803-7280   (BR)
HOME DEPOT OF CANADA INC
HOME DEPOT
(*Suby of* THE HOME DEPOT INC)
2980 Drinkwater Rd Unit 1, Duncan, BC, V9L 6C6
(250) 737-2360
Emp Here 80
SIC 5251 Hardware stores
Denise Milkovic

D-U-N-S 24-034-0661   (HQ)
ISLAND SAVINGS CREDIT UNION
ISLAND SAVINGS, A DIVISION OF FIRST WEST CREDIT UNION
499 Canada Ave Suite 300, Duncan, BC, V9L 1T7
(250) 748-4728
Emp Here 45   *Sales* 56,082,900
SIC 6062 State credit unions
Fred Zdan
Randy Bertsch
Jeff Wood
William Mccreadie

Pearl Graham
John Richmond
Sheila Service

D-U-N-S 24-996-2226   (HQ)
KHOWUTZUN DEVELOPMENT CORP
KDC
200 Cowichan Way, Duncan, BC, V9L 6P4

Sales 12,344,940
SIC 8741 Management services
Buz Martin
Stephanie Charlie
Garrett Elliott
Matthew Louie
William Seymour Sr
Maureen Tommy
Dora Wilson

D-U-N-S 20-259-0238   (HQ)
LMG INSURANCE BROKERS LTD
2640 Beverly St Suite 200, Duncan, BC, V9L 5C7
(250) 748-3200
Emp Here 10   *Sales* 28,834,040
SIC 6411 Insurance agents, brokers, and service
Daniel Lomas

D-U-N-S 25-270-1529   (BR)
LOBLAWS INC
REAL CANADIAN SUPERSTORE 1563
(*Suby of* LOBLAW COMPANIES LIMITED)
291 Cowichan Way Suite 1563, Duncan, BC, V9L 6P5
(250) 746-0529
Emp Here 250
SIC 5141 Groceries, general line
Steve Metcalfe

D-U-N-S 25-318-1481   (BR)
MCDONALD'S   RESTAURANTS   OF CANADA LIMITED
MCDONALD'S
(*Suby of* MCDONALD'S CORPORATION)
5883 Trans Canada Hwy, Duncan, BC, V9L 3R9
(250) 715-2370
Emp Here 100
SIC 5812 Eating places
Amber Battie

D-U-N-S 20-096-1522   (SL)
MOUNT SICKER LUMBER COMPANY LTD
7795 Mays Rd, Duncan, BC, V9L 6A8
(250) 746-4121
Emp Here 75   *Sales* 14,427,750
SIC 2411 Logging
George Fredrickson
Raymond Smith
Ian Batty
Richard Holman
Craig Fredrickson
Gerry Gammie

D-U-N-S 25-133-2904   (BR)
NATIONAL ASSOCIATION OF FRIENDSHIP CENTRES
HIIYE'YU LELUM FRIENDSHIP
5462 Trans Canada Hwy Unit 205, Duncan, BC, V9L 6W4
(250) 748-2242
Emp Here 76
SIC 8322 Individual and family services
Debbie Williams

D-U-N-S 25-507-1060   (SL)
PACIFIC ENERGY FIREPLACE PRODUCTS LTD
2975 Allenby Rd, Duncan, BC, V9L 6V8
(250) 748-1184
Emp Here 100   *Sales* 19,208,500
SIC 3433 Heating equipment, except electric
Paul Erickson

D-U-N-S 24-987-4533   (SL)
PRINGLE INSURANCE BROKERS
380 Trunk Rd Unit 1, Duncan, BC, V9L 2P6

(250) 748-3242
Emp Here 20   *Sales* 11,598,480
SIC 6411 Insurance agents, brokers, and service
George Schmidt

D-U-N-S 20-867-9548   (SL)
QUEEN MARGARET'S SCHOOL
660 Brownsey Ave, Duncan, BC, V9L 1C2
(250) 746-4185
Emp Here 115   *Sales* 11,398,685
SIC 8211 Elementary and secondary schools
Julie Scurr

D-U-N-S 25-154-7089   (SL)
VALLEY INTEGRATION TO ACTIVE LIVING SOCIETY
VITAL
80 Station St Suite 217, Duncan, BC, V9L 1M4
(250) 748-5899
Emp Here 45   *Sales* 17,883,630
SIC 8699 Membership organizations, nec
Makenna Rielly

D-U-N-S 24-887-4083   (HQ)
VAN ISLE INSURANCE SERVICES (1983) INC
471 Trans Canada Hwy, Duncan, BC, V9L 3R7

Sales 14,498,100
SIC 6411 Insurance agents, brokers, and service
Donald Hatton
Natalie Hatton

D-U-N-S 25-140-8969   (BR)
VANCOUVER ISLAND HEALTH AUTHORITY
COWICHAN DISTRICT HOSPITAL
(*Suby of* GOVERNMENT OF THE PROVINCE OF BRITISH COLUMBIA)
3045 Gibbins Rd, Duncan, BC, V9L 1E5
(250) 737-2030
Emp Here 4,500
SIC 8011 Offices and clinics of medical doctors
Brendan Carr

D-U-N-S 25-297-7624   (BR)
WAL-MART CANADA CORP
(*Suby of* WALMART INC.)
3020 Drinkwater Rd, Duncan, BC, V9L 6C6
(250) 748-2566
Emp Here 100
SIC 5311 Department stores
Mather Rick

Elkford, BC V0B

D-U-N-S 24-851-1177   (SL)
BEARSPAW CONTRACTING INC
2200 Balmer Dr Suite 2, Elkford, BC, V0B 1H0

Emp Here 145   *Sales* 61,296,865
SIC 1541 Industrial buildings and warehouses
Ian Benson
Len Gostick

D-U-N-S 24-320-8423   (BR)
TECK COAL LIMITED
FORDING RIVER OPERATIONS
(*Suby of* TECK RESOURCES LIMITED)
Gd, Elkford, BC, V0B 1H0
(250) 865-2271
Emp Here 520
SIC 1221 Bituminous coal and lignite-surface mining
Dean Runzer

D-U-N-S 20-385-8758   (SL)
TRANSCENDENT MINING & MOBILIZATION INC
4a Front St, Elkford, BC, V0B 1H0
(778) 521-5144
Emp Here 50   *Sales* 12,044,200

SIC 1629 Heavy construction, nec
Ian Benson
Bud Lynch

Enderby, BC V0E

D-U-N-S 24-881-4535   (HQ)
CENTRAL HARDWARE LTD
701 Bass Ave, Enderby, BC, V0E 1V2
(250) 838-6474
Sales 26,765,200
SIC 5211 Lumber and other building materials
Bruce Khler

D-U-N-S 24-608-0931   (SL)
NORTH ENDERBY TIMBER LTD
6261 Hwy 97a Rr 3, Enderby, BC, V0E 1V3
(250) 838-9668
Emp Here 100   *Sales* 15,586,300
SIC 2421 Sawmills and planing mills, general
Larry Poggemoeller

Errington, BC V0R

D-U-N-S 20-388-7252   (SL)
QUALITY FOODS LTD
(*Suby of* PATTISON, JIM GROUP INC)
1581 Alberni Hwy, Errington, BC, V0R 1V0
(250) 248-4004
Emp Here 1,100   *Sales* 211,710,400
SIC 5411 Grocery stores
Noel Hayward
Justin Schley

Fairmont Hot Springs, BC V0B

D-U-N-S 20-096-3254   (HQ)
FAIRMONT HOT SPRINGS RESORT LTD
5225 Fairmont Resort Rd Rr 1, Fairmont Hot Springs, BC, V0B 1L1
(250) 345-6070
Sales 17,147,650
SIC 7011 Hotels and motels
David Vessey

D-U-N-S 24-673-7050   (SL)
FAIRMONT VILLA MANAGEMENT
5247 Fairmont Creek Rd Rr 1, Fairmont Hot Springs, BC, V0B 1L1
(250) 345-6341
Emp Here 55   *Sales* 15,088,260
SIC 8741 Management services
David Dupont
Don Seable

Fanny Bay, BC V0R

D-U-N-S 20-802-3341   (SL)
MAC'S OYSTERS LTD
7162 Island Hwy S, Fanny Bay, BC, V0R 1W0
(250) 335-2129
Emp Here 70   *Sales* 20,543,390
SIC 5411 Grocery stores
Gordon Mclellan Sr
Gordon Mclellan Jr
Pamela Mclellan

D-U-N-S 25-506-5682   (SL)
NATURAL GLACIAL WATERS INC
8430 Berray Rd Rr 1, Fanny Bay, BC, V0R 1W0
(250) 335-9119
Emp Here 50   *Sales* 13,833,000
SIC 2899 Chemical preparations, nec
Alan Lai

Ivy Lai

D-U-N-S 24-582-0167   (SL)
TAYLOR SHELLFISH CANADA ULC
FANNY BAY OYSTERS
8260 Island Hwy S, Fanny Bay, BC, V0R 1W0
(250) 335-0125
Emp Here 50   *Sales* 13,707,600
SIC 5421 Meat and fish markets
Brian Yip

Fernie, BC V0B

D-U-N-S 24-298-2288   (SL)
357672 B.C. LTD
PARK PLACE LODGE
742 Hwy 3 Rr 5, Fernie, BC, V0B 1M5
(250) 423-6871
Emp Here 85   *Sales* 7,878,650
SIC 7011 Hotels and motels
Gotthardt Sombrowski
Gordon Sombrowski
Ingrid Sombrowski
Carmen Sombrowski
Arthur Sombrowski

D-U-N-S 20-828-0024   (SL)
COAL VALLEY MOTOR PRODUCTS LTD
16 Manitou Rd, Fernie, BC, V0B 1M5
(250) 423-9288
Emp Here 25   *Sales* 12,451,950
SIC 5511 New and used car dealers
Ralph Will

D-U-N-S 24-028-9053   (BR)
GOLDEN LIFE MANAGEMENT CORP
ROCKY MOUNTAIN VILLAGE
(*Suby of* GOLDEN LIFE MANAGEMENT CORP)
55 Cokato Rd Suite 206, Fernie, BC, V0B 1M4
(250) 423-4214
Emp Here 80
SIC 8059 Nursing and personal care, nec
Nancy Watson

D-U-N-S 24-312-6856   (BR)
INTERIOR HEALTH AUTHORITY
ELK VALLEY HOSPITAL
(*Suby of* INTERIOR HEALTH AUTHORITY)
1501 5 Ave, Fernie, BC, V0B 1M0
(250) 423-4453
Emp Here 100
SIC 8062 General medical and surgical hospitals
Karyn Morash

Fort Nelson, BC V0C

D-U-N-S 20-919-2223   (SL)
399837 BC LTD
FORT NELSON IGA
4823 50th Ave S, Fort Nelson, BC, V0C 1R0
(250) 774-2791
Emp Here 60   *Sales* 17,608,620
SIC 5411 Grocery stores
Douglas Andrews

D-U-N-S 20-537-5405   (SL)
COOPER BARGING SERVICE LTD
Gd, Fort Nelson, BC, V0C 1R0
(250) 774-3359
Emp Here 40   *Sales* 10,781,960
SIC 4449 Water transportation of freight
Michael P. Cooper
Milton J. Cooper
Cameron R. Cooper
Edward H. Cooper
Jennifer J. Cooper
Sheila B. Mould

D-U-N-S 24-395-8980   (HQ)

DALL CONTRACTING LTD
Gd, Fort Nelson, BC, V0C 1R0
(250) 774-7251
Emp Here 12   *Sales* 16,524,928
SIC 5171 Petroleum bulk stations and terminals
Randy Bassett

D-U-N-S 24-390-3908   (SL)
DECHANT CONSTRUCTION (WESTERN) LTD
(*Suby of* DECHANT CONSTRUCTION LTD)
4801 44 Ave, Fort Nelson, BC, V0C 1R0
(250) 775-6064
Emp Here 100   *Sales* 67,267,900
SIC 1389 Oil and gas field services, nec
Daniel Dechant
Doug Dechant
Wayne Dechant

D-U-N-S 20-354-7443   (SL)
FT NELSON BULK SALES LTD
Mile 293 Alaska Hwy, Fort Nelson, BC, V0C 1R0
(250) 774-7340
Emp Here 12   *Sales* 12,393,696
SIC 5172 Petroleum products, nec
Erin Hyderman

D-U-N-S 20-310-0656   (SL)
KLEDO CONSTRUCTION LTD
4301 Nahanni Dr, Fort Nelson, BC, V0C 1R0
(250) 774-2501
Emp Here 40   *Sales* 11,340,960
SIC 1611 Highway and street construction
Brent Doyle
Michael Nadoronzy

D-U-N-S 20-916-3026   (SL)
M & M RESOURCES INC
4901 44th Ave, Fort Nelson, BC, V0C 1R0
(250) 774-4862
Emp Here 150   *Sales* 37,866,300
SIC 1629 Heavy construction, nec
Michael Barrette
Kevin Mcnee

D-U-N-S 24-090-7550   (HQ)
SCHOOL DISTRICT #81 (FORT NELSON)
5104 Airport Dr, Fort Nelson, BC, V0C 1R0
(250) 774-2591
Emp Here 1   *Sales* 11,894,280
SIC 8211 Elementary and secondary schools
Margaret Anne Hall

D-U-N-S 24-805-0838   (SL)
TORQUE INDUSTRIAL LTD
5100 46 Ave, Fort Nelson, BC, V0C 1R0
(250) 233-8675
Emp Here 65   *Sales* 16,002,090
SIC 1799 Special trade contractors, nec
Roger Beaulieu

Fort St. James, BC V0J

D-U-N-S 24-509-0480   (SL)
APOLLO FOREST PRODUCTS LTD
2555 Tachie Rd, Fort St. James, BC, V0J 1P0
(250) 996-8297
Emp Here 150   *Sales* 30,992,550
SIC 0851 Forestry services
Brent Brandys

D-U-N-S 20-919-3445   (BR)
CONIFEX INC
(*Suby of* CONIFEX TIMBER INC)
300 Takla Rd, Fort St. James, BC, V0J 1P0
(250) 996-8241
Emp Here 200
SIC 2421 Sawmills and planing mills, general
Ray Helmkay

Fort St. John, BC V1J

D-U-N-S 24-583-0856   (SL)
13876 ENTERPRISES LTD
INDEPENDENT PLUMBING & HEATING SUPPLY
10020 93 Ave, Fort St. John, BC, V1J 1E2
(250) 785-6679
Emp Here 24   *Sales* 10,732,176
SIC 5074 Plumbing and heating equipment and supplies (hydronics)
Victor Moskalyk
Jerry Friesen
Robert Slavik
Audrey Carter

D-U-N-S 24-853-3804   (SL)
321124 B.C. LTD
HOME HARDWARE STORE #5075-4
9820 108 St, Fort St. John, BC, V1J 0A7
(250) 787-0371
Emp Here 55   *Sales* 14,720,860
SIC 5251 Hardware stores
Lorna Pomeroy
Douglas (Doug) Gallinger
Glen Pomeroy

D-U-N-S 24-583-4796   (HQ)
ACE INSTRUMENTS LTD
11207 Tahltan Rd, Fort St. John, BC, V1J 6G8
(250) 785-1207
Emp Here 70   *Sales* 40,377,210
SIC 5084 Industrial machinery and equipment
Dino Soucy

D-U-N-S 24-802-6580   (HQ)
AVENTUR ENERGY CORP
10493 Alder Cres, Fort St. John, BC, V1J 4M7
(250) 785-7093
Emp Here 25   *Sales* 15,985,250
SIC 1389 Oil and gas field services, nec
Terry Aven
Tracy Hunter
Sicily Aven

D-U-N-S 24-906-9493   (SL)
BANNERMAN ENTERPRISES INC
CANADIAN TIRE STORE
9820 93 Ave, Fort St. John, BC, V1J 6J8
(250) 787-1142
Emp Here 75   *Sales* 47,196,000
SIC 5531 Auto and home supply stores
Ross Bannerman

D-U-N-S 24-857-3508   (SL)
BRASS APPLE ENTERPRISES INC
9320 82a Ave, Fort St. John, BC, V1J 6S2

Emp Here 60   *Sales* 16,256,520
SIC 1521 Single-family housing construction
Robert Allan Kirschner

D-U-N-S 20-740-0974   (BR)
CANADIAN FOREST PRODUCTS LTD
CANFOR
(*Suby of* CANFOR CORPORATION)
9312 259 Rd Lcd Main, Fort St. John, BC, V1J 4M6
(250) 787-3600
Emp Here 200
SIC 5031 Lumber, plywood, and millwork
William Clewes

D-U-N-S 20-609-2731   (SL)
CASCADE SERVICES LTD
9619 81 Ave, Fort St. John, BC, V1J 6P6
(250) 785-0236
Emp Here 130   *Sales* 87,448,270
SIC 1389 Oil and gas field services, nec
Geoff Durion
Doug Marquardt

D-U-N-S 20-253-8224   (SL)
CHEBUCTO VENTURES CORP
TIM HORTONS
8911 117 Ave, Fort St. John, BC, V1J 6B8
(250) 787-7501
Emp Here 88   *Sales* 3,772,824

SIC 5812 Eating places
Ron Bowie
Julia Bowie

D-U-N-S 20-114-0832   (HQ)
COMPRESSION TECHNOLOGY INC
10911 89 Ave, Fort St. John, BC, V1J 6V2
(250) 787-8655
Emp Here 40   *Sales* 13,320,060
SIC 3563 Air and gas compressors
Gordon Humphrey

D-U-N-S 25-516-3024   (BR)
CORRPRO CANADA, INC
(*Suby of* AEGION CORPORATION)
8607 101 St, Fort St. John, BC, V1J 5K4
(250) 787-9100
Emp Here 1,500
SIC 8711 Engineering services
Dwayne Taylor

D-U-N-S 25-453-1619   (BR)
DEVON CANADA CORPORATION
DEVON CANADA
(*Suby of* DEVON ENERGY CORPORATION)
10514 87 Ave, Fort St. John, BC, V1J 5K7

Emp Here 80
SIC 1382 Oil and gas exploration services
Tip Johnson

D-U-N-S 20-829-3071   (SL)
ECOFOR CONSULTING LTD
9940 104 Ave, Fort St. John, BC, V1J 2K3
(250) 787-6009
Emp Here 49   *Sales* 10,582,494
SIC 8748 Business consulting, nec
Rob Paterson

D-U-N-S 24-064-2033   (HQ)
EPSCAN INDUSTRIES LTD
10012 94 Ave, Fort St. John, BC, V1J 5J6
(250) 787-9659
Sales 14,250,780
SIC 5084 Industrial machinery and equipment
Shane Stirling

D-U-N-S 25-417-6464   (SL)
FORT CITY CHRYSLER SALES LTD
FORT CITY CHRYSLER
8424 Alaska Rd, Fort St. John, BC, V1J 5L6
(250) 787-5220
Emp Here 24   *Sales* 11,953,872
SIC 5511 New and used car dealers
Dwight Bazin
Michael Vida

D-U-N-S 20-096-6430   (SL)
FORT MOTORS LTD
(*Suby of* KARMA HOLDINGS LTD)
11104 Alaska Rd, Fort St. John, BC, V1J 5T5
(250) 785-6661
Emp Here 56   *Sales* 35,239,680
SIC 5511 New and used car dealers
Brian Gentles

D-U-N-S 20-096-6463   (HQ)
FORT ST JOHN CO-OPERATIVE ASSOCIATION
10808 91 Ave, Fort St. John, BC, V1J 5R1
(250) 785-4471
Sales 15,492,120
SIC 5171 Petroleum bulk stations and terminals
Brian Johnston
Doug Sather
Mitchel Chilcott

D-U-N-S 24-336-6619   (SL)
FSJ OILFIELD SERVICES
MULLEN OILFIELD SERVICES LP, DIV OF
8140 Alaska Rd, Fort St. John, BC, V1J 0P3
(250) 785-8935
Emp Here 380   *Sales* 255,618,020
SIC 1389 Oil and gas field services, nec
Rick Henning
Roland Lessard

D-U-N-S 25-267-8768   (BR)
GREAT PACIFIC INDUSTRIES INC
OVERWAITEA FOOD GROUP
(*Suby of* PATTISON, JIM GROUP INC)
10345 100 St, Fort St. John, BC, V1J 3Z2
(250) 785-2985
Emp Here 90
SIC 5411 Grocery stores
Cory Butler

D-U-N-S 20-959-3529   (SL)
HOME HARDWARE BUILDING CENTRE
FORT ST. JOHN HOME HARDWARE BUILDING CENTRE
9820 108 St, Fort St. John, BC, V1J 0A7
(250) 787-0371
Emp Here 60   *Sales* 16,059,120
SIC 5251 Hardware stores
Douglas Gallinger

D-U-N-S 24-375-5894   (BR)
INTEROUTE CONSTRUCTION LTD
DGS ASTRO PAVING
9503 79th Ave, Fort St. John, BC, V1J 4J3
(250) 787-7283
Emp Here 100   *Sales* 1,134,096
SIC 1611 Highway and street construction
Darren Francis

D-U-N-S 24-398-3087   (BR)
JORDAN ENTERPRISES LIMITED
QUALITY INN NORTHERN GRAND HOTEL
(*Suby of* JORDAN ENTERPRISES LIMITED)
9830 100 Ave, Fort St. John, BC, V1J 1Y5
(250) 787-0521
Emp Here 100
SIC 7011 Hotels and motels
Jamie Lewis

D-U-N-S 20-383-6486   (BR)
LOUISIANA-PACIFIC CANADA LTD
(*Suby of* LOUISIANA-PACIFIC CORPORATION)
8220 259 Rd Site 13 Comp 14, Fort St. John, BC, V1J 4M6
(250) 263-6600
Emp Here 180
SIC 2431 Millwork
Jeremy Barton

D-U-N-S 20-067-0268   (SL)
MACENNA BUSINESS SERVICES CORP
MACENNA STAFFING SERVICES
10139 101 Ave 2nd Fl, Fort St. John, BC, V1J 2B4
(250) 785-8367
Emp Here 49   *Sales* 11,611,530
SIC 7361 Employment agencies
Leanne Mcarthur
Cameron Mcarthur

D-U-N-S 24-333-7768   (HQ)
MACRO ENTERPRISES INC
6807 100 Ave, Fort St. John, BC, V1J 4J2
(250) 785-0033
Sales 144,842,968
SIC 1623 Water, sewer, and utility lines
Frank Miles
Mike Nielsen
Ken Mastre
Don Stewart
Lars Nielsen
Mike Doll
Jeff Redmond
William Mcfetridge
Ronald Baker
Wayne Albo

D-U-N-S 25-386-8293   (SL)
MACRO INDUSTRIES INC
(*Suby of* MACRO ENTERPRISES INC)
7904 101 Ave, Fort St. John, BC, V1J 2A3
(250) 785-0033
Emp Here 80   *Sales* 53,814,320
SIC 1389 Oil and gas field services, nec
Frank Miles
Mike Nielsen

▲ Public Company   ■ Public Company Family Member   **HQ** Headquarters   **BR** Branch   **SL** Single Location

Don Stewart
Lars Nielsen
Mike Doll
Frank Miles
Mike Nielsen
William Mcfetridge
Wayne Albo
Jeff Redmond

D-U-N-S 20-301-5482   (SL)
MACRO PIPELINES INC
6807 100 Ave, Fort St. John, BC, V1J 4J2
(250) 785-0033
Emp Here 100   *Sales* 26,954,900
SIC 4619 Pipelines, nec
Frank Miles
Mike Nielsen

D-U-N-S 24-332-5263   (BR)
MCELHANNEY ASSOCIATES LAND SURVEYING LTD
MCELHANNEY LAND SURVEYORS
(*Suby of* MCELHANNEY ASSOCIATES LAND SURVEYING LTD)
8808 72 St, Fort St. John, BC, V1J 6M2
(250) 787-0356
Emp Here 600
SIC 8713 Surveying services
Walter Johnson

D-U-N-S 25-081-2237   (SL)
MURRAY AUTO GROUP FORT ST. JOHN LTD
MURRAY GM
11204 Alaska Rd, Fort St. John, BC, V1J 5T5
(250) 785-8005
Emp Here 75   *Sales* 47,196,000
SIC 5511 New and used car dealers
Clark Lang

D-U-N-S 20-338-2353   (SL)
MURRAY MOTORS FORT ST. JOHN LTD
11204 Alaska Rd, Fort St. John, BC, V1J 5T5
(250) 785-6661
Emp Here 49   *Sales* 24,405,822
SIC 5511 New and used car dealers
Daniel Holtmann

D-U-N-S 20-280-3313   (BR)
NINE ENERGY CANADA INC
IPS
(*Suby of* NINE ENERGY SERVICE, INC.)
9404 73 Ave, Fort St. John, BC, V1J 4H7
(250) 785-4210
Emp Here 111
SIC 1389 Oil and gas field services, nec
Bruce Mcdowell

D-U-N-S 20-096-7206   (HQ)
NORTH CARIBOO FLYING SERVICE LTD
NORTH CARIBOO AIR
9945 Caribou Way, Fort St. John, BC, V1J 4J2
(250) 787-0311
Emp Here 24   *Sales* 95,205,600
SIC 4512 Air transportation, scheduled
Daniel Wuthrich
Peter Scheiwiller
Randy Gee

D-U-N-S 20-897-3933   (HQ)
NORTH PEACE SAVINGS AND CREDIT UNION
10344 100 St, Fort St. John, BC, V1J 3Z1
(250) 787-0361
Emp Here 1   *Sales* 13,048,435
SIC 6062 State credit unions
Mitchel Chilcott

D-U-N-S 20-096-7255   (HQ)
NORTHERN METALIC SALES (F.S.J.) LTD
10407 Alaska Rd, Fort St. John, BC, V1J 1B1
(250) 787-0717
Sales 30,876,690
SIC 5085 Industrial supplies
Bruce Mitchell
Wayne Klassen

D-U-N-S 25-967-1902   (SL)

PEACE RIVER HYDRO PARTNERS CONSTRUCTION LTD
7007 269 Rd, Fort St. John, BC, V1J 4M7
(250) 263-9920
Emp Here 3,000   *Sales* 984,345,000
SIC 1629 Heavy construction, nec
Daniel Cuarter

D-U-N-S 25-873-6339   (BR)
PETRO-CANADA HIBERNIA PARTNERSHIP
PETRO CANADA
11527 Alaska Rd, Fort St. John, BC, V1J 6N2
(250) 787-8200
Emp Here 100
SIC 1311 Crude petroleum and natural gas
Bob Lawson

D-U-N-S 24-396-7965   (SL)
PIMM PRODUCTION SERVICES INC
10924 Alaska Rd, Fort St. John, BC, V1J 5T5
(250) 787-0808
Emp Here 40   *Sales* 16,774,200
SIC 6712 Bank holding companies
Darwin Pimm

D-U-N-S 20-169-8508   (SL)
POINTS NORTH CONTRACTING LTD
PNC
8011 93 St, Fort St. John, BC, V1J 6X1
(250) 787-5525
Emp Here 50   *Sales* 100,901,850
SIC 1389 Oil and gas field services, nec
Oran Trevor Hall

D-U-N-S 24-984-1677   (SL)
RAVEN CENTER HOLDINGS LTD
RAVEN OILFIELD RENTALS
49 Alaska Hwy, Fort St. John, BC, V1J 4H7
(250) 787-8474
Emp Here 37   *Sales* 10,810,253
SIC 7359 Equipment rental and leasing, nec
Randy Gee

D-U-N-S 24-929-8696   (SL)
RHYASON CONTRACTING LTD
7307 Bipa Rd E, Fort St. John, BC, V1J 4M6
(250) 785-0515
Emp Here 80   *Sales* 20,195,360
SIC 1623 Water, sewer, and utility lines
Greg Rhyason
Robin Cant

D-U-N-S 25-131-7137   (HQ)
SCHOOL DISTRICT NO. 60 (PEACE RIVER NORTH)
10112 105 Ave, Fort St. John, BC, V1J 4S4
(250) 262-6000
Emp Here 15   *Sales* 57,289,250
SIC 8211 Elementary and secondary schools
Larry Espe
Ida Campbell
Ernie Inglehard
Gordon Anderson
Heather Hannaford
Gary Gamble
Linda Sewell
Lynda Peterson

D-U-N-S 20-656-2477   (BR)
SCHOOL DISTRICT NO. 60 (PEACE RIVER NORTH)
NORTH PEACE SECONDARY SCHOOL
(*Suby of* SCHOOL DISTRICT NO. 60 (PEACE RIVER NORTH))
9304 86 St, Fort St. John, BC, V1J 6L9
(250) 785-4429
Emp Here 75
SIC 8211 Elementary and secondary schools
Randy Pauls

D-U-N-S 24-616-6883   (BR)
STONEWATER GROUP OF FRANCHISES
MR MIKE STEAKHOUSE
(*Suby of* STONEWATER GROUP OF FRANCHISES)
9324 Alaska Rd, Fort St. John, BC, V1J 6L5

(250) 262-4151
Emp Here 80
SIC 5812 Eating places
Jayson Alicor

D-U-N-S 24-685-7291   (BR)
SUNCOR ENERGY INC
(*Suby of* SUNCOR ENERGY INC)
11527 Alaska Rd, Fort St. John, BC, V1J 6N2
(250) 787-8200
Emp Here 100
SIC 2911 Petroleum refining
Rocky Patterson

D-U-N-S 20-616-3420   (SL)
SURERUS CONSTRUCTION & DEVELOPMENT LTD
9312 109 St, Fort St. John, BC, V1J 6G9
(250) 785-2423
Emp Here 60   *Sales* 11,481,240
SIC 7359 Equipment rental and leasing, nec
Brian Surerus

D-U-N-S 25-416-4437   (SL)
TRACKER CONTRACTING LTD
7648 100 Ave, Fort St. John, BC, V1J 1V9

Emp Here 60   *Sales* 15,146,520
SIC 1623 Water, sewer, and utility lines
Greg Wilson
Louise Wilson

D-U-N-S 25-136-5524   (HQ)
TROJAN SAFETY SERVICES LTD
11116 Tahltan Rd, Fort St. John, BC, V1J 7C4
(250) 785-9557
Emp Here 30   *Sales* 31,970,500
SIC 1389 Oil and gas field services, nec
Al Kirschner

D-U-N-S 20-515-7147   (BR)
WAL-MART CANADA CORP
WALMART
(*Suby of* WALMART INC.)
9007 96a St, Fort St. John, BC, V1J 7B6
(250) 261-5544
Emp Here 300
SIC 5311 Department stores

D-U-N-S 20-046-9729   (BR)
WSP CANADA INC
FOCUS SURVEYS
(*Suby of* AST TRUST COMPANY (CANADA))
10716 100 Ave, Fort St. John, BC, V1J 1Z3
(250) 787-0300
Emp Here 100
SIC 8713 Surveying services
Adam Brash

Fraser Lake, BC V0J

D-U-N-S 24-152-6698   (BR)
WEST FRASER MILLS LTD
FRASER LAKE SAWMILLS
(*Suby of* WEST FRASER TIMBER CO. LTD)
6626 Highway 16 E, Fraser Lake, BC, V0J 1S0
(250) 699-6235
Emp Here 250
SIC 2621 Paper mills
Scott Mcdougall

Galloway, BC V0B

D-U-N-S 20-096-8493   (HQ)
GALLOWAY LUMBER COMPANY LTD
GALLOWAY LUMBER
7325 Galloway Mill Rd, Galloway, BC, V0B 1T2
(250) 429-3496
Sales 11,542,200
SIC 2421 Sawmills and planing mills, general
Charles (Bud) Nelson

Garibaldi Highlands, BC V0N

D-U-N-S 25-141-8778   (SL)
563769 B.C. LTD
EXTRA FOODS
1900 Garibaldi Way, Garibaldi Highlands, BC, V0N 1T0
(604) 898-6810
Emp Here 45   *Sales* 12,336,840
SIC 5411 Grocery stores
Craig Woida

D-U-N-S 25-998-1595   (SL)
SEA TO SKY COURIER & FREIGHT LTD
38922 Mid Way Suite 1, Garibaldi Highlands, BC, V0N 1T0
(604) 892-8484
Emp Here 35   *Sales* 15,522,150
SIC 7389 Business services, nec
Kulvinder Kaila

Gibsons, BC V0N

D-U-N-S 20-921-2757   (SL)
AL'S POWER PLUS
921 Gibsons Way, Gibsons, BC, V0N 1V8
(604) 886-3700
Emp Here 49   *Sales* 12,399,891
SIC 5251 Hardware stores
Bob Frizzell

D-U-N-S 20-622-7167   (HQ)
GIBSONS BUILDING SUPPLIES LTD
(*Suby of* REEVES GBS INVESTMENTS LTD)
924 Gibsons Way, Gibsons, BC, V0N 1V7
(604) 886-8141
Emp Here 38   *Sales* 15,523,816
SIC 5211 Lumber and other building materials
Barrie Reeves
Marion Reeves

D-U-N-S 20-916-4706   (SL)
H. W. M. STORES LTD
SUPER VALU 23
900 Gibsons Way, Gibsons, BC, V0N 1V7
(604) 886-2424
Emp Here 50   *Sales* 13,707,600
SIC 5411 Grocery stores
Blane Hagedorn
Timothy Thompson

D-U-N-S 20-353-2163   (SL)
HORIZON EXPORTS INC
HALEY DODGE SUNSHINE COAST
1028 Gibsons Way, Gibsons, BC, V0N 1V7
(604) 886-3433
Emp Here 22   *Sales* 10,957,716
SIC 5511 New and used car dealers
Todd Macdonald
Joseph Haley

D-U-N-S 24-898-6168   (HQ)
SCHOOL DISTRICT NO. 46 (SUNSHINE COAST)
494 South Fletcher Rd, Gibsons, BC, V0N 1V0
(604) 886-8811
Emp Here 10   *Sales* 48,963,150
SIC 8211 Elementary and secondary schools
Deborah Palmer
Andrea Debucy
Silas White
Ken Sinnott
Lori Fielding
Fran Heppell
Dave Mewhort
Greg Russell
Jason Scott

D-U-N-S 25-261-6966   (HQ)
SUNSHINE COAST CREDIT UNION
985 Gibsons Way Rr 8, Gibsons, BC, V0N 1V8

▲ Public Company   ■ Public Company Family Member   **HQ** Headquarters   **BR** Branch   **SL** Single Location

(604) 740-2662
Emp Here 17   *Sales* 11,874,213
SIC 6062 State credit unions
Dale Eichar
Shelley Mcdade
Dawn Bezaire
Brian Beecham
Bernie Bennett
Rick Cooney

D-U-N-S 25-125-9842   (BR)
UNIFOR
CEP LOCAL 1119
(*Suby of* UNIFOR)
1045 Gibsons Way, Gibsons, BC, V0N 1V4
(604) 886-2722
Emp Here 530
SIC 8631 Labor organizations
Gerry Sauve

D-U-N-S 25-484-8054   (SL)
WESDAN HOLDINGS INC
IGA PLUS STORES NO 56
1100 Sunshine Coast Hwy, Gibsons, BC, V0N 1V7
(604) 886-3487
Emp Here 45   *Sales* 12,336,840
SIC 5411 Grocery stores
Bob Hoy

Gold River, BC V0P

D-U-N-S 24-553-6987   (BR)
WESTERN FOREST PRODUCTS INC
NOOTKA SOUND DRYLAND
(*Suby of* WESTERN FOREST PRODUCTS INC)
300 Western Dr, Gold River, BC, V0P 1G0
(250) 283-2961
Emp Here 175
SIC 2611 Pulp mills

Golden, BC V0A

D-U-N-S 25-750-6261   (SL)
GOLDEN FIRE JUMPERS LTD
1717 Moberly School Rd, Golden, BC, V0A 1H1
(250) 344-6464
Emp Here 50   *Sales* 10,580,650
SIC 0851 Forestry services
Matthew Ward

D-U-N-S 25-646-6160   (SL)
GOLDEN TEACHERS ASSOCIATION
912 11th Ave S, Golden, BC, V0A 1H0

Emp Here 100   *Sales* 26,296,459
SIC 8611 Business associations
Norman Mac Donald

D-U-N-S 25-484-6579   (SL)
INTERIOR HEALTH AUTHORITY
GOLDEN & DISTRICT GENERAL HOSPITAL
835 9th St N, Golden, BC, V0A 1H2
(250) 344-5271
Emp Here 106   *Sales* 11,774,480
SIC 8062 General medical and surgical hospitals
Norman Hatlevik

D-U-N-S 25-365-1335   (BR)
LOUISIANA-PACIFIC CANADA LTD
LOUISIANA-PACIFIC BUILDING PRODUCTS
(*Suby of* LOUISIANA-PACIFIC CORPORATION)
800 9th St N, Golden, BC, V0A 1H0
(250) 344-8800
Emp Here 300
SIC 2436 Softwood veneer and plywood
Bryce Piggot

D-U-N-S 20-798-2976   (SL)
LP ENGINEERED WOOD PRODUCTS LTD
LP GOLDEN
(*Suby of* LOUISIANA-PACIFIC CORPORATION)
1221 10th Ave N, Golden, BC, V0A 1H2
(250) 344-8800
Emp Here 350   *Sales* 97,436,500
SIC 2436 Softwood veneer and plywood
Leonard Pettman
John Mckercher

Grand Forks, BC V0H

D-U-N-S 24-069-4687   (SL)
BOUNDARY HOSPITAL
7649 22nd St, Grand Forks, BC, V0H 1H2
(250) 443-2100
Emp Here 140   *Sales* 15,551,200
SIC 8062 General medical and surgical hospitals
John Lucke
Garth Burnell

D-U-N-S 25-116-9363   (SL)
BRON & SONS NURSERY CO. LTD
3315 Carson Rd, Grand Forks, BC, V0H 1H4
(250) 442-2014
Emp Here 65   *Sales* 48,263,800
SIC 5193 Flowers and florists supplies
Vince Bron
Ed Bron

D-U-N-S 25-506-8223   (BR)
ROXUL INC
WESTERN FACILITY
(*Suby of* ROCKWOOL INTERNATIONAL A/S)
6526 Industrial Pkwy, Grand Forks, BC, V0H 1H0
(250) 442-5253
Emp Here 180
SIC 3296 Mineral wool
Bill Faminoff

D-U-N-S 25-454-7003   (HQ)
SCHOOL DISTRICT 51 BOUNDARY
1021 Central Ave, Grand Forks, BC, V0H 1H0
(250) 442-8258
Sales 24,779,750
SIC 8211 Elementary and secondary schools
Kevin Argue

Harrison Hot Springs, BC V0M

D-U-N-S 25-996-1886   (SL)
HARRISON HOT SPRINGS RESORT & SPA CORP
HARRISON HOT SPRINGS RESORT & SPA
(*Suby of* DELAWARE NORTH COMPANIES INCORPORATED)
100 Esplanade Ave, Harrison Hot Springs, BC, V0M 1K0
(604) 796-2244
Emp Here 325   *Sales* 31,092,100
SIC 7011 Hotels and motels
Jeremy Jacobs
Danny Crowell

Harrison Mills, BC V0M

D-U-N-S 20-034-7438   (SL)
PRETTY ESTATES LTD
SANDPIPER GOLF CLUB/ROWENAS INN ON THE RIVER
14282 Morris Valley Rd, Harrison Mills, BC, V0M 1L0
(604) 796-1000
Emp Here 75   *Sales* 7,117,425

SIC 7011 Hotels and motels
Elizabeth Faulkner

D-U-N-S 24-014-9695   (HQ)
WESTERN CANADIAN TIMBER PRODUCTS LTD
14250 Morris Valley Rd, Harrison Mills, BC, V0M 1L0
(604) 796-0314
Emp Here 35   *Sales* 14,427,750
SIC 2411 Logging
Brian Dorman
Don Bonasky
Rick Delver
Doug Hill

Hedley, BC V0X

D-U-N-S 20-839-5488   (SL)
HEDLEY IMPROVEMENT DISTRICT
HEDLEY VOLUNTEER FIRE DEPARTMENT
825 Rue Scott, Hedley, BC, V0X 1K0
(250) 292-8637
Emp Here 23   *Sales* 10,451,701
SIC 7389 Business services, nec
Lindsay Stone

Heffley Creek, BC V0E

D-U-N-S 20-180-7182   (SL)
19959 YUKON INC
SUN PEAKS GRAND HOTEL
3240 Village Way, Heffley Creek, BC, V0E 1Z1
(250) 578-6000
Emp Here 80   *Sales* 7,591,920
SIC 7011 Hotels and motels
Kent Murray

Heriot Bay, BC V0P

D-U-N-S 24-328-2931   (SL)
TULA FOUNDATION
1713 Hyacinthe Bay Rd, Heriot Bay, BC, V0P 1H0
(250) 285-2628
Emp Here 60   *Sales* 42,552,720
SIC 8699 Membership organizations, nec
Eric Peterson
Christina Mumck

D-U-N-S 20-955-7404   (HQ)
WALCAN SEAFOOD LTD
Gd, Heriot Bay, BC, V0P 1H0
(250) 285-3361
Sales 60,495,750
SIC 2091 Canned and cured fish and seafoods
Cameron Pirie
Norman Brown
Robert Wayne Eastland

Hope, BC V0X

D-U-N-S 20-992-2657   (BR)
FRASER HEALTH AUTHORITY
FRASER CANYON HOSPITAL
(*Suby of* GOVERNMENT OF THE PROVINCE OF BRITISH COLUMBIA)
1275 7th Ave, Hope, BC, V0X 1L4
(604) 869-5656
Emp Here 130
SIC 8011 Offices and clinics of medical doctors
Maureen Wood

D-U-N-S 20-146-5916   (SL)
GARDNER CHEVROLET OLDSMOBILE LTD
945 Water Ave, Hope, BC, V0X 1L0
(604) 869-2002
Emp Here 23   *Sales* 11,455,794
SIC 5511 New and used car dealers
C K Gardner

D-U-N-S 24-504-4052   (SL)
GARDNER CHEVROLET PONTIAC BUICK GMC LTD
945 Water St, Hope, BC, V0X 1L0
(604) 869-9511
Emp Here 35   *Sales* 17,432,730
SIC 5511 New and used car dealers
Keith Gardner
Richard Gardner

D-U-N-S 20-153-5726   (SL)
HEALTHSPACE INFORMATICS LTD
417 Wallace St Unit 7, Hope, BC, V0X 1L0

Emp Here 177   *Sales* 25,520,214
SIC 7371 Custom computer programming services
John Halstad
Joseph Willmott
Patricia Halsted
Andrew Price
Susan- Marie Price

D-U-N-S 25-685-2443   (BR)
NESTLE CANADA INC
NESTLE WATERS CANADA DIV
(*Suby of* NESTLE S.A.)
66700 Othello Rd, Hope, BC, V0X 1L1
(604) 860-4888
Emp Here 75
SIC 5149 Groceries and related products, nec
Ivan Graham

Houston, BC V0J

D-U-N-S 20-511-9779   (BR)
CANADIAN FOREST PRODUCTS LTD
CANFOR
(*Suby of* CANFOR CORPORATION)
1397 Morice River Forest Service Rd Rr 1, Houston, BC, V0J 1Z1
(250) 845-5200
Emp Here 350
SIC 2421 Sawmills and planing mills, general
Dennis Hotte

D-U-N-S 24-349-4403   (SL)
DH MANUFACTURING INC
1250 Hols Rd, Houston, BC, V0J 1Z1
(250) 845-3390
Emp Here 120   *Sales* 23,084,400
SIC 2499 Wood products, nec
Lynda Denise Hotte
Dustin Hotte

D-U-N-S 20-955-9251   (SL)
GROOT BROS. CONTRACTING LTD
3377 Thirteenth St Unit 3, Houston, BC, V0J 1Z0
(250) 845-0093
Emp Here 70   *Sales* 10,910,410
SIC 2411 Logging
Mark Groot
Kevin Groot

D-U-N-S 20-965-2838   (BR)
HUCKLEBERRY MINES LTD
(*Suby of* IMPERIAL METALS CORPORATION)
Gd, Houston, BC, V0J 1Z0
(604) 517-4723
Emp Here 220
SIC 1021 Copper ores
Randall Thompson

▲ Public Company   ■ Public Company Family Member   **HQ** Headquarters   **BR** Branch   **SL** Single Location

D-U-N-S 24-863-1413   (SL)
PACIFIC TRUCK & EQUIPMENT
PETER BILT OF HOUSTON BC
2226 North Nadina Ave, Houston, BC, V0J 1Z0
(250) 845-0061
Emp Here 30   *Sales* 14,250,780
SIC 5084 Industrial machinery and equipment
Lisa Tymkow

D-U-N-S 20-797-2167   (SL)
SULLIVAN MOTOR PRODUCTS LTD
SULLIVAN MOTORS
2760 Yellowhead Hwy Suite 16, Houston, BC, V0J 1Z0
(250) 845-2244
Emp Here 35   *Sales* 17,432,730
SIC 5511 New and used car dealers
John Sullivan

Hudson'S Hope, BC V0C

D-U-N-S 24-064-2017   (SL)
BUTLER RIDGE ENERGY SERVICES (2011) LTD
8908 Clarke Ave, Hudson'S Hope, BC, V0C 1V0
(250) 783-2363
Emp Here 40   *Sales* 10,122,360
SIC 5211 Lumber and other building materials
Richard Brown

Invermere, BC V0A

D-U-N-S 20-917-9766   (BR)
BOARD OF EDUCATION OF SCHOOL DISTRICT NO. 06 (ROCKY MOUNTAIN), THE
DAVID THOMPSON SECONDARY SCHOOL
1535 14th St Suite 4, Invermere, BC, V0A 1K4
(250) 342-9213
Emp Here 78
SIC 8211 Elementary and secondary schools
Darren Danyluk

D-U-N-S 20-744-1619   (HQ)
HELMER, MAX CONSTRUCTION LTD
1000 Panorama Dr Rr 7, Invermere, BC, V0A 1K7
(250) 342-6767
Sales 14,121,930
SIC 1542 Nonresidential construction, nec
Joe Helmer
Tony Helmer

D-U-N-S 20-097-7098   (SL)
INVERMERE HARDWARE & BUILDING SUPPLIES CO LTD
HOME HARDWARE INVERMERE
9980 Arrow Rd, Invermere, BC, V0A 1K2
(250) 342-6908
Emp Here 70   *Sales* 18,735,640
SIC 5211 Lumber and other building materials
Allen Miller
Lorraine Miller

D-U-N-S 24-978-3648   (SL)
IW RESORTS LIMITED PARTNERSHIP
PANORAMA MOUNTAIN VILLAGE
2030 Panorama Dr, Invermere, BC, V0A 1K0
(250) 342-6941
Emp Here 200   *Sales* 18,538,000
SIC 7011 Hotels and motels
Nancy Jankinson
Mark Woodburn

Kamloops, BC V1S

D-U-N-S 20-555-8161   (SL)
ALUMINUM CURTAINWALL SYSTEMS INC

1820 Kryczka Pl, Kamloops, BC, V1S 1S4
(250) 372-3600
Emp Here 100   *Sales* 19,208,500
SIC 3449 Miscellaneous Metalwork
Regan Loehr

D-U-N-S 25-287-5778   (BR)
COSTCO WHOLESALE CANADA LTD
COSTCO
(*Suby of* COSTCO WHOLESALE CORPORATION)
1675 Versatile Dr, Kamloops, BC, V1S 1W7
(250) 374-5336
Emp Here 240
SIC 5099 Durable goods, nec
Chris Carr

D-U-N-S 25-792-6857   (HQ)
DAWNAL QUICK SERVE LTD
MCDONALD'S RESTAURANT
1465 Trans Canada Hwy W, Kamloops, BC, V1S 1A1
(250) 374-1922
Emp Here 80   *Sales* 11,659,750
SIC 5812 Eating places

D-U-N-S 24-519-7913   (SL)
DESERT CARDLOCK FUEL SERVICES LIMITED
1885 Versatile Dr, Kamloops, BC, V1S 1C5
(250) 374-8144
Emp Here 13   *Sales* 13,426,504
SIC 5172 Petroleum products, nec
Scott Angstadt

D-U-N-S 25-301-2462   (BR)
HUDSON'S BAY COMPANY
BAY, THE
(*Suby of* HUDSON'S BAY COMPANY)
1320 Trans Canada Hwy W Suite 300, Kamloops, BC, V1S 1J1
(250) 372-8271
Emp Here 100
SIC 5311 Department stores
Al Avila

D-U-N-S 25-603-7094   (SL)
INTEGRATED PROACTION CORP
IPAC
1425 Hugh Allan Dr, Kamloops, BC, V1S 1J3
(250) 828-7977
Emp Here 50   *Sales* 22,174,500
SIC 7389 Business services, nec
Darryl Ketter
John Pellizzon

D-U-N-S 25-096-8666   (HQ)
IRL INTERNATIONAL TRUCK CENTRES LTD
1495 Iron Mask Rd, Kamloops, BC, V1S 1C8
(250) 372-1445
Emp Here 40   *Sales* 22,216,248
SIC 4212 Local trucking, without storage
Ian Dawson
Tom Barley

D-U-N-S 25-409-3750   (HQ)
WOODLAND EQUIPMENT INC
2015 Trans Canada Hwy W, Kamloops, BC, V1S 1A7
(250) 372-2855
Emp Here 15   *Sales* 15,242,740
SIC 5084 Industrial machinery and equipment
George Anderson
Donna L. Anderson

Kamloops, BC V2B

D-U-N-S 24-134-0322   (SL)
BUTLER AUTO SALES LTD
BUTLER AUTO & RV CENTRE
142 Tranquille Rd, Kamloops, BC, V2B 3G1
(250) 554-2518
Emp Here 35   *Sales* 17,432,730

SIC 5511 New and used car dealers
June Butler
Joe Butler

D-U-N-S 24-383-7817   (BR)
DAWNAL QUICK SERVE LTD
MCDONALD'S
(*Suby of* DAWNAL QUICK SERVE LTD)
661 Fortune Dr, Kamloops, BC, V2B 2K7
(250) 376-0222
Emp Here 100
SIC 5812 Eating places
Andrew Williams

D-U-N-S 24-535-0657   (SL)
KAMLOOPS HOME SUPPORT SERVICES ASSOCIATION
396 Tranquille Rd, Kamloops, BC, V2B 3G7
(250) 851-7550
Emp Here 135   *Sales* 10,366,920
SIC 8322 Individual and family services
Marian Mackinnon
Barb Smith
Dorothy Hungar
Evan Plommer
Lynn Hansen
Jim Fedorak
Betty Ann Kuhn
Sandra Jones
Gail Cameron

D-U-N-S 24-897-2762   (SL)
NICOLANI SERVICES LTD
PAUL LAKE HUSKY MARKET
995 Arlington Crt, Kamloops, BC, V2B 8T5
(250) 372-0451
Emp Here 25   *Sales* 12,451,950
SIC 5541 Gasoline service stations
Agostino Bossio

D-U-N-S 25-449-6615   (SL)
OBOR HOLDINGS LTD
ROBO CAR WASH
228 Tranquille Rd, Kamloops, BC, V2B 3G1
(250) 376-1710
Emp Here 30   *Sales* 14,942,340
SIC 5541 Gasoline service stations
Robert Phillips

D-U-N-S 24-233-0459   (SL)
OSPREY CARE INC
HAMLETS AT WESTSYDE, THE
3255 Overlander Dr, Kamloops, BC, V2B 0A5
(250) 579-9061
Emp Here 165   *Sales* 11,273,790
SIC 8059 Nursing and personal care, nec
Hendrik Van Ryk

D-U-N-S 24-930-9964   (HQ)
PRIMA ENTERPRISES LTD
1103 12th St Unit 102, Kamloops, BC, V2B 8A6
(250) 376-9554
Emp Here 10   *Sales* 21,835,800
SIC 8741 Management services
Gary Fridell

Kamloops, BC V2C

D-U-N-S 20-178-9398   (SL)
646371 B.C. LTD
SUN COUNTRY TOYOTA
1355 Cariboo Pl, Kamloops, BC, V2C 5Z3
(250) 828-7966
Emp Here 41   *Sales* 20,421,198
SIC 5511 New and used car dealers
Robert Splane
Michael Vida

D-U-N-S 25-113-6610   (SL)
ACRES ENTERPRISES LTD
971 Camosun Cres, Kamloops, BC, V2C 6G1
(250) 372-7456
Emp Here 65   *Sales* 13,252,395

SIC 6553 Cemetery subdividers and developers
Jason Paige

D-U-N-S 20-864-2371   (BR)
ARROW TRANSPORTATION SYSTEMS INC
(*Suby of* ARROW TRANSPORTATION SYSTEMS INC)
1805 Mission Flats Rd, Kamloops, BC, V2C 1A9
(250) 374-6715
Emp Here 100
SIC 4212 Local trucking, without storage
Kevin Gayfer

D-U-N-S 24-726-9934   (SL)
B. C. GAS INC.
910 Columbia St W, Kamloops, BC, V2C 1L2

Emp Here 6   *Sales* 18,635,142
SIC 4924 Natural gas distribution

D-U-N-S 24-374-2637   (SL)
B.C. LOTTOTECH INTERNATIONAL INC
(*Suby of* GOVERNMENT OF THE PROVINCE OF BRITISH COLUMBIA)
74 Seymour St W, Kamloops, BC, V2C 1E2
(250) 828-5500
Emp Here 200   *Sales* 18,990,600
SIC 7999 Amusement and recreation, nec
Vic Poleschuk

D-U-N-S 24-372-9506   (HQ)
BARTON, BLACK & ROBERTSON INSURANCE SERVICES LTD
206 Seymour St Unit 100, Kamloops, BC, V2C 6P5
(250) 314-6217
Emp Here 15   *Sales* 110,864,520
SIC 6411 Insurance agents, brokers, and service
Tom Douglas

D-U-N-S 24-535-4600   (HQ)
BRITISH COLUMBIA LOTTERY CORPORATION
DRIFTWOOD TICKET CENTRE
(*Suby of* GOVERNMENT OF THE PROVINCE OF BRITISH COLUMBIA)
74 Seymour St W, Kamloops, BC, V2C 1E2
(250) 828-5500
Emp Here 800   *Sales* 2,393,147,467
SIC 7993 Coin-operated amusement devices
Jim Lightbody
Peter Kappel
Brad Desmarais
Susan Dolinski
Kevin Gass
Amanda Hobson
Jamie Callahan
Rob Kroeker
Patrick Davis
Andrew Brown

D-U-N-S 20-182-5820   (HQ)
CASTLE FUELS (2008) INC
PETRO CANADA
1639 Trans Canada Hwy E, Kamloops, BC, V2C 3Z5
(250) 372-5035
Emp Here 18   *Sales* 31,430,025
SIC 5172 Petroleum products, nec
Robert Vandriel
Lisa Vandriel

D-U-N-S 24-777-1488   (SL)
CENTURY GLASS (85) LTD
APPLE AUTO GLASS
1110 Victoria St, Kamloops, BC, V2C 2C5
(250) 374-1274
Emp Here 50   *Sales* 12,652,950
SIC 5211 Lumber and other building materials
Dave Mitchell

D-U-N-S 25-678-9140   (HQ)
COOPER MARKET LTD
COOPER'S FOODS
(*Suby of* PATTISON, JIM GROUP INC)

---

804 Laval Cres, Kamloops, BC, V2C 5P3

Emp Here 11   Sales 105,855,200
SIC 5411 Grocery stores
Kirk Henderson
Nick Desmarais
Rod Bergen
Dennis Pedersen

D-U-N-S 25-773-1968   (BR)
DAWNAL QUICK SERVE LTD
MCDONALD'S RESTAURANTS
(Suby of DAWNAL QUICK SERVE LTD)
500 Notre Dame Dr Unit 800, Kamloops, BC,
V2C 6T6
(250) 314-3686
Emp Here 80
SIC 5812 Eating places
Cara Messum

D-U-N-S 20-110-7513   (HQ)
DAWSON CONSTRUCTION LIMITED
1212 Mcgill Rd, Kamloops, BC, V2C 6N6
(250) 374-3657
Sales 17,670,940
SIC 1611 Highway and street construction
Ian Dawson
Graham Dawson
Walter Coxon

D-U-N-S 20-427-3627   (SL)
DEARBORN MOTORS LTD
2555 Trans Canada Hwy E, Kamloops, BC,
V2C 4B1
(250) 372-7101
Emp Here 95   Sales 59,781,600
SIC 5511 New and used car dealers
Ronald Bacon
Michael Bacon

D-U-N-S 24-567-1339   (SL)
DESSERT CITY INVESTIGATIONS AND SE-
CURITY INC
LORMIT PROCESS SERVICE
6968 Furrer Rd, Kamloops, BC, V2C 4V9
(250) 828-8778
Emp Here 30   Sales 20,367,690
SIC 6211 Security brokers and dealers
Patrick Bodnard

D-U-N-S 24-319-0928   (BR)
DOMTAR INC
KAMLOOPS MILL
(Suby of DOMTAR LUXEMBOURG INVEST-
MENTS SARL)
2005 Mission Flats Rd, Kamloops, BC, V2C
5M7
(250) 434-6000
Emp Here 426
SIC 2421 Sawmills and planing mills, general
Carol Lapointe

D-U-N-S 25-014-9176   (BR)
EARL'S RESTAURANTS LTD
EARL'1
(Suby of EARL'S RESTAURANTS LTD)
1210 Summit Dr Suite 800, Kamloops, BC,
V2C 6M1
(250) 372-3275
Emp Here 75
SIC 5812 Eating places
Steve Faraday

D-U-N-S 20-006-7429   (BR)
FABRICLAND PACIFIC LIMITED
FABRICLAND
(Suby of FABRICLAND PACIFIC LIMITED)
2121 Trans Canada Hwy E, Kamloops, BC,
V2C 4A6
(250) 374-3360
Emp Here 100
SIC 5949 Sewing, needlework, and piece
goods
Warren Kimel

D-U-N-S 25-771-6563   (SL)
HOT SHOT TRUCKING (1990) LTD
BEST EXPRESS HOT SHOT TRUCKING

937 Laval Cres, Kamloops, BC, V2C 5P4
(250) 372-7651
Emp Here 24   Sales 10,643,760
SIC 7389 Business services, nec
Herman Vandegoode
Penny Vandegoode

D-U-N-S 20-097-9847   (SL)
INTERIOR PLUMBING AND HEATING LIM-
ITED
782 Laval Cres, Kamloops, BC, V2C 5P3
(250) 372-3441
Emp Here 50   Sales 11,046,700
SIC 1711 Plumbing, heating, air-conditioning
Chris Owen
Edward Jurista
Richard Owen

D-U-N-S 24-760-6510   (HQ)
INTERIOR ROADS LTD
1212 Mcgill Rd, Kamloops, BC, V2C 6N6
(250) 374-7238
Emp Here 4   Sales 82,028,750
SIC 1611 Highway and street construction
Ian Dawson
Tom Barley
Graham Dawson

D-U-N-S 20-548-9755   (HQ)
JASSUN HOLDINGS LTD
WESTCAN AUTO PARTS PLUS
874 Notre Dame Dr, Kamloops, BC, V2C 6L5
(250) 372-1991
Emp Here 1   Sales 12,383,310
SIC 5013 Motor vehicle supplies and new
parts
Ron Jhaj

D-U-N-S 20-586-4259   (SL)
KAMLOOPS DODGE CHRYSLER JEEP
LIMITED
2525 Trans Canada Hwy E, Kamloops, BC,
V2C 4A9
(250) 374-4477
Emp Here 44   Sales 21,915,432
SIC 5511 New and used car dealers
Brian Johnston
James Mcmanes

D-U-N-S 25-993-5877   (SL)
KAMLOOPS HYUNDAI
948 Notre Dame Dr, Kamloops, BC, V2C 6J2
(250) 851-9380
Emp Here 25   Sales 12,451,950
SIC 5511 New and used car dealers
Rod Cartier
Anthony Muzzillo

D-U-N-S 24-120-4270   (SL)
KAMLOOPS PROFESSIONAL MANAGE-
MENT GROUP
248 2nd Ave, Kamloops, BC, V2C 2C9
(250) 372-5542
Emp Here 40   Sales 10,462,120
SIC 6712 Bank holding companies
Lyle Backman
Nick Weiser

D-U-N-S 20-067-1233   (BR)
KAMLOOPS, THE CORPORATION OF THE
CITY OF
CANADA GAMES AQUATIC CENTRE
(Suby of KAMLOOPS, THE CORPORATION
OF THE CITY OF)
910 Mcgill Rd, Kamloops, BC, V2C 6N6
(250) 828-3655
Emp Here 100
SIC 7999 Amusement and recreation, nec
Eric Bientjes

D-U-N-S 20-735-8925   (HQ)
KB HOLDINGS LTD
PETRO-CANADA
411 10th Ave, Kamloops, BC, V2C 6J8
(250) 372-1734
Emp Here 10   Sales 24,903,900
SIC 5541 Gasoline service stations

David Marson
Wanda Macphee

D-U-N-S 24-007-7776   (SL)
KGHM AJAX MINING INC
124 Seymour St Suite 200, Kamloops, BC,
V2C 2E1
(250) 374-5446
Emp Here 50   Sales 11,671,750
SIC 1021 Copper ores
Marcin Mostowy
Jaroslaw Romanowski
Maciej Konski
Michael Mcinnis
Warner Uhl

D-U-N-S 24-824-1440   (BR)
KPMG LLP
(Suby of KPMG LLP)
206 Seymour St Suite 200, Kamloops, BC,
V2C 6P5
(250) 372-5581
Emp Here 85
SIC 8721 Accounting, auditing, and book-
keeping
Starr Carson

D-U-N-S 25-136-9393   (BR)
LOBLAWS INC
REAL CANADIAN SUPERSTORE
(Suby of LOBLAW COMPANIES LIMITED)
910 Columbia St W Suite 1522, Kamloops,
BC, V2C 1L2
(250) 371-6418
Emp Here 300
SIC 5411 Grocery stores
Glenn Gregory

D-U-N-S 25-273-1385   (BR)
LONDON DRUGS LIMITED
(Suby of H.Y. LOUIE CO. LIMITED)
450 Lansdowne St Suite 68, Kamloops, BC,
V2C 1Y3
(250) 372-0028
Emp Here 100
SIC 5912 Drug stores and proprietary stores
Jim Larsen

D-U-N-S 25-771-7652   (SL)
MCDONALD'S RESTAURANTS LTD
1751 Trans Canada Hwy E, Kamloops, BC,
V2C 3Z6
(250) 374-1718
Emp Here 80   Sales 3,641,520
SIC 5812 Eating places
Al Godza

D-U-N-S 20-329-1682   (SL)
NATURE'S FARE NATURAL FOODS INC
1350 Summit Dr Suite 5, Kamloops, BC, V2C
1T8
(250) 314-9560
Emp Here 40   Sales 10,966,080
SIC 5499 Miscellaneous food stores
Spencer Dobell

D-U-N-S 24-246-6171   (SL)
NORPAC CONSTRUCTION INC
5520 Campbell Creek Rd, Kamloops, BC, V2C
6V4
(778) 696-2434
Emp Here 46   Sales 15,333,318
SIC 1541 Industrial buildings and warehouses
Sandy Thomson
Chris Wouters

D-U-N-S 20-352-7239   (BR)
NORTHAM BEVERAGES LTD
(Suby of NORTHAM BEVERAGES LTD)
965 Mcgill Pl, Kamloops, BC, V2C 6N9
(250) 851-2543
Emp Here 87
SIC 2085 Distilled and blended liquors

D-U-N-S 25-898-7932   (SL)
OII OWNERSHIP IDENTIFICATION INC
1402 Mcgill Rd Suite 102, Kamloops, BC, V2C
1L3

(250) 314-9686
Emp Here 35   Sales 15,722,665
SIC 7389 Business services, nec
Robert Miller

D-U-N-S 25-360-0027   (HQ)
PATTISON, JIM BROADCAST GROUP LTD
COUNTRY 95.5 FM
(Suby of PATTISON, JIM GROUP INC)
460 Pemberton Ter, Kamloops, BC, V2C 1T5
(250) 372-3322
Emp Here 60   Sales 133,817,600
SIC 4832 Radio broadcasting stations
Rod Schween
Bill Dinicol
Mark Rogers
Bill Stovold
Ross Winters
Andrew Snook

D-U-N-S 20-097-7759   (BR)
POSTMEDIA NETWORK INC
KAMLOOPS DAILY NEWS, THE
(Suby of POSTMEDIA NETWORK CANADA
CORP)
393 Seymour St, Kamloops, BC, V2C 6P6

Emp Here 80
SIC 2711 Newspapers
Tim Shoults

D-U-N-S 20-209-2248   (SL)
RIVER CITY NISSAN
2405 Trans Canada Hwy E, Kamloops, BC,
V2C 4A9
(250) 377-8850
Emp Here 21   Sales 10,459,638
SIC 5511 New and used car dealers
Sean Turner

D-U-N-S 25-767-5681   (HQ)
RJAMES MANAGEMENT GROUP LTD
WESTERN STAR FREIGHTLINER
2072 Falcon Rd, Kamloops, BC, V2C 4J3
(250) 374-1431
Emp Here 50   Sales 62,928,000
SIC 5511 New and used car dealers
Robert James

D-U-N-S 25-773-1075   (SL)
ROYAL LEPAGE KAMLOOPS REALTY
HOME COTTAGE
322 Seymour St, Kamloops, BC, V2C 2G2
(250) 374-3022
Emp Here 40   Sales 10,870,240
SIC 6531 Real estate agents and managers
Albert Gatien

D-U-N-S 25-857-9648   (SL)
ROYAL LEPAGE-WESTWIN REALTY LTD
800 Seymour St, Kamloops, BC, V2C 2H5
(250) 819-3404
Emp Here 55   Sales 14,946,580
SIC 6531 Real estate agents and managers
Michael Mitchell

D-U-N-S 20-034-0920   (BR)
SCHOOL   DISTRICT   73   (KAM-
LOOPS/THOMPSON)
SOUTH KAMLOOPS SECONDARY SCHOOL
(Suby of SCHOOL DISTRICT 73 (KAM-
LOOPS/THOMPSON))
821 Munro St, Kamloops, BC, V2C 3E9
(250) 374-1405
Emp Here 130
SIC 8211 Elementary and secondary schools
Richard Kienlein

D-U-N-S 25-815-1273   (BR)
SCHOOL   DISTRICT   73   (KAM-
LOOPS/THOMPSON)
BUS GARAGE
(Suby of SCHOOL DISTRICT 73 (KAM-
LOOPS/THOMPSON))
710 Mcgill Rd, Kamloops, BC, V2C 0A2
(250) 372-5853
Emp Here 86
SIC 4173 Bus terminal and service facilities

Dave Mell

D-U-N-S 20-919-9173   (HQ)
SCHOOL DISTRICT 73 (KAM-LOOPS/THOMPSON)
1383 9th Ave, Kamloops, BC, V2C 3X7
(250) 374-0679
Emp Here 31   *Sales* 158,590,400
SIC 8211 Elementary and secondary schools
Kelvin Stretch
Terry Sullivan

D-U-N-S 20-098-2213   (SL)
SMITH CHEVROLET OLDSMOBILE LTD
950 Notre Dame Dr Suite 3310, Kamloops, BC, V2C 6J2
(250) 377-3302
Emp Here 65   *Sales* 40,903,200
SIC 5511 New and used car dealers
Michael Schreiner
Anthony Muzzillo

D-U-N-S 25-825-0666   (BR)
SOBEYS WEST INC
SAHALI MALL SAFEWAY
(*Suby of* EMPIRE COMPANY LIMITED)
945 Columbia St W, Kamloops, BC, V2C 1L5
(250) 374-2811
Emp Here 120
SIC 5411 Grocery stores
Dave Nemrava

D-U-N-S 20-368-3540   (SL)
SUMMIT SECURITY GROUP LTD
Gd Stn Main, Kamloops, BC, V2C 5K2

Emp Here 49   *Sales* 19,388,222
SIC 7381 Detective and armored car services
Jeff Defer

D-U-N-S 20-235-8417   (SL)
SUNRISE VEHICLE SALES LTD
RIVERSHORE CHRYSLER JEEP
2477 Trans Canada Hwy E, Kamloops, BC, V2C 4A9
(250) 372-5588
Emp Here 30   *Sales* 14,942,340
SIC 5511 New and used car dealers
Denis Lowe

D-U-N-S 24-314-8421   (SL)
THOMPSON RIVER VENEER PRODUCTS LIMITED
8405 Dallas Dr, Kamloops, BC, V2C 6X2
(250) 573-6002
Emp Here 55   *Sales* 10,580,350
SIC 2436 Softwood veneer and plywood
Ronnie Doman
Doug Webb

D-U-N-S 25-453-6667   (HQ)
THOMPSON RIVERS UNIVERSITY
805 Tru Way, Kamloops, BC, V2C 0C8
(250) 828-5000
Emp Here 1,676   *Sales* 137,217,057
SIC 8221 Colleges and universities
Alan Shaver

D-U-N-S 20-311-1083   (SL)
TRI CITY CANADA INC
150 Victoria St Suite 102, Kamloops, BC, V2C 1Z7
(250) 372-5576
Emp Here 50   *Sales* 23,536,550
SIC 1542 Nonresidential construction, nec
Casey Vandongen

D-U-N-S 24-356-9741   (HQ)
TVE INDUSTRIAL SERVICES LTD
60 Vicars Rd, Kamloops, BC, V2C 6A4
(250) 377-3533
Emp Here 300   *Sales* 63,712,800
SIC 1799 Special trade contractors, nec
Justin Currie
Grant Toutant
Wayne Welsh

D-U-N-S 24-247-5101   (SL)

UNDERWRITERS INSURANCE BROKERS (B.C.) LTD
UNDERWRITERS INSURANCE
310 Nicola St Unit 103, Kamloops, BC, V2C 2P5
(250) 374-2139
Emp Here 34   *Sales* 19,717,416
SIC 6411 Insurance agents, brokers, and service
Kevin Mcintyre
Carl Sulkowski
Mark Joly

D-U-N-S 20-919-9843   (HQ)
URBAN SYSTEMS LTD
286 St Paul St Suite 200, Kamloops, BC, V2C 6G4
(250) 374-8311
Emp Here 70   *Sales* 55,409,090
SIC 8711 Engineering services
Martin Bell
Steve Frith

D-U-N-S 20-575-1498   (SL)
ZIMMER WHEATON BUICK GMC LTD
(*Suby of* WHEATON, DON LTD)
685 Notre Dame Dr, Kamloops, BC, V2C 5N7
(250) 374-1148
Emp Here 55   *Sales* 34,610,400
SIC 5511 New and used car dealers
Robert E Zimmer

Kamloops, BC V2E

D-U-N-S 20-177-5082   (BR)
HOME DEPOT OF CANADA INC
HOME DEPOT
(*Suby of* THE HOME DEPOT INC)
1020 Hillside Dr, Kamloops, BC, V2E 2N1
(250) 371-4300
Emp Here 150
SIC 5251 Hardware stores
Craig Howaniec

D-U-N-S 24-345-3362   (HQ)
JUUSOLA, JACK SALES LTD
CANADIAN TIRE
1441 Hillside Dr, Kamloops, BC, V2E 1A9
(250) 374-3115
Emp Here 100   *Sales* 53,530,400
SIC 5251 Hardware stores
Jack Juusola

D-U-N-S 24-314-0584   (BR)
WAL-MART CANADA CORP
(*Suby of* WALMART INC.)
1055 Hillside Dr Unit 100, Kamloops, BC, V2E 2S5
(250) 374-1591
Emp Here 300
SIC 5311 Department stores
Tim Labermeyer

Kamloops, BC V2H

D-U-N-S 24-552-2008   (SL)
327989 BC LTD
HALSTON BRIDGE ESSO
1271 Salish Rd, Kamloops, BC, V2H 1P6
(250) 828-1515
Emp Here 30   *Sales* 14,942,340
SIC 5541 Gasoline service stations
Yvon Blanchard

D-U-N-S 24-495-4921   (HQ)
ABSORBENT PRODUCTS LTD
724 Sarcee St E, Kamloops, BC, V2H 1E7
(250) 372-1600
Sales 10,118,475
SIC 2048 Prepared feeds, nec
Peter Aylen

D-U-N-S 20-733-3670   (BR)
COMPAGNIE DES CHEMINS DE FER NATIONAUX DU CANADA
(*Suby of* COMPAGNIE DES CHEMINS DE FER NATIONAUX DU CANADA)
309 Cn Rd, Kamloops, BC, V2H 1K3
(250) 828-6331
Emp Here 375
SIC 4111 Local and suburban transit
Evelyn Fawsett

D-U-N-S 24-192-7461   (HQ)
COOL CREEK ENERGY LTD
ESSO - COOL CREEK
455 Dene Dr, Kamloops, BC, V2H 1J1
(250) 374-0614
Emp Here 25   *Sales* 21,105,225
SIC 5983 Fuel oil dealers
Lorne Esselink
Blair Mayer

D-U-N-S 20-695-9103   (SL)
GERICO FOREST PRODUCTS LTD
666 Athabasca St W, Kamloops, BC, V2H 1C4
(250) 374-0333
Emp Here 45   *Sales* 12,748,185
SIC 8741 Management services
George W. Hogg
Connie G. Wait

D-U-N-S 25-999-4531   (BR)
GREAT CANADIAN RAILTOUR COMPANY LTD
ROCKY MOUNTAINEER VACATION
525 Cn Rd, Kamloops, BC, V2H 1K3
(250) 314-0576
Emp Here 150
SIC 4725 Tour operators
Peter Casement

D-U-N-S 20-032-0047   (SL)
LYONS LANDSCAPING LTD
LYONS GARDEN CENTRE & LANDSCAPING
1271 Salish Rd, Kamloops, BC, V2H 1P6
(250) 374-6965
Emp Here 45   *Sales* 11,387,655
SIC 5261 Retail nurseries and garden stores
Colin Lyons

D-U-N-S 25-772-0581   (SL)
PROGRESSIVE RUBBER INDUSTRIES INC
597a Chilcotin Rd, Kamloops, BC, V2H 1G6
(250) 851-0611
Emp Here 38   *Sales* 18,050,988
SIC 5085 Industrial supplies
Erik Lynum
Thor Lynum

D-U-N-S 25-039-3480   (SL)
RICK KURZAC BUILDING MATERIALS LTD
HOME HARDWARE BUILDING CENTRE
1325 Josep Way, Kamloops, BC, V2H 1N6
(250) 377-7234
Emp Here 49   *Sales* 12,399,891
SIC 5211 Lumber and other building materials
Ryan Kurzac

D-U-N-S 20-002-0345   (SL)
SOUTHSTAR EQUIPMENT LTD
728 Tagish St, Kamloops, BC, V2H 1B7
(250) 828-7820
Emp Here 25   *Sales* 11,875,650
SIC 5082 Construction and mining machinery
Marcel R. Payeur
Jeffrey A. Rankel
Michael P. Sampietro
Michael A. Klopp
Jeremy E. Disher
John B. Matthews

D-U-N-S 20-113-2060   (HQ)
SUN RIVERS LIMITED PARTNERSHIP
1000 Clubhouse Dr, Kamloops, BC, V2H 1T9
(250) 828-9989
Sales 14,235,480
SIC 6552 Subdividers and developers, nec
Richard Siemens

George Schurian

D-U-N-S 20-879-6628   (BR)
TOLKO INDUSTRIES LTD
HEFFLEY CREEK, DIVISION OF
(*Suby of* AMERICAN INDUSTRIAL ACQUISITION CORPORATION)
6275 Old Hwy 5, Kamloops, BC, V2H 1T8
(250) 578-7212
Emp Here 200
SIC 2435 Hardwood veneer and plywood
Phil Dean

Kaslo, BC V0G

D-U-N-S 24-136-2045   (SL)
MEADOW CREEK CEDAR LTD
Gd, Kaslo, BC, V0G 1M0
(250) 366-4434
Emp Here 120   *Sales* 23,084,400
SIC 2421 Sawmills and planing mills, general
Albert Volpatti

Kelowna, BC V1P

D-U-N-S 20-098-3856   (HQ)
BIG WHITE SKI RESORT LTD
5315 Big White Rd, Kelowna, BC, V1P 1P4
(250) 765-3101
Sales 13,903,500
SIC 7011 Hotels and motels
Peter Schumann
Kate Davies

Kelowna, BC V1V

D-U-N-S 24-897-5542   (HQ)
CARSON AIR LTD
00-6197 Airport Way, Kelowna, BC, V1V 2S2
(250) 765-7776
Sales 12,990,160
SIC 4522 Air transportation, nonscheduled
Kevin Carson

D-U-N-S 24-313-8950   (SL)
FLAIR AIRLINES LTD
5795 Airport Way, Kelowna, BC, V1V 1S1
(250) 491-5513
Emp Here 75   *Sales* 24,356,550
SIC 4522 Air transportation, nonscheduled
James Rogers
Katharine Rogers

D-U-N-S 20-751-5276   (SL)
KELOWNA AMBASSADORS
680 Valley Rd Suite 25, Kelowna, BC, V1V 2J3
(250) 712-1634
Emp Here 65   *Sales* 29,690,331
SIC 7389 Business services, nec
A G E Sones

D-U-N-S 24-164-7411   (HQ)
KELOWNA FLIGHTCRAFT AIR CHARTER LTD
(*Suby of* RAINMAKER INDUSTRIES INC)
5655 Airport Way Suite 1, Kelowna, BC, V1V 1S1
(250) 491-5500
Emp Here 500   *Sales* 104,831,760
SIC 4512 Air transportation, scheduled
Barry Lapointe
Tracy Medve

D-U-N-S 24-787-1171   (HQ)
KELOWNA FLIGHTCRAFT LTD
KF AEROSPACE
5655 Airport Way Unit 1, Kelowna, BC, V1V 1S1

(250) 491-5500
Sales 317,352,000
SIC 4581 Airports, flying fields, and services
Barry Lapointe
Meryle Corbett

   D-U-N-S 24-120-4077   (SL)
KELOWNA INTERNATIONAL AIRPORT
5533 Airport Way Suite 1, Kelowna, BC, V1V 1S1
(250) 807-4300
Emp Here 32   *Sales* 10,392,128
SIC 4581 Airports, flying fields, and services
Sam Samaddar
Dave Fuller

   D-U-N-S 25-630-2548   (HQ)
MODU-LOC FENCE RENTALS LTD
FENCE GUYS, THE
240 Neave Rd, Kelowna, BC, V1V 2L9
(250) 491-4110
Emp Here 6   *Sales* 10,141,762
SIC 7353 Heavy construction equipment rental
Darren Rintoul
Don Rintoul

   D-U-N-S 20-812-4979   (SL)
OKANAGAN GENERAL PARTNER LIMITED
MONTANA KAMLOOPS
3333 University Way, Kelowna, BC, V1V 1V7
(250) 807-9851
Emp Here 75   *Sales* 3,453,465
SIC 5812 Eating places
Michael Brunki

Kelowna, BC V1W

   D-U-N-S 24-957-9871   (SL)
ARTHON INDUSTRIES LIMITED
1790 K.L.O. Rd Unit 9, Kelowna, BC, V1W 3P6
(250) 764-6144
Emp Here 50   *Sales* 10,206,500
SIC 1442 Construction sand and gravel
Kerry Leong
Guy Ferrari
Darren Bidulka

   D-U-N-S 20-177-0471   (BR)
BOARD OF EDUCATION OF SCHOOL DISTRICT NO. 23 (CENTRAL OKANAGAN), THE
K L O MIDDLE SCHOOL
(*Suby of* BOARD OF EDUCATION OF SCHOOL DISTRICT NO. 23 (CENTRAL OKANAGAN), THE)
3130 Gordon Dr, Kelowna, BC, V1W 3M4
(250) 870-5106
Emp Here 75
SIC 8211 Elementary and secondary schools
Raquel Steen

   D-U-N-S 24-370-2375   (HQ)
CATHOLIC INDEPENDENT SCHOOLS OF NELSON DIOCESE, THE
CIS
3665 Benvoulin Rd, Kelowna, BC, V1W 4M7
(250) 762-2905
Emp Here 10   *Sales* 14,867,850
SIC 8211 Elementary and secondary schools
Beverly A Pulyk

   D-U-N-S 24-084-6951   (SL)
JDS ENERGY & MINING INC
3200 Richter St Unit 206, Kelowna, BC, V1W 5K9
(250) 763-6369
Emp Here 65   *Sales* 17,831,580
SIC 8741 Management services
Jeff Stibbard

   D-U-N-S 25-910-0311   (SL)
MANTEO BEACH CLUB LTD
MANTEO RESORT
3766 Lakeshore Rd, Kelowna, BC, V1W 3L4

(250) 860-1031
Emp Here 100   *Sales* 9,489,900
SIC 7011 Hotels and motels
Adrian A J Block
Mike Maschek
Rod Voth

   D-U-N-S 20-912-6937   (HQ)
OKANAGAN REGIONAL LIBRARY DISTRICT
1430 K.L.O. Rd, Kelowna, BC, V1W 3P6
(250) 860-4652
Emp Here 36   *Sales* 15,852,600
SIC 8231 Libraries
Lesley Dieno
Jane Diamanti
Don Nettleton
Carol Williams

   D-U-N-S 20-098-7774   (SL)
STEWART BROTHERS NURSERIES LTD
4129 Spiers Rd, Kelowna, BC, V1W 4B5
(250) 764-2121
Emp Here 35   *Sales* 11,986,345
SIC 0181 Ornamental nursery products
Julie Crawford
William Stewart

   D-U-N-S 24-930-5327   (SL)
SUMMERHILL ESTATE WINERY CO
SUMMERHILL PYRAMID WINERY
4870 Chute Lake Rd Suite 1, Kelowna, BC, V1W 4M3
(250) 764-8000
Emp Here 40   *Sales* 11,965,200
SIC 5921 Liquor stores
Stephen Cipes

   D-U-N-S 24-371-5331   (SL)
SUTHERLAND HILLS REST HOME LTD
3081 Hall Rd, Kelowna, BC, V1W 2R5
(250) 860-2330
Emp Here 80   *Sales* 5,498,640
SIC 8051 Skilled nursing care facilities
Fritz Wirtz

   D-U-N-S 24-812-8964   (BR)
YMCA-YWCA OF THE CENTRAL OKANAGAN
H2O ADVENTURES + FITNESS CENTRE
(*Suby of* YMCA-YWCA OF THE CENTRAL OKANAGAN)
4075 Gordon Dr, Kelowna, BC, V1W 5J2
(250) 764-4040
Emp Here 140
SIC 7997 Membership sports and recreation clubs
Cory Krist

Kelowna, BC V1X

   D-U-N-S 25-939-9640   (SL)
0092584 B.C. LTD
KELOWNA TOYOTA
1200 Leathead Rd, Kelowna, BC, V1X 2K4
(250) 491-2475
Emp Here 35   *Sales* 17,432,730
SIC 5511 New and used car dealers
Jack Kofoed
Jamie Kaban

   D-U-N-S 20-748-8888   (SL)
0705507 BC LTD
KELOWNA HYUNDAI
3260 Highway 97 N, Kelowna, BC, V1X 5C1
(250) 491-9467
Emp Here 40   *Sales* 19,923,120
SIC 5511 New and used car dealers
Vaughn Wyant
Adrian Wyant

   D-U-N-S 24-858-4497   (SL)
0859710 B.C. LTD
LEXUS OF KELOWNA
2767 Highway 97 N, Kelowna, BC, V1X 4J8

(250) 448-0990
Emp Here 40   *Sales* 19,923,120
SIC 5511 New and used car dealers
Rick Sentes
David Dempster

   D-U-N-S 25-015-3848   (SL)
435809 B.C. LTD
KELOWNA MERCEDES BENZ
2580 Enterprise Way, Kelowna, BC, V1X 7X5
(250) 712-0505
Emp Here 50   *Sales* 24,903,900
SIC 5511 New and used car dealers
Rick Sentes
David Dempster

   D-U-N-S 25-625-8005   (HQ)
ANTHONY'S AUTO SALES INC
ANTHONY SUZUKI KELOWNA
2759 Highway 97 N, Kelowna, BC, V1X 4J8
(250) 861-6163
Emp Here 1   *Sales* 14,942,340
SIC 5511 New and used car dealers
Anthony Lunelli
Franca Lunelli

   D-U-N-S 25-653-6038   (SL)
BAR DEN FOODS LTD
MARKETPLACE I G A
590 Highway 33 W Unit 12, Kelowna, BC, V1X 6A8
(250) 762-9234
Emp Here 50   *Sales* 13,707,600
SIC 5411 Grocery stores
Dennis Mitchell

   D-U-N-S 25-932-6080   (BR)
BLACK PRESS GROUP LTD
CALENDAR, THE
(*Suby of* BLACK PRESS HOLDINGS LTD)
2495 Enterprise Way, Kelowna, BC, V1X 7K2
(250) 766-4688
Emp Here 75
SIC 2711 Newspapers
Karen Hill

   D-U-N-S 25-150-3777   (BR)
BOARD OF EDUCATION OF SCHOOL DISTRICT NO. 23 (CENTRAL OKANAGAN), THE
RUTLAND SENIOR SECONDARY SCHOOL
(*Suby of* BOARD OF EDUCATION OF SCHOOL DISTRICT NO. 23 (CENTRAL OKANAGAN), THE)
705 Rutland Rd N, Kelowna, BC, V1X 3B6
(250) 870-5134
Emp Here 100
SIC 8211 Elementary and secondary schools
Hugh Gloster

   D-U-N-S 24-716-5434   (HQ)
BOARD OF EDUCATION OF SCHOOL DISTRICT NO. 23 (CENTRAL OKANAGAN), THE
SCHOOL DISTRICT NO. 23 (CENTRAL OKANAGAN)
1040 Hollywood Rd S, Kelowna, BC, V1X 4N2
(250) 860-8888
Emp Here 30   *Sales* 170,402,134
SIC 8211 Elementary and secondary schools
Kevin Kaardal
Larry Paul
Eileen Sadlowski
Moyra Baxter
Deb Butler
Rolli Cacchioni
Julia Fraser
Chris Gorman
Lee Mossman
Lee-Ann Tiede

   D-U-N-S 25-231-7268   (BR)
BRICK WAREHOUSE LP, THE
BRICK, THE
(*Suby of* BRICK WAREHOUSE LP, THE)
948 Mccurdy Rd Suite 100, Kelowna, BC, V1X 2P7

(250) 765-2220
Emp Here 75
SIC 5712 Furniture stores
Tom St George

   D-U-N-S 24-551-8717   (SL)
BRICOR MECHANICAL LTD
ACE PLUMBING
1778 Baron Rd, Kelowna, BC, V1X 7G9
(250) 861-6696
Emp Here 80   *Sales* 18,645,200
SIC 1711 Plumbing, heating, air-conditioning
Brian Walters
Corallee Walters

   D-U-N-S 24-001-8940   (BR)
CACTUS RESTAURANTS LTD
CACTUS CLUB CAFE
(*Suby of* CACTUS RESTAURANTS LTD)
1575 Banks Rd Suite 200, Kelowna, BC, V1X 7Y8
(250) 763-6752
Emp Here 120
SIC 5812 Eating places
Kobryn Octwain

   D-U-N-S 24-371-0613   (SL)
CAMPION MARINE INC
200 Campion St, Kelowna, BC, V1X 7S8
(250) 765-7795
Emp Here 70   *Sales* 15,669,010
SIC 3732 Boatbuilding and repairing
Brock Elliot
Mark Elliott

   D-U-N-S 20-301-5060   (SL)
CARIBOO CENTRAL RAILROAD CONTRACTING LTD
307 Banks Rd Unit 209, Kelowna, BC, V1X 6A1
(778) 478-1745
Emp Here 50   *Sales* 12,044,200
SIC 1629 Heavy construction, nec
Blair Irwin
Gary Janzen
Mona Irwin

   D-U-N-S 20-813-8813   (SL)
CARIBOO PRESS PRINTING & PUBLISHING LTD
KELOWNA CAPITAL NEWS
2495 Enterprise Way, Kelowna, BC, V1X 7K2
(250) 763-3212
Emp Here 49   *Sales* 10,407,453
SIC 8748 Business consulting, nec
David Black

   D-U-N-S 25-229-6843   (SL)
CENTURY LANE KITCHENS INC.
800 Mccurdy Rd, Kelowna, BC, V1X 2P7
(250) 765-2366
Emp Here 30   *Sales* 13,415,220
SIC 5031 Lumber, plywood, and millwork
Donald Quiring
A. Ward Quering

   D-U-N-S 25-999-1487   (BR)
COCA-COLA REFRESHMENTS CANADA COMPANY
(*Suby of* THE COCA-COLA COMPANY)
406 Old Vernon Rd Suite 100, Kelowna, BC, V1X 4R2
(250) 491-3414
Emp Here 100
SIC 2086 Bottled and canned soft drinks

   D-U-N-S 25-287-5257   (BR)
COSTCO WHOLESALE CANADA LTD
COSTCO
(*Suby of* COSTCO WHOLESALE CORPORATION)
2479 Highway 97 N, Kelowna, BC, V1X 4J2
(250) 868-9515
Emp Here 250
SIC 5099 Durable goods, nec
Mike Gazso

   D-U-N-S 20-120-2207   (SL)

CRYSTAL MOUNTAIN RESORTS LTD
Gd Rpo Banks Centre, Kelowna, BC, V1X 4K3

Emp Here 100   *Sales* 9,489,900
SIC 7011 Hotels and motels
 Michel Morin
 David Tschanz
 Winston Tschanz
 Nico Tschanz

D-U-N-S 24-597-6402   (HQ)
DASKO HOLDINGS LTD
ORCHARD PARK CAR WASH
1830 Underhill St, Kelowna, BC, V1X 5P8
(250) 862-5242
Emp Here 17   *Sales* 21,395,520
SIC 5541 Gasoline service stations
 Dave Skoglund

D-U-N-S 20-384-4865   (SL)
DFC AUTO LTD
KELOWNA CHEVROLET
2350 Highway 97 N, Kelowna, BC, V1X 4H8
(250) 860-6000
Emp Here 65   *Sales* 40,903,200
SIC 5511 New and used car dealers
 Patrick Priestner

D-U-N-S 25-506-6847   (SL)
DOPPELMAYR CANADA LTD
567 Adams Rd, Kelowna, BC, V1X 7R9
(250) 765-3000
Emp Here 110   *Sales* 24,622,730
SIC 3799 Transportation equipment, nec
 Warren Sparks
 Andre Lamoureux

D-U-N-S 20-098-8186   (SL)
FOLK, DON CHEVROLET INC
2350 Highway 97 N, Kelowna, BC, V1X 4H8
(250) 860-6000
Emp Here 55   *Sales* 34,610,400
SIC 5511 New and used car dealers
 Donald Folk
 David Huber
 Jason Jones

D-U-N-S 24-931-1044   (HQ)
FRASERWAY RV GP LTD
COUNTRY R.V.
3732 Highway 97 N, Kelowna, BC, V1X 5C2
(250) 807-2898
Sales 25,171,200
SIC 5561 Recreational vehicle dealers
 James Epp

D-U-N-S 24-371-1868   (SL)
GOSTLIN, K E ENTERPRISES LTD
CANADIAN TIRE
1655 Leckie Rd, Kelowna, BC, V1X 6E4
(250) 860-4331
Emp Here 120   *Sales* 75,513,600
SIC 5531 Auto and home supply stores
 Keith Gostlin
 Andrea Gostlin

D-U-N-S 20-098-5000   (HQ)
GROWERS SUPPLY COMPANY LIMITED
2605 Acland Rd, Kelowna, BC, V1X 7J4
(250) 765-4500
Emp Here 21   *Sales* 38,611,040
SIC 5191 Farm supplies
 David Sloan
 Mae Shannon

D-U-N-S 25-067-5451   (SL)
HARMONY AUTO SALES LTD
HARMONY HONDA
2550 Enterprise Way, Kelowna, BC, V1X 7X5
(250) 860-6500
Emp Here 38   *Sales* 18,926,964
SIC 5511 New and used car dealers
 Manse Binkley

D-U-N-S 24-397-3596   (SL)
HARMONY PREMIUM MOTORS LTD
HARMONY ACURA
2552 Enterprise Way, Kelowna, BC, V1X 7X5

(250) 861-3003
Emp Here 22   *Sales* 10,957,716
SIC 5511 New and used car dealers
 Manse Binkley

D-U-N-S 24-595-0696   (SL)
HEARTWOOD MANUFACTURING LTD
251 Adams Rd, Kelowna, BC, V1X 7R1
(250) 765-4145
Emp Here 80   *Sales* 12,345,760
SIC 2521 Wood office furniture
 Tom Mclean
 Rick Jennens

D-U-N-S 25-171-5637   (BR)
HOME DEPOT OF CANADA INC
HOME DEPOT
(*Suby of* THE HOME DEPOT INC)
2515 Enterprise Way, Kelowna, BC, V1X 7K2
(250) 979-9501
Emp Here 150
SIC 5251 Hardware stores
 Tim Murray

D-U-N-S 20-384-0830   (HQ)
INSUL-WEST BUILDING MATERIALS LTD
BOYD DISTRIBUTORS
860 Mccurdy Rd, Kelowna, BC, V1X 2P7
(250) 807-2551
Emp Here 6   *Sales* 45,930,780
SIC 5039 Construction materials, nec
 Nina Halliwelll

D-U-N-S 25-015-3145   (BR)
KELOWNA CHRISTIAN CENTER SOCIETY
HERITAGE CHRISTIAN ONLINE SCHOOL
(*Suby of* KELOWNA CHRISTIAN CENTER
SOCIETY)
907 Badke Rd, Kelowna, BC, V1X 5Z5
(250) 862-2376
Emp Here 400
SIC 8661 Religious organizations

D-U-N-S 24-070-5954   (SL)
KELOWNA CHRYSLER DODGE JEEP
2440 Enterprise Way, Kelowna, BC, V1X 6X6
(250) 763-6121
Emp Here 64   *Sales* 40,273,920
SIC 5511 New and used car dealers
 Jeff Gilbert

D-U-N-S 25-067-1021   (SL)
KELOWNA FORD LINCOLN SALES LTD
2540 Enterprise Way, Kelowna, BC, V1X 7X5
(250) 868-2330
Emp Here 47   *Sales* 23,409,666
SIC 5511 New and used car dealers
 Norm Assam
 Sherry Schreiner
 Anita Assam

D-U-N-S 20-098-5661   (SL)
KELOWNA MOTORS LTD
MAZDA
2560 Enterprise Way, Kelowna, BC, V1X 7X5
(250) 762-2068
Emp Here 27   *Sales* 13,448,106
SIC 5511 New and used car dealers
 Brian August

D-U-N-S 20-378-0403   (SL)
KELOWNA NISSAN LTD
2741 Highway 97 N, Kelowna, BC, V1X 4J8
(250) 712-0404
Emp Here 80   *Sales* 50,342,400
SIC 5511 New and used car dealers
 Rick Sentes
 David Dempster

D-U-N-S 20-098-6958   (SL)
L & D PETCH CONTRACTING LTD
KETTLE VALLEY STONE DIV OF
204 Cambro Rd, Kelowna, BC, V1X 7T3
(250) 491-0405
Emp Here 40   *Sales* 17,886,960
SIC 5032 Brick, stone, and related material
 Lyle Jorde

D-U-N-S 24-681-4826   (SL)
LAKEVIEW MOTORS LP
OKANAGAN CHRYSLER JEEP DODGE
(*Suby of* AUTOCANADA INC)
2690 Highway 97 N, Kelowna, BC, V1X 4J4
(250) 763-5337
Emp Here 40   *Sales* 25,171,200
SIC 5511 New and used car dealers
 Dean Mcauley

D-U-N-S 25-678-7177   (SL)
LEATHEAD INVESTMENTS LTD
2727 Highway 97 N, Kelowna, BC, V1X 4J8
(250) 860-7700
Emp Here 80   *Sales* 50,342,400
SIC 5511 New and used car dealers
 Ron Jacobsen
 Shayne Jacobsen

D-U-N-S 24-732-6028   (SL)
NORELCO CABINETS LTD
677 Willow Park Rd Unit 2, Kelowna, BC, V1X
5H9
(250) 765-2121
Emp Here 120   *Sales* 23,084,400
SIC 2434 Wood kitchen cabinets
 Peter Raja

D-U-N-S 20-956-7747   (SL)
OAKRIDGE ACCOUNTING SERVICES LTD
(*Suby of* PATTISON, JIM GROUP INC)
2604 Enterprise Way Unit 1, Kelowna, BC,
V1X 7Y5
(250) 712-3800
Emp Here 86   *Sales* 17,860,910
SIC 8721 Accounting, auditing, and book-
keeping
 William Borthwick
 Roger Hamm

D-U-N-S 24-136-2391   (SL)
ORCHARD FORD SALES LTD
911 Stremel Rd, Kelowna, BC, V1X 5E6
(250) 860-1000
Emp Here 65   *Sales* 40,903,200
SIC 5511 New and used car dealers
 Norm Assam
 Daniel Assam

D-U-N-S 20-640-2161   (SL)
R 870 HOLDINGS LTD
BC UNDERGROUND
171 Commercial Dr Suite 203, Kelowna, BC,
V1X 7W2

Emp Here 50   *Sales* 11,008,400
SIC 1794 Excavation work
 Greg Cruikshanck

D-U-N-S 24-778-4408   (HQ)
RAYBURN'S MARINE WORLD LTD
2330 Enterprise Way, Kelowna, BC, V1X 4H7
(250) 860-4232
Emp Here 35   *Sales* 22,654,080
SIC 5551 Boat dealers
 Dale Koepke

D-U-N-S 20-359-2241   (SL)
SANDHER FRUIT PACKERS LTD
4525 Scotty Creek Rd, Kelowna, BC, V1X 6N3
(250) 491-9176
Emp Here 40   *Sales* 17,608,620
SIC 5431 Fruit and vegetable markets
 Sukhwinderjit K Sandher

D-U-N-S 24-372-3467   (SL)
SAWCHUK DEVELOPMENTS CO. LTD
486 Adams Rd, Kelowna, BC, V1X 7S1
(250) 765-3838
Emp Here 100   *Sales* 57,033,800
SIC 1542 Nonresidential construction, nec
 Larry Sawchuk

D-U-N-S 20-210-7897   (HQ)
SPRING FUEL DISTRIBUTORS INC
PETRO CANADA
275 Campion St, Kelowna, BC, V1X 7S9

(250) 491-0427
Emp Here 18   *Sales* 31,430,025
SIC 5172 Petroleum products, nec
 Donald Spring
 Carol Spring

D-U-N-S 24-798-0451   (HQ)
SUNCO DRYWALL LTD
330 Highway 33 W Unit 102, Kelowna, BC,
V1X 1X9
(250) 807-2270
Emp Here 8   *Sales* 23,140,754
SIC 1742 Plastering, drywall, and insulation
 Dennis Bigham
 Ronald Knight

D-U-N-S 20-689-1983   (SL)
TOTAL LEASE & TRUCK SALES LTD
ELITE AUTO CENTRE, DIV OF.
2655 Enterprise Way, Kelowna, BC, V1X 7Y6
(250) 712-0668
Emp Here 30   *Sales* 14,942,340
SIC 5511 New and used car dealers
 Greg Gaspari
 Korey Gaspari

D-U-N-S 20-169-3871   (BR)
TRANE CANADA ULC
TRANE NORTHWEST
(*Suby of* INGERSOLL-RAND PUBLIC LIM-
ITED COMPANY)
2260 Hunter Rd Suite 3, Kelowna, BC, V1X
7J8
(250) 491-4600
Emp Here 150
SIC 5075 Warm air heating and air condition-
ing
 Peter Hoemberg

D-U-N-S 24-141-9324   (BR)
WAL-MART CANADA CORP
(*Suby of* WALMART INC.)
1555 Banks Rd, Kelowna, BC, V1X 7Y8
(250) 860-8811
Emp Here 150
SIC 5311 Department stores
 Amell Bob

D-U-N-S 25-687-0932   (HQ)
YOUR DOLLAR STORE WITH MORE INC
160 Dougall Rd S Unit 200, Kelowna, BC, V1X
3J4
(250) 860-4225
Emp Here 27   *Sales* 11,704,551
SIC 5399 Miscellaneous general merchandise
 Russell Meszaros

Kelowna, BC V1Y

D-U-N-S 24-983-9556   (SL)
564549 ALBERTA LTD
1865 Dilworth Dr Suite 335, Kelowna, BC, V1Y
9T1
(250) 215-1143
Emp Here 25   *Sales* 10,660,201
SIC 6712 Bank holding companies
 Sylvia Grassl

D-U-N-S 24-316-3768   (SL)
ABOUGOUSH COLLISION INC
BOYD AUTOBODY AND GLASS
1960 Dayton St, Kelowna, BC, V1Y 7W6
(250) 868-2693
Emp Here 61   *Sales* 17,281,300
SIC 7532 Top and body repair and paint shops
 Methal Abougoush
 Gordie Abougoush
 Rick Mcgillivray

D-U-N-S 24-029-8869   (HQ)
ANDRE'S T.V. SALES & SERVICE LTD
ANDRE'S AUDIOTRONIC
2153 Springfield Rd, Kelowna, BC, V1Y 7X1
(250) 861-4101
Emp Here 5   *Sales* 13,944,180

SIC 5731 Radio, television, and electronic stores
Andre Blanleil Jr.

D-U-N-S 24-418-2486   (HQ)
ANODYNE ELECTRONICS HOLDING CORP
1925 Kirschner Rd Unit 15, Kelowna, BC, V1Y 4N7
(250) 763-1088
Emp Here 1   Sales 24,594,570
SIC 5065 Electronic parts and equipment, nec
David Veitch

D-U-N-S 24-388-4199   (SL)
ANODYNE ELECTRONICS MANUFACTURING CORP
(Suby of ANODYNE ELECTRONICS HOLDING CORP)
1925 Kirschner Rd Unit 15, Kelowna, BC, V1Y 4N7
(250) 763-1088
Emp Here 90   Sales 52,222,230
SIC 5065 Electronic parts and equipment, nec
David Veitch

D-U-N-S 20-703-0359   (BR)
ARAMARK ENTERTAINMENT SERVICES (CANADA) INC
(Suby of ARAMARK)
1223 Water St, Kelowna, BC, V1Y 9V1
(250) 979-0878
Emp Here 125
SIC 8742 Management consulting services
Annis Ha

D-U-N-S 24-881-6704   (HQ)
B.C. FASTENERS & TOOLS LTD
1960 Windsor Rd Suite 3, Kelowna, BC, V1Y 4R5
(250) 868-9222
Sales 16,150,884
SIC 5085 Industrial supplies
Gerald Miller
Tom Allison
Darcy Deck

D-U-N-S 20-098-3955   (HQ)
B.C. TREE FRUITS LIMITED
1473 Water St, Kelowna, BC, V1Y 1J6
(250) 470-4200
Emp Here 39   Sales 35,094,234
SIC 5148 Fresh fruits and vegetables
Greg Gauthier
Jim Elliot
Glenn Cross
John Bernard
Robert Dawson
Steven Day
Sam Dimaria
Joe Hart
Jack Machial
Malcolm Mitchell

D-U-N-S 20-297-6051   (BR)
BC CANCER FOUNDATION
BC CANCER AGENCY
399 Royal Ave, Kelowna, BC, V1Y 5L3
(250) 712-3900
Emp Here 250
SIC 8069 Specialty hospitals, except psychiatric
Sandra Broughton

D-U-N-S 20-359-9196   (HQ)
BC TREE FRUITS COOPERATIVE
1473 Water St, Kelowna, BC, V1Y 1J6
(250) 470-4200
Sales 70,092,540
SIC 5148 Fresh fruits and vegetables
Todd Mcmyn
Ross Dwhytie

D-U-N-S 24-346-4034   (SL)
BINGO KELOWNA CHANCES GAMING ENTERTAINMENT
CHANCES KELOWNA
1585 Springfield Rd, Kelowna, BC, V1Y 5V5

(250) 860-9577
Emp Here 120   Sales 11,394,360
SIC 7999 Amusement and recreation, nec
Stanley Walt

D-U-N-S 20-253-9545   (SL)
BLACK, SHARON RE/MAX KELOWNA
1553 Harvey Ave Suite 100, Kelowna, BC, V1Y 6G1
(250) 717-5040
Emp Here 49   Sales 13,316,044
SIC 6531 Real estate agents and managers
Rick Baker

D-U-N-S 25-151-0541   (BR)
BOARD OF EDUCATION OF SCHOOL DISTRICT NO. 23 (CENTRAL OKANAGAN), THE
KELOWNA SECONDARY
(Suby of BOARD OF EDUCATION OF SCHOOL DISTRICT NO. 23 (CENTRAL OKANAGAN), THE)
1079 Raymer Ave, Kelowna, BC, V1Y 4Z7
(250) 870-5105
Emp Here 130
SIC 8211 Elementary and secondary schools
Susana Brown

D-U-N-S 20-741-6772   (SL)
BRIDGES TRANSITIONS INC
BRIDGES
(Suby of XAP CORPORATION)
1726 Dolphin Ave Unit 205, Kelowna, BC, V1Y 9R9
(250) 869-4200
Emp Here 76   Sales 12,680,372
SIC 7372 Prepackaged software
Eddie Monnier

D-U-N-S 24-026-4387   (SL)
CANRIM PACKAGING LTD
1125 Richter St, Kelowna, BC, V1Y 2K6
(250) 762-3332
Emp Here 170   Sales 58,767,300
SIC 2085 Distilled and blended liquors
Douglas Gallagher
Helena Smith

D-U-N-S 20-919-3986   (HQ)
CAPRICMW INSURANCE SERVICES LTD
1500 Hardy St Suite 100, Kelowna, BC, V1Y 8H2
(250) 860-2426
Emp Here 150   Sales 1,993,363,680
SIC 6411 Insurance agents, brokers, and service
Tim Miller

D-U-N-S 25-015-3723   (HQ)
CENTRAL OKANAGAN BOYS & GIRLS CLUB
1434 Graham St, Kelowna, BC, V1Y 3A8
(250) 762-3914
Sales 431,580,300
SIC 8699 Membership organizations, nec
Geremy Welder

D-U-N-S 24-578-8278   (SL)
CENTRAL OKANAGAN CHILD DEVELOPMENT ASSOCIATION
1546 Bernard Ave, Kelowna, BC, V1Y 6R9
(250) 763-5100
Emp Here 70   Sales 49,644,840
SIC 8699 Membership organizations, nec
Wendy Salkowski

D-U-N-S 20-649-3715   (SL)
CENTURY 21 ASSURANCE REALTY LTD
251 Harvey Ave, Kelowna, BC, V1Y 6C2
(250) 869-0101
Emp Here 40   Sales 13,085,080
SIC 6531 Real estate agents and managers
Ken Wiebe

D-U-N-S 24-938-8950   (SL)
CHELTON TECHNOLOGIES CANADA LIMITED
(Suby of COBHAM PLC)
1925 Kirschner Rd Suite 14, Kelowna, BC,

V1Y 4N7
(250) 763-2232
Emp Here 160
SIC 3663 Radio and t.v. communications equipment

D-U-N-S 25-652-8498   (SL)
COLDWELL BANKER HORIZON REALTY LTD
COLDWELL BANKER HORIZON REALTY
1470 Harvey Ave Suite 14, Kelowna, BC, V1Y 9K8
(250) 860-7500
Emp Here 49   Sales 13,316,044
SIC 6531 Real estate agents and managers
Christina Raho

D-U-N-S 25-978-7729   (HQ)
CONTINENTAL NEWSPAPERS (CANADA) LTD
OKANAGAN VALLEY NEWSPAPER GROUP, THE
550 Doyle Ave, Kelowna, BC, V1Y 7V1
(250) 763-4000
Emp Here 200   Sales 42,630,280
SIC 2711 Newspapers
F David Radler
Melanie Radler

D-U-N-S 20-098-4284   (SL)
COOKSON MOTORS LTD
1150 Gordon Dr, Kelowna, BC, V1Y 3E4
(250) 763-2327
Emp Here 42   Sales 20,919,276
SIC 5511 New and used car dealers
Hugo Cookson Sr
D Hugo Cookson

D-U-N-S 24-566-3216   (SL)
CYPRESS MANAGEMENT LTD
537 Leon Ave Suite 200, Kelowna, BC, V1Y 2A9
(250) 763-4323
Emp Here 40   Sales 16,774,200
SIC 6712 Bank holding companies
Hilary Shirreff
Debbie Hardwick

D-U-N-S 25-506-9692   (SL)
DARGAL INTERLINE CRUISE & TOURS LTD
DARGAL INTERLINE
1632 Dickson Ave Suite 200, Kelowna, BC, V1Y 7T2
(250) 861-3223
Emp Here 45   Sales 17,341,200
SIC 4725 Tour operators
Darci Galati

D-U-N-S 20-273-6757   (HQ)
DECISIVE DIVIDEND CORPORATION
1674 Bertram St Unit 201, Kelowna, BC, V1Y 9G4
(250) 870-9146
Sales 28,802,569
SIC 6719 Holding companies, nec
James Paterson
David Redekop
Terry Edwards
Rick Torriero
Bruce Campbell
Michael Conway
Peter Jeffrey
Robert Louie
Warren Matheos
Tim Pirie

D-U-N-S 24-120-9613   (SL)
DEHL HOLDINGS LTD
1465 Ellis St Suite 100, Kelowna, BC, V1Y 2A3
(250) 762-5434
Emp Here 26   Sales 10,903,230
SIC 6712 Bank holding companies
David Pihl

D-U-N-S 24-248-4736   (SL)
DISNEY CANADA INC

DISNEY INTERACTIVE WORLD
(Suby of THE WALT DISNEY COMPANY)
1628 Dickson Ave Suite 500, Kelowna, BC, V1Y 9X1
(250) 868-8622
Emp Here 300   Sales 62,366,400
SIC 7374 Data processing and preparation
Jeffrey Axenty

D-U-N-S 20-072-9825   (BR)
DIVERSICARE CANADA MANAGEMENT SERVICES CO., INC
HAWTHORN PARK
(Suby of DCMS HOLDINGS INC)
867 K.L.O. Rd, Kelowna, BC, V1Y 9G5
(250) 861-6636
Emp Here 100
SIC 8361 Residential care
Gary Buckberry

D-U-N-S 25-014-9382   (BR)
DIVERSICARE REALTY INVESTMENTS LIMITED
HAWTHORN PK RETIREMENT COMMUNITY
867 K.L.O. Rd, Kelowna, BC, V1Y 9G5
(250) 861-6636
Emp Here 100
SIC 8361 Residential care
Gary Buckberry

D-U-N-S 24-329-5321   (SL)
EARL'S ON TOP RESTAURANT LTD
211 Bernard Ave, Kelowna, BC, V1Y 6N2
(250) 763-2777
Emp Here 100   Sales 4,551,900
SIC 5812 Eating places
Brad Atwood

D-U-N-S 20-359-1953   (SL)
EMIL ANDERSON CONSTRUCTION (EAC) INC
(Suby of PASS CONSTRUCTION CO. LTD)
907 Ethel St, Kelowna, BC, V1Y 2W1
(250) 762-9999
Emp Here 100   Sales 25,244,200
SIC 1611 Highway and street construction
Robert Hasell

D-U-N-S 20-052-5736   (SL)
ENVIROMECH INDUSTRIES INC
AGILITY FUEL SYSTEMS
(Suby of AGILITY FUEL SOLUTIONS HOLDINGS INC.)
2092 Enterprise Way Suite 100, Kelowna, BC, V1Y 6H7
(250) 765-1777
Emp Here 65   Sales 14,549,795
SIC 3714 Motor vehicle parts and accessories
Todd Sloan
Joseph Pike
Adam Robertson
Chris Forsberg

D-U-N-S 20-304-8764   (HQ)
EXC HOLDINGS LTD.
1631 Dickson Ave 10th Fl, Kelowna, BC, V1Y 0B5
(250) 448-0030
Emp Here 10   Sales 20,570,600
SIC 4214 Local trucking with storage
Jonathan Friesen
Jason David Siebenga

D-U-N-S 25-998-2163   (SL)
EXPEDIA CRUISESHIPCENTERS
EXPEDIA CRUISE SHIP CENTERS KELOWNA
1980 Cooper Rd Unit 106, Kelowna, BC, V1Y 8K5
(250) 763-2900
Emp Here 25   Sales 12,999,175
SIC 4724 Travel agencies
Cathy Francis

D-U-N-S 20-108-3169   (HQ)
FORTISBC INC
(Suby of FORTIS INC)

1975 Springfield Rd Suite 100, Kelowna, BC,
V1Y 7V7
(604) 576-7000
Emp Here 80   *Sales* 298,504,737
SIC 4911 Electric services
Roger A. Dall'antonia
Doyle Sam
Ian G. Lorimer
Cynthia Des Brisay
Douglas L. Stout
Dennis A. Swanson
Michael A. Leclair
Diane E. Roy
Diane E. Roy
Jody D. Drope

D-U-N-S 20-298-9166   (HQ)
FORTISBC PACIFIC HOLDINGS INC
(Suby of FORTIS INC)
1975 Springfield Rd Suite 100, Kelowna, BC,
V1Y 7V7
(250) 469-8000
Sales 1,359,748,000
SIC 4911 Electric services
John Walker
Michele Leeners

D-U-N-S 24-327-2544   (SL)
FWS PHARMACY SERVICES LTD
SHOPPERS DRUG MART
2271 Harvey Ave Suite 1360, Kelowna, BC,
V1Y 6H2
(250) 860-3764
Emp Here 55   *Sales* 13,438,040
SIC 5912 Drug stores and proprietary stores
Frank Strobel

D-U-N-S 20-860-9201   (BR)
GRANT THORNTON LLP
CAPSERVCO
(Suby of GRANT THORNTON LLP)
1633 Ellis St Suite 200, Kelowna, BC, V1Y
2A8
(250) 712-6800
Emp Here 75
SIC 8721 Accounting, auditing, and book-
keeping
Raymond Chabot

D-U-N-S 24-797-8547   (BR)
GREAT PACIFIC INDUSTRIES INC
SAVE-ON-FOODS
(Suby of PATTISON, JIM GROUP INC)
1876 Cooper Rd Suite 101, Kelowna, BC, V1Y
9N6
(250) 860-1444
Emp Here 130
SIC 5411 Grocery stores
Don Gandy

D-U-N-S 20-619-4441   (SL)
H & B INVESTMENTS LTD
LAKEVIEW MARKET
3033 Pandosy St, Kelowna, BC, V1Y 1W3
(250) 763-0819
Emp Here 50   *Sales* 13,707,600
SIC 5411 Grocery stores
Barbara Jones

D-U-N-S 20-806-4055   (HQ)
HUBER DEVELOPMENT LTD
PRESTIGE INN
516 Lawrence Ave, Kelowna, BC, V1Y 6L7
(250) 860-5858
Emp Here 50   *Sales* 139,132,800
SIC 1522 Residential construction, nec
Josef Huber
Anna Huber

D-U-N-S 25-301-2264   (BR)
HUDSON'S BAY COMPANY
(Suby of HUDSON'S BAY COMPANY)
2271 Harvey Ave Suite 1415, Kelowna, BC,
V1Y 6H3
(250) 860-2483
Emp Here 175
SIC 5311 Department stores
Scott Jeffrey

D-U-N-S 25-680-6696   (HQ)
INTERIOR HEALTH AUTHORITY
INVERMERE & DISTRICT HOSPITAL
505 Doyle Ave, Kelowna, BC, V1Y 0C5
(250) 862-4200
Emp Here 6,000   *Sales* 1,607,176,339
SIC 8062 General medical and surgical hospi-
tals
Chris Mazurkewich
Doug Cochrane
Susan Brown
Donna Lommer
Mike Ertel
Trevor Corneil
Mal Griffin
Jenn Goodwin
Norma Malanowich
Anne-Marie Visockas

D-U-N-S 20-317-3591   (BR)
INTERIOR HEALTH AUTHORITY
COTTONWOODS CARE CENTRE
(Suby of INTERIOR HEALTH AUTHORITY)
2255 Ethel St, Kelowna, BC, V1Y 2Z9
(250) 862-4100
Emp Here 478
SIC 8051 Skilled nursing care facilities
Jim Palfrey

D-U-N-S 24-333-8683   (HQ)
INTERIOR SAVINGS CREDIT UNION
678 Bernard Ave Suite 300, Kelowna, BC, V1Y
6P3
(250) 869-8300
Emp Here 25   *Sales* 102,818,650
SIC 6062 State credit unions
Barry Meckler
Elmer Epp
Rolli Cacchioni
Wendy Caban
Doug Findlater
Pauline Fleming
Brad Fossett
Don Grant
Jeff Holm
Bianca Ianfrancesco

D-U-N-S 25-653-3092   (SL)
INTERNET REALTY LTD
PRUDENTIAL KELOWNA PROPERTY
1101 Harvey Ave, Kelowna, BC, V1Y 6E8
(250) 762-9979
Emp Here 40   *Sales* 13,085,080
SIC 6531 Real estate agents and managers
John Adolf

D-U-N-S 25-315-7275   (BR)
**INVESTORS GROUP FINANCIAL SER-
VICES INC**
INVESTORS GROUP
(Suby of POWER CORPORATION DU
CANADA)
1628 Dickson Ave Suite 100, Kelowna, BC,
V1Y 9X1
(250) 762-3329
Emp Here 75
SIC 8742 Management consulting services
Paul Demay

D-U-N-S 24-523-0888   (SL)
KARIS SUPPORT SOCIETY
1849 Ethel St, Kelowna, BC, V1Y 2Z3
(250) 860-9507
Emp Here 30   *Sales* 11,922,420
SIC 8699 Membership organizations, nec
Stephen Krysko
Donara Krysko
Melissa Sargent

D-U-N-S 24-551-8089   (HQ)
KELDON ELECTRIC & DATA LTD
1909 Bredin Rd, Kelowna, BC, V1Y 7S9
(250) 861-4255
Emp Here 1   *Sales* 19,604,610
SIC 1731 Electrical work
Brian Yamaoka

D-U-N-S 20-523-3427   (SL)
**KELOWNA ROCKETS HOCKEY ENTER-
PRISES LTD**
KELOWNA ROCKETS HOCKEY CLUB
1223 Water St Suite 101, Kelowna, BC, V1Y
9V1
(250) 860-7825
Emp Here 40   *Sales* 16,949,200
SIC 7941 Sports clubs, managers, and pro-
moters
Bruce Hamilton

D-U-N-S 24-594-7551   (SL)
KRUEGER ELECTRICAL LTD
1027 Trench Pl Unit 100, Kelowna, BC, V1Y
9Y4
(250) 860-3905
Emp Here 67   *Sales* 14,594,543
SIC 1731 Electrical work
Peter Sherba
Oscar Krueger

D-U-N-S 20-166-6638   (SL)
**LODGING COMPANY RESERVATIONS LTD,
THE**
510 Bernard Ave Suite 200, Kelowna, BC, V1Y
6P1
(250) 979-3939
Emp Here 55   *Sales* 24,707,045
SIC 7389 Business services, nec
Christopher Pattie
Brian Pattie
Nicole Pattie
Tawnya Pattie

D-U-N-S 20-098-6271   (SL)
MERVYN MOTORS LIMITED
TURNER VOLKSWAGON & AUDI
1717 Harvey Ave, Kelowna, BC, V1Y 6G3
(250) 860-6278
Emp Here 41   *Sales* 20,421,198
SIC 5511 New and used car dealers
Edwin Turner

D-U-N-S 20-369-0573   (SL)
MISSION GROUP ENTERPRISES LTD
1631 Dickson Ave Suite 1000, Kelowna, BC,
V1Y 0B5
(250) 448-8810
Emp Here 40   *Sales* 12,754,760
SIC 1521 Single-family housing construction
Jonathan Friesen

D-U-N-S 20-424-5518   (SL)
**MONASHEE MANUFACTURING CORPO-
RATION LTD**
1247 Ellis St, Kelowna, BC, V1Y 1Z6
(250) 762-2646
Emp Here 74   *Sales* 16,428,074
SIC 3599 Industrial machinery, nec
Dale Armeneau

D-U-N-S 24-138-5587   (SL)
**NATURES FORMULAE HEALTH PROD-
UCTS LTD**
NATURES FORMULAE
2130 Leckie Pl Suite 300, Kelowna, BC, V1Y
7W7
(250) 717-5700
Emp Here 80   *Sales* 27,655,200
SIC 2023 Dry, condensed and evaporated
dairy products
Barbra Johnston

D-U-N-S 25-316-4842   (BR)
**NORTHLAND PROPERTIES CORPORA-
TION**
SANDMAN HOTEL & SUITES KELOWNA
(Suby of NORTHLAND PROPERTIES COR-
PORATION)
2130 Harvey Ave, Kelowna, BC, V1Y 6G8
(250) 860-6409
Emp Here 80
SIC 7011 Hotels and motels
Kelly Watt

D-U-N-S 25-653-3381   (SL)
NORWICH REAL ESTATE SERVICES INC

RE/MAX KELOWNA
1553 Harvey Ave Suite 100, Kelowna, BC,
V1Y 6G1
(250) 717-5000
Emp Here 140   *Sales* 58,644,460
SIC 6531 Real estate agents and managers
Jerry Redman

D-U-N-S 20-336-9533   (BR)
OKANAGAN COLLEGE
CONTINUING STUDIES
(Suby of OKANAGAN COLLEGE)
1000 K.L.O. Rd Unit A108, Kelowna, BC, V1Y
4X8
(250) 862-5480
Emp Here 200
SIC 7371 Custom computer programming ser-
vices
Dennis Silverstrone

D-U-N-S 20-993-7572   (HQ)
OKANAGAN COLLEGE
OC
1000 K.L.O. Rd, Kelowna, BC, V1Y 4X8
(250) 762-5445
Emp Here 647   *Sales* 88,658,810
SIC 8221 Colleges and universities
James Hamilton
Roy Daykin
Andrew Hay
Curtis Morcom
Charlotte Kushner
Christopher Derickson
Gloria Morgan
Blake Edwards
Shelley Cook
Juliette Cunningham

D-U-N-S 24-101-4575   (HQ)
OKANAGAN TREE FRUIT COOPERATIVE
880 Vaughan Ave, Kelowna, BC, V1Y 7E4
(250) 763-7003
Emp Here 50   *Sales* 11,091,816
SIC 0723 Crop preparation services for mar-
ket
Gary Schieck
Tom Macdonald

D-U-N-S 24-578-7031   (SL)
PUSHOR MITCHELL LLP
LEGUM MANAGEMENT
1665 Ellis St Suite 301, Kelowna, BC, V1Y
2B3
(250) 869-1100
Emp Here 85   *Sales* 13,090,935
SIC 8111 Legal services
Richard Pushor

D-U-N-S 20-982-0054   (SL)
QUALITY GREENS CANADA LTD
1889 Spall Rd Unit 101, Kelowna, BC, V1Y
4R2
(250) 763-8200
Emp Here 49   *Sales* 13,433,448
SIC 5431 Fruit and vegetable markets
Daisy Leslie-Orser

D-U-N-S 20-244-1577   (SL)
**R D I REFORESTATION & DEVELOPMENTS
INC**
534 Christleton Ave, Kelowna, BC, V1Y 5J2
(250) 470-1842
Emp Here 80   *Sales* 10,940,720
SIC 0851 Forestry services
Miles Sanoy

D-U-N-S 25-086-4204   (BR)
RG PROPERTIES LTD
(Suby of RG PROPERTIES LTD)
1223 Water St Suite 102, Kelowna, BC, V1Y
9V1
(250) 979-0888
Emp Here 150
SIC 7999 Amusement and recreation, nec

D-U-N-S 24-366-9335   (HQ)
RLK REALTY LTD
ROYAL LEPAGE

▲ Public Company   ■ Public Company Family Member   **HQ** Headquarters   **BR** Branch   **SL** Single Location

1890 Cooper Rd Unit 1, Kelowna, BC, V1Y 8B7
(250) 860-1100
Emp Here 190   *Sales* 84,516,000
SIC 6531 Real estate agents and managers
Francis Braam

D-U-N-S 24-019-1275   (BR)
S C RESTORATIONS LTD
(*Suby of* S C RESTORATIONS LTD)
1025 Trench Pl, Kelowna, BC, V1Y 9Y4
(250) 763-1556
Emp Here 100
SIC 7299 Miscellaneous personal service
Hans Caspers

D-U-N-S 25-659-1843   (HQ)
S C RESTORATIONS LTD
STUTTERS CONSTRUCTION RESTORATIONS
1216 St. Paul St Suite 201, Kelowna, BC, V1Y 2C8
(250) 832-9818
Emp Here 30   *Sales* 15,146,520
SIC 1629 Heavy construction, nec
Keith Stutters

D-U-N-S 24-078-7312   (SL)
SERENDIPITY CLOTHING CO
2903 Pandosy St Suite 102, Kelowna, BC, V1Y 1W1
(250) 861-4166
Emp Here 25   *Sales* 16,411,600
SIC 5963 Direct selling establishments
Roy Hulse

D-U-N-S 25-656-2257   (SL)
SLIZEK INC
ADVOCARE HEALTH SERVICES
1450 St. Paul St, Kelowna, BC, V1Y 2E6
(250) 861-3446
Emp Here 100   *Sales* 17,020,500
SIC 8049 Offices of health practitioner
Mary Manton
John T Manton

D-U-N-S 25-236-1035   (HQ)
SOUND WAVES ENTERTAINMENT NETWORK LTD
SW AUDIO VISUAL
1-325 Bay Ave, Kelowna, BC, V1Y 7S3
(250) 868-3333
Emp Here 70   *Sales* 66,629,600
SIC 7359 Equipment rental and leasing, nec
Calvin Mccarthy
Grant Mackeney

D-U-N-S 25-262-8771   (SL)
STATESMEN REALTY CORPORATION
SAGE EXECUTIVE GROUP
1980 Cooper Rd Suite 108, Kelowna, BC, V1Y 8K5
(250) 861-5122
Emp Here 45   *Sales* 14,720,715
SIC 6531 Real estate agents and managers
Nadine Westgate

D-U-N-S 20-098-7782   (HQ)
STOBER, AL CONSTRUCTION LTD
WK MANUFACTURING, DIV OF
1631 Dickson Ave Suite 1700, Kelowna, BC, V1Y 0B5
(250) 763-2305
Emp Here 12   *Sales* 16,401,000
SIC 6719 Holding companies, nec
Albert Stober
Mark Stober
Sandra Stober

D-U-N-S 20-098-7840   (HQ)
SUN-RYPE PRODUCTS LTD
1165 Ethel St, Kelowna, BC, V1Y 2W4
(250) 860-7973
Sales 194,954,000
SIC 2033 Canned fruits and specialties
Lesli Bradley
Amanda Burns
Warren Sarafinchan

Glen Clark
James Eccott
Michael J. Korenberg
James A. Pattison
Donald Selman
Douglas Souter

D-U-N-S 24-749-6698   (SL)
SYSTEMATIC MILL INSTALLATIONS LTD
1226 St. Paul St, Kelowna, BC, V1Y 2C8
(236) 420-4041
Emp Here 60   *Sales* 25,364,220
SIC 1541 Industrial buildings and warehouses
Clark Berry

D-U-N-S 20-966-5426   (SL)
TCB TRI-CITIES BUILDERS SUPPLY LTD
KELOWNA HOME HARDWARE BUILDING CENTRE
1650 Springfield Rd, Kelowna, BC, V1Y 5V4
(250) 763-5040
Emp Here 80   *Sales* 21,412,160
SIC 5251 Hardware stores
Paul Mccann

D-U-N-S 20-294-6559   (BR)
TEC THE EDUCATION COMPANY INC
CENTER FOR ARTS & TECHNOLOGY OKANAGAN
(*Suby of* TEC THE EDUCATION COMPANY INC)
1632 Dickson Ave Suite 100, Kelowna, BC, V1Y 7T2
(250) 860-2787
Emp Here 75
SIC 8222 Junior colleges
Peter Vigilante

D-U-N-S 24-390-4625   (HQ)
TROIKA VENTURES INC
1856 Ambrosi Rd Suite 114, Kelowna, BC, V1Y 4R9
(250) 869-4945
Sales 11,543,320
SIC 1522 Residential construction, nec
Renee Wasylyk
Bradley (Brad) Klassen
Brian Wall

D-U-N-S 25-862-2273   (BR)
URBAN SYSTEMS LTD
(*Suby of* URBAN SYSTEMS LTD)
1353 Ellis St Unit 304, Kelowna, BC, V1Y 1Z9
(250) 762-2517
Emp Here 400
SIC 8711 Engineering services
Geoff Blunden

D-U-N-S 25-413-9017   (SL)
VALOROSO FOODS (1996) LTD
1467 Sutherland Ave, Kelowna, BC, V1Y 5Y4
(250) 860-3631
Emp Here 24   *Sales* 20,053,848
SIC 5141 Groceries, general line
Lisa Valoroso
Joe Valoroso

D-U-N-S 25-657-1530   (SL)
VAN DEN ELZEN DEVELOPMENTS LTD
KELOWNA CYCLE
2949 Pandosy St Suite 103, Kelowna, BC, V1Y 1W1
(250) 769-5315
Emp Here 30   *Sales* 14,942,340
SIC 5541 Gasoline service stations
Marie Van Den Elzen
Ron Van Den Elzen
Mike Van Den Elzen
Linda Van Den Elzen

D-U-N-S 24-842-4801   (SL)
WATERPLAY SOLUTIONS CORP
1451 Ellis St Unit B, Kelowna, BC, V1Y 2A3
(250) 712-3393
Emp Here 60   *Sales* 17,834,520
SIC 4941 Water supply
Lisa Neilson

D-U-N-S 20-622-7597   (SL)
WESTWOOD FINE CABINETRY INC
2140 Leckie Pl, Kelowna, BC, V1Y 7W7
(250) 860-3900
Emp Here 180   *Sales* 34,626,600
SIC 2434 Wood kitchen cabinets
Bill Holland
Angela Norman
Susan Holland

D-U-N-S 20-015-2655   (HQ)
WMI MANUFACTURING CORP
1451 Ellis St, Kelowna, BC, V1Y 2A3
(250) 712-3393
Emp Here 16   *Sales* 19,568,160
SIC 3949 Sporting and athletic goods, nec
Jill White

Kelowna, BC V4V

D-U-N-S 25-528-8656   (HQ)
N.A.P. WINDOWS & DOORS LTD
8775 Jim Bailey Cres Unit B1, Kelowna, BC, V4V 2L7
(250) 762-5343
Sales 12,113,820
SIC 3089 Plastics products, nec
Frank Raponi
Albert Raponi

D-U-N-S 20-118-0239   (SL)
OKANAGAN NORTH GROWERS CO-OPERATIVE
9751 Bottom Wood Lake Rd, Kelowna, BC, V4V 1S7

Emp Here 180
SIC 0723 Crop preparation services for market

D-U-N-S 24-990-9334   (BR)
WASTE MANAGEMENT OF CANADA CORPORATION
(*Suby of* WASTE MANAGEMENT, INC.)
350 Beaver Lake Rd, Kelowna, BC, V4V 1S5
(250) 766-9100
Emp Here 75
SIC 4953 Refuse systems
Tim Teeple

D-U-N-S 25-731-6901   (SL)
WHITEWATER COMPOSITES LTD
FORMASHAPE
(*Suby of* 398314 B.C. LTD)
9505 Haldane Rd, Kelowna, BC, V4V 2K5
(250) 766-5152
Emp Here 80   *Sales* 14,337,520
SIC 3299 NonMetallic mineral products,
Douglas Heke
Geoffrey Chutter

Keremeos, BC V0X

D-U-N-S 20-398-4190   (SL)
LASSER PRODUCE LTD
601 Keremeos Bypass Rd, Keremeos, BC, V0X 1N1
(250) 506-0707
Emp Here 50   *Sales* 19,575,100
SIC 6799 Investors, nec
Sukhseev Lasser
Nabdeep Lasser
Jaswinder Lasser

D-U-N-S 24-671-1902   (SL)
SPORTSMANS CORNER GAS 2002
3162 10th Ave Ss 1, Keremeos, BC, V0X 1N1
(250) 499-7192
Emp Here 4   *Sales* 12,423,428
SIC 4925 Gas production and/or distribution
Kevin Cluett

D-U-N-S 20-306-0038   (SL)
SUNKATCHERS RV PARK COOPERATIVE
4155 Hwy 3, Keremeos, BC, V0X 1N1
(250) 499-2065
Emp Here 49   *Sales* 11,197,672
SIC 6111 Federal and federally sponsored credit agencies
Bruce Logan

Kimberley, BC V1A

D-U-N-S 25-074-9368   (SL)
CAMBODIA SUPPORT GROUP SOCIETY
135 Thompson St, Kimberley, BC, V1A 1T9
(250) 427-2159
Emp Here 49   *Sales* 19,800,803
SIC 8699 Membership organizations, nec

D-U-N-S 24-088-1482   (SL)
CHALET CHEVROLET OLDSMOBILE LTD
CHALET GM
1142 304th St, Kimberley, BC, V1A 3H6
(250) 427-4895
Emp Here 30   *Sales* 14,942,340
SIC 5511 New and used car dealers
James Fugina

D-U-N-S 25-620-7374   (SL)
INTERIOR HEALTH KIMBERLY SPECIAL CARE HOME
KIMBERLEY SPECIAL CARE HOME
386 2nd Ave, Kimberley, BC, V1A 2Z8
(250) 427-4807
Emp Here 80   *Sales* 4,739,760
SIC 8361 Residential care
Jeff Bedker

D-U-N-S 24-397-7290   (SL)
KIMBERLEY SEARCH & RESCUE SOCIETY
340 Spokane St, Kimberley, BC, V1A 2E8
(250) 427-5998
Emp Here 30   *Sales* 11,922,420
SIC 8699 Membership organizations, nec
Peter Reid

D-U-N-S 25-621-8389   (SL)
KIMBERLEY TEACHER'S ASSOCIATION
KTA OFFICE
144 Deer Park Ave Suite 201, Kimberley, BC, V1A 2J4
(250) 427-3113
Emp Here 49   *Sales* 11,451,055
SIC 8621 Professional organizations
Jerry Mcmahon

D-U-N-S 25-680-5896   (BR)
RESORTS OF THE CANADIAN ROCKIES INC
KIMBERLEY ALPINE RESORT
(*Suby of* RESORTS OF THE CANADIAN ROCKIES INC)
301 North Star Blvd, Kimberley, BC, V1A 2Y5
(250) 427-4881
Emp Here 200
SIC 7011 Hotels and motels
Andy Cohen

Kitimat, BC V8C

D-U-N-S 20-295-0759   (BR)
BOARD OF EDUCATION OF SCHOOL DISTRICT #82 (COAST M
THE BOARD OF EDUCATION OF SCHOOL DISTRICT #82 (COAST MOUNTAIN)
(*Suby of* BOARD OF EDUCATION OF SCHOOL DISTRICT #82 (COAST M)
1491 Kingfisher Ave N, Kitimat, BC, V8C 1E9
(250) 632-6174
Emp Here 80
SIC 8211 Elementary and secondary schools
Nancy Tormene

D-U-N-S 24-713-8063 (SL)
DAUDET CREEK CONTRACTING LTD
495 Quatsino Blvd, Kitimat, BC, V8C 2G7
(250) 632-4831
Emp Here 50   *Sales* 14,429,150
SIC 1522 Residential construction, nec
Shaun Oviatt

D-U-N-S 25-191-7332 (BR)
NORTHERN HEALTH AUTHORITY
KITIMAT GENERAL HOSPITAL
(*Suby of* NORTHERN HEALTH AUTHORITY)
920 Lahakas Blvd S, Kitimat, BC, V8C 2S3
(250) 632-2121
Emp Here 150
SIC 8062 General medical and surgical hospitals
Agnes Snow

D-U-N-S 24-137-2655 (BR)
RIO TINTO ALCAN INC
ALCAN PRIMARY METAL GROUP, DIV OF
(*Suby of* RIO TINTO PLC)
1 Smelter Site Rd, Kitimat, BC, V8C 2H2
(250) 639-8000
Emp Here 2,000
SIC 3334 Primary aluminum
Paul Henning

Lac La Hache, BC V0K

D-U-N-S 25-836-1385 (SL)
COUNTRY PRIME MEATS LTD
3171 97 Hwy, Lac La Hache, BC, V0K 1T1
(250) 396-4111
Emp Here 85   *Sales* 29,383,650
SIC 2011 Meat packing plants
Peter Springmann
Markus Springmann
Reinhard Springmann

D-U-N-S 25-389-2061 (HQ)
DWB CONSULTING SERVICES LTD
3361 Helena Lake Rd, Lac La Hache, BC, V0K 1T1
(250) 396-7208
Sales 10,619,850
SIC 8748 Business consulting, nec
David Bedford
Daniel Bedford

Ladysmith, BC V9G

D-U-N-S 20-099-3285 (HQ)
49TH PARALLEL GROCERY LIMITED
49TH PARALLEL GROCERY
1020 1st Ave, Ladysmith, BC, V9G 1A5
(250) 245-3221
Emp Here 97   *Sales* 51,945,429
SIC 5411 Grocery stores
Wayne L Richmond
Peter Richmond
Harmina Richmond
Kathy Richmond

D-U-N-S 24-311-4998 (SL)
HABENDUM HOLDING LTD
DAIRY QUEEN RESTAURANT
365 Davis Rd, Ladysmith, BC, V9G 1V1
(250) 245-3212
Emp Here 55   *Sales* 22,014,339
SIC 7383 News syndicates
Thomas Floyd

D-U-N-S 25-486-2071 (BR)
SCHOOL DISTRICT NO. 68 (NANAIMO-LADYSMITH)
LADYSMITH SECONDARY SCHOOL
(*Suby of* SCHOOL DISTRICT NO. 68 (NANAIMO-LADYSMITH))
710 6th Ave, Ladysmith, BC, V9G 1A1

---

(250) 245-3043
Emp Here 80
SIC 8211 Elementary and secondary schools
Steve Thompson

Lake Country, BC V4V

D-U-N-S 25-861-2811 (HQ)
CORAL BEACH FARMS LTD
JEALOUS FRUIT
16351 Carrs Landing Rd, Lake Country, BC, V4V 1A9
(250) 766-5393
Sales 487,385,000
SIC 2035 Pickles, sauces, and salad dressings
David Geen

D-U-N-S 24-324-3669 (BR)
OKANAGAN TREE FRUIT COOPERATIVE
OTFC
(*Suby of* OKANAGAN TREE FRUIT COOPERATIVE)
9751 Bottom Wood Lake Rd, Lake Country, BC, V4V 1S7

Emp Here 150
SIC 0723 Crop preparation services for market
Gary Schieck

D-U-N-S 25-097-3112 (HQ)
SNOWLINE ENTERPRISES LTD
PREMIUM CANADA
3121 Hill Rd Suite 214, Lake Country, BC, V4V 1G1
(250) 766-0068
Emp Here 18   *Sales* 18,988,970
SIC 5169 Chemicals and allied products, nec
Patrick Gallagher
Mario Russo
Sue Chapman

D-U-N-S 24-552-0812 (SL)
VOYAGER R.V. CENTRE LTD
9250 Highway 97, Lake Country, BC, V4V 1P9
(250) 766-4607
Emp Here 25   *Sales* 12,451,950
SIC 5561 Recreational vehicle dealers
Rodney Friesen
Bruce Schnnour
John Schat

Langley, BC V1M

D-U-N-S 20-304-6966 (SL)
425480 B.C. LTD
TMS TRANSPORTATION
9440 202 St Unit 117, Langley, BC, V1M 4A6
(604) 882-2550
Emp Here 80   *Sales* 11,855,360
SIC 4213 Trucking, except local
Robert Benedict
Allen Benedict

D-U-N-S 24-423-5128 (HQ)
4REFUEL CANADA LP
(*Suby of* 4REFUEL GP CORPORATION)
9440 202 St Suite 215, Langley, BC, V1M 4A6
(604) 513-0386
Emp Here 60   *Sales* 567,491,040
SIC 5172 Petroleum products, nec
Larry Rodo
Mike Mcgee

D-U-N-S 24-581-4277 (SL)
A 52 WAREHOUSE INC
20146 100a Ave Suite 2, Langley, BC, V1M 3G2
(604) 881-0251
Emp Here 60   *Sales* 12,342,360
SIC 4225 General warehousing and storage

Darren Andrew Hawrish
Kevin Paul Kirsten
Nicole May Burke
Paul Mccurry

D-U-N-S 24-838-4919 (SL)
AMAN ENTERPRISES 1989 LTD
20255 102 Ave, Langley, BC, V1M 4B4
(604) 513-0462
Emp Here 75   *Sales* 11,114,400
SIC 4213 Trucking, except local
Sukhjinder Sanghera
Kuldip Sanghera

D-U-N-S 25-126-9390 (SL)
APEX ALUMINUM EXTRUSIONS LTD
9767 201 St, Langley, BC, V1M 3E7
(604) 882-3542
Emp Here 70   *Sales* 16,340,450
SIC 3354 Aluminum extruded products
Thomas R. Martini

D-U-N-S 24-369-6945 (SL)
ARCHITECTURAL PRECAST STRUCTURES LTD
9844 199a St, Langley, BC, V1M 2X7
(604) 888-1968
Emp Here 82   *Sales* 20,293,606
SIC 1771 Concrete work
Claudio Corra
Phillip Toulusso

D-U-N-S 24-290-7236 (SL)
ARMAUR PLUMBING LTD
20085 100a Ave Unit 1, Langley, BC, V1M 3G4
(604) 888-1255
Emp Here 85   *Sales* 19,810,525
SIC 1711 Plumbing, heating, air-conditioning
Brent Kreklevich
Jay Chenier

D-U-N-S 20-695-6141 (SL)
BERMAN FALK INC
9499 198 St, Langley, BC, V1M 3B8
(604) 882-8903
Emp Here 29   *Sales* 19,037,456
SIC 5963 Direct selling establishments
Gary Berman
Paul Falk

D-U-N-S 24-995-8687 (BR)
BEST BUY CANADA LTD
(*Suby of* BEST BUY CO., INC.)
19890 92a Ave, Langley, BC, V1M 3A9
(604) 419-5500
Emp Here 150
SIC 5999 Miscellaneous retail stores, nec
Khalid Aberhouch

D-U-N-S 24-325-2538 (HQ)
BRITCO MANAGEMENT INC
BRITCO BUILDING SYSTEMS
20091 91a Ave Unit 100, Langley, BC, V1M 3A2
(604) 455-8000
Emp Here 10   *Sales* 23,084,400
SIC 2452 Prefabricated wood buildings
Richard Mcclymont
David Taft

D-U-N-S 25-216-5634 (HQ)
BRITISH PACIFIC TRANSPORT HOLDINGS LTD
SHADOW LINES
9975 199b St, Langley, BC, V1M 3G4
(604) 882-5880
Sales 16,401,000
SIC 6712 Bank holding companies
Robert Reid Jr

D-U-N-S 20-839-4010 (HQ)
CENTRA CONSTRUCTION GROUP LTD
20178 98 Ave, Langley, BC, V1M 3G1
(604) 882-5010
Emp Here 100   *Sales* 39,272,200
SIC 1751 Carpentry work
Garret Wall

D-U-N-S 24-952-0862 (SL)
CHEMICAL LIME COMPANY OF CANADA INC
102 B Avenue Suite 20303, Langley, BC, V1M 4B4
(604) 888-2575
Emp Here 40   *Sales* 13,093,760
SIC 2899 Chemical preparations, nec
Scott Hinds

D-U-N-S 20-749-0996 (SL)
COLLINS MANUFACTURING CO. LTD
(*Suby of* COLVAN ENTERPRISES LTD)
9835 199a St Suite 5, Langley, BC, V1M 2X7
(604) 888-2812
Emp Here 60   *Sales* 13,430,580
SIC 3713 Truck and bus bodies
Mike Sondergaard

D-U-N-S 24-373-8718 (BR)
EMERGENCY AND HEALTH SERVICES COMMISSION
HEALTHLINK BC
(*Suby of* EMERGENCY AND HEALTH SERVICES COMMISSION)
9440 202 St, Langley, BC, V1M 4A6
(604) 215-8103
Emp Here 100
SIC 8099 Health and allied services, nec

D-U-N-S 24-681-3232 (SL)
FASTIK LABEL & SUPPLY INC
9703 199a St, Langley, BC, V1M 2X7
(604) 882-6853
Emp Here 31   *Sales* 13,748,190
SIC 7389 Business services, nec
Bradley William Malchuk
Frederick Malchuk

D-U-N-S 20-786-3346 (SL)
FELXIA CORPORATION
19680 94a Ave, Langley, BC, V1M 3B7
(604) 513-1266
Emp Here 49   *Sales* 11,630,694
SIC 2621 Paper mills
Brigit Stefani

D-U-N-S 24-939-5955 (HQ)
GERMAN ADVERTISING ADVANTAGE INC, THE
TGAA
19770 94a Ave, Langley, BC, V1M 3B7
(604) 888-8008
Emp Here 15   *Sales* 12,622,840
SIC 5199 Nondurable goods, nec
Siegfried Haas

D-U-N-S 24-309-9038 (SL)
GOLDEN CROSSING CONSTRUCTORS JOINT VENTURE
20100 100a Ave, Langley, BC, V1M 3G4

Emp Here 50   *Sales* 10,580,750
SIC 1622 Bridge, tunnel, and elevated highway construction
Terry Cage
Michael Heerdt

D-U-N-S 20-162-8948 (HQ)
GREAT PACIFIC INDUSTRIES INC
OVERWAITEA FOOD GROUP
(*Suby of* PATTISON, JIM GROUP INC)
19855 92a Ave, Langley, BC, V1M 3B6
(604) 888-1213
Emp Here 200   *Sales* 2,694,496,000
SIC 5411 Grocery stores
Michael Korenberg
Rodney C Bergen
David G Bell
Nick Desmarais
James A Pattison
Darlene Hubbard

D-U-N-S 25-387-9845 (SL)
GREENSTAR PLANT PRODUCTS INC
9430 198 St, Langley, BC, V1M 3C8
(604) 882-7699
Emp Here 50   *Sales* 37,126,000

SIC 5191 Farm supplies
Douglas Pulver
Timothy Walker
Ronald Stern
Norman Drewlo

D-U-N-S 20-553-0236   (HQ)
HARDWOODS DISTRIBUTION INC
9440 202 St Unit 306, Langley, BC, V1M 4A6
(604) 881-1988
Sales 859,890,081
SIC 5031 Lumber, plywood, and millwork
Robert J. (Rob) Brown
Drew Dickinson
David Hughes
Lance R. Blanco
Jason R. West
Faiz Karmally
Peter M. Bull
Michelle Lewis
Jim Macaulay
E. Lawrence Sauder

D-U-N-S 25-359-8742   (HQ)
HARDWOODS SPECIALTY PRODUCTS LP
9440 202 St Suite 306, Langley, BC, V1M 4A6
(604) 881-1988
Emp Here 10   Sales 51,266,520
SIC 5031 Lumber, plywood, and millwork
Maurice Paquette
Daniel Besen
Garry Warner
Kevin Slabaugh
Robert Brown

D-U-N-S 24-778-1719   (HQ)
INTERPAC FOREST PRODUCTS LTD
9701 201 St, Langley, BC, V1M 3E7
(604) 881-2300
Emp Here 7   Sales 11,230,475
SIC 7389 Business services, nec
David Milne

D-U-N-S 20-800-4325   (HQ)
IRIS THE VISUAL GROUP WESTERN CANADA INC
IRIS-OPTOMISTRIS & OPTICIANS
(Suby of CANADIAN DEPOSITORY FOR SE-CURITIES LIMITED, THE)
9440 202 St Suite 315, Langley, BC, V1M 4A6
(604) 881-0353
Emp Here 16   Sales 47,888,288
SIC 5995 Optical goods stores
Francis Jean
Ronald Phillip
Randy Schuller

D-U-N-S 20-398-6315   (SL)
JD SWEID FOODS (2013) LTD
9696 199a St, Langley, BC, V1M 2X7
(800) 665-4355
Emp Here 160   Sales 55,310,400
SIC 2015 Poultry slaughtering and processing
Ronald Pollon
Clifford Pollon

D-U-N-S 24-732-3678   (HQ)
JORDAN ENTERPRISES LIMITED
QUALITY INN NORTHERN GRAND, THE
20111 93a Ave Suite 200, Langley, BC, V1M 4A9
(604) 888-8677
Emp Here 1   Sales 12,142,390
SIC 7011 Hotels and motels
Ralph Jordan

D-U-N-S 24-724-1425   (HQ)
JULIAN TILE INC
9688 203 St, Langley, BC, V1M 4B9
(604) 299-4085
Emp Here 34   Sales 16,059,120
SIC 5211 Lumber and other building materials
Joe Giusti
Renato Baldo
Steve Crnac

D-U-N-S 24-639-9828   (SL)

KNELSON RECOVERY SYSTEMS INTER-NATIONAL INC
19855 98 Ave, Langley, BC, V1M 2X5
(604) 888-4015
Emp Here 140   Sales 38,912,638
SIC 6712 Bank holding companies
Brett Knelson

D-U-N-S 20-621-5899   (HQ)
MAINLAND CONSTRUCTION MATERIALS ULC
9525 201 St Unit 317, Langley, BC, V1M 4A5
(604) 882-5650
Emp Here 10   Sales 20,073,900
SIC 5211 Lumber and other building materials
Kevin Spenst
Stephen P. Hardy

D-U-N-S 20-113-6843   (SL)
MARK-CREST FOODS LTD
19670 92a Ave Suite 100, Langley, BC, V1M 3B2
(604) 882-2066
Emp Here 45   Sales 12,336,840
SIC 5411 Grocery stores
Trent Glukler

D-U-N-S 24-310-7711   (SL)
MITSUI HOME CANADA INC
(Suby of MITSUI FUDOSAN CO., LTD.)
19680 94a Ave, Langley, BC, V1M 3B7
(604) 882-8415
Emp Here 80   Sales 53,351,360
SIC 4731 Freight transportation arrangement
Hiroshi Kuratsu
Tatsuya Suzuki
Douglas Smith

D-U-N-S 24-101-7263   (SL)
MODERN GROUNDS MAINTENANCE LTD
9702 216 St, Langley, BC, V1M 3J2
(604) 888-4999
Emp Here 30   Sales 14,121,930
SIC 1542 Nonresidential construction, nec
David Fialkowski

D-U-N-S 24-133-7641   (SL)
MUTUAL FIRE INSURANCE COMPANY OF BRITISH COLUMBIA, THE
9366 200a St Suite 201, Langley, BC, V1M 4B3
(604) 881-1250
Emp Here 10   Sales 61,859,470
SIC 6331 Fire, marine, and casualty insurance
Darin Lord Nessel
Don Hooge
Jake Bredenhof
Jason Christopherson
W.J. (Bill) Adams
Mike Bose
Sam Wind
John Pruim
Tako Van Popta
Dan Robinson

D-U-N-S 24-881-7777   (HQ)
NATIONAL TRUCK CENTRE INC
9758 203 St, Langley, BC, V1M 4B9
(604) 888-5577
Emp Here 5   Sales 62,928,000
SIC 5511 New and used car dealers
John Williams

D-U-N-S 20-275-3943   (SL)
NEWMARK CONSTRUCTION INC
NEWMARK GROUP
9525 201 St Unit 219, Langley, BC, V1M 4A5
(604) 371-3963
Emp Here 100   Sales 27,094,200
SIC 1521 Single-family housing construction
Mark Chandler

D-U-N-S 20-911-7407   (HQ)
NORCAN FLUID POWER LTD
NORCAN FLUID POWER 84
(Suby of BCB CORPORATE SERVICES LTD)
19650 Telegraph Trail, Langley, BC, V1M 3E5

(604) 881-7877
Sales 21,156,080
SIC 7699 Repair services, nec
Bill Dix

D-U-N-S 24-290-0793   (SL)
POWER DRYWALL (2005) LTD
19855 98 Ave, Langley, BC, V1M 2X5
(604) 626-4900
Emp Here 275   Sales 50,377,525
SIC 1742 Plastering, drywall, and insulation
Ronald Rosevear
Lorraine Rosevear

D-U-N-S 20-748-0377   (HQ)
PRIMEX MANUFACTURING LTD
(Suby of LIGHTHOUSE EQUITY PARTNERS LIMITED PARTNERSHIP)
20160 92a Ave, Langley, BC, V1M 3A4
(604) 881-7875
Sales 33,433,680
SIC 3089 Plastics products, nec
Bob Smart
Mark Campbell
Heinz Avendano
Craig East
Steve Hnatiuk
Joe Lucke
Dave Davelaar

D-U-N-S 25-850-9025   (SL)
R. R. PLETT TRUCKING LTD
19675 98 Ave, Langley, BC, V1M 2X5
(604) 513-9920
Emp Here 70   Sales 10,373,440
SIC 4213 Trucking, except local
Reginald Plett
Ann Plett

D-U-N-S 24-361-2665   (SL)
REMCAN PROJECTS LIMITED PARTNER-SHIP
20075 100a Ave Suite 2, Langley, BC, V1M 3G4
(604) 882-0840
Emp Here 500   Sales 164,057,500
SIC 1629 Heavy construction, nec
John Thwaites
Tom Winters
Jeff Swanson
Jason Thomas

D-U-N-S 20-125-9731   (SL)
RITE-WAY METALS LTD
20058 92a Ave, Langley, BC, V1M 3A4
(604) 882-7557
Emp Here 35   Sales 16,475,585
SIC 1542 Nonresidential construction, nec

D-U-N-S 24-311-1155   (SL)
RJMB RESTAURANTS LTD
MCDONALD'S RESTAURANT
20394 88 Ave, Langley, BC, V1M 2Y6
(604) 881-6220
Emp Here 110   Sales 5,007,090
SIC 5812 Eating places
Ronald Knight

D-U-N-S 20-278-9566   (SL)
SANGROUP INC
SAN INDUSTRIES, DIV OF
25583 88 Ave, Langley, BC, V1M 3N8
(604) 881-4848
Emp Here 50   Sales 12,652,950
SIC 5211 Lumber and other building materials
Abolghasem Saneinejad

D-U-N-S 24-802-4635   (HQ)
SAVE-ON-FOODS LIMITED PARTNERSHIP
URBAN FARE
19855 92a Ave, Langley, BC, V1M 3B6
(604) 888-1213
Emp Here 5   Sales 14,380,373
SIC 5411 Grocery stores
Michael Korenberg

D-U-N-S 25-451-5950   (BR)
SCHOOL DISTRICT NO. 35 (LANGLEY)

WALNUT GROVE SECONDARY SCHOOL
8919 Walnut Grove Dr, Langley, BC, V1M 2N7
(604) 882-0220
Emp Here 140
SIC 8211 Elementary and secondary schools
George Kozlovic

D-U-N-S 24-778-4440   (HQ)
SEPRO MINERAL SYSTEMS CORP
SYSTEMES MINERAUX DE SEPRO
(Suby of FALCON CONCENTRATORS LTD)
9850 201 St Unit 101a, Langley, BC, V1M 4A3
(604) 888-5568
Emp Here 30   Sales 11,100,050
SIC 3532 Mining machinery
Mark Van Kleek
Wolfgang Van Ommen
Steve Mcalister
Sinisa Ciric
Dave Hornick
Ken Kirk

D-U-N-S 20-273-2566   (SL)
SEYEM' QWANTLEN BUSINESS MANAGE-MENT LTD
23684 Gabriel Lane, Langley, BC, V1M 2S4
(604) 888-5556
Emp Here 49   Sales 13,881,357
SIC 8741 Management services
Derrick Mitchell

D-U-N-S 25-946-6183   (HQ)
SPECIALIZED PROPERTY EVALUATION CONTROL SERVICES LIMITED
SPECS
9525 201 St Suite 303, Langley, BC, V1M 4A5
(604) 882-8930
Emp Here 10   Sales 22,460,950
SIC 7389 Business services, nec
Dave Wallace
Andrew Ross
Jarett Finney
Mike Padua

D-U-N-S 25-215-8092   (SL)
TMS TRANSPORTATION MANAGEMENT SERVICES LTD
TMS
9975 199b St, Langley, BC, V1M 3G4
(604) 882-2550
Emp Here 100   Sales 13,097,000
SIC 6712 Bank holding companies
Robert Benedict
Dietmar Krause
Lawrence Flint
Allan Benedict

D-U-N-S 20-922-4588   (BR)
UAP INC
NAPA AUTO PARTS
(Suby of GENUINE PARTS COMPANY)
9325 200 St Unit 100, Langley, BC, V1M 3A7
(604) 513-9458
Emp Here 150
SIC 5013 Motor vehicle supplies and new parts
Jeff Trainor

D-U-N-S 24-825-0359   (BR)
UNIFIRST CANADA LTD
(Suby of UNIFIRST CORPORATION)
9189 196a St, Langley, BC, V1M 3B5
(604) 888-8119
Emp Here 80
SIC 7213 Linen supply
Courteney Stevenson

D-U-N-S 25-760-4538   (HQ)
VALLEY TRAFFIC SYSTEMS INC
(Suby of PKJ HOLDINGS LTD)
19689 Telegraph Trail, Langley, BC, V1M 3E6
(604) 513-0210
Sales 13,126,957
SIC 7389 Business services, nec
Philip Jackman

D-U-N-S 25-677-6238   (HQ)

VEDDER STEEL LTD
9663 199a St Unit 4, Langley, BC, V1M 2X7
(604) 882-0035
Emp Here 1   *Sales* 11,768,275
SIC 1542 Nonresidential construction, nec
Gerald Innes

D-U-N-S 25-409-4360   (HQ)
VITRUM HOLDINGS LTD
9739 201 St, Langley, BC, V1M 3E7
(604) 882-3513
Sales 109,652,700
SIC 6712 Bank holding companies
Gema Martini
Thomas Martini
Diana Lindgren

D-U-N-S 20-354-5215   (SL)
VITRUM INDUSTRIES LTD
(*Suby of* VITRUM HOLDINGS LTD)
9739 201 St, Langley, BC, V1M 3E7
(604) 882-3513
Emp Here 425   *Sales* 108,668,250
SIC 3231 Products of purchased glass
Thomas Martini
Gema Martine

D-U-N-S 20-117-1790   (HQ)
WESCO INDUSTRIES LTD
9663 199a St Unit 1, Langley, BC, V1M 2X7
(604) 881-3000
Emp Here 24   *Sales* 12,497,170
SIC 5085 Industrial supplies
Allison Arai
David Arai
Kaz Arai

D-U-N-S 24-857-0137   (SL)
WESTLAM INDUSTRIES LTD
CROWN 44
19755 98 Ave, Langley, BC, V1M 2X5
(604) 888-2894
Emp Here 80   *Sales* 12,469,040
SIC 2435 Hardwood veneer and plywood
Bud Sardone

D-U-N-S 20-102-7158   (HQ)
WINDSOR BUILDING SUPPLIES LTD
WINDSOR PLYWOOD
20039 96 Ave, Langley, BC, V1M 3C6
(604) 455-9663
Emp Here 45   *Sales* 869,387,250
SIC 6794 Patent owners and lessors
Randle Jones
Michael Bodnar
Curt Crego

D-U-N-S 20-959-0108   (HQ)
YOKOHAMA TIRE (CANADA) INC
(*Suby of* YOKOHAMA RUBBER COMPANY,
LIMITED, THE)
9325 200 St Suite 500, Langley, BC, V1M 3A7
(604) 546-9656
Emp Here 1   *Sales* 14,942,340
SIC 5531 Auto and home supply stores
Eric Dedoyard
Naoki Takeda

Langley, BC V2Y

D-U-N-S 24-824-0418   (SL)
BEVO FARMS LTD
(*Suby of* ZENABIS GLOBAL INC)
7170 Glover Rd, Langley, BC, V2Y 2R1
(604) 888-0420
Emp Here 75   *Sales* 12,676,875
SIC 0161 Vegetables and melons
Leo Benne
John Hoekstra

D-U-N-S 25-532-9435   (BR)
CANADA BREAD COMPANY, LIMITED
DEMPSTER BREAD, DIV OF
(*Suby of* GRUPO BIMBO, S.A.B. DE C.V.)

6350 203 St, Langley, BC, V2Y 1L9
(604) 532-8200
Emp Here 280
SIC 2051 Bread, cake, and related products
Donald Bagnall

D-U-N-S 25-154-3351   (HQ)
CLEARWEST SOLUTIONS INC
8700 200 St Suite 310, Langley, BC, V2Y 0G4
(604) 888-5050
Emp Here 8   *Sales* 10,419,200
SIC 5999 Miscellaneous retail stores, nec
David Ens

D-U-N-S 25-408-6903   (SL)
COAST SPAS MANUFACTURING INC
COAST SPAS
6315 202 St, Langley, BC, V2Y 1N1
(604) 514-8111
Emp Here 225   *Sales* 59,527,800
SIC 3999 Manufacturing industries, nec
Donald Elkington
Jatinder Sudhu

D-U-N-S 25-372-0742   (BR)
COSTCO WHOLESALE CANADA LTD
COSTCO WHOLESALE
(*Suby of* COSTCO WHOLESALE CORPO-
RATION)
20499 64 Ave, Langley, BC, V2Y 1N5
(604) 539-8901
Emp Here 250
SIC 5099 Durable goods, nec
Michael Thompson

D-U-N-S 25-218-6622   (HQ)
**CRESTWOOD ENGINEERING COMPANY
LTD**
TCS
6217 205 St, Langley, BC, V2Y 1N7
(604) 533-8675
Emp Here 1   *Sales* 18,210,750
SIC 5013 Motor vehicle supplies and new
parts
Robert Marshall
Jean Marshall

D-U-N-S 20-109-0581   (HQ)
DARVONDA NURSERIES LTD
6690 216 St, Langley, BC, V2Y 2N9
(604) 530-6889
Sales 13,232,596
SIC 0181 Ornamental nursery products
Byron Jansen
Tamara Jansen
Lawrence Jansen

D-U-N-S 24-316-1796   (BR)
FRASER HEALTH AUTHORITY
*BC CLINICAL AND SUPPORT SERVICES
SOCIETY*
(*Suby of* GOVERNMENT OF THE
PROVINCE OF BRITISH COLUMBIA)
8521 198a St, Langley, BC, V2Y 0A1
(604) 455-1300
Emp Here 400
SIC 8742 Management consulting services
Pat Veasey

D-U-N-S 20-801-1791   (SL)
FRASER VALLEY AUCTIONS (1983) LTD
21801 56 Ave, Langley, BC, V2Y 2M9
(604) 534-3241
Emp Here 15   *Sales* 18,155,955
SIC 5154 Livestock
Kenneth Pearson

D-U-N-S 24-448-5165   (SL)
G.A. VALLANCE HOLDINGS LIMITED
CANADIAN TIRE ASSOCIATE STORE
6312 200 St Suite 426, Langley, BC, V2Y 1A1
(604) 532-4411
Emp Here 100   *Sales* 62,928,000
SIC 5541 Gasoline service stations
George Vallance
Shirley Vallance

D-U-N-S 25-019-8009   (SL)
HOLESHOT MOTORSPORTS LTD
8867 201 St, Langley, BC, V2Y 0C8
(604) 882-3800
Emp Here 22   *Sales* 10,957,716
SIC 5571 Motorcycle dealers
Larry Visco
Daniel Reynolds

D-U-N-S 25-734-0711   (BR)
HOME DEPOT OF CANADA INC
HOME DEPOT
(*Suby of* THE HOME DEPOT INC)
6550 200 St, Langley, BC, V2Y 1P2
(604) 514-1788
Emp Here 250
SIC 5251 Hardware stores
Kevin Kappeli

D-U-N-S 24-446-9300   (HQ)
HOMELIFE BENCHMARK REALTY CORP
6323 197 St, Langley, BC, V2Y 1K8
(604) 530-4141
Emp Here 3   *Sales* 84,516,000
SIC 6531 Real estate agents and managers
Colin Dreyer
Rick Dubord
Robert Bontkes

D-U-N-S 20-276-9832   (SL)
IHAUL FREIGHT LTD
105-8047 199 St, Langley, BC, V2Y 0E2
(604) 594-4100
Emp Here 80   *Sales* 41,597,360
SIC 4731 Freight transportation arrangement
Harpreet Maroke
Rashminder Josan
Kanwardeep Rattanpaul

D-U-N-S 24-202-8137   (SL)
IRONCLAD METALS INC
6325 204 St Unit 312, Langley, BC, V2Y 3B3
(604) 539-0112
Emp Here 60   *Sales* 34,220,280
SIC 1542 Nonresidential construction, nec
Bruce Dick
Anthony Toews

D-U-N-S 24-337-1122   (BR)
**LANGLEY, CORPORATION OF THE TOWN-
SHIP OF**
*TOWNSHIP OF LANGLEY FIRE DEPART-
MENT*
(*Suby of* LANGLEY, CORPORATION OF THE
TOWNSHIP OF)
22170 50 Ave, Langley, BC, V2Y 2V4
(604) 532-7500
Emp Here 190
SIC 7389 Business services, nec
Stephen Gamble

D-U-N-S 20-921-1820   (HQ)
**M. VAN NOORT & SONS BULB COMPANY
LIMITED**
22264 No 10 Hwy, Langley, BC, V2Y 2K6
(604) 888-6555
Sales 37,126,000
SIC 5193 Flowers and florists supplies
Carl Van Noort

D-U-N-S 20-768-6742   (SL)
MAUREEN KLEIN
HERB & MAUREEN KLEIN
19925 Willowbrook Dr Unit 110, Langley, BC,
V2Y 1A7
(604) 530-0231
Emp Here 49   *Sales* 13,316,044
SIC 6531 Real estate agents and managers
Maureen Klein

D-U-N-S 20-806-6894   (HQ)
MOPAC AUTO SUPPLY LTD
MOPAC PERFORMANCE DISTRIBUTERS
19950 84 Ave Suite 596, Langley, BC, V2Y
3C2
(604) 881-4900
Emp Here 43   *Sales* 32,864,381

SIC 7538 General automotive repair shops
John Duda
Kathleen Duda
Rick Duda
Axel Ahrens

D-U-N-S 25-369-9284   (SL)
**MOTOR DEALER COUNCIL OF BRITISH
COLUMBIA**
*MOTOR VEHICLE SALES AUTHORITY OF
BRITISH COLUMBIA*
8029 199 St Suite 280, Langley, BC, V2Y 0E2
(604) 574-5050
Emp Here 46   *Sales* 18,281,044
SIC 8699 Membership organizations, nec
Ellen Laoha

D-U-N-S 20-350-9997   (SL)
NEWMARK GROUP INC
(*Suby of* NEWMARK HOLDINGS CORP)
20780 Willoughby Town Centre Dr Unit 300,
Langley, BC, V2Y 0M7
(604) 371-3963
Emp Here 47   *Sales* 22,406,874
SIC 1531 Operative builders
Mark Chandler

D-U-N-S 25-733-9143   (BR)
**PEPPERS, SAMMY J GOURMET GRILL
AND BAR**
(*Suby of* PEPPERS, SAMMY J GOURMET
GRILL AND BAR)
19925 Willowbrook Dr Suite 101, Langley, BC,
V2Y 1A7
(604) 514-0224
Emp Here 75
SIC 5812 Eating places
Mike Gardner

D-U-N-S 24-310-6791   (HQ)
PHARMASAVE DRUGS (NATIONAL) LTD
PHARMASAVE
8411 200 St Suite 201, Langley, BC, V2Y 0E7
(604) 455-2400
Emp Here 5   *Sales* 56,784,420
SIC 6794 Patent owners and lessors

D-U-N-S 20-956-3626   (HQ)
POWER TO CHANGE MINISTRIES
20385 64 Ave, Langley, BC, V2Y 1N5
(604) 514-2000
Emp Here 150   *Sales* 34,920,900
SIC 8661 Religious organizations
Hugh Little
Don Van Meer
Reg Allatt
Mark Peterson
Bruce Chandler
Don Voth
Lorne Plette
Leonard Buhler

D-U-N-S 24-897-4826   (HQ)
PREMIER SCHOOL AGENDAS LTD
*SCHOOL SPECIALTY CANADA PREMIER
AGENDAS*
20230 64 Ave Unit 103, Langley, BC, V2Y 1N3
(604) 857-1707
Emp Here 40   *Sales* 19,546,240
SIC 5999 Miscellaneous retail stores, nec
Dave Loeppky
Phil Minderhoud

D-U-N-S 24-326-4053   (BR)
**PREMIUM BRANDS OPERATING LIMITED
PARTNERSHIP**
GRIMM'S FINE FOODS
(*Suby of* PREMIUM BRANDS HOLDINGS
CORPORATION)
8621 201 St Suite 120, Langley, BC, V2Y 0G9
(866) 663-4746
Emp Here 180
SIC 2013 Sausages and other prepared
meats
Rick Grim

D-U-N-S 25-387-5959   (SL)

RE/MAX TREELAND REALTY (1992) LTD
6337 198 St Suite 101, Langley, BC, V2Y 2E3
(604) 533-3491
Emp Here 89   *Sales* 24,186,284
SIC 6531 Real estate agents and managers
Verne Gatzke

D-U-N-S 20-424-5245   (HQ)
REMPEL BROS. CONCRETE LTD
20353 64 Ave Unit 203, Langley, BC, V2Y 1N5
(604) 525-9344
Emp Here 25   *Sales* 35,843,800
SIC 3273 Ready-mixed concrete
James Brown
Stephen Roik
Robert Fairbank
Richard Lehingrat
Doug Blender
James Purcell
Bruce Luck
Richard Harper

D-U-N-S 20-115-4911   (HQ)
ROLLINS MACHINERY LIMITED
21869 56 Ave, Langley, BC, V2Y 2M9
(604) 533-0048
Emp Here 35   *Sales* 21,376,170
SIC 5084 Industrial machinery and equipment
Victor Rollins
Rod Graham

D-U-N-S 20-033-6746   (BR)
SCHOOL DISTRICT NO. 35 (LANGLEY)
LANGLEY SECONDARY SCHOOL
21405 56 Ave, Langley, BC, V2Y 2N1
(604) 534-7155
Emp Here 100
SIC 8211 Elementary and secondary schools
Dawn Tomlinson

D-U-N-S 25-271-1072   (BR)
SOBEYS WEST INC
SAFEWAY PHARMACY
(*Suby of* EMPIRE COMPANY LIMITED)
6153 200 St, Langley, BC, V2Y 1A2
(604) 530-6131
Emp Here 280
SIC 5411 Grocery stores
Lawrence Heisler

D-U-N-S 24-174-1284   (BR)
SODEXO CANADA LTD
(*Suby of* SODEXO)
7600 Glover Rd, Langley, BC, V2Y 1Y1
(604) 513-2009
Emp Here 80
SIC 5812 Eating places
Ray Young

D-U-N-S 25-968-7358   (SL)
SPORTS-CAN INSURANCE CONSUL-TANTS LTD
8411 200 St Suite 103, Langley, BC, V2Y 0E7
(604) 888-0050
Emp Here 18   *Sales* 13,057,902
SIC 6351 Surety insurance
Mark Woodall

D-U-N-S 24-320-4621   (BR)
STANDARD AERO LIMITED
(*Suby of* STANDARDAERO AVIATION HOLD-INGS, INC.)
21330 56 Ave Unit 48, Langley, BC, V2Y 0E5
(604) 514-0388
Emp Here 85
SIC 4581 Airports, flying fields, and services
Ranjeet Singh

D-U-N-S 20-867-5483   (BR)
SUTTON GROUP - WEST COAST REALTY
(*Suby of* SUTTON GROUP - WEST COAST REALTY)
19653 Willowbrook Dr Unit 156, Langley, BC, V2Y 1A5
(604) 533-3939
Emp Here 84
SIC 6361 Title insurance

Suzanne Carswell

D-U-N-S 20-314-4233   (SL)
TAG CONSTRUCTION LTD
21869 56 Ave Unit B, Langley, BC, V2Y 2M9
(604) 534-2685
Emp Here 60   *Sales* 15,146,520
SIC 1623 Water, sewer, and utility lines
Michael Grant

D-U-N-S 24-851-1599   (HQ)
TLTC HOLDINGS INC
6270 205 St, Langley, BC, V2Y 1N7
(604) 533-3294
Sales 18,042,970
SIC 2759 Commercial printing, nec
John Attayak

D-U-N-S 24-348-5567   (BR)
TORBRAM ELECTRIC SUPPLY CORPORA-TION
6360 202 St Suite 103, Langley, BC, V2Y 1N2
(604) 539-9331
Emp Here 90
SIC 5063 Electrical apparatus and equipment
Gareth Robertshaw

D-U-N-S 20-064-2606   (SL)
TREELAND REALTY LTD
RE/MAX TREELAND
6337 198 St Suite 101, Langley, BC, V2Y 2E3
(604) 533-3491
Emp Here 45   *Sales* 12,229,020
SIC 6531 Real estate agents and managers

D-U-N-S 24-134-9125   (SL)
TRINITY WESTERN UNIVERSITY
7600 Glover Rd, Langley, BC, V2Y 1Y1
(604) 888-7511
Emp Here 450   *Sales* 67,225,950
SIC 8221 Colleges and universities
Sheldon Perry
Jonathan Raymond
Dale Clark
Marilyn Crone

D-U-N-S 20-275-9648   (SL)
UTOPIA DAY SPAS & SALONS LTD
SPA UTOPIA & SALON
20486 64 Ave Unit 106, Langley, BC, V2Y 2V5
(604) 539-8772
Emp Here 90   *Sales* 6,875,730
SIC 7991 Physical fitness facilities
Awni Abu-Ulba

D-U-N-S 20-187-9975   (BR)
WAL-MART CANADA CORP
WALMART TIRE & LUBE EXPRESS
(*Suby of* WALMART INC.)
20202 66 Ave, Langley, BC, V2Y 1P3
(604) 539-5210
Emp Here 175
SIC 5531 Auto and home supply stores
Dean White

D-U-N-S 24-838-1071   (HQ)
WILLOW FUN WORLD LTD
WILLOW VIDEO GAMES
19609 Willowbrook Dr Unit 2, Langley, BC, V2Y 1A5
(604) 530-5324
Emp Here 10   *Sales* 13,013,550
SIC 5092 Toys and hobby goods and supplies
Steve Vilio
Eric Vilio
Glen Vilio

Langley, BC V2Z

D-U-N-S 20-773-8100   (SL)
C & K HAPPY FARMS LTD
22950 16 Ave, Langley, BC, V2Z 1K7
(604) 533-8307
Emp Here 31   *Sales* 10,739,436
SIC 0191 General farms, primarily crop

Yeong-Fang Kuo

D-U-N-S 24-310-0476   (SL)
COUNTRY LUMBER LTD
22538 Fraser Hwy, Langley, BC, V2Z 2T8
(604) 533-4447
Emp Here 110   *Sales* 107,171,820
SIC 5211 Lumber and other building materials
Ron Hann
Ken Humphrey
Bruce Vandanbrink
Brian Wierks
Glenn Jenkins
Scott Rexworthy
Ron Davidson

D-U-N-S 24-897-2507   (SL)
DOMAINE DE CHABERTON ESTATES LTD
CHABERTON ESTATE WINERY
1064 216 St, Langley, BC, V2Z 1R3
(604) 530-1736
Emp Here 50   *Sales* 11,242,750
SIC 2084 Wines, brandy, and brandy spirits
Eugene Kwan
Anthony Cheng

D-U-N-S 25-497-4033   (HQ)
HIGHLINE MUSHROOMS WEST LIMITED
3392 224 St, Langley, BC, V2Z 2G8
(604) 534-0278
Emp Here 50   *Sales* 25,353,750
SIC 0191 General farms, primarily crop
Aaron Hamer
Glenn Martin
Enda Walsh

D-U-N-S 20-087-5867   (BR)
LANGLEY, CORPORATION OF THE TOWN-SHIP OF
(*Suby of* LANGLEY, CORPORATION OF THE TOWNSHIP OF)
4700 224 St, Langley, BC, V2Z 1N4
(604) 532-7300
Emp Here 250
SIC 6111 Federal and federally sponsored credit agencies
Rene Payer

D-U-N-S 20-988-4381   (SL)
NICOMEKL ENHANCEMENT SOCIETY
5263 232 St, Langley, BC, V2Z 2P8
(604) 539-2486
Emp Here 49   *Sales* 18,890,431
SIC 0273 Animal aquaculture
Drew Waska

D-U-N-S 24-974-8260   (BR)
SCHOOL DISTRICT NO. 35 (LANGLEY)
D W POPPY SECONDARY SCHOOL
23752 52 Ave, Langley, BC, V2Z 2P3
(604) 530-2151
Emp Here 90
SIC 8211 Elementary and secondary schools
Balan Moorthy

D-U-N-S 20-766-2417   (SL)
TANSEY INSURANCE SERVICE LTD
4769 222 St Unit 103, Langley, BC, V2Z 3C1
(604) 539-7783
Emp Here 30   *Sales* 31,046,430
SIC 6311 Life insurance
Bill Tansey

D-U-N-S 20-862-3368   (SL)
UNDERCOVER WEAR FASHIONS & LIN-GERIE
4888 236 St, Langley, BC, V2Z 2S5

Emp Here 200   *Sales* 35,879,200
SIC 5632 Women's accessory and specialty stores
Yvonne Habart

Langley, BC V3A

D-U-N-S 24-291-1519   (SL)
414067 B.C. LTD
LANGLEY TOYOTATOWN
20622 Langley Bypass, Langley, BC, V3A 6K8
(604) 530-3156
Emp Here 60   *Sales* 33,082,720
SIC 5511 New and used car dealers
Scott Kemp
Thomas Kemp

D-U-N-S 25-150-6002   (SL)
598755 B.C. LTD
ACURA OF LANGLEY
20257 Langley Bypass, Langley, BC, V3A 6K9
(604) 539-2111
Emp Here 30   *Sales* 14,942,340
SIC 5511 New and used car dealers
Ajay Dalawri
Christian Dubois

D-U-N-S 20-004-9265   (SL)
APPLEWOOD MOTORS INC
APPLEWOOD KIA
(*Suby of* SCOCHI HOLDINGS INC)
19764 Langley Bypass, Langley, BC, V3A 7B1
(604) 533-7881
Emp Here 100   *Sales* 62,928,000
SIC 5511 New and used car dealers
Darren Graham

D-U-N-S 20-913-3636   (HQ)
BOARD OF EDUCATION OF SCHOOL DIS-TRICT NO. 35 (LANGLEY)
LANGLEY SCHOOL DISTRICT 35
4875 222 St, Langley, BC, V3A 3Z7
(604) 534-7891
Sales 218,061,800
SIC 8211 Elementary and secondary schools

D-U-N-S 24-931-1234   (SL)
CANDAN ENTERPRISES LTD
CANDAN RV CENTER
20257 Langley Bypass, Langley, BC, V3A 6K9
(604) 530-3645
Emp Here 30   *Sales* 14,942,340
SIC 5571 Motorcycle dealers
Steen Salomon
Anne Salomon

D-U-N-S 24-133-6023   (BR)
CKF INC
(*Suby of* SCOTIA INVESTMENTS LIMITED)
19878 57a Ave, Langley, BC, V3A 6G6
(604) 530-9121
Emp Here 150
SIC 2821 Plastics materials and resins
Rick Eberest

D-U-N-S 20-099-4853   (SL)
CROSS & NORMAN (1986) LTD
LANGLEY VOLKSWAGEN
20027 Fraser Hwy, Langley, BC, V3A 4E4
(604) 534-7927
Emp Here 23   *Sales* 11,455,794
SIC 5511 New and used car dealers

D-U-N-S 24-248-5308   (HQ)
DELCO FIREPLACES LTD
20679 Langley Bypass, Langley, BC, V3A 5E8
(604) 530-2166
Sales 17,809,960
SIC 5023 Homefurnishings
Eric Lewtas
Denise Lewtas

D-U-N-S 20-321-2766   (HQ)
DRYCO BUILDING SUPPLIES INC
5955 205a St, Langley, BC, V3A 8C4
(604) 533-2313
Emp Here 120   *Sales* 113,925,600
SIC 5039 Construction materials, nec
Jim Ritchie

D-U-N-S 25-414-2896   (HQ)
E.E. ENGRAVER'S EXPRESS INC
20381 62 Ave Suite 705, Langley, BC, V3A

5E6
(604) 533-3467
Emp Here 11   Sales 10,450,572
SIC 5087 Service establishment equipment
Bruce King

D-U-N-S 20-802-5866   (BR)
ECCO HEATING PRODUCTS LTD
ECCO MANUFACTURING
(*Suby of* ECCO HEATING PRODUCTS LTD)
19860 Fraser Hwy, Langley, BC, V3A 4C9
(604) 530-4151
Emp Here 100
SIC 3567 Industrial furnaces and ovens
Ken Nolan

D-U-N-S 24-034-4189   (SL)
EJ ENTERPRISE
HA-RA PRODUCTS CANADA
20179 56 Ave, Langley, BC, V3A 3Y6
(604) 514-2224
Emp Here 30   Sales 14,250,780
SIC 5084 Industrial machinery and equipment
Jeff Lyon

D-U-N-S 24-272-4748   (HQ)
FOREWEST HOLDINGS INC
PHARMASAVE DRUGS, DIV OF
5769 201a St Unit 169, Langley, BC, V3A 8H9
(604) 514-8303
Emp Here 14   Sales 70,266,275
SIC 5912 Drug stores and proprietary stores

D-U-N-S 20-528-5617   (SL)
GRAND CONSTRUCTION LTD
4539 210a St, Langley, BC, V3A 8Z3
(604) 530-1931
Emp Here 40   Sales 18,829,240
SIC 1542 Nonresidential construction, nec
Andrew Guran
Eric Guran

D-U-N-S 24-897-9361   (SL)
HOLLSHOP IMPORTS LTD
20215 62 Ave Unit 102, Langley, BC, V3A 5E6
(604) 533-8822
Emp Here 20   Sales 10,702,480
SIC 5141 Groceries, general line
Bram Eigenraam

D-U-N-S 25-301-2421   (BR)
HUDSON'S BAY COMPANY
(*Suby of* HUDSON'S BAY COMPANY)
19705 Fraser Hwy Suite 320, Langley, BC,
V3A 7E9
(604) 530-8434
Emp Here 170
SIC 5311 Department stores
Kapil Sharma

D-U-N-S 25-272-7474   (BR)
INSURANCE CORPORATION OF BRITISH COLUMBIA
I C B C
(*Suby of* GOVERNMENT OF THE PROVINCE OF BRITISH COLUMBIA)
6000 Production Way, Langley, BC, V3A 6L5
(604) 530-7111
Emp Here 100
SIC 6331 Fire, marine, and casualty insurance
Ian Wood

D-U-N-S 24-593-9194   (BR)
IPEX INC
IPEX MANAGEMENT
(*Suby of* ALIAXIS)
20460 Duncan Way, Langley, BC, V3A 7A3
(604) 534-8631
Emp Here 110
SIC 3088 Plastics plumbing fixtures
Terry Mintern

D-U-N-S 24-370-6405   (BR)
KWANTLEN POLYTECHNIC UNIVERSITY FOUNDATION
KWANTLEN POLYTECHNIC UNIVERSITY
(*Suby of* KWANTLEN POLYTECHNIC UNIVERSITY FOUNDATION)

20901 Langley Bypass, Langley, BC, V3A 8G9
(604) 599-2100
Emp Here 300
SIC 8222 Junior colleges
Skip Triplett

D-U-N-S 20-867-5918   (SL)
LANGLEY CARE SOCIETY
LANGLEY LODGE
5451 204 St, Langley, BC, V3A 5M9
(604) 530-2305
Emp Here 120   Sales 8,199,120
SIC 8051 Skilled nursing care facilities
Werner Pauls

D-U-N-S 24-502-7784   (SL)
LANGLEY TIMES PUBLISHING CO
20258 Fraser Hwy, Langley, BC, V3A 4E6
(604) 533-4157
Emp Here 85   Sales 13,942,295
SIC 2711 Newspapers
Dwayne Weidendorf

D-U-N-S 25-215-4208   (SL)
MAPLE LEAF DISPOSAL LTD
20380 Langley Bypass, Langley, BC, V3A 5E7
(604) 533-4993
Emp Here 70   Sales 17,999,170
SIC 4953 Refuse systems
Doug Mass

D-U-N-S 20-374-7691   (SL)
MARCON CONSTRUCTION LTD
5645 199 St, Langley, BC, V3A 1H9
(604) 530-5646
Emp Here 100   Sales 23,428,800
SIC 8742 Management consulting services
Marco Paolella

D-U-N-S 25-318-2067   (BR)
MCDONALD'S   RESTAURANTS   OF CANADA LIMITED
MCDONALD'S #8187
(*Suby of* MCDONALD'S CORPORATION)
19780 Fraser Hwy, Langley, BC, V3A 4C9
(604) 514-1820
Emp Here 110
SIC 5812 Eating places
Chris Stewart

D-U-N-S 20-114-2726   (HQ)
NATIONAL GLASS LTD
(*Suby of* Z. & R. HOLDINGS LTD)
5744 198 St, Langley, BC, V3A 7J2
(604) 530-2311
Sales 17,921,900
SIC 3231 Products of purchased glass
Martin Nixon
Rosette Yehia

D-U-N-S 20-800-9019   (SL)
NEWLANDS GOLF & COUNTRY CLUB LTD
21025 48 Ave, Langley, BC, V3A 3M3
(604) 534-3205
Emp Here 150   Sales 16,017,300
SIC 7299 Miscellaneous personal service
Judy Davies
Raoul Anderson

D-U-N-S 20-789-9811   (SL)
OLIVE GARDEN ITALIAN RESTAURANT
20080 Langley Bypass, Langley, BC, V3A 9J7
(604) 514-3499
Emp Here 130   Sales 6,063,070
SIC 5812 Eating places
Monique Gleig

D-U-N-S 24-657-0972   (HQ)
PACIFIC RADIATOR MFG. LTD
PACIFIC RADIATOR MFG
20579 Langley Bypass Suite 203, Langley, BC, V3A 5E8
(604) 534-7555
Sales 12,311,365
SIC 3714 Motor vehicle parts and accessories
Bob Friesen

D-U-N-S 24-446-7676   (HQ)

PACIFIC WEST SYSTEMS SUPPLY LTD
20109 Logan Ave, Langley, BC, V3A 4L5
(604) 530-7489
Emp Here 3   Sales 141,837,372
SIC 5039 Construction materials, nec
Jack Sentla

D-U-N-S 24-339-7648   (SL)
PRESTON   CHEVROLET   BUICK   GMC CADILLAC LTD
19990 Langley Bypass, Langley, BC, V3A 4Y1
(604) 534-4154
Emp Here 80   Sales 50,342,400
SIC 5511 New and used car dealers
Robert Wolfe
Peter Heppner

D-U-N-S 25-990-3185   (HQ)
PRO-LINE   CONSTRUCTION   MATERIALS LTD
20109 Logan Ave, Langley, BC, V3A 4L5
(604) 534-2060
Emp Here 4   Sales 18,781,308
SIC 5033 Roofing, siding, and insulation
Jack Sentla
Don Macaulay
Andy Mrak

D-U-N-S 24-939-3950   (SL)
R.D.M. ENTERPRISES LTD
20436 Fraser Hwy Unit 207, Langley, BC, V3A 4G2
(604) 530-6310
Emp Here 70   Sales 17,233,020
SIC 1794 Excavation work
Ron Madsen

D-U-N-S 24-982-6202   (SL)
RS LINE CONSTRUCTION INC
5680 Production Way, Langley, BC, V3A 4N4
(778) 278-7000
Emp Here 65   Sales 16,408,730
SIC 1623 Water, sewer, and utility lines
Robert Smith
Mitch Gunter

D-U-N-S 25-797-6720   (SL)
SCHMUNK GATT SMITH & ASSOCIATES
20334 56 Ave Suite 204, Langley, BC, V3A 3Y7
(604) 533-9813
Emp Here 10   Sales 10,348,810
SIC 6311 Life insurance
Robert Schmunk

D-U-N-S 20-013-2335   (HQ)
SCOCHI HOLDINGS INC
19820 Fraser Hwy, Langley, BC, V3A 4C9
(604) 533-7881
Emp Here 1   Sales 15,938,496
SIC 5511 New and used car dealers
Darren Graham

D-U-N-S 24-957-2942   (HQ)
SPECIALTY POLYMER COATINGS INC
(*Suby of* RPM INTERNATIONAL INC.)
20529 62 Ave Suite 104, Langley, BC, V3A 8R4
(604) 514-9711
Emp Here 27   Sales 16,189,197
SIC 2851 Paints and allied products
Jane Lang
George R Alliston
Sharon Alliston
Christopher Alliston
Robert Alliston

D-U-N-S 20-099-6148   (SL)
TECK CONSTRUCTION LTD
5197 216 St, Langley, BC, V3A 2N4
(604) 534-7917
Emp Here 40   Sales 18,829,240
SIC 1542 Nonresidential construction, nec
Alfons Tecklenborg
Marilyn Tecklenborg

D-U-N-S 20-384-8429   (SL)
TEL-PAL COMM INC

20316 56 Ave Suite 225, Langley, BC, V3A 3Y7
(250) 202-8770
Emp Here 1   Sales 216,021,149
SIC 4813 Telephone communication, except radio
Babar Romail

D-U-N-S 20-513-5130   (HQ)
THIESSEN EQUIPMENT LTD
20131 Logan Ave, Langley, BC, V3A 4L5
(604) 532-8611
Emp Here 12   Sales 26,126,430
SIC 5082 Construction and mining machinery
Lawrence R. Thiessen

D-U-N-S 24-778-4796   (HQ)
TRAVELAND LEISURE VEHICLES LTD
TRAVELAND RV SUPERCENTRE
20529 Langley Bypass, Langley, BC, V3A 5E8
(604) 530-8141
Sales 40,903,200
SIC 5561 Recreational vehicle dealers
Gordon Bird
Dale Howes

D-U-N-S 25-715-2009   (SL)
TRAVELAND R.V. RENTALS LTD
CANDAN R.V. CENTER
(*Suby of* TRAVELAND LEISURE VEHICLES LTD)
20257 Langley Bypass, Langley, BC, V3A 6K9
(604) 532-8128
Emp Here 25   Sales 15,732,000
SIC 5571 Motorcycle dealers
Gary Dumbrell

D-U-N-S 24-738-8668   (SL)
TRENDWEST
20258 Fraser Hwy Suite 104, Langley, BC, V3A 4E6
(604) 534-5044
Emp Here 35   Sales 11,587,667
SIC 5999 Miscellaneous retail stores, nec
Ken Kemp

D-U-N-S 24-888-1161   (SL)
VISION PLASTICS INC
5800 Production Way, Langley, BC, V3A 4N4
(604) 530-1882
Emp Here 60   Sales 12,113,820
SIC 3089 Plastics products, nec
Thomas Simmons

D-U-N-S 24-882-3403   (BR)
WELDCO-BEALES MFG. ALBERTA LTD
WELDCO-BEALES MANUFACTURING
(*Suby of* WELDCO-BEALES MFG. ALBERTA LTD)
5770 Production Way, Langley, BC, V3A 4N4
(604) 533-8933
Emp Here 120
SIC 3531 Construction machinery
John Folkers

D-U-N-S 20-799-7123   (HQ)
WESTERN OIL SERVICES LTD
19840 57a Ave, Langley, BC, V3A 6G6
(604) 514-4787
Emp Here 25   Sales 15,200,832
SIC 5084 Industrial machinery and equipment
Robin Bateman

D-U-N-S 24-136-0387   (SL)
WILLOWBROOK MOTORS LTD
WILLOWBROOK CHRYSLER
19611 Langley Bypass, Langley, BC, V3A 4K8
(604) 530-7361
Emp Here 30   Sales 14,942,340
SIC 5511 New and used car dealers
Douglas Seal

D-U-N-S 20-835-2331   (HQ)
YOUTH FOR CHRIST CANADA
19705 Fraser Hwy Unit 135, Langley, BC, V3A 7E9

Emp Here 1   Sales 19,870,700

▲ Public Company   ■ Public Company Family Member   **HQ** Headquarters   **BR** Branch   **SL** Single Location

SIC 8699 Membership organizations, nec
Shirley Loewen

D-U-N-S 24-349-2183   (HQ)
Z. & R. HOLDINGS LTD
5744 198 St, Langley, BC, V3A 7J2
(604) 530-2311
Sales 14,006,100
SIC 3231 Products of purchased glass
Marty Nixon

Langley, BC V3W

D-U-N-S 25-241-1439   (SL)
TCBC HOLDINGS INC
TIRECRAFT AUTO CENTER
26712 Bloucester Way Suite 203, Langley, BC,
V3W 3V6
(604) 626-4412
Emp Here 40   *Sales* 19,923,120
SIC 5531 Auto and home supply stores
Frank Endersty

Langley, BC V4W

D-U-N-S 20-110-9733   (HQ)
A.K. DRAFT SEAL LTD
DS GROUP, THE
100-4825 275 St, Langley, BC, V4W 0C7
(604) 451-1080
Emp Here 45   *Sales* 10,141,500
SIC 3442 Metal doors, sash, and trim
Christopher Kamensek

D-U-N-S 24-374-4323   (SL)
**ADVANCED BENDING TECHNOLOGIES
INC**
(*Suby of* ADVANTEC GLOBAL INNOVA-
TIONS INC)
27372 Gloucester Way, Langley, BC, V4W 4A1
(604) 856-6220
Emp Here 28   *Sales* 12,520,872
SIC 5051 Metals service centers and offices
Brad Miller
Rod Pare

D-U-N-S 25-814-6299   (SL)
ADVANCED STEEL STRUCTURES INC
5250 272 St, Langley, BC, V4W 1S3
(604) 626-4211
Emp Here 100   *Sales* 24,618,600
SIC 1791 Structural steel erection
Dennis Winton

D-U-N-S 20-257-2541   (SL)
AFD PROCESSING LTD
(*Suby of* ALLIANCE FREEZE DRY LTD)
5292 272 St, Langley, BC, V4W 1S3
(604) 856-3886
Emp Here 75   *Sales* 7,834,770
SIC 2034 Dried and dehydrated fruits, vegeta-
bles and soup mixes
Guang Xu
Yi Xing Wang

D-U-N-S 20-511-2931   (SL)
AGGRESSIVE TRANSPORT LTD
5111 272 St, Langley, BC, V4W 3Z2
(604) 626-4511
Emp Here 100   *Sales* 14,819,200
SIC 4213 Trucking, except local
Dave Macdonald

D-U-N-S 24-639-5826   (SL)
CANADIAN HEATING PRODUCTS INC
MONTIGO DELRAY
27342 Gloucester Way, Langley, BC, V4W 4A1
(604) 607-6422
Emp Here 60   *Sales* 11,525,100
SIC 3429 Hardware, nec
Daniel Binzer

D-U-N-S 25-417-8189   (BR)
CINTAS CANADA LIMITED
(*Suby of* CINTAS CORPORATION)
5293 272 St, Langley, BC, V4W 1P1
(604) 857-2281
Emp Here 160
SIC 7218 Industrial launderers
Rod Farquharson

D-U-N-S 20-806-0152   (HQ)
**CLEARVIEW HORTICULTURAL PROD-
UCTS INC**
5343a 264 St Suite 1, Langley, BC, V4W 1J7
(604) 856-6131
Sales 16,280,000
SIC 5992 Florists
Fred Wein Sr
Sidney Mary Wein
Frederick Wein Jr
Robert Wein

D-U-N-S 20-510-0365   (HQ)
**EDDI'S WHOLESALE GARDEN SUPPLIES
LTD**
(*Suby of* HYDROFARM, LLC)
5744 268 St, Langley, BC, V4W 0B2
(604) 607-4447
Emp Here 35   *Sales* 10,881,537
SIC 5261 Retail nurseries and garden stores
Edward Les
Diane Les

D-U-N-S 20-209-1612   (HQ)
EV LOGISTICS
5111 272 St, Langley, BC, V4W 3Z2
(604) 857-6750
Sales 110,628,600
SIC 4213 Trucking, except local
Dave Martin

D-U-N-S 20-554-0235   (BR)
EV LOGISTICS
EV LOGISTICS PERISHABLES
(*Suby of* EV LOGISTICS)
5111 272 St, Langley, BC, V4W 3Z2
(604) 857-6750
Emp Here 260
SIC 4225 General warehousing and storage

D-U-N-S 20-111-5789   (HQ)
FG DELI GROUP LTD
(*Suby of* PREMIUM BRANDS HOLDINGS
CORPORATION)
27101 56 Ave, Langley, BC, V4W 3Y4
(604) 607-7426
Emp Here 250   *Sales* 170,584,750
SIC 2011 Meat packing plants
Henning Freybe
Sven Freybe

D-U-N-S 25-234-3256   (BR)
**GENERAL MOTORS OF CANADA COM-
PANY**
GM OF CANADA LANGLEY
(*Suby of* GENERAL MOTORS COMPANY)
27475 58 Cres, Langley, BC, V4W 3W3
(604) 857-5277
Emp Here 75
SIC 5013 Motor vehicle supplies and new
parts
Terry Hnidy

D-U-N-S 24-929-5445   (HQ)
HARDY SALES (ALBERTA) LTD
27417 Gloucester Way, Langley, BC, V4W 3Z8
(604) 856-3911
Sales 29,245,195
SIC 5147 Meats and meat products
Steve Hardy

D-U-N-S 24-776-9292   (SL)
HARDY SALES LTD
HARDY SALES
27417 Gloucester Way, Langley, BC, V4W 3Z8
(604) 856-3911
Emp Here 30   *Sales* 25,067,310
SIC 5147 Meats and meat products

Steve Hardy
Gerry Hardy

D-U-N-S 24-696-3029   (HQ)
HUER FOODS INC
5543 275 St, Langley, BC, V4W 3X9
(604) 626-4888
Emp Here 25   *Sales* 25,067,310
SIC 5145 Confectionery
Ryan Storey

D-U-N-S 24-394-9331   (SL)
**IEM INDUSTRIAL ELECTRIC MFG.
(CANADA) INC**
IEM CANADA
(*Suby of* ABD EL & LARSON HOLDINGS,
LLC)
27353 58 Cres Unit 201, Langley, BC, V4W
3W7
(866) 302-9836
Emp Here 23   *Sales* 10,285,002
SIC 5063 Electrical apparatus and equipment
Edward Rossi
Doug Kristensen
Guy Anderson
Edward Herman

D-U-N-S 25-734-3871   (SL)
INFINITY SPORTS GROUP LTD, THE
27452 52 Ave, Langley, BC, V4W 4B2

Emp Here 30   *Sales* 15,616,260
SIC 5091 Sporting and recreation goods
Nigel Hogarth
James Prescott

D-U-N-S 25-974-4811   (SL)
INTERNATIONAL PLAY COMPANY INC
IPLAYCO
(*Suby of* PLAY PLANET SRL)
27353 58 Cres Unit 215, Langley, BC, V4W
3W7
(604) 607-1111
Emp Here 50   *Sales* 16,306,800
SIC 3949 Sporting and athletic goods, nec
Scott Forbes
Dave Romano

D-U-N-S 25-148-2030   (HQ)
IPLAYCO CORPORATION LTD
(*Suby of* PLAY PLANET SRL)
27353 58 Cres Unit 215, Langley, BC, V4W
3W7
(604) 607-1111
Sales 15,917,158
SIC 3949 Sporting and athletic goods, nec
Scott C Forbes
Max Liszkowski
David Romano
Muhanad Awad
Craig Williams
Shaun Kriel
Sultan Alhokair
Zaher Fattouh
Mel Barsky
John Plumpton

D-U-N-S 25-216-1401   (SL)
K-LINE TRAILERS LTD
27360 58 Cres, Langley, BC, V4W 3W7
(604) 856-7899
Emp Here 180   *Sales* 40,291,740
SIC 3715 Truck trailers
Les Knight
Alex Ma

D-U-N-S 25-219-6100   (SL)
KINETICS DRIVE SOLUTIONS INC
(*Suby of* ST ENGINEERING LAND SYS-
TEMS LTD.)
27489 56 Ave, Langley, BC, V4W 3X1
(604) 607-8877
Emp Here 75   *Sales* 16,788,225
SIC 3714 Motor vehicle parts and accessories
Chi Jui Mah
Gordon Osborn
Paul Dries

D-U-N-S 25-290-6516   (SL)
MADE-RITE MEAT PRODUCTS INC
26656 56 Ave, Langley, BC, V4W 3X5
(604) 607-8844
Emp Here 65   *Sales* 22,469,850
SIC 2013 Sausages and other prepared
meats
Norm Campbell
Douglas Campbell

D-U-N-S 25-655-5756   (HQ)
MTF MAINLAND DISTRIBUTORS INC
MTF PRICE MATTERS
(*Suby of* MVF INVESTMENT FUND INC)
26868 56 Ave Unit 101, Langley, BC, V4W
1N9
(604) 626-4465
Emp Here 40   *Sales* 41,068,600
SIC 5399 Miscellaneous general merchandise
Mark Funk
Norman Dyck
James Huth

D-U-N-S 24-557-9396   (HQ)
NORTHWEST TANK LINES INC
7025 272 St, Langley, BC, V4W 1R3
(604) 856-6666
Emp Here 10   *Sales* 14,819,200
SIC 4213 Trucking, except local
Thomas G. Blaney
Tony Mcmurchy

D-U-N-S 20-563-4251   (BR)
**OLDCASTLE BUILDING PRODUCTS
CANADA, INC**
*MATERIAUX DE CONSTRUCTION OLDCAS-
TLE CANADA INC, LES*
(*Suby of* CRH PUBLIC LIMITED COMPANY)
5075 275 St, Langley, BC, V4W 0A8
(604) 607-1300
Emp Here 130
SIC 3211 Flat glass
Chris Boswell

D-U-N-S 20-093-5203   (HQ)
OTTER FARM & HOME CO-OPERATIVE
OTTER CO-OP
3650 248 St, Langley, BC, V4W 1X7
(604) 607-6924
Emp Here 156   *Sales* 156,550,812
SIC 5191 Farm supplies
Jack Nicholson
Mike Will
Eduardo Fuentes
Kristin Zehnder
Bruno Accili

D-U-N-S 25-098-1594   (SL)
PACIFIC COAST DISTRIBUTION LTD
27433 52 Ave, Langley, BC, V4W 4B2
(604) 888-8489
Emp Here 55   *Sales* 28,598,185
SIC 4731 Freight transportation arrangement
Ted Pozniak

D-U-N-S 20-624-0335   (SL)
PAZMAC ENTERPRISES LTD
26777 Gloucester Way, Langley, BC, V4W 3X6
(604) 857-8838
Emp Here 70   *Sales* 15,540,070
SIC 3599 Industrial machinery, nec
Tim Walls

D-U-N-S 24-855-8389   (SL)
PEDRE CONTRACTORS LTD
26620 56 Ave Unit 101, Langley, BC, V4W 3X5
(604) 881-2411
Emp Here 50   *Sales* 12,044,200
SIC 1623 Water, sewer, and utility lines
Ronald H. Cicuto

D-U-N-S 20-802-8563   (HQ)
REGAL BELOIT CANADA ULC
THOMSON POWER SYSTEMS
(*Suby of* REGAL BELOIT CORPORATION)
4916 275 St, Langley, BC, V4W 0A3
(604) 888-0110
Emp Here 156   *Sales* 31,232,488

SIC 3625 Relays and industrial controls
Norm Schmidt

D-U-N-S 24-979-9040   (SL)
RELIABLE TUBE INC
26867 Gloucester Way, Langley, BC, V4W 3Y3
(604) 857-9861
Emp Here 24   *Sales* 10,732,176
SIC 5051 Metals service centers and offices
David Lyman
Ken Brenner
Robert Wharton

D-U-N-S 20-994-5864   (HQ)
RIMEX SUPPLY LTD
5929 274 St, Langley, BC, V4W 0B8
(604) 888-0025
Emp Here 80   *Sales* 116,340,000
SIC 3714 Motor vehicle parts and accessories
Derek Weston
Christopher Weston

D-U-N-S 20-958-6429   (HQ)
ROPAK CANADA INC
CAPILANO, DIV OF
(*Suby of* STONE CANYON INDUSTRIES
LLC)
5850 272 St, Langley, BC, V4W 3Z1
(604) 857-1177
Emp Here 150   *Sales* 119,406,000
SIC 3089 Plastics products, nec
Greg Toft
David A. Williams
James R. Dobell
Douglas Hugh Macdonald

D-U-N-S 25-416-5996   (SL)
SCAMP INDUSTRIES LTD
SCAMP TRANSPORT
26988 Gloucester Way, Langley, BC, V4W 3Y5
(604) 856-8211
Emp Here 104   *Sales* 21,393,424
SIC 4212 Local trucking, without storage
Stuart Campbell
Jay Campbell
Troy Campbell
Mark Dirksen
Rolf Guenther

D-U-N-S 24-656-9081   (SL)
SICOM INDUSTRIES LTD
27385 Gloucester Way, Langley, BC, V4W 3Z8
(604) 856-3455
Emp Here 67   *Sales* 21,794,864
SIC 3599 Industrial machinery, nec
Michael Chester

D-U-N-S 25-413-8464   (SL)
STUYVER'S BAKESTUDIO
27353 58 Cres Unit 101, Langley, BC, V4W
3W7
(604) 607-7760
Emp Here 60   *Sales* 20,741,400
SIC 2051 Bread, cake, and related products
Aziz Dossa

D-U-N-S 20-560-9642   (HQ)
TRITECH GROUP LTD
5413 271 St, Langley, BC, V4W 3Y7
(604) 607-8878
Emp Here 40   *Sales* 20,195,360
SIC 1629 Heavy construction, nec
Jack Gill

D-U-N-S 24-957-6760   (SL)
**UNIFIED ALLOYS (BRITISH COLUMBIA)
LTD**
(*Suby of* UNIFIED ALLOYS LTD)
26835 Gloucester Way, Langley, BC, V4W 3Y3
(604) 607-6750
Emp Here 25   *Sales* 14,937,660
SIC 5051 Metals service centers and offices
Darren Hansen

D-U-N-S 20-914-1357   (HQ)
WEST COAST MACHINERY LTD
SHEARFORCE EQUIPMENT
27050 Gloucester Way, Langley, BC, V4W 3Y5

(604) 855-5101
Sales 15,200,832
SIC 5082 Construction and mining machinery
Brad Dewit
Robert Beukema

Lantzville, BC V0R

D-U-N-S 20-266-0770   (SL)
CRUISEPLUS MANAGEMENT LTD
7143 Caillet Rd, Lantzville, BC, V0R 2H0
(250) 390-0220
Emp Here 45   *Sales* 17,341,200
SIC 4724 Travel agencies
David Frinton
Shelley Good

Likely, BC V0L

D-U-N-S 25-329-2890   (SL)
MOUNT POLLEY MINING CORPORATION
(*Suby of* IMPERIAL METALS CORPORA-
TION)
5720 Moorehead-Bootjack Rd, Likely, BC, V0L
1N0
(250) 790-2215
Emp Here 250   *Sales* 63,943,500
SIC 1041 Gold ores
Pierre Lebel
Brian Kynoch
Darb Dhillon
Randall Thompson
Sheila Colwill
Andre Deepwell
Don Parsons

Lillooet, BC V0K

D-U-N-S 24-650-6880   (SL)
COAST RANGE CONCRETE LTD
1011 Hwy 99 N, Lillooet, BC, V0K 1V0
(250) 256-7803
Emp Here 25   *Sales* 11,179,350
SIC 5032 Brick, stone, and related material

D-U-N-S 20-990-4478   (BR)
INTERIOR HEALTH AUTHORITY
LILLOOET HOSPITAL & HEALTH CENTER
(*Suby of* INTERIOR HEALTH AUTHORITY)
951 Murray St, Lillooet, BC, V0K 1V0
(250) 256-1300
Emp Here 80
SIC 8062 General medical and surgical hospi-
tals

Lions Bay, BC V0N

D-U-N-S 25-143-8685   (SL)
**FURRY CREEK GOLF & COUNTRY CLUB
INC**
150 Country Club Rd, Lions Bay, BC, V0N 2E0
(604) 896-2216
Emp Here 120   *Sales* 9,425,400
SIC 7992 Public golf courses
Sarah Cruse

Logan Lake, BC V0K

D-U-N-S 24-640-2986   (SL)
**TECK HIGHLAND VALLEY COPPER PART-
NERSHIP**
(*Suby of* TECK RESOURCES LIMITED)

Hwy 97c Highland Valley Copper Minesite, Lo-
gan Lake, BC, V0K 1W0
(250) 523-2443
Emp Here 1,250   *Sales* 319,717,500
SIC 1021 Copper ores
Chris J. Dechert
Rod Killough
Ronald J. Greenway

Mackenzie, BC V0J

D-U-N-S 20-522-3626   (BR)
CANADIAN FOREST PRODUCTS LTD
CANFOR MACKENZIE DIVISION
(*Suby of* CANFOR CORPORATION)
Mill Rd, Mackenzie, BC, V0J 2C0
(250) 997-3271
Emp Here 200
SIC 2421 Sawmills and planing mills, general
Cam Milne

D-U-N-S 25-795-2911   (BR)
EAST FRASER FIBER CO LTD
PARALLEL 55
(*Suby of* EAST FRASER FIBER CO LTD)
1000 Sheppard Rd, Mackenzie, BC, V0J 2C0
(250) 997-6360
Emp Here 100
SIC 2421 Sawmills and planing mills, general
Tony Lang

D-U-N-S 24-888-2318   (SL)
**MACKENZIE   CONSUMERS   CO-
OPERATIVE ASSOCIATION**
403 Mackenzie Blvd Suite 103, Mackenzie,
BC, V0J 2C0
(250) 997-3335
Emp Here 50   *Sales* 16,148,450
SIC 5411 Grocery stores
Wolf De Smet

D-U-N-S 24-424-4872   (SL)
MACKENZIE PULP MILL CORPORATION
(*Suby of* CAPITAL ASSETS HOLDINGS (L)
BERHAD)
1000 Coquawaldy Rd, Mackenzie, BC, V0J
2C0
(250) 997-2431
Emp Here 250   *Sales* 121,932,500
SIC 5084 Industrial machinery and equipment
Tanner Elton

D-U-N-S 20-209-2726   (SL)
**SNOWSHOE   MOUNTAIN   RESOURCES
CORP**
Gd, Mackenzie, BC, V0J 2C0
(250) 988-1325
Emp Here 5   *Sales* 15,529,285
SIC 4924 Natural gas distribution

Maple Ridge, BC V2W

D-U-N-S 24-016-6702   (SL)
ADVANCED FLOW SYSTEMS INC
(*Suby of* ADVANTEC GLOBAL INNOVA-
TIONS INC)
27222 Lougheed Hwy, Maple Ridge, BC, V2W
1M4
(604) 462-1514
Emp Here 300   *Sales* 84,263,100
SIC 3569 General industrial machinery, nec
Bradley Miller
Allan Nagy
Renay Nunninkhoven
Darren Toop

D-U-N-S 25-230-0199   (SL)
CANN-AMM EXPORTS INC
23638 River Rd Unit 1, Maple Ridge, BC, V2W
1B7
(604) 466-9121
Emp Here 40   *Sales* 20,821,680

SIC 5093 Scrap and waste materials
Darshan Sahsi

D-U-N-S 24-292-4116   (SL)
FRASER CEDAR PRODUCTS LTD
27400 Lougheed Hwy, Maple Ridge, BC, V2W
1L1
(604) 462-7335
Emp Here 200   *Sales* 38,474,000
SIC 2429 Special product sawmills, nec
Baljinder Gill

D-U-N-S 20-297-4130   (SL)
**FRASER RIVER MARINE TRANSPORTA-
TION LTD**
ALBION FERRY, THE
23888 River Rd, Maple Ridge, BC, V2W 1B7
(604) 463-3044
Emp Here 40   *Sales* 10,781,960
SIC 4449 Water transportation of freight
Dave Miller

D-U-N-S 24-027-6308   (BR)
**SCHOOL DISTRICT NO 42 (MAPLE RIDGE-
PITT MEADOWS)**
*ROBERTSON, SAMUEL TECHNICAL SEC-
ONDARY SCHOOL*
(*Suby of* SCHOOL DISTRICT NO 42 (MAPLE
RIDGE-PITT MEADOWS))
10445 245 St Suite 10445, Maple Ridge, BC,
V2W 2G4
(604) 466-8409
Emp Here 75
SIC 8211 Elementary and secondary schools
Michael Keenan

D-U-N-S 20-093-4826   (SL)
SEA FRESH FISH LTD
BRUCE'S COUNTRY MARKET
23963 Lougheed Hwy, Maple Ridge, BC, V2W
1J1
(604) 463-9817
Emp Here 85   *Sales* 24,945,545
SIC 5411 Grocery stores
Darrell Mceachern
Angus Mceachern
Glenna Murray

D-U-N-S 20-148-5294   (SL)
SOUTHCOAST MILLWORK LTD
23347 Mckay Ave, Maple Ridge, BC, V2W 1B9
(604) 467-0111
Emp Here 100   *Sales* 15,586,300
SIC 2431 Millwork
Alfred Loewen
Peter A. Shields

D-U-N-S 24-980-5391   (SL)
STEADFAST CEDAR PRODUCTS LTD
FRASER CEDAR PRODUCTS
27400 Lougheed Hwy, Maple Ridge, BC, V2W
1L1
(604) 462-7335
Emp Here 200   *Sales* 113,925,600
SIC 5031 Lumber, plywood, and millwork
Baljinder Gill

D-U-N-S 20-862-5293   (SL)
**SUPER DAVE'S GOLDEN EARS MOTORS
LTD**
MAPLE RIDGE HAUDAI
23213 Lougheed Hwy, Maple Ridge, BC, V2W
1C1
(604) 467-3401
Emp Here 32   *Sales* 15,938,496
SIC 5511 New and used car dealers
Vaughn Wyant
David Wyant

D-U-N-S 20-747-0753   (SL)
SURROUND TECHNOLOGIES INC
(*Suby of* ADVANTEC GLOBAL INNOVA-
TIONS INC)
27222 Lougheed Hwy, Maple Ridge, BC, V2W
1M4
(604) 462-8223
Emp Here 200   *Sales* 38,417,000
SIC 3499 Fabricated Metal products, nec

▲ Public Company   ■ Public Company Family Member   **HQ** Headquarters   **BR** Branch   **SL** Single Location

Brad Miller

D-U-N-S 20-863-2943   (SL)
VISTA RAILING SYSTEMS INC
BW VISTA RAILINGS
23282 River Rd, Maple Ridge, BC, V2W 1B6
(604) 467-5147
Emp Here 70   *Sales* 10,910,410
SIC 2431 Millwork
Derek Henrey

D-U-N-S 24-367-5733   (HQ)
WALDUN FOREST PRODUCTS LTD
9393 287 St, Maple Ridge, BC, V2W 1L1
(604) 462-8266
Emp Here 90   *Sales* 28,855,500
SIC 2429 Special product sawmills, nec
Curtis Walker
Kirk Nagy

Maple Ridge, BC V2X

D-U-N-S 20-832-6418   (SL)
CAPITAL WEST INSURANCE SERVICES
22785 Dewdney Trunk Rd, Maple Ridge, BC,
V2X 3K4
(604) 476-1227
Emp Here 20   *Sales* 11,598,480
SIC 6411 Insurance agents, brokers, and service
Melvin Gill

D-U-N-S 24-931-3545   (SL)
CORPORATE CLEANING SERVICES LTD
20285 Stewart Cres Suite 402, Maple Ridge,
BC, V2X 8G1
(604) 465-4699
Emp Here 84   *Sales* 7,528,836
SIC 7217 Carpet and upholstery cleaning
Robert Handel
Mark Sippola

D-U-N-S 24-837-4845   (SL)
E-ONE MOLI ENERGY (CANADA) LIMITED
(*Suby of* INTERNATIONAL CSRC INVESTMENT HOLDINGS CO.)
20000 Stewart Cres, Maple Ridge, BC, V2X
9E7
(604) 466-6654
Emp Here 65   *Sales* 12,378,730
SIC 3691 Storage batteries

D-U-N-S 20-175-9358   (SL)
**ENERGY WORKS CREATIVE HEALING
ARTS**
23085 118 Avenue, Maple Ridge, BC, V2X 3J7
(604) 817-9956
Emp Here 5   *Sales* 15,529,285
SIC 4924 Natural gas distribution

D-U-N-S 20-800-7653   (SL)
EPIC FOOD SERVICES INC
TIM HORTONS
22987 Dewdney Trunk Rd, Maple Ridge, BC,
V2X 3K8
(604) 466-0671
Emp Here 55   *Sales* 16,141,235
SIC 5461 Retail bakeries
Kim Anderson

D-U-N-S 25-021-1257   (BR)
FRASER HEALTH AUTHORITY
RIDGE MEADOWS HOSPITAL
(*Suby of* GOVERNMENT OF THE
PROVINCE OF BRITISH COLUMBIA)
11666 Laity St, Maple Ridge, BC, V2X 5A3
(604) 463-4111
Emp Here 1,000
SIC 8062 General medical and surgical hospitals

D-U-N-S 25-685-0371   (BR)
GREAT PACIFIC INDUSTRIES INC
SAVE-ON-FOODS
(*Suby of* PATTISON, JIM GROUP INC)

20395 Lougheed Hwy Suite 300, Maple
Ridge, BC, V2X 2P9
(604) 465-8665
Emp Here 140
SIC 5411 Grocery stores
Ralph Paragini

D-U-N-S 20-800-2626   (HQ)
HANEY BUILDERS SUPPLIES (1964) LTD
22740 Dewdney Trunk Rd, Maple Ridge, BC,
V2X 3K2
(604) 820-0444
Emp Here 1   *Sales* 12,652,950
SIC 5211 Lumber and other building materials
Robert Stinson
Thomas Stinson

D-U-N-S 20-619-5315   (SL)
HANEY BUILDERS' SUPPLIES (1971) LTD
(*Suby of* HANEY BUILDERS SUPPLIES
(1964) LTD)
22740 Dewdney Trunk Rd, Maple Ridge, BC,
V2X 3K2
(604) 463-6206
Emp Here 50   *Sales* 13,382,600
SIC 5211 Lumber and other building materials
Robert Stinson
Tom Stinson
Henry Tjart

D-U-N-S 20-375-0422   (SL)
HUTTON, B. MARKETING LTD
11969 200 St, Maple Ridge, BC, V2X 3M7
(604) 460-4664
Emp Here 80   *Sales* 50,342,400
SIC 5531 Auto and home supply stores
Bryan Hutton

D-U-N-S 24-290-3631   (HQ)
JOHNSTON, MEIER INSURANCE AGENCIES LTD
22367 Dewdney Trunk Rd, Maple Ridge, BC,
V2X 3J4
(604) 467-4184
Emp Here 35   *Sales* 982,443,528
SIC 6411 Insurance agents, brokers, and service
Bruce Johnston
Thomas Meier

D-U-N-S 20-620-5668   (SL)
JONES, MARV LTD
MARV JONES HONDA
20611 Lougheed Hwy, Maple Ridge, BC, V2X
2P9
(604) 465-5464
Emp Here 29   *Sales* 14,444,262
SIC 5511 New and used car dealers
Marvin Jones

D-U-N-S 20-863-0954   (HQ)
LORDCO PARTS LTD
LORDCO AUTO PARTS
22866 Dewdney Trunk Rd, Maple Ridge, BC,
V2X 3K6
(604) 467-1581
Emp Here 1   *Sales* 1,154,504,000
SIC 5531 Auto and home supply stores
Marlyn Coates
Tara Hammer
Samantha Coates
Ian Coates

D-U-N-S 25-001-4560   (SL)
MAPLE RIDGE PITT MEADOWS NEWS
22328 119 Ave, Maple Ridge, BC, V2X 2Z3
(604) 467-1122
Emp Here 17   *Sales* 11,159,888
SIC 5963 Direct selling establishments
Jim Coulter

D-U-N-S 24-696-4704   (HQ)
MAPLE RIDGE/PITT MEADOWS COMMUNITY SERVICES
MEALS ON WHEELS
11907 228 St, Maple Ridge, BC, V2X 8G8
(604) 467-6911
Emp Here 1   *Sales* 46,098,780

SIC 8699 Membership organizations, nec
Vicki Kipps

D-U-N-S 24-441-6413   (BR)
**MCDONALD'S RESTAURANTS OF
CANADA LIMITED**
MCDONALDS - MAPLE RIDGE
(*Suby of* MCDONALD'S CORPORATION)
20780 Lougheed Hwy, Maple Ridge, BC, V2X
2V6
(604) 463-7858
Emp Here 80
SIC 5812 Eating places

D-U-N-S 24-388-8794   (SL)
MR MOTORS LP
MAPLE RIDGE CHRYSLER
(*Suby of* AUTOCANADA INC)
11911 West St, Maple Ridge, BC, V2X 3M6
(604) 465-8931
Emp Here 150   *Sales* 94,392,000
SIC 5511 New and used car dealers
Mike Mcnulty

D-U-N-S 20-514-5795   (HQ)
R.S.T. INSTRUMENTS LTD
11545 Kingston St, Maple Ridge, BC, V2X 0Z5
(604) 540-1100
Sales 14,773,785
SIC 3826 Analytical instruments
Bruce Ripley
Robert Taylor
Jason Luty
Robert Kobetitch
Dean Polvi
Randy Scanks
Brian Nguyen

D-U-N-S 25-710-9389   (SL)
RIDGE MEADOWS RECYCLING SOCIETY
10092 236 St, Maple Ridge, BC, V2X 7G2
(604) 463-5545
Emp Here 62   *Sales* 19,772,420
SIC 4953 Refuse systems
Kim Day
Bill Elder
Ken Jacobsen
Julie Koehn

D-U-N-S 24-446-6777   (HQ)
**SCHOOL DISTRICT NO 42 (MAPLE RIDGE-
PITT MEADOWS)**
22225 Brown Ave, Maple Ridge, BC, V2X 8N6
(604) 463-4200
Emp Here 50   *Sales* 118,942,800
SIC 8211 Elementary and secondary schools
Jan Unwin
Wayne Jefferson

D-U-N-S 25-266-8728   (BR)
**SCHOOL DISTRICT NO 42 (MAPLE RIDGE-
PITT MEADOWS)**
WESTVIEW SECONDARY SCHOOL
(*Suby of* SCHOOL DISTRICT NO 42 (MAPLE
RIDGE-PITT MEADOWS))
20905 Wicklund Ave, Maple Ridge, BC, V2X
8E8
(604) 467-3481
Emp Here 110
SIC 8211 Elementary and secondary schools
Patricia Giesinger

D-U-N-S 25-453-3664   (BR)
**SCHOOL DISTRICT NO 42 (MAPLE RIDGE-
PITT MEADOWS)**
MAPLE RIDGE SECONDARY SCHOOL
(*Suby of* SCHOOL DISTRICT NO 42 (MAPLE
RIDGE-PITT MEADOWS))
21911 122 Ave, Maple Ridge, BC, V2X 3X2
(604) 463-4175
Emp Here 150
SIC 8211 Elementary and secondary schools
Trevor Connor

D-U-N-S 25-087-6679   (BR)
SOBEYS WEST INC
SAFEWAY STORE #0198

(*Suby of* EMPIRE COMPANY LIMITED)
20201 Lougheed Hwy Suite 300, Maple
Ridge, BC, V2X 2P6
(604) 460-7200
Emp Here 150
SIC 5411 Grocery stores
Stephen Enslen

D-U-N-S 24-491-9940   (HQ)
**STELMASCHUK, W. J. AND ASSOCIATES
LTD**
ADULT COMMUNITY ALTERNATIVE MEASURES PROGRAM
22470 Dewdney Trunk Rd Suite 510, Maple
Ridge, BC, V2X 5Z6

Emp Here 15   *Sales* 113,887,400
SIC 8399 Social services, nec
William Stelmaschuk

D-U-N-S 24-886-2729   (SL)
**STELMASCHUK, W.J. AND ASSOCIATES
LTD**
WJS CANADA
11491 Kingston St Suite 2, Maple Ridge, BC,
V2X 0Y6
(604) 465-5515
Emp Here 49   *Sales* 13,442,268
SIC 8741 Management services
Caroline Bonesky
Tim Beachy
Monty Chew
Ian Doyle
Cassie Mccaffrey

D-U-N-S 20-097-4228   (HQ)
WEST COAST MOTORS LTD
WEST COAST FORD LINCOLN
20370 Lougheed Hwy, Maple Ridge, BC, V2X
2P8
(604) 465-5481
Emp Here 1   *Sales* 37,756,800
SIC 5511 New and used car dealers
Michelle Jones-Ruppel
Ron Jones
Scott Jones

Maple Ridge, BC V4R

D-U-N-S 20-369-5002   (HQ)
AFX HOLDINGS CORP
14301 256 St Suite 302, Maple Ridge, BC,
V4R 0B9
(604) 380-4458
Sales 13,077,650
SIC 6712 Bank holding companies
Hassan Firouzbakht

D-U-N-S 25-020-9129   (BR)
**SCHOOL DISTRICT NO 42 (MAPLE RIDGE-
PITT MEADOWS)**
GARIBALDI SECONDARY SCHOOL
(*Suby of* SCHOOL DISTRICT NO 42 (MAPLE
RIDGE-PITT MEADOWS))
24789 Dewdney Trunk Rd, Maple Ridge, BC,
V4R 1X2
(604) 463-3500
Emp Here 80
SIC 8211 Elementary and secondary schools
Shannon Derinzy

Masset, BC V0T

D-U-N-S 20-099-8490   (SL)
DELMAS CO-OPERATIVE ASSOCIATION
1562 Main St, Masset, BC, V0T 1M0
(250) 626-3933
Emp Here 65   *Sales* 17,819,880
SIC 5411 Grocery stores
Richard Clairmount

D-U-N-S 25-834-6287   (SL)
OMEGA PACKING COMPANY LIMITED
2040 Harrison, Masset, BC, V0T 1M0
(250) 626-3391
Emp Here 169   *Sales* 58,421,610
SIC 2092 Fresh or frozen packaged fish
Bob Jongewaard

Meadow Creek, BC V0G

D-U-N-S 24-857-7541   (SL)
HAMILL CREEK TIMBER HOMES INC
(*Suby of* HAMILL CREEK TIMBERWRIGHTS
INC)
13440 Hwy 31, Meadow Creek, BC, V0G 1N0
(250) 366-4320
Emp Here 44   *Sales* 11,921,448
SIC 1522 Residential construction, nec
Dwight Smith
Debbie Smith

D-U-N-S 20-212-8372   (HQ)
HAMILL CREEK TIMBERWRIGHTS INC
13440 Hwy 31, Meadow Creek, BC, V0G 1N0
(250) 366-4320
Sales 11,508,332
SIC 6712 Bank holding companies
Dwight Smith
Debbie Smith

Merritt, BC V1K

D-U-N-S 20-152-2856   (BR)
ASPEN PLANERS LTD
(*Suby of* ASPEN PLANERS LTD)
1375 Houston St, Merritt, BC, V1K 1B8
(250) 378-9266
Emp Here 200
SIC 2421 Sawmills and planing mills, general
Joe Facey

D-U-N-S 24-750-9458   (HQ)
EMCON SERVICES INC
1121 Mcfarlane Way Unit 105, Merritt, BC,
V1K 1B9
(250) 378-4176
Emp Here 30   *Sales* 328,115,000
SIC 1611 Highway and street construction
Frank Rizzardo
Glenn Walsh

D-U-N-S 24-206-6889   (SL)
**MURRAY CHEVROLET PONTIAC BUICK
GMC MERRITT LIMITED PARTNERSHIP**
MURRAY GM MERRITT
2049 Nicola Ave, Merritt, BC, V1K 1B8
(250) 378-9255
Emp Here 28   *Sales* 13,946,184
SIC 5511 New and used car dealers
Scott Robertson
Jason Leech

D-U-N-S 24-456-8119   (SL)
NICOLA TRIBAL ASSOCIATION INC
2090 Coutlee Ave Unit 202, Merritt, BC, V1K
1B8
(250) 378-4235
Emp Here 50   *Sales* 13,716,600
SIC 8741 Management services
Neil Todd

D-U-N-S 25-173-3820   (HQ)
**SCHOOL DISTRICT NO 58 (NICOLA-
SIMILKAMEEN)**
1550 Chapman St, Merritt, BC, V1K 1B0
(250) 378-5161
Emp Here 1   *Sales* 31,718,080
SIC 8211 Elementary and secondary schools
Byron Robbie

D-U-N-S 24-824-4766   (BR)
TOLKO INDUSTRIES LTD

NICOLA VALLEY DIVISION
(*Suby of* AMERICAN INDUSTRIAL ACQUISI-
TION CORPORATION)
1750 Lindley Creek Rd, Merritt, BC, V1K 0A2
(250) 378-2224
Emp Here 200
SIC 2421 Sawmills and planing mills, general
David Bickerton

D-U-N-S 20-981-7183   (BR)
VSA HIGHWAY MAINTENANCE LTD
(*Suby of* VSA HIGHWAY MAINTENANCE
LTD)
2925 Pooley Ave, Merritt, BC, V1K 1C2
(250) 315-0166
Emp Here 100
SIC 1611 Highway and street construction
Blair Barr

D-U-N-S 24-319-5083   (BR)
WAL-MART CANADA CORP
WALMART
(*Suby of* WALMART INC.)
3900 Crawford Ave Suite 100, Merritt, BC, V1K
0A4
(250) 315-1366
Emp Here 120
SIC 5311 Department stores
Kareem Shalaby

Merville, BC V0R

D-U-N-S 20-938-4846   (SL)
ARBUTUS RV & MARINE SALES LTD
2603 Sackville Rd, Merville, BC, V0R 2M0
(250) 337-2174
Emp Here 24   *Sales* 11,953,872
SIC 5571 Motorcycle dealers
Jerry Eskes

Mill Bay, BC V0R

D-U-N-S 20-863-4212   (SL)
BRENTWOOD COLLEGE ASSOCIATION
BRENTWOOD COLLEGE SCHOOL
2735 Mt Baker Rd, Mill Bay, BC, V0R 2P1
(250) 743-5521
Emp Here 130   *Sales* 12,885,470
SIC 8211 Elementary and secondary schools
Arthur Crooks
Charles Woodward
Vern Fauth
Andrea Flaa
George Killy
Clyde Ogilvie

D-U-N-S 20-750-9048   (SL)
MILL BAY FIRE DEPARTMENT
2675 Lodgepole Rd, Mill Bay, BC, V0R 2P1
(250) 743-5563
Emp Here 30   *Sales* 13,476,570
SIC 7389 Business services, nec
Terry Culp

D-U-N-S 20-034-7339   (BR)
**SCHOOL DISTRICT NO. 79 (COWICHAN
VALLEY)**
FRANCES-KELSEY SECONDARY SCHOOL
953 Shawnigan-Mill Bay Rd, Mill Bay, BC, V0R
2P2
(250) 743-6916
Emp Here 80
SIC 8211 Elementary and secondary schools
Macleod Allan

Milner, BC V0X

D-U-N-S 20-100-1054   (SL)

**WESTGEN, WESTERN CANADA'S GENET-
ICS CENTRE**
6681 Glover Rd, Milner, BC, V0X 1T0
(604) 530-1141
Emp Here 35   *Sales* 51,369,220
SIC 5159 Farm-product raw materials, nec
Bradley (Brad) Howard
David Janssens
Carey Prinse
Tim Hofstra

Mission, BC V2V

D-U-N-S 20-853-9283   (SL)
662942 BC LTD
SHOPPERS DRUG MART
32530 Lougheed Hwy Suite 206, Mission, BC,
V2V 1A5
(604) 826-1244
Emp Here 40   *Sales* 10,118,160
SIC 5912 Drug stores and proprietary stores
Bradley Craig

D-U-N-S 20-100-1294   (HQ)
**ANGLO AMERICAN CEDAR PRODUCTS
LTD**
7160 Beatty Dr, Mission, BC, V2V 6B4
(604) 826-7185
Emp Here 20   *Sales* 70,064,244
SIC 5031 Lumber, plywood, and millwork
Gerald Clark
Peter Laslo
Patrick Guterres
Henry Friesen

D-U-N-S 25-104-7239   (SL)
B.C. CUSTOM CAR ASSOCIATION
MISSION RACE WAY PARK
32670 Dyke Rd, Mission, BC, V2V 4J5
(604) 826-6315
Emp Here 76   *Sales* 53,900,112
SIC 8699 Membership organizations, nec
Brian Nawyn
Ken Lowe

D-U-N-S 20-147-7168   (BR)
BLACK BOND BOOKS LTD
EDU KIDS (DIV OF)
(*Suby of* BLACK BOND BOOKS LTD)
32555 London Ave Suite 344, Mission, BC,
V2V 6M7
(604) 814-2650
Emp Here 619
SIC 5942 Book stores
Milena Raschpichler

D-U-N-S 24-579-5760   (SL)
CATHERWOOD TOWING LTD
32885 Mission Way Suite 101, Mission, BC,
V2V 6E4
(604) 826-9221
Emp Here 75   *Sales* 20,216,175
SIC 4492 Towing and tugboat service
Ernest Catherwood
Ervin Mihalicz

D-U-N-S 24-897-3216   (HQ)
**FRASER VALLEY BUILDING SUPPLIES
INC**
RONA
7072 Wren St, Mission, BC, V2V 2V9
(604) 820-1134
Emp Here 100   *Sales* 78,039,036
SIC 5039 Construction materials, nec
Ray Cyr
David J Nick
Ernest Nick
Terry Holland
Dirk Weymann

D-U-N-S 25-268-0087   (BR)
GREAT PACIFIC INDUSTRIES INC
SAVE-ON-FOODS
(*Suby of* PATTISON, JIM GROUP INC)

32555 London Ave Suite 400, Mission, BC,
V2V 6M7
(604) 826-9564
Emp Here 100
SIC 5411 Grocery stores
Dawn Haig

D-U-N-S 24-248-9243   (HQ)
**MISSION ASSOCIATION FOR COMMUNITY
LIVING**
33345 2nd Ave, Mission, BC, V2V 1K4
(604) 826-9080
Emp Here 120   *Sales* 7,778,122
SIC 8361 Residential care
Robert Keys

D-U-N-S 24-059-4718   (SL)
MISSION COMMUNITY FOUNDATION
Gd Lcd Main, Mission, BC, V2V 4J2
(604) 826-5322
Emp Here 26   *Sales* 10,332,764
SIC 8699 Membership organizations, nec
Shelley Clarkson

D-U-N-S 24-362-4884   (HQ)
**MISSION COMMUNITY SERVICES SOCI-
ETY**
33179 2nd Ave, Mission, BC, V2V 1J9
(604) 826-3634
Emp Here 44   *Sales* 10,009,425
SIC 8399 Social services, nec
Jenny Stevens
Marilynne Davis
Anthony Lapointe

D-U-N-S 20-147-3852   (HQ)
MR P'S & MR PET'S LTD
MR. PET'S
33560 1st Ave, Mission, BC, V2V 1H4
(604) 814-2994
Emp Here 35   *Sales* 19,546,240
SIC 5999 Miscellaneous retail stores, nec
Greg Penno

D-U-N-S 20-100-2235   (SL)
PIONEER GARAGE LIMITED
PIONEER CHRYSLER JEEP
33320 1st Ave, Mission, BC, V2V 1G8
(604) 462-7333
Emp Here 30   *Sales* 14,942,340
SIC 5511 New and used car dealers
Raymond Van Empel

D-U-N-S 24-446-2636   (SL)
PLEASANT VIEW HOUSING SOCIETY 1980
PLEASANT VIEW CARE HOME
7540 Hurd St Unit 101, Mission, BC, V2V 3H9
(604) 826-2176
Emp Here 100   *Sales* 6,856,600
SIC 8051 Skilled nursing care facilities
Judith Ray

D-U-N-S 20-299-3999   (BR)
SCHOOL DISTRICT #75 (MISSION)
MISSION SECONDARY SCHOOL
(*Suby of* SCHOOL DISTRICT #75 (MIS-
SION))
32939 7th Ave, Mission, BC, V2V 2C5
(604) 826-7191
Emp Here 100
SIC 8211 Elementary and secondary schools
Brian Tucker

D-U-N-S 24-640-1038   (HQ)
SCHOOL DISTRICT #75 (MISSION)
MISSION PUBLIC SCHOOLS
33046 4th Ave Suite 75, Mission, BC, V2V 1S5
(604) 826-6286
Sales 49,744,916
SIC 8211 Elementary and secondary schools
Angus Wilson
Corien Becker
Derek Welsh

D-U-N-S 20-299-3916   (BR)
SCHOOL DISTRICT #75 (MISSION)
HATZIC SECONDARY SCHOOL
(*Suby of* SCHOOL DISTRICT #75 (MIS-

SION))
34800 Dewdney Trunk Rd Suite 1, Mission, BC, V2V 5V6
(604) 826-3651
Emp Here 75
SIC 8211 Elementary and secondary schools
 Mike Malfesi

D-U-N-S 24-886-9687   (HQ)
V I P SOAP PRODUCTS LTD
32859 Mission Way, Mission, BC, V2V 6E4
(604) 820-8665
Sales 17,041,260
SIC 2841 Soap and other detergents
 Keith Bozman
 Tami Bozman

D-U-N-S 25-664-9216   (BR)
WAL-MART CANADA CORP
WALMART PHARMACIES
(*Suby of* WALMART INC.)
31956 Lougheed Hwy Suite 1119, Mission, BC, V2V 0C6
(604) 820-0048
Emp Here 150
SIC 5311 Department stores

Mission, BC V4S

D-U-N-S 24-394-9174   (SL)
CONVERGE CONSTRUCTION LTD
31413 Gill Ave Unit 108, Mission, BC, V4S 0C4
(604) 814-3401
Emp Here 25   *Sales* 10,761,748
SIC 1521 Single-family housing construction
 William Vroom
 Dwayne Vanderveen

D-U-N-S 24-373-5698   (SL)
J. BOND & SONS LTD
JBS
31413 Gill Ave Unit 103, Mission, BC, V4S 0C4
(604) 826-5391
Emp Here 52   *Sales* 11,544,052
SIC 3523 Farm machinery and equipment
 Justin Bond

Moberly Lake, BC V0C

D-U-N-S 24-468-5793   (SL)
4 EVERGREEN RESOURCES INC.
1717 Boucher Lake Rd, Moberly Lake, BC, V0C 1X0
(250) 788-7916
Emp Here 50   *Sales* 10,506,550
SIC 1389 Oil and gas field services, nec
 Henry Paquette

Nakusp, BC V0G

D-U-N-S 25-500-0309   (HQ)
ARROW AND SLOCAN LAKES COMMUNITY SERVICES
205 6 Ave Nw, Nakusp, BC, V0G 1R0
(250) 265-3674
Emp Here 10   *Sales* 11,341,650
SIC 8399 Social services, nec
 Ulli Mueller

Nanaimo, BC V9R

D-U-N-S 25-506-2044   (SL)
434870 B.C. LTD

HUB CITY FISHERIES
(*Suby of* PREMIUM BRANDS HOLDINGS CORPORATION)
262 Southside Dr, Nanaimo, BC, V9R 6Z5
(250) 753-4135
Emp Here 30   *Sales* 10,370,700
SIC 2092 Fresh or frozen packaged fish
 Roger Paquette

D-U-N-S 24-310-4478   (SL)
A C TAXI LTD
835 Old Victoria Rd, Nanaimo, BC, V9R 5Z9
(250) 754-9555
Emp Here 215   *Sales* 16,183,480
SIC 4111 Local and suburban transit
 Garry Smith
 Micheal Reeves

D-U-N-S 25-086-4766   (SL)
ACME FOOD CO, THE
14 Commercial St, Nanaimo, BC, V9R 5G2
(250) 753-0042
Emp Here 45   *Sales* 12,336,840
SIC 5411 Grocery stores
 Peter Ertsos

D-U-N-S 25-839-2133   (SL)
ANSWERPLUS COMMUNICATION SERVICES INC
ANSWERPLUS COMMUNICATIONS
235 Bastion St Suite 205, Nanaimo, BC, V9R 3A3
(250) 753-7587
Emp Here 35   *Sales* 15,522,150
SIC 7389 Business services, nec
 Doug Swift

D-U-N-S 20-100-3621   (SL)
BAKER SUPPLY LTD
33 Cliff St, Nanaimo, BC, V9R 5E6
(250) 754-6315
Emp Here 30   *Sales* 10,926,450
SIC 5013 Motor vehicle supplies and new parts
 William Baker

D-U-N-S 24-930-1151   (SL)
CARLSON, G. W. CONSTRUCTION LTD
78 Esplanade, Nanaimo, BC, V9R 4Y8

Emp Here 125   *Sales* 71,292,250
SIC 1542 Nonresidential construction, nec
 Gordon Carlson

D-U-N-S 20-100-4090   (HQ)
CENTRAL DRUG STORES LTD, THE
495 Dunsmuir St, Nanaimo, BC, V9R 6B9
(250) 753-6401
Emp Here 1   *Sales* 10,994,760
SIC 5912 Drug stores and proprietary stores
 Jordan Mark
 Cynthia Mcquillan
 Kevin Bourgeouis
 Russell Beales
 Richard Fukui

D-U-N-S 24-578-5597   (BR)
COAST HOTELS LIMITED
COAST BASTION INN
(*Suby of* OKABE CO., LTD.)
11 Bastion St, Nanaimo, BC, V9R 6E4
(250) 753-6601
Emp Here 90
SIC 7011 Hotels and motels
 Volker Grady

D-U-N-S 24-616-7097   (BR)
COASTAL COMMUNITY CREDIT UNION
(*Suby of* COASTAL COMMUNITY CREDIT UNION)
59 Wharf St Unit 220, Nanaimo, BC, V9R 2X3
(250) 716-2331
Emp Here 100
SIC 6062 State credit unions
 Deborah Edwards

D-U-N-S 24-534-5319   (HQ)
COASTAL COMMUNITY CREDIT UNION

59 Wharf St Suite 220, Nanaimo, BC, V9R 2X3
(250) 741-3200
Emp Here 80   *Sales* 61,693,491
SIC 6062 State credit unions
 Adrian Legin
 Mary Ashley
 Judy Fraser
 Lynne Fraser
 Richard Kerton
 Barbara Steele
 Susanne Jakobsen
 Evelyn Clark

D-U-N-S 25-939-6604   (SL)
COASTAL COMMUNITY INSURANCE AGENCIES LTD
(*Suby of* COASTAL COMMUNITY CREDIT UNION)
50 Tenth St Suite 111, Nanaimo, BC, V9R 6L1

Emp Here 30   *Sales* 25,441,800
SIC 6411 Insurance agents, brokers, and service
 Bob Bennie
 Lorne Purchase

D-U-N-S 24-626-2005   (SL)
COASTAL COMMUNITY INSURANCE SERVICES 2007 LTD
59 Wharf St Suite 220, Nanaimo, BC, V9R 2X3
(888) 741-1010
Emp Here 30   *Sales* 31,046,430
SIC 6311 Life insurance
 Robert Buckley

D-U-N-S 24-696-0009   (HQ)
COASTLAND WOOD INDUSTRIES LTD
84 Robarts St Suite 2, Nanaimo, BC, V9R 2S5
(250) 754-1962
Sales 64,029,700
SIC 2436 Softwood veneer and plywood
 Robert Shields
 Donald Mckay
 Duthie Welsford

D-U-N-S 24-551-0888   (HQ)
COMOX VALLEY DISTRIBUTION LTD
(*Suby of* REIMER CONSOLIDATED CORP)
140 Tenth St, Nanaimo, BC, V9R 6Z5
(250) 754-7773
Emp Here 64   *Sales* 13,930,048
SIC 4213 Trucking, except local
 Ken Hiebert

D-U-N-S 25-680-0699   (BR)
DAVEY TREE EXPERT CO. OF CANADA, LIMITED
DAVEY TREE SERVICES
(*Suby of* THE DAVEY TREE EXPERT COMPANY)
13 Victoria Cres Suite 20, Nanaimo, BC, V9R 5B9
(250) 755-1288
Emp Here 150
SIC 5261 Retail nurseries and garden stores
 Paul Pickles

D-U-N-S 24-521-1235   (SL)
E MADILL OFFICE CO
1400 Rocky Creek Way, Nanaimo, BC, V9R 5C8
(250) 754-1611
Emp Here 25   *Sales* 11,179,350
SIC 5044 Office equipment
 Ehren Madill

D-U-N-S 20-198-1797   (HQ)
GARDEN CITY WAREHOUSING & DISTRIBUTION LTD
RICHARDSON FOODS GROUP
839 Old Victoria Rd, Nanaimo, BC, V9R 5Z9
(250) 754-5447
Emp Here 43   *Sales* 45,956,735
SIC 5141 Groceries, general line
 Tom Richardson
 James Richardson
 John Bannerman

D-U-N-S 25-822-8097   (BR)
GREAT CANADIAN CASINOS INC
CASINO NANAIMO
(*Suby of* GREAT CANADIAN GAMING CORPORATION)
620 Terminal Ave, Nanaimo, BC, V9R 5E2
(250) 753-3033
Emp Here 200
SIC 7999 Amusement and recreation, nec
 Kwai Lam

D-U-N-S 24-493-1150   (SL)
H & W FOOD COUNTRY
CHASE RIVER COUNTRY GROCER
82 Twelfth St, Nanaimo, BC, V9R 6R6
(250) 753-7041
Emp Here 85   *Sales* 24,945,545
SIC 5411 Grocery stores
 Henry Zuynenburg
 Wally Large

D-U-N-S 25-181-2939   (SL)
INTER TRIBAL HEALTH AUTHORITY
534 Centre St, Nanaimo, BC, V9R 4Z3
(250) 753-0590
Emp Here 38   *Sales* 70,173,042
SIC 6324 Hospital and medical service plans
 Kelly Wadham

D-U-N-S 20-693-7844   (HQ)
ISLAND TIMBERLANDS LIMITED PARTNERSHIP
65 Front St, Nanaimo, BC, V9R 5H9
(250) 755-3500
Sales 100,336,200
SIC 7389 Business services, nec
 Darshan Sihota
 Mike Cass

D-U-N-S 25-181-5098   (BR)
JACE HOLDINGS LTD
THRIFTY FOODS NANAIMO
650 Terminal Ave Unit 3, Nanaimo, BC, V9R 5E2
(250) 754-6273
Emp Here 100   *Sales* 822,456
SIC 5411 Grocery stores
 Dan Zapotichny

D-U-N-S 24-292-7259   (HQ)
SCHOOL DISTRICT NO. 68 (NANAIMO-LADYSMITH)
395 Wakesiah Ave, Nanaimo, BC, V9R 3K6
(250) 754-5521
Emp Here 200   *Sales* 168,502,300
SIC 8211 Elementary and secondary schools
 Micheal Munro
 J. David Green
 Donna Allen

D-U-N-S 20-789-4853   (SL)
TILLICUM HAUS SOCIETY
602 Haliburton St, Nanaimo, BC, V9R 4W5
(250) 753-6578
Emp Here 40   *Sales* 15,896,560
SIC 8699 Membership organizations, nec
 Elliott Nielsen

D-U-N-S 20-801-4902   (HQ)
VANCOUVER ISLAND UNIVERSITY
MALASPINA UNIVERSITY-COLLEGE BOOKSTORE, DIV OF
90 Fifth St, Nanaimo, BC, V9R 1N1
(250) 753-3245
Emp Here 4   *Sales* 298,782,000
SIC 8221 Colleges and universities
 Ralph Nilson
 Edwin Deas
 Maria Frost

D-U-N-S 20-260-3614   (SL)
WE CARE HOME HEALTH SERVICES
2349 East Wellington Rd, Nanaimo, BC, V9R 6V7
(250) 740-0035
Emp Here 49   *Sales* 13,442,268
SIC 8741 Management services
 Joyce Lange

D-U-N-S 24-348-5823   (BR)
WESTERN FOREST PRODUCTS INC
NANAIMO SAWMILL
(*Suby of* WESTERN FOREST PRODUCTS INC)
31 Port Way, Nanaimo, BC, V9R 5L5
(250) 755-4600
Emp Here 130
SIC 2611 Pulp mills
Andy Vanger

D-U-N-S 25-366-8818   (BR)
WESTERN FOREST PRODUCTS INC
(*Suby of* WESTERN FOREST PRODUCTS INC)
495 Dunsmuir St Unit 201, Nanaimo, BC, V9R 6B9
(250) 734-4700
Emp Here 300
SIC 2621 Paper mills
Ian Donaldson

D-U-N-S 24-060-7940   (BR)
WESTERN FOREST PRODUCTS INC
DUKE POINT SAWMILL
(*Suby of* WESTERN FOREST PRODUCTS INC)
500 Duke Pt Rd, Nanaimo, BC, V9R 1K1
(250) 722-2533
Emp Here 200
SIC 2611 Pulp mills
Terry Charlton

Nanaimo, BC V9S

D-U-N-S 20-587-7798   (HQ)
BERK'S INTERTRUCK LTD
2230 Mccullough Rd, Nanaimo, BC, V9S 4M8
(250) 758-5217
Emp Here 33   *Sales* 32,093,280
SIC 5511 New and used car dealers
Brian Sabourin
Berkeley Sabourin
Dan Grubac

D-U-N-S 25-936-2804   (BR)
CANADIAN CORPS OF COMMISSION-AIRES NATIONAL OFFICE, THE
CANADIAN CORPS OF COMMISSION-AIRES MID ISLAND OPERATIONS
(*Suby of* CANADIAN CORPS OF COMMIS-SIONAIRES NATIONAL OFFICE, THE)
711 Northumberland Ave, Nanaimo, BC, V9S 5C5
(250) 754-1042
Emp Here 142
SIC 7381 Detective and armored car services
Behn Heiko

D-U-N-S 25-231-2699   (SL)
EDGEWOOD CHEMICAL DEPENDENCY TREATMENT CENTRE
2121 Boxwood Rd, Nanaimo, BC, V9S 4L2
(250) 751-0111
Emp Here 96   *Sales* 7,212,384
SIC 8093 Specialty outpatient clinics, nec
Lorne Hildebrand
Larry Waterman

D-U-N-S 25-193-0871   (SL)
ISLAND WEST COAST DEVELOPMENTS LTD
IWCD
2214 Mccullough Rd, Nanaimo, BC, V9S 4M8
(250) 756-9665
Emp Here 25   *Sales* 11,768,275
SIC 1542 Nonresidential construction, nec
Gregory Constable

D-U-N-S 20-100-5436   (SL)
JOHNSTON DRUG WHOLESALE LTD
JOHNSTON WHOLESALE
2286 Dorman Rd, Nanaimo, BC, V9S 5G2
(250) 758-3341
Emp Here 50   *Sales* 55,267,250

SIC 5122 Drugs, proprietaries, and sundries
Earl Johnston
Theresa Korney

D-U-N-S 25-485-9358   (SL)
KIWANIS VILLAGE LODGE
1221 Kiwanis Cres, Nanaimo, BC, V9S 5Y1
(250) 753-6471
Emp Here 100   *Sales* 6,856,600
SIC 8051 Skilled nursing care facilities
Virginia Ostrand

D-U-N-S 20-349-8329   (HQ)
MACK SALES & SERVICE OF NANAIMO LTD
2213 Mccullough Rd, Nanaimo, BC, V9S 4M7
(250) 758-0185
Emp Here 35   *Sales* 19,923,120
SIC 5511 New and used car dealers
Richard Mayer

D-U-N-S 25-688-2957   (SL)
MCGREGOR AND THOMPSON HARD-WARE LTD
1920 Boxwood Rd, Nanaimo, BC, V9S 5Y2
(250) 729-7888
Emp Here 30   *Sales* 13,415,220
SIC 5072 Hardware
Dave Shelton

D-U-N-S 24-319-5414   (SL)
NANAIMO DISTRICTY SENIOR CITIZENS HOUSING DEVELOPMENT SOCIETY
KIWANIS VILLAGE
1233 Kiwanis Cres, Nanaimo, BC, V9S 5Y1
(250) 740-2815
Emp Here 125   *Sales* 42,258,000
SIC 6531 Real estate agents and managers
Heiko Behn

D-U-N-S 20-100-6376   (HQ)
NANAIMO REALTY CO LTD
ROYAL LEPAGE-NANAIMO REALTY
2000 Island Hwy N Suite 275, Nanaimo, BC, V9S 5W3
(250) 713-0494
Emp Here 50   *Sales* 25,133,340
SIC 6531 Real estate agents and managers
Barry Clark
Allan Lupton
Ted Lewis

D-U-N-S 24-165-6289   (SL)
NANAIMO TRAVELLERS LODGE SOCIETY
1917 Northfield Rd, Nanaimo, BC, V9S 3B6
(250) 758-4676
Emp Here 140   *Sales* 7,071,020
SIC 8361 Residential care
Greg Gaudaur

D-U-N-S 25-913-8170   (BR)
POSTMEDIA NETWORK INC
NANAIMO DAILY NEWS
(*Suby of* POSTMEDIA NETWORK CANADA CORP)
2575 Mccullough Rd Suite B1, Nanaimo, BC, V9S 4M9

Emp Here 200
SIC 2711 Newspapers
Curt Duddy

D-U-N-S 25-415-3364   (SL)
PRAXIS TECHNICAL GROUP, INC
1618 Northfield Rd, Nanaimo, BC, V9S 3A9
(250) 756-7971
Emp Here 11   *Sales* 605,376,000
SIC 7371 Custom computer programming ser-vices
Brandan Millbank
Fong Millbank
Greg Millbank

D-U-N-S 25-097-9614   (SL)
SAYWELL CONTRACTING LTD
2599 Mccullough Rd Unit B, Nanaimo, BC, V9S 4M9
(250) 729-0197
Emp Here 60   *Sales* 34,220,280

SIC 1542 Nonresidential construction, nec
Sheldon Saywell

D-U-N-S 20-790-7424   (BR)
SCHOOL DISTRICT NO. 68 (NANAIMO-LADYSMITH)
WOODLAND SECONDARY SCHOOL
(*Suby of* SCHOOL DISTRICT NO. 68 (NANAIMO-LADYSMITH))
1270 Strathmore St, Nanaimo, BC, V9S 2L9
(250) 753-2271
Emp Here 75
SIC 8211 Elementary and secondary schools
Lee Venables

Nanaimo, BC V9T

D-U-N-S 24-985-4675   (SL)
1049054 B.C. LTD.
NISSAN OF NANAIMO
3612 Island Hwy N, Nanaimo, BC, V9T 1W2
(250) 756-1515
Emp Here 30   *Sales* 14,942,340
SIC 5511 New and used car dealers
Jimmy Rogers

D-U-N-S 20-417-9027   (SL)
CANADIAN TIRE
4585 Uplands Dr, Nanaimo, BC, V9T 6M8
(250) 585-5485
Emp Here 30   *Sales* 10,926,450
SIC 5014 Tires and tubes
Owen Billes

D-U-N-S 20-863-5383   (HQ)
DEVON TRANSPORT LTD
BUDGET CAR AND TRUCK RENTAL
2501 Kenworth Rd, Nanaimo, BC, V9T 3M4
(250) 729-2400
Emp Here 30   *Sales* 19,015,552
SIC 7514 Passenger car rental
Barrie Rogers
Greg Willmon

D-U-N-S 20-913-1267   (SL)
GRAEMOND HOLDINGS LTD
NANAIMO HONDA CARS
2535 Bowen Rd, Nanaimo, BC, V9T 3L2
(250) 758-3361
Emp Here 23   *Sales* 11,455,794
SIC 5511 New and used car dealers
Barry Robson
Judy Robson

D-U-N-S 25-267-8651   (BR)
GREAT PACIFIC INDUSTRIES INC
OVERWAITEA FOOD GROUP
(*Suby of* PATTISON, JIM GROUP INC)
3200 Island Hwy N, Nanaimo, BC, V9T 1W1
(250) 751-1414
Emp Here 100
SIC 5411 Grocery stores
Fred Masales

D-U-N-S 24-400-3059   (SL)
HARBOURVIEW AUTOHAUS LTD
VOLKSWAGEN
4921 Wellington Rd, Nanaimo, BC, V9T 2H5
(250) 751-1411
Emp Here 35   *Sales* 17,432,730
SIC 5511 New and used car dealers
John Wynia
Ron Young
Carol Wynia

D-U-N-S 25-818-4175   (SL)
HAVEN SOCIETYTRANSITION HOUSE
HAVEN SOCIETY
3200 Island Hwy Unit 38, Nanaimo, BC, V9T 6N4
(250) 756-2452
Emp Here 35   *Sales* 13,909,490
SIC 8699 Membership organizations, nec
Marilyn Chapman

D-U-N-S 25-514-2770   (BR)
HOME DEPOT OF CANADA INC
HOME DEPOT
(*Suby of* THE HOME DEPQT INC)
6555 Metral Dr, Nanaimo, BC, V9T 2L9
(250) 390-9093
Emp Here 230
SIC 5251 Hardware stores
Lorcan Byrne

D-U-N-S 25-094-6563   (BR)
HUDSON'S BAY COMPANY
(*Suby of* HUDSON'S BAY COMPANY)
6631 Island Hwy N Suite 1a, Nanaimo, BC, V9T 4T7
(250) 390-3141
Emp Here 130
SIC 5311 Department stores
Lee Nolan

D-U-N-S 24-979-6269   (SL)
INUKTUN SERVICES LTD
2569 Kenworth Rd Suite C, Nanaimo, BC, V9T 3M4
(250) 729-8080
Emp Here 51   *Sales* 11,322,051
SIC 3569 General industrial machinery, nec
Colin Dobell
Allen C Robinson
Roy Coles

D-U-N-S 24-312-1670   (HQ)
KELLAND PROPERTIES INC
QUALITY FOODS
2350 Delinea Pl, Nanaimo, BC, V9T 5L9
(250) 585-1482
Emp Here 60   *Sales* 96,232,000
SIC 5411 Grocery stores
Ken Schley
John Briuolo

D-U-N-S 20-100-5972   (SL)
MARSHALL, STEVE FORD LINCOLN LTD
3851 Shenton Rd Suite 3, Nanaimo, BC, V9T 2H1
(250) 758-7311
Emp Here 70   *Sales* 44,049,600
SIC 5511 New and used car dealers
Stephen Marshall

D-U-N-S 24-802-1268   (SL)
MIDISLAND HOLDINGS LTD
FAIRWAY MARKET GROCERY
4750 Rutherford Rd Suite 103, Nanaimo, BC, V9T 4K6
(250) 729-2611
Emp Here 45   *Sales* 12,336,840
SIC 5411 Grocery stores
Randy Richter

D-U-N-S 20-915-5993   (SL)
NANAIMO CHRYSLER LTD
4170 Wellington Rd, Nanaimo, BC, V9T 2H3
(250) 758-1191
Emp Here 35   *Sales* 17,432,730
SIC 5511 New and used car dealers
Brian Neal

D-U-N-S 24-682-3660   (SL)
ROBINSON, D. CONTRACTING LTD
4341 Boban Dr, Nanaimo, BC, V9T 5V9

Emp Here 30   *Sales* 14,121,930
SIC 1542 Nonresidential construction, nec
John Barker

D-U-N-S 25-181-2871   (BR)
SCHOOL DISTRICT NO. 68 (NANAIMO-LADYSMITH)
WELLINGTON SECONDARY SCHOOL
(*Suby of* SCHOOL DISTRICT NO. 68 (NANAIMO-LADYSMITH))
3135 Mexicana Rd, Nanaimo, BC, V9T 2W8
(250) 758-9191
Emp Here 85
SIC 8211 Elementary and secondary schools
Chad Lintott

▲ Public Company   ■ Public Company Family Member   **HQ** Headquarters   **BR** Branch   **SL** Single Location

D-U-N-S 25-848-7883   (BR)
SECURIGUARD SERVICES LIMITED
WEST GUARD SECURITY
(*Suby of* SECURIGUARD SERVICES LIMITED)
2520 Bowen Rd Suite 205, Nanaimo, BC, V9T 3L3
(250) 756-4452
Emp Here 180
SIC 7381 Detective and armored car services
Cory Parnall

D-U-N-S 25-893-0080   (BR)
SLEGG LIMITED PARTNERSHIP
SLEGG CONSTRUCTION
(*Suby of* GMS INC.)
4950 Jordan Ave, Nanaimo, BC, V9T 2H8
(250) 758-8329
Emp Here 100
SIC 5031 Lumber, plywood, and millwork
Xavier Terris

D-U-N-S 24-341-2827   (SL)
VANCOUVER ISLAND AUTO SALES LTD
HARRIS KIA
2575 Bowen Rd, Nanaimo, BC, V9T 3L4
(250) 751-1168
Emp Here 23   *Sales* 11,455,794
SIC 5511 New and used car dealers
John (Jack) Harris
David (Dave) Bare

D-U-N-S 24-725-7256   (HQ)
VANCOUVER ISLAND REGIONAL LIBRARY
6250 Hammond Bay Rd, Nanaimo, BC, V9T 6M9
(250) 758-4697
Emp Here 35   *Sales* 18,007,651
SIC 8231 Libraries
Rosemary Bonanno
Lis Pedersen
Joel Adams

D-U-N-S 24-773-2477   (SL)
VERSATILE LEASING
3851 Shenton Rd Suite 3, Nanaimo, BC, V9T 2H1
(250) 758-7311
Emp Here 49   *Sales* 24,405,822
SIC 5511 New and used car dealers
Emery Ebdrup

D-U-N-S 25-294-7460   (BR)
WAL-MART CANADA CORP
(*Suby of* WALMART INC.)
6801 Island Hwy N Suite 3059, Nanaimo, BC, V9T 6N8
(250) 758-0343
Emp Here 250
SIC 5311 Department stores

D-U-N-S 24-446-5175   (SL)
**WHEATON   PONTIAC   BUICK   GMC
(NANAIMO) LTD**
2590 Bowen Rd, Nanaimo, BC, V9T 3L3
(250) 758-2438
Emp Here 44   *Sales* 21,915,432
SIC 5511 New and used car dealers
Stephen Laird
Donald A Wheaton
William Wheaton
Michael Chappell

D-U-N-S 20-920-0562   (BR)
**WORKERS' COMPENSATION BOARD OF
BRITISH COLUMBIA**
WORKSAFE BC
(*Suby of* WORKERS' COMPENSATION BOARD OF BRITISH COLUMBIA)
4980 Wills Rd, Nanaimo, BC, V9T 6C6
(604) 273-2266
Emp Here 100
SIC 6331 Fire, marine, and casualty insurance
George Morfitt

Nanaimo, BC V9V

D-U-N-S 25-981-1482   (SL)
DAVE'S CRUISES
6490 Ptarmigan Way, Nanaimo, BC, V9V 1V7
(250) 390-1115
Emp Here 30   *Sales* 15,599,010
SIC 4724 Travel agencies
David Frinton

D-U-N-S 25-673-4369   (SL)
GWENAL HOLDINGS LTD
CANADIAN TIRE STORE
6900 Island Hwy N, Nanaimo, BC, V9V 1P6

Emp Here 110   *Sales* 69,220,800
SIC 5531 Auto and home supply stores
Alison Abbott

D-U-N-S 20-584-7127   (BR)
**NANAIMO SENIORS VILLAGE VENTURES
LTD**
6085 Uplands Dr, Nanaimo, BC, V9V 1T8
(250) 729-9524
Emp Here 200
SIC 6513 Apartment building operators

D-U-N-S 25-532-8171   (SL)
PARADISE ISLAND FOODS INC
PARADISE ISLAND CHEESE
6451 Portsmouth Rd, Nanaimo, BC, V9V 1A3
(800) 889-3370
Emp Here 60   *Sales* 20,741,400
SIC 2022 Cheese; natural and processed
Len Thomson
Kevin Thomson
Bonita Thomson

D-U-N-S 20-713-5950   (BR)
**SCHOOL DISTRICT NO. 68 (NANAIMO-
LADYSMITH)**
DOVER BAY SECONDARY SCHOOL
(*Suby of* SCHOOL DISTRICT NO. 68 (NANAIMO-LADYSMITH))
6135 Mcgirr Rd, Nanaimo, BC, V9V 1M1
(250) 756-4595
Emp Here 125
SIC 8211 Elementary and secondary schools
Robyn Gray

Nanaimo, BC V9X

D-U-N-S 25-093-2733   (BR)
CASCADES CANADA ULC
CASCADES RECOVERY+
(*Suby of* CASCADES INC)
800 Maughan Rd, Nanaimo, BC, V9X 1J2
(250) 722-3396
Emp Here 150
SIC 4953 Refuse systems
Doug Money

D-U-N-S 24-888-1260   (SL)
COPCAN CONTRACTING LTD
COPCAN CIVIL
(*Suby of* GREGSON HOLDINGS LTD)
1920 Balsam Rd, Nanaimo, BC, V9X 1T5
(250) 754-7260
Emp Here 45   *Sales* 11,078,370
SIC 1794 Excavation work
Dave Gregson
Marilyn Gregson

D-U-N-S 24-930-2423   (HQ)
GREGSON HOLDINGS LTD
1920 Balsam Rd, Nanaimo, BC, V9X 1T5
(250) 754-7260
Emp Here 30   *Sales* 29,542,320
SIC 1794 Excavation work
Bryan Gregson
Marilyn Gregson

D-U-N-S 24-531-7149   (SL)

HOLDFAST METALWORKS LTD
HOLDFAST
1061 Maughan Rd, Nanaimo, BC, V9X 1J2
(250) 591-7400
Emp Here 60   *Sales* 14,771,160
SIC 1799 Special trade contractors, nec
Nadeen Marie Bettney

D-U-N-S 20-912-8847   (SL)
INDUSTRIAL SCAFFOLD SERVICES L.P.
2076 Balsam Rd, Nanaimo, BC, V9X 1T5
(250) 591-3535
Emp Here 100   *Sales* 24,618,600
SIC 1799 Special trade contractors, nec
Brian Parton

D-U-N-S 24-523-6083   (SL)
JSK TRAFFIC CONTROL SERVICES INC
2005 Waring Rd, Nanaimo, BC, V9X 1V1
(250) 618-0232
Emp Here 30   *Sales* 13,304,700
SIC 7389 Business services, nec
Sharron Elliott

D-U-N-S 24-957-6307   (HQ)
MAYCO MIX LTD
(*Suby of* HEIDELBERGCEMENT AG)
1125 Cedar Rd, Nanaimo, BC, V9X 1K9
(250) 722-0064
Emp Here 26   *Sales* 20,122,830
SIC 5032 Brick, stone, and related material
Doug Blender

D-U-N-S 24-365-8759   (SL)
NANAIMO FOREST PRODUCTS LTD
HARMAC PACIFIC, DIV OF
1000 Wave Pl, Nanaimo, BC, V9X 1J2
(250) 722-3211
Emp Here 200   *Sales* 38,953,600
SIC 2611 Pulp mills
Levi Sampson
Bob Smiley
Chris Mellors
Malcolm Ciesek
Bryan Reid
Frank Crucil
Bob Bowden
Michelle Dunham
Ed Sampson
Gerry Tellier

D-U-N-S 25-830-7482   (HQ)
TILRAY CANADA LTD
TILRAY
(*Suby of* PRIVATEER HOLDINGS, INC.)
1100 Maughan Rd, Nanaimo, BC, V9X 1J2
(250) 722-3991
Sales 41,183,045
SIC 2833 Medicinals and botanicals
Michael Glen Blue
Christian Albert Groh

D-U-N-S 24-899-6886   (SL)
VMAC GLOBAL TECHNOLOGY INC
VMAC (VEHICLE MOUNTED AIR COMPRESSORS)
1333 Kipp Rd, Nanaimo, BC, V9X 1R3
(250) 740-3200
Emp Here 100   *Sales* 22,200,100
SIC 3563 Air and gas compressors
James Hogan
Dan Hutchinson

Nanoose Bay, BC V9P

D-U-N-S 25-903-3769   (SL)
PC 96 HOLDINGS LTD
NANOOSE BAY PETRO-CANADA
2345 Island Hwy E, Nanoose Bay, BC, V9P 9E2
(250) 468-7441
Emp Here 29   *Sales* 14,444,262
SIC 5541 Gasoline service stations
Doug Tombe

D-U-N-S 20-813-4697   (HQ)
S.A.D.E HOLDINGS LTD
NANOOSE BAY PETRO-CANADA
2345 Island Hwy E, Nanoose Bay, BC, V9P 9E2
(250) 468-7441
Emp Here 5   *Sales* 10,966,080
SIC 5411 Grocery stores
Doug Tombe

Nelson, BC V1L

D-U-N-S 20-100-8752   (SL)
CITY AUTO SERVICE LTD
NELSON CHRYSLER
803 Baker St, Nelson, BC, V1L 4J8
(250) 352-5346
Emp Here 27   *Sales* 13,448,106
SIC 5511 New and used car dealers
Grant Mcken
Patrick Renwick
Archie Mcken

D-U-N-S 25-620-4553   (BR)
HUBER DEVELOPMENT LTD
PRESTIGE LAKESIDE RESORT & CONVENTION CENTRE
(*Suby of* HUBER DEVELOPMENT LTD)
701 Lakeside Dr, Nelson, BC, V1L 6G3
(250) 352-7222
Emp Here 100
SIC 7011 Hotels and motels
Josef Huber

D-U-N-S 24-362-5352   (BR)
INTERIOR HEALTH AUTHORITY
KOOTENAY LAKE HOSPITAL
(*Suby of* INTERIOR HEALTH AUTHORITY)
3 View St Suite 426, Nelson, BC, V1L 2V1
(250) 352-3111
Emp Here 100
SIC 8062 General medical and surgical hospitals
Phalia Vesterback

D-U-N-S 20-512-7632   (SL)
JOHNNY'S BAKERY (1981) LTD
660 Baker St, Nelson, BC, V1L 4J4

Emp Here 21   *Sales* 17,547,117
SIC 5149 Groceries and related products, nec
Hans Speck
Werner Suter

D-U-N-S 24-694-6743   (SL)
KOOTENAY COUNTRY STORE CO-OP
295 Baker St, Nelson, BC, V1L 4H4
(250) 354-4077
Emp Here 65   *Sales* 17,819,880
SIC 5411 Grocery stores
Deirdrie Lang

D-U-N-S 24-206-7309   (SL)
KOOTENAY MADE NATURAL PRODUCTS
377 Baker St, Nelson, BC, V1L 4H6
(250) 352-2333
Emp Here 22   *Sales* 14,685,108
SIC 5963 Direct selling establishments
Debra Defiletif

D-U-N-S 24-980-4170   (HQ)
LOUIS MAGLIO ENTERPRISES LTD
MAGLIO BUILDING CENTRE
29 Government Rd, Nelson, BC, V1L 4L9
(250) 352-6661
Emp Here 2   *Sales* 13,382,600
SIC 5211 Lumber and other building materials
Dominic Maglio
Antonio Maglio

D-U-N-S 20-100-8687   (SL)
MAGLIO BUILDING CENTRE LTD
29 Government Rd, Nelson, BC, V1L 4L9
(250) 352-6661
Emp Here 40   *Sales* 10,706,080

SIC 5211 Lumber and other building materials
Antonio Maglio
Dominic Maglio

D-U-N-S 24-247-1274　　(SL)
MARBOR HOLDINGS LTD
HERITAGE INN
422 Vernon St, Nelson, BC, V1L 4E5
(250) 352-5331
Emp Here 80　　*Sales* 7,591,920
SIC 7011 Hotels and motels
David Martin
Sheila Martin

D-U-N-S 20-798-4266　　(SL)
NELSON BUILDING CENTRE LTD
NELSON HOME HARDWARE BUILDING CENTRE
101 Mcdonald Dr, Nelson, BC, V1L 6B9
(250) 352-1919
Emp Here 45　　*Sales* 11,387,655
SIC 5251 Hardware stores
Randy Horswill

D-U-N-S 24-696-5362　　(HQ)
NELSON CARES SOCIETY
521 Vernon St, Nelson, BC, V1L 4E9
(250) 352-6011
Sales 21,328,004
SIC 8399 Social services, nec
Jenny Robinson

D-U-N-S 24-099-2995　　(SL)
NELSON FORD SALES (2003) INC
623 Railway St, Nelson, BC, V1L 1H5
(250) 352-7202
Emp Here 23　　*Sales* 11,455,794
SIC 5511 New and used car dealers
Mike Priester
Russell Stocks

D-U-N-S 24-825-4203　　(HQ)
PACIFIC INSIGHT ELECTRONICS CORP
PACIFIC INSIGHT
(*Suby of* METHODE ELECTRONICS, INC)
1155 Insight Dr, Nelson, BC, V1L 5P5
(250) 354-1155
Emp Here 5　　*Sales* 93,859,585
SIC 3694 Engine electrical equipment
Cliff Semenick
Jonathan Fogg
Laurent Curtil
Doug Mann
Mike Medvec

D-U-N-S 25-294-7387　　(BR)
WAL-MART CANADA CORP
(*Suby of* WALMART INC.)
1000 Lakeside Dr, Nelson, BC, V1L 5Z4
(250) 352-3782
Emp Here 166
SIC 5311 Department stores
Janice Freure

D-U-N-S 24-872-4150　　(SL)
WEST KOOTENAY DISTRICT OFFICE
310 Ward St Suite 400, Nelson, BC, V1L 5S4
(250) 354-6521
Emp Here 30　　*Sales* 14,490,461
SIC 5082 Construction and mining machinery
Hugh Eberle

D-U-N-S 25-592-7956　　(SL)
WHITEWATER SKI RESORT LTD
602 Lake St, Nelson, BC, V1L 4C8
(250) 354-4944
Emp Here 120　　*Sales* 11,122,800
SIC 7011 Hotels and motels
Brian Cusack

D-U-N-S 20-733-6921　　(HQ)
YELLOWHEAD ROAD & BRIDGE (KOOTE-NAY) LTD
110 Cedar St, Nelson, BC, V1L 6H2
(250) 352-3242
Emp Here 1　　*Sales* 45,439,560
SIC 1611 Highway and street construction
Kevin Higgins

New Westminster, BC V3L

D-U-N-S 20-792-5152　　(HQ)
ABREY ENTERPRISES INC
MCDONALD'S
815 Mcbride Blvd, New Westminster, BC, V3L 2B9
(604) 718-1189
Emp Here 75　　*Sales* 9,327,800
SIC 5812 Eating places
Wendy Abraham

D-U-N-S 20-101-1699　　(BR)
ARMY & NAVY DEPT. STORE LIMITED
(*Suby of* ARMY & NAVY DEPT. STORE LIMITED)
502 Columbia St, New Westminster, BC, V3L 1B1
(604) 526-4661
Emp Here 100
SIC 5311 Department stores
Theresa Coppendale

D-U-N-S 24-594-3931　　(HQ)
AVOCETTE TECHNOLOGIES INC
422 Sixth St 2nd Flr, New Westminster, BC, V3L 3B2
(604) 395-6000
Emp Here 67　　*Sales* 15,786,956
SIC 7371 Custom computer programming services
Scott Ross
Mitchell Ngai

D-U-N-S 24-930-8347　　(SL)
AZURITE HOLDINGS LTD
225 Edworthy Way, New Westminster, BC, V3L 5G4
(604) 527-1120
Emp Here 36　　*Sales* 15,096,780
SIC 6712 Bank holding companies

D-U-N-S 24-136-9875　　(BR)
BANK OF MONTREAL
BMO
(*Suby of* BANK OF MONTREAL)
610 Sixth St Suite 125, New Westminster, BC, V3L 3C2
(604) 665-3770
Emp Here 100
SIC 6021 National commercial banks
Hilda Pascoa

D-U-N-S 24-248-9685　　(BR)
CANADA POST CORPORATION
(*Suby of* GOVERNMENT OF CANADA)
24 Ovens Ave, New Westminster, BC, V3L 1Z2
(604) 516-7802
Emp Here 100
SIC 4311 U.s. postal service
Sean Traverse

D-U-N-S 24-778-1925　　(BR)
CANADIAN FOREST PRODUCTS LTD
PANEL & FIBER, DIV OF
(*Suby of* CANFOR CORPORATION)
430 Canfor Ave, New Westminster, BC, V3L 5G2

Emp Here 140
SIC 2421 Sawmills and planing mills, general
William Clewes

D-U-N-S 20-052-3616　　(HQ)
COAST MOUNTAIN BUS COMPANY LTD
CMBC
(*Suby of* SOUTH COAST BRITISH COLUMBIA TRANSPORTATION AUTHORITY)
287 Nelson'S Crt Suite 700, New Westminster, BC, V3L 0E7
(778) 375-6400
Emp Here 300　　*Sales* 299,170,908
SIC 4111 Local and suburban transit
Doug Kelsey

Haydn Acheson
Kristin Dacre
Donald Mclellan

D-U-N-S 20-795-0189　　(HQ)
COAST POWERTRAIN LTD
420 Canfor Ave, New Westminster, BC, V3L 5G2
(604) 520-6125
Emp Here 29　　*Sales* 19,507,680
SIC 5531 Auto and home supply stores
Wilson Stewart

D-U-N-S 25-069-0096　　(BR)
CORPORATION OF THE CITY OF NEW WESTMINSTER
CANADA GAMES POOL
(*Suby of* CORPORATION OF THE CITY OF NEW WESTMINSTER)
65 Sixth Ave E, New Westminster, BC, V3L 4G6
(604) 526-4281
Emp Here 90
SIC 7999 Amusement and recreation, nec
Cidalia Martin

D-U-N-S 24-174-1193　　(BR)
CORPORATION OF THE CITY OF NEW WESTMINSTER
GLENBROOK FIRE HALL
(*Suby of* CORPORATION OF THE CITY OF NEW WESTMINSTER)
1 Sixth Ave E, New Westminster, BC, V3L 4G6
(604) 519-1000
Emp Here 100
SIC 7389 Business services, nec
Tim Armstrong

D-U-N-S 20-513-7193　　(HQ)
E.R. PROBYN LTD
601 Sixth St Unit 350, New Westminster, BC, V3L 3C1
(604) 526-8545
Emp Here 5　　*Sales* 76,270,250
SIC 7389 Business services, nec
Peter Fograscher
Jack Menzies
Norman Toews
Peter K Fograscher
James Probyn
Michael Pedersen
Edward R Probyn

D-U-N-S 20-802-7128　　(HQ)
GLENWOOD LABEL & BOX MFG. LTD
GLENWOOD LABELS
15 Braid St Suite 117, New Westminster, BC, V3L 5N7
(604) 522-6001
Emp Here 45　　*Sales* 13,633,760
SIC 2679 Converted paper products, nec
Walter Lawrence
Terry Lawrence
Geraldine Lawrence

D-U-N-S 24-881-7116　　(BR)
GOVERNING COUNCIL OF THE SALVATION ARMY IN CANADA, THE
GOVERNING COUNCIL OF THE SALVATION ARMY IN CANADA,
(*Suby of* GOVERNING COUNCIL OF THE SALVATION ARMY IN CANADA, THE)
409 Blair Ave, New Westminster, BC, V3L 4A4
(604) 522-7033
Emp Here 130
SIC 8361 Residential care
Joy Gibson

D-U-N-S 20-912-2902　　(SL)
HEALTH SCIENCES ASSOCIATION OF BRITISH COLUMBIA
HSA
180 Columbia St E, New Westminster, BC, V3L 0G7
(604) 517-0994
Emp Here 50　　*Sales* 13,545,256
SIC 8631 Labor organizations
Val Alery

Anne Davis
Derrick Hoyt
Joseph Sebastian
John Christopherson
Anita Bardal
Marg Beddis
Allen Peters
Janice Morrison
Mandi Ayers

D-U-N-S 24-641-3629　　(HQ)
HERCULES FORWARDING ULC
TRANSITAIRE HERCULES
151 Spruce St, New Westminster, BC, V3L 5E6
(604) 517-1331
Emp Here 21　　*Sales* 69,356,768
SIC 4731 Freight transportation arrangement
Martin Burnham
Amber Karlstedt
Melanie Burnham

D-U-N-S 24-070-6440　　(HQ)
JUSTICE INSTITUTE OF BRITISH COLUMBIA
JIBC
715 Mcbride Blvd, New Westminster, BC, V3L 5T4
(604) 525-5422
Emp Here 450　　*Sales* 35,862,358
SIC 8221 Colleges and universities
Michel Tarko
Douglas Eastwood
James Mcgregor
Laureen Styles
Kim Logan
James Christenson
Helen Dutch
Rowland Johnson
Robert Kroeker
Tamara Olding

D-U-N-S 24-493-4055　　(SL)
KIWANIS CARE SOCIETY (1979) OF NEW WESTMINSTER
KIWANIS CARE CENTRE
35 Clute St, New Westminster, BC, V3L 1Z5
(604) 525-6471
Emp Here 75　　*Sales* 5,142,450
SIC 8051 Skilled nursing care facilities
Shirley Browne
Lorrie Gerrard

D-U-N-S 20-554-3924　　(SL)
PF MEDIA GROUP INC
319 Governors Crt, New Westminster, BC, V3L 5S5
(604) 599-3876
Emp Here 25　　*Sales* 11,087,250
SIC 7389 Business services, nec
Jim Gee

D-U-N-S 24-839-6830　　(SL)
PROBYN LOG LTD
(*Suby of* E.R. PROBYN LTD)
601 Sixth St Unit 350, New Westminster, BC, V3L 3C1
(604) 526-8545
Emp Here 30　　*Sales* 13,476,570
SIC 7389 Business services, nec
Peter Fograscher
James Probyn
Edward Probyn

D-U-N-S 20-988-2344　　(SL)
RIVER'S REACH PUB INC
320 Sixth St, New Westminster, BC, V3L 3A8
(604) 777-0101
Emp Here 50　　*Sales* 14,956,500
SIC 5921 Liquor stores
George Petropavlis

D-U-N-S 24-839-5329　　(SL)
ROYAL CITY MANOR LTD
77 Jamieson Crt, New Westminster, BC, V3L 5P8
(604) 522-6699
Emp Here 170　　*Sales* 10,071,990

SIC 8361 Residential care
Margo Lupien

D-U-N-S 20-101-9445   (SL)
ROYAL CITY TAXI LTD
436 Rousseau St, New Westminster, BC, V3L
3R3
(604) 526-6666
Emp Here 100   *Sales* 14,819,200
SIC 4212 Local trucking, without storage
Jagjit Sandhar

D-U-N-S 24-456-5495   (SL)
ROYAL TOWERS HOTEL INC
PLANCY'S BAR & GRILL
(*Suby of* EMPRESS TOWERS LTD)
140 Sixth St, New Westminster, BC, V3L 2Z9
(604) 524-4689
Emp Here 93   *Sales* 8,620,170
SIC 7011 Hotels and motels
Roy Lisogar

D-U-N-S 24-346-7391   (BR)
**SOUTH COAST BRITISH COLUMBIA
TRANSPORTATION AUTHORITY**
TRANSIT POLICE
(*Suby of* SOUTH COAST BRITISH
COLUMBIA TRANSPORTATION AUTHOR-
ITY)
287 Nelson'S Crt Suite 300, New Westmin-
ster, BC, V3L 0E7
(604) 515-8300
Emp Here 175
SIC 4111 Local and suburban transit
Neil Dubord

D-U-N-S 25-109-1468   (HQ)
**SOUTH COAST BRITISH COLUMBIA
TRANSPORTATION AUTHORITY**
TRANSLINK
287 Nelson'S Crt Suite 400, New Westmin-
ster, BC, V3L 0E7
(778) 375-7500
Emp Here 245   *Sales* 1,591,971,957
SIC 4111 Local and suburban transit
Kevin Desmond
Cathy Mclay
Vivienne King
Haydn Acheson
Doug Lepard
Lorraine Cunningham
Janet Austin
Larry Beasley
Jim Chu
Sarah Clark

D-U-N-S 20-280-3813   (SL)
SWARTZ ENTERPRISES INC
804 Winthrop St, New Westminster, BC, V3L
4B1
(778) 859-5040
Emp Here 60   *Sales* 14,848,980
SIC 1771 Concrete work
Daniel Swartz

D-U-N-S 24-285-4327   (SL)
UNICORN SECURITY
624 Sixth St Unit 201, New Westminster, BC,
V3L 3C4
(604) 593-5454
Emp Here 16   *Sales* 10,862,768
SIC 6289 Security and commodity service

D-U-N-S 24-384-0431   (SL)
UPG PROPERTY GROUP INC
WESTMINSTER CENTRE
555 Sixth St Unit 330, New Westminster, BC,
V3L 5H1
(604) 525-8292
Emp Here 40   *Sales* 13,085,080
SIC 6531 Real estate agents and managers
Wayne Beattie

D-U-N-S 20-991-7921   (HQ)
WEST COAST TITLE SEARCH LTD
WEST COAST PROCESS SERVING
99 Sixth St, New Westminster, BC, V3L 5H8

(604) 659-8600
Emp Here 22   *Sales* 13,252,260
SIC 6541 Title abstract offices
Wayne Crookes

D-U-N-S 20-915-1877   (SL)
WINVAN PAVING LTD
220 Edworthy Way, New Westminster, BC,
V3L 5G5
(604) 522-3921
Emp Here 80   *Sales* 20,195,360
SIC 1611 Highway and street construction
Stanley Weismiller
Willie Weismiller
Carol Weismiller
Glen Weismiller
Norm Weismiller
Mike Weismiller

New Westminster, BC V3M

D-U-N-S 20-108-7046   (HQ)
AMES TILE & STONE LTD
(*Suby of* SPARGUS INDUSTRIES LTD)
415 Boyne St Suite 301, New Westminster,
BC, V3M 5K2
(604) 515-3486
Emp Here 10   *Sales* 42,722,100
SIC 5032 Brick, stone, and related material
Jack Ames
John C Ames
June Lillian Ames
John Moncrieff Ames
Saron Dos Remedios

D-U-N-S 25-246-9085   (SL)
AMIX MARINE PROJECTS LTD
AMIX GROUP
625 Agnes St Unit 425, New Westminster,
V3M 5Y4
(604) 516-0857
Emp Here 49   *Sales* 13,207,901
SIC 4499 Water transportation services,
William Jackson

D-U-N-S 24-856-1623   (HQ)
**BOARD OF SCHOOL TRUSTEES OF
SCHOOL DISTRICT #40 (NEW WEST-
MINSTER), THE**
*NEW WESTMINSTER SCHOOL DISTRICT
#40*
1001 Columbia St, New Westminster, BC,
V3M 1C4
(604) 517-6240
Emp Here 30   *Sales* 69,383,300
SIC 8211 Elementary and secondary schools
John Woudzia

D-U-N-S 20-283-1400   (HQ)
CENTURY GROUP LANDS CORPORATION
11 Eighth St 10th Fl, Anvil Centre, New West-
minster, BC, V3M 3N7
(604) 943-2203
Emp Here 40   *Sales* 101,419,200
SIC 6531 Real estate agents and managers
Sean Hodgins
Philip F. Posehn
Miro Armeen

D-U-N-S 20-585-1173   (HQ)
CENTURY HOLDINGS LTD
11 Eighth St, New Westminster, BC, V3M 3N7
(604) 943-2203
Emp Here 10   *Sales* 33,130,650
SIC 6512 Nonresidential building operators
John Brown
George Hodgins

D-U-N-S 25-014-8376   (HQ)
COAST TO COAST VIDEO SALES LTD
1109 Royal Ave, New Westminster, BC, V3M
1K4
(604) 525-9355
Emp Here 10   *Sales* 20,821,680
SIC 5099 Durable goods, nec

Roxanne Perry

D-U-N-S 20-887-5539   (HQ)
DOUGLAS COLLEGE
700 Royal Ave Unit 2814, New Westminster,
BC, V3M 5Z5
(604) 527-5400
Emp Here 60   *Sales* 94,163,050
SIC 8222 Junior colleges
Kathy Denton

D-U-N-S 24-382-3122   (SL)
FRASER RIVER PILE & DREDGE (GP) INC
(*Suby of* FRPD INVESTMENTS LIMITED
PARTNERSHIP)
1830 River Dr, New Westminster, BC, V3M
2A8
(604) 522-7971
Emp Here 195   *Sales* 63,982,425
SIC 1629 Heavy construction, nec
Sarah Clark
Mike Bevan-Pritchard
Tino Isola
Albert Low

D-U-N-S 24-382-3130   (HQ)
**FRPD INVESTMENTS LIMITED PARTNER-
SHIP**
1830 River Dr, New Westminster, BC, V3M
2A8
(604) 522-7971
Sales 49,226,190
SIC 1629 Heavy construction, nec
Tom Lively

D-U-N-S 20-401-6133   (SL)
FUN TALKING SOFTWARE LTD
713 Columbia St Suite 202, New Westminster,
BC, V3M 1B2
(778) 999-1658
Emp Here 100   *Sales* 17,731,100
SIC 7371 Custom computer programming ser-
vices
Alvin Shang

D-U-N-S 24-619-2202   (BR)
**GATEWAY CASINOS & ENTERTAINMENT
INC**
STARLIGHT CASINO
(*Suby of* GATEWAY CASINOS & ENTER-
TAINMENT INC)
350 Gifford St Suite 1, New Westminster, BC,
V3M 7A3
(604) 777-2946
Emp Here 600
SIC 7011 Hotels and motels

D-U-N-S 20-101-5336   (SL)
GRIFF BUILDING SUPPLIES LTD
340 Ewen Ave, New Westminster, BC, V3M
5B1
(877) 934-7433
Emp Here 40   *Sales* 17,886,960
SIC 5031 Lumber, plywood, and millwork
Stella Griffiths
Deborah White
Denise O'neill
Janet Gant

D-U-N-S 24-034-0612   (SL)
HARLOCK MURRAY UNDERWRITING LTD
HMU
960 Quayside Dr Unit 103, New Westminster,
BC, V3M 6G2
(604) 669-7745
Emp Here 14   *Sales* 25,853,226
SIC 6331 Fire, marine, and casualty insurance
Richard Race
Rob Wesseling
Geoffrey Parkinson
David Calibaba
Murray Goertzen
Trevor F. Hart
Erin Myre
Ardith Ralph

D-U-N-S 20-698-6908   (BR)
HUDSON'S BAY COMPANY

HOME OUTFITTERS
(*Suby of* HUDSON'S BAY COMPANY)
805 Boyd St, New Westminster, BC, V3M 5X2
(604) 525-7362
Emp Here 100
SIC 5311 Department stores
Julian Tejtar

D-U-N-S 24-371-1835   (SL)
KEY WEST FORD SALES LTD
301 Stewardson Way, New Westminster, BC,
V3M 2A5
(604) 239-7832
Emp Here 100   *Sales* 62,928,000
SIC 5511 New and used car dealers
Allan Backman
Lawrence Isfeld

D-U-N-S 20-087-3045   (BR)
KRUGER PRODUCTS L.P.
(*Suby of* KRUGER INC)
1625 Fifth Ave, New Westminster, BC, V3M
1Z7
(604) 522-7893
Emp Here 400
SIC 2621 Paper mills
Charles Stewart

D-U-N-S 24-976-2501   (BR)
LONDON DRUGS LIMITED
(*Suby of* H.Y. LOUIE CO. LIMITED)
60 Tenth St, New Westminster, BC, V3M 3X3
(604) 524-1326
Emp Here 100
SIC 5912 Drug stores and proprietary stores
Norman Hoff

D-U-N-S 24-827-4099   (BR)
LOWE'S COMPANIES CANADA, ULC
(*Suby of* LOWE'S COMPANIES, INC.)
1085 Tanaka Crt, New Westminster, BC, V3M
0G2
(604) 527-7239
Emp Here 175
SIC 5211 Lumber and other building materials
Federico Pagotto

D-U-N-S 20-656-1651   (SL)
MEIER INSURANCE AGENCIES LTD
602 Twelfth St, New Westminster, BC, V3M
4J2
(604) 777-9999
Emp Here 30   *Sales* 17,397,720
SIC 6411 Insurance agents, brokers, and service
David Nguyen

D-U-N-S 25-715-3825   (SL)
PROCARE HEALTH SERVICES INC
JUST CARE
624 Columbia St Suite 201, New Westminster,
BC, V3M 1A5
(604) 525-1234
Emp Here 100   *Sales* 17,020,500
SIC 8049 Offices of health practitioner
Diana Leclair

D-U-N-S 24-738-7983   (SL)
Q CONTACTS
640 Clarkson St, New Westminster, BC, V3M
1C8
(604) 717-4500
Emp Here 35   *Sales* 15,722,665
SIC 7389 Business services, nec

D-U-N-S 25-646-9636   (SL)
RIVER SEAFOODS INC
522 Seventh St Unit 320, New Westminster,
BC, V3M 5T5

Emp Here 45   *Sales* 10,118,475
SIC 2092 Fresh or frozen packaged fish
Launa M Groulx
Corrine L Bjork

D-U-N-S 20-587-0637   (SL)
ROYAL CITY FIRE SUPPLIES LTD
633 Twelfth St, New Westminster, BC, V3M

4J5
(604) 522-4240
Emp Here 22   *Sales* 11,451,924
SIC 5099 Durable goods, nec
  Glenn Gillard

D-U-N-S 20-796-7055   (BR)
SLEEP COUNTRY CANADA INC
(*Suby of* SLEEP COUNTRY CANADA HOLD-INGS INC)
805 Boyd St Suite 100, New Westminster, BC, V3M 5X2
(604) 515-9711
Emp Here 1,000
SIC 5712 Furniture stores
  Gilleis Terry

D-U-N-S 20-428-1380   (BR)
SOBEYS WEST INC
(*Suby of* EMPIRE COMPANY LIMITED)
800 Carnarvon St Suite 220, New Westminster, BC, V3M 0G3
(604) 522-2019
Emp Here 140
SIC 5411 Grocery stores
  Dan Braun

D-U-N-S 24-777-7733   (HQ)
SOUTHERN RAILWAY OF BRITISH COLUMBIA LIMITED
SRY
(*Suby of* WASHINGTON CANADIAN LTD)
2102 River Dr, New Westminster, BC, V3M 6S3
(604) 521-1851
Emp Here 170   *Sales* 73,460,528
SIC 4011 Railroads, line-haul operating
  Frank J Butzelaar
  Derek Ollmann
  Keith Nordin
  Emily Mak

D-U-N-S 24-974-8203   (BR)
SPECTRA GROUP OF GREAT RESTAURANTS INC, THE
NEW WESTMINSTER BOAT HOUSE
(*Suby of* MADISON PACIFIC PROPERTIES INC)
900 Quayside Dr, New Westminster, BC, V3M 6G1
(604) 525-3474
Emp Here 80
SIC 5812 Eating places
  Mark Pribula

D-U-N-S 24-309-2553   (BR)
UNIVERSAL PROTECTION SERVICE OF CANADA CO
LEGACY UNIVERSAL PROTECTION SERVICE
(*Suby of* UNIVERSAL PROTECTION GP, LLC)
627 Columbia St Suite 200a, New Westminster, BC, V3M 1A7
(604) 522-5550
Emp Here 100
SIC 7381 Detective and armored car services
  Steve Danelon

D-U-N-S 20-790-5519   (SL)
WESTMINSTER HOUSE SOCIETY
228 Seventh St, New Westminster, BC, V3M 3K3
(604) 524-5633
Emp Here 50   *Sales* 19,870,700
SIC 8699 Membership organizations, nec
  Scott Emerson
  Ron Argue
  Marie Murray
  Michelle Mix

North Saanich, BC V8L

D-U-N-S 20-732-6252   (BR)
COMPASS GROUP CANADA LTD

(*Suby of* COMPASS GROUP PLC)
1640 Electra Blvd Suite 123, North Saanich, BC, V8L 5V4
(250) 655-3718
Emp Here 100
SIC 5812 Eating places
  James Green

D-U-N-S 25-093-5116   (BR)
JACE HOLDINGS LTD
THRIFTY FOODS
1893 Mills Rd, North Saanich, BC, V8L 5S9
(250) 483-1709
Emp Here 300   *Sales* 2,140,496
SIC 5141 Groceries, general line
  Rob Tostowaryk

D-U-N-S 25-677-6428   (HQ)
VICTORIA AIRPORT AUTHORITY
1640 Electra Blvd Suite 201, North Saanich, BC, V8L 5V4
(250) 953-7500
Sales 14,190,412
SIC 4581 Airports, flying fields, and services
  Geoff Dickson
  James Crowley
  Eric Donald
  Marilyn Loveless
  Gordon Safarik
  Lynne Henderson
  Rod Dewar
  Wendy Everson
  Frank Leonard
  Cathie Ounsted

D-U-N-S 20-352-3667   (SL)
VIH AEROSPACE INC
1962 Canso Rd, North Saanich, BC, V8L 5V5
(250) 656-3987
Emp Here 39   *Sales* 12,665,406
SIC 4581 Airports, flying fields, and services
  Kenneth Norie

D-U-N-S 20-107-2964   (HQ)
VIH HELICOPTERS LTD
1962 Canso Rd, North Saanich, BC, V8L 5V5
(250) 656-3987
Sales 14,416,812
SIC 4522 Air transportation, nonscheduled
  Kenneth Norie
  Charlie Hodgins
  Jennifer Norie

D-U-N-S 20-271-0484   (SL)
YYJ FBO SERVICES LTD
SHELL AEROCENTRE
1962 Canso Rd Suite 101, North Saanich, BC, V8L 5V5
(250) 655-8833
Emp Here 13   *Sales* 16,343,613
SIC 5172 Petroleum products, nec
  Martin Childes

North Vancouver, BC V7H

D-U-N-S 20-102-7471   (SL)
ALLIED SHIPBUILDERS LTD
WESTERN MACHINE WORKS, A DIV OF
(*Suby of* LOAD LINE HOLDINGS LTD)
1870 Harbour Rd, North Vancouver, BC, V7H 1A1
(604) 929-2365
Emp Here 122   *Sales* 27,308,846
SIC 3731 Shipbuilding and repairing
  Malcolm Benzies Mclaren
  Douglas Baxter Mclaren
  James Dick Mclaren

D-U-N-S 20-429-3906   (HQ)
ALS CANADA LTD
ALS GROUP
(*Suby of* ALS LIMITED)
2103 Dollarton Hwy, North Vancouver, BC, V7H 0A7

(604) 984-0221
Emp Here 353   *Sales* 259,388,222
SIC 8734 Testing laboratories
  Tammy Moore
  Jill Bridgman
  Lisa Droppo
  David Taylor
  Genevieve Bertrand
  Heather Durham
  Nick Egarhos
  Ronald Foerster
  Angela Genge
  Anne Marie Giannetti

D-U-N-S 24-515-1295   (HQ)
AMER SPORTS CANADA INC
ARC'TERYX EQUIPMENT DIV.
2220 Dollarton Hwy Unit 110, North Vancouver, BC, V7H 1A8
(604) 960-3001
Emp Here 1,000   *Sales* 6,966,906,000
SIC 5091 Sporting and recreation goods
  Paul S Mckeown
  Paul Blanchette
  David Deasley

D-U-N-S 20-102-7802   (HQ)
B.A. BLACKTOP LTD
(*Suby of* VINCI)
111 Forester St Suite 201, North Vancouver, BC, V7H 0A6
(604) 985-0611
Emp Here 40   *Sales* 20,195,360
SIC 1611 Highway and street construction
  Rudy Ernst
  Bill Elphinstone

D-U-N-S 25-142-3893   (BR)
CHEMTRADE ELECTROCHEM INC
(*Suby of* CHEMTRADE LOGISTICS INCOME FUND)
100 Amherst Ave, North Vancouver, BC, V7H 1S4
(604) 929-1107
Emp Here 167
SIC 2899 Chemical preparations, nec
  Bernardine Leong

D-U-N-S 20-703-5564   (BR)
CHEMTRADE ELECTROCHEM INC
NEXEN CHEMICALS CANADA LTD PARTNERSHIP
(*Suby of* CHEMTRADE LOGISTICS INCOME FUND)
100 Amherst Ave, North Vancouver, BC, V7H 1S4
(604) 929-1107
Emp Here 167
SIC 2812 Alkalies and chlorine
  Richard Denton

D-U-N-S 24-232-1466   (SL)
CHUNG DAHM IMMERSION SCHOOL, VANCOUVER INC
CHUNG DAHM IMMERSION SCHOOL
2420 Dollarton Hwy, North Vancouver, BC, V7H 2Y1

Emp Here 100   *Sales* 16,312,417
SIC 8299 Schools and educational services, nec
  Simon Yoon

D-U-N-S 24-797-1062   (SL)
DARWIN CONSTRUCTION (CANADA) LTD
197 Forester St Suite 404, North Vancouver, BC, V7H 0A6
(604) 929-7944
Emp Here 40   *Sales* 18,829,240
SIC 1542 Nonresidential construction, nec
  David Webbe

D-U-N-S 20-913-9781   (HQ)
DB PERKS & ASSOCIATES LTD
COMMERCIAL AQUATIC SUPPLIES
2411 Dollarton Hwy Suite 102, North Vancouver, BC, V7H 0A3

(604) 980-2805
Sales 18,218,970
SIC 5091 Sporting and recreation goods
  Doug Perks

D-U-N-S 25-678-7359   (HQ)
JASTRAM HOLDINGS LTD
135 Riverside Dr, North Vancouver, BC, V7H 1T6
(604) 986-0714
Emp Here 1   *Sales* 10,462,120
SIC 6712 Bank holding companies
  Peter Doetsch

D-U-N-S 24-029-9321   (SL)
MILES INDUSTRIES LTD
VALOR FIREPLACES
2255 Dollarton Hwy Suite 190, North Vancouver, BC, V7H 3B1
(604) 984-3496
Emp Here 55   *Sales* 10,564,675
SIC 3429 Hardware, nec
  Paul Miles
  Martin Miles

D-U-N-S 20-010-0811   (HQ)
PEAK POTENTIALS TRAINING INC
2155 Dollarton Hwy Suite 130, North Vancouver, BC, V7H 3B2
(604) 083-3344
Sales 18,650,600
SIC 8742 Management consulting services
  Gail Balsillie

D-U-N-S 25-073-5446   (BR)
SCHOOL DISTRICT NO. 44 (NORTH VANCOUVER)
WINDSOR SECONDARY SCHOOL
(*Suby of* SCHOOL DISTRICT NO. 44 (NORTH VANCOUVER))
931 Broadview Dr, North Vancouver, BC, V7H 2E9
(604) 903-3700
Emp Here 110
SIC 8211 Elementary and secondary schools
  Adam Baumann

D-U-N-S 25-271-7061   (BR)
SOBEYS WEST INC
SAFEWAY
(*Suby of* EMPIRE COMPANY LIMITED)
1175 Mt Seymour Rd, North Vancouver, BC, V7H 2Y4
(604) 924-1302
Emp Here 100
SIC 5411 Grocery stores
  Nikko ..

D-U-N-S 24-261-8205   (SL)
SUSSEX FRANCHISE SYSTEMS INC.
SUSSEX INSURANCE
173 Forester St Unit 108, North Vancouver, BC, V7H 0A6
(604) 983-6955
Emp Here 30   *Sales* 17,397,720
SIC 6411 Insurance agents, brokers, and service
  Kenneth Armstrong
  Deborah Armstron
  Jason Armstron
  Brandon Armstrong

North Vancouver, BC V7J

D-U-N-S 24-566-6946   (SL)
ABLE COPIERS LTD
12 Orwell St, North Vancouver, BC, V7J 2G1
(604) 904-9858
Emp Here 57   *Sales* 13,926,696
SIC 5999 Miscellaneous retail stores, nec
  Kevin Riley

D-U-N-S 25-714-2661   (HQ)
BAY CITY INSURANCE SERVICES LTD
1199 Lynn Valley Rd Suite 121, North Vancou-

ver, BC, V7J 3H2
(604) 986-1155
Emp Here 4   *Sales* 21,201,500
SIC 6411 Insurance agents, brokers, and service
S. Gurnan
Len Noort

D-U-N-S 20-913-6548   (HQ)
CAPILANO UNIVERSITY
(*Suby of* GOVERNMENT OF THE PROVINCE OF BRITISH COLUMBIA)
2055 Purcell Way Suite 284, North Vancouver, BC, V7J 3H5
(604) 986-1911
Emp Here 797   *Sales* 31,559,191
SIC 8221 Colleges and universities
Kris Bulcroft
Richard Gale
Cindy Turner

D-U-N-S 20-520-8460   (SL)
CENTRE BAY YACHT STATION LTD
1103 Heritage Blvd, North Vancouver, BC, V7J 3G8
(604) 986-0010
Emp Here 100   *Sales* 26,155,300
SIC 6719 Holding companies, nec

D-U-N-S 24-379-5197   (SL)
FRONTIER-KEMPER CONSTRUCTORS ULC
SEYMOUR-CAP PARTNERSHIP
(*Suby of* TUTOR PERINI CORPORATION)
4400 Lillooet Rd, North Vancouver, BC, V7J 2H9
(604) 988-1665
Emp Here 150   *Sales* 40,538,400
SIC 1241 Coal mining services
Walter David Rogstab
Matt Johnson

D-U-N-S 24-750-1711   (HQ)
HIGH OUTPUT SPORTS CANADA INC
BOARDROOM SNOWBOARD SHOP, DIV OF
1465 Charlotte Rd, North Vancouver, BC, V7J 1H1
(604) 985-3933
Emp Here 24   *Sales* 36,437,940
SIC 5091 Sporting and recreation goods
Murray Fraser

D-U-N-S 20-189-8876   (BR)
HONEYWELL LIMITED
(*Suby of* HONEYWELL INTERNATIONAL INC.)
500 Brooksbank Ave, North Vancouver, BC, V7J 3S4
(604) 980-3421
Emp Here 250
SIC 2679 Converted paper products, nec

D-U-N-S 25-148-1750   (BR)
LOBLAWS INC
REAL CANADIAN SUPERSTORE
(*Suby of* LOBLAW COMPANIES LIMITED)
333 Seymour Blvd Suite 1560, North Vancouver, BC, V7J 2J4
(604) 904-5537
Emp Here 350
SIC 5411 Grocery stores
Christi Kropf

D-U-N-S 25-775-1094   (SL)
MANA ENERGY CONNECTION
431 Mountain Highway, North Vancouver, BC, V7J 2L1

Emp Here 5   *Sales* 15,529,285
SIC 4924 Natural gas distribution

D-U-N-S 20-622-9312   (HQ)
MCMILLAN, J.S. FISHERIES LTD
12 Orwell St, North Vancouver, BC, V7J 2G1
(604) 982-9207
Emp Here 50   *Sales* 69,138,000
SIC 2092 Fresh or frozen packaged fish
Barry Mcmillan

Colin Mcmillan
Christopher R. Mcmillan

D-U-N-S 20-803-4660   (SL)
NORTH SHORE PRIVATE HOSPITAL (1985) LTD
LYNN VALLEY CARE CENTRE
1070 Lynn Valley Rd Suite 321, North Vancouver, BC, V7J 1Z8
(604) 988-4181
Emp Here 139   *Sales* 9,530,674
SIC 8051 Skilled nursing care facilities
Abolhassan Sherkat
Afsar Sherkat

D-U-N-S 20-428-0705   (HQ)
OLYMPIC INTERNATIONAL AGENCIES LTD
344 Harbour Ave, North Vancouver, BC, V7J 2E9
(604) 986-1400
Emp Here 43   *Sales* 32,203,080
SIC 5075 Warm air heating and air conditioning
Michael Mahannah
Dana Meritt
Steve Johnston
Julian Howitt
Donovan Watts
Dan Mackay

D-U-N-S 20-114-6966   (HQ)
PACIFIC TOWING SERVICES LTD
PORT ALBERNI MARINE INDUSTRIES, DIV OF
14 Orwell St, North Vancouver, BC, V7J 2G1
(604) 990-0591
Emp Here 45   *Sales* 23,623,440
SIC 4492 Towing and tugboat service
Gordon Wilson
Jim Wilson
Marguerite Wilson

D-U-N-S 24-724-1086   (SL)
SACRE CONSULTANTS LTD
SACRE-DAVEY INNOVATIONS
315 Mountain Hwy, North Vancouver, BC, V7J 2K7
(604) 983-0305
Emp Here 103   *Sales* 18,410,117
SIC 8711 Engineering services
Christopher K Sacre
Gemma Sacre
Warren Johnson

D-U-N-S 20-377-8717   (BR)
SAVE-ON-FOODS LIMITED PARTNERSHIP
(*Suby of* SAVE-ON-FOODS LIMITED PARTNERSHIP)
1199 Lynn Valley Rd Unit 1221, North Vancouver, BC, V7J 3H2
(604) 980-4857
Emp Here 100
SIC 5411 Grocery stores
Kevin Smith

D-U-N-S 25-271-7020   (BR)
SOBEYS WEST INC
SAFEWAY PHARMACY
(*Suby of* EMPIRE COMPANY LIMITED)
1170 27th St E, North Vancouver, BC, V7J 1S1
(604) 988-7095
Emp Here 85
SIC 5411 Grocery stores
Jane Mcdow

D-U-N-S 20-307-3510   (BR)
SUNRISE NORTH SENIOR LIVING LTD
(*Suby of* WELLTOWER INC.)
980 Lynn Valley Rd, North Vancouver, BC, V7J 3V7
(604) 904-1226
Emp Here 100
SIC 8361 Residential care
Damien Mcgoldrick

D-U-N-S 24-312-8667   (SL)
SUNSHINE CABS LIMITED

1465 Rupert St, North Vancouver, BC, V7J 1G1
(604) 988-8888
Emp Here 80   *Sales* 4,389,760
SIC 4121 Taxicabs
Charnjint Jawanda
Gurdip Gill

D-U-N-S 20-052-2808   (SL)
T MACRAE FAMILY SALES LTD
CANADIAN TIRE
1350 Main St Suite 601, North Vancouver, BC, V7J 1C6
(604) 982-9101
Emp Here 140   *Sales* 64,561,560
SIC 5014 Tires and tubes
Todd Macrae

D-U-N-S 25-506-0048   (SL)
TERMEL INDUSTRIES LTD
1667 Railway St, North Vancouver, BC, V7J 1B5
(604) 984-9652
Emp Here 70   *Sales* 13,445,950
SIC 3499 Fabricated Metal products, nec
Clayton Kensley

D-U-N-S 25-612-6707   (HQ)
TOTAL SAFETY SERVICES INC
PACIFIC ENVIRONMENTAL CONSULTING
(*Suby of* TOTAL SAFETY U.S., INC.)
1336 Main St, North Vancouver, BC, V7J 1C3

Emp Here 40   *Sales* 11,714,400
SIC 8748 Business consulting, nec
David Mcconnach

D-U-N-S 25-388-8622   (SL)
VANCOUVER PILE DRIVING LTD
20 Brooksbank Ave, North Vancouver, BC, V7J 2B8
(604) 986-5911
Emp Here 125   *Sales* 31,555,250
SIC 1629 Heavy construction, nec
Gordon W. Carlson Sr.
Wayne Saunders
Gary Hamata

D-U-N-S 20-285-1143   (SL)
VPG REALTY INC
1233 Lynn Valley Rd Suite 159, North Vancouver, BC, V7J 0A1
(604) 770-4353
Emp Here 34   *Sales* 11,122,318
SIC 6531 Real estate agents and managers
Eric Langhjelm

D-U-N-S 20-117-3325   (HQ)
WESTERN STEVEDORING COMPANY LIMITED
(*Suby of* FRS CAPITAL CORP.)
15 Mountain Hwy, North Vancouver, BC, V7J 2J9
(604) 904-2800
Emp Here 400   *Sales* 277,888,800
SIC 4491 Marine cargo handling
Brad Eshleman
Dave Lucas
Dave Dunbar

D-U-N-S 25-714-4493   (BR)
WHITE SPOT LIMITED
WHITE SPOT RESTAURANT
(*Suby of* SHATO HOLDINGS LTD)
333 Brooksbank Ave Suite 1100, North Vancouver, BC, V7J 3S8
(604) 988-6717
Emp Here 90
SIC 5812 Eating places
Kelvin Lum

North Vancouver, BC V7K

D-U-N-S 20-298-9310   (BR)
SCHOOL DISTRICT NO. 44 (NORTH VAN-

COUVER)
ARGYLE SECONDARY SCHOOL
(*Suby of* SCHOOL DISTRICT NO. 44 (NORTH VANCOUVER))
1131 Frederick Rd, North Vancouver, BC, V7K 1J3
(604) 903-3300
Emp Here 100
SIC 8211 Elementary and secondary schools
Elizabeth Bell

North Vancouver, BC V7L

D-U-N-S 20-865-6363   (HQ)
COWI NORTH AMERICA LTD
400-138 13th St E, North Vancouver, BC, V7L 0E5
(604) 986-1222
Emp Here 49   *Sales* 10,724,340
SIC 8712 Architectural services
Simon Kim

D-U-N-S 24-622-7974   (SL)
DISTRICT OF NORTH VANCOUVER MUNICIPAL PU
NORTH VANCOUVER FIRE HALL OFFICE
165 13th St E, North Vancouver, BC, V7L 2L3
(604) 980-5021
Emp Here 49   *Sales* 22,011,731
SIC 7389 Business services, nec
Dan Pistilli

D-U-N-S 20-328-4547   (SL)
FLICKA GYM CLUB
123 23rd St E, North Vancouver, BC, V7L 3E2
(604) 985-7918
Emp Here 27   *Sales* 17,724,528
SIC 5961 Catalog and mail-order houses
Sarah Ahmati

D-U-N-S 20-713-9874   (SL)
HALL FILTER SERVICE (2013) LTD, LES
338 Esplanade E, North Vancouver, BC, V7L 1A4
(604) 986-5366
Emp Here 10   *Sales* 40,987,350
SIC 5085 Industrial supplies
Jason Kean
Bryce Zurowski

D-U-N-S 20-518-8717   (SL)
NEPTUNE BULK TERMINALS (CANADA) LTD
1001 Low Level Rd, North Vancouver, BC, V7L 1A7
(604) 985-7461
Emp Here 320   *Sales* 125,991,680
SIC 4491 Marine cargo handling
Claus Thornverg

D-U-N-S 20-584-7494   (HQ)
PANABO SALES LTD
233 1st St E, North Vancouver, BC, V7L 1B4
(604) 988-5051
Emp Here 20   *Sales* 10,177,120
SIC 5023 Homefurnishings
Ursula Mange

D-U-N-S 25-385-5381   (SL)
PT PAPERTECH INC
PAPERTECH
219 1st St E, North Vancouver, BC, V7L 1B4
(604) 990-1600
Emp Here 33   *Sales* 15,675,858
SIC 5084 Industrial machinery and equipment
Kari Hilden
Darlene Hilden

D-U-N-S 24-595-2866   (BR)
RICHARDSON INTERNATIONAL LIMITED
(*Suby of* RICHARDSON, JAMES & SONS, LIMITED)
375 Low Level Rd, North Vancouver, BC, V7L 1A7

(604) 987-8855
Emp Here 120
SIC 5153 Grain and field beans
 Phil Hulina

D-U-N-S 20-027-1430   (BR)
SCHOOL DISTRICT NO. 44 (NORTH VAN-COUVER)
SUTHERLAND SECONDARY SCHOOL
(*Suby of* SCHOOL DISTRICT NO. 44
(NORTH VANCOUVER))
1860 Sutherland Ave, North Vancouver,
V7L 4C2
(604) 903-3500
Emp Here 85
SIC 8211 Elementary and secondary schools
 Ray Bodnaruk

D-U-N-S 25-615-3347   (SL)
SEA AGRA SEAFOOD BROKERAGE LTD
SEA AGRA SEAFOOD JOINT VENTURE
1078 Adderley St, North Vancouver, BC, V7L
1T3
(604) 984-3303
Emp Here 7   *Sales* 27,421,695
SIC 5146 Fish and seafoods
 Ralph Shaw

D-U-N-S 24-551-7610   (SL)
SHYLO NURSING SERVICES LTD
1305 St. Georges Ave, North Vancouver, BC,
V7L 3J2
(604) 985-6881
Emp Here 120   *Sales* 9,365,760
SIC 8049 Offices of health practitioner
 Margot Ware

D-U-N-S 20-035-3519   (BR)
VANCOUVER COASTAL HEALTH
LIONS GATE HOSPITAL
(*Suby of* VANCOUVER COASTAL HEALTH)
231 15th St E, North Vancouver, BC, V7L 2L7
(604) 988-3131
Emp Here 100
SIC 8062 General medical and surgical hospitals
 Bruce Harber

D-U-N-S 25-680-0020   (HQ)
VANCOUVER COASTAL HEALTH
LIONS GATE HOSPITAL
231 15th St E, North Vancouver, BC, V7L 2L7
(604) 988-3131
Sales 182,171,200
SIC 8062 General medical and surgical hospitals
 David Ostrow
 Kip Woodward
 Orene Brown
 Paul Klimo
 John Mcdiarmid
 Karen Muller
 Barbara Brett
 Michael Hoole
 Judy Ageson
 Bill Bryden

North Vancouver, BC V7M

D-U-N-S 25-384-5390   (HQ)
89536 BC LTD
KEY INSURANCE SERVICES
132 Esplanade W Suite 200, North Vancouver,
BC, V7M 1A2
(604) 982-3100
Sales 35,618,520
SIC 6411 Insurance agents, brokers, and service
 Terry Clarke

D-U-N-S 24-289-2875   (HQ)
A & W FOOD SERVICES OF CANADA INC
A & W
171 Esplanade W Suite 300, North Vancouver,
BC, V7M 3K9

(604) 988-2141
Emp Here 95   *Sales* 83,717,005
SIC 5812 Eating places
 Paul Holland
 Susan Senecal
 Axel F. Rehkatsch
 Donald T. Leslie

D-U-N-S 20-182-4864   (SL)
A&W REVENUE ROYALTIES INCOME FUND
171 Esplanade W Suite 300, North Vancouver,
BC, V7M 3K9
(604) 988-2141
Emp Here 18,000   *Sales* 1,033,289,994
SIC 6722 Management investment, open-end
 Paul F.B. Hollands
 Susan D. Senecal
 Trish Sahlstrom
 Patricia A. Parente
 R. Neil Farmer
 Robert D. Fussey
 Nancy Wuttunee
 Angela Griffiths
 Brent Todd
 Tom Newitt

D-U-N-S 20-797-8487   (HQ)
BLUESHORE FINANCIAL CREDIT UNION
1250 Lonsdale Ave, North Vancouver, BC,
V7M 2H6
(604) 983-4500
Emp Here 150   *Sales* 80,199,707
SIC 6062 State credit unions
 Christopher Catliff
 William Keen
 Brian Atkins
 Dave Davenport
 Justin Webb
 Marni Johnson
 Bill Crawford
 Allan Achtemichuk
 Yuri Fulmer
 Peter Leitch

D-U-N-S 20-697-6735   (SL)
CANADIAN BIOENERGY CORPORATION
221 Esplanade W Suite 310, North Vancouver,
BC, V7M 3J3
(604) 947-0040
Emp Here 11   *Sales* 11,492,468
SIC 5172 Petroleum products, nec
 Adam Levine

D-U-N-S 20-801-7905   (SL)
CONCORD SALES LTD
CONCORD NATIONAL PACIFIC, DIV OF
1124 Lonsdale Ave Suite 400, North Vancouver,
BC, V7M 2H1
(604) 986-7341
Emp Here 50   *Sales* 41,778,850
SIC 5141 Groceries, general line
 Mike Donald
 Tony Luongo
 Roger Cunningham

D-U-N-S 24-866-8725   (HQ)
DAKERYN INDUSTRIES LTD
233 1st St W Suite 210, North Vancouver, BC,
V7M 1B3
(604) 986-0323
Sales 155,761,200
SIC 5031 Lumber, plywood, and millwork
 Robert Chimko
 David Wardle Jr.
 Christopher Sainas
 Ray Stewart
 Brad Taylor
 Brett Johnson

D-U-N-S 25-188-0634   (SL)
DIGI117 LTD
145 Chadwick Crt Suite 220, North Vancouver,
BC, V7M 3K1
(778) 772-4770
Emp Here 51   *Sales* 10,906,401
SIC 7372 Prepackaged software

Vadym Chernega

D-U-N-S 24-316-9278   (HQ)
FORTRESS GLOBAL ENTERPRISES INC
157 Chadwick Crt Fl 2, North Vancouver, BC,
V7M 3K2
(888) 820-3888
Emp Here 8   *Sales* 140,965,276
SIC 2611 Pulp mills
 Giovanni Iadeluca
 Marco Veilleux
 Kurt Loewen
 Joe Nemeth
 Mark Kirby
 Anil Wirasekara
 Chadwick Wasilenkoff
 Terrence P. Kavanagh
 Ezra M. Gardner
 Gerald Gaetz

D-U-N-S 24-455-3798   (SL)
HARTS SYSTEMS LTD
1200 Lonsdale Ave Suite 304, North Vancouver, BC, V7M 3H6
(604) 990-9101
Emp Here 50   *Sales* 10,692,550
SIC 7372 Prepackaged software
 David Allen

D-U-N-S 20-864-2157   (HQ)
INSURANCE CORPORATION OF BRITISH COLUMBIA
ICBC
(*Suby of* GOVERNMENT OF THE
PROVINCE OF BRITISH COLUMBIA)
151 Esplanade W, North Vancouver, BC, V7M
3H9
(604) 661-2800
Emp Here 1,500   *Sales* 4,705,051,859
SIC 6331 Fire, marine, and casualty insurance
 Nicolas Jimenez

D-U-N-S 20-963-7060   (SL)
INTEGRITY INSTALLATIONS LTD
INTEGRITY MECHANICAL
705 15th St W, North Vancouver, BC, V7M 1T2
(604) 988-3700
Emp Here 55   *Sales* 12,818,575
SIC 1711 Plumbing, heating, air-conditioning
 Scott Miller

D-U-N-S 25-506-1830   (SL)
KEITH PANEL SYSTEMS CO., LTD
KPS
40 Gostick Pl Suite 2, North Vancouver, BC,
V7M 3G3
(604) 987-4499
Emp Here 100   *Sales* 17,595,800
SIC 8712 Architectural services
 Paul Myers

D-U-N-S 25-613-3570   (SL)
KISA ENTERPRISES LTD
LONSDALE CHEVRON
2305 Lonsdale Ave, North Vancouver, BC,
V7M 2K9
(604) 986-0288
Emp Here 45   *Sales* 22,413,510
SIC 5541 Gasoline service stations
 Kim Conrad

D-U-N-S 25-681-0698   (SL)
LION ONE METALS LIMITED
311 1st St W, North Vancouver, BC, V7M 1B5
(604) 998-1250
Emp Here 46   *Sales* 11,765,604
SIC 1011 Iron ores
 Walter Berukoff
 Hamish Greig
 Stephen Mann
 Tony Young
 Richard Meli
 Kevin Puil
 John Robinson

D-U-N-S 20-622-4602   (SL)
OLYMPIC INDUSTRIES ULC
(*Suby of* FCTG HOLDINGS, INC.)

221 Esplanade W Suite 402, North Vancouver,
BC, V7M 3J8
(604) 985-2115
Emp Here 35   *Sales* 15,651,090
SIC 5031 Lumber, plywood, and millwork
 Gerry Pankratz
 David Smith
 Craig Johnston

D-U-N-S 20-992-4943   (HQ)
PITEAU ASSOCIATES ENGINEERING LTD
788 Copping St Suite 300, North Vancouver,
BC, V7M 3G6
(604) 986-8551
Emp Here 1   *Sales* 14,861,245
SIC 8999 Services, nec

D-U-N-S 20-805-0401   (HQ)
SCHOOL DISTRICT NO. 44 (NORTH VAN-COUVER)
NORTH VANCOUVER SCHOOL DISTRICT
2121 Lonsdale Ave, North Vancouver, BC,
V7M 2K6
(604) 903-3444
Emp Here 800   *Sales* 196,255,620
SIC 8211 Elementary and secondary schools
 John Lewis

D-U-N-S 20-188-6988   (SL)
VMS VENTURES INC
(*Suby of* ROYAL NICKEL CORPORATION)
200 Esplanade W Suite 500, North Vancouver,
BC, V7M 1A4
(604) 986-2020
Emp Here 10   *Sales* 14,373,787
SIC 1081 Metal mining services
 Richard Mark
 John A. Roozendaal
 Cheryl Messier
 Evan Sleeman
 Jay Butterworth
 Mark Fedikow
 Donald Whalen

D-U-N-S 25-419-0960   (HQ)
WORKING ENTERPRISES TRAVEL SER-VICES LTD
W.E. TRAVEL
233 1st St W Suite 430, North Vancouver, BC,
V7M 1B3
(604) 969-5585
Emp Here 12   *Sales* 16,118,977
SIC 4724 Travel agencies
 Gerald Roper
 Ian Sinclair
 David Levi
 Kenneth Georgetti

D-U-N-S 20-702-9245   (BR)
WORLEYPARSONSCORD LP
(*Suby of* WORLEYPARSONS LIMITED)
233 1st St W, North Vancouver, BC, V7M 1B3

Emp Here 200
SIC 8711 Engineering services
 Neil Campbell

North Vancouver, BC V7N

D-U-N-S 20-806-7868   (SL)
CREST REALTY LTD
RE/MAX CREST REALTY
2609 Westview Dr Suite 101, North Vancouver, BC, V7N 4M2
(604) 985-1321
Emp Here 100   *Sales* 27,175,600
SIC 6531 Real estate agents and managers
 John Lichtenwald

D-U-N-S 24-372-7302   (SL)
QUEENSDALE SUPERMARKET LTD
3030 Lonsdale Ave, North Vancouver, BC,
V7N 3J5
(604) 987-6644
Emp Here 45   *Sales* 12,336,840

SIC 5411 Grocery stores
Norman Harris

D-U-N-S 25-229-8468   (SL)
TEJAZZ MANAGEMENT SERVICES INC
CORPORATE CLASSICS CATERERS
4238 St. Pauls Ave, North Vancouver, BC,
V7N 1T5
(604) 986-9475
Emp Here 100   *Sales* 4,287,300
SIC 5812 Eating places
Rustam Teja
Habiba Teja

North Vancouver, BC V7P

D-U-N-S 24-134-0525   (SL)
0695602 BC LTD
WESTAQUA COMMODITY GROUP
998 Harbourside Dr Suite 211, North Vancouver, BC, V7P 3T2
(604) 988-3833
Emp Here 9   *Sales* 10,893,573
SIC 5153 Grain and field beans
Kelly Mills

D-U-N-S 24-824-1408   (HQ)
A C & D INSURANCE SERVICES LTD
1196 Marine Dr, North Vancouver, BC, V7P
1S8
(604) 985-0581
Sales 110,864,520
SIC 6411 Insurance agents, brokers, and service
Joseph Stonehouse

D-U-N-S 25-261-9457   (SL)
AGRICOM INTERNATIONAL INC
828 Harbourside Dr Suite 213, North Vancouver, BC, V7P 3R9
(604) 983-6922
Emp Here 7   *Sales* 10,273,844
SIC 5153 Grain and field beans
Tyler Thorpe

D-U-N-S 24-492-6796   (SL)
AMAKO CONSTRUCTION LTD
1000 3rd St W Suite 300, North Vancouver,
BC, V7P 3J6
(604) 990-6766
Emp Here 80   *Sales* 21,675,360
SIC 1522 Residential construction, nec
Amir Etemadi
David Silcock
Maryiam Etemadi

D-U-N-S 25-927-2011   (SL)
AMITY-COOINDA PACKAGING SERVICES
1070 Roosevelt Cres, North Vancouver, BC,
V7P 1M3
(604) 985-7491
Emp Here 25   *Sales* 11,087,250
SIC 7389 Business services, nec
Carol Hawthorn

D-U-N-S 20-695-6935   (SL)
ATLANTIA HOLDINGS INCORPORATED
949 3rd St W Suite 121, North Vancouver, BC,
V7P 3P7
(604) 985-7257
Emp Here 50   *Sales* 22,358,700
SIC 5045 Computers, peripherals, and software
Karim Salemohamed
Erin Wizenberg

D-U-N-S 20-109-4497   (HQ)
BCB CORPORATE SERVICES LTD
1000 14th St W Unit 100, North Vancouver,
BC, V7P 3P3
(778) 340-1060
Emp Here 6   *Sales* 23,707,440
SIC 8741 Management services
Wendy Mcdonald
Robert Macpherson

William Dix
Wendy-Penelope Omes
Gordon Steele
Wynn Powell
Darcy Rezac
Grace Mccarthy
Allan Skidmore
Scott Macpherson

D-U-N-S 20-051-8756   (SL)
BUGABOOS EYEWEAR (U.S.A) INC
758 Harbourside Dr, North Vancouver, BC,
V7P 3R7
(604) 924-2393
Emp Here 50   *Sales* 26,328,544
SIC 5099 Durable goods, nec
Don Martin

D-U-N-S 20-648-9556   (SL)
CAM CLARK FORD LINCOLN LTD
833 Automall Dr, North Vancouver, BC, V7P
3R8
(604) 980-3673
Emp Here 82   *Sales* 23,230,600
SIC 7532 Top and body repair and paint shops
Dick Lau

D-U-N-S 20-948-4018   (SL)
CANADIAN TRAVEL TEAM
935 Marine Dr Suite 304, North Vancouver,
BC, V7P 1S3
(604) 990-7370
Emp Here 49   *Sales* 25,478,383
SIC 4725 Tour operators
Carrie Ashman

D-U-N-S 25-414-4934   (SL)
CAPILANO VOLKSWAGEN INC
1151 Marine Dr, North Vancouver, BC, V7P
1T1
(604) 985-0694
Emp Here 72   *Sales* 45,308,160
SIC 5511 New and used car dealers
Hans Fruehauf
Anders Lau

D-U-N-S 20-515-1819   (SL)
**CARTER CHEVROLET CADILLAC BUICK
GMC NORTHSHORE LTD**
CARTER GM
800 Automall Dr, North Vancouver, BC, V7P
3R8
(604) 987-5231
Emp Here 74   *Sales* 46,566,720
SIC 5511 New and used car dealers
James Carter

D-U-N-S 20-797-6119   (HQ)
**COMMANDER WAREHOUSE EQUIPMENT
LTD**
930 1st St W Suite 119, North Vancouver, BC,
V7P 3N4
(604) 980-8511
Emp Here 10   *Sales* 23,751,300
SIC 5084 Industrial machinery and equipment
Earle Morriss
Chris Hall

D-U-N-S 20-038-1957   (BR)
**CORPORATION OF THE DISTRICT OF
WEST VANCOUVER, THE**
BLUE BUS
(*Suby of* CORPORATION OF THE DISTRICT
OF WEST VANCOUVER, THE)
221 Lloyd Ave, North Vancouver, BC, V7P
3M2
(604) 985-7777
Emp Here 100
SIC 4111 Local and suburban transit

D-U-N-S 24-342-9870   (HQ)
COUNTRY FURNITURE LTD
CANADIAN HERITAGE DESIGN
1365 Pemberton Ave, North Vancouver, BC,
V7P 2R6
(604) 985-9700
Emp Here 3   *Sales* 20,354,240
SIC 5021 Furniture

Brock Andrew
John Andrew

D-U-N-S 20-427-8055   (HQ)
DENNISON AUTO LTD
NORTH SHORE ACURA
828 Automall Dr, North Vancouver, BC, V7P
3R8
(604) 929-6736
Emp Here 30   *Sales* 40,903,200
SIC 5511 New and used car dealers
Barbara Gadallah
Fahim Gadallah

D-U-N-S 24-686-6920   (SL)
DESTINATION CHRYSLER LTD
1600 Marine Dr, North Vancouver, BC, V7P
1T9
(888) 461-4138
Emp Here 30   *Sales* 14,942,340
SIC 5511 New and used car dealers
Aziz Ahame

D-U-N-S 20-804-1350   (SL)
E. E. C. INDUSTRIES LIMITED
1237 Welch St, North Vancouver, BC, V7P
1B3
(604) 986-5633
Emp Here 67   *Sales* 21,851,112
SIC 3993 Signs and advertising specialties
Allan Buch
Henning Buch
Palle Buch

D-U-N-S 24-032-6926   (SL)
FIBRECO EXPORT INC
1209 Mckeen Ave, North Vancouver, BC, V7P
3H9
(604) 980-6543
Emp Here 25   *Sales* 13,013,550
SIC 5099 Durable goods, nec
Kerry Lige

D-U-N-S 20-112-0508   (SL)
HALSE-MARTIN CONSTRUCTION CO. LTD
1636 Mcguire Ave, North Vancouver, BC, V7P
3B1
(604) 980-4811
Emp Here 35   *Sales* 19,961,830
SIC 1542 Nonresidential construction, nec
Roy Reichgeld

D-U-N-S 25-640-0409   (BR)
HONDA CANADA INC
PACIFIC HONDA
(*Suby of* HONDA MOTOR CO., LTD.)
816 Automall Dr, North Vancouver, BC, V7P
3R8
(604) 984-0331
Emp Here 80
SIC 5511 New and used car dealers
Jerry Chenkin

D-U-N-S 20-705-8632   (SL)
KEG RESTAURANT
PARK ROYAL KEG
800 Marine Dr, North Vancouver, BC, V7P
1R8
(604)
Emp Here 100   *Sales* 4,551,900
SIC 5812 Eating places
Greg Dubois

D-U-N-S 24-760-4635   (HQ)
KIANI MOTORS LTD
PETRO CANADA
1980 Marine Dr, North Vancouver, BC, V7P
1V6
(604) 987-4490
Emp Here 5   *Sales* 24,903,900
SIC 5541 Gasoline service stations
Rashna Kianipour

D-U-N-S 24-249-2999   (SL)
MARINE PETROBULK LTD
10 Pemberton Ave, North Vancouver, BC, V7P
2R1
(604) 987-4415
Emp Here 12   *Sales* 12,393,696

SIC 5172 Petroleum products, nec
Tony Brewster
Ken Brewster

D-U-N-S 25-318-2117   (BR)
**MCDONALD'S RESTAURANTS OF
CANADA LIMITED**
MCDONALD'S #8486
(*Suby of* MCDONALD'S CORPORATION)
925 Marine Dr, North Vancouver, BC, V7P 1S2
(604) 985-6757
Emp Here 75
SIC 5812 Eating places
Jim Pike

D-U-N-S 25-318-2158   (BR)
**MCDONALD'S RESTAURANTS OF
CANADA LIMITED**
MCDONALD'S #8045
(*Suby of* MCDONALD'S CORPORATION)
1219 Marine Dr, North Vancouver, BC, V7P
1T3
(604) 904-4390
Emp Here 95
SIC 5812 Eating places
Kam Salahi

D-U-N-S 20-794-5965   (HQ)
MODERN NIAGARA VANCOUVER INC
(*Suby of* MODERN/NIAGARA GROUP INC)
788 Harbourside Dr Suite 200, North Vancouver, BC, V7P 3R7
(604) 980-4891
Emp Here 205   *Sales* 89,379,840
SIC 1711 Plumbing, heating, air-conditioning
Yves Perron
Kevin Collier

D-U-N-S 25-146-2511   (SL)
MORREY AUTO GROUP LTD
MORREY MAZDA
818 Automall Dr, North Vancouver, BC, V7P
3R8
(604) 984-9211
Emp Here 35   *Sales* 17,432,730
SIC 5511 New and used car dealers
Steve Morrey

D-U-N-S 24-417-9482   (HQ)
NAVIGATA COMMUNICATIONS 2009, INC
949 3rd St W Suite 121, North Vancouver, BC,
V7P 3P7
(604) 998-4490
Sales 45,237,456
SIC 4899 Communication services, nec
Kevin Erickson
Peter Legault

D-U-N-S 24-457-7227   (HQ)
NORSON CONSTRUCTION LLP
949 3rd St W Suite 221, North Vancouver, BC,
V7P 3P7
(604) 986-5681
Emp Here 35   *Sales* 21,182,895
SIC 1542 Nonresidential construction, nec
Terry Clayton
Norman Stevenson

D-U-N-S 20-958-0778   (SL)
PARK SHORE MOTORS LTD
835 Automall Dr, North Vancouver, BC, V7P
3R8
(604) 985-9344
Emp Here 35   *Sales* 17,432,730
SIC 5511 New and used car dealers
Horst Duess
Heather Duess

D-U-N-S 25-539-2706   (HQ)
PINECORE ENTERPRISES INC
828 Harbourside Dr Suite 117, North Vancouver, BC, V7P 3R9
(604) 990-9679
Sales 13,365,360
SIC 5199 Nondurable goods, nec
Peyman Ashkenani
Hussain Ashkenani

D-U-N-S 24-683-3164 (SL)
RED ROBIN RESTAURANT (CAPILANO) LTD
801 Marine Dr Suite 100, North Vancouver, BC, V7P 3K6

Emp Here 100   *Sales* 4,551,900
SIC 5812 Eating places
Bruce Fox

D-U-N-S 20-103-3446 (SL)
SCANDINAVIAN BUILDING MAINTENANCE LTD
245 Fell Ave Suite 101, North Vancouver, BC, V7P 2K1

Emp Here 450   *Sales* 14,552,213
SIC 7349 Building maintenance services, nec
John Petersen
Judy Petersen

D-U-N-S 20-587-3961 (BR)
SEASPAN ULC
GENERAL TOWING, DIV OF
(*Suby of* WASHINGTON CANADIAN LTD)
10 Pemberton Ave, North Vancouver, BC, V7P 2R1
(604) 988-3111
Emp Here 200
SIC 4492 Towing and tugboat service
Michael Crosby

D-U-N-S 20-573-4270 (HQ)
SEASPAN ULC
SEASPAN MARINE
(*Suby of* WASHINGTON CANADIAN LTD)
10 Pemberton Ave, North Vancouver, BC, V7P 2R1
(604) 988-3111
Emp Here 1,700   *Sales* 548,433,900
SIC 4492 Towing and tugboat service
Brian Carter
Frank Butzelaar
Kyle Washington
Paul Thomas
Joe O'rourke
Paul Hebson
Tim Page
Ian Brennan
Jim Corr
John Lyle

D-U-N-S 20-799-7420 (HQ)
SINCLAIR DENTAL CO. LTD
SINCLAIR DENTAL
900 Harbourside Dr, North Vancouver, BC, V7P 3T8
(604) 986-1544
Emp Here 100   *Sales* 240,908,400
SIC 5047 Medical and hospital equipment
Shahab Soltani
Amir Nowtash
Victor Michaud

D-U-N-S 20-998-9651 (HQ)
SUNTECH OPTICS INC
PUGABOOS
(*Suby of* ESSILORLUXOTTICA)
758 Harbourside Dr, North Vancouver, BC, V7P 3R7
(604) 929-8141
Sales 20,821,680
SIC 5099 Durable goods, nec
Debra Heck

D-U-N-S 24-069-0461 (HQ)
SURESPAN CONSTRUCTION LTD
(*Suby of* SURESPAN INVESTMENTS GROUP INC)
38 Fell Ave Suite 301, North Vancouver, BC, V7P 3S2
(604) 998-1133
Emp Here 15   *Sales* 37,866,300
SIC 1622 Bridge, tunnel, and elevated highway construction
Nigel Bester
Mark Rogers

D-U-N-S 25-329-5034 (HQ)
SURESPAN INVESTMENTS GROUP INC
38 Fell Ave Suite 301, North Vancouver, BC, V7P 3S2
(604) 998-1133
Emp Here 30   *Sales* 50,488,400
SIC 1622 Bridge, tunnel, and elevated highway construction
Nigel Bester
Vivian Bester

D-U-N-S 20-103-4378 (SL)
VANCOUVER SHIPYARDS CO. LTD
(*Suby of* WASHINGTON CANADIAN LTD)
10 Pemberton Avenue, North Vancouver, BC, V7P 2R1
(604) 988-6361
Emp Here 350   *Sales* 101,797,500
SIC 3731 Shipbuilding and repairing
Kyle Washington

D-U-N-S 20-238-0114 (SL)
VOLVO OF NORTH VANCOUVER
809 Automall Dr, North Vancouver, BC, V7P 3R8
(604) 986-9889
Emp Here 30   *Sales* 14,942,340
SIC 5511 New and used car dealers
Marc Goodman

D-U-N-S 25-714-3321 (BR)
WAL-MART CANADA CORP
(*Suby of* WALMART INC.)
925 Marine Dr Suite 3057, North Vancouver, BC, V7P 1S2
(604) 984-6830
Emp Here 200
SIC 5311 Department stores
Lloyd Lyson

D-U-N-S 24-579-9028 (HQ)
WEST COAST REALTY LTD
SUTTON GROUP
889 Harbourside Dr Suite 100, North Vancouver, BC, V7P 3S1
(604) 365-9120
Emp Here 150   *Sales* 67,022,240
SIC 6531 Real estate agents and managers
Edmond Shung

D-U-N-S 20-584-4822 (HQ)
WSP
(*Suby of* OPUS INTERNATIONAL CONSULTANTS LIMITED)
889 Harbourside Dr Suite 210, North Vancouver, BC, V7P 3S1
(604) 990-4800
Emp Here 50   *Sales* 16,476,850
SIC 8748 Business consulting, nec
Jack Lee

North Vancouver, BC V7R

D-U-N-S 24-764-3328 (SL)
CAPILANO SUSPENSION BRIDGE LTD
3735 Capilano Rd Suite 1889, North Vancouver, BC, V7R 4J1
(604) 985-7474
Emp Here 84   *Sales* 18,882,640
SIC 4724 Travel agencies
Nancy Stibbard

D-U-N-S 20-713-5526 (SL)
MARINO'S MARKET LTD
SUPER VALU
3230 Connaught Cres, North Vancouver, BC, V7R 0A5

Emp Here 40   *Sales* 10,966,080
SIC 5411 Grocery stores
Allan Belich
Bill Belich
Francis Belich
Tim Belich

D-U-N-S 24-496-2200 (SL)
QUICK SPORTS
4740 Capilano Rd, North Vancouver, BC, V7R 4K3

Emp Here 49   *Sales* 10,663,037
SIC 5941 Sporting goods and bicycle shops
Brandt Quick

D-U-N-S 20-285-0921 (SL)
RIVERSIDE RETIREMENT CENTRE LTD
4315 Skyline Dr, North Vancouver, BC, V7R 3G9
(604) 307-1104
Emp Here 500   *Sales* 32,141,000
SIC 8361 Residential care
Mary Mcdougall

D-U-N-S 20-591-0834 (BR)
SCHOOL DISTRICT NO. 44 (NORTH VANCOUVER)
HANDSWORTH SECONDARY SCHOOL
(*Suby of* SCHOOL DISTRICT NO. 44 (NORTH VANCOUVER))
1044 Edgewood Rd, North Vancouver, BC, V7R 1Y7
(604) 903-3600
Emp Here 80
SIC 8211 Elementary and secondary schools
David Obergaard

Okanagan Falls, BC V0H

D-U-N-S 24-898-4304 (SL)
UNIT ELECTRICAL ENGINEERING LTD
1406 Maple St, Okanagan Falls, BC, V0H 1R2
(250) 497-5254
Emp Here 86   *Sales* 16,378,012
SIC 3613 Switchgear and switchboard apparatus
Mark Burleigh

Oliver, BC V0H

D-U-N-S 25-136-5334 (SL)
BURROWING OWL VINEYARDS LTD
BURROWING OWL ESTATE WINERY
100 Burrowing Owl Pl, Oliver, BC, V0H 1T0
(250) 498-0620
Emp Here 55   *Sales* 12,367,025
SIC 2084 Wines, brandy, and brandy spirits
Christopher Wyse
James Wyse

D-U-N-S 24-191-8259 (SL)
CANADIAN TIRE
34017 97th St, Oliver, BC, V0H 1T0
(250) 498-8473
Emp Here 30   *Sales* 10,926,450
SIC 5014 Tires and tubes
Sarah Van Lange

D-U-N-S 20-798-8601 (SL)
DOUBLE O MARKETS LTD
SUPER VALUE 18
Gd, Oliver, BC, V0H 1T0

Emp Here 51   *Sales* 14,967,327
SIC 5411 Grocery stores
William Brogan

D-U-N-S 24-026-1987 (BR)
MARK ANTHONY PROPERTIES LTD
MISSION HILL FAMILY ESTATE
(*Suby of* PELECANUS HOLDINGS LTD)
7151 Sibco Landfill, Oliver, BC, V0H 1T0

Emp Here 200
SIC 6531 Real estate agents and managers
Sherry Casorso

D-U-N-S 24-805-5647 (SL)

D-U-N-S 24-496-2200 (SL)

NK'MIP VINEYARDS LTD
7357 Vineyard Rd, Oliver, BC, V0H 1T0
(250) 498-3552
Emp Here 40   *Sales* 13,698,680
SIC 0172 Grapes
Sam Baptist

D-U-N-S 24-154-9609 (SL)
SOUTH OKANAGAN GENERAL HOSPITAL
7139 362 Ave, Oliver, BC, V0H 1T0
(250) 498-5000
Emp Here 200   *Sales* 22,216,000
SIC 8062 General medical and surgical hospitals
Cindy Crane

Osoyoos, BC V0H

D-U-N-S 24-844-5541 (SL)
ANARCHIST MOUNTAIN FIRE DEPARTMENT
115 Grizzly Rd, Osoyoos, BC, V0H 1V6

Emp Here 25   *Sales* 11,419,358
SIC 7389 Business services, nec
Robert Burk

Panorama, BC V0A

D-U-N-S 24-849-0935 (SL)
PANORAMA MOUNTAIN VILLAGE INC
PANORAMA MOUNTAIN RESORT
2000 Panorama Dr, Panorama, BC, V0A 1T0
(250) 342-6941
Emp Here 200   *Sales* 19,133,600
SIC 7011 Hotels and motels
Steve Paccagnan
Don Archibald
Chad Jensen
Kenneth S Renton
Robert Ritchie
Ivan Smith
Ryan Thorogood
Elden Trach
Barry Travers

Parksville, BC V9P

D-U-N-S 24-457-9660 (SL)
AQUILA CEDAR PRODUCTS LTD
WEATHERWISE INDUSTRIES DIV OF
1282 Alberni Hwy, Parksville, BC, V9P 2C9
(250) 248-5922
Emp Here 40   *Sales* 17,886,960
SIC 5031 Lumber, plywood, and millwork
Lyle Stolz
Craig Hocking
Warren Bay
Pat Hyde
Dave Haynes

D-U-N-S 25-902-6185 (SL)
ARROWSMITH POTTERS GUILD
600 Alberni Hwy, Parksville, BC, V9P 1J9
(250) 954-1872
Emp Here 49   *Sales* 11,114,817
SIC 8399 Social services, nec
Barbara Strachen

D-U-N-S 24-312-0318 (SL)
ARROWSMITH REST HOME SOCIETY
ARROWSMITH LODGE
266 Moilliet St S Suite 1, Parksville, BC, V9P 1M9
(250) 947-9777
Emp Here 113   *Sales* 7,720,838
SIC 8051 Skilled nursing care facilities
David Mcdowell

D-U-N-S 25-415-6763   (SL)
EXPRESS CUSTOM TRAILERS MFG. INC
EXPRESS CUSTOM
1365 Alberni Hwy, Parksville, BC, V9P 2B9

Emp Here 70   Sales 15,540,070
SIC 3537 Industrial trucks and tractors
  Robert Ethier
  Sharon Ethier

D-U-N-S 25-133-8570   (SL)
FOOTPRINTS SECURITY PATROL INC
*FOOTPRINTS SECURITY GROUP, ISLAND
LOSS PREVENTION*
Gd, Parksville, BC, V9P 2G2
(250) 248-9117
Emp Here 45   Sales 20,214,855
SIC 7389 Business services, nec
  Simon Collery

D-U-N-S 20-022-3576   (SL)
KERR GROUP, THE
886 Wembley Rd Unit5, Parksville, BC, V9P
2E6
(250) 586-1100
Emp Here 200   Sales 83,777,800
SIC 6531 Real estate agents and managers
  Rod Kerr

D-U-N-S 20-038-4613   (SL)
**MAINROAD MID-ISLAND CONSTRUCTING
LTD**
435 Springhill Rd, Parksville, BC, V9P 2T2

Emp Here 45   Sales 12,758,580
SIC 1611 Highway and street construction
  Peter Ashcroft,

D-U-N-S 20-863-7413   (SL)
PARKSVILLE CHRYSLER
230 Shelly Rd, Parksville, BC, V9P 1V6
(250) 248-3281
Emp Here 40   Sales 19,923,120
SIC 5511 New and used car dealers
  Bruce Alexander

D-U-N-S 25-485-7873   (BR)
SCHOOL DISTRICT NO 69 (QUALICUM)
ECOLE BALLENAS SECONDARY SCHOOL
135 N Pym Rd, Parksville, BC, V9P 2H4
(250) 248-5721
Emp Here 90
SIC 8211 Elementary and secondary schools
  Rudy Terpstra

D-U-N-S 20-582-9117   (SL)
SHOPPERS DRUG MART
140 Island Hwy E, Parksville, BC, V9P 2G5
(250) 248-3521
Emp Here 40   Sales 10,118,160
SIC 5912 Drug stores and proprietary stores
  Mike Biagioni

D-U-N-S 24-155-7081   (SL)
TIGH-NA-MARA RESORTS LTD
TIGH-NA-MARA RESORT HOTEL
1155 Resort Dr, Parksville, BC, V9P 2E3
(250) 248-2072
Emp Here 190   Sales 17,611,100
SIC 7011 Hotels and motels
  Patricia Cocks
  Dant Hirsch
  Jackie Hirsch

D-U-N-S 24-345-6311   (BR)
**VANCOUVER ISLAND HEALTH AUTHOR-
ITY**
TRILLIUM LODGE
(*Suby of* GOVERNMENT OF THE
PROVINCE OF BRITISH COLUMBIA)
Gd, Parksville, BC, V9P 2G2
(250) 947-8230
Emp Here 150
SIC 8011 Offices and clinics of medical doc-
tors
  Gillian Forsyth

D-U-N-S 20-086-9845   (BR)

**VANCOUVER ISLAND HEALTH AUTHOR-
ITY**
HOME & COMMUNITY CARE SERVICES
(*Suby of* GOVERNMENT OF THE
PROVINCE OF BRITISH COLUMBIA)
180 Mccarter St Suite 100, Parksville, BC,
V9P 2H3
(250) 731-1315
Emp Here 175
SIC 8011 Offices and clinics of medical doc-
tors
  Robyn Monrufet

Peachland, BC V0H

D-U-N-S 25-930-0341   (HQ)
CO DARA VENTURES LTD
PETRO CANADA
5500 Clements Cres Suite 80, Peachland, BC,
V0H 1X5
(250) 767-9054
Emp Here 5   Sales 24,903,900
SIC 5541 Gasoline service stations
  Terry A. Newman

D-U-N-S 24-235-9037   (SL)
PEACHLAND FIRE & RESCUE SERVICE
4401 3rd St, Peachland, BC, V0H 1X7
(250) 767-2841
Emp Here 37   Sales 16,621,103
SIC 7389 Business services, nec
  Grant Topham

Pemberton, BC V0N

D-U-N-S 24-320-2301   (HQ)
682880 B.C. LTD
AC PETROLEUM
7338 Industrial Way, Pemberton, BC, V0N 2L0
(604) 894-6220
Emp Here 7   Sales 11,360,888
SIC 5172 Petroleum products, nec
  Norman Leblanc
  Patricia Leblanc

Penticton, BC V2A

D-U-N-S 20-378-0739   (SL)
0769510 B.C. LTD
PENTICTON HONDA
510 Duncan Ave W, Penticton, BC, V2A 7N1
(250) 492-0100
Emp Here 50   Sales 24,903,900
SIC 5511 New and used car dealers
  Rick Sentes
  David Dempster

D-U-N-S 24-554-4064   (SL)
0794856 B.C. LTD
PENTICTON HYUNDAI
448 Duncan Ave W, Penticton, BC, V2A 7N1
(250) 492-0205
Emp Here 25   Sales 12,451,950
SIC 5511 New and used car dealers
  Rick Sentes
  David Dempster

D-U-N-S 24-995-4389   (SL)
ACTION STEEL SALES (OKANAGAN) LTD
ACTION REBAR, DIV OF
2365 Barnes St, Penticton, BC, V2A 7K6
(250) 492-7822
Emp Here 25   Sales 11,179,350
SIC 5051 Metals service centers and offices
  Michael Nixon

D-U-N-S 25-485-9192   (SL)
APEX MOUNTAIN RESORT (1997) LTD

---

324 Strayhorse Rd, Penticton, BC, V2A 6J9
(250) 292-8222
Emp Here 150   Sales 14,242,950
SIC 7999 Amusement and recreation, nec
  Ted Garnett
  Brian Martin
  Dean Garnett
  James Shalman

D-U-N-S 25-483-2934   (HQ)
**ARGO ROAD MAINTENANCE (SOUTH
OKANAGAN) INC**
290 Waterloo Ave, Penticton, BC, V2A 7N3
(250) 493-6969
Emp Here 10   Sales 72,185,300
SIC 1611 Highway and street construction
  Harley Hook
  Case Van Diemen
  Robert Wills

D-U-N-S 24-374-1147   (SL)
BARLEY MILL PUB LTD, THE
*BARLEY MILL BREW PUB & SPORTS
BISTRO*
2460 Skaha Lake Rd, Penticton, BC, V2A 6E9
(250) 493-8000
Emp Here 35   Sales 10,469,550
SIC 5921 Liquor stores
  Harley Hatfield
  Lawrence Lund
  Kevin L Hatfield

D-U-N-S 20-100-8133   (HQ)
BERRY & SMITH TRUCKING LTD
301 Warren Ave E, Penticton, BC, V2A 3M1
(250) 492-4042
Emp Here 100   Sales 22,627,660
SIC 4213 Trucking, except local
  Matthew Berry
  Mark Berry
  Julie Berry
  Deborah Berry

D-U-N-S 20-691-0239   (HQ)
BPWOOD LTD
186 Nanaimo Ave W Unit 102, Penticton, BC,
V2A 1N4
(250) 493-9339
Emp Here 8   Sales 37,379,802
SIC 5031 Lumber, plywood, and millwork
  Paul Bouchard
  Steve Winstone
  Dan Bouchard

D-U-N-S 24-311-4774   (SL)
BROWN, BOB BUICK GMC LTD
1010 Westminster Ave W, Penticton, BC, V2A
1L6
(250) 493-7121
Emp Here 50   Sales 24,903,900
SIC 5511 New and used car dealers
  Robert Brown
  Martin Mcginn

D-U-N-S 24-317-3943   (BR)
GREAT PACIFIC INDUSTRIES INC
SAVE-ON-FOODS
(*Suby of* PATTISON, JIM GROUP INC)
2111 Main St Suite 161, Penticton, BC, V2A
6W6
(250) 492-2011
Emp Here 150
SIC 5411 Grocery stores
  Randall Bamford

D-U-N-S 24-455-6155   (SL)
GREYBACK CONSTRUCTION LTD
402 Warren Ave E, Penticton, BC, V2A 3M2
(250) 493-7972
Emp Here 100   Sales 57,033,800
SIC 1542 Nonresidential construction, nec
  Larry Kenyon
  Matt Kenyon

D-U-N-S 24-351-6841   (SL)
**HAMLETS AT PENTICTON RESIDENCE
INC, THE**
HAMLETS AT PENTICTON

---

103 Duncan Ave W, Penticton, BC, V2A 2Y3
(250) 490-8503
Emp Here 150   Sales 10,248,900
SIC 8059 Nursing and personal care, nec
  Andre Van Ryk
  Kasey Vandongen

D-U-N-S 25-538-9983   (SL)
HILLSIDE CELLARS WINERY LTD
HILLSIDE WINERY AND BISTRO
1350 Naramata Rd, Penticton, BC, V2A 8T6
(250) 493-6274
Emp Here 35   Sales 10,469,550
SIC 5921 Liquor stores
  Duncan Mcgowan

D-U-N-S 25-301-2504   (BR)
HUDSON'S BAY COMPANY
BAY, THE
(*Suby of* HUDSON'S BAY COMPANY)
2111 Main St Suite 160, Penticton, BC, V2A
6V1
(250) 493-1900
Emp Here 120
SIC 5311 Department stores
  Jerry Barsky

D-U-N-S 24-369-2357   (HQ)
INLAND CONTRACTING LTD
INLAND EQUIPMENT SALES
716 Okanagan Ave E, Penticton, BC, V2A 3K6
(250) 492-2626
Emp Here 45   Sales 14,176,200
SIC 1611 Highway and street construction
  David Kampe

D-U-N-S 24-595-3393   (SL)
KEIJ ENTERPRISES LTD
PENTICTON TOYOTA
2405 Skaha Lake Rd, Penticton, BC, V2A 6E8
(250) 493-1107
Emp Here 30   Sales 14,942,340
SIC 5511 New and used car dealers
  Hendrik Keij

D-U-N-S 24-245-0187   (HQ)
LOCATIONS WEST REALTY INC
*ROYAL LEPAGE-LOCATIONS WEST RE-
ALTY*
484 Main St, Penticton, BC, V2A 5C5
(250) 493-2244
Sales 13,587,800
SIC 6531 Real estate agents and managers
  Robin Agur
  Debrah Kozari
  Roger Love

D-U-N-S 25-556-6564   (SL)
MACMILLAN, DOUG ENTERPRISES LTD
CANADIAN TIRE
960 Railway St, Penticton, BC, V2A 8N2
(250) 492-3586
Emp Here 60   Sales 37,756,800
SIC 5531 Auto and home supply stores
  Doug Macmillan
  Lorraine Macmillan

D-U-N-S 25-046-9710   (SL)
MURRAY BUICK GMC PENTICTON
1010 Westminster Ave W, Penticton, BC, V2A
1L6
(250) 493-7121
Emp Here 49   Sales 24,405,822
SIC 5511 New and used car dealers
  Scott Robertson

D-U-N-S 25-195-9482   (SL)
NOR-MAR INDUSTRIES LTD
682 Okanagan Ave E, Penticton, BC, V2A 3K6
(250) 492-7866
Emp Here 68   Sales 30,546,892
SIC 7389 Business services, nec
  Gerry Turchak

D-U-N-S 20-168-1587   (SL)
OKANAGAN COLLEGE
583 Duncan Ave W, Penticton, BC, V2A 8E1

---

(250) 492-4305
Emp Here 100   *Sales* 25,349,000
SIC 8748 Business consulting, nec
Jacquie Dewarpine

D-U-N-S 20-104-1340   (SL)
PARKER'S CHRYSLER DODGE JEEP LTD
1765 Main St, Penticton, BC, V2A 5H1
(250) 492-2839
Emp Here 45   *Sales* 22,413,510
SIC 5511 New and used car dealers
Janet Parker
Rainer Wuthe

D-U-N-S 24-714-8620   (HQ)
PEERLESS LIMITED
575 Page Ave, Penticton, BC, V2A 6P3
(250) 492-0408
Sales 26,293,727
SIC 3715 Truck trailers
Andy Mceachern
Marc Berthiaume

D-U-N-S 25-227-1655   (HQ)
PENTICTON & DISTRICT COMMUNITY RE-SOURCES SOCIETY
330 Ellis St, Penticton, BC, V2A 4L7
(250) 492-5814
Emp Here 30   *Sales* 20,706,800
SIC 8399 Social services, nec
Heather Cooke
Mark Rutter
Terry Rolston
Anne Cossentine
Lise Ecclestone
Kathryn Lundman
John Mott
Sheilagh Seaton
Dave Stigant

D-U-N-S 20-865-3162   (SL)
PENTICTON AND DISTRICT SOCIETY FOR COMMUNITY LIVING
PDSCL
180 Industrial Ave W, Penticton, BC, V2A 6X9
(250) 493-0312
Emp Here 100   *Sales* 6,842,200
SIC 8322 Individual and family services
Tony Laing
Bill Barid
Wilma Perry

D-U-N-S 24-750-4046   (SL)
PENTICTON COURTYARD INN LTD
RAMADA INN & SUITES PENTICTON
1050 Eckhardt Ave W, Penticton, BC, V2A 2C3
(250) 492-8926
Emp Here 80   *Sales* 7,591,920
SIC 7011 Hotels and motels
Robin Agur
Randy Kowalchuk

D-U-N-S 20-748-9485   (SL)
PENTICTON FOUNDRY LTD
568 Dawson Ave, Penticton, BC, V2A 3N8
(250) 492-7043
Emp Here 57   *Sales* 10,339,116
SIC 3322 Malleable iron foundries
Brian Bendig

D-U-N-S 24-421-3034   (SL)
PENTICTON KIA
550 Duncan Ave W, Penticton, BC, V2A 7N1
(250) 276-1200
Emp Here 25   *Sales* 12,451,950
SIC 5511 New and used car dealers
David Newman
Joanna Newman

D-U-N-S 25-964-0886   (SL)
PETER'S BROS. CONSTRUCTION LTD
716 Okanagan Ave E, Penticton, BC, V2A 3K6
(250) 492-2626
Emp Here 75   *Sales* 18,933,150
SIC 1611 Highway and street construction
Joseph Cuzzocrea
Eric Peter Selles

D-U-N-S 20-196-6186   (SL)
PRO BUILDERS LTD
PENTICTON HOME HARDWARE BUILDING CENTRE
150 Fairview Pl, Penticton, BC, V2A 6A5
(250) 493-7844
Emp Here 90   *Sales* 24,088,680
SIC 5251 Hardware stores
Paul Mccann

D-U-N-S 24-559-1417   (HQ)
PRO BUILDING SUPPLY LTD
150 Fairview Pl, Penticton, BC, V2A 6A5
(250) 492-6635
Sales 57,334,200
SIC 5211 Lumber and other building materials
Paul Mccann
Elizabeth Watters

D-U-N-S 25-497-3043   (HQ)
SCHOOL DISTRICT NO 67 (OKANAGAN SKAHA)
425 Jermyn Ave, Penticton, BC, V2A 1Z4
(250) 770-7700
Emp Here 25   *Sales* 79,295,200
SIC 8211 Elementary and secondary schools
Wendy Hyer
Tott Manuel

D-U-N-S 20-065-5772   (SL)
SENTES CHEVROLET LTD
933 Westminster Ave W, Penticton, BC, V2A 1L1
(250) 493-2333
Emp Here 53   *Sales* 33,351,840
SIC 5511 New and used car dealers
Richard Sentes
David Dempster

D-U-N-S 24-881-2364   (SL)
SINGLA BROS. HOLDINGS LTD
567 Heather Rd Suite 32860, Penticton, BC, V2A 6N8
(250) 490-1700
Emp Here 40   *Sales* 12,754,760
SIC 1521 Single-family housing construction
Paul Singla
Bhushan Singla
Subhash Singla

D-U-N-S 24-535-1606   (SL)
SKAHA FORD INC
198 Parkway Pl, Penticton, BC, V2A 8G8
(250) 492-3800
Emp Here 65   *Sales* 40,903,200
SIC 5511 New and used car dealers
Richard Fuhr

D-U-N-S 24-320-2771   (SL)
STRUCTURLAM MASS TIMBER CORPO-RATION
2176 Government St, Penticton, BC, V2A 8B5
(250) 492-8912
Emp Here 200   *Sales* 38,474,000
SIC 2439 Structural wood members, nec
Hardy Wentzel
Bill Downing

D-U-N-S 20-865-2867   (HQ)
VALLEY COMFORT SYSTEMS INC
BLAZE KING
(*Suby of* DECISIVE DIVIDEND CORPORA-TION)
1290 Commercial Way, Penticton, BC, V2A 3H5
(250) 493-7444
Sales 11,752,155
SIC 3433 Heating equipment, except electric
Alan Murphy

D-U-N-S 24-594-5639   (HQ)
VALLEY FIRST CREDIT UNION
184 Main St, Penticton, BC, V2A 8G7
(250) 490-2720
Emp Here 30   *Sales* 68,320,400
SIC 6062 State credit unions
Harley Biddlecombe
Colleen Lister

Robert Mowat
Jackie Baron
Ramesh Rickhi

D-U-N-S 24-246-9484   (BR)
WAL-MART CANADA CORP
(*Suby of* WALMART INC.)
275 Green Ave W Suite 135, Penticton, BC, V2A 7J2
(250) 493-6681
Emp Here 250
SIC 5311 Department stores
Murray Mandzak

Pitt Meadows, BC V3Y

D-U-N-S 24-310-5087   (HQ)
EURO-RITE CABINETS LTD
19100 Airport Way Suite 212, Pitt Meadows, BC, V3Y 0E2
(604) 464-5060
Sales 21,605,080
SIC 2541 Wood partitions and fixtures
Bill Longman

D-U-N-S 25-217-8314   (SL)
GOLDEN EAGLE GOLF COURSES INC
GOLDEN EAGLE GOLF CLUB
21770 Ladner Rd, Pitt Meadows, BC, V3Y 1Z1
(604) 460-1871
Emp Here 90   *Sales* 6,875,730
SIC 7992 Public golf courses
Roberto Aquilini
Paolo Aquilini
Francesco Aquilini

D-U-N-S 25-678-1501   (SL)
HALO SAWMILL LIMITED PARTNERSHIP
17700 Fraser Dyke Rd, Pitt Meadows, BC, V3Y 0A7
(604) 465-0682
Emp Here 100   *Sales* 15,586,300
SIC 2421 Sawmills and planing mills, general
Rowland Price
Glen Franke

D-U-N-S 24-324-9435   (SL)
HOLLANDIA GREENHOUSES LTD
19731 Richardson Rd, Pitt Meadows, BC, V3Y 1Z1
(604) 460-1866
Emp Here 60   *Sales* 15,738,540
SIC 0181 Ornamental nursery products
John Duyvestyn

D-U-N-S 20-553-5318   (SL)
HOWE PRECISION INDUSTRIAL INC
11718 Harris Rd, Pitt Meadows, BC, V3Y 1Y6
(604) 460-2892
Emp Here 130   *Sales* 29,547,570
SIC 3823 Process control instruments
Yukun Du
Lina Hao

D-U-N-S 24-773-1842   (SL)
JUNGLE JAC'S PLAY CENTRE
19800 Lougheed Hwy Suite 115, Pitt Meadows, BC, V3Y 2W1
(604) 460-1654
Emp Here 49   *Sales* 10,722,376
SIC 3949 Sporting and athletic goods, nec
Darren Walker

D-U-N-S 25-368-7248   (BR)
LOBLAWS INC
REAL CANADIAN SUPERSTORE
(*Suby of* LOBLAW COMPANIES LIMITED)
19800 Lougheed Hwy Suite 201, Pitt Meadows, BC, V3Y 2W1
(604) 460-4319
Emp Here 350
SIC 5411 Grocery stores
Grant Sakabria

D-U-N-S 20-792-0864   (SL)

MARKETPLACE IGA 48
19150 Lougheed Hwy, Pitt Meadows, BC, V3Y 2H6

Emp Here 50   *Sales* 13,707,600
SIC 5411 Grocery stores
Jim Pattenden

D-U-N-S 24-326-9177   (SL)
MERCHANT'S EXPRESS LIMITED
19981 Richardson Rd, Pitt Meadows, BC, V3Y 1Z1
(604) 460-1971
Emp Here 75   *Sales* 11,114,400
SIC 4212 Local trucking, without storage
Les Cridland

D-U-N-S 24-777-8517   (SL)
PIROCHE PLANTS INC
20542 Mcneil Rd, Pitt Meadows, BC, V3Y 2T9
(604) 465-7101
Emp Here 70   *Sales* 51,976,400
SIC 5193 Flowers and florists supplies
Pierre Piroche
Setsuko Piroche

D-U-N-S 20-706-9829   (SL)
PROSNACK NATURAL FOODS INC
ELEVATE ME
(*Suby of* NATURALLY SPLENDID ENTER-PRISES LTD)
19100 Airport Way Unit 108, Pitt Meadows, BC, V3Y 0E2
(604) 465-0548
Emp Here 30   *Sales* 10,370,700
SIC 2032 Canned specialties
Douglas Mason
Craig Goodwin

D-U-N-S 24-369-7943   (SL)
PUREWAL BLUEBERRY FARMS LTD
13753 Hale Rd, Pitt Meadows, BC, V3Y 1Z1

Emp Here 50   *Sales* 17,123,350
SIC 0171 Berry crops
Malkiat Purewal
Gurjit Purewal
Charan Purewal

D-U-N-S 24-899-0962   (HQ)
RHEMA HEALTH PRODUCTS LIMITED
19055 Airport Way Unit 601, Pitt Meadows, BC, V3Y 0G4
(604) 516-0199
Sales 34,082,520
SIC 2833 Medicinals and botanicals
Carlo Szarillo
William Horie
John Tims

D-U-N-S 20-294-8126   (BR)
SCHOOL DISTRICT NO 42 (MAPLE RIDGE-PITT MEADOWS)
PITT MEADOWS SECONDARY SCHOOL
(*Suby of* SCHOOL DISTRICT NO 42 (MAPLE RIDGE-PITT MEADOWS))
19438 116b Ave, Pitt Meadows, BC, V3Y 1G1
(604) 465-7141
Emp Here 85
SIC 8211 Elementary and secondary schools
Mike Keenan

D-U-N-S 24-897-2549   (SL)
SWAN-E-SET BAY RESORT LTD
16651 Rannie Rd, Pitt Meadows, BC, V3Y 1Z1
(604) 465-9380
Emp Here 150   *Sales* 11,781,750
SIC 7997 Membership sports and recreation clubs
Naoya Fukui
Mitsuru Kani

D-U-N-S 24-033-5976   (SL)
TSANG, A.J. PHARMACY LTD
SHOPPERS DRUG MART - PITT MEADOWS
19150 Lougheed Hwy Suite 110, Pitt Meadows, BC, V3Y 2H6

(604) 465-8122
Emp Here 45   *Sales* 11,382,930
SIC 5912 Drug stores and proprietary stores
Angel Luo

D-U-N-S 24-557-9339   (SL)
WEST COAST IMPORT VEHICLES LTD
WEST COAST TOYOTA
19950 Lougheed Hwy, Pitt Meadows, BC, V3Y 2S9
(604) 465-3209
Emp Here 25   *Sales* 12,451,950
SIC 5511 New and used car dealers
Scott Jones

D-U-N-S 24-014-2476   (BR)
WINNERS MERCHANTS INTERNATIONAL L.P.
HOMESENSE
(*Suby of* THE TJX COMPANIES INC)
19800 Lougheed Hwy Suite 160, Pitt Meadows, BC, V3Y 2W1
(604) 465-4330
Emp Here 80
SIC 5651 Family clothing stores
Julie Jones

Port Alberni, BC V9Y

D-U-N-S 25-056-5678   (SL)
ALBERNI CHRYSLER LTD
ALBERNI CHRYSLER DODGE JEEP
2611 Port Alberni Hwy, Port Alberni, BC, V9Y 8P2
(250) 723-5331
Emp Here 26   *Sales* 12,950,028
SIC 5521 Used car dealers
Dennis See
Albert See Jr.

D-U-N-S 20-992-0151   (SL)
ALBERNI DISTRICT CO-OPERATIVE ASSOCIATION
4006 Johnston Rd, Port Alberni, BC, V9Y 5N3
(250) 724-0008
Emp Here 12   *Sales* 37,270,284
SIC 4925 Gas production and/or distribution
Patty Wangler

D-U-N-S 24-507-8196   (SL)
ALBERNI ECHO TOYOTA
2555 Port Alberni Hwy, Port Alberni, BC, V9Y 8P2
(250) 723-9448
Emp Here 30   *Sales* 14,942,340
SIC 5511 New and used car dealers
Dennis See

D-U-N-S 25-119-8784   (SL)
ATTIC, THE
4760 Johnston Rd, Port Alberni, BC, V9Y 5M3
(250) 723-2143
Emp Here 49   *Sales* 19,473,286
SIC 8699 Membership organizations, nec
Sylvia Broadfoot

D-U-N-S 25-538-4117   (BR)
CATALYST PAPER CORPORATION
PORT ALBERNI MILL
(*Suby of* CAPITAL ASSETS HOLDINGS (L) BERHAD)
4000 Stamp Ave, Port Alberni, BC, V9Y 5J7
(250) 723-2161
Emp Here 324
SIC 2621 Paper mills
Carlo Dalmonte

D-U-N-S 24-593-6133   (HQ)
COULSON AIRCRANE LTD
(*Suby of* COULSON FOREST PRODUCTS LIMITED)
4890 Cherry Creek Rd, Port Alberni, BC, V9Y 8E9
(250) 723-8118
Emp Here 20   *Sales* 41,381,590

SIC 4522 Air transportation, nonscheduled
Wayne Coulson

D-U-N-S 20-104-3312   (HQ)
COULSON FOREST PRODUCTS LIMITED
4890 Cherry Creek Rd, Port Alberni, BC, V9Y 8E9
(250) 723-8118
Sales 139,195,000
SIC 2411 Logging
Wayne Coulson
Susan Merivirta
Jim Messer

D-U-N-S 20-104-3429   (HQ)
DOLAN'S CONCRETE LTD
4779 Roger St, Port Alberni, BC, V9Y 3Z3
(250) 723-6442
Sales 15,203,916
SIC 5032 Brick, stone, and related material
Thomas Black
Brian Makenny

D-U-N-S 25-387-7005   (SL)
ECHO VILLAGE FOUNDATION
4200 10th Ave, Port Alberni, BC, V9Y 4X3
(250) 724-1090
Emp Here 150   *Sales* 9,642,300
SIC 8361 Residential care
Barb Stevenson

D-U-N-S 20-104-3635   (SL)
JONSSON, DENNIS MOTOR PRODUCTS LTD
3800 Johnston Rd, Port Alberni, BC, V9Y 5N7
(250) 723-3541
Emp Here 32   *Sales* 15,938,496
SIC 5511 New and used car dealers
Dennis Jonsson
Vinni Weening

D-U-N-S 25-384-9244   (BR)
KELLAND PROPERTIES INC
KELLAND FOODS LTD
(*Suby of* KELLAND PROPERTIES INC)
2943 10th Ave, Port Alberni, BC, V9Y 2N5
(250) 723-3397
Emp Here 100
SIC 5411 Grocery stores
Bill Flynn

D-U-N-S 20-311-0671   (SL)
NU BODY EQUIPMENT SALES LTD
5211 Compton Rd, Port Alberni, BC, V9Y 7B5
(778) 552-4540
Emp Here 54   *Sales* 12,273,606
SIC 3845 Electromedical equipment
Amanda Hall

D-U-N-S 20-868-0124   (HQ)
PORT ALBERNI ASSOCIATION FOR COMMUNITY LIVING
ARROWSMITH SERVICES
3008 2nd Ave, Port Alberni, BC, V9Y 1Y9
(250) 724-7155
Emp Here 80   *Sales* 70,921,200
SIC 8699 Membership organizations, nec
Dominic Rocco

D-U-N-S 25-254-3512   (SL)
RYDER CONTRACTING LTD
5700 Shoemaker Bay Rd, Port Alberni, BC, V9Y 8X8
(250) 736-1995
Emp Here 43   *Sales* 12,191,532
SIC 1611 Highway and street construction

D-U-N-S 25-288-5124   (BR)
SCHOOL DISTRICT #70 (ALBERNI) SCHOOL BOARD
ALBERNI DISTRICT SECONDARY SCHOOL
4000 Burde St, Port Alberni, BC, V9Y 3L6
(250) 724-3284
Emp Here 110
SIC 8211 Elementary and secondary schools
Jim Ansell

D-U-N-S 24-319-5034   (BR)

WAL-MART CANADA CORP
(*Suby of* WALMART INC.)
3355 Johnston Rd, Port Alberni, BC, V9Y 8K1
(250) 720-0912
Emp Here 120
SIC 5311 Department stores
Bill Robertson

D-U-N-S 24-620-7567   (HQ)
WALCO INDUSTRIES LTD
WALCO
(*Suby of* WALCO CONSULTING LTD)
6113 Beaver Creek Rd, Port Alberni, BC, V9Y 8X4
(250) 723-6919
Emp Here 4   *Sales* 10,285,240
SIC 4959 Sanitary services, nec
Charles Walcot
Phillip Edward Walcot

D-U-N-S 20-919-3028   (SL)
WEST COAST GENERAL HOSPITAL
(*Suby of* GOVERNMENT OF THE PROVINCE OF BRITISH COLUMBIA)
3949 Port Alberni Hwy, Port Alberni, BC, V9Y 4S1
(250) 731-1370
Emp Here 220   *Sales* 33,036,520
SIC 8062 General medical and surgical hospitals
Howard Waldner
Don Hubbard
David Kruyt
Vern Slaney
Johan Van De Sande
Matthew Watson
Jean Wheeler
Frank Carson
Michael Costello
Shelley Garside

D-U-N-S 24-205-1861   (SL)
WESTCOAST ENERGY VENTURES INC
4529 Melrose St, Port Alberni, BC, V9Y 1K7

Emp Here 5   *Sales* 15,529,285
SIC 4924 Natural gas distribution
R Fiedorek

D-U-N-S 20-869-5903   (BR)
WESTERN FOREST PRODUCTS INC
ALBERNI PACIFIC SAWMILL
(*Suby of* WESTERN FOREST PRODUCTS INC)
2500 1st Ave, Port Alberni, BC, V9Y 8H7
(250) 724-7438
Emp Here 300
SIC 2611 Pulp mills
Joel Holmes

D-U-N-S 25-671-5491   (BR)
WEYERHAEUSER COMPANY LIMITED
(*Suby of* WEYERHAEUSER COMPANY)
Gd Lcd Main, Port Alberni, BC, V9Y 7M3
(250) 724-6511
Emp Here 155
SIC 2421 Sawmills and planing mills, general

Port Alice, BC V0N

D-U-N-S 24-070-3798   (HQ)
NEUCEL SPECIALTY CELLULOSE LTD
(*Suby of* FULIDA GROUP HOLDING CO., LTD.)
300 Marine Drive, Port Alice, BC, V0N 2N0
(250) 284-3331
Emp Here 30   *Sales* 89,554,500
SIC 3081 Unsupported plastics film and sheet
Lauron Keiver

D-U-N-S 20-558-2898   (SL)
PORT ALICE SPECIALTY CELLULOSE INC
Po Box 2000, Port Alice, BC, V0N 2N0

Emp Here 346

SIC 2611 Pulp mills

Port Coquitlam, BC V3B

D-U-N-S 24-229-7591   (SL)
ALLWEST ELECTRIC LTD
110-2250 Fremont St, Port Coquitlam, BC, V3B 0M3
(604) 464-6200
Emp Here 250   *Sales* 58,877,250
SIC 1731 Electrical work
Anthony Ballazanna

D-U-N-S 24-621-0280   (HQ)
BENEFITS BY DESIGN INC
2755 Lougheed Hwy Suite 500, Port Coquitlam, BC, V3B 5Y9
(604) 464-0313
Emp Here 20   *Sales* 33,922,400
SIC 6411 Insurance agents, brokers, and service
Mike Mcclenahan
Ron Southward

D-U-N-S 25-831-4426   (BR)
COSTCO WHOLESALE CANADA LTD
COSTCO
(*Suby of* COSTCO WHOLESALE CORPORATION)
2370 Ottawa St, Port Coquitlam, BC, V3B 7Z1
(604) 552-2228
Emp Here 300
SIC 5099 Durable goods, nec
Steele Jones

D-U-N-S 24-818-2599   (HQ)
DOMINION LENDING CENTRES INC
2215 Coquitlam Ave Suite 16, Port Coquitlam, BC, V3B 1J6
(604) 696-1221
Sales 12,316,755
SIC 6162 Mortgage bankers and loan correspondents
Gary Mauris
Chris Kayat

D-U-N-S 24-802-8511   (SL)
FINGER FOOD STUDIOS INC
2755 Lougheed Hwy Suite 420, Port Coquitlam, BC, V3B 5Y9
(604) 475-0350
Emp Here 60   *Sales* 10,638,660
SIC 7371 Custom computer programming services
Ryan Peterson
Trent Shumay

D-U-N-S 20-209-2446   (BR)
HOME DEPOT OF CANADA INC
HOME DEPOT
(*Suby of* THE HOME DEPOT INC)
1069 Nicola Ave, Port Coquitlam, BC, V3B 8B2
(604) 468-3360
Emp Here 200
SIC 5251 Hardware stores
Ted Stevenson

D-U-N-S 25-664-6183   (SL)
HOPE DISTRIBUTION & SALES INC
CANADIAN TIRE
2125 Hawkins St Suite 609, Port Coquitlam, BC, V3B 0G6
(604) 468-6951
Emp Here 60   *Sales* 12,320,580
SIC 5311 Department stores
Ingmar Wilkens

D-U-N-S 25-152-3130   (SL)
INGREDIENTS PLUS DISTRIBUTION INC
585 Seaborne Ave Unit 2120, Port Coquitlam, BC, V3B 0M3
(604) 468-7146
Emp Here 10   *Sales* 12,103,970
SIC 5153 Grain and field beans

Richard Sand

D-U-N-S 24-492-4965   (SL)
LIGHTHEADED LIGHTING LTD
572 Nicola Pl Suite 1150, Port Coquitlam, BC, V3B 0K4
(604) 464-5644
Emp Here 65   *Sales* 12,378,730
SIC 3646 Commercial lighting fixtures
Norman David
Tony Salcito

D-U-N-S 20-104-6935   (SL)
METRO MOTORS LTD
2505 Lougheed Hwy, Port Coquitlam, BC, V3B 1B2
(604) 464-6631
Emp Here 100   *Sales* 62,928,000
SIC 5511 New and used car dealers
Michael Mckone
Layne Magnuson

D-U-N-S 25-260-6017   (SL)
MORREY NISSAN OF COQUITLAM LTD
MORREY INFINITY NISSAN OF COQUIT-LAM
(*Suby of* MORREY, G & L HOLDINGS LTD))
2710 Lougheed Hwy, Port Coquitlam, BC, V3B 6P2
(604) 464-1216
Emp Here 40   *Sales* 19,923,120
SIC 5511 New and used car dealers
Gary Morrey
Jason Morrey

D-U-N-S 20-967-0954   (SL)
REMAX SABRE REAL ESTATE GROUP LTD
REMAX
2748 Lougheed Hwy Suite 102, Port Coquitlam, BC, V3B 6P2
(604) 942-0606
Emp Here 70   *Sales* 19,022,920
SIC 6531 Real estate agents and managers
Verne Gatzke

D-U-N-S 25-451-3286   (BR)
SCHOOL DISTRICT NO. 43 (COQUITLAM)
TERRY FOX SECONDARY SCHOOL
(*Suby of* SCHOOL DISTRICT NO. 43 (COQUITLAM))
1260 Riverwood Gate, Port Coquitlam, BC, V3B 7Z5
(604) 941-5401
Emp Here 95
SIC 8211 Elementary and secondary schools
Heather Murphy

D-U-N-S 25-862-5540   (SL)
WESTWOOD CRUISESHIPCENTERS
2748 Lougheed Hwy Suite 304, Port Coquitlam, BC, V3B 6P2
(604) 464-7447
Emp Here 25   *Sales* 12,999,175
SIC 4724 Travel agencies
Don Adam

D-U-N-S 24-620-6494   (HQ)
WIMCO NURSERIES LTD
ART KNAPP PLANTLAND & FLORISTS
1300 Dominion Ave, Port Coquitlam, BC, V3B 8G7
(604) 942-7518
Emp Here 38   *Sales* 13,382,600
SIC 5261 Retail nurseries and garden stores
Wim Vander Zalm

Port Coquitlam, BC V3C

D-U-N-S 25-140-2780   (SL)
1002495 B.C. LTD
TRI CITY MITSUBISHI
2060 Oxford Connector, Port Coquitlam, BC, V3C 0A4
(604) 464-3330
Emp Here 43   *Sales* 21,417,354

SIC 5511 New and used car dealers
Jamie Arens
Larry Campeau

D-U-N-S 20-341-4503   (SL)
1079259 B.C. LTD
TRICITY MITSUBISHI
2060 Oxford Connector, Port Coquitlam, BC, V3C 0A4
(604) 464-3330
Emp Here 30   *Sales* 14,942,340
SIC 5511 New and used car dealers
James Arens
Tyler Atkins
Ray Van Empel

D-U-N-S 20-585-5265   (HQ)
AERCO INDUSTRIES LTD
201-1952 Kingsway Ave, Port Coquitlam, BC, V3C 6C2
(604) 431-6883
Emp Here 51   *Sales* 13,983,900
SIC 1711 Plumbing, heating, air-conditioning
Richard Alban

D-U-N-S 20-316-6525   (SL)
ALLIANCE SUPPLY LTD
1585 Broadway St Suite 104, Port Coquitlam, BC, V3C 2M7
(604) 944-4081
Emp Here 11   *Sales* 11,003,729
SIC 5051 Metals service centers and offices
John Lacey
Dan Solvey

D-U-N-S 24-551-8758   (HQ)
BARCLAY SALES LTD
1441 Kebet Way, Port Coquitlam, BC, V3C 6L3
(604) 945-1010
Emp Here 18   *Sales* 10,285,002
SIC 5074 Plumbing and heating equipment and supplies (hydronics)
Bruce Barclay
Lynn Barclay

D-U-N-S 24-418-0035   (BR)
BREWERS' DISTRIBUTOR LTD
(*Suby of* BREWERS' DISTRIBUTOR LTD)
1711 Kingsway Ave, Port Coquitlam, BC, V3C 0B6
(604) 927-4055
Emp Here 1,200
SIC 5181 Beer and ale
Peter Gill

D-U-N-S 24-042-3269   (HQ)
BRYMARK INSTALLATIONS GROUP INC
1648 Broadway St, Port Coquitlam, BC, V3C 2M8
(604) 944-1206
Sales 81,254,400
SIC 1711 Plumbing, heating, air-conditioning
Gordon Carlson
Bruce Smith

D-U-N-S 24-867-1919   (HQ)
CIMS LIMITED PARTNERSHIP
1610 Industrial Ave, Port Coquitlam, BC, V3C 6N3
(604) 472-4300
Emp Here 40   *Sales* 139,678,400
SIC 1541 Industrial buildings and warehouses
John Mclaughlin
Patrick Mcginley
Herb Gill
Dennis Thompson
Mike Mckay
Kelly Rayne
George Gemmell
Mike Miketon

D-U-N-S 24-887-3036   (SL)
CUSTOM AIR CONDITIONING LTD
1835 Broadway St, Port Coquitlam, BC, V3C 4Z1
(604) 945-7728
Emp Here 100   *Sales* 23,306,500
SIC 1711 Plumbing, heating, air-conditioning

Peter Harteveld
Peter Whiten

D-U-N-S 24-558-9155   (SL)
DESIGN ROOFING & SHEET METAL LTD
1385 Kingsway Ave, Port Coquitlam, BC, V3C 1S2
(604) 944-2977
Emp Here 75   *Sales* 16,337,175
SIC 1761 Roofing, siding, and sheetMetal work
Ian Wallace

D-U-N-S 20-377-5593   (HQ)
DYNAMIC ATTRACTIONS LTD
EMPIRE IRON WORKS
1515 Kingsway Ave, Port Coquitlam, BC, V3C 1S2
(604) 639-8200
Sales 49,237,200
SIC 1791 Structural steel erection
Allan Francis
Guy Nelson
Michael Martin

D-U-N-S 24-363-1335   (SL)
DYNAMIC INSTALLATIONS INC
1556 Kebet Way, Port Coquitlam, BC, V3C 5M5
(604) 464-7695
Emp Here 50   *Sales* 10,141,500
SIC 3462 Iron and steel forgings

D-U-N-S 20-199-7322   (SL)
DYNAMIC STRUCTURES LTD
(*Suby of* EMPIRE INDUSTRIES LTD)
1515 Kingsway Ave, Port Coquitlam, BC, V3C 1S2
(604) 941-9481
Emp Here 120   *Sales* 25,485,120
SIC 1791 Structural steel erection
Allan Francis
K. Guy Nelson
Michael Martin

D-U-N-S 25-219-6522   (SL)
EAGLE RIDGE MECHANICAL CONTRACTING LTD
1515 Broadway St Suite 116, Port Coquitlam, BC, V3C 6M2
(604) 941-1071
Emp Here 50   *Sales* 11,046,700
SIC 1711 Plumbing, heating, air-conditioning
Garth Moore
Greg Robertson

D-U-N-S 25-820-3165   (BR)
EARL'S RESTAURANTS LTD
EARL'S PORT COQUITLAM
(*Suby of* EARL'S RESTAURANTS LTD)
2850 Shaughnessy St Suite 5100, Port Coquitlam, BC, V3C 6K5
(604) 941-1733
Emp Here 200
SIC 5812 Eating places
Bobby Ewing

D-U-N-S 20-916-7659   (SL)
EARLS INDUSTRIES LTD
1616 Kebet Way, Port Coquitlam, BC, V3C 5W9
(604) 941-8388
Emp Here 35   *Sales* 16,625,910
SIC 5085 Industrial supplies
Stephen Coatta
Bruce Coatta

D-U-N-S 20-425-6275   (SL)
EDOKO FOOD IMPORTERS LTD
1335 Kebet Way, Port Coquitlam, BC, V3C 6G1
(604) 944-7332
Emp Here 35   *Sales* 29,245,195
SIC 5141 Groceries, general line
Neal Letourneau
Sigrun Letourneau
Dorothy Koltzenburg

D-U-N-S 20-916-1728   (SL)
ELLETT INDUSTRIES LTD
1575 Kingsway Ave, Port Coquitlam, BC, V3C 1S2
(604) 941-8211
Emp Here 110   *Sales* 21,129,350
SIC 3443 Fabricated plate work (boiler shop)
John Ellett
Geoffrey Birch

D-U-N-S 20-104-6307   (HQ)
ESCO LIMITED
(*Suby of* WEIR GROUP PLC(THE))
1855 Kingsway Ave, Port Coquitlam, BC, V3C 1T1
(604) 942-7261
Emp Here 190   *Sales* 154,726,120
SIC 3325 Steel foundries, nec
Larry Huget

D-U-N-S 20-292-8032   (HQ)
FIT FOODS LTD
1589 Kebet Way, Port Coquitlam, BC, V3C 6L5
(604) 464-3524
Emp Here 1   *Sales* 34,569,000
SIC 2087 Flavoring extracts and syrups, nec
James B. Mcmahon
Steven Badger

D-U-N-S 20-273-6591   (SL)
GLASTECH GLAZING CONTRACTORS LTD
1613 Kebet Way, Port Coquitlam, BC, V3C 5W9
(604) 941-9115
Emp Here 140   *Sales* 34,466,040
SIC 1793 Glass and glazing work
Warren Elmer
Mark Degoutiere

D-U-N-S 20-104-6489   (SL)
HARKEN TOWING CO. LTD
1990 Argue St, Port Coquitlam, BC, V3C 5K4
(604) 942-8511
Emp Here 70   *Sales* 19,831,000
SIC 7549 Automotive services, nec
Tim Mackenzie
Linda Mackensie

D-U-N-S 24-372-5293   (SL)
HIWAY FUEL SERVICES LTD
1485 Coast Meridian Rd Suite 200, Port Coquitlam, BC, V3C 5P1
(604) 552-8586
Emp Here 10   *Sales* 10,328,080
SIC 5172 Petroleum products, nec
Kelly Grehan

D-U-N-S 20-427-5614   (HQ)
HIWAY REFRIGERATION LTD
1462 Mustang Pl, Port Coquitlam, BC, V3C 6L2
(604) 944-0119
Sales 12,501,320
SIC 7623 Refrigeration service and repair
Kerry Winkler
Guff Muench
Gregory Doyle

D-U-N-S 25-072-9779   (BR)
INTERWRAP ULC
INTERWRAP INC
(*Suby of* OWENS CORNING)
1650 Broadway St Suite 101, Port Coquitlam, BC, V3C 2M8

Emp Here 130
SIC 3069 Fabricated rubber products, nec
Mohan Sidhu

D-U-N-S 24-931-7843   (HQ)
IOTRON INDUSTRIES CANADA INC
1425 Kebet Way, Port Coquitlam, BC, V3C 6L3
(604) 945-8838
Emp Here 20   *Sales* 20,781,605
SIC 8734 Testing laboratories
Tino Pereira
John Mackay
Sol Rauch

▲ Public Company   ■ Public Company Family Member   **HQ** Headquarters   **BR** Branch   **SL** Single Location

Bruce Hynds
Norman Mack Ritchie

D-U-N-S 20-915-3030 (HQ)
KONGSBERG MESOTECH LTD
(*Suby of* KONGSBERG GRUPPEN ASA)
1598 Kebet Way, Port Coquitlam, BC, V3C
5M5
(604) 464-8144
Emp Here 12   *Sales* 12,058,414
SIC 3812 Search and navigation equipment
Karen O'grady
Sumanjit Missan

D-U-N-S 24-120-5970 (HQ)
KOST KLIP MANUFACTURING LTD
(*Suby of* KOST KLIP INDUSTRIES LTD)
1611 Broadway St Unit 119, Port Coquitlam,
BC, V3C 2M7
(604) 468-7917
Sales 30,982,920
SIC 3993 Signs and advertising specialties
John Philippson
Tina Philippson

D-U-N-S 20-106-3588 (BR)
KOST KLIP MANUFACTURING LTD
(*Suby of* KOST KLIP INDUSTRIES LTD)
1611 Broadway St Unit 119, Port Coquitlam,
BC, V3C 2M7
(604) 468-1117
Emp Here 100
SIC 3993 Signs and advertising specialties
John Philittson

D-U-N-S 25-090-5291 (HQ)
LEVEL IT INSTALLATIONS LTD
1515 Broadway St Unit 804, Port Coquitlam,
BC, V3C 6M2
(604) 942-2022
Sales 10,232,235
SIC 1751 Carpentry work
Todd Isackson

D-U-N-S 24-620-0943 (BR)
LILYDALE INC
(*Suby of* SOFINA FOODS INC)
1910 Kingsway Ave, Port Coquitlam, BC, V3C
1S7
(604) 941-4041
Emp Here 400
SIC 2015 Poultry slaughtering and processing
Bill Vanderspek

D-U-N-S 24-058-0014 (SL)
LITCHFIELD & CO LTD
(*Suby of* LITCHFIELD HOLDINGS & MAN-
AGEMENT CORPORATION)
3046 Westwood St, Port Coquitlam, BC, V3C
3L7
(604) 464-7525
Emp Here 45   *Sales* 11,078,370
SIC 1795 Wrecking and demolition work
Wendy Litchfield

D-U-N-S 25-700-6317 (SL)
LIVE TO PLAY SPORTS
1465 Kebet Way, Port Coquitlam, BC, V3C 6L3
(604) 552-2930
Emp Here 49   *Sales* 25,506,558
SIC 5091 Sporting and recreation goods
John Williams

D-U-N-S 20-114-4334 (HQ)
LTP SPORTS GROUP INC
NORCO PERFORMANCE BIKES
1465 Kebet Way Suite B, Port Coquitlam, BC,
V3C 6L3
(604) 552-2930
Emp Here 75   *Sales* 24,622,730
SIC 3751 Motorcycles, bicycles and parts
Albert Lewis
Nathan L Zalkow
Samuel Zalkow
Marlene Lewis

D-U-N-S 24-164-6306 (SL)
MILLERS LANDING PUB LTD

CAT AND FIDDLE SPORTS BAR
1979 Brown St, Port Coquitlam, BC, V3C 2N4
(604) 941-8822
Emp Here 75   *Sales* 3,215,475
SIC 5813 Drinking places
Randy Doncaster
Brad Doncaster

D-U-N-S 24-389-3232 (SL)
NORCO MANAGEMENT LTD
1465 Kebet Way Suite B, Port Coquitlam, BC,
V3C 6L3
(604) 552-2930
Emp Here 110   *Sales* 24,622,730
SIC 3751 Motorcycles, bicycles and parts
Albert M Lewis
Nathan L Zalkow
Marlene Lewis
Samuel Zalkow

D-U-N-S 24-728-0071 (SL)
NORSTAN SALES LTD
1530 Kingsway Ave Suite 201, Port Coquitlam,
BC, V3C 6N6
(604) 257-5555
Emp Here 27   *Sales* 33,944,427
SIC 5172 Petroleum products, nec
Gerrad Parsons

D-U-N-S 20-865-7148 (SL)
NORTHERN GOLD FOODS LTD
1725 Coast Meridian Rd, Port Coquitlam, BC,
V3C 3T7
(604) 941-0731
Emp Here 50   *Sales* 11,242,750
SIC 2043 Cereal breakfast foods
Spencer Beach

D-U-N-S 20-619-6636 (SL)
NUTRI-NATION FUNCTIONAL FOODS INC
1560 Broadway St Suite 1110, Port Coquitlam,
BC, V3C 2M8
(604) 552-5549
Emp Here 140   *Sales* 75,810,200
SIC 2032 Canned specialties
Richard Schroeder
Melany Schroeder

D-U-N-S 20-057-9444 (HQ)
PACIFIC BLENDS LTD
1625 Kebet Way Unit 100, Port Coquitlam, BC,
V3C 5W9
(604) 945-4600
Sales 17,547,117
SIC 5149 Groceries and related products, nec
John Wells
Cameron Wells

D-U-N-S 20-104-7131 (HQ)
**PORT COQUITLAM BUILDING SUPPLIES
LTD**
POCO BUILDING SUPPLIES
2650 Mary Hill Rd, Port Coquitlam, BC, V3C
3B3
(604) 942-7282
Sales 17,886,960
SIC 5039 Construction materials, nec
Robert Galer
Jeffrey Galer
Christopher Galer

D-U-N-S 24-155-1977 (SL)
**PORT COQUITLAM SENIOR CITIZENS
HOUSING SOCIETY**
*HAWTHORNE SENIORS CARE COMMU-
NITY*
2111 Hawthorne Ave Suite 406, Port Coquit-
lam, BC, V3C 1W3
(604) 941-4051
Emp Here 230   *Sales* 14,784,860
SIC 8361 Residential care
Lenore Pickering
Walter Van Drimmelen
Gary Temlett
Jackie Harmer
Frank Findlay
Charlie Spriggs

D-U-N-S 24-150-1709 (SL)
PRESTIGE GLASS (2002) LTD
1353 Kebet Way, Port Coquitlam, BC, V3C
6G1
(604) 464-5015
Emp Here 80
SIC 1793 Glass and glazing work
Boris Sawicky

D-U-N-S 25-681-6356 (HQ)
QUALITY INSERTIONS LTD
1560 Broadway St Unit 2, Port Coquitlam, BC,
V3C 2M8
(604) 941-1942
Emp Here 1   *Sales* 16,937,920
SIC 7319 Advertising, nec
Richard Renaud
Louise Renaud

D-U-N-S 24-898-7349 (HQ)
RADIAL ENGINEERING LTD
1588 Kebet Way, Port Coquitlam, BC,, V3C
5M5
(604) 942-1001
Sales 17,046,675
SIC 3861 Photographic equipment and supplies
Peter Janis

D-U-N-S 24-030-1135 (SL)
RIDGE SHEET METAL LTD
2532 Davies Ave, Port Coquitlam, BC, V3C
2J9
(604) 942-0244
Emp Here 80   *Sales* 17,426,320
SIC 1761 Roofing, siding, and sheetMetal
work
John Danilkiewicz
Dave Danilkiewicz
Dan Beer

D-U-N-S 20-020-8705 (BR)
SCHOOL DISTRICT NO. 43 (COQUITLAM)
RIVERSIDE SECONDARY SCHOOL
(*Suby of* SCHOOL DISTRICT NO. 43 (CO-
QUITLAM))
2215 Reeve St, Port Coquitlam, BC, V3C 6K8
(604) 941-6053
Emp Here 130
SIC 8211 Elementary and secondary schools
Anthony Ciolfitto

D-U-N-S 20-705-0100 (BR)
SCHOOL DISTRICT NO. 43 (COQUITLAM)
MAINTAINANCE SHOP
(*Suby of* SCHOOL DISTRICT NO. 43 (CO-
QUITLAM))
1982 Kingsway Ave, Port Coquitlam, BC, V3C
1S5
(604) 941-5643
Emp Here 80
SIC 8211 Elementary and secondary schools

D-U-N-S 24-345-0041 (BR)
SYSCO CANADA, INC
SYSCO VANCOUVER
(*Suby of* SYSCO CORPORATION)
1346 Kingsway Ave, Port Coquitlam, BC, V3C
6G4
(604) 944-4410
Emp Here 500
SIC 5141 Groceries, general line
Doug Ramsay

D-U-N-S 24-552-2081 (SL)
TREND-TEX FABRICS INC
1317 Kebet Way, Port Coquitlam, BC, V3C
6G1
(604) 941-4620
Emp Here 26   *Sales* 12,956,372
SIC 5131 Piece goods and notions
Milton Jorgenson

D-U-N-S 24-350-4060 (HQ)
TRI-CITY TRANSITIONS SOCIETY
2540 Shaughnessy St Suite 200, Port Coquitlam, BC, V3C 3W4
(604) 941-7111
Emp Here 3   *Sales* 13,909,490

SIC 8699 Membership organizations, nec
Carol Metz Murray

D-U-N-S 24-139-1106 (SL)
VALLEY PERSONNEL LTD
WORK CENTER, THE
2509 Kingsway Ave, Port Coquitlam, BC, V3C
1T5

Emp Here 45   *Sales* 12,748,185
SIC 8741 Management services
Crystal Trouty

D-U-N-S 20-428-9029 (SL)
WESGAR INC
1634 Kebet Way Unit 1, Port Coquitlam, BC,
V3C 5W9
(604) 942-9558
Emp Here 160   *Sales* 30,733,600
SIC 3444 Sheet Metalwork
Keith Day
John Purdy
Allan D Laird

D-U-N-S 20-117-3192 (SL)
WESTERN SCALE CO LTD
1670 Kingsway Ave, Port Coquitlam, BC, V3C
3Y9
(604) 941-3474
Emp Here 55   *Sales* 12,210,055
SIC 3596 Scales and balances, except laboratory
David Frewin

D-U-N-S 20-743-3348 (SL)
YOUNGHUSBAND RESOURCES LTD
1628 Kebet Way Unit 100, Port Coquitlam,
V3C 5W9
(604) 466-1220
Emp Here 49   *Sales* 14,042,130
SIC 8741 Management services
Faye Younghusband

Port Hardy, BC V0N

D-U-N-S 25-329-1553 (BR)
MARINE HARVEST CANADA INC
(*Suby of* MARINE HARVEST NORTH AMER-
ICA INC)
7200 Cohoe Rd, Port Hardy, BC, V0N 2P0
(250) 949-9448
Emp Here 150
SIC 2091 Canned and cured fish and
seafoods
Dave Pashley

D-U-N-S 24-134-8655 (SL)
PACIFIC SEAFOODS INTERNATIONAL LTD
(*Suby of* HARDY BUOYS SMOKED FISH
INC)
9300 Trustee Rd, Port Hardy, BC, V0N 2P0
(250) 949-8781
Emp Here 40   *Sales* 33,423,080
SIC 5146 Fish and seafoods
Bruce Dirom
Carol Dirom

Port Mcneill, BC V0N

D-U-N-S 24-579-2536 (HQ)
LEMARE LAKE LOGGING LTD
3341 Mine Rd, Port Mcneill, BC, V0N 2R0
(250) 956-3123
Sales 69,597,500
SIC 2411 Logging
David Dutcyvich

D-U-N-S 25-123-6584 (SL)
PORT MCNEIL FOODS LTD
IGA
1705 Campbell Way Unit 44, Port Mcneill, BC,
V0N 2R0

▲ Public Company   ■ Public Company Family Member   **HQ** Headquarters   **BR** Branch   **SL** Single Location

(250) 956-4404
Emp Here 50   *Sales* 13,707,600
SIC 5411 Grocery stores
David Cote

D-U-N-S 20-093-5674   (HQ)
ROSBACK, R A ENTERPRISES LTD
SHOPRITE STORES
1700 Broughton Blvd, Port Mcneill, BC, V0N
2R0
(250) 956-3323
Emp Here 20   *Sales* 11,387,655
SIC 5251 Hardware stores
Ray Rosback
Clifford Rosback

D-U-N-S 24-311-7301   (HQ)
**WEST COAST HELICOPTERS MAINTE-
NANCE AND CONTRACTING LTD**
WEST COAST HELICOPTERS
1011 Airport Rd, Port Mcneill, BC, V0N 2R0
(250) 956-2244
Emp Here 20   *Sales* 12,990,160
SIC 4522 Air transportation, nonscheduled
Granger Avery
Peter Barratt
Terrence Dean Eissfeldt

Port Mellon, BC V0N

D-U-N-S 24-525-0969   (HQ)
**HOWE SOUND PULP & PAPER CORPORA-
TION**
(*Suby of* CAPITAL ASSETS HOLDINGS (L)
BERHAD)
3838 Port Mellon Hwy, Port Mellon, BC, V0N
2S0
(604) 884-5223
Sales 145,216,615
SIC 2611 Pulp mills
Mac Palmieri
Sugiarto Kardiman
Hardi Wardhana

Port Moody, BC V3H

D-U-N-S 24-128-4749   (SL)
COLWIN ELECTRIC GROUP
2829 Murray St, Port Moody, BC, V3H 1X3
(604) 461-2181
Emp Here 70   *Sales* 15,248,030
SIC 1731 Electrical work
John Parolin

D-U-N-S 20-650-8298   (SL)
FLAVELLE SAWMILL COMPANY LTD
(*Suby of* ASPEN PLANERS LTD)
2400 Murray St, Port Moody, BC, V3H 4H6
(604) 939-1141
Emp Here 90   *Sales* 17,313,300
SIC 2421 Sawmills and planing mills, general
George Kozznetsosf
David Gray

D-U-N-S 24-345-9547   (BR)
FRASER HEALTH AUTHORITY
TRI CITY HOME HEALTH
(*Suby of* GOVERNMENT OF THE
PROVINCE OF BRITISH COLUMBIA)
220 Brew St Suite 700, Port Moody, BC, V3H
0H6
(604) 777-7300
Emp Here 200
SIC 8742 Management consulting services
Lynn Dowsley

D-U-N-S 20-804-6805   (SL)
GORDON AULENBACK LTD
G A CHECKPOINT
3034 St Johns St, Port Moody, BC, V3H 2C5
(604) 461-3434
Emp Here 32   *Sales* 15,938,496

SIC 5571 Motorcycle dealers
Gordon Aulenback

D-U-N-S 20-646-6596   (SL)
JON WOOD
ROYAL LEPAGE SHOWCASE PLUS
3137 St Johns St, Port Moody, BC, V3H 2C8

Emp Here 80   *Sales* 21,740,480
SIC 6531 Real estate agents and managers
Paul Degraaf

D-U-N-S 20-101-8298   (SL)
PACIFIC COAST TERMINALS CO. LTD
PCT
(*Suby of* SULTRAN LTD)
2300 Columbia St, Port Moody, BC, V3H 5J9
(604) 939-7371
Emp Here 70   *Sales* 27,560,680
SIC 4491 Marine cargo handling
Wade Leslie
Andre Olivier

D-U-N-S 20-173-8895   (SL)
REICHHOLD INDUSTRIES LIMITED
50 Douglas St, Port Moody, BC, V3H 3L9
(604) 939-1181
Emp Here 150   *Sales* 42,603,150
SIC 2821 Plastics materials and resins

D-U-N-S 25-715-0458   (SL)
ROYAL LEPAGE STERLING REALTY
220 Brew St Suite 801, Port Moody, BC, V3H
0H6
(604) 421-1010
Emp Here 75   *Sales* 31,416,675
SIC 6531 Real estate agents and managers
Randy Ryalls

D-U-N-S 25-745-6327   (BR)
SCHOOL DISTRICT NO. 43 (COQUITLAM)
PORT MOODY SECONDARY SCHOOL
(*Suby of* SCHOOL DISTRICT NO. 43 (CO-
QUITLAM))
300 Albert St, Port Moody, BC, V3H 2M5
(604) 939-6656
Emp Here 125
SIC 8211 Elementary and secondary schools
Karen Jensen

D-U-N-S 20-713-4763   (BR)
SCHOOL DISTRICT NO. 43 (COQUITLAM)
HERITAGE WOODS SECONDARY SCHOOL
(*Suby of* SCHOOL DISTRICT NO. 43 (CO-
QUITLAM))
1300 David Ave, Port Moody, BC, V3H 5K6
(604) 461-8679
Emp Here 100
SIC 8211 Elementary and secondary schools
Doug Sheppard

Pouce Coupe, BC V0C

D-U-N-S 20-978-2361   (BR)
CARIBOU ROAD SERVICES LTD
CRS
5201 52nd Ave, Pouce Coupe, BC, V0C 2C0
(250) 786-5440
Emp Here 80
SIC 5082 Construction and mining machinery
Al Harwood

D-U-N-S 20-744-9828   (HQ)
H.F. NODES CONSTRUCTION LTD
5102 50 St, Pouce Coupe, BC, V0C 2C0
(250) 786-5474
Emp Here 1   *Sales* 25,576,400
SIC 1389 Oil and gas field services, nec
Herbert Nodes
Myrna Nodes
Joe Nodes

Powell River, BC V8A

D-U-N-S 24-347-2458   (BR)
CATALYST PAPER CORPORATION
POWELL RIVER MILL
(*Suby of* CAPITAL ASSETS HOLDINGS (L)
BERHAD)
5775 Ash Ave, Powell River, BC, V8A 4R3
(604) 483-3722
Emp Here 441
SIC 2621 Paper mills
Stew Gibson

D-U-N-S 24-372-6163   (SL)
MASSULLO MOTORS LIMITED
4493 Joyce Ave, Powell River, BC, V8A 3A8
(604) 485-7981
Emp Here 25   *Sales* 12,451,950
SIC 5511 New and used car dealers
Felix Massullo

D-U-N-S 20-068-3550   (SL)
**POWELL RIVER ASSOCIATION FOR COM-
MUNITY LIVING**
PRACL
4675 Marine Ave Unit 201, Powell River, BC,
V8A 2L2
(604) 485-4628
Emp Here 240   *Sales* 345,264,240
SIC 8699 Membership organizations, nec
Lilla Tipton

D-U-N-S 20-583-1584   (SL)
POWELL RIVER BUILDING SUPPLY LTD
RONA BUILDING CENTRE
4750 Joyce Ave, Powell River, BC, V8A 3B6
(604) 485-2791
Emp Here 42   *Sales* 10,628,478
SIC 5211 Lumber and other building materials
Patrick Hull

D-U-N-S 20-088-0529   (SL)
SILVERTIP SECURITY LTD
7100 Alberni St Suite 24, Powell River, BC,
V8A 5K9

Emp Here 20   *Sales* 13,578,460
SIC 6211 Security brokers and dealers

D-U-N-S 24-455-5061   (BR)
**VANCOUVER COASTAL HEALTH AUTHOR-
ITY**
OLIVE DEVAUD RESIDENCE
(*Suby of* GOVERNMENT OF THE
PROVINCE OF BRITISH COLUMBIA)
7105 Kemano St, Powell River, BC, V8A 1L8
(604) 485-9868
Emp Here 205
SIC 8361 Residential care
Ona Head

D-U-N-S 25-294-7866   (BR)
WAL-MART CANADA CORP
WAL-MART
(*Suby of* WALMART INC.)
7100 Alberni St Suite 23, Powell River, BC,
V8A 5K9
(604) 485-9811
Emp Here 110
SIC 5311 Department stores
Bonnie Goldstraw

D-U-N-S 20-045-0281   (SL)
**WEST COAST FISHCULTURE (LOIS LAKE)
LTD**
11060 Morton Rd, Powell River, BC, V8A 0L9
(604) 487-9200
Emp Here 47   *Sales* 18,119,393
SIC 0273 Animal aquaculture
Robert Walker
Bill Vanderfert

Prince George, BC V2K

D-U-N-S 20-896-4770   (HQ)

ALLNORTH CONSULTANTS LIMITED

2011 Prince George Pulpmill Rd, Prince
George, BC, V2K 5P5
(250) 614-7291
Emp Here 3   *Sales* 114,070,500
SIC 8748 Business consulting, nec
Darby Kreitz
Jeff Lawson
Thomas Sitar

D-U-N-S 25-484-1265   (BR)
**BOARD OF EDUCATION OF SCHOOL DIS-
TRICT NO. 57 (PRINCE GEORGE), THE**
KELLY ROAD SECONDARY SCHOOL
(*Suby of* BOARD OF EDUCATION OF
SCHOOL DISTRICT NO. 57 (PRINCE
GEORGE), THE)
4540 Handlen Rd, Prince George, BC, V2K
2J8
(250) 962-9271
Emp Here 130
SIC 8211 Elementary and secondary schools
Jane Kennedy

D-U-N-S 20-915-4371   (BR)
DIVERSIFIED TRANSPORTATION LTD
PACIFIC WESTERN TRANSPORTATION
(*Suby of* PACIFIC WESTERN TRANSPORTA-
TION LTD)
391 North Nechako Rd, Prince George, BC,
V2K 4K8
(250) 563-5431
Emp Here 113
SIC 4142 Bus charter service, except local
Jerry Pelletier

D-U-N-S 24-313-1823   (SL)
EXCEL TRANSPORTATION ALBERTA INC
333 Ongman Rd, Prince George, BC, V2K
4K9
(250) 563-7356
Emp Here 250   *Sales* 51,426,500
SIC 4212 Local trucking, without storage
Roy Dondale

D-U-N-S 20-801-8549   (SL)
EXCEL TRANSPORTATION INC
333 Ongman Rd, Prince George, BC, V2K
4K9
(250) 563-7356
Emp Here 150   *Sales* 30,855,900
SIC 4212 Local trucking, without storage
Ivan Andersen
Keith Andersen
Florent Foucher
Gordon Andersen
Roy Dondale

D-U-N-S 24-292-8349   (SL)
FARR INSTALLATIONS LTD
4912 Hart Hwy, Prince George, BC, V2K 3A1
(250) 962-0333
Emp Here 150   *Sales* 36,927,900
SIC 1791 Structural steel erection
Raymond Fortier

D-U-N-S 20-120-0230   (HQ)
GEOTECH DRILLING SERVICES LTD
5052 Hartway Dr, Prince George, BC, V2K
5B7
(250) 962-9041
Emp Here 80   *Sales* 59,339,568
SIC 1081 Metal mining services
Jody Lambert
Jason Oliver
Ryan Sanis
Nicole Toran

D-U-N-S 20-921-2260   (BR)
HUSKY ENERGY INC
(*Suby of* HUSKY ENERGY INC)
2542 Prince George Pulpmill Rd, Prince
George, BC, V2K 5P5

Emp Here 80
SIC 1311 Crude petroleum and natural gas
Greg Caltas

D-U-N-S 24-281-6114 (SL)
LO-BAR LOG TRANSPORT CO. LTD
8377 Hart Hwy, Prince George, BC, V2K 3B8
(250) 962-8644
Emp Here 100 *Sales* 15,586,300
SIC 2411 Logging
Greg Jacob

D-U-N-S 25-991-9090 (HQ)
PEROXYCHEM CANADA LTD
(Suby of PEROXYCHEM HOLDINGS, L.P.)
2147 Prince George Pulpmill Rd, Prince
George, BC, V2K 5P5
(250) 561-4200
Emp Here 50 *Sales* 13,833,000
SIC 2819 Industrial inorganic chemicals, nec
James A. Mcclung
Theodore H. Laws
Randall (Randy) S. Ellis
Joseph H. Netherland
Steven H Shapiro
Michael J Matymish
Charlotte M Smith
Robert Service

D-U-N-S 20-268-7463 (SL)
**PRINCE GEORGE SEARCH AND RESCUE
SOCIETY**
PGSAR
4057 Hart Hwy, Prince George, BC, V2K 2Z5
(250) 962-5544
Emp Here 49 *Sales* 19,473,286
SIC 8699 Membership organizations, nec
Ian Leitch
Sven Freitag

D-U-N-S 24-798-5682 (HQ)
**WESTERN INDUSTRIAL CONTRACTORS
LTD**
4912 Hart Hwy, Prince George, BC, V2K 3A1
(250) 962-6011
Emp Here 12 *Sales* 42,273,700
SIC 1541 Industrial buildings and warehouses
Ray Fortier
Brian Savage
John Pateman

D-U-N-S 25-798-2769 (BR)
YRB MANAGEMENT CORP
PARTS ON THE HART
(Suby of YRB MANAGEMENT CORP)
2424 Hart Hwy, Prince George, BC, V2K 2X8
(250) 614-7604
Emp Here 80
SIC 1611 Highway and street construction
Steven Macneil

Prince George, BC V2L

D-U-N-S 20-591-4364 (BR)
**BOARD OF EDUCATION OF SCHOOL DIS-
TRICT NO. 57 (PRINCE GEORGE), THE**
?COLE DUSHCESS PARK SECONDAIRE
(Suby of BOARD OF EDUCATION OF
SCHOOL DISTRICT NO. 57 (PRINCE
GEORGE), THE)
747 Winnipeg St, Prince George, BC, V2L 2V3
(250) 563-7124
Emp Here 100
SIC 8211 Elementary and secondary schools
Dolores Patenaude

D-U-N-S 24-152-8645 (HQ)
**BOARD OF EDUCATION OF SCHOOL DIS-
TRICT NO. 57 (PRINCE GEORGE), THE**
2100 Ferry Ave, Prince George, BC, V2L 4R5
(250) 561-6800
Emp Here 120 *Sales* 111,274,080
SIC 8211 Elementary and secondary schools
Marilyn Marquis-Forster
Allan Reed
Tim Bennett
Trish Perrin

Tony Cable
Bob Harris
Brenda Hooker
Sharel Warrington
Bruce Wiebe

D-U-N-S 20-226-2890 (SL)
BRAIN INJURED GROUP SOCIETY
P G BIG
1070 4th Ave, Prince George, BC, V2L 3J1
(250) 564-2447
Emp Here 45 *Sales* 17,883,630
SIC 8699 Membership organizations, nec
Allison Hagreen

D-U-N-S 24-866-9574 (HQ)
BRINK FOREST PRODUCTS LTD
2023 River Rd, Prince George, BC, V2L 5S8
(250) 564-0412
Sales 14,427,750
SIC 2421 Sawmills and planing mills, general
John Brink

D-U-N-S 20-747-8483 (BR)
CANADIAN FOREST PRODUCTS LTD
CANFOR ADMINISTRATION CENTRE
(Suby of CANFOR CORPORATION)
5162 Northwood Pulp Mill Rd, Prince George,
BC, V2L 4W2
(250) 962-3500
Emp Here 200
SIC 2421 Sawmills and planing mills, general
Debbie Brandner

D-U-N-S 24-930-7232 (HQ)
**CARRIER SEKANI FAMILY SERVICES SO-
CIETY**
987 4th Ave, Prince George, BC, V2L 3H7
(250) 562-3591
Emp Here 1 *Sales* 25,883,500
SIC 8399 Social services, nec
Warner Adam
Marilyn Teegee

D-U-N-S 24-838-2707 (SL)
CENTRE CITY REAL ESTATE INC
RE/MAX CENTRE CITY REALTY
1679 15th Ave, Prince George, BC, V2L 3X2
(250) 552-2757
Emp Here 43 *Sales* 14,066,461
SIC 6531 Real estate agents and managers
William Lynch
Nancy Lynch

D-U-N-S 24-730-9784 (HQ)
CHIEFTAIN AUTO PARTS (1987) INC
CHIEFTAIN WAREHOUSING
555 3rd Ave, Prince George, BC, V2L 3C2
(250) 562-1258
Emp Here 32 *Sales* 12,383,310
SIC 5013 Motor vehicle supplies and new
parts
Peter Heinze
Eileen Heinze

D-U-N-S 24-346-7292 (BR)
COAST HOTELS LIMITED
COAST HOTELS AND RESORTS
(Suby of OKABE CO., LTD.)
770 Brunswick St, Prince George, BC, V2L
2C2
(250) 563-0121
Emp Here 130
SIC 7011 Hotels and motels
Tony Arevalo

D-U-N-S 20-596-7990 (SL)
DHILLON FOOD SERVICES LTD
WHITE SPOT RESTAURANT
820 Victoria St, Prince George, BC, V2L 5P1
(250) 563-2331
Emp Here 80 *Sales* 3,641,520
SIC 5812 Eating places
Jas Dhillon

D-U-N-S 20-583-6802 (BR)
GLACIER MEDIA INC
PRINCE GEORGE CITIZENS NEWSPAPER

(Suby of GLACIER MEDIA INC)
150 Brunswick St, Prince George, BC, V2L
2B3
(250) 562-6666
Emp Here 100
SIC 2711 Newspapers
Hugh Nicholson

D-U-N-S 24-310-6242 (SL)
GREAT STEAK HOUSE INC, THE
KEG RESTAURANT
582 George St, Prince George, BC, V2L 1R7
(250) 563-1768
Emp Here 150 *Sales* 6,827,850
SIC 5812 Eating places
Kelly Nordin

D-U-N-S 25-388-6204 (HQ)
HIGHLAND CATERERS LTD
570 3rd Ave, Prince George, BC, V2L 3C3
(250) 563-5332
Sales 10,462,120
SIC 6712 Bank holding companies
Ed Theessen

D-U-N-S 24-958-0382 (BR)
HUDSON'S BAY COMPANY
BAY, THE
(Suby of HUDSON'S BAY COMPANY)
1600 15th Ave Suite 140, Prince George, BC,
V2L 3X3
(250) 563-0211
Emp Here 90
SIC 5311 Department stores
Giles Fernando

D-U-N-S 24-292-6038 (BR)
HUSKY OIL OPERATIONS LIMITED
HUSKY ENERGY
(Suby of HUSKY ENERGY INC)
2542 Pg Pulpmill Rd, Prince George, BC, V2L
4V4

Emp Here 79
SIC 2911 Petroleum refining
Roy Warnock

D-U-N-S 20-862-8180 (HQ)
INDUSTRIAL FORESTRY SERVICE LTD
1595 5th Ave, Prince George, BC, V2L 3L9
(250) 564-4115
Emp Here 50 *Sales* 10,256,925
SIC 0851 Forestry services
Rob Schuetz
Ken Steel
Barry Steel

D-U-N-S 24-249-2130 (HQ)
KEY LEASE CANADA LTD
NORTHERN TOYOTA
2005 Redwood St, Prince George, BC, V2L
2N5
(250) 564-7205
Sales 34,610,400
SIC 5511 New and used car dealers
Ken Leboe

D-U-N-S 20-797-0922 (SL)
LAKELAND MILLS LTD
(Suby of SINCLAR GROUP FOREST PROD-
UCTS LTD)
Gd, Prince George, BC, V2L 4V4
(250) 564-7976
Emp Here 175 *Sales* 33,664,750
SIC 2421 Sawmills and planing mills, general
Keith Andersen

D-U-N-S 20-712-5527 (HQ)
N R MOTORS LTD
NORTHERN RECREATION
805 1st Ave, Prince George, BC, V2L 2Y4
(250) 563-8891
Emp Here 46 *Sales* 11,640,714
SIC 5271 Mobile home dealers
Robert Nikkel
Marvina Nikkel

D-U-N-S 20-105-6132 (HQ)

**NORTHERN HARDWARE & FURNITURE
CO., LTD**
AMCO WHOLESALE
1386 3rd Ave, Prince George, BC, V2L 3E9
(250) 563-7161
Emp Here 45 *Sales* 14,720,860
SIC 5251 Hardware stores
Kelly Green
Hilliard Clare

D-U-N-S 24-151-1773 (HQ)
NORTHERN HEALTH AUTHORITY
PRINCE GEORGE REGIONAL HOSPITAL
299 Victoria St Suite 600, Prince George, BC,
V2L 5B8
(250) 565-2649
Emp Here 10 *Sales* 777,560,000
SIC 8062 General medical and surgical hospi-
tals
Cathy Ulrich
Mark De Croos
David Williams
Fraser Bell

D-U-N-S 20-548-0221 (SL)
NORTHERN ICE SUPPLY LTD
1835 1st Ave, Prince George, BC, V2L 2Y8
(778) 763-0945
Emp Here 26 *Sales* 19,305,520
SIC 5199 Nondurable goods, nec

D-U-N-S 24-491-7928 (SL)
**NORTHERN INTERIOR WOODWORKERS
HOLDING SOCIETY**
STEELWORKERS
1777 3rd Ave Suite 100, Prince George, BC,
V2L 3G7
(250) 563-7771
Emp Here 11 *Sales* 11,383,691
SIC 6371 Pension, health, and welfare funds
Frank Everitt

D-U-N-S 20-873-2458 (SL)
NORTHLAND MOTORS LP
NORTHLAND HYUNDAI
(Suby of AUTOCANADA INC)
2021 Highway 16 W, Prince George, BC, V2L
0A4
(250) 564-6663
Emp Here 28 *Sales* 17,619,840
SIC 5511 New and used car dealers
Steven Landry

D-U-N-S 25-771-6498 (SL)
NUMBER EIGHTY-EIGHT HOLDINGS LTD
NECHAKO BOTTLE DEPOT
1922 1st Ave, Prince George, BC, V2L 2Y9
(250) 562-3871
Emp Here 23 *Sales* 10,200,270
SIC 7389 Business services, nec
Rick Neufeld

D-U-N-S 25-778-3654 (SL)
PRINCE GEORGE HOSPICE SOCIETY
3089 Clapperton St, Prince George, BC, V2L
5N4
(250) 563-2551
Emp Here 30 *Sales* 11,922,420
SIC 8699 Membership organizations, nec
Donalda Carson

D-U-N-S 24-153-2514 (SL)
REGIONAL SECURITY SERVICES LTD
190 Victoria St, Prince George, BC, V2L 2J2
(250) 562-1215
Emp Here 70 *Sales* 27,697,460
SIC 7381 Detective and armored car services
Rodney Holmes

D-U-N-S 24-397-5625 (SL)
TABOR VIEW HOLDINGS LTD
505 4th Ave, Prince George, BC, V2L 3H2
(250) 563-8250
Emp Here 40 *Sales* 16,774,200
SIC 6712 Bank holding companies
George Hoover

D-U-N-S 20-749-7314 (SL)

WATSON, WAYNE CONSTRUCTION LTD
(*Suby of* 254358 BC LTD)
730 3rd Ave, Prince George, BC, V2L 3C5
(250) 562-8251
Emp Here 129   *Sales* 90,092,568
SIC 1542 Nonresidential construction, nec
Wayne Watson
Brian Savage
Carol Watson

D-U-N-S 25-887-6747   (BR)
WORKERS' COMPENSATION BOARD OF BRITISH COLUMBIA
WORKERS' COMPENSATION BOARD
(*Suby of* WORKERS' COMPENSATION BOARD OF BRITISH COLUMBIA)
1066 Vancouver St, Prince George, BC, V2L 5M4
(250) 561-3715
Emp Here 100
SIC 6331 Fire, marine, and casualty insurance
Julie Quartay

Prince George, BC V2M

D-U-N-S 25-169-3446   (SL)
AIMHI-PRINCE GEORGE ASSOCIATION FOR COMMUNITY LIVING
950 Kerry St, Prince George, BC, V2M 5A3
(250) 564-6408
Emp Here 250   *Sales* 47,551,750
SIC 8011 Offices and clinics of medical doctors
Guy Tremblay
Vince Scott
Lorelei (Dolly) Hilton
Paul Raines
Fred Nelson
Mary Parkin
Ruth Stanton
Brenda Peacock
Gary Godwin
Rory Summers

D-U-N-S 24-345-6329   (BR)
BOARD OF EDUCATION OF SCHOOL DISTRICT NO. 57 (PRINCE GEORGE), THE
PRINCE GEORGE SECONDARY SCHOOL
(*Suby of* BOARD OF EDUCATION OF SCHOOL DISTRICT NO. 57 (PRINCE GEORGE), THE)
2901 Griffiths Ave, Prince George, BC, V2M 2S7
(250) 562-6441
Emp Here 140
SIC 8211 Elementary and secondary schools
Sherry Thibault

D-U-N-S 25-260-2628   (SL)
C.I.F. CONSTRUCTION LTD
6171 Otway Rd, Prince George, BC, V2M 7B4
(250) 564-8174
Emp Here 100   *Sales* 42,273,700
SIC 1541 Industrial buildings and warehouses
Jack Fomenoff

D-U-N-S 24-291-3382   (SL)
ESTHER'S INN LTD
1151 Commercial Cres, Prince George, BC, V2M 6W6
(250) 562-4131
Emp Here 100   *Sales* 9,489,900
SIC 7011 Hotels and motels
Henry Creuzot
Esther Creuzot

D-U-N-S 24-682-7885   (SL)
KONA DRUGS LTD
SHOPPERS DRUG MART
737 Central St W, Prince George, BC, V2M 3C6
(250) 562-2311
Emp Here 60   *Sales* 14,659,680
SIC 5912 Drug stores and proprietary stores

D-U-N-S 20-210-8457   (BR)
MOXIE'S RESTAURANTS, LIMITED PARTNERSHIP
MOXIE'S CLASIC GROW RESTAURANT
1804 Central St E, Prince George, BC, V2M 3C3
(250) 564-4700
Emp Here 75
SIC 5812 Eating places
Elise Walle

D-U-N-S 24-385-7575   (BR)
NORTHERN HEALTH AUTHORITY
RAINBOW INTERMEDIATE CARE HOME
(*Suby of* NORTHERN HEALTH AUTHORITY)
1000 Liard Dr, Prince George, BC, V2M 3Z3
(250) 649-7293
Emp Here 300
SIC 8742 Management consulting services
Karen Calvert

D-U-N-S 20-105-6975   (SL)
PRINCE GEORGE MOTORS LTD
PG MOTORS
1331 Central St W, Prince George, BC, V2M 3E2
(250) 563-8111
Emp Here 65   *Sales* 40,903,200
SIC 5511 New and used car dealers
Craig Wood
Valerie Caouette

D-U-N-S 24-641-5533   (SL)
SIMON FRASER LODGE INC
(*Suby of* BURON HOLDINGS LTD)
2410 Laurier Cres, Prince George, BC, V2M 2B3
(250) 563-3413
Emp Here 120   *Sales* 8,199,120
SIC 8059 Nursing and personal care, nec
John Nicholls
Howard Addison

Prince George, BC V2N

D-U-N-S 20-175-2834   (BR)
CANADIAN FOREST PRODUCTS LTD
PRINCE GEORGE PULP & PAPER
(*Suby of* CANFOR CORPORATION)
2789 Pulp Mill Rd, Prince George, BC, V2N 2K3
(250) 563-0161
Emp Here 400
SIC 2421 Sawmills and planing mills, general
Peter Lovell

D-U-N-S 25-097-3885   (BR)
CANADIAN FOREST PRODUCTS LTD
CANFOR PULP
(*Suby of* CANFOR CORPORATION)
2533 Prince George Pulpmill Rd, Prince George, BC, V2N 2K3
(250) 563-0161
Emp Here 250
SIC 2421 Sawmills and planing mills, general
Peter Lovell

D-U-N-S 20-269-2943   (BR)
CANFOR PULP LTD
NORTHWOOD DIVISION
(*Suby of* CANFOR CORPORATION)
5353 Northwood Pulp Mill Rd, Prince George, BC, V2N 2K3
(250) 962-3666
Emp Here 500
SIC 2611 Pulp mills

D-U-N-S 20-023-5992   (SL)
CAPITAL BUILDING SUPPLIES LTD
RONA PRINCE GEORGE
4150 Cowart Rd, Prince George, BC, V2N 6H9
(250) 562-1125
Emp Here 50   *Sales* 22,358,700
SIC 5039 Construction materials, nec

Rod Bellmann

D-U-N-S 25-790-6057   (HQ)
CARRIER FOREST PRODUCTS LTD
4722 Continental Way, Prince George, BC, V2N 5S5
(250) 963-9664
Emp Here 60   *Sales* 19,980,090
SIC 3599 Industrial machinery, nec
William Michael Kordyban
Terry Kuzma

D-U-N-S 20-105-2321   (HQ)
CARRIER LUMBER LTD
4722 Continental Way, Prince George, BC, V2N 5S5
(250) 563-9271
Emp Here 20   *Sales* 83,517,000
SIC 2421 Sawmills and planing mills, general
William Michael Kordyban
Mary Kordyban

D-U-N-S 24-143-6653   (HQ)
CENTRAL BUILDERS' SUPPLY P.G. LIMITED
HOME HARDWARE
1501 Central St W, Prince George, BC, V2N 1P6
(250) 563-1538
Sales 27,477,905
SIC 1541 Industrial buildings and warehouses
Grant Skelly

D-U-N-S 20-911-8223   (HQ)
COLLEGE OF NEW CALEDONIA, THE
CNC
3330 22nd Ave, Prince George, BC, V2N 1P8
(250) 562-2131
Emp Here 800   *Sales* 46,674,291
SIC 8221 Colleges and universities
Henry Reiser
Tara Szerencsi
Robert Doney
Gillain Malfair
Mary Sjostrom
Dan Marcotte
Steve Nycholat
Vincent Prince
Sandra Ramsay

D-U-N-S 24-104-5926   (BR)
COMPAGNIE DES CHEMINS DE FER NATIONAUX DU CANADA
CN RAILWAY
(*Suby of* COMPAGNIE DES CHEMINS DE FER NATIONAUX DU CANADA)
1108 Industrial Way, Prince George, BC, V2N 5S1
(250) 561-4190
Emp Here 750
SIC 4111 Local and suburban transit
Doug Ryhorchuk

D-U-N-S 20-105-2743   (SL)
COOPER, R J CONSTRUCTION LTD
1937 Ogilvie St S, Prince George, BC, V2N 1X2
(250) 563-4649
Emp Here 23   *Sales* 10,826,813
SIC 1542 Nonresidential construction, nec
Brian Teschke

D-U-N-S 24-354-8943   (BR)
COSTCO WHOLESALE CANADA LTD
(*Suby of* COSTCO WHOLESALE CORPORATION)
2555 Range Rd Suite 158, Prince George, BC, V2N 4G8
(250) 561-0784
Emp Here 200
SIC 5099 Durable goods, nec
Mick Heise

D-U-N-S 20-902-5738   (BR)
DUCKS UNLIMITED CANADA
(*Suby of* DUCKS UNLIMITED CANADA)
7813 Renison Pl, Prince George, BC, V2N 3J2

(250) 964-3825
Emp Here 300
SIC 8999 Services, nec
Jeffrey Nelson

D-U-N-S 24-713-7297   (SL)
EDGEWATER HOLDINGS LTD
8545 Willow Cale Rd, Prince George, BC, V2N 6Z9
(250) 561-7061
Emp Here 50   *Sales* 22,174,500
SIC 7389 Business services, nec
Kent Cooper

D-U-N-S 20-176-7311   (BR)
HOME DEPOT OF CANADA INC
HOME DEPOT
(*Suby of* THE HOME DEPOT INC)
5959 O'Grady Rd, Prince George, BC, V2N 6Z5
(250) 906-3610
Emp Here 150
SIC 5251 Hardware stores
Adrian Pryce

D-U-N-S 24-309-4385   (SL)
IDL PROJECTS INC
1088 Great St, Prince George, BC, V2N 2K8
(250) 649-0561
Emp Here 1,250   *Sales* 872,990,000
SIC 1542 Nonresidential construction, nec
Dennis Schwab
Sheldon Boyes

D-U-N-S 24-957-3700   (SL)
J D T CONSTRUCTION LTD
9407 Penn Rd, Prince George, BC, V2N 5T6
(250) 561-2027
Emp Here 50   *Sales* 16,666,650
SIC 1541 Industrial buildings and warehouses
Daryl Kiland
Terry Schweda

D-U-N-S 24-897-4842   (SL)
J V LOGGING LTD
J.V. LOGGING LTD
9453 Rock Island Rd, Prince George, BC, V2N 5T4
(250) 561-2220
Emp Here 80   *Sales* 12,469,040
SIC 2411 Logging
Jimmy Allen Vaughan
Laura Vaughan

D-U-N-S 24-446-6744   (HQ)
JAMES WESTERN STAR TRUCK & TRAILER LTD
5239 Continental Way, Prince George, BC, V2N 5S5
(250) 561-0646
Sales 125,856,000
SIC 5511 New and used car dealers
Bryan James

D-U-N-S 24-797-2680   (SL)
LLOYD REFORESTATION LTD
13025 Woodland Rd, Prince George, BC, V2N 5B4

Emp Here 150   *Sales* 26,085,750
SIC 0781 Landscape counseling and planning
Alan Lloyd

D-U-N-S 20-808-3407   (HQ)
LOAD'EM UP PETROLEUMS LTD
PETRO CANADA
1064 Great St, Prince George, BC, V2N 2K8
(250) 562-8166
Emp Here 1   *Sales* 10,328,080
SIC 5171 Petroleum bulk stations and terminals
Gordon D Hamborg

D-U-N-S 20-795-5704   (BR)
LOBLAWS INC
REAL CANADIAN SUPERSTORE, THE
(*Suby of* LOBLAW COMPANIES LIMITED)
2155 Ferry Ave, Prince George, BC, V2N 5E8

---

(250) 960-1300
Emp Here 300
SIC 5411 Grocery stores
Chris Hotlood

D-U-N-S 25-839-8635 (BR)
MANITOULIN TRANSPORTATION
BANDSTRA TRANSPORTATION
(*Suby of* MANITOULIN TRANSPORTATION)
9499 Milwaukee Way, Prince George, BC, V2N 5T3
(250) 563-9138
Emp Here 90
SIC 4212 Local trucking, without storage
Ken Turner

D-U-N-S 20-793-0392 (SL)
MILESTEP PHARMACY SERVICES INC
SHOPPERS DRUG MART
5240 Domano Blvd Unit 470, Prince George, BC, V2N 4A1
(250) 964-1888
Emp Here 40 *Sales* 10,118,160
SIC 5912 Drug stores and proprietary stores
Steven Leong
Janice (Jan) Leong

D-U-N-S 25-094-2625 (SL)
NORTHERN ACREAGE SUPPLY LTD
4870 Continental Way, Prince George, BC, V2N 5S5
(250) 596-2273
Emp Here 20 *Sales* 10,000,000
SIC 5083 Farm and garden machinery
Alan Doode

D-U-N-S 24-876-7993 (SL)
NORTHERN ENERGY CONSTRUCTORS LTD
9368 Milwaukee Way Suite 101, Prince George, BC, V2N 5T3
(250) 562-8100
Emp Here 50 *Sales* 12,652,950
SIC 5211 Lumber and other building materials
Fritz Hausot

D-U-N-S 24-362-3050 (HQ)
NORTHERN INDUSTRIAL SALES B.C. LTD
NORTHERN INDUSTRIAL SALES
3526 Opie Cres, Prince George, BC, V2N 2P9
(250) 562-4435
Sales 45,127,470
SIC 5085 Industrial supplies
Timothy Macdonald
Wayne Gordon

D-U-N-S 24-317-4054 (HQ)
NORTHERN LINKWELL CONSTRUCTION LTD
2011 Pg Pulp Mill Rd, Prince George, BC, V2N 2K3
(250) 563-2844
Emp Here 1 *Sales* 80,388,175
SIC 1622 Bridge, tunnel, and elevated highway construction
Andrew Scott Purdey

D-U-N-S 25-104-8997 (HQ)
NORTHERN THUNDERBIRD AIR INC
NT AIR
(*Suby of* 580741 BRITISH COLUMBIA LTD)
4245 Hanger Rd Unit 100, Prince George, BC, V2N 4M6
(250) 963-9611
Emp Here 17 *Sales* 16,018,680
SIC 4522 Air transportation, nonscheduled
Doug Mccrea

D-U-N-S 20-338-3310 (SL)
NORTHTOWN AUTO LP
NORTHLAND CHRYSLER DODGE JEEP RAM
(*Suby of* AUTOCANADA INC)
2844 Recplace Dr, Prince George, BC, V2N 0G2
(250) 562-5254
Emp Here 120 *Sales* 75,513,600
SIC 5511 New and used car dealers

Kyle Bachman

D-U-N-S 20-560-6226 (SL)
NORTHWEST WOOD TREATERS LP
(*Suby of* CANWEL BUILDING MATERIALS GROUP LTD)
10553 Willow Cale Forest, Prince George, BC, V2N 4T7
(250) 963-9628
Emp Here 40 *Sales* 17,886,960
SIC 5039 Construction materials, nec
Steven Marshall

D-U-N-S 24-379-3002 (SL)
NORWELD MECHANICAL INSTALLATIONS INC
1416 Santa Fe Rd, Prince George, BC, V2N 5T5
(250) 562-6660
Emp Here 100 *Sales* 23,306,500
SIC 1711 Plumbing, heating, air-conditioning
Jeff Houghton

D-U-N-S 24-808-9851 (HQ)
PREMIUM TRUCK & TRAILER INC
FREIGHTLINER PRINCE GEORGE
1015 Great St, Prince George, BC, V2N 2K8
(250) 563-0696
Emp Here 60 *Sales* 75,513,600
SIC 5511 New and used car dealers
Tom Coffey

D-U-N-S 20-230-5681 (SL)
PRINCE GEORGE CASINO SUPPLY COMPANY INC
TREASURE COVE CASINO
2003 Highway 97 S, Prince George, BC, V2N 7A3
(250) 564-7070
Emp Here 200 *Sales* 18,990,600
SIC 7999 Amusement and recreation, nec
John Major
Shelley Major

D-U-N-S 20-105-7452 (SL)
ROLLING MIX CONCRETE (B.C) LTD
105 Foothill Blvd, Prince George, BC, V2N 2J8
(250) 563-9213
Emp Here 45 *Sales* 10,350,855
SIC 3273 Ready-mixed concrete
John Paolucci
Guido Di Stefano

D-U-N-S 20-328-5940 (SL)
ROYAL LEPAGE PRINCE GEORGE
3166 Massey Dr, Prince George, BC, V2N 2S9
(250) 564-4488
Emp Here 40 *Sales* 10,870,240
SIC 6531 Real estate agents and managers
Jim Mcneal

D-U-N-S 24-881-2844 (HQ)
RUSKIN CONSTRUCTION LTD
(*Suby of* NORTHERN LINKWELL CONSTRUCTION LTD)
2011 Pg Pulp Mill Rd, Prince George, BC, V2N 2K3
(250) 563-2800
Emp Here 20 *Sales* 80,716,290
SIC 1622 Bridge, tunnel, and elevated highway construction
Andrew Purdey

D-U-N-S 20-719-8172 (HQ)
SALEM CONTRACTING LTD
9097 Milwaukee Way, Prince George, BC, V2N 5T3
(250) 564-2244
Emp Here 1 *Sales* 22,813,520
SIC 1542 Nonresidential construction, nec
Monty Belsham
Rod Belsham

D-U-N-S 25-774-1793 (HQ)
SANDS BULK SALES LTD
SANDS BULK TRANSPORT
1059 Eastern St, Prince George, BC, V2N 5R8

(250) 563-2855
Emp Here 53 *Sales* 13,438,040
SIC 5983 Fuel oil dealers
Wayne Sands

D-U-N-S 20-911-9155 (SL)
SHOPPERS WHOLESALE FOOD COMPANY
1959 Nicholson St S, Prince George, BC, V2N 2Z9
(250) 562-6655
Emp Here 65 *Sales* 36,116,750
SIC 5141 Groceries, general line
Peter Sherba
Larry Hyette

D-U-N-S 24-346-7052 (SL)
SPECTRUM RESOURCE GROUP INC
3810 18th Ave, Prince George, BC, V2N 4V5
(250) 564-0383
Emp Here 100 *Sales* 23,428,800
SIC 8748 Business consulting, nec
Duane Maki
Dean Marshall

D-U-N-S 24-824-2120 (SL)
TWO RIVERS TRANSPORT
9408 Penn Rd, Prince George, BC, V2N 5T6

Emp Here 30 *Sales* 13,476,570
SIC 7389 Business services, nec
Clint Hunter

D-U-N-S 24-081-3704 (HQ)
UNIVERSAL RESTORATION SYSTEMS LTD
3675 Opie Cres, Prince George, BC, V2N 1B9
(250) 612-5177
Emp Here 35 *Sales* 20,320,650
SIC 1521 Single-family housing construction
Ken Zwiers

D-U-N-S 24-027-0780 (BR)
WAL-MART CANADA CORP
(*Suby of* WALMART INC.)
6565 Southridge Ave Suite 3651, Prince George, BC, V2N 6Z4
(250) 906-3203
Emp Here 200
SIC 5311 Department stores

D-U-N-S 24-979-6236 (HQ)
WESTCANA ELECTRIC INC
1643 Ogilvie St S, Prince George, BC, V2N 1W7
(250) 564-5800
Emp Here 41 *Sales* 13,069,740
SIC 1731 Electrical work
Scott Sherba

D-U-N-S 24-579-0043 (SL)
WOLFTEK INDUSTRIES INC
4944 Continental Way, Prince George, BC, V2N 5S5
(250) 561-1556
Emp Here 50 *Sales* 23,751,300
SIC 5084 Industrial machinery and equipment
Bruce Sutherland
Gerry Bergeron

D-U-N-S 20-059-5796 (HQ)
YOUNG, GARY AGENCIES LTD
ESSO BULK AGENT
1085 Great St, Prince George, BC, V2N 2K8
(250) 563-1725
Emp Here 13 *Sales* 19,623,352
SIC 5171 Petroleum bulk stations and terminals
Gary Young
Rhonda Young

Prince Rupert, BC V8J

D-U-N-S 20-981-9957 (SL)
CITY WEST CABLE & TELEPHONE CORP
CITY WEST

(*Suby of* CORPORATION OF THE CITY OF PRINCE RUPERT)
248 3rd Ave W, Prince Rupert, BC, V8J 1L1
(250) 624-2111
Emp Here 75 *Sales* 17,135,400
SIC 4899 Communication services, nec
William Craig

D-U-N-S 20-306-1296 (SL)
COAST INDUSTRIAL CONSTRUCTION LTD
110 1st Ave W Suite 260, Prince Rupert, BC, V8J 1A8
(250) 624-4327
Emp Here 25 *Sales* 14,592,140
SIC 1542 Nonresidential construction, nec
Mark Ignas

D-U-N-S 20-105-9441 (SL)
CREST HOTEL LTD
222 1st Ave W, Prince Rupert, BC, V8J 1A8
(250) 624-6771
Emp Here 75 *Sales* 7,117,425
SIC 7011 Hotels and motels
Gwyn Murray
Christina Smith

D-U-N-S 24-032-6504 (BR)
MCMILLAN, J.S. FISHERIES LTD
(*Suby of* MCMILLAN, J.S. FISHERIES LTD)
Gd Stn Main, Prince Rupert, BC, V8J 3P3
(250) 624-2146
Emp Here 100
SIC 2092 Fresh or frozen packaged fish
Jonathan Hunt

D-U-N-S 25-364-7838 (BR)
NORTHERN HEALTH AUTHORITY
PRINCE RUPERT REGIONAL HOSPITAL
(*Suby of* NORTHERN HEALTH AUTHORITY)
1305 Summit Ave, Prince Rupert, BC, V8J 2A6
(250) 624-2171
Emp Here 350
SIC 8062 General medical and surgical hospitals
Susan Beckerman

D-U-N-S 24-069-0362 (HQ)
NORTHERN SAVINGS CREDIT UNION
138 3rd Ave W, Prince Rupert, BC, V8J 1K8
(250) 627-3612
Emp Here 65 *Sales* 18,421,320
SIC 6062 State credit unions
Bill Nicholls

D-U-N-S 24-164-0275 (SL)
PRINCE RUPERT GRAIN LTD
(*Suby of* GLENCORE PLC)
Gd Stn Main, Prince Rupert, BC, V8J 3P3
(250) 627-8777
Emp Here 130 *Sales* 26,741,780
SIC 4221 Farm product warehousing and storage
Curt Vossen
Art Froehlich

D-U-N-S 24-074-4169 (HQ)
PRINCE RUPERT SCHOOL DISTRICT 52
634 6th Ave E, Prince Rupert, BC, V8J 1X1
(250) 624-6717
Sales 23,783,726
SIC 8211 Elementary and secondary schools
Sandra Jones
Cam Mcintyre
Kathy Gomez
Peter Edwards
Dave Garcia
Ken Minette

D-U-N-S 20-713-5000 (BR)
PRINCE RUPERT SCHOOL DISTRICT 52
(*Suby of* PRINCE RUPERT SCHOOL DISTRICT 52)
634 6th Ave E, Prince Rupert, BC, V8J 1X1
(250) 624-6717
Emp Here 500
SIC 8211 Elementary and secondary schools

Ken Minette

D-U-N-S 24-763-5670   (HQ)
QUICKLOAD CEF INC
1220 Ridley Island, Prince Rupert, BC, V8J 4P8
(250) 627-5623
Emp Here 10   *Sales* 12,999,175
SIC 4731 Freight transportation arrangement
Matt Holland

D-U-N-S 24-368-4586   (SL)
RIDLEY TERMINALS INC
(Suby of GOVERNMENT OF CANADA)
2110 Ridley Rd, Prince Rupert, BC, V8J 4H3
(250) 624-9511
Emp Here 115   *Sales* 45,278,260
SIC 4491 Marine cargo handling
Michael Mcphie
Marc Dulude
George Dorsey
Shiva Dean
Melanie Mackay
Catherine Wade
Liza Aboud

D-U-N-S 20-713-6219   (SL)
SHERMAN, L.E. MOTORS LTD
1001 Chamberlin Ave, Prince Rupert, BC, V8J 4J5
(250) 624-9171
Emp Here 21   *Sales* 10,459,638
SIC 5511 New and used car dealers
Larry Sherman

Princeton, BC V0X

D-U-N-S 25-773-9490   (SL)
KTW HOLDINGS LTD
VALLEYVIEW MOHAWK
580 Highway W, Princeton, BC, V0X 1W0
(250) 372-0451
Emp Here 30   *Sales* 14,942,340
SIC 5541 Gasoline service stations

D-U-N-S 24-866-4955   (HQ)
SBC FIREMASTER LTD
275 Copper Mountain Rd, Princeton, BC, V0X 1W0
(250) 295-7685
Emp Here 35   *Sales* 20,821,680
SIC 5099 Durable goods, nec
Brian Patton
Paul Patton

D-U-N-S 24-639-8770   (BR)
WEYERHAEUSER COMPANY LIMITED
(Suby of WEYERHAEUSER COMPANY)
201 Old Hedley Rd, Princeton, BC, V0X 1W0
(250) 295-3281
Emp Here 250
SIC 2421 Sawmills and planing mills, general
Jerry Micklos

Qualicum Beach, BC V9K

D-U-N-S 24-995-5865   (SL)
470695 BC LTD
QUALICUM BEACH SHELL
2712 Island Hwy W, Qualicum Beach, BC, V9K 2C4
(250) 752-3111
Emp Here 60   *Sales* 37,756,800
SIC 5541 Gasoline service stations
Valri Buggey

D-U-N-S 24-139-3300   (SL)
ARROWSMITH SEARCH & RESCUE
3241 Alberni Hwy, Qualicum Beach, BC, V9K 1Y6
(250) 752-7774
Emp Here 30   *Sales* 12,738,210

SIC 8999 Services, nec
Kent Meden

D-U-N-S 25-795-3679   (BR)
CANADIAN CANCER SOCIETY
(Suby of CANADIAN CANCER SOCIETY)
172 2 Ave W, Qualicum Beach, BC, V9K 1T7

Emp Here 75
SIC 8399 Social services, nec
Moreen Robertson

D-U-N-S 20-272-3768   (SL)
COAST REALTY GROUP (QUALICUM) LTD
689 Memorial Ave, Qualicum Beach, BC, V9K 1S8
(250) 752-3375
Emp Here 45   *Sales* 14,891,209
SIC 6531 Real estate agents and managers
Roland Wicket

D-U-N-S 25-937-4379   (BR)
VANCOUVER ISLAND HEALTH AUTHOR-ITY
EAGLE PARK HEALTH CARE FACILITY
(Suby of GOVERNMENT OF THE PROVINCE OF BRITISH COLUMBIA)
777 Jones St, Qualicum Beach, BC, V9K 2L1
(250) 947-8220
Emp Here 130
SIC 8011 Offices and clinics of medical doctors
Gill Forsyth

Queen Charlotte, BC V0T

D-U-N-S 25-676-8771   (SL)
GWAALAGAA NAAY CORPORATION
226 Hwy 16, Queen Charlotte, BC, V0T 1S1

Emp Here 30   *Sales* 18,878,400
SIC 5541 Gasoline service stations
Paula Lawson

Quesnel, BC V2J

D-U-N-S 20-868-3128   (HQ)
330542 BC LTD
REGENCY CHRYSLER
259 Mclean St, Quesnel, BC, V2J 2N8
(250) 992-9293
Emp Here 88   *Sales* 62,928,000
SIC 5511 New and used car dealers
Douglas Beckman

D-U-N-S 24-137-5260   (HQ)
C. & C. WOOD PRODUCTS LTD
1751 Quesnel-Hixon Rd, Quesnel, BC, V2J 5Z5
(250) 992-7471
Emp Here 1   *Sales* 23,084,400
SIC 2431 Millwork
Kristian Hayman
Miliana Celli
Mike Hayman

D-U-N-S 24-552-2503   (SL)
CARIBOO FOREST CONSULTANTS LTD
335 Vaughan St, Quesnel, BC, V2J 2T1

Emp Here 40   *Sales* 11,331,720
SIC 8741 Management services
Paul Galliazzo
Steve Curtis

D-U-N-S 20-575-6570   (SL)
CARIBOO PULP & PAPER COMPANY
50 North Star Rd, Quesnel, BC, V2J 3J6
(250) 992-0200
Emp Here 340   *Sales* 124,996,580
SIC 2611 Pulp mills
Edward (Ted) Seraphim

Raymond Ferris
Chris Virostek
Tom Theodorakis
Christopher Mciver

D-U-N-S 25-901-0502   (BR)
COLLEGE OF NEW CALEDONIA, THE
(Suby of COLLEGE OF NEW CALEDONIA, THE)
100 Campus Way, Quesnel, BC, V2J 7K1
(250) 991-7500
Emp Here 100
SIC 8222 Junior colleges
Chris Hartridge

D-U-N-S 24-390-9178   (SL)
DESUTTER INVESTMENTS INC
CANADIAN TIRE
570 Newman Rd, Quesnel, BC, V2J 6Z8
(250) 747-5275
Emp Here 50   *Sales* 24,903,900
SIC 5531 Auto and home supply stores
Darcy Desutter

D-U-N-S 20-268-7922   (SL)
FRASER RIVER CHEVROLET BUICK GMC LTD
FRASER RIVER GM
340 Carson Ave, Quesnel, BC, V2J 2B3
(250) 992-5515
Emp Here 23   *Sales* 11,455,794
SIC 5511 New and used car dealers
Brian Garland

D-U-N-S 24-566-7332   (HQ)
JHAJ HOLDINGS LTD
WEST-CAN AUTO PARTS
156 Malcolm Dr, Quesnel, BC, V2J 1E4
(604) 594-8800
Emp Here 13   *Sales* 44,049,600
SIC 5531 Auto and home supply stores
Darshan Jhaj
Ron Jhaj
Gurcharn Jhaj
Baljit (Bill) Jhaj

D-U-N-S 25-364-3845   (BR)
LOBLAWS INC
EXTRA FOODS
(Suby of LOBLAW COMPANIES LIMITED)
2335 Maple Dr E, Quesnel, BC, V2J 7J6
(250) 747-2803
Emp Here 130
SIC 5411 Grocery stores
Pat Bolitho

D-U-N-S 25-359-6415   (BR)
NORTHERN HEALTH AUTHORITY
BAKER, G.R. MEMORIAL HOSPITAL
(Suby of NORTHERN HEALTH AUTHORITY)
543 Front St, Quesnel, BC, V2J 2K7
(250) 985-5600
Emp Here 350
SIC 8062 General medical and surgical hospitals
Margaret Sadlon

D-U-N-S 25-838-7778   (SL)
QUESNEL CRAFTERS SOCIETY
CARIBOO KEEPSAKES
102 Carson Ave, Quesnel, BC, V2J 2A8
(250) 991-0419
Emp Here 65   *Sales* 15,881,320
SIC 5947 Gift, novelty, and souvenir shop
Diane Fletcher
Verna Teichroeb

D-U-N-S 25-811-9825   (BR)
SCHOOL DISTRICT #28
CORRELIEU SECONDARY SCHOOL
(Suby of SCHOOL DISTRICT #28)
850 Anderson Dr, Quesnel, BC, V2J 1G4
(250) 992-7007
Emp Here 80
SIC 8211 Elementary and secondary schools
Dennis Hawkins-Bogle

D-U-N-S 25-807-0853   (BR)

SCHOOL DISTRICT #28
QUESNEL SECONDARY SCHOOL
(Suby of SCHOOL DISTRICT #28)
585 Callanan St, Quesnel, BC, V2J 2V3
(250) 992-2131
Emp Here 80
SIC 8211 Elementary and secondary schools
Suzanne Bolin

D-U-N-S 24-312-2199   (HQ)
SCHOOL DISTRICT #28
QUESNEL SCHOOL DISTRICT
401 North Star Rd Suite 28, Quesnel, BC, V2J 5K2
(250) 992-8802
Sales 29,006,816
SIC 8211 Elementary and secondary schools
Sue-Ellen Miller

D-U-N-S 24-536-7818   (BR)
TOLKO INDUSTRIES LTD
QUEST WOOD DIVISION
(Suby of AMERICAN INDUSTRIAL ACQUISI-TION CORPORATION)
1879 Brownmiller Rd, Quesnel, BC, V2J 6R9
(250) 992-1700
Emp Here 250
SIC 2421 Sawmills and planing mills, general
Hank Randrup

D-U-N-S 20-862-1086   (SL)
TRU-WAY ENTERPRISES LTD
WEST CENTRAL PIPE DIV
135 Keis Ave, Quesnel, BC, V2J 3S1
(250) 992-8512
Emp Here 24   *Sales* 10,732,176
SIC 5074 Plumbing and heating equipment and supplies (hydronics)
Bert Keis
Larry Keis

D-U-N-S 24-855-9684   (HQ)
UNITED CONCRETE & GRAVEL LTD
1077 Carson Pit Rd, Quesnel, BC, V2J 7H2
(250) 992-7281
Emp Here 20   *Sales* 21,464,352
SIC 5032 Brick, stone, and related material
Dave Zacharias
Paul Zacharias

D-U-N-S 24-654-9997   (BR)
WAL-MART CANADA CORP
WALMART QUESNEL
(Suby of WALMART INC.)
890 Rita Rd, Quesnel, BC, V2J 7J3
(250) 747-4464
Emp Here 140
SIC 5311 Department stores

D-U-N-S 20-269-9047   (BR)
WEST FRASER MILLS LTD
QUESNEL PLYWOOD
(Suby of WEST FRASER TIMBER CO. LTD)
2000 Plywood Rd, Quesnel, BC, V2J 5W1
(250) 992-5511
Emp Here 300
SIC 2435 Hardwood veneer and plywood
Richard Brandson

D-U-N-S 24-694-5703   (BR)
WEST FRASER MILLS LTD
EUROCAN PULP & PAPER, DIV OF
(Suby of WEST FRASER TIMBER CO. LTD)
1250 Brownmiller Rd, Quesnel, BC, V2J 6P5
(250) 992-9244
Emp Here 450
SIC 5031 Lumber, plywood, and millwork
Christopher Finch

D-U-N-S 24-113-5735   (BR)
WEST FRASER MILLS LTD
QUESNEL MILL PLYWOOD
(Suby of WEST FRASER TIMBER CO. LTD)
1000 Plywood Rd, Quesnel, BC, V2J 3J5
(250) 991-7619
Emp Here 300
SIC 2421 Sawmills and planing mills, general
Chris Finch

▲ Public Company   ■ Public Company Family Member   **HQ** Headquarters   **BR** Branch   **SL** Single Location

D-U-N-S 20-189-2028   (BR)
WEST FRASER TIMBER CO. LTD
QUESNEL RIVER PULP
(*Suby of* WEST FRASER TIMBER CO. LTD)
1000 Finning Rd, Quesnel, BC, V2J 6A1
(250) 992-8919
Emp Here 130
SIC 2611 Pulp mills
Dave Needham

D-U-N-S 20-300-6382   (BR)
WEST FRASER TIMBER CO. LTD
WEST FRASER
(*Suby of* WEST FRASER TIMBER CO. LTD)
1250 Brownmiller Rd, Quesnel, BC, V2J 6P5
(250) 992-9244
Emp Here 500
SIC 5031 Lumber, plywood, and millwork
Chris Finch

D-U-N-S 24-681-5898   (SL)
YESNABY INVESTMENTS LTD
MCDONALD'S RESTAURANT
105 North Star Rd, Quesnel, BC, V2J 5K2
(250) 992-6868
Emp Here 100   *Sales* 4,287,300
SIC 5812 Eating places
Leigh Clarke
Lynda Clarke

Radium Hot Springs, BC V0A

D-U-N-S 25-973-6155   (HQ)
RADIUM RESORT INC
8100 Golf Course Rd, Radium Hot Springs,
BC, V0A 1M0
(250) 347-9311
Sales 10,996,300
SIC 7992 Public golf courses
William Newis

Revelstoke, BC V0E

D-U-N-S 20-400-5387   (SL)
AVALANCHE CANADA
1596 Illecillewaet Rd, Revelstoke, BC, V0E
2S1
(250) 837-2141
Emp Here 42   *Sales* 29,786,904
SIC 8699 Membership organizations, nec
Kevin Seel
Kevin Williams
Paul William Chatterton
Michael Mcmynn
Gilles Valade

D-U-N-S 20-645-7801   (BR)
CANADIAN PACIFIC RAILWAY COMPANY
(*Suby of* CANADIAN PACIFIC RAILWAY LIMITED)
420 Victoria Rd, Revelstoke, BC, V0E 2S0
(250) 837-8229
Emp Here 300
SIC 4011 Railroads, line-haul operating
Gerry Cook

D-U-N-S 25-290-9981   (SL)
DOWNIE TIMBER LTD
(*Suby of* DOWNIE STREET SAWMILLS LTD)
1621 Mill St, Revelstoke, BC, V0E 2S0
(250) 837-2222
Emp Here 180   *Sales* 34,626,600
SIC 2421 Sawmills and planing mills, general
Ron Torman

D-U-N-S 20-875-3330   (SL)
INTERIOR HEALTH
QUEEN VICTORIA HOSPITAL
1200 Newlands Rd Suite 5000, Revelstoke,
BC, V0E 2S1
(250) 837-2131
Emp Here 240   *Sales* 26,659,200

SIC 8062 General medical and surgical hospitals
Julie Lowes

D-U-N-S 24-363-7159   (SL)
RCU INSURANCE SERVICES LTD
(*Suby of* REVELSTOKE CREDIT UNION)
110 2nd St W, Revelstoke, BC, V0E 2S0
(250) 837-6291
Emp Here 10   *Sales* 10,348,810
SIC 6321 Accident and health insurance
Roberta Bobicki
Randy Driediger
David Raven

D-U-N-S 24-349-7869   (SL)
REVELSTOKE MOUNTAIN RESORT LIMITED PARTNERSHIP
2950 Camozzi Rd, Revelstoke, BC, V0E 2S3
(250) 814-0087
Emp Here 150   *Sales* 13,903,500
SIC 7011 Hotels and motels
Peter Greenway

D-U-N-S 24-535-0574   (HQ)
VIC VAN ISLE CONSTRUCTION LTD
LORTAP ENTERPRISES DIV OF
96 Cartier St, Revelstoke, BC, V0E 2S0
(250) 837-2919
Sales 34,220,280
SIC 1542 Nonresidential construction, nec
Lewis Hendrickson
Bruce Walker
Mario Lopez
Paul Jones

D-U-N-S 24-392-8293   (SL)
VVI CONSTRUCTION LTD
VIC VAN ISLE CONSTRUCTION
96 Cartier St, Revelstoke, BC, V0E 2S0
(250) 837-2919
Emp Here 150   *Sales* 40,641,300
SIC 1521 Single-family housing construction
Kenneth Hendrickson

Richmond, BC V6V

D-U-N-S 25-485-7071   (BR)
7-ELEVEN CANADA, INC
7-ELEVEN FOOD CENTER
(*Suby of* SEVEN & I HOLDINGS CO., LTD.)
3531 Viking Way Unit 7, Richmond, BC, V6V
1W1
(604) 273-2008
Emp Here 100
SIC 5411 Grocery stores
Brian Loney

D-U-N-S 20-573-0278   (SL)
A. & R. METAL INDUSTRIES LTD
2020 No. 6 Rd, Richmond, BC, V6V 1P1
(604) 276-2838
Emp Here 75   *Sales* 14,406,375
SIC 3441 Fabricated structural Metal
Stephen Johnston
Michael Cook
Greg Tooth

D-U-N-S 24-350-8848   (BR)
AEROTEK ULC
(*Suby of* ALLEGIS GROUP, INC.)
13575 Commerce Pky Suite 150, Richmond,
BC, V6V 2L1
(604) 244-1007
Emp Here 100
SIC 7361 Employment agencies
Christopher Boyd

D-U-N-S 20-638-6518   (HQ)
ALLIANCE TRAFFIC GROUP INC
2600 Viking Way, Richmond, BC, V6V 1N2
(604) 273-5220
Emp Here 3   *Sales* 140,470,680
SIC 7389 Business services, nec
Barry Sheahan

D-U-N-S 24-647-7376   (HQ)
ALLSCRIPTS CANADA CORPORATION
(*Suby of* ALLSCRIPTS HEALTHCARE SOLUTIONS, INC.)
13888 Wireless Way Suite 110, Richmond,
BC, V6V 0A3
(604) 273-4900
Emp Here 80   *Sales* 20,021,640
SIC 7372 Prepackaged software
Robert L Hawkins

D-U-N-S 20-748-2456   (HQ)
ANDRITZ AUTOMATION LTD
(*Suby of* ANDRITZ AG)
13700 International Pl Suite 100, Richmond,
BC, V6V 2X8
(604) 214-9248
Emp Here 55   *Sales* 14,076,640
SIC 8711 Engineering services
Milind Karkare
Greg Peters

D-U-N-S 20-291-6813   (HQ)
AP MARTIN PHARMACEUTICAL SUPPLIES LTD
13711 Mayfield Pl Unit 150, Richmond, BC,
V6V 2G9
(604) 273-8899
Sales 38,687,075
SIC 5122 Drugs, proprietaries, and sundries
Paul Fu
Martin Shen
Ruby Hari
Andrew Yu

D-U-N-S 24-311-3896   (SL)
APPLIED BIOLOGICAL MATERIALS INC
ABM
1-3671 Viking Way, Richmond, BC, V6V 2J5
(604) 247-2416
Emp Here 60   *Sales* 10,824,900
SIC 8731 Commercial physical research
Peter Peixiang Li
Gregory Chi-Yu Lee

D-U-N-S 24-369-5855   (SL)
ARODAL SERVICES LTD
2631 Viking Way Suite 248, Richmond, BC,
V6V 3B5
(604) 274-0477
Emp Here 100   *Sales* 4,020,900
SIC 7349 Building maintenance services, nec
Arden Peckenpaugh

D-U-N-S 24-166-9803   (HQ)
ARROW SPEED CONTROLS LIMITED
MGI TECHNOLOGIES, DIV OF
13851 Bridgeport Rd, Richmond, BC, V6V 1J6
(604) 321-4033
Emp Here 44   *Sales* 14,092,708
SIC 3625 Relays and industrial controls
John Oldham

D-U-N-S 20-958-6726   (SL)
ATLAS PAINTING & RESTORATIONS LTD
5020 No. 7 Rd, Richmond, BC, V6V 1R7
(604) 244-8244
Emp Here 32   *Sales* 15,063,392
SIC 1542 Nonresidential construction, nec
Maria Gled
Anton Gled

D-U-N-S 24-344-1792   (SL)
AUTO WEST INFINITI LTD
(*Suby of* M T K AUTO WEST LTD)
13720 Smallwood Pl, Richmond, BC, V6V
1W8

Emp Here 35   *Sales* 22,024,800
SIC 5511 New and used car dealers
Peter Sargent
Joachim Neumann
Leonard Fong

D-U-N-S 20-558-2765   (SL)
AZUMA FOODS (CANADA) CO., LTD
11451 Twigg Pl, Richmond, BC, V6V 3C9

(604) 325-1129
Emp Here 30   *Sales* 25,067,310
SIC 5146 Fish and seafoods
Toshinobu Azuma
Akimasa Pakuma
Kimiyuki Inamura

D-U-N-S 20-113-0226   (HQ)
BAKEMARK INGREDIENTS CANADA LIMITED
BAKEMARK CANADA
(*Suby of* MILL LUXEMBOURG HOLDINGS 1)
2480 Viking Way, Richmond, BC, V6V 1N2
(604) 303-1700
Emp Here 50   *Sales* 107,507,400
SIC 5149 Groceries and related products, nec
Jim Parker
Rick Barnes
Dave Ford

D-U-N-S 20-713-3849   (BR)
BOARD OF EDUCATION SCHOOL DISTRICT #38 (RICHMOND)
H J CAMBIE SECONDARY SCHOOL
(*Suby of* BOARD OF EDUCATION SCHOOL
DISTRICT #38 (RICHMOND))
4151 Jacombs Rd, Richmond, BC, V6V 1N7
(604) 668-6430
Emp Here 75
SIC 8211 Elementary and secondary schools
Rob Laing

D-U-N-S 24-640-9858   (SL)
BONICA PRECISION (CANADA) INC
3830 Jacombs Rd Unit 105, Richmond, BC,
V6V 1Y6
(604) 270-0812
Emp Here 25   *Sales* 13,013,550
SIC 5094 Jewelry and precious stones
Kenneth Ho

D-U-N-S 25-327-6703   (SL)
BROADCOM CANADA LTD
(*Suby of* BROADCOM INC.)
13711 International Pl Unit 200, Richmond,
BC, V6V 2Z8
(604) 233-8500
Emp Here 80   *Sales* 11,534,560
SIC 7371 Custom computer programming services
Henry Samueli

D-U-N-S 20-109-6708   (SL)
BULLDOG BAG LTD
13631 Vulcan Way, Richmond, BC, V6V 1K4
(604) 273-8021
Emp Here 150   *Sales* 29,215,200
SIC 2674 Bags: uncoated paper and multiwall
Irving Sirlin
Frank Sirlin
Marcia Sirlin

D-U-N-S 20-012-5792   (SL)
C2 MEDIA CANADA ULC
C2 MEDIA
14291 Burrows Rd, Richmond, BC, V6V 1K9
(604) 270-4000
Emp Here 62   *Sales* 10,169,674
SIC 2759 Commercial printing, nec
Marc Stahr
Ken Channon

D-U-N-S 24-338-0776   (SL)
CAM CLARK FORD RICHMOND LTD
13580 Smallwood Pl, Richmond, BC, V6V 2C1
(604) 273-7331
Emp Here 65   *Sales* 45,728,220
SIC 5531 Auto and home supply stores
Cameron Clark

D-U-N-S 20-866-5307   (HQ)
CANADA SCAFFOLD SUPPLY CO. LTD
11331 Twigg Pl, Richmond, BC, V6V 3C9
(604) 324-7691
Sales 16,327,225
SIC 3446 Architectural Metalwork
Sam Lazarian
Alice Lazarian

Siranoush Lazarian
Madeleine Lazarian

D-U-N-S 24-364-9188   (BR)
CANADIAN STANDARDS ASSOCIATION
CSA INTERNATIONAL
(*Suby of* CANADIAN STANDARDS ASSOCI-
ATION)
13799 Commerce Pky, Richmond, BC, V6V
2N9
(604) 273-4581
Emp Here 90
SIC 8734 Testing laboratories
Terry Nagy

D-U-N-S 24-375-6496   (BR)
CANEM SYSTEMS LTD
(*Suby of* STUART OLSON INC)
1600 Valmont Way Suite 100, Richmond, BC,
V6V 1Y4
(604) 273-1131
Emp Here 87
SIC 1731 Electrical work
Jack Morgadinho

D-U-N-S 24-930-3017   (HQ)
CANEM SYSTEMS LTD
(*Suby of* STUART OLSON INC)
13351 Commerce Pky Suite 1358, Richmond,
BC, V6V 2X7
(604) 214-8650
Emp Here 18   *Sales* 162,972,228
SIC 1731 Electrical work
Allen D. Miller
Doug Hale
Jeff Luccock
Julie Lee
Bill Oulton

D-U-N-S 20-872-6104   (SL)
CAPWORK LABORATORY INC
13982 Cambie Rd Suite 113, Richmond, BC,
V6V 2K2
(604) 233-7060
Emp Here 20   *Sales* 10,702,480
SIC 5149 Groceries and related products, nec
Vikey Fu

D-U-N-S 25-826-4105   (SL)
CARO ANALYTICAL SERVICES LTD
4011 Viking Way Unit 110, Richmond, BC,
V6V 2K9
(604) 279-1499
Emp Here 49   *Sales* 10,796,072
SIC 8734 Testing laboratories
Brent Nussato

D-U-N-S 24-275-0461   (BR)
CASCADES CANADA ULC
(*Suby of* CASCADES INC)
3300 Viking Way, Richmond, BC, V6V 1N6
(604) 273-7321
Emp Here 140
SIC 2653 Corrugated and solid fiber boxes
Frank Beyell

D-U-N-S 20-712-7044   (HQ)
CATHAY IMPORTERS 2000 LIMITED
12631 Vulcan Way, Richmond, BC, V6V 1J7
(604) 233-0050
Emp Here 1   *Sales* 15,616,260
SIC 5099 Durable goods, nec
Ko Ming Chong
Yuen Chong

D-U-N-S 24-344-8656   (BR)
CENTENNIAL FOODSERVICE
(*Suby of* PREMIUM BRANDS HOLDINGS
CORPORATION)
12759 Vulcan Way Unit 108, Richmond, BC,
V6V 3C8
(604) 273-5261
Emp Here 90
SIC 2011 Meat packing plants
Garth Mccann

D-U-N-S 24-341-9236   (HQ)
CLEVEST SOLUTIONS INC

13700 International Pl Suite 200, Richmond,
BC, V6V 2X8
(604) 214-9700
Sales 14,418,200
SIC 7371 Custom computer programming ser-
vices
Thomas Ligocki
Garnik Bobloyan
Paul Needham
David Trotter
Julien Marin
Carol Johnston
Ricardo Ferreyros
Lily Ligocki
Trevor Greene
Jim Thompson

D-U-N-S 24-493-1978   (HQ)
**COMET STRIP ENTERPRISES (CANADA)
LTD**
5375 Parkwood Pl Suite 1, Richmond, BC,
V6V 2N1
(604) 278-4005
Emp Here 30   *Sales* 31,232,520
SIC 5092 Toys and hobby goods and supplies
Frank Yeh
Alice Yeh

D-U-N-S 20-904-7609   (HQ)
CONETEC INVESTIGATIONS LTD
12140 Vulcan Way, Richmond, BC, V6V 1J8
(604) 273-4311
Sales 26,085,750
SIC 0711 Soil preparation services
David Woeller

D-U-N-S 20-393-8360   (SL)
CONGLOM INC
(*Suby of* CONGLOM INC)
11488 Eburne Way Unit 130, Richmond, BC,
V6V 3E1
(604) 629-1338
Emp Here 160   *Sales* 114,674,560
SIC 5141 Groceries, general line
Kelly Boulding

D-U-N-S 25-862-6712   (HQ)
**CONSEIL SCOLAIRE FRANCOPHONE DE
LA COLOMBIE-BRITANNIQUE**
*SCHOOL DISTRICT NO. 93 (CONSEIL SCO-
LAIRE FRANCOPHONE)*
13511 Commerce Pky Unit 100, Richmond,
BC, V6V 2J8
(604) 214-2600
Emp Here 24   *Sales* 68,389,225
SIC 8211 Elementary and secondary schools
Bertrand Dupain
Caroline Picard
Sylvain Allison
Kapka Djarova

D-U-N-S 24-142-7256   (SL)
CONTAINERWEST MANUFACTURING LTD
CONTAINERWEST
11660 Mitchell Rd, Richmond, BC, V6V 1T7
(604) 322-0533
Emp Here 35   *Sales* 16,625,910
SIC 5085 Industrial supplies
Dean Olund

D-U-N-S 24-378-6246   (HQ)
CORIX WATER SYSTEMS INC
1128 Burdette St, Richmond, BC, V6V 2Z3
(604) 273-4987
Emp Here 30   *Sales* 13,320,060
SIC 3589 Service industry machinery, nec
Brett Hodson
Hamish Cumming
Albert Low
Dietz Kellmann
Steve Little
Jack Touhey
Eric Van Roon

D-U-N-S 25-612-1831   (SL)
COWELL IMPORTS INC
LAND ROVER OF RICHMOND

5680 Parkwood Cres, Richmond, BC, V6V
0B5
(604) 273-6068
Emp Here 30   *Sales* 14,942,340
SIC 5511 New and used car dealers
Gary Cowell

D-U-N-S 20-527-1013   (HQ)
COWELL MOTORS LTD
AUDI OF RICHMOND
(*Suby of* G.E. COWELL HOLDINGS LTD)
5600 Parkwood Cres, Richmond, BC, V6V
0B5
(604) 279-9663
Sales 94,392,000
SIC 5511 New and used car dealers
Gary Cowell

D-U-N-S 24-996-8728   (HQ)
DATAWAVE SYSTEMS INC
(*Suby of* HI TECHNOLOGY CORP)
13575 Commerce Pky Suite 110, Richmond,
BC, V6V 2L1
(604) 295-1800
Emp Here 65   *Sales* 21,704,840
SIC 4813 Telephone communication, except
radio
Joshua Emanuel
William Turner
Larry Wetzel
Bob Stanchina
Debbie Camoia

D-U-N-S 20-187-5031   (SL)
DISCOVER ENERGY CORP
DISCOVER BATTERY
13511 Crestwood Pl Unit 4, Richmond, BC,
V6V 2E9
(778) 776-3288
Emp Here 21   *Sales* 49,378,090
SIC 5013 Motor vehicle supplies and new
parts
Darwin Sauer
Sang Jay Nam
Dean Smurthwaite

D-U-N-S 24-798-4982   (SL)
**EBCO METAL FINISHING LIMITED PART-
NERSHIP**
15200 Knox Way, Richmond, BC, V6V 3A6
(604) 244-1500
Emp Here 70   *Sales* 13,445,950
SIC 3479 Metal coating and allied services
Hugo Eppich
Gordon Eppich

D-U-N-S 20-343-8304   (SL)
ELCO FINE FOODS LTD
(*Suby of* NATIONAL IMPORTERS CANADA
LTD)
13100 Mitchell Rd Suite 120, Richmond, BC,
V6V 1M8
(604) 324-1551
Emp Here 20   *Sales* 16,711,540
SIC 5141 Groceries, general line
David L. Dueck
David C. Dueck
Daniel Maclean

D-U-N-S 20-248-1800   (HQ)
EYESTAR OPTICAL LTD
EYESTAR OPTICAL (RICHMOND CENTRE)
2639 Viking Way Unit 150, Richmond, BC,
V6V 3B7
(604) 303-9760
Emp Here 20   *Sales* 36,649,200
SIC 5995 Optical goods stores
Norman Kwan

D-U-N-S 24-491-3745   (SL)
FAIRWAY PRODUCTS INC
13611 Maycrest Way, Richmond, BC, V6V 2J4
(604) 278-1919
Emp Here 56   *Sales* 25,041,744
SIC 5072 Hardware
Francis Lee
Allen Lee

D-U-N-S 24-898-6374   (SL)
FINE CHOICE FOODS LTD
23111 Fraserwood Way, Richmond, BC, V6V
3B3
(604) 522-3110
Emp Here 45   *Sales* 10,118,475
SIC 2099 Food preparations, nec
Charles Lui
Eileen Wong

D-U-N-S 20-954-5180   (HQ)
**FLATIRON CONSTRUCTORS CANADA
LIMITED**
FLATIRON AECON JOINT VENTURE
(*Suby of* ACS, ACTIVIDADES DE CON-
STRUCCION Y SERVICIOS, SA)
4020 Viking Way Suite 210, Richmond, BC,
V6V 2L4
(604) 244-7343
Sales 295,631,615
SIC 1611 Highway and street construction
Blair Brandon
Javier Sevilla
Drew Phillips

D-U-N-S 24-939-2481   (SL)
FLUIDSEAL INC
13680 Bridgeport Rd Suite 5, Richmond, BC,
V6V 1V3
(604) 278-6808
Emp Here 180   *Sales* 87,791,400
SIC 5085 Industrial supplies
Nathan Hall
Dollard Leblanc

D-U-N-S 25-207-3374   (HQ)
G.E. COWELL HOLDINGS LTD
VOLKSWAGEN AUDI LANDROVER JAGUAR
13611 Smallwood Pl, Richmond, BC, V6V
1W8
(604) 273-3922
Emp Here 1   *Sales* 62,928,000
SIC 5511 New and used car dealers
Gary Cowell

D-U-N-S 20-012-2658   (SL)
GEA REFRIGERATION CANADA INC
(*Suby of* GEA GROUP AG)
2551 Viking Way Suite 150, Richmond, BC,
V6V 1N4
(604) 278-4118
Emp Here 90   *Sales* 41,403,960
SIC 5078 Refrigeration equipment and sup-
plies
Robert Laflamme

D-U-N-S 20-984-9806   (SL)
GOGO GEEK ENTERPRISES INC
13988 Cambie Rd Suite 373, Richmond, BC,
V6V 2K4
(604) 248-0782
Emp Here 30   *Sales* 13,415,220
SIC 5045 Computers, peripherals, and soft-
ware
Brad Moldowan

D-U-N-S 20-619-9960   (SL)
GOLDWOOD INDUSTRIES LTD
12691 Mitchell Rd, Richmond, BC, V6V 1M7
(604) 327-2935
Emp Here 84   *Sales* 22,482,768
SIC 5211 Lumber and other building materials
Jack Uppal
Cindy Bains
Pam Gill

D-U-N-S 24-931-7975   (SL)
**GRAND HALE MARINE PRODUCTS COM-
PANY LIMITED**
11551 Twigg Pl, Richmond, BC, V6V 2Y2
(604) 325-9393
Emp Here 100   *Sales* 83,557,700
SIC 5146 Fish and seafoods
Reginald Cheung
Francis Cheung
Pandora Cheung

D-U-N-S 24-400-3075   (HQ)

GREAT LITTLE BOX COMPANY LTD, THE
PARROT LABEL, DIV OF
11300 Twigg Pl, Richmond, BC, V6V 3C1
(604) 301-3700
Emp Here 190   *Sales* 95,585,620
SIC 2653 Corrugated and solid fiber boxes
  Robert Meggy
  Margaret Meggy

     D-U-N-S 24-024-4418   (SL)
HERBALAND NATURALS INC
13330 Maycrest Way, Richmond, BC, V6V 2J7
(604) 284-5050
Emp Here 55   *Sales* 15,216,300
SIC 2834 Pharmaceutical preparations
  Musharaf Syed
  Aisha Yang

     D-U-N-S 25-313-8853   (BR)
HOME DEPOT OF CANADA INC
HOME DEPOT
(*Suby of* THE HOME DEPOT INC)
2700 Sweden Way, Richmond, BC, V6V 2W8
(604) 303-7360
Emp Here 250
SIC 5251 Hardware stores

     D-U-N-S 20-359-2969   (HQ)
**ICONIX WATERWORKS LIMITED PART-
NERSHIP**
(*Suby of* ENTREPRISES MIRCA INC, LES)
1128 Burdette St, Richmond, BC, V6V 2Z3
(604) 273-4987
Emp Here 35   *Sales* 144,500,400
SIC 4941 Water supply
  Richard Clements

     D-U-N-S 24-788-2983   (SL)
IMAC ENTERPRISES CORP
DURA BAMBOO
11488 Eburne Way, Richmond, BC, V6V 3E1
(604) 324-8288
Emp Here 49   *Sales* 21,911,526
SIC 5031 Lumber, plywood, and millwork
  Anh Hai Pham

     D-U-N-S 24-163-0821   (HQ)
INTERCITY PACKERS LTD
ALBION FARMS AND FISHERIES
1900 No. 6 Rd, Richmond, BC, V6V 1W3
(604) 295-2010
Emp Here 90   *Sales* 86,005,920
SIC 5147 Meats and meat products
  Frank Geier
  Dean Noble
  Richard Wolowski
  Alisha Cieslak

     D-U-N-S 25-364-8539   (SL)
INTERLINE MOTOR FREIGHT INC
13562 Maycrest Way Suite 5108, Richmond,
BC, V6V 2J7

Emp Here 198   *Sales* 41,201,517
SIC 4212 Local trucking, without storage
  Harmon Bal

     D-U-N-S 20-150-6305   (SL)
ISLAND CITY BAKING COMPANY INC
12753 Vulcan Way Suite 105, Richmond, BC,
V6V 3C8
(604) 278-6979
Emp Here 140   *Sales* 48,396,600
SIC 2051 Bread, cake, and related products
  Carmelo Deluca

     D-U-N-S 20-171-6724   (HQ)
**JENSEN HUGHES CONSULTING CANADA
LTD**
(*Suby of* JENSEN HUGHES, INC.)
13900 Maycrest Way Unit 135, Richmond, BC,
V6V 3E2
(604) 295-4000
Emp Here 20   *Sales* 20,554,985
SIC 8711 Engineering services
  Peter Senez

     D-U-N-S 24-855-7159   (SL)

KAWAKI (CANADA) LTD
(*Suby of* KAWAKI CO., LTD.)
2500 Viscount Way, Richmond, BC, V6V 1N1
(604) 277-7158
Emp Here 50   *Sales* 17,284,500
SIC 2092 Fresh or frozen packaged fish
  Haruo Kato
  Toshihiko Kawai

     D-U-N-S 25-229-8369   (BR)
**KONICA MINOLTA BUSINESS SOLUTIONS
(CANADA) LTD**
KONICA MINOLTA
(*Suby of* KONICA MINOLTA, INC.)
21500 Westminster Hwy, Richmond, BC, V6V
2V1
(604) 276-1611
Emp Here 75
SIC 5044 Office equipment
  Alton Mick

     D-U-N-S 20-279-5071   (HQ)
LEVELTON CONSULTANTS LTD
12791 Clarke Pl Suite 150, Richmond, BC,
V6V 2H9
(604) 278-1411
Emp Here 75   *Sales* 33,960,410
SIC 8711 Engineering services
  Thomas Charles Cotton
  Nicholas Edgar Davis
  Neil Alexander Cumming

     D-U-N-S 25-738-9858   (SL)
LOKI MANAGEMENT SYSTEMS INC
(*Suby of* ZEROCHAOS, LLC)
13351 Commerce Pky Suite 1258, Richmond,
BC, V6V 2X7
(604) 249-5050
Emp Here 210,000
SIC 7371 Custom computer programming ser-
vices
  Richard Swann

     D-U-N-S 24-320-2842   (SL)
LUCID VISION LABS, INC
13200 Delf Pl Unit 130, Richmond, BC, V6V
2A2
(833) 465-8243
Emp Here 50   *Sales* 12,828,100
SIC 3861 Photographic equipment and supplies
  Rod Barman

     D-U-N-S 24-029-4249   (HQ)
MAR-CON WIRE BELT INC
2431 Vauxhall Pl, Richmond, BC, V6V 1Z5
(604) 278-8922
Sales 11,875,650
SIC 5084 Industrial machinery and equipment
  Michael Chiu

     D-U-N-S 20-691-4884   (HQ)
MARINE CANADA ACQUISITION INC
SEASTAR SOLUTIONS
(*Suby of* DOMETIC GROUP AB (PUBL))
3831 No. 6 Rd Suite 100, Richmond, BC, V6V
1P6
(604) 270-6899
Sales 78,571,570
SIC 8731 Commercial physical research
  Yvan Cote
  Eric Fetchko
  Ji Yoon
  Matthew Lozow

     D-U-N-S 20-176-6912   (HQ)
**MARINE CANADA ACQUISITION LIMITED
PARTNERSHIP**
SEASTAR SOLUTIONS
3831 No. 6 Rd, Richmond, BC, V6V 1P6
(604) 270-6899
Sales 99,724,710
SIC 3492 Fluid power valves and hose fittings
  Ji Yoon

     D-U-N-S 25-514-1459   (HQ)
MARQUISE FACILITIES CORPORATION
MARQUISE FACILITIES MANAGEMENT

13351 Commerce Pky Suite 1373, Richmond,
BC, V6V 2X7
(604) 214-8525
Sales 43,280,963
SIC 6512 Nonresidential building operators
  Ronald Floyd
  Ilona Kovacs

     D-U-N-S 24-311-0475   (HQ)
MAYNARDS LIQUIDATION GROUP INC
3331 Jacombs Rd, Richmond, BC, V6V 1Z6
(604) 876-6787
Emp Here 25   *Sales* 22,460,950
SIC 7389 Business services, nec
  Barry Scott

     D-U-N-S 24-846-7623   (SL)
MDA GEOSPATIAL SERVICES INC
(*Suby of* MAXAR TECHNOLOGIES INC.)
13800 Commerce Pkwy, Richmond, BC, V6V
2J3
(604) 278-3411
Emp Here 105   *Sales* 21,038,955
SIC 7335 Commercial photography
  Michael Greenley
  William Haworth
  Hitem Makim
  Michelle Kley

     D-U-N-S 24-387-6716   (SL)
MDA SYSTEMS HOLDINGS LTD
(*Suby of* MAXAR TECHNOLOGIES INC.)
13800 Commerce Pkwy, Richmond, BC, V6V
2J3
(604) 278-3411
Emp Here 4,800   *Sales* 1,216,752,000
SIC 8748 Business consulting, nec
  Howard Lance

     D-U-N-S 24-387-6708   (HQ)
MDA SYSTEMS LTD
(*Suby of* MAXAR TECHNOLOGIES INC.)
13800 Commerce Pkwy, Richmond, BC, V6V
2J3
(604) 278-3411
Sales 219,789,840
SIC 7373 Computer integrated systems de-
sign
  Daniel Friedmann
  Michael Rack
  William Mccombe
  Timothy M. Hascall

     D-U-N-S 25-975-4919   (BR)
**MING PAO NEWSPAPERS (CANADA) LIM-
ITED**
(*Suby of* MEDIA CHINESE INTERNATIONAL
LIMITED)
5368 Parkwood Pl, Richmond, BC, V6V 2N1
(604) 231-8998
Emp Here 125
SIC 2711 Newspapers
  Michael Liu

     D-U-N-S 25-910-2176   (SL)
MISTY MOUNTAIN INDUSTRIES LTD
MISTY MOUNTAIN SPECIALTIES
13900 Maycrest Way Suite 130, Richmond,
BC, V6V 3E2
(604) 273-8299
Emp Here 30   *Sales* 25,067,310
SIC 5148 Fresh fruits and vegetables
  David Lee

     D-U-N-S 20-114-1678   (SL)
MORTON CLARKE & CO. LTD
2551 No. 6 Rd Unit 1105, Richmond, BC, V6V
1P3
(604) 273-1055
Emp Here 40   *Sales* 20,821,680
SIC 5099 Durable goods, nec
  Paul Clarke

     D-U-N-S 25-363-7086   (SL)
**MUSTANG SURVIVAL HOLDINGS CORPO-
RATION**
3810 Jacombs Rd, Richmond, BC, V6V 1Y6

(604) 270-8631
Emp Here 300   *Sales* 110,922,687
SIC 6712 Bank holding companies
  Dwight Davies

     D-U-N-S 25-977-6144   (HQ)
NATIONAL IMPORTERS CANADA LTD
13100 Mitchell Rd Suite 120, Richmond, BC,
V6V 1M8
(604) 324-1551
Emp Here 100   *Sales* 86,005,920
SIC 5141 Groceries, general line
  David L. Dueck
  David C. Dueck

     D-U-N-S 25-839-4535   (SL)
NO 1 COLLISION (1993) INC
20 Vulcan Way Suite 124, Richmond, BC, V6V
1J8
(604) 231-9614
Emp Here 60   *Sales* 16,998,000
SIC 7532 Top and body repair and paint shops
  Gary Walker
  Scott Walker
  Lena Walker

     D-U-N-S 24-246-0616   (HQ)
NORSAT INTERNATIONAL INC
(*Suby of* HYTERA COMMUNICATIONS COR-
PORATION LIMITED)
4020 Viking Way Unit 110, Richmond, BC,
V6V 2N2
(604) 821-2800
Emp Here 70   *Sales* 34,279,560
SIC 3669 Communications equipment, nec
  Amiee Chan
  Arthur Chin

     D-U-N-S 25-998-2304   (SL)
NOVA EXPRESS MILLENNIUM INC
NOVEX NOVA EXPRESS
14271 Knox Way Suite 105, Richmond, BC,
V6V 2Z4
(604) 278-8044
Emp Here 35   *Sales* 15,522,150
SIC 7389 Business services, nec
  Ken Johnston
  R W Bob Garnett

     D-U-N-S 24-695-8003   (SL)
OCEANFOOD INDUSTRIES LIMITED
11520 Eburne Way, Richmond, BC, V6V 2G7
(604) 324-1666
Emp Here 50   *Sales* 41,778,850
SIC 5146 Fish and seafoods
  John Graham
  Shirley Graham

     D-U-N-S 20-178-6089   (BR)
OPENROAD AUTO GROUP LIMITED
OPENROAD LEXUS - RICHMOND
(*Suby of* OPENROAD AUTO GROUP LIM-
ITED)
5631 Parkwood Way, Richmond, BC, V6V
2M6
(604) 273-5533
Emp Here 100
SIC 5511 New and used car dealers
  Kirt Gill

     D-U-N-S 25-538-9645   (HQ)
OPENROAD AUTO GROUP LIMITED
RICHMOND LEXUS
13251 Smallwood Pl, Richmond, BC, V6V
1W8
(604) 273-3766
Emp Here 240   *Sales* 202,038,200
SIC 5511 New and used car dealers
  Christian Chia
  Bob Lukman

     D-U-N-S 25-235-8098   (HQ)
ORGANIKA HEALTH PRODUCTS INC
13480 Verdun Pl, Richmond, BC, V6V 1V2
(604) 277-3302
Emp Here 40   *Sales* 66,320,700
SIC 5122 Drugs, proprietaries, and sundries
  Thomas Chin

D-U-N-S 24-696-4217   (SL)
ORIGINAL ROOF MAINTAINER INC
CONTINENTAL ROOFING
16020 River Rd, Richmond, BC, V6V 1L6

Emp Here 65   Sales 14,158,885
SIC 1761 Roofing, siding, and sheetMetal work
Roger Cumming
Lee Eward

D-U-N-S 20-742-5112   (SL)
PACBLUE DIGITAL IMAGING INC
3551 Viking Way Unit 109, Richmond, BC, V6V 1W1
(604) 714-3288
Emp Here 1   Sales 17,573,092
SIC 7334 Photocopying and duplicating services
Jonathan Colley
Carol Colley

D-U-N-S 25-313-0637   (HQ)
PCL CONSTRUCTORS WESTCOAST INC
(*Suby of* PCL EMPLOYEES HOLDINGS LTD)
13911 Wireless Way Suite 310, Richmond, BC, V6V 3B9
(604) 241-5200
Sales 164,057,500
SIC 1629 Heavy construction, nec
Todd Craigen
David Filipchuk
Robert Holmberg

D-U-N-S 20-105-2797   (SL)
PHOTON CONTROL INC
13500 Verdun Pl Suite 130, Richmond, BC, V6V 1V2
(604) 900-3150
Emp Here 16   Sales 35,406,396
SIC 3841 Surgical and medical instruments
Nigel Hunton
Neil Mcdonnell
John Rydstrom
Nalini Mcintosh
Sal Akram
Chuck Cargile
Michele Klein
Ronan Mcgrath
Daniel Lee

D-U-N-S 25-976-8406   (SL)
PLUG CANADA INC
(*Suby of* PLUG POWER INC.)
13120 Vanier Pl, Richmond, BC, V6V 2J2
(604) 303-0050
Emp Here 85
SIC 8731 Commercial physical research
Christopher Reid

D-U-N-S 24-319-2817   (HQ)
PORTABLES EXHIBIT SYSTEMS LIMITED, THE
XIBITA
3551 Viking Way Suite 109, Richmond, BC, V6V 1W1
(604) 276-2366
Emp Here 50   Sales 26,090,880
SIC 3993 Signs and advertising specialties
Hanif Muljiani
Shafig Gulamani

D-U-N-S 24-345-3867   (SL)
PRIME BUILDING MAINTENANCE LTD
12800 Bathgate Way Unit 13, Richmond, BC, V6V 1Z4
(604) 270-7766
Emp Here 80   Sales 3,216,720
SIC 7349 Building maintenance services, nec
Parm Boparai

D-U-N-S 24-683-8812   (SL)
QUANTUM MURRAY-NWDD PARTNERSHIP
3600 Viking Way Suite 100, Richmond, BC, V6V 1N6
(604) 270-7388
Emp Here 700   Sales 228,005,400
SIC 4959 Sanitary services, nec

Wilf Marcq

D-U-N-S 24-370-5936   (HQ)
RAINCOAST BOOK DISTRIBUTION LTD
BOOK EXPRESS
2440 Viking Way, Richmond, BC, V6V 1N2
(604) 448-7100
Emp Here 83   Sales 66,826,800
SIC 5192 Books, periodicals, and newspapers
John Sawyer

D-U-N-S 20-621-0676   (HQ)
RALPH'S AUTO SUPPLY (B.C.) LTD
A-SCOTT DISCOUNT USED AUTO PARTS
12011 Mitchell Rd, Richmond, BC, V6V 1M7
(604) 572-5747
Emp Here 20   Sales 50,342,400
SIC 5531 Auto and home supply stores
Moira Lutar

D-U-N-S 24-657-0022   (SL)
RGM CHEMTECH INTERNATIONAL INC
CHEMTECH INTERNATIONAL
14351 Burrows Rd Suite 100, Richmond, BC, V6V 1K9
(604) 270-3320
Emp Here 40   Sales 11,066,400
SIC 2841 Soap and other detergents
Gary Mathews
Brendon Mathews

D-U-N-S 20-138-8563   (SL)
RICHELIEU CANADA LTD
PANEL PRODUCTS
2600 Viking Way, Richmond, BC, V6V 1N2
(604) 273-3108
Emp Here 40   Sales 17,886,960
SIC 5072 Hardware
Jan Ciarniello

D-U-N-S 20-115-3632   (SL)
RICHMOND BUILDING SUPPLIES CO. LTD
12231 Bridgeport Rd, Richmond, BC, V6V 1J4
(604) 278-9865
Emp Here 30   Sales 13,415,220
SIC 5039 Construction materials, nec
Peter Niebuhr
Dietrich Krause
Peter Krause

D-U-N-S 20-867-2147   (SL)
RICHMOND CHRYSLER DODGE JEEP LTD
5491 Parkwood Way, Richmond, BC, V6V 2M9
(604) 273-7521
Emp Here 75   Sales 47,196,000
SIC 5511 New and used car dealers
James Mcmanes
Gordon Moors

D-U-N-S 20-621-9735   (SL)
RICHMOND IMPORTS LTD
RICHMOND HONDA
13600 Smallwood Pl, Richmond, BC, V6V 1W8
(604) 207-1846
Emp Here 141   Sales 88,728,480
SIC 5511 New and used car dealers
Henning Brasso
Peter Brasso
John Poole
Robert Lee

D-U-N-S 24-000-6093   (SL)
RICHMOND INTERNATIONAL TECHNOLOGY CORP
DR. BATTERY
4460 Jacombs Rd Suite 102, Richmond, BC, V6V 2C5
(604) 273-8248
Emp Here 40   Sales 17,886,960
SIC 5063 Electrical apparatus and equipment
Kei Yip Huen
Fan Chun
Ricky Ho

D-U-N-S 25-611-5759   (SL)
RICHMOND NISSAN LTD

PAN PACIFIC NISSAN RICHMOND
13220 Smallwood Pl, Richmond, BC, V6V 1W8
(604) 273-1661
Emp Here 52   Sales 32,722,560
SIC 5511 New and used car dealers
Mark Akabori
Sylvester Tai
Rick Bentley

D-U-N-S 20-115-3889   (HQ)
RICHMOND PLYWOOD CORPORATION LIMITED
13911 Vulcan Way, Richmond, BC, V6V 1K7
(604) 278-9111
Sales 118,315,750
SIC 2436 Softwood veneer and plywood
Lakhvinder Dhillon
Gurnam Minhas

D-U-N-S 20-799-9996   (HQ)
RICHMOND STEEL RECYCLING LIMITED
11760 Mitchell Rd, Richmond, BC, V6V 1V8
(604) 324-4656
Emp Here 69   Sales 29,339,720
SIC 4953 Refuse systems
Harbinder Dhillon
Doug Hallson
John Rai
Nathan Billing
Laura Necochea

D-U-N-S 20-294-6732   (BR)
RICHMOND, CITY OF
CAMBIE COMMUNITY CENTRE
(*Suby of* RICHMOND, CITY OF)
12800 Cambie Rd, Richmond, BC, V6V 0A9
(604) 233-8399
Emp Here 100
SIC 8322 Individual and family services
Karen Maceachern

D-U-N-S 24-980-6761   (SL)
ROLAND CANADA LTD
(*Suby of* ROLAND CORPORATION)
5480 Parkwood Way, Richmond, BC, V6V 2M4
(604) 270-6626
Emp Here 50   Sales 26,027,100
SIC 5099 Durable goods, nec
Paul Mccabe
Kim Nunney
Laurie Gillespie
Hidekazu Tanaka

D-U-N-S 25-679-7069   (HQ)
SEVEN SEAS FISH CO. LTD
7 SEAS
12411 Vulcan Way, Richmond, BC, V6V 1J7
(604) 247-1266
Emp Here 200   Sales 157,677,520
SIC 5146 Fish and seafoods
George Heras
John Heras
Michael Heras

D-U-N-S 24-980-4279   (HQ)
SIERRA WIRELESS, INC
13811 Wireless Way, Richmond, BC, V6V 3A4
(604) 231-1100
Emp Here 417   Sales 193,602,000
SIC 4899 Communication services, nec
Kent Thexton
Jason Krause
Rene Link
Jim Ryan
Roy Maclean
Pierre Teyssier
Dan Schieler
Bill Seefeldt
David Mclennan
Philippe Guillemette

D-U-N-S 24-724-4882   (HQ)
SKANA FOREST PRODUCTS LTD
(*Suby of* J.C. BEVERIDGE EQUITIES LTD)
20800 Westminster Hwy Suite 1303, Rich-

mond, BC, V6V 2W3
Emp Here 20   Sales 10,732,176
SIC 5031 Lumber, plywood, and millwork
John Christopher Beveridge
Kent Beveridge

D-U-N-S 25-113-9549   (SL)
SS LASER TECH LTD
13560 Maycrest Way Unit 2115, Richmond, BC, V6V 2W9
(604) 821-0058
Emp Here 30   Sales 15,109,740
SIC 5112 Stationery and office supplies
Richard Soon

D-U-N-S 20-394-0650   (BR)
STANDARD AERO LIMITED
(*Suby of* STANDARDAERO AVIATION HOLDINGS, INC.)
20699 Westminster Hwy, Richmond, BC, V6V 1B3
(604) 273-6040
Emp Here 125
SIC 4581 Airports, flying fields, and services
Rick Stine

D-U-N-S 24-039-2386   (HQ)
STERLING SHOES LIMITED PARTNERSHIP
GIA SHOES
2580 Viscount Way, Richmond, BC, V6V 1N1
(604) 270-6640
Emp Here 30   Sales 68,615,250
SIC 5661 Shoe stores
Daniel Gumprich

D-U-N-S 24-355-3109   (BR)
STUART OLSON BUILDINGS LTD
BUILDINGS DIVISION
(*Suby of* STUART OLSON INC)
13777 Commerce Pky Suite 300, Richmond, BC, V6V 2X3
(604) 273-7765
Emp Here 125
SIC 1522 Residential construction, nec
Al Stowkowy

D-U-N-S 24-363-8488   (HQ)
TELDON MEDIA GROUP INC
TELDON PRINT MEDIA, DIV OF
12751 Vulcan Way Suite 100, Richmond, BC, V6V 3C8
(604) 231-3454
Emp Here 50   Sales 58,132,200
SIC 2752 Commercial printing, lithographic
Ryan Benn

D-U-N-S 20-116-4852   (HQ)
TERMINAL FOREST PRODUCTS LTD
MAINLAND SAWMILLS, DIV OF
12180 Mitchell Rd, Richmond, BC, V6V 1M8
(604) 717-1200
Emp Here 120   Sales 97,436,500
SIC 2421 Sawmills and planing mills, general
Darcy Johal
Asa Johal
Bruce Shaw

D-U-N-S 20-115-9787   (HQ)
THOMAS SKINNER & SON LIMITED
(*Suby of* 4628 HOLDINGS LTD)
13880 Vulcan Way, Richmond, BC, V6V 1K6
(604) 276-2131
Emp Here 50   Sales 47,502,600
SIC 5084 Industrial machinery and equipment
Paul Krainer
Vincent Khoo
Ross Mcdonald

D-U-N-S 24-805-1166   (SL)
TM CANADA ACQUISITION CORP
3831 No. 6 Rd, Richmond, BC, V6V 1P6
(604) 270-6899
Emp Here 43   Sales 11,246,779
SIC 6712 Bank holding companies
Ji Yoon
Matthew Lozow
Christopher Laitala

▲ Public Company   ■ Public Company Family Member   **HQ** Headquarters   **BR** Branch   **SL** Single Location

D-U-N-S 24-737-9451   (SL)
TOPVIEW TECHNOLOGY CORP
14488 Knox Way Unit 123, Richmond, BC,
V6V 2Z5
(604) 231-5858
Emp Here 50   *Sales* 10,233,650
SIC 3634 Electric housewares and fans
Michael Li

D-U-N-S 24-246-0822   (HQ)
TRAIL APPLIANCES LTD
3388 Sweden Way, Richmond, BC, V6V 0B2
(604) 233-2030
Emp Here 150   *Sales* 100,013,625
SIC 5722 Household appliance stores
Michael Broderick
Peter Broderick
Jane Frohlick

D-U-N-S 25-100-4305   (SL)
TRANS-PACIFIC TRADING LTD
TRAPA
(*Suby of* HAMPTON INVESTMENT COM-
PANY)
13091 Vanier Pl Unit 368, Richmond, BC, V6V
2J1
(604) 232-5400
Emp Here 32   *Sales* 14,309,568
SIC 5031 Lumber, plywood, and millwork
James Micheal Tyrer
Trent Gustafson

D-U-N-S 20-691-5139   (SL)
TRANSCONTINENTAL FLEXSTAR INC
FLEXSTAR PACKAGING
(*Suby of* TRANSCONTINENTAL INC)
13320 River Rd, Richmond, BC, V6V 1W7
(604) 273-9277
Emp Here 117   *Sales* 22,787,856
SIC 2671 Paper; coated and laminated pack-
aging
Brian Reid
Nelson Gentiletti
Marc Bray

D-U-N-S 20-102-0617   (HQ)
TREE ISLAND INDUSTRIES LTD
(*Suby of* TREE ISLAND STEEL LTD)
3933 Boundary Rd, Richmond, BC, V6V 1T8
(604) 524-3744
Emp Here 267   *Sales* 97,292,400
SIC 3496 Miscellaneous fabricated wire prod-
ucts
Dale Maclean
Amar Doman
Remy Stachowiak
Nancy Davies
Stephen Ogden
James Miller
Michael Fitch
Theodore Leja
Janine Waite
Sam Fleiser

D-U-N-S 20-188-7234   (HQ)
TREE ISLAND STEEL LTD
HALSTEEL
3933 Boundary Rd, Richmond, BC, V6V 1T8
(604) 524-3744
Emp Here 1,500   *Sales* 178,385,949
SIC 3496 Miscellaneous fabricated wire prod-
ucts
Dale Maclean
Nancy Davies
Stephen Ogden
Remy Stachowiak
Janine Waite
Amar Doman
Sam Fleiser
Harry Rosenfeld
Michael Fitch
Ted Leja

D-U-N-S 24-503-1059   (SL)
TRIATHLON LTD
(*Suby of* MAXAR TECHNOLOGIES INC.)
13800 Commerce Pkwy, Richmond, BC, V6V

2J3
(604) 233-5000
Emp Here 160   *Sales* 107,025,280
SIC 7389 Business services, nec
John Hornsby
Gordon Thiessen
Anil Wirasekara
Daniel E Freidmann

D-U-N-S 24-838-4174   (SL)
TRIMSEAL PLASTICS LTD
3511 Jacombs Rd, Richmond, BC, V6V 1Z8
(604) 278-3803
Emp Here 75   *Sales* 12,302,025
SIC 2782 Blankbooks and looseleaf binders
Daniel Siemens

D-U-N-S 25-216-0049   (SL)
TRISTAR CAP & GARMENT LTD
12671 Bathgate Way Unit 1, Richmond, BC,
V6V 1Y5
(604) 279-4287
Emp Here 30   *Sales* 14,949,660
SIC 5136 Men's and boy's clothing
Kantilal Kubar
Harish Kuber
Jagdish Kuber

D-U-N-S 25-326-2588   (SL)
TSC NURSERY SALES LIMITED
(*Suby of* 541488 BRITISH COLUMBIA LTD)
18071 Westminster Hwy, Richmond, BC, V6V
1B1
(604) 214-4575
Emp Here 26   *Sales* 19,305,520
SIC 5193 Flowers and florists supplies
Don Wilson
Trisha Wilson

D-U-N-S 24-855-5856   (SL)
TTC TECHNOLOGY CORP
13151 Vanier Pl Suite 150, Richmond, BC,
V6V 2J1
(604) 276-9884
Emp Here 48   *Sales* 12,314,976
SIC 3829 Measuring and controlling devices,
nec
David Warkentin
Jeff Finkelstein
William Cronin
Martin Gannon
George O'leary

D-U-N-S 24-245-9741   (HQ)
UNIPHARM WHOLESALE DRUGS LTD
2051 Van Dyke Pl Suite 100, Richmond, BC,
V6V 1X6
(604) 270-9745
Emp Here 60   *Sales* 77,374,150
SIC 5122 Drugs, proprietaries, and sundries
Derek Desrosiers
Stephen Mavety
Rossell Beales

D-U-N-S 25-143-0807   (HQ)
URBAN IMPACT RECYCLING LTD
URBAN SHREDDING SYSTEMS
15360 Knox Way, Richmond, BC, V6V 3A6
(604) 273-0089
Emp Here 40   *Sales* 10,285,240
SIC 4953 Refuse systems
Nicole T Stefenelli
Roderick Nicolls

D-U-N-S 20-558-2740   (SL)
UTSTARCOM CANADA COMPANY
4600 Jacombs Rd Suite 120, Richmond, BC,
V6V 3B1
(604) 276-0055
Emp Here 80   *Sales* 15,235,360
SIC 3663 Radio and t.v. communications
equipment
Peter Blackmore
Hong Liang Lu
Kent Toy

D-U-N-S 20-380-4377   (HQ)
VERSACOLD LOGISTICS SERVICES

(*Suby of* VERSA LP)
3371 No. 6 Rd, Richmond, BC, V6V 1P6
(604) 258-0350
Emp Here 60   *Sales* 391,738,500
SIC 4222 Refrigerated warehousing and stor-
age
Douglas Harrison
Aqshai Vasan
Mike Arcamone

D-U-N-S 25-328-8898   (SL)
VIVA PHARMACEUTICAL INC
13880 Viking Pl, Richmond, BC, V6V 1K8
(604) 718-0816
Emp Here 120   *Sales* 29,319,360
SIC 5912 Drug stores and proprietary stores
Jason Ko
Ivan Ko

D-U-N-S 24-313-3220   (HQ)
VOESTALPINE NORTRAK LTD
(*Suby of* VOESTALPINE AG)
5500 Parkwood Way, Richmond, BC, V6V
2M4
(604) 273-3030
Sales 11,790,220
SIC 3312 Blast furnaces and steel mills
Ludwig Freythe

D-U-N-S 24-558-8801   (HQ)
VOLCO ENTERPRISES LTD
VOLCO TIRES & WHEELS
12291 Bridgeport Rd, Richmond, BC, V6V 1J4
(604) 270-4727
Emp Here 7   *Sales* 12,451,950
SIC 5531 Auto and home supply stores
Roman Volpov
Sofia Volpov

D-U-N-S 24-073-8153   (HQ)
WAGONMASTER ENTERPRISES (BC) INC
12671 Bathgate Way Suite 3, Richmond, BC,
V6V 1Y5
(604) 270-2033
Sales 16,389,675
SIC 5013 Motor vehicle supplies and new
parts
William (Bill) Miller
Thomas Christian

D-U-N-S 24-072-7347   (SL)
WAH LOONG LTD
5388 Parkwood Pl, Richmond, BC, V6V 2N1
(604) 273-1688
Emp Here 38   *Sales* 31,751,926
SIC 5146 Fish and seafoods
Jonathan Choi
Eric Tang
Simon Tang

D-U-N-S 24-887-7334   (HQ)
WARTSILA CANADA, INCORPORATED
(*Suby of* WARTSILA OYJ ABP)
1771 Savage Rd, Richmond, BC, V6V 1R1
(604) 244-8181
Emp Here 80   *Sales* 30,218,805
SIC 3731 Shipbuilding and repairing
Tomas Ronn
Rumi Mistry
Aaron Gordon Bresnahan
Guido Barbazza

D-U-N-S 24-725-5607   (HQ)
**WENCO INTERNATIONAL MINING SYS-
TEMS LTD**
WENCO
13777 Commerce Pkwy Suite 100, Richmond,
BC, V6V 2X3
(604) 270-8277
Emp Here 85   *Sales* 17,301,840
SIC 7371 Custom computer programming ser-
vices
Andrew Pyne
Akio Hoshi

D-U-N-S 20-993-9024   (HQ)
WEXXAR PACKAGING INC
WEXXAR BEL

(*Suby of* PRO MACH, INC.)
13471 Vulcan Way, Richmond, BC, V6V 1K4
(604) 930-9300
Sales 37,740,170
SIC 3556 Food products machinery
William Chu

D-U-N-S 25-710-8886   (SL)
WIDE LOYAL DEVELOPMENT LTD
FLEXLIGHT
13160 Vanier Pl Suite 160, Richmond, BC,
V6V 2J2
(604) 303-0931
Emp Here 28   *Sales* 12,520,872
SIC 5063 Electrical apparatus and equipment
Louis Ko

D-U-N-S 20-866-4586   (SL)
YAO SUN LOONG KONG CHICKEN LTD
2391 Vauxhall Pl, Richmond, BC, V6V 1Z5

Emp Here 50   *Sales* 19,275,950
SIC 0259 Poultry and eggs, nec
David Leung

D-U-N-S 24-338-3267   (SL)
ZEUGMA SYSTEMS INC
13571 Commerce Pky Suite 250, Richmond,
BC, V6V 2R2
(604) 247-3250
Emp Here 80   *Sales* 14,783,840
SIC 4813 Telephone communication, except
radio
Andrew Harries
Justin Currie

Richmond, BC V6W

D-U-N-S 20-656-0968   (BR)
**ADESA AUCTIONS CANADA CORPORA-
TION**
ADESA VANCOUVER
(*Suby of* KAR AUCTION SERVICES, INC.)
7111 No. 8 Rd, Richmond, BC, V6W 1L9
(604) 232-4403
Emp Here 225
SIC 5012 Automobiles and other motor vehi-
cles
Cathy Rankine

D-U-N-S 24-696-5776   (BR)
AP INFRASTRUCTURE SOLUTIONS LP
(*Suby of* TREVLUC HOLDINGS LTD)
7900 Nelson Rd, Richmond, BC, V6W 1G4
(604) 278-9766
Emp Here 150
SIC 3312 Blast furnaces and steel mills
Ron Adams

D-U-N-S 20-646-7073   (BR)
AQUATERRA CORPORATION
CANADIAN SPRINGS WATER COMPANY
(*Suby of* COTT CORPORATION)
6560 Mcmillan Way, Richmond, BC, V6W 1L2
(604) 232-7610
Emp Here 100
SIC 5963 Direct selling establishments
Alain Lavallee

D-U-N-S 24-838-3499   (BR)
BIRD CONSTRUCTION COMPANY LIMITED
(*Suby of* BIRD CONSTRUCTION INC)
6900 Graybar Rd 2370, Richmond, BC,
V6W 0A5
(604) 271-4600
Emp Here 100
SIC 1542 Nonresidential construction, nec
Ken Nakagawa

D-U-N-S 20-249-7467   (HQ)
BOOTLEGGER CLOTHING INC
BOOTLEGGER
(*Suby of* 9383921 CANADA INC)
6651 Fraserwood Pl Unit 250, Richmond, BC,
V6W 1J3

(604) 276-8400
Emp Here 50   *Sales* 17,939,600
SIC 5621 Women's clothing stores
Shamsh Kassam
Keith D. Van Apeldoorn
Shawn Lewis
Neil Armstrong
Gerry Bachynski
Conrad Ledrew

D-U-N-S 24-392-6672   (HQ)
CADEX ELECTRONICS INC
22000 Fraserwood Way, Richmond, BC, V6W 1J6
(604) 231-7777
Emp Here 70   *Sales* 16,819,386
SIC 3825 Instruments to measure electricity
Isidor Buchmann
Paul Buchmann
Heidi Estrada
Mark Buchmann
Robert Buchmann
Thomas Buchmann

D-U-N-S 25-116-6005   (SL)
COAST 2000 TERMINALS LTD
16080 Portside Rd Suite 100, Richmond, BC, V6W 1M1
(604) 270-3625
Emp Here 90   *Sales* 13,337,280
SIC 4231 Trucking terminal facilities
Kevin Ouellette

D-U-N-S 20-255-4606   (BR)
COCA-COLA REFRESHMENTS CANADA COMPANY
(*Suby of* THE COCA-COLA COMPANY)
7200 Nelson Rd, Richmond, BC, V6W 1G4
(416) 424-6000
Emp Here 150
SIC 4225 General warehousing and storage
Glen Nightingale

D-U-N-S 24-679-3223   (SL)
COLIN PLOTKIN & SONS CONSULTING INC
12011 Riverside Way Suite 210, Richmond, BC, V6W 1K6
(604) 241-9639
Emp Here 10   *Sales* 10,348,810
SIC 6321 Accident and health insurance
Colin Plotkin
Darren Plotkin
Shaun Plotkin
Ricci Plotkin
Glenn Plotkin

D-U-N-S 24-174-6135   (HQ)
COMMERCIAL LOGISTICS INC
(*Suby of* CONTAINERWORLD FORWARDING SERVICES INC)
16133 Blundell Rd, Richmond, BC, V6W 0A3
(604) 276-1300
Emp Here 60   *Sales* 51,996,700
SIC 4731 Freight transportation arrangement
Dennis Chrismas

D-U-N-S 24-957-8220   (HQ)
CONTAINERWORLD FORWARDING SERVICES INC
16133 Blundell Rd, Richmond, BC, V6W 0A3
(604) 276-1300
Emp Here 240   *Sales* 110,722,640
SIC 4731 Freight transportation arrangement
Dennis Chrismas

D-U-N-S 24-457-0966   (HQ)
E.C.S. ELECTRICAL CABLE SUPPLY LTD
6900 Graybar Rd Unit 3135, Richmond, BC, V6W 0A5
(604) 207-1500
Emp Here 25   *Sales* 66,728,405
SIC 5063 Electrical apparatus and equipment
Mohamed Mohseni
Gordon Thursfield

D-U-N-S 25-533-4955   (HQ)
FLIR INTEGRATED IMAGING SOLUTIONS,

INC
(*Suby of* FLIR SYSTEMS, INC.)
12051 Riverside Way, Richmond, BC, V6W 1K7
(604) 242-9937
Sales 47,749,090
SIC 3559 Special industry machinery, nec
Vladimir Tucakov
Julie Marandjian
Michael Gibbons
Malcolm Steenburgh
Donald Murray

D-U-N-S 20-268-3330   (SL)
FLOWRIDER SURF LTD
6700 Mcmillan Way, Richmond, BC, V6W 1J7
(604) 273-1068
Emp Here 50   *Sales* 10,669,600
SIC 4412 Deep sea foreign transportation of freight
Geoffrey P Chutter

D-U-N-S 24-522-1994   (HQ)
FPS FOOD PROCESS SOLUTIONS CORPORATION
7431 Nelson Rd Unit 130, Richmond, BC, V6W 1G3
(604) 232-4145
Emp Here 25   *Sales* 60,361,400
SIC 3822 Environmental controls
Jeffrey Chang
Justin Lai
Kam Man Wong
Anna Lui

D-U-N-S 20-800-9399   (SL)
FRASER WHARVES LTD
(*Suby of* MITSUI & CO., LTD.)
13800 Steveston Hwy, Richmond, BC, V6W 1A8
(604) 277-1141
Emp Here 160   *Sales* 32,912,960
SIC 4226 Special warehousing and storage, nec
Yasao Uchiyama
Peter Liu

D-U-N-S 24-163-1985   (SL)
GEMINI PACKAGING LTD
12071 Jacobson Way Unit 150, Richmond, BC, V6W 1L5
(604) 278-3455
Emp Here 50   *Sales* 13,833,000
SIC 2841 Soap and other detergents
Timothy Stranks
Reginald Stranks
Dave Stranks

D-U-N-S 24-824-8940   (HQ)
HALO METRICS INC
21320 Gordon Way Unit 230, Richmond, BC, V6W 1J8
(604) 273-4456
Emp Here 15   *Sales* 13,415,220
SIC 5065 Electronic parts and equipment, nec
Sheryl Gillott

D-U-N-S 24-812-8824   (SL)
HARVEST FRASER RICHMOND ORGANICS LTD
HARVEST POWER
7028 York Rd, Richmond, BC, V6W 0B1
(604) 270-7500
Emp Here 120   *Sales* 83,436,000
SIC 5093 Scrap and waste materials
Sam Monaco

D-U-N-S 20-178-8747   (BR)
HUDSON'S BAY COMPANY
VANCOUVER LOGISTICS CENTER
(*Suby of* HUDSON'S BAY COMPANY)
18111 Blundell Rd, Richmond, BC, V6W 1L8
(604) 249-3000
Emp Here 400
SIC 4225 General warehousing and storage

D-U-N-S 25-682-1844   (SL)
HYP GOLF LTD

LIJA
21320 Gordon Way Unit 110, Richmond, BC, V6W 1J8
(604) 270-6060
Emp Here 25   *Sales* 12,458,050
SIC 5137 Women's and children's clothing
Linda Hipp
David Hipp
Ross Gurney

D-U-N-S 25-219-6951   (BR)
INGRAM MICRO INC
(*Suby of* HNA TECHNOLOGY CO., LTD.)
7451 Nelson Rd, Richmond, BC, V6W 1L7
(604) 276-8357
Emp Here 120
SIC 5045 Computers, peripherals, and software
Jeff Kennett

D-U-N-S 20-806-0483   (HQ)
INTERNATIONAL PACIFIC SALES LTD
22111 Fraserwood Way, Richmond, BC, V6W 1J5
(604) 273-7035
Emp Here 25   *Sales* 33,423,080
SIC 5141 Groceries, general line
Michael Driscoll

D-U-N-S 24-317-3015   (HQ)
MR. LUBE CANADA LIMITED PARTNERSHIP
6900 Graybar Rd Suite 2330, Richmond, BC, V6W 0A5
(604) 759-4300
Emp Here 26   *Sales* 46,459,980
SIC 6794 Patent owners and lessors
Stuart Suls
Bob Anderson
Pamela Lee
David Waterfall
Mike Cordoba
Kevin Giese
Greg C. Melville
Bill Ticknor
Greg Ticknor
Jan Ticknor

D-U-N-S 24-357-7850   (SL)
NUHEAT INDUSTRIES LIMITED
6900 Graybar Rd Suite 3105, Richmond, BC, V6W 0A5
(800) 778-9276
Emp Here 100   *Sales* 22,200,100
SIC 3567 Industrial furnaces and ovens
John C Ames
John Rose
David Orr

D-U-N-S 24-249-2106   (HQ)
OSSUR CANADA INC
6900 Graybar Rd Unit 2150, Richmond, BC, V6W 0A5
(604) 241-8152
Sales 12,500,895
SIC 3842 Surgical appliances and supplies
Jon Sigurdsson

D-U-N-S 24-684-6849   (HQ)
PRIMESOURCE BUILDING PRODUCTS CANADA CORPORATION
(*Suby of* PRIMESOURCE BUILDING PRODUCTS, INC.)
7431 Nelson Rd Suite 110, Richmond, BC, V6W 1G3
(604) 231-0473
Emp Here 30   *Sales* 97,546,000
SIC 5085 Industrial supplies
Michael Gibson
Mona Zinman
Ken Fishbein
Jerry Kegley

D-U-N-S 24-785-1780   (SL)
SALTWORKS TECHNOLOGIES INC
13800 Steveston Hwy, Richmond, BC, V6W 1A8

(604) 628-6508
Emp Here 75   *Sales* 17,571,600
SIC 8748 Business consulting, nec
Benjamin Sparrow
Joshua Zoshi
Malcolm Man
Xiangchun Yin

D-U-N-S 24-498-7777   (BR)
SCHNEIDER ELECTRIC CANADA INC
(*Suby of* SCHNEIDER ELECTRIC SE)
22171 Fraserwood Way, Richmond, BC, V6W 1J5
(604) 273-3711
Emp Here 100
SIC 1731 Electrical work

D-U-N-S 20-514-3352   (SL)
SIMARD WESTLINK INC
(*Suby of* ENTREPOTS SIMARD INC, LES)
16062 Portside Rd, Richmond, BC, V6W 1M1
(604) 231-8756
Emp Here 35   *Sales* 18,198,845
SIC 4731 Freight transportation arrangement
Denis Bertrand
Evangelos Manos

D-U-N-S 20-116-2773   (HQ)
STORK CRAFT MANUFACTURING INC
STORKCRAFT BABY
12033 Riverside Way Suite 200, Richmond, BC, V6W 1K6
(604) 274-5121
Emp Here 80   *Sales* 40,708,480
SIC 5021 Furniture
Gary Segal
James Moore

D-U-N-S 24-798-7464   (HQ)
SUN RICH FRESH FOODS INC
22151 Fraserwood Way, Richmond, BC, V6W 1J5
(604) 244-8800
Emp Here 500   *Sales* 584,862,000
SIC 2033 Canned fruits and specialties
Neville Israel
Jeff Pitchford
Steve Davies
Theresa Makelki
Brian Tieszen
Kim Tieszen

D-U-N-S 24-958-2503   (HQ)
T & T SUPERMARKET INC
OSAKA SUPERMARKET
(*Suby of* LOBLAW COMPANIES LIMITED)
21500 Gordon Way, Richmond, BC, V6W 1J8
(604) 276-9889
Emp Here 500   *Sales* 962,320,000
SIC 5411 Grocery stores
Cindy Lee
Eric Chao
Vivien Li

D-U-N-S 24-594-9581   (HQ)
TOYO TIRE CANADA INC
TOYO TIRES
(*Suby of* TOYO TIRE CORPORATION)
7791 Nelson Rd Unit 120, Richmond, BC, V6W 1G3
(604) 304-1941
Emp Here 33   *Sales* 40,273,920
SIC 5531 Auto and home supply stores
Shoji Hirao
Shabbir Mohammad
Matsaru Oda

D-U-N-S 24-838-0446   (SL)
TRANSWORLD IMPORTS INC
22071 Fraserwood Way Suite 100, Richmond, BC, V6W 1J5
(604) 272-3432
Emp Here 25   *Sales* 13,013,550
SIC 5099 Durable goods, nec
Isabella Briski

D-U-N-S 24-797-3605   (BR)
UPS SCS INC

UPS SCS, INC
(Suby of UNITED PARCEL SERVICE, INC.)
7451 Nelson Rd, Richmond, BC, V6W 1L7
(604) 270-9449
Emp Here 80
SIC 4731 Freight transportation arrangement
Michael Heath

D-U-N-S 24-161-7752   (HQ)
VANCOUVER FIRE PREVENTION SERVICE
CO. LTD
VANCOUVER ALARMS
(Suby of 355323 BC LTD)
22131 Fraserwood Way, Richmond, BC, V6W
1J5
(604) 232-3478
Sales 45,670,775
SIC 7382 Security systems services
Robert Baxter
Garth Baxter
Joslyn Alderson

D-U-N-S 20-915-8039   (SL)
WALES MCLELLAND CONSTRUCTION
COMPANY (1988) LIMITED
6211 Fraserwood Pl, Richmond, BC, V6W 1J2
(604) 638-1212
Emp Here 50   Sales 23,536,550
SIC 1542 Nonresidential construction, nec
Doug Scott
Tony Vigini
Sonny Wong
Kevin Armon

D-U-N-S 20-005-5635   (SL)
WATERMANIA
14300 Entertainment Blvd, Richmond, BC,
V6W 1K3
(604) 448-9616
Emp Here 200   Sales 18,990,600
SIC 7999 Amusement and recreation, nec
David Mcbride

D-U-N-S 24-207-1889   (SL)
WESTRAN PORTSIDE TERMINAL LIMITED
16060 Portside Rd, Richmond, BC, V6W 1M1
(604) 244-1975
Emp Here 49   Sales 10,456,208
SIC 4492 Towing and tugboat service
Mike Peters

D-U-N-S 24-696-7251   (HQ)
WHITEWATER WEST INDUSTRIES LTD
PRIME PLAY SYSTEMS, DIV OF
6700 Mcmillan Way, Richmond, BC, V6W 1J7
(604) 273-1068
Emp Here 120   Sales 104,295,000
SIC 5091 Sporting and recreation goods
Geoffrey Chutter
Ingrid Wray
Barbara Keys
Linda Heke

D-U-N-S 25-669-6316   (SL)
WINGSUM INTERNATIONAL TRADING INC
21331 Gordon Way Unit 3110, Richmond, BC,
V6W 1J9
(604) 370-3610
Emp Here 35   Sales 13,702,570
SIC 6799 Investors, nec
John Jiang

Richmond, BC V6X

D-U-N-S 20-549-5596   (SL)
0998236 B.C. LTD
4151 Hazelbridge Way Suite 1700, Richmond,
BC, V6X 4J7
(604) 288-1002
Emp Here 20   Sales 10,006,500
SIC 5137 Women's and children's clothing
Carmen Chan
Claudia Wai
Patrick S.H. Wong

D-U-N-S 24-326-3899   (SL)
663353 B.C. LTD
SHOPPERS DRUG MART
11800 Cambie Rd, Richmond, BC, V6X 1L5
(604) 278-9105
Emp Here 60   Sales 14,659,680
SIC 5912 Drug stores and proprietary stores
Alex Dar Santos

D-U-N-S 24-803-2562   (BR)
ABB INC
VENTYX, DIV
(Suby of ABB LTD)
10651 Shellbridge Way, Richmond, BC, V6X
2W8
(604) 207-6000
Emp Here 170
SIC 7372 Prepackaged software
Simon Jacobs

D-U-N-S 20-004-7264   (SL)
AIDUS INTERNATIONAL
2560 Shell Rd Unit 1048, Richmond, BC, V6X
0B8
(604) 304-7889
Emp Here 15   Sales 12,533,655
SIC 5149 Groceries and related products, nec

D-U-N-S 24-694-8095   (HQ)
ALIVE HEALTH CENTRE LTD
2680 Shell Rd Suite 228, Richmond, BC, V6X
4C9
(604) 273-6266
Emp Here 7   Sales 49,891,090
SIC 5499 Miscellaneous food stores
Alice Chung

D-U-N-S 20-806-5904   (SL)
ARBUTUS ROOFING & DRAINS (2006) LTD
4260 Vanguard Rd, Richmond, BC, V6X 2P5
(604) 272-7277
Emp Here 70   Sales 15,248,030
SIC 1761 Roofing, siding, and sheetMetal
work
Richard Ambrose

D-U-N-S 20-921-0363   (SL)
ARTHRITIS RESEARCH CENTRE SOCIETY
OF CANADA, THE
ARC
5591 No. 3 Rd, Richmond, BC, V6X 2C7
(604) 879-7511
Emp Here 40   Sales 11,389,880
SIC 8733 Noncommercial research organiza-
tions
Shauneen Kellner

D-U-N-S 25-509-9905   (SL)
ASLCHEM INTERNATIONAL INC
4871 Shell Rd Suite 1260, Richmond, BC,
V6X 3Z6
(604) 270-8824
Emp Here 40   Sales 17,886,960
SIC 5052 Coal and other minerals and ores
Eddie Au
Leon Leung

D-U-N-S 20-278-8543   (HQ)
AVENEX COATING TECHNOLOGIES INC
AVENEX
11938 Bridgeport Rd Unit 260, Richmond, BC,
V6X 1T2
(604) 716-4599
Emp Here 4   Sales 11,120,060
SIC 3089 Plastics products, nec
Gary Shokar

D-U-N-S 24-029-3639   (HQ)
AZ TRADING CO. LTD
AZ HOME AND GIFTS
7080 River Rd Suite 223, Richmond, BC, V6X
1X5
(604) 214-3600
Emp Here 37   Sales 12,216,400
SIC 5947 Gift, novelty, and souvenir shop
Mark Lang
Ernest Lang
Edwin Lang

D-U-N-S 24-939-1590   (SL)
BAYRIDGE TRANSPORT LTD
9900 River Dr, Richmond, BC, V6X 3S3
(604) 278-6622
Emp Here 85   Sales 12,596,320
SIC 4213 Trucking, except local
Bindy Sangara
Henry Hui

D-U-N-S 20-789-4143   (BR)
BIG HEARTS HOLDINGS LTD
CARE COUNTS HEALTH SERVICES
5760 Minoru Blvd Suite 203, Richmond, BC,
V6X 2A9
(604) 278-3318
Emp Here 100
SIC 8059 Nursing and personal care, nec
Victor De Castro

D-U-N-S 20-995-8537   (SL)
BLUNDELL SEAFOODS LTD
11351 River Rd, Richmond, BC, V6X 1Z6
(604) 270-3300
Emp Here 80   Sales 57,337,280
SIC 5146 Fish and seafoods
Ian Tak Yen Law

D-U-N-S 24-455-4390   (HQ)
BOSTON PIZZA INTERNATIONAL INC
10760 Shellbridge Way Unit 100, Richmond,
BC, V6X 3H1
(604) 270-1108
Emp Here 59   Sales 674,644,506
SIC 6794 Patent owners and lessors
George Melville
Michael E. Harbinson

D-U-N-S 20-175-9227   (HQ)
BOSTON PIZZA ROYALTIES INCOME FUND
10760 Shellbridge Way Unit 100, Richmond,
BC, V6X 3H1
(604) 270-1108
Sales 34,577,790
SIC 5812 Eating places
Jordan Holm
Joanne Forrester
Cavin Green
Jonathan Jeske
Robert Kirincic
Ian Thomas
Walter Treliving
Marc Guay
Paulina Hiebert
David L. Merrell

D-U-N-S 25-533-2090   (SL)
BRIGHT HARVEST ENTERPRISE INC
2620 Simpson Rd Suite 140, Richmond, BC,
V6X 2P9
(604) 278-6680
Emp Here 15   Sales 12,533,655
SIC 5141 Groceries, general line
Kwing Yui Ho
Eddie Ho
Ronald Ho
Johnny Ho

D-U-N-S 20-852-9391   (SL)
BUDGET RENT A CAR OF BC LTD
7080 River Rd Unit 203, Richmond, BC, V6X
1X5
(604) 678-1124
Emp Here 100   Sales 28,330,000
SIC 7514 Passenger car rental
Estella Lo

D-U-N-S 25-717-4110   (BR)
CACTUS RESTAURANTS LTD
CACTUS CLUB
(Suby of CACTUS RESTAURANTS LTD)
5500 No. 3 Rd, Richmond, BC, V6X 2C8
(604) 244-9969
Emp Here 80
SIC 5812 Eating places
Ed Miller

D-U-N-S 24-071-2542   (SL)
CANADIAN ROCKIE MATSUTAKE LTD

8740 Beckwith Rd Suite 110, Richmond, BC,
V6X 1V5

Emp Here 25   Sales 20,889,425
SIC 5141 Groceries, general line
Joe Chung

D-U-N-S 20-976-3296   (SL)
CANADIAN TIRE
3511 No. 3 Rd, Richmond, BC, V6X 2B8
(604) 273-2939
Emp Here 49   Sales 12,399,891
SIC 5251 Hardware stores
Dean Mccann

D-U-N-S 24-043-3875   (HQ)
CELLMART COMMUNICATIONS INC
5300 No. 3 Rd Suite 432, Richmond, BC, V6X
2X9
(604) 247-2355
Emp Here 7   Sales 11,087,880
SIC 4812 Radiotelephone communication
Benjamin Tsang
Anna Lee

D-U-N-S 24-657-6391   (HQ)
CHANGE HEALTHCARE CANADA COM-
PANY
(Suby of MCKESSON CORPORATION)
10711 Cambie Rd Suite 130, Richmond, BC,
V6X 3G5
(604) 279-5422
Sales 119,972,450
SIC 7371 Custom computer programming ser-
vices
Neil De Crescenzo
Fredrik Eliasson
Loretta Cecil

D-U-N-S 24-696-3011   (HQ)
CHOYS HOLDINGS INCORPORATED
FRESH CHOICE FOOD DISTRIBUTION &
SERVICES
(Suby of TOP MANAGEMENT INCORPO-
RATED)
4751 Shell Rd Suite 2, Richmond, BC, V6X
3H4
(604) 270-6882
Emp Here 40   Sales 12,092,058
SIC 5147 Meats and meat products
George Choy
Cecelia Choy

D-U-N-S 20-861-5641   (SL)
COAL ISLAND LTD
10991 Shellbridge Way Suite 310, Richmond,
BC, V6X 3C6
(604) 873-4312
Emp Here 200   Sales 38,474,000
SIC 2436 Softwood veneer and plywood
Robert Shields

D-U-N-S 25-730-9823   (SL)
COSMO MOTORS LTD
RICHMOND SUBARU
3511 No. 3 Rd, Richmond, BC, V6X 2B8
(604) 273-0333
Emp Here 70   Sales 44,049,600
SIC 5511 New and used car dealers
Tom Glenn
Mathew Clapperton

D-U-N-S 25-287-5216   (BR)
COSTCO WHOLESALE CANADA LTD
(Suby of COSTCO WHOLESALE CORPO-
RATION)
9151 Bridgeport Rd Suite 54, Richmond, BC,
V6X 3L9
(604) 270-3647
Emp Here 400
SIC 5099 Durable goods, nec
Scotty Ayton

D-U-N-S 25-091-7742   (SL)
CSI CHEMICAL COMPANY LTD
2560 Shell Rd Suite 3013, Richmond, BC,
V6X 0B8
(604) 278-1071
Emp Here 49   Sales 35,786,905

SIC 5169 Chemicals and allied products, nec
Johnny Dai
Brian Wu

D-U-N-S 24-696-1320   (SL)
DAN-JEN MECHANICAL LTD
11786 River Rd Suite 146, Richmond, BC,
V6X 3Z3
(604) 232-4545
Emp Here 50   *Sales* 11,046,700
SIC 1711 Plumbing, heating, air-conditioning
Robert Mchattie

D-U-N-S 24-837-5255   (SL)
DCH MOTORS LTD
RICHMOND ACURA
(*Suby of* DAH CHONG HONG HOLDINGS
LIMITED)
4211 No. 3 Rd, Richmond, BC, V6X 2C3
(604) 278-8999
Emp Here 57   *Sales* 35,868,960
SIC 5511 New and used car dealers
Henry Liang

D-U-N-S 24-825-5440   (HQ)
**DELTA TOUR AND TRAVEL SERVICES
(CANADA) INC**
DELTA TOUR VANCOUVER
(*Suby of* MING PAO NEWSPAPERS LIM-
ITED)
5611 Cooney Rd Suite 160, Richmond, BC,
V6X 3J6
(604) 233-0081
Emp Here 20   *Sales* 12,999,175
SIC 4724 Travel agencies
Eric Li
Kelvin Chu

D-U-N-S 24-246-4493   (HQ)
**DEVELOPMENTAL DISABILITIES ASSOCI-
ATION OF VANCOUVER-RICHMOND**
3851 Shell Rd Suite 100, Richmond, BC, V6X
2W2
(604) 273-9778
Sales 50,836,800
SIC 8322 Individual and family services
John Neilson
Louise Huber
Sue Swayne
Allyson Baker
Rob Bahd
Bill Adams
Ronda Karliner
Nancy Panchuk
Alanna Hendren
Bonnie Hunter

D-U-N-S 24-493-3602   (SL)
DIGITEL SYSTEMS INC
10851 Shellbridge Way Suite 110, Richmond,
BC, V6X 2W8
(604) 231-0101
Emp Here 33   *Sales* 10,744,800
SIC 5999 Miscellaneous retail stores, nec
Jerry Mckenzie
David Shaw

D-U-N-S 20-917-8839   (HQ)
DORSET REALTY GROUP CANADA LTD
DORSET REALTY GROUP
10451 Shellbridge Way Suite 215, Richmond,
BC, V6X 2W8
(604) 270-1711
Sales 25,133,340
SIC 6531 Real estate agents and managers
Damien Roussin
Ron Schuss

D-U-N-S 20-111-0798   (HQ)
EBCO INDUSTRIES LTD
7851 Alderbridge Way, Richmond, BC, V6X
2A4
(604) 278-5578
Sales 44,400,200
SIC 3599 Industrial machinery, nec
Richard Eppich
Umendra Mital
Pearl Lee

D-U-N-S 20-896-6270   (SL)
ELITE WEALTH MANAGEMENT INC
7080 River Rd Suite 241, Richmond, BC, V6X
1X5
(604) 276-8081
Emp Here 30   *Sales* 17,397,720
SIC 6411 Insurance agents, brokers, and service
Angela Fok

D-U-N-S 20-148-2564   (SL)
EMPIRE SUPERMARKET (2010) LTD
4600 No. 3 Rd Unit 111, Richmond, BC, V6X
2C2

Emp Here 49   *Sales* 13,433,448
SIC 5411 Grocery stores
Simon Hui

D-U-N-S 25-514-1384   (BR)
**EXECUTIVE HOTELS GENERAL PARTNER-
SHIP**
EXECUTIVE AIRPORT PLAZA
(*Suby of* EXECUTIVE HOTELS GENERAL
PARTNERSHIP)
7311 Westminster Hwy, Richmond, BC, V6X
1A3
(604) 278-5555
Emp Here 200
SIC 7011 Hotels and motels
Bruce Marks

D-U-N-S 20-586-2014   (HQ)
FABRICANA IMPORTS LTD
INTERIOR DELIGHTS
4591 Garden City Rd, Richmond, BC, V6X
2K4
(604) 273-5316
Emp Here 1   *Sales* 12,652,950
SIC 5211 Lumber and other building materials
Richard Megrian
Karen Megrian

D-U-N-S 20-748-4122   (SL)
FJORD PACIFIC MARINE INDUSTRIES LTD.
2400 Simpson Rd, Richmond, BC, V6X 2P9
(604) 270-3393
Emp Here 75   *Sales* 25,926,750
SIC 2091 Canned and cured fish and
seafoods
Don Pollard

D-U-N-S 24-626-2286   (SL)
GEAR PELLING INSURANCE LTD
7340 Westminster Hwy Suite 110, Richmond,
BC, V6X 1A1
(604) 276-2474
Emp Here 15   *Sales* 10,881,585
SIC 6321 Accident and health insurance
Andrew Tablotney

D-U-N-S 20-121-1831   (SL)
GLG LIFE TECH CORPORATION
10271 Shellbridge Way Suite 100, Richmond,
BC, V6X 2W8
(604) 285-2602
Emp Here 251   *Sales* 12,571,305
SIC 5122 Drugs, proprietaries, and sundries
Luke Zhang
Brian Palmieri
Paul Block
Qibin Wang
Kevin Li
Hong Zhao Guang
Sophia Leung
Liu Yingchun
Simon Springett

D-U-N-S 25-995-9906   (SL)
**GRAND PACIFIC TRAVEL & TRADE
(CANADA) CORP**
CANADIAN GRAND HOLIDAY
8877 Odlin Cres Suite 100, Richmond, BC,
V6X 3Z7
(604) 276-2616
Emp Here 40   *Sales* 20,798,680
SIC 4724 Travel agencies
Tony Wong

D-U-N-S 20-764-5722   (HQ)
GRAYMONT LIMITED
10991 Shellbridge Way Suite 200, Richmond,
BC, V6X 3C6
(604) 207-4292
Emp Here 7   *Sales* 854,442,000
SIC 5032 Brick, stone, and related material
William Dodge
Philip Graham
Kenneth J. Lahti
Stuart Wolfe
James H Cleave

D-U-N-S 25-365-1319   (BR)
GREAT CANADIAN CASINOS INC
RIVER ROCK CASINO RESORT
(*Suby of* GREAT CANADIAN GAMING COR-
PORATION)
8811 River Rd, Richmond, BC, V6X 3P8
(604) 247-8900
Emp Here 450
SIC 7999 Amusement and recreation, nec
William A. Dimma

D-U-N-S 20-912-8735   (HQ)
H-S TOOL & PARTS INC
2560 Simpson Rd Suite 140, Richmond, BC,
V6X 2P9
(604) 273-4743
Sales 11,366,390
SIC 4581 Airports, flying fields, and services
Hans Sarghie

D-U-N-S 20-918-6451   (SL)
HANSEN INDUSTRIES LTD
2871 Olafsen Ave, Richmond, BC, V6X 2R4
(604) 278-2223
Emp Here 55   *Sales* 10,564,675
SIC 3469 Metal stampings, nec
Edwin Beange

D-U-N-S 20-866-1215   (SL)
HODDER TUGBOAT CO. LTD
11171 River Rd, Richmond, BC, V6X 1Z6
(604) 273-2821
Emp Here 65   *Sales* 17,520,685
SIC 4492 Towing and tugboat service
Benjamin Wendland
Ian Wright

D-U-N-S 20-112-3064   (SL)
HODGSON, KING AND MARBLE LIMITED
4200 Vanguard Rd, Richmond, BC, V6X 2P4
(604) 247-2422
Emp Here 38   *Sales* 17,887,778
SIC 1542 Nonresidential construction, nec
Gary Maguire
John Whiteman

D-U-N-S 24-166-2287   (SL)
INTERNATIONAL STAGE LINES INC
4171 Vanguard Rd, Richmond, BC, V6X 2P6
(604) 270-6135
Emp Here 100   *Sales* 5,487,200
SIC 4142 Bus charter service, except local
George Pullman
Bob Myhre

D-U-N-S 25-069-2183   (SL)
INTERNATIONAL VINEYARD INC
4631 Shell Rd Suite 165, Richmond, BC, V6X
3M4
(604) 303-5778
Emp Here 50   *Sales* 11,242,750
SIC 2032 Canned specialties
Joshua Chan

D-U-N-S 20-322-2484   (SL)
IYINISIW MANAGEMENT INC
10551 Shellbridge Way Unit 100, Richmond,
BC, V6X 2W9
(604) 249-3969
Emp Here 50   *Sales* 16,666,650
SIC 1541 Industrial buildings and warehouses
Lawrence Ching
Michael Chen
Dipak Datta

D-U-N-S 24-372-4549   (HQ)
JTB INTERNATIONAL (CANADA) LTD
JTB CANADA
(*Suby of* JTB CORP.)
8899 Odlin Cres, Richmond, BC, V6X 3Z7
(604) 276-0300
Emp Here 50   *Sales* 40,013,520
SIC 4725 Tour operators
Andrew Shimizu
Amyn Khimji
Chiemi Nishinari
Toru Tsuthie

D-U-N-S 24-839-6855   (SL)
KANATA HOLDINGS LTD
ORCA SEAFOODS
11251 River Rd Unit 200, Richmond, BC, V6X
1Z6
(604) 273-6005
Emp Here 40   *Sales* 10,966,080
SIC 5421 Meat and fish markets
John Willcott

D-U-N-S 20-749-4097   (HQ)
KEG RESTAURANTS LTD
KEG STEAKHOUSE & BAR, THE
(*Suby of* RECIPE UNLIMITED CORPORA-
TION)
10100 Shellbridge Way, Richmond, BC, V6X
2W7
(604) 276-0242
Emp Here 62   *Sales* 377,775,900
SIC 5812 Eating places
David Aisenstat
Neil Maclean

D-U-N-S 25-412-8812   (SL)
KEG ROYALTIES INCOME FUND, THE
10100 Shellbridge Way, Richmond, BC, V6X
2W7
(604) 276-0242
Emp Here 5   *Sales* 22,483,789
SIC 6722 Management investment, open-end
David Aisenstat
Neil Maclean
Doug Smith
James Henderson
Christopher Charles Woodward
George Killy
Timothy Kerr

D-U-N-S 25-505-1401   (HQ)
**LION INTERNATIONAL TRAVEL SERVICE
CO LTD**
LION TOURS
110-4140 No. 3 Rd, Richmond, BC, V6X 2C2
(604) 231-8256
Emp Here 19   *Sales* 12,479,208
SIC 4724 Travel agencies
Albert Pei
Jason Wong
Vicki Ling
Frank Chen
William Wu

D-U-N-S 25-187-7171   (BR)
LOBLAWS INC
REAL CANADIAN SUPERSTORE
(*Suby of* LOBLAW COMPANIES LIMITED)
4651 No. 3 Rd Suite 1557, Richmond, BC,
V6X 2C4
(604) 233-2418
Emp Here 100
SIC 5141 Groceries, general line
Terry Maguire

D-U-N-S 24-142-0616   (SL)
LOCURETT ENTERPRISES LTD
5660 Minoru Blvd, Richmond, BC, V6X 2A9
(604) 273-1001
Emp Here 35   *Sales* 17,432,730
SIC 5521 Used car dealers
Frank Gelshon

D-U-N-S 25-715-5259   (SL)
**LONDON DRUGS INSURANCE SERVICES
LTD**
THE INSURANCE SERVICES DEPART-

MENT
5971 No. 3 Rd, Richmond, BC, V6X 3Y6
(604) 821-0808
Emp Here 25   *Sales* 21,201,500
SIC 6411 Insurance agents, brokers, and service
Joseph Fellner

D-U-N-S 20-512-3727   (SL)
M J FASHIONS LTD
8571 Bridgeport Rd, Richmond, BC, V6X 1R7
(604) 273-9233
Emp Here 60   *Sales* 29,899,320
SIC 5137 Women's and children's clothing
Yee Mei Fong
Candice Yuen

D-U-N-S 24-640-1095   (HQ)
M T K AUTO WEST LTD
AUTO WEST BMW
10780 Cambie Rd, Richmond, BC, V6X 1K8
(604) 233-0700
Emp Here 20   *Sales* 100,684,800
SIC 5511 New and used car dealers
Joachim Neumann
Pete Sargent
Leonard Fong

D-U-N-S 25-318-1747   (BR)
**MCDONALD'S   RESTAURANTS   OF
CANADA LIMITED**
MCDONALD'S
(*Suby of* MCDONALD'S CORPORATION)
8191 Alderbridge Way, Richmond, BC, V6X
3A9

Emp Here 85
SIC 5812 Eating places
Jason Cebuliak

D-U-N-S 24-370-9003   (SL)
**MENNONITE INTERMEDIATE CARE HOME
SOCIETY OF RICHMOND**
PINEGROVE PLACE
11331 Mellis Dr, Richmond, BC, V6X 1L8
(604) 278-1296
Emp Here 105   *Sales* 7,174,230
SIC 8051 Skilled nursing care facilities
Gordon Milner
Bruce Hynds

D-U-N-S 24-867-5696   (SL)
MONTALCO CABINETS (1991) LTD
2700 Simpson Rd Unit 125, Richmond, BC,
V6X 2P9
(604) 273-5105
Emp Here 50   *Sales* 12,652,950
SIC 5211 Lumber and other building materials
Herb Klassen
Erich Schellenberg

D-U-N-S 24-183-6001   (SL)
NATURE'S PATH BAKING INC
9100 Van Horne Way, Richmond, BC, V6X
1W3
(604) 248-8806
Emp Here 100   *Sales* 83,557,700
SIC 5149 Groceries and related products, nec
Arran Stphens

D-U-N-S 24-535-5821   (HQ)
NATURE'S PATH FOODS INC
(*Suby of* MANNA FOOD COMPANY LTD)
9100 Van Horne Way, Richmond, BC, V6X
1W3
(604) 248-8777
Sales 83,557,700
SIC 5149 Groceries and related products, nec
Arran Stephens
Ratana Stephens

D-U-N-S 24-335-9648   (SL)
NEWTYPE MOTORS LTD
NEWTYPE RICHMOND MITSUBISHI
(*Suby of* NEWTYPE AUTO GROUP LTD)
9200 Bridgeport Rd, Richmond, BC, V6X 1S1
(604) 231-9200
Emp Here 26   *Sales* 16,361,280

SIC 5511 New and used car dealers
Todd Ho

D-U-N-S 24-493-3664   (SL)
OVERSEAS AIR CARGO
10451 Shellbridge Way Suite 100, Richmond,
BC, V6X 2W8
(604) 734-8155
Emp Here 30   *Sales* 15,599,010
SIC 4729 Passenger transportation arrangement
Peter Hilton

D-U-N-S 24-162-0558   (HQ)
**OVERSEAS   CONTAINER   FORWARDING,
INC**
OCFLINK
10451 Shellbridge Way Unit 100, Richmond,
BC, V6X 2W8
(604) 734-8155
Sales 14,098,698
SIC 4731 Freight transportation arrangement
Peter Hilton
Sherry Babcock

D-U-N-S 24-804-0128   (HQ)
**PAPER EXCELLENCE CANADA HOLDINGS
CORPORATION**
(*Suby of* CAPITAL ASSETS HOLDINGS (L)
BERHAD)
10551 Shellbridge Way Suite 95, Richmond,
BC, V6X 2W9
(604) 232-2453
Emp Here 50   *Sales* 22,203,552
SIC 2611 Pulp mills
Hardi Wardhana
Bujung Wahab

D-U-N-S 20-748-1185   (HQ)
PARAMOUNT INDUSTRIES LTD
PARAMOUNT FURNITURE
5520 Minoru Blvd, Richmond, BC, V6X 2A9
(604) 273-0155
Sales 10,690,538
SIC 5712 Furniture stores
Moe Samuel

D-U-N-S 20-014-7176   (HQ)
PHELPS APARTMENT LAUNDRIES LTD
LAUNDRY PEOPLE
3640 No. 4 Rd Suite 1, Richmond, BC, V6X
2L7
(604) 257-8200
Emp Here 28   *Sales* 36,646,280
SIC 7359 Equipment rental and leasing, nec
William Ung
Stanley Saibil
Ellen Pan
Conchita Ung

D-U-N-S 24-137-0782   (HQ)
PHELPS LEASING LTD
BUDGET RENT-A-CAR
3640 No. 4 Rd, Richmond, BC, V6X 2L7
(604) 257-8230
Emp Here 20   *Sales* 16,998,000
SIC 7514 Passenger car rental
William (Bill) Ung
Olen Pan
Conafita Ung

D-U-N-S 20-532-9881   (SL)
POLARIS TRADING CORP
2030-10013 River Dr, Richmond, BC, V6X
0N2
(778) 834-2701
Emp Here 10   *Sales* 10,185,201
SIC 5199 Nondurable goods, nec
Lorenzo Ku
Harvin Uy

D-U-N-S 20-189-7555   (BR)
POSTMEDIA NETWORK INC
COLLEGE PRINTERS
(*Suby of* POSTMEDIA NETWORK CANADA
CORP)
7280 River Rd Suite 110, Richmond, BC, V6X
1X5

Emp Here 90
SIC 7374 Data processing and preparation
Ken Nelson

D-U-N-S 20-358-2747   (HQ)
PREMIUM BRANDS BAKERY GROUP INC
(*Suby of* PREMIUM BRANDS HOLDINGS
CORPORATION)
10991 Shellbridge Way, Richmond, BC, V6X
3C6
(604) 656-3100
Sales 13,369,232
SIC 5149 Groceries and related products, nec
Carmelo De Luca
An Nguyen
Doug Ramsay
William Kalutycz
George Paleologou

D-U-N-S 24-333-8337   (HQ)
**PREMIUM BRANDS HOLDINGS CORPO-
RATION**
10991 Shellbridge Way Unit 100, Richmond,
BC, V6X 3C6
(604) 656-3100
Sales 2,293,865,032
SIC 2099 Food preparations, nec
George Paleologou
Douglas Goss
William Kalutycz
Bruce Hodge
Johnny Ciampi
Kathleen Keller-Hobson
Hugh Mckinnon
John Zaplatynsky

D-U-N-S 20-746-1328   (HQ)
**PREMIUM BRANDS OPERATING LIMITED
PARTNERSHIP**
HARVEST MEATS
(*Suby of* PREMIUM BRANDS HOLDINGS
CORPORATION)
10991 Shellbridge Way Suite 100, Richmond,
BC, V6X 3C6
(604) 656-3100
Emp Here 65   *Sales* 28,692,270
SIC 2099 Food preparations, nec
George Paleologou
Douglas Goss
Donald Chiu
William D. Kalutycz

D-U-N-S 25-017-3838   (SL)
PRO-CLAIM RESTORATION LTD
PC FLOORING
5811 Cedarbridge Way Unit 150, Richmond,
BC, V6X 2A8
(604) 276-2483
Emp Here 42   *Sales* 24,356,808
SIC 6411 Insurance agents, brokers, and service
Anthony Scott
Lars Andstein

D-U-N-S 20-619-7782   (HQ)
PROGRESSIVE CONTRACTING LTD
5591 No. 3 Rd, Richmond, BC, V6X 2C7
(604) 273-6655
Sales 25,244,200
SIC 1623 Water, sewer, and utility lines
Milan Ilich
Maureen Ilich

D-U-N-S 25-236-7230   (SL)
PROTEC INSTALLATIONS GROUP
11720 Voyageur Way Suite 9, Richmond, BC,
V6X 3G9
(604) 278-3200
Emp Here 120   *Sales* 26,139,480
SIC 1731 Electrical work
Gary Woods

D-U-N-S 24-375-6785   (SL)
PROTRANS BC OPERATIONS LTD
(*Suby of* GROUPE SNC-LAVALIN INC)
9851 Van Horne Way, Richmond, BC, V6X
1W4

(604) 247-5757
Emp Here 170   *Sales* 12,796,240
SIC 4111 Local and suburban transit
Marc Devlin
Louise Pelletier
Charles Rate

D-U-N-S 24-536-8238   (SL)
QUE PASA MEXICAN FOODS LTD
9100 Van Horne Way, Richmond, BC, V6X
1W3
(866) 880-7284
Emp Here 119   *Sales* 41,137,110
SIC 2032 Canned specialties
Joe Zallen
Marie Zallen
Morris Zallen
Judy Zallen

D-U-N-S 24-777-1827   (HQ)
QUICK AS A WINK COURIER SERVICE LTD
QUICK TRANSLOAD
9300 Van Horne Way, Richmond, BC, V6X
1W3
(604) 276-8686
Sales 20,982,012
SIC 4212 Local trucking, without storage
Bindy Sangara

D-U-N-S 20-702-7439   (SL)
RAYMOND-CBE MACHINERY INC
11788 River Rd Suite 118, Richmond, BC,
V6X 1Z7

Emp Here 103   *Sales* 22,866,103
SIC 3561 Pumps and pumping equipment
Henry Zhou

D-U-N-S 24-578-4723   (HQ)
REDPATH FOODS INC
MAX'S BAKERY & DELICATESSEN
2560 Simpson Rd, Richmond, BC, V6X 2P9
(604) 873-1393
Emp Here 60   *Sales* 22,010,775
SIC 5461 Retail bakeries
Bruce Redpath
David Greeley

D-U-N-S 20-115-3608   (HQ)
RICHMOND AUTO BODY LTD
OPENROAD RICHMOND AUTO BODY
2691 No. 5 Rd, Richmond, BC, V6X 2S8
(604) 278-9158
Emp Here 22   *Sales* 15,581,500
SIC 7532 Top and body repair and paint shops
Randy Lowe
Robert Lowe
Joan Lowe

D-U-N-S 25-612-3134   (HQ)
RICHMOND HOSPITAL, THE
7000 Westminster Hwy, Richmond, BC, V6X
1A2
(604) 278-9711
Sales 16,662,000
SIC 8062 General medical and surgical hospitals
Patricia Bloom
Anne Chapotelle
Karen Hodgkins
Colleen Kason
Dolores Mattson

D-U-N-S 24-805-9206   (SL)
RICHMOND INN HOTEL LTD
SHERATON VANCOUVER AIRPORT HOTEL
(*Suby of* LARCO INVESTMENTS LTD)
7551 Westminster Hwy, Richmond, BC, V6X
1A3
(604) 273-7878
Emp Here 380   *Sales* 36,353,840
SIC 7011 Hotels and motels
Andy Loges
Brad Makagawa

D-U-N-S 20-653-4336   (SL)
SCIENTEK MEDICAL EQUIPMENT
11151 Bridgeport Rd, Richmond, BC, V6X

1T3

Emp Here 40   *Sales* 10,262,480
SIC 3841 Surgical and medical instruments
  Joaseph Jeyanayagan

  D-U-N-S 24-032-2367   (SL)
SNC-LAVALIN CONSTRUCTORS (PACIFIC) INC
RSL JOINT VENTURE
7400 River Rd Suite 160, Richmond, BC, V6X 1X6

Emp Here 45   *Sales* 14,999,985
SIC 1541 Industrial buildings and warehouses
  Denis Jasmin
  Janice Hu

  D-U-N-S 24-968-7724   (SL)
SUN SUI WAH SEAFOOD RESTAURANT
4940 No. 3 Rd Suite 102, Richmond, BC, V6X 3A5
(604) 273-8208
Emp Here 180   *Sales* 8,395,020
SIC 5812 Eating places
  Simon Chan
  Chan Chan Tang-Chung

  D-U-N-S 25-648-3629   (BR)
T & T SUPERMARKET INC
(*Suby of* LOBLAW COMPANIES LIMITED)
8181 Cambie Rd Suite 1000, Richmond, BC, V6X 3X9
(604) 284-5550
Emp Here 80
SIC 5411 Grocery stores
  Bill Fong

  D-U-N-S 20-913-8390   (BR)
T & T SUPERMARKET INC
(*Suby of* LOBLAW COMPANIES LIMITED)
3700 No. 3 Rd Suite 1000, Richmond, BC, V6X 3X2
(604) 276-8808
Emp Here 150
SIC 5411 Grocery stores
  Sonia Ma

  D-U-N-S 24-682-4804   (SL)
TETRA TECH OGD INC
(*Suby of* TETRA TECH, INC.)
10851 Shellbridge Way Suite 100, Richmond, BC, V6X 2W8
(604) 270-7728
Emp Here 250   *Sales* 49,282,750
SIC 8711 Engineering services
  Michael Cantor

  D-U-N-S 24-695-6437   (SL)
TOURLAND TRAVEL LTD
(*Suby of* JTB CORP.)
8899 Odlin Cres, Richmond, BC, V6X 3Z7
(604) 276-9592
Emp Here 45   *Sales* 23,398,515
SIC 4725 Tour operators
  Isao Onaga
  Hideo Nishi
  Gordon M. Craig

  D-U-N-S 25-735-6949   (SL)
TRANSATLANTIC ANGELS TRADING CO LTD
11482 River Rd, Richmond, BC, V6X 1Z7
(604) 231-1960
Emp Here 40   *Sales* 20,821,680
SIC 5093 Scrap and waste materials
  Nizar Jiwani

  D-U-N-S 24-335-9663   (SL)
TREND AUTO GROUP INC
11631 Bridgeport Rd, Richmond, BC, V6X 1T5
(604) 638-9899
Emp Here 50   *Sales* 24,903,900
SIC 5511 New and used car dealers
  Randy Purcell

  D-U-N-S 24-445-9376   (SL)
TRI-STAR SEAFOOD SUPPLY LTD

11751 Voyageur Way, Richmond, BC, V6X 3J4
(604) 273-3324
Emp Here 45   *Sales* 37,600,965
SIC 5146 Fish and seafoods
  Claude T Tchao
  Gregory Nelsen

  D-U-N-S 24-613-8788   (SL)
TRIDENT MILLWORK AND DISPLAY INDUSTRIES LTD
11140 River Rd, Richmond, BC, V6X 1Z5
(604) 276-2855
Emp Here 45   *Sales* 20,122,830
SIC 5031 Lumber, plywood, and millwork
  Elso Mion

  D-U-N-S 20-116-8564   (HQ)
UNIVAR CANADA LTD
TRUENORTH SPECIALTY PRODUCTS, DIV OF
(*Suby of* UNIVAR INC.)
9800 Van Horne Way, Richmond, BC, V6X 1W5
(604) 273-1441
Emp Here 85   *Sales* 520,964,300
SIC 5169 Chemicals and allied products, nec
  David Jukes
  Mike Hildebrand
  Neil Douglas
  Cheryl Winter
  Barry Mcgee
  Jeff Thomas
  Willy St. Cyr
  Peter Gupta
  Adam Iasenzaniro
  Chris Halberg

  D-U-N-S 25-054-5100   (HQ)
VANCOUVER AIRPORT CENTRE LIMITED
VANCOUVER AIRPORT MARRIOTT HOTEL
(*Suby of* LARCO INVESTMENTS LTD)
7571 Westminster Hwy, Richmond, BC, V6X 1A3
(604) 276-2112
Emp Here 120   *Sales* 18,538,000
SIC 7011 Hotels and motels
  Amin Lalji
  Vazir Kara

  D-U-N-S 24-421-5500   (BR)
VANCOUVER AIRPORT CENTRE LIMITED
HILTON
(*Suby of* LARCO INVESTMENTS LTD)
5911 Minoru Blvd, Richmond, BC, V6X 4C7
(604) 273-6336
Emp Here 110
SIC 7011 Hotels and motels

  D-U-N-S 20-001-2078   (SL)
VTECH ENGINEERING CANADA LTD
7671 Alderbridge Way Suite 200, Richmond, BC, V6X 1Z9
(604) 273-5131
Emp Here 80   *Sales* 14,076,640
SIC 8711 Engineering services
  Gordon Chow

  D-U-N-S 24-363-5914   (SL)
WESTERN CANADA STEEL & TECHNOLOGIES INC
5811 No. 3 Rd Unit 1807, Richmond, BC, V6X 4L7
(604) 247-1442
Emp Here 10   *Sales* 10,003,390
SIC 5051 Metals service centers and offices
  Vera Jorge

  D-U-N-S 25-482-9948   (BR)
WHITE SPOT LIMITED
WHITE SPOT RESTAURANT
(*Suby of* SHATO HOLDINGS LTD)
5880 No. 3 Rd, Richmond, BC, V6X 2E1
(604) 273-3699
Emp Here 75
SIC 5812 Eating places
  Roy Kurian

  D-U-N-S 24-374-0123   (HQ)

WORLD INSURANCE SERVICES LTD
7100 River Rd Unit 2, Richmond, BC, V6X 1X5

Emp Here 26   *Sales* 31,378,220
SIC 6411 Insurance agents, brokers, and service
  Lincoln Yeung
  Sanny Lai
  Trudy Babcock
  Steven Yee
  Ray Luk
  Peter Macdonald

Richmond, BC V6Y

  D-U-N-S 20-044-6982   (BR)
BOARD OF EDUCATION SCHOOL DISTRICT #38 (RICHMOND)
RICHMOND SECONDARY
(*Suby of* BOARD OF EDUCATION SCHOOL DISTRICT #38 (RICHMOND))
7171 Minoru Blvd, Richmond, BC, V6Y 1Z3
(604) 668-6400
Emp Here 97
SIC 8211 Elementary and secondary schools
  Darlene Macklam

  D-U-N-S 24-029-3183   (HQ)
BOARD OF EDUCATION SCHOOL DISTRICT #38 (RICHMOND)
RICHMOND SCHOOL BOARD
7811 Granville Ave, Richmond, BC, V6Y 3E3
(604) 668-6000
Emp Here 200   *Sales* 189,883,427
SIC 8211 Elementary and secondary schools
  Kenneth Morris
  Monica Pamer
  Mark De Mello
  Kathy Champion
  Ray Jung
  Michael Khoo
  Diane Brow
  Richard Hudson
  Clive Mason

  D-U-N-S 25-715-4930   (HQ)
GROUP CONNECT LTD, THE
CONNECT
8010 Saba Rd Suite 110, Richmond, BC, V6Y 4B2
(604) 821-1852
Emp Here 9   *Sales* 32,251,296
SIC 5999 Miscellaneous retail stores, nec
  Max Mintzberg
  Cyndi Mintzberg

  D-U-N-S 20-574-2042   (BR)
HUDSON'S BAY COMPANY
BAY, THE
(*Suby of* HUDSON'S BAY COMPANY)
6060 Minoru Blvd Suite 100, Richmond, BC, V6Y 1Y2
(604) 273-3844
Emp Here 310
SIC 5311 Department stores
  Li Hardy

  D-U-N-S 20-646-6430   (HQ)
INDUSTRY TRAINING AUTHORITY
ITA
(*Suby of* GOVERNMENT OF THE PROVINCE OF BRITISH COLUMBIA)
8100 Granville Ave Unit 800, Richmond, BC, V6Y 3T6
(604) 214-8700
Sales 77,333,185
SIC 7699 Repair services, nec
  Frank Pasacreta
  Allan Bruce
  Jack Davidson
  Tom Kirk

  D-U-N-S 25-243-1197   (SL)
LIN ROBERT SUTTON GROUP

9100 Blundell Rd Unit 550, Richmond, BC, V6Y 3X9
(604) 727-0917
Emp Here 48   *Sales* 13,044,288
SIC 6531 Real estate agents and managers
  Robert Lin

  D-U-N-S 24-289-8310   (SL)
NORTH AMERICAN AIR TRAVEL INSURANCE AGENTS LTD
TUGO
6081 No. 3 Rd 11 Fl Suite 1101, Richmond, BC, V6Y 2B2
(604) 276-9900
Emp Here 140   *Sales* 172,958,520
SIC 6321 Accident and health insurance
  Patrick Robinson
  Kathleen Starko
  Georgina Robinson

  D-U-N-S 25-244-4778   (SL)
PETTIPIECE HELEN SUTTON GROUP
9100 Blundell Rd Unit 550, Richmond, BC, V6Y 3X9
(604) 341-7997
Emp Here 47   *Sales* 12,772,532
SIC 6531 Real estate agents and managers
  Daniel Jones

  D-U-N-S 24-345-9539   (BR)
RICHMOND HOSPITAL, THE
VANCOUVER COASTAL HEALTH AUTHORITY
(*Suby of* RICHMOND HOSPITAL, THE)
6111 Minoru Blvd, Richmond, BC, V6Y 1Y4
(604) 244-5300
Emp Here 200
SIC 8059 Nursing and personal care, nec
  Swamy Revatta

  D-U-N-S 24-502-9657   (HQ)
RICHMOND PUBLIC LIBRARY BOARD
7700 Minoru Gate Suite 100, Richmond, BC, V6Y 1R8
(604) 231-6422
Emp Here 75
SIC 8231 Libraries
  Greg Buss

Richmond, BC V7A

  D-U-N-S 20-208-4864   (SL)
22 ENTERPRISES LTD
CHEVRON
11131 No. 5 Rd, Richmond, BC, V7A 4E8
(604) 204-0047
Emp Here 26   *Sales* 12,950,028
SIC 5541 Gasoline service stations
  Sean Holmes

  D-U-N-S 25-116-1972   (BR)
ACUREN GROUP INC
(*Suby of* ROCKWOOD SERVICE CORPORATION)
12271 Horseshoe Way, Richmond, BC, V7A 4V4
(604) 275-3800
Emp Here 90
SIC 3821 Laboratory apparatus and furniture
  Gerry Siebem

  D-U-N-S 20-033-3628   (BR)
BOARD OF EDUCATION SCHOOL DISTRICT #38 (RICHMOND)
MATHEW MCNAIR SECONDARY SCHOOL
(*Suby of* BOARD OF EDUCATION SCHOOL DISTRICT #38 (RICHMOND))
9500 No. 4 Rd, Richmond, BC, V7A 2Y9
(604) 668-6575
Emp Here 85
SIC 8211 Elementary and secondary schools
  Rose Sebellin

  D-U-N-S 24-445-8931   (SL)
BRIDGE ELECTRIC CORP

▲ Public Company   ■ Public Company Family Member   **HQ** Headquarters   **BR** Branch   **SL** Single Location

(*Suby of* GRANBY ENTERPRISES INC)
11091 Hammersmith Gate, Richmond, BC,
V7A 5E6
(604) 273-2744
Emp Here 130   *Sales* 23,940,630
SIC 1731 Electrical work
Duane Besse
Bradley Goodwin
Terry Lange

D-U-N-S 24-166-6825   (SL)
CENTRAL FOODS CO. LTD
12160 Horseshoe Way, Richmond, BC, V7A
4V5
(604) 271-9797
Emp Here 75   *Sales* 22,010,775
SIC 5431 Fruit and vegetable markets
William Wong

D-U-N-S 25-978-9337   (SL)
CLEAR PACIFIC TRADING LTD
12160 Horseshoe Way Suite 120, Richmond,
BC, V7A 4V5

Emp Here 35   *Sales* 29,245,195
SIC 5146 Fish and seafoods
Jackson Chan
Yoshiya Tateyama

D-U-N-S 24-340-2943   (BR)
COAST MOUNTAIN BUS COMPANY LTD
CMBC
(*Suby of* SOUTH COAST BRITISH
COLUMBIA TRANSPORTATION AUTHOR-
ITY)
11133 Coppersmith Way, Richmond, BC, V7A
5E8
(604) 277-7787
Emp Here 443
SIC 4142 Bus charter service, except local
Danny Wong

D-U-N-S 20-213-4388   (HQ)
CROWN CORRUGATED COMPANY
BOXMASTER, DIV OF
(*Suby of* CROWN PAPER GROUP INC.)
13911 Garden City Rd, Richmond, BC, V7A
2S5
(604) 277-7111
Emp Here 210   *Sales* 147,054,800
SIC 2653 Corrugated and solid fiber boxes
Colin Fernie
Joseph Beers
John Combatti
Fraser Macfadyen
Ted Lodge
Ernest Conrads
Dale Stahl

D-U-N-S 24-798-3562   (HQ)
DAN-D FOODS LTD
11760 Machrina Way, Richmond, BC, V7A
4V1
(604) 274-3263
Sales 54,312,505
SIC 5141 Groceries, general line
Dan On

D-U-N-S 24-760-6106   (HQ)
DDS WIRELESS INTERNATIONAL INC
11920 Forge Pl, Richmond, BC, V7A 4V9
(604) 241-1441
Emp Here 16   *Sales* 51,773,445
SIC 3663 Radio and t.v. communications
equipment
Scott Hardy
Roger Lines
Darren Schrader
Matt Scheuing
Erik Dysthe
Mark Joseph
Daniel Daviau
Sal Visca
Jp Leblanc
Jim Zadra

D-U-N-S 20-520-9377   (SL)
DELGADO FOODS INTERNATIONAL LIM-

ITED
12031 No. 5 Rd, Richmond, BC, V7A 4E9
(604) 241-8175
Emp Here 45   *Sales* 11,769,885
SIC 6712 Bank holding companies
Joe Zallen

D-U-N-S 24-534-6895   (SL)
ECHELON HOME PRODUCTS LTD
11120 Horseshoe Way Unit 120, Richmond,
BC, V7A 5H7
(604) 275-2210
Emp Here 30   *Sales* 13,415,220
SIC 5064 Electrical appliances, television and
radio
Vernon Daughney
Douglas Mcrobbie
Kevin Richardson

D-U-N-S 24-535-2497   (HQ)
EUROPEAN CREATIONS LTD
ALDILA BOUTIQUE
12240 Horseshoe Way Unit 14, Richmond,
BC, V7A 4X9
(604) 275-0440
Emp Here 1   *Sales* 29,899,320
SIC 5137 Women's and children's clothing
Hasan Sarihan
Gulay Sarihan

D-U-N-S 24-390-0714   (SL)
GREENFIELD PRODUCE LTD
KIN'S FARM MARKET
(*Suby of* KFM INVESTMENTS LTD)
12151 Horseshoe Way, Richmond, BC, V7A
4V4
(604) 272-2551
Emp Here 15   *Sales* 12,533,655
SIC 5148 Fresh fruits and vegetables
Kin Hun Leung

D-U-N-S 20-797-2597   (HQ)
HAAKON INDUSTRIES (CANADA) LTD
11851 Dyke Rd, Richmond, BC, V7A 4X8
(604) 273-0161
Emp Here 100   *Sales* 126,394,650
SIC 3585 Refrigeration and heating equip-
ment
Robert W. Hole

D-U-N-S 20-733-6210   (SL)
HAYDEN DIAMOND BIT INDUSTRIES LTD
12020 No. 5 Rd, Richmond, BC, V7A 4G1
(604) 341-6941
Emp Here 115   *Sales* 27,421,695
SIC 3532 Mining machinery
Hira Gaunder
Eric Hayden

D-U-N-S 24-394-6535   (HQ)
HEATHERBRAE BUILDERS CO. LTD
12371 Horseshoe Way Unit 140, Richmond,
BC, V7A 4X6
(604) 277-2315
Emp Here 300   *Sales* 209,517,600
SIC 1542 Nonresidential construction, nec
David Knight
Tim Knight
Greg Knight

D-U-N-S 24-394-5966   (SL)
IDEON PACKAGING
11251 Dyke Rd, Richmond, BC, V7A 0A1
(604) 524-0524
Emp Here 100   *Sales* 22,318,110
SIC 2653 Corrugated and solid fiber boxes
Tim Koutsandreas

D-U-N-S 20-732-1808   (SL)
J.R.S. AMENITIES LTD
11151 Horseshoe Way Unit 25, Richmond,
BC, V7A 4S5
(604) 244-7627
Emp Here 200   *Sales* 107,070,400
SIC 5046 Commercial equipment, nec
Susan Howard Memory

D-U-N-S 20-110-1979   (HQ)

JOSEPH S. CHOW LTD
11780 Hammersmith Way Suite 120, Richmond, BC, V7A 5E9
(604) 271-0255
Emp Here 25   *Sales* 20,889,425
SIC 5148 Fresh fruits and vegetables
Duncan Chow

D-U-N-S 25-089-0100   (HQ)
KIN'S FARM LTD
12151 Horseshoe Way, Richmond, BC, V7A
4V4
(604) 272-2551
Emp Here 5   *Sales* 97,473,376
SIC 5141 Groceries, general line
Kin Leung
Chie Leung

D-U-N-S 20-912-3389   (HQ)
KING MARKETING LTD
11121 Horseshoe Way Suite 148, Richmond,
BC, V7A 5G7
(604) 271-3455
Emp Here 8   *Sales* 11,714,400
SIC 8742 Management consulting services
Paul Crawford

D-U-N-S 20-280-2567   (HQ)
LAYFIELD CANADA LTD
11131 Hammersmith Gate, Richmond, BC,
V7A 5E6
(604) 275-5588
Sales 15,885,800
SIC 3081 Unsupported plastics film and sheet
Thomas Rose

D-U-N-S 20-082-9323   (HQ)
LAYFIELD GROUP LIMITED
11131 Hammersmith Gate, Richmond, BC,
V7A 5E6
(604) 275-5588
Emp Here 100   *Sales* 63,587,430
SIC 1731 Electrical work
Thomas Rose
Brian Fraser
Mark Rose
Mark Simpson

D-U-N-S 20-388-7430   (SL)
LIMSON CANADA, LTD
12411 Horseshoe Way, Richmond, BC, V7A
4X6
(604) 529-5275
Emp Here 12   *Sales* 233,516,400
SIC 6221 Commodity contracts brokers, dealers
David Gray

D-U-N-S 20-802-4591   (SL)
LONDON DRUGS EXECUTIVE
12151 Horseshoe Way, Richmond, BC, V7A
4V4
(604) 272-7400
Emp Here 49   *Sales* 12,394,746
SIC 5912 Drug stores and proprietary stores
Wynne Powell

D-U-N-S 20-514-1211   (HQ)
LONDON DRUGS LIMITED
(*Suby of* H.Y. LOUIE CO. LIMITED)
12251 Horseshoe Way, Richmond, BC, V7A
4X5
(604) 272-7400
Emp Here 350   *Sales* 1,284,759,000
SIC 5912 Drug stores and proprietary stores
Brandt Louie
Wynne Powell
Clint Mahlman
Laird Miller

D-U-N-S 24-359-7726   (BR)
NEUCEL SPECIALTY CELLULOSE LTD
(*Suby of* FULIDA GROUP HOLDING CO.,
LTD.)
11331 Coppersmith Way Suite 305, Rich-
mond, BC, V7A 5J9

Emp Here 350

SIC 3081 Unsupported plastics film and sheet

D-U-N-S 24-535-0723   (SL)
NIGHTINGALE ELECTRICAL LTD
11121 Horseshoe Way Suite 143, Richmond,
BC, V7A 5G7
(604) 275-0500
Emp Here 250   *Sales* 58,877,250
SIC 1731 Electrical work
Douglas Nightingale

D-U-N-S 25-365-2440   (HQ)
PEAK INNOVATIONS INC
11782 Hammersmith Way Unit 203, Rich-
mond, BC, V7A 5E2
(604) 448-8000
Sales 11,179,350
SIC 5039 Construction materials, nec
John Gross

D-U-N-S 20-703-7321   (SL)
PEAK PRODUCTS INTERNATIONAL INC
11782 Hammersmith Way Suite 203, Rich-
mond, BC, V7A 5E2
(604) 448-8000
Emp Here 1   *Sales* 10,483,875
SIC 6712 Bank holding companies
John Gross

D-U-N-S 25-677-5925   (HQ)
PEAK PRODUCTS MANUFACTURING INC
PEAK PRODUCTS
(*Suby of* PEAK INNOVATIONS INC)
11782 Hammersmith Way Unit 203, Rich-
mond, BC, V7A 5E2
(604) 448-8000
Sales 11,179,350
SIC 5039 Construction materials, nec
John Gross

D-U-N-S 20-351-9590   (SL)
PHASE ANALYZER COMPANY LTD
11168 Hammersmith Gate, Richmond, BC,
V7A 5H8
(604) 241-9568
Emp Here 100   *Sales* 22,728,900
SIC 3821 Laboratory apparatus and furniture
Gordon Chiu

D-U-N-S 24-069-9694   (SL)
PIONEER'S PUB LTD, THE
10111 No. 3 Rd Suite 200, Richmond, BC,
V7A 1W6
(604) 271-6611
Emp Here 36   *Sales* 10,768,680
SIC 5921 Liquor stores
Anthony Yurkovich

D-U-N-S 24-289-5795   (SL)
POLYNOVA INDUSTRIES INC
11480 Blacksmith Pl Unit 101, Richmond, BC,
V7A 4X1
(604) 277-1274
Emp Here 60   *Sales* 12,113,820
SIC 3086 Plastics foam products
Dennis Wong
Pradeep Sanganeria

D-U-N-S 25-218-7653   (HQ)
PORTOLA PACKAGING CANADA LTD.
(*Suby of* SILGAN HOLDINGS INC.)
12431 Horseshoe Way, Richmond, BC, V7A
4X6
(604) 272-5000
Emp Here 64   *Sales* 42,603,150
SIC 2821 Plastics materials and resins
Kevin Happer

D-U-N-S 20-577-2408   (SL)
**RICHMOND CHRISTIAN SCHOOL ASSOCI-
ATION**
10200 No. 5 Rd, Richmond, BC, V7A 4E5
(604) 272-5720
Emp Here 140   *Sales* 13,876,660
SIC 8211 Elementary and secondary schools
Roger Grose
Aza Nakagawa

D-U-N-S 24-309-1105   (SL)

▲ Public Company   ■ Public Company Family Member   **HQ** Headquarters   **BR** Branch   **SL** Single Location

RICHMOND COUNTRY CLUB
9100 Steveston Hwy, Richmond, BC, V7A 1M5
(604) 277-3141
Emp Here 100   *Sales* 7,854,500
SIC 7997 Membership sports and recreation clubs
Brian Davis
Myer A Goldgerg
David Berns
Stephen Cronk
Ron Fratkin
Grant Lapthorne
Lyall Levy
Ron Rozen
Alan Tobe
Simon Margolis

D-U-N-S 20-956-9995   (SL)
RICHMOND ELEVATOR MAINTENANCE LTD
12091 No. 5 Rd Suite 5, Richmond, BC, V7A 4E9
(604) 274-8440
Emp Here 103   *Sales* 25,357,158
SIC 1796 Installing building equipment
Vladimir Zachata
Irene Zachata

D-U-N-S 25-533-5051   (SL)
RICHWAY ENVIRONMENTAL TECHNOLOGIES LTD
11300 No. 5 Rd Suite 100, Richmond, BC, V7A 5J7
(604) 275-2201
Emp Here 25   *Sales* 11,875,650
SIC 5084 Industrial machinery and equipment
Leonard L Li
Eddie Man Wai Ho

D-U-N-S 24-776-9557   (HQ)
RONSONS SHOE STORES LTD
WALK WITH RONSON
12495 Horseshoe Way, Richmond, BC, V7A 4X6
(604) 270-9974
Sales 11,660,740
SIC 5661 Shoe stores
Mayer Aronson
Tony Aronson

D-U-N-S 20-202-7855   (SL)
SMART-TEK COMMUNICATIONS INC
130-11300 No. 5 Rd, Richmond, BC, V7A 5J7
(604) 718-1882
Emp Here 26   *Sales* 10,855,156
SIC 7382 Security systems services
Perry Law
Stephen Platt

D-U-N-S 25-218-9881   (SL)
ST. GENEVE FINE BEDLINENS LTD
11160 Silversmith Pl, Richmond, BC, V7A 5E4
(604) 272-3004
Emp Here 30   *Sales* 15,265,680
SIC 5023 Homefurnishings
Annette Delaplace

D-U-N-S 24-838-1105   (SL)
STEVESTON RESTAURANTS LTD
KEG SOUTH RICHMOND
11151 No. 5 Rd, Richmond, BC, V7A 4E8
(604) 272-1399
Emp Here 100   *Sales* 4,287,300
SIC 5812 Eating places
Kurt Landert
Robert Matheson

D-U-N-S 24-761-4423   (HQ)
T L D COMPUTERS INC
(*Suby of* H.Y. LOUIE CO. LIMITED)
12251 Horseshoe Way Unit 100, Richmond, BC, V7A 4V4
(604) 272-6000
Emp Here 50   *Sales* 16,268,210
SIC 5734 Computer and software stores
G. Wynne Powell
Brandt Louie

Clint Mahlman
Laird Miller
John Matyus
Nick Curalli

D-U-N-S 24-978-3390   (SL)
T N L INDUSTRIAL CONTRACTORS LTD
12391 Horseshoe Way Suite 130, Richmond, BC, V7A 4X6
(604) 278-7424
Emp Here 100   *Sales* 21,782,900
SIC 1731 Electrical work
Tony Greatbanks

D-U-N-S 25-685-3235   (BR)
TECK RESOURCES LIMITED
(*Suby of* TECK RESOURCES LIMITED)
12380 Horseshoe Way, Richmond, BC, V7A 4Z1
(778) 296-4900
Emp Here 80
SIC 8731 Commercial physical research
Pete Mayhew

D-U-N-S 20-012-7756   (HQ)
TURVEY FINANCIAL GROUP INC, THE
11388 No. 5 Rd Suite 110, Richmond, BC, V7A 4E7
(604) 279-8484
Sales 27,335,000
SIC 6712 Bank holding companies
Tania Mordaunt

D-U-N-S 20-702-3032   (SL)
VERY JAZZROO ENTERPRISES INCORPORATED
HOSPITALITY DESIGNS
11720 Horseshoe Way, Richmond, BC, V7A 4V5
(604) 248-1806
Emp Here 80   *Sales* 12,345,760
SIC 2599 Furniture and fixtures, nec
Ruben Cohen

D-U-N-S 20-116-1614   (SL)
WASTE-NOT RECYCLING AND DISPOSAL INC
12171 Horseshoe Way, Richmond, BC, V7A 4V4
(604) 273-0089
Emp Here 40   *Sales* 12,045,680
SIC 4953 Refuse systems
Thomas Lindsay
Gordon Pow

D-U-N-S 20-790-5154   (HQ)
WESTERN PROTECTION ALLIANCE INC
11771 Horseshoe Way Unit 1, Richmond, BC, V7A 4V4
(604) 271-7475
Emp Here 85   *Sales* 33,632,630
SIC 7381 Detective and armored car services
Robert Reeleder
Chris Valuven

D-U-N-S 24-881-2877   (HQ)
WING TAT GAME BIRD PACKERS INC
11951 Forge Pl, Richmond, BC, V7A 4V9
(604) 278-4450
Emp Here 40   *Sales* 20,798,680
SIC 4731 Freight transportation arrangement
Shung Tat Ng
Sung-Lap Ng
Michael Jung

D-U-N-S 20-273-3085   (HQ)
WISMETTAC ASIAN FOODS, INC
(*Suby of* NISHIMOTO CO., LTD.)
11388 No. 5 Rd Suite 130, Richmond, BC, V7A 4E7
(604) 303-8620
Emp Here 60   *Sales* 645,044,400
SIC 5141 Groceries, general line
Hitoshi Hashimoto
Toshiyuki Nishikawa

Richmond, BC V7B

D-U-N-S 20-347-5384   (HQ)
420877 B.C. LTD
FLYING FRESH
5200 Miller Rd Unit 2170, Richmond, BC, V7B 1L1
(604) 233-1377
Emp Here 30   *Sales* 14,613,930
SIC 4512 Air transportation, scheduled
Brendan Harnett
Krystal Harnett
Peter Christensen

D-U-N-S 24-214-6327   (BR)
AIR NORTH PARTNERSHIP
(*Suby of* AIR NORTH PARTNERSHIP)
1 3rd Suite 3135, Richmond, BC, V7B 1Y7
(604) 207-1165
Emp Here 120
SIC 4512 Air transportation, scheduled

D-U-N-S 20-109-4869   (HQ)
CATALYST PAPER CORPORATION
CROFTON, DIV OF
(*Suby of* CAPITAL ASSETS HOLDINGS (L) BERHAD)
3600 Lysander Lane Suite 200 Fl 2, Richmond, BC, V7B 1C3
(604) 247-4400
Emp Here 133   *Sales* 1,497,068,268
SIC 2621 Paper mills
Edward Dwyer
Lucas Mcleod
Sally Chan
James Hardt
Mark Petersen
Linda Champigny
Hamish Doughty

D-U-N-S 20-181-0483   (SL)
CATALYST PULP AND PAPER SALES INC
(*Suby of* CAPITAL ASSETS HOLDINGS (L) BERHAD)
3600 Lysander Lane 2nd Fl, Richmond, BC, V7B 1C3
(604) 247-4400
Emp Here 3,000   *Sales* 2,085,900,000
SIC 5099 Durable goods, nec
Brian Baarda
Jim Bayles
Pat Sakai

D-U-N-S 20-860-7528   (BR)
CENTRAL MOUNTAIN AIR LTD
(*Suby of* 580741 BRITISH COLUMBIA LTD)
4180 Agar Dr, Richmond, BC, V7B 1A3
(604) 207-0130
Emp Here 100
SIC 4512 Air transportation, scheduled
Eddy Soler

D-U-N-S 24-722-5113   (HQ)
CHC HELICOPTER HOLDING S.A.R.L.
HELI-ONE
(*Suby of* FRC FOUNDERS CORPORATION)
4740 Agar Dr, Richmond, BC, V7B 1A3
(604) 276-7500
Emp Here 45   *Sales* 1,408,725,528
SIC 4522 Air transportation, nonscheduled
Sylvain A Allard
Craig C Dobbin
Mark Dobbin
John J Kelly
Donald Carty
George Gillett Jr
Jack Mintz
Bob Reid
Guylaine Saucier
William Stinson

D-U-N-S 24-421-6276   (SL)
CHC HELICOPTERS CANADA INC
4740 Agar Dr, Richmond, BC, V7B 1A3
(604) 276-7500
Emp Here 1,400   *Sales* 373,769,200
SIC 4522 Air transportation, nonscheduled

William Amelio
Peter Bartolotta
Anthony Dinota
Mark Dobbin
Sylvain Allard
Greg Wyght

D-U-N-S 24-292-4785   (HQ)
CLS CATERING SERVICES LTD
(*Suby of* DEUTSCHE LUFTHANSA AG)
3560 Jericho Rd, Richmond, BC, V7B 1C2
(604) 273-4438
Emp Here 270   *Sales* 25,185,060
SIC 5812 Eating places
David Wainman

D-U-N-S 24-357-2450   (BR)
DELTA HOTELS LIMITED
DELTA VANCOUVER AIRPORT HOTEL
(*Suby of* GOVERNMENT OF THE PROVINCE OF BRITISH COLUMBIA)
3500 Cessna Dr, Richmond, BC, V7B 1C7
(604) 278-1241
Emp Here 240
SIC 8741 Management services
Gord Johnson

D-U-N-S 25-131-1536   (SL)
ESSO AVITAT INTERDEL AVIATION SERVICES INC
ESSO (IMPERIAL OIL)
5360 Airport Rd S, Richmond, BC, V7B 1B4
(604) 270-2222
Emp Here 25   *Sales* 31,430,025
SIC 5172 Petroleum products, nec
Derrick Watts

D-U-N-S 20-812-5356   (HQ)
EXCHANGE CORPORATION CANADA INC
ICE CURRENCY SERVICE
(*Suby of* LENLYN HOLDINGS LIMITED)
4831 Miller Rd Suite 206, Richmond, BC, V7B 1K7
(604) 656-1700
Emp Here 4   *Sales* 58,384,500
SIC 6099 Functions related to deposit banking
Shamir Desai
Nizar Tejani
Dan Northam
Hassan Tejani
Zulfikaralli Tejani
Firoz Tejani

D-U-N-S 24-308-4477   (BR)
FAIRMONT HOTELS & RESORTS INC
FAIRMONT VANCOUVER AIRPORT HOTEL
(*Suby of* ACCOR)
3111 Grant Mcconachie Way, Richmond, BC, V7B 0A6
(604) 207-5200
Emp Here 400
SIC 7011 Hotels and motels
Dan Mcgowan

D-U-N-S 24-797-4249   (BR)
FEDERAL EXPRESS CANADA CORPORATION
FEDEX SHIP CENTRE
(*Suby of* FEDEX CORPORATION)
3151 Aylmer Rd, Richmond, BC, V7B 1L5
(800) 463-3339
Emp Here 300
SIC 7389 Business services, nec

D-U-N-S 24-447-4631   (HQ)
HARBOUR AIR LTD
HARBOUR AIR SEAPLANES
4760 Inglis Dr, Richmond, BC, V7B 1W4
(604) 278-3478
Emp Here 30   *Sales* 20,134,748
SIC 4512 Air transportation, scheduled
Greg Mcdougal
Kenn Borek

D-U-N-S 24-421-2929   (HQ)
HELI-ONE CANADA ULC
4740 Agar Dr, Richmond, BC, V7B 1A3

▲ Public Company   ■ Public Company Family Member   **HQ** Headquarters   **BR** Branch   **SL** Single Location

(604) 276-7500
Emp Here 10   *Sales* 16,310,520
SIC 7699 Repair services, nec
Eddie Lane
Guy Borowski
Priscilla Shung
Rune Tallaksen

D-U-N-S 24-776-6553   (HQ)
HELIJET INTERNATIONAL INC
HELIJET
5911 Airport Rd S, Richmond, BC, V7B 1B5
(604) 273-4688
Emp Here 115   *Sales* 28,682,532
SIC 4522 Air transportation, nonscheduled
Daniel A. J. Sitnam
Rick Hill
Morris Forchuk
Karen Sabourin
Carla Kovacs
Brendan Mccormick
Jay Minter
Troy Macdonald
Frank Inouye
Tammi Lim

D-U-N-S 20-573-2613   (HQ)
HIGHLAND HELICOPTERS LTD
4240 Agar Dr, Richmond, BC, V7B 1A3
(604) 273-6161
Emp Here 25   *Sales* 20,023,350
SIC 4522 Air transportation, nonscheduled
April Lee O'brien
Audrey Diane Rendall
Robert Henry Jens
Kenneth Rudolph Jens

D-U-N-S 24-939-2200   (HQ)
INTERNATIONAL FASTLINE FORWARDING INC
5200 Miller Rd Suite 106, Richmond, BC, V7B 1K5
(604) 278-0191
Emp Here 1   *Sales* 17,678,878
SIC 4731 Freight transportation arrangement
Anthony Chan
Joe Chan
David Ng

D-U-N-S 25-978-8610   (SL)
LONDON AIR SERVICES LIMITED
(*Suby of* H.Y. LOUIE CO. LIMITED)
4580 Cowley Cres, Richmond, BC, V7B 1B8
(604) 272-8123
Emp Here 37   *Sales* 12,015,898
SIC 4512 Air transportation, scheduled
Wynne Powell
Brandt Louie

D-U-N-S 24-425-8526   (HQ)
MAPLE FREIGHT PARTNERSHIP
4871 Miller Rd Unit 1162, Richmond, BC, V7B 1K8
(604) 279-2525
Emp Here 12   *Sales* 10,399,340
SIC 4731 Freight transportation arrangement
Bonnie Chu

D-U-N-S 24-881-5110   (SL)
MILLER ROAD HOLDINGS LTD
PARK N FLY
6380 Miller Rd, Richmond, BC, V7B 1B3
(604) 270-9395
Emp Here 80   *Sales* 36,015,760
SIC 7521 Automobile parking
Sydney Belzberg
Brenton Kenny
Ray Mccarron
Eric Bresler
Samuel Bresler

D-U-N-S 25-676-5256   (SL)
MTU MAINTENANCE CANADA LTD
(*Suby of* MTU AERO ENGINES AG)
6020 Russ Baker Way, Richmond, BC, V7B 1B4
(604) 233-5700
Emp Here 300   *Sales* 26,908,800

SIC 7699 Repair services, nec
Helmut Neuper

D-U-N-S 24-716-5426   (HQ)
PACIFIC COASTAL AIRLINES LIMITED
4440 Cowley Cres Suite 204, Richmond, BC, V7B 1B8
(604) 273-8666
Emp Here 110   *Sales* 53,395,600
SIC 4512 Air transportation, scheduled
Daryl Smith
Quetin Smith
Ian Harris
David Rossi

D-U-N-S 24-320-2846   (HQ)
PINNACLE RENEWABLE ENERGY INC
3600 Lysander Ln Suite 350, Richmond, BC, V7B 1C3
(604) 270-9613
Emp Here 10   *Sales* 263,394,959
SIC 2448 Wood pallets and skids
Robert Mccurdy
Leroy Reitsma
Andrea Johnston
Scott Bax
Vaughan Bassett
Ranj Sangra
Erin Strong
Gregory Baylin
Pat Bell
Michael Lay

D-U-N-S 24-311-2976   (HQ)
PREFERRED SERVICE CUSTOM BROKERS INC
5980 Miller Rd Unit 115, Richmond, BC, V7B 1K2
(604) 270-6607
Emp Here 15   *Sales* 10,919,307
SIC 4731 Freight transportation arrangement
Jack Peterson
Dorothy Peterson

D-U-N-S 25-831-9433   (BR)
RECIPE UNLIMITED CORPORATION
(*Suby of* RECIPE UNLIMITED CORPORATION)
6260 Miller Rd, Richmond, BC, V7B 1B3
(604) 278-9144
Emp Here 600
SIC 5812 Eating places
Howard Yan

D-U-N-S 20-735-1417   (SL)
RICK HANSEN FOUNDATION
RICK HANSEN MAN IN MOTION FOUNDATION
3820 Cessna Dr Suite 300, Richmond, BC, V7B 0A2
(604) 295-8149
Emp Here 50   *Sales* 11,433,619
SIC 8699 Membership organizations, nec
Rick Hansen
Mike Reid
Carol Nelson
Brad Mccannell
Brad Brohman
Catherine Ruby
Doramy Ehling
Jo-Anne Nykilchyk
Tamara Vrooman
Sarah Mccarthy

D-U-N-S 20-585-6073   (HQ)
RUTHERFORD, WILLIAM L (BC) LTD
RUTHERFORD TERMINALS
(*Suby of* RUTHERFORD, WILLIAM L. LIMITED)
6086 Russ Baker Way Suite 125, Richmond, BC, V7B 1B4
(604) 273-8611
Emp Here 33   *Sales* 19,758,746
SIC 4731 Freight transportation arrangement
Larry Wiseman
Romas Krilavicius
Barton Ramsay

D-U-N-S 24-682-0443   (HQ)
SECURE FREIGHT SYSTEMS INC
SECURE FREIGHT
4871 Miller Rd Suite 1160, Richmond, BC, V7B 1K8
(604) 276-2369
Emp Here 13   *Sales* 12,999,175
SIC 4731 Freight transportation arrangement
Gordon Lam

D-U-N-S 24-320-4619   (BR)
STANDARD AERO LIMITED
(*Suby of* STANDARDAERO AVIATION HOLDINGS, INC.)
4551 Agar Dr, Richmond, BC, V7B 1A4
(604) 276-7600
Emp Here 309
SIC 4581 Airports, flying fields, and services

D-U-N-S 24-163-6679   (HQ)
SUMMIT INTERNATIONAL TRADE SERVICES INC
SUMMIT CUSTOM BROKERS
5200 Miller Rd Suite 2060, Richmond, BC, V7B 1L1
(604) 278-3551
Emp Here 8   *Sales* 11,959,241
SIC 4731 Freight transportation arrangement
Sharmaine Shultz
Steven Kendall
Elfrieda Kendall

D-U-N-S 20-852-3972   (BR)
SWISSPORT CANADA INC
(*Suby of* SWISSPORT CANADA INC)
Gd, Richmond, BC, V7B 1Y4
(604) 303-4550
Emp Here 750
SIC 4581 Airports, flying fields, and services

D-U-N-S 25-388-0769   (SL)
SYSCON JUSTICE SYSTEMS CANADA LTD
3600 Lysander Lane Suite 300, Richmond, BC, V7B 1C3
(604) 606-7650
Emp Here 65   *Sales* 13,900,315
SIC 7372 Prepackaged software
Mark Derraugh

D-U-N-S 24-930-7364   (HQ)
VANCOUVER AIRPORT AUTHORITY
YVR
3211 Grant Mcconachie Way, Richmond, BC, V7B 0A4
(604) 207-7077
Emp Here 347   *Sales* 415,728,566
SIC 4581 Airports, flying fields, and services
Craig Richmond
Glenn Mccoy
Michele Mawhinney
Don Ehrenholz
Steve Hankinson
Anne Murray
Lynette Dujohn
Scott Norris
Gerry Bruno
Annalisa King

D-U-N-S 24-333-0235   (HQ)
WDFG CANADA INC
WDFG
(*Suby of* EDIZIONE SRL)
3211 Grant Mcconachie Way, Richmond, BC, V7B 0A4
(604) 273-1708
Sales 41,068,600
SIC 5399 Miscellaneous general merchandise
Antoni Felany Bender
Daniel Montero
Donald M Dalik

D-U-N-S 25-327-5937   (HQ)
WEST COAST AIR LTD
4760 Inglis Dr, Richmond, BC, V7B 1W4
(604) 278-3478
Emp Here 10   *Sales* 40,046,700
SIC 4512 Air transportation, scheduled

Rick Baxter
Lindsay Hill
Greg Mcdougall
Peter Evans

D-U-N-S 20-980-1344   (BR)
WEST COAST AIR LTD
(*Suby of* WEST COAST AIR LTD)
5220 Airport Rd S, Richmond, BC, V7B 1B4

Emp Here 100
SIC 4512 Air transportation, scheduled

D-U-N-S 25-462-6653   (SL)
WESTCOAST GREEN ENERGY SYSTEMS LTD.
6880 Miller Rd, Richmond, BC, V7B 1L3
(604) 244-0421
Emp Here 5   *Sales* 15,529,285
SIC 4924 Natural gas distribution
Ian Mcintyre

D-U-N-S 24-344-3590   (BR)
WESTJET AIRLINES LTD
(*Suby of* WESTJET AIRLINES LTD)
3880 Grant Mcconachie Way Suite 4130, Richmond, BC, V7B 0A5
(604) 249-1165
Emp Here 200
SIC 4512 Air transportation, scheduled
Dan Geier

Richmond, BC V7C

D-U-N-S 20-574-9351   (SL)
CANADIAN ART PRINTS INC
(*Suby of* THE ART WINN/DEVON GROUP LTD)
6311 Westminster Hwy Unit 110, Richmond, BC, V7C 4V4
(604) 207-0165
Emp Here 51   *Sales* 30,047,109
SIC 5199 Nondurable goods, nec
Joseph Halby Krieger
Lisa Krieger

D-U-N-S 20-915-2854   (BR)
DARE FOODS LIMITED
(*Suby of* DARE FOODS LIMITED)
6751 Elmbridge Way, Richmond, BC, V7C 4N1
(604) 233-1117
Emp Here 100
SIC 2051 Bread, cake, and related products
Norm Knight

D-U-N-S 20-622-9650   (HQ)
PEERLESS, E.B. LTD
6651 Elmbridge Way Suite 130, Richmond, BC, V7C 5C2
(604) 279-9907
Emp Here 10   *Sales* 10,925,598
SIC 5088 Transportation equipment and supplies
Charles Hume
Myrtle Hume
Daniel Hume
Kenneth Hume
Derek Hume

D-U-N-S 24-031-7420   (SL)
PENTEL STATIONERY OF CANADA LIMITED
(*Suby of* PENTEL CO., LTD.)
5900 No. 2 Rd Suite 140, Richmond, BC, V7C 4R9
(604) 270-1566
Emp Here 24   *Sales* 12,087,792
SIC 5112 Stationery and office supplies
Takeshi Wada
Keima Horie
James Leith

D-U-N-S 20-115-1610   (SL)
QUILCHENA GOLF & COUNTRY CLUB

3551 Granville Ave, Richmond, BC, V7C 1C8
(604) 277-1101
Emp Here 100   *Sales* 7,854,500
SIC 7997 Membership sports and recreation clubs
Brian Taylor

D-U-N-S 25-100-5856   (SL)
RICHMOND INTERMEDIATE CARE SOCI-ETY
ROSEWOOD MANOR
6260 Blundell Rd, Richmond, BC, V7C 5C4
(604) 271-3590
Emp Here 150   *Sales* 10,248,900
SIC 8051 Skilled nursing care facilities
Ross Peters
Deborah Goegan
Marilyn Moxin

D-U-N-S 24-371-7480   (SL)
RICHMOND OLYMPIC OVAL CORPORA-TION
(*Suby of* RICHMOND, CITY OF)
6111 River Rd, Richmond, BC, V7C 0A2
(778) 296-1400
Emp Here 200   *Sales* 12,139,267
SIC 7999 Amusement and recreation, nec
George Duncan
Michael O'brien
Linda Sanderson
Dennis Skulsky
Victor Farmer
Wayne Duzita
Moray Keith
Stanley Wok
Umendra Mital
Anna Nyarady

D-U-N-S 24-240-8803   (SL)
SAMMI INTERNATIONAL TRADING LTD
6191 Westminster Hwy Unit 150, Richmond, BC, V7C 4V4
(778) 938-2277
Emp Here 24   *Sales* 16,723,440
SIC 6799 Investors, nec

D-U-N-S 20-293-9729   (SL)
STEELE DISTRIBUTORS INC
3351 Francis Rd, Richmond, BC, V7C 1J1
(604) 278-4569
Emp Here 120   *Sales* 70,699,080
SIC 5192 Books, periodicals, and newspapers
John Finne

D-U-N-S 25-144-2752   (SL)
THOMPSON COMMUNITY ASSOCIATION, THE
THOMPSON COMMUNITY CENTRE
5151 Granville Ave, Richmond, BC, V7C 1E6
(604) 238-8422
Emp Here 180   *Sales* 13,822,560
SIC 8322 Individual and family services
Marion Gray
Angela Lim
George Atkinson
Gerald Galasso

D-U-N-S 20-117-3176   (SL)
WESTERN RICE MILLS LTD
THIRD PLANET FOODS, DIV OF
6231 Westminster Hwy Unit 120, Richmond, BC, V7C 4V4
(604) 321-0338
Emp Here 35   *Sales* 29,245,195
SIC 5149 Groceries and related products, nec
Baldwin Chiang
John Chiang

D-U-N-S 25-072-1339   (HQ)
WESTMAR REALTY LTD
MACDONALD REALTERS WESTMAR
5188 Westminster Hwy Suite 203, Richmond, BC, V7C 5S7
(604) 506-5352
Sales 75,400,020
SIC 6531 Real estate agents and managers
Gary Craig

Glenn Temes

D-U-N-S 20-522-5746   (HQ)
WORKERS' COMPENSATION BOARD OF BRITISH COLUMBIA
WORKSAFE BC
6951 Westminster Hwy, Richmond, BC, V7C 1C6
(604) 231-8888
Emp Here 2,000   *Sales* 6,838,297,600
SIC 6331 Fire, marine, and casualty insurance
Brian Erickson
Ian Shaw
Wendy Strugnell

D-U-N-S 24-860-0061   (HQ)
WORKSAFEBC
6951 Westminster Hwy Suite 600, Richmond, BC, V7C 1C6
(604) 231-8888
Sales 6,838,297,600
SIC 6331 Fire, marine, and casualty insurance
Diana Miles

D-U-N-S 25-387-9134   (SL)
ZE POWERGROUP INC
5920 No. 2 Rd Suite 130, Richmond, BC, V7C 4R9
(604) 244-1469
Emp Here 100   *Sales* 12,477,600
SIC 8741 Management services
Zak El-Ramly
Aiman El-Ramly
Manal El-Ramly
Fran Rolon
Ian Gordon
Gary Hagerty
Jim Cowan
Alexey Melekhin
Olga Gorstenko

Richmond, BC V7E

D-U-N-S 24-470-2432   (SL)
ANGELS THERE FOR YOU
12031 2nd Ave Suite 100, Richmond, BC, V7E 3L6
(604) 271-4427
Emp Here 45   *Sales* 10,207,485
SIC 8399 Social services, nec
Patricia Cruz

D-U-N-S 20-980-0957   (BR)
BOARD OF EDUCATION SCHOOL DIS-TRICT #38 (RICHMOND)
BOYD SECONDARY SCHOOL
(*Suby of* BOARD OF EDUCATION SCHOOL DISTRICT #38 (RICHMOND))
9200 No. 1 Rd, Richmond, BC, V7E 6L5
(604) 668-6615
Emp Here 81
SIC 8211 Elementary and secondary schools
Barbara Raynor

D-U-N-S 20-914-0180   (BR)
BOARD OF EDUCATION SCHOOL DIS-TRICT #38 (RICHMOND)
STEVESTON LONDON SECONDARY SCHOOL
(*Suby of* BOARD OF EDUCATION SCHOOL DISTRICT #38 (RICHMOND))
6600 Williams Rd, Richmond, BC, V7E 1K5
(604) 668-6668
Emp Here 75
SIC 8211 Elementary and secondary schools
Jim Allison

D-U-N-S 20-713-3997   (BR)
BOARD OF EDUCATION SCHOOL DIS-TRICT #38 (RICHMOND)
MCMATH SECONDARY SCHOOL
(*Suby of* BOARD OF EDUCATION SCHOOL DISTRICT #38 (RICHMOND))
4251 Garry St, Richmond, BC, V7E 2T9

(604) 718-4050
Emp Here 80
SIC 8211 Elementary and secondary schools
Mike Charlton

D-U-N-S 25-672-8791   (SL)
FORUM NATIONAL INVESTMENTS LTD
SNOWBIRD VACATIONS INTERNATIONAL
13040 No. 2 Rd Suite 180a, Richmond, BC, V7E 2G1
(604) 275-2170
Emp Here 123   *Sales* 470,349
SIC 8699 Membership organizations, nec
Daniel Clozza
Martin Tutschek
Scott Mcmanus
Jeff Teeny
Chris Yergensen
Mike Barret
Kazunari Kohno

D-U-N-S 24-504-8012   (HQ)
HENLEY DEVELOPMENT CORP
STEVESTON MARINE & HARDWARE
3560 Moncton St, Richmond, BC, V7E 3A2
(604) 275-2317
Emp Here 1   *Sales* 12,847,296
SIC 5251 Hardware stores
Iqbal Ladha
Salim Ladha
Nura Ladha

D-U-N-S 24-154-9617   (HQ)
LU & SONS ENTERPRISE LTD
SUPER GROCER & PHARMACY
12051 No. 1 Rd Suite 604, Richmond, BC, V7E 1T5
(604) 274-7878
Sales 13,707,600
SIC 5411 Grocery stores
Sam Lu

D-U-N-S 24-120-0620   (SL)
MASTER SECURITY LTD
3580 Moncton St Suite 212, Richmond, BC, V7E 3A4
(604) 278-3024
Emp Here 30   *Sales* 11,870,340
SIC 7382 Security systems services
Dorin Cichcruc

D-U-N-S 20-747-9478   (HQ)
PACIFIC NET & TWINE LTD
3731 Moncton St, Richmond, BC, V7E 3A5
(604) 274-7238
Emp Here 14   *Sales* 10,410,840
SIC 5091 Sporting and recreation goods
Frank Nakashima
Herbert Nakashima
Gary Nakashima

D-U-N-S 20-988-1940   (BR)
RICHMOND, CITY OF
WEST RICHMOND COMMUNITY CENTRE
(*Suby of* RICHMOND, CITY OF)
9180 No. 1 Rd, Richmond, BC, V7E 6L5
(604) 238-8400
Emp Here 120
SIC 8322 Individual and family services

D-U-N-S 25-613-7670   (SL)
S O S CHILDREN'S VILLAGE SOCIETY
S O S TREASURE COTTAGE
3800 Moncton St, Richmond, BC, V7E 3A6
(604) 274-8866
Emp Here 100   *Sales* 13,345,900
SIC 8399 Social services, nec
Barbara High

D-U-N-S 20-322-7525   (SL)
TRUSTING INVESTMENT & CONSULTING CO., LTD
10891 Hogarth Dr, Richmond, BC, V7E 3Z9
(778) 321-7399
Emp Here 120   *Sales* 32,802,000
SIC 6719 Holding companies, nec
Liang Ji Zhuang

Roberts Creek, BC V0N

D-U-N-S 20-310-2652   (SL)
EON BUILDING SYSTEMS INC
Gd, Roberts Creek, BC, V0N 2W0

Emp Here 47   *Sales* 14,986,843
SIC 1521 Single-family housing construction
Brock Patrick O'byrne
Brad Montchar
Robert Milsted
Don Devor

Rosedale, BC V0X

D-U-N-S 25-500-6850   (HQ)
EMIL ANDERSON MAINTENANCE CO. LTD
CONSTRUCTION
(*Suby of* PASS CONSTRUCTION CO. LTD)
51160 Sache St, Rosedale, BC, V0X 1X0
(604) 794-7414
Emp Here 100   *Sales* 40,390,720
SIC 1611 Highway and street construction
Robert J. Hasell
Mike Jacobs

D-U-N-S 20-120-5569   (SL)
K AND L CONTRACTING
10704 Hwy 9, Rosedale, BC, V0X 1X1
(604) 794-0107
Emp Here 24   *Sales* 10,732,176
SIC 5032 Brick, stone, and related material
Lincoln John Douglas

D-U-N-S 25-956-4847   (SL)
QUALITREE PROPAGATORS INC
51546 Ferry Rd, Rosedale, BC, V0X 1X2
(604) 794-3375
Emp Here 40   *Sales* 29,700,800
SIC 5193 Flowers and florists supplies
Henk Rozendaal
Tony Van Oort
Gary Neels
William Neels
Gerrit Rozendaal

D-U-N-S 24-150-3770   (HQ)
TY-CROP MANUFACTURING LTD
TYCROP
9880 Mcgrath Rd, Rosedale, BC, V0X 1X0
(604) 794-7078
Emp Here 300   *Sales* 194,631,696
SIC 5013 Motor vehicle supplies and new parts
Gary Teichrob
Scott Mason
Dave Keck

Saanichton, BC V8M

D-U-N-S 24-132-9960   (SL)
ASL ENVIRONMENTAL SCIENCES INC
ASL AQFLOW
6703 Rajpur Pl Unit 1, Saanichton, BC, V8M 1Z5
(250) 656-0177
Emp Here 42   *Sales* 10,646,580
SIC 8748 Business consulting, nec
David Lemon
Rene Shave
Garry Borstad
John Marko
Jan Buermans

D-U-N-S 24-798-1392   (SL)
B & C FOOD DISTRIBUTORS LTD
6711 Butler Cres, Saanichton, BC, V8M 1Z7
(250) 544-2333
Emp Here 95   *Sales* 79,379,815

SIC 5147 Meats and meat products
Donald Bold
Raymond Degirolamo
Glenn Miskulin
Michael Degirolamo
Shawn Watts
Rolf Nelson

D-U-N-S 20-808-3225   (BR)
BALMORAL INVESTMENTS LTD
QUALITY INN
(*Suby of* BALMORAL INVESTMENTS LTD)
2476 Mount Newton Cross Rd, Saanichton,
BC, V8M 2B8
(250) 652-1146
Emp Here 100
SIC 7011 Hotels and motels
Ross Borland

D-U-N-S 20-995-4494   (HQ)
BENSON INDUSTRIES LIMITED
2201 Keating Cross Rd, Saanichton, BC, V8M
2A5
(250) 652-4417
Emp Here 50   *Sales* 12,504,050
SIC 2434 Wood kitchen cabinets

D-U-N-S 24-249-4706   (HQ)
BUTLER BROTHERS SUPPLIES LTD
1851 Keating Cross Rd Unit 101, Saanichton,
BC, V8M 1W9
(250) 652-1680
Sales 16,340,450
SIC 3273 Ready-mixed concrete
Brian Butler

D-U-N-S 25-978-7042   (HQ)
CAMACC SYSTEMS INC
2261 Keating Cross Rd Unit 200b, Saanichton,
BC, V8M 2A5
(250) 652-3406
Emp Here 16   *Sales* 24,594,570
SIC 5065 Electronic parts and equipment, nec
Ho Jin Kim
Dennis Law
Jim Immler
Steve Comber

D-U-N-S 24-694-7378   (HQ)
CAPITAL CITY PAVING LTD
6588 Bryn Rd, Saanichton, BC, V8M 1X6
(250) 652-3626
Emp Here 10   *Sales* 15,146,520
SIC 1611 Highway and street construction
David Howells
Anthony Russell Trace

D-U-N-S 24-030-3156   (HQ)
**EMERGENCY AND HEALTH SERVICES
COMMISSION**
BC AMBULANCE SERVICE
2261 Keating Cross Rd, Saanichton, BC, V8M
2A5
(250) 953-3298
Emp Here 100   *Sales* 112,428,000
SIC 4119 Local passenger transportation, nec
Lynda Cranston
Michael Macdougall
Boyd Bert
David Butcher
Murray Ramsden
Cathy Ulrich

D-U-N-S 24-120-3678   (HQ)
JACE HOLDINGS LTD
THRIFTY FOODS
(*Suby of* EMPIRE COMPANY LIMITED)
6649 Butler Cres, Saanichton, BC, V8M 1Z7
(250) 483-1600
Emp Here 400
SIC 5141 Groceries, general line

D-U-N-S 24-376-9937   (BR)
JACE HOLDINGS LTD
THRIFTY KITCHENS
6772 Kirkpatrick Cres, Saanichton, BC, V8M
1Z9

(250) 483-1616
Emp Here 100   *Sales* 822,456
SIC 5411 Grocery stores
Troy Archibald

D-U-N-S 20-166-4948   (SL)
LEVEL GROUND TRADING LTD
1757 Sean Hts, Saanichton, BC, V8M 0B3
(250) 544-0932
Emp Here 30   *Sales* 25,067,310
SIC 5149 Groceries and related products, nec
Hugo Ciro
Laurie Klassen

D-U-N-S 24-454-9671   (HQ)
M.D. CHARLTON CO. LTD
(*Suby of* UKE 2000 HOLDINGS LIMITED)
2200 Keating Cross Rd Suite E, Saanichton,
BC, V8M 2A6
(250) 652-5266
Emp Here 20   *Sales* 22,805,874
SIC 5049 Professional equipment, nec
Alec Rossa
Joan Rossa

D-U-N-S 20-865-4384   (HQ)
O.K. INDUSTRIES LTD
TAYCO PAVING COMPANY
6702 Rajpur Pl, Saanichton, BC, V8M 1Z5
(250) 652-9211
Emp Here 60   *Sales* 50,488,400
SIC 1611 Highway and street construction
Buncy Sangha
Ranjit Sangha
David Clark

D-U-N-S 20-372-9566   (SL)
P & R TRUCK CENTRE LTD
2005 Keating Cross Rd, Saanichton, BC, V8M
2A5
(250) 652-9139
Emp Here 60   *Sales* 16,998,000
SIC 7538 General automotive repair shops
D Polack

D-U-N-S 24-154-0855   (HQ)
P. & R. REPAIRS LTD
P & R WESTERN STAR TRUCKS
2005 Keating Cross Rd, Saanichton, BC, V8M
2A5
(250) 652-9139
Emp Here 55   *Sales* 12,342,360
SIC 4212 Local trucking, without storage
Pat Mcconnell

D-U-N-S 24-032-3089   (HQ)
**PENINSULA CONSUMER SERVICES CO-
OPERATIVE**
PENINSULA CO-OP
2132 Keating Cross Rd Unit 1, Saanichton,
BC, V8M 2A6
(250) 652-5752
Emp Here 100   *Sales* 150,085,520
SIC 5541 Gasoline service stations
Dave Hoy
Ron Gaudet

D-U-N-S 24-579-8590   (SL)
POWER MEASUREMENT LTD
SCHNEIDER ELECTRIC
(*Suby of* SCHNEIDER ELECTRIC SE)
2195 Keating Cross Rd, Saanichton, BC, V8M
2A5
(250) 652-7100
Emp Here 360   *Sales* 98,773,200
SIC 3825 Instruments to measure electricity
Jacques Van Campen
Richard Stetler

D-U-N-S 20-698-5892   (HQ)
POWER MEASUREMENT, INC
SCHNEIDER ELECTRIC
(*Suby of* SCHNEIDER ELECTRIC SE)
2195 Keating Cross Rd, Saanichton, BC, V8M
2A5
(250) 652-7100
Sales 96,029,500
SIC 3825 Instruments to measure electricity

Jackie Trump
Jacques Van Campen

D-U-N-S 20-120-2004   (SL)
REDLEN TECHNOLOGIES INC
1763 Sean Hts Unit 123, Saanichton, BC, V8M
0A5
(250) 656-5411
Emp Here 55   *Sales* 10,474,310
SIC 3674 Semiconductors and related devices
Glenn Bindley
Ralph Turfus
Bob Armstrong
Glenn Bindley
Colin C. Harris
Jeromy Xue
Eric Erikson
Jim Balcom

D-U-N-S 20-713-5679   (BR)
SCHOOL DISTRICT 63 (SAANICH)
STELLY'S SECONDARY SCHOOL
1627 Stellys Cross Rd, Saanichton, BC, V8M
1S8
(250) 652-4401
Emp Here 100
SIC 8211 Elementary and secondary schools
Bruce Frith

D-U-N-S 24-798-2143   (SL)
SHERWOOD INDUSTRIES LTD
6782 Oldfield Rd, Saanichton, BC, V8M 2A3
(250) 652-6080
Emp Here 100   *Sales* 19,208,500
SIC 3433 Heating equipment, except electric
Thomas O'connor
Cherbel Yousief
Dan Marcil

D-U-N-S 24-374-3754   (SL)
SHERWOOD MARINE CENTRE LTD
6771 Oldfield Rd, Saanichton, BC, V8M 2A2
(250) 652-6520
Emp Here 26   *Sales* 12,950,028
SIC 5551 Boat dealers
Barry Sherwood
Muriel Sherwood
Bill Sherwood

D-U-N-S 20-333-0845   (SL)
SHERWOOD YACHT SALES
6771 Oldfield Rd, Saanichton, BC, V8M 2A2
(250) 652-5445
Emp Here 30   *Sales* 13,304,700
SIC 7389 Business services, nec
Barry Sherwood

D-U-N-S 24-797-0304   (SL)
SPECIFIC MECHANICAL SYSTEMS LTD
6848 Kirkpatrick Cres, Saanichton, BC, V8M
1Z9
(250) 652-2111
Emp Here 75   *Sales* 16,650,075
SIC 3556 Food products machinery
Philip Zacharias
William Cummings
Trevor Harmon

D-U-N-S 20-699-1452   (HQ)
UKE 2000 HOLDINGS LIMITED
2200 Keating Cross Rd Unit E, Saanichton,
BC, V8M 2A6
(250) 652-5266
Emp Here 2   *Sales* 26,830,440
SIC 5049 Professional equipment, nec
Alec Rossa
Joan Rossa

D-U-N-S 20-119-9353   (SL)
VANTREIGHT FARMS
8277 Central Saanich Rd, Saanichton, BC,
V8M 1T7
(250) 652-7777
Emp Here 30   *Sales* 22,275,600
SIC 5191 Farm supplies
Ian Vantreight

Salmo, BC V0G

D-U-N-S 25-768-9778   (HQ)
SUTCO CONTRACTING LTD
8561 Hwy 6, Salmo, BC, V0G 1Z0
(250) 357-2612
Emp Here 50   *Sales* 16,456,480
SIC 4212 Local trucking, without storage
Chris Sutherland
Melanie Sutherland

Salmon Arm, BC V1E

D-U-N-S 24-335-1389   (HQ)
ASKEW'S ENTERPRISES LTD
ASKEW'S FOOD
111 Lakeshore Dr Ne, Salmon Arm, BC, V1E
4N3
(250) 832-2668
Sales 28,701,750
SIC 6712 Bank holding companies
David Askew
Colleen Davis

D-U-N-S 20-424-4263   (HQ)
ASKEW'S FOOD SERVICE LTD
ASKEW'S FOODS
(*Suby of* ASKEW'S ENTERPRISES LTD)
111 Lakeshore Dr Ne, Salmon Arm, BC, V1E
4N3
(250) 832-2064
Emp Here 55   *Sales* 30,815,085
SIC 5411 Grocery stores
David Askew
Colleen Davis

D-U-N-S 20-106-8640   (SL)
BRABY MOTORS LTD
1250 Trans Canada Hwy Sw, Salmon Arm,
BC, V1E 1T1
(250) 832-8053
Emp Here 32   *Sales* 15,938,496
SIC 5511 New and used car dealers
Derrrick Braby
Michael Braby

D-U-N-S 20-334-9050   (SL)
CANADIAN TIRE ASSOCIATE STORE LTD
2090 10 Ave Sw, Salmon Arm, BC, V1E 0E1
(250) 832-5474
Emp Here 49   *Sales* 24,405,822
SIC 5531 Auto and home supply stores
Justin Mondor

D-U-N-S 20-315-5957   (SL)
D & K CROSS SALES LTD.
CANADIAN TIRE NO 482
1151 10 Ave Sw Suite 300, Salmon Arm, BC,
V1E 1T3
(250) 832-9600
Emp Here 80   *Sales* 21,412,160
SIC 5251 Hardware stores
David Samuel Cross
Karen Joan Cross

D-U-N-S 24-174-1953   (BR)
DOEPKER INDUSTRIES LTD
(*Suby of* DOEPKER INDUSTRIES LTD)
5301 40 Ave Se, Salmon Arm, BC, V1E 1X1

Emp Here 100
SIC 3715 Truck trailers
Paul Cairney

D-U-N-S 25-735-1908   (BR)
FEDERATED CO-OPERATIVES LIMITED
(*Suby of* FEDERATED CO-OPERATIVES
LIMITED)
8160 Trans Can Hwy Ne, Salmon Arm, BC,
V1E 2S6
(250) 833-1200
Emp Here 200
SIC 2436 Softwood veneer and plywood

Darrell Embley

D-U-N-S 24-370-2719   (SL)
HOBAN CONSTRUCTION LTD
HOBAN EQUIPMENT
5121 46 Ave Se, Salmon Arm, BC, V1E 1X2
(250) 832-8831
Emp Here 60   *Sales* 15,146,520
SIC 1611 Highway and street construction
Clayton Hoban
Penny Hoban

D-U-N-S 20-551-1947   (SL)
HOBAN EQUIPMENT LTD
2691 13 Ave Sw, Salmon Arm, BC, V1E 3K1
(250) 832-8831
Emp Here 100   *Sales* 25,244,200
SIC 1611 Highway and street construction
Clayton Hoban

D-U-N-S 24-144-4095   (HQ)
JACOBSON FORD SALES LTD
450 Trans Canada Hwy Sw, Salmon Arm, BC, V1E 1S9
(250) 832-2101
Emp Here 5   *Sales* 40,903,200
SIC 5511 New and used car dealers
Michael Vandermeer
Mark R Schneider

D-U-N-S 25-360-5471   (SL)
R.P. JOHNSON CONSTRUCTION LTD
CENTENOKA PARK MALL
360 Trans Canada Hwy Sw Suite 317, Salmon Arm, BC, V1E 1B6
(250) 832-9731
Emp Here 200   *Sales* 44,174,200
SIC 6512 Nonresidential building operators
Douglas Johnson
Lance Johnson

D-U-N-S 25-388-2997   (SL)
SALMON ARM CHEV BUICK GMC LTD
SALMON ARM GM
3901 11 Ave Ne, Salmon Arm, BC, V1E 2S2
(250) 832-6066
Emp Here 35   *Sales* 17,432,730
SIC 5511 New and used car dealers
Mark Bannister

D-U-N-S 24-578-1349   (HQ)
SALMON ARM SAVINGS AND CREDIT UNION
370 Lakeshore Dr Ne, Salmon Arm, BC, V1E 1E4
(250) 832-8011
Emp Here 80   *Sales* 23,741,339
SIC 6062 State credit unions
Michael Wagner
June Stewart
Richard Chmilar

D-U-N-S 24-247-5960   (BR)
SOBEYS WEST INC
CANADA SAFEWAY NO. 171
(*Suby of* EMPIRE COMPANY LIMITED)
360 Trans Canada Hwy Sw Unit 1, Salmon Arm, BC, V1E 1B4
(250) 832-8086
Emp Here 85
SIC 5411 Grocery stores
Dave Nemrava

D-U-N-S 24-867-5647   (SL)
VALID MANUFACTURING LTD
5320 48 Ave Se, Salmon Arm, BC, V1E 1X2
(250) 832-6477
Emp Here 120   *Sales* 20,627,282
SIC 3716 Motor homes
Gerald Clancy

Salt Spring Island, BC V8K

D-U-N-S 24-456-7749   (SL)
123 ENTERPRISES LTD

COUNTRY GROCER SALTSPRING
374 Lower Ganges Rd, Salt Spring Island, BC, V8K 2V7
(250) 537-4144
Emp Here 70   *Sales* 20,543,390
SIC 5411 Grocery stores
Paul Large
Leigh Large

D-U-N-S 20-567-0792   (SL)
CANADIAN FEDERATION OF UNIVERSITY WOMEN
Gd, Salt Spring Island, BC, V8K 2W1

Emp Here 46   *Sales* 10,434,318
SIC 8399 Social services, nec
Margaret Baker

D-U-N-S 24-150-2251   (SL)
GREENWOODS ELDERCARE SOCIETY
133 Blain Rd, Salt Spring Island, BC, V8K 1Z9
(250) 537-5561
Emp Here 49   *Sales* 11,114,817
SIC 8399 Social services, nec
Andrew Brown

D-U-N-S 20-512-1742   (SL)
MOUAT'S TRADING CO. LTD
MOUAT'S HOME HARDWARE
106 Fulford-Ganges Rd, Salt Spring Island, BC, V8K 2S3
(250) 537-5551
Emp Here 54   *Sales* 11,088,522
SIC 5399 Miscellaneous general merchandise
Kevin Bell
Thomas Toynbee
Kenneth Almond
Daniel Bell
Nicola Bell
Micheal Bell
Gerald Bell

Savona, BC V0K

D-U-N-S 24-679-2811   (HQ)
SAVONA SPECIALTY PLYWOOD CO. LTD
(*Suby of* ASPEN PLANERS LTD)
7273 Kamloops Lake Dr, Savona, BC, V0K 2J0
(250) 373-5600
Sales 35,773,920
SIC 5031 Lumber, plywood, and millwork
Surinder Ghog
David Hugh Gray

Sechelt, BC V0N

D-U-N-S 20-881-3795   (SL)
COAST STORAGE & CONTAINERS LTD
5674 Teredo St Suite 102, Sechelt, BC, V0N 3A0
(604) 883-2444
Emp Here 10   *Sales* 16,453,017
SIC 7359 Equipment rental and leasing, nec
Vaughan Anthony Kooyman
Daniel Freedman

D-U-N-S 20-175-7940   (SL)
ENDRESS SALES AND DISTRIBUTION LTD
CANADIAN TIRE
4380 Sunshine Coast Hwy Rr 1, Sechelt, BC, V0N 3A1
(604) 885-6611
Emp Here 50   *Sales* 24,903,900
SIC 5531 Auto and home supply stores
Jeff Endress

D-U-N-S 20-865-8344   (SL)
SOUTH COAST FORD SALES LTD
5606 Wharf Rd, Sechelt, BC, V0N 3A0
(604) 885-3281
Emp Here 23   *Sales* 11,455,794

SIC 5511 New and used car dealers
Robert William Copping

D-U-N-S 20-124-7942   (SL)
SUNSHINE COAST ASSOCIATION FOR COMMUNITY LIVING
5711 Mermaid St Suite 105, Sechelt, BC, V0N 3A3
(604) 885-7455
Emp Here 40   *Sales* 15,896,560
SIC 8699 Membership organizations, nec
Glen Mclughan

D-U-N-S 20-621-9461   (HQ)
TRAIL BAY DEVELOPMENTS LTD
CLAYTON'S HERITAGE MARKET
5755 Cowrie St Suite 1, Sechelt, BC, V0N 3A0
(604) 885-9812
Emp Here 1   *Sales* 26,412,930
SIC 5411 Grocery stores
Neil Clayton
John Clayton
Richard Clayton

Sicamous, BC V0E

D-U-N-S 25-678-7003   (SL)
PARKLAND BUILDING SUPPLIES (1998) LTD
PARKLAND
1125 Eagle Pa Way Rr 2, Sicamous, BC, V0E 2V2
(250) 836-2514
Emp Here 30   *Sales* 13,415,220
SIC 5039 Construction materials, nec
Brian Tancock
Janet Tancock

Sidney, BC V8L

D-U-N-S 25-101-3322   (HQ)
AXYS TECHNOLOGIES INC
2035 Mills Rd W, Sidney, BC, V8L 5X2
(250) 655-5850
Sales 10,074,384
SIC 8748 Business consulting, nec
Peggy Sue Reily
David Thomas
Peter Berrang
Paul Erickson

D-U-N-S 25-754-0567   (HQ)
BEACON COMMUNITY SERVICES
9860 Third St, Sidney, BC, V8L 4R2
(250) 658-6407
Sales 719,930,500
SIC 8699 Membership organizations, nec
Isobel Mackenzie

D-U-N-S 20-119-3794   (HQ)
NICHOLSON MANUFACTURING LTD
(*Suby of* KADANT INC.)
9896 Galaran Rd, Sidney, BC, V8L 4K4
(250) 656-3131
Sales 26,640,120
SIC 3553 Woodworking machinery
Douglas Jeffrey
Jeffrey Powell
Jonathan Painter

D-U-N-S 20-588-4190   (HQ)
PHILBROOK'S BOATYARD LTD
TOWER MILLWORKS, DIV OF
2324 Harbour Rd, Sidney, BC, V8L 2P6
(250) 656-1157
Emp Here 65   *Sales* 20,145,870
SIC 3732 Boatbuilding and repairing
Harold Irwin
Andrew Irwin

D-U-N-S 25-290-6953   (SL)
RMW HOLDINGS LTD

2066 Henry Ave W, Sidney, BC, V8L 5Y1
(250) 656-5314
Emp Here 2   *Sales* 10,141,500
SIC 3441 Fabricated structural Metal

D-U-N-S 20-119-6896   (SL)
SCOTT PLASTICS LTD
2065 Henry Ave W, Sidney, BC, V8L 5Z6
(250) 656-8102
Emp Here 121   *Sales* 23,242,285
SIC 3429 Hardware, nec
Ian Scott
Kevin Scott
Robin Richardson
Almeda Scott

D-U-N-S 25-215-4638   (HQ)
SEAFIRST INSURANCE BROKERS LTD
9769 Fifth St Suite A2, Sidney, BC, V8L 2X1
(250) 656-9886
Emp Here 5   *Sales* 21,201,500
SIC 6411 Insurance agents, brokers, and service
Douglas Strong
Douglas Guedes

D-U-N-S 24-995-8588   (SL)
SGS AXYS ANALYTICAL SERVICES LTD
2045 Mills Rd W, Sidney, BC, V8L 5X2
(250) 655-5800
Emp Here 118   *Sales* 37,726,606
SIC 8734 Testing laboratories
Arun Deshpande
John Cosgrove
Steven Dorry
Marcel Costa

D-U-N-S 20-624-2059   (HQ)
SIDNEY TIRE LTD
SIDNEY TIRE & AUTO SERVICE
9817 Resthaven Dr, Sidney, BC, V8L 3E7
(250) 656-5544
Emp Here 16   *Sales* 15,938,496
SIC 5531 Auto and home supply stores
Hendrikus Vissers
Nick Lansdorp
Herbert Vissers

D-U-N-S 20-993-6749   (HQ)
SLEGG LIMITED PARTNERSHIP
WSB TITAN, DIV OF
(*Suby of* GMS INC.)
2030 Malaview Ave W, Sidney, BC, V8L 5X6
(250) 656-1125
Emp Here 40   *Sales* 85,444,200
SIC 5031 Lumber, plywood, and millwork
Timothy Urquhart
Ronald Slegg
Robert Slegg

D-U-N-S 25-271-0918   (BR)
SOBEYS WEST INC
SAVE ON FOODS
(*Suby of* EMPIRE COMPANY LIMITED)
2345 Beacon Ave, Sidney, BC, V8L 1W9
(250) 656-2735
Emp Here 80
SIC 5411 Grocery stores
Justine Mcgregor

D-U-N-S 20-713-0329   (SL)
VANISLE MARINA CO. LTD
(*Suby of* SIDNEY MARINA CO. LTD)
2320 Harbour Rd, Sidney, BC, V8L 2P6
(250) 656-1138
Emp Here 63   *Sales* 24,804,612
SIC 4493 Marinas
Mark Dickinson
Allan Dickinson

D-U-N-S 20-693-7745   (HQ)
VICTORIAN EPICURE INC
EPICURE SELECTIONS
10555 West Saanich Rd, Sidney, BC, V8L 6A8
(250) 656-5751
Sales 83,557,700
SIC 5149 Groceries and related products, nec

Sylvie Rochette

D-U-N-S 20-584-8013   (SL)
VIKING AIR LIMITED
(*Suby of* WESTERKIRK CAPITAL INC)
1959 De Havilland Way, Sidney, BC, V8L 5V5
(250) 656-7227
Emp Here 455   *Sales* 132,336,750
SIC 3728 Aircraft parts and equipment, nec
David Curtis
Peter Winters
Bradley Douglas
Terry Cunningham
Lawrence Pentland

Skookumchuck, BC V0B

D-U-N-S 24-254-9421   (BR)
DCT CHAMBERS TRUCKING LTD
GLEN TRANSPORT, DIV OF
(*Suby of* DCT CHAMBERS TRUCKING LTD)
4631 Farstad Way Rr 1, Skookumchuck, BC,
V0B 2E0
(250) 422-3535
Emp Here 86
SIC 4212 Local trucking, without storage
Scott Henderson

D-U-N-S 20-305-9035   (SL)
SKOOKUMCHUCK PULP INC
SKOOKUMCHUCK PULP MILL
(*Suby of* CAPITAL ASSETS HOLDINGS (L)
BERHAD)
4501 Farstad Way, Skookumchuck, BC, V0B
2E0
(250) 422-3261
Emp Here 300   *Sales* 110,291,100
SIC 2611 Pulp mills
Andy Reyes
Gavin Baxter
Jonathan Tan

Smithers, BC V0J

D-U-N-S 20-572-7787   (HQ)
AWG NORTHERN INDUSTRIES INC
3424 16 Hwy E Rr 6, Smithers, BC, V0J 2N6
(250) 847-9211
Emp Here 20   *Sales* 28,050,750
SIC 8741 Management services
Daniel Young
Laura Stanton
Doug Peters

D-U-N-S 24-899-6498   (HQ)
**BANDSTRA TRANSPORTATION SYSTEMS
LTD**
3394 Hwy 16 E, Smithers, BC, V0J 2N0
(250) 847-2057
Emp Here 35   *Sales* 36,615,668
SIC 4213 Trucking, except local
John Jr Bandstra
Beverley Bandstra
Christina Bandstra
Jack Bandstra
Ronald Bandstra
Tiffany Bandstra
Richard Bandstra
Karen Bandstra
Phillip Bandstra
Sharon Bandstra

D-U-N-S 20-957-5547   (SL)
BULKLEY VALLEY HEALTH COUNCIL
BULKLEY VALLEY DISTRICT HOSPITAL
3950 8 Ave, Smithers, BC, V0J 2N0
(250) 847-2611
Emp Here 130   *Sales* 14,440,400
SIC 8062 General medical and surgical hospitals
Shirley Butchart

D-U-N-S 25-216-8646   (HQ)
CENTRAL MOUNTAIN AIR LTD
(*Suby of* 580741 BRITISH COLUMBIA LTD)
6431 Airport Rd, Smithers, BC, V0J 2N2
(250) 877-5000
Emp Here 60   *Sales* 79,338,000
SIC 4512 Air transportation, scheduled
Douglas Ellwood Mccrea
Lindsay Clougher

D-U-N-S 25-160-1696   (SL)
**COAST MOUNTAIN CHEVROLET PONTIAC
BUICK GMC LTD**
COAST MOUNTAIN GM
4038 16 Hwy E Rr 6, Smithers, BC, V0J 2N6
(250) 847-2214
Emp Here 22   *Sales* 10,957,716
SIC 5511 New and used car dealers
Dennis Groves

D-U-N-S 24-931-4097   (HQ)
HY-TECH DRILLING LTD
2715 Tatlow Rd, Smithers, BC, V0J 2N5
(250) 847-9301
Emp Here 50   *Sales* 11,671,750
SIC 1081 Metal mining services
Harvey Tremblay
Corry Tremblay

D-U-N-S 20-981-7100   (BR)
SCHOOL DISTRICT NO. 54 (BULKLEY VALLEY)
3377 Third Ave, Smithers, BC, V0J 2N3
(250) 847-4846
Emp Here 400
SIC 8211 Elementary and secondary schools

D-U-N-S 20-591-3663   (BR)
**SMITHERS SCHOOL BOARD DISTRICT #54
(BULKLEY VALLEY)**
SMITHERS SECONDARY SCHOOL
4408 Third Ave, Smithers, BC, V0J 2N3
(250) 847-2231
Emp Here 90
SIC 8211 Elementary and secondary schools
Jaksun Grice

D-U-N-S 24-363-3893   (BR)
SOBEYS WEST INC
SMITHERS SAFEWAY
(*Suby of* EMPIRE COMPANY LIMITED)
3664 16 Hwy E, Smithers, BC, V0J 2N6
(250) 847-4744
Emp Here 130
SIC 5411 Grocery stores
Floyd Krishan

D-U-N-S 24-368-5377   (BR)
WEST FRASER MILLS LTD
PACIFIC INLAND RESOURCES, DIV OF
(*Suby of* WEST FRASER TIMBER CO. LTD)
2375 Tatlow Rd, Smithers, BC, V0J 2N5
(250) 847-2656
Emp Here 250
SIC 2421 Sawmills and planing mills, general
Dean Macdonald

D-U-N-S 20-814-5875   (SL)
WET'SUWET'EN TREATY OFFICE
3873 1st Ave, Smithers, BC, V0J 2N0
(250) 847-3630
Emp Here 33   *Sales* 13,114,662
SIC 8699 Membership organizations, nec
Debbie Pierre

Sooke, BC V9Z

D-U-N-S 25-229-6199   (SL)
LOGAN GROUP PARTNERSHIP
VILLAGE FOOD MARKETS
6661 Sooke Rd Suite 103, Sooke, BC, V9Z
0A1
Emp Here 90   *Sales* 26,412,930

SIC 5411 Grocery stores
Scott Logan

D-U-N-S 20-803-1653   (SL)
OTTER POINT FIRE DEPARTMENT
3727 Otter Point Rd, Sooke, BC, V9Z 0K1
(250) 642-6211
Emp Here 25   *Sales* 11,230,475
SIC 7389 Business services, nec
Kevin Brehart

Sparwood, BC V0B

D-U-N-S 24-128-2347   (BR)
JOY GLOBAL (CANADA) LTD
KOMATSU MINING
(*Suby of* KOMATSU LTD.)
749 Douglas Fir Rd Suite 618, Sparwood, BC,
V0B 2G0
(250) 433-4100
Emp Here 80
SIC 3532 Mining machinery
Steve Droste

D-U-N-S 25-360-9085   (BR)
TECK COAL LIMITED
LINE CREEK OPERATIONS
(*Suby of* TECK RESOURCES LIMITED)
Gd, Sparwood, BC, V0B 2G0
(250) 425-2555
Emp Here 530
SIC 1221 Bituminous coal and lignite-surface
mining
Marcia Smith

D-U-N-S 20-552-8180   (BR)
TECK COAL LIMITED
COAL MOUNTAIN OPERATIONS
(*Suby of* TECK RESOURCES LIMITED)
2261 Corbin Rd, Sparwood, BC, V0B 2G0
(250) 425-6305
Emp Here 320
SIC 1221 Bituminous coal and lignite-surface
mining
Nick Burt

D-U-N-S 24-367-8856   (BR)
TECK COAL LIMITED
ELKVIEW OPERATIONS
(*Suby of* TECK RESOURCES LIMITED)
Gd, Sparwood, BC, V0B 2G0
(250) 425-8325
Emp Here 1,060
SIC 1221 Bituminous coal and lignite-surface
mining
Larry Davey

D-U-N-S 24-390-4534   (SL)
TERCON CONSTRUCTION LTD
610 Douglas Fir, Sparwood, BC, V0B 2G0

Emp Here 40   *Sales* 11,340,960
SIC 1611 Highway and street construction
Milan Soucek
Joseph Hanna

Squamish, BC V8B

D-U-N-S 24-679-0898   (SL)
CARBON ENGINEERING LTD
37321 Galbraith Rd, Squamish, BC, V8B 0A2
(778) 386-1457
Emp Here 45   *Sales* 12,449,700
SIC 2813 Industrial gases
Steve Oldham
Susan Koch
David Keith

D-U-N-S 24-361-3390   (SL)
MILLER CAPILANO MAINTENANCE CORPORATION

(*Suby of* MILLER GROUP INC)
38921 Midway, Squamish, BC, V8B 0J5
(604) 892-1010
Emp Here 50   *Sales* 12,622,100
SIC 1611 Highway and street construction
Blair Mcarthur
W Barrie Brayford
Barry Drummond
Steven Drummond

D-U-N-S 24-072-8360   (HQ)
SCHOOL DISTRICT NO. 48 (HOWE SOUND)
37866 2nd Ave, Squamish, BC, V8B 0A2
(604) 892-3421
Emp Here 30   *Sales* 44,603,550
SIC 8211 Elementary and secondary schools
Richard Erickson
John Hetherington
Nancy Edwards

D-U-N-S 25-018-3969   (HQ)
SEA TO SKY COMMUNITY HEALTH COUNCIL
SQUAMISH GENERAL HOSPITAL
(*Suby of* GOVERNMENT OF THE
PROVINCE OF BRITISH COLUMBIA)
38140 Behrner Dr, Squamish, BC, V8B 0J3
(604) 892-9337
Emp Here 200   *Sales* 25,437,320
SIC 8062 General medical and surgical hospitals
Brian Kines
Gloria Healy
Kathryn Kiltatrick

D-U-N-S 25-325-4866   (SL)
SEA TO SKY FORD SALES LTD
SEA TO SKY FORD
1100 Commercial Pl, Squamish, BC, V8B 0S7
(604) 892-3673
Emp Here 30   *Sales* 14,942,340
SIC 5511 New and used car dealers
Donald Carson
Enzo Milia

D-U-N-S 20-101-3112   (SL)
SEA TO SKY HELI RIGGING LTD
Gd, Squamish, BC, V8B 0J2

Emp Here 45   *Sales* 14,613,930
SIC 4522 Air transportation, nonscheduled
David Nagle

D-U-N-S 20-623-2159   (SL)
SQUAMISH TERMINALS LTD
(*Suby of* FRS CAPITAL CORP.)
37500 Third Ave, Squamish, BC, V8B 0B1
(604) 892-3511
Emp Here 110   *Sales* 43,309,640
SIC 4491 Marine cargo handling
Russ Peters

D-U-N-S 24-319-5117   (BR)
WAL-MART CANADA CORP
WAL-MART
(*Suby of* WALMART INC.)
39210 Discovery Way Suite 1015, Squamish,
BC, V8B 0N1
(604) 815-4625
Emp Here 120
SIC 5311 Department stores

Stewart, BC V0T

D-U-N-S 24-327-0142   (SL)
MORE CORE DIAMOND DRILLING SERVICES LTD
EXPLORATION DRILLING
2511 Hwy 37a, Stewart, BC, V0T 1W0
(250) 636-9156
Emp Here 75   *Sales* 18,463,950
SIC 1799 Special trade contractors, nec
Sean Patrick Pownall

▲ Public Company   ■ Public Company Family Member   **HQ** Headquarters   **BR** Branch   **SL** Single Location

Summerland, BC V0H

D-U-N-S 24-593-4005   (HQ)
HAGENS TRAVEL (1957 OPERATIONS) LTD
HAGEN'S TRAVEL & CRUISES
13606 Kelly Ave, Summerland, BC, V0H 1Z0
(250) 494-5202
Emp Here 1   *Sales* 17,158,911
SIC 4724 Travel agencies
  Michael Scott-Iversen

D-U-N-S 25-066-7193   (SL)
I.G.A. PLUS SUMMERLAND NO 155
7519 Prairie Valley Rd, Summerland, BC, V0H 1Z4
(250) 494-4376
Emp Here 40   *Sales* 10,966,080
SIC 5411 Grocery stores
  Dennis Candy

D-U-N-S 24-071-2497   (SL)
SUN-VIEW INDUSTRIES LTD
SUN-VIEW POWDER COATING
15915 Bentley Pl, Summerland, BC, V0H 1Z3
(250) 494-1327
Emp Here 24   *Sales* 11,953,872
SIC 5561 Recreational vehicle dealers
  David Miller
  Kent Miller
  Sherry Campbell
  Lorraine Miller

Sun Peaks, BC V0E

D-U-N-S 20-365-3829   (SL)
NIPPON CABLE (CANADA) HOLDINGS LTD
SUN PEAKS RESORT
1280 Alpine Rd Rr 1, Sun Peaks, BC, V0E 5N0
(250) 578-7232
Emp Here 250   *Sales* 23,917,000
SIC 7011 Hotels and motels
  Darcy Alexander
  Masayoshi Ohkubo
  Shungo Ohkubo

Surrey, BC V3R

D-U-N-S 20-622-0642   (SL)
APPLEWOOD NISSAN INC
15257 Fraser Hwy, Surrey, BC, V3R 3P3
(604) 589-1775
Emp Here 24   *Sales* 12,451,950
SIC 5511 New and used car dealers
  Glen Daman

D-U-N-S 25-723-7979   (HQ)
CENTRAL CITY BREWERS & DISTILLERS LTD
11411 Bridgeview Dr, Surrey, BC, V3R 0C2
(604) 588-2337
Sales 24,432,800
SIC 5921 Liquor stores
  Darryll Frost
  Tim Barnes
  Daryl Hrynkiw

D-U-N-S 24-120-7310   (BR)
COMPAGNIE DES CHEMINS DE FER NA-TIONAUX DU CANADA
(*Suby of* COMPAGNIE DES CHEMINS DE FER NATIONAUX DU CANADA)
13477 116 Ave, Surrey, BC, V3R 6W4
(604) 589-6552
Emp Here 150
SIC 4111 Local and suburban transit
  Derrick Colasimone

D-U-N-S 24-694-2940   (SL)
CONCEPT 2000 REAL ESTATE (1989) IN-

CORPORATED
REMAX 2000 REALTY
15127 100 Ave Suite 103, Surrey, BC, V3R 0N9
(604) 583-2000
Emp Here 100   *Sales* 27,175,600
SIC 6531 Real estate agents and managers
  Verne Gatzke

D-U-N-S 24-797-3852   (SL)
CROSSTOWN METAL INDUSTRIES LTD
13133 115 Ave Suite 100, Surrey, BC, V3R 2V8
(604) 589-3133
Emp Here 50   *Sales* 10,141,500
SIC 3444 Sheet Metalwork
  Randy Popowich

D-U-N-S 24-492-1268   (SL)
D.G.S. CONSTRUCTION COMPANY LTD
13761 116 Ave Unit A101, Surrey, BC, V3R 0T2
(604) 584-2214
Emp Here 30   *Sales* 14,121,930
SIC 1542 Nonresidential construction, nec
  George Rossi
  Dennis Rossi

D-U-N-S 20-641-6559   (SL)
DOLO INVESTIGATIONS LTD
10090 152 St Suite 408, Surrey, BC, V3R 8X8
(604) 951-1600
Emp Here 50   *Sales* 22,174,500
SIC 7389 Business services, nec
  Thomas Dolo

D-U-N-S 20-690-9603   (HQ)
E CARE CONTACT CENTERS LTD
15225 104 Ave Suite 400, Surrey, BC, V3R 6Y8
(604) 587-6200
Emp Here 20   *Sales* 334,454,000
SIC 7389 Business services, nec
  Kim Dethomas

D-U-N-S 20-918-4910   (SL)
FLAG CHEVROLET-CHEVROLET TRUCK LTD
15250 104 Ave, Surrey, BC, V3R 6N8
(604) 584-7411
Emp Here 75   *Sales* 47,196,000
SIC 5511 New and used car dealers
  Sherrold Haddad
  Janet Lea

D-U-N-S 20-741-4363   (SL)
FREEWAY IMPORTS LTD
FREEWAY MAZDA
15420 104 Ave, Surrey, BC, V3R 1N8
(604) 583-7121
Emp Here 50   *Sales* 24,903,900
SIC 5511 New and used car dealers
  Rodney Alan Vines
  Grant Hansen
  Dean Hamilton

D-U-N-S 24-372-0948   (SL)
GLOBAL AGRICULTURE TRANS-LOADING INC
11678 130 St, Surrey, BC, V3R 2Y3
(604) 580-1786
Emp Here 45   *Sales* 17,341,200
SIC 4789 Transportation services, nec
  Bikramajit Sangha
  Amrik Sangha

D-U-N-S 20-565-0067   (SL)
GUILDFORD VENTURES LTD
SHERATON VANCOUVER GUILDFORD HOTEL
15269 104 Ave, Surrey, BC, V3R 1N5
(604) 582-9288
Emp Here 200   *Sales* 18,538,000
SIC 7011 Hotels and motels
  Azim Jamal
  Firoz Alibhai Kassam

D-U-N-S 24-536-3387   (SL)

HALLMARK FORD SALES LIMITED
10025 152 St, Surrey, BC, V3R 4G6
(604) 584-1222
Emp Here 72   *Sales* 45,308,160
SIC 5511 New and used car dealers
  Jeff Hall
  Richard Hall

D-U-N-S 25-760-3043   (SL)
HAWTHORNE PARK INC
MCDONALD'S RESTAURANTS
14476 104 Ave, Surrey, BC, V3R 1L9
(604) 587-1040
Emp Here 100   *Sales* 4,287,300
SIC 5812 Eating places
  Leanne Grunau
  Christine Vit

D-U-N-S 20-621-8901   (BR)
HUDSON'S BAY COMPANY
THE BAY
(*Suby of* HUDSON'S BAY COMPANY)
1400 Guildford Town Ctr, Surrey, BC, V3R 7B7
(604) 588-2111
Emp Here 200
SIC 5311 Department stores
  Connie Savicevic

D-U-N-S 25-272-7458   (BR)
INSURANCE CORPORATION OF BRITISH COLUMBIA
I C B C
(*Suby of* GOVERNMENT OF THE PROVINCE OF BRITISH COLUMBIA)
10262 152a St, Surrey, BC, V3R 6T8
(604) 584-3211
Emp Here 125
SIC 6331 Fire, marine, and casualty insurance
  Kellee Irwin

D-U-N-S 25-967-5846   (SL)
LANKI INVESTIGATIONS INC
9547 152 St Suite 113, Surrey, BC, V3R 5Y5
(604) 930-0399
Emp Here 30   *Sales* 17,397,720
SIC 6411 Insurance agents, brokers, and service
  Guy Lanki

D-U-N-S 24-311-2562   (BR)
LONDON DRUGS LIMITED
(*Suby of* H.Y. LOUIE CO. LIMITED)
2340 Guildford Town Ctr, Surrey, BC, V3R 7B9
(604) 588-7881
Emp Here 115
SIC 5912 Drug stores and proprietary stores
  Meena Nahal

D-U-N-S 24-327-0134   (SL)
MACKENZIE SAWMILL LTD
11732 130 St, Surrey, BC, V3R 2Y3
(604) 580-4500
Emp Here 120   *Sales* 23,084,400
SIC 2421 Sawmills and planing mills, general
  Rob Sohi

D-U-N-S 25-318-1705   (BR)
MCDONALD'S RESTAURANTS OF CANADA LIMITED
MCDONALD'S #8159
(*Suby of* MCDONALD'S CORPORATION)
10250 152 St, Surrey, BC, V3R 6N7
(604) 587-3380
Emp Here 120
SIC 5812 Eating places
  Katelyn Harvey

D-U-N-S 25-318-1713   (BR)
MCDONALD'S RESTAURANTS OF CANADA LIMITED
MCDONALD'S #8485
(*Suby of* MCDONALD'S CORPORATION)
1000 Guildford Town Ctr, Surrey, BC, V3R 7C3

Emp Here 100
SIC 5812 Eating places

D-U-N-S 20-378-1711   (SL)
MERCEDES-BENZ SURREY
(*Suby of* OPEN ROAD AUTO GROUP LTD)
15508 104 Ave, Surrey, BC, V3R 1N8
(604) 581-7662
Emp Here 58   *Sales* 36,498,240
SIC 5511 New and used car dealers
  Jeremy Schaab

D-U-N-S 24-579-3021   (SL)
METRO-CAN CONSTRUCTION LTD
10470 152 St Suite 520, Surrey, BC, V3R 0Y3
(604) 583-1174
Emp Here 50   *Sales* 14,429,150
SIC 1522 Residential construction, nec
  Don Voth
  Dennis Schwab

D-U-N-S 24-072-5739   (HQ)
OVERLAND WEST FREIGHT LINES LTD
11398 Bridgeview Dr, Surrey, BC, V3R 0C2
(604) 888-6300
Emp Here 20   *Sales* 20,570,600
SIC 4213 Trucking, except local
  Ryan Robinson
  Carl Levesque
  Rob Croteau
  Steve Lauridsen

D-U-N-S 20-190-6190   (SL)
PARK PLACE SENIORS LIVING INC
HILTON VILLA CARE CENTRE
(*Suby of* PARK PLACE SENIORS LIVING)
13525 Hilton Rd, Surrey, BC, V3R 5J3
(604) 588-3424
Emp Here 700   *Sales* 47,828,200
SIC 8051 Skilled nursing care facilities
  Al Jina
  Jenny Jina

D-U-N-S 24-797-2107   (SL)
PARTNERS YOUR SECRETARIAL SOLUTIONS
14680 110 Ave, Surrey, BC, V3R 2A8
(604) 588-9926
Emp Here 49   *Sales* 10,548,962
SIC 7338 Secretarial and court reporting

D-U-N-S 20-049-3000   (HQ)
PREMIER BATHROOMS CANADA LTD
PREMIER CARE IN BATHING
14716 104 Ave, Surrey, BC, V3R 1M3
(604) 588-9688
Emp Here 75   *Sales* 21,412,160
SIC 5211 Lumber and other building materials
  Iain Whyte
  Philip Barnes
  Dave Harmon

D-U-N-S 20-157-7041   (SL)
PRO DRAFT INC
14727 108 Ave Unit 205, Surrey, BC, V3R 1V9
(604) 589-6425
Emp Here 25   *Sales* 11,087,250
SIC 7389 Business services, nec
  Tony Zepedo

D-U-N-S 25-369-3659   (BR)
PWC MANAGEMENT SERVICES LP
(*Suby of* PRICEWATERHOUSECOOPERS LLP)
10190 152a St 3 Fl, Surrey, BC, V3R 1J7
(604) 806-7000
Emp Here 900
SIC 8721 Accounting, auditing, and book-keeping
  John Delucchi

D-U-N-S 24-163-7081   (SL)
RIVER CABLE LTD
11406 132a St, Surrey, BC, V3R 7S2
(604) 580-4636
Emp Here 10   *Sales* 10,003,390
SIC 5051 Metals service centers and offices
  Kirk Mackenzie

D-U-N-S 25-768-0868   (BR)

RRGB RESTAURANTS CANADA INC
(*Suby of* RRGB RESTAURANTS CANADA INC)
10237 152 St, Surrey, BC, V3R 4G6
(604) 930-2415
Emp Here 100
SIC 5812 Eating places
 Paul Breda

D-U-N-S 20-797-6507   (HQ)
SCHILL INSURANCE BROKERS LTD
15127 100 Ave Unit 302, Surrey, BC, V3R 0N9
(604) 585-4445
Emp Here 9   *Sales* 184,774,200
SIC 6411 Insurance agents, brokers, and service
 Al Schill

D-U-N-S 20-590-7566   (BR)
SCHOOL DISTRICT NO. 36 (SURREY)
SCHOOL DISTRICT NO 36 (SURREY)
(*Suby of* SCHOOL DISTRICT NO. 36 (SURREY))
10719 150 St, Surrey, BC, V3R 4C8
(604) 585-2566
Emp Here 100
SIC 8211 Elementary and secondary schools
 Andrew Shook

D-U-N-S 20-026-9111   (BR)
SCHOOL DISTRICT NO. 36 (SURREY)
SCHOOL DISTRICT NO 36 (SURREY)
(*Suby of* SCHOOL DISTRICT NO. 36 (SURREY))
15350 99 Ave, Surrey, BC, V3R 0R9
(604) 581-5500
Emp Here 90
SIC 8211 Elementary and secondary schools
 Ken Hignell

D-U-N-S 20-058-9393   (SL)
SILVER STAR AUTO MB INC
SILVER STAR MERCEDES-BENZ
15508 104 Ave, Surrey, BC, V3R 1N8
(604) 581-7806
Emp Here 30   *Sales* 14,942,340
SIC 5511 New and used car dealers
 George Taubenfligel
 Stanley Shenker

D-U-N-S 25-413-9744   (SL)
SURREY IMPORTS LTD
SURREY HONDA
15291 Fraser Hwy, Surrey, BC, V3R 3P3
(604) 583-7421
Emp Here 70   *Sales* 44,049,600
SIC 5511 New and used car dealers
 Henning Brasso
 Cathleen Brasso

D-U-N-S 25-294-8666   (BR)
WAL-MART CANADA CORP
WALMART
(*Suby of* WALMART INC.)
1000 Guildford Town Ctr, Surrey, BC, V3R 7C3
(604) 581-1932
Emp Here 350
SIC 5311 Department stores

Surrey, BC V3S

D-U-N-S 24-750-1364   (HQ)
328633 BC LTD
WOLFE'S LANGLEY MAZDA
19265 Langley Bypass, Surrey, BC, V3S 6K1
(604) 534-0181
Sales 21,417,354
SIC 5511 New and used car dealers
 Gordon Wolfe
 Mike Hacquard

D-U-N-S 20-376-5297   (SL)
ACCORD LOGISTICS LTD
17660 65a Ave Unit 207, Surrey, BC, V3S 5N4

(604) 331-9515
Emp Here 7   *Sales* 12,956,329
SIC 4731 Freight transportation arrangement
 Howard Breslaw
 Kuldip Dhaliwal
 Gurdeep Dhaliwal
 Christopher Hawrysh

D-U-N-S 24-824-0616   (HQ)
ACCORD TRANSPORTATION LTD
17665 66a Ave Suite 801, Surrey, BC, V3S 2A7
(604) 575-7500
Emp Here 35   *Sales* 11,313,830
SIC 4213 Trucking, except local
 Kuldip Dhaliwal
 Howard Breslaw
 Gurdeep Dhaliwal
 Jagdeep Dhaliwal

D-U-N-S 24-312-3890   (HQ)
ACTTON SUPER-SAVE GAS STATIONS LTD
SUPER SAVE GAS
19395 Langley Bypass, Surrey, BC, V3S 6K1
(604) 533-4423
Sales 14,444,262
SIC 5541 Gasoline service stations
 William Vandekerkove

D-U-N-S 25-231-2392   (SL)
ACTTON TRANSPORT LTD
19395 Langley Bypass, Surrey, BC, V3S 6K1
(604) 533-4423
Emp Here 110   *Sales* 22,627,660
SIC 4213 Trucking, except local
 William Vandekerkhove
 Doug Vandekerkove

D-U-N-S 20-371-9872   (SL)
AE CONCRETE PRODUCTS INC
(*Suby of* HEADWATER EQUITY PARTNERS INC)
19060 54 Ave, Surrey, BC, V3S 8E5
(604) 576-1808
Emp Here 90   *Sales* 13,313,610
SIC 3272 Concrete products, nec
 Ian Graham
 Zia Waraich

D-U-N-S 25-216-7739   (SL)
BIGRIDGE BREWING CORPORATION
5580 152 St, Surrey, BC, V3S 5J9
(604) 574-2739
Emp Here 100   *Sales* 34,569,000
SIC 2082 Malt beverages
 Mark James

D-U-N-S 24-725-2109   (HQ)
BRITISH COLUMBIA CONSERVATION FOUNDATION, THE
17564 56a Ave Suite 206, Surrey, BC, V3S 1G3
(604) 576-1433
Emp Here 138   *Sales* 30,992,550
SIC 0971 Hunting, trapping, game propagation
 Terry O'brien
 John Holdstock
 Carmen Purdy
 Deborah Gibson

D-U-N-S 25-360-0290   (BR)
CANADIAN UTILITY CONSTRUCTION CORP
(*Suby of* QUANTA SERVICES, INC.)
6739 176 St Unit 1, Surrey, BC, V3S 4G6
(604) 576-9358
Emp Here 100
SIC 1623 Water, sewer, and utility lines
 Russell Wintersgill

D-U-N-S 24-700-7839   (SL)
CASINO TROPICAL PLANTS LTD.
4148 184th St, Surrey, BC, V3S 0R5
(604) 576-1156
Emp Here 30   *Sales* 10,274,010
SIC 0179 Fruits and tree nuts, nec
 George Sachinids

D-U-N-S 25-598-5806   (HQ)
CELLCOM WIRELESS INC
ROGERS WIRELESS
17650 66a Ave, Surrey, BC, V3S 4S4
(604) 575-1700
Emp Here 35   *Sales* 39,982,600
SIC 4899 Communication services, nec
 Kenneth Mitchell
 Diane Mary Mitchell

D-U-N-S 20-336-7479   (BR)
CITY OF SURREY, THE
ENGINNERING OPERATIONS
(*Suby of* CITY OF SURREY, THE)
6651 148 St Fl 3, Surrey, BC, V3S 3C7
(604) 591-4152
Emp Here 200
SIC 8711 Engineering services
 Robert Costanzo

D-U-N-S 25-160-1456   (HQ)
COASTAL PACIFIC XPRESS INC
5355 152 St Suite 105, Surrey, BC, V3S 5A5
(604) 575-4200
Sales 16,456,480
SIC 4213 Trucking, except local
 James Mickey
 Gwen Parsons

D-U-N-S 20-110-3967   (SL)
COLUMBIA PLASTICS LTD
19320 60 Ave, Surrey, BC, V3S 3M2
(604) 530-9990
Emp Here 50   *Sales* 10,094,850
SIC 3089 Plastics products, nec
 Greg Howard
 Ian Howard

D-U-N-S 20-044-0902   (SL)
D.W.P. DISTRIBUTORS LTD
CHEVRON
5504 176 St, Surrey, BC, V3S 4C3
(604) 576-2961
Emp Here 24   *Sales* 30,172,824
SIC 5172 Petroleum products, nec
 William Poppy

D-U-N-S 20-863-2018   (HQ)
DAMS FORD LINCOLN SALES LTD
19330 Langley Bypass, Surrey, BC, V3S 7R2
(604) 532-9921
Sales 125,856,000
SIC 5511 New and used car dealers
 Gordon Dams
 Gordon Dams Jr

D-U-N-S 24-695-1859   (HQ)
DELTA CONTROLS INC
17850 56 Ave, Surrey, BC, V3S 1C7
(604) 574-9444
Emp Here 180   *Sales* 84,874,500
SIC 3613 Switchgear and switchboard apparatus
 Brian Goodchild
 Raymond Rae
 John Nicholls
 Erchard Dobler
 Chris Wong
 Timo Kinna
 Lee Dickson
 Grant Calhoun
 Alan Waddell
 Una De Boer

D-U-N-S 24-289-4574   (SL)
DIXON HEATING & SHEET METAL LTD
17741 65a Ave Unit 101, Surrey, BC, V3S 1Z8
(604) 576-0585
Emp Here 43   *Sales* 10,021,795
SIC 1711 Plumbing, heating, air-conditioning
 Chris Dixon
 Susan Dixon

D-U-N-S 24-110-7168   (HQ)
DOUGLAS LAKE EQUIPMENT LIMITED PARTNERSHIP
DOUGLAS LAKE EQUIPMENT

17924 56 Ave, Surrey, BC, V3S 1C7
(604) 576-7506
Emp Here 1   *Sales* 29,983,320
SIC 7353 Heavy construction equipment rental
 Garry Frelick

D-U-N-S 24-855-6243   (SL)
ELTEX ENTERPRISES 2002 LTD
18927 62b Ave, Surrey, BC, V3S 8S3
(604) 599-5088
Emp Here 80   *Sales* 12,990,480
SIC 1742 Plastering, drywall, and insulation
 James Hatch
 Ralph Wilcott

D-U-N-S 24-309-0529   (HQ)
ESC AUTOMATION INC
5265 185a St Suite 100, Surrey, BC, V3S 7A4
(604) 574-7790
Emp Here 50   *Sales* 23,751,300
SIC 5084 Industrial machinery and equipment
 Brian Goodchild
 Raymond Rae

D-U-N-S 24-672-8018   (HQ)
EXCELL BATTERY COMPANY
18525 53 Ave Suite 133, Surrey, BC, V3S 7A4
(604) 575-5011
Emp Here 12   *Sales* 19,675,656
SIC 5063 Electrical apparatus and equipment
 Mark Kroeker
 Brian Larsen

D-U-N-S 20-864-6398   (SL)
FRASER CITY MOTORS LTD
LANGLEY CHRYSLER
19418 Langley Bypass, Surrey, BC, V3S 7R2
(604) 534-5355
Emp Here 50   *Sales* 24,903,900
SIC 5511 New and used car dealers
 Michael Trotman

D-U-N-S 24-029-1476   (SL)
G & M STEEL SERVICE LTD
5980 Enterprise Way, Surrey, BC, V3S 6S8
(604) 530-0117
Emp Here 70   *Sales* 17,233,020
SIC 1791 Structural steel erection
 Giovanni (John) Dinicola
 Araceli Romero

D-U-N-S 24-777-4730   (SL)
GLOBAL PLASTICS
MERFIN PLASTICS
19440 Enterprise Way, Surrey, BC, V3S 6J9
(604) 514-0600
Emp Here 150   *Sales* 23,828,700
SIC 3089 Plastics products, nec
 Matthew Friesen
 Brad Friesen

D-U-N-S 20-864-7743   (HQ)
GOLD KEY AUTOMOTIVE LTD
19545 Langey Bypass, Surrey, BC, V3S 6K1
(604) 534-7431
Sales 62,928,000
SIC 5511 New and used car dealers
 William Sie
 Tracey Mcrae

D-U-N-S 20-428-8849   (SL)
GOLD KEY PONTIAC BUICK (1984) LTD
(*Suby of* GOLD KEY AUTOMOTIVE LTD)
19545 Langley Bypass, Surrey, BC, V3S 6K1
(604) 534-7431
Emp Here 100   *Sales* 62,928,000
SIC 5511 New and used car dealers
 William Sie

D-U-N-S 24-202-7092   (SL)
GOLD KEY SALES AND LEASE LTD
(*Suby of* GOLD KEY AUTOMOTIVE LTD)
19545 Langey Bypass, Surrey, BC, V3S 6K1
(604) 534-7431
Emp Here 80   *Sales* 50,342,400
SIC 5511 New and used car dealers

Bill Sie
Mary Sie

D-U-N-S 25-215-5056   (HQ)
HALKIN TOOL LTD
17819 66 Ave, Surrey, BC, V3S 7X1
(604) 574-9799
Emp Here 70   *Sales* 21,129,350
SIC 3469 Metal stampings, nec
Edward Hilton
Steve Hilton

D-U-N-S 24-309-1605   (SL)
HARPO ENTERPRISES
MCDONALD'S
17960 56 Ave, Surrey, BC, V3S 1C7
(604) 575-1690
Emp Here 75   *Sales* 3,413,925
SIC 5812 Eating places
James Harper

D-U-N-S 24-979-7895   (SL)
HOMELIFE BENCHMARK TITUS REALTY
105-5477 152 St, Surrey, BC, V3S 5A5
(604) 575-5262
Emp Here 90   *Sales* 24,458,040
SIC 6531 Real estate agents and managers
Robert Timmath

D-U-N-S 25-978-3900   (HQ)
INDEPENDENT SUPPLY COMPANY INC
19505 56 Ave Unit 104, Surrey, BC, V3S 6K3
(604) 298-4472
Emp Here 17   *Sales* 33,123,168
SIC 5078 Refrigeration equipment and supplies
Brian Nixon
Keith Werner
Rudy Wieschorster
Ray Newstad
Sheri Pusch

D-U-N-S 24-320-7839   (SL)
INTERCONTINENTAL TRUCK BODY (B.C.) INC
INTERCONTINENTAL TRUCK BODY
5285 192 St, Surrey, BC, V3S 8E5
(604) 576-2971
Emp Here 75   *Sales* 16,788,225
SIC 3713 Truck and bus bodies
Nathan Van Seters
John Van Seters
Phil Van Dyke

D-U-N-S 24-310-4981   (SL)
INTERNATIONAL TENTNOLOGY CORP
TENTNOLOGY CO
15427 66 Ave, Surrey, BC, V3S 2A1
(604) 597-8368
Emp Here 75   *Sales* 10,250,550
SIC 2394 Canvas and related products
Gery Warner
Suzanne Warner

D-U-N-S 25-290-7233   (SL)
JEEM HOLDINGS LTD
19060 54 Ave, Surrey, BC, V3S 8E5
(604) 576-1808
Emp Here 80   *Sales* 20,924,240
SIC 6712 Bank holding companies
James Mcausland
Edward Pentland

D-U-N-S 24-313-0655   (SL)
JONKER AUTO LTD
JONKER HONDA
19515 Langley Bypass, Surrey, BC, V3S 6K1
(604) 530-6281
Emp Here 30   *Sales* 14,942,340
SIC 5511 New and used car dealers
Karel Jonker

D-U-N-S 24-947-1538   (SL)
KADANT CANADA CORP
KADANT CARMANAH DESIGN
(*Suby of* KADANT INC.)
15050 54a Ave Unit 8, Surrey, BC, V3S 5X7

(604) 299-3431
Emp Here 75   *Sales* 16,650,075
SIC 3569 General industrial machinery, nec
Michael Colwell
Michael Mckenney
Sandra Lambert
Deborah Selwwod
Robert Mcnicol
Christopher Macey
Thomas Martin
Daniel Walsh
Clayton Cox
Jonathan Painter

D-U-N-S 20-790-1732   (SL)
KAROB FOODS LTD
MARKETPLACE IGA 73
17710 56 Ave Suite 10, Surrey, BC, V3S 1C7

Emp Here 40   *Sales* 10,966,080
SIC 5411 Grocery stores
Robert Neufeld

D-U-N-S 20-873-2466   (SL)
LANGLEY HYUNDAI LTD
LANGLEY MOTOR SPORTS
19459 Langley Bypass, Surrey, BC, V3S 6K1
(604) 539-8549
Emp Here 25   *Sales* 12,451,950
SIC 5511 New and used car dealers
Jane Dubuc

D-U-N-S 24-354-6954   (HQ)
LEWIS-PATRICK INVESTMENTS LTD
6320 148 St, Surrey, BC, V3S 3C4
(604) 598-9930
Sales 19,134,500
SIC 6712 Bank holding companies
Ivan Harmatny
Ronald Mcneil

D-U-N-S 25-679-8299   (HQ)
LMS MANAGEMENT LTD
(*Suby of* LEWIS-PATRICK INVESTMENTS LTD)
6320 148 St, Surrey, BC, V3S 3C4
(604) 598-9930
Emp Here 70   *Sales* 18,463,950
SIC 1791 Structural steel erection
Ronald Mcneil
Ivan Harmatny
Darryl Hebert

D-U-N-S 24-356-8669   (SL)
LOTUS TERMINALS LTD
18833 52 Ave, Surrey, BC, V3S 8E5
(604) 534-1119
Emp Here 75   *Sales* 11,114,400
SIC 4213 Trucking, except local
Saran Bal

D-U-N-S 24-930-4825   (SL)
LUTHERN SENIOR CITIZEN HOUSING SOCIETY
ZION PARK MANOR
5939 180 St, Surrey, BC, V3S 4L2
(604) 576-2891
Emp Here 175   *Sales* 11,957,050
SIC 8051 Skilled nursing care facilities
Glenn Peschke
Tom Crump

D-U-N-S 25-361-7385   (HQ)
MAINROAD CONTRACTING LTD
17474 56 Ave, Surrey, BC, V3S 1C3
(604) 575-7020
Sales 27,768,620
SIC 1611 Highway and street construction
Douglas A Bjornson

D-U-N-S 25-108-7185   (HQ)
MAINROAD EAST KOOTENAY CONTRACTING LTD
17474 56 Ave, Surrey, BC, V3S 1C3
(604) 575-7020
Emp Here 40   *Sales* 25,244,200
SIC 1611 Highway and street construction
David A. Zerr

Doug Bjornson
Dale Routley

D-U-N-S 20-654-8443   (HQ)
MAINROAD HOWE SOUND CONTRACTING LTD
17474 56 Ave, Surrey, BC, V3S 1C3
(604) 575-7020
Sales 16,408,730
SIC 1611 Highway and street construction
Peter Ashbroft
Doug Bjornson

D-U-N-S 24-340-7629   (SL)
MAINROAD LOWER MAINLAND CONTRACTING LTD
17474 56 Ave, Surrey, BC, V3S 1C3
(604) 575-7021
Emp Here 50   *Sales* 12,622,100
SIC 1611 Highway and street construction
David Zerr

D-U-N-S 24-373-4886   (SL)
MANSONVILLE PLASTICS (B.C.) LIMITED
19402 56 Ave, Surrey, BC, V3S 6K4
(604) 534-8626
Emp Here 80   *Sales* 22,132,800
SIC 2821 Plastics materials and resins

D-U-N-S 24-886-5094   (HQ)
MBG BUILDINGS INC
17957 55 Ave Suite 102, Surrey, BC, V3S 6C4
(604) 574-6600
Sales 15,567,760
SIC 1541 Industrial buildings and warehouses
Steve Triance
Jonathan Triance
Trent Warkentin

D-U-N-S 25-310-9441   (BR)
MCDONALD'S   RESTAURANTS   OF CANADA LIMITED
MCDONALD'S
(*Suby of* MCDONALD'S CORPORATION)
15574 Fraser Hwy, Surrey, BC, V3S 2V9
(604) 507-7900
Emp Here 130
SIC 5812 Eating places
Richard Ellis

D-U-N-S 24-558-2010   (SL)
MEGA CRANES LTD
6330 148 St, Surrey, BC, V3S 3C4
(604) 599-4200
Emp Here 40   *Sales* 17,739,600
SIC 7389 Business services, nec
Kerry Hawley
Kelly Peterson

D-U-N-S 25-747-6986   (HQ)
MEGA HAIR GROUP INC, THE
MEGA HAIR & CARE
6448 148 St Suite 107, Surrey, BC, V3S 7G7
(604) 599-6800
Emp Here 10   *Sales* 18,152,940
SIC 7231 Beauty shops
Mark Banicevic
Malejne Soligo

D-U-N-S 20-153-2657   (HQ)
METIS PROVINCIAL COUNCIL OF BRITISH COLUMBIA
METIS NATION BRITISH COLUMBIA
103-5668 192 St, Surrey, BC, V3S 2V7
(604) 557-5851
Emp Here 20   *Sales* 13,941,950
SIC 8748 Business consulting, nec
Clara Morindalcol
Lissa Smith
Dale Drown

D-U-N-S 24-751-6839   (SL)
NEWS THE CLASSIFIED
5450 152 St, Surrey, BC, V3S 5J9
(604) 575-5555
Emp Here 35   *Sales* 26,425,290
SIC 5192 Books, periodicals, and newspapers

David Black

D-U-N-S 24-314-1850   (SL)
NORTHCOAST BUILDING PRODUCTS LTD
14682 66 Ave, Surrey, BC, V3S 1Z9
(604) 597-8884
Emp Here 35   *Sales* 15,651,090
SIC 5039 Construction materials, nec
Ronald Sargeant

D-U-N-S 20-048-9404   (SL)
NORTHWEST WASTE SYSTEMS INC
19500 56 Ave, Surrey, BC, V3S 6K4
(604) 539-1900
Emp Here 50   *Sales* 15,231,490
SIC 4953 Refuse systems
Mark O'hara

D-U-N-S 20-131-4970   (SL)
NUCOR ENVIRONMENTAL SOLUTIONS LTD
5250 185a St Suite 2, Surrey, BC, V3S 7A4
(604) 575-4721
Emp Here 49   *Sales* 11,480,112
SIC 8748 Business consulting, nec
Jim Dumelie

D-U-N-S 25-696-7514   (SL)
NUEST SERVICES LTD
SERVICEMASTER
17858 66 Ave, Surrey, BC, V3S 7X1
(604) 888-1588
Emp Here 100   *Sales* 4,020,900
SIC 7349 Building maintenance services, nec
Rico Ardanaz
Glen Sheepwash

D-U-N-S 20-017-0251   (HQ)
NURMANN HOLDINGS LTD
HAMPTON INN & SUITES
19500 Langley Bypass, Surrey, BC, V3S 7R2
(604) 530-6545
Emp Here 30   *Sales* 14,830,400
SIC 7011 Hotels and motels
Abdulhamid Tejpar
Abdulla Tejpar

D-U-N-S 25-173-6765   (HQ)
ORCA SPECIALTY FOODS LTD
17350 56 Ave Suite 4, Surrey, BC, V3S 1C3
(604) 574-6722
Sales 38,025,900
SIC 2091 Canned and cured fish and seafoods
David Mckinnon
Robert Probert

D-U-N-S 25-678-4729   (SL)
OTTO MOBILE VANCOUVER
17535 55b Ave, Surrey, BC, V3S 5V2

Emp Here 30   *Sales* 14,942,340
SIC 5561 Recreational vehicle dealers
Rick Knappe

D-U-N-S 20-178-9752   (SL)
PACE PROCESSING AND PRODUCT DEVELOPMENT LTD
19495 55 Ave Suite 107, Surrey, BC, V3S 8P7
(604) 539-9201
Emp Here 110   *Sales* 91,913,470
SIC 5149 Groceries and related products, nec
Sean Darrah
Jansen Blyth

D-U-N-S 25-613-7381   (HQ)
PACIFIC RIM INDUSTRIAL INSULATION LTD
19510 55 Ave Unit 2, Surrey, BC, V3S 8P7
(604) 543-8178
Sales 10,554,765
SIC 1742 Plastering, drywall, and insulation
Paul Smith
Susan Smith

D-U-N-S 24-523-0987   (SL)
PACK FRESH FOODS LTD
(*Suby of* ORCA SPECIALTY FOODS LTD)

17350 56 Ave Suite 3, Surrey, BC, V3S 1C3
(604) 574-6720
Emp Here 45   *Sales* 15,556,050
SIC 2091 Canned and cured fish and seafoods
David Mckinnon

D-U-N-S 20-159-8393   (HQ)
PETROVALUE PRODUCTS CANADA INC
19402 54 Ave Unit 104, Surrey, BC, V3S 7H9
(604) 576-0004
Emp Here 8   *Sales* 16,343,613
SIC 5172 Petroleum products, nec
Peter Coleman
Joel Siebenga
Jeremy Nichols
Lorraine Bridden

D-U-N-S 20-838-7865   (SL)
PMC BUILDERS & DEVELOPERS LTD
19414 Enterprise Way, Surrey, BC, V3S 6J9
(604) 534-1822
Emp Here 34   *Sales* 10,841,546
SIC 1521 Single-family housing construction
Daryll Stewart

D-U-N-S 20-011-7476   (HQ)
PUNJAB MILK FOODS INC
6308 146 St, Surrey, BC, V3S 3A4
(604) 594-9190
Sales 20,741,400
SIC 2021 Creamery butter
Gurpreet Arneja
Vineet Taneja

D-U-N-S 24-504-1868   (HQ)
QUALITY CRAFT LTD
(*Suby of* COLLINS CO., LTD.)
17750 65a Ave Unit 301, Surrey, BC, V3S 5N4
(604) 575-5550
Emp Here 23   *Sales* 50,170,472
SIC 5023 Homefurnishings
John Brice
Dennis Hale
Joanne Devost
Archie Gardner

D-U-N-S 24-939-7498   (SL)
RAINTREE LUMBER SPECIALTIES LTD
(*Suby of* E.R. PROBYN LTD)
5390 192 St, Surrey, BC, V3S 8E5
(604) 574-0444
Emp Here 100
SIC 2421 Sawmills and planing mills, general
Vince Carnovale
Eric Van Wagbinigin
Edward Probyn

D-U-N-S 20-102-5624   (HQ)
RELIANCE FOUNDRY CO. LTD
6450 148 St Unit 207, Surrey, BC, V3S 7G7
(604) 547-0460
Emp Here 13   *Sales* 11,179,350
SIC 5051 Metals service centers and offices
Brent Done
Brad Done

D-U-N-S 24-956-9963   (HQ)
REST-WELL MATTRESS COMPANY LTD
SPRING AIR
14922 54a Ave, Surrey, BC, V3S 5X7
(604) 576-2339
Sales 15,432,200
SIC 2515 Mattresses and bedsprings
Troy Zanatta

D-U-N-S 20-047-1345   (SL)
RMC READY-MIX LTD
19275 54 Ave, Surrey, BC, V3S 8E5
(604) 574-1164
Emp Here 60   *Sales* 14,006,100
SIC 3273 Ready-mixed concrete
Gary Whipple

D-U-N-S 20-124-8924   (SL)
ROBERTSON CONSTRUCTION LTD
ROBERTSON DRYWALL SERVICES

17802 66 Ave Unit 101a, Surrey, BC, V3S 7X1
(778) 574-4455
Emp Here 120   *Sales* 19,485,720
SIC 1742 Plastering, drywall, and insulation
Garth Robertson
Sandra Robertson

D-U-N-S 24-881-6571   (SL)
S-304 HOLDINGS LTD
JONKER NISSAN
19505 Langley Bypass, Surrey, BC, V3S 6K1
(604) 534-7957
Emp Here 27   *Sales* 13,448,106
SIC 5511 New and used car dealers
Karel Jonker

D-U-N-S 20-590-9588   (BR)
SCHOOL DISTRICT NO. 36 (SURREY)
SCHOOL DISTRICT NO 36 (SURREY)
(*Suby of* SCHOOL DISTRICT NO. 36 (SURREY))
7940 156 St, Surrey, BC, V3S 3R3
(604) 597-2301
Emp Here 100
SIC 8211 Elementary and secondary schools
Susan Knox

D-U-N-S 20-966-5517   (BR)
SCHOOL DISTRICT NO. 36 (SURREY)
SCHOOL DISTRICT NO 36 (SURREY)
(*Suby of* SCHOOL DISTRICT NO. 36 (SURREY))
6151 180 St, Surrey, BC, V3S 4L5
(604) 574-7407
Emp Here 90
SIC 8211 Elementary and secondary schools
Allan Buggie

D-U-N-S 24-556-6067   (SL)
SIMPLY THE BEST GOURMET PRODUCTS
17665 66a Ave Suite 110, Surrey, BC, V3S 2A7
(604) 576-9395
Emp Here 12   *Sales* 10,026,924
SIC 5149 Groceries and related products, nec

D-U-N-S 20-117-7339   (SL)
SOUTHRIDGE BUILDING SUPPLIES LTD
17444 56 Ave, Surrey, BC, V3S 1C3
(604) 576-2113
Emp Here 25   *Sales* 11,179,350
SIC 5039 Construction materials, nec
Terrence Deane
Jamey Deane
Wilma Deane
Kevin Deane
Anthony Deane
Jeremy Deane

D-U-N-S 20-076-7411   (BR)
SUNRISE POULTRY PROCESSORS LTD
(*Suby of* SUNRISE POULTRY PROCESSORS LTD)
17565 65a Ave, Surrey, BC, V3S 7B6
(604) 596-9505
Emp Here 100
SIC 5147 Meats and meat products
Peter Shoor

D-U-N-S 24-867-1703   (HQ)
SUPER-SAVE ENTERPRISES LTD
SUPER SAVE PROPANE
19395 Langley Bypass, Surrey, BC, V3S 6K1
(604) 533-4423
Emp Here 23   *Sales* 40,314,120
SIC 5984 Liquefied petroleum gas dealers
William Vandekerhove
Philip Vandekerhove

D-U-N-S 24-898-8982   (SL)
SUPERIOR CITY SERVICES LTD
15151 64 Ave, Surrey, BC, V3S 1X9
(604) 591-3434
Emp Here 30   *Sales* 12,580,650
SIC 6712 Bank holding companies
Raymond Ng

D-U-N-S 20-393-2210   (SL)

TELEDYNE QUANTITATIVE IMAGING CORPORATION
19535 56 Ave Suite 101, Surrey, BC, V3S 6K3
(604) 530-5800
Emp Here 40   *Sales* 10,262,480
SIC 3861 Photographic equipment and supplies
Jonathan Mason

D-U-N-S 25-099-3680   (SL)
TELEDYNE QUANTITATIVE IMAGING CORPORATION
19535 56 Ave Suite 101, Surrey, BC, V3S 6K3
(604) 530-5800
Emp Here 40   *Sales* 10,262,480
SIC 3861 Photographic equipment and supplies
Robert Mehrabian
Silvio Favrin
Edwin Roks

D-U-N-S 24-887-9835   (HQ)
TERUS CONSTRUCTION LTD
(*Suby of* BOUYGUES)
15288 54a Ave Unit 300, Surrey, BC, V3S 6T4
(604) 575-3689
Sales 196,869,000
SIC 1611 Highway and street construction
Lorne Davies
Louis Gabanna
Greg King
Robert Cote

D-U-N-S 24-330-5856   (HQ)
TMG LOGISTICS INC
14722 64 Ave Unit 9, Surrey, BC, V3S 1X7
(604) 598-3680
Emp Here 1   *Sales* 15,427,950
SIC 4213 Trucking, except local
Jaspreet Mangat
Bruce Tremblay
Jag Singh

D-U-N-S 24-824-8007   (SL)
VIADUCT SHEET METAL LTD
18787 52 Ave, Surrey, BC, V3S 8E5
(604) 575-1600
Emp Here 60   *Sales* 13,983,900
SIC 1711 Plumbing, heating, air-conditioning
Mark Halborsen
Dan Taillefer
Miles Heck

D-U-N-S 20-059-0664   (SL)
VOYAGEUR SOAP & CANDLE COMPANY LTD
19257 Enterprise Way Suite 14, Surrey, BC, V3S 6J8
(604) 530-8979
Emp Here 36   *Sales* 11,784,384
SIC 2841 Soap and other detergents
Robert Knowles

D-U-N-S 20-117-2715   (HQ)
WESTERN EQUIPMENT LTD
5219 192 St Unit 114, Surrey, BC, V3S 4P6
(604) 574-3311
Emp Here 21   *Sales* 34,676,898
SIC 5085 Industrial supplies
Ian Morriss
Earle Morriss

D-U-N-S 24-445-5242   (HQ)
WESTOWER COMMUNICATIONS LTD
(*Suby of* EXCHANGE INCOME CORPORATION)
17886 55 Ave, Surrey, BC, V3S 6C8
(604) 576-4755
Emp Here 29   *Sales* 118,121,400
SIC 1623 Water, sewer, and utility lines
Peter Jeffrey
Calvin Payne
S Roy Jeffrey

D-U-N-S 24-799-0203   (SL)
ZINETTI FOOD PRODUCTS LTD
17760 66 Ave, Surrey, BC, V3S 7X1

(604) 574-2028
Emp Here 60   *Sales* 20,741,400
SIC 2038 Frozen specialties, nec
Maurizio Zinetti

Surrey, BC V3T

D-U-N-S 20-572-7183   (HQ)
7-ELEVEN CANADA, INC
(*Suby of* SEVEN & I HOLDINGS CO., LTD.)
13450 102 Ave Suite 2400, Surrey, BC, V3T 0C3
(604) 586-0711
Emp Here 120   *Sales* 1,251,016,000
SIC 5411 Grocery stores
Joseph M Depinto
Stanley Reynolds
Jack Stout
Chris Tanco
Rankin Gasaway
Scott Hintz

D-U-N-S 20-102-5079   (SL)
99 TRUCK PARTS & INDUSTRIAL EQUIPMENT LTD
12905 King George Blvd, Surrey, BC, V3T 2T1
(604) 580-1677
Emp Here 22   *Sales* 10,957,716
SIC 5531 Auto and home supply stores
Douglas Milner
Dane Wheating

D-U-N-S 24-777-6958   (HQ)
APEX COMMUNICATIONS INC
APEX WIRELESS
13734 104 Ave Suite 201, Surrey, BC, V3T 1W5
(604) 583-6685
Emp Here 20   *Sales* 19,546,240
SIC 5999 Miscellaneous retail stores, nec
Andrew Westlund

D-U-N-S 24-957-1332   (SL)
BOLIVAR HOLDINGS LTD
HOCKEY SHOP, THE
10280 City Pky, Surrey, BC, V3T 4C2
(604) 589-8299
Emp Here 60   *Sales* 14,659,680
SIC 5941 Sporting goods and bicycle shops
Rod Bolivar
Kristie Whiddington
Ken Whiddington

D-U-N-S 25-079-2173   (SL)
BOUYGUES ENERGIES AND SERVICES CANADA LIMITED
(*Suby of* BOUYGUES)
9801 King George Blvd Unit 125, Surrey, BC, V3T 5H5
(604) 585-3358
Emp Here 180   *Sales* 22,459,680
SIC 8741 Management services
Jatinder Heer

D-U-N-S 20-358-9361   (SL)
CDI EDUCATION (ALBERTA) LIMITED PARTNERSHIP
13401 108 Ave Suite 360, Surrey, BC, V3T 5T3
(604) 915-7288
Emp Here 300   *Sales* 29,735,700
SIC 8211 Elementary and secondary schools
David Kwong

D-U-N-S 20-804-1665   (HQ)
COAST CAPITAL SAVINGS FEDERAL CREDIT UNION
COAST CAPITAL
9900 King George Blvd Suite 800, Surrey, BC, V3T 0K7
(604) 517-7400
Emp Here 100   *Sales* 463,884,130
SIC 6062 State credit unions
Calvin Macinnis
Helen Blackburn

Bob Armstrong
Bill Cooke
Robin Chakrabarti
Mary Jordan
Valerie Lambert
Frank Leonard
Nancy Mckenzie
Christian Morrison

D-U-N-S 20-401-5932   (BR)
COAST CAPITAL SAVINGS FEDERAL CREDIT UNION
EQUIPMENT FINANCE DEPARTMENT
(*Suby of* COAST CAPITAL SAVINGS FEDERAL CREDIT UNION)
9900 King George Blvd 4th Fl, Surrey, BC, V3T 0K7
(778) 945-3225
Emp Here 75
SIC 6159 Miscellaneous business credit institutions
Michael Fox

D-U-N-S 20-797-9410   (HQ)
COMMUNITY SAVINGS CREDIT UNION
13450 102 Ave Suite 1600, Surrey, BC, V3T 5X3
(604) 654-2000
Emp Here 25   *Sales* 12,810,075
SIC 6062 State credit unions
Doug Eveneshen
Ken Hodge
Colleen Jordan
Ken Isomura
David Tones
Robin Medeko
Eric Doomberg

D-U-N-S 20-904-6759   (SL)
CORE SECURITY GROUP INC
CORE SECURITY
13456 108 Ave, Surrey, BC, V3T 2K1
(604) 583-2673
Emp Here 35   *Sales* 13,848,730
SIC 7381 Detective and armored car services
Charlena Radic

D-U-N-S 24-121-0140   (BR)
FRASER HEALTH AUTHORITY
GATEWAY HOME HOUSE
(*Suby of* GOVERNMENT OF THE PROVINCE OF BRITISH COLUMBIA)
13401 108th Ave Suite 1500, Surrey, BC, V3T 5T3
(604) 953-4950
Emp Here 100
SIC 8059 Nursing and personal care, nec

D-U-N-S 20-153-2871   (HQ)
FRASER HEALTH AUTHORITY
(*Suby of* GOVERNMENT OF THE PROVINCE OF BRITISH COLUMBIA)
13450 102 Ave Suite 400, Surrey, BC, V3T 0H1
(604) 587-4600
Emp Here 12,000   *Sales* 2,880,229,035
SIC 8062 General medical and surgical hospitals
Victoria Lee
Cameron Brine
Linda Dempster
Martin Lavoie
Laurie Leith
David Thompson
Naseem Nuraney
Roy Morton
Gregor Mcwalter
Brenda Liggett

D-U-N-S 20-864-8329   (SL)
GUILDFORD MOTORS INC
GUILDFORD VOLKSWAGEN
13820 104 Ave, Surrey, BC, V3T 1W9
(604) 584-1304
Emp Here 33   *Sales* 16,436,574
SIC 5511 New and used car dealers
William Wu

D-U-N-S 25-067-3683   (SL)
KASA SUPPLY LTD
13237 King George Blvd, Surrey, BC, V3T 2T3
(604) 581-5815
Emp Here 30   *Sales* 11,959,815
SIC 5039 Construction materials, nec
Sarbjit Sahota
Sunraj Gaehri

D-U-N-S 20-563-4137   (BR)
MCELHANNEY CONSULTING SERVICES LTD
(*Suby of* MCELHANNEY SERVICES LTD)
13450 102 Ave Suite 2300, Surrey, BC, V3T 5X3
(604) 596-0391
Emp Here 100
SIC 8748 Business consulting, nec
Gary Tencha

D-U-N-S 25-386-5976   (SL)
SAFE SOFTWARE INC
9639 137a St Suite 1200, Surrey, BC, V3T 0M1
(604) 501-9985
Emp Here 88   *Sales* 18,818,888
SIC 7372 Prepackaged software
Don Murray
Dale Lutz
Darice Lutz
Alice Bush

D-U-N-S 24-134-4808   (BR)
SCHOOL DISTRICT NO. 36 (SURREY)
SCHOOL DISTRICT NO 36 (SURREY)
(*Suby of* SCHOOL DISTRICT NO. 36 (SURREY))
10441 132 St, Surrey, BC, V3T 3V3
(604) 588-6934
Emp Here 100
SIC 8211 Elementary and secondary schools
Raj Puri

D-U-N-S 25-125-8257   (SL)
SECURITY RESOURCE GROUP INC
10252 City Pky Suite 301, Surrey, BC, V3T 4C2
(604) 951-3388
Emp Here 35   *Sales* 13,848,730
SIC 7381 Detective and armored car services
Blair Ross

D-U-N-S 24-725-1879   (HQ)
SURREY PUBLIC LIBRARY
SURREY LIBRARY
10350 University Dr 3rd Floor, Surrey, BC, V3T 4B8
(604) 598-7300
Emp Here 10   *Sales* 15,852,600
SIC 8231 Libraries
Beth Barlow

D-U-N-S 20-278-7552   (SL)
TRAVELLERS FINANCE LTD
800-9900 King George Blvd, Surrey, BC, V3T 0K7
(604) 293-0202
Emp Here 65   *Sales* 14,556,165
SIC 6159 Miscellaneous business credit institutions
Roberto Cortese
Wayne Berg
Gary Thompson
James Case
Pehlaj Malhotra
Donald Coutler

D-U-N-S 20-865-7304   (HQ)
WESTMINSTER SAVINGS CREDIT UNION
13450 102 Ave Suite 1900, Surrey, BC, V3T 5Y1
(604) 517-0100
Emp Here 60   *Sales* 68,320,400
SIC 6062 State credit unions
Gavin Toy
Maury Kask
Brian Rogers
Tj Schmaltz

Greg Oyhenart
Mary Falconer

D-U-N-S 24-368-9593   (SL)
WHALLEY & DISTRICT SENIOR CITIZEN HOUSING SOCIETY
KINSMEN PLACE LODGE
13333 Old Yale Rd, Surrey, BC, V3T 5A2
(604) 588-0445
Emp Here 140   *Sales* 9,565,640
SIC 8059 Nursing and personal care, nec
Terry Mcleod
Brian Garard
Art Hildebrant
Ted Rieder
Len Selby

D-U-N-S 25-170-0639   (SL)
WILLIAMS, DAVE & PAT SALES LTD
CANADIAN TIRE
13665 102 Ave Suite 489, Surrey, BC, V3T 1N7
(604) 583-8473
Emp Here 75   *Sales* 47,196,000
SIC 5531 Auto and home supply stores
Dave Williams

Surrey, BC V3V

D-U-N-S 24-724-2985   (SL)
A I INDUSTRIES
12349 104 Ave, Surrey, BC, V3V 3H2
(604) 583-2171
Emp Here 60   *Sales* 11,525,100
SIC 3441 Fabricated structural Metal
Amin Walji
Karim Walji
Kalim Walji

D-U-N-S 24-805-5902   (HQ)
ADVANCE PALLET & CRATE LTD
(*Suby of* ADVANCE LUMBER REMANUFACTURING LTD)
12184 Old Yale Rd, Surrey, BC, V3V 3X5
(888) 791-2323
Sales 10,442,821
SIC 2448 Wood pallets and skids
Jaspinder Brar

D-U-N-S 20-804-4644   (HQ)
ALLIED BLOWER & SHEET METAL LTD
12224 103a Ave, Surrey, BC, V3V 3G9
(604) 930-7000
Emp Here 60   *Sales* 28,557,576
SIC 1796 Installing building equipment
Barrie Forbes
Erkki Rautianinen
Bruce Wendel

D-U-N-S 20-441-2787   (HQ)
ARTEK GROUP LIMITED, THE
ARTEK VANCOUVER, DIV OF
12140 103a Ave, Surrey, BC, V3V 7Y9
(604) 584-2131
Emp Here 50   *Sales* 85,550,700
SIC 1542 Nonresidential construction, nec
William Tymkiw

D-U-N-S 20-099-9316   (HQ)
ASPEN PLANERS LTD
12745 116 Ave, Surrey, BC, V3V 7H9
(604) 580-2781
Emp Here 125   *Sales* 83,517,000
SIC 2421 Sawmills and planing mills, general
Surinder Ghog
Nad Shan
David Gray
Tom Chambers

D-U-N-S 24-104-1628   (BR)
BC CANCER FOUNDATION
13750 96 Ave, Surrey, BC, V3V 1Z2
(604) 930-2098
Emp Here 250

SIC 8621 Professional organizations
Andrea Coogan

D-U-N-S 24-335-5505   (BR)
CATALYST PAPER CORPORATION
SURREY DISTRIBUTION CENTRE
(*Suby of* CAPITAL ASSETS HOLDINGS (L) BERHAD)
10555 Timberland Rd, Surrey, BC, V3V 3T3
(604) 953-0373
Emp Here 88
SIC 2621 Paper mills
Avril Loft

D-U-N-S 20-992-5494   (HQ)
CENTRE FOR CHILD DEVELOPMENT OF THE LOWER MAINLAND, THE
CENTRE FOR CHILD DEVELOPMENT, THE
9460 140 St, Surrey, BC, V3V 5Z4
(604) 584-1361
Emp Here 115   *Sales* 9,215,040
SIC 8322 Individual and family services
Diana Diggle
Harold Pugash
Jann Richardson
Norm Sherritt
Rob Shirreff
Lyn Stringer
Marilyn Watts
Zosia Ettenberg
Dave Goodwin
Martin Hyatt

D-U-N-S 20-916-8517   (SL)
CORVETTE SPECIALTIES AUTO GROUP LTD
CORVETTE PARTS WORLD WIDE
11180 Scott Rd, Surrey, BC, V3V 8B8
(604) 580-8388
Emp Here 25   *Sales* 12,451,950
SIC 5511 New and used car dealers
Bruce Iggulden
Glen Iggulden

D-U-N-S 25-739-2261   (SL)
DIVISION 2 CONTRACTING LTD
10553 120 St, Surrey, BC, V3V 4G4
(604) 589-4663
Emp Here 40   *Sales* 12,045,680
SIC 4953 Refuse systems
Paul Bovell

D-U-N-S 25-932-6643   (BR)
FIRSTCANADA ULC
FIRST STUDENT
(*Suby of* FIRSTGROUP PLC)
12079 103a Ave, Surrey, BC, V3V 3G7
(604) 583-7060
Emp Here 127
SIC 4151 School buses

D-U-N-S 25-539-4025   (BR)
GEORGIA-PACIFIC CANADA LP
(*Suby of* KOCH INDUSTRIES, INC.)
12509 116 Ave, Surrey, BC, V3V 3S6
(604) 209-6588
Emp Here 90
SIC 3275 Gypsum products
Marcel Tack

D-U-N-S 25-234-3876   (BR)
HOME DEPOT OF CANADA INC
HOME DEPOT
(*Suby of* THE HOME DEPOT INC)
12701 110 Ave, Surrey, BC, V3V 3J7
(604) 580-2159
Emp Here 170
SIC 5251 Hardware stores
Wilfrid Meloche

D-U-N-S 20-554-3320   (SL)
IDC DISTRIBUTION SERVICES LTD
10550 Timberland Rd, Surrey, BC, V3V 7Z1
(604) 812-5048
Emp Here 30   *Sales* 15,599,010
SIC 4789 Transportation services, nec
Fran Dundas

D-U-N-S 20-371-4282   (SL)
LARK PROJECTS LTD
13737 96 Ave Suite 1500, Surrey, BC, V3V 0C6
(604) 576-2935
Emp Here 70   *Sales* 39,866,050
SIC 1542 Nonresidential construction, nec
Larry Fisher

D-U-N-S 25-318-1556   (BR)
MCDONALD'S RESTAURANTS OF CANADA LIMITED
MCDONALD'S #8249
(*Suby of* MCDONALD'S CORPORATION)
12930 96 Ave, Surrey, BC, V3V 6A8
(604) 587-3390
Emp Here 100
SIC 5812 Eating places
Christopher Chia

D-U-N-S 20-113-9987   (HQ)
MILL & TIMBER PRODUCTS LTD
(*Suby of* ASPEN PLANERS LTD)
12770 116 Ave, Surrey, BC, V3V 7H9
(604) 580-2781
Sales 56,210,000
SIC 5211 Lumber and other building materials
Surinder Ghog
Tom Chambers
David Gray
Nad Shan

D-U-N-S 25-215-9793   (HQ)
PACIFIC COAST EXPRESS LIMITED
10299 Grace Rd, Surrey, BC, V3V 3V7
(604) 582-3230
Emp Here 50   *Sales* 18,513,540
SIC 4213 Trucking, except local
John Assman

D-U-N-S 24-802-8438   (BR)
PEPSICO CANADA ULC
FRITO LAY CANADA
(*Suby of* PEPSICO, INC.)
11811 103a Ave, Surrey, BC, V3V 0B5
(604) 587-8300
Emp Here 300
SIC 5145 Confectionery
Dave Kang

D-U-N-S 25-653-5576   (BR)
PROVINCIAL HEALTH SERVICES AUTHORITY
BC CANCER, PART OF THE PROVINCIAL HEALTH SERVICES AUTHORITY
(*Suby of* PROVINCIAL HEALTH SERVICES AUTHORITY)
13750 96 Ave, Surrey, BC, V3V 1Z2
(604) 930-2098
Emp Here 240
SIC 8069 Specialty hospitals, except psychiatric
Noorjeen Hassam

D-U-N-S 20-739-1207   (SL)
QUALIFIED CONTRACTORS LTD
12788 Ross Pl, Surrey, BC, V3V 6E1
(604) 951-8677
Emp Here 60   *Sales* 16,256,520
SIC 1522 Residential construction, nec
Harvey Shoker

D-U-N-S 20-300-1912   (HQ)
SCHNITZER STEEL CANADA LTD
(*Suby of* SCHNITZER STEEL INDUSTRIES, INC.)
12195 Musqueam Dr, Surrey, BC, V3V 3T2
(604) 580-0251
Sales 52,054,200
SIC 5093 Scrap and waste materials
Richard Peach
Steven Heiskell
Thomas Klauer
Tom Maun
Brandon Peele
Richard Josephson

D-U-N-S 20-914-2017   (HQ)
SCHOOL DISTRICT NO. 36 (SURREY)
14033 92 Ave, Surrey, BC, V3V 0B7
(604) 596-7733
Emp Here 100   *Sales* 544,833,239
SIC 8211 Elementary and secondary schools
Laurie Larsen
Terry Allen
Bob Holmes
Laurae Mcnally
Garry Thind
Gary Tymoschuk
Shawn Wilson

D-U-N-S 25-194-8162   (BR)
SONEPAR CANADA INC
TEXCAN, DIV OF
(*Suby of* SOCIETE DE NEGOCE ET DE PARTICIPATION)
10449 120 St, Surrey, BC, V3V 4G4
(604) 528-3700
Emp Here 120
SIC 5063 Electrical apparatus and equipment

D-U-N-S 24-805-6905   (SL)
TWO SMALL MEN WITH BIG HEARTS MOVING (B.C.) CORPORATION
11180 Scott Rd, Surrey, BC, V3V 8B8
(604) 581-1616
Emp Here 25   *Sales* 51,426,500
SIC 4214 Local trucking with storage
Glen Buckler

D-U-N-S 20-116-9703   (HQ)
VAN-KAM FREIGHTWAYS LTD
VAN-KAM FREIGHTWAYS
10155 Grace Rd, Surrey, BC, V3V 3V7
(604) 582-7451
Emp Here 220   *Sales* 110,628,600
SIC 4213 Trucking, except local
Rory Anthony Henry
Robert James Henry

D-U-N-S 20-979-0257   (BR)
VITRAN EXPRESS CANADA INC
(*Suby of* TFI INTERNATIONAL INC)
10077 Grace Rd, Surrey, BC, V3V 3V7
(604) 582-4500
Emp Here 300
SIC 4213 Trucking, except local
Rick Garnett

D-U-N-S 24-360-6139   (HQ)
WILLIAMS MACHINERY LIMITED PARTNERSHIP
10240 Grace Rd, Surrey, BC, V3V 3V6
(604) 930-3300
Emp Here 20   *Sales* 30,876,690
SIC 5084 Industrial machinery and equipment
Shane Otteson

Surrey, BC V3W

D-U-N-S 20-794-8084   (HQ)
0756271 B.C. LTD
MIDWAY TIRE EXCEL
13412 72 Ave, Surrey, BC, V3W 2N8
(604) 591-6064
Emp Here 25   *Sales* 37,756,800
SIC 5531 Auto and home supply stores
Mark Endersby
Ian Endersby

D-U-N-S 20-978-2114   (SL)
302084 B.C. LTD
CENTURY PACIFIC FOUNDRY
8239 128 St, Surrey, BC, V3W 4G1
(604) 596-9984
Emp Here 70   *Sales* 18,308,710
SIC 6712 Bank holding companies
Heinz Hasselmann

D-U-N-S 20-013-4158   (HQ)
428675 BC LTD

NEWTON SQUARE BINGO COUNTRY
7093 King George Blvd Suite 401a, Surrey, BC, V3W 5A2
(604) 590-3230
Emp Here 50   *Sales* 11,202,320
SIC 7999 Amusement and recreation, nec
Alan Dyck

D-U-N-S 25-104-7007   (HQ)
A & M VENTURES LTD
12448 82 Ave Suite 201, Surrey, BC, V3W 3E9
(604) 597-9058
Sales 17,767,750
SIC 6712 Bank holding companies
Arnold Badke
Ed Fujii
Bill Lee
Ray Janzen
Andrew Baker

D-U-N-S 24-839-0544   (SL)
A - 1 BUILDING SUPPLIES LTD
8683 132 St, Surrey, BC, V3W 4P1
(604) 599-3822
Emp Here 50   *Sales* 22,358,700
SIC 5032 Brick, stone, and related material
Jerry Badhan
Kalwinder Kang

D-U-N-S 24-851-6259   (SL)
ACANA CAPITAL CORP
8338 120 St Suite 200, Surrey, BC, V3W 3N4
(604) 592-6881
Emp Here 50   *Sales* 15,943,450
SIC 1521 Single-family housing construction
Eugene Beukman
Jamie Lewin
Ravinder Binpal
Brian Findlay

D-U-N-S 24-980-4956   (SL)
ACME GLASS LTD
8335 129 St, Surrey, BC, V3W 0A6
(604) 543-8777
Emp Here 50   *Sales* 15,943,450
SIC 1521 Single-family housing construction
Lakhi Sahota

D-U-N-S 25-929-5269   (SL)
ACTIVE FIRE & SAFETY SERVICES LTD
12110 86 Ave, Surrey, BC, V3W 3H7
(604) 590-0149
Emp Here 50   *Sales* 26,027,100
SIC 5099 Durable goods, nec
Harjit Sangha

D-U-N-S 20-013-9876   (HQ)
ALL WEATHER PRODUCTS LTD
ROOFING STORE, THE
(*Suby of* BEACON ROOFING SUPPLY, INC.)
12510 82 Ave, Surrey, BC, V3W 3E9
(604) 572-8088
Emp Here 2   *Sales* 12,073,698
SIC 5033 Roofing, siding, and insulation
Ken Lillejord
Robert Kaethler

D-U-N-S 20-428-5712   (HQ)
APLIN & MARTIN CONSULTANTS LTD
MURRAY & ASSOCIATES
(*Suby of* A & M VENTURES LTD)
12448 82 Ave Suite 201, Surrey, BC, V3W 3E9
(604) 597-9189
Emp Here 100   *Sales* 17,595,800
SIC 8711 Engineering services
Edward Fujii
William Lee
Raymond Janzen
Andrew Baker

D-U-N-S 24-839-9404   (HQ)
ASSOCIATED HEALTH SYSTEMS INC
AHS
8145 130 St Unit 6, Surrey, BC, V3W 7X4
(604) 591-8012
Emp Here 10   *Sales* 12,520,872
SIC 5047 Medical and hospital equipment

James (Jim) Rikley
Arthur (Art) Forsyth

D-U-N-S 24-372-0828   (HQ)
B & W INSURANCE AGENCIES
8434 120 St Suite 108, Surrey, BC, V3W 7S2
(604) 591-7891
Emp Here 7   *Sales* 48,013,134
SIC 6331 Fire, marine, and casualty insurance
Ken Wilson
Tammy Stamnes

D-U-N-S 25-978-4858   (SL)
B.C. FASTENERS & TOOLS (2000) LTD
12824 78 Ave Unit 101, Surrey, BC, V3W 8E7
(604) 599-5455
Emp Here 25   *Sales* 11,875,650
SIC 5085 Industrial supplies
Thomas Allison
Gerry Miller

D-U-N-S 24-034-5256   (HQ)
BAILEY WEST INC
(*Suby of* BAILEY-HUNT LIMITED)
7715 129a St, Surrey, BC, V3W 6A2
(604) 590-5100
Sales 10,141,500
SIC 3444 Sheet Metalwork
David Hunt
David Mcconach

D-U-N-S 20-551-9676   (SL)
BASALITE CONCRETE PRODUCTS-VANCOUVER ULC
(*Suby of* PACIFIC COAST BUILDING PRODUCTS, INC.)
8650 130 St, Surrey, BC, V3W 1G1
(604) 596-3844
Emp Here 45   *Sales* 10,504,575
SIC 3272 Concrete products, nec
Weber Scott

D-U-N-S 24-798-4842   (HQ)
BAYWEST MANAGEMENT CORPORATION
(*Suby of* ASSOCIATIONS, INC.)
13468 77 Ave, Surrey, BC, V3W 6Y3
(604) 591-6060
Emp Here 5   *Sales* 49,019,280
SIC 6531 Real estate agents and managers
Bruce Friesen

D-U-N-S 20-865-1141   (HQ)
BC BIOMEDICAL LABORATORIES LTD
7455 130 St, Surrey, BC, V3W 1H8
(604) 507-5000
Emp Here 200   *Sales* 244,478,250
SIC 8071 Medical laboratories
Douglas Buchanan
Jatinder Bhan
John O'connell
Douglas Morrison
Walter Amann
David Reich

D-U-N-S 25-361-8078   (HQ)
BEACHCOMBER HOT TUBS GROUP
13245 Comber Way, Surrey, BC, V3W 5V8
(604) 502-4733
Emp Here 180   *Sales* 52,913,600
SIC 3999 Manufacturing industries, nec
Keith Scott

D-U-N-S 20-702-7496   (HQ)
BEACHCOMBER HOT TUBS INC
13245 Comber Way, Surrey, BC, V3W 5V8
(604) 591-8611
Sales 111,248,000
SIC 5091 Sporting and recreation goods
Keith Morris Scott
Almero Vanwyk

D-U-N-S 24-121-2153   (BR)
BELFOR (CANADA) INC
BELFOR PROPERTY & RESTORATION
(*Suby of* BELFOR HOLDINGS INC.)
7677d 132 St, Surrey, BC, V3W 4M8
(604) 599-9980
Emp Here 200

SIC 1799 Special trade contractors, nec
Drew Ivans

D-U-N-S 20-109-8373　　(HQ)
CAM CHAIN CO. LTD
CAN-AM CHAINS
8355 128 St, Surrey, BC, V3W 4G1
(604) 599-1522
Emp Here 55　　*Sales* 12,485,525
SIC 3462 Iron and steel forgings
Robert B. Gibb
Robert A. Gibb

D-U-N-S 24-012-8970　　(SL)
CANADIAN TIRE ASSOCIATE STORE
7599 King George Blvd, Surrey, BC, V3W 5A8
(604) 572-3739
Emp Here 80　　*Sales* 50,342,400
SIC 5531 Auto and home supply stores
Glen Reddemann

D-U-N-S 20-915-4699　　(HQ)
CEDAR GROVE BUILDING PRODUCTS LTD
CEDAR GROVE ROOFING SUPPLY
8073 132 St, Surrey, BC, V3W 4N5
(604) 590-3106
Emp Here 14　　*Sales* 13,382,600
SIC 5211 Lumber and other building materials
D. Houtman

D-U-N-S 24-008-2722　　(SL)
CENTURY 21 COASTAL REALTY LTD
12837 76 Ave Suite 217, Surrey, BC, V3W 2V3
(604) 599-4888
Emp Here 127　　*Sales* 53,198,903
SIC 6531 Real estate agents and managers
Tarsem Thind
Harpreet Purba

D-U-N-S 20-573-3462　　(SL)
CENTURY PACIFIC FOUNDRY LTD
8239 128 St, Surrey, BC, V3W 4G1
(604) 596-7451
Emp Here 50　　*Sales* 11,671,750
SIC 3325 Steel foundries, nec
Heinz Hasselmann

D-U-N-S 24-887-9983　　(HQ)
CHRISTIAN & MISSIONARY ALLIANCE - CANADIAN PACIFIC DISTRICT
7565 132 St Suite 107, Surrey, BC, V3W 1K5

Emp Here 7　　*Sales* 26,030,750
SIC 8661 Religious organizations
David Hearn
Robert Rose
Shelby Thiessen

D-U-N-S 24-957-7271　　(HQ)
COAST BUILDING SUPPLIES LTD
8484 128 St Unit 100, Surrey, BC, V3W 4G3
(604) 590-0055
Sales 20,122,830
SIC 5032 Brick, stone, and related material
Amrik Sangha
Altaf (Ben) Azad
Jaswant Chahal

D-U-N-S 20-623-7554　　(HQ)
CONVOY SUPPLY LTD
(*Suby of* HOLDING SOPREMA)
8183 130 St, Surrey, BC, V3W 7X4
(604) 591-5381
Emp Here 55　　*Sales* 208,483,848
SIC 5039 Construction materials, nec
Alma Garnett
Pierre-Etienne Bindschedler
Richard Voyer

D-U-N-S 25-679-7309　　(SL)
COSMACEUTICAL RESEARCH LAB INC
12920 84 Ave, Surrey, BC, V3W 1K7
(604) 590-1373
Emp Here 40　　*Sales* 11,066,400
SIC 2844 Toilet preparations
Ruth Ghuman

D-U-N-S 25-287-5331　　(BR)

COSTCO WHOLESALE CANADA LTD
COSTCO
(*Suby of* COSTCO WHOLESALE CORPORATION)
7423 King George Blvd Suite 55, Surrey, BC, V3W 5A8
(604) 596-7435
Emp Here 265
SIC 5099 Durable goods, nec
Mark Johnson

D-U-N-S 20-282-7010　　(SL)
CROWN BUILDING SUPPLIES LTD
7550 132 St Unit 10, Surrey, BC, V3W 4M7
(604) 591-5555
Emp Here 50　　*Sales* 22,358,700
SIC 5039 Construction materials, nec
Gary Sangha

D-U-N-S 24-877-4031　　(SL)
CYPRESS SECURITY (2013) INC
7028 120 St Suite 203, Surrey, BC, V3W 3M8
(778) 564-4088
Emp Here 100　　*Sales* 39,567,800
SIC 7381 Detective and armored car services
Jasbir Gill

D-U-N-S 25-722-9898　　(SL)
DELTA SUNSHINE TAXI (1972) LTD
12837 76 Ave Unit 203, Surrey, BC, V3W 2V3
(604) 594-5444
Emp Here 150　　*Sales* 11,290,800
SIC 4121 Taxicabs
Maheshinder Sidhu

D-U-N-S 20-369-7628　　(SL)
DIANNE WATTS CAMPAIGN, THE
7327 137 St Unit 307, Surrey, BC, V3W 1A4

Emp Here 70　　*Sales* 19,459,522
SIC 8651 Political organizations
Dianne Watts

D-U-N-S 24-898-7257　　(SL)
DIVERSECITY COMMUNITY RESOURCES SOCIETY
13455 76 Ave, Surrey, BC, V3W 2W3
(604) 597-0205
Emp Here 80　　*Sales* 10,676,720
SIC 8399 Social services, nec
Karen Ayres
Linda Howard
Baldev Sarahan

D-U-N-S 20-795-9008　　(SL)
DOUBLE V CONSTRUCTION LTD
(*Suby of* DOUBLE V DEVELOPMENTS LTD)
13303 78 Ave Suite 406, Surrey, BC, V3W 5B9
(604) 590-3131
Emp Here 21　　*Sales* 11,977,098
SIC 1542 Nonresidential construction, nec
Shane Van Vliet

D-U-N-S 24-167-1189　　(HQ)
DURADEK CANADA LIMITED
DURADEK
8288 129 St, Surrey, BC, V3W 0A6
(604) 591-5594
Sales 11,179,350
SIC 5039 Construction materials, nec
John David Ogilvie
Robert Bruce Ogilvie

D-U-N-S 24-350-4342　　(HQ)
EAGLE CINEMATRONICS INC
CINEMATRONIX
8299 129 St Unit 104, Surrey, BC, V3W 0A6
(604) 592-5511
Emp Here 9　　*Sales* 11,451,924
SIC 5099 Durable goods, nec
Kevin Eagle

D-U-N-S 24-578-7668　　(SL)
EAGLEPICHER ENERGY PRODUCTS ULC
EAGLEPICHER MEDICAL POWER
(*Suby of* EAGLEPICHER TECHNOLOGIES, LLC)
13136 82a Ave, Surrey, BC, V3W 9Y6

(604) 543-4350
Emp Here 125　　*Sales* 35,502,625
SIC 2819 Industrial inorganic chemicals, nec
James Hong

D-U-N-S 25-825-4267　　(BR)
EARL'S RESTAURANTS LTD
EARL'S STRAWBERRY HILL
(*Suby of* EARL'S RESTAURANTS LTD)
7236 120 St, Surrey, BC, V3W 3M9

Emp Here 85
SIC 5812 Eating places
Eric Holland

D-U-N-S 20-069-7238　　(SL)
ECHO BRAND MANAGEMENT LTD
8065 130 St, Surrey, BC, V3W 7X4
(604) 590-4020
Emp Here 30　　*Sales* 15,616,260
SIC 5099 Durable goods, nec
Greg Forrester

D-U-N-S 25-625-4111　　(BR)
EDENVALE RESTORATION SPECIALISTS LTD
EDENVALE RESTORATION SPECIALISTS
13260 78 Ave Unit 24, Surrey, BC, V3W 0H6
(604) 590-1440
Emp Here 100
SIC 1521 Single-family housing construction
Allen Booth

D-U-N-S 20-293-6621　　(SL)
EWOS CANADA LTD
EWOS
(*Suby of* CARGILL, INCORPORATED)
7721 132 St, Surrey, BC, V3W 4M8
(604) 591-6368
Emp Here 75　　*Sales* 25,926,750
SIC 2048 Prepared feeds, nec
Jason Mann

D-U-N-S 20-973-2432　　(SL)
EXPRESS-IT DELIVERY SERVICES (2002) INC
13350 Comber Way, Surrey, BC, V3W 5V9
(604) 543-7800
Emp Here 25　　*Sales* 11,087,250
SIC 7389 Business services, nec
Lyle Dewan

D-U-N-S 25-498-6904　　(SL)
FIRST CANADIAN MESSENGER SERVICE INC
13350 Comber Way, Surrey, BC, V3W 5V9
(604) 590-3301
Emp Here 35　　*Sales* 15,522,150
SIC 7389 Business services, nec
Richard Charles Diamond

D-U-N-S 25-450-9441　　(SL)
FRASERVIEW CEDAR PRODUCTS LTD
6630 144 St, Surrey, BC, V3W 5R5
(604) 590-3355
Emp Here 100　　*Sales* 15,586,300
SIC 2499 Wood products, nec
Gary Gill
Amritpal Gill
Balwant Gill

D-U-N-S 24-321-3373　　(HQ)
FRUITICANA PRODUCE LTD
7676 129a St, Surrey, BC, V3W 4H7
(604) 502-0005
Emp Here 120　　*Sales* 107,507,400
SIC 5148 Fresh fruits and vegetables
Tony Singh

D-U-N-S 25-754-0963　　(SL)
GUILDFORD CAB (1993) LTD
SURREY METRO TAXI
8299 129 St Unit 101, Surrey, BC, V3W 0A6
(604) 585-8888
Emp Here 120　　*Sales* 9,032,640
SIC 4121 Taxicabs
Surinder Attwal
Don Guilbault

Jaswant Gill
Talwinder Singh Sohal

D-U-N-S 25-754-2951　　(BR)
HOME DEPOT OF CANADA INC
HOME DEPOT
(*Suby of* THE HOME DEPOT INC)
7350 120 St, Surrey, BC, V3W 3M9
(604) 590-2796
Emp Here 200
SIC 5999 Miscellaneous retail stores, nec

D-U-N-S 24-938-3506　　(HQ)
I.C.C. INTEGRATED CONSTRUCTION CONCEPTS LTD
12960 84 Ave Suite 310, Surrey, BC, V3W 1K7
(604) 599-0706
Emp Here 20　　*Sales* 11,666,655
SIC 1541 Industrial buildings and warehouses
Eldon Ortlieb
Peter Krause

D-U-N-S 25-538-0578　　(HQ)
ICON SALON SYSTEMS LTD
13361 78 Ave Suite 610, Surrey, BC, V3W 5B9
(604) 591-2339
Emp Here 1　　*Sales* 15,447,982
SIC 5131 Piece goods and notions
Kent Gold
Art Ericson
Michael Blanchard

D-U-N-S 25-272-7375　　(BR)
INSURANCE CORPORATION OF BRITISH COLUMBIA
ICBC
(*Suby of* GOVERNMENT OF THE PROVINCE OF BRITISH COLUMBIA)
13665 68 Ave, Surrey, BC, V3W 0Y6
(604) 597-7600
Emp Here 130
SIC 6331 Fire, marine, and casualty insurance
Ian Wood

D-U-N-S 25-328-9565　　(SL)
INTERNATIONAL CASTINGS & SUPPLIES LTD
ICS
12383 83a Ave, Surrey, BC, V3W 9Y7
(604) 596-4961
Emp Here 28　　*Sales* 12,520,872
SIC 5051 Metals service centers and offices
Mark Pipke

D-U-N-S 24-798-7352　　(SL)
JOHN VOLKEN ACADEMY SOCIETY
PRICEPRO
6911 King George Blvd, Surrey, BC, V3W 5A1
(604) 594-1700
Emp Here 40　　*Sales* 15,896,560
SIC 8699 Membership organizations, nec
John Volken
Bilhar Koonar

D-U-N-S 24-787-2922　　(BR)
KEG RESTAURANTS LTD
KEG STEAKHOUSE & BAR, THE
(*Suby of* RECIPE UNLIMITED CORPORATION)
7948 120 St, Surrey, BC, V3W 3N2
(604) 591-6161
Emp Here 120
SIC 5812 Eating places
Dave Mortensen

D-U-N-S 24-359-3154　　(SL)
KHALSA SCHOOL
6933 124 St, Surrey, BC, V3W 3W6
(604) 591-2248
Emp Here 172　　*Sales* 23,333,520
SIC 8299 Schools and educational services, nec
Jasbir Singh Bhatia

D-U-N-S 20-120-2512　　(SL)
KIEF MUSIC LTD
13139 80 Ave Suite 1, Surrey, BC, V3W 3B1

Emp Here 30   *Sales* 15,616,260
SIC 5099 Durable goods, nec
 Fred Kief

   D-U-N-S 20-113-0564   (SL)
KOBELT MANUFACTURING CO. LTD
(Suby of BOW RIVER CAPITAL PARTNERS
LLC*)*
8238 129 St, Surrey, BC, V3W 0A6
(604) 572-3935
Emp Here 62   *Sales* 13,878,266
SIC 3732 Boatbuilding and repairing
 Dave Bockhold
 Ben Sykora

   D-U-N-S 20-271-8789   (SL)
KTC INDUSTRIAL ENGINEERING LTD
12877 76 Ave Suite 218, Surrey, BC, V3W 1E6
(604) 592-3123
Emp Here 40   *Sales* 13,333,320
SIC 1541 Industrial buildings and warehouses
 Jan Karnik
 Jim Mcmahon

   D-U-N-S 24-309-5809   (HQ)
**KWANTLEN POLYTECHNIC UNIVERSITY
FOUNDATION**
12666 72 Ave, Surrey, BC, V3W 2M8
(604) 599-2000
Emp Here 500   *Sales* 224,086,500
SIC 8221 Colleges and universities
 Scott Nicoll
 Alan Davis
 Salvador Ferreras

   D-U-N-S 24-363-2960   (SL)
LMS LIMITED PARTNERSHIP
7452 132 St, Surrey, BC, V3W 4M7
(604) 598-9930
Emp Here 65   *Sales* 16,002,090
SIC 1791 Structural steel erection
 Ron Mcneil
 Norm Streu
 Greg Hubbard
 Michael Schutz

   D-U-N-S 25-270-1339   (BR)
LOBLAWS INC
REAL CANADIAN SUPERSTORE 1521
(Suby of LOBLAW COMPANIES LIMITED*)*
7550 King George Blvd Suite 1, Surrey, BC,
V3W 2T2

Emp Here 400
SIC 5141 Groceries, general line
 Gerald Munts

   D-U-N-S 20-994-3927   (HQ)
LYNUM MANAGEMENT RESOURCES INC
LYNUM PROGRESSIVE INDUSTRIES
8456 129a St Unit 17, Surrey, BC, V3W 1A2
(604) 594-0100
Emp Here 8   *Sales* 26,830,440
SIC 5049 Professional equipment, nec
 Thor Lynum

   D-U-N-S 20-102-0179   (HQ)
M.A. STEWART & SONS LTD
12900 87 Ave, Surrey, BC, V3W 3H9
(604) 594-8431
Emp Here 37   *Sales* 33,251,820
SIC 5085 Industrial supplies
 John Makarchuk

   D-U-N-S 24-658-5590   (HQ)
M.J.M. FURNITURE CENTRE LTD
13570 77 Ave, Surrey, BC, V3W 6Y3
(604) 596-9901
Emp Here 3   *Sales* 13,944,180
SIC 5712 Furniture stores
 Manjit Jaswal
 Jagit Jaswal

   D-U-N-S 20-396-8560   (SL)
MAINLAND CIVIL SITE SERVICES INC
12899 80 Ave Unit 206, Surrey, BC, V3W 0E6

(604) 591-5599
Emp Here 85   *Sales* 21,457,570
SIC 1623 Water, sewer, and utility lines
 Gary Dhaliwal
 Joel Grams

   D-U-N-S 20-115-1065   (SL)
**MURRAY LATTA PROGRESSIVE MACHINE
INC**
8717 132 St, Surrey, BC, V3W 4P1
(604) 599-9598
Emp Here 145   *Sales* 40,727,165
SIC 3569 General industrial machinery, nec

   D-U-N-S 24-309-8647   (SL)
NATIONAL HYDRONICS LTD
12178 86 Ave, Surrey, BC, V3W 3H7
(604) 591-6106
Emp Here 50   *Sales* 11,046,700
SIC 1711 Plumbing, heating, air-conditioning
 Michael Vesterback
 Richard Musil
 Ronald Jassmann

   D-U-N-S 24-333-2793   (BR)
NAV CANADA
(Suby of NAV CANADA*)*
7421 135 St, Surrey, BC, V3W 0M8
(604) 775-9534
Emp Here 600
SIC 4899 Communication services, nec
 Margot Spronk

   D-U-N-S 20-749-5862   (SL)
NEWTON'S HI QUALITY MEATS LTD
12481 80 Ave, Surrey, BC, V3W 3A4
(604) 596-1528
Emp Here 35   *Sales* 29,245,195
SIC 5147 Meats and meat products
 Peter Steinfeld
 Merle Steinfeld

   D-U-N-S 24-153-1375   (SL)
NORTH STAR PATROL (1996) LTD
12981 80 Ave, Surrey, BC, V3W 3B1

Emp Here 100   *Sales* 39,567,800
SIC 7381 Detective and armored car services
 Kenneth Robertson

   D-U-N-S 25-113-4003   (SL)
**NORWOOD MANUFACTURING CANADA
INC**
8519 132 St, Surrey, BC, V3W 4N8

Emp Here 50   *Sales* 13,833,000
SIC 2844 Toilet preparations
 Daryl Martini
 Spencer Sheinin

   D-U-N-S 24-837-8531   (SL)
OASIS WINDOWS LTD
7677 134 St, Surrey, BC, V3W 9E9
(604) 597-5033
Emp Here 25   *Sales* 11,179,350
SIC 5031 Lumber, plywood, and millwork
 Barjinder Singh Sidhu

   D-U-N-S 24-454-9234   (HQ)
PACIFIC RIM FLOORING LTD
PACIFIC RIM FLOOR SUPPLIES
13375 76 Ave Suite 101, Surrey, BC, V3W 6J3
(604) 591-3431
Emp Here 1   *Sales* 33,584,496
SIC 5023 Homefurnishings
 David Arthur
 Roger Collins
 Roger Lu
 Matthew Saunders

   D-U-N-S 20-862-3660   (SL)
PACIFIC SALMON INDUSTRIES INC
SCANNER ENTERPRISES
8305 128 St, Surrey, BC, V3W 4G1
(604) 501-7600
Emp Here 40   *Sales* 33,423,080
SIC 5146 Fish and seafoods
 Michael Sato

 Virginia Sato

   D-U-N-S 24-148-1048   (SL)
PARM'S PRESCRIPTIONS LTD
SHOPPERS DRUG MART
12080 Nordel Way Suite 101, Surrey, BC,
V3W 1P6
(604) 543-8155
Emp Here 50   *Sales* 12,647,700
SIC 5912 Drug stores and proprietary stores
 Parm Dhami

   D-U-N-S 25-364-1534   (SL)
PLANET DRUGS DIRECT INC
7455 132 St Suite 100, Surrey, BC, V3W 1J8
(604) 501-6902
Emp Here 200   *Sales* 48,865,600
SIC 5961 Catalog and mail-order houses
 Vaughn Hodson

   D-U-N-S 24-855-9601   (HQ)
**PLAYTIME COMMUNITY GAMING CEN-
TRES INC**
7445 132 St Suite 1001, Surrey, BC, V3W 1J8
(604) 590-2577
Emp Here 12   *Sales* 18,990,600
SIC 7999 Amusement and recreation, nec
 Joe Nellis

   D-U-N-S 24-777-2031   (SL)
POWERTECH LABS INC
(Suby of GOVERNMENT OF THE
PROVINCE OF BRITISH COLUMBIA*)*
12388 88 Ave, Surrey, BC, V3W 7R7
(604) 590-7500
Emp Here 200   *Sales* 28,164,733
SIC 8734 Testing laboratories
 Raymond Lings

   D-U-N-S 20-176-3633   (SL)
PRUDENTIAL TRANSPORTATION LTD
8138 128 St Unit 239, Surrey, BC, V3W 1R1
(604) 543-2147
Emp Here 100   *Sales* 14,819,200
SIC 4212 Local trucking, without storage
 Rex D'souza

   D-U-N-S 20-972-3423   (HQ)
**R. DIAMOND GROUP OF COMPANIES LTD,
THE**
DIAMOND DELIVERY SERVICES
13350 Comber Way, Surrey, BC, V3W 5V9
(604) 591-8641
Emp Here 20   *Sales* 18,198,845
SIC 4731 Freight transportation arrangement
 Richard Diamond

   D-U-N-S 24-798-2135   (SL)
RAILCRAFT (2010) INTERNATIONAL INC
13272 Comber Way, Surrey, BC, V3W 5V9
(604) 543-7245
Emp Here 81   *Sales* 15,558,885
SIC 3446 Architectural Metalwork
 Neill Baker
 Bilma Baker

   D-U-N-S 25-818-3649   (SL)
**REGENCY INTERMEDIATE CARE FACILI-
TIES INC**
NEWTON REGENCY CARE HOME
13855 68 Ave, Surrey, BC, V3W 2G9
(604) 597-9333
Emp Here 80   *Sales* 5,206,000
SIC 8361 Residential care
 Cora Bueza

   D-U-N-S 20-102-5764   (SL)
ROBAR INDUSTRIES LTD
12945 78 Ave, Surrey, BC, V3W 2X8
(604) 591-8811
Emp Here 100   *Sales* 23,343,500
SIC 3321 Gray and ductile iron foundries
 Jackie Vey
 Michelle Charleston

   D-U-N-S 24-995-2094   (SL)
**SATNAM EDUCATION SOCIETY OF
BRITISH COLUMBIA**

KHALSA SCHOOL
6933 124 St, Surrey, BC, V3W 3W6

Emp Here 100   *Sales* 12,012,900
SIC 8299 Schools and educational services,
nec
 Jarnail Manhas
 Aniljit Singh
 Satwant Singh
 Kewal Singh
 Ripdalman Singh Malik

   D-U-N-S 24-073-7817   (SL)
SCANNER ENTERPRISES (1982) INC
8305 128 St, Surrey, BC, V3W 4G1
(604) 591-2908
Emp Here 60   *Sales* 20,741,400
SIC 2092 Fresh or frozen packaged fish
 Virginia Sato

   D-U-N-S 20-301-3169   (BR)
SCHOOL DISTRICT NO. 36 (SURREY)
SCHOOL DISTRICT NO 36 (SURREY)
(Suby of SCHOOL DISTRICT NO. 36 (SUR-
REY)*)*
12600 66 Ave, Surrey, BC, V3W 2A8
(604) 597-5234
Emp Here 100
SIC 8211 Elementary and secondary schools
 Jim Lamond

   D-U-N-S 20-139-6491   (BR)
SCHOOL DISTRICT NO. 36 (SURREY)
SCHOOL DISTRICT NO 36 (SURREY)
(Suby of SCHOOL DISTRICT NO. 36 (SUR-
REY)*)*
12772 88 Ave, Surrey, BC, V3W 3J9
(604) 502-5710
Emp Here 100
SIC 8211 Elementary and secondary schools
 Rick Ryan

   D-U-N-S 20-033-3206   (BR)
SCHOOL DISTRICT NO. 36 (SURREY)
ELLIS, THOMAS G. CENTRE
(Suby of SCHOOL DISTRICT NO. 36 (SUR-
REY)*)*
6700 144 St, Surrey, BC, V3W 5R5
(604) 572-0500
Emp Here 200
SIC 4173 Bus terminal and service facilities
 Lance Nordling

   D-U-N-S 24-974-8609   (BR)
SCHOOL DISTRICT NO. 36 (SURREY)
SCHOOL DISTRICT NO 36 (SURREY)
(Suby of SCHOOL DISTRICT NO. 36 (SUR-
REY)*)*
12870 72 Ave, Surrey, BC, V3W 2M9
(604) 594-5458
Emp Here 100
SIC 8211 Elementary and secondary schools
 Dennis Hugh

   D-U-N-S 20-115-8474   (HQ)
SHANAHAN'S LIMITED PARTNERSHIP
13139 80 Ave, Surrey, BC, V3W 3B1
(604) 591-5111
Emp Here 85   *Sales* 213,610,500
SIC 5039 Construction materials, nec
 Gerrit Mey
 William Peter Mey
 Mike Barnes
 Gerald Mey
 Joan Toews

   D-U-N-S 24-292-6673   (HQ)
SMITH CAMERON PUMP SOLUTIONS INC
SMITH CAMERON PROCESS SOLUTIONS
13478 78 Ave Unit 1, Surrey, BC, V3W 8J6
(604) 596-5522
Emp Here 25   *Sales* 14,010,984
SIC 5084 Industrial machinery and equipment
 Tom Kramer

   D-U-N-S 25-482-9328   (BR)
SOBEYS WEST INC

SAFEWAY, DIV
(*Suby of* EMPIRE COMPANY LIMITED)
7165 138 St, Surrey, BC, V3W 7T9
(604) 594-4515
Emp Here 100
SIC 5411 Grocery stores
Farzin Rawji

D-U-N-S 25-723-9822   (BR)
SOBEYS WEST INC
SAFEWAY
(*Suby of* EMPIRE COMPANY LIMITED)
7450 120 St, Surrey, BC, V3W 3M9
(604) 594-7341
Emp Here 180
SIC 5411 Grocery stores
Reno Pozzobon

D-U-N-S 20-911-4326   (SL)
SOLARIS PHARMACEUTICALS INC
8322 130 St Suite 201, Surrey, BC, V3W 8J9
(778) 218-2655
Emp Here 50   *Sales* 12,647,700
SIC 5912 Drug stores and proprietary stores
Amarjit Mann

D-U-N-S 24-837-9604   (SL)
SUNRISE KITCHENS LTD
13375 Comber Way, Surrey, BC, V3W 5V8
(604) 597-0364
Emp Here 110   *Sales* 16,975,420
SIC 2541 Wood partitions and fixtures
Paul Bhogal
Sohan Singh Bhogal

D-U-N-S 24-369-2829   (HQ)
SUNRISE POULTRY PROCESSORS LTD
SUNRISE FARMS
13538 73 Ave, Surrey, BC, V3W 2R6
(604) 596-9505
Sales 268,061,750
SIC 2015 Poultry slaughtering and processing
Peter Shoore

D-U-N-S 24-329-4456   (SL)
SUPREME CHAIN LOGISTICS LTD
8277 129 St Unit 201, Surrey, BC, V3W 0A6
(604) 585-1415
Emp Here 60   *Sales* 31,198,020
SIC 4731 Freight transportation arrangement
Sukhdeep Brar

D-U-N-S 24-448-3038   (SL)
SURREY GYMNASTIC SOCIETY
13940 77 Ave, Surrey, BC, V3W 5Z4
(604) 594-2442
Emp Here 30   *Sales* 11,922,420
SIC 8699 Membership organizations, nec
Sandra Smith
Lisa Webb

D-U-N-S 24-672-6285   (SL)
SURTEK INDUSTRIES INC
13018 84 Ave Unit 4, Surrey, BC, V3W 1L2
(604) 590-2235
Emp Here 60   *Sales* 11,426,520
SIC 3679 Electronic components, nec
Vijay Tharmarajah

D-U-N-S 24-329-4464   (SL)
SYNERGY TRUCKING LTD
7184 120 St Suite 190, Surrey, BC, V3W 0M6
(604) 598-3498
Emp Here 50   *Sales* 25,998,350
SIC 4731 Freight transportation arrangement
Paul Nahal

D-U-N-S 25-171-2196   (HQ)
TAPESTRY REALTY LTD
ROYAL GROUP TAPESTRY REALTY
13049 76 Ave Suite 104, Surrey, BC, V3W 2V7

Sales 27,227,785
SIC 6531 Real estate agents and managers
Sandy Rakhra
Sam Rakhra

D-U-N-S 24-897-7977   (HQ)

TRANS CONTINENTAL TEXTILE RECY-CLING LTD
13120 78a Ave, Surrey, BC, V3W 1P4
(604) 592-2845
Sales 10,285,240
SIC 4953 Refuse systems
Patricia Penrose

D-U-N-S 20-152-7566   (SL)
UNICITY NETWORK CANADA, LTD
7495 132 St Suite 1007, Surrey, BC, V3W 1J8

Emp Here 20   *Sales* 22,478,711
SIC 5122 Drugs, proprietaries, and sundries

D-U-N-S 24-040-2839   (SL)
UPPAL BUILDING SUPPLIES LTD
7846 128 St, Surrey, BC, V3W 4E8
(604) 594-4142
Emp Here 52   *Sales* 13,917,904
SIC 5211 Lumber and other building materials
Jagtar Uppal

D-U-N-S 20-921-0322   (SL)
VANCOUVER PARTYWORKS INTERAC-TIVE CO INC
VANCOUVER PARTYWORKS
8473 124 St Unit 13, Surrey, BC, V3W 9G4
(604) 599-5541
Emp Here 95   *Sales* 18,178,630
SIC 7359 Equipment rental and leasing, nec
Garnett Pawliw

D-U-N-S 24-330-0527   (BR)
WAL-MART CANADA CORP
(*Suby of* WALMART INC.)
12451 88 Ave, Surrey, BC, V3W 1P8
(604) 597-7117
Emp Here 200
SIC 5311 Department stores
Dean White

D-U-N-S 20-104-4703   (SL)
WALDIE, D.S. HOLDINGS INCORPORATED
CANADIAN TIRE
8140 120 St, Surrey, BC, V3W 3N3

Emp Here 30   *Sales* 14,942,340
SIC 5531 Auto and home supply stores
Doug Waldie

D-U-N-S 24-805-1174   (HQ)
WESTPRO INFRASTRUCTURE LTD
(*Suby of* INGENIUM GROUP INC)
8241 129 St, Surrey, BC, V3W 0A6
(604) 592-9767
Emp Here 10   *Sales* 23,536,550
SIC 1542 Nonresidential construction, nec
Joel Nauss

D-U-N-S 24-491-8462   (SL)
XL IRONWORKS
12720 82 Ave, Surrey, BC, V3W 3G1
(604) 596-1747
Emp Here 60   *Sales* 14,771,160
SIC 1791 Structural steel erection
Slivano Patrignani
Richard Hounslow

Surrey, BC V3X

D-U-N-S 25-243-5081   (SL)
GET IT DONE DEMOLITION & DISPOSAL
12224 Boundary Dr N, Surrey, BC, V3X 1Z5
(604) 916-1388
Emp Here 45   *Sales* 11,078,370
SIC 1795 Wrecking and demolition work

D-U-N-S 20-590-9463   (BR)
SCHOOL DISTRICT NO. 36 (SURREY)
SCHOOL DISTRICT NO 36 (SURREY)
(*Suby of* SCHOOL DISTRICT NO. 36 (SUR-REY))
6248 144 St, Surrey, BC, V3X 1A1

(604) 543-8749
Emp Here 100
SIC 8211 Elementary and secondary schools
Raj Puri

Surrey, BC V3Z

D-U-N-S 24-681-2163   (HQ)
4499034 CANADA INC
TRYDOR INDUSTRIES
(*Suby of* WESCO INTERNATIONAL, INC.)
19275 25 Ave, Surrey, BC, V3Z 3X1
(604) 542-4773
Emp Here 23   *Sales* 14,756,742
SIC 5063 Electrical apparatus and equipment
Murray Leimert

D-U-N-S 24-153-2761   (HQ)
A & A CONTRACT CUSTOMS BROKERS LTD
120 176 St Suite 101, Surrey, BC, V3Z 9S2
(604) 538-1042
Emp Here 110   *Sales* 81,460,228
SIC 4731 Freight transportation arrangement
Graham Robins Jr

D-U-N-S 25-992-1070   (HQ)
A.R. THOMSON GROUP
3420 189 St, Surrey, BC, V3Z 1A7
(604) 507-6050
Emp Here 22   *Sales* 31,771,600
SIC 3053 Gaskets; packing and sealing de-vices
James Thomson
Allan R Thomson

D-U-N-S 20-342-5962   (SL)
ABSOLUTE RESULTS MARKETING SYS-TEMS INC
(*Suby of* ABSOLUTE RESULTS PRODUC-TIONS LTD)
2677 192 St Unit 104, Surrey, BC, V3Z 3X1
(888) 751-7171
Emp Here 92
SIC 7311 Advertising agencies
Gordon Swail

D-U-N-S 20-747-8749   (HQ)
ABSOLUTE RESULTS PRODUCTIONS LTD
ABSOLUTE RESULTS
2677 192 St Unit 104, Surrey, BC, V3Z 3X1
(888) 751-7171
Sales 14,057,280
SIC 8748 Business consulting, nec
Jeffrey Williams

D-U-N-S 20-108-5404   (SL)
ADVANCE WIRE PRODUCTS LTD
AWP
19095 24 Ave Suite 19095, Surrey, BC, V3Z 3S9
(604) 541-4666
Emp Here 70   *Sales* 10,802,540
SIC 2599 Furniture and fixtures, nec
Mary Murphy
Ronald Le Boutillier

D-U-N-S 25-629-2624   (SL)
AGM BEEF FARMS LTD
GRANDMAISON BEEF FARMS
5175 184 St, Surrey, BC, V3Z 1B5
(604) 576-8318
Emp Here 28   *Sales* 10,794,532
SIC 0212 Beef cattle, except feedlots
Alain Grandmaison

D-U-N-S 25-126-8095   (SL)
ALCA DISTRIBUTION INC
2153 192 St Unit 4, Surrey, BC, V3Z 3X2
(604) 635-3901
Emp Here 20   *Sales* 10,006,500
SIC 5137 Women's and children's clothing
Douglas Jonathan Fulton
Loretta Gail Fulton

D-U-N-S 24-672-3688   (HQ)
ANIPET ANIMAL SUPPLIES INC
19038 24 Ave, Surrey, BC, V3Z 3S9
(604) 536-3367
Emp Here 115   *Sales* 76,590,670
SIC 5199 Nondurable goods, nec
Larry Kellington
Grant Hadland
Heather Kellington

D-U-N-S 20-798-3891   (SL)
AQUIFORM DISTRIBUTORS LTD
STAWARM, DIV OF
19296 25 Ave, Surrey, BC, V3Z 3X1
(604) 541-0500
Emp Here 24   *Sales* 12,493,008
SIC 5091 Sporting and recreation goods
Franco Rasera

D-U-N-S 20-094-9428   (HQ)
B & B CONTRACTING LTD
B & B CONTRACTING GROUP
3077 188 St Suite 100, Surrey, BC, V3Z 9V5
(604) 539-7200
Sales 11,114,400
SIC 4212 Local trucking, without storage
Gary Bailey
Bickerton Kelly
Bruce Fraser

D-U-N-S 24-598-4096   (SL)
BAY HILL CONTRACTING LTD
19122 21 Ave, Surrey, BC, V3Z 3M3
(604) 536-3306
Emp Here 80   *Sales* 17,426,320
SIC 1731 Electrical work
Robert Burns

D-U-N-S 25-387-6445   (HQ)
BEKINS MOVING AND STORAGE (CANADA) LTD
3779 190 St, Surrey, BC, V3Z 0P6
(604) 270-1120
Sales 14,399,420
SIC 4214 Local trucking with storage
Larry Rosenberg

D-U-N-S 20-114-4164   (SL)
BLUE PINE ENTERPRISES LTD
18960 34a Ave, Surrey, BC, V3Z 1A7
(604) 535-3026
Emp Here 120   *Sales* 20,868,600
SIC 0782 Lawn and garden services
Mike Lalonde

D-U-N-S 24-192-7578   (SL)
CANADIAN AUTOMATED BANK MA-CHINES INC
17637 1 Ave Suite 101, Surrey, BC, V3Z 9S1
(866) 538-2982
Emp Here 50   *Sales* 22,358,700
SIC 5044 Office equipment
J Glen Todd
Gregory L Timm

D-U-N-S 24-111-9197   (HQ)
CARSON CUSTOM BROKERS LIMITED
CARSON FREIGHT SYSTEMS
17735 1 Ave Suite 260, Surrey, BC, V3Z 9S1
(604) 538-4966
Emp Here 32   *Sales* 53,351,360
SIC 4731 Freight transportation arrangement
Richard Carson
Thomas Fisher
Carmine Cesari
Paula Carson
Robert Walker
Ray Carson
Tyler Carson

D-U-N-S 20-109-7847   (HQ)
CB SUPPLIES LTD
3325 190 St, Surrey, BC, V3Z 1A7
(604) 535-5088
Emp Here 10   *Sales* 60,648,160
SIC 5074 Plumbing and heating equipment and supplies (hydronics)

Warren Lowe

D-U-N-S 25-507-5947   (HQ)
CLOVERDALE INVESTMENTS LTD
2630 Croydon Dr Ste 400, Surrey, BC, V3Z
6T3
(604) 594-6211
Emp Here 2   *Sales* 237,580,850
SIC 6712 Bank holding companies
Walter Vogle
Noelle Vogle

D-U-N-S 20-102-2621   (HQ)
CLOVERDALE PAINT INC
(*Suby of* CLOVERDALE INVESTMENTS LTD)
2630 Croydon Dr Unit 400, Surrey, BC, V3Z
6T3
(604) 596-6261
Emp Here 85   *Sales* 444,645,000
SIC 2851 Paints and allied products
Walter Vogel
Noelle Vogel
Timothy Vogel
Alan Laird
Robert Mair
Thomas Braden

D-U-N-S 24-414-3736   (HQ)
CORLIVING DISTRIBUTION LTD
CORPORATE IMAGES
2252 190 St, Surrey, BC, V3Z 3W7
(604) 542-7650
Sales 33,075,640
SIC 5021 Furniture
Chris Helser

D-U-N-S 24-418-0886   (SL)
CRYSTAL CONSULTING INC
2677 192 St Unit 108, Surrey, BC, V3Z 3X1
(778) 294-4425
Emp Here 150   *Sales* 29,454,150
SIC 1751 Carpentry work
Ajit Sangha
Kuldeep Chohan
Garry Sangha

D-U-N-S 24-980-0624   (HQ)
CUSTOM HOUSE ULC
WESTERN UNION BUSINESS SOLUTIONS
(*Suby of* THE WESTERN UNION COMPANY)
409-2626 Croydon Dr, Surrey, BC, V3Z 0S8
(604) 560-8060
Emp Here 100   *Sales* 168,653,008
SIC 6099 Functions related to deposit banking
Kerry Agiasotis
Ian Taylor
Brian Harris
Jacqueline Keogh
Adam Tiberi
Cecilia Watts
Tony Crivelli
Kenneth Timbers
Scott Smith
Tristan Van Der Vijver

D-U-N-S 24-839-4199   (HQ)
D. & A.'S PET FOOD 'N MORE LTD
19347 24 Ave Unit 105, Surrey, BC, V3Z 3S9
(604) 591-5990
Emp Here 7   *Sales* 13,024,000
SIC 5999 Miscellaneous retail stores, nec
David Mackay
Andrew Mackay

D-U-N-S 24-116-2861   (SL)
D.J. DRILLING (2004) LTD
19286 24 Ave Unit 104, Surrey, BC, V3Z 3M3
(604) 541-1362
Emp Here 60   *Sales* 14,006,100
SIC 1081 Metal mining services
David Schussler

D-U-N-S 25-625-4095   (HQ)
E.B. HORSMAN & SON LTD
19295 25 Ave, Surrey, BC, V3Z 3X1
(778) 545-9916
Emp Here 35   *Sales* 145,061,750

SIC 5063 Electrical apparatus and equipment
Timothy Horsman

D-U-N-S 20-119-9366   (SL)
EVERGREEN HERBS LTD
3727 184 St, Surrey, BC, V3Z 1B8
(604) 576-2567
Emp Here 60   *Sales* 50,134,620
SIC 5148 Fresh fruits and vegetables
Ron Brar
Tj Brar

D-U-N-S 24-806-6128   (SL)
FASTEEL INDUSTRIES LTD
19176 21 Ave, Surrey, BC, V3Z 3M3
(604) 542-8881
Emp Here 30   *Sales* 13,415,220
SIC 5051 Metals service centers and offices
Brian Mckenny
Donald Mckenny

D-U-N-S 20-275-9015   (SL)
GALLAGHER BROS CONTRACTORS LTD
19140 28 Ave Unit 114, Surrey, BC, V3Z 6M3
(604) 531-3156
Emp Here 70   *Sales* 11,366,670
SIC 1742 Plastering, drywall, and insulation
Daniel Gallagher

D-U-N-S 25-228-7586   (HQ)
GARAVENTA (CANADA) LTD
(*Suby of* AMD PRIVATSTIFTUNG)
18920 36 Ave, Surrey, BC, V3Z 0P6
(604) 594-0422
Emp Here 170   *Sales* 66,142,000
SIC 3999 Manufacturing industries, nec
Vincent Sciamanna

D-U-N-S 24-081-1617   (SL)
GREENWAY FARMS LTD
5040 160 St Suite 5040, Surrey, BC, V3Z 1E8
(604) 574-1564
Emp Here 50   *Sales* 17,123,350
SIC 0161 Vegetables and melons
Bill Singh
Ricky Sandhu

D-U-N-S 25-972-7191   (SL)
GROUPHEALTH BENEFIT SOLUTIONS
2626 Croydon Dr Suite 200, Surrey, BC, V3Z
0S8
(604) 542-4100
Emp Here 411   *Sales* 1,950,648,744
SIC 6411 Insurance agents, brokers, and service
Matt Houghton

D-U-N-S 24-361-7292   (BR)
HOME DEPOT OF CANADA INC
HOME DEPOT
(*Suby of* THE HOME DEPOT INC)
2525 160 St, Surrey, BC, V3Z 0C8
(604) 542-3520
Emp Here 150
SIC 5251 Hardware stores
Peg Hunter

D-U-N-S 25-483-5432   (SL)
INTERNATIONAL HERBS (B.C.) LTD
(*Suby of* ATLAS PRODUCE SUPPLY LTD)
4151 184 St, Surrey, BC, V3Z 1B7
(604) 576-2345
Emp Here 75   *Sales* 53,753,700
SIC 5149 Groceries and related products, nec
Rick Brar
Tim Quat

D-U-N-S 24-586-9933   (SL)
JACOB BROS CONSTRUCTION INC
3399 189 St, Surrey, BC, V3Z 1A7
(604) 541-0303
Emp Here 250   *Sales* 82,028,750
SIC 1611 Highway and street construction
Jason Jacob
Todd Jacob
Scott Jacob

D-U-N-S 20-751-6324   (HQ)

JACOB BROS. ASSET CO. LTD
3399 189 St, Surrey, BC, V3Z 1A7
(604) 541-0303
Emp Here 50   *Sales* 50,488,400
SIC 1611 Highway and street construction
Jason Jacob
Scott Jacob
Todd Jacob

D-U-N-S 25-180-1072   (SL)
K.D.S. CONSTRUCTION LTD
16250 20 Ave, Surrey, BC, V3Z 9M8
(604) 535-8152
Emp Here 50   *Sales* 23,536,550
SIC 1542 Nonresidential construction, nec
Kelly Shannon
Marvin Kale

D-U-N-S 24-320-4373   (HQ)
KAHUNAVERSE SPORTS GROUP INC
19036 22 Ave Suite 101, Surrey, BC, V3Z 3S6
(604) 536-2441
Emp Here 10   *Sales* 132,107,000
SIC 5091 Sporting and recreation goods
Gord Querin
Craig Preece
Lamberto Balducci
Dean Longstaff
Paul Michaud
Michael Hamm
Scott Neiles

D-U-N-S 24-037-0127   (BR)
KEG RESTAURANTS LTD
MORGAN CREEK KEG
(*Suby of* RECIPE UNLIMITED CORPORA-
TION)
15180 32 Ave Divers, Surrey, BC, V3Z 3M1
(604) 542-9733
Emp Here 120
SIC 5812 Eating places
Eduardo Tolentino

D-U-N-S 24-426-1371   (SL)
KIM'S FARM
4186 176 St, Surrey, BC, V3Z 1C3
(604) 649-7938
Emp Here 40   *Sales* 13,698,680
SIC 0119 Cash grains, nec
Kim Tam Cho
Bo Kan Cho

D-U-N-S 24-551-5262   (SL)
KUZCO LIGHTING INC
19054 28 Ave Suite 19054, Surrey, BC, V3Z
6M3
(604) 538-7162
Emp Here 55   *Sales* 24,594,570
SIC 5063 Electrical apparatus and equipment
Nathan Yang

D-U-N-S 24-534-9287   (SL)
MERCANA FURNITURE & DECOR LTD
3250 189 St, Surrey, BC, V3Z 1A7
(604) 596-1668
Emp Here 90   *Sales* 45,797,040
SIC 5023 Homefurnishings
Merlin Smith
Maureen Smith

D-U-N-S 20-863-3826   (HQ)
MORGAN CREEK TROPICALS LTD
4148 184 St, Surrey, BC, V3Z 1B7
(604) 576-1156
Sales 22,275,600
SIC 5193 Flowers and florists supplies
George Sachinidis

D-U-N-S 20-584-8919   (SL)
MUD BAY NURSERIES LTD
ART KNAPP PLANTLAND
4391 King George Blvd, Surrey, BC, V3Z 1G6
(604) 596-9201
Emp Here 40   *Sales* 10,122,360
SIC 5261 Retail nurseries and garden stores
Marty Vanderzalm
Jamie Vanderzalm

Kerry Vanderzalm
Lonnie Vanderzalm

D-U-N-S 24-881-3909   (HQ)
NORTHSTAR REALTY LTD
ROYAL LEPAGE NORTHSTAR REALTY
15272 Croydon Dr Suite 118, Surrey, BC, V3Z
0Z5
(604) 597-1664
Sales 12,229,020
SIC 6531 Real estate agents and managers
Wayne Gervan

D-U-N-S 24-132-0311   (SL)
NORTHWEST SHEET METAL LTD
19159 33 Ave, Surrey, BC, V3Z 1A1
(604) 542-9536
Emp Here 75   *Sales* 16,337,175
SIC 1761 Roofing, siding, and sheetMetal
work
Dave Antchak

D-U-N-S 24-681-5716   (HQ)
NOVA POLE INTERNATIONAL INC
2579 188 St, Surrey, BC, V3Z 2A1
(604) 881-0090
Sales 13,465,900
SIC 2499 Wood products, nec
Sandra Atkins
Chandru Narwani
Rajwinder Johal
Fawzy Morcos

D-U-N-S 20-114-5000   (HQ)
O.K. TIRE STORES INC
19082 21 Ave, Surrey, BC, V3Z 3M3
(604) 542-7999
Emp Here 50   *Sales* 72,156,500
SIC 5531 Auto and home supply stores
George Grose
Darryl Croft
Nelson Gray
Marc Audet
Colin Fraser
Tim Togeretz
Mark Franklin
Dick Graham
Jules Bolduc
Dave Cote

D-U-N-S 24-314-0670   (HQ)
PACIFIC CUSTOMS BROKERS LTD
17637 1 Ave Suite 101, Surrey, BC, V3Z 9S1
(604) 538-1566
Emp Here 70   *Sales* 51,996,700
SIC 4731 Freight transportation arrangement
Glenn Todd
Barry Davidson

D-U-N-S 24-566-3935   (HQ)
**PAN AMERICAN NURSERY PRODUCTS
INC**
5151 152 St, Surrey, BC, V3Z 1G9
(604) 576-8641
Emp Here 90   *Sales* 82,482,260
SIC 5193 Flowers and florists supplies
Margie Van Zanten
Edward Van Zanten
Robert Van Zanten
Donald Williamson

D-U-N-S 20-120-6281   (SL)
PENGUIN MEAT SUPPLY LTD
(*Suby of* PREMIUM BRANDS HOLDINGS
CORPORATION)
19195 33 Ave Unit 1, Surrey, BC, V3Z 1A1
(604) 531-1447
Emp Here 60   *Sales* 50,134,620
SIC 5147 Meats and meat products
Steve Levis

D-U-N-S 20-147-1138   (SL)
POTTERS FARM & NURSERY INC
POTTERS
19158 48 Ave, Surrey, BC, V3Z 1B2
(604) 576-5011
Emp Here 44   *Sales* 11,134,596

SIC 5261 Retail nurseries and garden stores
Edward Bernard Holden
William Stuart Ringer

D-U-N-S 24-504-4227   (SL)
PRECISION PULLEY & IDLER INC
PPI CANADA
(*Suby of* PRECISION, INC.)
3388 190 St, Surrey, BC, V3Z 1A7
(604) 560-8188
Emp Here 54   *Sales* 12,248,208
SIC 3429 Hardware, nec
Roger Brown
Craig Wilson
Monica Xia

D-U-N-S 24-356-0922   (SL)
RADIUS GLOBAL SOLUTIONS INC
RADIUS LOGISTICS
2455 192 St Suite 108, Surrey, BC, V3Z 3X1
(604) 541-1910
Emp Here 30   *Sales* 11,560,800
SIC 4731 Freight transportation arrangement
Roger Harrison
Deanie Hiles
Clayton Leech

D-U-N-S 25-229-1380   (SL)
RAVEN ROOFING LTD
18988 34a Ave, Surrey, BC, V3Z 1A7
(604) 531-9619
Emp Here 60   *Sales* 13,069,740
SIC 1761 Roofing, siding, and sheetMetal
work
Neil Rook

D-U-N-S 24-364-9469   (SL)
ROOTS ORGANIC INC
3585 184 St, Surrey, BC, V3Z 1B8
(604) 576-2567
Emp Here 50   *Sales* 41,778,850
SIC 5148 Fresh fruits and vegetables
Tejinder Brar

D-U-N-S 25-964-0308   (HQ)
SAGINAW ENTERPRISES LTD
SAGINAW BAKERIES
2520 190 St Suite 102, Surrey, BC, V3Z 3W6
(604) 385-2520
Emp Here 1   *Sales* 24,198,300
SIC 2051 Bread, cake, and related products
Denny Blue
Cheryl Blue

D-U-N-S 24-866-7040   (SL)
SHAIR SALES LTD
TIP TOP PARTS
3557 190 St Unit 101, Surrey, BC, V3Z 0P6
(604) 514-7005
Emp Here 29   *Sales* 13,775,754
SIC 5087 Service establishment equipment
James Gair
Colleen Gair

D-U-N-S 24-133-2543   (SL)
STAR MARKETING LTD
3289 190 St, Surrey, BC, V3Z 1A7
(778) 574-0778
Emp Here 37   *Sales* 30,916,349
SIC 5141 Groceries, general line
Randy Gaudette
Dennis Hunt
Kyle Leslie

D-U-N-S 20-187-5072   (HQ)
STARLINE WINDOWS (2001) LTD
19091 36 Ave, Surrey, BC, V3Z 0P6
(604) 882-5100
Emp Here 225   *Sales* 170,888,400
SIC 5031 Lumber, plywood, and millwork
Ron Martini

D-U-N-S 20-555-8633   (SL)
STARLINE WINDOWS LTD
19091 36 Ave, Surrey, BC, V3Z 0P6
(604) 882-5100
Emp Here 150   *Sales* 28,812,750

SIC 3442 Metal doors, sash, and trim
Renato Martini

D-U-N-S 20-273-7883   (SL)
SURREY FARMS COMPANY
5180 152 St, Surrey, BC, V3Z 1G9
(604) 574-1390
Emp Here 30   *Sales* 10,274,010
SIC 0191 General farms, primarily crop
Charan Rai

D-U-N-S 24-737-1318   (SL)
TRI-METAL FABRICATORS
19150 21 Ave, Surrey, BC, V3Z 3M3
(604) 531-5518
Emp Here 60   *Sales* 11,525,100
SIC 3499 Fabricated Metal products, nec
Guiseppe Toso
Craig Ono
Patrick Toso
Steve Eden
Paul Rouillard

D-U-N-S 24-320-1219   (SL)
TWG CANADA CONSOLIDATED INC
19350 22 Ave, Surrey, BC, V3Z 3S6
(604) 547-2100
Emp Here 80   *Sales* 17,760,080
SIC 3531 Construction machinery
James Zoretich
Lee Charlson
Soma Somasundaram

D-U-N-S 24-995-2961   (SL)
VAN GOGH DESIGNS FURNITURE LTD
19178 34a Ave, Surrey, BC, V3Z 1A7
(604) 372-3001
Emp Here 90   *Sales* 13,888,980
SIC 2512 Upholstered household furniture
Amarjit Dhindsa
Jaswant Dhindsa
Kamaljit Gill

D-U-N-S 24-034-5561   (SL)
VANGA PRODUCTS (PLASTICS) INC
2330 190 St Suite 102, Surrey, BC, V3Z 3W7
(604) 538-4088
Emp Here 50   *Sales* 10,094,850
SIC 3089 Plastics products, nec
Robert Hall
Bill Van Gaalen
Gerard Van Gaalen
Elizabeth Van Gaalen

D-U-N-S 24-599-1992   (BR)
WAL-MART CANADA CORP
WALMART
(*Suby of* WALMART INC.)
2355 160 St, Surrey, BC, V3Z 9N6
(604) 541-9015
Emp Here 420
SIC 5311 Department stores
Drew Cashmore

D-U-N-S 24-639-5776   (SL)
WEST COAST DUTY FREE STORE LTD
111 176 St Suite 1, Surrey, BC, V3Z 9S4
(604) 538-3222
Emp Here 80   *Sales* 16,427,440
SIC 5399 Miscellaneous general merchandise
Gary Holowaychuk
Randy Holowaychuk
Coreen Holowaychuk

D-U-N-S 20-832-6772   (HQ)
WESTLAND INSURANCE GROUP LTD
2121 160 St Suite 200, Surrey, BC, V3Z 9N6
(604) 543-7788
Emp Here 200   *Sales* 4,746,104,000
SIC 6411 Insurance agents, brokers, and ser-
vice
Jason Wubs
Jetsko Wubs
Matthew Wubs
Geoff Belair
Jo-Ann Mcgillivary
Carolyn Nichols

Anthea Smith
Philip Tapley
Colin Thompson
Donna Townson

D-U-N-S 25-949-2155   (HQ)
**WESTLAND INSURANCE LIMITED PART-
NERSHIP**
2121 160 St Unit 200, Surrey, BC, V3Z 9N6
(604) 543-7788
Emp Here 35   *Sales* 664,454,560
SIC 6411 Insurance agents, brokers, and ser-
vice
Jeff Webbs
Colin Thompson
Matt Wubs
Andy Luiten

Surrey, BC V4A

D-U-N-S 20-563-2958   (BR)
ALLDRITT DEVELOPMENT LIMITED
NORDIC RESORT
2055 152 St Suite 300, Surrey, BC, V4A 4N7
(604) 536-5525
Emp Here 100
SIC 6552 Subdividers and developers, nec
Jim Wong

D-U-N-S 24-141-8649   (HQ)
BLACK BOND BOOKS LTD
15562 24 Ave Unit 1, Surrey, BC, V4A 2J5
(604) 536-4444
Emp Here 12   *Sales* 14,171,024
SIC 5942 Book stores
Catherine Jesson
Mel Jesson

D-U-N-S 20-639-5068   (SL)
CLARK, RON AND ASSOCIATES (2006) INC
2195 King George Blvd, Surrey, BC, V4A 5A3

Emp Here 25   *Sales* 11,768,275
SIC 1542 Nonresidential construction, nec
Ronald Clark

D-U-N-S 25-193-1408   (SL)
EARL'S RESTAURANT (WHITE ROCK) LTD
1767 152 St Suite 7, Surrey, BC, V4A 4N3

Emp Here 80   *Sales* 3,641,520
SIC 5812 Eating places
Alan Merriman

D-U-N-S 25-241-5638   (SL)
ETHEREAL NAIL & BEAUTY
1688 152 St Unit 107, Surrey, BC, V4A 4N2
(604) 531-6889
Emp Here 10   *Sales* 10,003,390
SIC 5051 Metals service centers and offices
Jeffrey Tran

D-U-N-S 20-056-3299   (SL)
GOLD KEY SALES & SERVICES LTD
GOLD KEY VOLKSWAGEN
2092 152 St, Surrey, BC, V4A 4N8
(604) 536-7212
Emp Here 25   *Sales* 12,451,950
SIC 5511 New and used car dealers
William Sie

D-U-N-S 25-513-2516   (HQ)
GUNGNIR RESOURCES INC
1688 152 St Suite 404, Surrey, BC, V4A 4N2
(604) 683-0484
Emp Here 4   *Sales* 1,988,828,317
SIC 1041 Gold ores
Jari Paaki
Christopher Robbins
Todd Keast
Garett Macdonald

D-U-N-S 20-796-3547   (SL)
HUGH & MCKINNON REALTY LTD

(*Suby of* DOUGLAS CAPITAL CORPORA-
TION)
14007 16 Ave, Surrey, BC, V4A 1P9
(604) 531-1909
Emp Here 40   *Sales* 10,870,240
SIC 6531 Real estate agents and managers
Bruce Robinson
Greg Long

D-U-N-S 24-996-3315   (HQ)
KELSO TECHNOLOGIES INC
13966 18b Ave, Surrey, BC, V4A 8J1
(250) 764-3618
Emp Here 5   *Sales* 12,716,596
SIC 3743 Railroad equipment
James Bond
Kathy Love
Anthony (Tony) Andrukaitis
Richard Lee
Peter R. Hughes
Phillip (Phil) Dyer
Paul Cass
Laura B. Roach
Jesse V. Crews

D-U-N-S 20-307-3114   (SL)
LIFESTYLE OPERATIONS LP
WHITECLIFF
15501 16 Ave, Surrey, BC, V4A 9M5
(604) 538-7227
Emp Here 65   *Sales* 14,356,615
SIC 6513 Apartment building operators
Sherry Fossum
Derek Saywell

D-U-N-S 25-411-9910   (SL)
MAJESTIC GOLD CORP
1688 152nd St Suite 306, Surrey, BC, V4A
4N2
(604) 560-9060
Emp Here 15   *Sales* 33,804,198
SIC 1041 Gold ores
Stephen Kenwood
James Mackie
Gengshu Miao
Shaohui Chen
John Campbell
Shou Wu Chen
David Duval

D-U-N-S 24-448-1727   (SL)
RE/MAX COLONIAL PACIFIC REALTY
15414 24 Ave, Surrey, BC, V4A 2J3
(604) 541-4850
Emp Here 41   *Sales* 13,412,207
SIC 6531 Real estate agents and managers
Al Hippsley

D-U-N-S 20-960-8004   (SL)
ROYAL WEST COAST PENINSULA, THE
PENINSULA RETIREMENT RESIDENCE
2088 152 St Suite 402, Surrey, BC, V4A 9Z4
(604) 538-2033
Emp Here 49   *Sales* 11,412,639
SIC 6513 Apartment building operators
Rob Gillis

D-U-N-S 20-033-3701   (BR)
SCHOOL DISTRICT NO. 36 (SURREY)
SCHOOL DISTRICT NO 36 (SURREY)
(*Suby of* SCHOOL DISTRICT NO. 36 (SUR-
REY))
15751 16 Ave, Surrey, BC, V4A 1S1
(604) 531-8354
Emp Here 95
SIC 8211 Elementary and secondary schools
Ken Hignell

D-U-N-S 24-974-8336   (BR)
SCHOOL DISTRICT NO. 36 (SURREY)
SCHOOL DISTRICT NO 36 (SURREY)
(*Suby of* SCHOOL DISTRICT NO. 36 (SUR-
REY))
1785 148 St, Surrey, BC, V4A 4M6
(604) 536-2131
Emp Here 150
SIC 8211 Elementary and secondary schools

Claudine Bunyan

D-U-N-S 20-033-7454   (BR)
SCHOOL DISTRICT NO. 36 (SURREY)
SCHOOL DISTRICT NO 36 (SURREY)
(*Suby of* SCHOOL DISTRICT NO. 36 (SURREY))
13484 24 Ave, Surrey, BC, V4A 2G5
(604) 538-6678
Emp Here 85
SIC 8211 Elementary and secondary schools
Bruce Filsinger

D-U-N-S 25-479-9075   (SL)
SEMIAHMOO HOUSE SOCIETY
15306 24 Ave, Surrey, BC, V4A 2J1
(604) 536-1242
Emp Here 250   *Sales* 19,198,000
SIC 8322 Individual and family services
Jane Mackinnon
Michael Boni
Rod Pennington
John Groom
Glen Ross
Doug Tennant
Patti Robinson

D-U-N-S 25-271-7269   (BR)
SOBEYS WEST INC
FRIENDLY OCEAN PARK SAFEWAY
(*Suby of* EMPIRE COMPANY LIMITED)
12825 16 Ave, Surrey, BC, V4A 1N5
(604) 531-3422
Emp Here 130
SIC 5411 Grocery stores
Jim Farina

D-U-N-S 24-887-2814   (SL)
SOUTH SURREY HOTEL LTD
BEST WESTERN PACIFIC INN
1160 King George Blvd, Surrey, BC, V4A 4Z2
(604) 535-1432
Emp Here 150   *Sales* 13,903,500
SIC 7011 Hotels and motels
Fareed Pirani

D-U-N-S 25-001-2221   (SL)
TERASEN GAS LTD
2310 King George Boulevard, Surrey, BC, V4A 5A5
(604) 536-2956
Emp Here 5   *Sales* 15,529,285
SIC 4923 Gas transmission and distribution

D-U-N-S 24-397-6912   (SL)
WHITE ROCK CHRISTIAN ACADEMY SOCIETY
2265 152 St, Surrey, BC, V4A 4P1
(604) 531-9186
Emp Here 40   *Sales* 15,896,560
SIC 8699 Membership organizations, nec
Trish Stobbe

D-U-N-S 25-151-9435   (HQ)
ZENABIS GLOBAL INC
1688 152 St Suite 205, Surrey, BC, V4A 4N2
(604) 888-0420
Sales 25,579,091
SIC 8422 Botanical and zoological gardens
Jack Benne
Leo Benne
John Hoekstra
J. Green
Donald Fairholm
Natascha Kiernan
Daniel Burns
Andrew Grieve
Manoj (Monty) Sikka
Adam Spears

Surrey, BC V4N

D-U-N-S 20-383-4655   (SL)
1001432 B.C. LTD

SURREY GOLF CLUB
7700 168 St, Surrey, BC, V4N 0E1
(604) 576-8224
Emp Here 75   *Sales* 5,729,775
SIC 7992 Public golf courses
Jeong Ho Lee

D-U-N-S 24-445-7164   (HQ)
ADP DISTRIBUTORS INC
KINETIC MOTORSPORT
18940 94 Ave Suite 100, Surrey, BC, V4N 4X5
(604) 888-3726
Emp Here 64   *Sales* 53,650,300
SIC 5084 Industrial machinery and equipment
Alan Meikle
Ron Wiebe

D-U-N-S 24-725-6035   (SL)
AGGRESSIVE TUBE BENDING INC
ATB
9750 188 St, Surrey, BC, V4N 3M2
(604) 882-4872
Emp Here 50   *Sales* 10,141,500
SIC 3498 Fabricated pipe and fittings
Robert Georgison
Peter Diesing
Yuri Tofini

D-U-N-S 24-070-7612   (HQ)
ALDER AUTO PARTS LTD
19414 96 Ave Suite 3, Surrey, BC, V4N 4C2
(604) 888-3722
Emp Here 11   *Sales* 16,436,574
SIC 5531 Auto and home supply stores
John Feddersen
Steve Fedderson

D-U-N-S 25-611-9405   (SL)
BARNSTON ISLAND HERB CORPORATION
148 Barnston Island, Surrey, BC, V4N 4R1
(604) 581-8017
Emp Here 10   *Sales* 12,103,970
SIC 5159 Farm-product raw materials, nec
Peter Hoffmann

D-U-N-S 24-293-2838   (SL)
BEVCO SALES INTERNATIONAL INC
BEVCO
9354 194 St, Surrey, BC, V4N 4E9
(604) 888-1455
Emp Here 25   *Sales* 11,875,650
SIC 5084 Industrial machinery and equipment
Brian Fortier
Donna Fortier

D-U-N-S 20-102-2415   (HQ)
BURNABY LAKE GREENHOUSES LTD
17250 80 Ave, Surrey, BC, V4N 6J6
(604) 576-2088
Sales 117,055,200
SIC 5083 Farm and garden machinery
Herb Van Der Ende
John Van Der Ende
Cornelius Van Der Ende
Robert Van Der Ende
A C Van Der Ende
Ken Van Der Ende
Herb J Van Der Ende

D-U-N-S 25-914-0333   (BR)
BURNABY LAKE GREENHOUSES LTD
(*Suby of* BURNABY LAKE GREENHOUSES LTD)
17250 80 Ave, Surrey, BC, V4N 6J6
(604) 576-2088
Emp Here 250
SIC 0181 Ornamental nursery products
Robert Vanderende

D-U-N-S 20-714-1607   (HQ)
BUY-LOW FOODS LTD
G & H MARKETING ENTERPRISE
(*Suby of* PATTISON, JIM GROUP INC)
19580 Telegraph Trail, Surrey, BC, V4N 4H1
(604) 888-1121
Emp Here 200   *Sales* 307,942,400
SIC 5411 Grocery stores

Daniel Bregg
Sam Corea
Atanu Dalal

D-U-N-S 25-050-4826   (SL)
CANWEST WIRE ROPE INC
9323 194 St Suite 200, Surrey, BC, V4N 4G1

Emp Here 12   *Sales* 12,004,068
SIC 5051 Metals service centers and offices
Art Go

D-U-N-S 20-639-5233   (HQ)
CBS PARTS LTD
9505 189 St Suite 9505, Surrey, BC, V4N 5L8
(604) 888-1944
Emp Here 50   *Sales* 29,501,415
SIC 5013 Motor vehicle supplies and new parts
Richard Spitke
Frederick Allen Hopton
Kevin Hopton
Robyn Spitzke-Kent

D-U-N-S 25-648-1813   (HQ)
CHECKWELL SOLUTIONS CORPORATION
BACKCHECK DIV OF
(*Suby of* STERLING INFOSYSTEMS, INC.)
19433 96 Ave Suite 200, Surrey, BC, V4N 4C4
(604) 506-4663
Emp Here 154   *Sales* 82,967,850
SIC 8748 Business consulting, nec
Dean Drysdale
Dave Dinesen
Brian Ward-Hall
Henk Berends

D-U-N-S 24-207-3687   (SL)
CHOHAN CARRIERS LTD
15760 110 Ave, Surrey, BC, V4N 4Z1
(604) 888-1855
Emp Here 100   *Sales* 14,819,200
SIC 4213 Trucking, except local
Kuljit Chohan
Sunny Chohan

D-U-N-S 24-457-3945   (SL)
COBRA ELECTRIC LTD
9688 190 St, Surrey, BC, V4N 3M9
(604) 594-1633
Emp Here 100   *Sales* 21,782,900
SIC 1731 Electrical work
Murray Berry

D-U-N-S 20-112-3122   (HQ)
CULLEN DIESEL POWER LTD
9300 192 St, Surrey, BC, V4N 3R8
(604) 888-1211
Emp Here 110   *Sales* 109,739,250
SIC 5084 Industrial machinery and equipment
Robert Allan Cullen

D-U-N-S 20-110-6366   (HQ)
CUMMINS WESTERN CANADA LIMITED PARTNERSHIP
18452 96 Ave, Surrey, BC, V4N 3P8
(604) 882-5000
Emp Here 120   *Sales* 365,797,500
SIC 5084 Industrial machinery and equipment
Mike Angus
Kerry Winkler
Bill Lapp
Kim Kelly
Lorraine Christensen
Larry Fendrick
Peter Young

D-U-N-S 24-695-1651   (HQ)
CWS INDUSTRIES (MFG) CORP
19490 92 Ave, Surrey, BC, V4N 4G7
(604) 888-9008
Sales 84,263,100
SIC 3531 Construction machinery
Earl Hirtz
Kenneth Clasby
James Hewett
Stephen Wright

D-U-N-S 20-702-1705   (SL)
CWS VENTURES INC
19490 92 Ave, Surrey, BC, V4N 4G7
(604) 888-9008
Emp Here 150   *Sales* 33,685,829
SIC 3531 Construction machinery
Earl Hirtz

D-U-N-S 25-506-7076   (HQ)
DE DUTCH PANNEKOEK HOUSE RESTAURANTS INC
8484 162 St Suite 108, Surrey, BC, V4N 1B4
(604) 543-3101
Emp Here 7   *Sales* 18,813,870
SIC 6794 Patent owners and lessors
William Kenneth Waring

D-U-N-S 20-359-6077   (SL)
DSI CANADA CIVIL, LTD
19433 96 Ave Suite 103, Surrey, BC, V4N 4C4
(604) 888-8818
Emp Here 34   *Sales* 14,886,063
SIC 5039 Construction materials, nec
Joseph Li
Kerry Allen
Nicholas Moses

D-U-N-S 20-488-0191   (SL)
EUREST-TERASEN GAS-633
16705 Fraser Hwy, Surrey, BC, V4N 0E7

Emp Here 5   *Sales* 15,529,285
SIC 4923 Gas transmission and distribution

D-U-N-S 24-369-2717   (BR)
FIRST TRUCK CENTRE INC
FIRST TRUCK CENTRE VANCOUVER
(*Suby of* FIRST INDUSTRIES CORPORATION)
18688 96 Ave, Surrey, BC, V4N 3P9
(604) 888-1424
Emp Here 85
SIC 5012 Automobiles and other motor vehicles
Roman Tomica

D-U-N-S 20-183-0754   (SL)
FLEETWOOD PLACE HOLDINGS LTD
16011 83 Ave, Surrey, BC, V4N 0N2
(604) 590-6860
Emp Here 60   *Sales* 16,401,000
SIC 6712 Bank holding companies
Michael Ahmon
Kevin Ahmon
Betty Zuilan Ahmon
Betty Y. Ahmon

D-U-N-S 20-325-3695   (SL)
FLUXWERX ILLUMINATION INC
FLUXWERX
(*Suby of* POWER CORPORATION DU CANADA)
9255 194 St, Surrey, BC, V4N 4G1
(604) 549-9379
Emp Here 150   *Sales* 28,566,300
SIC 3648 Lighting equipment, nec
Scott Santoro
Reuben Bartlett
Nikki Loeppke

D-U-N-S 24-995-3860   (HQ)
FORTISBC ENERGY INC
(*Suby of* FORTIS INC)
16705 Fraser Hwy, Surrey, BC, V4N 0E8
(604) 576-7000
Emp Here 300   *Sales* 939,388,923
SIC 4923 Gas transmission and distribution
Roger Dall'antonia
Ian Lorimer
Doyle Sam
Cynthia Des Brisay
Jody Drope
Diane Roy
Douglas Stout
Dennis Swanson
Brenda Eaton
Ida J. Goodreau

▲ Public Company   ■ Public Company Family Member   **HQ** Headquarters   **BR** Branch   **SL** Single Location

D-U-N-S 24-373-4936 (SL)
FREYBE GOURMET CHEF LTD
(*Suby of* PREMIUM BRANDS HOLDINGS CORPORATION)
19405 94 Ave, Surrey, BC, V4N 4E6
(604) 856-5221
Emp Here 42   Sales 14,518,980
SIC 2038 Frozen specialties, nec
Sven Freybe
Henning Freybe

D-U-N-S 20-993-4777 (SL)
HARDING FORKLIFT SERVICES LTD
18623 96 Ave, Surrey, BC, V4N 3P6
(604) 888-1412
Emp Here 30   Sales 14,250,780
SIC 5084 Industrial machinery and equipment
Peter Harding
Cheryl Harding

D-U-N-S 20-584-6215 (HQ)
HIGHLAND FOUNDRY LTD
(*Suby of* CANERECTOR INC)
9670 187 St, Surrey, BC, V4N 3N6
(604) 888-8444
Sales 23,580,440
SIC 3325 Steel foundries, nec
Garth Mckay

D-U-N-S 24-987-6082 (SL)
ICG PROPANE INC.
19433 96 Ave Suite 200, Surrey, BC, V4N 4C4

Emp Here 6   Sales 18,635,142
SIC 4924 Natural gas distribution

D-U-N-S 24-803-4253 (HQ)
ILTA GRAIN INC
8427 160 St, Surrey, BC, V4N 0V6
(604) 597-5060
Emp Here 17   Sales 219,789,240
SIC 5153 Grain and field beans
Anthony Daniel Burneski
Gerald Donkersgoed
Paul Taggar

D-U-N-S 20-076-4348 (HQ)
IMASCO MINERALS INC
IMASCO
19287 98a Ave, Surrey, BC, V4N 4C8
(604) 888-3848
Emp Here 38   Sales 12,545,330
SIC 3299 NonMetallic mineral products,

D-U-N-S 20-112-5150 (HQ)
INDUSTRIAL EQUIPMENT MANUFACTURING LTD
IEM
19433 96 Ave Unit 109, Surrey, BC, V4N 4C4
(604) 513-9930
Sales 11,371,530
SIC 3535 Conveyors and conveying equipment
John Hards
Joseph Wurz

D-U-N-S 20-568-5030 (SL)
LANTRAX LOGISTICS LTD
19272 96 Ave Suite 10, Surrey, BC, V4N 4C1
(604) 526-8729
Emp Here 18   Sales 10,412,467
SIC 4731 Freight transportation arrangement
Rod Wainwright
Robert Hillmer

D-U-N-S 24-957-9400 (SL)
LASER VALLEY TECHNOLOGIES CORP
9761 192 St Unit 1, Surrey, BC, V4N 4C7
(604) 888-7085
Emp Here 30   Sales 13,415,220
SIC 5045 Computers, peripherals, and software
Perry M Niehaus
Keith Falardeau
Rita Niehaus

D-U-N-S 20-621-6590 (HQ)

M.G. CHEMICALS LTD
9347 193 St, Surrey, BC, V4N 4E7
(604) 888-3084
Emp Here 1   Sales 23,253,048
SIC 5065 Electronic parts and equipment, nec
Howard Clark
Robert Clark

D-U-N-S 24-162-1051 (HQ)
MAC CHAIN COMPANY LIMITED
9445 193a St, Surrey, BC, V4N 4N5
(604) 888-1229
Emp Here 25   Sales 18,782,528
SIC 5411 Grocery stores
Kevin Mcfarland
Andrew Mcfarland
Thomas James Mcfarland
Stephen Tan

D-U-N-S 20-271-5967 (SL)
MAC INDUSTRIES LTD
9445 193a St, Surrey, BC, V4N 4N5
(604) 513-4536
Emp Here 25   Sales 11,179,350
SIC 5051 Metals service centers and offices
Kevin Mcfarland
Andrew Mcfarland
Thomas Mcfarland
Thomas Hickey

D-U-N-S 24-446-6751 (SL)
MCALLISTER INDUSTRIES LTD
9678 186 St, Surrey, BC, V4N 3N7
(604) 888-1871
Emp Here 35   Sales 14,250,780
SIC 5085 Industrial supplies
David C. Dueck
Ted Parker

D-U-N-S 20-425-5566 (HQ)
MCLAREN, P. D. LIMITED
9725 192 St Unit 104, Surrey, BC, V4N 4C7
(604) 371-3732
Emp Here 20   Sales 12,309,300
SIC 1799 Special trade contractors, nec
John Allen

D-U-N-S 20-048-4016 (SL)
NEW WAVE CRUISE SHIP CENTRES
15957 84 Ave Suite 102, Surrey, BC, V4N 0W7
(604) 572-9500
Emp Here 35   Sales 18,198,845
SIC 4724 Travel agencies
Barbara Addy

D-U-N-S 20-795-7283 (HQ)
NEW-LINE PRODUCTS LTD
NEW-LINE HOSE & FITTINGS
9415 189 St Unit 1, Surrey, BC, V4N 5L8
(604) 455-5400
Emp Here 56   Sales 38,002,080
SIC 5085 Industrial supplies
Kenneth Goller
Jason Goller
Justin Goller

D-U-N-S 24-863-1553 (SL)
PAC BRAKE MANUFACTURING
19594 96 Ave, Surrey, BC, V4N 4C3
(604) 882-0183
Emp Here 49   Sales 30,834,720
SIC 5531 Auto and home supply stores

D-U-N-S 20-114-6503 (SL)
PACBRAKE COMPANY
19594 96 Ave, Surrey, BC, V4N 4C3
(604) 882-0183
Emp Here 49   Sales 17,907,440
SIC 3714 Motor vehicle parts and accessories
Vincent Meneely
Dennis Marander
Jennifer Singleton

D-U-N-S 25-135-7075 (SL)
PACIFIC NORTHERN CARRIERS LTD
15760 110 Ave, Surrey, BC, V4N 4Z1
(604) 592-9630
Emp Here 6   Sales 18,635,142

SIC 4923 Gas transmission and distribution

D-U-N-S 25-236-6315 (SL)
PACIFIC PENTECOSTAL EDUCATION AND COMMUNICATION SOCIETY
PACIFIC ACADEMY
10238 168 St, Surrey, BC, V4N 1Z4
(604) 581-0132
Emp Here 120   Sales 11,894,280
SIC 8211 Elementary and secondary schools
Diane Stone
Rev. Gordon Mcdonald
Dan Lowndes
Brad Miller
Mary Pattison
David Schellenberg
Rodney Bergen
Clark Hollands

D-U-N-S 20-051-5935 (SL)
PARAGON REMEDIATION GROUP LTD
ENVIRO-VAC
8815 Harvie Rd, Surrey, BC, V4N 4B9
(604) 513-1324
Emp Here 99   Sales 56,463,462
SIC 1542 Nonresidential construction, nec
James Klassen
Steven Parks
Michael Baker
Greg Peterson
Raymond Zonbag

D-U-N-S 24-155-5788 (SL)
PENTCO INDUSTRIES INC
PHASE TWO DOORS, DIV OF
9274 194 St, Surrey, BC, V4N 4E9
(604) 888-0508
Emp Here 80   Sales 15,708,880
SIC 1751 Carpentry work
Ian Jackson
John P. Mcnulty

D-U-N-S 20-513-3531 (HQ)
PETERBILT PACIFIC INC
(*Suby of* PATTISON, JIM GROUP INC)
19470 96 Ave, Surrey, BC, V4N 4C2
(604) 888-1411
Emp Here 60   Sales 117,759,408
SIC 5511 New and used car dealers
Donald Pasiuk
Terry Pasiuk
Leanne Schroeder

D-U-N-S 25-733-1710 (SL)
PORT KELLS NURSERIES LTD
18730 88 Ave, Surrey, BC, V4N 5T1
(604) 882-1344
Emp Here 40   Sales 13,698,680
SIC 0161 Vegetables and melons
Rene Duineveld

D-U-N-S 25-677-9745 (BR)
RONA INC
RONA HOME CENTRE FLEETWOOD
(*Suby of* LOWE'S COMPANIES, INC.)
16659 Fraser Hwy, Surrey, BC, V4N 0E7
(604) 576-2955
Emp Here 90
SIC 5211 Lumber and other building materials
Al Shamley

D-U-N-S 25-228-9517 (SL)
SANDPIPER CONTRACTING LTD
9342 194 St, Surrey, BC, V4N 4E9
(604) 888-8484
Emp Here 50   Sales 12,044,200
SIC 1623 Water, sewer, and utility lines
Rino Dinicolo
Mario Dinicolo
Colleen Kott

D-U-N-S 20-047-8357 (BR)
SCHOOL DISTRICT NO. 36 (SURREY)
SCHOOL DISTRICT NO 36 (SURREY)
(*Suby of* SCHOOL DISTRICT NO. 36 (SURREY))
15945 96 Ave, Surrey, BC, V4N 2R8

(604) 581-4433
Emp Here 100
SIC 8211 Elementary and secondary schools
Darren Bedard

D-U-N-S 20-297-2555 (BR)
SCHOOL DISTRICT NO. 36 (SURREY)
SCHOOL DISTRICT NO 36 (SURREY)
(*Suby of* SCHOOL DISTRICT NO. 36 (SURREY))
16060 108 Ave, Surrey, BC, V4N 1M1
(604) 582-9231
Emp Here 130
SIC 8211 Elementary and secondary schools
Andrew Holland

D-U-N-S 20-801-4522 (SL)
SOUTHWEST CONTRACTING LTD
9426 192 St, Surrey, BC, V4N 3R9
(604) 888-5221
Emp Here 75   Sales 18,933,150
SIC 1623 Water, sewer, and utility lines
Scott Maccara
Rudy Froese
Kevin Ronning

D-U-N-S 20-557-5777 (SL)
SYBER CONCRETE FORMING LTD
18812 96 Ave Unit 11, Surrey, BC, V4N 3R1
(604) 513-5717
Emp Here 85   Sales 21,036,055
SIC 1771 Concrete work
Steve Beaton
Anna Balluff

D-U-N-S 25-679-4660 (HQ)
TEAL CEDAR PRODUCTS LTD
STAG TIMBER, DIV OF
17897 Triggs Rd, Surrey, BC, V4N 4M8
(604) 587-8700
Emp Here 375   Sales 167,034,000
SIC 2429 Special product sawmills, nec
Thomas Jones
Richard Jones

D-U-N-S 24-132-8264 (SL)
VCS VALLEY CUT STEEL CORP
VALLEY CUT STEEL
9515 190 St Suite 4, Surrey, BC, V4N 3S1
(604) 513-8866
Emp Here 12   Sales 12,004,068
SIC 5051 Metals service centers and offices
Eric Taylor

D-U-N-S 20-184-8707 (HQ)
VENTURIS CAPITAL CORPORATION
19433 96 Ave Unit 102, Surrey, BC, V4N 4C4
(604) 607-8000
Emp Here 76   Sales 91,615,700
SIC 7359 Equipment rental and leasing, nec
Tom Leavitt
Brian Leavitt

D-U-N-S 20-919-1543 (SL)
WELLONS CANADA CORP
(*Suby of* WELLONS, INC.)
19087 96 Ave, Surrey, BC, V4N 3P2
(604) 888-0122
Emp Here 180   Sales 39,960,180
SIC 3567 Industrial furnaces and ovens
Patrick Thornton
Dave Fitzgerald

D-U-N-S 24-839-3985 (SL)
WESTCOAST MOULDING & MILLWORK LIMITED
18810 96 Ave, Surrey, BC, V4N 3R1
(604) 513-1138
Emp Here 45   Sales 11,387,655
SIC 5211 Lumber and other building materials
Peter Fograscher
Norm Toews
John Hutton

D-U-N-S 24-035-4444 (SL)
WESTERN GASCO CYLINDERS LTD
18925 94 Ave Unit 4, Surrey, BC, V4N 4X5

(604) 513-4429
Emp Here 35   *Sales* 11,396,000
SIC 5999 Miscellaneous retail stores, nec
Stuart Younger

D-U-N-S 25-215-7888   (SL)
WINDSOR SECURITY LIMITED
10833 160 St Suite 626, Surrey, BC, V4N 1P3
(604) 689-7588
Emp Here 150   *Sales* 3,937,500
SIC 7381 Detective and armored car services
Andrew Mroz

Surrey, BC V4P

D-U-N-S 24-204-5925   (SL)
3248 KING GEORGE HWY HOLDINGS LTD
CHOICES MARKET SOUTH SURREY
3248 King George Blvd, Surrey, BC, V4P 1A5
(604) 541-3902
Emp Here 100   *Sales* 29,347,700
SIC 5499 Miscellaneous food stores
Mark Vickars

D-U-N-S 24-806-0899   (SL)
BERO INVESTMENTS LTD
KING GEORGE NISSAN
14948 32 Ave, Surrey, BC, V4P 3R5
(604) 536-3644
Emp Here 22   *Sales* 10,957,716
SIC 5511 New and used car dealers
Bernie Rosenblatt

D-U-N-S 25-419-1083   (HQ)
GEORDY RENTALS INC
BUDGET CAR & TRUCK RENTALS
2576 King George Blvd, Surrey, BC, V4P 1H5
(604) 668-7230
Emp Here 10   *Sales* 62,928,000
SIC 5521 Used car dealers
Kevin Golka

D-U-N-S 20-992-1097   (SL)
KING GEORGE CARRIAGE LTD
WHITE ROCK HONDA
2466 King George Blvd, Surrey, BC, V4P 1H5
(604) 536-2884
Emp Here 35   *Sales* 17,432,730
SIC 5511 New and used car dealers
Paul Billing
Dixie Billing

D-U-N-S 20-396-5731   (SL)
MURRAY AUTO GROUP POCK LP
MURRAY HYUNDAI WHITE ROCK
3150 King George Blvd, Surrey, BC, V4P 1A2
(604) 538-7022
Emp Here 30   *Sales* 14,942,340
SIC 5511 New and used car dealers
Tom Pasemko

D-U-N-S 24-694-3260   (SL)
OCEAN PARK FORD SALES LTD
3050 King George Blvd, Surrey, BC, V4P 1A2
(604) 531-8883
Emp Here 78   *Sales* 49,083,840
SIC 5511 New and used car dealers
Ronald Ford

D-U-N-S 25-658-3337   (SL)
OCEAN PARK MECHANICAL INC
2428 King George Blvd Suite 102, Surrey, BC,
V4P 1H5
(604) 536-2363
Emp Here 85   *Sales* 19,810,525
SIC 1711 Plumbing, heating, air-conditioning
Roger Hendrix

D-U-N-S 24-773-1867   (SL)
**PACIFICA RESORT LIVING RETIREMENT,
THE**
THE PACIFICA
2525 King George Blvd, Surrey, BC, V4P 0C8
(604) 535-9194
Emp Here 50   *Sales* 11,645,550

SIC 6513 Apartment building operators
Robert Gilles

D-U-N-S 20-120-6265   (SL)
PEACE ARCH MOTORS LTD
PEACE ARCH TOYOTA
3174 King George Blvd, Surrey, BC, V4P 1A2
(604) 531-2916
Emp Here 55   *Sales* 34,610,400
SIC 5511 New and used car dealers
Alan Bines
Grant Hansen

D-U-N-S 25-169-9914   (SL)
TYSACH HIGGINS LTD
CANADIAN TIRE
3059 152 St Suite 485, Surrey, BC, V4P 3K1
(604) 542-4326
Emp Here 50   *Sales* 18,210,750
SIC 5014 Tires and tubes
Paul Wilson

D-U-N-S 20-868-3771   (SL)
WHITE ROCK CHRYSLER LTD
HALEY DODGE
3050 King George Blvd Unit 7, Surrey, BC,
V4P 1A2
(604) 531-9156
Emp Here 46   *Sales* 22,911,588
SIC 5511 New and used car dealers
Brian Haley
Joseph M Haley
Carolyn Haley

D-U-N-S 20-237-6633   (SL)
WHITEROCK CHRYSLER JEEP LIMITED
3050 King George Blvd, Surrey, BC, V4P 1A2
(604) 531-9156
Emp Here 45   *Sales* 22,413,510
SIC 5511 New and used car dealers
Joseph Haley

Taylor, BC V0C

D-U-N-S 25-191-0741   (BR)
CANADIAN FOREST PRODUCTS LTD
CANFOR - TAYLOR
(*Suby of* CANFOR CORPORATION)
8300 Cherry Ave E, Taylor, BC, V0C 2K0
(250) 789-9300
Emp Here 110
SIC 2421 Sawmills and planing mills, general
Bert Eisler

Terrace, BC V8G

D-U-N-S 24-761-6865   (HQ)
141187 VENTURES LTD
*NECHAKO NORTHCOAST CONSTRUC-
TION TERRACE*
5720 16 Hwy W, Terrace, BC, V8G 0C6
(250) 638-1881
Sales 30,293,040
SIC 1611 Highway and street construction
John Ryan
Peter Lansdowne
William Hooker
Blaine Scott

D-U-N-S 24-024-4124   (HQ)
**BILLABONG ROAD & BRIDGE MAINTE-
NANCE INC**
(*Suby of* 141187 VENTURES LTD)
5630 16 Hwy W, Terrace, BC, V8G 0C6
(250) 638-7918
Emp Here 75   *Sales* 23,981,990
SIC 1611 Highway and street construction
John Ryan

D-U-N-S 25-485-6834   (HQ)
BOARD OF EDUCATION OF SCHOOL DIS-

TRICT #82 (COAST M
SUWILAAWKS COMMUNITY SCHOOL
3430 Sparks St, Terrace, BC, V8G 2V3
(250) 638-0306
Sales 99,119,000
SIC 8211 Elementary and secondary schools
Barry Pinkhurst

D-U-N-S 20-521-3429   (SL)
BRYAN, J GASCON INVESTMENTS INC
CANADIAN TIRE 486
5100 16 Hwy W Suite 486, Terrace, BC, V8G
5S5
(250) 635-7178
Emp Here 103   *Sales* 27,568,156
SIC 5251 Hardware stores
J Gascon

D-U-N-S 24-031-9020   (HQ)
COAST MOUNTAIN COLLEGE
5331 Mcconnell Ave, Terrace, BC, V8G 4X2
(250) 635-6511
Emp Here 200   *Sales* 37,347,750
SIC 8221 Colleges and universities
Stephanie Forsyth
Cathay Sousa

D-U-N-S 25-072-6577   (SL)
KITSUMKALUM TEMPLE GAS BAR
14309 Hwy 16e, Terrace, BC, V8G 0A6
(250) 635-0017
Emp Here 26   *Sales* 12,950,028
SIC 5541 Gasoline service stations
Ernie Gerow

D-U-N-S 24-897-2861   (SL)
KRISINGER DRUG LTD
SHOPPERS DRUG MART
4647 Lakelse Ave Suite 102, Terrace, BC, V8G
1R3
(250) 635-7261
Emp Here 45   *Sales* 11,382,930
SIC 5912 Drug stores and proprietary stores
Manuela Krisinger

D-U-N-S 20-107-9951   (SL)
MACCARTHY MOTORS (TERRACE) LTD
5004 16 Hwy W, Terrace, BC, V8G 5S5
(250) 635-4941
Emp Here 34   *Sales* 16,934,652
SIC 5511 New and used car dealers
Gary Maccarthy
Marilyn Cooper
Ed Mcewan
James Mcewen

D-U-N-S 20-977-5381   (SL)
NORTHWEST FUELS LIMITED
5138 Keith Ave, Terrace, BC, V8G 1K9
(250) 635-2066
Emp Here 75   *Sales* 94,290,075
SIC 5172 Petroleum products, nec
Doug Ames

D-U-N-S 20-490-5665   (SL)
SPECTRA ENERGY
4716 Lazelle Ave Suite 210, Terrace, BC, V8G
1T2

Emp Here 5   *Sales* 15,529,285
SIC 4924 Natural gas distribution

D-U-N-S 20-794-5577   (HQ)
TERRACE TOTEM FORD SALES LTD
4631 Keith Ave, Terrace, BC, V8G 1K3
(250) 635-4978
Emp Here 50   *Sales* 37,756,800
SIC 5511 New and used car dealers
Kevin Kennedy
Mitchell Shinde
Shane Dejong

D-U-N-S 24-813-5431   (BR)
VALARD CONSTRUCTION LTD
(*Suby of* QUANTA SERVICES, INC.)
3120 Braun St, Terrace, BC, V8G 5N9

Emp Here 100

SIC 1623 Water, sewer, and utility lines

D-U-N-S 24-080-1642   (BR)
WAL-MART CANADA CORP
(*Suby of* WALMART INC.)
4427 16 Hwy W, Terrace, BC, V8G 5L5
(250) 615-4728
Emp Here 150
SIC 5311 Department stores
Tabatha Foxe

Thornhill, BC V8G

D-U-N-S 20-512-3532   (SL)
BEAR CREEK CONTRACTING LTD
3550 16 Hwy E, Thornhill, BC, V8G 5J3
(250) 635-4345
Emp Here 150   *Sales* 30,485,480
SIC 1629 Heavy construction, nec
Ian Munson
Gail Munson
Ron Burton

D-U-N-S 20-918-7848   (SL)
**THORNHILL VOLUNTEER FIREFIGHTERS
ASSOCIATION**
3128 16 Hwy E, Thornhill, BC, V8G 4N8
(250) 638-1466
Emp Here 42   *Sales* 16,691,388
SIC 8699 Membership organizations, nec
Gerald Prosser

Tofino, BC V0R

D-U-N-S 20-084-0218   (BR)
CERMAQ CANADA LTD
MAIN STREAM
(*Suby of* MC OCEAN HOLDINGS LIMITED)
61 4th St, Tofino, BC, V0R 2Z0
(250) 725-1255
Emp Here 200
SIC 2048 Prepared feeds, nec
Doug Knuson

D-U-N-S 25-164-0892   (SL)
CREATIVE SALMON COMPANY LTD
612 Campbell St, Tofino, BC, V0R 2Z0
(250) 725-2884
Emp Here 50   *Sales* 19,275,950
SIC 0273 Animal aquaculture
Jack Waterfield
Todd Waterfield
Chohachi Kashima
Tetsuo Yamagiwa

D-U-N-S 20-960-6958   (SL)
TOFINO RESORT + MARINA INC
634 Campbell St, Tofino, BC, V0R 2Z0
(250) 725-3277
Emp Here 80   *Sales* 7,591,920
SIC 7011 Hotels and motels
Willie Mitchelle

D-U-N-S 25-328-4590   (SL)
WICKANINNISH INN LIMITED
500 Osprey Lane, Tofino, BC, V0R 2Z0
(250) 725-3106
Emp Here 150   *Sales* 13,903,500
SIC 7011 Hotels and motels
Charles Mcdiarmid
Bruce Mcdiarmid
Howard Mcdiarmid

Trail, BC V1R

D-U-N-S 25-523-4882   (SL)
593130 BC LTD
ALLGARD SECURITY SERVICES

▲ Public Company   ■ Public Company Family Member   **HQ** Headquarters   **BR** Branch   **SL** Single Location

1200 Second Ave, Trail, BC, V1R 1L6
(250) 364-2253
Emp Here 30   *Sales* 13,069,740
SIC 1731 Electrical work
William R Lee

D-U-N-S 24-838-3952   (HQ)
ANNABLE FOODS LTD
FERRARO FOODS
850 Farwell St, Trail, BC, V1R 3T8
(250) 368-3363
Emp Here 80   *Sales* 44,021,550
SIC 5411 Grocery stores
James Ferraro
David Ferraro
Danny Ferraro

D-U-N-S 20-510-0886   (HQ)
BENSON B A & SON LTD
BENSON OIL
266 1st Ave, Trail, BC, V1R 4V2
(250) 368-6428
Emp Here 9   *Sales* 10,328,080
SIC 5171 Petroleum bulk stations and terminals
Albert Benson
Connie Benson

D-U-N-S 20-873-1385   (SL)
CHAMPION CHEVROLET BUICK GMC LTD
2880 Highway Dr, Trail, BC, V1R 2T3
(250) 368-9134
Emp Here 23   *Sales* 11,455,794
SIC 5511 New and used car dealers
Marc Cabana

D-U-N-S 20-868-3839   (HQ)
KOOTENAY SAVINGS CREDIT UNION
1101 Dewdney Ave Suite 106, Trail, BC, V1R 4T1
(250) 368-2686
Emp Here 14   *Sales* 44,866,320
SIC 6062 State credit unions
Brent Tremblay
Nick Ogloff
John Loo
Judy Aldridge
Forrest Drinnan
Helga Boker
Walter Bottcheer
Phyllis Stone

D-U-N-S 20-208-5077   (SL)
MCAULEY'S NOFRILLS
8100 3b Hwy Suite 142, Trail, BC, V1R 4N7
(250) 368-8577
Emp Here 57   *Sales* 16,728,189
SIC 5411 Grocery stores
Blair Mcauley

D-U-N-S 25-399-7480   (HQ)
SCHOOL DISTRICT NO. 20 (KOOTENAY-COLUMBIA)
2001 Third Ave, Trail, BC, V1R 1R6
(250) 368-6434
Emp Here 12   *Sales* 34,691,650
SIC 8211 Elementary and secondary schools
Teri Ferworn
Rosann Brunton
Natalie Verigin

D-U-N-S 20-874-5732   (SL)
T & L GREGORINI ENTERPRISES INC
CANADIAN TIRE
8238 3b Hwy, Trail, BC, V1R 4W4
(250) 364-3333
Emp Here 45   *Sales* 22,413,510
SIC 5531 Auto and home supply stores
Terry Gregorini

D-U-N-S 20-108-1627   (BR)
TECK METALS LTD
(*Suby of* TECK RESOURCES LIMITED)
25 Aldridge Ave, Trail, BC, V1R 4L8
(250) 364-4222
Emp Here 1,500
SIC 1081 Metal mining services

Mike Martin

D-U-N-S 24-026-1433   (BR)
WAL-MART CANADA CORP
WALMART
(*Suby of* WALMART INC.)
1601 Marcolin Dr Suite 1011, Trail, BC, V1R 4Y1
(250) 364-1802
Emp Here 100
SIC 5311 Department stores

D-U-N-S 24-319-1108   (BR)
WAL-MART CANADA CORP
WAL-MART
(*Suby of* WALMART INC.)
1601 Marcolin Dr Suite 1011, Trail, BC, V1R 4Y1
(250) 364-2688
Emp Here 120
SIC 5311 Department stores

D-U-N-S 20-306-7418   (SL)
WARFIELD FIRE DEPARTMENT
555 Schofield Hwy, Trail, BC, V1R 2G7
(250) 368-9300
Emp Here 25   *Sales* 11,230,475
SIC 7389 Business services, nec
Gabby Libertore

D-U-N-S 24-290-6980   (SL)
WEST KOOTENAY MECHANICAL (2001) LTD
8131 Old Waneta Rd, Trail, BC, V1R 4X1
(250) 364-1541
Emp Here 60   *Sales* 13,983,900
SIC 1711 Plumbing, heating, air-conditioning
John Balfour

D-U-N-S 20-048-0627   (BR)
WOOD CANADA LIMITED
(*Suby of* JOHN WOOD GROUP P.L.C.)
1385 Cedar Ave, Trail, BC, V1R 4C3
(250) 368-2400
Emp Here 110
SIC 8711 Engineering services
Eric Macfarlane

Tumbler Ridge, BC V0C

D-U-N-S 24-332-5966   (HQ)
LAPRAIRIE CRANE LTD
Gd, Tumbler Ridge, BC, V0C 2W0
(250) 242-5561
Emp Here 30   *Sales* 22,174,500
SIC 7389 Business services, nec
Scott Laprairie
Cliff Laprairie

Ucluelet, BC V0R

D-U-N-S 24-641-2191   (BR)
OAK BAY MARINA LTD
CANADIAN PRINCESS RESORT
(*Suby of* OAK BAY HOLDINGS LTD)
1943 Peninsula Rd, Ucluelet, BC, V0R 3A0
(250) 726-7771
Emp Here 150
SIC 7011 Hotels and motels
Brian Clarkson

Union Bay, BC V0R

D-U-N-S 20-621-6830   (SL)
BAYNES SOUND OYSTER LTD
5848 Island Hwy, Union Bay, BC, V0R 3B0
(250) 335-2111
Emp Here 15   *Sales* 12,533,655
SIC 5146 Fish and seafoods

Joe Tarnowski
Joanne Tarnowski
Janet Morrison
Joe Tarnowski Jr

D-U-N-S 24-550-1841   (SL)
HORNBY ISLAND NEW HORIZONS
1765 Sollans, Union Bay, BC, V0R 3B0
(250) 335-0385
Emp Here 49   *Sales* 22,381,941
SIC 7389 Business services, nec
Christl Hansen

Valemount, BC V0E

D-U-N-S 20-970-8189   (HQ)
YELLOWHEAD HELICOPTERS LTD
3010 Selwyn Rd, Valemount, BC, V0E 2Z0
(250) 566-4401
Emp Here 21   *Sales* 11,366,390
SIC 4522 Air transportation, nonscheduled
Garry Forman

Van Anda, BC V0N

D-U-N-S 25-216-8281   (SL)
TEXADA QUARRYING LTD
(*Suby of* LAFARGEHOLCIM LTD)
2 Airport Rd, Van Anda, BC, V0N 3K0
(604) 486-7627
Emp Here 80   *Sales* 21,620,480
SIC 1422 Crushed and broken limestone
Andrea Balse

Vancouver, BC V5C

D-U-N-S 25-728-8423   (SL)
MDE ENTERPRISES LTD
MDE ELECTRICAL MECHANICAL CONTRACTORS
3947 Graveley St, Vancouver, BC, V5C 3T4
(604) 291-1995
Emp Here 100   *Sales* 21,782,900
SIC 1731 Electrical work
Mel Di Nunno

Vancouver, BC V5K

D-U-N-S 20-109-3531   (HQ)
A. BOSA & CO. LTD
BOSA FOODS
1465 Kootenay St, Vancouver, BC, V5K 4Y3
(604) 253-5578
Sales 18,382,694
SIC 5141 Groceries, general line
Bruno Benedet Jr
Louie Brushcetta
Bruno Benedet Sr

D-U-N-S 24-312-5411   (SL)
ALBI BEVERAGES LIMITED
3440 Bridgeway, Vancouver, BC, V5K 1B6

Emp Here 19   *Sales* 10,167,356
SIC 5149 Groceries and related products, nec
Iain Bell

D-U-N-S 24-723-8371   (SL)
AUTOMATION ONE BUSINESS SYSTEMS INC
1365 Boundary Rd, Vancouver, BC, V5K 4T9
(604) 233-7702
Emp Here 40   *Sales* 17,886,960
SIC 5044 Office equipment
John Achtem

Sylvia Achtem
Neil Achtem

D-U-N-S 24-370-8880   (HQ)
BELFOR (CANADA) INC
BELFOR RESTORATION SERVICES
(*Suby of* BELFOR HOLDINGS INC.)
3300 Bridgeway, Vancouver, BC, V5K 1H9
(604) 432-1123
Emp Here 175   *Sales* 223,844,304
SIC 1799 Special trade contractors, nec
William Cook
Joe Ciolino
Sheldon Yellen

D-U-N-S 24-577-9764   (SL)
CON-WEST CONTRACTING LTD
1311 Kootenay St Suite 250, Vancouver, BC, V5K 4Y3
(604) 294-5067
Emp Here 60   *Sales* 15,146,520
SIC 1629 Heavy construction, nec
Giovanni (John) Marinelli
Antonio Marinelli

D-U-N-S 25-096-5464   (SL)
E-COMM EMERGENCY COMMUNICATIONS FOR SOUTHWEST BRITISH COLUMBIA INCORPORATED
E-COMM
3301 Pender St E, Vancouver, BC, V5K 5J3
(604) 215-5000
Emp Here 400   *Sales* 91,388,800
SIC 4899 Communication services, nec
Ken Shymanski
Daphne Corbett

D-U-N-S 20-068-3428   (SL)
HASTINGS ENTERTAINMENT INC
HASTINGS RACECOURSE & CASINO
(*Suby of* GREAT CANADIAN GAMING CORPORATION)
188 Renfrew St N, Vancouver, BC, V5K 3N8
(604) 254-1631
Emp Here 300   *Sales* 24,755,100
SIC 7948 Racing, including track operation
Vicky Heese

D-U-N-S 20-006-4157   (BR)
LITTLE MOUNTAIN RESIDENTIAL CARE & HOUSING SOCIETY
ADANAC PARK LODGE
(*Suby of* LITTLE MOUNTAIN RESIDENTIAL CARE & HOUSING SOCIETY)
851 Boundary Rd, Vancouver, BC, V5K 4T2
(604) 299-7567
Emp Here 110
SIC 8051 Skilled nursing care facilities
Cristian Farquharson

D-U-N-S 25-070-3717   (HQ)
OPTIONS FOR SEXUAL HEALTH
3550 Hastings St E, Vancouver, BC, V5K 2A7
(604) 731-4252
Emp Here 10   *Sales* 15,154,600
SIC 8093 Specialty outpatient clinics, nec
Greg Smith
Suzie Soman

D-U-N-S 20-861-6540   (SL)
PACIFIC NATIONAL EXHIBITION
PNE
2901 Hastings St E, Vancouver, BC, V5K 5J1
(604) 253-2311
Emp Here 1,700   *Sales* 147,390,000
SIC 7999 Amusement and recreation, nec
Michael Mcdaniel
Roger Gil
Raymond Louie
Patrice Impey
David Mclellan
Sadhu Johnston
Peter Kuran
Richard Saunders
Cheryl Prepchuk
Nancy Wright

D-U-N-S 20-802-0743   (SL)
T A F CONSTRUCTION LTD
2620 Hastings St E, Vancouver, BC, V5K 1Z6
(604) 254-1111
Emp Here 55   Sales 31,368,590
SIC 1542 Nonresidential construction, nec
Fortunata Dalla-Zanna

D-U-N-S 24-761-2468   (SL)
THOMAS, J.O. & ASSOCIATES LTD
1370 Kootenay St, Vancouver, BC, V5K 4R1
(604) 291-6340
Emp Here 50   Sales 10,619,850
SIC 8748 Business consulting, nec
Jim Thomas

D-U-N-S 24-389-3059   (SL)
WOLFE MOTORS LTD
WOLFE AUTOMOTIVE FAMILY
1595 Boundary Rd, Vancouver, BC, V5K 5C4
(604) 293-1311
Emp Here 100   Sales 62,928,000
SIC 5511 New and used car dealers
Frank Evan Wolfe
Dixie J Woodcock
John Douglas Wolfe

Vancouver, BC V5L

D-U-N-S 24-839-5220   (SL)
347942 B. C. LTD
CHONG LEE SEA FOOD
57 Lakewood Dr, Vancouver, BC, V5L 4W4
(604) 251-9168
Emp Here 58   Sales 17,021,666
SIC 5421 Meat and fish markets
Vincent Wong

D-U-N-S 24-033-7394   (SL)
A.T. STORRS LTD
1353 Pender St E, Vancouver, BC, V5L 1V7
(800) 561-5800
Emp Here 28   Sales 14,575,176
SIC 5094 Jewelry and precious stones
Andrew Storrs
Patricia Storrs

D-U-N-S 24-723-7597   (HQ)
ALL CITY IMPORTERS LTD
1290 Odlum Dr, Vancouver, BC, V5L 3L9
(604) 251-1045
Emp Here 10   Sales 12,533,655
SIC 5141 Groceries, general line
Sylvia Chen

D-U-N-S 20-109-1147   (HQ)
BEATTY FLOORS LTD
BURRITT BROS. CARPET
(Suby of 508348 B.C. LTD.)
1840 Pandora St, Vancouver, BC, V5L 1M7
(604) 254-9571
Emp Here 20   Sales 16,690,685
SIC 1752 Floor laying and floor work, nec

D-U-N-S 20-007-5083   (HQ)
BRYAN'S FASHIONS LTD
1950 Franklin St, Vancouver, BC, V5L 1R2
(604) 255-1890
Emp Here 10   Sales 31,188,750
SIC 5621 Women's clothing stores
Brian Rosner

D-U-N-S 25-195-4095   (SL)
CANADA YOUTH ORANGE NETWORK INC
CYONI
1638 Pandora St, Vancouver, BC, V5L 1L6
(604) 254-7733
Emp Here 50   Sales 11,242,750
SIC 2086 Bottled and canned soft drinks
Tom Nowicki

D-U-N-S 20-104-2707   (HQ)
CENTRE SKATEBOARD DISTRIBUTION LTD
CENTRE DISTRIBUTION

1486 E Pender St, Vancouver, BC, V5L 1V8
(604) 629-0000
Sales 10,410,840
SIC 5091 Sporting and recreation goods
Joosef Itkonen
Robert Boyce
Gerry Mckay
Colin Mckay

D-U-N-S 20-748-5293   (SL)
COLUMBIA CONTAINERS LTD
2319 Commissioner St, Vancouver, BC, V5L 1A4
(604) 254-9461
Emp Here 24   Sales 11,400,624
SIC 5084 Industrial machinery and equipment
Randy Ferrario

D-U-N-S 24-037-2842   (SL)
CORE ENERGY RECOVERY SOLUTIONS INC
1455 Georgia St E, Vancouver, BC, V5L 2A9
(604) 488-1132
Emp Here 65   Sales 14,934,010
SIC 8731 Commercial physical research
James Dean

D-U-N-S 24-505-0869   (SL)
DOLLAR FOOD MFG INC
1410 Odlum Dr, Vancouver, BC, V5L 4X7
(604) 253-1422
Emp Here 40   Sales 10,966,080
SIC 5411 Grocery stores
Kelly Chow
Yon Lin Chow

D-U-N-S 24-682-1417   (SL)
DONALD'S MARKET LTD
2342 Hastings St E, Vancouver, BC, V5L 1V5
(604) 254-3014
Emp Here 43   Sales 11,788,536
SIC 5411 Grocery stores
Donald Joe

D-U-N-S 24-162-7710   (SL)
DRAKE TOWING LTD
1553 Powell St, Vancouver, BC, V5L 5C3
(604) 251-3344
Emp Here 50   Sales 10,131,450
SIC 7549 Automotive services, nec
Dale Clearwater

D-U-N-S 24-725-9534   (HQ)
EVERGREEN INTERNATIONAL FOOD-STUFFS LTD
1944 Franklin St, Vancouver, BC, V5L 1R2
(604) 253-8835
Sales 16,711,540
SIC 5146 Fish and seafoods
Jack Lai

D-U-N-S 24-888-1336   (SL)
FANTASTIC-T KNITTERS INC
1374 Venables St, Vancouver, BC, V5L 2G4
(604) 255-8883
Emp Here 80   Sales 39,865,760
SIC 5136 Men's and boy's clothing
Lawrence Lau
Joseph Wong

D-U-N-S 20-312-5356   (SL)
FUSION CINE SALES & RENTALS INC
FUSION CINE
(Suby of 965591 ALBERTA LTD)
1469 Venables St, Vancouver, BC, V5L 2G1
(604) 879-0003
Emp Here 25   Sales 11,179,350
SIC 5065 Electronic parts and equipment, nec
Byron Drinkle

D-U-N-S 20-622-2085   (SL)
HALLMARK POULTRY PROCESSORS LTD
1756 Pandora St, Vancouver, BC, V5L 1M1
(604) 254-9885
Emp Here 400   Sales 194,954,000
SIC 2015 Poultry slaughtering and processing
Clifford Pollon

D-U-N-S 25-939-9798   (HQ)
KETTLE FRIENDSHIP SOCIETY
1725 Venables St, Vancouver, BC, V5L 2H3
(604) 251-2856
Emp Here 20   Sales 19,870,700
SIC 8699 Membership organizations, nec
Nancy Keough

D-U-N-S 20-113-0671   (SL)
KOO, JIM M. PRODUCE LTD
KOO, JIM WHOLESALE PRODUCE
777 Clark Dr, Vancouver, BC, V5L 3J3
(604) 253-6622
Emp Here 20   Sales 10,702,480
SIC 5148 Fresh fruits and vegetables
Teanna Koo

D-U-N-S 20-114-0167   (HQ)
MILLS PRINTING & STATIONERY CO. LTD
MILLS BASICS
1111 Clark Dr, Vancouver, BC, V5L 3K5
(604) 254-7211
Sales 25,182,900
SIC 5112 Stationery and office supplies
Brad Mills
Blair Mills
Doug Robinson
Donald Mills
Joan Mills

D-U-N-S 20-575-0599   (HQ)
OCEANFOOD SALES LIMITED
1909 Hastings St E, Vancouver, BC, V5L 1T5
(604) 255-1414
Emp Here 11   Sales 13,369,232
SIC 5146 Fish and seafoods
John Graham

D-U-N-S 24-367-7085   (HQ)
PLUM CLOTHING LTD
PLUM
1543 Venables St, Vancouver, BC, V5L 2G8
(604) 254-5034
Emp Here 8   Sales 13,454,700
SIC 5651 Family clothing stores
Kathleen (Katie) O'brien
Edward (Ed) Desroches

D-U-N-S 24-393-1925   (SL)
RAPID ELECTRIC VEHICLES INC
1570 Clark Dr, Vancouver, BC, V5L 3L3

Emp Here 25   Sales 12,661,377
SIC 5531 Auto and home supply stores
Jay Giraud

D-U-N-S 25-215-6617   (SL)
RELAXUS PRODUCTS LTD
FUN FEED, DIV OF
1590 Powell St, Vancouver, BC, V5L 1H3
(604) 879-3895
Emp Here 25   Sales 11,179,350
SIC 5047 Medical and hospital equipment
Ron Kline
Eugene Schwartz

D-U-N-S 20-257-0495   (SL)
SAAM SMIT CANADA INC
2285 Commissioner St, Vancouver, BC, V5L 1A8
(604) 255-1133
Emp Here 50   Sales 13,477,450
SIC 4492 Towing and tugboat service
Frans Tjallingii
Beverley Vlassopoulos
Peter Byland
Arjen Van Dijk

D-U-N-S 20-162-6335   (SL)
SEARCHLIGHT SYSTEMS LTD
1395 Frances St, Vancouver, BC, V5L 1Z1
(604) 255-4620
Emp Here 70   Sales 12,411,770
SIC 7371 Custom computer programming services
Gary Procknow

D-U-N-S 20-802-3978   (HQ)

SERVICE CORPORATION INTERNATIONAL (CANADA) LIMITED
MOUNT PLEASANT SIMMONS & MCBRIDE CHAPEL
(Suby of SERVICE CORPORATION INTERNATIONAL)
1835 Hastings St E, Vancouver, BC, V5L 1T3
(604) 806-4100
Emp Here 8   Sales 22,334,304
SIC 7261 Funeral service and crematories
John Gordon
Curtis Briggs
Melisa Chow

D-U-N-S 24-358-2223   (SL)
SILVERBIRCH NO. 41 OPERATIONS LIMITED PARTNERSHIP
CANNERY SEAFOOD RESTAURANT
(Suby of SILVERBIRCH HOTELS AND RESORTS LIMITED PARTNERSHIP)
2205 Commissioner St, Vancouver, BC, V5L 1A4

Emp Here 80
SIC 5812 Eating places
Robert Pratt
Jean Turcotte
Douglas Lantz

D-U-N-S 20-014-6327   (HQ)
SMALL POTATOES URBAN DELIVERY INC
SPUD
1660 Hastings St E, Vancouver, BC, V5L 1S6
(604) 215-7783
Emp Here 60   Sales 107,507,400
SIC 5149 Groceries and related products, nec
Peter Von Stolk
Joel Solomon
Peter Day
John Sereda

D-U-N-S 24-653-9436   (HQ)
SMIT MARINE CANADA INC
2285 Commissioner St, Vancouver, BC, V5L 1A8
(604) 255-1133
Emp Here 49   Sales 27,560,680
SIC 4492 Towing and tugboat service
Frans Tjallingii
Beverley Vlassopoulos
Peter Byland
Arjen Van Dijk

D-U-N-S 25-519-0139   (SL)
TACORPORATION RESTAURANT LTD
LA MEZCALERIA
1622 Commercial Dr Unit A, Vancouver, BC, V5L 3Y4
(604) 559-8226
Emp Here 80   Sales 3,429,840
SIC 5812 Eating places
Marcelo Ramirez
Alfonso Sanz

D-U-N-S 24-887-5452   (SL)
ULTRA-TECH CLEANING SYSTEMS LTD
1420 Adanac St Suite 201, Vancouver, BC, V5L 2C3
(604) 253-4698
Emp Here 115   Sales 3,676,320
SIC 7349 Building maintenance services, nec
Sukru Yigit

D-U-N-S 20-865-5316   (SL)
UNITED MARITIME SUPPLIERS INC
1854 Franklin St, Vancouver, BC, V5L 1P8
(604) 255-6525
Emp Here 24   Sales 11,400,624
SIC 5088 Transportation equipment and supplies
Steven Kravariotis

D-U-N-S 20-116-9315   (HQ)
VANCOUVER QUILTING MANUFACTURING LTD
(Suby of MAXWELL FABRICS LTD)
188 Victoria Dr, Vancouver, BC, V5L 4C3

---

(604) 253-7744
Emp Here 40   *Sales* 26,909,388
SIC 5131 Piece goods and notions
Larry Garaway
Darlene Ames

D-U-N-S 24-328-9667   (SL)
VANCOUVER TAXI LTD
790 Clark Dr, Vancouver, BC, V5L 3J2
(604) 871-1111
Emp Here 300   *Sales* 16,864,200
SIC 4121 Taxicabs
Kashmir S Nahal
Mojtaba Nasimi
Navdeep Atwal
Hamid Anwar
Bhajan Johal
Dalbag Johal

D-U-N-S 24-368-3455   (HQ)
VERSACOLD CANADA CORPORATION
2115 Commissioner St Suite 1, Vancouver,
BC, V5L 1A6
(604) 255-4656
Emp Here 3   *Sales* 210,194,340
SIC 4222 Refrigerated warehousing and stor-
age
Joel Smith

D-U-N-S 24-351-0901   (HQ)
**VERSACOLD INTERNATIONAL CORPORA-
TION**
2115 Commissioner St Suite 1, Vancouver,
BC, V5L 1A6
(604) 255-4656
Emp Here 3   *Sales* 829,714,500
SIC 4222 Refrigerated warehousing and stor-
age
Paul Campbell
Michele (Mike) Arcamone

D-U-N-S 24-536-4591   (HQ)
WESTERN MARINE COMPANY
1494 Powell St, Vancouver, BC, V5L 5B5
(604) 253-7721
Sales 29,263,800
SIC 5088 Transportation equipment and sup-
plies
Bill Falk
Alan Stovell
Daan Hengeveld

Vancouver, BC V5M

D-U-N-S 25-054-1596   (SL)
534422 B.C. LTD
*CANADA WEST VETERINARY SPECIAL-
ISTS AND CRITICAL CARE HOSPITAL*
1988 Kootenay St, Vancouver, BC, V5M 4Y3
(604) 294-2629
Emp Here 126   *Sales* 21,912,030
SIC 0742 Veterinary services, specialties
Terri Schiller
Laurence Braun
Alan Kuzma
Greg Starrak
Nick Sharp

D-U-N-S 24-493-6050   (SL)
ACTIVE NETWORK LTD, THE
(*Suby of* PAPAY HOLDCO, LLC)
2925 Virtual Way Suite 310, Vancouver, BC,
V5M 4X5
(800) 661-1196
Emp Here 145   *Sales* 20,906,390
SIC 7371 Custom computer programming ser-
vices
Alex Barnetson

D-U-N-S 24-509-2486   (BR)
AMER SPORTS CANADA INC
ARC'TERYX EQUIPMENT DIV.
2770 Bentall St, Vancouver, BC, V5M 4H4
(604) 960-3001
Emp Here 100

SIC 3949 Sporting and athletic goods, nec
Boyd White

D-U-N-S 20-646-0656   (HQ)
ART INSTITUTE OF VANCOUVER INC, THE
ART INSTITUTE OF VANCOUVER, THE
(*Suby of* THE DREAM CENTER FOUNDA-
TION A CALIFORNIA NONPROFIT CORPO-
RATION)
2665 Renfrew St, Vancouver, BC, V5M 0A7
(604) 683-9200
Sales 29,878,200
SIC 8221 Colleges and universities
Brian Parker

D-U-N-S 24-558-6490   (HQ)
ASSOCIATED ENGINEERING (B.C.) LTD
(*Suby of* ASHCO SHAREHOLDERS INC)
2889 12th Ave E Suite 500, Vancouver, BC,
V5M 4T5
(604) 293-1411
Emp Here 100   *Sales* 35,747,800
SIC 8711 Engineering services
Kerry Rudd
Martin Jobke
Donna Bonk

D-U-N-S 24-227-9987   (BR)
BELL MOBILITE INC
BELL MOBILITY INC
(*Suby of* BCE INC)
2925 Virtual Way Suite 400, Vancouver, BC,
V5M 4X5
(604) 678-4160
Emp Here 500
SIC 4899 Communication services, nec
Blaik Kirby

D-U-N-S 25-485-7147   (BR)
**BOARD OF EDUCATION OF SCHOOL DIS-
TRICT NO. 39 (VANCOUVER), THE**
*VANCOUVER TECHNICAL SECONDARY
SCHOOL*
(*Suby of* BOARD OF EDUCATION OF
SCHOOL DISTRICT NO. 39 (VANCOUVER),
THE)
2600 Broadway E, Vancouver, BC, V5M 1Y5
(604) 713-8215
Emp Here 77
SIC 8211 Elementary and secondary schools
Annette Vey-Chilton

D-U-N-S 24-824-5300   (HQ)
CHEMETICS INC
(*Suby of* JACOBS ENGINEERING GROUP
INC.)
2930 Virtual Way Suite 200, Vancouver, BC,
V5M 0A5
(604) 734-1200
Emp Here 170   *Sales* 53,225,370
SIC 8711 Engineering services
Andrew Barr
Nicole Von Keutz
Andrew Berryman

D-U-N-S 20-801-6329   (SL)
CHILDREN'S FOUNDATION, THE
KENNEDY HOUSE
2750 18th Ave E, Vancouver, BC, V5M 4W8
(604) 434-9101
Emp Here 100   *Sales* 13,345,900
SIC 8399 Social services, nec
Dennis Dandeneau

D-U-N-S 20-644-1342   (BR)
**COMPAGNIE DE TELEPHONE BELL DU
CANADA OU BELL CANADA, LA**
BELL MOBILITY
(*Suby of* BCE INC)
2980 Virtual Way, Vancouver, BC, V5M 4X3

Emp Here 400
SIC 5963 Direct selling establishments
Jeff Gau

D-U-N-S 24-348-3711   (SL)
COPPERLEAF TECHNOLOGIES INC
2920 Virtual Way Suite 140, Vancouver, BC,

V5M 0C4
(604) 639-9700
Emp Here 120   *Sales* 17,301,840
SIC 7371 Custom computer programming ser-
vices
Judith Hess
Boudewijn Neijens
Miranda Alldritt
Chris Allen
Kevin Ishiguro
Phil Jones
Bill Dal
Phil Jones
Barry Quart

D-U-N-S 20-592-6111   (SL)
CRAWFORD MARINE SERVICES
2985 Virtual Way Suite 280, Vancouver, BC,
V5M 4X7
(604) 436-2277
Emp Here 30   *Sales* 14,942,340
SIC 5541 Gasoline service stations
Harris Harding

D-U-N-S 20-049-2291   (SL)
DEELEY, TREV MOTORCYCLES (1991) LTD
(*Suby of* FRED DEELEY LIMITED)
1875 Boundary Rd, Vancouver, BC, V5M 3Y7
(604) 291-1875
Emp Here 50   *Sales* 24,903,900
SIC 5571 Motorcycle dealers
Malcolm Hunter
Donald James

D-U-N-S 24-996-2705   (SL)
EXTRA FOODS & DRUGS LTD
3189 Grandview Hwy, Vancouver, BC, V5M
2E9
(604) 439-5402
Emp Here 15   *Sales* 12,533,655
SIC 5141 Groceries, general line
Richard L Leigh
John Zeller
John Thompson
Stewart Green
Serge Darkazanli
Marian Burrows

D-U-N-S 25-635-0851   (BR)
G4S CASH SOLUTIONS (CANADA) LTD
GROUP 4 SECURICOR
(*Suby of* G4S PLC)
2743 Skeena St Suite 200, Vancouver, BC,
V5M 4T1

Emp Here 300
SIC 7381 Detective and armored car services
Dallas Duke

D-U-N-S 25-107-2187   (BR)
G4S CASH SOLUTIONS (CANADA) LTD
GROUP FOR SUCURICOR
(*Suby of* G4S PLC)
2743 Skeena St, Vancouver, BC, V5M 4T1

Emp Here 250
SIC 7381 Detective and armored car services
Helen Parris

D-U-N-S 20-111-7652   (SL)
GIZELLA PASTRY ULC
(*Suby of* C.H. GUENTHER & SON LLC)
3436 Lougheed Hwy, Vancouver, BC, V5M
2A4
(604) 253-5220
Emp Here 100   *Sales* 34,569,000
SIC 2051 Bread, cake, and related products
Tom Spicker
Andrew Mann

D-U-N-S 25-123-7293   (HQ)
**HEALTH EMPLOYERS ASSOCIATION OF
BRITISH COLUMBIA**
2889 12th Ave E Suite 300, Vancouver, BC,
V5M 4T5
(604) 736-5909
Sales 23,411,100
SIC 8621 Professional organizations

Michael Mcmillan
Tony Collins
Audra Fediurek
Adrienne Hook
Lyn Kocher
Ingrid Otto
Matt Prescott
Moninder Singh
Roy Thorpe-Doward
Betsy Gibbons

D-U-N-S 25-320-4929   (HQ)
HEALTHCARE BENEFIT TRUST
350-2889 12th Ave E, Vancouver, BC, V5M
4T5
(604) 736-2087
Emp Here 63   *Sales* 19,011,750
SIC 8748 Business consulting, nec
Donnie Wing
Sarah Hoffman

D-U-N-S 24-750-8377   (BR)
INTACT INSURANCE COMPANY
ING INSURANCE
(*Suby of* INTACT FINANCIAL CORPORA-
TION)
2955 Virtual Way Suite 400, Vancouver, BC,
V5M 4X6
(604) 891-5400
Emp Here 130
SIC 6411 Insurance agents, brokers, and ser-
vice
Jill Manuel

D-U-N-S 24-030-6837   (SL)
ITALIAN FOLK SOCIETY OF BC, THE
ITALIAN CULTURAL CENTRE SOCIETY
3075 Slocan St, Vancouver, BC, V5M 3E4
(604) 430-3337
Emp Here 90   *Sales* 12,859,110
SIC 8641 Civic and social associations
Luca Citton
Deanna Lythgo
Mauro Vescera
Giorgio Gasparro
Rabio Rasotto
Giulio Recchioni
Edda Onesti
Michael Cuccione
Joe Finamore
Mike Lombardi

D-U-N-S 20-562-7495   (SL)
IWA-FOREST INDUSTRY PENSION PLAN
2955 Virtual Way Suite 150, Vancouver, BC,
V5M 4X6
(604) 433-6310
Emp Here 50   *Sales* 51,744,050
SIC 6371 Pension, health, and welfare funds
Dawn Becker

D-U-N-S 24-694-6222   (SL)
JESSEL, BRIAN AUTOSPORT INC
BRIAN JESSEL BMW
(*Suby of* JESSEL, BRIAN HOLDINGS INC)
2311 Boundary Rd, Vancouver, BC, V5M 4W5
(604) 222-7788
Emp Here 150   *Sales* 94,392,000
SIC 5511 New and used car dealers
Brian Jessel

D-U-N-S 24-333-9897   (HQ)
JESSEL, BRIAN HOLDINGS INC
2311 Boundary Rd, Vancouver, BC, V5M 4W5
(604) 222-7788
Emp Here 1   *Sales* 41,002,500
SIC 6712 Bank holding companies
Brian Jessel

D-U-N-S 24-340-8221   (HQ)
KLOHN CRIPPEN BERGER HOLDINGS LTD
2955 Virtual Way Suite 500, Vancouver, BC,
V5M 4X6
(604) 669-3800
Emp Here 2   *Sales* 109,652,700
SIC 6712 Bank holding companies
Bryan Watts

D-U-N-S 24-101-1316   (HQ)
KLOHN CRIPPEN BERGER LTD
(*Suby of* KLOHN CRIPPEN BERGER HOLD-INGS LTD)
2955 Virtual Way Suite 500, Vancouver, BC,
V5M 4X6
(604) 669-3800
Emp Here 214   *Sales* 99,748,286
SIC 8711 Engineering services
 Len Murray
 Alex Sy
 Ryan Douglas
 Bob Chambers
 Dave Mack
 Daisy Lee
 Chris Langton
 Stuart Forbes

D-U-N-S 25-270-1388   (BR)
LOBLAWS INC
REAL CANADIAN SUPERSTORE
(*Suby of* LOBLAW COMPANIES LIMITED)
3185 Grandview Hwy, Vancouver, BC, V5M
2E9
(604) 439-5479
Emp Here 460
SIC 5141 Groceries, general line
 Carlo Fierro

D-U-N-S 24-798-4131   (HQ)
NINTENDO OF CANADA LTD
(*Suby of* NINTENDO CO., LTD.)
2925 Virtual Way Suite 150, Vancouver, BC,
V5M 4X5
(604) 279-1600
Emp Here 50   *Sales* 31,232,520
SIC 5092 Toys and hobby goods and supplies
 Ronald Bertram

D-U-N-S 24-311-8874   (HQ)
ON SIDE RESTORATION SERVICES LTD
3157 Grandview Hwy, Vancouver, BC, V5M
2E9
(604) 293-1596
Emp Here 200   *Sales* 148,663,200
SIC 1799 Special trade contractors, nec
 Craig Hogarth
 Michael Tyrer

D-U-N-S 24-682-0252   (BR)
OTIS CANADA, INC
(*Suby of* UNITED TECHNOLOGIES CORPO-RATION)
2788 Rupert St, Vancouver, BC, V5M 3T7
(604) 412-3400
Emp Here 100
SIC 3534 Elevators and moving stairways
 Scott Calkins

D-U-N-S 25-168-4247   (HQ)
PACIFIC COMMUNITY RESOURCES SOCI-ETY
2830 Grandview Hwy Suite 201, Vancouver,
BC, V5M 2C9
(604) 412-7950
Emp Here 5   *Sales* 17,742,280
SIC 8322 Individual and family services
 Ingrid Kastens
 Steven Atkinson
 David Piltman
 Michelle Shaw
 Laura Jamieson
 Eva Ho
 William Mcmichael
 Bruce Johnstone
 Jeremy Wright
 Larry Adams

D-U-N-S 20-300-0919   (HQ)
PARIS ORTHOTICS LTD
3630 1st Ave E, Vancouver, BC, V5M 1C3
(604) 301-2150
Sales 38,639,130
SIC 3842 Surgical appliances and supplies
 Paul Paris
 Gary Jewula
 Stephen Paris

 Renee Paris

D-U-N-S 20-022-8216   (BR)
PR SENIORS HOUSING MANAGEMENT LTD
RENFREW CARE CENTER
(*Suby of* PR SENIORS HOUSING MANAGE-MENT LTD)
1880 Renfrew St, Vancouver, BC, V5M 3H9
(604) 255-7723
Emp Here 200
SIC 8051 Skilled nursing care facilities
 Lorraine Coffin

D-U-N-S 24-390-4153   (SL)
PUR BRANDS INC
2642 Nootka St, Vancouver, BC, V5M 3M5
(604) 299-5045
Emp Here 30   *Sales* 25,067,310
SIC 5149 Groceries and related products, nec
 Frank Devries

D-U-N-S 24-492-7166   (HQ)
QUARTECH SYSTEMS LIMITED
2889 12th Ave E Suite 650, Vancouver, BC,
V5M 4T5
(604) 291-9686
Emp Here 50   *Sales* 17,731,100
SIC 7371 Custom computer programming ser-vices
 David Marshall
 Paul Huffington
 William O'brien

D-U-N-S 25-723-8162   (SL)
RAND & FOWLER INSURANCE LTD
2323 Boundary Rd Suite 101, Vancouver, BC,
V5M 4V8
(604) 298-4222
Emp Here 40   *Sales* 23,196,960
SIC 6411 Insurance agents, brokers, and ser-vice
 Brad Jefferson

D-U-N-S 25-912-2117   (SL)
RENFREW PARK COMMUNITY ASSOCIA-TION
RENFREW PARK COMMUNITY CENTRE
2929 22nd Ave E, Vancouver, BC, V5M 2Y3
(604) 257-8388
Emp Here 80   *Sales* 5,473,760
SIC 8322 Individual and family services
 Lily Dong

D-U-N-S 20-116-8093   (HQ)
UNIVCO INVESTMENTS LTD
2835 12th Ave E, Vancouver, BC, V5M 4P9
(604) 253-4000
Emp Here 40   *Sales* 33,538,050
SIC 5074 Plumbing and heating equipment
and supplies (hydronics)
 David Reed
 Jeff Reed

D-U-N-S 20-280-6865   (HQ)
VARD MARINE INC
2930 Virtual Way Suite 180, Vancouver, BC,
V5M 0A5
(604) 216-3360
Sales 11,618,035
SIC 8711 Engineering services
 David Mcmillan
 Steinar Nerbovik
 Eero Makinen

Vancouver, BC V5N

D-U-N-S 20-111-3123   (SL)
FAMOUS FOODS MARKETS LTD
FAMOUS FOODS
1595 Kingsway Unit 101, Vancouver, BC, V5N
2R8
(604) 872-3019
Emp Here 60   *Sales* 17,608,620
SIC 5411 Grocery stores

 Cameron Bruce
 Ross Gibson

D-U-N-S 20-867-3905   (HQ)
GOLD KEY INSURANCE SERVICES LTD
4038 Knight St, Vancouver, BC, V5N 5Y7
(604) 325-1241
Emp Here 10   *Sales* 25,441,800
SIC 6411 Insurance agents, brokers, and ser-vice
 Raghbir Bhinder
 Sharn Bhinder

D-U-N-S 20-104-8506   (SL)
GREATER VANCOUVER ASSOCIATE STORES LTD
CANADIAN TIRE
2220 Kingsway, Vancouver, BC, V5N 2T7

Emp Here 49   *Sales* 24,405,822
SIC 5531 Auto and home supply stores
 Mike Maciver

D-U-N-S 24-856-0245   (HQ)
IMMIGRANT SERVICES SOCIETY OF BRITISH COLUMBIA, THE
ISS
2610 Victoria Dr, Vancouver, BC, V5N 4L2
(604) 684-2561
Emp Here 120   *Sales* 34,166,220
SIC 8399 Social services, nec
 Catherine Der
 Shawqi Rashad
 Patricia Woroch
 Manchan Sonachansingh
 Marian Dewitt
 Janet Gartner
 Jennifer Hyndman
 Howard Leong

D-U-N-S 24-026-7026   (BR)
M.O.S.A.I.C. MULTI-LINGUAL ORIENTA-TION SERVICE ASSOCIATION FOR IMMI-GRANT COMMUNITIES
(*Suby of* M.O.S.A.I.C. MULTI-LINGUAL ORI-ENTATION SERVICE ASSOCIATION FOR IM-MIGRANT COMMUNITIES)
2555 Commercial Dr Suite 312, Vancouver,
BC, V5N 4C1
(604) 708-3905
Emp Here 100
SIC 8322 Individual and family services
 Jas Hundle

D-U-N-S 24-558-3653   (HQ)
MAXIMS BAKERY LTD
3596 Commercial St, Vancouver, BC, V5N
4E9
(604) 876-8266
Emp Here 35   *Sales* 44,021,550
SIC 5461 Retail bakeries
 Yuen Hung Lai
 Steve Yuen
 Richie Lai

D-U-N-S 25-318-1911   (BR)
MCDONALD'S RESTAURANTS OF CANADA LIMITED
MCDONALD'S 8067
(*Suby of* MCDONALD'S CORPORATION)
2021 Kingsway, Vancouver, BC, V5N 2T2
(604) 718-1060
Emp Here 80
SIC 5812 Eating places
 Prasad Aarti

D-U-N-S 24-400-2648   (HQ)
MULTIPLE REALTY LTD
2298 Kingsway, Vancouver, BC, V5N 5M9
(604) 434-8843
Emp Here 130   *Sales* 77,754,720
SIC 6531 Real estate agents and managers
 John Ma
 Randy Wong

D-U-N-S 25-013-1661   (HQ)
PACIFIC LEGAL EDUCATION ASSOCIA-

TION
P.L.E.A.
3894 Commercial St, Vancouver, BC, V5N
4G2
(604) 871-0450
Sales 16,565,440
SIC 8399 Social services, nec
 Allan Howard
 Ann Alexander
 Stewart Smith
 Timothy Agg
 Jennifer Lawrence
 Nikki Nagy
 Michelle Francis
 Michael Jeffreys
 Rory Cleave
 Ray Hartley

D-U-N-S 25-664-2547   (BR)
REVERA LONG TERM CARE INC
LAKEVIEW CARE CENTRE
(*Suby of* GOVERNMENT OF CANADA)
3490 Porter St, Vancouver, BC, V5N 5W4
(604) 874-2803
Emp Here 100
SIC 8051 Skilled nursing care facilities
 Susan Rushton

D-U-N-S 25-271-7285   (BR)
SOBEYS WEST INC
SAFEWAY
(*Suby of* EMPIRE COMPANY LIMITED)
1780 Broadway E, Vancouver, BC, V5N 1W3
(604) 873-0225
Emp Here 170
SIC 5411 Grocery stores
 Peter Lemon

Vancouver, BC V5P

D-U-N-S 25-266-8777   (BR)
BOARD OF EDUCATION OF SCHOOL DIS-TRICT NO. 39 (VANCOUVER), THE
DAVID THOMPSON SECONDARY SCHOOL
(*Suby of* BOARD OF EDUCATION OF
SCHOOL DISTRICT NO. 39 (VANCOUVER),
THE)
1755 55th Ave E, Vancouver, BC, V5P 1Z7
(604) 713-8278
Emp Here 90
SIC 8211 Elementary and secondary schools
 Alex Grant

D-U-N-S 20-080-6623   (HQ)
GREIG ASSOCIATES X-RAY, ULTRA-SOUND AND MAMMOGRAPHY INC
5732 Victoria Dr, Vancouver, BC, V5P 3W6
(604) 321-6769
Emp Here 68   *Sales* 19,277,520
SIC 8011 Offices and clinics of medical doc-tors
 Connie Siu
 Philip Switzer

D-U-N-S 20-378-2586   (SL)
INTERNATIONAL ORNITHOLOGICAL CONGRESS 2018 ORGANIZING SOCIETY
IOC2018
7190 Duff St, Vancouver, BC, V5P 4B3
(604) 218-9138
Emp Here 210   *Sales* 54,128,213
SIC 8748 Business consulting, nec
 Robert Elner
 Andrew Huang

D-U-N-S 24-308-7678   (SL)
KRYTON CANADA CORPORATION
1645 E Kent Ave North, Vancouver, BC, V5P
2S8
(604) 324-8280
Emp Here 45   *Sales* 20,122,830
SIC 5039 Construction materials, nec
 Kari Yuers
 Kevin Yuers

D-U-N-S 20-114-4292 (SL)
NORTHERN BUILDING SUPPLY LTD
1640 E Kent Ave South, Vancouver, BC, V5P
2S7
(604) 321-6141
Emp Here 40   *Sales* 17,886,960
SIC 5031 Lumber, plywood, and millwork
John Thomas
Gordon Thomas
Alexander Thomas

D-U-N-S 24-504-6180 (BR)
PROVIDENCE HEALTH CARE SOCIETY
HOLY FAMILY HOSPITAL
(*Suby of* PROVIDENCE HEALTH CARE SO-
CIETY)
7801 Argyle St, Vancouver, BC, V5P 3L6
(604) 321-2661
Emp Here 400
SIC 8062 General medical and surgical hospi-
tals
Karen Chiang

Vancouver, BC V5R

D-U-N-S 24-153-1516 (SL)
B C FEDERATION OF LABOUR (CLC)
5118 Joyce St Suite 200, Vancouver, BC, V5R
4H1
(604) 430-1421
Emp Here 25   *Sales* 46,166,475
SIC 6371 Pension, health, and welfare funds
Jim Sinclair
Angela Schira

D-U-N-S 25-612-3753 (SL)
**BRITISH COLUMBIA CENTRE FOR ABIL-
ITY ASSOCIATION**
CHILDREN'S CENTRE FOR ABILITY
2805 Kingsway, Vancouver, BC, V5R 5H9
(604) 451-5511
Emp Here 176   *Sales* 13,336,048
SIC 8093 Specialty outpatient clinics, nec
Shawqi Rashed
Lesley Bainbridge
Maureen Flangan
Tracy Wong
Richard Mayede
Stephen Flamer
Martin Wittman
Alan Kenney
Harriet Mann
Catalina Rodriguez

D-U-N-S 20-358-1392 (SL)
**BRITISH COLUMBIA FEDERATION OF RE-
TIRED UNION MEMBERS**
5118 Joyce St Suite 200, Vancouver, BC, V5R
4H1
(604) 688-4565
Emp Here 19   *Sales* 19,662,739
SIC 6371 Pension, health, and welfare funds
Diane Wood

D-U-N-S 25-664-7579 (HQ)
**COLLINGWOOD   NEIGHBOURHOOD
HOUSE SOCIETY**
*COLLINGWOOD   NEIGHBOURHOOD
HOUSE*
5288 Joyce St, Vancouver, BC, V5R 6C9
(604) 435-0323
Emp Here 15   *Sales* 11,341,650
SIC 8399 Social services, nec
Jennifer Gray-Grant

D-U-N-S 24-333-3197 (SL)
INTRA ENERGY BC INC
3665 Kingsway Suite 300, Vancouver, BC,
V5R 5W2

Emp Here 30   *Sales* 34,666,950
SIC 4924 Natural gas distribution

D-U-N-S 24-798-5518 (HQ)

**M.O.S.A.I.C. MULTI-LINGUAL ORIENTA-
TION SERVICE ASSOCIATION FOR IMMI-
GRANT COMMUNITIES**
M.O.S.A.I.C
5575 Boundary Rd, Vancouver, BC, V5R 2P9
(604) 254-9626
Emp Here 1   *Sales* 31,060,200
SIC 8399 Social services, nec
Eyob Naizghi
Elizabeth Briemberg

D-U-N-S 20-113-6611 (SL)
MR. SPORT HOTEL HOLDINGS LTD
RAMADA HOTEL & SUITES
3484 Kingsway Suite 101, Vancouver, BC,
V5R 5L6
(604) 433-8255
Emp Here 100   *Sales* 9,489,900
SIC 7011 Hotels and motels
Zulfikar Nathoo

D-U-N-S 24-346-3036 (BR)
ROYAL PACIFIC REALTY CORP
ROYAL PACIFIC REALTY GROUP
(*Suby of* ROYAL PACIFIC REALTY CORP)
3107 Kingsway, Vancouver, BC, V5R 5J9
(604) 439-0068
Emp Here 280
SIC 6531 Real estate agents and managers
Edward Fung

D-U-N-S 20-986-6230 (SL)
SINGGA ENTERPRISES INC
3373 Kingsway, Vancouver, BC, V5R 5K6

Emp Here 20   *Sales* 10,174,797
SIC 5137 Women's and children's clothing
Hamza Ahmed

D-U-N-S 24-345-0405 (BR)
**VANCOUVER COASTAL HEALTH AUTHOR-
ITY**
*EVERGREEN COMMUNITY HEALTH CEN-
TRE*
(*Suby of* GOVERNMENT OF THE
PROVINCE OF BRITISH COLUMBIA)
3425 Crowley Dr, Vancouver, BC, V5R 6G3
(604) 872-2511
Emp Here 150
SIC 8322 Individual and family services
Christine Tang

D-U-N-S 25-181-9327 (SL)
**VANCOUVER DODGEBALL LEAGUE SOCI-
ETY**
*INTERNATIONAL DODGEBALL ASSOCIA-
TION*
5695 Aberdeen St, Vancouver, BC, V5R 4M5
(604) 353-7892
Emp Here 34   *Sales* 13,668,572
SIC 8699 Membership organizations, nec
Kevin Bao

D-U-N-S 20-799-8303 (HQ)
YMCA OF GREATER VANCOUVER, THE
5055 Joyce St Suite 300, Vancouver, BC, V5R
6B2
(604) 681-9622
Emp Here 60   *Sales* 310,602,000
SIC 8399 Social services, nec
Stephen Butz
Moray Keiths
Dennis Skulsky
John Willson
Howard Young
Mary Beck
Marty Reynolds
James Bond
Bob Chan Kent
Jeff Devins

Vancouver, BC V5S

D-U-N-S 20-265-3911 (BR)

**BOARD OF EDUCATION OF SCHOOL DIS-
TRICT NO. 39 (VANCOUVER), THE**
KILLARNEY SECONDARY SCHOOL
(*Suby of* BOARD OF EDUCATION OF
SCHOOL DISTRICT NO. 39 (VANCOUVER),
THE)
6454 Killarney St, Vancouver, BC, V5S 2X7
(604) 713-8950
Emp Here 123
SIC 8211 Elementary and secondary schools
Robert Moro

D-U-N-S 20-798-7181 (HQ)
**FAIR HAVEN UNITED CHURCH HOMES,
THE**
2720 48th Ave E, Vancouver, BC, V5S 1G7
(604) 433-2939
Emp Here 80   *Sales* 10,285,120
SIC 8361 Residential care
Carol Mothersill
John Gowan
Sonja Mcmahon

D-U-N-S 24-267-2996 (SL)
FIRST GROCERY LTD
EXTRA FOODS
7190 Kerr St, Vancouver, BC, V5S 4W2
(604) 433-0434
Emp Here 45   *Sales* 12,336,840
SIC 5411 Grocery stores
Dave Sawatsky
Jim Nielsen

D-U-N-S 25-754-8792 (SL)
**M. KOPERNIK (NICOLAUS COPERNICUS)
FOUNDATION**
THE KOPERNIK LODGE
3150 Rosemont Dr, Vancouver, BC, V5S 2C9
(604) 438-2474
Emp Here 95   *Sales* 5,628,465
SIC 8361 Residential care
Timothy Motyka

D-U-N-S 20-114-4144 (HQ)
NORTH ARM TRANSPORTATION LTD
2582 E Kent Ave South, Vancouver, BC, V5S
2H8
(604) 321-9171
Sales 56,574,045
SIC 5172 Petroleum products, nec
Henry Gino Stradiotti
Michael Stradiotti

D-U-N-S 24-370-6082 (SL)
ROYAL ARCH MASONIC HOMES SOCIETY
*ROYAL ARCH MASONIC HOME AND SE-
NIORS APARTMENTS*
7850 Champlain Cres Suite 252, Vancouver,
BC, V5S 4C7
(604) 437-7343
Emp Here 150   *Sales* 10,248,900
SIC 8051 Skilled nursing care facilities
Gregory Runzer

D-U-N-S 25-892-8175 (BR)
WEYERHAEUSER COMPANY LIMITED
K3 SPECIALTIES
(*Suby of* WEYERHAEUSER COMPANY)
3650 E Kent Ave S, Vancouver, BC, V5S 2J2

Emp Here 80
SIC 2421 Sawmills and planing mills, general
Mylee Powell

Vancouver, BC V5T

D-U-N-S 20-712-6293 (SL)
ALPHA SPORTSWEAR LIMITED
112 6th Ave E, Vancouver, BC, V5T 1J5
(604) 873-2621
Emp Here 40   *Sales* 19,932,880
SIC 5137 Women's and children's clothing
George Agazarian
Robert Ian Moodie

D-U-N-S 25-215-8423 (HQ)
ANN-LOUISE JEWELLERS LTD
TIME BOUTIQUE
(*Suby of* KUNG'S MANUFACTORY LTD)
18 2nd Ave E, Vancouver, BC, V5T 1B1
(604) 873-6341
Emp Here 30   *Sales* 43,979,040
SIC 5944 Jewelry stores
Jimmy Chen
Marie Chen
Colin Chen

D-U-N-S 24-509-1686 (SL)
AQUINOX PHARMACEUTICALS INC
887 Great Northern Way Suite 450, Vancou-
ver, BC, V5T 4T5
(604) 629-9223
Emp Here 6   *Sales* 25,000,000
SIC 5912 Drug stores and proprietary stores
David J. Main
Kamran Alam
Gary Bridger
Daniel Levitt
Richard Levy
Kelvin Neu
Sean Nolan
Robert E. Pelzer
Todd Simpson

D-U-N-S 20-864-1571 (HQ)
**ASSOCIATION OF NEIGHBOURHOOD
HOUSES OF BRITISH COLUMBIA**
3102 Main St Suite 203, Vancouver, BC, V5T
3G7
(604) 875-9111
Emp Here 2   *Sales* 14,593,097
SIC 8399 Social services, nec
Debra Bryant

D-U-N-S 24-980-2810 (SL)
B I V PUBLICATIONS LTD
BUSINESS IN VANCOUVER
102 4th Ave E, Vancouver, BC, V5T 1G2
(604) 669-8500
Emp Here 70   *Sales* 11,481,890
SIC 2711 Newspapers
Paul Harris
Thomas Siba

D-U-N-S 24-408-2694 (SL)
**BOYS AND GIRLS CLUBS FOUNDATION
OF SOUTH COAST BC**
*BOYS AND GIRLS CLUBS OF SOUTH
COAST BC*
2875 St. George St, Vancouver, BC, V5T 3R8
(604) 879-6554
Emp Here 400   *Sales* 82,827,200
SIC 8399 Social services, nec
Carolyn Tuckwell

D-U-N-S 20-992-0057 (HQ)
**BOYS' AND GIRLS' CLUBS OF GREATER
VANCOUVER**
2875 St. George St, Vancouver, BC, V5T 3R8
(604) 879-9118
Emp Here 55   *Sales* 10,366,920
SIC 8322 Individual and family services
David Bruce
Lothar Fabian
Terry Holland
Tracy Cooke

D-U-N-S 20-957-7568 (BR)
BRINK'S CANADA LIMITED
(*Suby of* THE BRINK'S COMPANY)
247 1st Ave E, Vancouver, BC, V5T 1A7
(604) 875-6221
Emp Here 100
SIC 7381 Detective and armored car services
Darin Reid

D-U-N-S 20-805-8727 (HQ)
**BRITISH COLUMBIA SOCIETY FOR THE
PREVENTION OF CRUELTY TO ANIMALS,
THE**
BC SPCA
1245 7th Ave E, Vancouver, BC, V5T 1R1

---

(604) 681-7271
Emp Here 15   *Sales* 11,353,520
SIC 8699 Membership organizations, nec
Craig J. Daniell
Joshua Wheeloch
Cindy Soules
Marylee Davies
J. Kristen Bryson
Eric Stebner
Vicky Renneberg

D-U-N-S 24-725-6456   (SL)
BUSTERS TOWING 1987 LTD
104 1st Ave E, Vancouver, BC, V5T 1A4
(604) 685-8181
Emp Here 1   *Sales* 68,665,315
SIC 7549 Automotive services, nec
Spencer Shrump

D-U-N-S 24-641-0948   (SL)
CORPORATE ELECTRIC LIMITED
2233 Quebec St, Vancouver, BC, V5T 3A1
(604) 879-0551
Emp Here 60   *Sales* 13,069,740
SIC 1731 Electrical work
Jason Killins

D-U-N-S 24-793-4347   (SL)
DESTINATION AUTO SALES INC
KINGSWAY HONDA
368 Kingsway, Vancouver, BC, V5T 3J6
(604) 873-3676
Emp Here 30   *Sales* 14,942,340
SIC 5511 New and used car dealers
David Wilson
Vincent Lau

D-U-N-S 24-136-2342   (SL)
EMILY CARR UNIVERSITY OF ART & DE-SIGN
520 1st Ave E, Vancouver, BC, V5T 0H2
(604) 844-3800
Emp Here 240   *Sales* 32,558,400
SIC 8299 Schools and educational services, nec
Ronald Burnett

D-U-N-S 25-781-8377   (SL)
EXCEL TIRE CENTRES INC
615 Kingsway, Vancouver, BC, V5T 3K5
(604) 876-1225
Emp Here 9   *Sales* 15,193,652
SIC 5531 Auto and home supply stores
Al Knowles

D-U-N-S 20-111-3784   (HQ)
FINNING INTERNATIONAL INC
UNIVERSAL MACHINERY SERVICES, DIV OF
565 Great Northern Way Suite 300, Vancouver, BC, V5T 0H8
(604) 331-4816
Emp Here 897   *Sales* 5,303,681,592
SIC 5084 Industrial machinery and equipment
L. Scott Thomson
David W. Cummings
Chad Hiley
Anna P. Marks
Jane Murdoch
Steven M. Nielsen
Harold Kvisle
Vicki Avril
Marcelo Awad
James E.C. Carter

D-U-N-S 24-523-6216   (HQ)
HOOTSUITE INC
UBERVU
5 8th Ave E, Vancouver, BC, V5T 1R6
(604) 681-4668
Emp Here 550   *Sales* 207,888,000
SIC 7374 Data processing and preparation
Ryan Holmes
Matthew Handford
Philippe Renon
Bob Elliott
Diraj Goel

Garry Tauss
Jeff Lieberman
Ryan Sweeney
Sara Clemens
Greg Twinney

D-U-N-S 20-572-8793   (HQ)
KUNG'S MANUFACTORY LTD
18 2nd Ave E, Vancouver, BC, V5T 1B1
(604) 873-6341
Emp Here 30   *Sales* 173,825,000
SIC 5094 Jewelry and precious stones
Jimmy Chen
Marie Chen

D-U-N-S 25-099-8564   (HQ)
LIBERTY WINE MERCHANTS LTD
291 2nd Ave E Suite 100, Vancouver, BC, V5T 1B8
(604) 739-7801
Emp Here 10   *Sales* 14,956,500
SIC 5921 Liquor stores
Robert Simpson
S. Paul Simpson

D-U-N-S 20-584-1463   (HQ)
MANTIQUE FASHIONS LTD
MANTIQUE
5 5th Ave E, Vancouver, BC, V5T 1G7
(604) 736-7161
Emp Here 12   *Sales* 25,115,440
SIC 5621 Women's clothing stores
Gino Cuglietta
Louisa Tsui

D-U-N-S 24-939-4065   (HQ)
MARK ANTHONY GROUP INC
MISSION HILL FAMILY ESTATE
(*Suby of* PELECANUS HOLDINGS LTD)
887 Great Northern Way Suite 500, Vancouver, BC, V5T 4T5
(888) 394-1122
Emp Here 125   *Sales* 243,692,500
SIC 2084 Wines, brandy, and brandy spirits
Anthony Von Mandl
Timothy Howley
Victor Giacomin

D-U-N-S 24-329-9633   (HQ)
MARK ANTHONY PROPERTIES LTD
(*Suby of* PELECANUS HOLDINGS LTD)
887 Great Northern Way Suite 101, Vancouver, BC, V5T 4T5
(604) 263-9994
Emp Here 100   *Sales* 109,652,700
SIC 6719 Holding companies, nec
Anthony Von Mandl
Victor Giacomin

D-U-N-S 24-163-2827   (HQ)
MICRO COM SYSTEMS LTD
27 7th Ave E, Vancouver, BC, V5T 1M4
(604) 872-6771
Sales 26,953,140
SIC 7389 Business services, nec
Craig Hollingum
Victor Suos

D-U-N-S 20-114-0563   (SL)
MODER, JAMES R. CRYSTAL CHANDE-LIER (CANADA) LTD
JAMES R MODER CRYSTAL CHANDELIER
106 7th Ave E, Vancouver, BC, V5T 1M6
(604) 879-0934
Emp Here 65   *Sales* 12,378,730
SIC 3645 Residential lighting fixtures
James Rudy Moder

D-U-N-S 20-714-1862   (HQ)
MOUNTAIN EQUIPMENT CO-OPERATIVE
MEC
1077 Great Northern Way, Vancouver, BC, V5T 1E1
(604) 707-3300
Emp Here 300   *Sales* 364,998,639
SIC 5941 Sporting goods and bicycle shops
David Labistour
Ellen Pekeles

Sandy Treagus

D-U-N-S 20-280-6519   (SL)
OAK AND FORT CORP
OAK + FORT
7 6th Ave E Unit 200, Vancouver, BC, V5T 1J3
(604) 559-6911
Emp Here 100   *Sales* 17,939,600
SIC 5651 Family clothing stores
Min Kang

D-U-N-S 25-115-1155   (HQ)
PELECANUS HOLDINGS LTD
887 Great Northern Way Suite 101, Vancouver, BC, V5T 4T5
(604) 263-9994
Sales 73,034,500
SIC 5169 Chemicals and allied products, nec
Anthony Von Mandl

D-U-N-S 25-159-4750   (SL)
PROTEC DENTAL LABORATORIES LTD
38 1st Ave E, Vancouver, BC, V5T 1A1
(604) 873-8000
Emp Here 130   *Sales* 8,621,000
SIC 8072 Dental laboratories

D-U-N-S 20-886-1331   (SL)
PROTEC ORTHODONTIC LABORATORIES LTD
38 1st Ave E, Vancouver, BC, V5T 1A1
(604) 734-8966
Emp Here 120   *Sales* 9,365,760
SIC 8072 Dental laboratories
Hillary Currie

D-U-N-S 25-362-4795   (BR)
PROVIDENCE HEALTH CARE SOCIETY
MOUNT SAINT JOSEPH HOSPITAL
(*Suby of* PROVIDENCE HEALTH CARE SO-CIETY)
3080 Prince Edward St, Vancouver, BC, V5T 3N4
(604) 877-8302
Emp Here 1,000
SIC 8062 General medical and surgical hospitals
Akber Mathani

D-U-N-S 20-115-1022   (HQ)
RALPH'S RADIO LTD
220 1st Ave E, Vancouver, BC, V5T 1A5
(604) 879-4281
Emp Here 1   *Sales* 13,111,740
SIC 5013 Motor vehicle supplies and new parts

D-U-N-S 25-597-9908   (HQ)
RBDS RUBBISH BOYS DISPOSAL SER-VICE INC
1-800-GOT-JUNK ?
887 Great Northern Way Suite 301, Vancouver, BC, V5T 4T5
(604) 731-5782
Emp Here 2   *Sales* 11,570,895
SIC 4953 Refuse systems
Brian Scudamore

D-U-N-S 20-796-6532   (HQ)
REGENCY AUTO INVESTMENTS INC
REGENCY GROUP CANADA
401 Kingsway, Vancouver, BC, V5T 3K1
(604) 879-8411
Emp Here 61   *Sales* 50,342,400
SIC 5511 New and used car dealers
Amir Ahamed
Aleem Ahamed

D-U-N-S 20-357-3022   (SL)
REGENCY LEXUS TOYOTA INC
401 Kingsway, Vancouver, BC, V5T 3K1
(604) 879-6241
Emp Here 25   *Sales* 12,451,950
SIC 5511 New and used car dealers
Amir Ahammad

D-U-N-S 20-702-2828   (HQ)
SAJE NATURAL BUSINESS INC

SAJE NATURAL WELLNESS
22 5th Ave E Suite 500, Vancouver, BC, V5T 1G8
(877) 275-7253
Emp Here 75   *Sales* 73,034,500
SIC 5169 Chemicals and allied products, nec
Kate Ross-Leblanc
Jean-Pierre Leblanc
Jamie Moore

D-U-N-S 24-346-9504   (SL)
SUGOI PERFORMANCE APPAREL LIM-ITED PARTNERSHIP
144 7th Ave E, Vancouver, BC, V5T 1M6
(604) 875-0887
Emp Here 200   *Sales* 27,334,800
SIC 2329 Men's and boy's clothing, nec
Anthony Reznick

D-U-N-S 24-996-8710   (SL)
TAMODA APPAREL INC
319 2nd Ave E Suite 315, Vancouver, BC, V5T 1B9
(604) 877-2282
Emp Here 160   *Sales* 134,005,280
SIC 5136 Men's and boy's clothing
Charles Tan

D-U-N-S 20-995-2605   (HQ)
TEAMSTERS UNION LOCAL NO. 213
490 Broadway E Suite 464, Vancouver, BC, V5T 1X3
(604) 874-3654
Emp Here 24   *Sales* 11,773,500
SIC 8631 Labor organizations
Raymond (Ray) Zigmont
Donald (Don) Mcgill

D-U-N-S 25-533-3148   (SL)
TG INDUSTRIES INC
107 3rd Ave E, Vancouver, BC, V5T 1C7
(604) 872-6676
Emp Here 30   *Sales* 13,304,700
SIC 7389 Business services, nec
Thompson Chu
Ida Chu

D-U-N-S 20-294-6679   (SL)
UNITED NATURALS INC
2416 Main St Unit 132, Vancouver, BC, V5T 3E2
(604) 999-9999
Emp Here 90   *Sales* 24,899,400
SIC 2833 Medicinals and botanicals
Steve Curtis

D-U-N-S 24-334-2743   (BR)
UNIVERSITY OF BRITISH COLUMBIA, THE
DEPARTMENT OF RADIOLOGY
(*Suby of* UNIVERSITY OF BRITISH COLUMBIA, THE)
950 10th Ave E Rm 3350, Vancouver, BC, V5T 2B2

Emp Here 83
SIC 8221 Colleges and universities
Bruce Forster

D-U-N-S 24-326-1232   (BR)
VANCOUVER COASTAL HEALTH AUTHOR-ITY
VANCOUVER DETOX CENTRE
(*Suby of* GOVERNMENT OF THE PROVINCE OF BRITISH COLUMBIA)
377 2nd Ave E, Vancouver, BC, V5T 1B9
(604) 658-1253
Emp Here 75
SIC 8062 General medical and surgical hospitals
Margaret Sampson

D-U-N-S 20-864-0425   (HQ)
VANCOUVER COMMUNITY COLLEGE
1155 Broadway E Suite 2713, Vancouver, BC, V5T 4V5
(604) 871-7000
Sales 172,247,823
SIC 8221 Colleges and universities

Gordon Barefoot
Dale Dorn

Vancouver, BC V5V

D-U-N-S 24-074-4557   (SL)
CLARKDALE MOTORS LTD
CLARKDALE VOLKSWAGEN
4575 Main St, Vancouver, BC, V5V 3R4
(604) 872-5431
Emp Here 75   *Sales* 47,196,000
SIC 5511 New and used car dealers
Denis Barnard

D-U-N-S 20-110-4874   (SL)
CONTINENTAL SAUSAGE CO. LTD
3585 Main St, Vancouver, BC, V5V 3N4
(604) 874-0332
Emp Here 20   *Sales* 10,702,480
SIC 5147 Meats and meat products
Max Kohler

D-U-N-S 24-247-8381   (SL)
DEAFBLIND SERVICES SOCIETY OF BRITISH COLUMBIA
3369 Fraser St Suite 212, Vancouver, BC, V5V 4C2

Emp Here 49   *Sales* 19,800,803
SIC 8699 Membership organizations, nec

D-U-N-S 24-957-3726   (HQ)
LEGEND REAL ESTATE GROUP LTD
LEGEND GROUP
4728 Main St, Vancouver, BC, V5V 3R7
(604) 879-8989
Sales 27,646,674
SIC 6531 Real estate agents and managers
Gina Lin

D-U-N-S 24-536-4070   (HQ)
LITTLE MOUNTAIN NEIGHBOURHOOD HOUSE SOCIETY
3981 Main St, Vancouver, BC, V5V 3P3
(604) 879-7104
Sales 10,009,425
SIC 8399 Social services, nec
Eduardo Aragon

D-U-N-S 24-980-9583   (SL)
PERPETUAL HOLDINGS LTD
3473 Fraser St, Vancouver, BC, V5V 4C3
(604) 874-4228
Emp Here 136   *Sales* 37,175,600
SIC 6712 Bank holding companies
Alex Nam

D-U-N-S 25-375-2133   (HQ)
PERPETUAL INSURANCE SERVICES LTD
3479 Fraser St Suite 3473, Vancouver, BC, V5V 4C3
(604) 606-8118
Emp Here 20   *Sales* 33,922,400
SIC 6411 Insurance agents, brokers, and service
Alex Nam

Vancouver, BC V5W

D-U-N-S 25-312-8532   (SL)
AMEX FRASERIDGE REALTY
6325 Fraser St Suite 200, Vancouver, BC, V5W 3A3
(604) 322-3272
Emp Here 258   *Sales* 87,220,512
SIC 6531 Real estate agents and managers
Ranjan Sharman

D-U-N-S 24-750-7171   (HQ)
LITTLE MOUNTAIN RESIDENTIAL CARE & HOUSING SOCIETY
LITTLE MOUNTAIN PLACE

330 36th Ave E, Vancouver, BC, V5W 3Z4
(604) 325-2298
Emp Here 100   *Sales* 17,081,500
SIC 8051 Skilled nursing care facilities
Angela Johnston
Claire Prescott

Vancouver, BC V5X

D-U-N-S 24-141-9530   (HQ)
AERO TRADING CO LTD
8592 Fraser St Suite 200, Vancouver, BC, V5X 3Y3
(604) 327-6331
Emp Here 20   *Sales* 16,711,540
SIC 5146 Fish and seafoods
Munikazu Yamagishi

D-U-N-S 25-650-4556   (SL)
ALTIMA CONTRACTING LTD
8029 Fraser St, Vancouver, BC, V5X 3X5
(604) 327-5977
Emp Here 70   *Sales* 11,366,670
SIC 1742 Plastering, drywall, and insulation
Paul Athwal

D-U-N-S 25-327-9814   (HQ)
ANGEL SEAFOODS LTD
8475 Fraser St, Vancouver, BC, V5X 3Y1
(604) 254-2824
Emp Here 38   *Sales* 40,107,696
SIC 5146 Fish and seafoods
Kinji Matsuyama
Robert Matsuyama

D-U-N-S 24-916-3978   (SL)
B C FUNDRAISERS
8278 Manitoba St, Vancouver, BC, V5X 3A2

Emp Here 30   *Sales* 11,922,420
SIC 8699 Membership organizations, nec
Douglas Nelson

D-U-N-S 25-236-6711   (SL)
B. & C. LIST (1982) LTD
ALBERTA LEGAL & SERVICES DIRECTORY
8278 Manitoba St, Vancouver, BC, V5X 3A2
(604) 482-3100
Emp Here 80   *Sales* 13,122,160
SIC 2721 Periodicals
Shirley Hyman
Barry Hyman
Jack Hyman

D-U-N-S 20-553-3982   (HQ)
BAINS TRAVEL LIMITED
CRUISE CONCEPT
6550 Fraser St, Vancouver, BC, V5X 3T3
(604) 324-2277
Emp Here 16   *Sales* 11,439,274
SIC 4724 Travel agencies
Paul Bains

D-U-N-S 20-109-2988   (SL)
BLUE BOY MOTOR HOTEL LTD
QUALITY INN AIRPORT
(*Suby of* 342548 B.C. LTD)
725 Marine Dr Se, Vancouver, BC, V5X 2T9
(604) 321-6611
Emp Here 75
SIC 7011 Hotels and motels
Mahedi Hirji
Salim Merali
Zulfikar (Zool) Nathoo
Bahadurali Alibhai

D-U-N-S 24-837-5859   (SL)
BROWN BROS MANAGEMENT LTD
270 Marine Dr Se, Vancouver, BC, V5X 2S6
(604) 321-5100
Emp Here 110   *Sales* 69,220,800
SIC 5511 New and used car dealers
Thomas Brown

D-U-N-S 24-166-6528   (HQ)

C.G. INDUSTRIAL SPECIALTIES LTD
CGIS
558 E Kent Ave South, Vancouver, BC, V5X 4V6
(604) 263-1671
Emp Here 14   *Sales* 13,300,728
SIC 5085 Industrial supplies
Ross Waters
David Friesen

D-U-N-S 20-806-6092   (SL)
CAMBIE ROOFING CONTRACTORS LTD
CAMBIE ROOFING & DRAINAGE CONTRACTORS
1367 E Kent Ave North, Vancouver, BC, V5X 4T6
(604) 261-1111
Emp Here 90   *Sales* 19,604,610
SIC 1761 Roofing, siding, and sheetMetal work
Knute Skujins
Richard Skujins

D-U-N-S 20-918-0629   (HQ)
CANADIAN GRAPHICS WEST INC
8285 Main St, Vancouver, BC, V5X 3L7
(604) 324-1246
Emp Here 35   *Sales* 29,899,320
SIC 5136 Men's and boy's clothing
Peter Jim

D-U-N-S 24-073-3154   (HQ)
CANTU BATHROOMS & HARDWARE LTD
8351 Ontario St, Vancouver, BC, V5X 3E8
(604) 688-1252
Emp Here 29   *Sales* 15,651,090
SIC 5074 Plumbing and heating equipment and supplies (hydronics)
Michael Bull

D-U-N-S 24-212-2422   (SL)
CHUNG HING CO. LTD
8595 Fraser St, Vancouver, BC, V5X 3Y1
(604) 324-7411
Emp Here 30   *Sales* 25,067,310
SIC 5141 Groceries, general line
Raymond Lui
Roger Mak

D-U-N-S 24-101-4674   (HQ)
COAST WHOLESALE APPLIANCES INC
8488 Main St, Vancouver, V5X 4W8
(604) 321-6644
Emp Here 12   *Sales* 73,343,325
SIC 5722 Household appliance stores
Maurice Paquette
Stephen Bellringer
James Willoughby
Bradley Romo
Michael Fiorini
Jim Mather
Stephen Raben
Jack Peck
Harlow B. Burrows
Gordon Howie

D-U-N-S 24-247-1704   (SL)
CORPORATE COURIERS LOGISTICS ULC
8350 Prince Edward St, Vancouver, BC, V5X 3R9

Emp Here 200   *Sales* 133,781,600
SIC 7389 Business services, nec
Donald Mccarthy
Lutcya Mccarthy

D-U-N-S 20-116-0421   (HQ)
DANIADOWN QUILTS LTD
DANIADOWN HOME
1270 Marine Dr Se, Vancouver, BC, V5X 2V9
(604) 324-8766
Emp Here 38   *Sales* 20,916,270
SIC 5719 Miscellaneous homefurnishings
Mary Vang Andersen
Lisa Vang Andersen
Katherine Vang Andersen
Margaret Vang Andersen

D-U-N-S 25-618-7147   (BR)
DUECK CHEVROLET BUICK CADILLAC GMC LIMITED
DUECK AUTO GROUP TIRE STORE
(*Suby of* DUECK CHEVROLET BUICK CADILLAC GMC LIMITED)
400 Marine Dr Se, Vancouver, BC, V5X 4X2
(604) 324-7222
Emp Here 200
SIC 5012 Automobiles and other motor vehicles
Stuart Haskins

D-U-N-S 20-587-3748   (HQ)
DUECK CHEVROLET BUICK CADILLAC GMC LIMITED
DUECK GM
400 Marine Dr Se, Vancouver, BC, V5X 4X2
(604) 324-7222
Sales 125,856,000
SIC 5511 New and used car dealers
Moray Keith
Jack Galbraith
Stuart Haskins

D-U-N-S 25-261-8004   (SL)
GOLDEN GLOBE CONSTRUCTION LTD
8380 St. George St Unit 103, Vancouver, BC, V5X 3S7
(604) 261-3936
Emp Here 40   *Sales* 12,754,760
SIC 1521 Single-family housing construction
Amin Imani
Payam Imani

D-U-N-S 24-797-6046   (BR)
HOWE SOUND PULP & PAPER CORPORATION
WESTCOAST CELLUFIBRE, DIV OF
(*Suby of* CAPITAL ASSETS HOLDINGS (L) BERHAD)
8501 Ontario St, Vancouver, BC, V5X 4W2
(604) 301-3300
Emp Here 200
SIC 2421 Sawmills and planing mills, general
John Hruby

D-U-N-S 20-112-8717   (HQ)
KEIR SURGICAL LTD
(*Suby of* PACIFIC SURGICAL HOLDINGS LTD)
408 E Kent Ave South Suite 126, Vancouver, BC, V5X 2X7
(604) 261-9596
Emp Here 26   *Sales* 22,358,700
SIC 5047 Medical and hospital equipment
Michael Fish

D-U-N-S 24-321-2433   (SL)
KIA SOUTH VANCOUVER
396 Marine Dr Sw, Vancouver, BC, V5X 2R6
(604) 326-6868
Emp Here 50   *Sales* 24,903,900
SIC 5511 New and used car dealers
Rich Orzol

D-U-N-S 24-855-9791   (HQ)
MARINE CHRYSLER DODGE JEEP LTD
450 Marine Dr Se, Vancouver, BC, V5X 4V2
(604) 321-1236
Sales 34,610,400
SIC 5511 New and used car dealers
Edward Warkentin
Carolyne Smith

D-U-N-S 24-856-4838   (HQ)
MATAKANA SCAFFOLDING B.C. INC
1085 E Kent Ave North Suite 122, Vancouver, BC, V5X 4V9
(604) 873-5140
Sales 20,433,438
SIC 1799 Special trade contractors, nec
Paul Roche
Nick Shaw
Darren O'leary

D-U-N-S 20-259-6990   (HQ)
NEW AGE SPORTS INC

NIKE
8206 Ontario St Suite 200, Vancouver, BC, V5X 3E3
(604) 324-9943
Emp Here 15   *Sales* 10,880,650
SIC 5941 Sporting goods and bicycle shops
Paul Dusanj

D-U-N-S 24-797-8786   (SL)
OCEAN WEST CONSTRUCTION LTD
1083 E Kent Ave North Unit 113, Vancouver, BC, V5X 4V9
(604) 324-3531
Emp Here 47   *Sales* 13,563,401
SIC 1522 Residential construction, nec
Gorm Damborg

D-U-N-S 20-114-6727   (HQ)
PACIFIC METALS LIMITED
PACIFIC METALS RECYCLING INTERNATIONAL
8360 Ontario St, Vancouver, BC, V5X 3E5
(604) 327-1148
Sales 18,218,970
SIC 5093 Scrap and waste materials
Mark Lotzkar
Rod Lotzkar

D-U-N-S 20-256-3284   (HQ)
PACIFIC SURGICAL HOLDINGS LTD
408 E Kent Ave South Suite 126, Vancouver, BC, V5X 2X7
(604) 261-9596
Sales 44,717,400
SIC 5047 Medical and hospital equipment
Michael Fish

D-U-N-S 24-980-7785   (SL)
PACIFIC VEND DISTRIBUTORS LTD
(*Suby of* FEDER HOLDINGS (1994) LTD)
8250 Fraser St, Vancouver, BC, V5X 3X6
(604) 324-2164
Emp Here 28   *Sales* 14,575,176
SIC 5099 Durable goods, nec
Samuel Feder
Karl Feder

D-U-N-S 20-922-7334   (SL)
POLO SECURITY SERVICES LTD
7251 Fraser St, Vancouver, BC, V5X 3V8
(604) 321-4046
Emp Here 350   *Sales* 9,187,500
SIC 7381 Detective and armored car services
Paul Gopol

D-U-N-S 20-115-1255   (HQ)
PURDY, R.C. CHOCOLATES LTD
PURDY'S CHOCOLATES
8330 Chester St, Vancouver, BC, V5X 3Y7
(604) 454-2777
Emp Here 150   *Sales* 219,323,250
SIC 2066 Chocolate and cocoa products
Karen Flavelle

D-U-N-S 24-290-7186   (SL)
RATANA INTERNATIONAL LTD
8310 Manitoba St, Vancouver, BC, V5X 3A5
(604) 321-6776
Emp Here 70   *Sales* 35,619,920
SIC 5021 Furniture
David Leung
Yolanda Leung
Godfrey Leung

D-U-N-S 25-737-4892   (SL)
SEASIA FOODS LTD
8310 Prince Edward St, Vancouver, BC, V5X 3R9
(604) 618-8680
Emp Here 26   *Sales* 21,725,002
SIC 5149 Groceries and related products, nec
Stanley Uy
Steve Uy

D-U-N-S 24-828-4184   (HQ)
SKRETTING CANADA INC
1370 E Kent Ave South, Vancouver, BC, V5X 2Y2

(604) 325-0302
Sales 34,569,000
SIC 2048 Prepared feeds, nec
Trevor Stanley

D-U-N-S 25-220-3328   (BR)
SKRETTING CANADA INC
SKRETTING DIV.
1370 E Kent Ave South, Vancouver, BC, V5X 2Y2
(604) 325-0302
Emp Here 95
SIC 2048 Prepared feeds, nec
Ron Gowan

D-U-N-S 24-312-0339   (BR)
SOFINA FOODS INC
FLETCHER'S FINE FOODS DIV OF
(*Suby of* SOFINA FOODS INC)
8385 Fraser St, Vancouver, BC, V5X 3X8
(604) 668-5800
Emp Here 300
SIC 2011 Meat packing plants
Les Cowley

D-U-N-S 20-623-7927   (SL)
SOUTHSIDE NISSAN LTD
290 Marine Dr Sw, Vancouver, BC, V5X 2R5
(604) 324-4644
Emp Here 40   *Sales* 19,923,120
SIC 5511 New and used car dealers

D-U-N-S 24-320-0081   (SL)
SRS VICTORIA REALTY
7291 Fraser St, Vancouver, BC, V5X 3V8
(604) 263-3033
Emp Here 40   *Sales* 10,870,240
SIC 6531 Real estate agents and managers
Satnam Bains

D-U-N-S 20-813-5579   (SL)
STAR LABOUR SUPPLY LTD
426e 59th Ave E, Vancouver, BC, V5X 1Y1
(604) 325-1027
Emp Here 300   *Sales* 22,408,200
SIC 7361 Employment agencies
Gurpal Birak

D-U-N-S 24-492-0344   (SL)
SYSCO FOUR SEASONS PRODUCE LTD
127 E Kent Ave North, Vancouver, BC, V5X 2X5

Emp Here 60   *Sales* 50,134,620
SIC 5141 Groceries, general line
Ron Chan
Bert Koning

D-U-N-S 24-762-1576   (BR)
TERMINAL FOREST PRODUCTS LTD
MAINLAND SAWMILL
(*Suby of* TERMINAL FOREST PRODUCTS LTD)
8708 Yukon St, Vancouver, BC, V5X 2Y9
(604) 327-6344
Emp Here 110
SIC 2421 Sawmills and planing mills, general
Kovlaske Albert

D-U-N-S 25-716-3154   (SL)
UNIVERSAL FOOD & PAPER PRODUCTS LTD
8595 Fraser St, Vancouver, BC, V5X 3Y1
(604) 324-0331
Emp Here 35   *Sales* 16,625,910
SIC 5087 Service establishment equipment
Stephen Lui

D-U-N-S 25-951-0436   (SL)
URBAN WOOD WASTE RECYCLERS LTD
URBAN II RECYCLERS & TOOLS
110 69th Ave E, Vancouver, BC, V5X 4K6

Emp Here 53   *Sales* 13,379,426
SIC 1629 Heavy construction, nec
Sean Mabberley

D-U-N-S 20-117-4000   (HQ)
WHITE SPOT LIMITED

WHITE SPOT RESTAURANT
(*Suby of* SHATO HOLDINGS LTD)
1126 Marine Dr Se, Vancouver, BC, V5X 2V7
(604) 321-6631
Emp Here 45   *Sales* 127,276,600
SIC 5812 Eating places
Warren Erhart
Peter Toigo
Kelvin Lum
Larry Bell
Frank Price

Vancouver, BC V5Y

D-U-N-S 20-812-4987   (SL)
0781337 B.C. LTD
BEAT 94.5 FM
380 2nd Ave W Suite 300, Vancouver, BC, V5Y 1C8
(604) 699-2328
Emp Here 60   *Sales* 11,087,880
SIC 4832 Radio broadcasting stations
James Stuart

D-U-N-S 24-324-7413   (BR)
ALSCO CANADA CORPORATION
ALSCO UNIFORM & LINEN SERVICE
(*Suby of* ALSCO INC.)
5 4th Ave W, Vancouver, BC, V5Y 1G2
(604) 876-3272
Emp Here 160
SIC 7213 Linen supply
Tim Harmer

D-U-N-S 24-797-4611   (HQ)
ANDREWS & GEORGE COMPANY LIMITED
125 3rd Ave W, Vancouver, BC, V5Y 1E6
(604) 876-0466
Sales 36,765,388
SIC 5149 Groceries and related products, nec
John Harrison

D-U-N-S 25-450-6165   (SL)
ARDENT SPORTSWEAR INCORPORATED
125 3rd Ave W, Vancouver, BC, V5Y 1E6
(604) 879-3268
Emp Here 60   *Sales* 29,899,320
SIC 5136 Men's and boy's clothing
Raymond Wong
Wendy Wong
Jimmy Chen

D-U-N-S 20-390-1415   (SL)
ATCO GAS
115 3rd Ave W, Vancouver, BC, V5Y 1E6

Emp Here 5   *Sales* 15,529,285
SIC 4924 Natural gas distribution

D-U-N-S 24-320-4406   (SL)
BLACK STREET PRODUCTIONS LTD
2339 Columbia St Suite 202, Vancouver, BC, V5Y 3Y3
(604) 257-4720
Emp Here 200   *Sales* 17,832,600
SIC 7812 Motion picture and video production
Harvey Kahn

D-U-N-S 24-338-8605   (SL)
BLACKSTONE PRODUCTIONS INC
112 6th Ave W, Vancouver, BC, V5Y 1K6
(604) 623-3369
Emp Here 80   *Sales* 7,133,040
SIC 7812 Motion picture and video production
Micah Gardener
Kirk Shaw

D-U-N-S 25-786-4678   (HQ)
BTY CONSULTANCY GROUP INC
B T Y GROUP
2288 Manitoba St, Vancouver, BC, V5Y 4B5
(604) 734-3126
Emp Here 20   *Sales* 23,428,800
SIC 8742 Management consulting services
Joseph Rekab

D-U-N-S 24-536-1720   (SL)
C-W AGENCIES INC
2020 Yukon St, Vancouver, BC, V5Y 3N8
(604) 879-9080
Emp Here 350   *Sales* 76,980,050
SIC 8732 Commercial nonphysical research

D-U-N-S 25-680-9492   (SL)
CANADIAN OVERSEAS MARKETING CORPORATION
2020 Yukon St, Vancouver, BC, V5Y 3N8

Emp Here 300   *Sales* 60,111,300
SIC 7331 Direct mail advertising services

D-U-N-S 24-456-1064   (HQ)
CANTRAV SERVICES INC
22 2nd Ave W, Vancouver, BC, V5Y 1B3
(604) 708-2500
Emp Here 25   *Sales* 10,973,280
SIC 8741 Management services
George Bartel

D-U-N-S 24-578-3121   (SL)
CDC CONSTRUCTION LTD
16 4th Ave W Suite 300, Vancouver, BC, V5Y 1G3
(604) 873-6656
Emp Here 30   *Sales* 14,121,930
SIC 1542 Nonresidential construction, nec
Donald Livingston
Warren Gotch
Chris Holman

D-U-N-S 20-110-7117   (HQ)
DANICA IMPORTS LTD
348 7th Ave W, Vancouver, BC, V5Y 1M4
(604) 255-6150
Emp Here 50   *Sales* 25,951,656
SIC 5023 Homefurnishings
Rodney Benson
Jeremy Braude
Sushil Arora

D-U-N-S 24-375-0408   (SL)
DELUXE VANCOUVER LTD
50 2nd Ave W, Vancouver, BC, V5Y 1B3
(604) 872-7000
Emp Here 150   *Sales* 13,374,450
SIC 7812 Motion picture and video production
Richard Cederlund

D-U-N-S 24-551-7420   (HQ)
DOMINION BLUEPRINT & REPROGRAPHICS LTD
(*Suby of* BINGHAM HOLDINGS LTD)
99 6th Ave W, Vancouver, BC, V5Y 1K2
(604) 681-7501
Sales 12,491,716
SIC 7334 Photocopying and duplicating services
John Bingham, Sr
John Bingham Jr
Jean Bingham

D-U-N-S 24-329-5656   (SL)
EDDIE'S HANG-UP DISPLAY LTD
60 3rd Ave W, Vancouver, BC, V5Y 1E4
(604) 708-3100
Emp Here 40   *Sales* 29,700,800
SIC 5199 Nondurable goods, nec
Stephen Gaerber
Allen Gaerber
Morris Gaerber

D-U-N-S 20-321-5900   (SL)
GENER8 MEDIA CORP
177 7th Ave W Suite 200, Vancouver, BC, V5Y 1L8
(604) 669-8885
Emp Here 200   *Sales* 17,832,600
SIC 7819 Services allied to motion pictures
Paul Becker
Ben Breckenridge

D-U-N-S 24-930-2266   (HQ)
GLACIER MEDIA INC
2188 Yukon St, Vancouver, BC, V5Y 3P1

▲ Public Company   ■ Public Company Family Member   **HQ** Headquarters   **BR** Branch   **SL** Single Location

(604) 872-8565
Emp Here 190   *Sales* 142,805,190
SIC 2721 Periodicals
Jonathon J.L. Kennedy
Mark Melville
Bill Whitelaw
Craig Roberts
Peter Kvarnstrom
Orest Smysnuik
Sam Grippo
Bruce Aunger
Chris Heming
Tim Mcelvaine

D-U-N-S 24-340-6688   (HQ)
GLACIER PUBLICATIONS LIMITED PART-NERSHIP
SCOTT'S DIRECTORIES, DIV OF
(*Suby of* GLACIER MEDIA INC)
1970 Alberta St, Vancouver, BC, V5Y 3X4
(604) 708-3291
Emp Here 15   *Sales* 96,887,000
SIC 2711 Newspapers
Scott Stoilen

D-U-N-S 24-378-9083   (HQ)
GVIC COMMUNICATIONS CORP
303 5th Ave W, Vancouver, BC, V5Y 1J6
(604) 638-2451
Sales 15,020,038
SIC 4813 Telephone communication, except radio
Jonathon J.L. Kennedy
Mark Melville
Orest E. Smysnuik
Bruce W. Aunger
Donald J. Ross
Richard Whittall

D-U-N-S 24-312-8741   (SL)
IG IMAGE GROUP INC
IMAGE GROUP
34 2nd Ave W, Vancouver, BC, V5Y 1B3
(604) 873-3333
Emp Here 22   *Sales* 16,335,440
SIC 5199 Nondurable goods, nec
Laura Hansen
Gillian Smith

D-U-N-S 20-011-6213   (HQ)
LANGARA COLLEGE
100 49th Ave W, Vancouver, BC, V5Y 2Z6
(604) 323-5511
Emp Here 500   *Sales* 155,114,300
SIC 8221 Colleges and universities
David Ross
Lane Trotter
Anne Lippert
David Bowra
Deanna Douglas
Barry Coulson

D-U-N-S 20-746-3548   (HQ)
LEADING BRANDS OF CANADA, INC
NORTH AMERICAN BOTTLING
(*Suby of* LEADING BRANDS, INC)
33 8th Ave W Unit 101, Vancouver, BC, V5Y 1M8
(604) 685-5200
Emp Here 20   *Sales* 34,569,000
SIC 2086 Bottled and canned soft drinks
Ralph Douglas Mcrae

D-U-N-S 24-825-5481   (HQ)
MADISON PACIFIC PROPERTIES INC
389 6 Ave W, Vancouver, BC, V5Y 1L1
(604) 732-6540
Emp Here 8   *Sales* 24,252,656
SIC 6719 Holding companies, nec
Marvin Haasen
Rob Hackett
Nathan Worbets
Dino Di Marco
Sam Grippo
Michael W Delesalle
Peter Bonner
Mark Elliott

D-U-N-S 20-270-1850   (SL)
METHOD STUDIOS
(*Suby of* MACANDREWS & FORBES INCOR-PORATED)
50 2nd Ave W, Vancouver, BC, V5Y 1B3
(604) 874-8700
Emp Here 100   *Sales* 8,916,300
SIC 7819 Services allied to motion pictures
Millie Cox

D-U-N-S 25-216-5394   (SL)
MP DESIGN INC
MP LIGHTING
16 4th Ave W, Vancouver, BC, V5Y 1G3
(604) 708-1184
Emp Here 50   *Sales* 10,233,650
SIC 3648 Lighting equipment, nec
Mirek Pospisil
Jirina Nyznerova

D-U-N-S 20-521-2827   (SL)
MUNICIPAL INSURANCE ASSOCIATION OF BRITISH COLUMBIA
MIABC
429 2nd Ave W Unit 200, Vancouver, BC, V5Y 1E3
(604) 683-6266
Emp Here 14   *Sales* 14,488,334
SIC 6351 Surety insurance
Thomas Barnes
Mitchell Kenyon

D-U-N-S 24-133-9402   (SL)
NO LIMITS SPORTSWEAR INC
68 5th Ave W, Vancouver, BC, V5Y 1H6
(604) 431-7330
Emp Here 50   *Sales* 24,916,100
SIC 5137 Women's and children's clothing
Paul Mccurry

D-U-N-S 20-114-6818   (SL)
PACIFIC PARTS LTD
110 5th Ave W, Vancouver, BC, V5Y 1H7
(604) 879-1481
Emp Here 32   *Sales* 11,654,880
SIC 5013 Motor vehicle supplies and new parts
Wayne Hoskins
Marnie Copeland

D-U-N-S 24-881-8825   (SL)
SKYLAND TRAVEL INC
ESCAPES.CA
445 6th Ave W Suite 100, Vancouver, BC, V5Y 1L3
(604) 685-6885
Emp Here 30   *Sales* 15,599,010
SIC 4724 Travel agencies
Tomoko Shimada

D-U-N-S 24-578-4475   (HQ)
SLS GROUP INDUSTRIES INC
SPECIFIED LIGHTING SYSTEMS
22 2nd Ave W Suite 2, Vancouver, BC, V5Y 1B3
(604) 874-2226
Emp Here 38   *Sales* 17,886,960
SIC 5063 Electrical apparatus and equipment
Bruce Howitt

D-U-N-S 20-699-1502   (HQ)
STP PUBLICATIONS LIMITED PARTNER-SHIP
STP SPECIALTY TECHNICAL PUBLISHERS
2188 Yukon St, Vancouver, BC, V5Y 3P1
(604) 983-3434
Emp Here 56   *Sales* 14,106,322
SIC 2721 Periodicals
Steve Britten
Jonathon Kennedy
Orest Smysnuik

D-U-N-S 25-898-8716   (SL)
TALLGRASS NATURAL HEALTH LTD
TALLGRASS
375 5th Ave W Suite 201, Vancouver, BC, V5Y 1J6

(604) 709-0101
Emp Here 32   *Sales* 35,371,040
SIC 5122 Drugs, proprietaries, and sundries
Matthew Breech
Tracey Iu

D-U-N-S 25-117-4025   (SL)
UNION OF BC PERFORMERS
UBCP/ACTRA
380 2nd Ave W Unit 300, Vancouver, BC, V5Y 1C8
(604) 689-0727
Emp Here 40   *Sales* 15,646,320
SIC 8631 Labor organizations
Howard Storey

Vancouver, BC V5Z

D-U-N-S 20-352-4186   (SL)
1127770 B.C. LTD
777 Broadway W, Vancouver, BC, V5Z 4J7

Emp Here 1,398   *Sales* 761,009,648
SIC 5047 Medical and hospital equipment
Ralph Vasquez

D-U-N-S 20-293-5040   (HQ)
20/20 PROPERTIES INC
638 Millbank, Vancouver, BC, V5Z 4B7
(604) 620-3130
Sales 13,578,460
SIC 6211 Security brokers and dealers
John Murphy

D-U-N-S 24-798-3869   (SL)
360641 BC LTD
KIRIN SEAFOOD RESTAURANT
555 12th Ave W Unit 201, Vancouver, BC, V5Z 3X7
(604) 879-8038
Emp Here 100   *Sales* 4,287,300
SIC 5812 Eating places
Dominic Leung
Swan Leung

D-U-N-S 20-357-2826   (SL)
640039 BC LTD
SHOPPERS DRUG MART 263
885 Broadway W Suite 263, Vancouver, BC, V5Z 1J9
(604) 708-1135
Emp Here 55   *Sales* 13,438,040
SIC 5912 Drug stores and proprietary stores
James Ng

D-U-N-S 20-260-1428   (HQ)
ALZHEIMER SOCIETY OF B.C.
828 8th Ave W Suite 300, Vancouver, BC, V5Z 1E2
(604) 681-6530
Sales 53,512,640
SIC 7389 Business services, nec
Christine Penney
Nicole Bertrand
Maria Howard

D-U-N-S 20-766-9607   (HQ)
AMERICAN CUMO MINING CORPORATION
638 Millbank Rd, Vancouver, BC, V5Z 4B7
(604) 689-7902
Emp Here 6   *Sales* 90,726,862
SIC 1044 Silver ores
Shaun Dykes
John Moeller
Brett Kagetsu
Joseph Baird
Thomas Conway
Trevor Burns

D-U-N-S 24-682-7398   (SL)
ANDREWS REALTY LTD
RE/MAX REAL ESTATE SERVICES
650 41st Ave W Suite 410, Vancouver, BC, V5Z 2M9
(604) 263-2823
Emp Here 115   *Sales* 48,172,235

SIC 6531 Real estate agents and managers
David Andrews

D-U-N-S 25-452-2816   (BR)
BAYSHORE HEALTHCARE LTD.
BAYSHORE HEALTHCARE LTD
(*Suby of* BAYSHORE HEALTHCARE LTD.)
555 12th Ave W Unit 410, Vancouver, BC, V5Z 3X7
(604) 873-2545
Emp Here 250
SIC 8082 Home health care services
Christopher Clark

D-U-N-S 25-912-6852   (BR)
BOARD OF EDUCATION OF SCHOOL DISTRICT NO. 39 (VANCOUVER), THE
ERIC HAMBER SECONDARY SCHOOL
(*Suby of* BOARD OF EDUCATION OF SCHOOL DISTRICT NO. 39 (VANCOUVER), THE)
5025 Willow St Suite 39, Vancouver, BC, V5Z 3S1
(604) 713-8927
Emp Here 120
SIC 8211 Elementary and secondary schools
Alex Grant

D-U-N-S 25-408-1326   (SL)
BRITISH COLUMBIA CENTRE FOR DISEASE CONTROL AND PREVENTION SOCIETY BRANCH
(*Suby of* PROVINCIAL HEALTH SERVICES AUTHORITY)
655 12th Ave W, Vancouver, BC, V5Z 4R4
(604) 660-0584
Emp Here 305   *Sales* 43,951,720
SIC 8011 Offices and clinics of medical doctors
Sue Murphy

D-U-N-S 24-134-9539   (HQ)
BRITISH COLUMBIA TEACHER'S FEDERATION
550 6th Ave W Suite 100, Vancouver, BC, V5Z 4P2
(604) 871-2283
Sales 35,116,650
SIC 8621 Professional organizations
Glen Hansman
Teri Mooring

D-U-N-S 20-304-4727   (SL)
BRITISH COLUMBIA'S CHILDREN'S HOSPITAL FOUNDATION
BC CHILDREN'S HOSPITAL FOUNDATION (BCCHF)
938 28th Ave W, Vancouver, BC, V5Z 4H4
(604) 875-2444
Emp Here 100   *Sales* 85,387,733
SIC 8699 Membership organizations, nec
Teri Nicholas
Hitesh Kothary
Maria Faccio
Lillian Hum
Zdenka Buric
Donald Lindsay
Mike Brankston
Robin Dhir
Lisa Hudson
Darrell Jones

D-U-N-S 24-204-2682   (HQ)
CACTUS CAFE BARLOW LTD
CACTUS CLUB CAFE
(*Suby of* CACTUS RESTAURANTS LTD)
550 Broadway W, Vancouver, BC, V5Z 0E9
(604) 714-2025
Emp Here 14   *Sales* 34,979,250
SIC 5812 Eating places
Richard Jaffray

D-U-N-S 25-168-4858   (HQ)
CACTUS RESTAURANTS LTD
550 Broadway W Suite 201, Vancouver, BC, V5Z 0E9
(604) 714-2025
Emp Here 14   *Sales* 34,979,250

▲ Public Company   ■ Public Company Family Member   **HQ** Headquarters   **BR** Branch   **SL** Single Location

SIC 5812 Eating places
Richard Jaffray
Scott Morison

D-U-N-S 25-018-4553　(BR)
CANADIAN CANCER SOCIETY
BC AND YUKON DIVISION, THE
(*Suby of* CANADIAN CANCER SOCIETY)
565 10th Ave W Suite 44, Vancouver, BC, V5Z 4J4
(604) 879-9131
Emp Here 77
SIC 7389 Business services, nec
Barbara Kaminsky

D-U-N-S 24-455-7567　(HQ)
CATHOLIC INDEPENDENT SCHOOLS OF VANCOUVER ARCHDIOCESE, THE
CATHOLIC SCHOOL BOARD
4885 Saint John Paul Ii Way, Vancouver, BC, V5Z 0G3
(604) 683-9331
Emp Here 15　*Sales* 93,710,700
SIC 8661 Religious organizations
Stephen Jensen
Patrick Chisholm

D-U-N-S 24-246-1940　(SL)
CENTRE FOR MOLECULAR MEDICINE AND THERAPEUTIC
950 28th Ave W Suite 3109, Vancouver, BC, V5Z 4H4
(604) 875-3535
Emp Here 49　*Sales* 10,454,542
SIC 8732 Commercial nonphysical research
Michael Hayden

D-U-N-S 25-094-3669　(HQ)
CIBT EDUCATION GROUP INC
777 Broadway W Unit 1200, Vancouver, BC, V5Z 4J7
(604) 871-9909
Emp Here 8　*Sales* 42,791,665
SIC 6282 Investment advice
Toby Chu
Dennis Huang
Morris Chen
May Hsu
Troy Rice
Shane Weir
Tony David
Derek Feng

D-U-N-S 20-081-4684　(SL)
CKWX NEWS
NEWS 1130
2440 Ash St Suite 1130, Vancouver, BC, V5Z 4J6
(604) 873-2599
Emp Here 49　*Sales* 19,388,222
SIC 7383 News syndicates
Treena Wood

D-U-N-S 20-957-8699　(SL)
CRESSEY DEVELOPMENT CORPORATION
555 8th Ave W Suite 200, Vancouver, BC, V5Z 1C6
(604) 683-1256
Emp Here 80　*Sales* 21,675,360
SIC 1522 Residential construction, nec
Norman Cressey
Scott Cressey

D-U-N-S 20-322-7806　(SL)
EASTSIDE GAMES INC
555 12th Ave W Suite 550, Vancouver, BC, V5Z 3X7
(604) 568-5051
Emp Here 45　*Sales* 10,365,300
SIC 5734 Computer and software stores
Jason Bailey
Josh Nilson

D-U-N-S 25-566-1956　(SL)
ENERGY HEALING VANCOUVER - KIM U-MING
900 8th Ave W, Vancouver, BC, V5Z 1E5
(604) 790-6400
Emp Here 5　*Sales* 15,529,285

SIC 4924 Natural gas distribution

D-U-N-S 25-453-1437　(BR)
EVANGELICAL LUTHERAN CHURCH IN CANADA
OAKRIDGE LUTHERAN CHURCH
(*Suby of* EVANGELICAL LUTHERAN CHURCH IN CANADA)
585 41st Ave W, Vancouver, BC, V5Z 2M7
(604) 261-2442
Emp Here 90
SIC 8661 Religious organizations
Sheila Hamilton

D-U-N-S 20-133-5788　(SL)
FALSE CREEK SURGICAL CENTRE INC
555 8th Ave W Suite 600, Vancouver, BC, V5Z 1C6
(604) 739-9695
Emp Here 102　*Sales* 16,385,892
SIC 8011 Offices and clinics of medical doctors
Mark Godley
Susan Rafter
Toni Massolin

D-U-N-S 24-168-7339　(SL)
GEORGIA PACIFIC REALTY CORPORATION
601 Broadway W Unit 200, Vancouver, BC, V5Z 4C2
(604) 222-8585
Emp Here 49　*Sales* 16,029,223
SIC 6531 Real estate agents and managers
Kevin Chiang

D-U-N-S 24-866-4047　(SL)
GLOBESPAN TRAVEL LTD
FLY GLOBESPAN
(*Suby of* THE GLOBESPAN GROUP PLC)
660 Leg In Boot Sq Unit C, Vancouver, BC, V5Z 4B3
(604) 879-6466
Emp Here 20　*Sales* 10,399,340
SIC 4724 Travel agencies
Jim Whyte

D-U-N-S 24-361-7318　(BR)
HOME DEPOT OF CANADA INC
HOME DEPOT
(*Suby of* THE HOME DEPOT INC)
2388 Cambie St, Vancouver, BC, V5Z 2T8
(604) 675-1260
Emp Here 100
SIC 5251 Hardware stores

D-U-N-S 25-301-2546　(BR)
HUDSON'S BAY COMPANY
BAY, THE
(*Suby of* HUDSON'S BAY COMPANY)
650 41st Ave W, Vancouver, BC, V5Z 2M9
(604) 261-3311
Emp Here 200
SIC 5311 Department stores
Dave Wilkinson

D-U-N-S 25-453-0033　(SL)
JEWISH COMMUNITY CENTRE OF GREATER VANCOUVER
950 41st Ave W, Vancouver, BC, V5Z 2N7
(604) 257-5111
Emp Here 100　*Sales* 6,842,200
SIC 8322 Individual and family services
Alvin Wasserman
Rick Nelson

D-U-N-S 24-457-6716　(BR)
LONDON DRUGS LIMITED
(*Suby of* H.Y. LOUIE CO. LIMITED)
525 Broadway W, Vancouver, BC, V5Z 1E6
(604) 448-4804
Emp Here 200
SIC 5912 Drug stores and proprietary stores
Doreen Phone

D-U-N-S 25-186-5499　(HQ)
PLATINUM PROPERTIES GROUP CORP
777 Broadway W Suite 707, Vancouver, BC,

V5Z 4J7
(604) 638-3300
Emp Here 1　*Sales* 10,862,768
SIC 6211 Security brokers and dealers
Chance Lee

D-U-N-S 25-195-7833　(SL)
PLAZA 500 HOTELS LTD
500 12th Ave W, Vancouver, BC, V5Z 1M2
(604) 873-1811
Emp Here 100　*Sales* 9,489,900
SIC 7011 Hotels and motels
Azim Bobad
Xzim Popat

D-U-N-S 20-917-0174　(BR)
PROVIDENCE HEALTH CARE SOCIETY
YOUVILLE RESIDENCE
(*Suby of* PROVIDENCE HEALTH CARE SOCIETY)
4950 Heather St Suite 321, Vancouver, BC, V5Z 3L9
(604) 261-9371
Emp Here 100
SIC 8059 Nursing and personal care, nec
Dianne Doyle

D-U-N-S 24-207-0444　(BR)
PROVINCIAL HEALTH SERVICES AUTHORITY
BC CANCER, PART OF THE PROVINCIAL HEALTH SERVICES AUTHORITY
(*Suby of* PROVINCIAL HEALTH SERVICES AUTHORITY)
570 7th Ave W Suite 100, Vancouver, BC, V5Z 4S6
(604) 707-5800
Emp Here 180
SIC 8731 Commercial physical research
Victor Ling

D-U-N-S 20-376-9653　(BR)
PROVINCIAL HEALTH SERVICES AUTHORITY
BC CANCER, A PART OF THE PROVINCIAL HEALTH SERVICES AUTHORITY
(*Suby of* PROVINCIAL HEALTH SERVICES AUTHORITY)
600 10th Ave W, Vancouver, BC, V5Z 4E6
(604) 675-8251
Emp Here 3,000
SIC 8069 Specialty hospitals, except psychiatric
Francois Benard

D-U-N-S 24-596-8263　(HQ)
PURE FREEDOM YYOGA WELLNESS INC
YYOGA
575 8th Ave W Suite 500, Vancouver, BC, V5Z 0C4
(604) 736-6002
Emp Here 1　*Sales* 14,002,900
SIC 7999 Amusement and recreation, nec
Terry Mcbride
Matt Fraser
Kim Wilson

D-U-N-S 20-108-6212　(BR)
ROGERS MEDIA INC
JACK- FM 96.9
(*Suby of* ROGERS COMMUNICATIONS INC)
2440 Ash St, Vancouver, BC, V5Z 4J6
(604) 872-2557
Emp Here 100
SIC 4832 Radio broadcasting stations
Al Ford

D-U-N-S 20-803-3365　(HQ)
ROMAN CATHOLIC ARCHDIOCESE OF VANCOUVER, THE
4885 Saint John Paul Ii Way, Vancouver, BC, V5Z 0G3
(604) 683-0281
Emp Here 986　*Sales* 104,123,000
SIC 8661 Religious organizations

D-U-N-S 20-574-7843　(HQ)
SHATO HOLDINGS LTD

4088 Cambie St Suite 300, Vancouver, BC, V5Z 2X8
(604) 874-5533
Emp Here 2,500　*Sales* 2,193,054,000
SIC 6712 Bank holding companies
Elizabeth Toigo
Larry Bell
Frank Price
Peter R Toigo Jr
Ronald Toigo
Sultan Thiara

D-U-N-S 25-968-7168　(SL)
SILK HOLIDAYS INC
4012 Cambie St, Vancouver, BC, V5Z 2X8

Emp Here 25　*Sales* 12,999,175
SIC 4724 Travel agencies
Paulus Ng

D-U-N-S 24-839-5576　(SL)
SILKWAY TRAVEL & DESTINATION MANAGEMENT INC
SILKWAY TRAVEL & CRUISE
4018 Cambie St Suite 4012, Vancouver, BC, V5Z 2X8

Emp Here 45　*Sales* 23,398,515
SIC 4725 Tour operators
Paulus Ng
Kathy Ng

D-U-N-S 20-775-0220　(SL)
SIMBA TECHNOLOGIES INCORPORATED
(*Suby of* MAGNITUDE SOFTWARE, INC.)
938 8th Ave W, Vancouver, BC, V5Z 1E5
(604) 633-0008
Emp Here 164　*Sales* 23,645,848
SIC 7371 Custom computer programming services
Chris Ney
Lou Guercia
Tony Fisher

D-U-N-S 20-556-1785　(BR)
SOBEYS WEST INC
OAKRIDGE SAFEWAY
(*Suby of* EMPIRE COMPANY LIMITED)
650 41st Ave W, Vancouver, BC, V5Z 2M9
(604) 263-5502
Emp Here 100
SIC 5411 Grocery stores
Darcy Edge

D-U-N-S 25-003-6381　(BR)
SOBEYS WEST INC
SAFEWAY
(*Suby of* EMPIRE COMPANY LIMITED)
990 King Edward Ave W, Vancouver, BC, V5Z 2E2
(604) 733-0073
Emp Here 135
SIC 5411 Grocery stores
Lemon Peter

D-U-N-S 24-249-7667　(HQ)
SPENCE DIAMONDS LTD
550 6th Ave W Suite 410, Vancouver, BC, V5Z 1A1
(604) 739-9928
Emp Here 35　*Sales* 18,324,600
SIC 5944 Jewelry stores
Douglas Spence
Sean Jones
Faheem Gwadry

D-U-N-S 20-918-8747　(SL)
ST JUDE'S ANGLICAN HOME SOCIETY
810 27th Ave W, Vancouver, BC, V5Z 2G7
(604) 874-3200
Emp Here 90　*Sales* 6,170,940
SIC 8051 Skilled nursing care facilities
Katharyn Sainty
Dorothy Watts

D-U-N-S 20-114-5781　(BR)
STEMCELL TECHNOLOGIES CANADA INC
STEMSOFT SOFTWARE

▲ Public Company　■ Public Company Family Member　**HQ** Headquarters　**BR** Branch　**SL** Single Location

(*Suby of* STEMCELL TECHNOLOGIES CANADA INC)
570 7th Ave W Suite 400, Vancouver, BC, V5Z 1B3
(604) 877-0713
Emp Here 200
SIC 8733 Noncommercial research organizations
Allen Eaves

D-U-N-S 20-124-9443 (BR)
UNIVERSITY OF BRITISH COLUMBIA, THE
DEPARTMENT OF ORTHOPAEDICS
(*Suby of* UNIVERSITY OF BRITISH COLUMBIA, THE)
2775 Laurel St 11 Fl, Vancouver, BC, V5Z 1M9
(604) 875-4192
Emp Here 172
SIC 8221 Colleges and universities
Bassam A. Masri

D-U-N-S 25-417-2885 (SL)
UNIWELL INTERNATIONAL ENTERPRISES CORP
999 Broadway W Suite 880, Vancouver, BC, V5Z 1K5
(604) 730-2877
Emp Here 8 *Sales* 26,144,576
SIC 5063 Electrical apparatus and equipment
Steve J Nam
Sue Nam

D-U-N-S 25-450-6439 (BR)
VANCOUVER COASTAL HEALTH AUTHORITY
G F STRONG REHABILITATION CENTRE
(*Suby of* GOVERNMENT OF THE PROVINCE OF BRITISH COLUMBIA)
4255 Laurel St, Vancouver, BC, V5Z 2G9
(604) 734-1313
Emp Here 500
SIC 8093 Specialty outpatient clinics, nec
Nitin Khare

D-U-N-S 24-761-9518 (BR)
VANCOUVER COASTAL HEALTH AUTHORITY
VANCOUVER GENERAL HOSPITAL
(*Suby of* GOVERNMENT OF THE PROVINCE OF BRITISH COLUMBIA)
855 12th Ave W Suite 101, Vancouver, BC, V5Z 1M9
(604) 875-4111
Emp Here 230
SIC 8062 General medical and surgical hospitals
Jim Pattison

D-U-N-S 24-364-4569 (BR)
VANCOUVER COASTAL HEALTH AUTHORITY
CENTRE FOR HIP HEALTH AND MOBILITY
(*Suby of* GOVERNMENT OF THE PROVINCE OF BRITISH COLUMBIA)
2635 Laurel St, Vancouver, BC, V5Z 1M9
(604) 675-2575
Emp Here 100
SIC 8733 Noncommercial research organizations
Ander Stesanson

D-U-N-S 20-914-9371 (BR)
VANCOUVER COASTAL HEALTH AUTHORITY
RESEARCH INSTITUTE
(*Suby of* GOVERNMENT OF THE PROVINCE OF BRITISH COLUMBIA)
2647 Willow St Rm 100, Vancouver, BC, V5Z 1M9
(604) 875-4372
Emp Here 500
SIC 8733 Noncommercial research organizations
Karen Donaldson

D-U-N-S 25-664-9807 (BR)
WHITE SPOT LIMITED
WHITE SPOT RESTAURANT

(*Suby of* SHATO HOLDINGS LTD)
650 41st Ave W Suite 613a, Vancouver, BC, V5Z 2M9
(604) 261-2820
Emp Here 80
SIC 5812 Eating places
Viberta Croy

D-U-N-S 24-665-5877 (SL)
WINDERMERE CARE CENTRE INC
900 12th Ave W Suite 811, Vancouver, BC, V5Z 1N3
(604) 736-8676
Emp Here 40 *Sales* 11,940,225
SIC 8059 Nursing and personal care, nec
Dan Mcdonald
Alex Valera

Vancouver, BC V6A

D-U-N-S 25-234-3645 (SL)
480412 B.C. LTD
NORTH AMERICAN PRODUCE SALES
645 Malkin Ave, Vancouver, BC, V6A 3V7
(604) 255-6684
Emp Here 35 *Sales* 29,245,195
SIC 5148 Fresh fruits and vegetables
Dennis Tom

D-U-N-S 24-619-2327 (SL)
541823 BC LTD
RENNIE MARKETING SYSTEMS
51 Pender St E, Vancouver, BC, V6A 1S9
(604) 682-2088
Emp Here 35 *Sales* 11,449,445
SIC 6531 Real estate agents and managers
Bob Rennie

D-U-N-S 24-249-5752 (SL)
ACTION ELECTRIC LTD
1277 Georgia St E, Vancouver, BC, V6A 2A9
(604) 734-9146
Emp Here 100 *Sales* 21,782,900
SIC 1731 Electrical work
Willy Disler

D-U-N-S 20-650-7142 (SL)
AGAPE STREET MINISTRY
887 Keefer St, Vancouver, BC, V6A 1Y8
(604) 215-4115
Emp Here 49 *Sales* 19,473,286
SIC 8699 Membership organizations, nec
Daniel Dobin

D-U-N-S 24-350-1272 (SL)
ALLIANCE GRAIN TERMINAL LTD
1155 Stewart St, Vancouver, BC, V6A 4H4
(604) 254-4414
Emp Here 75 *Sales* 11,114,400
SIC 4221 Farm product warehousing and storage
David Cushner

D-U-N-S 24-365-0392 (HQ)
APPNOVATION TECHNOLOGIES INC
190 Alexander St Suite 600, Vancouver, BC, V6A 1B5
(604) 568-0313
Emp Here 150 *Sales* 15,567,760
SIC 7374 Data processing and preparation
Arnold Leung
Tim Welsch
Paul Crookshanks
Sherborne Pao
Clarence Lee

D-U-N-S 24-392-2346 (HQ)
ARITZIA INC
611 Alexander St Suite 118, Vancouver, BC, V6A 1E1
(604) 251-3132
Emp Here 13 *Sales* 596,454,672
SIC 5651 Family clothing stores
Brian Hill
Jennifer Wong

Pippa Morgan
Karen Kwan
Jed Paulson
Todd Ingledew
Kevin Callaghan
John Currie
Ryan Holmes
David Labistour

D-U-N-S 25-716-3121 (HQ)
ARITZIA LP
(*Suby of* ARITZIA INC)
611 Alexander St Suite 118, Vancouver, BC, V6A 1E1
(604) 251-3132
Emp Here 300 *Sales* 99,804,000
SIC 5621 Women's clothing stores
Brian James Hill
Jennifer Wong

D-U-N-S 20-827-6282 (HQ)
ATIRA PROPERTY MANAGEMENT INC
405 Powell St, Vancouver, BC, V6A 1G7
(604) 439-8848
Emp Here 87 *Sales* 24,415,548
SIC 8741 Management services
Janice Abbott

D-U-N-S 20-052-0596 (SL)
AURORA BIOMED INC
1001 Pender St E, Vancouver, BC, V6A 1W2
(604) 215-8700
Emp Here 50 *Sales* 11,734,800
SIC 8731 Commercial physical research
Dong Liang
Fay Liang

D-U-N-S 24-939-0642 (SL)
AURORA INSTRUMENTS LTD
1001 Pender St E, Vancouver, BC, V6A 1W2
(604) 215-8700
Emp Here 50 *Sales* 12,828,100
SIC 3821 Laboratory apparatus and furniture
Dong Liang

D-U-N-S 25-450-6850 (HQ)
BOSS BAKERY & RESTAURANT LTD, THE
BOSS BAKERY & RESTAURANT
532 Main St, Vancouver, BC, V6A 2T9
(604) 683-3860
Emp Here 30 *Sales* 16,141,235
SIC 5461 Retail bakeries
Yuet Kwan Lai
Chris Cheng
Steve C.W. Yuen
Jason Lai

D-U-N-S 24-165-5901 (HQ)
BRITISH COLUMBIA MARITIME EMPLOYERS ASSOCIATION
BCMEA
349 Railway St Suite 500, Vancouver, BC, V6A 1A4
(604) 688-1155
Emp Here 60 *Sales* 29,433,750
SIC 8631 Labor organizations
Terry A Duggan

D-U-N-S 24-886-9760 (SL)
CAN-AM PRODUCE & TRADING LTD
886 Malkin Ave, Vancouver, BC, V6A 2K7
(604) 253-8834
Emp Here 29 *Sales* 24,231,733
SIC 5148 Fresh fruits and vegetables
Roberto Su
Jack Chan
Jim Su
Pauline Chan
Steve Chan
Robert Chan
Garry Mah

D-U-N-S 20-647-5506 (HQ)
CANADIAN FISHING COMPANY LIMITED, THE
GOLD SEAL
(*Suby of* PATTISON, JIM GROUP INC)
301 Waterfront Rd E, Vancouver, BC, V6A 0B3

(604) 681-0211
Emp Here 60 *Sales* 1,146,745,600
SIC 5146 Fish and seafoods
Dan Nomura
Mark Cornell

D-U-N-S 24-695-5553 (SL)
CITY-CORE MESSENGER SERVICES LTD
1185 Grant St, Vancouver, BC, V6A 2J7
(604) 254-9218
Emp Here 25 *Sales* 11,087,250
SIC 7389 Business services, nec
Edward Chu

D-U-N-S 25-236-2116 (SL)
DAI TOKU HOLDINGS COMPANY LTD
1575 Vernon Dr, Vancouver, BC, V6A 3P8
(604) 253-5111
Emp Here 1 *Sales* 13,339,203
SIC 6712 Bank holding companies
Tony Hieda

D-U-N-S 20-051-5596 (SL)
DISCOVERY ISLANDS ORGANICS LTD
DISCOVERY ORGANICS
880 Malkin Ave, Vancouver, BC, V6A 2K6
(604) 299-1684
Emp Here 50 *Sales* 41,778,850
SIC 5149 Groceries and related products, nec
Anne Moss
Randy Hooper

D-U-N-S 20-176-5547 (SL)
DP WORLD (CANADA) INC
DP WORLD VANCOUVER
(*Suby of* DP WORLD PLC)
777 Centennial Rd, Vancouver, BC, V6A 1A3
(604) 255-5151
Emp Here 600 *Sales* 208,416,600
SIC 4491 Marine cargo handling
Ryan Uy

D-U-N-S 25-529-1379 (SL)
DUECK PONTIAC BUICK GMC LIMITED
888 Terminal Ave, Vancouver, BC, V6A 0A9
(604) 675-7900
Emp Here 40 *Sales* 19,923,120
SIC 5511 New and used car dealers
Moray Keith
Bradley Cruickshank

D-U-N-S 24-798-5914 (SL)
FLASH COURIER SERVICES INC
1213 Frances St, Vancouver, BC, V6A 1Z4
(604) 689-3278
Emp Here 75 *Sales* 33,691,425
SIC 7389 Business services, nec
Erik Bjorklund

D-U-N-S 20-512-4019 (SL)
FON-TILE CORPORATION LIMITED
FONTILE KITCHEN & BATH
270 Terminal Ave, Vancouver, BC, V6A 2L6
(604) 683-9358
Emp Here 34 *Sales* 15,203,916
SIC 5032 Brick, stone, and related material
Gary Kershaw

D-U-N-S 20-183-1463 (SL)
FRESH DIRECT PRODUCE LTD
(*Suby of* HAMMOND, KENNEDY, WHITNEY & COMPANY, INC.)
890 Malkin Ave, Vancouver, BC, V6A 2K6
(604) 255-1330
Emp Here 40 *Sales* 33,423,080
SIC 5148 Fresh fruits and vegetables
Davis Yung
Jozef Hubburmin
Albert Lum
Danny Tsang

D-U-N-S 25-388-2773 (HQ)
FRESHPOINT VANCOUVER LTD
FRESHPOINT
(*Suby of* SYSCO CORPORATION)
1020 Malkin Ave, Vancouver, BC, V6A 3S9
(604) 253-1551
Emp Here 150 *Sales* 225,765,540

SIC 5148 Fresh fruits and vegetables
Kent Shoemaker
Larry Brown
Wayne Walling
Bryan Uyesugi
Michael Nichols
Mark Sanders
Drew Yurko
Brian Sturgeon

D-U-N-S 20-734-0428   (SL)
GAYA CANADA ENTERPRISE LTD
GAYA
1868 Glen Dr Suite 232, Vancouver, BC, V6A 4K4
(604) 738-0971
Emp Here 25   *Sales* 12,667,579
SIC 5137 Women's and children's clothing
Ralph-Charles Goodwin

D-U-N-S 20-261-4780   (SL)
GCT CANADA LIMITED PARTNERSHIP
(*Suby of* GCT GLOBAL CONTAINER TERMINALS INC)
1285 Franklin St, Vancouver, BC, V6A 1J9
(604) 267-5200
Emp Here 1,614   *Sales* 560,640,654
SIC 4491 Marine cargo handling
Stephen Edwards
Eric Waltz

D-U-N-S 24-995-6582   (SL)
GREATER VANCOUVER FOOD BANK SOCIETY
1150 Raymur Ave, Vancouver, BC, V6A 3T2
(604) 876-3601
Emp Here 28   *Sales* 10,044,574
SIC 8399 Social services, nec
Aart Hess
Craig Edwards
Iryn Vekay

D-U-N-S 25-662-0550   (BR)
GREYHOUND CANADA TRANSPORTATION ULC
(*Suby of* FIRSTGROUP PLC)
1150 Station St Unit 200, Vancouver, BC, V6A 4C7
(604) 683-8133
Emp Here 100
SIC 4131 Intercity and rural bus transportation
David Mell

D-U-N-S 25-107-0223   (SL)
GRIFFIN TRANSPORTATION SERVICES INC
873 Hastings St E, Vancouver, BC, V6A 1R8
(604) 628-4474
Emp Here 75   *Sales* 4,115,400
SIC 4119 Local passenger transportation, nec
Ninindar Grewal
Mark Mahedy

D-U-N-S 24-821-2974   (SL)
HERSCHEL SUPPLY COMPANY LTD
611 Alexander St Suite 327, Vancouver, BC, V6A 1E1
(800) 307-5597
Emp Here 50   *Sales* 37,126,000
SIC 5199 Nondurable goods, nec
Jamie Cormack
Jason Cormack
Lyndon Cormack

D-U-N-S 25-514-3174   (BR)
HOME DEPOT OF CANADA INC
HOME DEPOT
(*Suby of* THE HOME DEPOT INC)
900 Terminal Ave, Vancouver, BC, V6A 4G4
(604) 608-1423
Emp Here 300
SIC 5251 Hardware stores
Ryan Laird

D-U-N-S 24-247-7172   (HQ)
INPROHEAT INDUSTRIES LIMITED
(*Suby of* INDUSTRIAL PROCESS HEAT ENGINEERING LTD.)

680 Raymur Ave, Vancouver, BC, V6A 2R1
(604) 254-0461
Emp Here 19   *Sales* 12,520,872
SIC 5051 Metals service centers and offices
Steven Panz

D-U-N-S 20-177-8987   (SL)
INVENTURE SOLUTIONS INC
(*Suby of* VANCOUVER CITY SAVINGS CREDIT UNION)
183 Terminal Ave, Vancouver, BC, V6A 4G2
(604) 877-7000
Emp Here 130   *Sales* 21,690,110
SIC 7379 Computer related services, nec
Garry Smith
Tony Fernandes
Andy Jones-Cox
Rob Church
Jesse Breaker
Stewart Shum

D-U-N-S 20-112-6414   (SL)
J & K POULTRY LTD
771 Cordova St E, Vancouver, BC, V6A 1M2
(604) 253-8292
Emp Here 25   *Sales* 20,889,425
SIC 5144 Poultry and poultry products
Colin Wosk

D-U-N-S 20-803-5022   (SL)
KARO DESIGN VANCOUVER INC
611 Alexander St Suite 308, Vancouver, BC, V6A 1E1
(604) 255-6100
Emp Here 23   *Sales* 10,332,037
SIC 7389 Business services, nec
Ellen Randall
Joe Strasser
Barry Marshall

D-U-N-S 25-956-0043   (BR)
LANTIC INC
ROGERS SUGAR LTD
(*Suby of* ROGERS SUGAR INC)
123 Rogers St, Vancouver, BC, V6A 3N2
(604) 253-1131
Emp Here 185
SIC 2062 Cane sugar refining
Doug Emek

D-U-N-S 20-260-3536   (SL)
LAROSA FINE FOODS INC
855 Terminal Ave, Vancouver, BC, V6A 2M9
(604) 688-8306
Emp Here 40   *Sales* 33,423,080
SIC 5141 Groceries, general line
Rod Terry
Emily Nakai

D-U-N-S 24-445-8477   (SL)
LARRIVEE, JEAN GUITARS LTD
LARRIVEE GUITARS
780 Cordova St E, Vancouver, BC, V6A 1M3

Emp Here 65   *Sales* 21,198,840
SIC 3931 Musical instruments
Jean Larrivee
Wendy Larrivee

D-U-N-S 24-153-3884   (HQ)
LEKIU POULTRY (2006) LTD
458 Prior St, Vancouver, BC, V6A 2E5
(604) 681-1999
Emp Here 11   *Sales* 10,702,480
SIC 5144 Poultry and poultry products
Austin Kang
Nathan Kang

D-U-N-S 20-749-1531   (BR)
LONG & MCQUADE LIMITED
LONG & MCQUADE MUSICAL INSTRUMENTS
(*Suby of* LONG HOLDINGS INC)
368 Terminal Ave, Vancouver, BC, V6A 3W9
(604) 734-4886
Emp Here 94
SIC 5736 Musical instrument stores
Chad Roberts

D-U-N-S 25-692-0018   (HQ)
LOOKOUT THE EMERGENCY AID SOCIETY
429 Alexander St, Vancouver, BC, V6A 1C6
(604) 255-2347
Emp Here 12   *Sales* 18,399,130
SIC 8361 Residential care
Karen O'shannacery
Stanley Pukesh
Allan Mitchell
Anne Marie Perks
Leonard Levy

D-U-N-S 24-683-3057   (SL)
MAN-KWONG ENTERPRISES LTD
KUM SING POULTRY
1233 Glen Dr, Vancouver, BC, V6A 3M8
(604) 254-3688
Emp Here 20   *Sales* 10,702,480
SIC 5144 Poultry and poultry products
Hubert Yiu

D-U-N-S 25-679-7564   (HQ)
MAVI JEANS INC
580 Industrial Ave, Vancouver, BC, V6A 2P3
(604) 708-2373
Emp Here 35   *Sales* 36,875,828
SIC 5136 Men's and boy's clothing
Arkun Durmaz
Ersin Akarlilar

D-U-N-S 25-452-2915   (BR)
MCDONALD'S RESTAURANTS OF CANADA LIMITED
MCDONALD'S
(*Suby of* MCDONALD'S CORPORATION)
1527 Main St, Vancouver, BC, V6A 2W5
(604) 718-1075
Emp Here 100
SIC 5812 Eating places
John Lamb

D-U-N-S 20-113-8393   (HQ)
MCGREGOR & THOMPSON HARDWARE LTD
(*Suby of* SPEYSIDE EQUITY FUND I LP)
1250 Georgia St E, Vancouver, BC, V6A 2B1
(604) 253-8252
Emp Here 45   *Sales* 108,110,340
SIC 5072 Hardware
James W Mcgregor
Ken Newcombe
Mike Longhi
Ray Hazledine

D-U-N-S 25-372-1666   (SL)
METALOGIX SOFTWARE CORP
(*Suby of* FRANCISCO PARTNERS MANAGEMENT, L.P.)
55 Cordova St E Suite 604, Vancouver, BC, V6A 0A5
(604) 677-4636
Emp Here 60   *Sales* 10,010,820
SIC 7372 Prepackaged software

D-U-N-S 24-120-1826   (HQ)
MOE'S CLASSIC RUGS & HOME ACCESSORIES LTD
MOE'S HOME COLLECTION
1728 Glen Dr, Vancouver, BC, V6A 4L5
(604) 688-0633
Emp Here 5   *Sales* 19,693,920
SIC 5963 Direct selling establishments
Mohammad Samieian

D-U-N-S 20-327-2455   (SL)
MONSTERCAT INC
MONSTERCAT
380 Railway St, Vancouver, BC, V6A 4E3
(519) 729-2179
Emp Here 32   *Sales* 14,191,680
SIC 7389 Business services, nec
Ari Paunonen

D-U-N-S 20-351-9702   (SL)
PACIFIC RESTAURANT SUPPLY, INC
1020 Cordova St E, Vancouver, BC, V6A 4A3

(604) 216-2566
Emp Here 45   *Sales* 20,122,830
SIC 5046 Commercial equipment, nec
Jason Evanow
Luke Evanow
Jason Gilron

D-U-N-S 24-614-1345   (HQ)
PARK GEORGIA INSURANCE AGENCIES LTD
(*Suby of* PARK GEORGIA PROPERTIES LTD)
180 Pender St E Unit 200, Vancouver, BC, V6A 1T3
(604) 688-2323
Emp Here 30   *Sales* 25,441,800
SIC 6411 Insurance agents, brokers, and service
Brian Hui
Ernest Hui
Preston Lai

D-U-N-S 25-681-1753   (HQ)
PENFOLDS ROOFING INC
1262 Vernon Dr, Vancouver, BC, V6A 4C9
(604) 254-4663
Sales 13,069,740
SIC 1761 Roofing, siding, and sheetMetal work

D-U-N-S 24-825-5283   (HQ)
PLENTY STORES INC
PLENTY
1352 Vernon Dr, Vancouver, BC, V6A 3P7
(604) 733-4484
Emp Here 9   *Sales* 14,351,680
SIC 5651 Family clothing stores
Murat Imren

D-U-N-S 25-736-3911   (SL)
PRIMCORP SECURITY LTD
211 Georgia St E Suite 303, Vancouver, BC, V6A 1Z6
(604) 801-6899
Emp Here 20   *Sales* 13,578,460
SIC 6211 Security brokers and dealers
Daniel Lee

D-U-N-S 25-099-9026   (SL)
RADICAL ENTERTAINMENT INC
(*Suby of* ACTIVISION BLIZZARD, INC.)
369 Terminal Ave, Vancouver, BC, V6A 4C4
(604) 688-0606
Emp Here 191
SIC 7371 Custom computer programming services
Wendy Robillard

D-U-N-S 24-349-6226   (HQ)
RAINCITY HOUSING AND SUPPORT SOCIETY
191 Alexander St, Vancouver, BC, V6A 1B8
(604) 662-7023
Emp Here 150   *Sales* 13,822,801
SIC 8699 Membership organizations, nec
Mark Smith

D-U-N-S 20-115-6015   (HQ)
RUSSELL FOOD EQUIPMENT LIMITED
RUSSELL HENDRIX FOODSERVICE EQUIPMENT
(*Suby of* BLUE POINT CAPITAL PARTNERS LLC)
1255 Venables St, Vancouver, BC, V6A 3X6
(604) 253-6611
Emp Here 55   *Sales* 160,605,600
SIC 5046 Commercial equipment, nec
Charley Geiger
Mike Kane
Mark Morris
Tom Pitera
Lawrence Vander Baaren
Stephen Robert Viau

D-U-N-S 24-163-8568   (SL)
RUSTAN METALS LTD
630 Raymur Ave, Vancouver, BC, V6A 3L2

Emp Here 10   *Sales* 10,171,635

▲ Public Company   ■ Public Company Family Member   **HQ** Headquarters   **BR** Branch   **SL** Single Location

SIC 5052 Coal and other minerals and ores
Ruby Stretton
Stan Stretton
Martin Stretton

D-U-N-S 20-805-3728   (SL)
S & K NG ENTERPRISES LTD
NEW TOWN BAKERY & RESTAURANT
158 Pender St E, Vancouver, BC, V6A 1T3
(604) 689-7835
Emp Here 46   *Sales* 12,610,992
SIC 5461 Retail bakeries
Kwok Choi Ng
Susan Ng

D-U-N-S 25-856-9706   (SL)
**SAVE OUR LIVING ENVIRONMENT SOCI-
ETY (S.O.L.E.)**
UNITED WE CAN
39 Hastings St E, Vancouver, BC, V6A 1M9
(604) 681-0001
Emp Here 35   *Sales* 15,722,665
SIC 7389 Business services, nec
Gerry Martin

D-U-N-S 24-070-5343   (HQ)
SHIGS ENTERPRISES LTD
FUJIYA FISH MARKET
450 Alexander St, Vancouver, BC, V6A 1C5
(604) 251-9093
Emp Here 7   *Sales* 21,130,344
SIC 5421 Meat and fish markets
Jeffrey Matsuda

D-U-N-S 20-080-6714   (SL)
SMARTDESIGN GROUP (CANADA) LTD
1150 Station St Suite 102, Vancouver, BC,
V6A 4C7
(604) 662-7015
Emp Here 25   *Sales* 11,087,250
SIC 7389 Business services, nec
Nicholas F Baker
Neal Sims
Emily Woeste
Alan Dieckmann

D-U-N-S 24-578-5118   (SL)
STAR LIMOUSINE SERVICE LTD
328 Industrial Ave, Vancouver, BC, V6A 2P3
(604) 685-5600
Emp Here 60   *Sales* 16,998,000
SIC 7514 Passenger car rental
Randy Snider

D-U-N-S 25-215-2400   (HQ)
STEMCELL TECHNOLOGIES CANADA INC
1618 Station St, Vancouver, BC, V6A 1B6
(604) 877-0713
Sales 39,762,940
SIC 2836 Biological products, except diagnos-
tic
Allen Eaves

D-U-N-S 24-008-4132   (SL)
STERLING HEALTH SERVICES CORP
1188 Quebec St Suite 1402, Vancouver, BC,
V6A 4B3
(604) 261-2616
Emp Here 49   *Sales* 13,881,357
SIC 8741 Management services
Donna Moroz

D-U-N-S 24-031-7800   (SL)
**STRATHCONA COMMUNITY CENTRE AS-
SOCIATION (1972)**
STRATHCONA COMMUNITY CENTRE
601 Keefer St, Vancouver, BC, V6A 3V8
(604) 713-1838
Emp Here 100   *Sales* 6,842,200
SIC 8322 Individual and family services
Liza Tam
Patricia Badiir

D-U-N-S 20-116-3359   (HQ)
SUNRISE MARKETS INC
SUNRISE SOYA FOODS
729 Powell St, Vancouver, BC, V6A 1H5

(604) 253-2326
Emp Here 200   *Sales* 121,846,250
SIC 2099 Food preparations, nec
Peter Joe
Winnie Joe
Jenny Joe
Sally Joe

D-U-N-S 20-116-4845   (SL)
TERMINAL FRUIT & PRODUCE LTD
PRODUCE TERMINAL, THE
788 Malkin Ave, Vancouver, BC, V6A 2K2
(604) 251-3383
Emp Here 45   *Sales* 37,600,965
SIC 5148 Fresh fruits and vegetables
Phillip Wong
Kurt Louie

D-U-N-S 25-273-9370   (SL)
TRIUMPH FASHIONS LTD
1275 Venables St Suite 300, Vancouver, BC,
V6A 2E4
(604) 254-6969
Emp Here 50   *Sales* 24,916,100
SIC 5137 Women's and children's clothing
Kinny Cheung

D-U-N-S 25-089-6933   (SL)
TRUMPS FOOD INTEREST LTD
TRUMP'S
646 Powell St, Vancouver, BC, V6A 1H4
(604) 732-8473
Emp Here 35   *Sales* 29,245,195
SIC 5142 Packaged frozen goods
Heather Angel

D-U-N-S 20-573-9659   (SL)
UNITED POULTRY CO LTD
534 Cordova St E, Vancouver, BC, V6A 1L7
(604) 255-9308
Emp Here 80   *Sales* 66,846,160
SIC 5144 Poultry and poultry products
Clifford Pollon
Dave Pollon

D-U-N-S 20-992-7318   (SL)
UNITOW SERVICES (1978) LTD
1717 Vernon Dr, Vancouver, BC, V6A 3P8
(604) 659-1225
Emp Here 45   *Sales* 18,414,500
SIC 7549 Automotive services, nec
Gary Tarantino

D-U-N-S 24-658-7737   (SL)
VAN-WHOLE PRODUCE LTD
VAN-WHOLE PRODUCE
(*Suby of* PATTISON, JIM GROUP INC)
830 Malkin Ave, Vancouver, BC, V6A 2K2
(604) 251-3330
Emp Here 230   *Sales* 42,407,630
SIC 4225 General warehousing and storage
Dan Bregg
Leonard Jang
Benjamin Shuen

D-U-N-S 20-796-2259   (HQ)
**VANCOUVER CITY SAVINGS CREDIT
UNION**
VANCITY CREDIT UNION
183 Terminal Ave, Vancouver, BC, V6A 4G2
(604) 877-7013
Emp Here 20   *Sales* 341,602,000
SIC 6062 State credit unions
Tamara Vrooman
Dave Mowat
Patrice Pratt
Elain Duvall
Catharine Mccreary
Doug Soo
Doreen Braverman
Ian Gill
Reva Dester
Lisa Barrett

D-U-N-S 20-117-7248   (BR)
**VANCOUVER COASTAL HEALTH AUTHOR-
ITY**
DOWNTOWN COMMUNITY HEALTH CLINIC

(*Suby of* GOVERNMENT OF THE
PROVINCE OF BRITISH COLUMBIA)
569 Powell St, Vancouver, BC, V6A 1G8
(604) 255-3151
Emp Here 100
SIC 8011 Offices and clinics of medical doc-
tors
Monica Stein

D-U-N-S 24-029-2714   (SL)
VILLA CATHAY CARE HOME SOCIETY
970 Union St, Vancouver, BC, V6A 3V1
(604) 254-5621
Emp Here 130   *Sales* 8,882,380
SIC 8059 Nursing and personal care, nec
Harry Fan
Shou Hsin Hsu
Edward Yeung
Anthony Fan

D-U-N-S 20-958-7872   (SL)
WATERFRONT EMPLOYERS OF B.C.
349 Railway St Suite 400, Vancouver, BC, V6A
1A4
(604) 689-7184
Emp Here 80   *Sales* 13,347,760
SIC 7374 Data processing and preparation
Tom Teasdale

D-U-N-S 20-117-2145   (HQ)
WEST COAST REDUCTION LTD
ALBERTA PROCESSING CO.
(*Suby of* RUFUS HOLDINGS LTD)
1292 Venables St, Vancouver, BC, V6A 4B4
(604) 255-9301
Emp Here 125   *Sales* 207,138,625
SIC 2077 Animal and marine fats and oils
Gordon Diamond
Barry Glotman
Humphry Koch

D-U-N-S 24-371-2593   (SL)
WINNER SPORTSWEAR LTD
1223 Frances St, Vancouver, BC, V6A 1Z4
(604) 253-0411
Emp Here 150   *Sales* 26,909,400
SIC 5651 Family clothing stores
Tony Yiu

D-U-N-S 20-623-6168   (SL)
YEN BROS. FOOD SERVICE LTD
1988 Vernon Dr, Vancouver, BC, V6A 3Y6
(604) 255-6522
Emp Here 85   *Sales* 71,024,045
SIC 5148 Fresh fruits and vegetables
Eddie Yen
Edward Yen

Vancouver, BC V6B

D-U-N-S 20-521-0839   (SL)
540806 BC LTD
DTZ BARNICKEY
475 Georgia St W Suite 800, Vancouver, BC,
V6B 4M9
(604) 684-7117
Emp Here 36   *Sales* 15,096,780
SIC 6719 Holding companies, nec
John Steven Caldwell

D-U-N-S 20-191-8518   (HQ)
**ACCENTURE BUSINESS SERVICES FOR
UTILITIES INC**
(*Suby of* ACCENTURE INC)
510 Georgia St W Suite 2075, Vancouver, BC,
V6B 0M3
(604) 646-5000
Sales 187,164,000
SIC 8741 Management services
William Morris

D-U-N-S 25-687-1666   (BR)
ACCENTURE INC
(*Suby of* ACCENTURE INC)
401 Georgia St W Suite 1500, Vancouver, BC,

V6B 5A1
(604) 646-5000
Emp Here 400
SIC 8741 Management services
Syed Hussain

D-U-N-S 24-594-6892   (HQ)
ALLIED HOTEL PROPERTIES INC
(*Suby of* ALLIED HOLDINGS LTD)
515 Pender St W Suite 300, Vancouver, BC,
V6B 6H5
(604) 669-5335
Emp Here 50   *Sales* 11,078,903
SIC 7011 Hotels and motels
Peter Y.L. Eng
Michael F. Chan
Dennis Ng
Patrick K. Kong
Syed Abu Bakar Bin Syed Mohsin Almohdzar
Francis Wong
T. Lloyd Callahan

D-U-N-S 20-865-7254   (BR)
AON REED STENHOUSE INC
(*Suby of* AON PLC)
401 Georgia St W Suite 1200, Vancouver, BC,
V6B 5A1
(604) 688-4442
Emp Here 180
SIC 6411 Insurance agents, brokers, and ser-
vice
Steve Van Halst

D-U-N-S 24-750-8658   (SL)
APEX REFORESTATION LTD
Gd Stn Terminal, Vancouver, BC, V6B 3P7
(604) 736-0063
Emp Here 200   *Sales* 50,698,000
SIC 8748 Business consulting, nec
Marc Hobday

D-U-N-S 24-595-1926   (HQ)
AQUILINI INVESTMENT GROUP INC
HIGHLINER INN
800 Griffiths Way, Vancouver, BC, V6B 6G1
(604) 687-8813
Emp Here 15   *Sales* 19,401,811
SIC 6512 Nonresidential building operators
Luigi Aquilini
Francesco Aquilini
Paolo Aquilini
Roberto Aquilini

D-U-N-S 24-677-5287   (BR)
**ARAMARK ENTERTAINMENT SERVICES
(CANADA) INC**
ARAMARK ENTERTAINMENT SERVICES
(*Suby of* ARAMARK)
800 Griffiths Way, Vancouver, BC, V6B 6G1
(604) 780-7623
Emp Here 100
SIC 8742 Management consulting services
Jeffrey Kennedy

D-U-N-S 20-066-8861   (HQ)
ARMY & NAVY DEPT. STORE LIMITED
ARMY & NAVY
74 Cordova St W, Vancouver, BC, V6B 1C9
(604) 683-9660
Emp Here 16   *Sales* 68,448,600
SIC 5311 Department stores
Jacqueline Cohen
Marlene Cohen

D-U-N-S 20-108-8309   (BR)
ARMY & NAVY DEPT. STORE LIMITED
(*Suby of* ARMY & NAVY DEPT. STORE LIM-
ITED)
27 Hastings St W Suite 25, Vancouver, BC,
V6B 1G5
(604) 682-6644
Emp Here 150
SIC 5311 Department stores
Rosa Fernandez

D-U-N-S 20-689-9333   (SL)
ASENTUS CONSULTING GROUP LTD
(*Suby of* GP STRATEGIES CORPORATION)

1286 Homer St Suite 200, Vancouver, BC, V6B 2Y5
(604) 609-9993
Emp Here 45   *Sales* 12,344,940
SIC 8741 Management services
Jules Campeau

D-U-N-S 20-122-6581   (SL)
ATAC RESOURCES LTD
510 Hastings St W Suite 1016, Vancouver, BC, V6B 1L8
(604) 687-2522
Emp Here 10   *Sales* 23,875,490
SIC 1041 Gold ores
Graham N. Downs
Matthew Keevil
Julia Lane
Glenn Yeadon
Larry Donaldson
Ian Talbot
Douglas O. Goss
Robert C. Carne
Don Poirier
Bruce Youngman

D-U-N-S 20-116-7132   (SL)
ATLANTIC HOTELS PARTNERSHIP
510 Hastings St W, Vancouver, BC, V6B 1L8
(604) 687-8813
Emp Here 500   *Sales* 47,834,000
SIC 7011 Hotels and motels
Roberto Aquilini
Paolo Aquilini
Francesco Aquilini

D-U-N-S 25-976-5618   (HQ)
AUSENCO ENGINEERING CANADA INC
855 Homer St, Vancouver, BC, V6B 2W2
(604) 684-9311
Sales 35,747,800
SIC 8711 Engineering services
Zimi Meka
Chris King
Clint Donkin
Ron Douglas
Matthew Mcgowan
Linda Cochrane
Tania Leil O'brien
Greg Lane
Joel Cawker
Gordon Grams

D-U-N-S 20-382-9056   (HQ)
AUSTRALIS CAPITAL INC.
510 Seymour St Suite 900, Vancouver, BC, V6B 3J5

Sales 29,844,315
SIC 5122 Drugs, proprietaries, and sundries

D-U-N-S 20-966-6739   (SL)
AVC INSURANCE SERVICES INC
INTEGRATED PLANNING GROUP
650 Georgia St W Suite 11588, Vancouver, BC, V6B 4N8
(604) 685-6431
Emp Here 49   *Sales* 11,480,112
SIC 8742 Management consulting services
Sue Jerkins

D-U-N-S 24-316-6662   (HQ)
AVIGILON CORPORATION
(Suby of MOTOROLA SOLUTIONS, INC.)
555 Robson St 3rd Fl, Vancouver, BC, V6B 3K9
(604) 629-5182
Emp Here 90   *Sales* 408,629,000
SIC 3651 Household audio and video equipment
Alexander Fernandes
Joel Schuster
James Henderson
Mahesh Saptharishi
Ric Leong
Murray Teylin
Mike Mcknight
Fred Withers

Murray Tevlin
Wan Jung

D-U-N-S 25-978-3454   (HQ)
BLAST RADIUS INC
(Suby of WPP PLC)
509 Richards St, Vancouver, BC, V6B 2Z6
(604) 647-6500
Emp Here 180   *Sales* 83,155,200
SIC 7374 Data processing and preparation
Gurval Caer
Lee Feldman

D-U-N-S 25-373-0519   (HQ)
BRITISH COLUMBIA HYDRO AND POWER AUTHORITY
BC HYDRO
(Suby of GOVERNMENT OF THE PROVINCE OF BRITISH COLUMBIA)
333 Dunsmuir St, Vancouver, BC, V6B 5R3
(604) 224-9376
Emp Here 350   *Sales* 3,957,525,591
SIC 4911 Electric services
W.J. Brad Bennett
James M. Brown
Janine North
John C.W. Ritchie
Bill Adsit
James P. Halton
John Knappett
Valerie Lambert
Tracy Redies
Jack Weisgerber

D-U-N-S 25-978-3991   (HQ)
BUILDDIRECT.COM TECHNOLOGIES INC
401 Georgia St W Suite 2200, Vancouver, BC, V6B 5A1
(604) 662-8100
Emp Here 50   *Sales* 113,925,600
SIC 5039 Construction materials, nec
Dan Park
Robert Thomas Banks
John Sotham
Andrew Lugsdin
Robert Banks
Roger Hardy
Jim Orlando
Howard Gwin
Maria Pacella
William Robinson

D-U-N-S 20-912-8958   (SL)
BULL, HOUSSER & TUPPER LLP
510 Georgia St W Suite 1800, Vancouver, BC, V6B 0M3
(604) 687-6575
Emp Here 250   *Sales* 51,469,000
SIC 8111 Legal services
Herb Isherwood

D-U-N-S 24-372-2480   (SL)
BUYATAB ONLINE INC
(Suby of FLEETCOR TECHNOLOGIES, INC.)
B1 788 Beatty St, Vancouver, BC, V6B 2M1
(604) 678-3275
Emp Here 62   *Sales* 15,148,336
SIC 5961 Catalog and mail-order houses
Johann Tergesen
Greg Barret
Matias Marquez

D-U-N-S 25-057-1205   (HQ)
BWIRELESS COMMUNICATIONS INC
555 Robson St Unit 1, Vancouver, BC, V6B 1A6
(604) 689-8488
Emp Here 1   *Sales* 16,280,000
SIC 5999 Miscellaneous retail stores, nec
Emil Bosnjak

D-U-N-S 24-957-7974   (HQ)
CAMPBELL TRAVEL LTD
181 Keefer Pl Suite 201, Vancouver, BC, V6B 6C1
(604) 688-2913
Emp Here 35   *Sales* 18,198,845
SIC 4724 Travel agencies

Isabella Fung

D-U-N-S 20-915-7916   (SL)
CANADA TOUR SYSTEM INC
510 Hastings St W Suite 1308, Vancouver, BC, V6B 1L8
(604) 681-9747
Emp Here 25   *Sales* 12,999,175
SIC 4724 Travel agencies
Kazuya Noguchi
Tomoo Mitsueda

D-U-N-S 20-109-8993   (BR)
CANADIAN BROADCASTING CORPORATION
CBC
(Suby of GOVERNMENT OF CANADA)
700 Hamilton St, Vancouver, BC, V6B 2R5
(604) 662-6000
Emp Here 500
SIC 4832 Radio broadcasting stations
Rae Hull

D-U-N-S 24-535-0566   (HQ)
CANADIAN NORTHERN SHIELD INSURANCE COMPANY
CNS
(Suby of RSA INSURANCE GROUP PLC)
555 Hastings St W Unit 1900, Vancouver, BC, V6B 4N6
(604) 662-2900
Emp Here 89   *Sales* 664,454,560
SIC 6411 Insurance agents, brokers, and service
Ken Keenan
Alexander Patton
Beckie Scarrow

D-U-N-S 25-314-0800   (HQ)
CANADIAN WESTERN TRUST COMPANY
(Suby of CANADIAN WESTERN BANK)
750 Cambie St Suite 300, Vancouver, BC, V6B 0A2
(604) 685-2081
Emp Here 40   *Sales* 11,844,000
SIC 6091 Nondeposit trust facilities
Jack Donald
Larry Pollack
Rod Sorbo

D-U-N-S 20-982-5384   (SL)
CANUCKS CENTRE FOR BC HOCKEY, THE
800 Griffiths Way Suite 4, Vancouver, BC, V6B 6G1
(604) 899-7770
Emp Here 200   *Sales* 15,709,000
SIC 7997 Membership sports and recreation clubs
Mike Gillis

D-U-N-S 24-359-1257   (SL)
CANUCKS SPORTS & ENTERTAINMENT CORPORATION
800 Griffiths Way, Vancouver, BC, V6B 6G1
(604) 899-7400
Emp Here 50   *Sales* 21,186,500
SIC 7941 Sports clubs, managers, and promoters
Francesco Aquilini
Roberto Aquilini
Paolo Aquilini

D-U-N-S 24-931-6720   (HQ)
CAPSTONE MINING CORP
510 Georgia St W Suite 2100, Vancouver, BC, V6B 0M3
(604) 684-8894
Emp Here 18   *Sales* 415,887,000
SIC 1081 Metal mining services
Darren M. Pylot
Wendy King
Cindy Burnett
Albert Garcia Iii
Jason Howe
Cindy L. Burnett
Raman Randhawa
Gillian Mccombie
Brad Mercer

James Slattery

D-U-N-S 24-139-9877   (SL)
CCL PROPERTIES LTD
J J BARNICKE
475 Georgia St W Suite 800, Vancouver, BC, V6B 4M9
(604) 684-7117
Emp Here 45   *Sales* 14,720,715
SIC 6531 Real estate agents and managers
Scott Primrose

D-U-N-S 25-625-3808   (SL)
CERTIFIED GENERAL ACCOUNTANTS ASSOCIATION OF BRITISH COLUMBIA
CGA-BC
555 Hastings St W Suite 800, Vancouver, BC, V6B 4N6
(604) 872-7222
Emp Here 150   *Sales* 35,116,650
SIC 8621 Professional organizations
Lori Mathison

D-U-N-S 20-351-9111   (SL)
CHARTERED PROFESSIONAL ACCOUNTANTS OF BRITISH COLUMBIA
CPABC
555 Hastings St W Unit 800, Vancouver, BC, V6B 4N5
(604) 872-7222
Emp Here 115   *Sales* 26,922,765
SIC 8621 Professional organizations
Lori Mathison
Amy Lam
Sabine Rouques

D-U-N-S 20-112-2947   (SL)
CHINA EDUCATION RESOURCES INC
515 Pender St W Suite 300, Vancouver, BC, V6B 6H5
(604) 331-2388
Emp Here 53   *Sales* 11,863,341
SIC 5999 Miscellaneous retail stores, nec
Chengfeng Zhou
Chi Tak Hon
Lian Li
Li Wang

D-U-N-S 20-911-6375   (HQ)
CITY CENTRE CARE SOCIETY
415 Pender St W, Vancouver, BC, V6B 1V2
(604) 681-9111
Emp Here 110   *Sales* 10,248,900
SIC 8051 Skilled nursing care facilities
Seamus O'melinn

D-U-N-S 20-911-9239   (HQ)
COAST UNDERWRITERS LTD
(Suby of RSA INSURANCE GROUP PLC)
650 Georgia St W Unit 2690, Vancouver, BC, V6B 4N7
(604) 683-5631
Sales 64,633,065
SIC 6331 Fire, marine, and casualty insurance
Kevan Gielty

D-U-N-S 24-457-9769   (SL)
COLUMBIA COLLEGE
555 Seymour St Suite 500, Vancouver, BC, V6B 3H6
(604) 683-8360
Emp Here 100   *Sales* 11,263,600
SIC 8221 Colleges and universities
Trevor Toone

D-U-N-S 24-325-0417   (SL)
COLUMBUS GOLD CORP
1090 Hamilton St, Vancouver, BC, V6B 2R9
(604) 634-0970
Emp Here 50   *Sales* 119,377,450
SIC 1041 Gold ores
Robert Giustra
Rock Lefrancois
Blaine Monaghan
Warren Beil
Jorge Martinez
Andrew Yau
Russell Ball

Peter L. Gianulis
Marie-Helene Berard
Oleg Pelevin

D-U-N-S 20-393-3403 (HQ)
COMARK HOLDINGS INC
(*Suby of* 9383921 CANADA INC)
650 Georgia St W Suite 2900, Vancouver, BC,
V6B 4N8
(604) 646-3790
Sales 260,759,980
SIC 6712 Bank holding companies
Shamsh Kassam
Neil Armstrong
Gerry Bachynski
Neville Lewis
Shaun Lewis
Keith Van Apeldoorn

D-U-N-S 24-762-9608 (SL)
CONTACT SERVICES INC
128 Pender St W Flr 6-7, Vancouver, BC, V6B
1R8
(604) 688-5523
Emp Here 49   *Sales* 10,582,494
SIC 8748 Business consulting, nec
Riaz Pisani

D-U-N-S 24-984-1151 (SL)
CONTINUING LEGAL EDUC, THE
845 Cambie St Suite 500, Vancouver, BC, V6B
4Z9
(604) 669-3544
Emp Here 45   *Sales* 10,516,275
SIC 8621 Professional organizations
Ron Frison

D-U-N-S 24-354-8935 (BR)
COSTCO WHOLESALE CANADA LTD
COSTCO
(*Suby of* COSTCO WHOLESALE CORPO-
RATION)
605 Expo Blvd, Vancouver, BC, V6B 1V4
(604) 622-5050
Emp Here 150
SIC 5099 Durable goods, nec
Derek Campbell

D-U-N-S 20-367-8706 (HQ)
COVENANT HOUSE VANCOUVER
326 Pender St W, Vancouver, BC, V6B 1T1
(604) 647-4480
Emp Here 5   *Sales* 13,345,900
SIC 8399 Social services, nec
Krista Thompson

D-U-N-S 24-336-2030 (SL)
**DAVID SULLIVAN GROUP OF COMPANIES
LTD, THE**
489 Robson St, Vancouver, BC, V6B 6L9
(604) 684-5714
Emp Here 60   *Sales* 17,608,620
SIC 5411 Grocery stores
David Sullivan

D-U-N-S 20-813-3723 (SL)
**DAVIE STREET MANAGEMENT SERVICES
LTD**
OPUS HOTEL
322 Davie St, Vancouver, BC, V6B 5Z6
(604) 642-6787
Emp Here 100   *Sales* 9,489,900
SIC 7011 Hotels and motels
Nicholas Gandossi

D-U-N-S 25-979-7975 (BR)
DELTA HOTELS LIMITED
DELTA VANCOUVER SUITE HOTEL
(*Suby of* GOVERNMENT OF THE
PROVINCE OF BRITISH COLUMBIA)
550 Hastings St W, Vancouver, BC, V6B 1L6
(604) 689-8188
Emp Here 120
SIC 7011 Hotels and motels
Peter Catarino

D-U-N-S 20-031-5961 (HQ)
EARL'S RESTAURANTS CARRELL LTD

EARL'S RESTAURANTS
425 Carrall St Unit 200, Vancouver, BC, V6B
6E3
(604) 646-4880
Sales 13,881,357
SIC 8741 Management services
Stan Fuller
Mohamed Jessa

D-U-N-S 20-650-2432 (SL)
EDGEWATER MANAGEMENT INC
EDGEWATER CASINO
750 Pacific Blvd Suite 311, Vancouver, BC,
V6B 5E7
(604) 687-3343
Emp Here 800   *Sales* 76,534,400
SIC 7011 Hotels and motels
Gary Jackson
Christopher Jackson

D-U-N-S 20-111-1333 (HQ)
ELECTRIC POWER EQUIPMENT LIMITED
1285 Homer St, Vancouver, BC, V6B 2Z2
(604) 682-4221
Emp Here 15   *Sales* 19,044,200
SIC 3625 Relays and industrial controls
Roy Bartholomew

D-U-N-S 25-664-5276 (HQ)
GEVITY CONSULTING INC
GEVITY
375 Water St Suite 350, Vancouver, BC, V6B
5C6
(604) 608-1779
Sales 22,814,100
SIC 8748 Business consulting, nec
Leon Salvail
Sacha Mallais
Charles Hill
Martin Pearce
Tracy Forbes
Zen Tharani
Anushka Premji-Osman
Marc Koehn
Sacha Mallais

D-U-N-S 20-286-4377 (SL)
GLOBAL PACIFIC RESOURCES INC
134 Abbott St Suite 500, Vancouver, BC, V6B
2K4
(604) 685-4411
Emp Here 10   *Sales* 46,008,576
SIC 5099 Durable goods, nec
David Honing

D-U-N-S 20-015-5286 (HQ)
GLOBAL RELAY COMMUNICATIONS INC
GLOBAL RELAY
220 Cambie St Fl 2, Vancouver, BC, V6B 2M9
(604) 484-6630
Emp Here 250   *Sales* 92,286,500
SIC 7371 Custom computer programming ser-
vices
Warren Roy
Shannon Rogers
Bryan Young
Kelvin Ng
Joyce Hung
Eric Parusel
Lu Vo
Glenn Rogers
Simon Edgett
Stephen Lazenby

D-U-N-S 25-068-6250 (SL)
**GOTHAM STEAKHOUSE & COCKTAIL BAR
LIMITED PARTNERSHIP**
HYS STEAKHOUSE
615 Seymour St, Vancouver, BC, V6B 3K3
(604) 605-8282
Emp Here 80   *Sales* 3,641,520
SIC 5813 Drinking places
David Aisenstat

D-U-N-S 25-662-0410 (BR)
**GOVERNING COUNCIL OF THE SALVA-
TION ARMY IN CANADA, THE**
GOVERNING COUNCIL OF THE SALVATION

ARMY IN CANADA,
(*Suby of* GOVERNING COUNCIL OF THE
SALVATION ARMY IN CANADA, THE)
555 Homer St Suite 703, Vancouver, BC, V6B
1K8
(604) 681-3405
Emp Here 100
SIC 8322 Individual and family services
George Perkins

D-U-N-S 24-899-0848 (BR)
GRANT THORNTON LLP
CAPSERVCO
(*Suby of* GRANT THORNTON LLP)
333 Seymour St Suite 1600, Vancouver, BC,
V6B 0A4
(604) 687-2711
Emp Here 109
SIC 8721 Accounting, auditing, and book-
keeping
Monique Samson

D-U-N-S 24-244-7936 (SL)
HARPER GREY LLP
650 Georgia St W Suite 3200, Vancouver, BC,
V6B 4P7
(604) 687-0411
Emp Here 162   *Sales* 17,962,884
SIC 8111 Legal services
Steven Abramson
Richard Bereti
Salman Bhura
Kimberly Jakeman
Guy Brown
John Brown
William Clark
Karen Douglas
Cameron Elder
Maureen Lundell

D-U-N-S 25-972-5620 (SL)
HENRIQUEZ PARTNERS
HENRIQUEZ PARTNERS ARCHITECTS
598 Georgia St W, Vancouver, BC, V6B 2A3
(604) 687-5681
Emp Here 62   *Sales* 14,973,930
SIC 8621 Professional organizations
Gregory Henriquez
Patricia Tewfik

D-U-N-S 24-682-2274 (HQ)
HORTON TRADING LTD
ELAN DATAMAKERS, DIV OF
788 Beatty St Suite 307, Vancouver, BC, V6B
2M1
(604) 688-8521
Emp Here 80   *Sales* 20,855,875
SIC 7374 Data processing and preparation
John T Horton
Warwick J Reid
Gerry Mcnee
Marshall M Soule

D-U-N-S 25-500-9177 (BR)
HOTEL SASKATCHEWAN (1990) LTD
SCC GROUP
(*Suby of* HOTEL SASKATCHEWAN (1990)
LTD)
1118 Homer St Suite 425, Vancouver, BC,
V6B 6L5

Emp Here 80
SIC 7011 Hotels and motels
Becky Hu

D-U-N-S 20-107-8867 (BR)
HSBC BANK CANADA
(*Suby of* HSBC HOLDINGS PLC)
401 Georgia St W Suite 1300, Vancouver, BC,
V6B 5A1
(604) 668-4682
Emp Here 90
SIC 8742 Management consulting services
Greg Todd

D-U-N-S 20-509-2653 (HQ)
HY'S OF CANADA LTD
HY'S STEAKHOUSE & COCKTAIL BAR

128 Pender St W Unit 303, Vancouver, BC,
V6B 1R8
(604) 684-3311
Emp Here 8   *Sales* 25,651,450
SIC 5812 Eating places
Neil Aisenstat
Sam Belzberg
Barbara Aisenstat

D-U-N-S 25-713-1714 (SL)
I-CORP SECURITY SERVICES LTD
1040 Hamilton St Suite 303, Vancouver, BC,
V6B 2R9
(604) 687-8645
Emp Here 150   *Sales* 3,937,500
SIC 7381 Detective and armored car services
Gordon Baker
Reynold Comeault

D-U-N-S 24-678-9064 (HQ)
ICEBREAKER MERINO CLOTHING INC
21 Water St Suite 502, Vancouver, BC, V6B
1A1
(778) 328-9666
Sales 26,909,400
SIC 5651 Family clothing stores
Justin Walford

D-U-N-S 25-984-8273 (HQ)
ILSC (VANCOUVER) INC
*INTERNATIONAL LANGUAGE SCHOOLS
OF CANADA*
555 Richards St, Vancouver, BC, V6B 2Z5
(604) 689-9095
Emp Here 120   *Sales* 18,314,100
SIC 8299 Schools and educational services,
nec
Paul Zysman

D-U-N-S 20-120-3668 (HQ)
**IMPERIAL PARKING CANADA CORPORA-
TION**
IMPARK
(*Suby of* GATES GROUP CAPITAL PART-
NERS, LLC)
601 Cordova St W Suite 300, Vancouver, BC,
V6B 1G1
(604) 681-7311
Emp Here 500   *Sales* 313,936,000
SIC 7521 Automobile parking
Herbert W Anderson Jr
Walter G Stuelpe
Bryan L Wallner
Allan C Copping
Stephen M.G. Richards
Andrew E Saxton
Daniel J Brickman
Anthony Mosse
Paul Clough
Leonard Shavel

D-U-N-S 24-957-7347 (SL)
INCOGNITO SOFTWARE SYSTEMS INC
375 Water St Suite 500, Vancouver, BC, V6B
5C6
(604) 688-4332
Emp Here 103   *Sales* 17,185,241
SIC 7372 Prepackaged software
Stephane Bourque

D-U-N-S 24-504-7519 (HQ)
INTERNATIONAL CELLARS INC
1122 Mainland St Suite 200, Vancouver, BC,
V6B 5L1
(604) 689-5333
Emp Here 12   *Sales* 11,170,404
SIC 5182 Wine and distilled beverages
Michael Shuster
Norman J Gladstone

D-U-N-S 24-031-9426 (HQ)
INTRAWEST ULC
BLUE MOUNTAIN RESORT
(*Suby of* HAWK HOLDING COMPANY, LLC)
375 Water St Suite 710, Vancouver, BC, V6B
5C6
(604) 695-8200
Emp Here 75   *Sales* 794,044,400

SIC 7011 Hotels and motels
Brian Collins
Trevor Bruno
Sky Foules
Travis Mayer
David Blaiklock
Randal A. Nardone
Hugh Smythe
Andrew Stotesbury
Michael Forsayeth

D-U-N-S 24-373-0657   (HQ)
ITC CONSTRUCTION CANADA INC
ITC CONSTRUCTION GROUP
564 Beatty St Suite 800, Vancouver, BC, V6B
2L3
(604) 685-0111
Emp Here 40   *Sales* 57,033,800
SIC 1542 Nonresidential construction, nec
Peter Rezansoff
Doug Macfarlane

D-U-N-S 20-255-5975   (SL)
KABUNI TECHNOLOGIES INC
WHOLE NEW HOME
375 Water St Suite 200, Vancouver, BC, V6B
0M9
(778) 686-2243
Emp Here 30   *Sales* 19,693,920
SIC 5961 Catalog and mail-order houses
Neil Patel

D-U-N-S 24-578-4152   (SL)
LINDSAY KENNEY LLP
401 Georgia St W Suite 1800, Vancouver, BC,
V6B 5A1
(604) 687-1323
Emp Here 100   *Sales* 11,088,200
SIC 8111 Legal services
Kelvin R. Stephens
Michael J. Jackson
John J. Kim
Jan L. Lindsay
Brad T. Martyniuk
Gregory S. Miller
Carmen Place
Kirk Poje
Frank Potts
Deborah H. Taylor

D-U-N-S 25-308-5760   (SL)
LINDSAY LLP
564 Beatty St Suite 1000, Vancouver, BC, V6B
2L3
(778) 945-5188
Emp Here 21   *Sales* 38,779,839
SIC 6311 Life insurance
John B. Arnesen
Vanessa Gauthier
Christopher Hope
Michael J. Jackson
John J. Kim
Jan Lindsay
Richard Lindsay

D-U-N-S 20-955-1956   (HQ)
LODGING OVATIONS CORP
(*Suby of* HAWK HOLDING COMPANY, LLC)
375 Water St Suite 326, Vancouver, BC, V6B
5C6
(604) 938-9999
Sales 13,716,600
SIC 8741 Management services
James Gibbons
Ron Zimmer
Rene Cardinal
Barb Jackson

D-U-N-S 24-152-1590   (SL)
**LSBC CAPTIVE INSURANCE COMPANY
LTD**
THE LAW SOCIETY OF BRITISH COLUMBIA
845 Cambie St Suite 800, Vancouver, BC, V6B
4Z9
(604) 669-2533
Emp Here 180   *Sales* 384,654,240
SIC 6351 Surety insurance

Timothy Mcgee

D-U-N-S 24-796-5739   (SL)
MAGNUM PROJECTS LTD
128 Pender St W Suite 401, Vancouver, BC,
V6B 1R8
(604) 569-3900
Emp Here 40   *Sales* 16,774,200
SIC 6719 Holding companies, nec
George Wong

D-U-N-S 24-372-5108   (HQ)
MAPLE FUN TOURS LTD
997 Seymour St Suite 610, Vancouver, BC,
V6B 3M1
(604) 683-5244
Emp Here 22   *Sales* 17,678,878
SIC 4724 Travel agencies
William Bessho
Tomoko Bessho

D-U-N-S 20-180-1292   (SL)
MAXIMIZER SOFTWARE INC
60 Smithe St Unit 260, Vancouver, BC, V6B
0P5
(604) 601-8000
Emp Here 87   *Sales* 14,515,689
SIC 7372 Prepackaged software
Terence Hui
John Caputo
William Anderson
Joseph Hui
Kam Sandhu
Enzo Dimichele
Mark Skapinker
Tom Bennett
Richard Whittall
Kevin Armitage

D-U-N-S 25-216-7747   (HQ)
MAYFAIR PROPERTIES LTD
HAMPTON INN & SUITES
111 Robson St, Vancouver, BC, V6B 6P5
(604) 681-0868
Emp Here 30   *Sales* 15,757,300
SIC 7011 Hotels and motels
Akber Kassam
Zack Bhatia

D-U-N-S 20-642-4389   (BR)
**MCDONALD'S   RESTAURANTS   OF
CANADA LIMITED**
MCDONALD'S #8646
(*Suby of* MCDONALD'S CORPORATION)
86 Pender St W Unit 1001, Vancouver, BC,
V6B 6N8
(604) 718-1165
Emp Here 80
SIC 5812 Eating places
Nielne Chand

D-U-N-S 24-350-2262   (HQ)
**MCELHANNEY ASSOCIATES LAND SUR-
VEYING LTD**
858 Beatty St Suite 200, Vancouver, BC, V6B
1C1
(604) 683-8521
Emp Here 50   *Sales* 26,810,850
SIC 8713 Surveying services
John Blair
James (Jim) Christie

D-U-N-S 20-353-2085   (HQ)
**MCELHANNEY CONSULTING SERVICES
LTD**
MCELHANNEY
(*Suby of* MCELHANNEY SERVICES LTD)
858 Beatty St Suite 200, Vancouver, BC, V6B
1C1
(604) 683-8521
Emp Here 10   *Sales* 63,372,500
SIC 8748 Business consulting, nec
Chris Newcomb

D-U-N-S 24-838-1659   (HQ)
METASOFT SYSTEMS INC
353 Water St Suite 300, Vancouver, BC, V6B
1B8

(604) 683-6711
Emp Here 75   *Sales* 12,255,470
SIC 7371 Custom computer programming ser-
vices
Trevor Skillen

D-U-N-S 25-092-6271   (HQ)
MOGO FINANCE TECHNOLOGY INC
MOGO
401 Georgia St W Suite 2100, Vancouver, BC,
V6B 5A1
(604) 659-4380
Emp Here 6   *Sales* 46,454,216
SIC 6153 Short-term business credit institu-
tions, except agricultural
David Feller
Gregory Feller
Matthew Bosrock
Minhas Mohamed
Praveen Varshney

D-U-N-S 25-330-0776   (HQ)
NASCO SERVICES INC
(*Suby of* CROCODILE LABOUR SERVICES
INC)
128 Pender St W Suite 205, Vancouver, BC,
V6B 1R8
(604) 683-2512
Emp Here 17   *Sales* 149,388,000
SIC 7361 Employment agencies
David James
Jennifer Wickham
Bronwen O'hara
Shelley Johnson

D-U-N-S 20-176-5943   (SL)
NEXT LEVEL GAMES INC
208 Robson St, Vancouver, BC, V6B 6A1
(604) 484-6111
Emp Here 70   *Sales* 22,829,520
SIC 3944 Games, toys, and children's vehicles
Doug Tronsgard

D-U-N-S 20-337-1658   (HQ)
NORTHAM BEVERAGES LTD
68 Water St Unit 501, Vancouver, BC, V6B
1A4
(604) 731-2900
Emp Here 23   *Sales* 38,025,900
SIC 2085 Distilled and blended liquors
Bruce Dean

D-U-N-S 24-887-8753   (HQ)
NORZINC LTD
650 Georgia St W Suite 1710, Vancouver, BC,
V6B 4N9
(604) 688-2001
Emp Here 13   *Sales* 53,968,314
SIC 1031 Lead and zinc ores
Don Macdonald
Michael Vande Guchte
Steve Dawson
Joseph Lanzon
David Harpley
Trevor Cunningham
Alan B. Taylor
John Warwick
Malcolm Ja Swallow
Ian Ward

D-U-N-S 24-368-6433   (HQ)
NOVELION THERAPEUTICS INC
510 West Georgia St Suite 1800, Vancouver,
BC, V6B 0M3
(877) 764-3131
Sales 130,432,000
SIC 2834 Pharmaceutical preparations
Ben Harshbarger
Michael Price
Linda Buono
Mark Corrigan
Suzanne Bruhn
John Orloff
Stephen L. Sabba
Donald K. Stern
John C. Thomas

D-U-N-S 20-271-7252   (SL)

ONNI AIRWAYS LTD
550 Robson St Unit 300, Vancouver, BC, V6B
2B7
(604) 602-7711
Emp Here 165   *Sales* 44,792,260
SIC 4512 Air transportation, scheduled
Rossano De Cotiis
Morris De Cotiis

D-U-N-S 25-306-0748   (HQ)
OPEN ROAD AUTO GROUP LTD
1039 Hamilton St, Vancouver, BC, V6B 5T4

Sales 62,928,000
SIC 5511 New and used car dealers

D-U-N-S 25-417-2265   (SL)
**ORCA BAY ARENA LIMITED PARTNER-
SHIP**
ORCA BAY SPORTS & ENTERTAINMENT
800 Griffiths Way, Vancouver, BC, V6B 6G1
(604) 899-7400
Emp Here 200   *Sales* 27,135,400
SIC 6512 Nonresidential building operators
Chris Zimmerman
John Mccaw

D-U-N-S 24-558-3000   (HQ)
PACIFIC DOCUMENT EXCHANGE LTD
PDX COURIER
(*Suby of* ALL-CAN EXPRESS LTD)
111 Smithe St, Vancouver, BC, V6B 4Z8
(604) 684-3336
Sales 20,214,855
SIC 7389 Business services, nec
Tom Uhreniuk
Dorothy Klug

D-U-N-S 25-229-8328   (HQ)
PERKINS + WILL ARCHITECTS CO
1220 Homer St, Vancouver, BC, V6B 2Y5
(604) 684-5446
Emp Here 1   *Sales* 12,317,060
SIC 8712 Architectural services
Peter Busby

D-U-N-S 25-998-5232   (SL)
**PINNACLE   INTERNATIONAL   MANAGE-
MENT INC**
*VANCOUVER   MARRIOTT   PINNACLE
DOWNTOWN*
911 Homer St Suite 300, Vancouver, BC, V6B
2W6
(604) 602-7747
Emp Here 250   *Sales* 23,917,000
SIC 7011 Hotels and motels
Michael Decotiis

D-U-N-S 25-267-6838   (SL)
PNI DIGITAL MEDIA ULC
(*Suby of* SYCAMORE PARTNERS MANAGE-
MENT, L.P.)
425 Carrall St Suite 100, Vancouver, BC, V6B
6E3
(604) 893-8955
Emp Here 350   *Sales* 64,600,550
SIC 7371 Custom computer programming ser-
vices
Cameron Lawrence

D-U-N-S 20-316-6756   (SL)
PUBLIC OUTREACH CONSULTANCY INC
207 Hastings St W Suite 1005, Vancouver,
BC, V6B 1H7
(604) 800-3730
Emp Here 503   *Sales* 153,455,743
SIC 7389 Business services, nec
John Finlay
Bryan Mckinnon

D-U-N-S 25-988-2934   (SL)
QUARTERDECK BREWING CO LTD
STEAMWORKS BREWING CO
601 Cordova St W, Vancouver, BC, V6B 1G1
(604) 689-9151
Emp Here 80   *Sales* 3,429,840
SIC 5812 Eating places
Eli Gershkovitch

▲ Public Company   ■ Public Company Family Member   **HQ** Headquarters   **BR** Branch   **SL** Single Location

Soren Rasmussen

D-U-N-S 20-299-2348   (SL)
RECYCLING COUNCIL OF BRITISH COLUMBIA
RCBC
119 Pender St W Suite 10, Vancouver, BC, V6B 1S5
(604) 683-6009
Emp Here 9   *Sales* 65,941,243
SIC 8999 Services, nec
  Lynn Bailey
  Brock Macdonalds
  Anna Rochelle

D-U-N-S 25-974-8507   (SL)
RELIC ENTERTAINMENT, INC
THQ CANADA
(*Suby of* SEGA SAMMY HOLDINGS INC.)
1040 Hamilton St Suite 400, Vancouver, BC, V6B 2R9
(604) 801-6577
Emp Here 47   *Sales* 10,050,997
SIC 7372 Prepackaged software
  Ron Moravek
  Roy Tessler
  James Kennedy
  Teri Manby

D-U-N-S 24-967-4685   (SL)
RHYTHM & HUES STUDIOS
(*Suby of* RHYTHM AND HUES, INC.)
401 Georgia St W Suite 500, Vancouver, BC, V6B 5A1
(604) 288-8745
Emp Here 91   *Sales* 8,113,833
SIC 7819 Services allied to motion pictures
  John Hughes
  Pauline Ts'o
  Keith Goldfarb
  Janice Taylor

D-U-N-S 24-567-3512   (SL)
RICHARDS BUELL SUTTON LLP
RBS LAWYERS
401 Georgia St W Suite 700, Vancouver, BC, V6B 5A1
(604) 682-3664
Emp Here 80   *Sales* 12,320,880
SIC 8111 Legal services
  Jeffrey Lowe
  Scott Macdonald
  Angela Spanjers

D-U-N-S 24-321-3894   (SL)
ROCKHAVEN RESOURCES LTD
510 Hastings St W Suite 1016, Vancouver, BC, V6B 1L8
(604) 688-2568
Emp Here 10   *Sales* 23,875,490
SIC 1041 Gold ores
  Matthew A. Turner
  Glenn R. Yeadon
  Larry Donaldson
  Ian J. Talbot
  Robert C. Carne
  Randy C. Turner
  R. Allan Doherty
  David G. Skoglund
  Bradley J. Shisler
  Bruce Youngman

D-U-N-S 20-552-9543   (HQ)
ROSEDALE ON ROBSON SUITE HOTEL (2018) INC
838 Hamilton St, Vancouver, BC, V6B 6A2
(604) 689-8033
Sales 16,401,000
SIC 6712 Bank holding companies
  Yin Kau Pang

D-U-N-S 24-246-9054   (HQ)
S.U.C.C.E.S.S. (ALSO KNOWN AS UNITED CHINESE COMMUNITY ENRICHMENT SERVICES SOCIETY)
S.U.C.C.E.S.S.
28 Pender St W, Vancouver, BC, V6B 1R6

(604) 684-1628
Emp Here 20   *Sales* 15,530,100
SIC 8399 Social services, nec
  William Siu
  Glenn Wong
  Grace Wong
  Jenny Wong
  Roger Wong
  Clarence Cheng
  Joseph Chu
  Herman Kan
  Kenneth Li
  Lawrence Woo

D-U-N-S 20-369-7933   (SL)
SAL MARKETING INC
IA PACIFIC MARKETING
(*Suby of* INDUSTRIELLE ALLIANCE, ASSURANCE ET SERVICES FINANCIERS INC)
2165 Broadway W, Vancouver, BC, V6B 5H6
(604) 737-3816
Emp Here 200   *Sales* 427,393,600
SIC 6351 Surety insurance
  Alnoor Jiwani
  Azmina Karim-Bondy
  Luc Samson

D-U-N-S 24-798-2093   (HQ)
SELECT WINE MERCHANTS LTD
SELECT WINE AND SPIRITS
1122 Mainland St Suite 470, Vancouver, BC, V6B 5L1
(604) 687-8199
Emp Here 30   *Sales* 55,852,020
SIC 5182 Wine and distilled beverages
  Pierre Doise
  Werner Schonberger
  Alan Langley

D-U-N-S 24-346-4075   (BR)
SIMON FRASER UNIVERSITY
SIMON FRASER UNIVERSITY BOOKSTORE
(*Suby of* SIMON FRASER UNIVERSITY)
555 Hastings St W Suite 17u, Vancouver, BC, V6B 4N5
(778) 782-5235
Emp Here 100
SIC 5942 Book stores
  Rudy Hoogey

D-U-N-S 20-557-6478   (BR)
SLAVE LAKE PULP CORPORATION
(*Suby of* WEST FRASER TIMBER CO. LTD)
858 Beatty St Suite 501, Vancouver, BC, V6B 1C1
(604) 895-2700
Emp Here 100
SIC 2611 Pulp mills
  Tyler Warman

D-U-N-S 20-296-3484   (SL)
SNAP HOME FINANCE CORP
538 Cambie St, Vancouver, BC, V6B 2N7
(866) 282-2384
Emp Here 60   *Sales* 14,057,280
SIC 8742 Management consulting services
  David Nickel

D-U-N-S 20-985-0713   (SL)
SOFTLANDING SOLUTIONS INC
555 Hastings St W Suite 1605, Vancouver, BC, V6B 4N6
(604) 633-1410
Emp Here 45   *Sales* 10,542,960
SIC 8748 Business consulting, nec
  Shaun Roberts
  Andrew Sobieski
  Izabella Sobieska
  Mahmood Jaffer
  Salma Jaffer

D-U-N-S 24-826-5287   (HQ)
STERN PARTNERS INC
(*Suby of* BELGRAVIA INVESTMENTS LIMITED)
650 Georgia St W Unit 2900, Vancouver, BC, V6B 4N8

(604) 681-8817
Sales 10,183,845
SIC 6211 Security brokers and dealers
  Ronald Stern
  Norm Drewlo
  Shamsh Kassam

D-U-N-S 24-265-6231   (SL)
STIGAN MEDIA INC
55 Water Street, Vancouver, BC, V6B 1A1
(778) 379-0888
Emp Here 49   *Sales* 10,374,476
SIC 7311 Advertising agencies
  Sandro Federico

D-U-N-S 25-504-4646   (SL)
STRATEGIC METALS LTD
510 Hastings St W Suite 1016, Vancouver, BC, V6B 1L8
(604) 687-2522
Emp Here 10   *Sales* 23,875,490
SIC 1081 Metal mining services
  W. Douglas Eaton
  Richard Drechsler
  Glenn R. Yeadon
  Larry Donaldson
  Ian Talbot
  Bruce A. Youngman
  Lee A. Groat
  Bruce J. Kenway
  Gordon Davis
  Ryan Schedler

D-U-N-S 24-778-2881   (HQ)
SUTTON GROUP REALTY SERVICES LTD
1080 Mainland St Suite 206, Vancouver, BC, V6B 2T4
(604) 568-1005
Emp Here 27   *Sales* 20,904,300
SIC 6794 Patent owners and lessors
  Scott Shaw
  Edmond Shung
  Lance Tracey

D-U-N-S 24-384-2973   (SL)
SWIFT POWER CORP
55 Water St Suite 608, Vancouver, BC, V6B 1A1
(604) 637-6393
Emp Here 20   *Sales* 10,393,100
SIC 4911 Electric services
  Alexi Zawadzki
  Ross Maclachlan
  David Turner

D-U-N-S 25-691-7980   (BR)
T & T SUPERMARKET INC
(*Suby of* LOBLAW COMPANIES LIMITED)
179 Keefer Pl, Vancouver, BC, V6B 6L4
(604) 899-8836
Emp Here 100
SIC 5411 Grocery stores
  Michael Chan

D-U-N-S 25-792-3560   (SL)
TEACH AWAY INC
896 Cambie St Suite 301, Vancouver, BC, V6B 2P6
(604) 628-1822
Emp Here 49   *Sales* 13,442,268
SIC 8741 Management services
  Rene Frey

D-U-N-S 20-558-7657   (SL)
TELIGENCE (CANADA) LTD
(*Suby of* TELIGENCE CORPORATION)
303 Pender St W Unit 300, Vancouver, BC, V6B 1T3
(604) 629-6055
Emp Here 250   *Sales* 28,050,750
SIC 8741 Management services
  Robert Madigan
  Cameron Sobolik
  Peter Gill
  Ivelina Vladimirova

D-U-N-S 20-539-6625   (HQ)
TELUS COMMUNICATIONS INC

TELUS BUSINESS SOLUTIONS
(*Suby of* TELUS CORPORATION)
510 West Georgia St 7th Fl, Vancouver, BC, V6B 0M3
(888) 493-2007
Emp Here 1,800   *Sales* 9,032,688,000
SIC 4899 Communication services, nec
  Darren Entwistle
  John Gossling
  Joe Natale
  Josh Blair
  John Manley
  William Mackinnon
  Stockwell Day

D-U-N-S 25-677-5016   (HQ)
TELUS CORPORATION
510 West Georgia St Fl 8, Vancouver, BC, V6B 0M3
(604) 697-8044
Emp Here 500   *Sales* 10,685,447,690
SIC 4899 Communication services, nec
  Darren Entwistle
  Josh Blair
  Doug French
  Eros Spadotto
  Francois Gratton
  Sandy Mcintosh
  Tony Geheran
  Jeffrey Puritt
  R.H. (Dick) Auchinleck
  Raymond T. Chan

D-U-N-S 24-952-3494   (SL)
TIDES CANADA INITIATIVES SOCIETY
163 Hastings St W Suite 400, Vancouver, BC, V6B 1H5
(604) 647-6611
Emp Here 33   *Sales* 13,114,662
SIC 8699 Membership organizations, nec
  Ross Mcmillan
  Elissa Beckett

D-U-N-S 20-801-2138   (HQ)
TOM LEE MUSIC CO. LTD
650 Georgia St W Suite 310, Vancouver, BC, V6B 4N7
(604) 685-2521
Emp Here 20   *Sales* 41,832,540
SIC 5736 Musical instrument stores
  Henry Lee

D-U-N-S 20-120-1683   (SL)
TRIALTO WINE GROUP LTD
1260 Hamilton St Suite 300, Vancouver, BC, V6B 2S8
(778) 331-8999
Emp Here 54   *Sales* 31,747,464
SIC 5182 Wine and distilled beverages
  Rick Toller
  Richard Ditmar
  Derrick Armstrong
  Jim Robinson

D-U-N-S 25-138-4962   (HQ)
TWINKLE ENTERPRISES LTD
308 Water St, Vancouver, BC, V6B 1B6

Sales 14,850,400
SIC 5199 Nondurable goods, nec
  Li-Fen Wang
  Chiang-Ho Lui

D-U-N-S 20-512-2240   (SL)
USTRI CANADA INC
QA LABS, DIV OF
1122 Mainland St Suite 470, Vancouver, BC, V6B 5L1

Emp Here 120   *Sales* 17,502,229
SIC 7371 Custom computer programming services
  Wolfgang Strigel
  Cecilia Furia Cesar

D-U-N-S 25-715-3197   (BR)
VANCITY COMMUNITY INVESTMENT BANK

(*Suby of* VANCOUVER CITY SAVINGS CREDIT UNION)
401 Hastings St W Suite 401, Vancouver, BC, V6B 1L5
(604) 708-7800
Emp Here 140
SIC 6021 National commercial banks
Linda Crompton

D-U-N-S 25-681-9830   (BR)
VANCOUVER COMMUNITY COLLEGE
CITY CENTRE CAMPUS
(*Suby of* VANCOUVER COMMUNITY COLLEGE)
250 Pender St W Suite 358, Vancouver, BC, V6B 1S9
(604) 443-8484
Emp Here 1,050
SIC 8221 Colleges and universities
Dale Dorn

D-U-N-S 25-734-0471   (SL)
VANCOUVER ENGLISH CENTRE INC
250 Smithe St, Vancouver, BC, V6B 1E7

Emp Here 75   *Sales* 12,031,950
SIC 8299 Schools and educational services, nec

D-U-N-S 24-824-5391   (HQ)
VANCOUVER FILM SCHOOL LIMITED
198 Hastings St W Suite 200, Vancouver, BC, V6B 1H2
(604) 685-5808
Emp Here 30   *Sales* 56,977,200
SIC 8299 Schools and educational services, nec
James Griffin
Richard Appleby
Marty Hasselbach

D-U-N-S 20-798-4790   (SL)
VANCOUVER HOCKEY LIMITED PARTNERSHIP
800 Griffiths Way, Vancouver, BC, V6B 6G1
(604) 899-4600
Emp Here 75   *Sales* 6,534,600
SIC 7941 Sports clubs, managers, and promoters
Stan Mccammon

D-U-N-S 20-865-7502   (HQ)
VANCOUVER PUBLIC LIBRARY FOUNDATION
350 Georgia St W, Vancouver, BC, V6B 6B1
(604) 331-3603
Emp Here 500   *Sales* 55,484,100
SIC 8231 Libraries
Terry Salman
Sally Warren

D-U-N-S 20-866-0167   (HQ)
VANCOUVER SYMPHONY SOCIETY
VANCOUVER SYMPHONY ORCHESTRA
843 Seymour St Suite 500, Vancouver, BC, V6B 3L4
(604) 684-9100
Sales 17,078,682
SIC 7929 Entertainers and entertainment groups
Fred Withers
Judith Korbin
Kelly Tweeddale
Diane Hodgins
Etienne Bruson
Debra Finlay
Michael Fish
Cathy Grant
Hein Poulus

D-U-N-S 20-947-2484   (SL)
VANCOUVER WHITECAPS FC L.P.
VANCOUVER WHITECAPS
375 Water St Suite 550, Vancouver, BC, V6B 5C6
(604) 669-9283
Emp Here 130   *Sales* 10,841,350
SIC 7941 Sports clubs, managers, and pro-

moters
Robert Lenarduzzi
Don Ford

D-U-N-S 25-537-2344   (HQ)
VERIS GOLD CORP
688 Hastings St W Suite 900, Vancouver, BC, V6B 1P1
(604) 688-9427
Sales 105,123,114
SIC 1081 Metal mining services
Francois Marland
Shaun Heinrichs
Graham Dickson
Cameron Paterson
Todd Johnson
Joanne Jobin
Graham Scott

D-U-N-S 20-322-7913   (SL)
VISIER SOLUTIONS INC
(*Suby of* VISIER, INC.)
858 Beatty St Suite 400, Vancouver, BC, V6B 1C1
(778) 331-6950
Emp Here 200   *Sales* 28,836,400
SIC 7371 Custom computer programming services
John Swartz
Ryan Wong
Fionna Song

D-U-N-S 25-328-5811   (SL)
WASSERMAN & PARTNERS ADVERTISING INC
1020 Mainland St Unit 160, Vancouver, BC, V6B 2T5
(604) 684-1111
Emp Here 50   *Sales* 10,586,200
SIC 7311 Advertising agencies
Alvin Wasserman
Andeen Pitt
Doug Conn
Tim Dundon

D-U-N-S 24-798-2705   (SL)
WEST COAST SIGHTSEEING LTD
200-110 Cambie St, Vancouver, BC, V6B 2M8
(604) 451-1600
Emp Here 150   *Sales* 11,290,800
SIC 4141 Local bus charter service
Robert Safrata

D-U-N-S 20-426-8163   (HQ)
WEST FRASER MILLS LTD
(*Suby of* WEST FRASER TIMBER CO. LTD)
858 Beatty St Suite 501, Vancouver, BC, V6B 1C1
(604) 895-2700
Emp Here 42   *Sales* 1,893,052,000
SIC 2421 Sawmills and planing mills, general
Henry Ketcham
Robert Phillips
Janice Rennie
Edward Seraphim
Martti Solin
Rodger Hutchinson
Harald Ludwig
Duncan Gibson
William Peters Ketcham
Clark Binkley

D-U-N-S 20-120-8675   (HQ)
WEST FRASER TIMBER CO. LTD
858 Beatty St Suite 501, Vancouver, BC, V6B 1C1
(604) 895-2700
Emp Here 295   *Sales* 4,638,068,036
SIC 5031 Lumber, plywood, and millwork
Edward Seraphim
Raymond Ferris
Sean Mclaren
Larry Gardner
Keith Carter
Brian Balkwill
Chuck Watkins
Chris Virostek

Christopher Mciver
James Gorman

D-U-N-S 25-326-5516   (HQ)
WESTCOAST ENGLISH LANGUAGE CENTER LIMITED
GLOBAL VILLAGE
888 Cambie St, Vancouver, BC, V6B 2P6
(604) 684-1010
Emp Here 1   *Sales* 13,214,190
SIC 8299 Schools and educational services, nec

D-U-N-S 24-826-7270   (HQ)
WESTERN CANADA WILDERNESS COMMITTEE
WILDERNESS COMMITTEE
341 Water St, Vancouver, BC, V6B 1B8
(604) 609-3752
Emp Here 20   *Sales* 11,888,996
SIC 8999 Services, nec
Kevin Bell
Jennifer Campagnolo
Paul Morgan
Joseph Foy
Mathew Jong
Heidi Sherwood
Ross Muirhead
Thomas Perry
Robert Broughton
Alice Eaton

D-U-N-S 20-609-8324   (SL)
WHITECAPS FOOTBALL CLUB LTD
375 Water St Suite 550, Vancouver, BC, V6B 5C6
(604) 669-9283
Emp Here 30   *Sales* 12,859,128
SIC 7941 Sports clubs, managers, and promoters
Robert Lenarduzzi

D-U-N-S 20-194-1643   (BR)
WOOD CANADA LIMITED
AMEC EARTH & EVIRONMENTAL DIVISION
(*Suby of* JOHN WOOD GROUP P.L.C.)
111 Dunsmuir St Suite 400, Vancouver, BC, V6B 5W3
(604) 664-4315
Emp Here 600
SIC 8711 Engineering services
Steve Toews

D-U-N-S 24-535-9138   (SL)
YALETOWN HOUSE SOCIETY
1099 Cambie St, Vancouver, BC, V6B 5A8
(604) 689-0022
Emp Here 120   *Sales* 8,199,120
SIC 8051 Skilled nursing care facilities
Carol Creighton
Jim Ferguson
Margaret Fraser
Ardis Julian
Terry Mcgauley
Doug Page
David Scammells

Vancouver, BC V6C

D-U-N-S 20-131-9619   (SL)
10SHEET SERVICES INC
BENCH
(*Suby of* BENCH ACCOUNTING, INC.)
717 Pender St W Unit 200, Vancouver, BC, V6C 1G9
(888) 760-1940
Emp Here 250   *Sales* 46,213,250
SIC 8721 Accounting, auditing, and bookkeeping
Ian Crosby
Adam Saint
Felicia Bochicchio
Emily Key
Gibson Turley

D-U-N-S 24-823-7794   (SL)
1987 THE TRAVEL GROUP LTD
TRAVEL GROUP, THE
890 Pender St W Suite 330, Vancouver, BC, V6C 1J9
(604) 681-6345
Emp Here 22   *Sales* 11,439,274
SIC 4724 Travel agencies
David Elmy

D-U-N-S 24-422-6614   (SL)
299 BURRARD HOTEL LIMITED PARTNERSHIP
FAIRMONT PACIFIC RIM
1038 Canada Pl, Vancouver, BC, V6C 0B9
(604) 695-5300
Emp Here 200   *Sales* 18,538,000
SIC 7011 Hotels and motels
Philip Barnes

D-U-N-S 24-760-6887   (SL)
801 WEST GEORGIA LTD
801 Georgia St W, Vancouver, BC, V6C 1P7
(604) 682-5566
Emp Here 100   *Sales* 9,489,900
SIC 7011 Hotels and motels
Bruce Langereis
Kenneth Henry J Bowden

D-U-N-S 20-585-2239   (SL)
885 PROFESSIONAL MANAGEMENT LIMITED PARTNERSHIP
885 Georgia St W Suite 900, Vancouver, BC, V6C 3H1
(604) 687-5700
Emp Here 124   *Sales* 13,749,368
SIC 8111 Legal services
Doug Howard
Alex Petrenko
David Buchanan

D-U-N-S 24-368-6453   (SL)
ABATTIS BIOCEUTICALS CORP
625 Howe St Suite 1200, Vancouver, BC, V6C 2T6

Emp Here 50   *Sales* 11,734,800
SIC 8731 Commercial physical research
Robert Abenante
Francesco Paolini
Patrick Mitchell
Peter Gordon
Cedric Wilson

D-U-N-S 20-425-5384   (SL)
ACGI SHIPPING INC
900 Hastings St W Suite 1100, Vancouver, BC, V6C 1E5
(604) 683-4221
Emp Here 52   *Sales* 27,038,284
SIC 4731 Freight transportation arrangement
Blake Pottinger
Erich Billung-Meyer
Cesare D'amico

D-U-N-S 25-408-7463   (HQ)
AFRICA OIL CORP
885 Georgia St W Suite 2000, Vancouver, BC, V6C 3E8
(604) 689-7842
Sales 10,919,420
SIC 1382 Oil and gas exploration services
Keith Hill
Paul Martinez
Mark Dingley
Tim Thomas
Ian Gibbs
John Vraig
Gary Guidry
Bryan Benitz
Andrew Bartlett
Kimberley Wood

D-U-N-S 24-329-3750   (SL)
AFTON OPERATING CORPORATION
(*Suby of* TECK RESOURCES LIMITED)
3300 Burrard St, Vancouver, BC, V6C 0B3

(604) 699-4000
Emp Here 150   *Sales* 38,366,100
SIC 1021 Copper ores
Robert Scott
Michel Filion
Ronald Millos
Karen Dunfee
Scott Wilson
John Gingell

D-U-N-S 24-334-1083   (SL)
ALIANZA MINERALS LTD
325 Howe St Suite 410, Vancouver, BC, V6C 1Z7
(604) 687-3520
Emp Here 50   *Sales* 10,206,500
SIC 1041 Gold ores
Jason Weber
Winnie Wong
Mark T. Brown
John Wilson
Marc G. Blythe
Craig Lindsay

D-U-N-S 24-338-6799   (HQ)
ALIO GOLD INC
700 West Pender St Suite 507, Vancouver, BC, V6C 1G8
(604) 682-4002
Sales 104,527,000
SIC 1041 Gold ores
Mark Backens
Ian Harcus
Markus Felderer
Bryan Coates
George Brack
Stephen Lang
Paula Rogers
Jose Alberto Vizquerra-Benavides
John Mansanti
Tim Baker

D-U-N-S 20-305-1073   (HQ)
AMERICAN HOTEL INCOME PROPERTIES REIT LP
AHIP
925 Georgia St W Suite 800, Vancouver, BC, V6C 3L2
(604) 630-3134
Sales 52,163,235
SIC 6798 Real estate investment trusts
John O'neill
Bruce Pittet
Anne Yu
Martin Pinsker
Jamie Kokoska
Robert F. O'neill
Tamara L. Lawson
W. Michael Murphy
Minaz B. Abji
Elizabeth Walters

D-U-N-S 25-167-3067   (SL)
AMERIGO RESOURCES LTD
355 Burrard St Suite 1260, Vancouver, BC, V6C 2G8
(604) 681-2802
Emp Here 299   *Sales* 136,833,000
SIC 1021 Copper ores
Rob Henderson
Aurora Davidson
Kimberly Thomas
Klaus Zeitler
Robert Gayton
Sidney Robinson
George Ireland
Alberto Salas

D-U-N-S 25-385-2131   (HQ)
ANGIOTECH PHARMACEUTICALS, INC
355 Burrard St Suite 1100, Vancouver, BC, V6C 2G8
(604) 221-7676
Emp Here 7   *Sales* 278,367,848
SIC 8731 Commercial physical research
John R. Barr
Victor Diaz

Dan Sutherby
Janet Hart
Jeffrey D. Goldberg
Kurt M. Cellar
Bradley S. Karro
Donald M. Casey
Omar Vaishnavi
Richard A. Packer

D-U-N-S 24-378-4282   (SL)
ARCO RESOURCES CORP
570 Granville St Suite 1200, Vancouver, BC, V6C 3P1
(604) 689-8336
Emp Here 50   *Sales* 10,206,500
SIC 1081 Metal mining services
Warren Mcintyre
Simon Anderson
Jeff Sheremeta
Robert Mcmorran
John Sutherland

D-U-N-S 24-858-3200   (SL)
ARIZONA SILVER EXPLORATION INC
750 West Pender St Suite 804, Vancouver, BC, V6C 2T7
(604) 833-4278
Emp Here 500   *Sales* 1,193,774,500
SIC 1041 Gold ores
Greg Hahn
Dong H Shim
Mike Stark
David Vincent
Scott Hean
Joe Charland

D-U-N-S 20-102-7687   (HQ)
ARROW TRANSPORTATION SYSTEMS INC
999 Hastings St W Suite 1300, Vancouver, BC, V6C 2W2
(604) 324-1333
Emp Here 35   *Sales* 102,853,000
SIC 4213 Trucking, except local
Jack Charles Jr
Archie Campbell
Brian Charles

D-U-N-S 25-188-4388   (SL)
ATICO MINING CORPORATION
543 Granville St Unit 501, Vancouver, BC, V6C 1X8
(604) 633-9022
Emp Here 593   *Sales* 54,599,946
SIC 1021 Copper ores
Fernando E. Ganoza
Luis D. Ganoza
Jorge Ganoza
Michael Winn
Mario Szotlender
Luis F. Saenz
Bill Tsang
Joseph A. Salas

D-U-N-S 20-174-0607   (SL)
ATIMI SOFTWARE INC
800 Pender St W Suite 800, Vancouver, BC, V6C 2V6
(778) 372-2800
Emp Here 50   *Sales* 10,692,550
SIC 7372 Prepackaged software
Steven Gully

D-U-N-S 24-881-3164   (SL)
ATLATSA RESOURCES CORPORATION
666 Burrard St Suite 1700, Vancouver, BC, V6C 2X8
(604) 631-1300
Emp Here 3,390   *Sales* 91,297,896
SIC 1081 Metal mining services
Harold Motaung
Boipelo Lekubo
Joel Kesler
Bava Reddy
Tumelo Motsisi
Andile Mabizela
Fikile Tebogo De Buck
Colin Wayne Clarke

D-U-N-S 24-424-4976   (HQ)
AURCANA CORPORATION
789 Pender St W Suite 850, Vancouver, BC, V6C 1H2
(604) 331-9333
Emp Here 7   *Sales* 22,252,338
SIC 1021 Copper ores
Kevin Drover
Kevin Francis
Donna Moroney
Salvador Huerta
Brian Briggs
Jose Manuel Borquez
Jose Manuel
Michael Gross
Dave Kaplan
Elliot Rothstein

D-U-N-S 20-575-2322   (HQ)
AVINO SILVER & GOLD MINES LTD
570 Granville St Suite 900, Vancouver, BC, V6C 3P1
(604) 682-3701
Sales 34,116,000
SIC 1044 Silver ores
David Wolfin
Gary Robertson
Dorothy Chin
Nathan Harte
Carlos Rodriguez
Peter Latta
Jasman Yee
Peter Bojtos
Ronald Andrews

D-U-N-S 24-206-8182   (BR)
BANK OF NOVA SCOTIA, THE
SCOTIA BANK
(*Suby of* BANK OF NOVA SCOTIA, THE)
409 Granville St Unit 700, Vancouver, BC, V6C 1T2
(604) 630-4000
Emp Here 80
SIC 6021 National commercial banks
Linda Salminen

D-U-N-S 25-297-0918   (BR)
BANK OF NOVA SCOTIA, THE
SCOTIABANK
(*Suby of* BANK OF NOVA SCOTIA, THE)
815 Hastings St W Suite 300, Vancouver, BC, V6C 1B4

Emp Here 100
SIC 6021 National commercial banks
Brent Diewold

D-U-N-S 24-672-5287   (BR)
BDO CANADA LIMITED
BDO DUNWOODY
(*Suby of* BDO CANADA LIMITED)
925 Georgia St W Suite 600, Vancouver, BC, V6C 3L2
(604) 688-5421
Emp Here 150
SIC 8721 Accounting, auditing, and bookkeeping
Nancy Grant

D-U-N-S 24-672-4645   (BR)
BDO CANADA LLP
VANCOUVER ACCOUNTING
(*Suby of* BDO CANADA LLP)
925 Georgia St W Suite 600, Vancouver, BC, V6C 3L2
(604) 688-5421
Emp Here 200
SIC 8721 Accounting, auditing, and bookkeeping
David Mceown

D-U-N-S 24-764-3369   (SL)
BLUESTONE RESOURCES INC
800 Pender St W Unit 1020, Vancouver, BC, V6C 2V6
(604) 646-4534
Emp Here 8   *Sales* 19,100,392
SIC 1041 Gold ores

Darren Klinck
John Robins
David Gunning
Stephen Williams
David Cass
Jeff Reinson
Peter Hemstead
Penny Johnson
Zara Boldt
Leo Hathaway

D-U-N-S 24-387-7821   (HQ)
BONTERRA RESOURCES INC
200 Burrard St Suite 1680, Vancouver, BC, V6C 3L6
(604) 678-5308
Sales 11,937,745
SIC 1041 Gold ores
Navjit Dhaliwal
Dale Ginn
Peter A Ball
Joseph Meager
Greg Gibson
Robert Gagnon
Allan J Folk
Richard Boulay
Tina Ouellette

D-U-N-S 25-106-8060   (BR)
BORDEN LADNER GERVAIS LLP
BLG
(*Suby of* BORDEN LADNER GERVAIS LLP)
200 Burrard St Suite 1200, Vancouver, BC, V6C 3L6
(604) 687-5744
Emp Here 350
SIC 8111 Legal services

D-U-N-S 25-731-1472   (SL)
BOSA CONSTRUCTION INC
(*Suby of* BOSA ENTERPRISE CORPORATION)
838 Hastings St W Unit 1100, Vancouver, BC, V6C 0A6
(604) 299-1363
Emp Here 200   *Sales* 54,188,400
SIC 1522 Residential construction, nec
Robert Bosa
Colin Bosa

D-U-N-S 24-324-3636   (HQ)
BOSA ENTERPRISE CORPORATION
838 Hastings St W Suite 1100, Vancouver, BC, V6C 0A6
(604) 299-1363
Emp Here 1   *Sales* 109,652,700
SIC 6712 Bank holding companies
Robert Bosa

D-U-N-S 25-533-8659   (HQ)
BOSA PROPERTIES INC
838 Hastings St W Suite 1201, Vancouver, BC, V6C 0A6
(604) 299-1363
Emp Here 10   *Sales* 159,404,760
SIC 6733 Trusts, nec
Colin Bosa
Robert Bosa
Dale Bosa

D-U-N-S 24-129-7162   (BR)
BOSA PROPERTIES INC
(*Suby of* BOSA PROPERTIES INC)
838 W Hastings St, Vancouver, BC, V6C 2X1
(604) 412-0313
Emp Here 100
SIC 6531 Real estate agents and managers
Doug Watson

D-U-N-S 20-382-9754   (SL)
BRITISH COLUMBIA COLLEGE OF NURSING PROFESSIONALS
200 Granville St Suite 900, Vancouver, BC, V6C 1S4
(604) 742-6200
Emp Here 140   *Sales* 32,775,540
SIC 8621 Professional organizations

Cynthia Johansen

D-U-N-S 24-033-4698   (HQ)
BRITISH COLUMBIA CORPS OF COMMISSIONAIRES
COMMISSIONAIRES BC
595 Howe St Unit 801, Vancouver, BC, V6C
2T5
(604) 646-3330
Emp Here 1   *Sales* 42,000,000
SIC 7381 Detective and armored car services
Allen F. Batchelar
Darrell Dean

D-U-N-S 24-958-1398   (HQ)
BROADRIDGE SOFTWARE LIMITED
BROADRIDGE FINANCIAL SOLUTION
(*Suby of* BROADRIDGE FINANCIAL SOLUTIONS, INC.)
510 Burrard St Suite 600, Vancouver, BC, V6C
3A8
(604) 687-2133
Emp Here 65   *Sales* 12,513,525
SIC 7374 Data processing and preparation
Kirk Delis
Michael Dignam
Adam Amsterdam

D-U-N-S 20-055-0353   (SL)
CAMROVA RESOURCES INC
890 W Pender Suite 600, Vancouver, BC, V6C
1J9
(604) 685-2323
Emp Here 506   *Sales* 674,453
SIC 1481 NonMetallic mineral services
C. Thomas Ogryzlo
David Dreisinger
Kris Misir
Wolf Seidler
Peter M. Clausi

D-U-N-S 24-371-4813   (SL)
CANADA PLACE CORPORATION
CANADA PLACE
(*Suby of* GOVERNMENT OF CANADA)
999 Canada Pl Suite 100, Vancouver, BC,
V6C 3E1
(604) 775-7200
Emp Here 49   *Sales* 13,937,413
SIC 6512 Nonresidential building operators
Mike Shardlow
Robin Wilson
Andrew Mann

D-U-N-S 25-281-4454   (BR)
CANADIAN CORPS OF COMMISSIONAIRES NATIONAL OFFICE, THE
BC CORPS OF COMMISSIONAIRES
(*Suby of* CANADIAN CORPS OF COMMISSIONAIRES NATIONAL OFFICE, THE)
595 Howe St Suite 801, Vancouver, BC, V6C
2T5
(604) 646-3330
Emp Here 650
SIC 7381 Detective and armored car services
Ken Walker

D-U-N-S 20-349-4047   (HQ)
CANADIAN DEVELOPMENT CONSULTANTS INTERNATIONAL INC
CDCI
541 Howe St Unit 200, Vancouver, BC, V6C
2C2
(604) 633-1849
Emp Here 30   *Sales* 14,935,060
SIC 8732 Commercial nonphysical research
Anthony Brace
Michael Brace

D-U-N-S 24-750-5282   (BR)
CANADIAN WESTERN BANK
(*Suby of* CANADIAN WESTERN BANK)
666 Burrard St 22nd Fl, Vancouver, BC, V6C
2X8
(604) 669-0081
Emp Here 500
SIC 6021 National commercial banks
Kathy Smith

D-U-N-S 20-429-6800   (SL)
CGL-GRS SWISS CANADIAN GEM LAB INC
409 Granville St Suite 510, Vancouver, BC,
V6C 1T2
(604) 687-0091
Emp Here 47   *Sales* 10,355,416
SIC 8734 Testing laboratories
Branko Deljanin

D-U-N-S 24-930-6390   (SL)
COAST MOUNTAIN GEOLOGICAL LTD
625 Howe St Suite 488, Vancouver, BC, V6C
2T6
(604) 681-0209
Emp Here 40   *Sales* 12,219,200
SIC 8999 Services, nec
Gary Schellenberg
Chris Basil

D-U-N-S 20-804-4156   (HQ)
COLLIERS MACAULAY NICOLLS INC
COLLIERS INTERNATIONAL CANADA
(*Suby of* COLLIERS INTERNATIONAL GROUP INC)
200 Granville St Unit 19, Vancouver, BC, V6C
1S4
(604) 681-4111
Emp Here 100   *Sales* 1,419,868,800
SIC 6531 Real estate agents and managers
David Bowden
Scott Addison
Lex Perry

D-U-N-S 25-832-0209   (SL)
COLUMBUS LINE CANADA INC
HAMBURGSUD
900 Hastings St W Suite 600, Vancouver, BC,
V6C 1E5

Emp Here 49   *Sales* 13,433,448
SIC 5411 Grocery stores
Debrah Bateman

D-U-N-S 24-297-8760   (SL)
COMEX FOOD PRODUCTION INC
LA TAQUERIA PINCHE TACO SHOP
586 Hornby St, Vancouver, BC, V6C 2E7
(604) 971-4745
Emp Here 130   *Sales* 5,917,470
SIC 5812 Eating places
Marcelo Ramirez

D-U-N-S 20-153-2392   (HQ)
CONSEJO DE PROMOCION TURISTICA DE MEXICO S.A. DE C.A.
MEXICO TOURISM BOARD
999 Hastings St W Suite 1110, Vancouver,
BC, V6C 2W2

Emp Here 1   *Sales* 15,273,446
SIC 7389 Business services, nec
Salvador Dominguez Diaz

D-U-N-S 25-385-2024   (SL)
CONTINENTAL MINERALS CORPORATION
(*Suby of* JINCHUAN GROUP CO., LTD.)
800 Pender St W Suite 1020, Vancouver, BC,
V6C 2V6
(604) 684-6365
Emp Here 100   *Sales* 238,754,900
SIC 1081 Metal mining services
Gerald S. Panneton
David J. Copeland
Marchand Snyman

D-U-N-S 24-357-4675   (HQ)
COPPER MOUNTAIN MINING CORPORATION
700 Pender St W Suite 1700, Vancouver, BC,
V6C 1G8
(604) 682-2992
Emp Here 50   *Sales* 224,412,596
SIC 1021 Copper ores
Gilmour Clausen
Peter Holbek
Richard Klue
Letitia Wong

Lance Newman
Rodney A. (Rod) Shier
Don Strickland
James C. (Jim) O'rourke
Bruce Aunger
Al Cloke

D-U-N-S 24-696-7442   (SL)
CORAL GOLD RESOURCES LTD
570 Granville St Suite 900, Vancouver, BC,
V6C 3P1
(604) 682-3701
Emp Here 10   *Sales* 23,875,490
SIC 1081 Metal mining services
David Wolfin
Malcolm Davidson
Dorothy Chin
Ron Andrews
Gary Robertson
Andrew Kaplan

D-U-N-S 24-358-0755   (HQ)
CORO MINING CORP
625 Howe St Suite 1280, Vancouver, BC, V6C
2T6
(604) 682-5546
Sales 97,889,509
SIC 1021 Copper ores
Luis Albano Tondo
Sergio L. Rivera
Nicholas Bias
Leonardo Araya Muoz
Colin Kinley
Petra Decher
Tim Petterson
Michael Haworth
Alan Stephens

D-U-N-S 24-313-7838   (HQ)
CRH MEDICAL CORPORATION
999 Canada Pl Suite 578, Vancouver, BC,
V6C 3E1
(604) 633-1440
Sales 112,749,380
SIC 3841 Surgical and medical instruments
Edward Wright
Richard Bear
Mitchel Guttenplan
Anthony F. Holler
David A. Johnson
Todd Patrick
Ian Webb

D-U-N-S 20-265-0263   (SL)
CURALEAF HOLDINGS, INC
666 Burrard St Suite 1700, Vancouver, BC,
V6C 2X8
(604) 218-4766
Emp Here 1   *Sales* 77,057,000
SIC 1081 Metal mining services
Joseph Lusardi
Matthew Harrell
Keisha Brice
Gretchen Mccarthy
Greg Schaan
Peter Clateman
Jessie Kater
Chris Melillo
Robert Winnicki
Ed Conklin

D-U-N-S 25-229-7866   (SL)
CYBERLINK PACIFIC TELECOMMUNICATIONS LIMITED
888 Dunsmuir St Suite 868, Vancouver, BC,
V6C 3K4
(604) 708-9688
Emp Here 140   *Sales* 31,986,080
SIC 4899 Communication services, nec
Nicholas J L Tominson
Keith Ross Harisson
Virginia W M Lam
Mary Y Ng
David Tat Wai Wong

D-U-N-S 24-163-3882   (HQ)
DAVIS LLP

666 Burrard St Suite 2800, Vancouver, BC,
V6C 2Z7
(604) 687-9444
Emp Here 1   *Sales* 82,350,400
SIC 8111 Legal services
Paul R. Albi
Warren H. Downs
P. Anthony Mcarthur
Mark A. Schmidt

D-U-N-S 24-151-6780   (HQ)
DAVIS MANAGEMENT LTD
DAVIS AND COMPANY
666 Burrard St Suite 2800, Vancouver, BC,
V6C 2Z7
(604) 687-9444
Sales 49,910,400
SIC 8741 Management services
Paul Albi
P. Anthony Mcarthur

D-U-N-S 24-931-5011   (SL)
DEANS KNIGHT CAPITAL MANAGEMENT LTD
999 Hastings St W Suite 730, Vancouver, BC,
V6C 2W2
(604) 669-0212
Emp Here 15   *Sales* 10,450,155
SIC 6722 Management investment, open-end
Wayne Deans
Doug Knight
Craig Langdon

D-U-N-S 24-837-5164   (BR)
DENTONS CANADA LLP
(*Suby of* DENTONS CANADA LLP)
250 Howe St Suite 2000, Vancouver, BC, V6C
3R8
(604) 687-4460
Emp Here 125
SIC 8111 Legal services
Lori Mathison

D-U-N-S 24-996-4370   (SL)
DIVERSIFIED ROYALTY CORP
510 Burrard St Suite 902, Vancouver, BC, V6C
3A8
(604) 235-3146
Emp Here 50   *Sales* 20,248,146
SIC 4953 Refuse systems
Sean Morrison
Lawrence Haber
Greg Gutmanis
Lawrence Haber
Johnny Ciampi
Paula Rogers
Anita Anand
Garry Herdler
Lorraine Mclachlan

D-U-N-S 24-824-6563   (SL)
EASTFIELD RESOURCES LTD
325 Howe St Suite 110, Vancouver, BC, V6C
1Z7
(604) 681-7913
Emp Here 50   *Sales* 10,206,500
SIC 1081 Metal mining services
William Morton
David Douglas
Glen Garratt
Don Sharp
Paul Way
Al Scott

D-U-N-S 24-938-4421   (HQ)
ELDORADO GOLD CORPORATION
ELD
550 Burrard St 1188 Bentall 5, Vancouver, BC,
V6C 2B5
(604) 687-4018
Emp Here 358   *Sales* 459,016,000
SIC 1041 Gold ores
George Burns
Philip Yee
Paul Skayman
Timothy Garvin
Jason Cho
Shane Williams

Cara Allaway
Peter Lewis
Andor Lips
Lisa Ower

D-U-N-S 20-635-7803   (HQ)
EMX ROYALTY CORPORATION
543 Granville St Suite 501, Vancouver, BC,
V6C 1X8
(604) 688-6390
Sales 16,111,251
SIC 1481 NonMetallic mineral services
David M. Cole
Lori Pavle
Scott Close
Jan Steiert
Christina Cepeliauskas
Eric Jensen
Thomas G. Mair
Jefferey C. Edelen
Michael D Winn
Brian E Bayley

D-U-N-S 25-747-7836   (HQ)
ENERGOLD DRILLING CORP
543 Granville St Suite 1100, Vancouver,
V6C 1X8
(604) 681-9501
Emp Here 50   Sales 63,740,458
SIC 1081 Metal mining services
Frederick W. Davidson
Jerry C Huang
James H. Coleman
Michael J. Beley
Wayne D. Lenton
Mark Corra
Alastair Mcbain
Richard Thomas
Nicols F Rodrigo
Brian Bertram

D-U-N-S 24-366-8485   (HQ)
EQUINOX GOLD CORP
700 West Pender St Suite 1501, Vancouver,
BC, V6C 1G8
(604) 558-0560
Sales 30,159,000
SIC 1021 Copper ores
Christian Milau
Gregory D. Smith
Jim Currie
Peter J. Hardie
Scott Heffernan
Sebastian D'amici
Rhylin Bailie
Kevin Scott
Kylie Dickson
Ross J. Beaty

D-U-N-S 20-369-1142   (HQ)
ERO COPPER CORP
625 Howe St Suite 1050, Vancouver, BC,
2T6
(604) 449-9244
Sales 233,105,000
SIC 1021 Copper ores
David Strang
Christopher Noel Dunn
Michal Romanowski
Pablo Mejia-Herrera
Jonathan Singh
Anthea Bath
Makko Defilippo
Deepk Hundal
Matthew Wubs
John Wright

D-U-N-S 24-888-1476   (HQ)
EUROMAX RESOURCES LTD
595 Howe St 10 Fl, Vancouver, BC, V6C 2T5
(604) 669-5999
Emp Here 12   Sales 11,671,750
SIC 1081 Metal mining services
Varshan Gokool
Patrick Forward
Nikola Gulev
Tim Morgan-Wynne

Martyn Konig
Raymond Threlkeld
James Burke
Nicolas Treand
Ivan Vutov

D-U-N-S 24-930-3686   (BR)
FAIRMONT HOTELS & RESORTS INC
(Suby of ACCOR)
900 Canada Pl, Vancouver, BC, V6C 3L5
(604) 691-1991
Emp Here 412
SIC 7011 Hotels and motels
Francis Parkinson

D-U-N-S 24-866-7701   (BR)
FAIRMONT HOTELS & RESORTS INC
FAIRMONT HOTEL VANCOUVER, THE
(Suby of ACCOR)
900 Georgia St W, Vancouver, BC, V6C 2W6
(604) 684-3131
Emp Here 500
SIC 7011 Hotels and motels
Michael Pye

D-U-N-S 24-030-5185   (BR)
FASKEN MARTINEAU DUMOULIN LLP
(Suby of FASKEN MARTINEAU DUMOULIN
LLP)
550 Burrard St Suite 2900, Vancouver, BC,
V6C 0A3
(604) 631-3131
Emp Here 140
SIC 8111 Legal services
William Westeringh

D-U-N-S 20-917-9076   (BR)
FINANCIERE BANQUE NATIONALE INC
NATIONAL BANK FINANCIAL
(Suby of FINANCIERE BANQUE NATIONALE
INC)
666 Burrard St Suite 100, Vancouver, BC,
2X8
(604) 623-6777
Emp Here 110
SIC 6211 Security brokers and dealers
John Clemens

D-U-N-S 25-165-3361   (SL)
FIRST BAUXITE CORPORATION
595 Howe St Suite 206, Vancouver, BC, V6C
2T5

Emp Here 5   Sales 11,937,745
SIC 1081 Metal mining services
Alan Roughead
William White
Larry Washow
Lee A. Graber
Mason Hills

D-U-N-S 24-860-8416   (HQ)
FIRST MAJESTIC SILVER CORP
925 Georgia St W Suite 1800, Vancouver,
V6C 3L2
(604) 688-3033
Emp Here 20   Sales 300,929,000
SIC 1044 Silver ores
Keith Neumeyer
Raymond Polman
Connie Lillico
Douglas Penrose
Robert Mccallum
David Shaw
Marjorie Co

D-U-N-S 25-504-9546   (HQ)
FIRST QUANTUM MINERALS LTD
543 Granville St 14th Fl, Vancouver, BC, V6C
1X8
(604) 688-6577
Emp Here 9   Sales 3,966,000,000
SIC 1021 Copper ores
Philip K. R. Pascall
Clive Newall
Hannes Meyer
Peter St. George
Andrew Adams

Paul Brunner
Robert Harding
Kathleen Hogenson
Simon Scott

D-U-N-S 25-406-5824   (SL)
FORAN MINING CORPORATION
409 Granville St Suite 904, Vancouver, BC,
V6C 1T2
(604) 488-0008
Emp Here 5   Sales 11,937,745
SIC 1081 Metal mining services
Patrick Soares
Tim Thiessen
Roger March
Darren Morcombe
Sharon Dowdall
Maurice Tagami
David Petroff
Mario Grossi

D-U-N-S 25-687-8000   (HQ)
FORTUNA SILVER MINES INC
200 Burrard St Suite 650, Vancouver, BC, V6C
3L6
(604) 484-4085
Sales 263,296,000
SIC 1044 Silver ores
Jorge Ganoza
Simon Ridgway
Manuel Ruiz-Conejo
Jose Pacora
David Volkert
Eric Chapman
Gordon Jang
Mario Szotlender
David Farrell
David Laing

D-U-N-S 20-992-2988   (BR)
FOUR SEASONS HOTELS LIMITED
FOUR SEASONS HOTEL VANCOUVER,
THE
(Suby of CASCADE INVESTMENT, L.L.C.)
791 Georgia St W, Vancouver, BC, V6C 2T4
(604) 689-9333
Emp Here 450
SIC 7011 Hotels and motels
Jason Waterlow

D-U-N-S 25-092-3575   (HQ)
FULCRUM CAPITAL PARTNERS INC
885 Georgia St W Suite 1020, Vancouver,
V6C 3E8
(604) 631-8088
Emp Here 5   Sales 11,237,200
SIC 6159 Miscellaneous business credit insti-
tutions
Neil Johansen
John Philip
Michael Berkson
Greg Collings
Paul Eldridge
Paul Rowe
Lindsay Wilson
Johan Lemmer

D-U-N-S 24-952-6695   (SL)
FUSION PROJECT MANAGEMENT LTD
850 Hastings St W Suite 800, Vancouver, BC,
V6C 1E1
(604) 629-0469
Emp Here 46   Sales 14,667,974
SIC 1521 Single-family housing construction
Nicholas E. Boyd

D-U-N-S 20-575-6211   (SL)
**GE CANADA EQUIPMENT FINANCING AND
CAPITALIST FUNDS**
400 Burrard St Suite 1050, Vancouver, BC,
V6C 3A6

Emp Here 15   Sales 15,523,215
SIC 6351 Surety insurance
Dean Shillington

D-U-N-S 24-761-6357   (HQ)
GENESIS METALS CORP

409 Granville St Suite 1500, Vancouver, BC,
V6C 1T2
(604) 602-1440
Sales 14,006,100
SIC 1041 Gold ores
Brian Groves
Jeff Sundar
Shawn Khunkhun
Adrian Fleming
John Florek
Robert Scott
Keenan Hohol
Andre Liboiron

D-U-N-S 25-067-6814   (SL)
**GLOBAL MINING MANAGEMENT CORPO-
RATION**
999 Canada Pl Suite 654, Vancouver, BC,
V6C 3E1
(604) 689-8765
Emp Here 40   Sales 10,973,280
SIC 8741 Management services
Greg Scenton

D-U-N-S 24-312-9033   (HQ)
GOLD STANDARD VENTURES CORP
815 Hastings St W Suite 610, Vancouver, BC,
V6C 1B4
(604) 687-2766
Sales 23,875,490
SIC 1041 Gold ores
Jonathan Awde
Glenn Kumoi
Michael Waldkirch
Don Harris
Mark Laffoon
Steven Koehler
William Threlkeld
Jamie Strauss
Bruce Mcleod
Robert Mcleod

D-U-N-S 24-980-3982   (HQ)
GOLDCORP CANADA LTD
MUSSELWHITE MINES
(Suby of NEWMONT GOLDCORP CORPO-
RATION)
666 Burrard St Suite 3400, Vancouver, BC,
V6C 2X8
(604) 696-3000
Emp Here 40   Sales 5,491,362,700
SIC 1041 Gold ores
Steven P Reid
Lindsay Hall

D-U-N-S 25-366-2670   (HQ)
**GOLDEN ARROW RESOURCES CORPO-
RATION**
837 Hastings St W Unit 312, Vancouver, BC,
V6C 3N6
(604) 687-1828
Sales 11,937,745
SIC 1081 Metal mining services
Joseph Grosso
Brian Mcewen
Nikolaos Cacos
Connie Norman
David Terry
John B. Gammon
Louis P. Salley
Alf Hills
Darren C. Urquhart

D-U-N-S 20-188-7754   (SL)
GOLDEN QUEEN MINING CO. LTD
580 Hornby St Suite 880, Vancouver, BC, V6C
3B6
(604) 417-7952
Emp Here 223   Sales 58,403,000
SIC 1041 Gold ores
Guy Le Bel
Brenda Dayton
Paul Blythe
Bryan Coates
Bernard Guarnera

D-U-N-S 20-652-8692   (SL)

GOLDEN REIGN RESOURCES LTD
595 Howe St Suite 501, Vancouver, BC, V6C
2T5
(604) 685-4655
Emp Here 10   *Sales* 23,875,490
SIC 1081 Metal mining services
Kevin Bullock
Kim Evans
Zoran Pudar
Akiba Leisman
Abraham Jonker
Rael Lipson
John Conlon
William Meyer
Len Dennis
Michele Pillon

D-U-N-S 20-304-4912   (HQ)
GOVIEX URANIUM INC
999 Canada Pl Suite 654, Vancouver, BC,
V6C 3E1
(604) 681-5529
Sales 14,067,570
SIC 1094 Uranium-radium-vanadium ores
Daniel Major
Govind Friedland
Lei Wang
Matthew Lechtzier
Christopher Wallace
Robert Hanson
Benoit La Salle
Anthony Abbenante
David Cates

D-U-N-S 25-388-7491   (BR)
GOWLING WLG (CANADA) LLP
GOWLINGS
(*Suby of* GOWLING WLG (CANADA) LLP)
550 Burrard St Suite 2300, Vancouver, BC,
V6C 2B5
(604) 683-6498
Emp Here 100
SIC 8111 Legal services
Shane Sturkoff

D-U-N-S 24-461-9193   (HQ)
GREAT PACIFIC ENTERPRISES INC
COROPLAST DIV
(*Suby of* PATTISON, JIM GROUP INC)
1067 Cordova St W Unit 1800, Vancouver, BC,
V6C 1C7
(604) 688-6764
Emp Here 5   *Sales* 525,386,400
SIC 3081 Unsupported plastics film and sheet
James Pattison
Nick Demarais
Michael Korenberg
Rod Bergen
David Bell
Bryan Barrington Foote

D-U-N-S 25-484-3162   (HQ)
GREAT PANTHER MINING LIMITED
200 Granville St Suite 1330, Vancouver, BC,
V6C 1S4
(604) 608-1766
Sales 59,434,000
SIC 1081 Metal mining services
James Bannantine
Matthew Wunder
Jim Zadra
Robert W. Garnett
Nicole Sheri Adshead-Bell
Robert A. Archer
Peter John Jennings
Kenneth W. Major
Jeffrey R. Mason
W. J. Mullin

D-U-N-S 20-956-2883   (SL)
**GREATER VANCOUVER CONVENTION
AND VISITORS BUREAU**
TOURISM VANCOUVER
200 Burrard St Suite 210, Vancouver, BC, V6C
3L6
(604) 682-2222
Emp Here 75   *Sales* 50,168,100

SIC 7389 Business services, nec
Rick Antonson
John Sandor
Ken Cretney
Steve Mcnally
Patti Smolen
Gordon Johnson
Dennis Skulsky
Robert Lindsay
Nicholas Gandossi
Ted Lee

D-U-N-S 20-369-1097   (HQ)
GROUP ELEVEN RESOURCES CORP
400 Burrard St Suite 1050, Vancouver, BC,
V6C 3A6
(604) 630-8839
Emp Here 5   *Sales* 47,750,980
SIC 1031 Lead and zinc ores
Bart Jaworski
John P. Barry
Spiros Cacos
Sheryl Dhillon
Shaun Heinrichs
David Furlong
Daniel Macinnis
Alessandro Bitelli
Brendan Cahill

D-U-N-S 20-562-8386   (SL)
GVP HOLDIGS INC
200 Burrard St Suite 1200, Vancouver, BC,
V6C 3L6
(604) 525-3900
Emp Here 500
SIC 6712 Bank holding companies
Garry Peters

D-U-N-S 25-716-2701   (HQ)
H.I.S. CANADA INC
(*Suby of* H.I.S. CO., LTD.)
636 Hornby St, Vancouver, BC, V6C 2G2
(604) 685-3524
Emp Here 30   *Sales* 20,798,680
SIC 4724 Travel agencies
Hideo Hatano
Hikaru Wada

D-U-N-S 24-329-2443   (SL)
HANWEI ENERGY SERVICES CORP
595 Howe St Suite 902, Vancouver, BC, V6C
2T5
(604) 685-2239
Emp Here 123   *Sales* 5,690,037
SIC 2679 Converted paper products, nec
Fulai Lang
Graham R. Kwan
Yucai (Rick) Huang
Joanne Yan
William G. Paine
S. Randall Smallbone
Malcolm Clay

D-U-N-S 24-128-8997   (BR)
HARBOUR AIR LTD
(*Suby of* HARBOUR AIR LTD)
1055 Canada Pl Unit 1, Vancouver, BC, V6C
0C3
(604) 233-3501
Emp Here 350
SIC 4512 Air transportation, scheduled
Alicia Schwarz

D-U-N-S 24-369-0716   (HQ)
HAYWOOD SECURITIES INC
(*Suby of* HAYWOOD CAPITAL CORPORA-
TION)
200 Burrard St Suite 700, Vancouver, BC, V6C
3L6
(604) 697-7100
Emp Here 195   *Sales* 231,895,500
SIC 6211 Security brokers and dealers
John Tognetti
Robert C. Blanchard
David B. Elliott
David John Shepherd
Charles Dunlap

Robert Disbrow
David Lyall
Eric Savics
John Rybinski
Kerry Smith

D-U-N-S 24-760-5132   (HQ)
HECLA QUEBEC INC
HECLA QUEBEC - CASA BERARDI
(*Suby of* HECLA MINING COMPANY)
800 Pender St W Suite 970, Vancouver, BC,
V6C 2V6
(604) 682-6201
Emp Here 5   *Sales* 127,887,000
SIC 1081 Metal mining services
Phillips S Baker
Lindsay A Hall
Lawrence P Radford
David C Sienko
Luke Russell

D-U-N-S 24-616-4490   (SL)
HIS INTERNATIONAL TOURS BC INC
636 Hornby St, Vancouver, BC, V6C 2G2
(604) 685-3524
Emp Here 30   *Sales* 11,560,800
SIC 4724 Travel agencies
Hiroshi Jiesumasac

D-U-N-S 20-202-7533   (SL)
HOLLAND AMERICA LINE
WORLD WIDE SHORE SERVICES
999 Canada Pl Suite 200, Vancouver, BC,
V6C 3C1
(604) 683-5776
Emp Here 204   *Sales* 136,045,968
SIC 4724 Travel agencies
Cathleen Collins

D-U-N-S 20-912-2209   (BR)
HOLT, RENFREW & CIE, LIMITEE
HOLT RENFREW
737 Dunsmuir St, Vancouver, BC, V6C 1N5
(604) 681-3121
Emp Here 400
SIC 5311 Department stores
Dana Hall

D-U-N-S 20-780-5768   (BR)
HOLT, RENFREW & CIE, LIMITEE
HOLT RENFREW
737 Dunsmuir St, Vancouver, BC, V6C 1N5
(604) 681-3121
Emp Here 660
SIC 5621 Women's clothing stores
Craig Duncan

D-U-N-S 20-369-3981   (SL)
**HOTEL GEORGIA (OP) LIMITED PARTNER-
SHIP**
ROSEWOOD HOTEL GEORGIA
801 Georgia St W, Vancouver, BC, V6C 1P7
(604) 682-5566
Emp Here 275   *Sales* 26,308,700
SIC 7011 Hotels and motels
Azim Jamal

D-U-N-S 20-800-5330   (HQ)
HSBC BANK CANADA
(*Suby of* HSBC HOLDINGS PLC)
885 Georgia St W, Vancouver, BC, V6C 3G1
(604) 685-1000
Emp Here 300   *Sales* 1,496,441,070
SIC 6021 National commercial banks
Sandra Stuart
Larry Tomei
Kim Toews
Linda Seymour
Jason Henderson
Georgia Stavridis
Sophia Tsui
Kimberly Flood
Josee Turcotte
Gerhardt Samwell

D-U-N-S 24-931-1077   (SL)
HSBC CAPITAL (CANADA) INC
(*Suby of* HSBC HOLDINGS PLC)

885 Georgia St W Suite 1100, Vancouver, BC,
V6C 3E8
(604) 631-8088
Emp Here 25   *Sales* 23,479,425
SIC 6211 Security brokers and dealers
David F Mullen
Johan Lemmer
Craig Shearer

D-U-N-S 20-391-8149   (HQ)
HUACHANGDA CANADA HOLDINGS INC
2800 Park Pl 666 Burrard St, Vancouver, BC,
V6C 2Z7

Sales 219,305,400
SIC 6712 Bank holding companies
Tao Liu

D-U-N-S 20-112-4302   (BR)
HUDSON'S BAY COMPANY
BAY, THE
(*Suby of* HUDSON'S BAY COMPANY)
674 Granville St Suite 9999, Vancouver, BC,
V6C 1Z6
(604) 681-6211
Emp Here 1,300
SIC 5311 Department stores
Dana Hall

D-U-N-S 24-317-3825   (HQ)
IBC ADVANCED ALLOYS CORP
570 Granville St Unit 1200, Vancouver, BC,
V6C 3P1
(604) 685-6263
Emp Here 50   *Sales* 15,715,000
SIC 3351 Copper rolling and drawing
David R. Heinz
David Anderson
Rajeev Jain
James Malone
Simon J. Anderson
C. Geoffrey Hampson
Jerry Michael Jarvis
Mark Smith

D-U-N-S 20-180-6572   (HQ)
IMPERIAL METALS CORPORATION
580 Hornby St Suite 200, Vancouver, BC, V6C
3B6
(604) 669-8959
Emp Here 30   *Sales* 273,047,872
SIC 1041 Gold ores
Brian Kynoch
Sophie Hsia
Darb Dhillon
Randall Thompson
Jim Miller-Tait
Sheila Colwill
Andre Deepwell
Don Parsons
Pierre Lebel
Larry Moeller

D-U-N-S 24-386-5677   (HQ)
INNERGEX RENEWABLE ENERGY INC
888 Dunsmuir St Suite 1100, Vancouver, BC,
V6C 3K4
(604) 669-4999
Sales 400,263,000
SIC 4911 Electric services
Michel Letellier
Jean Perron
Richard Blanchet
Renaud De Batz
Peter Grover
Francois Hebert
Jean-Francois Neault
Yves Baribeault
Anne Cliche
Claude Chartrand

D-U-N-S 20-315-5668   (BR)
INTACT INSURANCE COMPANY
(*Suby of* INTACT FINANCIAL CORPORA-
TION)
999 Hastings St W Suite 1100, Vancouver,
BC, V6C 2W2

(604) 891-5400
Emp Here 360
SIC 6331 Fire, marine, and casualty insurance
Rick Howe

D-U-N-S 20-913-7314   (HQ)
INTEGRAL GROUP INC
200 Granville St Suite 180, Vancouver, BC,
V6C 1S4
(604) 687-1800
Emp Here 72   *Sales* 23,306,500
SIC 1711 Plumbing, heating, air-conditioning
Conrad Schartau
Goran Ostojic
Heidi Mathena
Rodney Roberts
Ali Nazari
Stuart Hood
Christine Jeffery

D-U-N-S 20-371-1770   (HQ)
**INTERNATIONAL PETROLEUM CORPORA-
TION**
885 Georgia St W Suite 2000, Vancouver,
V6C 3E8
(604) 689-7842
Emp Here 149   *Sales* 454,443,000
SIC 1311 Crude petroleum and natural gas
Mike Nicholson
Chris Hogue
Ed Sobel
Rebecca Gordon
Daniel Fitzgerald
Ryan Adair
Jeffrey Fountain
Christophe Nerguararian
Lukas Lundin
C. Ashley Heppenstall

D-U-N-S 24-983-3088   (HQ)
**INTRINSYC TECHNOLOGIES CORPORA-
TION**
885 Dunsmuir St 3rd Fl, Vancouver, BC, V6C
1N5
(604) 801-6461
Emp Here 17   *Sales* 25,681,727
SIC 7371 Custom computer programming ser-
vices
Tracy Rees
Mark Waldenberg
Cliff Morton
Victor Gonzalez
George Reznik
George Duguay
Howard Speaks
Michael W. Bird
Daniel S. Marks
Jeff Macdonald

D-U-N-S 20-114-9148   (HQ)
**IQMETRIX SOFTWARE DEVELOPMENT
CORP**
READY TO PAY
250 Howe St Suite 1210, Vancouver, BC, V6C
3R8
(866) 476-3874
Sales 17,199,167
SIC 7371 Custom computer programming ser-
vices
Christopher Krywulak
Gregory Krywulak

D-U-N-S 24-198-5604   (HQ)
ISODIOL INTERNATIONAL INC
200 Granville St Suite 2710, Vancouver, BC,
V6C 1S4
(604) 409-4409
Sales 355,959,000
SIC 5961 Catalog and mail-order houses
Marcos Agramont
Aman Parmar
Soheil Samimi
Bryan Loree

D-U-N-S 20-258-5410   (HQ)
IVANHOE MINES LTD
999 Canada Pl Suite 654, Vancouver, BC,
V6C 3E1

(604) 688-6630
Emp Here 50   *Sales* 196,945,980
SIC 1061 Ferroalloy ores, except vanadium
Lars-Eric Johansson
Tony Giardini
Mark Farren
Marna Cloete
Patricia Makhesha
Louis Watum
Robert Friedland
Egizio Bianchini
Ian Cockerill
William Hayden

D-U-N-S 24-940-2264   (HQ)
JIM PATTISON ENTERPRISES LTD
1067 Cordova St W Unit 1800, Vancouver, BC,
V6C 1C7
(604) 688-6764
Emp Here 2   *Sales* 91,739,648
SIC 5142 Packaged frozen goods
Michael Korenberg
James A Pattison
David Bell
Nicolas (Nick) Desmarais
P. Nicholas Geer
David Schellenberg

D-U-N-S 24-761-1804   (SL)
KGHM AJAX MINING INC
800 Pender St W Suite 615, Vancouver, BC,
V6C 2V6
(604) 682-0301
Emp Here 50   *Sales* 10,206,500
SIC 1021 Copper ores
Ian Macneily

D-U-N-S 24-070-4544   (HQ)
KNIGHT PIESOLD LTD
750 Pender St W Suite 1400, Vancouver, BC,
V6C 2T8
(604) 685-0543
Sales 11,437,270
SIC 8711 Engineering services
Andre Niewenhuizen
Ken Brouwer

D-U-N-S 20-919-3754   (HQ)
LAWSON LUNDELL LLP
925 Georgia St W Suite 1600, Vancouver, BC,
V6C 3L2
(604) 685-3456
Emp Here 190   *Sales* 48,380,860
SIC 8111 Legal services
L Neil Marshall
Murray T A Campbell
David A Allard
Gregory T W Bowden
Chris W Sanderson
Maureen E Baird
Brian D Fulton
J Martin Kyle
A W Carpenter
Irving D Laskin

D-U-N-S 20-272-2893   (SL)
LAYER 7 TECHNOLOGIES INC
(*Suby of* BROADCOM INC.)
885 Georgia St W Suite 500, Vancouver, BC,
V6C 3E8
(604) 681-9377
Emp Here 130   *Sales* 18,743,660
SIC 7371 Custom computer programming ser-
vices
Paul Rochester
Praveen Gupta
Dimitri Sirota

D-U-N-S 24-030-3102   (HQ)
LED MEDICAL DIAGNOSTICS INC
LED DENTAL
580 Hornby St Suite 810, Vancouver, BC, V6C
3B6
(604) 434-4614
Emp Here 13   *Sales* 14,215,812
SIC 3843 Dental equipment and supplies
David Gane
Lamar Roberts

Darryl Yea
Joel Leetzow
Stephen Sweeney
James Topham

D-U-N-S 20-118-7502   (HQ)
LEDCOR CMI LTD
LEDCOR CIVIL/MINING
(*Suby of* 280818 ALBERTA LTD)
1067 Cordova St W Unit 1200, Vancouver, BC,
V6C 1C7
(604) 681-7500
Sales 11,671,750
SIC 1481 NonMetallic mineral services
David Lede
Clifford Lederd

D-U-N-S 20-105-5691   (HQ)
LEDCOR CONSTRUCTION LIMITED
(*Suby of* 280818 ALBERTA LTD)
1067 Cordova St W Suite 1200, Vancouver,
BC, V6C 1C7
(604) 681-7500
Emp Here 150   *Sales* 174,598,000
SIC 1542 Nonresidential construction, nec
David Lede
Peter Hrdlitschka
Jim Logan

D-U-N-S 25-678-4174   (HQ)
LEDCOR HOLDINGS INC
(*Suby of* 280818 ALBERTA LTD)
1067 Cordova St W Suite 1200, Vancouver,
BC, V6C 1C7
(604) 681-7500
Emp Here 6   *Sales* 262,492,000
SIC 1611 Highway and street construction
David Lede
Clifford Lede
Leroy Sonnenberg
Ronald Stevenson

D-U-N-S 20-117-7651   (HQ)
LEDCOR INDUSTRIES INC
LEDCOR GROUP
(*Suby of* 280818 ALBERTA LTD)
1067 Cordova St W Suite 1200, Vancouver,
BC, V6C 1C7
(604) 681-7500
Emp Here 800   *Sales* 262,492,000
SIC 1611 Highway and street construction
David Lede
Clifford Lede
Leroy Sonnenberg

D-U-N-S 24-164-9008   (HQ)
LEGAL SERVICES SOCIETY
(*Suby of* GOVERNMENT OF THE
PROVINCE OF BRITISH COLUMBIA)
510 Burrard St Suite 400, Vancouver, BC, V6C
3A8
(604) 601-6200
Emp Here 20   *Sales* 76,506,562
SIC 8111 Legal services

D-U-N-S 24-131-4025   (SL)
LEITH WHEELER FIXED INCOME FUND
400 Burrard St Suite 1500, Vancouver, BC,
V6C 3A6
(604) 683-3391
Emp Here 49   *Sales* 41,243,261
SIC 6722 Management investment, open-end
Kim Gilliland

D-U-N-S 24-493-4204   (SL)
**LEITH WHEELER INVESTMENT COUNSEL
LTD**
LEITH WHEELER
400 Burrard St Suite 1500, Vancouver, BC,
V6C 3A6
(604) 683-3391
Emp Here 85   *Sales* 79,830,045
SIC 6282 Investment advice
Jim Gilliland
Gordon Gibbons
Cecilia Wong
William Wheeler

D-U-N-S 24-825-1480   (HQ)
LEVON RESOURCES LTD
LVN
666 Burrard St Suite 500, Vancouver, BC, V6C
2X8
(604) 682-2991
Sales 16,712,843
SIC 1081 Metal mining services
Ron Tremblay
Vic Chevillon
Christina Boddy
Daniel Vickerman
Joanne Odette
Ed Karr
Lee Bowles

D-U-N-S 24-359-9441   (HQ)
LIONS GATE ENTERTAINMENT CORP
250 Howe St Fl 20, Vancouver, BC, V6C 3R8
(877) 848-3866
Sales 4,129,100,000
SIC 7812 Motion picture and video production
Jon Feltheimer
Michael Burns
Steve Beeks
Brian Goldsmith
Wayne Levin
James Barge
Gordon Crawford
Arthur Evrensel
Emily Fine
Sir Lucian Grainge

D-U-N-S 25-290-9296   (BR)
LIVERTON HOTELS INTERNATIONAL INC
METROPOLITAN HOTEL VANCOUVER
(*Suby of* LIVERTON HOTELS INTERNA-
TIONAL INC)
645 Howe St, Vancouver, BC, V6C 2Y9
(604) 687-1122
Emp Here 200
SIC 7011 Hotels and motels
Kari Costkela

D-U-N-S 20-300-2381   (SL)
LOGINRADIUS INC
815 Hastings St W Suite 801, Vancouver, BC,
V6C 1B4
(844) 625-8889
Emp Here 60   *Sales* 10,638,660
SIC 7371 Custom computer programming ser-
vices
Rakesh Soni
Deepak Gupta
Ousama Haffar
William Lin

D-U-N-S 25-167-8801   (SL)
LOS ANDES COPPER LTD
355 Burrard St Suite 1260, Vancouver, BC,
V6C 2G8
(604) 681-2802
Emp Here 5   *Sales* 11,937,745
SIC 1021 Copper ores
Antony Amberg
Aurora Davidson
Klaus Zeitler
Francis O'kelly
Francisco Covarrubias
Paul Miquel
Gonzalo Delaveau
Eduardo Covarrubias

D-U-N-S 24-350-1793   (HQ)
LUCARA DIAMOND CORP
885 Georgia St W Suite 2000, Vancouver,
V6C 3E8
(604) 689-7842
Sales 176,191,000
SIC 1499 Miscellaneous nonMetallic minerals,
except fuels
Eira Thomas
John Armstrong
Zara Boldt
Ayesha Hira
Lukas H. Lundin
Paul K Conibear

Brian Edgar
Marie Inkster
Cathrine Mcleod-Seltzer
Richard P. Clark

D-U-N-S 24-101-4229   (SL)
LUNDIN GOLD INC
885 Georgia St W Suite 2000, Vancouver, BC,
V6C 3E8
(604) 689-7842
Emp Here 1,645   *Sales* 420,748,230
SIC 1041 Gold ores
Ron F. Hochstein
Alessandro Bitelli
Nathan Monash
David Dicaire
Sheila Colman
Chester See
Iliana Rodriguez
Lukas Lundin
Carmel Daniele
Ian Gibbs

D-U-N-S 24-163-2025   (BR)
**MACQUARIE CAPITAL MARKETS CANADA
LTD**
BLACKMONT CAPITAL
(*Suby of* MACQUARIE GROUP LIMITED)
550 Burrard St Suite 500, Vancouver, BC, V6C
2B5
(604) 605-3944
Emp Here 160
SIC 6211 Security brokers and dealers
Nevin Shernick

D-U-N-S 24-797-6665   (BR)
MARSH CANADA LIMITED
(*Suby of* MARSH & MCLENNAN COMPA-
NIES, INC.)
550 Burrard St Suite 800, Vancouver, BC, V6C
2K1
(604) 685-3765
Emp Here 180
SIC 6411 Insurance agents, brokers, and ser-
vice
Denisse Munoz

D-U-N-S 20-385-8998   (SL)
**MASTERCARD TECHNOLOGIES CANADA
ULC**
(*Suby of* MASTERCARD INCORPORATED)
475 Howe St Suite 2000, Vancouver, BC, V6C
2B3
(604) 800-3711
Emp Here 106
SIC 7371 Custom computer programming ser-
vices
Michel Giasson
Derek Houg

D-U-N-S 24-235-2815   (SL)
MAVERIX METALS INC
510 Burrard St Suite 575, Vancouver, BC, V6C
3A8
(604) 449-9290
Emp Here 10   *Sales* 25,814,131
SIC 1499 Miscellaneous nonMetallic minerals,
except fuels
Dan O'flaherty
Geoff Burns
Brent Bonney
Doug Ward
Matt Fargey
Chris Barnes
David Scott
Rob Doyle
J.C. Stefan Spicer
Blake Rhodes

D-U-N-S 20-623-3199   (HQ)
MAXAR TECHNOLOGIES LTD
(*Suby of* MAXAR TECHNOLOGIES INC.)
200 Burrard St Suite 1570, Vancouver, BC,
V6C 3L6
(604) 974-5275
Emp Here 20   *Sales* 1,631,200,000
SIC 7371 Custom computer programming ser-

vices
Howard L. Lance
Angela Lau
Michelle Kley
Andrea Bortner
Stephanie Georges
Timothy H. Hascall
Jeff Robertson
Walter S. Scott
Marcy Steinke
Bruce W. Stephenson

D-U-N-S 20-995-5640   (BR)
MERCER (CANADA) LIMITED
MMC
(*Suby of* MARSH & MCLENNAN COMPA-
NIES, INC.)
550 Burrard St Suite 900, Vancouver, BC, V6C
3S8
(604) 683-6761
Emp Here 100
SIC 8999 Services, nec
John Cosby

D-U-N-S 24-647-6642   (HQ)
MERCER INTERNATIONAL INC
700 Pender St W Suite 1120, Vancouver, BC,
V6C 1G8
(604) 684-1099
Emp Here 17   *Sales* 1,457,718,000
SIC 2611 Pulp mills
Jimmy S.H. Lee
David M. Gandossi
David Ure
Brian Merwin
Wolfram Ridder
David Cooper
Eric Heine
Genevieve Stannus
Adolf Koppensteiner
Eric Lauritzen

D-U-N-S 20-800-9514   (HQ)
MERCER PEACE RIVER PULP LTD
DMI
510 Burrard St Suite 700, Vancouver, BC, V6C
3A8
(604) 684-4326
Emp Here 16   *Sales* 117,643,840
SIC 2611 Pulp mills
Yasu Amakusa

D-U-N-S 20-348-1494   (HQ)
METALLA ROYALTY & STREAMING LTD
543 Granville St Suite 501, Vancouver, BC,
V6C 1X8
(604) 696-0741
Sales 11,197,050
SIC 6159 Miscellaneous business credit insti-
tutions
Brett Heath
Drew Clark
Kim Casswell
Bill Tsang
Lawrence Roulston
Frank Hanagarne Jr
Alexander Molyneux
E.B Tucker

D-U-N-S 20-635-4367   (HQ)
METHANEX CORPORATION
200 Burrard St Suite 1800, Vancouver, BC,
V6C 3M1
(604) 661-2600
Emp Here 810   *Sales* 3,931,847,000
SIC 2869 Industrial organic chemicals, nec
John Floren
Brad W. Boyd
Ian P. Cameron
Kevin L. Henderson
Michael J. (Mike) Herz
Vanessa L. James
Thomas M. Hamilton
Bruce Aitken
Douglas Arnell
Howard R. Balloch

D-U-N-S 24-850-7472   (HQ)
MIDAS GOLD CORP
999 Hastings St W Suite 890, Vancouver, BC,
V6C 2W2
(778) 724-4700
Sales 85,951,764
SIC 1041 Gold ores
Stephen Quin
Darren Morgans
Liz Monger
Peter Nixon
Keith Allred
Jamie Donovan
Brad Doores
Michael Bogert
Marcelo Kim
Donald Young

D-U-N-S 20-425-5582   (HQ)
MITSUBISHI CANADA LIMITED
(*Suby of* MITSUBISHI CORPORATION)
200 Granville St Suite 2800, Vancouver, BC,
V6C 1G6
(604) 654-8000
Sales 14,756,742
SIC 5051 Metals service centers and offices
Hisashi Ikeda
David Lim
Daisuke Kajikawa
Hidemoto Mizuhara
Haruhiko Sato

D-U-N-S 20-914-0813   (HQ)
NACEL PROPERTIES LTD
925 Georgia St W Suite 800, Vancouver, BC,
V6C 3L2
(604) 685-7789
Sales 13,252,260
SIC 6513 Apartment building operators
Norman Cressey

D-U-N-S 25-733-5273   (SL)
**NATURE TRUST OF BRITISH COLUMBIA,
THE**
888 Dunsmuir St Suite 500, Vancouver, BC,
V6C 3K4
(604) 924-9771
Emp Here 36   *Sales* 15,285,852
SIC 8999 Services, nec
Douglas Walker

D-U-N-S 20-340-6467   (SL)
NEOS CANADA SERVICES ULC
355 Burrard St Suite 1800, Vancouver, BC,
V6C 2G8
(604) 682-7737
Emp Here 49   *Sales* 10,415,671
SIC 1382 Oil and gas exploration services
James Hollis

D-U-N-S 25-415-0477   (SL)
NETNATION COMMUNICATIONS INC
(*Suby of* LJ2 & CO., LLC)
550 Burrard St Suite 200, Vancouver, BC, V6C
2B5
(604) 688-8946
Emp Here 80   *Sales* 18,277,760
SIC 4899 Communication services, nec
Joseph Kibur
Jag Gillan
Grey Shenk
Rebecca Mccolough

D-U-N-S 20-296-1439   (SL)
NEVADA ENERGY METALS INC
789 Pender St W Suite 1220, Vancouver, BC,
V6C 1H2
(604) 428-5690
Emp Here 197   *Sales* 53,240,432
SIC 1479 Chemical and fertilizer mining
Rick Wilson
Tina Whyte
Tim Fernback
Robert Guanzon
Ali H. Alizadeh
Jay Oness

D-U-N-S 24-454-8939   (SL)

NEW GUINEA GOLD CORPORATION
595 Howe St Suite 900, Vancouver, BC, V6C
2T5
(604) 689-1515
Emp Here 51   *Sales* 121,764,999
SIC 1081 Metal mining services
Greg Heaney
Brian Koster
Ben Graham
Ces Le Wago
Arthur Alexander
Lachlan Mcintosh

D-U-N-S 25-533-4732   (SL)
NEW PACIFIC METALS CORP
200 Granville St Suite 1378, Vancouver, BC,
V6C 1S4
(604) 633-1368
Emp Here 10   *Sales* 23,875,490
SIC 1021 Copper ores
Rui Feng
Gordon Neal
Hongen Ma
Alex Zhang
Jalen Yuan
Jack Austin
Greg Hawkins
David Kong
Martin Wafforn
John Mccluskey

D-U-N-S 20-291-2895   (SL)
NEWCASTLE GOLD LTD
(*Suby of* EQUINOX GOLD CORP)
800 Pender St W Suite 730, Vancouver, BC,
V6C 2V6
(250) 925-2713
Emp Here 21   *Sales* 50,138,529
SIC 1041 Gold ores
Gerald Panneton
Richard Warke
Marc Leduc
Louis Dionne
Lenard Boggio
R. Stuart Angus
Jacques Mcmullen

D-U-N-S 24-861-4133   (HQ)
NGEX RESOURCES INC
885 Georgia St W Suite 2000, Vancouver, BC,
V6C 3E8
(604) 689-7842
Sales 35,813,235
SIC 1021 Copper ores
Wojtek A. Wodzicki
Bob Carmichael
Jamie Beck
Joyce Ngo
Julie Kemp
Lukas H. Lundin
William A. Rand
David F. Mullen
Jack Lundin
Cheri Pedersen

D-U-N-S 25-536-2162   (HQ)
NICOLA MINING INC
355 Burrard St Suite 1000, Vancouver, BC,
V6C 2G8
(604) 683-8604
Sales 262,630,390
SIC 1044 Silver ores
Peter Espig
Warwick Bay
Frank Hogel
Doug F. Robinson
Paul Johnston

D-U-N-S 25-533-0151   (SL)
**NORTH AMERICAN TUNGSTEN CORPO-
RATION LTD**
400 Burrard St Suite 1680, Vancouver, BC,
V6C 3A6
(604) 638-7440
Emp Here 207   *Sales* 52,945,218
SIC 1081 Metal mining services
Kurt Heikkila

▲ **Public Company**   ■ **Public Company Family Member**   **HQ** Headquarters   **BR** Branch   **SL** Single Location

Dennis M. Lindahl
Allan Krasnick
Ronald Erickson
Brian Abraham

D-U-N-S 20-257-1964   (HQ)
NOVA METRIX GROUND MONITORING (CANADA) LTD
WESTBAY INSTRUMENTS DIV OF
666 Burrard St Suite 1700, Vancouver, BC, V6C 2X8
(604) 430-4272
Sales 11,769,885
SIC 6712 Bank holding companies
Janet Barbookles

D-U-N-S 20-183-9250   (HQ)
NOVAGOLD RESOURCES INC
ALASKA GOLD
789 W Pender St Suite 720, Vancouver, BC, V6C 1H2
(604) 669-6227
Emp Here 15   *Sales* 12,788,700
SIC 1041 Gold ores
Gregory A. Lang
Ron Rimelman
David Ottewell
Richard Williams
Melanie Hennessey
David Deisley
Tricia Pannier
Thomas Kaplan
Sharon Dowdall
Igor Levental

D-U-N-S 20-918-7694   (SL)
OCEAN PACIFIC HOTELS LTD
PAN PACIFIC VANCOUVER HOTEL
999 Canada Pl Suite 300, Vancouver, BC, V6C 3B5
(604) 662-8111
Emp Here 400   *Sales* 38,267,200
SIC 7011 Hotels and motels
Majid Mangalji
Fereed Mangalji

D-U-N-S 20-509-6670   (HQ)
ODLUM BROWN LIMITED
250 Howe St Suite 1100, Vancouver, BC, V6C 3S9
(604) 669-1600
Emp Here 130   *Sales* 187,835,400
SIC 6211 Security brokers and dealers
Debra Hewson
Mark Srdanovic

D-U-N-S 20-153-2665   (SL)
OMNI WARRANTY CORP
355 Burrard St Suite 350, Vancouver, BC, V6C 2G8
(604) 806-5300
Emp Here 50   *Sales* 51,744,050
SIC 6351 Surety insurance
Adam Hill

D-U-N-S 24-034-4627   (HQ)
ORCA GOLD INC
885 Georgia St W Suite 2000, Vancouver, BC, V6C 3E8
(604) 689-7842
Sales 143,252,940
SIC 1041 Gold ores
Richard Clark
Hugh Stuart
Glenn Kondo
Kevin Ross
Alexander Davidson
Robert Chase
David Field
Derek White

D-U-N-S 25-399-8801   (HQ)
P SUN'S ENTERPRISES (VANCOUVER) LTD
HOTEL CLARION GRAND PACIFIC
885 Georgia St W, Vancouver, BC, V6C 3E8
(604) 643-7939
Emp Here 1   *Sales* 11,122,800

SIC 7011 Hotels and motels
Naoaki Sun
Jackson Lam
Keith Burrell
Derek Winnett

D-U-N-S 25-215-5098   (HQ)
PACNET SERVICES LTD
595 Howe St 4 Fl, Vancouver, BC, V6C 2T5
(604) 689-0399
Sales 28,024,560
SIC 6099 Functions related to deposit banking
Rosanne Day

D-U-N-S 24-371-2064   (HQ)
PAN AMERICAN SILVER CORP
625 Howe St Suite 1440, Vancouver, BC, V6C 2T6
(604) 684-1175
Emp Here 4,500   *Sales* 784,495,000
SIC 1044 Silver ores
Michael Steinmann
Steve Busby
Robert Doyle
Andres Dasso
George Greer
Martin Wafforn
Sean Mcaleer
Christopher Emerson
Ross J. Beaty
Michael Carroll

D-U-N-S 20-584-8054   (SL)
PARKING CORPORATION OF VANCOUVER, THE
EASY PARK
(*Suby of* VANCOUVER, CITY OF)
700 Pender St W Suite 209, Vancouver, BC, V6C 1G8
(604) 682-6744
Emp Here 100   *Sales* 45,019,700
SIC 7521 Automobile parking
Mel Mckinney
Nadia Gargaro

D-U-N-S 25-498-4321   (HQ)
PATTISON, JIM ENTERTAINMENT LTD
RIPLEY'S BELIEVE IT OR NOT
1067 Cordova St W Suite 1800, Vancouver, BC, V6C 1C7
(604) 688-6764
Sales 15,729,000
SIC 8412 Museums and art galleries
James Pattison
Michael Korenberg
Glen Clark
David Bell
Nick Desmarais

D-U-N-S 24-161-4965   (HQ)
PATTISON, JIM GROUP INC
1067 Cordova St W Suite 1800, Vancouver, BC, V6C 1C7
(604) 688-6764
Sales 19,049,316,000
SIC 5511 New and used car dealers
James Pattison
Glen Clark
Mark Kaplan
Edward Meyer
William R Fatt
Dieter W Jentsch
Michael Korenberg
Robert G Miller
Jim Pattison Jr

D-U-N-S 20-622-7506   (HQ)
PATTISON, JIM INDUSTRIES LTD
PATTISON SIGN GROUP DIV OF
(*Suby of* PATTISON, JIM GROUP INC)
1067 Cordova St W Suite 1800, Vancouver, BC, V6C 1C7
(604) 688-6764
Emp Here 30   *Sales* 750,427,600
SIC 5511 New and used car dealers
James Pattison
David Bell

Nick Desmarais
Ryan Barrington-Foot

D-U-N-S 24-324-4006   (SL)
PENDER NDI LIFE SCIENCES FUND (VCC) INC
ADVANTAGE LIFE SCIENCE FUND II
885 Georgia St W Suite 200, Vancouver, BC, V6C 3E8
(604) 688-1511
Emp Here 25   *Sales* 16,973,075
SIC 6211 Security brokers and dealers
David Roberts
Cameron Belsher
James Miller

D-U-N-S 24-620-7039   (HQ)
PEOPLES TRUST COMPANY/COMPAGNIE DE FIDUCIE PEOPLES
888 Dunsmuir St Suite 1400, Vancouver, BC, V6C 3K4
(604) 683-2881
Emp Here 34   *Sales* 13,899,843
SIC 6021 National commercial banks
Derek Peddlesden
Bill Moffat
Samson Lim
Darren Kozol
Neil Allen
Jo-Anne Morefield
Michael Andrews
Howard Anson
Andrew Bury
David Ghermezian

D-U-N-S 24-447-6701   (HQ)
PI FINANCIAL CORP
666 Burrard St Suite 1900, Vancouver, BC, V6C 3N1
(604) 664-2900
Emp Here 130   *Sales* 426,941,400
SIC 6211 Security brokers and dealers
Max Meier
John T Eymann
Jean-Paul Bachellerie
Lawrence Mcquid
Teresa M Sheehan
Bert Quattrociocchi
Richard Thomas
Andrew Murray

D-U-N-S 20-099-7877   (SL)
PLATINUM GROUP METALS LTD
550 Burrard St Suite 788, Vancouver, BC, V6C 2B5
(604) 899-5450
Emp Here 320   *Sales* 81,847,680
SIC 1041 Gold ores
R. Michael Jones
Kris Begic
Frank R. Hallam
Iain Mclean
Timothy Marlow
Diana Walters
Stuart Harshaw

D-U-N-S 24-000-9287   (BR)
POSTMEDIA NETWORK INC
(*Suby of* POSTMEDIA NETWORK CANADA CORP)
200 Granville St Suite 1, Vancouver, BC, V6C 3N3
(604) 605-2000
Emp Here 500
SIC 2711 Newspapers
Rod Phillips

D-U-N-S 20-347-9316   (BR)
POSTMEDIA NETWORK INC
PACIFIC NEWSPAPER GROUP DIV OF
(*Suby of* POSTMEDIA NETWORK CANADA CORP)
200 Granville St Suite 1, Vancouver, BC, V6C 3N3
(604) 605-2000
Emp Here 100
SIC 2711 Newspapers

D-U-N-S 24-347-2128   (HQ)
PREMIER MARINE INSURANCE MANAGERS GROUP (WEST) INC
(*Suby of* CO-OPERATORS GENERAL INSURANCE COMPANY)
625 Howe St Suite 300, Vancouver, BC, V6C 2T6
(604) 669-5211
Emp Here 45   *Sales* 81,537,588
SIC 6331 Fire, marine, and casualty insurance
Nat Moreira
Troy Moreira
Henry John

D-U-N-S 25-995-4592   (BR)
PRICEWATERHOUSECOOPERS LLP
(*Suby of* PRICEWATERHOUSECOOPERS LLP)
250 Howe St Suite 700, Vancouver, BC, V6C 3S7
(604) 806-7000
Emp Here 600
SIC 8721 Accounting, auditing, and bookkeeping
John Webster

D-U-N-S 25-676-5900   (HQ)
PROPHECY DEVELOPMENT CORP
409 Granville St Suite 1610, Vancouver, BC, V6C 1T2
(604) 569-3661
Sales 479,643,000
SIC 1221 Bituminous coal and lignite-surface mining
John Lee
Bekzod Kasimov
Michael Drozd
Danniel Oosterman
Greg Hall
Harald Batista
Masa Igata
Daniel Fidock
Irina Plavutska

D-U-N-S 24-225-6555   (BR)
PRT GROWING SERVICES LTD
(*Suby of* PRT GROWING SERVICES LTD)
355 Burrard St Suite 410, Vancouver, BC, V6C 2G8

Emp Here 505
SIC 7389 Business services, nec
Mike Wood

D-U-N-S 25-957-0083   (HQ)
PUBLIC GUARDIAN AND TRUSTEE OF BRITISH COLUMBIA
808 Hastings St W Suite 700, Vancouver, BC, V6C 3L3
(604) 660-4444
Sales 1,181,501,000
SIC 6733 Trusts, nec
Catherine Romanko

D-U-N-S 20-299-7474   (HQ)
PURE MULTI-FAMILY REIT LP
925 Georgia St W Suite 910, Vancouver, BC, V6C 3L2
(604) 681-5959
Sales 26,120,160
SIC 6531 Real estate agents and managers
Stephen Evans
Samantha Adams
Scott Shillington

D-U-N-S 20-344-2363   (HQ)
QUADREAL PROPERTY GROUP LIMITED PARTNERSHIP
(*Suby of* GOVERNMENT OF THE PROVINCE OF BRITISH COLUMBIA)
666 Burrard St Suite 800, Vancouver, BC, V6C 2X8
(604) 975-9500
Emp Here 100   *Sales* 37,187,040
SIC 6531 Real estate agents and managers
Dennis Lopez
Remco Deal

Jonathan Dubois-Phillips
Susan Maclaurin
Rosemary Feenan
Cheryl Gray
Neil Lacheur
Doug Reid
Rebecca Catley
Roger Chouinard

D-U-N-S 24-798-7373 (HQ)
RAYMOND JAMES LTD
(Suby of RAYMOND JAMES FINANCIAL, INC.)
925 Georgia St W Suite 2100, Vancouver, BC, V6C 3L2
(604) 659-8000
Emp Here 150 Sales 587,468,600
SIC 6211 Security brokers and dealers
Paul Allison
Mario Addeo
Peter Kahnert
Lloyd Costley
Thomas Raidl
Richard Rousseau
Sybil Verch
Kevin Whelly
Tom Williams
Mike Westcott

D-U-N-S 24-760-7174 (HQ)
RED EAGLE MINING CORPORATION
666 Burrard St Suite 2348, Vancouver, BC, V6C 2X8
(604) 638-2545
Emp Here 10 Sales 47,573,964
SIC 1041 Gold ores
Ian Slater
Patrick Balit
Dave Thomas
Judy A. Mccall
Chui Wong
Robert Bell
Robert Pease
Jay Sujir

D-U-N-S 20-015-3760 (HQ)
RETHINK COMMUNICATIONS INC
470 Granville St Suite 700, Vancouver, BC, V6C 1V5
(604) 685-8911
Emp Here 90 Sales 24,674,976
SIC 4899 Communication services, nec
Thomas Shepansky
Chris Staples
Ian Grais

D-U-N-S 20-366-4979 (SL)
RIO2 LIMITED
355 Burrard St Suite 1260, Vancouver, BC, V6C 2G8
(604) 260-2696
Emp Here 10 Sales 23,875,490
SIC 1041 Gold ores
Alex Black
Klaus Zeitler
Jose Luis Martinez
Kathryn Johnson
Tim Williams
Enrique Garay
Andrew Cox
Ian Dreyer
Alejandra Gomez
Sidney Robinson

D-U-N-S 20-279-1851 (SL)
ROOSTER ENERGY LTD
666 Burrard St Suite 1700, Vancouver, BC, V6C 2X8
(604) 574-7558
Emp Here 1 Sales 33,325,288
SIC 7371 Custom computer programming services
Kenneth Tamplain Jr
Chester Morrison Jr
Leroy Guidry Jr
Tod Darcey

D-U-N-S 24-370-4731 (SL)
ROTARY CLUB OF VANCOUVER
475 Howe St Suite 315, Vancouver, BC, V6C 2B3
(604) 685-0481
Emp Here 150 Sales 31,060,200
SIC 8399 Social services, nec
Bill Dauphinee

D-U-N-S 20-296-7175 (SL)
S & E LIMITED PARTNERSHIP
666 Burrard St Suite 1700, Vancouver, BC, V6C 2X8
(604) 631-1300
Emp Here 90 Sales 13,860,990
SIC 8111 Legal services
Jim Foo

D-U-N-S 24-374-4450 (SL)
SAFEMAP INTERNATIONAL INC
SAFEMAP
666 Burrard St Suite 500, Vancouver, BC, V6C 3P6
(604) 642-6110
Emp Here 45 Sales 10,542,960
SIC 8748 Business consulting, nec
Cornelius Pitzer

D-U-N-S 24-657-1079 (SL)
SAGIT INVESTMENT MANAGEMENT LTD
789 Pender St W Suite 900, Vancouver, BC, V6C 1H2

Emp Here 16 Sales 11,146,832
SIC 6722 Management investment, open-end
Raoul Tsakok
Ernest Cheung
Don Lyons

D-U-N-S 24-366-8451 (HQ)
SANDSTORM GOLD LTD
400 Burrard St Suite 1400, Vancouver, BC, V6C 3G2
(604) 689-0234
Emp Here 5 Sales 50,632,000
SIC 1041 Gold ores
Nolan Watson
David Awram
Tom Bruington
Adam Spencer
George Darling
Keith Laskowski
Ron Ho
Erfan Kazemi
David E. De Witt
John P. A. Budreski

D-U-N-S 24-977-2851 (HQ)
SANTACRUZ SILVER MINING LTD
580 Hornby St Suite 880, Vancouver, BC, V6C 3B6
(604) 569-1609
Sales 11,396,000
SIC 1044 Silver ores
Arturo Prestamo
Robert Mcmorran
Carlos Alberto Silva Ramos
Roland Lohner
Larry Okada
Federico Villaseor

D-U-N-S 20-014-0536 (SL)
SCANLINE VFX INC
580 Granville St, Vancouver, BC, V6C 1W6
(604) 683-6822
Emp Here 170 Sales 15,157,710
SIC 7819 Services allied to motion pictures
Stephan Trojansky
Danielle Plantec

D-U-N-S 20-057-9337 (HQ)
SEASPAN SHIP MANAGEMENT LTD
(Suby of SEASPAN CORPORATION)
200 Granville St Suite 2600, Vancouver, BC, V6C 1S4
(604) 638-2575
Sales 18,716,400
SIC 8741 Management services

Gerry Wang
David Batchelder
Kyle Washington
Sai Chu

D-U-N-S 24-682-0117 (SL)
SECURED SECURITY GROUP (INTERNATIONAL) LIMITED
3555 Burrard St Suite 1400, Vancouver, BC, V6C 2G8
(604) 385-1555
Emp Here 60 Sales 23,740,680
SIC 7381 Detective and armored car services
Balraj Jouhal
Neetu Jouhal

D-U-N-S 20-336-8431 (SL)
SELECT SANDS CORP
850 Hastings St W Suite 310, Vancouver, BC, V6C 1E1
(604) 639-4533
Emp Here 7 Sales 11,866,359
SIC 1446 Industrial sand
Zigurds Vitols
Rasool Mohammad
Darren Urquhart
Daniel A. Gillett
Steven H. Goldman
Douglas Turnbull
John Kime

D-U-N-S 25-674-1562 (HQ)
SHAMARAN PETROLEUM CORP
885 Georgia St W Suite 2000, Vancouver, BC, V6C 3E8
(604) 689-7842
Sales 69,600,000
SIC 1382 Oil and gas exploration services
Adel Chaouch
Chris Bruijnzeels
Keith Hill
Terry Allen
Mike Ebsary
Brian Edgar
Brenden Johnstone

D-U-N-S 20-734-6730 (SL)
SHORE TO SEA SERVICES LLS
999 Canada Pl, Vancouver, BC, V6C 3C1
(604) 775-7200
Emp Here 50 Sales 10,669,600
SIC 4491 Marine cargo handling
Paul Mitchell

D-U-N-S 20-345-7437 (HQ)
SIERRA ONCOLOGY, INC
885 West Georgia St Suite 2150, Vancouver, BC, V6C 3E8
(604) 558-6536
Sales 42,011,739
SIC 8731 Commercial physical research
Nick Glover
Keith Anderson
Wendy Chapman
Diane Gardiner
Emma Mccann
Gregg Smith
Sukhi Jagpal
Christian Hassig
Barbara Klencke
Mark Kowalski

D-U-N-S 25-533-1498 (SL)
SILVERCORP METALS INC
200 Granville St Suite 1378, Vancouver, BC, V6C 1S4
(604) 669-9397
Emp Here 10 Sales 170,039,000
SIC 1044 Silver ores
Rui Feng
Lorne Waldman
Derek Liu
Yikang Liu
Paul Simpson
David Kong
Marina A. Katusa

D-U-N-S 20-294-4385 (BR)

SIMON FRASER UNIVERSITY
BEEDIE SCHOOL OF BUSINESS
(Suby of SIMON FRASER UNIVERSITY)
500 Granville St, Vancouver, BC, V6C 1W6
(778) 782-5013
Emp Here 100
SIC 8244 Business and secretarial schools
Danny Shapiro

D-U-N-S 24-446-0929 (SL)
SINGLETON URQUHART LLP
925 Georgia St W Suite 1200, Vancouver, BC, V6C 3L2
(604) 682-7474
Emp Here 140 Sales 15,523,480
SIC 8111 Legal services
John Singleton

D-U-N-S 20-364-9389 (HQ)
SKIDMORE DEVELOPMENT GROUP LTD
837 Hastings St W Suite 715, Vancouver, BC, V6C 3N6
(604) 757-7461
Sales 22,394,100
SIC 6159 Miscellaneous business credit institutions
Thomas Skidmore

D-U-N-S 24-373-7590 (HQ)
SMYTHE RATCLIFFE LLP
355 Burrard St Suite 700, Vancouver, BC, V6C 2G8
(604) 687-1231
Emp Here 68 Sales 16,614,800
SIC 8721 Accounting, auditing, and bookkeeping
Aaron Henshaw
Larry Vicic
Perry Munton
Kevin Nishi
Anita Johnson
Terry Rogers

D-U-N-S 25-408-9089 (SL)
SOPHOS INC
(Suby of SOPHOS GROUP PLC)
580 Granville St Suite 400, Vancouver, BC, V6C 1W6
(604) 484-6400
Emp Here 190 Sales 27,394,580
SIC 7371 Custom computer programming services
Steve Munford
Jim Zadra

D-U-N-S 20-193-7674 (HQ)
SOUTHGOBI RESOURCES LTD
250 Howe St 20th Floor, Vancouver, BC, V6C 3R8
(604) 762-6783
Emp Here 62 Sales 103,804,000
SIC 1081 Metal mining services
Shougao Wang
Tao Zhang
Allison Snetsinger
Weiguo Zhang
Aiming Guo
Mao Sun
Yingbin Ian He
Jin Lan Quan
Wen (Wayne) Yao
Zhiwei Chen

D-U-N-S 20-844-8576 (SL)
ST TOURING CANADA LTD
SCENIC TOURS
900 Georgia St W, Vancouver, BC, V6C 2W6
(604) 689-1553
Emp Here 80 Sales 41,597,360
SIC 4725 Tour operators
Lisa Mccaskill
Rhonda Gauthier

D-U-N-S 25-532-9195 (SL)
STARCORE INTERNATIONAL MINES LTD
580 Hornby St Suite 750, Vancouver, BC, V6C 3B6

(604) 602-4935
Emp Here 69   *Sales* 20,442,973
SIC 1041 Gold ores
Robert Eadie
Cory Kent
Gary Arca
Salvador Garcia
Ken Sumanik
Federico Villasenor
Tanya Lutzke
Jordan Estra

D-U-N-S 20-574-8163   (HQ)
TECK RESOURCES LIMITED
550 Burrard St Suite 3300, Vancouver, BC,
V6C 0B3
(604) 699-4000
Emp Here 5,000   *Sales* 9,524,793,528
SIC 1021 Copper ores
Donald R. Lindsay
Dale E. Andres
Alex Christopher
Andrew Golding
Kieron Mcfadyen
Ronald Millos
Andrew Milner
H. Fraser Phillips
Peter Rozee
Robin B. Sheremeta

D-U-N-S 24-961-1757   (SL)
TECK-BULLMOOSE COAL INC
(*Suby of* TECK RESOURCES LIMITED)
550 Burrard St Suite 3300, Vancouver, BC,
V6C 0B3
(604) 699-4000
Emp Here 505   *Sales* 242,219,715
SIC 1221 Bituminous coal and lignite-surface
mining
Kieth Steeves
John Taylor
Larry Mackwood
Karen Dunfee
Norman Keevil
Michael Lipkewich
Richard Mundie
Ron Millos
Howard Chu

D-U-N-S 24-881-8809   (HQ)
TEEKAY SHIPPING (CANADA) LTD
(*Suby of* TEEKAY CORPORATION)
550 Burrard St Suite 2000, Vancouver, BC,
V6C 2K2
(604) 683-3529
Sales 78,744,800
SIC 4412 Deep sea foreign transportation of
freight
Kenneth Hvid
Arthur Bensler
David Wong
Brian Fortier

D-U-N-S 20-806-5631   (SL)
TERMINAL CITY CLUB INC
837 Hastings St W Suite 100, Vancouver, BC,
V6C 1B6
(604) 488-8970
Emp Here 130   *Sales* 187,018,130
SIC 8699 Membership organizations, nec
David Long
James Pike
Alistair Black
David Cottrell
Dennis Evans
Sidney Fattedad
Frank Lo
Larry Nelson
Lisa Ohara
Kelvin Stephens

D-U-N-S 25-533-1092   (HQ)
TIO NETWORKS CORP
(*Suby of* PAYPAL HOLDINGS, INC.)
250 Howe St Unit 1550, Vancouver, BC, V6C
3R8
(604) 298-4636
Emp Here 27   *Sales* 28,175,310

SIC 6211 Security brokers and dealers
Hamed Shahbazi
Allan M. Adler
Kenneth A. Cawkell
Reid Drury
Talal Yassin
Arjan Shutte
Bill Burnham

D-U-N-S 20-354-7310   (SL)
TITAN MINING CORPORATION
999 Canada Pl Unit 555, Vancouver, BC, V6C
3C1
(604) 687-1717
Emp Here 50   *Sales* 119,377,450
SIC 1031 Lead and zinc ores
Richard Warke
Donald R. Taylor
Purni Parikh
Jacqueline Allison
Scott Burkett
Kevin Torpy
John Boehner
Lenard Boggio
Gregory Clark
James Gowans

D-U-N-S 24-447-6610   (SL)
TOKYU CANADA CORPORATION
PAN PACIFIC HOTEL
999 Canada Pl Suite 515, Vancouver, BC,
V6C 3E1

Emp Here 400
SIC 7011 Hotels and motels

D-U-N-S 24-325-4989   (SL)
TRIMETALS MINING INC
580 Hornby St Suite 880, Vancouver, BC, V6C
3B6
(604) 639-4523
Emp Here 50   *Sales* 119,377,450
SIC 1081 Metal mining services
Matias Herrero
Randall L. Moore
Felipe Malbran
Killian Ruby
Robert Van Doorn
Antonio Canton
Tina Woodside
Roman Mironchik
Victor Dario

D-U-N-S 25-387-7690   (HQ)
TURQUOISE HILL RESOURCES LTD
200 Granville St Suite 354, Vancouver, BC,
V6C 1S4
(604) 688-5755
Sales 1,180,022,000
SIC 1081 Metal mining services
Ulf Quellmann
Dustin S. Isaacs
Luke Colton
Jo-Anne Dudley
Peter Gillin
James Gill
Russel Robertson
Maryse Saint-Laurent
Stephen Jones
Alan Chirgwin

D-U-N-S 24-333-1118   (HQ)
UNISYNC CORP
885 West Georgia St Suite 1328, Vancouver,
BC, V6C 3E8
(778) 370-1725
Emp Here 5   *Sales* 58,818,710
SIC 2339 Women's and misses' outerwear,
nec
Carmin Garofalo
Douglas F. Good
Richard Smith
Bruce W. Aunger
Darryl R. Eddy
Joseph M. Gantz
Joel R. Mclean
C. O'brian

D-U-N-S 24-339-1443   (HQ)
URTHECAST CORP
1055 Canada Pl Unit 33, Vancouver, BC, V6C
0C3
(604) 265-6266
Emp Here 63   *Sales* 11,852,167
SIC 8713 Surveying services
Don Osborne
Peter Duggan
Sai Chu
George Tyc
Adam Vore
Pirmin Luond
Jack Shannon
Andreas Georghiou
Mark Piegza
Mac Evans

D-U-N-S 24-374-6463   (SL)
VALORE METALS CORP
800 Pender St W Suite 1020, Vancouver, BC,
V6C 2V6
(604) 646-4527
Emp Here 6   *Sales* 14,325,294
SIC 1094 Uranium-radium-vanadium ores
Jim Paterson
Jeffrey Dare
Robert J. Scott
Dale Wallster
Jim Malone
Garth Kirkham

D-U-N-S 24-292-5931   (HQ)
**VANCITY COMMUNITY INVESTMENT
BANK**
(*Suby of* VANCOUVER CITY SAVINGS
CREDIT UNION)
815 Hastings St W Suite 401, Vancouver, BC,
V6C 1B4
(604) 708-7800
Emp Here 350   *Sales* 107,313,200
SIC 6021 National commercial banks
Tamara Vrooman
Virginia Weiler
William Knight
Doug Brownridge
Chris Dobrzanski
Alexandra Wilson
Jay-Ann Gilfoy

D-U-N-S 24-334-9599   (SL)
VANCOUVER BAY CLUBS LTD
STEVE NASH SPORTS CLUB
610 Granville St Suite 201, Vancouver, BC,
V6C 3T3
(604) 682-5213
Emp Here 75   *Sales* 10,502,175
SIC 7999 Amusement and recreation, nec
Don Harbich

D-U-N-S 24-996-2317   (HQ)
**VANCOUVER BULLION AND CURRENCY
EXCHANGE LTD**
VBCE
800 Pender St W Suite 120, Vancouver, BC,
V6C 2V6
(604) 685-1008
Emp Here 25   *Sales* 13,818,000
SIC 6099 Functions related to deposit banking
Tony Ma

D-U-N-S 24-362-4892   (HQ)
**VANCOUVER CAREER COLLEGE (BURN-
ABY) INC**
CDI COLLEGE
(*Suby of* CHUNG FAMILY HOLDINGS INC)
400 Burrard St Suite 1800, Vancouver, BC,
V6C 3A6
(604) 915-7288
Sales 29,735,700
SIC 8211 Elementary and secondary schools
Peter Chung

D-U-N-S 20-116-8820   (SL)
VANCOUVER CLUB, THE
915 Hastings St W, Vancouver, BC, V6C 1C6
(604) 685-9321
Emp Here 70   *Sales* 10,001,530

SIC 8641 Civic and social associations
Philip Ireland
Steven Cannizzaro

D-U-N-S 24-358-1688   (HQ)
VANCOUVER FRASER PORT AUTHORITY
PORT METRO VANCOUVER
(*Suby of* GOVERNMENT OF CANADA)
999 Canada Pl Suite 100, Vancouver, BC,
V6C 3T4
(604) 665-9000
Emp Here 100   *Sales* 69,472,200
SIC 4491 Marine cargo handling
Judy Rogers
Robin Silvester
Sandra Case
Chief Clarence Louie
Victor Pang

D-U-N-S 20-867-5525   (SL)
VARSHNEY CAPITAL CORPORATION
925 Georgia St W Suite 1304, Vancouver, BC,
V6C 3L2
(604) 684-2181
Emp Here 15   *Sales* 10,183,845
SIC 6282 Investment advice
Hari Varshney
Peeyush Varshney
Praveen Varshney

D-U-N-S 24-640-9734   (HQ)
VENTURES WEST MANAGEMENT INC
999 Hastings St W Suite 400, Vancouver, BC,
V6C 2W2

Emp Here 19   *Sales* 20,207,490
SIC 6799 Investors, nec
Robin Louis
Ted Anderson
Samuel Znaimer
Barry Gekiere
David Berkowitz
Howard Riback

D-U-N-S 25-416-6010   (SL)
**WATERBORNE UNDERWRITING SER-
VICES LTD**
(*Suby of* THE SHIPOWNERS' MUTUAL PRO-
TECTION AND INDEMNITY ASSOCIATION
(LUXEMBOURG) ASSOC.ASSUR.MUT.)
409 Granville St Suite 1157, Vancouver, BC,
V6C 1T2

Emp Here 6   *Sales* 11,079,954
SIC 6331 Fire, marine, and casualty insurance
Francis Fyfe
Rosemary Adams
Simon Swallow
Les Jourdain

D-U-N-S 24-131-9198   (HQ)
WESTERNONE INC
925 Georgia St W Suite 910, Vancouver, BC,
V6C 3L2
(604) 678-4042
Emp Here 100   *Sales* 62,372,604
SIC 6722 Management investment, open-end
Peter Blake
Geoff Shorten
Geraldine Prior
Jason Gray
Carlos Yam
Robert W. King
T. Richard Turner
J. Lee Matheson

D-U-N-S 25-400-0243   (HQ)
**WESTSHORE TERMINALS INVESTMENT
CORPORATION**
1067 Cordova St W Suite 1800, Vancouver,
BC, V6C 1C7
(604) 946-4491
Emp Here 1   *Sales* 275,470,766
SIC 6722 Management investment, open-end
Glenn Dudar
Angela Morfitt
David Honsberger

Greg Andrew
Joost Van Woerden
Peter Prince-Wright

D-U-N-S 24-314-2481   (SL)
WILSON BANWELL INTERNATIONAL INC
355 Burrard St Suite 1600, Vancouver, BC, V6C 2G8
(604) 689-1717
Emp Here 3   *Sales* 33,348,700
SIC 6712 Bank holding companies
William Barker
Greg Banwell
Robert Wilson

D-U-N-S 20-309-7972   (SL)
YEUNG, GAYNOR C. LAW CORPORATION
WHITELAW TWINING
200 Granville St Suite 2400, Vancouver, BC, V6C 1S4
(604) 682-5466
Emp Here 95   *Sales* 14,631,045
SIC 8111 Legal services
Gaynor Yeung

D-U-N-S 20-588-0164   (HQ)
YOUNG WOMEN'S CHRISTIAN ASSOCIA-TION
Y W C A
535 Hornby St, Vancouver, BC, V6C 2E8
(604) 895-5800
Emp Here 100   *Sales* 30,613,760
SIC 7011 Hotels and motels
Janet Austin
Helen Ghabel
Arthur Mills
Marnie Marley

D-U-N-S 20-991-6134   (BR)
YOUNG WOMEN'S CHRISTIAN ASSOCIA-TION
(*Suby of* YOUNG WOMEN'S CHRISTIAN AS-SOCIATION)
535 Hornby St Suite 100, Vancouver, BC, V6C 2E8
(604) 895-5777
Emp Here 100
SIC 8641 Civic and social associations
Janet Austin

D-U-N-S 24-593-8766   (HQ)
ZLC FINANCIAL GROUP LTD
666 Burrard St Suite 1200, Vancouver, BC, V6C 2X8
(604) 684-3863
Emp Here 40   *Sales* 42,403,000
SIC 6411 Insurance agents, brokers, and ser-vice
Marc Zlotnik
Marty Zlotnik
Garry Zlotnik
Peter Lamb

Vancouver, BC V6E

D-U-N-S 24-134-6563   (SL)
3MC INVESTMENTS LTD
1030 Georgia St W Suite 1700, Vancouver, BC, V6E 2Y3
(604) 602-1887
Emp Here 50   *Sales* 14,164,650
SIC 8741 Management services
David Spear

D-U-N-S 24-134-7827   (SL)
462388 BC LTD
GRAND ADEX MANAGEMENT
1095 Pender St W Suite 1000, Vancouver, BC, V6E 2M6
(604) 662-3838
Emp Here 40   *Sales* 13,085,080
SIC 6531 Real estate agents and managers
Terrence Hui

D-U-N-S 20-329-6236   (HQ)

A THINKING APE ENTERTAINMENT LTD
1132 Alberni St Unit 200, Vancouver, BC, V6E 1A5
(604) 682-7773
Sales 10,638,660
SIC 7371 Custom computer programming ser-vices
Kenshi Arasaki
Eric Diep

D-U-N-S 25-187-1018   (SL)
AB PALISADES LIMITED PARTNERSHIP
ZIN RESTAURANT & LOUNGE
1277 Robson St, Vancouver, BC, V6E 1C2
(604) 688-0461
Emp Here 150   *Sales* 13,903,500
SIC 7011 Hotels and motels
Tom Waithe

D-U-N-S 24-680-6371   (SL)
ACADIAN TIMBER CORP
1055 Georgia St W Suite 1800, Vancouver, BC, V6E 0B6
(604) 661-9143
Emp Here 92   *Sales* 75,694,968
SIC 5082 Construction and mining machinery
Mark Bishop
Matthew Gross
Marcia A. Mckeague
Luc Ouellet
Mabel Wong
Kevin Topolniski
Benjamin Vaughan
Phil Brown
Reid Carter
David Mann

D-U-N-S 24-206-5873   (SL)
ACTIVESTATE SOFTWARE INC
1177 Hastings St W Unit 1000, Vancouver, BC, V6E 2K3
(778) 786-1100
Emp Here 50   *Sales* 10,692,550
SIC 7372 Prepackaged software
Bart Copeland
Maria Chu
David Roberts
Kelly Edmison

D-U-N-S 24-297-2127   (BR)
ALTUS GROUP LIMITED
(*Suby of* ALTUS GROUP LIMITED)
1055 West Georgia St Suite 2500, Vancouver, BC, V6E 0B6
(604) 683-5591
Emp Here 80
SIC 6722 Management investment, open-end
Pedro Tavares

D-U-N-S 20-302-2207   (HQ)
ARDENTON CAPITAL CORPORATION
ARDENTON FINANCIAL
1021 West Hastings St Unit 2400, Vancouver, BC, V6E 0C3
(604) 833-4899
Sales 389,194,000
SIC 6162 Mortgage bankers and loan corre-spondents
James Livingstone

D-U-N-S 20-978-1934   (HQ)
ASANKO GOLD INC
1066 Hastings St W Suite 680, Vancouver, BC, V6E 3X2
(604) 683-8193
Emp Here 24   *Sales* 161,918,000
SIC 1011 Iron ores
Greg Mccunn
Frederick Attakumah
Fausto Di Trapani
Josephat Zvaipa
Mike Begg
Charles Amoah
Colin Steyn
Gordon J. Fretwell
Marcel De Groot
Michael Price

D-U-N-S 24-368-2593   (HQ)
AURORA CANNABIS INC
1199 Hastings St W Suite 1500, Vancouver, BC, V6E 3T5

Emp Here 10   *Sales* 43,055,419
SIC 2833 Medicinals and botanicals
Terry Booth
Steve Dobler
Cameron Battley
Glen Ibbott
Allan Cleiren
Jillian Swainson
Neil Belot
Darryl Vleeming
Debra Wilson
Darren Karasiuk

D-U-N-S 24-390-1662   (HQ)
AURYN RESOURCES INC
1199 Hastings St W Suite 600, Vancouver, BC, V6E 3T5
(778) 729-0600
Emp Here 15   *Sales* 40,588,333
SIC 1081 Metal mining services
Shawn Wallace
Ivan Bebek
Russell Starr
Michael Henrichsen
Michael Kosowan
Steve Cook
Gordon Fretwell
Antonio Arribas
Daniel Mccoy

D-U-N-S 20-959-7236   (BR)
AXA ASSURANCES INC
AXA PACIFIC INSURANCE
(*Suby of* AXA ASSURANCES INC)
1090 Georgia St W Suite 1350, Vancouver, BC, V6E 3V7

Emp Here 160
SIC 6311 Life insurance
Bob Kozak

D-U-N-S 20-551-1996   (HQ)
BD CANADA LTD
COBS BREAD
(*Suby of* BAKERS DELIGHT HOLDINGS LTD.)
1100 Melville St Unit 210, Vancouver, BC, V6E 4A6
(604) 296-3500
Emp Here 30   *Sales* 96,232,000
SIC 5461 Retail bakeries
Braeden Lord
Roger Gillespie

D-U-N-S 25-998-5034   (HQ)
BFL CANADA INSURANCE SERVICES INC
(*Suby of* FIRST LION HOLDINGS INC)
1177 Hastings St W Suite 200, Vancouver, BC, V6E 2K3
(604) 669-9600
Emp Here 100   *Sales* 1,186,526,000
SIC 6411 Insurance agents, brokers, and ser-vice
Bradley Potter
Barry Lorenzetti

D-U-N-S 20-382-4383   (SL)
BPRE SAINT LOUIS HOLDINGS, LIMITED PARTNERSHIP
1075 Georgia St W Suite 2010, Vancouver, BC, V6E 3C9
(604) 806-3350
Emp Here 50   *Sales* 13,077,650
SIC 6712 Bank holding companies
Mark Scott
Michael Wong

D-U-N-S 25-538-7821   (SL)
CANAF INVESTMENTS INC
CANAF
1111 Melville St Bureau 1100, Vancouver, BC, V6E 3V6

(604) 283-6110
Emp Here 10   *Sales* 14,673,658
SIC 1221 Bituminous coal and lignite-surface mining
Christopher Way
Rebecca Williams
Richard Skeith
David Way
Kevin Corrigan

D-U-N-S 20-703-8725   (HQ)
CANWEL BUILDING MATERIALS GROUP LTD
1055 Georgia St W Suite 1100, Vancouver, BC, V6E 0B6
(604) 432-1400
Emp Here 135   *Sales* 978,933,322
SIC 5039 Construction materials, nec
Amar S. Doman
Marc Seguin
David Stojni
Michel Parent
Julie Wong
Michel Walsh
James Code
Tom Donaldson
Kelvin Dushnisky
Sam Fleiser

D-U-N-S 24-797-6244   (HQ)
CANWEL BUILDING MATERIALS LTD
SUREWOOD FOREST PRODUCTS, DIV OF
(*Suby of* CANWEL BUILDING MATERIALS GROUP LTD)
1055 West Georgia St Suite 1100, Vancouver, BC, V6E 3P3
(604) 432-1400
Emp Here 62   *Sales* 398,739,600
SIC 5039 Construction materials, nec
Amar Doman
Marc Seguin
R.S. (Rob) Doman
Julie Wong
James Code

D-U-N-S 25-991-0883   (BR)
CBRE LIMITEE
CBRE LIMITED
(*Suby of* CBRE LIMITED PARTNERSHIP)
1021 Hastings St W Suite 2500, Vancouver, BC, V6E 0C3
(604) 319-1374
Emp Here 80
SIC 6531 Real estate agents and managers
Jim Szabo

D-U-N-S 24-181-1970   (HQ)
CENGEA SOLUTIONS INC
(*Suby of* TRIMBLE INC.)
1188 Georgia St W Suite 560, Vancouver, BC, V6E 4A2
(604) 697-6400
Emp Here 23   *Sales* 10,344,514
SIC 7372 Prepackaged software
K. Garry Rasmussen
Darcy Bennett
Kenneth Moen

D-U-N-S 24-227-5258   (SL)
CGTV GAMES LTD
1199 Pender St W Suite 800, Vancouver, BC, V6E 2R1

Emp Here 73   *Sales* 13,161,401
SIC 7371 Custom computer programming ser-vices
David Mathewson
Robert Carlsson

D-U-N-S 20-110-1730   (HQ)
CHEVRON CANADA LIMITED
CHEVRON CANADA RESOURCES
(*Suby of* CHEVRON CORPORATION)
1050 Pender St W Suite 1200, Vancouver, BC, V6E 3T4
(604) 668-5300
Emp Here 350   *Sales* 1,340,300,000
SIC 2911 Petroleum refining

▲ Public Company   ■ Public Company Family Member   **HQ** Headquarters   **BR** Branch   **SL** Single Location

Jeff Gustavos
Alan Dunlop
Steven Parker

D-U-N-S 24-270-3971   (SL)
CHEVRON CORP.
1050 Pender St W Suite 1200, Vancouver, BC,
V6E 3T4
(604) 668-5671
Emp Here 5   *Sales* 15,529,285
SIC 4923 Gas transmission and distribution
C. Mar

D-U-N-S 20-291-6631   (SL)
CITY OFFICE REIT, INC
1075 Georgia St W Suite 2010, Vancouver,
BC, V6E 3C9
(604) 806-3366
Emp Here 500   *Sales* 129,484,000
SIC 6798 Real estate investment trusts
James Farrar
Greg Tylee
Anthony Maretic
John Mclernon
William Flatt
Sabah Mirza
Mark Murski
Stephen Shraiberg
John Sweet

D-U-N-S 24-390-8766   (SL)
COAST FRASER ENTERPRISES LTD
1177 West Hastings St Suite 2101, Vancouver, BC, V6E 2K3
(604) 498-1110
Emp Here 25   *Sales* 11,179,350
SIC 5031 Lumber, plywood, and millwork
Frank Hui
Hong Bian

D-U-N-S 20-712-8125   (HQ)
COAST HOTELS LIMITED
COAST HOTELS AND RESORTS
(*Suby of* OKABE CO., LTD.)
1090 Georgia St W Suite 900, Vancouver, BC,
V6E 3V7
(604) 682-7982
Emp Here 60   *Sales* 86,101,200
SIC 7011 Hotels and motels
Noriaki Matsumoto
Victor Komoda
Pia Collins
Linda Hagen
Mark Hope
Manny Ilao
Sarah Kirby Yung
Wendy Lamont

D-U-N-S 25-193-3586   (BR)
COMPAGNIE DE TELEPHONE BELL DU CANADA OU BELL CANADA, LA
(*Suby of* BCE INC)
1066 Hastings St W Suite 1500, Vancouver,
BC, V6E 3X2
(604) 484-1010
Emp Here 100
SIC 4899 Communication services, nec
Greg Maffei

D-U-N-S 25-719-4324   (HQ)
CONNOR, CLARK & LUNN FINANCIAL GROUP
1111 Georgia St W Suite 2200, Vancouver,
BC, V6E 4M3
(604) 685-4465
Sales 43,988,600
SIC 8732 Commercial nonphysical research
Larry Lunn
Phillip Cotterill
Brian Eby
Gordon Macdougall
Gary Baker

D-U-N-S 24-491-7514   (HQ)
CONNOR, CLARK & LUNN INVESTMENT MANAGEMENT LTD
1111 Georgia St W Unit 2300, Vancouver, BC,

V6E 4M3
(604) 685-2020
Emp Here 100   *Sales* 247,626,012
SIC 6282 Investment advice
Larry R. Lunn
Patrick Robitaille
Steve Affleck
Andrew Lefevre
Gordon H. Macdougall
Warren Stoddart
Martin Gerber
Phillip Cotterill
Brian Eby
Gary Baker

D-U-N-S 24-313-0148   (SL)
CORE GOLD INC
1166 Alberni St Suite 1201, Vancouver, BC,
V6E 3Z3
(604) 345-4822
Emp Here 513   *Sales* 27,270,000
SIC 1041 Gold ores
Mark Bailey
Sam Wong
Gregg J. Sedun
Keith Piggott
Javier Reyes
Leonard Clough

D-U-N-S 20-248-4270   (SL)
CORINEX COMMUNICATIONS CORP
CORINEX COMMUNICATION
1090 Pender St W Suite 1000, Vancouver, BC,
V6E 2N7
(604) 692-0520
Emp Here 180   *Sales* 34,279,560
SIC 3669 Communications equipment, nec
Peter Sobotka
Norbert Benko
Sam Shi

D-U-N-S 24-308-9880   (HQ)
CORIX INFRASTRUCTURE INC
CORIX GROUP OF COMPANIES
1188 Georgia St W Suite 1160, Vancouver,
BC, V6E 4A2
(604) 697-6700
Emp Here 120   *Sales* 839,574,173
SIC 6712 Bank holding companies
Brett Hodson
Gordon Barefoot
Susan Paish
Garry Thompson
Lincoln Webb
Peter Restler
John Reid

D-U-N-S 24-308-4410   (HQ)
CORIX UTILITIES INC
(*Suby of* CORIX INFRASTRUCTURE INC)
1188 Georgia St W Suite 1160, Vancouver,
BC, V6E 4A2
(604) 697-6700
Emp Here 2   *Sales* 25,244,200
SIC 1623 Water, sewer, and utility lines
Brett Hodson

D-U-N-S 20-799-1733   (HQ)
CREDENTIAL FINANCIAL INC
1111 Georgia St W Suite 800, Vancouver, BC,
V6E 4T6
(604) 714-3800
Sales 36,465,975
SIC 8741 Management services
Don Rolfe
John Ebsary
Kenn Lalonde
John Thompson
Norman Ayoub
Bob Hague
Stephen Bolton
David Mortimer
Sid Bildfell
Ian Glassford

D-U-N-S 24-356-7620   (HQ)
CREDENTIAL FINANCIAL STRATEGIES

INC
CREDENTIAL
1111 Georgia St W Suite 800, Vancouver, BC,
V6E 4T6
(604) 742-8259
Emp Here 40   *Sales* 16,599,034
SIC 8742 Management consulting services
Doce Tomic
Rick Sielski
Bruce West
Russ Fast
Christ Catliff
Yasmin Lalani
Marcel Schroder
Randal Biberdorf
Marilyn Brennan
Gavin Toy

D-U-N-S 25-497-8786   (HQ)
CREDENTIAL SECURITIES INC
CSI
(*Suby of* CREDENTIAL FINANCIAL INC)
1111 Georgia St W Suite 800, Vancouver, BC,
V6E 4T6
(604) 714-3900
Emp Here 20   *Sales* 384,247,260
SIC 6211 Security brokers and dealers
Don Rolfe
John G M Fries
Lothar Fabian
Helen Elizabeth Blackburn

D-U-N-S 20-191-1000   (HQ)
CRUISESHIPCENTERS   INTERNATIONAL INC
1055 Hastings St W Suite 400, Vancouver,
BC, V6E 2E9
(604) 685-1221
Emp Here 78   *Sales* 358,187,547
SIC 6794 Patent owners and lessors
Michael Drever
Rob Jacoby
Julie Wong

D-U-N-S 24-957-4591   (SL)
DALE   MATHESON   CARR-HILTON LABONTE LLP
DMCL CHARTTERED PROFENSSIONAL ACCOUNTANT
1140 Pender St W Suite 1500, Vancouver, BC,
V6E 4G1
(604) 687-4747
Emp Here 200   *Sales* 41,537,000
SIC 8721 Accounting, auditing, and bookkeeping
Alvin Dale
Fraser Ross

D-U-N-S 24-641-8263   (HQ)
DASSAULT SYSTEMES CANADA SOFTWARE INC
GEMCOM SOFTWARE INTERNATIONAL
(*Suby of* DASSAULT SYSTEMES)
1066 Hastings St W Suite 1100, Vancouver,
BC, V6E 3X1
(604) 684-6550
Emp Here 75   *Sales* 57,672,800
SIC 7371 Custom computer programming services
Richard M. Moignard
Eric Palmer

D-U-N-S 20-587-9588   (SL)
DAVIDSON & SONS CUSTOMS BROKERS LTD
(*Suby of* DAVIDSON & SONS VENTURES LTD)
1188 Georgia St W Suite 1220, Vancouver,
BC, V6E 4A2
(604) 681-5132
Emp Here 30   *Sales* 15,599,010
SIC 4731 Freight transportation arrangement
Barry Davidson
William F Davidson

D-U-N-S 25-152-9509   (SL)
DRAKE MEDOX HEALTH SERVICES (VAN-

COUVER) INC
DRAKE MEDOX HEALTH SERVICES
1166 Alberni St Suite 802, Vancouver, BC,
V6E 3Z3
(604) 682-2801
Emp Here 50   *Sales* 11,581,650
SIC 8621 Professional organizations
Bruce Chutka

D-U-N-S 25-536-2071   (SL)
DYLAN RYAN TELESERVICES
1177 Hastings St W Suite 411, Vancouver,
BC, V6E 2K3

Emp Here 100   *Sales* 45,094,896
SIC 7389 Business services, nec
Stephen Greenspoon

D-U-N-S 24-796-8324   (SL)
EASTERN PLATINUM LIMITED
EASTPLATS
1188 Georgia St W Suite 1080, Vancouver,
BC, V6E 4A2
(604) 800-8200
Emp Here 7   *Sales* 16,712,843
SIC 1081 Metal mining services
Diana Hu
Rowland Wallenius
Andrea Zhang
George Dorin
Michael Cosic
Bielin Shi
Nigel K Dentoom

D-U-N-S 25-321-9786   (BR)
ECONOMICAL MUTUAL INSURANCE COMPANY
(*Suby of* ECONOMICAL MUTUAL INSURANCE COMPANY)
1055 Georgia St W Suite 1900, Vancouver,
BC, V6E 0B6
(800) 951-6665
Emp Here 97
SIC 6331 Fire, marine, and casualty insurance
Gary Horga

D-U-N-S 25-194-5309   (SL)
ELASTIC PATH SOFTWARE INC
745 Thurlow St Unit 1400, Vancouver, BC,
V6E 0C5
(604) 408-8078
Emp Here 120   *Sales* 17,301,840
SIC 7371 Custom computer programming services
Harry Chemko
Gord Janzen
Peter Lukomskyj
Sean Skamnes
Peter Ford
Mark Miller
Darin Archer
Sal Visca
Brenton Brown

D-U-N-S 25-357-5336   (SL)
ENTREE GOLD INC
1066 Hastings St W Suite 1650, Vancouver,
BC, V6E 3X1
(604) 687-4777
Emp Here 130   *Sales* 310,381,370
SIC 1081 Metal mining services
Greg Crowe
Lindsay Bottomer
James Harris
Peter Meredith
Mark Bailey
Michael Howard

D-U-N-S 24-354-7911   (HQ)
EXCELSIOR MINING CORP
1140 Pender St W Suite 1240, Vancouver, BC,
V6E 4G1
(604) 681-8030
Emp Here 5   *Sales* 71,626,470
SIC 1021 Copper ores
Stephen Twyerould
Rebecca Sawyer

Jj Jennex
Sheila Paine
Carlo Valente
Roland Goodgame
Mark J. Morabito
Lord Robin Renwick
Michael Haworth
Jim Kolbe

D-U-N-S 24-798-9940   (SL)
FAIRMONT SHIPPING (CANADA) LIMITED
1112 Pender St W Suite 300, Vancouver, BC,
V6E 2S1
(604) 685-3318
Emp Here 50   *Sales* 25,998,350
SIC 4731 Freight transportation arrangement
Steven Ho

D-U-N-S 25-681-6760   (HQ)
FAMILY INSURANCE SOLUTIONS INC
(*Suby of* ECONOMICAL MUTUAL INSUR-
ANCE COMPANY)
1177 Hastings St W Suite 1400, Vancouver,
BC, V6E 2K3
(604) 687-2655
Sales 129,341,940
SIC 6411 Insurance agents, brokers, and ser-
vice
John Preston
Joanne Challen

D-U-N-S 25-360-8566   (BR)
FLUOR CANADA LTD
FLUOR DANIEL
(*Suby of* FLUOR CORPORATION)
1075 Georgia St W Suite 700, Vancouver, BC,
V6E 4M7
(604) 488-2000
Emp Here 400
SIC 8711 Engineering services
Norene Hanes

D-U-N-S 25-612-4488   (SL)
**FORTES, JOE SEAFOOD & CHOP HOUSE
LTD**
777 Thurlow St, Vancouver, BC, V6E 3V5
(604) 669-1940
Emp Here 115   *Sales* 5,363,485
SIC 5812 Eating places
Wilbert (Bud) Kanke

D-U-N-S 24-798-1798   (HQ)
FORTISBC HOLDINGS INC
(*Suby of* FORTIS INC)
1111 Georgia St W Suite 1000, Vancouver,
BC, V6E 4M3
(604) 443-6525
Emp Here 200   *Sales* 2,940,938,562
SIC 4923 Gas transmission and distribution
John C Walker
David Bennett
Roger Dall'antonia
Cynthia Des Brisay
Michele Leeners
Tom Loski
Michael Mulcahy
Doyle Sam
Douglas Stout
Stanley Marshall

D-U-N-S 25-530-9171   (SL)
FPX NICKEL CORP
1155 W Pender St Suite 725, Vancouver, BC,
V6E 2P4
(604) 681-8600
Emp Here 100   *Sales* 23,343,500
SIC 1061 Ferroalloy ores, except vanadium
Martin Turenne
J. Christopher Mitchell
Peter M. D. Bradshaw
William H. Myckatyn
John A. Mcdonald
Rob Pease
Peter Marshall
James S. Gilbert

D-U-N-S 20-379-8806   (SL)

FUM MEDIA CORP
1151 Georgia St W Suite 3205, Vancouver,
BC, V6E 0B3
(778) 859-5882
Emp Here 5   *Sales* 10,000,000
SIC 7311 Advertising agencies
Minh Dang
Simon Yang

D-U-N-S 20-116-1882   (SL)
G2 OCEAN SHIPPING (CANADA) LTD
(*Suby of* GEARBULK HOLDING AG)
1111 Hastings St W Suite 900, Vancouver,
BC, V6E 2J3
(604) 661-2020
Emp Here 25   *Sales* 12,999,175
SIC 4731 Freight transportation arrangement
Rune Birkeland

D-U-N-S 24-352-2591   (SL)
GATEWAY SECURITIES INC
1177 Hastings St W Suite 168, Vancouver,
BC, V6E 2K3

Emp Here 31   *Sales* 21,400,592
SIC 6211 Security brokers and dealers
Mark Lotz
Jason Chen

D-U-N-S 24-195-3764   (SL)
GEKKO SYSTEMS INC
(*Suby of* GEKKO SYSTEMS PTY LTD)
1112 Pender St W Suite 908, Vancouver, BC,
V6E 2S1
(604) 681-2288
Emp Here 150   *Sales* 73,159,500
SIC 5082 Construction and mining machinery
Gregory Rasmussen

D-U-N-S 20-610-9527   (HQ)
GENERAL CREDIT SERVICES INC
1201 West Pender St Suite 400, Vancouver,
BC, V6E 2V2
(604) 688-6097
Emp Here 12   *Sales* 16,937,920
SIC 7322 Adjustment and collection services
Peter Sorrentino
Heidi Roszmann

D-U-N-S 20-279-1240   (HQ)
GIBRALTAR MINES LTD
(*Suby of* TASEKO MINES LIMITED)
1040 Georgia St W, Vancouver, BC, V6E 4H1
(778) 373-4533
Emp Here 600   *Sales* 166,253,100
SIC 1081 Metal mining services
Russell Hallbauer
Ronald Thiessen
Stuart Mcdonald

D-U-N-S 25-508-6183   (HQ)
GOLDGROUP MINING INC
1166 Alberni St Suite 1502, Vancouver, BC,
V6E 3Z3
(604) 682-1943
Emp Here 2   *Sales* 21,093,000
SIC 1041 Gold ores
Keith Piggott
Anthony Balic
Javier Montano
Javier Reyes
Corry J. Silbernagel
Harry Burgess

D-U-N-S 24-787-4238   (SL)
GOLDMINING INC
1030 W Georgia St Suite 1830, Vancouver,
BC, V6E 2Y3
(604) 630-1000
Emp Here 5   *Sales* 11,937,745
SIC 1041 Gold ores
Garnet Dawson
Amir Adnani
Paulo Pereira
Jeff Wright
Pat Obara
Mario Garnero

Herb Dhaliwal
David Kong
Gloria Ballesta

D-U-N-S 20-693-0179   (HQ)
GOLDSTRIKE RESOURCES LTD
1130 W Pender St Suite 1010, Vancouver, BC,
V6E 4A4
(604) 681-1820
Emp Here 6   *Sales* 33,425,686
SIC 1041 Gold ores
Terrence King
John Kuehne
Lucy Zhang
William Chornobay
Reimer Koch
Lawrence Dick

D-U-N-S 25-104-9912   (HQ)
GOLFBC HOLDINGS INC
*GALLAGHERS CANYON GOLF COURSE
(KELOWNA)*
1030 Georgia St W Suite 1800, Vancouver,
BC, V6E 2Y3
(604) 681-8700
Emp Here 20   *Sales* 52,671,500
SIC 7992 Public golf courses
Caleb Chan
Tom Chan
Donald Lee

D-U-N-S 24-447-8616   (SL)
GRANVILLE WEST GROUP LTD
1075 Georgia St W Suite 1425, Vancouver,
BC, V6E 3C9
(604) 687-5570
Emp Here 25   *Sales* 16,973,075
SIC 6282 Investment advice
John Humphries
Lorne Wilson
Ian Dixon
Paul B Shaw

D-U-N-S 20-229-5361   (BR)
**GREAT-WEST LIFE ASSURANCE COM-
PANY, THE**
(*Suby of* POWER CORPORATION DU
CANADA)
1075 Georgia St W Suite 900, Vancouver, BC,
V6E 4N4
(604) 646-1200
Emp Here 160
SIC 6321 Accident and health insurance
Trent Yochin

D-U-N-S 24-392-9804   (SL)
GROWTH WORKS LTD
2600-1055 Georgia St W, Vancouver, BC, V6E
0B6
(604) 688-9631
Emp Here 20   *Sales* 13,578,460
SIC 6211 Security brokers and dealers
David Levi

D-U-N-S 25-672-0426   (HQ)
GROWTHWORKS CAPITAL LTD
1055 Georgia St W Suite 2600, Vancouver,
BC, V6E 0B6
(604) 633-1418
Emp Here 50   *Sales* 82,595,520
SIC 6799 Investors, nec
David Levi

D-U-N-S 20-379-5760   (SL)
GSL HOLDINGS LTD
GSL GROUP
1177 W Hastings St Suite 2088, Vancouver,
BC, V6E 2K3
(604) 688-8999
Emp Here 50   *Sales* 16,356,350
SIC 6531 Real estate agents and managers
Graham Lee

D-U-N-S 24-647-6956   (HQ)
H.R.A. INVESTMENTS LTD
HRA DIAMONDS
1021 Hastings St W Unit 2300, Vancouver,
BC, V6E 0C3

(604) 669-9562
Emp Here 24   *Sales* 13,013,550
SIC 5094 Jewelry and precious stones
Uri Ariel
Sara Ariel

D-U-N-S 24-166-2386   (SL)
HARO PARK CENTRE SOCIETY
1233 Haro St, Vancouver, BC, V6E 3Y5
(604) 687-5584
Emp Here 200   *Sales* 12,856,400
SIC 8361 Residential care
Cathrine Kohm
Margery Evjen

D-U-N-S 20-273-1779   (BR)
HATCH LTD
(*Suby of* HATCHCOS HOLDINGS LTD)
1066 Hastings St W Suite 400, Vancouver,
BC, V6E 3X1
(604) 689-5767
Emp Here 135
SIC 8711 Engineering services
Margaret Jennings

D-U-N-S 24-291-7573   (SL)
HEMISPHERE ENERGY CORPORATION
905 W Pender St Suite 501, Vancouver, BC,
V6E 2E9
(604) 685-9255
Emp Here 10   *Sales* 13,461,192
SIC 1382 Oil and gas exploration services
Don Simmons
Andrew Arthur
Ashley Ramsden-Wood
Dorlyn Evanic
Ian Duncan
Charles O'sullivan
Frank S. Borowicz
Bruce Mcintyre
Gregg Vernon
Richard Wyman

D-U-N-S 25-100-8868   (BR)
HOLLYBURN PROPERTIES LIMITED
(*Suby of* HOLLYBURN PROPERTIES LIM-
ITED)
1160 Haro St Suite 101, Vancouver, BC, V6E
1E2
(604) 685-8525
Emp Here 200
SIC 6513 Apartment building operators
Allan Wassel

D-U-N-S 25-500-6843   (HQ)
HUB FINANCIAL (BC) INC, THE
1185 Georgia St W Suite 800, Vancouver, BC,
V6E 4E6
(604) 684-0086
Emp Here 28   *Sales* 295,638,720
SIC 6411 Insurance agents, brokers, and ser-
vice
Terri Diflorio

D-U-N-S 25-418-0698   (SL)
HUNTER DICKINSON INC
HDI
1040 Georgia St W Suite 1500, Vancouver,
BC, V6E 4H8
(604) 684-6365
Emp Here 75   *Sales* 17,507,625
SIC 1081 Metal mining services
Ronald Thiessen
Robert Dickinson
David Copeland
Scott Cousens

D-U-N-S 24-787-1163   (BR)
IBI GROUP
(*Suby of* IBI GROUP)
1285 Pender St W Suite 700, Vancouver, BC,
V6E 4B1
(604) 683-8797
Emp Here 130
SIC 8712 Architectural services
Ronald Eagleston

D-U-N-S 24-850-7621   (SL)

IDC WORLDSOURCE INSURANCE NET-WORK INC
1075 Georgia St W, Vancouver, BC, V6E 3C9
(604) 689-8289
Emp Here 61   *Sales* 112,646,199
SIC 6351 Surety insurance
Paul Brown
Ron Madzia

D-U-N-S 20-279-4947   (SL)
INCA ONE GOLD CORP
1140 West Pender Suite 850, Vancouver, BC, V6E 4G1
(604) 568-4877
Emp Here 7   *Sales* 12,916,572
SIC 3339 Primary nonferrous Metals, nec
Bruce Bragagnolo
Edward Kelly
Mark St.John Wright
Rodney Stevens
Adrian Morger
Rafael Rossi
Kevin Hart

D-U-N-S 24-995-1005   (SL)
INLAND PACIFIC RESOURCES INC
(*Suby of* CORIX INFRASTRUCTURE INC)
1188 Georgia St W Suite 1160, Vancouver, BC, V6E 4A2
(604) 697-6700
Emp Here 2,000
SIC 1623 Water, sewer, and utility lines
Brett Hodson

D-U-N-S 24-696-7384   (SL)
INSURANCE COUNCIL OF BRITISH COLUMBIA
1040 Georgia St W Suite 300, Vancouver, BC, V6E 4H1
(604) 688-0321
Emp Here 26   *Sales* 22,049,560
SIC 6411 Insurance agents, brokers, and service
Daniel Swanlund

D-U-N-S 24-658-6143   (HQ)
INTEGRA GOLD CORP
CORPORATION D'OR INTEGRA
(*Suby of* ELDORADO GOLD CORPORATION)
1055 Georgia St W Unit 2270, Vancouver, BC, V6E 0B6
(604) 629-0891
Emp Here 1   *Sales* 131,315,195
SIC 1081 Metal mining services
Stephen De Jong
H. Thiboutot
Andree St-Germain
Langis St-Pierre
Francois Chabot
Jacques Simoneau
George Salamis
Robert Bryce
Charles Oliver
Petra Decher

D-U-N-S 24-155-2397   (HQ)
INTERNATIONAL CONFERENCE SERVICES LTD
ICS
1201 Pender St W Suite 300, Vancouver, BC, V6E 2V2
(604) 681-2153
Emp Here 19   *Sales* 24,707,045
SIC 7389 Business services, nec
Mathias Posch
Iain Mackay

D-U-N-S 24-846-2439   (SL)
INTERWORX PLANNING AND DESIGN
1140 Pender St W Suite 600, Vancouver, BC, V6E 4G1
(604) 806-6255
Emp Here 30   *Sales* 13,476,570
SIC 7389 Business services, nec
Crystal Matthews

D-U-N-S 24-455-3186   (HQ)

INTERWRAP ULC
(*Suby of* OWENS CORNING)
1177 Hastings St W Suite 1818, Vancouver, BC, V6E 2K3
(800) 567-9727
Sales 17,529,120
SIC 2671 Paper; coated and laminated packaging
Robert Milne
Baldev Shokar

D-U-N-S 24-202-8095   (HQ)
IPSOS CORP
(*Suby of* IPSOS)
1285 Pender St W Suite 200, Vancouver, BC, V6E 4B1
(778) 373-5000
Sales 381,225,176
SIC 8732 Commercial nonphysical research
Didier Truchot
Andrew Cochrane

D-U-N-S 20-562-7636   (HQ)
IPSOS LIMITED PARTNERSHIP
(*Suby of* IPSOS)
1700-1075 Georgia St W, Vancouver, BC, V6E 3C9
(778) 373-5000
Emp Here 100   *Sales* 329,914,500
SIC 8732 Commercial nonphysical research
Gary Bennewies

D-U-N-S 24-234-7342   (HQ)
IPSOS-INSIGHT CORPORATION
(*Suby of* IPSOS)
1075 Georgia St W Unit 1700, Vancouver, BC, V6E 3C9
(778) 373-5000
Emp Here 8   *Sales* 23,753,844
SIC 8732 Commercial nonphysical research
Bidier Truchot
Gary L Bennewies

D-U-N-S 20-797-8719   (HQ)
JARDINE LLOYD THOMPSON CANADA INC
(*Suby of* JARDINE LLOYD THOMPSON GROUP LTD)
1111 Georgia St W Suite 1600, Vancouver, BC, V6E 4G2
(604) 682-4211
Emp Here 85   *Sales* 1,139,064,960
SIC 6411 Insurance agents, brokers, and service
Mark Drummond Brady
David Richards

D-U-N-S 24-619-2442   (SL)
JORDAN CAPITAL MARKETS INC
1075 Georgia St W Suite 1920, Vancouver, BC, V6E 3C9
(778) 373-4091
Emp Here 26   *Sales* 17,651,998
SIC 6211 Security brokers and dealers
Mark Redcliffe

D-U-N-S 20-448-5531   (SL)
JOSTLE CORPORATION
1090 West Georgia St Suite 1200, Vancouver, BC, V6E 3V7
(604) 566-9520
Emp Here 68   *Sales* 12,057,148
SIC 7371 Custom computer programming services
Bradley Francis Palmer

D-U-N-S 24-826-0171   (SL)
K92 MINING INC
1090 Georgia St W Suite 488, Vancouver, BC, V6E 3V7
(236) 521-0584
Emp Here 221   *Sales* 53,160,754
SIC 1041 Gold ores
John Lewins
Warren Uyen
David Medilek
Chris Muller
Nancy La Couvee

Justin Blanchet
Stuart Angus
Mark Eaton
Saurabh Handa
Graham Wheelock

D-U-N-S 20-065-9550   (SL)
KBK NO 51 VENTURES LTD
CARMANA PLAZA
1128 Alberni St, Vancouver, BC, V6E 4R6
(604) 683-1399
Emp Here 50   *Sales* 11,323,700
SIC 6513 Apartment building operators
Benett Mak

D-U-N-S 24-376-9531   (HQ)
KIEWIT/FLATIRON GENERAL PARTNERSHIP
1111 Georgia St W Suite 1410, Vancouver, BC, V6E 4M3

Emp Here 5   *Sales* 57,033,800
SIC 1542 Nonresidential construction, nec
Frank Margitan
Louis Chapdelaine

D-U-N-S 24-535-4840   (SL)
KINCORA COPPER LIMITED
1199 West Hastings St Suite 800, Vancouver, BC, V6E 3T5
(604) 283-1722
Emp Here 50   *Sales* 119,377,450
SIC 1021 Copper ores
Jonathan (Sam) Spring
John Holliday
Anthony Jackson
Peter Leaman
Cameron Mcrae
Ray Nadarajah
Lewis Marks

D-U-N-S 24-897-7134   (HQ)
KINTETSU INTERNATIONAL EXPRESS (CANADA) INC
(*Suby of* KINTETSU INTERNATIONAL EXPRESS (U.S.A.), INC.)
1140 Pender St W Suite 910, Vancouver, BC, V6E 4G1
(778) 328-9754
Emp Here 40   *Sales* 34,678,384
SIC 4724 Travel agencies
Hiaeo Adachi

D-U-N-S 20-193-6684   (SL)
KOOTENAY SILVER INC
1075 W Georgia St Suite 1650, Vancouver, BC, V6E 3C9
(604) 601-5650
Emp Here 8   *Sales* 19,100,392
SIC 1061 Ferroalloy ores, except vanadium
James M. Mcdonald
Tom Richards
Rajwant Kang
Kenneth Berry
Brian Groves
Nathaniel Jon Morda
Andrea Zaradic
Tony Reda

D-U-N-S 25-369-1760   (BR)
LEDCOR CONSTRUCTION LIMITED
LEDCOR SPECIAL PROJECTS
(*Suby of* 280818 ALBERTA LTD)
1055 Hastings St W Suite 1500, Vancouver, BC, V6E 2E9
(604) 646-2493
Emp Here 100
SIC 1542 Nonresidential construction, nec
Ray Brown

D-U-N-S 20-303-7882   (SL)
LGM FINANCIAL SERVICES INC
1021 Hastings St W Unit 400, Vancouver, BC, V6E 0C3
(604) 806-5300
Emp Here 128   *Sales* 607,501,312
SIC 6411 Insurance agents, brokers, and ser-

vice
Adam Hill
Jeffrey Fallowfield
Drew Collier
Gad Campbell
Fob Fink
Charles Hotel
Eduarda Mcwhirter
Chrintine Rybas
Jim Steffler
Brent Heath

D-U-N-S 20-387-6982   (HQ)
LIBERTY GOLD CORP
1055 Hastings St W Suite 1900, Vancouver, BC, V6E 2E9
(604) 632-4677
Sales 23,875,490
SIC 1041 Gold ores
Cal Everett
Moira Smith
Joanna Bailey
Jim Lincoln
Mark O'dea
Rob Pease
Donald Mcinnes
Sean Tetzlaff

D-U-N-S 24-657-6367   (HQ)
LISTEL CANADA LTD
LISTEL WHISTLER HOTEL
(*Suby of* LISTEL GROUP)
1300 Robson St, Vancouver, BC, V6E 1C5
(604) 684-8461
Emp Here 10   *Sales* 10,195,900
SIC 7011 Hotels and motels
Tao Zhou
Hiro Suzuki

D-U-N-S 24-445-6133   (BR)
LONDON LIFE, COMPAGNIE D'ASSURANCE-VIE
LONDON LIFE INSURANCE COMPANY
(*Suby of* POWER CORPORATION DU CANADA)
1111 Georgia St W Suite 1200, Vancouver, BC, V6E 4M3
(604) 685-6521
Emp Here 85
SIC 6311 Life insurance
Reid Ncgruer

D-U-N-S 20-550-4629   (HQ)
LUMERICAL INC
1095 Pender St W Suite 1700, Vancouver, BC, V6E 2M6
(604) 733-9006
Sales 10,692,550
SIC 7372 Prepackaged software
Michael Newland
James Pond
Todd Kleckner
Adam Reid

D-U-N-S 25-105-7394   (HQ)
MAN ENERGY SOLUTIONS CANADA LTD
(*Suby of* VOLKSWAGEN AG)
1177 Hastings St W Suite 1930, Vancouver, BC, V6E 2K3
(604) 235-2254
Emp Here 29   *Sales* 15,669,540
SIC 5084 Industrial machinery and equipment
Christian Mueller
Manish Jethra
Michael Pflueger
Thomas Leander

D-U-N-S 20-297-2845   (HQ)
MANNING ELLIOTT LLP
1050 Pender St W 11th Fl, Vancouver, BC, V6E 3S7
(604) 714-3600
Emp Here 70   *Sales* 29,075,900
SIC 8721 Accounting, auditing, and bookkeeping
Alden Aumann
Ryan Ayre

Joseph Bonvillain
Abbe Chivers

D-U-N-S 20-360-0374   (SL)
MASON RESOURCES CORP
1066 Hastings St W Suite 1650, Vancouver,
BC, V6E 3X1
(604) 673-2001
Emp Here 11   *Sales* 26,263,039
SIC 1021 Copper ores
Stephen Scott
Duane Lo
Robert Cinits
Susan Mcleod
Alan R Edwards
Mark H Bailey
Geoffrey Chater
James L Harris

D-U-N-S 25-107-1247   (SL)
MAX RESOURCE CORP
1095 W Pender St Suite 1188, Vancouver, BC,
V6E 2M6
(604) 365-1522
Emp Here 65   *Sales* 15,173,275
SIC 1041 Gold ores
Brett Matich
Stuart Rogers
Paul John
John Theobald
Alexander Helmel

D-U-N-S 20-993-5105   (SL)
MCLELLAN'S SUPERMARKET LTD
SUPERVALU 48
1255 Davie St, Vancouver, BC, V6E 1N4
(604) 688-0911
Emp Here 50   *Sales* 13,707,600
SIC 5411 Grocery stores
Ross Mclellan

D-U-N-S 20-703-9731   (BR)
MCMILLAN LLP
(*Suby of* MCMILLAN LLP)
1055 Georgia St W Suite 1500, Vancouver,
BC, V6E 4N7
(604) 689-9111
Emp Here 250
SIC 8111 Legal services
Sandra Knowler

D-U-N-S 24-031-9293   (HQ)
METRO PARKING LTD
1078 Pender St W, Vancouver, BC, V6E 2N7
(604) 682-6754
Emp Here 11   *Sales* 46,370,291
SIC 7521 Automobile parking
Sat Khantura

D-U-N-S 20-118-9508   (HQ)
MICHAEL HILL JEWELLER (CANADA) LTD
(*Suby of* MICHAEL HILL INTERNATIONAL
LIMITED)
1090 Pender St W Suite 530, Vancouver, BC,
V6E 2N7
(604) 913-3114
Emp Here 7   *Sales* 31,762,640
SIC 5944 Jewelry stores
Emma Hill

D-U-N-S 20-112-2517   (HQ)
MONUMENT MINING LIMITED
1100 Melville St Suite 1580, Vancouver, BC,
V6E 4A6
(604) 638-1661
Sales 19,250,000
SIC 1081 Metal mining services
Robert F. Baldock
Cathy Zhai
Zaidi Harun
Graham Dickson
Mark Richard Gasson
Michael John Kitney
Rhett Brans

D-U-N-S 20-523-9077   (SL)
MT SERVICES LIMITED PARTNERSHIP
MCCARTHY TETARAULT LAW OFFICES

745 Thurlow St Unit 2400, Vancouver, BC,
V6E 0C5
(604) 643-7100
Emp Here 150   *Sales* 16,632,300
SIC 8111 Legal services
Sven Milelli

D-U-N-S 20-585-9747   (HQ)
NEVSUN RESOURCES LTD
1066 Hastings St W Suite 1750, Vancouver,
BC, V6E 3X1
(604) 623-4700
Sales 289,397,000
SIC 1081 Metal mining services
Peter Kukielski
Ryan Macwilliam
Joseph Giuffre
Scott Trebilcock
Cara Allaway
Marc Blythe
Peter Manojlovic
Jerzy Orzechowski
Todd Romaine
Ian Pearce

D-U-N-S 24-724-9584   (SL)
NEW WORLD HOTELS LTD
*RENAISSANCE VANCOUVER HOTEL HAR-
BOURSIDE*
1133 Hastings St W, Vancouver, BC, V6E 3T3
(604) 689-9211
Emp Here 200   *Sales* 19,133,600
SIC 7011 Hotels and motels
Karl Daniel Heininger
Patrick M Gaffney
Heidi Fuerst
Brad Hornbacher
Samuel Siu
Amy Chan
Daniel Wong

D-U-N-S 20-321-6510   (HQ)
NEXGEN ENERGY LTD
1021 Hastings St W Suite 3150, Vancouver,
BC, V6E 0C3
(604) 428-4112
Sales 10,230,960
SIC 1094 Uranium-radium-vanadium ores
Leigh Curyer
Travis Mcpherson
James Hatley
Troy Boisjoli
Bruce Sprague
Christopher Mcfadden
Trevor Thiele
Craig Parry
Richard Patricio
Warrem Gilman

D-U-N-S 24-805-8430   (HQ)
NIPPON TRAVEL AGENCY CANADA LTD
N T A
(*Suby of* WEST JAPAN RAILWAY COMPANY)
1199 Pender St W Suite 370, Vancouver, BC,
V6E 2R1
(604) 685-4663
Sales 15,599,010
SIC 4725 Tour operators
Hiroshi Iwasaki

D-U-N-S 20-285-4832   (HQ)
NORDSTROM CANADA RETAIL, INC
NORDSTROM
(*Suby of* NORDSTROM, INC.)
745 Thurlow St Suite 2400, Vancouver, BC,
V6E 0C5

Emp Here 1   *Sales* 76,054,000
SIC 5311 Department stores
Erik Nordstrom
Andy Dickerf
Robert Sari
Robert Campbell

D-U-N-S 24-888-2375   (SL)
NORTH AMERICAN NICKEL INC
1055 West Hastings St Suite 2200, Vancou-

ver, BC, V6E 2E9
(604) 770-4334
Emp Here 5   *Sales* 11,937,745
SIC 1061 Ferroalloy ores, except vanadium
Keith Morrison
Mark Fedikow
Sarah-Wenjia Zhu
John Sabine
Gilbert Clark
Douglas E. Ford
Christopher Messina

D-U-N-S 24-620-3830   (HQ)
NORTHERN DYNASTY MINERALS LTD
1040 West Georgia St 15th Fl, Vancouver, BC,
V6E 4H1
(604) 684-6365
Emp Here 10   *Sales* 12,788,700
SIC 1021 Copper ores
Ronald W Thiessen
Bruce Jenkins
Stephen Hodgson
Sean Magee
Doug Allen
Trevor Thomas
Mark Peters
Robert A Dickinson
Desmond Balakrishnan
Steven Decker

D-U-N-S 24-368-2767   (SL)
NORTHERN VERTEX MINING CORP
1075 W Georgia St Suite 1650, Vancouver,
BC, V6E 3C9
(604) 601-3656
Emp Here 7   *Sales* 16,712,843
SIC 1081 Metal mining services
Kenneth E. Berry
Christopher Park
Joseph Bardswich
James Mcdonald
Michael John Haworth
David Farrell

D-U-N-S 20-554-2637   (HQ)
NRG RESEARCH GROUP INC
1100 Melville St Suite 1380, Vancouver, BC,
V6E 4A6
(604) 681-0381
Emp Here 10   *Sales* 24,193,730
SIC 8732 Commercial nonphysical research
Jon Johnson
Adam Di Paula

D-U-N-S 24-996-3950   (SL)
OAK MARITIME (CANADA) INC
(*Suby of* OAK MARITIME (H.K.) INC. LIM-
ITED)
1111 Georgia St W Suite 1500, Vancouver,
BC, V6E 4M3
(604) 689-8083
Emp Here 30   *Sales* 15,599,010
SIC 4731 Freight transportation arrangement
Fred Tsai
Jack Hsu
Steve Hsu

D-U-N-S 20-015-8629   (SL)
**OCEANWORKS INTERNATIONAL CORPO-
RATION**
100-535 Thurlow St, Vancouver, BC, V6E 0C8
(604) 398-4998
Emp Here 90   *Sales* 17,287,650
SIC 3429 Hardware, nec
Rodney W. Stanley
James G. English
Glen Viau
Ray Coufal

D-U-N-S 25-725-8533   (HQ)
ONE WEST HOLDINGS LTD
(*Suby of* ADEX SECURITIES INC)
1095 Pender St W Suite 900, Vancouver, BC,
V6E 2M6
(604) 681-8882
Sales 10,194,150
SIC 6553 Cemetery subdividers and develop-

ers
Terrence Hui
Dennis Au-Yeung
Mitchell Gropper

D-U-N-S 24-860-9547   (HQ)
ORACLE MINING CORP
1090 Georgia St W Suite 250, Vancouver, BC,
V6E 3V7
(604) 689-9282
Emp Here 8   *Sales* 127,887,000
SIC 1041 Gold ores
Alan Edwards
Paul England
Derek Price
Gregory K. Liller
Mark Forsyth
Michael Tardiff

D-U-N-S 24-088-2758   (HQ)
PACIFIC BIOENERGY CORPORATION
1111 Hastings St W Suite 780, Vancouver,
BC, V6E 2J3
(604) 602-1099
Sales 23,424,390
SIC 5099 Durable goods, nec
Donald Steele
Wayne Young

D-U-N-S 20-187-1600   (SL)
PACIFIC LINK MINING CORP
1055 Georgia St W Suite 2772, Vancouver,
BC, V6E 0B6

Emp Here 50   *Sales* 14,832,400
SIC 6799 Investors, nec
Ken Cai
Jennifer Trevitt
Scott Davis
Michael D. Doggett

D-U-N-S 24-395-5192   (SL)
PACIFIC NORTHERN GAS (N.E.) LTD
1185 Georgia St W Suite 950, Vancouver, BC,
V6E 4E6
(604) 691-5680
Emp Here 35   *Sales* 40,444,775
SIC 4924 Natural gas distribution
R.G. Dyce
D.G. Unruh
G.B. Weeres

D-U-N-S 20-376-1193   (SL)
PACIFIC NORTHERN GAS LTD
Suite 2550 1066 Hastings St W, Vancouver,
BC, V6E 3X2
(604) 697-9221
Emp Here 5   *Sales* 15,529,285
SIC 4923 Gas transmission and distribution
Greg Weeres

D-U-N-S 24-321-4496   (HQ)
PEACE RIVER COAL INC
(*Suby of* ANGLO AMERICAN PLC)
1055 Hastings St W Suite 1900, Vancouver,
BC, V6E 2E9

Emp Here 20   *Sales* 11,671,750
SIC 1221 Bituminous coal and lignite-surface
mining
Trevor Hulme
Pat C Devlin

D-U-N-S 20-052-8086   (HQ)
POLARIS MATERIALS CORPORATION
(*Suby of* U.S. CONCRETE, INC.)
1055 Georgia St W Suite 2740, Vancouver,
BC, V6E 4N4
(604) 915-5000
Sales 15,674,848
SIC 1442 Construction sand and gravel
Scott Dryden
Tyson Mackay
Rob Mcintosh
Richard Williams
Keven Wasylyshyn

D-U-N-S 24-898-2597   (HQ)

POTTINGER GAHERTY ENVIRONMENTAL CONSULTANTS LTD
1185 Georgia St W Suite 1200, Vancouver, BC, V6E 4E6
(604) 682-3707
Emp Here 58   *Sales* 16,400,160
SIC 8748 Business consulting, nec
  Edmund Pottinger
  William Gaherty
  Susan Wilkins
  Harvey Fung

D-U-N-S 24-313-3191   (SL)
PURE ENERGY MINERALS LIMITED
1111 Georgia St Suite 1400, Vancouver, BC, V6E 3M3
(604) 608-6611
Emp Here 10   *Sales* 13,512,800
SIC 1479 Chemical and fertilizer mining
  Patrick Highsmith
  Walter Weinig
  Paul Zink
  Mary Little
  Scott Shellhaas
  Michael Dake
  Frank Wells

D-U-N-S 25-217-1772   (SL)
QUATERRA RESOURCES INC
1199 Hastings St W Suite 1100, Vancouver, BC, V6E 3T5
(855) 681-9059
Emp Here 169   *Sales* 43,225,806
SIC 1021 Copper ores
  Thomas C. Patton
  Gerald Prosalendis
  Roy Wilkes
  Terry Eyton
  John R. Kerr
  Lei Wang

D-U-N-S 24-680-2164   (SL)
QUICKMOBILE INC
(*Suby of* PAPAY HOLDCO, LLC)
1177 Hastings St W Suite 2600, Vancouver, BC, V6E 2K3
(604) 875-0403
Emp Here 100   *Sales* 14,418,200
SIC 7371 Custom computer programming services
  Craig Hughes
  Roohshan Divecha
  David Smith
  Roohshan Divecha

D-U-N-S 25-681-4948   (HQ)
RADIANT COMMUNICATIONS CORP
1050 Pender St W Suite 1600, Vancouver, BC, V6E 4T3
(604) 257-0500
Emp Here 47   *Sales* 15,993,040
SIC 4813 Telephone communication, except radio
  Ted Chislett
  Chuck Leighton
  Craig White
  Jason Leeson
  Dan Tung
  Sam Ketcham
  Kelly Edmison
  Johnny Ciampi
  Greg Gutmanis

D-U-N-S 25-235-5375   (HQ)
RG PROPERTIES LTD
1177 Hastings St W Suite 2088, Vancouver, BC, V6E 2K3
(604) 688-8999
Emp Here 750   *Sales* 167,544,900
SIC 6553 Cemetery subdividers and developers
  Graham S Lee
  Robert H Lee
  William H Levine
  Alvin G Poettcker
  Robert C Wong
  Victor J Yang

Jack Austin

D-U-N-S 20-797-3868   (SL)
ROBERT LEE LTD
1177 Hastings St W Suite 517, Vancouver, BC, V6E 2K3
(604) 669-7733
Emp Here 40   *Sales* 11,539,960
SIC 6512 Nonresidential building operators
  Robert Lee
  Derek Lee

D-U-N-S 24-312-9066   (SL)
ROCHESTER RESOURCES LTD
1090 W Georgia St Suite 1305, Vancouver, BC, V6E 3V7
(604) 685-9316
Emp Here 200   *Sales* 5,444,774
SIC 1081 Metal mining services
  Eduardo Luna Arellano
  Nicholas Demare
  Jose Silva
  Joseph M. Keane
  Marc Cernovitch
  Michael Magrum

D-U-N-S 25-217-2176   (SL)
SALMAN PARTNERS INC
1095 Pender St W Suite 1702, Vancouver, BC, V6E 2M6

Emp Here 31   *Sales* 16,467,417
SIC 6211 Security brokers and dealers
  Terry Salman
  Alan Herrington
  Victor Chan
  Rahim Rajwani
  Gina Holliday
  Julina Wong

D-U-N-S 20-263-3462   (BR)
SAP CANADA INC
SAP
(*Suby of* SAP SE)
1095 Pender St W Suite 400, Vancouver, BC, V6E 2M6
(604) 647-8888
Emp Here 100
SIC 7371 Custom computer programming services
  David Galloway

D-U-N-S 24-826-0866   (BR)
SAVE-ON-FOODS LIMITED PARTNERSHIP
URBAN FARE
(*Suby of* SAVE-ON-FOODS LIMITED PARTNERSHIP)
1133 Alberni St, Vancouver, BC, V6E 4T9
(604) 648-2053
Emp Here 120
SIC 5411 Grocery stores
  Jason Molosci

D-U-N-S 20-547-7974   (BR)
SCHENKER OF CANADA LIMITED
SCHENKER LOGISTICS
(*Suby of* BUNDESREPUBLIK DEUTSCHLAND)
1030 Georgia St W Suite 3a, Vancouver, BC, V6E 2Y3
(604) 688-8511
Emp Here 150
SIC 4731 Freight transportation arrangement
  Claude Germain

D-U-N-S 24-367-6038   (HQ)
SHAFER - HAGGART LTD
(*Suby of* 6695512 HOLDINGS CORPORATION)
1100 Melville St Suite 938, Vancouver, BC, V6E 4A6
(604) 669-5512
Emp Here 25   *Sales* 25,067,310
SIC 5149 Groceries and related products, nec
  Clive Lonsdale
  Brian Dougall
  Dennis Linfoot
  Barbara Rocca

Angel Cheng

D-U-N-S 25-327-5382   (HQ)
SHAFER COMMODITIES INC
(*Suby of* 6695512 HOLDINGS CORPORATION)
1100 Melville St Suite 938, Vancouver, BC, V6E 4A6
(604) 669-5512
Emp Here 4   *Sales* 11,880,320
SIC 5191 Farm supplies
  Jan Leishman
  Dennis Linfoot
  Brian Dougall
  Clive Lonsdale

D-U-N-S 24-371-9937   (HQ)
SIERRA SYSTEMS GROUP INC
(*Suby of* NIPPON TELEGRAPH AND TELEPHONE CORPORATION)
1177 Hastings St W Suite 2500, Vancouver, BC, V6E 2K3
(604) 688-1371
Emp Here 60   *Sales* 151,634,000
SIC 7379 Computer related services, nec
  Calvin Yonker
  Gaylyn Lawton
  Patricia Kaiser

D-U-N-S 20-569-1699   (HQ)
SILVERBIRCH HOTELS AND RESORTS LIMITED PARTNERSHIP
1188 Georgia St W Unit 1640, Vancouver, BC, V6E 4A2
(604) 646-2447
Sales 11,714,400
SIC 8742 Management consulting services
  Jonathan Korol
  Robert Pratt
  Kevin Grayston
  Sharon Mackay
  Giri Rajamahendran
  Mark Medland
  Jiri Rumlena
  Rachel Koller
  Gaetan Brunnelle
  David Mcquinn

D-U-N-S 24-302-6739   (HQ)
SKEENA SAWMILLS LTD
1030 West Georgia St Suite 1518, Vancouver, BC, V6E 2Y3
(604) 800-5990
Sales 21,160,700
SIC 2421 Sawmills and planing mills, general
  Teddy Cui
  Shenwei Wu

D-U-N-S 25-680-6795   (BR)
SNC-LAVALIN INC
(*Suby of* GROUPE SNC-LAVALIN INC)
745 Thurlow St Suite 500, Vancouver, BC, V6E 0C5
(604) 662-3555
Emp Here 300
SIC 8711 Engineering services
  Tim Burke

D-U-N-S 25-681-1191   (HQ)
SPANISH MOUNTAIN GOLD LTD
1095 Pender St W Suite 1120, Vancouver, BC, V6E 2M6
(604) 601-3651
Sales 19,100,392
SIC 1081 Metal mining services
  Larry Yau
  Morris Beattie
  Judy Stoeterau
  Christopher Lattanzi
  James Clare
  Donald Coxe
  James Rogers
  Sharon Ng

D-U-N-S 25-963-9466   (SL)
SPECTRUM MANAGEMENT LTD
1166 Alberni St Suite 501, Vancouver, BC, V6E 3Z3

(604) 682-1388
Emp Here 100   *Sales* 4,020,900
SIC 7349 Building maintenance services, nec
  William Ng

D-U-N-S 24-558-3885   (HQ)
SRK CONSULTING (CANADA) INC
1066 Hastings St W Suite 2200, Vancouver, BC, V6E 3X1
(604) 681-4196
Sales 191,003,920
SIC 1081 Metal mining services
  Andrew Barrett
  Darrell Sandison
  Cameron Scott
  Peter Healey

D-U-N-S 20-259-3331   (SL)
TARGETED MICROWAVE SOLUTIONS INC
1066 Hastings St W Suite 2300, Vancouver, BC, V6E 3X2
(778) 995-5833
Emp Here 1,000   *Sales* 227,289,000
SIC 3822 Environmental controls
  Gurminder Sangha
  Ian Hume
  Lawrence Siegel

D-U-N-S 25-385-2107   (HQ)
TASEKO MINES LIMITED
1040 Georgia St W 15th Fl, Vancouver, BC, V6E 4H1
(778) 373-4533
Emp Here 18   *Sales* 260,688,535
SIC 1081 Metal mining services
  Russell Hallbauer
  Stuart Mcdonald
  Brian Battison
  Scott Jones
  Robert Rotzinger
  Brian Bergot
  Richard Tremblay
  John W. Mcmanus
  Bryce Hamming
  Ronald W. Thiessen

D-U-N-S 24-861-2970   (HQ)
TELSON MINING CORPORATION
1111 Melville St Suite 1000, Vancouver, BC, V6E 3V6
(604) 684-8071
Sales 26,347,648
SIC 1041 Gold ores
  Jose Antonio Balderas
  Ralph Shearing
  Enrique Margalef
  Yao Sun
  Arturo Bonillas
  Rory Godinho

D-U-N-S 24-319-3971   (HQ)
TERRACO GOLD CORP
1055 Hastings St W Suite 2390, Vancouver, BC, V6E 2E9
(604) 443-3830
Emp Here 5   *Sales* 47,750,980
SIC 1041 Gold ores
  Todd L. Hilditch
  Charlie Sulfrian
  Kathleen Jones-Bartels
  Bryan Mckenzie
  Richard F. Delong
  William Lamb
  Alfred F. Fischer
  Zahir Dhanani

D-U-N-S 20-021-6500   (HQ)
TIMBERWEST FOREST COMPANY
TIMBERWEST
1055 Georgia St W Suite 2300, Vancouver, BC, V6E 0B6
(604) 654-4600
Sales 14,463,190
SIC 0831 Forest products
  Brenda Blue

D-U-N-S 25-539-2003   (HQ)
TIMBERWEST FOREST CORP

(Suby of TWF ACQUSITION CORPORATION)
2000-1055 Hastings St W, Vancouver, BC, V6E 2E9
(604) 654-4600
Emp Here 20   Sales 56,319,300
SIC 5099 Durable goods, nec
Jeffery Zweig
Brian Baarda
Rob Gough
Benjamin Lee

D-U-N-S 24-889-0006   (HQ)
TINKA RESOURCES LIMITED
1090 Georgia St W Suite 1305, Vancouver, BC, V6E 3V7
(604) 685-9316
Emp Here 2   Sales 42,975,882
SIC 1031 Lead and zinc ores
Graham Donald Carman
Alvaro Fernandez-Baca
Mariana Bermudez
Nick Demare
Benedict Mckeown
Mary L. Little
Pieter Britz

D-U-N-S 24-682-1222   (HQ)
TREVALI MINING CORPORATION
1199 Hastings St W Unit 1400, Vancouver, BC, V6E 3T5
(604) 488-1661
Emp Here 23   Sales 402,589,000
SIC 1031 Lead and zinc ores
Mark Cruise
Ricus Grimbeek
Jessica Mcdonald
Dan Isserow
Alex Terentiew
Joanne Thomopoulos
Steven Molnar
Russell Ball
Anton Drescher
Chris Eskdale

D-U-N-S 24-726-2058   (SL)
TRIAL LAWYERS ASSOCIATION OF BRITISH COLUMBIA
TLABC
1100 Melville St Suite 1111, Vancouver, BC, V6E 4A6
(604) 682-5343
Emp Here 68   Sales 16,423,020
SIC 8621 Professional organizations
Carla Terzariol

D-U-N-S 24-737-1896   (SL)
UNIGLOBE TRAVEL INTERNATIONAL LIMITED
1199 Pender St W Suite 900, Vancouver, BC, V6E 2R1
(604) 718-2600
Emp Here 100   Sales 66,689,200
SIC 4724 Travel agencies
U. Gary Charlwood

D-U-N-S 24-367-1237   (HQ)
VANCOUVER CONDOMINIUM SERVICES LTD
(Suby of FIRSTSERVICE CORPORATION)
1281 Georgia St W Suite 400, Vancouver, BC, V6E 3J7
(604) 684-6291
Sales 11,180,254
SIC 6519 Real property lessors, nec
Gerrard E Fanaken
Linda Van Os
Desmond Chao

D-U-N-S 20-651-5640   (SL)
VANCOUVER EXTENDED STAY LTD
1288 Georgia St W Unit 101, Vancouver, BC, V6E 4R3
(604) 891-6100
Emp Here 25   Sales 11,087,250
SIC 7389 Business services, nec
Lise Labreche

D-U-N-S 24-669-3233   (SL)
VANCOUVER MARRIOTT PINNACLE DOWNTOWN HOTEL
SHOW CASE RESTAURANT
1128 Hastings St W, Vancouver, BC, V6E 4R5
(604) 684-1128
Emp Here 30   Sales 13,304,700
SIC 7389 Business services, nec
Mike Decotiis

D-U-N-S 20-302-5213   (SL)
VERTEX ONE ASSET MANAGEMENT INC
1021 Hastings St W Suite 3200, Vancouver, BC, V6E 0C3
(604) 681-5787
Emp Here 22   Sales 11,686,554
SIC 6282 Investment advice
Jeff Mccord
Matthew Wood
John Theissen

D-U-N-S 25-387-7815   (SL)
WARRINGTON PROPERTY GROUP INCORPORATED, THE
WARRINGTON PCI MANAGEMENT
1030 Georgia St W Suite 1700, Vancouver, BC, V6E 2Y3
(604) 602-1887
Emp Here 32   Sales 10,468,064
SIC 6531 Real estate agents and managers
David Coon
Malena Coon

D-U-N-S 25-234-8958   (SL)
WEALTH MINERALS LTD
1177 Hastings St W Suite 2300, Vancouver, BC, V6E 2K3
(604) 331-0096
Emp Here 9   Sales 21,487,941
SIC 1041 Gold ores
Henk Van Alphen
Tim Mccutcheon
Marla Ritchie
Gordon Neal
Stefan Schauss
Xiaohuan (Juan) Tang
David Cross

D-U-N-S 24-593-0784   (SL)
WENTWORTH HOTELS LTD
LODEN HOTEL
(Suby of AMACON PROPERTY MANAGEMENT SERVICES INC)
1177 Melville St, Vancouver, BC, V6E 0A3
(604) 669-5060
Emp Here 160   Sales 14,830,400
SIC 7011 Hotels and motels
Wesley Joe

D-U-N-S 24-312-2785   (HQ)
WESBILD HOLDINGS LTD
WESBILD SHOPPING CENTRES
1055 W Georgia St Suite 2600, Vancouver, BC, V6E 3P3
(604) 694-8800
Emp Here 20   Sales 15,460,970
SIC 6512 Nonresidential building operators
Kevin Layden
Hassan Khosrowshahi
Maryam Khosrowshahi
Nezhat Khosrowshahi
Golnar Khosrowshahi
Behzad Khosrowshahi

D-U-N-S 24-358-1092   (SL)
WEST KIRKLAND MINING INC
1100 Melville St Suite 838, Vancouver, BC, V6E 4A6
(604) 685-8311
Emp Here 20   Sales 47,750,980
SIC 1041 Gold ores
R. Michael Jones
Frank Hallam
Sandy Mcvey
Pierre Lebel
Kevin Falcon

D-U-N-S 24-326-3667   (SL)
WESTERN COPPER AND GOLD CORPORATION
1040 Georgia St W Fl 15, Vancouver, BC, V6E 4H1
(604) 684-9497
Emp Here 11   Sales 26,263,039
SIC 1081 Metal mining services
Paul West-Sells
Julien Francois
Cameron Brown
Chris Donaldson
Dale Corman
Robert Gayton
Klaus Zeitler
David Williams
Archie Lang

D-U-N-S 25-361-5736   (HQ)
WESTERN FOREST PRODUCTS INC
800-1055 Georgia St W, Vancouver, BC, V6E 0B6
(604) 648-4500
Emp Here 40   Sales 907,220,663
SIC 2611 Pulp mills
Don Demens
Stephen Williams
Bruce Alexander
Rick Forgaard
Don Mcgregor
Shannon Janzen
Jennifer Foster
Brad Kirkbride
Rob Regner
Alyce Harper

D-U-N-S 24-318-6892   (SL)
WESTERN PACIFIC ACCEPTANCE CORPORATION
VERSAPAY
1199 Pender St W Suite 510, Vancouver, BC, V6E 2R1
(604) 678-3230
Emp Here 30   Sales 13,304,700
SIC 7389 Business services, nec
Mark H Lachance
Michael Gokturk
Kevin Short
Jon De Vos

D-U-N-S 20-371-5185   (HQ)
WESTERN RESOURCES CORP
1111 Georgia St W Suite 1400, Vancouver, BC, V6E 4M3
(604) 689-9378
Sales 35,813,235
SIC 1081 Metal mining services
Bill Xue
Matthew Wood
Jerry Zhang
George Gao
James Moore
Geoffrey Chang
Qinglong Xia
Wang Yingping
Jennifer Fang

D-U-N-S 24-196-3718   (SL)
WESTPARK PARKING SERVICES (2015) INC
WESTPARK
1140 Pender St W Suite 1310, Vancouver, BC, V6E 4G1
(604) 669-7275
Emp Here 105   Sales 47,270,685
SIC 7521 Automobile parking
John Laires
Gerry Marchiafava
Eric Fabia

D-U-N-S 25-687-2631   (HQ)
WEYERHAEUSER COMPANY LIMITED
WEYERHAEUSER AVIATION
(Suby of WEYERHAEUSER COMPANY)
1140 Pender St W Suite 440, Vancouver, BC, V6E 4G1

(604) 661-8000
Emp Here 200   Sales 1,154,220,000
SIC 2421 Sawmills and planing mills, general
Alfred Dzida
Devin Stockfish

D-U-N-S 25-230-4662   (HQ)
WHEATON PRECIOUS METALS CORP
1021 Hastings St W Suite 3500, Vancouver, BC, V6E 0C3
(604) 684-9648
Sales 794,012,000
SIC 1044 Silver ores
Randy Smallwood
Douglas Holtby
Patrick Drouin
Haytham Hodaly
Gary Brown
Curt Bernardi
George Brack
John Brough
R. Peter Gillin
Chantal Gosselin

D-U-N-S 24-130-1394   (HQ)
WORKING OPPORTUNITY FUND (EVCC) LTD
1055 Georgia St W Suite 260, Vancouver, BC, V6E 0B6
(604) 633-1418
Emp Here 13   Sales 84,021,477
SIC 6722 Management investment, open-end
David Levi
Murray Munro
Dean Drysdale
Julia Levy
Lori A Mayhew
Graeme Mcfarlane
Kenneth Neumann
Barry O'neill
Cynthia C Oliver
Angela Schira

D-U-N-S 20-510-6313   (BR)
XEROX CANADA LTD
XEROX
(Suby of XEROX CORPORATION)
1055 Georgia St W, Vancouver, BC, V6E 0B6
(604) 668-2300
Emp Here 250
SIC 5044 Office equipment
Diana Wyley

D-U-N-S 24-166-6270   (SL)
YCO CORPORATE INVESTMENTS LTD
EDWARDS KENNY & BRAY LLP
1040 Georgia St W Suite 1900, Vancouver, BC, V6E 4H3
(604) 689-1811
Emp Here 70   Sales 18,308,710
SIC 6719 Holding companies, nec
David S. Allman

Vancouver, BC V6G

D-U-N-S 20-621-9487   (SL)
0319637 B.C. LTD
FISH HOUSE IN STANLEY PARK, THE
(Suby of SILVERBIRCH HOTELS AND RESORTS LIMITED PARTNERSHIP)
8901 Stanley Park Dr, Vancouver, BC, V6G 3E2

Emp Here 80   Sales 3,641,520
SIC 5812 Eating places
Wilbert G Kanke

D-U-N-S 24-134-6530   (SL)
239188 BC LTD
ALDRICH PEARS ASSOCIATES
1455 Georgia St W Suite 400, Vancouver, BC, V6G 2T3
(604) 669-7044
Emp Here 40   Sales 17,739,600

SIC 7389 Business services, nec
Isaac Marshall

D-U-N-S 25-719-2013   (SL)
A POWER INTERNATIONAL TRADING COMPANY
JANG MO JIB KOREAN RESTAURANT
1575 Robson St, Vancouver, BC, V6G 1C3
(604) 872-0712
Emp Here 90   *Sales* 4,096,710
SIC 5812 Eating places
Kil Bong Moon

D-U-N-S 20-915-8732   (HQ)
BEST WESTERN SANDS HOTEL
BEST WESTERN VERNON LODGE HOTEL
(*Suby of* ROSEN FOUNDATION LTD)
1755 Davie St, Vancouver, BC, V6G 1W5
(604) 682-1831
Emp Here 88   *Sales* 52,617,400
SIC 7011 Hotels and motels
Dallas Worthington

D-U-N-S 20-622-0063   (HQ)
BLUE TREE HOTELS INVESTMENT (CANADA), LTD
WESTIN BAYSHORE VANCOUVER, THE
1601 Bayshore Dr, Vancouver, BC, V6G 2V4
(604) 682-3377
Emp Here 100   *Sales* 76,534,400
SIC 7011 Hotels and motels
Yasutaro Saito
Toru Hirano
Hiroaki Okamoto
Hirofumi Matsunaga

D-U-N-S 25-216-6392   (HQ)
CALKINS & BURKE HOLDINGS LTD
1500 Georgia St W Suite 800, Vancouver, BC, V6G 2Z6
(604) 669-3741
Emp Here 58   *Sales* 20,741,400
SIC 2092 Fresh or frozen packaged fish
David Calkins
Michael Calkins

D-U-N-S 20-109-8241   (HQ)
CALKINS & BURKE LIMITED
ARROW PACKING COMPANY
(*Suby of* CALKINS & BURKE HOLDINGS LTD)
1500 Georgia St W Suite 800, Vancouver, BC, V6G 2Z6
(604) 669-3741
Emp Here 58   *Sales* 50,134,620
SIC 5146 Fish and seafoods
David Calkins
Blair Calkins
Michael Calkins

D-U-N-S 25-341-6507   (HQ)
CANNON DESIGN ARCHITECTURE INC
1500 Georgia St W Suite 710, Vancouver, BC, V6G 2Z6
(250) 388-0115
Emp Here 20   *Sales* 17,873,900
SIC 8712 Architectural services
Robert Johnston

D-U-N-S 20-019-2958   (HQ)
CEI - ARCHITECTURE PLANNING INTERIORS
1500 Georgia St W Suite 500, Vancouver, BC, V6G 2Z6
(604) 687-1898
Emp Here 50   *Sales* 11,618,035
SIC 8712 Architectural services
William Locking
Richard Boles
John Scott

D-U-N-S 24-996-7464   (BR)
COAST HOTELS LIMITED
COAST PLAZA AT STANLEY PARK
(*Suby of* OKABE CO., LTD.)
1763 Comox St, Vancouver, BC, V6G 1P6
(604) 688-7711
Emp Here 80

SIC 7011 Hotels and motels
Linda Hagen

D-U-N-S 24-939-4487   (HQ)
CUSTOMPLAN FINANCIAL ADVISORS INC
1500 Georgia St W Suite 1900, Vancouver, BC, V6G 2Z6
(604) 687-7773
Emp Here 1   *Sales* 14,265,264
SIC 8741 Management services
Karl Krokosinski

D-U-N-S 24-897-7589   (SL)
DEGELDER CONSTRUCTION CO. (2010) LTD
1455 Georgia St W Suite 100, Vancouver, BC, V6G 2T3
(604) 688-1515
Emp Here 24   *Sales* 11,297,544
SIC 1542 Nonresidential construction, nec
Michael Degelder
Patricia Degelder

D-U-N-S 25-678-1873   (HQ)
DIAMOND PARKING LTD
DIAMOND PARKING SERVICES
(*Suby of* DIAMOND PARKING SERVICES, LLC)
817 Denman St, Vancouver, BC, V6G 2L7
(604) 681-8797
Emp Here 37   *Sales* 38,266,745
SIC 7521 Automobile parking
Joel Diamond
Jon Diamond
Ian Bailey
Robert Watson
Dave Bailey

D-U-N-S 24-120-0661   (HQ)
FULMER DEVELOPMENT CORPORATION, THE
MR MIKE'S
1500 Georgia St W Suite 1290, Vancouver, BC, V6G 2Z6
(604) 558-5492
Sales 60,630,700
SIC 5812 Eating places
Kaye Alison Fulmer
Yuri Leith Fulmer
Darren D Flintoff

D-U-N-S 25-325-8982   (SL)
GLOBAL GATEWAY CORP
EMPIRE LANDMARK HOTEL
(*Suby of* ASIA STANDARD HOTEL (HOLDINGS) LIMITED)
1400 Robson St, Vancouver, BC, V6G 1B9
(604) 566-2688
Emp Here 120   *Sales* 11,480,160
SIC 7011 Hotels and motels
Johnny Tsang

D-U-N-S 24-456-2427   (HQ)
HOLLYBURN PROPERTIES (ALBERTA) LTD
(*Suby of* HOLLYBURN PROPERTIES LIMITED)
1640 Alberni St Suite 300, Vancouver, BC, V6G 1A7
(604) 926-7345
Emp Here 12   *Sales* 13,252,260
SIC 6513 Apartment building operators
Stephen Sander
Paul Sander

D-U-N-S 24-714-8372   (HQ)
KASIAN ARCHITECTURE INTERIOR DESIGN AND PLANNING LTD
1500 Georgia St W Suite 1685, Vancouver, BC, V6G 2Z6
(604) 683-4145
Emp Here 65   *Sales* 49,282,750
SIC 8712 Architectural services
Donald Kasian
Bill Chomik
Ian Sinclair
Michael Mcdonald

Wojciech Brus
Mehb Jessa

D-U-N-S 20-758-2610   (HQ)
KERNAGHAN, S J ADJUSTERS LIMITED
1445 Georgia St W Suite 300, Vancouver, BC, V6G 2T3
(604) 688-5651
Emp Here 15   *Sales* 110,864,520
SIC 6411 Insurance agents, brokers, and service
Patti M. Kernaghan
Stanley Kernaghan
Agnes Kernaghan

D-U-N-S 25-709-9663   (BR)
LONDON DRUGS LIMITED
(*Suby of* H.Y. LOUIE CO. LIMITED)
1650 Davie St, Vancouver, BC, V6G 1V9
(604) 448-4850
Emp Here 100
SIC 5912 Drug stores and proprietary stores
Lorne Pederson

D-U-N-S 20-575-8568   (BR)
MCDONALD'S RESTAURANTS OF CANADA LIMITED
MCDONALD'S #8578
(*Suby of* MCDONALD'S CORPORATION)
1701 Robson St, Vancouver, BC, V6G 1C9
(604) 718-1020
Emp Here 80
SIC 5812 Eating places
Meliza Devera

D-U-N-S 20-564-4904   (HQ)
NAVIGATA COMMUNICATIONS LIMITED
(*Suby of* NAVIGATA COMMUNICATIONS 2009, INC)
1550 Alberni St Suite 300, Vancouver, BC, V6G 1A5
(604) 990-2000
Emp Here 96   *Sales* 27,416,640
SIC 4899 Communication services, nec
Peter Legault
John Warta
Don Potts
Owen J. Gilbert
Glen Gregory
Tim Sansom

D-U-N-S 20-864-3767   (SL)
OCEAN WISE CONSERVATION ASSOCIATION
VANCOUVER AQUARIUM GIFT SHOP
845 Stanley Park Dr, Vancouver, BC, V6G 3E2
(604) 659-3400
Emp Here 400   *Sales* 53,362,400
SIC 8422 Botanical and zoological gardens
John Nightingale
Randy Pratt
Derral Moriyama
Cathy Imrie
Brian Hanna
Mary Buttery
Rizwan Gehlen
Barbara Atkinson
Christian Baxter
Karam Bayrakal

D-U-N-S 24-887-6690   (HQ)
PROSPECT POINT HOLDINGS LTD
2099 Beach Ave, Vancouver, BC, V6G 1Z4
(604) 669-2737
Sales 19,134,500
SIC 6712 Bank holding companies
George Frankel

D-U-N-S 24-073-3014   (HQ)
SECURIGUARD SERVICES LIMITED
1445 Georgia St W, Vancouver, BC, V6G 2T3
(604) 685-6011
Emp Here 65   *Sales* 28,875,000
SIC 7381 Detective and armored car services
Darcy Kernaghan
Lorna Clamp
David Long

D-U-N-S 25-506-8207   (HQ)
SEQUOIA COMPANY OF RESTAURANTS INC
CARDERO'S RESTAURANT
1583 Coal Harbour Quay, Vancouver, BC, V6G 3E7
(604) 687-5684
Sales 18,655,600
SIC 5812 Eating places
Brent Davies

D-U-N-S 25-146-8716   (BR)
SEQUOIA COMPANY OF RESTAURANTS INC
SAND BAR, THE
(*Suby of* SEQUOIA COMPANY OF RESTAURANTS INC)
1583 Coal Harbour Quay, Vancouver, BC, V6G 3E7
(604) 687-5684
Emp Here 100
SIC 5812 Eating places
Mike Deas

D-U-N-S 25-271-6998   (BR)
SOBEYS WEST INC
(*Suby of* EMPIRE COMPANY LIMITED)
1766 Robson St, Vancouver, BC, V6G 1E2
(604) 683-0202
Emp Here 75
SIC 5411 Grocery stores
Gwen Evans

D-U-N-S 20-702-7603   (BR)
SOBEYS WEST INC
(*Suby of* EMPIRE COMPANY LIMITED)
1641 Davie St, Vancouver, BC, V6G 1W1
(604) 669-8131
Emp Here 100
SIC 5411 Grocery stores
Steve Hodgewide

D-U-N-S 24-979-6132   (SL)
TASKTOP TECHNOLOGIES INCORPORATED
1500 Georgia St W Suite 1100, Vancouver, BC, V6G 2Z6
(778) 588-6896
Emp Here 70   *Sales* 31,302,180
SIC 5045 Computers, peripherals, and software
Mik Kersten
Neelan Choksi
Simon Bodymore
Nicole Bryan
Bruce Mcdonald
Sarah Elkins
Adrian Jones
John Kapral
Gail Murphy
John Thornton

D-U-N-S 20-307-0297   (SL)
TELIPHONE CORP
TELIPHONE NAVAIGATA WESTEL
1550 Alberni St 3rd Fl, Vancouver, BC, V6G 1A5
(604) 990-2000
Emp Here 120   *Sales* 27,416,640
SIC 4899 Communication services, nec
Benoit Laliberte

D-U-N-S 25-982-4089   (SL)
TRIMARK HEALTHCARE SERVICES LTD
1500 Georgia St W Suite 1300, Vancouver, BC, V6G 2Z6
(604) 425-2208
Emp Here 60   *Sales* 16,459,920
SIC 8741 Management services
Ted Chu

D-U-N-S 24-081-3761   (SL)
UNIGLOBE ONE TRAVEL INC
1444 Alberni St Suite 300, Vancouver, BC, V6G 2Z4
(604) 688-3551
Emp Here 180   *Sales* 120,040,560
SIC 4724 Travel agencies

Samantha Howl

D-U-N-S 24-367-3563   (HQ)
UNIGLOBE VISION TRAVEL GROUP INC
1444 Alberni St Suite 300, Vancouver, BC,
V6G 2Z4
(604) 688-3551
Sales 17,678,878
SIC 4724 Travel agencies
Irv Benjamin Wight
Paul Verhoeff
Alain Leprise
Rob Lindsay
Paul Knickerbocker
Jackie Lafontaine

D-U-N-S 20-801-9398   (HQ)
WESTERN PACIFIC MARINE LTD
501 Denman St, Vancouver, BC, V6G 2W9
(604) 681-5199
Sales 57,089,980
SIC 4482 Ferries
Graham Clarke

D-U-N-S 20-374-7832   (SL)
**YOUNG ENTREPRENEUR LEADERSHIP
LAUNCHPAD (YELL)**
1500 Georgia St W Unit 1250, Vancouver, BC,
V6G 2Z6
(778) 808-4641
Emp Here 200   *Sales* 287,720,200
SIC 8699 Membership organizations, nec
Judy Brooks
Amitpal Sandhu
Punit Dhillon
Sarah Lubik
Val Litwin
Rattan Bagga
David Cameron

Vancouver, BC V6H

D-U-N-S 25-850-8274   (SL)
ACCENT CRUISES.CA
1676 Duranleau St Suite 100, Vancouver, BC,
V6H 3S4
(604) 688-8072
Emp Here 40   *Sales* 20,798,680
SIC 4725 Tour operators
Ken Milne

D-U-N-S 24-866-8014   (HQ)
ALLEN-FELDMAN HOLDINGS LTD
1505 2nd Ave W Suite 200, Vancouver, BC,
V6H 3Y4
(604) 734-5945
Emp Here 1   *Sales* 11,741,940
SIC 6712 Bank holding companies
Bruce Allen
Sam Feldman

D-U-N-S 20-372-8519   (HQ)
ALTERNATE HEALTH CORP.
1485 6th Ave W Suite 309, Vancouver, BC,
V6H 4G1
(604) 569-4969
Sales 10,384,823
SIC 7372 Prepackaged software
Michael Murphy
Jade Green
Jay Briggs
James Griffiths
Chris Boling
Howard W. Mann
J. Bernard Rice
James E. Tykoliz
Michael Klipper
Jeff Langenbach

D-U-N-S 20-800-7153   (HQ)
BELMONT PROPERTIES
1401 Broadway W Suite 302, Vancouver, BC,
V6H 1H6
(604) 736-2841
Sales 11,237,200

SIC 6141 Personal credit institutions

D-U-N-S 20-959-8804   (HQ)
**BRITISH COLUMBIA'S CHILDRENS HOSPI-
TAL**
4480 Oak St Suite B321, Vancouver, BC, V6H
3V4
(604) 875-2345
Sales 244,376,000
SIC 8069 Specialty hospitals, except psychi-
atric
John Tegenfeldt
Lorna Tomlinson
Jarvis Hoult
Ann Sutherland-Bowl
Faye Whightman

D-U-N-S 20-588-6372   (SL)
**BRITISH COLUMBIA'S WOMEN'S HOSPI-
TAL AND HEALTH CENTRE FOUNDATION**
4500 Oak St Rm D310, Vancouver, BC, V6H
3N1
(604) 875-2270
Emp Here 26   *Sales* 11,679,694
SIC 7389 Business services, nec
Laurie Clarke

D-U-N-S 24-246-7140   (SL)
**BROADWAY PENTECOSTAL CARE ASSO-
CIATION**
BROADWAY PENTECOSTAL LODGE
1377 Lamey'S Mill Rd, Vancouver, BC, V6H
3S9
(604) 733-1441
Emp Here 110   *Sales* 7,515,860
SIC 8051 Skilled nursing care facilities
David Lade
Mark Perry
Irene Hamming
Cary Skidmore
John Puddell
Peter Lade
Bob Loose
Ross Hughs

D-U-N-S 25-507-5822   (HQ)
**CHILDREN'S & WOMEN'S HEALTH CEN-
TRE OF BRITISH COLUMBIA BRANCH**
(*Suby of* PROVINCIAL HEALTH SERVICES
AUTHORITY)
4500 Oak St, Vancouver, BC, V6H 3N1
(604) 875-2424
Emp Here 2,000   *Sales* 433,212,000
SIC 8069 Specialty hospitals, except psychi-
atric
Lynda Cranston

D-U-N-S 24-656-9529   (HQ)
**CHILDREN'S ARTS UMBRELLA ASSOCIA-
TION**
ARTS UMBRELLA
1286 Cartwright St, Vancouver, BC, V6H 3R8
(604) 681-5268
Sales 20,349,000
SIC 8299 Schools and educational services,
nec
Lucille Pacey

D-U-N-S 20-621-9446   (HQ)
CHRISTOFFERSEN, READ JONES LTD
RJC ENGINEERS
1285 Broadway W Unit 300, Vancouver, BC,
V6H 3X8
(604) 738-0048
Emp Here 70   *Sales* 34,854,105
SIC 8711 Engineering services
Norman R. Webster

D-U-N-S 24-249-6339   (SL)
**D & H GROUP CHARTERED ACCOUN-
TANTS**
1333 Broadway W, Vancouver, BC, V6H 4C1
(604) 731-5881
Emp Here 54   *Sales* 11,214,990
SIC 8721 Accounting, auditing, and book-
keeping
Bruce Mcfarlane

Dennis Louie
Larry Bisaro
Michael Louie
Michael Nakanishi
Tom Hamar
Brant Brondin

D-U-N-S 24-127-9178   (SL)
FELDMAN AGENCY INC, THE
1505 2nd Ave W Suite 200, Vancouver, BC,
V6H 3Y4
(604) 734-5945
Emp Here 150   *Sales* 22,471,950
SIC 7922 Theatrical producers and services
Samuel Feldman
Vinny Cinquemani
Shaw Saltzerg
Jeff Craib
Doug Cucheron
Linda Mccann

D-U-N-S 24-373-3391   (SL)
GAGE-BABCOCK & ASSOCIATES LTD
1195 Broadway W Suite 228, Vancouver, BC,
V6H 3X5
(604) 732-3751
Emp Here 26   *Sales* 11,679,694
SIC 7389 Business services, nec
Randall Kovacs
Gordon Richards
Anthony Godwin

D-U-N-S 20-113-1927   (SL)
GORDON LATHAM LIMITED
LATHAMS
1060 8th Ave W Suite 100, Vancouver, BC,
V6H 1C4
(604) 683-2321
Emp Here 95   *Sales* 22,141,175
SIC 1711 Plumbing, heating, air-conditioning
Kenneth Pearce
Carol Pearce
Robert Flipse

D-U-N-S 20-914-0045   (HQ)
**HEART AND STROKE FOUNDATION OF BC
& YUKON**
1212 Broadway W Unit 200, Vancouver, BC,
V6H 3V2
(604) 736-4088
Emp Here 40   *Sales* 16,565,440
SIC 8399 Social services, nec
Barbara Harwood
John Jackson
Carol Jillings
Ed Kry
Mike Riley
Michael E. Riley
John Cairns
Penny Hicks
Joyce Resin
Alan Peretz

D-U-N-S 20-863-2901   (HQ)
HEFFEL GALLERY LIMITED
HEFFEL FINE ART AUCTION HOUSE
2247 Granville St, Vancouver, BC, V6H 3G1
(604) 732-6505
Emp Here 14   *Sales* 10,781,256
SIC 7389 Business services, nec
David Heffel
Robert Heffel

D-U-N-S 24-317-1753   (HQ)
HIGHTECH SALES COACH INC
1338 Broadway W Suite 305, Vancouver, BC,
V6H 1H2
(604) 731-1377
Sales 22,174,500
SIC 7389 Business services, nec
Bill O'drowsky
Rick Huffman

D-U-N-S 20-117-1258   (SL)
INSPIRATION FURNITURE INC
1275 6th Ave W, Vancouver, BC, V6H 1A6
(604) 730-1275
Emp Here 50   *Sales* 11,517,000

SIC 5712 Furniture stores
Steen Skaaning

D-U-N-S 25-908-5033   (SL)
INVENTA SALES & PROMOTIONS INC
INVENTA
1401 8th Ave W Suite 210, Vancouver, BC,
V6H 1C9
(604) 687-0544
Emp Here 50   *Sales* 10,383,700
SIC 8743 Public relations services
Geoff Cribbs
Brent Nichols
David Nichols

D-U-N-S 20-112-8014   (HQ)
JORDANS INTERIORS LTD
JORDANS
(*Suby of* JORDANS RUGS LTD)
1470 Broadway W, Vancouver, BC, V6H 1H4
(604) 733-1174
Emp Here 20   *Sales* 23,240,300
SIC 5712 Furniture stores
David Jordan-Knox
Keith Bradbury

D-U-N-S 20-112-8030   (HQ)
JORDANS RUGS LTD
STYLE SOLUTIONS, DIV OF
1470 Broadway W, Vancouver, BC, V6H 1H4
(604) 733-1174
Emp Here 60   *Sales* 64,008,720
SIC 5713 Floor covering stores
David Jordan-Knox
James Jordan-Knox
Craig Jordan-Knox

D-U-N-S 24-837-9034   (BR)
KEG RESTAURANTS LTD
KEG STEAKHOUSE & BAR, THE
(*Suby of* RECIPE UNLIMITED CORPORA-
TION)
1499 Anderson St, Vancouver, BC, V6H 3R5
(604) 685-4735
Emp Here 90
SIC 5812 Eating places
Brad Patterson

D-U-N-S 20-594-1391   (SL)
KINETIC CAPITAL PARTNERS
1195 Broadway W Suite 500, Vancouver, BC,
V6H 3X5
(604) 692-2530
Emp Here 25   *Sales* 20,934,106
SIC 6722 Management investment, open-end
Frank Barker
Dallas Ross

D-U-N-S 25-385-3816   (SL)
MEINHARDT FINE FOODS INC
3002 Granville St, Vancouver, BC, V6H 3J8
(604) 732-4405
Emp Here 100   *Sales* 29,347,700
SIC 5411 Grocery stores
Linda Meinhardt

D-U-N-S 24-736-0261   (SL)
MOSAIC SIMON FRASER HOLDINGS LTD
2609 Granville St Unit 500, Vancouver, BC,
V6H 3H3
(604) 685-3888
Emp Here 100   *Sales* 20,388,300
SIC 6553 Cemetery subdividers and develop-
ers
Chris Barbati
Chris White

D-U-N-S 24-290-7640   (SL)
MUSTEL RESEARCH GROUP LTD
1505 2nd Ave W Unit 402, Vancouver, BC,
V6H 3Y4
(604) 733-4213
Emp Here 70   *Sales* 14,935,060
SIC 8732 Commercial nonphysical research
Evi Mustel
Jami Koehl

D-U-N-S 25-756-3726   (HQ)

POLYGON HOMES LTD
(Suby of WINCHESTER INVESTMENTS LTD)
1333 Broadway W Suite 900, Vancouver, BC, V6H 4C2
(604) 877-1131
Sales 13,077,650
SIC 6712 Bank holding companies
Neil Chrystal
Micheal Audain

D-U-N-S 24-824-2984   (SL)
PREMIER SECURITY INC
1055 Broadway W Suite 603, Vancouver, BC, V6H 1E2
(604) 739-1893
Emp Here 175   *Sales* 4,593,750
SIC 7381 Detective and armored car services
Martin Parker

D-U-N-S 20-799-2751   (SL)
REAL ESTATE BOARD OF GREATER VAN-COUVER
VANCOUVER REAL ESTATE BOARD
2433 Spruce St, Vancouver, BC, V6H 4C8
(604) 730-3000
Emp Here 82   *Sales* 21,206,430
SIC 8611 Business associations
Robert K. Wallace
W. Dave Watt
Jake Moldowan

D-U-N-S 24-641-4429   (HQ)
REM TEK ENTERPRISES LTD
BROOKE RADIOLOGY & ASSOCIATES
3195 Granville St Suite 218, Vancouver, BC, V6H 3K2
(604) 733-6345
Emp Here 40   *Sales* 13,716,600
SIC 8741 Management services
Marian Kean
Kathryn Jenkins
Barbara Dolden
Patricia Wan
Anna Williamson

D-U-N-S 24-152-1368   (HQ)
SUKI'S BEAUTY BAZAAR LTD
SUKI'S INTERNATIONAL HAIR DESIGN
3157 Granville St, Vancouver, BC, V6H 3K1
(604) 738-2127
Emp Here 54   *Sales* 11,746,020
SIC 7231 Beauty shops
Tsukiko Takagi

D-U-N-S 24-310-9055   (HQ)
UNIGLOBE TRAVEL (WESTERN CANADA) INC
UNIGLOBE WESTERN CANADA REGION
2695 Granville St Suite 600, Vancouver, BC, V6H 3H4
(604) 602-3470
Emp Here 12   *Sales* 12,542,580
SIC 6794 Patent owners and lessors
Laurie Radloff
Dennis Hop
Paul Verhoeff
Darol Hamilton
Ron Russell

D-U-N-S 24-088-1677   (HQ)
ZYMEWORKS INC
1385 8th Ave W Suite 540, Vancouver, BC, V6H 3V9
(604) 678-1388
Sales 53,019,000
SIC 8733 Noncommercial research organizations
Ali Tehrani
Anthony J. Polverino
John Babcook
Mark Hollywood
Neil Klompas
Diana Hausman
David Kai Yuen Poon
Surjit Dixit
Jennifer Kaufmann-Shaw

Wajida Leclerc

Vancouver, BC V6J

D-U-N-S 25-718-1677   (SL)
4TH & BURRARD ESSO SERVICE
TIM HORTONS
1790 4th Ave W, Vancouver, BC, V6J 1M1

Emp Here 25   *Sales* 12,451,950
SIC 5541 Gasoline service stations
Mahir Nibber

D-U-N-S 20-619-9135   (SL)
A B C PHOTOCOLOUR PRODUCTS LTD
1618 4th Ave W, Vancouver, BC, V6J 1L9
(604) 736-7017
Emp Here 33   *Sales* 13,057,374
SIC 7384 Photofinish laboratories
Eddie Lee
Robin Kearns
Peter Bentley
Norman Williams

D-U-N-S 25-419-1984   (SL)
AIRLINER MOTOR HOTEL (1972) LTD
HOWARD JOHNSON HOTEL
2233 Burrard St Suite 309, Vancouver, BC, V6J 3H9

Emp Here 126   *Sales* 5,735,394
SIC 5813 Drinking places
David Greywal

D-U-N-S 20-797-4254   (HQ)
ALLWEST INSURANCE SERVICES LTD
2-1855 Burrard St, Vancouver, BC, V6J 3G9
(604) 736-1969
Emp Here 45   *Sales* 221,729,040
SIC 6411 Insurance agents, brokers, and service
Paul Zalesky

D-U-N-S 20-425-1920   (SL)
ARBUTUS CLUB, THE
2001 Nanton Ave, Vancouver, BC, V6J 4A1
(604) 266-7166
Emp Here 150   *Sales* 11,781,750
SIC 7997 Membership sports and recreation clubs
Brent Elkington
Dale Cadeau
Allen Whitchelo

D-U-N-S 24-641-0070   (SL)
B+H CHIL DESIGN
1706 1st Ave W Suite 400, Vancouver, BC, V6J 0E4
(604) 688-8571
Emp Here 47   *Sales* 20,844,030
SIC 7389 Business services, nec
Linda Negrin-Webb

D-U-N-S 20-005-4943   (SL)
BERRIS MANGAN CHARTERED ACCOUNTANTS
1827 5th Ave W, Vancouver, BC, V6J 1P5

Emp Here 54   *Sales* 11,344,881
SIC 8721 Accounting, auditing, and bookkeeping
Micheal Berris
Patrick Mangan
Kent Elliot
Dennis Shikaze
John Galbraith
Brent Axworthy
Dino Infanti

D-U-N-S 20-229-5783   (HQ)
BMW STORE LTD, THE
2040 Burrard St, Vancouver, BC, V6J 3H5
(604) 659-3200
Sales 62,928,000
SIC 5511 New and used car dealers

Dan Field
John Field

D-U-N-S 20-803-9594   (HQ)
BOARD OF EDUCATION OF SCHOOL DISTRICT NO. 39 (VANCOUVER), THE
VANCOUVER BOARD OF EDUCATION
1580 Broadway W, Vancouver, BC, V6J 5K8
(604) 713-5000
Emp Here 200   *Sales* 437,734,302
SIC 8211 Elementary and secondary schools
Joy Alexander
Patti Bacchus
Fraser Ballantyne
Ken Clement
Janet Fraser
Ken Denike
Mike Lombardi
Penny Noble
Cherie Payne
Christopher Richardson

D-U-N-S 20-355-1940   (SL)
BOARD OF SCHOOL TRUSTEES
1580 Broadway W, Vancouver, BC, V6J 5K8
(604) 713-5000
Emp Here 200   *Sales* 19,823,800
SIC 8211 Elementary and secondary schools
Mike Lombardi
Janet Fraser
Joy Alexander
Patti Bacchus
Fraser Ballantyne
Penny Noble
Christopher Richardson
Stacy Robertson
Allan Wong

D-U-N-S 20-917-3228   (HQ)
BRITISH COLUMBIA MEDICAL ASSOCIATION (CANADIAN MEDICAL ASSOCIATION - B.C. DIVISION)
DOCTORS OF BC
1665 Broadway W Suite 115, Vancouver, BC, V6J 5A4
(604) 736-5551
Sales 11,852,647
SIC 8621 Professional organizations

D-U-N-S 24-939-7332   (SL)
BURRARD IMPORTS LTD
BURRARD ACURA AUTO PLAZA
2430 Burrard St, Vancouver, BC, V6J 5L3
(604) 736-8890
Emp Here 52   *Sales* 32,722,560
SIC 5511 New and used car dealers
William Tse

D-U-N-S 20-789-8888   (BR)
CACTUS RESTAURANTS LTD
CACTUS CLUB CAFE
(Suby of CACTUS RESTAURANTS LTD)
1530 Broadway W, Vancouver, BC, V6J 5K9
(604) 733-0434
Emp Here 100
SIC 5812 Eating places
Barry Jorgen

D-U-N-S 24-492-0260   (HQ)
CARTER MOTOR CARS LTD
CARTER HONDA
2390 Burrard St, Vancouver, BC, V6J 3J1
(604) 736-2821
Emp Here 35   *Sales* 72,367,200
SIC 5511 New and used car dealers
Joe Mitchell

D-U-N-S 20-515-1637   (BR)
CHILDREN'S & WOMEN'S HEALTH CENTRE OF BRITISH COLUMBIA BRANCH
(Suby of PROVINCIAL HEALTH SERVICES AUTHORITY)
1770 7th Ave W Suite 260, Vancouver, BC, V6J 4Y6
(604) 733-6721
Emp Here 150
SIC 8721 Accounting, auditing, and book-

keeping
Nozer Kanga

D-U-N-S 24-778-1552   (HQ)
COLLEGE OF REGISTERED NURSES OF BC
CRNBC
2855 Arbutus St, Vancouver, BC, V6J 3Y8
(604) 736-7331
Sales 19,321,200
SIC 8621 Professional organizations
Cynthia Johansen

D-U-N-S 20-864-7875   (HQ)
COMOR SPORTS CENTRE LTD
COMOR-GO PLAY OUTSIDE
1793 4th Ave W, Vancouver, BC, V6J 1M2
(604) 734-0212
Emp Here 1   *Sales* 29,319,360
SIC 5941 Sporting goods and bicycle shops
Steve Curell

D-U-N-S 25-215-7995   (HQ)
CORREVIO PHARMA CORP
(Suby of CIPHER PHARMACEUTICALS INC)
1441 Creekside Dr 6 Fl, Vancouver, BC, V6J 4S7
(604) 677-6905
Sales 24,489,840
SIC 8731 Commercial physical research
Mark H. Corrigan
W. James Oshea
Justin A. Renz
Arthur H. Willms
Richard M. Glickman
Vanda De Cian
William Hunter
Robert James Meyer
David Dean
Hugues Sachot

D-U-N-S 25-691-9143   (SL)
CULINARY CAPERS CATERING INC
1545 3rd Ave W, Vancouver, BC, V6J 1J8
(604) 875-0123
Emp Here 150   *Sales* 6,827,850
SIC 5812 Eating places
Debra Lykkemark

D-U-N-S 24-957-6604   (HQ)
DENCAN RESTAURANTS INC
DENNY'S RESTAURANT
(Suby of NORTHLAND PROPERTIES CORPORATION)
1755 Broadway W Suite 310, Vancouver, BC, V6J 4S5
(604) 730-6620
Emp Here 35   *Sales* 69,958,500
SIC 5812 Eating places
R.Thomas Gaglardi
Bobby Naicker
Bob Gaglardi

D-U-N-S 24-855-7258   (BR)
EARL'S RESTAURANTS LTD
EARL'S
(Suby of EARL'S RESTAURANTS LTD)
1601 Broadway W, Vancouver, BC, V6J 1W9
(604) 736-5663
Emp Here 120
SIC 5812 Eating places
Brad Billick

D-U-N-S 25-719-5727   (SL)
EIGEN DEVELOPMENT LTD
1807 10th Ave W Suite 300, Vancouver, BC, V6J 2A9
(604) 484-0211
Emp Here 40   *Sales* 21,248,280
SIC 6289 Security and commodity service
Shaune Stoddard

D-U-N-S 25-723-3387   (SL)
EPI ENVIRONMENTAL PRODUCTS INC
1788 Broadway W Suite 801, Vancouver, BC, V6J 1Y1
(604) 738-6281
Emp Here 30   *Sales* 21,910,350

SIC 5169 Chemicals and allied products, nec
Joseph G Gho
Henry Poon

D-U-N-S 20-160-9448   (SL)
EXECUTIVE WAITER RESOURCES INC
1975 16th Ave W, Vancouver, BC, V6J 2M5
(604) 689-0640
Emp Here 49   *Sales* 11,611,530
SIC 7361 Employment agencies
Christopher Monk

D-U-N-S 24-670-4337   (SL)
FAMILY CENTRED PRACTICES GROUP INC
1820 Fir St Unit 210, Vancouver, BC, V6J 3B1
(604) 736-0094
Emp Here 48   *Sales* 10,195,056
SIC 8748 Business consulting, nec
Tina Linton

D-U-N-S 24-626-2245   (SL)
FRAMERS CHOICE
1695 2nd Ave W, Vancouver, BC, V6J 1H3
(604) 732-8477
Emp Here 30   *Sales* 15,265,680
SIC 5023 Homefurnishings
Richard Allan

D-U-N-S 24-493-1085   (SL)
GOLDILOCKS BAKE SHOP (CANADA) INC
1606 Broadway W, Vancouver, BC, V6J 1X6
(604) 736-2464
Emp Here 50   *Sales* 13,707,600
SIC 5461 Retail bakeries
Leslie Wong
Freddie Go
Mary Jane Yee

D-U-N-S 24-006-3557   (SL)
I B S INTEGRATED BUSINESS SERVICES
1632 6th Ave W, Vancouver, BC, V6J 1R3
(604) 714-1100
Emp Here 48   *Sales* 21,825,357
SIC 5065 Electronic parts and equipment, nec
Don Nelder

D-U-N-S 24-726-2017   (HQ)
INTERCITY EQUITY CORPORATION
1847 Broadway W Suite 104, Vancouver, BC, V6J 1Y6
(604) 731-6541
Emp Here 1   *Sales* 24,593,740
SIC 6411 Insurance agents, brokers, and service
Jack Meier

D-U-N-S 25-539-0619   (SL)
IRIDIA MEDICAL INC
1644 3rd Ave W, Vancouver, BC, V6J 1K2
(604) 685-4747
Emp Here 49   *Sales* 17,700,613
SIC 8049 Offices of health practitioner
Allan Holmes
Vern Biccum
Thomas Puddicombe

D-U-N-S 25-679-9347   (HQ)
LULULEMON ATHLETICA CANADA INC
LULULEMON
1818 Cornwall Ave Suite 400, Vancouver, BC, V6J 1C7
(604) 732-6124
Emp Here 800   *Sales* 3,288,319,000
SIC 2339 Women's and misses' outerwear, nec
Calvin Mcdonald
Glenn Murphy
Celeste Burgoyne
Michael Casey
Kathryn Henry
Jon Mcneill
Martha Morfitt
David Mussafer
Tricia Patrick
Emily White

D-U-N-S 20-241-5688   (SL)

MACDONALD COMMECIAL REAL ESTATE SERVICES LTD
SOUTH GRANVILLE BUSINESS CENTRE
(*Suby of* MACDONALD REALTY LTD)
1827 5th Ave W, Vancouver, BC, V6J 1P5
(604) 736-5611
Emp Here 44   *Sales* 10,870,240
SIC 6531 Real estate agents and managers
Anthony Letvinchuk

D-U-N-S 20-651-7752   (HQ)
MACDONALD REALTY LTD
MACDONALD COMMERCIAL
1827 5th Ave W, Vancouver, BC, V6J 1P5
(604) 736-5611
Sales 111,903,600
SIC 8742 Management consulting services
Anthony Letvinchuk

D-U-N-S 25-051-4346   (SL)
MAINFRAME ENTERTAINMENT INC
(*Suby of* WOW UNLIMITED MEDIA INC)
2025 Broadway W Suite 200, Vancouver, BC, V6J 1Z6
(604) 714-2600
Emp Here 260
SIC 7812 Motion picture and video production
Katherine Tam

D-U-N-S 20-086-5553   (HQ)
MAX WRIGHT REAL ESTATE CORPORATION
SOTHEBY'S INTERNATIONAL REALTY CANADA
1672 2nd Ave W, Vancouver, BC, V6J 1H4
(604) 632-3300
Emp Here 40   *Sales* 41,888,900
SIC 6531 Real estate agents and managers
Ross Mccredie

D-U-N-S 20-146-6088   (SL)
MCL MOTOR CARS 1992 INC
1718 3rd Ave W, Vancouver, BC, V6J 1K4
(604) 736-7911
Emp Here 30   *Sales* 14,942,340
SIC 5511 New and used car dealers
Steven Ho

D-U-N-S 24-311-1460   (BR)
MOLSON BREWERIES OF CANADA LIMITED
MOLSON COORS BREWING COMPANY
(*Suby of* MOLSON COORS BREWING COMPANY)
1550 Burrard St, Vancouver, BC, V6J 3G5
(604) 664-1786
Emp Here 300
SIC 2082 Malt beverages

D-U-N-S 24-839-1716   (BR)
MOLSON CANADA 2005
MOLSON BREWERIES
(*Suby of* MOLSON COORS BREWING COMPANY)
1550 Burrard St, Vancouver, BC, V6J 3G5
(604) 664-1786
Emp Here 325
SIC 2082 Malt beverages
Blair Shier

D-U-N-S 24-579-5265   (HQ)
NEMETZ, ARNOLD & ASSOCIATES LTD
2009 4th Ave W, Vancouver, BC, V6J 1N3
(604) 736-6562
Emp Here 40   *Sales* 10,557,480
SIC 8711 Engineering services
Arnold Nemetz
Steven Nemetz

D-U-N-S 20-911-7670   (HQ)
NORTHLAND PROPERTIES CORPORATION
SANDMAN INNS
1755 Broadway W Suite 310, Vancouver, BC, V6J 4S5
(604) 730-6610
Emp Here 60   *Sales* 861,012,000
SIC 7011 Hotels and motels

Robert Gaglardi
Thomas Gaglardi
Shamlin Pillay

D-U-N-S 20-514-1034   (SL)
OPEN SOLUTIONS DATAWEST INC
1770 Burrard St Suite 300, Vancouver, BC, V6J 3G7
(604) 734-7494
Emp Here 80   *Sales* 18,743,040
SIC 8742 Management consulting services
Barry Cleaver
Kenneth Saunders
Andrew S. Saunders

D-U-N-S 24-445-9301   (SL)
OPEN SOLUTIONS DTS INC
1441 Creekside Dr Suite 300, Vancouver, BC, V6J 4S7
(604) 714-1848
Emp Here 20   *Sales* 30,032,460
SIC 7372 Prepackaged software
Colin Brown
Michael Kelso

D-U-N-S 20-995-3819   (HQ)
OPUS FRAMING LTD
OPUS FRAMING & ART SUPPLIES
1677 2nd Ave W, Vancouver, BC, V6J 1H3
(604) 736-7535
Emp Here 40   *Sales* 39,092,480
SIC 5999 Miscellaneous retail stores, nec
David Van Berckel
Simon Chow
Scott Cronshaw

D-U-N-S 20-868-1841   (SL)
POST MODERN SOUND INC
1722 2nd Ave W, Vancouver, BC, V6J 1H6
(604) 736-7474
Emp Here 30   *Sales* 13,304,700
SIC 7389 Business services, nec
Menashe Arbel
Mark Scott

D-U-N-S 25-718-4606   (BR)
QUINTERRA PROPERTY MAINTENANCE INC
(*Suby of* QUINTERRA PROPERTY MAINTENANCE INC)
1681 Chestnut St Suite 400, Vancouver, BC, V6J 4M6
(604) 689-1800
Emp Here 2,700
SIC 7349 Building maintenance services, nec
David Weakley

D-U-N-S 24-167-0918   (HQ)
SAWARNE LUMBER CO. LTD
1770 Burrard St Suite 280, Vancouver, BC, V6J 3G7
(604) 324-4666
Emp Here 75   *Sales* 17,313,300
SIC 2421 Sawmills and planing mills, general
Sawarne Sangara
Terry Sangara
Davy Sangara
Kerry Sangara
Kirpy Sangara

D-U-N-S 20-801-6303   (SL)
SEYMOUR MEDICAL CLINIC, THE
1530 7th Ave W Suite 200, Vancouver, BC, V6J 1S3
(604) 738-2151
Emp Here 70   *Sales* 11,245,220
SIC 8011 Offices and clinics of medical doctors
Ronald D Bennett
W Peter House
James K Lai
Paul M Leung
Margaret E M Moss
Bruce Noble
Roy J Oakey
Roy A Saunders
Paul E Wilson
Blake Newton Wright

D-U-N-S 24-995-3548   (HQ)
SIMPLY COMPUTING INC
1690 Broadway W Suite 203, Vancouver, BC, V6J 1X6
(604) 714-1450
Emp Here 30   *Sales* 11,620,150
SIC 5734 Computer and software stores
Gordon Mcormond

D-U-N-S 24-881-8239   (HQ)
SLR CONSULTING (CANADA) LTD
(*Suby of* SLR GLOBAL LUX SARL)
1620 8th Ave W Suite 200, Vancouver, BC, V6J 1V4
(604) 738-2500
Emp Here 65   *Sales* 27,883,900
SIC 8748 Business consulting, nec
Faramarz Bogzaran
Steven Numata
Ruth Ann Pierce
James Malick
Richard Johnson

D-U-N-S 24-419-1271   (HQ)
SMARTDESIGN GROUP KTBS INC
1788 5th Ave W Suite 300, Vancouver, BC, V6J 1P2
(604) 662-7015
Sales 11,230,475
SIC 7389 Business services, nec
Nicholas F Baker

D-U-N-S 24-292-8448   (HQ)
SNOW COVERS SPORTS INC
SNOW COVERS
(*Suby of* SKIIS LTD)
1701 3rd Ave W, Vancouver, BC, V6J 1K7
(604) 738-3715
Emp Here 22   *Sales* 12,460,728
SIC 5941 Sporting goods and bicycle shops
Paul Montgomery

D-U-N-S 24-068-7814   (HQ)
SPEEDI GOURMET CO LTD
ORANGE JULIUS
(*Suby of* SENIOR ENTERPRISES LTD)
1650 4th Ave W, Vancouver, BC, V6J 1L9
(604) 731-8877
Emp Here 4   *Sales* 11,659,750
SIC 5812 Eating places
David Vaillencourt
Jack Senior
Elenor Senior
Lyle Knott
Michael Senior

D-U-N-S 25-597-8140   (SL)
STOWE, LESLEY FINE FOODS LTD
EXECUTIVE CHEF
1685 5th Ave W, Vancouver, BC, V6J 1N5

Emp Here 20   *Sales* 10,702,480
SIC 5149 Groceries and related products, nec
Lesley Stowe

D-U-N-S 20-804-2499   (SL)
VANCOUVER LAWN TENNIS AND BADMINTON CLUB
1630 15th Ave W, Vancouver, BC, V6J 2K7
(604) 731-9411
Emp Here 80   *Sales* 6,283,600
SIC 7997 Membership sports and recreation clubs
Janis Ostling

D-U-N-S 20-868-4951   (BR)
WAWANESA MUTUAL INSURANCE COMPANY, THE
(*Suby of* WAWANESA MUTUAL INSURANCE COMPANY, THE)
1985 Broadway W Suite 400, Vancouver, BC, V6J 4Y3
(800) 665-2778
Emp Here 115
SIC 6331 Fire, marine, and casualty insurance
Graham Haigh

D-U-N-S 25-917-1668   (SL)

WESTSIDE NURSING SERVICES LTD
1892 Broadway W Suite 200, Vancouver, BC,
V6J 1Y9
(604) 261-9161
Emp Here 40   *Sales* 11,331,720
SIC 8741 Management services
Kristen Nordli

D-U-N-S 20-188-6103   (HQ)
WOW UNLIMITED MEDIA INC
RAINMAKER STUDIOS
2025 Broadway W Suite 200, Vancouver, BC,
V6J 1Z6
(604) 714-2600
Sales 59,608,261
SIC 7812 Motion picture and video production
Michael Hirsh
Steve Hendry
Marc Bertrand
Steve Hendry
Craig Graham
Fred Seibert
Bob Ezrin
Mike Cosentino
John Vandervelde

D-U-N-S 25-146-8617   (HQ)
X O TOURS CANADA LTD
1788 Broadway W Unit 600, Vancouver, BC,
V6J 1Y1
(604) 738-6188
Emp Here 20   *Sales* 11,439,274
SIC 4725 Tour operators
Ronnie Chem
Hung Chih Chen
Li Hsing Chen

D-U-N-S 20-028-1214   (SL)
ZAD HOLDINGS LTD
CANADIAN FLOORING & RENOVATIONS
1903 Broadway W, Vancouver, BC, V6J 1Z3
(604) 739-4477
Emp Here 4   *Sales* 10,640,742
SIC 1752 Floor laying and floor work, nec
Nader Kianzad

Vancouver, BC V6K

D-U-N-S 25-068-7530   (HQ)
0561768 B.C. LTD
PARTHENON SUPERMARKET
3080 Broadway W, Vancouver, BC, V6K 2H1
(604) 733-4191
Sales 26,738,464
SIC 5141 Groceries, general line
Kyriakos Katsanikakis
Paula Lebraron

D-U-N-S 24-856-4346   (HQ)
2627 W 16TH AVENUE HOLDINGS LTD
2627 16th Ave W, Vancouver, BC, V6K 3C2
(604) 736-0009
Sales 58,695,400
SIC 5411 Grocery stores
Wayne Lockhart
Lloyd Lockhart

D-U-N-S 25-365-5310   (BR)
**BOARD OF EDUCATION OF SCHOOL DIS-
TRICT NO. 39 (VANCOUVER), THE**
KITSILANO SECONDARY SCHOOL
(*Suby of* BOARD OF EDUCATION OF
SCHOOL DISTRICT NO. 39 (VANCOUVER),
THE)
2706 Trafalgar St, Vancouver, BC, V6K 2J6
(604) 713-8961
Emp Here 109
SIC 8211 Elementary and secondary schools
Ranjit Bains

D-U-N-S 24-897-9536   (HQ)
DAVID SUZUKI FOUNDATION, THE
2211 4th Ave W Unit 219, Vancouver, BC, V6K
4S2

(604) 732-4228
Sales 13,909,490
SIC 8699 Membership organizations, nec
Tara Cullis
Peter Steele

D-U-N-S 20-364-5986   (SL)
IDEA PARTNER MARKETING INC, THE
*TAPESTRY AT THE O'KEEFE - ARBUTUS
WALK*
2799 Yew St, Vancouver, BC, V6K 4W2
(604) 736-1640
Emp Here 50   *Sales* 11,323,700
SIC 6513 Apartment building operators
Sam Zeigoun

D-U-N-S 25-384-9210   (SL)
KINDRED CONSTRUCTION LTD
2150 Broadway W Unit 308, Vancouver, BC,
V6K 4L9
(604) 736-4847
Emp Here 70   *Sales* 19,203,240
SIC 8741 Management services
Richard Reid
Briony Reid

D-U-N-S 20-110-6606   (HQ)
LENS & SHUTTER CAMERAS LTD
2902 Broadway W Suite 201, Vancouver, BC,
V6K 2G8

Emp Here 1   *Sales* 17,102,960
SIC 5946 Camera and photographic supply
stores
Stephen Good
Ronald Booth

D-U-N-S 24-579-0944   (SL)
NORTHWEST LOGISTICS INC
(*Suby of* CANADIAN LOGISTICS SYSTEMS
LIMITED)
2906 Broadway W Suite 260, Vancouver, BC,
V6K 2G8
(604) 731-8001
Emp Here 25   *Sales* 12,999,175
SIC 4785 Inspection and fixed facilities
Edward Truman

D-U-N-S 24-166-4648   (HQ)
RENSHAW TRAVEL LTD
RENSHAW TRAVEL & CRUISE CENTER
2175 4th Ave W, Vancouver, BC, V6K 1N7
(604) 838-1008
Emp Here 1   *Sales* 15,599,010
SIC 4724 Travel agencies
Donald Renshaw Jr

D-U-N-S 20-913-9039   (HQ)
SERENA FASHIONS LTD
BELLISSIMA
2700 Broadway W, Vancouver, BC, V6K 2G4
(604) 733-8508
Emp Here 12   *Sales* 16,145,640
SIC 5621 Women's clothing stores
John Kwei
Serena Kwei

D-U-N-S 25-271-7111   (BR)
SOBEYS WEST INC
CANADA SAFEWAY
(*Suby of* EMPIRE COMPANY LIMITED)
2733 Broadway W, Vancouver, BC, V6K 2G5
(604) 732-5030
Emp Here 100
SIC 5411 Grocery stores
Joy Mcdow

D-U-N-S 25-140-1683   (SL)
ST. JOHN'S SCHOOL SOCIETY
ST JOHN'S SCHOOL
2215 10th Ave W, Vancouver, BC, V6K 2J1
(604) 732-4434
Emp Here 80   *Sales* 7,426,080
SIC 8211 Elementary and secondary schools
David Dale-Johnson
Anu Khanna
Doris Orr
Shiuman Ho

D-U-N-S 20-272-4246   (HQ)
TRAVEL MASTERS INC
TRAVEL MASTERS PRINCE ALBERT
2678 Broadway W Suite 200, Vancouver, BC,
V6K 2G3
(604) 659-4150
Emp Here 24   *Sales* 18,198,845
SIC 4724 Travel agencies
Neil Mcmahon

Vancouver, BC V6L

D-U-N-S 20-031-6698   (BR)
**BOARD OF EDUCATION OF SCHOOL DIS-
TRICT NO. 39 (VANCOUVER), THE**
*BOARD OF EDUCATION OF SCHOOL DIS-
TRICT NO. 39 (VANC*
(*Suby of* BOARD OF EDUCATION OF
SCHOOL DISTRICT NO. 39 (VANCOUVER),
THE)
2250 Eddington Dr, Vancouver, BC, V6L 2E7
(604) 713-8974
Emp Here 80
SIC 8211 Elementary and secondary schools
Angela Haveman

D-U-N-S 24-345-9489   (BR)
REVERA INC
ARBUTUS CARE CENTRE
(*Suby of* GOVERNMENT OF CANADA)
4505 Valley Dr, Vancouver, BC, V6L 2L1
(604) 261-4292
Emp Here 200
SIC 8051 Skilled nursing care facilities
Clayton Beverley

Vancouver, BC V6M

D-U-N-S 24-856-8685   (SL)
BALANCED FINANCIAL SERVICES LTD
2309 41st Ave W Suite 202, Vancouver, BC,
V6M 2A3
(604) 261-8509
Emp Here 21   *Sales* 11,155,347
SIC 6282 Investment advice
Jan Giezen
Fran Goldberg
Robert Paulett
Earle Yasin
Brian Goss
Michael Conrad

D-U-N-S 20-147-2219   (HQ)
BEAUMONT STANLEY INC
BLUE RUBY
2125 41st Ave W, Vancouver, BC, V6M 1Z3
(604) 266-9177
Emp Here 15   *Sales* 29,319,360
SIC 5944 Jewelry stores
Nancy Hill

D-U-N-S 20-202-7806   (BR)
**BOARD OF EDUCATION OF SCHOOL DIS-
TRICT NO. 39 (VANCOUVER), THE**
MAGEE SECONDARY SCHOOL
(*Suby of* BOARD OF EDUCATION OF
SCHOOL DISTRICT NO. 39 (VANCOUVER),
THE)
6360 Maple St, Vancouver, BC, V6M 4M2
(604) 713-8200
Emp Here 100
SIC 8211 Elementary and secondary schools
Alec Macinnes

D-U-N-S 20-920-0096   (SL)
**JEWISH HOME FOR THE AGED OF
BRITISH COLUMBIA**
LOUIS BRIER HOME & HOSPITAL, DIV OF
1055 41st Ave W, Vancouver, BC, V6M 1W9
(604) 261-9376
Emp Here 300   *Sales* 20,497,800

SIC 8051 Skilled nursing care facilities
David Dunn

D-U-N-S 20-112-9228   (HQ)
KERRISDALE CAMERAS LTD
2170 41st Ave W, Vancouver, BC, V6M 1Z5
(604) 263-3221
Emp Here 5   *Sales* 10,880,650
SIC 5946 Camera and photographic supply
stores
Robert Hudson
Jay Hudson

D-U-N-S 20-196-7283   (SL)
KERRISDALE LUMBER CO LTD
6191 West Boulevard, Vancouver, BC, V6M
3X3
(604) 261-4274
Emp Here 50   *Sales* 12,652,950
SIC 5211 Lumber and other building materials
Mark Perry

D-U-N-S 24-311-2141   (BR)
LONDON DRUGS LIMITED
(*Suby of* H.Y. LOUIE CO. LIMITED)
2091 42nd Ave W Suite 10, Vancouver, BC,
V6M 2B4
(604) 448-1036
Emp Here 100
SIC 5912 Drug stores and proprietary stores
Bob Thompson

D-U-N-S 20-802-1139   (HQ)
MACDONALD REALTY (1974) LTD
2105 38th Ave W Suite 208, Vancouver, BC,
V6M 1R8
(604) 263-1911
Emp Here 1   *Sales* 46,077,790
SIC 6531 Real estate agents and managers
Lynn Hsu
Kai Leung

D-U-N-S 24-370-4079   (HQ)
PARK GEORGIA REALTY LTD
(*Suby of* PARK GEORGIA PROPERTIES
LTD)
5701 Granville St Suite 201, Vancouver, BC,
V6M 4J7
(604) 261-7275
Emp Here 5   *Sales* 67,612,800
SIC 6531 Real estate agents and managers
Ernest Hui
Brian Hui
Mimie Hui
Stan Choi

D-U-N-S 20-112-3663   (HQ)
PROTECH HOME MEDICAL CORP
PATIENT HOME MONITORING
5626 Larch St Suite 202, Vancouver, BC, V6M
4E1
(877) 811-9690
Sales 108,058,357
SIC 3845 Electromedical equipment
Casey Hoyt
Mike Moore
Greg Crawford
Michael Dalsin
Roger Greene
Nitin Kaushal

D-U-N-S 25-686-1717   (SL)
PROVIDENT SECURITY CORP
2309 41st Ave W Suite 400, Vancouver, BC,
V6M 2A3
(604) 664-1087
Emp Here 150   *Sales* 3,937,500
SIC 7381 Detective and armored car services
Michael Jagger

D-U-N-S 20-112-2694   (SL)
REID'S DRY GOODS LTD
HILLS OF KERRISDALE
2125 41st Ave W, Vancouver, BC, V6M 1Z3
(604) 266-9177
Emp Here 100   *Sales* 17,939,600
SIC 5651 Family clothing stores
Ross Hill

Kathleen Hill
Nancy Hill
James Hill

D-U-N-S 25-219-4915   (SL)
STERN REALTY (1994) LTD
COLDWELL BANKER PREMIER REALTY
6272 East Boulevard, Vancouver, BC, V6M
3V7
(604) 266-1364
Emp Here 50   *Sales* 16,356,350
SIC 6531 Real estate agents and managers
Sheila Stern
Marline Kolterhoff

D-U-N-S 24-150-3465   (SL)
VANCOUVER COLLEGE LIMITED
5400 Cartier St, Vancouver, BC, V6M 3A5
(604) 261-4285
Emp Here 137   *Sales* 12,717,162
SIC 8211 Elementary and secondary schools
David Hardy
Kelly Latimer

D-U-N-S 25-068-7779   (BR)
VANCOUVER, CITY OF
VANDUSEN BOTANICAL GARDEN
(*Suby of* VANCOUVER, CITY OF)
5251 Oak St, Vancouver, BC, V6M 4H1
(604) 257-8666
Emp Here 100
SIC 8422 Botanical and zoological gardens
Guy Pottinger

D-U-N-S 24-325-4963   (SL)
ZINCORE METALS INC
5626 Larch St Suite 202, Vancouver, BC, V6M
4E1
(604) 669-6611
Emp Here 50   *Sales* 10,206,500
SIC 1031 Lead and zinc ores
Jorge Benavides
Adam Ho
David Black
Roman Friedrich

Vancouver, BC V6N

D-U-N-S 20-705-1009   (SL)
MARKET PLACE IGA
3535 41st Ave W, Vancouver, BC, V6N 3E7
(604) 261-2423
Emp Here 80   *Sales* 23,478,160
SIC 5411 Grocery stores
Steve Stojkovic

D-U-N-S 25-712-9312   (BR)
REVERA INC
CROFTON MANOR
(*Suby of* GOVERNMENT OF CANADA)
2803 41st Ave W Suite 110, Vancouver, BC,
V6N 4B4
(604) 263-0921
Emp Here 110
SIC 8361 Residential care
Marilyn Harris

D-U-N-S 20-573-1755   (SL)
**SHAUGHNESSY GOLF AND COUNTRY
CLUB**
4300 Marine Dr Sw, Vancouver, BC, V6N 4A6
(604) 266-4141
Emp Here 80   *Sales* 6,283,600
SIC 7997 Membership sports and recreation
clubs
Kathleen Bech
Carolyn Wark
Graham Wilson
Hiroko Ainsworth
Peter Birks
Ron Emerson
Iain Harris
David Kraemer
Ronald Larter

Derek Mullan

Vancouver, BC V6P

D-U-N-S 25-612-2706   (SL)
0844212 BC LTD
*SUTTON GROUP - WEST LANGARA RE-
ALTY*
7547 Cambie St, Vancouver, BC, V6P 3H6
(604) 618-0646
Emp Here 100   *Sales* 41,888,900
SIC 6531 Real estate agents and managers
Greg Rahn

D-U-N-S 24-797-7960   (HQ)
AUTHENTIC T-SHIRT COMPANY ULC, THE
SANMAR CANADA
850 Kent Ave South W, Vancouver, BC, V6P
3G1
(778) 732-0258
Emp Here 40   *Sales* 47,340,590
SIC 5136 Men's and boy's clothing

D-U-N-S 24-974-6322   (BR)
**BOARD OF EDUCATION OF SCHOOL DIS-
TRICT NO. 39 (VANCOUVER), THE**
*SIR WINSTON CHURCHILL SECONDARY
SCHOOL*
(*Suby of* BOARD OF EDUCATION OF
SCHOOL DISTRICT NO. 39 (VANCOUVER),
THE)
7055 Heather St, Vancouver, BC, V6P 3P7
(604) 713-8189
Emp Here 100
SIC 8211 Elementary and secondary schools
Kevin Land

D-U-N-S 25-459-1837   (HQ)
**BUREAU   VERITAS   COMMODITIES
CANADA LTD**
ACME ANALYTICAL LABORATORIES
(*Suby of* BUREAU VERITAS)
9050 Shaughnessy St, Vancouver, BC, V6P
6E5
(604) 253-3158
Sales 51,020,500
SIC 8734 Testing laboratories
John Landau
Michael Toy
Joselito Alviar

D-U-N-S 20-109-9199   (HQ)
CANADIAN FOREST PRODUCTS LTD
*CANFOR RESEARCH & DEVELOPMENT
CENTRE*
(*Suby of* CANFOR CORPORATION)
1700 75th Ave W Unit 100, Vancouver, BC,
V6P 6G2
(604) 661-5241
Emp Here 120   *Sales* 695,975,000
SIC 2421 Sawmills and planing mills, general

D-U-N-S 20-109-9686   (HQ)
CANFOR CORPORATION
1700 75th Ave W Suite 100, Vancouver, BC,
V6P 6G2
(604) 661-5241
Sales 3,824,169,729
SIC 2421 Sawmills and planing mills, general
Donald Kayne
David M. Calabrigo
Mark Feldinger
Stephen Mackie
Alan Nicholl
Kevin Pankratz
Patrick Elliott
Katy Player
Bob Hayes
David Trent

D-U-N-S 20-702-9682   (HQ)
CANFOR PULP PRODUCTS INC
(*Suby of* CANFOR CORPORATION)
1700 75th Ave W Unit 230, Vancouver, BC,
V6P 6G2

(604) 661-5241
Emp Here 6   *Sales* 1,041,859,579
SIC 2621 Paper mills
Donald B. Kayne
Brett R Robinson
Alan Nicholl
David Calabrigo
Mark Feldinger
Kevin Pankratz
Stephen Mackie
David Trent
Martin Pudlas
Peter Hart

D-U-N-S 25-539-6996   (BR)
CERIDIAN CANADA LTD
(*Suby of* FOUNDATION HOLDINGS, INC.)
1200 73rd Ave W Suite 1400, Vancouver, BC,
V6P 6G5
(604) 267-6200
Emp Here 80
SIC 8721 Accounting, auditing, and book-
keeping
Liz Massey

D-U-N-S 25-932-7526   (BR)
CESL LIMITED
CESL ENGINEERING
(*Suby of* TECK RESOURCES LIMITED)
8898 Heather St Unit 107, Vancouver, BC,
V6P 3S8

Emp Here 120
SIC 8731 Commercial physical research
Jennifer Defreyne

D-U-N-S 25-485-7402   (SL)
COLUMBUS LONG TERM CARE SOCIETY
COLUMBUS RESIDENCE
704 69th Ave W, Vancouver, BC, V6P 2W3
(604) 321-4405
Emp Here 115   *Sales* 7,392,430
SIC 8361 Residential care
Tom Wilson
Joe Apolonia
Armand Girody
Dale Clements

D-U-N-S 20-110-8891   (SL)
DON DOCKSTEADER MOTORS LTD
*VOLVO & SUBARU SALES PARTS & SER-
VICES*
8530 Cambie St, Vancouver, BC, V6P 6N6
(604) 323-2200
Emp Here 105   *Sales* 66,074,400
SIC 5511 New and used car dealers
Donald Docksteader
Paul Docksteader
Tennyson Choo
Murry Carle

D-U-N-S 24-448-5785   (SL)
ETD BUILDING MAINTENANCE LTD
9001 Shaughnessy St, Vancouver, BC, V6P
6R9
(604) 327-2555
Emp Here 200   *Sales* 6,393,600
SIC 7349 Building maintenance services, nec
Randy Zimmerman
Martin Zimmerman

D-U-N-S 24-866-8188   (HQ)
HELIFOR INDUSTRIES LIMITED
HELIFOR
1200 73rd Ave W Suite 828, Vancouver, BC,
V6P 6G5
(604) 269-2000
Emp Here 6   *Sales* 10,195,610
SIC 2411 Logging
Gary Laidlaw
Michael Ackerfeldt

D-U-N-S 24-073-7551   (HQ)
HERITAGE OFFICE FURNISHINGS LTD
1588 Rand Ave, Vancouver, BC, V6P 3G2
(604) 688-2381
Emp Here 115   *Sales* 34,860,450
SIC 5712 Furniture stores

Pat Hill
Ross Wheatley
Rick Scurfield
Paul Mccrea

D-U-N-S 20-338-7977   (HQ)
INTERVISTAS CONSULTING INC
(*Suby of* STICHTING HASKONINGDHV)
1200 73rd Ave W Suite 550, Vancouver, BC,
V6P 6G5
(604) 717-1800
Emp Here 38   *Sales* 12,122,890
SIC 8742 Management consulting services
Gerry Bruno

D-U-N-S 20-587-9901   (SL)
JANA AND COMPANY IMPORTS
8680 Cambie St, Vancouver, BC, V6P 6M9
(604) 688-3657
Emp Here 40   *Sales* 19,932,880
SIC 5137 Women's and children's clothing
Max Fugman

D-U-N-S 24-544-8782   (HQ)
JMAX GLOBAL DISTRIBUTORS INC
8680 Cambie St, Vancouver, BC, V6P 6M9
(604) 688-3657
Emp Here 3   *Sales* 32,889,252
SIC 5137 Women's and children's clothing
David Fugman
Max Fugman
Michael Alan Fugman

D-U-N-S 24-724-4973   (BR)
LEHIGH HANSON MATERIALS LIMITED
LEHIGH MATERIALS
(*Suby of* HEIDELBERGCEMENT AG)
8955 Shaughnessy St, Vancouver, BC, V6P
3Y7
(604) 261-6225
Emp Here 80
SIC 5032 Brick, stone, and related material
Loren Donnelly

D-U-N-S 25-327-9012   (HQ)
LUSH HANDMADE COSMETICS LTD
LUSH FRESH HANDMADE COSMETICS
8688 Cambie St, Vancouver, BC, V6P 6M6
(604) 638-3632
Emp Here 3   *Sales* 144,064,980
SIC 2844 Toilet preparations
Mark Wolverton
Graham Brown
Andy Mcnevin

D-U-N-S 20-955-5833   (HQ)
LUSH MANUFACTURING LTD
(*Suby of* LUSH COSMETICS LIMITED)
8680 Cambie St, Vancouver, BC, V6P 6M9
(888) 733-5874
Emp Here 20   *Sales* 13,833,000
SIC 2844 Toilet preparations
Mark Wolverton
Graham Brown

D-U-N-S 20-429-3120   (SL)
MACLURES CABS (1984) LTD
1275 75th Ave W, Vancouver, BC, V6P 3G4
(604) 683-6666
Emp Here 200   *Sales* 15,054,400
SIC 4121 Taxicabs
Rajinder Sangra

D-U-N-S 24-641-1847   (SL)
MARINE DRIVE IMPORTED CARS LTD
VANCOUVER HONDA
850 Marine Dr Sw, Vancouver, BC, V6P 5Z1
(604) 324-6632
Emp Here 50   *Sales* 31,464,000
SIC 5511 New and used car dealers
William Tse

D-U-N-S 25-539-4116   (HQ)
MAXWELL FABRICS LTD
8811 Laurel St Unit 113, Vancouver, BC, V6P
3V9
(604) 253-7744
Emp Here 30   *Sales* 19,336,528

SIC 5023 Homefurnishings
Larry Garaway
Darlene Ann Ames
Maxwell Garaway

D-U-N-S 24-682-8941   (HQ)
MONTCALM VENTURES LTD
BUDGET CAR SALES
1404 Marine Dr Sw, Vancouver, BC, V6P 5Z9
(604) 261-3343
Emp Here 24   Sales 36,498,240
SIC 5521 Used car dealers
Sydney Belzberg
Irwin Riback

D-U-N-S 24-319-4672   (SL)
**NORSWAY INVESTMENTS & CONSUL-
TANTS INC**
KEYNOR SPRING MANUFACTURING
8563 Selkirk St, Vancouver, BC, V6P 4J1
(604) 267-1307
Emp Here 100   Sales 19,208,500
SIC 3495 Wire springs
Raymond Shao

D-U-N-S 24-162-6555   (SL)
PACIFIC BINDERY SERVICES LTD
870 Kent Ave South W, Vancouver, BC, V6P
6Y6
(604) 873-4291
Emp Here 75   Sales 12,302,025
SIC 2789 Bookbinding and related work
Bradley Clement

D-U-N-S 24-930-3785   (SL)
**PREMIER   ELECTION   SOLUTIONS
CANADA ULC**
(Suby of DIEBOLD NIXDORF, INCORPO-
RATED)
1200 73rd Ave W Suite 350, Vancouver, BC,
V6P 6G5
(604) 261-6313
Emp Here 129
SIC 7371 Custom computer programming ser-
vices
Robert J Urosevich

D-U-N-S 20-115-1214   (HQ)
PUDDIFOOT, W. H. LTD
1566 Rand Ave, Vancouver, BC, V6P 3G2
(604) 263-0971
Emp Here 15   Sales 10,177,120
SIC 5023 Homefurnishings
John Puddifoot
Jason Puddifoot

D-U-N-S 24-860-9018   (SL)
RESPONSE BIOMEDICAL CORP
RBM
1781 75th Ave W, Vancouver, BC, V6P 6P2
(604) 456-6010
Emp Here 56   Sales 11,592,486
SIC 5047 Medical and hospital equipment
Barbara Kinnaird
Angela Carter
Megan Eastwood
Mark Nah
Anastasios Tsonis
Jonathan Wang
Liu Hui
Caroline Chan
Ken Xu

D-U-N-S 24-097-7793   (HQ)
SING TAO (CANADA) LIMITED
(Suby of TORSTAR CORPORATION)
8508 Ash St, Vancouver, BC, V6P 3M2
(604) 321-1111
Emp Here 3   Sales 21,815,591
SIC 2711 Newspapers
Calvin Wong

D-U-N-S 24-749-7878   (HQ)
**SING TAO NEWSPAPERS (CANADA 1988)
LIMITED**
(Suby of SING TAO NEWS CORPORATION
LIMITED)
8508 Ash St, Vancouver, BC, V6P 3M2

(604) 909-1122
Sales 82,482,260
SIC 5192 Books, periodicals, and newspapers
Carol Peddie
Calvin Wong

D-U-N-S 24-855-6672   (SL)
SMITH BROS. & WILSON (B.C.) LTD
SBW
8729 Aisne St, Vancouver, BC, V6P 3P1
(604) 324-1155
Emp Here 60   Sales 25,364,220
SIC 1541 Industrial buildings and warehouses
Tim Harrington
Don Langner
Murray Saunders
Bill Cann

D-U-N-S 20-919-2397   (SL)
STERLING NEWSPAPERS GROUP
1200 73rd Ave W Suite 920, Vancouver, BC,
V6P 6G5
(604) 732-4443
Emp Here 68   Sales 50,491,360
SIC 5192 Books, periodicals, and newspapers
David Radler

D-U-N-S 20-521-1266   (BR)
SUNRISE NORTH SENIOR LIVING LTD
*SUNRISE ASSISTED LIVING & SUNRISE OF
VANCOUVER*
(Suby of WELLTOWER INC.)
999 57th Ave W, Vancouver, BC, V6P 6Y9
(604) 261-5799
Emp Here 100
SIC 8361 Residential care
Damien Mcgoldrick

D-U-N-S 24-637-0923   (BR)
**VANCOUVER COASTAL HEALTH AUTHOR-
ITY**
PEARSON, GEORGE CENTRE
(Suby of GOVERNMENT OF THE
PROVINCE OF BRITISH COLUMBIA)
700 57th Ave W Suite 909, Vancouver, BC,
V6P 1S1
(604) 321-3231
Emp Here 200
SIC 8331 Job training and related services
Romilda Ang

D-U-N-S 25-505-5733   (SL)
W.D.I. SERVICES LTD
HERITAGE GROUP OF COMPANIES
1588 Rand Ave, Vancouver, BC, V6P 3G2
(604) 263-2739
Emp Here 100   Sales 14,819,200
SIC 4225 General warehousing and storage
Laurence Daws

D-U-N-S 20-328-6310   (SL)
WANG, JOHN C
SUPTON LAMGRA REALITY
7547 Cambie St, Vancouver, BC, V6P 3H6
(604) 322-3000
Emp Here 49   Sales 13,316,044
SIC 6531 Real estate agents and managers
Greg Rahn

D-U-N-S 25-289-2955   (HQ)
WESTPORT FUEL SYSTEMS INC
1750 75th Ave W Suite 101, Vancouver, BC,
V6P 6G2
(604) 718-2000
Emp Here 150   Sales 270,283,000
SIC 3519 Internal combustion engines, nec

D-U-N-S 24-420-7994   (HQ)
WESTPORT LIGHT DUTY INC
(Suby of WESTPORT FUEL SYSTEMS INC)
1750 75th Ave W Suite 101, Vancouver, BC,
V6P 6G2
(604) 718-2000
Sales 22,200,100
SIC 3519 Internal combustion engines, nec
M.A. (Jill) Bodkin
Nancy Gougarty

D-U-N-S 20-117-3655   (HQ)

WESTPORT MANUFACTURING CO LTD
1122 Marine Dr Sw, Vancouver, BC, V6P 5Z3
(604) 261-9326
Emp Here 20   Sales 15,034,140
SIC 2391 Curtains and draperies
Terry Balfour
Winnie Yan
Paul Graham
Kern Chiu

D-U-N-S 24-377-0539   (HQ)
WESTPORT POWER INC
(Suby of WESTPORT FUEL SYSTEMS INC)
1750 75th Ave W Suite 101, Vancouver, BC,
V6P 6G2
(604) 718-2000
Sales 82,967,850
SIC 8748 Business consulting, nec
David Johnson
James Arthurs
Ashoka Achutan

D-U-N-S 24-124-9619   (SL)
ZABER TECHNOLOGIES INC
605 Kent Ave North W Unit 2, Vancouver, BC,
V6P 6T7
(604) 569-3780
Emp Here 60   Sales 11,426,520
SIC 3625 Relays and industrial controls
Rob Steves

Vancouver, BC V6R

D-U-N-S 20-007-5559   (BR)
**BOARD OF EDUCATION OF SCHOOL DIS-
TRICT NO. 39 (VANCOUVER), THE**
LORD BYNG SECONDARY SCHOOL
(Suby of BOARD OF EDUCATION OF
SCHOOL DISTRICT NO. 39 (VANCOUVER),
THE)
3939 16th Ave W, Vancouver, BC, V6R 3C9
(604) 713-8171
Emp Here 100
SIC 8211 Elementary and secondary schools
Annette Vey-Chilton

D-U-N-S 25-453-5834   (HQ)
BUNTAIN INSURANCE AGENCIES LTD
3707 10th Ave W, Vancouver, BC, V6R 2G5
(604) 224-2373
Emp Here 7   Sales 18,657,320
SIC 6411 Insurance agents, brokers, and ser-
vice
James Robert Buntain
Lois Jean Buntain

D-U-N-S 25-013-2115   (HQ)
CANADIAN LOGISTICS SYSTEMS LIMITED
3433 Broadway W Suite 201, Vancouver, BC,
V6R 2B4
(604) 731-8001
Sales 12,999,175
SIC 4785 Inspection and fixed facilities
Edward Truman

D-U-N-S 25-634-9564   (SL)
ROYAL VANCOUVER YACHT CLUB
3811 Point Grey Rd, Vancouver, BC, V6R 1B3
(604) 224-1344
Emp Here 140   Sales 10,996,300
SIC 7997 Membership sports and recreation
clubs
Carmen Derricott

D-U-N-S 25-384-5754   (SL)
**WEST   POINT   GREY   INDEPENDENT
SCHOOL SOCIETY**
WEST POINT GREY ACADEMY
4125 8th Ave W, Vancouver, BC, V6R 4P9
(604) 222-8750
Emp Here 88   Sales 8,168,688
SIC 8211 Elementary and secondary schools
Clive Austin

D-U-N-S 20-436-7076   (HQ)

YGGDRASIL HOLDINGS LTD.
4550 Langara Ave, Vancouver, BC, V6R 1C8

Sales 10,462,120
SIC 6712 Bank holding companies
Antoine Moret

Vancouver, BC V6S

D-U-N-S 25-539-0353   (SL)
49 NORTH MECHANICAL LTD
3641 29th Ave W Suite 201, Vancouver, BC,
V6S 1T5
(604) 224-7604
Emp Here 50   Sales 11,046,700
SIC 1711 Plumbing, heating, air-conditioning
Calvin Matt
Shane Matt

D-U-N-S 20-587-3581   (SL)
STONG'S MARKETS LTD
STONG'S EXPRESS
4560 Dunbar St, Vancouver, BC, V6S 2G6
(604) 266-1401
Emp Here 110   Sales 32,282,470
SIC 5411 Grocery stores
Cori Bonina

D-U-N-S 20-551-7191   (SL)
UBC PROPERTIES INVESTMENTS LTD
UBC PROPERTIES TRUST
(Suby of UNIVERSITY OF BRITISH
COLUMBIA, THE)
3313 Shrum Lane Unit 200, Vancouver, BC,
V6S 0C8
(604) 731-3103
Emp Here 30   Sales 1,818,003,067
SIC 6553 Cemetery subdividers and develop-
ers
Aubrey Kelly
Donald Matheson
Avtar Bains
Brad Bennett
Andrew Bibby
Sandra Cawley
Caleb Chan
Robert Fung
Robert Lee
Rob Macdonald

Vancouver, BC V6T

D-U-N-S 20-351-7060   (SL)
**FOREST ENGINEERING RESEARCH INSTI-
TUTE**
2601 East Mall, Vancouver, BC, V6T 1Z4
(604) 228-1555
Emp Here 40   Sales 11,389,880
SIC 8733 Noncommercial research organiza-
tions
John Mann

D-U-N-S 24-391-0705   (BR)
FPINNOVATIONS
FORINTEK, DIV OF
(Suby of FPINNOVATIONS)
2665 East Mall, Vancouver, BC, V6T 1Z4
(604) 224-3221
Emp Here 150
SIC 8731 Commercial physical research

D-U-N-S 20-976-3288   (SL)
MICHAEL SMITH LABORATORIES
2185 East Mall Suite 301, Vancouver, BC, V6T
1Z4
(604) 822-4838
Emp Here 300   Sales 68,926,200
SIC 8731 Commercial physical research
Darlene Crowe
Stephen Macdonald

D-U-N-S 20-730-4580   (SL)
MOTION METRICS INTERNATIONAL CORP
2389 Health Sciences Mall Unit 101, Vancouver, BC, V6T 1Z3
(604) 822-5848
Emp Here 50   *Sales* 10,206,500
SIC 1081 Metal mining services
  Shahram Tafazoli

D-U-N-S 20-867-2055   (SL)
REGENT COLLEGE
5800 University Blvd, Vancouver, BC, V6T 2E4
(604) 224-3245
Emp Here 130   *Sales* 19,420,830
SIC 8221 Colleges and universities
  Jeffery P Greenman

D-U-N-S 20-986-4284   (SL)
SAUDER SCHOOL OF BUSINESS
2053 Main Mall Suite 402, Vancouver, BC, V6T 1Z2
(604) 822-8391
Emp Here 150   *Sales* 27,975,900
SIC 8742 Management consulting services
  Dan Muzyka

D-U-N-S 24-367-8802   (HQ)
TRIUMF
CANADA'S NATIONAL LABORATORY FOR PARTICLE AND NUCLEAR PHYSICS
4004 Wesbrook Mall, Vancouver, BC, V6T 2A3
(604) 222-1047
Emp Here 300   *Sales* 55,324,347
SIC 8733 Noncommercial research organizations
  Jonathan Bagger
  Reiner Kruecken
  Robert Laxdal
  Reiner Kruecken
  Anne Louise Aboud

D-U-N-S 25-068-8090   (SL)
U B C TRAFFIC OFFICE
PARKING AND ACCESS CONTROL SERVICES
2075 Wesbrook Mall Suite 204, Vancouver, BC, V6T 1Z1
(604) 822-6786
Emp Here 95   *Sales* 42,768,715
SIC 7521 Automobile parking
  Danny Ho

D-U-N-S 24-558-2911   (SL)
U.G.C.C. HOLDINGS INC
UNIVERSITY GOLF CLUB
5185 University Blvd, Vancouver, BC, V6T 1X5
(604) 224-1018
Emp Here 75   *Sales* 5,729,775
SIC 7997 Membership sports and recreation clubs
  David Ho
  Edward Lau
  Michael Mather
  David Chu

D-U-N-S 20-369-5478   (BR)
UNIVERSITY OF BRITISH COLUMBIA, THE
UBC ENGINEERING
(*Suby of* UNIVERSITY OF BRITISH COLUMBIA, THE)
2332 Main Mall Suite 5000, Vancouver, BC, V6T 1Z4
(604) 822-0895
Emp Here 91
SIC 8221 Colleges and universities
  James Olson

D-U-N-S 20-369-4393   (BR)
UNIVERSITY OF BRITISH COLUMBIA, THE
SCHOOL OF NURSING
(*Suby of* UNIVERSITY OF BRITISH COLUMBIA, THE)
2211 Wesbrook Mall Rm T201, Vancouver, BC, V6T 2B5
(604) 822-7417
Emp Here 144
SIC 8221 Colleges and universities

  Elizabeth Saewyc

D-U-N-S 20-981-6656   (BR)
UNIVERSITY OF BRITISH COLUMBIA, THE
DEPARTMENT OF MATHEMATICS
(*Suby of* UNIVERSITY OF BRITISH COLUMBIA, THE)
1984 Mathematics Rd Rm 121, Vancouver, BC, V6T 1Z2
(604) 822-2666
Emp Here 107
SIC 8221 Colleges and universities
  Philip Loewen

D-U-N-S 20-979-0323   (BR)
UNIVERSITY OF BRITISH COLUMBIA, THE
WALTER H GAGE RESIDENCE
(*Suby of* UNIVERSITY OF BRITISH COLUMBIA, THE)
5959 Student Union Blvd, Vancouver, BC, V6T 1K2
(604) 822-1000
Emp Here 75
SIC 8221 Colleges and universities
  Rane Hakami

D-U-N-S 20-104-5981   (BR)
UNIVERSITY OF BRITISH COLUMBIA, THE
SAUDER SCHOOL OF BUSINESS
(*Suby of* UNIVERSITY OF BRITISH COLUMBIA, THE)
2053 Main Mall Suite 247, Vancouver, BC, V6T 1Z2
(604) 822-8500
Emp Here 228
SIC 8221 Colleges and universities
  Daniel Nuzyka

D-U-N-S 20-153-2707   (BR)
UNIVERSITY OF BRITISH COLUMBIA, THE
INSTITUTE FOR COMPUTING, INFORMATION & COGNITIVE SYSTEMS
(*Suby of* UNIVERSITY OF BRITISH COLUMBIA, THE)
2366 Main Mall Unit 289, Vancouver, BC, V6T 1Z4
(604) 822-6894
Emp Here 130
SIC 8221 Colleges and universities
  Robert Rohling

D-U-N-S 24-894-4717   (BR)
UNIVERSITY OF BRITISH COLUMBIA, THE
DEPARTMENT OF BOTANY
(*Suby of* UNIVERSITY OF BRITISH COLUMBIA, THE)
6270 University Blvd Rm 3200, Vancouver, BC, V6T 1Z4
(604) 822-2133
Emp Here 200
SIC 8221 Colleges and universities
  Sean Graham

D-U-N-S 24-765-2345   (BR)
UNIVERSITY OF BRITISH COLUMBIA, THE
FACULTY MEDICINE
(*Suby of* UNIVERSITY OF BRITISH COLUMBIA, THE)
2194 Health Sciences Mall Unit 317, Vancouver, BC, V6T 1Z6
(604) 822-2421
Emp Here 150
SIC 8221 Colleges and universities
  Dermot Kelleher

D-U-N-S 24-765-2287   (BR)
UNIVERSITY OF BRITISH COLUMBIA, THE
INTSTITUTE FOR GENDER, RACE, SEXUALITY AND SOCIAL JUSTICE
(*Suby of* UNIVERSITY OF BRITISH COLUMBIA, THE)
1873 East Mall Rm 1097, Vancouver, BC, V6T 1Z1
(604) 822-9171
Emp Here 75
SIC 8221 Colleges and universities
  Denise Ferriera Da Silva

D-U-N-S 24-765-2188   (BR)
UNIVERSITY OF BRITISH COLUMBIA, THE
DJAVAD MOWAFAGHIAN CENTRE FOR BRAIN HEALTH
(*Suby of* UNIVERSITY OF BRITISH COLUMBIA, THE)
2215 Wesbrook Mall 3rd Fl, Vancouver, BC, V6T 1Z3
(604) 822-1388
Emp Here 200
SIC 8221 Colleges and universities
  Brian Macvicar

D-U-N-S 20-300-7476   (BR)
UNIVERSITY OF BRITISH COLUMBIA, THE
ENGLISH LANGUAGE INSTITUTE
(*Suby of* UNIVERSITY OF BRITISH COLUMBIA, THE)
2121 West Mall, Vancouver, BC, V6T 1Z4
(604) 822-1555
Emp Here 75
SIC 8221 Colleges and universities
  Andrew Scales

D-U-N-S 20-375-0976   (BR)
UNIVERSITY OF BRITISH COLUMBIA, THE
DEPARTMENT OF ASIAN STUDIES
(*Suby of* UNIVERSITY OF BRITISH COLUMBIA, THE)
1871 West Mall Unit 607, Vancouver, BC, V6T 1Z2
(604) 822-0019
Emp Here 78
SIC 8221 Colleges and universities
  Ross King

D-U-N-S 24-336-7633   (BR)
UNIVERSITY OF BRITISH COLUMBIA, THE
SCHOOL OF KINESIOLOGY
(*Suby of* UNIVERSITY OF BRITISH COLUMBIA, THE)
6081 University Blvd Rm 210, Vancouver, BC, V6T 1Z1
(604) 822-9192
Emp Here 85
SIC 8221 Colleges and universities
  Robert Boushel

D-U-N-S 20-789-3806   (BR)
UNIVERSITY OF BRITISH COLUMBIA, THE
FACULTY OF DENTISTRY, THE
(*Suby of* UNIVERSITY OF BRITISH COLUMBIA, THE)
2194 Health Sciences Mall, Vancouver, BC, V6T 1Z6
(604) 822-5773
Emp Here 100
SIC 8221 Colleges and universities
  Mary Macdougall

D-U-N-S 20-717-4900   (BR)
UNIVERSITY OF BRITISH COLUMBIA, THE
PETER A. ALLARD SCHOOL OF LAW
(*Suby of* UNIVERSITY OF BRITISH COLUMBIA, THE)
1822 East Mall, Vancouver, BC, V6T 1Y1
(604) 822-2275
Emp Here 85
SIC 8221 Colleges and universities

D-U-N-S 20-797-5301   (HQ)
UNIVERSITY OF BRITISH COLUMBIA, THE
UBC BOOKSTORE
2329 West Mall, Vancouver, BC, V6T 1Z4
(604) 822-2211
Emp Here 10,000   *Sales* 1,818,003,067
SIC 8221 Colleges and universities
  Santa J. Ono

D-U-N-S 20-360-1224   (BR)
UNIVERSITY OF BRITISH COLUMBIA, THE
DEPT OF COMPUTER SCIENCE
(*Suby of* UNIVERSITY OF BRITISH COLUMBIA, THE)
2366 Main Mall Suite 201, Vancouver, BC, V6T 1Z4
(604) 822-3061
Emp Here 100

SIC 8221 Colleges and universities
  Chen Greif

D-U-N-S 24-334-6405   (BR)
VANCOUVER COASTAL HEALTH AUTHORITY
(*Suby of* GOVERNMENT OF THE PROVINCE OF BRITISH COLUMBIA)
2211 Wesbrook Mall, Vancouver, BC, V6T 2B5
(604) 822-7121
Emp Here 500
SIC 8062 General medical and surgical hospitals
  Nitin Khare

D-U-N-S 25-096-9623   (SL)
WEBCT EDUCATIONAL TECHNOLOGIES CORPORATION
(*Suby of* BLACKBOARD NETHERLANDS COOPERATIE U.A.)
2389 Health Sciences Mall Suite 2, Vancouver, BC, V6T 1Z3
(604) 221-0558
Emp Here 102
SIC 7371 Custom computer programming services
  Carol Vallone
  John Giordano

Vancouver, BC V6X

D-U-N-S 24-312-9934   (SL)
PEEKABOO BEANS INC
11120 Bridgeport Rd Unit 170, Vancouver, BC, V6X 1T2
(604) 279-2326
Emp Here 271   *Sales* 2,107,538
SIC 2369 Girl's and children's outerwear, nec
  Traci Costa
  Nikki Mayer
  Darrell Kopke
  Sarah Bundy

D-U-N-S 24-136-6228   (SL)
WORLD WIDE ENTERPRISES LIMITED
10991 Shellbridge Way Ste 490, Vancouver, BC, V6X 3C6

Emp Here 150
SIC 5961 Catalog and mail-order houses

Vancouver, BC V6Z

D-U-N-S 20-575-8803   (SL)
1110 HOWE HOLDINGS INCORPORATED
HOLIDAY INN VANCOUVER DOWNTOWN HOTEL
1110 Howe St, Vancouver, BC, V6Z 1R2
(604) 684-2151
Emp Here 80   *Sales* 7,591,920
SIC 7011 Hotels and motels
  Kris Szylowski

D-U-N-S 24-977-1395   (HQ)
955 BAY STREET HOSPITALITY INC
SUTTON PLACE HOTEL TORONTO, THE
(*Suby of* NORTHLAND PROPERTIES CORPORATION)
845 Burrard St, Vancouver, BC, V6Z 2K6
(604) 682-5511
Emp Here 5   *Sales* 86,101,200
SIC 7011 Hotels and motels
  Charles Woo
  Christopher Ho

D-U-N-S 24-874-7859   (HQ)
ACL SERVICES LTD
GALVANIZE
980 Howe St Suite 1500, Vancouver, BC, V6Z 0C8
(604) 669-4225
Sales 39,129,476

SIC 7371 Custom computer programming services
 Laurie Schultz
 Keith Cerny
 Kathy Enros
 Jose Aleman
 Dan Zitting
 Sean Zuberbier
 Brendan Quigley
 Harald Will
 Eric Patel
 Greg Wolfe

D-U-N-S 20-689-5059   (SL)
AMERICAN PAPER EXPORT INC
1080 Howe St Unit 506, Vancouver, BC, V6Z 2T1
(604) 298-7092
Emp Here 8   *Sales* 46,848,523
SIC 5113 Industrial and personal service paper
 Sadruddin Budhwani
 Rahil Budhwani
 Shamsuddin Budhwani
 Soile Weaver

D-U-N-S 25-679-1856   (BR)
AON CANADA INC
AON INSURANCE MANAGERS
(*Suby of* AON PLC)
900 Howe St, Vancouver, BC, V6Z 2M4
(604) 688-4442
Emp Here 200
SIC 6411 Insurance agents, brokers, and service
 Harry Venselaar

D-U-N-S 20-867-2576   (BR)
AVIVA INSURANCE COMPANY OF CANADA
(*Suby of* GENERAL ACCIDENT PLC)
1125 Howe St Suite 1100, Vancouver, BC, V6Z 2Y6
(604) 669-2626
Emp Here 150
SIC 6331 Fire, marine, and casualty insurance
 Lien Diep

D-U-N-S 25-684-5686   (SL)
BC CENTRE FOR EXCELLENCE IN HIV AIDS
1081 Burrard St Suite 608, Vancouver, BC, V6Z 1Y6
(604) 806-8477
Emp Here 150   *Sales* 32,991,450
SIC 8732 Commercial nonphysical research
 Julio Montaner

D-U-N-S 25-681-0748   (BR)
BELL MEDIA INC
C I V T
(*Suby of* BCE INC)
750 Burrard St Suite 300, Vancouver, BC, V6Z 2V6
(604) 608-2868
Emp Here 200
SIC 4833 Television broadcasting stations
 Tom Haberstroh

D-U-N-S 24-383-4723   (BR)
BELL MEDIA INC
CKST AM
(*Suby of* BCE INC)
969 Robson St Unit 500, Vancouver, BC, V6Z 1X5
(604) 871-9000
Emp Here 160
SIC 4832 Radio broadcasting stations
 James Stuart

D-U-N-S 20-426-0269   (SL)
BLACK TOP CABS LTD
777 Pacific St, Vancouver, BC, V6Z 2R7
(604) 683-4567
Emp Here 60   *Sales* 37,756,800
SIC 5541 Gasoline service stations
 Dalwara Sidhu

D-U-N-S 24-249-1041   (HQ)
C.B. CONSTANTINI LTD
910-980 Howe St, Vancouver, BC, V6Z 0C8
(604) 669-1212
Emp Here 15   *Sales* 22,994,730
SIC 6799 Investors, nec
 Alfred Constantini

D-U-N-S 20-799-5077   (SL)
CENTURY PLAZA LTD
CENTURY PLAZA HOTEL
(*Suby of* EMPRESS TOWERS LTD)
1015 Burrard St, Vancouver, BC, V6Z 1Y5
(604) 687-0575
Emp Here 210   *Sales* 20,090,280
SIC 7011 Hotels and motels
 Sergio Cocchia
 Wendy Lisogar

D-U-N-S 24-696-8069   (SL)
CHATEAU GRANVILLE INC
BEST WESTERN PLUS CHATEAU GRANVILLE HOTEL
1100 Granville St, Vancouver, BC, V6Z 2B6
(604) 669-7070
Emp Here 100   *Sales* 9,489,900
SIC 7011 Hotels and motels
 Amir Virani

D-U-N-S 24-418-5174   (BR)
CINEPLEX ODEON CORPORATION
SCOTIABANK THEATRE VANCOUVER
(*Suby of* CINEPLEX INC)
900 Burrard St, Vancouver, BC, V6Z 3G5
(604) 630-1407
Emp Here 130
SIC 7832 Motion picture theaters, except drive-in
 Ken Mont

D-U-N-S 20-259-1285   (HQ)
CONCERT INFRASTRUCTURE LTD
1190 Hornby St, Vancouver, BC, V6Z 2K5
(604) 688-9460
Emp Here 140   *Sales* 187,835,400
SIC 6211 Security brokers and dealers
 Brian Mccauley

D-U-N-S 25-162-0266   (HQ)
CONCERT PROPERTIES LTD
1190 Hornby St, Vancouver, BC, V6Z 2K5
(604) 688-9460
Emp Here 69   *Sales* 47,328,960
SIC 6531 Real estate agents and managers
 David R Podmore
 Brian Mccauley
 Daniel Jarvis

D-U-N-S 25-235-0798   (SL)
CONCERT REAL ESTATE CORPORATION
1190 Hornby St, Vancouver, BC, V6Z 2K5
(604) 688-9460
Emp Here 125   *Sales* 19,771,500
SIC 6553 Cemetery subdividers and developers
 David Podmore

D-U-N-S 24-032-2776   (HQ)
CROSBY PROPERTY MANAGEMENT LTD
777 Hornby St Suite 600, Vancouver, BC, V6Z 1S4
(604) 683-8900
Emp Here 65   *Sales* 16,565,325
SIC 6513 Apartment building operators
 Jane Thorne
 Les Porter

D-U-N-S 20-937-2957   (BR)
EARL'S RESTAURANTS CARRELL LTD
EARL'S RESTAURANTS
(*Suby of* EARL'S RESTAURANTS CARRELL LTD)
905 Hornby St, Vancouver, BC, V6Z 1V3
(604) 682-6700
Emp Here 120
SIC 5812 Eating places
 Peter Collins

D-U-N-S 24-979-3373   (BR)
ELITE INSURANCE COMPANY
CTU ELITE
(*Suby of* GENERAL ACCIDENT PLC)
1125 Howe St Suite 1100, Vancouver, BC, V6Z 2Y6
(604) 669-2626
Emp Here 150
SIC 6411 Insurance agents, brokers, and service
 Nadya Rahim

D-U-N-S 20-749-2554   (HQ)
EMPRESS TOWERS LTD
1015 Burrard St Suite 403, Vancouver, BC, V6Z 1Y5
(604) 682-4246
Sales 41,002,500
SIC 6712 Bank holding companies
 Roy Lisogar
 Wendy Lisogar
 Jill Seeley

D-U-N-S 20-585-6925   (SL)
FERNANDO'S RESTAURANT LTD
LA BODEGA RESTAURANT
1277 Howe St, Vancouver, BC, V6Z 1R3

Emp Here 26   *Sales* 10,903,230
SIC 6712 Bank holding companies
 Francisco Rivas
 Jose Rivas
 Sharon Rivas
 Maria Victoria Rivas

D-U-N-S 25-052-1184   (HQ)
FLIGHT CENTRE TRAVEL GROUP (CANADA) INC
FLIGHT CENTRE CANADA
(*Suby of* FLIGHT CENTRE TRAVEL GROUP LIMITED)
980 Howe St Suite 700, Vancouver, BC, V6Z 0C8
(604) 682-5202
Emp Here 300   *Sales* 646,541,130
SIC 4724 Travel agencies
 John Beauvais
 Kim Knapp
 Mark Wilkie
 Graham Turner

D-U-N-S 20-588-4737   (HQ)
FLUEVOG, JOHN BOOTS & SHOES LTD
JOHN FLUEVOG SHOES
(*Suby of* FLUEVOG, JOHN VANCOUVER LTD)
837 Granville St, Vancouver, BC, V6Z 1K7
(604) 688-5245
Emp Here 25   *Sales* 12,557,720
SIC 5661 Shoe stores
 John Fluevog

D-U-N-S 25-216-0973   (HQ)
FLUEVOG, JOHN VANCOUVER LTD
837 Granville St, Vancouver, BC, V6Z 1K7
(604) 688-2828
Emp Here 50   *Sales* 43,861,080
SIC 6712 Bank holding companies
 John Fluevog

D-U-N-S 24-867-0432   (HQ)
GREAT CANADIAN RAILTOUR COMPANY LTD
ROCKY MOUNTAINEER VACATIONS
980 Howe St, Vancouver, BC, V6Z 1N9
(604) 606-7200
Emp Here 100   *Sales* 108,745,450
SIC 4725 Tour operators
 Peter R B Armstrong
 Laura Lee Armstrong
 Mike Phillips
 Mackenzie Norris
 Sam Gudewill
 Jeffrey Lipman
 Nick Hafner
 Al Duerr
 Jim Dinning

D-U-N-S 24-392-8376   (SL)
HELIFOR CANADA CORP
815 Hornby St Suite 406, Vancouver, BC, V6Z 2E6

Emp Here 115   *Sales* 22,122,550
SIC 2411 Logging
 Gary Mcdermid

D-U-N-S 20-295-1612   (SL)
ISTUARY INNOVATION LABS INC
1125 Howe St 8th Fl, Vancouver, BC, V6Z 2K8

Emp Here 60   *Sales* 10,638,660
SIC 7371 Custom computer programming services
 Yian Sun

D-U-N-S 24-725-7306   (BR)
LONDON DRUGS LIMITED
(*Suby of* H.Y. LOUIE CO. LIMITED)
710 Granville St, Vancouver, BC, V6Z 1E4
(604) 448-4002
Emp Here 140
SIC 5912 Drug stores and proprietary stores
 Daryl Agrle

D-U-N-S 20-179-0909   (BR)
MILLER THOMSON LLP
(*Suby of* MILLER THOMSON LLP)
840 Howe St Suite 1000, Vancouver, BC, V6Z 2M1
(604) 687-2242
Emp Here 160
SIC 8111 Legal services
 Peter Mcarthur

D-U-N-S 24-726-2165   (SL)
MURRICK INSURANCE SERVICES LTD
1045 Howe St Suite 925, Vancouver, BC, V6Z 2A9
(604) 688-5158
Emp Here 22   *Sales* 12,758,328
SIC 6411 Insurance agents, brokers, and service
 Gloria Murphy
 Floyd Murphy

D-U-N-S 24-897-0287   (HQ)
NECHAKO REAL ESTATE LTD
CENTURY 21 IN TOWN REALTY
421 Pacific St, Vancouver, BC, V6Z 2P5
(604) 685-5951
Emp Here 75   *Sales* 35,605,565
SIC 6531 Real estate agents and managers
 Michael La Prairie
 Heather La Prairie

D-U-N-S 24-694-8194   (SL)
NEWDALE HOLDINGS INC
QUALITY HOTEL
1335 Howe St, Vancouver, BC, V6Z 1R7

Emp Here 65   *Sales* 17,000,945
SIC 6719 Holding companies, nec
 Najmudin Lalji
 Mehrunissa Lalji
 Firoz Lalji

D-U-N-S 25-435-0437   (HQ)
OCEANAGOLD CORPORATION
777 Hornby Street Suite 1910, Vancouver, BC, V6Z 1S4
(604) 235-3360
Emp Here 950   *Sales* 724,413,000
SIC 1081 Metal mining services
 Michael Wilkes
 Scott Mcqueen
 Mark Cadzow
 Michael Holmes
 Craig Feebrey
 Yuwen Ma
 Cody Whipperman
 Sharon Flynn
 Liang Tang
 James Askew

D-U-N-S 20-555-7866   (BR)

OMNICOM CANADA CORP
DDB CANADA
(*Suby of* OMNICOM GROUP INC.)
777 Hornby St Suite 1600, Vancouver, BC,
V6Z 2T3
(604) 687-7911
Emp Here 120
SIC 7311 Advertising agencies
  Frank Palmer

  D-U-N-S 25-972-7139   (HQ)
ONACTUATE CONSULTING INC.
ONACTUATE
777 Hornby St Suite 600, Vancouver, BC, V6Z
2H7
(604) 506-3435
Emp Here 130
SIC 8748 Business consulting, nec
  Sharan Oberoi

  D-U-N-S 24-279-9831   (HQ)
PERSONNEL DEPARTMENT LTD, THE
980 Howe St Unit 201, Vancouver, BC, V6Z
0C8
(604) 685-3530
Emp Here 225   *Sales* 76,228,000
SIC 7361 Employment agencies
  Paul Tournier
  Julia Ng
  Linda Higgs
  Leslie Meingast

  D-U-N-S 24-868-3104   (HQ)
PETAQUILLA MINERALS LTD
777 Hornby St Suite 1230, Vancouver, BC,
V6Z 1S4

Emp Here 840   *Sales* 428,165,676
SIC 1041 Gold ores
  Rodrigo Esquivel
  Joao Manuel
  Andrew J. Ramcharan
  David Kaplan
  Ezequiel Sirotinsky
  Lazaro Rodriguez
  Richard Fifer
  Cristobal Colon De Carvajal
  Raul Ferrer
  Pedro Pablo Permuy

  D-U-N-S 24-444-2005   (SL)
PROMPTON REAL ESTATE SERVICES INC
179 Davie St Suite 201, Vancouver, BC, V6Z
2Y1
(604) 899-2333
Emp Here 40   *Sales* 13,085,080
SIC 6531 Real estate agents and managers
  Costas Papadopoulos

  D-U-N-S 25-676-6353   (HQ)
PROVIDENCE HEALTH CARE SOCIETY
HOLY FAMILY HOSPITAL
1081 Burrard St, Vancouver, BC, V6Z 1Y6
(604) 682-2344
Emp Here 2,800   *Sales* 588,724,000
SIC 8062 General medical and surgical hospitals
  Dianne Doyle
  Mary Procter
  Janet Brown
  Stephen Jensen
  Margaret Vickers
  Tom Murphy
  Elaine Moonen
  Henry Ewanchuk
  Michal Crean
  Michael Miller

  D-U-N-S 25-372-4215   (HQ)
PROVINCIAL HEALTH SERVICES AUTHORITY
1380 Burrard St Suite 700, Vancouver, BC,
V6Z 2H3
(604) 675-7400
Emp Here 100   *Sales* 2,229,120,000
SIC 8099 Health and allied services, nec
  Carl Roy

Tim Manning
Linda Lupini
Thomas Chan

  D-U-N-S 20-176-4326   (HQ)
RESPONSETEK NETWORKS CORP
RESPONSETEK
969 Robson St Suite 320, Vancouver, BC, V6Z
2V7
(604) 484-2900
Sales 10,692,550
SIC 7372 Prepackaged software
  Syed Hasan
  Andrew Price

  D-U-N-S 20-939-0793   (SL)
RSVP CUSTOMER CARE CENTRES INC
1265 Howe St Suite 201, Vancouver, BC, V6Z
1R3
(604) 682-2001
Emp Here 120   *Sales* 80,268,960
SIC 7389 Business services, nec
  Gary Stevens

  D-U-N-S 20-515-0027   (SL)
SKY BAR LTD
938 Howe St Suite 615, Vancouver, BC, V6Z
1N9
(604) 697-0990
Emp Here 100   *Sales* 4,551,900
SIC 5812 Eating places

  D-U-N-S 20-027-1469   (SL)
THE PERSONNEL DEPARTMENT LTD
TPD
980 Howe St Unit 201, Vancouver, BC, V6Z
0C8
(604) 685-3530
Emp Here 49   *Sales* 13,442,268
SIC 8741 Management services
  Leslie Meingast

  D-U-N-S 20-584-4327   (SL)
VANCOUVER ART GALLERY ASSOCIATION, THE
750 Hornby St, Vancouver, BC, V6Z 2H7
(604) 662-4700
Emp Here 80   *Sales* 7,309,520
SIC 8412 Museums and art galleries
  Kathleen Bartels

  D-U-N-S 20-509-6969   (HQ)
WALL FINANCIAL CORPORATION
SHERATON VANCOUVER WALL CENTRE
1088 Burrard St, Vancouver, BC, V6Z 2R9
(604) 331-1000
Emp Here 70   *Sales* 230,180,229
SIC 7011 Hotels and motels
  Bruno Wall
  Peter Ufford
  Sascha Voth
  Joanne Liu
  Robert King
  Barton Finlay
  David E Gruber
  Michael Redekop

  D-U-N-S 24-456-1577   (SL)
WEDGEWOOD VILLAGE ESTATES LTD
WEDGEWOOD HOTEL, THE
845 Hornby St, Vancouver, BC, V6Z 1V1
(604) 689-7777
Emp Here 110   *Sales* 10,195,900
SIC 7011 Hotels and motels
  Elpie Jackson

  D-U-N-S 25-976-2276   (SL)
WESTBERG HOLDINGS INC
HOWARD JOHNSON
1176 Granville St, Vancouver, BC, V6Z 1L8
(604) 688-8701
Emp Here 100   *Sales* 9,489,900
SIC 7011 Hotels and motels
  Micheal Pixner

  D-U-N-S 25-372-8935   (BR)
**WINNERS MERCHANTS INTERNATIONAL
L.P.**

WINNERS
(*Suby of* THE TJX COMPANIES INC)
798 Granville St Suite 300, Vancouver, BC,
V6Z 3C3
(604) 683-1058
Emp Here 80
SIC 5651 Family clothing stores
  Helen Abdulla

  D-U-N-S 24-375-7155   (BR)
WSP CANADA GROUP LIMITED
(*Suby of* AST TRUST COMPANY (CANADA))
1000-840 Howe St, Vancouver, BC, V6Z 2M1
(604) 685-9381
Emp Here 120
SIC 8711 Engineering services
  Tim Stanley

Vancouver, BC V7V

  D-U-N-S 20-393-8282   (SL)
EUROHOUSE CONSTRUCTION INC
2474 Marine Dr W, Vancouver, BC, V7V 1L1
(604) 354-6325
Emp Here 55   *Sales* 14,901,810
SIC 1521 Single-family housing construction
  Vladimir Botnari

Vancouver, BC V7X

  D-U-N-S 20-269-0293   (HQ)
1005199 B.C. LTD
555 Burrard St Suite 600, Vancouver, BC, V7X
1M8
(604) 559-4322
Sales 14,429,644
SIC 6141 Personal credit institutions
  Michael Galpin
  Cody Green
  Stephen Brown
  Shannon Friesen
  Tyler Thielmann
  Rick Dhami
  Chris Reynolds

  D-U-N-S 24-154-1192   (HQ)
ABBARCH ARCHITECTURE INC
505 Burrard St Suite 1830, Vancouver, BC,
V7X 1M6
(604) 669-6041
Emp Here 55   *Sales* 21,448,680
SIC 8712 Architectural services
  Jeremy Woolf
  David O'sheehan
  Kenneth Grotsky
  Michael Burton-Brown
  Michelle Beggs
  Daryl Hutchinson
  Robert Smith
  Sarah Emmerson

  D-U-N-S 25-219-7835   (HQ)
ABSOLUTE SOFTWARE CORPORATION
ABSOLUTE
1055 Dunsmuir St Suite 1400, Vancouver, BC,
V7X 1K8
(604) 730-9851
Emp Here 207   *Sales* 93,621,832
SIC 7371 Custom computer programming services

  D-U-N-S 24-365-7595   (HQ)
**ACCIONA INFRASTRUCTURE CANADA
INC**
(*Suby of* ACCIONA, SA)
595 Burrard St Suite 2000, Vancouver, BC,
V7X 1J1
(604) 622-6550
Emp Here 50   *Sales* 139,678,400
SIC 1541 Industrial buildings and warehouses
  Jose Manuel Entrecanales

Darren Sokoloski
Jeffrey Merrick
Vincent Blasa
Francisco Adalberto Claudio-Vazquez

  D-U-N-S 20-954-7806   (SL)
AINSWORTH ENGINEERED CANADA LIMITED PARTNERSHIP
(*Suby of* NORBORD INC)
1055 Dunsmuir St Suite 3194, Vancouver, BC,
V7X 1L3
(604) 661-3200
Emp Here 600   *Sales* 145,938,600
SIC 3491 Industrial valves
  James Lake
  Robert Feustel

  D-U-N-S 20-956-2284   (HQ)
ALEXCO RESOURCE CORP
555 Burrard St Two Bentall Centre Suite 1225,
Vancouver, BC, V7X 1M9
(604) 633-4888
Emp Here 110   *Sales* 15,071,068
SIC 1041 Gold ores
  Clynton Nauman
  Brad Thrall
  Alan Mconie
  Gordon Wong
  James Harrington
  Michael Clark
  Richard Zimmer
  Terry Krepiakevich
  Elaine Sanders
  Rick Van Nieuwenhuys

  D-U-N-S 24-175-7157   (HQ)
ANNEX CONSULTING GROUP INC
555 Burrard St Suite 950, Vancouver, BC, V7X
1M8
(604) 638-8878
Emp Here 50   *Sales* 37,674,212
SIC 8742 Management consulting services
  Stacey Cerniuk

  D-U-N-S 20-702-1820   (HQ)
ANTHEM ACQUISITION LTD
Suite 1100 Bentall Iv, 1055 Dunsmuir St, Vancouver, BC, V7X 1K8
(604) 689-3040
Sales 29,322,230
SIC 6531 Real estate agents and managers
  Eric Carlson

  D-U-N-S 25-287-7691   (HQ)
ANTHEM WORKS LTD
ANTHEM INDUSTRIAL, A DIV OF
(*Suby of* ANTHEM ACQUISITION LTD)
1055 Dunsmuir Street, Vancouver, BC, V7X
1K8
(604) 689-3040
Emp Here 60   *Sales* 11,862,900
SIC 6553 Cemetery subdividers and developers
  Eric Carlson
  David Ferguson

  D-U-N-S 25-384-5283   (HQ)
ATLANTIC GOLD CORPORATION
595 Burrard St Suite 3083, Vancouver, BC,
V7X 1L3
(604) 689-5564
Sales 97,285,231
SIC 1479 Chemical and fertilizer mining
  Steven Dean
  Maryse Belanger
  Alastair Tiver
  Chris Batalha
  Tony Woodfine
  David Black
  Wally Bucknell
  Donald Siemens
  William Armstrong
  Ryan Beedie

  D-U-N-S 25-928-1418   (HQ)
AXIS INSURANCE MANAGERS INC
AXIS INSURANCE GROUP
(*Suby of* VERTICAL INSURANCE GROUP

LTD)
555 Burrard St. Box 275 Unit 400, Vancouver, BC, V7X 1M8
(604) 731-5328
Emp Here 31   *Sales* 96,082,584
SIC 6411 Insurance agents, brokers, and service
  Brian Andrews
  Clive Bird
  Ashley Murphy

D-U-N-S 24-366-3601   (HQ)
B2GOLD CORP
595 Burrard St Suite 3100, Vancouver, BC, V7X 1L7
(604) 681-8371
Emp Here 400   *Sales* 1,225,061,000
SIC 1041 Gold ores
  Clive Johnson
  Roger Richer
  Michael Cinnamond
  Tom Garagan
  Dennis Stansbury
  William Lytle
  Ian Maclean
  Dale Craig
  Eduard Bartz
  Brian Scott

D-U-N-S 20-112-2327   (HQ)
BENTALLGREENOAK (CANADA) LIMITED PARTNERSHIP
1055 Dunsmuir St Suite 1800, Vancouver, BC, V7X 1B1
(604) 661-5000
Emp Here 1   *Sales* 46,094,400
SIC 6531 Real estate agents and managers
  Gary Whitelaw
  Paul Zembla
  Tony Astles
  Richard Crofts
  Malcolm Leitch
  Mike Andrews
  Keith Major
  Sharon Oster
  Kenneth Bacon
  John O'bryan

D-U-N-S 24-313-2987   (BR)
BENTALLGREENOAK (CANADA) LIMITED PARTNERSHIP
(*Suby of* BENTALLGREENOAK (CANADA) LIMITED PARTNERSHIP)
1055 Dunsmuir St Suite 1800, Vancouver, BC, V7X 1L3
(604) 646-2800
Emp Here 300
SIC 6531 Real estate agents and managers
  Darcy Brabbian

D-U-N-S 24-824-6852   (BR)
BLAKE, CASSELS & GRAYDON LLP
(*Suby of* BLAKE, CASSELS & GRAYDON LLP)
595 Burrard St Suite 2600, Vancouver, BC, V7X 1L3
(604) 631-3300
Emp Here 140
SIC 8111 Legal services
  Nancy Sartene

D-U-N-S 20-565-9972   (SL)
BLUETREE HOMES LTD
1055 Dunsmuir St Suite 2000, Vancouver, BC, V7X 1L5
(604) 648-1800
Emp Here 49   *Sales* 15,887,368
SIC 1521 Single-family housing construction
  Peter Wesik

D-U-N-S 20-377-2595   (SL)
CANADA DRIVES LTD
GDC AUTOMOTIVE SERVICES
(*Suby of* 1005199 B.C. LTD)
555 Burrard St Suite 600, Vancouver, BC, V7X 1M8
(888) 865-6402
Emp Here 200   *Sales* 37,344,150

SIC 6141 Personal credit institutions
  Michael Galpin
  Cody Green
  Stephen Brown

D-U-N-S 24-861-1766   (SL)
CENTRAL SUN MINING INC
(*Suby of* B2GOLD CORP)
595 Burrard St Suite 3100, Vancouver, BC, V7X 1L7
(604) 681-8371
Emp Here 350
SIC 1081 Metal mining services
  Roger Richer
  Clive Johnson
  Mark Corra

D-U-N-S 20-053-2856   (HQ)
CHINA GOLD INTERNATIONAL RESOURCES CORP LTD
505 Burrard St Suite 660, Vancouver, BC, V7X 1M4
(604) 609-0598
Emp Here 100   *Sales* 570,570,000
SIC 1081 Metal mining services
  Liangyou Jiang
  Lianzhong Sun
  Xin Song
  Jerry Xie
  Lisheng Zhang
  Shiliang Guan
  Xiangdong Jiang
  Yunfei Chen
  Gregory Hall
  John King Burns

D-U-N-S 24-343-9846   (SL)
CHINA KELI ELECTRIC COMPANY LTD
555 Burrard St Suite 900, Vancouver, BC, V7X 1M8

Emp Here 150   *Sales* 8,242,066
SIC 3679 Electronic components, nec
  Lou Meng Cheong
  Sou Wa Wong
  Tze Fung Philip Lo
  George Dorin
  Jian Wen Wu
  Yan Zhang

D-U-N-S 25-999-9191   (HQ)
COSCO SHIPPING LINES (CANADA) INC
COSCO
(*Suby of* CHINA COSCO SHIPPING CORPORATION LIMITED)
1055 Dunsmuir St Suite 2288, Vancouver, BC, V7X 1K8
(604) 689-8989
Emp Here 30   *Sales* 22,835,992
SIC 4491 Marine cargo handling
  Qimin Liu

D-U-N-S 24-317-6158   (HQ)
COUNTERPATH CORPORATION
505 Burrard St Suite 300, Vancouver, BC, V7X 1M3
(604) 320-3344
Emp Here 20   *Sales* 12,381,741
SIC 7379 Computer related services, nec
  David Karp
  Todd Carothers
  Michael Doyle
  Rahim Rehmat
  Jim O'brein
  Damian Wallace
  Jim Bergamini
  John Wigboldus
  Bruce Ford
  Terence Matthews

D-U-N-S 24-167-9591   (BR)
DELOITTE LLP
DELOITTE MANAGEMENT SERVICES
(*Suby of* DELOITTE LLP)
1055 Dunsmuir St Suite 2800, Vancouver, BC, V7X 1P4
(604) 669-4466
Emp Here 400

SIC 8721 Accounting, auditing, and bookkeeping

D-U-N-S 24-165-3963   (HQ)
ELSWOOD INVESTMENT CORPORATION
1055 Dunsmuir St Suite 3500, Vancouver, BC, V7X 1H3
(604) 691-9100
Sales 183,485,518
SIC 6712 Bank holding companies
  William Sauder
  Lawrence Sauder

D-U-N-S 24-980-1770   (SL)
ENDEAVOUR FINANCIAL LTD
595 Burrard St Suite 3123, Vancouver, BC, V7X 1J1
(604) 685-4554
Emp Here 21   *Sales* 14,257,383
SIC 6211 Security brokers and dealers
  Neil Woodyer
  Frank Giustra

D-U-N-S 24-866-9087   (HQ)
GLOBAL SECURITIES CORPORATION
3 Bentall Ctr Suite 1100, Vancouver, BC, V7X 1C4
(604) 689-5400
Emp Here 80
SIC 6211 Security brokers and dealers
  Douglas Garrod
  Arthur Smolensky
  Aline Smolensky
  Duncan Boggs

D-U-N-S 24-144-4335   (BR)
GLOBAL SECURITIES CORPORATION
595 Burrard St, Vancouver, BC, V7X 1C4
(604) 689-5400
Emp Here 100
SIC 6211 Security brokers and dealers
  Natalie Dahl

D-U-N-S 20-889-8759   (BR)
GORE MUTUAL INSURANCE COMPANY
(*Suby of* GORE MUTUAL INSURANCE COMPANY)
505 Burrard St Unit 1780, Vancouver, BC, V7X 1M6
(604) 682-0998
Emp Here 210
SIC 6331 Fire, marine, and casualty insurance
  Kevin Mcneil

D-U-N-S 24-417-2552   (SL)
IDM MINING LTD
555 Burrard St Suite 1800, Vancouver, BC, V7X 1M9
(604) 681-5672
Emp Here 9   *Sales* 21,487,941
SIC 1041 Gold ores
  Robert Mcleod
  Ryan Weymark
  Susan Neale
  Michael Mcphie
  David Parker
  Andrew Farncomb
  Duncan Middlemiss
  Andree St-Germain
  Terry Harbort

D-U-N-S 20-621-3688   (HQ)
INTERFOR CORPORATION
INTERFOR
1055 Dunsmuir St Suite 3500, Vancouver, BC, V7X 1H7
(604) 689-6800
Emp Here 30   *Sales* 1,657,640,816
SIC 2421 Sawmills and planing mills, general
  Duncan Davies
  Lawrence Sauder
  Martin Juravsky
  Ian Fillinger
  Mark Stock
  Bart Bender
  Richard Slaco
  Xenia Kritsos
  Jeane Hull

  Tom Milroy

D-U-N-S 25-677-2161   (HQ)
JOEY TOMATO'S
505 Burrard St Unit 950, Vancouver, BC, V7X 1M5
(604) 699-5639
Emp Here 513   *Sales* 23,925,807
SIC 5812 Eating places
  Jeffrey Fuller
  Kent Fowler
  Stan Fuller
  Stewart Fuller

D-U-N-S 20-365-3647   (HQ)
LEAGOLD MINING CORPORATION
595 Burrard St Suite 3043, Vancouver, BC, V7X 1J1
(604) 398-4505
Emp Here 100   *Sales* 193,694,000
SIC 1041 Gold ores
  Neil Woodyer
  Doug Bowlby
  Doug Reddy
  Richard Thomas
  Cornelius Lourens
  Peter Burger
  Harpreet Dhaliwal
  Kelly Boychuk
  Jeff Leung
  Bernadette Dsilva

D-U-N-S 25-674-3196   (SL)
LITHIUM X ENERGY CORP
595 Burrard St Suite 3123, Vancouver, BC, V7X 1J1
(604) 609-6138
Emp Here 8   *Sales* 19,100,392
SIC 1081 Metal mining services
  Paul Matysek
  Brian Paes-Braga
  Eduardo Morales
  William Randall
  Bassam Moubarak
  Harry Pokrandt
  David Raffa
  Michele Ashby

D-U-N-S 24-357-0988   (HQ)
MARLIN GOLD MINING LTD
595 Burrard St Suite 2833, Vancouver, BC, V7X 1J1
(604) 646-1580
Emp Here 10   *Sales* 54,263,433
SIC 1041 Gold ores
  Akiba Leisman
  Cesar Gonzalez
  Jesse Munoz
  Scott Kelly
  Guillermo Kaelin
  John Pontius

D-U-N-S 20-115-6981   (HQ)
METRIE CANADA LTD
METRIE
(*Suby of* ELSWOOD INVESTMENT CORPORATION)
1055 Dunsmuir St Suite 3500, Vancouver, BC, V7X 1H3
(604) 691-9100
Emp Here 10   *Sales* 139,195,000
SIC 2431 Millwork
  Greg Stoner
  Kent Bowie
  Pamela Campbell

D-U-N-S 24-796-7479   (BR)
MNP LLP
(*Suby of* MNP LLP)
1055 Dunsmuir Suite 2300, Vancouver, BC, V7X 1J1
(604) 639-0001
Emp Here 100
SIC 8721 Accounting, auditing, and bookkeeping
  Kyle Mackenzie

D-U-N-S 25-538-3572   (BR)

MORNEAU SHEPELL LTD
SHEPPELL FGI DIV OF
(*Suby of* MORNEAU SHEPELL INC)
505 Burrard St Unit 1070, Vancouver, BC, V7X 1M5
(604) 642-5200
Emp Here 100
SIC 8999 Services, nec
Norah Joyce

D-U-N-S 20-758-8955　　(HQ)
NORTHBRIDGE INDEMNITY INSURANCE CORPORATION
(*Suby of* FAIRFAX FINANCIAL HOLDINGS LIMITED)
595 Burrard St Suite 1500, Vancouver, BC, V7X 1G4
(604) 683-5511
Emp Here 178　　*Sales* 949,220,800
SIC 6411 Insurance agents, brokers, and service
Ronald Schwab
Timothy R. Ius
Stewart Woo

D-U-N-S 20-994-2254　　(HQ)
OMICRON ARCHITECTURE ENGINEERING CONSTRUCTION LTD
(*Suby of* OMICRON CANADA INC)
595 Burrard St, Vancouver, BC, V7X 1M7
(604) 632-3350
Emp Here 160　　*Sales* 35,747,800
SIC 8712 Architectural services
William Tucker

D-U-N-S 24-391-9136　　(HQ)
OMICRON CANADA INC
595 Burrard St, Vancouver, BC, V7X 1M7
(604) 632-3350
Emp Here 158　　*Sales* 35,747,800
SIC 8712 Architectural services
William Tucker
Cameron Kemp

D-U-N-S 24-327-8178　　(SL)
OMICRON CONSTRUCTION MANAGEMENT LTD
595 Burrard St, Vancouver, BC, V7X 1L4
(604) 632-3350
Emp Here 37　　*Sales* 17,417,047
SIC 1542 Nonresidential construction, nec
Cameron Kemp
Bill Tucker
George Sawatzky

D-U-N-S 25-538-8621　　(SL)
OMICRON CONSULTING GROUP
595 Burrard St, Vancouver, BC, V7X 1L4
(604) 632-3350
Emp Here 150　　*Sales* 104,758,800
SIC 1541 Industrial buildings and warehouses
Cameron Kemp
George Sawatzky
Bill Tucker
Bruce Knapp
Greg Richardson
Doug Vincent
Sally Mills
Lori Billson
Kevin Hanvey
Andy Kohler

D-U-N-S 20-865-1539　　(SL)
OWEN BIRD LAW CORPORATION
595 Burrard St Suite 2900, Vancouver, BC, V7X 1J5
(604) 688-0401
Emp Here 100　　*Sales* 15,401,100
SIC 8111 Legal services
William E Irland
D Barry Kirkham
J David Dunn
Robin C Macfarlane
Douglas R Johnson

D-U-N-S 24-373-5594　　(SL)
PARKLANE VENTURES LTD

PARKLANE HOMES
1055 Dunsmuir St Suite 2000, Vancouver, BC, V7X 1L5
(604) 648-1800
Emp Here 54　　*Sales* 11,009,682
SIC 6553 Cemetery subdividers and developers
Peter Wesik
Vincent Cheung

D-U-N-S 20-268-2027　　(SL)
PRETIUM EXPLORATION INC
(*Suby of* PRETIUM RESOURCES INC)
1055 Dunsmuir St Suite 2300, Vancouver, BC, V7X 1L4
(604) 558-1784
Emp Here 500　　*Sales* 127,887,000
SIC 1041 Gold ores
Joseph Ovsenek
Robert Quartermain
Tom Yip
Grant Bond

D-U-N-S 24-684-3549　　(HQ)
PRETIUM RESOURCES INC
1055 Dunsmuir St Suite 2300 Four Bentall Ctr, Vancouver, BC, V7X 1L4
(604) 558-1784
Sales 454,556,000
SIC 1041 Gold ores
Joseph J. Ovsenek
Tom S.Q. Yip
Michelle Romero
Kenneth Mcnaughton
Warwick Board
David Prins
Robert A. Quartermain
George Paspalas
Peter Birkey
David Smith

D-U-N-S 20-384-4485　　(HQ)
PUNA OPERATIONS INC
1055 Dunsmuir St, Vancouver, BC, V7X 1G4
(604) 689-3846
Sales 1,339,414,989
SIC 1031 Lead and zinc ores
Gregory Martin
Matthew Langford

D-U-N-S 25-975-5445　　(HQ)
QTRADE CANADA INC
QTRADE FINANCIAL GROUP
505 Burrard St Suite 1920, Vancouver, BC, V7X 1M6
(604) 605-4111
Sales 140,876,550
SIC 6211 Security brokers and dealers
Scott Gibner

D-U-N-S 25-990-9760　　(SL)
QTRADE SECURITIES INC
(*Suby of* QTRADE CANADA INC)
505 Burrard St Suite 1920, Vancouver, BC, V7X 1M6
(604) 605-4199
Emp Here 35　　*Sales* 15,722,665
SIC 7389 Business services, nec
Scott Robert Gibner
Joseph Edward Meehan
Neil M Mccammon
Elaine Davison

D-U-N-S 20-279-4129　　(SL)
RENAISSANCE OIL CORP
595 Burrard St Suite 3123, Vancouver, BC, V7X 1J1
(604) 536-3637
Emp Here 10　　*Sales* 18,967,137
SIC 1382 Oil and gas exploration services
Craig Steinke
Kevin Smith
Carlos Camacho
Carlos Escribano
Carol Law
Carmen Etchart
Ian Telfer

Gordon Keep
Eskandar Maleki
Allan Folk

D-U-N-S 24-351-5496　　(SL)
RHYOLITE RESOURCES LTD
595 Burrard St Suite 1703, Vancouver, BC, V7X 1J1
(604) 488-8717
Emp Here 20　　*Sales* 14,006,100
SIC 1041 Gold ores
Richard Graham
Sandra Lee
John Downes
Demetrius Pohl
Mike Basha

D-U-N-S 20-201-7252　　(HQ)
RUSORO MINING LTD
595 Burrard St Suite 3123, Vancouver, BC, V7X 1J1
(604) 609-6110
Sales 25,577,400
SIC 1041 Gold ores
Andre Agapov
Vladimir Agapov
Jay Kaplowitz
Abraham Stein
Peter Hediger
Gordon Keep

D-U-N-S 25-993-4946　　(SL)
SHAPE MARKETING CORP
(*Suby of* SHAPE PROPERTIES (BTCR) CORP)
505 Burrard St Suite 2020, Vancouver, BC, V7X 1M6
(604) 681-2358
Emp Here 60　　*Sales* 25,133,340
SIC 6531 Real estate agents and managers
John Horton

D-U-N-S 25-093-3186　　(HQ)
SHAPE PROPERTIES (BTCR) CORP
505 Burrard St Suite 2020, Vancouver, BC, V7X 1M6
(604) 681-2358
Sales 67,612,800
SIC 6531 Real estate agents and managers
John Horton
Graeme Johnson
Darren Kwiatkowski
Brad Stokes

D-U-N-S 20-957-6875　　(SL)
SHAW SABEY & ASSOCIATES LTD
555 Burrard St Suite 1275, Vancouver, BC, V7X 1M9
(604) 689-2441
Emp Here 60　　*Sales* 110,864,520
SIC 6411 Insurance agents, brokers, and service
Alex Meier
Victor Montagliani
Nadene Beemish
Kari Montes
Jeffrey Mccann

D-U-N-S 20-115-9365　　(HQ)
SSR MINING INC
1055 Dunsmuir St Suite 800, Vancouver, BC, V7X 1G4
(604) 689-3846
Emp Here 100　　*Sales* 420,675,000
SIC 1044 Silver ores
Paul Benson
Gregory Martin
Kevin O'kane
W. John Decooman
Nadine Block
Gustavo Herrero
Michael Anglin
Brian Booth
Beverlee Park
Richard Paterson

D-U-N-S 24-850-0675　　(SL)
THORSTEINSSONS

595 Burrard St Suite 49123, Vancouver, BC, V7X 1J2
(604) 689-1261
Emp Here 100　　*Sales* 8,962,900
SIC 7291 Tax return preparation services
David Thompson

D-U-N-S 20-292-6353　　(SL)
WESGROUP PROPERTIES LIMITED PARTNERSHIP
WESGROUP PROPERTIES
1055 Dunsmuir St Suite 910, Vancouver, BC, V7X 1J1
(604) 632-1727
Emp Here 50　　*Sales* 14,424,950
SIC 6512 Nonresidential building operators
Peeter Wesik

Vancouver, BC V7Y

D-U-N-S 25-484-6066　　(SL)
AHBL MANAGEMENT LIMITED PARTNERSHIP
ALEXANDER HOLBURN BEAUDIN & LANG
700 Georgia St W Suite 2700, Vancouver, BC, V7Y 1K8
(604) 688-1351
Emp Here 195　　*Sales* 24,331,320
SIC 8741 Management services
David Gooderham

D-U-N-S 24-120-5004　　(SL)
ALEXANDER HOLBURN BEAUDIN & LANG LLP
AHBL MANAGEMENT
700 Georgia St W Suite 2700, Vancouver, BC, V7Y 1B8
(604) 484-1700
Emp Here 185　　*Sales* 20,513,170
SIC 8111 Legal services
William Holburn
Stuart Lang
Richard Saul
Michael Ragona
James Dowler

D-U-N-S 24-343-9879　　(SL)
ANDEANGOLD LTD
701 Georgia St W Suite 1500, Vancouver, BC, V7Y 1K8
(604) 608-6172
Emp Here 50　　*Sales* 11,671,750
SIC 1081 Metal mining services
Alexander Pena Bottcher
John E. Bolanos
Alberto E. Paz
Graham H. Scott
Michael P. Cachia
Thomas Kelly
William Francis Lindqvist

D-U-N-S 20-993-7494　　(BR)
ARITZIA LP
(*Suby of* ARITZIA INC)
701 Georgia St W Suite 53d, Vancouver, BC, V7Y 1K8
(604) 681-9301
Emp Here 120
SIC 5621 Women's clothing stores
Jennifer Luney

D-U-N-S 25-682-2685　　(HQ)
BEACON UNDERWRITING LTD
CAN-SURE UNDERWRITING
(*Suby of* HELLMAN & FRIEDMAN LLC)
700 Georgia St W Suite 1488, Vancouver, BC, V7Y 1K8
(604) 685-6533
Emp Here 5　　*Sales* 36,933,180
SIC 6331 Fire, marine, and casualty insurance
Cameron Copeland

D-U-N-S 24-037-3584　　(HQ)
CAN-SURE UNDERWRITING LTD
(*Suby of* HELLMAN & FRIEDMAN LLC)

700 Georgia St W Suite 1488, Vancouver, BC,
V7Y 1A1
(604) 685-6533
Emp Here 10   *Sales* 61,770,900
SIC 6351 Surety insurance
 Cameron Copeland
 Bruce Mackinnon
 Tommy Truong
 Martin Lynch
 Ed Quek
 Brent Lexier

D-U-N-S 20-799-3759   (HQ)
CANACCORD GENUITY CORP
(*Suby of* CANACCORD GENUITY GROUP
INC)
609 Granville St Suite 2200, Vancouver, BC,
V7Y 1H2
(604) 643-7300
Emp Here 500   *Sales* 1,707,765,600
SIC 6211 Security brokers and dealers
 Dan Davieu

D-U-N-S 20-188-1559   (HQ)
CANACCORD GENUITY GROUP INC
609 Granville St Van Unit 2200, Vancouver,
BC, V7Y 1H2
(604) 643-7300
Emp Here 345   *Sales* 669,518,331
SIC 6211 Security brokers and dealers
 Dan Daviau
 David Kassie
 Alexis De Rosnay
 Don Macfayden
 Adrian Pelosi
 Stuart Raftus
 Charles Bralver
 Massimo Carello
 Kalpana Desai
 Michael Harris

D-U-N-S 24-367-0812   (HQ)
CONIFEX TIMBER INC
700 West Georgia St Suite 980, Vancouver,
BC, V7Y 1B6
(604) 216-2949
Emp Here 50   *Sales* 507,866,782
SIC 2421 Sawmills and planing mills, general
 Ken Shields
 Hans Thur
 Adam Infanti
 Brett Bray
 Jordan Neeser
 Sandy Ferguson
 Pat Bell
 Michael Costello
 Jim Jia
 George Judd

D-U-N-S 25-715-2694   (BR)
CORUS ENTERTAINMENT INC
CFMI-FM
(*Suby of* CORUS ENTERTAINMENT INC)
700 Georgia St W Suite 2000, Vancouver, BC,
V7Y 1K8
(604) 687-5177
Emp Here 168
SIC 4832 Radio broadcasting stations
 Dustin Collins

D-U-N-S 25-014-1736   (BR)
CORUS ENTERTAINMENT INC
AM730
(*Suby of* CORUS ENTERTAINMENT INC)
700 Georgia St W Suite 2000, Vancouver, BC,
V7Y 1K8
(604) 687-5177
Emp Here 120
SIC 4832 Radio broadcasting stations
 Lou Del Gobbo

D-U-N-S 25-615-4683   (BR)
CORUS ENTERTAINMENT INC
CKNY-FM
(*Suby of* CORUS ENTERTAINMENT INC)
700 Georgia St W Suite 2000, Vancouver, BC,
V7Y 1K8

(604) 687-5177
Emp Here 130
SIC 4832 Radio broadcasting stations
 Dustin Collins

D-U-N-S 20-795-9081   (BR)
CUSHMAN & WAKEFIELD ULC
CUSHMAN & WAKEFIELD LTD
(*Suby of* CUSHMAN & WAKEFIELD PLC)
700 Georgia St W, Vancouver, BC, V7Y 1K8
(604) 683-3111
Emp Here 100
SIC 6531 Real estate agents and managers
 Randy Swant

D-U-N-S 24-681-6433   (SL)
**DAVIDSON & COMPANY CHARTERED AC-
COUNTANTS LLP**
609 Grandville St Suite 1200, Vancouver, BC,
V7Y 1G6
(604) 687-0947
Emp Here 60   *Sales* 12,545,100
SIC 8721 Accounting, auditing, and book-
keeping
 William (Bill) Davidson

D-U-N-S 24-939-0006   (HQ)
ENDEAVOUR SILVER CORP
609 Granville St Suite 1130, Vancouver, BC,
V7Y 1G5
(604) 685-9775
Emp Here 15   *Sales* 150,509,000
SIC 1041 Gold ores
 Bradford J. Cooke
 Geoff Handley
 Godfrey J. Walton
 Christine West
 Luis Castro Valdez
 Dale Mah
 Manuel Echevarria
 Nicholas Shakesby
 Lorena Aguilar
 Galina Meleger

D-U-N-S 20-919-1621   (BR)
ERNST & YOUNG LLP
(*Suby of* ERNST & YOUNG LLP)
700 Georgia St W Suite 2200, Vancouver, BC,
V7Y 1K8
(604) 891-8200
Emp Here 400
SIC 8721 Accounting, auditing, and book-
keeping
 Fred Withers

D-U-N-S 20-689-2429   (SL)
FARONICS CORPORATION
FARONICS
609 Granville St Suite 1400, Vancouver, BC,
V7Y 1G5
(604) 637-3333
Emp Here 100   *Sales* 17,731,100
SIC 7371 Custom computer programming ser-
vices
 Farid Ali
 Randy K Lomnes

D-U-N-S 20-775-2408   (HQ)
FARRIS, VAUGHAN, WILLS & MURPHY LLP
700 Georgia St W Suite 25, Vancouver, BC,
V7Y 1K8
(604) 684-9151
Emp Here 80   *Sales* 14,414,660
SIC 8111 Legal services
 A. Keith Mitchell
 Dominic A. Petraroia
 Jay R. Cathcart
 Jay R. Cathcart

D-U-N-S 24-520-9366   (SL)
FREEGOLD VENTURES LIMITED
700 Georgia St W Suite 888, Vancouver, BC,
V7Y 1K8
(604) 662-7307
Emp Here 10   *Sales* 23,875,490
SIC 1081 Metal mining services
 Kristina Walcott
 Alvin W. Jackson

 Gordon Steblin
 David A. Knight
 Gary Moore
 Garnet Dawson
 Greg Hanks
 Glen Dickson
 Ron Ewing
 Reagan Glazier

D-U-N-S 24-856-7604   (BR)
KPMG LLP
(*Suby of* KPMG LLP)
777 Dunsmuir St Suite 900, Vancouver, BC,
V7Y 1K3
(604) 691-3000
Emp Here 800
SIC 8721 Accounting, auditing, and book-
keeping
 Jonathan Kallner

D-U-N-S 20-804-3039   (SL)
MILLENNUIM MANAGEMENT CORP
609 Granville St Suite 1600, Vancouver, BC,
V7Y 1C3
(604) 669-1322
Emp Here 15   *Sales* 10,355,125
SIC 6211 Security brokers and dealers
 Peter Malek

D-U-N-S 24-856-4994   (HQ)
**MOBIFY RESEARCH AND DEVELOPMENT
INC**
725 Granville St Suite 420, Vancouver, BC,
V7Y 1C6
(866) 502-5880
Sales 12,255,470
SIC 7371 Custom computer programming ser-
vices
 Igor Faletski
 Kirk Hasley
 James Sherrett
 Peter Mclachlan
 John Boxall
 Candace Meagher

D-U-N-S 20-082-0295   (BR)
NORDSTROM CANADA RETAIL, INC
NORDSTROM PACIFIC CENTRE
(*Suby of* NORDSTROM, INC.)
799 Robson St, Vancouver, BC, V7Y 0A2
(604) 699-2100
Emp Here 80
SIC 5311 Department stores

D-U-N-S 24-358-1050   (SL)
RYE PATCH GOLD CORP
(*Suby of* ALIO GOLD INC)
701 West Georgia St Suite 1500, Vancouver,
BC, V7Y 1C6
(604) 638-1588
Emp Here 20   *Sales* 10,802,406
SIC 1041 Gold ores
 William Howald
 Tony Wood
 Bernard Poznanski
 Jonathan Challis
 Charles Russell
 Timothy Baker

D-U-N-S 25-046-1816   (SL)
TRILOGY METALS INC
609 Granville St Suite 1150, Vancouver, BC,
V7Y 1G5
(604) 638-8088
Emp Here 30   *Sales* 71,626,470
SIC 1021 Copper ores
 Rick Van Nieuwenhuyse
 Robert Jacko
 Patrick Donnelly
 Elaine Sanders
 Tony S. Giardini
 Gregory Lang
 Kalidas Madhavpeddi
 Gerald Mcconnell
 William Hayden
 Diana Walters

D-U-N-S 25-818-0108   (BR)

WESTERN FOREST PRODUCTS INC
(*Suby of* WESTERN FOREST PRODUCTS
INC)
700 Georgia St W Suite 510, Vancouver, BC,
V7Y 1K8

Emp Here 100
SIC 2421 Sawmills and planing mills, general
 Lorne Holman

D-U-N-S 24-351-4705   (HQ)
WOLVERTON SECURITIES LTD
777 Dunsmuir St Suite 1700, Vancouver, BC,
V7Y 1J5
(604) 622-1000
Emp Here 100   *Sales* 27,975,900
SIC 8742 Management consulting services
 Brent Wolverton
 Ellen Paterson

Vancouver, BC V8W

D-U-N-S 20-132-0254   (HQ)
APPSONTIME TECHNOLOGIES LTD
AOT TECHNOLOGIES
320-645 Fort St, Vancouver, BC, V8W 1G2
(778) 433-1268
Sales 13,354,416
SIC 8748 Business consulting, nec
 George Philip
 Praveen Ramathandran

Vanderhoof, BC V0J

D-U-N-S 25-993-3856   (SL)
ADVANCED MILLWRIGHT SERVICES LTD
AMS
971 Hwy 16, Vanderhoof, BC, V0J 3A1
(250) 567-5756
Emp Here 75   *Sales* 18,463,950
SIC 1796 Installing building equipment
 Tim Johnson

D-U-N-S 20-337-9115   (BR)
BID GROUP TECHNOLOGIES LTD
BID GROUP TECHNOLOGIES LTD
(*Suby of* BID GROUP TECHNOLOGIES LTD)
3446 Mountain View Rd, Vanderhoof, BC, V0J
3A2
(250) 567-2578
Emp Here 116
SIC 3441 Fabricated structural Metal
 David Fehr

D-U-N-S 25-415-4719   (HQ)
**BOARD OF EDUCATION OF SCHOOL DIS-
TRICT NO. 91 (NECHAKO LAKE), THE**
*SCHOOL DISTRICT NO. 91 (NECHAKO
LAKE)*
153 Connaught St E, Vanderhoof, BC, V0J
3A0
(250) 567-2284
Emp Here 25   *Sales* 43,242,065
SIC 8211 Elementary and secondary schools
 Eugene Marks
 Darlene Turner
 Steve Davis
 Nadine Frenkel
 Lynda Maertz
 Lucille Duncan
 Tim Maertz
 Tom Bulmer
 Adele Gooding

D-U-N-S 20-735-2738   (BR)
CANADIAN FOREST PRODUCTS LTD
CANFOR - PLATEAU
(*Suby of* CANFOR CORPORATION)
1399 Bearhead Rd, Vanderhoof, BC, V0J 3A2
(250) 567-4725
Emp Here 283

SIC 2421 Sawmills and planing mills, general
Dwayne Klassen

D-U-N-S 20-117-7078   (HQ)
FOUR RIVERS CO-OPERATIVE
188 East Stewart St, Vanderhoof, BC, V0J 3A0
(250) 567-4414
Emp Here 65   *Sales* 125,720,100
SIC 5171 Petroleum bulk stations and terminals
Kenneth Loper
Kimberley Mcivor
Godfrey (Bud) Pye
Rene Jones
Henry Dyck
Marje Makow
Colleen Erickson
Caeser Isiboro
Nirmal Barmar

D-U-N-S 20-748-9865   (SL)
L. & M. LUMBER LTD
1241 Hwy 16 W, Vanderhoof, BC, V0J 3A0
(250) 567-4701
Emp Here 73   *Sales* 16,206,073
SIC 3553 Woodworking machinery
Mike Manojlovic
Toreall Scott
Keith Anderson
Maryella Larsen
Bill Stewart

D-U-N-S 20-620-3796   (SL)
NECHAKO LUMBER CO. LTD
1241 Hwy 16 W, Vanderhoof, BC, V0J 3A0
(250) 567-4701
Emp Here 88   *Sales* 16,928,560
SIC 2421 Sawmills and planing mills, general
Manojlo (Mike) Manojlovic
Ivan Andersen
William Stewart
Lloyd Larsen

Vernon, BC V1B

D-U-N-S 24-633-4366   (SL)
0809021 B.C. LTD
VERNON NISSAN
6417 Hwy 97, Vernon, BC, V1B 3R4
(250) 542-0371
Emp Here 30   *Sales* 14,942,340
SIC 5511 New and used car dealers
Rick Sentes
David Dempster

D-U-N-S 25-670-4776   (SL)
351684 BC LTD
SUNSHINE HONDA
6425 Hwy 97, Vernon, BC, V1B 3R4
(250) 545-0531
Emp Here 30   *Sales* 14,942,340
SIC 5511 New and used car dealers
Peter Dubetz

D-U-N-S 25-313-0470   (SL)
BIG D PRODUCTS LTD
THE PADDOCK
7861 Hwy 97 Suite 1, Vernon, BC, V1B 3R9

Emp Here 97   *Sales* 49,359,032
SIC 5023 Homefurnishings
Darryl R.C. O'brian
Karin O'brian

D-U-N-S 20-117-7698   (SL)
BUTCHER BOYS ENTERPRISES LTD
BUTCHER BOYS FOOD MARKET
4803 Pleasant Valley Rd, Vernon, BC, V1B 3L7
(250) 542-2968
Emp Here 40   *Sales* 10,966,080
SIC 5411 Grocery stores
Paul Guidi

D-U-N-S 24-682-3397   (HQ)
GREAT WEST EQUIPMENT LTD
123 L & A Cross Rd, Vernon, BC, V1B 3S1
(250) 549-4232
Emp Here 35   *Sales* 53,650,300
SIC 5084 Industrial machinery and equipment
Ross Davidson
Roger Dobie
Colin Matejka
Earl Shipmaker

D-U-N-S 25-677-2328   (BR)
IRL INTERNATIONAL TRUCK CENTRES LTD
(*Suby of* IRL INTERNATIONAL TRUCK CENTRES LTD)
7156 Meadowlark Rd, Vernon, BC, V1B 3R6
(877) 463-0292
Emp Here 75
SIC 5511 New and used car dealers
Williams Lake

D-U-N-S 20-058-2604   (HQ)
KINGFISHER BOATS INC
8160 Highland Rd, Vernon, BC, V1B 3W6
(250) 545-9171
Sales 25,597,825
SIC 3732 Boatbuilding and repairing
Byron Bolton
Bradley Armstrong
Sheryl Bolton

D-U-N-S 24-312-2231   (HQ)
MORMAK INVESTMENTS LTD
8140 Becketts Rd, Vernon, BC, V1B 3V3
(250) 542-7350
Emp Here 18   *Sales* 14,250,780
SIC 5084 Industrial machinery and equipment
Robert Mohr

D-U-N-S 25-503-4522   (BR)
NORTH OKANAGAN REGIONAL HEALTH BOARD
VERNON INTERIOR HEALTH
1440 14 Ave, Vernon, BC, V1B 2T1
(250) 549-5700
Emp Here 100
SIC 8011 Offices and clinics of medical doctors
Lesly Mcmillan

D-U-N-S 20-187-4232   (BR)
OKANAGAN RESTORATION SERVICES LTD
(*Suby of* OKANAGAN RESTORATION SERVICES LTD)
6236 Pleasant Valley Rd, Vernon, BC, V1B 3R3
(250) 542-3470
Emp Here 75
SIC 1629 Heavy construction, nec
Terry Moorhouse

Vernon, BC V1H

D-U-N-S 25-218-9667   (SL)
LAKERS GOLF CLUB INC, THE
7000 Cummins Rd, Vernon, BC, V1H 1M2
(250) 260-1050
Emp Here 25   *Sales* 10,483,875
SIC 6712 Bank holding companies
Kerry Korberg
Kevin Korberg

D-U-N-S 24-067-3905   (SL)
LAWDAN INVESTMENTS LTD
A & W
683 Commonage Rd, Vernon, BC, V1H 1G3
(250) 542-1707
Emp Here 50   *Sales* 24,903,900
SIC 5541 Gasoline service stations
Lawrence Brown
Dana Brown

D-U-N-S 25-924-8466   (SL)

NIGHT HAWK SECURITY LTD
9095 Tronson Rd, Vernon, BC, V1H 1E2

Emp Here 33   *Sales* 13,057,374
SIC 7381 Detective and armored car services
Brenda- Mae Thurston

D-U-N-S 25-811-9767   (BR)
SCHOOL DISTRICT NO 22 (VERNON)
CLARENCE FULTON SECONDARY SCHOOL
(*Suby of* SCHOOL DISTRICT NO 22 (VERNON))
2301 Fulton Rd, Vernon, BC, V1H 1Y1
(250) 545-1348
Emp Here 80
SIC 8211 Elementary and secondary schools
Ken Gatzke

Vernon, BC V1T

D-U-N-S 20-276-6150   (SL)
0127494 B.C. LTD
VERNON HYUNDAI
4608 27 St, Vernon, BC, V1T 4Y6
(250) 275-4004
Emp Here 50   *Sales* 24,903,900
SIC 5511 New and used car dealers
Vaughn Wyant
Adrian Wyant
John Bokitch

D-U-N-S 25-652-9553   (SL)
30TH STREET LIQUOR STORE LTD
2901 30 St, Vernon, BC, V1T 5C9
(250) 545-5800
Emp Here 70   *Sales* 17,102,960
SIC 5921 Liquor stores
Joe Tarnowski

D-U-N-S 24-994-9967   (SL)
421042 BC LTD
887 Fairweather Rd, Vernon, BC, V1T 8T8
(250) 542-5481
Emp Here 75   *Sales* 16,337,175
SIC 1731 Electrical work
David Borden

D-U-N-S 20-692-2705   (SL)
616536 B.C. LTD
HOME BUILDING CENTRE VERNON
4601 27 St, Vernon, BC, V1T 4Y8
(250) 545-5384
Emp Here 65   *Sales* 17,397,380
SIC 5211 Lumber and other building materials
John Kehler
Gary Gilchrist

D-U-N-S 25-267-6705   (HQ)
ACUTRUSS INDUSTRIES (1996) LTD
2003 43 St, Vernon, BC, V1T 6K7
(250) 545-3215
Emp Here 41   *Sales* 11,542,200
SIC 2439 Structural wood members, nec
David Marcoux
Barry Schick

D-U-N-S 24-911-3838   (HQ)
BANNISTER CHEVROLET BUICK GMC VERNON INC
BANNISTER GM VERNON
4703 27 St, Vernon, BC, V1T 4Y8
(250) 542-2647
Emp Here 1   *Sales* 24,903,900
SIC 5511 New and used car dealers
J. Lyn Bannister
Joanne Bannister

D-U-N-S 25-067-5196   (HQ)
BARON INSURANCE AGENCIES GROUP INC
BARON INSURANCE BROKER GROUP
(*Suby of* WESTLAND INSURANCE GROUP LTD)
5301 25 Ave Suite 119, Vernon, BC, V1T 9R1

(250) 545-6565
Emp Here 10   *Sales* 22,897,620
SIC 6411 Insurance agents, brokers, and service
Barry Amies
Patricia Kinghorn
Helena Chambers
Donna Amies
Chuck Melanson

D-U-N-S 24-761-3748   (HQ)
BEACHCOMBER HOME & LEISURE LTD
5309 26 St, Vernon, BC, V1T 7G4
(250) 542-3399
Emp Here 20   *Sales* 15,265,680
SIC 5021 Furniture
Dennis Melvin
Shawn Melvin
Kent Melvin
Bryce Melvin

D-U-N-S 24-798-1954   (BR)
BEST WESTERN SANDS HOTEL
R P B HOLDINGS LTD
(*Suby of* ROSEN FOUNDATION LTD)
3914 32 St, Vernon, BC, V1T 5P1
(250) 545-3755
Emp Here 124
SIC 7011 Hotels and motels
Heeson Domay

D-U-N-S 24-368-7431   (SL)
CHAPMAN MECHANICAL LTD
CHAPMAN FIRE PROTECTION A DIVISION OF
901 Waddington Dr, Vernon, BC, V1T 9E2
(250) 545-9040
Emp Here 70   *Sales* 16,314,550
SIC 1711 Plumbing, heating, air-conditioning
Mark Chapman
Dawn Chapman
Brad Chapman

D-U-N-S 20-117-7516   (HQ)
CORBETT OFFICE EQUIPMENT LTD
3306 30 Ave, Vernon, BC, V1T 2C8
(250) 549-2236
Emp Here 20   *Sales* 12,073,698
SIC 5044 Office equipment
Wayne Armbrust

D-U-N-S 24-289-4780   (HQ)
DCT CHAMBERS TRUCKING LTD
600 Waddington Dr, Vernon, BC, V1T 8T6
(250) 549-2157
Sales 17,485,010
SIC 4212 Local trucking, without storage
Arthur Chambers
David Chambers
Mona Chambers

D-U-N-S 25-670-4362   (BR)
DENCAN RESTAURANTS INC
DENNY'S RESTAURANT
(*Suby of* NORTHLAND PROPERTIES CORPORATION)
4201 32 St Suite 6501, Vernon, BC, V1T 5P3
(250) 542-0079
Emp Here 75
SIC 5812 Eating places
Shawna Predushewski

D-U-N-S 24-120-6549   (HQ)
DOWNTOWN REALTY LTD
ROYAL LEPAGE DOWNTOWN
4007 32 St, Vernon, BC, V1T 5P2
(250) 260-0453
Emp Here 49   *Sales* 27,227,785
SIC 6531 Real estate agents and managers
Raley Twyford
Paulette Web
Peter Nicolson
Mimi Stehle

D-U-N-S 20-609-6666   (SL)
FISHER, DEBBIE & LOCHHEAD, DAN
RE/MAX VERNON
5603 27 St, Vernon, BC, V1T 8Z5

(250) 549-4161
Emp Here 45   *Sales* 12,229,020
SIC 6531 Real estate agents and managers
Debbie Fisher

D-U-N-S 25-485-9705   (SL)
GATEBY CARE FACILITY
3000 Gateby Pl, Vernon, BC, V1T 8V8
(250) 545-4456
Emp Here 90   *Sales* 6,170,940
SIC 8051 Skilled nursing care facilities
Sue Gubbels

D-U-N-S 20-919-1139   (SL)
HILLTOP SALES & SERVICE LTD
HILLTOP SUBARU/VERNON HYUNDAI
4407 27 St, Vernon, BC, V1T 4Y5
(250) 542-2324
Emp Here 50   *Sales* 24,903,900
SIC 5511 New and used car dealers
Vaughn Wyant

D-U-N-S 24-344-7708   (BR)
HOME DEPOT OF CANADA INC
(*Suby of* THE HOME DEPOT INC)
5501 Anderson Way, Vernon, BC, V1T 9V1
(250) 550-1600
Emp Here 100
SIC 5251 Hardware stores
Sarah Qadeer

D-U-N-S 20-117-8472   (BR)
HUDSON'S BAY COMPANY
THE BAY
(*Suby of* HUDSON'S BAY COMPANY)
4900 27 St Suite 10, Vernon, BC, V1T 2C7
(250) 545-5331
Emp Here 130
SIC 5311 Department stores
Rein Nurmosoo

D-U-N-S 20-809-9692   (SL)
JUST REWARDS MANAGEMENT LTD
ALLAN FRANCIS & PRINGLE
3009 28 St Suite B, Vernon, BC, V1T 4Z7
(250) 542-1177
Emp Here 24   *Sales* 10,064,520
SIC 6712 Bank holding companies
Nick Vlahos

D-U-N-S 24-137-1095   (HQ)
KAL TIRE LTD
1540 Kalamalka Lake Rd, Vernon, BC, V1T 6V2
(250) 542-2366
Emp Here 300   *Sales* 1,178,248,470
SIC 5014 Tires and tubes
Robert Foord
Robert Kehler
John Mullin
Mark Bachelor
Robert Wallis
Kenneth Chaun
Keneth Finch
Mike Kreuger

D-U-N-S 25-273-1419   (BR)
LONDON DRUGS LIMITED
(*Suby of* H.Y. LOUIE CO. LIMITED)
4400 32 St Suite 700, Vernon, BC, V1T 9H2
(250) 549-1551
Emp Here 110
SIC 5912 Drug stores and proprietary stores
Lou Dugal

D-U-N-S 20-117-9108   (SL)
MONAHAN AGENCY LTD
2506 41 St, Vernon, BC, V1T 6J9
(250) 545-3235
Emp Here 30   *Sales* 22,275,600
SIC 5192 Books, periodicals, and newspapers
Thomas R. Monahan Jr

D-U-N-S 24-396-4231   (SL)
MQN INTERIORS LTD
3313 32 Ave Suite 100, Vernon, BC, V1T 2E1
(250) 542-1199
Emp Here 25   *Sales* 11,087,250

SIC 7389 Business services, nec
Dora Anderson
Brian Quiring
Vicki Topping

D-U-N-S 24-695-9571   (SL)
NIXON WENGER LLP
2706 30 Ave Suite 301, Vernon, BC, V1T 2B6
(250) 542-5353
Emp Here 80   *Sales* 8,870,560
SIC 8111 Legal services
Paul Nixon, Q.C.
Jonathan Jones
Gary Weatherill, Q.C.
Douglas Lemiski
Kent Burnham
Michael Yawney
Phil Dyck
Christopher Alveberg
James Cotter
William Dick

D-U-N-S 24-881-3750   (HQ)
PODOLLAN'S CONSTRUCTION LTD
2201 11 Ave Suite 205, Vernon, BC, V1T 8V7
(250) 545-7752
Emp Here 10   *Sales* 17,007,067
SIC 6512 Nonresidential building operators
David Podollan

D-U-N-S 25-833-0166   (BR)
SCHOOL DISTRICT NO 22 (VERNON)
W L SEATON SECONDARY SCHOOL
(*Suby of* SCHOOL DISTRICT NO 22 (VERNON))
2701 41 Ave, Vernon, BC, V1T 6X3
(250) 542-3361
Emp Here 75
SIC 8211 Elementary and secondary schools
Jackie Kersey

D-U-N-S 25-483-1266   (BR)
SCHOOL DISTRICT NO 22 (VERNON)
VERNON SECONDARY SCHOOL
(*Suby of* SCHOOL DISTRICT NO 22 (VERNON))
2303 18 St, Vernon, BC, V1T 3Z9
(250) 545-0701
Emp Here 100
SIC 8211 Elementary and secondary schools
Malcolm Reid

D-U-N-S 24-246-5003   (HQ)
SCHOOL DISTRICT NO 22 (VERNON)
OKANAGAN LANDING ELEMENTARY
1401 15 St, Vernon, BC, V1T 8S8
(250) 542-3331
Emp Here 50   *Sales* 123,898,750
SIC 8211 Elementary and secondary schools
Mary Jo O'keefe
Len Anderson
Shirley Spiller
Bill Turanski
Steve Connor
Mitzi Fortin

D-U-N-S 25-683-4318   (SL)
SERVICE QUALITY MEASUREMENT GROUP INC
SQM GROUP
3126 31 Ave Suite 301, Vernon, BC, V1T 2H1
(800) 446-2095
Emp Here 75   *Sales* 16,001,850
SIC 8732 Commercial nonphysical research
Mike Desmarais
Lisa Desmarais

D-U-N-S 25-215-3796   (BR)
SLEEMAN BREWERIES LTD
OKANAGAN SPRING BREWERY
(*Suby of* SAPPORO HOLDINGS LIMITED)
2808 27 Ave, Vernon, BC, V1T 9K4
(250) 542-2337
Emp Here 120
SIC 2082 Malt beverages
Michael Hertel

D-U-N-S 24-593-8683   (BR)

SOBEYS WEST INC
SAFEWAY LOCAL
(*Suby of* EMPIRE COMPANY LIMITED)
4300 32 St, Vernon, BC, V1T 9H1
(250) 542-2627
Emp Here 125
SIC 5411 Grocery stores
Sindhi Petrosky

D-U-N-S 24-837-9844   (SL)
TOLKO FOREST PRODUCTS LTD
(*Suby of* TIMBER INVESTMENTS LTD)
3000 28 St, Vernon, BC, V1T 9W9
(250) 545-4411
Emp Here 2,500   *Sales* 695,975,000
SIC 2421 Sawmills and planing mills, general
Brad Thorlakson
J. Allan Thorlakson
John Thorlakson
Trevor Jahnig
Tanya Wicks
Hardy Wentzel

D-U-N-S 24-776-6306   (HQ)
TOLKO INDUSTRIES LTD
HEFFLEY CREEK, DIV OF
(*Suby of* AMERICAN INDUSTRIAL ACQUISITION CORPORATION)
3000 28 St, Vernon, BC, V1T 1W1
(250) 545-4411
Emp Here 180   *Sales* 1,391,950,000
SIC 2421 Sawmills and planing mills, general
Brad Thorlakson
Mike Harkies
Trevor Jahnig
Jim Baskerville
Tanya Wick
Bob Fleet
Pino Pucci
James Allan Thorlakson
John Thorlakson
Norm Chow

D-U-N-S 20-548-8864   (HQ)
TOLKO MARKETING AND SALES LTD
TMS
(*Suby of* AMERICAN INDUSTRIAL ACQUISITION CORPORATION)
3000 28 St, Vernon, BC, V1T 9W9
(250) 545-4411
Sales 44,717,400
SIC 5031 Lumber, plywood, and millwork
Bradley Thorlakson
Pino Pucci
Trevor Jahnig

D-U-N-S 25-269-7412   (SL)
TRI STAR GAS MART (1992) LTD
TRI STAR GAS MART
3308 48 Ave, Vernon, BC, V1T 3R6
(250) 558-7800
Emp Here 200   *Sales* 125,856,000
SIC 5541 Gasoline service stations
Gary Vandekerkhove
Lynne Vandekerkhove

D-U-N-S 25-388-5875   (SL)
TURNER, GRANT C. T. ENTERPRISES INC
CANADIAN TIRE NO 361
Suite 345 4900 27 St, Vernon, BC, V1T 7G7
(250) 549-2131
Emp Here 40   *Sales* 10,122,360
SIC 5251 Hardware stores
Grant Turner

D-U-N-S 24-613-2609   (SL)
UPI GLASS INC
UNIVERSAL PACKAGING
(*Suby of* HIGHLAND ESTATES LTD)
1810 Kosmina Rd, Vernon, BC, V1T 8T2
(250) 549-1323
Emp Here 50   *Sales* 22,460,950
SIC 7389 Business services, nec
Steve Pelkey

D-U-N-S 24-898-8701   (HQ)
VALHALLA PURE OUTFITTERS INC

2700 30 Ave, Vernon, BC, V1T 2B6
(250) 542-9800
Emp Here 5   *Sales* 24,432,800
SIC 5941 Sporting goods and bicycle shops
David Harley

D-U-N-S 24-558-6339   (SL)
VANTAGEONE FINANCIAL CORP
3108 33 Ave, Vernon, BC, V1T 2N7
(250) 260-4513
Emp Here 49   *Sales* 13,316,044
SIC 6531 Real estate agents and managers
Devin Lukens

D-U-N-S 25-670-4966   (SL)
VERNON CHRYSLER DODGE LTD
VERNON DODGE JEEP
4607 27 St, Vernon, BC, V1T 4Y8
(250) 545-2261
Emp Here 43   *Sales* 21,417,354
SIC 5511 New and used car dealers
Brian Johnston
James David Mcmanes

D-U-N-S 25-603-9272   (SL)
VERNON INSURANCE SERVICES INC
3118 32 Ave, Vernon, BC, V1T 2L9
(250) 549-3074
Emp Here 23   *Sales* 19,505,380
SIC 6411 Insurance agents, brokers, and service
Donalda Marshall

D-U-N-S 20-719-9592   (BR)
WAL-MART CANADA CORP
WALMART
(*Suby of* WALMART INC.)
2200 58 Ave Suite 3169, Vernon, BC, V1T 9T2
(250) 558-0425
Emp Here 100
SIC 5311 Department stores
John Binn

D-U-N-S 20-119-4151   (SL)
WATKIN MOTORS PARTNERSHIP
MARJAK LEASING
4602 27 St, Vernon, BC, V1T 4Y6
(250) 260-3411
Emp Here 65   *Sales* 40,903,200
SIC 5511 New and used car dealers
Bruce Blankley
Ross Blankley

D-U-N-S 24-397-8330   (HQ)
WESTWOOD ELECTRIC LTD
WESTWOOD INDUSTRIAL ELECTRIC
887 Fairweather Rd, Vernon, BC, V1T 8T8
(250) 542-5481
Emp Here 10   *Sales* 11,562,432
SIC 1623 Water, sewer, and utility lines
Darryl Chekerda
Jason Mccormick
Mark Zaino
Jason Mccormick

Victoria, BC V8N

D-U-N-S 20-041-9005   (BR)
BOARD OF EDUCATION OF SCHOOL DISTRICT NO. 61 (GREATER VICTORIA)
MOUNT DOUGLAS SECONDARY SCHOOL
(*Suby of* BOARD OF EDUCATION OF SCHOOL DISTRICT NO. 61 (GREATER VICTORIA))
3970 Gordon Head Rd, Victoria, BC, V8N 3X3
(250) 477-6977
Emp Here 100
SIC 8211 Elementary and secondary schools
Shawn Boulding

D-U-N-S 25-959-2350   (SL)
CENTURY 21 QUEENSWOOD REALTY LTD
2558 Sinclair Rd, Victoria, BC, V8N 1B8
(250) 477-1100
Emp Here 45   *Sales* 14,720,715

SIC 6531 Real estate agents and managers
Chris Markham

D-U-N-S 20-697-7667   (BR)
HOME DEPOT OF CANADA INC
HOME DEPOT
(*Suby of* THE HOME DEPOT INC)
3986 Shelbourne St, Victoria, BC, V8N 3E3
(250) 853-5350
Emp Here 80
SIC 5251 Hardware stores
Carl Eaton

D-U-N-S 20-119-4065   (SL)
O & P SUPERMARKETS LTD
PEPPERS FOOD STORE
3829 Cadboro Bay Rd, Victoria, BC, V8N 4G1
(250) 477-6513
Emp Here 55   *Sales* 16,141,235
SIC 5411 Grocery stores
John Davits

D-U-N-S 20-073-9642   (BR)
**VANCOUVER ISLAND HEALTH AUTHOR-
ITY**
*QUEEN ALEXANDRA CENTRE FOR CHIL-
DREN*
(*Suby of* GOVERNMENT OF THE
PROVINCE OF BRITISH COLUMBIA)
2400 Arbutus Rd, Victoria, BC, V8N 1V7
(250) 519-5390
Emp Here 400
SIC 8011 Offices and clinics of medical doc-
tors
Schactman Chuck

D-U-N-S 25-025-3283   (SL)
WEAVER, J & D HOLDINGS LTD
CANADIAN TIRE
3993 Cedar Hill Rd, Victoria, BC, V8N 4M9
(250) 721-1125
Emp Here 50   *Sales* 24,903,900
SIC 5531 Auto and home supply stores
John Weaver

Victoria, BC V8P

D-U-N-S 20-033-7116   (BR)
**BOARD OF EDUCATION OF SCHOOL DIS-
TRICT NO. 61 (GREATER VICTORIA)**
REYNOLDS SECONDARY
(*Suby of* BOARD OF EDUCATION OF
SCHOOL DISTRICT NO. 61 (GREATER VIC-
TORIA))
3963 Borden St, Victoria, BC, V8P 3H9
(250) 479-1696
Emp Here 100
SIC 8211 Elementary and secondary schools
Allana Charleston

D-U-N-S 20-912-2084   (HQ)
CAMOSUN COLLEGE
3100 Foul Bay Rd, Victoria, BC, V8P 5J2
(250) 370-3550
Sales 176,281,380
SIC 8221 Colleges and universities
Peter Baillie
Elizabeth Ashton
Ann Moskow
Louise Oetting
John Overall
David Reagan
Maureen Duncan
Alan Danesh
Stacy Kuiack
Tracey Kalimeris

D-U-N-S 24-930-4759   (SL)
CANAWAY HOLDINGS LTD
FAIRWAY MARKET #4
(*Suby of* FAIRWAY HOLDINGS (1994) LTD)
3651 Shelbourne St Suite 4, Victoria, BC, V8P
4H1
(250) 477-2218
Emp Here 60   *Sales* 17,608,620

SIC 5411 Grocery stores
Don Yuen
Robert Jay

D-U-N-S 25-092-0712   (SL)
CENTRE FOR GLOBAL STUDIES, THE
CFG
3800 Finnerty Rd Suite 3800, Victoria, BC,
V8P 5C2
(250) 472-4990
Emp Here 30   *Sales* 11,922,420
SIC 8699 Membership organizations, nec
Christopher Yeomans

D-U-N-S 24-069-1626   (HQ)
DFH REAL ESTATE LTD
3914 Shelbourne St, Victoria, BC, V8P 4J1
(250) 477-7291
Emp Here 11   *Sales* 37,700,010
SIC 6531 Real estate agents and managers
Megan John

D-U-N-S 24-245-2266   (SL)
LUTHER COURT SOCIETY
1525 Cedar Hill Cross Rd, Victoria, BC, V8P
5M1
(250) 477-7241
Emp Here 80   *Sales* 5,485,280
SIC 8051 Skilled nursing care facilities
Karen Johnson-Lessrud

D-U-N-S 24-457-8472   (HQ)
MEGSON FITZPATRICK INC
3561 Shelbourne St, Victoria, BC, V8P 4G8
(250) 595-5212
Emp Here 72   *Sales* 151,514,844
SIC 6411 Insurance agents, brokers, and ser-
vice
David Fitzpatrick
Michael Megson

D-U-N-S 25-965-7518   (BR)
RECREATION OAK BAY
HENDERSON CENTRE
2291 Cedar Hill Cross Rd, Victoria, BC, V8P
5H9
(250) 370-7200
Emp Here 100
SIC 7999 Amusement and recreation, nec
Ronanne Mcconnchie

D-U-N-S 24-715-6503   (HQ)
REVENUEWIRE INC
3962 Borden St Suite 102, Victoria, BC, V8P
3H8
(250) 590-2273
Sales 15,397,200
SIC 6099 Functions related to deposit banking
Bobbi Leach
Sue Connors
Trevor Wingert
William Ng
Kim Krenzler
Laura Callow

D-U-N-S 20-801-7319   (HQ)
**ST. MICHAELS UNIVERSITY SCHOOL SO-
CIETY**
SMUS
3400 Richmond Rd, Victoria, BC, V8P 4P5
(250) 592-2411
Emp Here 155   *Sales* 26,927,083
SIC 8211 Elementary and secondary schools
David Angus
Tom Rigos
Robert Snowden

D-U-N-S 20-956-7957   (HQ)
UNIVERSITY OF VICTORIA
ADVANCEMENT SERVICES
3800 Finnerty Rd, Victoria, BC, V8P 5C2
(250) 721-7211
Sales 548,563,752
SIC 8221 Colleges and universities
Jamie L Cassels
Jack Falk
Gayle Gorrill
Valerie Kuehne

Gayle Gorrill
David Castle

D-U-N-S 20-296-0790   (BR)
UNIVERSITY OF VICTORIA
DIVISION OF CONTINUING STUDIES
(*Suby of* UNIVERSITY OF VICTORIA)
3800a Finnerty Rd Suite 168, Victoria, BC,
V8P 5C2
(250) 721-6673
Emp Here 130
SIC 8221 Colleges and universities
Wayne Brunsdon

D-U-N-S 20-351-4872   (SL)
**UNIVERSITY OF VICTORIA STUDENTS'
SOCIETY**
3800 Finnerty Rd Rm B128, Victoria, BC, V8P
5C2
(250) 472-4317
Emp Here 200   *Sales* 41,413,600
SIC 8399 Social services, nec
Dale Robertson
Erin Ewart
Noor Chasib
Mackenzie Cumberland
Kaitlin Fortier
Pierre-Paul Angelblazer
Anmol Swaich
Nicholas Chen
Karina Dhillon
Christopher Dickey

D-U-N-S 25-825-8763   (SL)
VICTORIA FUJIYA FOODS LTD
3624 Shelbourne St, Victoria, BC, V8P 4H2
(250) 598-3711
Emp Here 40   *Sales* 10,966,080
SIC 5411 Grocery stores
Koji Hayashi

Victoria, BC V8R

D-U-N-S 20-555-1885   (HQ)
BLACK PRESS GROUP LTD
CARIBOO PRESS
(*Suby of* BLACK PRESS HOLDINGS LTD)
3175 Beach Dr, Victoria, BC, V8R 6L7
(250) 480-3220
Emp Here 120   *Sales* 297,636,864
SIC 2711 Newspapers
David Black

D-U-N-S 24-369-2928   (HQ)
DEVON PROPERTIES LTD
2067 Cadboro Bay Rd Suite 201, Victoria, BC,
V8R 5G4
(250) 595-7000
Sales 22,087,100
SIC 6513 Apartment building operators
David Craig
Reed Kipp

D-U-N-S 25-069-6366   (SL)
MAYFAIR VILLAGE FOODS
FAIRWAY MARKET NO.6
2187 Oak Bay Ave Unit 101, Victoria, BC, V8R
1G1
(250) 592-8911
Emp Here 50   *Sales* 13,707,600
SIC 5411 Grocery stores
Don Yuen

D-U-N-S 25-362-4035   (BR)
**PROVINCIAL HEALTH SERVICES AUTHOR-
ITY**
*BC CANCER, PART OF THE PROVINCIAL
HEALTH SERVICES AUTHORITY*
(*Suby of* PROVINCIAL HEALTH SERVICES
AUTHORITY)
2410 Lee Ave, Victoria, BC, V8R 6V5
(250) 519-5500
Emp Here 100
SIC 8399 Social services, nec
Anne Burgess

D-U-N-S 20-652-3792   (SL)
ROYAL JUBILEE HOSPITAL AUXILIARY
1952 Bay St, Victoria, BC, V8R 1J8
(250) 370-8496
Emp Here 50   *Sales* 11,895,050
SIC 8742 Management consulting services
Marilyn Webb
Marion Gray
Dianne Roy
Darlene Macdonald

D-U-N-S 24-136-3670   (SL)
UPLANDS MOTORING COMPANY LTD
LANSDOWNE AUTO SERVICE CENTRE
3095 Shelbourne St, Victoria, BC, V8R 4M9
(250) 592-2444
Emp Here 22   *Sales* 10,957,716
SIC 5541 Gasoline service stations
Gary Bryant
Marsha Fric

D-U-N-S 25-082-9553   (HQ)
**VANCOUVER ISLAND HEALTH AUTHOR-
ITY**
ISLAND HEALTH
(*Suby of* GOVERNMENT OF THE
PROVINCE OF BRITISH COLUMBIA)
1952 Bay St, Victoria, BC, V8R 1J8
(250) 519-7700
Emp Here 500   *Sales* 1,931,050,400
SIC 8011 Offices and clinics of medical doc-
tors
Brendan Carr
Catherine Claiter-Larsen
Jeremy Etherington
Kim Kerrone
Catherine Mackay
Kathy Macneil
James Hanson
Toni O'keeffe

D-U-N-S 25-072-6585   (SL)
VICTORIA HOSPICE SOCIETY
1952 Bay St, Victoria, BC, V8R 1J8
(250) 370-8715
Emp Here 80   *Sales* 5,485,280
SIC 8051 Skilled nursing care facilities
Wayne Peterson
Roderick Braithwaite
Fraser Black

Victoria, BC V8S

D-U-N-S 24-989-3186   (BR)
BAYSHORE HEALTHCARE LTD.
BAYSHORE HEALTHCARE LTD
(*Suby of* BAYSHORE HEALTHCARE LTD.)
1512 Fort St, Victoria, BC, V8S 5J2
(250) 370-2253
Emp Here 75
SIC 8082 Home health care services
Stasia Hartley

D-U-N-S 24-694-3427   (HQ)
GLENLYON-NORFOLK SCHOOL SOCIETY
801 Bank St, Victoria, BC, V8S 4A8
(250) 370-6801
Emp Here 128   *Sales* 14,867,850
SIC 8211 Elementary and secondary schools
Christopher Denford
Glenn Zederayko

D-U-N-S 20-310-2426   (SL)
OAK BAY BEACH HOTEL LIMITED
SNUG PUB
1175 Beach Dr, Victoria, BC, V8S 2N2
(250) 598-4556
Emp Here 100   *Sales* 9,489,900
SIC 7011 Hotels and motels
Kevin Walker
Michelle Le Sage

D-U-N-S 20-119-4180   (HQ)
OAK BAY MARINA LTD

▲ Public Company   ■ Public Company Family Member   **HQ** Headquarters   **BR** Branch   **SL** Single Location

APRIL POINT LODGE
(Suby of OAK BAY HOLDINGS LTD)
1327 Beach Dr, Victoria, BC, V8S 2N4
(250) 370-6509
Emp Here 80   *Sales* 86,840,250
SIC 4493 Marinas
Robert Wright
Graeme Bryson
Lana Denoni

D-U-N-S 20-866-3229   (SL)
VICTORIA GOLF CLUB
1110 Beach Dr, Victoria, BC, V8S 2M9
(250) 598-4224
Emp Here 90   *Sales* 7,069,050
SIC 7997 Membership sports and recreation
clubs
Scott Kolb
Susan Klemola

Victoria, BC V8T

D-U-N-S 24-317-6349   (SL)
0743398 B.C. LTD
STEEL PACIFIC RECYCLING
307 David St, Victoria, BC, V8T 5C1
(250) 381-5865
Emp Here 50   *Sales* 83,613,500
SIC 7389 Business services, nec
Brian Begert
Andrew Ketch

D-U-N-S 20-391-5124   (SL)
0859291 B.C. LTD
CHEK
780 Kings Rd, Victoria, BC, V8T 5A2
(250) 480-3732
Emp Here 100   *Sales* 18,479,800
SIC 4833 Television broadcasting stations
Rob Jermaine

D-U-N-S 24-359-2560   (SL)
1712318 ONTARIO LIMITED
THREE POINT MOTORS
2546 Government St, Victoria, BC, V8T 4P7
(250) 385-1408
Emp Here 34   *Sales* 16,934,652
SIC 5511 New and used car dealers
Sylvester Chuang
Peter Trzewik

D-U-N-S 25-505-6756   (SL)
260304 BC LTD
PAYNES MARINE
2120 Quadra St, Victoria, BC, V8T 4C5
(250) 382-7722
Emp Here 30   *Sales* 14,250,780
SIC 5088 Transportation equipment and supplies
John Simson

D-U-N-S 20-176-4714   (HQ)
443696 B.C. LTD
MEDICHAIR VICTORIA
1856 Quadra St, Victoria, BC, V8T 4B9
(250) 384-8000
Emp Here 23   *Sales* 11,179,350
SIC 5047 Medical and hospital equipment
Paul Fogh-Dohmsmidt
Ronald Nagel
Dan Webb
Jane Fogh-Dohmsmidt

D-U-N-S 20-118-0866   (SL)
ACME SUPPLIES LTD
(Suby of BUNZL PUBLIC LIMITED COM-
PANY)
2311 Government St, Victoria, BC, V8T 4P4
(250) 383-8822
Emp Here 38   *Sales* 18,050,988
SIC 5087 Service establishment equipment
Richard Impett
Robin Impett

D-U-N-S 24-326-3964   (BR)
AGROPUR COOPERATIVE
ISLAND FARMS
(Suby of AGROPUR COOPERATIVE)
2220 Dowler Pl, Victoria, BC, V8T 4H3
(250) 360-5200
Emp Here 300
SIC 5143 Dairy products, except dried or
canned
Art Paulo

D-U-N-S 20-292-4895   (HQ)
BAMBORA INC
2659 Douglas St Suite 302, Victoria, BC, V8T
4M3
(250) 472-2326
Sales 13,716,600
SIC 8741 Management services
Johan Tjarnberg
Ryan Stewart
Tor Patrik Gothlin

D-U-N-S 25-096-8039   (SL)
BC PENSION CORPORATION
MUNICIPAL PENSION PLAN
(Suby of GOVERNMENT OF THE
PROVINCE OF BRITISH COLUMBIA)
2995 Jutland Rd, Victoria, BC, V8T 5J9
(250) 356-8548
Emp Here 400   *Sales* 49,611,412
SIC 6371 Pension, health, and welfare funds
Laura Nashman
Wayne Jefferson
Weldon Cowan
Carl Fischer
Dale Lauber
John Mazure
Mary Procter
David Vipond
Gary Yee

D-U-N-S 25-149-5750   (HQ)
BCIMC REALTY CORPORATION
2950 Jutland Rd Unit 300, Victoria, BC, V8T
5K2
(778) 410-7100
Sales 304,257,600
SIC 6531 Real estate agents and managers
Gordon Fyfe
Dean Atkins
David Woodward
Steve Barnett

D-U-N-S 24-310-7539   (SL)
BELFRY THEATRE SOCIETY, THE
BELFRY ARTS CENTRE
1291 Gladstone Ave, Victoria, BC, V8T 1G5
(250) 385-6815
Emp Here 70   *Sales* 10,595,830
SIC 7922 Theatrical producers and services
Patrick Stewart
Mary Desprez

D-U-N-S 20-118-2458   (SL)
BLUE BIRD CABS LTD
2612 Quadra St, Victoria, BC, V8T 4E4
(250) 382-2222
Emp Here 220   *Sales* 16,559,840
SIC 4121 Taxicabs
Kenny Hundal

D-U-N-S 25-486-2360   (BR)
**BOARD OF EDUCATION OF SCHOOL DIS-
TRICT NO. 61 (GREATER VICTORIA)**
VICTORIA HIGH SCHOOL
(Suby of BOARD OF EDUCATION OF
SCHOOL DISTRICT NO. 61 (GREATER VIC-
TORIA))
1260 Grant St, Victoria, BC, V8T 1C2
(250) 388-5456
Emp Here 75
SIC 8211 Elementary and secondary schools
Steven Benette

D-U-N-S 25-532-4667   (HQ)
CAPITAL IRON (1997) LTD
1900 Store St, Victoria, BC, V8T 4R4

(250) 385-9703
Emp Here 70   *Sales* 20,073,900
SIC 5251 Hardware stores
Michael Black

D-U-N-S 20-774-7424   (SL)
CENTRAL VICTORIA SECURITY LTD
SECURITY GROUP
612 Garbally Rd, Victoria, BC, V8T 2K2

Emp Here 40   *Sales* 16,093,313
SIC 7381 Detective and armored car services
Grant Breiland

D-U-N-S 20-118-4272   (SL)
CHEW EXCAVATING LTD
575 Gorge Rd E, Victoria, BC, V8T 2W5
(250) 386-7586
Emp Here 100   *Sales* 24,618,600
SIC 1794 Excavation work
Bruce Dyck
John Heraghty
Kim Johson
Shirley Chew

D-U-N-S 24-447-1215   (HQ)
COAST CLAIM SERVICE LTD
2727 Quadra St Suite 6, Victoria, BC, V8T 4E5
(250) 386-3111
Emp Here 9   *Sales* 27,985,980
SIC 6411 Insurance agents, brokers, and ser-
vice
John D Prissick

D-U-N-S 20-551-1590   (HQ)
COLUMBIA ENERGY INC
2659 Douglas St Suite 200, Victoria, BC, V8T
4M3
(250) 474-3533
Sales 31,058,570
SIC 4924 Natural gas distribution
Jim Smith
Bruce Nagel

D-U-N-S 20-653-4260   (HQ)
CRIDGE CENTRE FOR THE FAMILY, THE
1307 Hillside Ave Suite 414, Victoria, BC, V8T
0A2
(250) 384-8058
Emp Here 75   *Sales* 9,599,000
SIC 8322 Individual and family services
David Rand
Mary-Ethel Audrey
Mike Kridge
Shelley Morris
Rosemary Smith

D-U-N-S 24-137-4487   (HQ)
DODD'S FURNITURE LTD
715 Finlayson St, Victoria, BC, V8T 2T4
(250) 388-6663
Emp Here 25   *Sales* 17,662,628
SIC 5712 Furniture stores
Gurdial Dodd

D-U-N-S 20-236-2005   (HQ)
**FIRST ISLAND ARMOURED TRANSPORT
(1998) LTD**
DVA SECURITY GROUP
612 Garbally Rd, Victoria, BC, V8T 2K2
(250) 920-7114
Emp Here 1   *Sales* 11,870,340
SIC 7381 Detective and armored car services
Grant Breiland
Murray Marchak

D-U-N-S 24-340-1325   (BR)
GLACIER MEDIA INC
TIMES COLONIST
(Suby of GLACIER MEDIA INC)
2621 Douglas St, Victoria, BC, V8T 4M2
(250) 380-5211
Emp Here 300
SIC 2711 Newspapers
Peter Baillie

D-U-N-S 20-700-8280   (HQ)
GSL FAMILY TRUST

780 Topaz Ave, Victoria, BC, V8T 2M1
(250) 384-3003
Sales 10,628,478
SIC 5211 Lumber and other building materials
George Joseph Linger
Suzette Marie Linger

D-U-N-S 24-531-1837   (SL)
HAZMASTERS ENVIRONMENTAL INC
575 Hillside Ave, Victoria, BC, V8T 1Y8
(250) 384-0025
Emp Here 30   *Sales* 15,616,260
SIC 5099 Durable goods, nec
Dan Nickel

D-U-N-S 20-048-0726   (HQ)
HEALTH VENTURES LTD
LIFESTYLE MARKETS
2950 Douglas St Suite 180, Victoria, BC, V8T
4N4
(250) 384-3388
Sales 12,885,144
SIC 5499 Miscellaneous food stores
Carmine Sparanese

D-U-N-S 25-266-6987   (SL)
HOME AND COMMUNITY CARE ACCESS
1947 Cook St, Victoria, BC, V8T 3P7
(250) 388-2273
Emp Here 49   *Sales* 11,480,112
SIC 8742 Management consulting services
Penny Martin

D-U-N-S 24-071-9559   (HQ)
**ILLUMINATIONS LIGHTING SOLUTIONS
LTD**
2885 Quesnel St, Victoria, BC, V8T 4K2
(250) 382-5483
Emp Here 1   *Sales* 11,179,350
SIC 5063 Electrical apparatus and equipment
Robert Macritchie
Wendy Macritchie

D-U-N-S 25-315-5303   (BR)
**INSURANCE CORPORATION OF BRITISH
COLUMBIA**
ICBC
(Suby of GOVERNMENT OF THE
PROVINCE OF BRITISH COLUMBIA)
425 Dunedin St, Victoria, BC, V8T 5H7
(250) 480-5600
Emp Here 80
SIC 6331 Fire, marine, and casualty insurance
John Story

D-U-N-S 20-058-6068   (HQ)
MAXIMUM EXPRESS & FREIGHT LTD
576 Hillside Ave Unit 3, Victoria, BC, V8T 1Y9
(250) 721-5170
Emp Here 21   *Sales* 12,417,720
SIC 7389 Business services, nec
Al Hasham
Harmesh Chumber

D-U-N-S 25-969-5153   (SL)
MCDONALD'S RESTAURANTS LTD
1644 Hillside Ave, Victoria, BC, V8T 2C5

Emp Here 100   *Sales* 4,551,900
SIC 5812 Eating places
Ryan Jagt

D-U-N-S 24-594-8328   (HQ)
NATIONAL MONEY MART COMPANY
MONEY MART
(Suby of DFC GLOBAL CORP.)
401 Garbally Rd, Victoria, BC, V8T 5M3
(250) 595-5211
Emp Here 300   *Sales* 282,580,980
SIC 6099 Functions related to deposit banking
Melanie Latoski

D-U-N-S 24-329-1812   (SL)
**OAK BAY KIWANIS HEALTH CARE SOCI-
ETY**
KIWANIS PAVILLION, THE
3034 Cedar Hill Rd, Victoria, BC, V8T 3J3

(250) 598-2022
Emp Here 140   *Sales* 26,628,980
SIC 8011 Offices and clinics of medical doctors
Derek Rennie
Stephen Gorman
Gary Weir

D-U-N-S 24-362-5022   (HQ)
PHOENIX HUMAN SERVICES ASSOCIATION
1824 Store St, Victoria, BC, V8T 4R4
(250) 383-4821
Emp Here 100   *Sales* 6,813,892
SIC 8361 Residential care
George Klukowski

D-U-N-S 24-134-1700   (BR)
POSTMEDIA NETWORK INC
CH TELEVISION
(*Suby of* POSTMEDIA NETWORK CANADA CORP)
780 Kings Rd, Victoria, BC, V8T 5A2
(250) 383-2435
Emp Here 110
SIC 4833 Television broadcasting stations
Ron Eberle

D-U-N-S 24-593-5267   (SL)
S G POWER PRODUCTS LTD
S G POWER
730 Hillside Ave, Victoria, BC, V8T 1Z4
(250) 382-8291
Emp Here 30   *Sales* 14,942,340
SIC 5551 Boat dealers
Bernard Simpson

D-U-N-S 20-192-7907   (HQ)
SHERET, ANDREW HOLDINGS LIMITED
721 Kings Rd, Victoria, BC, V8T 1W4
(250) 386-7744
Emp Here 20   *Sales* 96,609,240
SIC 5074 Plumbing and heating equipment and supplies (hydronics)
Brian Findlay
Ed Pratt
Eric Findlay

D-U-N-S 20-119-7209   (HQ)
SHERET, ANDREW LIMITED
SPLASHES BATH & KITCHEN CENTRE, A DIV OF
(*Suby of* SHERET, ANDREW HOLDINGS LIMITED)
740 Hillside Ave Suite 401, Victoria, BC, V8T 1Z4
(250) 386-7744
Emp Here 25   *Sales* 115,011,000
SIC 5074 Plumbing and heating equipment and supplies (hydronics)
Brian Findlay
David R. Broad
George Hill

D-U-N-S 24-798-0621   (SL)
SOLBAKKEN AND ASSOCIATES
990 Hillside Ave Suite 201, Victoria, BC, V8T 2A1
(250) 590-5211
Emp Here 49   *Sales* 10,245,165
SIC 8721 Accounting, auditing, and bookkeeping
Erik Solbakken

D-U-N-S 24-455-2139   (SL)
STM SPORTS TRADE MALL LTD
SPORTS TRADERS - VICTORIA
508 Discovery St, Victoria, BC, V8T 1G8
(250) 383-6443
Emp Here 40   *Sales* 10,880,650
SIC 5941 Sporting goods and bicycle shops
Al Mellett
Terrance R. Mellett

D-U-N-S 25-819-9470   (SL)
TRADERS INTERNATIONAL FRANCHISE MANAGEMENT INC
508 Discovery St, Victoria, BC, V8T 1G8

Emp Here 40   *Sales* 15,660,080
SIC 6794 Patent owners and lessors
Al Mellett

D-U-N-S 24-136-6327   (HQ)
VAN'ISLE WINDOWS LTD
404 Hillside Ave, Victoria, BC, V8T 1Y7
(250) 383-7128
Emp Here 38   *Sales* 10,122,360
SIC 5211 Lumber and other building materials
Richard Niblock
Wing Li

D-U-N-S 20-994-2523   (SL)
ZOMEL HOLDINGS LTD
HONDA CITY
506 Finlayson St, Victoria, BC, V8T 5C8
(250) 388-6921
Emp Here 56   *Sales* 35,239,680
SIC 5511 New and used car dealers
Dick Graham

Victoria, BC V8V

D-U-N-S 25-624-0214   (SL)
AUDI AUTOHAUS
1101 Yates St, Victoria, BC, V8V 3N1
(250) 590-5849
Emp Here 23   *Sales* 11,455,794
SIC 5511 New and used car dealers
Carl Munroe

D-U-N-S 25-485-9382   (BR)
BAPTIST HOUSING MINISTRIES SOCIETY, THE
MOUNT EDWARDS COURT CARE HOME
(*Suby of* BAPTIST HOUSING MINISTRIES SOCIETY, THE)
1002 Vancouver St Suite 112, Victoria, BC, V8V 3V8
(250) 384-1313
Emp Here 80
SIC 8361 Residential care
Carol Larsen

D-U-N-S 20-651-5392   (SL)
BECKLEY FARM LODGE FOUNDATION
BECKLEY FARM LODGE SOCIETY
530 Simcoe St, Victoria, BC, V8V 4W4
(250) 381-4421
Emp Here 85   *Sales* 5,828,110
SIC 8051 Skilled nursing care facilities
Melanie Henning

D-U-N-S 20-130-7613   (SL)
CLACE HOLDINGS LTD
MARKET ON YATES, THE
903 Yates St, Victoria, BC, V8V 3M4
(250) 381-6000
Emp Here 100   *Sales* 29,347,700
SIC 5411 Grocery stores
Ernie Skinner
Carol Anne Skinner

D-U-N-S 24-518-8391   (SL)
CVS CRUISE VICTORIA LTD
CVS SIGHT SEEING
185 Dallas Rd, Victoria, BC, V8V 1A1
(250) 386-8652
Emp Here 35   *Sales* 13,487,600
SIC 4725 Tour operators
Gary Gale

D-U-N-S 20-118-5543   (HQ)
DANIELS ELECTRONICS LTD
CODAN RADIO COMMUNICATIONS
(*Suby of* CODAN LIMITED)
43 Erie St, Victoria, BC, V8V 1P8
(250) 382-8268
Sales 13,330,940
SIC 3669 Communications equipment, nec
Robert Small

D-U-N-S 25-532-2760   (HQ)

DEVELUS SYSTEMS INC
PROCURA
1112 Fort St Suite 600, Victoria, BC, V8V 3K8
(250) 388-0880
Emp Here 45   *Sales* 12,976,380
SIC 7371 Custom computer programming services

D-U-N-S 24-319-5547   (SL)
ENSIGN CHRYSLER DODGE JEEP LTD
1061 Yates St, Victoria, BC, V8V 3M5
(250) 386-2981
Emp Here 40   *Sales* 19,923,120
SIC 5511 New and used car dealers
Peter Kulyk
E.A. Knight
Kevin Knight

D-U-N-S 24-838-9629   (SL)
F.A.S. SEAFOOD PRODUCERS LTD
27 Erie St, Victoria, BC, V8V 1P8
(250) 383-7764
Emp Here 50   *Sales* 10,580,650
SIC 0912 Finfish
Robert Fraumeni

D-U-N-S 24-387-2103   (SL)
FINEST AT SEA OCEAN PRODUCTS LIMITED
27 Erie St, Victoria, BC, V8V 1P8
(250) 383-7760
Emp Here 125   *Sales* 43,211,250
SIC 2092 Fresh or frozen packaged fish
Bob Fraumeni

D-U-N-S 24-292-8273   (SL)
FRIENDSHIP DEVELOPMENTS LTD
HUNTINGDON HOTEL & SUITES
330 Quebec St, Victoria, BC, V8V 1W3
(250) 381-3456
Emp Here 75   *Sales* 7,117,425
SIC 7011 Hotels and motels
Rita Roy

D-U-N-S 25-235-3586   (BR)
HARBOUR TOWERS LIMITED PARTNERSHIP
HARBOUR TOWERS HOTEL AND SUITES
345 Quebec St, Victoria, BC, V8V 1W4
(250) 385-2405
Emp Here 100
SIC 7011 Hotels and motels
Tracey Sims

D-U-N-S 24-457-6740   (SL)
LUM & SON FINE FOODS LTD
WELLBURN'S FINE FOODS
1058 Pandora Ave, Victoria, BC, V8V 3P5
(250) 384-3543
Emp Here 40   *Sales* 10,966,080
SIC 5411 Grocery stores
Victor Lum
Ed Lum
Lee Lum

D-U-N-S 24-368-1798   (SL)
MARIE ESTHER SOCIETY, THE
MOUNT ST MARY HOSPITAL
861 Fairfield Rd Suite 317, Victoria, BC, V8V 5A9
(250) 480-3100
Emp Here 200   *Sales* 22,216,000
SIC 8069 Specialty hospitals, except psychiatric
Colleen Black

D-U-N-S 24-996-6615   (SL)
NEWPORT REALTY LTD
1144 Fort St, Victoria, BC, V8V 3K8
(250) 385-2033
Emp Here 65   *Sales* 17,664,140
SIC 6531 Real estate agents and managers
John Hayes
Jack Petrie

D-U-N-S 25-982-2182   (SL)
OMBUDSPERSON OF B C
947 Fort St, Victoria, BC, V8V 3K3

(250) 387-5855
Emp Here 60   *Sales* 40,134,480
SIC 7389 Business services, nec
Jay Chalke

D-U-N-S 20-011-7369   (BR)
P SUN'S ENTERPRISES (VANCOUVER) LTD
HOTEL GRAND PACIFIC
(*Suby of* P SUN'S ENTERPRISES (VANCOUVER) LTD)
463 Belleville St, Victoria, BC, V8V 1X3
(250) 386-0450
Emp Here 180
SIC 7011 Hotels and motels
Reid James

D-U-N-S 20-146-6146   (SL)
PACIFIC MOTOR SALES AND SERVICE LTD
PACIFIC MAZDA
1060 Yates St, Victoria, BC, V8V 3M6
(250) 385-5747
Emp Here 30   *Sales* 14,942,340
SIC 5511 New and used car dealers
Michail Stevulak

D-U-N-S 25-907-7220   (BR)
PAUL'S RESTAURANTS LTD
LAUREL POINT INN
(*Suby of* PAUL'S RESTAURANTS LTD)
680 Montreal St, Victoria, BC, V8V 1Z8
(250) 412-3194
Emp Here 200
SIC 7011 Hotels and motels
Scott Hoadley

D-U-N-S 24-761-8754   (HQ)
PRT GROWING SERVICES LTD
1006 Fort St Unit 101, Victoria, BC, V8V 3K4
(250) 381-1404
Emp Here 280   *Sales* 194,954,000
SIC 2068 Salted and roasted nuts and seeds
Robert A. Miller
Owen Davies
Herb Markgraf
Rob Maxwell

D-U-N-S 25-147-4938   (HQ)
ROBINS PARKING SERVICES LTD
U-PARK ENTERPRISES
1102 Fort St Suite 196, Victoria, BC, V8V 3K8
(250) 382-4411
Emp Here 12   *Sales* 16,002,090
SIC 1799 Special trade contractors, nec
Dan Sawchuk
Debra Anney

D-U-N-S 25-994-1417   (SL)
S & V PLANNING CORPORATION
968 Meares St, Victoria, BC, V8V 3J4
(250) 388-6774
Emp Here 20   *Sales* 14,508,780
SIC 6311 Life insurance
Dennis Smith

D-U-N-S 24-569-9579   (SL)
VICTORIA FIREFIGHTERS SOCIETY
1234 Yates St, Victoria, BC, V8V 3M8
(250) 384-1122
Emp Here 45   *Sales* 10,743,750
SIC 8611 Business associations
Mike Beaulac

D-U-N-S 25-153-7650   (SL)
VICTORIA FIREMAN'S MUTUAL BENEFIT SOCIETY
1234 Yates St, Victoria, BC, V8V 3M8

Emp Here 49   *Sales* 11,012,456
SIC 6141 Personal credit institutions
Robert Marshall

D-U-N-S 25-903-5061   (HQ)
WCG INTERNATIONAL CONSULTANTS LTD
(*Suby of* PROVIDENCE SERVICE CORPORATION)
915 Fort St, Victoria, BC, V8V 3K3

▲ Public Company   ■ Public Company Family Member   **HQ** Headquarters   **BR** Branch   **SL** Single Location

(250) 389-0699
Emp Here 20   *Sales* 12,697,980
SIC 7361 Employment agencies
Elizabeth Ferguson
Bob Skene
John Parker
Tania Bennett

D-U-N-S 20-705-7758   (SL)
WORLDMARK AT VICTORIA
120 Kingston St, Victoria, BC, V8V 1V4
(250) 386-8555
Emp Here 30   *Sales* 13,476,570
SIC 7389 Business services, nec
David Martin

Victoria, BC V8W

D-U-N-S 24-764-2168   (SL)
ANGEL STAR HOLDINGS LTD
CHATEAU VICTORIA HOTEL & SUITES
740 Burdett Ave Suite 1901, Victoria, BC, V8W 1B2
(250) 382-4221
Emp Here 110   *Sales* 10,195,900
SIC 7011 Hotels and motels
Clive Piercy

D-U-N-S 24-882-0222   (SL)
AQUACULTURE DEVELOPMENT BRANCH
3rd Fl, Victoria, BC, V8W 2Z7

Emp Here 49   *Sales* 11,480,112
SIC 8748 Business consulting, nec
Al Casteldine

D-U-N-S 20-695-0490   (SL)
ARBUTUS COVE ENTERPRISES INC
650 Herald St, Victoria, BC, V8W 1S7
(250) 598-1387
Emp Here 7   *Sales* 13,497,730
SIC 5146 Fish and seafoods
Robert Husband
Steven Klees

D-U-N-S 24-106-4612   (BR)
ATLIFIC INC
VICTORIA MARRIOTT INNER HARBOUR, THE
728 Humboldt St, Victoria, BC, V8W 3Z5
(250) 480-3800
Emp Here 150
SIC 7011 Hotels and motels
Stephen Roughly

D-U-N-S 24-030-8957   (HQ)
BRITISH COLUMBIA FERRY SERVICES INC
BC FERRIES
(*Suby of* B.C. FERRY AUTHORITY, THE)
1321 Blanshard St Suite 500, Victoria, BC, V8W 0B7
(250) 381-1401
Emp Here 600   *Sales* 715,631,813
SIC 4482 Ferries
Mark Collins
Janet Carson
Cynthia Lukaitis
Jamie Marshall
Mark Wilson
Alana Gallagher

D-U-N-S 25-172-3813   (HQ)
BRITISH COLUMBIA INVESTMENT MANAGEMENT CORPORATION
BCIMC
(*Suby of* GOVERNMENT OF THE PROVINCE OF BRITISH COLUMBIA)
750 Pandora Ave, Victoria, BC, V8W 0E4
(778) 410-7100
Emp Here 151   *Sales* 331,590,396
SIC 6722 Management investment, open-end
Gordon Fyfe
Stefan Dunatov
Daniel Garant

Norine Hale
Shauna Lukaitis
David Morhart
Jim Pittman
Lincoln Webb
Peter Milburn
Paul Finch

D-U-N-S 20-807-1670   (HQ)
BROWN BROS. AGENCIES LIMITED
1125 Blanshard St, Victoria, BC, V8W 2H7
(250) 385-8771
Emp Here 49   *Sales* 101,625,810
SIC 6411 Insurance agents, brokers, and service
Thomas Sowler
Gordon Brown
David Brown

D-U-N-S 24-695-2659   (SL)
CAUSEWAY RESTAURANTS LTD
MILESTONES RESTAURANT
812 Wharf St, Victoria, BC, V8W 1T3
(250) 381-2244
Emp Here 80   *Sales* 3,641,520
SIC 5812 Eating places
Peter Bonner
Wayne Holm
Bob Roe
Karl Busch

D-U-N-S 24-647-4753   (HQ)
CHINTZ & COMPANY DECORATIVE FURNISHINGS INC
CHINTZ & COMPANY
1720 Store St, Victoria, BC, V8W 1V5
(250) 381-2404
Emp Here 30   *Sales* 34,860,450
SIC 5719 Miscellaneous homefurnishings
Nicole Degoutiere
Ronald Netolitzky

D-U-N-S 20-302-0529   (SL)
COLLINS BARROW VICTORIA LTD
645 Fort St Suite 540, Victoria, BC, V8W 1G2
(250) 386-0500
Emp Here 55   *Sales* 11,499,675
SIC 8721 Accounting, auditing, and bookkeeping
William Camden
Deron Freer

D-U-N-S 20-910-9722   (SL)
DND HMCS HURON
Gd Stn Csc, Victoria, BC, V8W 2L9
(250) 363-5482
Emp Here 50   *Sales* 10,669,600
SIC 4499 Water transportation services,
Mike Palka

D-U-N-S 20-238-9339   (SL)
DRAYCOR CONSTRUCTION LTD
Gd Stn Csc, Victoria, BC, V8W 2L9
(250) 391-9899
Emp Here 55   *Sales* 14,901,810
SIC 1521 Single-family housing construction
Kent Sheldrake
Kevin Parker

D-U-N-S 25-957-6361   (BR)
EARL'S RESTAURANTS LTD
EARL'S RESTAURANTS
(*Suby of* EARL'S RESTAURANTS LTD)
1703 Blanshard St, Victoria, BC, V8W 2J8

Emp Here 80
SIC 5812 Eating places
Maria Toby

D-U-N-S 20-275-9387   (HQ)
ENCOREFX INC
517 Fort St Fl 2, Victoria, BC, V8W 1E7
(250) 412-5253
Emp Here 5   *Sales* 17,766,000
SIC 6099 Functions related to deposit banking
Peter Gustavson
Paul Lennox
Philip Gans

Briony Bayer
Marlene Tripple

D-U-N-S 20-867-4622   (SL)
EXECUTIVE HOUSE LTD
BARTHOLOMEWS BAR & GRILL
777 Douglas St, Victoria, BC, V8W 2B5
(250) 388-5111
Emp Here 80   *Sales* 7,591,920
SIC 7011 Hotels and motels
Derryck Jackson
Edwin Popham
Anne Jackson

D-U-N-S 25-026-6269   (BR)
FAIRMONT HOTELS & RESORTS INC
FAIRMONT EMPRESS, THE
(*Suby of* ACCOR)
721 Government St, Victoria, BC, V8W 1W5
(250) 384-8111
Emp Here 450
SIC 7011 Hotels and motels
Don Sennerty

D-U-N-S 24-445-7594   (HQ)
GREATER VICTORIA VISITORS & CONVENTION BUREAU
TOURISM VICTORIA
31 Bastion Sq, Victoria, BC, V8W 1J1
(250) 414-6999
Emp Here 22   *Sales* 10,861,830
SIC 8611 Business associations
Lorinda Staples

D-U-N-S 24-616-6974   (SL)
HAILEY MANAGEMENT LTD
1070 Douglas St Suite 800, Victoria, BC, V8W 2C4
(250) 388-5421
Emp Here 28   *Sales* 11,741,940
SIC 6712 Bank holding companies
Bruce Hallsor

D-U-N-S 24-593-5796   (HQ)
HENDRY SWINTON MCKENZIE INSURANCE SERVICES INC
830 Pandora Ave, Victoria, BC, V8W 1P4
(250) 388-5555
Sales 18,557,568
SIC 6411 Insurance agents, brokers, and service
Brad Hendry
Ross Mckenzie

D-U-N-S 20-118-9800   (BR)
HUDSON'S BAY COMPANY
(*Suby of* HUDSON'S BAY COMPANY)
1150 Douglas St Suite 1, Victoria, BC, V8W 2C8
(250) 385-1311
Emp Here 300
SIC 5311 Department stores
Adele Matte

D-U-N-S 20-866-6649   (SL)
IRISH TIMES PUB CO LTD
IRISH TIMES PUB
1200 Government St, Victoria, BC, V8W 1Y3
(250) 383-5531
Emp Here 80   *Sales* 3,641,520
SIC 5813 Drinking places
Matthew Macneil
Gordon Mccormick
Nels Dugstad

D-U-N-S 24-839-2169   (HQ)
ISLAND ACOUSTICS (OAK BAY) INC
ISLAND HEARING SERVICES
645 Fort St Unit 309, Victoria, BC, V8W 1G2
(250) 385-3103
Emp Here 93
SIC 5999 Miscellaneous retail stores, nec
Marke Hambley

D-U-N-S 25-994-1433   (BR)
ISLAND PUBLISHERS LTD
BLACK PRESS
(*Suby of* ISLAND PUBLISHERS LTD)

---

818 Broughton St, Victoria, BC, V8W 1E4
(250) 480-0755
Emp Here 150
SIC 2711 Newspapers
Andrew Burchill Lynch

D-U-N-S 24-137-9908   (HQ)
ISLAND PUBLISHERS LTD
LADYSMITH CHRONICLE
818 Broughton St, Victoria, BC, V8W 1E4
(250) 480-0755
Emp Here 100   *Sales* 81,385,080
SIC 2711 Newspapers
Mark Warner

D-U-N-S 24-824-1481   (BR)
KPMG LLP
KPMG MSLP
(*Suby of* KPMG LLP)
730 View St Suite 800, Victoria, BC, V8W 3Y7
(250) 480-3500
Emp Here 90
SIC 8721 Accounting, auditing, and bookkeeping
Chuck Burkett

D-U-N-S 20-554-5713   (HQ)
LATITUDE GEOGRAPHICS GROUP LTD
1117 Wharf St Unit 300, Victoria, BC, V8W 1T7
(250) 381-8130
Sales 16,580,930
SIC 7371 Custom computer programming services
Steven Myhill-Jones
David Stevenson

D-U-N-S 25-898-7833   (HQ)
MALATEST, R. A. & ASSOCIATES LTD
MALATEST ASSOCIATES
858 Pandora Ave, Victoria, BC, V8W 1P4
(250) 384-2770
Emp Here 78   *Sales* 52,786,320
SIC 8732 Commercial nonphysical research
Robert Malatest
Colleen Malatest

D-U-N-S 20-316-5170   (SL)
METALAB DESIGN LTD
524 Yates St Suite 101, Victoria, BC, V8W 1K8

Emp Here 76   *Sales* 17,801,837
SIC 7374 Data processing and preparation
Richard Ward
Andrew Wilkinson
Dan Bowerman
Stephanie Ito

D-U-N-S 24-369-1487   (HQ)
NATIONAL HEARING SERVICES INC
ISLAND HEARING SERVICES
(*Suby of* SONOVA HOLDING AG)
1007 Langley St Suite 301, Victoria, BC, V8W 1V7
(250) 413-2100
Emp Here 50   *Sales* 55,061,100
SIC 5999 Miscellaneous retail stores, nec
Craig Cameron
Paul Thompson

D-U-N-S 25-908-0997   (SL)
OLIVE THE SENSES
1701 Douglas St Unit 9, Victoria, BC, V8W 0C1
(250) 590-8418
Emp Here 12   *Sales* 10,026,924
SIC 5149 Groceries and related products, nec

D-U-N-S 25-913-8998   (SL)
PACIFICA HOUSING ADVISORY ASSOCIATION
827 Fisgard St, Victoria, BC, V8W 1R9
(250) 385-2131
Emp Here 90   *Sales* 37,700,010
SIC 6531 Real estate agents and managers
Dean Fortin

D-U-N-S 25-222-5979   (SL)

RESEARCH UNIVERSITIES' COUNCIL OF BRITISH COLUMBIA, THE
RUCBC
880 Douglas St Suite 400, Victoria, BC, V8W 2B7
(250) 480-4859
Emp Here 50   *Sales* 11,714,400
SIC 8742 Management consulting services
  Robin Ciceri

D-U-N-S 24-155-2785   (HQ)
ROYAL AND MCPHERSON THEATRES SOCIETY
1005 Broad St Unit 302, Victoria, BC, V8W 2A1
(250) 361-0800
Emp Here 8   *Sales* 13,567,700
SIC 6512 Nonresidential building operators
  Lloyd Fitzsimonds
  Roy Hanson
  Terry Waller
  Mike Wagnell
  Judith Scott
  Colleen Craig
  Maureen Barker
  Dawn Cameron
  Pam Copley
  Alastair Cousland

D-U-N-S 24-838-7110   (BR)
SIERRA SYSTEMS GROUP INC
(*Suby of* NIPPON TELEGRAPH AND TELEPHONE CORPORATION)
737 Courtney St, Victoria, BC, V8W 1C3
(250) 385-1535
Emp Here 150
SIC 7379 Computer related services, nec

D-U-N-S 20-341-1368   (SL)
STOCKSY UNITED CO-OP
560 Johnson St Suite 320, Victoria, BC, V8W 3C6
(250) 590-7308
Emp Here 30   *Sales* 11,745,060
SIC 6794 Patent owners and lessors
  Brianna Wettlaufer

D-U-N-S 24-493-6118   (SL)
STRATA CORPORATION # 962
VICTORIA REGENT HOTEL
1234 Wharf St Suite 962, Victoria, BC, V8W 3H9
(250) 386-2211
Emp Here 40   *Sales* 10,870,240
SIC 6531 Real estate agents and managers
  Bruce Bradburn
  Peter Fothergill-Payne
  Robert Grace
  Earl Wilde

D-U-N-S 20-119-8082   (SL)
STRATHCONA HOTEL OF VICTORIA LTD
STRATHCONA HOTEL
919 Douglas St, Victoria, BC, V8W 2C2
(250) 383-7137
Emp Here 150   *Sales* 6,995,850
SIC 5813 Drinking places
  Kirk Olson
  Grant Olson
  Craig Olson

D-U-N-S 24-806-7050   (SL)
SWANS ENTERPRISES LTD
SWANS SUITE HOTELS
506 Pandora Ave Suite 203, Victoria, BC, V8W 1N6
(250) 361-3310
Emp Here 85   *Sales* 3,869,115
SIC 5813 Drinking places
  Janina Ceglarz

D-U-N-S 20-119-9148   (SL)
UNION CLUB OF BRITISH COLUMBIA
805 Gordon St, Victoria, BC, V8W 1Z6
(250) 384-1151
Emp Here 70   *Sales* 16,906,050
SIC 8621 Professional organizations
  David Hammonds

D-U-N-S 24-371-0902   (HQ)
VICTORIA COOL AID SOCIETY, THE
749 Pandora Ave Suite 102, Victoria, BC, V8W 1N9
(250) 380-2663
Emp Here 20   *Sales* 16,937,253
SIC 8399 Social services, nec
  Kathy Stinson

D-U-N-S 25-069-7059   (SL)
VICTORIA WOMEN IN NEED SOCIETY
785 Pandora Ave, Victoria, BC, V8W 1N9
(250) 480-4006
Emp Here 50   *Sales* 11,341,650
SIC 8399 Social services, nec
  Claire Yazganoglu

D-U-N-S 25-084-8728   (BR)
WATER   STREET   (VANCOUVER) SPAGHETTI CORP
OLD SPAGHETTI FACTORY, THE
(*Suby of* WATER STREET (VANCOUVER) SPAGHETTI CORP)
703 Douglas St, Victoria, BC, V8W 2B4
(250) 381-8444
Emp Here 130
SIC 5812 Eating places
  Michael Gonzalez

D-U-N-S 24-374-0297   (HQ)
YMCA-YWCA OF GREATER VICTORIA
851 Broughton St, Victoria, BC, V8W 1E5
(250) 386-7511
Emp Here 150   *Sales* 28,531,050
SIC 8011 Offices and clinics of medical doctors
  Jennifer (Jennie) Edgecombe

Victoria, BC V8X

D-U-N-S 24-837-7848   (HQ)
ACCENT INNS INC
(*Suby of* FARMER INDUSTRIES GROUP INC)
3233 Maple St, Victoria, BC, V8X 4Y9
(250) 475-7500
Emp Here 9   *Sales* 17,220,240
SIC 7011 Hotels and motels
  Terry Farmer
  Mandy Farmer
  Murray Farmer
  Brian Scroggs
  Joan Murrell
  John Mcmanaman
  David Splawski

D-U-N-S 25-931-9903   (HQ)
ADANAC RECOVERY LTD
BOTTLE DEPOT, THE
3961 Quadra St, Victoria, BC, V8X 1J7
(250) 727-7480
Emp Here 1   *Sales* 17,968,760
SIC 7389 Business services, nec
  Darcy Hipwell

D-U-N-S 20-210-7863   (HQ)
BISHOP OF VICTORIA CORPORATION SOLE
ROMAN CATHOLIC DIOCESE OF VICTORIA
4044 Nelthorpe St Suite 1, Victoria, BC, V8X 2A1
(250) 479-1331
Emp Here 16   *Sales* 10,772,700
SIC 8661 Religious organizations
  Richard Gagnon

D-U-N-S 24-345-2067   (SL)
BROADMEAD CARE SOCIETY
REST HAVEN LODGE
4579 Chatterton Way, Victoria, BC, V8X 4Y7
(250) 656-0717
Emp Here 75   *Sales* 5,142,450
SIC 8051 Skilled nursing care facilities
  Gary Zachary

D-U-N-S 24-761-1759   (BR)
CANADIAN CORPS OF COMMISSIONAIRES NATIONAL OFFICE, THE
COMMISSIONAIRES
(*Suby of* CANADIAN CORPS OF COMMISSIONAIRES NATIONAL OFFICE, THE)
928 Cloverdale Ave, Victoria, BC, V8X 2T3
(250) 727-7755
Emp Here 1,000
SIC 7381 Detective and armored car services
  Stan Verran

D-U-N-S 25-138-5928   (HQ)
CATHOLIC INDEPENDENT SCHOOLS, DIOCESE OF VICTORIA
ST. PATRICK'S ELEMENTARY SCHOOL
4044 Nelthorpe St Suite 1, Victoria, BC, V8X 2A1
(250) 727-6893
Emp Here 120   *Sales* 14,867,850
SIC 8211 Elementary and secondary schools
  Beverly Pulyk

D-U-N-S 24-392-6040   (HQ)
CHEROVAN HOLDINGS LTD
4400 Chatterton Way Suite 301, Victoria, BC, V8X 5J2
(250) 881-7878
Emp Here 1   *Sales* 13,077,650
SIC 6712 Bank holding companies
  Darcy Kray

D-U-N-S 24-236-2304   (BR)
COAST CAPITAL REAL ESTATE LTD
(*Suby of* COAST CAPITAL REAL ESTATE LTD)
4460 Chatterton Way Suite 110, Victoria, BC, V8X 5J2
(250) 477-5353
Emp Here 142
SIC 6531 Real estate agents and managers
  Bill Ethier

D-U-N-S 25-189-5608   (BR)
CORPORATION OF THE DISTRICT OF SAANICH, THE
SAANICH FIRE DEPARTMENT
(*Suby of* CORPORATION OF THE DISTRICT OF SAANICH, THE)
760 Vernon Ave, Victoria, BC, V8X 2W6
(250) 475-5500
Emp Here 100
SIC 7389 Business services, nec

D-U-N-S 24-446-7528   (SL)
DURWEST HOLDINGS LTD
(*Suby of* CHEROVAN HOLDINGS LTD)
4400 Chatterton Way Suite 301, Victoria, BC, V8X 5J2
(250) 881-7878
Emp Here 50   *Sales* 13,716,600
SIC 8741 Management services
  Darcy Kray
  Carl Novak

D-U-N-S 20-806-3354   (HQ)
HARBORD INSURANCE SERVICES LTD
805 Cloverdale Ave Suite 150, Victoria, BC, V8X 2S9
(250) 388-5533
Emp Here 26   *Sales* 25,441,800
SIC 6411 Insurance agents, brokers, and service
  Philip C. M. Holmes

D-U-N-S 24-762-1709   (SL)
ISLANDS WEST MANUFACTURERS LTD
4247 Douglas St, Victoria, BC, V8X 3Y7
(250) 727-0744
Emp Here 85   *Sales* 71,024,045
SIC 5148 Fresh fruits and vegetables
  Wayne Fatt
  Ian Fatt

D-U-N-S 25-314-5999   (HQ)
J.B. PRECISION ENGINES & PARTS LTD
J.B. GROUP WAREHOUSE
3340 Oak St, Victoria, BC, V8X 1R1

(250) 475-2520
Emp Here 12   *Sales* 30,834,720
SIC 5531 Auto and home supply stores
  Edward B.B. Cuppage

D-U-N-S 20-703-1456   (BR)
JACE HOLDINGS LTD
THRIFTY FOODS
3475 Quadra St Suite 13, Victoria, BC, V8X 1G8
(250) 382-2751
Emp Here 200   *Sales* 2,140,496
SIC 5141 Groceries, general line
  Shawn Parkhouse

D-U-N-S 24-577-9970   (HQ)
KINETIC CONSTRUCTION LTD
(*Suby of* GYLES INVESTMENTS LTD)
862 Cloverdale Ave Suite 201, Victoria, BC, V8X 2S8
(250) 381-6331
Emp Here 20   *Sales* 68,440,560
SIC 1542 Nonresidential construction, nec
  Tom Plumb
  Mark Liudzius

D-U-N-S 24-805-4202   (SL)
LIFEPLAN FINANCIAL SERVICES GROUP INC
3960 Quadra St Suite 101, Victoria, BC, V8X 4A3
(250) 727-7197
Emp Here 98   *Sales* 22,960,224
SIC 8742 Management consulting services
  David W. C. Bulinckx
  Leeanna M Bulinckx

D-U-N-S 20-584-7999   (SL)
MANN, DON EXCAVATING LTD
4098 Lochside Dr, Victoria, BC, V8X 2C8
(250) 479-8283
Emp Here 135   *Sales* 33,235,110
SIC 1794 Excavation work
  Stephen Mann
  Steve Mann
  Jordan Mann

D-U-N-S 20-045-9886   (SL)
MCTAVISH INSURANCE AGENCIES LTD
4430 Chatterton Way, Victoria, BC, V8X 5J2
(905) 898-0361
Emp Here 25   *Sales* 21,201,500
SIC 6411 Insurance agents, brokers, and service
  William Mctavish

D-U-N-S 24-841-4497   (SL)
PACIFIC RIM EXTERIORS
831 Shamrock St, Victoria, BC, V8X 2V1
(250) 686-8738
Emp Here 40   *Sales* 12,754,760
SIC 1521 Single-family housing construction
  Fairmont Pacific Rim

D-U-N-S 20-119-7415   (SL)
PARK PACIFIC LUMBERWORLD LTD
3955 Quadra St, Victoria, BC, V8X 1J7
(250) 479-7151
Emp Here 50   *Sales* 12,652,950
SIC 5211 Lumber and other building materials
  David F Flaig
  Robert Mcadams
  Clive Piercy

D-U-N-S 25-127-9386   (BR)
RRGB RESTAURANTS CANADA INC
RED ROBIN
(*Suby of* RRGB RESTAURANTS CANADA INC)
800 Tolmie Ave, Victoria, BC, V8X 3W4
(250) 386-4440
Emp Here 100
SIC 5812 Eating places
  Mark Edmunds

D-U-N-S 25-271-5503   (BR)
SHAW COMMUNICATIONS INC
SHAW CABLE
(*Suby of* SHAW COMMUNICATIONS INC)

▲ Public Company   ■ Public Company Family Member   **HQ** Headquarters   **BR** Branch   **SL** Single Location

861 Cloverdale Ave, Victoria, BC, V8X 4S7
(250) 475-5655
Emp Here 100
SIC 4841 Cable and other pay television services
Jeffery Mooney

D-U-N-S 20-801-6832   (SL)
ST. MARGARET'S SCHOOL
1080 Lucas Ave, Victoria, BC, V8X 3P7
(250) 479-7171
Emp Here 100   *Sales* 9,282,600
SIC 8211 Elementary and secondary schools
Julie Collins

D-U-N-S 25-261-3476   (SL)
TRADEX FOODS INC
3960 Quadra St Unit 410, Victoria, BC, V8X 4A3
(250) 479-1355
Emp Here 20   *Sales* 36,759,300
SIC 5146 Fish and seafoods
Robert Reierson
Irving Choran
Patrick Giordano

Victoria, BC V8Y

D-U-N-S 25-902-6763   (SL)
CORDOVA BAY GOLF COURSE LTD
BILL MATTICK'S RESTAURANT & LOUNGE
5333 Cordova Bay Rd, Victoria, BC, V8Y 2L3
(250) 658-4445
Emp Here 75   *Sales* 5,729,775
SIC 7992 Public golf courses
Mohan Jawl

D-U-N-S 20-052-0355   (SL)
FULL CIRCLE ENERGY HEALING
994 Abbey Rd, Victoria, BC, V8Y 1L2
(778) 350-3260
Emp Here 5   *Sales* 15,529,285
SIC 4924 Natural gas distribution

D-U-N-S 25-984-8042   (BR)
SCHOOL DISTRICT 63 (SAANICH)
CLAREMONT SECONDARY SCHOOL
4980 Wesley Rd, Victoria, BC, V8Y 1Y9
(250) 686-5221
Emp Here 100
SIC 8211 Elementary and secondary schools
Bruce Frith

D-U-N-S 20-823-9819   (SL)
TASK ENGINEERING LTD
5141 Cordova Bay Rd, Victoria, BC, V8Y 2K1
(250) 590-2440
Emp Here 50   *Sales* 11,279,628
SIC 7363 Help supply services
Andy Kyfiuk

Victoria, BC V8Z

D-U-N-S 24-312-3684   (SL)
6 MILE BAKERY & DELI LTD
3950 Carey Rd, Victoria, BC, V8Z 4E2
(250) 727-7737
Emp Here 30   *Sales* 25,067,310
SIC 5149 Groceries and related products, nec
John Warman
Debbie King
Tracey Hebden

D-U-N-S 24-457-7185   (SL)
BEST COST FOOD LTD
FAIRWAY MARKET
(*Suby of* FAIRWAY HOLDINGS (1994) LTD)
3555 Douglas St, Victoria, BC, V8Z 3L6

Emp Here 180   *Sales* 34,643,520
SIC 5411 Grocery stores

Don Yuen
Tam Chew
Doug Yuen

D-U-N-S 25-026-7499   (BR)
BOARD OF EDUCATION OF SCHOOL DISTRICT NO. 61 (GREATER VICTORIA)
SPECTRUM COMMUNITY SCHOOL
(*Suby of* BOARD OF EDUCATION OF SCHOOL DISTRICT NO. 61 (GREATER VICTORIA))
957 Burnside Rd W, Victoria, BC, V8Z 6E9
(250) 479-8271
Emp Here 100
SIC 8211 Elementary and secondary schools
Judy Harrison

D-U-N-S 24-245-5962   (HQ)
BOARD OF EDUCATION OF SCHOOL DISTRICT NO. 61 (GREATER VICTORIA)
556 Boleskine Rd, Victoria, BC, V8Z 1E8
(250) 475-3212
Emp Here 100   *Sales* 160,315,634
SIC 8211 Elementary and secondary schools

D-U-N-S 20-915-2235   (SL)
BOLZANO HOLDINGS LTD
STARLINE WINDOW
477 Boleskine Rd, Victoria, BC, V8Z 1E7
(250) 475-1441
Emp Here 5   *Sales* 19,237,000
SIC 2431 Millwork
Ron Martine

D-U-N-S 25-513-2748   (HQ)
BRIDGE, P.R. SYSTEMS LTD
BRIDGE SYSTEMS
455 Banga Pl Suite 108, Victoria, BC, V8Z 6X5
(250) 475-3766
Emp Here 48   *Sales* 13,069,740
SIC 1731 Electrical work
Peter A Bridge
Douglas M Vincent

D-U-N-S 20-576-1059   (HQ)
BUDGET RENT-A-CAR OF VICTORIA LTD
BUDGET CAR & TRUCK RENTAL
3657 Harriet Rd, Victoria, BC, V8Z 3T1
(250) 953-5300
Emp Here 25   *Sales* 16,148,100
SIC 7514 Passenger car rental
Judith S Scott

D-U-N-S 20-118-3589   (HQ)
CAMPBELL CONSTRUCTION LTD
(*Suby of* FAREY HOLDINGS LTD)
559 Kelvin Rd, Victoria, BC, V8Z 1C4
(250) 475-1300
Sales 102,660,840
SIC 1542 Nonresidential construction, nec
Kenneth Farey
Archie Campbell

D-U-N-S 24-492-1664   (SL)
CANPRO CONSTRUCTION LTD
555 Dupplin Rd, Victoria, BC, V8Z 1C2
(250) 475-0975
Emp Here 40   *Sales* 18,829,240
SIC 1542 Nonresidential construction, nec
Donald (Don) Wagnor
John Burkard

D-U-N-S 24-491-4297   (HQ)
E. ROKO DISTRIBUTORS LTD
646 Alpha St, Victoria, BC, V8Z 1B2
(250) 381-2552
Emp Here 5   *Sales* 19,675,656
SIC 5072 Hardware
Roko Kliman
Eva Kliman

D-U-N-S 24-044-7339   (HQ)
ESIT ADVANCED SOLUTIONS INC
(*Suby of* DXC TECHNOLOGY COMPANY)
4464 Markham St Suite 2200, Victoria, BC, V8Z 7X8
(250) 405-4500
Sales 114,323,990

SIC 8748 Business consulting, nec
Ross Davidson
Nataly Mayrand

D-U-N-S 24-077-8717   (BR)
EUROLINE WINDOWS INC
(*Suby of* EUROLINE WINDOWS INC)
3352 Tennyson Ave, Victoria, BC, V8Z 3P6
(250) 383-8465
Emp Here 100
SIC 5031 Lumber, plywood, and millwork
Kyle Gordon

D-U-N-S 25-368-3122   (HQ)
GENOLOGICS LIFE SCIENCES SOFTWARE INC
4464 Markham St Suite 2302, Victoria, BC, V8Z 7X8
(250) 483-7011
Sales 10,092,740
SIC 7371 Custom computer programming services
Michael Ball
James Degreef
Paul Ford
Don Listwin
Joe Timlin
Steven Peter William Hnatiuk
Tristan Orpin

D-U-N-S 20-048-4694   (BR)
GOLDER ASSOCIATES LTD
(*Suby of* GOLDER ASSOCIATES CORPORATION)
3795 Carey Rd Fl 2, Victoria, BC, V8Z 6T8
(250) 881-7372
Emp Here 75
SIC 8711 Engineering services
Jeff Bailey

D-U-N-S 24-958-0309   (BR)
HUDSON'S BAY COMPANY
THE BAY MAYFAIR
(*Suby of* HUDSON'S BAY COMPANY)
3125 Douglas St, Victoria, BC, V8Z 3K3
(250) 386-3322
Emp Here 250
SIC 5311 Department stores
Adele Matte

D-U-N-S 24-980-0756   (SL)
JAMES EVANS AND ASSOCIATES LTD
JEA PENSION SYSTEMS SOLUTIONS
4464 Markham St Suite 1205, Victoria, BC, V8Z 7X8
(250) 380-3811
Emp Here 100   *Sales* 8,759,265
SIC 7371 Custom computer programming services
James O Evans
Gail Evans
Christine Bowles

D-U-N-S 24-247-6091   (SL)
KNIGHT, CONTRACTING LTD
37 Cadillac Ave, Victoria, BC, V8Z 1T3
(250) 475-2595
Emp Here 30   *Sales* 14,121,930
SIC 1542 Nonresidential construction, nec
Wayne Knight

D-U-N-S 25-101-0278   (SL)
MONTANA'S COOKHOUSE
315 Burnside Rd W, Victoria, BC, V8Z 7L6
(250) 978-9333
Emp Here 77   *Sales* 3,504,963
SIC 5812 Eating places
Kevin White

D-U-N-S 25-266-8694   (HQ)
OAK LANE ENTERPRISES LTD
ROYAL OAK COUNTRY GROCERY
4420 West Saanich Rd, Victoria, BC, V8Z 3E9
(250) 708-3900
Emp Here 1   *Sales* 32,282,470
SIC 5411 Grocery stores
Mark Wilson

D-U-N-S 20-957-5026   (HQ)
OUGHTRED COFFEE & TEA LTD
(*Suby of* OUGHTRED COFFEE & TEA LTD)
723b Vanalman Ave, Victoria, BC, V8Z 3B6
(250) 384-7444
Emp Here 14   *Sales* 11,230,475
SIC 7389 Business services, nec
John Oughtred

D-U-N-S 25-991-3473   (HQ)
OUTSET MEDIA CORPORATION
4226 Commerce Cir Unit 106, Victoria, BC, V8Z 6N6
(250) 592-7374
Emp Here 14   *Sales* 16,136,802
SIC 5092 Toys and hobby goods and supplies
David Manga

D-U-N-S 20-180-6242   (HQ)
POSSCAN SYSTEMS INC
4243 Glanford Ave Suite 100, Victoria, BC, V8Z 4B9
(250) 380-5020
Emp Here 1   *Sales* 13,415,220
SIC 5065 Electronic parts and equipment, nec
Al Chartrand
Robert Price

D-U-N-S 24-457-5551   (HQ)
PRICE'S ALARM SYSTEMS (2009) LTD
PRICE'S BURGLAR STOP
4243 Glanford Ave Unit 100, Victoria, BC, V8Z 4B9
(250) 384-4104
Sales 42,757,400
SIC 5999 Miscellaneous retail stores, nec
Robert Price
Kevin Price
Peggy Price

D-U-N-S 25-069-7380   (HQ)
RED BARN COUNTRY MARKET LTD
RED BARN MARKET
(*Suby of* RB MARKET LTD)
751 Vanalman Ave, Victoria, BC, V8Z 3B8
(250) 479-6817
Emp Here 50   *Sales* 39,619,395
SIC 5411 Grocery stores
Peter Hansen
Samuel R Schwabe
Ashley Bourque
Russ Benwell

D-U-N-S 24-777-5133   (HQ)
ROGERS' CHOCOLATES LTD
SAM'S DELI
4253 Commerce Cir, Victoria, BC, V8Z 4M2
(250) 384-7021
Emp Here 25   *Sales* 44,939,700
SIC 2064 Candy and other confectionery products
Steve Parkhill
Bjorn Bjornson

D-U-N-S 20-794-9975   (SL)
RYAN COMPANY LIMITED
RYAN VENDING
723a Vanalman Ave, Victoria, BC, V8Z 3B6
(250) 388-4254
Emp Here 50   *Sales* 32,823,200
SIC 5962 Merchandising machine operators
Robert M. Oughtred
William Oughtred
Glen Jackson

D-U-N-S 25-920-8627   (BR)
SPECTRA GROUP OF GREAT RESTAURANTS INC, THE
ROMANO'S MACARONI GRILL
(*Suby of* MADISON PACIFIC PROPERTIES INC)
3195 Douglas St, Victoria, BC, V8Z 3K3

Emp Here 90
SIC 5812 Eating places
Kim Hong

D-U-N-S 20-119-7712   (SL)

SPEEDWAY MOTORS LTD
(Suby of 355676 B.C. LTD)
3329 Douglas St, Victoria, BC, V8Z 3L2
(250) 386-6650
Emp Here 45   *Sales* 28,317,600
SIC 5511 New and used car dealers
Roy Passmore

D-U-N-S 24-141-9188   (HQ)
STARFISH PRODUCT ENGINEERING INC
STARFISH MEDICAL
455 Boleskine Rd, Victoria, BC, V8Z 1E7
(250) 388-3537
Emp Here 100   *Sales* 29,547,570
SIC 3841 Surgical and medical instruments
Scott Phillips

D-U-N-S 25-651-3714   (SL)
THREE AMIGO'S BEAUTY SUPPLY CO LTD
ALLIANCE BEAUTY COMPANY
555 Ardersier Rd Unit A8, Victoria, BC, V8Z 1C8
(250) 475-3099
Emp Here 24   *Sales* 11,400,624
SIC 5087 Service establishment equipment
Duane Lobson
Gregory Lobson

D-U-N-S 20-575-5077   (SL)
THURBER MANAGEMENT LTD
4396 West Saanich Rd Suite 100, Victoria, BC, V8Z 3E9
(250) 727-2201
Emp Here 110   *Sales* 13,725,360
SIC 8741 Management services
Nathan Tidarney

D-U-N-S 25-453-7418   (HQ)
TOM HARRIS CELLULAR LTD
3680 Uptown Blvd Unit 209, Victoria, BC, V8Z 0B9
(250) 360-0606
Emp Here 10   *Sales* 30,541,000
SIC 5999 Miscellaneous retail stores, nec
Jack Harris
Greg Marriette
Thomas Harris
John R. Harris

D-U-N-S 20-032-1169   (HQ)
TOTAL DELIVERY SYSTEMS INC
450 Banga Pl, Victoria, BC, V8Z 6X5
(250) 382-9110
Emp Here 100   *Sales* 167,227,000
SIC 7389 Business services, nec
Chris Chater
Bob Polmateer

D-U-N-S 25-829-5963   (BR)
VANCOUVER ISLAND HEALTH AUTHORITY
VICTORIA GENERAL HOSPITAL
(Suby of GOVERNMENT OF THE PROVINCE OF BRITISH COLUMBIA)
1 Hospital Way, Victoria, BC, V8Z 6R5
(250) 370-8355
Emp Here 500
SIC 8011 Offices and clinics of medical doctors
Howard Waldner

D-U-N-S 24-914-5343   (HQ)
VECIMA NETWORKS INC
SPECTRUM SIGNAL PROCESSING BY VECIMA, DIV OF
771 Vanalman Ave Suite 201, Victoria, BC, V8Z 3B8
(250) 881-1982
Emp Here 460   *Sales* 53,161,738
SIC 3663 Radio and t.v. communications equipment
Sumit Kumar
David Hobb
Laird Froese
Mark Briggs
Richard Blenkinsop
Colin Howlett

Mark Depietro
Lindsay Ryerson
Peter Torn
John Hanna

D-U-N-S 20-118-3902   (HQ)
VICTORIA FORD ALLIANCE LTD
SUBURBAN MOTORS
3377 Douglas St, Victoria, BC, V8Z 3L4
(250) 475-2255
Emp Here 75   *Sales* 84,952,800
SIC 5511 New and used car dealers
Sherman F B Carson
James Carson
Leonard Carson
Donald Carson

D-U-N-S 24-662-1663   (BR)
WAL-MART CANADA CORP
WALMART
(Suby of WALMART INC.)
3460 Saanich Rd Suite 3109, Victoria, BC, V8Z 0B9
(250) 475-3356
Emp Here 485
SIC 5311 Department stores
Brad Bester

D-U-N-S 20-976-7040   (SL)
WESCOR CONTRACTING LTD
3368 Tennyson Ave, Victoria, BC, V8Z 3P6
(250) 475-8882
Emp Here 49   *Sales* 23,065,819
SIC 1542 Nonresidential construction, nec
Richard Green

D-U-N-S 20-912-1896   (SL)
WILLE DODGE CHRYSLER LTD
3240 Douglas St, Victoria, BC, V8Z 3K7
(250) 475-3511
Emp Here 70   *Sales* 44,049,600
SIC 5511 New and used car dealers
Monica Wille

D-U-N-S 25-917-0777   (HQ)
WILSON'S TRANSPORTATION LTD
YYJ AIRPORT SHUTTLE
4196 Glanford Ave, Victoria, BC, V8Z 4B6
(250) 475-3235
Sales 11,290,800
SIC 4142 Bus charter service, except local
John Wilson

Victoria, BC V9A

D-U-N-S 25-927-7416   (HQ)
ABEBOOKS INC
ABEBOOKS EUROPE GMBH
(Suby of AMAZON.COM, INC.)
655 Tyee Rd Suite 500, Victoria, BC, V9A 6X5
(250) 412-3200
Emp Here 100   *Sales* 73,644,875
SIC 5192 Books, periodicals, and newspapers
Glenn Bromley

D-U-N-S 25-312-8490   (HQ)
ARCHIPELAGO MARINE RESEARCH LTD
525 Head St Suite 1, Victoria, BC, V9A 5S1
(250) 383-4535
Emp Here 50   *Sales* 39,589,740
SIC 8732 Commercial nonphysical research
Shawn Stebbins
Howard Mcelderry
Brian Emmett

D-U-N-S 20-713-5414   (BR)
BOARD OF EDUCATION OF SCHOOL DISTRICT NO. 61 (GREATER VICTORIA)
ESQUIMALT HIGH SCHOOL
(Suby of BOARD OF EDUCATION OF SCHOOL DISTRICT NO. 61 (GREATER VICTORIA))
847 Colville Rd, Victoria, BC, V9A 4N9
(250) 382-9226
Emp Here 75

SIC 8211 Elementary and secondary schools
Colin Roberts

D-U-N-S 24-317-4070   (BR)
CARMANAH TECHNOLOGIES CORPORATION
(Suby of CARMANAH TECHNOLOGIES CORPORATION)
203 Harbour Rd Suite 4, Victoria, BC, V9A 3S2
(250) 380-0052
Emp Here 100
SIC 5074 Plumbing and heating equipment and supplies (hydronics)
Genevieve St Dennis

D-U-N-S 25-989-6157   (HQ)
CARMANAH TECHNOLOGIES CORPORATION
250 Bay St, Victoria, BC, V9A 3K5
(250) 380-0052
Sales 27,770,000
SIC 3648 Lighting equipment, nec
John Simmons
Jim Meekison
Sara Elford
Terry Holland
Evan Brown

D-U-N-S 20-165-3990   (SL)
CFB ESQUIMALT MILITARY FAMILY RESOURCE CENTRE
ESQUIMALT MFRC
1505 Esquimalt Rd, Victoria, BC, V9A 7N2
(250) 363-8628
Emp Here 45   *Sales* 10,207,485
SIC 8399 Social services, nec
Gaynor Jackson

D-U-N-S 24-247-8758   (HQ)
COAST CAPITAL INSURANCE SERVICES LTD
(Suby of WESTERN FINANCIAL GROUP INC)
1499 Admirals Rd, Victoria, BC, V9A 2P8
(250) 483-7000
Emp Here 3   *Sales* 328,681,966
SIC 6411 Insurance agents, brokers, and service
Don Coulter
Bill Cooke
David Gaskin
Bob Armstrong
Robin Chakrabarti
Mary Jordan
Valerie Lambert
Frank Leonard
Christian Morrison
Chris Trumpy

D-U-N-S 24-085-3163   (SL)
COMPASSIONATE RESOURCE WAREHOUSE
831 Devonshire Rd Suite 2, Victoria, BC, V9A 4T5
(250) 381-4483
Emp Here 49   *Sales* 19,473,286
SIC 8699 Membership organizations, nec
Dell Wergeland

D-U-N-S 20-699-9091   (BR)
DELTA HOTELS LIMITED
(Suby of GOVERNMENT OF THE PROVINCE OF BRITISH COLUMBIA)
45 Songhees Rd, Victoria, BC, V9A 6T3
(250) 360-2999
Emp Here 214
SIC 7011 Hotels and motels
Kimberly Hughes

D-U-N-S 24-371-6198   (SL)
DOWNS CONSTRUCTION LTD
870 Devonshire Rd, Victoria, BC, V9A 4T6
(250) 384-1390
Emp Here 54   *Sales* 30,798,252
SIC 1542 Nonresidential construction, nec
William Downs

Stephen Downs

D-U-N-S 20-118-7051   (HQ)
FAIRWAY HOLDINGS (1994) LTD
FAIRWAY MARKET #1
272 Gorge Rd W, Victoria, BC, V9A 1M7
(250) 385-4814
Emp Here 100   *Sales* 125,294,064
SIC 5411 Grocery stores
Don Yuen
Doug Yuen

D-U-N-S 25-507-0815   (SL)
FARMER CONSTRUCTION LTD
360 Harbour Rd, Victoria, BC, V9A 3S1
(250) 388-5121
Emp Here 250   *Sales* 174,598,000
SIC 1542 Nonresidential construction, nec
Gerrit Vink
David Evans
Paul Gray
Dave Haydar

D-U-N-S 24-353-5445   (HQ)
FARMER INDUSTRIES GROUP INC
360a Harbour Rd, Victoria, BC, V9A 3S1
(250) 360-1511
Emp Here 1   *Sales* 82,605,034
SIC 6712 Bank holding companies
Murray Farmer

D-U-N-S 25-149-3680   (BR)
GOVERNING COUNCIL OF THE SALVATION ARMY IN CANADA, THE
GOVERNING COUNCIL OF THE SALVATION ARMY IN CANADA,
(Suby of GOVERNING COUNCIL OF THE SALVATION ARMY IN CANADA, THE)
952 Arm St, Victoria, BC, V9A 4G7
(250) 385-3422
Emp Here 132
SIC 8051 Skilled nursing care facilities
Larry Jennings

D-U-N-S 25-968-1138   (SL)
K A R INDUSTRIES LIMITED
CANADIAN TIRE
1519 Admirals Rd, Victoria, BC, V9A 2P8
(250) 381-3111
Emp Here 49   *Sales* 24,405,822
SIC 5531 Auto and home supply stores
Kim Raynhoudt

D-U-N-S 20-139-9693   (SL)
KARDEL CONSULTING SERVICES INC
2951 Tillicum Rd Unit 209, Victoria, BC, V9A 2A6
(250) 382-5959
Emp Here 220   *Sales* 19,637,640
SIC 8049 Offices of health practitioner
Karl Egner

D-U-N-S 20-119-3307   (HQ)
MONK OFFICE SUPPLY LTD
800 Viewfield Rd, Victoria, BC, V9A 4V1
(800) 735-3433
Emp Here 60   *Sales* 30,212,390
SIC 5712 Furniture stores
James Mckenzie
Ross Hill

D-U-N-S 24-620-1685   (SL)
RELIABLE CONTROLS CORPORATION
RELIABLE CONTROLS
120 Hallowell Rd, Victoria, BC, V9A 7K2
(250) 475-2036
Emp Here 90   *Sales* 17,139,780
SIC 3625 Relays and industrial controls
Roland Laird
James Puritch
Thomas Zaban
Juliana Yu
Vince Palmer

D-U-N-S 24-308-6647   (HQ)
SELECT MORTGAGE CORP
VERICO SELECT MORTGAGE
1497 Admirals Rd Suite 205, Victoria, BC, V9A

2P8
(250) 483-1373
Emp Here 28   *Sales* 16,347,693
SIC 6162 Mortgage bankers and loan corre-
spondents
Don Barr
Jeff Parkin

D-U-N-S 24-899-2661   (SL)
VICTORIA SHIPYARDS CO. LTD
(*Suby of* WASHINGTON CANADIAN LTD)
825 Admirals Rd, Victoria, BC, V9A 2P1
(250) 380-1602
Emp Here 500   *Sales* 145,425,000
SIC 3731 Shipbuilding and repairing
Kyle Washington
Kevin Irvine
Roland Webb
Steve Frasher

Victoria, BC V9B

D-U-N-S 20-021-3585   (SL)
ALLTERRA CONSTRUCTION LTD
2158 Millstream Rd, Victoria, BC, V9B 6H4
(250) 658-3772
Emp Here 50   *Sales* 11,008,400
SIC 1794 Excavation work
Raymond Lam
Todd Mizuik

D-U-N-S 20-100-3662   (HQ)
BALMORAL INVESTMENTS LTD
COMFORT INN & SUITES
101 Island Hwy, Victoria, BC, V9B 1E8
(250) 388-7807
Emp Here 30   *Sales* 28,700,400
SIC 7011 Hotels and motels
Dominic Petraroia
Anita Simo
Maria Petraroia

D-U-N-S 20-137-0215   (HQ)
COLDSTAR SOLUTIONS INC
937 Dunford Ave Unit 1, Victoria, BC, V9B 2S4
(250) 391-7425
Sales 16,456,480
SIC 4212 Local trucking, without storage
Kelly Hawes
Kathryn Frankfurter
Trevor Sawkins

D-U-N-S 25-831-9458   (BR)
COSTCO WHOLESALE CANADA LTD
(*Suby of* COSTCO WHOLESALE CORPO-
RATION)
799 Mccallum Rd, Victoria, BC, V9B 6A2
(250) 391-1151
Emp Here 200
SIC 5099 Durable goods, nec
Phillip Coates

D-U-N-S 20-813-4689   (HQ)
DARVIC ENTERPRISES LTD
PETRO CANADA
2435 Millstream Rd, Victoria, BC, V9B 3R5
(250) 391-6082
Emp Here 7   *Sales* 24,903,900
SIC 5541 Gasoline service stations
Darren Macdonald

D-U-N-S 24-824-7892   (SL)
DRANE, STEVE MOTERCYCLES LTD
2940 Ed Nixon Terr, Victoria, BC, V9B 0B2
(250) 475-1345
Emp Here 22   *Sales* 10,957,716
SIC 5571 Motorcycle dealers
Steve Drane

D-U-N-S 20-118-4223   (SL)
E88TLC90 HOLDINGS LTD
WESTERN FOODS
772 Goldstream Ave, Victoria, BC, V9B 2X3
(250) 478-8306
Emp Here 40   *Sales* 10,966,080

SIC 5411 Grocery stores
Charles Low
Theresa Low
Edward Low
Laura Lum

D-U-N-S 24-594-4996   (HQ)
EVERGREEN INDUSTRIES LTD
ALPINE DISPOSAL & RECYCLING
1045 Dunford Ave, Victoria, BC, V9B 2S4
(250) 474-5145
Emp Here 35   *Sales* 12,856,550
SIC 4953 Refuse systems
Stewart Young
Robert Ruygrok

D-U-N-S 24-247-0466   (HQ)
**FTS FOREST TECHNOLOGY SYSTEMS
LTD**
FTS
1065 Henry Eng Pl, Victoria, BC, V9B 6B2
(250) 478-5561
Sales 10,474,310
SIC 3669 Communications equipment, nec
David Illing

D-U-N-S 25-684-7443   (BR)
HOME DEPOT OF CANADA INC
HOME DEPOT
(*Suby of* THE HOME DEPOT INC)
2400 Millstream Rd, Victoria, BC, V9B 3R3
(250) 391-6001
Emp Here 200
SIC 5251 Hardware stores
Erik Penno

D-U-N-S 24-311-5701   (SL)
ISLAND VIEW CONSTRUCTION LTD
2780 Veterans Memorial Pky Suite 210, Victoria, BC, V9B 3S6

Emp Here 41   *Sales* 13,293,512
SIC 1521 Single-family housing construction
Michael Volk
Dan Pawluk

D-U-N-S 20-958-7989   (SL)
JENNER CHEVROLET BUICK GMC LTD
1730 Island Hwy, Victoria, BC, V9B 1H8
(250) 474-1211
Emp Here 50   *Sales* 10,131,450
SIC 7538 General automotive repair shops
Jack Jenner
Michael Bohonos

D-U-N-S 24-776-7569   (HQ)
LEKKER FOOD DISTRIBUTORS LTD
2670 Wilfert Rd, Victoria, BC, V9B 5Z3
(250) 388-0377
Sales 18,382,694
SIC 5147 Meats and meat products
Richard Van Wiltenburg
Maureen Van Wiltenburg

D-U-N-S 25-273-1534   (BR)
LONDON DRUGS LIMITED
(*Suby of* H.Y. LOUIE CO. LIMITED)
1907 Sooke Rd, Victoria, BC, V9B 1V8
(250) 474-0900
Emp Here 100
SIC 5912 Drug stores and proprietary stores
Richard Thompson

D-U-N-S 24-372-3459   (SL)
PSC NATURAL FOODS LTD
(*Suby of* HORIZON DISTRIBUTORS LTD)
2924 Jacklin Rd Suite 117, Victoria, BC, V9B
3Y5
(250) 386-3880
Emp Here 46   *Sales* 38,436,542
SIC 5141 Groceries, general line
Ronald Francisco
Don Rector
Thomas Van Williams

D-U-N-S 25-528-0943   (SL)
ROYAL ROADS UNIVERSITY
RRU

2005 Sooke Rd, Victoria, BC, V9B 5Y2
(250) 391-2511
Emp Here 400   *Sales* 44,977,867
SIC 8221 Colleges and universities
Allan Cahoon
Stephen Grundy
Dan Tulip
Wayne Strandlund
Liz Bicknell
Kathleen Birney
Manpreet Dhillon
Bruce Donaldson
Sandy Gray
Charles Krusekopf

D-U-N-S 20-383-5560   (BR)
SAVE-ON-FOODS LIMITED PARTNERSHIP
(*Suby of* SAVE-ON-FOODS LIMITED PART-
NERSHIP)
759 Mccallum Rd, Victoria, BC, V9B 6A2
(250) 475-3157
Emp Here 100
SIC 5411 Grocery stores
Paul Anacleto

D-U-N-S 24-537-0192   (SL)
SCANSA CONSTRUCTION LTD
2089 Millstream Rd Unit 203, Victoria, BC,
V9B 6H4
(250) 478-5222
Emp Here 60   *Sales* 15,146,520
SIC 1623 Water, sewer, and utility lines
Kory Gronnestad

D-U-N-S 20-713-5513   (BR)
SCHOOL DISTRICT NO 62 (SOOKE)
BELMONT SECONDARY SCHOOL
(*Suby of* SCHOOL DISTRICT NO 62
(SOOKE))
3067 Jacklin Rd, Victoria, BC, V9B 3Y7
(250) 478-5501
Emp Here 120
SIC 8211 Elementary and secondary schools
Ray Miller

D-U-N-S 25-325-7109   (HQ)
SCHOOL DISTRICT NO 62 (SOOKE)
3143 Jacklin Rd, Victoria, BC, V9B 5R1
(250) 474-9800
Emp Here 46   *Sales* 118,942,800
SIC 8211 Elementary and secondary schools
Wendy Hobbs
Bob Phillips
Don Brown
Rob Gordy
Denise Riley
Dianna Seaton
Margot Swinburnson

D-U-N-S 20-321-6754   (BR)
SYSCO CANADA, INC
NORTH DOUGLAS SYSCO
(*Suby of* SYSCO CORPORATION)
2881 Amy Rd, Victoria, BC, V9B 0B2
(250) 475-3333
Emp Here 250
SIC 5141 Groceries, general line

D-U-N-S 20-749-5904   (SL)
SYSCO VICTORIA, INC
(*Suby of* SYSCO CORPORATION)
2881 Amy Rd, Victoria, BC, V9B 0B2
(250) 475-3333
Emp Here 250   *Sales* 179,179,000
SIC 5141 Groceries, general line
Bruce Pascoe

D-U-N-S 20-791-9742   (SL)
TIM CURRY SALES LIMITED
CANADIAN TIRE
855 Langford Pky, Victoria, BC, V9B 4V5
(250) 474-2291
Emp Here 75   *Sales* 15,400,725
SIC 5311 Department stores
Tim Curry

D-U-N-S 24-725-2430   (SL)

TRIPLE CROWN FOODS LTD
FAIRWAY MARKET 3
2945 Jacklin Rd Suite 200, Victoria, BC, V9B
5E3
(250) 478-8998
Emp Here 90   *Sales* 26,412,930
SIC 5411 Grocery stores
Don Yuen
Doug Yuen
Brian Young

D-U-N-S 24-797-0114   (SL)
**VAN ISLE BRICKLOK SURFACING & LAND-
SCAPE SUPPLIES LTD**
BRICKLOK SURFACING
2717 Peatt Rd Suite 101, Victoria, BC, V9B
3V2
(250) 382-5012
Emp Here 50   *Sales* 14,176,200
SIC 1611 Highway and street construction
Brad Mitchell
Harold Bloomenthal

D-U-N-S 20-915-2946   (BR)
**VANCOUVER ISLAND HEALTH AUTHOR-
ITY**
PRIORY, THE
(*Suby of* GOVERNMENT OF THE
PROVINCE OF BRITISH COLUMBIA)
567 Goldstream Ave, Victoria, BC, V9B 2W4
(250) 370-5790
Emp Here 150
SIC 8051 Skilled nursing care facilities
Linda Mae Ross

D-U-N-S 24-325-9699   (SL)
WARDILL, J.A. ENTERPRISES INC
SHOPPERS DRUG MART
2945 Jacklin Rd Suite 300, Victoria, BC, V9B
5E3
(250) 474-1114
Emp Here 50   *Sales* 12,647,700
SIC 5912 Drug stores and proprietary stores
Jeffrey Wardill

D-U-N-S 20-707-9331   (SL)
**WEST SHORE PARKS AND RECREATION
SOCIETY**
JUAN DE FUCA RECREATION CENTRE
1767 Island Hwy, Victoria, BC, V9B 1J1
(250) 478-8384
Emp Here 170   *Sales* 16,142,010
SIC 7999 Amusement and recreation, nec
Grant Brown

Victoria, BC V9C

D-U-N-S 20-118-4892   (SL)
LOMBARD PRE-CAST INC
(*Suby of* LANGLEY CONCRETE & TILE LTD)
661 Lombard Dr, Victoria, BC, V9C 3Y9
(250) 478-9581
Emp Here 40   *Sales* 10,706,080
SIC 5211 Lumber and other building materials
Mark Omelaniec

D-U-N-S 24-773-1511   (SL)
SAFEHAVEN NURSING & SERVICES INC
3700 Ridge Pond Dr, Victoria, BC, V9C 4M8
(250) 477-8339
Emp Here 45   *Sales* 12,748,185
SIC 8741 Management services
Jesse Schulte
Laura Schulte

D-U-N-S 20-027-0929   (BR)
SCHOOL DISTRICT NO 62 (SOOKE)
DUNSMUIR MIDDLE SCHOOL
(*Suby of* SCHOOL DISTRICT NO 62
(SOOKE))
3341 Painter Rd, Victoria, BC, V9C 2J1
(250) 478-5548
Emp Here 75
SIC 8211 Elementary and secondary schools

Darren Russell

D-U-N-S 25-359-9310 (BR)
SLEGG DEVELOPMENTS LTD
(*Suby of* SLEGG DEVELOPMENTS LTD)
2901 Sooke Rd, Victoria, BC, V9C 3W7
(250) 386-3667
Emp Here 150
SIC 5031 Lumber, plywood, and millwork
Steve Slegg

D-U-N-S 24-072-9632 (HQ)
WEST BAY MECHANICAL LTD
584 Ledsham Rd, Victoria, BC, V9C 1J8
(250) 478-8532
Sales 13,983,900
SIC 1711 Plumbing, heating, air-conditioning
Ken Rozon
Morey Rozon
Ralph Rozon
Ray Rozon

Victoria, BC V9E

D-U-N-S 20-705-8160 (SL)
INTEGRITY WALL SYSTEMS INC
1371 Courtland Ave, Victoria, BC, V9E 2C5
(250) 480-5500
Emp Here 80 *Sales* 18,592,240
SIC 5714 Drapery and upholstery stores
Joe Frenette

D-U-N-S 25-456-9312 (SL)
PYE CONSTRUCTION LTD
1647 Little Rd, Victoria, BC, V9E 2E3
(250) 384-2662
Emp Here 50 *Sales* 16,666,650
SIC 1541 Industrial buildings and warehouses
Bill Johnson
Wayne Pye
Barry Scroggs
Lyle Scroggs

West Kelowna, BC V1Z

D-U-N-S 20-278-5473 (HQ)
ALPINE AEROTECH LIMITED PARTNER-SHIP
(*Suby of* WINTER PARK RESORT)
1260 Industrial Rd, West Kelowna, BC, V1Z 1G5
(250) 769-6344
Emp Here 95 *Sales* 21,845,992
SIC 4581 Airports, flying fields, and services
Jeffrey Denomme
Cherie Handvold
Sarah Groff

D-U-N-S 20-074-4084 (HQ)
ALPINE HELICOPTERS INC
(*Suby of* HAWK HOLDING COMPANY, LLC)
1295 Industrial Rd, West Kelowna, BC, V1Z 1G4
(250) 769-4111
Sales 32,037,360
SIC 4522 Air transportation, nonscheduled
Dave Gubbles
Craig Cousins

D-U-N-S 20-806-7066 (SL)
BYLANDS NURSERIES LTD
1600 Byland Rd, West Kelowna, BC, V1Z 1H6
(250) 769-7272
Emp Here 60 *Sales* 15,738,540
SIC 0181 Ornamental nursery products
John Byland

D-U-N-S 25-942-6252 (SL)
KELOWNA TRUCK & R.V. LTD
KELOWNA RV
1780 Byland Rd, West Kelowna, BC, V1Z 1A9

(250) 769-1000
Emp Here 21 *Sales* 10,459,638
SIC 5571 Motorcycle dealers
Randy Woodside

D-U-N-S 20-578-1243 (SL)
WESTWOOD FIBRE PRODUCTS INC
(*Suby of* VIRIDIS ENERGY INC)
2677 Kyle Rd Suite E, West Kelowna, BC, V1Z 2M9
(250) 769-1427
Emp Here 30 *Sales* 15,616,260
SIC 5099 Durable goods, nec
Cliff Ramsay

West Kelowna, BC V4T

D-U-N-S 20-120-2173 (HQ)
GORMAN BROS. LUMBER LTD
3900 Dunfield Rd, West Kelowna, BC, V4T 1W4
(250) 768-5131
Emp Here 250 *Sales* 83,517,000
SIC 2421 Sawmills and planing mills, general
Ronald Bruce Gorman
James Ross Gorman
Kathryn Vernon

D-U-N-S 20-733-3290 (SL)
LANG'S VENTURES INC
LVI DIGITAL GROUP & LVI TECHNOLOGY GROUP
3099 Shannon Lake Rd Suite 105, West Kelowna, BC, V4T 2M2
(250) 768-7055
Emp Here 80 *Sales* 21,999,236
SIC 7629 Electrical repair shops

D-U-N-S 25-690-6009 (SL)
PACIFIC WILDCAT RESOURCES CORP
2300 Carrington Rd Suite 110, West Kelowna, BC, V4T 2N6
(250) 768-0009
Emp Here 50 *Sales* 11,671,750
SIC 1081 Metal mining services
Francis Donald O'sullivan
Malcolm Carson
Christopher J. Lalor
Yunis Shaik
David Warwick Anderson

West Vancouver, BC V7P

D-U-N-S 24-120-5541 (HQ)
CAPILANO HIGHWAY SERVICES COMPANY
118 Bridge Rd, West Vancouver, BC, V7P 3R2
(604) 983-2411
Sales 14,176,200
SIC 1611 Highway and street construction
Barry Drummond

D-U-N-S 25-613-3034 (BR)
EARL'S RESTAURANTS LTD
EARL'S TIN PALACE
(*Suby of* EARL'S RESTAURANTS LTD)
303 Marine Dr, West Vancouver, BC, V7P 3J8

Emp Here 150
SIC 5812 Eating places
John Hawkins

D-U-N-S 25-389-2301 (HQ)
HILBAR ENTERPRISES INC
118 Bridge Rd, West Vancouver, BC, V7P 3R2
(604) 983-2411
Sales 14,214,200
SIC 6712 Bank holding companies
Barry Drummond

West Vancouver, BC V7S

D-U-N-S 24-193-3451 (SL)
492632 BC LTD
WEST COAST SIGHT SEEING
1412 Sandhurst Pl, West Vancouver, BC, V7S 2P3
(604) 451-1600
Emp Here 45 *Sales* 17,341,200
SIC 4725 Tour operators
Rudolph Tize

D-U-N-S 20-009-7116 (BR)
BOARD OF SCHOOL TRUSTEES OF SCHOOL DISTRICT NO. 45
SENTINEL SECONDARY SCHOOL
1250 Chartwell Dr, West Vancouver, BC, V7S 2R2
(604) 981-1130
Emp Here 85
SIC 8211 Elementary and secondary schools
Mike Finch

D-U-N-S 24-931-2695 (HQ)
COLLINGWOOD SCHOOL SOCIETY
COLLINGWOOD SCHOOL
70 Morven Dr, West Vancouver, BC, V7S 1B2
(604) 925-3331
Sales 18,832,610
SIC 8211 Elementary and secondary schools
Rodger Wright
Cal Buss
Chris Stafleu

D-U-N-S 20-288-5471 (BR)
COLLINGWOOD SCHOOL SOCIETY
COLLINGWOOD SCHOOL WENTWORTH.
(*Suby of* COLLINGWOOD SCHOOL SOCIETY)
2605 Wentworth Ave, West Vancouver, BC, V7S 3H4
(604) 925-8375
Emp Here 150
SIC 8211 Elementary and secondary schools
Ian Kennedy

D-U-N-S 20-619-9614 (SL)
HOLLYBURN COUNTRY CLUB
950 Cross Creek Rd, West Vancouver, BC, V7S 2S5
(604) 922-0161
Emp Here 170 *Sales* 13,352,650
SIC 7997 Membership sports and recreation clubs
Bruce Adanac
Christy Wilson

D-U-N-S 25-078-3156 (SL)
MULGRAVE INDEPENDENT SCHOOL SOCIETY
MULGRAVE SCHOOL
2330 Cypress Bowl Lane, West Vancouver, BC, V7S 3H9
(604) 922-3223
Emp Here 85 *Sales* 7,890,210
SIC 8211 Elementary and secondary schools
Tony Macoun

D-U-N-S 24-557-1455 (SL)
STARLITE ILLUMINATION INC
81 Deep Dene Rd, West Vancouver, BC, V7S 1A1
(604) 926-4808
Emp Here 25 *Sales* 11,087,250
SIC 7389 Business services, nec
Tim Johnson

West Vancouver, BC V7T

D-U-N-S 20-646-5580 (SL)
BABESKIN BODYCARE INC
HEALTH MEGAMALL
815 Margaree Pl, West Vancouver, BC, V7T 2J5

(604) 922-1883
Emp Here 25 *Sales* 27,633,625
SIC 5122 Drugs, proprietaries, and sundries
Kamran Victory

D-U-N-S 20-191-1638 (BR)
BEST BUY CANADA LTD
FUTURE SHOP
(*Suby of* BEST BUY CO., INC.)
2100 Park Royal S, West Vancouver, BC, V7T 2W4
(604) 913-3336
Emp Here 120
SIC 5731 Radio, television, and electronic stores
Skyler Bell

D-U-N-S 24-369-2837 (HQ)
C. WALKER GROUP INC
WALKER GROUP, THE
1455 Bellevue Ave Suite 300, West Vancouver, BC, V7T 1C3
(604) 922-6563
Emp Here 25 *Sales* 13,716,600
SIC 8741 Management services
Charles Walker
Beverley Walker

D-U-N-S 20-826-8933 (SL)
FIRST NATIONS FINANCIAL MANAGEMENT BOARD
100 Park Royal S Suite 905, West Vancouver, BC, V7T 1A2
(604) 925-6665
Emp Here 50 *Sales* 11,895,050
SIC 8742 Management consulting services
Harold Calla

D-U-N-S 20-354-4986 (HQ)
FIRST NATIONS HEALTH AUTHORITY
100 Park Royal S Suite 501, West Vancouver, BC, V7T 1A2
(604) 693-6500
Sales 327,554,363
SIC 8011 Offices and clinics of medical doctors
Joe Gallagher
Greg Shea
John Mah
Kim Humpheys
Joseph Mendez
Sonia Isaac-Mann
Tally Bains
Michelle Degroot
Harmony Johnson
Richard Jock

D-U-N-S 20-553-6209 (BR)
HOME DEPOT OF CANADA INC
(*Suby of* THE HOME DEPOT INC)
840 Main St Suite E1, West Vancouver, BC, V7T 2Z3
(604) 913-2630
Emp Here 100
SIC 5251 Hardware stores
Tony Main

D-U-N-S 24-957-9327 (BR)
HUDSON'S BAY COMPANY
BAY, THE
(*Suby of* HUDSON'S BAY COMPANY)
725 Park Royal N, West Vancouver, BC, V7T 1H9
(604) 925-1411
Emp Here 225
SIC 5311 Department stores
Jeff James

D-U-N-S 24-324-3198 (SL)
JAFFSONS HOLDINGS LTD
100 Park Royal S Suite 300, West Vancouver, BC, V7T 1A2
(604) 925-2700
Emp Here 2,200 *Sales* 804,119,800
SIC 6719 Holding companies, nec
Amin Lalji
Mansoor Lalji
Bill Moore

D-U-N-S 25-365-5294   (HQ)
LARCO HOSPITALITY INC
100 Park Royal S Unit 300, West Vancouver,
BC, V7T 1A2
(604) 925-2700
Sales 18,538,000
SIC 7011 Hotels and motels
Jim Nesbitt
Tim Mashford
Mark Mccue

D-U-N-S 24-030-2778   (HQ)
LARCO INVESTMENTS LTD
MAPLE LEAF SELF STORAGE
100 Park Royal S Suite 300, West Vancouver,
BC, V7T 1A2
(604) 925-2700
Sales 27,335,000
SIC 6719 Holding companies, nec

D-U-N-S 25-977-9072   (HQ)
MACPHERSON, PAUL & ASSOCIATES LTD
1010 Duchess Ave, West Vancouver, BC, V7T
1G9
(604) 925-0609
Emp Here 1   *Sales* 10,233,650
SIC 3669 Communications equipment, nec
Paul R Macpherson

D-U-N-S 24-567-0229   (HQ)
WGI MANUFACTURING INC
DIAMOND-KOTE
(*Suby of* C. WALKER GROUP INC)
1455 Bellevue Ave Suite 300, West Vancouver, BC, V7T 1C3
(604) 922-6563
Emp Here 30   *Sales* 17,041,260
SIC 2842 Polishes and sanitation goods
Charles Walker
Scott Walker

D-U-N-S 24-594-2909   (SL)
WGI SERVICE PLAN DIVISION INC
W3 SOLUTIONS
(*Suby of* C. WALKER GROUP INC)
1455 Bellevue Ave Suite 300, West Vancouver, BC, V7T 1C3
(604) 922-6563
Emp Here 101   *Sales* 215,833,768
SIC 6351 Surety insurance
Charles Walker
Beverly Walker

D-U-N-S 20-512-9190   (BR)
WHITE SPOT LIMITED
WHITE SPOT RESTAURANT
(*Suby of* SHATO HOLDINGS LTD)
752 Marine Dr Unit 1108, West Vancouver,
BC, V7T 1A6
(604) 922-4520
Emp Here 79
SIC 5812 Eating places
Milton Sorokin

D-U-N-S 20-554-3981   (HQ)
WHOLE FOODS MARKET CANADA INC
(*Suby of* AMAZON.COM, INC.)
925 Main St, West Vancouver, BC, V7T 2Z3
(604) 678-0500
Emp Here 50   *Sales* 29,347,700
SIC 5411 Grocery stores
Jorge Sosa

D-U-N-S 20-015-8165   (SL)
WORLD WIDE WARRANTY INC
1455 Bellevue Ave Suite 300, West Vancouver, BC, V7T 1C3
(604) 922-0305
Emp Here 10   *Sales* 10,468,669
SIC 6351 Surety insurance
Scott Walker
Charles S Walker
John S Burns
Shannon Walker
Phil Macdonnell
Robert W. Garnett

D-U-N-S 20-477-9243   (SL)

XEVA MORTGAGE
1455 Bellevue Ave Suite 213, West Vancouver, BC, V7T 1C3

Emp Here 45   *Sales* 10,113,480
SIC 6163 Loan brokers

West Vancouver, BC V7V

D-U-N-S 25-612-0973   (SL)
ANGELL HASMAN & ASSOCIATES REALTY LTD
1544 Marine Dr Suite 203, West Vancouver,
BC, V7V 1H8
(604) 921-1188
Emp Here 60   *Sales* 16,305,360
SIC 6531 Real estate agents and managers
Malcolm Hasman
Allan Angell

D-U-N-S 24-938-4140   (SL)
ARCAN DEVELOPMENTS LTD
WEST VANCOUVER CARE CENTRE
1675 27th St, West Vancouver, BC, V7V 4K9
(604) 925-1247
Emp Here 105   *Sales* 8,592,465
SIC 8069 Specialty hospitals, except psychiatric
Archie Woodworth
Candace Woodworth
Carrie Woodworth
Courtenay Woodworth

D-U-N-S 25-100-8819   (BR)
HOLLYBURN PROPERTIES LIMITED
(*Suby of* HOLLYBURN PROPERTIES LIMITED)
250 18th St, West Vancouver, BC, V7V 3V5
(604) 926-7345
Emp Here 100
SIC 6513 Apartment building operators
Frank Aldermir

D-U-N-S 25-613-4883   (SL)
PRUDENTIAL SUSSEX REALTY
2397 Marine Dr, West Vancouver, BC, V7V
1K9
(604) 913-4068
Emp Here 110   *Sales* 46,077,790
SIC 6531 Real estate agents and managers
Gordon Harmon

D-U-N-S 20-798-0939   (SL)
RUSCO ENTERPRISES LTD
2410 Marine Dr, West Vancouver, BC, V7V
1L1
(604) 925-9095
Emp Here 45   *Sales* 14,349,105
SIC 1521 Single-family housing construction
Russell Hollingsworth

D-U-N-S 25-369-3709   (HQ)
SCHOOL DISTRICT NO. 45 (WEST VANCOUVER)
1075 21st St Suite 45, West Vancouver, BC,
V7V 4A9
(604) 981-1000
Emp Here 25   *Sales* 60,678,991
SIC 8211 Elementary and secondary schools
Chris Kennedy
Kim Martin
Julia Leiterman
Carolyn Broady
Dave Stevenson
Nicole Brown
Sheelah Donahue
Pieter Dorsman

D-U-N-S 24-345-6360   (BR)
SCHOOL DISTRICT NO. 45 (WEST VANCOUVER)
WEST VANCOUVER SECONDARY SCHOOL
(*Suby of* SCHOOL DISTRICT NO. 45 (WEST VANCOUVER))

1750 Mathers Ave, West Vancouver, BC, V7V
2G7
(604) 981-1100
Emp Here 150
SIC 8211 Elementary and secondary schools
Steve Rauh

D-U-N-S 20-310-3960   (BR)
VANCOUVER, CITY OF
WEST VANCOUVER MEMORIAL LIBRARY
(*Suby of* VANCOUVER, CITY OF)
1950 Marine Dr, West Vancouver, BC, V7V
1J8
(604) 925-7400
Emp Here 80
SIC 8231 Libraries

D-U-N-S 20-915-3758   (SL)
WEST VAN FLORIST LTD
WEST VAN FLORIST HOME AND GARDEN
1821 Marine Dr, West Vancouver, BC, V7V
1J7
(604) 922-4171
Emp Here 40   *Sales* 13,024,000
SIC 5992 Florists
Robert Harrington
Wendy Harrington

West Vancouver, BC V7W

D-U-N-S 20-115-8177   (HQ)
SERVICE DRUG LTD
PHARMASAVE #214
5331 Headland Dr, West Vancouver, BC, V7W
3C6
(604) 926-5331
Emp Here 40   *Sales* 12,647,700
SIC 5912 Drug stores and proprietary stores

D-U-N-S 25-271-6956   (BR)
SOBEYS WEST INC
SAFEWAY PHARMACY
(*Suby of* EMPIRE COMPANY LIMITED)
5385 Headland Dr, West Vancouver, BC, V7W
3C7
(604) 926-2034
Emp Here 110
SIC 5411 Grocery stores
Glen Evans

D-U-N-S 20-796-7472   (HQ)
TOTEM COVE HOLDINGS INC
5776 Marine Dr, West Vancouver, BC, V7W
2S2
(604) 921-7434
Emp Here 20   *Sales* 11,321,058
SIC 4493 Marinas
Robert Welch
Mike Depfyffer
Fred Macdonald
Peter Welch
Barry Sutton

Westbank, BC V4T

D-U-N-S 20-271-9407   (BR)
DISTRICT OF WEST KELOWNA
DISTRICT OF WEST KELOWNA FIRE DEPARTMENT
(*Suby of* DISTRICT OF WEST KELOWNA)
3651 Old Okanagan Hwy, Westbank, BC, V4T
1P6
(250) 769-1640
Emp Here 90
SIC 7389 Business services, nec
Wayne Schnitzler

D-U-N-S 20-337-7072   (SL)
OKANAGAN NATION AQUATIC ENTERPRISES LTD
3535 Old Okanagan Hwy Unit 104, Westbank,
BC, V4T 3L7

(778) 754-8001
Emp Here 90   *Sales* 12,308,310
SIC 0921 Fish hatcheries and preserves
Pauline Terbasket
Keith Crow
Jonathan Kruger
Byron Louie
Clarence Louie
Robert Louie
Harvey Mcleod
Charlotte Mitchell

D-U-N-S 24-593-7321   (SL)
WESTBANK FIRST NATION PINE ACRES HOME
PINE ACRES HOME
1902 Pheasant Lane, Westbank, BC, V4T 2H4
(250) 768-7676
Emp Here 85   *Sales* 5,035,995
SIC 8361 Residential care
Robert Louie
Jo-Ann Derrickson

Whistler, BC V0N

D-U-N-S 24-311-3362   (SL)
ALIK ENTERPRISES LTD
ARAXI RESTAURANT & BAR
4222 Village Sq, Whistler, BC, V0N 1B4
(604) 932-4540
Emp Here 80   *Sales* 3,641,520
SIC 5812 Eating places
Jack Evrensel

D-U-N-S 24-725-4030   (SL)
ALPINE ELECTRIC LTD
1085 Millar Creek Rd Suite 3, Whistler, BC,
V0N 1B1

Emp Here 60   *Sales* 13,069,740
SIC 1731 Electrical work
Andrew Tacilauskas
Jamie Yetman

D-U-N-S 25-066-7722   (SL)
BIG RED DOG INC
EXTREMELY CANADIAN ADVENTURES & PROMOTIONS
4122 Village Green Suite 5, Whistler, BC, V0N
1B4
(604) 938-9656
Emp Here 30   *Sales* 15,599,010
SIC 4725 Tour operators
Peter Smart

D-U-N-S 25-264-8964   (SL)
CANADIAN WILDERNESS ADVENTURES LTD
4545 Blackcomb Way, Whistler, BC, V0N 1B4
(604) 938-1554
Emp Here 49   *Sales* 24,405,822
SIC 5571 Motorcycle dealers
Dennis Van Dongen

D-U-N-S 25-979-2018   (SL)
GREEN LAKE PROJECTS INC
NICKLAUS NORTH GOLF COURSE
8080 Nicklaus Blvd N, Whistler, BC, V0N 1B0
(604) 938-9898
Emp Here 150   *Sales* 11,781,750
SIC 7997 Membership sports and recreation clubs
Caleb Chan
Donald Lee
Tom Chan

D-U-N-S 25-997-3014   (SL)
OHR WHISTLER MANAGEMENT LTD
WESTIN RESORT & SPA
4090 Whistler Way, Whistler, BC, V0N 1B4
(604) 905-5000
Emp Here 400   *Sales* 38,267,200
SIC 7011 Hotels and motels
John O'neill
Norman Dowad

Robert O'neill

D-U-N-S 24-658-8750   (SL)
PANZEX VANCOUVER INC
THE ORIGINAL RISTORANTE
4270 Mountain Sq, Whistler, BC, V0N 1B4
(604) 932-6945
Emp Here 75   *Sales* 3,215,475
SIC 5812 Eating places
Lawrence Black
Willy Jang

D-U-N-S 20-977-7585   (SL)
PATENT PENDING IDEAS
1200 Alpha Lake Rd Suite 205c, Whistler, BC,
V0N 1B1
(604) 905-6485
Emp Here 49   *Sales* 10,374,476
SIC 7336 Commercial art and graphic design
Chris Armstrong

D-U-N-S 24-837-9075   (SL)
SNOWLINE RESTAURANTS INC
KEG AT THE MOUNTAIN
4429 Sundial Pl, Whistler, BC, V0N 1B4
(604) 932-5151
Emp Here 80   *Sales* 3,641,520
SIC 5812 Eating places
David Patriquin

D-U-N-S 25-969-8884   (SL)
VISION WEST DEVELOPMENT LTD
VISION PACIFIC
6717 Crabapple Dr, Whistler, BC, V0N 1B6
(604) 932-5275
Emp Here 40   *Sales* 12,754,760
SIC 1521 Single-family housing construction
Tim Regan

D-U-N-S 25-505-0478   (HQ)
WHISTLER & BLACKCOMB MOUNTAIN
RESORTS LIMITED
GARBANZO BIKE & BEAN
4545 Blackcomb Way Rr 4, Whistler, BC, V0N
1B4
(604) 932-3141
Sales 95,668,000
SIC 7011 Hotels and motels
Pete Fonntag

Whistler, BC V8E

D-U-N-S 20-650-4149   (SL)
BEVENDALE ENTERPRISES LTD
1380 Alpha Lake Rd Suite 4, Whistler, BC,
V8E 0H9
(604) 932-5506
Emp Here 60   *Sales* 17,608,620
SIC 5411 Grocery stores
Sandy Carrico

D-U-N-S 24-119-6609   (SL)
BLACKCOMB SKIING ENTERPRISES LIM-
ITED PARTNERSHIP
4545 Blackcomb Way, Whistler, BC, V8E 0X9
(604) 932-3141
Emp Here 1,300   *Sales* 124,368,400
SIC 7011 Hotels and motels
Ross Meacher

D-U-N-S 24-025-0899   (SL)
CREEKSIDE MARKET INC
2071 Lake Placid Rd Suite 305, Whistler, BC,
V8E 0B6
(604) 938-9301
Emp Here 45   *Sales* 12,336,840
SIC 5411 Grocery stores
Jerry Marsh

D-U-N-S 24-806-0204   (BR)
FAIRMONT HOTELS & RESORTS INC
(*Suby of* ACCOR)
4599 Chateau Blvd, Whistler, BC, V8E 0Z5
(604) 938-8000
Emp Here 600

SIC 7011 Hotels and motels
Jennifer Fox

D-U-N-S 20-610-9246   (HQ)
FS WHISTLER HOLDINGS LIMITED
*FOUR SEASONS RESORT AND RESI-
DENCES WHISTLER*
4591 Blackcomb Way, Whistler, BC, V8E 0Y4
(604) 935-3400
Sales 23,917,000
SIC 7011 Hotels and motels
Kathleen Taylor
Randolph Weisz
Jennifer Elfenbein

D-U-N-S 25-361-2402   (BR)
FS WHISTLER HOLDINGS LIMITED
FOUR SEASONS RESIDENCES
(*Suby of* FS WHISTLER HOLDINGS LIM-
ITED)
4591 Blackcomb Way, Whistler, BC, V8E 0Y4
(604) 935-3400
Emp Here 300
SIC 7011 Hotels and motels
Arthur Davies

D-U-N-S 25-827-0610   (BR)
GOLFBC HOLDINGS INC
DEN AT NICKLAUS NORTH
(*Suby of* GOLFBC HOLDINGS INC)
8080 Nicklaus North Blvd, Whistler, BC, V8E
1J7
(604) 938-9898
Emp Here 100
SIC 5812 Eating places
Jeff Ciecko

D-U-N-S 25-116-2640   (BR)
INTRAWEST RESORT CLUB GROUP
EMBARC WHISTLER
(*Suby of* HAWK HOLDING COMPANY, LLC)
4580 Chateau Blvd, Whistler, BC, V8E 0Z6
(604) 938-3030
Emp Here 115
SIC 7011 Hotels and motels
Lisa Davis

D-U-N-S 24-931-4485   (BR)
LISTEL CANADA LTD
LISTEL HOTEL
(*Suby of* LISTEL GROUP)
4121 Village Green, Whistler, BC, V8E 1H2
(604) 932-1133
Emp Here 110
SIC 7011 Hotels and motels
Doug Andrews

D-U-N-S 24-856-0666   (SL)
NESTERS MARKET LTD
(*Suby of* PATTISON, JIM GROUP INC)
7019 Nesters Rd, Whistler, BC, V8E 0X1
(604) 932-3545
Emp Here 55   *Sales* 16,141,235
SIC 5411 Grocery stores
Brian Kerr
Martha Heintzman
Ken Beatty
Elaine Kerr

D-U-N-S 20-653-6919   (SL)
OLD SPAGHETTI FACTORY (WHISTLER)
LTD
4154 Village Green, Whistler, BC, V8E 1H1
(604) 938-1015
Emp Here 75   *Sales* 3,413,925
SIC 5812 Eating places
Marlys Clemiss

D-U-N-S 25-023-6882   (SL)
SUMMIT SKI LIMITED
(*Suby of* INTRAWEST EUROPE HOLDINGS
SARL)
4293 Mountain Sq Unit 118, Whistler, BC, V8E
1B8
(604) 932-6225
Emp Here 60   *Sales* 14,659,680
SIC 5941 Sporting goods and bicycle shops
Ian Van Gruen

David Reid
Brett Milner

D-U-N-S 25-934-8688   (SL)
WHISTLER CONNECTION TOUR & TRAVEL
SERVICES LTD
WHISTLER CONNECTION
8056 Nesters Rd, Whistler, BC, V8E 0G4
(604) 938-9711
Emp Here 45   *Sales* 17,341,200
SIC 4725 Tour operators
William Murray
Stephanie Murray

D-U-N-S 25-514-0774   (SL)
WHISTLER MOUNTAIN RESORT LIMITED
PARTNERSHIP
WHISTLER & BLACKCOMB MOUNTAINS
4545 Blackcomb Way, Whistler, BC, V8E 0X9
(604) 932-3141
Emp Here 200   *Sales* 18,538,000
SIC 7011 Hotels and motels
Randy Goodwin

D-U-N-S 24-143-8720   (SL)
WHISTLER PLATINUM RESERVATIONS
204 4230 Gateway Dr, Whistler, BC, V8E 0Z8
(604) 932-0100
Emp Here 38   *Sales* 19,758,746
SIC 4725 Tour operators
Damian Saw
Corrine Harris

D-U-N-S 24-578-2586   (HQ)
WHISTLER REAL ESTATE COMPANY LIM-
ITED, THE
4308 Main St Suite 17, Whistler, BC, V8E 1A9
(604) 932-5538
Emp Here 40   *Sales* 12,229,020
SIC 6531 Real estate agents and managers
Patrick Kelly

D-U-N-S 24-247-9905   (SL)
WHISTLER RESORT ASSOCIATION
WHISTLER GOLF CLUB
4010 Whistler Way, Whistler, BC, V8E 1J2
(604) 664-5625
Emp Here 100   *Sales* 13,684,566
SIC 8743 Public relations services
Barrett Fisher
Karen Playfair
Karen Goodwin
Louise Walker
Norman Mastalir
Duane Hepditch
Dave Brownlie
Saad Hasan
Stuart Rempel
Tony Cary-Barnard

D-U-N-S 25-928-6003   (SL)
WHISTLER TAXI LTD
SEA TO SKY
1080 Millar Creek Rd Suite 201, Whistler, BC,
V8E 0S7
(604) 932-4430
Emp Here 80   *Sales* 4,389,760
SIC 4121 Taxicabs
Eric Larsen

D-U-N-S 24-233-4410   (SL)
WW HOTELS (WHISTLER) LIMITED PART-
NERSHIP
HILTON WHISTLER RESORT & SPA
4050 Whistler Way, Whistler, BC, V8E 1H9
(604) 932-1982
Emp Here 200   *Sales* 18,538,000
SIC 7011 Hotels and motels
Scott De Savoye

White Rock, BC V4B

D-U-N-S 25-612-0882   (SL)
527758 B.C. LTD

OCEAN BEACH HOTEL, THE
14995 Marine Dr Suite 6, White Rock, BC,
V4B 1C3

Emp Here 35   *Sales* 10,469,550
SIC 5921 Liquor stores
Tony Veltri

D-U-N-S 25-068-2853   (SL)
ANNETTE'S KEEPSAKES
Gd, White Rock, BC, V4B 5L5
(604) 538-5890
Emp Here 35   *Sales* 18,525,391
SIC 5099 Durable goods, nec
Annette Symonds

D-U-N-S 24-792-7358   (SL)
APPLE SECURITY INC
15216 North Bluff Rd Suite 604, White Rock,
BC, V4B 0A7
(604) 507-9577
Emp Here 49   *Sales* 21,731,010
SIC 7389 Business services, nec
Steve Harvester

D-U-N-S 20-624-1754   (SL)
AZARGA METALS CORP
15782 Marine Dr Unit 1, White Rock, BC, V4B
1E6
(604) 536-2711
Emp Here 103   *Sales* 245,917,547
SIC 1021 Copper ores
Michael Hopley
Alexander Yakubchuk
Doris Meyer
Dan O'brien
Alexander Molyneux
Vladimir Pakhomov
Blake Steele
Trevor Steel

D-U-N-S 24-362-8661   (HQ)
AZARGA URANIUM CORP
15782 Marine Dr Unit 1, White Rock, BC, V4B
1E6
(604) 536-2711
Sales 64,463,823
SIC 1081 Metal mining services
Blake Steele
John Mays
Dan O'brien
Doris Meyer
Glenn Catchpole
Joseph Havlin
Todd Hilditch
Sandra Mackay
Matthew O'kane

D-U-N-S 20-334-7518   (SL)
BOATHOUSE RESTAURANTS OF CANADA
14935 Marine Dr, White Rock, BC, V4B 1C3
(604) 536-7320
Emp Here 120   *Sales* 5,462,280
SIC 5812 Eating places
Kelly Gordon

D-U-N-S 24-397-7902   (HQ)
CANADIAN METAL AND FIBRE LTD
HILLTOP PETRO CANADA
1392 Johnston Rd, White Rock, BC, V4B 3Z2
(604) 535-2793
Emp Here 5   *Sales* 24,903,900
SIC 5541 Gasoline service stations
Gary Baghela

D-U-N-S 20-911-5682   (SL)
EVERGREEN BAPTIST HOME
1550 Oxford St, White Rock, BC, V4B 3R5
(604) 536-3344
Emp Here 125   *Sales* 8,540,750
SIC 8051 Skilled nursing care facilities
Catherine Rutter

Williams Lake, BC V2G

D-U-N-S 24-887-3150   (SL)
ATLANTIC POWER (WILLIAMS LAKE) LTD
(*Suby of* ATLANTIC POWER CORPORA-TION)
4455 Mackenzie Ave N, Williams Lake, BC, V2G 5E8
(250) 392-6394
Emp Here 32   *Sales* 20,051,648
SIC 4911 Electric services
  Mark Blezard

D-U-N-S 24-537-7200   (HQ)
AXIS FAMILY RESOURCES LTD
321 Second Ave N, Williams Lake, BC, V2G 2A1
(250) 392-1000
Emp Here 10   *Sales* 11,341,650
SIC 8399 Social services, nec
  Ann Smith

D-U-N-S 20-120-7461   (SL)
CARIBOO CHEVROLET BUICK GMC LTD
CARIBOO GM
370 Mackenzie Ave S, Williams Lake, BC, V2G 1C7
(250) 392-7185
Emp Here 34   *Sales* 16,934,652
SIC 5511 New and used car dealers
  Brian Garland
  Tom White
  Conrad Pinette
  Roger Tarion

D-U-N-S 20-873-1070   (SL)
CARIBOO CHEVROLET OLDSMOBILE PONTIAC BUICK GMC LTD
370 Mackenzie Ave S, Williams Lake, BC, V2G 1C7
(250) 392-7185
Emp Here 35   *Sales* 17,432,730
SIC 5511 New and used car dealers
  Brian Garland

D-U-N-S 24-135-5080   (SL)
CARIBOO MEMORIAL HOSPITAL
517 Sixth Ave N Suite 401, Williams Lake, BC, V2G 2G8
(250) 392-4411
Emp Here 270   *Sales* 29,991,600
SIC 8062 General medical and surgical hospitals
  Polly Chalifoux
  Allison Ruault

D-U-N-S 24-292-1070   (SL)
CHUCK'S AUTO SUPPLY LTD
861 Mackenzie Ave S, Williams Lake, BC, V2G 3X8
(250) 398-7012
Emp Here 30   *Sales* 10,926,450
SIC 5013 Motor vehicle supplies and new parts
  Marcel Therrien
  Fred Manchur

D-U-N-S 24-212-2273   (SL)
CPM FOODS LTD
MCDONALDS RESTAURANT
1324 Broadway Ave S, Williams Lake, BC, V2G 4N2
(250) 392-4919
Emp Here 95   *Sales* 24,847,535
SIC 6712 Bank holding companies
  James (Jim) Knowles

D-U-N-S 20-510-5307   (SL)
GUSTAFSON'S AUTO SERVICE LTD
122 Broadway Ave N, Williams Lake, BC, V2G 2X8
(250) 392-2305
Emp Here 36   *Sales* 17,930,808
SIC 5511 New and used car dealers
  Kerry Gustafson

D-U-N-S 20-172-5533   (SL)
GUSTAFSON'S AUTOMOBILE CO LTD
GUSTAFSON'S KIA
122 Broadway Ave N, Williams Lake, BC, V2G 2X8
(250) 392-3035
Emp Here 30   *Sales* 14,942,340
SIC 5511 New and used car dealers
  Kerry Gustafson

D-U-N-S 20-120-7388   (SL)
HEARTLAND MOTORS LIMITED
HEARTLAND TOYOTA
106 Broadway Ave N, Williams Lake, BC, V2G 2X7
(250) 392-3225
Emp Here 21   *Sales* 10,459,638
SIC 5521 Used car dealers
  Ed Leidl
  Randy Beatson
  Jacine Chappell
  Bill Cornish

D-U-N-S 20-120-7727   (SL)
LAKE CITY FORD SALES INC
800 Broadway Ave N, Williams Lake, BC, V2G 3P4
(250) 392-4455
Emp Here 40   *Sales* 19,923,120
SIC 5511 New and used car dealers
  Warren Lux

D-U-N-S 25-088-3543   (BR)
LOBLAWS INC
WHOLESALE CLUB
(*Suby of* LOBLAW COMPANIES LIMITED)
1000 South Lakeside Dr, Williams Lake, BC, V2G 3A6
(250) 305-2150
Emp Here 80
SIC 5141 Groceries, general line
  Andrea Moleschi

D-U-N-S 25-262-5959   (HQ)
PIONEER LOG HOMES OF BRITISH COLUMBIA LTD
351 Hodgson Rd, Williams Lake, BC, V2G 3P7
(250) 392-5577
Sales 32,513,040
SIC 1521 Single-family housing construction
  Bryan Reid
  Marcel Therrien

D-U-N-S 24-535-1507   (HQ)
SCHOOL DISTRICT NO 27 (CARIBOO-CHILCOTIN)
350 Second Ave N, Williams Lake, BC, V2G 1Z9
(250) 398-3800
Sales 49,701,226
SIC 8211 Elementary and secondary schools
  Mark Wintjes

D-U-N-S 20-587-7186   (HQ)
TASCO SUPPLIES LTD
CARIBOO STEEL CENTRE
336 Mackenzie Ave N, Williams Lake, BC, V2G 1N7
(250) 392-6232
Emp Here 31   *Sales* 18,050,988
SIC 5085 Industrial supplies
  Richard Weil

D-U-N-S 25-195-4483   (BR)
TOLKO INDUSTRIES LTD
SODA CREEK DIVISION
(*Suby of* AMERICAN INDUSTRIAL ACQUISI-TION CORPORATION)
5000 Soda Creek Rd, Williams Lake, BC, V2G 5E4
(250) 398-3600
Emp Here 250
SIC 2421 Sawmills and planing mills, general
  Ryan Oliver

D-U-N-S 20-795-7564   (BR)
WEST FRASER MILLS LTD
(*Suby of* WEST FRASER TIMBER CO. LTD)
4255 Rottacker Rd, Williams Lake, BC, V2G 5E4
(250) 392-7784
Emp Here 200

SIC 2421 Sawmills and planing mills, general
  D'arcy Henderson

D-U-N-S 20-120-8006   (BR)
WEST FRASER MILLS LTD
WILLIAMS LAKE PLYWOOD
(*Suby of* WEST FRASER TIMBER CO. LTD)
4200 Mackenzie Ave N, Williams Lake, BC, V2G 1N4
(250) 392-7731
Emp Here 350
SIC 2421 Sawmills and planing mills, general
  David Walgren

Woss, BC V0N

D-U-N-S 24-372-8300   (BR)
CANADIAN FOREST PRODUCTS LTD
ENGLEWOOD LOGGING, DIV OF
(*Suby of* CANFOR CORPORATION)
Gd, Woss, BC, V0N 3P0
(250) 281-2300
Emp Here 250
SIC 2421 Sawmills and planing mills, general
  John Holmes

Wynndel, BC V0B

D-U-N-S 20-120-9533   (SL)
WYNNDEL BOX & LUMBER COMPANY LTD
1140 Winlaw Rd, Wynndel, BC, V0B 2N1
(250) 866-5231
Emp Here 100   *Sales* 15,586,300
SIC 2421 Sawmills and planing mills, general
  Michael Wigen

▲ Public Company   ■ Public Company Family Member   **HQ** Headquarters   **BR** Branch   **SL** Single Location

Alexander, MB R0K

D-U-N-S 20-834-9159   (SL)
DEERBOINE COLONY FARMS LTD
DEERBOINE COLONY OF HUTTERIAN BRETHREN TRUST
Gd, Alexander, MB, R0K 0A0
(204) 728-7383
Emp Here 100   *Sales* 26,230,900
SIC 0119 Cash grains, nec
 Mel Hofer
 Thomas Hofer
 Christian Wurtz

Altona, MB R0G

D-U-N-S 20-000-1774   (HQ)
FRIESENS CORPORATION
FRIESEN PRINTERS
1 Printers Way, Altona, MB, R0G 0B0
(204) 324-6401
Emp Here 511   *Sales* 14,403,938
SIC 2732 Book printing
 Chad Friesen
 Curwin Friesen
 Curt Letkeman
 Doug Symington

D-U-N-S 20-000-2053   (HQ)
GOLDEN WEST BROADCASTING
THE EAGLE 94.1 FM SWIFT CURRENT SK
125 Centre Ave W Suite 201, Altona, MB, R0G 0B0
(204) 324-6464
Emp Here 60   *Sales* 45,694,400
SIC 4832 Radio broadcasting stations
 Elmer Hildebrand
 Lyndon Friesen

D-U-N-S 20-837-2946   (HQ)
RED RIVER VALLEY MUTUAL INSURANCE COMPANY
245 Centre Ave E, Altona, MB, R0G 0B0
(204) 324-6434
Emp Here 35   *Sales* 82,294,857
SIC 6411 Insurance agents, brokers, and service
 Brian Esau
 Geoff Branson
 Lyndon Friesen
 Alvin Ginter
 Rob Hamelynck
 Ray Loewen
 Garth Reimer
 Darrel Penner
 Catherine Kloepfer
 Monique Vielfaure-Mackenzie

D-U-N-S 20-502-3802   (SL)
THINK4D INC
511 Industrial Dr, Altona, MB, R0G 0B0
(204) 324-6401
Emp Here 35   *Sales* 15,522,150
SIC 7389 Business services, nec
 Chad Friesens
 Michael Fehr

D-U-N-S 20-436-2545   (SL)
WEST PARK MOTORS LTD
248 Centre Ave Se Ss 3, Altona, MB, R0G 0B3
(204) 324-6494
Emp Here 29   *Sales* 14,444,262
SIC 5511 New and used car dealers
 Ray Loewen

Angusville, MB R0J

D-U-N-S 24-967-3336   (SL)
GLANBIA NUTRITIONALS (CANADA) INC

PIZZEY'S NUTRITIONAL
(*Suby of* GLANBIA PUBLIC LIMITED COMPANY)
190 Main St S, Angusville, MB, R0J 0A0
(204) 773-2575
Emp Here 50   *Sales* 37,126,000
SIC 5191 Farm supplies
 Linda Pizzey
 Glenn Pizzey

Arborg, MB R0C

D-U-N-S 24-171-9384   (SL)
ARBORG & DISTRICT HEALTH CENTER
Gd, Arborg, MB, R0C 0A0
(204) 376-5247
Emp Here 100   *Sales* 11,108,000
SIC 8062 General medical and surgical hospitals
 Ruby Tretiak

D-U-N-S 24-428-1176   (SL)
DIEMO MACHINE WORKS INC
Hwy 326 N, Arborg, MB, R0C 0A0
(204) 364-2404
Emp Here 90   *Sales* 19,980,090
SIC 3523 Farm machinery and equipment
 Jacob Wiebe
 Les Loewen
 George Wiebe

D-U-N-S 20-000-2418   (HQ)
INTERLAKE CONSUMERS CO-OPERATIVE LIMITED
253 Main St, Arborg, MB, R0C 0A0
(204) 376-5245
Emp Here 37   *Sales* 113,148,090
SIC 5171 Petroleum bulk stations and terminals
 Reg Perry
 Robin Toni
 Andrea Sweetland
 Brian Fjeldsted
 Doreen Lindell
 Greg Lupal
 Clayton Tompkins

D-U-N-S 25-289-0934   (BR)
INTERLAKE REGIONAL HEALTH AUTHORITY INC
ARBORG PERSONAL CARE HOME
233 St Phillips Dr, Arborg, MB, R0C 0A0
(204) 376-5226
Emp Here 75
SIC 8051 Skilled nursing care facilities
 Dorothy Froman

D-U-N-S 24-236-9155   (SL)
JOHNSON, S. S. SEEDS LTD
Gd, Arborg, MB, R0C 0A0
(204) 376-5228
Emp Here 25   *Sales* 18,563,000
SIC 5191 Farm supplies
 Brian Johnson
 Keith Johnson
 Lorne Johnson
 June Christopherson

D-U-N-S 24-115-8732   (HQ)
VIDIR MACHINE INC
8126 Rd 138 North, Arborg, MB, R0C 0A0
(204) 364-2442
Sales 23,761,828
SIC 3399 Primary Metal products
 Peter Dueck
 Sid Dueck

Arden, MB R0J

D-U-N-S 20-834-8854   (SL)
RIVERSIDE HUTTERIAN MUTUAL CORPO-

RATION
RIVERSIDE POULTRY FARM
Gd, Arden, MB, R0J 0B0
(204) 368-2444
Emp Here 116   *Sales* 29,404,840
SIC 8748 Business consulting, nec
 John J Hofer
 David Hofer

Argyle, MB R0C

D-U-N-S 24-036-5320   (SL)
NEW HAVEN COLONY FARMS LTD
82080 Rd 1 E, Argyle, MB, R0C 0B0
(204) 467-8790
Emp Here 88   *Sales* 17,412,384
SIC 8661 Religious organizations
 Michael Wollman
 Jacob Waldner
 David Wollmann

Ashern, MB R0C

D-U-N-S 24-883-4806   (SL)
ASHERN GARAGE LTD
ASHERN SERVICE
2 Main St, Ashern, MB, R0C 0E0
(204) 768-2835
Emp Here 35   *Sales* 17,432,730
SIC 5541 Gasoline service stations
 Diane Price

D-U-N-S 20-647-6280   (BR)
INTERLAKE REGIONAL HEALTH AUTHORITY INC
LAKESHORE HEALTH CENTER
1 Steenson Dr, Ashern, MB, R0C 0E0
(204) 768-2461
Emp Here 100
SIC 8062 General medical and surgical hospitals
 Linda Fisson

Bagot, MB R0H

D-U-N-S 24-883-5084   (SL)
ASPENHEIM COLONY FARMS LTD
ASPENHEIM COLONY OF HUTTERIAN BRETHREN - TRUST
Gd, Bagot, MB, R0H 0E0
(204) 274-2782
Emp Here 30   *Sales* 10,274,010
SIC 0191 General farms, primarily crop
 Ben Waldner
 Rueben Waldner
 Jacob Waldner

D-U-N-S 20-329-7395   (SL)
RIVER VALLEY SPECIALTY FARMS INC
Gd, Bagot, MB, R0H 0E0
(204) 274-2467
Emp Here 70   *Sales* 18,361,630
SIC 0161 Vegetables and melons
 James Kuhl

Baldur, MB R0K

D-U-N-S 24-852-9281   (SL)
TRI-LEAF COLONY OF HUTTERIAN BRETHREN
Gd, Baldur, MB, R0K 0B0
(204) 535-2274
Emp Here 95   *Sales* 24,919,355
SIC 0191 General farms, primarily crop
 Jacob Waldner Sr

Beausejour, MB R0E

D-U-N-S 20-000-3812   (HQ)
BEAUSEJOUR CONSUMERS CO-OPERATIVE LIMITED
605 Park Ave, Beausejour, MB, R0E 0C0
(204) 268-2605
Emp Here 57   *Sales* 56,286,135
SIC 5171 Petroleum bulk stations and terminals
 Les Howard
 Richard Kuffner
 Dan Bergson
 Robert Carmichael
 Ernie Chalus
 Wayne Wittmeier
 Rhonda Friesen
 Diane Einarson

D-U-N-S 25-653-4777   (SL)
MELNICK MOTORS LTD
1012 Park Ave, Beausejour, MB, R0E 0C0
(204) 268-1514
Emp Here 26   *Sales* 12,950,028
SIC 5511 New and used car dealers
 Jeffrey Melnick
 Thecla Melnick

D-U-N-S 20-836-9413   (BR)
NORTH EASTMAN HEALTH ASSOCIATION INC
BEAUSEJOUR HEALTH CENTRE
151 1 St S, Beausejour, MB, R0E 0C0
(204) 268-1076
Emp Here 175
SIC 8062 General medical and surgical hospitals
 Brenda Neufeld

D-U-N-S 20-278-3655   (HQ)
SUNRISE SCHOOL DIVISION
344 2nd St N, Beausejour, MB, R0E 0C0
(204) 268-6500
Emp Here 20   *Sales* 74,339,250
SIC 8211 Elementary and secondary schools
 Wayne Leckie
 Diane Duma
 Al Tymko

D-U-N-S 25-176-8024   (BR)
SUNRISE SCHOOL DIVISION
EDWARD SCHREYER SCHOOL
(*Suby of* SUNRISE SCHOOL DIVISION)
85 5th St S, Beausejour, MB, R0E 0C0
(204) 268-2423
Emp Here 92
SIC 8211 Elementary and secondary schools
 Cathy Tymco

Birtle, MB R0M

D-U-N-S 25-134-8231   (HQ)
PARK WEST SCHOOL DIVISION
1161 St Clare St N, Birtle, MB, R0M 0C0
(204) 842-2100
Emp Here 19   *Sales* 19,922,919
SIC 8211 Elementary and secondary schools
 Gerald Puhach

D-U-N-S 20-000-5650   (HQ)
TWIN VALLEY CO-OP LTD
861 Vine St, Birtle, MB, R0M 0C0
(204) 842-3387
Emp Here 15   *Sales* 29,347,700
SIC 5411 Grocery stores
 Dwayne Moncur
 John Bonnell
 Mark Morton
 Mike Heneghan
 Garth Butcher
 Lawson Ashcroft

Blumenort, MB R0A

D-U-N-S 24-804-0078   (HQ)
4117638 MANITOBA LTD
SOUTH EAST PALLET AND WOOD PRODUCTS
94 Penner Dr S, Blumenort, MB, R0A 0C0
(204) 346-9314
Emp Here 2   *Sales* 10,185,201
SIC 2448 Wood pallets and skids
  Darrel Penner
  Ron Gerardy
  Reginald Penner
  Randall Penner

D-U-N-S 24-748-7523   (HQ)
A.G. PENNER FARM SERVICES LTD
10 Penner Dr, Blumenort, MB, R0A 0C0
(204) 326-3781
Sales 19,954,550
SIC 6712 Bank holding companies
  Reginald Penner
  Darrel Penner
  Randy Penner

D-U-N-S 20-710-2757   (BR)
GRANNY'S POULTRY COOPERATIVE (MANITOBA) LTD
(*Suby of* GRANNY'S POULTRY COOPERATIVE (MANITOBA) LTD)
4 Penner, Blumenort, MB, R0A 0C0
(204) 452-6315
Emp Here 350
SIC 2015 Poultry slaughtering and processing
  Carry Vadeboncoeur

D-U-N-S 20-000-5833   (HQ)
K.K. PENNER TIRE CENTERS INC
39 Penner Dr, Blumenort, MB, R0A 0C0
(204) 326-6419
Emp Here 27   *Sales* 24,903,900
SIC 5531 Auto and home supply stores
  Mike Warkentin
  Irene Penner
  Gerald Penner

D-U-N-S 24-747-7649   (HQ)
PENN-CO CONSTRUCTION CANADA LTD
(*Suby of* ERNEST G. PENNER INVESTMENTS LTD)
25 Penner Dr, Blumenort, MB, R0A 0C0
(204) 326-1341
Sales 28,516,900
SIC 1542 Nonresidential construction, nec
  Ernest G Penner
  Dan Reimer
  Dave Caron

D-U-N-S 25-539-5659   (HQ)
PENN-CO CONSTRUCTION INT'L LTD
(*Suby of* ERNEST G. PENNER INVESTMENTS LTD)
16 Centre Ave, Blumenort, MB, R0A 0C0
(204) 326-1341
Emp Here 1   *Sales* 28,516,900
SIC 1542 Nonresidential construction, nec
  Ernest G. Penner

D-U-N-S 25-539-5618   (SL)
PENN-CO CONSTRUCTION LTD
PENNER PROPERTIES WEST
24 Centre Ave, Blumenort, MB, R0A 0C0
(204) 326-1341
Emp Here 25   *Sales* 10,483,875
SIC 6712 Bank holding companies
  Ernest G. Penner
  Robert Froese

D-U-N-S 25-067-1492   (HQ)
STEVE'S LIVESTOCK TRANSPORTATION (BLUMENORT) LTD
BISON VIEW TRAILERS
214 Center Ave Ss 10, Blumenort, MB, R0A 0C1
(204) 326-6380
Sales 25,096,132

SIC 4212 Local trucking, without storage
  Steven Brant

Boissevain, MB R0K

D-U-N-S 20-000-5965   (SL)
DU-RITE MOTORS LIMITED
237 Mill Rd, Boissevain, MB, R0K 0E0
(204) 534-2929
Emp Here 20   *Sales* 10,000,000
SIC 5083 Farm and garden machinery
  George Dyck

D-U-N-S 20-001-6020   (HQ)
GOODON, IRVIN INDUSTRIES LTD
GOODON INDUSTRIES
Hwy 10, Boissevain, MB, R0K 0E0
(204) 534-2468
Emp Here 1   *Sales* 17,110,140
SIC 1542 Nonresidential construction, nec
  Bryan Tyerman
  Irvin Goodon
  Robert Dyck

Brandon, MB R7A

D-U-N-S 24-368-1256   (SL)
5517509 MANITOBA LTD
THE GREEN SPOT
1329 Rosser Ave E, Brandon, MB, R7A 7J2
(204) 728-7540
Emp Here 52   *Sales* 13,917,904
SIC 5261 Retail nurseries and garden stores
  Bernie Whetter

D-U-N-S 25-361-5173   (BR)
ALLSTREAM BUSINESS INC
(*Suby of* ZAYO GROUP HOLDINGS, INC.)
517 18th St, Brandon, MB, R7A 5Y9
(204) 225-5687
Emp Here 150
SIC 4899 Communication services, nec

D-U-N-S 20-149-6291   (HQ)
B.O.B. HEADQUARTERS INC
658 18th St Unit 2, Brandon, MB, R7A 5B4
(204) 728-7470
Emp Here 16   *Sales* 11,816,352
SIC 5961 Catalog and mail-order houses
  Robert Ritchot

D-U-N-S 20-065-3165   (HQ)
BEHLEN INDUSTRIES LP
(*Suby of* TREVLUC HOLDINGS LTD)
927 Douglas St, Brandon, MB, R7A 7B3
(204) 728-1188
Sales 174,598,000
SIC 1541 Industrial buildings and warehouses
  Sean Lepper

D-U-N-S 20-190-5275   (BR)
BELL MTS INC
(*Suby of* BCE INC)
517 18th St, Brandon, MB, R7A 5Y9
(204) 727-4500
Emp Here 480
SIC 4841 Cable and other pay television services
  Florence Payne

D-U-N-S 24-232-5256   (HQ)
BRANDON CLINIC MEDICAL CORPORATION
620 Dennis St, Brandon, MB, R7A 5E7
(204) 728-4440
Emp Here 1   *Sales* 21,873,805
SIC 8011 Offices and clinics of medical doctors
  Jean Deong
  Ravi Shunmugam
  Pieter Vanrensburg

D-U-N-S 20-807-6484   (SL)
BRANDON COMMUNITY OPTIONS INC
136 11th St, Brandon, MB, R7A 4J4
(204) 571-5770
Emp Here 200   *Sales* 13,684,400
SIC 8322 Individual and family services
  Brenda Elmes

D-U-N-S 25-162-7394   (BR)
BRANDON SCHOOL DIVISION, THE
CROCUS PLAINS REGIONAL SECONDARY SCHOOL
(*Suby of* BRANDON SCHOOL DIVISION, THE)
1930 1st St, Brandon, MB, R7A 6Y6
(204) 729-3900
Emp Here 80
SIC 8211 Elementary and secondary schools
  Chad Cobbe

D-U-N-S 24-497-8532   (HQ)
BRANDON SCHOOL DIVISION, THE
1031 6th St, Brandon, MB, R7A 4K5
(204) 729-3100
Emp Here 60   *Sales* 84,331,043
SIC 8211 Elementary and secondary schools
  Kevin Zabowski
  James Murray

D-U-N-S 20-554-0052   (BR)
BRANDON, CITY OF
BRANDON POLICE SERVICE
(*Suby of* BRANDON, CITY OF)
1020 Victoria Ave, Brandon, MB, R7A 1A9
(204) 729-2345
Emp Here 120
SIC 7381 Detective and armored car services
  Ian Grant

D-U-N-S 20-944-6715   (SL)
CANCADE COMPANY LIMITED
1651 12th St, Brandon, MB, R7A 7L1
(204) 728-4450
Emp Here 185   *Sales* 41,070,185
SIC 3523 Farm machinery and equipment
  Darrel Phiessen
  Darcy Oakden

D-U-N-S 20-746-9227   (HQ)
CANDO RAIL SERVICES LTD
CANDO TIE DEPOT
740 Rosser Ave Suite 400, Brandon, MB, R7A 0K9
(204) 725-2627
Emp Here 50   *Sales* 50,488,400
SIC 1629 Heavy construction, nec
  Gordon Peters

D-U-N-S 24-241-8247   (SL)
CAPITAL S ENTERPRISES LTD
CAPITAL S AUTO SALES
Gd, Brandon, MB, R7A 5Y1
(204) 730-0097
Emp Here 25   *Sales* 12,451,950
SIC 5521 Used car dealers
  Scott Dowslaugh

D-U-N-S 20-946-6937   (HQ)
CHILD & FAMILY SERVICES OF WESTERN MANITOBA
(*Suby of* PROVINCE OF MANITOBA)
800 Mctavish Ave, Brandon, MB, R7A 7L4
(204) 726-6030
Emp Here 75   *Sales* 16,894,240
SIC 8322 Individual and family services
  David Mcgregor
  Tracy Baker
  James Burkart

D-U-N-S 24-373-6951   (HQ)
CHRISTIE SCHOOL SUPPLY MANITOBA
CHRISTIE'S OFFICE PLUS
705 Pacific Ave, Brandon, MB, R7A 0H8
(204) 727-1423
Emp Here 25   *Sales* 10,506,104
SIC 5943 Stationery stores
  Donald Green

D-U-N-S 24-717-3453   (SL)
CUMMING & DOBBIE (1986) LTD
3000 Victoria Ave E, Brandon, MB, R7A 7L2
(204) 726-0790
Emp Here 80   *Sales* 19,694,880
SIC 1794 Excavation work
  Richard Osterbeck
  Wayne Osterbeck
  Sean Osterbeck

D-U-N-S 24-258-8952   (SL)
DILLABOUGH, D M HOLDINGS LIMITED
1655 18th St, Brandon, MB, R7A 5C6
Emp Here 163   *Sales* 33,470,909
SIC 5399 Miscellaneous general merchandise
  Donald Dillabough

D-U-N-S 24-376-3976   (BR)
GOVERNING COUNCIL OF THE SALVATION ARMY IN CANADA, THE
DINSDALE PERSONAL CARE HOME
(*Suby of* GOVERNING COUNCIL OF THE SALVATION ARMY IN CANADA, THE)
510 6th St, Brandon, MB, R7A 3N9
(204) 727-3636
Emp Here 100
SIC 8051 Skilled nursing care facilities
  Wilson Perrin

D-U-N-S 25-372-4611   (BR)
HOME DEPOT OF CANADA INC
HOME DEPOT
(*Suby of* THE HOME DEPOT INC)
801 18th St N, Brandon, MB, R7A 7S1
(204) 571-3300
Emp Here 112
SIC 5251 Hardware stores
  Curtis Williams

D-U-N-S 20-035-6843   (BR)
IMARKETING SOLUTIONS GROUP INC
(*Suby of* IMARKETING SOLUTIONS GROUP INC)
800 Rosser Ave Suite D7, Brandon, MB, R7A 6N5
(204) 727-4242
Emp Here 150
SIC 8399 Social services, nec
  Peter Boland

D-U-N-S 25-085-0658   (SL)
INTERIOR IMAGES LIMITED
1440 Rosser Ave Unit 1, Brandon, MB, R7A 0M4
(204) 726-8282
Emp Here 35   *Sales* 15,522,150
SIC 7389 Business services, nec
  Candace Sigurdson

D-U-N-S 24-346-0974   (SL)
J. GRANT WALLACE HOLDINGS LTD
CANADIAN TIRE
1655 18th St, Brandon, MB, R7A 5C6
(204) 728-7120
Emp Here 135   *Sales* 27,721,305
SIC 5399 Miscellaneous general merchandise
  Grant Wallace

D-U-N-S 25-999-3582   (SL)
KAR-BASHER MANITOBA LTD
WESMAN SALVAGE
855 49th St E, Brandon, MB, R7A 7R2
(204) 726-8080
Emp Here 24   *Sales* 12,493,008
SIC 5093 Scrap and waste materials
  Blair Waldzogel

D-U-N-S 20-835-5263   (SL)
KEYSTONE AGRICULTURE & RECREATION CENTRE INC
KEYSTONE CENTRE
1175 18th St Unit 1, Brandon, MB, R7A 7C5
(204) 726-3500
Emp Here 150   *Sales* 100,336,200
SIC 7389 Business services, nec
  Dan Robertson
  Ken Fitzpatrick

D-U-N-S 24-372-9014   (SL)
KOCH FERTILIZER CANADA, ULC
(*Suby of* KOCH INDUSTRIES, INC.)
1400 17th St E, Brandon, MB, R7A 7C4
(204) 729-2900
Emp Here 220   *Sales* 97,821,900
SIC 2873 Nitrogenous fertilizers
Lawrence Hlobik
Lindsay Kaspik

D-U-N-S 24-329-4639   (BR)
LOBLAWS INC
REAL CANADIAN SUPERSTORE
(*Suby of* LOBLAW COMPANIES LIMITED)
920 Victoria Ave, Brandon, MB, R7A 1A7
(204) 729-4600
Emp Here 200
SIC 5411 Grocery stores
Douglas Barber

D-U-N-S 25-685-0249   (BR)
MAPLE LEAF FOODS INC
MAPLE LEAF PORK
(*Suby of* MAPLE LEAF FOODS INC)
6355 Richmond Ave E, Brandon, MB, R7A
7M5
(204) 571-2500
Emp Here 2,186
SIC 2011 Meat packing plants
Leo Collins

D-U-N-S 25-120-3626   (HQ)
MARSH, GLENDA PHARMACY LTD
SHOPPERS DRUG MART
809 18th St, Brandon, MB, R7A 5B8
(204) 729-8100
Emp Here 30   *Sales* 15,881,320
SIC 5912 Drug stores and proprietary stores
Glenda Marsh

D-U-N-S 25-517-8824   (BR)
MENNONITE CENTRAL COMMITTEE CANADA
BRANDON MCC TRIFTH SHOP
(*Suby of* MENNONITE CENTRAL COMMIT-
TEE CANADA)
414 Pacific Ave, Brandon, MB, R7A 0H5
(204) 727-1162
Emp Here 200
SIC 5932 Used merchandise stores
Shelly Burrows

D-U-N-S 20-082-8692   (BR)
MNP LLP
(*Suby of* MNP LLP)
1401 Princess Ave, Brandon, MB, R7A 7L7
(204) 727-0661
Emp Here 100
SIC 8721 Accounting, auditing, and book-
keeping
William Pugh

D-U-N-S 20-759-6495   (SL)
MURRAY AUTO GROUP BRANDON LTD
MURRAY CHEVROLET CADILLAC
1500 Richmond Ave, Brandon, MB, R7A 7E3
(204) 728-0130
Emp Here 85   *Sales* 53,488,800
SIC 5511 New and used car dealers
Andrew Murray
Douglas Murray
Chris Murray
Paul Murray
Dan Murray
Mildred Murray

D-U-N-S 20-584-8294   (SL)
PATMAN LTD
927 Douglas St, Brandon, MB, R7A 7B3
(204) 728-1188
Emp Here 112   *Sales* 23,260,720
SIC 8721 Accounting, auditing, and book-
keeping
Gary Edwards

D-U-N-S 24-655-7763   (BR)
PAUL'S HAULING LTD
(*Suby of* PAUL'S HAULING LTD)

1515 Richmond Ave E, Brandon, MB, R7A
7A3
(204) 728-5785
Emp Here 150
SIC 4213 Trucking, except local
Bill Hall

D-U-N-S 20-338-2973   (BR)
PFIZER CANADA SRI
PFIZER CANADA ULC
(*Suby of* C.P. PHARMACEUTICALS INTER-
NATIONAL C.V.)
720 17th St E, Brandon, MB, R7A 7H2
(204) 728-1511
Emp Here 150
SIC 2834 Pharmaceutical preparations

D-U-N-S 25-518-0507   (BR)
PRAIRIE MOUNTAIN HEALTH
RIDEAU PARK PERSONAL CARE HOME
(*Suby of* PRAIRIE MOUNTAIN HEALTH)
525 Victoria Ave E, Brandon, MB, R7A 6S9
(204) 578-2670
Emp Here 115
SIC 8059 Nursing and personal care, nec
Cheryl Bourdeau D""hui

D-U-N-S 24-037-3365   (SL)
PRECISION HOLDINGS LTD
PRECISION TOYOTA
404 18th St N, Brandon, MB, R7A 7P3
(204) 725-0508
Emp Here 40   *Sales* 19,923,120
SIC 5511 New and used car dealers
Ronald Ball

D-U-N-S 20-569-8046   (HQ)
QUINTAINE, P & SON LTD
Gd, Brandon, MB, R7A 5Y5
(204) 729-8565
Emp Here 1   *Sales* 60,175,372
SIC 5154 Livestock
James H Quintaine
Deborah Quintaine

D-U-N-S 24-545-7924   (HQ)
REDFERN ENTERPRISES INC
922 Douglas St, Brandon, MB, R7A 7B2
(204) 725-8580
Sales 25,148,200
SIC 6712 Bank holding companies
Raymond Redfern
Beverley Redfern

D-U-N-S 20-711-5429   (HQ)
REDFERN FARM SERVICES LTD
(*Suby of* REDFERN ENTERPRISES INC)
922 Douglas St, Brandon, MB, R7A 7B2
(204) 725-8580
Emp Here 12   *Sales* 44,595,815
SIC 5261 Retail nurseries and garden stores
Raymond Redfern
Beverly Redfern

D-U-N-S 24-224-8602   (SL)
ROYAL LEPAGE MARTIN-LIBERTY REALTY LTD
920 Victoria Ave, Brandon, MB, R7A 1A7

Emp Here 45   *Sales* 14,720,715
SIC 6531 Real estate agents and managers
Miriam Mc Leod

D-U-N-S 24-387-4406   (SL)
SHAPE FOODS, INC
2001 Victoria Ave E, Brandon, MB, R7A 7L2
(204) 727-3529
Emp Here 60   *Sales* 50,134,620
SIC 5141 Groceries, general line
Vernon Snidal
Stuart Kidd
Glen William Ager
Daniel Sierens

D-U-N-S 20-757-5531   (SL)
SPRING VALLEY COLONY FARMS LTD
SPRING VALLEY HUTTERIAN COLONY
Gd, Brandon, MB, R7A 5Y4

(204) 728-3830
Emp Here 63   *Sales* 16,525,467
SIC 0119 Cash grains, nec
Henry Hofer
Sam Hofer

D-U-N-S 24-034-9662   (HQ)
SUPER THRIFTY DRUGS CANADA LTD
381 Park Ave E Unit F, Brandon, MB, R7A 7A5
(204) 728-1522
Emp Here 20   *Sales* 12,394,746
SIC 5912 Drug stores and proprietary stores
Joss March
Greg Skura
Tom Bush
Bryan Ferguson

D-U-N-S 24-890-1618   (BR)
TRICAN WELL SERVICE LTD
(*Suby of* TRICAN WELL SERVICE LTD)
59 Limestone Rd, Brandon, MB, R7A 7L5

Emp Here 80
SIC 1389 Oil and gas field services, nec
Curtis Nerlien

D-U-N-S 25-297-6980   (BR)
WAL-MART CANADA CORP
(*Suby of* WALMART INC.)
903 18th St N, Brandon, MB, R7A 7S1
(204) 726-5821
Emp Here 300
SIC 5311 Department stores
Michael Humenny

D-U-N-S 24-231-2619   (SL)
WESTMAN REGIONAL LABORATORY SERVICES INC
WESTMAN LABORATORY
150 Mctavish Ave E Suite 1, Brandon, MB,
R7A 7H8
(204) 578-4440
Emp Here 150   *Sales* 48,895,650
SIC 8071 Medical laboratories
Carol Brown

D-U-N-S 24-883-7585   (SL)
WHEAT BELT EQUIPMENT LTD
10 Campbell'S Trailer Crt, Brandon, MB, R7A
5Y5
(204) 725-2273
Emp Here 20   *Sales* 10,000,000
SIC 5083 Farm and garden machinery
Neil Adriaansen

D-U-N-S 20-001-0858   (HQ)
WHEAT CITY CONCRETE PRODUCTS LTD
MID WESTERN REDI-MIX 1980
4801 Victoria Ave E, Brandon, MB, R7A 7L2
(204) 725-5600
Emp Here 30   *Sales* 10,753,140
SIC 3273 Ready-mixed concrete
William Cumming
Dave Nicol
Garth W. Cumming
Walter Bradley
Wes Norosky

D-U-N-S 20-385-2140   (BR)
XPLORNET COMMUNICATIONS INC
NETSET COMMUNICATION
(*Suby of* BARRETT CORPORATION)
5 Granite Rd, Brandon, MB, R7A 7V2
(204) 578-7840,
Emp Here 80
SIC 4813 Telephone communication, except
radio

D-U-N-S 20-379-9239   (BR)
XPLORNET COMMUNICATIONS INC
NETSET COMMUNICATIONS
(*Suby of* BARRETT CORPORATION)
5 Granite Rd, Brandon, MB, R7A 7V2
(204) 578-7840
Emp Here 85
SIC 4813 Telephone communication, except
radio
Robbie Zetariuk

D-U-N-S 24-112-6739   (SL)
YOUNG MEN'S CHRISTIAN ASSOCIATION OF BRANDON, THE
YMCA BRANDON
231 8th St, Brandon, MB, R7A 3X2
(204) 727-5456
Emp Here 150   *Sales* 215,790,150
SIC 8699 Membership organizations, nec
Tayona Johans
Lon Cullen

Brandon, MB R7B

D-U-N-S 24-113-4717   (SL)
35790 MANITOBA LTD
KEG, THE
1836 Brandon Ave, Brandon, MB, R7B 3G8
(204) 725-4223
Emp Here 80   *Sales* 3,641,520
SIC 5812 Eating places
David Schaworski

D-U-N-S 20-436-6413   (SL)
ATOM-JET INDUSTRIES (2002) LTD
2110 Park Ave, Brandon, MB, R7B 0R9
(204) 728-8590
Emp Here 100   *Sales* 22,200,100
SIC 3599 Industrial machinery, nec
Barry Larocque

D-U-N-S 24-747-7045   (SL)
BRANDON CHRYSLER DODGE (1987) LTD
3250 Victoria Ave, Brandon, MB, R7B 3Y4
(204) 728-3396
Emp Here 30   *Sales* 10,926,450
SIC 5013 Motor vehicle supplies and new
parts
Pat Larkin
Dean Larkin

D-U-N-S 20-517-1866   (BR)
BRANDON SCHOOL DIVISION, THE
VINCENT MASSEY HIGH SCHOOL
(*Suby of* BRANDON SCHOOL DIVISION,
THE)
715 Mcdiarmid Dr, Brandon, MB, R7B 2H7
(204) 729-3170
Emp Here 85
SIC 8211 Elementary and secondary schools
Bruce Shamray

D-U-N-S 24-039-3470   (HQ)
CENTURY 21 WESTMAN REALTY LTD.
2915 Victoria Ave, Brandon, MB, R7B 2N6
(204) 725-0555
Emp Here 28   *Sales* 11,141,996
SIC 6531 Real estate agents and managers
Ray Brownlee
Bill Crossman
Maurice Torr

D-U-N-S 25-682-5902   (HQ)
GENESIS HOSPITALITY INC
VICTORIA INN
3550 Victoria Ave, Brandon, MB, R7B 2R4
(204) 725-1532
Emp Here 120   *Sales* 81,317,800
SIC 7011 Hotels and motels
William Grenier
Kevin Swark
Vionell Jacobson
Gary Buckley

D-U-N-S 24-851-3301   (HQ)
GUILD INSURANCE BROKERS INC
2830 Victoria Ave, Brandon, MB, R7B 3X1
(204) 729-4949
Emp Here 28   *Sales* 27,985,980
SIC 6411 Insurance agents, brokers, and ser-
vice
Darryl Andrews
Fern O'donnell

D-U-N-S 20-948-8659   (SL)
HILLCREST PLACE HOLDINGS LTD

HILLCREST PLACE PERSONAL CARE
930 26th St Suite 104, Brandon, MB, R7B 2B8
(204) 728-6690
Emp Here 140   *Sales* 9,599,240
SIC 8051 Skilled nursing care facilities
Kathy Traill
Patrick Kelleher

D-U-N-S 20-948-8352   (HQ)
K.A.S.A. HOLDINGS LTD
MCDONALDS RESTAURANT
1907 Richmond Ave, Brandon, MB, R7B 0T4
(204) 725-2244
Emp Here 80   *Sales* 9,794,190
SIC 5812 Eating places
George Sheard

D-U-N-S 24-426-3745   (SL)
MAZER IMPLEMENTS
R G MAZER GROUP
1908 Currie Blvd, Brandon, MB, R7B 4E7
(204) 728-2244
Emp Here 35   *Sales* 11,396,000
SIC 5999 Miscellaneous retail stores, nec
Patricia Mazer Holdings Ltd

D-U-N-S 24-422-5558   (HQ)
MAZERGROUP LTD
1908 Currie Blvd, Brandon, MB, R7B 4E7
(204) 728-2244
Emp Here 35   *Sales* 48,865,600
SIC 5999 Miscellaneous retail stores, nec
Robert Mazer

D-U-N-S 25-321-4456   (BR)
REVERA INC
VALLEYVIEW CARE CENTRE
(Suby of GOVERNMENT OF CANADA)
3015 Victoria Ave Suite 219, Brandon, MB,
R7B 2K2
(204) 728-2030
Emp Here 140
SIC 8051 Skilled nursing care facilities
Mona Koroscil

D-U-N-S 20-806-2427   (BR)
SOBEYS CAPITAL INCORPORATED
SOBEYS STORE# 5138
(Suby of EMPIRE COMPANY LIMITED)
3409 Victoria Ave, Brandon, MB, R7B 2L8
(204) 727-3443
Emp Here 100
SIC 5411 Grocery stores
Ken Mcfarlin

D-U-N-S 25-522-2788   (BR)
SOBEYS CAPITAL INCORPORATED
SOBEYS WESTEND
(Suby of EMPIRE COMPANY LIMITED)
3409 Victoria Ave, Brandon, MB, R7B 2L8
(204) 727-3443
Emp Here 95
SIC 5411 Grocery stores
Ken Mcfarlan

D-U-N-S 25-272-1691   (SL)
SOUTHWEST AUTO CENTRE LTD
FORMAN HONDA
2080 Currie Blvd, Brandon, MB, R7B 4E7
(204) 728-8740
Emp Here 33   *Sales* 16,436,574
SIC 5511 New and used car dealers
Kent Forman

D-U-N-S 24-038-6631   (HQ)
WESTMAN MEDIA COOPERATIVE LTD
WESTMAN COMMUNICATIONS GROUP
1906 Park Ave, Brandon, MB, R7B 0R9
(204) 725-4300
Emp Here 80   *Sales* 21,019,424
SIC 4841 Cable and other pay television ser-
vices
David Baxter

Brandon, MB R7C

D-U-N-S 25-678-4687   (SL)
4236009 MANITOBA LTD
KELLEHER FORD SALES
1445 18th St N Suite 1445, Brandon, MB, R7C
1A6
(204) 728-8554
Emp Here 68   *Sales* 42,791,040
SIC 5511 New and used car dealers
John Kelleher

D-U-N-S 24-631-1302   (HQ)
73502 MANITOBA LIMITED
MAR-DEE ENTERPRISES
1873 1st St N, Brandon, MB, R7C 1A9
(204) 728-4554
Emp Here 12   *Sales* 40,230,432
SIC 5171 Petroleum bulk stations and terminals
Mario Floresco

D-U-N-S 24-852-4571   (SL)
J.W. VENTURES INC
SMITTY'S RESTAURANT
1790 Highland Ave, Brandon, MB, R7C 1A7
(204) 571-3152
Emp Here 75   *Sales* 3,413,925
SIC 5812 Eating places
Jeff Crooks
Royce Brooking
Glen Jackson

Brookdale, MB R0K

D-U-N-S 20-945-8462   (HQ)
SPRUCEWOOD COLONY FARMS LTD
Gd, Brookdale, MB, R0K 0G0
(204) 354-2318
Sales 22,296,265
SIC 0191 General farms, primarily crop
Joseph Wollmans

Carberry, MB R0K

D-U-N-S 20-834-8490   (HQ)
RIVERBEND COLONY LTD
Gd, Carberry, MB, R0K 0H0
(204) 834-3141
Emp Here 1   *Sales* 24,623,360
SIC 2439 Structural wood members, nec
John Hofer
Michael Hofer

Carman, MB R0G

D-U-N-S 24-851-7690   (SL)
**BOYNE VALLEY HOSTEL CORPORATION,
THE**
BOYNE LODGE PERSONAL CARE HOME
120 4th Ave Sw Rr 3, Carman, MB, R0G 0J0
(204) 745-6715
Emp Here 110   *Sales* 7,071,020
SIC 8361 Residential care
Sylvia Ptashnik

D-U-N-S 24-169-8935   (HQ)
LINEAR GRAIN INC
LINEAR GRAIN CROP INPUTS, DIV OF
67 Center Ave W, Carman, MB, R0G 0J0
(204) 745-6747
Sales 29,353,840
SIC 5153 Grain and field beans
Ross Mcknight
Sandra Mcknight

Cartier, MB R4K

D-U-N-S 20-838-9429   (SL)
LAKESIDE COLONY LTD
5600 Assiniboine Rd, Cartier, MB, R4K 1C3
(204) 864-2710
Emp Here 95   *Sales* 10,382,455
SIC 0762 Farm management services
Joshua Hofer
Garry Hofer
Sam Hofer

Cartwright, MB R0K

D-U-N-S 24-236-8520   (HQ)
WILLOW CREEK COLONY FARMS LTD
Gd, Cartwright, MB, R0K 0L0
(204) 529-2178
Sales 12,210,055
SIC 3537 Industrial trucks and tractors
John Hofer Sr
Paul Hofer
John Hofer Jr

Churchill, MB R0B

D-U-N-S 20-947-1465   (SL)
**CHURCHILL REGIONAL HEALTH AUTHOR-
ITY INC**
CHURCHILL RHA
162 Laverendrye Ave, Churchill, MB, R0B 0E0
(204) 675-8881
Emp Here 100   *Sales* 10,213,300
SIC 8062 General medical and surgical hospi-
tals
Verna Flett

D-U-N-S 25-672-0152   (SL)
HUDSON BAY PORT COMPANY
1 Axworthy Way, Churchill, MB, R0B 0E0
(204) 675-8823
Emp Here 75   *Sales* 29,529,300
SIC 4491 Marine cargo handling
Shane Hutchins

Cross Lake, MB R0B

D-U-N-S 24-346-4729   (BR)
CROSS LAKE EDUCATION AUTHORITY
MIKISEW MIDDLE SCHOOL
(Suby of CROSS LAKE EDUCATION AU-
THORITY)
Gd, Cross Lake, MB, R0B 0J0
(204) 676-3030
Emp Here 100
SIC 8211 Elementary and secondary schools
Anna Mekay

Cypress River, MB R0K

D-U-N-S 24-036-8357   (SL)
CYPRESS COLONY FARMS LTD
Gd, Cypress River, MB, R0K 0P0
(204) 743-2185
Emp Here 50   *Sales* 19,275,950
SIC 0291 General farms, primarily animals
Joseph Hofer
David Hofer

Darlingford, MB R0G

D-U-N-S 20-834-9621   (SL)

PEMBINA COLONY FARMS LTD
Gd, Darlingford, MB, R0G 0L0
(204) 246-2182
Emp Here 115
SIC 7389 Business services, nec
Paul Maendel
David Hofer

Dauphin, MB R7N

D-U-N-S 20-292-9654   (SL)
COOLEY, DEAN MOTORS LTD
COOLEY, DEAN GM
1600 Main St S, Dauphin, MB, R7N 3B3
(204) 638-4026
Emp Here 55   *Sales* 15,581,500
SIC 7538 General automotive repair shops
Dean Cooley

D-U-N-S 20-001-4496   (HQ)
**DAUPHIN CONSUMERS COOPERATIVE
LTD**
DAUPHIN CO-OP
18 3rd Ave Ne, Dauphin, MB, R7N 0Y6
(204) 638-6003
Emp Here 64   *Sales* 53,306,890
SIC 5411 Grocery stores
Drake Mcmurphy
Eric Irwin

D-U-N-S 24-562-4668   (SL)
**DAUPHIN GENERAL HOSPITAL FOUNDA-
TION, THE**
(Suby of DAUPHIN REGIONAL HEALTH
CENTRE)
625 3rd St Sw, Dauphin, MB, R7N 1R7
(204) 638-3010
Emp Here 150   *Sales* 19,727,250
SIC 8641 Civic and social associations
Curt Gullet

D-U-N-S 24-455-4619   (SL)
DAUPHIN PERSONAL CARE HOME INC
(Suby of DAUPHIN REGIONAL HEALTH
CENTRE)
625 3rd St Sw, Dauphin, MB, R7N 1R7
(204) 638-3010
Emp Here 75
SIC 8059 Nursing and personal care, nec
Glenda Short
Melodie Powell

D-U-N-S 20-945-2267   (HQ)
DAUPHIN REGIONAL HEALTH CENTRE
625 3rd St Sw, Dauphin, MB, R7N 1R7
(204) 638-3010
Sales 33,324,000
SIC 8062 General medical and surgical hospi-
tals
Curt Gullett

D-U-N-S 24-428-8841   (SL)
FORMAN FORD SALES LIMITED
36 2nd Ave Nw, Dauphin, MB, R7N 1H2
(204) 622-3673
Emp Here 39   *Sales* 19,425,042
SIC 5511 New and used car dealers
Barry Forman

D-U-N-S 20-612-6229   (HQ)
**MCMUNN & YATES BUILDING SUPPLIES
LTD**
288 2 Ave Ne, Dauphin, MB, R7N 0Z9
(204) 638-5303
Emp Here 20   *Sales* 127,928,150
SIC 6712 Bank holding companies
Jason Yates

D-U-N-S 20-945-5971   (HQ)
MOUNTAIN VIEW SCHOOL DIVISION
182519 Sw, Dauphin, MB, R7N 3B3
(204) 638-3001
Emp Here 25   *Sales* 54,515,450
SIC 8211 Elementary and secondary schools

Floyd Martin
Bart Michaleski

D-U-N-S 20-709-7135   (BR)
MOUNTAIN VIEW SCHOOL DIVISION
DAUPHIN REGIONAL COMPREHENSIVE SECONDARY SCHOOL
(*Suby of* MOUNTAIN VIEW SCHOOL DIVISION)
330 Mountain Rd, Dauphin, MB, R7N 2V6
(204) 638-4629
Emp Here 100
SIC 8211 Elementary and secondary schools
Norman Casavant

D-U-N-S 20-292-4846   (HQ)
PARKLAND REGIONAL HEALTH AUTHORITY INC
625 3rd St Sw, Dauphin, MB, R7N 1R7
(204) 638-2118
Emp Here 50   *Sales* 311,024,000
SIC 8062 General medical and surgical hospitals

D-U-N-S 25-678-1428   (SL)
RITZ MACHINE WORKS INC
507 1st Ave Se, Dauphin, MB, R7N 2Z8
(204) 638-1633
Emp Here 50   *Sales* 10,141,500
SIC 3443 Fabricated plate work (boiler shop)
Richard Ilnisky
Thomas Zaporzan

D-U-N-S 20-002-0063   (SL)
STRILKIWSKI CONTRACTING LTD
Gd Lcd Main, Dauphin, MB, R7N 2T3
(204) 638-9304
Emp Here 75   *Sales* 18,933,150
SIC 1611 Highway and street construction
Gerald Strilkiwski
Harvey Strilkiwski
Lisa Saunders

D-U-N-S 20-269-1957   (SL)
SYDOR FARM EQUIPMENT LTD
JOHN DEERE DEALER
Gd, Dauphin, MB, R7N 2T3
(204) 638-6443
Emp Here 45   *Sales* 21,376,170
SIC 5083 Farm and garden machinery
Don Tarrant

D-U-N-S 25-297-7509   (BR)
WAL-MART CANADA CORP
(*Suby of* WALMART INC.)
1450 Main St S Unit A, Dauphin, MB, R7N 3H4
(204) 638-4808
Emp Here 80
SIC 5311 Department stores

Decker, MB R0M

D-U-N-S 24-229-5491   (HQ)
DECKER COLONY FARMS LTD
DECKER COLONY OF HUTTERIAN BRETHREN TRUST
Gd, Decker, MB, R0M 0K0
(204) 764-2481
Sales 14,426,995
SIC 0191 General farms, primarily crop
Sam Waldner
Raymond Walder
Jacob Waldner

Dugald, MB R0E

D-U-N-S 20-378-0556   (SL)
LX CONSTRUCTION INC
G&B PORTABLE FABRIC BUILDINGS
68132 Highway 212, Dugald, MB, R0E 0K0
(204) 898-8453
Emp Here 40   *Sales* 12,754,760

SIC 1521 Single-family housing construction
Alex Lentowich
Ryan Hunter
Brad Shambel
Ash Khan

East St Paul, MB R2E

D-U-N-S 24-776-0259   (HQ)
CANADIAN GUIDE RAIL CORPORATION
MONTEFERRO AMERICA
2840 Wenzel St, East St Paul, MB, R2E 1E7
(204) 222-2142
Emp Here 75   *Sales* 29,187,720
SIC 3441 Fabricated structural Metal

D-U-N-S 20-760-1436   (SL)
LUDWICK CATERING LTD
3184 Birds Hill Rd, East St Paul, MB, R2E 1H1
(204) 668-8091
Emp Here 100   *Sales* 4,287,300
SIC 5812 Eating places
Carol Aitkenhead
Rose Ludwick

Ebb And Flow, MB R0L

D-U-N-S 25-360-1066   (HQ)
EBB AND FLOW FIRST NATION EDUCATION AUTHORITY
Po Box 160, Ebb And Flow, MB, R0L 0R0
(204) 448-2438
Emp Here 3   *Sales* 11,894,280
SIC 8211 Elementary and secondary schools
Arlene Mousseau

D-U-N-S 20-651-7935   (BR)
EBB AND FLOW FIRST NATION EDUCATION AUTHORITY
EBB AND FLOW SCHOOL
(*Suby of* EBB AND FLOW FIRST NATION EDUCATION AUTHORITY)
Gd, Ebb And Flow, MB, R0L 0R0
(204) 448-2012
Emp Here 80
SIC 8211 Elementary and secondary schools
Paul Monchka

Edwin, MB R0H

D-U-N-S 20-588-7370   (SL)
ARROWHEAD DEVELOPMENT CORPORATION
LONG PLAIN FIRST NATION
101 Yellowquill Trail W, Edwin, MB, R0H 0G0
(204) 252-2731
Emp Here 50   *Sales* 24,903,900
SIC 5541 Gasoline service stations
Tim Daniel

Elgin, MB R0K

D-U-N-S 24-115-5498   (SL)
SOURIS RIVER COLONY FARMS LTD
Gd, Elgin, MB, R0K 0T0

Emp Here 91
SIC 7389 Business services, nec
Michael E Waldner
George Wipf

Elie, MB R0H

D-U-N-S 24-851-5900   (SL)
HURON COLONY FARMS LTD
64082 Road 17w, Elie, MB, R0H 0H0
(204) 353-2704
Emp Here 56   *Sales* 14,689,304
SIC 0119 Cash grains, nec
Joseph Waldner
James Waldner

D-U-N-S 20-759-5109   (SL)
IBERVILLE FARMS LTD
Gd, Elie, MB, R0H 0H0
(204) 864-2058
Emp Here 40   *Sales* 10,492,360
SIC 0191 General farms, primarily crop
Alvin Gross
Paul Gross
Conrad Gross
Andrew Gross
Jonathan Gross

D-U-N-S 25-532-9856   (SL)
JAMES VALLEY COLONY FARMS LTD
(*Suby of* JAMES VALLEY HUTTERIAN MUTUAL CORPORATION)
100 James Valley Rd, Elie, MB, R0H 0H0
(204) 353-2827
Emp Here 120   *Sales* 20,283,000
SIC 0191 General farms, primarily crop
John Hoffer
David T Hoffer
Edward Hoffer

D-U-N-S 25-408-9006   (HQ)
MILLTOWN COLONY FARMS LTD
Gd, Elie, MB, R0H 0H0
(204) 353-2838
Sales 110,076,900
SIC 5153 Grain and field beans
Jake Waldner
Joe Kleinsasser

D-U-N-S 25-416-5020   (SL)
MILLTOWN METAL SHOP LTD
(*Suby of* MILLTOWN COLONY FARMS LTD)
Gd, Elie, MB, R0H 0H0
(204) 353-2741
Emp Here 75   *Sales* 137,368,275
SIC 5153 Grain and field beans
Jake Waldner
Joe Kleinsasser

D-U-N-S 20-834-9688   (SL)
WALDHEIM COLONY FARMS LTD
16025 Rd 58 Nw, Elie, MB, R0H 0H0
(204) 353-2473
Emp Here 105   *Sales* 21,694,785
SIC 0291 General farms, primarily animals
Samuel Waldner
Tom Waldner
Joshua Stahl

D-U-N-S 20-434-3180   (SL)
WILF'S ELIE FORD SALES LTD
Hwy 1, Elie, MB, R0H 0H0
(204) 353-2481
Emp Here 31   *Sales* 15,440,418
SIC 5511 New and used car dealers
Wilf Legault
Alice Legault

Elm Creek, MB R0G

D-U-N-S 24-608-7886   (HQ)
CLEARVIEW COLONY LTD
CUSTOM MARBLE
(*Suby of* WHITESHELL COLONY FARMS LTD)
Gd, Elm Creek, MB, R0G 0N0
(204) 436-2187
Sales 22,750,420
SIC 5211 Lumber and other building materials
Ronald Gross

Henry Gross

D-U-N-S 20-001-7309   (SL)
ELM CREEK CO-OPERATIVE OIL & SUPPLIES LTD
43 Church Ave, Elm Creek, MB, R0G 0N0
(204) 436-2493
Emp Here 25   *Sales* 25,820,200
SIC 5171 Petroleum bulk stations and terminals
Dave Henderson
Ron De Ruiter
Matthew Tkachyk
Gayle Wolfram
Joanne Gilbraith
Michelle Lepp
Willie Schroeder
Larry Perrin
Phil Schmidt

Elma, MB R0E

D-U-N-S 20-743-1326   (SL)
SUN GRO HORTICULTURE CANADA LTD
SUN GRO HORTICULTURE PROCESSING
Gd, Elma, MB, R0E 0Z0
(204) 426-2121
Emp Here 750   *Sales* 309,831,750
SIC 1499 Miscellaneous nonMetallic minerals, except fuels
Mitch Weaver
Jon Dawson
Douglas Allen
Rodrick Senft
John T Goldsmith

Erickson, MB R0J

D-U-N-S 24-329-1023   (HQ)
WEST REGION CHILD AND FAMILY SERVICES COMMITTEE INCORPORATED
Gd, Erickson, MB, R0J 0P0
(204) 636-6100
Sales 13,345,900
SIC 8399 Social services, nec
Stella Bone

Eriksdale, MB R0C

D-U-N-S 20-946-3744   (HQ)
LAKESHORE SCHOOL DIVISION
23 Second Ave, Eriksdale, MB, R0C 0W0
(204) 739-2101
Emp Here 18   *Sales* 22,797,370
SIC 8211 Elementary and secondary schools
Marlene Michno

Ethelbert, MB R0L

D-U-N-S 20-730-0547   (SL)
PODOLSKI HONEY FARMS
119 Main St W, Ethelbert, MB, R0L 0T0
(204) 742-3555
Emp Here 26   *Sales* 10,023,494
SIC 0279 Animal specialties, nec
Ed Podolski

Falcon Beach, MB R0E

D-U-N-S 24-914-1008   (SL)
FALCON BAKERY
21 Park Blvd, Falcon Beach, MB, R0E 0N0

(204) 349-8993
Emp Here 25   *Sales* 21,131,365
SIC 5149 Groceries and related products, nec
Karen Persoage

Fisher Branch, MB R0C

D-U-N-S 24-611-5948   (SL)
FISHER BRANCH CO-OP GAS B
22 Cache, Fisher Branch, MB, R0C 0Z0
(204) 372-6202
Emp Here 27   *Sales* 22,560,579
SIC 5141 Groceries, general line
Jim Cruikshank

D-U-N-S 20-551-6193   (SL)
POLAR FOODS INC
Gd, Fisher Branch, MB, R0C 0Z0
(204) 372-6132
Emp Here 26   *Sales* 21,725,002
SIC 5149 Groceries and related products, nec
Nathan Golas

D-U-N-S 20-001-8646   (SL)
UKRAINIAN FARMERS CO-OPERATIVE LIMITED
22 Tache St, Fisher Branch, MB, R0C 0Z0
(204) 372-6202
Emp Here 30   *Sales* 30,984,240
SIC 5171 Petroleum bulk stations and terminals
Robert Schreyer
Gordie Wevursky
Shannon Pyziak
James Cruikshank
Wayne Imlah
Richard Woloshyn
Ron Gagulak

Flin Flon, MB R8A

D-U-N-S 20-068-2180   (SL)
600038 SASKATCHEWAN LTD
EDDIE'S FAMILY FOODS
557 South Hudson St, Flin Flon, MB, R8A 1E1
(306) 688-3426
Emp Here 44   *Sales* 12,062,688
SIC 5411 Grocery stores
Gregory Phair
Leanne Phair

D-U-N-S 20-464-8757   (SL)
HUDBAY MINERALS INC
Gd Stn Main, Flin Flon, MB, R8A 1N9
(204) 687-2385
Emp Here 50   *Sales* 11,671,750
SIC 1081 Metal mining services
David Garofalo
Kenneth Stowe
Alan Hibben
Warren Holmes
Wesley Voorheis
Thomas Goodman
Bruce Barraclough
Alan Lenczner
John Knowles

D-U-N-S 20-001-9289   (BR)
HUDBAY MINERALS INC
HUDBAY MINERALS INC
(*Suby of* HUDBAY MINERALS INC)
Gd, Flin Flon, MB, R8A 1N9
(204) 687-2385
Emp Here 1,500
SIC 1021 Copper ores
Eugene Lei

D-U-N-S 20-275-2960   (HQ)
NORTHERN REGIONAL HEALTH AUTHORITY
84 Church St, Flin Flon, MB, R8A 1L8

(204) 687-1300
Sales 185,843,167
SIC 8062 General medical and surgical hospitals
Helga Bryant
Hussam Azzam
Rusty Beardy
Wanda Reader
Joy Tetlock
Rajinder Thethy
Marion Ellis
Lois Moberly
Ingrid Olson
Douglas Lauvstad

Gilbert Plains, MB R0L

D-U-N-S 25-125-2920   (SL)
GILBERT PLAINS HEALTH CENTRE INC
100 Cutforth St N, Gilbert Plains, MB, R0L 0X0
(204) 548-2161
Emp Here 55   *Sales* 12,853,225
SIC 8621 Professional organizations
Joan Gryba

Gillam, MB R0B

D-U-N-S 20-038-3805   (HQ)
FOX LAKE CREE NATION
103 Fox Lake Dr, Gillam, MB, R0B 0L0
(204) 953-2760
Emp Here 30   *Sales* 15,242,740
SIC 8399 Social services, nec
Clara Mcleod
Jennifer Neepin
Walter Spence

Gimli, MB R0C

D-U-N-S 25-681-2009   (BR)
BETEL HOME FOUNDATION
96 1st Ave, Gimli, MB, R0C 1B1
(204) 642-5556
Emp Here 90
SIC 8051 Skilled nursing care facilities
Brenna Raemer

D-U-N-S 20-002-2150   (SL)
CHUDD'S CHRYSLER LTD
231 Gd, Gimli, MB, R0C 1B0
(204) 642-8555
Emp Here 30   *Sales* 14,942,340
SIC 5511 New and used car dealers
Edward Chudd
Carmen Chen
Michael Chudd
Kim Like
Kevin Chudd

D-U-N-S 20-946-0427   (SL)
DORING ENTERPRISES INC
SOBEYS
94 7th Ave, Gimli, MB, R0C 1B1
(204) 642-5995
Emp Here 75   *Sales* 22,010,775
SIC 5411 Grocery stores
Ingvar Karvelson
Kara Peiluck
Doriane Johnson

D-U-N-S 24-036-7300   (HQ)
EVERGREEN SCHOOL DIVISION
RIVERTON EARLY MIDDLE YEARS SCHOOL
140 Centre Ave W, Gimli, MB, R0C 1B1
(204) 642-6260
Emp Here 10   *Sales* 24,779,750
SIC 8211 Elementary and secondary schools

Charles (Charlie) Grieve
Paul Cuthbert
Cheryl Zelenitsky

D-U-N-S 24-230-0473   (SL)
FAROEX LTD
FAROEX COMPOSITE TECHNOLOGIES
(*Suby of* NANOXPLORE INC)
123 Anson St, Gimli, MB, R0C 1B1
(204) 642-6400
Emp Here 50   *Sales* 11,671,750
SIC 3299 NonMetallic mineral products,
Bertrand Cote

D-U-N-S 20-002-2259   (SL)
GIESBRECHT & SONS LTD
Gd, Gimli, MB, R0C 1B0
(204) 642-5133
Emp Here 23   *Sales* 11,455,794
SIC 5511 New and used car dealers
John K Giesbrecht Sr

D-U-N-S 24-114-4823   (HQ)
GIMLI COMMUNITY HEALTH CENTRE
JOHNSON MEMORIAL HOSPITAL
120 6th Ave, Gimli, MB, R0C 1B0
(204) 642-5116
Sales 10,213,300
SIC 8062 General medical and surgical hospitals
Lori Wahoski

Ginew, MB R0A

D-U-N-S 20-064-0147   (SL)
GINEW WELLNESS CENTRE
Gd, Ginew, MB, R0A 2R0
(204) 427-2384
Emp Here 79   *Sales* 12,691,034
SIC 8011 Offices and clinics of medical doctors
Sherrie Thomas
Ken Henry
Grace Hage
Joanne Hayden
Martha Larocque
Sherrie-Anne Thomas

Gladstone, MB R0J

D-U-N-S 24-232-5223   (SL)
GLADSTONE AUCTION MART LTD
Gd, Gladstone, MB, R0J 0T0
(204) 385-2537
Emp Here 17   *Sales* 20,576,749
SIC 5154 Livestock
Ken Waddell
Garth Jarvis
Les Foxon
Vern Mcgowan

D-U-N-S 24-546-5414   (HQ)
PINE CREEK SCHOOL DIVISION
25 Brown St, Gladstone, MB, R0J 0T0
(204) 385-2216
Emp Here 10   *Sales* 19,823,800
SIC 8211 Elementary and secondary schools
Jodi Joss

D-U-N-S 24-392-6032   (BR)
REGIONAL HEALTH AUTHORITY - CENTRAL MANITOBA INC
SEVEN REGIONS HEALTH CENTRE
(*Suby of* REGIONAL HEALTH AUTHORITY - CENTRAL MANITOBA INC)
24 Mill St, Gladstone, MB, R0J 0T0
(204) 385-2968
Emp Here 160
SIC 8062 General medical and surgical hospitals
Joann Egilson

Glenella, MB R0J

D-U-N-S 20-948-4591   (SL)
GRASS RIVER COLONY FARMS LTD
GRASS RIVER COLONY OF HUTTERIAN BRETHREN
Gd, Glenella, MB, R0J 0V0
(204) 352-4286
Emp Here 40   *Sales* 15,420,760
SIC 0241 Dairy farms
Joseph Waldner
Calvin Waldner
Corney Waldner

Grand Rapids, MB R0C

D-U-N-S 24-495-4942   (SL)
POWER SUPPLY GRAND RAPIDS GS
Gd, Grand Rapids, MB, R0C 1E0
(204) 639-4138
Emp Here 40   *Sales* 25,064,560
SIC 4911 Electric services
Brian Fox

Grande Pointe, MB R5A

D-U-N-S 20-954-9364   (HQ)
KEYSTONE WESTERN INC
594 Bernat Rd, Grande Pointe, MB, R5A 1H5
(204) 256-0800
Emp Here 65   *Sales* 26,741,780
SIC 4213 Trucking, except local
Norman Curtis
Bob Roulston

Graysville, MB R0G

D-U-N-S 20-834-9266   (SL)
ROSE VALLEY COLONY LTD
Gd, Graysville, MB, R0G 0T0
(204) 828-3338
Emp Here 30   *Sales* 10,274,010
SIC 0191 General farms, primarily crop
David D Waldner
Ed Waldner

Grunthal, MB R0A

D-U-N-S 25-124-4562   (SL)
GRUNTHAL LIVESTOCK AUCTION MART LIMITED
Gd, Grunthal, MB, R0A 0R0
(204) 434-6519
Emp Here 80   *Sales* 18,155,955
SIC 5154 Livestock
Robert Krentz
Henry Penner
Gordon Krentz

D-U-N-S 25-950-9636   (SL)
MENNO HOME FOR THE AGED
235 Park St, Grunthal, MB, R0A 0R0
(204) 434-6496
Emp Here 80   *Sales* 4,739,760
SIC 8361 Residential care
Maria Krentz

D-U-N-S 24-883-2800   (SL)
TRISTAR DAIRY CENTRE LTD
26147 Wiens Rd, Grunthal, MB, R0A 0R0
(204) 434-6801
Emp Here 30   *Sales* 14,250,780
SIC 5083 Farm and garden machinery

Cliff Bakx
Rosemarie Bakx

Hamiota, MB R0M

D-U-N-S 25-826-5404   (SL)
CATTLEX LTD
Gd, Hamiota, MB, R0M 0T0
(204) 764-2471
Emp Here 20   *Sales* 24,207,940
SIC 5154 Livestock

Hartney, MB R0M

D-U-N-S 20-321-3376   (BR)
MAZERGROUP LTD
(*Suby of* MAZERGROUP LTD)
Gd, Hartney, MB, R0M 0X0
(204) 858-2000
Emp Here 200
SIC 5999 Miscellaneous retail stores, nec
Bruce Evans

Headingley, MB R4H

D-U-N-S 25-370-1395   (HQ)
68235 MANITOBA LTD
TERRACO
5461 Portage Ave Unit B, Headingley, MB, R4H 1H8
(204) 885-8120
Emp Here 10   *Sales* 37,126,000
SIC 5191 Farm supplies

D-U-N-S 20-013-0153   (SL)
AMC FORM TECHNOLOGIES
35 Headingley St, Headingley, MB, R4H 0A8
(204) 633-8800
Emp Here 45   *Sales* 12,044,340
SIC 5211 Lumber and other building materials

D-U-N-S 25-794-9149   (HQ)
BEST BUY HOUSING INC
BEST BUY MOBILE HOMES
4250 Portage Ave, Headingley, MB, R4H 1C6
(204) 895-2393
Emp Here 20   *Sales* 10,706,080
SIC 5211 Lumber and other building materials
Donald Sawatsky

D-U-N-S 20-175-2487   (SL)
DYTERRA CORPORATION
7501 Wilkes Ave, Headingley, MB, R4H 1B8
(204) 885-8260
Emp Here 27   *Sales* 12,825,702
SIC 5083 Farm and garden machinery
Pat Beavis

D-U-N-S 20-545-3751   (HQ)
MANITOBA FIRST NATIONS EDUCATION RESOURCE CENTRE INC
4820 Portage Ave, Headingley, MB, R4H 1C8
(204) 831-1224
Emp Here 20   *Sales* 12,417,264
SIC 8748 Business consulting, nec
Lorne Keeper
Rebecca Ross
Nora Murdoch

D-U-N-S 20-350-2737   (SL)
WAWASUM ENERGY INC
200 Alpine Way Unit 135, Headingley, MB, R4H 0B7
(204) 299-9400
Emp Here 49   *Sales* 11,803,316
SIC 1623 Water, sewer, and utility lines
Reginald Beardy
Ralph Beardy

Headingley, MB R4J

D-U-N-S 20-837-4702   (SL)
STURGEON CREEK COLONY FARMS LTD
STURGEON CREEK WELDING
1069 Road 63, Headingley, MB, R4J 1C1
(204) 633-2196
Emp Here 120   *Sales* 23,079,360
SIC 7692 Welding repair
Joey Maendal
Joe Maendel

High Bluff, MB R0H

D-U-N-S 24-040-2719   (SL)
SOMMERFELD COLONY FARMS LTD
Gd, High Bluff, MB, R0H 0K0
(204) 243-2453
Emp Here 40   *Sales* 15,420,760
SIC 0213 Hogs
Mike Hofer, Jr
John Hofer
Levi Hofer

Hodgson, MB R0C

D-U-N-S 20-269-2021   (SL)
MARBLE RIDGE FARMS LTD
RIDGEMAR
Gd, Hodgson, MB, R0C 1N0
(204) 372-6438
Emp Here 50   *Sales* 25,998,350
SIC 4731 Freight transportation arrangement
Nathan Hofer
Darren Waldner
Darius Hofer

Ile Des Chenes, MB R0A

D-U-N-S 24-205-4331   (SL)
TITAN ENVIRONMENTAL CONTAINMENT LTD
777 Quest Blvd, Ile Des Chenes, MB, R0A 0T1
(204) 878-3955
Emp Here 100   *Sales* 28,049,774
SIC 1629 Heavy construction, nec
Brett Burkard
Kelly Sitarz
Juice Lambert
Derek Bishop

D-U-N-S 25-329-5695   (SL)
VANDERMEER GREENHOUSES LTD
21065 Dumaine Rd, Ile Des Chenes, MB, R0A 0T0
(204) 878-3420
Emp Here 22   *Sales* 16,335,440
SIC 5193 Flowers and florists supplies
Leonard Vandermeer
Lori Vandermeer

Killarney, MB R0K

D-U-N-S 24-607-3845   (SL)
KILLARNEY AUCTION MART LTD
2 17 W Suite 27, Killarney, MB, R0K 1G0
(204) 523-8477
Emp Here 14   *Sales* 16,945,558
SIC 5154 Livestock
Scott Campbell

D-U-N-S 24-387-3127   (BR)
PRAIRIE MOUNTAIN HEALTH

TRI-LAKE HEALTH CENTRE
(*Suby of* PRAIRIE MOUNTAIN HEALTH)
86 Ellice Dr, Killarney, MB, R0K 1G0
(204) 523-4661
Emp Here 140
SIC 8062 General medical and surgical hospitals
Deb Rey

D-U-N-S 24-172-3998   (HQ)
TURTLE MOUNTAIN SCHOOL DIVISION
435 Williams Ave, Killarney, MB, R0K 1G0
(204) 523-7531
Emp Here 15   *Sales* 19,823,800
SIC 8211 Elementary and secondary schools
Larry Rainnie
Shirley Highfield
Brad Heide
Kathy Siatecki
Samatha Cole
William Korchinski
Rhonda Coupland
Gordon Wooley
Gail Patterson
Darrell Desrosiers

Kola, MB R0M

D-U-N-S 24-748-7861   (SL)
T. L. PENNER MANAGEMENT LTD
Hwy 257 E, Kola, MB, R0M 1B0
(204) 556-2265
Emp Here 25   *Sales* 11,768,275
SIC 1542 Nonresidential construction, nec
Travis Penner

La Broquerie, MB R0A

D-U-N-S 25-327-2520   (HQ)
HYLIFE LTD
SPRINGHILL FARMS
5 Fabas St, La Broquerie, MB, R0A 0W0
(204) 424-5359
Emp Here 40   *Sales* 72,315,950
SIC 0291 General farms, primarily animals
Donald Janzen
Claude Vielfaure

La Salle, MB R0G

D-U-N-S 25-892-5718   (HQ)
VOMAR INDUSTRIES INC
TANK TRADERS, DIV OF
Gd, La Salle, MB, R0G 1B0
(204) 736-4288
Emp Here 25   *Sales* 13,438,040
SIC 5984 Liquefied petroleum gas dealers
Marcel Vouriot

Lac Du Bonnet, MB R0E

D-U-N-S 20-529-9811   (SL)
TANTALUM MINING CORPORATION OF CANADA LIMITED
TANCO
(*Suby of* CABOT CORPORATION)
Bernic Lake, Lac Du Bonnet, MB, R0E 1A0
(204) 884-2400
Emp Here 140   *Sales* 334,256,860
SIC 1061 Ferroalloy ores, except vanadium
Alistair Gibb

Letellier, MB R0G

D-U-N-S 24-717-2455   (HQ)
B S I INSURANCE BROKERS LTD
BARNABE & SAURETTE INSURANCE BROKERS
16 3rd Avenue East, Letellier, MB, R0G 1C0
(204) 737-2471
Emp Here 13   *Sales* 142,276,134
SIC 6411 Insurance agents, brokers, and service
Richard Barnabe

D-U-N-S 25-385-4905   (SL)
SEED-EX INC
SEED-EX
Gd, Letellier, MB, R0G 1C0
(204) 737-2000
Emp Here 20   *Sales* 10,702,480
SIC 5149 Groceries and related products, nec
Roger Barnabe
Susan Barnabe

Lockport, MB R1A

D-U-N-S 24-883-3329   (SL)
DOMTEK INC
Gd Stn Lockport, Lockport, MB, R1A 3R9
(204) 981-1266
Emp Here 32   *Sales* 14,309,568
SIC 5039 Construction materials, nec
Rodney Mancini
Joyce Mancini

Lorette, MB R0A

D-U-N-S 24-968-3962   (HQ)
DIVISION SCOLAIRE FRANCO-MANITOBAINE
1263 Dawson Rd, Lorette, MB, R0A 0Y0
(204) 878-9399
Emp Here 50   *Sales* 99,119,000
SIC 8211 Elementary and secondary schools
Dennis Ferre
Annette Grenier Tetrault

D-U-N-S 20-871-5453   (SL)
LORETTE MARKET PLACE LIMITED
11 Laramee Dr, Lorette, MB, R0A 0Y0
(204) 878-2510
Emp Here 40   *Sales* 10,966,080
SIC 5411 Grocery stores
Darcy Davis

Lowe Farm, MB R0G

D-U-N-S 20-002-9387   (SL)
LOWE FARM CO-OP SERVICES (1959) LTD
LOWE FARM CO-OP
78 Main St, Lowe Farm, MB, R0G 1E0
(204) 746-8476
Emp Here 14   *Sales* 14,459,312
SIC 5171 Petroleum bulk stations and terminals
Joanne Paetkau
Dennis Rempel
Jerry Brown
Peter J. Falk
Matthew Almey

Lundar, MB R0C

D-U-N-S 25-327-2603   (HQ)
SIGFUSSON NORTHERN LTD
50 Swan Creek Dr, Lundar, MB, R0C 1Y0

(204) 762-5500
Emp Here 60   *Sales* 25,244,200
SIC 1629 Heavy construction, nec
  Wayne Stewart
  Dwayne Sigfusson
  Wade Sigfusson
  Grant Sigfusson
  Warren Sigfusson
  Larry Erickson

Marius, MB R0H

D-U-N-S 24-774-5904   (SL)
SANDY BAY SCHOOL
ISAAC BEAULIEU MEMORIAL SCHOOL
Gd, Marius, MB, R0H 0T0
(204) 843-2407
Emp Here 160   *Sales* 15,859,040
SIC 8211 Elementary and secondary schools
  Rene Roulette
  Waltrina Maccyver

Marquette, MB R0H

D-U-N-S 20-003-0948   (SL)
**MARQUETTE CONSUMERS COOPERA-
TIVE LIMITED**
Gd, Marquette, MB, R0H 0V0
(204) 375-6570
Emp Here 20   *Sales* 20,656,160
SIC 5171 Petroleum bulk stations and termi-
nals
  Brian Penner
  Armin Friesen
  Paul Heller
  Lawrence Paton
  Glen Macmillan
  Paul Hueging
  Bernie Elskamp
  Martin Keen

Mccreary, MB R0J

D-U-N-S 24-229-7034   (SL)
MCCREARY ALONSA HEALTH CENTRE
613 Government Rd, Mccreary, MB, R0J 1B0
(204) 835-2482
Emp Here 75   *Sales* 11,725,950
SIC 8099 Health and allied services, nec
  Roger Mitchell

D-U-N-S 25-671-0054   (SL)
OAK RIDGE MEATS LIMITED
1055 Boundary Rd, Mccreary, MB, R0J 1B0
(204) 835-2365
Emp Here 19   *Sales* 10,167,356
SIC 5147 Meats and meat products
  Gilbert Kohlman
  Lorne Nagorski

D-U-N-S 24-171-4880   (HQ)
TURTLE RIVER SCHOOL DIVISION
808 Burrows Rd, Mccreary, MB, R0J 1B0
(204) 835-2067
Emp Here 10   *Sales* 15,859,040
SIC 8211 Elementary and secondary schools
  Richard Bidzinski
  Gwen Mclean

Medora, MB R0M

D-U-N-S 20-922-5122   (SL)
VANDAELE SEEDS LTD
Gd, Medora, MB, R0M 1K0

(204) 665-2384
Emp Here 50   *Sales* 37,126,000
SIC 5191 Farm supplies
  Calvin Vandaele
  Mark Vandaele
  Robert Vandaele

Melita, MB R0M

D-U-N-S 24-345-6113   (BR)
PRAIRIE MOUNTAIN HEALTH
MELITA HEALTH CENTER
(*Suby of* PRAIRIE MOUNTAIN HEALTH)
147 Summit St, Melita, MB, R0M 1L0
(204) 522-8197
Emp Here 100
SIC 8062 General medical and surgical hospi-
tals
  William Bryant

D-U-N-S 20-875-4221   (HQ)
**SOUTHWEST HORIZON SCHOOL DIVI-
SION**
Gd, Melita, MB, R0M 1L0
(204) 483-6292
Emp Here 20   *Sales* 19,823,800
SIC 8211 Elementary and secondary schools
  Dale Peake
  Brian Spurrill
  Glynn Warnica
  Rhonda Dickenson
  Lynn Cory
  Bill Warren
  Irv Skelton

Minnedosa, MB R0J

D-U-N-S 20-003-2753   (HQ)
HERITAGE CO-OP 1997 LTD
120 Main St, Minnedosa, MB, R0J 1E0
(204) 867-2295
Emp Here 51   *Sales* 48,116,000
SIC 5411 Grocery stores
  Ken Jenner
  Richard Lemoing
  Katharine Kingdon
  Mel Birmingham
  Larry Chemerika
  Bill Moorehead

D-U-N-S 24-171-8360   (BR)
MORRIS INDUSTRIES LTD
(*Suby of* MORRIS INDUSTRIES LTD)
284 6th Ave Nw, Minnedosa, MB, R0J 1E0
(204) 867-2713
Emp Here 75
SIC 3523 Farm machinery and equipment
  Todd Sereachny

D-U-N-S 20-797-1644   (BR)
PRAIRIE MOUNTAIN HEALTH
(*Suby of* PRAIRIE MOUNTAIN HEALTH)
334 1st St Sw, Minnedosa, MB, R0J 1E0
(204) 867-2701
Emp Here 150
SIC 8062 General medical and surgical hospi-
tals
  Kowaluc Gail

Moosehorn, MB R0C

D-U-N-S 20-003-3199   (SL)
**MOOSEHORN CONSUMERS COOPERA-
TIVE LTD**
1 Main St, Moosehorn, MB, R0C 2E0
(204) 768-2770
Emp Here 38   *Sales* 39,246,704
SIC 5171 Petroleum bulk stations and termi-

nals
  Kathy Price
  Adrain Shabaga
  Dan Meisner
  Bev Klatt
  Ernie Kebel
  Elmer Nickel
  David Gall
  Stacy Meisner

Morden, MB R6M

D-U-N-S 24-967-2858   (BR)
3M CANADA COMPANY
(*Suby of* 3M/COMPANY)
400 Route 100, Morden, MB, R6M 1Z9
(204) 822-6284
Emp Here 200
SIC 2821 Plastics materials and resins
  Kent Brkak

D-U-N-S 24-376-9911   (HQ)
5274398 MANITOBA LTD
CROSS COUNTRY MANUFACTURING
418 South Railway St Suite 2, Morden, MB,
R6M 2G2
(204) 822-9509
Sales 22,384,300
SIC 3715 Truck trailers
  Jon Doerksen
  Timothy Klassen

D-U-N-S 25-145-4096   (BR)
BUHLER INDUSTRIES INC
MORDEN DIVISION
(*Suby of* ROSTSELMASH, PAO)
301 Mountain St S, Morden, MB, R6M 1X7
(204) 822-4467
Emp Here 250
SIC 3523 Farm machinery and equipment
  Vern Snidal

D-U-N-S 24-039-7125   (SL)
DECOR CABINETS LTD
DECOR CABINET COMPANY
200 Route 100, Morden, MB, R6M 1Y4
(204) 822-6151
Emp Here 420   *Sales* 33,470,684
SIC 2434 Wood kitchen cabinets
  Larry Dyck
  Abram Dyck

D-U-N-S 24-967-8921   (HQ)
ED'S TIRE SERVICE (1993) LTD
ED'S OK TIRE
(*Suby of* ED'S TIRE SERVICE LTD)
80 Thornhill St, Morden, MB, R6M 1C7

Emp Here 5   *Sales* 12,950,028
SIC 5531 Auto and home supply stores
  Ed Wiebe
  Rita Wiebe

D-U-N-S 20-003-3462   (SL)
GARDEN CITY CHRYSLER PLYMOUTH LTD
GARDEN CITY CHRYSLER JEEP
220 Stephen St, Morden, MB, R6M 1T4
(204) 822-6296
Emp Here 21   *Sales* 10,459,638
SIC 5511 New and used car dealers
  Esther Freisen
  Grace Warkentin
  Max Freisen

D-U-N-S 24-354-1161   (HQ)
GREENVALLEY EQUIPMENT INC
25016 Road 25w Highway 3 E, Morden, MB,
R6M 2B9
(204) 325-7742
Emp Here 35   *Sales* 16,858,632
SIC 5999 Miscellaneous retail stores, nec
  Glen Kehler
  Ernie Kehler

D-U-N-S 24-497-6924   (SL)

HURON WINDOW CORPORATION
345 Mountain St S, Morden, MB, R6M 1J5
(204) 822-6281
Emp Here 50   *Sales* 22,358,700
SIC 5031 Lumber, plywood, and millwork
  Victor Fehr

D-U-N-S 20-834-5892   (SL)
MIAMI COLONY FARMS LTD
Gd Stn Main, Morden, MB, R6M 1A1
(204) 435-2447
Emp Here 106   *Sales* 27,804,754
SIC 0191 General farms, primarily crop
  Levi Hofer
  Edwin Hofer

D-U-N-S 24-851-1867   (HQ)
RIMER ALCO NORTH AMERICA INC
RANA MEDICAL
205 Stephen St, Morden, MB, R6M 1V2
(204) 822-6595
Emp Here 22   *Sales* 12,216,400
SIC 5999 Miscellaneous retail stores, nec
  Earl Gardiner
  George Lacey
  Kalvin Lewis

D-U-N-S 20-758-6280   (SL)
TABOR HOME INC
450 Loren Dr, Morden, MB, R6M 0E2
(204) 822-4848
Emp Here 120   *Sales* 8,199,120
SIC 8051 Skilled nursing care facilities
  Wilf Warhentin
  Irvin Wiebe

D-U-N-S 24-546-2452   (HQ)
WESTERN SCHOOL DIVISION
75 Thornhill St Unit 4, Morden, MB, R6M 1P2
(204) 822-4448
Sales 24,779,750
SIC 8211 Elementary and secondary schools
  Stephen Ross
  Ken Klassen

Morris, MB R0G

D-U-N-S 25-288-4598   (SL)
BARTEL BULK FREIGHT INC
BARTEL FREIGHT
405 Stampede Dr, Morris, MB, R0G 1K0
(204) 746-2053
Emp Here 75   *Sales* 11,114,400
SIC 4213 Trucking, except local
  Chester Bartel
  Lynnford Bartel

D-U-N-S 20-947-3263   (SL)
BRANDT, PAUL TRUCKING LTD
226 Station St S, Morris, MB, R0G 1K0
(204) 746-2555
Emp Here 95   *Sales* 19,542,070
SIC 4213 Trucking, except local
  Kerry Brandt
  William Brandt
  Tracy Brandt

D-U-N-S 24-265-0000   (SL)
HORIZON AGRO INC
(*Suby of* HORIZON AGRO HOLDINGS INC)
1086 Horizon Rd, Morris, MB, R0G 1K0
(204) 746-2026
Emp Here 12   *Sales* 17,612,304
SIC 5153 Grain and field beans
  Arthur Dueck
  Lawrence Dueck

D-U-N-S 20-689-5554   (SL)
NORSTAR INDUSTRIES LTD
27157 Hwy 422, Morris, MB, R0G 1K0
(204) 746-8200
Emp Here 75   *Sales* 16,650,075
SIC 3532 Mining machinery
  Ray Waldner

Cameron Cornelsen

D-U-N-S 20-832-4913   (SL)
OAK BLUFF COLONY FARMS LTD
OAK BLUFF COLONY OF HUTTERIAN BRETHREN
Gd, Morris, MB, R0G 1K0
(204) 746-2122
Emp Here 80   *Sales* 20,984,720
SIC 0191 General farms, primarily crop
Jacob Maendel
Sam Waldner
Jake Maendel

D-U-N-S 24-883-2875   (HQ)
R H A CENTRAL MANITOBA INC.
MORRIS GENERAL HOSPITAL
215 Railroad Ave E, Morris, MB, R0G 1K0
(204) 746-2301
Emp Here 175   *Sales* 25,548,400
SIC 8062 General medical and surgical hospitals
Brad Street

D-U-N-S 24-112-3942   (HQ)
RED RIVER VALLEY SCHOOL DIVISION
233 Main St, Morris, MB, R0G 1K0
(204) 746-2317
Emp Here 18   *Sales* 37,665,220
SIC 8211 Elementary and secondary schools
Kelly Barkman
Alma Mitchell

Neepawa, MB R0J

D-U-N-S 20-835-6311   (HQ)
BEAUTIFUL PLAINS SCHOOL DIVISION
213 Mountain Ave, Neepawa, MB, R0J 1H0
(204) 476-2387
Emp Here 50   *Sales* 23,937,540
SIC 8211 Elementary and secondary schools
Gorth Hunter
Gordon Olmstead
Debbie Rea
Sharon Biehn
Richard Manns
Garth Hunter
Bonnie Snezyk
John Douglas
Ray Kulbacki

D-U-N-S 24-630-1865   (SL)
HYLIFE FOODS LP
(*Suby of* HYLIFE LTD)
623 Main St E, Neepawa, MB, R0J 1H0
(204) 476-3393
Emp Here 600   *Sales* 292,431,000
SIC 2011 Meat packing plants
Don Janzen
Claude Vielfaure
Denis Vielfaure
Howard Siemens
Bill Teichrow
Grant Lazaruk

D-U-N-S 24-362-8851   (BR)
HYLIFE LTD
SPRINGHILL FARMS
(*Suby of* HYLIFE LTD)
623 Main St E, Neepawa, MB, R0J 1H0
(204) 476-3624
Emp Here 350
SIC 2011 Meat packing plants
Chris Baker

D-U-N-S 25-011-3503   (SL)
NEEPAWA HEALTH CENTRE
500 Hospital St, Neepawa, MB, R0J 1H0
(204) 476-2394
Emp Here 120   *Sales* 13,329,600
SIC 8062 General medical and surgical hospitals
Judy Gabler

D-U-N-S 20-948-6901   (HQ)
NEEPAWA-GLADSTONE COOPERATIVE LIMITED
32 Main St E, Neepawa, MB, R0J 1H0
(204) 476-2328
Emp Here 85   *Sales* 65,057,402
SIC 5541 Gasoline service stations
Brian Hedley
Raymond Kulbacki
Bruce Gilmore
Gerald Mcgowan
John Forke
Aleki Tomoniko
Mark Sumner
Jason Sumner
Chris Scott

D-U-N-S 20-838-5666   (HQ)
SPRING HILL COLONY FARMS LTD
30 Township 15 Rg Suite 15, Neepawa, MB, R0J 1H0
(204) 476-2715
Sales 22,469,850
SIC 2013 Sausages and other prepared meats
John Hofer
Michael Wollmann

Nelson House, MB R0B

D-U-N-S 24-690-8032   (HQ)
NELSON HOUSE EDUCATION AUTHORITY, INC
8 Bay Rd, Nelson House, MB, R0B 1A0
(204) 484-2095
Emp Here 94   *Sales* 8,725,644
SIC 8211 Elementary and secondary schools
Ernesta Rivais
Susan Kobliski
Edna Moore
Lena Dysart
Ryan Linklater
Ed Primrose

New Bothwell, MB R0A

D-U-N-S 20-003-5533   (SL)
BOTHWELL CHEESE INC
61 Main St N, New Bothwell, MB, R0A 1C0
(204) 388-4666
Emp Here 60   *Sales* 20,741,400
SIC 2022 Cheese; natural and processed
Ivan Balenovic
Wally Smith

Newton Siding, MB R0H

D-U-N-S 20-003-5707   (SL)
NEWTON ENTERPRISES (1983)
RONA BUILDING CENTRE
1 Main St, Newton Siding, MB, R0H 0X0
(204) 267-2211
Emp Here 85   *Sales* 22,750,420
SIC 5211 Lumber and other building materials
Bradley Dick
Warren Bracken
Wayne Klippenstein

D-U-N-S 24-852-5255   (SL)
SUNNYSIDE COLONY LTD
SUNNYSIDE COLONY OF HUTTERIAN TRUST
Gd, Newton Siding, MB, R0H 0X0
(204) 267-2812
Emp Here 44   *Sales* 15,068,548
SIC 0191 General farms, primarily crop
Michael Waldner

Zackarius Kleinsasser
Cornelius Waldner

Ninette, MB R0K

D-U-N-S 24-967-8517   (SL)
WELLWOOD COLONY FARMS LTD
Gd, Ninette, MB, R0K 1R0
(204) 776-2130
Emp Here 50   *Sales* 17,123,350
SIC 0119 Cash grains, nec
Lawrence (Larry) Waldner
Robert Hofer

Niverville, MB R0A

D-U-N-S 25-217-9312   (SL)
3084761 MANITOBA LTD
WILLIAM DYCK & SONS (1993)
262 Main St, Niverville, MB, R0A 1E0
(204) 883-2327
Emp Here 40   *Sales* 10,122,360
SIC 5211 Lumber and other building materials
Carl Fast

D-U-N-S 25-506-0816   (SL)
C & G VILLAGE INN
2193 Hwy 59, Niverville, MB, R0A 1E0
(204) 388-4283
Emp Here 20   *Sales* 10,129,102
SIC 5541 Gasoline service stations
Claire Depauw
Gary Depauw

D-U-N-S 25-098-5223   (SL)
EXCEL PLAYGREEN GROUP INC
18 3 Ave S, Niverville, MB, R0A 1E0
(204) 388-9250
Emp Here 50   *Sales* 19,275,950
SIC 0213 Hogs
Dan Klippenstein
Anthony Lenchyshyn

D-U-N-S 25-231-2020   (SL)
SPECTIS MOULDERS INC
100 Cedar Dr, Niverville, MB, R0A 1E0
(204) 388-6700
Emp Here 100   *Sales* 27,666,000
SIC 2821 Plastics materials and resins
Kenton Pilek
Eric Will

Norway House, MB R0B

D-U-N-S 20-709-9974   (BR)
FRONTIER SCHOOL DIVISION
HELEN BETTY OSBORNE ININIW EDUCATION RESOURCE CENTRE
(*Suby of* FRONTIER SCHOOL DIVISION)
1 Rossville Rd, Norway House, MB, R0B 1B0
(204) 359-4100
Emp Here 1,005
SIC 8211 Elementary and secondary schools
Agnes Mowat

D-U-N-S 24-915-3131   (BR)
NORTH WEST COMPANY LP, THE
NORTHERN STORES
(*Suby of* NORTH WEST COMPANY LP, THE)
Gd, Norway House, MB, R0B 1B0
(204) 359-6258
Emp Here 80
SIC 5411 Grocery stores
Shamus Acdonel

Oak Bluff, MB R4G

D-U-N-S 24-882-4989   (HQ)
AMBASSADOR MECHANICAL L.P.
(*Suby of* MOSAIC CAPITAL CORPORATION)
400 Fort Whyte Way Unit 110, Oak Bluff, MB, R4G 0B1
(204) 231-1094
Emp Here 135   *Sales* 40,627,200
SIC 1711 Plumbing, heating, air-conditioning
Claude Cloutier
Colin Cloutier
Harold Kunich
Alan Fowler

D-U-N-S 24-751-4958   (SL)
BAYVIEW CONSTRUCTION LTD
4000 Mcgillivray Blvd, Oak Bluff, MB, R4G 0B5
(204) 254-7761
Emp Here 250   *Sales* 82,028,750
SIC 1611 Highway and street construction
Blake Karchuk
Joel Martens

D-U-N-S 25-976-7960   (SL)
C.L. MALACH COMPANY (1997) LTD
3501 Mcgillivray Blvd, Oak Bluff, MB, R4G 0B5
(204) 895-8002
Emp Here 88   *Sales* 16,903,480
SIC 3444 Sheet Metalwork
Bruce Mcivor

D-U-N-S 20-003-7232   (HQ)
ENNS BROTHERS LTD
400 Fort Whyte Way Unit 310, Oak Bluff, MB, R4G 0B1
(204) 895-0212
Sales 56,576,680
SIC 5083 Farm and garden machinery
Victor Enns
David Enns
Bob Enns

D-U-N-S 24-203-7245   (HQ)
FXR FACTORY RACING INC
155 Oakland Rd, Oak Bluff, MB, R4G 0A4
(204) 736-4406
Sales 17,441,270
SIC 5136 Men's and boy's clothing
Milton Reimer

D-U-N-S 20-002-0709   (HQ)
KLEYSEN GROUP LTD
(*Suby of* MULLEN GROUP LTD)
2800 Mcgillivray Blvd, Oak Bluff, MB, R4G 0B4
(204) 488-5550
Emp Here 225   *Sales* 55,314,300
SIC 4213 Trucking, except local
Jeff Kleysen

D-U-N-S 25-108-1295   (SL)
NEW HOPE TRANSPORT LTD
170 Agri Park Rd, Oak Bluff, MB, R4G 0A5

Emp Here 130   *Sales* 26,741,780
SIC 4213 Trucking, except local
Jake Peters
John Peters

D-U-N-S 24-607-5717   (HQ)
PRE-CON BUILDERS LTD
405 Fort Whyte Way Suite 100, Oak Bluff, MB, R4G 0B1
(204) 633-2515
Sales 21,136,850
SIC 1541 Industrial buildings and warehouses
Robin Lee
Jeff Hawryluk

D-U-N-S 24-027-5045   (SL)
ROCKY ROAD RECYCLING LTD
4154 Mcgillivray Blvd, Oak Bluff, MB, R4G 0B5
(204) 832-7802
Emp Here 100   *Sales* 25,244,200
SIC 1611 Highway and street construction
Blake Karschuk

D-U-N-S 25-106-5009   (SL)

SUPERIOR TRUSS CO LTD
(Suby of 4834772 MANITOBA LTD)
165 Industrial Rd, Oak Bluff, MB, R4G 0A5
(204) 888-7663
Emp Here 690
SIC 2439 Structural wood members, nec
Vince Ryz

Oak Lake, MB R0M

D-U-N-S 20-435-1159   (SL)
LEWIS CATTLE OILER CO. LTD
Gd, Oak Lake, MB, R0M 1P0
(204) 855-2775
Emp Here 30   Sales 22,275,600
SIC 5191 Farm supplies
Garry Morcombe
Debbie Morcombe

Oak River, MB R0K

D-U-N-S 20-691-6806   (HQ)
OAK RIVER COLONY FARMS LTD
Gd, Oak River, MB, R0K 1T0
(204) 566-2359
Sales 10,409,013
SIC 0213 Hogs
Joseph Wurtz
Albert Hofer

Oakbank, MB R0E

D-U-N-S 20-875-4064   (BR)
NORTH EASTMAN HEALTH ASSOCIATION INC
KIN PLACE HEALTH COMPLEX
689 Main St, Oakbank, MB, R0E 1J2
(204) 444-2227
Emp Here 150
SIC 8011 Offices and clinics of medical doctors
Karen Stevens-Chambers

Oakville, MB R0H

D-U-N-S 25-345-1264   (SL)
BRANTWOOD COLONY FARMS LTD
Gd, Oakville, MB, R0H 0Y0
(204) 267-2527
Emp Here 86   Sales 22,558,574
SIC 0119 Cash grains, nec
John Waldner
Johnny Waldner Jr.

D-U-N-S 20-834-9209   (SL)
GRAND COLONY FARMS LTD
GRAND COLONY OF HUTTERIAN BRETHREN TRUST
20125 Road 57n, Oakville, MB, R0H 0Y0
(204) 267-2292
Emp Here 33   Sales 11,301,411
SIC 0139 Field crops, except cash grain
Michael Waldner
Jerry Stahl

D-U-N-S 25-011-3578   (SL)
NORQUAY HOLDING CO LTD
23042 Road 68n, Oakville, MB, R0H 0Y0
(204) 267-2139
Emp Here 15   Sales 18,155,955
SIC 5154 Livestock
Elie Walner

Onanole, MB R0J

D-U-N-S 20-838-4941   (SL)
ELKHORN RANCH & RESORT LTD
ELKHORN RESORT SPA & CONFERENCE CENTRE
3 Mooswa Dr E, Onanole, MB, R0J 1N0
(204) 848-2802
Emp Here 80   Sales 7,591,920
SIC 7011 Hotels and motels
Ian Sarna
Gary Buckley

Opaskwayak, MB R0B

D-U-N-S 25-826-5586   (SL)
PAS IGA 1979 FOOD PRODUCTS LTD, THE
PAS IGA, THE
Hwy 10 N, Opaskwayak, MB, R0B 2J0

Emp Here 45   Sales 12,336,840
SIC 5411 Grocery stores
Howard Young

D-U-N-S 20-310-6674   (HQ)
PASKWAYAK BUSINESS DEVELOMENT CORPORATION LTD
Hwy 10 N, Opaskwayak, MB, R0B 2J0
(204) 627-7200
Emp Here 8   Sales 10,667,900
SIC 8732 Commercial nonphysical research
Russell Constant
Garth Flett
Mike Bignell
Rhonda Norman
Eric Sanderson
Gary Cook
Rosina Hester

Otterburne, MB R0A

D-U-N-S 20-758-1513   (HQ)
PROVIDENCE UNIVERSITY COLLEGE AND THEOLOGICAL SEMINARY
10 College Cres, Otterburne, MB, R0A 1G0
(204) 433-7488
Emp Here 1   Sales 19,420,830
SIC 8221 Colleges and universities
August Konkel
Antoinette Van Kuik
David Johnson
Mark Little
Jamie Heide

D-U-N-S 20-303-8047   (SL)
SCHRIEMER FAMILY FARM LTD
33096 Rat River Rd, Otterburne, MB, R0A 1G0
(204) 299-9708
Emp Here 35   Sales 11,986,345
SIC 0161 Vegetables and melons
Trevor Schriemer
Grace Raap

Peguis, MB R0C

D-U-N-S 24-040-4103   (SL)
PEGUIS SCHOOL BOARD
Gd, Peguis, MB, R0C 3J0
(204) 645-2648
Emp Here 250   Sales 24,779,750
SIC 8211 Elementary and secondary schools
Edwin Mccorrister
Eugene Stevenson
Sharon Stevenson

Petersfield, MB R0C

D-U-N-S 25-313-1056   (SL)
NETLEY COLONY LTD
NETLEY MILL WORK
897 Henry Rd, Petersfield, MB, R0C 2L0
(204) 738-2828
Emp Here 87   Sales 11,898,033
SIC 0213 Hogs
Chris Hofer
Simon Hofer

Pierson, MB R0M

D-U-N-S 20-003-8164   (SL)
EDWARD CONSUMERS COOPERATIVE LTD
13 Broadway St, Pierson, MB, R0M 1S0
(204) 634-2418
Emp Here 20   Sales 20,656,160
SIC 5171 Petroleum bulk stations and terminals
David Wowk
Ron White
Tony Mcmechan
Ed Arnt
Bill Kennedy
Allan Philip
Trevor Copithorne
Adam Mcgreogor
Grant Phillip
Jason Wickman

Pilot Mound, MB R0G

D-U-N-S 25-764-7289   (BR)
ROCK LAKE HEALTH DISTRICT FOUNDATION INC
ROCK LAKE PERSONAL CARE HOME
(Suby of ROCK LAKE HEALTH DISTRICT FOUNDATION INC)
115 Brown St Apt 27, Pilot Mound, MB, R0G 1P0
(204) 825-2246
Emp Here 110
SIC 8361 Residential care

Pinawa, MB R0E

D-U-N-S 20-834-8961   (BR)
ATOMIC ENERGY OF CANADA LIMITED
AECL WHITE SHELL LABORATORY
(Suby of GOVERNMENT OF CANADA)
Gd, Pinawa, MB, R0E 1L0
(204) 753-2311
Emp Here 250
SIC 2819 Industrial inorganic chemicals, nec
Grant Koroll

Pine Falls, MB R0E

D-U-N-S 24-040-4152   (HQ)
SAGKEENG EDUCATION AUTHORITY
Gd, Pine Falls, MB, R0E 1M0
(204) 367-4109
Emp Here 1   Sales 25,752,210
SIC 8621 Professional organizations
Eva Courchene

Plum Coulee, MB R0G

D-U-N-S 20-832-4244   (HQ)
BLUMENGART COLONY FARMS LTD
Gd, Plum Coulee, MB, R0G 1R0
(204) 829-3687
Sales 26,230,900
SIC 0191 General farms, primarily crop
Isaac Waldner

Portage La Prairie, MB R1N

D-U-N-S 20-948-5200   (SL)
AIRPORT COLONY OF HUTTERIAN BRETHREN TRUST
Gd Lcd Main, Portage La Prairie, MB, R1N 3A7
(204) 274-2422
Emp Here 82   Sales 21,509,338
SIC 0191 General farms, primarily crop
Andrew Hofer
Tomas Maendel
Jake Hofer

D-U-N-S 20-648-2148   (BR)
CANAD CORPORATION LTD
AALTO'S FAMILY DINING
(Suby of CANAD CORPORATION LTD)
2401 Saskatchewan Ave W, Portage La Prairie, MB, R1N 4A6
(204) 857-9745
Emp Here 100
SIC 7011 Hotels and motels
Jeff Bemarcke

D-U-N-S 25-103-8287   (SL)
DOUGLAS CAMPBELL LODGE
150 9th St Se, Portage La Prairie, MB, R1N 3T6
(204) 239-6006
Emp Here 80   Sales 17,669,680
SIC 6513 Apartment building operators
Cindy Joel

D-U-N-S 24-468-9022   (SL)
DUNN, CRAIG PONTIAC BUICK GMC LTD
DUNN, CRAIG MOTOR CITY
2345 Sissons Dr, Portage La Prairie, MB, R1N 3P1
(204) 239-5770
Emp Here 42   Sales 20,919,276
SIC 5511 New and used car dealers
Craig Dunn
Douglas Murray

D-U-N-S 20-837-7598   (SL)
E. F. MOON CONSTRUCTION LTD
1200 Lorne Ave E, Portage La Prairie, MB, R1N 4A2
(204) 857-7871
Emp Here 50   Sales 12,044,200
SIC 1622 Bridge, tunnel, and elevated highway construction
Mark Moon
Darrell Jack Meseyton

D-U-N-S 20-834-6072   (SL)
FAIRHOLME COLONY FARMS LTD
FAIRHOLME COLONY OF HUTTERIAN BRETHREN-TRUST
E 27-9-8 S, Portage La Prairie, MB, R1N 3B9
(204) 252-2225
Emp Here 75   Sales 8,196,675
SIC 0762 Farm management services
Chris Maendel
Wayne Maendel
Cameron Maendel

D-U-N-S 24-883-5001   (SL)
GOOD HOPE COLONY FARMS LTD
GOOD HOPE COLONY OF HUTTERIAN BRETHREN-TRUST
Gd Lcd Main, Portage La Prairie, MB, R1N 3A7

---

(204) 252-2334
Emp Here 86   *Sales* 14,536,150
SIC 0191 General farms, primarily crop
Benjamin Waldner

D-U-N-S 25-414-5188   (HQ)
HI-TEC INDUSTRIES INC
1000 6th Ave Ne, Portage La Prairie, MB, R1N
0B4
(204) 239-4270
Sales 33,300,150
SIC 3523 Farm machinery and equipment
John Dueck
Cornelius Dueck
Ben Dueck

D-U-N-S 24-966-5316   (HQ)
**MANITOBA AGRICULTURAL SERVICES
CORPORATION**
(*Suby of* PROVINCE OF MANITOBA)
50 24th St Nw Suite 400, Portage La Prairie,
MB, R1N 3V9
(204) 239-3499
Emp Here 35   *Sales* 238,404,500
SIC 6159 Miscellaneous business credit institutions
Neil Hamilton
John Plohman
Jim Lewis

D-U-N-S 20-006-7593   (HQ)
MUNRO FARM SUPPLIES LTD
Gd Lcd Main, Portage La Prairie, MB, R1N
3A7
(204) 857-8741
Emp Here 28   *Sales* 16,059,120
SIC 5261 Retail nurseries and garden stores
Ronald Helwer

D-U-N-S 20-834-6908   (SL)
NEW ROSEDALE COLONY FARMS LTD
NEW ROSEDALE FEED MILL
(*Suby of* NEW ROSEDALE HOLDING COMPANY LTD)
Gd Lcd Main, Portage La Prairie, MB, R1N
3B7
(204) 252-2727
Emp Here 50   *Sales* 13,115,450
SIC 0191 General farms, primarily crop
Arnie Mandeal
James Mandeal

D-U-N-S 24-607-7606   (SL)
NORQUAY NURSERIES LTD
Gd Lcd Main 28168 1 Hwy E, Portage La
Prairie, MB, R1N 3B2
(204) 239-6507
Emp Here 21   *Sales* 15,592,920
SIC 5193 Flowers and florists supplies
William Bruinooge

D-U-N-S 24-105-0058   (SL)
NORTHERN BREEZE FARMS LTD
NORTHERN BREEZE COLONY
Gd Lcd Main, Portage La Prairie, MB, R1N
3A7
(204) 239-4396
Emp Here 35   *Sales* 13,493,165
SIC 0212 Beef cattle, except feedlots
Mike Waldner
Ernie Waldner
David Hofer

D-U-N-S 20-834-6312   (SL)
POPLAR POINT COLONY FARMS LTD
94 River Rd W, Portage La Prairie, MB, R1N
3C4
(204) 267-2560
Emp Here 77   *Sales* 20,197,793
SIC 0191 General farms, primarily crop
Joe Waldner
Amos Waldner
Rueben Waldner

D-U-N-S 20-833-0936   (HQ)
PORTAGE LA PRAIRIE MUTUAL INSURANCE CO, THE
PORTAGE MUTUAL INSURANCE
749 Saskatchewan Ave E, Portage La Prairie,

MB, R1N 0L3
(204) 857-3415
Emp Here 82   *Sales* 854,298,720
SIC 6411 Insurance agents, brokers, and service
Randy L Clark
John G Mitchell
Tom W Mccartney
Doug Pedden
Hugh G Owens
Dennis W Thompson

D-U-N-S 25-687-4116   (SL)
PORTAGE TRANSPORT INC
PORTAGE TRANSPORT 1998
1450 Lorne Ave E, Portage La Prairie, MB,
R1N 4A2
(204) 239-6451
Emp Here 70   *Sales* 19,831,000
SIC 7538 General automotive repair shops
Bernie Driedger
Liz Driedger

D-U-N-S 24-520-0399   (BR)
REGIONAL HEALTH AUTHORITY - CENTRAL MANITOBA INC
PORTAGE DISTRICT GENERAL HOSPITAL
(*Suby of* REGIONAL HEALTH AUTHORITY -
CENTRAL MANITOBA INC)
524 5th St Se, Portage La Prairie, MB, R1N
3A8
(204) 239-2211
Emp Here 275
SIC 8062 General medical and surgical hospitals
Pat Nodrick

D-U-N-S 20-291-7142   (SL)
RICHARDSON MILLING LIMITED
(*Suby of* RICHARDSON, JAMES & SONS,
LIMITED)
1 Can-Oat Dr, Portage La Prairie, MB, R1N
3W1
(204) 857-9700
Emp Here 500   *Sales* 915,788,500
SIC 5153 Grain and field beans
Hartley Richardson

D-U-N-S 20-702-9179   (HQ)
SIMPLOT CANADA (II) LIMITED
J.R. SIMPLOT COMPANY (FOOD)
Hwy 1 W & Simplot Rd, Portage La Prairie,
MB, R1N 3A4
(204) 857-1400
Sales 112,098,550
SIC 2099 Food preparations, nec
Scott Simplot
Garrett Lofto
Gay Simplot
Ted Simplot
Steve Beebe
Richard Hormaechea
John Otter
J.D. Simplot
Terry Uhling

D-U-N-S 25-250-0967   (SL)
VISIONS OF INDEPENDENCE INC.
20 Saskatchewan Ave W, Portage La Prairie,
MB, R1N 0L9
(204) 239-6698
Emp Here 49   *Sales* 19,473,286
SIC 8699 Membership organizations, nec
Irene Boyse

D-U-N-S 25-055-0431   (SL)
**W.R.A. ENTERPRISES PORTAGE LA
PRAIRIE LTD**
SOBEYS
2100 Saskatchewan Ave W, Portage La
Prairie, MB, R1N 0P3
(204) 857-4700
Emp Here 100   *Sales* 29,347,700
SIC 5411 Grocery stores
Robert Smith

D-U-N-S 25-498-2515   (BR)

WAL-MART CANADA CORP
WALMART #3069
(*Suby of* WALMART INC.)
2348 Sissons Dr, Portage La Prairie, MB, R1N
0G5
(204) 857-5011
Emp Here 125
SIC 5311 Department stores
Gerry Tkachuk

Red Sucker Lake, MB R0B

D-U-N-S 20-649-7385   (SL)
**RED SUCKER LAKE HEALTH AUTHORITY
INC**
Gd, Red Sucker Lake, MB, R0B 1H0
(204) 469-5229
Emp Here 24   *Sales* 24,837,144
SIC 6324 Hospital and medical service plans
Ron Monias

Richer, MB R0E

D-U-N-S 20-546-2851   (SL)
PREMIER HORTICULTURE LTD
302 North, Richer, MB, R0E 1S0
(204) 422-8805
Emp Here 70   *Sales* 103,928,347
SIC 5159 Farm-product raw materials, nec
Janie Mclennan

Riding Mountain, MB R0J

D-U-N-S 20-834-6734   (SL)
PARK VIEW COLONY FARMS LTD
Gd, Riding Mountain, MB, R0J 1T0
(204) 967-2492
Emp Here 128   *Sales* 28,271,488
SIC 6513 Apartment building operators
Danny Waldner

Rivers, MB R0K

D-U-N-S 24-851-8698   (SL)
HANGAR FARMS INC
Rivers Air Base, Rivers, MB, R0K 1X0

Emp Here 40   *Sales* 13,698,680
SIC 0191 General farms, primarily crop
Larry Friesen

D-U-N-S 25-959-0586   (BR)
**RIVERDALE HEALTH SERVICES DISTRICT
FOUNDATION INC**
RIVERDALE HEALTH CENTRE
(*Suby of* RIVERDALE HEALTH SERVICES
DISTRICT FOUNDATION INC)
512 Quebec St, Rivers, MB, R0K 1X0
(204) 328-5321
Emp Here 75
SIC 8062 General medical and surgical hospitals
Greg Paddock

Riverton, MB R0C

D-U-N-S 20-384-0186   (SL)
CANADIAN FISH GUYS
390 Reggie Leach Dr, Riverton, MB, R0C 2R0
(204) 378-5510
Emp Here 30   *Sales* 11,565,570
SIC 0273 Animal aquaculture

Murray Olafson

D-U-N-S 24-630-6724   (SL)
ERICKSON CONSTRUCTION (1975) LTD
Gd, Riverton, MB, R0C 2R0

Emp Here 50   *Sales* 14,176,200
SIC 1611 Highway and street construction
John (Craig) Erickson

D-U-N-S 20-012-8127   (HQ)
EROSIONCONTROLBLANKET.COM INC
1 Broadway Ave, Riverton, MB, R0C 2R0
(204) 378-5610
Sales 17,439,786
SIC 5039 Construction materials, nec
Mark Myrowich

Roblin, MB R0L

D-U-N-S 24-546-4185   (SL)
65548 MANITOBA LTD
W D LIVESTOCK
Gd, Roblin, MB, R0L 1P0
(204) 937-2106
Emp Here 12   *Sales* 14,524,764
SIC 5154 Livestock
Brad Welcher
Barry Welcher
Ruth Welcher

D-U-N-S 25-841-5983   (SL)
**CARDEAGER FORD SALES SERVICE &
AUTO BODY LTD**
CARDEAGER AUTO BODY
Gd, Roblin, MB, R0L 1P0
(204) 937-8386
Emp Here 25   *Sales* 12,451,950
SIC 5511 New and used car dealers
Hubert Carriere
Wanda Carriere

D-U-N-S 24-343-2924   (BR)
PARKLAND REGIONAL HEALTH AUTHORITY INC
ROBLIN DISTRICT HEALTH CENTRE
(*Suby of* PARKLAND REGIONAL HEALTH
AUTHORITY INC)
Gd, Roblin, MB, R0L 1P0
(204) 937-2142
Emp Here 135
SIC 8062 General medical and surgical hospitals
Cheryl Jerome

D-U-N-S 20-004-3123   (SL)
ROBLIN FOREST PRODUCTS LTD
83 N Hwy, Roblin, MB, R0L 1P0
(204) 937-2103
Emp Here 30   *Sales* 13,415,220
SIC 5031 Lumber, plywood, and millwork
Larry Cousins

Rosenort, MB R0G

D-U-N-S 20-004-3701   (HQ)
MIDLAND MANUFACTURING LIMITED
36 Main St E, Rosenort, MB, R0G 1W0
(204) 746-2348
Sales 22,384,300
SIC 3713 Truck and bus bodies
Ervin Friesen
Leroy Friesen
Elmer Dueck
Erika Friesen

D-U-N-S 24-818-0861   (HQ)
WESTFIELD INDUSTRIES LTD
74 Hwy 205 E, Rosenort, MB, R0G 1W0
(204) 746-2396
Emp Here 270   *Sales* 88,195,378

▲ Public Company   ■ Public Company Family Member   **HQ** Headquarters   **BR** Branch   **SL** Single Location

SIC 3523 Farm machinery and equipment
Gary Anderson
Steve Somerfeld

Rosser, MB R0H

D-U-N-S 24-848-1835   (SL)
4TRACKS LTD
374 Eagle Dr, Rosser, MB, R0H 1E0

Emp Here 160   *Sales* 32,912,960
SIC 4212 Local trucking, without storage
Adam Singh

D-U-N-S 24-235-9677   (HQ)
ARCTIC BEVERAGES LP
(*Suby of* TRIBAL COUNCILS INVESTMENT
GROUP OF MANITOBA LTD)
107 Mountain View Rd Unit 2, Rosser, MB,
R0H 1E0
(204) 633-8686
Emp Here 35   *Sales* 65,175,006
SIC 5149 Groceries and related products, nec
Allan Mcleod

D-U-N-S 20-945-7480   (SL)
ARNASON INDUSTRIES LTD
9094 Hwy 1, Rosser, MB, R0H 1E0
(204) 633-2567
Emp Here 125   *Sales* 31,555,250
SIC 1623 Water, sewer, and utility lines
Brett Arnason
Barry Arnason
Lana Arnason

Russell, MB R0J

D-U-N-S 24-266-2526   (HQ)
BRENDONN HOLDINGS LTD
RUSSELL PETRO-CANADA CENTRE
Junction Of Hwy Suite 16, Russell, MB, R0J
1W0
(204) 773-2268
Emp Here 20   *Sales* 47,773,638
SIC 5171 Petroleum bulk stations and termi-
nals
Brent Shuya
Donna Shuya

D-U-N-S 20-732-9876   (SL)
RUSSELL HEALTH CENTRE
426 Alexandria Ave, Russell, MB, R0J 1W0
(204) 773-2125
Emp Here 80   *Sales* 18,743,040
SIC 8742 Management consulting services
Norma Holmes

D-U-N-S 25-670-8694   (SL)
SUNRIDGE FORAGE LTD
15 2128 Nw, Russell, MB, R0J 1W0

Emp Here 18   *Sales* 13,365,360
SIC 5191 Farm supplies
Garry Halwas
Ronald Halwas

Sanford, MB R0G

D-U-N-S 24-883-4210   (SL)
VERMILLION FARMS LTD
Gd, Sanford, MB, R0G 2J0
(204) 736-2787
Emp Here 50   *Sales* 17,123,350
SIC 0191 General farms, primarily crop
Hardy Wipf
Elie Hoser

Selkirk, MB R1A

D-U-N-S 24-223-1541   (BR)
3177743 MANITOBA LTD
BOSTON PIZZA
(*Suby of* 3177743 MANITOBA LTD)
1018 Manitoba Ave, Selkirk, MB, R1A 4M2
(204) 785-7777
Emp Here 80
SIC 5812 Eating places
Steve Lam

D-U-N-S 25-518-8831   (SL)
ACL SELKIRK INC
ACL
306 Jemima St, Selkirk, MB, R1A 1X1
(204) 482-5435
Emp Here 48   *Sales* 15,102,336
SIC 8699 Membership organizations, nec

D-U-N-S 20-005-6232   (HQ)
AMSCO CAST PRODUCTS (CANADA) INC
(*Suby of* TONUX INC)
35 Mercy St, Selkirk, MB, R1A 1N5
(204) 482-4442
Emp Here 4   *Sales* 18,138,800
SIC 3325 Steel foundries, nec
Eddie Chung

D-U-N-S 20-114-8397   (BR)
AMSCO CAST PRODUCTS (CANADA) INC
(*Suby of* TONUX INC)
35 Mercy St, Selkirk, MB, R1A 1N5
(204) 482-4442
Emp Here 100
SIC 3325 Steel foundries, nec

D-U-N-S 25-262-6023   (BR)
BLACK CAT WEAR PARTS LTD
(*Suby of* TONUX INC)
71 Railway St, Selkirk, MB, R1A 4L4
(204) 482-9046
Emp Here 91
SIC 3531 Construction machinery
Dick Buxton

D-U-N-S 20-180-2324   (BR)
GERDAU AMERISTEEL CORPORATION
(*Suby of* METALURGICA GERDAU S/A.)
27 Main St, Selkirk, MB, R1A 1P6
(204) 482-3241
Emp Here 500
SIC 3312 Blast furnaces and steel mills
Gavin Tobin

D-U-N-S 25-417-5227   (BR)
GERDAU AMERISTEEL CORPORATION
GERDAU AMERSTEEL MANITOBA METALS
(*Suby of* METALURGICA GERDAU S/A.)
1 Railway St, Selkirk, MB, R1A 2B3
(204) 482-6701
Emp Here 120
SIC 5093 Scrap and waste materials
Kevin Higgs

D-U-N-S 24-428-6407   (BR)
**INTERLAKE REGIONAL HEALTH AUTHOR-
ITY INC**
SELKIRK & DISTRICT GENERAL HOSPITAL
120 Easton Drive, Selkirk, MB, R1A 2M2
(204) 482-5800
Emp Here 100
SIC 8062 General medical and surgical hospi-
tals
Dianne Mestdagh

D-U-N-S 20-709-8026   (BR)
LORD SELKIRK SCHOOL DIVISION, THE
*LORD SELKIRK REGIONAL COMPREHEN-
SIVE SECONDARY SCHOOL*
(*Suby of* LORD SELKIRK SCHOOL DIVI-
SION, THE)
221 Mercy St, Selkirk, MB, R1A 2C8
(204) 482-6926
Emp Here 250
SIC 8211 Elementary and secondary schools

Scott Kwasnitza

D-U-N-S 20-834-6460   (HQ)
LORD SELKIRK SCHOOL DIVISION, THE
205 Mercy St, Selkirk, MB, R1A 2C8
(204) 482-5942
Emp Here 25   *Sales* 118,942,800
SIC 8211 Elementary and secondary schools
Bruce Cairns

D-U-N-S 25-217-3075   (SL)
MORSTAR HOLDINGS LTD
HARRIS CHEV-OLDS
230 Main St, Selkirk, MB, R1A 1R9

Emp Here 21   *Sales* 10,459,638
SIC 5511 New and used car dealers
Bruce Harris

D-U-N-S 25-269-5531   (SL)
PENNY POWER HARDWARE LTD
*SELKIRK HOME HARDWARE BUILDING
CENTRE*
917 Manitoba Ave, Selkirk, MB, R1A 3T7
(204) 785-2773
Emp Here 90   *Sales* 24,088,680
SIC 5251 Hardware stores
Richard Borthistle
Lenora Borthistle

D-U-N-S 24-395-0305   (SL)
PHARMAPLUS #4950
366 Main St, Selkirk, MB, R1A 2J7
(204) 482-6003
Emp Here 25   *Sales* 16,411,600
SIC 5961 Catalog and mail-order houses
Mark Juvonen

D-U-N-S 20-835-4498   (SL)
RED RIVER MANOR INC
RED RIVER PLACE NURSING HOME
133 Manchester Ave, Selkirk, MB, R1A 0B5
(204) 482-3036
Emp Here 145   *Sales* 9,921,190
SIC 8322 Individual and family services
Melvin S. Fages

D-U-N-S 20-874-8249   (SL)
ROB WILLITTS SALES LTD
CANADIAN TIRE ASSOCIATE STORES
1041 Manitoba Ave Suite 447, Selkirk, MB,
R1A 3T7
(204) 482-8473
Emp Here 75   *Sales* 27,316,125
SIC 5014 Tires and tubes
Rob Willitts

D-U-N-S 24-737-7968   (HQ)
RPM ENTERPRISES LTD
PETRO CANADA
395 Main St, Selkirk, MB, R1A 1T9
(204) 482-4131
Emp Here 5   *Sales* 24,903,900
SIC 5541 Gasoline service stations
Richard Marchak

D-U-N-S 20-813-0802   (SL)
**SELKIRK CHEVROLET PONTIAC BUICK
GMC LTD**
SELKIRK GM
1010 Manitoba Ave, Selkirk, MB, R1A 3T7
(204) 482-1010
Emp Here 45   *Sales* 22,413,510
SIC 5541 Gasoline service stations
Donald Walters

D-U-N-S 25-522-2168   (SL)
SELKIRK CHRYSLER (MB) LTD
SELKIRK CHRYSLER JEEP
1011 Manitoba Ave, Selkirk, MB, R1A 3T7
(204) 482-4151
Emp Here 24   *Sales* 11,953,872
SIC 5511 New and used car dealers
Andy Rewucki
Lorraine Cahill

D-U-N-S 25-272-0099   (BR)
SOBEYS WEST INC

SAFEWAY
(*Suby of* EMPIRE COMPANY LIMITED)
318 Manitoba Ave, Selkirk, MB, R1A 0Y7
(204) 482-5775
Emp Here 100
SIC 5411 Grocery stores
Fred Kriegl

D-U-N-S 20-758-6504   (SL)
STEELTOWN FORD SALES 1980 LTD
933 Manitoba Ave, Selkirk, MB, R1A 3T7
(888) 485-3230
Emp Here 44   *Sales* 21,915,432
SIC 5511 New and used car dealers
Jason Sargent

D-U-N-S 24-608-2358   (HQ)
SUNOVA CREDIT UNION LIMITED
(*Suby of* BRIO INSURANCE)
233 Main St, Selkirk, MB, R1A 1S1
(204) 785-7625
Emp Here 50   *Sales* 29,742,944
SIC 6062 State credit unions
Edward Bergen
Curtis Fines
Jeff Erickson
Chad Willis
Kevin Beresford
Huguette Dandeneau
Justin Evenden
Chris Kinghorn
Lesli Malegus
Lindy Norris

D-U-N-S 24-630-1121   (SL)
TUDOR HOUSE LTD
800 Manitoba Ave, Selkirk, MB, R1A 2C9
(204) 482-6601
Emp Here 80   *Sales* 5,485,280
SIC 8051 Skilled nursing care facilities
Marvin H Benson
Pauline A Martyniw
K Anita Clayton
John Iwan Martyniw
Myrtle Barnett
Arthur Barnett
John Ashley Martyniw

Shoal Lake, MB R0J

D-U-N-S 20-003-5608   (SL)
S. H. DAYTON LTD
144 Industrial Rd, Shoal Lake, MB, R0J 1Z0
(204) 759-2065
Emp Here 24   *Sales* 14,672,940
SIC 5083 Farm and garden machinery
Keith Martin
Peter Baydak
Calvin Harrison

D-U-N-S 20-834-9597   (SL)
**SHOAL LAKE-STRATHCLAIR HEALTH
CENTRE**
524 Mary St, Shoal Lake, MB, R0J 1Z0
(204) 759-2336
Emp Here 100   *Sales* 10,213,300
SIC 8062 General medical and surgical hospi-
tals
Roseanne Yaremchuk

D-U-N-S 24-520-2692   (HQ)
SOLOMON, M.J. LTD
MURRAY'S FARM SUPPLIES
124 Industrial Park Rd, Shoal Lake, MB, R0J
1Z0
(204) 759-2626
Emp Here 1   *Sales* 11,880,320
SIC 5191 Farm supplies
Duane Kent

Somerset, MB R0G

D-U-N-S 20-947-4709   (SL)
EVERGREEN COLONY LTD
Gd, Somerset, MB, R0G 2L0
(204) 744-2596
Emp Here 45   *Sales* 17,348,355
SIC 0212 Beef cattle, except feedlots
Joe Waldner
Paul Waldner
Elie Waldner Sr

D-U-N-S 24-104-8193   (SL)
KAMSLEY COLONY LTD
KAMSLEY COLONY FARMS
Gd, Somerset, MB, R0G 2L0
(204) 744-2706
Emp Here 50   *Sales* 19,275,950
SIC 0291 General farms, primarily animals
David Hofer

Souris, MB R0K

D-U-N-S 20-285-2018   (HQ)
PRAIRIE MOUNTAIN HEALTH
192 1st Ave W, Souris, MB, R0K 2C0
(204) 483-5000
Emp Here 20   *Sales* 436,111,201
SIC 8011 Offices and clinics of medical doctors
Penny Gilson

D-U-N-S 20-948-5390   (SL)
SOURIS DISTRICT HOSPITAL & AMBULANCE SERVICE
155 Brindle Ave E, Souris, MB, R0K 2C0
(204) 483-2121
Emp Here 150   *Sales* 16,662,000
SIC 8062 General medical and surgical hospitals
Marilyn Macgregor

Southport, MB R0H

D-U-N-S 25-678-7532   (HQ)
REGIONAL HEALTH AUTHORITY - CENTRAL MANITOBA INC
SEVEN REGIONS HEALTH CENTRE
180 Centennaire Dr, Southport, MB, R0H 1N1
(204) 428-2720
Emp Here 40   *Sales* 377,672,000
SIC 8062 General medical and surgical hospitals
Connie Gretsinger
Albert Schmidt
Celine Beaudette
Eric Cameron
Ralph Cibula
Nobert Delaquis
Ted Fransen
Roger Kirouac
Jeannie Marion
Daren Vandenbussche

Sperling, MB R0G

D-U-N-S 25-204-9671   (HQ)
SPERLING INDUSTRIES LTD
51 Station Sr, Sperling, MB, R0G 2M0
(204) 626-3401
Sales 22,141,175
SIC 1711 Plumbing, heating, air-conditioning
Russell Nicolajsen
Jeff Nicolajsen

Springfield, MB R2C

D-U-N-S 20-229-0289   (SL)
3728111 MANITOBA LTD
EASTSIDE INDUSTRIAL COATINGS
2262 Springfield Rd Bldg A, Springfield, MB, R2C 2Z2
(204) 654-1955
Emp Here 90   *Sales* 15,232,230
SIC 1721 Painting and paper hanging
Lynn Brick
Chad Brick

D-U-N-S 20-833-0357   (HQ)
ACRYLON PLASTICS INC
(Suby of TECHNOLOGY MANAGEMENT INC*)*
2954 Day St, Springfield, MB, R2C 2Z2
(204) 669-2224
Emp Here 80   *Sales* 15,885,800
SIC 3089 Plastics products, nec
Craig Mcintosh

D-U-N-S 20-120-2848   (HQ)
ANDE CAPITAL CORP
(Suby of TREVLUC HOLDINGS LTD)*
2976 Day St, Springfield, MB, R2C 2Z2
(204) 777-5345
Emp Here 20   *Sales* 102,440,400
SIC 6712 Bank holding companies
Paul Cunningham
Gary Edwards
Edna Edwards
Russ Edwards
Mike Froese

D-U-N-S 24-112-8263   (SL)
KILDONAN VENTURES LTD
KILDONAN AUTO & TRUCK PARTS
2850 Day St, Springfield, MB, R2C 2Z2

Emp Here 40   *Sales* 14,568,600
SIC 5013 Motor vehicle supplies and new parts
David C Blayden
Jeffery G Williams

D-U-N-S 25-533-6547   (SL)
PARKWEST PROJECTS LTD
1077 Oxford St W, Springfield, MB, R2C 2Z2
(204) 654-9314
Emp Here 25   *Sales* 11,768,275
SIC 1542 Nonresidential construction, nec
Randy Clegg
Grant Clegg
Warren Sigfusson

D-U-N-S 25-409-5086   (SL)
PERIMETER INDUSTRIES LTD
2262 Springfield Rd Suite 5, Springfield, MB, R2C 2Z2
(204) 988-2140
Emp Here 70   *Sales* 13,633,760
SIC 2653 Corrugated and solid fiber boxes
Richard Defehr
Gerald Loewen
Leona Defehr
Charlotte Defehr
Martens Duhoux

D-U-N-S 24-914-1276   (HQ)
TREVLUC HOLDINGS LTD
2976 Day St, Springfield, MB, R2C 2Z2
(204) 777-5345
Emp Here 1   *Sales* 413,492,700
SIC 3448 Prefabricated Metal buildings and components
Paul Cunningham

D-U-N-S 20-299-1584   (SL)
WESTMAN STEEL INC
(Suby of TREVLUC HOLDINGS LTD)*
2976 Day St, Springfield, MB, R2C 2Z2
(204) 777-5345
Emp Here 200   *Sales* 38,417,000
SIC 3444 Sheet Metalwork
Paul Cunningham
Michael Froese

D-U-N-S 20-149-8065   (HQ)
WESTMAN STEEL INDUSTRIES
(Suby of TREVLUC HOLDINGS LTD)*
2976 Day St, Springfield, MB, R2C 2Z2
(204) 777-5345
Sales 28,115,140
SIC 3312 Blast furnaces and steel mills
Derek Neil

D-U-N-S 20-558-1130   (HQ)
WGI WESTMAN GROUP INC
(Suby of TREVLUC HOLDINGS LTD)*
2976 Day St, Springfield, MB, R2C 2Z2
(204) 777-5345
Emp Here 12   *Sales* 486,462,000
SIC 3441 Fabricated structural Metal
Paul Cunningham
Michael Froese
Gary Edwards

Springfield, MB R2E

D-U-N-S 20-008-7393   (HQ)
GILLIS QUARRIES LIMITED
2895 Wenzel St, Springfield, MB, R2E 1H4
(204) 222-2242
Emp Here 10   *Sales* 11,671,750
SIC 1411 Dimension stone
Keith Gillis
Douglas Gillis

Springfield, MB R2J

D-U-N-S 20-248-2196   (SL)
IRONCLAD DEVELOPMENTS INC
57158 Symington Road 20e Unit 101, Springfield, MB, R2J 4L6
(204) 777-1972
Emp Here 100   *Sales* 20,388,300
SIC 6553 Cemetery subdividers and developers
Ryan Van Damme

D-U-N-S 20-945-1335   (SL)
NDL CONSTRUCTION LTD
83 Symington Ln S, Springfield, MB, R2J 3R8
(204) 255-7300
Emp Here 50   *Sales* 28,516,900
SIC 1542 Nonresidential construction, nec
Harold Barg
Peter Barg
Jonathan Barg

St Andrews, MB R1A

D-U-N-S 24-034-8862   (HQ)
CUSTOM HELICOPTERS LTD
(Suby of EXCHANGE INCOME CORPORATION*)*
706 South Gate Rd, St Andrews, MB, R1A 3P8
(204) 338-7953
Emp Here 35   *Sales* 16,237,700
SIC 4522 Air transportation, nonscheduled
Jade Hamsen
Brian Hawes

D-U-N-S 24-916-6570   (HQ)
FORT DISTRIBUTORS LTD
938 Mcphillips Rd, St Andrews, MB, R1A 4E7
(204) 785-2180
Emp Here 23   *Sales* 19,719,315
SIC 5169 Chemicals and allied products, nec
Grant Jehle
Hans Jehle
Louise Jehle

D-U-N-S 20-000-2970   (HQ)

NORTHWAY AVIATION LTD
SASAGINNIGAK FISHING LODGE
501 Airline Rd, St Andrews, MB, R1A 3P4
(204) 339-2310
Sales 12,990,160
SIC 4522 Air transportation, nonscheduled
Marilyn Johnson
Veronica Johnson

St Claude, MB R0G

D-U-N-S 25-386-3211   (BR)
PARMALAT CANADA INC
(Suby of PARMALAT SPA)*
9 Provincial Rd Suite 240, St Claude, MB, R0G 1Z0
(204) 379-2571
Emp Here 100
SIC 2026 Fluid milk
Doug Head

D-U-N-S 25-705-1144   (SL)
TALLBOYS GRILL & PUB
10 Pth 2, St Claude, MB, R0G 1Z0
(204) 379-2491
Emp Here 30   *Sales* 14,942,340
SIC 5541 Gasoline service stations
Pat Massinon

St Jean Baptiste, MB R0G

D-U-N-S 20-515-6180   (SL)
NUVISION COMMODITIES INC
49 Elevator Rd, St Jean Baptiste, MB, R0G 2B0
(204) 758-3401
Emp Here 14   *Sales* 16,945,558
SIC 5153 Grain and field beans
Daniel Sabourin
Terry Sabourin

St Leon, MB R0G

D-U-N-S 20-292-7968   (HQ)
PEMBINA CONSUMERS CO-OP (2000) LTD
61 Main St, St Leon, MB, R0G 2E0
(204) 744-2228
Emp Here 4   *Sales* 40,147,800
SIC 5251 Hardware stores
Kevin Cutting

St Pierre Jolys, MB R0A

D-U-N-S 25-919-8299   (BR)
SOUTHERN HEALTH-SANTE SUD
DESALABERRY DISTRICT HEALTH CENTRE
(Suby of SOUTHERN HEALTH-SANTE SUD)*
354 Prefontaine Ave, St Pierre Jolys, MB, R0A 1V0
(204) 433-7611
Emp Here 80
SIC 8062 General medical and surgical hospitals
Madeleine Baril

Ste Anne, MB R5H

D-U-N-S 24-366-4815   (HQ)
CAISSE POPULAIRE LA PRAIRIE LTEE
130 Centrale Ave, Ste Anne, MB, R5H 1J3

---

(204) 422-8896
Emp Here 17   *Sales* 13,508,968
SIC 6062 State credit unions
Leo Leclair
Pierre Gagne
Joel Rondeau

Ste Rose Du Lac, MB R0L

D-U-N-S 24-851-1748   (SL)
BODNAR DRILLING LTD
23 Delaurier Dr, Ste Rose Du Lac, MB, R0L
1S0
(204) 447-2755
Emp Here 50   *Sales* 10,206,500
SIC 1481 NonMetallic mineral services
Nick Bodnar

D-U-N-S 24-234-7888   (SL)
STE ROSE AUCTION MART LTD
Gd, Ste Rose Du Lac, MB, R0L 1S0
(204) 447-2266
Emp Here 15   *Sales* 18,155,955
SIC 5154 Livestock
Don Masson
Myles Masson

D-U-N-S 25-482-6928   (SL)
STE ROSE GENERAL HOSPITAL
540 3rd Ave E, Ste Rose Du Lac, MB, R0L 1S0
(204) 447-2131
Emp Here 80   *Sales* 8,170,640
SIC 8062 General medical and surgical hospitals
Anthony Fraser

Steinbach, MB R5G

D-U-N-S 20-113-8661   (SL)
4498411 MANITOBA LTD
LINKS AT QUARRY OAK GOLF & COUNTRY CLUB (2002), THE
Gd, Steinbach, MB, R5G 1L8
(204) 326-4653
Emp Here 75   *Sales* 5,729,775
SIC 7992 Public golf courses
Allen Scott
Jj Lyons
Ken Sewell

D-U-N-S 24-851-5686   (HQ)
ASSOCIATION FOR COMMUNITY LIVING-STEINBACH BRANCH INC
395 Main St, Steinbach, MB, R5G 1Z4
(204) 326-7539
Sales 352,457,245
SIC 8699 Membership organizations, nec
Ed Barkman

D-U-N-S 20-569-2221   (HQ)
BARKMAN CONCRETE LTD
152 Brandt St, Steinbach, MB, R5G 0R2
(204) 326-3445
Emp Here 80   *Sales* 44,717,400
SIC 5032 Brick, stone, and related material
Lorne P Barkman
Allan Barkman
Brian Pries

D-U-N-S 25-039-9388   (HQ)
BRIO INSURANCE
13 Brandt St Suite 1, Steinbach, MB, R5G 0C2
(204) 326-3870
Sales 57,280,002
SIC 6411 Insurance agents, brokers, and service

D-U-N-S 20-613-7200   (HQ)
C.P. LOEWEN ENTERPRISES LTD
LOEWEN WINDOWS
(*Suby of* C4SJ DEVELOPMENTS INC)
77 Pth 52 W, Steinbach, MB, R5G 1B2

(204) 326-6446
Emp Here 540   *Sales* 145,938,600
SIC 3444 Sheet Metalwork
Al Babiuk
Clyde Loewen
Steven Kreitz

D-U-N-S 20-429-7054   (SL)
CENTRA GAS MANITOBA INC.
175 North Front Dr, Steinbach, MB, R5G 1X3
(204) 326-9805
Emp Here 5   *Sales* 15,529,285
SIC 4924 Natural gas distribution
Ernie Hiebert

D-U-N-S 20-004-5078   (HQ)
CLEARVIEW CONSUMER CO-OP LTD
365 Pth 12 N, Steinbach, MB, R5G 1V1
(204) 346-2667
Emp Here 20   *Sales* 58,695,400
SIC 5411 Grocery stores
Henry Nickel
Calvin Dyck
Menno Plett

D-U-N-S 20-005-9541   (SL)
DIAMOND READY MIX CONCRETE LTD
DIAMOND CONSTRUCTION
399 Pth 12 N, Steinbach, MB, R5G 1V1
(204) 326-3456
Emp Here 50   *Sales* 22,358,700
SIC 5032 Brick, stone, and related material
Theodore Falk
Robert Giesbrecht

D-U-N-S 24-747-7607   (HQ)
E.G. PENNER BUILDING CENTRES LTD
PENN-CO TOOL RENTALS
(*Suby of* ERNEST G. PENNER INVESTMENTS LTD)
200 Park Rd W, Steinbach, MB, R5G 1A1
(204) 326-1325
Sales 40,147,800
SIC 5211 Lumber and other building materials
Ernest Penner
Dave Caron

D-U-N-S 24-325-3791   (SL)
EPP'S PHARMACY LTD
SHOPPERS DRUG MART 545
382 Main St, Steinbach, MB, R5G 1Z3
(204) 326-3747
Emp Here 60   *Sales* 14,659,680
SIC 5912 Drug stores and proprietary stores
Hans Epp
Valrae Hans

D-U-N-S 20-005-9608   (SL)
FAIRWAY FORD SALES LTD
FAIRWAY SPECIALTY VEHICLES
236 Main St, Steinbach, MB, R5G 1Y6
(204) 326-3412
Emp Here 60   *Sales* 37,756,800
SIC 5511 New and used car dealers
Ronald Loeppky
Robert Banman

D-U-N-S 24-375-8166   (SL)
FUNK'S TOYOTA LTD
FUNK MOTORS
57 Pth 12 N, Steinbach, MB, R5G 1T3
(204) 326-9808
Emp Here 32   *Sales* 15,938,496
SIC 5511 New and used car dealers
Peter Funk
Betty Funk

D-U-N-S 25-272-4463   (BR)
HANOVER SCHOOL DIVISION
STEINBACH REGIONAL SECONDARY SCHOOL
(*Suby of* HANOVER SCHOOL DIVISION)
190 Mckenzie Ave, Steinbach, MB, R5G 0P1
(204) 326-6426
Emp Here 100
SIC 8211 Elementary and secondary schools
Luis Reis

D-U-N-S 20-834-1362   (HQ)
HANOVER SCHOOL DIVISION
5 Chrysler Gate, Steinbach, MB, R5G 0E2
(204) 326-6471
Emp Here 30   *Sales* 77,252,970
SIC 8211 Elementary and secondary schools
Ken Klassen
Kevin Heide
Randy Hildebrand
Marilyn Plett
Ed Durksen
Karen Peters
Ron Falk
Ruby Wiens
Lynn Barkman
Gerry Klassen

D-U-N-S 25-705-0757   (SL)
HARVEST INSURANCE AGENCY LTD
304 Main St, Steinbach, MB, R5G 1Z1
(204) 326-2323
Emp Here 21   *Sales* 12,178,404
SIC 6411 Insurance agents, brokers, and service
Gerald Banman

D-U-N-S 24-170-1119   (SL)
HARVEST INVESTMENTS LTD
HARVEST HONDA
144 Pth 12 N, Steinbach, MB, R5G 1T4
(204) 326-1311
Emp Here 26   *Sales* 12,950,028
SIC 5511 New and used car dealers
Gordon Kreutzer
Doug Kreutzer

D-U-N-S 24-387-8704   (SL)
JTI TRUCKING
33 Clear Springs Rd E, Steinbach, MB, R5G 1V2
(866) 346-1673
Emp Here 62   *Sales* 12,753,772
SIC 4213 Trucking, except local
Ike Bueckert

D-U-N-S 20-918-8957   (SL)
LEDINGHAM PONTIAC BUICK GMC
LEDINGHAM GM
200 Pth 12 N, Steinbach, MB, R5G 1T6
(204) 326-3451
Emp Here 76   *Sales* 47,825,280
SIC 5511 New and used car dealers
Jason Ledingham
Kent Ledingham

D-U-N-S 24-314-1822   (BR)
LOBLAWS INC
EXTRA FOODS
(*Suby of* LOBLAW COMPANIES LIMITED)
276 Main St, Steinbach, MB, R5G 1Y8
(204) 346-6304
Emp Here 80
SIC 5411 Grocery stores
Al Hallson

D-U-N-S 24-325-8964   (BR)
LOBLAWS INC
REAL CANADIAN SUPERSTORES
(*Suby of* LOBLAW COMPANIES LIMITED)
130 Pth 12 N, Steinbach, MB, R5G 1T4
(204) 320-4101
Emp Here 250
SIC 5411 Grocery stores
Nancy Urquhart

D-U-N-S 24-968-2998   (SL)
NURKKALA, HJ INVESTMENTS
CANADIAN TIRE
131 Pth 12 N, Steinbach, MB, R5G 1T5
(204) 326-3436
Emp Here 90   *Sales* 56,635,200
SIC 5531 Auto and home supply stores
Hannu J Nurkkala

D-U-N-S 20-006-0036   (HQ)
PENNER INTERNATIONAL INC
20 Pth 12 N, Steinbach, MB, R5G 1B7

(204) 326-3487
Emp Here 538   *Sales* 103,990,884
SIC 4213 Trucking, except local
Allen Penner

D-U-N-S 20-006-0093   (SL)
REIMER FARM SUPPLIES LTD
DEER COUNTRY EQUIPMENT
340 Pth 12 N, Steinbach, MB, R5G 1T6
(204) 326-1305
Emp Here 45   *Sales* 21,376,170
SIC 5083 Farm and garden machinery
Alex Loewen

D-U-N-S 24-546-1686   (SL)
REST HAVEN NURSING HOME OF STEINBACH INC
REST HAVEN NURSING HOME
185 Woodhaven Ave Suite 175, Steinbach, MB, R5G 1K7
(204) 326-2206
Emp Here 115   *Sales* 7,857,490
SIC 8051 Skilled nursing care facilities
David Driedger
Henry Klassen

D-U-N-S 24-207-5369   (BR)
SOBEYS CAPITAL INCORPORATED
STEINBACH GARDEN MARKET
(*Suby of* EMPIRE COMPANY LIMITED)
178 Pth 12 N Unit 1, Steinbach, MB, R5G 1T7
(204) 326-1316
Emp Here 150
SIC 5411 Grocery stores
Cliff Salk

D-U-N-S 20-739-7907   (BR)
SOBEYS WEST INC
SAFEWAY FOOD & DRUG
(*Suby of* EMPIRE COMPANY LIMITED)
143 Pth 12 N, Steinbach, MB, R5G 1T5
(204) 346-1555
Emp Here 90
SIC 5411 Grocery stores
Lana Boyechko

D-U-N-S 24-232-9837   (SL)
SOUTHEASTERN FARM EQUIPMENT LTD
300 Pth 12 N, Steinbach, MB, R5G 1T6
(204) 326-9834
Emp Here 36   *Sales* 11,721,600
SIC 5999 Miscellaneous retail stores, nec
Edward Peterson
Corey Plett
Russell Plett

D-U-N-S 20-781-1188   (BR)
SOUTHERN HEALTH-SANTE SUD
BETHESDA HOSPITAL
(*Suby of* SOUTHERN HEALTH-SANTE SUD)
316 Henry St, Steinbach, MB, R5G 0P9
(204) 326-6411
Emp Here 300
SIC 8062 General medical and surgical hospitals
Jan Gunness

D-U-N-S 20-571-7184   (SL)
SPACE AGE TIRE LTD
KAL-TIRE
8 Pth 52 W, Steinbach, MB, R5G 1X7
(204) 326-6039
Emp Here 21   *Sales* 10,459,638
SIC 5531 Auto and home supply stores
Gary Reimer
Marilyn Reimer

D-U-N-S 25-095-9319   (HQ)
STEINBACH CREDIT UNION LIMITED
305 Main St, Steinbach, MB, R5G 1B1
(204) 326-3495
Emp Here 200   *Sales* 46,970,275
SIC 6062 State credit unions
Glenn Friesen
Ted Falk
Reg Penner
Russ Fast
Carl Doerksen

Doris Martens
Alan Barkman
Abe Hiebert
Sleg Peters
Bryan Rempel

D-U-N-S 24-231-8640   (SL)
STEINBACH DODGE CHRYSLER LTD
208 Main St, Steinbach, MB, R5G 1Y6
(204) 326-4461
Emp Here 45   *Sales* 22,413,510
SIC 5511 New and used car dealers
W A Jim Neustaedter
Paul Neustaedter
Phyllis Neustaedter

D-U-N-S 24-417-9912   (SL)
SUPER SPLASH AUTO CLEANING LTD
SHELL
53 Pth 12 N, Steinbach, MB, R5G 1T3
(204) 326-3474
Emp Here 25   *Sales* 12,451,950
SIC 5541 Gasoline service stations
Stella Unrau
Wes Unrau

D-U-N-S 25-363-8043   (SL)
W S MACHINING & FABRICATION INC
49 Life Sciences Pky, Steinbach, MB, R5G
2G7
(204) 326-5444
Emp Here 125   *Sales* 27,750,125
SIC 3599 Industrial machinery, nec
Joseph Waldner

D-U-N-S 24-917-1687   (SL)
WIELER ENTERPRISES LTD
COUNTRYSIDE FARMS
88 Millwork Dr, Steinbach, MB, R5G 1V9
(204) 326-4313
Emp Here 50   *Sales* 20,967,750
SIC 6712 Bank holding companies
Peter Wieler

Stonewall, MB R0C

D-U-N-S 25-731-2314   (HQ)
2982651 MANITOBA LIMITED
HALLMARK CARD SHOP
333 Main St Suite 17, Stonewall, MB, R0C 2Z0
(204) 467-8113
Emp Here 4   *Sales* 18,813,256
SIC 5947 Gift, novelty, and souvenir shop
Vern Appleyard

D-U-N-S 25-835-8365   (BR)
BEARSKIN LAKE AIR SERVICE LP
BEARSKIN AIRLINES
(*Suby of* EXCHANGE INCOME CORPORA-
TION)
585 6th Ave S, Stonewall, MB, R0C 2Z0

Emp Here 300
SIC 8299 Schools and educational services,
nec

D-U-N-S 20-838-5302   (HQ)
DUCKS UNLIMITED CANADA
CONSERVING CANADA'S WETLANDS
1 Mallard Bay Hwy Suite 220, Stonewall, MB,
R0C 2Z0
(204) 467-3000
Emp Here 80   *Sales* 96,976,610
SIC 8999 Services, nec
James.E Couch
Karla Guyn
David C Blom
Mac Dunfield
James Couch
Mauri Rutherford
David Blom
Marcy Sullivan
James Fortune
Gregory Siekaniec

D-U-N-S 25-679-3563   (BR)
**INTERLAKE REGIONAL HEALTH AUTHOR-
ITY INC**
RIVERTON COMMUNITY HEALTH OFFICE
68 Main St, Stonewall, MB, R0C 2Z0
(204) 378-2460
Emp Here 100
SIC 8062 General medical and surgical hospi-
tals
Brian Magnusson

D-U-N-S 24-036-6278   (HQ)
INTERLAKE SCHOOL DIVISION
192 2nd Ave N, Stonewall, MB, R0C 2Z0
(204) 467-5100
Sales 49,559,500
SIC 8211 Elementary and secondary schools
Allen Leiman

D-U-N-S 24-818-1125   (SL)
SPRUCE TOP LUMBER SALES LTD
11 Tony'S Trail, Stonewall, MB, R0C 2Z0
(204) 467-1915
Emp Here 6   *Sales* 13,718,466
SIC 5031 Lumber, plywood, and millwork
Ross Mollberg
Lori Mollberg

D-U-N-S 24-882-5507   (SL)
STONEWALL GROCERS LIMITED, THE
STONEWALL FAMILY FOODS
330 3rd Ave S Unit 3, Stonewall, MB, R0C 2Z0
(204) 467-5553
Emp Here 47   *Sales* 12,885,144
SIC 5411 Grocery stores
David Kalynuk

D-U-N-S 24-844-8107   (BR)
SUNOVA CREDIT UNION LIMITED
(*Suby of* BRIO INSURANCE)
410 Centre Ave, Stonewall, MB, R0C 2Z0
(204) 467-5574
Emp Here 150
SIC 6062 State credit unions

Swan River, MB R0L

D-U-N-S 20-066-1536   (SL)
FORMO MOTORS LTD
1550 Main St, Swan River, MB, R0L 1Z0
(204) 734-4577
Emp Here 25   *Sales* 12,451,950
SIC 5511 New and used car dealers
Elmer Formo
Lauretta Formo

D-U-N-S 24-338-5502   (BR)
**PARKLAND REGIONAL HEALTH AUTHOR-
ITY INC**
SWAN RIVER HEALTH CENTRE
(*Suby of* PARKLAND REGIONAL HEALTH
AUTHORITY INC)
1011 Main St E, Swan River, MB, R0L 1Z0
(204) 734-3441
Emp Here 200
SIC 8062 General medical and surgical hospi-
tals
Shannon Bresky

D-U-N-S 20-520-5768   (SL)
POWELL MOTORS LTD
804 Main St E, Swan River, MB, R0L 1Z0
(204) 734-3464
Emp Here 30   *Sales* 14,942,340
SIC 5511 New and used car dealers
David Powell
Marion Powell

D-U-N-S 24-426-3034   (SL)
SWAN RIVER FRIENDSHIP CENTRE INC
1413 Main St, Swan River, MB, R0L 1Z0
(204) 734-9301
Emp Here 35   *Sales* 13,909,490
SIC 8699 Membership organizations, nec

Elbert Chartand

D-U-N-S 25-750-7590   (HQ)
SWAN VALLEY AGENCIES LTD
COOK & COOKE INSURANCE BROKERS
922 Main St E, Swan River, MB, R0L 1Z0
(204) 734-9421
Emp Here 11   *Sales* 17,809,260
SIC 6411 Insurance agents, brokers, and ser-
vice
Clifford Cook
Douglas Cooke
Curtis Cook
Kent Cook

D-U-N-S 20-006-1943   (HQ)
**SWAN VALLEY CONSUMERS COOPERA-
TIVE LIMITED**
811 Main St E, Swan River, MB, R0L 1Z0
(204) 734-3431
Emp Here 100   *Sales* 25,873,218
SIC 5399 Miscellaneous general merchandise
Larry Terhorst
Preston Hartwig
Rick Achter
Sharon Alford
Brenda Bielik
Don Hagman
Lorna Munro
Jodi Proctor
John Sandborn

D-U-N-S 25-094-5800   (BR)
SWAN VALLEY SCHOOL DIVISION
*SWAN VALLEY REGIONAL SECONDARY
SCHOOL*
1483 3rd St N, Swan River, MB, R0L 1Z0
(204) 734-4511
Emp Here 90
SIC 8211 Elementary and secondary schools
Henry Barkowski

Teulon, MB R0C

D-U-N-S 20-832-4186   (SL)
INTERLAKE COLONY FARMS LTD
Gd, Teulon, MB, R0C 3B0
(204) 886-2107
Emp Here 40   *Sales* 13,698,680
SIC 0191 General farms, primarily crop
Hardy Hofer
Sam Hofer

D-U-N-S 20-274-1687   (BR)
**INTERLAKE REGIONAL HEALTH AUTHOR-
ITY INC**
TEULON HUNTER MEMORIAL HOSPITAL
162 3 Ave Se, Teulon, MB, R0C 3B0
(204) 886-2108
Emp Here 80
SIC 8062 General medical and surgical hospi-
tals
Margaret Medwid

D-U-N-S 20-583-6914   (SL)
NORTHERN FREEDOM INC
Po Box 510, Teulon, MB, R0C 3B0
(204) 886-2552
Emp Here 80   *Sales* 27,655,200
SIC 2015 Poultry slaughtering and processing
Darren Salkeld

The Pas, MB R9A

D-U-N-S 24-968-4887   (HQ)
74829 MANITOBA LTD
DOAK'S BULK FIELD
945 Garden Ave, The Pas, MB, R9A 1L6
(204) 623-2581
Emp Here 5   *Sales* 12,393,696
SIC 5171 Petroleum bulk stations and termi-

nals
Kelvin Doak

D-U-N-S 20-691-2110   (SL)
**ASENESKAK CASINO LIMITED PARTNER-
SHIP**
Gd Stn Main, The Pas, MB, R9A 1K2
(204) 627-2250
Emp Here 134   *Sales* 12,723,702
SIC 7999 Amusement and recreation, nec
Suzanne Barbeau-Bracegirdle
Darcy Bolton

D-U-N-S 24-426-7654   (SL)
**BEAVER AIR SERVICES LIMITED PART-
NERSHIP**
BEAVER AIR SERVICES
2 Grace Lake Rd, The Pas, MB, R9A 1M3
(204) 623-7160
Emp Here 60   *Sales* 16,018,680
SIC 4512 Air transportation, scheduled
John Fondse

D-U-N-S 20-346-4276   (HQ)
**CANADIAN KRAFT PAPER INDUSTRIES
LIMITED**
(*Suby of* AMERICAN INDUSTRIAL ACQUISI-
TION CORPORATION)
Hwy 10 N, The Pas, MB, R9A 1L4
(204) 623-7411
Sales 110,291,100
SIC 2621 Paper mills
Leonard Levi
Ron Trehogan
Edward Mahood
Terry Hamilton

D-U-N-S 20-002-9882   (SL)
DOAK'S PETROLEUM LTD
945 Gordon Ave, The Pas, MB, R9A 1L6
(204) 623-2581
Emp Here 16   *Sales* 16,524,928
SIC 5171 Petroleum bulk stations and termi-
nals
Wayne Doak

D-U-N-S 25-417-6068   (SL)
HUDSON BAY RAILWAY COMPANY
OMNITRACK
(*Suby of* THE BROE COMPANIES INC)
728 Bignel Ave, The Pas, MB, R9A 1L8
(204) 627-2007
Emp Here 92   *Sales* 6,925,024
SIC 4111 Local and suburban transit
Tanya Pidskalny

D-U-N-S 24-039-7042   (HQ)
KELSEY SCHOOL DIVISION
322 Edwards Ave, The Pas, MB, R9A 1R4
(204) 623-6421
Sales 19,823,800
SIC 8211 Elementary and secondary schools
Jennette Freese

D-U-N-S 20-758-7205   (SL)
MORRISH HOLDINGS LTD
GRUB BOX
Gd Stn Main, The Pas, MB, R9A 1K2
(204) 623-6469
Emp Here 55   *Sales* 16,141,235
SIC 5411 Grocery stores
Gary Morrish
Florence Morrish

D-U-N-S 20-295-3274   (SL)
**MURRAY MOTORS THE PAS LIMITED
PARTNERSHIP**
212 Larose Ave, The Pas, MB, R9A 1L1
(204) 623-3481
Emp Here 31   *Sales* 15,440,418
SIC 5511 New and used car dealers
Frank Lang

D-U-N-S 25-235-5466   (HQ)
NORTHLAND FORD SALES LTD
Highway 10 S, The Pas, MB, R9A 1K9
(204) 623-4350
Emp Here 30   *Sales* 24,903,900

SIC 5511 New and used car dealers
Dale Bigelow

D-U-N-S 20-945-6607   (SL)
PAS HEALTH COMPLEX INC, THE
ST ANTHONYS GENERAL HOSPITAL
67 1st St W, The Pas, MB, R9A 1K4
(204) 623-6431
Emp Here 325   *Sales* 36,101,000
SIC 8062 General medical and surgical hospitals
Drew Lockhart

D-U-N-S 24-174-8164   (BR)
TOLKO INDUSTRIES LTD
TOLKO MANITOBA SOLID WOOD DIVISION
(*Suby of* AMERICAN INDUSTRIAL ACQUISITION CORPORATION)
Hwy 10 N, The Pas, MB, R9A 1S1
(204) 623-7411
Emp Here 300
SIC 2499 Wood products, nec
Dave Neufeld

D-U-N-S 25-116-8159   (BR)
TOLKO INDUSTRIES LTD
TOLKO MANITOBA KRAFT PAPERS, DIV OF
(*Suby of* AMERICAN INDUSTRIAL ACQUISITION CORPORATION)
Hwy 10 N, The Pas, MB, R9A 1L4
(204) 623-7411
Emp Here 360
SIC 2674 Bags: uncoated paper and multiwall
Blair Rydberg

D-U-N-S 20-006-3360   (HQ)
TWIN MOTORS LTD
1637 Gordon Ave, The Pas, MB, R9A 1L1
(204) 623-6402
Emp Here 30   *Sales* 22,413,510
SIC 5511 New and used car dealers
Murray Haukaas

D-U-N-S 20-545-9261   (HQ)
UNIVERSITY COLLEGE OF THE NORTH
(*Suby of* PROVINCE OF MANITOBA)
436 7th St E, The Pas, MB, R9A 1M7
(204) 627-8500
Emp Here 110   *Sales* 42,359,810
SIC 8221 Colleges and universities
Konrad Jonasson
Dwight Botting
William Schaffer

Thompson, MB R8N

D-U-N-S 20-006-3758   (SL)
4001966 MANITOBA LTD
LA FURLANE CONSTRUCTION (1999)
176 Hayes Rd, Thompson, MB, R8N 1M4
(204) 677-4548
Emp Here 50   *Sales* 16,666,650
SIC 1541 Industrial buildings and warehouses
David Brenton

D-U-N-S 24-325-4211   (SL)
5043680 MANITOBA INC
SHOPPERS DRUG MART
17 Selkirk Ave Suite 549, Thompson, MB, R8N 0M5
(204) 778-8391
Emp Here 40   *Sales* 10,118,160
SIC 5912 Drug stores and proprietary stores
Kerri Rotizen

D-U-N-S 20-078-2303   (BR)
MACDONALD, SR JOHN HUGH MEMORIAL HOSTEL
MACDONALD YOUTH SERVICES
(*Suby of* MACDONALD, SR JOHN HUGH MEMORIAL HOSTEL)
83 Churchill Dr Suite 204, Thompson, MB, R8N 0L6
(204) 677-7870
Emp Here 80

SIC 8399 Social services, nec
Dave Kuhl

D-U-N-S 24-607-9305   (SL)
ROCK COUNTRY CHEVROLET BUICK GMC LTD
MCKAY GM
121 Nelson Rd, Thompson, MB, R8N 0B7
(204) 778-7081
Emp Here 29   *Sales* 14,444,262
SIC 5511 New and used car dealers
Randy Mckay
Monique Mckay

D-U-N-S 20-434-4840   (SL)
SMOOK CONTRACTORS LTD
(*Suby of* MULLEN GROUP LTD)
101 Hayes Rd, Thompson, MB, R8N 1M3
(204) 677-1560
Emp Here 180   *Sales* 45,439,560
SIC 1629 Heavy construction, nec
Edward Smook
Christopher Smook

D-U-N-S 24-966-8989   (SL)
THOMPSON FORD SALES LTD
15 Station Rd, Thompson, MB, R8N 0N6
(204) 778-6386
Emp Here 32   *Sales* 15,938,496
SIC 5511 New and used car dealers
Kevin Kelleher

D-U-N-S 25-313-8754   (BR)
VALE CANADA LIMITED
(*Suby of* VALE S/A)
1 Plant Rd, Thompson, MB, R8N 1P3
(204) 778-2211
Emp Here 1,400
SIC 1061 Ferroalloy ores, except vanadium
Lovro Paulic

D-U-N-S 20-614-1624   (BR)
WAL-MART CANADA CORP
(*Suby of* WALMART INC.)
300 Mystery Lake Rd Suite 3102, Thompson, MB, R8N 0M2
(204) 778-4669
Emp Here 200
SIC 5311 Department stores
Jeff Proulx

Tourond, MB R0A

D-U-N-S 20-758-6298   (SL)
SUNCREST COLONY FARMS LTD
43051 Suncrest Rd, Tourond, MB, R0A 2G0
(204) 433-7853
Emp Here 65   *Sales* 17,050,085
SIC 0191 General farms, primarily crop
Kenneth Mandel
John Kleinsasser
Joe Kleinsasser Jr

Treherne, MB R0G

D-U-N-S 20-006-5597   (SL)
METCALFE'S GARAGE LTD
Hwy 2 E, Treherne, MB, R0G 2V0
(204) 723-2175
Emp Here 23   *Sales* 11,455,794
SIC 5511 New and used car dealers
Neil Metcalfe
Patricia Metcalfe
Barbara Metcalfe

Virden, MB R0M

D-U-N-S 20-832-9318   (HQ)

ANDREW AGENCIES LTD
322 7th Ave S, Virden, MB, R0M 2C0
(204) 748-2734
Emp Here 15   *Sales* 230,967,750
SIC 6411 Insurance agents, brokers, and service
Scott Andrew
Blair Andrew

D-U-N-S 20-519-4889   (HQ)
BRUCE'S FOUR SEASONS (1984) LTD
FOUR SEASONS SALES
Transcanada Hwy N, Virden, MB, R0M 2C0
(204) 748-1539
Sales 31,464,000
SIC 5561 Recreational vehicle dealers
Peter Dillon
Don Gray
Rob Denolf

D-U-N-S 20-946-9386   (HQ)
FORT LA BOSSE SCHOOL DIVISION
523 9th Ave, Virden, MB, R0M 2C0
(204) 748-2692
Emp Here 1   *Sales* 49,559,500
SIC 8211 Elementary and secondary schools
Kent Reid

D-U-N-S 25-103-4542   (BR)
PRAIRIE MOUNTAIN HEALTH
VIRDEN HEALTH CENTRE
(*Suby of* PRAIRIE MOUNTAIN HEALTH)
480 King St E, Virden, MB, R0M 2C0
(204) 748-1230
Emp Here 150
SIC 8062 General medical and surgical hospitals
Georgina Henuset

D-U-N-S 24-372-2852   (HQ)
SUNRISE CREDIT UNION LIMITED
220 7th Ave S, Virden, MB, R0M 2C0
(204) 748-2907
Emp Here 32   *Sales* 24,561,760
SIC 6062 State credit unions
Harry Bowler
Tayona Johnas
Tony Keown

D-U-N-S 20-006-6603   (HQ)
VALLEYVIEW CONSUMERS CO-OP LTD
250 Princess St W, Virden, MB, R0M 2C0
(204) 748-2520
Emp Here 50   *Sales* 22,010,775
SIC 5411 Grocery stores

D-U-N-S 24-546-2510   (HQ)
VIRDEN MAINLINE MOTOR PRODUCTS LIMITED
Hwy 1 W, Virden, MB, R0M 2C0
(204) 748-3811
Emp Here 40   *Sales* 24,903,900
SIC 5511 New and used car dealers
Gerald Merrifield
Donald Campbell

Vita, MB R0A

D-U-N-S 24-656-3506   (HQ)
SMOOK FUELS LTD
Hwy 201, Vita, MB, R0A 2K0
(204) 425-3997
Emp Here 7   *Sales* 15,492,120
SIC 5171 Petroleum bulk stations and terminals
Dennis Smook

D-U-N-S 20-833-6396   (BR)
SOUTHERN HEALTH-SANTE SUD
VITA AND DISTRICT HEALTH CENTRE
(*Suby of* SOUTHERN HEALTH-SANTE SUD)
217 1st Ave, Vita, MB, R0A 2K0
(204) 425-3325
Emp Here 80

SIC 8062 General medical and surgical hospitals
Ken Wersch

Wabowden, MB R0B

D-U-N-S 24-335-9242   (BR)
CANICKEL MINING LIMITED
CROWFLIGHT MINERALS
(*Suby of* CANICKEL MINING LIMITED)
Gd, Wabowden, MB, R0B 1S0
(204) 689-2972
Emp Here 150
SIC 1081 Metal mining services
Paul Keller

Wawanesa, MB R0K

D-U-N-S 24-914-7091   (HQ)
GREEN ACRES COLONY LTD
Gd, Wawanesa, MB, R0K 2G0
(204) 824-2627
Sales 17,837,012
SIC 0191 General farms, primarily crop
Paul Waldner
Harry Waldner
Ernest Hofer

Wellwood, MB R0K

D-U-N-S 25-680-0764   (SL)
SPUD PLAINS FARMS LTD
12 14w Ne Suite 32, Wellwood, MB, R0K 2H0
(204) 834-3866
Emp Here 9   *Sales* 10,893,573
SIC 5159 Farm-product raw materials, nec
Paul Adriaansen

West St Paul, MB R2P

D-U-N-S 24-654-5420   (SL)
SUBTERRANEAN (MANITOBA) LTD
(*Suby of* M. J. MIGNACCA HOLDINGS LTD)
6 St Paul Blvd, West St Paul, MB, R2P 2W5
(204) 775-8291
Emp Here 50   *Sales* 12,622,100
SIC 1629 Heavy construction, nec
Peter Mignacca
Gordon Benson

West St Paul, MB R2V

D-U-N-S 25-230-4407   (SL)
J. C. PAVING LTD
3000 Main St Unit 7, West St Paul, MB, R2V 4Z3
(204) 989-4700
Emp Here 150   *Sales* 37,866,300
SIC 1611 Highway and street construction
John Teixeira
Maria Teixeira

West St Paul, MB R4A

D-U-N-S 24-630-5569   (SL)
MIDDLECHURCH HOME OF WINNIPEG INC
280 Balderstone Rd, West St Paul, MB, R4A 4A6

(204) 339-1947
Emp Here 300   *Sales* 20,497,800
SIC 8051 Skilled nursing care facilities
  Laurie Kuivenhoven
  Laurie Holgate

Winkler, MB R6W

D-U-N-S 24-428-9567   (HQ)
3490051 MANITOBA LTD
PARKSIDE HOME BUILDING CENTRE
880 Memorial Dr, Winkler, MB, R6W 0M6
(204) 325-9133
Sales 10,122,360
SIC 5211 Lumber and other building materials
  Henry Enns

D-U-N-S 24-419-9704   (HQ)
ACCESS CREDIT UNION LIMITED
23111 Pth 14 Unit 2, Winkler, MB, R6W 4B4
(204) 331-1612
Emp Here 10   *Sales* 42,700,250
SIC 6062 State credit unions
  Larry Davey

D-U-N-S 20-593-9098   (SL)
ACRYLON PLASTICS MB (1983) INC
355 Airport Dr, Winkler, MB, R6W 0J9
(204) 325-9569
Emp Here 63   *Sales* 12,719,511
SIC 3089 Plastics products, nec
  Ron Funk

D-U-N-S 24-718-4112   (HQ)
CANADIAN LUMBER LTD
139 North Railway Ave, Winkler, MB, R6W 1J4
(204) 325-5319
Emp Here 25   *Sales* 14,453,208
SIC 5211 Lumber and other building materials
  Henry Friesen

D-U-N-S 20-549-0407   (SL)
CANAGRO EXPORTS INC
24084 Hwy 3 E, Winkler, MB, R6W 4B1
(204) 325-5090
Emp Here 37   *Sales* 17,575,962
SIC 5083 Farm and garden machinery
  Justin Taylor
  Melissa Vencatasamy
  Sheila Taylor

D-U-N-S 20-000-4610   (SL)
CELERITY BUILDERS LTD
Gd, Winkler, MB, R6W 4B3
(204) 362-4003
Emp Here 40   *Sales* 10,837,680
SIC 1522 Residential construction, nec

D-U-N-S 24-115-9755   (SL)
CENTENNIAL SUPPLY LTD
PETRO CANADA
526 Centennial St, Winkler, MB, R6W 1J4
(204) 325-8261
Emp Here 18   *Sales* 18,590,544
SIC 5171 Petroleum bulk stations and terminals
  Laurence Braun

D-U-N-S 25-676-4317   (SL)
COMMERCIAL WELDING LTD
130 Canada St, Winkler, MB, R6W 0J3
(204) 325-4195
Emp Here 115   *Sales* 48,172,235
SIC 6531 Real estate agents and managers
  Bob Toews

D-U-N-S 24-427-3157   (SL)
CONVEY-ALL INDUSTRIES INC
(*Suby of* TREVLUC HOLDINGS LTD)
130 Canada St, Winkler, MB, R6W 0J3
(204) 325-4195
Emp Here 130   *Sales* 28,860,130
SIC 3523 Farm machinery and equipment
  Bob Toews

D-U-N-S 25-372-0569   (SL)

DELANEY HOLDINGS INC
200 Pacific St, Winkler, MB, R6W 0K2
(204) 325-7376
Emp Here 150   *Sales* 27,208,200
SIC 3321 Gray and ductile iron foundries
  David Reid

D-U-N-S 25-607-5789   (SL)
ELIAS WOODWORKING AND MANUFAC-TURING LTD
ACORN CONTINENTAL HARDWOODS
275 Badger Rd, Winkler, MB, R6W 0K5
(204) 325-9962
Emp Here 200   *Sales* 38,474,000
SIC 2431 Millwork
  Ralph Fehr

D-U-N-S 24-917-0085   (HQ)
ENS, PHILIPP R LTD
301 Roblin Blvd, Winkler, MB, R6W 4C4
(204) 325-4361
Emp Here 1   *Sales* 127,928,150
SIC 6712 Bank holding companies
  Philipp R Ens

D-U-N-S 25-272-4505   (BR)
GARDEN VALLEY SCHOOL DIVISION
GARDEN VALLEY COLLEGIATE
(*Suby of* GARDEN VALLEY SCHOOL DIVISION)
Garden Valley Collegiate, Winkler, MB, R6W 4C8
(204) 325-8008
Emp Here 100
SIC 8211 Elementary and secondary schools
  Scott Jantzen

D-U-N-S 25-011-4402   (HQ)
GARDEN VALLEY SCHOOL DIVISION
750 Triple E Blvd, Winkler, MB, R6W 0M7
(204) 325-8335
Sales 44,603,550
SIC 8211 Elementary and secondary schools
  Terry Penner

D-U-N-S 24-571-6022   (SL)
GENERAL METAL FABRICATION LTD
269 Manitoba Rd, Winkler, MB, R6W 0J8
(204) 325-9374
Emp Here 80   *Sales* 21,747,360
SIC 7692 Welding repair
  Gerald Bauman
  Timothy Bauman
  Leon Bauman

D-U-N-S 20-832-8773   (HQ)
GRANDEUR HOUSING LTD
401 Pembina Ave E, Winkler, MB, R6W 4B9
(204) 325-9558
Sales 42,157,500
SIC 5211 Lumber and other building materials
  William J. Siemens
  Andrew Nickel
  Rod Fehr
  Mary Anne Siemens
  Colleen Bueckert
  Scott Fehr

D-U-N-S 20-174-0557   (SL)
HEARTLAND FRESH PAK INC
Gd Stn Main, Winkler, MB, R6W 4A3
(204) 325-6948
Emp Here 24   *Sales* 10,643,760
SIC 7389 Business services, nec
  Kenneth Penner

D-U-N-S 20-006-8328   (SL)
HOMETOWN SERVICE LTD
690 Memorial Dr, Winkler, MB, R6W 0M6
(204) 325-4777
Emp Here 25   *Sales* 12,451,950
SIC 5511 New and used car dealers
  Alvin Derksen
  Ronald Derksen
  Bob Derksen
  Dennis Derksen

D-U-N-S 20-267-1314   (SL)

ICON TECHNOLOGIES LTD
ICON DIRECT
925 Roblin Blvd E, Winkler, MB, R6W 0N2
(204) 325-1081
Emp Here 45   *Sales* 12,449,700
SIC 2821 Plastics materials and resins
  John Loewen

D-U-N-S 24-819-5513   (SL)
INTEGRA CASTINGS INC
200 Pacific St, Winkler, MB, R6W 0K2
(204) 325-7376
Emp Here 150   *Sales* 27,208,200
SIC 3321 Gray and ductile iron foundries
  James Umlah

D-U-N-S 20-613-0981   (HQ)
JANZEN CHEVROLET BUICK GMC LTD
145 Boundary Trail, Winkler, MB, R6W 0L7
(204) 325-9511
Emp Here 40   *Sales* 37,756,800
SIC 5511 New and used car dealers
  Jake Janzen
  Paul Janzen
  Margaret Janzen

D-U-N-S 20-006-8435   (HQ)
KROEKER FARMS LIMITED
777 Circle K Dr, Winkler, MB, R6W 0K7
(204) 325-4333
Emp Here 100   *Sales* 16,902,500
SIC 0134 Irish potatoes
  Wayne Rempel
  Grant Thiessen
  Donald Kroeker
  Gerald Bock
  Edwin James Kroeker
  Jeff Thiessen
  Edwin Kroeger
  Wally Kroeker
  Mervyn Kroeker

D-U-N-S 24-654-0884   (SL)
LOAD LINE INCORPORATED
LOAD LINE MANUFACTURING
9081 Hwy 32, Winkler, MB, R6W 4B7
(204) 325-4798
Emp Here 78   *Sales* 17,459,754
SIC 3715 Truck trailers
  Jake Friesen
  Jake Friesen Jr
  Willy Fehr

D-U-N-S 20-948-5739   (BR)
MONARCH INDUSTRIES LIMITED
(*Suby of* MERIT CAPITAL PARTNERS IV, L.L.C.)
280 Monarch Dr, Winkler, MB, R6W 0J6
(204) 325-4393
Emp Here 250
SIC 3321 Gray and ductile iron foundries

D-U-N-S 20-946-2043   (SL)
SALEM HOME INC
165 15th St, Winkler, MB, R6W 1T8
(204) 325-4316
Emp Here 200   *Sales* 13,665,200
SIC 8051 Skilled nursing care facilities
  Sherry Janzen

D-U-N-S 25-327-6620   (HQ)
SCHWEITZER-MAUDUIT CANADA, INC
(*Suby of* SCHWEITZER-MAUDUIT INTERNATIONAL, INC.)
340 Airport Dr, Winkler, MB, R6W 0J9
(204) 325-7986
Sales 11,686,080
SIC 2621 Paper mills
  Joseph Hogue
  Pete Thompson
  Dean Graham

D-U-N-S 20-256-3933   (SL)
SOLUTIONS
777 Norquay Dr, Winkler, MB, R6W 2S2
(204) 325-1006
Emp Here 30   *Sales* 15,109,740

SIC 5112 Stationery and office supplies
  Dennis Kehler

D-U-N-S 20-518-1910   (SL)
SOUTHERN MANITOBA POTATO CO. LTD
(*Suby of* S.M.P. HOLDINGS INC)
375 North Railway Ave, Winkler, MB, R6W 1J4
(204) 325-4318
Emp Here 50   *Sales* 13,115,450
SIC 0134 Irish potatoes
  John Kuhl
  Keith Kuhl

D-U-N-S 25-831-7767   (BR)
TRIPLE E CANADA LTD
LODE KING INDUSTRIES, DIV. OF
(*Suby of* ENS, PHILIPP R LTD)
135 Canada St, Winkler, MB, R6W 0J3
(204) 325-4345
Emp Here 250
SIC 3792 Travel trailers and campers
  Lloyd Elias

D-U-N-S 20-759-6883   (HQ)
TRIPLE E CANADA LTD
TRIPLE E RV, DIV OF
(*Suby of* ENS, PHILIPP R LTD)
301 Roblin Blvd, Winkler, MB, R6W 4C4
(204) 325-4361
Emp Here 150   *Sales* 93,406,560
SIC 3711 Motor vehicles and car bodies
  Terry Elias
  Philipp R Ens
  Andy Schmidt
  Robert Hucal
  Lloyd Elias

D-U-N-S 24-316-9070   (BR)
WAL-MART CANADA CORP
WINKLER WALMART
(*Suby of* WALMART INC.)
1000 Navigator Rd, Winkler, MB, R6W 0L8
(204) 325-4160
Emp Here 130
SIC 5311 Department stores
  Johnny Elias

D-U-N-S 24-546-2635   (SL)
WIEBE, DR. C.W. MEDICAL CORPORATION
385 Main St, Winkler, MB, R6W 1J2
(204) 325-4312
Emp Here 55   *Sales* 10,193,700
SIC 8011 Offices and clinics of medical doctors
  C Jacob Jr

D-U-N-S 20-436-4780   (SL)
WINKLER BUILDING SUPPLIES (1981) LTD
WBS CONSTRUCTION
570 Centennial St Unit 300, Winkler, MB, R6W 1J4
(204) 325-4336
Emp Here 30   *Sales* 14,121,930
SIC 1542 Nonresidential construction, nec
  Alvin Thiessen
  Harv Thiessen

D-U-N-S 20-519-7163   (SL)
WINKLER MEATS LTD
270 George Ave, Winkler, MB, R6W 3M4
(204) 325-9593
Emp Here 64   *Sales* 33,423,080
SIC 5147 Meats and meat products
  Warren Dyck

Winnipeg, MB R2C

D-U-N-S 20-257-6179   (HQ)
4L COMMUNICATIONS INC
1555 Regent Ave W Suite T58, Winnipeg, MB, R2C 4J2
(204) 927-6363
Emp Here 10   *Sales* 14,659,680
SIC 5999 Miscellaneous retail stores, nec
  Al Koop

D-U-N-S 24-853-0573   (SL)
5465461 MANITOBA INC
SHOAL LAKE WILD RICE
28 Christopher St, Winnipeg, MB, R2C 2Z2
(204) 989-7696
Emp Here 20   *Sales* 24,207,940
SIC 5153 Grain and field beans
  Murray Ratuski

D-U-N-S 20-355-4084   (SL)
AFTERMARKET PARTS COMPANY LLC, THE
(*Suby of* NFI GROUP INC)
630 Kernaghan Ave Door 76, Winnipeg, MB, R2C 5G1
(800) 665-2637
Emp Here 100   *Sales* 22,384,300
SIC 3711 Motor vehicles and car bodies
  Brian Dewsnup

D-U-N-S 25-362-7210   (SL)
ALC - AUTO LIST OF CANADA INC
AUTO LIST OF CANADA
823 Regent Ave W, Winnipeg, MB, R2C 3A7
(204) 224-0636
Emp Here 50   *Sales* 24,903,900
SIC 5521 Used car dealers
  Ishwar Thawani

D-U-N-S 24-309-9913   (BR)
AMSTED CANADA INC
GRIFFIN CANADA
(*Suby of* AMSTED INDUSTRIES INCORPORATED)
104 Regent Ave E, Winnipeg, MB, R2C 0C1
(204) 222-4252
Emp Here 200
SIC 3462 Iron and steel forgings
  Don Grant

D-U-N-S 20-252-1423   (HQ)
AMSTED CANADA INC
GRIFFIN CANADA
(*Suby of* AMSTED INDUSTRIES INCORPORATED)
2500 Day St, Winnipeg, MB, R2C 3A4
(204) 222-4252
Sales 51,078,510
SIC 3462 Iron and steel forgings
  Mark Shirley
  Jacques Contois

D-U-N-S 24-275-8894   (SL)
BISON FIRE PROTECTION INC
35 Boys Rd, Winnipeg, MB, R2C 2Z2
(204) 237-3473
Emp Here 77   *Sales* 9,482,268
SIC 7389 Business services, nec
  Robert Read

D-U-N-S 20-910-0499   (SL)
BISON FIRE PROTECTION INC
35 Boys Rd, Winnipeg, MB, R2C 2Z2
(204) 237-3473
Emp Here 80   *Sales* 35,937,520
SIC 7389 Business services, nec

D-U-N-S 25-659-9945   (SL)
BRADLEY STEEL PROCESSORS INC
1201 Regent Ave W, Winnipeg, MB, R2C 3B2
(204) 987-2080
Emp Here 200   *Sales* 38,417,000
SIC 3441 Fabricated structural Metal
  Ossama Abou Zeid

D-U-N-S 20-613-3621   (SL)
BRUNSWICK ENTERPRISES LIMITED
BRUNSWICK STEEL
125 Bismarck St, Winnipeg, MB, R2C 2Z2
(204) 224-1472
Emp Here 70   *Sales* 31,302,180
SIC 5051 Metals service centers and offices
  Grant Copp
  Justin Copp
  Christine Dockter

D-U-N-S 25-289-3045   (BR)
CANAD CORPORATION OF MANITOBA

LTD
CANAD TRANSCONA INN
826 Regent Ave W, Winnipeg, MB, R2C 3A8
(204) 224-1681
Emp Here 100
SIC 7011 Hotels and motels
  Jason Hopps

D-U-N-S 24-318-0242   (HQ)
CASERA CREDIT UNION LIMITED
1300 Plessis Rd, Winnipeg, MB, R2C 2Y6
(204) 958-6300
Emp Here 4   *Sales* 11,699,288
SIC 6062 State credit unions
  Brent Thomas
  Dave Abel
  Barb Anderson
  Ian Blomeley
  Gary Esslinger
  John Gottfried
  Martin Johnson
  Bev Lafrance
  Grace Page

D-U-N-S 25-107-2567   (HQ)
CHAMOIS CAR WASH CORP, THE
85 Reenders Dr, Winnipeg, MB, R2C 5E8
(204) 669-9700
Sales 28,330,000
SIC 7542 Carwashes
  David Watson

D-U-N-S 25-152-3148   (BR)
COMPAGNIE DES CHEMINS DE FER NATIONAUX DU CANADA
CN EQUIPMENT
(*Suby of* COMPAGNIE DES CHEMINS DE FER NATIONAUX DU CANADA)
150 Pandora Ave W, Winnipeg, MB, R2C 4H5
(204) 235-2626
Emp Here 550
SIC 4789 Transportation services, nec
  Claude Courchaine

D-U-N-S 25-288-9639   (BR)
COSTCO WHOLESALE CANADA LTD
COSTCO
(*Suby of* COSTCO WHOLESALE CORPORATION)
1499 Regent Ave W, Winnipeg, MB, R2C 4M4
(204) 654-4214
Emp Here 178
SIC 5099 Durable goods, nec
  Spencer Cottee

D-U-N-S 20-757-9723   (SL)
EQUINOX INDUSTRIES LTD
401 Chrislind St, Winnipeg, MB, R2C 5G4
(204) 633-7564
Emp Here 92   *Sales* 21,476,020
SIC 3299 NonMetallic mineral products,
  Daniel Putter
  David Putter

D-U-N-S 20-518-5705   (HQ)
FRESHWATER FISH MARKETING CORPORATION
1199 Plessis Rd, Winnipeg, MB, R2C 3L4
(204) 983-6600
Emp Here 46   *Sales* 52,154,550
SIC 2092 Fresh or frozen packaged fish
  David Bevan
  Stan Lazar
  Durga Liske
  Paul Cater
  Stan Lazar
  Ron Ballantyne
  Bert Buckley
  Angus Gardiner
  Gail Wood
  Peter Beatty

D-U-N-S 20-836-1881   (SL)
FRONTIER AUTOMOTIVE INC
FRONTIER TOYOTA
1486 Regent Ave W, Winnipeg, MB, R2C 3A8

(204) 944-6600
Emp Here 65   *Sales* 40,903,200
SIC 5511 New and used car dealers
  Marcel Thompson
  Valerie Thompson

D-U-N-S 20-834-3319   (SL)
GAUTHIER CHRYSLER DODGE JEEP
(*Suby of* RANJOY SALES & LEASING LTD)
1375 Regent Ave W, Winnipeg, MB, R2C 3B2
(204) 661-8999
Emp Here 65   *Sales* 40,903,200
SIC 5511 New and used car dealers
  Randy Gauthier

D-U-N-S 20-519-9870   (HQ)
GENERAL SCRAP PARTNERSHIP
135 Bismarck St, Winnipeg, MB, R2C 2W3
(877) 495-6314
Emp Here 120   *Sales* 173,825,000
SIC 5093 Scrap and waste materials
  Blair Waldvogel

D-U-N-S 24-113-1333   (HQ)
GRANNY'S POULTRY COOPERATIVE (MANITOBA) LTD
GRANNY'S FINEST
750 Pandora Ave E, Winnipeg, MB, R2C 4G5
(204) 488-2230
Emp Here 55   *Sales* 127,706,751
SIC 2015 Poultry slaughtering and processing
  Craig Evans
  Rod Harder
  Darcy Ballance
  Jason Wortzman
  Andrea Thomson
  Orville Friesen
  Wayne Urbonas
  Barclay Uruski
  Ken Reimer
  Darren Kornelsen

D-U-N-S 20-721-4763   (SL)
GRANNY'S POULTRY COOPERATIVE (MANITOBA) LTD
750 Pandora Ave E, Winnipeg, MB, R2C 4G5
(204) 925-6260
Emp Here 50   *Sales* 26,756,200
SIC 5144 Poultry and poultry products
  Barclay Uruski

D-U-N-S 20-694-1390   (SL)
HERD NORTH AMERICA INC
2168 Springfield Rd, Winnipeg, MB, R2C 2Z2
(204) 222-0880
Emp Here 120   *Sales* 26,861,160
SIC 3714 Motor vehicle parts and accessories
  Mark Daudet

D-U-N-S 25-095-5606   (BR)
HOME DEPOT OF CANADA INC
HOME DEPOT
(*Suby of* THE HOME DEPOT INC)
1590 Regent Ave W, Winnipeg, MB, R2C 3B4
(204) 654-5400
Emp Here 200
SIC 5251 Hardware stores
  Brent Ballantyne

D-U-N-S 20-548-7119   (SL)
HUTCHISON, W A LTD
CANADIAN TIRE ASSOCIATE STORE
1519 Regent Ave W, Winnipeg, MB, R2C 4M4
(204) 667-2454
Emp Here 130   *Sales* 26,694,590
SIC 5399 Miscellaneous general merchandise
  William Alan Hutchison
  Patricia Hutchison

D-U-N-S 20-293-0009   (SL)
INTERNET COURIER MESSENGER SERVICES
1137 Pandora Ave W, Winnipeg, MB, R2C 1N4

Emp Here 25   *Sales* 11,087,250
SIC 7389 Business services, nec
  Bert Morton

D-U-N-S 20-648-0337   (HQ)
KITCHEN CRAFT OF CANADA
KITCHEN CRAFT
(*Suby of* FORTUNE BRANDS HOME & SECURITY, INC.)
1180 Springfield Rd, Winnipeg, MB, R2C 2Z2
(204) 224-3211
Emp Here 1,300   *Sales* 626,377,500
SIC 2434 Wood kitchen cabinets
  Vic Lukic
  Darin Dieleman
  Jack Laninga

D-U-N-S 20-191-5977   (SL)
LAKESIDE AUTOMOTIVE GROUP LTD
VICKAR MITSUBISHI
950 Regent Ave W, Winnipeg, MB, R2C 3A8
(204) 667-9200
Emp Here 38   *Sales* 13,840,170
SIC 5012 Automobiles and other motor vehicles
  Stephen Vickar

D-U-N-S 24-654-8499   (SL)
MARTEL BROS LTD
359 Pandora Ave W, Winnipeg, MB, R2C 1M6
(204) 233-2022
Emp Here 28   *Sales* 10,790,080
SIC 4731 Freight transportation arrangement
  Robert David Martel
  Carol Martel

D-U-N-S 20-923-8299   (BR)
MCDONALD'S RESTAURANTS OF CANADA LIMITED
MCDONALD'S
(*Suby of* MCDONALD'S CORPORATION)
15 Reenders Dr, Winnipeg, MB, R2C 5K5
(204) 949-3221
Emp Here 83
SIC 5812 Eating places
  Karena Henderson

D-U-N-S 20-276-0963   (HQ)
MEDI-QUOTE INSURANCE BROKERS INC
505 Pandora Ave W, Winnipeg, MB, R2C 1M8
(204) 947-9210
Sales 25,441,800
SIC 6411 Insurance agents, brokers, and service
  Lori Yorke

D-U-N-S 25-809-3533   (BR)
MOXIE'S RESTAURANTS, LIMITED PARTNERSHIP
MOXIE'S BAR AND GRILL
1615 Regent Ave W Suite 200, Winnipeg, MB, R2C 5C6
(204) 654-3345
Emp Here 140
SIC 5812 Eating places
  Tyler Macphearson

D-U-N-S 20-434-2059   (HQ)
MUNRO, HUGH CONSTRUCTION LTD
61053 Hwy 207, Winnipeg, MB, R2C 2Z2
(204) 224-9218
Emp Here 20   *Sales* 84,950,400
SIC 1794 Excavation work
  Colleen Munro

D-U-N-S 20-571-5469   (HQ)
NEW FLYER INDUSTRIES CANADA ULC
(*Suby of* NFI GROUP INC)
711 Kernaghan Ave Suite 3, Winnipeg, MB, R2C 3T4
(204) 224-1251
Emp Here 150   *Sales* 610,785,000
SIC 3711 Motor vehicles and car bodies
  Paul Soubry
  Hans Peper
  Colin Pewarchuk
  Glenn Asham
  Brian Tobin
  V James Sardo
  Wayne M E Mcleod
  John Marinucci

D-U-N-S 24-333-1332   (HQ)
NFI GROUP INC
711 Kernaghan Ave, Winnipeg, MB, R2C 3T4
(204) 224-1251
Emp Here 1,019   *Sales* 2,519,021,000
SIC 3711 Motor vehicles and car bodies
Paul Soubry
Glenn Asham
Paul Smith
David White
Janice Harper
Colin Pewarchuk
Kevin Wood
Margaret Lewis
Chris Stoddart
Brian Tobin

D-U-N-S 20-548-0390   (SL)
NORCRAFT CANADA CORPORATION
NORCRAFT COMPANIES LP
1980 Springfield Rd, Winnipeg, MB, R2C 2Z2
(204) 222-9888
Emp Here 105   *Sales* 20,168,925
SIC 3429 Hardware, nec
Dieter Loewen
Keith Berrard

D-U-N-S 24-426-5450   (SL)
NORTHERN BLOWER INC
(*Suby of* CANERECTOR INC)
901 Regent Ave W, Winnipeg, MB, R2C 2Z8
(204) 222-4216
Emp Here 65   *Sales* 31,702,450
SIC 5084 Industrial machinery and equipment
Neal Boyd

D-U-N-S 20-010-6581   (HQ)
PRINCESS AUTO LTD
475 Panet Rd, Winnipeg, MB, R2C 2Z1
(204) 667-4630
Emp Here 300   *Sales* 674,520,000
SIC 5251 Hardware stores
Robert Tallman
Mark Breslauer
Ken Kumar
Harold Romanychyn
Robert Hucal

D-U-N-S 25-533-8642   (HQ)
PRINCESS GROUP INC
475 Panet Rd, Winnipeg, MB, R2C 2Z1
(204) 667-4630
Emp Here 2   *Sales* 453,333,650
SIC 5251 Hardware stores
Robert Tallman
Harold Romanychyn

D-U-N-S 20-338-2130   (BR)
QUICK TRANSFER LTD
(*Suby of* 65238 MANITOBA LTD)
766 Pandora Ave E Unit 200, Winnipeg, MB,
R2C 3A6
(204) 786-6011
Emp Here 90
SIC 4214 Local trucking with storage

D-U-N-S 25-713-3082   (BR)
RED LOBSTER HOSPITALITY LLC
OLIVE GARDEN
51 Reenders Dr, Winnipeg, MB, R2C 5E8
(204) 661-8129
Emp Here 80
SIC 5812 Eating places
Jason Chapman

D-U-N-S 25-504-8027   (SL)
RED RIVER AIR BRAKE INC
171 Gunn Rd, Winnipeg, MB, R2C 2Z8
(204) 231-4111
Emp Here 25   *Sales* 12,999,175
SIC 4789 Transportation services, nec
Darlene Keller
Andrew Keller

D-U-N-S 25-890-5025   (SL)
REENDERS CAR WASH LTD
CHAMOIS, THE

(*Suby of* CHAMOIS CAR WASH CORP, THE)
85 Reenders Dr, Winnipeg, MB, R2C 5E8
(204) 669-9700
Emp Here 100   *Sales* 45,019,700
SIC 7542 Carwashes
David Watson

D-U-N-S 25-268-0897   (BR)
RIVER EAST TRANSCONA SCHOOL DIVISION
MURDOCH MACKAY COLLEGIATE
(*Suby of* RIVER EAST TRANSCONA
SCHOOL DIVISION)
260 Redonda St, Winnipeg, MB, R2C 1L6
(204) 958-6460
Emp Here 85
SIC 8211 Elementary and secondary schools
John Muller

D-U-N-S 20-760-0847   (HQ)
S & L PROPERTIES LTD
REGENT SHELL
605 Regent Ave W, Winnipeg, MB, R2C 1R9
(204) 222-9431
Emp Here 5   *Sales* 22,413,510
SIC 5541 Gasoline service stations
Steve Blaney

D-U-N-S 25-271-9927   (BR)
SOBEYS WEST INC
KILDONAN CROSSING SAFEWAY
(*Suby of* EMPIRE COMPANY LIMITED)
1615 Regent Ave W Unit 500, Winnipeg, MB,
R2C 5C6
(204) 663-6862
Emp Here 100
SIC 5411 Grocery stores
Brent Harrison

D-U-N-S 25-786-6145   (BR)
SOBEYS WEST INC
(*Suby of* EMPIRE COMPANY LIMITED)
105 Pandora Ave E, Winnipeg, MB, R2C 0A1
(204) 222-6878
Emp Here 75
SIC 5411 Grocery stores
Mike Scott

D-U-N-S 24-916-7883   (SL)
SONAL BACHU PHARMACY LTD
SHOPPER'S DRUG MART
1555 Regent Ave W Unit 32t, Winnipeg, MB,
R2C 4J2
(204) 661-8068
Emp Here 45   *Sales* 11,382,930
SIC 5912 Drug stores and proprietary stores
Sonal Purohit

D-U-N-S 20-049-8728   (SL)
SOR HOLDINGS LTD
SATURN ISUZU OF REGENT
1364 Regent Ave W, Winnipeg, MB, R2C 3A8
(204) 667-9993
Emp Here 37   *Sales* 18,428,886
SIC 5511 New and used car dealers
Al Johnson

D-U-N-S 24-372-1370   (HQ)
STRUCTURAL COMPOSITE TECHNOLOGIES LTD
(*Suby of* JELKO INC)
100 Hoka St Unit 200, Winnipeg, MB, R2C
3N2
(204) 668-9320
Sales 10,753,140
SIC 3299 NonMetallic mineral products,
John Zadro

D-U-N-S 20-003-6853   (SL)
SUBURBAN CENTRE & AUTO SERVICE LTD
LEE RIVER TRANSPORT
130 Transport Rd, Winnipeg, MB, R2C 2Z2
(204) 953-6200
Emp Here 42   *Sales* 13,986,711
SIC 4213 Trucking, except local
Randy Belluk

Laurie Belluk

D-U-N-S 24-691-9500   (HQ)
TRAPPERS TRANSPORT LTD
1300 Redonda St, Winnipeg, MB, R2C 2Z2
(204) 697-7647
Sales 25,713,250
SIC 4213 Trucking, except local
Daniel Omeniuk
Ian Fordyce

D-U-N-S 20-835-1262   (SL)
VICKAR COMMUNITY CHEVROLET LTD
964 Regent Ave W, Winnipeg, MB, R2C 3A8
(204) 661-8391
Emp Here 120   *Sales* 75,513,600
SIC 5511 New and used car dealers
Larry Vickar

D-U-N-S 24-169-9024   (HQ)
WYATT NU TREND INSURANCE AGENCY LTD
WYATT INSURANCE & FINANCIAL
138 Regent Ave W, Winnipeg, MB, R2C 1P9
(204) 222-3221
Sales 184,774,200
SIC 6411 Insurance agents, brokers, and service
Andrew Clinsky

Winnipeg, MB R2E

D-U-N-S 20-257-0870   (SL)
JEHOVAH'S WITNESSES EAST ST PAUL CONGREGATION
KINGDOM HALL OF JEHOVAH'S WITNESSES
3760 Andrews Rd, Winnipeg, MB, R2E 1C2
(204) 654-1829
Emp Here 100   *Sales* 10,772,700
SIC 8661 Religious organizations
Jerry Kozum

Winnipeg, MB R2G

D-U-N-S 24-318-9086   (HQ)
CASANA FURNITURE COMPANY LTD
(*Suby of* PALLISER FURNITURE HOLDINGS
LTD)
90 Lexington Pk, Winnipeg, MB, R2G 4H2
(204) 988-3189
Emp Here 5   *Sales* 12,212,544
SIC 5021 Furniture
Roger Friesen
Philip Klassen
Ben Horch
Arthur Defehr
Peter Tielmann
Reginald Kliewer

D-U-N-S 24-036-8753   (SL)
CONCORD PROJECTS LTD
(*Suby of* PAETKAU HOLDINGS LTD)
1277 Henderson Hwy Suite 200, Winnipeg,
MB, R2G 1M3
(204) 339-1651
Emp Here 15   *Sales* 37,025,943
SIC 1541 Industrial buildings and warehouses
Theodore Paetkau

D-U-N-S 24-378-0504   (SL)
DEFEHR FURNITURE (2009) LTD
DEFEHR FURNITURE
(*Suby of* FRANK DEFEHR HOLDINGS LTD)
125 Furniture Park, Winnipeg, MB, R2G 1B9
(204) 988-5630
Emp Here 405   *Sales* 31,135,520
SIC 2511 Wood household furniture
Philip Klassen
Andrew Defehr
Michael Defehr

Irene Loewen
Richard Defehr

D-U-N-S 25-056-6486   (HQ)
DONWOOD MANOR PERSONAL CARE HOME INC
171 Donwood Dr, Winnipeg, MB, R2G 0V9
(204) 668-4410
Sales 12,298,680
SIC 8051 Skilled nursing care facilities
James Heinrichs

D-U-N-S 24-425-3154   (HQ)
EQ3 LTD
170 Furniture Park, Winnipeg, MB, R2G 1B9
(204) 957-8018
Emp Here 30   *Sales* 61,341,690
SIC 5712 Furniture stores
Peter Tielmann
Jim Hunt
Mark Letain

D-U-N-S 20-334-3793   (HQ)
FRANK DEFEHR HOLDINGS LTD
125 Furniture Park, Winnipeg, MB, R2G 1B9
(204) 988-5630
Sales 75,706,100
SIC 2599 Furniture and fixtures, nec
Andrew Defehr
Frank Defehr
Joanne Duhourx-Defehr
Richard Defehr

D-U-N-S 24-616-4193   (BR)
HEALTHCARE INSURANCE RECIPROCAL OF CANADA
HIROC
(*Suby of* HEALTHCARE INSURANCE RECIPROCAL OF CANADA)
1200 Rothesay St, Winnipeg, MB, R2G 1T7
(204) 943-4125
Emp Here 100
SIC 6411 Insurance agents, brokers, and service
Susan Bowen

D-U-N-S 25-311-2825   (BR)
MCDONALD'S RESTAURANTS OF CANADA LIMITED
MCDONALD'S
(*Suby of* MCDONALD'S CORPORATION)
1460 Henderson Hwy, Winnipeg, MB, R2G
1N4
(204) 949-6074
Emp Here 110
SIC 5812 Eating places
Perry Cox

D-U-N-S 24-819-8194   (SL)
OAKWOOD CONSTRUCTION SERVICES LTD
20 Burnett Ave, Winnipeg, MB, R2G 1C1
(204) 661-8415
Emp Here 60   *Sales* 16,459,920
SIC 8741 Management services

D-U-N-S 24-037-3415   (SL)
OAKWOOD ROOFING AND SHEET METAL CO. LTD
20 Burnett Ave, Winnipeg, MB, R2G 1C1
(204) 237-8361
Emp Here 130   *Sales* 16,004,877
SIC 1761 Roofing, siding, and sheetMetal
work
Harry Bosma

D-U-N-S 24-333-1076   (HQ)
PALLISER FURNITURE HOLDINGS LTD
70 Lexington Pk, Winnipeg, MB, R2G 4H2
(866) 444-0777
Emp Here 5   *Sales* 632,330,570
SIC 6712 Bank holding companies
Arthur Defehr
David Defehr
Reginald Kliewer
Darren Stevenson
Leona Defehr

▲ Public Company   ■ Public Company Family Member   **HQ** Headquarters   **BR** Branch   **SL** Single Location

D-U-N-S 20-308-6236   (HQ)
PALLISER FURNITURE UPHOLSTERY HOLDINGS LTD
(*Suby of* PALLISER FURNITURE HOLDINGS LTD)
70 Lexington Pk, Winnipeg, MB, R2G 4H2
(204) 988-5600
Emp Here 1,175
SIC 2512 Upholstered household furniture
Cary Benson
Cathy Gillespie
Lorri Kelley
Heather Goertzen
Arthur Defehr
Reginald Kliewer
Bryan Rach
Andrew Willms

D-U-N-S 24-377-8391   (HQ)
PALLISER FURNITURE UPHOLSTERY LTD
(*Suby of* PALLISER FURNITURE HOLDINGS LTD)
70 Lexington Pk, Winnipeg, MB, R2G 4H2
(204) 988-5600
Emp Here 30   *Sales* 122,465,750
SIC 2512 Upholstered household furniture
Arthur Defehr
Cary Benson
Bryan Andrew
Heather Goertzen
Cathy Gillespie
Lorri Kelley
Andrew Willms
Reginald Kliewer

D-U-N-S 20-555-3378   (BR)
RIVER EAST TRANSCONA SCHOOL DIVISION
RIVER EAST COLLEGIATE
(*Suby of* RIVER EAST TRANSCONA SCHOOL DIVISION)
295 Sutton Ave, Winnipeg, MB, R2G 0T1
(204) 338-4611
Emp Here 100
SIC 8211 Elementary and secondary schools
Diana Posthumus

D-U-N-S 20-292-9324   (SL)
ROYAL LEPAGE PRIME REAL ESTATE
1877 Henderson Hwy, Winnipeg, MB, R2G 1P4
(204) 989-7900
Emp Here 80   *Sales* 33,511,120
SIC 6531 Real estate agents and managers
John Froese

D-U-N-S 20-513-4302   (SL)
SPRINGFIELD INDUSTRIES LTD
125 Furniture Park, Winnipeg, MB, R2G 1B9

Emp Here 50   *Sales* 13,993,213
SIC 2821 Plastics materials and resins
Richard De Fehr
Shannon Loewenn
Andrew De Fehr
David Loewenn
Daniel Loewenn

D-U-N-S 20-945-4792   (HQ)
SPRINGHILL LUMBER WHOLESALE LTD
1820 De Vries Ave, Winnipeg, MB, R2G 3S8
(204) 661-1055
Sales 31,329,540
SIC 5039 Construction materials, nec
Paul Waldner
Mike Price
Don Henzel

D-U-N-S 24-112-4700   (SL)
WOODLAND SUPPLY & MFG. CO.
867 Mcleod Ave, Winnipeg, MB, R2G 0Y4
(204) 668-0079
Emp Here 140   *Sales* 26,931,800
SIC 2431 Millwork
George Bock Jr
George Bock Sr

Winnipeg, MB R2H

D-U-N-S 20-700-7522   (BR)
AG GROWTH INTERNATIONAL INC
WESTEEL DIVISION
(*Suby of* AG GROWTH INTERNATIONAL INC)
450 Rue Desautels, Winnipeg, MB, R2H 3E6
(204) 233-7133
Emp Here 340
SIC 3443 Fabricated plate work (boiler shop)
Bruce Allen

D-U-N-S 25-117-7655   (HQ)
ARCHDIOCESE OF ST BONIFACE, THE
CACR DE ST BONIFACE
151 De La Cathedrale Ave, Winnipeg, MB, R2H 0H6
(204) 237-9851
Emp Here 35   *Sales* 26,551,365
SIC 8661 Religious organizations
Emilius Goulet

D-U-N-S 24-113-9245   (HQ)
CAISSE POPULAIRE DE SAINT-BONIFACE LIMITEE, LA
205 Provencher Blvd Suite 100, Winnipeg, MB, R2H 0G4
(204) 237-8874
Sales 51,289,150
SIC 8742 Management consulting services
Gilbert Dube
Normand Collet
Richard Bosch
Joe Rondeau

D-U-N-S 20-946-2530   (SL)
COLLEGE DE SAINT-BONIFACE
200 De La Cathedrale Ave, Winnipeg, MB, R2H 0H7
(204) 233-0210
Emp Here 200   *Sales* 29,878,200
SIC 8221 Colleges and universities
Raymonde Gagne
Normand Collet
Charlotte Walkty

D-U-N-S 20-226-4987   (SL)
DATA PROBE INC
297 St Mary'S Rd, Winnipeg, MB, R2H 1J5

Emp Here 150   *Sales* 33,373,554
SIC 8732 Commercial nonphysical research
Lauren Gervais
Bev Everett
Dorothy Fontaine

D-U-N-S 25-289-2781   (BR)
DIVISION SCOLAIRE FRANCO-MANITOBAINE
COLLEGE LOUIS RIEL
(*Suby of* DIVISION SCOLAIRE FRANCO-MANITOBAINE)
585 Rue St Jean Baptiste, Winnipeg, MB, R2H 2Y2
(204) 237-8927
Emp Here 86
SIC 8221 Colleges and universities
Marc Roy

D-U-N-S 24-037-1117   (SL)
MBS RESIDENCE INC
213 St Mary'S Rd Suite 9, Winnipeg, MB, R2H 1J2
(204) 233-5363
Emp Here 43   *Sales* 10,015,173
SIC 6513 Apartment building operators

D-U-N-S 25-310-9102   (BR)
MCDONALD'S RESTAURANTS OF CANADA LIMITED
MCDONALD'S
(*Suby of* MCDONALD'S CORPORATION)
77 Goulet St, Winnipeg, MB, R2H 0R5
(204) 949-6018
Emp Here 80

SIC 5812 Eating places
Krystal Walker

D-U-N-S 25-326-6134   (HQ)
MOMENTUM HEALTHWARE, INC
131 Provencher Blvd Suite 308, Winnipeg, MB, R2H 0G2
(204) 231-3836
Sales 10,050,997
SIC 7372 Prepackaged software
Raymond Lafond
Peter Falk
Rod Kamins

D-U-N-S 24-567-8177   (SL)
NETWORK SOUTH ENTERPRISES
188 Goulet St, Winnipeg, MB, R2H 0R8
(204) 474-1959
Emp Here 49   *Sales* 22,011,731
SIC 7389 Business services, nec
Shelly Gall

D-U-N-S 20-570-7391   (SL)
NORWOOD HOTEL CO LTD
WOOD TAVERN AND GRILL
112 Marion St, Winnipeg, MB, R2H 0T1
(204) 233-4475
Emp Here 110   *Sales* 10,195,900
SIC 7011 Hotels and motels
Robert Sparrow
Brian Sparrow

D-U-N-S 25-713-4163   (SL)
PARENTY REITMEIER INC
123b Marion St, Winnipeg, MB, R2H 0T3
(204) 237-3737
Emp Here 34   *Sales* 15,078,660
SIC 7389 Business services, nec
Jean-Pierre Parenty
Diane Lauraine Reitmeier
Linda Parenty

D-U-N-S 24-882-5622   (SL)
POWERLAND COMPUTERS LTD
170 Marion St, Winnipeg, MB, R2H 0T4
(204) 237-3800
Emp Here 93   *Sales* 21,613,479
SIC 5734 Computer and software stores
Wes Penner
Ashley Penner

D-U-N-S 24-363-0857   (BR)
RGIS CANADA ULC
(*Suby of* THE BLACKSTONE GROUP L P)
196 Tache Ave Unit 5, Winnipeg, MB, R2H 1Z6
(204) 774-0013
Emp Here 250
SIC 7389 Business services, nec
Hanlei Sun

D-U-N-S 20-049-0311   (SL)
SPRINGS OF LIVING WATER CHRISTIAN ACADEMY INC
SPRINGS CHRISTIAN ACADEMY ELEMENTARY SCHOOL CAMPUS
261 Youville St, Winnipeg, MB, R2H 2S7
(204) 231-3640
Emp Here 80   *Sales* 7,426,080
SIC 8211 Elementary and secondary schools
Darcy Bayne

D-U-N-S 20-838-9361   (SL)
ST. BONIFACE GENERAL HOSPITAL
409 Tache Ave, Winnipeg, MB, R2H 2A6
(204) 233-8563
Emp Here 3,000   *Sales* 329,438,597
SIC 8062 General medical and surgical hospitals
Michel Tetreault
Robert Gannon
Ken Lamoureux
Vic Schroeder
Marvelle Mcpherson
Allen Grant

D-U-N-S 24-630-7383   (HQ)
ULTRACUTS LTD

167 St Mary'S Rd, Winnipeg, MB, R2H 1J1
(204) 231-0110
Emp Here 200   *Sales* 712,897,545
SIC 6794 Patent owners and lessors
Meril Rivard

D-U-N-S 20-947-1341   (BR)
WESTERN INVENTORY SERVICE LTD
WIS INTERNATIONAL
(*Suby of* ARES CAPITAL CORPORATION)
73 Goulet St, Winnipeg, MB, R2H 0R5
(204) 669-6505
Emp Here 120
SIC 7389 Business services, nec
Mario Fontes

Winnipeg, MB R2J

D-U-N-S 24-776-0663   (SL)
2474761 MANITOBA LTD
WINNIPEG SPORT & LEISURE
1272 Dugald Rd, Winnipeg, MB, R2J 0H2
(204) 987-5640
Emp Here 30   *Sales* 14,942,340
SIC 5561 Recreational vehicle dealers
Daniel Boone

D-U-N-S 25-779-2283   (SL)
2851262 MANITOBA LTD
DART MESSENGER & COURIER SERVICE
393 Dawson Rd N, Winnipeg, MB, R2J 0S8
(204) 988-3278
Emp Here 73   *Sales* 10,818,016
SIC 4212 Local trucking, without storage
Robert Morton
Norman Matlashewski

D-U-N-S 24-364-4809   (SL)
5177007 MANITOBA LTD
CANADA DRUGS CUSTOMER CARE
24 Terracon Pl Suite 467, Winnipeg, MB, R2J 4G7
(204) 654-5194
Emp Here 125   *Sales* 30,541,000
SIC 5961 Catalog and mail-order houses
Kris Thorkelson

D-U-N-S 24-362-4850   (SL)
6089585 CANADA LTD
NUCO SERVICES
500 Camiel Sys St, Winnipeg, MB, R2J 4K2
(204) 663-2866
Emp Here 40   *Sales* 18,829,240
SIC 1542 Nonresidential construction, nec
Rich Magliozzi

D-U-N-S 20-324-8448   (SL)
ACR CANADA CORPORATION
AMERICAN CUSTOM ROTOMOLDING
(*Suby of* TECHNOLOGY MANAGEMENT INC)
122 Paquin Rd, Winnipeg, MB, R2J 3V4
(204) 669-2345
Emp Here 90   *Sales* 25,561,890
SIC 2821 Plastics materials and resins
Craig Mcintosh

D-U-N-S 25-384-4880   (SL)
ALI ARC INDUSTRIES LP
(*Suby of* BARTLEY GROUP HOLDINGS LIMITED)
155 Elan Blvd, Winnipeg, MB, R2J 4H1
(204) 253-6080
Emp Here 50   *Sales* 11,192,150
SIC 3714 Motor vehicle parts and accessories
David Harrald
Robert Bartley

D-U-N-S 20-612-4273   (HQ)
ALL-FAB BUILDING COMPONENTS INC
OLYMPIC BUILDING SUPPLIES, DIV OF
1755 Dugald Rd, Winnipeg, MB, R2J 0H3
(204) 661-8880
Sales 86,300,900

SIC 2431 Millwork
Blaine Reimer
John Reimer
Gary Roehr
William Fast

D-U-N-S 20-004-5284   (SL)
ARNE'S WELDING LTD
ARNE'S TRAILER SALES
835 Mission St, Winnipeg, MB, R2J 0A4
(204) 233-7111
Emp Here 130   *Sales* 29,099,590
SIC 3715 Truck trailers
Geral Bouthard
Michael Rosembaum
Douglas L. Harvey

D-U-N-S 20-004-5292   (HQ)
ARNOLD BROS. TRANSPORT LTD
739 Lagimodiere Blvd, Winnipeg, MB, R2J
0T8
(204) 257-6666
Emp Here 200   *Sales* 92,190,500
SIC 4213 Trucking, except local
Fred Arnold
Gary Arnold
Dennis Balzer

D-U-N-S 20-711-6195   (HQ)
BEAVER BUS LINES LIMITED
339 Archibald St, Winnipeg, MB, R2J 0W6
(204) 989-7007
Emp Here 77   *Sales* 6,398,120
SIC 4142 Bus charter service, except local
John Fehr
Mary Fehr
Sandra Janzen

D-U-N-S 24-655-9314   (SL)
BITUMINEX LIMITED
29 Terracon Pl, Winnipeg, MB, R2J 4B3
(204) 237-6253
Emp Here 45   *Sales* 13,147,605
SIC 7359 Equipment rental and leasing, nec
Dennis Cruise

D-U-N-S 20-004-5524   (SL)
BOCKSTAEL CONSTRUCTION LIMITED
100 Paquin Rd Unit 200, Winnipeg, MB, R2J
3V4
(204) 233-7135
Emp Here 50   *Sales* 23,536,550
SIC 1542 Nonresidential construction, nec
John Bockstael
Carmine Militano
Dan Bockstael
Nick Bockstael

D-U-N-S 24-519-6076   (SL)
BORETTA CONSTRUCTION 2002 LTD
1383 Dugald Rd, Winnipeg, MB, R2J 0H3
(204) 237-7375
Emp Here 30   *Sales* 14,121,930
SIC 1542 Nonresidential construction, nec
Gregory Fast
William Charles (Bill) Canners
Feliciana (Fely) De Leon

D-U-N-S 24-967-0894   (SL)
**BORLAND CONSTRUCTION (1989) LIM-
ITED**
(*Suby of* LADCO COMPANY LIMITED)
751 Lagimodiere Blvd, Winnipeg, MB, R2J
0T8
(204) 255-6444
Emp Here 60   *Sales* 15,146,520
SIC 1611 Highway and street construction
Alan A. Borger
Ralph J. Borger
John Henry Borger
Gerald D. Borger

D-U-N-S 24-967-5661   (SL)
BRIDGES, DAVID INC
CHAMP INDUSTRIES
(*Suby of* CANERECTOR INC)
360 Dawson Rd N, Winnipeg, MB, R2J 0S7

(204) 233-0500
Emp Here 65   *Sales* 11,790,220
SIC 3399 Primary Metal products
Claudia Bridges
Lise Baker

D-U-N-S 20-855-2112   (HQ)
CABELA'S RETAIL CANADA INC
CABELA'S CANADA
(*Suby of* BASS PRO GROUP, LLC)
25 De Baets St, Winnipeg, MB, R2J 4G5
(204) 788-4867
Emp Here 200   *Sales* 48,865,600
SIC 5941 Sporting goods and bicycle shops
Brian Linneman

D-U-N-S 25-671-2340   (BR)
**CANAD CORPORATION OF MANITOBA
LTD**
CANADA INNS WINDSORS PARK
1034 Elizabeth Rd, Winnipeg, MB, R2J 1B3
(204) 253-2641
Emp Here 200
SIC 7011 Hotels and motels
Christopher Miller

D-U-N-S 20-566-0553   (HQ)
CANADA DRUGS LTD
CANADADRUGS.COM
16 Terracon Pl, Winnipeg, MB, R2J 4G7

Emp Here 5   *Sales* 39,092,480
SIC 5912 Drug stores and proprietary stores
Kris Thorkelson

D-U-N-S 20-366-3984   (SL)
CARFAIR COMPOSITES INC
(*Suby of* NFI GROUP INC)
692 Mission St, Winnipeg, MB, R2J 0A3
(204) 233-0671
Emp Here 300   *Sales* 76,707,000
SIC 3299 NonMetallic mineral products,
Neil Carlson

D-U-N-S 24-036-0628   (HQ)
CARNEIL GROUP LTD, THE
1035 Mission St, Winnipeg, MB, R2J 0A4
(204) 233-0671
Sales 51,811,980
SIC 1721 Painting and paper hanging
Neil Carlson

D-U-N-S 20-012-2120   (SL)
COLOR AD PACKAGING LTD
200 Beghin Ave, Winnipeg, MB, R2J 3W2
(204) 777-7770
Emp Here 200   *Sales* 31,771,600
SIC 3086 Plastics foam products
Chip Batten
Andrew Chang
Dawn Zifarelli

D-U-N-S 20-518-5416   (HQ)
CON-PRO INDUSTRIES CANADA LTD
765 Marion St, Winnipeg, MB, R2J 0K6
(204) 233-3717
Emp Here 25   *Sales* 23,536,550
SIC 1542 Nonresidential construction, nec
Donald Wayne Snodgrass

D-U-N-S 24-608-4693   (SL)
CUSTOM CASTINGS LIMITED
2015 Dugald Rd, Winnipeg, MB, R2J 0H3
(204) 663-9142
Emp Here 80   *Sales* 18,674,800
SIC 3365 Aluminum foundries
Mark Striepe
Herb Striepe

D-U-N-S 20-570-9611   (HQ)
DYNAMIC MACHINE CORPORATION
1407 Dugald Rd, Winnipeg, MB, R2J 0H3
(204) 982-4900
Emp Here 45   *Sales* 17,760,080
SIC 3599 Industrial machinery, nec
Joe Mcevoy
Richard Van Den Broek

D-U-N-S 25-325-4528   (SL)
EAST SIDE VENTILATION LTD
EAST SIDE VENTILATION
11 Durand Rd, Winnipeg, MB, R2J 3T1
(204) 667-8700
Emp Here 130   *Sales* 16,051,354
SIC 1711 Plumbing, heating, air-conditioning
Rick Levesque
Brian Derksen
James Derksen
Kurt Derksen

D-U-N-S 20-008-9506   (SL)
ERNST HANSCH CONSTRUCTION LTD
3 Terracon Pl, Winnipeg, MB, R2J 4B3
(204) 233-7881
Emp Here 22   *Sales* 10,356,082
SIC 1542 Nonresidential construction, nec
Vladimir Hlas
Norbert Hansch

D-U-N-S 20-004-6126   (SL)
FAIRWAY COACHLINES INC
339 Archibald St, Winnipeg, MB, R2J 0W6
(204) 989-7007
Emp Here 100   *Sales* 5,487,200
SIC 4131 Intercity and rural bus transportation
John Fehr Jr

D-U-N-S 25-106-6148   (SL)
FOXRIDGE HOMES (MANITOBA) LTD
30 Speers Rd, Winnipeg, MB, R2J 1L9
(204) 488-7578
Emp Here 70   *Sales* 18,965,940
SIC 1522 Residential construction, nec
David Freisen

D-U-N-S 20-571-4520   (SL)
FRANK FAIR INDUSTRIES LTD
(*Suby of* NFI GROUP INC)
400 Archibald St, Winnipeg, MB, R2J 0W9
(204) 237-7987
Emp Here 130   *Sales* 29,099,590
SIC 3713 Truck and bus bodies
Rafael Gomez

D-U-N-S 20-005-9590   (HQ)
FRIENDLY FAMILY FARMS LTD
500 Dawson Rd N, Winnipeg, MB, R2J 0T1
(204) 231-5151
Emp Here 2   *Sales* 26,230,900
SIC 0191 General farms, primarily crop
Marshall Freed
Sam Freed

D-U-N-S 20-832-5977   (HQ)
FRONTIER SCHOOL DIVISION
30 Speers Rd, Winnipeg, MB, R2J 1L9
(204) 775-9741
Emp Here 50   *Sales* 148,678,500
SIC 8211 Elementary and secondary schools
Gerald Cattani
Gordon Shead

D-U-N-S 20-023-8645   (BR)
FRONTIER SCHOOL DIVISION
MOSAKAHIKAN SCHOOL
(*Suby of* FRONTIER SCHOOL DIVISION)
30 Speers Rd, Winnipeg, MB, R2J 1L9
(204) 775-9741
Emp Here 87
SIC 8211 Elementary and secondary schools
Dan Ehman

D-U-N-S 20-759-4565   (SL)
G N R TRAVEL CENTRE LTD
G N R CAMPING WORLD RV CENTRE
1370 Dugald Rd, Winnipeg, MB, R2J 0H2
(204) 233-4478
Emp Here 30   *Sales* 14,942,340
SIC 5561 Recreational vehicle dealers
Gilbert Robert
Jeannine Robert
Kevin Betzold
Jim Gorrie

D-U-N-S 20-757-3098   (SL)

**GATEWAY CONSTRUCTION & ENGINEER-
ING LTD**
434 Archibald St, Winnipeg, MB, R2J 0X5
(204) 233-8550
Emp Here 40   *Sales* 18,829,240
SIC 1542 Nonresidential construction, nec
Carson Rist
Wesley Rist
Seno W. Rist

D-U-N-S 25-832-2072   (SL)
GIRTON MANAGEMENT LTD
CANADIAN TIRE ASSOCIATE STORE
157 Vermillion Rd Suite 266, Winnipeg, MB,
R2J 3Z7
(204) 254-5169
Emp Here 125   *Sales* 25,667,875
SIC 5399 Miscellaneous general merchandise
Ronald Lapointe
Jay Crowley

D-U-N-S 20-008-8961   (SL)
**GUERTIN COATINGS, SEALANTS AND
POLYMERS LTD**
(*Suby of* CLOVERDALE INVESTMENTS LTD)
50 Panet Rd, Winnipeg, MB, R2J 0R9
(204) 237-0241
Emp Here 75   *Sales* 21,301,575
SIC 2851 Paints and allied products
Phillip Guertin

D-U-N-S 25-099-0751   (SL)
HAMS MARKETING SERVICES CO-OP INC
750 Marion St, Winnipeg, MB, R2J 0K4
(204) 233-4991
Emp Here 23   *Sales* 33,756,916
SIC 5154 Livestock
Perry Mohr
John Preun

D-U-N-S 24-916-7750   (HQ)
I.D.C. WHOLESALE INC
I.D.C. COMMUNICATIONS
1385 Niakwa Rd E, Winnipeg, MB, R2J 3T3
(204) 254-8282
Emp Here 33   *Sales* 66,728,405
SIC 5065 Electronic parts and equipment, nec
Lorne Plett
David Penner
Mary Ann Penner
Ingrid Plett

D-U-N-S 24-677-0890   (HQ)
INDUSTRIAL METALS (2011)
550 Messier St, Winnipeg, MB, R2J 0G5
(204) 233-1908
Sales 13,013,550
SIC 5093 Scrap and waste materials
Calum Hughes
Clifford Chisick

D-U-N-S 20-647-9826   (HQ)
INDUSTRIAL TRUCK SERVICE LTD
89 Durand Rd, Winnipeg, MB, R2J 3T1
(204) 663-9325
Emp Here 26   *Sales* 19,476,066
SIC 5084 Industrial machinery and equipment
John David Monteith
Gisela Monteith
David J. Monteith
Sandra Hawman

D-U-N-S 20-517-9146   (SL)
INTERGRAPHICS DECAL LIMITED
180 De Baets St, Winnipeg, MB, R2J 3W6
(204) 958-9570
Emp Here 75   *Sales* 8,226,509
SIC 2759 Commercial printing, nec
Conrad Desender
Yvonne Marie Desender

D-U-N-S 20-210-5412   (SL)
J & S HOLDINGS INC
TIM HORTONS
1040 Beaverhill Blvd Suite 1, Winnipeg, MB,
R2J 4B1
(204) 255-8431
Emp Here 60   *Sales* 17,608,620

SIC 5461 Retail bakeries
Jeff Taweel

D-U-N-S 20-519-7999   (SL)
JADE TRANSPORT LTD
(*Suby of* 2741688 MANITOBA LTD)
963 Dugald Rd, Winnipeg, MB, R2J 0G8
(204) 233-3566
Emp Here 100   *Sales* 20,570,600
SIC 4212 Local trucking, without storage
Larry Dyck
Greg Arndt

D-U-N-S 25-386-8152   (HQ)
JANICO INVESTMENTS LTD
PETRO CANADA
928 Marion St, Winnipeg, MB, R2J 0K8
(204) 949-7281
Emp Here 16   *Sales* 42,744,834
SIC 5171 Petroleum bulk stations and terminals
Murray Wedlake
Glen Poapst

D-U-N-S 20-116-3438   (SL)
KRAUS GLOBAL LTD
25 Paquin Rd, Winnipeg, MB, R2J 3V9
(204) 663-3601
Emp Here 75   *Sales* 16,788,225
SIC 3728 Aircraft parts and equipment, nec
Ossama Abouzeid
Donald Keatch
Ross Devisser
Scott Bailey
Dev Patel
Bill Cassell
Penny Topolnitsky
Harold Heide
D William Easton
Eric Stefanson

D-U-N-S 24-656-1419   (HQ)
LABELS UNLIMITED INC
67 Archibald St, Winnipeg, MB, R2J 0V7
(204) 233-4444
Sales 11,671,750
SIC 2679 Converted paper products, nec
Larry Chartrand

D-U-N-S 24-654-1924   (HQ)
LADCO COMPANY LIMITED
LAKEWOOD AGENCIES
40 Lakewood Blvd Suite 200, Winnipeg, MB, R2J 2M7
(204) 982-5959
Emp Here 30   *Sales* 65,623,000
SIC 1629 Heavy construction, nec
Alan A Borger
Ralph J Borger
J Henry Borger
Gerald D Borger
Gary T Brazzell
Mark Kneale

D-U-N-S 24-968-4093   (SL)
LEXAR INTERNATIONAL LTD
16 Mazenod Rd Suite 3, Winnipeg, MB, R2J 4H2
(204) 661-9000
Emp Here 25   *Sales* 18,563,000
SIC 5199 Nondurable goods, nec
Ronald L Saltel

D-U-N-S 20-064-3398   (BR)
LOUIS RIEL SCHOOL DIVISION
SHAMROCK ELEMENTARY SCHOOL
(*Suby of* LOUIS RIEL SCHOOL DIVISION)
831 Beaverhill Blvd, Winnipeg, MB, R2J 3K1
(204) 257-0637
Emp Here 80
SIC 8211 Elementary and secondary schools
Sheena Braun

D-U-N-S 20-004-7074   (SL)
LOVEDAY MUSHROOM FARMS LTD
556 Mission St, Winnipeg, MB, R2J 0A2
(204) 233-4378
Emp Here 125   *Sales* 21,128,125

SIC 0182 Food crops grown under cover
Frederick Loveday
Burton Loveday
Betty Loveday

D-U-N-S 24-852-0975   (BR)
MAPLE LEAF FOODS INC
ROTHSAY RENDERING, DIV OF
(*Suby of* MAPLE LEAF FOODS INC)
607 Dawson Rd N Suite 555, Winnipeg, MB, R2J 0T2
(204) 233-7347
Emp Here 80
SIC 2048 Prepared feeds, nec
Glen Gratton

D-U-N-S 24-630-6567   (BR)
MAPLE LEAF FOODS INC
MAPLE LEAF CONSUMER FOODS
(*Suby of* MAPLE LEAF FOODS INC)
870 Lagimodiere Blvd Suite 23, Winnipeg, MB, R2J 0T9
(204) 233-2421
Emp Here 400
SIC 2011 Meat packing plants
Jim Scott

D-U-N-S 25-318-1226   (BR)
MCDONALD'S RESTAURANTS OF CANADA LIMITED
MCDONALD'S #8394
(*Suby of* MCDONALD'S CORPORATION)
65 Vermillion Rd, Winnipeg, MB, R2J 3W7
(204) 949-6015
Emp Here 80
SIC 5812 Eating places

D-U-N-S 25-948-4103   (BR)
MCPHILLIPS LIMITED PARTNERSHIP
PERKIN'S FAMILY RESTAURANT
(*Suby of* MCPHILLIPS LIMITED PARTNERSHIP)
123 Vermillion Rd, Winnipeg, MB, R2J 4A9
(204) 253-1928
Emp Here 120
SIC 5812 Eating places
James Hunter

D-U-N-S 20-009-9463   (HQ)
MELET PLASTICS INC
34 De Baets St, Winnipeg, MB, R2J 3S9
(204) 667-6635
Emp Here 75   *Sales* 23,987,558
SIC 3089 Plastics products, nec
Bill Senton

D-U-N-S 20-010-1087   (HQ)
MONARCH INDUSTRIES LIMITED
LION HYDRAULICS
(*Suby of* MERIT CAPITAL PARTNERS IV, L.L.C.)
51 Burmac Rd, Winnipeg, MB, R2J 4J3
(204) 786-7921
Emp Here 350   *Sales* 140,438,500
SIC 3593 Fluid power cylinders and actuators
Gene Dunn
Roy Cook
Dan O'rourke
Bo Blundell

D-U-N-S 24-320-7797   (SL)
MONARCH INVESTMENTS LTD
51 Burmac Rd, Winnipeg, MB, R2J 4J3
(204) 786-7921
Emp Here 1   *Sales* 97,949,520
SIC 3369 Nonferrous foundries, nec
Donald Streuber

D-U-N-S 24-968-3798   (HQ)
NATIONAL SHIPPERS & RECEIVERS INC
TRANSPORT EASE & MANAGEMENT SERVICES
45 Beghin Ave Suite 7, Winnipeg, MB, R2J 4B9
(204) 222-6289
Emp Here 30   *Sales* 18,198,845
SIC 4731 Freight transportation arrangement

Elmer Thiessen

D-U-N-S 20-004-7397   (SL)
NELSON RIVER CONSTRUCTION INC
101 Dawson Rd N, Winnipeg, MB, R2J 0S6
(204) 949-8700
Emp Here 300   *Sales* 98,434,500
SIC 1611 Highway and street construction
Gordon Lee
Louis G Bouvier
Ervin Petkau

D-U-N-S 25-388-4415   (BR)
NEW FLYER INDUSTRIES CANADA ULC
NEW FLYER PARTS & PUBLICATIONS
(*Suby of* NFI GROUP INC)
25 De Baets St, Winnipeg, MB, R2J 4G5
(204) 982-8400
Emp Here 200
SIC 3711 Motor vehicles and car bodies
Hans Peper

D-U-N-S 24-034-8854   (SL)
OLYMPIC BUILDING SYSTEMS LTD
WAHKEHEKUN BUILDING SUPPLIES DIV
1783 Dugald Rd, Winnipeg, MB, R2J 0H3
(204) 661-8600
Emp Here 30   *Sales* 13,415,220
SIC 5039 Construction materials, nec
Blaine Reimer
Garry Roehr
John Reimer
William Fast

D-U-N-S 20-004-7579   (SL)
PARAMOUNT WINDOWS INC
105 Panet Rd, Winnipeg, MB, R2J 0S1
(204) 233-4966
Emp Here 75   *Sales* 15,142,275
SIC 3089 Plastics products, nec
Bernie Dudeck
Ken Dudeck
Tim Dudeck

D-U-N-S 24-571-6444   (BR)
PARMALAT CANADA INC
(*Suby of* PARMALAT SPA)
330 Mazenod Rd, Winnipeg, MB, R2J 4L2
(204) 654-6455
Emp Here 102
SIC 2026 Fluid milk
Ray Sinclair

D-U-N-S 24-818-7197   (SL)
PHASON INC
2 Terracon Pl, Winnipeg, MB, R2J 4G7
(204) 233-1400
Emp Here 25   *Sales* 11,179,350
SIC 5065 Electronic parts and equipment, nec
Tim Wilton
Norm Mathews

D-U-N-S 24-113-5094   (HQ)
POLARIS INDUSTRIES LTD
(*Suby of* POLARIS INDUSTRIES INC.)
50 Prairie Way, Winnipeg, MB, R2J 3J8
(204) 925-7100
Sales 21,852,900
SIC 5012 Automobiles and other motor vehicles
Tom Tiller
Norman Sukkau

D-U-N-S 20-434-0491   (SL)
PREMIER PRINTING LTD
1 Beghin Ave, Winnipeg, MB, R2J 3X5
(204) 663-9000
Emp Here 114   *Sales* 18,699,078
SIC 2752 Commercial printing, lithographic
William Gortemaker

D-U-N-S 24-607-8125   (HQ)
QSI INTERIORS LTD
120 Terracon Pl, Winnipeg, MB, R2J 4G7
(204) 235-0710
Emp Here 8   *Sales* 59,170,693
SIC 1742 Plastering, drywall, and insulation

Dean Vereschagin

D-U-N-S 24-314-6979   (SL)
QUALITY EDGE CONVERTING LTD
94 Durand Rd, Winnipeg, MB, R2J 3T2
(204) 256-4115
Emp Here 30   *Sales* 13,415,220
SIC 5049 Professional equipment, nec
Dwayne Riel

D-U-N-S 24-546-9796   (HQ)
RED RIVER COOPERATIVE LTD
CO-OP GAS BAR
10 Prairie Way, Winnipeg, MB, R2J 3J8
(204) 631-4600
Emp Here 15   *Sales* 343,464,940
SIC 5541 Gasoline service stations
Doug Wiebe
Murray Dehn
Gordon Grainger
Paul Bustard
Marcel Daeninck
Fred Homann
Judy Yeo
Greg Reiter

D-U-N-S 25-417-3982   (HQ)
RIDLEY INC
RIDLEY FEED OPERATIONS
(*Suby of* FAIRFAX FINANCIAL HOLDINGS LIMITED)
34 Terracon Pl, Winnipeg, MB, R2J 4G7
(204) 956-1717
Emp Here 6   *Sales* 441,570,810
SIC 2048 Prepared feeds, nec
Steven J. Vanroekel
Bradley P. Martin
Mark D. Nelson
Denis Daudet
Michael Hudspith
Robert E. Frost
K. Bruce Campbell
Wayne Harden
Brian Hayward
Larry J. Martin

D-U-N-S 20-294-1340   (HQ)
RIDLEY MF INC
EMF NUTRITION
715 Marion St, Winnipeg, MB, R2J 0K6
(204) 233-1112
Emp Here 10   *Sales* 44,939,700
SIC 2048 Prepared feeds, nec
Scott Miller

D-U-N-S 24-333-1548   (BR)
ROYAL CANADIAN MINT
(*Suby of* GOVERNMENT OF CANADA)
520 Lagimodiere Blvd, Winnipeg, MB, R2J 3E7
(204) 983-6400
Emp Here 450
SIC 5094 Jewelry and precious stones
Mark Neuendorff

D-U-N-S 25-022-3609   (HQ)
SPRINGS OF LIVING WATER CENTRE INC
SPRINGS CHURCH
595 Lagimodiere Blvd Suite 1, Winnipeg, MB, R2J 3X2
(204) 233-7003
Emp Here 61   *Sales* 17,700,910
SIC 8661 Religious organizations
Leon Fontaine
Abram Thiessen
Richard (Dick) Penner

D-U-N-S 25-408-6069   (HQ)
STAR BUILDING MATERIALS (ALBERTA) LTD
(*Suby of* QUALICO GROUP LTD)
16 Speers Rd, Winnipeg, MB, R2J 1L8
(204) 233-8687
Emp Here 1   *Sales* 26,765,200
SIC 5211 Lumber and other building materials
Brian Hastings
Ruth Hastings

Gerry Cadrin

D-U-N-S 24-967-8749   (HQ)
STAR BUILDING MATERIALS LTD
STAR TRUSS, DIV OF
(*Suby of* QUALICO GROUP LTD)
16 Speers Rd Suite 118, Winnipeg, MB, R2J
1L8
(204) 233-8687
Emp Here 80   *Sales* 40,147,800
SIC 5211 Lumber and other building materials
Ruth Hastings
Brian Hastings

D-U-N-S 24-968-3541   (HQ)
STURGEON TIRE (1993) LTD
STURGEON TIRE
791 Marion St, Winnipeg, MB, R2J 0K6
(204) 987-9566
Emp Here 20   *Sales* 20,031,825
SIC 5014 Tires and tubes
Jonathan Feldman
Ashley Leibl

D-U-N-S 25-976-5865   (SL)
TRANSCONA ROOFING (2000) LTD
992 Dugald Rd, Winnipeg, MB, R2J 0G9
(204) 233-3716
Emp Here 60   *Sales* 13,069,740
SIC 1761 Roofing, siding, and sheetMetal
work
Ronald C Simard
Paul A Simard

D-U-N-S 20-011-6259   (SL)
TRANSCONA TRAILER SALES LTD
1330 Dugald Rd, Winnipeg, MB, R2J 0H2
(204) 237-7272
Emp Here 25   *Sales* 12,451,950
SIC 5561 Recreational vehicle dealers
Garth Bromley
Terry Bromley

D-U-N-S 20-523-1033   (SL)
UNIVERSAL DRUG STORE LTD
1329 Niakwa Rd E Unit 9, Winnipeg, MB, R2J
3T4
(204) 255-9911
Emp Here 120   *Sales* 29,319,360
SIC 5961 Catalog and mail-order houses
Jeremy Cockerill
Jeff Uhl

D-U-N-S 25-362-3839   (SL)
VANTAGE FOODS (MB) INC
(*Suby of* WESTAR FOODS LTD)
41 Paquin Rd, Winnipeg, MB, R2J 3V9
(204) 667-9903
Emp Here 130   *Sales* 44,939,700
SIC 2011 Meat packing plants
Gary Haley

D-U-N-S 20-514-3196   (BR)
VANTAGE FOODS INC
(*Suby of* WESTAR FOODS LTD)
41 Paquin Rd, Winnipeg, MB, R2J 3V9
(204) 667-9903
Emp Here 150   *Sales* 44,939,700
SIC 2011 Meat packing plants
Mary Shananon

D-U-N-S 24-607-9859   (HQ)
VITA HEALTH PRODUCTS INC
(*Suby of* KKR & CO. INC.)
150 Beghin Ave, Winnipeg, MB, R2J 3W2
(204) 661-8386
Emp Here 485   *Sales* 165,797,000
SIC 2833 Medicinals and botanicals
Rachel Cahill
Stephanie Haverstick
Steven J. Conboy
Joseph Looney
Harvey Kamil

D-U-N-S 20-011-8776   (HQ)
WEST END TIRE (1990) LTD
1991 Dugald Rd, Winnipeg, MB, R2J 0H3

(204) 663-9037
Emp Here 42   *Sales* 42,791,040
SIC 5531 Auto and home supply stores
Andre Collet
Gisele Collet

D-U-N-S 20-165-3313   (BR)
**WINNIPEG REGIONAL HEALTH AUTHOR-
ITY, THE**
NUTRITION & FOOD SERVICES
(*Suby of* WINNIPEG REGIONAL HEALTH
AUTHORITY, THE)
345 De Baets St, Winnipeg, MB, R2J 3V6
(204) 654-5100
Emp Here 205
SIC 8099 Health and allied services, nec
Kathleen Richardson

D-U-N-S 20-922-6112   (BR)
XPLORNET COMMUNICATIONS INC
(*Suby of* BARRETT CORPORATION)
275 De Baets St Suite 4, Winnipeg, MB, R2J
4A8
(204) 669-7007
Emp Here 300
SIC 4813 Telephone communication, except
radio
Doug Downie

Winnipeg, MB R2K

D-U-N-S 20-007-1595   (HQ)
AUTOLINE PRODUCTS LTD
675 Golspie St, Winnipeg, MB, R2K 2V2
(204) 668-8242
Emp Here 62   *Sales* 16,650,075
SIC 3592 Carburetors, pistons, piston rings
and valves
Cyril Russell

D-U-N-S 20-836-0198   (SL)
**BETHANIA MENNONITE PERSONAL CARE
HOME INC**
1045 Concordia Ave, Winnipeg, MB, R2K 3S7
(204) 667-0795
Emp Here 350   *Sales* 22,498,700
SIC 8361 Residential care
Anita Kampen
Tony Driedger

D-U-N-S 20-569-7428   (SL)
BUILDERS FURNITURE LTD
695 Washington Ave, Winnipeg, MB, R2K 1M4
(204) 668-0783
Emp Here 65   *Sales* 10,030,930
SIC 2541 Wood partitions and fixtures
Greg Patenaude

D-U-N-S 20-013-1980   (BR)
CASCADES CANADA ULC
CASCADES BOXBOARD GROUP, DIV OF
(*Suby of* CASCADES INC)
531 Golspie St, Winnipeg, MB, R2K 2T9
(204) 667-6600
Emp Here 240
SIC 2657 Folding paperboard boxes

D-U-N-S 20-758-9649   (SL)
CONCORDIA HOSPITAL
1095 Concordia Ave, Winnipeg, MB, R2K 3S8
(204) 667-1560
Emp Here 1,100   *Sales* 122,188,000
SIC 8062 General medical and surgical hospi-
tals
Henry Tessmann
Les Janzen
Elizabeth Wall

D-U-N-S 24-914-8917   (SL)
**FIRST CHOICE COURIER & MESSENGER
LTD**
704 Watt St, Winnipeg, MB, R2K 2S7
(204) 661-3668
Emp Here 42   *Sales* 18,626,580
SIC 7389 Business services, nec

Harvey Chemerika

D-U-N-S 20-834-7617   (HQ)
GORDON HOTELS & MOTOR INNS LTD
CURTIS GORDON MOTOR HOTEL
1011 Henderson Hwy, Winnipeg, MB, R2K
2M2
(204) 334-4355
Sales 14,274,260
SIC 7011 Hotels and motels
Lawrence Jocelyn
Donald Stewart

D-U-N-S 20-029-3968   (SL)
**GRAPHIC PACKAGING INTERNATIONAL
CANADA ULC**
(*Suby of* GRAPHIC PACKAGING HOLDING
COMPANY)
531 Golspie St, Winnipeg, MB, R2K 2T9
(204) 667-6600
Emp Here 140   *Sales* 27,267,520
SIC 2631 Paperboard mills
Herp Cielhaver

D-U-N-S 25-369-3642   (HQ)
JELD-WEN OF CANADA LTD
JELD-WEN WINDOWS & DOORS
(*Suby of* JELD-WEN HOLDING, INC.)
485 Watt St, Winnipeg, MB, R2K 2R9
(204) 694-6012
Emp Here 100   *Sales* 288,555,000
SIC 2431 Millwork
Barry J Homrighaus
Bill Donaldson

D-U-N-S 25-386-1389   (BR)
LOBLAWS INC
REAL-CANADIAN SUPERSTORES
(*Suby of* LOBLAW COMPANIES LIMITED)
1035 Gateway Rd Suite 1512, Winnipeg, MB,
R2K 4C1
(204) 987-7534
Emp Here 200
SIC 5141 Groceries, general line
Pat Scoular

D-U-N-S 20-814-5420   (SL)
POLAR RAY-O-MAX WINDOWS LTD
672 Kimberly Ave, Winnipeg, MB, R2K 0Y2
(204) 956-6555
Emp Here 100   *Sales* 20,189,700
SIC 3089 Plastics products, nec
Phil Tait

D-U-N-S 20-010-6540   (HQ)
PRICE INDUSTRIES LIMITED
E.H. PRICE DIVISION
638 Raleigh St, Winnipeg, MB, R2K 3Z9
(204) 669-4220
Emp Here 700   *Sales* 3,405,234,000
SIC 3496 Miscellaneous fabricated wire prod-
ucts
Gerald Price
Rick Geyson
Graig Brown

D-U-N-S 25-090-0008   (SL)
RIVER EAST PERSONAL CARE HOME LTD
1375 Molson St, Winnipeg, MB, R2K 4K8
(204) 668-7460
Emp Here 160   *Sales* 10,970,560
SIC 8059 Nursing and personal care, nec
Michael Baron

D-U-N-S 20-946-0336   (HQ)
**RIVER EAST TRANSCONA SCHOOL DIVI-
SION**
589 Roch St, Winnipeg, MB, R2K 2P7
(204) 667-7130
Emp Here 65   *Sales* 218,061,800
SIC 8211 Elementary and secondary schools
Dennis Pottage
Vince Mariani
Robert Fraser

D-U-N-S 25-272-3762   (BR)
**RIVER EAST TRANSCONA SCHOOL DIVI-
SION**

KILDONAN-EAST COLLEGIATE
(*Suby of* RIVER EAST TRANSCONA
SCHOOL DIVISION)
845 Concordia Ave, Winnipeg, MB, R2K 2M6
(204) 667-2960
Emp Here 125
SIC 8211 Elementary and secondary schools
Darwin Macfarlane

D-U-N-S 25-369-8914   (BR)
**RIVER EAST TRANSCONA SCHOOL DIVI-
SION**
SALISBURY MORSE PLACE SCHOOL
(*Suby of* RIVER EAST TRANSCONA
SCHOOL DIVISION)
795 Prince Rupert Ave, Winnipeg, MB, R2K
1W6
(204) 668-9304
Emp Here 90
SIC 8211 Elementary and secondary schools
Marjorie Millman

D-U-N-S 20-555-3386   (BR)
**RIVER EAST TRANSCONA SCHOOL DIVI-
SION**
MILES MACDONELL COLLEGIATE
(*Suby of* RIVER EAST TRANSCONA
SCHOOL DIVISION)
757 Roch St, Winnipeg, MB, R2K 2R1
(204) 667-1103
Emp Here 85
SIC 8211 Elementary and secondary schools
Vivien Laurie

D-U-N-S 25-957-7971   (BR)
RONA INC
HOME & GARDEN BY RONA
(*Suby of* LOWE'S COMPANIES, INC.)
775 Panet Rd, Winnipeg, MB, R2K 4C6
(204) 663-7389
Emp Here 250
SIC 5211 Lumber and other building materials
Tammy Kondryshyn

D-U-N-S 20-835-3771   (HQ)
ROYAL SPORTS SHOP LTD
650 Raleigh St, Winnipeg, MB, R2K 3Z9
(204) 668-4584
Emp Here 30   *Sales* 14,659,680
SIC 5941 Sporting goods and bicycle shops
John H Haasbeek
Gerald Haasbeek

D-U-N-S 24-028-1415   (BR)
SOBEYS CAPITAL INCORPORATED
SOBEYS
(*Suby of* EMPIRE COMPANY LIMITED)
965 Henderson Hwy, Winnipeg, MB, R2K 2M2
(204) 338-0349
Emp Here 150
SIC 5411 Grocery stores
Jeff Clendenan

D-U-N-S 20-011-3751   (SL)
**STANDARD MANUFACTURERS SERVICES
LTD**
STANDARD HEAT TREATING
691 Golspie St, Winnipeg, MB, R2K 2V3
(204) 956-6300
Emp Here 90   *Sales* 42,752,340
SIC 5084 Industrial machinery and equipment
Rolf Gretschmann

D-U-N-S 24-336-6445   (BR)
**WINNIPEG REGIONAL HEALTH AUTHOR-
ITY, THE**
ACCESS RIVER EAST
(*Suby of* WINNIPEG REGIONAL HEALTH
AUTHORITY, THE)
975 Henderson Hwy, Winnipeg, MB, R2K 4L7
(204) 938-5000
Emp Here 200
SIC 8093 Specialty outpatient clinics, nec
Christine Duprat

▲ Public Company   ■ Public Company Family Member   **HQ** Headquarters   **BR** Branch   **SL** Single Location

Winnipeg, MB R2L

D-U-N-S 20-007-0142   (HQ)
ALLMAR INC
ALLMAR INTERNATIONAL
287 Riverton Ave, Winnipeg, MB, R2L 0N2
(204) 668-1000
Emp Here 43   *Sales* 156,647,700
SIC 5039 Construction materials, nec
 Edwin Redekopp
 Arthur Redekopp
 Ron Jonkman
 Brad Miles
 Paul Porco

D-U-N-S 20-007-0266   (HQ)
ALSIP'S INDUSTRIAL PRODUCTS LTD
1 Cole Ave, Winnipeg, MB, R2L 1J3
(204) 667-3330
Emp Here 27   *Sales* 13,415,220
SIC 5039 Construction materials, nec
 Frank Wayne Alsip
 Bradley Alsip
 Jason Alsip

D-U-N-S 20-833-6917   (SL)
CORREIA ENTERPRISES LTD
BEE CLEAN CENTRAL
375 Nairn Ave, Winnipeg, MB, R2L 0W8
(204) 668-4420
Emp Here 7,000   *Sales* 223,776,000
SIC 7349 Building maintenance services, nec
 Joe Correia

D-U-N-S 24-882-4823   (SL)
FOCUS MOTORS LIMITED
FOCUS HYUNDAI
1066 Nairn Ave, Winnipeg, MB, R2L 0Y4
(204) 663-3814
Emp Here 24   *Sales* 11,953,872
SIC 5511 New and used car dealers
 John Carey
 Tom Carey

D-U-N-S 24-653-7625   (HQ)
MIDLAND FOODS (WINNIPEG), INC
GOLDEN GATE SEAFOOD
900 Nairn Ave, Winnipeg, MB, R2L 0X8
(204) 663-3883
Sales 25,067,310
SIC 5146 Fish and seafoods
 Tim Chu
 Louisa Chu Young
 Thomas Lai

D-U-N-S 24-571-5289   (SL)
NAIRN VACUUM & APPLIANCE
929 Nairn Ave, Winnipeg, MB, R2L 0X9
(204) 668-4901
Emp Here 58   *Sales* 13,479,374
SIC 5722 Household appliance stores
 Krishna Goolcharan

D-U-N-S 20-011-0096   (HQ)
NORDSTRONG EQUIPMENT LIMITED
(*Suby of* CANERECTOR INC)
5 Chester St, Winnipeg, MB, R2L 1W5
(204) 667-1553
Emp Here 85   *Sales* 43,895,700
SIC 5083 Farm and garden machinery
 Terry Milnes
 Cecil Hawkins
 Maynard Young

D-U-N-S 20-552-7950   (SL)
ORTYNSKY AUTOMOTIVE COMPANY LTD
ORTYNSKY, TERRY KIA
980 Nairn Ave, Winnipeg, MB, R2L 0Y2
(204) 654-0440
Emp Here 27   *Sales* 13,448,106
SIC 5511 New and used car dealers

D-U-N-S 25-678-1063   (SL)
ORTYNSKY NISSAN LTD
980 Nairn Ave, Winnipeg, MB, R2L 0Y2

(204) 669-0791
Emp Here 26   *Sales* 12,950,028
SIC 5511 New and used car dealers
 Terry Ortynsky

D-U-N-S 24-034-3561   (SL)
PRO FAB SUNROOMS LTD
342 Nairn Ave, Winnipeg, MB, R2L 0W9
(204) 668-3544
Emp Here 67   *Sales* 12,869,695
SIC 3448 Prefabricated Metal buildings and components
 Stephen Kisil

D-U-N-S 24-333-8956   (BR)
QSI INTERIORS LTD
(*Suby of* QSI INTERIORS LTD)
975 Thomas Ave Unit 1, Winnipeg, MB, R2L 1P7
(204) 953-1200
Emp Here 75
SIC 1742 Plastering, drywall, and insulation
 Pat Lee

Winnipeg, MB R2M

D-U-N-S 25-483-8220   (SL)
A LEADER BUILDING CLEANING SERVICES OF CANADA LTD
894 St Mary'S Rd, Winnipeg, MB, R2M 3R1
(204) 255-4000
Emp Here 285   *Sales* 9,110,880
SIC 7349 Building maintenance services, nec
 Sam Elharouni

D-U-N-S 20-115-3049   (SL)
AIL CANADA
1549 St Mary'S Rd Suite 101, Winnipeg, MB, R2M 5G9
(204) 942-9477
Emp Here 34   *Sales* 62,786,406
SIC 6311 Life insurance

D-U-N-S 20-643-7373   (SL)
CARA FOODS
MONTANA'S COOKHOUSE SALOON
1221 St Mary'S Rd, Winnipeg, MB, R2M 5L5
(204) 254-2128
Emp Here 80   *Sales* 3,641,520
SIC 5812 Eating places
 Michelle Field
 Rod Greening

D-U-N-S 24-914-0864   (HQ)
CENTURY 21 CARRIE REALTY LTD
CENTURY 21 CARRIE.COM
1046 St Mary'S Rd, Winnipeg, MB, R2M 5S6
(204) 987-2100
Emp Here 50   *Sales* 31,416,675
SIC 6531 Real estate agents and managers
 Gerry Carriere
 Raymond Carriere
 George Bohemier

D-U-N-S 25-514-2812   (BR)
HOME DEPOT OF CANADA INC
HOME DEPOT
(*Suby of* THE HOME DEPOT INC)
1999 Bishop Grandin Blvd, Winnipeg, MB, R2M 5S1
(204) 253-7649
Emp Here 200
SIC 5251 Hardware stores
 Bill Lennie

D-U-N-S 24-968-5652   (SL)
HOUGHTAM ENTERPRISES
MOXIE'S RESTAURANT
1225 St Mary'S Rd Suite 49, Winnipeg, MB, R2M 5E5
(204) 257-1132
Emp Here 90   *Sales* 3,858,570
SIC 5812 Eating places
 Brad Houghton
 Darin Amies

D-U-N-S 20-517-3086   (BR)
LOUIS RIEL SCHOOL DIVISION
DAKOTA COLLEGIATE INSTITUTE
(*Suby of* LOUIS RIEL SCHOOL DIVISION)
661 Dakota St, Winnipeg, MB, R2M 3K3
(204) 256-4366
Emp Here 100
SIC 8211 Elementary and secondary schools
 Jill Mathez

D-U-N-S 25-362-2955   (HQ)
LOUIS RIEL SCHOOL DIVISION
LOUIS RIEL SCHOOL DIVISION BOARD OFFICE
900 St Mary'S Rd, Winnipeg, MB, R2M 3R3
(204) 257-7827
Emp Here 10   *Sales* 194,174,121
SIC 8211 Elementary and secondary schools
 Marna Kenny
 Christian Michalik

D-U-N-S 25-144-2463   (BR)
LOUIS RIEL SCHOOL DIVISION
GLENLAWN COLLEGIATE INSTITUTE
(*Suby of* LOUIS RIEL SCHOOL DIVISION)
770 St Mary'S Rd, Winnipeg, MB, R2M 3N7
(204) 233-3263
Emp Here 100
SIC 8211 Elementary and secondary schools
 Irene Nordheim

D-U-N-S 24-040-4434   (SL)
MANITOBA BAPTIST HOME SOCIETY INC
MEADOWOOD MANOR
577 St Anne'S Rd, Winnipeg, MB, R2M 3G5
(204) 257-2394
Emp Here 100   *Sales* 6,856,600
SIC 8051 Skilled nursing care facilities
 Charles Kunze

D-U-N-S 24-915-8650   (SL)
NORVAN ENTERPRISES (1982) LTD
246 Dunkirk Dr, Winnipeg, MB, R2M 3W9
(204) 257-0373
Emp Here 75   *Sales* 3,215,475
SIC 5812 Eating places
 Norman Van Elslander
 Margaret Van Elslander

D-U-N-S 20-814-5560   (SL)
R M KOMAR ENTERPRISES LIMITED
ST. MARY'S CO-OP
1621 St Mary'S Rd, Winnipeg, MB, R2M 3W8
(204) 254-4955
Emp Here 22   *Sales* 10,957,716
SIC 5541 Gasoline service stations
 Scott Amstrong

D-U-N-S 25-021-6942   (HQ)
RE/MAX PERFORMANCE REALTY
942 St Mary'S Rd, Winnipeg, MB, R2M 3R5
(204) 255-4204
Emp Here 1   *Sales* 37,700,010
SIC 6531 Real estate agents and managers
 Aaron Joseph
 Tom Fulton

D-U-N-S 24-575-0935   (SL)
ROYAL LEPAGE TOP PRODUCERS
1549 St Mary'S Rd Suite 6, Winnipeg, MB, R2M 5G9
(204) 989-6900
Emp Here 40   *Sales* 10,870,240
SIC 6531 Real estate agents and managers
 Glenn Ponomarenko

D-U-N-S 20-050-3089   (BR)
SOBEYS CAPITAL INCORPORATED
ST ANNES SOBEYS
(*Suby of* EMPIRE COMPANY LIMITED)
1939 Bishop Grandin Blvd, Winnipeg, MB, R2M 5S1
(204) 255-5064
Emp Here 192
SIC 5411 Grocery stores
 Randy Leclerc

D-U-N-S 20-836-9215   (SL)

ST AMANT INC
440 River Rd, Winnipeg, MB, R2M 3Z9
(204) 256-4301
Emp Here 1,500   *Sales* 102,489,000
SIC 8059 Nursing and personal care, nec
 Carl Stevens
 Paulette Perrault
 Harry Casey

D-U-N-S 25-289-0975   (BR)
WAL-MART CANADA CORP
(*Suby of* WALMART INC.)
1225 St Mary'S Rd Suite 54, Winnipeg, MB, R2M 5E6
(204) 256-7027
Emp Here 300
SIC 5311 Department stores
 Douglas Hall

D-U-N-S 25-270-1495   (SL)
WESTFAIR FOODS LTD
REAL CANADIAN SUPERSTORE
215 St Anne'S Rd, Winnipeg, MB, R2M 2Z9
(204) 258-2419
Emp Here 45   *Sales* 12,336,840
SIC 5411 Grocery stores
 Robert Bernard

Winnipeg, MB R2N

D-U-N-S 24-776-2198   (SL)
MOM'S PANTRY PRODUCTS LTD
JIM E' LEONIE
3241 St Mary'S Rd, Winnipeg, MB, R2N 4B4
(204) 954-2060
Emp Here 20   *Sales* 10,702,480
SIC 5142 Packaged frozen goods
 Leonie Olcen
 Maureen Wiebe
 Glenn Olcen

D-U-N-S 24-427-8172   (SL)
ODD FELLOWS & REBEKAHS PERSONAL CARE HOMES INC
GOLDEN LINKS LODGE
2280 St Mary'S Rd, Winnipeg, MB, R2N 3Z6
(204) 257-9947
Emp Here 130   *Sales* 8,882,380
SIC 8051 Skilled nursing care facilities
 Mary Knight
 Herman Nikkel

D-U-N-S 20-165-3008   (BR)
SOBEYS CAPITAL INCORPORATED
ST VITAL GARDEN MARKET IGA
(*Suby of* EMPIRE COMPANY LIMITED)
1500 Dakota St Suite 1, Winnipeg, MB, R2N 3Y7
(204) 253-3663
Emp Here 100
SIC 5411 Grocery stores
 Keith Mcdougall

D-U-N-S 24-546-1546   (SL)
VISTA PARK LODGE
144 Novavista Dr, Winnipeg, MB, R2N 1P8
(204) 257-6688
Emp Here 130   *Sales* 9,982,960
SIC 8322 Individual and family services
 Melvin S Fages

D-U-N-S 24-349-7034   (BR)
WINNIPEG REGIONAL HEALTH AUTHORITY, THE
RIVER PARK GARDENS
(*Suby of* WINNIPEG REGIONAL HEALTH AUTHORITY, THE)
735 St Anne'S Rd, Winnipeg, MB, R2N 0C4
(204) 255-9073
Emp Here 100
SIC 8361 Residential care
 Linda Norton

▲ Public Company   ■ Public Company Family Member   **HQ** Headquarters   **BR** Branch   **SL** Single Location

Winnipeg, MB R2P

D-U-N-S 20-074-8460   (HQ)
CANAD CORPORATION LTD
AALTO'S FAMILY DINING
930 Jefferson Ave Suite 3, Winnipeg, MB, R2P 1W1
(204) 697-1495
Emp Here 30   *Sales* 15,599,010
SIC 4724 Travel agencies
  Leo Ledohowski
  Dan Lussier

D-U-N-S 20-072-7873   (HQ)
CANAD CORPORATION OF MANITOBA LTD
CANAD INNS EXPRESS FORT GARRY (CELEBRATIONS, ALLEY CATZ, THE BEACH NIGHT CLUB)
930 Jefferson Ave Suite 3, Winnipeg, MB, R2P 1W1
(204) 697-1495
Emp Here 35   *Sales* 172,202,400
SIC 7011 Hotels and motels
  Leon Norman Ledohowski

D-U-N-S 20-711-9702   (HQ)
CUBEX LIMITED
42 St Paul Blvd, Winnipeg, MB, R2P 2W5
(204) 336-0008
Sales 35,626,950
SIC 5082 Construction and mining machinery
  H H Kitch Wilson
  William E J Wilson

D-U-N-S 24-375-5832   (SL)
MAPLES PERSONAL CARE HOME (1982) LTD
500 Mandalay Dr, Winnipeg, MB, R2P 1V4
(204) 632-8570
Emp Here 205   *Sales* 14,006,830
SIC 8051 Skilled nursing care facilities
  Ed Pollock
  Fred Bohna
  Michael Baron

D-U-N-S 25-127-9626   (BR)
SEVEN OAKS SCHOOL DIVISION
MAPLES COLLEGIATE
(*Suby of* SEVEN OAKS SCHOOL DIVISION)
1330 Jefferson Ave, Winnipeg, MB, R2P 1L3
(204) 632-6641
Emp Here 133
SIC 8211 Elementary and secondary schools
  Blair Peppler

D-U-N-S 25-288-5132   (SL)
ST. JOSEPH'S RESIDENCE INC
1149 Leila Ave, Winnipeg, MB, R2P 1S6
(204) 697-8031
Emp Here 150   *Sales* 10,248,900
SIC 8059 Nursing and personal care, nec
  Charles Gagne

Winnipeg, MB R2R

D-U-N-S 20-164-5921   (HQ)
4131827 MANITOBA LTD
WATERITE TECHNOLOGIES
75 Meridian Dr Unit 3, Winnipeg, MB, R2R 2V9
(204) 786-1604
Emp Here 17   *Sales* 15,651,090
SIC 5074 Plumbing and heating equipment and supplies (hydronics)
  Paul Jacuzzi

D-U-N-S 20-042-0607   (HQ)
625056 SASKATCHEWAN LTD
PETRO CANADA
1050 Keewatin St, Winnipeg, MB, R2R 2E2
(204) 694-0085
Emp Here 5   *Sales* 13,707,600

SIC 5411 Grocery stores
  Bev Gardner
  Deb Gardner

D-U-N-S 25-417-4295   (HQ)
CADORATH AEROSPACE INC
(*Suby of* CADORATH HOLDINGS INC)
2070 Logan Ave, Winnipeg, MB, R2R 0H9
(204) 633-2707
Sales 13,430,580
SIC 3728 Aircraft parts and equipment, nec
  Gerald J. Cadorath
  Gerald O. Cadorath

D-U-N-S 24-519-5847   (BR)
CANADIAN LINEN AND UNIFORM SERVICE CO
(*Suby of* ARAMARK)
1860 King Edward St, Winnipeg, MB, R2R 0N2
(204) 633-7261
Emp Here 150
SIC 7213 Linen supply

D-U-N-S 25-137-1134   (HQ)
CARTE INTERNATIONAL INC
(*Suby of* CROCUS INVESTMENT FUND)
1995 Logan Ave, Winnipeg, MB, R2R 0H8
(204) 633-7220
Emp Here 305   *Sales* 87,703,650
SIC 3612 Transformers, except electric
  Brian Klaponski
  Gary Mowat

D-U-N-S 25-170-9200   (SL)
CONNEXION TRUCK CENTRE LTD
440 Oak Point Hwy, Winnipeg, MB, R2R 1V3
(204) 633-3333
Emp Here 45   *Sales* 22,413,510
SIC 5511 New and used car dealers
  Kenneth Cranwill
  Gilles Bouchard
  Marshall Love

D-U-N-S 20-837-3415   (HQ)
DENRAY TIRE LTD
344 Oak Point Hwy, Winnipeg, MB, R2R 1V1
(204) 632-7339
Emp Here 4   *Sales* 14,132,790
SIC 3011 Tires and inner tubes
  Derek Braun
  Brad Braun
  Dennis Braun

D-U-N-S 20-152-1809   (HQ)
DIXON GROUP CANADA LIMITED
2200 Logan Ave, Winnipeg, MB, R2R 0J2
(204) 633-5650
Emp Here 1   *Sales* 78,036,800
SIC 5084 Industrial machinery and equipment
  Cam Phang
  Julian Huby

D-U-N-S 20-007-8897   (HQ)
FORT GARRY INDUSTRIES LTD
FGI
2525 Inkster Blvd Unit 2, Winnipeg, MB, R2R 2Y4
(204) 632-8261
Emp Here 100   *Sales* 239,800,080
SIC 5013 Motor vehicle supplies and new parts
  Richard Spitzke
  Robyn Spitzke
  Chris Spitzke
  Jeff Carriere

D-U-N-S 24-883-7049   (HQ)
FREIGHTLINER MANITOBA LTD
2058 Logan Ave, Winnipeg, MB, R2R 0H9
(204) 694-3000
Emp Here 74   *Sales* 59,781,600
SIC 5511 New and used car dealers
  Barry Talbot
  Ken Talbot
  Rod Snyder
  Braden Kulchycki

D-U-N-S 20-137-0546   (SL)
FRESH HEMP FOODS LTD
MANITOBA HARVEST
69 Eagle Dr, Winnipeg, MB, R2R 1V4
(204) 953-0233
Emp Here 150   *Sales* 51,853,500
SIC 2032 Canned specialties
  Michael Fata
  John Durkin
  Barry Tomiski

D-U-N-S 24-426-8483   (HQ)
GARDEWINE GROUP INC
GARDEWINE NORTH
(*Suby of* MULLEN GROUP LTD)
60 Eagle Dr, Winnipeg, MB, R2R 1V5
(204) 633-5795
Emp Here 50   *Sales* 666,892,000
SIC 4731 Freight transportation arrangement
  Darin Downey
  Alex Shewtchenko

D-U-N-S 25-118-8520   (HQ)
KENORA FOREST PRODUCTS LTD
RYAN FOREST PRODUCTS, DIV OF
(*Suby of* PRENDIVILLE CORPORATION)
165 Ryan St, Winnipeg, MB, R2R 0N9
(204) 989-9600
Sales 19,237,000
SIC 2421 Sawmills and planing mills, general
  Maureen Prendiville
  James Prendiville
  Michael Prendiville

D-U-N-S 20-945-6565   (SL)
LOWE MECHANICAL SERVICES LTD
72 Park Lane Ave, Winnipeg, MB, R2R 0K2
(204) 233-3292
Emp Here 95   *Sales* 22,141,175
SIC 1711 Plumbing, heating, air-conditioning
  Jennifer Lowe

D-U-N-S 25-011-0855   (BR)
MCDONALD'S RESTAURANTS OF CANADA LIMITED
MCDONALD'S
(*Suby of* MCDONALD'S CORPORATION)
994 Keewatin St, Winnipeg, MB, R2R 2V1
(204) 949-6079
Emp Here 78
SIC 5812 Eating places
  Amit Thamik

D-U-N-S 25-328-7114   (HQ)
MILLER ENVIRONMENTAL CORPORATION
1803 Hekla Ave, Winnipeg, MB, R2R 0K3
(204) 925-9600
Emp Here 14   *Sales* 10,542,371
SIC 4953 Refuse systems

D-U-N-S 20-948-7016   (HQ)
MOORE INDUSTRIAL LTD
MI CONSTRUCTION SUPPLY
169 Omands Creek Blvd, Winnipeg, MB, R2R 1V9
(204) 632-4092
Emp Here 29   *Sales* 26,601,456
SIC 5084 Industrial machinery and equipment
  Gary Moore
  Leah Anne Moore

D-U-N-S 24-917-2263   (HQ)
NORTHERN CARTAGE LIMITED
NORTHERN LOGISTICS, DIV OF
60 Eagle Dr Suite 204, Winnipeg, MB, R2R 1V5
(204) 633-5795
Emp Here 30   *Sales* 30,855,900
SIC 4213 Trucking, except local
  Paul Albrechtsen

D-U-N-S 20-647-6848   (SL)
OAK POINT SERVICE
272 Oak Point Hwy, Winnipeg, MB, R2R 1V1
(204) 633-9435
Emp Here 70   *Sales* 19,831,000
SIC 7538 General automotive repair shops

  John Albrechtsen

D-U-N-S 20-010-4776   (HQ)
PAUL'S HAULING LTD
250 Oak Point Hwy, Winnipeg, MB, R2R 1V1
(204) 633-4330
Emp Here 115   *Sales* 55,314,300
SIC 4213 Trucking, except local
  Paul Albrechtsen
  Rodney Corbett
  Gordon Beazley

D-U-N-S 24-320-3598   (HQ)
PAYNE TRANSPORTATION LTD
(*Suby of* MT-NU OPERATING COMPANY INC)
435 Lucas Ave, Winnipeg, MB, R2R 2S9
(204) 953-1400
Sales 15,854,300
SIC 6712 Bank holding companies
  Tom Payne Jr
  Pauline Wiebe Peters
  Jason Mcnicholl

D-U-N-S 20-944-6079   (HQ)
PETERBILT MANITOBA LTD
PETERBILT MANITOBA PACLEASE
1895 Brookside Blvd, Winnipeg, MB, R2R 2Y3
(204) 633-0071
Emp Here 75   *Sales* 56,635,200
SIC 5511 New and used car dealers
  Douglas Danylchuk

D-U-N-S 25-315-6822   (SL)
POLYTUBES (MAN) INC
1803 Hekla Ave, Winnipeg, MB, R2R 0K3

Emp Here 200   *Sales* 92,008,800
SIC 5074 Plumbing and heating equipment and supplies (hydronics)
  Mary Mccaffery

D-U-N-S 25-533-8535   (HQ)
PRENDIVILLE CORPORATION
165 Ryan St, Winnipeg, MB, R2R 0N9
(204) 989-9600
Sales 12,652,950
SIC 5211 Lumber and other building materials
  Maureen Patricia Prendiville
  Michael Lawrence Prendiville
  James Ailbe Prendiville

D-U-N-S 20-278-6729   (SL)
PRICE MECHANICAL LIMITED
(*Suby of* PRICE INDUSTRIES LIMITED)
404 Egesz St, Winnipeg, MB, R2R 1X5
(204) 633-4808
Emp Here 90   *Sales* 20,975,850
SIC 1711 Plumbing, heating, air-conditioning
  Gerald V Price

D-U-N-S 24-519-7843   (SL)
RUSS PATERSON LTD
NORTHERN MEAT SERVICE
49 Omands Creek Blvd, Winnipeg, MB, R2R 2V2
(204) 985-5400
Emp Here 35   *Sales* 29,245,195
SIC 5147 Meats and meat products
  Russ Paterson

D-U-N-S 24-559-2118   (HQ)
RW CONSUMER PRODUCTS LTD
200 Omands Creek Blvd, Winnipeg, MB, R2R 1V7
(204) 786-6873
Emp Here 60   *Sales* 19,881,470
SIC 2834 Pharmaceutical preparations
  Henry A De Ruiter
  Bernice Ryzowski
  Vincent P Pileggi
  Deanne Downey

D-U-N-S 20-836-5197   (SL)
SATURN INDUSTRIES LTD
37 Sylvan Way, Winnipeg, MB, R2R 2B9
(204) 633-1529
Emp Here 24   *Sales* 10,732,176

SIC 5072 Hardware
John Lang
Kathy Lang
Keith Fisher

D-U-N-S 24-230-0184 (SL)
SIERRA MESSENGER & COURIER SER-VICE LTD
SIERRA MESSENGER & COURIER
165 Ryan St, Winnipeg, MB, R2R 0N9
(204) 632-8920
Emp Here 30 *Sales* 13,304,700
SIC 7389 Business services, nec
Barry Bruce

D-U-N-S 25-271-7822 (BR)
SOBEYS WEST INC
BURROWS & KEEWATIN SAFEWAY
(*Suby of* EMPIRE COMPANY LIMITED)
850 Keewatin St Suite 12, Winnipeg, MB, R2R 0Z5
(204) 632-6763
Emp Here 100
SIC 5411 Grocery stores
Len Bergunder

D-U-N-S 20-718-2523 (BR)
TOROMONT INDUSTRIES LTD
CATERPILLAR
(*Suby of* TOROMONT INDUSTRIES LTD)
140 Inksbrook Dr, Winnipeg, MB, R2R 2W3
(204) 453-4343
Emp Here 120
SIC 7699 Repair services, nec
John Mccallum

D-U-N-S 24-330-9544 (BR)
TST SOLUTIONS L.P.
TST PORTER, DIV OF
(*Suby of* TST SOLUTIONS L.P.)
1987 Brookside Blvd, Winnipeg, MB, R2R 2Y3
(204) 697-5795
Emp Here 500
SIC 4231 Trucking terminal facilities
Bob Senkow

D-U-N-S 20-689-7733 (HQ)
WATERITE, INC
200 Discovery Place Unit 5, Winnipeg, MB, R2R 0P7
(204) 786-1604
Emp Here 9 *Sales* 13,320,060
SIC 3589 Service industry machinery, nec
Paul Jacuzzi
Jo-Anne Duncan
Terry Mee

D-U-N-S 20-434-2869 (HQ)
WES-T-RANS COMPANY
515 Oak Point Hwy, Winnipeg, MB, R2R 1V2
(204) 633-9282
Emp Here 53 *Sales* 14,773,638
SIC 3714 Motor vehicle parts and accessories
John Williams

D-U-N-S 25-236-2512 (SL)
WINNIPEG EQUIPMENT SALES LTD
BEAVER TRUCK CENTER
33 Oak Point Hwy, Winnipeg, MB, R2R 0T8
(204) 632-9100
Emp Here 75 *Sales* 27,316,125
SIC 5012 Automobiles and other motor vehicles
Barry Searcy

D-U-N-S 25-022-4094 (BR)
WINNIPEG SCHOOL DIVISION
STANLEY KNOWLES SCHOOL
(*Suby of* WINNIPEG SCHOOL DIVISION)
2424 King Edward St, Winnipeg, MB, R2R 2R2
(204) 694-0483
Emp Here 96
SIC 8211 Elementary and secondary schools
John Drzystek

Winnipeg, MB R2V

D-U-N-S 25-678-9769 (SL)
3881793 MANITOBA LTD
SOBEY'S RIVERGROVE
2575 Main St, Winnipeg, MB, R2V 4W3
(204) 334-1211
Emp Here 135 *Sales* 39,619,395
SIC 5411 Grocery stores
Timothy Ward
Kimberly Ward

D-U-N-S 24-428-7322 (SL)
61401 MANITOBA LTD
MAIN STREET IGA
1650 Main St, Winnipeg, MB, R2V 1Y9
(204) 339-0213
Emp Here 78 *Sales* 22,891,206
SIC 5411 Grocery stores
William O'leary

D-U-N-S 20-571-7994 (BR)
ARMTEC INC
ARMTEC
(*Suby of* TREVLUC HOLDINGS LTD)
2500 Ferrier St, Winnipeg, MB, R2V 4P6
(204) 338-9311
Emp Here 80
SIC 3312 Blast furnaces and steel mills
Don Grant

D-U-N-S 24-032-4538 (SL)
AUTOWEST INC
2150 Mcphillips St, Winnipeg, MB, R2V 3C8
(204) 632-7135
Emp Here 24 *Sales* 11,953,872
SIC 5521 Used car dealers
Lawrence Isfeld

D-U-N-S 25-659-8251 (SL)
BLEAK HOUSE SENIOR'S CENTRE
1637 Main St, Winnipeg, MB, R2V 1Y8
(204) 338-4723
Emp Here 40 *Sales* 15,896,560
SIC 8699 Membership organizations, nec
Roger Lorkeau

D-U-N-S 24-968-3426 (BR)
CANAD CORPORATION OF CANADA INC
CANAD INNS GARDEN CITY
2100 Mcphillips St, Winnipeg, MB, R2V 3T9
(204) 633-0024
Emp Here 200
SIC 7011 Hotels and motels
Rob Roberts

D-U-N-S 25-668-4119 (SL)
COMPLETE CARE INC
1801 Main St, Winnipeg, MB, R2V 2A2
(204) 949-5090
Emp Here 100 *Sales* 6,873,300
SIC 8051 Skilled nursing care facilities
Aaron Nudler

D-U-N-S 24-114-2363 (HQ)
DON'S PHOTO SHOP LTD
LABWORKS, THE
1839 Main St, Winnipeg, MB, R2V 2A4
(204) 942-7887
Emp Here 35 *Sales* 20,767,880
SIC 5946 Camera and photographic supply stores
Donald Godfrey
Michael Godfrey
Tamara Warwick
Judith Godfrey

D-U-N-S 20-007-9077 (SL)
GAUTHIER, JIM CHEVROLET LTD
1400 Mcphillips St, Winnipeg, MB, R2V 4G6
(204) 697-1400
Emp Here 145 *Sales* 91,245,600
SIC 5511 New and used car dealers
James E Gauthier
Randy Gauthier
William Huntly

D-U-N-S 20-512-5763 (SL)
GAUTHIER, JIM PONTIAC BUICK GMC LTD
GAUTHIER, JIM COLLISION CENTRE, DIV OF
2400 Mcphillips St, Winnipeg, MB, R2V 4J6
(204) 633-8833
Emp Here 80 *Sales* 22,664,000
SIC 7515 Passenger car leasing
Jim Gauthier
Randy Gauthier

D-U-N-S 20-556-0647 (BR)
HOME DEPOT OF CANADA INC
HOME DEPOT
(*Suby of* THE HOME DEPOT INC)
845 Leila Ave, Winnipeg, MB, R2V 3J7
(204) 336-5530
Emp Here 75
SIC 5251 Hardware stores
Ken Yackel

D-U-N-S 25-270-1149 (BR)
LOBLAWS INC
REAL CANADIAN SUPERSTORE #1505
(*Suby of* LOBLAW COMPANIES LIMITED)
2132 Mcphillips St, Winnipeg, MB, R2V 3C8
(204) 631-6250
Emp Here 300
SIC 5411 Grocery stores
Marilyn Wright

D-U-N-S 24-234-2285 (HQ)
MARYMOUND INC
MARYMOUND SCHOOL
442 Scotia St, Winnipeg, MB, R2V 1X4
(204) 338-7971
Sales 62,120,400
SIC 8399 Social services, nec
Ian Hughes

D-U-N-S 25-311-2908 (BR)
MCDONALD'S RESTAURANTS OF CANADA LIMITED
MCDONALD'S
(*Suby of* MCDONALD'S CORPORATION)
847 Leila Ave, Winnipeg, MB, R2V 3J7
(204) 949-6066
Emp Here 98
SIC 5812 Eating places
Lisa Bjornson

D-U-N-S 25-385-3501 (SL)
MCPHILLIPS HOLDINGS (WINNIPEG) LTD
MCPHILLIPS TOYOTA
2425 Mcphillips St, Winnipeg, MB, R2V 4J7
(204) 338-7985
Emp Here 35 *Sales* 17,432,730
SIC 5511 New and used car dealers
James Cornwall
Karin Weise

D-U-N-S 20-010-4545 (SL)
PARKSIDE FORD LINCOLN LTD
2000 Main St, Winnipeg, MB, R2V 2B8
(204) 339-2000
Emp Here 80 *Sales* 50,342,400
SIC 5511 New and used car dealers
Campbell Maciver

D-U-N-S 24-039-7380 (HQ)
REIDER INSURANCE SERVICES
1399 Mcphillips St, Winnipeg, MB, R2V 3C4
(204) 334-4319
Emp Here 7 *Sales* 11,598,480
SIC 6411 Insurance agents, brokers, and service
Morley M Reider

D-U-N-S 20-011-0393 (HQ)
SALISBURY HOUSE OF CANADA LTD
(*Suby of* 4328796 MANITOBA LTD)
787 Leila Ave, Winnipeg, MB, R2V 3J7
(204) 594-7257
Emp Here 100 *Sales* 32,647,300
SIC 5812 Eating places
Costas Ataliotis
Patrick Panchuk

Earl Barish
Lorne Saifer
Hersh Wolch
Harris Liontas

D-U-N-S 24-235-8158 (SL)
SEVEN OAKS GENERAL HOSPITAL
2300 Mcphillips St, Winnipeg, MB, R2V 3M3
(204) 632-7133
Emp Here 1,400 *Sales* 155,512,000
SIC 8062 General medical and surgical hospitals
Carrie Solmudson
Dave Magura
Monique Constant
Stuart Greenfield
Louise Evaschesen

D-U-N-S 25-096-7676 (BR)
SEVEN OAKS SCHOOL DIVISION
SEVEN OAKS SCHOOL DIVISION MET SCHOOL
(*Suby of* SEVEN OAKS SCHOOL DIVISION)
711 Jefferson Ave, Winnipeg, MB, R2V 0P7
(204) 336-5050
Emp Here 80
SIC 8211 Elementary and secondary schools
Adair Warren

D-U-N-S 20-838-8363 (HQ)
SEVEN OAKS SCHOOL DIVISION
830 Powers St, Winnipeg, MB, R2V 4E7
(204) 586-8061
Emp Here 20 *Sales* 112,327,004
SIC 8211 Elementary and secondary schools
Evelyn Mysaiw
Wayne Shimizu
Edward Ploszay

D-U-N-S 24-232-9365 (HQ)
TEN TEN SINCLAIR HOUSING INC
1010 Sinclair St, Winnipeg, MB, R2V 3H7
(204) 339-9268
Emp Here 5 *Sales* 11,249,350
SIC 8361 Residential care
Donna Collins
Debbie Van Ettinger
Heather Korol

D-U-N-S 24-686-6318 (SL)
TIM HORTONS
2500 Main St, Winnipeg, MB, R2V 4Y1
(204) 334-3126
Emp Here 49 *Sales* 13,433,448
SIC 5461 Retail bakeries
William Martens

D-U-N-S 24-369-2055 (HQ)
UKRAINIAN CATHOLIC ARCHEPARCHY OF WINNIPEG
STS PETER & PAUL UKRANIAN CATHOLIC CHURCH
233 Scotia St, Winnipeg, MB, R2V 1V7
(204) 338-7801
Emp Here 16 *Sales* 17,492,664
SIC 8661 Religious organizations
Lawrence Huculak

D-U-N-S 25-294-8419 (BR)
WAL-MART CANADA CORP
(*Suby of* WALMART INC.)
2370 Mcphillips St Suite 3118, Winnipeg, MB, R2V 4J6
(204) 334-2273
Emp Here 300
SIC 5311 Department stores
Barry Pederson

D-U-N-S 25-313-5271 (SL)
WINNIPEG C MOTORS LP
EASTERN CHRYSLER DODGE JEEP
(*Suby of* AUTOCANADA INC)
1900 Main St, Winnipeg, MB, R2V 3S9
(204) 339-2011
Emp Here 82 *Sales* 51,600,960
SIC 5511 New and used car dealers
Joseph Rewucki

Marietta Rewucki
Andy Rewucki

Winnipeg, MB R2W

D-U-N-S 24-608-0410 (SL)
B. D. R. SERVICES LTD
11 Yard St, Winnipeg, MB, R2W 5J6
(204) 586-8227
Emp Here 50   *Sales* 11,046,700
SIC 1711 Plumbing, heating, air-conditioning
David Skromeda

D-U-N-S 24-380-5335 (SL)
B.U.I.L.D. BUILDING URBAN INDUSTRIES FOR LOCAL DEVELOPMENT INC
WARM UP WINNIPEG
765 Main St Unit 200, Winnipeg, MB, R2W 3N5
(204) 943-5981
Emp Here 100   *Sales* 27,094,200
SIC 1521 Single-family housing construction
Shaun Loney

D-U-N-S 24-545-9334 (HQ)
BAGOS BUN BAKERY LTD
SON'S BAKERY
232 Jarvis Ave, Winnipeg, MB, R2W 3A1
(204) 586-8409
Emp Here 1   *Sales* 42,554,165
SIC 5461 Retail bakeries
Harvey Goldman
Steven Baldinger

D-U-N-S 24-348-6573 (SL)
BLUE MOOSE CLOTHING COMPANY LTD
MANITOBAH MUKLUKS
90 Sutherland Ave Unit 100, Winnipeg, MB, R2W 3C7
(204) 783-2557
Emp Here 70   *Sales* 16,340,450
SIC 3143 Men's footwear, except athletic
Sean Mccormick

D-U-N-S 25-961-7330 (SL)
BRASS WORKS LTD
511 Jarvis Ave, Winnipeg, MB, R2W 3A8
(204) 582-3737
Emp Here 75   *Sales* 17,507,625
SIC 3312 Blast furnaces and steel mills
Irvin Koch

D-U-N-S 25-369-8302 (BR)
CITY BREAD CO. LTD, THE
(*Suby of* M.I.H. HOLDINGS LTD)
238 Dufferin Ave, Winnipeg, MB, R2W 2X6
(204) 586-8409
Emp Here 100
SIC 2051 Bread, cake, and related products
Harvey Goldman

D-U-N-S 24-171-0367 (HQ)
CITY BREAD CO. LTD, THE
(*Suby of* M.I.H. HOLDINGS LTD)
232 Jarvis Ave, Winnipeg, MB, R2W 3A1
(204) 586-8409
Emp Here 1   *Sales* 34,569,000
SIC 2051 Bread, cake, and related products
Harvey Goldman

D-U-N-S 20-042-5176 (SL)
DICKIE-DEE ICE CREAM VENDING BIKES & TRUCKS
530 Dufferin Ave, Winnipeg, MB, R2W 2Y6
(204) 586-5218
Emp Here 40   *Sales* 10,966,080
SIC 5451 Dairy products stores
Jeff Hubka

D-U-N-S 25-679-0858 (SL)
E.K. CONSTRUCTION 2000 LTD
11 Yard St, Winnipeg, MB, R2W 5J6
(204) 589-8387
Emp Here 30   *Sales* 14,121,930
SIC 1542 Nonresidential construction, nec

Ernst Keller
Janice Grubert

D-U-N-S 24-335-1017 (HQ)
EMPIRE INDUSTRIES LTD
717 Jarvis Ave, Winnipeg, MB, R2W 3B4
(204) 589-9300
Emp Here 37   *Sales* 106,846,138
SIC 3441 Fabricated structural Metal
Guy Nelson
Allan Francis
Michael Martin
Ian Macdonald
Jack Chang
Bob Marshall
Terry Quinn
James Chui

D-U-N-S 25-505-2722 (SL)
GARDEN GROVE DISTRIBUTION (2013) LTD
440 Jarvis Ave, Winnipeg, MB, R2W 3A6

Emp Here 40   *Sales* 33,423,080
SIC 5148 Fresh fruits and vegetables
Andrew Maitland

D-U-N-S 20-008-9027 (SL)
GUNN'S HOMEMADE CAKES & PASTRY LTD
GUNN'S BAKERY
247 Selkirk Ave, Winnipeg, MB, R2W 2L5
(204) 582-2364
Emp Here 70   *Sales* 58,490,390
SIC 5149 Groceries and related products, nec
Bernard Gunn
Arthur Gunn

D-U-N-S 20-569-1298 (SL)
KOCH STAINLESS PRODUCTS LTD
511 Jarvis Ave, Winnipeg, MB, R2W 3A8
(204) 586-8364
Emp Here 60   *Sales* 11,525,100
SIC 3499 Fabricated Metal products, nec
Irvin Koch

D-U-N-S 24-630-3382 (HQ)
MA MAWI-WI-CHI-ITATA CENTRE INC
445 King St, Winnipeg, MB, R2W 2C5
(204) 925-0300
Sales 18,636,120
SIC 8399 Social services, nec
George Munroe
Sandra Lagimodiere
Gerald Slater
Myrtle Thomas
Anita Flett
Norma Lagimodiere
Verna Mcivor
Robert Coorchene
Don Robinson
Albert Mcleod

D-U-N-S 24-848-4706 (SL)
MANITOBA HYDRO UTILITY SERVICES LIMITED
(*Suby of* PROVINCE OF MANITOBA)
35 Sutherland Ave, Winnipeg, MB, R2W 3C5
(204) 360-5660
Emp Here 100   *Sales* 66,890,800
SIC 7389 Business services, nec
Victor H Schroeder
David Friesen
Phil Dorion
Gerard Jennissen
Garry Leach
Michael Spence
Kenneth Paupanekis
Leslie Turnbell
William Fraser

D-U-N-S 25-204-8624 (SL)
MARINER NEPTUNE FISH & SEAFOOD COMPANY LTD
472 Dufferin Ave, Winnipeg, MB, R2W 2Y6
(204) 589-5341
Emp Here 42   *Sales* 35,094,234

SIC 5146 Fish and seafoods
John Alexander
Evan Page
Russell Page
Kelly Page
Rudi Mccowan

D-U-N-S 20-302-2744 (SL)
MOUNT CARMEL CLINIC
886 Main St, Winnipeg, MB, R2W 5L4
(204) 582-2311
Emp Here 190   *Sales* 36,139,330
SIC 8011 Offices and clinics of medical doctors
Jeremy Akerstream
Bobbette Shoffner
Al Shpeller

D-U-N-S 24-036-3911 (SL)
PARR METAL FABRICATORS LTD
(*Suby of* EMPIRE INDUSTRIES LTD)
717 Jarvis Ave, Winnipeg, MB, R2W 3B4
(204) 586-8121
Emp Here 27   *Sales* 12,825,702
SIC 5085 Industrial supplies
Campbell Mcintyre

D-U-N-S 25-659-9523 (SL)
SEED WINNIPEG INC
80 Salter St, Winnipeg, MB, R2W 4J6
(204) 927-9935
Emp Here 34   *Sales* 10,697,488
SIC 8699 Membership organizations, nec
Cindy Coker

D-U-N-S 24-374-9900 (SL)
UKRAINIAN FRATERNAL SOCIETY OF CANADA
235 Mcgregor St, Winnipeg, MB, R2W 4W5
(204) 586-4482
Emp Here 12   *Sales* 12,418,572
SIC 6311 Life insurance
Boris Salamon

D-U-N-S 24-116-1603 (SL)
WINNIPEG OLD COUNTRY SAUSAGE LTD
MANITOBA SAUSAGE
691 Dufferin Ave, Winnipeg, MB, R2W 2Z3
(204) 589-8331
Emp Here 45   *Sales* 10,118,475
SIC 2013 Sausages and other prepared meats
Ken Werner

D-U-N-S 20-709-7499 (BR)
WINNIPEG SCHOOL DIVISION
ST. JOHN HIGH SCHOOL
(*Suby of* WINNIPEG SCHOOL DIVISION)
401 Church Ave, Winnipeg, MB, R2W 1C4
(204) 589-4374
Emp Here 150
SIC 8211 Elementary and secondary schools
Doug Taylor

Winnipeg, MB R2X

D-U-N-S 24-390-8782 (HQ)
3225537 NOVA SCOTIA LIMITED
WILSON AUTO ELECTRIC
(*Suby of* BBB INDUSTRIES, LLC)
90 Hutchings St Unit B, Winnipeg, MB, R2X 2X1
(204) 272-2880
Emp Here 50   *Sales* 36,421,500
SIC 5013 Motor vehicle supplies and new parts
Mike Silva

D-U-N-S 20-515-1686 (SL)
4093879 CANADA LTD
1771 Inkster Blvd, Winnipeg, MB, R2X 1R3
(204) 982-5783
Emp Here 2,600   *Sales* 950,323,400
SIC 6712 Bank holding companies

Peter Nygard

D-U-N-S 24-373-0210 (SL)
7062001 CANADA LIMITED
WINNIPEG MOTOR EXPRESS
1180 Fife St, Winnipeg, MB, R2X 2N6
(204) 633-8161
Emp Here 55   *Sales* 12,914,688
SIC 4212 Local trucking, without storage
Brian Page

D-U-N-S 24-266-6741 (HQ)
A.D. RUTHERFORD INTERNATIONAL INC
1355 Mountain Ave Suite 301, Winnipeg, MB, R2X 3B6
(204) 633-7207
Emp Here 18   *Sales* 12,999,175
SIC 4731 Freight transportation arrangement
Royal Unruh

D-U-N-S 20-011-8917 (HQ)
ANTEX WESTERN LTD
1340 Church Ave, Winnipeg, MB, R2X 1G4
(204) 633-4815
Emp Here 100   *Sales* 35,326,350
SIC 1752 Floor laying and floor work, nec
Michael Kolas
Joseph Ng
Brian Fedorchuk
Bryan Demarcke
Ken Klohn
Salvadore Maida

D-U-N-S 20-810-4794 (HQ)
ARCTIC CO-OPERATIVES LIMITED
NORTHERN IMAGES, THE
1645 Inkster Blvd, Winnipeg, MB, R2X 2W7
(204) 697-1625
Emp Here 80   *Sales* 58,300,704
SIC 5099 Durable goods, nec
Rod Wilson
Glenn D Willliams
Mary Nirlungayuk

D-U-N-S 25-205-1826 (SL)
BENTLEYS OF LONDON SLACKS LTD
1309 Mountain Ave, Winnipeg, MB, R2X 2Y1
(204) 786-6081
Emp Here 1,500   *Sales* 205,011,000
SIC 2339 Women's and misses' outerwear, nec
Stephen Freed

D-U-N-S 20-006-0184 (HQ)
BIG FREIGHT SYSTEMS INC
BIG FREIGHT WAREHOUSING
(*Suby of* DASEKE, INC.)
10 Hutchings St, Winnipeg, MB, R2X 2X1
(204) 772-3434
Emp Here 1   *Sales* 47,939,060
SIC 4213 Trucking, except local
Gary Coleman
Paul Petrick

D-U-N-S 20-385-4328 (HQ)
BROCK WHITE CANADA ULC
879 Keewatin St, Winnipeg, MB, R2X 2S7
(204) 694-3600
Emp Here 50   *Sales* 44,717,400
SIC 5039 Construction materials, nec
Greg Hanson
Mitchell Williams

D-U-N-S 24-038-3950 (SL)
CANADA WEST SHOE MANUFACTURING INC
CANADA WEST BOOT FACTORY OUTLET
1250 Fife St, Winnipeg, MB, R2X 2N6
(204) 632-4110
Emp Here 66   *Sales* 11,840,136
SIC 5661 Shoe stores
William M Moorby
Ted Moorby
Paul Moorby
William E Moorby Jr

D-U-N-S 24-113-2695 (HQ)
CELCO CONTROLS LTD

(*Suby* of HIGH ROAD CAPITAL PARTNERS SARL)
78 Hutchings St, Winnipeg, MB, R2X 3B1
(204) 788-1677
Emp Here 50   *Sales* 14,283,150
SIC 3613 Switchgear and switchboard apparatus
Clay Derrett

D-U-N-S 24-914-5392   (BR)
COCA-COLA CANADA BOTTLING LIMITED
(*Suby* of COCA-COLA CANADA BOTTLING LIMITED)
1331 Inkster Blvd, Winnipeg, MB, R2X 1P6
(204) 633-2590
Emp Here 250
SIC 2086 Bottled and canned soft drinks
David Kavalench

D-U-N-S 24-775-1969   (HQ)
CORMER GROUP INDUSTRIES INC
CORMER AEROSPACE
33 Bentall St, Winnipeg, MB, R2X 2Z7
(204) 987-6400
Emp Here 80   *Sales* 15,162,040
SIC 3728 Aircraft parts and equipment, nec
Andrew Corner

D-U-N-S 25-171-2576   (SL)
DEWPOINT BOTTLING COMPANY LTD
WORLD OF WATER
326 Keewatin St, Winnipeg, MB, R2X 2R9
(204) 774-7770
Emp Here 18   *Sales* 11,816,352
SIC 5963 Direct selling establishments
Jack Davidson
Shirley Davidson

D-U-N-S 20-119-5562   (HQ)
DOORTECH MFG. AND DISTRIBUTION LTD
530 Sheppard St, Winnipeg, MB, R2X 2P8
(204) 633-7133
Emp Here 25   *Sales* 13,862,394
SIC 5031 Lumber, plywood, and millwork
Frederick (Fred) Perrier
Jocelyn Perrier
Gerhard Epp

D-U-N-S 24-966-6165   (HQ)
ENDURAPAK INC
55 Plymouth St, Winnipeg, MB, R2X 2V5
(204) 947-1383
Emp Here 105   *Sales* 23,372,160
SIC 2673 Bags: plastic, laminated, and coated
Jay Cumbers
Wayne M Pestaluky
Clayton Matthes
Bruce Macdonald

D-U-N-S 20-309-6961   (SL)
EPAK INC
55 Plymouth St, Winnipeg, MB, R2X 2V5
(204) 947-1383
Emp Here 50   *Sales* 12,037,155
SIC 3081 Unsupported plastics film and sheet
Jay Cumbers
Bruce Macdonald

D-U-N-S 20-053-2682   (HQ)
FP CANADIAN NEWSPAPERS LIMITED PARTNERSHIP
WINNIPEG FREE PRESS
1355 Mountain Ave, Winnipeg, MB, R2X 3B6
(204) 697-7000
Sales 122,077,620
SIC 2711 Newspapers
Ronald Stern
Daniel Koshowski
Harvey Secter

D-U-N-S 24-630-9496   (HQ)
FREED & FREED INTERNATIONAL LTD
1309 Mountain Ave, Winnipeg, MB, R2X 2Y1
(204) 786-6081
Sales 10,933,920
SIC 2311 Men's and boy's suits and coats

D-U-N-S 20-758-8740   (HQ)
GASPARD & SONS (1963) LIMITED
(*Suby* of 63254 MANITOBA LTD)
1266 Fife St, Winnipeg, MB, R2X 2N6
(204) 949-5700
Sales 17,084,250
SIC 2389 Apparel and accessories, nec
Inge Gaspard

D-U-N-S 24-390-1811   (SL)
GASPARD LP
1266 Fife St, Winnipeg, MB, R2X 2N6
(204) 949-5700
Emp Here 350   *Sales* 92,867,250
SIC 2389 Apparel and accessories, nec
Roddy Premsukh
Valerie Morgan
David Blatt

D-U-N-S 20-397-4886   (SL)
GASPARD REGALIA INC
GASPARD
(*Suby* of BRADDOCK HOLDINGS LLC)
1266 Fife St, Winnipeg, MB, R2X 2N6
(204) 949-5700
Emp Here 100   *Sales* 7,068,493
SIC 5137 Women's and children's clothing
Rob Martins
Arlene Furst

D-U-N-S 24-882-7461   (SL)
ICE CREAM UNLIMITED INC
CAKES UNLIMITED
55 Plymouth St, Winnipeg, MB, R2X 2V5

Emp Here 120   *Sales* 42,180,490
SIC 2053 Frozen bakery products, except bread
Wesley Jakilazek
Gordon Andrushuk

D-U-N-S 25-328-8542   (BR)
IMPRIMERIES TRANSCONTINENTAL INC
TRANSCONTINENTAL PRINTING INC
(*Suby* of TRANSCONTINENTAL INC)
1615 Inkster Blvd, Winnipeg, MB, R2X 1R2
(204) 988-9476
Emp Here 100
SIC 2752 Commercial printing, lithographic
Peters Jo

D-U-N-S 20-711-2921   (SL)
INDUSTRIAL RUBBER SUPPLY (1995) LTD
55 Dunlop Ave, Winnipeg, MB, R2X 2V2
(204) 694-4444
Emp Here 80   *Sales* 22,132,800
SIC 2822 Synthetic rubber
William John Magalas
Scott Magalas
Kevin Magalas

D-U-N-S 24-859-8539   (HQ)
KRAUS CANADA LP
1551 Church Ave Suite 167, Winnipeg, MB, R2X 1G7
(204) 633-1020
Sales 86,305,200
SIC 5023 Homefurnishings
Shaun Davies

D-U-N-S 20-012-0509   (HQ)
LIFETOUCH CANADA INC
(*Suby* of SHUTTERFLY, INC.)
1410 Mountain Ave Unit 1, Winnipeg, MB, R2X 0A4
(204) 977-3475
Emp Here 218   *Sales* 76,270,250
SIC 7384 Photofinish laboratories
Paul Harmel
Bruce Nicholson
Andy Vanderzalm
Randolph Pladson
Ted Koenecke
James Campbell
John Anderson
Richard Erickson
Donald Goldfus

P. Robert Larson

D-U-N-S 20-009-6840   (SL)
M.J. ROOFING & SUPPLY LTD
(*Suby* of WILLMAN, LARRY HOLDINGS LTD)
909 Jarvis Ave, Winnipeg, MB, R2X 0A1
(204) 586-8411
Emp Here 120   *Sales* 26,139,480
SIC 1761 Roofing, siding, and sheetMetal work
Larry Willman
Sandra Willman

D-U-N-S 25-116-1857   (SL)
MAGNUM OIL (MB) LTD
450 Sheppard St, Winnipeg, MB, R2X 2P8
(204) 594-0440
Emp Here 12   *Sales* 12,393,696
SIC 5172 Petroleum products, nec
Keith L Micklash
Lorraine Micklash
Keith A (Manny) Micklash

D-U-N-S 20-009-8739   (HQ)
MAYERS PACKAGING LTD
50 Mandalay Dr, Winnipeg, MB, R2X 2Z2
(204) 774-1651
Emp Here 12   *Sales* 12,591,450
SIC 5113 Industrial and personal service paper
Jodi Cristall
Lorne Cristall

D-U-N-S 20-010-0386   (SL)
MIKKELSEN-COWARD & CO LTD
1615 Inkster Blvd, Winnipeg, MB, R2X 1R2
(204) 694-8900
Emp Here 80   *Sales* 18,645,200
SIC 1711 Plumbing, heating, air-conditioning
Mitchel Zajac
Michael Zajac

D-U-N-S 20-010-1806   (SL)
NALEWAY FOODS LTD.
233 Hutchings St, Winnipeg, MB, R2X 2R4
(204) 633-6535
Emp Here 80   *Sales* 9,108,749
SIC 2038 Frozen specialties, nec
Richard Lyles
Winston Ho Fatt

D-U-N-S 20-347-1677   (SL)
NOR'WEST CO-OP COMMUNITY HEALTH CENTRE, INC
785 Keewatin St, Winnipeg, MB, R2X 3B9
(204) 938-5900
Emp Here 140   *Sales* 26,628,980
SIC 8011 Offices and clinics of medical doctors
Nancy Heinrichs

D-U-N-S 20-515-1603   (HQ)
NYGARD INTERNATIONAL PARTNERSHIP
NYGARD FASHIONS
1771 Inkster Blvd, Winnipeg, MB, R2X 1R3
(204) 982-5000
Emp Here 450   *Sales* 249,510,000
SIC 5621 Women's clothing stores
Peter J Nygard
James Bennett
Denise Lapointe

D-U-N-S 20-005-1639   (HQ)
OLD DUTCH FOODS LTD
100 Bentall St, Winnipeg, MB, R2X 2Y5
(204) 632-0249
Emp Here 100   *Sales* 584,862,000
SIC 2096 Potato chips and similar snacks
Steven Aanenson
Eric Aanenson
Bonna Jean Bateman

D-U-N-S 24-655-4323   (SL)
POLYCAST INDUSTRIAL PRODUCTS LTD
POLYCAST INTERNATIONAL
486 Sheppard St, Winnipeg, MB, R2X 2P8
(204) 632-5428
Emp Here 50   *Sales* 10,233,650

SIC 3677 Electronic coils and transformers
Paul Magel
Leah Magel
Beryl Magel

D-U-N-S 20-010-6383   (SL)
PRATTS LIMITED
PRATTS WHOLESALE
(*Suby* of GREENVALE HOLDINGS LTD)
101 Hutchings St, Winnipeg, MB, R2X 2V4
(204) 949-2800
Emp Here 600   *Sales* 353,495,400
SIC 5194 Tobacco and tobacco products
Leonard Baranyk
Lenny Baranyk
Jason Baranyk
Jeffrey Baranyk
Tom Tetlock
Ed Holowaty
Kim Peters
Grant Avery
Mark Poklar

D-U-N-S 24-852-4357   (SL)
PRIORITY RESTORATION SERVICES LTD
1300 Church Ave, Winnipeg, MB, R2X 1G4
(204) 783-3344
Emp Here 120   *Sales* 5,747,451
SIC 1541 Industrial buildings and warehouses
Richard Hutchings

D-U-N-S 25-998-1447   (SL)
PROGRESS RAIL TRANSCANADA CORPORATION
(*Suby* of CATERPILLAR INC.)
478 Mcphillips St Suite 300, Winnipeg, MB, R2X 2G8
(204) 934-4307
Emp Here 300   *Sales* 72,969,300
SIC 3462 Iron and steel forgings
William Ainsworth
David Roeder
Chris Ross
Bernard Garney
Robert Powell
J Duane Cantrell

D-U-N-S 20-834-7070   (HQ)
PROLIFIC GRAPHICS INC
PROLIFIC GROUP
150 Wyatt Rd, Winnipeg, MB, R2X 2X6
(204) 694-2300
Emp Here 110   *Sales* 26,244,320
SIC 2752 Commercial printing, lithographic
Albert Alexandruk
Thomas Wilton

D-U-N-S 20-435-2736   (SL)
PROTELEC LTD
1450 Mountain Ave Unit 200, Winnipeg, MB, R2X 3C4
(204) 949-1417
Emp Here 60   *Sales* 23,740,680
SIC 7382 Security systems services
Rial Black
Alan K Rogers

D-U-N-S 20-945-0428   (SL)
QUALITY VENDING & COFFEE SERVICES LTD
91 Plymouth St, Winnipeg, MB, R2X 2V5
(204) 233-2405
Emp Here 36   *Sales* 23,632,704
SIC 5962 Merchandising machine operators
Clayton Lawrence
Darryl Jackson

D-U-N-S 25-450-2230   (SL)
REMAX ASSOCIATES
1060 Mcphillips St, Winnipeg, MB, R2X 2K9
(204) 989-9000
Emp Here 40   *Sales* 10,870,240
SIC 6531 Real estate agents and managers
Judith Meckling

D-U-N-S 24-466-5881   (SL)
SHAPE INDUSTRIES INC

255 Hutchings St, Winnipeg, MB, R2X 2R4
(204) 947-0409
Emp Here 60   *Sales* 14,006,100
SIC 3399 Primary Metal products
Ryan Smith

D-U-N-S 24-819-1439   (SL)
SHARE CORPORATION CANADA LTD
1691 Church Ave, Winnipeg, MB, R2X 2Y7
(204) 633-8553
Emp Here 55   *Sales* 40,168,975
SIC 5169 Chemicals and allied products, nec
Dianna Kiely

D-U-N-S 24-034-8235   (BR)
SOBEYS CAPITAL INCORPORATED
SOBEYS WEST
(*Suby of* EMPIRE COMPANY LIMITED)
1800 Inkster Blvd, Winnipeg, MB, R2X 2Z5
(204) 632-7100
Emp Here 250
SIC 5141 Groceries, general line
Ken Mitchler

D-U-N-S 24-346-5353   (BR)
SOBEYS CAPITAL INCORPORATED
(*Suby of* EMPIRE COMPANY LIMITED)
1870 Burrows Ave, Winnipeg, MB, R2X 3C3
(204) 697-1997
Emp Here 160
SIC 5411 Grocery stores
Annette Stevens

D-U-N-S 20-011-0286   (HQ)
ST JOHN'S MUSIC LTD
1570 Church Ave, Winnipeg, MB, R2X 1G8
(204) 694-1818
Emp Here 18   *Sales* 32,768,823
SIC 5736 Musical instrument stores
Mark Yusishen
Janet Lynn Watson

D-U-N-S 25-387-6981   (SL)
SUPERIOR HEATING & AIR CONDITION-
ING/ST. JAMES SHEET METAL LTD
1600 Church Ave, Winnipeg, MB, R2X 1G8
(204) 697-5666
Emp Here 51   *Sales* 11,109,279
SIC 1731 Electrical work
David Smith

D-U-N-S 24-229-3322   (SL)
VAW SYSTEMS LTD
1300 Inkster Blvd, Winnipeg, MB, R2X 1P5
(204) 697-7770
Emp Here 90   *Sales* 17,139,780
SIC 3625 Relays and industrial controls
Dan Sierens

D-U-N-S 24-429-2314   (HQ)
WHITE-WOOD DISTRIBUTORS LTD
WHITE-WOOD FOREST PRODUCTS
119 Plymouth St, Winnipeg, MB, R2X 2T3
(204) 982-9450
Emp Here 21   *Sales* 10,881,537
SIC 5211 Lumber and other building materials
Gloria Yusishen
Brian Conn

D-U-N-S 25-289-5206   (SL)
WINNIPEG MOTOR EXPRESS INC
1180 Fife St, Winnipeg, MB, R2X 2N6

Emp Here 200
SIC 4213 Trucking, except local

D-U-N-S 25-892-6146   (BR)
WINNIPEG SCHOOL DIVISION
SISLER HIGH SCHOOL
(*Suby of* WINNIPEG SCHOOL DIVISION)
1360 Redwood Ave, Winnipeg, MB, R2X 0Z1
(204) 589-8321
Emp Here 135
SIC 8211 Elementary and secondary schools
George Heshka

D-U-N-S 20-012-1242   (HQ)
YETMAN'S LTD

949 Jarvis Ave, Winnipeg, MB, R2X 0A1
(204) 586-8046
Sales 19,001,040
SIC 5083 Farm and garden machinery
Norman Yetman
Keith Yetman
Earl Yetman

D-U-N-S 25-415-5047   (HQ)
YRC FREIGHT CANADA COMPANY
(*Suby of* YRC WORLDWIDE INC.)
1400 Inkster Blvd, Winnipeg, MB, R2X 1R1
(204) 958-5000
Emp Here 300   *Sales* 165,942,900
SIC 4213 Trucking, except local
Thomas O'connor
Phil Gaines
Richard Bronk
Christopher Masoner
Mark Boehmer
Terry Gerrond
Leah Dawson
Joseph Pec

Winnipeg, MB R2Y

D-U-N-S 20-690-6773   (BR)
ALL SENIORS CARE LIVING CENTRES
LTD
STURGEON CREEK RETIREMENT RESI-
DENCE
(*Suby of* ALL SENIORS CARE HOLDINGS
INC)
10 Hallonquist Dr Suite 318, Winnipeg, MB,
R2Y 2M5
(204) 885-1415
Emp Here 75
SIC 8361 Residential care
Heather Mutcheson

D-U-N-S 25-484-7668   (BR)
GOVERNING COUNCIL OF THE SALVA-
TION ARMY IN CANADA, THE
GOVERNING COUNCIL OF THE SALVATION
ARMY IN CANADA,
(*Suby of* GOVERNING COUNCIL OF THE
SALVATION ARMY IN CANADA, THE)
811 School Rd, Winnipeg, MB, R2Y 0S8
(204) 888-3311
Emp Here 185
SIC 8322 Individual and family services
Wilson Perrin

D-U-N-S 20-272-3730   (HQ)
ISCO CANADA, INC
(*Suby of* ISCO INDUSTRIES, INC.)
2901 Sturgeon Rd, Winnipeg, MB, R2Y 2L9
(204) 831-8625
Emp Here 9   *Sales* 15,675,858
SIC 5085 Industrial supplies
James Kirchborfer
Mark Kirchborfer
Murray Glen Henderson

D-U-N-S 24-243-2024   (SL)
STURGEON CREEK RETIREMENT RESI-
DENCE II
707 Setter St Suite 136, Winnipeg, MB, R2Y
0A4
(204) 885-0303
Emp Here 49   *Sales* 11,412,639
SIC 6513 Apartment building operators
Michael Heart

Winnipeg, MB R3A

D-U-N-S 24-917-2818   (SL)
2792924 MANITOBA LTD
BUNTY'S BUBBLE BATH
228 Isabel St, Winnipeg, MB, R3A 1G9

Emp Here 23   *Sales* 11,455,794
SIC 5541 Gasoline service stations
Amarjit Apee Panchhi

D-U-N-S 20-702-2026   (HQ)
3851401 CANADA INC
555 Logan Ave, Winnipeg, MB, R3A 0S4
(204) 788-4249
Sales 27,335,000
SIC 6712 Bank holding companies
Ronald Stern

D-U-N-S 25-408-7620   (HQ)
AGI CCAA INC
ARCTIC GLACIER
(*Suby of* THE CARLYLE GROUP L P)
625 Henry Ave, Winnipeg, MB, R3A 0V1
(204) 772-2473
Emp Here 70   *Sales* 536,123,500
SIC 2097 Manufactured ice
Fred Smagorinsky
Brent Bonvarlez
Richard Scott
Garth Wadell
Pierre Fortier

D-U-N-S 24-032-8851   (SL)
ANIMIKII OZOSON CHILD AND FAMILY
SERVICES INC
313 Pacific Ave Unit 3, Winnipeg, MB, R3A
0M2
(204) 944-0040
Emp Here 50   *Sales* 11,341,650
SIC 8399 Social services, nec
Bonnie Kocsis

D-U-N-S 20-007-6123   (HQ)
CANADIAN FOOTWEAR (1982) LTD
128 Adelaide St, Winnipeg, MB, R3A 0W5
(204) 944-7463
Emp Here 25   *Sales* 11,660,740
SIC 5661 Shoe stores
Brian Scharfstein
Pamela Cipryk

D-U-N-S 24-337-8606   (SL)
DIASER MANAGEMENT (2006) LTD
268 Ellen St, Winnipeg, MB, R3A 1A7
(204) 943-8855
Emp Here 45   *Sales* 21,182,895
SIC 1542 Nonresidential construction, nec
Hans Boge

D-U-N-S 25-386-6966   (SL)
DIRECT FOCUS MARKETING COMMUNI-
CATIONS INC
DIRECT FOCUS
315 Pacific Ave, Winnipeg, MB, R3A 0M2
(204) 947-6912
Emp Here 80   *Sales* 18,743,040
SIC 8743 Public relations services
Martin Hofer
Michael Li

D-U-N-S 24-883-5399   (SL)
IMMIGRANT AND REFUGEE COMMUNITY
ORGANIZATION OF MANITOBA INC
95 Ellen St, Winnipeg, MB, R3A 1S8
(204) 943-8765
Emp Here 40   *Sales* 10,870,240
SIC 6531 Real estate agents and managers
Mike Dudar
Dorota Blumczynska

D-U-N-S 24-851-3236   (SL)
MANITOBA CLINIC MEDICAL CORPORA-
TION
MANITOBA CLINIC
790 Sherbrook St Suite 503, Winnipeg, MB,
R3A 1M3
(204) 774-6541
Emp Here 120   *Sales* 22,824,840
SIC 8011 Offices and clinics of medical doc-
tors
Victor Dekorompay
Ron Monson
David Connor

David Meyrowitz
Jeff Grapenstine
George Matthew
Dimitrios Balageorge

D-U-N-S 20-613-9271   (SL)
RABER GLOVE MFG. CO. LTD
560 Mcdermot Ave, Winnipeg, MB, R3A 0C1
(204) 786-2469
Emp Here 57   *Sales* 13,305,795
SIC 3111 Leather tanning and finishing
Howard Raber

D-U-N-S 20-010-8561   (HQ)
RICHLU SPORTSWEAR MFG. LTD
85 Adelaide St, Winnipeg, MB, R3A 0V9
(204) 942-3494
Sales 27,334,800
SIC 2329 Men's and boy's clothing, nec
David Rich

D-U-N-S 20-834-7658   (HQ)
SANATORIUM BOARD OF MANITOBA
LUNG ASSOCIATION OF MANITOBA
629 Mcdermot Ave, Winnipeg, MB, R3A 1P6
(204) 774-5501
Emp Here 3   *Sales* 10,332,037
SIC 7389 Business services, nec
Carmelle Mulaire
Margaret Bernhardt-Lowdon

D-U-N-S 24-916-7370   (SL)
SAXON LEATHER LTD
310 Ross Ave, Winnipeg, MB, R3A 0L4
(204) 956-4011
Emp Here 50   *Sales* 10,880,650
SIC 5948 Luggage and leather goods stores
Len Hirsch

D-U-N-S 20-827-6159   (SL)
SIMARIL INC
321 Mcdermot Ave Suite 402, Winnipeg, MB,
R3A 0A3
(204) 788-4366
Emp Here 50   *Sales* 11,937,500
SIC 8611 Business associations
Daryn Turcotte
Kara Mandryk

D-U-N-S 20-948-3411   (HQ)
SOCIETY FOR MANITOBANS WITH DIS-
ABILITIES INC
825 Sherbrook St, Winnipeg, MB, R3A 1M5
(204) 975-3010
Emp Here 90   *Sales* 9,698,944
SIC 8093 Specialty outpatient clinics, nec
Phil Romaniuk

D-U-N-S 25-486-0307   (HQ)
VOLUNTEER ENTERPRISES OF THE
HEALTH SCIENCES CENTRE INC
GUILDY'S
820 Sherbrook St Suite Ms210, Winnipeg,
MB, R3A 1R9
(204) 787-7313
Emp Here 1   *Sales* 11,739,080
SIC 5499 Miscellaneous food stores

D-U-N-S 25-207-4364   (HQ)
WESTERN GLOVE WORKS
SILVER JEANS CO, DIV OF
555 Logan Ave, Winnipeg, MB, R3A 0S4
(204) 788-4249
Sales 75,377,970
SIC 5137 Women's and children's clothing
Robert Silver
Ronald Stern
Michael Silver

D-U-N-S 20-011-9121   (SL)
WESTERN GLOVE WORKS LTD
(*Suby of* 3851401 CANADA INC)
555 Logan Ave, Winnipeg, MB, R3A 0S4
(204) 788-4249
Emp Here 100   *Sales* 7,469,400
SIC 7363 Help supply services
Robert Silver
Christina Love

Ronald Stern

D-U-N-S 20-011-9279   (HQ)
WESTERN REPAIR & SALES INC
WR DISPLAY & PACKAGING
500 Higgins Ave, Winnipeg, MB, R3A 0B1
(204) 925-7900
Emp Here 30   *Sales* 15,722,665
SIC 7389 Business services, nec
Ken Walford
Darlene Walford

D-U-N-S 24-171-3106   (HQ)
WINNIPEG PANTS & SPORTSWEAR MFG. LTD
RICHLU MANUFACTURING
(*Suby of* RICHLU SPORTSWEAR MFG. LTD)
85 Adelaide St, Winnipeg, MB, R3A 0V9
(204) 942-3494
Emp Here 150   *Sales* 32,069,586
SIC 2326 Men's and boy's work clothing
David Rich
Gavin Rich
Reva Lerner
Barry Rich
Dorothy Kotler
Beverly Rosove

D-U-N-S 20-052-4812   (BR)
WINNIPEG REGIONAL HEALTH AUTHORITY, THE
HEALTH SCIENCES CENTRE (DIV OF)
(*Suby of* WINNIPEG REGIONAL HEALTH AUTHORITY, THE)
820 Sherbrook St Suite 543, Winnipeg, MB, R3A 1R9
(204) 774-6511
Emp Here 1,500
SIC 8062 General medical and surgical hospitals
John Horne

D-U-N-S 20-875-4122   (BR)
WINNIPEG REGIONAL HEALTH AUTHORITY, THE
(*Suby of* WINNIPEG REGIONAL HEALTH AUTHORITY, THE)
490 Hargrave St, Winnipeg, MB, R3A 0X7
(204) 940-2665
Emp Here 130
SIC 8093 Specialty outpatient clinics, nec
Theresa Perdonic

Winnipeg, MB R3B

D-U-N-S 25-718-7328   (HQ)
(C.C.A.) COMMERCIAL CREDIT ADJUSTERS LTD
300-317 Donald St, Winnipeg, MB, R3B 2H6
(204) 958-5850
Emp Here 120   *Sales* 30,055,650
SIC 7322 Adjustment and collection services
Kevin Deblaera

D-U-N-S 25-668-1719   (SL)
4659555 MANITOBA LTD
PERFECT PLACEMENT SYSTEMS, DIV OF
328 King St Suite A, Winnipeg, MB, R3B 3H4
(204) 989-5820
Emp Here 900   *Sales* 67,224,600
SIC 7361 Employment agencies
Norman William Kyliuk

D-U-N-S 24-907-3891   (HQ)
ABORIGINAL PEOPLE'S TELEVISION NETWORK INCORPORATED
APTN
339 Portage Ave, Winnipeg, MB, R3B 2C3
(204) 947-9331
Sales 29,701,360
SIC 4833 Television broadcasting stations
Jean Larose
Mike Metatawabin
Daniel Vandal

Deborah Ann Charles
Donna Wuttunee
Shirley Adamson
Brian Smith
Kerry Assiniwe
Jamie Veilleux
David Mcleod

D-U-N-S 20-810-3668   (SL)
ACCENT CARE HOME & HOSPITAL HEALTH SERVICES INC
420 Notre Dame Ave, Winnipeg, MB, R3B 1R1
(204) 783-9888
Emp Here 49   *Sales* 16,029,223
SIC 6531 Real estate agents and managers
Neilson Arruda

D-U-N-S 20-514-5506   (BR)
ADECCO EMPLOYMENT SERVICES LIMITED
ADECCO
(*Suby of* ADECCO GROUP AG)
228 Notre Dame Ave, Winnipeg, MB, R3B 1N7

Emp Here 105
SIC 7361 Employment agencies
Colin Soockton

D-U-N-S 20-571-8299   (BR)
AIR CANADA
(*Suby of* AIR CANADA)
355 Portage Ave Suite 3850, Winnipeg, MB, R3B 0J6
(204) 941-2684
Emp Here 600
SIC 4512 Air transportation, scheduled
Kymberley Shwaluke

D-U-N-S 24-852-1387   (SL)
ASSEMBLY OF MANITOBA CHIEFS SECRETARIAT INC
275 Portage Ave Suite 200, Winnipeg, MB, R3B 2B3
(204) 956-0610
Emp Here 140   *Sales* 43,690,360
SIC 8651 Political organizations
Ron Evans

D-U-N-S 24-368-6768   (SL)
B & L HOMES FOR CHILDREN LTD
470 Notre Dame Ave Suite 200, Winnipeg, MB, R3B 1R5
(204) 774-6089
Emp Here 80   *Sales* 10,676,720
SIC 8399 Social services, nec
Bruce Bertrand-Meadows
Shelley Bertrand-Meadows

D-U-N-S 20-010-1384   (SL)
BEN MOSS JEWELLERS WESTERN CANADA LTD
BEN MOSS JEWELLERS
201 Portage Ave Suite 300, Winnipeg, MB, R3B 3K6
(204) 947-6682
Emp Here 450   *Sales* 82,591,650
SIC 5944 Jewelry stores
Brent Trepel

D-U-N-S 20-436-4822   (HQ)
BORDER GROUP OF COMPANIES INC, THE
BORDER GLASS & ALUMINUM
53 Higgins Ave, Winnipeg, MB, R3B 0A8
(204) 957-7200
Sales 11,525,100
SIC 3442 Metal doors, sash, and trim
Paul Borys
Don Borys
David Borys

D-U-N-S 24-882-5200   (SL)
CANADIAN ARTISTS' REPRESENTATION (MANITOBA) INC
100 Arthur St Suite 407, Winnipeg, MB, R3B 1H3
(204) 943-7211
Emp Here 91   *Sales* 36,164,674

SIC 8699 Membership organizations, nec
Maeganvun Wong

D-U-N-S 20-570-8423   (HQ)
CANADIAN GOODWILL INDUSTRIES CORP
GOODWILL
70 Princess St, Winnipeg, MB, R3B 1K2
(204) 943-6435
Emp Here 32   *Sales* 102,140,671
SIC 8699 Membership organizations, nec
Douglas Mckechnie
Jack Watts
Bruce Down
Allan Graham
Donald Haddock

D-U-N-S 20-834-5686   (SL)
CANOLA COUNCIL OF CANADA
167 Lombard Ave Unit 400, Winnipeg, MB, R3B 0T6
(204) 982-2100
Emp Here 30   *Sales* 13,476,570
SIC 7389 Business services, nec
Patti Miller

D-U-N-S 20-837-9677   (SL)
CAVALIER CANDIES LTD
185 Bannatyne Ave, Winnipeg, MB, R3B 0R4
(204) 957-8777
Emp Here 45   *Sales* 10,118,475
SIC 2064 Candy and other confectionery products
Walter Fletcher

D-U-N-S 20-519-0726   (BR)
CIBC WORLD MARKETS INC
CIBC WOOD GUNDY
(*Suby of* CANADIAN IMPERIAL BANK OF COMMERCE)
1 Lombard Pl Suite 1000, Winnipeg, MB, R3B 3N9
(204) 942-0311
Emp Here 85
SIC 6211 Security brokers and dealers
Richard Cruise

D-U-N-S 20-835-6279   (SL)
CREDIT UNION CENTRAL OF MANITOBA LIMITED
317 Donald St Suite 400, Winnipeg, MB, R3B 2H6
(204) 985-4700
Emp Here 400   *Sales* 78,677,544
SIC 8611 Business associations
Garth Manness
Russell Fast
Alexander Sandy Wallace
Al Morin
Alex Eggie

D-U-N-S 20-515-4409   (SL)
DESTINATION WINNIPEG INC
259 Portage Ave Suite 300, Winnipeg, MB, R3B 2A9
(204) 943-1970
Emp Here 24   *Sales* 10,781,256
SIC 7389 Business services, nec
Stuart Duncan

D-U-N-S 20-844-9608   (BR)
FAIRMONT HOTELS & RESORTS INC
FAIRMONT WINNIPEG
(*Suby of* ACCOR)
2 Lombard Pl, Winnipeg, MB, R3B 0Y3
(204) 957-1350
Emp Here 250
SIC 7011 Hotels and motels
Jennifer Fox

D-U-N-S 20-948-6505   (SL)
FAMILY DYNAMICS
393 Portage Ave Suite 401, Winnipeg, MB, R3B 3H6
(204) 947-1401
Emp Here 180   *Sales* 13,822,560
SIC 8322 Individual and family services
Millie Braun

D-U-N-S 20-707-4506   (HQ)
FARMLINK MARKETING SOLUTIONS
93 Lombard Ave Suite 110, Winnipeg, MB, R3B 3B1
(877) 376-5465
Sales 14,057,280
SIC 8748 Business consulting, nec
Mark Lepp

D-U-N-S 25-993-1785   (BR)
FINANCIERE BANQUE NATIONALE INC
(*Suby of* FINANCIERE BANQUE NATIONALE INC)
200 Waterfront Dr Suite 400, Winnipeg, MB, R3B 3P1
(204) 925-2250
Emp Here 100
SIC 6021 National commercial banks
Reagan Kintrachuk

D-U-N-S 20-259-0022   (HQ)
G3 CANADA LIMITED
423 Main St Suite 800, Winnipeg, MB, R3B 1B3
(204) 983-0239
Emp Here 50   *Sales* 20,570,600
SIC 4221 Farm product warehousing and storage
Don Chapman
Brita Chell
Don Macdonald
Janice Watson
Brett Malkoske
Thomas Price

D-U-N-S 25-892-1485   (SL)
IMMIGRANT WOMEN'S ASSOCIATION OF MANITOBA INC
IWAM
515 Portage Ave, Winnipeg, MB, R3B 2E9

Emp Here 16   *Sales* 16,558,096
SIC 6311 Life insurance
Beatrice Watson

D-U-N-S 24-242-6083   (HQ)
IMPACT SECURITY GROUP INC
456 Main St 2nd Fl, Winnipeg, MB, R3B 1B6
(866) 385-7037
Sales 19,687,500
SIC 7381 Detective and armored car services
Ronald D'errico

D-U-N-S 24-428-4006   (BR)
IMPERIAL PARKING CANADA CORPORATION
IMPARK
(*Suby of* GATES GROUP CAPITAL PARTNERS, LLC)
136 Market Ave Suite 2, Winnipeg, MB, R3B 0P4
(204) 943-3578
Emp Here 125
SIC 7521 Automobile parking
Bert Treller

D-U-N-S 24-852-1775   (HQ)
INTERNATIONAL INSTITUTE FOR SUSTAINABLE DEVELOPMENT
IISD
111 Lombard Ave Suite 325, Winnipeg, MB, R3B 0T4
(204) 958-7700
Emp Here 54   *Sales* 35,471,520
SIC 8733 Noncommercial research organizations
Thomas Scott Vaughan
Grace Mota

D-U-N-S 25-506-0980   (SL)
JAMEL METALS INC
316 Notre Dame Ave, Winnipeg, MB, R3B 1P4
(204) 947-3066
Emp Here 25   *Sales* 13,013,550
SIC 5093 Scrap and waste materials
Jacob Lazareck
Melvin Lazareck

D-U-N-S 24-027-4675 (SL)
KISQUARED CORPORATION
388 Donald St Suite 226, Winnipeg, MB, R3B 2J4
(204) 989-8002
Emp Here 50   *Sales* 10,667,900
SIC 8732 Commercial nonphysical research
Katherine Devine

D-U-N-S 20-550-9743 (HQ)
KORE WIRELES CANADA INC
93 Lombard Ave Suite 412, Winnipeg, MB, R3B 3B1
(204) 954-2888
Emp Here 50   *Sales* 20,562,480
SIC 4899 Communication services, nec
Craig Kozlowski

D-U-N-S 25-301-5473 (BR)
KPMG LLP
(*Suby of* KPMG LLP)
1 Lombard Pl Unit 2000, Winnipeg, MB, R3B 0X3
(204) 957-1770
Emp Here 100
SIC 8721 Accounting, auditing, and book-keeping
Austin Abas

D-U-N-S 20-351-7875 (SL)
LAWMARK CAPITAL INC
179 Mcdermot Ave Unit 301, Winnipeg, MB, R3B 0S1
(204) 942-1138
Emp Here 50   *Sales* 16,356,350
SIC 6531 Real estate agents and managers
Mark Buleziuk

D-U-N-S 20-517-5628 (BR)
LEGER MARKETING INC
(*Suby of* LEGER MARKETING INC)
35 King St Suite 5, Winnipeg, MB, R3B 1H4
(204) 885-7570
Emp Here 105
SIC 8732 Commercial nonphysical research
Hidie Allison

D-U-N-S 20-930-2777 (HQ)
LEVY'S LEATHERS LIMITED
190 Disraeli Fwy, Winnipeg, MB, R3B 2Z4
(204) 957-5139
Emp Here 66   *Sales* 22,966,832
SIC 5948 Luggage and leather goods stores
Dennis Levy

D-U-N-S 25-499-8180 (HQ)
LIONS CLUB OF WINNIPEG HOUSING CENTRES
320 Sherbrook St, Winnipeg, MB, R3B 2W6
(204) 784-1240
Emp Here 197   *Sales* 12,856,400
SIC 8361 Residential care
Laurel Ann Kalupar

D-U-N-S 20-758-4475 (SL)
LIONS CLUB OF WINNIPEG SENIOR CITI-ZENS HOME
LIONS MANOR
320 Sherbrook St, Winnipeg, MB, R3B 2W6
(204) 784-1240
Emp Here 280   *Sales* 17,998,960
SIC 8361 Residential care
John Sinclair
Dan Burton

D-U-N-S 20-436-3899 (HQ)
LUKE'S MACHINERY CO. LTD
318 Notre Dame Ave, Winnipeg, MB, R3B 1P5
(204) 943-3421
Emp Here 17   *Sales* 10,450,572
SIC 5084 Industrial machinery and equipment
Melvin Lazareck
Jacob Lazareck

D-U-N-S 20-651-4924 (BR)
MA MAWI-WI-CHI-ITATA CENTRE INC
(*Suby of* MA MAWI-WI-CHI-ITATA CENTRE INC)

443 Spence St, Winnipeg, MB, R3B 2R8
(204) 925-0348
Emp Here 230
SIC 8699 Membership organizations, nec
Patricia Desjarlas

D-U-N-S 24-852-1007 (SL)
MANITOBA CHAMBERS OF COMMERCE, THE
227 Portage Ave, Winnipeg, MB, R3B 2A6
(204) 948-0100
Emp Here 49   *Sales* 10,360,168
SIC 8611 Business associations
Graham Starmer
Rita Chahal

D-U-N-S 20-835-3821 (HQ)
MANITOBA METIS FEDERATION INC
150 Henry Ave Suite 300, Winnipeg, MB, R3B 0J7
(204) 586-8474
Emp Here 50   *Sales* 19,137,650
SIC 8651 Political organizations
David Chartrand

D-U-N-S 24-231-9739 (SL)
NEW WEST METALS INC
13 Higgins Ave, Winnipeg, MB, R3B 0A3
(204) 949-0967
Emp Here 18   *Sales* 18,006,102
SIC 5051 Metals service centers and offices
Kevin Kessler

D-U-N-S 24-818-1851 (HQ)
ONLINE ENTERPRISES INC
ONLINE BUSINESS SYSTEMS
115 Bannatyne Ave Suite 200, Winnipeg, MB, R3B 0R3
(204) 982-0200
Emp Here 121   *Sales* 43,190,082
SIC 7371 Custom computer programming ser-vices
Charles K Loewen
Scott Sanders
Lynne Black
Tim Siemens

D-U-N-S 20-010-4594 (HQ)
PARRISH & HEIMBECKER, LIMITED
MINOTERIES P&H, LES
201 Portage Ave Suite 1400, Winnipeg, MB, R3B 3K6
(204) 956-2030
Emp Here 25   *Sales* 2,241,850,248
SIC 5153 Grain and field beans

D-U-N-S 20-010-4891 (SL)
PEERLESS GARMENTS LTD
(*Suby of* NEWPORT PRIVATE WEALTH INC)
515 Notre Dame Ave, Winnipeg, MB, R3B 1R9

Emp Here 200   *Sales* 27,334,800
SIC 2325 Men's and boys' trousers and slacks
Albert Eltassi

D-U-N-S 20-106-7720 (BR)
POSTMEDIA NETWORK INC
POSTMEDIA BUSINESS TECHNOLOGY
(*Suby of* POSTMEDIA NETWORK CANADA CORP)
300 Carlton St 6th Fl, Winnipeg, MB, R3B 2K6
(204) 926-4600
Emp Here 200
SIC 7299 Miscellaneous personal service
Lorna Macleod

D-U-N-S 25-961-7975 (BR)
PRICEWATERHOUSECOOPERS LLP
(*Suby of* PRICEWATERHOUSECOOPERS LLP)
1 Lombard Pl Suite 2300, Winnipeg, MB, R3B 0X6
(204) 926-2400
Emp Here 180
SIC 8721 Accounting, auditing, and book-keeping
Glen Dyrda

D-U-N-S 20-051-9846 (SL)
QUNARA INC
136 Market Ave Suite 8, Winnipeg, MB, R3B 0P4
(204) 925-0050
Emp Here 230   *Sales* 52,548,560
SIC 4813 Telephone communication, except radio
Dave Rourke

D-U-N-S 25-297-3193 (BR)
RBC DOMINION SECURITIES INC
(*Suby of* ROYAL BANK OF CANADA)
201 Portage Ave Suite 3100, Winnipeg, MB, R3B 3K6
(204) 982-3450
Emp Here 134
SIC 6211 Security brokers and dealers
Alan Dunnett

D-U-N-S 20-193-7567 (HQ)
REIMER CONSOLIDATED CORP
201 Portage Ave Suite 2900, Winnipeg, MB, R3B 3K6
(204) 958-5300
Emp Here 1   *Sales* 10,462,120
SIC 6712 Bank holding companies
Donald S. Reimer

D-U-N-S 20-948-6950 (HQ)
REIMER EXPRESS ENTERPRISES LTD
201 Portage Ave Suite 2900, Winnipeg, MB, R3B 3K6
(204) 958-5000
Sales 10,934,000
SIC 6712 Bank holding companies
Donald S. Reimer
Douglas M. Reimer
James S. Reimer
Anne Reimer
Kelly Reimer

D-U-N-S 20-613-2490 (HQ)
REIMER WORLD CORP
(*Suby of* REIMER CONSOLIDATED CORP)
201 Portage Ave Suite 2900, Winnipeg, MB, R3B 3K6
(204) 958-5300
Emp Here 40   *Sales* 10,973,280
SIC 8741 Management services
Donald Reimer
Anne Reimer

D-U-N-S 24-174-7760 (SL)
RESOLUTE TECHNOLOGY SOLUTIONS INC
433 Main St Suite 600, Winnipeg, MB, R3B 1B3
(204) 927-3520
Emp Here 50   *Sales* 10,619,850
SIC 8748 Business consulting, nec
Rodney Devos

D-U-N-S 20-165-3545 (BR)
REVERA INC
PARKVIEW PLACE-CENTRAL PARK LODGES
(*Suby of* GOVERNMENT OF CANADA)
440 Edmonton St, Winnipeg, MB, R3B 2M4
(204) 942-5291
Emp Here 300
SIC 8059 Nursing and personal care, nec
Don Solar

D-U-N-S 20-010-8488 (HQ)
RICHARDSON INTERNATIONAL LIMITED
RICHARDSON PIONEER GRAIN
(*Suby of* RICHARDSON, JAMES & SONS, LIMITED)
1 Lombard Pl Suite 2800, Winnipeg, MB, R3B 0X3
(204) 934-5961
Emp Here 400   *Sales* 3,113,680,900
SIC 5153 Grain and field beans
Curt Vossen
Hartley T Richardson
Don Solman
Robert G Puchniak

Sandi J. Mielitz
G. David Richardson
Serge Darkazanli
W. James Benidickson
David A. Dyck
Michael D. Walter

D-U-N-S 20-088-3379 (HQ)
RICHARDSON OILSEED LIMITED
(*Suby of* RICHARDSON, JAMES & SONS, LIMITED)
1 Lombard Pl Suite 2800, Winnipeg, MB, R3B 0X3
(204) 934-5961
Emp Here 20   *Sales* 116,972,400
SIC 2079 Edible fats and oils
Curt R. Vossen
Patrick Van Osch

D-U-N-S 20-010-5575 (HQ)
RICHARDSON PIONEER LIMITED
(*Suby of* RICHARDSON, JAMES & SONS, LIMITED)
1 Lombard Pl Suite 2700, Winnipeg, MB, R3B 0X8
(204) 934-5961
Emp Here 100   *Sales* 915,788,500
SIC 5153 Grain and field beans
Hartley T Richardson
Curtis R Vossen
Robert J Miles
James A Richardson
Nick W Fox
David G Brown
Bruce Sobkow
Robert G Puchniak
Wallace Mccain

D-U-N-S 25-399-4982 (HQ)
RICHARDSON, JAMES & SONS, LIMITED
3000 One Lombard Pl, Winnipeg, MB, R3B 0Y1
(204) 953-7970
Emp Here 20   *Sales* 2,747,365,500
SIC 5153 Grain and field beans
Hartley T. Richardson
Carolyn A. Hursh

D-U-N-S 20-288-6149 (HQ)
ROGERS WEST GROUP INCORPORATED
ROGERS WEST
201 Portage Ave Suite 1800, Winnipeg, MB, R3B 3K6
(204) 800-0202
Sales 13,167,936
SIC 8741 Management services
Jason Rogers

D-U-N-S 24-608-6722 (HQ)
SAMETCO AUTO INC
BUCK'S AUTO PARTS
233 Portage Ave Suite 200, Winnipeg, MB, R3B 2A7
(204) 925-7278
Emp Here 1   *Sales* 19,923,120
SIC 5531 Auto and home supply stores
Blair Waldvogel

D-U-N-S 24-496-1249 (SL)
SPECIAL OLYMPICS MANITOBA, INC
145 Pacific Ave Suite 304, Winnipeg, MB, R3B 2Z6
(204) 925-5628
Emp Here 27   *Sales* 10,730,178
SIC 8699 Membership organizations, nec
Jennifer Campbell

D-U-N-S 20-699-7947 (BR)
STANTEC ARCHITECTURE LTD
STANTEC CONSULTING
(*Suby of* STANTEC INC)
500 / 311 Portage Ave, Winnipeg, MB, R3B 2B9
(204) 489-5900
Emp Here 300
SIC 8712 Architectural services
Eric Wiens

▲ Public Company   ■ Public Company Family Member   **HQ** Headquarters   **BR** Branch   **SL** Single Location

D-U-N-S 24-037-9540   (BR)
STANTEC CONSULTING LTD
(*Suby of* STANTEC INC)
311 Portage Ave Unit 500, Winnipeg, MB, R3B 2B9
(204) 489-5900
Emp Here 250
SIC 8711 Engineering services
  Eric Wiens

D-U-N-S 20-651-8909   (SL)
TEEN CHALLENGE OF CENTRAL CANADA INC
414 Edmonton St, Winnipeg, MB, R3B 2M2
(204) 949-9484
Emp Here 33   *Sales* 23,403,996
SIC 8699 Membership organizations, nec
  Steve Paulson
  Chris Lowes
  Daniel Emond
  Robby Ahuja
  Mike Friesen

D-U-N-S 24-420-0726   (BR)
TETRA TECH CANADA INC
(*Suby of* TETRA TECH, INC.)
161 Portage Ave E Suite 400, Winnipeg, MB, R3B 0Y4
(204) 954-6800
Emp Here 122
SIC 8711 Engineering services
  Dean Stewart

D-U-N-S 20-706-1180   (SL)
TETREM CAPITAL MANAGEMENT LTD
201 Portage Ave Suite 1910, Winnipeg, MB, R3B 3K6
(204) 975-2865
Emp Here 15   *Sales* 10,450,155
SIC 6722 Management investment, open-end
  Daniel Bubis
  Louis Junior Damianidis

D-U-N-S 24-171-0045   (HQ)
TUNDRA OIL & GAS LIMITED
(*Suby of* RICHARDSON, JAMES & SONS, LIMITED)
1 Lombard Pl Suite 1700, Winnipeg, MB, R3B 0X3
(204) 934-5850
Emp Here 35   *Sales* 135,946,779
SIC 1382 Oil and gas exploration services
  Ken Neufeld
  Jane Mactaggart
  Murray Hanstead
  James A Richardson
  Hartley T. Richardson
  Michael E. Guttormson
  Graeme G. Phipps
  Daniel Maclean
  David J. Boone

D-U-N-S 20-833-7535   (SL)
UNITED WAY OF WINNIPEG
580 Main St, Winnipeg, MB, R3B 1C7
(204) 477-5360
Emp Here 50   *Sales* 11,341,650
SIC 8399 Social services, nec
  Connie Walker
  Beverly Passey

D-U-N-S 20-758-7916   (HQ)
UNIVERSITY OF WINNIPEG, THE
515 Portage Ave, Winnipeg, MB, R3B 2E9
(204) 786-7811
Emp Here 805   *Sales* 99,658,393
SIC 8221 Colleges and universities
  Annette Trimbee
  Neil Besner
  James Currie
  Michael Emslie
  Laurel Repski
  Jino Distasio

D-U-N-S 24-630-5528   (SL)
VIEWPOINTS RESEARCH LTD
115 Bannatyne Ave Suite 404, Winnipeg, MB,

R3B 0R3
(204) 988-9253
Emp Here 74   *Sales* 15,788,492
SIC 8732 Commercial nonphysical research
  Ginny Devine
  Leslie Turnbull

D-U-N-S 20-759-1835   (SL)
W. H. ESCOTT COMPANY LIMITED
BROKERAGE SERVICES, DIV OF
(*Suby of* MAY, J. K. INVESTMENTS LTD)
95 Alexander Ave, Winnipeg, MB, R3B 2Y8
(204) 942-5127
Emp Here 25   *Sales* 11,230,475
SIC 7389 Business services, nec
  Raymond Prokopchuk
  James Burt
  Marilyn Burt
  Jennifer Burnett

D-U-N-S 20-385-5072   (HQ)
WELLINGTON-ALTUS PRIVATE WEALTH INC
201 Portage Avee 3rd Fl, Winnipeg, MB, R3B 3K6
(888) 315-8729
Emp Here 10   *Sales* 11,714,400
SIC 8742 Management consulting services
  Charles Spiring
  Rodger Gray
  Paul Greene
  Andrew Greene
  Laurie Bonten
  Paul Jelec
  Ben Kizemchuk
  Elaine Knotek-Holmes
  Michael Micheff
  Brian Hayward

D-U-N-S 24-309-3593   (SL)
WINNIPEG CIVIC EMPLOYEES BENEFITS PROGRAM, THE
WCEBP
317 Donald St Suite 5, Winnipeg, MB, R3B 2H6
(204) 986-2522
Emp Here 32   *Sales* 59,093,088
SIC 6371 Pension, health, and welfare funds
  Glenda Willis

D-U-N-S 20-056-6177   (HQ)
WINNIPEG REGIONAL HEALTH AUTHORITY, THE
HEALTH SCIENCES CENTRE, DIV OF
650 Main St 4th Fl, Winnipeg, MB, R3B 1E2
(204) 926-7000
Emp Here 245   *Sales* 3,110,240,000
SIC 8062 General medical and surgical hospitals
  Real Cloutier
  Karen Dunlop
  Derek Johannson
  Alaa Awadalla
  Bill Baines
  Jan Byrd
  Dawn Daudrich
  Victor Giesbrecht
  Raquel Godin
  Stuart Greenfield

D-U-N-S 20-948-7644   (SL)
WINNIPEG SYMPHONY ORCHESTRA INC
555 Main St Rm 1020, Winnipeg, MB, R3B 1C3
(204) 949-3950
Emp Here 121   *Sales* 18,127,373
SIC 7929 Entertainers and entertainment groups
  Trudy Schroeder
  John Bacon
  Dorothy Dobbie
  Muriel Smith
  Ed Martens

D-U-N-S 20-520-6642   (HQ)
WYNWARD INSURANCE GROUP
1 Lombard Pl Suite 1240, Winnipeg, MB, R3B

0V9
(204) 943-0721
Emp Here 39   *Sales* 76,595,916
SIC 6331 Fire, marine, and casualty insurance
  Darryl Levy
  Gary Dyson
  Frank (Ted) Williams
  Cheryl Madden
  C.R. Vossen
  Sandy Mielits
  A.B. Paterson
  W.S. Parrish
  L. Penner
  J.W. Zacharias

D-U-N-S 20-758-4764   (HQ)
YOUNG MEN'S AND YOUNG WOMEN'S CHRISTIAN ASSOCIATION OF WINNIPEG INCORPORATED, THE
YMCA-YWCA WINNIPEG
301 Vaughan St, Winnipeg, MB, R3B 2N7
(204) 661-9474
Emp Here 100   *Sales* 65,757,500
SIC 8641 Civic and social associations
  Dave Young
  Bill Simundson
  Pamela Wright
  Dave Angus

D-U-N-S 20-569-1652   (HQ)
YOUNG, GEO H & CO LTD
GHY INTERNATIONAL
167 Lombard Ave Unit 809, Winnipeg, MB, R3B 3H8
(204) 947-6851
Emp Here 65   *Sales* 80,027,040
SIC 4731 Freight transportation arrangement
  Richard Riess
  Charles Riess
  Carol-Ann Kjartanson
  Reynold Martens

Winnipeg, MB R3C

D-U-N-S 20-613-5527   (SL)
1379025 ONTARIO LIMITED
BEST WESTERN CHARTERHOUSE HOTELS
330 York Ave Suite 508, Winnipeg, MB, R3C 0N9
(204) 942-0101
Emp Here 75   *Sales* 7,117,425
SIC 7011 Hotels and motels
  John Anderson

D-U-N-S 24-661-3645   (SL)
1700 MANAGEMENT CORPORATION
FILLMORE RILEY LLP
360 Main St Suite 1700, Winnipeg, MB, R3C 3Z3
(204) 956-2970
Emp Here 49   *Sales* 13,881,357
SIC 8741 Management services
  Glen Peters

D-U-N-S 20-364-6468   (HQ)
24-7 INTOUCH INC
240 Kennedy St 2nd Fl, Winnipeg, MB, R3C 1T1
(800) 530-1121
Emp Here 300   *Sales* 106,778,350
SIC 7389 Business services, nec
  Greg Fettes
  Jeff Fettes
  Mitul Kotecha
  Shane Kozlowich
  Steve Muise
  Matt Wheatley
  Brent Stevenson
  Deanne Harrison
  Teri Miller
  Ambrosio Ringor

D-U-N-S 24-967-7428   (SL)

3031632 MANITOBA INC
HOTEL FORT GARRY
(*Suby of* GROUPE LABERGE INC)
222 Broadway, Winnipeg, MB, R3C 0R3
(204) 942-8251
Emp Here 175   *Sales* 16,220,750
SIC 7011 Hotels and motels
  Richard Bel
  Gilles Laberge

D-U-N-S 25-097-3849   (BR)
ADESA AUCTIONS CANADA CORPORATION
ADESA WINNIPEG
(*Suby of* KAR AUCTION SERVICES, INC.)
Hwy 7 N, Winnipeg, MB, R3C 2E6
(204) 697-4400
Emp Here 200
SIC 5012 Automobiles and other motor vehicles
  Gregg Maidment

D-U-N-S 24-334-8344   (SL)
ALL IN WESTU CAPITAL CORPORATION
360 Main St Suite 400, Winnipeg, MB, R3C 3Z3
(204) 947-1200
Emp Here 25   *Sales* 17,420,250
SIC 6799 Investors, nec
  Cornelius Martens
  Edward Larry Warkentin
  Armin Martens
  Victor Jakob Thielmann
  Wayne Townsend
  Allan Mcleod

D-U-N-S 20-543-5881   (SL)
AMT MANAGEMENT SERVICES
360 Main St Suite 3000, Winnipeg, MB, R3C 4G1
(204) 957-4868
Emp Here 100   *Sales* 23,428,800
SIC 8742 Management consulting services
  Deborah Greenlay

D-U-N-S 20-617-0607   (HQ)
ARTIS REAL ESTATE INVESTMENT TRUST
ARTIS REIT
220 Portage Ave Suite 600, Winnipeg, MB, R3C 0A5
(204) 947-1250
Emp Here 20   *Sales* 388,807,773
SIC 6722 Management investment, open-end
  Armin Martens
  Dave Johnson
  Dennis Wong
  Frank Sherlock
  Kim Riley
  Jaclyn Koenig
  Ida Albo
  Steven Joyce
  Ron Rimer
  Lauren Zucker

D-U-N-S 20-364-4716   (SL)
ARTIS US HOLDINGS II GP, INC
ARTIS REIT
360 Main St Suite 300, Winnipeg, MB, R3C 3Z3
(204) 947-1250
Emp Here 120   *Sales* 16,281,240
SIC 6519 Real property lessors, nec
  Armin Martens

D-U-N-S 20-836-8662   (HQ)
ASSINIBOINE CREDIT UNION LIMITED, THE
200 Main St 6th Fl, Winnipeg, MB, R3C 1A8
(204) 958-8588
Emp Here 40   *Sales* 34,160,200
SIC 6062 State credit unions
  Allan Morin
  Mona Forsen
  Garry Mitchell
  Gerry Campbell

D-U-N-S 20-837-3035   (SL)

BALMORAL HALL - SCHOOL FOR GIRLS
630 Westminster Ave, Winnipeg, MB, R3C 3S1
(204) 784-1600
Emp Here 85   *Sales* 7,890,210
SIC 8211 Elementary and secondary schools
  Sheila Hunter

D-U-N-S 25-295-8681   (BR)
BANK OF NOVA SCOTIA, THE
SCOTIABANK
(*Suby of* BANK OF NOVA SCOTIA, THE)
200 Portage Ave, Winnipeg, MB, R3C 2R7
(204) 985-3011
Emp Here 150
SIC 6021 National commercial banks
  Nita Jobanputra

D-U-N-S 20-648-7691   (BR)
BDO CANADA LLP
WINNIPEG ACCOUNTING
(*Suby of* BDO CANADA LLP)
200 Graham Ave Suite 700, Winnipeg, MB, R3C 4L5
(204) 956-7200
Emp Here 100
SIC 8721 Accounting, auditing, and book-keeping
  Russell Paradoski

D-U-N-S 25-678-4091   (BR)
BELL MEDIA INC
CTV WINNIPEG
(*Suby of* BCE INC)
345 Graham Ave Suite 400, Winnipeg, MB, R3C 5S6
(204) 788-3300
Emp Here 95
SIC 4833 Television broadcasting stations
  Mark Maheu

D-U-N-S 20-370-6770   (HQ)
BELL MTS INC
(*Suby of* BCE INC)
333 Main St, Winnipeg, MB, R3C 4E2
(204) 225-5687
Emp Here 1   *Sales* 1,107,860,728
SIC 4841 Cable and other pay television services
  Dan Mckeen

D-U-N-S 25-230-2047   (BR)
BMO NESBITT BURNS INC
(*Suby of* BMO NESBITT BURNS INC)
360 Main St Suite 1400, Winnipeg, MB, R3C 3Z3
(204) 949-2183
Emp Here 140
SIC 6211 Security brokers and dealers
  Mrcolin Ryan

D-U-N-S 24-967-8640   (HQ)
BROWNSTONE INVESTMENT PLANNING INC
444 St Mary Ave Suite 1122, Winnipeg, MB, R3C 3T1
(204) 944-9911
Emp Here 13   *Sales* 13,280,175
SIC 6282 Investment advice
  Joe Silva
  Murray Kipling

D-U-N-S 24-717-9773   (HQ)
C & T RENTALS & SALES LTD
116 Wheatfield Rd, Winnipeg, MB, R3C 2E6
(204) 594-7368
Emp Here 13   *Sales* 11,875,650
SIC 5082 Construction and mining machinery
  Ed Dwyer

D-U-N-S 24-764-5062   (HQ)
CAMBRIAN CREDIT UNION LIMITED
ACHIEVA FINANCIAL DIV OF
225 Broadway, Winnipeg, MB, R3C 5R4
(204) 925-2600
Emp Here 40   *Sales* 74,614,316
SIC 6062 State credit unions
  Tom Bryk

Jim Grapentine
Bruce Fink
Ken Lamoureux
Paul Holden
Rose Marie Couture
Alan Curd
Howard Falk
Cindy Genyk
Judy Mathieson

D-U-N-S 24-618-2260   (SL)
CANADA MANITOBA BUSINESS SERVICE CENTRE
240 Graham Ave Suite 250, Winnipeg, MB, R3C 0J7
(204) 984-2272
Emp Here 25   *Sales* 10,615,175
SIC 8999 Services, nec
  Jean Gaultier

D-U-N-S 20-948-1829   (SL)
CANADIAN INTERNATIONAL GRAINS INSTITUTE
303 Main St Suite 1000, Winnipeg, MB, R3C 3G7
(204) 983-5344
Emp Here 45   *Sales* 10,542,960
SIC 8743 Public relations services
  Joanne Buth

D-U-N-S 25-961-8510   (BR)
CANADIAN UNION OF PUBLIC EMPLOY-EES
CUPE LOCAL 2153
(*Suby of* CANADIAN UNION OF PUBLIC EM-PLOYEES)
275 Broadway Suite 403b, Winnipeg, MB, R3C 4M6
(204) 942-6524
Emp Here 400
SIC 8631 Labor organizations
  Kevin Baldwin

D-U-N-S 20-007-6727   (HQ)
CARGILL LIMITED
CARGILL NUTRENA FEEDS
(*Suby of* CARGILL, INCORPORATED)
240 Graham Ave Suite 300, Winnipeg, MB, R3C 0J7
(204) 947-0141
Emp Here 200   *Sales* 18,315,770,000
SIC 5153 Grain and field beans
  Leonard Penner
  Julian Hatherell
  Jeffrey Johnston
  Wayne Teddy

D-U-N-S 25-532-9369   (HQ)
CERIDIAN CANADA LTD
(*Suby of* FOUNDATION HOLDINGS, INC.)
125 Garry St, Winnipeg, MB, R3C 3P2
(204) 947-9400
Emp Here 350   *Sales* 228,684,000
SIC 7361 Employment agencies
  David Mackay
  Paul Elliott
  John Cardella
  Cande Dandele
  Scott Kitching
  Sandy Lovell
  Suzy Hester

D-U-N-S 24-763-6181   (SL)
CIVIL SERVICE SUPERANNUATION BOARD
444 St Mary Ave Suite 1200, Winnipeg, MB, R3C 3T1
(204) 946-3200
Emp Here 49   *Sales* 90,486,291
SIC 6371 Pension, health, and welfare funds
  Al Morin

D-U-N-S 20-948-0342   (HQ)
CMS CREATIVE MANAGEMENT SERVICES LIMITED
330 St Mary Ave Suite 750, Winnipeg, MB, R3C 3Z5

(204) 944-0789
Emp Here 1   *Sales* 10,973,280
SIC 8741 Management services
  Abraham Simkin

D-U-N-S 20-253-3407   (SL)
COMPASS FINANCIAL
428 Portage Ave Suite 204, Winnipeg, MB, R3C 0E2
(204) 940-3950
Emp Here 15   *Sales* 10,450,155
SIC 6722 Management investment, open-end
  Glen Gibbing

D-U-N-S 20-613-8554   (HQ)
CONTINENTAL TRAVEL BUREAU LTD
222 Osborne St N, Winnipeg, MB, R3C 1V4
(204) 989-8575
Emp Here 26   *Sales* 17,158,911
SIC 4724 Travel agencies
  Daryl Silver
  Jocelyn Silver

D-U-N-S 20-833-7493   (SL)
CONVENTION CENTRE CORPORATION, THE
WINNIPEG CONVENTION CENTRE
375 York Ave Suite 243, Winnipeg, MB, R3C 3J3
(204) 956-1720
Emp Here 120   *Sales* 80,268,960
SIC 7389 Business services, nec
  Klaus Lahr
  Zivan Saper

D-U-N-S 24-116-3930   (SL)
CREDIT UNION DEPOSIT GUARANTEE CORPORATION
200 Graham Ave Suite 390, Winnipeg, MB, R3C 4L5
(204) 942-8480
Emp Here 18   *Sales* 18,627,858
SIC 6399 Insurance carriers, nec
  William (Bill) Saunders
  Irvin Wiebe
  Wally Cherski
  Carol King
  Judy Holden
  Ron Pozernick
  Walter Mackay

D-U-N-S 20-188-2383   (BR)
DELTA HOTELS LIMITED
DELTA WINNIPEG
(*Suby of* GOVERNMENT OF THE PROVINCE OF BRITISH COLUMBIA)
350 St Mary Ave, Winnipeg, MB, R3C 3J2
(204) 944-7278
Emp Here 250
SIC 7011 Hotels and motels
  Joan Enns

D-U-N-S 20-875-4163   (HQ)
DIAGNOSTIC SERVICES OF MANITOBA INC
155 Carlton St Suite 1502, Winnipeg, MB, R3C 3H8
(204) 926-8005
Sales 12,477,600
SIC 8741 Management services
  Jim Slater
  Marie Perchotte
  Hussam Azzam

D-U-N-S 24-655-1071   (SL)
DOME INSURANCE CORP LTD
(*Suby of* ROYAL CANADIAN SECURITIES LIMITED)
240 Graham Ave Suite 800, Winnipeg, MB, R3C 0J7
(204) 947-2835
Emp Here 6   *Sales* 11,079,954
SIC 6331 Fire, marine, and casualty insurance
  Richard R Bracken
  Douglas D Everett
  P Jane Everett
  N Ashleigh Everett
  Kate M Everett

D-U-N-S 20-570-1881   (HQ)
DOMO GASOLINE CORPORATION LTD
(*Suby of* ROYAL CANADIAN SECURITIES LIMITED)
270 Fort St, Winnipeg, MB, R3C 1E5
(204) 943-5920
Emp Here 25   *Sales* 279,967,220
SIC 5541 Gasoline service stations
  Douglas C. Everette
  Bruce Chwartacki
  Richard Bracken
  Sarah Everette
  Ashleigh Everette

D-U-N-S 24-520-6888   (SL)
DOWNTOWN WATCH
DOWNTOWN WINNIPEG BIZ
426 Portage Ave Suite 101, Winnipeg, MB, R3C 0C9
(204) 958-4620
Emp Here 49   *Sales* 11,698,750
SIC 8611 Business associations
  Stefano Grande

D-U-N-S 25-168-5830   (BR)
EARL'S RESTAURANTS LTD
EARL'S
(*Suby of* EARL'S RESTAURANTS LTD)
191 Main St, Winnipeg, MB, R3C 1A7
(204) 989-0103
Emp Here 175
SIC 5812 Eating places
  Lisa Frederick

D-U-N-S 20-008-0075   (SL)
EBD ENTERPRISES INC
29 Roy Roche Dr, Winnipeg, MB, R3C 2E6
(204) 633-1657
Emp Here 100   *Sales* 14,819,200
SIC 4213 Trucking, except local
  Bruce Danylchuk

D-U-N-S 24-496-6446   (HQ)
ENTERPRISE PROPERTY GROUP (MAN) INC
O & Y ENTERPRISE
330 Portage Ave Unit 1000, Winnipeg, MB, R3C 0C4
(204) 947-2242
Emp Here 3   *Sales* 10,326,728
SIC 6531 Real estate agents and managers
  Doug Mcdonald

D-U-N-S 25-297-1551   (BR)
ERNST & YOUNG INC
(*Suby of* ERNST & YOUNG INC)
360 Main St Suite 2700, Winnipeg, MB, R3C 4G9
(204) 947-6519
Emp Here 100
SIC 8721 Accounting, auditing, and book-keeping
  Inga Sheane

D-U-N-S 24-385-3582   (HQ)
EXPERT CUSTOMS BROKERS
2595 Inkster Blvd, Winnipeg, MB, R3C 2E6
(204) 633-1200
Emp Here 24   *Sales* 14,039,109
SIC 4731 Freight transportation arrangement
  Wayne Boiteau

D-U-N-S 24-113-6845   (HQ)
FEDERATED INSURANCE COMPANY OF CANADA
(*Suby of* FAIRFAX FINANCIAL HOLDINGS LIMITED)
255 Commerce Drive, Winnipeg, MB, R3C 3C9
(204) 786-6431
Emp Here 130   *Sales* 553,474,712
SIC 6331 Fire, marine, and casualty insurance
  Wayne Connely
  Kenneth Tresoor
  Rick Hurlin

D-U-N-S 20-759-8061   (SL)
FILLMORE RILEY LLP

360 Main St Suite 1700, Winnipeg, MB, R3C
3Z3
(204) 956-2970
Emp Here 90   *Sales* 13,860,990
SIC 8111 Legal services
Glen Peters
Ronald Ade

D-U-N-S 24-173-3344   (SL)
FINE LINE COMMUNICATIONS LTD
FINELINE SOLUTIONS
290 Garry St, Winnipeg, MB, R3C 1H3
(204) 947-9520
Emp Here 115   *Sales* 21,448,190
SIC 8742 Management consulting services
Polly Craik
David Rattray
Maximilian Panzo

D-U-N-S 24-351-3541   (SL)
FORT GARRY FIRE TRUCKS LTD
53 Bergen Cutoff Rd, Winnipeg, MB, R3C 2E6
(204) 594-3473
Emp Here 115   *Sales* 25,741,945
SIC 3711 Motor vehicles and car bodies
Richard Suche
Tony Brelis
Jim Peters
Brian Nash

D-U-N-S 25-115-5511   (HQ)
FRANTIC FILMS CORPORATION
220 Portage Ave Suite 1300, Winnipeg, MB,
R3C 0A5
(204) 949-0070
Emp Here 75   *Sales* 9,403,700
SIC 7819 Services allied to motion pictures
Chris Bond
Ken Zorniak

D-U-N-S 24-236-0360   (SL)
GREAT PLAINS RAIL CONTRACTORS INC
(*Suby of* UNIVERSAL RAIL SYSTEMS INC)
Gd, Winnipeg, MB, R3C 2G1
(204) 633-0135
Emp Here 40   *Sales* 10,097,680
SIC 1629 Heavy construction, nec
Jason Crawford
Daniel Jacques
Neil Johansen
Odette Bock

D-U-N-S 20-844-9343   (BR)
**GREAT-WEST LIFE ASSURANCE COM-
PANY, THE**
(*Suby of* POWER CORPORATION DU
CANADA)
60 Osborne St N, Winnipeg, MB, R3C 1V3
(204) 946-8100
Emp Here 3,000
SIC 6311 Life insurance

D-U-N-S 20-570-0313   (HQ)
**GREAT-WEST LIFE ASSURANCE COM-
PANY, THE**
(*Suby of* POWER CORPORATION DU
CANADA)
100 Osborne St N, Winnipeg, MB, R3C 1V3
(204) 946-1190
Emp Here 2,775   *Sales* 16,336,933,200
SIC 6324 Hospital and medical service plans

D-U-N-S 24-608-3885   (HQ)
GREAT-WEST LIFECO INC
(*Suby of* POWER CORPORATION DU
CANADA)
100 Osborne St N, Winnipeg, MB, R3C 1V3
(204) 946-1190
Sales 28,552,961,700
SIC 6311 Life insurance
Paul A. Mahon
Philip Armstrong
Graham Bird
Sharon Geraghty
Garry Macnicholas
Grace M. Palombo
Ross J. Petersmeyer

Nancy D. Russell
Anne C. Sonnen
Raman Srivastava

D-U-N-S 20-944-9859   (BR)
HATCH LTD
ACRES MANITOBA
(*Suby of* HATCHCOS HOLDINGS LTD)
500 Portage Ave Suite 600, Winnipeg, MB,
R3C 3Y8
(204) 786-8751
Emp Here 90
SIC 8711 Engineering services
Neil Fergusson

D-U-N-S 20-118-3766   (HQ)
**HEALTHCARE EMPLOYEES PENSION
PLAN - MANITOBA**
HEPP
200 Graham Ave Suite 900, Winnipeg, MB,
R3C 4L5
(204) 942-6591
Sales 55,593,810
SIC 6371 Pension, health, and welfare funds
Winston Maharaj
Grant D. Slater
Bob Romphf
Gerry Gattinger
Gloria O'rourke
Brian Ellis

D-U-N-S 24-572-6278   (BR)
HUDSON'S BAY COMPANY
BAY, THE
(*Suby of* HUDSON'S BAY COMPANY)
450 Portage Ave, Winnipeg, MB, R3C 0E7
(204) 783-2112
Emp Here 400
SIC 5311 Department stores
Desiree Blackmore

D-U-N-S 20-759-2536   (HQ)
IGM FINANCIAL INC
(*Suby of* POWER CORPORATION DU
CANADA)
447 Portage Ave, Winnipeg, MB, R3C 3B6
(204) 943-0361
Sales 2,463,127,223
SIC 6211 Security brokers and dealers
Jeffrey Carney
Luke Gould
Cynthia Currie
Rhonda Goldberg
Doug Milne
Blaine Shewchuk
Mike Dibden
Jeffrey Orr
Henri-Paul Rousseau
Marc A. Bibeau

D-U-N-S 20-757-3262   (HQ)
INLAND AUDIO VISUAL LIMITED
INLAND AV
422 Lucas Ave, Winnipeg, MB, R3C 2E6
(204) 786-6521
Emp Here 33   *Sales* 21,782,900
SIC 1731 Electrical work
Kim Edward Werbowski
James Alexander Werbowski

D-U-N-S 20-558-1163   (SL)
INN AT THE FORKS LP
75 Forks Market Rd, Winnipeg, MB, R3C 0A2
(204) 942-6555
Emp Here 150   *Sales* 13,903,500
SIC 7011 Hotels and motels
Robert (Bob) Sparrow
Ross Greeve
Kathy Greeve

D-U-N-S 24-916-2892   (HQ)
**INVESTORS GROUP FINANCIAL SER-
VICES INC**
GROUPE INVESTORS
(*Suby of* POWER CORPORATION DU
CANADA)
447 Portage Ave, Winnipeg, MB, R3C 3B6

(204) 943-0361
Emp Here 1   *Sales* 12,477,600
SIC 8741 Management services
Sonya Reiss
Mark Kinzel
Gould Luke
Todd D. Asman
Esther Bast
Michael Dibden
Ian Lawrence

D-U-N-S 24-691-2323   (HQ)
INVESTORS GROUP INC
(*Suby of* POWER CORPORATION DU
CANADA)
447 Portage Ave, Winnipeg, MB, R3C 3B6
(204) 943-0361
Emp Here 500   *Sales* 5,836,925,000
SIC 6722 Management investment, open-end
Sharon L. Hodgson
John S. Mccallum
Jacques Parisien
Marcel R. Coutu
Jeffrey R. Carney
Paul Desmarais
Andre Desmarais
Jeffrey Orr
Susan Doniz
Claude Genereux

D-U-N-S 24-130-4943   (SL)
**INVESTORS TACTICAL ASSET ALLOCA-
TION FUND**
447 Portage Ave, Winnipeg, MB, R3C 3B6
(204) 957-7383
Emp Here 40   *Sales* 33,494,570
SIC 6722 Management investment, open-end
Dom Grestoni

D-U-N-S 20-554-4955   (BR)
IPSOS LIMITED PARTNERSHIP
IPSOS REID
(*Suby of* IPSOS)
185 Carlton St Fl 4, Winnipeg, MB, R3C 3J1
(204) 949-3100
Emp Here 80
SIC 8732 Commercial nonphysical research
Glenn Gumany

D-U-N-S 25-116-0289   (HQ)
KEE WEST AUTO CARRIERS INC
12-15-2 Epm, Winnipeg, MB, R3C 2E6
(204) 774-2937
Emp Here 105   *Sales* 21,599,130
SIC 4213 Trucking, except local
Ken Konrad
Melanie Dickin

D-U-N-S 25-219-3941   (BR)
KEG RESTAURANTS LTD
KEG STEAKHOUSE & BAR, THE
(*Suby of* RECIPE UNLIMITED CORPORA-
TION)
115 Garry St, Winnipeg, MB, R3C 1G5
(204) 942-7619
Emp Here 140
SIC 5812 Eating places
Laurent Chapdelaine

D-U-N-S 25-095-2462   (SL)
KENMAR FOOD SERVICES LTD
PONY CORRAL RESTAURANT & BAR
444 St Mary Ave Suite 135, Winnipeg, MB,
R3C 3T1
(204) 942-4414
Emp Here 1   *Sales* 11,659,750
SIC 5812 Eating places
Peter Ginakes

D-U-N-S 20-188-7515   (SL)
LAKEVIEW HOTEL INVESTMENT CORP
185 Carlton St Suite 600, Winnipeg, MB, R3C
3J1
(204) 947-1161
Emp Here 24   *Sales* 13,385,615
SIC 6726 Investment offices, nec
Keith Levit
Chris K Miller

Avrum Senensky
Rudy Beyer
Lloyd Baker
Sean Shore

D-U-N-S 25-329-9713   (HQ)
LAKEVIEW MANAGEMENT INC
*FOUR POINTS SHERATON INTERNA-
TIONAL*
185 Carlton St Suite 600, Winnipeg, MB, R3C
3J1
(204) 947-1161
Emp Here 40   *Sales* 28,700,400
SIC 7011 Hotels and motels
Keith Levit
Yetta Levit

D-U-N-S 24-966-5357   (HQ)
**LEGAL AID SERVICES SOCIETY OF MANI-
TOBA**
LEGALI AID MANITOBA
(*Suby of* PROVINCE OF MANITOBA)
294 Portage Ave Unit 402, Winnipeg, MB, R3C
0B9
(204) 985-8500
Emp Here 30   *Sales* 13,305,840
SIC 8111 Legal services
Mario Santos
Gil Clifford
Robin Dwarka

D-U-N-S 20-000-2871   (SL)
LEO'S SALES & SERVICE LTD
Sturgeon Rd & Hwy 101, Winnipeg, MB, R3C
2E6
(204) 694-4978
Emp Here 22   *Sales* 10,450,572
SIC 5083 Farm and garden machinery
Gerald Grandmont
George Grandmont
Phillip Grandmont

D-U-N-S 25-659-9077   (BR)
**LIONS CLUB OF WINNIPEG PLACE FOR
SENIOR CITIZENS INC**
LIONS PLACE
610 Portage Ave Suite 1214, Winnipeg, MB,
R3C 0G5
(204) 784-1236
Emp Here 360
SIC 8361 Residential care
Helmut Epp

D-U-N-S 24-679-8503   (HQ)
MACKENZIE INC
(*Suby of* POWER CORPORATION DU
CANADA)
447 Portage Ave, Winnipeg, MB, R3C 3B6
(204) 943-0361
Sales 27,335,000
SIC 6719 Holding companies, nec
Andre Desmarais
Marc A. Bibeau
Henri-Paul Rousseau
Marcel R. Coutu
Gregory D. Tretiak
Gary A. Doer
Jeffrey R. Carney
Claude Genereux
Sharon L. Hodgson
Paul Desmarais Jr.

D-U-N-S 24-971-4973   (HQ)
**MANITOBA GOVERNMENT AND GENERAL
EMPLOYEES UNION**
MGEU
275 Broadway Suite 601, Winnipeg, MB, R3C
4M6
(204) 982-6438
Emp Here 1   *Sales* 21,584,750
SIC 8631 Labor organizations
Peter Olfert

D-U-N-S 20-568-9045   (HQ)
**MANITOBA HYDRO-ELECTRIC BOARD,
THE**
MANITOBA HYDRO
(*Suby of* PROVINCE OF MANITOBA)

360 Portage Ave Suite 6, Winnipeg, MB, R3C 0G8
(204) 360-3311
Emp Here 750   *Sales* 1,771,333,343
SIC 4911 Electric services
Robert B Brennan
Vince A Warden
Ken M Tennenhouse
Victor H Schroeder

D-U-N-S 24-229-3744   (HQ)
MANITOBA NURSES' UNION
275 Broadway Unit 301, Winnipeg, MB, R3C 4M6
(204) 942-1320
Emp Here 3   *Sales* 11,734,740
SIC 8631 Labor organizations
Sandi Mowat
Janice Grift
Sudhir Sadhua

D-U-N-S 20-838-1103   (HQ)
MANITOBA PUBLIC INSURANCE CORPORATION, THE
(*Suby of* PROVINCE OF MANITOBA)
234 Donald St Suite 912, Winnipeg, MB, R3C 4A4
(204) 985-7000
Emp Here 700   *Sales* 268,217,500
SIC 8743 Public relations services
Marilyn Mclaren
Jake Janzen
Kerry Bittner
Kathy Kalinowsky
Heather Reichert

D-U-N-S 24-267-6112   (HQ)
MARWEST GROUP OF COMPANIES LTD
360 Main St Suite 300, Winnipeg, MB, R3C 3Z3
(204) 947-1200
Emp Here 20   *Sales* 13,077,650
SIC 6712 Bank holding companies
Cornelius Martens
Peter Martens
Armin Martens
William Martens

D-U-N-S 24-232-4788   (HQ)
MAXIM TRANSPORTATION SERVICES INC
MAXIM TRUCK & TRAILER
1860 Brookside Blvd, Winnipeg, MB, R3C 2E6
(204) 790-6599
Emp Here 135   *Sales* 317,488,600
SIC 5511 New and used car dealers
Douglas Harvey
Cliff Kolson
Gerry Mcmillan

D-U-N-S 24-426-4297   (HQ)
MAY, J. K. INVESTMENTS LTD
SCOTT BATHGATE
149 Pioneer Ave, Winnipeg, MB, R3C 0H2
(204) 943-8525
Sales 125,425,300
SIC 5145 Confectionery
Marilyn L Burt
James Burt

D-U-N-S 20-837-2870   (SL)
MILNE, D. R. & COMPANY LTD
MILNCO INSURANCE
330 St Mary Ave Suite 210, Winnipeg, MB, R3C 3Z5
(204) 949-7000
Emp Here 25   *Sales* 14,498,100
SIC 6411 Insurance agents, brokers, and service
Daniel R. Milne
Rosemary Henderson

D-U-N-S 20-838-6326   (HQ)
MISERICORDIA GENERAL HOSPITAL
MISERICORDIA HEALTH CENTRE
99 Cornish Ave Suite 370, Winnipeg, MB, R3C 1A2
(204) 774-6581
Sales 115,283,200

SIC 8011 Offices and clinics of medical doctors
Caroline De Kayster

D-U-N-S 20-834-0836   (HQ)
MONTROSE MORTGAGE CORPORATION LTD
200 Graham Ave Suite 1110, Winnipeg, MB, R3C 4L5
(204) 982-1110
Emp Here 12   *Sales* 10,338,224
SIC 6162 Mortgage bankers and loan correspondents
Michael Nesbitt
Jack Mcdiarmid
Richard Brownscombe
Holly Dreger

D-U-N-S 20-010-2796   (HQ)
NORTH AMERICAN LUMBER LIMITED
205 Fort St Suite 200, Winnipeg, MB, R3C 1E3
(204) 942-8121
Emp Here 150   *Sales* 40,147,800
SIC 5211 Lumber and other building materials
William G Konantz
Martha Peever

D-U-N-S 24-655-1055   (HQ)
NORTH WEST COMPANY INC, THE
NORTHERN
77 Main St, Winnipeg, MB, R3C 1A3
(204) 943-0881
Emp Here 500   *Sales* 1,503,838,464
SIC 5311 Department stores
Edward Kennedy
Christie Frazier-Coleman
Craig Gilpin
John King
Amanda E. Sutton
Daniel Mcconnell
Beth Millard-Hales
Michael Beaulieu
Steve Boily
Gary Merasty

D-U-N-S 24-338-7292   (HQ)
NORTH WEST COMPANY LP, THE
NORTHERN
77 Main St, Winnipeg, MB, R3C 1A3
(204) 943-0881
Emp Here 391   *Sales* 921,813,698
SIC 6712 Bank holding companies
Edward S. Kennedy
John D.King
Gary Merasty
Beth Millard-Hales

D-U-N-S 24-345-1965   (BR)
NRG RESEARCH GROUP INC
(*Suby of* NRG RESEARCH GROUP INC)
360 Main St Suite 1910, Winnipeg, MB, R3C 3Z3
(204) 989-8999
Emp Here 200
SIC 8732 Commercial nonphysical research
Hu Gett

D-U-N-S 20-875-4189   (SL)
OFFICE OF THE FIRE COMMISSIONER
401 York Ave Unit 508, Winnipeg, MB, R3C 0P8
(204) 945-3322
Emp Here 115   *Sales* 20,554,985
SIC 8711 Engineering services
Dave Schafer

D-U-N-S 20-152-6113   (SL)
OMNITRAX CANADA INC
(*Suby of* THE BROE COMPANIES INC)
155 Carlton St Suite 300, Winnipeg, MB, R3C 3H8
(204) 947-0033
Emp Here 280
SIC 4011 Railroads, line-haul operating
Brad Chase

D-U-N-S 25-289-9935   (SL)

OSBORNE HOUSE INC
Gd, Winnipeg, MB, R3C 2H6
(204) 942-7373
Emp Here 50   *Sales* 11,341,650
SIC 8399 Social services, nec
Barbara Judt
Debbie Young
Carol Ellerback

D-U-N-S 20-049-2502   (HQ)
PATERSON GLOBALFOODS INC
PATERSON GRAIN
333 Main St 22nd Fl, Winnipeg, MB, R3C 4E2
(204) 956-2090
Emp Here 100   *Sales* 732,630,800
SIC 5153 Grain and field beans
Andrew B Paterson
Donald H Price
Murray R Dickson
Harry T Ethans
James W Burns
Ted Biyea
Hugh L Ross

D-U-N-S 24-914-2357   (HQ)
PENNER, LARRY ENTERPRISES INC
PENNER OIL
29 Mountain View, Winnipeg, MB, R3C 2E6
(204) 989-4300
Sales 44,002,035
SIC 5172 Petroleum products, nec
Larry Penner

D-U-N-S 20-727-1136   (SL)
PITBLADO LLP
COORDINATED MANAGEMENT SERVICES
360 Main St Suite 2500, Winnipeg, MB, R3C 4H6
(204) 956-0560
Emp Here 140   *Sales* 15,523,480
SIC 8111 Legal services
Bruce King
Paul Sheedy

D-U-N-S 24-851-9837   (HQ)
PRAIRIE RESEARCH ASSOCIATES PRA INC
363 Broadway Unit 500, Winnipeg, MB, R3C 3N9
(204) 987-2030
Emp Here 10   *Sales* 21,335,800
SIC 8732 Commercial nonphysical research
Gregory Mason
Kerry Dangerfield
Rita Gunn

D-U-N-S 24-498-0405   (SL)
PRATT MCGARRY INC
COLLIERS INTERNATIONAL
305 Broadway Suite 500, Winnipeg, MB, R3C 3J7
(204) 943-1600
Emp Here 45   *Sales* 14,720,715
SIC 6531 Real estate agents and managers
Wayne Pratt
Brian Taillieu
John Prall
Chris Cleverley

D-U-N-S 20-072-3729   (SL)
PUBLIC TRUSTEE OFFICE
155 Carlton St Suite 500, Winnipeg, MB, R3C 5R9
(204) 945-2700
Emp Here 20   *Sales* 10,109,180
SIC 6733 Trusts, nec
Anne Bolton

D-U-N-S 24-113-6035   (HQ)
ROYAL CANADIAN SECURITIES LIMITED
240 Graham Ave Suite 800, Winnipeg, MB, R3C 0J7
(204) 947-2835
Emp Here 10   *Sales* 288,626,000
SIC 5541 Gasoline service stations
Richard Bracken
Douglas Everett

N Ashley Everett
Sarah Everett
Judy Wakefield

D-U-N-S 24-040-2826   (SL)
ROYAL WINNIPEG BALLET, THE
380 Graham Ave, Winnipeg, MB, R3C 4K2
(204) 956-0183
Emp Here 150   *Sales* 15,897,600
SIC 7922 Theatrical producers and services
David Reid

D-U-N-S 20-814-2757   (SL)
SCOTIA PRIVATE CLIENT GROUP
200 Portage Ave Suite 845, Winnipeg, MB, R3C 3X2
(204) 985-3104
Emp Here 22   *Sales* 11,686,554
SIC 6211 Security brokers and dealers
Jean Sikomas

D-U-N-S 20-011-1094   (HQ)
SCOTT-BATHGATE LTD
NUTTY CLUB
(*Suby of* MAY, J. K. INVESTMENTS LTD)
149 Pioneer Ave, Winnipeg, MB, R3C 0H2
(204) 943-8525
Emp Here 10   *Sales* 125,425,300
SIC 5145 Confectionery
James C Burt
Angus Mcdowell
Marilyn Burt
Maurice Mearon

D-U-N-S 24-115-4632   (HQ)
SOUTHEAST RESOURCE DEVELOPMENT COUNCIL CORP
360 Broadway, Winnipeg, MB, R3C 0T6
(204) 956-7500
Sales 41,413,600
SIC 8399 Social services, nec
Valerie Flett
Inderjit Roopra
Alfred Everette
John Thunder
Joe Owen

D-U-N-S 25-961-1317   (SL)
STEVENSON ADVISORS LTD
ROYAL LEPAGE/STEVENSON ADVISORS
260 St Mary Ave Unit 200, Winnipeg, MB, R3C 0M6
(204) 956-1901
Emp Here 80   *Sales* 21,740,480
SIC 6531 Real estate agents and managers
Martin Mcgarry
Patrick Hamilton

D-U-N-S 20-913-3417   (BR)
SYMCOR INC
(*Suby of* SYMCOR INC)
195 Fort St, Winnipeg, MB, R3C 3V1
(204) 924-5819
Emp Here 100
SIC 7374 Data processing and preparation
Carol Gregoire

D-U-N-S 20-584-5444   (SL)
TEACHERS RETIREMENT ALLOWANCES FUND BOARD
TRAF
25 Forks Market Rd Suite 330, Winnipeg, MB, R3C 4S8
(204) 949-0048
Emp Here 34   *Sales* 62,786,406
SIC 6371 Pension, health, and welfare funds
Jeffrey Norton

D-U-N-S 20-250-5400   (SL)
TN ARENA LIMITED PARTNERSHIP
345 Graham Ave, Winnipeg, MB, R3C 5S6
(204) 987-7825
Emp Here 100   *Sales* 8,712,800
SIC 7941 Sports clubs, managers, and promoters
Jim Ludlow

D-U-N-S 20-006-6645   (HQ)

TRANSX LTD
CANXPRESS
(Suby of COMPAGNIE DES CHEMINS DE FER NATIONAUX DU CANADA)
2595 Inkster Blvd, Winnipeg, MB, R3C 2E6
(204) 632-6694
Emp Here 1,500   *Sales* 460,952,500
SIC 4213 Trucking, except local
Louie Tolaini
James Zacharias
Dereck Lachaine
Michael Jones

D-U-N-S 24-913-9643   (HQ)
TRANSX TRANSPORT INC
2595 Inkster Blvd Suite 2, Winnipeg, MB, R3C 2E6
(204) 632-6694
Emp Here 3   *Sales* 308,559,000
SIC 4213 Trucking, except local
Louis Tolaini
Tina Jones
Lia Banville

D-U-N-S 20-551-8165   (SL)
TRUE NORTH SPORTS & ENTERTAINMENT LIMITED
MTS CENTRE
345 Graham Ave, Winnipeg, MB, R3C 5S6
(204) 987-7825
Emp Here 102   *Sales* 8,506,290
SIC 7941 Sports clubs, managers, and promoters
Jim Ludlow

D-U-N-S 20-731-1635   (SL)
VISIONS OF INDEPENDENCE INC
190 Sherbrook St, Winnipeg, MB, R3C 2B6
(204) 453-5982
Emp Here 70   *Sales* 129,266,130
SIC 6321 Accident and health insurance
Sue Cirelaard

D-U-N-S 24-655-4786   (HQ)
WAWANESA LIFE INSURANCE COMPANY, THE
(Suby of WAWANESA MUTUAL INSURANCE COMPANY, THE)
200 Main St Suite 400, Winnipeg, MB, R3C 1A8
(204) 985-3940
Emp Here 78   *Sales* 156,898,086
SIC 6311 Life insurance
Jeff Goy
Patricia Horncastle

D-U-N-S 20-760-1832   (HQ)
WAWANESA MUTUAL INSURANCE COMPANY, THE
191 Broadway Suite 900, Winnipeg, MB, R3C 3P1
(204) 985-3923
Emp Here 217   *Sales* 2,324,108,821
SIC 6331 Fire, marine, and casualty insurance
Jeff Goy
K. E. Hartry
G. J. Timlick
E.T. Johnston
J. E. Carradice
M. K. Nemeth
C. R. Loeppky
C.M. Low
K. P. Boyd
C. J. Jardine

D-U-N-S 20-832-3998   (HQ)
WESTERN CANADA LOTTERY CORPORATION
125 Garry St Suite 1000, Winnipeg, MB, R3C 4J1
(204) 942-8217
Emp Here 140   *Sales* 18,207,000
SIC 7999 Amusement and recreation, nec
David Lob
Paul Erickson

D-U-N-S 24-229-3280   (HQ)

WINNIPEG CLINIC
425 St Mary Ave, Winnipeg, MB, R3C 0N2
(204) 957-1900
Emp Here 198   *Sales* 38,041,400
SIC 8011 Offices and clinics of medical doctors
Glenn Large

D-U-N-S 24-805-3782   (SL)
WINNIPEG JETS HOCKEY CLUB LIMITED PARTNERSHIP
WINNIPEG JETS HOCKEY CLUB
345 Graham Ave, Winnipeg, MB, R3C 5S6
(204) 987-7825
Emp Here 100   *Sales* 8,712,800
SIC 7941 Sports clubs, managers, and promoters
Mark Chipman

D-U-N-S 25-706-0913   (SL)
WINNIPEG LIVESTOCK SALES LTD
Gd, Winnipeg, MB, R3C 2E6
(204) 694-8328
Emp Here 35   *Sales* 51,369,220
SIC 5154 Livestock
Murray Couch
Jim Christie
Barry Anderson

Winnipeg, MB R3E

D-U-N-S 24-967-3732   (SL)
3075487 MANITOBA LTD
N R G MANAGEMENT
1124 Sanford St, Winnipeg, MB, R3E 2Z9
(204) 788-4117
Emp Here 60   *Sales* 13,983,900
SIC 1711 Plumbing, heating, air-conditioning
William Rodger

D-U-N-S 25-681-9772   (SL)
3885136 MANITOBA ASSOCIATION INC
CALVARY PLACE PERSONAL CARE HOME
1325 Erin St, Winnipeg, MB, R3E 3R6
(204) 943-4424
Emp Here 140   *Sales* 9,565,640
SIC 8051 Skilled nursing care facilities
Wayne Bolman
Gerhard Epp

D-U-N-S 24-556-6471   (SL)
5126614 MANITOBA INC
SK SECURITY SERVICES
857 Sargent Ave Unit 2, Winnipeg, MB, R3E 0C5
(204) 772-4135
Emp Here 45   *Sales* 17,805,510
SIC 7381 Detective and armored car services
Bonnie Donald

D-U-N-S 25-997-2714   (SL)
6119701 MANITOBA LTD
WINMAR WINNIPEG
1574 Erin St, Winnipeg, MB, R3E 2T1
(204) 255-5005
Emp Here 35   *Sales* 11,160,415
SIC 1521 Single-family housing construction
Bryan Dudek
Scott Rose

D-U-N-S 20-278-0474   (SL)
8948399 CANADA INC
SUR-SEAL PACKAGING
1425 Whyte Ave Unit 200, Winnipeg, MB, R3E 1V7
(204) 832-8001
Emp Here 30   *Sales* 13,304,700
SIC 7389 Business services, nec
Randy Graham

D-U-N-S 20-711-7979   (HQ)
ABCO SUPPLY & SERVICE LTD
(Suby of ABCO HOLDINGS LTD)
1346 Spruce St, Winnipeg, MB, R3E 2V7

(204) 633-8071
Sales 28,807,876
SIC 1711 Plumbing, heating, air-conditioning
Robert Di Lazaro
Bob Munz

D-U-N-S 20-759-8939   (SL)
ANCAST INDUSTRIES LTD
(Suby of ROBERT G. MCBAIN INVESTMENTS LTD)
1350 Saskatchewan Ave, Winnipeg, MB, R3E 0L2
(204) 786-7911
Emp Here 190   *Sales* 34,463,720
SIC 3322 Malleable iron foundries
Clyde Mcbain
Robert Mcbain

D-U-N-S 24-666-4713   (SL)
BEAUSEJOUR TOWN FIRE HALL
1369 Erin St, Winnipeg, MB, R3E 2S7
(204) 792-8627
Emp Here 27   *Sales* 12,332,906
SIC 7389 Business services, nec

D-U-N-S 20-838-8470   (BR)
BLACK & MCDONALD LIMITED
(Suby of BLACK & MCDONALD GROUP LIMITED)
401 Weston St Suite A, Winnipeg, MB, R3E 3H4
(204) 774-4403
Emp Here 90
SIC 1711 Plumbing, heating, air-conditioning
J. Mcdonald

D-U-N-S 20-269-4902   (SL)
CANADIAN SCIENCE CENTRE FOR HUMAN AND ANIMAL HEALTH
(Suby of GOVERNMENT OF CANADA)
1015 Arlington St Suite A1010, Winnipeg, MB, R3E 3P6
(204) 789-6001
Emp Here 400   *Sales* 81,632,800
SIC 8733 Noncommercial research organizations
Stella Chausse
David Butler-Jones

D-U-N-S 20-385-9009   (HQ)
CANCERCARE MANITOBA
675 Mcdermot Ave Unit 4025, Winnipeg, MB, R3E 0V9
(204) 787-2197
Sales 129,144,660
SIC 8069 Specialty hospitals, except psychiatric
Sri Navaratnam
Louis Bailey

D-U-N-S 20-758-0960   (HQ)
CANCERCARE MANITOBA FOUNDATION INC
(Suby of PROVINCE OF MANITOBA)
675 Mcdermot Ave Suite 1160, Winnipeg, MB, R3E 0V9
(204) 787-4143
Emp Here 647   *Sales* 133,315,996
SIC 8069 Specialty hospitals, except psychiatric
Dhali Dhaliwal
Arnold Naimark
Greg Tallon
Alyson Kennedy
Barb Lillie

D-U-N-S 20-007-6586   (SL)
CANTOR'S GROCERY LTD
1445 Logan Ave, Winnipeg, MB, R3E 1S1
(204) 774-1679
Emp Here 45   *Sales* 12,336,840
SIC 5411 Grocery stores
Ed Cantor
Oscar Cantor

D-U-N-S 25-507-3108   (SL)
CAPITOL STEEL CORPORATION
1355 Saskatchewan Ave, Winnipeg, MB, R3E

3K4
(204) 889-9980
Emp Here 50   *Sales* 10,141,500
SIC 3441 Fabricated structural Metal
Jeff Ganczar

D-U-N-S 20-852-9458   (BR)
CHILDREN'S HOSPITAL FOUNDATION OF MANITOBA INC, TH
MANITOBA INSTITUTE OF CHILD HEALTH
(Suby of CHILDREN'S HOSPITAL FOUNDATION OF MANITOBA INC, TH)
715 Mcdermot Ave Suite 513, Winnipeg, MB, R3E 3P4
(204) 789-3968
Emp Here 100
SIC 8733 Noncommercial research organizations
Karen Sparrow

D-U-N-S 24-693-5477   (SL)
COMMUNITY RESPITE SERVICE
CRS
1155 Notre Dame Ave, Winnipeg, MB, R3E 3G1
(204) 953-2400
Emp Here 49   *Sales* 11,114,817
SIC 8399 Social services, nec
Michelle Hammond

D-U-N-S 20-008-0133   (HQ)
CROWN CAP (1987) LTD
1130 Wall St, Winnipeg, MB, R3E 2R9
(204) 775-7740
Emp Here 1   *Sales* 10,250,550
SIC 2353 Hats, caps, and millinery
Paul Leinburd

D-U-N-S 20-711-6054   (SL)
DAVIAN CONSTRUCTION LTD
740 Logan Ave, Winnipeg, MB, R3E 1M9
(204) 783-7251
Emp Here 36   *Sales* 16,946,316
SIC 1542 Nonresidential construction, nec
Ian Balcain
Sheila Balcain

D-U-N-S 24-818-5019   (BR)
DHL EXPRESS (CANADA) LTD
(Suby of DEUTSCHE POST AG)
130 Midland St Unit 2, Winnipeg, MB, R3E 3R3
(855) 345-7447
Emp Here 80
SIC 7389 Business services, nec
Todd Billington

D-U-N-S 20-050-4186   (SL)
DUFFY'S TAXI (1996) LTD
1100 Notre Dame Ave, Winnipeg, MB, R3E 0N8
(204) 925-0101
Emp Here 154   *Sales* 11,591,888
SIC 4121 Taxicabs
Gurcharan Singh

D-U-N-S 20-008-5157   (HQ)
FINMAC LUMBER LIMITED
945 Elgin Ave, Winnipeg, MB, R3E 1B3
(204) 786-7694
Emp Here 20   *Sales* 22,358,700
SIC 5031 Lumber, plywood, and millwork
William Mcgregor
Bruce Mcgregor

D-U-N-S 20-322-2716   (SL)
FROST FIGHTER INC
(Suby of HEADWATER EQUITY PARTNERS INC)
1500 Notre Dame Ave Unit 100, Winnipeg, MB, R3E 0P9
(204) 775-8252
Emp Here 35   *Sales* 15,651,090
SIC 5075 Warm air heating and air conditioning
Nicole Clancy
Derek Wipzky

D-U-N-S 25-097-6826   (SL)
G2 LOGISTICS INC
944 Henry Ave, Winnipeg, MB, R3E 3L2
(204) 633-8989
Emp Here 32   *Sales* 16,638,944
SIC 4731 Freight transportation arrangement
Jonathan Gershman
Darryl Gershman

D-U-N-S 20-880-1717   (BR)
HALTON RECYCLING LTD
DISTRIBUTION OF HOLTON RECYCLING
(*Suby of* HALTON RECYCLING LTD)
1029 Henry Ave, Winnipeg, MB, R3E 1V6
(204) 772-0770
Emp Here 100
SIC 4953 Refuse systems
Frank Andie

D-U-N-S 20-011-8545   (HQ)
INNOVAIR INDUSTRIAL LIMITED
150 Mcphillips St, Winnipeg, MB, R3E 2J9
(204) 772-9476
Emp Here 30   *Sales* 19,001,040
SIC 5084 Industrial machinery and equipment
Arthur B Cockshott
Grant Cockshott
Joan Cockshott

D-U-N-S 20-282-1542   (BR)
INTERNATIONAL ASSOCIATION OF HEAT & FROST INSULATORS & ALLIED WORKERS
LOCAL 99
(*Suby of* INTERNATIONAL ASSOCIATION OF HEAT & FROST INSULATORS & ALLIED WORKERS)
946 Elgin Ave Suite 99, Winnipeg, MB, R3E 1B4
(204) 694-0726
Emp Here 150
SIC 8631 Labor organizations

D-U-N-S 20-009-2385   (HQ)
JACKSON, GEORGE N. LIMITED
1139 Mcdermot Ave, Winnipeg, MB, R3E 0V2
(204) 786-3821
Emp Here 75   *Sales* 73,159,500
SIC 5087 Service establishment equipment
Robert Bowes Jackson
Robert Douglas Jackson
Donald Kerr
Herbert Lorne
William Kenneth Jackson

D-U-N-S 24-265-6643   (HQ)
KITTSON INVESTMENTS LTD
SINGLETONS PROFESSIONAL FAMILY HAIR CARE
1450 Wellington Ave, Winnipeg, MB, R3E 0K5
(204) 772-3999
Emp Here 6   *Sales* 13,881,660
SIC 7231 Beauty shops
Scott Mcghie
Robert Mcghie

D-U-N-S 25-682-7577   (HQ)
LITZ, R. & SONS COMPANY LIMITED
LITZ CRANE RENTALS
277 Mcphillips St, Winnipeg, MB, R3E 2K7
(204) 783-7979
Sales 66,629,600
SIC 7359 Equipment rental and leasing, nec
William Litz Jr

D-U-N-S 25-369-5175   (BR)
LOBLAWS INC
REAL CANADIAN SUPERSTORE
(*Suby of* LOBLAW COMPANIES LIMITED)
1385 Sargent Ave, Winnipeg, MB, R3E 3P8
(204) 784-7901
Emp Here 300
SIC 5141 Groceries, general line
Cliff Faeit

D-U-N-S 24-691-9054   (SL)
MACKOW INDUSTRIES

1395 Whyte Ave, Winnipeg, MB, R3E 1V7
(204) 774-8323
Emp Here 50   *Sales* 10,141,500
SIC 3499 Fabricated Metal products, nec
Bob Mackow

D-U-N-S 24-321-7374   (SL)
MID CANADIAN INDUSTRIES
HERTZ
1577 Erin St, Winnipeg, MB, R3E 2T2
(204) 925-6600
Emp Here 50   *Sales* 14,165,000
SIC 7514 Passenger car rental
R M Chipman

D-U-N-S 20-248-5546   (SL)
MONDETTA CANADA, INC
MONDETTA CLOTHING CO
(*Suby of* MONDETTA PERFORMANCE GEAR, ULC)
1109 Winnipeg Ave, Winnipeg, MB, R3E 0S2
(204) 786-1700
Emp Here 80   *Sales* 60,648,160
SIC 5136 Men's and boy's clothing
Ashish Modha
Prashant Modha
Rajeed Bahl
Nish Verma

D-U-N-S 20-613-3175   (SL)
MWG APPAREL CORP
MID-WEST GARMENT
1147 Notre Dame Ave, Winnipeg, MB, R3E 3G1
(204) 774-2561
Emp Here 200   *Sales* 27,334,800
SIC 2321 Men's and boy's furnishings
Sam Klapman
Hartley Klapman
Brian Gibson

D-U-N-S 20-010-2192   (HQ)
NATURAL BAKERY LTD
769 Henry Ave, Winnipeg, MB, R3E 1V2
(204) 783-7344
Sales 29,347,700
SIC 5461 Retail bakeries
Rennie Balciunas
Danny Balciunas

D-U-N-S 20-010-5252   (HQ)
PERTH SERVICES LTD
PERTH'S
765 Wellington Ave Suite 1, Winnipeg, MB, R3E 0J1
(204) 697-6100
Emp Here 32   *Sales* 26,908,800
SIC 7211 Power laundries, family and commercial
Stewart Leibl

D-U-N-S 20-758-5548   (SL)
REHABILITATION CENTRE FOR CHILDREN INC
(*Suby of* PROVINCE OF MANITOBA)
1155 Notre Dame Ave, Winnipeg, MB, R3E 3G1
(204) 452-4311
Emp Here 100   *Sales* 5,924,700
SIC 8361 Residential care
Gayle Restall
Cheryl Susinski

D-U-N-S 24-883-6913   (SL)
SI ALARMS LIMITED
1380 Notre Dame Ave Unit 200, Winnipeg, MB, R3E 0P7
(204) 231-1606
Emp Here 21   *Sales* 11,155,347
SIC 6211 Security brokers and dealers
Joe Putaro

D-U-N-S 20-651-7760   (BR)
SOBEYS WEST INC
LUCERNE FOODS BREAD PLANT
(*Suby of* EMPIRE COMPANY LIMITED)
1525 Erin St, Winnipeg, MB, R3E 2T2

(204) 775-0344
Emp Here 90
SIC 2051 Bread, cake, and related products
Jorge Feldmen

D-U-N-S 25-161-0569   (SL)
STEPHEN GROUP INC., THE
765 Wellington Ave, Winnipeg, MB, R3E 0J1
(204) 697-6100
Emp Here 118   *Sales* 12,746,211
SIC 7215 Coin-operated laundries and cleaning
Terrell Stephen
Jason Comin

D-U-N-S 20-800-4254   (BR)
UNIVERSITY OF MANITOBA THE
MANITOBA INSTITUTE OF CELL BIOLOGY
(*Suby of* PROVINCE OF MANITOBA)
675 Mcdermot Ave Suite 5008, Winnipeg, MB, R3E 0V9
(204) 787-2137
Emp Here 135
SIC 8221 Colleges and universities
Leigh Murphy

D-U-N-S 20-758-4707   (HQ)
UNIVERSITY OF MANITOBA,THE
(*Suby of* PROVINCE OF MANITOBA)
727 Mcdermot Ave Suite 408, Winnipeg, MB, R3E 3P5
(204) 474-9668
Emp Here 300   *Sales* 783,778,930
SIC 8221 Colleges and universities
Jeff Lieberman
Rafi Mohammed
David Barnard

D-U-N-S 20-520-7400   (SL)
WINNIPEG BUILDING & DECORATING LTD
1586 Wall St, Winnipeg, MB, R3E 2S4
(204) 942-6121
Emp Here 35   *Sales* 11,160,415
SIC 1521 Single-family housing construction
David Macangus
Brian Thiessen

D-U-N-S 24-336-6742   (BR)
WINNIPEG REGIONAL HEALTH AUTHORITY, THE
WINNIPEG REGIONAL HEALTH AUTHORITY
(*Suby of* WINNIPEG REGIONAL HEALTH AUTHORITY, THE)
720 Mcdermot Ave Rm Ad301, Winnipeg, MB, R3E 0T3
(204) 787-1165
Emp Here 245
SIC 8062 General medical and surgical hospitals
Glenn Mclennan

D-U-N-S 25-892-6179   (BR)
WINNIPEG SCHOOL DIVISION
SARGENT PARK SCHOOL
(*Suby of* WINNIPEG SCHOOL DIVISION)
2 Sargent Park Pl, Winnipeg, MB, R3E 0V8
(204) 775-8985
Emp Here 80
SIC 8211 Elementary and secondary schools
Luba Krosney

D-U-N-S 20-832-5688   (HQ)
WINNIPEG SCHOOL DIVISION
1577 Wall St E, Winnipeg, MB, R3E 2S5
(204) 775-0231
Emp Here 1   *Sales* 308,574,574
SIC 8211 Elementary and secondary schools
Pauline Clarke
Rene Appelmans
Brad Corbett
Julie Smerchanski
Rob Riel
Chris Rhodes
Julie Millar

D-U-N-S 24-329-9463   (BR)
WINNIPEG SCHOOL DIVISION

BUILDING DEPARTMENT
(*Suby of* WINNIPEG SCHOOL DIVISION)
1395 Spruce St Suite 1, Winnipeg, MB, R3E 2V8
(204) 786-0344
Emp Here 120
SIC 8211 Elementary and secondary schools
George Heaph

D-U-N-S 20-709-7507   (BR)
WINNIPEG SCHOOL DIVISION
TECHNICAL VOCATIONAL HIGH SCHOOL
(*Suby of* WINNIPEG SCHOOL DIVISION)
1555 Wall St, Winnipeg, MB, R3E 2S2
(204) 786-1401
Emp Here 100
SIC 8211 Elementary and secondary schools
Gordon C Crook

D-U-N-S 25-055-1231   (BR)
WINNIPEG SCHOOL DIVISION
DANIEL MCINTYRE COLLEGIATE INSTITUTE
(*Suby of* WINNIPEG SCHOOL DIVISION)
720 Alverstone St, Winnipeg, MB, R3E 2H1
(204) 783-7131
Emp Here 91
SIC 8211 Elementary and secondary schools
L Belmore

Winnipeg, MB R3G

D-U-N-S 24-171-9871   (HQ)
3600106 MANITOBA INC
PISTON RING SERVICE SUPPLY
660 Wall St Suite 843, Winnipeg, MB, R3G 2T3
(204) 783-0816
Emp Here 70   *Sales* 119,900,040
SIC 5013 Motor vehicle supplies and new parts
James Tennant
John Tennant

D-U-N-S 20-006-9607   (HQ)
ADVANCE ELECTRONICS LTD
ADVANCED AUDIO & VIDEO
1300 Portage Ave, Winnipeg, MB, R3G 0V1
(204) 786-6541
Emp Here 100   *Sales* 41,535,760
SIC 5999 Miscellaneous retail stores, nec
Arnold Frieman
Myra Frieman

D-U-N-S 24-852-1999   (HQ)
BIRD CONSTRUCTION COMPANY
OMSAC DEVELOPMENTS, DIV OF
1055 Erin St, Winnipeg, MB, R3G 2X1
(204) 775-7141
Emp Here 50   *Sales* 104,758,800
SIC 1542 Nonresidential construction, nec
Dom Constantini
Paul Charette

D-U-N-S 24-267-4356   (SL)
BRYJON ENTERPRISES LTD
U-RENT-IT BANQUET & PARTY CENTRE
925 Milt Stegall Dr, Winnipeg, MB, R3G 3H7
(204) 786-8756
Emp Here 60   *Sales* 11,481,240
SIC 7359 Equipment rental and leasing, nec
Sheldon Glass
Sandra Glass
Bryan Glass
Jonathan Glass

D-U-N-S 24-572-3028   (SL)
CANADIAN CORPS OF COMMISSIONAIRES (MANITOBA AND NORTHWESTERN ONTARIO DIVISION)
290 Burnell St, Winnipeg, MB, R3G 2A7
(204) 942-5993
Emp Here 400   *Sales* 10,500,000
SIC 7381 Detective and armored car services

Robert Chmara
Robert Dowe
Thomas W. Reimer
George Elliott

D-U-N-S 20-008-1925 (BR)
CASCADES CANADA ULC
NORAMPAC, DIV OF
(*Suby of* CASCADES INC)
680 Wall St, Winnipeg, MB, R3G 2T8
(204) 786-5761
Emp Here 120
SIC 2653 Corrugated and solid fiber boxes
Jason Pufahl

D-U-N-S 20-007-7303 (SL)
CENTRAL TRANSPORT REFRIGERATION (MAN.) LTD
CTR AUTO/INDUSTRIAL SUPPLY
986 Wall St Suite 480, Winnipeg, MB, R3G 2V3
(204) 772-2481
Emp Here 41 *Sales* 18,334,134
SIC 5078 Refrigeration equipment and supplies
Donald Harvey

D-U-N-S 24-418-2874 (BR)
CINEPLEX ODEON CORPORATION
SILVERCITY POLO PARK
(*Suby of* CINEPLEX INC)
817 St James St, Winnipeg, MB, R3G 3L9
(204) 774-1001
Emp Here 140
SIC 7832 Motion picture theaters, except drive-in
Brad Phill

D-U-N-S 24-387-8654 (SL)
D & S FURNITURE GALLERIES LTD
LA-Z-BOY FURNITURE
1425 Ellice Ave, Winnipeg, MB, R3G 0G3
(204) 783-8500
Emp Here 50 *Sales* 11,517,000
SIC 5712 Furniture stores
David Sykora

D-U-N-S 25-329-1629 (SL)
ENGLAND, PAUL SALES LTD
CANADIAN TIRE
750 St James St, Winnipeg, MB, R3G 3J7
(204) 943-0311
Emp Here 150 *Sales* 30,801,450
SIC 5399 Miscellaneous general merchandise
Paul England

D-U-N-S 24-348-6722 (SL)
FABRIS-MILANO GROUP LTD, THE
1035 Erin St, Winnipeg, MB, R3G 2X1
(204) 783-7179
Emp Here 50 *Sales* 11,369,150
SIC 1752 Floor laying and floor work, nec
Rick Watts

D-U-N-S 20-913-7780 (BR)
G4S CASH SOLUTIONS (CANADA) LTD
(*Suby of* G4S PLC)
994 Wall St, Winnipeg, MB, R3G 2V3
(204) 774-6883
Emp Here 100
SIC 7381 Detective and armored car services
Chris Moerkerk

D-U-N-S 25-514-2853 (BR)
HOME DEPOT OF CANADA INC
HOME DEPOT
(*Suby of* THE HOME DEPOT INC)
727 Empress St, Winnipeg, MB, R3G 3P5
(204) 779-0703
Emp Here 250
SIC 5251 Hardware stores
Lance Sidor

D-U-N-S 20-698-6627 (BR)
HUDSON'S BAY COMPANY
BAY, THE
(*Suby of* HUDSON'S BAY COMPANY)
1485 Portage Ave, Winnipeg, MB, R3G 0W4

(204) 975-3228
Emp Here 200
SIC 5311 Department stores
Brian Read

D-U-N-S 25-716-5258 (SL)
K.B. BORISENKO PHARMACY LTD
SHOPPERS DRUG MART
1485 Portage Ave Suite 178, Winnipeg, MB, R3G 0W4
(204) 775-2478
Emp Here 50 *Sales* 12,647,700
SIC 5912 Drug stores and proprietary stores
Kelly Borisenko

D-U-N-S 20-837-1062 (SL)
KLINIC INC
KLINIC COMMUNITY HEALTH CENTRE
870 Portage Ave, Winnipeg, MB, R3G 0P1
(204) 784-4090
Emp Here 102 *Sales* 7,832,784
SIC 8322 Individual and family services
Nicole Chammartin

D-U-N-S 20-570-1162 (SL)
KROMAR PRINTING LTD
725 Portage Ave, Winnipeg, MB, R3G 0M8
(204) 775-8721
Emp Here 100 *Sales* 16,402,700
SIC 2752 Commercial printing, lithographic
Jack Cohen
Joseph Cohen

D-U-N-S 20-946-2514 (SL)
LANDAU FORD LINCOLN SALES LIMITED
555 Empress St, Winnipeg, MB, R3G 3H1
(204) 772-2411
Emp Here 80 *Sales* 50,342,400
SIC 5511 New and used car dealers
Leonard Friesen
Robert Friesen

D-U-N-S 20-836-8779 (HQ)
MANITOBA MOTOR LEAGUE, THE
CAA MANITOBA
870 Empress St, Winnipeg, MB, R3G 3H3
(204) 262-6115
Emp Here 100 *Sales* 287,720,200
SIC 8699 Membership organizations, nec
Michael Mager
June James

D-U-N-S 20-009-7988 (HQ)
MAPLE LEAF CONSTRUCTION LTD
777 Erin St, Winnipeg, MB, R3G 2W2
(204) 783-7091
Emp Here 50 *Sales* 16,408,730
SIC 1611 Highway and street construction
Barry Brown
Jack Fitzpatrick
Blake Fitzpatrick
Kevin Brown
Erin Fitzpatrick
Garrett Fitzpatrick

D-U-N-S 20-049-9593 (BR)
MCDONALD'S RESTAURANTS OF CANADA LIMITED
MCDONALD'S RESTAURANTS
(*Suby of* MCDONALD'S CORPORATION)
1440 Ellice Ave, Winnipeg, MB, R3G 0G4
(204) 949-5123
Emp Here 100
SIC 5812 Eating places
Mark Napu

D-U-N-S 20-947-8254 (HQ)
MML CLUB SERVICES LTD
CAA (MANITOBA)
870 Empress St, Winnipeg, MB, R3G 3H3
(204) 262-6131
Emp Here 1 *Sales* 25,998,350
SIC 4724 Travel agencies
Mike Mager
David Hughes
Alice Poyser

D-U-N-S 20-924-0907 (SL)

MOXIE'S CLASSIC GRILL
1485 Portage Ave Suite 234, Winnipeg, MB, R3G 0W4
(204) 783-1840
Emp Here 100 *Sales* 4,551,900
SIC 5812 Eating places
Brett Coward

D-U-N-S 24-682-4262 (HQ)
NAYLOR (CANADA), INC
1200 Portage Ave Suite 200, Winnipeg, MB, R3G 0T5
(204) 975-0415
Emp Here 194 *Sales* 38,754,800
SIC 2721 Periodicals
Michael Moss
Bob Hitesman
Chris Coldwell
Craig Gansky
Brent Naylor

D-U-N-S 20-759-5398 (HQ)
PHOENIX ENTERPRISES LTD
BROADWAY CONSTRUCTION, DIV OF
500 St James St, Winnipeg, MB, R3G 3J4
(204) 956-2233
Emp Here 10 *Sales* 50,709,600
SIC 6531 Real estate agents and managers
Saul Morantz
Richard Morantz
Ron Penner
Maria Da Ponte
Joanne Roer
Jenna Pollins
Martin Morentz

D-U-N-S 20-010-7035 (SL)
QUEST METAL PRODUCTS LTD
889 Erin St, Winnipeg, MB, R3G 2W6
(204) 786-2403
Emp Here 65 *Sales* 14,430,065
SIC 3589 Service industry machinery, nec
Roy Cuddeford

D-U-N-S 25-663-6333 (BR)
RED LOBSTER HOSPITALITY LLC
OLIVE GARDEN
1544 Portage Ave, Winnipeg, MB, R3G 0W9
(204) 783-9434
Emp Here 120
SIC 5812 Eating places
William Trochimiuk

D-U-N-S 24-440-3825 (BR)
RED LOBSTER HOSPITALITY LLC
1540 Portage Ave, Winnipeg, MB, R3G 0W9
(204) 783-9434
Emp Here 100
SIC 5812 Eating places
Andrew Fajardo

D-U-N-S 20-007-1041 (SL)
ROBINSON LIGHTING LTD
NORBURN LIGHTING & BATH CENTRE
995 Milt Stegall Dr, Winnipeg, MB, R3G 3H7
(204) 784-0099
Emp Here 55 *Sales* 12,782,165
SIC 5719 Miscellaneous homefurnishings
Brett Robinson

D-U-N-S 24-265-4788 (SL)
S. A. M. (MANAGEMENT) INC
200-1080 Portage Ave, Winnipeg, MB, R3G 3M3
(204) 942-0991
Emp Here 42 *Sales* 11,413,752
SIC 6531 Real estate agents and managers
Ken Murdoch
Ken Todd

D-U-N-S 25-271-7798 (BR)
SOBEYS WEST INC
POLO PARK SAFEWAY
(*Suby of* EMPIRE COMPANY LIMITED)
1485 Portage Ave Suite 160e, Winnipeg, MB, R3G 0W4
(204) 775-6348
Emp Here 200

SIC 5411 Grocery stores
Steven Burd

D-U-N-S 20-347-1685 (BR)
SOUTHERN FIRST NATIONS NETWORK OF CARE
ALL NATIONS COORDINATED RESPONSE NETWORK (ANCR)
835 Portage Ave, Winnipeg, MB, R3G 0N6
(204) 944-4200
Emp Here 140
SIC 8322 Individual and family services
Sandie Stoker

D-U-N-S 24-775-5366 (HQ)
UNIGRAPHICS LIMITED
488 Burnell St, Winnipeg, MB, R3G 2B4
(204) 784-1030
Emp Here 2 *Sales* 11,481,890
SIC 2732 Book printing
Kevin Polley

D-U-N-S 20-944-5071 (HQ)
UNITED FOOD & COMMERCIAL WORKERS LOCAL NO. 832
1412 Portage Ave, Winnipeg, MB, R3G 0V5
(204) 786-5055
Emp Here 46 *Sales* 20,799,850
SIC 8631 Labor organizations
Robert Ziegler
Jeff Traeger

D-U-N-S 20-838-5948 (HQ)
UNITED HEALTH SERVICES CORPORATION
MANITOBA BLUE CROSS
599 Empress St, Winnipeg, MB, R3G 3P3
(204) 775-0151
Sales 534,242,000
SIC 6324 Hospital and medical service plans
Andrew Yorke
Lois Fjeldsted
William Olson
Ted Bartman
William Christie
Lindsay Du Val
Neil Craton
Richard Ashdown
Irene Giesbrecht
Kerry Hawkins

D-U-N-S 20-011-7190 (SL)
VALOUR DECORATING (1988) LTD
889 Wall St, Winnipeg, MB, R3G 2T9
(204) 786-5875
Emp Here 60 *Sales* 10,154,820
SIC 1721 Painting and paper hanging
Karl Loepp
Rolf Langelotz

D-U-N-S 25-451-1322 (BR)
WAL-MART CANADA CORP
(*Suby of* WALMART INC.)
1001 Empress St, Winnipeg, MB, R3G 3P8
(204) 284-6900
Emp Here 200
SIC 5311 Department stores
Drew Cashmore

D-U-N-S 20-861-0548 (SL)
WESTERN FINANCIAL GROUP INC
H.E.D. INSURANCE AND RISK SERVICES
777 Portage Ave, Winnipeg, MB, R3G 0N3
(204) 943-0331
Emp Here 120 *Sales* 221,729,040
SIC 6411 Insurance agents, brokers, and service
Grant Ostir

D-U-N-S 24-845-0769 (SL)
WESTERN LIFE ASSURANCE COMPANY
WESTERN LIFE
(*Suby of* WESTERN FINANCIAL GROUP INC)
717 Portage Ave 4th Floor, Winnipeg, MB, R3G 0M8
(204) 786-6431
Emp Here 40 *Sales* 49,416,720

SIC 6311 Life insurance
  John Paisley
  Bruce Ratzlaff
  Ray Novog
  Dave Derksen
  Eric Salsberg
  John Varnell
  Winslow W Bennett
  Paul Fink

  D-U-N-S 20-612-8597   (SL)
WESTERN MESSENGER & TRANSFER LIMITED
839 Ellice Ave, Winnipeg, MB, R3G 0C3
(204) 987-7020
Emp Here 60   *Sales* 26,953,140
SIC 7389 Business services, nec
  Tom Elendiuk
  Bob Taylor

  D-U-N-S 25-892-6153   (BR)
WINNIPEG SCHOOL DIVISION
GORDON BELL HIGH SCHOOL
(*Suby of* WINNIPEG SCHOOL DIVISION)
3 Borrowman Pl, Winnipeg, MB, R3G 1M6
(204) 774-5401
Emp Here 140
SIC 8211 Elementary and secondary schools
  Arlene Skull

  D-U-N-S 24-241-7801   (SL)
ZEIDCO INC
FOOD FAIR
905 Portage Ave, Winnipeg, MB, R3G 0P3
(204) 987-8840
Emp Here 50   *Sales* 13,707,600
SIC 5411 Grocery stores
  Husni Zeid

Winnipeg, MB R3H

  D-U-N-S 20-613-9248   (SL)
191191 CANADA LTD
ST. JAMES VOLKSWAGEN
(*Suby of* AUTOCANADA INC)
670 Century St, Winnipeg, MB, R3H 0A1
(204) 788-1100
Emp Here 70   *Sales* 44,049,600
SIC 5511 New and used car dealers
  Russell Saladin
  Rick Hetherington

  D-U-N-S 20-346-4136   (SL)
7169311 MANITOBA LTD
FLOWER FACTORY, THE
975 Sherwin Rd Unit 1, Winnipeg, MB, R3H 0T8
(855) 838-7852
Emp Here 74   *Sales* 43,597,766
SIC 5193 Flowers and florists supplies
  Kim Hannam
  Maxine Hannam
  Tyler Specula

  D-U-N-S 24-747-7227   (HQ)
AERO RECIP. (CANADA) LTD
540 Marjorie St, Winnipeg, MB, R3H 0S9
(204) 788-4765
Sales 14,613,930
SIC 4581 Airports, flying fields, and services
  Alvin Joseph Gregorash

  D-U-N-S 24-098-8746   (BR)
AIR CANADA
(*Suby of* AIR CANADA)
2000 Wellington Ave Rm 222, Winnipeg, MB, R3H 1C1
(204) 788-6953
Emp Here 150
SIC 4581 Airports, flying fields, and services
  Patty Whitehill

  D-U-N-S 24-103-8715   (BR)
AIR CANADA

(*Suby of* AIR CANADA)
2020 Sargent Ave, Winnipeg, MB, R3H 0E1
(204) 788-7871
Emp Here 100
SIC 4581 Airports, flying fields, and services
  David Yewdall

  D-U-N-S 25-750-5545   (BR)
AIR CANADA PILOTS ASSOCIATION
(*Suby of* AIR CANADA PILOTS ASSOCIATION)
2000 Wellington Ave Suite 124a, Winnipeg, MB, R3H 1C1
(204) 779-0736
Emp Here 3,500
SIC 8641 Civic and social associations
  Janis Kazor

  D-U-N-S 20-613-7374   (SL)
AIRLINER MOTOR HOTEL (1972) LTD
QUALITY INN AIRLINER
1740 Ellice Ave, Winnipeg, MB, R3H 0B3
(204) 775-7131
Emp Here 125   *Sales* 11,586,250
SIC 7011 Hotels and motels
  Nizar Kaszam

  D-U-N-S 24-318-5225   (BR)
AIRPORT TERMINAL SERVICES CANADIAN COMPANY
(*Suby of* AIRPORT TERMINAL SERVICES INC)
2000 Wellington Ave Suite 221, Winnipeg, MB, R3H 1C1

Emp Here 110
SIC 4581 Airports, flying fields, and services
  Jim Lane

  D-U-N-S 24-608-0089   (SL)
ALLCO ELECTRICAL LTD
930 Bradford St, Winnipeg, MB, R3H 0N5
(204) 697-1000
Emp Here 60   *Sales* 13,069,740
SIC 1731 Electrical work
  Ian Hendry
  Dale Hendry
  Norm Mohr
  Perry Schenkeveld

  D-U-N-S 25-543-4102   (SL)
AMPHENOL TECHNICAL PRODUCTS INTERNATIONAL CO
(*Suby of* AMPHENOL CORPORATION)
2110 Notre Dame Ave, Winnipeg, MB, R3H 0K1
(204) 697-2222
Emp Here 125   *Sales* 35,364,375
SIC 3679 Electronic components, nec
  Martin Loeffler
  Edward C. Wetmore
  Edward Jespen
  Jamie Fraser

  D-U-N-S 20-007-0514   (HQ)
ANCHOR CONSTRUCTION INDUSTRIAL PRODUCTS LTD
1810 Dublin Ave, Winnipeg, MB, R3H 0H3
(204) 633-0064
Emp Here 29   *Sales* 23,253,048
SIC 5072 Hardware
  Fil Fileccia

  D-U-N-S 20-041-5698   (SL)
ARCANE HORIZON INC
1313 Border St Unit 62, Winnipeg, MB, R3H 0X4
(204) 897-5482
Emp Here 49   *Sales* 11,698,750
SIC 8611 Business associations
  Don Mcpherson

  D-U-N-S 20-335-3958   (HQ)
ATLAS GRAHAM FURGALE LTD
1725 Sargent Ave, Winnipeg, MB, R3H 0C5
(204) 775-4451
Sales 10,941,200
SIC 3991 Brooms and brushes

  Tim Macgregor
  James Graham

  D-U-N-S 20-106-7316   (SL)
AVION SERVICES CORP
2000 Wellington Ave Suite 503, Winnipeg, MB, R3H 1C1
(204) 784-5800
Emp Here 150   *Sales* 3,937,500
SIC 7381 Detective and armored car services
  Shelley Tataryn
  Robert Edgar

  D-U-N-S 24-519-3107   (HQ)
BALCO INC
ARTISTS EMPORIUM
1610 St James St, Winnipeg, MB, R3H 0L2
(204) 772-2421
Emp Here 19   *Sales* 14,850,400
SIC 5199 Nondurable goods, nec
  Janeen Balenovic
  Ivan Balenovic

  D-U-N-S 20-947-8221   (HQ)
BEE MAID HONEY LIMITED
625 Roseberry St, Winnipeg, MB, R3H 0T4
(204) 786-8977
Emp Here 45   *Sales* 56,819,236
SIC 5149 Groceries and related products, nec
  Guy Chartier
  Neil Secht
  Bill Bygarski Jr

  D-U-N-S 24-414-9175   (HQ)
BEST WEST PET FOODS INC
PET FOOD WAREHOUSE
(*Suby of* BURRETT CAPITAL CORPORATION)
1150 St James St, Winnipeg, MB, R3H 0K7
(204) 783-0952
Emp Here 7   *Sales* 15,881,320
SIC 5999 Miscellaneous retail stores, nec
  Philip Burrett

  D-U-N-S 20-519-1612   (HQ)
BISON TRANSPORT INC
(*Suby of* JANPHER INVESTMENTS INC)
1001 Sherwin Rd, Winnipeg, MB, R3H 0T8
(204) 833-0000
Emp Here 950   *Sales* 313,447,700
SIC 4213 Trucking, except local
  Robert Penner
  Donald Streuber
  Damiano Coniglio
  Jeff Pries
  Steve Zokvic
  Norm Sneyd
  Rod Hendrickson
  Michael Ludwick

  D-U-N-S 20-835-4068   (HQ)
BOARD OF GOVERNOR'S OF RED RIVER COLLEGE, THE
RRC
(*Suby of* PROVINCE OF MANITOBA)
2055 Notre Dame Ave, Winnipeg, MB, R3H 0J9
(204) 632-3960
Emp Here 750   *Sales* 161,368
SIC 8222 Junior colleges
  Stephanie Forsyth
  Richard Lennon
  Cathy Woods
  Catherine Rushton

  D-U-N-S 20-193-8664   (HQ)
BOYD GROUP INCOME FUND
1745 Ellice Ave, Winnipeg, MB, R3H 1A6
(204) 895-1244
Sales 1,413,566,845
SIC 7532 Top and body repair and paint shops
  Brock Bulbuck
  Timothy O'day
  Narendra Pathipati
  Allan Davis
  Dave Brown
  Sally Savoia

  Gene Dunn
  Robert Gross
  Violet A.M. Konkle

  D-U-N-S 20-779-2735   (SL)
BRISTOL AEROSPACE LIMITED
MAGELLAN AEROSPACE, WINNIPEG
(*Suby of* MAGELLAN AEROSPACE CORPORATION)
660 Berry St, Winnipeg, MB, R3H 0S5
(204) 775-8331
Emp Here 625   *Sales* 181,781,250
SIC 3728 Aircraft parts and equipment, nec
  James Butyniec
  Donald Boitson
  Brett Habington
  Nelson Kalin
  Dave O'connor
  Elena Milantoni

  D-U-N-S 25-999-0455   (HQ)
BUHLER FURNITURE INC
IDEAL GLASS
700 King Edward St, Winnipeg, MB, R3H 1B4
(204) 775-7799
Sales 29,166,858
SIC 2511 Wood household furniture
  Douglas Buhler

  D-U-N-S 25-313-8762   (SL)
BUSINESS FURNISHINGS (1996) LTD
BF WORKPLACE
1741 Wellington Ave, Winnipeg, MB, R3H 0G1
(204) 489-4191
Emp Here 28   *Sales* 14,102,424
SIC 5112 Stationery and office supplies
  Dennis Riley
  Stephen Hicks

  D-U-N-S 24-038-6656   (HQ)
CALM AIR INTERNATIONAL LP
930 Ferry Rd, Winnipeg, MB, R3H 0Y8
(204) 778-6471
Emp Here 40   *Sales* 142,808,400
SIC 4512 Air transportation, scheduled
  Gary Bell

  D-U-N-S 24-426-1087   (SL)
CARBERRY INTERNATIONAL SPORTS INC
CARBERRY INTERNATIONAL
820 Bradford St, Winnipeg, MB, R3H 0N5
(204) 632-4222
Emp Here 21   *Sales* 10,931,382
SIC 5091 Sporting and recreation goods
  Douglas Carberry

  D-U-N-S 25-517-7859   (SL)
CARDINAL CAPITAL MANAGEMENT INC
1780 Wellington Ave Suite 506, Winnipeg, MB, R3H 1B3
(204) 783-0716
Emp Here 23   *Sales* 15,615,229
SIC 6282 Investment advice
  Timothy Burt
  Brian Shaw

  D-U-N-S 20-025-5839   (SL)
COMMUNITY THERAPY SERVICES INC
1555 St James St Unit 201, Winnipeg, MB, R3H 1B5
(204) 949-0533
Emp Here 80   *Sales* 56,736,960
SIC 8699 Membership organizations, nec
  Irwin Corobow

  D-U-N-S 20-052-1628   (HQ)
COMPUTER BOULEVARD INC
1250 St James St Unit B, Winnipeg, MB, R3H 0L1
(204) 775-3202
Emp Here 1   *Sales* 22,358,700
SIC 5045 Computers, peripherals, and software
  George Yung

  D-U-N-S 20-005-0128   (HQ)
CONSOLIDATED TURF EQUIPMENT (1965) LTD

986 Powell Ave, Winnipeg, MB, R3H 0H6
(204) 633-7276
Emp Here 18   *Sales* 16,150,884
SIC 5083 Farm and garden machinery
William D. Watson
R. Gordon Fogg

D-U-N-S 20-005-0136   (HQ)
CONTROLLED ENVIRONMENTS LIMITED
CONVIRON
590 Berry St, Winnipeg, MB, R3H 0R9
(204) 786-6451
Sales 43,211,814
SIC 3821 Laboratory apparatus and furniture
Steven Kroft
Robert Sobra
John Proven
Andrew Kunz

D-U-N-S 25-260-0317   (SL)
CORPORATE SECURITY SUPPLY LTD
URBAN TACTICAL
891 Century St Suite A, Winnipeg, MB, R3H 0M3
(204) 989-1000
Emp Here 65   *Sales* 33,835,230
SIC 5099 Durable goods, nec
Christopher Gray
Geoff Gray
Glenda Gray

D-U-N-S 25-920-5672   (HQ)
COSIMO MINNELLA INVESTMENTS INC
SALON CENTRE
1680 Notre Dame Ave Unit 7, Winnipeg, MB, R3H 1H6
(204) 786-0001
Emp Here 20   *Sales* 14,725,806
SIC 5087 Service establishment equipment
Cosimo Minnella

D-U-N-S 25-287-5414   (BR)
COSTCO WHOLESALE CANADA LTD
(*Suby of* COSTCO WHOLESALE CORPORATION)
1315 St James St Suite 57, Winnipeg, MB, R3H 0K9
(204) 788-4415
Emp Here 175
SIC 5099 Durable goods, nec
Mrrick Hucik

D-U-N-S 25-890-3731   (SL)
DIVA DELIGHTS INC
548 King Edward St, Winnipeg, MB, R3H 1H8
(204) 885-4376
Emp Here 45   *Sales* 12,336,840
SIC 5461 Retail bakeries
Angela Husmann

D-U-N-S 20-946-5582   (HQ)
DOWLING INSURANCE BROKERS INC
1045 St James St Unit A, Winnipeg, MB, R3H 1B1
(204) 949-2600
Emp Here 16   *Sales* 101,625,810
SIC 6411 Insurance agents, brokers, and service
Charles Dowling
Curtis Wyatt
Debbie Wyatt

D-U-N-S 24-265-6916   (SL)
DUFORT INDUSTRIES LTD
999 King Edward St Unit 6, Winnipeg, MB, R3H 0R1
(204) 633-3381
Emp Here 25   *Sales* 12,451,950
SIC 5551 Boat dealers
Maurice Dufort
Gil Dufort
Claude Dufort

D-U-N-S 20-008-2469   (HQ)
DUHA COLOR SERVICES LIMITED
DUHA GROUP
750 Bradford St, Winnipeg, MB, R3H 0N3

(204) 786-8961
Emp Here 250   *Sales* 67,820,900
SIC 2752 Commercial printing, lithographic
Emeric John (Rick) Duha
Duncan Theodore Duha
Gwendolyn Ann Duha
Philis Duha

D-U-N-S 24-968-1438   (HQ)
ELITE COMMUNICATIONS INC
585 Century St, Winnipeg, MB, R3H 0W1
(204) 989-2995
Emp Here 40   *Sales* 10,163,890
SIC 4899 Communication services, nec
Scott Greer

D-U-N-S 25-152-2686   (SL)
ELLEMENT CONSULTING GROUP
503-1780 Wellington Ave, Winnipeg, MB, R3H 1B3
(204) 954-7300
Emp Here 34   *Sales* 35,185,954
SIC 6371 Pension, health, and welfare funds
Dennis Ellement

D-U-N-S 24-175-7629   (SL)
EPIC OPPORTUNITIES INC
1644 Dublin Ave, Winnipeg, MB, R3H 0X5
(204) 982-4673
Emp Here 250   *Sales* 19,198,000
SIC 8322 Individual and family services
Jeannette Delong

D-U-N-S 20-699-0215   (HQ)
EXCHANGE INCOME CORPORATION
1067 Sherwin Rd, Winnipeg, MB, R3H 0T8
(204) 982-1857
Emp Here 17   *Sales* 912,293,882
SIC 8249 Vocational schools, nec
Michael Pyle
Duncan Jessiman
Carmele Peter
David White
Dianne Spencer
Darryl Bergman
Darwin Sparrow
Adam Terwin
Gary Filmon
Donald Streuber

D-U-N-S 24-380-3322   (SL)
FALCON CAPITAL CORPORATION
590 Berry St, Winnipeg, MB, R3H 0R9
(204) 786-6451
Emp Here 100   *Sales* 26,155,300
SIC 6719 Holding companies, nec
Steven Kroft

D-U-N-S 20-008-4895   (BR)
FEDERATED CO-OPERATIVES LIMITED
(*Suby of* FEDERATED CO-OPERATIVES LIMITED)
1615 King Edward St, Winnipeg, MB, R3H 0R7
(204) 633-8950
Emp Here 206
SIC 5141 Groceries, general line
Ken Mc Cullough

D-U-N-S 20-008-5355   (HQ)
FLORISTS SUPPLY LTD
(*Suby of* FLORACO HOLDINGS INC)
35 Airport Rd, Winnipeg, MB, R3H 0V5
(800) 665-7378
Emp Here 40   *Sales* 74,252,000
SIC 5193 Flowers and florists supplies
Laurie Nesbitt
John Forsyth
Jack Cahill

D-U-N-S 20-139-8653   (SL)
FOUR POINTS HOTEL SHERATON WINNIPEG INTERNATIONAL AIRPORT
1999 Wellington Ave, Winnipeg, MB, R3H 1H5
(204) 775-5222
Emp Here 76   *Sales* 7,212,324
SIC 7011 Hotels and motels
John Pisker

D-U-N-S 24-348-6409   (BR)
G4S SECURE SOLUTIONS (CANADA) LTD
(*Suby of* G4S PLC)
530 Century St Suite 231, Winnipeg, MB, R3H 0Y4
(204) 774-0005
Emp Here 200
SIC 7381 Detective and armored car services
Thor Goodmanson

D-U-N-S 24-915-8015   (SL)
INTEGRATED MESSAGING INC
550 Berry St, Winnipeg, MB, R3H 0R9

Emp Here 100   *Sales* 22,847,200
SIC 4899 Communication services, nec
Merrill Shulman
Sheldon Stoller
Lesia Stoller
Shayna Shulman

D-U-N-S 24-533-9549   (SL)
JCA INDUSTRIES INC
JCA ELECTRONICS
118 King Edward St E, Winnipeg, MB, R3H 0N8
(204) 415-1104
Emp Here 85   *Sales* 4,572,822
SIC 3625 Relays and industrial controls
John Anderson
Darcy Cook

D-U-N-S 24-375-2789   (HQ)
JOHNSTON GROUP INC
1051 King Edward St, Winnipeg, MB, R3H 0R4
(204) 774-6677
Sales 60,837,600
SIC 8748 Business consulting, nec
David Johnston

D-U-N-S 25-385-9094   (SL)
JOSEPH & COMPANY LTD
ATLAS GRAHAM
1725 Sargent Ave, Winnipeg, MB, R3H 0C5
(204) 775-4451
Emp Here 65   *Sales* 21,198,840
SIC 3991 Brooms and brushes
Joseph Graham

D-U-N-S 20-434-6985   (HQ)
JOSTENS CANADA LTD
(*Suby of* CHAMP ACQUISITION CORPORATION)
1643 Dublin Ave, Winnipeg, MB, R3H 0G9
(204) 783-1310
Emp Here 40   *Sales* 32,613,600
SIC 3961 Costume jewelry
Robert K Sigurdson
Janice Marsch

D-U-N-S 24-318-8708   (HQ)
KREVCO LIFESTYLES INC
700 Berry St, Winnipeg, MB, R3H 0S6
(204) 786-6957
Sales 31,232,520
SIC 5091 Sporting and recreation goods
Don Carson

D-U-N-S 25-538-9827   (BR)
LOBLAWS INC
REAL CANADIAN WHOLESALE CLUB
(*Suby of* LOBLAW COMPANIES LIMITED)
1725 Ellice Ave, Winnipeg, MB, R3H 1A6
(204) 775-8280
Emp Here 100
SIC 5141 Groceries, general line
Lyle Wicklund

D-U-N-S 25-386-1256   (SL)
MACK SALES & SERVICE OF MANITOBA LTD
385 Eagle Dr, Winnipeg, MB, R3H 0G7
(204) 772-0316
Emp Here 42   *Sales* 20,919,276
SIC 5511 New and used car dealers
John Letwin

D-U-N-S 20-613-1450   (HQ)
MACMOR INDUSTRIES LTD
1175 Sherwin Rd, Winnipeg, MB, R3H 0V1
(204) 786-5891
Emp Here 40   *Sales* 32,196,528
SIC 5072 Hardware
Jean-Marc Roy
Gisele Roy
Mike Baessler

D-U-N-S 20-015-4677   (BR)
MAGELLAN AEROSPACE LIMITED
MAGELLAN AEROSPACE, WINNIPEG, A DIV OF
(*Suby of* MAGELLAN AEROSPACE CORPORATION)
660 Berry St, Winnipeg, MB, R3H 0S5
(204) 775-8331
Emp Here 700
SIC 3728 Aircraft parts and equipment, nec
Don Boitson

D-U-N-S 20-005-1241   (HQ)
MANITOBA COOPERATIVE HONEY PRODUCERS LIMITED
BEEMAID HONEY
625 Roseberry St, Winnipeg, MB, R3H 0T4
(204) 783-2240
Emp Here 31   *Sales* 26,738,464
SIC 5149 Groceries and related products, nec
Phil Veldhuis

D-U-N-S 20-944-4744   (HQ)
MARSHALL FABRICS LTD
NORTHWEST FABRICS
575 Berry St, Winnipeg, MB, R3H 0S2
(204) 783-1939
Emp Here 3   *Sales* 24,916,100
SIC 5131 Piece goods and notions
Marshall Etkin
Gary O'shawnessy

D-U-N-S 20-072-3828   (BR)
PEPSI BOTTLING GROUP (CANADA), ULC, THE
PEPSICO BEVERAGES CANADA
(*Suby of* PBG INVESTMENT (LUXEMBOURG) SARL)
1850 Ellice Ave, Winnipeg, MB, R3H 0B8
(204) 784-0600
Emp Here 300
SIC 2086 Bottled and canned soft drinks
Dwayne Mcarthur

D-U-N-S 24-685-9909   (HQ)
PERIMETER AVIATION LP
626 Ferry Rd, Winnipeg, MB, R3H 0T7
(204) 786-7031
Emp Here 380   *Sales* 190,411,200
SIC 4522 Air transportation, nonscheduled
Denis Lavallee

D-U-N-S 24-546-4854   (SL)
PETALS WEST INC
975 Sherwin Rd Unit 1, Winnipeg, MB, R3H 0T8
(204) 786-1801
Emp Here 80   *Sales* 59,401,600
SIC 5193 Flowers and florists supplies
Kim Hannam
Maxine Hannam
Tyler Specula
Aaron Paintner

D-U-N-S 20-757-6950   (HQ)
PRAIRIE COMMUNICATIONS LTD
PRAIRIE MOBILE COMMUNICATIONS
1305 King Edward St, Winnipeg, MB, R3H 0R6
(204) 632-7800
Emp Here 25   *Sales* 12,047,200
SIC 5999 Miscellaneous retail stores, nec
Kimberly Bishop
Murray Ronald

D-U-N-S 24-914-3488   (HQ)
PRIME FASTENERS (MANITOBA) LIMITED

1501 King Edward St, Winnipeg, MB, R3H 0R8
(204) 633-6624
Emp Here 25   *Sales* 47,502,600
SIC 5084 Industrial machinery and equipment
Brian Gingera

D-U-N-S 24-718-2181   (HQ)
PRO-DATA INC
1560 St James St, Winnipeg, MB, R3H 0L2
(204) 779-9960
Emp Here 14   *Sales* 17,886,960
SIC 5045 Computers, peripherals, and software
Gil Guertin
Cameron Janzen
Michael Kutz
Richard Lumsden

D-U-N-S 25-532-6696   (SL)
QUALITY CLASSROOMS INC
840 Bradford St, Winnipeg, MB, R3H 0N5
(204) 775-6566
Emp Here 24   *Sales* 12,087,792
SIC 5112 Stationery and office supplies
Matthew Todd

D-U-N-S 20-273-8837   (BR)
QUICK TRANSFER LTD
(*Suby of* 65238 MANITOBA LTD)
1680 Sargent Ave, Winnipeg, MB, R3H 0C2
(204) 786-6011
Emp Here 75
SIC 4214 Local trucking with storage
Ralph Mueller

D-U-N-S 24-356-8875   (SL)
R.J.R. INVESTMENTS LTD
670 Century St, Winnipeg, MB, R3H 0A1
(204) 788-1100
Emp Here 70   *Sales* 44,049,600
SIC 5511 New and used car dealers
Russell Saladin

D-U-N-S 25-388-5883   (SL)
RELIANCE PRODUCTS LTD
(*Suby of* BODTKER GROUP OF COMPANIES LTD)
1093 Sherwin Rd, Winnipeg, MB, R3H 1A4
(204) 633-4403
Emp Here 130   *Sales* 26,027,442
SIC 3089 Plastics products, nec
Nils Bodtker
Linda Friesen

D-U-N-S 24-265-0737   (BR)
REXEL CANADA ELECTRICAL INC
WESTBURNE ELECTRIC
(*Suby of* REXEL)
1650 Notre Dame Ave Unit 1, Winnipeg, MB, R3H 0Y7
(204) 954-9900
Emp Here 100
SIC 5063 Electrical apparatus and equipment
John Hildebrandt

D-U-N-S 20-010-8942   (HQ)
ROBINSON, B.A. CO. LTD
BCP PLUMBING SUPPLIES, DIV OF
619 Berry St, Winnipeg, MB, R3H 0S2
(204) 784-0150
Emp Here 25   *Sales* 186,720,750
SIC 5074 Plumbing and heating equipment and supplies (hydronics)
J Ross Robinson
Shea Robinson

D-U-N-S 24-851-6023   (BR)
RUSSEL METALS INC
RUSSEL METALS NORTH WINNIPEG
(*Suby of* RUSSEL METALS INC)
1359 St James St, Winnipeg, MB, R3H 0K9

Emp Here 90
SIC 5051 Metals service centers and offices
Greh Ozog

D-U-N-S 20-009-6600   (HQ)

SHIPPAM & ASSOCIATES INC
865 King Edward St, Winnipeg, MB, R3H 0P8
(204) 925-3696
Sales 19,305,520
SIC 5199 Nondurable goods, nec
Brian Shippam
Scott Shippam

D-U-N-S 24-571-4662   (HQ)
SIRCO CLEANERS (1980) LTD
KEATS BROTHERS (DIV OF)
1393 Border St Unit 5, Winnipeg, MB, R3H 0N1
(204) 831-8551
Emp Here 1   *Sales* 10,955,175
SIC 5169 Chemicals and allied products, nec
Stan Keats
Ron Keats

D-U-N-S 25-372-2094   (BR)
STANDARD AERO LIMITED
(*Suby of* STANDARDAERO AVIATION HOLDINGS, INC.)
570 Ferry Rd Suite 4, Winnipeg, MB, R3H 0T7

Emp Here 100
SIC 7538 General automotive repair shops
Kerry Boucher

D-U-N-S 20-836-9863   (HQ)
STANDARD AERO LIMITED
(*Suby of* STANDARDAERO AVIATION HOLDINGS, INC.)
33 Allen Dyne Rd, Winnipeg, MB, R3H 1A1
(204) 775-9711
Emp Here 1,200   *Sales* 493,328,000
SIC 7538 General automotive repair shops
Russell Ford
Mike Scott
Tony Brancato
Kerry O'sullivan

D-U-N-S 24-173-4128   (HQ)
SUNPLY CORPORATION
WINDSOR PLYWOOD
(*Suby of* JOHNER'S LTD)
551 Century St, Winnipeg, MB, R3H 0L8
(204) 786-5555
Sales 10,706,080
SIC 5211 Lumber and other building materials
Jarl Johner
Jarl (Ed) Johner
Jeffry Johner

D-U-N-S 25-414-3449   (SL)
TRYTON INVESTMENT COMPANY LIMITED
590 Berry St, Winnipeg, MB, R3H 0R9
(204) 772-7110
Emp Here 130   *Sales* 29,547,570
SIC 3821 Laboratory apparatus and furniture
Richard H. Kroft
Sabina Willborn

D-U-N-S 24-035-4845   (SL)
VERSATECH INDUSTRIES INC
500 Madison St, Winnipeg, MB, R3H 0L4
(204) 956-9700
Emp Here 5   *Sales* 11,313,764
SIC 4953 Refuse systems
Richard Doyle

D-U-N-S 20-005-2850   (SL)
VICTORIA INN WINNIPEG INC
(*Suby of* GENESIS HOSPITALITY INC)
1808 Wellington Ave, Winnipeg, MB, R3H 0G3
(204) 786-4801
Emp Here 200   *Sales* 18,538,000
SIC 7011 Hotels and motels
Mike Roziere
William Greiner

D-U-N-S 20-007-3411   (SL)
VOLTAGE POWER LTD
1313 Border St Unit 26, Winnipeg, MB, R3H 0X4
(204) 594-1140
Emp Here 150   *Sales* 37,866,300

SIC 1623 Water, sewer, and utility lines
Jody Rideout
Grant Petersen
Grant Sigfusson
Warren Sigfusson
Wayne Stewart
Lonnie Eirickson

D-U-N-S 25-389-2871   (SL)
WINNIPEG AIRPORTS AUTHORITY INC
2000 Wellington Ave Rm 249, Winnipeg, MB, R3H 1C2
(204) 987-9400
Emp Here 280   *Sales* 88,858,560
SIC 4581 Airports, flying fields, and services
Barry Rempel
Arthur Mauro
Michael Rodyniuk
Catherine Kloepfer
Warren Thompson
Carl Havixbeck
Geoffery Elliott
Elaine Cowan
Jim Carr
Shirley Render

Winnipeg, MB R3J

D-U-N-S 20-570-6369   (HQ)
APPELT'S JEWELLERY LTD
APPELT'S DIAMONDS
305 Madison St Unit C, Winnipeg, MB, R3J 1H9
(204) 774-2829
Emp Here 15   *Sales* 10,880,650
SIC 5944 Jewelry stores
Albert Appelt
Jeff Appelt

D-U-N-S 25-660-5502   (BR)
BAYSHORE HEALTHCARE LTD.
BAYSHORE HEALTHCARE LTD
(*Suby of* BAYSHORE HEALTHCARE LTD.)
1700 Ness Ave, Winnipeg, MB, R3J 3Y1
(204) 943-7124
Emp Here 150
SIC 8049 Offices of health practitioner
Dona Marie Johnson

D-U-N-S 24-820-0214   (HQ)
BOEING CANADA OPERATIONS LTD
BOEING CANADA WINNIPEG, DIV OF
(*Suby of* THE BOEING COMPANY)
99 Murray Park Rd, Winnipeg, MB, R3J 3M6
(204) 888-2300
Sales 436,275,000
SIC 3728 Aircraft parts and equipment, nec
Bob Cantwell
Amy May

D-U-N-S 20-004-9773   (HQ)
BORDER CHEMICAL COMPANY LIMITED
2147 Portage Ave, Winnipeg, MB, R3J 0L4
(204) 837-1383
Emp Here 3   *Sales* 17,893,323
SIC 2819 Industrial inorganic chemicals, nec
Patricia Smerchanski
Kenneth Gray
Brian P. Hurst
R.G. Smerchanski
Paul A. Godard

D-U-N-S 25-725-5687   (SL)
CANADIAN CANOLA GROWERS ASSOCIATION
CANADA LIVESTOCK ADVANCE ASSOCIATION
1661 Portage Ave Suite 400, Winnipeg, MB, R3J 3T7
(204) 788-0090
Emp Here 42   *Sales* 10,861,830
SIC 8611 Business associations
Bob Wilson
Janet Morgan

Allan Bedard
Richard White
Wayne Bacon

D-U-N-S 20-196-0437   (SL)
CLEMENT FOODS LTD
PORTAGE AVENUE FAMILY FOODS
1881 Portage Ave, Winnipeg, MB, R3J 0H3
(204) 988-4810
Emp Here 80   *Sales* 23,478,160
SIC 5411 Grocery stores
Rheal Clement

D-U-N-S 24-718-2496   (SL)
DIMATEC INC
DIAMOND DRILLING TOOLS & PRECISION MACHINING
180 Cree Cres, Winnipeg, MB, R3J 3W1
(204) 832-2828
Emp Here 80   *Sales* 38,002,080
SIC 5084 Industrial machinery and equipment
Ivor Perry

D-U-N-S 20-944-9719   (HQ)
DISCOVERY CANADA MERCHANDISERS LTD
LANCER GRAPHICS SYSTEMS
311 Saulteaux Cres, Winnipeg, MB, R3J 3C7
(204) 885-7792
Sales 28,501,560
SIC 5084 Industrial machinery and equipment
James Challis

D-U-N-S 20-041-5052   (HQ)
DOHENY SECURITIES LIMITED
1661 Portage Ave Suite 702, Winnipeg, MB, R3J 3T7
(204) 925-1250
Sales 13,578,460
SIC 6282 Investment advice
Brian Gertenstein

D-U-N-S 25-417-6878   (SL)
ENDURON INC
150 Cree Cres, Winnipeg, MB, R3J 3W1
(204) 885-2580
Emp Here 140   *Sales* 26,891,900
SIC 3499 Fabricated Metal products, nec
Richard Klassen

D-U-N-S 24-775-0029   (BR)
EXTENDICARE INC
EXTENDICARE OAKVIEW PLACE
(*Suby of* EXTENDICARE INC)
2395 Ness Ave, Winnipeg, MB, R3J 1A5
(204) 888-3005
Emp Here 300
SIC 8051 Skilled nursing care facilities
Teery Vanbocquestal

D-U-N-S 20-543-6103   (SL)
FAMILY FOODS PORTAGE AVENUE
1881 Portage Ave, Winnipeg, MB, R3J 0H3
(204) 988-4810
Emp Here 50   *Sales* 13,707,600
SIC 5411 Grocery stores
Rheal Clement

D-U-N-S 20-238-8281   (SL)
FAST AIR LTD
FAST AIR EXECUTIVE AVIATION SERVICES
80 Hangar Line Rd, Winnipeg, MB, R3J 3Y7
(204) 982-7240
Emp Here 50   *Sales* 16,237,700
SIC 4512 Air transportation, scheduled
Dylan Henry Fast

D-U-N-S 25-506-7555   (SL)
G.R.R. HOLDINGS LTD
KEG STEAKHOUSE & BAR
2553 Portage Ave, Winnipeg, MB, R3J 0P3
(204) 885-5275
Emp Here 140   *Sales* 6,372,660
SIC 5812 Eating places
Gordon Howard

D-U-N-S 25-652-0974   (BR)
GORDON HOTELS & MOTOR INNS LTD

ASSINIBOINE GORDON INN ON THE PARK
(*Suby of* GORDON HOTELS & MOTOR INNS
LTD)
1975 Portage Ave, Winnipeg, MB, R3J 0J9
(204) 888-4806
Emp Here 75
SIC 7011 Hotels and motels
 Brian Kruk

 D-U-N-S 25-011-5888   (HQ)
HUB INTERNATIONAL MANITOBA
HORIZON INSURANCE
1661 Portage Ave Suite 500, Winnipeg, MB,
R3J 3T7
(204) 988-4800
Emp Here 25   *Sales* 230,967,750
SIC 6411 Insurance agents, brokers, and ser-
vice
 Michael Leipsic
 Peter Leipsic

 D-U-N-S 25-315-7382   (BR)
**INVESTORS GROUP FINANCIAL SER-
VICES INC**
(*Suby of* POWER CORPORATION DU
CANADA)
1661 Portage Ave Suite 702, Winnipeg, MB,
R3J 3T7
(204) 786-2708
Emp Here 80
SIC 8741 Management services
 Don Courcelles

 D-U-N-S 20-520-1460   (SL)
KELLY WESTERN SERVICES LTD
KELLY WESTERN JET CENTRE
30 Hangar Line Rd, Winnipeg, MB, R3J 3Y7
(204) 948-9500
Emp Here 20   *Sales* 20,656,160
SIC 5172 Petroleum products, nec
 Gordon Peters

 D-U-N-S 24-953-1815   (BR)
LADCO COMPANY LIMITED
HOLIDAY INN AIRPORT WEST
(*Suby of* LADCO COMPANY LIMITED)
2520 Portage Ave, Winnipeg, MB, R3J 3T6
(204) 885-4478
Emp Here 200
SIC 7011 Hotels and motels

 D-U-N-S 20-613-9263   (HQ)
MACDON INDUSTRIES LTD
(*Suby of* LINAMAR CORPORATION)
680 Moray St, Winnipeg, MB, R3J 3S3
(204) 885-5590
Sales 154,482,350
SIC 3523 Farm machinery and equipment
 Ken Ross
 Neil Scott Macdonald
 Gene Fraser
 Kiera Young

 D-U-N-S 24-748-8067   (HQ)
MANITOBA TEACHERS' SOCIETY, THE
191 Harcourt St, Winnipeg, MB, R3J 3H2
(204) 888-7961
Sales 17,389,080
SIC 8621 Professional organizations
 Paul Olson

 D-U-N-S 24-683-2773   (HQ)
**METIS CHILD, FAMILY AND COMMUNITY
SERVICES AGENCY INC**
*METIS CHILD, FAMILY AND COMMUNITY
SERVICES*
2000 Portage Ave, Winnipeg, MB, R3J 0K1
(204) 927-6960
Sales 19,870,700
SIC 8699 Membership organizations, nec
 Greg Besant

 D-U-N-S 24-519-4717   (HQ)
NATIONAL DEVELOPMENTS LTD
220 Saulteaux Cres, Winnipeg, MB, R3J 3W3
(204) 889-5430
Emp Here 10   *Sales* 14,924,470

SIC 6512 Nonresidential building operators
 Philip Kives

 D-U-N-S 25-974-9331   (BR)
NAV CANADA
CANADA WINNIPEG AREA CONTROL
(*Suby of* NAV CANADA)
777 Moray St, Winnipeg, MB, R3J 3W8
(204) 983-8566
Emp Here 300
SIC 3812 Search and navigation equipment
 Dan Pickard

 D-U-N-S 24-334-0499   (SL)
SAN GOLD CORPORATION
1661 Portage Ave Unit 212, Winnipeg, MB,
R3J 3T7
(204) 772-9149
Emp Here 405   *Sales* 103,588,470
SIC 1041 Gold ores
 R. Dale Ginn
 Torben Jensen
 Gestur Kristjansson
 Gregory Gibson
 Mandeep Rai
 Robert Brennan
 Michael Anderson
 Steven Harapiak

 D-U-N-S 20-837-5972   (HQ)
**ST. JAMES-ASSINIBOIA SCHOOL DIVI-
SION**
2574 Portage Ave, Winnipeg, MB, R3J 0H8
(204) 888-7951
Emp Here 40   *Sales* 108,807,000
SIC 8211 Elementary and secondary schools
 Brett Lough
 Michael J Friesen
 Ron Weston
 Bruce Alexander
 Peter Carney
 Craig Mcgregor
 Sandra Paterson-Greene
 Bruce Chegus
 Linda Archer
 Kelly De Groot

 D-U-N-S 24-037-1658   (SL)
SUNWEST SCREEN GRAPHICS LTD
277 Cree Cres, Winnipeg, MB, R3J 3X4
(204) 888-0003
Emp Here 95   *Sales* 15,582,565
SIC 2759 Commercial printing, nec
 Subhas Chandar

 D-U-N-S 20-005-0227   (SL)
VISCOUNT GORT MOTOR HOTEL LTD
VISCOUNT GORT HOTEL
1670 Portage Ave, Winnipeg, MB, R3J 0C9
(204) 775-0451
Emp Here 100   *Sales* 9,269,000
SIC 7011 Hotels and motels
 Philip Kives
 Fred Hehirchuk
 Theodore Kives

 D-U-N-S 24-360-1403   (BR)
WE CARE HEALTH SERVICES INC
(*Suby of* WE CARE HEALTH SERVICES INC)
1661 Portage Ave Suite 209, Winnipeg, MB,
R3J 3T7
(204) 987-3044
Emp Here 175
SIC 8051 Skilled nursing care facilities
 Tiffany Hopkins

 D-U-N-S 20-947-7355   (HQ)
WINPAK LTD
WPK
100 Saulteaux Cres, Winnipeg, MB, R3J 3T3
(204) 889-1015
Emp Here 601   *Sales* 889,641,000
SIC 3081 Unsupported plastics film and sheet
 Olivier Y. Muggli
 Mustafa Bilgen
 James C. Holland
 Sharon K. Hooper

 Timothy L. Johnson
 David J. Stacey
 Larry A. Warelis
 Antti Aarnio-Wihuri
 Juha M Hellgren
 Martti Aarnio-Wihuri

Winnipeg, MB R3K

 D-U-N-S 20-005-2488   (SL)
178011 CANADA INC
RIVER CITY FORD SALES
3636 Portage Ave, Winnipeg, MB, R3K 0Z8
(204) 837-3636
Emp Here 51   *Sales* 32,093,280
SIC 5511 New and used car dealers
 Cameron Clark

 D-U-N-S 24-468-4320   (SL)
178023 CANADA LTD
3965 Portage Ave Suite 100, Winnipeg, MB,
R3K 2H4
(204) 837-4000
Emp Here 75   *Sales* 47,196,000
SIC 5511 New and used car dealers
 Carl Eisbrenner

 D-U-N-S 20-812-5133   (SL)
4695900 MANITOBA LTD
AUTO GALLERY OF WINNIPEG
3777 Portage Ave, Winnipeg, MB, R3K 0X6
(204) 895-3777
Emp Here 35   *Sales* 17,432,730
SIC 5521 Used car dealers
 Gord Pedersen

 D-U-N-S 20-651-8560   (SL)
BIRCHWOOD HONDA WEST
3965 Portage Ave Suite 75, Winnipeg, MB,
R3K 2H5
(204) 888-4542
Emp Here 40   *Sales* 19,923,120
SIC 5511 New and used car dealers
 Mike Dobush

 D-U-N-S 24-818-2008   (SL)
BIRCHWOOD PONTIAC BUICK LIMITED
BIRCHWOOD CHEVROLET BUICK GMC
3965 Portage Ave Unit 40, Winnipeg, MB, R3K
2H1
(204) 837-5811
Emp Here 72   *Sales* 45,308,160
SIC 5511 New and used car dealers
 Mark Chipman
 Stephen Chipman
 Steve Chipman

 D-U-N-S 24-523-3759   (HQ)
BOYD GROUP HOLDINGS INC
(*Suby of* BOYD GROUP INCOME FUND)
3570 Portage Ave, Winnipeg, MB, R3K 0Z8
(204) 895-1244
Emp Here 1   *Sales* 70,321,664
SIC 7538 General automotive repair shops
 Brock Bulbuck
 Gene Dunn
 Allan Davis
 Sally Savioa
 Robert Gross
 Timothy O'day
 Dave Brown

 D-U-N-S 25-539-2128   (HQ)
BOYD GROUP INC, THE
BOYD AUTOBODY & GLASS
(*Suby of* BOYD GROUP INCOME FUND)
3570 Portage Ave, Winnipeg, MB, R3K 0Z8
(204) 895-1244
Emp Here 80   *Sales* 70,231,968
SIC 7532 Top and body repair and paint shops
 Brock Bulbuck
 Allan Davis
 Dave Brown
 Robert Gross

 Timothy O'day
 Sally Savioa
 Gene Dunn

 D-U-N-S 25-301-8006   (BR)
CARTER, DWAYNE ENTERPRISES LTD
MCDONALD'S
(*Suby of* CARTER, DWAYNE ENTERPRISES
LTD)
3401 Portage Ave, Winnipeg, MB, R3K 0W9
(204) 949-6022
Emp Here 100
SIC 5812 Eating places
 Russ Shine

 D-U-N-S 20-435-3692   (SL)
JLV ENTERPRISES
VOLVO WINNIPEG
3965 Portage Ave Unit 10, Winnipeg, MB, R3K
2G8
(204) 452-0756
Emp Here 25   *Sales* 12,451,950
SIC 5511 New and used car dealers
 Steve Chipman

 D-U-N-S 20-433-8594   (SL)
KIRKFIELD HOTEL LIMITED
KIRKFIELD MOTOR HOTEL
3317 Portage Ave, Winnipeg, MB, R3K 0W8
(204) 837-1314
Emp Here 35   *Sales* 10,469,550
SIC 5921 Liquor stores
 Keith Dangerfield

 D-U-N-S 25-719-2351   (BR)
LOBLAWS INC
REAL CANADIAN SUPERSTORE
(*Suby of* LOBLAW COMPANIES LIMITED)
3193 Portage Ave, Winnipeg, MB, R3K 0W4
(204) 831-3528
Emp Here 270
SIC 5399 Miscellaneous general merchandise
 John Honke

 D-U-N-S 24-852-4787   (HQ)
LUTHERAN CHURCH-CANADA
3074 Portage Ave, Winnipeg, MB, R3K 0Y2
(204) 895-3433
Emp Here 9   *Sales* 15,618,450
SIC 8661 Religious organizations
 Ralph Mayan
 Dwayne Cleave

 D-U-N-S 20-049-9601   (SL)
MANDEX CORPORATION
MCDOUGALL AUTO SUPERSTORE
3081 Portage Ave, Winnipeg, MB, R3K 0W4

Emp Here 50   *Sales* 24,903,900
SIC 5521 Used car dealers
 Jorgen Nelson

 D-U-N-S 24-967-4482   (SL)
MANITOBA JOCKEY CLUB INC
ASSINIBOIA DOWNS
3975 Portage Ave, Winnipeg, MB, R3K 2E9
(204) 885-3330
Emp Here 150   *Sales* 12,509,250
SIC 7948 Racing, including track operation
 Harvey Warner

 D-U-N-S 20-835-3920   (SL)
**MEDI-VAN TRANSPORTATION SPECIAL-
ISTS INC**
MEDI-VAN
284 Rouge Rd, Winnipeg, MB, R3K 1K2
(204) 982-0790
Emp Here 90   *Sales* 4,938,480
SIC 4111 Local and suburban transit
 Brian Yaholkoski
 Ian Mcdougall
 Greg Leiman

 D-U-N-S 20-557-9886   (BR)
REVERA INC
HERITAGE LODGE PERSONAL CARE
(*Suby of* GOVERNMENT OF CANADA)
3555 Portage Ave, Winnipeg, MB, R3K 0X2

 ▲ Public Company   ■ Public Company Family Member   **HQ** Headquarters   **BR** Branch   **SL** Single Location

(204) 888-7940
Emp Here 110
SIC 8051 Skilled nursing care facilities
 Farr Bobbi

D-U-N-S 20-806-2443   (BR)
SOBEYS CAPITAL INCORPORATED
SOBEYS STORE 5104
(*Suby of* EMPIRE COMPANY LIMITED)
3635 Portage Ave, Winnipeg, MB, R3K 2G6
(204) 832-8605
Emp Here 100
SIC 5411 Grocery stores
 Scott Innes

D-U-N-S 20-838-7415   (SL)
ST. CHARLES COUNTRY CLUB
100 Country Club Blvd, Winnipeg, MB, R3K
1Z3
(204) 889-4444
Emp Here 90   *Sales* 7,069,050
SIC 7997 Membership sports and recreation
clubs
 Cameron Gray

D-U-N-S 24-736-0428   (SL)
TN ICEPLEX LIMITED PARTNERSHIP
MTS ICEPLEX
3969 Portage Ave, Winnipeg, MB, R3K 1W4

Emp Here 75   *Sales* 10,502,175
SIC 7999 Amusement and recreation, nec
 Rick Bochinski

D-U-N-S 20-561-0681   (SL)
VBALLS TARGET SYSTEMS INC
COMBATBALL
51 Allard Ave, Winnipeg, MB, R3K 0S8

Emp Here 60   *Sales* 19,568,160
SIC 3949 Sporting and athletic goods, nec
 Barry Belog

D-U-N-S 25-058-2400   (BR)
WAL-MART CANADA CORP
(*Suby of* WALMART INC.)
3655 Portage Ave, Winnipeg, MB, R3K 2G6
(204) 897-3410
Emp Here 115
SIC 5311 Department stores
 Roger Tam

D-U-N-S 24-818-6009   (SL)
WINNIPEG DODGE CHRYSLER LTD
WINNIPEG DODGE CHRYSLER JEEP
3965 Portage Ave Unit 90, Winnipeg, MB, R3K
2H3
(204) 774-4444
Emp Here 90   *Sales* 56,635,200
SIC 5511 New and used car dealers
 Walt Morris

D-U-N-S 20-705-4284   (SL)
WLT HOLDINGS LTD
WOODHAVEN LEXUS TOYOTA
3965 Portage Ave Suite 70, Winnipeg, MB,
R3K 2H8
(204) 889-3700
Emp Here 65   *Sales* 40,903,200
SIC 5511 New and used car dealers
 Marilou Capiendo

D-U-N-S 20-913-8168   (BR)
**YOUNG MEN'S AND YOUNG WOMEN'S
CHRISTIAN ASSOCIATION OF WINNIPEG
INCORPORATED, THE**
(*Suby of* YOUNG MEN'S AND YOUNG
WOMEN'S CHRISTIAN ASSOCIATION OF
WINNIPEG INCORPORATED, THE)
3550 Portage Ave, Winnipeg, MB, R3K 0Z8
(204) 889-8052
Emp Here 75
SIC 8641 Civic and social associations
 Hildebrand Angela

Winnipeg, MB R3L

D-U-N-S 20-518-1022   (SL)
285 PEMBINA INC
285 Pembina Hwy, Winnipeg, MB, R3L 2E1
(204) 284-0802
Emp Here 100   *Sales* 41,888,900
SIC 6531 Real estate agents and managers
 Henry Neudorf

D-U-N-S 24-308-4105   (SL)
ARCHANGEL FIREWORKS INC
104 Pembina Hwy, Winnipeg, MB, R3L 2C8
(204) 943-3332
Emp Here 38   *Sales* 12,372,800
SIC 5999 Miscellaneous retail stores, nec
 Kelly Guille

D-U-N-S 24-916-6398   (SL)
DELBIGIO, KEN PHARMACY LTD
SHOPPERS DRUG MART
43 Osborne St, Winnipeg, MB, R3L 1Y2
(204) 958-7000
Emp Here 50   *Sales* 12,647,700
SIC 5912 Drug stores and proprietary stores
 Ken Delbigio

D-U-N-S 24-035-1114   (HQ)
**HEART AND STROKE FOUNDATION OF
MANITOBA INC**
6 Donald St Suite 200, Winnipeg, MB, R3L
0K6
(204) 949-2000
Emp Here 36   *Sales* 18,417,979
SIC 7389 Business services, nec
 Debbie Brown

D-U-N-S 25-087-6927   (HQ)
HOLTMANN, J. HOLDINGS INC
*VITA HEALTH NATURAL FOOD STORES OF
MANITOBA*
106 Osborne St Suite 200, Winnipeg, MB, R3L
1Y5
(204) 984-9561
Emp Here 4   *Sales* 10,143,624
SIC 5499 Miscellaneous food stores
 John Holtmann

D-U-N-S 20-377-9756   (SL)
**MURRAY MOTOR SALES WINNIPEG LIM-
ITED PARTNERSHIP**
MURRAY CHRYSLER DODGE JEEP RAM
300 Pembina Hwy, Winnipeg, MB, R3L 2E2
(204) 284-6650
Emp Here 94   *Sales* 59,152,320
SIC 5511 New and used car dealers
 Daniel Murray

D-U-N-S 24-718-2926   (SL)
**PAQUIN ENTERTAINMENT GROUP INC,
THE**
468 Stradbrook Ave, Winnipeg, MB, R3L 0J9
(204) 988-1120
Emp Here 24   *Sales* 10,643,760
SIC 7389 Business services, nec
 Gilles Paquin
 Hartley Richardson

D-U-N-S 24-113-6969   (SL)
PEMBINA PROMOTIONS INC
PEM BRAND DIVISION
421 Mulvey Ave, Winnipeg, MB, R3L 0R6
(204) 453-4132
Emp Here 30   *Sales* 22,275,600
SIC 5199 Nondurable goods, nec
 Linda Affleck
 Teresa Kirlin
 Dennis Affleck
 Dennis Elchuk

D-U-N-S 20-010-7084   (SL)
QUINTEX SERVICES LTD
*QUINTEX UNIFORM & MAT RENTAL SER-
VICE*
332 Nassau St N, Winnipeg, MB, R3L 0R8
(204) 477-6600
Emp Here 80   *Sales* 8,542,560

SIC 7213 Linen supply
 David R Quinton
 Janette Millar
 Roger Loewen
 Paul Radley
 Mark Hutcheson

D-U-N-S 24-265-3533   (SL)
RIVERVIEW HEALTH CENTRE INC
1 Morley Ave, Winnipeg, MB, R3L 2P4
(204) 478-6203
Emp Here 850   *Sales* 44,723,978
SIC 8051 Skilled nursing care facilities
 Norman R Kasian
 Romeo Daley
 Marilyn Kapitany
 Vince Cerasani

D-U-N-S 24-348-6656   (HQ)
**SHELTER CANADIAN PROPERTIES LIM-
ITED**
2600 Seven Evergreen Place, Winnipeg, MB,
R3L 2T3
(204) 475-9090
Sales 426,941,400
SIC 6282 Investment advice
 Arni Thorsteinson

D-U-N-S 24-914-2647   (HQ)
**SHELTER CANADIAN PROPERTIES LIM-
ITED**
(*Suby of* 2668921 MANITOBA LTD)
7 Evergreen Pl Suite 2600, Winnipeg, MB,
R3L 2T3
(204) 474-5975
Emp Here 75   *Sales* 40,703,100
SIC 6513 Apartment building operators
 Arni Thorsteinson
 Richard Blair
 Kenneth Dando

D-U-N-S 24-206-5923   (BR)
SOBEYS WEST INC
OSBORNE & KYLEMORE SAFEWAY
(*Suby of* EMPIRE COMPANY LIMITED)
655 Osborne St, Winnipeg, MB, R3L 2B7
(204) 475-0793
Emp Here 150
SIC 5411 Grocery stores
 Brad Muttern

D-U-N-S 25-138-5456   (BR)
WINNIPEG SCHOOL DIVISION
CHURCHILL HIGH SCHOOL
(*Suby of* WINNIPEG SCHOOL DIVISION)
510 Hay St, Winnipeg, MB, R3L 2L6
(204) 474-1301
Emp Here 90
SIC 8211 Elementary and secondary schools
 D Miller

Winnipeg, MB R3M

D-U-N-S 20-049-9668   (HQ)
3867359 MANITOBA INC
MIDAS
584 Pembina Hwy Suite 204, Winnipeg, MB,
R3M 3X7
(204) 925-3840
Emp Here 2   *Sales* 16,998,000
SIC 7538 General automotive repair shops
 Greg Ware

D-U-N-S 24-325-8485   (HQ)
4834772 MANITOBA LTD
600 Pembina Hwy, Winnipeg, MB, R3M 2M5

Sales 221,132,945
SIC 6712 Bank holding companies
 Thomas Matthews

D-U-N-S 24-231-2882   (SL)
AUTO HAUS FORT GARRY (1981) LTD
AUTO HAUS VOLKSWAGEN
660 Pembina Hwy, Winnipeg, MB, R3M 2M5

---

(204) 284-7520
Emp Here 65   *Sales* 40,903,200
SIC 5511 New and used car dealers
 Kevin Knight
 Keith Single

D-U-N-S 20-835-6170   (SL)
**CONVALESCENT HOME OF WINNIPEG,
THE**
276 Hugo St N, Winnipeg, MB, R3M 2N6
(204) 453-4663
Emp Here 98   *Sales* 6,719,468
SIC 8051 Skilled nursing care facilities
 Carol Allen

D-U-N-S 20-758-9615   (HQ)
**COUGHLIN, GUY INSURANCE AGENCY
LTD**
COUGHLIN INSURANCE BROKERS
1170 Taylor Ave Unit 4, Winnipeg, MB, R3M
3Z4
(204) 953-4600
Emp Here 10   *Sales* 12,720,900
SIC 6411 Insurance agents, brokers, and ser-
vice
 Guy Coughlin
 Marlene Coughlin
 Ken Coughlin
 Robert Coughlin
 Brian Coughlin
 Donna Kommishon

D-U-N-S 25-313-3805   (SL)
**DIAMOND ATHLETIC MEDICAL SUPPLIES
INC**
75 Poseidon Bay Unit 185, Winnipeg, MB,
R3M 3E4
(204) 488-7820
Emp Here 30   *Sales* 13,415,220
SIC 5047 Medical and hospital equipment
 Gerald Diamond
 Ben Diamond

D-U-N-S 24-669-6624   (SL)
FORT ROUGE AUTO SALES
680 Pembina Hwy, Winnipeg, MB, R3M 2M5
(877) 792-9521
Emp Here 25   *Sales* 12,451,950
SIC 5521 Used car dealers
 Frank Torchia

D-U-N-S 24-966-5217   (HQ)
KILKENNY REAL ESTATE LTD
SUTTON GROUP-KILKENNY REAL ESTATE
663 Stafford St, Winnipeg, MB, R3M 2X7
(204) 475-9130
Emp Here 1   *Sales* 13,316,044
SIC 6531 Real estate agents and managers
 Blaine Campbell

D-U-N-S 24-322-9841   (SL)
MAGELLAN VACATION INC
730 Taylor Ave, Winnipeg, MB, R3M 2K8
(204) 992-5215
Emp Here 30   *Sales* 11,560,800
SIC 4724 Travel agencies
 Andrew Vignuzzi

D-U-N-S 25-305-4902   (BR)
**MCDONALD'S RESTAURANTS OF
CANADA LIMITED**
MCDONALD'S 8031
(*Suby of* MCDONALD'S CORPORATION)
425 Nathaniel St Suite 1187, Winnipeg, MB,
R3M 3X1
(204) 949-6031
Emp Here 80
SIC 5812 Eating places
 Tash Teech

D-U-N-S 25-831-9318   (BR)
**MCMUNN & YATES BUILDING SUPPLIES
LTD**
MCDIARMID LUMBER HOME CENTRES
(*Suby of* MCMUNN & YATES BUILDING SUP-
PLIES LTD)
600 Pembina Hwy, Winnipeg, MB, R3M 2M5

▲ Public Company   ■ Public Company Family Member   **HQ** Headquarters   **BR** Branch   **SL** Single Location

(204) 940-4040
Emp Here 88
SIC 5211 Lumber and other building materials
Stan White

D-U-N-S 24-116-3401   (SL)
MENNONITE BRETHREN CHURCH OF MANITOBA, THE
M B CHURCH OF MANITOBA
1310 Taylor Ave, Winnipeg, MB, R3M 3Z6
(204) 415-0670
Emp Here 113   *Sales* 11,765,899
SIC 8661 Religious organizations
Dan Block

D-U-N-S 25-993-4573   (HQ)
PAVILION FINANCIAL CORPORATION
1001 Corydon Ave Suite 300, Winnipeg, MB, R3M 0B6
(204) 954-5103
Emp Here 20   *Sales* 23,562,630
SIC 8741 Management services
Daniel Friedman
Martin Weinberg
Gary Buckley
Patrick Belland
Meril Rivard
Michael Beasley
Greg Fettes
Lord Charles Cecil

D-U-N-S 24-915-8494   (BR)
REVERA INC
POSEIDON CARE CENTRE
(*Suby of* GOVERNMENT OF CANADA)
70 Poseidon Bay Suite 504, Winnipeg, MB, R3M 3E5
(204) 452-6204
Emp Here 300
SIC 8051 Skilled nursing care facilities
Marg Fisher

D-U-N-S 20-759-8442   (HQ)
SMITH AGENCY LIMITED
929 Corydon Ave Suite 3, Winnipeg, MB, R3M 0W8
(204) 287-2872
Sales 29,322,230
SIC 6531 Real estate agents and managers
Dennis Clinton

D-U-N-S 24-206-5931   (BR)
SOBEYS WEST INC
GRANT PARK PLAZA SAFEWAY
(*Suby of* EMPIRE COMPANY LIMITED)
1120 Grant Ave, Winnipeg, MB, R3M 2A6
(204) 452-7197
Emp Here 150
SIC 5411 Grocery stores

D-U-N-S 25-952-3041   (SL)
T.F.G. (1987) LTD
PIZZA HOTLINE
834 Corydon Ave Suite 1, Winnipeg, MB, R3M 0Y2

Emp Here 30   *Sales* 11,745,060
SIC 6794 Patent owners and lessors
Jerry Cianflonne

D-U-N-S 25-097-1504   (HQ)
THE KITCHING GROUP (CANADA) INC.
KITCHEN GROUP, THE
747 Corydon Ave Suite B, Winnipeg, MB, R3M 0W5

Emp Here 3   *Sales* 27,335,000
SIC 6712 Bank holding companies
Deborah Kitching

D-U-N-S 24-322-7282   (SL)
TIM HORTONS
570 Pembina Hwy, Winnipeg, MB, R3M 2M5
(204) 452-2531
Emp Here 40   *Sales* 10,966,080
SIC 5461 Retail bakeries
Greg Mikolajek

D-U-N-S 25-417-0624   (HQ)

W.O.W. HOSPITALITY CONCEPTS INC
529 Wellington Cres 3rd Fl, Winnipeg, MB, R3M 0A1
(204) 942-1090
Emp Here 12   *Sales* 24,955,200
SIC 8741 Management services
Douglas Stephen
Janet Cunningham
James Armstrong

D-U-N-S 25-026-4637   (BR)
WINNIPEG SCHOOL DIVISION
GRANT PARK HIGH SCHOOL
(*Suby of* WINNIPEG SCHOOL DIVISION)
450 Nathaniel St, Winnipeg, MB, R3M 3E3
(204) 452-3112
Emp Here 170
SIC 8211 Elementary and secondary schools
S Anderson

D-U-N-S 25-011-5532   (BR)
WINNIPEG SCHOOL DIVISION
KELVIN HIGH SCHOOL
(*Suby of* WINNIPEG SCHOOL DIVISION)
155 Kingsway, Winnipeg, MB, R3M 0G3
(204) 474-1492
Emp Here 110
SIC 8211 Elementary and secondary schools
Jim Brown

Winnipeg, MB R3N

D-U-N-S 24-125-5715   (SL)
4395612 MANITOBA LTD
ROYAL LEPAGE DYNAMIC
1450 Corydon Ave Suite 2, Winnipeg, MB, R3N 0J3
(204) 989-5000
Emp Here 70   *Sales* 19,022,920
SIC 6531 Real estate agents and managers
Rick Preston

D-U-N-S 24-882-7644   (HQ)
C & R VENTURES INC
HARVEST BAKERY & DELI
1857 Grant Ave Suite A, Winnipeg, MB, R3N 1Z2
(204) 489-1086
Emp Here 1   *Sales* 12,336,840
SIC 5461 Retail bakeries
Glenn Wilde
Andy Kostynuik
Jo-Al Wilde
Debra Kostynuik

D-U-N-S 25-055-1181   (SL)
CANADIAN CENTER FOR CHILD PROTECTION INC
CHILD FIND MANITOBA
615 Academy Rd, Winnipeg, MB, R3N 0E7
(204) 945-5735
Emp Here 33   *Sales* 13,114,662
SIC 8699 Membership organizations, nec
Lianna Mcdonald

D-U-N-S 25-721-4080   (SL)
COLDWELL BANKER NATIONAL PREFERRED PROPERTIES
1530 Taylor Ave Suite 6, Winnipeg, MB, R3N 1Y1
(204) 985-4300
Emp Here 60   *Sales* 16,305,360
SIC 6531 Real estate agents and managers
David Moffatt

D-U-N-S 24-630-3069   (HQ)
GISELLE'S PROFESSIONAL SKIN CARE LTD
1700 Corydon Ave Unit 13, Winnipeg, MB, R3N 0K1

Emp Here 22   *Sales* 13,347,750
SIC 7231 Beauty shops
Daphne Petrakos

Winnipeg, MB R3P

D-U-N-S 20-006-8773   (HQ)
A A A ALARM SYSTEMS LTD
A A A ALARM SYSTEMS WINNIPEG
180 Nature Park Way, Winnipeg, MB, R3P 0X7
(204) 949-0078
Emp Here 50   *Sales* 14,594,543
SIC 1731 Electrical work
William Fraser

D-U-N-S 20-570-8902   (BR)
AECOM CANADA LTD
SWAN HILLS TREATMENT CENTER
(*Suby of* AECOM)
99 Commerce Dr, Winnipeg, MB, R3P 0Y7
(204) 477-5381
Emp Here 146
SIC 8711 Engineering services
Ron Typliski

D-U-N-S 25-532-7819   (HQ)
AG GROWTH INTERNATIONAL INC
BATCO MANUFACTURING, DIV OF
198 Commerce Dr, Winnipeg, MB, R3P 0Z6
(204) 489-1855
Emp Here 100   *Sales* 706,296,342
SIC 3496 Miscellaneous fabricated wire products
Tim Close
Steve Sommerfeld
Craig Wilson
Nicolle Parker
Dan Donner
George Vis
Ron Braun
Paul Brisebois
Shane Knutson
Gurcan Kocdag

D-U-N-S 24-376-3786   (SL)
AGI-METAL FAB
(*Suby of* AG GROWTH INTERNATIONAL INC)
198 Commerce Dr, Winnipeg, MB, R3P 0Z6
(204) 489-1855
Emp Here 135   *Sales* 25,931,475
SIC 3441 Fabricated structural Metal
Gary Anderson
John Gergely

D-U-N-S 20-267-6839   (HQ)
ARXIUM INC
96 Nature Park Way, Winnipeg, MB, R3P 0X8
(204) 943-0066
Emp Here 80   *Sales* 71,336,200
SIC 3845 Electromedical equipment
Niels Erik Hansen
Edouard Van Humbeck
Randy Howorth
Thomas Doherty
Olivier Martin
Ravee Navaretnam
Kathy Goertzen

D-U-N-S 24-424-1142   (SL)
ASSINIBOINE PARK CONSERVANCY INC
55 Pavilion Cres, Winnipeg, MB, R3P 2N6
(204) 927-6002
Emp Here 500   *Sales* 719,300,500
SIC 8699 Membership organizations, nec
Margaret Redmond
Leanne Burkowski

D-U-N-S 20-294-0920   (BR)
CABELA'S RETAIL CANADA INC
CABELA'S CANADA
(*Suby of* BASS PRO GROUP, LLC)
580 Sterling Lyon Pky, Winnipeg, MB, R3P 1E9
(204) 786-8966
Emp Here 150
SIC 5941 Sporting goods and bicycle shops

D-U-N-S 20-165-3156   (SL)

CANADIAN MENNONITE UNIVERSITY
500 Shaftesbury Blvd, Winnipeg, MB, R3P 2N2
(204) 487-3300
Emp Here 200   *Sales* 29,878,200
SIC 8221 Colleges and universities
Gordon Epp-Fransen
Gerald Gerbrandt

D-U-N-S 24-807-8289   (HQ)
CONFIDENCE MANAGEMENT LTD
(*Suby of* FWS HOLDINGS LTD)
275 Commerce Dr, Winnipeg, MB, R3P 1B3
(204) 487-2500
Emp Here 50   *Sales* 18,716,400
SIC 8741 Management services
Rick Chale
Michael Evans
Douglas Patrick
Carl Doerksen

D-U-N-S 24-037-5048   (SL)
DIRECT ACTION IN SUPPORT OF COMMUNITY HOMES INCORPORATED
117 Victor Lewis Dr Unit 1, Winnipeg, MB, R3P 1J6
(204) 987-1550
Emp Here 750   *Sales* 48,211,500
SIC 8361 Residential care
Jack Mutter
Wayne Forbes
Judy Wakeford
Karen Fonseth
Brenda Martinussen
Lesley Hamilton
Debra Roach
Chris Noonan
Nadeen Haverstock
Scott Smith

D-U-N-S 25-611-6422   (SL)
DUFRESNE GROUP INC, THE
116 Nature Park Way, Winnipeg, MB, R3P 0X8
(204) 989-9898
Emp Here 30   *Sales* 15,265,680
SIC 5021 Furniture
Mark Dufresne
Michael Linton

D-U-N-S 25-846-3066   (SL)
ENNS BROTHERS LTD
55 Rothwell Rd, Winnipeg, MB, R3P 2M5
(204) 475-3667
Emp Here 30   *Sales* 14,250,780
SIC 5083 Farm and garden machinery
Ray Bouchard

D-U-N-S 24-375-0189   (BR)
EXTENDICARE (CANADA) INC
EXTENDICARE TUXEDO VILLA
(*Suby of* EXTENDICARE INC)
2060 Corydon Ave, Winnipeg, MB, R3P 0N3
(204) 889-2650
Emp Here 253
SIC 8051 Skilled nursing care facilities

D-U-N-S 20-268-7679   (HQ)
FARMERS EDGE INC
25 Rothwell Rd, Winnipeg, MB, R3P 2M5
(204) 452-3131
Sales 38,023,500
SIC 8748 Business consulting, nec
Wade Barnes

D-U-N-S 20-004-8064   (HQ)
FWS CONSTRUCTION LTD
(*Suby of* FWS HOLDINGS LTD)
275 Commerce Dr, Winnipeg, MB, R3P 1B3
(204) 487-2500
Emp Here 63   *Sales* 31,705,275
SIC 1541 Industrial buildings and warehouses
Richard Chale
Michael Evans
Douglas Patrick
Troy Valgardson

D-U-N-S 25-679-8547   (HQ)

FWS HOLDINGS LTD
275 Commerce Dr, Winnipeg, MB, R3P 1B3
(204) 487-2500
Emp Here 30   *Sales* 209,517,600
SIC 1542 Nonresidential construction, nec
Donald Price
Douglas Petrick
Ray Bisson
Carl Doerksen
Eric Stefanson
Len Penner
George Depres
Troy Valgardson

D-U-N-S 24-248-7663   (BR)
GORDON FOOD SERVICE CANADA LTD
(*Suby of* GORDON FOOD SERVICE, INC.)
310 Sterling Lyon Pky, Winnipeg, MB, R3P
0Y2
(204) 224-0134
Emp Here 250
SIC 5141 Groceries, general line
Dale Moldenhauer

D-U-N-S 24-581-5860   (SL)
KALSHEA COMMODITIES INC
42 Parkroyal Bay, Winnipeg, MB, R3P 1P2
(204) 272-3773
Emp Here 10   *Sales* 12,103,970
SIC 5153 Grain and field beans
Darwin Hamilton
Deborah Hamilton
Shea Hamilton

D-U-N-S 25-452-4747   (SL)
LINDEN CHRISTIAN SCHOOL INC
877 Wilkes Ave, Winnipeg, MB, R3P 1B8
(204) 989-6730
Emp Here 120   *Sales* 11,894,280
SIC 8211 Elementary and secondary schools
Robert Charach

D-U-N-S 24-631-0619   (SL)
MACCHIA ENTERPRISES LTD
AURA
43 Newbury Cres, Winnipeg, MB, R3P 0V6
(204) 255-7181
Emp Here 120   *Sales* 12,813,840
SIC 7231 Beauty shops
Rocco Macchia
Josephine Macchia
Gennaro Macchia

D-U-N-S 20-718-2739   (SL)
MANITOBA HYDRO INTERNATIONAL LTD
(*Suby of* PROVINCE OF MANITOBA)
211 Commerce Dr, Winnipeg, MB, R3P 1A3
(204) 480-5200
Emp Here 100   *Sales* 12,477,600
SIC 8741 Management services
Shawna Pachal

D-U-N-S 24-172-2388   (SL)
MCCAINE ELECTRIC LTD
(*Suby of* STUART OLSON INC)
106 Lowson Cres, Winnipeg, MB, R3P 2H8
(204) 786-2435
Emp Here 140   *Sales* 32,971,260
SIC 1731 Electrical work
Kem Smith

D-U-N-S 20-918-5607   (BR)
PEMBINA TRAILS SCHOOL DIVISION, THE
SHAFTESBURY HIGH SCHOOLA
(*Suby of* PEMBINA TRAILS SCHOOL DIVI-
SION, THE)
2240 Grant Ave, Winnipeg, MB, R3P 0P7
(204) 888-5898
Emp Here 80
SIC 8211 Elementary and secondary schools
Stan Wiebe

D-U-N-S 24-351-3962   (HQ)
PEOPLE CORPORATION
1403 Kenaston Blvd, Winnipeg, MB, R3P 2T5
(204) 940-3933
Emp Here 20   *Sales* 84,462,521

SIC 8742 Management consulting services
Laurie Goldberg
Bonnie Chwartacki
Brevan Canning
Lisa Villani
Paul Asmundson
Dennis Stwner
Scott C. Anderson
Richard Leipsic
Eric Stefanson

D-U-N-S 24-392-4797   (SL)
PINNACLE AUTO SALES
MERCEDES BENZ WINNIPEG
23 Rothwell Rd, Winnipeg, MB, R3P 2M5
(204) 667-2467
Emp Here 25   *Sales* 12,451,950
SIC 5511 New and used car dealers
Bruce Danylchuk
Doug Danylchuk

D-U-N-S 25-176-4205   (HQ)
POLYWEST LTD
3700 Mcgillivray Blvd Unit B, Winnipeg, MB,
R3P 5S3
(204) 924-8265
Emp Here 15   *Sales* 11,875,650
SIC 5084 Industrial machinery and equipment
Thomas E. Northam
Thomas Smith

D-U-N-S 20-010-6466   (HQ)
PRENDIVILLE INDUSTRIES LTD
NORWEST MANUFACTURING
(*Suby of* PRENDIVILLE CORPORATION)
986 Lorimer Blvd Unit 5, Winnipeg, MB, R3P
0Z8
(204) 989-9600
Emp Here 15   *Sales* 28,855,500
SIC 2431 Millwork
Maureen Patricia Prendiville
James Ailbe Prendiville
Michael Lawrence Prendiville

D-U-N-S 20-835-2919   (SL)
PRITCHARD METALFAB INC
PRITCHARD ENGINEERING
110 Lowson Cres, Winnipeg, MB, R3P 2H8
(204) 784-7600
Emp Here 60   *Sales* 11,525,100
SIC 3499 Fabricated Metal products, nec
Mike Best

D-U-N-S 24-852-1820   (SL)
R.J. O'BRIEN & ASSOCIATES CANADA INC
RJO CANADA ONLINE, DIV OF
(*Suby of* R.J. O'BRIEN HOLDINGS, INC.)
195 Commerce Dr, Winnipeg, MB, R3P 1A2
(204) 594-1440
Emp Here 20   *Sales* 10,624,140
SIC 6211 Security brokers and dealers
Keith Riddock
Lora-Lee Miller

D-U-N-S 25-417-4436   (SL)
SIRIUS BENEFIT PLANS INC
(*Suby of* PEOPLE CORPORATION)
1403 Kenaston Blvd, Winnipeg, MB, R3P 2T5
(204) 488-7600
Emp Here 24   *Sales* 20,353,440
SIC 6411 Insurance agents, brokers, and ser-
vice
Edward Melna

D-U-N-S 20-350-6873   (BR)
SOBEYS CAPITAL INCORPORATED
KENASTON SOBEYS
(*Suby of* EMPIRE COMPANY LIMITED)
1660 Kenaston Blvd, Winnipeg, MB, R3P 2M6
(204) 489-7007
Emp Here 170
SIC 5411 Grocery stores
Sean O'malia

D-U-N-S 25-271-7830   (BR)
SOBEYS WEST INC
TUXEDO SAFEWAY

(*Suby of* EMPIRE COMPANY LIMITED)
2025 Corydon Ave Suite 150, Winnipeg, MB,
R3P 0N5
(204) 489-6498
Emp Here 100
SIC 5411 Grocery stores
Ken Mcfarlin

D-U-N-S 20-690-4794   (SL)
**STERLING O&G INTERNATIONAL CORPO-
RATION**
AESHU PROPANE
99 Royal Crest Dr, Winnipeg, MB, R3P 2R1
(204) 952-1505
Emp Here 64   *Sales* 15,636,992
SIC 5984 Liquefied petroleum gas dealers
Govind Thawani

D-U-N-S 25-137-8746   (SL)
SWAGELOK CENTRAL CANADA
118 Commerce Dr, Winnipeg, MB, R3P 0Z6
(204) 633-4446
Emp Here 23   *Sales* 10,925,598
SIC 5085 Industrial supplies
Sean Unrau

D-U-N-S 24-363-7183   (HQ)
TDG FURNITURE INC
DUFRESNE FURNITURE & APPLIANCES
116 Nature Park Way, Winnipeg, MB, R3P 0X8
(204) 989-9898
Emp Here 75   *Sales* 213,362,400
SIC 5712 Furniture stores
Mark Dufresne
Michael Linton

D-U-N-S 24-749-8350   (SL)
TRANSAMERICAS TRADING INC
TRANSAMERICAS BUSINESS GROUP
1248 Wilkes Ave, Winnipeg, MB, R3P 1C2
(204) 831-3663
Emp Here 42   *Sales* 31,185,840
SIC 5193 Flowers and florists supplies
Fernando Jativa

D-U-N-S 25-366-8453   (SL)
URBANMINE INC
72 Rothwell Rd, Winnipeg, MB, R3P 2H7
(204) 774-0192
Emp Here 38   *Sales* 19,780,596
SIC 5093 Scrap and waste materials
Mark Chisick
Alex Goodman
Adam Chisick

D-U-N-S 20-179-8183   (BR)
WAL-MART CANADA CORP
(*Suby of* WALMART INC.)
1665 Kenaston Blvd, Winnipeg, MB, R3P 2M4
(204) 488-2052
Emp Here 300
SIC 5311 Department stores
Brent Tokarchuk

D-U-N-S 20-375-0836   (SL)
WALLACE INTERNATIONAL LTD
WALLACE PERIMETER SECURITY
115 Lowson Cres, Winnipeg, MB, R3P 1A6
(204) 452-2700
Emp Here 100   *Sales* 23,343,500
SIC 3312 Blast furnaces and steel mills
Kori Buhler

D-U-N-S 20-390-8421   (SL)
WALLACE PERIMETER SECURITY
115 Lowson Cres, Winnipeg, MB, R3P 1A6
(866) 300-1110
Emp Here 50   *Sales* 10,141,500
SIC 3446 Architectural Metalwork
Kori Buhler

D-U-N-S 20-385-1584   (SL)
WAM MOTORS GP INC
AUDI WINNIPEG
(*Suby of* AUTOCANADA INC)
485 Sterling Lyon Pky, Winnipeg, MB, R3P
2S8

(204) 284-2834
Emp Here 50   *Sales* 31,464,000
SIC 5511 New and used car dealers
Michael Rawluck
David Pestrak
Gerald Boiteau

D-U-N-S 24-231-3856   (SL)
WESTLAND PLASTICS LTD
PRAIRIE PRIDE
12 Rothwell Rd, Winnipeg, MB, R3P 2H7
(204) 488-6075
Emp Here 50   *Sales* 10,094,850
SIC 3089 Plastics products, nec
Thomas Wilton

D-U-N-S 25-256-4385   (SL)
WINSUN DISTRIBUTING
2025 Corydon Ave Suite 267, Winnipeg, MB,
R3P 0N5
(204) 888-1873
Emp Here 30   *Sales* 19,693,920
SIC 5963 Direct selling establishments
Darren Lewis

D-U-N-S 24-916-4302   (HQ)
ZOOLOGICAL SOCIETY OF MANITOBA
ASSINIBOINE PARK CONSERVANCY
54 Zoo Dr, Winnipeg, MB, R3P 2N8
(204) 982-0660
Sales 140,132,952
SIC 6732 Trusts: educational, religious, etc.
Kevin Turner
Peggy May
Mike Stevens
Roger Wight
Tim Kist

Winnipeg, MB R3R

D-U-N-S 25-271-7715   (BR)
SOBEYS WEST INC
CHARLESWOOD SAFEWAY
(*Suby of* EMPIRE COMPANY LIMITED)
3900 Grant Ave Suite 20, Winnipeg, MB, R3R
3C2
(204) 837-5339
Emp Here 126
SIC 5411 Grocery stores
John Laudeldinsky

D-U-N-S 20-836-6062   (SL)
**WEST PARK MANOR PERSONAL CARE
HOME INC**
3199 Grant Ave, Winnipeg, MB, R3R 1X2
(204) 889-3330
Emp Here 210   *Sales* 14,348,460
SIC 8051 Skilled nursing care facilities
Kenneth D Reimche
Charles Toop
Ken Wiebe

Winnipeg, MB R3S

D-U-N-S 24-466-5725   (SL)
ELMHURST LATHING AND DRYWALL LTD
3160 Wilkes Ave, Winnipeg, MB, R3S 1A7
(204) 889-8238
Emp Here 100   *Sales* 16,238,100
SIC 1742 Plastering, drywall, and insulation
Rick Kippen
Rod Kippen
Terry Kippen

Winnipeg, MB R3T

D-U-N-S 20-011-9493   (BR)
2104225 ONTARIO LTD
2104225 ONTARIO LTD

(*Suby of* GEORGE WESTON LIMITED)
1485 Chevrier Blvd, Winnipeg, MB, R3T 1Y7
(416) 252-7323
Emp Here 150
SIC 2051 Bread, cake, and related products
Bratt Robinson

D-U-N-S 24-375-5092   (SL)
4665181 MANITOBA LTD
ICUC MODERATION SERVICES
2855 Pembina Hwy Suite 35, Winnipeg, MB,
R3T 2H5
(800) 710-2713
Emp Here 130   *Sales* 28,592,590
SIC 8732 Commercial nonphysical research
Keith Bilous

D-U-N-S 24-654-6030   (HQ)
75040 MANITOBA LTD
WINNIPEG HONDA
1717 Waverley St Unit 900, Winnipeg, MB,
R3T 6A9
(204) 261-9580
Sales 24,903,900
SIC 5511 New and used car dealers
Ashok Dilawri
Annu Dilawri
Glenn Damon

D-U-N-S 20-280-0967   (SL)
ACCURATE DORWIN INC
1535 Seel Ave, Winnipeg, MB, R3T 1C6
(204) 982-4640
Emp Here 80   *Sales* 18,674,800
SIC 3229 Pressed and blown glass, nec
Richard Brodeur
Terrance W. Johnstone
Robert M. Johnstone

D-U-N-S 25-668-5140   (SL)
ANIKA HOLDINGS INC
CROWN ACURA
1700 Waverley St Suite B, Winnipeg, MB, R3T
5V7
(204) 269-9551
Emp Here 35   *Sales* 17,432,730
SIC 5511 New and used car dealers
Ashok Dilawri

D-U-N-S 24-887-9546   (HQ)
ARCHITECTURE49 INC
(*Suby of* AST TRUST COMPANY (CANADA))
1600 Buffalo Pl, Winnipeg, MB, R3T 6B8
(204) 477-1260
Emp Here 15   *Sales* 27,704,545
SIC 8712 Architectural services
Scott Stirton
J. Albert Paquette
Glen Klym
Andre Desautels
Bruno Verenini

D-U-N-S 24-376-6037   (BR)
ATLIFIC INC
HOLIDAY INN WINNIPEG SOUTH
1330 Pembina Hwy, Winnipeg, MB, R3T 2B4
(204) 452-4747
Emp Here 125
SIC 7011 Hotels and motels
Michael Gore

D-U-N-S 20-042-0268   (SL)
AUTOTOWN SALES CORPORATION
1717 Waverley St Suite 400, Winnipeg, MB,
R3T 6A9
(204) 269-1600
Emp Here 22   *Sales* 10,957,716
SIC 5521 Used car dealers
Evan Titchkosky

D-U-N-S 24-967-7253   (HQ)
BUHLER INDUSTRIES INC
(*Suby of* ROSTSELMASH, PAO)
1260 Clarence Ave, Winnipeg, MB, R3T 1T2
(204) 661-8711
Sales 220,455,496
SIC 3523 Farm machinery and equipment
Yury Ryazanov

Maxim Loktionov
Chad Gray
Willy Janzen
Grant Adolph
Dmitry Udras
Konstantin Babkin
John Buhler
Oleg Gorbunov

D-U-N-S 20-648-3757   (BR)
BUHLER INDUSTRIES INC
(*Suby of* ROSTSELMASH, PAO)
1260 Clarence Ave Suite 112, Winnipeg, MB,
R3T 1T2
(204) 661-8711
Emp Here 200
SIC 3523 Farm machinery and equipment
Grant Adolph

D-U-N-S 24-628-3147   (SL)
BUHLER VERSATILE INC
(*Suby of* ROSTSELMASH, PAO)
1260 Clarence Ave, Winnipeg, MB, R3T 1T2
(204) 284-6100
Emp Here 300   *Sales* 84,263,100
SIC 3523 Farm machinery and equipment

D-U-N-S 20-072-2523   (BR)
**CANAD CORPORATION OF MANITOBA
LTD**
CANADA INN EXPRESS FORT GARY
1792 Pembina Hwy, Winnipeg, MB, R3T 2G2
(204) 269-6955
Emp Here 85
SIC 7011 Hotels and motels
Joe Sacco

D-U-N-S 20-517-8734   (SL)
CANADIAN TOOL & DIE LTD
CTD
(*Suby of* GATSCHUFF HOLDINGS INC)
1331 Chevrier Blvd, Winnipeg, MB, R3T 1Y4
(204) 453-6833
Emp Here 240   *Sales* 58,375,440
SIC 3469 Metal stampings, nec
James Umlah

D-U-N-S 20-334-1839   (SL)
CANFARM PULSE INC
1427 Somerville Ave, Winnipeg, MB, R3T 1C3
(204) 298-3595
Emp Here 5   *Sales* 29,852,272
SIC 5153 Grain and field beans
Gabriel Schujman
Sergio Alejandro Vaca Contreras

D-U-N-S 25-890-3681   (SL)
CANTERRA SEEDS (2002) LTD
(*Suby of* CANTERRA SEEDS HOLDINGS
LTD)
1475 Chevrier Blvd Unit 201, Winnipeg, MB,
R3T 1Y7
(204) 988-9750
Emp Here 15   *Sales* 11,137,800
SIC 5191 Farm supplies
Ron Gorst
Fred Greig
Joe Dales
Greg Andrukow
Lloyd Affleck
James Wilson
Ken Nelson

D-U-N-S 20-702-1986   (HQ)
CANTERRA SEEDS HOLDINGS LTD
1475 Chevrier Blvd Unit 201, Winnipeg, MB,
R3T 1Y7
(204) 988-9750
Sales 24,129,144
SIC 5191 Farm supplies
David Hansen
Gerry Cantin
Jim Bagshaw
Brent Derkatch
Sheena Pitura
Lloyd Affleck
Jim Wilson

Ryan Baldwin
Antoine Colombo
Joe Dales

D-U-N-S 20-007-8673   (HQ)
COGHLAN'S LTD
121 Irene St, Winnipeg, MB, R3T 4C7
(204) 284-9550
Sales 14,575,176
SIC 5091 Sporting and recreation goods
Robert Coghlan
Gail Coghlan

D-U-N-S 20-276-1003   (BR)
CONGEBEC LOGISTIQUE INC
WESTCO
(*Suby of* CONGEBEC LOGISTIQUE INC)
1555 Chevrier Blvd Unit A, Winnipeg, MB, R3T
1Y7
(204) 475-5570
Emp Here 100
SIC 4222 Refrigerated warehousing and stor-
age
Daryl Doubleday

D-U-N-S 20-613-6780   (SL)
CONVENTRY MOTORS LIMITED
GERRY GORDON'S MAZDA
1717 Waverley St Unit 520, Winnipeg, MB,
R3T 6A9
(204) 475-3982
Emp Here 35   *Sales* 17,432,730
SIC 5511 New and used car dealers
W Gerry Gordon

D-U-N-S 25-974-8197   (SL)
CROWN NISSAN
1717 Waverley St Suite 700, Winnipeg, MB,
R3T 6A9
(204) 269-4685
Emp Here 30   *Sales* 14,942,340
SIC 5511 New and used car dealers
Nick Guffeii

D-U-N-S 24-116-9036   (HQ)
CURTIS CARPETS LTD
(*Suby of* 66295 MANITOBA LTD)
1280 Pembina Hwy, Winnipeg, MB, R3T 2B2
(204) 452-8100
Sales 11,517,000
SIC 5713 Floor covering stores
Wayne Curtis
Jerry Sherby

D-U-N-S 24-775-8022   (HQ)
CWB NATIONAL LEASING INC
NATIONAL LEASING
(*Suby of* CANADIAN WESTERN BANK)
1525 Buffalo Pl, Winnipeg, MB, R3T 1L9
(204) 954-9000
Emp Here 230   *Sales* 166,531,050
SIC 6159 Miscellaneous business credit insti-
tutions
Michael Dubowec
Jackie Lowe
Miles Macdonell
Grant Shaw
Chris Noonan
Janice Boulet
Arthur Anhalt
Alex Mackay
Colin Tirschmann
Tom Pundyk

D-U-N-S 25-415-5286   (HQ)
CWS LOGISTICS LTD
1664 Seel Ave, Winnipeg, MB, R3T 4X5
(204) 474-2278
Emp Here 100   *Sales* 24,684,720
SIC 4225 General warehousing and storage
Lee Stange

D-U-N-S 25-261-3617   (SL)
DILAWRI HOLDINGS INC
SUNSHINE TOYOTA
1700 Waverley St Suite C, Winnipeg, MB, R3T
5V7

(204) 269-1572
Emp Here 28   *Sales* 13,946,184
SIC 5511 New and used car dealers
Ashok Dilawri
Annu Dilawri

D-U-N-S 20-519-8401   (BR)
DILLON CONSULTING LIMITED
(*Suby of* DILLON CONSULTING LIMITED)
1558 Willson Pl, Winnipeg, MB, R3T 0Y4
(204) 453-2301
Emp Here 80
SIC 8711 Engineering services
Karen Peters

D-U-N-S 20-310-4349   (SL)
**DMT DEVELOPMENT SYSTEMS GROUP
INC**
1 Research Rd Unit 500, Winnipeg, MB, R3T
6E3
(204) 927-1800
Emp Here 75   *Sales* 13,298,325
SIC 7371 Custom computer programming ser-
vices
Glen Demetrioff

D-U-N-S 20-712-0742   (HQ)
DUNN-RITE FOOD PRODUCTS LTD
(*Suby of* SUNRISE POULTRY PROCES-
SORS LTD)
199 Hamelin St, Winnipeg, MB, R3T 0P2
(204) 452-8379
Sales 150,510,360
SIC 5144 Poultry and poultry products
Rico Deneen

D-U-N-S 25-341-7760   (BR)
EARL'S RESTAURANTS LTD
(*Suby of* EARL'S RESTAURANTS LTD)
2005 Pembina Hwy, Winnipeg, MB, R3T 5W7

Emp Here 120
SIC 5812 Eating places
Kevin Byrne

D-U-N-S 24-325-3783   (SL)
ECONOMY DRUGS LTD
SHOPPERS DRUG MART
2211 Pembina Hwy, Winnipeg, MB, R3T 2H1
(204) 269-8113
Emp Here 40   *Sales* 10,118,160
SIC 5912 Drug stores and proprietary stores
Stuart Bellingham

D-U-N-S 20-350-8049   (HQ)
EMERGENT BIOSOLUTIONS CANADA INC
(*Suby of* EMERGENT BIOSOLUTIONS INC.)
155 Innovation Dr, Winnipeg, MB, R3T 5Y3
(204) 275-4200
Emp Here 330   *Sales* 144,487,350
SIC 5122 Drugs, proprietaries, and sundries
Adam Havey
Sean Kirk
Christopher Sinclair
Barbara Solow
Steven Rambo
Eric Burt
Daniel Abdun-Nabi

D-U-N-S 24-968-5959   (SL)
**FIRST GENERAL SERVICES (WINNIPEG)
LTD**
125 Fennoll St Unit 1, Winnipeg, MB, R3T 0M2
(204) 477-0560
Emp Here 43   *Sales* 36,466,580
SIC 6411 Insurance agents, brokers, and ser-
vice
James Drew Bayes
Karen Bayes
Kristen Bayes
Bradley Koster
Marian (Joyce) Bayes

D-U-N-S 20-008-5363   (HQ)
FLOFORM INDUSTRIES LTD
FLOFORM COUNTERTOPS
125 Hamelin St, Winnipeg, MB, R3T 3Z1

(204) 474-2334
Sales 30,864,400
SIC 2541 Wood partitions and fixtures
Edward Sherrit
Marnie Sherritt

D-U-N-S 24-327-9887   (HQ)
FRONTIER SUPPLY CHAIN SOLUTIONS INC
(*Suby of* C2 CAPITAUX INC)
555 Hervo St Ste 10, Winnipeg, MB, R3T 3L6
(204) 784-4800
Emp Here 13   *Sales* 23,398,515
SIC 4731 Freight transportation arrangement
Michael Butterfield
Darold Snell
John Quirke

D-U-N-S 20-192-5992   (BR)
GENERAL MILLS CANADA CORPORATION
(*Suby of* GENERAL MILLS, INC.)
1555 Chevrier Blvd Suite B, Winnipeg, MB, R3T 1Y7
(204) 477-8338
Emp Here 90
SIC 2099 Food preparations, nec
Henry Van Der Ley

D-U-N-S 24-520-1975   (SL)
HARDWOOD FOREST PRODUCTS CO LTD
1213 Chevrier Blvd, Winnipeg, MB, R3T 1Y4
(204) 981-1490
Emp Here 30   *Sales* 13,415,220
SIC 5031 Lumber, plywood, and millwork
Douglas Broeska

D-U-N-S 25-236-7750   (HQ)
JOHN BUHLER INC
(*Suby of* ROSTSELMASH, PAO)
1260 Clarence Ave, Winnipeg, MB, R3T 1T2
(204) 661-8711
Emp Here 300   *Sales* 280,877,000
SIC 3523 Farm machinery and equipment
John Buhler
Larry Schroeder
Osama Abouzeid

D-U-N-S 24-820-0180   (HQ)
KONTZAMANIS   GRAUMANN   SMITH MACMILLAN INC
KGS GROUP
865 Waverley St Suite 300, Winnipeg, MB, R3T 5P4
(204) 896-1209
Emp Here 200   *Sales* 68,995,850
SIC 8711 Engineering services
Demetrios Kontzamanis
Helmut Graumann
David Macmillan
Bert Smith

D-U-N-S 25-058-2616   (BR)
LOBLAWS INC
REAL CANADIAN SUPERSTORE
(*Suby of* LOBLAW COMPANIES LIMITED)
80 Bison Dr Suite 1509, Winnipeg, MB, R3T 4Z7
(204) 275-4118
Emp Here 300
SIC 5411 Grocery stores
John Davidson

D-U-N-S 25-892-2772   (SL)
MANITOBAN NEWSPAPER PUBLICATIONS CORPORATION, THE
MANITOBAN, THE
105 University Cres, Winnipeg, MB, R3T 2N5
(204) 474-6535
Emp Here 22   *Sales* 16,335,440
SIC 5192 Books, periodicals, and newspapers
Omar Al Ramlawi

D-U-N-S 20-011-6176   (SL)
MCNAUGHT PONTIAC BUICK CADILLAC GMC LTD
MCNAUGHT MOTORS
1717 Waverley St Unit 1000, Winnipeg, MB, R3T 6A9

(204) 786-3811
Emp Here 60   *Sales* 37,756,800
SIC 5511 New and used car dealers
Gordon Mcnaught Sr

D-U-N-S 25-681-2710   (HQ)
MEDICURE INC
1250 Waverley St Suite 2, Winnipeg, MB, R3T 6C6
(204) 487-7412
Emp Here 10   *Sales* 22,067,868
SIC 2834 Pharmaceutical preparations
Albert D. Friesen
Neil Owens
Jamie Gowryluk
Reuben Saba
Arnold Naimark
Peter Quick
Brent Fawkes
Gerald P. Mcdole
James Kinley

D-U-N-S 20-832-5928   (HQ)
MENNONITE   CENTRAL   COMMITTEE CANADA
TEN THOUSAND VILLAGES
134 Plaza Dr, Winnipeg, MB, R3T 5K9
(204) 261-6381
Emp Here 43   *Sales* 46,390,114
SIC 8399 Social services, nec
Donald G Peters
Neil Janzen
Ron Janzen

D-U-N-S 20-183-3048   (HQ)
MFI FOOD CANADA LTD
INOVATECH EGG PRODUCTS, DIV OF
70 Irene St, Winnipeg, MB, R3T 4E1
(204) 453-6613
Emp Here 160   *Sales* 69,138,000
SIC 2015 Poultry slaughtering and processing
J. Hugh Wiebe
Gregg Ostrander

D-U-N-S 24-206-7234   (SL)
MID-TOWN FORD SALES LIMITED
1717 Waverley St Suite 100, Winnipeg, MB, R3T 6A9
(204) 284-7650
Emp Here 65   *Sales* 40,903,200
SIC 5511 New and used car dealers
Robert Fridfinnson

D-U-N-S 20-613-1278   (HQ)
MONDO FOODS CO. LTD
LA GROTTA DEL FORMAGGIO
40 Otter St, Winnipeg, MB, R3T 4J7
(204) 453-7722
Emp Here 24   *Sales* 83,557,700
SIC 5143 Dairy products, except dried or canned
Ugo A De Nardi
Maria De Nardi

D-U-N-S 20-565-7448   (HQ)
MONSANTO CANADA INC
(*Suby of* BAYER AG)
1 Research Rd Suite 900, Winnipeg, MB, R3T 6E3
(204) 985-1000
Emp Here 25   *Sales* 47,327,000
SIC 0181 Ornamental nursery products
Michael Mcguire
Lisa Safarian

D-U-N-S 20-010-1400   (HQ)
MOTOR COACH INDUSTRIES LIMITED
(*Suby of* NFI GROUP INC)
1475 Clarence Ave, Winnipeg, MB, R3T 1T5
(204) 284-5360
Emp Here 1,500   *Sales* 698,040,000
SIC 3711 Motor vehicles and car bodies
Richard A. Heller
Timothy Nalepka
Sandra Morison

D-U-N-S 25-660-5270   (SL)
MURRAY AUTO GROUP WINNIPEG LTD

MURRAY CHEVROLET HUMMER
1700 Waverley St Suite C, Winnipeg, MB, R3T 5V7
(204) 261-6200
Emp Here 160   *Sales* 100,684,800
SIC 5511 New and used car dealers
Daniel Murray
A.C. Murray
Doug Murray
Paul Murray
Chris Murray

D-U-N-S 20-388-9779   (SL)
PARIAN LOGISTICS INC
1530 Gamble Pl, Winnipeg, MB, R3T 1N6
(204) 885-4200
Emp Here 150   *Sales* 30,855,900
SIC 4212 Local trucking, without storage
Neil Armstrong
Gerry Bachynski
Shamsh Kassam

D-U-N-S 24-805-7049   (BR)
PARKER HANNIFIN CANADA
ELECTRONIC CONTROLS, DIV OF
(*Suby of* PARKER-HANNIFIN CORPORATION)
1305 Clarence Ave, Winnipeg, MB, R3T 1T4
(204) 452-6776
Emp Here 600
SIC 3625 Relays and industrial controls
Randy Howorth

D-U-N-S 25-196-1835   (HQ)
PAYWORKS INC
1565 Willson Pl, Winnipeg, MB, R3T 4H1
(204) 779-0537
Emp Here 80   *Sales* 35,306,450
SIC 8721 Accounting, auditing, and bookkeeping
Barbara Gamey
Jp Perron
Rob Sterling
Kevin Sokolowski
Mike Leon
Mark Johannson
Patrick Hood
Jim Butler
Michael Derksen

D-U-N-S 20-833-2213   (SL)
PEMBINA CARE SERVICES LTD
GOLDEN DOOR GERIATRIC CENTRE
1679 Pembina Hwy, Winnipeg, MB, R3T 2G6
(204) 269-6308
Emp Here 80   *Sales* 5,206,000
SIC 8361 Residential care
David Pollock

D-U-N-S 20-047-0867   (BR)
PEMBINA TRAILS SCHOOL DIVISION, THE
ACADIA JUNIOR HIGH SCHOOL
(*Suby of* PEMBINA TRAILS SCHOOL DIVISION, THE)
175 Killarney Ave, Winnipeg, MB, R3T 3B3
(204) 269-6210
Emp Here 78
SIC 8211 Elementary and secondary schools
Troy Scott

D-U-N-S 20-945-4487   (SL)
PHLYN HOLDINGS LTD
(*Suby of* CARLETON HATCHERIES LTD)
199 Hamelin St, Winnipeg, MB, R3T 0P2
(204) 452-8379
Emp Here 210   *Sales* 150,510,360
SIC 5144 Poultry and poultry products
Enrico Emil Bertschinger
Frank Doerksen Funk
Mario Marcel Bertschinger
Ursula Bertschinger
Frank Lavitt

D-U-N-S 25-678-1725   (SL)
PM CANADA INC
PROFITMASTER CANADA
(*Suby of* CONSTELLATION SOFTWARE

INC)
135 Innovation Dr Unit 300, Winnipeg, MB, R3T 6A8
(204) 889-5320
Emp Here 43   *Sales* 19,228,482
SIC 5045 Computers, peripherals, and software
Don Kroeker

D-U-N-S 24-130-8506   (HQ)
POLLARD BANKNOTE INCOME FUND
140 Otter St, Winnipeg, MB, R3T 0M8
(204) 474-2323
Emp Here 1   *Sales* 317,217,032
SIC 3999 Manufacturing industries, nec
John Pollard
Rob Rose

D-U-N-S 24-580-7420   (HQ)
POLLARD BANKNOTE LIMITED
140 Otter St, Winnipeg, MB, R3T 0M8
(204) 474-2323
Emp Here 500   *Sales* 251,589,795
SIC 2679 Converted paper products, nec
Douglas Pollard
John Pollard
Jennifer Westbury
Robert Young
Robert Rose
Riva Richard
Paul Franzmann
Pedro Melo
Lawrence Pollard
Gordon Pollard

D-U-N-S 24-232-9803   (SL)
PRIORITY ELECTRONICS LTD
55 Trottier Bay, Winnipeg, MB, R3T 3R3
(204) 284-0164
Emp Here 79   *Sales* 35,326,746
SIC 5065 Electronic parts and equipment, nec
Blaine Henderson

D-U-N-S 20-010-6649   (HQ)
PRITCHARD   ENGINEERING   COMPANY LIMITED
PRITCHARD INDUSTRIAL, DIV OF
100 Otter St, Winnipeg, MB, R3T 0M8
(204) 452-2344
Sales 42,752,340
SIC 5084 Industrial machinery and equipment
Phillip Hildebrand
Alan K Johnstone

D-U-N-S 24-115-6983   (HQ)
PRO AUTO LTD
PRO BODY PARTS
1761 Pembina Hwy Unit 3, Winnipeg, MB, R3T 2G6
(204) 982-3020
Emp Here 20   *Sales* 69,173,100
SIC 5013 Motor vehicle supplies and new parts
David Provinciano

D-U-N-S 25-674-8724   (SL)
R.S. HARRIS TRANSPORT LTD
555 Hervo St Unit 15, Winnipeg, MB, R3T 3L6
(204) 255-2700
Emp Here 100   *Sales* 14,819,200
SIC 4213 Trucking, except local
Robert S Harris

D-U-N-S 24-324-6035   (SL)
RAZIR TRANSPORT SERVICES LTD
1460 Clarence Ave Suite 204, Winnipeg, MB, R3T 1T6
(204) 489-2258
Emp Here 45   *Sales* 18,241,472
SIC 4213 Trucking, except local
Karandeep Grewal
Amandeep Grewal

D-U-N-S 24-914-0112   (SL)
ROBLIN ATHLETIC INC
ROBLIN FOOTWEAR
1457 Chevrier Blvd Suite A, Winnipeg, MB, R3T 1Y7

(204) 477-5100
Emp Here 20   *Sales* 10,006,500
SIC 5139 Footwear
Rodmond Roblin Sr
Charles Dufferin Roblin

D-U-N-S 20-286-4799   (BR)
RONA INC
ACE CANADA
(*Suby of* LOWE'S COMPANIES, INC.)
1530 Gamble Pl Suite 453, Winnipeg, MB,
R3T 1N6

Emp Here 200
SIC 5191 Farm supplies
Robert Hagborg

D-U-N-S 25-205-4341   (SL)
RTDS TECHNOLOGIES INC
100-150 Innovation Dr, Winnipeg, MB, R3T
2E1
(204) 989-9700
Emp Here 71   *Sales* 15,762,071
SIC 3571 Electronic computers
Rick Kuffel
Trevor Maguire
Rudi Wierckx
James Giesbrecht
Neil Mackenzie

D-U-N-S 20-212-7267   (BR)
RUSSEL METALS INC
(*Suby of* RUSSEL METALS INC)
1510 Clarence Ave, Winnipeg, MB, R3T 1T6
(204) 475-8584
Emp Here 100
SIC 1791 Structural steel erection
Marion Britton

D-U-N-S 25-450-1901   (BR)
SALISBURY HOUSE OF CANADA LTD
SALISBURY HOUSE
(*Suby of* 4328796 MANITOBA LTD)
1941 Pembina Hwy, Winnipeg, MB, R3T 2G7

Emp Here 100
SIC 5812 Eating places
Earl Barish

D-U-N-S 24-498-8056   (SL)
SCM ADJUSTERS CANADA LTD.
1479 Buffalo Pl Suite 200, Winnipeg, MB, R3T
1L7
(204) 985-1777
Emp Here 45   *Sales* 38,804,550
SIC 6411 Insurance agents, brokers, and service
Drew Knox

D-U-N-S 24-607-6228   (HQ)
SEARCY TRUCKING LTD
UNIVERSAL RELOAD DIV
(*Suby of* JANPHER INVESTMENTS INC)
1470 Chevrier Blvd, Winnipeg, MB, R3T 1Y6
(204) 475-8411
Sales 19,336,364
SIC 4213 Trucking, except local
Norman Blagden

D-U-N-S 20-719-7109   (SL)
SMARTREND SUPPLY LTD
MARKTRAND MANUFACTURING GROUP
1249 Clarence Ave Unit 9, Winnipeg, MB, R3T
1T4
(204) 489-7237
Emp Here 24   *Sales* 12,493,008
SIC 5099 Durable goods, nec
Kevin Smith

D-U-N-S 25-271-9935   (BR)
SOBEYS WEST INC
SAFEWAY
(*Suby of* EMPIRE COMPANY LIMITED)
1319 Pembina Hwy, Winnipeg, MB, R3T 2B6
(204) 284-0973
Emp Here 100
SIC 5411 Grocery stores
Howard Lutman

D-U-N-S 20-192-7741   (BR)
**SONOCO FLEXIBLE PACKAGING CANADA
CORPORATION**
(*Suby of* SONOCO PRODUCTS COMPANY)
1664 Seel Ave, Winnipeg, MB, R3T 4X5

Emp Here 160
SIC 2759 Commercial printing, nec
Chris Parker

D-U-N-S 20-325-8223   (SL)
SOUTHEAST PERSONAL CARE HOME INC
SOUTHEAST PERSONAL CARE HOME
1265 Lee Blvd, Winnipeg, MB, R3T 2M3
(204) 269-7111
Emp Here 80   *Sales* 4,900,320
SIC 8052 Intermediate care facilities
Jean Foster

D-U-N-S 25-507-1151   (SL)
ST JOHN'S-RAVENSCOURT SCHOOL
400 South Dr, Winnipeg, MB, R3T 3K5
(204) 504-3110
Emp Here 125   *Sales* 12,389,875
SIC 8211 Elementary and secondary schools
Stephen Johnson

D-U-N-S 20-133-9640   (HQ)
SUPER AUTO CENTRE INC
2028 Pembina Hwy, Winnipeg, MB, R3T 2G8
(204) 269-8444
Emp Here 10   *Sales* 54,023,640
SIC 7549 Automotive services, nec
Marge Laidlaw

D-U-N-S 20-011-4775   (SL)
SUPER-LITE LIGHTING LTD
SUPER-LITE
1040 Waverley St, Winnipeg, MB, R3T 0P3
(204) 989-7277
Emp Here 38   *Sales* 16,992,612
SIC 5063 Electrical apparatus and equipment
Simon Simkin
Stuart Pudavick
Allan Hochman

D-U-N-S 24-717-2422   (BR)
SYSCO CANADA, INC
SYSCO FOOD SERVICES OF WINNIPEG
(*Suby of* SYSCO CORPORATION)
1570 Clarence Ave, Winnipeg, MB, R3T 1T6
(204) 478-4000
Emp Here 200
SIC 5411 Grocery stores
Blair Schmidt

D-U-N-S 20-011-5665   (HQ)
TESHMONT CONSULTANTS INC
TESHMONT
1190 Waverley St, Winnipeg, MB, R3T 0P4
(204) 284-8100
Emp Here 2   *Sales* 37,281,918
SIC 6712 Bank holding companies
R.D. (Ralph) Kurth
B.K. (Brian) Benediktson
Timothy P. Gelbar
Robert Livet
Donald Belliveau
Eric Wiens

D-U-N-S 20-316-0007   (SL)
TESHMONT CONSULTANTS LP
(*Suby of* TESHMONT CONSULTANTS INC)
1190 Waverley St, Winnipeg, MB, R3T 0P4
(204) 284-8100
Emp Here 75
SIC 8711 Engineering services
R.D (Ralp) Kurth
B.K (Brian) Benediktson

D-U-N-S 20-948-7313   (HQ)
**UNIVERSITY OF MANITOBA STUDENTS
UNION**
UMSU
81 University Cres Suite 101, Winnipeg, MB,
R3T 4W9
(204) 474-8678
Sales 26,303,000

SIC 8641 Civic and social associations
Al Turnbull

D-U-N-S 24-345-0462   (BR)
UNIVERSITY OF MANITOBA THE
I.H. ASPER SCHOOL OF BUSINESS
(*Suby of* PROVINCE OF MANITOBA)
181 Freedman Cres Suite 121, Winnipeg, MB,
R3T 5V4
(204) 474-6200
Emp Here 100
SIC 8221 Colleges and universities

D-U-N-S 20-948-7685   (SL)
VICTORIA GENERAL HOSPITAL
2340 Pembina Hwy, Winnipeg, MB, R3T 2E8
(204) 269-3570
Emp Here 1,200   *Sales* 133,296,000
SIC 8062 General medical and surgical hospitals
James (Jim) Gordon
Kelvin Shepherd

D-U-N-S 24-546-2882   (SL)
WALL GRAIN HANDLING SYSTEMS LTD
WALL GRAIN
1460 Chevrier Blvd Unit 202, Winnipeg, MB,
R3T 1Y6
(204) 269-7616
Emp Here 25   *Sales* 11,875,650
SIC 5084 Industrial machinery and equipment
David Wall
Denise Wall

D-U-N-S 20-184-1652   (HQ)
WAREHOUSE ONE CLOTHING LTD
WAREHOUSE ONE - THE JEAN STORE
1530 Gamble Pl, Winnipeg, MB, R3T 1N6
(204) 885-4200
Emp Here 70   *Sales* 62,304,480
SIC 5651 Family clothing stores
Shansh Kassam
Neil Armstrong
Stephanie Graham

D-U-N-S 20-833-1439   (SL)
**WINNIPEG HUMANE SOCIETY FOR THE
PREVENTION CRUELTY TO ANIMALS**
SPCA
45 Hurst Way, Winnipeg, MB, R3T 0R3
(204) 982-2021
Emp Here 120   *Sales* 172,632,120
SIC 8699 Membership organizations, nec
Nancy Mcquade

D-U-N-S 20-758-2750   (BR)
XEROX CANADA LTD
DOCUMENT COMPANY, THE
(*Suby of* XEROX CORPORATION)
895 Waverley St, Winnipeg, MB, R3T 5P4
(204) 488-5100
Emp Here 100
SIC 5044 Office equipment
Mansel Belyea

Winnipeg, MB R3V

D-U-N-S 24-027-5359   (SL)
5195684 MANITOBA INC
RED RIVER CO OPERATIVE
3357 Pembina Hwy, Winnipeg, MB, R3V 1A2
(204) 261-3014
Emp Here 26   *Sales* 12,950,028
SIC 5541 Gasoline service stations
Richard M Tabak

D-U-N-S 20-758-8518   (SL)
**BEHAVIOURAL HEALTH FOUNDATION
INC, THE**
MALE YOUTH SERVICES
35 De La Digue Ave, Winnipeg, MB, R3V 1M7
(204) 269-3430
Emp Here 103   *Sales* 7,909,576
SIC 8322 Individual and family services

Jean Doucha

D-U-N-S 20-647-7267   (HQ)
BRETT-YOUNG SEEDS LIMITED
BRETTYOUNG
(*Suby of* JALO MANAGEMENT INC)
Hwy 330 And Hwy 100 Sw Corner, Winnipeg,
MB, R3V 1L5
(204) 261-7932
Emp Here 100   *Sales* 129,897,980
SIC 5191 Farm supplies
Calvin Sonntag
Andrew Steiman
Lloyd Dyck

D-U-N-S 24-372-5657   (SL)
**BRETT-YOUNG SEEDS LIMITED PARTNER-
SHIP**
Gd, Winnipeg, MB, R3V 1L5
(204) 261-7932
Emp Here 150   *Sales* 88,373,850
SIC 5191 Farm supplies
Lloyd Dyck

D-U-N-S 24-427-8479   (SL)
ST NORBERT LODGES LTD
ST ADOLPHE PERSONAL CARE HOME
50 St Pierre St, Winnipeg, MB, R3V 1J6
(204) 269-4538
Emp Here 170   *Sales* 11,656,220
SIC 8051 Skilled nursing care facilities
Michael Brousseau
David Brousseau

Winnipeg, MB R3X

D-U-N-S 24-976-4429   (SL)
B. & K. INTERNATIONAL CORPORATION
34 Waterfront Rd, Winnipeg, MB, R3X 1L2
(204) 654-4785
Emp Here 10   *Sales* 12,307,544
SIC 5159 Farm-product raw materials, nec
Bruno Burnichon

D-U-N-S 20-005-4773   (SL)
GUERTIN EQUIPMENT LTD
35 Melnick Rd, Winnipeg, MB, R3X 1V5
(204) 255-0260
Emp Here 30   *Sales* 14,250,780
SIC 5083 Farm and garden machinery
Michael Guertin

D-U-N-S 24-819-5166   (HQ)
**QUALICO DEVELOPMENTS (WINNIPEG)
LTD**
(*Suby of* QUALICO GROUP LTD)
1 Dr. David Friesen Dr, Winnipeg, MB, R3X
0G8
(204) 233-2451
Sales 73,101,800
SIC 6712 Bank holding companies
Brian Hastings
Ron Reimer

D-U-N-S 24-607-3357   (HQ)
QUALICO DEVELOPMENTS CANADA LTD
QUALICO
(*Suby of* QUALICO GROUP LTD)
1 Dr. David Friesen Dr, Winnipeg, MB, R3X
0G8
(204) 233-2451
Emp Here 200   *Sales* 731,018,000
SIC 6712 Bank holding companies
Kevin Van
Brian Hastings

D-U-N-S 20-721-4896   (SL)
RAINBOW DAY NURSERY INC
445 Island Shore Blvd Unit 11, Winnipeg, MB,
R3X 2B4
(204) 256-0672
Emp Here 100   *Sales* 5,936,900
SIC 8351 Child day care services
Diane Hale

D-U-N-S 24-702-5091   (HQ)
STREETSIDE DEVELOPMENT CORPORA-TION
(*Suby of* QUALICO GROUP LTD)
1 Dr. David Friesen Dr, Winnipeg, MB, R3X 0G8
(204) 233-2451
Sales 11,543,320
SIC 1522 Residential construction, nec
Ruth Hastings
Brian Hastings

Winnipeg, MB R3Y

D-U-N-S 20-387-8512   (SL)
10022441 MANITOBA LTD
KELLER WILLIAMS REAL ESTATE SER-VICES
15 Scurfield Blvd, Winnipeg, MB, R3Y 1G3
(204) 615-7333
Emp Here 39   *Sales* 12,757,953
SIC 6531 Real estate agents and managers
Antonio Martone
Tessie Martone

D-U-N-S 24-775-9541   (HQ)
2302659 MANITOBA LTD
URBAN TRAIL
59 Scurfield Blvd Suite 9, Winnipeg, MB, R3Y 1V2
(204) 925-6880
Emp Here 12   *Sales* 22,394,457
SIC 5661 Shoe stores
Dave Quark
Albert Krahn
Doug Quark
Tom Quark
Kristy Krahn
Ryan James Krahn

D-U-N-S 20-720-9490   (HQ)
4549440 MANITOBA LTD
VERICO ONE-LINK MORTGAGE AND FI-NANCIAL
99 Scurfield Blvd Unit 100, Winnipeg, MB, R3Y 1Y1
(204) 954-7620
Emp Here 45   *Sales* 10,113,480
SIC 6162 Mortgage bankers and loan corre-spondents
Nadine Coubrough
Marty Coubrough

D-U-N-S 24-882-7743   (SL)
APOTEX FERMENTATION INC
50 Scurfield Blvd, Winnipeg, MB, R3Y 1G4
(204) 989-6830
Emp Here 90   *Sales* 25,561,890
SIC 2834 Pharmaceutical preparations
Mila Sailer
Craig R Baxter

D-U-N-S 24-607-4173   (SL)
BYLES, A. S. SUPPLIES LIMITED
CANADIAN TIRE
(*Suby of* BYCO ENTERPRISES INC)
1711 Kenaston Blvd, Winnipeg, MB, R3Y 1V5
(204) 269-9630
Emp Here 75   *Sales* 15,400,725
SIC 5311 Department stores
Adrian S. Byles

D-U-N-S 20-042-4658   (SL)
CALABRIA MARKET & DELI INC
139 Scurfield Blvd, Winnipeg, MB, R3Y 1L6
(204) 487-1700
Emp Here 38   *Sales* 10,417,776
SIC 5411 Grocery stores
Dereck Wozny

D-U-N-S 24-344-7674   (BR)
COSTCO WHOLESALE CANADA LTD
COSTCO
(*Suby of* COSTCO WHOLESALE CORPO-RATION)
2365 Mcgillivray Blvd Suite 1, Winnipeg, MB, R3Y 0A1
(204) 487-5100
Emp Here 225
SIC 5399 Miscellaneous general merchandise
Barry Lane

D-U-N-S 20-702-3925   (BR)
EMERGENT BIOSOLUTIONS CANADA INC
(*Suby of* EMERGENT BIOSOLUTIONS INC.)
26 Henlow Bay, Winnipeg, MB, R3Y 1G4
(204) 275-4200
Emp Here 200
SIC 8731 Commercial physical research
Jeff Lamothe

D-U-N-S 25-098-9944   (HQ)
EPIC INFORMATION SOLUTIONS INC
1730 Mcgillivray Blvd, Winnipeg, MB, R3Y 1A1
(204) 453-2300
Emp Here 49   *Sales* 22,358,700
SIC 5045 Computers, peripherals, and soft-ware
Glen Leblanc
Mirko Bibic
Michel Lalande

D-U-N-S 24-679-0617   (SL)
FWS COMMERCIAL PROJECTS LTD
(*Suby of* FWS HOLDINGS LTD)
475 Dovercourt Dr, Winnipeg, MB, R3Y 1G4
(204) 487-2500
Emp Here 50   *Sales* 28,516,900
SIC 1542 Nonresidential construction, nec
Richard Chale
Michael Evans
Douglas Petrick
Troy Valgardson

D-U-N-S 24-571-2609   (BR)
GRAND & TOY LIMITED
(*Suby of* OFFICE DEPOT, INC.)
15 Scurfield Blvd, Winnipeg, MB, R3Y 1V4
(204) 284-5100
Emp Here 85
SIC 5943 Stationery stores
Audrey Stewar

D-U-N-S 24-382-9681   (HQ)
IC GROUP INC
383 Dovercourt Dr, Winnipeg, MB, R3Y 1G4
(204) 487-5000
Emp Here 55   *Sales* 11,190,360
SIC 8743 Public relations services
Duncan Mccready
Marc Caron
Mike Svetkoff

D-U-N-S 25-077-7117   (SL)
J & D PENNER LTD
2560 Mcgillivray Blvd, Winnipeg, MB, R3Y 1G5
(204) 895-8602
Emp Here 55   *Sales* 13,884,310
SIC 1611 Highway and street construction
Richard (Dick) Penner
Jacob Penner

D-U-N-S 24-852-2245   (BR)
KEG RESTAURANTS LTD
KEG STEAKHOUSE & BAR, THE
(*Suby of* RECIPE UNLIMITED CORPORA-TION)
2034 Mcgillivray Blvd, Winnipeg, MB, R3Y 1V5
(204) 477-5300
Emp Here 200
SIC 5812 Eating places
Scott Stephen

D-U-N-S 24-916-7875   (SL)
M. D. STEELE CONSTRUCTION LTD
193 Henlow Bay, Winnipeg, MB, R3Y 1G4
(204) 488-7070
Emp Here 30   *Sales* 17,110,140
SIC 1542 Nonresidential construction, nec

Kurt Wegner
John Elands
Shawn Legault
Peter Plaza
Richard Wilson
Clarence Catellier
Sherry Macleod
Pat Lusty
Tony Dinella
Russ Dueck

D-U-N-S 20-229-3168   (BR)
MCDONALD'S RESTAURANTS OF CANADA LIMITED
MCDONALD'S
(*Suby of* MCDONALD'S CORPORATION)
1725 Kenaston Blvd, Winnipeg, MB, R3Y 1V5
(204) 949-5128
Emp Here 100
SIC 5812 Eating places
Mark Storey

D-U-N-S 24-374-9553   (HQ)
NORTH/SOUTH CONSULTANTS INC
83 Scurfield Blvd, Winnipeg, MB, R3Y 1G4
(204) 284-3366
Emp Here 50   *Sales* 12,885,840
SIC 8748 Business consulting, nec
Stuart Davies
Gail Davies

D-U-N-S 24-037-4736   (HQ)
PEMBINA TRAILS SCHOOL DIVISION, THE
181 Henlow Bay, Winnipeg, MB, R3Y 1M7
(204) 488-1757
Emp Here 100   *Sales* 172,863,536
SIC 8211 Elementary and secondary schools
Ted Fransen
Craig Stahlke
Jacquie Field
Karen Velthuys

D-U-N-S 25-535-8830   (HQ)
PIC CANADA LTD
(*Suby of* PIC USA, INC.)
99 Scurfield Blvd Unit 161, Winnipeg, MB, R3Y 1Y1
(204) 927-7120
Emp Here 2   *Sales* 21,301,575
SIC 2834 Pharmaceutical preparations
Chris Stener

D-U-N-S 24-265-2113   (SL)
THOMAS DESIGN BUILDERS LTD
TDB
2395 Mcgillivray Blvd Unit C, Winnipeg, MB, R3Y 1G6
(204) 989-5400
Emp Here 31   *Sales* 14,592,661
SIC 1542 Nonresidential construction, nec
Jeffery Miller
Trevor Miller
Ronald Miller

D-U-N-S 24-748-8521   (SL)
TO-LE-DO FOODSERVICE REALTY HOLD-INGS LTD
TO-LE-DO FOODSERVICE
2430 Mcgillivray Blvd, Winnipeg, MB, R3Y 1G6
(204) 487-3340
Emp Here 44   *Sales* 36,765,388
SIC 5147 Meats and meat products
Leigh Young
Barbara Young

D-U-N-S 24-264-6891   (HQ)
VECTOR CONSTRUCTION LTD
(*Suby of* VECTOR MANAGEMENT LTD)
474 Dovercourt Dr, Winnipeg, MB, R3Y 1G4
(204) 489-6300
Emp Here 30   *Sales* 36,627,484
SIC 1771 Concrete work
Robert Spriggs

D-U-N-S 20-758-2800   (HQ)
VECTOR MANAGEMENT LTD
474 Dovercourt Dr, Winnipeg, MB, R3Y 1G4

(204) 489-6300
Emp Here 10   *Sales* 30,485,480
SIC 1611 Highway and street construction
Donald Whitmore
Robert Spriggs
Florence Whitmore

D-U-N-S 25-451-8673   (SL)
VISTA MEDICAL LTD
55 Henlow Bay Unit 3, Winnipeg, MB, R3Y 1G4
(204) 949-7678
Emp Here 40   *Sales* 10,262,480
SIC 3841 Surgical and medical instruments
Andrew Frank

D-U-N-S 24-171-4849   (SL)
WESTLAND CONSTRUCTION LTD
(*Suby of* PBG HOLDINGS INC)
475 Dovercourt Dr Unit 1, Winnipeg, MB, R3Y 1G4
(204) 633-6272
Emp Here 50   *Sales* 21,136,850
SIC 1541 Industrial buildings and warehouses
Peter Grose

D-U-N-S 24-545-9987   (HQ)
WINNIPEG TECHNICAL COLLEGE
130 Henlow Bay, Winnipeg, MB, R3Y 1G4
(204) 989-6500
Sales 11,263,600
SIC 8222 Junior colleges
Doug Kurtz
Karen Velthuys
Laureen Goodridge

Winnipeg, MB R4G

D-U-N-S 24-859-5972   (SL)
PBL PROJECTS LP
405 Fort Whyte Way Unit 100, Winnipeg, MB, R4G 0B1
(204) 633-2515
Emp Here 80   *Sales* 45,627,040
SIC 1542 Nonresidential construction, nec
Jeff Hawryluk
Robin Lee

Winnipeg, MB S7K

D-U-N-S 24-172-5910   (HQ)
T. & D. ENTERPRISES LTD
WESCAN ELECTRICAL MECHANICAL SER-VICES
1546 Saskatchewan Ave, Winnipeg, MB, S7K 1P7
(204) 786-3384
Sales 32,674,350
SIC 1731 Electrical work
Terrance Henry
Dirk Kleinholz
Dennis Johnston

Woodlands, MB R0C

D-U-N-S 20-652-8460   (SL)
NORTHQUIP INC
ARROWQUIP
141 Railway Ave, Woodlands, MB, R0C 3H0
(866) 383-7827
Emp Here 60   *Sales* 28,501,560
SIC 5083 Farm and garden machinery
Andrew Firth
Phil Filth
Jennifer Langrell
Jerry Langrell

▲ Public Company   ■ Public Company Family Member   **HQ** Headquarters   **BR** Branch   **SL** Single Location

Acadieville, NB E4Y

D-U-N-S 24-672-8245   (SL)
SNJ FORESTERIE
4016 Route 480, Acadieville, NB, E4Y 2B7
(506) 775-2895
Emp Here 49   *Sales* 10,369,037
SIC 0851 Forestry services
Steven Guimont

Anderson Road, NB E7G

D-U-N-S 25-525-9699   (SL)
H. E. FORESTRY LTD
1990 Route 380, Anderson Road, NB, E7G
4C1
(506) 356-2310
Emp Here 25   *Sales* 11,725,125
SIC 5989 Fuel dealers, nec
Dale Eccleston
Darlene Shirley

Anse-Bleue, NB E8N

D-U-N-S 25-092-0696   (BR)
BARRY GROUP INC
BARRY GROUP
(*Suby of* BARRY GROUP INC)
12 Allee Frigault, Anse-Bleue, NB, E8N 2J2

Emp Here 125
SIC 5421 Meat and fish markets
Michelle Gauvin

Atholville, NB E3N

D-U-N-S 20-018-5593   (SL)
CENTRAL GARAGE LTD
CHRYSLER JEEP
76 Rue Notre Dame, Atholville, NB, E3N 3Z2
(506) 753-7731
Emp Here 48   *Sales* 23,907,744
SIC 5511 New and used car dealers
Guy Cormier
Denis Cormier
Roger Cormier
Pauline Cormier

D-U-N-S 24-391-8385   (SL)
GAUDREAU, MARC INC
CANADIAN TIRE
384 Old Val D'Amour Rd, Atholville, NB, E3N
4E3
(506) 789-0220
Emp Here 45   *Sales* 22,413,510
SIC 5531 Auto and home supply stores
Marc Gaudreau

D-U-N-S 20-194-2609   (SL)
GESTION ROGER THERIAULT
CANADIAN TIRE
384 Old Val D'Amour Rd, Atholville, NB, E3N
4E3
(506) 789-0230
Emp Here 25   *Sales* 12,451,950
SIC 5531 Auto and home supply stores
Roger Theriault

D-U-N-S 20-732-0511   (SL)
VISION FORD INC
105 Sister Green Rd, Atholville, NB, E3N 5C5
(506) 753-5001
Emp Here 24   *Sales* 11,953,872
SIC 5511 New and used car dealers
Lucien Leblanc

D-U-N-S 24-318-0796   (BR)
WAL-MART CANADA CORP
WALMART
(*Suby of* WALMART INC.)
4 Rue Jagoe, Atholville, NB, E3N 5C3
(506) 753-7105
Emp Here 150
SIC 5311 Department stores
Scott Munroe

Aulac, NB E4L

D-U-N-S 24-956-0814   (SL)
BENICK SERVICES INC
AULAC IRVING BIG STOP
170 Aulac Rd, Aulac, NB, E4L 2X2
(506) 536-1339
Emp Here 70   *Sales* 44,049,600
SIC 5541 Gasoline service stations
William J. Allen

Baie-Sainte-Anne, NB E9A

D-U-N-S 20-018-5890   (SL)
BAIE STE-ANNE CO-OPERATIVE LTD
5575 Route 117, Baie-Sainte-Anne, NB, E9A
1E6
(506) 228-4211
Emp Here 31   *Sales* 10,012,039
SIC 5411 Grocery stores
Pierre Turbide
Robert Martin

D-U-N-S 24-931-9310   (BR)
TOURBIERES BERGER LTEE, LES
BERGER PEATMOSS
(*Suby of* TOURBIERES BERGER LTEE, LES)
4188 Route 117, Baie-Sainte-Anne, NB, E9A
1R7

Emp Here 100
SIC 1499 Miscellaneous nonMetallic minerals,
except fuels
Daniel Lebel

Balmoral, NB E8E

D-U-N-S 24-189-8675   (HQ)
ALPA EQUIPMENT COMPANY LIMITED
ALPA EQUIPMENT
258 Drapeau St, Balmoral, NB, E8E 1H3
(506) 826-2717
Emp Here 40   *Sales* 45,127,470
SIC 5082 Construction and mining machinery
Armand Landry
Serge Landry
Linda Landry-Firth

D-U-N-S 25-363-9041   (SL)
BALMORAL SAVE EASY
647 Des Pionniers Ave, Balmoral, NB, E8E
1B3
(506) 826-2545
Emp Here 40   *Sales* 10,966,080
SIC 5411 Grocery stores
Gilles Leclair

D-U-N-S 24-309-8147   (SL)
SCIERIES ADRIEN ARSENEAULT LTEE
47 Du Moulin St, Balmoral, NB, E8E 1H6

Emp Here 35   *Sales* 15,651,090
SIC 5031 Lumber, plywood, and millwork
Allain Arseneault

Bas-Cap-Pele, NB E4N

D-U-N-S 24-723-1301   (SL)
P & E MANUFACTURING LTD
1524 Route 950, Bas-Cap-Pele, NB, E4N 1A9
(506) 577-4356
Emp Here 22   *Sales* 10,957,716
SIC 5551 Boat dealers
James Belliveau
Roland Belliveau

Bas-Caraquet, NB E1W

D-U-N-S 20-288-8186   (SL)
**PECHERIES BAS-CARAQUET FISHERIES
INC**
2270 Industrielle St, Bas-Caraquet, NB, E1W
5Z2
(506) 727-3632
Emp Here 49   *Sales* 11,017,895
SIC 2092 Fresh or frozen packaged fish
Rudy Lebreton

Bathurst, NB E2A

D-U-N-S 25-946-4303   (BR)
ATLANTIC WHOLESALERS LTD
REAL ATLANTIC SUPERSTORE, THE
(*Suby of* LOBLAW COMPANIES LIMITED)
700 St. Peter Ave, Bathurst, NB, E2A 2Y7
(506) 547-3180
Emp Here 178
SIC 5411 Grocery stores
Margaret Astle

D-U-N-S 25-401-1489   (SL)
BATHURST FINE CARS INC
BATHURST HONDA
2300 St. Peter Ave, Bathurst, NB, E2A 7K2
(506) 548-4569
Emp Here 23   *Sales* 11,455,794
SIC 5511 New and used car dealers
Marc Frenette

D-U-N-S 25-828-8083   (BR)
BATHURST, CITY OF
K C IRVING REGIONAL CENTRE
(*Suby of* BATHURST, CITY OF)
14 Sean Couturier Ave, Bathurst, NB, E2A
6X2
(506) 549-3300
Emp Here 100
SIC 7999 Amusement and recreation, nec
Marc Boudreau

D-U-N-S 20-444-8500   (HQ)
BAYSIDE CHRYSLER DODGE LTD
1374 St. Peter Ave, Bathurst, NB, E2A 3A5
(506) 546-6606
Emp Here 1   *Sales* 18,926,964
SIC 5511 New and used car dealers
Evan Moffitt
Jason Moffitt

D-U-N-S 24-123-5071   (BR)
**CONNECT NORTH AMERICA CORPORA-
TION**
275 Main St Suite 600, Bathurst, NB, E2A 1A9
(506) 545-9450
Emp Here 95
SIC 7389 Business services, nec
Lori Roy

D-U-N-S 25-241-9502   (BR)
CONSEIL SCOLAIRE DISTRICT NO 5
ECOLE SECONDAIRE NEPISIGUIT
915 St. Anne St, Bathurst, NB, E2A 6X1
(506) 547-2785
Emp Here 115   *Sales* 396,535
SIC 8211 Elementary and secondary schools
Paul Thibodeau

D-U-N-S 24-755-8752   (HQ)
EDDY GROUP LIMITED
EDDY WHOLESALE
660 St. Anne St, Bathurst, NB, E2A 2N6
(506) 546-6631
Emp Here 40   *Sales* 64,406,160
SIC 5074 Plumbing and heating equipment
and supplies (hydronics)
Kenneth R Eddy
Robyn Eddy
Keith Assaff
Darryl Eddy
Jody Mcdonald

D-U-N-S 25-686-7201   (SL)
**FOYER NOTRE-DAME DE LOURDES INC,
LE**
2055 Vallee Lourdes Dr, Bathurst, NB, E2A
4P8
(506) 549-5085
Emp Here 140   *Sales* 8,999,480
SIC 8361 Residential care
Paul Sonier

D-U-N-S 24-637-3955   (SL)
GESTION GILLES CHARTRAND INC
CANADIAN TIRE
520 St. Peter Ave, Bathurst, NB, E2A 2Y7
(506) 547-8120
Emp Here 75   *Sales* 47,196,000
SIC 5531 Auto and home supply stores
Gilles Chartrand

D-U-N-S 24-127-3796   (SL)
HATHEWAY LIMITED
1030 St. Anne St, Bathurst, NB, E2A 6X2
(506) 546-4464
Emp Here 40   *Sales* 19,923,120
SIC 5511 New and used car dealers
Ian Hatheway
David Hatheway

D-U-N-S 24-472-1049   (SL)
R. G. MC. GROUP LIMITED
MCDONALDS FAMILY RESTAURANT
620 St. Peter Ave, Bathurst, NB, E2A 2Y7
(506) 548-9555
Emp Here 110   *Sales* 5,007,090
SIC 5812 Eating places
Ronald Mclellan
Gail Mclellan

D-U-N-S 24-421-8181   (HQ)
REGIONAL HEALTH AUTHORITY A
275 Main St Suite 600, Bathurst, NB, E2A 1A9
(506) 544-2188
Sales 111,080,000
SIC 8062 General medical and surgical hospi-
tals
Jill Lanteigne

D-U-N-S 24-318-5340   (BR)
REGIONAL HEALTH AUTHORITY A
CHALEUR REGIONAL HOSPITAL
(*Suby of* REGIONAL HEALTH AUTHORITY
A)
1750 Sunset Dr, Bathurst, NB, E2A 4L7
(506) 544-3000
Emp Here 900
SIC 8062 General medical and surgical hospi-
tals
Aldeoda Losier

D-U-N-S 20-365-3345   (SL)
**ROGER'S ELECTRIC MOTOR SERVICE
(1998) LTD**
ROGER'S ELECTRIC AND MACHINE
1990 Connolly Ave, Bathurst, NB, E2A 4W7
(506) 548-8711
Emp Here 30   *Sales* 14,250,780
SIC 5084 Industrial machinery and equipment
Todd Morrison

D-U-N-S 24-628-8328   (HQ)
ROY CONSULTANTS GROUP LTD
ROY CONSULTANTS
(*Suby of* 603414 NB INC)
548 King Ave, Bathurst, NB, E2A 1P7

(506) 546-4484
Emp Here 50   ·   *Sales* 17,595,800
SIC 8711 Engineering services
Rejean Boudreau
Michel Dusresne

D-U-N-S 24-878-7442   (SL)
STEVE DOUCET PHARMACUETICAL INC
SHOPPERS DRUG MART
939 St. Peter Ave, Bathurst, NB, E2A 2Z3
(506) 547-8023
Emp Here 40   *Sales* 10,118,160
SIC 5912 Drug stores and proprietary stores
Steve Doucet

D-U-N-S 20-018-8050   (SL)
STOTHART AUTOMOTIVE INC
335 Murray Ave, Bathurst, NB, E2A 1T4
(506) 548-8988
Emp Here 25   *Sales* 12,451,950
SIC 5511 New and used car dealers
Daryll Stothart
Sharon Stothart

D-U-N-S 25-185-2570   (SL)
TITAN ACADIE BATHURST (2013) INC, LE
TITAN ACADIE BATHURST
14 Sean Couturier Ave, Bathurst, NB, E2A 6X2
(506) 549-3300
Emp Here 40   *Sales* 16,949,200
SIC 7941 Sports clubs, managers, and promoters
Serge Theriault
Gilles Cormier

D-U-N-S 24-993-4548   (HQ)
VITALITE HEALTH NETWORK
EDMUNDSTON REGIONAL HOSPITAL
275 Main St Suite 600, Bathurst, NB, E2A 1A9
(506) 544-2133
Sales 164,953,800
SIC 8062 General medical and surgical hospitals
Pierre Verret

D-U-N-S 24-097-9042   (BR)
WAL-MART CANADA CORP
WALMART
(*Suby of* WALMART INC.)
900 St. Anne St, Bathurst, NB, E2A 6X2
(506) 546-0500
Emp Here 130
SIC 5311 Department stores
Scott Munro

Bay Du Vin, NB E1N

D-U-N-S 20-135-7006   (SL)
BERGER PEAT MOSS ENR
BERGER MIX
149 Bay Du Vin River Rd, Bay Du Vin, NB, E1N 5P4
(800) 463-5582
Emp Here 54   *Sales* 14,453,208
SIC 5261 Retail nurseries and garden stores
Denis Lebel

Bayside, NB E5B

D-U-N-S 20-251-1176   (SL)
FUNDY STEVEDORING INC
140 Champlain Prom, Bayside, NB, E5B 2Y2
(506) 529-8821
Emp Here 49   *Sales* 10,456,208
SIC 4491 Marine cargo handling
Maureen Worrell

D-U-N-S 25-149-2187   (SL)
JAMER MATERIALS LIMITED
3019 Route 127, Bayside, NB, E5B 2S4

(506) 529-1117
Emp Here 40   *Sales* 17,886,960
SIC 5032 Brick, stone, and related material
Miller Esson

Belledune, NB E8G

D-U-N-S 24-336-6718   (SL)
SANCON CONTRACTING LTD
SANCON COMMISSIONING
4621 Main St, Belledune, NB, E8G 2L3
(506) 507-2222
Emp Here 40   *Sales* 12,754,760
SIC 1521 Single-family housing construction
Dennis Killoran

D-U-N-S 25-154-2478   (SL)
TRA MARITIMES
FOODLAND
3917 Main St, Belledune, NB, E8G 2K3

Emp Here 45   *Sales* 13,206,465
SIC 5411 Grocery stores

Berry Mills, NB E1G

D-U-N-S 20-016-0815   (BR)
MILLER PAVING LIMITED
INDUSTRIAL COLD MILLING, DIV OF
(*Suby of* MILLER GROUP INC)
2276 Route 128, Berry Mills, NB, E1G 4K4
(506) 857-0112
Emp Here 130
SIC 1611 Highway and street construction
Calvin Flight

D-U-N-S 20-807-7219   (SL)
MILLER WASTE SYSTEMS INC
(*Suby of* MILLER GROUP INC)
2276 Route 128, Berry Mills, NB, E1G 4K4
(506) 855-9783
Emp Here 170   *Sales* 54,214,700
SIC 4953 Refuse systems
Ronald Mckinnon
Frank Arsenault

D-U-N-S 25-135-6259   (SL)
WESTMORLAND-ALBERT SOLID WASTE CORPORATION
2024 Route 128, Berry Mills, NB, E1G 4K6
(506) 877-1050
Emp Here 55   *Sales* 17,540,050
SIC 4953 Refuse systems
Bill Slater
Norman Crossman
Yvan Gautreau
Ron Boudreau
Harley Tingley

Berwick, NB E5P

D-U-N-S 24-000-5947   (SL)
615317 NB INC
BTN ATLANTIC
(*Suby of* BROOKDALE TREELAND NURSERIES LIMITED)
891 Route 880, Berwick, NB, E5P 3H5
(506) 433-6168
Emp Here 25   *Sales* 18,563,000
SIC 5193 Flowers and florists supplies
Ryan Somerville

Blacks Harbour, NB E5H

D-U-N-S 25-361-6825   (BR)

CONNORS BROS. CLOVER LEAF SEAFOODS COMPANY
CONNOR BROS., DIV OF
(*Suby of* CLOVER LEAF HOLDINGS COMPANY)
180 Brunswick St, Blacks Harbour, NB, E5H 1G6
(506) 456-3391
Emp Here 700
SIC 5146 Fish and seafoods
Wayne Ingeresoll

D-U-N-S 24-994-4380   (HQ)
COOKE AQUACULTURE INC
(*Suby of* COOKE INC)
874 Main St, Blacks Harbour, NB, E5H 1E6
(506) 456-6600
Emp Here 30   *Sales* 268,602,100
SIC 0912 Finfish
Glenn Cooke
Michael Cooke

D-U-N-S 20-369-4419   (HQ)
COOKE INC
669 Main St, Blacks Harbour, NB, E5H 1K1
(506) 456-6600
Sales 268,602,100
SIC 0912 Finfish
Glen Cooke

D-U-N-S 24-790-2216   (HQ)
KELLY COVE SALMON LTD
OAK BAY HATCHERY
(*Suby of* COOKE INC)
874 Main St, Blacks Harbour, NB, E5H 1E6
(506) 456-6600
Sales 20,741,400
SIC 2092 Fresh or frozen packaged fish
Glen Cooke
Gifford Cooke
Peter Buck
Michael Cooke

D-U-N-S 24-314-4420   (HQ)
TRUE NORTH SALMON CO. LTD
HERITAGE SALMON
(*Suby of* COOKE INC)
669 Main St, Blacks Harbour, NB, E5H 1K1
(506) 456-6600
Emp Here 20   *Sales* 170,584,750
SIC 2092 Fresh or frozen packaged fish
Glenn Cooke
Gifford Cooke
Michael Cooke

D-U-N-S 24-320-1301   (SL)
TRUE NORTH SALMON LIMITED PARTNERSHIP
669 Main St, Blacks Harbour, NB, E5H 1K1
(506) 456-6610
Emp Here 20   *Sales* 170,584,750
SIC 2092 Fresh or frozen packaged fish
Gifford Cooke

Bouctouche, NB E4S

D-U-N-S 20-549-5351   (SL)
BOUCTOUCHE PHARMACY LTD
PHARMASAVE
30 Irving Blvd Suite 200, Bouctouche, NB, E4S 3L2
(506) 743-2434
Emp Here 49   *Sales* 12,394,746
SIC 5912 Drug stores and proprietary stores

D-U-N-S 24-382-1167   (BR)
CAISSE POPULAIRE KENT-SUD LTEE
CAISSE POPULAIRE DE BOUCTOUCHE
(*Suby of* CAISSE POPULAIRE KENT-SUD LTEE)
196 Irving Blvd, Bouctouche, NB, E4S 3L7
(506) 576-6666
Emp Here 150
SIC 6062 State credit unions

Elmo Caissie

D-U-N-S 25-105-3369   (SL)
CO-OPERATIVE DE BOUCTOUCHE LTD , (LA)
191 Irving Blvd, Bouctouche, NB, E4S 3K3
(506) 743-1960
Emp Here 80   *Sales* 23,478,160
SIC 5411 Grocery stores
Sylvie Dallaire
Don Auffrey

D-U-N-S 20-023-3570   (BR)
DISTRICT SCOLAIRE 11
DISTRICT SCOLAIRE FRANCOPHONE SUD
37 Av Richard, Bouctouche, NB, E4S 3T5
(506) 743-7200
Emp Here 75
SIC 8211 Elementary and secondary schools
Ken Therrien

D-U-N-S 24-333-2603   (BR)
IRVING, J. D. LIMITED
KENT HOMES
(*Suby of* IRVING, J. D. LIMITED)
28 Ch Du Couvent, Bouctouche, NB, E4S 3B9
(506) 743-2481
Emp Here 150
SIC 2452 Prefabricated wood buildings
Steve Wheeler

D-U-N-S 20-932-3955   (SL)
MANOIR SAINT-JEAN BAPTISTE INC
5 Av Richard, Bouctouche, NB, E4S 3T2
(506) 743-7344
Emp Here 85   *Sales* 5,035,995
SIC 8361 Residential care
Ian Drapeau
Gilles Hebert

D-U-N-S 20-340-1237   (SL)
MILLS AQUACULTURE INC
5 Rue Mills, Bouctouche, NB, E4S 3S3

Emp Here 20   *Sales* 10,702,480
SIC 5146 Fish and seafoods
Norm Leblan

D-U-N-S 20-618-7650   (HQ)
MILLS SEA FOOD LTD
5 Rue Mills, Bouctouche, NB, E4S 3S3

Sales 69,138,000
SIC 2092 Fresh or frozen packaged fish
Steven Mills
Marie Allain

D-U-N-S 24-956-3727   (SL)
PAYS DE LA SAGOUINE INC, LE
57 Rue Acadie, Bouctouche, NB, E4S 2T7
(506) 743-1400
Emp Here 211   *Sales* 18,293,700
SIC 7999 Amusement and recreation, nec
Leo-Paul Leblanc
Pierre-Marcel Desjardins

D-U-N-S 20-023-8272   (SL)
PHARE DES SERVICES COMMUNAUTAIRES INC, LE
68 Av De La Riviere, Bouctouche, NB, E4S 3A7
(506) 743-7377
Emp Here 100   *Sales* 6,842,200
SIC 8322 Individual and family services
Stephane Demers
Colette Lacroix

D-U-N-S 25-358-6341   (HQ)
SYSTEMAIR INC
(*Suby of* SYSTEMAIR AB)
50 Kanalflakt Way Route, Bouctouche, NB, E4S 3M5
(506) 743-9500
Emp Here 125   *Sales* 44,400,200
SIC 3564 Blowers and fans
Gerald Engstrom
Roland Mazerolle
Alan Graham

Brunswick Mines, NB E2A

D-U-N-S 24-379-0545   (SL)
FORNEBU LUMBER COMPANY INC
BATHURST LUMBER, DIV OF
5060 Route 430, Brunswick Mines, NB, E2A
6W6
(506) 547-8690
Emp Here 200   *Sales* 38,474,000
SIC 2421 Sawmills and planing mills, general
Joerk Rimmasch
David Wright
Tim Beaulieu

Campbellton, NB E3N

D-U-N-S 24-994-6336   (SL)
056186 N.B. INC
PHARMACIE JEAN COUTU
101 Water St, Campbellton, NB, E3N 1B2
(506) 759-8547
Emp Here 40   *Sales* 10,118,160
SIC 5912 Drug stores and proprietary stores
Brigitte Arseneault
Marc Carriere
Joanne Lebourque

D-U-N-S 20-813-9030   (SL)
CAMPBELLTON NURSING HOME INC
VILLAGE, THE
101 Dover St, Campbellton, NB, E3N 3K6
(506) 789-7350
Emp Here 120   *Sales* 8,199,120
SIC 8051 Skilled nursing care facilities
Jack Renault
Ken Murray

D-U-N-S 25-241-6730   (BR)
CONSEIL SCOLAIRE DISTRICT NO 5
*POLYVALENTE   ROLAND-PEPIN   HIGH
SCHOOL*
45a Rue Du Village, Campbellton, NB, E3N
3G4
(506) 789-2250
Emp Here 75   *Sales* 396,535
SIC 8211 Elementary and secondary schools
Gilles Lurette

D-U-N-S 20-058-9716   (SL)
EASTERN RAILWAY SERVICES
205 Roseberry St, Campbellton, NB, E3N 2H4
(506) 753-0462
Emp Here 40   *Sales* 15,592,928
SIC 4789 Transportation services, nec
Gill Richard

D-U-N-S 20-932-3070   (HQ)
RESTIGOUCHE HEALTH AUTHORITY
CAMPBELLTON REGIONAL HOSPITAL
189 Lily Lake Rd, Campbellton, NB, E3N 3H3
(506) 789-5000
Emp Here 800   *Sales* 135,739,760
SIC 8062 General medical and surgical hospitals
Dan Arsenault
Jean Boulay

D-U-N-S 24-130-4906   (SL)
RESTIGOUCHE MOTORS LTD
RESTIGOUCHE TOYOTA
388 Dover St, Campbellton, NB, E3N 3M7
(506) 753-5019
Emp Here 21   *Sales* 10,459,638
SIC 5511 New and used car dealers
Pierre Bourgoin
Lorraine Ahier
Yvette Bourgoin

D-U-N-S 24-118-0566   (BR)
SNC-LAVALIN INC
SLP CUSTOMER SUPPORT
(Suby of GROUPE SNC-LAVALIN INC)

88 Sr Green Rd Suite 101, Campbellton, NB,
E3N 3Y6
(506) 759-6350
Emp Here 100
SIC 6798 Real estate investment trusts
Jon F Miller

D-U-N-S 25-309-1797   (BR)
SOBEYS CAPITAL INCORPORATED
SOBEYS
(Suby of EMPIRE COMPANY LIMITED)
140 Roseberry St, Campbellton, NB, E3N 2G9
(506) 753-5339
Emp Here 100
SIC 5411 Grocery stores
Marcel Sevoie

D-U-N-S 24-893-9139   (SL)
V.C. RENOVATION
103 Vanier St, Campbellton, NB, E3N 1T8
(506) 753-6273
Emp Here 49   *Sales* 13,276,158
SIC 1521 Single-family housing construction

Cap-Pele, NB E4N

D-U-N-S 20-019-1344   (HQ)
CAPE BALD PACKERS, LIMITED
2618 Ch Acadie, Cap-Pele, NB, E4N 1E3
(506) 577-4316
Emp Here 200   *Sales* 143,343,200
SIC 5146 Fish and seafoods
Doris Losier
Matthieu Landry

D-U-N-S 24-262-1332   (SL)
SEA TIDE IMPORT & EXPORT LTD
SEA TIDE GROUND FISH PLANT
45 Rue Cormier, Cap-Pele, NB, E4N 1N8
(506) 577-4070
Emp Here 50   *Sales* 11,242,750
SIC 2092 Fresh or frozen packaged fish
Gerard Cormier
Nicole Cormier

D-U-N-S 24-262-3528   (SL)
THERMALITE PRODUCTS INC
2598 Ch Acadie, Cap-Pele, NB, E4N 1E3
(506) 577-4351
Emp Here 140   *Sales* 22,240,120
SIC 3086 Plastics foam products
Victor Landry

D-U-N-S 20-741-5829   (HQ)
WESTMORLAND FISHERIES LTD
64 Gautreau St, Cap-Pele, NB, E4N 1V3
(506) 577-4325
Sales 185,206,300
SIC 2091 Canned and cured fish and
seafoods
Russel Jacob
Michael Jacob

Caraquet, NB E1W

D-U-N-S 20-446-2477   (HQ)
BELLE BAY PRODUCTS LTD
BELLE BAY PRODUCTS
10 Rue Du Quai, Caraquet, NB, E1W 1B6
(506) 727-4414
Sales 34,569,000
SIC 2092 Fresh or frozen packaged fish
Valmond Chiasson
Rheal Leblanc
Alie A Lebouthillier

D-U-N-S 20-019-1666   (SL)
COMEAU, C. L. CO, LTD
117 Boul St-Pierre O, Caraquet, NB, E1W 1B6
(506) 727-3411
Emp Here 32   *Sales* 26,738,464

SIC 5141 Groceries, general line
Henri Mourant
Normand Mourant
Andy Power
Estelle Landry
Robert Nadeau
Muriel Comeau

D-U-N-S 20-019-1831   (HQ)
**COOPERATIVE DE CARAQUET LIMITEE,
LA**
121 Boul St-Pierre O, Caraquet, NB, E1W 1B6
(506) 727-1930
Emp Here 97   *Sales* 35,217,240
SIC 5411 Grocery stores
Gabriel Legere
Michel Rail
Nicole Landry
Marcel Garbie
Anick Lanteigne
Rose-Marie Gionet
Joseph Lanteigne
Rene Chiasson

D-U-N-S 25-298-9447   (HQ)
**EDITIONS DE L'ACADIE NOUVELLE (1984)
LTEE, LES**
ACADIE NOUVELLE
476 Boul St-Pierre O, Caraquet, NB, E1W 1A3
(800) 561-2255
Sales 10,661,755
SIC 2711 Newspapers
Clarence Lebreton
Marcel Lanteigne
Armand Caron
Monique Leger
Michel Leblanc
Germain Blanchard
Yvon Lanteigne
Fernand Rioux

D-U-N-S 25-287-1637   (HQ)
**FEDERATION DES CAISSES POPULAIRE
ACADIENNES INC, LA**
295 Boul St-Pierre O, Caraquet, NB, E1W 1A4
(506) 726-4000
Sales 31,598,185
SIC 6062 State credit unions
Camille Theriault
Brian Comeau
Rene Legacy
Roland Lebouthillier
Simonne Godin
Pierre Doiron

D-U-N-S 24-912-8802   (SL)
ICHIBOSHI L.P.C LTD
24 Rue Du Quai, Caraquet, NB, E1W 1B6
(506) 727-0807
Emp Here 250   *Sales* 121,846,250
SIC 2092 Fresh or frozen packaged fish
Masazeumi Okada

D-U-N-S 24-189-1423   (SL)
LANDRY ASPHALTE LTEE
14 Rue Du Portage, Caraquet, NB, E1W 1A8
(506) 727-6551
Emp Here 50   *Sales* 14,176,200
SIC 1611 Highway and street construction
Ivan Landry
Monik Noel

D-U-N-S 24-912-7747   (HQ)
PNEUS DU BOULEVARD LTEE
461 Boul St-Pierre O, Caraquet, NB, E1W 1A3
(506) 727-7488
Emp Here 9   *Sales* 11,455,794
SIC 5531 Auto and home supply stores
Yves Mourant
Andre Landry
Conrad Lambert

D-U-N-S 25-109-0957   (SL)
VILLA BEAUSEJOUR INC
253 Boul St-Pierre O, Caraquet, NB, E1W 1A4
(506) 726-2744
Emp Here 75   *Sales* 4,443,525

SIC 8361 Residential care
Roger Landry
Aldoria Cormier

D-U-N-S 24-946-6603   (SL)
VILLAG HISTORIQUE ACADIEN
14311 Route 11, Caraquet, NB, E1W 1B7
(506) 726-2600
Emp Here 49   *Sales* 19,473,286
SIC 8699 Membership organizations, nec
Sylvain Godwin

Centreville, NB E7K

D-U-N-S 20-446-1644   (SL)
B.W.S. MANUFACTURING LTD
EZ-2-LOAD
29 Hawkins Rd, Centreville, NB, E7K 1A4
(506) 276-4567
Emp Here 100   *Sales* 19,236,900
SIC 3715 Truck trailers
Hugo St-Cyr
Randall Mcdougall

D-U-N-S 24-324-2216   (SL)
HSF FOODS LTD
741 Central St Suite 501, Centreville, NB, E7K
2M4
(506) 276-3621
Emp Here 75   *Sales* 14,901,300
SIC 2099 Food preparations, nec
Benjamin Brake

Charlo, NB E8E

D-U-N-S 25-355-5890   (HQ)
DESIGN BUILT MECHANICAL INC
168 Craig Rd, Charlo, NB, E8E 2J6
(506) 684-2765
Emp Here 55   *Sales* 23,050,200
SIC 3441 Fabricated structural Metal
Luc Bernard
Lise Bernard
Charles Bernard

D-U-N-S 25-525-1423   (SL)
L.C.L. EXCAVATION (2006) INC
214 Craig Rd, Charlo, NB, E8E 2J2
(506) 684-3453
Emp Here 70   *Sales* 17,233,020
SIC 1794 Excavation work
Luc Levesque
Charles Levesque

Chipman, NB E4A

D-U-N-S 20-751-8858   (SL)
CHIPMAN OUTREACH INC
12 Civic Crt, Chipman, NB, E4A 2H9
(506) 339-5639
Emp Here 49   *Sales* 11,451,055
SIC 8621 Professional organizations
Carolyn Lemon

D-U-N-S 24-498-7454   (BR)
IRVING, J. D. LIMITED
SCALE HOUSE MILL YARD
(Suby of IRVING, J. D. LIMITED)
290 Main St, Chipman, NB, E4A 2M7
(506) 339-7910
Emp Here 200
SIC 2421 Sawmills and planing mills, general

D-U-N-S 20-271-9456   (BR)
IRVING, J. D. LIMITED
(Suby of IRVING, J. D. LIMITED)
290 Main St, Chipman, NB, E4A 2M7
(506) 339-7900
Emp Here 200

SIC 5211 Lumber and other building materials
Jim Lawless

Clair, NB E7A

D-U-N-S 20-619-0266   (SL)
CLAIR INDUSTRIAL DEVELOPMENT CORPORATION LTD
LATHS WASKA
14 Av 2 Ieme Industriel, Clair, NB, E7A 2B1
(506) 992-2152
Emp Here 88   *Sales* 16,928,560
SIC 2429 Special product sawmills, nec
Tierre Michoud
Jean-Louis Levasseur
Paul Levasseur
Jacques Levasseur
Pierre Levasseur
Guy Levasseur

D-U-N-S 24-472-0488   (SL)
CONFECTION B L INC
681 Rue Principale, Clair, NB, E7A 2H3
(506) 992-3602
Emp Here 65   *Sales* 12,948,260
SIC 2335 Women's, junior's, and misses' dresses
Gilles Blanchette
Claudette Blanchette

D-U-N-S 20-938-9969   (BR)
IRVING, J. D. LIMITED
(*Suby of* IRVING, J. D. LIMITED)
632 Rue Principale, Clair, NB, E7A 2H2
(506) 992-9068
Emp Here 150
SIC 2426 Hardwood dimension and flooring mills
Denis Dube

Coal Creek, NB E4A

D-U-N-S 25-500-1026   (HQ)
ARMSTRONG'S COMMUNICATION LTD
380 Salmon River Mouth Rd, Coal Creek, NB, E4A 2T7
(506) 339-6066
Emp Here 6   *Sales* 14,640,086
SIC 7382 Security systems services
Gary Armstrong

Cocagne, NB E4R

D-U-N-S 20-618-2545   (HQ)
ATLANTIC ROOFERS LIMITED
118 Ch Cocagne Cross, Cocagne, NB, E4R 2J2
(506) 576-6683
Emp Here 30   *Sales* 16,337,175
SIC 1761 Roofing, siding, and sheetMetal work
Arthur Allain

Cormier-Village, NB E4P

D-U-N-S 20-555-9383   (SL)
DANGO INC
725 Route 945 Suite A, Cormier-Village, NB, E4P 5Y4
(506) 533-6272
Emp Here 25   *Sales* 11,230,475
SIC 7389 Business services, nec
Allain Leger

Coteau Road, NB E8T

D-U-N-S 20-020-6522   (HQ)
SCOTT CANADA LTD
1571 Route 310, Coteau Road, NB, E8T 3K7
(506) 344-2225
Emp Here 50   *Sales* 18,917,920
SIC 1499 Miscellaneous nonMetallic minerals, except fuels
Gilles Hache
Lison Hache
Stephane Chiasson

Dalhousie, NB E8C

D-U-N-S 25-879-0922   (SL)
DALHOUSIE NURSING HOME INC
296 Victoria St Unit 1, Dalhousie, NB, E8C 2R8
(506) 684-7800
Emp Here 140   *Sales* 9,599,240
SIC 8051 Skilled nursing care facilities
Alden Appleby
Diane Leger

Dieppe, NB E1A

D-U-N-S 24-955-7083   (SL)
041216 NB LTD
SPRUCE GROVE BUILDING CLEANERS
376 Rue Champlain, Dieppe, NB, E1A 1P3
(506) 858-5085
Emp Here 100   *Sales* 4,020,900
SIC 7349 Building maintenance services, nec
Donat Arsenault
Serge Leblanc

D-U-N-S 24-723-4743   (SL)
055841 NB LTD
ACURA OF MONCTON
1170 Av Aviation, Dieppe, NB, E1A 9A3
(506) 853-1116
Emp Here 22   *Sales* 10,957,716
SIC 5511 New and used car dealers
Susan Peters

D-U-N-S 24-912-7226   (HQ)
ACADIA DRYWALL SUPPLIES LTD
521 Boul Ferdinand, Dieppe, NB, E1A 7G1
(506) 858-1319
Emp Here 20   *Sales* 11,179,350
SIC 5032 Brick, stone, and related material
Marcel Girouard

D-U-N-S 24-931-8775   (SL)
ACADIAN CONSTRUCTION (1991) LTD
671 Boul Malenfant Suite 2, Dieppe, NB, E1A 5T8
(506) 857-1909
Emp Here 25   *Sales* 60,648,160
SIC 1542 Nonresidential construction, nec
David Savoie

D-U-N-S 24-204-9273   (SL)
ALLIANCE SEAFOOD INCORPORATED
621 Ch Gauvin, Dieppe, NB, E1A 1M7
(506) 854-5800
Emp Here 6   *Sales* 13,779,234
SIC 2092 Fresh or frozen packaged fish
Pierre Nadeau

D-U-N-S 20-289-9741   (HQ)
ALTIMAX COURIER (2006) LIMITED
274 Boul Dieppe, Dieppe, NB, E1A 6P8
(866) 258-4629
Emp Here 15   *Sales* 25,605,483
SIC 7389 Business services, nec
Wes Penwarden
Gregory Keating

Kevin Butler

D-U-N-S 20-006-3647   (HQ)
ARCHIDIOCESE DE MONCTON
CENTRE DIOCESAN
452 Rue Amirault, Dieppe, NB, E1A 1G3
(506) 857-9531
Emp Here 18   *Sales* 10,772,700
SIC 8661 Religious organizations
Andre Richard
Jaques Doiron

D-U-N-S 24-723-2374   (HQ)
ATLANTIC ALARM & SOUND LTD
489 Av Acadie Suite 200, Dieppe, NB, E1A 1H7
(506) 853-9315
Emp Here 15   *Sales* 12,748,968
SIC 6211 Security brokers and dealers
Louis Bourgeois
Charles Leblanc
Darrell Turple
Donald Belliveau

D-U-N-S 20-549-0329   (SL)
ATLANTIC MOTORS LTD
ATLANTIC MAZDA
665 Boul Ferdinand, Dieppe, NB, E1A 7G1
(506) 852-8225
Emp Here 21   *Sales* 10,459,638
SIC 5511 New and used car dealers
John Smith

D-U-N-S 24-129-2713   (SL)
BONTE FOODS LIMITED
(*Suby of* TRUCORP INVESTMENTS LIMITED)
615 Rue Champlain, Dieppe, NB, E1A 7Z7
(506) 857-0025
Emp Here 140   *Sales* 48,396,600
SIC 2011 Meat packing plants
Michael Whittaker
Claude Pothier

D-U-N-S 24-320-1979   (SL)
CABOT MANUFACTURING ULC
521 Boul Ferdinand, Dieppe, NB, E1A 7G1
(506) 386-2868
Emp Here 70   *Sales* 16,340,450
SIC 3275 Gypsum products
Marcel Girouard

D-U-N-S 24-878-6998   (HQ)
CAPTAIN DAN'S INC
463 Champlain St, Dieppe, NB, E1A 1P2
(506) 872-7621
Emp Here 196   *Sales* 60,648,160
SIC 2092 Fresh or frozen packaged fish
Normand Leblanc

D-U-N-S 20-017-4761   (HQ)
CAVENDISH AGRI SERVICES LIMITED
(*Suby of* IRVING, J. D. LIMITED)
100 Midland Dr, Dieppe, NB, E1A 6X4
(506) 858-7777
Emp Here 13   *Sales* 26,765,200
SIC 5261 Retail nurseries and garden stores
Robert K Irving
James K Irving
John E Irving
Arthur L Irving
Robert Higson

D-U-N-S 20-562-7669   (HQ)
CAVENDISH FARMS CORPORATION
CAVENDISH PRODUCE, DIV OF
(*Suby of* IRVING, J. D. LIMITED)
100 Midland Dr, Dieppe, NB, E1A 6X4
(506) 858-7777
Emp Here 100   *Sales* 537,537,000
SIC 5142 Packaged frozen goods
Robert Irving
Paul Landry

D-U-N-S 24-343-3091   (SL)
DIEPPE AUTO LTEE/LTD
600 Rue Champlain, Dieppe, NB, E1A 1P4

---

(506) 857-0444
Emp Here 21   *Sales* 10,459,638
SIC 5511 New and used car dealers
Rheal Hebert
Gerald Randall

D-U-N-S 20-375-0963   (SL)
DISTRICT SCOLAIRE FRANCOPHONE SUD
425 Rue Champlain, Dieppe, NB, E1A 1P2
(506) 856-3333
Emp Here 800   *Sales* 79,295,200
SIC 8211 Elementary and secondary schools
Paul Demers

D-U-N-S 25-875-7814   (HQ)
DITECH PAINT CO. LTD
DITECH TESTING
561 Boul Ferdinand, Dieppe, NB, E1A 7G1
(506) 384-8197
Sales 14,951,310
SIC 7699 Repair services, nec
Jason Gildart
Daniel Leblanc

D-U-N-S 20-254-3000   (SL)
EXIT REALTY ASSOCIATES
260 Rue Champlain, Dieppe, NB, E1A 1P3
(506) 382-3948
Emp Here 60   *Sales* 16,305,360
SIC 6531 Real estate agents and managers
Paul Arsenault

D-U-N-S 20-278-9579   (SL)
FUNDY DRYWALL LTD
FUNDY CONSTRUCTION
91 Rue Englehart, Dieppe, NB, E1A 8K2
(506) 383-6466
Emp Here 80   *Sales* 12,990,480
SIC 1742 Plastering, drywall, and insulation
Mario Allain

D-U-N-S 25-920-3321   (SL)
GREATER MONCTON INTERNATIONAL AIRPORT AUTHORITY INC
GREATER MONCTON INTERNATIONAL AIRPORT
777 Av Aviation Unit 12, Dieppe, NB, E1A 7Z5
(506) 856-5444
Emp Here 45   *Sales* 13,262,838
SIC 4581 Airports, flying fields, and services
Bernard F. Leblanc
Jacques Fournier
Chris Farmer
Natasha Ostaff
Christopher D. Bacich
Nancy Whipp
Maurice Richard
Andre Pelletier
Gil Meredith
Brian Donaghy

D-U-N-S 25-167-4602   (HQ)
IRVING CONSUMER PRODUCTS LIMITED
(*Suby of* IRVING, J. D. LIMITED)
100 Prom Midland, Dieppe, NB, E1A 6X4
(506) 858-7777
Emp Here 275   *Sales* 330,873,300
SIC 2679 Converted paper products, nec
James K Irving
Robert Irving
Bruce Drost

D-U-N-S 25-369-6066   (HQ)
IRVING PERSONAL CARE LIMITED
(*Suby of* IRVING, J. D. LIMITED)
100 Prom Midland, Dieppe, NB, E1A 6X4
(506) 857-7713
Emp Here 125   *Sales* 251,259,900
SIC 5137 Women's and children's clothing
Robert K Irving
James K Irving
Arthur L Irving
John E Irving
James D Irving
John F Irving
Kenneth Irving

D-U-N-S 25-184-7000   (BR)
IRVING, J. D. LIMITED
IRVING TISSUE
(*Suby of* IRVING, J. D. LIMITED)
100 Prom Midland, Dieppe, NB, E1A 6X4
(506) 859-5757
Emp Here 198
SIC 2679 Converted paper products, nec
Scott Jungles

D-U-N-S 25-952-5769   (BR)
IRVING, J. D. LIMITED
IRVING CONSUMER PRODUCTS
(*Suby of* IRVING, J. D. LIMITED)
102 Rue Dawson, Dieppe, NB, E1A 0C1
(506) 859-5018
Emp Here 195
SIC 2621 Paper mills
Michel Morin

D-U-N-S 20-052-7708   (HQ)
ISLAND HOLDINGS LTD
(*Suby of* IRVING, J. D. LIMITED)
100 Midland Dr, Dieppe, NB, E1A 6X4
(506) 858-7777
Sales 10,702,480
SIC 5148 Fresh fruits and vegetables
James K Irving

D-U-N-S 24-831-7281   (HQ)
LANTECH DRILLING SERVICES INC
(*Suby of* FORAGE ORBIT GARANT INC)
398 Dover Ch, Dieppe, NB, E1A 7L6
(506) 853-9131
Emp Here 30   *Sales* 11,671,750
SIC 1499 Miscellaneous nonMetallic minerals, except fuels
John G Leblanc

D-U-N-S 24-386-5644   (HQ)
LION BRIDGE LTD
(*Suby of* HIG CAPITAL MANAGEMENT, INC.)
10 Rue Dawson, Dieppe, NB, E1A 6C8
(506) 859-5200
Emp Here 78   *Sales* 142,477,404
SIC 7389 Business services, nec
Lawrence Rogers

D-U-N-S 20-401-5262   (SL)
MAPLEBRAINS TECHNOLOGIES INC
842 Gauvin Rd, Dieppe, NB, E1A 1N1
(506) 899-1526
Emp Here 185   *Sales* 46,895,650
SIC 8748 Business consulting, nec
Mehul Vyas

D-U-N-S 25-687-0361   (BR)
MASTER PACKAGING INC
(*Suby of* MASTER PACKAGING INC)
333 Boul Adelard-Savoie, Dieppe, NB, E1A 7G9
(506) 389-3737
Emp Here 140
SIC 2653 Corrugated and solid fiber boxes
Mike Auffrey

D-U-N-S 20-589-8109   (HQ)
MIDLAND TRANSPORT LIMITED
MIDLAND COURIER
(*Suby of* IRVING, J. D. LIMITED)
100 Midland Dr, Dieppe, NB, E1A 6X4
(506) 858-5555
Emp Here 150   *Sales* 331,885,800
SIC 4213 Trucking, except local
Robert Irving
Jim Irving
Shane Esson

D-U-N-S 20-792-6689   (SL)
PHARMACIE DENNIS ABUD PHARMACY INC
JEAN COUTU
123 Rue Champlain, Dieppe, NB, E1A 1N5
(506) 859-1990
Emp Here 55   *Sales* 13,438,040
SIC 5912 Drug stores and proprietary stores
Dennis Abud

D-U-N-S 25-335-5226   (BR)
PROVINCE OF NEW BRUNSWICK
NEW BRUNSWICK COMMUNITY COLLEGE
(*Suby of* PROVINCE OF NEW BRUNSWICK)
505 Rue Du College, Dieppe, NB, E1A 6X2
(506) 856-2200
Emp Here 150
SIC 8221 Colleges and universities
Pauline Guay

D-U-N-S 20-059-4005   (SL)
SHOPPERS DRUG MART
477 Rue Paul Suite 181, Dieppe, NB, E1A 4X5
(506) 857-0820
Emp Here 70   *Sales* 17,102,960
SIC 5912 Drug stores and proprietary stores
Deirdre O'briain

D-U-N-S 20-278-9454   (BR)
SYSCO CANADA, INC
(*Suby of* SYSCO CORPORATION)
611 Boul Ferdinand, Dieppe, NB, E1A 7G1
(506) 857-6000
Emp Here 107
SIC 5141 Groceries, general line
Maillet Maurice

D-U-N-S 24-669-5464   (HQ)
TRC HYDRAULICS INC
855 Rue Champlain, Dieppe, NB, E1A 1P6
(506) 853-1986
Emp Here 47   *Sales* 45,846,620
SIC 5084 Industrial machinery and equipment
Terrence Coyle
Terrence Coyle Jr
Neil Duncan
Jacqueline Coyle
Ruth Leblanc

D-U-N-S 20-814-1077   (SL)
TRIANGLE KITCHEN LTD
DOVER WOODS CABINETRY (DIV OF)
679 Rue Babin, Dieppe, NB, E1A 5M7
(506) 858-5855
Emp Here 75   *Sales* 14,727,075
SIC 1751 Carpentry work
Roger Fournier
Fernande Fournier

D-U-N-S 20-023-2049   (HQ)
UNIVERSAL TRUCK & TRUCK TRAILER
925 Rue Champlain, Dieppe, NB, E1A 5T6
(506) 857-2222
Sales 24,903,900
SIC 5511 New and used car dealers
James K. Irving
David Jamieson
William Maclean

D-U-N-S 24-120-3186   (SL)
WADE, R.S. HEALTH CARE LTD
SHOPPERS DRUG MART
18 Rue Champlain Unit 1, Dieppe, NB, E1A 1N3
(506) 389-1680
Emp Here 40   *Sales* 10,118,160
SIC 5912 Drug stores and proprietary stores
Rosemary Wade

Dipper Harbour, NB E5J

D-U-N-S 20-618-3246   (HQ)
COASTAL ENTERPRISES LTD
MISTY HARBOUR SEAFOOD
(*Suby of* 507806 N.B. LTD)
48 Dipper Harbour Rd, Dipper Harbour, NB, E5J 1X2
(506) 659-2781
Emp Here 8   *Sales* 12,533,655
SIC 5146 Fish and seafoods
Richard Thompson
Andrew Thompson
Shirley Chartier

D-U-N-S 20-932-3492   (SL)
FUNDY BAY ENTERPRISES LTD
FUNDY BAY SEAFOOD
65 Dipper Harbour Rd, Dipper Harbour, NB, E5J 1X3
(506) 659-2890
Emp Here 250   *Sales* 179,179,000
SIC 5146 Fish and seafoods
Jardine Janes
Linda Janes
Daryn Janes
Jeffrey Janes

Doaktown, NB E9C

D-U-N-S 24-932-9806   (BR)
IRVING, J. D. LIMITED
(*Suby of* IRVING, J. D. LIMITED)
120 South Rd, Doaktown, NB, E9C 1H2
(506) 365-1020
Emp Here 130
SIC 2421 Sawmills and planing mills, general
Marco Theriault

Douglas Harbour, NB E4B

D-U-N-S 25-758-9739   (SL)
HUNTER'S ONE STOP LTD
2046 Route 690, Douglas Harbour, NB, E4B 1Y7
(506) 385-2292
Emp Here 24   *Sales* 11,953,872
SIC 5541 Gasoline service stations
Eldon Hunter

Dsl De Drummond, NB E3Y

D-U-N-S 25-244-3114   (SL)
TOBIQUE FARMS OPERATING (2012) LIMITED
2424 Route 108, Dsl De Drummond, NB, E3Y 2K7
(506) 553-9913
Emp Here 24   *Sales* 20,053,848
SIC 5148 Fresh fruits and vegetables
Henk Tepper
Berend Tepper

Dufferin Charlotte Co, NB E3L

D-U-N-S 24-340-4373   (SL)
CHARLOTTE COUNTY CHEVROLET BUICK GMC LTD
137 Route 170, Dufferin Charlotte Co, NB, E3L 3X5
(506) 466-0640
Emp Here 24   *Sales* 11,953,872
SIC 5511 New and used car dealers
Andrew Moffitt
Joan Clark

Edmundston, NB E3V

D-U-N-S 20-106-8629   (SL)
050537 N.B. LTEE
EDMUNDSTON HONDA
475 Rue Victoria, Edmundston, NB, E3V 2K7
(506) 739-7716
Emp Here 33   *Sales* 16,436,574
SIC 5511 New and used car dealers
Pierre-Paul Levesque

D-U-N-S 25-097-4193   (HQ)
ALIMENTATION LIGILICA LTEE
PIZZA DELIGHT
180 Boul Hebert, Edmundston, NB, E3V 2S7
(506) 735-3544
Emp Here 2   *Sales* 14,002,900
SIC 7999 Amusement and recreation, nec
Louis Ouellet
Bernard Cyr

D-U-N-S 24-103-1637   (SL)
AT LIMITED PARTNERSHIP
ACADIAN TIMBER EDMUNDSTON DIV OF
365 Ch Canada, Edmundston, NB, E3V 1W2
(506) 737-2345
Emp Here 200   *Sales* 113,925,600
SIC 5031 Lumber, plywood, and millwork
Daniel Ringuette

D-U-N-S 20-019-6301   (HQ)
BREAU, RAYMOND LTD
JEAN COUTU PHARMACY #59
131 Rue De L'Eglise, Edmundston, NB, E3V 1J9
(506) 735-5559
Emp Here 1   *Sales* 19,546,240
SIC 5912 Drug stores and proprietary stores
Paul Breau
Claude Doiron

D-U-N-S 25-881-0852   (SL)
CERCUEILS ALLIANCE CASKETS INC
ST LAWRENCE CASKET
355 Du Pouvoir Ch, Edmundston, NB, E3V 4K1
(506) 739-6226
Emp Here 125   *Sales* 40,767,000
SIC 3995 Burial caskets
Paul Michaud
Rino Caissey

D-U-N-S 20-573-2543   (BR)
COMPAGNIE DES CHEMINS DE FER NATIONAUX DU CANADA
(*Suby of* COMPAGNIE DES CHEMINS DE FER NATIONAUX DU CANADA)
194 Rue St-Francois, Edmundston, NB, E3V 1E9
(506) 735-1201
Emp Here 100
SIC 4011 Railroads, line-haul operating

D-U-N-S 25-241-8207   (BR)
DISTRICT SCOLAIRE 3
CITE DES JEUNES A.-M. SORMANY D'EDMUNDSTON
(*Suby of* DISTRICT SCOLAIRE 3)
300 Rue Martin, Edmundston, NB, E3V 0G9
(506) 735-2008
Emp Here 150
SIC 8211 Elementary and secondary schools
Bertin Lang

D-U-N-S 25-241-4297   (HQ)
DISTRICT SCOLAIRE 3
298 Rue Martin Suite 3, Edmundston, NB, E3V 5E5
(506) 737-4567
Emp Here 29   *Sales* 88,909,743
SIC 8211 Elementary and secondary schools
Yvan Guerette
Denise Querry

D-U-N-S 20-019-6574   (SL)
DUBE AUTO SALES LIMITED
454 Rue Victoria, Edmundston, NB, E3V 2K5

Emp Here 25   *Sales* 12,451,950
SIC 5511 New and used car dealers
Edward Dube
Marie-Mai Dube

D-U-N-S 20-811-7325   (SL)
EDMUNDSTON AUTO LTD. - EDMUNDSTON AUTO LTEE
EDMUNDSTON TOYOTA
121 Ch Canada, Edmundston, NB, E3V 1V7

---

(506) 735-4741
Emp Here 23   *Sales* 11,455,794
SIC 5511 New and used car dealers
Luc P. Nadeau
Charles Albert

D-U-N-S 20-019-6418   (SL)
G & M CHEVROLET-CADILLAC LTD
605 Rue Victoria, Edmundston, NB, E3V 3M8
(506) 735-3331
Emp Here 32   *Sales* 15,938,496
SIC 5511 New and used car dealers
Gerald Toner
Maurice Lafrance

D-U-N-S 20-930-6224   (SL)
GALLANT ENTERPRISES LTD
194 Rue St-Francois Suite 210, Edmundston,
NB, E3V 1E9
(506) 739-9390
Emp Here 45   *Sales* 23,424,390
SIC 5093 Scrap and waste materials
James Gallant
Ben Gallant
Vicky Gallant

D-U-N-S 24-316-1952   (BR)
IPL INC
(*Suby of* PLASTIQUES IPL INC)
20 Rue Boyd, Edmundston, NB, E3V 4H4
(506) 739-9559
Emp Here 240
SIC 3089 Plastics products, nec
Pierre Hebert

D-U-N-S 24-129-0071   (HQ)
JEAN C. DUPONT LTEE
260 Ch Canada, Edmundston, NB, E3V 1W1
(506) 739-8343
Emp Here 20   *Sales* 15,938,496
SIC 5531 Auto and home supply stores
Charlyne Dupont
Francis Dupont
Yves Dupont

D-U-N-S 20-812-9684   (SL)
OUELLETTE, RONALD INC
SHOPPERS DRUG MART
160 Boul Hebert, Edmundston, NB, E3V 2S7
(506) 735-8459
Emp Here 53   *Sales* 12,949,384
SIC 5912 Drug stores and proprietary stores
Ronald Ouellette

D-U-N-S 20-188-2672   (HQ)
PROVINCIAL BANDAG TIRES LTD
PNEUS MIRACO, DIV DE
410 Rue St-Francois, Edmundston, NB, E3V
1G6
(506) 735-6136
Emp Here 17   *Sales* 21,247,500
SIC 7534 Tire retreading and repair shops

D-U-N-S 25-359-4709   (SL)
RBI PLASTIQUE INC
6 Av Crabtree, Edmundston, NB, E3V 3K5
(506) 739-9180
Emp Here 85   *Sales* 23,516,100
SIC 2821 Plastics materials and resins
Michel Lebel

D-U-N-S 20-005-9512   (BR)
**SERVICE D'AIDE A LA FAMILLE EDMUND-
STON GRAND SAULT INC**
13 Rue Dugal, Edmundston, NB, E3V 1X4
(506) 737-8000
Emp Here 250
SIC 8741 Management services
Murielle Bourgeois

D-U-N-S 20-019-7606   (SL)
**SUPER MARCHE DONAT THERIAULT LIMI-
TEE**
MAGASIN I G A
570 Rue Victoria, Edmundston, NB, E3V 3N1
(506) 735-1860
Emp Here 110   *Sales* 32,282,470
SIC 5411 Grocery stores

Jean-Eudes Theriault
Daniel Theriault

D-U-N-S 24-123-3498   (SL)
TWEEDIE BRUNSWICK & LAVESQUE
36 Rue De L'Eglise, Edmundston, NB, E3V
1J2
(506) 735-5515
Emp Here 12   *Sales* 12,418,572
SIC 6331 Fire, marine, and casualty insurance
Debbie Rioux

D-U-N-S 24-422-1847   (HQ)
TWIN RIVERS PAPER COMPANY INC
27 Rue Rice, Edmundston, NB, E3V 1S9
(506) 735-5551
Emp Here 350   *Sales* 202,200,350
SIC 2621 Paper mills
Tim Lowe
Jean-Pierre Grenon
Wayne Gosse

D-U-N-S 24-120-3806   (BR)
WAL-MART CANADA CORP
(*Suby of* WALMART INC.)
805 Rue Victoria Suite 1033, Edmundston,
NB, E3V 3T3
(506) 735-8412
Emp Here 75
SIC 5311 Department stores
Stephanie Leveille

Edmundston, NB E7C

D-U-N-S 20-019-7630   (SL)
VIOLETTE MOTORS LTD
70 Chief Joanna Blvd Mmfn, Edmundston, NB,
E7C 0C1
(506) 737-9520
Emp Here 24   *Sales* 11,953,872
SIC 5521 Used car dealers
Michel Violette
Philip Violette
Pauline Violette
Marc Violette

Eel River Bar First Nation, NB E8C

D-U-N-S 24-327-7196   (SL)
OSPREY TRUCK STOP
2 Martin Dr, Eel River Bar First Nation, NB,
E8C 3C7
(506) 685-8210
Emp Here 30   *Sales* 14,942,340
SIC 5541 Gasoline service stations
Holly Labillois

Escuminac, NB E9A

D-U-N-S 20-349-5791   (SL)
BAIE STE-ANNE SEAFOODS (2014) INC
143 Ch Escuminac Point, Escuminac, NB,
E9A 1V6
(506) 228-4444
Emp Here 150   *Sales* 51,853,500
SIC 2091 Canned and cured fish and
seafoods
Paulin Savoie

D-U-N-S 24-605-6295   (SL)
**O'NEILL, RAYMOND & SON FISHERIES
LTD**
221 Ch Escuminac Point, Escuminac, NB,
E9A 1V6
(506) 228-4794
Emp Here 200   *Sales* 69,138,000
SIC 2091 Canned and cured fish and
seafoods
Raymond O'neill

Florenceville-Bristol, NB E7K

D-U-N-S 20-987-0377   (SL)
MOUNTAIN VIEW PACKERS LTD
9112 Route 130, Florenceville-Bristol, NB,
E7K 2R2
(506) 392-6017
Emp Here 35   *Sales* 29,245,195
SIC 5148 Fresh fruits and vegetables
Byron Mcgrath

Florenceville-Bristol, NB E7L

D-U-N-S 20-019-5857   (SL)
CARLETON CO-OPERATIVE LIMITED
8818 Main St, Florenceville-Bristol, NB, E7L
3G2
(506) 392-5587
Emp Here 62   *Sales* 16,997,424
SIC 5411 Grocery stores
Kenneth Ferguson

D-U-N-S 20-018-9173   (SL)
H. J. CRABBE & SONS, LTD
CRABBE LUMBER
6 Lockharts Mill Rd, Florenceville-Bristol,
E7L 2R2
(506) 392-5563
Emp Here 40   *Sales* 17,886,960
SIC 5031 Lumber, plywood, and millwork
Donald Crabbe
Ray Crabbe

D-U-N-S 24-877-8722   (HQ)
MCCAIN FERTILIZERS LIMITED
MCCAIN PRODUCE, DIV OF
(*Suby of* MCCAIN FOODS GROUP INC)
9109 Route 130, Florenceville-Bristol, NB,
E7L 1Y8
(506) 392-2810
Emp Here 14   *Sales* 25,245,680
SIC 5191 Farm supplies
Dan Moore
Steven Mccain

D-U-N-S 25-539-4967   (HQ)
MCCAIN FOODS GROUP INC
MCCAIN FOODS CANADA
8800 Main St, Florenceville-Bristol, NB, E7L
1B2
(506) 392-5541
Emp Here 5   *Sales* 19,495,400,000
SIC 2037 Frozen fruits and vegetables
Allison Mccain
Max Koeune
Andrew Mccain
Scott Mccain
J-P Bisnaire
Jacques Bougie
Victor Young
Janet Plaut Giesselman

D-U-N-S 20-180-8354   (SL)
MCCAIN INTERNATIONAL INC
(*Suby of* MCCAIN FOODS GROUP INC)
8734 Main St Unit 3, Florenceville-Bristol, NB,
E7L 3G6
(506) 392-5541
Emp Here 75   *Sales* 25,926,750
SIC 2037 Frozen fruits and vegetables
Kai Bockmann

D-U-N-S 24-831-4783   (HQ)
MCCAIN PRODUCE INC
(*Suby of* MCCAIN FOODS GROUP INC)
8734 Main St Unit 1, Florenceville-Bristol, NB,
E7L 3G6
(506) 392-3036
Emp Here 30   *Sales* 84,572,488
SIC 5148 Fresh fruits and vegetables
Vernon Thomas

Fredericton, NB E3A

D-U-N-S 20-287-2862   (BR)
ANGLOPHONE WEST SCHOOL DISTRICT
LEO HAYES HIGH SCHOOL
(*Suby of* ANGLOPHONE WEST SCHOOL
DISTRICT)
499 Cliffe St, Fredericton, NB, E3A 9P5
(506) 457-6898
Emp Here 160
SIC 8211 Elementary and secondary schools
Brad Sturgeon

D-U-N-S 24-124-0030   (SL)
ATLANTIC RETIREMENT CONCEPTS INC
WINDSOR COURT
10 Barton Cres Suite 504, Fredericton, NB,
E3A 5S3
(506) 450-7088
Emp Here 150   *Sales* 33,130,650
SIC 6513 Apartment building operators
Cam Rabaey

D-U-N-S 20-183-1935   (SL)
BRUNSWICK VALLEY LUMBER INC
367 Main St Suite 1, Fredericton, NB, E3A 1E6
(506) 457-1900
Emp Here 40   *Sales* 17,886,960
SIC 5031 Lumber, plywood, and millwork
Michael Jennings
Michael Youssef
Paul Bessery
Peter Macwilliam
Jeffrey Cabral

D-U-N-S 24-605-7665   (SL)
CAPABLE BUILDING CLEANING LTD
158 Clark St, Fredericton, NB, E3A 2W7
(506) 458-9343
Emp Here 80   *Sales* 3,216,720
SIC 7349 Building maintenance services, nec
Jennifer Wishart

D-U-N-S 20-929-8934   (SL)
DEVON LUMBER CO. LTD
DEVON LUMBER
200 Gibson St, Fredericton, NB, E3A 4E3
(506) 457-7123
Emp Here 50   *Sales* 22,358,700
SIC 5031 Lumber, plywood, and millwork
Harry Gill

D-U-N-S 25-710-8282   (SL)
E & L DRUGS LTD
SHOPPERS DRUG MART
269 Main St, Fredericton, NB, E3A 1E1
(506) 451-1550
Emp Here 55   *Sales* 13,438,040
SIC 5912 Drug stores and proprietary stores
Glenn Jackson

D-U-N-S 25-363-3499   (BR)
**LUXURY HOTELS INTERNATIONAL OF
CANADA, ULC**
*MARRIOTT REGIONAL WORLD WIDE
RESERVATIONS CANADA ADMINISTRA-
TION OFFICES*
(*Suby of* MARRIOTT INTERNATIONAL, INC.)
102 Main St Unit 16, Fredericton, NB, E3A
9N6

Emp Here 300
SIC 7389 Business services, nec
Anne Bauldereau

D-U-N-S 20-812-7266   (SL)
MACLEAN'S SPORTS LTD
489 Union St, Fredericton, NB, E3A 3M9
(506) 450-6090
Emp Here 30   *Sales* 14,942,340
SIC 5571 Motorcycle dealers
Brian Maclean
Angus Maclean
Aileen Maclean

D-U-N-S 20-515-7733   (BR)

NEW BRUNSWICK POWER CORPORA-TION
(*Suby of* PROVINCE OF NEW BRUNSWICK)
239 Gilbert St, Fredericton, NB, E3A 0J6
(506) 458-4308
Emp Here 150
SIC 4911 Electric services
 Barb Hairs

D-U-N-S 20-120-7433   (HQ)
PHOENIX PETROLEUM LTD
400 Thompson Dr, Fredericton, NB, E3A 9X2
(506) 459-6260
Emp Here 41   *Sales* 74,143,940
SIC 1542 Nonresidential construction, nec
 Kevin Nicklin
 Marcia Nicklin

D-U-N-S 25-991-1220   (HQ)
PLAZACORP RETAIL PROPERTIES LTD
PLAZA RETAIL REIT
98 Main St, Fredericton, NB, E3A 9N6
(506) 451-1826
Emp Here 7   *Sales* 81,887,904
SIC 6719 Holding companies, nec
 Michael A. Zakuta
 Jamie Petrie
 Peter Mackenzie
 Floriana Cipollone
 Kimberly Strange
 Earl Brewer
 Stephen Johnson
 Edouard Babineau
 Barbara Trenholm
 Denis Losier

D-U-N-S 25-088-3139   (SL)
SEMEGEN, MICHEL HOLDINGS LTD
CANADIAN TIRE
75 Two Nations Xg Suite 337, Fredericton, NB, E3A 0T3
(506) 450-8933
Emp Here 75   *Sales* 47,196,000
SIC 5531 Auto and home supply stores
 Michel Semegen
 Allan Killam

D-U-N-S 25-309-1201   (BR)
SOBEYS CAPITAL INCORPORATED
SOBEYS
(*Suby of* EMPIRE COMPANY LIMITED)
463 Brookside Dr Suite 349, Fredericton, NB, E3A 8V4
(506) 450-7109
Emp Here 115
SIC 5411 Grocery stores
 Paul Nielsen

D-U-N-S 20-749-3508   (SL)
ST MARY'S ECONOMIC DEVELOPMENT CORP
ST MARY'S SUPERMARKET
150 Cliffe St, Fredericton, NB, E3A 0A1
(506) 452-9367
Emp Here 160   *Sales* 46,956,320
SIC 5411 Grocery stores
 Nathan Paul
 David Chisholm

D-U-N-S 25-359-3008   (SL)
ST MARY'S ECONOMIC DEVELOPMENT CORPORATION
ST MARY'S ENTERTAINMENT CENTRE
185 Gabriel Dr, Fredericton, NB, E3A 5V9
(506) 462-9300
Emp Here 80   *Sales* 11,202,320
SIC 7999 Amusement and recreation, nec
 Walter Brooks
 Anthony Gabriel
 Arthur Bear

D-U-N-S 20-372-7073   (SL)
ST. MARY'S RETAIL SALES
150 Cliffe St, Fredericton, NB, E3A 0A1
(506) 452-9367
Emp Here 65   *Sales* 19,076,005
SIC 5411 Grocery stores

 Candice Paul

D-U-N-S 24-329-8622   (BR)
WAL-MART CANADA CORP
WALMART
(*Suby of* WALMART INC.)
125 Two Nations Xg Suite 1067, Fredericton, NB, E3A 0T3

Emp Here 200
SIC 5311 Department stores
 Robert Wicks

D-U-N-S 25-078-5839   (SL)
WHEELS & DEALS LTD
402 Saint Marys St, Fredericton, NB, E3A 8H5
(506) 459-6832
Emp Here 30   *Sales* 14,942,340
SIC 5521 Used car dealers
 James Gilbert
 Dawna Gilbert

D-U-N-S 25-747-9451   (SL)
WINDSOR COURT RETIREMENT RESI-DENCE LIMITED PARTNERSHIP
10 Barton Cres Suite 421, Fredericton, NB, E3A 5S3
(506) 450-7088
Emp Here 85   *Sales* 18,774,035
SIC 6513 Apartment building operators
 Camiel Rabaey

D-U-N-S 20-811-5634   (SL)
YORK MANOR INC
YORK MANOR NURSING HOME
100 Sunset Dr Suite 121, Fredericton, NB, E3A 1A3
(506) 444-3880
Emp Here 210   *Sales* 14,348,460
SIC 8051 Skilled nursing care facilities
 Cathy Bowlen
 Bill Alexander
 Ken Mcgeorge

Fredericton, NB E3B

D-U-N-S 25-880-9748   (SL)
053944 NB INC
BREWBAKER'S
546 King St Suite A, Fredericton, NB, E3B 1E6
(506) 459-0067
Emp Here 47   *Sales* 12,885,144
SIC 5461 Retail bakeries
 James W Ross
 Kelly Grant

D-U-N-S 20-578-0666   (SL)
A. K. HOLDINGS INC
HOWARD JOHNSON
958 Prospect St, Fredericton, NB, E3B 2T8
(506) 462-4444
Emp Here 30   *Sales* 13,304,700
SIC 7389 Business services, nec
 Kamal Mostosa

D-U-N-S 24-371-4347   (SL)
ACCREON INC
414 York St, Fredericton, NB, E3B 3P7
(506) 452-0551
Emp Here 85   *Sales* 19,914,480
SIC 8748 Business consulting, nec
 Neil Russon
 Trevor Cookson

D-U-N-S 24-933-0036   (HQ)
ADI GROUP INC
1133 Regent St Suite 300, Fredericton, NB, E3B 3Z2
(506) 452-9000
Sales 73,101,800
SIC 6712 Bank holding companies
 Hollis Cole
 Andrew Steves

D-U-N-S 20-548-9818   (HQ)

ADI LIMITED
(*Suby of* ADI GROUP INC)
1133 Regent St Suite 300, Fredericton, NB, E3B 3Z2
(506) 452-9000
Emp Here 160   *Sales* 49,282,750
SIC 8711 Engineering services
 Hollis B. Cole
 Paul D. Morrisson
 G. A. Robinson

D-U-N-S 25-350-5218   (BR)
ANGLOPHONE WEST SCHOOL DISTRICT
FREDERICTON HIGH SCHOOL
(*Suby of* ANGLOPHONE WEST SCHOOL DISTRICT)
300 Priestman St, Fredericton, NB, E3B 6J8
(506) 453-5435
Emp Here 200
SIC 8211 Elementary and secondary schools
 Shane Thomas

D-U-N-S 20-375-0950   (HQ)
ANGLOPHONE WEST SCHOOL DISTRICT
1135 Prospect St, Fredericton, NB, E3B 3B9
(506) 453-5454
Sales 11,398,685
SIC 8211 Elementary and secondary schools
 Catherine Blaney

D-U-N-S 20-354-8990   (SL)
AQUILNI GROUP PROPERTIES LP
CROWN PLAZA FREDERICTON LORD BEAVER BROOK HOTEL, DIV OF
(*Suby of* AQUILINI INVESTMENT GROUP INC)
659 Queen St, Fredericton, NB, E3B 1C3
(506) 455-3371
Emp Here 215   *Sales* 20,568,620
SIC 7011 Hotels and motels
 Robert Aquilini

D-U-N-S 25-139-0977   (HQ)
ASTRAL MEDIA RADIO ATLANTIC INC
K93FM
206 Rookwood Ave, Fredericton, NB, E3B 2M2
(506) 451-9111
Emp Here 50   *Sales* 18,479,800
SIC 4832 Radio broadcasting stations
 Jacques Parisien
 Patrick Brennan

D-U-N-S 20-019-8158   (HQ)
AUTO MACHINERY AND GENERAL SUP-PLY COMPANY, LIMITED
EASTERN AUTOMOTIVE WAREHOUSING, DIV OF
50 Whiting Rd, Fredericton, NB, E3B 5V5
(506) 453-1600
Sales 20,031,825
SIC 5013 Motor vehicle supplies and new parts
 Ronald Vaughan
 Dorothy Vaughan
 Douglas Vaughan
 David Vaughan

D-U-N-S 20-813-1433   (SL)
BARRY PHARMACY LTD
SHOPPERS DRUG MART
1040 Prospect St Suite 172, Fredericton, NB, E3B 3C1
(506) 451-1567
Emp Here 70   *Sales* 17,102,960
SIC 5912 Drug stores and proprietary stores
 Brian Barry

D-U-N-S 20-618-9623   (HQ)
BIRD, J.W. AND COMPANY LIMITED
BIRD STAIRS
(*Suby of* BIRD-STAIRS LTD)
670 Wilsey Rd, Fredericton, NB, E3B 7K4
(506) 453-9915
Emp Here 45   *Sales* 42,481,530
SIC 5039 Construction materials, nec
 Geoffrey Munn

 Lewis Somers

D-U-N-S 24-832-6142   (HQ)
BIRD-STAIRS LTD
670 Wilsey Rd, Fredericton, NB, E3B 7K4
(506) 453-9915
Sales 58,024,700
SIC 5063 Electrical apparatus and equipment
 Geoffrey Munn
 Brian Moore
 Eric Pineault
 William Johnston
 Ernest Lean

D-U-N-S 20-019-8950   (HQ)
CLARK, J & SON LIMITED
CLARK'S CHEVROLET CADILLAC
820 Prospect St, Fredericton, NB, E3B 4Z2
(506) 452-1010
Sales 32,093,280
SIC 5511 New and used car dealers
 John Clark Jr

D-U-N-S 25-742-4606   (SL)
CLARK, JIM MOTORS LTD
CLARK TOYOTA
35 Alison Blvd, Fredericton, NB, E3B 4Z9
(506) 452-2200
Emp Here 30   *Sales* 14,942,340
SIC 5511 New and used car dealers
 James Clark

D-U-N-S 20-791-2796   (BR)
COMCARE (CANADA) LIMITED
(*Suby of* COMCARE (CANADA) LIMITED)
168 Brunswick St, Fredericton, NB, E3B 1G6

Emp Here 100
SIC 8059 Nursing and personal care, nec
 Bonnie Colpitts

D-U-N-S 20-800-4494   (BR)
CORPORATION OF THE CITY OF FREDER-ICTON
FIRE DEPARTMENT
(*Suby of* CORPORATION OF THE CITY OF FREDERICTON)
520 York St, Fredericton, NB, E3B 3R2
(506) 460-2020
Emp Here 113
SIC 1389 Oil and gas field services, nec
 Paul Fleming

D-U-N-S 25-095-4948   (BR)
DELTA HOTELS LIMITED
(*Suby of* GOVERNMENT OF THE PROVINCE OF BRITISH COLUMBIA)
1133 Regent St, Fredericton, NB, E3B 3Z2

Emp Here 280
SIC 8741 Management services
 Sarah Holyoke

D-U-N-S 25-672-1457   (SL)
DELTA HOTELS NO. 32 LIMITED PARTNER-SHIP
DELTA FREDERICTON
225 Woodstock Rd, Fredericton, NB, E3B 2H8
(506) 451-7929
Emp Here 175   *Sales* 16,220,750
SIC 7011 Hotels and motels
 Sara Holyoke

D-U-N-S 25-150-6994   (SL)
ENBRIDGE GAS NEW BRUNSWICK INC
(*Suby of* ENBRIDGE INC)
440 Wilsey Rd Suite 101, Fredericton, NB, E3B 7G5
(506) 444-7773
Emp Here 100   *Sales* 182,976,600
SIC 4924 Natural gas distribution
 Arunas Pleckaitis
 Denis Losier
 Glenn Beaumont
 James Grant
 William Ramos
 David Charleson

D-U-N-S 25-150-8271   (SL)
ENBRIDGE GAS NEW BRUNSWICK LIMITED PARTNERSHIP
440 Wilsey Rd Suite 101, Fredericton, NB, E3B 7G5
(506) 444-7773
Emp Here 80
SIC 4922 Natural gas transmission
Arunas Pleckaitis
Andrew Harrington
Mark Butler
Mark Boyce
James Schultz
Stephen Letwin

D-U-N-S 24-858-2343   (BR)
EXP SERVICES INC
(*Suby of* EXP GLOBAL INC)
1133 Regent St Suite 300, Fredericton, NB, E3B 3Z2
(506) 452-9000
Emp Here 110
SIC 8711 Engineering services
Richard Smith

D-U-N-S 20-036-7451   (SL)
FREDERICTON REGION SOLID WASTE COMMISSION
1775 Wilsey Rd, Fredericton, NB, E3B 7K4
(506) 453-9930
Emp Here 40   *Sales* 12,045,680
SIC 4953 Refuse systems
Gordon Wilson
John Bigger

D-U-N-S 24-574-5633   (SL)
FREDERICTON SOUTH NURSING HOME INC
PINE GROVE NURSING HOME
521 Woodstock Rd, Fredericton, NB, E3B 2J2
(506) 444-3400
Emp Here 100   *Sales* 6,856,600
SIC 8051 Skilled nursing care facilities
Cheryl Wiggins

D-U-N-S 20-178-3482   (BR)
GDI SERVICES (CANADA) LP
(*Suby of* GDI SERVICES AUX IMMEUBLES INC)
475 Wilsey Rd, Fredericton, NB, E3B 7K1
(506) 453-1404
Emp Here 400
SIC 7349 Building maintenance services, nec
Michael Brewer

D-U-N-S 20-618-5142   (SL)
GUITARD, CHARLES MERCHANDISING LTD
CANADIAN TIRE
1110 Smythe St, Fredericton, NB, E3B 3H6
(506) 450-8920
Emp Here 110   *Sales* 50,726,940
SIC 5014 Tires and tubes
Charles Guitard

D-U-N-S 20-446-0422   (SL)
HILLSIDE NISSAN LTD
FREDERICTON NISSAN
580 Prospect St, Fredericton, NB, E3B 6G9
(506) 458-9423
Emp Here 22   *Sales* 10,957,716
SIC 5511 New and used car dealers
J.J. Kennedy

D-U-N-S 20-005-0438   (SL)
JOBS UNLIMITED INC
YORK STREET COURIER
1079 York St, Fredericton, NB, E3B 3S4
(506) 458-9380
Emp Here 55   *Sales* 24,707,045
SIC 7389 Business services, nec
Abdel Fattah

D-U-N-S 25-181-6930   (SL)
KIL INVESTMENTS LTD
DIPLOMAT RESTAURANT, THE
251 Woodstock Rd, Fredericton, NB, E3B 2H8

(506) 457-4386
Emp Here 75   *Sales* 3,413,925
SIC 5812 Eating places
David Kileel Jr.

D-U-N-S 20-020-0376   (SL)
L & A METALWORKS INC
1968 Lincoln Rd, Fredericton, NB, E3B 8M7
(506) 458-1100
Emp Here 50   *Sales* 10,141,500
SIC 3499 Fabricated Metal products, nec
Harry Evans
Laurie Leger

D-U-N-S 24-533-4875   (SL)
MAPLE LEAF HOMES INC
655 Wilsey Rd, Fredericton, NB, E3B 7K3
(506) 459-1335
Emp Here 400   *Sales* 76,948,000
SIC 2452 Prefabricated wood buildings
Jacques Roy

D-U-N-S 20-094-7286   (SL)
MCDONALD'S RESTAURANTS
MCDONALD'S
1177 Prospect St, Fredericton, NB, E3B 3B9
(506) 444-6231
Emp Here 100   *Sales* 4,551,900
SIC 5812 Eating places
Kristy Roberts

D-U-N-S 24-322-4685   (SL)
MOORE ENTERPRISES INC
WENDY'S
1050 Woodstock Rd, Fredericton, NB, E3B 7R8
(506) 450-3778
Emp Here 100   *Sales* 4,551,900
SIC 5812 Eating places
Daniel Morre

D-U-N-S 20-337-6124   (HQ)
NEW BRUNSWICK COMMUNITY COLLEGE (NBCC)
(*Suby of* PROVINCE OF NEW BRUNSWICK)
284 Smythe St, Fredericton, NB, E3B 3C9
(888) 796-6222
Emp Here 100   *Sales* 1,791,014
SIC 8221 Colleges and universities
Marilyn Luscombe

D-U-N-S 20-815-7826   (HQ)
NEW BRUNSWICK LIQUOR CORPORATION
ALCOOL NB LIQUOR
(*Suby of* PROVINCE OF NEW BRUNSWICK)
170 Wilsey Rd, Fredericton, NB, E3B 5J1
(506) 452-6826
Emp Here 100   *Sales* 327,620,757
SIC 5921 Liquor stores
Rachelle Gagnon
Brian Harriman
Bradford Cameron
Reid Reid
Paul Henderson
Mike Jenkins
Pierre Lafrance
Jocelyn Hachey
Arthur Doyle
Louella Woods

D-U-N-S 24-878-1924   (SL)
NEW BRUNSWICK MUNICIPAL FINANCE CORPORATION
(*Suby of* PROVINCE OF NEW BRUNSWICK)
670 King St Rm 376, Fredericton, NB, E3B 1G1
(506) 453-2515
Emp Here 1   *Sales* 24,726,169
SIC 6111 Federal and federally sponsored credit agencies
Jane Garbutt
Leonard Lee-White
Catherine Mosher

D-U-N-S 20-310-9814   (HQ)
NEW BRUNSWICK POWER CORPORATION

(*Suby of* PROVINCE OF NEW BRUNSWICK)
515 King St, Fredericton, NB, E3B 1E7
(506) 458-4444
Sales 1,118,401,075
SIC 4911 Electric services
Gaetan Thomas
Ed Barrett

D-U-N-S 20-752-0961   (SL)
PERPETUAL SECURITY CORPORATION
880 Hanwell Rd Unit 203, Fredericton, NB, E3B 6A3
(506) 457-1458
Emp Here 25   *Sales* 10,437,650
SIC 7382 Security systems services
Michael Durley

D-U-N-S 20-351-9731   (SL)
PROFESSIONAL ABORIGINAL TESTING ORGANIZATION INC
PLATO
(*Suby of* PROFESSIONAL QUALITY ASSURANCE LTD)
231 Regent St Suite 301, Fredericton, NB, E3B 3W8
(506) 455-7725
Emp Here 57   *Sales* 10,630,842
SIC 8742 Management consulting services
Keith Mcintosh
Scott Kennedy

D-U-N-S 20-312-0782   (HQ)
PROFESSIONAL QUALITY ASSURANCE LTD
PQA
231 Regent St Suite 104, Fredericton, NB, E3B 3W8
(506) 455-7725
Sales 15,666,504
SIC 8742 Management consulting services
Keith Mcintosh

D-U-N-S 25-308-6656   (BR)
REGIONAL HEALTH AUTHORITY NB
NEW BRUNSWICK EXTRA MURAL PROGRAM
(*Suby of* PROVINCE OF NEW BRUNSWICK)
700 Priestman St, Fredericton, NB, E3B 3B7
(506) 452-5800
Emp Here 92
SIC 8051 Skilled nursing care facilities
Sylvie Arsenau

D-U-N-S 24-387-8613   (HQ)
REGIONAL HEALTH AUTHORITY NB
HORIZON HEALTH NETWORK
(*Suby of* PROVINCE OF NEW BRUNSWICK)
180 Woodbridge St, Fredericton, NB, E3B 4R3
(506) 623-5500
Emp Here 1,000   *Sales* 893,794,100
SIC 8062 General medical and surgical hospitals
Karen Mcgrath
Jean Daigle
Gary Foley
Geri Geldart
Edouard Hendriks
Margaret Melanson
Janet Hogan
Andrea Seymour

D-U-N-S 20-812-5393   (HQ)
ROSS VENTURES LTD
BREWBAKERS
35 Colter Crt, Fredericton, NB, E3B 1X7
(506) 453-1800
Emp Here 10   *Sales* 14,221,850
SIC 6512 Nonresidential building operators
James Ross

D-U-N-S 25-732-9953   (SL)
S W C RECYCLING
760 Wilsey Rd, Fredericton, NB, E3B 7K4
(506) 453-9931
Emp Here 40   *Sales* 10,285,240
SIC 4953 Refuse systems
Robert Macdowell

D-U-N-S 25-241-7274   (BR)
SCHOOL BOARD DISTRICT 01
ECOLE STE ANNE
715 Priestman St, Fredericton, NB, E3B 5W7
(506) 453-3991
Emp Here 80   *Sales* 396,535
SIC 8211 Elementary and secondary schools
Vincent Thibeau

D-U-N-S 24-943-6452   (BR)
SOBEYS CAPITAL INCORPORATED
SOBEYS
(*Suby of* EMPIRE COMPANY LIMITED)
1150 Prospect St, Fredericton, NB, E3B 3C1
(506) 458-8891
Emp Here 125
SIC 5411 Grocery stores
Daniel Lowther

D-U-N-S 20-059-5739   (HQ)
ST. THOMAS UNIVERSITY
STU
51 Dineen Dr College Hill, Fredericton, NB, E3B 5G3
(506) 452-0640
Emp Here 15   *Sales* 48,552,075
SIC 8221 Colleges and universities
Micheal Higgins

D-U-N-S 20-020-1630   (SL)
SUTHERLAND EQUIPMENT LTD
SUTHERLAND HONDA
911 Hanwell Rd, Fredericton, NB, E3B 9Z1
(506) 452-1155
Emp Here 39   *Sales* 19,425,042
SIC 5511 New and used car dealers
Dave Lenihan
Stephen Lenihan
Lori Lenihan

D-U-N-S 20-346-3252   (SL)
TELEDYNE CARIS, INC.
(*Suby of* TELEDYNE TECHNOLOGIES INC)
115 Waggoners Lane, Fredericton, NB, E3B 2L4
(506) 458-8533
Emp Here 100
SIC 7371 Custom computer programming services

D-U-N-S 24-101-2678   (BR)
TOROMONT INDUSTRIES LTD
(*Suby of* TOROMONT INDUSTRIES LTD)
165 Urquhart Cres, Fredericton, NB, E3B 8K4
(506) 452-6651
Emp Here 75
SIC 5082 Construction and mining machinery
John Mcintyre

D-U-N-S 24-124-6367   (BR)
UNITED PARCEL SERVICE CANADA LTD
UPS
(*Suby of* UNITED PARCEL SERVICE, INC.)
900 Hanwell Rd, Fredericton, NB, E3B 6A2
(506) 447-3601
Emp Here 500
SIC 4513 Air courier services
Shelley Gares

D-U-N-S 24-339-4087   (SL)
UNIVERSAL SYSTEMS LTD
CARIS
829 Woodstock Rd, Fredericton, NB, E3B 7R7
(506) 458-8533
Emp Here 150   *Sales* 41,002,500
SIC 6712 Bank holding companies
Salem Masry

D-U-N-S 20-107-7133   (BR)
UNIVERSITY OF NEW BRUNSWICK
PHYSICAL PLANT
(*Suby of* UNIVERSITY OF NEW BRUNSWICK)
767 Kings College Rd, Fredericton, NB, E3B 5A3
(506) 453-4889
Emp Here 130
SIC 7382 Security systems services

▲ Public Company   ■ Public Company Family Member   **HQ** Headquarters   **BR** Branch   **SL** Single Location

Jeff Smythe

D-U-N-S 20-813-0260   (HQ)
UNIVERSITY OF NEW BRUNSWICK
UNB
3 Bailey Dr, Fredericton, NB, E3B 5A3
(506) 453-4666
Emp Here 1,600   *Sales* 373,477,500
SIC 8221 Colleges and universities
Eddy Campbell
Eric Cook
David Burns
Sharon Simms
Derek Lister
Keith Miller
Rick Didsbury

D-U-N-S 20-293-7673   (SL)
UNIVERSITY PRESS OF NEW BRUNSWICK
DAILY GLEANER
984 Prospect St, Fredericton, NB, E3B 2T8
(506) 452-6671
Emp Here 120   *Sales* 19,683,240
SIC 2711 Newspapers
Eric Lawson

D-U-N-S 20-285-4402   (SL)
VAST-AUTO DISTRIBUTION ATLANTIC LTD
AUTO MACHINERY
50 Whiting Rd, Fredericton, NB, E3B 5V5
(506) 453-1600
Emp Here 47   *Sales* 17,118,105
SIC 5015 Motor vehicle parts, used
John Del Vasto
David Vaughan

D-U-N-S 25-973-7641   (SL)
VESTCOR INVESTMENT MANAGEMENT CORPORATION, THE
VIMC
(*Suby of* PROVINCE OF NEW BRUNSWICK)
440 King St Suite 581, Fredericton, NB, E3B 5H8
(506) 444-5800
Emp Here 48   *Sales* 63,761,904
SIC 6733 Trusts, nec
John A. Sinclair
Inge Despres
Jan Imeson
Jon Spinney
Brent Henry
Michael Walton
Wiktor Afkanaf
Donna Bovolaneas
David Losier
Tim Mawhinney

D-U-N-S 24-188-8817   (SL)
VICTORY MEAT MARKET LTD
334 King St, Fredericton, NB, E3B 1E3
(506) 458-8480
Emp Here 50   *Sales* 41,778,850
SIC 5147 Meats and meat products
Harry Chippin
Seth Chippin

D-U-N-S 24-190-1909   (SL)
WILSON INSURANCE LTD
404 Queen St, Fredericton, NB, E3B 1B6
(506) 458-8505
Emp Here 46   *Sales* 26,676,504
SIC 6411 Insurance agents, brokers, and service
David Wilson
Allan Hughson
Michael Toole
Elizabeth Wilson

D-U-N-S 20-742-1983   (SL)
WOOD MOTORS (1972) LIMITED
WOOD MOTORS FORD
880 Prospect St, Fredericton, NB, E3B 2T8
(506) 452-6611
Emp Here 62   *Sales* 39,015,360
SIC 5511 New and used car dealers
Edward Seymour
Garrett Seymour

D-U-N-S 24-439-4248   (SL)
YORK FINANCIAL SERVICES INC.
INDUSTRIAL-ALLIANCE LIFE INS
440 York St, Fredericton, NB, E3B 3P7
(506) 443-7776
Emp Here 18   *Sales* 10,438,632
SIC 6411 Insurance agents, brokers, and service
Alden Kaley

Fredericton, NB E3C

D-U-N-S 20-550-7697   (SL)
609173 N.B. LTD
FREDERICTON HYUNDAI
1165 Hanwell Rd, Fredericton, NB, E3C 1A5
(506) 450-0800
Emp Here 31   *Sales* 15,440,418
SIC 5511 New and used car dealers
Gerald O'leary
Aubrey Ward
David O'leary

D-U-N-S 20-971-7235   (SL)
612111 NB LTD
SUMMIT DODGE JEEP CHRYSLER
505 Bishop Dr, Fredericton, NB, E3C 2M6
(506) 454-3634
Emp Here 25   *Sales* 12,451,950
SIC 5511 New and used car dealers
John James (Jj) Kennedy

D-U-N-S 24-130-1191   (HQ)
ARROW CONSTRUCTION PRODUCTS LIMITED
50 Gervais Crt, Fredericton, NB, E3C 1L4
(506) 458-9610
Emp Here 10   *Sales* 16,992,612
SIC 5039 Construction materials, nec
Edgar Goguen
Neil Rodgers

D-U-N-S 20-052-6262   (HQ)
BULLETPROOF SOLUTIONS INC
25 Alison Blvd, Fredericton, NB, E3C 2N5
(506) 452-8558
Sales 13,280,175
SIC 6211 Security brokers and dealers
Steven Burns
Timothy Hawkins
Ian Donald
Robert Buchanan

D-U-N-S 20-742-0670   (SL)
CALDWELL & ROSS LIMITED
195 Doak Rd, Fredericton, NB, E3C 2E6
(506) 453-1333
Emp Here 55   *Sales* 13,884,310
SIC 1611 Highway and street construction
Paul Demerchant
Donald Demerchant

D-U-N-S 24-573-2029   (SL)
COREY NUTRITION COMPANY INC
COREY FEED MILLS
136 Hodgson Rd, Fredericton, NB, E3C 2G4
(506) 444-7744
Emp Here 30   *Sales* 10,370,700
SIC 2048 Prepared feeds, nec
Lee Corey
Jane Corey

D-U-N-S 20-019-9057   (HQ)
COVEY OFFICE GROUP INC
COVEY BASICS
250 Alison Blvd, Fredericton, NB, E3C 0A9
(506) 458-8333
Emp Here 30   *Sales* 25,182,900
SIC 5112 Stationery and office supplies
David Mcmullin
Stuart Blair
Dean Morgan

D-U-N-S 20-618-3568   (SL)

FAIRVIEW PLYMOUTH CHRYSLER LTD
FAIRVIEW CHRYSLER JEEP
1065 Hanwell Rd, Fredericton, NB, E3C 1A5
(506) 458-8955
Emp Here 45   *Sales* 22,413,510
SIC 5511 New and used car dealers
Roy Kennedy

D-U-N-S 20-930-0953   (SL)
FREDERICTON DIRECT CHARGE CO-OPERATIVE LIMITED
170 Doak Rd, Fredericton, NB, E3C 2G2
(506) 453-1300
Emp Here 240   *Sales* 70,434,480
SIC 5411 Grocery stores
Edward Hanscomb
Sheldon Palk
Deborah Macneil
Sharon Nussey
Marilyn Scott
Cindy Riley
Janice Mcintyre
Maurice Boucher

D-U-N-S 20-815-5218   (SL)
FREDERICTON MOTOR INN LTD
FREDERICTON INN
1315 Regent St, Fredericton, NB, E3C 1A1
(506) 455-1430
Emp Here 75   *Sales* 7,117,425
SIC 7011 Hotels and motels
John Waite

D-U-N-S 24-723-2150   (HQ)
GEMTEC LIMITED
191 Doak Rd, Fredericton, NB, E3C 2E6
(506) 453-1025
Emp Here 40   *Sales* 12,511,730
SIC 8711 Engineering services
Paul Mcneil
Corey Keats
Shaun Pelkey

D-U-N-S 24-361-7243   (BR)
HOME DEPOT OF CANADA INC
HOME DEPOT
(*Suby of* THE HOME DEPOT INC)
1450 Regent St, Fredericton, NB, E3C 0A4
(506) 462-9460
Emp Here 100
SIC 5251 Hardware stores
Duane Ackerman

D-U-N-S 25-499-3090   (SL)
IRVING TRANSPORTATION SERVICES LIMITED
71 Alison Blvd, Fredericton, NB, E3C 2N5

Emp Here 50   *Sales* 10,454,250
SIC 8721 Accounting, auditing, and bookkeeping
James D. Irving
John F. Irving
Arthur L. Irving
John E. Irving
Kenneth Irving
Arthur I. Irving Jr.

D-U-N-S 20-235-1321   (SL)
MONTEITH VENTURES INC
FREDERICTON KIA
433 Bishop Dr, Fredericton, NB, E3C 2M6
(506) 455-2277
Emp Here 22   *Sales* 10,957,716
SIC 5511 New and used car dealers
Scott Amos

D-U-N-S 24-340-9893   (SL)
O'LEARY BUICK GMC LTD
1135 Hanwell Rd, Fredericton, NB, E3C 1A5
(506) 453-7000
Emp Here 48   *Sales* 23,907,744
SIC 5511 New and used car dealers
Gerald O'leary
Aubrey Ward

D-U-N-S 24-186-3067   (SL)

RITCHIE, KEVIN A LTD
RITCHIE'S CARPET WAREHOUSE
1250 Hanwell Rd, Fredericton, NB, E3C 1A7
(506) 458-8588
Emp Here 45   *Sales* 10,365,300
SIC 5713 Floor covering stores
Kevin Ritchie

D-U-N-S 20-116-3529   (SL)
SPRINGHILL CONSTRUCTION LIMITED
940 Springhill Rd, Fredericton, NB, E3C 1R5
(506) 452-0044
Emp Here 40   *Sales* 13,333,320
SIC 1541 Industrial buildings and warehouses
Geoff Colter

D-U-N-S 25-758-8822   (SL)
UNITED AUTO SALES & SERVICE LTD
FREDERICTON VOLKSWAGEN
14 Avonlea Crt, Fredericton, NB, E3C 1N8
(506) 454-2886
Emp Here 21   *Sales* 10,459,638
SIC 5511 New and used car dealers
Thor Olesen
Robert Ricketts

D-U-N-S 25-297-7749   (BR)
WAL-MART CANADA CORP
(*Suby of* WALMART INC.)
1399 Regent St, Fredericton, NB, E3C 1A3
(506) 452-1511
Emp Here 200
SIC 5311 Department stores
Greg Steeves

D-U-N-S 24-096-4783   (HQ)
WALLACE EQUIPMENT LTD
25 Gillis Rd, Fredericton, NB, E3C 2G3
(506) 458-8380
Emp Here 20   *Sales* 38,002,080
SIC 5084 Industrial machinery and equipment
Lee Macpherson
Neil Cogsley
Nancy Didiodato

Fredericton, NB E3G

D-U-N-S 24-573-9370   (SL)
AQUA-POWER CLEANERS (1979) LTD
SERVICEMASTER CLEAN
65 Royal Parkway, Fredericton, NB, E3G 0J9
(506) 458-1113
Emp Here 140   *Sales* 4,475,520
SIC 7349 Building maintenance services, nec
Christopher Brown
John Brown
Robert Sweeney

Grand Manan, NB E5G

D-U-N-S 20-931-8633   (SL)
M. G. FISHERIES LTD
7 Norman Rd, Grand Manan, NB, E5G 2G5
(506) 662-3696
Emp Here 50   *Sales* 41,778,850
SIC 5146 Fish and seafoods
Jenny Green

D-U-N-S 25-814-8550   (SL)
ROLAND'S SEA VEGETABLES
174 Hill Rd, Grand Manan, NB, E5G 4C4
(506) 662-3468
Emp Here 20   *Sales* 16,711,540
SIC 5149 Groceries and related products, nec
Sandy Flagg

Grand-Barachois, NB E4P

D-U-N-S 20-939-5974   (SL)
SHORELINE LUBE DISTRIBUTION INC
55 Ch Raymel, Grand-Barachois, NB, E4P 7M7
(506) 577-4440
Emp Here 12   *Sales* 12,393,696
SIC 5172 Petroleum products, nec
Maurice Hebert
Nadine Hebert

Grand-Sault/Grand Falls, NB E3Y

D-U-N-S 24-393-9415   (SL)
GESTION GIACOMO D'AMICO INC
CANADIAN TIRE
383 Ch Madawaska, Grand-Sault/Grand Falls, NB, E3Y 1A4
(506) 473-3550
Emp Here 40   *Sales* 19,923,120
SIC 5531 Auto and home supply stores
Giacomo D'amico

D-U-N-S 20-020-3636   (SL)
SENECHAL, EMILE ET FILS LTEE
190 Ch Industriel, Grand-Sault/Grand Falls, NB, E3Y 3V3
(506) 473-2392
Emp Here 60   *Sales* 14,006,100
SIC 2674 Bags: uncoated paper and multiwall
Yves Senechal
Nathalie Senechal Cyr

Grand-Sault/Grand Falls, NB E3Z

D-U-N-S 20-811-6327   (HQ)
ALLIANCE ASSURANCE INC
166 Boul Broadway Suite 200, Grand-Sault/Grand Falls, NB, E3Z 2J9
(506) 473-9400
Emp Here 15   *Sales* 101,625,810
SIC 6411 Insurance agents, brokers, and service
Patrick Durepos
A. M. Lily Durepos
Mike St-Onge
Rolf Spanganberg
Denis Durepos

D-U-N-S 20-115-7067   (HQ)
CAISSE POPULAIRE LA VALLEE LTEE
181 Boul Broadway, Grand-Sault/Grand Falls, NB, E3Z 2J8
(506) 473-3660
Emp Here 24   *Sales* 15,156,100
SIC 6062 State credit unions
Paul Leclerc
Donald Dufour

D-U-N-S 20-020-3370   (SL)
MCCLURE, F. & SONS LTD
55 Rue Ouellette, Grand-Sault/Grand Falls, NB, E3Z 0A6
(506) 473-2024
Emp Here 28   *Sales* 13,946,184
SIC 5521 Used car dealers
Donald Mcclure
Jacques Mcclure

D-U-N-S 20-020-3404   (HQ)
MICHAUD PETROLEUM INC
866 Boul Everard H Daigle, Grand-Sault/Grand Falls, NB, E3Z 3C8
(506) 473-1197
Emp Here 8   *Sales* 18,760,200
SIC 5983 Fuel oil dealers
Hermel Michaud
Manon Gagne
Marie-Anne Michaud
Gilbert Michaud

D-U-N-S 20-020-3453   (SL)

NORTHERN CONSTRUCTION AND SUPPLIERS LTD
534 West River Rd, Grand-Sault/Grand Falls, NB, E3Z 3E7
(506) 473-1822
Emp Here 60   *Sales* 15,146,520
SIC 1611 Highway and street construction
Edward Belanger

D-U-N-S 24-677-8604   (SL)
NORTHERN CONSTRUCTION INC
554 West River Rd, Grand-Sault/Grand Falls, NB, E3Z 3E7
(506) 473-1822
Emp Here 45   *Sales* 12,758,580
SIC 1611 Highway and street construction
Edward Belanger

D-U-N-S 24-933-0424   (SL)
RENDEZ-VOUS CHRYSLER LTD
795 Boul Everard H Daigle, Grand-Sault/Grand Falls, NB, E3Z 3C7
(506) 473-5000
Emp Here 35   *Sales* 17,432,730
SIC 5511 New and used car dealers
Daniel Levesque
Leo D Levesque

D-U-N-S 20-020-3743   (SL)
TONER CHEVROLET BUICK GMC LTD
877 Boul Everard H Daigle, Grand-Sault/Grand Falls, NB, E3Z 3C7
(506) 473-2727
Emp Here 30   *Sales* 18,878,400
SIC 5511 New and used car dealers
Gerald Toner

D-U-N-S 24-186-2192   (SL)
VIOLETTE LTEE
VIOLETTEFORD
157 Madawaska Rd, Grand-Sault/Grand Falls, NB, E3Z 3E8
(506) 473-1770
Emp Here 25   *Sales* 12,451,950
SIC 5511 New and used car dealers
Robert Violette
Sylvia Violette

D-U-N-S 25-331-0197   (BR)
VITALITE HEALTH NETWORK
GRAND FALLS GENERAL HOSPITAL
(*Suby of* VITALITE HEALTH NETWORK)
625 Boul Everard H Daigle, Grand-Sault/Grand Falls, NB, E3Z 2R9
(506) 473-7555
Emp Here 200
SIC 8062 General medical and surgical hospitals
Solange Bosse

Hampton, NB E5N

D-U-N-S 24-606-5452   (SL)
SNOW, DR. V. A. CENTRE INC
54 Demille Crt Suite 14, Hampton, NB, E5N 5S7
(506) 832-6210
Emp Here 80   *Sales* 5,485,280
SIC 8051 Skilled nursing care facilities
George Stevens

Hanwell, NB E3C

D-U-N-S 24-993-5446   (SL)
056729 N.B. LTD
FRESH CHOICE
18 Divot Dr, Hanwell, NB, E3C 0L2
(506) 457-0305
Emp Here 20   *Sales* 10,702,480
SIC 5148 Fresh fruits and vegetables
Eric Peabody

Katherine Bridges
John Mickie

D-U-N-S 24-123-2730   (SL)
BRUN-WAY HIGHWAYS OPERATIONS INC
1754 Route 640, Hanwell, NB, E3C 2B2
(506) 474-7750
Emp Here 60   *Sales* 15,146,520
SIC 1611 Highway and street construction
Christina Costy
Charlie Rate
J Marc Devlin

D-U-N-S 24-932-9822   (HQ)
HAWKINS TRUCK MART LTD
PETERBILT ATLANTIC
125 Greenview Dr, Hanwell, NB, E3C 0E4
(506) 452-7946
Emp Here 32   *Sales* 39,015,360
SIC 5511 New and used car dealers
Tim Hawkins
Tom Dykeman
Craig Allen

D-U-N-S 25-986-3082   (SL)
JARDINE AUCTIONEERS INC
1849 Route 640, Hanwell, NB, E3C 2A7
(506) 454-4400
Emp Here 23   *Sales* 10,200,270
SIC 7389 Business services, nec
Frank Jardine
John Jardine
Stephanie Jordan

D-U-N-S 20-618-1786   (HQ)
MCFADZEN HOLDINGS LIMITED
KINGSWOOD FAMILY ENTERTAINMENT
31 Kingswood Way, Hanwell, NB, E3C 2L4
(506) 443-3331
Emp Here 1   *Sales* 62,833,350
SIC 6531 Real estate agents and managers
Ernest J. Mcfadzen
Brian Johnson

D-U-N-S 24-994-4745   (SL)
MEASURAND INC
2111 Route 640, Hanwell, NB, E3C 1M7
(506) 462-9119
Emp Here 40   *Sales* 10,262,480
SIC 3827 Optical instruments and lenses
Lee Danisch
Scott Thomson

Hartland, NB E7P

D-U-N-S 20-020-4691   (SL)
AITON DRUG COMPANY, LIMITED
20 Aiton Cres, Hartland, NB, E7P 2H2
(506) 375-4469
Emp Here 17   *Sales* 18,790,865
SIC 5122 Drugs, proprietaries, and sundries
Charles D Pooley
Sandra Pooley
Kimberly Pooley

D-U-N-S 25-101-1557   (SL)
BETCO ENTERPRISES LTD
120 Mclean Ave, Hartland, NB, E7P 2K5
(506) 375-4671
Emp Here 28   *Sales* 13,180,468
SIC 1542 Nonresidential construction, nec
Jeff Foster
Rachel Foster

D-U-N-S 20-020-4733   (SL)
CRAIG MANUFACTURING LTD
96 Mclean Ave, Hartland, NB, E7P 2K5
(506) 375-4493
Emp Here 175   *Sales* 33,614,875
SIC 3441 Fabricated structural Metal
John Craig
Benjamin Craig
Betty Lou Craig

D-U-N-S 20-020-4758   (HQ)

DAY & ROSS INC
DAY & ROSS TRANSPORTATION GROUP
(*Suby of* MCCAIN FOODS GROUP INC)
398 Main St, Hartland, NB, E7P 1C6
(506) 375-4401
Emp Here 100   *Sales* 460,952,500
SIC 4213 Trucking, except local
Bill Doherty
Kevin Chase
Patrick Potter
Mark Osborne
Luc Marcoux

D-U-N-S 24-261-0541   (SL)
PALMER ATLANTIC INSURANCE LTD
PALMER ATLANTIC
(*Suby of* ARTHUR J. GALLAGHER & CO.)
538 Main St Unit 1, Hartland, NB, E7P 2N5
(506) 375-7500
Emp Here 24   *Sales* 20,353,440
SIC 6411 Insurance agents, brokers, and service
Joseph Palmer
Shelley Palmer

D-U-N-S 25-241-4214   (BR)
SCHOOL DISTRICT 14
HARTLAND COMMUNITY SCHOOL
217 Rockland Rd, Hartland, NB, E7P 0A2
(506) 375-3000
Emp Here 80   *Sales* 396,535
SIC 8211 Elementary and secondary schools
Angela James

D-U-N-S 20-549-1210   (SL)
VALLEY EQUIPMENT LIMITED
289 Mclean Ave, Hartland, NB, E7P 2K7
(506) 375-4412
Emp Here 75   *Sales* 47,196,000
SIC 5511 New and used car dealers
Peter Cook

Haut-Lameque, NB E8T

D-U-N-S 25-088-3774   (SL)
LAROCQUE, CHRISTIAN SERVICES LTEE
5106 Route 113, Haut-Lameque, NB, E8T 3L4
(506) 344-7077
Emp Here 100   *Sales* 14,819,200
SIC 4212 Local trucking, without storage
Christian Larocque
Guy Duguay
Remi Larocque

D-U-N-S 20-023-6099   (BR)
SUN GRO HORTICULTURE CANADA LTD
FPM PEAT MOSS
(*Suby of* SUN GRO HORTICULTURE DISTRIBUTION INC.)
4492 Route 113, Haut-Lameque, NB, E8T 3L3
(506) 336-2229
Emp Here 85
SIC 5159 Farm-product raw materials, nec
Andre Fafard

Havelock, NB E4Z

D-U-N-S 25-115-0819   (SL)
GRAYMONT (NB) INC
(*Suby of* GRAYMONT LIMITED)
4634 Route 880, Havelock, NB, E4Z 5K8
(506) 534-2311
Emp Here 45   *Sales* 10,504,575
SIC 1422 Crushed and broken limestone
Andre Van Agten
William Dodge
Kenneth Lahti
Graham Weir

▲ Public Company   ■ Public Company Family Member   HQ Headquarters   BR Branch   SL Single Location

Holmesville, NB E7J

D-U-N-S 24-862-5290   (SL)
L.F.OAKES & SONS LTD.
259 Mcelroy Rd, Holmesville, NB, E7J 2J4

Emp Here 30   *Sales* 10,274,010
SIC 0134 Irish potatoes
Jeff Furrow

Inkerman, NB E8P

D-U-N-S 24-129-6375   (HQ)
BASQUE, GILLES SALES LTD
UNISELECT
878 Route 113, Inkerman, NB, E8P 1C9
(506) 336-4738
Emp Here 14   *Sales* 11,290,665
SIC 5013 Motor vehicle supplies and new parts
Gilles Basque
Brian Basque

Jacksonville, NB E7M

D-U-N-S 20-931-6538   (HQ)
BMG HOLDINGS LTD
(*Suby of* BARRETT CORPORATION)
32 Sawyer Rd, Jacksonville, NB, E7M 3B7
(506) 328-8853
Emp Here 25   *Sales* 46,848,780
SIC 5091 Sporting and recreation goods
Malcolm Barrett
William Barrett
Edward Barrett

D-U-N-S 24-340-5172   (SL)
CULBERSON, RALPH B & SONS LTD
682 Route 560, Jacksonville, NB, E7M 3J8
(506) 328-4366
Emp Here 30   *Sales* 10,274,010
SIC 0134 Irish potatoes
Roy Culberson
Murray Culberson

D-U-N-S 24-756-3257   (SL)
MCCONNELL TRANSPORT LIMITED
208 Route 590, Jacksonville, NB, E7M 3R7
(506) 325-2211
Emp Here 150   *Sales* 30,855,900
SIC 4213 Trucking, except local
Larry Mcconnell

D-U-N-S 24-629-3138   (SL)
PIONEER TRANSPORT INC
208 Route 590, Jacksonville, NB, E7M 3R7
(506) 325-2211
Emp Here 98   *Sales* 5,377,456
SIC 4131 Intercity and rural bus transportation
Larry Mcconnell

D-U-N-S 24-574-0964   (SL)
RICHWIL TRUCK CENTRE LTD
314 Lockhart Mill Rd, Jacksonville, NB, E7M 3S4
(506) 328-9379
Emp Here 33   *Sales* 16,436,574
SIC 5511 New and used car dealers
Richard Wilson

D-U-N-S 20-812-9189   (SL)
VALLEY REFRIGERATION & AIR CONDITIONING LTD
35 Kinney Rd, Jacksonville, NB, E7M 3G1
(506) 325-2204
Emp Here 50   *Sales* 11,046,700
SIC 1711 Plumbing, heating, air-conditioning
William Barrett
Ed Barrett

D-U-N-S 20-566-5180   (SL)
XPLORNET LIMITED
300 Lockhart Mill Rd, Jacksonville, NB, E7M 5C3
(506) 328-1274
Emp Here 100   *Sales* 18,479,800
SIC 4813 Telephone communication, except radio
Edward Barrett
Malcolm Barrett
William Barrett

Juniper, NB E7L

D-U-N-S 24-204-9869   (BR)
NORBORD INDUSTRIES INC
(*Suby of* NORBORD INC)
137 Juniper Rd, Juniper, NB, E7L 1G8
(506) 246-1125
Emp Here 120
SIC 2431 Millwork
Steve Dickinson

Keswick Ridge, NB E6L

D-U-N-S 24-629-0290   (BR)
NEW BRUNSWICK POWER CORPORATION
MACTAQUAC GENERATING STATION
(*Suby of* PROVINCE OF NEW BRUNSWICK)
451 Route 105, Keswick Ridge, NB, E6L 1B2
(506) 462-3800
Emp Here 75
SIC 4911 Electric services
Marcel Chaffe

Killarney Road, NB E3G

D-U-N-S 24-423-8494   (HQ)
ENVIREM ORGANICS INC
274 Route 148, Killarney Road, NB, E3G 9E2
(506) 459-3464
Sales 21,625,744
SIC 2875 Fertilizers, mixing only
Robert Kiely

Lakeville-Westmorland, NB E1H

D-U-N-S 24-878-4845   (HQ)
CARTER BROTHERS LTD
1797 Route 134, Lakeville-Westmorland, NB, E1H 1A1
(506) 383-9150
Emp Here 50   *Sales* 20,195,360
SIC 1623 Water, sewer, and utility lines
John Carter
Corinne Keenan

Lameque, NB E8T

D-U-N-S 24-955-6861   (BR)
REGIONAL HEALTH AUTHORITY A
HOPITAL DE LAMEQUE
(*Suby of* REGIONAL HEALTH AUTHORITY A)
29 Rue De L'Hopital, Lameque, NB, E8T 1C5
(506) 344-2261
Emp Here 100
SIC 8062 General medical and surgical hospitals
Rose-Marie Chiasson Goupil

D-U-N-S 20-020-6639   (SL)
SOCIETE CO-OPERATIVE DE LAMEQUE LTEE, LA
68 Rue Principale, Lameque, NB, E8T 1M6
(506) 344-2206
Emp Here 63   *Sales* 11,028,906
SIC 5399 Miscellaneous general merchandise
Paul Lanteigne
Gaston Paulin

Lansdowne, NB E7L

D-U-N-S 20-814-1937   (SL)
DONNELLY FARMS LTD
40 Stockford Rd, Lansdowne, NB, E7L 4K4
(506) 375-4564
Emp Here 75   *Sales* 10,669,918
SIC 4213 Trucking, except local
Dwayne Donnelly

Le Goulet, NB E8S

D-U-N-S 24-574-7084   (SL)
NAGEOIRE LTEE, LA
144 Ch Du Havre, Le Goulet, NB, E8S 2H1
(506) 336-8808
Emp Here 80   *Sales* 66,846,160
SIC 5146 Fish and seafoods
Roger Bulger
Albert Bulger
Alfred Bulger

Lincoln, NB E3B

D-U-N-S 20-011-1867   (SL)
FREDERICTON INTERNATIONAL AIRPORT AUTHORITY INC
2570 Route 102 Unit 22, Lincoln, NB, E3B 9G1
(506) 460-0920
Emp Here 63   *Sales* 10,392,128
SIC 4581 Airports, flying fields, and services
Johanne Gallant
Andrew Steeves
Meredith Boyle
Alvin Nason
Blake Anderson
Lily Fraser
Mary Goggin
Anthony Knight
Kenneth Kyle
Karina Leblanc

D-U-N-S 24-383-9235   (SL)
LEADING EDGE GEOMATICS LTD
AERIAL SURVEY
2398 Route 102 Hwy, Lincoln, NB, E3B 7G1
(506) 446-4403
Emp Here 38   *Sales* 17,070,322
SIC 7389 Business services, nec
Bruce Hogan
William Kidman
William Lowry
Mike Oliver
Yong Kwon
Francois Laflamme
Kristian Valenta

D-U-N-S 20-446-2832   (SL)
SCOTT'S NURSERY LTD
2192 Route 102, Lincoln, NB, E3B 8N1
(506) 458-9208
Emp Here 35   *Sales* 25,988,200
SIC 5193 Flowers and florists supplies
George Scott

Lorne, NB E8G

D-U-N-S 25-363-0677   (SL)
HOMETOWN COMMUNICATIONS
97 Pine St, Lorne, NB, E8G 1M6

Emp Here 26   *Sales* 11,679,694
SIC 7389 Business services, nec
Donna Hilliard

Lower Kintore, NB E7H

D-U-N-S 20-814-4642   (SL)
VICTORIA GLEN MANOR INC
30 Beech Glen Rd, Lower Kintore, NB, E7H 1J9
(506) 273-4885
Emp Here 75   *Sales* 5,154,975
SIC 8051 Skilled nursing care facilities
Cheryl Reed

Lower St Marys, NB E3A

D-U-N-S 20-295-1906   (HQ)
NATURALLY FIT SUPPLEMENTS INC
125 Route 105, Lower St Marys, NB, E3A 8P8
(506) 451-8707
Emp Here 6   *Sales* 33,423,080
SIC 5149 Groceries and related products, nec
Spencer Court

Maugerville, NB E3A

D-U-N-S 24-582-0472   (SL)
HOLLAND, E. CONTRACTING INC
HOLLAND POWER SERVICES
272 Route 105, Maugerville, NB, E3A 8G2
(506) 472-0649
Emp Here 202   *Sales* 47,572,818
SIC 1731 Electrical work
Lyle Earl Holland

Mcadam, NB E6J

D-U-N-S 20-081-8347   (SL)
WAUKLEHEGAN MANOR INC
MCADAM OUTREACH FOR SENIORS PROGRAM
11 Saunders Rd, Mcadam, NB, E6J 1K9
(506) 784-6303
Emp Here 84   *Sales* 7,783,860
SIC 8322 Individual and family services
Frank Carroll
Debi Bourque

Mcleods, NB E3N

D-U-N-S 20-019-5030   (SL)
PRODUCTIONS AGRICOLES OUELLET, LES
RIVERVIEW POULTRY
1119 Route 280, Mcleods, NB, E3N 5W6
(506) 753-3736
Emp Here 14   *Sales* 11,698,078
SIC 5144 Poultry and poultry products
Jean-Paul Ouellet

Meductic, NB E6H

D-U-N-S 20-445-2783   (HQ)
SABIAN LTD
219 Main St, Meductic, NB, E6H 2L5
(506) 272-2019
Sales 39,136,320
SIC 3931 Musical instruments
Armand Zildjian
James Hargrove
Michael Connell
Peter Crocco

Memramcook, NB E4K

D-U-N-S 20-003-6874   (SL)
BSM SERVICES (1998) LTD
948 Ch Royal, Memramcook, NB, E4K 1Y8
(506) 862-0810
Emp Here 50   *Sales* 11,046,700
SIC 1711 Plumbing, heating, air-conditioning
Michel Gaudet
Gilles Leblanc
Mathieu Landry

D-U-N-S 24-342-4405   (SL)
VERGER BELLIVEAU ORCHARD LTD
1209 Rue Principale, Memramcook, NB, E4K 2S6
(506) 758-0295
Emp Here 20   *Sales* 10,702,480
SIC 5148 Fresh fruits and vegetables
Louis Bourgeois
Robert Bourgeois

Mill Cove, NB E4C

D-U-N-S 24-338-7743   (SL)
MILL COVE NURSING HOME INC
5647 Route 105, Mill Cove, NB, E4C 3A5

Emp Here 117   *Sales* 7,994,142
SIC 8051 Skilled nursing care facilities
Jason Dickson

Minto, NB E4B

D-U-N-S 25-502-7468   (SL)
TIRE RECYCLING ATLANTIC CANADA CORPORATION
TRACC
149 Industrial Park Rd, Minto, NB, E4B 3A6
(506) 327-4355
Emp Here 30   *Sales* 14,942,340
SIC 5531 Auto and home supply stores
John Leonard

Miramichi, NB E1N

D-U-N-S 25-897-3866   (SL)
CANADIAN CORRECTIONAL MANAGEMENT INC
(*Suby of* THE GEO GROUP INC)
4 Airport Dr, Miramichi, NB, E1N 3W4
(506) 624-2160
Emp Here 150   *Sales* 3,937,500
SIC 7381 Detective and armored car services
George Zoley
Mary Maher
Brian Evans
David Lever

D-U-N-S 20-282-1344   (BR)
DEW ENGINEERING AND DEVELOPMENT ULC
(*Suby of* KEYSTONE HOLDINGS LLC)

99 General Manson Way, Miramichi, NB, E1N 6K6
(506) 778-8000
Emp Here 100
SIC 3795 Tanks and tank components

D-U-N-S 25-409-9773   (HQ)
HEBERT'S RECYCLING INC
53 Walsh Ave, Miramichi, NB, E1N 3A5
(506) 773-1880
Emp Here 1   *Sales* 17,999,170
SIC 4953 Refuse systems
Kevin Sargent

D-U-N-S 25-887-1664   (SL)
KERR, WILLIAM J LTD
365 Wellington St, Miramichi, NB, E1N 1P6

Emp Here 35   *Sales* 16,475,585
SIC 1542 Nonresidential construction, nec
William Kerr

D-U-N-S 20-618-9581   (HQ)
KINGSTON FUELS LTD
249 Duke St, Miramichi, NB, E1N 1J5
(506) 773-6426
Emp Here 7   *Sales* 22,512,240
SIC 5983 Fuel oil dealers
Leonard Kingston
Roberta Whalen
Weldon Kingston

D-U-N-S 20-287-2565   (SL)
MIRAMICHI SENIOR CITIZENS HOME INC
1400 Water St, Miramichi, NB, E1N 1A4
(506) 778-6810
Emp Here 110   *Sales* 7,542,260
SIC 8051 Skilled nursing care facilities
Margaret Manderson

D-U-N-S 24-128-7309   (SL)
MOUNT SAINT JOSEPH NURSING HOME
51 Lobban Ave, Miramichi, NB, E1N 2W8
(506) 622-5091
Emp Here 200   *Sales* 13,665,200
SIC 8051 Skilled nursing care facilities
Debbie Walls
Jack Barry
Robert E Stewart
Kim Arsenault

D-U-N-S 20-788-4607   (BR)
PROVINCE OF NEW BRUNSWICK
NEW BRUNSWICK COMMUNITY COLLEGE
(*Suby of* PROVINCE OF NEW BRUNSWICK)
80 University Ave, Miramichi, NB, E1N 0C6
(506) 778-6000
Emp Here 75
SIC 8221 Colleges and universities
Karen White-O'connell

Miramichi, NB E1V

D-U-N-S 20-822-4378   (BR)
AGROPUR COOPERATIVE
NARTEL
(*Suby of* AGROPUR COOPERATIVE)
256 Lawlor Lane, Miramichi, NB, E1V 3Z9
(506) 627-7720
Emp Here 250
SIC 5143 Dairy products, except dried or canned
Joey Cotroneo

D-U-N-S 20-731-9117   (SL)
AUTO LAC INC
CANADIAN TIRE MIRAMICHI
2491 King George Hwy, Miramichi, NB, E1V 6W3
(506) 773-9448
Emp Here 60   *Sales* 12,320,580
SIC 5399 Miscellaneous general merchandise
Anne Macdonald

D-U-N-S 24-393-0471   (SL)

CEDM TOWER LTD
CANADIAN TIRE
2491 King George Hwy, Miramichi, NB, E1V 6W3
(506) 773-9446
Emp Here 45   *Sales* 22,413,510
SIC 5531 Auto and home supply stores
Charlie Tower

D-U-N-S 20-815-4831   (SL)
CHECKPOINT GMC PONTIAC BUICK LTD
349 King George Hwy, Miramichi, NB, E1V 1L2
(506) 622-7091
Emp Here 22   *Sales* 13,844,160
SIC 5511 New and used car dealers
Gerald Toner

D-U-N-S 20-575-9314   (BR)
ICT CANADA MARKETING INC
SYKES
(*Suby of* SYKES ENTERPRISES INCORPORATED)
408 King George Hwy, Miramichi, NB, E1V 1L4
(506) 836-9050
Emp Here 250
SIC 7389 Business services, nec
Robert Morley

D-U-N-S 24-993-8093   (SL)
JARDINE SECURITY LTD
107 Tardy Ave, Miramichi, NB, E1V 3Y8
(506) 622-2787
Emp Here 80   *Sales* 31,654,240
SIC 7381 Detective and armored car services
Douglas Jardine

D-U-N-S 20-932-7337   (SL)
MIRAMICHI CHRYSLER DODGE JEEP INC
1155 King George Hwy, Miramichi, NB, E1V 5J7
(506) 622-3900
Emp Here 23   *Sales* 11,455,794
SIC 5511 New and used car dealers
Bert Mcintyre

D-U-N-S 20-021-7172   (SL)
MORRIS WHOLESALE LTD
DEALS 4 U
125 Petrie St, Miramichi, NB, E1V 1S4
(506) 836-9012
Emp Here 21   *Sales* 17,547,117
SIC 5141 Groceries, general line
Gerald Morris
Jeffrey Morris

D-U-N-S 20-021-7263   (HQ)
NORTHUMBERLAND COOPERATIVE LIMITED
NORTHUMBERLAND DAIRY
256 Lawlor Lane, Miramichi, NB, E1V 3Z9
(506) 627-7720
Emp Here 150   *Sales* 103,707,000
SIC 2026 Fluid milk
Jack Christie
John Macdiarmid

D-U-N-S 20-298-2893   (SL)
ROUSSEL TOYOTA
ROUSSEL MOTORS
323 King George Hwy, Miramichi, NB, E1V 1L2
(506) 622-1867
Emp Here 25   *Sales* 12,451,950
SIC 5511 New and used car dealers
Michel Roussel

D-U-N-S 24-629-7816   (SL)
SKYCO INC
SKY-TEC SATELLITE
734 King George Hwy, Miramichi, NB, E1V 1P8
(506) 622-8890
Emp Here 70   *Sales* 19,028,940
SIC 7699 Repair services, nec
Kevin Macdonald
Kelley Macdonald

D-U-N-S 20-813-6069   (HQ)
SUNNY CORNER ENTERPRISES INC
259 Dalton Ave, Miramichi, NB, E1V 3C4
(506) 622-5600
Emp Here 50   *Sales* 74,525,343
SIC 1711 Plumbing, heating, air-conditioning
Gordon Lavoie
Eugene Nowlan
William Schenkels
Jolyon Hunter

D-U-N-S 25-357-6631   (SL)
TOWNE SALES AND SERVICE LIMITED
2227 King George Hwy, Miramichi, NB, E1V 6N1
(506) 622-9020
Emp Here 45   *Sales* 22,413,510
SIC 5511 New and used car dealers
Hal Somers

D-U-N-S 24-375-7460   (SL)
UMOE SOLAR NEW BRUNSWICK INC
345 Curtis Rd, Miramichi, NB, E1V 3R7

Emp Here 100   *Sales* 23,343,500
SIC 2621 Paper mills
David Wright
Joerk Rimmasch
Oystein Oyehaug

D-U-N-S 24-120-3517   (BR)
WAL-MART CANADA CORP
(*Suby of* WALMART INC.)
200 Douglastown Blvd, Miramichi, NB, E1V 7T9
(506) 778-8224
Emp Here 200
SIC 5311 Department stores
Shelly Vance

Moncton, NB E1A

D-U-N-S 24-804-5049   (HQ)
ASHKYLE LTD
LEON'S FURNITURE
101 Lewisville Rd, Moncton, NB, E1A 2K5
(506) 859-6969
Emp Here 25   *Sales* 10,458,135
SIC 5712 Furniture stores
Darren Leon

D-U-N-S 20-814-2083   (SL)
CAN-AM MOTORS LTD
CAN-AM CHRYSLER
40 Morton Ave, Moncton, NB, E1A 3H9
(506) 852-8210
Emp Here 25   *Sales* 12,451,950
SIC 5511 New and used car dealers
James Toogood

D-U-N-S 20-812-1178   (HQ)
ELMWOOD HARDWARE LTD
HOME HARDWARE
257 Elmwood Dr, Moncton, NB, E1A 1X4
(506) 858-8100
Emp Here 40   *Sales* 26,765,200
SIC 5211 Lumber and other building materials
Alvin Leger
Rachelle Leger

D-U-N-S 25-881-3559   (BR)
ICT CANADA MARKETING INC
(*Suby of* SYKES ENTERPRISES INCORPORATED)
459 Elmwood Dr, Moncton, NB, E1A 2X2

Emp Here 220
SIC 8732 Commercial nonphysical research
Tom Loberto

D-U-N-S 24-914-9548   (SL)
MCBUNS BAKERY
122 Shediac Rd, Moncton, NB, E1A 2R9
(506) 858-1700
Emp Here 49   *Sales* 11,017,895

▲ Public Company   ■ Public Company Family Member   **HQ** Headquarters   **BR** Branch   **SL** Single Location

SIC 2051 Bread, cake, and related products
Steven Buckler

D-U-N-S 20-004-6741 (SL)
O'BRIAIN DRUGS LTD
SHOPPERS DRUG MART
320 Elmwood Dr, Moncton, NB, E1A 6V2
(506) 383-8303
Emp Here 45   *Sales* 11,382,930
SIC 5912 Drug stores and proprietary stores
Deirdre Kyle

D-U-N-S 25-087-7420 (SL)
PUMP HOUSE BREWERY LTD
131 Mill Rd, Moncton, NB, E1A 6R1
(506) 854-2537
Emp Here 60   *Sales* 13,491,300
SIC 2082 Malt beverages
Shaun Fraser
Lilia Fraser

D-U-N-S 24-189-0409 (SL)
TAYLOR FORD SALES LTD
TAYLOR FORD LINCOLN
10 Lewisville Rd, Moncton, NB, E1A 2K2
(506) 857-2300
Emp Here 106   *Sales* 66,703,680
SIC 5511 New and used car dealers
Terry Taylor
Maureen Taylor
Paul Leblanc

D-U-N-S 24-472-0009 (SL)
TRI PROVINCE ENTERPRISES (1984) LTD
158 Toombs St, Moncton, NB, E1A 3A5
(506) 858-8110
Emp Here 38   *Sales* 16,992,612
SIC 5051 Metals service centers and offices
Bruce Nowlan
Mark Nowlan
Pearl Nowlan

D-U-N-S 20-813-6846 (HQ)
UNIVERSITE DE MONCTON
18 Av Antonine-Maillet, Moncton, NB, E1A 3E9
(506) 858-4000
Emp Here 636   *Sales* 113,797,491
SIC 8221 Colleges and universities
Yvon Fontaine
Jacques Paul Coutier
Richard Saillant
Neil Boucher
Daniel Godbout
Guy Richard

D-U-N-S 20-743-1917 (SL)
VILLA DU REPOS INC
125 Murphy Ave, Moncton, NB, E1A 8V2
(506) 857-3560
Emp Here 125   *Sales* 8,035,250
SIC 8361 Residential care
John Lyons
Eldor Leblanc

Moncton, NB E1C

D-U-N-S 24-131-8583 (HQ)
501479 NB LTD
SOUNDS FANTASTIC
48 Bonaccord St, Moncton, NB, E1C 5K7
(506) 857-0000
Emp Here 1   *Sales* 15,571,001
SIC 5736 Musical instrument stores
Jeffrey Kelly
Kevin Cormier

D-U-N-S 20-631-1664 (HQ)
A.P.M. LIMITED
96 King St, Moncton, NB, E1C 4M6
(506) 857-3838
Emp Here 16   *Sales* 36,421,500
SIC 5013 Motor vehicle supplies and new parts
Douglas J Squires

William (Bill) Carter

D-U-N-S 20-555-2727 (HQ)
ACADIAN COACH LINES LP
300 Main St Unit B2-2, Moncton, NB, E1C 1B9

Emp Here 82
SIC 4142 Bus charter service, except local
Carrie Cormier

D-U-N-S 24-350-4334 (HQ)
AMBULANCE NEW BRUNSWICK INC
NEW BRUNSWICK EMS FLEET CENTRE
(*Suby of* PROVINCE OF NEW BRUNSWICK)
210 John St Suite 101, Moncton, NB, E1C 0B8
(506) 872-6500
Emp Here 100   *Sales* 82,639,837
SIC 4119 Local passenger transportation, nec
Alan Stephen
Shirley Neville

D-U-N-S 25-370-0942 (BR)
AMERICA ONLINE CANADA INC
AOL CANADA
(*Suby of* VERIZON COMMUNICATIONS INC.)
11 Ocean Limited Way, Moncton, NB, E1C 0H1

Emp Here 350
SIC 4899 Communication services, nec
Bernadette Kenny

D-U-N-S 20-177-1776 (BR)
AQUILINI INVESTMENT GROUP INC
CROWNE PLAZA MONCTON DOWNTOWN
(*Suby of* AQUILINI INVESTMENT GROUP INC)
1005 Main St, Moncton, NB, E1C 1G9
(506) 854-6340
Emp Here 100
SIC 7011 Hotels and motels
Shawn Warman

D-U-N-S 20-742-0316 (HQ)
ASSUMPTION MUTUAL LIFE INSURANCE COMPANY
ASSUMPTION LIFE
770 Main St, Moncton, NB, E1C 1E7
(506) 853-6040
Sales 138,238,657
SIC 6311 Life insurance
Denis Losier
Gilles Leblanc
Georges Marcoux
Robert Moreau
Yves Arseneau
Denis Larocque
Philippe Desrosiers
Jacques Valotaire
Andree Savoie
Nathalie Godbout

D-U-N-S 20-742-2312 (HQ)
ASSUMPTION PLACE LIMITED
770 Main St, Moncton, NB, E1C 1E7
(506) 853-5420
Emp Here 12   *Sales* 19,215,777
SIC 6512 Nonresidential building operators
Denis Losier

D-U-N-S 25-402-6313 (SL)
ASURION CANADA, INC
(*Suby of* NEW ASURION CORPORATION)
11 Ocean Limited Way, Moncton, NB, E1C 0H1
(506) 386-9200
Emp Here 500   *Sales* 167,272,000
SIC 4899 Communication services, nec
Rick Taweel
Donna Cooke

D-U-N-S 20-813-8552 (HQ)
ATLANTIC LOTTERY CORPORATION INC
922 Main St, Moncton, NB, E1C 8W6
(506) 867-5800
Emp Here 320   *Sales* 854,510,956
SIC 7999 Amusement and recreation, nec

Michelle Carinci
C. Sean O'connor
Patricia Mella
Terry Paddon
Patrick Daigle
John E. Mallory
Paul Jelley
Marie Mullally
Charles F. Cox
Kevin Breen

D-U-N-S 20-021-3155 (HQ)
ATLANTIC RETAIL CO-OPERATIVES FEDERATION
CO-OP ATLANTIC
123 Halifax St, Moncton, NB, E1C 9R6
(506) 858-6000
Emp Here 300   *Sales* 521,769,248
SIC 5141 Groceries, general line
Michael Oulton
George Trueman
Margaret Herbert
Bertha Campbell
Adelard Cormier
Marcel Garvie
Wayne Lee
Mary Macdonald

D-U-N-S 24-334-4749 (BR)
BELL ALIANT REGIONAL COMMUNICATIONS INC
(*Suby of* BCE INC)
27 Alma St, Moncton, NB, E1C 4Y2
(506) 860-8655
Emp Here 80
SIC 4899 Communication services, nec
Nicole Gallant

D-U-N-S 24-248-9016 (SL)
BEST BUY MEDICAL SUPPLIES INC
211 Bromley Ave Suite 7, Moncton, NB, E1C 5V5
(506) 851-1644
Emp Here 35   *Sales* 15,651,090
SIC 5047 Medical and hospital equipment
Dan Robichaud

D-U-N-S 20-742-0399 (HQ)
BLUE CROSS LIFE INSURANCE COMPANY OF CANADA
644 Main St Suite 500, Moncton, NB, E1C 1E2
(506) 853-1811
Sales 44,319,816
SIC 6311 Life insurance
James Gilligan
Irene Richard
Pat Howe
Paul Dowie
Arnie Shaw
Andrew Yorke
Gilles Lepage
Pierre-Yves Julien
Arnie Arnott
Eric Howatt

D-U-N-S 25-526-9706 (HQ)
BRUNSWICK NEWS INC
TIMES & TRANSCRIPT
(*Suby of* IRVING, J. D. LIMITED)
939 Main St, Moncton, NB, E1C 8P3
(506) 859-4900
Emp Here 400   *Sales* 106,575,700
SIC 2711 Newspapers
A L Irving
J E Irving
J K Irving

D-U-N-S 20-021-1159 (BR)
CANADA BREAD COMPANY, LIMITED
MAPLE LEAF
(*Suby of* GRUPO BIMBO, S.A.B. DE C.V.)
235 Botsford St, Moncton, NB, E1C 4X9
(506) 857-9158
Emp Here 130
SIC 2051 Bread, cake, and related products
Rick Smith

D-U-N-S 20-573-1925 (BR)
CANADIAN BROADCASTING CORPORATION
(*Suby of* GOVERNMENT OF CANADA)
250 Archibald St, Moncton, NB, E1C 8N8

Emp Here 260
SIC 4832 Radio broadcasting stations
Richard Simeons

D-U-N-S 20-181-9781 (SL)
CHANTALE'S BED & BREAKFAST INC
1234 Main St, Moncton, NB, E1C 1H7

Emp Here 1   *Sales* 29,739,290
SIC 6712 Bank holding companies

D-U-N-S 20-748-9308 (BR)
CO-OPERATORS GENERAL INSURANCE COMPANY
(*Suby of* CO-OPERATORS GENERAL INSURANCE COMPANY)
10 Record St, Moncton, NB, E1C 0B2
(506) 853-1215
Emp Here 250
SIC 6311 Life insurance
Carry Mcrory

D-U-N-S 25-849-3816 (BR)
COMCARE (CANADA) LIMITED
COMCARE HEALTH SERVICES
(*Suby of* COMCARE (CANADA) LIMITED)
30 Gordon St Suite 105, Moncton, NB, E1C 1L8
(506) 853-9112
Emp Here 80
SIC 7363 Help supply services
Nancy Sills

D-U-N-S 20-812-5120 (HQ)
COREY CRAIG LTD
TIM HORTONS
713 Main St, Moncton, NB, E1C 1E3
(506) 856-8050
Emp Here 9   *Sales* 37,311,200
SIC 5812 Eating places
Gary O'neill

D-U-N-S 20-609-1550 (SL)
CROWNE PLAZA MONCTON DOWNTOWN HOTEL
1005 Main St, Moncton, NB, E1C 1G9
(506) 854-6340
Emp Here 90   *Sales* 8,540,910
SIC 7011 Hotels and motels
Gerald Normandeau

D-U-N-S 25-100-0113 (BR)
D&B COMPANIES OF CANADA ULC, THE
D & B COMPANIES OF CANADA LTD, THE
(*Suby of* STAR PARENT, LP)
1234 Main St Suite 2001, Moncton, NB, E1C 1H7
(506) 867-2000
Emp Here 135
SIC 7323 Credit reporting services

D-U-N-S 20-300-0992 (SL)
DENIS OFFICE SUPPLIES
123 Lutz St, Moncton, NB, E1C 5E8
(506) 853-8920
Emp Here 25   *Sales* 12,591,450
SIC 5112 Stationery and office supplies
John Leblanc

D-U-N-S 24-122-8092 (SL)
ESTATE MORTGAGE INC
ESTATE MORGAGE CENTER
19 Katherine Ave, Moncton, NB, E1C 7M7
(506) 855-5626
Emp Here 24   *Sales* 12,748,968
SIC 6211 Security brokers and dealers
Joe Daley

D-U-N-S 20-732-2673 (BR)
FIRST CANADIAN TITLE COMPANY LIMITED
(*Suby of* FIRST AMERICAN FINANCIAL

CORPORATION)
1234 Main St Suite 2001, Moncton, NB, E1C
1H7
(506) 383-6326
Emp Here 80
SIC 6411 Insurance agents, brokers, and service
Christine Francis

D-U-N-S 20-918-0202   (HQ)
FUNDY ENERGY LIMITED
BLAKENY FUELS
132 Beaverbrook St, Moncton, NB, E1C 9S8
(506) 857-3283
Emp Here 20   *Sales* 10,285,002
SIC 5074 Plumbing and heating equipment
and supplies (hydronics)
Mike Nazair
James Gould
Normand Leblanc
Lorenzo Leger
Claude Simmoneau

D-U-N-S 20-289-6044   (SL)
GESTION REMI GAUTHIER INC
CANADIAN TIRE
1106 Mountain Rd, Moncton, NB, E1C 2T3
(506) 852-2970
Emp Here 45   *Sales* 22,413,510
SIC 5531 Auto and home supply stores
Mike Marcier

D-U-N-S 24-993-9885   (SL)
HEALTHCONNECT INC
210 John St Suite 200, Moncton, NB, E1C 0B8
(506) 384-8020
Emp Here 40   *Sales* 17,739,600
SIC 7389 Business services, nec
Marcel Gervais
Vera Gervais

D-U-N-S 20-177-0695   (BR)
HOME DEPOT OF CANADA INC
HOME DEPOT
(*Suby of* THE HOME DEPOT INC)
235 Mapleton Rd, Moncton, NB, E1C 0G9
(506) 853-8150
Emp Here 100
SIC 5251 Hardware stores
Mark Stubbs

D-U-N-S 25-685-2112   (BR)
HUDSON'S BAY COMPANY
BAY, THE
(*Suby of* HUDSON'S BAY COMPANY)
1100 Main St, Moncton, NB, E1C 1H4

Emp Here 200
SIC 5311 Department stores

D-U-N-S 20-649-6270   (BR)
ICT CANADA MARKETING INC
(*Suby of* SYKES ENTERPRISES INCORPORATED)
1234 Main St Suite 2001, Moncton, NB, E1C
1H7

Emp Here 100
SIC 4899 Communication services, nec

D-U-N-S 20-918-8999   (BR)
INNVEST REAL ESTATE INVESTMENT TRUST
DELTA BEAUSEJOUR
(*Suby of* INNVEST REAL ESTATE INVESTMENT TRUST)
750 Main St, Moncton, NB, E1C 1E6
(506) 854-4344
Emp Here 100
SIC 7011 Hotels and motels
George Kosziwka

D-U-N-S 24-317-9236   (SL)
LOUNSBURY AUTOMOTIVE LIMITED
(*Suby of* LOUNSBURY COMPANY LIMITED)
2155 West Main St, Moncton, NB, E1C 9P2
(506) 857-4300
Emp Here 400   *Sales* 230,900,800

SIC 5511 New and used car dealers
Larry Nelson
Edward Mcnally
Dennis Dickie
Michael Jenkins

D-U-N-S 25-293-2397   (BR)
LOUNSBURY COMPANY LIMITED
LOUNSBURY CHEV OLDS
(*Suby of* LOUNSBURY COMPANY LIMITED)
2155 Main St W, Moncton, NB, E1C 9P2
(506) 857-4300
Emp Here 100
SIC 5511 New and used car dealers
Kendall Underhill

D-U-N-S 24-382-7222   (BR)
LUXURY HOTELS INTERNATIONAL OF CANADA ULC
LUXURY HOTELS INTERNATIONAL OF CANADA, ULC
(*Suby of* MARRIOTT INTERNATIONAL, INC.)
600 Main St, Moncton, NB, E1C 0M6
(506) 854-7100
Emp Here 100
SIC 7011 Hotels and motels
Darlene Power

D-U-N-S 20-743-4549   (HQ)
MAJOR DRILLING GROUP INTERNATIONAL INC
111 St. George St Suite 100, Moncton, NB,
E1C 1T7
(506) 857-8636
Emp Here 27   *Sales* 225,683,575
SIC 1481 NonMetallic mineral services
Denis Larocque
Marc Landry
Kelly Johnson
Larry Pisto
John Davies
Ben Graham
Andrew Mclaughlin
David Balser
David B. Tennant
David Fennell

D-U-N-S 20-742-0910   (SL)
MARITIME DOOR & WINDOW LTD
118 Albert St, Moncton, NB, E1C 1B2
(506) 857-8108
Emp Here 60   *Sales* 11,781,660
SIC 1751 Carpentry work
Mike Mann

D-U-N-S 24-120-1438   (BR)
MEDAVIE INC
(*Suby of* MEDAVIE INC)
644 Main St, Moncton, NB, E1C 1E2
(506) 853-1811
Emp Here 100
SIC 6321 Accident and health insurance
Peter Kent

D-U-N-S 20-743-4333   (HQ)
MEDAVIE INC
MEDAVIE BLUE CROSS
644 Main St, Moncton, NB, E1C 1E2
(506) 853-1811
Emp Here 700   *Sales* 3,632,845,600
SIC 6321 Accident and health insurance
Tim Coolen
Matt Crossman
Erik Sande
Paula Poirier
John Ferguson
Greg Bambury
John Diamond
Gerry Schriemer
Marian Walsh
Daniel Marcil

D-U-N-S 25-077-4361   (HQ)
MONCTON YOUTH RESIDENCES INC
536 Mountain Rd, Moncton, NB, E1C 2N5
(506) 869-6333
Emp Here 10   *Sales* 23,672,700

SIC 8641 Civic and social associations
Mel Kennah

D-U-N-S 25-880-8591   (BR)
NUMERIS
(*Suby of* NUMERIS)
1234 Main St Suite 600, Moncton, NB, E1C
1H7
(506) 859-7700
Emp Here 170
SIC 8732 Commercial nonphysical research
Linda Taylor

D-U-N-S 24-833-3916   (SL)
PERSONNEL SEARCH LTD
883 Main St, Moncton, NB, E1C 1G5
(506) 857-2156
Emp Here 300   *Sales* 22,408,200
SIC 7361 Employment agencies

D-U-N-S 24-832-1960   (HQ)
PLEXUS CONNECTIVITY SOLUTIONS LTD
(*Suby of* J. A. AUSTIN ASSOCIATES LIMITED)
225 Barker St, Moncton, NB, E1C 0M4
(506) 859-1514
Emp Here 22   *Sales* 11,980,595
SIC 1731 Electrical work
John Austin

D-U-N-S 24-932-4765   (SL)
RALLYE MOTORS LTD
RALLYE MOTORS HYUNDAI
199 Carson Dr, Moncton, NB, E1C 0K4
(506) 852-8200
Emp Here 24   *Sales* 11,953,872
SIC 5511 New and used car dealers
Chris Darrach

D-U-N-S 24-363-0659   (BR)
RGIS CANADA ULC
(*Suby of* THE BLACKSTONE GROUP L P)
236 St George St, Moncton, NB, E1C 1W1
(506) 382-9146
Emp Here 106
SIC 7389 Business services, nec
Charlene Ward

D-U-N-S 25-241-8660   (BR)
SCHOOL DISTRICT 2
MONCTON HIGH SCHOOL
(*Suby of* SCHOOL DISTRICT 2)
207 Church St, Moncton, NB, E1C 5A3
(506) 856-3439
Emp Here 110
SIC 8211 Elementary and secondary schools
Michael Belong

D-U-N-S 24-943-6262   (BR)
SOBEYS CAPITAL INCORPORATED
SOBEYS
(*Suby of* EMPIRE COMPANY LIMITED)
1380 Mountain Rd, Moncton, NB, E1C 2T8
(506) 858-8283
Emp Here 180
SIC 5411 Grocery stores
Darlene Johnson

D-U-N-S 20-248-9899   (SL)
TRANSPORT SOLUTIONS
883 Main St, Moncton, NB, E1C 1G5
(506) 857-1095
Emp Here 120   *Sales* 8,963,280
SIC 7361 Employment agencies
Lynn Breau

D-U-N-S 25-418-0334   (BR)
UNITED PARCEL SERVICE CANADA LTD
UPS
(*Suby of* UNITED PARCEL SERVICE, INC.)
1 Factory Lane Suite 200, Moncton, NB, E1C
9M3
(506) 877-4929
Emp Here 250
SIC 7389 Business services, nec
Craig Isaac

D-U-N-S 25-134-0295   (BR)

UNITED PARCEL SERVICE CANADA LTD
UPS
(*Suby of* UNITED PARCEL SERVICE, INC.)
77 Foundry St, Moncton, NB, E1C 5H7
(506) 877-6657
Emp Here 200
SIC 4212 Local trucking, without storage
Tammy Bilodeau

D-U-N-S 24-932-0573   (HQ)
VITALITE HEALTH NETWORK
DR. GEORGES-L.-DUMONT UNIVERSITY HOSPITAL CENTRE (DGLDUHC)
330 Av Universite, Moncton, NB, E1C 2Z3
(506) 862-4000
Emp Here 1,500   *Sales* 277,700,000
SIC 8062 General medical and surgical hospitals
Gilles Lanteigne

D-U-N-S 24-103-2171   (BR)
WAL-MART CANADA CORP
(*Suby of* WALMART INC.)
25 Plaza Blvd Suite 3659, Moncton, NB, E1C
0G3
(506) 853-7394
Emp Here 215
SIC 5311 Department stores
Gregory Steeves

D-U-N-S 24-122-1311   (BR)
WE CARE HEALTH SERVICES INC
WE CARE HOME HEALTH SERVICES
(*Suby of* WE CARE HEALTH SERVICES INC)
236 St George St Suite 110, Moncton, NB,
E1C 1W1
(506) 384-2273
Emp Here 84
SIC 8093 Specialty outpatient clinics, nec
Greg Mckim

D-U-N-S 20-932-2999   (SL)
WILDWOOD CABINETS LTD
PRECISION COUNTERTOPS
400 Collishaw St, Moncton, NB, E1C 0B4
(506) 858-9219
Emp Here 150   *Sales* 13,411,170
SIC 2541 Wood partitions and fixtures
Romeo Goguen
Daniel Bourque
Lucie Dugas

Moncton, NB E1E

D-U-N-S 20-444-7460   (SL)
ACADIA MOTORS LTD
ACADIA TOYOTA
22 Baig Blvd, Moncton, NB, E1E 1C8
(506) 857-8611
Emp Here 60   *Sales* 37,756,800
SIC 5511 New and used car dealers
Sam Girvan

D-U-N-S 24-188-8346   (HQ)
ACTION CAR AND TRUCK ACCESSORIES INC
ACTION CAR AND TRUCK ACCESSORIES
200 Horsman Rd, Moncton, NB, E1E 0E8
(506) 857-8786
Emp Here 20   *Sales* 69,173,100
SIC 5013 Motor vehicle supplies and new parts
John Chamberlaine

D-U-N-S 20-393-7219   (SL)
ANIMAL SAFETY PUBLICATIONS
295 English Dr, Moncton, NB, E1E 0J3
(506) 858-7807
Emp Here 80   *Sales* 16,937,920
SIC 7311 Advertising agencies
Mark Fenety

D-U-N-S 20-020-9294   (HQ)
APEX INDUSTRIES INC
APEX GARAGE STORE

(*Suby of* APEX INC)
100 Millennium Blvd, Moncton, NB, E1E 2G8
(506) 867-1600
Emp Here 180   *Sales* 55,943,130
SIC 3442 Metal doors, sash, and trim
 H Jack Stultz
 Stephen Stultz
 Keith Parlee

D-U-N-S 20-445-7709   (HQ)
ARMOUR TRANSPORT INC
ARMOUR TRANSPORTATION SYSTEMS
(*Suby of* ARMOUR TRANSPORTATION SYS-
TEMS INC)
689 Edinburgh Dr, Moncton, NB, E1E 2L4
(506) 857-0205
Emp Here 800   *Sales* 295,009,600
SIC 4213 Trucking, except local
 Wesley Armour
 Patricia Armour
 Ralston Armour
 Victoria Armour
 Norm Bourque
 Alban Gaudet
 Mike Gaudet
 David Miller
 Ken Mutter
 Don Rawle

D-U-N-S 24-360-4787   (HQ)
**ARMOUR TRANSPORTATION SYSTEMS
INC**
689 Edinburgh Dr, Moncton, NB, E1E 2L4
(506) 857-0205
Emp Here 500   *Sales* 731,018,000
SIC 6712 Bank holding companies
 Wesley Armour
 Ralston Armour
 Norm Bourque
 Alban Gaudet
 Mike Gaudet
 David Miller
 Don Rawle
 Wayne Wood
 David Creighton
 Ken Mutter

D-U-N-S 20-390-3356   (SL)
ATIS LP
ALLSCO WINDOWS AND DOORS
70 Rideout St, Moncton, NB, E1E 1E2
(506) 853-8080
Emp Here 120   *Sales* 68,355,360
SIC 5039 Construction materials, nec
 Robert Doyon

D-U-N-S 20-743-3251   (HQ)
**ATLANTIC BAPTIST SENIOR CITIZENS
HOMES INC**
GRANITE COURT
35 Atlantic Baptist Ave, Moncton, NB, E1E
4N3
(506) 858-7870
Emp Here 2   *Sales* 182,754,500
SIC 6712 Bank holding companies
 Mark Cameron

D-U-N-S 20-813-2522   (HQ)
ATLANTIC COMPRESSED AIR LTD
484 Edinburgh Dr, Moncton, NB, E1E 2L1
(506) 858-9500
Emp Here 20   *Sales* 11,875,650
SIC 5084 Industrial machinery and equipment
 Richard Eusanio
 Carole Landry
 Tom Bourgeois

D-U-N-S 25-495-5552   (BR)
ATLANTIC WHOLESALERS LTD
REAL ATLANTIC SUPERSTORE, THE
(*Suby of* LOBLAW COMPANIES LIMITED)
100 Baig Blvd, Moncton, NB, E1E 1C8
(506) 852-2000
Emp Here 150
SIC 5141 Groceries, general line
 Jeffery Holly

D-U-N-S 20-933-2162   (SL)
BAIG BLVD MOTORS INC
MONCTON HONDA
1820 Main St, Moncton, NB, E1E 4S7
(506) 857-2950
Emp Here 47   *Sales* 23,409,666
SIC 5511 New and used car dealers
 John Brushett
 Fred Taylor
 Ron Girouard

D-U-N-S 20-287-2847   (BR)
BAYSHORE HEALTHCARE LTD.
BAYSHORE HEALTHCARE LTD
(*Suby of* BAYSHORE HEALTHCARE LTD.)
50 Driscoll Cres Suite 201, Moncton, NB, E1E
3R8
(506) 857-9992
Emp Here 79
SIC 8082 Home health care services
 Karen Fullerton

D-U-N-S 24-356-5707   (BR)
CASCADES CANADA ULC
NORAMPAC, DIV OF
(*Suby of* CASCADES INC)
232 Baig Blvd, Moncton, NB, E1E 1C8
(506) 869-2200
Emp Here 150
SIC 2653 Corrugated and solid fiber boxes

D-U-N-S 20-617-5499   (SL)
CHAMPLAIN MOTORS LIMITED
CHAMPLAIN NISSAN
1810 Main St, Moncton, NB, E1E 4S7
(506) 857-1800
Emp Here 27   *Sales* 13,448,106
SIC 5511 New and used car dealers
 Daniel Casey
 Terry Gibson

D-U-N-S 24-262-4088   (BR)
**COMPAGNIE DES CHEMINS DE FER NA-
TIONAUX DU CANADA**
CN ATLANTIC ZONE
(*Suby of* COMPAGNIE DES CHEMINS DE
FER NATIONAUX DU CANADA)
255 Hump Yard Rd, Moncton, NB, E1E 4S3
(506) 853-2866
Emp Here 150
SIC 4231 Trucking terminal facilities
 Derrick Colasimone

D-U-N-S 20-814-9716   (HQ)
CONTROLS & EQUIPMENT LTD
185 Millennium Blvd, Moncton, NB, E1E 2G7
(506) 857-8836
Emp Here 40   *Sales* 28,261,080
SIC 1731 Electrical work
 Patrick Manning
 Christopher Stevens
 Troy Vautour
 George Mayo
 Darrell Clattenburg
 David Nugent

D-U-N-S 20-290-0176   (BR)
COUNTERFORCE CORPORATION
(*Suby of* UNITED TECHNOLOGIES CORPO-
RATION)
1077 St George Blvd, Moncton, NB, E1E 4C9
(506) 862-5500
Emp Here 200
SIC 7382 Security systems services
 Sandy Hislop

D-U-N-S 20-341-2952   (SL)
DAJO HOLDINGS LTD
RALLYE MOTORS CHRYSLER
1810 Main St, Moncton, NB, E1E 4S7
(506) 852-8210
Emp Here 30   *Sales* 14,942,340
SIC 5511 New and used car dealers
 Chris Darrach

D-U-N-S 20-548-8414   (HQ)
EASTERN FENCE LIMITED

(*Suby of* NEW BRUNSWICK WIRE FENCE
COMPANY LIMITED)
80 Henri Dunant St, Moncton, NB, E1E 1E6
(506) 857-8141
Emp Here 10   *Sales* 14,771,160
SIC 1799 Special trade contractors, nec
 James Kelly Sr
 James Kelly Jr
 Ross Jackson

D-U-N-S 20-806-0751   (SL)
**EXTREME WINDOW AND ENTRANCE SYS-
TEMS INC**
80 Loftus St, Moncton, NB, E1E 2N2
(506) 384-3667
Emp Here 67   *Sales* 13,527,099
SIC 3089 Plastics products, nec
 Darren Bannister
 Phyllis Bannister

D-U-N-S 20-913-4035   (BR)
FAIRMONT HOTELS & RESORTS INC
(*Suby of* ACCOR)
2081 Main St, Moncton, NB, E1E 1J2
(506) 877-3025
Emp Here 300
SIC 7389 Business services, nec
 Pascale Lebrasseur

D-U-N-S 24-803-7533   (HQ)
FANCY POKKET CORPORATION
1220 St George Blvd, Moncton, NB, E1E 4K7
(506) 853-7299
Sales 12,336,840
SIC 5461 Retail bakeries
 Mike Taimane
 Nadia Taimane

D-U-N-S 25-410-5927   (HQ)
**FENETY MARKETING SERVICES (AT-
LANTIC) LTD**
295 English Dr, Moncton, NB, E1E 0J3
(800) 561-4422
Sales 29,199,235
SIC 7389 Business services, nec
 Mark Fenety

D-U-N-S 25-179-4889   (HQ)
FERO WASTE & RECYCLING INC
203 Desbrisay Ave, Moncton, NB, E1E 0G7
(506) 855-3376
Emp Here 22   *Sales* 25,713,100
SIC 4953 Refuse systems
 Joyce Pischiutta
 Albino Pischiutta

D-U-N-S 24-628-7049   (SL)
GREYSTONE ENERGY SYSTEMS INC
(*Suby of* GREYSTONE INDUSTRIES LTD)
150 English Dr, Moncton, NB, E1E 4G7
(506) 853-3057
Emp Here 78   *Sales* 17,728,542
SIC 3822 Environmental controls
 Robin Drummond
 Scott Mackinnon
 Brian Kent
 Steve Wheeler
 Lucas Steeves
 Francinis Basque
 Sima Eskandari
 Jeff Ayer
 Mary Helen Mcdonald
 Michael Campbell

D-U-N-S 24-994-2905   (HQ)
GREYSTONE INDUSTRIES LTD
150 English Dr, Moncton, NB, E1E 4G7
(506) 853-3057
Emp Here 1   *Sales* 17,955,831
SIC 3822 Environmental controls
 William Robblee
 Barbara Robblee

D-U-N-S 24-913-2499   (SL)
**KENNETH E. SPENCER MEMORIAL HOME
INC, THE**
(*Suby of* ATLANTIC BAPTIST SENIOR CITI-

ZENS HOMES INC)
35 Atlantic Baptist Ave, Moncton, NB, E1E
4N3
(506) 858-7870
Emp Here 205   *Sales* 14,006,830
SIC 8051 Skilled nursing care facilities
 Barbara Cook
 Richard Steeves

D-U-N-S 24-317-9228   (SL)
**LOUNSBURY HEAVY-DUTY TRUCK LIM-
ITED**
(*Suby of* LOUNSBURY COMPANY LIMITED)
725 St George Blvd, Moncton, NB, E1E 2C2
(506) 857-4345
Emp Here 100   *Sales* 19,232,800
SIC 7699 Repair services, nec
 Edward D Mcnally

D-U-N-S 20-813-2787   (SL)
MACDONALD BUICK GMC CADILLAC LTD
111 Baig Blvd, Moncton, NB, E1E 1C9
(506) 853-6202
Emp Here 95   *Sales* 59,781,600
SIC 5511 New and used car dealers
 Douglas Macdonald
 Scott Langin
 Robert D Macdonald
 Dana Steeves

D-U-N-S 24-341-2509   (SL)
MARITIME EXHAUST LTD
IDEAL MUFFLER, DIV OF
191 Henri Dunant St Unit 4, Moncton, NB, E1E
1E4
(506) 857-8733
Emp Here 25   *Sales* 12,451,950
SIC 5511 New and used car dealers
 Robert Tingley
 Dale Tingley
 Donna Blacklock

D-U-N-S 24-386-3680   (SL)
METAL CORE ATLANTIC INC
180 Edinburgh Dr Suite 1, Moncton, NB, E1E
2K7
(506) 854-2673
Emp Here 12   *Sales* 12,004,068
SIC 5051 Metals service centers and offices
 Daniel Rinzler

D-U-N-S 20-021-3676   (SL)
MODERN CONSTRUCTION (1983) LTD
MONCTON CRUSHED STONE
(*Suby of* MODERN BUILDING SYSTEM LTD)
275 Salisbury Rd, Moncton, NB, E1E 4N1
(506) 853-8853
Emp Here 150   *Sales* 40,538,400
SIC 1429 Crushed and broken stone, nec
 James Steeves
 David Holt

D-U-N-S 25-483-2538   (BR)
MONCTON, CITY OF
CODIAC TRANSIT
(*Suby of* MONCTON, CITY OF)
140 Millennium Blvd, Moncton, NB, E1E 2G8
(506) 857-2008
Emp Here 86
SIC 4131 Intercity and rural bus transportation
 John Allain

D-U-N-S 20-268-6791   (BR)
MONCTON, CITY OF
*MONCTON FIRE DEPT ADMINISTRATION
OFFICE*
(*Suby of* MONCTON, CITY OF)
800 St George Blvd, Moncton, NB, E1E 2C7
(506) 857-8800
Emp Here 120
SIC 7389 Business services, nec
 Nadine Leblanc

D-U-N-S 24-541-5174   (SL)
NEW BRUNSWICK OIL BURNER TECH
555 Edinburgh Dr Suite 4, Moncton, NB, E1E
4E3

Emp Here 5   *Sales* 15,790,468
SIC 4924 Natural gas distribution
 Gary Wilson

   D-U-N-S 20-021-3973   (HQ)
**NEW BRUNSWICK WIRE FENCE COM-
PANY LIMITED**
80 Henri Dunant St, Moncton, NB, E1E 1E6
(506) 857-8141
Emp Here 20   *Sales* 62,659,080
SIC 5039 Construction materials, nec
 James Kelly Jr
 James S Kelly Sr
 Ross Jackson

   D-U-N-S 20-929-7910   (SL)
NEWCO CONSTRUCTION LTD
50 Rooney Cres, Moncton, NB, E1E 4M3
(506) 857-8710
Emp Here 30   *Sales* 17,110,140
SIC 1542 Nonresidential construction, nec
 Stephen Eagles
 Raymond Green

   D-U-N-S 20-812-7050   (SL)
PEOPLES PARK TOWER INC
960 St George Blvd Suite 144, Moncton, NB,
E1E 3Y3
(506) 857-8872
Emp Here 70   *Sales* 15,460,970
SIC 6513 Apartment building operators
 Leo Leblanc
 Norma Tomiczek
 Marcel Garvie
 Wayne Lee
 Paul-Emile Legere

   D-U-N-S 20-021-4690   (BR)
**PEPSI BOTTLING GROUP (CANADA), ULC,
THE**
PEPSICO BEVERAGES CANADA
(*Suby of* PBG INVESTMENT (LUXEM-
BOURG) SARL)
220 Henri Dunant St, Moncton, NB, E1E 1E6
(506) 853-4010
Emp Here 125
SIC 2086 Bottled and canned soft drinks
 Kim Carpenter

   D-U-N-S 20-742-8715   (HQ)
PLANT HOPE ADJUSTERS LTD
16 Coronation Dr, Moncton, NB, E1E 2X1
(506) 853-8500
Emp Here 20   *Sales* 37,314,640
SIC 6411 Insurance agents, brokers, and ser-
vice
 Frederick R Plant
 Raymond Aucoin
 Luc Bourque
 Ronald Dunn
 Gilbert Fournier
 Michel Roy

   D-U-N-S 24-628-7148   (BR)
POLE STAR TRANSPORT INCORPORATED
POLE STAR LONG HAUL
(*Suby of* ARMOUR TRANSPORTATION SYS-
TEMS INC)
689 Edinburgh Dr, Moncton, NB, E1E 2L4
(506) 859-7025
Emp Here 100
SIC 4213 Trucking, except local
 Wes Armour

   D-U-N-S 24-421-4560   (SL)
RALLYE MOTORS MITSUBISHI
1837 Main St, Moncton, NB, E1E 1H6
(506) 857-8677
Emp Here 40   *Sales* 19,923,120
SIC 5511 New and used car dealers
 Chris Darrach

   D-U-N-S 24-932-3924   (SL)
RAYAN INVESTMENTS LTD
NEIGHBORHOOD RECYCLING
1635 Berry Mills Rd, Moncton, NB, E1E 4R7

(506) 858-1600
Emp Here 60   *Sales* 19,134,600
SIC 4953 Refuse systems
 Murray L Cruickshank
 Anne Cruickshank

   D-U-N-S 24-912-8901   (SL)
ROADWAY SYSTEMS LIMITED
64 Rooney Cres, Moncton, NB, E1E 4M3
(506) 384-3069
Emp Here 60   *Sales* 11,087,880
SIC 4899 Communication services, nec
 Terry Rickard

   D-U-N-S 20-020-9997   (HQ)
ROBERT K. BUZZELL LIMITED
ATLANTIC AIR-COOLED ENGINES DIV
254 Horsman Rd, Moncton, NB, E1E 0E8
(506) 853-0936
Emp Here 45   *Sales* 21,156,080
SIC 7699 Repair services, nec
 Robert Buzzell
 Jennifer Buzzell

   D-U-N-S 24-261-9773   (SL)
ROYAL DOORS LTD
105 Henri Dunant St, Moncton, NB, E1E 1E4
(506) 857-4075
Emp Here 90   *Sales* 24,088,680
SIC 5211 Lumber and other building materials
 Dan Everson

   D-U-N-S 24-131-8369   (HQ)
SCHOOL DISTRICT 2
1077 St George Blvd, Moncton, NB, E1E 4C9
(506) 856-3222
Emp Here 40   *Sales* 168,502,300
SIC 8211 Elementary and secondary schools
 Karen Branscombe

   D-U-N-S 24-318-7874   (BR)
SITEL CANADA CORPORATION
CLIENTLOGIC
320c Edinburgh Dr, Moncton, NB, E1E 2L1

Emp Here 600
SIC 7389 Business services, nec
 Laurie Nouasri

   D-U-N-S 20-446-3087   (SL)
TOYS FOR BIG BOYS LTD
633 Salisbury Rd, Moncton, NB, E1E 1B9
(506) 858-8088
Emp Here 35   *Sales* 17,432,730
SIC 5571 Motorcycle dealers
 Frederick (Larry) Northrup

   D-U-N-S 24-262-7370   (SL)
TWINPAK ATLANTIC INC
66 English Dr, Moncton, NB, E1E 4G1
(506) 857-8116
Emp Here 53   *Sales* 10,700,541
SIC 3089 Plastics products, nec
 Jason Nyman

   D-U-N-S 20-608-6659   (HQ)
UAP/NAPA AUTO PARTS INC
325 Edinburgh Dr, Moncton, NB, E1E 4A6
(506) 857-1111
Emp Here 1   *Sales* 37,756,800
SIC 5531 Auto and home supply stores
 William Boudiler

   D-U-N-S 20-081-8321   (SL)
**VICTORIAN ORDER OF NURSES NEW
BRUNSWICK BRANCH INC**
VON
1077 St George Blvd Suite 310, Moncton, NB,
E1E 4C9

Emp Here 150   *Sales* 11,505,150
SIC 8082 Home health care services
 Marg Boak

   D-U-N-S 20-812-8801   (SL)
WALKER INVESTIGATION BUREAU LTD
1765 Main St, Moncton, NB, E1E 1H3
(506) 857-8343
Emp Here 180   *Sales* 4,725,000

SIC 7381 Detective and armored car services
 Derek Weldon

   D-U-N-S 25-207-5247   (BR)
**WAWANESA MUTUAL INSURANCE COM-
PANY, THE**
(*Suby of* WAWANESA MUTUAL INSURANCE
COMPANY, THE)
1010 St George Blvd, Moncton, NB, E1E 4R5
(506) 853-1010
Emp Here 76
SIC 6331 Fire, marine, and casualty insurance
 Sharon Gates

Moncton, NB E1G

   D-U-N-S 25-483-6489   (BR)
ATLANTIC WHOLESALERS LTD
REAL ATLANTIC SUPERSTORE
(*Suby of* LOBLAW COMPANIES LIMITED)
89 Trinity Dr, Moncton, NB, E1G 2J7
(506) 383-4919
Emp Here 160
SIC 5411 Grocery stores
 Terry Kyle

   D-U-N-S 24-224-6911   (SL)
BTK INVESTMENTS LIMITED
PETRO CANADA
2600 Mountain Rd, Moncton, NB, E1G 3T6
(506) 859-6000
Emp Here 30   *Sales* 14,942,340
SIC 5541 Gasoline service stations
 Darell Lefrense

   D-U-N-S 25-859-4050   (BR)
**CANADIAN CORPS OF COMMISSION-
AIRES NATIONAL OFFICE, THE**
(*Suby of* CANADIAN CORPS OF COMMIS-
SIONAIRES NATIONAL OFFICE, THE)
41 Mecca Dr, Moncton, NB, E1G 1B7
(506) 384-2020
Emp Here 120
SIC 7381 Detective and armored car services
 Ronald Harris

   D-U-N-S 20-187-4612   (SL)
CHERRYFIELD CONTRACTING LTD
1050 Mclaughlin Dr, Moncton, NB, E1G 3R2

Emp Here 55   *Sales* 14,117,827
SIC 1623 Water, sewer, and utility lines
 George Mcintosh
 Fraser Frizzell

   D-U-N-S 25-097-2106   (BR)
COSTCO WHOLESALE CANADA LTD
(*Suby of* COSTCO WHOLESALE CORPO-
RATION)
25 Trinity Dr Suite 217, Moncton, NB, E1G 2J7
(506) 858-7959
Emp Here 130
SIC 5399 Miscellaneous general merchandise
 Stephen Sheel

   D-U-N-S 20-753-6314   (BR)
DAY & ROSS INC
(*Suby of* MCCAIN FOODS GROUP INC)
623 Mapleton Rd, Moncton, NB, E1G 2K5
(866) 329-7677
Emp Here 100
SIC 4213 Trucking, except local
 Jeff Pearson

   D-U-N-S 20-735-5707   (SL)
**EXPEDIA CRUISE SHIP CENTRE MONC-
TON**
1633 Mountain Rd Suite 13, Moncton, NB,
E1G 1A5
(506) 386-7447
Emp Here 49   *Sales* 25,478,383
SIC 4724 Travel agencies
 Justin Brown

   D-U-N-S 20-748-9845   (SL)

**GREAT NORTHERN AUCTION COMPANY
LTD**
2131 Route 128, Moncton, NB, E1G 4K5
(506) 382-2777
Emp Here 30   *Sales* 13,304,700
SIC 7389 Business services, nec
 Sean Liptay

   D-U-N-S 20-021-2876   (HQ)
LOUNSBURY COMPANY LIMITED
1655 Mountain Rd, Moncton, NB, E1G 1A5
(506) 857-4385
Emp Here 11   *Sales* 230,900,800
SIC 5511 New and used car dealers
 Larry Nelson
 Edward Mcnally
 Clarence Aube
 Warren Rayworth
 Michael Jenkins

   D-U-N-S 24-669-6389   (HQ)
MONDART HOLDINGS LIMITED
DISCOUNT CAR & TRUCK RENTALS
1543 Mountain Rd, Moncton, NB, E1G 1A3
(506) 857-2309
Sales 15,014,900
SIC 7514 Passenger car rental
 Terry Taylor
 Paul Leblanc

   D-U-N-S 20-543-5766   (SL)
NORTHEND PHARMACY LTD
SHOPPERS DRUG MART
1633 Mountain Rd, Moncton, NB, E1G 1A5
(506) 858-0055
Emp Here 40   *Sales* 10,118,160
SIC 5912 Drug stores and proprietary stores
 Ken Kyle

   D-U-N-S 25-134-5344   (SL)
POWER PLUS TECHNOLOGY INC
LUMAC BIG SCOOP
2731 Mountain Rd, Moncton, NB, E1G 2W5
(506) 857-9212
Emp Here 40   *Sales* 19,923,120
SIC 5541 Gasoline service stations
 Jason Lutes

   D-U-N-S 20-274-3345   (SL)
PROTEM HEALTH SERVICES INC
2069 Mountain Rd, Moncton, NB, E1G 1B1
(506) 852-9652
Emp Here 45   *Sales* 10,685,025
SIC 8099 Health and allied services, nec
 Chris Wallace

   D-U-N-S 24-523-0938   (SL)
**SONCO GAMING NEW BRUNSWICK LIM-
ITED PARTNERSHIP**
CASINO NEW NOUVEAU-BRUNSWICK
(*Suby of* GREAT CANADIAN GAMING COR-
PORATION)
21 Casino Dr, Moncton, NB, E1G 0R7
(506) 859-7770
Emp Here 350   *Sales* 33,483,800
SIC 7011 Hotels and motels
 Dan Wilson

Moncton, NB E1H

   D-U-N-S 24-994-0826   (HQ)
AL-PACK ENTERPRISES LTD
(*Suby of* AL-PACK HOLDINGS LTD)
60 Commerce St, Moncton, NB, E1H 0A5
(506) 852-4262
Emp Here 58   *Sales* 11,686,080
SIC 2653 Corrugated and solid fiber boxes
 Louis Leblanc

   D-U-N-S 24-368-5802   (HQ)
AL-PACK HOLDINGS LTD
60 Commerce St, Moncton, NB, E1H 0A5
(506) 852-4262
Emp Here 2   *Sales* 26,953,140
SIC 7389 Business services, nec

▲ Public Company   ■ Public Company Family Member   **HQ** Headquarters   **BR** Branch   **SL** Single Location

Louis Leblanc

D-U-N-S 24-319-9804   (HQ)
EAST COAST INTERNATIONAL TRUCKS INC
(*Suby of* NAVISTAR INTERNATIONAL CORPORATION)
100 Urquhart Ave, Moncton, NB, E1H 2R5
(506) 857-2857
Emp Here 55   *Sales* 29,501,415
SIC 5012 Automobiles and other motor vehicles
David Lockhart
Patti Moore
Mark Lockhart

D-U-N-S 20-043-0581   (SL)
GREEN DIAMOND EQUIPMENT
70 Commerce St, Moncton, NB, E1H 0A5
(506) 388-3337
Emp Here 300   *Sales* 146,319,000
SIC 5083 Farm and garden machinery
Tina Sears

D-U-N-S 25-136-6204   (BR)
IGT CANADA SOLUTIONS ULC
(*Suby of* B&D HOLDING SPA)
328 Urquhart Ave, Moncton, NB, E1H 2R6
(506) 878-6000
Emp Here 400
SIC 0971 Hunting, trapping, game propagation

D-U-N-S 24-323-6101   (HQ)
IGT CANADA SOLUTIONS ULC
(*Suby of* B&D HOLDING SPA)
328 Urquhart Ave, Moncton, NB, E1H 2R6
(506) 878-6000
Emp Here 100   *Sales* 65,227,200
SIC 3999 Manufacturing industries, nec
Victor Duarte
A. Lavaz Watson

D-U-N-S 25-393-3139   (HQ)
KELTIC TRANSPORTATION INC
90 Macnaughton Ave, Moncton, NB, E1H 3L9
(506) 854-1233
Emp Here 157   *Sales* 41,141,200
SIC 4213 Trucking, except local
Noel Mullins
Chris Steeves
Mike Clements
Vickey Watters

D-U-N-S 24-804-1501   (SL)
MARITIME HYDRAULIC REPAIR CENTRE (1997) LTD
355 Macnaughton Ave, Moncton, NB, E1H 2J9
(506) 858-0393
Emp Here 68   *Sales* 18,485,256
SIC 7699 Repair services, nec
Kim Carruthers

D-U-N-S 20-017-1895   (BR)
MATRIX LOGISTICS SERVICES LIMITED
MATRIX
(*Suby of* MATRIX LOGISTICS SERVICES LIMITED)
10 Deware Dr Suite 1, Moncton, NB, E1H 2S6
(506) 863-1300
Emp Here 100
SIC 4225 General warehousing and storage
Bill Mitton

D-U-N-S 24-993-8283   (SL)
ROLLY'S WHOLESALE LTD
CAPITAL FOOD SERVICE
10 Macnaughton Ave, Moncton, NB, E1H 3L9
(506) 859-7110
Emp Here 45   *Sales* 33,413,400
SIC 5194 Tobacco and tobacco products
Roland Drisdelle
Victor Meisner

D-U-N-S 20-555-5472   (BR)
SYSCO CANADA, INC
SYSCO FOOD SERVICES OF ATLANTIC CANADA

(*Suby of* SYSCO CORPORATION)
460 Macnaughton Ave, Moncton, NB, E1H 2K1
(866) 447-9726
Emp Here 100
SIC 5141 Groceries, general line
Maurice Maillet

D-U-N-S 20-459-5506   (SL)
ULTRAMAR BUSINESS & HOME ENERGY
335 Macnaughton Ave, Moncton, NB, E1H 2J9
(506) 855-2424
Emp Here 5   *Sales* 15,529,285
SIC 4924 Natural gas distribution

D-U-N-S 25-530-1848   (HQ)
WHITEHILL TECHNOLOGIES INC
260 Macnaughton Ave, Moncton, NB, E1H 2J8

Emp Here 100   *Sales* 28,836,400
SIC 7371 Custom computer programming services
Paul Mcspurren

Mundleville, NB E4W

D-U-N-S 25-501-9010   (SL)
ROCKWOOD TRANSPORTATION CO. LTD
(*Suby of* J & S LUMBER CO LTD)
909 Route 495, Mundleville, NB, E4W 2M8
(506) 523-9813
Emp Here 70   *Sales* 17,233,020
SIC 1794 Excavation work
James Ferguson

Nackawic, NB E6G

D-U-N-S 20-337-4269   (SL)
AV GROUP NB INC
(*Suby of* ADITYA BIRLA MANAGEMENT CORPORATION PRIVATE LIMITED)
103 Pinder Rd, Nackawic, NB, E6G 1W4
(506) 575-3314
Emp Here 360   *Sales* 132,349,320
SIC 2611 Pulp mills
Mike O'blenis
Paul Jack
Vishnu Sharma
Kevin Larlee
Krishna Khaitan

Neguac, NB E9G

D-U-N-S 25-242-0716   (SL)
CENTRE SCOLAIRE COMMUNAUTAIRE LA FONTAINE
700 Rue Principale, Neguac, NB, E9G 1N4
(506) 776-3808
Emp Here 80   *Sales* 7,426,080
SIC 8211 Elementary and secondary schools
Jean-Pierre Devost

D-U-N-S 24-114-5569   (BR)
DISTRICT SCOLAIRE FRANCOPHONE NORD-EST
CSC LA FONTAINE
700 Rue Principale, Neguac, NB, E9G 1N4
(506) 776-3808
Emp Here 80
SIC 8299 Schools and educational services, nec
Denis Losier

D-U-N-S 24-471-9373   (HQ)
LEGRESLEY, FRANCOIS LTEE/LTD
NEGUAC HOME HARDWARE BUILDING CENTRE
790 Rue Principale, Neguac, NB, E9G 1N5

(506) 776-8334
Emp Here 15   *Sales* 10,122,360
SIC 5251 Hardware stores
Paul Lebreton
Nicole Lebreton

Nigadoo, NB E8K

D-U-N-S 24-340-5883   (SL)
POISSONERIE ARSENEAU FISH MARKET LTEE/LTD
221 Rue Principale, Nigadoo, NB, E8K 3S8
(506) 783-2195
Emp Here 50   *Sales* 41,778,850
SIC 5142 Packaged frozen goods
Jean-Paul Arseneau
Roger Arseneau

Northampton, NB E7N

D-U-N-S 25-500-8468   (HQ)
JOLLY FARMER PRODUCTS INC
56 Crabbe Rd, Northampton, NB, E7N 1R6
(506) 325-3850
Sales 30,424,500
SIC 0181 Ornamental nursery products
James Darrow
Peter Darrow
Samuel Keeler
Elisabeth Ann Keeler
Sarah Eversfield

Northern Harbour, NB E5V

D-U-N-S 25-974-4894   (HQ)
PATUREL INTERNATIONAL COMPANY
349 Northern Harbour Rd, Northern Harbour, NB, E5V 1G6
(506) 747-1888
Emp Here 125   *Sales* 55,310,400
SIC 2092 Fresh or frozen packaged fish
Stuart Mckay
Bernard Leblanc
Michael Tourkistas
Spiros Tourkakis

Notre-Dame, NB E4V

D-U-N-S 24-261-3990   (SL)
ALLAIN EQUIPMENT MANUFACTURING LTD
577 Route 535, Notre-Dame, NB, E4V 2K4
(506) 576-6436
Emp Here 60   *Sales* 13,320,060
SIC 3599 Industrial machinery, nec
Bruno Lagace

D-U-N-S 24-834-1190   (SL)
FUTURE DOORS LTD
4009 Route 115, Notre-Dame, NB, E4V 2G2
(506) 576-9769
Emp Here 60   *Sales* 11,781,660
SIC 1751 Carpentry work
Lionel Boucher

Oak Bay, NB E3L

D-U-N-S 20-739-6438   (SL)
BORDER INVESTIGATION AND SECURITY INC
303 Route 170, Oak Bay, NB, E3L 3Y2

(506) 466-6303
Emp Here 15   *Sales* 10,183,845
SIC 6211 Security brokers and dealers
Brent Macdougall

D-U-N-S 20-814-9070   (SL)
MOFFITT DODGE CHRYSLER LTD
205 Route 170, Oak Bay, NB, E3L 3X7
(506) 466-3061
Emp Here 25   *Sales* 12,451,950
SIC 5511 New and used car dealers
Ralph Moffitt
Eva Moffitt
Ed Mackie
Carolyn Frost

Old Ridge, NB E3L

D-U-N-S 20-814-1390   (HQ)
R.E.M. TRANSPORT LTD
4 Hall Rd, Old Ridge, NB, E3L 5E1
(506) 466-2918
Sales 11,313,830
SIC 4213 Trucking, except local
Dion Cull
Samantha Kinney
Graydon Murphy
Michael Bishop

Oromocto, NB E2V

D-U-N-S 25-986-2795   (BR)
ATLANTIC WHOLESALERS LTD
REAL ATLANTIC SUPERSTORE, THE
(*Suby of* LOBLAW COMPANIES LIMITED)
1198 Onondaga St, Oromocto, NB, E2V 1B8
(506) 357-5982
Emp Here 140
SIC 5411 Grocery stores
Gary Murphy

D-U-N-S 20-741-3811   (SL)
FITCHCO ENTERPRISES INC
CANADIAN TIRE
345 Miramichi Rd, Oromocto, NB, E2V 4T4
(506) 357-3304
Emp Here 49   *Sales* 24,405,822
SIC 5531 Auto and home supply stores
Gary Fitch

D-U-N-S 20-198-3850   (SL)
M & L PHARMACY LTD
SHOPPERS DRUG MART
1198 Onondaga St Suite 16, Oromocto, NB, E2V 1B8
(506) 357-8435
Emp Here 46   *Sales* 11,635,884
SIC 5912 Drug stores and proprietary stores
Micheal Shaw

D-U-N-S 20-287-8208   (SL)
MRDC OPERATIONS CORPORATION
MRDC
203 Av Black Watch, Oromocto, NB, E2V 4L7
(506) 357-1240
Emp Here 45   *Sales* 12,758,580
SIC 1611 Highway and street construction
Normon Clouston
Mike Park

D-U-N-S 20-786-9277   (SL)
MULDER'S MEAT MARKET (1983) LTD
1400 Onondaga St, Oromocto, NB, E2V 2H6
(506) 357-8862
Emp Here 20   *Sales* 10,702,480
SIC 5147 Meats and meat products
Jerry Mulder

D-U-N-S 25-241-7639   (BR)
SCHOOL DISTRICT 17
OROMOCTO HIGH SCHOOL
25 Mackenzie Ave, Oromocto, NB, E2V 1K4

---

(506) 357-4015
Emp Here 100   *Sales* 396,535
SIC 8211 Elementary and secondary schools
Donna Shirley

D-U-N-S 24-532-5964   (BR)
SOBEYS CAPITAL INCORPORATED
SOBEYS DISTRIBUTION CENTRE
(*Suby of* EMPIRE COMPANY LIMITED)
1 Lewis St, Oromocto, NB, E2V 4K5
(506) 357-9831
Emp Here 165
SIC 5411 Grocery stores
Todd Fast

D-U-N-S 25-769-8639   (HQ)
TIM HORTONS
280 Restigouche Rd, Oromocto, NB, E2V 2G9
(506) 446-9343
Emp Here 20   *Sales* 12,885,144
SIC 5461 Retail bakeries
David Moore

D-U-N-S 24-122-7730   (BR)
VALCOM CONSULTING GROUP INC
(*Suby of* MACPHERSON, PAUL & ASSO-
CIATES LTD)
281 Restigouche Rd Suite 204, Oromocto,
NB, E2V 2H2
(506) 357-5835
Emp Here 110
SIC 8748 Business consulting, nec
Charlie Richer

Penobsquis, NB E4G

D-U-N-S 20-812-4206   (SL)
ROYAL GARDENS LIMITED
AVON VALLEY FLORAL
(*Suby of* AVON VALLEY FLORAL INC)
30 Royal Gardens Rd, Penobsquis, NB, E4G
2C5
(506) 433-2030
Emp Here 65   *Sales* 38,295,335
SIC 5193 Flowers and florists supplies
Malcolm Isnor
J Thomas Macquarrie
Doug Mcarthur

D-U-N-S 24-755-5436   (SL)
**VIC PROGRESSIVE DIAMOND DRILLING
INC**
12992 Route 114 Hwy, Penobsquis, NB, E4G
2Z9
(506) 433-6139
Emp Here 75   *Sales* 18,463,950
SIC 1799 Special trade contractors, nec
Viateur Fournier
Laura Araneda
Victoria Fournier
Ian Fournier

Perth-Andover, NB E7H

D-U-N-S 24-120-2618   (SL)
ATLANTIC POTATO DISTRIBUTORS LTD
42 Industrial Park St, Perth-Andover, NB, E7H
2J2
(506) 273-6501
Emp Here 50   *Sales* 41,778,850
SIC 5148 Fresh fruits and vegetables
Ralph Hanscome
Nancy Hanscome

Petit-Cap, NB E4N

D-U-N-S 24-131-5647   (SL)
BOTSFORD FISHERIES LTD
2112 Route 950, Petit-Cap, NB, E4N 2J8

(506) 577-4327
SIC 5146 Fish and seafoods
Janice Ryan
Clement Leblanc
William Leblanc
Bernice Leblanc

D-U-N-S 25-359-4295   (SL)
BRUN FISHERIES LTD
73 Ch De L'Ile, Petit-Cap, NB, E4N 2G6
(506) 577-1157
Emp Here 30   *Sales* 25,067,310
SIC 5146 Fish and seafoods
Fernand Noel
Andrea Despres

Petitcodiac, NB E4Z

D-U-N-S 24-655-2025   (SL)
BRUNSWICK HINO INC
20 Smith St, Petitcodiac, NB, E4Z 4W1
(506) 756-2250
Emp Here 40   *Sales* 19,923,120
SIC 5511 New and used car dealers
Derek Burgess

D-U-N-S 20-814-9393   (SL)
**BURGESS TRANSPORTATION SERVICES
INC**
20 Smith St, Petitcodiac, NB, E4Z 4W1
(506) 756-2250
Emp Here 60   *Sales* 12,342,360
SIC 4213 Trucking, except local
Derek Burgess
Trevor Burgess
Scott Burgess

D-U-N-S 20-021-9004   (SL)
FAWCETT, H. A. & SON LIMITED
FAWCETT LUMBER
2 King St Suite 2, Petitcodiac, NB, E4Z 4L2
(506) 756-3366
Emp Here 200   *Sales* 38,474,000
SIC 2421 Sawmills and planing mills, general
George Fawcett
Tim Fawcett
Robert Fawcett
Henry Fawcett

Plaster Rock, NB E7G

D-U-N-S 24-736-1723   (BR)
TWIN RIVERS PAPER COMPANY INC
(*Suby of* TWIN RIVERS PAPER COMPANY
INC)
31 Renous Rd Suite 36, Plaster Rock, NB,
E7G 4B5
(506) 356-4132
Emp Here 200
SIC 2421 Sawmills and planing mills, general
John Grenon

D-U-N-S 24-858-1428   (SL)
**WORLD POND HOCKEY CHAMPIONSHIP
INC**
159 Main St, Plaster Rock, NB, E7G 2H2
(506) 356-6070
Emp Here 200   *Sales* 16,679,000
SIC 7941 Sports clubs, managers, and pro-
moters
Danny Braun

Port Elgin, NB E4M

D-U-N-S 24-341-5643   (HQ)
ATLANTIC ALL-WEATHER WINDOWS LTD
ATLANTIC WINDOWS
49 East Main St, Port Elgin, NB, E4M 2X9

(506) 538-2361
Emp Here 175   *Sales* 54,926,760
SIC 3089 Plastics products, nec
Robert Miller
Bruce Burdock

Quispamsis, NB E2E

D-U-N-S 20-298-0780   (BR)
**ANGLOPHONE SOUTH SCHOOL DISTRICT
(ASD-S)**
KENNEBECASIS VALLEY HIGH SCHOOL
(*Suby of* ANGLOPHONE SOUTH SCHOOL
DISTRICT (ASD-S))
398 Hampton Rd, Quispamsis, NB, E2E 4V5
(506) 847-6200
Emp Here 110
SIC 8211 Elementary and secondary schools
Peter Smith

D-U-N-S 25-867-4076   (HQ)
BRODY COMPANY LTD, THE
GREAT CANADIAN DOLLAR STORE
199 Hampton Rd Suite 606, Quispamsis, NB,
E2E 4L9
(506) 849-4123
Emp Here 15   *Sales* 76,054,000
SIC 5399 Miscellaneous general merchandise
Kevin Kane

Rexton, NB E4W

D-U-N-S 20-619-1199   (SL)
WARREN READY-MIX LTD
CONCRETE SOLUTIONS, DIV OF
58 California Rd, Rexton, NB, E4W 1W8
(506) 523-4240
Emp Here 125   *Sales* 22,402,375
SIC 3273 Ready-mixed concrete
Vaughn Sturgeon

D-U-N-S 24-831-4031   (SL)
WARREN TRANSPORT LTD
58 California Rd, Rexton, NB, E4W 1W8

Emp Here 104   *Sales* 21,393,424
SIC 4213 Trucking, except local
Vaughan Sturgeon

Richibucto, NB E4W

D-U-N-S 20-022-0564   (SL)
COOPERATIVE CARTIER LTEE, LA
25 Boul Cartier Unit 105, Richibucto, NB, E4W
3W7
(506) 523-4461
Emp Here 50   *Sales* 16,148,450
SIC 5411 Grocery stores
Laurent Brideau
Paul Leblanc

D-U-N-S 20-936-2458   (SL)
DOIRON, RENEE
8 Rue Centennial, Richibucto, NB, E4W 3X2
(506) 523-9403
Emp Here 20   *Sales* 11,598,480
SIC 6411 Insurance agents, brokers, and ser-
vice
Renee Doiron

D-U-N-S 20-187-8365   (SL)
GLOBAL WINDOW SOLUTIONS INC
GLOBAL WINDOWS AND DOORS
128 Rue Industrial, Richibucto, NB, E4W 4A4
(506) 523-4900
Emp Here 80   *Sales* 16,151,760
SIC 3089 Plastics products, nec
Scott Targett
Ola Johnson

Allan Doyle

D-U-N-S 25-859-1817   (SL)
HAVRE COMMUNAUTAIRE INC, LE
17 Commerciale, Richibucto, NB, E4W 3X5
(506) 523-6790
Emp Here 100   *Sales* 6,873,300
SIC 8051 Skilled nursing care facilities
Emile Chevarie

D-U-N-S 24-684-6864   (HQ)
IMPERIAL MANUFACTURING GROUP INC
40 Industrial Park St, Richibucto, NB, E4W
4A4
(506) 523-9117
Emp Here 500   *Sales* 243,231,000
SIC 3444 Sheet Metalwork
Bradley Spencer
Steve Finlay
Dean Kochalka
Omer Babineau
Patrick Magee

Riverview, NB E1B

D-U-N-S 20-313-1821   (BR)
ATLANTIC WHOLESALERS LTD
RIVERVIEW SUPERSTORE
(*Suby of* LOBLAW COMPANIES LIMITED)
425 Coverdale Rd, Riverview, NB, E1B 3K3
(506) 387-5992
Emp Here 200
SIC 5411 Grocery stores

D-U-N-S 20-191-7171   (BR)
**CONCENTRIX TECHNOLOGIES SERVICES
(CANADA) LIMITED**
(*Suby of* SYNNEX CORPORATION)
720 Coverdale Rd, Riverview, NB, E1B 3L8
(506) 860-5900
Emp Here 700
SIC 4899 Communication services, nec
Valerie D''amours

D-U-N-S 20-811-6707   (SL)
DOWNEY BUILDING SUPPLIES LTD
DOWNEY HOME HARDWARE
1106 Cleveland Ave, Riverview, NB, E1B 5V8
(506) 388-2240
Emp Here 52   *Sales* 13,917,904
SIC 5211 Lumber and other building materials
Stephen Downey

D-U-N-S 20-429-1949   (SL)
ICG PROPANE
63 Goldsboro Ave, Riverview, NB, E1B 4E9

Emp Here 5   *Sales* 15,709,144
SIC 4924 Natural gas distribution

D-U-N-S 20-191-3162   (BR)
ICT CANADA MARKETING INC
(*Suby of* SYKES ENTERPRISES INCORPO-
RATED)
720 Coverdale Rd Unit 9, Riverview, NB, E1B
3L8

Emp Here 600
SIC 7389 Business services, nec
Mark Alpern

D-U-N-S 25-401-7908   (BR)
NAV CANADA
(*Suby of* NAV CANADA)
222 Old Coach Rd, Riverview, NB, E1B 4G2
(613) 563-5588
Emp Here 250
SIC 7389 Business services, nec
Steve Hunt

D-U-N-S 24-943-6387   (BR)
SOBEYS CAPITAL INCORPORATED
SOBEYS #736
(*Suby of* EMPIRE COMPANY LIMITED)
1160 Findlay Blvd, Riverview, NB, E1B 0J6

▲ Public Company   ■ Public Company Family Member   **HQ** Headquarters   **BR** Branch   **SL** Single Location

(506) 386-4616
Emp Here 100
SIC 5411 Grocery stores
David Watts

Roachville, NB E4G

D-U-N-S 24-339-7585   (SL)
DAIRY FARMERS OF NEW BRUNSWICK
29 Milk Board Rd, Roachville, NB, E4G 2G7
(506) 432-4330
Emp Here 14   *Sales* 98,016,829
SIC 5143 Dairy products, except dried or canned
Paul Gaunce
Riant'jan Dykstra

D-U-N-S 24-473-4794   (HQ)
DAIRYTOWN PROCESSING LTD
49 Milk Board Rd, Roachville, NB, E4G 2G7
(506) 432-1950
Emp Here 49   *Sales* 30,420,720
SIC 2026 Fluid milk
Derek Roberts
Jim Ryan
Alex Henderson
James Walker
Pierre Laviolette
Vernon Black

D-U-N-S 20-812-9726   (HQ)
R & G TRANSPORT LTD
EAGLE TRANSPORTATION SYSTEMS, A DIV OF
(*Suby of* DAIRYTOWN PROCESSING LTD)
16 Milk Board Rd, Roachville, NB, E4G 2G8
(506) 432-9128
Sales 14,399,420
SIC 4213 Trucking, except local
Reginald Parlee

Rogersville, NB E4Y

D-U-N-S 20-022-1513   (SL)
COOPERATIVE DE ROGERSVILLE LIMITEE, LA
28 Boucher St, Rogersville, NB, E4Y 1X5
(506) 775-6131
Emp Here 36   *Sales* 11,626,884
SIC 5411 Grocery stores
Sylvain Thebeau
Fernand Gaudet
Paulette Maillet

D-U-N-S 24-187-4619   (SL)
FINNIGAN GREENHOUSE PRODUCE LTD
MR TOMATO
11021 Rue Principale, Rogersville, NB, E4Y 2L7
(506) 775-6042
Emp Here 20   *Sales* 10,702,480
SIC 5148 Fresh fruits and vegetables
Patrice Finnigan
Lise Finnigan

D-U-N-S 20-022-1505   (SL)
GALLANT, RAYMOND & SONS LTD
LE GALLANT RESTAURANT
11055 Rue Principale, Rogersville, NB, E4Y 2L8
(506) 775-2797
Emp Here 25   *Sales* 12,451,950
SIC 5531 Auto and home supply stores
Terry Gallant
Raymond Gallant

Rothesay, NB E2E

D-U-N-S 20-742-2924   (SL)

KENNEBECASIS DRUGS LTD
GUARDIAN DRUGS
1a Marr Rd, Rothesay, NB, E2E 3L4
(506) 847-7581
Emp Here 46   *Sales* 11,635,884
SIC 5912 Drug stores and proprietary stores
James Hutton
R Patrick Goguen
Ivan Ho

D-U-N-S 24-714-4525   (SL)
KENNEBECASIS VALLEY FIRE DEPT
7 Campbell Dr, Rothesay, NB, E2E 5B6
(506) 848-6601
Emp Here 40   *Sales* 17,968,760
SIC 7389 Business services, nec

D-U-N-S 24-205-1428   (SL)
R & L CONVENIENCE ENTERPRISES INC
ROUTE 1 BIGSTOP
1 Ellis Dr, Rothesay, NB, E2E 1A1
(506) 847-1603
Emp Here 75   *Sales* 22,010,775
SIC 5411 Grocery stores
Raymond Campbell
Louise Campbell

D-U-N-S 24-131-7874   (SL)
ROTHESAY COLLEGIATE SCHOOL, THE
ROTHESAY NETHERWOOD SCHOOL
40 College Hill Rd, Rothesay, NB, E2E 5H1
(506) 847-8224
Emp Here 75   *Sales* 6,961,950
SIC 8211 Elementary and secondary schools
Paul Mclellan

D-U-N-S 24-943-6015   (BR)
SOBEYS CAPITAL INCORPORATED
SOBEYS 495
(*Suby of* EMPIRE COMPANY LIMITED)
140a Hampton Rd, Rothesay, NB, E2E 2R1
(506) 847-5697
Emp Here 140
SIC 5411 Grocery stores
Don Gass

Sackville, NB E4L

D-U-N-S 25-298-8274   (SL)
3135772 CANADA INC
ENTERPRISES FAWCETT, DIV OF
73 Lorne St, Sackville, NB, E4L 4A2

Emp Here 45   *Sales* 10,504,575
SIC 3322 Malleable iron foundries
D Michael Wheaton

D-U-N-S 20-393-2959   (HQ)
ATLANTIC INDUSTRIES LIMITED
32 York St, Sackville, NB, E4L 4R4
(506) 364-4600
Emp Here 5   *Sales* 10,948,845
SIC 3499 Fabricated Metal products, nec
Mike Wilson

D-U-N-S 20-588-6406   (BR)
MONERIS SOLUTIONS CORPORATION
(*Suby of* MONERIS SOLUTIONS CORPORATION)
2 Charlotte St, Sackville, NB, E4L 3S8
(506) 364-1920
Emp Here 225
SIC 8231 Libraries

D-U-N-S 20-812-2614   (SL)
MOUNT ALLISON UNIVERSITY
65 York St, Sackville, NB, E4L 1E4
(506) 364-2269
Emp Here 1,435   *Sales* 214,376,085
SIC 8221 Colleges and universities
Robert M. Campbell
Robert Inglis

D-U-N-S 20-108-8932   (BR)
REGIONAL HEALTH AUTHORITY NB

SACKVILLE MEMORIAL HOSPITAL
(*Suby of* PROVINCE OF NEW BRUNSWICK)
8 Main St, Sackville, NB, E4L 4A3
(506) 364-4100
Emp Here 155
SIC 8062 General medical and surgical hospitals
Emily Doucette

D-U-N-S 24-532-3266   (SL)
UNITED CHURCH HOME FOR SENIOR CITIZENS INC, THE
DREW NURSING HOME
165 Main St, Sackville, NB, E4L 4S2
(506) 364-4900
Emp Here 180   *Sales* 12,298,680
SIC 8051 Skilled nursing care facilities
Deborah Sears
Ruth Flanagan
Linda Leroux

D-U-N-S 24-994-4166   (HQ)
WILSON WREATH CO LTD
11 Squire St, Sackville, NB, E4L 4K8

Emp Here 3   *Sales* 10,941,200
SIC 3999 Manufacturing industries, nec
Peter Hess
Tanya Hess

Saint John, NB E2H

D-U-N-S 25-381-2689   (SL)
059884 N.B. INC
BROOKVILLE MANUFACTURING COMPANY
1360 Rothesay Rd, Saint John, NB, E2H 2J1
(506) 633-1200
Emp Here 30   *Sales* 13,415,220
SIC 5032 Brick, stone, and related material

D-U-N-S 20-814-9575   (SL)
MITCHELL MCCONNELL INSURANCE LIMITED
FOREMOST UNDERWRITERS
660 Rothesay Ave Suite 344, Saint John, NB, E2H 2H4
(506) 634-7200
Emp Here 24   *Sales* 20,353,440
SIC 6411 Insurance agents, brokers, and service
Christopher Bourque

Saint John, NB E2J

D-U-N-S 20-956-1377   (SL)
011810 N.B. LIMITED
IRVING PAPER
(*Suby of* IRVING, J. D. LIMITED)
435 Bayside Dr, Saint John, NB, E2J 1B2
(506) 633-3333
Emp Here 310   *Sales* 113,967,470
SIC 2679 Converted paper products, nec
James K Irving
James D Irving
Robert K Irving

D-U-N-S 24-804-6070   (HQ)
045502 N. B. LTD
DOBSON CHRYSLER DODGE JEEP
312 Rothesay Ave, Saint John, NB, E2J 2B9
(506) 634-6060
Sales 22,413,510
SIC 5511 New and used car dealers
Daniel Dobson
Derek Dobson
Rose Dobson

D-U-N-S 25-684-8185   (HQ)
500323 (N.B.) LTD
EAST COAST MOVING & STORAGE

---

406 Grandview Ave, Saint John, NB, E2J 4N1
(506) 642-6683
Emp Here 15   *Sales* 12,342,360
SIC 4225 General warehousing and storage
Wayne Marshall

D-U-N-S 20-693-2787   (SL)
616813 N.B. LTD
ON THE VINE MEAT & PRODUCE
1350 Hickey Rd, Saint John, NB, E2J 5C9
(506) 657-8463
Emp Here 59   *Sales* 17,315,143
SIC 5411 Grocery stores
Mandy Fillmore

D-U-N-S 25-257-2813   (SL)
ADRA SALES INC
CANADIAN TIRE ASSOCIATES STORE 254
400 Westmorland Rd Suite 254, Saint John, NB, E2J 2G4
(506) 634-2606
Emp Here 100   *Sales* 36,421,500
SIC 5014 Tires and tubes
Adam Pustowka

D-U-N-S 25-077-8276   (SL)
ATLANTIC WALLBOARD LIMITED PARTNERSHIP
IRVING WALLBOARD
30 Jervis Lane, Saint John, NB, E2J 0A9
(506) 633-3311
Emp Here 95   *Sales* 173,827,770
SIC 4924 Natural gas distribution
Jenna Hazeleon

D-U-N-S 24-912-9800   (BR)
ATLANTIC WHOLESALERS LTD
ATLANTIC SUPERSTORE, THE
(*Suby of* LOBLAW COMPANIES LIMITED)
168 Rothesay Ave, Saint John, NB, E2J 2B5
(506) 648-1320
Emp Here 130
SIC 5411 Grocery stores
Dave Parker

D-U-N-S 24-359-2032   (SL)
BAYSIDE POWER L.P.
(*Suby of* EMERA INCORPORATED)
509 Bayside Dr, Saint John, NB, E2J 1B4
(506) 694-1400
Emp Here 25   *Sales* 15,665,350
SIC 4911 Electric services
Steven Sairther

D-U-N-S 20-618-4954   (HQ)
BAYVIEW TRUCKS & EQUIPMENT LTD
NAGLE LEASING & RENTALS
315 Mcallister Dr, Saint John, NB, E2J 2S8
(800) 561-9911
Emp Here 43   *Sales* 72,367,200
SIC 5511 New and used car dealers
Michael Nagle Jr
Jane Nagle
Lisa Mclaughlin

D-U-N-S 24-533-5625   (SL)
BLT FOODS LTD
DAIRY QUEEN BRAZIER
499 Rothesay Ave, Saint John, NB, E2J 2C6
(506) 633-1098
Emp Here 125   *Sales* 5,689,875
SIC 5812 Eating places
Robert Dewar
Timothy Dewar
Lester Dewar

D-U-N-S 24-339-7858   (SL)
BRETT CHEVROLET CADILLAC
183 Rothesay Ave, Saint John, NB, E2J 2B4
(506) 634-5555
Emp Here 80   *Sales* 50,342,400
SIC 5511 New and used car dealers
Ian Brett
Glen Gibbons

D-U-N-S 20-813-3611   (HQ)
CAA ATLANTIC LIMITED
378 Westmorland Rd, Saint John, NB, E2J

2G4
(506) 634-1400
Emp Here 20   *Sales* 39,006,660
SIC 8699 Membership organizations, nec
Steve Mccall

D-U-N-S 24-341-4547   (SL)
CENTENNIAL PONTIAC BUICK GMC LTD
160 Rothesay Ave, Saint John, NB, E2J 2B5
(506) 634-2020
Emp Here 62   *Sales* 39,015,360
SIC 5511 New and used car dealers
Stephen C Downey
Robert M Downey

D-U-N-S 20-022-5605   (HQ)
CLEAR VIEW HOME FURNISHINGS LTD
LEON'S FURNITURE
428 Rothesay Ave, Saint John, NB, E2J 2C4
(506) 634-1966
Sales 13,479,374
SIC 5712 Furniture stores
Robert Northrup

D-U-N-S 20-198-3835   (SL)
COVE VIEW PHARMACY INC
SHOPPERS DRUG MART
407 Westmorland Rd Suite 194, Saint John,
NB, E2J 3S9
(506) 636-7777
Emp Here 40   *Sales* 10,118,160
SIC 5912 Drug stores and proprietary stores
Greg Mcintyre

D-U-N-S 20-022-5852   (SL)
CROSBY MOLASSES COMPANY LIMITED
327 Rothesay Ave, Saint John, NB, E2J 2C3
(506) 634-7515
Emp Here 60   *Sales* 50,134,620
SIC 5149 Groceries and related products, nec
James Crosby

D-U-N-S 24-736-9882   (HQ)
**DISTINCTIVE AUTOBODY & COLLISON
CENTER LTD**
LOCH LOMOND MITSUBISHI
1265 Loch Lomond Rd, Saint John, NB, E2J
3V4
(506) 634-1765
Sales 11,455,794
SIC 5511 New and used car dealers
Randy Defazio

D-U-N-S 24-369-2196   (HQ)
DOWNEY FORD SALES LTD
DOWNEY'S SALES & SERVICE DIV OF
35 Consumers Dr, Saint John, NB, E2J 4Z7
(506) 632-6519
Emp Here 4   *Sales* 10,459,638
SIC 5511 New and used car dealers
Stephen Downey

D-U-N-S 20-022-6975   (SL)
FLOOD, JOHN & SONS (1961) LIMITED
32 Frederick St, Saint John, NB, E2J 2A9
(506) 634-1112
Emp Here 30   *Sales* 14,121,930
SIC 1542 Nonresidential construction, nec
Roderick Flood

D-U-N-S 20-933-2386   (SL)
FUNDY MOTORS (1995) LTD
FUNDY HONDA
160 Rothesay Ave, Saint John, NB, E2J 2B5
(506) 633-1333
Emp Here 56   *Sales* 35,239,680
SIC 5511 New and used car dealers
Ian Bret
Paul Mifsud
Julie Kingston

D-U-N-S 24-605-3110   (SL)
GULF OPERATORS LTD
(*Suby of* IRVING, J. D. LIMITED)
633 Bayside Dr, Saint John, NB, E2J 1B4
(506) 633-0116
Emp Here 150   *Sales* 49,217,250
SIC 1629 Heavy construction, nec

James D Irving

D-U-N-S 24-101-5176   (BR)
HOME DEPOT OF CANADA INC
HOME DEPOT
(*Suby of* THE HOME DEPOT INC)
55 Lcd Crt, Saint John, NB, E2J 5E5
(506) 632-9440
Emp Here 100
SIC 5251 Hardware stores
Jay Romhild

D-U-N-S 20-812-4263   (SL)
INDUSTRIAL SECURITY LIMITED
(*Suby of* IRVING, J. D. LIMITED)
635 Bayside Dr, Saint John, NB, E2J 1B4
(506) 648-3060
Emp Here 25   *Sales* 3,150,000
SIC 7381 Detective and armored car services
James K Irving

D-U-N-S 20-136-4127   (BR)
IRVING, J. D. LIMITED
CHANDLER SALES
(*Suby of* IRVING, J. D. LIMITED)
225 Thorne Ave, Saint John, NB, E2J 1W8
(506) 658-8000
Emp Here 97
SIC 5021 Furniture
Jeannot Richard

D-U-N-S 25-994-5033   (SL)
J A T INVESTMENTS INC
LITTLE CAESARS
535 Westmorland Rd Suite 3, Saint John, NB,
E2J 3T3
(506) 649-2002
Emp Here 25   *Sales* 16,411,600
SIC 5963 Direct selling establishments
Jin Charters

D-U-N-S 24-342-0080   (HQ)
KING MAZDA INC
440 Rothesay Ave, Saint John, NB, E2J 2C4
(506) 634-8370
Sales 18,878,400
SIC 5511 New and used car dealers
Troy Northrup

D-U-N-S 20-742-0688   (SL)
LOCH LOMOND VILLA INC
185 Loch Lomond Rd, Saint John, NB, E2J
3S3
(506) 643-7175
Emp Here 350   *Sales* 23,914,100
SIC 8051 Skilled nursing care facilities
Gordon Burnett
Cindy Donovan

D-U-N-S 20-617-5010   (HQ)
MARITIME SOD LTD
MILLSTREAM NURSERY
1101 Bayside Dr, Saint John, NB, E2J 4Y2
(506) 634-8540
Emp Here 45   *Sales* 20,984,720
SIC 0181 Ornamental nursery products
Robert Arseneau
William Arseneau

D-U-N-S 20-158-9113   (SL)
NORBULK SHIPPING NB LTD
120 Mcdonald St Unit 135, Saint John, NB,
E2J 1M5
(506) 657-7555
Emp Here 49   *Sales* 11,698,750
SIC 8611 Business associations
Neil Graham

D-U-N-S 24-369-2451   (HQ)
PETRO SERVICE LIMITED
(*Suby of* SKYLINE HOLDINGS INCORPO-
RATED)
11 Mcilveen Dr, Saint John, NB, E2J 4Y6
(506) 632-1000
Sales 28,976,586
SIC 5085 Industrial supplies
John Irving

D-U-N-S 20-377-3309   (SL)
PORT CITY WATER PARTNERS
380 Bayside Dr Suite 101, Saint John, NB,
E2J 4Y8
(506) 645-9070
Emp Here 30   *Sales* 57,977,298
SIC 1629 Heavy construction, nec
Andrew Reid

D-U-N-S 20-918-6795   (SL)
RST INDUSTRIES LIMITED
(*Suby of* IRVING, J. D. LIMITED)
485 Mcallister Dr, Saint John, NB, E2J 2S8
(506) 634-8800
Emp Here 100   *Sales* 20,570,600
SIC 4213 Trucking, except local
Scott Gillis

D-U-N-S 20-022-5555   (SL)
SAINT JOHN TRANSIT COMMISSION
(*Suby of* SAINT JOHN, CITY OF)
55 Mcdonald St, Saint John, NB, E2J 0C7
(506) 658-4710
Emp Here 90   *Sales* 6,774,480
SIC 4111 Local and suburban transit
Frank Mccarey
Christopher Titus

D-U-N-S 24-243-9409   (SL)
SAINT JOHN VOLKSWAGEN
297 Rothesay Ave, Saint John, NB, E2J 2C1
(506) 658-1313
Emp Here 28   *Sales* 13,946,184
SIC 5511 New and used car dealers
Jonathan Kennedy

D-U-N-S 20-617-4666   (HQ)
SANCTON GROUP INC
SANCTON EQUIPMENT
85 Mcilveen Dr, Saint John, NB, E2J 4Y6
(506) 635-8500
Emp Here 12   *Sales* 12,825,702
SIC 5084 Industrial machinery and equipment
Clark Sancton
Thomas Sancton
Jeff Martin

D-U-N-S 25-242-1201   (BR)
SCHOOL DISTRICT 8
SIMONDS HIGH SCHOOL
1490 Hickey Rd, Saint John, NB, E2J 4E7
(506) 658-5367
Emp Here 80   *Sales* 396,535
SIC 8211 Elementary and secondary schools
Gary Keating

D-U-N-S 24-187-8834   (BR)
SOBEYS CAPITAL INCORPORATED
SOBEYS #692
(*Suby of* EMPIRE COMPANY LIMITED)
519 Westmorland Rd, Saint John, NB, E2J
3W9
(506) 633-1187
Emp Here 200
SIC 5411 Grocery stores
Paul Barter

D-U-N-S 25-664-7363   (HQ)
SPRINGER INVESTMENTS LTD
TIM HORTONS
97 Loch Lomond Rd, Saint John, NB, E2J 1X6
(506) 847-9168
Emp Here 25   *Sales* 35,217,240
SIC 5461 Retail bakeries
Gary Springer

D-U-N-S 20-548-7739   (HQ)
SUNBURY TRANSPORT LIMITED
(*Suby of* IRVING, J. D. LIMITED)
485 Mcallister Dr, Saint John, NB, E2J 2S8
(800) 786-2878
Emp Here 80   *Sales* 24,684,720
SIC 4213 Trucking, except local
James Irving
Wayne Power
Neil Hossack

D-U-N-S 24-130-3916   (HQ)

TECHNICO INC
(*Suby of* APPLUS SERVICES SA.)
299 Mcilveen Dr, Saint John, NB, E2J 4Y6
(506) 633-1300
Sales 48,161,376
SIC 7389 Business services, nec
Paul Galloway

D-U-N-S 25-294-8468   (BR)
WAL-MART CANADA CORP
(*Suby of* WALMART INC.)
450 Westmorland Rd Suite 3091, Saint John,
NB, E2J 4Z2
(506) 634-6600
Emp Here 250
SIC 5311 Department stores
Kevin Cantwell

Saint John, NB E2K

D-U-N-S 20-742-9127   (HQ)
501420 NB INC
ROYAL LEPAGE ATLANTIC
71 Paradise Row, Saint John, NB, E2K 3H6
(506) 644-8095
Emp Here 31   *Sales* 101,419,200
SIC 6531 Real estate agents and managers
Carl Sherwood
Ralph Stephen

D-U-N-S 20-175-6280   (BR)
AIR CANADA
(*Suby of* AIR CANADA)
1 Air Canada Way, Saint John, NB, E2K 0B1

Emp Here 250
SIC 7389 Business services, nec
Mario Di Rienzo

D-U-N-S 25-680-1247   (HQ)
**ANGLOPHONE SOUTH SCHOOL DISTRICT
(ASD-S)**
490 Woodward Ave, Saint John, NB, E2K 5N3
(506) 658-5300
Emp Here 120   *Sales* 109,030,900
SIC 8211 Elementary and secondary schools
Zoe Watson
John Macdonald

D-U-N-S 24-574-2234   (HQ)
APOLLO MEDICAL LTD
MEDICHAIR
379 Somerset St, Saint John, NB, E2K 2Y5
(506) 693-3330
Emp Here 9   *Sales* 12,073,698
SIC 5047 Medical and hospital equipment
James Mclaughlin
Lynne Mclaughlin
Bob Mclaughlin

D-U-N-S 25-985-8983   (BR)
ATLANTIC WHOLESALERS LTD
MILLEDGEVILLE SUPERSTORE
(*Suby of* LOBLAW COMPANIES LIMITED)
650 Somerset St, Saint John, NB, E2K 2Y7
(506) 658-6054
Emp Here 120
SIC 5411 Grocery stores
Lionel Duguay

D-U-N-S 20-311-3423   (BR)
BAYSHORE HEALTHCARE LTD.
BAYSHORE HEALTHCARE LTD
(*Suby of* BAYSHORE HEALTHCARE LTD.)
600 Main St Suite C150, Saint John, NB, E2K
1J5
(506) 633-9588
Emp Here 140
SIC 8082 Home health care services
Tina Learmouth

D-U-N-S 24-316-6647   (HQ)
**BELL ALIANT REGIONAL COMMUNICA-
TIONS INC**
BELL CANADA

(Suby of BCE INC)
1 Brunswick Pl Suite 1800, Saint John, NB, E2K 1B5
(800) 665-6000
Emp Here 100   Sales 2,509,080,000
SIC 4899 Communication services, nec
Karen H. Sheriff
Edward Reevey
Robert Dexter
George Cope
Siim Vanaselja
Martine Turcotte
Louis Tanguay
David Wells

D-U-N-S 20-606-0241   (SL)
CHATEAU DE CHAMPLAIN
300 Boars Head Rd Suite 119, Saint John, NB, E2K 5C2
(506) 633-1195
Emp Here 24   Sales 20,353,440
SIC 6411 Insurance agents, brokers, and service
Tom Smith

D-U-N-S 20-608-4399   (SL)
CHURCH OF ST. JOHN & ST. STEPHEN HOME INC, THE
130 University Ave, Saint John, NB, E2K 4K3
(506) 643-6001
Emp Here 120   Sales 8,227,920
SIC 8051 Skilled nursing care facilities
Claire Driscoll
Shelle Wilkins

D-U-N-S 20-022-8328   (HQ)
COAST TIRE & AUTO SERVICE LTD
130 Somerset St Suite 150, Saint John, NB, E2K 2X4
(506) 674-9620
Emp Here 30   Sales 173,175,600
SIC 5531 Auto and home supply stores
Ronald Outerbridge
Jack Jacobs
Peter Coleman
John Correia
Robin Hunter
Michael Cosentino
Arch Cook
Gerald Mcmackin
James Coulter

D-U-N-S 20-549-1673   (BR)
IBM CANADA LIMITED
(Suby of INTERNATIONAL BUSINESS MACHINES CORPORATION)
400 Main St Suite 1000, Saint John, NB, E2K 4N5
(506) 646-4000
Emp Here 100
SIC 7389 Business services, nec
Vivian Sailsman

D-U-N-S 25-373-2853   (HQ)
ICT CANADA MARKETING INC
(Suby of SYKES ENTERPRISES INCORPORATED)
400 Main St Suite 2004, Saint John, NB, E2K 4N5
(506) 653-9050
Emp Here 2   Sales 2,541,850,400
SIC 7389 Business services, nec
Robert Foley
Ruth-Anne Foley
Gerry Doiron

D-U-N-S 20-311-4780   (SL)
INMAR PROMOTIONS - CANADA INC.
MILLENNIUM1 PROMOTIONAL SERVICES
(Suby of ABRY PARTNERS, INC.)
661 Millidge Ave, Saint John, NB, E2K 2N7
(506) 632-1400
Emp Here 150   Sales 100,336,200
SIC 7389 Business services, nec
Don Moffatt
Tom Band
Jennie Bradley

Michael Morrison

D-U-N-S 24-342-9792   (SL)
KENNEBEC MANOR INC
475 Woodward Ave, Saint John, NB, E2K 4N1
(506) 632-9628
Emp Here 97   Sales 6,650,902
SIC 8051 Skilled nursing care facilities
Ken Corkum
Judy Lane

D-U-N-S 25-483-2561   (BR)
MAC'S FOODS LTD
DELUXE FRENCH FRIES
(Suby of MAC'S FOODS LTD)
5 Wellesley Ave, Saint John, NB, E2K 2V1
(506) 642-2424
Emp Here 100
SIC 5812 Eating places
Irene Connlley

D-U-N-S 20-027-3518   (SL)
MARITIME RESCUE & MEDICAL ACADEMY INC
7 Foster Thurston Dr, Saint John, NB, E2K 5J4
(506) 672-3389
Emp Here 49   Sales 20,805,743
SIC 8999 Services, nec
Scott O Brain

D-U-N-S 20-022-9219   (SL)
MARQUE CONSTRUCTION LIMITED
400 Chesley Dr, Saint John, NB, E2K 5L6
(506) 634-1144
Emp Here 100   Sales 27,433,200
SIC 8741 Management services
Hans Klohn
John E Irving
Arthur L Irving Sr.

D-U-N-S 20-122-8066   (SL)
MAXIM 2000 INC
555 Somerset St Unit 208, Saint John, NB, E2K 4X2
(506) 652-9292
Emp Here 45   Sales 21,182,895
SIC 1542 Nonresidential construction, nec
Louis Tiller
Pat Hanlon

D-U-N-S 24-913-0568   (HQ)
MAXIM CONSTRUCTION INC
555 Somerset St Unit 208, Saint John, NB, E2K 4X2
(506) 652-9292
Emp Here 20   Sales 28,516,900
SIC 1542 Nonresidential construction, nec
Pat Hanlon
Lewis Tiller

D-U-N-S 20-299-1084   (HQ)
MCPORT CITY FOOD SERVICES LIMITED
MACDONALDS RESTAURANTS
399 Main St, Saint John, NB, E2K 1J3
(506) 657-4381
Emp Here 25   Sales 40,552,200
SIC 8741 Management services
Mike Shulze

D-U-N-S 25-672-7793   (SL)
NIGHT SHIFT ANSWERING SERVICE LTD, THE
DIRECTOR'S CHOICE
600 Main St Suite 201, Saint John, NB, E2K 1J5
(506) 637-7010
Emp Here 70   Sales 31,445,330
SIC 7389 Business services, nec
Gary Darychuk
Mary Stewart

D-U-N-S 20-023-0175   (HQ)
OCEAN STEEL & CONSTRUCTION LTD
OSCO
400 Chesley Dr, Saint John, NB, E2K 5L6
(506) 632-2600
Emp Here 60   Sales 38,417,000
SIC 3441 Fabricated structural Metal

Hans O. Klohn
John F. Irving

D-U-N-S 25-242-1474   (BR)
SCHOOL DISTRICT 8
HARBOUR VIEW HIGH SCHOOL
305 Douglas Ave, Saint John, NB, E2K 1E5
(506) 658-5359
Emp Here 80   Sales 396,535
SIC 8211 Elementary and secondary schools
David Morgan

D-U-N-S 25-359-7058   (BR)
SEABOARD LIQUID CARRIERS LIMITED
SEABOARD TRANSPORT GROUP
(Suby of SEABOARD LIQUID CARRIERS LIMITED)
120 Ashburn Rd, Saint John, NB, E2K 5J5
(506) 652-7070
Emp Here 110
SIC 4213 Trucking, except local
Gordon Mcintyre

D-U-N-S 24-380-6762   (HQ)
SKYLINE HOLDINGS INCORPORATED
331 Chesley Dr, Saint John, NB, E2K 5P2

Sales 146,319,000
SIC 5085 Industrial supplies
John K.F. Irving

D-U-N-S 24-187-8891   (BR)
SOBEYS CAPITAL INCORPORATED
(Suby of EMPIRE COMPANY LIMITED)
149 Lansdowne Ave Suite 233, Saint John, NB, E2K 2Z9
(506) 652-4470
Emp Here 120
SIC 5411 Grocery stores
Tim Barton

D-U-N-S 20-279-1984   (BR)
SOURCE ATLANTIC LIMITED
THORNES
(Suby of SKYLINE HOLDINGS INCORPORATED)
331 Chesley Dr, Saint John, NB, E2K 5P2
(506) 632-1000
Emp Here 106
SIC 5084 Industrial machinery and equipment

D-U-N-S 20-605-8906   (HQ)
SOURCE ATLANTIC LIMITED
INDUSTRIAL SUPPLIES
(Suby of SKYLINE HOLDINGS INCORPORATED)
331 Chesley Dr, Saint John, NB, E2K 5P2
(506) 635-7711
Emp Here 100   Sales 146,319,000
SIC 5084 Industrial machinery and equipment
John K. F. Irving
Steve Drummond

D-U-N-S 20-023-1694   (HQ)
STRESCON LIMITED
400 Chesley Dr Suite 3, Saint John, NB, E2K 5L6
(506) 633-8877
Emp Here 50   Sales 35,843,800
SIC 3272 Concrete products, nec
Hans O. Klohn
Hans W. Klohn Sr
John K Irving
Donald Isnor

D-U-N-S 20-023-1371   (HQ)
T. S. SIMMS & CO. LIMITED
SIMMS
560 Main St Suite 320, Saint John, NB, E2K 1J5
(506) 635-6330
Emp Here 1   Sales 29,352,240
SIC 3991 Brooms and brushes
Thomas Simms
Phillip Jones

D-U-N-S 24-790-4659   (HQ)
YMCA OF GREATER SAINT JOHN INC, THE

191 Churchill Blvd, Saint John, NB, E2K 3E2
(506) 693-9622
Emp Here 1   Sales 17,079,900
SIC 7999 Amusement and recreation, nec
Shelley Reinhart
Shailo Boucher
Marie Rackley

Saint John, NB E2L

D-U-N-S 24-122-0693   (HQ)
ALL SEA ATLANTIC LTD
ALL-SEA UNDERWATER SOLUTIONS
9 Lower Cove Loop, Saint John, NB, E2L 1W7
(506) 632-3483
Emp Here 1   Sales 44,921,900
SIC 7389 Business services, nec
Kent Grass

D-U-N-S 20-933-2428   (HQ)
ANDERSON-MCTAGUE & ASSOCIATES LTD
(Suby of HELLMAN & FRIEDMAN LLC)
154 Prince William St, Saint John, NB, E2L 2B6
(506) 632-5020
Emp Here 1   Sales 33,922,400
SIC 6411 Insurance agents, brokers, and service
Charles Mctague
Charles A Mctague
Christopher J Mctague

D-U-N-S 20-609-0420   (SL)
ANDERSON-MCTAGUE INSURANCE AGENCY
158 Prince William St, Saint John, NB, E2L 2B6
(506) 632-5000
Emp Here 35   Sales 29,682,100
SIC 6411 Insurance agents, brokers, and service
Charles Mctague

D-U-N-S 20-743-2824   (SL)
ANGUS-MILLER LTD
40 Wellington Row, Saint John, NB, E2L 3H3
(506) 633-7000
Emp Here 30   Sales 17,397,720
SIC 6411 Insurance agents, brokers, and service
Grant Kimball

D-U-N-S 20-548-7424   (HQ)
ATLANTIC TOWING LIMITED
(Suby of IRVING, J. D. LIMITED)
300 Union St Suite 2, Saint John, NB, E2L 4Z2
(506) 648-2750
Sales 78,744,800
SIC 4492 Towing and tugboat service
James Irving
Arthur L Irving
John Irving

D-U-N-S 20-073-8974   (BR)
BELL ALIANT REGIONAL COMMUNICATIONS INC
(Suby of BCE INC)
Gd, Saint John, NB, E2L 4K2
(506) 658-7169
Emp Here 800
SIC 4899 Communication services, nec
Erick Poiriei

D-U-N-S 20-549-5708   (SL)
BRAXCO LIMITED
SCOTSBURN DAIRY GROUP
130 Station St, Saint John, NB, E2L 3H6
(506) 633-9040
Emp Here 50   Sales 13,707,600
SIC 5411 Grocery stores
Earle Branscombe
Mel Macconnell

D-U-N-S 20-509-8796   (BR)

CANADA REVENUE AGENCY
CANADA REVENUE AGENCY SAINT JOHN PSO
(*Suby of* GOVERNMENT OF CANADA)
126 Prince William St, Saint John, NB, E2L 2B6
(506) 636-4623
Emp Here 300
SIC 8721 Accounting, auditing, and bookkeeping
Kerry-Lynne D Findlay

D-U-N-S 20-382-2325 (SL)
CARNAGHAN THORNE INSURANCE GROUP INC.
10 Crown St, Saint John, NB, E2L 2X5
(506) 634-1177
Emp Here 19 *Sales* 13,783,341
SIC 6311 Life insurance
Myles Hall

D-U-N-S 20-549-5047 (HQ)
COASTAL TRANSPORT LIMITED
22 Germain St Suite 104, Saint John, NB, E2L 2E5
(506) 642-0520
Emp Here 8 *Sales* 13,477,450
SIC 4482 Ferries
Murray Ryder

D-U-N-S 20-181-5268 (SL)
DEBLY ENTERPRISES LIMITED
170 Ashburn Rd, Saint John, NB, E2L 3T5
(506) 696-2936
Emp Here 160 *Sales* 40,390,720
SIC 1611 Highway and street construction
Majid R. Debly
Kimberly Debly

D-U-N-S 24-187-0955 (BR)
DELTA HOTELS LIMITED
(*Suby of* GOVERNMENT OF THE PROVINCE OF BRITISH COLUMBIA)
39 King St, Saint John, NB, E2L 4W3
(506) 648-1981
Emp Here 175
SIC 8741 Management services
Paulette Hicks

D-U-N-S 24-382-9004 (SL)
EMERA BRUNSWICK PIPELINE COMPANY LTD
BRUNSWICK PIPELINE
(*Suby of* EMERA INCORPORATED)
1 Germain St Suite 1102, Saint John, NB, E2L 4V1
(506) 693-4214
Emp Here 8 *Sales* 24,846,856
SIC 4922 Natural gas transmission
Ed Kacer
John Macisaan

D-U-N-S 25-355-8274 (HQ)
GENESYS LABORATORIES CANADA INC
(*Suby of* PERMIRA ADVISERS LLP)
50 Smythe St Suite 2000, Saint John, NB, E2L 0B8
(506) 637-3900
Sales 14,541,868
SIC 7372 Prepackaged software
Chris Magee
Warren O'donnell

D-U-N-S 24-738-8564 (HQ)
GLOBAL CONVENTION SERVICES LTD
48 Broad St, Saint John, NB, E2L 1Y5
(506) 658-0506
Emp Here 17 *Sales* 22,174,500
SIC 7389 Business services, nec
Mark Howes
Christopher Howes

D-U-N-S 20-022-8153 (HQ)
GRAND FOREST HOLDINGS INCORPORATED
(*Suby of* IRVING, J. D. LIMITED)
300 Union St, Saint John, NB, E2L 4Z2

(506) 635-6666
Emp Here 15 *Sales* 1,838,185,000
SIC 2611 Pulp mills
James Kenneth Irving
Arthur L Irving
John E Irving
James D Irving
David Jamieson
William C Maclean
Robert K Irving
John F Irving
Kenneth C Irving
Arthur L Irving Jr

D-U-N-S 20-317-0360 (HQ)
GREENERGY FUELS CANADA INC
(*Suby of* BCP IV UK FUEL HOLDINGS II LIMITED)
107 Germain St Suite 300, Saint John, NB, E2L 2E9
(506) 632-1650
Sales 13,936,200
SIC 6799 Investors, nec
Andrew Owens
Paul Bateson
Kirby Tremblay
Michael Healey
Adam Traeger

D-U-N-S 20-022-7742 (SL)
HAYWARD & WARWICK LIMITED
TACKLES
85 Princess St, Saint John, NB, E2L 1K5
(506) 653-9066
Emp Here 35 *Sales* 17,809,960
SIC 5023 Homefurnishings
Mark Hayward
David Hayward
Royden Mckillop

D-U-N-S 24-372-8701 (SL)
HIGHLANDS BLENDING & PACKAGING G.P.
COASTAL BLENDING & PACKAGING
555 Courtenay Causeway, Saint John, NB, E2L 4E6
(506) 632-7000
Emp Here 69 *Sales* 18,647,664
SIC 2992 Lubricating oils and greases
Kevin Boyle

D-U-N-S 24-374-0631 (HQ)
HIGHLANDS FUEL DELIVERY G.P.
IRVING ENERGY DISTRIBUTION & MARKETING
201 Crown St, Saint John, NB, E2L 5E5
(506) 202-2000
Emp Here 150 *Sales* 921,563,200
SIC 4924 Natural gas distribution
Darren Gillis
Jim Sepanski

D-U-N-S 20-269-9435 (BR)
HIGHLANDS FUEL DELIVERY G.P.
IRVING OIL
(*Suby of* HIGHLANDS FUEL DELIVERY G.P.)
10 Sydney St, Saint John, NB, E2L 5E6
(506) 202-2000
Emp Here 300
SIC 4924 Natural gas distribution
Jonathan Mckenzie

D-U-N-S 25-412-4332 (BR)
HILTON CANADA CO.
HILTON
(*Suby of* HILTON WORLDWIDE HOLDING LLP)
1 Market Sq, Saint John, NB, E2L 4Z6
(506) 693-8484
Emp Here 120
SIC 7011 Hotels and motels
Tammy Leblanc

D-U-N-S 25-108-9181 (HQ)
INNOVATIA INC
1 Germain St, Saint John, NB, E2L 4V1
(506) 640-4000
Emp Here 250 *Sales* 125,637,030

SIC 8748 Business consulting, nec
Roxanne Fairweather
David Grebenc
John Gruyter
Robert Keefe

D-U-N-S 25-195-1935 (SL)
IRVING ENERGY SERVICES LIMITED
10 Sydney St, Saint John, NB, E2L 5E6
(506) 202-2000
Emp Here 30 *Sales* 93,175,710
SIC 4924 Natural gas distribution
Michael Wennberg

D-U-N-S 25-973-3350 (SL)
IRVING FOREST PRODUCTS LIMITED
300 Union St Suite 5777, Saint John, NB, E2L 4Z2
(506) 632-7777
Emp Here 400 *Sales* 227,851,200
SIC 5031 Lumber, plywood, and millwork
Karl Hansen
Arthur Irving

D-U-N-S 24-833-2413 (HQ)
IRVING FOREST SERVICES LIMITED
(*Suby of* IRVING, J. D. LIMITED)
300 Union St 11th Fl, Saint John, NB, E2L 4Z2
(506) 634-4242
Sales 11,714,400
SIC 8742 Management consulting services
James Kenneth Irving

D-U-N-S 24-374-0607 (HQ)
IRVING OIL COMMERCIAL G.P.
IOC
10 Sydney St, Saint John, NB, E2L 5E6
(506) 202-2000
Sales 23,111,300
SIC 4925 Gas production and/or distribution
Ian Whitcomb
Sarah Irving
Kevin Dumaresque
Kevin Scott
Darren Gillis
Jennifer Beach
John Laidlaw
Kelley Greer White
Jeff Matthews
Dale Cooper

D-U-N-S 20-742-4029 (HQ)
IRVING OIL LIMITED
IRVING ENERGY
10 Sydney St, Saint John, NB, E2L 5E6
(506) 202-2000
Emp Here 500 *Sales* 1,584,904,750
SIC 2911 Petroleum refining
Arthur L. Irving
Ian W. Whitcomb
Mark Sherman
Sarah J. Irving
John D. Laidlaw
John K.F. Irving
John M. Cassaday
Sarah E. Nash
Bruce G. Waterman
V. Maureen Kempston-Darkes

D-U-N-S 24-325-3452 (HQ)
IRVING PULP & PAPER, LIMITED
(*Suby of* IRVING, J. D. LIMITED)
300 Union St, Saint John, NB, E2L 4Z2
(506) 632-7777
Sales 123,158,395
SIC 2621 Paper mills
Robert Irving
Karl Hansen

D-U-N-S 20-022-8138 (HQ)
IRVING, J. D. LIMITED
KENT BUILDING SUPPLIES, DIV OF
300 Union St Suite 5, Saint John, NB, E2L 4Z2
(506) 632-7777
Emp Here 1,200 *Sales* 2,885,550,000
SIC 2421 Sawmills and planing mills, general

D-U-N-S 20-562-7628 (SL)
JARDINE BROOK HOLDINGS LIMITED
300 Union St, Saint John, NB, E2L 4Z2
(506) 632-5110
Emp Here 100 *Sales* 26,155,300
SIC 6712 Bank holding companies
Bruce Drost

D-U-N-S 20-692-9296 (SL)
MARINER PARTNERS INC
1 Germain St 18 Fl, Saint John, NB, E2L 4V1
(506) 642-9000
Emp Here 78 *Sales* 8,234,950
SIC 7371 Custom computer programming services
Curtis Howe
Mark Savoie
Robert Justason
Andrew Harrigan

D-U-N-S 20-354-4556 (SL)
MARITIME HOME IMPROVEMENT LIMITED
CENTRAL BUILDING SUPPLIES
300 Union St, Saint John, NB, E2L 4Z2
(506) 632-4100
Emp Here 400 *Sales* 112,420,000
SIC 5211 Lumber and other building materials
Maureen Hourihan

D-U-N-S 20-444-7692 (SL)
O'BRIEN ELECTRIC CO LTD
79 Marsh St, Saint John, NB, E2L 5R1

Emp Here 150 *Sales* 32,674,350
SIC 1731 Electrical work
Patrick O'brien
Eric Blanchard
Michael O'brien

D-U-N-S 20-376-7629 (SL)
ORION MANAGEMENT & CONSTRUCTION INC
479 Rothesay Ave, Saint John, NB, E2L 4G7
(506) 634-5717
Emp Here 50 *Sales* 23,809,148
SIC 1542 Nonresidential construction, nec
Troy Northrup

D-U-N-S 24-573-8661 (SL)
SAINT JOHN AQUATIC CENTRE COMMISSION
CANADA GAMES AQUATIC CENTRE
50 Union St, Saint John, NB, E2L 1A1
(506) 658-4715
Emp Here 200 *Sales* 18,990,600
SIC 7999 Amusement and recreation, nec
Karen Irwin

D-U-N-S 25-400-4690 (BR)
STEWART MCKELVEY STIRLING SCALES
(*Suby of* STEWART MCKELVEY STIRLING SCALES)
44 Chipman Hill Suite 1000, Saint John, NB, E2L 2A9
(506) 632-1970
Emp Here 80
SIC 8111 Legal services
Catherine Lahey

D-U-N-S 20-813-0146 (BR)
UNIVERSITY OF NEW BRUNSWICK
UNIVERSITY OF NEW BRUNSWICK SAINT JOHN
(*Suby of* UNIVERSITY OF NEW BRUNSWICK)
100 Tucker Park Rd, Saint John, NB, E2L 4L5
(506) 648-5500
Emp Here 300
SIC 8221 Colleges and universities
Tom Condon

D-U-N-S 24-670-2468 (SL)
WOODLAND IMPROVEMENTS CORP
300 Union St, Saint John, NB, E2L 4Z2
(506) 632-7777
Emp Here 90 *Sales* 14,027,670
SIC 2421 Sawmills and planing mills, general
J K Irving

D-U-N-S 25-095-5366   (HQ)
WORKPLACE HEALTH, SAFETY & COMPENSATION COMMISSION OF NEW BRUNSWICK
WHSCC
1 Portland St, Saint John, NB, E2L 3X9
(506) 632-2200
Emp Here 100   *Sales* 235,080,631
SIC 6331 Fire, marine, and casualty insurance
Douglas Stanley
Roberta Dugas
Conrad Pitre

D-U-N-S 20-297-2118   (HQ)
WYNDHAM WORLDWIDE CANADA INC
(*Suby of* WYNDHAM DESTINATIONS, INC.)
180 Crown St Suite 200, Saint John, NB, E2L 2X7
(506) 646-2700
Sales 274,166,400
SIC 4899 Communication services, nec
Susan Steeves
Henry R Silverman

Saint John, NB E2M

D-U-N-S 24-263-2776   (SL)
BROOKVILLE CARRIERS VAN LIMITED PARTNERSHIP
65 Alloy Dr, Saint John, NB, E2M 7S9
(506) 633-7555
Emp Here 154
SIC 4213 Trucking, except local

D-U-N-S 20-753-5191   (SL)
C E P LOCAL 30
1216 Sand Cove Rd Unit 15, Saint John, NB, E2M 5V8
(506) 635-5786
Emp Here 235   *Sales* 66,928,470
SIC 8631 Labor organizations
Eric Thorne

D-U-N-S 24-994-7797   (SL)
CARLETON KIRK LODGE NURSING HOME
2 Carleton Kirk Pl, Saint John, NB, E2M 5B8
(506) 643-7040
Emp Here 105   *Sales* 7,174,230
SIC 8051 Skilled nursing care facilities
Tim Stevens
Linda Morais

D-U-N-S 24-132-1199   (SL)
CENTRACARE
414 Bay St, Saint John, NB, E2M 7L4
(506) 649-2550
Emp Here 100   *Sales* 9,691,100
SIC 8063 Psychiatric hospitals
Bea Leblanc

D-U-N-S 24-338-5564   (SL)
CONSUMERS COMMUNITY CO-OP
RIVER ROAD CO-OP
3300 Westfield Rd, Saint John, NB, E2M 7A4

Emp Here 39   *Sales* 10,691,928
SIC 5411 Grocery stores
Phillip Duffley

D-U-N-S 20-295-1877   (HQ)
CUSTOM FABRICATORS & MACHINISTS LIMITED
(*Suby of* IRVING, J. D. LIMITED)
45 Gifford Rd, Saint John, NB, E2M 5K7
(506) 648-2226
Emp Here 1   *Sales* 44,400,200
SIC 3599 Industrial machinery, nec
James D. Irving
James K. Irving
Robert K. Irving

D-U-N-S 24-370-4454   (BR)
ENVIROSYSTEMS INCORPORATED
ATLANTIC INDUSTRIAL CLEANERS, DIV OF

(*Suby of* REVOLUTION ENVIRONMENTAL SOLUTIONS LP)
55 Stinson Dr, Saint John, NB, E2M 7E3
(506) 652-9178
Emp Here 100
SIC 7349 Building maintenance services, nec
Sean Macdonald

D-U-N-S 25-258-6813   (SL)
FAIRVILLE CONSTRUCTION LTD
12 Linton Rd, Saint John, NB, E2M 5V4
(506) 635-1573
Emp Here 50   *Sales* 14,176,200
SIC 1611 Highway and street construction
Brian Cunningham
Larry Dunlop
Paul Cole
Cindy Swetnam

D-U-N-S 20-814-0959   (BR)
FLEETWAY INC
(*Suby of* FLEETWAY INC)
45 Gifford Rd, Saint John, NB, E2M 5K7
(506) 635-7733
Emp Here 200
SIC 7363 Help supply services
Christine Risk

D-U-N-S 25-356-8638   (HQ)
HUESTIS INSURANCE & ASSOCIATES LTD
HUESTIS INSURANCE
11 Lloyd St, Saint John, NB, E2M 4N4
(506) 635-1515
Emp Here 11   *Sales* 110,864,520
SIC 6411 Insurance agents, brokers, and service
David Huestis

D-U-N-S 20-812-8173   (HQ)
HUESTIS INSURANCE GROUP
METRO INSURANCE SERVICES
11 Lloyd St, Saint John, NB, E2M 4N4
(506) 635-1515
Emp Here 10   *Sales* 1,181,779,896
SIC 6411 Insurance agents, brokers, and service
David Huestis

D-U-N-S 20-294-9939   (SL)
IRVING, J. D. LIMITED
(*Suby of* IRVING, J. D. LIMITED)
45 Gifford Rd, Saint John, NB, E2M 5K7
(506) 635-5555
Emp Here 150   *Sales* 49,972,200
SIC 7353 Heavy construction equipment rental
James D. Irving
James K. Irving
Robert K. Irving
M. Ross Langley
William Maclean

D-U-N-S 24-363-8439   (BR)
LAIDLAW CARRIERS VAN LP
BROOKVILLE CARRIERS VAN, DIV OF
(*Suby of* LAIDLAW CARRIERS VAN LP)
65 Alloy Dr, Saint John, NB, E2M 7S9
(506) 648-0499
Emp Here 75
SIC 4213 Trucking, except local
Susan Court

D-U-N-S 24-784-8182   (SL)
MA FEENER SALES LTD
885 Fairville Blvd, Saint John, NB, E2M 5T9
(506) 635-1711
Emp Here 49   *Sales* 24,816,298
SIC 5531 Auto and home supply stores
Mike Feener

D-U-N-S 20-022-9805   (HQ)
MOOSEHEAD BREWERIES LIMITED
HOP CITY BREWING CO
89 Main St W, Saint John, NB, E2M 3H2
(506) 635-7000
Emp Here 250   *Sales* 134,030,875
SIC 2082 Malt beverages

Bruce Mccubbin
Derek Oland
Andrew Oland
Patrick Oland
Jim Eagles
Matthew Johnston
Wayne Arsenult
Paul Mcgraw

D-U-N-S 25-355-4646   (HQ)
NEW BRUNSWICK SOUTHERN RAILWAY COMPANY LIMITED
NB SOUTHERN
11 Gifford Rd, Saint John, NB, E2M 4X8
(506) 632-6314
Emp Here 50   *Sales* 27,946,940
SIC 4011 Railroads, line-haul operating
James K Irving
Arthur L Irving

D-U-N-S 20-335-1072   (SL)
OLSENS MEAT & PRODUCE LTD
391 Lancaster Ave, Saint John, NB, E2M 2L3
(506) 657-0000
Emp Here 35   *Sales* 29,245,195
SIC 5147 Meats and meat products
Robert Olsen
Allen Olsen

D-U-N-S 20-813-9899   (SL)
POWER COMMISSION OF THE CITY OF SAINT JOHN
SAINT JOHN ENERGY
325 Simms St, Saint John, NB, E2M 3L6
(506) 658-5252
Emp Here 95   *Sales* 98,465,436
SIC 4911 Electric services
Eric Marr
Marta Kelly
Chris Titus
Bernard Desmond
Elizabeth Gormley

D-U-N-S 25-309-1128   (BR)
SOBEYS CAPITAL INCORPORATED
SOBEYS 576
(*Suby of* EMPIRE COMPANY LIMITED)
1 Plaza Ave, Saint John, NB, E2M 0C2
(506) 674-1460
Emp Here 125
SIC 5411 Grocery stores
Terry Ells

D-U-N-S 20-391-8305   (HQ)
TERRAEX HOLDINGS INC
1942 Manawagonish Rd, Saint John, NB, E2M 5H5
(506) 672-4422
Sales 10,462,120
SIC 6712 Bank holding companies
Michael Francis

D-U-N-S 24-129-4925   (SL)
WEST SIDE PHARMACY INC
SHOPPERS DRUG MART
667 Fairville Blvd, Saint John, NB, E2M 3W2
(506) 636-7740
Emp Here 50   *Sales* 12,647,700
SIC 5912 Drug stores and proprietary stores
Julie Humphrey
Lisa Zwicker

D-U-N-S 20-108-9534   (BR)
WORKPLACE HEALTH, SAFETY & COMPENSATION COMMISSION OF NEW BRUNSWICK
WORKERS REHABILITATION CENTER
(*Suby of* WORKPLACE HEALTH, SAFETY & COMPENSATION COMMISSION OF NEW BRUNSWICK)
3700 Westfield Rd, Saint John, NB, E2M 5Z4
(506) 738-8411
Emp Here 100
SIC 8011 Offices and clinics of medical doctors
Douglas Stanley

Saint John, NB E2R

D-U-N-S 20-022-4830   (SL)
BOURQUE INDUSTRIAL LTD
85 Industrial Dr, Saint John, NB, E2R 1A4
(506) 633-7740
Emp Here 85   *Sales* 8,566,479
SIC 3499 Fabricated Metal products, nec
John Bourque

D-U-N-S 24-534-3637   (HQ)
GARDNER ELECTRIC LTD
875 Bayside Dr, Saint John, NB, E2R 1A3
(506) 634-3918
Emp Here 70   *Sales* 35,506,127
SIC 1731 Electrical work
Wendell Jones
Jeffrey Gardner

Saint-Andre, NB E3Y

D-U-N-S 20-531-7659   (SL)
RIOUX, GILBERT M & FILS LTEE
GM RIOUX
855 Route 108, Saint-Andre, NB, E3Y 4A5
(506) 473-1764
Emp Here 40   *Sales* 15,414,400
SIC 4731 Freight transportation arrangement
Rejean Rioux

Saint-Antoine, NB E4V

D-U-N-S 24-573-7218   (SL)
SOCIETE D'HABITATION DE ST-ANTOINE INC
FOYER SAINT-ANTOINE
7 De L'Eglise Ave, Saint-Antoine, NB, E4V 1L6
(506) 525-4040
Emp Here 46   *Sales* 12,619,272
SIC 8741 Management services
Marcel Henri
Gilles Ouellette
Bernice Leger

Saint-Antoine Sud, NB E4V

D-U-N-S 20-932-0340   (HQ)
RENAUD FURNITURE LTD
4327 Route 115, Saint-Antoine Sud, NB, E4V 2Z4
(506) 525-2493
Emp Here 3   *Sales* 15,265,680
SIC 5021 Furniture
Andrea Leblanc

Saint-Francois-De-Madawaska, NB E7A

D-U-N-S 24-187-7299   (SL)
DISTRIBUTION WESTCO INC
9 Rue Westco, Saint-Francois-De-Madawaska, NB, E7A 1A5
(506) 992-3112
Emp Here 15   *Sales* 11,137,800
SIC 5191 Farm supplies
Rodrigue Nadeau
Alban Boulay
Bertin Cyr
Yvon Cyr
Albert Bouchard
Rino Lavasseur

D-U-N-S 20-009-5904   (SL)
GROUPE WESTCO INC

9 Rue Westco, Saint-Francois-De-Madawaska, NB, E7A 1A5
(506) 992-3112
Emp Here 100 *Sales* 29,347,700
SIC 5499 Miscellaneous food stores
Bertin Cyr
Rino Levasseur
Albert Bouchard
Rodrigue Nadeau
Yvon Cyr
Tom Soucy

D-U-N-S 25-065-8341 (BR)
MAPLE LODGE FARMS LTD
NADEAU FERME AVICOLE
(*Suby of* MAPLE LODGE HOLDING CORPORATION)
2222 Commerciale St, Saint-Francois-De-Madawaska, NB, E7A 1B6
(506) 992-2192
Emp Here 300
SIC 2015 Poultry slaughtering and processing

Saint-Isidore, NB E8M

D-U-N-S 20-548-7382 (HQ)
ST. ISIDORE ASPHALT LTD
19 Rue Duclos, Saint-Isidore, NB, E8M 1N3
(506) 358-6345
Sales 50,488,400
SIC 1611 Highway and street construction
Richard Losier

Saint-Jacques, NB E7B

D-U-N-S 25-380-8497 (HQ)
BOISE ALLJOIST LTD
(*Suby of* BOISE CASCADE COMPANY)
70 Rue Industrielle, Saint-Jacques, NB, E7B 1T1
(506) 735-3561
Sales 28,855,500
SIC 2499 Wood products, nec
Thom Lovlien
Tom Corrik

Saint-Leolin, NB E4P

D-U-N-S 20-023-5497 (SL)
COOPERATIVE DE SHEDIAC LIMITEE, LA
335 Main St, Saint-Leolin, NB, E4P 2B1
(506) 532-4441
Emp Here 125 *Sales* 36,684,625
SIC 5411 Grocery stores
Jean Claude Bertin
Conrad Grant

Saint-Leonard, NB E7E

D-U-N-S 24-789-9669 (SL)
CONFECTION 4E DIMENSION LTEE
11 Rue Industrielle, Saint-Leonard, NB, E7E 2A9
(506) 423-7660
Emp Here 80 *Sales* 15,936,320
SIC 2337 Women's and misses' suits and coats
Michel St-Amand
Guylaine Fecteau

D-U-N-S 24-573-3423 (SL)
FOYER NOTRE-DAME DE SAINT-LEONARD INC
604 Rue Principale, Saint-Leonard, NB, E7E 2H5

Emp Here 75 *Sales* 4,443,525
SIC 8361 Residential care
Marcelle Fafard Godbout
Denis Michaud

D-U-N-S 20-378-5332 (SL)
G T I BROKER GROUP INC
177 Rue St-Jean, Saint-Leonard, NB, E7E 2B3
(506) 423-7777
Emp Here 45 *Sales* 26,398,828
SIC 6411 Insurance agents, brokers, and service
John Stevens
Dennis Daigle

Saint-Louis-De-Kent, NB E4X

D-U-N-S 25-290-8884 (SL)
VILLA MARIA INC
19 Rue Du College, Saint-Louis-De-Kent, NB, E4X 1C2
(506) 876-3488
Emp Here 100 *Sales* 6,856,600
SIC 8051 Skilled nursing care facilities
Louis Arsenault

Saint-Quentin, NB E8A

D-U-N-S 24-186-3760 (SL)
ATELIER GERARD BEAULIEU INC
164 Rue Mgr-Martin E, Saint-Quentin, NB, E8A 1W1
(506) 235-2243
Emp Here 50 *Sales* 10,141,500
SIC 3443 Fabricated plate work (boiler shop)
Marc Beaulieu
Linda Tharest

D-U-N-S 24-128-5758 (SL)
CO-OPERATIVE DE SAINT-QUENTIN LTEE
145 Rue Canada, Saint-Quentin, NB, E8A 1J4
(506) 235-2083
Emp Here 50 *Sales* 13,707,600
SIC 5411 Grocery stores
Jacqueline Beaulieu

D-U-N-S 24-994-4786 (HQ)
GROUPE SAVOIE INC
251 Route 180, Saint-Quentin, NB, E8A 2K9
(506) 235-2228
Emp Here 500 *Sales* 167,034,000
SIC 2421 Sawmills and planing mills, general
Jean-Claude Savoie
Nathalie Savoie
Alain Bosse
Jason Somers
Vincent Caron
Jonathan Levesque
Gilles Boucher

D-U-N-S 20-741-6140 (SL)
NORTH AMERICAN FOREST PRODUCTS LTD
MATERIAUX PARENT, DIV OF
40 Labrie Ch, Saint-Quentin, NB, E8A 2E1
(506) 235-2873
Emp Here 150 *Sales* 28,855,500
SIC 2421 Sawmills and planing mills, general
Pierre Parent
Sylvia Gauthier

Saint-Simon, NB E8P

D-U-N-S 20-285-2984 (SL)
BOLERO SHELLFISH PROCESSING INC
(*Suby of* CONSULTRANS INTERNATIONAL LTEE)

1324 Route 335, Saint-Simon, NB, E8P 2B2
(506) 727-5217
Emp Here 150 *Sales* 51,853,500
SIC 2091 Canned and cured fish and seafoods
Gabriel Elbaz

Sainte-Anne-De-Kent, NB E4S

D-U-N-S 25-412-9992 (SL)
RICHARD, B. A. LTEE
374 Ch Cote Sainte-Anne, Sainte-Anne-De-Kent, NB, E4S 1M6
(506) 743-6198
Emp Here 300 *Sales* 146,215,500
SIC 2091 Canned and cured fish and seafoods
Marcel Richard
Bernard Richard
Emilia Richard

Sainte-Rosette, NB E8K

D-U-N-S 24-913-6003 (SL)
ROJAC ENTREPRISES INC
1671 Ch Nicholas-Denys, Sainte-Rosette, NB, E8K 3J9

Emp Here 24 *Sales* 10,732,176
SIC 5031 Lumber, plywood, and millwork
Robert Arseneau

Salisbury, NB E4J

D-U-N-S 24-607-0791 (SL)
LAVOIE, J. P. & SONS LTD
SALISBURY IRVING BIG STOP
2986 Fredericton Rd, Salisbury, NB, E4J 2G1
(506) 372-3333
Emp Here 95 *Sales* 4,072,935
SIC 5812 Eating places
Paul Lavoie
Francis Lavoie

Scoudouc, NB E4P

D-U-N-S 24-805-3563 (SL)
OCEAN PIER INC
20 Pattison St, Scoudouc, NB, E4P 3R4
(506) 532-3010
Emp Here 75 *Sales* 25,926,750
SIC 2092 Fresh or frozen packaged fish
Michel Breau

D-U-N-S 24-129-5922 (SL)
SEASIDE CHEVROLET LIMITED
(*Suby of* LOUNSBURY COMPANY LIMITED)
13 Harbour View Dr, Scoudouc, NB, E4P 3L5
(506) 532-6666
Emp Here 40 *Sales* 25,171,200
SIC 5511 New and used car dealers
Michael Jenkins

D-U-N-S 20-020-9492 (HQ)
SPRINGWALL SLEEP PRODUCTS INC
MACGREGOR SLEEP PRODUCTS
211 Parker Rd, Scoudouc, NB, E4P 3P7
(506) 532-4481
Emp Here 75 *Sales* 23,148,300
SIC 2515 Mattresses and bedsprings
Boyd Kay
Robert Kay
Greg Kay
Dale Black

D-U-N-S 25-502-3541 (SL)
WEST-WOOD INDUSTRIES LTD
NORWOOD WINDOW & DOOR, DIV. OF
249 Parker Rd, Scoudouc, NB, E4P 3P8
(506) 532-0908
Emp Here 230 *Sales* 131,014,440
SIC 5039 Construction materials, nec
Leandre Cormier

Shediac, NB E4P

D-U-N-S 24-393-1313 (SL)
BENNETT, KEN ENTERPRISES INC
CANADIAN TIRE
173 Main St, Shediac, NB, E4P 2A5
(506) 533-9788
Emp Here 40 *Sales* 19,923,120
SIC 5531 Auto and home supply stores
Ken Bennett

D-U-N-S 20-742-5190 (SL)
GLENWOOD KITCHENS LTD
191 Main St, Shediac, NB, E4P 2A5
(506) 532-4491
Emp Here 115 *Sales* 22,122,550
SIC 2434 Wood kitchen cabinets
James Mckenna

D-U-N-S 24-805-1807 (SL)
PHARMACIE LEBLANC, PIERRE INC
JEAN COUTU PHARMACY #130
338 Main St, Shediac, NB, E4P 2E5
(506) 532-4410
Emp Here 40 *Sales* 10,118,160
SIC 5912 Drug stores and proprietary stores
Pierre Leblanc

D-U-N-S 20-023-5653 (SL)
SHEDIAC LOBSTER SHOP LTD
261 Main St, Shediac, NB, E4P 2A6
(506) 532-4302
Emp Here 125 *Sales* 89,589,500
SIC 5146 Fish and seafoods
Gilles Maillet

D-U-N-S 24-556-7487 (BR)
SOBEYS CAPITAL INCORPORATED
SOBEYS
(*Suby of* EMPIRE COMPANY LIMITED)
183 Main St Suite 738, Shediac, NB, E4P 2A5
(506) 532-0842
Emp Here 150
SIC 5411 Grocery stores
Mario Savoie

D-U-N-S 20-742-6370 (SL)
VILLA PROVIDENCE SHEDIAC INC
403 Main St, Shediac, NB, E4P 2B9
(506) 532-4484
Emp Here 190 *Sales* 12,981,940
SIC 8051 Skilled nursing care facilities
Yvon Belliveau

Shediac Cape, NB E4P

D-U-N-S 24-994-9512 (SL)
RIGEL SHIPPING CANADA INC
3521 Route 134, Shediac Cape, NB, E4P 3G6
(506) 533-9000
Emp Here 100 *Sales* 14,819,200
SIC 4213 Trucking, except local
Brian Ritchie

Shippagan, NB E8S

D-U-N-S 20-760-8287 (SL)
COASTAL ZONE RESEARCH INSTITUTE INC

232b Av De L'Eglise, Shippagan, NB, E8S 1J2
(506) 336-6600
Emp Here 40   *Sales* 10,062,920
SIC 8733 Noncommercial research organizations
  Jocelyne Roy Vienneau
  Gastien Godin

D-U-N-S 20-814-6043   (HQ)
JIFFY PRODUCTS (N.B.) LTD
(*Suby of* JOHAN G OLSEN AS)
125 Rue Parc Industriel, Shippagan, NB, E8S 1X9
(506) 336-2284
Sales 29,215,200
SIC 2655 Fiber cans, drums, and similar products
  Zoel Gautreau
  John Hanson
  Arsten Knutson

D-U-N-S 24-670-4399   (SL)
PECHERIES F.N. FISHERIES LTD
99 15e Rue, Shippagan, NB, E8S 1E2

Emp Here 200   *Sales* 69,138,000
SIC 2092 Fresh or frozen packaged fish
  Lorenzo Noel
  Yolande Noel
  Albanie Noel
  Joseph Noel
  Mathurin Noel

D-U-N-S 25-841-4523   (SL)
PESE PECHE INC
140 1re Rue, Shippagan, NB, E8S 1A4
(506) 336-1400
Emp Here 45   *Sales* 19,957,050
SIC 7389 Business services, nec
  Johncharle Hache

D-U-N-S 24-126-3891   (SL)
RESIDENCES MGR CHIASSON INC, LES
130j Boul J D Gauthier, Shippagan, NB, E8S 1N8
(506) 336-3266
Emp Here 130   *Sales* 8,913,580
SIC 8051 Skilled nursing care facilities
  Anne Marie Richardson Chiasson

Smithfield, NB E6K

D-U-N-S 25-165-9181   (SL)
FEENEY R.A. LOGGING & TRUCKING LTD
9 New Market Bye Rd, Smithfield, NB, E6K 2T9

Emp Here 45   *Sales* 19,957,050
SIC 7389 Business services, nec
  Richard A Feeney

St Andrews, NB E5B

D-U-N-S 20-665-7160   (BR)
FAIRMONT HOTELS & RESORTS INC
(*Suby of* ACCOR)
184 Adolphus St, St Andrews, NB, E5B 1T7
(506) 529-3004
Emp Here 200
SIC 7231 Beauty shops
  Chris Cahilo

D-U-N-S 25-292-4915   (BR)
FAIRMONT HOTELS & RESORTS INC
(*Suby of* ACCOR)
184 Adolphus St, St Andrews, NB, E5B 1T7
(506) 529-8823
Emp Here 250
SIC 7011 Hotels and motels
  Judy Adams

St Stephen, NB E3L

D-U-N-S 20-020-8437   (BR)
ARAUCO CANADA LIMITED
ARAUCO NORTH AMERICA
(*Suby of* INVERSIONES ANGELINI Y COMPANIA LIMITADA)
151 Church St, St Stephen, NB, E3L 5H1
(506) 466-2370
Emp Here 250
SIC 5039 Construction materials, nec
  David Moffatt

D-U-N-S 20-741-4256   (SL)
CANADIAN TIRE ASSOCIATE STORE
250 King St, St Stephen, NB, E3L 2E5
(506) 466-4110
Emp Here 45   *Sales* 22,413,510
SIC 5531 Auto and home supply stores
  Terry Leitch

D-U-N-S 25-871-9798   (SL)
CHARLOTTE COUNTY HUMANE RESOURCES INC
KINDRED HOME CARE
15 Marks St, St Stephen, NB, E3L 2A9
(506) 466-5081
Emp Here 50   *Sales* 14,164,650
SIC 8741 Management services
  Paul English

D-U-N-S 20-742-3229   (SL)
DAY, GUY R. & SON LIMITED
EXIT REALTY CHARLOTTE COUNTY
78 Milltown Blvd, St Stephen, NB, E3L 1G6
(506) 466-3330
Emp Here 23   *Sales* 13,338,252
SIC 6411 Insurance agents, brokers, and service
  Brandon Mcgee
  Darryl Spires
  Lorraine Day-Richard
  Raymond Day

D-U-N-S 20-023-4094   (HQ)
GANONG BROS., LIMITED
1 Chocolate Dr, St Stephen, NB, E3L 2X5
(506) 465-5600
Emp Here 300   *Sales* 158,400,125
SIC 2064 Candy and other confectionery products
  David Ganong
  J. Terry Arthurs
  Jean-Marc Lefebvre
  Dana Branscombe
  Greg Fash
  Cathy Hastey
  Douglas Ettinger

D-U-N-S 20-651-7380   (SL)
LINCOURT MANOR INC
1 Chipman St, St Stephen, NB, E3L 2W9
(506) 466-7855
Emp Here 89   *Sales* 6,117,237
SIC 8051 Skilled nursing care facilities
  Jane Lyons

D-U-N-S 25-984-8737   (BR)
LOBLAWS INC
REAL CANADIAN SUPERSTORE
(*Suby of* LOBLAW COMPANIES LIMITED)
195 King St, St Stephen, NB, E3L 2E4
(506) 465-1457
Emp Here 130
SIC 5411 Grocery stores
  Tarry Hancock

St Thomas, NB E7P

D-U-N-S 20-285-1358   (BR)
COVERED BRIDGE POTATO CHIP COMPANY INC

(*Suby of* COVERED BRIDGE POTATO CHIP COMPANY INC)
149 St Thomas Rd, St Thomas, NB, E7P 2X6
(506) 375-2447
Emp Here 100
SIC 4225 General warehousing and storage
  Jody Mclauthlin

Stanley, NB E6B

D-U-N-S 20-930-9723   (HQ)
STANLEY MUTUAL INSURANCE COMPANY
32 Irishtown Rd, Stanley, NB, E6B 1B6
(506) 367-2273
Emp Here 11   *Sales* 62,786,406
SIC 6331 Fire, marine, and casualty insurance
  John Garwood
  William Smith
  Arthur Wilson

Sussex, NB E4E

D-U-N-S 20-297-1714   (BR)
ANGLOPHONE SOUTH SCHOOL DISTRICT (ASD-S)
SUSSEX REGIONAL HIGH SCHOOL
(*Suby of* ANGLOPHONE SOUTH SCHOOL DISTRICT (ASD-S))
55 Leonard Dr, Sussex, NB, E4E 2P8
(506) 432-2017
Emp Here 92
SIC 8211 Elementary and secondary schools
  Lori Wall

D-U-N-S 20-086-6031   (BR)
ATLANTIC WHOLESALERS LTD
SUSSEX SUPER VALUE
(*Suby of* LOBLAW COMPANIES LIMITED)
10 Lower Cove Rd, Sussex, NB, E4E 0B7
(506) 433-9820
Emp Here 90
SIC 5411 Grocery stores
  Dave Aresanault

D-U-N-S 25-690-5175   (SL)
DRURY'S TRANSFER REG'D
160 Stewart Ave, Sussex, NB, E4E 2G2

Emp Here 100   *Sales* 20,570,600
SIC 4212 Local trucking, without storage
  Westley Armour

D-U-N-S 24-472-5313   (HQ)
FUNDY MUTUAL INSURANCE LTD
1022 Main St, Sussex, NB, E4E 2M3
(506) 432-1535
Emp Here 15   *Sales* 81,252,996
SIC 6331 Fire, marine, and casualty insurance
  John Crealock
  John Robinson
  Jim Wilson

D-U-N-S 20-022-4566   (SL)
G. E. BARBOUR INC
165 Stewart Ave, Sussex, NB, E4E 3H1
(506) 432-2300
Emp Here 120   *Sales* 41,482,800
SIC 2099 Food preparations, nec
  Sylvia Macvey
  Jeff Martin
  Gary Lajoie

D-U-N-S 24-418-4367   (SL)
GEORGE, JS ENTERPRISES LTD
CANADIAN TIRE
138 Main St Suite 17, Sussex, NB, E4E 3E1
(506) 433-3201
Emp Here 35   *Sales* 17,432,730
SIC 5531 Auto and home supply stores
  Steve George

D-U-N-S 24-532-4603   (SL)
KIWANIS NURSING HOME INC
11 Bryant Dr, Sussex, NB, E4E 2P3
(506) 432-3118
Emp Here 90   *Sales* 6,170,940
SIC 8051 Skilled nursing care facilities
  Keri Marr

D-U-N-S 20-742-7923   (SL)
M.M.H. PRESTIGE HOMES INC
PRESTIGE HOMES
14 Industrial Dr, Sussex, NB, E4E 2R8
(506) 433-9130
Emp Here 150   *Sales* 28,855,500
SIC 2452 Prefabricated wood buildings
  Dean Robertson

D-U-N-S 25-357-1947   (HQ)
MRS. DUNSTER'S (1996) INC
30 Leonard Dr, Sussex, NB, E4E 5T5
(506) 433-9333
Emp Here 83   *Sales* 7,508,479
SIC 2051 Bread, cake, and related products
  Blair Hyslop
  Rosalyn Hyslop

D-U-N-S 20-023-7477   (HQ)
NELSON MONUMENTS LTD
23 Western St, Sussex, NB, E4E 1E7
(506) 432-9000
Emp Here 30   *Sales* 14,652,000
SIC 5999 Miscellaneous retail stores, nec
  Bernard Imbeault
  Inouk Imbeault

D-U-N-S 24-329-9257   (BR)
WAL-MART CANADA CORP
(*Suby of* WALMART INC.)
80 Main St, Sussex, NB, E4E 1Y6
(506) 432-9333
Emp Here 200
SIC 5311 Department stores
  Chris Redmond

Sussex Corner, NB E4E

D-U-N-S 20-023-6958   (SL)
BROWN'S PAVING LTD
20 Plant Rd, Sussex Corner, NB, E4E 2W9
(506) 433-4721
Emp Here 42   *Sales* 11,908,008
SIC 1611 Highway and street construction
  Wallace Brown Jr
  Corey Mcallister

Tabusintac, NB E9H

D-U-N-S 20-023-7931   (SL)
HEVECO LTD
4534 Route 11, Tabusintac, NB, E9H 1J4
(506) 779-9277
Emp Here 55   *Sales* 12,838,925
SIC 1499 Miscellaneous nonMetallic minerals, except fuels
  Bernad-George Mecking
  Rolf Mecking
  Hans Mecking

Tilley Road, NB E8M

D-U-N-S 24-313-1989   (SL)
PENNISULA FOODS
514 Route 365, Tilley Road, NB, E8M 1P4
(506) 358-6366
Emp Here 49   *Sales* 11,017,895
SIC 2037 Frozen fruits and vegetables
  Daniel Losier

▲ Public Company   ■ Public Company Family Member   **HQ** Headquarters   **BR** Branch   **SL** Single Location

Titusville, NB E5N

D-U-N-S 24-835-6185   (HQ)
JOANS HOME SUPPORT CARE
1815 Route 860 Suite 860, Titusville, NB, E5N 3V6
(506) 832-0369
Emp Here 1   *Sales* 10,248,900
SIC 8059 Nursing and personal care, nec
Joan Mitchell

Tracadie-Sheila, NB E1X

D-U-N-S 25-897-3395   (BR)
ATLANTIC WHOLESALERS LTD
TRACADIE FOOD WAREHOUSE
(*Suby of* LOBLAW COMPANIES LIMITED)
3409 Rue Principale Suite 31, Tracadie-Sheila, NB, E1X 1C7
(506) 393-1155
Emp Here 120
SIC 5411 Grocery stores
Lisette Godin

D-U-N-S 24-262-3080   (SL)
COOPERATIVE REGIONALE DE LA BAIE LTEE, LA
3430 Rue Principale, Tracadie-Sheila, NB, E1X 1C8
(506) 395-1700
Emp Here 75   *Sales* 20,561,400
SIC 5411 Grocery stores
Roger St-Coeur
Leonce Lauzier
Jacqueline Blanchard Sonier

D-U-N-S 20-385-9629   (SL)
DISTRICT SCOLAIRE FRANCOPHONE NORD-EST
3376 Rue Principale, Tracadie-Sheila, NB, E1X 1A4
(506) 394-3400
Emp Here 700   *Sales* 69,383,300
SIC 8211 Elementary and secondary schools
Pierre Lavoie

D-U-N-S 20-814-0504   (BR)
DISTRICT SCOLAIRE FRANCOPHONE NORD-EST
POLY BALENPE WA LOSOER
585 Rue De L'Eglise, Tracadie-Sheila, NB, E1X 1B1
(506) 394-3508
Emp Here 100   *Sales* 396,535
SIC 8211 Elementary and secondary schools
Belmont St.-Tierre

D-U-N-S 20-710-0517   (BR)
DISTRICT SCOLAIRE FRANCOPHONE NORD-EST
ECOLE POLYVALENTE
585 Church St, Tracadie-Sheila, NB, E1X 1G5
(506) 394-3500
Emp Here 90   *Sales* 396,535
SIC 8211 Elementary and secondary schools
Bernard St Pierre

D-U-N-S 25-524-8718   (SL)
ENTREPRISES A & R SAVOIE ET FILS LTEE, LES
MAISONS SUPREME HOMES
2650 Rue Principale, Tracadie-Sheila, NB, E1X 1A1
(506) 395-6997
Emp Here 100   *Sales* 26,765,200
SIC 5211 Lumber and other building materials
Aristide Savoie
Robert Savoie

D-U-N-S 20-749-7236   (SL)
GLOUCESTER CONSTRUCTION LTD
4260 Rue Principale, Tracadie-Sheila, NB, E1X 1B9

Emp Here 30   *Sales* 14,359,443
SIC 1542 Nonresidential construction, nec
Stephane Mcgraw

D-U-N-S 20-742-6784   (SL)
GROUPE BELLE-ILE INC
3113 Rue Principale, Tracadie-Sheila, NB, E1X 1A2
(506) 395-3374
Emp Here 20   *Sales* 10,702,480
SIC 5146 Fish and seafoods
Paul Boudreau
Ronald Guinard

D-U-N-S 20-445-7329   (SL)
HATHEWAY (TRACADIE) LIMITED
HATHEWAY FORD
3318 Rue Lachapelle, Tracadie-Sheila, NB, E1X 1G5
(506) 395-2208
Emp Here 25   *Sales* 12,451,950
SIC 5511 New and used car dealers
David Hatheway
Ian Hatheway

D-U-N-S 25-168-8867   (SL)
LEMAY, G & S HOLDINGS INC
CANADIAN TIRE
450 Rue Du Moulin Suite 491, Tracadie-Sheila, NB, E1X 1A4
(506) 395-4313
Emp Here 40   *Sales* 19,923,120
SIC 5531 Auto and home supply stores
Gerald Lemay

D-U-N-S 20-084-0747   (SL)
MCCRAM INC
MCDONALD'S RESTAURANT
3458 Rue Principale, Tracadie-Sheila, NB, E1X 1C8
(506) 394-1111
Emp Here 140   *Sales* 6,372,660
SIC 5812 Eating places
Chantale Cormier

D-U-N-S 20-741-5977   (SL)
MCGRAW ET FRERE LIMITEE
PONTIAC BUICK GMC
2892 Rue Principale, Tracadie-Sheila, NB, E1X 1A2
(506) 395-2263
Emp Here 40   *Sales* 19,923,120
SIC 5511 New and used car dealers
Leopold Mcgraw

D-U-N-S 25-499-7695   (SL)
MQM QUALITY MANUFACTURING LTD
2676 Commerce St, Tracadie-Sheila, NB, E1X 1G5
(506) 395-7777
Emp Here 60   *Sales* 14,771,160
SIC 1791 Structural steel erection
Kenneth Pitre
Gerald Pitre
Leopold Theriault

D-U-N-S 25-090-9959   (BR)
REGIONAL HEALTH AUTHORITY A
CENTRE HOSPITALIER DE TRACADIE
(*Suby of* REGIONAL HEALTH AUTHORITY A)
400 Rue Des Hospitalieres, Tracadie-Sheila, NB, E1X 1G5
(506) 394-3000
Emp Here 280
SIC 8062 General medical and surgical hospitals
Odette Robichaud

Tracyville, NB E5L

D-U-N-S 24-804-7862   (HQ)
ASHMORE LIMITED
3307 Route 101, Tracyville, NB, E5L 1N7

(506) 459-7777
Sales 16,401,000
SIC 6712 Bank holding companies
Ross Creelman

D-U-N-S 24-129-5369   (HQ)
MARWOOD LTD
(*Suby of* ASHMORE LIMITED)
3307 Route 101, Tracyville, NB, E5L 1N7
(506) 459-7777
Emp Here 275   *Sales* 111,356,000
SIC 2499 Wood products, nec
Michael O'donnell
Harry Foreman
Danny Goodine
David Harris
Glen Warman
Ross Creelman

Upper Cape, NB E4M

D-U-N-S 24-755-3142   (SL)
SOUTH SHORE TRADING CO. LTD
36 John A Trenholm Rd, Upper Cape, NB, E4M 2R6
(506) 538-7619
Emp Here 25   *Sales* 20,889,425
SIC 5146 Fish and seafoods
Mitchell Feigenbaum

Utopia, NB E5C

D-U-N-S 24-831-5350   (BR)
IRVING, J. D. LIMITED
LAKE UTOPIA PAPER
(*Suby of* IRVING, J. D. LIMITED)
600 Route 785, Utopia, NB, E5C 2K4
(506) 755-3384
Emp Here 145
SIC 2679 Converted paper products, nec
Mark Mofagar

Val-Comeau, NB E1X

D-U-N-S 20-342-4783   (SL)
THAI UNION CANADA INC
PECHERIES DE CHEZ-NOUS, LES
78 Rue Du Quai, Val-Comeau, NB, E1X 4L1
(506) 395-3292
Emp Here 100   *Sales* 34,569,000
SIC 2092 Fresh or frozen packaged fish
Francois Benoit

Val-Doucet, NB E8R

D-U-N-S 20-752-4724   (SL)
BBT TRANSPORT LTD
1999 Ch Val-Doucet, Val-Doucet, NB, E8R 1Z5
(506) 764-8004
Emp Here 30   *Sales* 11,560,800
SIC 4731 Freight transportation arrangement
Bruno Theriault

D-U-N-S 20-362-8016   (SL)
COOPERATIVE NOTRE-DAME LIMITEE , LA
2616 Ch Val-Doucet, Val-Doucet, NB, E8R 1Z2
(506) 764-3394
Emp Here 40   *Sales* 10,966,080
SIC 5411 Grocery stores
Adjutor Belanger

Waterford, NB E4E

D-U-N-S 24-877-9936   (SL)
POLEY MOUNTAIN RESORTS LTD
69 Poley Mountain Rd, Waterford, NB, E4E 4Y2
(506) 433-7653
Emp Here 170   *Sales* 15,757,300
SIC 7011 Hotels and motels
Charles Keith
William (Bill) Anderson
Audrey Chapman
Leonard Lee White
Peter Jobe

Waterville Carleton Co, NB E7P

D-U-N-S 24-342-4194   (SL)
DEDICATED FREIGHT CARRIERS INC
634 Route 590, Waterville Carleton Co, NB, E7P 1B7
(506) 375-1010
Emp Here 75   *Sales* 38,997,525
SIC 4731 Freight transportation arrangement
Mike Oakes

Woodstock, NB E7M

D-U-N-S 20-429-2884   (SL)
ATLANTIC SPEEDY PROPANE
668 Main St, Woodstock, NB, E7M 2C8

Emp Here 5   *Sales* 15,709,144
SIC 4924 Natural gas distribution

D-U-N-S 25-086-2471   (BR)
ATLANTIC WHOLESALERS LTD
REAL ATLANTIC SUPERSTORE, THE
(*Suby of* LOBLAW COMPANIES LIMITED)
350 Connell St, Woodstock, NB, E7M 5G8
(506) 328-1100
Emp Here 120
SIC 5411 Grocery stores
Lester Oakes

D-U-N-S 24-889-3224   (HQ)
AYR MOTOR EXPRESS INC
46 Poplar St, Woodstock, NB, E7M 4G2
(506) 325-2205
Emp Here 200   *Sales* 47,939,060
SIC 4213 Trucking, except local
Joe Keenan

D-U-N-S 24-190-2337   (HQ)
BARRETT CORPORATION
DIXIE SALES CANADA
300 Lockhart Mill Rd, Woodstock, NB, E7M 6B9
(506) 328-8853
Emp Here 15   *Sales* 556,240,000
SIC 5091 Sporting and recreation goods
Harold Reiter
William Barrett
Edward Barrett
Bruce Barr
J W Bud Bird
Earl Lande
Lyle Huston
P Brian Neill
Peter Porteous
Frank Mckenna

D-U-N-S 24-670-6881   (SL)
CLARK OIL CO. LTD
Gd Stn Main, Woodstock, NB, E7M 6B9
(506) 328-3243
Emp Here 12   *Sales* 12,393,696
SIC 5172 Petroleum products, nec
Peter Leighton Clark
Janet Clark

D-U-N-S 24-755-6996   (SL)
COREY FORD LTD
336 Connell St, Woodstock, NB, E7M 5E2
(506) 328-8828
Emp Here 35   *Sales* 17,432,730
SIC 5511 New and used car dealers
  Aubrey Corey

D-U-N-S 25-368-8956   · (SL)
CUMMINGS PHARMACY LTD
SHOPPERS DRUG MART
370 Connell St, Woodstock, NB, E7M 5G9
(506) 328-8801
Emp Here 50   *Sales* 12,647,700
SIC 5912 Drug stores and proprietary stores

D-U-N-S 24-338-6588   (SL)
**CYV CHEVROLET PONTIAC BUICK GMC
LTD**
324 Connell St, Woodstock, NB, E7M 5E2
(506) 799-0110
Emp Here 30   *Sales* 14,942,340
SIC 5511 New and used car dealers
  Robert Toner

D-U-N-S 20-568-2821   (HQ)
FRANCHISE MANAGEMENT INC
FMI GROUP
417 Connell St Suite 7, Woodstock, NB, E7M
5G5
(506) 328-4631
Sales 279,834,000
SIC 5812 Eating places
  Dwight F Fraser
  Greg Walton

D-U-N-S 20-342-3512   (SL)
K & J PECK SALES LTD
CANADIAN TIRE
388 Connell St, Woodstock, NB, E7M 5G9
(506) 328-3353
Emp Here 43   *Sales* 10,881,537
SIC 5251 Hardware stores
  Kevin Peck

D-U-N-S 24-393-0497   (SL)
LANDRY, CLAUDE INVESTMENTS INC
CANADIAN TIRE
388 Connell St, Woodstock, NB, E7M 5G9
(506) 328-3353
Emp Here 40   *Sales* 19,923,120
SIC 5531 Auto and home supply stores
  Claude Landry

D-U-N-S 24-943-6379   (BR)
SOBEYS CAPITAL INCORPORATED
SOBEYS 846
(*Suby of* EMPIRE COMPANY LIMITED)
370 Connell St Unit 11, Woodstock, NB, E7M
5G9
(506) 328-6819
Emp Here 150
SIC 5411 Grocery stores
  Daniel Lowther

D-U-N-S 24-534-3579   (SL)
TANN PAPER LIMITED
(*Suby of* EURASIA INVEST HOLDING AG)
149 Heller Rd, Woodstock, NB, E7M 1X3
(506) 325-9100
Emp Here 47   *Sales* 10,971,445
SIC 2621 Paper mills
  Stephen Smith
  Darren Farell

D-U-N-S 24-756-0816   (SL)
VAN NELLE CANADA LIMITED
(*Suby of* IMPERIAL BRANDS PLC)
147 Heller Rd, Woodstock, NB, E7M 1X4
(506) 325-1930
Emp Here 50   *Sales* 11,671,750
SIC 2655 Fiber cans, drums, and similar products
  Graham Bolt
  Ted King

D-U-N-S 24-319-5182   (BR)
WAL-MART CANADA CORP

WALMART
(*Suby of* WALMART INC.)
430 Connell St, Woodstock, NB, E7M 5R5
(506) 324-8099
Emp Here 120
SIC 5311 Department stores
  Meredith Noseworthy

D-U-N-S 25-672-4311   (HQ)
XPLORNET COMMUNICATIONS INC
XPLORNET
(*Suby of* BARRETT CORPORATION)
300 Lockhart Mill Rd, Woodstock, NB, E7M
6B5
(506) 328-8853
Emp Here 150   *Sales* 100,363,200
SIC 4813 Telephone communication, except radio
  William Barrett
  Edward Barrett

Arnolds Cove, NL A0B

D-U-N-S 20-561-1754   (SL)
ICEWATER SEAFOODS INC
24 High Liner Ave, Arnolds Cove, NL, A0B 1A0
(709) 463-2445
Emp Here 250   *Sales* 121,846,250
SIC 2091 Canned and cured fish and seafoods
Bruce Wareham

Baie Verte, NL A0K

D-U-N-S 20-012-2729   (SL)
GUY J BAILEY LTD
6 Highway 412, Baie Verte, NL, A0K 1B0
(709) 532-4642
Emp Here 40   *Sales* 11,340,960
SIC 1611 Highway and street construction
Scott Bailey
Kent Bailey
Ivan Bailey
Pearl Bailey

D-U-N-S 24-320-4190   (SL)
RAMBLER METALS AND MINING CANADA LIMITED
RAMBLER MINES
(*Suby of* RAMBLER METALS AND MINING PLC)
309 410 William Chipp Bldg Hwy, Baie Verte, NL, A0K 1B0
(709) 800-1929
Emp Here 23   *Sales* 54,913,627
SIC 1081 Metal mining services
Norm Williams
Tim Slater
Peter Mercer
Tim Sanford
Brad Mills
Mark Sander
Glenn Poulter
Belinda Labatte
Terrell Iver Ackerman
Eason Cong Chen

Bay Roberts, NL A0A

D-U-N-S 24-449-7905   (HQ)
ATLANTIC GROCERY DISTRIBUTORS LIMITED
(*Suby of* POWELL'S SUPERMARKET LIMITED)
1 Hope Ave, Bay Roberts, NL, A0A 1G0
(709) 786-9720
Sales 78,838,760
SIC 5141 Groceries, general line
David Powell
Isabel Powell

D-U-N-S 20-690-3234   (SL)
CAD CONSTRUCTION LTD
19 Sawdust Road, Bay Roberts, NL, A0A 1G0

Emp Here 25   *Sales* 11,768,275
SIC 1542 Nonresidential construction, nec

D-U-N-S 25-703-1088   (BR)
COMPASSION HOME CARE INC
COMPASSION HOME HEALTH SERVICES
(*Suby of* COMPASSION HOME CARE INC)
Gd, Bay Roberts, NL, A0A 1G0
(709) 786-8677
Emp Here 100
SIC 8322 Individual and family services
Diane Strickland

D-U-N-S 25-058-6567   (BR)

LOBLAW COMPANIES LIMITED
DOMINION STORES #906
(*Suby of* LOBLAW COMPANIES LIMITED)
Gd, Bay Roberts, NL, A0A 1G0
(709) 786-6001
Emp Here 85
SIC 5411 Grocery stores
Shawn Higden

D-U-N-S 20-012-4014   (HQ)
POWELL'S SUPERMARKET LIMITED
160 Conception Bay Hwy Suite 152, Bay Roberts, NL, A0A 1G0
(709) 786-2101
Emp Here 35   *Sales* 24,945,545
SIC 5411 Grocery stores
Isabel Powell
David Powell

D-U-N-S 20-582-4118   (SL)
ROW, TED
RE/MAX EAST COAST REALTY
164 Conception Bay Hwy, Bay Roberts, NL, A0A 1G0
(709) 786-2310
Emp Here 100   *Sales* 41,888,900
SIC 6531 Real estate agents and managers
Ted Row

Benoits Cove, NL A0L

D-U-N-S 24-912-3357   (SL)
ALLEN'S FISHERIES LIMITED
151 Main Rd, Benoits Cove, NL, A0L 1A0
(709) 789-3139
Emp Here 200   *Sales* 21,888,210
SIC 2092 Fresh or frozen packaged fish
Craig Allen
Richard Allen

Bishops Falls, NL A0H

D-U-N-S 24-877-7039   (SL)
HI-POINT INDUSTRIES (1991) LTD
141 Sunset Dr, Bishops Falls, NL, A0H 1C0
(709) 258-6274
Emp Here 15   *Sales* 18,155,955
SIC 5159 Farm-product raw materials, nec
William Butler

D-U-N-S 24-502-6070   (SL)
TIM HORTONS
8 Trans Canada Hwy, Bishops Falls, NL, A0H 1C0
(709) 258-2156
Emp Here 45   *Sales* 12,336,840
SIC 5461 Retail bakeries
Lisa Brenton

Bonavista, NL A0C

D-U-N-S 24-827-5542   (BR)
OCEAN CHOICE INTERNATIONAL
(*Suby of* OCEAN CHOICE INTERNATIONAL)
28 Campbell St Suite 10, Bonavista, NL, A0C 1B0
(709) 468-7840
Emp Here 100
SIC 5421 Meat and fish markets
Curtis Fisher

Botwood, NL A0H

D-U-N-S 20-020-7491   (BR)
CENTRAL REGIONAL HEALTH AUTHOR-

ITY
TWOMEY, DR HUGH HEALTH CARE CENTRE
(*Suby of* PROVINCE OF NEWFOUNDLAND & LABRADOR)
25 Pleasantview Rd, Botwood, NL, A0H 1E0
(709) 257-2874
Emp Here 170
SIC 8051 Skilled nursing care facilities
Doug Prince

Burnt Islands Blp, NL A0M

D-U-N-S 20-548-4090   (HQ)
KING'S, ERIC FISHERIES LIMITED
17 Plant Rd Suite 15, Burnt Islands Blp, NL, A0M 1B0
(709) 698-3421
Emp Here 134
SIC 2091 Canned and cured fish and seafoods
Gertrude King

Cape Broyle, NL A0A

D-U-N-S 24-449-2716   (SL)
CAPE BROYLE SEA PRODUCTS LIMITED
(*Suby of* FORMANDENS DEPARTEMENT)
Gd, Cape Broyle, NL, A0A 1P0
(709) 432-2400
Emp Here 60   *Sales* 20,741,400
SIC 2092 Fresh or frozen packaged fish
Maurice Murphy

Carbonear, NL A1Y

D-U-N-S 24-340-9849   (SL)
GOFF FISHERIES LIMITED
GOFF FISHERIES
5 Blueberry Cres, Carbonear, NL, A1Y 1A6
(709) 596-7155
Emp Here 100   *Sales* 14,002,900
SIC 7999 Amusement and recreation, nec
Ed Goff

D-U-N-S 25-366-5178   (BR)
ICT CANADA MARKETING INC
(*Suby of* SYKES ENTERPRISES INCORPORATED)
80 Powell Dr, Carbonear, NL, A1Y 1A5

Emp Here 260
SIC 7389 Business services, nec
Dan Fraser

D-U-N-S 25-717-9879   (BR)
WAL-MART CANADA CORP
(*Suby of* WALMART INC.)
120 Columbus Dr, Carbonear, NL, A1Y 1B3
(709) 596-5009
Emp Here 100
SIC 5311 Department stores

Catalina, NL A0C

D-U-N-S 20-023-5500   (SL)
BARRY GROUP INC
ATLANTIC MARINE PRODUCTS
(*Suby of* BARRY GROUP INC)
Gd, Catalina, NL, A0C 1J0
(709) 469-2849
Emp Here 35   *Sales* 18,218,970
SIC 5093 Scrap and waste materials
William Barry

Cavendish, NL A0B

D-U-N-S 20-756-4704   (SL)
VIKING FUR INC
160 Main Rd, Cavendish, NL, A0B 1J0
(709) 588-2820
Emp Here 30   *Sales* 11,565,570
SIC 0271 Fur-bearing animals and rabbits
Peter Noer
Erik Dalsager
Betty Tuck

Channel-Port-Aux-Basques, NL A0M

D-U-N-S 25-725-3815   (BR)
MARINE ATLANTIC INC
(*Suby of* GOVERNMENT OF CANADA)
Gd, Channel-Port-Aux-Basques, NL, A0M 1C0
(709) 695-4200
Emp Here 150
SIC 4482 Ferries
Jim Anderson

Churchill Falls, NL A0R

D-U-N-S 20-852-1364   (SL)
CHURCHILL FALL LABRADOR CORPORATION
Gd, Churchill Falls, NL, A0R 1A0
(709) 925-8298
Emp Here 220   *Sales* 149,572,280
SIC 4911 Electric services
Andrew Macneil

Clarenville, NL A5A

D-U-N-S 20-907-6033   (HQ)
ATLANTICA DIVERSIFIED TRANSPORTATION SYSTEMS
ADTS
5 Myers Ave, Clarenville, NL, A5A 1T5
(709) 466-7052
Emp Here 13   *Sales* 17,485,010
SIC 4213 Trucking, except local
Gordon Peddle
Lavern Peddle
Phyllis Peddle

D-U-N-S 24-205-0131   (BR)
BARRY GROUP INC
ATLANTIC SHELLFISH
(*Suby of* BARRY GROUP INC)
1 Masonic Terrace, Clarenville, NL, A5A 1N2
(709) 466-7186
Emp Here 700
SIC 2092 Fresh or frozen packaged fish
Kay Ryan

D-U-N-S 20-449-3324   (SL)
CLARENVILLE AREA CONSUMERS CO-OPERATIVE SOCIETY LTD
238 Memorial Dr, Clarenville, NL, A5A 1N9
(709) 466-2622
Emp Here 90   *Sales* 24,673,680
SIC 5411 Grocery stores
Craig Pardy
Wendy Brinstone

D-U-N-S 24-804-3366   (SL)
CROSS, DR G B MEMORIAL HOSPITAL
(*Suby of* EASTERN REGIONAL INTEGRATED HEALTH AUTHORITY)
67 Manitoba Dr, Clarenville, NL, A5A 1K3
(709) 466-3411
Emp Here 900   *Sales* 99,972,000

SIC 8062 General medical and surgical hospitals
Roy Manuel
Frank Crews

D-U-N-S 20-013-0730   (SL)
DECKER MOTORS LIMITED
DECKER AUTO RECREATION MARINE
(*Suby of* DECKER MOTORS (1982) LIMITED)
245 Memorial Dr, Clarenville, NL, A5A 1R4
(709) 466-2394
Emp Here 28   *Sales* 17,619,840
SIC 5511 New and used car dealers
Gary Decker

D-U-N-S 24-955-8404   (SL)
EASTERN FOUNDRY LIMITED
3 Wharf Rd Suite 147, Clarenville, NL, A5A 2B2
(709) 466-3814
Emp Here 15   *Sales* 15,005,085
SIC 5051 Metals service centers and offices
Austin Burry
Catherine Burry

D-U-N-S 20-013-0821   (HQ)
MERCER'S MARINE EQUIPMENT LIMITED
MERCER'S MARINE EQUIPMENT
210 Marine Dr, Clarenville, NL, A5A 1L8
(709) 466-7430
Emp Here 3   *Sales* 19,001,040
SIC 5088 Transportation equipment and supplies
Philip Mercer
Scott Mercer
Joanne Mercer

D-U-N-S 20-165-0954   (HQ)
O M B PARTS & INDUSTRIAL LTD
OK TIRE
7 Blackmore Ave Suite 1, Clarenville, NL, A5A 1B8
(709) 466-6491
Emp Here 1   *Sales* 11,953,872
SIC 5531 Auto and home supply stores
Owen Blundon
Marlene Blundon

D-U-N-S 24-390-9012   (SL)
SEARS, WC HOLDINGS INC
CANADIAN TIRE
27 Manitoba Dr, Clarenville, NL, A5A 1K3
(709) 466-8080
Emp Here 40   *Sales* 19,923,120
SIC 5531 Auto and home supply stores
Williams Sears

Clarkes Beach, NL A0A

D-U-N-S 24-736-5757   (SL)
NEWFOUNDLAND EGGS, INC
1 Roaches Line, Clarkes Beach, NL, A0A 1W0
(709) 528-4595
Emp Here 20   *Sales* 10,702,480
SIC 5144 Poultry and poultry products
Joey Smallwood

Coleys Point South, NL A0A

D-U-N-S 20-012-3495   (HQ)
AVALON COAL SALT & OIL LTD
AVALON SALT
69 Coley'S Pt N, Coleys Point South, NL, A0A 1X0
(709) 753-4000
Emp Here 14   *Sales* 12,415,865
SIC 5169 Chemicals and allied products, nec
Eric Dawe
Peter Dawe
Ellen Dawe
Elizabeth Earle

Patricia Lemon
Lois Oates

Conception Bay South, NL A1W

D-U-N-S 20-717-5311   (SL)
HURLEY SLATE WORKS COMPANY INC
250 Minerals Rd, Conception Bay South, NL, A1W 5A2
(709) 834-2320
Emp Here 50   *Sales* 11,671,750
SIC 3281 Cut stone and stone products
John Hurley
Bertha Hurley

Conception Bay South, NL A1X

D-U-N-S 25-299-3779   (BR)
SOBEYS CAPITAL INCORPORATED
SOBEYS #590
(*Suby of* EMPIRE COMPANY LIMITED)
350 Conception Bay Hwy, Conception Bay South, NL, A1X 7A3
(709) 834-9052
Emp Here 150
SIC 5411 Grocery stores
Paul Hessernan

Conche, NL A0K

D-U-N-S 25-997-1625   (SL)
CONCHE SEAFOODS LTD
(*Suby of* FORMANDENS DEPARTEMENT)
2 Hambour Dr, Conche, NL, A0K 1Y0
(709) 622-4111
Emp Here 20   *Sales* 16,711,540
SIC 5146 Fish and seafoods
Derrick Philpott

Corner Brook, NL A2H

D-U-N-S 24-449-1684   (HQ)
A-LINE ATLANTIC INC
A-LINE GREETING CARDS
43 Maple Valley Rd Suite 6, Corner Brook, NL, A2H 6T3
(709) 634-1280
Emp Here 100   *Sales* 146,568,275
SIC 5112 Stationery and office supplies
Harvey Fradsham
Norma Fradsham

D-U-N-S 20-191-1158   (HQ)
ACADEMY CANADA INC
25 Park Dr, Corner Brook, NL, A2H 7H8
(709) 637-2130
Emp Here 17   *Sales* 12,885,470
SIC 8244 Business and secretarial schools
Clyde Pike
Michael Barrett
Lisa Sheehan
Walter Vincent
Richard Squire
Paul White
Albert Wareham
Ted Burden

D-U-N-S 24-314-8108   (BR)
ATLANTIC MINERALS LIMITED
ATLANTIC READY-MIX, DIV OF
22 Commercial St, Corner Brook, NL, A2H 2V2
(709) 634-8255
Emp Here 130
SIC 1422 Crushed and broken limestone

William Fitzpatrick

D-U-N-S 20-606-6537   (SL)
ATLANTIC READY MIX
280 Humber Rd, Corner Brook, NL, A2H 7H1
(709) 634-1885
Emp Here 35   *Sales* 15,651,090
SIC 5032 Brick, stone, and related material
Robert Mcginn

D-U-N-S 20-548-0353   (HQ)
B & B SALES LIMITED
27 Union St, Corner Brook, NL, A2H 5P9
(709) 639-8991
Emp Here 15   *Sales* 12,825,702
SIC 5087 Service establishment equipment
Keith Berkshire
Norma Berkshire
Raymond Berkshire Jr

D-U-N-S 24-994-9272   (HQ)
BARRY GROUP INC
415 Griffin Dr, Corner Brook, NL, A2H 3E9
(709) 785-7387
Emp Here 4   *Sales* 516,035,520
SIC 5146 Fish and seafoods
William Barry
James Barry
David Middleton
Joseph Barry

D-U-N-S 20-013-2355   (SL)
BUGDEN, E L LIMITED
199 Riverside Dr, Corner Brook, NL, A2H 4A1
(709) 634-6177
Emp Here 30   *Sales* 25,067,310
SIC 5141 Groceries, general line
Craig Bugden
Kent Bugden
John Bugden
Gary Bugden
Paul Bugden
Carolyn Bugden

D-U-N-S 24-932-1738   (HQ)
CITY MOTORS A LIMITED PARTNERSHIP
CITY CHRYSLER
119 O'Connell Dr, Corner Brook, NL, A2H 5M6
(709) 637-1000
Emp Here 50   *Sales* 39,015,360
SIC 5511 New and used car dealers
Rosemary O'reilly

D-U-N-S 20-013-2231   (HQ)
CORNER BROOK PULP AND PAPER LIMITED
DEER LAKE POWER COMPANY DIV OF
(*Suby of* KRUGER INC)
1 Mills Rd, Corner Brook, NL, A2H 6B9
(709) 637-3104
Emp Here 264   *Sales* 113,599,833
SIC 2621 Paper mills
Joseph Kruger Ii
George J Bunze
Walter Mlynaryk
Donald Cayouette
Pierre Duhamel

D-U-N-S 20-013-2769   (HQ)
DAWE, STAN LTD
191 Riverside Dr, Corner Brook, NL, A2H 2N2
(709) 639-9131
Sales 16,059,120
SIC 5211 Lumber and other building materials
Gerald Dawe
David Dawe
Harold Dawe
Robert Tony Dawe

D-U-N-S 20-449-7085   (HQ)
DENNIS CHEVROLET PONTIAC BUICK GMC LTD
24 Confederation Dr, Corner Brook, NL, A2H 6G7
(709) 634-8248
Sales 37,127,520
SIC 5511 New and used car dealers
Les W Dennis

Richard Dennis
Maureen Dennis
Heather Collins
Rosemary Eldridge

D-U-N-S 20-351-3486   (SL)
EASTERN DOOR LOGISTICS INC
3 Church St, Corner Brook, NL, A2H 2Z4
(709) 639-2479
Emp Here 70   *Sales* 16,590,105
SIC 8742 Management consulting services
Martin Sadkin

D-U-N-S 20-013-3429   (HQ)
HUMBER MOTORS LIMITED
HUMBER MOTORS FORD
8 Mount Bernard Ave, Corner Brook, NL, A2H 0C6
(709) 634-4371
Emp Here 50   *Sales* 33,981,120
SIC 5511 New and used car dealers
Derek Young
Judy Young

D-U-N-S 24-260-2761   (SL)
JAGO AUTO LTD
WESTERN TOYOTA
31 Confederation Dr, Corner Brook, NL, A2H 0A6
(709) 639-7575
Emp Here 40   *Sales* 19,923,120
SIC 5511 New and used car dealers
Michelle Melendy
Goldie Melendy

D-U-N-S 24-335-5885   (BR)
LOBLAWS INC
DOMINION CORNER BROOK
(*Suby of* LOBLAW COMPANIES LIMITED)
5 Murphy Sq Suite 926, Corner Brook, NL, A2H 1R4
(709) 634-9450
Emp Here 100
SIC 5411 Grocery stores
Kevin Shea

D-U-N-S 20-335-2377   (SL)
ROBERT G. AYLWARD SALES LTD
CANADIAN TIRE ASSOCIATE STORE
4 Murphy Sq Unit 185, Corner Brook, NL, A2H 1R4
(709) 634-8531
Emp Here 95   *Sales* 59,781,600
SIC 5531 Auto and home supply stores
Robert Aylward

D-U-N-S 25-299-3811   (BR)
SOBEYS CAPITAL INCORPORATED
SOBEY'S 861
(*Suby of* EMPIRE COMPANY LIMITED)
1 Mount Bernard Ave Suite 861, Corner Brook, NL, A2H 6Y5
(709) 639-7193
Emp Here 79
SIC 5411 Grocery stores
Max Paddock

D-U-N-S 20-779-6574   (HQ)
SPEEDY AUTOMOTIVE LIMITED
92 Broadway, Corner Brook, NL, A2H 4C8
(709) 639-8929
Emp Here 15   *Sales* 10,926,450
SIC 5013 Motor vehicle supplies and new parts
Ronald Gunson

D-U-N-S 20-607-5439   (SL)
SUMMERSIDE LIONS CENTRE
19 Park Dr, Corner Brook, NL, A2H 4T4
(709) 783-2616
Emp Here 30   *Sales* 12,122,941
SIC 8699 Membership organizations, nec
Frank Payne

D-U-N-S 24-317-1845   (BR)
WAL-MART CANADA CORP
WALMART
(*Suby of* WALMART INC.)

▲ Public Company   ■ Public Company Family Member   **HQ** Headquarters   **BR** Branch   **SL** Single Location

16 Murphy Sq, Corner Brook, NL, A2H 1R4
(709) 634-2310
Emp Here 130
SIC 5311 Department stores
Morley Ford

D-U-N-S 24-932-7933   (SL)
WESTERN BUILDING LTD
25 Poplar Rd, Corner Brook, NL, A2H 4T6
(709) 634-3163
Emp Here 40   *Sales* 10,122,360
SIC 5211 Lumber and other building materials
Lloyd Piercey

D-U-N-S 20-984-2061   (HQ)
WESTERN REGIONAL INTEGRATED HEALTH AUTHORITY, THE
1 Brookfield Ave, Corner Brook, NL, A2H 6J7
(709) 637-5000
Emp Here 1,800   *Sales* 333,240,000
SIC 8062 General medical and surgical hospitals
Susan Gillam

D-U-N-S 25-498-2846   (SL)
WINDJAMMER INVESTMENTS INC
FAIRWAY HONDA
30 Confederation Dr, Corner Brook, NL, A2H 6T2
(709) 634-8881
Emp Here 30   *Sales* 14,942,340
SIC 5511 New and used car dealers
Corey Stone

Cottlesville, NL A0G

D-U-N-S 25-676-1537   (BR)
BREAKWATER FISHERIES LIMITED
(*Suby of* BREAKWATER FISHERIES LIMITED)
23 Hill View Dr, Cottlesville, NL, A0G 1S0

Emp Here 200
SIC 2092 Fresh or frozen packaged fish
Kenny White

Deer Lake, NL A8A

D-U-N-S 20-013-5796   (HQ)
SHEARS, W BRYANT LIMITED
SHEARS BUILDING SUPPLIES
201 Nicholsville Rd, Deer Lake, NL, A8A 1W5
(709) 635-2186
Emp Here 22   *Sales* 20,122,830
SIC 5039 Construction materials, nec
Boyd Shears
Margaret Gould

Dover, NL A0G

D-U-N-S 25-897-5879   (BR)
BARRY GROUP INC
CRIMSON TIDE FISHERIES
(*Suby of* BARRY GROUP INC)
Gd, Dover, NL, A0G 1X0
(709) 537-5888
Emp Here 150
SIC 2091 Canned and cured fish and seafoods
James Payne

Eastport, NL A0G

D-U-N-S 24-956-3453   (SL)
HAPPY ADVENTURE SEA PRODUCTS

(1991) LIMITED
Plant Rd, Eastport, NL, A0G 1Z0
(709) 677-2612
Emp Here 75   *Sales* 25,926,750
SIC 2092 Fresh or frozen packaged fish
Geoffrey Moss
Eugene Moss
Beulah Moss
Donna Moss

Fogo, NL A0G

D-U-N-S 20-348-2245   (BR)
FOGO ISLAND CO-OPERATIVE SOCIETY LIMITED
(*Suby of* FOGO ISLAND CO-OPERATIVE SOCIETY LIMITED)
22-24 Garrison Rd, Fogo, NL, A0G 2B0
(709) 266-2448
Emp Here 75
SIC 2092 Fresh or frozen packaged fish
Phillip Barnes

Freshwater Pb, NL A0B

D-U-N-S 25-393-7684   (SL)
ARGENTIA FREEZERS & TERMINALS LIMITED
Gd, Freshwater Pb, NL, A0B 1W0
(709) 227-5603
Emp Here 60   *Sales* 12,342,360
SIC 4222 Refrigerated warehousing and storage
Jerone Mcgrath

Gander, NL A1V

D-U-N-S 24-621-2497   (SL)
AAS CO OF NFLD ULC
AIR CONTROL AVIATION
1000 James Blvd, Gander, NL, A1V 2V4
(709) 256-8043
Emp Here 45   *Sales* 14,613,930
SIC 4581 Airports, flying fields, and services
Dion Faulkner

D-U-N-S 20-906-0128   (SL)
AIRCONSOL AVIATION SERVICES ULC
(*Suby of* ALLIED AVIATION LLC.)
Gd Lcd Main, Gander, NL, A1V 1W4
(709) 256-3042
Emp Here 65   *Sales* 81,718,065
SIC 5172 Petroleum products, nec
Robert Rose
Alice R. Nicholas

D-U-N-S 25-607-6274   (SL)
CANADIAN COURIER LTD
DOOLEY'S TRUCKING
20 Av Roe, Gander, NL, A1V 0H5
(709) 256-3528
Emp Here 29   *Sales* 11,175,440
SIC 4731 Freight transportation arrangement
Barry Warren
Kay Warren

D-U-N-S 20-729-1865   (SL)
CROSSROADS PONTIAC BUICK LIMITED
295 Airport Blvd, Gander, NL, A1V 1Y9
(709) 651-3500
Emp Here 21   *Sales* 10,459,638
SIC 5511 New and used car dealers
Eric Clarke
David Clarke

D-U-N-S 20-013-8451   (SL)
GANDER CONSUMERS CO-OPERATIVE SOCIETY LIMITED

GANDER CONSUMERS CO-OP
72 Elizabeth Dr, Gander, NL, A1V 1J8
(709) 256-4843
Emp Here 63   *Sales* 17,271,576
SIC 5411 Grocery stores
Morley Goodyear

D-U-N-S 20-013-8790   (HQ)
JIM PENNEY LIMITED
KELLY FORD
105 Laurell Rd, Gander, NL, A1V 0A9
(709) 256-4821
Emp Here 30   *Sales* 22,413,510
SIC 5511 New and used car dealers
Corey Kelly

D-U-N-S 20-608-2542   (BR)
NEWFOUNDLAND AND LABRADOR ENGLISH SCHOOL DISTRICT
GANDER ACADEMY
(*Suby of* NEWFOUNDLAND AND LABRADOR ENGLISH SCHOOL DISTRICT)
55 Fraser Rd, Gander, NL, A1V 1K8
(709) 256-8531
Emp Here 80
SIC 8211 Elementary and secondary schools
Duane Smith

D-U-N-S 20-987-7729   (SL)
SIMMONS AUTO SALES & SERVICE LIMITED
SIMMONS HONDA
461 James Blvd, Gander, NL, A1V 2V4
(709) 256-3415
Emp Here 27   *Sales* 13,448,106
SIC 5511 New and used car dealers
Robert Steel

D-U-N-S 20-555-7718   (BR)
WAL-MART CANADA CORP
(*Suby of* WALMART INC.)
55 Av Roe, Gander, NL, A1V 0H6
(709) 256-7581
Emp Here 200
SIC 5311 Department stores
Carl Dibbons

Glenwood, NL A0G

D-U-N-S 24-324-6696   (SL)
BEAVER BROOK ANTIMONY MINE INC
Gd, Glenwood, NL, A0G 2K0
(709) 679-5866
Emp Here 85   *Sales* 202,941,665
SIC 1099 Metal ores, nec
Bertin Bourgoin
Peter Dimmell
Ronald Goguen
Joseph Martin
Patrick Fernet

Glovertown, NL A0G

D-U-N-S 24-339-8703   (SL)
NORTHSIDE MARINE LTD
GLOVERTOWN SHIPYARDS
300 Main St N, Glovertown, NL, A0G 2L0
(709) 533-6792
Emp Here 25   *Sales* 10,483,875
SIC 6712 Bank holding companies
Leon Dowden
Harvey Humby

Goulds, NL A1S

D-U-N-S 20-013-9780   (SL)
BIDGOOD'S WHOLESALE LIMITED
BIDGOOD'S SUPERMARKET

355 Main Rd, Goulds, NL, A1S 1J9
(709) 368-3125
Emp Here 95   *Sales* 27,880,315
SIC 5411 Grocery stores
Rick Bidgood

D-U-N-S 20-087-6675   (SL)
D W I SERVICE LIMITED
738 Main Rd, Goulds, NL, A1S 1J2
(709) 745-7054
Emp Here 50   *Sales* 19,268,000
SIC 4789 Transportation services, nec
Gerard Fennelly

Grand Bank, NL A0E

D-U-N-S 25-298-7813   (BR)
CLEARWATER SEAFOODS LIMITED PARTNERSHIP
CLEARWATER SEAFOOD
(*Suby of* THORNVALE HOLDINGS LIMITED)
1 Plant Rd, Grand Bank, NL, A0E 1W0
(709) 832-1550
Emp Here 200
SIC 5146 Fish and seafoods
Colin Macdonald

D-U-N-S 20-020-7301   (BR)
EASTERN REGIONAL INTEGRATED HEALTH AUTHORITY
BLUE CREST INTERFAITH HOME
(*Suby of* EASTERN REGIONAL INTEGRATED HEALTH AUTHORITY)
1 Seniors Pl, Grand Bank, NL, A0E 1W0
(709) 832-1660
Emp Here 100
SIC 8051 Skilled nursing care facilities
Shirley Rose

Grand Falls-Windsor, NL A2A

D-U-N-S 20-985-8166   (SL)
BLUEBIRD INVESTMENTS LIMITED
12 Duggan St, Grand Falls-Windsor, NL, A2A 2K6
(709) 489-5403
Emp Here 25   *Sales* 31,387,470
SIC 1542 Nonresidential construction, nec
Owen Young
Dave Perry
Ann Young
Anne Perry

D-U-N-S 20-787-4939   (HQ)
CENTRAL REGIONAL HEALTH AUTHORITY
A.M. GUY MEMORIAL HEALTH CENTRE
(*Suby of* PROVINCE OF NEWFOUNDLAND & LABRADOR)
50 Union St, Grand Falls-Windsor, NL, A2A 2E1
(709) 292-2500
Emp Here 500   *Sales* 316,415,170
SIC 8062 General medical and surgical hospitals
Rosemarie Goodyear
Jeff Cole
Sean Tulk
Terry Ings
John Kattenbusch
Stephanie Power

D-U-N-S 24-393-9480   (HQ)
DUNGEY, D.B. HOLDINGS INC
CANADIAN TIRE
8 Cromer Ave, Grand Falls-Windsor, NL, A2A 1X2
(709) 489-9270
Emp Here 50   *Sales* 44,049,600
SIC 5531 Auto and home supply stores
David B Dungey

▲ Public Company   ■ Public Company Family Member   **HQ** Headquarters   **BR** Branch   **SL** Single Location

D-U-N-S 20-017-1734   (HQ)
MARSH MOTORS CHRYSLER LIMITED
Gd, Grand Falls-Windsor, NL, A2A 2J9
(709) 489-2151
Emp Here 3   *Sales* 12,950,028
SIC 5511 New and used car dealers
 Paul Marsh
 Richard Marsh
 Paul Marsh

D-U-N-S 20-017-1825   (HQ)
RIFF'S LIMITED
2 Hardy Ave, Grand Falls-Windsor, NL, A2A 2P9
(709) 489-5631
Emp Here 13   *Sales* 20,534,300
SIC 5311 Department stores
 Ivar Riff

D-U-N-S 20-547-8605   (HQ)
RIVERVIEW MOTORS LIMITED
RIVERVIEW MOTORS
75 Lincoln Rd, Grand Falls-Windsor, NL, A2A 1N3
(709) 489-2138
Emp Here 1   *Sales* 19,923,120
SIC 5511 New and used car dealers
 Frank Howard
 Thelma Howard

D-U-N-S 25-297-5958   (BR)
WAL-MART CANADA CORP
(*Suby of* WALMART INC.)
19 Cromer Ave, Grand Falls-Windsor, NL, A2A 2K5
(709) 489-5739
Emp Here 185
SIC 5311 Department stores
 Anthony Brake

Grand Falls-Windsor, NL A2B

D-U-N-S 25-985-4651   (SL)
EXPLOITS WELDING & MACHINE SHOP LTD
2 Queensway, Grand Falls-Windsor, NL, A2B 1J3
(709) 489-5618
Emp Here 77   *Sales* 13,816,033
SIC 3599 Industrial machinery, nec
 Chad Stuckless
 Marjorie Stuckless

Happy Valley-Goose Bay, NL A0P

D-U-N-S 20-337-8807   (SL)
AIR BOREALIS LIMITED PARTNERSHIP
1 Centralia Dr, Happy Valley-Goose Bay, NL, A0P 1C0
(709) 576-1800
Emp Here 122   *Sales* 32,571,316
SIC 4512 Air transportation, scheduled
 Tom Randell

D-U-N-S 20-283-2291   (BR)
ASTALDI CANADA INC
(*Suby of* FIN.AST. SRL)
358 Hamilton River Rd, Happy Valley-Goose Bay, NL, A0P 1C0
(709) 896-4470
Emp Here 1,000
SIC 1541 Industrial buildings and warehouses
 Sante Astaldi

D-U-N-S 20-779-5485   (SL)
BENNETT'S LIMITED
BENNETT'S ULTRAMAR
165 Hamilton River Rd, Happy Valley-Goose Bay, NL, A0P 1E0
(709) 896-5024
Emp Here 30   *Sales* 14,942,340
SIC 5541 Gasoline service stations

 George Bennett
 Elaine Bennett
 Darrell Bennett
 Sonya Bennett

D-U-N-S 20-779-0841   (HQ)
HAMILTON STORES LIMITED
PARKS STORE
445 Hamilton River Rd, Happy Valley-Goose Bay, NL, A0P 1S0
(709) 896-5451
Emp Here 50   *Sales* 11,088,522
SIC 5399 Miscellaneous general merchandise
 Herbert Woodward
 Kay Woodward

D-U-N-S 24-524-1596   (SL)
INNU MIKUN INC
Gd Stn, Happy Valley-Goose Bay, NL, A0P 1C0
(709) 896-5521
Emp Here 80   *Sales* 21,358,240
SIC 4512 Air transportation, scheduled
 Brain Chafe
 Robert Halliday
 Tom Randell
 Kelvin Ash
 Virginia Collins
 David Hart Jr

D-U-N-S 24-449-6956   (HQ)
LABRADOR INUIT DEVELOPMENT CORPORATION
LIDC
6 Royal St Unit 2, Happy Valley-Goose Bay, NL, A0P 1E0
(709) 896-8505
Emp Here 6   *Sales* 10,462,120
SIC 6719 Holding companies, nec
 James Thornborne
 Chris Webb
 Davis Clinton
 Stephanie Normore

D-U-N-S 20-014-1968   (HQ)
LABRADOR MOTORS LIMITED
(*Suby of* PETERCO LIMITED)
12 Loring Dr, Happy Valley-Goose Bay, NL, A0P 1C0
(709) 896-2452
Emp Here 34   *Sales* 42,161,760
SIC 5511 New and used car dealers
 Peter Woodward
 Melvin Woodward
 Sybil Woodward

D-U-N-S 20-908-2569   (HQ)
LABRADOR SCHOOL BOARD
16 Strathcona St, Happy Valley-Goose Bay, NL, A0P 1E0
(709) 896-7220
Emp Here 120   *Sales* 22,849,470
SIC 8211 Elementary and secondary schools
 Bruce Vey
 George Michelau
 Goronwy Price
 Glenn Andrews
 Patricia Loder
 Heather Leriche

D-U-N-S 24-450-5780   (SL)
NEWFOUNDLAND MULTI-FOODS LIMITED
MULTI-FOODS
(*Suby of* NOR-LAB LIMITED)
43 Aspen Rd, Happy Valley-Goose Bay, NL, A0P 1C0
(709) 896-3543
Emp Here 12   *Sales* 10,026,924
SIC 5142 Packaged frozen goods
 Andrew Hewitt
 Andrew Warr
 Charles Warr
 Bob Warr
 Burt Warr
 Don Warr

D-U-N-S 25-778-6855   (HQ)

NOR-LAB LIMITED
MAXWELL'S II
8 London St, Happy Valley-Goose Bay, NL, A0P 1E0
(709) 896-3795
Emp Here 17   *Sales* 28,409,618
SIC 5145 Confectionery
 Charles Warr Jr
 Robert Warr
 Bertram Warr
 Donald Warr
 Sandra Warr
 Gloria Warr

D-U-N-S 20-756-2542   (SL)
RIDEOUT LABRADOR LIMITED
RIDEOUT TOOL & MACHINE
Gd, Happy Valley-Goose Bay, NL, A0P 1C0
(709) 754-2240
Emp Here 49   *Sales* 23,276,274
SIC 5084 Industrial machinery and equipment
 Raymond Rideout
 Harry Rideout

D-U-N-S 25-503-7517   (BR)
SERCO CANADA INC
SERCO FACILITIES MANAGEMENT
(*Suby of* SERCO GROUP PLC)
271 Canadian Forces, Happy Valley-Goose Bay, NL, A0P 1C0
(709) 896-6946
Emp Here 350
SIC 8741 Management services
 Dusty Miller

D-U-N-S 20-449-7861   (SL)
TERRINGTON CONSUMERS CO-OPERATIVE SOCIETY LIMITED
1 Abbott Dr, Happy Valley-Goose Bay, NL, A0P 1E0
(709) 896-5737
Emp Here 50   *Sales* 16,148,450
SIC 5411 Grocery stores
 Fred Humber
 David Tipping

D-U-N-S 25-494-7252   (HQ)
TORNGAIT SERVICES INC
TSI
215 Hamilton River Rd, Happy Valley-Goose Bay, NL, A0P 1E0
(709) 896-5431
Sales 19,185,592
SIC 1629 Heavy construction, nec
 R.J. Robert Kieley

D-U-N-S 25-828-7747   (SL)
TORNGAT REGIONAL HOUSING ASSOCIATION
436 Hamilton Rd, Happy Valley-Goose Bay, NL, A0P 1C0
(709) 896-8126
Emp Here 40   *Sales* 10,870,240
SIC 6531 Real estate agents and managers
 Margaret Fox

D-U-N-S 24-448-9209   (HQ)
UNIVERSAL HELICOPTERS (NFLD) LIMITED
82 Winnipeg St, Happy Valley-Goose Bay, NL, A0P 1C0
(709) 896-2444
Sales 11,691,144
SIC 4522 Air transportation, nonscheduled
 Harry Steele
 Peter Steele
 Geoff Goodyear
 Norman Noseworthy
 Paul Williams
 Ross Vardy

D-U-N-S 20-987-5541   (SL)
WOODWARD'S LIMITED
16 Loring Dr, Happy Valley-Goose Bay, NL, A0P 1C0
(709) 896-2421
Emp Here 35   *Sales* 11,366,390

SIC 4581 Airports, flying fields, and services
 Melvin Woodward
 Peter Woodward
 Sybil Woodward

D-U-N-S 20-014-2180   (HQ)
WOODWARD'S OIL LIMITED
16 Loring Dr, Happy Valley-Goose Bay, NL, A0P 1C0
(709) 896-2421
Sales 41,295,825
SIC 5983 Fuel oil dealers
 Peter Woodward
 Melvin Woodward
 Dennis White
 Fred Constantine
 Roy Osmond

Harbour Grace, NL A0A

D-U-N-S 20-449-9081   (SL)
GREENSPAR WHOLESALE LIMITED
125 Harvey St, Harbour Grace, NL, A0A 2M0
(709) 596-3538
Emp Here 33   *Sales* 24,503,160
SIC 5199 Nondurable goods, nec
 Bruce Sparkes
 David Sheppard
 Daniel Green Jr

Hillview, NL A0E

D-U-N-S 24-625-8920   (SL)
GAMBO DRUGS LIMITED
Gd, Hillview, NL, A0E 2A0
(709) 546-2460
Emp Here 30   *Sales* 19,693,920
SIC 5961 Catalog and mail-order houses
 Karl Reid

Holyrood, NL A0A

D-U-N-S 25-308-4719   (BR)
NEWFOUNDLAND & LABRADOR HYDRO
(*Suby of* PROVINCE OF NEWFOUNDLAND & LABRADOR)
1 Thermal Plant Rd, Holyrood, NL, A0A 2R0
(709) 229-7441
Emp Here 120
SIC 4911 Electric services
 Jeff Vincent

Jacksons Arm, NL A0K

D-U-N-S 20-189-7530   (SL)
NORTHERN SHRIMP COMPANY LTD
Gd, Jacksons Arm, NL, A0K 3H0

Emp Here 120   *Sales* 41,482,800
SIC 2092 Fresh or frozen packaged fish
 Martin Sullivan

Jerseyside, NL A0B

D-U-N-S 20-642-6264   (SL)
EDWARD COLLINS CONTRACTING LIMITED
2 Guy St, Jerseyside, NL, A0B 2G0
(709) 227-5509
Emp Here 70   *Sales* 39,923,660
SIC 1542 Nonresidential construction, nec
 Edward Collins

Francis (Frank) Collins
Theresa Collins

Joe Batts Arm, NL A0G

D-U-N-S 20-384-0434 (SL)
SHOREFAST SOCIAL ENTERPRISES INC
181 Main St, Joe Batts Arm, NL, A0G 2X0
(709) 658-3444
Emp Here 145 *Sales* 13,440,050
SIC 7011 Hotels and motels
Zita Cobb
Alan Cobb
Anthony Cobb

L'Anse Au Loup, NL A0K

D-U-N-S 24-260-4668 (HQ)
LABRADOR FISHERMEN'S UNION SHRIMP COMPANY LIMITED
LABRADOR FISHERMAN'S COMPANY
46 Waterfront Rd, L'Anse Au Loup, NL, A0K 3L0
(709) 927-5816
Emp Here 5 *Sales* 192,517,075
SIC 2092 Fresh or frozen packaged fish
Frank Flynn
Dwight Russell
Harrison Campbell
Lester Letto
Kevin Normore
Morley Normore
Donald Kippenhuck
Wade Dyson

La Scie, NL A0K

D-U-N-S 24-524-1703 (BR)
COLD NORTH SEAFOODS LIMITED
(*Suby of* COLD NORTH SEAFOODS LIMITED)
2 Water St, La Scie, NL, A0K 3M0

Emp Here 80
SIC 2092 Fresh or frozen packaged fish
Chris Weir

D-U-N-S 25-977-8702 (SL)
O/L ENTERPRISES INC
Gd, La Scie, NL, A0K 3M0
(709) 675-2085
Emp Here 80 *Sales* 14,783,840
SIC 4832 Radio broadcasting stations
Larry Butt
Rhoda Butt

Labrador City, NL A2V

D-U-N-S 24-994-5460 (SL)
175042 CANADA INC
G.S.C. CRANE OPERATIONS
2 First Ave, Labrador City, NL, A2V 2K5
(709) 282-3910
Emp Here 35 *Sales* 10,225,915
SIC 7353 Heavy construction equipment rental
Yvon-Robert Gagnon

D-U-N-S 25-360-5729 (SL)
ALLARD DISTRIBUTING LIMITED
ALLARD
208 Humphry Rd, Labrador City, NL, A2V 2K7
(709) 944-5144
Emp Here 35 *Sales* 44,002,035
SIC 5172 Petroleum products, nec

Gilles Allard
Hilda Allard
Denis Allard

D-U-N-S 24-426-9291 (SL)
BUYNFLY FOOD LIMITED
IGA BUY N' FLY
208 Humber Ave, Labrador City, NL, A2V 1K9
(709) 944-4003
Emp Here 75 *Sales* 22,010,775
SIC 5411 Grocery stores
Pete Cornick
Alec Snow
Bill Gidge

D-U-N-S 25-954-2889 (SL)
CANADIAN TIRE
500 Vanier Ave, Labrador City, NL, A2V 2W7
(709) 944-7740
Emp Here 30 *Sales* 10,926,450
SIC 5014 Tires and tubes
Mark Lawrence

D-U-N-S 20-449-5089 (SL)
CAROL AUTOMOBILE LIMITED
55 Avalon Dr, Labrador City, NL, A2V 1K3
(709) 944-2000
Emp Here 34 *Sales* 16,934,652
SIC 5511 New and used car dealers
Mario Cayouette
Michel Cayouette

D-U-N-S 20-548-2797 (SL)
CAROL WABUSH CO-OP SOCIETY LIMITED
COMMUNITY CONSUMERS COOP
500 Vanier Ave, Labrador City, NL, A2V 2W7

Emp Here 38 *Sales* 12,414,965
SIC 5411 Grocery stores
Carson Gibson

D-U-N-S 24-373-7025 (BR)
COMPAGNIE MINIERE IOC INC
IRON ORE COMPANY OF CANADA
(*Suby of* RIO TINTO PLC)
2 Avalon Dr, Labrador City, NL, A2V 2Y6
(709) 944-8400
Emp Here 1,500
SIC 1011 Iron ores
Chantal Lavoie

D-U-N-S 24-858-2889 (SL)
DEXTER MINING INC
(*Suby of* MUNICIPAL ENTERPRISES LIMITED)
1001 Luce St, Labrador City, NL, A2V 2K7
(709) 944-2995
Emp Here 49 *Sales* 12,063,114
SIC 1794 Excavation work
Eirc Testiens
David Wood
Harold Thomas
Ken Thomas
Ken Maclean

D-U-N-S 24-319-5109 (BR)
WAL-MART CANADA CORP
WALMART
(*Suby of* WALMART INC.)
500 Vanier Ave Suite 1035, Labrador City, NL, A2V 2W7
(709) 944-3378
Emp Here 120
SIC 5311 Department stores
Corey Legge

Lewisporte, NL A0G

D-U-N-S 20-779-3886 (HQ)
COASTAL SHIPPING LIMITED
128 Main St, Lewisporte, NL, A0G 3A0
(709) 535-6944
Sales 86,840,250

SIC 4424 Deep sea domestic transportation of freight
Peter Woodward
Roy Osmondand

D-U-N-S 24-388-9305 (SL)
LABRADOR MARINE INC
111 Main St Suite 502, Lewisporte, NL, A0G 3A0
(709) 535-0810
Emp Here 250 *Sales* 166,723,000
SIC 4731 Freight transportation arrangement
Dennis White

D-U-N-S 20-907-5738 (SL)
LEWISPORTE AREA CONSUMERS CO-OP SOCIETY LTD
LEWISPORTE AREA CO-OP
423 Main St Suite 415, Lewisporte, NL, A0G 3A0
(709) 535-6728
Emp Here 32 *Sales* 10,335,008
SIC 5411 Grocery stores
Owen Brinson

D-U-N-S 20-150-4987 (SL)
LEWISPORTE CO-OP LTD
465 Main St, Lewisporte, NL, A0G 3A0
(709) 535-6728
Emp Here 44 *Sales* 12,062,688
SIC 5411 Grocery stores
Owen Brinson

D-U-N-S 20-642-6025 (HQ)
NOTRE DAME AGENCIES LIMITED
NOTRE DAME CASTLE BUILDING CENTRES
391 Main St, Lewisporte, NL, A0G 3A0
(709) 535-8691
Emp Here 25 *Sales* 48,006,540
SIC 5712 Furniture stores
Cluny Sheppard
Tina Belbin
Golda Sheppard
Jennifer Welsh
Ann Marie Hodder
Lorna Sargent
Scott Belbin
Kirk Hodder

Main Brook, NL A0K

D-U-N-S 20-323-0768 (SL)
NORTHERN LIGHTS SEAFOOD INC
44 Waters St Suite 40, Main Brook, NL, A0K 3N0
(709) 865-3333
Emp Here 30 *Sales* 25,067,310
SIC 5146 Fish and seafoods
Andy Schnare

Marystown, NL A0E

D-U-N-S 20-016-5736 (HQ)
AYLWARDS (1986) LIMITED
AYLWARDS HOME CENTRE
200 Atlantic St Suite 192, Marystown, NL, A0E 2M0
(709) 279-2202
Emp Here 25 *Sales* 16,594,424
SIC 5251 Hardware stores
Ronald Aylward
Daniel Aylward
Andrew Aylward
Jack Forsey

D-U-N-S 20-985-1591 (HQ)
SOUTH COAST INSURANCE AGENCY LIMITED
227 Atlantic St, Marystown, NL, A0E 2M0
(709) 279-3200
Emp Here 19 *Sales* 22,897,620

SIC 6411 Insurance agents, brokers, and service
Gordon Hickman
Kelly Hickman
Marie Hickman

Millertown, NL A0H

D-U-N-S 20-739-6123 (BR)
TECK RESOURCES LIMITED
DUCK POND OPERATIONS
(*Suby of* TECK RESOURCES LIMITED)
32 Rte 370, Millertown, NL, A0H 1V0
(709) 852-2195
Emp Here 250
SIC 1081 Metal mining services
Larry Bartlett

Milltown, NL A0H

D-U-N-S 25-686-7185 (BR)
NEWFOUNDLAND & LABRADOR HYDRO
(*Suby of* PROVINCE OF NEWFOUNDLAND & LABRADOR)
1 Kemp Boggy Road, Milltown, NL, A0H 1W0
(709) 882-2551
Emp Here 100
SIC 4911 Electric services
Legeson Kearley

Mount Pearl, NL A1N

D-U-N-S 20-011-8556 (SL)
AAA PRECISION TIRE AND AUTOMOTIVE
86 Clyde Ave, Mount Pearl, NL, A1N 4S2
(709) 747-9595
Emp Here 45 *Sales* 28,317,600
SIC 5511 New and used car dealers

D-U-N-S 25-100-6961 (HQ)
ASCO CANADA LIMITED
ASCO
10 Corisande Dr, Mount Pearl, NL, A1N 5A4
(709) 748-7800
Emp Here 2 *Sales* 18,513,540
SIC 4225 General warehousing and storage
Robert Crosbie

D-U-N-S 20-113-7705 (SL)
ATLANTIC TRAILER & EQUIPMENT LTD
8 Lintros Pl, Mount Pearl, NL, A1N 5K2
(709) 745-3260
Emp Here 20 *Sales* 10,000,000
SIC 5083 Farm and garden machinery
Rick Power
Steve Power

D-U-N-S 20-987-3322 (HQ)
BAE-NEWPLAN GROUP LIMITED
(*Suby of* GROUPE SNC-LAVALIN INC)
1133 Topsail Rd, Mount Pearl, NL, A1N 5G2
(709) 368-0118
Sales 13,196,850
SIC 8711 Engineering services
Albert Williams
Elwood Reid

D-U-N-S 25-543-2957 (SL)
BARTLETT, H J ELECTRIC INC
51 Dundee Ave Unit 1, Mount Pearl, NL, A1N 4R6
(709) 747-2204
Emp Here 70 *Sales* 15,248,030
SIC 1731 Electrical work
Harry Bartlett

D-U-N-S 24-228-4318 (BR)
BELL ALIANT REGIONAL COMMUNICA-

TIONS INC
(Suby of BCE INC)
760 Topsail Rd Suite 2110, Mount Pearl, NL,
A1N 3J5
(709) 739-2122
Emp Here 450
SIC 4899 Communication services, nec
Penny Harding

D-U-N-S 24-422-8354   (HQ)
BRITISH CONFECTIONERY COMPANY (1982) LIMITED
7 Panther Pl, Mount Pearl, NL, A1N 5B7
(709) 747-2377
Sales 19,407,850
SIC 6712 Bank holding companies
David Connolly
Gerald Connolly Jr

D-U-N-S 20-986-1202   (HQ)
BROWNE'S AUTO SUPPLIES LIMITED
1075 Topsail Rd, Mount Pearl, NL, A1N 5G1
(709) 364-9397
Emp Here 12   *Sales* 11,953,872
SIC 5511 New and used car dealers
Neil Browne
Annette Browne
Sheila Browne
John Browne

D-U-N-S 25-709-5323   (SL)
CANADIAN AUTO RECYCLING LIMITED
AUTO PARTS NETWORK
6 Corey King Dr, Mount Pearl, NL, A1N 0A2
(709) 747-2000
Emp Here 30   *Sales* 14,942,340
SIC 5531 Auto and home supply stores
Glenn Hickey

D-U-N-S 25-266-4263   (HQ)
CAPITAL CRANE LIMITED
20 Sagona Ave, Mount Pearl, NL, A1N 4R2
(709) 748-8888
Emp Here 45   *Sales* 16,265,090
SIC 7353 Heavy construction equipment rental
Danny King
Miguel Finn

D-U-N-S 24-967-5005   (SL)
CGI DEVELOPMENT INC
20 Sagona Ave, Mount Pearl, NL, A1N 4R2
(709) 748-8888
Emp Here 82   *Sales* 22,217,244
SIC 1521 Single-family housing construction
Dan King

D-U-N-S 20-449-6582   (HQ)
CITY TIRE & AUTO CENTRE LIMITED
GOODYEAR
1123 Topsail Rd, Mount Pearl, NL, A1N 5G2
(709) 364-6808
Emp Here 26   *Sales* 28,330,000
SIC 7538 General automotive repair shops
Everett Blackwood
Colin Blackwood

D-U-N-S 24-833-9335   (HQ)
COASTAL MARINE LIMITED
COASTAL OUTDOORS
1256 Topsail Rd, Mount Pearl, NL, A1N 5E8
(709) 747-0159
Emp Here 21   *Sales* 20,766,240
SIC 5551 Boat dealers
Kevin King

D-U-N-S 20-907-6884   (HQ)
COHEN'S HOME FURNISHINGS LIMITED
SIMMONS MATTRESS GALLERY
(Suby of BELL, CHARLES R. LIMITED)
24 Glencoe Dr, Mount Pearl, NL, A1N 4P6
(709) 739-6631
Emp Here 15   *Sales* 46,480,600
SIC 5712 Furniture stores
Andrew Bell
Richard Yabsley

D-U-N-S 24-476-6163   (HQ)

COLD NORTH SEAFOODS LIMITED
157 Glencoe Dr Suite 200, Mount Pearl, NL,
A1N 4S7
(709) 368-9953
Emp Here 50   *Sales* 41,778,850
SIC 5146 Fish and seafoods
Terry Daley

D-U-N-S 24-722-8414   (HQ)
COMPUSULT LIMITED
COMPUSULT
40 Bannister St, Mount Pearl, NL, A1N 1W1
(709) 745-7914
Emp Here 45   *Sales* 10,638,660
SIC 7371 Custom computer programming services
Barry O'rourke
Paul Mitten

D-U-N-S 25-244-8761   (SL)
DATA WIRING SOLUTIONS INC
1170 Topsail Rd Suite 3, Mount Pearl, NL,
A1N 5E8
(709) 747-2150
Emp Here 49   *Sales* 11,803,316
SIC 1623 Water, sewer, and utility lines
Shawn Kersey

D-U-N-S 24-352-6881   (BR)
EASTERN REGIONAL INTEGRATED HEALTH AUTHORITY
EASTERN HEALTH
(Suby of EASTERN REGIONAL INTEGRATED HEALTH AUTHORITY)
760 Topsail Rd, Mount Pearl, NL, A1N 3J5
(709) 752-4534
Emp Here 400
SIC 8062 General medical and surgical hospitals
Chris Al'grady

D-U-N-S 20-755-8953   (SL)
GENOA DESIGN INTERNATIONAL LTD
117 Glencoe Dr Suite 201, Mount Pearl, NL,
A1N 4S7
(709) 368-0669
Emp Here 68   *Sales* 11,965,144
SIC 8711 Engineering services
Leonard Pecore
Gina Pecore
Darren Letto
Kyran Pennell
Phillip Genge

D-U-N-S 20-799-1964   (SL)
INDEPENDENT DOCKSIDE GRADING INC
19 Old Placentia Rd, Mount Pearl, NL, A1N
4P4
(709) 364-5473
Emp Here 87   *Sales* 24,647,100
SIC 7549 Automotive services, nec
Jean Cooper
Howard Scott
Cris Daley

D-U-N-S 24-347-7457   (BR)
INMARSAT SOLUTIONS (CANADA) INC
34 Glencoe Dr, Mount Pearl, NL, A1N 4S8

Emp Here 125
SIC 5065 Electronic parts and equipment, nec
Levy May

D-U-N-S 24-913-2838   (HQ)
INMARSAT SOLUTIONS (CANADA) INC
34 Glencoe Dr, Mount Pearl, NL, A1N 4P6
(709) 724-5400
Emp Here 272   *Sales* 91,999,600
SIC 4899 Communication services, nec
Alison Horrocks
Sharon Forsey
David Thornhill
Roger Butt

D-U-N-S 20-268-3954   (BR)
IRVING, J. D. LIMITED
KENT HOME IMPROVEMENT WAREHOUSE

(Suby of IRVING, J. D. LIMITED)
60 Old Placentia Rd, Mount Pearl, NL, A1N
4Y1
(709) 748-3500
Emp Here 130
SIC 5211 Lumber and other building materials
Jackie Hopkins

D-U-N-S 20-985-3035   (HQ)
K&D PRATT GROUP INC
INDUSTRIAL SALES AND SERVICES
(Suby of JENNIKER HOLDINGS INC)
126 Glencoe Dr, Mount Pearl, NL, A1N 4S9
(709) 722-5690
Emp Here 45   *Sales* 29,926,638
SIC 5085 Industrial supplies
Andrew Bell
Jeffrey Macpherson
Shawn Tobin

D-U-N-S 25-715-6364   (SL)
KARISS ENTERPRISES LIMITED
DONOVANS IRVING
65 Clyde Ave, Mount Pearl, NL, A1N 4R8
(709) 745-3403
Emp Here 35   *Sales* 17,432,730
SIC 5541 Gasoline service stations
Kariss Lidstone
Sheila Reid

D-U-N-S 24-649-3261   (SL)
KENT JB FR COUNCIL 6638
7 Greenwood Cres, Mount Pearl, NL, A1N
2C1
(709) 781-6638
Emp Here 49   *Sales* 10,825,766
SIC 1711 Plumbing, heating, air-conditioning
Peter Furlong

D-U-N-S 20-279-0929   (SL)
MADSEN DIESEL & TURBINE INC
141 Glencoe Dr, Mount Pearl, NL, A1N 4S7
(709) 726-6774
Emp Here 30   *Sales* 14,250,780
SIC 5084 Industrial machinery and equipment
A. Geoffrey Pearcey
Jason B Pearcey

D-U-N-S 25-612-5139   (SL)
MASONIC PARK INC
100 Masonic Dr, Mount Pearl, NL, A1N 3K5

Emp Here 80   *Sales* 7,413,200
SIC 8322 Individual and family services
Marie Evens

D-U-N-S 20-548-4439   (HQ)
N.C.H. HOLDINGS LIMITED
N C HUTTON
14 Clyde Ave, Mount Pearl, NL, A1N 4S1
(709) 368-2131
Emp Here 1   *Sales* 10,524,169
SIC 6512 Nonresidential building operators
Noel Hutton
Christopher Hutton
Ronalda Hutton
Joanne Gray

D-U-N-S 20-050-8310   (SL)
NEWFOUNDLAND & LABRADOR SAFETY COUNCIL INC
SAFETY SERVICES NL
3 Moffatt Rd, Mount Pearl, NL, A1N 5B9
(709) 754-0210
Emp Here 50   *Sales* 11,714,400
SIC 8748 Business consulting, nec
Len Leriche

D-U-N-S 24-832-1135   (SL)
NEWFOUNDLAND HVAC LIMITED
16 Thomas Byrne Dr, Mount Pearl, NL, A1N
0E1
(709) 738-7700
Emp Here 45   *Sales* 10,487,925
SIC 1711 Plumbing, heating, air-conditioning
Darren Moss

D-U-N-S 25-370-5156   (SL)

OCEANEERING CANADA LIMITED
23 Dundee Ave, Mount Pearl, NL, A1N 4R6
(709) 570-7072
Emp Here 85   *Sales* 14,956,430
SIC 8711 Engineering services
J Jay Collins

D-U-N-S 24-450-7240   (HQ)
P.S. ATLANTIC LIMITED
PAINT SHOP, THE
102 Clyde Ave, Mount Pearl, NL, A1N 4S2
(709) 747-5432
Sales 20,790,560
SIC 5198 Paints, varnishes, and supplies
Paul Burt
Paula Bennett
Robert Payne

D-U-N-S 20-345-2479   (HQ)
RIVERBEND FREIGHT SERVICES LIMITED
26 Kyle Ave, Mount Pearl, NL, A1N 4R5
(709) 368-1773
Emp Here 1   *Sales* 28,598,185
SIC 4731 Freight transportation arrangement
Gordon Peddle

D-U-N-S 20-016-3145   (HQ)
ROYAL GARAGE LIMITED, THE
DODGE CITY
709 Topsail Rd, Mount Pearl, NL, A1N 3N4
(709) 748-2110
Emp Here 50   *Sales* 62,928,000
SIC 5511 New and used car dealers
Charles Elton Jr
Patrick Broderick
Stephen A. Elton

D-U-N-S 20-211-0446   (BR)
SCHLUMBERGER CANADA LIMITED
SCHLUMBERGER-OIL FIELD SERVICES DIV OF
2 Panther Pl, Mount Pearl, NL, A1N 5B1
(709) 748-7900
Emp Here 200
SIC 1389 Oil and gas field services, nec
Ruth Graham

D-U-N-S 20-250-8060   (SL)
SERENITY NURSING AND HOME SUPPORT SERVICES LTD
SERENITY HOME CARE
2 Glendale Ave, Mount Pearl, NL, A1N 1M9
(709) 364-9688
Emp Here 115   *Sales* 7,885,090
SIC 8059 Nursing and personal care, nec
Elizabeth Jones
Douglas Jones

D-U-N-S 25-124-5494   (BR)
SNC-LAVALIN INC
BAE NEWPLAN
(Suby of GROUPE SNC-LAVALIN INC)
1090 Topsail Rd, Mount Pearl, NL, A1N 5E7
(709) 368-0118
Emp Here 80
SIC 8711 Engineering services
Cliss Johnston

D-U-N-S 24-259-2970   (BR)
SOBEYS CAPITAL INCORPORATED
SYSCO FOOD SERVICES ATLANTIC
(Suby of EMPIRE COMPANY LIMITED)
10 Old Placentia Rd, Mount Pearl, NL, A1N
4P5
(709) 748-1200
Emp Here 120
SIC 5148 Fresh fruits and vegetables
Heber Prince

D-U-N-S 20-607-4895   (SL)
SOCIETY OF SAINT VINCENT DE PAUL
110 Ashford Dr, Mount Pearl, NL, A1N 3L6
(709) 747-3320
Emp Here 30   *Sales* 12,122,941
SIC 8699 Membership organizations, nec
Alexis Baksi

D-U-N-S 20-324-5659   (SL)

SOLACE POWER INC.
1118 Topsail Rd Suite 201, Mount Pearl, NL,
A1N 5E7
(709) 745-6099
Emp Here 22   *Sales* 13,785,508
SIC 4911 Electric services
  Michael Gotlieb
  Kris Mcneil
  Neil Chailk
  Gordon Conlin

D-U-N-S 20-182-6257   (BR)
SYSCO CANADA, INC
SYSCO FOOD SERVICES OF ATLANTIC CANADA
(*Suby of* SYSCO CORPORATION)
10 Old Placentia Rd, Mount Pearl, NL, A1N 4P5
(709) 748-1200
Emp Here 100
SIC 5142 Packaged frozen goods
  Jim Mcguire

D-U-N-S 25-713-8495   (BR)
TOROMONT INDUSTRIES LTD
BATTLEFIELD EQUIPMENT RENTAL, DIV OF
(*Suby of* TOROMONT INDUSTRIES LTD)
24 Third St, Mount Pearl, NL, A1N 2A5
(709) 282-5537
Emp Here 80
SIC 5082 Construction and mining machinery
  Terry Dyczkowsky

D-U-N-S 24-449-9760   (SL)
WADDEN, F.J. & SONS LIMITED
WADDEN F J FOOD SERVICE DIV OF
51 Glencoe Dr, Mount Pearl, NL, A1N 4S6
(709) 364-1444
Emp Here 60   *Sales* 43,002,960
SIC 5145 Confectionery
  Patrick W Wadden
  William Wadden
  Peter Rose

D-U-N-S 24-257-6353   (BR)
WAL-MART CANADA CORP
(*Suby of* WALMART INC.)
60 Merchant Dr, Mount Pearl, NL, A1N 5J5
(709) 364-4214
Emp Here 200
SIC 5311 Department stores
  Edward Walsh

D-U-N-S 24-336-7120   (HQ)
WLB SERVICES LIMITED
MAGICUTS
54 O'Flaherty Cres, Mount Pearl, NL, A1N 4M1
(709) 747-2340
Emp Here 2   *Sales* 13,347,750
SIC 7231 Beauty shops
  James Woodman
  Shirley Boone-Fraser
  Brenda Woodman

Nain, NL A0P

D-U-N-S 24-955-9592   (SL)
TORNGAIT UJAGANNIAVINGIT CORPORATION
TUC
(*Suby of* LABRADOR INUIT DEVELOPMENT CORPORATION)
2 Morhdt Rd, Nain, NL, A0P 1L0
(709) 922-2143
Emp Here 110
SIC 3281 Cut stone and stone products
  Richard Pamak

Newtown, NL A0G

D-U-N-S 20-781-1485   (SL)
BARBOUR LIVING HERITAGE VILLAGE
Gd, Newtown, NL, A0G 3L0
(709) 536-3220
Emp Here 65   *Sales* 46,098,780
SIC 8699 Membership organizations, nec
  Judy Stagg

Norris Point, NL A0K

D-U-N-S 25-331-0676   (BR)
WESTERN REGIONAL INTEGRATED HEALTH AUTHORITY, THE
BONNE BAY HEALTH CENTRE
(*Suby of* WESTERN REGIONAL INTEGRATED HEALTH AUTHORITY, THE)
Gd, Norris Point, NL, A0K 3V0
(709) 458-2211
Emp Here 100
SIC 8062 General medical and surgical hospitals
  Meta Kennedy

Paradise, NL A1L

D-U-N-S 24-826-2941   (SL)
ACAN WINDOWS INC
ACAN WINDOWS AND DOORS
1641 Topsail Rd, Paradise, NL, A1L 1V1

Emp Here 100   *Sales* 20,189,700
SIC 3089 Plastics products, nec
  Tae (Ted) Kwon

D-U-N-S 25-496-7342   (SL)
B & B LINE CONSTRUCTION LTD
FIBRECOM
1274 Kenmount Rd, Paradise, NL, A1L 1N3
(709) 722-1112
Emp Here 45   *Sales* 10,839,780
SIC 1623 Water, sewer, and utility lines
  James (Jim) O'leary

D-U-N-S 20-003-6825   (SL)
EASTERN EXPRESS LTD
21 St. Anne'S Cres, Paradise, NL, A1L 3W1
(709) 754-8855
Emp Here 40   *Sales* 17,739,600
SIC 7389 Business services, nec
  James May
  Marie May

D-U-N-S 25-701-9828   (SL)
ENVIRO CLEAN (NFLD.) LIMITED
POWER VAC DISASTER KLEENUP
(*Suby of* BELFOR HOLDINGS INC.)
155 Mcnamara Dr, Paradise, NL, A1L 0A7
(709) 781-3264
Emp Here 80   *Sales* 2,557,440
SIC 7349 Building maintenance services, nec
  Henry Power
  Paul Black
  Paul Conrad
  Carney Flynn
  Mark Genge

D-U-N-S 24-126-9893   (HQ)
PENNECON ENERGY HYDRAULIC SYSTEMS LIMITED
(*Suby of* PENNECON ENERGY LTD)
2 Maverick Pl, Paradise, NL, A1L 0H6
(709) 726-3490
Emp Here 26   *Sales* 13,320,258
SIC 7699 Repair services, nec
  Paul Stanley

D-U-N-S 25-264-8246   (SL)
PRIDE PAK NFLD LTD
107 Mcnamara Dr, Paradise, NL, A1L 0A7

---

(709) 782-8000
Emp Here 20   *Sales* 10,702,480
SIC 5148 Fresh fruits and vegetables
  Greg Karr

Petty Harbour, NL A0A

D-U-N-S 24-877-5835   (SL)
PEERLESS FISH COMPANY LIMITED
Gd, Petty Harbour, NL, A0A 3H0
(709) 747-1521
Emp Here 50   *Sales* 41,778,850
SIC 5146 Fish and seafoods
  Gary Hearn

Placentia, NL A0B

D-U-N-S 24-345-6030   (BR)
EASTERN REGIONAL INTEGRATED HEALTH AUTHORITY
PLACENTIA HEALTH CENTRE
(*Suby of* EASTERN REGIONAL INTEGRATED HEALTH AUTHORITY)
1 Corrigan Pl, Placentia, NL, A0B 2Y0
(709) 227-2061
Emp Here 187
SIC 8051 Skilled nursing care facilities
  Sandra Gear

D-U-N-S 20-261-7106   (SL)
PROVINCIAL READY MIX INC
36 Prince William Dr, Placentia, NL, A0B 2Y0
(709) 227-2727
Emp Here 49   *Sales* 14,140,567
SIC 1522 Residential construction, nec
  Morgan O'reilly

D-U-N-S 24-380-2183   (SL)
TACAMOR INC
1 Augusta Pl, Placentia, NL, A0B 2Y0

Emp Here 49   *Sales* 51,562,035
SIC 6351 Surety insurance
  Ken Hann

Plate Cove West, NL A0C

D-U-N-S 20-119-1058   (SL)
FURLONG BROTHERS LIMITED
Gd, Plate Cove West, NL, A0C 2E0
(709) 545-2251
Emp Here 100   *Sales* 34,569,000
SIC 2092 Fresh or frozen packaged fish
  Michael F Furlong
  Michael Furlong
  Samuel Furlong

Port Au Choix, NL A0K

D-U-N-S 20-264-6816   (BR)
OCEAN CHOICE INTERNATIONAL
OCI
(*Suby of* OCEAN CHOICE INTERNATIONAL)
7476 Fisher St, Port Au Choix, NL, A0K 4C0
(709) 861-3506
Emp Here 180
SIC 2092 Fresh or frozen packaged fish
  Richard Roberts

Port Au Port, NL A0N

D-U-N-S 20-814-1304   (BR)

ATLANTIC MINERALS LIMITED
ATLANTIC READY MIX
Gd, Port Au Port, NL, A0N 1T0
(709) 644-2447
Emp Here 100
SIC 1011 Iron ores
  David Mc Issaz

D-U-N-S 20-223-9310   (SL)
KENDALL'S FISHERY LIMITED
Gd, Port Au Port, NL, A0N 1T0
(709) 642-5711
Emp Here 25   *Sales* 20,889,425
SIC 5146 Fish and seafoods
  Patricia Kendall

Port De Grave, NL A0A

D-U-N-S 20-264-8176   (BR)
NU SEA PRODUCTS INC
Main Rd, Port De Grave, NL, A0A 3J0
(709) 786-6302
Emp Here 200
SIC 2091 Canned and cured fish and seafoods
  Jeff Gulliford

Portugal Cove-St Philips, NL A1M

D-U-N-S 24-994-9660   (SL)
KELLOWAY CONSTRUCTION LIMITED
1388 Portugal Cove Rd, Portugal Cove-St Philips, NL, A1M 3J9
(709) 895-6532
Emp Here 100   *Sales* 4,020,900
SIC 7349 Building maintenance services, nec
  Terry Kelloway

Riverhead Harbour Grace, NL A0A

D-U-N-S 25-119-4791   (HQ)
WESTERN PETROLEUM NEWFOUNDLAND LIMITED
WESTERN PETROLEUM
4 Riverhead Center Unit 2, Riverhead Harbour Grace, NL, A0A 3P0
(709) 596-4181
Sales 37,756,800
SIC 5541 Gasoline service stations
  Luke Reynolds
  Ivan Cassell

South Brook Gb, NL A0J

D-U-N-S 25-982-7590   (SL)
EDDY'S RESTAURANT SERVICES LTD
Gd, South Brook Gb, NL, A0J 1S0
(709) 657-2590
Emp Here 30   *Sales* 14,942,340
SIC 5541 Gasoline service stations
  Wallace Mckay

Southern Harbour Pb, NL A0B

D-U-N-S 20-908-5265   (SL)
PARSONS TRUCKING LIMITED
1 Main St, Southern Harbour Pb, NL, A0B 3H0
(709) 463-8540
Emp Here 65   *Sales* 13,370,890
SIC 4212 Local trucking, without storage
  Kevin Parsons
  Rosanne Flight

▲ Public Company   ■ Public Company Family Member   HQ Headquarters   BR Branch   SL Single Location

Beverley Green
Sean Parsons
Michelle Morgan
Terrence Parsons
Lindy Parsons, Jr
Lana Parsons
Michael Parsons
Lindy Parsons, Sr

Springdale, NL A0J

D-U-N-S 20-755-9506   (SL)
SPRINGDALE FOREST RESOURCES INC
406 Little Bay Rd, Springdale, NL, A0J 1T0
(709) 673-4695
Emp Here 80   *Sales* 10,940,720
SIC 0851 Forestry services
Dennis Young

St Albans, NL A0H

D-U-N-S 24-676-9280   (SL)
NORTHERN HARVEST SEA FARMS NEW-FOUNDLAND LTD
183 Main St, St Albans, NL, A0H 2E0
(709) 538-3231
Emp Here 80   *Sales* 27,655,200
SIC 2092 Fresh or frozen packaged fish
Douglas Caines
Larry Ingalls
Norman Stavis
Mike Atkinson

St Georges, NL A0N

D-U-N-S 20-449-5642   (HQ)
CENTRAL SERVICE STATION LIMITED
160 Flatbay Junction Rd, St Georges, NL, A0N 1Z0
(709) 647-3500
Sales 10,097,680
SIC 1611 Highway and street construction
David Callahan
Sadie Callahan
Claudette Callahan

St Judes, NL A8A

D-U-N-S 20-759-1715   (SL)
EASTWOOD FOREST PRODUCTS INC
112 Trans Canada Hwy, St Judes, NL, A8A 3A1
(709) 635-7280
Emp Here 30   *Sales* 13,415,220
SIC 5031 Lumber, plywood, and millwork
Darcy Major

St Lawrence, NL A0E

D-U-N-S 20-398-2459   (BR)
OCEAN CHOICE INTERNATIONAL
OCEAN CHOICE INTERNATIONAL L.P.
(*Suby of* OCEAN CHOICE INTERNATIONAL)
69 Water St W, St Lawrence, NL, A0E 2V0
(709) 873-2798
Emp Here 100
SIC 2092 Fresh or frozen packaged fish
Gary Pike

St Anthony, NL A0K

D-U-N-S 20-985-7796   (HQ)
MAURICE'S SERVICE CENTRE LIMITED
MAIN STREET ULTRAMART
4 Barn Rd, St. Anthony, NL, A0K 4S0
(709) 454-3434
Sales 23,450,250
SIC 5983 Fuel oil dealers
Maurice Simmonds

St. John'S, NL A1A

D-U-N-S 20-988-4014   (SL)
AFONSO GROUP LIMITED
14 Robin Hood Bay Rd, St. John'S, NL, A1A 5V3
(709) 576-6070
Emp Here 30   *Sales* 13,476,570
SIC 7389 Business services, nec
Stephen Chafe

D-U-N-S 20-015-4839   (HQ)
BAINE JOHNSTON CORPORATION
410 East White Hills Rd, St. John'S, NL, A1A 5J7
(709) 576-1780
Emp Here 15   *Sales* 41,002,500
SIC 6712 Bank holding companies
Christopher Collingwood
Robert Collingwood
Gilbert Dalton

D-U-N-S 24-955-6341   (SL)
BATTERY MANAGEMENT INC
BATTERY HOTEL & SUITES
100 Signal Hill Rd, St. John'S, NL, A1A 1B3

Emp Here 80   *Sales* 7,591,920
SIC 7011 Hotels and motels
Bruce Pretty
Alan Connelly
Terry Tucker

D-U-N-S 20-100-7684   (BR)
BLACK & MCDONALD LIMITED
(*Suby of* BLACK & MCDONALD GROUP LIMITED)
29 Ottawa St, St. John'S, NL, A1A 2R9
(709) 896-2639
Emp Here 100
SIC 1711 Plumbing, heating, air-conditioning
George Dalton

D-U-N-S 24-754-6757   (HQ)
BREEN'S ENTERPRISES LIMITED
BREEN'S ULTRAMAR
104 Charter Ave, St. John'S, NL, A1A 1P2
(709) 726-9040
Emp Here 17   *Sales* 11,788,536
SIC 5461 Retail bakeries
John Breen
Judy Breen

D-U-N-S 25-304-8409   (BR)
CARLSON WAGONLIT CANADA
CARLSON WAGONLIT
(*Suby of* CARLSON WAGONLIT CANADA)
92 Elizabeth Ave, St. John'S, NL, A1A 1W7
(709) 726-2900
Emp Here 80
SIC 4724 Travel agencies
Stephen Outerbridge

D-U-N-S 20-052-9597   (SL)
CONCRETE PRODUCTS LIMITED
260 East White Hills Rd, St. John'S, NL, A1A 5J7
(709) 368-3171
Emp Here 45   *Sales* 10,350,855
SIC 3273 Ready-mixed concrete
Douglas Tipton

D-U-N-S 20-287-7986   (BR)
COSTCO WHOLESALE CANADA LTD

(*Suby of* COSTCO WHOLESALE CORPORATION)
28 Stavanger Dr, St. John'S, NL, A1A 5E8
(709) 738-8610
Emp Here 145
SIC 5141 Groceries, general line
Frank Chizlet

D-U-N-S 24-473-1733   (HQ)
COUGAR HELICOPTERS INC
10 Av Jetstream, St. John'S, NL, A1A 0R7
(709) 758-4800
Emp Here 200   *Sales* 72,990,960
SIC 4522 Air transportation, nonscheduled
Kenneth Norie
Hank Williams

D-U-N-S 25-411-5876   (SL)
CROSBIE SALAMIS LIMITED
80 Hebron Way, St. John'S, NL, A1A 0L9
(709) 722-5377
Emp Here 150   *Sales* 36,927,900
SIC 1799 Special trade contractors, nec
Robert Crosbie
Heather Conway
Matthew Follett
G. Mark Collett

D-U-N-S 20-547-7003   (HQ)
HARVEY'S TRAVEL LTD
92 Elizabeth Ave, St. John'S, NL, A1A 1W7
(709) 726-2900
Emp Here 23   *Sales* 80,027,040
SIC 4724 Travel agencies
Stephen Outerbridge
Peter Outerbridge
John Outerbridge

D-U-N-S 24-449-4480   (HQ)
HUNT'S TRANSPORT LIMITED
168 Major'S Path, St. John'S, NL, A1A 5A1
(709) 747-4868
Emp Here 38   *Sales* 16,456,480
SIC 4213 Trucking, except local
Greer Hunt

D-U-N-S 24-737-7125   (SL)
KCA DEUTAG DRILLING CANADA INC
45 Hebron Way Suite 201, St. John'S, NL, A1A 0P9
(709) 778-6200
Emp Here 100   *Sales* 31,970,500
SIC 1381 Drilling oil and gas wells
David Fong

D-U-N-S 24-705-1428   (SL)
M & M OFFSHORE LTD
(*Suby of* M & M ENGINEERING LIMITED)
456 Logy Bay Rd, St. John'S, NL, A1A 5C6
(709) 726-9112
Emp Here 75   *Sales* 14,406,375
SIC 3443 Fabricated plate work (boiler shop)
Geoff Wells
Chris King

D-U-N-S 20-985-6962   (SL)
MARSHALL, JAMES B ENTERPRISES LTD
CANADIAN TIRE ASSOC STORE
60 Elizabeth Ave Suite 144, St. John'S, NL, A1A 1W4
(709) 722-1860
Emp Here 90   *Sales* 56,635,200
SIC 5531 Auto and home supply stores
James Marshall
Carolyn Marshall

D-U-N-S 20-195-8613   (BR)
METRO ONTARIO INC
METRO
(*Suby of* METRO INC)
55 Stavanger Dr, St. John'S, NL, A1A 5E8
(709) 576-3576
Emp Here 100
SIC 5411 Grocery stores
John Pritchett

D-U-N-S 20-648-5372   (SL)
NEWFOUNDLAND SALES & MARKETING

INC
(*Suby of* ACOSTA INC.)
18 Argyle St Unit 201, St. John'S, NL, A1A 1V3
(709) 722-6706
Emp Here 12   *Sales* 10,026,924
SIC 5141 Groceries, general line
Wade Tetford
Heather Yetman

D-U-N-S 24-259-3978   (SL)
OLOINGSIGH DRUGS LIMITED
SHOPPERS DRUG MART
141 Torbay Rd, St. John'S, NL, A1A 2H1
(709) 722-6270
Emp Here 40   *Sales* 10,118,160
SIC 5912 Drug stores and proprietary stores
John Lynch

D-U-N-S 24-203-5751   (SL)
ORPHAN INDUSTRIES LIMITED
45 Pepperrell Rd, St. John'S, NL, A1A 5N8
(709) 726-6820
Emp Here 50   *Sales* 11,671,750
SIC 3312 Blast furnaces and steel mills
Glenn Byrne
Jason Fudge
Jerry Byrne

D-U-N-S 20-449-1310   (HQ)
P.F. COLLINS CUSTOMS BROKER LIMITED
P.F. COLLINS INTERNATIONAL TRADE SOLUTIONS
(*Suby of* SCRC HOLDINGS INC)
251 East White Hills Rd Unit 100, St. John'S, NL, A1A 5X7
(709) 726-7596
Emp Here 90   *Sales* 70,023,660
SIC 4731 Freight transportation arrangement
Raymond Collins
Susan Collins
Gerry Mayo
Sharlene Goobie

D-U-N-S 24-994-4984   (SL)
PAL AERO SERVICES LTD
TORBAY AERO SERVICES
(*Suby of* EXCHANGE INCOME CORPORATION)
Hangar No 4 St John'S International Airport, St. John'S, NL, A1A 5B5
(709) 576-4615
Emp Here 20   *Sales* 25,144,020
SIC 5172 Petroleum products, nec
Carl Riches

D-U-N-S 25-768-1866   (HQ)
PAL AEROSPACE LTD
(*Suby of* EXCHANGE INCOME CORPORATION)
St. Johns International Airport, Hangar 1, St. John'S, NL, A1A 5B5
(709) 576-1800
Sales 12,990,160
SIC 4581 Airports, flying fields, and services
Bill Madore

D-U-N-S 20-320-1587   (HQ)
PAL AIRLINES LTD.
PROVINCIAL AIRLINES
(*Suby of* EXCHANGE INCOME CORPORATION)
St Johns International Airport, St. John'S, NL, A1A 5B5
(709) 576-1800
Sales 222,146,400
SIC 4512 Air transportation, scheduled
Thomas Collingwood
Augustus Ollerhead
Robert Halliday
Brian Chafe
William Madore

D-U-N-S 25-363-7318   (HQ)
PROVINCIAL AEROSPACE LTD
(*Suby of* EXCHANGE INCOME CORPORATION)

Hangar No 1 St John'S International Airport, St. John'S, NL, A1A 5B5
(709) 576-1800
Emp Here 100   *Sales* 162,876,000
SIC 3721 Aircraft
 Brian Chafe
 Lisa Sparkes
 Michael Sangster
 Andrew Perry
 Jake Trainor

D-U-N-S 20-908-4250   (HQ)
PROVINCIAL AIRLINES LIMITED
(*Suby of* EXCHANGE INCOME CORPORA-TION)
Hangar No 4 St John'S International Airport, St. John'S, NL, A1A 5B5
(709) 576-1800
Emp Here 400   *Sales* 158,676,000
SIC 4512 Air transportation, scheduled
 Thomas Collingwood
 Augustus Ollerhead
 Derek Scott
 Tim Vaillancourt
 Robert Halliday
 Brian Chafe

D-U-N-S 24-450-1151   (HQ)
PUGLISEVICH CREWS & SERVICES LIM-ITED
PCSL
611 Torbay Rd Unit 1, St. John'S, NL, A1A 5J1
(709) 722-2744
Sales 10,185,201
SIC 7361 Employment agencies
 Valmhor Puglisevich
 Pheresa Puglisevich
 Frances Puglisevich

D-U-N-S 24-804-2749   (HQ)
SCOTIA RECYCLING (NL) LIMITED
55 Elizabeth Ave Ste 49, St. John'S, NL, A1A 1W9
(709) 579-7466
Emp Here 20   *Sales* 63,782,000
SIC 4953 Refuse systems
 Charles Flight

D-U-N-S 25-703-5089   (BR)
SOBEYS CAPITAL INCORPORATED
(*Suby of* EMPIRE COMPANY LIMITED)
10 Elizabeth Ave Suite 744, St. John'S, NL, A1A 5L4
(709) 753-3402
Emp Here 150
SIC 5411 Grocery stores
 Wayne Smart

D-U-N-S 25-331-0833   (SL)
ST. JOHN'S INTERNATIONAL AIRPORT AUTHORITY
100 World Parkway Suite 1, St. John'S, NL, A1A 5T2
(709) 758-8500
Emp Here 65   *Sales* 36,896,282
SIC 4581 Airports, flying fields, and services
 Keith Collins
 Art Cheeseman
 Glen Mahon
 Marie Manning
 Janet Obrien
 Laura Cooper
 Frank Wyse
 Tom Williams
 Robert Gosse
 Roger Butt

D-U-N-S 20-986-4453   (SL)
ST. JOHN'S YOUNG MEN'S AND YOUNG WOMEN'S CHRISTIAN ASSOCIATION
ST. JOHN'S YMCA-YWCA
34 New Cove Rd, St. John'S, NL, A1A 2B8
(709) 754-2960
Emp Here 70   *Sales* 10,001,530
SIC 8641 Civic and social associations
 Jason Brown

D-U-N-S 24-805-2334   (HQ)
STEERS INSURANCE LIMITED
99 Airport Rd Unit 201, St. John'S, NL, A1A 4Y3
(709) 722-1532
Sales 110,864,520
SIC 6411 Insurance agents, brokers, and ser-vice
 Wayne Sharpe

D-U-N-S 25-357-4230   (HQ)
VALE NEWFOUNDLAND & LABRADOR LIMITED
VALVE
(*Suby of* VALE S/A)
18 Hebron Way Level 2 Kmk Place, St. John'S, NL, A1A 0L9
(709) 758-8888
Sales 262,492,000
SIC 1629 Heavy construction, nec
 Eduardo Bartolomeo
 Jose Maurcio Pereira Coelho
 Luciano Siani Pires

D-U-N-S 24-802-4734   (HQ)
WHITE HILLS PROPERTY INC
(*Suby of* SCRC HOLDINGS INC)
251 East White Hills Rd Suite 100, St. John'S, NL, A1A 5X7
(709) 726-7596
Sales 14,246,085
SIC 6519 Real property lessors, nec
 Raymond Collins
 Bernard Collins
 Brian Collins
 Susan Collins

D-U-N-S 20-779-6517   (HQ)
WORKPLACE HEALTH SAFETY & COM-PENSATION COMMISSION OF NEW-FOUNDLAND AND LABRADOR
(*Suby of* PROVINCE OF NEWFOUNDLAND & LABRADOR)
148 Forest Rd Unit 146, St. John'S, NL, A1A 1E6
(709) 778-1000
Emp Here 190   *Sales* 261,701,405
SIC 6331 Fire, marine, and casualty insurance
 Tom Mahoney
 Brenda Greenslade
 Eric Bartlett
 Ann Martin
 Paul Kavanagh
 Leslie Galway

St. John'S, NL A1B

D-U-N-S 20-984-5890   (SL)
11336 NEWFOUNDLAND INC
TOYOTA PLAZA
73 Kenmount Rd, St. John'S, NL, A1B 3P8
(709) 753-4051
Emp Here 90   *Sales* 56,635,200
SIC 5511 New and used car dealers
 Daniel Penney

D-U-N-S 25-673-7701   (HQ)
ALTIUS MINERALS CORPORATION
38 Duffy Pl 2nd Fl, St. John'S, NL, A1B 4M5
(709) 576-3440
Sales 31,192,107
SIC 1081 Metal mining services
 Brian Dalton
 John A Baker
 Chad Wells
 Donald Warr
 Fred Mifflin
 Jamie Strauss
 Anna Stylianides
 Roger Lace
 Andre Gaumond
 Ben Lewis

D-U-N-S 25-737-1260   (BR)

AMEC FOSTER WHEELER INC
(*Suby of* JOHN WOOD GROUP P.L.C.)
133 Crosbie Rd, St. John'S, NL, A1B 1H3
(709) 724-1900
Emp Here 150
SIC 7373 Computer integrated systems de-sign
 Albert Peach

D-U-N-S 24-804-2442   (HQ)
AVALON FORD SALES 1996 LIMITED
AVALON FORD SALES
80 Wyatt Blvd, St. John'S, NL, A1B 3N9
(709) 754-7500
Emp Here 110   *Sales* 78,660,000
SIC 5511 New and used car dealers
 David Wilkins
 David Drodge

D-U-N-S 25-697-0617   (SL)
BENNETT RESTAURANT LTD
MCDONALD'S RESTAURANT
54 Kenmount Rd, St. John'S, NL, A1B 1W2
(709) 754-1254
Emp Here 95   *Sales* 4,324,305
SIC 5812 Eating places
 Kathy Bennett

D-U-N-S 24-449-2641   (SL)
BILL MATTHEWS' AUTOHAUS LIMITED
MATTHEWS, BILL VOLKSWAGEN AUDI
575 Kenmount Rd, St. John'S, NL, A1B 3P9
(709) 726-4424
Emp Here 25   *Sales* 12,451,950
SIC 5511 New and used car dealers
 William Matthews

D-U-N-S 20-015-5380   (HQ)
BRITISH CONFECTIONERY COMPANY LIMITED
BRITISH GROUP OF COMPANIES, THE
(*Suby of* BRITISH CONFECTIONERY COM-PANY (1982) LIMITED)
187 Kenmount Rd Suite 2, St. John'S, NL, A1B 3P9
(709) 747-2377
Sales 13,633,760
SIC 2679 Converted paper products, nec
 Blair Connolly

D-U-N-S 25-983-2632   (BR)
C A PIPPY PARK COMMISSION
ADMIRAL'S GREEN CLUB HOUSE, THE
(*Suby of* C A PIPPY PARK COMMISSION)
460 Allandale Rd, St. John'S, NL, A1B 4E8
(709) 753-7110
Emp Here 80
SIC 7992 Public golf courses
 Ric Mercer

D-U-N-S 24-932-6950   (HQ)
C-CORE
1 Morrissey Rd, St. John'S, NL, A1B 3X5
(709) 864-8354
Emp Here 82   *Sales* 16,086,510
SIC 8711 Engineering services
 Charles Randell
 David J. Oake
 Susan Kennedy
 Desmond Power
 Murray Brown
 David Murrin
 Paul Adlakha
 Joseph Chamberland
 Carolyn Walters

D-U-N-S 24-932-3544   (SL)
CABOT FORD LINCOLN SALES LIMITED
177 Kenmount Rd, St. John'S, NL, A1B 3P9
(709) 722-6600
Emp Here 65   *Sales* 40,903,200
SIC 5511 New and used car dealers
 Frank Clarke

D-U-N-S 25-738-0972   (SL)
CALL CENTRE INC, THE
TELELINK CALL CENTRE
5 Pippy Pl Suite 7, St. John'S, NL, A1B 3X2

(709) 722-3730
Emp Here 90   *Sales* 40,429,710
SIC 7389 Business services, nec
 Barbara Ryan
 Sydney Ryan
 Cindy Roma

D-U-N-S 24-309-8709   (BR)
CANADIAN BROADCASTING CORPORA-TION
CBC TV
(*Suby of* GOVERNMENT OF CANADA)
95 University Ave, St. John'S, NL, A1B 1Z4
(709) 576-5000
Emp Here 100
SIC 4833 Television broadcasting stations
 Diane Humber

D-U-N-S 25-703-2441   (SL)
CANADIAN CORPS OF COMMISSION-AIRES (NEWFOUNDLAND)
207a Kenmount Rd, St. John'S, NL, A1B 3P9
(709) 754-0757
Emp Here 220   *Sales* 5,775,000
SIC 7381 Detective and armored car services
 Brian Furlong

D-U-N-S 24-712-2161   (HQ)
CANADIAN ULTRAMAR COMPANY
(*Suby of* VALERO ENERGY CORPORATION)
39 Pippy Pl, St. John'S, NL, A1B 3X2
(709) 754-1880
Emp Here 25   *Sales* 599,982,453
SIC 5983 Fuel oil dealers
 Jean Bernier
 Curtis Anastasio
 Jennifer Overend
 Steve Blank
 Marcel Dupuis
 Paul Renaulds
 John Pye
 Lillian Crawford

D-U-N-S 25-494-7500   (SL)
CANSHIP UGLAND LTD
1315 Topsail Rd, St. John'S, NL, A1B 3N4
(709) 782-3333
Emp Here 400   *Sales* 157,489,600
SIC 4424 Deep sea domestic transportation of freight
 Marco Ahrens

D-U-N-S 24-258-8135   (HQ)
CAPITAL MOTORS LIMITED
CAPITAL HYUNDAI
479 Kenmount Rd, St. John'S, NL, A1B 3P9
(709) 726-0288
Sales 50,342,400
SIC 5511 New and used car dealers
 Frank Howard

D-U-N-S 24-257-4416   (SL)
CAPITAL READY MIX LIMITED
(*Suby of* PENNECON LIMITED)
Trans Canada Hwy, St. John'S, NL, A1B 3N4
(709) 364-5008
Emp Here 125   *Sales* 22,402,375
SIC 3273 Ready-mixed concrete
 Larry Puddister
 Jerry White

D-U-N-S 20-031-1137   (SL)
CHANCELLOR PARK INC
270 Portugal Cove Rd Suite 219, St. John'S, NL, A1B 4N6
(709) 754-1165
Emp Here 123   *Sales* 8,433,618
SIC 8051 Skilled nursing care facilities
 Gloria Parsons
 Barry Parsons

D-U-N-S 20-369-7581   (SL)
CHIMO CONSTRUCTION (2014) LIMITED
136 Crosbie Rd Suite 409, St. John'S, NL, A1B 3K3
(709) 739-5900
Emp Here 25   *Sales* 14,258,450
SIC 1542 Nonresidential construction, nec

Ronald Hickey
Karl Green
Alexander Crosbie
Timothy Crosbie
Robert Crosbie
Chynthia Crosbie

D-U-N-S 20-421-9885   (HQ)
CHURCHILL FALLS (LABRADOR) CORPO-
RATION LIMITED
(*Suby of* PROVINCE OF NEWFOUNDLAND
& LABRADOR)
500 Columbus Dr, St. John'S, NL, A1B 4K7
(709) 737-1450
Emp Here 2   *Sales* 211,865,472
SIC 4911 Electric services
Ed Martin
Derrick Sturge

D-U-N-S 24-450-1201   (HQ)
CROSBIE JOB INSURANCE LIMITED
1 Crosbie Pl Suite 201, St. John'S, NL, A1B
3Y8
(709) 726-5414
Emp Here 1   *Sales* 33,922,400
SIC 6411 Insurance agents, brokers, and ser-
vice
Jim Crosbie
Wayne Ralph
Basil Crosbie

D-U-N-S 20-015-8947   (HQ)
HARVEY & COMPANY LIMITED
(*Suby of* PROVINCIAL INVESTMENTS INC)
88 Kenmount Rd, St. John'S, NL, A1B 3R1
(709) 738-8911
Emp Here 2   *Sales* 19,001,040
SIC 5084 Industrial machinery and equipment
Roger Pike

D-U-N-S 20-015-9127   (HQ)
HICKMAN MOTORS LIMITED
85 Kenmount Rd, St. John'S, NL, A1B 3P8
(709) 726-6990
Emp Here 200   *Sales* 202,038,200
SIC 5511 New and used car dealers
Albert Hickman
Albert Junior (Bert) Hickman
Gary Bishop
Howard Hickman

D-U-N-S 25-365-8702   (BR)
HOME DEPOT OF CANADA INC
HOME DEPOT
(*Suby of* THE HOME DEPOT INC)
70 Kelsey Dr, St. John'S, NL, A1B 5C7
(709) 570-2400
Emp Here 100
SIC 5251 Hardware stores
Pam Browne

D-U-N-S 20-114-3810   (SL)
HOWARD MOTORS INC
CAPITAL SUBARU
46 Kenmount Rd, St. John'S, NL, A1B 1W2
(709) 726-9900
Emp Here 24   *Sales* 11,953,872
SIC 5511 New and used car dealers
Frank Howard

D-U-N-S 20-765-1253   (SL)
IMPORT AUTO PLAZA INC
CARMAX
475 Kenmount Rd, St. John'S, NL, A1B 3P9
(709) 579-6487
Emp Here 23   *Sales* 11,455,794
SIC 5521 Used car dealers
Frank Howard

D-U-N-S 25-298-5031   (BR)
JOHNSON INC
(*Suby of* RSA INSURANCE GROUP PLC)
95 Elizabeth Ave, St. John'S, NL, A1B 1R6
(709) 737-1500
Emp Here 600
SIC 6411 Insurance agents, brokers, and ser-
vice
Ken Bennett

D-U-N-S 20-692-6391   (SL)
JSM ELECTRICAL LTD
28 Duffy Pl, St. John'S, NL, A1B 4M5
(709) 754-3666
Emp Here 75   *Sales* 16,337,175
SIC 1731 Electrical work
Jim Murray

D-U-N-S 25-148-0877   (SL)
KENMOUNT MOTORS INC
CITY HONDA
547 Kenmount Rd, St. John'S, NL, A1B 3P9
(709) 579-1999
Emp Here 50   *Sales* 24,903,900
SIC 5511 New and used car dealers
Ches Penney Jr
Ches Penney Sr

D-U-N-S 25-064-9530   (HQ)
KEYCORP INC
303 Thorburn Rd, St. John'S, NL, A1B 4R1
(709) 753-2284
Emp Here 7   *Sales* 89,822,628
SIC 6794 Patent owners and lessors
Ralph Tucker
Gwen Tucker

D-U-N-S 20-761-0176   (SL)
L & L MCCAW HOLDINGS LTD
CANADIAN TIRE
50 Kelsey Dr, St. John'S, NL, A1B 5C7
(709) 722-5530
Emp Here 100   *Sales* 62,928,000
SIC 5531 Auto and home supply stores
Larry Mccaw

D-U-N-S 20-278-5739   (SL)
LABRADOR-ISLAND LINK LIMITED PART-
NERSHIP
500 Columbus Dr, St. John'S, NL, A1B 0C9
(709) 737-4860
Emp Here 20   *Sales* 10,393,100
SIC 4911 Electric services
James Keating

D-U-N-S 24-912-6467   (HQ)
LEGROW, CAL INSURANCE LIMITED
189 Higgins Line, St. John'S, NL, A1B 4N4
(709) 722-3282
Emp Here 28   *Sales* 110,864,520
SIC 6411 Insurance agents, brokers, and ser-
vice
Jeff Legrow

D-U-N-S 24-260-8339   (HQ)
M5 MARKETING COMMUNICATIONS INC
42 O'Leary Ave, St. John'S, NL, A1B 2C7
(709) 753-5559
Emp Here 60   *Sales* 19,035,245
SIC 7311 Advertising agencies
Gary Wadden
Derrick Langdon
George Battcott

D-U-N-S 20-272-6191   (BR)
MEMORIAL UNIVERSITY OF NEWFOUND-
LAND
QUEEN ELIZABETH LL LIBRARY
(*Suby of* MEMORIAL UNIVERSITY OF NEW-
FOUNDLAND)
234 Elizabeth Ave, St. John'S, NL, A1B 3Y1
(709) 864-8000
Emp Here 100
SIC 8231 Libraries
Susan Cleyle

D-U-N-S 20-779-0155   (SL)
METRO GENERAL INSURANCE CORPO-
RATION LIMITED
20 Crosbie Pl, St. John'S, NL, A1B 3Y8

Emp Here 20   *Sales* 14,508,780
SIC 6331 Fire, marine, and casualty insurance
Hayley J. Wilson

D-U-N-S 20-779-2102   (HQ)
MUNN'S INSURANCE LIMITED
121 Kelsey Dr Suite 100, St. John'S, NL, A1B

0L2
(709) 726-8627
Emp Here 20   *Sales* 33,922,400
SIC 6411 Insurance agents, brokers, and ser-
vice
Ian Munn
Ches Dowden
John Nolan

D-U-N-S 24-373-2281   (HQ)
NALCOR ENERGY
(*Suby of* PROVINCE OF NEWFOUNDLAND
& LABRADOR)
500 Columbus Dr, St. John'S, NL, A1B 4K7
(709) 737-1440
Sales 609,541,445
SIC 4911 Electric services
Stan Marshall
Brendad Paddick
Gilbert Bennett
John Macisaac
Jim Keating
Derrick Sturge
Chris Kieley
Mike Roberts
Peter Hickman
Rob Henderson

D-U-N-S 20-287-3733   (SL)
NALCOR ENERGY MARKETING CORPO-
RATION
500 Columbus Dr, St. John'S, NL, A1B 0P5
(709) 737-1491
Emp Here 30   *Sales* 18,798,420
SIC 4911 Electric services
James Haynes
Greg Jones

D-U-N-S 20-555-6702   (BR)
NATIONAL RESEARCH COUNCIL CANADA
(*Suby of* GOVERNMENT OF CANADA)
Gd, St. John'S, NL, A1B 3T5
(709) 772-4939
Emp Here 120
SIC 8732 Commercial nonphysical research
David Murrin

D-U-N-S 24-378-8192   (SL)
NEWFOUNDLAND & LABRADOR CENTRE
FOR HEALTH INFORMATION
(*Suby of* PROVINCE OF NEWFOUNDLAND
& LABRADOR)
70 O'Leary Ave, St. John'S, NL, A1B 2C7
(709) 752-6000
Emp Here 159   *Sales* 23,622,053
SIC 8011 Offices and clinics of medical doc-
tors
Stephen Clark
Paul Caines
Gillian Sweeney
Don Macdonald
Kris Aubrey-Bassler
Jerry Vink
Ted Dawe
Elye Bruce
Allan Bradley
Fred Cahill

D-U-N-S 20-449-0254   (HQ)
NEWFOUNDLAND & LABRADOR HYDRO
(*Suby of* PROVINCE OF NEWFOUNDLAND
& LABRADOR)
500 Columbus Dr, St. John'S, NL, A1B 4K7
(709) 737-1400
Emp Here 300   *Sales* 1,008,883,200
SIC 4911 Electric services
Jim Haynes
Dawn Dalley
Terry Gardiner
Jennifer Williams
Lisa Hutchens
Ron Leblanc
Geoff Young

D-U-N-S 20-794-2421   (BR)
NEWFOUNDLAND CAPITAL CORPORA-
TION LIMITED

STEEL COMMUNICATION
(*Suby of* GROUPE STINGRAY INC)
391 Kenmount Rd, St. John'S, NL, A1B 3P9
(709) 726-5590
Emp Here 100
SIC 4832 Radio broadcasting stations
Mike Murphy

D-U-N-S 24-260-5699   (HQ)
NEWFOUNDLAND LABRADOR LIQUOR
CORPORATION
(*Suby of* PROVINCE OF NEWFOUNDLAND
& LABRADOR)
90 Kenmount Rd, St. John'S, NL, A1B 3R1
(709) 724-1100
Emp Here 105   *Sales* 255,874,160
SIC 5921 Liquor stores
Steve Winter
Andrea Marshall
Dick Mccrate
Marjorie Gaulton
Brian Mccormack
Craig Martin

D-U-N-S 20-016-1628   (HQ)
NEWFOUNDLAND POWER INC
(*Suby of* FORTIS INC)
55 Kenmount Rd, St. John'S, NL, A1B 3P8
(709) 737-5600
Emp Here 200   *Sales* 497,138,333
SIC 4911 Electric services
Peter Alteen
Gary Murray
Paige London
Brian Mechenton
Derek Mercer
Lorne Henderson
Peter Feehan
Trina White
David Manning
Juliet O'brien

D-U-N-S 24-492-4598   (SL)
NORTH ATLANTIC
ORANGE STORE
86 Thorburn Rd, St. John'S, NL, A1B 3M3
(709) 738-5542
Emp Here 11   *Sales* 11,360,888
SIC 5172 Petroleum products, nec
Dominica Tuff

D-U-N-S 20-765-1147   (HQ)
NORTH ATLANTIC PETROLEUM LIMITED
29 Pippy Pl, St. John'S, NL, A1B 3X2
(709) 579-5831
Emp Here 10   *Sales* 22,358,700
SIC 5074 Plumbing and heating equipment
and supplies (hydronics)
Yong-Ho Cho

D-U-N-S 24-604-8292   (HQ)
NORTH ATLANTIC REFINING LIMITED
NORTH ATLANTIC PETROLEUM
(*Suby of* SILVERPEAK STRATEGIC PART-
NERS LP)
29 Pippy Pl, St. John'S, NL, A1B 3X2
(709) 463-8811
Emp Here 600   *Sales* 1,172,762,500
SIC 2911 Petroleum refining
Brent Jones
Changkoo Kang
Kiyuong Kim
Kanghyun Shin

D-U-N-S 24-831-9600   (HQ)
NOTRE DAME SEAFOODS INC
(*Suby of* PROVINCIAL INVESTMENTS INC)
88 Kenmount Rd, St. John'S, NL, A1B 3R1
(709) 758-0034
Emp Here 2   *Sales* 121,846,250
SIC 2092 Fresh or frozen packaged fish
Roger Pike
Jason Eveleigh

D-U-N-S 24-359-8088   (HQ)
OCEAN CHOICE INTERNATIONAL
OCI

1315 Topsail Rd, St. John'S, NL, A1B 3N4
(709) 782-6244
Emp Here 40   *Sales* 423,420,800
SIC 5421 Meat and fish markets
Martin Sullivan
Blaine Sullivan
Karen Parsons

D-U-N-S 20-052-2709   (HQ)
PENNECON LIMITED
1309 Topsail Rd, St. John'S, NL, A1B 3N4
(709) 782-3404
Emp Here 5   *Sales* 105,734,000
SIC 6159 Miscellaneous business credit institutions
David Mitchell
Edward Murphy
Jerry David White
Larry Puddister
Chesley Penney

D-U-N-S 20-779-5014   (HQ)
PENTECOSTAL ASSEMBLIES OF NEW-FOUNDLAND AND LABRADOR CORPO-RATION
57 Thorburn Rd, St. John'S, NL, A1B 3M2
(709) 753-6314
Emp Here 20   *Sales* 27,071,980
SIC 8661 Religious organizations
Paul Foster
Clarence Buckle
Barry Grimes
Robert Dewling

D-U-N-S 24-877-8417   (HQ)
PERSONA COMMUNICATIONS INC
AMAZING PERSONA, THE
(*Suby of* TIDNISH HOLDINGS LIMITED)
17 Duffy Pl, St. John'S, NL, A1B 4M7
(709) 754-3775
Sales 163,926,560
SIC 4841 Cable and other pay television services
John Bragg
Charles P. Hutchings
David Hoffman
Richard Cecchetto
George Revie

D-U-N-S 20-970-7004   (BR)
PITNEY BOWES OF CANADA LTD
(*Suby of* PITNEY BOWES INC.)
31 Pippy Pl, St. John'S, NL, A1B 3X2

Emp Here 100
SIC 5044 Office equipment
Mohamed Razalia

D-U-N-S 24-878-0595   (HQ)
PROVINCIAL INVESTMENTS INC
88 Kenmount Rd, St. John'S, NL, A1B 3R1
(709) 758-0002
Emp Here 1   *Sales* 182,754,500
SIC 6719 Holding companies, nec
Roger W Pike

D-U-N-S 25-320-8557   (BR)
PUROLATOR INC
(*Suby of* GOVERNMENT OF CANADA)
16 Duffy Pl, St. John'S, NL, A1B 4M5
(709) 579-5671
Emp Here 75
SIC 4731 Freight transportation arrangement
Pye Fonda

D-U-N-S 24-420-3860   (SL)
RESEARCH & DEVELOPMENT COR-PORATION OF NEWFOUNDLAND AND LABRADOR
RDC
(*Suby of* PROVINCE OF NEWFOUNDLAND & LABRADOR)
68 Portugal Cove Rd, St. John'S, NL, A1B 2L9
(709) 758-0913
Emp Here 32   *Sales* 17,266,676
SIC 8732 Commercial nonphysical research
Glenn Janes

Jacqueline Sheppard
Alan Brown
Lawrence Cochrane
Gary Dinn
Ray Gosine
Kari Kveseth
Terry-Lynn Young
Paul Morris
Geoff Hudson

D-U-N-S 20-016-2980   (HQ)
RIDEOUT TOOL AND MACHINE INC
222 Kenmount Rd, St. John'S, NL, A1B 3R2
(709) 754-2240
Emp Here 25   *Sales* 11,921,040
SIC 5084 Industrial machinery and equipment
Raymond Rideout
Harry Rideout
Christopher Rideout
Janet Rideout
Craig Rideout
Craig Rideout

D-U-N-S 20-779-0528   (SL)
ST. JOHN'S TRANSPORTATION COMMIS-SION
METROBUS
(*Suby of* CITY OF ST. JOHN'S)
25 Messenger Dr, St. John'S, NL, A1B 0H6
(709) 570-2020
Emp Here 116   *Sales* 8,731,552
SIC 4111 Local and suburban transit
Jason Hussey

D-U-N-S 20-295-8187   (BR)
STANTEC CONSULTING LTD
(*Suby of* STANTEC INC)
141 Kelsey Dr, St. John'S, NL, A1B 0L2
(709) 576-1458
Emp Here 100
SIC 8711 Engineering services
Wendy Worford

D-U-N-S 25-094-8312   (BR)
SUNCOR ENERGY INC
PETRO-CANADA
(*Suby of* SUNCOR ENERGY INC)
140 Kelsey Dr, St. John'S, NL, A1B 0T2
(709) 778-3500
Emp Here 150
SIC 1389 Oil and gas field services, nec
William Fleming

D-U-N-S 24-754-9272   (HQ)
SUPERCARS INC
PENNEY MAZDA
220 Kenmount Rd, St. John'S, NL, A1B 3T2
(709) 726-8555
Emp Here 57   *Sales* 39,015,360
SIC 5511 New and used car dealers
Chesley Penney
Daniel Penney

D-U-N-S 25-703-5352   (SL)
SUTTON GROUP-CAPITAL REALTY LTD
451 Kenmount Rd, St. John'S, NL, A1B 3P9
(709) 726-6262
Emp Here 50   *Sales* 16,356,350
SIC 6531 Real estate agents and managers
Calvin Ollerhead

D-U-N-S 24-663-6158   (SL)
TAMARACK GEOGRAPHIC TECHNOLO-GIES LTD.
303 Thorburn Rd Suite 302, St. John'S, NL, A1B 4R1
(709) 726-1046
Emp Here 49   *Sales* 11,693,522
SIC 8731 Commercial physical research
Collin Taylor

D-U-N-S 20-472-8905   (SL)
TECHNIPFMC CANADA LTD
(*Suby of* TECHNIPFMC PLC)
131 Kelsey Dr, St. John'S, NL, A1B 0L2
(709) 724-1851
Emp Here 449   *Sales* 245,140,979

SIC 1382 Oil and gas exploration services
Jason Muise
Scott Bittner
Guillaume Groisard
Cornelis Nicolaas
Martin Zonneveld

D-U-N-S 20-987-3017   (SL)
TERRA NOVA MOTORS LIMITED
TERRA NOVA
595 Kenmount Rd, St. John'S, NL, A1B 3P9
(709) 364-4130
Emp Here 80   *Sales* 50,342,400
SIC 5511 New and used car dealers
Douglas Russell
Alex Traverse

D-U-N-S 20-003-7377   (SL)
TLC NURSING AND HOME CARE SER-VICES LIMITED
TLC
25 Anderson Ave, St. John'S, NL, A1B 3E4
(709) 726-3473
Emp Here 200   *Sales* 24,955,200
SIC 8741 Management services
Christopher Carew
Sylvia Carew

D-U-N-S 20-310-9780   (BR)
TRA ATLANTIC
63 Glencoe Dr, St. John'S, NL, A1B 4A5
(709) 364-7771
Emp Here 99   *Sales* 440,403
SIC 4213 Trucking, except local
Tony Hickey

D-U-N-S 20-351-3957   (SL)
ULTIMATE DRIVING COMPANY INC, THE
120 Kenmount Rd, St. John'S, NL, A1B 3R2
(709) 754-3269
Emp Here 40   *Sales* 19,923,120
SIC 5531 Auto and home supply stores
Frank Howard
Jon Howard

D-U-N-S 20-779-6319   (HQ)
UNIFUND ADJUSTING INC
68 Portugal Cove Rd, St. John'S, NL, A1B 2L9
(709) 737-1680
Emp Here 20   *Sales* 21,201,500
SIC 6411 Insurance agents, brokers, and service
Chuan C. Huang
Gerard Corkran

D-U-N-S 20-786-1175   (BR)
WAL-MART CANADA CORP
(*Suby of* WALMART INC.)
75 Kelsey Dr, St. John'S, NL, A1B 0C7
(709) 722-6707
Emp Here 100
SIC 5311 Department stores

D-U-N-S 20-987-6333   (HQ)
WEDGWOOD INSURANCE LIMITED
85 Thorburn Rd Suite 102, St. John'S, NL, A1B 3M2
(709) 753-3210
Emp Here 80   *Sales* 110,864,520
SIC 6411 Insurance agents, brokers, and service
Geoffery Wedgwood
Thomas Hickey

St. John'S, NL A1C

D-U-N-S 25-224-0619   (SL)
ARCHEAN RESOURCES LTD
140 Water St Suite 903, St. John'S, NL, A1C 6H6
(709) 758-1700
Emp Here 200   *Sales* 477,509,800
SIC 1081 Metal mining services
Albert Chislett
Chris Verbiski

Douglas Hurst
Ray Jenner
Douglas Silver

D-U-N-S 24-640-5653   (SL)
ATLANTIC CUSTOM BROKERS
233 Duckworth St Suite 301, St. John'S, NL, A1C 1G8
(709) 745-8700
Emp Here 49   *Sales* 25,478,383
SIC 4731 Freight transportation arrangement
Karen Myers

D-U-N-S 25-496-0925   (HQ)
BLUEDROP PERFORMANCE LEARNING INC
18 Prescott St, St. John'S, NL, A1C 3S4
(709) 739-9000
Sales 15,335,917
SIC 3699 Electrical equipment and supplies, nec
Emad Rizkalla
Bernard (Bernie) Beckett
John Moores
Derrick Rowe
Tom Astle
Paul Sparkles
Andres Youngman

D-U-N-S 24-257-2881   (HQ)
CITY HOTELS LIMITED
HOTEL COURTENEY BAY
251 Empire Ave Suite 103, St. John'S, NL, A1C 3H9
(709) 738-3989
Emp Here 6   *Sales* 28,700,400
SIC 7011 Hotels and motels
Pat Aylward
Steve Sparkes

D-U-N-S 24-436-7020   (SL)
DOWNHOME SHOPPE AND GALLERY
303 Water St, St. John'S, NL, A1C 1B9
(709) 722-2970
Emp Here 49   *Sales* 13,316,044
SIC 6531 Real estate agents and managers
Ron Young

D-U-N-S 20-267-7928   (SL)
EAST COAST CATERING LIMITED
30 Queen'S Rd, St. John'S, NL, A1C 2A5
(709) 576-1741
Emp Here 150   *Sales* 100,336,200
SIC 7389 Business services, nec
Michael Deley
Audrey O'rielly

D-U-N-S 20-845-5019   (BR)
EASTERN REGIONAL INTEGRATED HEALTH AUTHORITY
ST CLAIRE MERCY HOSPITAL
(*Suby of* EASTERN REGIONAL INTE-GRATED HEALTH AUTHORITY)
154 Lemarchant Rd, St. John'S, NL, A1C 5B8
(709) 777-6300
Emp Here 5,000
SIC 8062 General medical and surgical hospitals
Lynn Sparkes

D-U-N-S 20-779-3241   (HQ)
ECLIPSE STORES INC
ECLIPSE
354 Water St Suite 401, St. John'S, NL, A1C 1C4
(709) 722-0311
Emp Here 20   *Sales* 37,426,500
SIC 5621 Women's clothing stores
Cyril Bulgin
Pamela Bulgin

D-U-N-S 24-257-7229   (SL)
HARVEY'S OIL LIMITED
HARVEY'S HOME HEAT
87 Water St, St. John'S, NL, A1C 1A5
(709) 726-1680
Emp Here 42   *Sales* 19,698,210
SIC 5983 Fuel oil dealers

▲ Public Company   ■ Public Company Family Member   **HQ** Headquarters   **BR** Branch   **SL** Single Location

Susan Patten
Robert French
Robert Patten
Rene Lemire
Claude Simoneau

D-U-N-S 20-015-8939   (HQ)
HARVEY, A. & COMPANY LIMITED
HARVEY'S AUTO CARRIERS
60 Water St, St. John'S, NL, A1C 1A3
(709) 576-4761
Sales 78,744,800
SIC 4491 Marine cargo handling
Susan Patten
Robert Patten
James Peddigrew
Maureen Meaney
Margart Patten
John Patten
James Chalker

D-U-N-S 24-832-5698   (SL)
**HIBERNIA MANAGEMENT AND DEVELOP-
MENT COMPANY LTD**
100 New Gower St Suite 1000, St. John'S, NL,
A1C 6K3

Emp Here 150   *Sales* 100,901,850
SIC 1382 Oil and gas exploration services
Paul Phelan
Brenda Clark
James Bates
Glenn Scott
Alan Brown
Jan Dejong

D-U-N-S 24-257-9936   (SL)
HOTEL NEWFOUNDLAND (1982)
FAIRMONT NEWFOUNDLAND, THE
Cavendish Sq, St. John'S, NL, A1C 5W8
(709) 726-4980
Emp Here 220   *Sales* 20,391,800
SIC 7011 Hotels and motels
Armand A Agabab

D-U-N-S 25-675-7097   (BR)
HUSKY OIL OPERATIONS LIMITED
HUSKY ENERGY
(*Suby of* HUSKY ENERGY INC)
351 Water St, St. John'S, NL, A1C 1C2
(709) 724-3900
Emp Here 150
SIC 1311 Crude petroleum and natural gas
Ruud Zoon

D-U-N-S 25-285-9491   (HQ)
JOHNSON CORPORATION, THE
(*Suby of* RSA INSURANCE GROUP PLC)
10 Factory Lane, St. John'S, NL, A1C 6H5
(709) 737-1500
Emp Here 1   *Sales* 372,982,200
SIC 6411 Insurance agents, brokers, and ser-
vice
George Anderson
Kenneth M. Bennett
Nick Creatura
Guy Dufresne
Simon Lee
Robert Mcfarlane
Shelly Miller
Rowan Saunders

D-U-N-S 20-548-0445   (HQ)
JOHNSON INC
UNIFUND ASSURANCE COMPANY
(*Suby of* RSA INSURANCE GROUP PLC)
10 Factory Lane, St. John'S, NL, A1C 6H5
(888) 737-1680
Emp Here 125   *Sales* 351,224,905
SIC 6411 Insurance agents, brokers, and ser-
vice
Kenneth Bennett
Roy Mercer
Donald Sword
Phillip Wilson
Rowan Saunders

D-U-N-S 25-363-6153   (BR)
KEG RESTAURANTS LTD
KEG STEAKHOUSE & BAR, THE
(*Suby of* RECIPE UNLIMITED CORPORA-
TION)
135 Harbour Dr, St. John'S, NL, A1C 6N6
(709) 726-4534
Emp Here 100
SIC 5812 Eating places
Ron Varley

D-U-N-S 20-815-1944   (HQ)
MARINE ATLANTIC INC
(*Suby of* GOVERNMENT OF CANADA)
10 Fort William Pl Suite 302, St. John'S, NL,
A1C 1K4
(709) 772-8957
Emp Here 7   *Sales* 322,698,369
SIC 4482 Ferries
Murray Hupman
Paul Trissin
Shawn Leamon
John Lochhead
Rhonda Green
Janie Bussey
Brent Chaffey
Owen Fitzgerald
Gary O'brien
Craig Priddle

D-U-N-S 25-846-7794   (BR)
**MEMORIAL UNIVERSITY OF NEWFOUND-
LAND**
FISHERIES AND MARINE INSTITUTE
(*Suby of* MEMORIAL UNIVERSITY OF NEW-
FOUNDLAND)
155 Ridge Road, St. John'S, NL, A1C 5R3
(709) 778-0483
Emp Here 600
SIC 8222 Junior colleges
Bill Chislett

D-U-N-S 20-779-3415   (HQ)
**MEMORIAL UNIVERSITY OF NEWFOUND-
LAND**
MUN BOOK STORE
208 Elizabeth Ave, St. John'S, NL, A1C 5S7
(709) 637-6298
Emp Here 3,080   *Sales* 492,521,545
SIC 8221 Colleges and universities
Christopher Loomis
Reela Tremblay
Ray Gosine

D-U-N-S 25-514-0220   (SL)
**MEMORIAL UNIVERSITY OF NEWFOUND-
LAND STUDENTS UNION**
MUNSU
1 Arctic Pl, St. John'S, NL, A1C 5S7

Emp Here 100   *Sales* 14,287,900
SIC 8641 Civic and social associations
Jessica Mccormick

D-U-N-S 20-100-1299   (BR)
MOLSON CANADA 2005
MOLSON COORS CANADA
(*Suby of* MOLSON COORS BREWING COM-
PANY)
131 Circular Rd, St. John'S, NL, A1C 2Z9
(709) 726-1786
Emp Here 101
SIC 2082 Malt beverages
Shaun Kennedy

D-U-N-S 20-907-7601   (HQ)
**NEWFOUNDLAND & LABRADOR CREDIT
UNION LIMITED**
240 Water St, St. John'S, NL, A1C 1B7
(709) 722-5824
Emp Here 30   *Sales* 15,351,100
SIC 6062 State credit unions
Allison Chaytor-Loveys
Raymond Piercey
Daniel Lavallee
Maureen Singleton
Owen Grimes

Nelson Larson
Don Brown
Keith Garland
Pat Cullins

D-U-N-S 20-987-5368   (HQ)
**NEWFOUNDLAND & LABRADOR LEGAL
AID COMMISSION**
(*Suby of* PROVINCE OF NEWFOUNDLAND
& LABRADOR)
251 Empire Ave Suite 200, St. John'S, NL,
A1C 3H9
(709) 753-7860
Emp Here 10   *Sales* 12,320,880
SIC 8111 Legal services
Newman Petten

D-U-N-S 25-709-3260   (SL)
NEWFOUNDLAND PERSONNEL INC
3 Queen St, St. John'S, NL, A1C 4K2
(709) 579-3400
Emp Here 49   *Sales* 11,611,530
SIC 7363 Help supply services
Phil Wheln

D-U-N-S 24-259-2392   (BR)
OCEANEX INC
(*Suby of* OCEANEX INC)
701 Kent Fort William Place, St. John'S, NL,
A1C 1K4
(709) 722-6280
Emp Here 350
SIC 4424 Deep sea domestic transportation of
freight
Glenn Etchegary

D-U-N-S 20-327-4576   (HQ)
OCEANEX INC
OCEANEX GLOBAL LOGISTICS
10 Fort William Pl Suite 701, St. John'S, NL,
A1C 1K4
(709) 758-0382
Emp Here 100   *Sales* 138,944,400
SIC 4424 Deep sea domestic transportation of
freight
Captain Sidney J. Hynes
Lori Caines
Menashe Grinshpan
Patrick Madigan
Dan Buffery

D-U-N-S 20-012-3339   (HQ)
QUINLAN BROTHERS LIMITED
215 Water St Suite 302, St. John'S, NL, A1C
6C9
(709) 739-6960
Sales 389,908,000
SIC 2092 Fresh or frozen packaged fish
Patrick Quinlan
Donald Quinlan
Wayne Quinlan

D-U-N-S 25-982-7855   (SL)
**ST. JOHN'S SPORTS & ENTERTAINMENT
LTD**
ST JOHN'S CONVENTION CENTRE
(*Suby of* CITY OF ST. JOHN'S)
50 New Gower St, St. John'S, NL, A1C 1J3
(709) 758-1111
Emp Here 200   *Sales* 18,990,600
SIC 7999 Amusement and recreation, nec
William Thistle
Carolyn Dooling

D-U-N-S 20-758-7606   (HQ)
TALON ENERGY SERVICES INC
215 Water St Suite 301, St. John'S, NL, A1C
6C9
(709) 739-8450
Emp Here 25   *Sales* 163,791,300
SIC 1389 Oil and gas field services, nec
Terry King
Gregory Drodge
Robyn King
Keith Way
Barry Whelan
Mike Dewling

D-U-N-S 25-965-3939   (HQ)
UNIFUND ASSURANCE COMPANY
(*Suby of* RSA INSURANCE GROUP PLC)
10 Factory Lane, St. John'S, NL, A1C 6H5
(709) 737-1500
Sales 459,448,120
SIC 6331 Fire, marine, and casualty insurance
Kenneth Bennett
Roy Mercer

D-U-N-S 20-705-0555   (SL)
WILDS AT SALMONIER RIVER INC, THE
THE WILDS
299 Salmonier Line, St. John'S, NL, A1C 5L7
(709) 229-5444
Emp Here 75   *Sales* 5,729,775
SIC 7992 Public golf courses
Eric Coombs
Glen Robatham
Ed Drover
Gerry Bishop

D-U-N-S 24-140-2028   (SL)
WOOD GROUP PSN CANADA INC
(*Suby of* JOHN WOOD GROUP P.L.C.)
277 Water St, St. John'S, NL, A1C 6L3
(709) 778-4000
Emp Here 140   *Sales* 25,023,460
SIC 8711 Engineering services
David Kemp

St. John'S, NL A1E

D-U-N-S 20-985-8927   (HQ)
ANTHONY INSURANCE INCORPORATED
35 Blackmarsh Rd, St. John'S, NL, A1E 1S4
(709) 758-5500
Emp Here 80   *Sales* 184,774,200
SIC 6411 Insurance agents, brokers, and ser-
vice
Rex Anthony
David Anthony
Mathieu Lamy
Johanne Cassis

D-U-N-S 20-781-0420   (BR)
AXA ASSURANCES INC
(*Suby of* AXA ASSURANCES INC)
35 Blackmarsh Rd, St. John'S, NL, A1E 1S4
(709) 726-8974
Emp Here 80
SIC 6311 Life insurance
Lloyd King

D-U-N-S 24-604-6122   (HQ)
BARNES, D.F. LIMITED
22 Sudbury St, St. John'S, NL, A1E 2V1
(709) 579-5041
Sales 10,141,500
SIC 3441 Fabricated structural Metal
Jerry Byrne
Glenn Byrne

D-U-N-S 20-015-5828   (SL)
BEARTOOTH HOLDINGS LIMITED
689 Water St, St. John'S, NL, A1E 1B5
(709) 726-6932
Emp Here 35   *Sales* 29,245,195
SIC 5147 Meats and meat products
Paul Campbell

D-U-N-S 20-015-5414   (HQ)
BROOKFIELD ICE CREAM LIMITED
SCOTSBURN
314 Lemarchant Rd, St. John'S, NL, A1E 1R2
(709) 738-4652
Sales 102,350,850
SIC 2024 Ice cream and frozen deserts
Gerald Smith
Bernard Sparrow

D-U-N-S 20-015-5448   (HQ)
BROWNING HARVEY LIMITED
BEAVER LODGE

15 Ropewalk Lane, St. John'S, NL, A1E 4P1
(709) 579-4116
Emp Here 95   *Sales* 44,594,010
SIC 2086 Bottled and canned soft drinks
Susan Patten
John Patten

D-U-N-S 24-101-3908   (SL)
CENTRE FOR MARINE CNG INC
130 Southside Rd, St. John'S, NL, A1E 0A2

Emp Here 6   *Sales* 18,948,562
SIC 4924 Natural gas distribution

D-U-N-S 20-015-6586   (HQ)
COLONIAL GARAGE & DISTRIBUTORS LIMITED
SYDNEY AUTO PARTS DIVISION
355 Hamilton Ave, St. John'S, NL, A1E 1K1
(709) 579-4011
Emp Here 50   *Sales* 50,726,940
SIC 5013 Motor vehicle supplies and new parts
Douglas Elton Sr
William Elton
Douglas Squires

D-U-N-S 24-683-4647   (SL)
D.F. BARNES SERVICES LIMITED
(*Suby of* J.V. DRIVER CORPORATION INC)
22 Sudbury St, St. John'S, NL, A1E 2V1
(709) 579-5041
Emp Here 150   *Sales* 27,208,200
SIC 3312 Blast furnaces and steel mills
Glenn Byrnes
Charles Mervin Sanders
Jason Fudge
William Elkington

D-U-N-S 20-015-7238   (HQ)
DICKS AND COMPANY LIMITED
385 Empire Ave, St. John'S, NL, A1E 1W6
(709) 579-5111
Emp Here 68   *Sales* 18,592,240
SIC 5712 Furniture stores
James Austin
Barry Tilley

D-U-N-S 20-117-7974   (HQ)
DISTRIBUTION GROUP INCORPORATED
99 Blackmarsh Rd, St. John's, NL, A1E 1S6
(709) 579-2151
Sales 40,245,660
SIC 5046 Commercial equipment, nec
Edwin Stratton
Michelle Hollett

D-U-N-S 24-705-7896   (HQ)
FISH FOOD & ALLIED WORKERS
FFAW/CAW
368 Hamilton Ave, St. John'S, NL, A1E 1K2
(709) 576-7276
Emp Here 25   *Sales* 11,773,500
SIC 8631 Labor organizations
Earle Mccurdy
David Decker
William Broderick
Gregory Pretty

D-U-N-S 24-755-2193   (HQ)
FORTIS INC
5 Springdale St Suite 1100, St. John'S, NL, A1E 0E4
(709) 737-2800
Emp Here 13   *Sales* 6,360,475,780
SIC 4911 Electric services
Barry V. Perry
James P. Laurito
Phonse J. Delaney
Gary J. Smith
David G Hutchens
James R Reid
Stephanie A Amaimo
Karen J Gosse
Karen M. Mccarthy
Regan Odea

D-U-N-S 24-878-2559   (HQ)
FORTIS PROPERTIES CORPORATION
FORTIS HOSPITALITY SVC DIV OF
(*Suby of* FORTIS INC)
5 Springdale St Suite 1100, St. John'S, NL, A1E 0E4
(709) 737-2800
Emp Here 225   *Sales* 94,973,900
SIC 6512 Nonresidential building operators
Nora Duke
Linda Inkpen
H Stanley Marshall
David Norris
Bruce Chafe

D-U-N-S 20-985-7242   (HQ)
G.J. CAHILL & COMPANY (1979) LIMITED
240 Waterford Bridge Rd, St. John'S, NL, A1E 1E2
(709) 368-2125
Emp Here 65   *Sales* 176,631,750
SIC 1731 Electrical work
Fred Cahill

D-U-N-S 20-393-2579   (HQ)
GRANITE DEPARTMENT STORE INC
PIPERS DEPARTMENT STORES
681 Topsail Rd, St. John'S, NL, A1E 2E3
(709) 368-2416
Emp Here 11   *Sales* 15,567,760
SIC 5311 Department stores
Jamie Allister

D-U-N-S 24-431-0996   (SL)
HISTORIC SITES ASSOCIATION OF NEW-FOUNDLAND AND LABRADOR INC
HERITAGE SHOP
10 Forbes St Suite 204, St. John'S, NL, A1E 3L5
(709) 753-5515
Emp Here 50   *Sales* 35,460,600
SIC 8699 Membership organizations, nec
John Butler
Andrea Macdonald
Ian Wallace
Margo Connors
Bob Constantine
Leeann Montgomery
Mandy White
Crystal Braye
Jeff Green
Robert Driscoll

D-U-N-S 20-690-6633   (SL)
ISKUETEU, LIMITED PARTNERSHIP
240 Waterford Bridge Rd, St. John'S, NL, A1E 1E2
(709) 747-4209
Emp Here 259   *Sales* 60,996,831
SIC 1731 Electrical work
Sandy Connors
Fred Cahill

D-U-N-S 24-450-2712   (SL)
J.B. HAND & SONS LIMITED
690 Topsail Rd, St. John'S, NL, A1E 2E2
(709) 364-2300
Emp Here 30   *Sales* 15,616,260
SIC 5099 Durable goods, nec
Leonard Hand
Thomas Hand
Denise Hand
Barbara Byrne
Frederick Hand

D-U-N-S 24-258-3763   (HQ)
KENNY ENTERPRISES LIMITED
MARIES MINI MART
462 Topsail Rd, St. John'S, NL, A1E 2C2
(709) 364-3207
Emp Here 9   *Sales* 33,749,855
SIC 5411 Grocery stores
Richard Kenny
Marie Kenny

D-U-N-S 25-622-3751   (BR)
LABATT BREWING COMPANY LIMITED

(*Suby of* ANHEUSER-BUSCH INBEV)
60 Leslie St, St. John'S, NL, A1E 2V8
(709) 579-0121
Emp Here 100
SIC 2082 Malt beverages
Edison Bagdy

D-U-N-S 20-016-0802   (HQ)
MCLOUGHLAN SUPPLIES LIMITED
LIGHTING WORLD
24 Blackmarsh Rd Suite 22, St. John'S, NL, A1E 1S3
(709) 576-4091
Emp Here 28   *Sales* 21,911,526
SIC 5063 Electrical apparatus and equipment
Ann Mcloughlan

D-U-N-S 24-247-7680   (BR)
MEDIAS TRANSCONTINENTAL INC
TELEGRAM, THE
(*Suby of* TRANSCONTINENTAL INC)
430 Topsail Rd Suite 86, St. John'S, NL, A1E 4N1
(709) 364-6300
Emp Here 100
SIC 2711 Newspapers
Charles Stacey

D-U-N-S 20-197-3604   (SL)
MILL LANE ENTERPRISES
807 Water St, St. John'S, NL, A1E 1C4

Emp Here 40   *Sales* 10,285,240
SIC 4953 Refuse systems
Susan Duff

D-U-N-S 20-016-1073   (HQ)
MODERN BUSINESS EQUIPMENT LIMITED
172 Hamilton Ave, St. John'S, NL, A1E 1J5
(709) 579-2147
Emp Here 27   *Sales* 12,047,200
SIC 5999 Miscellaneous retail stores, nec
Christopher Mallard
Cyril Mallard
Alice Mallard

D-U-N-S 20-778-9140   (HQ)
NEWFOUNDLAND AND LABRADOR HOUSING CORPORATION
NEWFOUNDLAND LABRADOR HOUSING
(*Suby of* PROVINCE OF NEWFOUNDLAND & LABRADOR)
2 Canada Dr, St. John'S, NL, A1E 0A1
(709) 724-3000
Emp Here 197   *Sales* 115,110
SIC 6531 Real estate agents and managers
Len Simms
Tom Lawrence
Janette Loveless
Thomas Baker
Olive Blake
Barbara Cull
Daniel Mccann
Rhonda Neary
Verna Northcott
Kimberley Anne Stroud

D-U-N-S 20-639-9920   (HQ)
PENNECON ENERGY LTD
650 Water St, St. John'S, NL, A1E 1B9
(709) 726-5888
Sales 16,459,920
SIC 8741 Management services
Donald Noseworthy

D-U-N-S 24-207-6318   (SL)
PENNECON ENERGY MARINE BASE LTD
(*Suby of* PENNECON LIMITED)
650 Water St, St. John'S, NL, A1E 1B9
(709) 334-2820
Emp Here 45   *Sales* 14,705,196
SIC 4491 Marine cargo handling
Chesley D Penney
Larry Puddister
Paul Stanley
Christian Somerton

D-U-N-S 20-642-9516   (HQ)

PENNECON TECHNICAL SERVICES LTD
(*Suby of* PENNECON LIMITED)
650 Water St, St. John'S, NL, A1E 1B9
(709) 726-4554
Emp Here 50   *Sales* 19,106,950
SIC 7694 Armature rewinding shops
Larry Puddister
Paul Stanley
Maggie Smith
Jerry White

D-U-N-S 20-449-6897   (HQ)
PUDDISTER TRADING COMPANY LIMITED
23 Springdale St, St. John'S, NL, A1E 2P9
(709) 722-4000
Sales 13,477,450
SIC 4424 Deep sea domestic transportation of freight
Arthur Puddister

D-U-N-S 20-016-2873   (SL)
PURITY FACTORIES LIMITED
96 Blackmarsh Rd, St. John'S, NL, A1E 1S8
(709) 579-2035
Emp Here 75   *Sales* 25,926,750
SIC 2051 Bread, cake, and related products
Doug Spurrell

D-U-N-S 20-037-2758   (SL)
RED OAK CATERING INC
50 Hamlyn Rd Suite 466, St. John'S, NL, A1E 5X7
(709) 368-6808
Emp Here 85   *Sales* 3,644,205
SIC 5812 Eating places
John Rogers
David Kannenberg

D-U-N-S 20-115-5087   (SL)
SANI PRO INC
(*Suby of* DISTRIBUTION GROUP INCORPORATED)
99 Blackmarsh Rd, St. John'S, NL, A1E 1S6
(709) 579-2151
Emp Here 30   *Sales* 13,415,220
SIC 5046 Commercial equipment, nec
Edwin Stratton
H John Mcdonald
Ray Smallwood
Stephen Sparkes
R Wayne Myles

D-U-N-S 25-299-3654   (BR)
SOBEYS CAPITAL INCORPORATED
SOBEYS
(*Suby of* EMPIRE COMPANY LIMITED)
45 Ropewalk Lane, St. John'S, NL, A1E 4P1
(709) 739-8663
Emp Here 200
SIC 5411 Grocery stores
Doug Lynch

D-U-N-S 20-022-6905   (BR)
SOBEYS CAPITAL INCORPORATED
(*Suby of* EMPIRE COMPANY LIMITED)
470 Topsail Rd Suite 340, St. John'S, NL, A1E 2C3
(709) 748-1250
Emp Here 128
SIC 5411 Grocery stores
Fintan White

D-U-N-S 20-045-4291   (SL)
ST JOHN'S NATIVE FRIENDSHIP CENTRE ASSOCIATION
SJNFC
716 Water St, St. John'S, NL, A1E 1C1
(709) 726-5902
Emp Here 50   *Sales* 11,341,650
SIC 8399 Social services, nec
Christopher Sheppard

D-U-N-S 24-789-7283   (SL)
ST. JOHN'S DOCKYARD LIMITED
NEWDOCK
475 Water St, St. John'S, NL, A1E 6B5
(709) 758-6800
Emp Here 100   *Sales* 22,384,300

SIC 3731 Shipbuilding and repairing
Chesley Penney
Robert Butt
Fred Taylor

D-U-N-S 20-333-8199   (SL)
TEEKAY (ATLANTIC) MANAGEMENT ULC
TEEKAY
(Suby of TEEKAY CORPORATION)
5 Springdale St Suite 105, St.   John'S, NL,
A1E 0E4
(855) 485-9351
Emp Here 49   Sales 13,207,901
SIC 4412 Deep sea foreign transportation of
freight
Peter Evensen

D-U-N-S 25-671-9584   (SL)
TERRA NOVA FOODS INC
(Suby of DISTRIBUTION GROUP INCORPO-
RATED)
49 James Lane, St. John'S, NL, A1E 3H3
(709) 579-2121
Emp Here 55   Sales 39,419,380
SIC 5142 Packaged frozen goods
Edwin W Stratton
Stephen Sparkes
Ray Smallwood
R Wayne Myles
H John Mcdonald

D-U-N-S 24-912-3571   (SL)
TRIWARE TECHNOLOGIES INC
76 Brookfield Rd, St. John'S, NL, A1E 3T9
(709) 579-5000
Emp Here 25   Sales 11,179,350
SIC 5045 Computers, peripherals, and soft-
ware
Arthur Stanley
Wallace O'neill

D-U-N-S 20-544-5625   (SL)
VITAL PHARMACY INC
SHOPPERS DRUG MART
250 Lemarchant Rd, St. John'S, NL, A1E 1P7
(709) 739-9751
Emp Here 40   Sales 10,118,160
SIC 5912 Drug stores and proprietary stores
Susan Gillingham

D-U-N-S 20-986-3687   (SL)
WAY'S PHARMACY LIMITED
SHOPPERS DRUG MART
390 Topsail Rd, St. John'S, NL, A1E 2B8
(709) 368-6084
Emp Here 50   Sales 12,647,700
SIC 5912 Drug stores and proprietary stores
Scott Way

St. John'S, NL A1N

D-U-N-S 25-690-2917   (SL)
FARRELLS EXCAVATING LTD
2700 Trans-Canada Hwy, St. John'S, NL, A1N
3C8
(709) 745-5904
Emp Here 85   Sales 20,925,810
SIC 1794 Excavation work
William Farrell
Clarence Kent

Stephenville, NL A2N

D-U-N-S 20-738-3337   (SL)
BAY ST GEORGE RESIDENTIAL SUPPORT
30b Atlantic Ave, Stephenville, NL, A2N 2E9
(709) 643-9762
Emp Here 40   Sales 10,870,240
SIC 6531 Real estate agents and managers
Paul Byrne

D-U-N-S 20-987-8990   (HQ)

COLLEGE OF THE NORTH ATLANTIC
CNA
(Suby of PROVINCE OF NEWFOUNDLAND
& LABRADOR)
432 Massachusetts Dr, Stephenville, NL, A2N
3C1
(709) 643-7868
Emp Here 50   Sales 124,889,940
SIC 8222 Junior colleges
Bruce Hollett
Elizabeth Kidd
Geoff Peters

D-U-N-S 25-894-8744   (SL)
COMMUNITY EDUCATION NETWORK INC
*COMMUNITY EDUCATION NETWORK FOR
SOUTH WESTERN NEWFOUNDLAND*
31 Gallant St, Stephenville, NL, A2N 2B5
(709) 643-4891
Emp Here 50   Sales 11,341,650
SIC 8399 Social services, nec
Sharon Park

D-U-N-S 25-672-6563   (BR)
FOCENCO LIMITED
COLEMAN'S FOOD CENTRE STORES
(Suby of COLEMAN MANAGEMENT SER-
VICES LIMITED)
127 Main St Suite 125, Stephenville, NL, A2N
1J5
(709) 643-2885
Emp Here 85
SIC 5411 Grocery stores
Mondella Stacey

D-U-N-S 20-984-2731   (HQ)
FOCENCO LIMITED
WESTERN WHOLESALERS, DIV OF
(Suby of COLEMAN MANAGEMENT SER-
VICES LIMITED)
383 Connecticut Dr, Stephenville, NL, A2N
2Y6
(709) 637-6600
Emp Here 30   Sales 86,608,800
SIC 5411 Grocery stores
Frank Coleman
Mike Coleman
Bob Coleman
Bill Coleman
Darrell Oram

D-U-N-S 20-449-3308   (SL)
**INDIAN   HEAD   CONSUMERS   CO-
OPERATIVE SOCIETY LTD**
50 Carolina Ave, Stephenville, NL, A2N 2S3
(709) 643-5675
Emp Here 47   Sales 12,885,144
SIC 5411 Grocery stores
Gordon Aucoin
Denise Mcisaac
Wayne Lee
Cator Best
Lori Foley
Ernest Romaine
Theresa Mcdonald
Tony White

D-U-N-S 25-169-1143   (BR)
LOBLAW FINANCIAL HOLDINGS INC
DOMINION 925
(Suby of LOBLAW COMPANIES LIMITED)
62 Prince Rupert Dr, Stephenville, NL, A2N
3W7
(709) 643-0862
Emp Here 100
SIC 5411 Grocery stores
Edmund Mckay

D-U-N-S 20-582-9695   (BR)
WAL-MART CANADA CORP
(Suby of WALMART INC.)
42 Queen St, Stephenville, NL, A2N 3A7
(709) 643-5018
Emp Here 125
SIC 5311 Department stores

D-U-N-S 20-985-6319   (BR)

**WESTERN   REGIONAL   INTEGRATED
HEALTH AUTHORITY, THE**
SIR THOMAS RODDICK HOSPITAL
(Suby of WESTERN REGIONAL INTE-
GRATED HEALTH AUTHORITY, THE)
142 Minnesota Dr, Stephenville, NL, A2N 3X9
(709) 643-5111
Emp Here 300
SIC 8062 General medical and surgical hospi-
tals
Catherine Mcdonald

D-U-N-S 20-796-2726   (SL)
**WESTERN   REGIONAL   INTERGREATED
HEALTH AUTHORITY**
WESTERN HEALTH
149 Montana Dr, Stephenville, NL, A2N 2T4
(709) 643-8608
Emp Here 50   Sales 11,820,082
SIC 8621 Professional organizations
Susan Ford

Twillingate, NL A0G

D-U-N-S 20-908-4359   (SL)
**NOTRE DAME BAY MEMORIAL HEALTH
CENTER**
Gd, Twillingate, NL, A0G 4M0
(709) 884-2131
Emp Here 145   Sales 16,106,600
SIC 8062 General medical and surgical hospi-
tals
Victor Shea

Wabush, NL A0R

D-U-N-S 24-895-0813   (SL)
ESCO LIMITED
(Suby of WEIR GROUP PLC(THE))
21 Second Ave, Wabush, NL, A0R 1B0
(709) 282-3660
Emp Here 50   Sales 11,671,750
SIC 3325 Steel foundries, nec
Maria Oram

D-U-N-S 25-152-3759   (SL)
R.M. & S. COMPANY LIMITED
RESISTANT MATERIAL AND SUPPLY
(Suby of DCL HOLDINGS LIMITED)
1 Commercial St, Wabush, NL, A0R 1B0
(709) 282-3644
Emp Here 60   Sales 28,501,560
SIC 5085 Industrial supplies
Dennis Langdon

Whitbourne, NL A0B

D-U-N-S 20-705-6321   (BR)
**PROVINCE   OF   NEWFOUNDLAND   &
LABRADOR**
*NEWFOUNDLAND & LABRADOR YOUTH
CENTRE*
(Suby of PROVINCE OF NEWFOUNDLAND
& LABRADOR)
Bond Rd, Whitbourne, NL, A0B 3K0
(709) 759-2471
Emp Here 150
SIC 8322 Individual and family services
Trudy Smith

Winterton, NL A0B

D-U-N-S 20-017-2047   (SL)
GREEN, E J & COMPANY LTD
287 Main St, Winterton, NL, A0B 3M0

(709) 583-2670
Emp Here 45   Sales 10,118,475
SIC 2092 Fresh or frozen packaged fish
Derek Green
Doris Harnum

Witless Bay, NL A0A

D-U-N-S 25-650-6585   (HQ)
C MAR SERVICES (CANADA) LTD
20 Bear Cove Rd, Witless Bay, NL, A0A 4K0
(709) 334-2033
Emp Here 4   Sales 20,463,264
SIC 8741 Management services
Denis Mair

Behchoko, NT X0E

D-U-N-S 24-358-6646 (SL)
TLI CHO CONSTRUCTION LTD
(*Suby of* BEHCHO KO DEVELOPMENT CORPORATION)
Gd, Behchoko, NT, X0E 0Y0
(867) 766-4909
Emp Here 45 *Sales* 12,192,390
SIC 1521 Single-family housing construction
James Golchert

Fort Liard, NT X0G

D-U-N-S 24-930-0369 (SL)
BEAVER ENTERPRISES LIMITED PARTNERSHIP
BEAVER ENTERPRISES
Gd, Fort Liard, NT, X0G 0A0
(867) 770-2203
Emp Here 200 *Sales* 50,488,400
SIC 1611 Highway and street construction
Shane Parrish

Fort Smith, NT X0E

D-U-N-S 24-939-7837 (HQ)
AURORA COLLEGE
(*Suby of* GOVERNMENT OF THE NORTHWEST TERRITORIES)
50 Conibear Cres, Fort Smith, NT, X0E 0P0
(867) 872-7000
Emp Here 100 *Sales* 26,062,268
SIC 8221 Colleges and universities
Jane Arychuk

D-U-N-S 24-584-8437 (SL)
NORTHWESTERN AIR LEASE LTD
Hangar 1, Fort Smith, NT, X0E 0P0
(867) 872-2216
Emp Here 74 *Sales* 24,031,796
SIC 4512 Air transportation, scheduled
Terry Harrold
Brian Harrold

D-U-N-S 24-929-1436 (SL)
TDC CONTRACTING LTD
BUMPER TO BUMPER
1 Breynat St, Fort Smith, NT, X0E 0P0
(867) 872-2458
Emp Here 19 *Sales* 19,623,352
SIC 5171 Petroleum bulk stations and terminals
Glen Freund
Marie Swanson

Hay River, NT X0E

D-U-N-S 24-809-6141 (HQ)
BASSETT PETROLEUM DISTRIBUTORS LTD
BLUEWAVE ENERGY
43013 Mackenzie Hwy, Hay River, NT, X0E 0R9
(867) 874-8500
Emp Here 38 *Sales* 62,860,050
SIC 5171 Petroleum bulk stations and terminals
Stephen Bassett
Georgina Bassett

D-U-N-S 25-230-2922 (HQ)
BUFFALO AIRWAYS LTD
25 Industrial Dr, Hay River, NT, X0E 0R6
(867) 874-3333
Emp Here 1 *Sales* 20,023,350

SIC 4512 Air transportation, scheduled
Wilson Mcbryan

D-U-N-S 20-268-8933 (SL)
HAY RIVER HEALTH & SOCIAL SERVICES AUTHORITY
3 Gaetz Dr, Hay River, NT, X0E 0R8
(867) 874-7100
Emp Here 185 *Sales* 38,307,580
SIC 8399 Social services, nec
Al Woods
Merle Engel
Sheryl Courtoreille

D-U-N-S 20-032-3090 (SL)
KING MANUFACTURING
9 Aspen Rd, Hay River, NT, X0E 0R6
(867) 874-2373
Emp Here 22 *Sales* 10,571,610
SIC 5085 Industrial supplies
Russell King

D-U-N-S 20-971-0342 (HQ)
KINGLAND FORD SALES LTD
KINGLAND TRUCK & WELDING
922 Mackenzie Hwy Ss 22, Hay River, NT, X0E 0R8

Sales 81,806,400
SIC 5511 New and used car dealers
Russell King
Arlene Mills
Spencer King
Tamara Powder

D-U-N-S 24-809-8089 (HQ)
MIDNIGHT MECHANICAL LIMITED
MIDNIGHT PETROLEUM
42099 Mackenzie Hwy, Hay River, NT, X0E 0R9
(867) 874-2201
Emp Here 7 *Sales* 56,574,045
SIC 5172 Petroleum products, nec
Jean-Marc Miltenberger
Leah Miltenberger

D-U-N-S 20-391-8243 (HQ)
NORTHWEST TERRITORIES HYDRO CORPORATION
NT HYDRO
(*Suby of* GOVERNMENT OF THE NORTHWEST TERRITORIES)
4 Capital Dr Ss 98 Suite 98, Hay River, NT, X0E 1G2
(867) 874-5200
Sales 115,578,580
SIC 4911 Electric services
Lew Voytilla
Leon Courneya

D-U-N-S 24-880-5616 (SL)
NORTHWEST TERRITORIES LIQUOR COMMISSION
(*Suby of* GOVERNMENT OF THE NORTHWEST TERRITORIES)
31 Capital Dr Suite 201, Hay River, NT, X0E 1G2
(867) 874-8700
Emp Here 8 *Sales* 52,998,000
SIC 5921 Liquor stores
Peter Maher

D-U-N-S 20-506-6475 (HQ)
NORTHWEST TERRITORIES POWER CORPORATION
(*Suby of* GOVERNMENT OF THE NORTHWEST TERRITORIES)
4 Capital Dr Ss 98 Suite 98, Hay River, NT, X0E 1G2
(867) 874-5200
Emp Here 55 *Sales* 115,578,580
SIC 4911 Electric services
Leon Courneya
Lew Voytilla

D-U-N-S 24-853-8332 (SL)
ROWE'S CONSTRUCTION LTD
25 Studney Dr, Hay River, NT, X0E 0R6

(867) 874-3243
Emp Here 100 *Sales* 25,244,200
SIC 1629 Heavy construction, nec
Michael Rowe

D-U-N-S 20-897-7389 (HQ)
WESCLEAN NORTHERN SALES LTD
15 Industrial Dr, Hay River, NT, X0E 0R6
(867) 875-5100
Emp Here 28 *Sales* 14,725,806
SIC 5087 Service establishment equipment
Bradley Mapes

Inuvik, NT X0E

D-U-N-S 20-059-5028 (HQ)
ARCTIC DOVE LIMITED
ESSO BULK AGENT
8 Tank Farm Rd, Inuvik, NT, X0E 0T0
(867) 777-3226
Emp Here 9 *Sales* 12,393,696
SIC 5171 Petroleum bulk stations and terminals
Paul Wiedemann

D-U-N-S 20-183-5274 (SL)
ARCTIC OIL & GAS SERVICES INC
AOGS
(*Suby of* INUVIALUIT REGIONAL CORPORATION)
170 Mackenzie Rd, Inuvik, NT, X0E 0T0
(867) 777-8700
Emp Here 100 *Sales* 4,551,900
SIC 5812 Eating places
Sam Daher

D-U-N-S 24-293-6458 (HQ)
INUVIALUIT DEVELOPMENT CORPORATION
IDC
(*Suby of* INUVIALUIT REGIONAL CORPORATION)
107 Mackenzie Rd 3rd Fl, Inuvik, NT, X0E 0T0
(867) 777-7000
Sales 56,101,500
SIC 8741 Management services
Bradley Carpenter
Ellice Schneider
Fred Abbott
Patrick Gruben
Kenneth Ruben
Keith Anderson
Harry Elias

D-U-N-S 20-576-0106 (SL)
INUVIK GAS LTD
107 Mackenzie Rd Suite 102, Inuvik, NT, X0E 0T0
(867) 777-3422
Emp Here 12 *Sales* 37,270,284
SIC 4924 Natural gas distribution
Gerald B Roy
Patricia M Newson
Michael Dever
George Seens

D-U-N-S 24-866-4054 (HQ)
NORTHWEST TERRITORY HEALTH AND SOCIAL SERVICES AUTHORITY-BDR
285 Mackenzie Rd, Inuvik, NT, X0E 0T0
(867) 777-8000
Emp Here 125 *Sales* 36,154,283
SIC 8062 General medical and surgical hospitals
Arlene Jorgensen
Roger Israel

D-U-N-S 24-492-8495 (SL)
STANTON DISTRIBUTING CO LTD
STANTON DISTRIBUTING & LIQUOR OPERATIONS
(*Suby of* INUVIALUIT REGIONAL CORPORATION)
49 Navy Rd, Inuvik, NT, X0E 0T0

(867) 777-4381
Emp Here 47 *Sales* 39,272,119
SIC 5141 Groceries, general line
Rino Driscoll

Norman Wells, NT X0E

D-U-N-S 20-052-5181 (HQ)
NORTH-WRIGHT AIRWAYS LTD
(*Suby of* 2140047 CANADA LTD)
2200, Norman Wells, NT, X0E 0V0
(867) 587-2288
Emp Here 35 *Sales* 20,798,680
SIC 4724 Travel agencies
Warren Wright
Carolyn Wright

Yellowknife, NT X1A

D-U-N-S 25-105-2403 (SL)
994421 N.W.T. LTD
NORTHERN FOOD SERVICES
353a Old Airport Rd, Yellowknife, NT, X1A 3T4
(867) 873-5338
Emp Here 19 *Sales* 10,167,356
SIC 5141 Groceries, general line
Pietro Bertolini
Jack Walker

D-U-N-S 25-360-6297 (SL)
994486 N.W.T LTD
STOCK POT, LE
Gd Lcd Main, Yellowknife, NT, X1A 2L8
(867) 873-5600
Emp Here 85 *Sales* 3,869,115
SIC 5812 Eating places
Pierre Lepage

D-U-N-S 20-741-7598 (SL)
ADVANCED MEDICAL SOLUTIONS INC
233 Utsingi Dr, Yellowknife, NT, X1A 0E7
(866) 578-9111
Emp Here 70 *Sales* 31,302,180
SIC 5047 Medical and hospital equipment
Sean Ivens

D-U-N-S 24-766-5888 (SL)
AIR TINDI LTD
28 Mitchell Dr, Yellowknife, NT, X1A 2H5
(867) 669-8200
Emp Here 109 *Sales* 29,100,602
SIC 4522 Air transportation, nonscheduled
Alex Arychuk
Peter Arychuk
Teri Arychuk
Sheila Arychuk

D-U-N-S 24-389-2333 (HQ)
ARCAN GROUP INC
112 Taltheilei Dr, Yellowknife, NT, X1A 0E9
(867) 873-2520
Emp Here 6 *Sales* 40,476,176
SIC 1542 Nonresidential construction, nec
Jon White
James Kimble Doyle
Duncan Cooke
Caelin Cameron
Dean Hudson
Ron Jordan
Nelson Madsen
Jonathan Noel

D-U-N-S 24-065-5535 (SL)
ARCTIC HOLDINGS & LEASING LTD
135 Kam Lake Rd, Yellowknife, NT, X1A 0G3
(867) 920-4844
Emp Here 40 *Sales* 11,340,960
SIC 1611 Highway and street construction
Rod Hedelberd

D-U-N-S 20-512-3362 (SL)
ARSLANIAN CUTTING WORKS NWT LTD

106 Archibald St, Yellowknife, NT, X1A 2P4
(867) 873-0138
Emp Here 48   *Sales* 10,503,552
SIC 3915 Jewelers' materials and lapidary work
Chahe Arslanian
Robert Bies
Ronen Basal
Shlomo Drazin

    D-U-N-S 24-358-6570   (HQ)
BEHCHO KO DEVELOPMENT CORPORATION
25 Stanton Plaza, Yellowknife, NT, X1A 2P3
(867) 920-7288
Sales 32,865,525
SIC 5169 Chemicals and allied products, nec
Kathy Macdonald

    D-U-N-S 25-507-5202   (HQ)
DIAVIK DIAMOND MINES (2012) INC
(Suby of RIO TINTO PLC)
5201 50 Ave Suite 300, Yellowknife, NT, X1A 3S9
(867) 669-6500
Emp Here 31   *Sales* 286,697,646
SIC 1499 Miscellaneous nonMetallic minerals, except fuels
Nigel Steward
Marie-Christine Dupont
Boitumelo Patrick

    D-U-N-S 25-955-9180   (BR)
DISCOVERY AIR INC
126 Crystal Ave, Yellowknife, NT, X1A 2P3
(867) 873-5350
Emp Here 200   *Sales* 575,061
SIC 4522 Air transportation, nonscheduled
Gilbert Bennett

    D-U-N-S 24-673-3638   (HQ)
DOMINION DIAMOND CORPORATION
(Suby of WASHINGTON CORPORATIONS)
4920 52 St Unit 900, Yellowknife, NT, X1A 3T1
(867) 669-6100
Emp Here 1   *Sales* 1,134,034,300
SIC 5094 Jewelry and precious stones
Patrick Evans
Brendan Hall
Matthew Quinlan
Chantal Lavoie
Elliot Holland
James Pounds
James Gowans
Graham Glow
Thomas Andruskevich
Trudy Curran

    D-U-N-S 25-326-5359   (HQ)
DOMINION DIAMOND EKATI ULC
DOMINION DIAMOND MINES
(Suby of WASHINGTON CORPORATIONS)
4920 52 St Suite 900, Yellowknife, NT, X1A 3A3
(867) 669-9292
Emp Here 50   *Sales* 826,218,000
SIC 1499 Miscellaneous nonMetallic minerals, except fuels
Chantal Lavoie

    D-U-N-S 25-160-6695   (SL)
EK'ATI SERVICES LTD
(Suby of OIL STATES INTERNATIONAL, INC.)
4910 50 Ave, Yellowknife, NT, X1A 3S5
(867) 873-8873
Emp Here 90
SIC 5812 Eating places
Gary Fortier
Neil Mcfadden

    D-U-N-S 24-523-0701   (HQ)
GREAT SLAVE HELICOPTERS LTD
GSH
106 Dickens St, Yellowknife, NT, X1A 3T2.
(867) 873-2081
Emp Here 25   *Sales* 14,683,790

SIC 4522 Air transportation, nonscheduled
Mark Mcgowan
Corey Taylor
Brian Merker

    D-U-N-S 24-948-3194   (SL)
KBL ENVIRONMENTAL LTD
17 Cameron Rd, Yellowknife, NT, X1A 0E8
(867) 873-5263
Emp Here 46   *Sales* 13,852,532
SIC 4953 Refuse systems
John Oakfield

    D-U-N-S 25-459-4133   (SL)
KO ENERGY
4902 45 St, Yellowknife, NT, X1A 1K5
(867) 447-3457
Emp Here 5   *Sales* 15,790,468
SIC 4924 Natural gas distribution

    D-U-N-S 24-850-3497   (SL)
MATONABEE PETROEUM LTD
117 Kam Lake Rd, Yellowknife, NT, X1A 0G3
(867) 873-4001
Emp Here 11   *Sales* 11,360,888
SIC 5171 Petroleum bulk stations and terminals
Shawn Delany

    D-U-N-S 25-110-1267   (HQ)
MATONABEE PETROLEUM LTD
PETRO-CANADA
Po Box 2697 Stn Main, Yellowknife, NT, X1A 2R1
(867) 873-4001
Emp Here 3   *Sales* 27,658,422
SIC 5171 Petroleum bulk stations and terminals
Shawn Delaney

    D-U-N-S 20-825-5369   (SL)
NAHANNI CONSTRUCTION LTD
100 Nahanni Dr, Yellowknife, NT, X1A 0E8
(867) 873-2975
Emp Here 120   *Sales* 68,440,560
SIC 1542 Nonresidential construction, nec
Robert Morgan
Dwight Peart

    D-U-N-S 20-745-2178   (HQ)
NORTHERN NEWS SERVICES LTD
YELLOWKNIFER, THE
5108 50 St, Yellowknife, NT, X1A 1S2
(867) 873-4031
Emp Here 61   *Sales* 11,317,863
SIC 2711 Newspapers
Jack Sigvaldason
Michael Scott

    D-U-N-S 25-207-3333   (SL)
NORTHLAND UTILITIES (YELLOWKNIFE) LTD
(Suby of ATCO LTD)
481 Range Lake Rd, Yellowknife, NT, X1A 3R9
(867) 873-4865
Emp Here 17   *Sales* 10,652,438
SIC 4911 Electric services
Don Brat

    D-U-N-S 20-807-6331   (HQ)
NORTHWEST TERRITORIES NON-PROFIT HOUSING CORPORATION
SOCIAL HOUSING PROGRAMS
(Suby of GOVERNMENT OF THE NORTHWEST TERRITORIES)
Gd Lcd Main, Yellowknife, NT, X1A 2L8
(867) 873-7873
Emp Here 49   *Sales* 83,587,884
SIC 6531 Real estate agents and managers
David Stewart

    D-U-N-S 24-098-4414   (BR)
NORTHWESTEL INC
(Suby of BCE INC)
5201 50 Ave, Yellowknife, NT, X1A 3S9
(867) 920-3500
Emp Here 100

SIC 4899 Communication services, nec
John Mabilog

    D-U-N-S 24-361-3267   (BR)
NUNASTAR PROPERTIES INC
EXPLORER HOTEL, THE
4825 49th Ave, Yellowknife, NT, X1A 2R3
(867) 873-3531
Emp Here 90
SIC 7011 Hotels and motels
Karl-Hainz Schafers

    D-U-N-S 25-399-5542   (SL)
POLAR EXPLOSIVES LTD
(Suby of INCITEC PIVOT LIMITED)
349 Old Airport Rd Suite 104, Yellowknife, NT, X1A 3X6
(867) 880-4613
Emp Here 540   *Sales* 362,994,480
SIC 5169 Chemicals and allied products, nec
Brad Rhude
Yves Tremblay

    D-U-N-S 20-537-8854   (HQ)
RTL- ROBINSON ENTERPRISES LTD
350 Old Airport Rd, Yellowknife, NT, X1A 3T4
(867) 873-6271
Emp Here 80   *Sales* 30,855,900
SIC 4213 Trucking, except local
Tom Kenny
Shawn Mcmillan

    D-U-N-S 25-329-1033   (SL)
RYFAN ELECTRIC LTD
9 Nahanni Dr, Yellowknife, NT, X1A 0E8
(867) 765-6100
Emp Here 125   *Sales* 27,228,625
SIC 1731 Electrical work
Richard Bolivar
David Tucker
Darren Fraser

    D-U-N-S 20-897-7108   (HQ)
STANTON TERRITORIAL HEALTH AUTHORITY
STANTON TERRITORIAL HOSPITAL
(Suby of GOVERNMENT OF THE NORTHWEST TERRITORIES)
550 Byrne Rd, Yellowknife, NT, X1A 2N1
(867) 669-4111
Emp Here 475   *Sales* 56,984,640
SIC 8062 General medical and surgical hospitals
Brenda Fitzgerald
Kay Lewis

    D-U-N-S 20-057-8156   (SL)
SUMMIT AIR LTD
(Suby of 280818 ALBERTA LTD)
100 Dickens St, Yellowknife, NT, X1A 3T2
(867) 873-4464
Emp Here 150   *Sales* 40,046,700
SIC 4522 Air transportation, nonscheduled
Myles Cane

    D-U-N-S 24-392-6313   (HQ)
SUMMIT HELICOPTERS LTD
(Suby of 280818 ALBERTA LTD)
27 Yellowknife Airport 100 Dickins St, Yellowknife, NT, X1A 3T2
(867) 765-5969
Sales 16,237,700
SIC 4522 Air transportation, nonscheduled
Rob Mauracher
Paul Henry
Keith Palmer

    D-U-N-S 24-088-5954   (HQ)
T.C. ENTERPRISES LTD
5013 48 St, Yellowknife, NT, X1A 1N4
(867) 669-8300
Emp Here 5   *Sales* 12,147,905
SIC 6519 Real property lessors, nec
Anthony Chang
Elaine Grundy

    D-U-N-S 20-153-8167   (SL)
TLI CHO LOGISTICS INC

25 Stanton Plaza, Yellowknife, NT, X1A 2N6
(867) 920-7288
Emp Here 250   *Sales* 47,166,524
SIC 8742 Management consulting services
Darrell Matchett
Bettyanne Nickerson

    D-U-N-S 20-874-6953   (SL)
W.J. PARISEAU SALES LTD
CANADIAN TIRE
328 Old Airport Rd, Yellowknife, NT, X1A 3T3
(867) 873-2403
Emp Here 70   *Sales* 44,049,600
SIC 5531 Auto and home supply stores
Warren Pariseau

    D-U-N-S 20-088-5452   (BR)
WAL-MART CANADA CORP
WALMART
(Suby of WALMART INC.)
313 Old Airport Rd, Yellowknife, NT, X1A 3T3
(867) 873-4545
Emp Here 100
SIC 5311 Department stores
Terry Andre

    D-U-N-S 25-417-5938   (SL)
WORKERS' SAFETY AND COMPENSATION COMMISSION OF THE NORTHWEST TERRITORIES AND NUNAVUT
W S C C
5022 49 St, Yellowknife, NT, X1A 3R8
(867) 920-3888
Emp Here 130   *Sales* 44,348,890
SIC 6331 Fire, marine, and casualty insurance
Dave Grundy
Dave Tucker

    D-U-N-S 25-977-2549   (SL)
YELLOWKNIFE CHRYSLER LTD
340 Old Airport Rd, Yellowknife, NT, X1A 3T3
(867) 873-4222
Emp Here 35   *Sales* 17,432,730
SIC 551 i New and used car dealers
Connie Dentinger

    D-U-N-S 24-584-4394   (SL)
YELLOWKNIFE DIRECT CHARGE CO-OPERATIVE LIMITED
321 Old Airport Rd, Yellowknife, NT, X1A 3T3
(867) 873-5770
Emp Here 80   *Sales* 21,932,160
SIC 5411 Grocery stores
Benjamin Walker
Mark Needham
John Argue
John Monroe

    D-U-N-S 25-842-6576   (SL)
YELLOWKNIFE INN LTD
ATITUDES RESTAURANT & BISTRO, L'
5010 49th St, Yellowknife, NT, X1A 2N4
(867) 873-2601
Emp Here 75   *Sales* 3,413,925
SIC 5812 Eating places
Derek Carmody

    D-U-N-S 24-928-4936   (HQ)
YELLOWKNIFE PUBLIC DENOMINATIONAL DISTRICT EDUCATION AUTHORITY
YELLOWKNIFE CATHOLIC SCHOOLS
5124 49 St, Yellowknife, NT, X1A 1P8
(867) 766-7400
Emp Here 16   *Sales* 17,841,420
SIC 8211 Elementary and secondary schools
Debra Kruger
Claudia Parker
Mike Huvenaars

    D-U-N-S 20-088-5221   (BR)
YOUNG WOMEN'S CHRISTIAN ASSOCIATION OF CANADA, THE
YWCA YELLOWKNIFE
(Suby of YOUNG WOMEN'S CHRISTIAN ASSOCIATION OF CANADA, THE)
5004 50th Ave, Yellowknife, NT, X1A 2P3

(867) 920-2777
Emp Here 120
SIC 7011 Hotels and motels
 Lyda Fuller

Amherst, NS B4H

D-U-N-S 25-265-2458   (BR)
AMHERST, TOWN OF
(*Suby of* AMHERST, TOWN OF)
98 Victoria St E, Amherst, NS, B4H 1X6
(902) 667-7743
Emp Here 100
SIC 4953 Refuse systems
Jason Macdonald

D-U-N-S 24-343-4461   (HQ)
ARCHWAY INSURANCE INC
81 Victoria St E, Amherst, NS, B4H 1X7
(902) 667-0800
Emp Here 11   *Sales* 33,922,400
SIC 6411 Insurance agents, brokers, and service
Garry Stack
Mike Stack
Gina Mcsetridge

D-U-N-S 25-181-8738   (BR)
ATLANTIC WHOLESALERS LTD
REAL ATLANTIC SUPERSTORE
(*Suby of* LOBLAW COMPANIES LIMITED)
126 Albion St S, Amherst, NS, B4H 2X3
(902) 661-0703
Emp Here 150
SIC 5411 Grocery stores
James Walker

D-U-N-S 20-113-2540   (SL)
C-VISION LIMITED
21 Tantramar Cres, Amherst, NS, B4H 4S8
(902) 667-1228
Emp Here 110   *Sales* 20,948,620
SIC 3672 Printed circuit boards
Charles A. Cartmill
Curtis Cartmill
David Scott

D-U-N-S 20-024-1073   (HQ)
CASEY CONCRETE LIMITED
96 Park St, Amherst, NS, B4H 2R7
(902) 667-3395
Emp Here 20   *Sales* 11,671,750
SIC 3273 Ready-mixed concrete
Bruce Casey
Earl Casey

D-U-N-S 24-994-6872   (SL)
CGW AUTOMOTIVE GROUP LIMITED
AMHERST TOYOTA
34 Lord Amherst Dr, Amherst, NS, B4H 4W6
(902) 667-8348
Emp Here 29   *Sales* 14,444,262
SIC 5511 New and used car dealers
Tracy Pye-Roberts
Garry Pye
Brent Macgrath
Glenn Roberts

D-U-N-S 20-022-6538   (HQ)
EPC INDUSTRIES LIMITED
POLYCELLO
12 Tupper Blvd, Amherst, NS, B4H 4S7
(902) 667-7241
Sales 62,976,550
SIC 2759 Commercial printing, nec
Stephen Emmerson
Robert Adamczyk
Craig Evans
George Landes
Ray Bristol

D-U-N-S 25-991-4380   (BR)
GEM HEALTH CARE GROUP LIMITED
GABLES LODGE
(*Suby of* GEM HEALTH CARE GROUP LIMITED)
260 Church St, Amherst, NS, B4H 3C9
(902) 667-3501
Emp Here 115
SIC 8051 Skilled nursing care facilities

Kathleen Maltby

D-U-N-S 20-026-4059   (HQ)
HARRISON, C. ERNEST & SONS LIMITED
HARRISON HOME BUILDING CENTRES
404 Macdonald Rd, Amherst, NS, B4H 3Y4
(902) 667-3306
Emp Here 45   *Sales* 24,088,680
SIC 5211 Lumber and other building materials
Rodrick Harrison
Raymond Harrison
Craig Harrison
Donald Harrison
Gary Harrison

D-U-N-S 20-024-1248   (SL)
HATHEWAY, JIM FORD SALES LIMITED
76 Robert Angus Dr, Amherst, NS, B4H 4R7
(902) 667-6000
Emp Here 32   *Sales* 15,938,496
SIC 5511 New and used car dealers
James (Jim) Hatheway

D-U-N-S 25-362-2815   (SL)
MARITIME PRIDE EGGS INC
50 Tantramar Cres, Amherst, NS, B4H 0A1
(800) 563-2246
Emp Here 40   *Sales* 33,423,080
SIC 5144 Poultry and poultry products
Hans Kristensen
Michael Gauvin

D-U-N-S 20-913-3946   (BR)
NOVA SCOTIA HEALTH AUTHORITY
(*Suby of* NOVA SCOTIA, PROVINCE OF)
18 Albion St S, Amherst, NS, B4H 2W3
(902) 661-1090
Emp Here 100
SIC 8062 General medical and surgical hospitals
Jackie Cooke

D-U-N-S 24-393-2337   (SL)
SOEHNER SALES LIMITED
CANADIAN TIRE
152 Albion St S, Amherst, NS, B4H 4H4
(902) 667-7218
Emp Here 60   *Sales* 37,756,800
SIC 5531 Auto and home supply stores
Kevin Soehner

D-U-N-S 25-400-6034   (SL)
STENEK CORPORATION
40 Tantramar Cres, Amherst, NS, B4H 0A1

Emp Here 75   *Sales* 33,538,050
SIC 5043 Photographic equipment and supplies
Michael Korenberg
Ryan Barrington-Foote
Nick Desmarais

D-U-N-S 20-024-2295   (SL)
TANTRAMAR CHEVROLET BUICK GMC (2009) LIMITED
TANTRAMAR CHEVROLET
88 Robert Angus Dr, Amherst, NS, B4H 4R7
(902) 667-9975
Emp Here 43   *Sales* 21,417,354
SIC 5511 New and used car dealers
Douglas Mcdonald
Donald Furlong

D-U-N-S 25-635-1966   (BR)
UNITED STEELWORKERS OF AMERICA
(*Suby of* UNITED STEELWORKERS)
10 Tantramar Pl, Amherst, NS, B4H 2A1
(902) 667-0727
Emp Here 182
SIC 8631 Labor organizations
Bruce Feruguson

D-U-N-S 24-346-7359   (BR)
VICTORIAN ORDER OF NURSES FOR CANADA
VON CUMBERLAND DISTRICT
(*Suby of* VICTORIAN ORDER OF NURSES FOR CANADA)

43 Prince Arthur St, Amherst, NS, B4H 1V8
(902) 667-8796
Emp Here 160
SIC 8082 Home health care services
Wendy Macdonald

D-U-N-S 24-121-2492   (BR)
WAL-MART CANADA CORP
(*Suby of* WALMART INC.)
46 Robert Angus Dr, Amherst, NS, B4H 4R7
(902) 661-3476
Emp Here 100
SIC 5311 Department stores
Shelley Broader

D-U-N-S 24-533-8918   (HQ)
WALDALE MANUFACTURING LIMITED
17 Tantramar Cres, Amherst, NS, B4H 4J6
(902) 667-3307
Sales 14,406,375
SIC 3469 Metal stampings, nec
Linda Long

Antigonish, NS B2G

D-U-N-S 24-186-3042   (SL)
ACTION MANAGEMENT SERVICES INC
23 Main St, Antigonish, NS, B2G 2B3
(902) 863-3200
Emp Here 60   *Sales* 17,066,220
SIC 6512 Nonresidential building operators
John Webb
John T Webb

D-U-N-S 24-399-9484   (SL)
CENTRAL HOME IMPROVEMENT WAREHOUSE
35 Market St, Antigonish, NS, B2G 3B5
(902) 863-6882
Emp Here 40   *Sales* 12,754,760
SIC 1521 Single-family housing construction
Steve Smith

D-U-N-S 25-362-5784   (HQ)
EAST COAST CREDIT UNION LIMITED
257 Main St, Antigonish, NS, B2G 2C1

Emp Here 9   *Sales* 19,139,197
SIC 6062 State credit unions
Ken Shea
Caroline Dicki

D-U-N-S 20-933-3061   (HQ)
GOVERNORS OF ST FRANCIS XAVIER UNIVERSITY
1 West St, Antigonish, NS, B2G 2W5
(902) 863-3300
Sales 1,643,301,000
SIC 8221 Colleges and universities
Kent Mcdonald

D-U-N-S 25-411-6510   (SL)
HOME DOCTOR LIMITED, THE
HIGHLAND CELLULAR
3067 Highway 104 Unit C, Antigonish, NS, B2G 2K5
(902) 735-9100
Emp Here 40   *Sales* 13,024,000
SIC 5999 Miscellaneous retail stores, nec
Mark Worth
Timothy Mahoney

D-U-N-S 20-005-4638   (SL)
M & N CROWELL PHARMACY SERVICES LTD
SHOPPERS DRUG MART
303 Main St Suite 143, Antigonish, NS, B2G 2C3
(902) 863-6522
Emp Here 40   *Sales* 10,118,160
SIC 5912 Drug stores and proprietary stores
Margie Crowell

D-U-N-S 25-325-0583   (SL)
NATIONAL PHILATELIC CENTRE

75 St Ninian St, Antigonish, NS, B2G 2R8
(902) 863-6550
Emp Here 75   *Sales* 18,324,600
SIC 5961 Catalog and mail-order houses
Heather Gillis

D-U-N-S 20-024-3533   (SL)
NOVA CONSTRUCTION CO. LTD
3098 Highway 104, Antigonish, NS, B2G 2K3
(902) 863-4004
Emp Here 150   *Sales* 40,641,300
SIC 1521 Single-family housing construction
Donald W. Chisholm
Carl Hartigan

D-U-N-S 20-781-9558   (SL)
R.K. MACDONALD NURSING HOME CORPORATION
64 Pleasant St, Antigonish, NS, B2G 1W7
(902) 863-2578
Emp Here 150   *Sales* 10,248,900
SIC 8051 Skilled nursing care facilities
Lorna Crocker

D-U-N-S 24-932-2199   (SL)
SHIRLEY, STEWART A ENTERPRISES LIMITED
CANADIAN TIRE
133 Church St Suite 1, Antigonish, NS, B2G 2E3
(902) 863-4753
Emp Here 60   *Sales* 37,756,800
SIC 5531 Auto and home supply stores
Stewart A Shirley
Margaret Shirley

D-U-N-S 25-299-3175   (BR)
SOBEYS CAPITAL INCORPORATED
SOBEYS # 596
(*Suby of* EMPIRE COMPANY LIMITED)
151 Church St, Antigonish, NS, B2G 2E2
(902) 863-6022
Emp Here 100
SIC 5411 Grocery stores
Darlene Harris

D-U-N-S 24-705-8720   (BR)
SODEXO CANADA LTD
(*Suby of* SODEXO)
Gd, Antigonish, NS, B2G 2W5
(902) 867-2491
Emp Here 90
SIC 5812 Eating places

D-U-N-S 24-245-6064   (SL)
ST. FRANCIS XAVIER UNIVERSITY
COADY INTERNATIONAL INSTITUTE
5005 Chapel Sq, Antigonish, NS, B2G 2W5
(902) 863-3300
Emp Here 100   *Sales* 92,449,587
SIC 8211 Elementary and secondary schools
Kent Macdonald
Kevin Wamsley
Andrew Beckett
June Webber
Murray Kyte
Mike Boyd
Mary Lou O'reilly
Andrew Beckett

D-U-N-S 25-241-0055   (BR)
STRAIT REGIONAL CENTRE FOR EDUCATION, THE
STRAIT REGIONAL SCHOOL BOARD
(*Suby of* STRAIT REGIONAL CENTRE FOR EDUCATION, THE)
105 Braemore Ave, Antigonish, NS, B2G 1L3
(902) 863-1620
Emp Here 75
SIC 8211 Elementary and secondary schools
Wanda Fougere

D-U-N-S 24-317-1860   (BR)
WAL-MART CANADA CORP
WALMART
(*Suby of* WALMART INC.)
50 Market St, Antigonish, NS, B2G 3B4

(902) 867-1279
Emp Here 150
SIC 5311 Department stores
Troy Dunnett

Arcadia, NS B0W

D-U-N-S 20-932-8012   (SL)
HERVIC ENTERPRISES LTD
2896 Melbourne Rd Rr 1, Arcadia, NS, B0W
1B0
(902) 742-3981
Emp Here 25   *Sales* 20,889,425
SIC 5146 Fish and seafoods
Herman Saulnier
Eric Saulnier
Carroll Saulnier
Ivan Saulnier

D-U-N-S 20-929-3133   (SL)
WM.R.MURPHY FISHERIES LTD
52 Wharf Rd Little River Harbour, Arcadia, NS,
B0W 1B0
(902) 663-4301
Emp Here 50   *Sales* 11,242,750
SIC 2091 Canned and cured fish and
seafoods
William Murphy
Christopher Murphy
Glen Murphy

Arichat, NS B0E

D-U-N-S 24-377-1131   (SL)
**GREEN ISLAND DISTRIBUTORS PART-
NERSHIP**
616 Lower Rd, Arichat, NS, B0E 1A0
(902) 226-2633
Emp Here 50   *Sales* 11,242,750
SIC 2091 Canned and cured fish and
seafoods
Brian Sampson
Edgar Sampson

D-U-N-S 24-473-4513   (SL)
PREMIUM SEAFOODS LIMITED
PREMIUM SEAFOOD GROUP
449 Veterans Memorial Dr, Arichat, NS, B0E
1A0
(902) 226-3474
Emp Here 30   *Sales* 25,067,310
SIC 5146 Fish and seafoods
Edgar Samson

D-U-N-S 25-964-2650   (BR)
THORNVALE HOLDINGS LIMITED
(*Suby of* THORNVALE HOLDINGS LIMITED)
441 Cape Auget Rd, Arichat, NS, B0E 1A0
(902) 226-3510
Emp Here 75
SIC 4222 Refrigerated warehousing and stor-
age
David George

Auburn, NS B0P

D-U-N-S 20-921-0207   (BR)
**ANNAPOLIS VALLEY REGIONAL SCHOOL
BOARD**
WEST KINGS DISTRICT HIGH SCHOOL
(*Suby of* NOVA SCOTIA, PROVINCE OF)
1941 Hwy 1, Auburn, NS, B0P 1A0
(902) 847-4440
Emp Here 75
SIC 8211 Elementary and secondary schools
Barry Squires

Avonport, NS B0P

D-U-N-S 24-341-3028   (HQ)
MERKS FARMS LIMITED
VALLEY TRANSFER
2250 Gaspereau River Rd, Avonport, NS, B0P
1B0
(902) 542-4200
Sales 12,596,320
SIC 4213 Trucking, except local
John Merks
Andre Merks

Baddeck, NS B0E

D-U-N-S 20-906-1654   (SL)
ALDERWOOD CORPORATION
ALDERWOOD REST HOME
42 Jones St, Baddeck, NS, B0E 1B0
(902) 295-2644
Emp Here 110   *Sales* 7,071,020
SIC 8361 Residential care
Arlene Morrison

D-U-N-S 24-833-7891   (SL)
**MACAULAY, SCOTT INVESTMENTS LIM-
ITED**
INVERARY INN & GLENGHORM RESORT
368 Shore Rd, Baddeck, NS, B0E 1B0
(902) 295-3500
Emp Here 180   *Sales* 49,203,000
SIC 6719 Holding companies, nec
Scott Macaulay

D-U-N-S 24-028-4867   (HQ)
MIDWAY MOTORS LTD
2499 Cabot Trail, Baddeck, NS, B0E 1B0
(902) 295-2290
Emp Here 17   *Sales* 14,942,340
SIC 5511 New and used car dealers
John A. Macdonald
Gordon Macdonald

D-U-N-S 24-261-2034   (SL)
ST ANNS LOBSTER GALLEY LIMITED
51943 Cabot Trail, Baddeck, NS, B0E 1B0
(902) 295-3100
Emp Here 21   *Sales* 17,547,117
SIC 5146 Fish and seafoods
Jack Thiele

Barrington Passage, NS B0W

D-U-N-S 20-527-9107   (SL)
GERRET ENTERPRISES INCORPORATED
XSEALENT SEAFOOD COMPANY
58 Boundary St, Barrington Passage, NS,
B0W 1G0
(902) 745-3899
Emp Here 40   *Sales* 33,423,080
SIC 5146 Fish and seafoods
Terry Zinck
Reginald Leblanc

D-U-N-S 24-186-9239   (HQ)
I. DEVEAU FISHERIES LIMITED
I. DEVEAU FISHERIES CSI, DIV OF
508 Hwy 330 Ne, Barrington Passage, NS,
B0W 1G0
(902) 745-2877
Emp Here 20   *Sales* 33,423,080
SIC 5146 Fish and seafoods
Burton German
Joel German

D-U-N-S 24-943-5942   (BR)
SOBEYS CAPITAL INCORPORATED
SOBEYS 323
(*Suby of* EMPIRE COMPANY LIMITED)
3552 Hwy 3, Barrington Passage, NS, B0W

1G0
(902) 637-3063
Emp Here 99
SIC 5411 Grocery stores
Collin Gates

D-U-N-S 20-024-5637   (SL)
WILSON'S SHOPPING CENTRE LIMITED
HOME HARDWARE BUILDING CENTRE
3536 Hwy 3, Barrington Passage, NS, B0W
1G0
(902) 637-2300
Emp Here 70   *Sales* 16,268,210
SIC 5712 Furniture stores
David Wilson
Michael Wilson

Barss Corner, NS B0R

D-U-N-S 20-273-5635   (SL)
G.A.R. TREE FARMS LTD
595 Farmington Rd, Barss Corner, NS, B0R
1A0
(902) 644-3415
Emp Here 40   *Sales* 29,700,800
SIC 5199 Nondurable goods, nec
George Rhodenizer

Bedford, NS B4A

D-U-N-S 25-173-6385   (BR)
ATLANTIC WHOLESALERS LTD
(*Suby of* LOBLAW COMPANIES LIMITED)
1650 Bedford Hwy, Bedford, NS, B4A 4J7
(902) 832-3117
Emp Here 200
SIC 5411 Grocery stores
Neil Macmillan

D-U-N-S 20-550-3787   (HQ)
BANC PROPERTIES LIMITED
30 Damascus Rd Suite 215, Bedford, NS, B4A
0C1
(902) 461-6450
Emp Here 10   *Sales* 62,833,350
SIC 6531 Real estate agents and managers
Besim Halef
Nadia Halef

D-U-N-S 24-608-6818   (SL)
BEDFORD LIONS CLUB
36 Holland Ave, Bedford, NS, B4A 1L9
(902) 835-0862
Emp Here 28   *Sales* 11,314,744
SIC 8699 Membership organizations, nec
George Churney

D-U-N-S 24-524-6785   (SL)
CANADIAN TIRE
150 Damascus Rd, Bedford, NS, B4A 0E5
(902) 835-1060
Emp Here 45   *Sales* 22,413,510
SIC 5531 Auto and home supply stores
Chris Keating

D-U-N-S 24-956-0384   (SL)
**CHADWICK FOOD SERVICE MANAGE-
MENT INCORPORATED**
200 Waterfront Dr Suite 225, Bedford, NS,
B4A 4J4

Emp Here 85   *Sales* 3,869,115
SIC 5812 Eating places
Bruce Chadwick

D-U-N-S 20-123-1052   (HQ)
CLEARWATER SEAFOODS HOLDINGS INC
CLEARWATER SEAFOODS
(*Suby of* THORNVALE HOLDINGS LIMITED)
757 Bedford Hwy, Bedford, NS, B4A 3Z7
(902) 443-0550
Emp Here 300   *Sales* 486,563,505

SIC 2092 Fresh or frozen packaged fish
Ian Smith
Teresa Fortney
Christine A. Penney
Dieter Gautschi
Tony Jabbour
Roy Cunningham
Colin Macdonald
John Risley
Mickey Macdonald
Brendan Paddick

D-U-N-S 24-705-5841   (HQ)
**CLEARWATER SEAFOODS LIMITED PART-
NERSHIP**
*CLEARWATER ARCTIC SURF CLAM COM-
PANY, DIV OF*
(*Suby of* THORNVALE HOLDINGS LIMITED)
757 Bedford Hwy, Bedford, NS, B4A 3Z7
(902) 443-0550
Sales 731,077,500
SIC 2092 Fresh or frozen packaged fish
Ian D. Smith
Teresa Fortney
Dieter Gautschi
Roy Cunningham

D-U-N-S 20-022-6157   (HQ)
**DEXTER CONSTRUCTION COMPANY LIM-
ITED**
(*Suby of* MUNICIPAL ENTERPRISES LIM-
ITED)
927 Rocky Lake Dr, Bedford, NS, B4A 2T7
(902) 835-3381
Sales 164,057,500
SIC 1611 Highway and street construction
Carl B Potter
Hugh Smith
Raphael Potter
Cecil Vance
David Wood

D-U-N-S 20-248-1214   (HQ)
ELCORA ADVANCED MATERIALS CORP
275 Rocky Lake Dr Suite 10, Bedford, NS,
B4A 2T3
(902) 802-8847
Sales 18,917,920
SIC 1499 Miscellaneous nonMetallic minerals,
except fuels
Troy Grant
Guy Bourgeois
Ian Flint
Theo Van De Linde
Shane Beattie
Denis Choquette

D-U-N-S 20-905-7793   (HQ)
HEALTH ASSOCIATION OF NOVA SCOTIA
2 Dartmouth Rd, Bedford, NS, B4A 2K7
(902) 832-8500
Emp Here 56   *Sales* 18,728,880
SIC 8621 Professional organizations
Mary Lee
Marjorie Sullivan
Ron Williams
Patricia Bates
Jim Wyatt
Steve Hemenway
Ed Kinley
Jason Shannon
Sandra Bauld
Ron Horrocks

D-U-N-S 24-386-8119   (SL)
LUCKETT RETAIL MANAGEMENT INC
PETE'S
1595 Bedford Hwy Suite 122, Bedford, NS,
B4A 3Y4
(902) 835-4997
Emp Here 275   *Sales* 52,927,600
SIC 5411 Grocery stores
Diane Hamilton

D-U-N-S 20-781-2215   (HQ)
MARSH ADJUSTMENT BUREAU LIMITED
1550 Bedford Hwy Suite 711, Bedford, NS,

▲ Public Company   ■ Public Company Family Member   **HQ** Headquarters   **BR** Branch   **SL** Single Location

B4A 1E6
(902) 469-3537
Emp Here 1   *Sales* 101,625,810
SIC 6411 Insurance agents, brokers, and service
Greg Clarke
Brian Gough

D-U-N-S 20-027-5923   (SL)
MINAS BASIN PULP AND POWER COMPANY LIMITED
(*Suby of* SCOTIA INVESTMENTS LIMITED)
3 Bedford Hills Rd, Bedford, NS, B4A 1J5
(902) 835-7100
Emp Here 145   *Sales* 53,307,365
SIC 2631 Paperboard mills
George Bishop
Scott Travers
Barbara E Moores
David Hennigar
Bruce Jodrey

D-U-N-S 24-340-2013   (HQ)
MUNICIPAL ENTERPRISES LIMITED
ROCKY LAKE QUARY, DIV OF
927 Rocky Lake Dr, Bedford, NS, B4A 2T3
(902) 835-3381
Emp Here 250   *Sales* 837,687,500
SIC 2951 Asphalt paving mixtures and blocks
Carl Potter
Harold Johnson
Hugh Smith
Ken Maclean
David Pangman
Raphael Potter
David Wood
Cecil Vance

D-U-N-S 24-965-9256   (SL)
NAMIBIA CRITICAL METALS INC
1550 Bedford Hwy Suite 802, Bedford, NS, B4A 1E6
(902) 835-8760
Emp Here 1,100   *Sales* 281,351,400
SIC 1081 Metal mining services
Pine Van Wyk
Gerald J. Mcconnell
Donald M. Burton
Darrin Campbell
Janice A. Stairs
Adrian T. Hickey
Steve E. Kapp
William L. Price
Scott Swinden

D-U-N-S 25-412-6923   (HQ)
NOVA SCOTIA SOCIETY FOR THE PREVENTION OF CRUELTY
NOVA SCOTIA SPCA
1600 Bedford Hwy Suite 422, Bedford, NS, B4A 1E8
(902) 835-4798
Emp Here 3   *Sales* 15,896,560
SIC 8699 Membership organizations, nec
Sean Kelly

D-U-N-S 20-206-3199   (SL)
OUR NEIGHBOURHOOD LIVING SOCIETY
15 Dartmouth Rd Suite 210, Bedford, NS, B4A 3X6
(902) 835-8826
Emp Here 90   *Sales* 5,332,230
SIC 8361 Residential care
Jim Snair
Wynn Wilson
Barry Macaskill
Karen Millar

D-U-N-S 20-852-7494   (SL)
PACRIM HOSPITALITY SERVICES INC
INTERGY RESERVATION & E-MARKETING SOLUTIONS, DIV OF
30 Damascus Rd Suite 201, Bedford, NS, B4A 0C1
(902) 404-7474
Emp Here 75   *Sales* 9,358,200
SIC 8741 Management services

W. Glenn Squires
Tracy Sherren
Michael Jackson
Charles Wright
Edward C. Good
Francesco Aquilini

D-U-N-S 20-328-5804   (SL)
PNL INTERNATIONAL TRADING INC
1496 Bedford Hwy Suite 212, Bedford, NS, B4A 1E5
(902) 307-2117
Emp Here 2   *Sales* 65,645,502
SIC 5146 Fish and seafoods
Changbeom Nam
Naomi Chaung Ngai

D-U-N-S 24-319-1934   (HQ)
REDSPACE INC
1595 Bedford Hwy Suite 168, Bedford, NS, B4A 3Y4
(902) 444-3490
Sales 20,329,662
SIC 7371 Custom computer programming services
Mike Johnston
Angela Johnston

D-U-N-S 20-363-3545   (HQ)
SCOTIA INVESTMENTS LIMITED
3 Bedford Hills Rd, Bedford, NS, B4A 1J5
(902) 835-7100
Sales 438,610,800
SIC 6712 Bank holding companies
Archie W. Macpherson
George E. Bishop
Michele L. Gerrard
E. Barbara Moores
Wesley G. Armour
Jesse C. Brotz
Bo Fears
Kristin Harris
Daryl W. Langille
Jeffrey T. Jodrey

D-U-N-S 24-574-1574   (HQ)
THORNVALE HOLDINGS LIMITED
CLEARWATER FINE FOODS
757 Bedford Hwy, Bedford, NS, B4A 3Z7
(902) 443-0550
Sales 90,094,616
SIC 6712 Bank holding companies
John Risley
Colin Macdonald
Stan Spavold

D-U-N-S 24-329-4324   (SL)
UCORE RARE METALS INC
210 Waterfront Dr Suite 106, Bedford, NS, B4A 0H3
(902) 482-5214
Emp Here 170   *Sales* 70,228,530
SIC 1481 NonMetallic mineral services
James Mckenzie
Peter Manuel
Mark Macdonald
Randy Macgillivray
Michael Schrider
Pat Ryan
Jaroslav Dostal
Steven Meister
Geoff Clarke
Reed Izatt

D-U-N-S 24-329-9265   (BR)
WAL-MART CANADA CORP
(*Suby of* WALMART INC.)
141 Damascus Rd, Bedford, NS, B4A 0C2
(902) 865-4000
Emp Here 200
SIC 5311 Department stores

D-U-N-S 24-188-6266   (SL)
WHITE BURGESS LANGILLE INMAN
WBLI CHARTERED ACCOUNTANTS
26 Union St 2nd Flr, Bedford, NS, B4A 2B5
(902) 835-7333
Emp Here 56   *Sales* 11,708,760

SIC 8721 Accounting, auditing, and bookkeeping
Brian Burgess
Brad Langille
Jerry Inman
Kirk Higgins

Bedford, NS B4B

D-U-N-S 24-956-5615   (SL)
ALUMITECH ARCHITECTURAL GLASS & METAL LIMITED
(*Suby of* ALUMITECH HOLDINGS LIMITED)
170 Bluewater Rd, Bedford, NS, B4B 1G9
(902) 832-1200
Emp Here 50   *Sales* 12,309,300
SIC 1799 Special trade contractors, nec
Norsat Eblaghi

D-U-N-S 24-342-3589   (SL)
AMIRIX SYSTEMS INC
VEMCO, DIV OF
20 Angus Morton Dr, Bedford, NS, B4B 0L9
(902) 450-1700
Emp Here 78   *Sales* 14,854,476
SIC 3674 Semiconductors and related devices
Sandra Greer
Douglas Pincock
John Sullivan

D-U-N-S 25-982-9885   (SL)
ATLANTIC MOBILITY PRODUCTS LIMITED PARTNERSHIP
ATLANTIC MOBILITY PRODUCTS
200 Bluewater Rd Unit 1, Bedford, NS, B4B 1G9
(902) 481-6699
Emp Here 68   *Sales* 30,407,832
SIC 5065 Electronic parts and equipment, nec
Darin Mclean

D-U-N-S 20-555-7650   (BR)
BUREAU VERITAS CANADA (2019) INC
MAXXAM ANALYTICS INTERNATIONAL CORPORATION
(*Suby of* BUREAU VERITAS)
200 Bluewater Rd Suite 201, Bedford, NS, B4B 1G9
(902) 420-0203
Emp Here 85
SIC 8731 Commercial physical research
Hartwell Murray

D-U-N-S 20-279-6801   (BR)
HALIFAX HERALD LIMITED, THE
THE CHRONICLE HERALD
(*Suby of* HALIFAX HERALD LIMITED, THE)
311 Bluewater Rd, Bedford, NS, B4B 1Z9
(902) 426-2811
Emp Here 80
SIC 2711 Newspapers
Mike Murtha

D-U-N-S 25-871-6612   (BR)
HALIFAX REGIONAL SCHOOL BOARD
CHARLES P ALLEN HIGH SCHOOL
(*Suby of* HALIFAX REGIONAL SCHOOL BOARD)
200 Innovation Dr, Bedford, NS, B4B 0G4
(902) 832-8964
Emp Here 99
SIC 8211 Elementary and secondary schools
Stephanie Bird

D-U-N-S 20-347-7893   (SL)
HOSTESS FOOD PRODUCTS
230 Bluewater Rd, Bedford, NS, B4B 1G9
(902) 832-2865
Emp Here 50   *Sales* 11,242,750
SIC 2096 Potato chips and similar snacks
Marc Guay

D-U-N-S 20-374-8223   (SL)
INNOVASEA MARINE SYSTEMS CANADA INC

VEMCO
20 Angus Morton Dr, Bedford, NS, B4B 0L9
(902) 450-1700
Emp Here 111   *Sales* 21,139,062
SIC 3669 Communications equipment, nec
Mark Jollymore
Karen Mckay
Robert Orr
David Kelly
Roly Morris
George Nardi

D-U-N-S 24-831-8065   (SL)
PIVOTAL POWER INC
DRS PIVOTAL POWER
(*Suby of* LEONARDO SPA)
150 Bluewater Rd, Bedford, NS, B4B 1G9
(902) 835-7268
Emp Here 85   *Sales* 16,187,570
SIC 3621 Motors and generators
George Mullally
Roger Sexauer
Nina Laserson Dunn
Richard Schneider
Mark Newman
Robert Mehmel

D-U-N-S 25-495-2732   (HQ)
RCS CONSTRUCTION INCORPORATED
26 Topsail Crt, Bedford, NS, B4B 1K5
(902) 468-6757
Emp Here 35   *Sales* 57,033,800
SIC 1542 Nonresidential construction, nec
Douglas Doucet
Chris Baldwin
Brendan Nobes
Dena Hueston

D-U-N-S 24-803-6964   (BR)
SLH TRANSPORT INC
SLH TRANSPORT
(*Suby of* HOLDING CANADIAN AMERICAN TRANSPORTATION C.A.T. INC)
347 Bluewater Rd, Bedford, NS, B4B 1Y3
(902) 832-4900
Emp Here 176
SIC 4213 Trucking, except local
Bill Oakley

D-U-N-S 24-309-1068   (SL)
VISTACARE COMMUNICATIONS SERVICES OF CANADA INC
200 Bluewater Rd Unit 201, Bedford, NS, B4B 1G9
(902) 444-7404
Emp Here 310   *Sales* 70,826,320
SIC 4899 Communication services, nec
Wayne Gillian
Sean Reyno

Belliveau Cove, NS B0W

D-U-N-S 24-831-8180   (SL)
INNOVATIVE FISHERY PRODUCTS INCORPORATED
3569 1 Hwy, Belliveau Cove, NS, B0W 1J0
(902) 837-5163
Emp Here 50   *Sales* 11,242,750
SIC 2091 Canned and cured fish and seafoods
Marc Blinn
Victor Mcguire
Douglas Bertram
Scott Bertram

Belnan, NS B2S

D-U-N-S 25-952-1151   (SL)
CORES WORLDWIDE INCORPORATED
674 Highway 214, Belnan, NS, B2S 2N2

---

(902) 883-1611
Emp Here 24   *Sales* 11,400,624
SIC 5084 Industrial machinery and equipment
Andrew G. Ryan
Douglas R. Lesbirel

Berwick, NS B0P

D-U-N-S 25-410-6057   (HQ)
ANNAPOLIS VALLEY REGIONAL SCHOOL BOARD
ANNAPOLIS EAST ELEMENTARY SCHOOL
(*Suby of* NOVA SCOTIA, PROVINCE OF)
121 Orchard St Rr 3, Berwick, NS, B0P 1E0
(902) 538-4600
Emp Here 60   *Sales* 105,101,242
SIC 8211 Elementary and secondary schools
Margo Tait

D-U-N-S 20-930-8550   (HQ)
FRASER SUPPLIES (1980) LIMITED
FRASERS PRO HOME CENTRE
4147 Main Hwy, Berwick, NS, B0P 1E0
(902) 538-3183
Emp Here 50   *Sales* 12,652,950
SIC 5211 Lumber and other building materials
Raymond Parsons
Sue Macarthur
Paul Parsons
Dorothy Parsons

D-U-N-S 24-130-2843   (SL)
KINGS COUNTY SENIOR CITIZENS HOME CORP
GRAND VIEW MANOR
110a Commercial St Rr 1, Berwick, NS, B0P 1E0
(902) 538-3118
Emp Here 220   *Sales* 15,031,720
SIC 8051 Skilled nursing care facilities
Graham Hardy

D-U-N-S 20-728-5727   (HQ)
KINGS MUTUAL INSURANCE COMPANY, THE
220 Commercial St, Berwick, NS, B0P 1E0
(902) 538-3187
Emp Here 16   *Sales* 11,018,556
SIC 6411 Insurance agents, brokers, and service
Daniel Lister
Doreen Maclellan
David Davies

D-U-N-S 25-785-6203   (HQ)
WHEATON, GARNET FARM LIMITED
518 Shaw Rd Rr 3, Berwick, NS, B0P 1E0
(902) 538-9793
Sales 24,402,315
SIC 5712 Furniture stores
Garnet A Wheaton
Kay L Wheaton

D-U-N-S 24-574-4248   (SL)
WILLOWDALE FARMS INCORPORATED
72 Chase Rd Rr 1, Berwick, NS, B0P 1E0
(902) 538-7324
Emp Here 55   *Sales* 14,426,995
SIC 0191 General farms, primarily crop
Mitchell Fillmore
David Fillmore
Ian Blenkharn

Blockhouse, NS B0J

D-U-N-S 20-524-4205   (SL)
NOVA SCOTIA BUILDING SUPPLIES (1982) LIMITED
459 Hwy 3, Blockhouse, NS, B0J 1E0
(902) 624-8328
Emp Here 36   *Sales* 16,098,264
SIC 5039 Construction materials, nec

Harold Mills
Wayne Nelson
Robert Mills

Bridgewater, NS B4V

D-U-N-S 20-268-9928   (SL)
3302775 NOVA SCOTIA LTD
SOUTH SHORE CHEVROLET
15133 Hebbville Rd, Bridgewater, NS, B4V 2W4
(902) 543-2493
Emp Here 40   *Sales* 19,923,120
SIC 5511 New and used car dealers
Robert Steele

D-U-N-S 25-791-2030   (BR)
ATLANTIC WHOLESALERS LTD
REAL ATLANTIC SUPERSTORE, THE
(*Suby of* LOBLAW COMPANIES LIMITED)
21 Davison Dr, Bridgewater, NS, B4V 3K8
(902) 543-1809
Emp Here 200
SIC 5411 Grocery stores
Shelley Blanchard

D-U-N-S 25-079-4146   (SL)
BRIDGEWATER PHARMACY LIMITED
BRIDGEWATER PHARMASAVE
215 Dominion St, Bridgewater, NS, B4V 2K7
(902) 543-3418
Emp Here 50   *Sales* 12,647,700
SIC 5912 Drug stores and proprietary stores

D-U-N-S 20-729-0792   (SL)
CARROLL SOUTH SHORE MOTORS INC
CARROLL SOUTH SORE GM
Gd Lcd Main, Bridgewater, NS, B4V 2V8
(902) 543-2493
Emp Here 32   *Sales* 15,938,496
SIC 5511 New and used car dealers
Scott Carroll
John Carroll

D-U-N-S 24-994-7318   (HQ)
G.E.'S ALL TRUCKING LIMITED
385 York St, Bridgewater, NS, B4V 3K1

Sales 16,625,910
SIC 5084 Industrial machinery and equipment
Graham Winterbourne

D-U-N-S 24-832-0137   (SL)
GOW'S HARDWARE LIMITED
GOW'S HOME HARDWARE & FURNITURE
76 High St, Bridgewater, NS, B4V 1V8
(902) 543-7121
Emp Here 60   *Sales* 16,059,120
SIC 5251 Hardware stores
Peter Gow

D-U-N-S 24-573-9271   (SL)
HILLSIDE PINES HOME FOR SPECIAL CARE SOCIETY
77 Exhibition Dr, Bridgewater, NS, B4V 3K6
(902) 543-1525
Emp Here 78   *Sales* 5,348,148
SIC 8051 Skilled nursing care facilities
Marisa Eisner

D-U-N-S 20-727-5843   (BR)
MICHELIN AMERIQUE DU NORD (CANADA) INC
MICHELIN NORTH AMERICA
(*Suby of* COMPAGNIE GENERALE DES ETABLISSEMENTS MICHELIN)
233 Logan Rd, Bridgewater, NS, B4V 3T3
(902) 543-8141
Emp Here 100
SIC 3011 Tires and inner tubes
Matthew Huet

D-U-N-S 25-299-0007   (BR)
NOVA SCOTIA, PROVINCE OF
LUNENBURG CAMPUS

(*Suby of* NOVA SCOTIA, PROVINCE OF)
75 High St, Bridgewater, NS, B4V 1V8
(902) 543-4608
Emp Here 75
SIC 8221 Colleges and universities
Craig Collins

D-U-N-S 20-706-6320   (BR)
RESOLVE CORPORATION
197 Dufferin St Suite 100, Bridgewater, NS, B4V 2G9
(902) 541-3600
Emp Here 600
SIC 8742 Management consulting services
Cindy Smith

D-U-N-S 25-826-6337   (BR)
SOBEYS CAPITAL INCORPORATED
(*Suby of* EMPIRE COMPANY LIMITED)
349 Lahave St Suite 322, Bridgewater, NS, B4V 2T6
(902) 543-9244
Emp Here 130
SIC 5411 Grocery stores
Rick Crowell

D-U-N-S 20-024-9670   (HQ)
SOUTH SHORE READY MIX LIMITED
SOUTH SHORE SAND & GRAVEL
1896 King St, Bridgewater, NS, B4V 2W9
(902) 543-4639
Emp Here 45   *Sales* 16,807,320
SIC 3273 Ready-mixed concrete
Lloyd Bonang
Betty Bonang

D-U-N-S 20-700-5252   (HQ)
SOUTH SHORE REGIONAL SCHOOL BOARD
ASPOTOGAN CONSOLIDATED ELEMENTARY SCHOOL
(*Suby of* NOVA SCOTIA, PROVINCE OF)
69 Wentzell Dr, Bridgewater, NS, B4V 0A2
(902) 543-2468
Emp Here 50   *Sales* 100,755,282
SIC 8211 Elementary and secondary schools
Nancy Pynch-Worthylake
Wade Tattrie
Tina Munro
Barry Butler
Steve Prest

D-U-N-S 24-606-0073   (SL)
STACY'S AUTO RANCH LIMITED
BRIDGEWATER HONDA
366 Dufferin St, Bridgewater, NS, B4V 2H2
(902) 212-0024
Emp Here 23   *Sales* 11,455,794
SIC 5511 New and used car dealers
Scott Carroll

D-U-N-S 24-121-7103   (BR)
WAL-MART CANADA CORP
(*Suby of* WALMART INC.)
60 Pine Grove Rd, Bridgewater, NS, B4V 4H2
(902) 543-8680
Emp Here 160
SIC 5311 Department stores
Carol Ann Storzuk

Brookfield, NS B0N

D-U-N-S 20-443-8956   (BR)
LAFARGE CANADA INC
(*Suby of* LAFARGEHOLCIM LTD)
87 Cement Plant Rd, Brookfield, NS, B0N 1C0
(902) 673-2281
Emp Here 100
SIC 2891 Adhesives and sealants
Frederick Bolduc

Brooklyn, NS B0J

D-U-N-S 25-109-8596   (SL)
BROOKLYN POWER CORPORATION
(*Suby of* EMERA INCORPORATED)
65 Bowater Mersey Hauling Rd, Brooklyn, NS, B0J 1H0
(902) 354-2299
Emp Here 28   *Sales* 17,545,192
SIC 4911 Electric services
Bradley H. Pelley
Stephen Fairweathe
Dave Pickles
Ian Clark

D-U-N-S 20-170-2128   (SL)
BROOKLYN VOLUNTEER FIRE DEPARTMENT
995 Hwy 215, Brooklyn, NS, B0J 1H0
(902) 757-2043
Emp Here 29   *Sales* 13,027,351
SIC 7389 Business services, nec
Mark Dearman

Caledonia, NS B0T

D-U-N-S 20-781-1407   (SL)
NORTH QUEENS NURSING HOME INC
9565 Highway 8, Caledonia, NS, B0T 1B0
(902) 682-2553
Emp Here 75   *Sales* 4,443,525
SIC 8361 Residential care
John Budgell
Joy Boyle

Cambridge, NS B0P

D-U-N-S 20-543-2078   (SL)
BROWN, DAVID UNITED LTD
761 Cambridge Rd, Cambridge, NS, B0P 1G0
(902) 538-8088
Emp Here 80   *Sales* 11,855,360
SIC 4213 Trucking, except local
David S Brown

D-U-N-S 20-025-0561   (SL)
ROSCOE CONSTRUCTION LIMITED
5765 Highway 1, Cambridge, NS, B0P 1G0
(902) 538-8080
Emp Here 50   *Sales* 23,536,550
SIC 1542 Nonresidential construction, nec
Kenneth Roscoe
Dave Logie
Elaine Roscoe

D-U-N-S 20-754-6198   (SL)
VALLEY SEARCH & RESCUE
5876 Hwy 1 Bldg 2, Cambridge, NS, B0P 1G0

Emp Here 49   *Sales* 20,805,743
SIC 8999 Services, nec
Shane Buttler

Chester, NS B0J

D-U-N-S 20-025-1569   (HQ)
CHESTER PHARMACY LTD
CHESTER PHARMASAVE
3785 Hwy 3, Chester, NS, B0J 1J0
(902) 275-3518
Sales 15,392,664
SIC 5912 Drug stores and proprietary stores

D-U-N-S 20-207-3198   (SL)
CHESTER VOLUNTEER FIRE DEPARTMENT
149 Central St, Chester, NS, B0J 1J0

▲ Public Company   ■ Public Company Family Member   **HQ** Headquarters   **BR** Branch   **SL** Single Location

(902) 275-5113
Emp Here 50   *Sales* 22,460,950
SIC 7389 Business services, nec
  Everett Hiltz

D-U-N-S 24-186-0238   (SL)
G.N. PLASTICS COMPANY LIMITED
GN THERMOFORMING EQUIPMENT
345 Old Trunk 3, Chester, NS, B0J 1J0
(902) 275-3571
Emp Here 104   *Sales* 23,088,104
SIC 3559 Special industry machinery, nec

D-U-N-S 25-365-1251   (BR)
LOUISIANA-PACIFIC CANADA LTD
(*Suby of* LOUISIANA-PACIFIC CORPORA-
TION)
2005 Highway 14, Chester, NS, B0J 1J0
(902) 275-3556
Emp Here 350
SIC 2493 Reconstituted wood products
  Jo Ann Grant

D-U-N-S 25-061-6182   (SL)
MACCOUL INVESTMENTS LIMITED
211 Duke St, Chester, NS, B0J 1J0
(902) 275-3262
Emp Here 23   *Sales* 12,217,761
SIC 6282 Investment advice
  Danny Maccoul

D-U-N-S 20-341-0337   (SL)
MDINA ENTERPRISES LTD
*SALES BEACON PRODUCTIVITY SOLU-
TIONS*
121 Duke St Suite 49, Chester, NS, B0J 1J0
(855) 855-3180
Emp Here 85   *Sales* 19,914,480
SIC 8742 Management consulting services

D-U-N-S 24-993-8648   (SL)
**SHOREHAM VILLAGE SENIOR CITIZENS
ASSOCIATION**
*SHOREHAM VILLAGE HOME FOR SPECIAL
CARE*
50 Shoreham Village Cres, Chester, NS, B0J
1J0
(902) 275-5631
Emp Here 130   *Sales* 9,982,960
SIC 8322 Individual and family services
  Angela Lohnes
  Brian Selig

Cheticamp, NS B0E

D-U-N-S 24-516-0861   (SL)
CHETICAMP COOP LTD.
15081 Cabot Trail Rd, Cheticamp, NS, B0E
1H0
(902) 224-2066
Emp Here 40   *Sales* 17,886,960
SIC 5039 Construction materials, nec
  Camille Maillet
  Bertie Leblanc
  Paulette Larade
  Gloria Lefort
  James Chiasson
  Denis Larade
  Louis Deveau

D-U-N-S 24-913-1194   (BR)
**INVERNESS MUNICIPAL HOUSING COR-
PORATION**
FOYER PERE FISET
(*Suby of* INVERNESS MUNICIPAL HOUSING
CORPORATION)
15092 Cabot Trail Rd, Cheticamp, NS, B0E
1H0
(902) 224-2087
Emp Here 100
SIC 8051 Skilled nursing care facilities
  Mona Poirier

Church Point, NS B0W

D-U-N-S 20-024-6841   (HQ)
BELLIVEAU MOTORS LIMITED
1484 Highway 1, Church Point, NS, B0W 1M0
(902) 769-0706
Emp Here 24   *Sales* 18,926,964
SIC 5511 New and used car dealers
  Richard Robicheau
  Claude Belliveau

D-U-N-S 20-781-0102   (HQ)
UNIVERSITE SAINTE-ANNE
1695 Rte 1, Church Point, NS, B0W 1M0
(902) 769-2114
Sales 19,420,830
SIC 8221 Colleges and universities
  Andre Roberge

Clarks Harbour, NS B0W

D-U-N-S 20-282-5295   (SL)
3274876 NOVA SCOTIA LIMITED
ATLANTIC CHICAN SEAFOOD
55 Orion Wharf Rd, Clarks Harbour, NS, B0W
1P0
(902) 745-2943
Emp Here 60   *Sales* 50,134,620
SIC 5146 Fish and seafoods
  Shang Long He

D-U-N-S 24-471-5595   (SL)
ATKINSON, LEO G FISHERIES LIMITED
89 Daniels Head Rd Rr 1, Clarks Harbour, NS,
B0W 1P0
(902) 745-3047
Emp Here 20   *Sales* 10,702,480
SIC 5146 Fish and seafoods
  Leo G Atkinson
  Martha Atkinson

D-U-N-S 20-025-1031   (SL)
SABLE FISH PACKERS (1988) LIMITED
377 Daniels Head Rd, Clarks Harbour, NS,
B0W 1P0
(902) 745-2500
Emp Here 40   *Sales* 13,827,600
SIC 2091 Canned and cured fish and
seafoods
  Brian Blades
  Paul Blades

Cleveland, NS B0E

D-U-N-S 25-413-2491   (BR)
**GUYSBOROUGH ANTIGONISH STRAIT
HEALTH AUTHORITY**
STRAIT RICHMOND HOSPITAL
(*Suby of* NOVA SCOTIA, PROVINCE OF)
138 Hospital Rd, Cleveland, NS, B0E 1J0
(902) 625-3230
Emp Here 110
SIC 8062 General medical and surgical hospi-
tals
  Melissa Robertson

Coldbrook, NS B4N

D-U-N-S 24-131-3972   (HQ)
EASSONS TRANSPORT LIMITED
ETL LOGISTICS, DIV OF
(*Suby of* EASSON, WILLIAM & SONS LIM-
ITED)
1505 Harrington Rd, Coldbrook, NS, B4N 3V7
(902) 679-1153
Emp Here 20   *Sales* 44,490,360
SIC 4213 Trucking, except local

Paul Easson
Thomas Easson

Coldbrook, NS B4R

D-U-N-S 25-516-4865   (SL)
2463103 NOVA SCOTIA LTD
VALLEY VOLKSWAGEN
7181 Highway 1, Coldbrook, NS, B4R 1A2
(902) 678-2155
Emp Here 25   *Sales* 12,451,950
SIC 5511 New and used car dealers
  Harvey Mapplebeck

D-U-N-S 20-050-0986   (SL)
**FREEDOM FINANCIAL SERVICES INCOR-
PORATED**
115 Coldbrook Village Park Dr, Coldbrook,
NS, B4R 1B9
(902) 681-1100
Emp Here 50   *Sales* 11,895,050
SIC 8742 Management consulting services
  Thomas Busch

D-U-N-S 20-027-8760   (HQ)
SCOTIAN GOLD CO-OPERATIVE LIMITED
FARM SUPPLY, DIV OF
2900 Lovett Rd, Coldbrook, NS, B4R 1A6
(902) 679-2191
Emp Here 10   *Sales* 50,134,620
SIC 5148 Fresh fruits and vegetables
  David Parrish
  William Spurr
  Dennis Macpherson

Collingwood Corner, NS B0M

D-U-N-S 20-025-2930   (HQ)
BRAGG LUMBER COMPANY LIMITED
(*Suby of* TIDNISH HOLDINGS LIMITED)
1536 Wyvrn Rd, Collingwood Corner, NS,
B0M 1E0
(902) 686-3254
Sales 33,805,000
SIC 0171 Berry crops
  John Bragg
  David Hoffman
  George Caines
  Geoffrey C Baldwin

Cornwallis, NS B0S

D-U-N-S 25-112-7627   (SL)
DIAMOND DIVERSIFIED INDUSTRIES LTD
FOAM WORX
55 Bren St, Cornwallis, NS, B0S 1H0
(902) 638-8616
Emp Here 49   *Sales* 10,722,376
SIC 3993 Signs and advertising specialties
  Heather Garner
  Lawrence Garner

Coxheath, NS B1L

D-U-N-S 20-012-7978   (SL)
**SENTRY SECURITY AND INVESTIGATIONS
INC**
1225 Coxheath Rd, Coxheath, NS, B1L 1B4
(902) 574-3276
Emp Here 27   *Sales* 10,683,306
SIC 7381 Detective and armored car services

Currys Corner, NS B0N

D-U-N-S 25-401-8377   (BR)
NOVA SCOTIA HEALTH AUTHORITY
HANTS COMMUNITY HOSPITAL
(*Suby of* NOVA SCOTIA, PROVINCE OF)
89 Payzant, Currys Corner, NS, B0N 2T0
(902) 798-8351
Emp Here 200
SIC 8062 General medical and surgical hospi-
tals
  Bob Smith

D-U-N-S 20-031-4086   (SL)
REDDEN, C. I. LTD
WINDSOR HOME HARDWARE
50 Empire Lane, Currys Corner, NS, B0N 2T0
(902) 798-3222
Emp Here 45   *Sales* 11,387,655
SIC 5251 Hardware stores
  Jeffrey Redden

Dartmouth, NS B2V

D-U-N-S 25-134-0733   (BR)
ATLANTIC WHOLESALERS LTD
REAL ATLANTIC SUPERSTORE, THE
(*Suby of* LOBLAW COMPANIES LIMITED)
920 Cole Harbour Rd, Dartmouth, NS, B2V
2J5
(902) 462-4500
Emp Here 100
SIC 5411 Grocery stores
  Darren Mathews

D-U-N-S 25-787-4420   (SL)
TREATY ENTERPRISES
TREATY GAS
600 Caldwell Rd, Dartmouth, NS, B2V 2S8
(902) 434-7777
Emp Here 33   *Sales* 16,436,574
SIC 5541 Gasoline service stations
  Kathy Fiander

Dartmouth, NS B2W

D-U-N-S 20-939-7871   (SL)
219 AUTOMOTIVE INC
MACPHEE FORD
580 Portland St, Dartmouth, NS, B2W 2M3
(902) 434-7700
Emp Here 75   *Sales* 47,196,000
SIC 5511 New and used car dealers
  Al Macphee

D-U-N-S 25-359-1358   (SL)
2207412 NOVA SCOTIA LTD
FORBES CHEVROLET
580 Portland St, Dartmouth, NS, B2W 2M3
(902) 434-4000
Emp Here 120   *Sales* 75,513,600
SIC 5511 New and used car dealers
  Michael Macdonald

D-U-N-S 24-946-6348   (SL)
3067419 NOVA SCOTIA LIMITED
STEELE MAZDA
15 Lansing Crt, Dartmouth, NS, B2W 0K3
(902) 462-6600
Emp Here 40   *Sales* 19,923,120
SIC 5511 New and used car dealers
  Patrick Lawrence

D-U-N-S 20-915-3746   (SL)
ANGUS G FOODS INC
MCDONALD'S RESTAURANT
588 Portland St, Dartmouth, NS, B2W 2M3
(902) 435-3181
Emp Here 85   *Sales* 3,869,115
SIC 5812 Eating places
  Peter Macisaac

▲ Public Company   ■ Public Company Family Member   **HQ** Headquarters   **BR** Branch   **SL** Single Location

D-U-N-S 24-473-0438   (HQ)
ATLANTIC FABRICS LIMITED
114 Woodlawn Rd, Dartmouth, NS, B2W 2S7
(902) 434-1440
Emp Here 20   *Sales* 17,102,960
SIC 5949 Sewing, needlework, and piece goods
Katherine Dean
Dennis Dean

D-U-N-S 20-335-1783   (SL)
CAISSIECO ENTERPRISES LTD
CANADIAN TIRE, DIV OF
24 Forest Hills Pky, Dartmouth, NS, B2W 6E4
(902) 462-6100
Emp Here 100   *Sales* 24,432,800
SIC 5999 Miscellaneous retail stores, nec
Julie Caissie

D-U-N-S 24-189-5796   (SL)
COMMUNITY BUILDERS INC
COLE HARBOUR PLACE
51 Forest Hills Pky Suite 1, Dartmouth, NS, B2W 6C6
(902) 464-5100
Emp Here 136   *Sales* 10,682,120
SIC 7997 Membership sports and recreation clubs
Cathy Burgess
Donald Kyte

D-U-N-S 20-025-4241   (HQ)
CONRAD BROTHERS LIMITED
31 Cono Dr, Dartmouth, NS, B2W 3Y2
(902) 435-3233
Sales 11,671,750
SIC 3281 Cut stone and stone products
Kimberley Conrad
Rodney Conrad
Brent Conrad
Glenna Conrad
Brian Conrad
Scott Conrad

D-U-N-S 25-982-9430   (BR)
CONSOLIDATED RESTAURANTS LIMITED
STEAK & STEIN RESTAURANT
(*Suby of* CONSOLIDATED RESTAURANTS LIMITED)
620 Portland St, Dartmouth, NS, B2W 2M3
(902) 434-8814
Emp Here 75
SIC 5812 Eating places
Cheryl Smith

D-U-N-S 24-228-2007   (SL)
DARTMOUTH MOTORS LP
DARTMOUTH CHRYSLER DODGE JEEP RAM
(*Suby of* AUTOCANADA INC)
61 Athorpe Dr, Dartmouth, NS, B2W 1K9
(902) 469-9050
Emp Here 77   *Sales* 34,665,169
SIC 7532 Top and body repair and paint shops
Doug Wilson

D-U-N-S 24-205-4729   (SL)
KA'LE BAY SEAFOODS LTD
501 Main St, Dartmouth, NS, B2W 4K1
(902) 842-9454
Emp Here 65   *Sales* 22,469,850
SIC 2092 Fresh or frozen packaged fish
James N. Kennedy

D-U-N-S 20-234-7527   (HQ)
MAJA HOLDINGS LTD
TIM HORTONS
4 Forest Hills Pky Suite 317, Dartmouth, NS, B2W 5G7
(902) 462-2032
Emp Here 40   *Sales* 22,010,775
SIC 5461 Retail bakeries
Jim Clarkson

D-U-N-S 24-832-3412   (HQ)
MCCARTHY'S ROOFING LIMITED
850 Main St, Dartmouth, NS, B2W 3V1

(902) 469-2260
Sales 28,317,770
SIC 1761 Roofing, siding, and sheetMetal work
George H Mccarthy

D-U-N-S 25-154-5570   (HQ)
NIMA VANI ENTERPRISES LIMITED
PAY A DOLLAR STORE
1 Matthew Francis Crt, Dartmouth, NS, B2W 6A1

Emp Here 5   *Sales* 15,400,725
SIC 5399 Miscellaneous general merchandise
Michael Mirpuri
Nisha Mirpuri

D-U-N-S 20-548-7825   (HQ)
O'REGAN PROPERTIES LIMITED
O'REGAN'S AUTOMOTIVE GROUP
60 Baker Dr Unit A, Dartmouth, NS, B2W 6L4
(902) 464-9550
Emp Here 20   *Sales* 201,029,950
SIC 6719 Holding companies, nec
Sean O'regan
Patrick O'regan
Stephen O'regan
David Cruikshank

D-U-N-S 24-261-0301   (SL)
O'REGAN'S NISSAN DARTMOUTH LTD
60 Baker Dr Unit C, Dartmouth, NS, B2W 6L4
(902) 469-8484
Emp Here 40   *Sales* 19,923,120
SIC 5511 New and used car dealers
Sean O'regan

D-U-N-S 20-759-3539   (SL)
RENEX INC
RENOVATIONEXPERTS.COM
73 Tacoma Dr Suite 800, Dartmouth, NS, B2W 3Y6

Emp Here 100   *Sales* 8,962,900
SIC 7299 Miscellaneous personal service
Craig Lucas
Chris Payne
Lorraine Kotyk

D-U-N-S 25-173-6153   (BR)
SOBEYS CAPITAL INCORPORATED
SOBEYS
(*Suby of* EMPIRE COMPANY LIMITED)
612 Main St Suite 622, Dartmouth, NS, B2W 5M5
(902) 433-0140
Emp Here 190
SIC 5411 Grocery stores
Grahmn Slaunwhite

D-U-N-S 25-362-2492   (BR)
SOBEYS CAPITAL INCORPORATED
(*Suby of* EMPIRE COMPANY LIMITED)
4 Forest Hills Pky, Dartmouth, NS, B2W 5G7
(902) 435-3909
Emp Here 80
SIC 5411 Grocery stores
Paul Keinick

D-U-N-S 20-727-6908   (SL)
STEELE CHEVROLET BUICK GMC CADILLAC
636 Portland St, Dartmouth, NS, B2W 2M3
(902) 434-4100
Emp Here 150   *Sales* 94,392,000
SIC 5511 New and used car dealers
Robert Steele
Debbie O'connor

D-U-N-S 20-298-3347   (SL)
SUTTON GROUP PROFESSIONAL REALTY
73 Tacoma Dr Suite 800, Dartmouth, NS, B2W 3Y6
(902) 223-1399
Emp Here 38   *Sales* 10,326,728
SIC 6531 Real estate agents and managers
Alan Hennigar

D-U-N-S 24-994-7938   (HQ)

TAYLOR FLOORING LIMITED
114 Woodlawn Rd Suite 257, Dartmouth, NS, B2W 2S7
(902) 435-3567
Emp Here 33   *Sales* 11,517,000
SIC 5713 Floor covering stores
Scott Brookfield

D-U-N-S 24-449-8226   (SL)
WILKINS LIMITED
PORTLAND STREET HONDA
36 Baker Dr, Dartmouth, NS, B2W 6K1
(902) 435-3330
Emp Here 53   *Sales* 33,351,840
SIC 5511 New and used car dealers
Gilbert Wilkins
Maureen Wilkins

Dartmouth, NS B2X

D-U-N-S 24-471-8458   (SL)
ATLANTIC CAR STEREO LIMITED
26 Lakecrest Dr, Dartmouth, NS, B2X 1T8
(902) 435-0600
Emp Here 24   *Sales* 11,953,872
SIC 5531 Auto and home supply stores
Scott Maclean

D-U-N-S 20-904-5996   (SL)
COMMERCIAL CLEANING SERVICES LIMITED
SERVICE MASTER CONTRACT SERVICE ATLANTIC
(*Suby of* LOOMIS MANAGEMENT SERVICES LTD)
166 Braemar Dr, Dartmouth, NS, B2X 2T3
(902) 435-9500
Emp Here 75   *Sales* 2,397,600
SIC 7349 Building maintenance services, nec
Gordon Loomis
Carmel Loomis

D-U-N-S 20-151-1685   (SL)
MIC-MAC BEVERAGE ROOM LIMITED
MICMAC BAR & GRILL
219 Waverley Rd, Dartmouth, NS, B2X 2C3
(902) 434-7600
Emp Here 45   *Sales* 12,336,840
SIC 5411 Grocery stores
Terrance Legoffic

D-U-N-S 25-010-5285   (BR)
SECURITAS CANADA LIMITED
(*Suby of* SECURITAS AB)
175 Main St Suite 201, Dartmouth, NS, B2X 1S1
(902) 434-2442
Emp Here 300
SIC 5999 Miscellaneous retail stores, nec
Roger Miller

D-U-N-S 25-298-1121   (BR)
SOBEYS CAPITAL INCORPORATED
SOBEYS #772
(*Suby of* EMPIRE COMPANY LIMITED)
100 Main St Suite 250, Dartmouth, NS, B2X 1R5
(902) 434-6696
Emp Here 170
SIC 5411 Grocery stores
Trevor Negus

Dartmouth, NS B2Y

D-U-N-S 25-627-4705   (HQ)
BELMONT FINANCIAL GROUP INC, THE
33 Alderney Dr Unit 7th, Dartmouth, NS, B2Y 2N4
(902) 465-5687
Sales 25,441,800
SIC 6411 Insurance agents, brokers, and service

Kevin Hollis

D-U-N-S 20-727-2444   (HQ)
CHARM JEWELRY LIMITED
CHARM DIAMOND CENTRES
140 Portland St, Dartmouth, NS, B2Y 1J1
(902) 463-7177
Emp Here 50   *Sales* 128,475,900
SIC 5944 Jewelry stores
Richard Calder
Troy Calder
Sharon Calder

D-U-N-S 20-049-1841   (SL)
CHEEP INSURANCE
Gd, Dartmouth, NS, B2Y 3Y3
(902) 463-1675
Emp Here 26   *Sales* 22,049,560
SIC 6411 Insurance agents, brokers, and service

D-U-N-S 25-175-4982   (BR)
CONCENTRIX TECHNOLOGIES SERVICES (CANADA) LIMITED
(*Suby of* SYNNEX CORPORATION)
375 Pleasant St Suite 103, Dartmouth, NS, B2Y 4N4
(902) 428-9999
Emp Here 300
SIC 4899 Communication services, nec
Shawn Maclean

D-U-N-S 25-590-5960   (BR)
CROTHALL SERVICES CANADA INC
CENTRAL LAUNDRY & LINEN SERVICES
300 Pleasant St Suite 10, Dartmouth, NS, B2Y 3S3
(902) 464-3115
Emp Here 120
SIC 7219 Laundry and garment services, nec
Allan Vail

D-U-N-S 24-342-8034   (SL)
DARTMOUTH SENIOR CARE SOCIETY
OAKWOOD TERRACE
10 Mount Hope Ave, Dartmouth, NS, B2Y 4K1
(902) 469-3702
Emp Here 160   *Sales* 10,932,160
SIC 8051 Skilled nursing care facilities
Al Bennett
Pam Murray
Elgie Carmichael
Anthony Fagg

D-U-N-S 24-130-0383   (SL)
DOMINION DIVING LIMITED
7 Canal St, Dartmouth, NS, B2Y 2W1
(902) 434-5120
Emp Here 48   *Sales* 21,287,520
SIC 7389 Business services, nec
Barry Robin Lohnes
Matthew Lohnes

D-U-N-S 24-994-9033   (HQ)
DOWN EAST HOSPITALITY INCORPORATED
TIM HORTONS
335 Prince Albert Rd Suite 1, Dartmouth, NS, B2Y 1N7
(902) 434-7500
Emp Here 100   *Sales* 5,643,319
SIC 5812 Eating places
Steve Breed

D-U-N-S 20-279-2818   (HQ)
FALCK SAFETY SERVICES CANADA INCORPORATED
20 Orion Crt Suite 1, Dartmouth, NS, B2Y 4W6
(902) 466-7878
Emp Here 40   *Sales* 14,057,280
SIC 8748 Business consulting, nec
Joel Carroll
Paul Douglas

D-U-N-S 24-789-6574   (BR)
HERSHEY CANADA INC
MOIRS DIV OF

(*Suby of* HERSHEY COMPANY)
375 Pleasant St, Dartmouth, NS, B2Y 4N4

Emp Here 700
SIC 2064 Candy and other confectionery products
 Loris Jarvis

D-U-N-S 20-352-7320   (SL)
HORIZON MARITIME SERVICES LTD
101 Research Dr, Dartmouth, NS, B2Y 4T6
(902) 468-2341
Emp Here 50   *Sales* 11,848,500
SIC 7361 Employment agencies
 Sean Leet
 Steve Widmeyer

D-U-N-S 25-537-0710   (HQ)
MARITIME PRESSUREWORKS LIMITED
41 Estates Rd, Dartmouth, NS, B2Y 4K3
(902) 468-8461
Emp Here 30   *Sales* 11,539,680
SIC 7699 Repair services, nec
 Richard Dunham

D-U-N-S 20-781-0003   (SL)
OCEAN CONTRACTORS LIMITED
204 Cono Dr, Dartmouth, NS, B2Y 3Y9
(902) 435-1291
Emp Here 200   *Sales* 50,488,400
SIC 1611 Highway and street construction
 John Flemming
 Bryant Deveaux

D-U-N-S 24-956-3529   (HQ)
PRIME MATERIAL HANDLING EQUIPMENT LIMITED
1 Canal St, Dartmouth, NS, B2Y 2W1
(902) 468-1210
Emp Here 28   *Sales* 42,277,314
SIC 5084 Industrial machinery and equipment
 Dwayne Smithers
 Andrew Hyson

D-U-N-S 20-695-3528   (HQ)
SMITHERS INTERNATIONAL LIMITED
1 Canal St, Dartmouth, NS, B2Y 2W1
(902) 465-3400
Emp Here 1   *Sales* 129,024,677
SIC 6712 Bank holding companies
 Alfred Smithers

D-U-N-S 20-905-7926   (BR)
SOBEYS CAPITAL INCORPORATED
SOBEYS #776
(*Suby of* EMPIRE COMPANY LIMITED)
551 Portland St, Dartmouth, NS, B2Y 4B1
(902) 469-8396
Emp Here 195
SIC 5411 Grocery stores
 Dhru Hughson

D-U-N-S 20-123-4189   (SL)
SURVIVAL SYSTEMS HOLDING LIMITED
20 Orion Crt Suite 1, Dartmouth, NS, B2Y 4W6
(902) 466-7878
Emp Here 105   *Sales* 73,006,500
SIC 5099 Durable goods, nec
 Albert Bohemier
 Ian Crowe

D-U-N-S 20-002-8111   (SL)
SYDAX DEVELOPMENTS LIMITED
SMITTY'S
300 Prince Albert Rd, Dartmouth, NS, B2Y 4J2
(902) 468-8817
Emp Here 117   *Sales* 5,325,723
SIC 5812 Eating places
 Michael Jonstone
 Gregory Johnstone

D-U-N-S 20-720-1570   (HQ)
ULTRA ELECTRONICS CANADA INC
HERMES ELECTRONICS
(*Suby of* ULTRA ELECTRONICS HOLDINGS PLC)

40 Atlantic St, Dartmouth, NS, B2Y 4N2
(902) 466-7491
Sales 96,029,500
SIC 3812 Search and navigation equipment
 Rakesh Sharma
 Carlos Santiago
 Douglas Randol
 Iwan Jemczyk
 Mary Waldner
 Alan Barker
 Andrew Norman Hamment
 Paul Dean

D-U-N-S 24-524-1778   (HQ)
ULTRA ELECTRONICS MARITIME SYSTEMS INC
(*Suby of* ULTRA ELECTRONICS HOLDINGS PLC)
40 Atlantic St, Dartmouth, NS, B2Y 4N2
(902) 466-7491
Sales 60,826,725
SIC 3679 Electronic components, nec
 Bernard Mills

D-U-N-S 20-552-1482   (BR)
ULTRA ELECTRONICS MARITIME SYSTEMS INC
(*Suby of* ULTRA ELECTRONICS HOLDINGS PLC)
40 Atlantic St, Dartmouth, NS, B2Y 4N2
(902) 466-7491
Emp Here 125
SIC 3679 Electronic components, nec
 Doug Burd

Dartmouth, NS B3A

D-U-N-S 25-357-6714   (SL)
1937225 NOVA SCOTIA LIMITED
METRO SUZUKI
224 Wyse Rd, Dartmouth, NS, B3A 1M9
(902) 466-0086
Emp Here 30   *Sales* 14,942,340
SIC 5511 New and used car dealers
 Eric J Corkum

D-U-N-S 20-021-1196   (BR)
AVIVA CANADA INC
(*Suby of* GENERAL ACCIDENT PLC)
99 Wyse Rd Suite 1600, Dartmouth, NS, B3A 4S5
(902) 460-3100
Emp Here 146
SIC 6411 Insurance agents, brokers, and service
 Gordon Murray

D-U-N-S 24-533-1020   (SL)
BOYNECLARKE LLP
BOYNE CLARKE NS LAW
99 Wyse Rd Suite 600, Dartmouth, NS, B3A 4S5
(902) 469-9500
Emp Here 180   *Sales* 19,958,760
SIC 8111 Legal services
 Tom Boyne
 Richey Clarke
 John Young
 David Bright
 Gordon Proudfoot
 Cyril Randall
 Matthew Napier
 Debbie Conrad
 David Coles

D-U-N-S 20-813-1664   (SL)
D.M. SERVANT PHARMACY LIMITED
SHOPPERS DRUG MART
21 Micmac Blvd Suite 129, Dartmouth, NS, B3A 4K6
(902) 463-3321
Emp Here 64   *Sales* 15,636,992
SIC 5912 Drug stores and proprietary stores
 Dorothy Servant

D-U-N-S 25-483-1316   (SL)
DARTMOUTH SPORTSPLEX COMMUNITY ASSOCIATION
DARTMOUTH SPORTSPLEX
110 Wyse Rd, Dartmouth, NS, B3A 1M2
(902) 464-2600
Emp Here 180   *Sales* 14,138,100
SIC 7997 Membership sports and recreation clubs
 Bob Quigley

D-U-N-S 24-217-2463   (HQ)
ERDENE RESOURCE DEVELOPMENT CORPORATION
99 Wyse Rd Suite 1480, Dartmouth, NS, B3A 4S5
(902) 423-6419
Emp Here 9   *Sales* 52,526,078
SIC 1081 Metal mining services
 Peter C. Akerley
 Michael Macdonald
 Michael Gillis
 Jon Lyons
 Bilguun Ankhbayar
 Dawson Brisco
 D. Suzan Frazer
 Darryn Broderick
 Robert Jenkins
 Layton Croft

D-U-N-S 25-241-2531   (BR)
HALIFAX REGIONAL SCHOOL BOARD
DARTMOUTH HIGH SCHOOL
(*Suby of* HALIFAX REGIONAL SCHOOL BOARD)
95 Victoria Rd, Dartmouth, NS, B3A 1V2
(902) 464-2457
Emp Here 90
SIC 8211 Elementary and secondary schools
 Eartha Monard

D-U-N-S 20-728-9018   (HQ)
HALIFAX-DARTMOUTH BRIDGE COMMISSION
HALIFAX HARBOUR BRIDGES
(*Suby of* NOVA SCOTIA, PROVINCE OF)
125 Wyse Rd, Dartmouth, NS, B3A 4K9
(902) 463-2800
Sales 23,766,467
SIC 4785 Inspection and fixed facilities
 Steven Snider
 Michael Mcfeters
 Wayne Mason
 Vicki Harnish
 Bill Book
 Doug Skinner
 Janet Macmillan

D-U-N-S 25-358-3777   (SL)
MANGA HOTELS (DARTMOUTH) INC
HOLIDAY INN HARBOURVIEW
(*Suby of* MANGA HOTELS INC)
101 Wyse Rd, Dartmouth, NS, B3A 1L9
(902) 463-1100
Emp Here 100   *Sales* 9,269,000
SIC 7011 Hotels and motels
 Sukhdev Toor

D-U-N-S 25-298-1048   (BR)
SOBEYS CAPITAL INCORPORATED
(*Suby of* EMPIRE COMPANY LIMITED)
6 Primrose St, Dartmouth, NS, B3A 4C5
(902) 463-2910
Emp Here 100
SIC 5411 Grocery stores
 Troy Strand

Dartmouth, NS B3B

D-U-N-S 20-011-0117   (SL)
3043177 NOVA SCOTIA LIMITED
FRONTIER TECHNOLOGIES
61 Raddall Ave, Dartmouth, NS, B3B 1T4

(902) 446-3940
Emp Here 100   *Sales* 17,731,100
SIC 7374 Data processing and preparation
 Raymond Kerr
 Rodney Kerr

D-U-N-S 24-101-3056   (SL)
3100477 NOVA SCOTIA LIMITED
EXIT REALTY METRO
110 Garland Ave Unit 201, Dartmouth, NS, B3B 0A7
(902) 405-3948
Emp Here 60   *Sales* 16,305,360
SIC 6531 Real estate agents and managers
 Sterling Stephens

D-U-N-S 24-313-6319   (SL)
3102597 NOVA SCOTIA LIMITED
WADE ATLANTIC
109 Ilsley Ave Unit 1, Dartmouth, NS, B3B 1S8
(902) 429-5002
Emp Here 90   *Sales* 15,836,220
SIC 8712 Architectural services
 John Day

D-U-N-S 20-383-3736   (SL)
3307862 NOVA SCOTIA LIMITED
NATIONWIDE LOGISTICS
132 Trider Cres Suite 2, Dartmouth, NS, B3B 1R6
(800) 371-8022
Emp Here 30   *Sales* 11,755,239
SIC 4731 Freight transportation arrangement
 Greg Easton

D-U-N-S 24-641-0323   (SL)
353903 ONTARIO LTD.
161 Joseph Zatzman Dr, Dartmouth, NS, B3B 1M7
(902) 463-0101
Emp Here 45   *Sales* 21,376,170
SIC 5082 Construction and mining machinery
 Kent Connell

D-U-N-S 24-188-9856   (HQ)
98599 CANADA LTD
WACKY'S CARPET & FLOOR CENTRE
30 Akerley Blvd, Dartmouth, NS, B3B 1N1
(902) 481-1010
Emp Here 25   *Sales* 11,517,000
SIC 5713 Floor covering stores
 D. Scott Brookfield
 Cheryl Inman

D-U-N-S 24-187-4254   (HQ)
ACADIAN SEAPLANTS LIMITED
30 Brown Ave, Dartmouth, NS, B3B 1X8
(902) 468-2840
Sales 133,393,500
SIC 2875 Fertilizers, mixing only
 Jean Paul Deveau
 Louis E Deveau

D-U-N-S 20-444-5688   (SL)
ACHESON, A.J. SALES LIMITED
CANADIAN TIRE
(*Suby of* ACHESON, ALAN J. LIMITED)
30 Lamont Terr, Dartmouth, NS, B3B 0B5
(902) 434-2823
Emp Here 135   *Sales* 84,952,800
SIC 5531 Auto and home supply stores
 Alan J Acheson

D-U-N-S 25-394-1793   (HQ)
ACHESON, ALAN J. LIMITED
CANADIAN TIRE
30 Lamont Terr, Dartmouth, NS, B3B 0B5
(902) 434-2823
Sales 62,255,790
SIC 5014 Tires and tubes
 Alan J Acheson

D-U-N-S 20-108-9989   (BR)
ADP CANADA CO
ADP DEALER SERVICES
(*Suby of* AUTOMATIC DATA PROCESSING, INC.)
130 Eileen Stubbs Ave Unit 22, Dartmouth, NS, B3B 2C4

(800) 668-8441
Emp Here 289
SIC 8721 Accounting, auditing, and book-keeping
Randall Hipson

D-U-N-S 24-573-4884   (HQ)
ADVANCED ENERGY MANAGEMENT LTD
AEM
60 Dorey Ave Suite 103, Dartmouth, NS, B3B 0B1
(902) 453-4498
Emp Here 18   *Sales* 36,577,002
SIC 5084 Industrial machinery and equipment
Blaine Mayo
Richard Mann

D-U-N-S 24-931-9542   (SL)
ADVANCED PRECISION MACHINING AND FABRICATION LIMITED
70 Thornhill Dr, Dartmouth, NS, B3B 1S3
(902) 468-5653
Emp Here 75   *Sales* 16,650,075
SIC 3599 Industrial machinery, nec
John Fitzpatrick
Chris Fitzpatrick

D-U-N-S 20-939-6006   (SL)
ADVANTAGE COURIER SYSTEMS LIMITED
1 Gurholt Dr, Dartmouth, NS, B3B 1J8
(902) 444-1511
Emp Here 25   *Sales* 11,087,250
SIC 7389 Business services, nec
Jeffrey Worton

D-U-N-S 25-382-5392   (BR)
ADVANTAGE PERSONNEL LTD
(*Suby of* ADVANTAGE PERSONNEL LTD)
75 Akerley Blvd Unit S, Dartmouth, NS, B3B 1R7
(902) 468-5624
Emp Here 125
SIC 7361 Employment agencies
David Wells

D-U-N-S 20-009-6431   (SL)
ALTIMAX COURIER (2006) LIMITED
132 Trider Cres, Dartmouth, NS, B3B 1R6
(902) 460-6006
Emp Here 58   *Sales* 26,054,702
SIC 7389 Business services, nec
Wesley Penwarden

D-U-N-S 20-729-5163   (HQ)
ALWEATHER WINDOWS & DOORS LIMITED
27 Troop Ave, Dartmouth, NS, B3B 2A7
(902) 468-2605
Emp Here 9   *Sales* 12,652,950
SIC 5211 Lumber and other building materials
Brian Macphee

D-U-N-S 20-728-3672   (HQ)
AMCA SALES LIMITED
1000 Windmill Rd Suite 22, Dartmouth, NS, B3B 1L7
(902) 468-1501
Sales 62,668,275
SIC 5141 Groceries, general line
Paul Armstrong

D-U-N-S 24-877-9084   (SL)
AMEC BLACK & MCDONALD LIMITED
11 Frazee Ave, Dartmouth, NS, B3B 1Z4
(902) 474-3700
Emp Here 118   *Sales* 25,703,822
SIC 1731 Electrical work
Julie Hebert
Mark Healy
W. Ian Mcdonald
Neil Bruce

D-U-N-S 25-401-6835   (BR)
ARMOUR TRANSPORT INC
ARMOUR TRANSPORTATION SYSTEMS
(*Suby of* ARMOUR TRANSPORTATION SYSTEMS INC)
80 Guildford Ave, Dartmouth, NS, B3B 0G3

(902) 468-8855
Emp Here 200
SIC 4213 Trucking, except local
Brad Price

D-U-N-S 24-669-6025   (HQ)
ATLANTIC BUSINESS INTERIORS LIMITED
(*Suby of* TAR INVESTMENTS LIMITED)
30 Troop Ave, Dartmouth, NS, B3B 1Z1
(902) 468-3200
Emp Here 45   *Sales* 38,164,200
SIC 5021 Furniture
Thomas Rose
Goerge Mitchell
Holland Peter
Dave Clarke

D-U-N-S 24-658-7401   (SL)
ATLANTIC PRIVATE PROTECTION SERVICE
7 Mellor Ave Unit 12, Dartmouth, NS, B3B 0E8
(902) 468-9002
Emp Here 49   *Sales* 19,388,222
SIC 7381 Detective and armored car services
Dan Barry

D-U-N-S 24-761-2711   (SL)
ATLANTICA DIVERSIFIED TRANSPORTATION SYSTEMS INC
ADTS
10 Morris Dr Unit 19, Dartmouth, NS, B3B 1K8

Emp Here 150   *Sales* 100,033,800
SIC 4731 Freight transportation arrangement

D-U-N-S 24-326-7759   (HQ)
ATLANTICA MECHANICAL CONTRACTORS INCORPORATED
LIFE SAFETY SYSTEMS, DIV OF
(*Suby of* G.J. CAHILL & COMPANY (1979) LIMITED)
9 Ralston Ave, Dartmouth, NS, B3B 1H5
(902) 468-2300
Sales 67,712,000
SIC 1711 Plumbing, heating, air-conditioning
Thomas Vincent

D-U-N-S 20-287-6525   (SL)
BARRY, D F & ASSOCIATES INC
7 Mellor Ave Unit 12, Dartmouth, NS, B3B 0E8
(902) 468-9001
Emp Here 70   *Sales* 31,445,330
SIC 7389 Business services, nec
Daniel Barry

D-U-N-S 24-363-5567   (BR)
BEST BUY CANADA LTD
BEST BUY
(*Suby of* BEST BUY CO., INC.)
119 Gale Terr, Dartmouth, NS, B3B 0C4
(902) 468-0075
Emp Here 130
SIC 5731 Radio, television, and electronic stores
Hatim A. Tyabji

D-U-N-S 25-571-8306   (SL)
BIRCHGROVE CAPITAL CORPORATION LTD
7 Mellor Ave Unit 1, Dartmouth, NS, B3B 0E8
(902) 453-9300
Emp Here 49   *Sales* 16,029,223
SIC 6531 Real estate agents and managers
Ron Basque

D-U-N-S 24-186-1574   (BR)
BLACK & MCDONALD LIMITED
(*Suby of* BLACK & MCDONALD GROUP LIMITED)
60 Cutler Ave, Dartmouth, NS, B3B 0J6
(902) 468-3101
Emp Here 250
SIC 1711 Plumbing, heating, air-conditioning
Charles Savoie

D-U-N-S 20-781-1597   (HQ)
BLUE WATER AGENCIES LIMITED
BLUE WATER GROUP

40 Topple Dr, Dartmouth, NS, B3B 1L6
(902) 468-4900
Emp Here 50   *Sales* 68,282,200
SIC 5088 Transportation equipment and supplies
Patrick Wilson
David Babin
Shannon Pye-Wilson
Robert Skaggs
Peter Michalak
Peter Mackay
Ashley Levy

D-U-N-S 24-393-5389   (HQ)
BLUEWAVE ENERGY LTD
(*Suby of* PARKLAND FUEL CORPORATION)
30 Oland Crt, Dartmouth, NS, B3B 1V2
(902) 481-0515
Emp Here 65   *Sales* 230,900,800
SIC 5541 Gasoline service stations
Shaun Peesker

D-U-N-S 20-026-5379   (BR)
BRINK'S CANADA LIMITED
(*Suby of* THE BRINK'S COMPANY)
19 Ilsley Ave, Dartmouth, NS, B3B 1L5
(902) 468-7124
Emp Here 90
SIC 7381 Detective and armored car services
Sharon Curnew

D-U-N-S 20-547-3692   (BR)
CANADIAN LINEN AND UNIFORM SERVICE CO
QUEBEC LINGE
(*Suby of* ARAMARK)
41 Thornhill Dr Suite 136, Dartmouth, NS, B3B 1R9
(902) 468-2155
Emp Here 95
SIC 7213 Linen supply
Tracy Mackenzie

D-U-N-S 25-099-0132   (HQ)
CANADIAN MARITIME ENGINEERING LIMITED
90 Thornhill Dr, Dartmouth, NS, B3B 1S3
(902) 468-1888
Emp Here 80   *Sales* 22,866,103
SIC 3599 Industrial machinery, nec
Anthony Kennedy
Raymond Gallant
Bob Deveaux
Doug Anderson

D-U-N-S 25-261-6842   (BR)
CANADIAN RED CROSS SOCIETY, THE
HOME PARTNERS
(*Suby of* CANADIAN RED CROSS SOCIETY, THE)
133 Troop Ave, Dartmouth, NS, B3B 2A7
(902) 496-0103
Emp Here 85
SIC 8059 Nursing and personal care, nec
Ismael Aquino

D-U-N-S 20-727-9506   (SL)
CHERUBINI METAL WORKS LIMITED
570 Av Wilkinson, Dartmouth, NS, B3B 0J4
(902) 468-5630
Emp Here 275   *Sales* 90,231,625
SIC 1622 Bridge, tunnel, and elevated highway construction
Danilo Gasparetto
Renato Gasparetto

D-U-N-S 24-310-7419   (HQ)
CHORUS AVIATION INC
3 Spectacle Lake Dr, Dartmouth, NS, B3B 1W8
(902) 873-5000
Sales 1,100,153,074
SIC 4512 Air transportation, scheduled
Joseph D. Randell
Tyrone Cotie
Nathalie Megann
Jolene Mahody

Laurel Clark
Dennis Lopes
Gary Osborne
James Bruce Peddle
Richard H. Mccoy
Gary M. Collins

D-U-N-S 25-089-7451   (HQ)
CLASSIC FREIGHT SYSTEMS (2011) LIMITED
CLASSIC FREIGHT
50 Joseph Zatzman Dr, Dartmouth, NS, B3B 1N8
(902) 481-3701
Emp Here 5   *Sales* 13,370,890
SIC 4213 Trucking, except local
Blair Clark
Danilo Gasparetto
Renato Gasparetto

D-U-N-S 20-630-8736   (HQ)
CLEVE'S SPORTING GOODS LIMITED
30 Thornhill Dr, Dartmouth, NS, B3B 1S1
(902) 468-1885
Emp Here 40   *Sales* 40,378,140
SIC 5941 Sporting goods and bicycle shops
Eric Bezanson
Kevin Bezanson
Anne Bezanson

D-U-N-S 24-588-5645   (SL)
CLUETT HOLDINGS INC
629 Windmill Rd, Dartmouth, NS, B3B 1B6
(902) 466-5328
Emp Here 30   *Sales* 12,792,241
SIC 6712 Bank holding companies
Roy Wilson Cluett

D-U-N-S 20-987-2605   (HQ)
COASTAL DOOR & FRAME INC
DOORTECH, DIV OF
(*Suby of* L & M ENTERPRISES LIMITED)
40 Raddall Ave, Dartmouth, NS, B3B 1T2
(902) 468-2333
Emp Here 29   *Sales* 15,651,090
SIC 5039 Construction materials, nec
Susan Andrea
Thane Stevens
Scott Stevens
Chris Sangster

D-U-N-S 25-590-6000   (BR)
COMPASS GROUP CANADA LTD
CHARTWELLS
(*Suby of* COMPASS GROUP PLC)
10 Morris Dr Suite 35, Dartmouth, NS, B3B 1K8
(902) 466-0150
Emp Here 100
SIC 5963 Direct selling establishments
Greg Osborne

D-U-N-S 25-749-4872   (BR)
CORUS MEDIA HOLDINGS INC
GLOBAL TELEVISION
(*Suby of* SHAW COMMUNICATIONS INC)
14 Akerley Blvd, Dartmouth, NS, B3B 1J3
(902) 481-7400
Emp Here 85
SIC 4833 Television broadcasting stations
Bill Albert

D-U-N-S 20-116-3050   (SL)
CUMBERLAND PAVING AND CONTRACTING
8 Moore Rd, Dartmouth, NS, B3B 1J2
(902) 832-9062
Emp Here 49   *Sales* 13,892,676
SIC 1611 Highway and street construction
Graham Clark

D-U-N-S 24-245-8417   (SL)
DARTMOUTH CROSSING LIMITED
34 Logiealmond Close, Dartmouth, NS, B3B 0C8
(902) 445-8883
Emp Here 300
SIC 7389 Business services, nec

Robert Green
Glenn Munro
Tracy Butler
Marcus Bertagnolli
Jennifer Starkey

D-U-N-S 24-832-0731   (SL)
DIGICON BUILDING CONTROL SOLUTIONS LIMITED
201 Brownlow Ave Unit 11, Dartmouth, NS, B3B 1W2
(902) 468-2633
Emp Here 22   *Sales* 10,450,572
SIC 5084 Industrial machinery and equipment
Leslie Beal
Kathy Walton-Beal
Real Awdet

D-U-N-S 20-727-3194   (SL)
DOMINION BIOLOGICALS LIMITED
(*Suby of* IVD HOLDINGS INC)
5 Isnor Dr, Dartmouth, NS, B3B 1M1
(902) 468-3992
Emp Here 40   *Sales* 11,066,400
SIC 2836 Biological products, except diagnostic
Patrick Waddy

D-U-N-S 20-190-6463   (HQ)
DORA CONSTRUCTION LIMITED
60 Dorey Ave Suite 101, Dartmouth, NS, B3B 0B1
(902) 468-2941
Emp Here 1   *Sales* 57,033,800
SIC 1542 Nonresidential construction, nec
John Young
Donald Macdonald

D-U-N-S 24-955-8180   (SL)
DSS AVIATION INC
HELICOPTER SURVIVAL RESCUE SERVICES
71 Wright Ave, Dartmouth, NS, B3B 1H4
(902) 444-3788
Emp Here 23   *Sales* 11,972,466
SIC 5099 Durable goods, nec
Douglas Thomas

D-U-N-S 20-023-5377   (BR)
ECONOMICAL MUTUAL INSURANCE COMPANY
(*Suby of* ECONOMICAL MUTUAL INSURANCE COMPANY)
238a Brownlow Ave Suite 310, Dartmouth, NS, B3B 2B4
(902) 835-6214
Emp Here 100
SIC 6331 Fire, marine, and casualty insurance
Dan Spears

D-U-N-S 25-128-0876   (SL)
EFFICIENCY NOVA SCOTIA CORP
EFFICIENCY E1 SERVICES
230 Brownlow Ave Suite 300, Dartmouth, NS, B3B 0G5
(902) 470-3500
Emp Here 49   *Sales* 11,480,112
SIC 8748 Business consulting, nec
Stephen Macdonald

D-U-N-S 25-501-2858   (HQ)
EMC EMERGENCY MEDICAL CARE INCORPORATED
EMC
(*Suby of* MEDAVIE INC)
239 Brownlow Ave Suite 300, Dartmouth, NS, B3B 2B2
(902) 832-8320
Emp Here 10   *Sales* 50,592,600
SIC 4119 Local passenger transportation, nec
Arnold Rovers
Doug Sabean
Paula Poirier
Jeff Fraser

D-U-N-S 25-628-7947   (BR)
EMCO CORPORATION
SANDALE UTILITY PRODUCTS

(*Suby of* HAJOCA CORPORATION)
111 Wright Ave, Dartmouth, NS, B3B 1K6
(902) 555-7744
Emp Here 101
SIC 5074 Plumbing and heating equipment and supplies (hydronics)
Glen Smith

D-U-N-S 25-244-8642   (HQ)
ENVIROSYSTEMS INCORPORATED
ATLANTIC INDUSTRIAL CLEANERS, DIV OF
(*Suby of* REVOLUTION ENVIRONMENTAL SOLUTIONS LP)
11 Brown Ave, Dartmouth, NS, B3B 1Z7
(902) 481-8008
Emp Here 100   *Sales* 1,352,027,625
SIC 2992 Lubricating oils and greases
Todd Moser
Glen Sivec
Ryan Reid
Took Whitely
Stephen Fletcher

D-U-N-S 20-184-8418   (BR)
EXCO TECHNOLOGIES LIMITED
NEOCON INTERNATIONAL
(*Suby of* EXCO TECHNOLOGIES LIMITED)
35 Akerley Blvd, Dartmouth, NS, B3B 1J7
(902) 468-6663
Emp Here 100
SIC 3089 Plastics products, nec
Patrick Ryan

D-U-N-S 24-320-5262   (SL)
EXIT REALTY OPTIMUM
1 Gloster Crt, Dartmouth, NS, B3B 1X9
(902) 444-3948
Emp Here 37   *Sales* 10,054,972
SIC 6531 Real estate agents and managers
Wayne Cochrane

D-U-N-S 20-025-4969   (SL)
FAIRLEY & STEVENS LIMITED
FAIRLEY & STEVENS FORD LINCOLN
580 Windmill Rd, Dartmouth, NS, B3B 1B5
(902) 468-6271
Emp Here 55   *Sales* 34,610,400
SIC 5511 New and used car dealers
Charles Giffin
Robert Charlton

D-U-N-S 20-523-9809   (SL)
FARNELL PACKAGING LIMITED
30 Ilsley Ave, Dartmouth, NS, B3B 1L3
(902) 468-9378
Emp Here 165   *Sales* 32,136,720
SIC 2673 Bags: plastic, laminated, and coated
Donald Farnell
Hilding Christianson
Amy Farnell
Judith S. Farnell

D-U-N-S 24-340-3144   (SL)
FOCAL TECHNOLOGIES CORPORATION
MOOG COMPONENTS GROUP
(*Suby of* MOOG INC.)
77 Frazee Ave, Dartmouth, NS, B3B 1Z4
(902) 468-2263
Emp Here 180   *Sales* 50,924,700
SIC 3621 Motors and generators
John R Scannell
Craig Bowers
Michael Glister
Timothy P Balkin

D-U-N-S 24-206-9982   (SL)
FOREIGNEXCHANGE TRANSLATIONS CANADA, INC
10 Morris Dr Unit 40, Dartmouth, NS, B3B 1K8
(902) 468-5553
Emp Here 45   *Sales* 19,957,050
SIC 7389 Business services, nec
Andres Heuberger

D-U-N-S 24-528-1899   (SL)

FOUNDERS INSURANCE GROUP INC.
250 Brownlow Ave Suite 18, Dartmouth, NS, B3B 1W9
(902) 468-3529
Emp Here 25   *Sales* 21,201,500
SIC 6411 Insurance agents, brokers, and service
Suzanne Mclelan

D-U-N-S 25-149-3821   (SL)
G. D. BROKERAGE INC
21 Williams Ave Unit 4, Dartmouth, NS, B3B 1X3
(902) 468-1777
Emp Here 20   *Sales* 10,702,480
SIC 5141 Groceries, general line
Deborah Crowell
Gary Crowell

D-U-N-S 20-955-7490   (SL)
G3 GALVANIZING LIMITED
160 Joseph Zatzman Dr, Dartmouth, NS, B3B 1P1
(902) 468-1040
Emp Here 50   *Sales* 10,141,500
SIC 3479 Metal coating and allied services
Darren S Nantes
David G Nantes

D-U-N-S 20-169-4937   (BR)
GDI SERVICES (CANADA) LP
(*Suby of* GDI SERVICES AUX IMMEUBLES INC)
202 Brownlow Ave, Dartmouth, NS, B3B 1T5
(902) 468-3103
Emp Here 90
SIC 7349 Building maintenance services, nec
Michael Brewer

D-U-N-S 24-593-7409   (SL)
GTL TRANSPORTATION INC
115 Trider Cres, Dartmouth, NS, B3B 1V6
(902) 468-3100
Emp Here 105   *Sales* 21,599,130
SIC 4213 Trucking, except local
Stephanie Clowes
Ronald Clowes

D-U-N-S 24-319-1843   (HQ)
GUILDFORDS (2005) INC
(*Suby of* NSM ACQUISITION COMPANY LIMITED)
25 Guildford Ave, Dartmouth, NS, B3B 0H5
(902) 481-7900
Emp Here 20   *Sales* 12,178,575
SIC 1742 Plastering, drywall, and insulation
Darren Nantes
Gregory Mombourquette
William Brown

D-U-N-S 24-834-0150   (BR)
HALIFAX REGIONAL MUNICIPALITY
METRO TRANSIT
(*Suby of* NOVA SCOTIA, PROVINCE OF)
200 Ilsley Ave, Dartmouth, NS, B3B 1V1
(902) 490-6614
Emp Here 576
SIC 4111 Local and suburban transit
Paul Mcdaniel

D-U-N-S 25-395-3780   (HQ)
HALIFAX REGIONAL SCHOOL BOARD
33 Spectacle Lake Dr, Dartmouth, NS, B3B 1X7
(902) 464-2000
Emp Here 200   *Sales* 365,409,362
SIC 8211 Elementary and secondary schools
Dave Wright
Cindy Littlefair

D-U-N-S 20-930-2413   (HQ)
HEAD SHOPPE COMPANY LIMITED, THE
GOLDEN CLIPPER, THE
10 Thorne Ave, Dartmouth, NS, B3B 1Y5
(902) 455-1504
Emp Here 15   *Sales* 18,925,856
SIC 7231 Beauty shops
Peter Mahoney

Sherry Mills

D-U-N-S 25-525-7842   (HQ)
HERCULES SLR INC
SPARTAN INDUSTRIAL MARINE
520 Windmill Rd, Dartmouth, NS, B3B 1B3
(902) 482-3125
Emp Here 40   *Sales* 256,905,220
SIC 5051 Metals service centers and offices
Giannous D Giannou
Peter Wong

D-U-N-S 20-175-8526   (HQ)
HERITAGE GAS LIMITED
(*Suby of* ALTAGAS LTD)
238 Brownlow Ave Suite 200, Dartmouth, NS, B3B 1Y2
(902) 466-2003
Sales 102,466,896
SIC 4924 Natural gas distribution
David Wright
John Hawkins
Zeda Redden
Michel Sarrouy

D-U-N-S 24-342-2362   (BR)
HGS CANADA INC
OLS
(*Suby of* HINDUJA GLOBAL SOLUTIONS LIMITED)
250 Brownlow Ave Suite 11, Dartmouth, NS, B3B 1W9
(902) 481-9475
Emp Here 125
SIC 7389 Business services, nec

D-U-N-S 20-004-0694   (BR)
HOME DEPOT OF CANADA INC
HOME DEPOT TOOL RENTAL
(*Suby of* THE HOME DEPOT INC)
40 Finnian Row, Dartmouth, NS, B3B 0B6
(902) 460-4700
Emp Here 100
SIC 5251 Hardware stores
Mark Wagner

D-U-N-S 20-026-9207   (HQ)
HOYT'S MOVING & STORAGE LIMITED
HOYT'S SPECIALTY SERVICES, DIV OF
320 Wright Ave Unit 12, Dartmouth, NS, B3B 0B3
(902) 876-8202
Emp Here 30   *Sales* 69,142,875
SIC 4213 Trucking, except local
Donald Campbell

D-U-N-S 24-755-5519   (HQ)
INSTALL-A-FLOR LIMITED
BURNSIDE FLOORING DIV OF
31 Sterns Crt, Dartmouth, NS, B3B 1W7
(902) 468-3111
Emp Here 15   *Sales* 11,517,000
SIC 5713 Floor covering stores
Larry Gibson
Patricia Gibson

D-U-N-S 25-673-8972   (BR)
INTACT INSURANCE COMPANY
(*Suby of* INTACT FINANCIAL CORPORATION)
20 Hector Gate Suite 200, Dartmouth, NS, B3B 0K3
(902) 420-1732
Emp Here 170
SIC 6331 Fire, marine, and casualty insurance
Allen Blair

D-U-N-S 24-190-3053   (SL)
INTERPROVINCIAL MEAT SALES LIMITED
(*Suby of* PREMIUM BRANDS HOLDINGS CORPORATION)
65 Thornhill Dr, Dartmouth, NS, B3B 1R9
(902) 468-5884
Emp Here 12   *Sales* 10,026,924
SIC 5142 Packaged frozen goods
John Koivu
Paul Maceachern
Steve Gilbert

▲ Public Company   ■ Public Company Family Member   **HQ** Headquarters   **BR** Branch   **SL** Single Location

D-U-N-S 24-449-6725   (HQ)
JAZZ AVIATION LP
AIR CANADA EXPRESS
3 Spectacle Lake Dr Suite 100, Dartmouth,
NS, B3B 1W8
(902) 873-5000
Emp Here 650   *Sales* 1,555,024,800
SIC 4512 Air transportation, scheduled
Joseph D. Randell
Gary Osborne
Kal Rebin
Franco Giampa
Rick Flynn
Jolene Mahody

D-U-N-S 20-781-3056   (HQ)
L & M ENTERPRISES LIMITED
STEVENS GROUP MANAGEMENT
20 Macdonald Ave, Dartmouth, NS, B3B 1C5
(902) 468-8040
Emp Here 20   *Sales* 109,652,700
SIC 6712 Bank holding companies
Thane Stevens
Scott Stevens
Chris Sangster

D-U-N-S 25-674-3188   (BR)
LAWTON'S DRUG STORES LIMITED
LAWTON'S DRUGS WHOLESALE DIV
(*Suby of* EMPIRE COMPANY LIMITED)
81 Thornhill Dr, Dartmouth, NS, B3B 1R9
(902) 468-4637
Emp Here 95
SIC 5122 Drugs, proprietaries, and sundries
John Duggan

D-U-N-S 20-026-4851   (HQ)
LAWTON'S DRUG STORES LIMITED
LAWTONS HOME HEALTH CARE
(*Suby of* EMPIRE COMPANY LIMITED)
236 Brownlow Ave Suite 270, Dartmouth, NS,
B3B 1V5
(902) 468-1000
Emp Here 100   *Sales* 330,366,600
SIC 5912 Drug stores and proprietary stores
Michael Medline
Doug Nathanson
Vivek Sood
Michael Vels

D-U-N-S 20-027-0023   (HQ)
LAWTON'S INCORPORATED
(*Suby of* EMPIRE COMPANY LIMITED)
236 Brownlow Ave Suite 270, Dartmouth, NS,
B3B 1V5
(902) 468-1000
Emp Here 75   *Sales* 293,659,200
SIC 5912 Drug stores and proprietary stores
Bill Mcewan
Jane Mcdow

D-U-N-S 20-390-1863   (HQ)
LINDSAY CONSTRUCTION LIMITED
134 Eileen Stubbs Ave Unit 105, Dartmouth,
NS, B3B 0A9
(902) 468-5000
Emp Here 50   *Sales* 42,273,700
SIC 1541 Industrial buildings and warehouses
Dan Jones
Jeff Skinner
Marc Dixon
Howie Doiron
Andy Knowles
George Collins

D-U-N-S 20-852-7403   (BR)
LOCKHEED MARTIN CANADA INC
(*Suby of* LOCKHEED MARTIN CORPORA-
TION)
1000 Windmill Rd, Dartmouth, NS, B3B 1L7
(902) 468-3399
Emp Here 100
SIC 5065 Electronic parts and equipment, nec
William Goodall

D-U-N-S 20-782-1604   (SL)
LVM / MARITIME TESTING LIMITED

EARTHTECH ENGINEERING
97 Troop Ave, Dartmouth, NS, B3B 2A7
(902) 468-6486
Emp Here 100   *Sales* 17,873,900
SIC 8711 Engineering services
Marc Verreault
Jean Aubuchon

D-U-N-S 20-008-6575   (SL)
MACKIE MOVING SYSTEMS
30 Gurholt Dr, Dartmouth, NS, B3B 1J9
(902) 481-2041
Emp Here 200   *Sales* 41,141,200
SIC 4213 Trucking, except local
Rob Thompson

D-U-N-S 20-278-8808   (SL)
**MARITIME PAPER PRODUCTS LIMITED
PARTNERSHIP**
25 Borden Ave, Dartmouth, NS, B3B 1C7
(902) 468-5353
Emp Here 50   *Sales* 11,806,931
SIC 2653 Corrugated and solid fiber boxes
Gary Johnson

D-U-N-S 24-833-0052   (SL)
**MASTER MERCHANT SYSTEMS SOFT-
WARE LIMITED**
202 Brownlow Ave Suite 700, Dartmouth, NS,
B3B 1T5
(902) 496-9500
Emp Here 50   *Sales* 22,358,700
SIC 5045 Computers, peripherals, and soft-
ware
Russell Brannon
Adam Baggs
Mike Abbot
Bryan Babineau
Doug Hamilton

D-U-N-S 20-350-4022   (SL)
METOCEAN TELEMATICS LIMITED
21 Thornhill Dr, Dartmouth, NS, B3B 1R9
(902) 468-2505
Emp Here 80   *Sales* 15,235,360
SIC 3679 Electronic components, nec
Anthony Chedrawy
Jonathan Zinck

D-U-N-S 20-727-6718   (BR)
MIDLAND TRANSPORT LIMITED
(*Suby of* IRVING, J. D. LIMITED)
31 Simmonds Dr, Dartmouth, NS, B3B 1R4
(902) 494-5555
Emp Here 150
SIC 4212 Local trucking, without storage
Richard Calvin

D-U-N-S 24-128-4827   (HQ)
MILLER TIRE SERVICES LTD
16 Gloria Mccluskey Ave, Dartmouth, NS, B3B
2C2
(902) 431-7733
Emp Here 30   *Sales* 23,673,975
SIC 5014 Tires and tubes
Brian Miller
Christopher Miller
Corey Miller

D-U-N-S 20-449-4520   (HQ)
MITCHELL AGENCIES LIMITED
CONCORD NATIONAL
55 Weston Crt, Dartmouth, NS, B3B 2C8
(902) 468-8990
Emp Here 11   *Sales* 20,889,425
SIC 5141 Groceries, general line
Douglas Eard
Ian Osmond

D-U-N-S 24-912-5584   (HQ)
MMP OFFICE INTERIORS INCORPORATED
OFFICE INTERIORS
656 Windmill Rd Suite 1, Dartmouth, NS, B3B
1B8
(902) 422-4011
Emp Here 90   *Sales* 25,564,330
SIC 5712 Furniture stores
James Mills

Ted Malpage

D-U-N-S 25-095-0834   (SL)
**MOBIA TECHNOLOGY INNOVATIONS IN-
CORPORATED**
340 Wright Ave Unit 13, Dartmouth, NS, B3B
0B3
(902) 468-8000
Emp Here 130   *Sales* 29,701,360
SIC 4899 Communication services, nec
Robert Lane

D-U-N-S 20-079-5784   (HQ)
NATURE'S WAY OF CANADA LIMITED
(*Suby of* SCHWABE INTERNATIONAL
GMBH)
15 Garland Ave Unit 4, Dartmouth, NS, B3B
0A6
(902) 334-1468
Emp Here 10   *Sales* 35,371,040
SIC 5122 Drugs, proprietaries, and sundries
Stephen Chiasson
Mike Winkler
Rene Leclerc
Chad Wiegand

D-U-N-S 24-955-9568   (HQ)
NEWCAP INC
NEWCAP RADIO
(*Suby of* GROUPE STINGRAY INC)
8 Basinview Dr, Dartmouth, NS, B3B 1G4
(902) 468-7557
Emp Here 17   *Sales* 301,089,600
SIC 4832 Radio broadcasting stations
Robert Steele
Scott Weatherby
Harry R. Steele

D-U-N-S 24-129-2945   (HQ)
NEWFOUND TRADING LIMITED
11 Morris Dr Suite 206, Dartmouth, NS, B3B
1M2
(902) 468-7100
Sales 93,364,880
SIC 4731 Freight transportation arrangement
Steinar Engeset
Shawn Frank

D-U-N-S 20-907-6702   (HQ)
**NEWFOUNDLAND CAPITAL CORPORA-
TION LIMITED**
(*Suby of* GROUPE STINGRAY INC)
8 Basinview Dr, Dartmouth, NS, B3B 1G4
(902) 468-7557
Emp Here 19   *Sales* 267,635,200
SIC 4832 Radio broadcasting stations
Robert G. Steele
Scott Broderick
Steve Jones
Richard Davis
Scott Weatherby
Ian S. Lurie
Harry R. Steele
Michael Macdonald
David Matheson
Allen Macphee

D-U-N-S 20-027-2011   (HQ)
NORTHEAST EQUIPMENT LIMITED
135 Joseph Zatzman Dr, Dartmouth, NS, B3B
1W1
(902) 468-7473
Emp Here 20   *Sales* 13,415,220
SIC 5074 Plumbing and heating equipment
and supplies (hydronics)
Wayne Loxdale
Glenn Loxdale

D-U-N-S 24-955-9113   (HQ)
**NORTHEASTERN INVESTIGATIONS IN-
CORPORATED**
NORTHEASTERN PROTECTION SERVICE
202 Brownlow Ave Suite 1, Dartmouth, NS,
B3B 1T5
(902) 435-1336
Emp Here 85   *Sales* 4,200,000
SIC 7381 Detective and armored car services
Mark Joseph

Roger Miller
Rebecca Joseph

D-U-N-S 20-607-0810   (SL)
NORTHWOOD HOMECARE LTD
130 Eileen Stubbs Ave Suite 19n, Dartmouth,
NS, B3B 2C4
(902) 425-2273
Emp Here 90   *Sales* 7,494,480
SIC 8082 Home health care services
John Verlinden

D-U-N-S 20-780-8122   (HQ)
NOVA ENTERPRISES LIMITED
NOVA TRUCK CENTRES
670 Av Wilkinson, Dartmouth, NS, B3B 0J4
(902) 468-5900
Emp Here 51   *Sales* 74,255,040
SIC 5511 New and used car dealers
Peter Macgillivray
Rod Mackay

D-U-N-S 25-174-5816   (HQ)
NUBODY'S FITNESS CENTRES INC
51 Raddall Ave, Dartmouth, NS, B3B 1T6
(902) 468-8920
Emp Here 25   *Sales* 19,866,000
SIC 7991 Physical fitness facilities
Dean Hartman

D-U-N-S 24-833-1076   (SL)
OCEANSIDE EQUIPMENT LIMITED
181 Joseph Zatzman Dr Unit 12, Dartmouth,
NS, B3B 1R5
(902) 468-4844
Emp Here 26   *Sales* 12,350,676
SIC 5085 Industrial supplies
Martin Greg Maloney
Gary Sullivan

D-U-N-S 25-099-7475   (HQ)
OFFICE INTERIORS
(*Suby of* MMP OFFICE INTERIORS INCOR-
PORATED)
656 Windmill Rd, Dartmouth, NS, B3B 1B8
(902) 422-4011
Emp Here 35   *Sales* 44,717,400
SIC 5044 Office equipment
James Mills
Keith Skiffington
Robert Wallace

D-U-N-S 20-364-0545   (SL)
ONE WIND SERVICES INC
4 Macdonald Ave, Dartmouth, NS, B3B 1C5
(902) 482-8687
Emp Here 75   *Sales* 14,424,600
SIC 7699 Repair services, nec
Paul Pynn

D-U-N-S 24-913-5773   (SL)
PARK PLACE CENTRE LIMITED
PARK PLACE RAMADA PLAZA HOTEL
(*Suby of* ARMOUR GROUP LIMITED, THE)
240 Brownlow Ave, Dartmouth, NS, B3B 1X6
(902) 468-8888
Emp Here 120   *Sales* 11,122,800
SIC 7011 Hotels and motels
Armour Mccrea
Doug Macisaac

D-U-N-S 20-027-3647   (HQ)
PARTS FOR TRUCKS, INC
PARTS FOR TRUCKS SERVICE CENTRE
15 Macdonald Ave, Dartmouth, NS, B3B 1C6
(902) 468-6100
Emp Here 100   *Sales* 129,123,120
SIC 5013 Motor vehicle supplies and new
parts
Corey Miller
Brent Miller

D-U-N-S 25-673-5499   (HQ)
PC MEDIC INCORPORATED
50 Akerley Blvd Suite 12, Dartmouth, NS, B3B
1R8
(902) 468-7237
Emp Here 13   *Sales* 15,651,090

▲ Public Company   ■ Public Company Family Member   **HQ** Headquarters   **BR** Branch   **SL** Single Location

SIC 5045 Computers, peripherals, and software
Ho-Sing Tom
Konstantinos Klironomos

D-U-N-S 25-563-1335   (HQ)
PINCHIN LEBLANC ENVIRONMENTAL LIMITED
42 Dorey Ave, Dartmouth, NS, B3B 0B1
(902) 461-9999
Emp Here 1   *Sales* 14,057,280
SIC 8748 Business consulting, nec
Ronald Leblanc
Scott Mcarthy
Dave Carter
Donald Pinchin

D-U-N-S 20-031-4524   (HQ)
POLE STAR TRANSPORT INCORPORATED
ARMOUR TRANSPORT
(*Suby of* ARMOUR TRANSPORTATION SYSTEMS INC)
80 Guildford Ave, Dartmouth, NS, B3B 0G3
(902) 468-8855
Emp Here 100   *Sales* 64,533,350
SIC 4213 Trucking, except local
Wesley Armour
Ruth Leblanc
Brad Price
Steve Lowe
Kenny O'hearn

D-U-N-S 24-471-3368   (SL)
PRECISION BIOLOGIC INC
140 Eileen Stubbs Ave, Dartmouth, NS, B3B 0A9
(800) 267-2796
Emp Here 50   *Sales* 22,358,700
SIC 5049 Professional equipment, nec
Paul Empey
Michael Scott

D-U-N-S 24-211-1572   (SL)
PREMIERE EXECUTIVE SUITES ATLANTIC LIMITED
(*Suby of* SOUTHWEST PROPERTIES LIMITED)
250 Brownlow Ave, Dartmouth, NS, B3B 1W9
(902) 420-1333
Emp Here 45   *Sales* 12,799,665
SIC 6512 Nonresidential building operators
Suzanne Bachur

D-U-N-S 24-341-8837   (SL)
PRO CYCLE LIMITED
360 Higney Ave, Dartmouth, NS, B3B 0L4
(902) 468-2518
Emp Here 30   *Sales* 14,942,340
SIC 5571 Motorcycle dealers
John Larson
James Dunsworth
Peter Dunsworth
David Munroe

D-U-N-S 24-766-8200   (HQ)
PROPERTY VALUATION SERVICES CORPORATION
238 Brownlow Ave Suite 200, Dartmouth, NS, B3B 1Y2
(902) 476-2748
Sales 22,011,731
SIC 7389 Business services, nec
Kathy Gillis

D-U-N-S 20-727-5124   (BR)
PUROLATOR INC
(*Suby of* GOVERNMENT OF CANADA)
220 Joseph Zatzman Dr, Dartmouth, NS, B3B 1P4
(902) 468-1611
Emp Here 100
SIC 7389 Business services, nec
Tom Mcmenamon

D-U-N-S 20-025-4571   (HQ)
QUALITY CONCRETE INC
(*Suby of* L & M ENTERPRISES LIMITED)
20 Macdonald Ave, Dartmouth, NS, B3B 1C5

(902) 468-8040
Emp Here 20   *Sales* 21,864,718
SIC 3273 Ready-mixed concrete
Daryl Cail
Scott Stevens
Thane Stevens
Chris Sangster

D-U-N-S 20-023-7787   (SL)
RE/MAX NOVA REAL ESTATE
BIRCHGROW REALTY
7 Mellor Ave Unit 1, Dartmouth, NS, B3B 0E8
(902) 478-0991
Emp Here 45   *Sales* 12,229,020
SIC 6531 Real estate agents and managers
Elvin Chaisson

D-U-N-S 24-190-1438   (HQ)
REGIONAL RESIDENTIAL SERVICES SOCIETY
202 Brownlow Ave Suite Lkd1, Dartmouth, NS, B3B 1T5
(902) 465-4022
Emp Here 15   *Sales* 30,855,360
SIC 8361 Residential care
Brenda Dixon

D-U-N-S 24-341-7367   (HQ)
RKO STEEL LIMITED
85 Macdonald Ave, Dartmouth, NS, B3B 1T8
(902) 468-1322
Sales 19,208,500
SIC 3441 Fabricated structural Metal
Ian Oulton
Patricia Cunningham
Tom Skinner
Stewart Clark
Steve Arklie

D-U-N-S 24-472-0090   (SL)
RODNEY ENTERPRISES LIMITED
20 Raddall Ave, Dartmouth, NS, B3B 1T2
(902) 468-2601
Emp Here 25   *Sales* 18,563,000
SIC 5199 Nondurable goods, nec
Ronald Jefferson
Tim Pedersen

D-U-N-S 25-645-5627   (BR)
ROYAL & SUN ALLIANCE INSURANCE COMPANY OF CANADA
(*Suby of* RSA INSURANCE GROUP PLC)
50 Garland Ave Suite 101, Dartmouth, NS, B3B 0A3
(902) 493-1500
Emp Here 150
SIC 6331 Fire, marine, and casualty insurance

D-U-N-S 25-884-6591   (SL)
SAFETY FIRST CONTRACTING (1995) LTD
SAFETY FIRST-SFC
116 Thorne Ave, Dartmouth, NS, B3B 1Z2
(902) 464-0889
Emp Here 260   *Sales* 73,557,900
SIC 3669 Communications equipment, nec
James Macdonald
Edward Hennessey

D-U-N-S 24-191-2039   (SL)
SAFETY SERVICES NOVA SCOTIA
201 Brownlow Ave Unit 1, Dartmouth, NS, B3B 1W2
(902) 454-9621
Emp Here 111   *Sales* 28,137,390
SIC 8748 Business consulting, nec
David Powers
Jeff Brett
Jackie Norman
Dave Shannon
Chris Goudge

D-U-N-S 20-906-7966   (HQ)
SCOTIA RECYCLING LIMITED
(*Suby of* SCOTIA INVESTMENTS LIMITED)
5 Brown Ave, Dartmouth, NS, B3B 1Z7
(902) 468-5650
Emp Here 16   *Sales* 52,147,500
SIC 5093 Scrap and waste materials

George Bishop
Dwight Whynot
Joe Lord
Barbara Moores
David Hennigar
Bruce Jodrey

D-U-N-S 20-444-5993   (HQ)
SEABOARD LIQUID CARRIERS LIMITED
SEABOARD TRANSPORT GROUP
721 Wilkinson Ave, Dartmouth, NS, B3B 0H4
(902) 468-4447
Emp Here 100   *Sales* 138,285,750
SIC 4212 Local trucking, without storage
Mark Shannon
Joel Shannon
Bob Macquarrie
David Macdonald
Todd Stauffer
Jim Dibbin
Ryan Conrod
Mike Cannavino

D-U-N-S 24-833-9913   (HQ)
SEAMASTERS SERVICES LIMITED
SEA GLASS INDUSTRIES, DIV OF
647 Windmill Rd, Dartmouth, NS, B3B 1B7
(902) 468-5967
Emp Here 35   *Sales* 19,923,120
SIC 5551 Boat dealers
John Mills
William L. Ryan

D-U-N-S 25-999-6507   (BR)
SOURCE ATLANTIC LIMITED
HYDRAULICS, RIGGING & RUBBER
(*Suby of* SKYLINE HOLDINGS INCORPORATED)
14 Akerley Blvd, Dartmouth, NS, B3B 1J3
(902) 494-5377
Emp Here 250
SIC 5999 Miscellaneous retail stores, nec

D-U-N-S 25-286-0564   (HQ)
SPARTAN ATHLETIC PRODUCTS LIMITED
SPARTAN FITNESS EQUIPMENT
10 Morris Dr Unit 13, Dartmouth, NS, B3B 1K8
(902) 482-0330
Emp Here 10   *Sales* 10,410,840
SIC 5091 Sporting and recreation goods
John William Lewis
Christopher Cluett
Carol Smith
Robert Warwick
Kevin Swicker
Steven Mcneil

D-U-N-S 20-810-1829   (HQ)
STEELE AUTO GROUP LIMITED
8 Basinview Dr, Dartmouth, NS, B3B 1G4
(902) 454-3185
Sales 24,903,900
SIC 5511 New and used car dealers
Rob Steele

D-U-N-S 20-008-9634   (SL)
STEELE VOLKSWAGEN LIMITED
696 Windmill Rd, Dartmouth, NS, B3B 2A5
(902) 468-6411
Emp Here 31   *Sales* 15,440,418
SIC 5511 New and used car dealers
Robert Steele

D-U-N-S 24-669-5670   (HQ)
STELLAR INDUSTRIAL SALES LIMITED
FLEXSTAR
520 Windmill Rd, Dartmouth, NS, B3B 1B3
(902) 468-5499
Emp Here 17   *Sales* 14,250,780
SIC 5085 Industrial supplies
Chris Giannou
Chris Maher

D-U-N-S 25-627-4309   (BR)
STOCK TRANSPORTATION LTD
(*Suby of* NATIONAL EXPRESS GROUP PLC)
51 Frazee Ave, Dartmouth, NS, B3B 1Z4

(902) 481-8400
Emp Here 350
SIC 4151 School buses
Troy Phinney

D-U-N-S 24-669-9888   (SL)
STRICTLY SALES & SERVICE INC
STRICTLY HYDRAULICS
125 Trider Cres, Dartmouth, NS, B3B 1V6
(902) 468-5308
Emp Here 22   *Sales* 10,450,572
SIC 5084 Industrial machinery and equipment
Douglas Lively
Ian Lively

D-U-N-S 25-411-4614   (HQ)
TANGRAM SURFACES INC
CENTURA FLOOR & WALL FASHIONS
66 Wright Ave, Dartmouth, NS, B3B 1H3
(902) 468-7679
Emp Here 28   *Sales* 17,886,960
SIC 5032 Brick, stone, and related material
Peter Maddalena
John Walsh
Evelyn Maddelano
Brian Cowie

D-U-N-S 24-955-7364   (HQ)
TAR INVESTMENTS LIMITED
ATLANTIC BUSINESS INTERIOR
30 Troop Ave, Dartmouth, NS, B3B 1Z1
(902) 468-3200
Sales 18,870,975
SIC 6719 Holding companies, nec
Thomas Rose
Garry Stewart

D-U-N-S 25-816-9770   (SL)
TIM DEALER SERVICES INCORPORATED
250 Brownlow Ave Suite 7, Dartmouth, NS, B3B 1W9
(902) 468-7177
Emp Here 87   *Sales* 15,426,057
SIC 7371 Custom computer programming services
Richard Macdonald
Pierre Cote

D-U-N-S 20-371-1817   (BR)
TOROMONT INDUSTRIES LTD
TOROMONT CAT (MARITIMES)
(*Suby of* TOROMONT INDUSTRIES LTD)
175 Akerley Blvd, Dartmouth, NS, B3B 3Z6
(902) 468-0581
Emp Here 310
SIC 5082 Construction and mining machinery

D-U-N-S 20-444-4376   (HQ)
TRUEFOAM LIMITED
11 Mosher Dr, Dartmouth, NS, B3B 1L8
(902) 468-5440
Emp Here 50   *Sales* 29,441,720
SIC 5211 Lumber and other building materials
Deborah Coles

D-U-N-S 20-717-3774   (HQ)
TUDHOPE CARTAGE LIMITED
(*Suby of* SEABOARD LIQUID CARRIERS LIMITED)
4 Vidito Dr, Dartmouth, NS, B3B 1P9
(902) 468-4447
Emp Here 20   *Sales* 20,570,600
SIC 4213 Trucking, except local
Mark Shannon

D-U-N-S 20-139-8679   (SL)
VANITY FASHIONS LIMITED
34 Payzant Ave, Dartmouth, NS, B3B 1Z6
(902) 468-6763
Emp Here 35   *Sales* 18,218,970
SIC 5094 Jewelry and precious stones
Brian Schwartz

D-U-N-S 25-297-7467   (BR)
WAL-MART CANADA CORP
(*Suby of* WALMART INC.)
90 Lamont Terr, Dartmouth, NS, B3B 0B5
(902) 461-4474
Emp Here 249

SIC 5311 Department stores
Kenny Macdonald

D-U-N-S 20-702-7934   (BR)
XEROX CANADA LTD
DOCUMENT COMPANY, THE
(Suby of XEROX CORPORATION)
215-237 Brownlow Ave, Dartmouth, NS, B3B
2C6
(902) 470-3000
Emp Here 146
SIC 5044 Office equipment
Cameron Bruce

D-U-N-S 25-689-8131   (SL)
XL ELECTRIC LIMITED
118 Cutler Ave, Dartmouth, NS, B3B 0J6
(902) 468-7708
Emp Here 60   *Sales* 13,069,740
SIC 1731 Electrical work
Nicole Soontiens
Ilona Macalpine

D-U-N-S 24-991-0972   (BR)
**YARMOUTH ASSOCIATION FOR COMMU-
NITY RESIDENTIAL OPTIONS**
1 Gloster Crt, Dartmouth, NS, B3B 1X9
(902) 832-0433
Emp Here 101
SIC 8322 Individual and family services
Kevin Walker

Debert, NS B0M

D-U-N-S 24-671-1618   (BR)
HOME HARDWARE STORES LIMITED
*HOME HARDWARE DISTRIBUTION CEN-
TRE*
*(Suby of HOME HARDWARE STORES LIM-
ITED)*
336 Lancaster Cres, Debert, NS, B0M 1G0
(902) 662-2800
Emp Here 200
SIC 5211 Lumber and other building materials
Pamela Mcewing

D-U-N-S 24-126-5396   (SL)
KOHLTECH INTERNATIONAL LIMITED
*PETER KOHLER WINDOWS & ENTRANCE
SYSTEMS*
583 Macelmon Rd, Debert, NS, B0M 1G0
(902) 662-3100
Emp Here 400   *Sales* 76,948,000
SIC 2431 Millwork
Kevin Pelley
Carl Ballard

D-U-N-S 20-782-7502   (SL)
MASSTOWN MARKET LIMITED
10622 Highway 2, Debert, NS, B0M 1G0
(902) 662-2816
Emp Here 110   *Sales* 32,282,470
SIC 5431 Fruit and vegetable markets
Eric Jennings
Laurie Jennings
Priscilla Jennings

D-U-N-S 20-937-5666   (HQ)
**NEWPORT CUSTOM METAL FABRICA-
TIONS INC**
*(Suby of UNITED STATES STOVE COM-
PANY)*
114 Lancaster Cres Lot 208, Debert, NS, B0M
1G0
(902) 662-3840
Emp Here 45   *Sales* 14,430,065
SIC 3585 Refrigeration and heating equip-
ment
Kenneth Johnson
Jim Johnson
Nancy Newport

D-U-N-S 24-124-6524   (BR)
SOBEYS CAPITAL INCORPORATED
SOBEYS ATLANTIC

(Suby of EMPIRE COMPANY LIMITED)
246 Lancaster Cres, Debert, NS, B0M 1G0
(902) 752-8371
Emp Here 100
SIC 5411 Grocery stores
Dave Goodwin

Digby, NS B0V

D-U-N-S 25-082-5973   (BR)
ATLANTIC WHOLESALERS LTD
ATLANTIC SUPERSTORE, THE
(Suby of LOBLAW COMPANIES LIMITED)
470 Warwick St, Digby, NS, B0V 1A0
(902) 245-4108
Emp Here 95
SIC 5411 Grocery stores
Butch Reitzel

D-U-N-S 24-832-8320   (SL)
BIRCH STREET SEAFOODS LTD
31 Birch St, Digby, NS, B0V 1A0
(902) 245-6551
Emp Here 32   *Sales* 26,738,464
SIC 5142 Packaged frozen goods
Janice Oliver
Alan Frankland
William Cottreau

D-U-N-S 25-882-4739   (SL)
BROAD COVE FISHERIES
1631 Culloden Rd, Digby, NS, B0V 1A0
(902) 532-7301
Emp Here 40   *Sales* 33,423,080
SIC 5146 Fish and seafoods
Fred Comeau

D-U-N-S 20-907-3162   (SL)
**DIGBY TOWN AND MUNICIPAL HOUSING
CORPORATION, THE**
TIDEVIEW TERRACE
74 Pleasant St, Digby, NS, B0V 1A0
(902) 245-4718
Emp Here 49   *Sales* 13,442,268
SIC 8741 Management services
Debra Boudreau

D-U-N-S 20-986-8769   (HQ)
**FAIRWAY INSURANCE SERVICES INCOR-
PORATED**
104 Montague Row, Digby, NS, B0V 1A0
(902) 245-4741
Emp Here 29   *Sales* 138,580,650
SIC 6411 Insurance agents, brokers, and ser-
vice
Sarah Amirault
Keith Amirault
Jana Amirault

D-U-N-S 20-780-7959   (HQ)
GIDNEY FISHERIES LIMITED
136 Dakin Park Rd, Digby, NS, B0V 1A0
(902) 834-2775
Sales 11,881,518
SIC 5146 Fish and seafoods
Barry Gidney
Robert Macdonald

D-U-N-S 20-813-6812   (HQ)
**LEBLANC, GUY ENTERPRISES (1984) LIM-
ITED**
GUY FRENCHY'S OF DIGBY
343 Conway Rd, Digby, NS, B0V 1A0
(902) 245-2211
Emp Here 14   *Sales* 51,390,360
SIC 5932 Used merchandise stores
Guy Leblanc
Delma Leblanc

D-U-N-S 25-412-3847   (BR)
NOVA SCOTIA HEALTH AUTHORITY
DIGBY GENERAL HOSPITAL
(Suby of NOVA SCOTIA, PROVINCE OF)
75 Warwick St, Digby, NS, B0V 1A0

(902) 245-2501
Emp Here 140
SIC 8062 General medical and surgical hospi-
tals
Hubert D'entremont

D-U-N-S 20-390-3328   (SL)
SCOTIA HARVEST INC
O'NEIL FISHERIES
144 Water St, Digby, NS, B0V 1A0
(902) 245-6528
Emp Here 100   *Sales* 83,557,700
SIC 5146 Fish and seafoods
Jean Guy D'entremont

Dominion, NS B1G

D-U-N-S 20-754-5943   (SL)
DOMINION HAWKS CLUB
28 Lower Mitchell Ave, Dominion, NS, B1G
1L2
(902) 849-0414
Emp Here 49   *Sales* 19,800,803
SIC 8699 Membership organizations, nec
John Stefura

East Mountain, NS B6L

D-U-N-S 20-031-0308   (SL)
WILSON EQUIPMENT LIMITED
66 Atlantic Central Dr, East Mountain, NS, B6L
2A3
(902) 895-1611
Emp Here 40   *Sales* 19,001,040
SIC 5082 Construction and mining machinery
Peter Fahey

Eastern Passage, NS B3G

D-U-N-S 20-781-7115   (HQ)
AUTOPORT LIMITED
*(Suby of COMPAGNIE DES CHEMINS DE
FER NATIONAUX DU CANADA)*
1180 Main Rd, Eastern Passage, NS, B3G
0B5
(902) 465-6050
Emp Here 130   *Sales* 82,971,450
SIC 4226 Special warehousing and storage,
nec
Sean Finn
Hunt Cary Iv
Bernd Beyer

D-U-N-S 25-683-0613   (SL)
H & H FISHERIES LIMITED
FISH BASKET, THE
100 Government Wharf Rd, Eastern Passage,
NS, B3G 1M5

Emp Here 30   *Sales* 25,067,310
SIC 5146 Fish and seafoods

D-U-N-S 24-130-5390   (SL)
OCEAN VIEW MANOR SOCIETY
1909 Caldwell Rd, Eastern Passage, NS, B3G
1M4

Emp Here 200   *Sales* 13,665,200
SIC 8051 Skilled nursing care facilities
Dion Mouland
Linda Judge
Mary Wile
James Young
Becky Kent
Beth Floyd
Debbie Mumford
Brian Cox
Valerie Wadden

Edwardsville, NS B2A

D-U-N-S 20-933-4424   (SL)
CAPE BRETON BEVERAGES LIMITED
65 Harbour Dr, Edwardsville, NS, B2A 4T7
(902) 564-4536
Emp Here 50   *Sales* 11,242,750
SIC 2086 Bottled and canned soft drinks
M. Andre Cote
James Chisholm
Stanley Macdonald
John Maclean

D-U-N-S 24-761-8239   (SL)
**EAST COAST METAL FABRICATION (2015)
INC**
LSF
10 Marine Dr, Edwardsville, NS, B2A 4S6
(902) 564-5600
Emp Here 50   *Sales* 10,206,500
SIC 3312 Blast furnaces and steel mills
James Kehoe
Joe Hines

D-U-N-S 24-378-8663   (SL)
SUPREME TANK INCORPORATED
26 Harbour Dr, Edwardsville, NS, B2A 4T4
(902) 564-9504
Emp Here 50   *Sales* 23,450,250
SIC 5984 Liquefied petroleum gas dealers
Brian Young

Elmsdale, NS B2S

D-U-N-S 25-706-4105   (HQ)
**ASSOCIATED MARITIME PHARMACIES
LIMITED**
PHARMASAVE
269 Highway 214 Unit 2, Elmsdale, NS, B2S
1K1
(902) 883-8018
Emp Here 50   *Sales* 19,546,240
SIC 5912 Drug stores and proprietary stores

D-U-N-S 20-743-4700   (BR)
ATLANTIC WHOLESALERS LTD
REAL ATLANTIC SUPERSTORE, THE
(Suby of LOBLAW COMPANIES LIMITED)
295 Highway 214, Elmsdale, NS, B2S 2L1
(902) 883-1180
Emp Here 80
SIC 5411 Grocery stores
Rod Noble

D-U-N-S 24-605-2047   (SL)
BASIN CONTRACTING LIMITED
100 Bedrock Lane, Elmsdale, NS, B2S 2B1
(902) 883-2235
Emp Here 90   *Sales* 22,719,780
SIC 1611 Highway and street construction
Fred Benere

D-U-N-S 20-008-2711   (SL)
CANADIAN TIRE
269 Highway 214, Elmsdale, NS, B2S 1K1
(902) 883-1771
Emp Here 30   *Sales* 10,926,450
SIC 5014 Tires and tubes

D-U-N-S 20-780-7462   (SL)
ELMSDALE LANDSCAPING LIMITED
113 Elmsdale Rd, Elmsdale, NS, B2S 1K7
(902) 883-2291
Emp Here 115   *Sales* 12,568,235
SIC 0782 Lawn and garden services
Dennis Coupar
George Coupar

D-U-N-S 20-188-2797   (SL)
ELMSDALE SOD FARMS LIMITED
113 Elmsdale Rd, Elmsdale, NS, B2S 1K7
(902) 883-2291
Emp Here 30   *Sales* 10,274,010

▲ Public Company   ■ Public Company Family Member   **HQ** Headquarters   **BR** Branch   **SL** Single Location

SIC 0181 Ornamental nursery products
George Coupar
Murray Coupar

D-U-N-S 24-804-1477   (BR)
SOBEYS CAPITAL INCORPORATED
SOBEYS #660
(*Suby of* EMPIRE COMPANY LIMITED)
269 Highway 214 Unit 1, Elmsdale, NS, B2S
1K1
(902) 883-8111
Emp Here 180
SIC 5411 Grocery stores
Troy Strang

Enfield, NS B2T

D-U-N-S 24-123-1575   (BR)
AIR CANADA
(*Suby of* AIR CANADA)
1 Bell Blvd Suite 7, Enfield, NS, B2T 1K2
(902) 873-2350
Emp Here 100
SIC 4581 Airports, flying fields, and services
Brad Murray

D-U-N-S 25-973-5330   (SL)
**HALIFAX INTERNATIONAL AIRPORT AU-
THORITY**
1 Bell Blvd Fl 3, Enfield, NS, B2T 1K2
(902) 873-4422
Emp Here 145   *Sales* 68,932,358
SIC 4581 Airports, flying fields, and services
Peter J E Mcdonough
J Robert Winters
Wadih M Fares
Cheryl Newcombe
Michele A Wood-Tweel
Jeffrey R Hunt

D-U-N-S 24-381-3727   (SL)
HUDSON GROUP CANADA, INC
THE HUDSON GROUP
1 Bell Blvd Suite 1621, Enfield, NS, B2T 1K2
(902) 873-3282
Emp Here 60   *Sales* 14,659,680
SIC 5947 Gift, novelty, and souvenir shop
Joseph Didomizio
Jay Marshall
James Cowan

D-U-N-S 24-789-8315   (BR)
PRATT & WHITNEY CANADA CIE
(*Suby of* PRATT AERO LIMITED PARTNER-
SHIP)
189 Pratt Whitney Pk, Enfield, NS, B2T 1L1
(902) 873-4241
Emp Here 500
SIC 3724 Aircraft engines and engine parts
John Saabas

Eskasoni, NS B1W

D-U-N-S 25-394-4318   (BR)
ESKASONI SCHOOL BOARD
*ESKASONI ELEMENTARY & MIDDLE
SCHOOL*
(*Suby of* ESKASONI SCHOOL BOARD)
4645 Shore Rd, Eskasoni, NS, B1W 1K3
(902) 379-2825
Emp Here 100
SIC 8211 Elementary and secondary schools
Cameron Frost

D-U-N-S 24-356-0351   (HQ)
ESKASONI SCHOOL BOARD
4645 Shore Rd, Eskasoni, NS, B1W 1K3
(902) 379-2507
Emp Here 8   *Sales* 14,867,850
SIC 8211 Elementary and secondary schools
Elizabeth Primo

Fall River, NS B2T

D-U-N-S 20-568-9289   (BR)
HALIFAX REGIONAL SCHOOL BOARD
LOCKVIEW HIGH SCHOOL
(*Suby of* HALIFAX REGIONAL SCHOOL
BOARD)
148 Lockview Rd, Fall River, NS, B2T 1J1
(902) 860-6000
Emp Here 89
SIC 8211 Elementary and secondary schools
Bernie Maceachern

Falmouth, NS B0P

D-U-N-S 20-026-0677   (HQ)
AVON VALLEY FLORAL INC
AVON VALLEY FLORAL
285 Town Rd Rr 2, Falmouth, NS, B0P 1L0
(902) 798-8381
Emp Here 100   *Sales* 26,230,900
SIC 0181 Ornamental nursery products
Kevin White
Kevin Matheson

D-U-N-S 20-026-0750   (SL)
POTHIER MOTORS LTD
18 Falmouth Back Rd, Falmouth, NS, B0P 1L0
(877) 286-0154
Emp Here 38   *Sales* 18,926,964
SIC 5511 New and used car dealers
John Pothier

Fletchers Lake, NS B2T

D-U-N-S 24-471-9816   (SL)
BARRACUDA HEATING SERVICE LTD
152 Holland Rd, Fletchers Lake, NS, B2T 1A1
(902) 576-3020
Emp Here 49   *Sales* 10,825,766
SIC 1711 Plumbing, heating, air-conditioning
Chris Stevens

Fortress Of Louisbourg, NS B1C

D-U-N-S 25-503-2864   (SL)
**FORTRESS OF LOUISBOURG ASSOCIA-
TION**
259 Park Service Rd, Fortress Of Louisbourg,
NS, B1C 2L2
(902) 733-2280
Emp Here 50   *Sales* 12,216,400
SIC 5947 Gift, novelty, and souvenir shop
Mitch Mcnutt

Glace Bay, NS B1A

D-U-N-S 20-208-0276   (SL)
A & E WARDELL LTD
CANADIAN TIRE
130 Reserve St, Glace Bay, NS, B1A 4W5
(902) 842-0077
Emp Here 35   *Sales* 17,432,730
SIC 5531 Auto and home supply stores
Adrian Wardell

D-U-N-S 24-443-1933   (SL)
ARGENT FISHERIES (2007) LIMITED
501 Main St, Glace Bay, NS, B1A 4X5
(902) 849-1005
Emp Here 49   *Sales* 10,369,037
SIC 0912 Finfish
Eliot Lieberman

D-U-N-S 25-614-5509   (BR)
ATLANTIC WHOLESALERS LTD
REAL ATLANTIC SUPERSTORE, THE
(*Suby of* LOBLAW COMPANIES LIMITED)
155 Reserve St, Glace Bay, NS, B1A 4W3
(902) 842-9609
Emp Here 108
SIC 5411 Grocery stores
Fred Bourgeois

D-U-N-S 20-073-1920   (SL)
CANADIAN TIRE ASSOCIATES STORE
*CANADIAN TIRE 229 GLACE BAY NOVA
SCOTIA*
130 Reserve St, Glace Bay, NS, B1A 4W5
(902) 842-0700
Emp Here 40   *Sales* 10,122,360
SIC 5251 Hardware stores
Gordon Mcdonald

D-U-N-S 20-026-2541   (HQ)
MEDICAL HALL (1978) LIMITED
MEDICAL HALL PHARMASAVE
135 Commercial St, Glace Bay, NS, B1A 3B9
(902) 849-6552
Sales 11,382,930
SIC 5912 Drug stores and proprietary stores

D-U-N-S 20-933-4101   (SL)
SEAVIEW MANOR CORPORATION
275 South St, Glace Bay, NS, B1A 1W6
(902) 849-7300
Emp Here 130   *Sales* 8,882,380
SIC 8051 Skilled nursing care facilities
Shirley Harvey
Leonard Stevenson
Allison Macdermitt

D-U-N-S 20-514-2552   (BR)
STREAM INTERNATIONAL CANADA ULC
STREAM
(*Suby of* SYNNEX CORPORATION)
95 Union St, Glace Bay, NS, B1A 2P6
(902) 842-3800
Emp Here 909
SIC 7389 Business services, nec
Maureen Latham

Goffs, NS B2T

D-U-N-S 24-851-6218   (SL)
**AIT WORLDWIDE LOGISTICS (CANADA),
INC**
(*Suby of* AIT WORLDWIDE LOGISTICS,
INC.)
588 Barnes Dr, Goffs, NS, B2T 1K3
(902) 873-5285
Emp Here 50   *Sales* 16,237,700
SIC 4512 Air transportation, scheduled
Alan Spencer
Rory Macarty
Lee Davison
Adam Lovett

D-U-N-S 25-367-5292   (BR)
ASPLUNDH CANADA ULC
ASPLUNDH TREE SERVICE ULC
(*Suby of* ASPLUNDH TREE EXPERT, LLC)
645 Pratt And Whitney Dr Suite 1, Goffs, NS,
B2T 0H4
(902) 468-8733
Emp Here 80
SIC 7299 Miscellaneous personal service
Steven Christiansen

D-U-N-S 24-773-1131   (SL)
ATLANTIC SKY SERVICE
647 Barnes Dr, Goffs, NS, B2T 1K3
(902) 873-3575
Emp Here 49   *Sales* 15,912,946
SIC 4522 Air transportation, nonscheduled
Dennis Figueiredo

D-U-N-S 24-317-5176   (BR)

**L-3 COMMUNICATIONS ELECTRONIC SYS-
TEMS INC**
249 Aerotech Dr, Goffs, NS, B2T 1K3
(902) 873-2000
Emp Here 159   *Sales* 741,765
SIC 3812 Search and navigation equipment
Stewart Downing

D-U-N-S 24-203-9050   (HQ)
WORLD LINK FOOD DISTRIBUTORS INC
209 Aerotech Dr Unit 10-12b, Goffs, NS, B2T
1K3
(902) 423-0787
Sales 15,040,386
SIC 5146 Fish and seafoods
Georges Jobert
Sara Liu
Paul Shore

Goodwood, NS B3T

D-U-N-S 24-913-0089   (SL)
**COASTAL RESTORATIONS & MASONRY
LIMITED**
8 Mills Dr, Goodwood, NS, B3T 1P3
(902) 876-8333
Emp Here 100   *Sales* 24,748,300
SIC 1771 Concrete work
Brice Morash
Beverly Morash

Goshen, NS B0H

D-U-N-S 24-669-5431   (SL)
**NORTH EASTERN CHRISTMAS TREE AS-
SOCIATION**
799 South River Lake Rd, Goshen, NS, B0H
1M0
(902) 783-2430
Emp Here 20   *Sales* 14,850,400
SIC 5199 Nondurable goods, nec
David Sweet
Donald Macmillan
Jim Webber
Norman Macisaac

Great Village, NS B0M

D-U-N-S 20-206-2860   (SL)
**ATLANTIC HIGHWAYS MANAGEMENT
CORPORATION LIMITED**
TOLL PLAZA COBEQUID PASS
209 Cobequid Pass, Great Village, NS, B0M
1L0
(902) 668-2211
Emp Here 37   *Sales* 14,258,320
SIC 4785 Inspection and fixed facilities
Wayne Crossan

D-U-N-S 25-734-1743   (SL)
BALAMORE FARM LTD
9036 Highway 2, Great Village, NS, B0M 1L0
(902) 668-2005
Emp Here 30   *Sales* 10,274,010
SIC 0191 General farms, primarily crop
Joseph Cooper

Greenfield, NS B0T

D-U-N-S 20-026-3515   (SL)
FREEMAN, HARRY AND SON LIMITED
FREEMAN LUMBER
4804 Meedway River Rd, Greenfield, NS, B0T
1E0

---

(902) 685-2792
Emp Here 100   *Sales* 44,717,400
SIC 5031 Lumber, plywood, and millwork
 Charles Freeman
 Richard Freeman

Greenwood, NS B0P

D-U-N-S 24-393-9605   (SL)
ANE STEWART LTD
CANADIAN TIRE
730 Central Ave, Greenwood, NS, B0P 1N0
(902) 765-6338
Emp Here 60   *Sales* 37,756,800
SIC 5531 Auto and home supply stores
 Darell Stewart

D-U-N-S 25-689-7067   (HQ)
AVERY'S FARM MARKETS LIMITED
619 Central Ave, Greenwood, NS, B0P 1R0
(902) 765-0224
Emp Here 5   *Sales* 38,152,010
SIC 5431 Fruit and vegetable markets
 Stephen Avery
 Elizabeth Avery

Hacketts Cove, NS B3Z

D-U-N-S 20-522-8976   (HQ)
NAUTEL LIMITED
(*Suby of* NAUTEL CAPITAL CORPORATION INC)
10089 Peggys Cove Rd Hwy 333, Hacketts Cove, NS, B3Z 3J4
(902) 823-3900
Sales 28,566,300
SIC 3663 Radio and t.v. communications equipment
 Kevin Rodgers
 Michael Morris
 Darlene Fowlow

Halifax, NS B3H

D-U-N-S 20-793-6589   (BR)
ARAMARK CANADA LTD.
(*Suby of* ARAMARK)
923 Robie St, Halifax, NS, B3H 3C3
(902) 420-5599
Emp Here 150
SIC 5812 Eating places
 Joe Makary

D-U-N-S 24-932-1936   (HQ)
ATLANTIC PROVINCES SPECIAL EDUCATION AUTHORITY
APSEA
5940 South St, Halifax, NS, B3H 1S6
(902) 423-8469
Sales 26,762,130
SIC 8211 Elementary and secondary schools
 Bertram R. Tulk
 Heather Conrad

D-U-N-S 25-891-4605   (BR)
ATLANTIC WHOLESALERS LTD
BARRINGTON MARKET SUPERSTORE
(*Suby of* LOBLAW COMPANIES LIMITED)
1075 Barrington St, Halifax, NS, B3H 4P1
(902) 492-3240
Emp Here 200
SIC 5411 Grocery stores
 Darren Hillier

D-U-N-S 20-728-1478   (BR)
COMMONWEALTH HOSPITALITY LTD
HOLIDAY INN
(*Suby of* WXI/WWH PARALLEL AMALCO (ONTARIO) LTD)

1980 Robie St, Halifax, NS, B3H 3G5
(902) 423-1161
Emp Here 120
SIC 7011 Hotels and motels
 David Clark

D-U-N-S 20-779-9404   (HQ)
DALHOUSIE UNIVERSITY
6299 South St, Halifax, NS, B3H 4J1
(902) 494-2211
Sales 846,078,000
SIC 8221 Colleges and universities
 Richard Florizone
 Carolyn Watters
 John Newhook
 Ian Nason
 Peter Fardy

D-U-N-S 20-063-8141   (BR)
DALHOUSIE UNIVERSITY
DEPARTMENT OF ANATOMY
(*Suby of* DALHOUSIE UNIVERSITY)
5850 College St Unit 13b, Halifax, NS, B3H 1X5
(902) 494-6850
Emp Here 75
SIC 8221 Colleges and universities
 William Baldridge

D-U-N-S 20-346-9846   (BR)
DALHOUSIE UNIVERSITY
FACULTY OF ARTS AND SOCIAL SCIENCES
(*Suby of* DALHOUSIE UNIVERSITY)
6135 University Ave Rm 3030, Halifax, NS, B3H 4P9
(902) 494-1440
Emp Here 200
SIC 8221 Colleges and universities

D-U-N-S 20-346-6537   (BR)
DALHOUSIE UNIVERSITY
FACULTY OF MEDICINE
(*Suby of* DALHOUSIE UNIVERSITY)
1276 South Park St Rm 225, Halifax, NS, B3H 2Y9
(902) 473-7736
Emp Here 300
SIC 8221 Colleges and universities
 Romesh Shukla

D-U-N-S 24-572-9397   (SL)
HALIFAX GRAIN ELEVATOR LIMITED
951 South Bland St, Halifax, NS, B3H 4S6
(902) 421-1714
Emp Here 15   *Sales* 22,015,380
SIC 5153 Grain and field beans
 Allen Stevens

D-U-N-S 24-532-2631   (SL)
HALIFAX PORT AUTHORITY
1215 Marginal Rd, Halifax, NS, B3H 4P8
(902) 426-8222
Emp Here 70   *Sales* 30,193,788
SIC 4491 Marine cargo handling
 Karen Oldfield
 Hector Jacques
 Thomas Hayes
 Paul MacIsaac
 Krista Dempsey
 David Cameron
 Diana Dalton
 Jim Spatz
 Anne Soucie
 Carole-Ann Miller

D-U-N-S 24-750-7473   (BR)
HALIFAX REGIONAL SCHOOL BOARD
CITADEL HIGH
(*Suby of* HALIFAX REGIONAL SCHOOL BOARD)
1855 Trollope St, Halifax, NS, B3H 0A4
(902) 491-4444
Emp Here 98
SIC 8211 Elementary and secondary schools
 Debbie Rowsell

D-U-N-S 20-606-5554   (SL)

HALIFAX STUDENT HOUSING SOCIETY
1094 Wellington St, Halifax, NS, B3H 2Z9
(902) 494-6888
Emp Here 45   *Sales* 17,883,630
SIC 8699 Membership organizations, nec
 Christine Ryan

D-U-N-S 20-589-5899   (SL)
HALTERM LIMITED
(*Suby of* MACQUARIE INFRASTRUCTURE CORPORATION)
577 Marginal Rd, Halifax, NS, B3H 4P6
(902) 421-1778
Emp Here 225   *Sales* 78,156,225
SIC 4491 Marine cargo handling
 Doug Rose
 Paul Brigley

D-U-N-S 25-580-5590   (SL)
HOTEL N.S. OWNERSHIP LIMITED PARTNERSHIP
WESTIN NOVA SCOTIAN HOTEL, THE
1181 Hollis St Suite 1, Halifax, NS, B3H 2P6
(902) 421-1000
Emp Here 225   *Sales* 21,525,300
SIC 7011 Hotels and motels
 Gido Kerpel

D-U-N-S 20-072-4719   (SL)
IWK HEALTH CENTRE CHARITABLE FOUNDATIONS
5855 Spring Garden Rd Suite B220, Halifax, NS, B3H 4S2
(902) 470-8085
Emp Here 28   *Sales* 11,127,592
SIC 8699 Membership organizations, nec
 Jennifer Gillivan

D-U-N-S 20-781-8089   (SL)
LOGISTEC STEVEDORING (NOVA SCOTIA) INC.
(*Suby of* LOGISTEC CORPORATION)
1096 Marginal Rd Suite 208, Halifax, NS, B3H 4N4
(902) 422-7483
Emp Here 75   *Sales* 29,529,300
SIC 4491 Marine cargo handling
 Anthony Steele

D-U-N-S 20-257-3739   (SL)
MAKE-A-WISH FOUNDATION (OF THE) ATLANTIC PROVINCES
5991 Spring Garden Rd Suite 705, Halifax, NS, B3H 1Y6
(902) 466-9474
Emp Here 50   *Sales* 19,870,700
SIC 8699 Membership organizations, nec
 Gerald Walsh
 Josh Santimaw
 Beth Cole
 Veronica Hunt
 Dennis Graves
 Owen Macneil
 Craig Sampson
 Paul Griffith
 Robert Thacker
 Cathy Deagle-Gammon

D-U-N-S 20-728-6089   (HQ)
NOVA SCOTIA HEALTH AUTHORITY
QUEEN ELIZABETH II HEALTH SCIENCES CENTRE
(*Suby of* NOVA SCOTIA, PROVINCE OF)
1276 South Park St Suite 1278, Halifax, NS, B3H 2Y9
(902) 473-5117
Emp Here 200   *Sales* 1,332,960,000
SIC 8062 General medical and surgical hospitals
 Steve Parker
 George Unsworth
 Janet Knox
 Allan Horsburgh
 Lindsay Peach
 Tricia Cochrane
 Tim Guest
 Paula Bond

Lynne Harrigan
Colin Stevenson

D-U-N-S 25-783-4614   (BR)
NOVA SCOTIA HEALTH AUTHORITY
HALIFAX INFIRMARY
(*Suby of* NOVA SCOTIA, PROVINCE OF)
1278 Tower Rd, Halifax, NS, B3H 2Y9
(902) 473-1787
Emp Here 2,000
SIC 8062 General medical and surgical hospitals
 Janet Knox

D-U-N-S 20-782-0895   (HQ)
SAINT MARY'S UNIVERSITY
SMU
923 Robie St Suite 210, Halifax, NS, B3H 3C3
(902) 420-5400
Emp Here 2,530   *Sales* 112,320,955
SIC 8221 Colleges and universities
 Robert Summerby-Murray
 Malcolm Butler
 Gabrielle Morrison
 Esther Enns
 Michelle Wood-Tweel
 Scott Norton
 Alan Abraham Jr
 Paul Baxter
 Barb Bel
 Greg Dickie

D-U-N-S 24-877-7781   (BR)
SOBEYS CAPITAL INCORPORATED
SOBEYS #574
(*Suby of* EMPIRE COMPANY LIMITED)
1120 Queen St, Halifax, NS, B3H 2R9
(902) 422-7605
Emp Here 200
SIC 5411 Grocery stores
 Bill Moulton

D-U-N-S 20-000-2185   (SL)
TERRAN NETWORKS CORP.
5503 Atlantic St, Halifax, NS, B3H 1G5
(902) 497-1191
Emp Here 45   *Sales* 11,545,290
SIC 3825 Instruments to measure electricity

D-U-N-S 25-286-9714   (HQ)
UNIVERSAL PROPERTY MANAGEMENT LIMITED
UNIVERSAL PROPERTIES
1190 Barrington St 4th Floor, Halifax, NS, B3H 2R4
(902) 425-8877
Emp Here 125   *Sales* 27,608,875
SIC 6513 Apartment building operators
 Menachem Suissa

D-U-N-S 24-325-1639   (SL)
UNIVERSITY OF KING'S COLLEGE
6350 Coburg Rd, Halifax, NS, B3H 2A1
(902) 422-1271
Emp Here 200   *Sales* 18,561,663
SIC 8221 Colleges and universities
 William Lehey

D-U-N-S 20-703-6430   (BR)
VIA RAIL CANADA INC
(*Suby of* GOVERNMENT OF CANADA)
1161 Hollis St, Halifax, NS, B3H 2P6
(902) 494-7900
Emp Here 300
SIC 4111 Local and suburban transit

Halifax, NS B3J

D-U-N-S 25-574-1472   (SL)
ARGYLE COBBLERS LTD
ECONOMY SHOE SHOP
1663 Argyle St, Halifax, NS, B3J 2B5
(902) 492-3018
Emp Here 150   *Sales* 6,827,850
SIC 5812 Eating places

Victor Syperek
David Henry

D-U-N-S 24-127-1659   (SL)
ATLANTIC BUILDING CLEANING LIMITED
1505 Barrington St Suite 1310, Halifax, NS,
B3J 3K5
(902) 420-1497
Emp Here 175   *Sales* 23,976,000
SIC 7349 Building maintenance services, nec
Robert Crozier
Bud Bird
Mario Levasseur

D-U-N-S 25-891-4415   (HQ)
ATLANTIC CATCH DATA LIMITED
ACD
1801 Hollis St Suite 1220, Halifax, NS, B3J
3N4
(902) 422-4745
Emp Here 96   *Sales* 27,274,680
SIC 3823 Process control instruments
Gregory Connor

D-U-N-S 20-905-2232   (HQ)
ATLANTIC PILOTAGE AUTHORITY
(*Suby of* GOVERNMENT OF CANADA)
1791 Barrington St Suite 1801, Halifax, NS,
B3J 3K9
(902) 426-2550
Sales 20,216,175
SIC 4499 Water transportation services,
L. Anne Galbraith
Peter Macarthur
Sean Griffiths

D-U-N-S 24-361-2129   (SL)
ATRIUM GROUP INC, THE
PETE'S EUROPEAN DELI
1515 Dresden Row, Halifax, NS, B3J 4B1
(902) 425-5700
Emp Here 50   *Sales* 13,707,600
SIC 5431 Fruit and vegetable markets
Peter Luckett
Dianne Hamilton

D-U-N-S 24-621-1259   (SL)
**BARRINGTON CONSULTING GROUP IN-
CORPORATED, THE**
1326 Barrington St, Halifax, NS, B3J 1Z1
(902) 491-4462
Emp Here 51   *Sales* 13,990,932
SIC 8741 Management services
Andrew Creaser

D-U-N-S 20-194-0041   (BR)
**BELL ALIANT REGIONAL COMMUNICA-
TIONS INC**
(*Suby of* BCE INC)
1505 Barrington St Suite 1102, Halifax, NS,
B3J 3K5
(902) 487-4609
Emp Here 711
SIC 4899 Communication services, nec
Louis Tanguay

D-U-N-S 24-309-0052   (HQ)
**BELL ALIANT REGIONAL COMMUNICA-
TIONS, LIMITED PARTNERSHIP**
XWAVE, DIV OF
1505 Barrington St, Halifax, NS, B3J 3K5
(888) 214-7896
Emp Here 50   *Sales* 3,345,440,000
SIC 4899 Communication services, nec
Frederick Crooks
Glen Leblanc

D-U-N-S 24-804-9710   (SL)
BRULE HOLDINGS LTD
*YOUR FATHER'S MOUSTACHE PUB &
EATERY*
5686 Spring Garden Rd, Halifax, NS, B3J 1H5
(902) 423-6766
Emp Here 75   *Sales* 19,616,475
SIC 6712 Bank holding companies
John O'hearn
Shaun O'hearn

D-U-N-S 24-705-8761   (SL)
CAMBRIDGE SUITES LIMITED, THE
1601 Lower Water St Suite 700, Halifax, NS,
B3J 3P6
(902) 421-1601
Emp Here 200   *Sales* 18,538,000
SIC 7011 Hotels and motels
Frank Medjuck
Ralph Medjuck

D-U-N-S 20-716-4893   (BR)
**CANADIAN BROADCASTING CORPORA-
TION**
CBC
(*Suby of* GOVERNMENT OF CANADA)
5600 Sackville St, Halifax, NS, B3J 1L2
(902) 420-4483
Emp Here 300
SIC 4832 Radio broadcasting stations
Susan Mitton

D-U-N-S 20-819-3979   (HQ)
**CANADIAN-BRITISH CONSULTING GROUP
LIMITED**
CBCL
1489 Hollis St, Halifax, NS, B3J 3M5
(902) 421-7241
Emp Here 29   *Sales* 81,874,016
SIC 6712 Bank holding companies
John Flewelling

D-U-N-S 20-321-6353   (BR)
CAPSERVCO LIMITED PARTNERSHIP
(*Suby of* CAPSERVCO LIMITED PARTNER-
SHIP)
2000 Barrington St Suite 1100, Halifax, NS,
B3J 3K1
(902) 421-1734
Emp Here 100
SIC 8721 Accounting, auditing, and book-
keeping
Michelle Moody

D-U-N-S 20-630-9072   (HQ)
CBCL LIMITED
(*Suby of* CANADIAN-BRITISH CONSULTING
GROUP LIMITED)
1489 Hollis St, Halifax, NS, B3J 3M5
(902) 421-7241
Emp Here 180   *Sales* 53,621,700
SIC 8711 Engineering services
Michael Macdonald
Walter Strachan

D-U-N-S 25-607-5896   (BR)
CENTENNIAL HOTELS LIMITED
LORD NELSON HOTEL & SUITES
(*Suby of* CENTENNIAL HOTELS LIMITED)
1515 South Park St, Halifax, NS, B3J 2L2
(902) 423-6331
Emp Here 80
SIC 7011 Hotels and motels
Etai Markowski

D-U-N-S 20-651-2688   (BR)
CENTENNIAL HOTELS LIMITED
CAMBRIDGE SUITES HOTEL
(*Suby of* CENTENNIAL HOTELS LIMITED)
1583 Brunswick St, Halifax, NS, B3J 3P5
(902) 420-0555
Emp Here 85
SIC 7011 Hotels and motels
John Duggan

D-U-N-S 20-282-4868   (SL)
CHICO'S FAS CANADA, CO.
(*Suby of* CHICO'S FAS, INC.)
1959 Upper Water St Suite 900, Halifax, NS,
B3J 3N2
(888) 855-4986
Emp Here 50   *Sales* 11,043,550
SIC 6512 Nonresidential building operators
Sean Mccartney
Austin Williams
Anthony Maldonado
Francisco Fuentes
Kevin Schockling

L. Susan Faw
Ann Joyce
Eivind Kolemainen
David Oliver
Andrea Hirst

D-U-N-S 24-227-7676   (BR)
CITCO (CANADA) INC
(*Suby of* CITCO (CANADA) INC)
5151 George St Suite 700, Halifax, NS, B3J
1M5
(902) 442-4242
Emp Here 150
SIC 8741 Management services
Scott Montreuil

D-U-N-S 24-790-8432   (HQ)
COACH STORES CANADA CORPORATION
COACH
(*Suby of* TAPESTRY, INC.)
1959 Upper Water St Suite 900, Halifax, NS,
B3J 3N2
(866) 995-9956
Emp Here 1   *Sales* 24,951,000
SIC 5632 Women's accessory and specialty
stores
Leonard Todd Khan
Susan Vo
David Edward Howard
Caroline De Rooy
Nancy Axilrod
Katia Devita
Kevin G. Willis
Alan Siegal
Carl Tremblay

D-U-N-S 24-514-4857   (SL)
**COLES RETIREMENT PLANNING CON-
SULTANTS**
2000 Barrington St, Halifax, NS, B3J 3K1
(902) 423-0350
Emp Here 18   *Sales* 10,438,632
SIC 6411 Insurance agents, brokers, and ser-
vice
Keith Coles

D-U-N-S 20-929-5849   (BR)
COMPASS GROUP CANADA LTD
(*Suby of* COMPASS GROUP PLC)
1800 Argyle St Suite 401, Halifax, NS, B3J
3N8

Emp Here 120
SIC 5812 Eating places
Chris Rowarth

D-U-N-S 20-791-3828   (HQ)
COPERNICUS STUDIOS INC
1226 Hollis St Suite 100, Halifax, NS, B3J 1T6
(902) 474-5194
Sales 12,738,210
SIC 8999 Services, nec
Juan Cruz Baldassarre
Paul Rigg
Andrew Holland
Murray Bain

D-U-N-S 25-384-8949   (HQ)
CORRIDOR RESOURCES INC
5475 Spring Garden Rd Suite 301, Halifax,
NS, B3J 3T2
(902) 429-4511
Emp Here 1   *Sales* 12,845,280
SIC 1321 Natural gas liquids
Steve Moran
Lisette Hachey
J. Douglas Foster
Phillip Knoll
Norman Miller
Robert Penner
Martin Frass-Ehrfeld
James S. Mckee

D-U-N-S 24-329-4670   (HQ)
COX & PALMER
1959 Upper Water St Suite 1100, Halifax, NS,
B3J 3N2

(902) 491-4118
Emp Here 20   *Sales* 11,088,200
SIC 8111 Legal services
Daniel F Gallivan
Michael S Ryan

D-U-N-S 25-370-7624   (BR)
CROMBIE DEVELOPMENTS LIMITED
HALIFAX DEVELOPMENTS
(*Suby of* EMPIRE COMPANY LIMITED)
2000 Barrington St Suite 1210, Halifax, NS,
B3J 3K1

Emp Here 200
SIC 6512 Nonresidential building operators
Terry Doran

D-U-N-S 20-389-9377   (SL)
DASH HUDSON INC
1668 Barrington St Unit 600, Halifax, NS, B3J
2A2
(902) 298-2795
Emp Here 68   *Sales* 14,541,868
SIC 7372 Prepackaged software
Thomas Rankin
Patrick Keefe
Tomasz Niewiarowski
Paul Gauthier
George Mcculloch
Dianne Hatcher

D-U-N-S 20-906-1068   (BR)
**DELOITTE & TOUCHE MANAGEMENT
CONSULTANTS**
(*Suby of* DELOITTE & TOUCHE MANAGE-
MENT CONSULTANTS)
1969 Upper Water St Suite 1500, Halifax, NS,
B3J 3R7
(902) 422-8541
Emp Here 100
SIC 8741 Management services
Andre Vincent

D-U-N-S 24-188-1325   (BR)
DELOITTE LLP
(*Suby of* DELOITTE LLP)
1969 Upper Water St Suite 1500, Halifax, NS,
B3J 3R7
(902) 422-8541
Emp Here 100
SIC 8721 Accounting, auditing, and book-
keeping
Matthew Harris

D-U-N-S 25-361-6544   (HQ)
DHX MEDIA LTD
1478 Queen St, Halifax, NS, B3J 2H7
(902) 423-0260
Emp Here 15   *Sales* 222,222,909
SIC 7812 Motion picture and video production
Michael Patrick Donovan
Josh Scherba
Joe Tedesco
Tara Talbot
Peter Byrne
Roz Nowicki
David Andrew Regan
Mark Gregory Gosine
Anne Loi
Douglas Lamb

D-U-N-S 20-780-2497   (SL)
DYMAXION RESEARCH LIMITED
DYMAXION COMPUTER SALES
5515 Cogswell St, Halifax, NS, B3J 1R2
(902) 422-1973
Emp Here 45   *Sales* 10,365,300
SIC 5734 Computer and software stores
Peter Mason
Robert Brown
Nick Jupp

D-U-N-S 20-052-3392   (HQ)
EMERA ENERGY INCORPORATED
EMERGY ENERGY SERVICES
(*Suby of* EMERA INCORPORATED)
1223 Lower Water St, Halifax, NS, B3J 3S8

▲ Public Company   ■ Public Company Family Member   **HQ** Headquarters   **BR** Branch   **SL** Single Location

(902) 474-7800
Emp Here 8   *Sales* 184,961,920
SIC 4911 Electric services
Judy Steele
Ian Johnston
Sandi Hennequin
Dave Bezanson
Brent Dreger
Scott Fortuna
Mark Christie
Paul Laberge

D-U-N-S 24-853-5390   (HQ)
EMERA INCORPORATED
1223 Lower Water St, Halifax, NS, B3J 3S8
(902) 450-0507
Emp Here 20   *Sales* 4,945,857,448
SIC 4911 Electric services
Scott Balfour
Bob Hanf
Dan Muldoon
Sarah Macdonald
Wayne O'connor
Greg Blunden
Mike Roberts
Jackie Sheppard
Sylvia Chrominska
Henry Demone

D-U-N-S 25-297-1718   (BR)
ERNST & YOUNG INC
(*Suby of* ERNST & YOUNG INC)
1871 Hollis St Unit 500, Halifax, NS, B3J 0C3
(902) 420-1080
Emp Here 90
SIC 8721 Accounting, auditing, and bookkeeping
Trent Henry

D-U-N-S 20-221-2254   (HQ)
ESIT CANADA ENTERPRISE SERVICES CO
(*Suby of* DXC TECHNOLOGY COMPANY)
1969 Upper Water St, Halifax, NS, B3J 3R7
(902) 000-0000
Emp Here 885   *Sales* 933,460,500
SIC 5734 Computer and software stores
Arif Manji
Sonia Price

D-U-N-S 20-368-9133   (SL)
EVENTS EAST GROUP
1800 Argyle St P.O. Box 955, Halifax, NS, B3J 3N8
(902) 421-8686
Emp Here 100   *Sales* 22,087,100
SIC 6512 Nonresidential building operators
Carrie Cussons

D-U-N-S 25-562-6277   (SL)
FEDERATED BUILDING SERVICES LIMITED
1505 Barrington St Suite 1310, Halifax, NS, B3J 3K5

Emp Here 80   *Sales* 3,270,821
SIC 7349 Building maintenance services, nec
Janet Crozier
Margaret Bird

D-U-N-S 24-199-7226   (SL)
FORTUNE BAY CORP
1969 Upper Water St Suite 2001, Halifax, NS, B3J 3R7
(902) 442-1421
Emp Here 400   *Sales* 102,309,600
SIC 1041 Gold ores
Wade K. Dawe
Sarah Oliver
Derrick Gill
Michael Gross

D-U-N-S 24-678-1640   (HQ)
GOGOLD RESOURCES INC
2000 Barrington St Suite 1301, Halifax, NS, B3J 3K1
(902) 482-1998
Emp Here 5   *Sales* 17,045,000
SIC 1044 Silver ores

Bradley Langille
Dana Hatfield
Anis Nehme
Terence F. Coughlan
Phillip Gaunce
George F. Waye
Terrence R. Cooper

D-U-N-S 24-671-1030   (HQ)
GRAFTONS CONNOR PROPERTY INC
1741 Grafton St, Halifax, NS, B3J 2C6
(902) 454-9344
Emp Here 100
SIC 5813 Drinking places
Gary Hurst
Ed Raymond

D-U-N-S 20-646-1126   (BR)
GRANT THORNTON LLP
(*Suby of* GRANT THORNTON LLP)
2000 Barrington St Suite 1100, Halifax, NS, B3J 3K1
(902) 421-1734
Emp Here 150
SIC 8721 Accounting, auditing, and bookkeeping
Michelle Williams

D-U-N-S 25-094-4196   (SL)
GROWTHWORKS ENTERPRISES LTD
1801 Hollis St Suite 310, Halifax, NS, B3J 3N4
(902) 423-9367
Emp Here 33   *Sales* 30,992,841
SIC 6211 Security brokers and dealers
Brent W Barrie
Stephen Rankin
Richard Coles
William Eeuwes
Robert Steele
Diane Macdiarmid
Anita Fifield

D-U-N-S 25-364-5378   (SL)
HALIFAX DEVELOPMENTS
CROMBIE REIT
2000 Barrington St Suite 1210, Halifax, NS, B3J 3K1
(902) 429-3660
Emp Here 100   *Sales* 27,433,200
SIC 8741 Management services
Mike Samson
Lynn Cosgrove

D-U-N-S 20-813-4676   (HQ)
HARDMAN GROUP LIMITED, THE
1226 Hollis St, Halifax, NS, B3J 1T6
(902) 429-3743
Emp Here 20   *Sales* 10,836,784
SIC 6553 Cemetery subdividers and developers
William N Hardman
William B Hardman
Clayton Hardman
Shirley Hardman

D-U-N-S 20-524-0070   (HQ)
I.H. MATHERS & SON LIMITED
1525 Birmingham St, Halifax, NS, B3J 2J6
(902) 429-5680
Emp Here 30   *Sales* 13,477,450
SIC 4491 Marine cargo handling
Harry I Mathers
Melissa J Mathers
Bernard Prevost
Brian Lane

D-U-N-S 24-790-0459   (SL)
JACK FRIDAY'S LIMITED
MY APARTMENT
1740 Argyle St, Halifax, NS, B3J 2B6
(902) 454-9344
Emp Here 85   *Sales* 3,869,115
SIC 5812 Eating places
Gary Hurst
Ed Raymond
John O'hearn

D-U-N-S 24-932-5077   (SL)

JAMIESON PHARMACY LTD
SHOPPERS DRUG MART
5524 Spring Garden Rd, Halifax, NS, B3J 1G5
(902) 429-2400
Emp Here 50   *Sales* 12,647,700
SIC 5912 Drug stores and proprietary stores
David Jamieson
Celia Jamieson

D-U-N-S 20-275-2978   (SL)
LEADON (BARRINGTON) OPERATIONS LP
DELTA HOTELS BY MARRIOTT BARRINGTON
1875 Barrington St, Halifax, NS, B3J 3L6
(902) 429-7410
Emp Here 100   *Sales* 9,489,900
SIC 7011 Hotels and motels
Corey Cheek

D-U-N-S 20-389-1374   (SL)
LEADON (HALIFAX) OPERATIONS LP
HOTEL HALIFAX
1990 Barrington St, Halifax, NS, B3J 1P2
(902) 425-6700
Emp Here 130   *Sales* 10,613,428
SIC 7011 Hotels and motels
Borden Mosher

D-U-N-S 20-728-8887   (HQ)
MARITIME TRAVEL INC
BAY TRAVEL, THE
2000 Barrington St Suite 202, Halifax, NS, B3J 3K1
(902) 420-1554
Emp Here 61   *Sales* 202,068,818
SIC 4724 Travel agencies
Robert Dexter
Gary Gaudry
Angela Dexter
Deanna Skinner
Julie Gaudry

D-U-N-S 20-905-9435   (HQ)
MARTEC LIMITED
(*Suby of* LLOYD'S REGISTER OF SHIPPING TRUST CORPORATION LIMITED)
1888 Brunswick St Suite 400, Halifax, NS, B3J 3J8
(902) 425-5101
Emp Here 40   *Sales* 11,245,824
SIC 8748 Business consulting, nec
Magnus Wollstrum
Mervyn Earl Norwood
James L Warner
James P Warner

D-U-N-S 20-782-2016   (HQ)
MCINNES COOPER
1969 Upper Water St Suite 1300, Halifax, NS, B3J 3R7
(902) 425-6500
Emp Here 200   *Sales* 61,762,800
SIC 8111 Legal services
Eric Ledrew
Malcolm D Boyle
Joseph A F Macdonald
John Kulik
Bernard F Miller
George T H Cooper
George W Macdonald
Eric Durnford
Robert G Belliveau
Peter Mclellan

D-U-N-S 24-354-3043   (SL)
MILLS COMPANY LIMITED
(*Suby of* MILLS COMPANY HOLDINGS LIMITED)
5486 Spring Garden Rd, Halifax, NS, B3J 1G4

Emp Here 60   *Sales* 10,763,760
SIC 5621 Women's clothing stores
Michael Macdonald
Ross Mcneil
James Dickson
Darin Mclean
Angie Taiani

D-U-N-S 24-756-5229   (SL)
NEW PALACE CABARET LIMITED, THE
1721 Brunswick St, Halifax, NS, B3J 2G4
(902) 420-0015
Emp Here 75   *Sales* 3,413,925
SIC 5813 Drinking places
Jehad Khoury

D-U-N-S 25-395-6353   (SL)
NORTHERN FIBRE TERMINAL INCORPORATED
1869 Upper Water St, Halifax, NS, B3J 1S9
(902) 422-3030
Emp Here 50   *Sales* 11,671,750
SIC 2611 Pulp mills
Anthony Mee
David Bassendale

D-U-N-S 24-994-3614   (HQ)
NOVA SCOTIA BUSINESS INC
(*Suby of* NOVA SCOTIA, PROVINCE OF)
1800 Argyle St Suite 701, Halifax, NS, B3J 3N8
(902) 424-6650
Sales 14,556,165
SIC 6111 Federal and federally sponsored credit agencies
Stephen Lund
J.D. (Jim) Eisenhauer
Sean Murray
Stuart Rath
Lois Dyer Mann
Nancy Tower

D-U-N-S 24-131-1513   (SL)
NOVA SCOTIA COLLEGE OF ART AND DESIGN
NSCAD UNIVERSITY
5163 Duke St, Halifax, NS, B3J 3J6
(902) 444-9600
Emp Here 190   *Sales* 16,649,725
SIC 8221 Colleges and universities
David B Smith
Peter Flemming

D-U-N-S 20-905-9609   (SL)
NOVA SCOTIA HEARING AND SPEECH CENTRES
5657 Spring Garden Rd Suite 401, Halifax, NS, B3J 3R4
(902) 492-8289
Emp Here 120   *Sales* 26,749,440
SIC 8099 Health and allied services, nec
D Lynn Fraser
Hal Boon

D-U-N-S 24-766-8168   (SL)
NOVA SCOTIA PENSION SERVICES CORPORATION
1949 Upper Water St Suite 400, Halifax, NS, B3J 3N3
(902) 424-5070
Emp Here 50   *Sales* 61,770,900
SIC 6371 Pension, health, and welfare funds
Steven R. Wolff
Kim Blinn
Elizabeth Vandenberg
Christine Tate
Alan Tottman
Chris Huestis

D-U-N-S 20-443-2637   (HQ)
NOVA SCOTIA POWER INCORPORATED
(*Suby of* EMERA INCORPORATED)
1223 Lower Water St, Halifax, NS, B3J 3S8
(902) 428-6221
Emp Here 600   *Sales* 1,513,324,800
SIC 4911 Electric services
Karen Hutt
Judith Ferguson
Paul Casey
Sasha Irving
David Landrigan
Claudette Porter
Mark Sidebottom
Scott Balfour
Lee Bragg

Sandra Greer

D-U-N-S 24-340-6584 (SL)
NOVACOS BUILDING CLEANING LTD
1505 Barrington St Suite 1310, Halifax, NS,
B3J 3K5

Emp Here 196   *Sales* 6,371,110
SIC 7349 Building maintenance services, nec
Mario Lavasseur

D-U-N-S 20-374-6479 (SL)
NS POWER ENERGY MARKETING INCOR-PORATED
1223 Lower Water St, Halifax, NS, B3J 3S8
(902) 428-6496
Emp Here 20   *Sales* 10,513,472
SIC 4911 Electric services
Karen Hutt
Mark Sidebottom
Judith Ferguson
Paul Casey
David Landrigan
Christopher Smith
Sara Phinney
Stephen Aftanas
Laura Gillham
Murray Fichten

D-U-N-S 24-168-2640 (HQ)
NTT DATA CANADA, INC
(*Suby of* NIPPON TELEGRAPH AND TELE-PHONE CORPORATION)
2000 Barrington St Suite 300, Halifax, NS, B3J 3K1
(902) 422-6036
Emp Here 700   *Sales* 216,620,000
SIC 7379 Computer related services, nec
John W. Mcclain
Lawrence Whelan
John Gillis
Sue Churchill

D-U-N-S 25-232-6442 (SL)
P.G. HOTEL LTD
PRINCE GEORGE HOTEL
1725 Market St, Halifax, NS, B3J 3N9
(902) 425-1986
Emp Here 130   *Sales* 12,049,700
SIC 7011 Hotels and motels
Scott Travis
Mani Suissa
Lindlynda Suissa

D-U-N-S 20-930-4799 (BR)
PRICEWATERHOUSECOOPERS LLP
PWC DEBT SOLUTIONS
(*Suby of* PRICEWATERHOUSECOOPERS LLP)
1601 Lower Water St Suite 400, Halifax, NS, B3J 3P6
(902) 491-7400
Emp Here 90
SIC 8721 Accounting, auditing, and book-keeping
Mike Anaka

D-U-N-S 24-335-9952 (HQ)
PRIMERO GOLD CANADA INC
(*Suby of* FIRST MAJESTIC SILVER CORP)
1969 Upper Water St Suite 2001, Halifax, NS, B3J 3R7
(902) 422-1421
Emp Here 220   *Sales* 58,828,020
SIC 1041 Gold ores
Wade Dawe
Jennifer Nicholson
Howard Bird
Jon Legatto
Dana Hatfiled
Daniel Gallivan

D-U-N-S 24-227-4335 (SL)
QUEEN ELIZABETH II HEALTH SCIENCES CENTRE FOUNDATION
QEII HEALTH SCIENCES CENTRE FOUN-DATION
5657 Spring Garden Rd Suite 3005, Halifax,

NS, B3J 3R4
(902) 334-1546
Emp Here 30   *Sales* 10,031,140
SIC 8399 Social services, nec
William Bean
Mike Hurley
Julie Mackean
Nancy Maccready-Williams
Dale Godsoe
Bruce Marchand
Jamie O'neil
Carolyn Booth
Scott Brookfield
Sharon Calder

D-U-N-S 20-561-9450 (BR)
QUEST SOFTWARE CANADA INC
(*Suby of* FRANCISCO PARTNERS MANAGE-MENT, L.P.)
5151 George St, Halifax, NS, B3J 1M5
(902) 442-5800
Emp Here 104
SIC 7372 Prepackaged software
Allison Mcmillan

D-U-N-S 24-670-5503 (HQ)
RELIANCE OFFSHORE CANADA INC
1525 Birmingham St, Halifax, NS, B3J 2J6
(902) 429-1255
Sales 10,457,160
SIC 7361 Employment agencies
Brian Lane

D-U-N-S 25-139-7709 (SL)
RJF HEALTHCARE SERVICES LTD
5657 Spring Garden Rd Unit 700, Halifax, NS, B3J 3R4
(902) 425-4031
Emp Here 300   *Sales* 26,778,600
SIC 8049 Offices of health practitioner
Ruby Felix

D-U-N-S 25-532-2240 (HQ)
ROYAL HOST INC
(*Suby of* HOLLOWAY LODGING CORPORA-TION)
1809 Barrington St Suite 1108, Halifax, NS, B3J 3K8
(902) 470-4500
Emp Here 10   *Sales* 95,668,000
SIC 7011 Hotels and motels
Michael Rapps
Blair Cook
George Armoyan
David Dingwall
Keith Maher

D-U-N-S 25-577-4036 (SL)
SILVERBIRCH NO. 15 OPERATIONS LIM-ITED PARTNERSHIP
HAMPTON INN AND HOMEWOOD SUITES HALIFAX DOWNTOWN, THE
1960 Brunswick St, Halifax, NS, B3J 2G7
(902) 422-1391
Emp Here 85   *Sales* 7,618,465
SIC 7299 Miscellaneous personal service
Trevor Morgan
Irvin Nicholson

D-U-N-S 24-231-8371 (SL)
SNAP TOGETHER PRODUCTIONS
5091 Terminal Rd, Halifax, NS, B3J 3Y1
(902) 422-6287
Emp Here 70   *Sales* 12,935,860
SIC 4833 Television broadcasting stations
Tracey Jardine

D-U-N-S 25-315-6442 (BR)
SNC-LAVALIN INC
(*Suby of* GROUPE SNC-LAVALIN INC)
5657 Spring Garden Rd Suite 200, Halifax, NS, B3J 3R4
(902) 492-4544
Emp Here 80
SIC 8711 Engineering services
Brian Decoste

D-U-N-S 24-832-5789 (HQ)

STEWART MCKELVEY STIRLING SCALES
SMSS
1959 Upper Water St Suite 900, Halifax, NS, B3J 3N2
(902) 420-3200
Emp Here 150   *Sales* 22,176,400
SIC 8111 Legal services
John M Rogers
James Dickinson

D-U-N-S 20-920-0620 (BR)
SYMCOR INC
(*Suby of* SYMCOR INC)
1580 Grafton St, Halifax, NS, B3J 2C2
(902) 404-4606
Emp Here 200
SIC 4226 Special warehousing and storage, nec
Paula Matthews

D-U-N-S 24-512-9614 (HQ)
TRADE CENTRE LIMITED
ATLANTIC CANADA WORLD TRADE CEN-TRE
(*Suby of* NOVA SCOTIA, PROVINCE OF)
1800 Argyle St Suite 801, Halifax, NS, B3J 3N8
(902) 421-8686
Sales 40,703,100
SIC 6512 Nonresidential building operators
Scott Furguson
Carrie Cussons
Colette Curran
Nina Kressler
Robert Logan
Ralph Williams
Darrell Hardy
Grant Macdonald
Peggy Dooley
Gordon Gillis

D-U-N-S 24-665-8009 (HQ)
UNISYS CANADA INC
(*Suby of* UNISYS CORPORATION)
1809 Barrington St Suite 600, Halifax, NS, B3J 3K8
(902) 704-5340
Emp Here 70   *Sales* 55,371,900
SIC 7371 Custom computer programming ser-vices
Gregory Bergman
Mary Joynt
Paul Oliver

D-U-N-S 20-780-9575 (SL)
VENTURES ENTERPRISES LTD
1525 Birmingham St, Halifax, NS, B3J 2J6
(902) 429-5680
Emp Here 45   *Sales* 12,982,455
SIC 6512 Nonresidential building operators
Harry Mathers

D-U-N-S 20-009-1408 (HQ)
WINDMILL CROSSING LIMITED
SOUTHWEST PROPERTIES
1475 Lower Water St Suite 100, Halifax, NS, B3J 3Z2
(902) 422-6412
Emp Here 100   *Sales* 41,888,900
SIC 6531 Real estate agents and managers
Gordon Lang

D-U-N-S 20-781-0169 (HQ)
WORKERS COMPENSATION BOARD OF NOVA SCOTIA
WORKSAFE NOVA SCOTIA
5668 South St, Halifax, NS, B3J 1A6
(902) 491-8999
Emp Here 300
SIC 6331 Fire, marine, and casualty insurance

D-U-N-S 24-338-3361 (SL)
YOUNG WOMEN'S CHRISTIAN ASSOCIA-TION
YWCA OF HALIFAX
1239 Barrington St, Halifax, NS, B3J 1Y3
(902) 423-6162
Emp Here 40   *Sales* 15,896,560

SIC 8699 Membership organizations, nec
Brenda Sanderson
Sue Wolstenholma

D-U-N-S 20-008-2147 (SL)
ZEPHYR MINERALS LTD
1959 Upper Water St Suite 1300, Halifax, NS, B3J 3N2
(902) 446-4189
Emp Here 10   *Sales* 23,613,863
SIC 1081 Metal mining services
Loren Komperdo
David Felderhof
Sean Tufford
Suzan Frazer
John Clark
G.W. (Will) Felderhof
Scott Rhodenizer
David Grand

Halifax, NS B3K

D-U-N-S 20-444-4145 (HQ)
2187878 NOVA SCOTIA LIMITED
CITY MAZDA
2672 Robie St, Halifax, NS, B3K 4N8
(902) 453-4115
Sales 22,413,510
SIC 5511 New and used car dealers
Stephen Scarff
Patricia Scarff

D-U-N-S 20-719-5962 (SL)
3025052 NOVA SCOTIA LIMITED
VOLVO OF HALIFAX
3363 Kempt Rd, Halifax, NS, B3K 4X5
(902) 453-2110
Emp Here 36   *Sales* 13,111,740
SIC 5012 Automobiles and other motor vehi-cles
Maryjean Denicola

D-U-N-S 25-580-5152 (SL)
3039214 NOVA SCOTIA LIMITED
STEELE HYUNDAI
3625 Kempt Rd, Halifax, NS, B3K 4X6
(902) 454-1000
Emp Here 26   *Sales* 12,950,028
SIC 5511 New and used car dealers
Robert G Steele
Chris Watt

D-U-N-S 20-112-9116 (HQ)
3041518 NOVA SCOTIA LIMITED
STEELE FORD LINCOLN
3773 Windsor St, Halifax, NS, B3K 0A2
(902) 453-1130
Emp Here 80   *Sales* 78,660,000
SIC 5511 New and used car dealers
Robert Steele

D-U-N-S 20-385-4612 (SL)
AMBASSATOURS LIMITED
AMBASSATOURS GRAYLINE
(*Suby of* ATLANTIC AMBASSATOURS LIM-ITED)
6575 Bayne St, Halifax, NS, B3K 0H1
(902) 423-6242
Emp Here 250   *Sales* 6,384,474
SIC 4725 Tour operators
Dennis Campbell
Mary Dempster
Sean Buckland

D-U-N-S 24-877-6510 (HQ)
ATLANTIC AMBASSATOURS LIMITED
AMBASSATOURS GRAY LINE
6575 Bayne St, Halifax, NS, B3K 0H1
(902) 423-6242
Sales 15,054,400
SIC 4111 Local and suburban transit
Dennis Campbell
Mary Dempster
Sean Buckland

D-U-N-S 24-850-1418   (HQ)
ATLANTIC CENTRAL
6074 Lady Hammond Rd Suite B, Halifax, NS,
B3K 2R7
(902) 453-0680
Emp Here 1   *Sales* 185,312,700
SIC 6351 Surety insurance
Michael Lennard

D-U-N-S 20-815-1837   (SL)
ATLANTIC TOURS LIMITED
2631 King St, Halifax, NS, B3K 4T7
(902) 423-6242
Emp Here 27   *Sales* 14,201,709
SIC 4725 Tour operators
Dennis Campbell
Paul Emmons
Gary Powell
Brian Gillif

D-U-N-S 20-207-3974   (BR)
BELL MEDIA INC
CTV ATLANTIC
(*Suby of* BCE INC)
2885 Robie St, Halifax, NS, B3K 5Z4
(902) 453-4000
Emp Here 100
SIC 4833 Television broadcasting stations
Trent Mcgranth

D-U-N-S 25-572-1847   (SL)
BERKELEY HOLDINGS LIMITED
BERKELEY GLADSTONE RIDGE
2633 Gladstone St Suite 312, Halifax, NS,
B3K 4W3
(902) 492-3700
Emp Here 151   *Sales* 33,351,521
SIC 6513 Apartment building operators
Diane Campbell
David Campbell

D-U-N-S 25-401-9359   (HQ)
**BRAGG COMMUNICATIONS INCORPO-
RATED**
EASTLINK
(*Suby of* TIDNISH HOLDINGS LIMITED)
6080 Young St Suite 800, Halifax, NS, B3K
5L2
(902) 453-2800
Emp Here 50   *Sales* 501,816,000
SIC 4841 Cable and other pay television ser-
vices
Lee Bragg
John Bragg
Deborah Shaffner
Jim Fitzgerald
Richard Cecchetto
David Hoffman
David Caldwell
Jeff Gillham
George Caines
Geofferey Baldwin

D-U-N-S 20-380-0250   (SL)
BROTHERS MEAT LIMITED
2665 Agricola St, Halifax, NS, B3K 4C7
(902) 455-8774
Emp Here 21   *Sales* 17,842,239
SIC 5147 Meats and meat products
Crystal Kelebrat

D-U-N-S 24-228-1371   (SL)
CALL-US INFO LTD
(*Suby of* INTERVIEWING SERVICE OF
AMERICA, LLC)
6009 Quinpool Rd, Halifax, NS, B3K 5J7

Emp Here 90
SIC 7389 Business services, nec
Connie Ruben

D-U-N-S 25-164-7285   (SL)
**CELLULAR CONCEPTS OF NOVA SCOTIA
LIMITED**
3232 Barrington St, Halifax, NS, B3K 2X7
(902) 423-0167
Emp Here 38   *Sales* 12,372,800

SIC 5999 Miscellaneous retail stores, nec
Neil Muir

D-U-N-S 25-542-6025   (HQ)
CHARLTOM RESTAURANTS LIMITED
WENDY'S
3630 Kempt Rd, Halifax, NS, B3K 4X8
(902) 832-2103
Emp Here 3   *Sales* 13,991,700
SIC 5812 Eating places
Thomas Cahill
Charles Ramia

D-U-N-S 20-002-6131   (BR)
CREDIT UNION CENTRAL OF CANADA
CREDIT UNION CENTRAL NOVA SCOTIA
(*Suby of* CREDIT UNION CENTRAL OF
CANADA)
6074 Lady Hammond Rd, Halifax, NS, B3K
2R7
(902) 453-0680
Emp Here 150
SIC 6062 State credit unions
Brenda O'connor

D-U-N-S 20-781-9152   (HQ)
**CREDIT UNION CENTRAL OF NOVA SCO-
TIA**
ATLANTIC CENTRAL
6074 Lady Hammond Rd, Halifax, NS, B3K
2R7
(902) 453-0680
Emp Here 143   *Sales* 227,702,080
SIC 6289 Security and commodity service
Bernie O'neill
Sharon Arnold
Richard Parker
David Maclean

D-U-N-S 20-468-3218   (SL)
CUNARD COURT HIGHRISE
2065 Brunswick St Suite 1706, Halifax, NS,
B3K 5T8
(902) 407-8845
Emp Here 47   *Sales* 13,563,401
SIC 1522 Residential construction, nec
Douglas Mathews

D-U-N-S 20-781-4401   (SL)
DONPAT INVESTMENTS LIMITED
*COLONIAL COLLISION CENTRE/ COLO-
NIAL HONDA*
2657 Robie St, Halifax, NS, B3K 4N9
(902) 453-1940
Emp Here 98   *Sales* 61,669,440
SIC 5511 New and used car dealers
Christopher Megaffin
Michael Megaffin
David Prosser

D-U-N-S 24-132-0928   (SL)
**EDMONDS LANDSCAPE & CONSTRUC-
TION SERVICES LIMITED**
EDMONDS CONSTRUCTION SERVICES
2675 Clifton St, Halifax, NS, B3K 4V4
(902) 453-5500
Emp Here 50   *Sales* 15,057,100
SIC 4959 Sanitary services, nec
Roger Edmonds

D-U-N-S 25-792-9190   (BR)
FARMERS CO-OPERATIVE DAIRY LIMITED
FARMERS DAIRY
Gd, Halifax, NS, B3K 5Y6

Emp Here 350
SIC 5143 Dairy products, except dried or
canned

D-U-N-S 20-026-8738   (HQ)
**HALIFAX SEED COMPANY INCORPO-
RATED**
5860 Kane St, Halifax, NS, B3K 2B7
(902) 454-7456
Emp Here 1   *Sales* 37,126,000
SIC 5191 Farm supplies
Paul Tregunno
Warren Tregunno

Emily Tregunno

D-U-N-S 20-026-9041   (SL)
HILLCREST VOLKSWAGON (1979) LTD
3154 Robie St, Halifax, NS, B3K 4P9
(902) 453-2790
Emp Here 67   *Sales* 42,161,760
SIC 5511 New and used car dealers
Roy Velemirovich
Anne Velemirovich

D-U-N-S 24-126-7020   (SL)
HMC COMMUNICATIONS INC
ANSWER 365
2829 Agricola St, Halifax, NS, B3K 4E5
(902) 453-0700
Emp Here 40   *Sales* 17,739,600
SIC 7389 Business services, nec
William Tucker

D-U-N-S 25-541-0763   (HQ)
IRVING SHIPBUILDING INC
HALIFAX SHIPYARD, DIV OF
3099 Barrington St, Halifax, NS, B3K 2X6
(902) 423-9271
Emp Here 5   *Sales* 261,765,000
SIC 3731 Shipbuilding and repairing
James D. Irving
Kevin M. Mccoy

D-U-N-S 25-995-9104   (BR)
IRVING SHIPBUILDING INC
HALIFAX SHIPYARD, DIV OF
(*Suby of* IRVING SHIPBUILDING INC)
3099 Barrington St, Halifax, NS, B3K 5M7
(902) 423-9271
Emp Here 300
SIC 3731 Shipbuilding and repairing
Steve Durrell

D-U-N-S 20-311-3543   (BR)
**IZAAK WALTON KILLAM HEALTH CENTRE,
THE**
*RESEARCH SERCVICES, DEPARTMENT
OF*
(*Suby of* NOVA SCOTIA, PROVINCE OF)
Gd, Halifax, NS, B3K 6R8
(902) 470-6682
Emp Here 3,200
SIC 8731 Commercial physical research
Kathleen Leadon

D-U-N-S 20-931-6348   (HQ)
**IZAAK WALTON KILLAM HEALTH CENTRE,
THE**
IWK HEALTH CENTRE
(*Suby of* NOVA SCOTIA, PROVINCE OF)
5980 University Ave, Halifax, NS, B3K 6R8
(902) 470-8888
Emp Here 3,500   *Sales* 223,441,330
SIC 8069 Specialty hospitals, except psychi-
atric
Krista Jangaard
Steve Ashton

D-U-N-S 24-736-4651   (HQ)
K-RIGHT COMMUNICATIONS LIMITED
EASTLINK
(*Suby of* TIDNISH HOLDINGS LIMITED)
6080 Young St, Halifax, NS, B3K 5L2
(902) 484-2800
Sales 34,270,800
SIC 4841 Cable and other pay television ser-
vices
Lee Bragg
John Bragg
Deborah Shaffner
David Hoffman
Richard Cecchetto
Jim Fitzgerald
Geoffrey Baldwin
George Caines

D-U-N-S 20-333-4701   (HQ)
**KILLAM APARTMENT REAL ESTATE IN-
VESTMENT TRUST**
KILLAM APARTMENT REIT

3700 Kempt Rd Suite 100, Halifax, NS, B3K
4X8
(902) 453-9000
Sales 163,718,950
SIC 6798 Real estate investment trusts
Philip Fraser
Robert Richardson
Ruth Buckle
Michael Mclean
Pamela Crowell
Erin Cleveland
Colleen Mccarville
Jeremy Jackson
Dale Noseworthy
Robert G. Kay

D-U-N-S 20-112-6732   (HQ)
KILLAM PROPERTIES INC
(*Suby of* KILLAM APARTMENT REAL ES-
TATE INVESTMENT TRUST)
3700 Kempt Rd Suite 100, Halifax, NS, B3K
4X8
(902) 453-9000
Emp Here 25   *Sales* 27,135,400
SIC 6513 Apartment building operators
Philip D Fraser
Robert G Richardson
Ruth Buckle
Colleen Mccarville
Erin Cleveland
Pamela Crowell
Jeremy Jackson
Michael Mclean
Dale Noseworthy

D-U-N-S 20-782-9607   (HQ)
**LEAGUE SAVINGS & MORTGAGE COM-
PANY**
(*Suby of* CREDIT UNION CENTRAL OF
NOVA SCOTIA)
6074 Lady Hammond Rd, Halifax, NS, B3K
2R7
(902) 453-4220
Emp Here 32   *Sales* 11,237,200
SIC 6162 Mortgage bankers and loan corre-
spondents
Bernie O'neil
Marion Garlick

D-U-N-S 20-904-8990   (SL)
LUNG ASSOCIATION OF NOVA SCOTIA
6331 Lady Hammond Rd Suite 200, Halifax,
NS, B3K 2S2
(902) 443-8141
Emp Here 26   *Sales* 10,332,764
SIC 8699 Membership organizations, nec
Louis Brill

D-U-N-S 20-021-3148   (HQ)
MARITIME BEAUTY SUPPLY CO LTD
3695 Barrington St, Halifax, NS, B3K 2Y3
(902) 429-8510
Emp Here 22   *Sales* 64,380,360
SIC 5087 Service establishment equipment
J Maurice Doucet

D-U-N-S 25-286-0473   (HQ)
**METROPOLITAIN REGIONAL HOUSING
AUTHORITY**
2131 Gottingen St, Halifax, NS, B3K 5Z7
(902) 420-6000
Emp Here 1   *Sales* 17,638,010
SIC 6513 Apartment building operators
Armand Pinard
Patricia Lawrence

D-U-N-S 25-574-1290   (SL)
MYTON PROJECT MANAGEMENT LIMITED
5555 Young St, Halifax, NS, B3K 1Z7

Emp Here 30   *Sales* 14,121,930
SIC 1542 Nonresidential construction, nec
William Nycum

D-U-N-S 24-662-1762   (BR)
NOVA SCOTIA COMMUNITY COLLEGE
NSCC ONLINE LEARNING

(Suby of NOVA SCOTIA, PROVINCE OF)
5685 Leeds St, Halifax, NS, B3K 2T3
(902) 491-3387
Emp Here 2,000
SIC 8221 Colleges and universities
 Don Bureaux

 D-U-N-S 20-728-9158   (HQ)
NOVA SCOTIA COMMUNITY COLLEGE
(Suby of NOVA SCOTIA, PROVINCE OF)
5685 Leeds St, Halifax, NS, B3K 2T3
(902) 491-6701
Emp Here 300   *Sales* 169,082,391
SIC 8222 Junior colleges
 Don Bureaux
 Monica Foster
 Anna Burke
 Roslind Penfound
 Catherine Maclean
 Glenda Barrett

 D-U-N-S 20-057-0880   (SL)
O'REGAN HALIFAX LIMITED
O'REGAN'S TOYOTA HALIFAX
3575 Kempt Rd, Halifax, NS, B3K 4X6
(902) 453-2331
Emp Here 50   *Sales* 24,903,900
SIC 5511 New and used car dealers
 Sean O'regan
 Pat O'regan
 Stephen M. O'regan
 Christopher D. Hubley

 D-U-N-S 20-781-9210   (SL)
O'REGAN I-N LIMITED
NISSAN HALIFAX
3461 Kempt Rd, Halifax, NS, B3K 5T7
(902) 453-2020
Emp Here 40   *Sales* 19,923,120
SIC 5521 Used car dealers
 Sean O'regan
 Christopher Hubley
 Patrick O'regan
 Mary O'regan
 Kathleen O'regan
 Stephen O'regan

 D-U-N-S 20-387-3034   (HQ)
PORSCHE CANADIAN INVESTMENT ULC
3367 Kempt Rd, Halifax, NS, B3K 4X5
(902) 453-8800
Sales 62,928,000
SIC 5511 New and used car dealers

 D-U-N-S 20-939-6840   (SL)
QUEST - A SOCIETY FOR ADULT SUP-PORT AND REHABILITATION
2131 Gottingen St Suite 101, Halifax, NS, B3K 5Z7
(902) 490-7200
Emp Here 75   *Sales* 4,443,525
SIC 8361 Residential care
 Laura Arthurs
 Cindy White

 D-U-N-S 24-532-6111   (SL)
R.C.R INVESTMENTS LIMITED
6009 Quinpool Rd Suite 300, Halifax, NS, B3K 5J7
(902) 454-8533
Emp Here 450   *Sales* 164,479,050
SIC 6712 Bank holding companies
 Robert Risley

 D-U-N-S 20-174-2157   (HQ)
RCR HOSPITALITY GROUP LIMITED
6009 Quinpool Rd Suite 300, Halifax, NS, B3K 5J7
(902) 454-8533
Emp Here 1   *Sales* 11,659,750
SIC 5812 Eating places
 Robert Risley

 D-U-N-S 24-342-6574   (HQ)
ROBIE & KEMPT SERVICES LIMITED
TIM HORTONS
(Suby of 2361927 NOVA SCOTIA LIMITED)
3630 Kempt Rd, Halifax, NS, B3K 4X8

(902) 832-2103
Emp Here 5   *Sales* 11,659,750
SIC 5812 Eating places
 Thomas Cahill
 Brent Stratton

 D-U-N-S 20-809-9767   (SL)
SAINT LEONARD'S SOCIETY OF NOVA SCOTIA
5506 Cunard St Suite 101, Halifax, NS, B3K 1C2
(902) 406-3631
Emp Here 65   *Sales* 46,098,780
SIC 8699 Membership organizations, nec
 Laurie Edwards
 Colin Mclean
 Lindsay Cross
 Mike Myett
 Melinda Countway
 Sean Lewis
 Jamie O'neill
 David Pangman
 Meghan Laing
 Jeremy Jackson

 D-U-N-S 20-930-3197   (SL)
SAINT VINCENT'S NURSING HOME
2080 Windsor St Suite 509, Halifax, NS, B3K 5B2
(902) 429-0550
Emp Here 250   *Sales* 16,070,500
SIC 8361 Residential care
 Kristin Schmitz
 Peggy Gorman

 D-U-N-S 20-631-6325   (SL)
SCOTIA FUELS LIMITED
6380 Lady Hammond Rd, Halifax, NS, B3K 2S3
(902) 453-2121
Emp Here 35   *Sales* 16,415,175
SIC 5983 Fuel oil dealers
 Jim Lawley
 Gordon Lawley
 James Farquhar Sr

 D-U-N-S 20-608-8978   (SL)
SMITH & SCOTT STEAKHOUSE LIMITED
STEAK AND STEIN STEAK HOUSE
6061 Young St, Halifax, NS, B3K 2A3
(902) 454-8814
Emp Here 100   *Sales* 4,551,900
SIC 5812 Eating places
 John Scott

 D-U-N-S 24-471-3723   (BR)
SOBEYS CAPITAL INCORPORATED
SOBEYS STORE
(Suby of EMPIRE COMPANY LIMITED)
2651 Windsor St Suite 554, Halifax, NS, B3K 5C7
(902) 455-8508
Emp Here 80
SIC 5411 Grocery stores
 Jay Allen

 D-U-N-S 25-088-3634   (BR)
STAPLES CANADA ULC
STAPLES THE BUSINESS DEPOT
(Suby of SYCAMORE PARTNERS MANAGE-MENT, L.P.)
2003 Gottingen St, Halifax, NS, B3K 3B1
(902) 474-5100
Emp Here 75
SIC 5943 Stationery stores
 Doug Baker

 D-U-N-S 24-760-2878   (HQ)
SUPERLINE FUELS (2009) LIMITED
3479 Barrington St Suite 3451, Halifax, NS, B3K 2X8
(902) 429-0740
Emp Here 10   *Sales* 37,716,030
SIC 5172 Petroleum products, nec
 James D Eisenhauer
 Graham Eisenhauer
 Valerie Rowlands

 D-U-N-S 24-338-7545   (SL)
TWIN CITY ALARMS LIMITED
TWIN CITY ELECTRIC
6371 Lady Hammond Rd, Halifax, NS, B3K 2S2
(902) 455-0645
Emp Here 70   *Sales* 15,248,030
SIC 1731 Electrical work
 John Mccurdy

 D-U-N-S 20-031-0316   (HQ)
WILSON FUEL CO. LIMITED
WILSON'S GAS STOP
3617 Barrington St Suite 289, Halifax, NS, B3K 2Y3
(902) 429-3835
Emp Here 45   *Sales* 591,136,500
SIC 5172 Petroleum products, nec
 Ian Wilson
 Stephen Curry
 Steven Wilson
 Judy Winter

Halifax, NS B3L

 D-U-N-S 24-609-4887   (HQ)
3025906 NOVA SCOTIA LIMITED
PETRO CANADA
6389 Quinpool Rd, Halifax, NS, B3L 1A6
(902) 424-1397
Emp Here 5   *Sales* 24,903,900
SIC 5541 Gasoline service stations
 Joanne Walker
 Hassan Headayati

 D-U-N-S 20-336-6062   (SL)
AFFINIO INC
2717 Joseph Howe Dr Suite 300, Halifax, NS, B3L 4T9
(866) 991-3263
Emp Here 50   *Sales* 11,517,000
SIC 5734 Computer and software stores
 Timothy Burke

 D-U-N-S 20-929-7035   (HQ)
ATLANTIC WHOLESALERS LTD
SAVE EASY
(Suby of LOBLAW COMPANIES LIMITED)
3711 Joseph Howe Dr, Halifax, NS, B3L 4H8
(902) 468-8866
Emp Here 71   *Sales* 2,117,104,000
SIC 5411 Grocery stores
 Mark Butler
 F Thomas Cogswell
 David Bragg

 D-U-N-S 25-295-3914   (BR)
BAYSHORE HEALTHCARE LTD.
BAYSHORE HEALTHCARE LTD
(Suby of BAYSHORE HEALTHCARE LTD.)
7071 Bayers Rd Suite 237, Halifax, NS, B3L 2C2
(902) 425-7683
Emp Here 120
SIC 8059 Nursing and personal care, nec
 Ann Fontaine

 D-U-N-S 25-183-0311   (HQ)
BLUE OCEAN CONTACT CENTERS INC
(Suby of I.M.P. GROUP INTERNATIONAL IN-CORPORATED)
7051 Bayers Rd Suite 400, Halifax, NS, B3L 4V2
(902) 722-3300
Emp Here 500
SIC 7389 Business services, nec
 Andrew O'brien
 Patricia Isnor
 Julie Briggs
 Kim Campbell
 Mike Hasler
 Susan Preiss
 Cathy Biddulph
 Amy Bennett

 John Doan

 D-U-N-S 24-342-9750   (HQ)
BOONE FOOD SERVICES LIMITED
A & W
6960 Mumford Rd Suite 300, Halifax, NS, B3L 4P1
(902) 453-5330
Emp Here 7   *Sales* 16,790,040
SIC 5812 Eating places
 Winston Boone
 Michael Boone
 Charles Miles

 D-U-N-S 20-106-8843   (SL)
CANADIAN TIRE ASSOCIATE STORE
6203 Quinpool Rd Suite 44, Halifax, NS, B3L 4P6
(902) 422-4598
Emp Here 40   *Sales* 10,122,360
SIC 5251 Hardware stores
 Mary Watson

 D-U-N-S 25-174-9347   (BR)
COMCARE (CANADA) LIMITED
COMCARE HEALTH SERVICES
(Suby of COMCARE (CANADA) LIMITED)
7071 Bayers Rd Suite 1151, Halifax, NS, B3L 2C2
(902) 453-0838
Emp Here 250
SIC 8051 Skilled nursing care facilities
 Jackie Nunn

 D-U-N-S 20-342-7497   (SL)
FARES CONSTRUCTION LTD
3480 Joseph Howe Dr Suite 500, Halifax, NS, B3L 0B5
(902) 457-6676
Emp Here 50   *Sales* 22,556,400
SIC 1522 Residential construction, nec
 Wadih Fares
 Darren Rodgers

 D-U-N-S 20-176-0506   (HQ)
G.B.S. COMMUNICATIONS INC
TELUS
3480 Joseph Howe Dr Unit 200, Halifax, NS, B3L 0B5
(902) 431-1100
Emp Here 5   *Sales* 29,472,888
SIC 4899 Communication services, nec
 Eli Hage

 D-U-N-S 25-193-0764   (HQ)
GRAYBAR CANADA LIMITED
GRAYBAR CANADA
(Suby of GRAYBAR ELECTRIC COMPANY, INC.)
3600 Joseph Howe Dr, Halifax, NS, B3L 4H7
(902) 457-8787
Emp Here 80   *Sales* 333,642,025
SIC 5063 Electrical apparatus and equipment
 Brian Thomas
 Peter Horncastle
 Mike Williamson
 Roberta Whalen
 Amanda Canning

 D-U-N-S 20-106-6870   (HQ)
GRAYBAR ELECTRIC CANADA LIMITED
(Suby of GRAYBAR ELECTRIC COMPANY, INC.)
3600 Joseph Howe Dr, Halifax, NS, B3L 4H7
(902) 443-8311
Emp Here 2   *Sales* 290,123,500
SIC 5063 Electrical apparatus and equipment
 Peter Horncastle
 Michael Williamson

 D-U-N-S 24-129-6011   (SL)
H.R.D.A. ENTERPRISES LIMITED
STONE HEARTH BAKERY, DIV OF
7071 Bayers Rd Suite 5009, Halifax, NS, B3L 2C2
(902) 454-2851
Emp Here 60   *Sales* 15,427,860
SIC 4953 Refuse systems

Ron Singer
Mark Lever
Eric Crowell
Michael White

D-U-N-S 20-906-6422   (SL)
HALIFAX GOLF & COUNTRY CLUB, LIMITED
ASHBURN GOLF CLUB
3250 Joseph Howe Dr, Halifax, NS, B3L 4G1
(902) 443-8260
Emp Here 100   *Sales* 7,854,500
SIC 7997 Membership sports and recreation clubs
Bert Frizzel

D-U-N-S 24-186-1996   (HQ)
HALIFAX HERALD LIMITED, THE
HEADLINE PROMOTIONAL PRODUCTS
2717 Joseph Howe Dr Suite 101, Halifax, NS, B3L 4T9
(902) 426-2811
Emp Here 300   *Sales* 77,509,600
SIC 2711 Newspapers
Mark Lever
Sarah Dennis
Heather Dennis
Bryan Duffy

D-U-N-S 25-301-2678   (BR)
HUDSON'S BAY COMPANY
BAY, THE
(*Suby of* HUDSON'S BAY COMPANY)
7067 Chebucto Rd Suite 111, Halifax, NS, B3L 4R5

Emp Here 140
SIC 5311 Department stores
Louise Smith

D-U-N-S 20-026-9330   (HQ)
I.M.P. GROUP INTERNATIONAL INCORPORATED
2651 Joseph Howe Dr, Halifax, NS, B3L 4T1
(902) 453-2400
Emp Here 75   *Sales* 1,110,732,000
SIC 4581 Airports, flying fields, and services
Kenneth C. Rowe
Stephen K. Plummer
Kirk A. Rowe
Stephen K. Rowe
Raymond P. Mccormick
J. Darrell Taylor
Rick Benwell
Rob Burns
Robert Radchuck
Gilles Ouimet

D-U-N-S 20-932-5588   (HQ)
I.M.P. GROUP LIMITED
CAN-MED HEALTHCARE
(*Suby of* I.M.P. GROUP INTERNATIONAL INCORPORATED)
2651 Joseph Howe Dr Suite 400, Halifax, NS, B3L 4T1
(902) 453-2400
Emp Here 90   *Sales* 1,459,819,200
SIC 4581 Airports, flying fields, and services
Kenneth Rowe
Stephen Plummer
J. Darrell Taylor
Raymond Mccormick
Kirk Rowe
Stephen Rowe
Rick Benwell
Robert Radchuck
Gilles Ouimet
Daniel Sullivan

D-U-N-S 24-832-1643   (SL)
IMMIGRANT SERVICES ASSOCIATION OF NOVA SCOTIA
ISANS
6960 Mumford Rd Suite 2120, Halifax, NS, B3L 4P1
(902) 423-3607
Emp Here 125   *Sales* 16,439,375

SIC 8641 Civic and social associations
Gerry Mills
Claudette Legault

D-U-N-S 20-905-1333   (SL)
J M S PHARMACY SERVICE INC
SHOPPERS DRUG MART
3430 Joseph Howe Dr Suite 138, Halifax, NS, B3L 4H7
(902) 443-6084
Emp Here 48   *Sales* 12,141,792
SIC 5912 Drug stores and proprietary stores
Wayne Little

D-U-N-S 25-359-3206   (BR)
LOBLAW PROPERTIES LIMITED
ATLANTIC WHOLESALERS
(*Suby of* LOBLAW COMPANIES LIMITED)
3711 Joseph Howe Dr, Halifax, NS, B3L 4H8

Emp Here 80
SIC 5411 Grocery stores
Rusty Lambke

D-U-N-S 24-345-6170   (BR)
MELOCHE MONNEX INC
(*Suby of* TORONTO-DOMINION BANK, THE)
6940 Mumford Rd Suite 301, Halifax, NS, B3L 0B7
(902) 420-1112
Emp Here 105
SIC 6331 Fire, marine, and casualty insurance
Rachel Shano

D-U-N-S 20-364-1019   (HQ)
NOVA LEAP HEALTH CORP
7071 Bayers Rd Suite 5003, Halifax, NS, B3L 2C2
(902) 401-9480
Sales 10,362,179
SIC 8059 Nursing and personal care, nec
Chris Dobbin
Dana Hatfield
Michael Okeefe
Wayne Myles
Megan Spidle
Michael Gremley

D-U-N-S 24-670-3904   (HQ)
SENTINEL DRUGS LIMITED
DRUGSTORE PHARMACY, THE
(*Suby of* LOBLAW COMPANIES LIMITED)
3711 Joseph Howe Dr, Halifax, NS, B3L 4H8
(902) 468-8866
Emp Here 15   *Sales* 91,768,500
SIC 5912 Drug stores and proprietary stores
John Lederer
Peter Mulroy

D-U-N-S 24-189-5986   (HQ)
STANHOPE SIMPSON INSURANCE LIMITED
3845 Joseph Howe Dr Suite 300, Halifax, NS, B3L 4H9
(902) 454-8641
Emp Here 26   *Sales* 22,897,620
SIC 6411 Insurance agents, brokers, and service
Victor Stanhope
Donald Mcdermaid
Victoria Stanhope
Steve Bates

D-U-N-S 20-731-8671   (BR)
WAL-MART CANADA CORP
WALMART
(*Suby of* WALMART INC.)
6990 Mumford Rd Suite 3636, Halifax, NS, B3L 4W4
(902) 454-7990
Emp Here 150
SIC 5311 Department stores
George King

Halifax, NS B3M

D-U-N-S 25-176-4569   (SL)
BOURQUE SECURITY SERVICES NS
176 Bedford Hwy, Halifax, NS, B3M 2J8
(902) 832-2456
Emp Here 20   *Sales* 13,578,460
SIC 6289 Security and commodity service
Jamie Creelman

D-U-N-S 24-670-4225   (SL)
FAIRVIEW COVE AUTO LIMITED
ATLANTIC ACURA
30 Bedford Hwy, Halifax, NS, B3M 2J2
(902) 457-1555
Emp Here 30   *Sales* 14,942,340
SIC 5511 New and used car dealers
Bruce Hill

D-U-N-S 24-956-6001   (HQ)
FISHERMAN'S MARKET INTERNATIONAL INCORPORATED
TRASK LOBSTERS
607 Bedford Hwy, Halifax, NS, B3M 2L6
(902) 443-3474
Emp Here 100   *Sales* 100,340,240
SIC 5146 Fish and seafoods
Frederick Greene
David Macleod

D-U-N-S 25-366-7844   (SL)
HOMELIFE ATLANTIC
233 Bedford Hwy, Halifax, NS, B3M 2J9
(902) 457-4000
Emp Here 37   *Sales* 12,103,699
SIC 6531 Real estate agents and managers
Francis Macdonald

D-U-N-S 25-754-4056   (SL)
INDEPENDENT ARMOURED TRANSPORT ATLANTIC INC
287 Lacewood Dr Unit 103, Halifax, NS, B3M 3Y7
(902) 450-1396
Emp Here 60   *Sales* 23,740,680
SIC 7381 Detective and armored car services
Lawrence Conrad
Donald Boudreau

D-U-N-S 20-051-1066   (SL)
INDEPENDENT SECURITY SERVICES ATLANTIC (ISS) INC
ISS
287 Lacewood Dr Unit 103, Halifax, NS, B3M 3Y7
(902) 450-1396
Emp Here 87   *Sales* 34,423,986
SIC 7381 Detective and armored car services
Lawrence Conrad

D-U-N-S 20-780-8932   (HQ)
MOUNT SAINT VINCENT UNIVERSITY
MOUNT SAINT VINCENT
166 Bedford Hwy, Halifax, NS, B3M 2J6
(902) 457-6788
Sales 70,506,500
SIC 8221 Colleges and universities
Mary Bluechardt
Dr. Elizabeth Church
Brian Jessop
Kelly Gallant

D-U-N-S 25-746-4776   (HQ)
PACRIM DEVELOPMENTS INC
HOLIDAY INN EXPRESS-MONCTON
117 Kearney Lake Rd Suite 11, Halifax, NS, B3M 4N9
(902) 457-0144
Emp Here 30   *Sales* 37,232,200
SIC 6552 Subdividers and developers, nec
Guy Lam
Edward Good
Glenn Squires
Malcom Bell

D-U-N-S 20-524-1649   (HQ)
SCOTIA TIRE SERVICES LIMITED
267 Bedford Hwy, Halifax, NS, B3M 2K5

(902) 443-3150
Emp Here 9   *Sales* 15,938,496
SIC 5531 Auto and home supply stores
John Darrell Robinson
John Douglas Robinson
Marilyn Robinson

D-U-N-S 24-804-8258   (BR)
SHANNEX INCORPORATED
MAPLE STONE
(*Suby of* SHANNEX INCORPORATED)
245 Main Ave, Halifax, NS, B3M 1B7
(902) 443-1971
Emp Here 250
SIC 8051 Skilled nursing care facilities

D-U-N-S 20-027-3845   (HQ)
SHAW GROUP LIMITED, THE
255 Lacewood Dr Suite 100c, Halifax, NS, B3M 4G2
(902) 457-0689
Emp Here 15   *Sales* 140,629,500
SIC 3251 Brick and structural clay tile
Dean Robertson
Brady Hawley
Lindsay Hawker
Carol Macmillan
Wesley Armour
Adam Randell
Terence Bird
Bill Black
Fred Cahill
Bert Frizzell

D-U-N-S 24-706-1252   (SL)
SHOPPERS DRUG MART
278 Lacewood Dr Suite 136, Halifax, NS, B3M 3N8
(902) 443-5214
Emp Here 42   *Sales* 10,624,068
SIC 5912 Drug stores and proprietary stores
Brent Evans

D-U-N-S 24-338-0748   (HQ)
SISTERS OF CHARITY
MOUNT ST VINCENT MOTHER HOUSE
215 Seton Rd, Halifax, NS, B3M 0C9
(902) 406-8100
Emp Here 150   *Sales* 72,886,100
SIC 8661 Religious organizations

D-U-N-S 24-943-6056   (BR)
SOBEYS CAPITAL INCORPORATED
SOBEYS
(*Suby of* EMPIRE COMPANY LIMITED)
287 Lacewood Dr Suite 644, Halifax, NS, B3M 3Y7
(902) 457-2102
Emp Here 200
SIC 5411 Grocery stores
Maurice Berrigan

D-U-N-S 24-790-2935   (SL)
STEELE CHRYSLER PLYMOUTH LIMITED
44 Bedford Hwy, Halifax, NS, B3M 2J2
(902) 454-7341
Emp Here 60   *Sales* 37,756,800
SIC 5511 New and used car dealers
Robert Steele

D-U-N-S 24-832-7546   (SL)
WEICKERT, C & R ENTERPRISES LTD
CANADIAN TIRE ASSOC STORE 465
10 Radcliffe Dr Suite 465, Halifax, NS, B3M 4K7
(902) 823-2499
Emp Here 90   *Sales* 56,635,200
SIC 5531 Auto and home supply stores
Carlo Weickert
Rebecca Weickert
Jeffery Weickert
Jason Weickert

Halifax, NS B3N

▲ Public Company   ■ Public Company Family Member   **HQ** Headquarters   **BR** Branch   **SL** Single Location

D-U-N-S 20-025-9854 (SL)
GATEWAY INSURANCE BROKERS LTD
GATEWAY INSURANCE GROUP
371 St Margarets Bay Rd Suite 101, Halifax,
NS, B3N 1J8
(902) 431-9300
Emp Here 25   *Sales* 14,498,100
SIC 6411 Insurance agents, brokers, and service
  Keith Dexter

D-U-N-S 25-577-3749 (BR)
GEM HEALTH CARE GROUP LIMITED
GLADES LODGE
(*Suby of* GEM HEALTH CARE GROUP LIMITED)
25 Alton Dr, Halifax, NS, B3N 1M1
(902) 477-1777
Emp Here 140
SIC 8051 Skilled nursing care facilities
  Bonnie Griffin

Halifax, NS B3P

D-U-N-S 20-026-6740 (HQ)
CROWELLS PHARMACY LTD
PHARMASAVE
205 Herring Cove Rd Suite 505, Halifax, NS,
B3P 1L1
(902) 477-4650
Emp Here 1   *Sales* 10,118,160
SIC 5912 Drug stores and proprietary stores

D-U-N-S 24-755-5915 (HQ)
GEM HEALTH CARE GROUP LIMITED
MIRA NURSING HOME
15 Shoreham Lane Suite 101, Halifax, NS,
B3P 2R3
(902) 429-6227
Emp Here 8   *Sales* 27,330,400
SIC 8051 Skilled nursing care facilities
  Syed Hussain
  Gloria Hussain
  Jim Balcom

D-U-N-S 25-991-4620 (BR)
GEM HEALTH CARE GROUP LIMITED
GEM MANAGEMENT HOLDINGS
(*Suby of* GEM HEALTH CARE GROUP LIMITED)
15 Shoreham Lane Suite 101, Halifax, NS,
B3P 2R3
(902) 429-6227
Emp Here 700
SIC 6712 Bank holding companies
  Syed Hussain

D-U-N-S 20-781-9889 (HQ)
HALIFAX REGIONAL WATER COMMISSION
HALIFAX WATER
450 Cowie Hill Rd, Halifax, NS, B3P 2V3
(902) 490-4840
Sales 60,270,840
SIC 4941 Water supply
  Carl Yates
  Blaine Rooney

D-U-N-S 24-722-5295 (SL)
MELVILLE LODGE LIMITED PARTNERSHIP
50 Shoreham Lane, Halifax, NS, B3P 2R3
(902) 479-1030
Emp Here 140   *Sales* 9,565,640
SIC 8051 Skilled nursing care facilities
  Syed Hussain

D-U-N-S 24-878-6170 (SL)
ORB FACTORY LIMITED, THE
ORB TOYS
225 Herring Cove Rd, Halifax, NS, B3P 1L3
(902) 477-9570
Emp Here 100   *Sales* 52,054,200
SIC 5092 Toys and hobby goods and supplies
  Steven Kay
  Paul Higgins

D-U-N-S 20-004-0728 (BR)
SOBEYS CAPITAL INCORPORATED
SOBEYS
(*Suby of* EMPIRE COMPANY LIMITED)
279 Herring Cove Rd, Halifax, NS, B3P 1M2
(902) 477-2817
Emp Here 130
SIC 5411 Grocery stores
  Mark Guthro

Halifax, NS B3R

D-U-N-S 24-789-6350 (SL)
BLUNDEN CONSTRUCTION (1995) LIMITED
519 Herring Cove Rd, Halifax, NS, B3R 1X3
(902) 477-2531
Emp Here 50   *Sales* 16,666,650
SIC 1541 Industrial buildings and warehouses
  Douglas Blunden
  Walter Dann

D-U-N-S 20-106-8686 (SL)
CANADIAN TIRE
16 Dentith Rd, Halifax, NS, B3R 2H9
(902) 477-5608
Emp Here 45   *Sales* 11,387,655
SIC 5251 Hardware stores
  Lewanda Le Pierre

D-U-N-S 24-424-2678 (SL)
FATHOM FISH & SEAFOOD INC
339 Herring Cove Suite 215, Halifax, NS, B3R 1V5
(902) 407-0700
Emp Here 8   *Sales* 32,261,850
SIC 5146 Fish and seafoods

D-U-N-S 24-339-4376 (SL)
KURT RYAN PHARMACY SERVICES LTD
SHOPPERS DRUG MART
315 Herring Cove Rd, Halifax, NS, B3R 1V5
(902) 477-1210
Emp Here 65   *Sales* 15,881,320
SIC 5912 Drug stores and proprietary stores
  Kurt Ryan

Halifax, NS B3S

D-U-N-S 20-026-8571 (SL)
2178320 CANADA LTD
HALIFAX CHRYSLER DODGE JEEP
12 Lakelands Blvd, Halifax, NS, B3S 1S8
(902) 454-2369
Emp Here 60   *Sales* 37,756,800
SIC 5511 New and used car dealers
  Andrew Macphee
  Mary Macphee

D-U-N-S 24-187-7166 (HQ)
ALYRIN OPERATIONS LTD
TIM HORTONS
10 Ragged Lake Blvd Suite 8, Halifax, NS,
B3S 1C2
(902) 450-0056
Emp Here 30   *Sales* 12,336,840
SIC 5461 Retail bakeries
  John Mays

D-U-N-S 25-590-0268 (BR)
ATLANTIC WHOLESALERS LTD
REAL ATLANTIC SUPERSTORE, THE
(*Suby of* LOBLAW COMPANIES LIMITED)
210 Chain Lake Dr, Halifax, NS, B3S 1C5
(902) 450-5317
Emp Here 200
SIC 5411 Grocery stores
  Dave Dauphinee

D-U-N-S 24-878-4761 (HQ)
AVONDALE CONSTRUCTION LIMITED
49 Hobsons Lake Dr, Halifax, NS, B3S 0E4

---

(902) 876-1818
Emp Here 6   *Sales* 30,227,914
SIC 1542 Nonresidential construction, nec
  Bill Garnett

D-U-N-S 24-095-2960 (SL)
BLUEDROP SIMULATION SERVICES INC
(*Suby of* BLUEDROP PERFORMANCE LEARNING INC)
36 Solutions Dr Suite 300, Halifax, NS, B3S 1N2
(800) 563-3638
Emp Here 140   *Sales* 40,719,000
SIC 3728 Aircraft parts and equipment, nec
  Andrew Day
  Carolyn Goddout
  Jay Konduros
  Chris Lewis
  George Chiarucci

D-U-N-S 24-389-2049 (HQ)
BLUEDROP TRAINING & SIMULATION INC
(*Suby of* BLUEDROP PERFORMANCE LEARNING INC)
36 Solutions Dr Suite 300, Halifax, NS, B3S 1N2
(800) 563-3638
Sales 22,384,300
SIC 3728 Aircraft parts and equipment, nec
  Emad Rizkalla
  Jean-Claude Siew
  John Moores
  Barbarie Palmer
  Wayne Shaddock

D-U-N-S 24-756-6193 (SL)
C & D CLEANING & SECURITY SERVICES LIMITED
106 Chain Lake Dr Unit 2a, Halifax, NS, B3S 1A8
(902) 450-5654
Emp Here 125   *Sales* 3,996,000
SIC 7349 Building maintenance services, nec
  Eric Gay
  Ralph Creelman
  Terry Creelman

D-U-N-S 25-528-2162 (BR)
COSTCO WHOLESALE CANADA LTD
COSTCO WHOLESALE STORE # 519
(*Suby of* COSTCO WHOLESALE CORPORATION)
230 Chain Lake Dr, Halifax, NS, B3S 1C5
(902) 450-1078
Emp Here 180
SIC 5099 Durable goods, nec
  Diane Sacre

D-U-N-S 24-931-9500 (HQ)
DAVIS STRAIT FISHERIES LIMITED
71 Mcquade Lake Cres, Halifax, NS, B3S 1C4
(902) 450-5115
Sales 68,517,314
SIC 5146 Fish and seafoods
  Grant Stonehouse

D-U-N-S 24-334-8575 (SL)
DWS DATA WIRING SOLUTIONS INC
127 Chain Lake Dr Unit 1, Halifax, NS, B3S 1B3
(902) 445-9473
Emp Here 80   *Sales* 15,235,360
SIC 3651 Household audio and video equipment
  Shawn Kersey
  Hugh Macleod

D-U-N-S 24-629-4045 (SL)
EISENHAUER INSURANCE INCORPORATED
362 Lacewood Dr Suite 205, Halifax, NS, B3S 1M7
(902) 454-5888
Emp Here 22   *Sales* 12,758,328
SIC 6411 Insurance agents, brokers, and service
  Robert Eisenhauer
  Patricia Eisenhauer

D-U-N-S 24-122-3853 (SL)
ENVIROBATE INC
93 Susie Lake Cres, Halifax, NS, B3S 1C3
(902) 832-0820
Emp Here 140   *Sales* 44,647,400
SIC 4959 Sanitary services, nec
  Robert Macdonald
  Carl Lang

D-U-N-S 24-605-9646 (HQ)
FLEETWAY INC
FLEETWAY FACILITIES SERVICES
84 Chain Lake Dr Suite 200, Halifax, NS, B3S 1A2
(902) 494-5700
Emp Here 75   *Sales* 54,211,025
SIC 8711 Engineering services
  James K Irving
  John E. Irving
  Arthur L. Irving
  James D. Irving
  Norman Brown
  W. David Jamieson
  Bruce A. Drost
  William Mclean
  John F. Irving
  Kenneth Irving

D-U-N-S 20-710-2950 (BR)
HALIFAX REGIONAL SCHOOL BOARD
HALIFAX WEST HIGHSCHOOL
(*Suby of* HALIFAX REGIONAL SCHOOL BOARD)
283 Thomas Raddall Dr, Halifax, NS, B3S 1R1
(902) 457-8900
Emp Here 112
SIC 8211 Elementary and secondary schools

D-U-N-S 24-329-7814 (HQ)
HOLLOWAY LODGING CORPORATION
106-145 Hobson Lake Dr, Halifax, NS, B3S 0H9
(902) 404-3499
Sales 81,812,852
SIC 7011 Hotels and motels
  Jane Rafuse
  Felix Seiler
  Michael Rapps
  Marc Staniloff
  Richard Grimaldi
  Dustin Haw
  David Wood

D-U-N-S 25-098-8359 (BR)
HOME DEPOT OF CANADA INC
(*Suby of* THE HOME DEPOT INC)
368 Lacewood Dr, Halifax, NS, B3S 1L8
(902) 457-3480
Emp Here 160
SIC 5211 Lumber and other building materials
  Brian Drane

D-U-N-S 24-373-8254 (HQ)
LED ROADWAY LIGHTING LTD
115 Chain Lake Dr Suite 201, Halifax, NS, B3S 1B3
(902) 450-2222
Emp Here 30   *Sales* 33,327,350
SIC 3648 Lighting equipment, nec
  Charles Cartmill

D-U-N-S 24-804-0792 (HQ)
MARITIME BROADCASTING SYSTEM LIMITED
CJCB
90 Lovett Lake Crt Suite 101, Halifax, NS, B3S 0H6
(902) 425-1225
Emp Here 12   *Sales* 93,673,520
SIC 4832 Radio broadcasting stations
  Robert L. Pace
  Owen Barnhill

D-U-N-S 20-028-4562 (SL)
MORTGAGEATLANTIC
14 Mcquade Lake Cres Unit 202, Halifax, NS,
B3S 1B6

---

(902) 493-3326
Emp Here 15   *Sales* 10,301,793
SIC 6211 Security brokers and dealers
Dean Sabourin

D-U-N-S 20-931-1372   (HQ)
NOVA SCOTIA LIQUOR CORPORATION
(*Suby of* NOVA SCOTIA, PROVINCE OF)
93 Chain Lake Dr, Halifax, NS, B3S 1A3
(902) 450-6752
Emp Here 150   *Sales* 498,036,337
SIC 5921 Liquor stores
Bret Mitchell
George Mclellan
Roddy Macdonald
Tim Pellerin
Liz Cody
John Mackinnon
James Wilson
Paul Kent
Kim Brooks
Michele Mckenzie

D-U-N-S 20-030-9565   (HQ)
ROSS, JOHN AND SONS LIMITED
171 Chain Lake Dr, Halifax, NS, B3S 1B3
(902) 450-5633
Emp Here 45   *Sales* 31,232,520
SIC 5093 Scrap and waste materials
Norman Ross
Jonathan Ross
Mark Monette
Tina Weir
Jing Xie

D-U-N-S 25-380-7440   (HQ)
SAMUEL & CO. APPAREL LIMITED
127 Chain Lake Dr Unit 9, Halifax, NS, B3S 1B3
(902) 454-7093
Emp Here 20   *Sales* 22,424,500
SIC 5621 Women's clothing stores
Nancy Holmes

D-U-N-S 24-931-8494   (HQ)
SHANNEX INCORPORATED
ARMVIEW ESTATES
48 Lovett Lake Crt, Halifax, NS, B3S 1B8
(902) 454-7499
Emp Here 30   *Sales* 68,326,000
SIC 8051 Skilled nursing care facilities
Joseph Shannon
Jason Shannon

D-U-N-S 24-533-8330   (HQ)
SHERLOCK CLOTHING LIMITED
PSEUDIO
127 Chain Lake Dr Unit 9, Halifax, NS, B3S 1B3
(902) 454-7098
Sales 17,939,600
SIC 5651 Family clothing stores
Rodney Hatcher
Arianna Card

D-U-N-S 25-175-0337   (BR)
SIR CORP
JACK ASTOR'S BAR & GRILL
(*Suby of* SIR CORP)
184 Chain Lake Dr, Halifax, NS, B3S 1C5
(902) 450-1370
Emp Here 82
SIC 5812 Eating places
Steven Macpherson

D-U-N-S 24-419-9514   (BR)
TRANSCONTINENTAL INC
(*Suby of* TRANSCONTINENTAL INC)
11 Ragged Lake Blvd, Halifax, NS, B3S 1R3
(902) 450-5611
Emp Here 100
SIC 2752 Commercial printing, lithographic

D-U-N-S 25-498-3026   (BR)
WAL-MART CANADA CORP
(*Suby of* WALMART INC.)
220 Chain Lake Dr, Halifax, NS, B3S 1C5
(902) 450-5570
Emp Here 200

SIC 5311 Department stores
Jim Laycock

Hammonds Plains, NS B3Z

D-U-N-S 24-262-7768   (BR)
I.M.P. GROUP LIMITED
IMP ELECTRONIC SYSTEMS
(*Suby of* I.M.P. GROUP INTERNATIONAL INCORPORATED)
3101 Hammonds Plains Rd, Hammonds Plains, NS, B3Z 1H7
(902) 835-4433
Emp Here 110
SIC 4581 Airports, flying fields, and services
David Meagher

Hammonds Plains, NS B4B

D-U-N-S 25-361-5900   (BR)
MARWOOD LTD
CAPE COD WOOD SIDINGS DIV OF
(*Suby of* ASHMORE LIMITED)
1948 Hammonds Plains Rd, Hammonds Plains, NS, B4B 1P4
(902) 835-9629
Emp Here 110
SIC 2421 Sawmills and planing mills, general
Gordon Stewart

Hantsport, NS B0P

D-U-N-S 20-027-5857   (HQ)
CKF INC
(*Suby of* SCOTIA INVESTMENTS LIMITED)
48 Prince St, Hantsport, NS, B0P 1P0
(902) 684-3231
Emp Here 350   *Sales* 147,108,192
SIC 3086 Plastics foam products
George Bishop

Havre Boucher, NS B0H

D-U-N-S 24-856-2675   (SL)
MSM CONSTRUCTION SERVICES LTD
(*Suby of* NSM ACQUISITION COMPANY LIMITED)
12575 Highway 4, Havre Boucher, NS, B0H 1P0
(902) 234-3202
Emp Here 57   *Sales* 12,416,253
SIC 1761 Roofing, siding, and sheetMetal work
Darren Nantes
Gregory Mombourquette
William Brown

D-U-N-S 20-365-3597   (HQ)
NSM ACQUISITION COMPANY LIMITED
12575 Highway 4, Havre Boucher, NS, B0H 1P0
(902) 234-3202
Sales 13,077,650
SIC 6712 Bank holding companies
Darren S. Nantes
Gregory Mombourquette
William Brown

Hebbville, NS B4V

D-U-N-S 20-369-9111   (SL)
BRIDGEWATER MAZDA

15230 Highway 3, Hebbville, NS, B4V 6X5
(902) 530-9666
Emp Here 34   *Sales* 16,934,652
SIC 5511 New and used car dealers
James Saunders
Peter Saunders
Steven Saunders

Herring Cove, NS B3R

D-U-N-S 24-955-5061   (SL)
LUMBER MART LIMITED
751 Herring Cove Rd, Herring Cove, NS, B3R 1Y9
(902) 477-6500
Emp Here 25   *Sales* 11,179,350
SIC 5039 Construction materials, nec
Fred O'hearn

Hubbards, NS B0J

D-U-N-S 25-308-6151   (SL)
FREEWHEELING ADVENTURES INCORPORATED
FREEWHEELING ADVENTURES
2070 Highway 329, Hubbards, NS, B0J 1T0
(902) 857-3600
Emp Here 26   *Sales* 13,519,142
SIC 4724 Travel agencies
Philip Guest
Catherine Guest

Hunts Point, NS B0T

D-U-N-S 20-443-6257   (HQ)
WHITE POINT HOLDINGS LIMITED
WHITE POINT BEACH RESORT
75 White Point Rd Suite 2, Hunts Point, NS, B0T 1G0
(902) 354-2711
Sales 23,234,750
SIC 6712 Bank holding companies
Robert Risley
Douglas Fawthrop

Inverness, NS B0E

D-U-N-S 24-188-4444   (HQ)
INVERNESS MUNICIPAL HOUSING CORPORATION
INVERARY MANOR
72 Maple St, Inverness, NS, B0E 1N0
(902) 258-2842
Emp Here 92   *Sales* 9,001,800
SIC 8051 Skilled nursing care facilities
Michael Macdougall

Isaacs Harbour, NS B0H

D-U-N-S 20-447-1706   (SL)
EXXONMOBIL
Gd, Isaacs Harbour, NS, B0H 1S0
(902) 387-3000
Emp Here 5   *Sales* 15,529,285
SIC 4924 Natural gas distribution

Kemptville, NS B5A

D-U-N-S 20-322-5271   (SL)

3092983 NOVA SCOTIA LIMITED
877 Highway 203, Kemptville, NS, B5A 5R3
(902) 761-2334
Emp Here 5   *Sales* 15,310,260
SIC 5146 Fish and seafoods
Lery D'eon

Kentville, NS B4N

D-U-N-S 20-256-5412   (SL)
3188192 NOVA SCOTIA INCORPORATED
KENTVILLE MAZDA
971 Park St, Kentville, NS, B4N 3X1
(902) 678-3323
Emp Here 25   *Sales* 12,451,950
SIC 5511 New and used car dealers
Michael Landry
Lisa Landry

D-U-N-S 24-524-3956   (BR)
ANNAPOLIS VALLEY DISTRICT HEALTH AUTHORITY
(*Suby of* NOVA SCOTIA, PROVINCE OF)
150 Exhibition St, Kentville, NS, B4N 5E3
(902) 678-7381
Emp Here 100
SIC 8062 General medical and surgical hospitals
Janet Knox

D-U-N-S 24-952-8014   (SL)
ANNAPOLIS VALLEY WORK ACTIVITY SOCIETY
11 Opportunity Lane, Kentville, NS, B4N 3V7
(902) 679-2755
Emp Here 30   *Sales* 20,904,300
SIC 6733 Trusts, nec
Shawna Sequeira

D-U-N-S 25-099-6287   (SL)
APPLE VALLEY FOODS INCORPORATED
14 Calkin Dr, Kentville, NS, B4N 1J5
(902) 679-4701
Emp Here 150   *Sales* 51,853,500
SIC 2051 Bread, cake, and related products
Jeff Sarsfield

D-U-N-S 25-865-9127   (HQ)
CAPITAL PAPER PRODUCTS LIMITED
27 Calkin Dr, Kentville, NS, B4N 3V7
(902) 678-6767
Emp Here 1   *Sales* 12,087,792
SIC 5113 Industrial and personal service paper
Jeff Zettler
Sharon Calder

D-U-N-S 20-394-0619   (SL)
JEFFREY BEST MOTORS INCORPORATED
KENTVILLE TOYOTA
843 Park St, Kentville, NS, B4N 3V7
(902) 678-6000
Emp Here 33   *Sales* 16,436,574
SIC 5511 New and used car dealers
Bryan Illsley
Joshua Macgrath
Andrew Pye

D-U-N-S 20-287-4355   (SL)
KENTVILLE CHRYSLER DODGE JEEP (2005) INC
800 Park St, Kentville, NS, B4N 3V7
(902) 678-2134
Emp Here 30   *Sales* 14,942,340
SIC 5511 New and used car dealers
Jon Carey
Shawn Carey

D-U-N-S 24-189-5846   (HQ)
MACDONALD CHISHOLM INCORPORATED
6 Masters Ave, Kentville, NS, B4N 2N6
(902) 678-6277
Emp Here 5   *Sales* 35,618,520

SIC 6411 Insurance agents, brokers, and service
Michael Brien
Ronald L French
George L Eye

D-U-N-S 24-579-3471   (BR)
NOVA SCOTIA HEALTH AUTHORITY
AVH CHIPMAN
(*Suby of* NOVA SCOTIA, PROVINCE OF)
5 Chipman Dr, Kentville, NS, B4N 3V7
(902) 365-1700
Emp Here 100
SIC 8062 General medical and surgical hospitals
Dan Pulsifer

D-U-N-S 20-027-8570   (SL)
PALMETER'S COUNTRY HOME (1986) LTD
EVERGREENS HOMES FOR SPECIAL CARE
655 Park St, Kentville, NS, B4N 3V7
(902) 678-7355
Emp Here 120   *Sales* 8,227,920
SIC 8051 Skilled nursing care facilities
Fred Houghton

D-U-N-S 20-027-8273   (BR)
PEPSICO CANADA ULC
FRITO LAY CANADA
(*Suby of* PEPSICO, INC.)
Gd, Kentville, NS, B4N 3W9
(902) 681-6183
Emp Here 200
SIC 2096 Potato chips and similar snacks
Cummings Karen

D-U-N-S 20-102-7575   (BR)
PEPSICO CANADA ULC
FRITO LAY CANADA
(*Suby of* PEPSICO, INC.)
59 Warehouse Rd, Kentville, NS, B4N 3W9
(902) 681-2923
Emp Here 100
SIC 2096 Potato chips and similar snacks
Ralph Comeau

D-U-N-S 25-331-4488   (SL)
PLANTERS EQUIPMENT LIMITED
JOHN DEERE
Gd, Kentville, NS, B4N 3V6
(902) 678-5555
Emp Here 1   *Sales* 12,216,400
SIC 5999 Miscellaneous retail stores, nec
Earl Kidston
Jeffrey Griffin
Dale Townsend
Robert Atkinson
Raymond Parsons

D-U-N-S 24-832-7918   (SL)
SLIPP, SCOTT NISSAN LIMITED
975 Park St, Kentville, NS, B4N 4H8
(902) 679-4000
Emp Here 26   *Sales* 12,950,028
SIC 5521 Used car dealers
Scott Slipp
Raymond Sacrey

D-U-N-S 20-009-1077   (SL)
VALLEY FORD LIMITED
898 Park St, Kentville, NS, B4N 3V7
(902) 678-1330
Emp Here 28   *Sales* 13,946,184
SIC 5511 New and used car dealers
Peter Simmons

D-U-N-S 24-738-7251   (SL)
VAN MEEKEREN FARMS LTD
237 Thorpe Rd, Kentville, NS, B4N 3V7
(902) 678-2366
Emp Here 44   *Sales* 36,765,388
SIC 5148 Fresh fruits and vegetables
Stephen Van Meekeren
Michael Meekeren

D-U-N-S 20-654-7742   (BR)
VON CANADA FOUNDATION

VON COMMITTEE SUPPORT
46 Chipman Dr Suite 1, Kentville, NS, B4N 3V7
(902) 678-1733
Emp Here 200
SIC 8621 Professional organizations
John Doe

D-U-N-S 20-027-8836   (HQ)
WORKPLACE ESSENTIALS LTD
59 Webster St, Kentville, NS, B4N 1H6
(902) 678-6106
Emp Here 22   *Sales* 21,371,952
SIC 5021 Furniture
Leigh Morrison
Ian Morrison

D-U-N-S 24-452-3155   (SL)
XERIUM CANADA INC
CORPORATION WEAVEXX
650 Park St, Kentville, NS, B4N 3W6
(902) 678-7311
Emp Here 100   *Sales* 18,340,300
SIC 2211 Broadwoven fabric mills, cotton
David Pretty
Michael F. Bly
Clifford E. Pietrafitta
David James

Kingston, NS B0P

D-U-N-S 20-027-8968   (HQ)
ARMSTRONG, O.H. LIMITED
1478 Park St, Kingston, NS, B0P 1R0
(902) 765-3311
Sales 83,557,700
SIC 5147 Meats and meat products
Jerry Hiltz

D-U-N-S 20-208-7388   (HQ)
J.D.I. VENTURES LIMITED
GREENWOOD PETRO CANADA
957 Central Ave, Kingston, NS, B0P 1R0

Emp Here 5   *Sales* 24,903,900
SIC 5541 Gasoline service stations
John Ives

D-U-N-S 25-503-7434   (SL)
MID-VALLEY CONSTRUCTION (1997) LIMITED
15096 Highway 1, Kingston, NS, B0P 1R0
(902) 765-6312
Emp Here 50   *Sales* 15,943,450
SIC 1521 Single-family housing construction
Craig Parsons
John Parsons

Lahave, NS B0R

D-U-N-S 24-574-2127   (HQ)
LAHAVE SEAFOODS LIMITED
3371 Hwy 331, Lahave, NS, B0R 1C0
(902) 688-2773
Sales 10,118,475
SIC 2091 Canned and cured fish and seafoods
David Himmelman

Lakeside, NS B3T

D-U-N-S 20-706-6353   (BR)
COCA-COLA CANADA BOTTLING LIMITED
(*Suby of* COCA-COLA CANADA BOTTLING LIMITED)
20 Lakeside Park Dr, Lakeside, NS, B3T 1L8
(902) 876-8661
Emp Here 100

SIC 2086 Bottled and canned soft drinks
Jeff Brown

D-U-N-S 20-026-6294   (BR)
COCA-COLA LTD
COCA-COLA BOTTLING
(*Suby of* THE COCA-COLA COMPANY)
20 Lakeside Park Dr, Lakeside, NS, B3T 1L8
(902) 876-8661
Emp Here 100
SIC 5149 Groceries and related products, nec

D-U-N-S 20-026-5346   (SL)
D. R. BRENTON LIMITED
DON BRENTON'S FIRE PROTECTION
2 Lakeside Park Dr Unit 5, Lakeside, NS, B3T 1L7
(902) 876-7879
Emp Here 23   *Sales* 11,972,466
SIC 5099 Durable goods, nec
Melissa Brenton
Matthew Brenton

D-U-N-S 20-014-6590   (HQ)
EMERA UTILITY SERVICES INCORPORATED
CABLECOM DIV.
(*Suby of* EMERA INCORPORATED)
31 Dominion Cres, Lakeside, NS, B3T 1M3
(902) 832-7999
Emp Here 143   *Sales* 32,674,350
SIC 1731 Electrical work
Craig Sutherland
Peter Murray
Scott Lafleur
Phil Stevens

D-U-N-S 20-003-7013   (SL)
MIRROR NOVA SCOTIA LIMITED
(*Suby of* MUNICIPAL ENTERPRISES LIMITED)
600 Otter Lake Dr, Lakeside, NS, B3T 2E2
(902) 453-3490
Emp Here 75   *Sales* 18,933,150
SIC 1629 Heavy construction, nec
Kurt Jacobs

D-U-N-S 25-356-6079   (BR)
RUSSEL METALS INC
RUSSEL METALS - ATLANTIC
(*Suby of* RUSSEL METALS INC)
28 Lakeside Park Dr, Lakeside, NS, B3T 1A3
(902) 876-7861
Emp Here 80
SIC 5051 Metals service centers and offices
Greg Bryant

D-U-N-S 20-607-3913   (SL)
SCOTIA FOODSERVICE LTD
EASTERN FOOD SERVICE
4 Dominion Cres, Lakeside, NS, B3T 1M1
(902) 876-2356
Emp Here 35   *Sales* 29,245,195
SIC 5141 Groceries, general line
Jerry Hilthz

D-U-N-S 24-877-5389   (BR)
SYSCO CANADA, INC
SYSCO FOOD SERVICES OF ATLANTIC CANADA
(*Suby of* SYSCO CORPORATION)
1 Duck Pond Rd Suite 1, Lakeside, NS, B3T 1M5
(902) 876-2311
Emp Here 250
SIC 5812 Eating places
Greg Davis

Lantz, NS B2S

D-U-N-S 24-207-9643   (BR)
SHAW GROUP LIMITED, THE
1101 Highway 2, Lantz, NS, B2S 1M9
(902) 883-2201
Emp Here 300

SIC 3251 Brick and structural clay tile
Bert Frizzell

Larrys River, NS B0H

D-U-N-S 20-213-9833   (SL)
TOR BAY FISHERIES LIMITED
472 Tor Bay Branch Rd, Larrys River, NS, B0H 1T0
(902) 525-2423
Emp Here 40   *Sales* 17,739,600
SIC 7389 Business services, nec
Willard Grover
Elizabeth Grover

Lawrencetown., NS B0S

D-U-N-S 24-472-2195   (BR)
NOVA SCOTIA, PROVINCE OF
NOVA SCOTIA COMMUNITY COLLEGE
(*Suby of* NOVA SCOTIA, PROVINCE OF)
50 Elliott Rd Suite 1, Lawrencetown., NS, B0S 1M0
(902) 584-2226
Emp Here 91
SIC 8222 Junior colleges
Jim Stanley

D-U-N-S 24-386-4431   (SL)
VALLEY INDUSTRIES (2007) LTD
BLUELINE NEW HOLLAND
110 Lawrencetown Lane, Lawrencetown., NS, B0S 1M0
(902) 584-2211
Emp Here 37   *Sales* 12,047,200
SIC 5999 Miscellaneous retail stores, nec
Eric Bent
Jacqueline Bent

Little River, NS B0V

D-U-N-S 24-487-7200   (SL)
L.J. ROBICHEAU & SON FISHERIES LIMITED
219 Shore Rd, Little River, NS, B0V 1C0
(902) 834-2792
Emp Here 45   *Sales* 10,118,475
SIC 2092 Fresh or frozen packaged fish
Cecil Robicheau
Llewellyn Robicheau

Liverpool, NS B0T

D-U-N-S 20-028-0642   (SL)
MERSEY SEAFOODS LIMITED
26 Bristol Ave, Liverpool, NS, B0T 1K0
(902) 354-3467
Emp Here 120   *Sales* 86,005,920
SIC 5146 Fish and seafoods
William Murphy

D-U-N-S 24-342-7382   (SL)
QUEENS HOME FOR SPECIAL CARE SOCIETY
QUEENS MANOR
20 Hollands Dr, Liverpool, NS, B0T 1K0
(902) 354-3451
Emp Here 80   *Sales* 4,739,760
SIC 8361 Residential care
Bob Mconnell
Tara Smith

D-U-N-S 24-943-5868   (BR)
SOBEYS CAPITAL INCORPORATED
SOBEYS 588

(Suby of EMPIRE COMPANY LIMITED)
180 Bristol Ave, Liverpool, NS, B0T 1K0
(902) 354-4225
Emp Here 100
SIC 5411 Grocery stores
 Robert Myers

D-U-N-S 24-357-6589   (BR)
**SOUTH SHORE DISTRICT HEALTH AU-
THORITY**
QUEENS GENERAL HOSPITAL
(Suby of NOVA SCOTIA, PROVINCE OF)
175 School St, Liverpool, NS, B0T 1K0
(902) 354-5785
Emp Here 128
SIC 8069 Specialty hospitals, except psychi-
atric
 Debra Doucette

Lockeport, NS B0T

D-U-N-S 24-804-1121   (BR)
THORNVALE HOLDINGS LIMITED
PIERCE FISHERIES
(Suby of THORNVALE HOLDINGS LIMITED)
68 Water St, Lockeport, NS, B0T 1L0
(902) 656-2413
Emp Here 225
SIC 2092 Fresh or frozen packaged fish
 Mike Roy

Louisbourg, NS B1C

D-U-N-S 25-978-8768   (SL)
A & L SEAFOODS LIMITED
20 Minto St, Louisbourg, NS, B1C 1L1
(902) 733-2900
Emp Here 90   *Sales* 75,201,930
SIC 5146 Fish and seafoods
 Pat Quinlan
 Lloyd Lamey
 Joseph Anthony
 Dereck Philpott

D-U-N-S 24-605-8176   (SL)
J K MARINE SERVICES LIMITED
5 Commercial St, Louisbourg, NS, B1C 1B5
(902) 733-2739
Emp Here 60   *Sales* 50,134,620
SIC 5146 Fish and seafoods
 James Kennedy

D-U-N-S 24-628-7726   (SL)
LOUISBOURG SEAFOODS LTD
3 Commercial St, Louisbourg, NS, B1C 1B5
(902) 733-2079
Emp Here 70   *Sales* 24,198,300
SIC 2091 Canned and cured fish and
seafoods
 James Kennedy

Lower East Pubnico, NS B0W

D-U-N-S 24-190-9324   (SL)
PUBNICO TRAWLERS LIMITED
ALYSSA FOODS, DIV OF
155 Hwy 3, Lower East Pubnico, NS, B0W
2A0
(902) 762-3202
Emp Here 20   *Sales* 10,702,480
SIC 5141 Groceries, general line
 George Cunningham
 Patricia Cunningham

Lower Onslow, NS B6L

D-U-N-S 20-028-1707   (SL)
MACLEOD'S FARM MACHINERY LIMITED
12412 Hwy 2, Lower Onslow, NS, B6L 5E3
(902) 662-2516
Emp Here 25   *Sales* 11,875,650
SIC 5083 Farm and garden machinery
 Carson Macleod
 Dwayne Langille
 Mark Maclellan
 John A. Macdonald

Lower Prospect, NS B3T

D-U-N-S 20-242-8491   (SL)
EAST COAST OUTFITTERS
2017 Lower Prospect Rd, Lower Prospect,
NS, B3T 1Y8
(902) 624-0334
Emp Here 30   *Sales* 15,599,010
SIC 4725 Tour operators
 David Adler

Lower Sackville, NS B4C

D-U-N-S 24-606-6088   (SL)
**A.C. DISPENSING EQUIPMENT INCORPO-
RATED**
SURESHOT DISPENSING SYSTEMS
100 Dispensing Way, Lower Sackville, NS,
B4C 4H2
(902) 865-9602
Emp Here 110   *Sales* 24,420,110
SIC 3585 Refrigeration and heating equip-
ment
 Michael Duck
 David Macaulay
 Ian Tramble
 Ian Maclean
 Cameron Haygarth
 Ian Tramble
 Deanna Mackinnon

D-U-N-S 24-894-1218   (SL)
AA MUNRO INSURANCE
209 Cobequid Rd, Lower Sackville, NS, B4C
3P3
(902) 864-2510
Emp Here 15   *Sales* 15,523,215
SIC 6311 Life insurance
 Aneill Maccaull

D-U-N-S 24-705-1105   (HQ)
**ARCHIE'S SACKVILLE BOTTLE EX-
CHANGE LIMITED**
446 Sackville Dr, Lower Sackville, NS, B4C
2R8
(902) 865-9010
Emp Here 21   *Sales* 11,230,475
SIC 7389 Business services, nec
 Bradley O'connell

D-U-N-S 25-629-5445   (SL)
CARS R US LTD
183 Sackville Dr, Lower Sackville, NS, B4C
2R5
(902) 864-1109
Emp Here 30   *Sales* 14,942,340
SIC 5521 Used car dealers
 Gary Shea
 Evelyn Shea

D-U-N-S 20-028-2002   (HQ)
PAYZANT BUILDING PRODUCTS LIMITED
PAYZANT HOME CENTRE
250 Sackville Dr, Lower Sackville, NS, B4C
2R4
(902) 864-0000
Emp Here 85   *Sales* 26,765,200
SIC 5211 Lumber and other building materials
 John Payzant

 James Payzant
 Jeff Payzant
 John L Payzant
 Andrew Payzant

D-U-N-S 24-955-7844   (SL)
SACKVILLE SPORTS STADIUM
409 Glendale Dr, Lower Sackville, NS, B4C
2T6
(902) 252-4000
Emp Here 150   *Sales* 14,242,950
SIC 7999 Amusement and recreation, nec
 Michael Bird

D-U-N-S 24-964-9661   (SL)
STRONGEST FAMILIES INSTITUTE
267 Cobequid Rd Suite 200, Lower Sackville,
NS, B4C 4E6
(902) 442-9520
Emp Here 42   *Sales* 11,959,374
SIC 8733 Noncommercial research organiza-
tions
 Patrick Mcgrath

Lower Sackville, NS B4E

D-U-N-S 24-670-7665   (BR)
ATLANTIC WHOLESALERS LTD
REAL ATLANTIC SUPERSTORE, THE
(Suby of LOBLAW COMPANIES LIMITED)
745 Sackville Dr, Lower Sackville, NS, B4E
2R2
(902) 864-2299
Emp Here 300
SIC 5411 Grocery stores
 Chris Cluett

D-U-N-S 25-891-6261   (BR)
ICT CANADA MARKETING INC
I C T GROUP
(Suby of SYKES ENTERPRISES INCORPO-
RATED)
800 Sackville Dr, Lower Sackville, NS, B4E
1R8
(902) 869-9050
Emp Here 200
SIC 7389 Business services, nec
 Jackie Fritz

D-U-N-S 25-298-1162   (BR)
SOBEYS CAPITAL INCORPORATED
SOBEYS #670
(Suby of EMPIRE COMPANY LIMITED)
752 Sackville Dr Suite 670, Lower Sackville,
NS, B4E 1R7
(902) 865-5057
Emp Here 200
SIC 5411 Grocery stores
 Jeff Thorsen

Lower Truro, NS B6L

D-U-N-S 25-769-7797   (HQ)
TREATY ENTERPRISE INC
TREATY ENTERTAINMENT
10 Treaty Trail, Lower Truro, NS, B6L 1V9
(902) 897-2650
Emp Here 50   *Sales* 29,347,700
SIC 5411 Grocery stores
 Jack Paul

Lower Wedgeport, NS B0W

D-U-N-S 20-906-6018   (HQ)
MURPHY, R & K ENTERPRISES LIMITED
2871 Highway 334, Lower Wedgeport, NS,
B0W 2B0
(902) 663-2503
Sales 12,533,655

SIC 5146 Fish and seafoods
 Roland Murphy

D-U-N-S 20-271-8243   (SL)
OCEAN LEADER FISHERIES LIMITED
138 Jacquard Rd, Lower Wedgeport, NS,
B0W 2B0
(902) 663-4579
Emp Here 50   *Sales* 11,372,962
SIC 2092 Fresh or frozen packaged fish
 Milton Leblanc
 Allen Hansen

Lower West Pubnico, NS B0W

D-U-N-S 20-444-6355   (SL)
INSHORE FISHERIES LIMITED
95 Dennis Point Rd, Lower West Pubnico, NS,
B0W 2C0
(902) 762-2522
Emp Here 70   *Sales* 10,432,201
SIC 2092 Fresh or frozen packaged fish

Lower Woods Harbour, NS B0W

D-U-N-S 25-688-8389   (HQ)
TWIN SEAFOOD LIMITED
6689 Wood Harbour Rd, Lower Woods Har-
bour, NS, B0W 2E0
(902) 723-9003
Sales 10,026,924
SIC 5146 Fish and seafoods
 Margaret Atkinson
 Arley Atkinson

Lunenburg, NS B0J

D-U-N-S 20-388-6713   (SL)
ABCO INDUSTRIES INC
81 Tannery Rd, Lunenburg, NS, B0J 2C0
(902) 634-8821
Emp Here 57   *Sales* 12,654,057
SIC 3569 General industrial machinery, nec
 John Meisner
 Gregory Huskilson
 Jason Huskilson
 Michael Huskilson

D-U-N-S 24-506-7272   (SL)
ABCO INDUSTRIES LIMITED
81 Tannery Rd, Lunenburg, NS, B0J 2C0
(902) 634-8821
Emp Here 60   *Sales* 13,320,060
SIC 3556 Food products machinery
 Eifen Hauer
 John Meisner

D-U-N-S 25-789-9732   (SL)
FRANCIS FOODSTORE LTD
LUNENBURG SAVE EASY
143 Victoria Rd, Lunenburg, NS, B0J 2C0
(902) 634-3751
Emp Here 44   *Sales* 12,062,688
SIC 5411 Grocery stores
 David Francis

D-U-N-S 20-027-1849   (HQ)
HIGH LINER FOODS INCORPORATED
HIGH LINER
100 Battery Pt, Lunenburg, NS, B0J 2C0
(902) 634-8811
Emp Here 250   *Sales* 1,048,531,000
SIC 2092 Fresh or frozen packaged fish
 Rod Hepponstall
 Paul Jewer
 Paul Snow
 Tim Rorabeck
 Craig Murray

Chris Mulder
Henry Demone
Alan Bell
Joan Chow
Jim G. Covelluzzi

D-U-N-S 20-630-7761   (HQ)
LUNENBURG FOUNDRY & ENGINEERING LIMITED
LUNENBERG INDUSTRIAL FOUNDRY & ENGINEERING
53 Falkland St, Lunenburg, NS, B0J 2C0
(902) 634-8827
Sales 13,430,580
SIC 3731 Shipbuilding and repairing
 Peter J. Kinley
 David Allen
 Craig Buffett
 Shona E. Kinley Mckeen
 Edward Kinley

D-U-N-S 20-728-6543   (SL)
LUNENBURG HOME FOR SPECIAL CARE CORP
HARBOURVIEW HAVEN
25 Blockhouse Hill Rd, Lunenburg, NS, B0J 2C0
(902) 634-8836
Emp Here 200   *Sales* 13,713,200
SIC 8051 Skilled nursing care facilities
 Ed Pomeroy

D-U-N-S 24-956-6902   (HQ)
STELIA AEROSPACE NORTH AMERICA INC
STELIA NORTH AMERICA
(*Suby of* AIRBUS SE)
71 Hall St, Lunenburg, NS, B0J 2C0
(902) 634-8448
Emp Here 416   *Sales* 127,974,000
SIC 3728 Aircraft parts and equipment, nec
 Claude Baril
 David Aulenback
 Mark Olivella
 Michael Snow
 Jim Eisenhauer
 Xavier Flory
 Cedric Gautier
 Alain Tropis
 Guillaume Vuillermoz

D-U-N-S 24-394-6253   (SL)
TERRA BEATA FARMS LTD
161 Monk Point Rd, Lunenburg, NS, B0J 2C0
(902) 634-4435
Emp Here 22   *Sales* 18,382,694
SIC 5149 Groceries and related products, nec
 David Ernst
 Evelyn Ernst

D-U-N-S 24-756-5096   (BR)
THORNVALE HOLDINGS LIMITED
CLEARWATER DEEP SEA TRAWLERS
(*Suby of* THORNVALE HOLDINGS LIMITED)
240 Montague St, Lunenburg, NS, B0J 2C0
(902) 634-8049
Emp Here 300
SIC 2092 Fresh or frozen packaged fish
 Mike Pittman

D-U-N-S 24-669-7346   (HQ)
WEST NOVA FUELS LIMITED
HUBBARD, C. FUELS
73 Falkland St, Lunenburg, NS, B0J 2C0
(902) 634-3835
Emp Here 15   *Sales* 72,917,658
SIC 5172 Petroleum products, nec
 James Eisenhauer
 Gaetan Morel
 Ralph S. Chancey
 Valerie Rowlands
 John Meisner

Mabou, NS B0E

D-U-N-S 24-124-4354   (SL)
VAN ZUTPHEN, J & T CONSTRUCTION INC
ZUTPHEN CONTRACTORS
10442 Hwy 19 Sw, Mabou, NS, B0E 1X0
(902) 945-2300
Emp Here 49   *Sales* 13,892,676
SIC 1611 Highway and street construction
 Vincent Van Zutphen
 Leonard Van Zutphen

D-U-N-S 25-223-0321   (HQ)
ZUTPHEN CONTRACTORS INC
10442 Highway 19, Mabou, NS, B0E 1X0
(902) 945-2300
Sales 27,080,460
SIC 1794 Excavation work

Mahone Bay, NS B0J

D-U-N-S 20-904-6713   (HQ)
MAHONE INSURANCE GROUP INC
201 Main St, Mahone Bay, NS, B0J 2E0
(902) 624-9600
Emp Here 15   *Sales* 21,201,500
SIC 6411 Insurance agents, brokers, and service
 Wade Barry
 Shelley Burgoyne Barry

D-U-N-S 24-471-3095   (HQ)
RPS COMPOSITES INC
MARITIME FIBERGLASS FABRICATORS
(*Suby of* SOUTHFIELD CAPITAL ADVISORS, LLC)
740 Main St S, Mahone Bay, NS, B0J 2E0
(902) 624-8383
Emp Here 20   *Sales* 35,796,600
SIC 3299 NonMetallic mineral products,
 David Hilchey
 Darren Stillman
 Manfred Schaper
 David Brunson
 Andrew Cook
 Andrew Levison

Maitland, NS B0N

D-U-N-S 24-473-0354   (SL)
COX BROS. POULTRY FARM LIMITED
7520 215 Hwy, Maitland, NS, B0N 1T0
(902) 261-2823
Emp Here 30   *Sales* 11,565,570
SIC 0259 Poultry and eggs, nec
 Ross Cox
 Barbara Dalrymple

Merigomish, NS B0K

D-U-N-S 24-832-4444   (SL)
J & K FISHERY (2001) LIMITED
Gd, Merigomish, NS, B0K 1G0

Emp Here 20   *Sales* 10,702,480
SIC 5146 Fish and seafoods
 Norman Leblanc

Meteghan, NS B0W

D-U-N-S 20-906-8766   (SL)
VILLA ACADIENNE INC
8403 Hwy 1, Meteghan, NS, B0W 2J0
(902) 645-2065
Emp Here 135   *Sales* 9,224,010

SIC 8051 Skilled nursing care facilities
 Eric Pothier
 Lucille Maillet

D-U-N-S 24-789-6970   (SL)
YARMOUTH SEA PRODUCTS LTD
HIGH LINE NETS & GEAR
Gd, Meteghan, NS, B0W 2J0
(902) 645-2417
Emp Here 90   *Sales* 46,848,780
SIC 5091 Sporting and recreation goods
 Steven Corkum

Meteghan Centre, NS B0W

D-U-N-S 20-281-1865   (BR)
RIVERSIDE LOBSTER INTERNATIONAL INC
(*Suby of* RIVERSIDE LOBSTER INTERNATIONAL INC)
11 John Thibodeau Rd, Meteghan Centre, NS, B0W 2K0
(902) 645-3455
Emp Here 175
SIC 2092 Fresh or frozen packaged fish

D-U-N-S 20-280-7236   (HQ)
RIVERSIDE LOBSTER INTERNATIONAL INC
11 John Thibodeau Rd, Meteghan Centre, NS, B0W 2K0
(902) 645-3433
Emp Here 35   *Sales* 75,240,300
SIC 2092 Fresh or frozen packaged fish
 David Deveau
 Serge Mccauley

Meteghan River, NS B0W

D-U-N-S 25-395-3707   (HQ)
CONSEIL SCOLAIRE ACADIEN PROVINCIAL
CENTRE SCOLAIRE ETOILE DE L'ACADIE
(*Suby of* NOVA SCOTIA, PROVINCE OF)
9248 Route 1, Meteghan River, NS, B0W 2L0
(902) 769-5458
Emp Here 30   *Sales* 50,695,358
SIC 8211 Elementary and secondary schools
 Kenneth Gaudet
 Jeanelle D' Entremont
 Michael Comeau
 Janine Saulnier
 Margaret Gillespie
 Norman Decelles
 Stephane Bertrand
 Brent Surette
 Francois Rouleau
 Jerry Thibeau

D-U-N-S 20-028-4677   (SL)
THERIAULT, A. F. & SON LTD
9027 Main Hwy, Meteghan River, NS, B0W 2L0
(902) 645-2327
Emp Here 150   *Sales* 33,576,450
SIC 3731 Shipbuilding and repairing
 Arthur Theriault
 Ernest Theriault
 Russell Theriault
 Larry Theriault

Middle Musquodoboit, NS B0N

D-U-N-S 20-780-5052   (HQ)
TAYLOR LUMBER COMPANY LIMITED
12111 Hwy 224 Rr 4, Middle Musquodoboit, NS, B0N 1X0

(902) 384-2444
Sales 14,720,860
SIC 5211 Lumber and other building materials
 Robert Taylor
 Connie Taylor

Middle Sackville, NS B4E

D-U-N-S 20-053-6372   (SL)
KEIZER'S COLLISION CENTRE
1682 Sackville Dr, Middle Sackville, NS, B4E 3A9
(902) 865-7311
Emp Here 49   *Sales* 13,881,700
SIC 7532 Top and body repair and paint shops

Middle West Pubnico, NS B0W

D-U-N-S 24-188-2158   (HQ)
VERNON D'EON FISHING SUPPLIES LTD
373 Route 335, Middle West Pubnico, NS, B0W 2M0
(902) 762-2217
Emp Here 20   *Sales* 10,017,448
SIC 5941 Sporting goods and bicycle shops
 Marc-Andre Robichaud
 Gilles Robichaud
 Lloyd D'eon
 Brian Surette

Middleton, NS B0S

D-U-N-S 24-320-4860   (SL)
ALLEN, A.W. HOMES LIMITED
166 Commercial St, Middleton, NS, B0S 1P0
(902) 825-4854
Emp Here 25   *Sales* 11,367,373
SIC 5072 Hardware
 Nick Bentley

D-U-N-S 20-028-5070   (SL)
BRUCE CHEVROLET PONTIAC BUICK GMC LIMITED
BRUCE GM
394 Main St, Middleton, NS, B0S 1P0
(902) 825-3494
Emp Here 45   *Sales* 22,413,510
SIC 5511 New and used car dealers
 Leslie George Barker
 Justin Barker

Mill Village, NS B0J

D-U-N-S 24-933-1091   (SL)
RBN FISHERIES LIMITED
65 Newell Rd, Mill Village, NS, B0J 2H0
(902) 677-2491
Emp Here 100   *Sales* 83,557,700
SIC 5146 Fish and seafoods
 Jane Newell
 Brian Newell

Mulgrave, NS B0E

D-U-N-S 25-092-3120   (BR)
BREAKWATER FISHERIES LIMITED
(*Suby of* BREAKWATER FISHERIES LIMITED)
13311 Hwy 104 Auld'S Cove, Mulgrave, NS, B0E 2G0

Emp Here 400

SIC 5146 Fish and seafoods
Randy Barnes

D-U-N-S 20-190-8121   (BR)
DSM NUTRITIONAL PRODUCTS CANADA INC
(Suby of KONINKLIJKE DSM N.V.)
39 England Dr, Mulgrave, NS, B0E 2G0
(902) 747-3500
Emp Here 140
SIC 2077 Animal and marine fats and oils
Daan Verkoeijen

D-U-N-S 24-129-3463   (SL)
MARTIN MARIETTA MATERIALS CANADA LIMITED
(Suby of MARTIN MARIETTA MATERIALS INC)
266 Lower Quarrie Rd, Mulgrave, NS, B0E 2G0
(902) 747-2882
Emp Here 100   Sales 56,962,800
SIC 5032 Brick, stone, and related material
Anthony Dirico
Michael Shea

Musquodoboit Harbour, NS B0J

D-U-N-S 24-189-8154   (SL)
TWIN OAKS SENIOR CITIZENS ASSOCIATION
BIRCHES NURSING HOME, THE
7702 # 7 Hwy, Musquodoboit Harbour, NS, B0J 2L0
(902) 889-3474
Emp Here 75   Sales 4,443,525
SIC 8361 Residential care
Rhonda Marks

New Glasgow, NS B2H

D-U-N-S 20-009-2141   (SL)
3213695 NOVA SCOTIA LIMITED
ATLANTIC DODGE
300 Westville Rd, New Glasgow, NS, B2H 2J5
(902) 752-8321
Emp Here 26   Sales 12,950,028
SIC 5511 New and used car dealers
John Macneil
Christian Barrett

D-U-N-S 20-411-8926   (SL)
A AND W RESTAURANT
A&W
689 Westville Rd, New Glasgow, NS, B2H 2J6

Emp Here 101   Sales 4,789,765
SIC 5812 Eating places
Steven Forbes

D-U-N-S 24-705-0768   (SL)
ABERCROMBIE VOLUNTEER FIRE DEPT
ABERCROMBI FIRE HALL
Gd Lcd Main, New Glasgow, NS, B2H 5C9
(902) 752-4248
Emp Here 30   Sales 13,476,570
SIC 7389 Business services, nec
Arnold Fitzgerald

D-U-N-S 20-727-1503   (SL)
BATTIST, GERALD TRUCKING LIMITED
2559 Granton Rd Suite 3, New Glasgow, NS, B2H 5C6
(902) 396-1398
Emp Here 70   Sales 10,373,440
SIC 4212 Local trucking, without storage
Gerald Battist
Kay Langille
Brandon Battist

D-U-N-S 24-946-6314   (SL)
BURKE'S AUTO SALES

2757 Westville Rd, New Glasgow, NS, B2H 5C6
(902) 755-2522
Emp Here 25   Sales 12,451,950
SIC 5511 New and used car dealers
Gary Burke

D-U-N-S 20-580-7626   (SL)
CENTRAL HOME IMPROVEMENT WAREHOUSE
610 River Rd E, New Glasgow, NS, B2H 3S1
(902) 755-2555
Emp Here 49   Sales 13,276,158
SIC 1521 Single-family housing construction
Stephen Smith

D-U-N-S 24-333-7974   (SL)
CROMBIE REAL ESTATE INVESTMENT TRUST
610 East River Rd Suite 200, New Glasgow, NS, B2H 3S2
(902) 755-8100
Emp Here 330   Sales 314,346,236
SIC 6798 Real estate investment trusts
Donald Clow
Glenn Hynes
Cheryl Fraser
John Barnoski
Trevor Lee
Ken Turple
Brady Landry
Jeff Downs
Steve Cleroux
Terry Doran

D-U-N-S 20-101-7972   (SL)
DEPARTMENT OF COMMUNITY SERVICES CHILD WELFARE
161 Terra Cotta Dr, New Glasgow, NS, B2H 6B6
(902) 755-5950
Emp Here 50   Sales 22,460,950
SIC 7389 Business services, nec
Margaret Macfarlane'lei

D-U-N-S 20-781-7156   (SL)
GLEN HAVEN MANOR CORPORATION
739 East River Rd, New Glasgow, NS, B2H 5E9
(902) 752-2588
Emp Here 280   Sales 19,131,280
SIC 8051 Skilled nursing care facilities
Lisa Smith

D-U-N-S 25-673-7446   (SL)
HERRON CHEVROLET PONTIAC BUICK GMC LIMITED
465 Westville Rd, New Glasgow, NS, B2H 2J6
(902) 752-1534
Emp Here 35   Sales 17,432,730
SIC 5511 New and used car dealers
Bruce Herron

D-U-N-S 20-287-5519   (BR)
ICT CANADA MARKETING INC
(Suby of SYKES ENTERPRISES INCORPORATED)
690 East River Rd, New Glasgow, NS, B2H 3S1
(902) 755-9050
Emp Here 100
SIC 7389 Business services, nec
Rodney Parr

D-U-N-S 20-638-6604   (SL)
K F C
674 East River Rd, New Glasgow, NS, B2H 3S1
(902) 752-8184
Emp Here 18   Sales 11,816,352
SIC 5963 Direct selling establishments
Allison Macleod

D-U-N-S 20-028-7845   (HQ)
MACKAY, J. J. CANADA LIMITED
MACKAY METERS
(Suby of 137954 CANADA LTD)
1342 Abercrombie Road, New Glasgow, NS,

B2H 5C6
(902) 752-5124
Emp Here 75   Sales 29,547,570
SIC 3824 Fluid meters and counting devices
George Mackay

D-U-N-S 20-287-3787   (HQ)
MARITIME INNS & RESORTS INCORPORATED
MARITIME INNS AND RESORTS
(Suby of MINGO FAMILY TRUST)
174 Archimedes St, New Glasgow, NS, B2H 2T6
(902) 752-5644
Emp Here 5   Sales 18,538,000
SIC 7011 Hotels and motels
Donald E Mingo

D-U-N-S 24-350-1926   (BR)
MARITIME STEEL AND FOUNDRIES LIMITED
379 Glasgow St, New Glasgow, NS, B2H 5C3

Emp Here 80   Sales 408,260
SIC 3325 Steel foundries, nec
Russ Bagnuolo

D-U-N-S 20-227-0906   (HQ)
MICHELIN AMERIQUE DU NORD (CANADA) INC
(Suby of COMPAGNIE GENERALE DES ETABLISSEMENTS MICHELIN)
2863 Granton Rd, New Glasgow, NS, B2H 5C6
(888) 871-4444
Emp Here 150   Sales 368,923,200
SIC 5014 Tires and tubes
R. Jeff Maclean
Scott A. Clark
Joan E. Martin
Catherine Mckean

D-U-N-S 20-987-2589   (SL)
SHANNON, BRENDA CONTRACTS LIMITED
DAVE'S COMMERCIAL CLEANING
130 George St, New Glasgow, NS, B2H 2K6

Emp Here 100   Sales 4,020,900
SIC 7349 Building maintenance services, nec
Brenda Shannon
David Shannon

D-U-N-S 25-298-0883   (BR)
SOBEYS CAPITAL INCORPORATED
SOBEYS
(Suby of EMPIRE COMPANY LIMITED)
38 George St Suite 652, New Glasgow, NS, B2H 2K1
(902) 752-6258
Emp Here 140
SIC 5411 Grocery stores
David Macdonald

D-U-N-S 20-728-6253   (HQ)
STONE'S SUPERIOR HOMES LIMITED
STONE'S R V & HOME CENTRE
2689 Westville Rd, New Glasgow, NS, B2H 5C6
(902) 752-3164
Emp Here 21   Sales 11,953,872
SIC 5571 Motorcycle dealers
Kim Stone
Anne T Stone

D-U-N-S 20-029-3165   (SL)
STRIGHT-MACKAY LIMITED
209 Terra Cotta Dr, New Glasgow, NS, B2H 6A8
(902) 928-1900
Emp Here 29   Sales 13,775,754
SIC 5088 Transportation equipment and supplies
Peter Bennett

D-U-N-S 25-953-5573   (SL)
SUMMER STREET INDUSTRIES INC
72 Park St, New Glasgow, NS, B2H 5B8

(902) 755-1745
Emp Here 150   Sales 7,239,450
SIC 8331 Job training and related services
Rob Roy
Bob Bennett
Sharon Darroch

D-U-N-S 20-801-1002   (BR)
SWENSON, LARRY ENTERPRISES LTD
WALLMART MCDONALDS
(Suby of SWENSON, LARRY ENTERPRISES LTD)
689 Westville Rd, New Glasgow, NS, B2H 2J6
(902) 752-6442
Emp Here 80
SIC 5812 Eating places

D-U-N-S 20-335-1809   (SL)
TOM MARA ENTERPRISE LIMITED
CANADIAN TIRE ASSOCIATE STORE
699 Westville Rd, New Glasgow, NS, B2H 2J6
(902) 755-5581
Emp Here 75   Sales 47,196,000
SIC 5531 Auto and home supply stores
Thomas (Tom) Mara

D-U-N-S 25-294-7429   (BR)
WAL-MART CANADA CORP
(Suby of WALMART INC.)
713 Westville Rd Suite 3061, New Glasgow, NS, B2H 2J6
(902) 928-0008
Emp Here 200
SIC 5311 Department stores
Kevin Forward

D-U-N-S 20-631-5467   (HQ)
WEEKS, S.W. CONSTRUCTION LIMITED
186 Terra Cotta Dr, New Glasgow, NS, B2H 5W5
(902) 755-3777
Sales 50,488,400
SIC 1611 Highway and street construction
Stephen Weeks
Audrey Weeks
Larry Kellock

New Minas, NS B4N

D-U-N-S 25-658-4616   (BR)
ATLANTIC WHOLESALERS LTD
ATLANTIC SUPERSTORE
(Suby of LOBLAW COMPANIES LIMITED)
9064 Commercial St, New Minas, NS, B4N 3E4
(902) 681-0665
Emp Here 150
SIC 5411 Grocery stores
Darlene George

D-U-N-S 24-128-1161   (SL)
BONNYMAN MITSUBISHI
BONNYMAN AUTOMOTIVE
29 Crescent Dr, New Minas, NS, B4N 3G7

Emp Here 21   Sales 10,459,638
SIC 5511 New and used car dealers
Matthew Bonnyman
James G. Bonnyman
Karen Munro

D-U-N-S 20-028-8843   (SL)
CORNWALLIS CHEVROLET BUICK GMC LIMITED
9184 Commercial St, New Minas, NS, B4N 3E5
(902) 681-8300
Emp Here 33   Sales 16,436,574
SIC 5511 New and used car dealers
Jamie O. Williams
Phyllis Plant

D-U-N-S 20-339-2142   (SL)
DEREK HUTCHISON SALES LIMITED
CANADIAN TIRE

▲ Public Company   ■ Public Company Family Member   HQ Headquarters   BR Branch   SL Single Location

9212 Commercial St, New Minas, NS, B4N
5J5
(902) 681-4576
Emp Here 80   *Sales* 21,412,160
SIC 5251 Hardware stores
  Derek Hutchinson
  Catherine Hutchison

D-U-N-S 24-994-8589   (HQ)
NOVA INDUSTRIAL SUPPLIES LIMITED
NOVA WELDING SUPPLIES, DIV OF
1006 Nova Dr, New Minas, NS, B4N 3X7
(902) 681-1665
Emp Here 13   *Sales* 17,575,962
SIC 5084 Industrial machinery and equipment
  Greg Trefry

D-U-N-S 24-943-5900   (BR)
SOBEYS CAPITAL INCORPORATED
SOBEYS #747
(*Suby of* EMPIRE COMPANY LIMITED)
9256 Commercial St, New Minas, NS, B4N
4A9
(902) 681-3723
Emp Here 150
SIC 5411 Grocery stores
  John Rideout

D-U-N-S 20-120-0206   (BR)
TRANSCONTINENTAL INC
KENTVILLE PUBLISHING
(*Suby of* TRANSCONTINENTAL INC)
9185 Commercial St Suite 2, New Minas, NS,
B4N 3G1
(902) 681-2121
Emp Here 125
SIC 2711 Newspapers
  Richard Jones

D-U-N-S 24-120-9936   (BR)
WAL-MART CANADA CORP
(*Suby of* WALMART INC.)
9097 Commercial St Suite 3738, New Minas,
NS, B4N 3E6
(902) 681-4271
Emp Here 200
SIC 5311 Department stores
  Max Noseworthy

New Waterford, NS B1H

D-U-N-S 20-907-4061   (SL)
MAPLE HILL MANOR SOCIETY INC
700 King St, New Waterford, NS, B1H 3Z5
(902) 862-6495
Emp Here 110   *Sales* 7,515,860
SIC 8051 Skilled nursing care facilities
  Kathy Macphee

D-U-N-S 24-629-1751   (SL)
**NEW WATERFORD HOMECARE SERVICE
SOCIETY**
3390 Plummer Ave, New Waterford, NS, B1H
1Y9
(902) 862-7554
Emp Here 102   *Sales* 21,120,936
SIC 8399 Social services, nec
  Janet Wilcox

D-U-N-S 20-523-4842   (HQ)
PARAMOUNT PHARMACIES LIMITED
MIDTOWN PHARMASAVE
3435 Plummer Ave Suite 529, New Waterford,
NS, B1H 1Z4
(902) 862-7186
Emp Here 25   *Sales* 18,324,600
SIC 5912 Drug stores and proprietary stores

North Sydney, NS B0A

D-U-N-S 24-926-1009   (SL)
COPOL   INTERNATIONAL   LTD.-

PACKAGING FILMS
69 Hartigan Dr, North Sydney, NS, B0A 1H0
(902) 794-9685
Emp Here 50   *Sales* 10,094,850
SIC 3081 Unsupported plastics film and sheet
  John O'donnell
  Denis Lanoe

North Sydney, NS B2A

D-U-N-S 20-321-2725   (BR)
ATLANTIC WHOLESALERS LTD
ATLANTIC SUPERSTORE
(*Suby of* LOBLAW COMPANIES LIMITED)
125 King St Suite 321, North Sydney, NS, B2A
3S1
(902) 794-7111
Emp Here 100
SIC 5411 Grocery stores
  Fred Bourgeois

D-U-N-S 24-955-4619   (SL)
G AND G WHITE HOWLEY PHARMACY LTD
SHOPPERS DRUG MART
131 King St Suite 148, North Sydney, NS, B2A
3S1
(902) 794-7211
Emp Here 41   *Sales* 10,371,114
SIC 5912 Drug stores and proprietary stores
  Tanya Howley

D-U-N-S 24-670-6261   (SL)
M. V. OSPREY LTD
P.O. Box 188 Stn Main, North Sydney, NS,
B2A 3M3
(902) 794-1600
Emp Here 75   *Sales* 10,256,925
SIC 0913 Shellfish
  Scott Nichols
  Gilbert Linstead
  Frank Flynn

D-U-N-S 20-556-0175   (BR)
MAGNA MECHANICAL INC
PRECISION FINISHED COMPONENTS
65 Memorial Dr, North Sydney, NS, B2A 0B9

Emp Here 300   *Sales* 377,782
SIC 3714 Motor vehicle parts and accessories
  Marc Leclerc

D-U-N-S 24-705-1329   (BR)
MARINE ATLANTIC INC
(*Suby of* GOVERNMENT OF CANADA)
355 Purves St, North Sydney, NS, B2A 3V2
(902) 794-5200
Emp Here 300
SIC 4482 Ferries
  Len Rhyno

D-U-N-S 20-904-6606   (SL)
**NORTHSIDE COMMUNITY GUEST HOME
SOCIETY**
11 Queen St, North Sydney, NS, B2A 1A2
(902) 794-4733
Emp Here 230   *Sales* 15,714,980
SIC 8051 Skilled nursing care facilities
  Donald Brown

D-U-N-S 20-059-2553   (SL)
UPSOURCE CANADA CORP
(*Suby of* UPSOURCE, INC.)
116 King St Unit 9a, North Sydney, NS, B2A
3R7

Emp Here 65   *Sales* 14,850,680
SIC 4899 Communication services, nec
  Joan Chaput

Oldham, NS B2T

D-U-N-S 20-025-9950   (SL)

LEDWIDGE LUMBER COMPANY LIMITED
195 Old Post Rd, Oldham, NS, B2T 1E2
(902) 883-9889
Emp Here 72   *Sales* 11,222,136
SIC 2421 Sawmills and planing mills, general
  James Ledwidge
  Douglas Ledwidge

Oxford, NS B0M

D-U-N-S 20-443-9152   (HQ)
OXFORD FROZEN FOODS LIMITED
(*Suby of* TIDNISH HOLDINGS LIMITED)
4881 Main St, Oxford, NS, B0M 1P0
(902) 447-2320
Emp Here 500   *Sales* 292,431,000
SIC 2037 Frozen fruits and vegetables
  John Bragg
  Ragnar Kamp
  Milton Wood
  Matthew Bragg

Petit De Grat, NS B0E

D-U-N-S 20-287-7515   (BR)
**CONSEIL SCOLAIRE ACADIEN PROVIN-
CIAL**
(*Suby of* NOVA SCOTIA, PROVINCE OF)
3435 Rte 206, Petit De Grat, NS, B0E 2L0
(902) 226-5232
Emp Here 500
SIC 8211 Elementary and secondary schools
  Francois Rouleau

D-U-N-S 20-827-9328   (SL)
PETIT DE GRAT PACKERS LIMITED
24 Hwy 206, Petit De Grat, NS, B0E 2L0
(902) 226-0029
Emp Here 100   *Sales* 34,569,000
SIC 2091 Canned and cured fish and
seafoods
  Edgar Samson
  Brian Samson
  Michel Brun
  Tom Burton

Pictou, NS B0K

D-U-N-S 20-728-0157   (HQ)
**ADVOCATE PRINTING AND PUBLISHING
COMPANY LIMITED**
ADVOCATE SIGNS AND BANNERS
Gd, Pictou, NS, B0K 1H0
(902) 485-1990
Emp Here 150   *Sales* 32,805,400
SIC 2731 Book publishing
  Sean Murray
  Shirley Murray
  Jill Murray

D-U-N-S 20-631-4429   (SL)
KING FREIGHT LINES LIMITED
131 Harris Rd, Pictou, NS, B0K 1H0
(902) 485-8077
Emp Here 100   *Sales* 14,819,200
SIC 4213 Trucking, except local
  John Macdonald
  Judy Macdonald

D-U-N-S 24-671-0818   (HQ)
PARTNERS CONSTRUCTION LIMITED
PARTNERS INDUSTRIAL CRANE RENTAL
Gd, Pictou, NS, B0K 1H0
(902) 485-4576
Emp Here 30   *Sales* 11,481,240
SIC 7353 Heavy construction equipment
rental
  Moodie Mansour

D-U-N-S 20-029-3157   (BR)
SOBEYS CAPITAL INCORPORATED
SOBEYS
(*Suby of* EMPIRE COMPANY LIMITED)
239 West River Rd, Pictou, NS, B0K 1H0
(902) 485-5841
Emp Here 106
SIC 5411 Grocery stores
  Jill Mcallum

Point Edward, NS B2A

D-U-N-S 25-990-7210   (SL)
A.B. MECHANICAL LIMITED
35 Rudderham Rd, Point Edward, NS, B2A
4V4
(902) 567-3897
Emp Here 60   *Sales* 13,983,900
SIC 1711 Plumbing, heating, air-conditioning
  Carson Mugford
  Brian Macleod
  Ian Macsween
  Donald Gillis
  Christopher Brace
  Shane Clarke
  Travis Campbell
  George Bennett
  Andrew Stewart
  Terry Kelly

Port Hawkesbury, NS B9A

D-U-N-S 20-352-6863   (SL)
CANSO FORD SALES (2005) LIMITED
9 Macintosh Rd, Port Hawkesbury, NS, B9A
3K4
(902) 625-1338
Emp Here 30   *Sales* 14,942,340
SIC 5541 Gasoline service stations
  Larry Mackeigan
  Glenn Mackeigan
  Wayne Mackay

D-U-N-S 20-207-8858   (SL)
**MACDONALD, R & G ENTERPRISES LIM-
ITED**
TIM HORTONS
603 Reeves St, Port Hawkesbury, NS, B9A
2R8
(902) 625-1199
Emp Here 60   *Sales* 17,608,620
SIC 5461 Retail bakeries
  Ronald Macdonald

D-U-N-S 20-324-7770   (SL)
**PORT HAWKESBURY PAPER LIMITED
PARTNERSHIP**
(*Suby of* BELGRAVIA INVESTMENTS LIM-
ITED)
120 Pulp Mill Rd Point Tupper Industrial Park,
Port Hawkesbury, NS, B9A 1A1
(902) 625-2460
Emp Here 320   *Sales* 117,643,840
SIC 2621 Paper mills
  Ronald Stern
  Wayne Nystrom
  Shawn Lewis
  Neil 4e Gelder
  Brian Konen
  Shamsh Kassam

D-U-N-S 24-804-4224   (BR)
SOBEYS CAPITAL INCORPORATED
SOBEYS #704
(*Suby of* EMPIRE COMPANY LIMITED)
622 Reeves St Unit 1, Port Hawkesbury,
B9A 2R7
(902) 625-1242
Emp Here 95
SIC 5411 Grocery stores
  Butler Brad

D-U-N-S 25-380-6202   (HQ)
STRAIT REGIONAL CENTRE FOR EDUCA-TION, THE
304 Pitt St Unit 2, Port Hawkesbury, NS, B9A 2T9
(902) 625-2191
Emp Here 27   *Sales* 63,835,190
SIC 8211 Elementary and secondary schools
Ford Rice
Terry Doyle
Francine Boudreau
Jamie Samson
Annee Peters
Basil Johnson
Brian Murray
Jim Austin
Joanne Reddick
Lian Parsons

D-U-N-S 24-932-0458   (SL)
SUPERPORT MARINE SERVICES LIMITED
30 Water St, Port Hawkesbury, NS, B9A 3L1
(902) 625-3375
Emp Here 60   *Sales* 15,146,520
SIC 1629 Heavy construction, nec
Leslie Macintyre
Susan Phelan

D-U-N-S 25-498-3307   (BR)
WAL-MART CANADA CORP
(*Suby of* WALMART INC.)
47 Paint St Unit 17, Port Hawkesbury, NS, B9A 3J9
(902) 625-0954
Emp Here 100
SIC 5311 Department stores
Shamus Greening

Port Hood, NS B0E

D-U-N-S 25-867-4951   (SL)
HOME SUPPORT CENTRAL SOCIETY
30 Water St, Port Hood, NS, B0E 2W0
(902) 787-3449
Emp Here 90   *Sales* 6,170,940
SIC 8059 Nursing and personal care, nec
Cindy Macdonald

D-U-N-S 24-832-2117   (SL)
J & T VAN ZUTPHEN CONSTRUCTION IN-CORPORATED
10442 Southwest Mabou, Port Hood, NS, B0E 2W0
(902) 945-2300
Emp Here 80   *Sales* 13,974,653
SIC 1623 Water, sewer, and utility lines

Port La Tour, NS B0W

D-U-N-S 24-755-2482   (SL)
CAPE BREEZE SEAFOODS LIMITED
3203 Main Rd, Port La Tour, NS, B0W 2T0
(902) 768-2550
Emp Here 50   *Sales* 11,242,750
SIC 2092 Fresh or frozen packaged fish
Roland Murphy

Port Morien, NS B1B

D-U-N-S 20-029-4544   (HQ)
HOPKINS, H LIMITED
11 Breakwater St, Port Morien, NS, B1B 1Y5
(902) 737-2244
Emp Here 12   *Sales* 50,134,620
SIC 5146 Fish and seafoods
Clifford Hopkins
Glen Hopkins
William Hopkins

Port Williams, NS B0P

D-U-N-S 25-139-0022   (SL)
ATLANTIC POULTRY INCORPORATED
791 Belcher St Suite 1, Port Williams, NS, B0P 1T0
(902) 678-1335
Emp Here 165   *Sales* 34,091,805
SIC 0259 Poultry and eggs, nec
Ian Blenkharn

D-U-N-S 25-193-6399   (SL)
HILLATON FOODS LIMITED
1853 Saxon St, Port Williams, NS, B0P 1T0
(902) 582-3343
Emp Here 100   *Sales* 34,569,000
SIC 2034 Dried and dehydrated fruits, vegeta-bles and soup mixes
John Bragg

Prime Brook, NS B1L

D-U-N-S 25-364-3621   (BR)
CAPE BRETON-VICTORIA REGIONAL SCHOOL BOARD
TRANSPORTATION SCHOOL BUSSING
(*Suby of* NOVA SCOTIA, PROVINCE OF)
999 Gabarus Hwy, Prime Brook, NS, B1L 1E5
(902) 562-4595
Emp Here 100
SIC 8211 Elementary and secondary schools
Paul Oldford

Pubnico, NS B0W

D-U-N-S 20-176-2791   (BR)
COMEAU'S SEA FOODS LIMITED
SEA LIFE FISHERIES
(*Suby of* MRC HOLDINGS LIMITED)
Gd, Pubnico, NS, B0W 2W0
(902) 762-3333
Emp Here 120
SIC 2092 Fresh or frozen packaged fish
Francois Cormier

D-U-N-S 20-223-8460   (SL)
TIDAL ORGANICS INCORPORATED
2433 Highway Unit 3, Pubnico, NS, B0W 2W0
(902) 762-3525
Emp Here 200   *Sales* 117,831,800
SIC 5191 Farm supplies
Tim Kaiser

Pugwash, NS B0K

D-U-N-S 20-558-8770   (SL)
BASIC SPIRIT INCORPORATED
73 Water St, Pugwash, NS, B0K 1L0
(902) 243-3390
Emp Here 25   *Sales* 18,563,000
SIC 5199 Nondurable goods, nec
Bonnie Bond
John Caraberis

D-U-N-S 24-803-3631   (SL)
CUMBERLAND SENIOR CARE CORPORA-TION
EAST CUMBERLAND LODGE
262 Church St, Pugwash, NS, B0K 1L0
(902) 243-2504
Emp Here 90   *Sales* 5,856,750
SIC 8361 Residential care
Kathy Redmond
Rose Mary Donkin

D-U-N-S 20-906-2991   (HQ)

SUNSET RESIDENTIAL & REHABILITA-TION SERVICES INCORPORATED
SUNSET COMMUNITY
140 Sunset Lane, Pugwash, NS, B0K 1L0
(902) 243-2571
Sales 11,892,170
SIC 8361 Residential care
Mary Ellen Pittoello
Julie Matheson

Salt Springs, NS B0K

D-U-N-S 20-280-7301   (SL)
RMSENERGY DALHOUSIE MOUNTAIN GP INC
1383 Mount Thom Rd, Salt Springs, NS, B0K 1P0
(902) 925-9463
Emp Here 50   *Sales* 31,330,700
SIC 4911 Electric services
Jason Lester
Reuben Burge
P. Jane Gavan
Michael Kosiancic
Gavin Ingram
Uwe Roeper

Sambro, NS B3V

D-U-N-S 24-878-6824   (SL)
IVY FISHERIES LTD
3762 Old Sambro Rd, Sambro, NS, B3V 1G1

Emp Here 12   *Sales* 10,026,924
SIC 5146 Fish and seafoods
Avery Henneberry
Wesley Henneberry
Marcel Henneberry
Clark Henneberry
Lewis Henneberry
Libby Henneberry

D-U-N-S 20-930-2959   (SL)
SAMBRO FISHERIES LIMITED
40 Lennys Lane, Sambro, NS, B3V 1L5
(902) 868-2140
Emp Here 20   *Sales* 10,702,480
SIC 5146 Fish and seafoods
Donald Hark

Saulnierville, NS B0W

D-U-N-S 20-029-6804   (HQ)
CLARENCE ENTERPRISES LIMITED
CLARENCE SHOPPING MART
10029 Highway 1, Saulnierville, NS, B0W 2Z0
(902) 769-3458
Emp Here 1   *Sales* 10,966,080
SIC 5411 Grocery stores
Aline Comeau

D-U-N-S 20-029-6838   (HQ)
COMEAU'S SEA FOODS LIMITED
FRANKLAND CANNING CO, DIV OF
(*Suby of* MRC HOLDINGS LIMITED)
60 Saulnierville Rd, Saulnierville, NS, B0W 2Z0
(902) 769-2101
Emp Here 175   *Sales* 38,984,400
SIC 2092 Fresh or frozen packaged fish
Marcel Comeau
Bernardin Comeau
Raymond Tucker
Danny Webber

D-U-N-S 24-832-0202   (SL)
COMEAUVILLE SEAFOOD PRODUCTS LIMITED

Gd, Saulnierville, NS, B0W 2Z0
(902) 769-2266
Emp Here 20   *Sales* 10,702,480
SIC 5146 Fish and seafoods
Elaine Comeau
Eric Comeau
Gilles Comeau

Scotchtown, NS B1H

D-U-N-S 24-246-2492   (SL)
SCOTCHTOWN VOLUNTEER FIRE DE-PARTMENT
11 Catherine St, Scotchtown, NS, B1H 3B3
(902) 862-8362
Emp Here 29   *Sales* 13,027,351
SIC 7389 Business services, nec
Harold Williams

Scotsburn, NS B0K

D-U-N-S 20-288-5190   (SL)
SCOTSBURN LUMBER LTD
(*Suby of* CAPITAL ASSETS HOLDINGS (L) BERHAD)
65 Condon Rd, Scotsburn, NS, B0K 1R0
(902) 485-8041
Emp Here 75   *Sales* 14,427,750
SIC 2421 Sawmills and planing mills, general
Hui-Lun Chneg
Gilbert Carre
Andreas Kammenos

Shag Harbour, NS B0W

D-U-N-S 24-472-9042   (SL)
SMITH, EMERY FISHERIES LIMITED
5309 Hwy 3, Shag Harbour, NS, B0W 3B0
(902) 723-2115
Emp Here 25   *Sales* 20,889,425
SIC 5146 Fish and seafoods
Monty Smith

Shelburne, NS B0T

D-U-N-S 20-029-4635   (SL)
KENNEY & ROSS LIMITED
6493 Shore Rd Rr 3, Shelburne, NS, B0T 1W0
(902) 637-2616
Emp Here 50   *Sales* 13,833,000
SIC 2899 Chemical preparations, nec
Robert Norland
Richard Norland
Robert Welland
Eric Norland
Raymond Jacquard
Jody Crook

D-U-N-S 25-412-3888   (BR)
NOVA SCOTIA HEALTH AUTHORITY
ROSEWAY HOSPITAL
(*Suby of* NOVA SCOTIA, PROVINCE OF)
1606 Lake Rd, Shelburne, NS, B0T 1W0
(902) 875-3011
Emp Here 130
SIC 8062 General medical and surgical hospi-tals
Jodi Ybarra

D-U-N-S 20-907-0846   (SL)
ROSEWAY MANOR INCORPORATED
1604 Lake Rd, Shelburne, NS, B0T 1W0
(902) 875-4707
Emp Here 101   *Sales* 6,492,482
SIC 8361 Residential care

Elizabeth Acker
Sharon Callan

D-U-N-S 25-543-7774 (HQ)
SOBEYS INC
SOBEYS
(*Suby of* EMPIRE COMPANY LIMITED)
115 King St, Shelburne, NS, B0T 1W0
(902) 752-8371
Emp Here 500 *Sales* 19,163,076,970
SIC 5411 Grocery stores
Michael Medline
Michael Vels
Clinton Keay
Lyne Castonguay
Vivek Sood
Pierre St-Laurent
Simon Gagne
Doug Nathanson
Sarah Joyce
L. Jane Mcdow

D-U-N-S 20-729-7649 (SL)
VEN-REZ PRODUCTS LIMITED
380 Sandy Point Rd, Shelburne, NS, B0T 1W0
(902) 875-3178
Emp Here 70 *Sales* 10,802,540
SIC 2531 Public building and related furniture
Bert Frizzell
John Greer
Michael A Kontak
Dan Gibson

Sherbrooke, NS B0J

D-U-N-S 24-191-3391 (SL)
LOCHIEL ENTERPRISES LIMITED
ST MARY'S RIVER SMOKEHOUSES
8000 Highway 7, Sherbrooke, NS, B0J 3C0
(902) 522-2005
Emp Here 65 *Sales* 22,469,850
SIC 2091 Canned and cured fish and seafoods
George Newell

D-U-N-S 24-832-4071 (SL)
SHERBROOKE RESTORATION COMMISSION
SHERBROOKE VILLAGE COMPANY STORE
(*Suby of* NOVA SCOTIA, PROVINCE OF)
42 Main St, Sherbrooke, NS, B0J 3C0
(902) 522-2400
Emp Here 80 *Sales* 2,338,913
SIC 8412 Museums and art galleries
Steven Phleming

Springhill, NS B0M

D-U-N-S 24-261-3867 (BR)
HIGH-CREST ENTERPRISES LIMITED
HIGH-CREST SPRINGHILL
(*Suby of* HIGH-CREST ENTERPRISES LIMITED)
11 Sproul St, Springhill, NS, B0M 1X0
(902) 597-2797
Emp Here 90
SIC 8051 Skilled nursing care facilities
Conrad Leblanc

D-U-N-S 20-025-6378 (HQ)
NATIONAL GYPSUM (CANADA) LTD
(*Suby of* SPANGLER COMPANIES, INC.)
1707 Highway 2, Springhill, NS, B0M 1X0
(902) 758-3256
Emp Here 77 *Sales* 24,863,552
SIC 1499 Miscellaneous nonMetallic minerals, except fuels
Thomas C. Nelson
Patrick Mills

D-U-N-S 20-589-4215 (BR)

ROPAK CANADA INC
ROPAK PACKAGING - NORTHEAST DIVISON
(*Suby of* STONE CANYON INDUSTRIES LLC)
29 Memorial Cres, Springhill, NS, B0M 1X0
(902) 597-3787
Emp Here 110
SIC 3089 Plastics products, nec
David Macdonald

D-U-N-S 25-900-4992 (SL)
SPRINGHILL GROUND SEARCH AND RESCUE (EMO)
Gd, Springhill, NS, B0M 1X0
(902) 597-3866
Emp Here 35 *Sales* 14,861,245
SIC 8999 Services, nec
Rodney Stewart
Brian Guthro
Michael Macpherson

D-U-N-S 20-029-6135 (SL)
SURRETTE BATTERY COMPANY LIMITED
1 Station Rd, Springhill, NS, B0M 1X0
(902) 597-3767
Emp Here 55 *Sales* 10,474,310
SIC 3691 Storage batteries
James Surrette
John David Surrette
Virginia Archibald

St Andrews, NS B0H

D-U-N-S 24-605-7095 (HQ)
SCOTT AND STEWART FORESTRY CONSULTANTS LIMITED
2267 Antigonish Guysborough Rd, St Andrews, NS, B0H 1X0
(902) 863-5508
Sales 11,714,400
SIC 8748 Business consulting, nec
Ralph Stewart
Chuck Bowers
Shaun Scott

Stellarton, NS B0K

D-U-N-S 24-339-8898 (HQ)
3-D AUTO PARTS LTD
17 Bridge Ave, Stellarton, NS, B0K 0A2
(902) 752-9370
Emp Here 26 *Sales* 16,990,560
SIC 5531 Auto and home supply stores
Dennis Vint

D-U-N-S 24-605-4555 (SL)
BIG 8 BEVERAGES LIMITED
(*Suby of* EMPIRE COMPANY LIMITED)
120 North Foord St, Stellarton, NS, B0K 0A2
(902) 755-6333
Emp Here 35 *Sales* 12,099,150
SIC 2086 Bottled and canned soft drinks
Michael Medline

D-U-N-S 24-472-8978 (HQ)
CONNORS TRANSFER LIMITED
39 Connors Ln, Stellarton, NS, B0K 0A2
(902) 752-1142
Emp Here 35 *Sales* 39,495,552
SIC 4213 Trucking, except local
Lauchie Connors
Glenn Connors
Robert Small
Robert Small
Donald Macgillivray

D-U-N-S 20-782-7767 (HQ)
CROMBIE DEVELOPMENTS LIMITED
HIGHFIELD SQUARE
(*Suby of* EMPIRE COMPANY LIMITED)

115 King St, Stellarton, NS, B0K 1S0
(902) 755-4440
Emp Here 30 *Sales* 61,054,650
SIC 6512 Nonresidential building operators
Donald Clow
Frank C Sobey

D-U-N-S 25-527-4243 (HQ)
EASTERN SIGN-PRINT LIMITED
(*Suby of* EMPIRE COMPANY LIMITED)
125 North Foord St, Stellarton, NS, B0K 0A2
(902) 752-2722
Sales 12,794,106
SIC 2752 Commercial printing, lithographic
Bill Mcewan
Thomas Steele

D-U-N-S 20-030-0069 (HQ)
EMPIRE COMPANY LIMITED
115 King St, Stellarton, NS, B0K 1S0
(902) 752-8371
Emp Here 30 *Sales* 17,501,984,953
SIC 5149 Groceries and related products, nec
Michael Medline
Clinton Keay
Doug Nelson
L. Jane Mcdow
Michael Vels
James M. Dickson
Cynthia Devine
Sharon Driscoll
Gregory Josefowicz
Sue Lee

D-U-N-S 20-347-0737 (BR)
NOVA SCOTIA COMMUNITY COLLEGE
NOVA SCOTIA COMMUNITY COLLEGE PICTOU CAMPUS
(*Suby of* NOVA SCOTIA, PROVINCE OF)
39 Acadia Ave, Stellarton, NS, B0K 1S0
(902) 752-2002
Emp Here 110
SIC 8222 Junior colleges

D-U-N-S 25-542-0895 (HQ)
PROUDFOOTS INCORPORATED
PROUDFOOTS HOME HARDWARE
130 Vista Dr, Stellarton, NS, B0K 1S0
(902) 752-4600
Emp Here 25 *Sales* 17,397,380
SIC 5251 Hardware stores
James Proudfoot
Kendell Proudfoot
James E Proudfoot Sr
John A Proudfoot

D-U-N-S 24-318-7130 (BR)
PROUDFOOTS INCORPORATED
PROUDFOOTS HOME HARDWARE BUILDING CENTER
130 Vista Dr, Stellarton, NS, B0K 0A2
(902) 752-1500
Emp Here 75
SIC 5251 Hardware stores
Kendall Proudfoot

D-U-N-S 24-606-1998 (SL)
RIVERVIEW HOME CORPORATION
ADULT RESIDENTIAL CENTRE
24 Riverview Lane, Stellarton, NS, B0K 0A2
(902) 755-4884
Emp Here 200 *Sales* 12,856,400
SIC 8361 Residential care
Patricia Bland

D-U-N-S 20-172-3236 (HQ)
SOBEYS CAPITAL INCORPORATED
(*Suby of* EMPIRE COMPANY LIMITED)
115 King St, Stellarton, NS, B0K 0A2
(902) 752-8371
Emp Here 200 *Sales* 32,968,936,000
SIC 5141 Groceries, general line
Michael Medline
Karen Mccaskill
Michael Vels

D-U-N-S 24-315-7307 (SL)

SQI HOLDINGS II INC
(*Suby of* EMPIRE COMPANY LIMITED)
115 King St, Stellarton, NS, B0K 0A2
(902) 752-8371
Emp Here 4,000 *Sales* 1,462,036,000
SIC 6712 Bank holding companies
William Mcewen

D-U-N-S 24-807-6809 (SL)
TRA STELLARTON
Gd, Stellarton, NS, B0K 1S0
(902) 752-1525
Emp Here 49 *Sales* 40,943,273
SIC 5141 Groceries, general line
Barry Dixon

D-U-N-S 20-030-0515 (SL)
WEARWELL GARMENTS LIMITED
WEARWELL
126 Acadia Ave, Stellarton, NS, B0K 1S0
(902) 752-4190
Emp Here 100 *Sales* 49,832,200
SIC 5136 Men's and boy's clothing
Sterling Maclean

Sydney, NS B1L

D-U-N-S 25-860-6987 (SL)
CAPE BRETON COUNTY HOMEMAKERS AGENCY
5 Detheridge Dr Suite 1, Sydney, NS, B1L 1B8
(902) 562-5003
Emp Here 135 *Sales* 9,224,010
SIC 8059 Nursing and personal care, nec
Sharon Crane

D-U-N-S 24-124-1848 (SL)
FIRST STRIKE SECURITY & INVESTIGATION LTD
2145 Kings Rd, Sydney, NS, B1L 1C2
(902) 539-9991
Emp Here 65 *Sales* 25,719,070
SIC 7381 Detective and armored car services
William Gosse

Sydney, NS B1M

D-U-N-S 24-130-9061 (SL)
CAPE BRETON UNIVERSITY
1250 Grand Lake Rd, Sydney, NS, B1M 1A2
(902) 539-5300
Emp Here 350 *Sales* 49,253,656
SIC 8221 Colleges and universities
Dale Keefe
Gordon Macinnis
Robert Sampson
Mark Shannon
Annette Verschuren

D-U-N-S 25-334-5326 (SL)
NOVA SCOTIA COMMUNITY COLLEGE MARCONI CAMPUS
1240 Grand Lake Rd, Sydney, NS, B1M 1A2
(902) 563-2450
Emp Here 140 *Sales* 20,914,740
SIC 8221 Colleges and universities
Dave Maclean

Sydney, NS B1N

D-U-N-S 24-913-0386 (SL)
CAPE CARE SERVICES (1996) LTD
(*Suby of* NEW DAWN ENTERPRISES LIMITED)
4 Dryden Ave, Sydney, NS, B1N 3K4
(902) 562-2444
Emp Here 80 *Sales* 10,676,720
SIC 8399 Social services, nec

▲ Public Company ■ Public Company Family Member **HQ** Headquarters **BR** Branch **SL** Single Location

Marie Macdonald
Ora Mcmanus

Sydney, NS B1P

D-U-N-S 20-429-6781   (SL)
ATLANTIC SPEEDY PROPANE
546 George St, Sydney, NS, B1P 1K7

Emp Here 5   *Sales* 15,709,144
SIC 4924 Natural gas distribution

D-U-N-S 25-400-3296   (HQ)
**CAPE BRETON DISTRICT HEALTH AU-
THORITY**
CAPE BRETON REGIONAL HOSPITAL
(*Suby of* NOVA SCOTIA, PROVINCE OF)
1482 George St, Sydney, NS, B1P 1P3
(902) 567-8000
Emp Here 1,000   *Sales* 269,487,797
SIC 8062 General medical and surgical hospi-
tals
John Malcom
Yvon Leblanc

D-U-N-S 24-471-5462   (HQ)
**CAPE BRETON ISLAND HOUSING AU-
THORITY**
18 Dolbin St, Sydney, NS, B1P 1S5
(902) 539-8520
Sales 11,210,556
SIC 8399 Social services, nec
Joan Mckeough

D-U-N-S 20-906-6984   (HQ)
**CAPE BRETON-VICTORIA REGIONAL
SCHOOL BOARD**
(*Suby of* NOVA SCOTIA, PROVINCE OF)
275 George St, Sydney, NS, B1P 1J7
(902) 564-8293
Emp Here 35   *Sales* 169,106,655
SIC 8211 Elementary and secondary schools
George Boudreau
Lorne Green
Joan Currie

D-U-N-S 25-244-3122   (BR)
DELTA HOTELS LIMITED
(*Suby of* GOVERNMENT OF THE
PROVINCE OF BRITISH COLUMBIA)
300 Esplanade St, Sydney, NS, B1P 1A7
(902) 562-7500
Emp Here 80
SIC 8741 Management services
Paulette Jolley

D-U-N-S 24-379-8175   (HQ)
DIRECT TRAFFIC CONTROL INC
180 Charlotte St, Sydney, NS, B1P 1C5
(902) 564-8402
Emp Here 1   *Sales* 10,781,256
SIC 7389 Business services, nec
Linda Tweedie

D-U-N-S 20-932-9952   (SL)
FIDDLEHEAD AUTO SALES LIMITED
70 Dodd St, Sydney, NS, B1P 1T6
(902) 539-0771
Emp Here 22   *Sales* 10,957,716
SIC 5511 New and used car dealers

D-U-N-S 20-780-6670   (SL)
HILLMAN'S TRANSFER LIMITED
(*Suby of* ARMOUR TRANSPORTATION SYS-
TEMS INC)
1159 Upper Prince St, Sydney, NS, B1P 5P8
(902) 564-8113
Emp Here 60   *Sales* 12,342,360
SIC 4213 Trucking, except local
Edward Hillman
Shauna Ley

D-U-N-S 25-370-8234   (BR)
HOME DEPOT OF CANADA INC

(*Suby of* THE HOME DEPOT INC)
50 Sydney Port Access Rd, Sydney, NS, B1P
7H2
(902) 564-3250
Emp Here 100
SIC 5251 Hardware stores
Brent Kerr

D-U-N-S 20-287-5485   (BR)
ICT CANADA MARKETING INC
(*Suby of* SYKES ENTERPRISES INCORPO-
RATED)
325 Vulcan Ave, Sydney, NS, B1P 5X1

Emp Here 363
SIC 7389 Business services, nec
Tom Kenzlie

D-U-N-S 25-541-1084   (HQ)
JONELJIM INVESTMENTS LIMITED
STEPHENS BUILDING SUPPLIES
199 Townsend St, Sydney, NS, B1P 5E4
(902) 564-5554
Emp Here 25   *Sales* 17,932,684
SIC 5211 Lumber and other building materials
James Kehoe
Roma Kehoe

D-U-N-S 20-523-6573   (SL)
**MACINTYRE CHEVROLET CADILLAC LIM-
ITED**
101 Disco St, Sydney, NS, B1P 5V7
(902) 564-4491
Emp Here 40   *Sales* 19,923,120
SIC 5511 New and used car dealers
Floyd Macintyre
Shaun Macintyre

D-U-N-S 20-906-4955   (HQ)
**MACLEOD-LORWAY FINANCIAL GROUP
LIMITED**
MORASH INSURANCE
215 Charlotte St, Sydney, NS, B1P 1C4
(902) 539-6666
Emp Here 30   *Sales* 129,341,940
SIC 6411 Insurance agents, brokers, and ser-
vice
Stuart Macleod

D-U-N-S 20-631-3801   (SL)
MAY, RON PONTIAC BUICK GMC LTD
303 Welton St, Sydney, NS, B1P 5S3
(902) 539-6494
Emp Here 45   *Sales* 22,413,510
SIC 5511 New and used car dealers
Ron May

D-U-N-S 24-348-0865   (BR)
MEDIAS TRANSCONTINENTAL S.E.N.C.
THE CAPE BRETON POST
(*Suby of* MEDIAS TRANSCONTINENTAL
S.E.N.C.)
255 George St, Sydney, NS, B1P 1J7
(902) 564-5451
Emp Here 90
SIC 2711 Newspapers
Shaun Robinson

D-U-N-S 20-929-3018   (HQ)
NEW DAWN ENTERPRISES LIMITED
106 Townsend St, Sydney, NS, B1P 5E1
(902) 539-9560
Sales 11,341,650
SIC 8399 Social services, nec
Rankin Macsween

D-U-N-S 24-705-6104   (BR)
NOVA CAPITAL INCORPORATED
CENTRAL HOME IMPROVEMENT, DIV OF
(*Suby of* NOVA CAPITAL INCORPORATED)
530 Grand Lake Rd, Sydney, NS, B1P 5T4
(902) 562-7000
Emp Here 100
SIC 5211 Lumber and other building materials
Bobby Joseph

D-U-N-S 24-913-0394   (SL)
PLAZA FORD SALES LIMITED

(*Suby of* MERCER INVESTMENTS LIMITED)
33 Terminal Rd, Sydney, NS, B1P 7B3
(902) 567-1616
Emp Here 38   *Sales* 23,912,640
SIC 5511 New and used car dealers
Gordon A Mercer
Regis Mcdonald
Shaun Macdonald

D-U-N-S 20-272-7033   (SL)
PROTOCASE INCORPORATED
45 DRIVES
46 Wabana Crt, Sydney, NS, B1P 0B9
(866) 849-3911
Emp Here 217   *Sales* 52,781,127
SIC 3499 Fabricated Metal products, nec
Stephen Lilley
Douglas Milburn
Ora Mcmanus
Darren Gallop

D-U-N-S 20-607-3871   (SL)
SCHWARTZ & CO LTD
SCHWARTZ FURNITURE SHOWROOMS
325 Vulcan Ave, Sydney, NS, B1P 5X1
(902) 539-4404
Emp Here 60   *Sales* 13,944,180
SIC 5712 Furniture stores
Brian Purchase

D-U-N-S 20-030-4178   (HQ)
SCHWARTZ & COMPANY (2006) LIMITED
RENTAL RIGHT
30 Reeves St, Sydney, NS, B1P 3C5
(902) 539-4404
Emp Here 39   *Sales* 15,106,195
SIC 5712 Furniture stores
Brian Purchase

D-U-N-S 24-834-0770   (SL)
SCOTIA CHRYSLER INC
325 Welton St, Sydney, NS, B1P 5S3
(902) 539-2280
Emp Here 45   *Sales* 22,413,510
SIC 5511 New and used car dealers
Bob Hawkins

D-U-N-S 25-614-5244   (BR)
**SCOTSBURN CO-OPERATIVE SERVICES
LIMITED**
SCOTSBURN DAIRY GROUP
1120 Upper Prince St, Sydney, NS, B1P 5P6

Emp Here 120   *Sales* 635,325
SIC 2026 Fluid milk
Katie Paruch

D-U-N-S 24-263-5514   (BR)
SOBEYS CAPITAL INCORPORATED
(*Suby of* EMPIRE COMPANY LIMITED)
272b Prince St, Sydney, NS, B1P 5K6
(902) 562-1762
Emp Here 115
SIC 5411 Grocery stores
Kevin Rogers

D-U-N-S 20-030-0879   (HQ)
SYDCO FUELS LIMITED
452 George St, Sydney, NS, B1P 1K3
(902) 539-6444
Sales 10,787,115
SIC 5983 Fuel oil dealers
Allen Pace

D-U-N-S 20-394-1609   (SL)
SYDNEY CALL CENTRE INC, THE
(*Suby of* TMONE, LLC)
90 Inglis St Unit A005, Sydney, NS, B1P 1W8
(877) 707-0365
Emp Here 500
SIC 4899 Communication services, nec
Mark Marlowe

D-U-N-S 24-913-2846   (SL)
TREIT HOLDINGS 21 INC
CAMBRIDGE SUITES HOTEL SYDNEY
(*Suby of* CENTENNIAL HOTELS LIMITED)

380 Esplanade St, Sydney, NS, B1P 1B1
(902) 562-6500
Emp Here 75   *Sales* 6,951,750
SIC 7011 Hotels and motels
Arni Clayton Thorsteinson
Richard Nelson Blair

D-U-N-S 25-294-8781   (BR)
WAL-MART CANADA CORP
(*Suby of* WALMART INC.)
800 Grand Lake Rd, Sydney, NS, B1P 6S9
(902) 562-1110
Emp Here 200
SIC 5311 Department stores
Sharon Faulkner

D-U-N-S 20-929-5583   (HQ)
WILSON'S INVESTMENTS LIMITED
TIM HORTONS
197 Charlotte St Suite 203, Sydney, NS, B1P
1C4
(902) 564-4399
Emp Here 8   *Sales* 57,739,200
SIC 5461 Retail bakeries
Gary Wilson
Karen Wilson

Sydney, NS B1S

D-U-N-S 20-030-5811   (HQ)
1015605 SALES LIMITED
LLOYD MACDONALD NISSAN
1124 Kings Rd, Sydney, NS, B1S 1C8
(902) 562-1298
Emp Here 1   *Sales* 34,610,400
SIC 5511 New and used car dealers
Christopher Macdonald
James Macdonald
Mark Macdonald
Ronald Macdonald

D-U-N-S 25-612-7622   (BR)
ATLANTIC WHOLESALERS LTD
REAL ATLANTIC SUPERSTORE, THE
(*Suby of* LOBLAW COMPANIES LIMITED)
1225 Kings Rd, Sydney, NS, B1S 1E1
(902) 539-7657
Emp Here 140
SIC 5411 Grocery stores
Kenny Fraser

D-U-N-S 20-813-8800   (SL)
COMMUNITY LODGE INCORPORATED
COVE GUEST HOME, THE
320 Alexandra St, Sydney, NS, B1S 2G1
(902) 539-5267
Emp Here 200   *Sales* 12,856,400
SIC 8361 Residential care
Carl Rideout
Reg Bonner

D-U-N-S 24-832-0582   (SL)
HIGGINS FAMILY PHARMACY LTD
SHOPPERS DRUG MART #149
1174 Kings Rd Suite 149, Sydney, NS, B1S
1C9
(902) 539-8111
Emp Here 40   *Sales* 10,118,160
SIC 5912 Drug stores and proprietary stores
Terry Higgins

D-U-N-S 20-630-1525   (SL)
**JONELJIM CONCRETE CONSTRUCTION
(1994) LIMITED**
90 Riverview Dr, Sydney, NS, B1S 1N5
(902) 567-2400
Emp Here 100   *Sales* 57,033,800
SIC 1542 Nonresidential construction, nec
James Kehoe
Everett Knickle

D-U-N-S 25-612-6996   (SL)
**MACGILLIVRAY, R.C. GUEST HOME SOCI-
ETY**

25 Xavier Dr, Sydney, NS, B1S 2R9
(902) 539-6110
Emp Here 160   *Sales* 10,932,160
SIC 8051 Skilled nursing care facilities
Gerald Miller
Germaine Macdonald
John Coffey

D-U-N-S 20-013-3101   (HQ)
MUNICIPAL CAPITAL INCORPORATED
19 Macrae Ave, Sydney, NS, B1S 1M1
(902) 564-4541
Sales 40,538,400
SIC 1422 Crushed and broken limestone
David Mackenna

D-U-N-S 20-030-5886   (SL)
MUNICIPAL READY-MIX LIMITED
(*Suby of* MUNICIPAL CAPITAL INCORPO-
RATED)
19 Macrae Ave, Sydney, NS, B1S 1M1
(902) 564-4541
Emp Here 140   *Sales* 25,090,660
SIC 3273 Ready-mixed concrete
David Mackenna
Robert Youden
Paul Yurchesyn

D-U-N-S 24-833-3577   (SL)
RAMSAY'S AUTO SALES LIMITED
RAMSAY'S HONDA
229 Kings Rd, Sydney, NS, B1S 1A5
(902) 539-0112
Emp Here 27   *Sales* 13,448,106
SIC 5511 New and used car dealers
Lisa Ramsay
John Ramsay
Michelle Marsh
David Ramsay

D-U-N-S 25-294-8740   (BR)
WAL-MART CANADA CORP
WAL-MART
(*Suby of* WALMART INC.)
65 Keltic Dr, Sydney, NS, B1S 1P4
(902) 562-3353
Emp Here 200
SIC 5311 Department stores
Kevin Cantwell

Sydney Mines, NS B1V

D-U-N-S 20-795-2388   (SL)
SYDNEY MINES FIRE DEPARTMENT
4 Elliot St, Sydney Mines, NS, B1V 3G1
(902) 736-2298
Emp Here 26   *Sales* 11,679,694
SIC 7389 Business services, nec
John Nugent

Trenton, NS B0K

D-U-N-S 24-782-7496   (SL)
**CUSTOM MARINE DESIGN & SUPPLY LIM-
ITED**
29 Greens Point Rd, Trenton, NS, B0K 1X0
(902) 752-2827
Emp Here 25   *Sales* 12,451,950
SIC 5551 Boat dealers
Robert Hawboldt

D-U-N-S 24-593-2558   (SL)
DSME TRENTON LTD
DSTN
34 Powerplant Rd, Trenton, NS, B0K 1X0
(902) 753-7777
Emp Here 100   *Sales* 19,208,500
SIC 3441 Fabricated structural Metal
Marvyn C Robar

D-U-N-S 20-030-7015   (SL)

**HIGGINS, ROBERT (1984) COMPANY LIM-
ITED**
HIGGINS CONSTRUCTION
205 Main St, Trenton, NS, B0K 1X0
(902) 755-5515
Emp Here 30   *Sales* 14,121,930
SIC 1542 Nonresidential construction, nec
J Royce Williston

D-U-N-S 20-102-5983   (BR)
NOVA SCOTIA POWER INCORPORATED
(*Suby of* EMERA INCORPORATED)
108 Power Plant Rd, Trenton, NS, B0K 1X0
(902) 755-5811
Emp Here 150
SIC 4911 Electric services
Dion Antle

D-U-N-S 20-906-7289   (SL)
RAM HERITAGE LTD
29 Greens Point Rd, Trenton, NS, B0K 1X0
(902) 752-6934
Emp Here 36   *Sales* 15,096,780
SIC 6712 Bank holding companies
Robert Hawboldt
Sharon Hawboldt

D-U-N-S 20-287-7309   (BR)
UNITED STEELWORKERS OF AMERICA
(*Suby of* UNITED STEELWORKERS)
1 Diamond St, Trenton, NS, B0K 1X0

Emp Here 1,201
SIC 8631 Labor organizations
Dave Fanning

Truro, NS B2N

D-U-N-S 25-640-3197   (SL)
2891379 CANADA INC
CANADIAN TIRE
90 Robie St, Truro, NS, B2N 1L1
(902) 897-4466
Emp Here 80   *Sales* 50,342,400
SIC 5531 Auto and home supply stores
Richard Johnson
Janice Johnson

D-U-N-S 20-151-1222   (SL)
3032948 NOVA SCOTIA LIMITED
*HOLIDAY INN HOTEL & CONFERENCE
CENTRE*
437 Prince St, Truro, NS, B2N 1E6
(902) 895-1651
Emp Here 80   *Sales* 7,591,920
SIC 7011 Hotels and motels
Susan Scharpegge

D-U-N-S 20-384-0462   (SL)
3278724 NOVA SCOTIA LIMITED
CENTURY HONDA
126 Main St, Truro, NS, B2N 4G9
(902) 897-1700
Emp Here 25   *Sales* 12,451,950
SIC 5511 New and used car dealers
Ronald Macgillivray

D-U-N-S 20-539-7058   (SL)
AFFORDABLE FUELS
362 Willow St, Truro, NS, B2N 5A5
(902) 895-4328
Emp Here 5   *Sales* 15,529,285
SIC 4924 Natural gas distribution

D-U-N-S 20-030-7247   (HQ)
ANDY'S TIRE SHOP LIMITED
146 Robie St, Truro, NS, B2N 1L1
(902) 897-1669
Emp Here 10   *Sales* 14,942,340
SIC 5531 Auto and home supply stores
Mike Langille

D-U-N-S 25-184-3132   (SL)
AUTO MOTION LIMITED
568 Prince St, Truro, NS, B2N 1G3

(902) 893-2288
Emp Here 45   *Sales* 20,122,830
SIC 5065 Electronic parts and equipment, nec
Floyd Gaetz

D-U-N-S 20-030-7528   (SL)
BLAIKIES DODGE CHRYSLER LIMITED
28 Waddell St, Truro, NS, B2N 4A2
(902) 893-4381
Emp Here 30   *Sales* 14,942,340
SIC 5511 New and used car dealers
Duane Rath
Stuart Rath

D-U-N-S 24-188-9039   (SL)
BURMAC MANAGEMENT LIMITED
710 Prince St, Truro, NS, B2N 1G6

Emp Here 40   *Sales* 11,539,960
SIC 6512 Nonresidential building operators
Lorne Macdougall
James W Stanley

D-U-N-S 20-906-2934   (HQ)
CALDWELL-ROACH AGENCIES LIMITED
CALDWELL ROACH INSURANCE
643 Prince St, Truro, NS, B2N 1G5
(902) 893-4204
Emp Here 16   *Sales* 26,289,860
SIC 6411 Insurance agents, brokers, and ser-
vice
Rodney Jones
Gregory Roach

D-U-N-S 20-589-5097   (BR)
CASEY CONCRETE LIMITED
(*Suby of* CASEY CONCRETE LIMITED)
69 Glenwood Dr, Truro, NS, B2N 1E9
(902) 895-1618
Emp Here 125
SIC 3273 Ready-mixed concrete
Earl Casey

D-U-N-S 20-030-7692   (SL)
CAVANAGH'S FOOD MARKET LIMITED
86 Main St, Truro, NS, B2N 4G6

Emp Here 40   *Sales* 10,966,080
SIC 5411 Grocery stores
Lloyd Cavanagh
Jean Cavanagh

D-U-N-S 20-310-9350   (SL)
**CENTRAL NOVA SCOTIA CIVIC CENTER
SOCIETY**
RATH EASTLINK COMMUNITY CENTER
625 Abenaki Rd, Truro, NS, B2N 0G6
(902) 893-2224
Emp Here 49   *Sales* 11,698,750
SIC 8611 Business associations
Jim Lambert

D-U-N-S 25-242-0690   (BR)
**CHIGNECTO CENTRAL REGIONAL
SCHOOL BOARD**
COBEQUID EDUCATIONAL CENTRE
(*Suby of* CHIGNECTO CENTRAL REGIONAL
SCHOOL BOARD)
34 Lorne St, Truro, NS, B2N 3K3
(902) 896-5700
Emp Here 125
SIC 8211 Elementary and secondary schools
Bill Kaulbach

D-U-N-S 24-129-7373   (HQ)
**CHIGNECTO CENTRAL REGIONAL
SCHOOL BOARD**
60 Lorne St, Truro, NS, B2N 3K3
(902) 897-8900
Emp Here 2,717   *Sales* 156,793,650
SIC 8211 Elementary and secondary schools
Gary Adams
Trudy Thompson
Marilyn Murray
Valerie Gauthier
Herb Steeves
Allison Mcgrath

D-U-N-S 25-410-5802   (HQ)
CLARENCE FARM SERVICES LIMITED
J & P FARM SERVICES & SADDLERY
70 Industrial Ave, Truro, NS, B2N 6V2
(902) 895-5434
Emp Here 50   *Sales* 24,198,300
SIC 2048 Prepared feeds, nec
Frank Van Gestel
Joel M. Henderson

D-U-N-S 20-030-7783   (SL)
**COLCHESTER CO-OPERATIVE SERVICES
LIMITED**
COLCHESTER CO-OP
339 Willow St Suite A, Truro, NS, B2N 5A6
(902) 893-9470
Emp Here 46   *Sales* 12,610,992
SIC 5411 Grocery stores
Jeff Yuill
Sherri Holman

D-U-N-S 25-650-9076   (SL)
**COLCHESTER RESIDENTIAL SERVICES
SOCIETY**
CRSS
35 Commercial St Suite 201, Truro, NS, B2N
3H9
(902) 893-4273
Emp Here 140   *Sales* 10,750,880
SIC 8322 Individual and family services
Shannon Mclellan
Judy Baird

D-U-N-S 25-702-3726   (BR)
DALHOUSIE UNIVERSITY
FACULTY OF AGRICULTURE
(*Suby of* DALHOUSIE UNIVERSITY)
62 Cumming Dr, Truro, NS, B2N 5E3
(902) 893-6600
Emp Here 400
SIC 8221 Colleges and universities
Angela Barrett-Jewers

D-U-N-S 20-248-4341   (BR)
DARLING INTERNATIONAL CANADA INC
ROTHSAY
(*Suby of* DARLING INGREDIENTS INC.)
169 Lower Truro Rd, Truro, NS, B2N 5C1
(902) 895-2801
Emp Here 100
SIC 4953 Refuse systems

D-U-N-S 25-720-1343   (BR)
**DEXTER CONSTRUCTION COMPANY LIM-
ITED**
PAVING BUILDING ROADS
(*Suby of* MUNICIPAL ENTERPRISES LIM-
ITED)
44 Meadow Dr, Truro, NS, B2N 5V4
(902) 895-6952
Emp Here 200
SIC 1611 Highway and street construction
Danny Clifton

D-U-N-S 20-703-1050   (HQ)
ECP L.P.
50 Abbey Ave, Truro, NS, B2N 6W4
(902) 895-1686
Emp Here 120   *Sales* 38,953,600
SIC 2671 Paper; coated and laminated pack-
aging
Steve Fawkes

D-U-N-S 20-905-5771   (HQ)
FUNDY GRINDING & MACHINING LIMITED
FUNDY GRINDING MACHINE TOOL SALES
9 Farnham Rd, Truro, NS, B2N 2X6
(902) 893-4274
Emp Here 10   *Sales* 11,875,650
SIC 5084 Industrial machinery and equipment
David Drummond
James Croft

D-U-N-S 24-471-5371   (HQ)
FUNDY TEXTILE & DESIGN LIMITED
189 Industrial Ave, Truro, NS, B2N 6V3
(902) 897-0010
Emp Here 76   *Sales* 10,933,920

SIC 2326 Men's and boy's work clothing
Friedel Moser

D-U-N-S 20-786-2017   (BR)
GEM HEALTH CARE GROUP LIMITED
MIRA, THE
(Suby of GEM HEALTH CARE GROUP LIMITED)
426 Young St, Truro, NS, B2N 7B1
(902) 895-8715
Emp Here 135
SIC 8059 Nursing and personal care, nec
Lynn Smith

D-U-N-S 20-030-8203   (SL)
GLENGARRY MOTEL AND RESTAURANT LIMITED
BEST WESTERN GLENGARRY
150 Willow St, Truro, NS, B2N 4Z6
(902) 893-4311
Emp Here 75   Sales 7,117,425
SIC 7011 Hotels and motels
Murray Nicholson
Judith A Nicholson

D-U-N-S 24-187-5590   (HQ)
GRINNER'S FOOD SYSTEMS LIMITED
GRECO PIZZA & DONAIR
(Suby of TRUCORP INVESTMENTS LIMITED)
105 Walker St, Truro, NS, B2N 4B1
(902) 893-4141
Sales 129,055,500
SIC 6794 Patent owners and lessors
Guy Soucy
William Hay

D-U-N-S 20-929-5955   (HQ)
HOLLIS FORD INC
266 Robie St, Truro, NS, B2N 1L1
(902) 895-5000
Sales 15,938,496
SIC 5511 New and used car dealers
Al Hollis
Rick Hollis

D-U-N-S 25-107-6766   (HQ)
INLAND TECHNOLOGIES CANADA INCORPORATED
(Suby of INTEC INVESTMENT HOLDINGS INC)
14 Queen St, Truro, NS, B2N 2A8
(902) 895-6346
Emp Here 12   Sales 18,688,460
SIC 4581 Airports, flying fields, and services
Roger Langille

D-U-N-S 24-472-9794   (HQ)
INTEC INVESTMENT HOLDINGS INC
ATLANTIC LUBRICANTS
9 Commercial St, Truro, NS, B2N 3H8
(902) 895-6346
Emp Here 10   Sales 95,205,600
SIC 4581 Airports, flying fields, and services
James G Bagnell
Stuart P Rath

D-U-N-S 24-831-7760   (BR)
INTERTAPE POLYMER INC
ENGINEERED COATED PRODUCTS
(Suby of GROUPE INTERTAPE POLYMER INC, LE)
50 Abbey Ave, Truro, NS, B2N 6W4

Emp Here 450
SIC 2221 Broadwoven fabric mills, manmade
Carol Fan

D-U-N-S 24-879-1865   (HQ)
ISLAND BEACH COMPANY CLOTHING & GRAPHICS INCORPORATED
82 Purdy Dr, Truro, NS, B2N 5W8
(902) 897-0560
Emp Here 8   Sales 10,763,760
SIC 5651 Family clothing stores
Charles Clerk

D-U-N-S 20-030-8666   (HQ)

KERR CONTROLS LIMITED
125 Polymer Rd, Truro, NS, B2N 7A7
(902) 895-9285
Emp Here 16   Sales 44,717,400
SIC 5075 Warm air heating and air conditioning
David Wilson
David Wilson
Trevor Pitcher

D-U-N-S 20-287-2094   (BR)
LOBLAW PROPERTIES LIMITED
TRURO SUPERSTORE
(Suby of LOBLAW COMPANIES LIMITED)
46 Elm St, Truro, NS, B2N 3H6
(902) 895-4306
Emp Here 200
SIC 5411 Grocery stores
Joe Gould

D-U-N-S 24-188-4121   (HQ)
MACKAY'S TRUCK & TRAILER CENTER LIMITED
MACKAY'S VOLVO TRUCK CENTER
124 Lower Truro Rd, Truro, NS, B2N 5E8
(902) 895-0511
Emp Here 1   Sales 14,568,600
SIC 5012 Automobiles and other motor vehicles
David Mackay

D-U-N-S 20-030-8872   (HQ)
MACQUARRIES DRUGS LIMITED
MACQUARRIES PHARMASAVE
920 Prince St Suite 513, Truro, NS, B2N 1H5
(902) 896-1600
Sales 43,131,195
SIC 5912 Drug stores and proprietary stores

D-U-N-S 20-030-8906   (SL)
MARGOLIANS MARITIMES LIMITED
TIMBER RIDGE OUTFITTERS
65 Inglis Pl Suite 49, Truro, NS, B2N 4B5

Emp Here 71   Sales 14,579,353
SIC 5311 Department stores
Robert Sidler

D-U-N-S 20-813-2014   (SL)
MCLEOD SAFETY SERVICES LTD
30 Upham Dr, Truro, NS, B2N 6W5
(902) 897-7233
Emp Here 50   Sales 12,828,100
SIC 3812 Search and navigation equipment
Ron Mcleod

D-U-N-S 24-341-7990   (SL)
NORTHEAST NUTRITION INC
(Suby of COOKE INC)
494 Willow St, Truro, NS, B2N 6X8
(902) 893-9449
Emp Here 45   Sales 15,556,050
SIC 2048 Prepared feeds, nec
Glenn Cooke
Kris Nicholls
Matthew Miller

D-U-N-S 25-366-7893   (HQ)
RESOURCE RECOVERY FUND BOARD, INCORPORATED
RRFB NOVA SCOTIA
(Suby of NOVA SCOTIA, PROVINCE OF)
35 Commercial St Suite 400, Truro, NS, B2N 3H9
(902) 895-7732
Emp Here 24   Sales 40,304,474
SIC 4953 Refuse systems
William Ring
Jerome Paris
Richard Ramsay
Einar Christensen
Bill Karsten
Ray Cote
Richie Cotton
Tim Dietrich
Charles Eastman
Gary Johnson

D-U-N-S 20-020-1283   (HQ)
SANSOM EQUIPMENT LIMITED
EAST COAST POWER SYSTEMS
100 Upham Dr, Truro, NS, B2N 6W8
(902) 895-2885
Emp Here 13   Sales 16,625,910
SIC 5084 Industrial machinery and equipment
James Wilson
David Sansom
Grant Sansom
Christopher Huyghue
Duane Webber

D-U-N-S 25-640-3122   (BR)
SHANNEX INCORPORATED
CEDARSTONE ENHANCED CARE
(Suby of SHANNEX INCORPORATED)
378 Young St, Truro, NS, B2N 7H2
(902) 895-2891
Emp Here 150
SIC 8051 Skilled nursing care facilities
Kim Power

D-U-N-S 25-935-1935   (BR)
SOBEYS CAPITAL INCORPORATED
(Suby of EMPIRE COMPANY LIMITED)
985 Prince St, Truro, NS, B2N 1H7
(902) 895-9579
Emp Here 100
SIC 5411 Grocery stores
Tom Buffett

D-U-N-S 24-943-5983   (BR)
SOBEYS CAPITAL INCORPORATED
SOBEYS #594
(Suby of EMPIRE COMPANY LIMITED)
68 Robie St Suite 594, Truro, NS, B2N 1L2
(902) 893-9388
Emp Here 160
SIC 5411 Grocery stores
Ron Rushton

D-U-N-S 20-030-9805   (HQ)
STANFIELD'S LIMITED
HARVEY WOODS
(Suby of COBEQUID INVESTMENTS LTD)
1 Logan St, Truro, NS, B2N 5C2
(902) 895-5406
Emp Here 340   Sales 99,500,625
SIC 2322 Men's and boy's underwear and nightwear
F. Thomas Stanfield
Jon D.F Stanfield
Peter Porteous
Ryan Butcher
Ian Covert
Cheryl Smith
G. Allan Henley
Mike Lee
Brian Hebb
Mark Collins

D-U-N-S 24-684-6617   (HQ)
TANDUS CENTIVA LIMITED
(Suby of SOCIETE INVESTISSEMENT DECONINCK)
435 Willow St Suite 30, Truro, NS, B2N 6T2
(902) 895-5491
Emp Here 250   Sales 94,601,200
SIC 2273 Carpets and rugs
Len Ferro
Stephen Houck

D-U-N-S 25-073-4209   (BR)
TANDUS FLOORING LIMITED
(Suby of SOCIETE INVESTISSEMENT DECONINCK)
Gd Rpo Prince, Truro, NS, B2N 5B5
(902) 895-5491
Emp Here 340
SIC 2273 Carpets and rugs

D-U-N-S 25-643-2642   (SL)
TRURO AND DISTRICT LIONS CLUB
1100 Prince St, Truro, NS, B2N 1J1
(902) 893-4773
Emp Here 30   Sales 11,922,420

SIC 8699 Membership organizations, nec
Clarence Daye

D-U-N-S 25-638-3530   (BR)
VICTORIAN ORDER OF NURSES FOR CANADA
VON COLCHESTER EAST HANTS DISTRICT
(Suby of VICTORIAN ORDER OF NURSES FOR CANADA)
30 Duke St Suite 5, Truro, NS, B2N 2A1
(902) 893-3803
Emp Here 200
SIC 8082 Home health care services
Carol Curley

D-U-N-S 24-120-9423   (BR)
WAL-MART CANADA CORP
(Suby of WALMART INC.)
140 Wade Rd, Truro, NS, B2N 7H3
(902) 893-5582
Emp Here 80
SIC 5311 Department stores
Jane Ghrelfall

D-U-N-S 24-776-2201   (SL)
WYNN PARK VILLA LIMITED
32 Windsor Way, Truro, NS, B2N 0B4
(902) 843-3939
Emp Here 90   Sales 5,332,230
SIC 8361 Residential care
James Boyle
Louise Boyle
Sheila Peck
Bill Boyle

Truro Heights, NS B6L

D-U-N-S 20-301-2062   (HQ)
MBW COURIER INCORPORATED
142 Parkway Dr, Truro Heights, NS, B6L 1N8
(902) 895-5120
Sales 40,429,710
SIC 7389 Business services, nec
Barry Mitchell

D-U-N-S 24-975-9770   (HQ)
NATIVE COUNCIL OF NOVA SCOTIA
129 Truro Heights Rd, Truro Heights, NS, B6L 1X2
(902) 895-1523
Emp Here 30   Sales 10,401,702
SIC 8651 Political organizations
Grace Conrad

Tusket, NS B0W

D-U-N-S 20-906-9533   (SL)
POTTIER'S GENERAL STORES LIMITED
CARLS GROCERY (DIV OF)
8175 Hwy 3, Tusket, NS, B0W 3M0
(902) 648-2212
Emp Here 38   Sales 10,417,776
SIC 5411 Grocery stores
Greg Pottier

D-U-N-S 20-443-7032   (SL)
TUSKET SALES & SERVICE LIMITED
TUSKET FORD
4143 Gavel Rd, Tusket, NS, B0W 3M0
(902) 648-2600
Emp Here 65   Sales 18,414,500
SIC 7532 Top and body repair and paint shops
Hubert Pothier
Phyllis Pothier
Donald Pothier

Upper Brookside, NS B6L

D-U-N-S 20-348-3755   (SL)
LKQ UPPER BROOKSIDE INC
(Suby of LKQ TIRE AND RECYCLING)
466 Brookside Rd, Upper Brookside, NS, B6L
2B3
(902) 897-0252
Emp Here 38   *Sales* 23,912,640
SIC 5531 Auto and home supply stores
 Robert Wagman

Upper Tantallon, NS B3Z

D-U-N-S 24-393-2469   (SL)
D & L GUITARD SALES INC
CANADIAN TIRE
5130 St Margarets Bay Rd, Upper Tantallon,
NS, B3Z 1E2
(902) 826-2800
Emp Here 49   *Sales* 12,399,891
SIC 5251 Hardware stores
 David Guitard

Wallace, NS B0K

D-U-N-S 20-246-6517   (SL)
AQUASHELL HOLDINGS INC
13915 Route 6, Wallace, NS, B0K 1Y0
(902) 257-2920
Emp Here 55   *Sales* 19,012,950
SIC 2092 Fresh or frozen packaged fish
 Frank De Waard
 Tracey De Waard

D-U-N-S 25-099-4944   (SL)
FOX HARB'R DEVELOPMENT LIMITED
FOX HARB'R RESORT
1337 Fox Harbour Rd, Wallace, NS, B0K 1Y0
(902) 257-1801
Emp Here 150   *Sales* 13,903,500
SIC 7011 Hotels and motels
 Steven Joyce
 Kevin Toth
 Ronald Joyce

Waterville, NS B0P

D-U-N-S 20-930-6505   (HQ)
**KINGS REGIONAL REHABILITATION CEN-
TRE**
1349 County Rd, Waterville, NS, B0P 1V0
(902) 538-3103
Sales 67,574,700
SIC 8069 Specialty hospitals, except psychi-
atric
 Betty Mattson
 John Fuller
 Bert Greene
 Warden Fred Whalen
 Eric Smith
 Wayne Atwater
 Ted Palmer

D-U-N-S 24-187-1292   (BR)
**MICHELIN   AMERIQUE   DU   NORD
(CANADA) INC**
*(Suby of COMPAGNIE GENERALE DES
ETABLISSEMENTS MICHELIN)*
866 Randolph Rd, Waterville, NS, B0P 1V0
(902) 535-3675
Emp Here 1,200
SIC 3089 Plastics products, nec
 Oliveir Cochateux

D-U-N-S 25-369-7486   (BR)
**MICHELIN   AMERIQUE   DU   NORD
(CANADA) INC**
(Suby of COMPAGNIE GENERALE DES

ETABLISSEMENTS MICHELIN)
866 Randolph Rd, Waterville, NS, B0P 1V0
(902) 538-8021
Emp Here 500
SIC 5014 Tires and tubes
 Grant Ferguson

Waverley, NS B2R

D-U-N-S 25-964-6867   (BR)
MUNICIPAL CONTRACTING LIMITED
*(Suby of MUNICIPAL ENTERPRISES LIM-
ITED)*
927 Rocky Lake Dr, Waverley, NS, B2R 1S1
(902) 835-3381
Emp Here 1,500
SIC 1611 Highway and street construction
 Carl Potter

D-U-N-S 24-533-8181   (HQ)
MUNICIPAL CONTRACTING LIMITED
DEXTER CONSTRUCTION COMPANY
*(Suby of MUNICIPAL ENTERPRISES LIM-
ITED)*
927 Rocky Lake Dr, Waverley, NS, B2R 1S1
(902) 835-3381
Sales 25,244,200
SIC 1611 Highway and street construction
 Carl Potter
 Raphael Potter
 Hugh Smith
 Cecil Vance

D-U-N-S 20-259-4235   (BR)
**SHANNAHAN'S INVESTIGATION SECU-
RITY LIMITED**
30 Brookfalls Crt, Waverley, NS, B2R 1J2
(902) 873-4536
Emp Here 105
SIC 7381 Detective and armored car services
 Heather Shannahan

Wedgeport, NS B0W

D-U-N-S 20-931-3451   (SL)
SCHOONER SEAFOODS LIMITED
51 Doucet Wharf Rd, Wedgeport, NS, B0W
3P0
(902) 663-2521
Emp Here 120   *Sales* 41,482,800
SIC 2091 Canned and cured fish and
seafoods
 Roland Murphy

West Pubnico, NS B0W

D-U-N-S 20-729-8969   (SL)
D'ENTREMONT, PAUL MARINE LTD
PAUL'S MARINE
2616 Hwy 3, West Pubnico, NS, B0W 3S0
(902) 762-3301
Emp Here 24   *Sales* 11,953,872
SIC 5541 Gasoline service stations
 Julie Muise

Westport, NS B0V

D-U-N-S 20-728-4340   (HQ)
D.B. KENNEY FISHERIES LIMITED
301 Water St, Westport, NS, B0V 1H0
(902) 839-2023
Emp Here 40   *Sales* 83,557,700
SIC 5146 Fish and seafoods
 Daniel Kenney Jr
 Teresa Kenney

Westville, NS B0K

D-U-N-S 20-028-8728   (SL)
HIGHLAND FORD SALES LIMITED
35 Balodis Dr, Westville, NS, B0K 2A0
(902) 396-2020
Emp Here 35   *Sales* 17,432,730
SIC 5511 New and used car dealers
 Eric Barker

Weymouth, NS B0W

D-U-N-S 24-878-3664   (SL)
**LEWIS MOULDINGS & WOOD SPECIAL-
TIES LIMITED**
134 Fort Point Rd, Weymouth, NS, B0W 3T0
(902) 837-7393
Emp Here 65   *Sales* 10,131,095
SIC 2431 Millwork
 Stewart Lewis
 Dwayne Ford
 Jamieson Lewis

Whycocomagh, NS B0E

D-U-N-S 20-782-2354   (HQ)
A.A. MUNRO INSURANCE BROKERS INC
9492 Trans Canada Hwy, Whycocomagh, NS,
B0E 3M0
(902) 756-2700
Emp Here 10   *Sales* 11,598,480
SIC 6411 Insurance agents, brokers, and ser-
vice
 Harley Maccaull

D-U-N-S 24-913-1731   (SL)
SIRCOM LODGE #66
MASONIC TEMPLE
Gd, Whycocomagh, NS, B0E 3M0
(902) 756-3262
Emp Here 160   *Sales* 21,042,400
SIC 8641 Civic and social associations
 Hugh Macphail
 Frederick E. Matthews

Windsor, NS B0N

D-U-N-S 25-503-7327   (BR)
**ANNAPOLIS VALLEY REGIONAL SCHOOL
BOARD**
AVON VIEW HIGH SCHOOL
(Suby of NOVA SCOTIA, PROVINCE OF)
225 Payzant Dr, Windsor, NS, B0N 2T0
(902) 792-6740
Emp Here 90
SIC 8211 Elementary and secondary schools
 Peter Johnston

D-U-N-S 25-133-9602   (BR)
ATLANTIC WHOLESALERS LTD
ATLANTIC SUPERSTORE
(Suby of LOBLAW COMPANIES LIMITED)
11 Cole Dr, Windsor, NS, B0N 2T0
(902) 798-9537
Emp Here 110
SIC 5411 Grocery stores
 Colin Hanson

D-U-N-S 24-360-2930   (BR)
CGC INC
FUNDY GYPSUM COMPANY, DIV OF
*(Suby of USG NETHERLANDS GLOBAL
HOLDINGS B.V.)*
Gd, Windsor, NS, B0N 2T0
(902) 798-4676
Emp Here 100

SIC 1499 Miscellaneous nonMetallic minerals,
except fuels
 Michael Bishop

D-U-N-S 20-650-7340   (SL)
EVANGELINE SECURITIES LIMITED
1051 King St, Windsor, NS, B0N 2T0
(902) 792-1035
Emp Here 33   *Sales* 17,529,831
SIC 6211 Security brokers and dealers
 Trevor Hughes
 Paul King
 Barbara Huges

D-U-N-S 20-905-3594   (SL)
**HANTS COUNTY RESIDENCE FOR SE-
NIOR CITIZENS**
DYKELAND LODGE
124 Cottage St, Windsor, NS, B0N 2T0
(902) 798-8346
Emp Here 200   *Sales* 13,713,200
SIC 8051 Skilled nursing care facilities
 Emily Samson

D-U-N-S 20-443-9830   (HQ)
NOVA INTERNATIONAL LIMITED
4449 Highway 1 Rr 2, Windsor, NS, B0N 2T0
(902) 798-9544
Emp Here 1   *Sales* 16,150,884
SIC 5082 Construction and mining machinery
 Wayne Forrest
 David Lothian
 Carol Ann Forrest

D-U-N-S 25-185-2786   (SL)
OULTON FUELS LTD
1699 King St, Windsor, NS, B0N 2T0
(902) 798-1118
Emp Here 15   *Sales* 15,492,120
SIC 5172 Petroleum products, nec

D-U-N-S 24-943-6189   (BR)
SOBEYS CAPITAL INCORPORATED
SOBEYS #672
(Suby of EMPIRE COMPANY LIMITED)
50 Empire Lane Wentworth Rd, Windsor, NS,
B0N 2T0
(902) 798-0992
Emp Here 120
SIC 5411 Grocery stores
 Jeff Cross

D-U-N-S 20-765-1485   (SL)
USG CANADIAN MINING LTD
FUNDY GYPSUM COMPANY, A DIV OF
669 Wentworth Rd, Windsor, NS, B0N 2T0
(902) 798-4676
Emp Here 150   *Sales* 41,007,912
SIC 1499 Miscellaneous nonMetallic minerals,
except fuels
 Michael Bishop

D-U-N-S 24-789-5535   (SL)
**WINDSOR ELMS VILLAGE FOR CONTINU-
ING CARE SOCIETY**
590 King St, Windsor, NS, B0N 2T0
(902) 798-2251
Emp Here 173   *Sales* 11,820,398
SIC 8051 Skilled nursing care facilities
 Sherry Keen
 Maxine Phinney
 Michael J Simmons
 Donald Mcleod
 Les Haley
 Gerald Raymond
 Andy Woolaver
 John Strum
 Steve Goodwin
 Jeff Williams

Windsor Junction, NS B2T

D-U-N-S 24-339-6785   (HQ)
MARID INDUSTRIES LIMITED

---

99 Windsor Junction Rd, Windsor Junction, NS, B2T 1G7
(902) 860-1138
Sales 24,618,600
SIC 1791 Structural steel erection
John Parke
Tina Lane
Greg Schofield
Tim Houtmsa

Wolfville, NS B4P

D-U-N-S 20-780-7710   (SL)
ACADIA STUDENTS' UNION INC
CAJUN'S CLOTHING STORE
30 Highland Ave, Wolfville, NS, B4P 1Y7
(902) 585-2110
Emp Here 80   *Sales* 98,833,440
SIC 6321 Accident and health insurance
Ian Morrison

D-U-N-S 20-300-5025   (BR)
ANNAPOLIS VALLEY REGIONAL SCHOOL BOARD
HORTON HIGH SCHOOL
(*Suby of* NOVA SCOTIA, PROVINCE OF)
75 Greenwich Rd S, Wolfville, NS, B4P 2R2
(902) 542-6060
Emp Here 75
SIC 8211 Elementary and secondary schools
Brad Stokes

D-U-N-S 20-392-9864   (SL)
CHURCH BREWING COMPANY LTD, THE
329 Main St, Wolfville, NS, B4P 1C8
(902) 818-8277
Emp Here 70   *Sales* 15,739,850
SIC 2082 Malt beverages
Steven Haysom
Matthew Hayson

D-U-N-S 20-031-4334   (HQ)
COCHRANE, D. ROSS PHARMACY LIMITED
COCHRANE'S PHARMASAVE
442 Main St, Wolfville, NS, B4P 1E2
(902) 542-3624
Emp Here 30   *Sales* 12,647,700
SIC 5912 Drug stores and proprietary stores

D-U-N-S 20-647-1448   (SL)
FOUNDERS INSURANCE GROUP INC
260 Main St, Wolfville, NS, B4P 1C4

Emp Here 35   *Sales* 20,297,340
SIC 6411 Insurance agents, brokers, and service
Don Abbey

D-U-N-S 20-729-3945   (SL)
OLD ORCHARD INN LIMITED
153 Greenwich Rd S, Wolfville, NS, B4P 2R2
(902) 542-5751
Emp Here 90   *Sales* 8,540,910
SIC 7011 Hotels and motels
Donald Wallace
Greg Wallace

D-U-N-S 20-631-3462   (SL)
RAFUSE BUILDING SUPPLIES (1977) LTD
RAFUSE HOME HARDWARE BUILDING CENTRE
200 Dykeland St, Wolfville, NS, B4P 1A2
(902) 542-2211
Emp Here 84   *Sales* 22,482,768
SIC 5211 Lumber and other building materials
Donna Bishop
Raymond Bishop

D-U-N-S 20-906-5812   (SL)
WOLFVILLE NURSING HOMES LIMITED
THE ELMS, THE DIV OF
601 Main St Suite 2, Wolfville, NS, B4P 1E9
(902) 542-2429
Emp Here 100   *Sales* 6,873,300

SIC 8051 Skilled nursing care facilities
Deanna Macdonald
Paul Macdonald

D-U-N-S 20-206-2621   (SL)
WOLFVILLE VOLUNTEER FIRE DEPARTMENT
355 Main St, Wolfville, NS, B4P 1A1
(902) 542-5635
Emp Here 43   *Sales* 19,316,417
SIC 7389 Business services, nec
Todd Crowell

Yarmouth, NS B5A

D-U-N-S 25-299-0080   (HQ)
2231737 NOVA SCOTIA LIMITED
MOTOR MART
45 Starrs Rd, Yarmouth, NS, B5A 2T2
(902) 742-7191
Emp Here 75   *Sales* 53,488,800
SIC 5511 New and used car dealers
Patricia Sullivan

D-U-N-S 24-726-9926   (SL)
ATLANTIC SPEEDY PROPANE
65a Starrs Rd, Yarmouth, NS, B5A 2T2
(902) 742-8305
Emp Here 5   *Sales* 15,529,285
SIC 4924 Natural gas distribution

D-U-N-S 20-630-3786   (SL)
CHEBOGUE FISHERIES LIMITED
98 Cliff St, Yarmouth, NS, B5A 3J9
(902) 742-9157
Emp Here 125   *Sales* 25,713,250
SIC 4213 Trucking, except local
Gladys Leblanc

D-U-N-S 24-747-7875   (BR)
CLEVE'S SPORTING GOODS LIMITED
(*Suby of* CLEVE'S SPORTING GOODS LIMITED)
76 Starrs Rd, Yarmouth, NS, B5A 2T5
(902) 742-8135
Emp Here 75
SIC 5941 Sporting goods and bicycle shops
Douglas Clark

D-U-N-S 24-706-1054   (SL)
DELMAR CONSTRUCTION LIMITED
77 Parade St Suite 1, Yarmouth, NS, B5A 3B3
(902) 742-4672
Emp Here 28   *Sales* 13,180,468
SIC 1542 Nonresidential construction, nec
Mark Bourque
Charlene Bourque

D-U-N-S 24-262-8758   (SL)
G & B SMITH FISHERIES LIMITED
50 Route 304, Yarmouth, NS, B5A 4J8
(902) 742-5478
Emp Here 50   *Sales* 37,126,000
SIC 5199 Nondurable goods, nec
Gerald Smith
Patricia Goodwin
David Fevens

D-U-N-S 20-727-9803   (SL)
IMO FOODS LIMITED
26 Water St, Yarmouth, NS, B5A 1K9
(902) 742-3519
Emp Here 75   *Sales* 25,926,750
SIC 2091 Canned and cured fish and seafoods
Phillip Leblanc
Joseph Macdonald

D-U-N-S 20-031-6479   (HQ)
MACDONALD CHISHOLM INC
MACDONALD CHISHOLM TRASK INSURANCE
(*Suby of* MACDONALD CHISHOLM INCORPORATED)
396 Main St Suite 100, Yarmouth, NS, B5A

1E9
(902) 742-3531
Emp Here 17   *Sales* 249,445,170
SIC 6411 Insurance agents, brokers, and service
Michael Brien

D-U-N-S 24-357-1366   (HQ)
MURRAY MOTORS YARMOUTH LIMITED PARTNERSHIP
MURRAY GM
45 Starrs Rd, Yarmouth, NS, B5A 2T2
(902) 742-7191
Emp Here 53   *Sales* 40,903,200
SIC 5511 New and used car dealers
Daniel Murray
Douglas Murray
Thomas (Tom) Demille

D-U-N-S 24-473-4877   (SL)
QUALITY SEAFOODS LIMITED
306 Hilton Rd, Yarmouth, NS, B5A 4A6
(902) 742-9238
Emp Here 20   *Sales* 10,702,480
SIC 5146 Fish and seafoods
Neil Leblanc
Gladys Leblanc

D-U-N-S 25-257-4769   (SL)
SCOTIA GARDEN SEAFOOD INCORPORATED
112 Water St, Yarmouth, NS, B5A 1L5
(902) 742-2411
Emp Here 25   *Sales* 20,889,425
SIC 5146 Fish and seafoods
Timothy Kaiser
Earle Kaiser

D-U-N-S 20-031-6289   (SL)
SPEARS & MACLEOD PHARMACY LIMITED
PHARMASAVE #519
333 Main St Suite 519, Yarmouth, NS, B5A 1E5
(902) 742-7825
Emp Here 40   *Sales* 10,118,160
SIC 5912 Drug stores and proprietary stores

D-U-N-S 24-187-5327   (HQ)
STRICTLY LOBSTER LIMITED
72 Water St, Yarmouth, NS, B5A 1K9
(902) 742-6272
Sales 12,533,655
SIC 5146 Fish and seafoods
Robert Newell

D-U-N-S 24-185-8828   (SL)
TIDAL VIEW MANOR
64 Vancouver St, Yarmouth, NS, B5A 2P5

Emp Here 150   *Sales* 10,248,900
SIC 8051 Skilled nursing care facilities
Sandra Boudreau
Gordon Wood

D-U-N-S 20-079-4464   (BR)
TOULON DEVELOPMENT CORPORATION
YARMOUTH MALL ADMINISTRATION
(*Suby of* TOULON DEVELOPMENT CORPORATION)
76 Starrs Rd, Yarmouth, NS, B5A 2T5
(902) 742-9518
Emp Here 500
SIC 7299 Miscellaneous personal service
Linda Deveau

D-U-N-S 25-871-7180   (HQ)
TRI-COUNTY REGIONAL SCHOOL BOARD
EVELYN RICHARDSON MEMORIAL ELEMENTARY SCHOOL
79 Water St, Yarmouth, NS, B5A 1L4
(902) 749-5696
Emp Here 40   *Sales* 49,559,500
SIC 8211 Elementary and secondary schools
Lisa Doucet
Tanya Forrest
Paul Ash

D-U-N-S 20-782-6660   (SL)
TRI-STAR INDUSTRIES LIMITED
TRI-STAR GRAPHICS
88 Forest St, Yarmouth, NS, B5A 4G6
(902) 742-2355
Emp Here 65   *Sales* 14,549,795
SIC 3711 Motor vehicles and car bodies
Colin Murphy

D-U-N-S 20-931-3337   (HQ)
VAUGHNE ASSURANCE LIMITED
379 Main St, Yarmouth, NS, B5A 1G1
(902) 742-2000
Emp Here 15   *Sales* 21,201,500
SIC 6411 Insurance agents, brokers, and service
Glenna Boudreau

D-U-N-S 24-348-1350   (BR)
WAL-MART CANADA CORP
WALMART
(*Suby of* WALMART INC.)
108 Starrs Rd, Yarmouth, NS, B5A 2T5
(902) 749-2306
Emp Here 120
SIC 5311 Department stores
Jean Thornton

Arviat, NU X0C

D-U-N-S 24-037-0338   (HQ)
ESKIMO POINT LUMBER SUP-PLY/AIRPORT SERVICES LTD
Gd, Arviat, NU, X0C 0E0
(867) 857-2752
Emp Here 50   *Sales* 27,880,315
SIC 5411 Grocery stores
 Ryan St. John
 Don St. John

D-U-N-S 25-500-5233   (HQ)
NUNAVUT ARCTIC COLLEGE
Gd, Arviat, NU, X0C 0E0
(867) 857-8600
Emp Here 25   *Sales* 11,263,600
SIC 8221 Colleges and universities
 Michael Shouldice

Baker Lake, NU X0C

D-U-N-S 24-663-5416   (SL)
NUNAVUT POWER CORPORATION
(*Suby of* NUNAVUT, GOVERNMENT OF)
2nd Floor Gn Building, Baker Lake, NU, X0C 0A0
(867) 793-4200
Emp Here 180   *Sales* 122,377,320
SIC 4911 Electric services
 Peter Ma

D-U-N-S 25-456-5476   (HQ)
QULLIQ ENERGY CORPORATION
NUNAVUT ENERGY CENTRE
(*Suby of* NUNAVUT, GOVERNMENT OF)
Gd, Baker Lake, NU, X0C 0A0
(866) 710-4200
Emp Here 36   *Sales* 107,120,375
SIC 4911 Electric services
 Bruno Pereira
 Elijah Evaluarjuk

Cambridge Bay, NU X0B

D-U-N-S 20-719-6627   (HQ)
KITNUNA CORPORATION
10 Omilik St, Cambridge Bay, NU, X0B 0C0
(867) 983-7500
Emp Here 78   *Sales* 35,932,645
SIC 1541 Industrial buildings and warehouses
 Jim Hughes
 Wilf Wilcox
 Charlie Lyall
 Fred Hunt
 Clare Basle

D-U-N-S 25-895-6713   (SL)
KITNUNA PROJECTS INC
(*Suby of* KITNUNA CORPORATION)
10 Omilik St, Cambridge Bay, NU, X0B 0C0
(867) 983-7500
Emp Here 50   *Sales* 12,856,550
SIC 4953 Refuse systems
 Pat Lyall
 Fred Hunt
 Charlie Lyall
 Clare Basler
 Jennifer Anawak

Igloolik, NU X0A

D-U-N-S 20-838-1947   (SL)
IGLOOLIK CO-OPERATIVE LIMITED
Gd, Igloolik, NU, X0A 0L0

(867) 934-8958
Emp Here 50   *Sales* 16,148,450
SIC 5411 Grocery stores
 Maurice Arnatsiaq
 Johnny Kublu

Iqaluit, NU X0A

D-U-N-S 24-203-6635   (SL)
ALMIQ CONTRACTING LTD
1340 Ulu Lane, Iqaluit, NU, X0A 0H0
(867) 975-2225
Emp Here 200   *Sales* 54,188,400
SIC 1521 Single-family housing construction
 Charles Des Lauriers

D-U-N-S 20-922-5817   (HQ)
KUDLIK CONSTRUCTION LTD
1519 Federal Rd, Iqaluit, NU, X0A 0H0
(867) 979-1166
Sales 114,067,600
SIC 1542 Nonresidential construction, nec
 Real Moreau

D-U-N-S 24-101-9835   (HQ)
NUNASI CORPORATION
1104 Inuksugait Plaza Suite 210, Iqaluit, NU, X0A 0H0
(867) 979-8920
Emp Here 1   *Sales* 62,388,000
SIC 8741 Management services
 Archie Angnakak
 Greg Cayen
 Cathy Munroe

D-U-N-S 25-192-9527   (SL)
NUNAVIT TEST CASE 1 CANADA
Po Box 1211, Iqaluit, NU, X0A 0H0
(867) 979-1000
Emp Here 150   *Sales* 5,645
SIC 6712 Bank holding companies

D-U-N-S 24-318-8419   (BR)
NUNAVUT ARCTIC COLLEGE
NUNATTA CAMPUS
(*Suby of* NUNAVUT ARCTIC COLLEGE)
Gd, Iqaluit, NU, X0A 0H0
(867) 979-7200
Emp Here 100
SIC 8211 Elementary and secondary schools
 Louise Flaherty

D-U-N-S 24-993-0595   (HQ)
NUNAVUT TUNNGAVIK INCORPORATED
921 Queen Elizabeth Way Ii Suite 301, Iqaluit, NU, X0A 0H0
(867) 975-4900
Sales 10,887,984
SIC 8399 Social services, nec
 Aluki Kotierk
 James Eetoolook
 Jack Anawak
 Charlie Evalik
 Joe Kaludjak
 Stanley Adjuk
 Okalik Eegeesiak
 George Eckalook

D-U-N-S 24-491-2192   (HQ)
QIKIQTANI INUIT ASSOCIATION
Gd, Iqaluit, NU, X0A 0H0
(867) 975-8400
Sales 79,123,055
SIC 8699 Membership organizations, nec
 P.J. Akeeagok
 Olayuk Akesuk
 Joe Attagutaluk
 Inutiq Iqaqrialu
 Simon Nattaq
 Harry Alookie
 Liza Ningiuk
 Tommy Akavak
 Paul Amagoalik
 Abraham Qammaniq

Rankin Inlet, NU X0C

D-U-N-S 20-100-3295   (SL)
HAMLET OF RANKIN
Gd, Rankin Inlet, NU, X0C 0G0
(867) 645-2895
Emp Here 49   *Sales* 11,698,750
SIC 8611 Business associations
 Justin Merritt

D-U-N-S 20-172-3751   (SL)
PULAARVIK KABLU FRIENDSHIP CENTRE
Gd, Rankin Inlet, NU, X0C 0G0
(867) 645-2600
Emp Here 49   *Sales* 11,114,817
SIC 8399 Social services, nec
 George Dunkerley

▲ Public Company   ■ Public Company Family Member   **HQ** Headquarters   **BR** Branch   **SL** Single Location

Acton, ON L7J

D-U-N-S 24-345-2500   (BR)
BEATTY FOODS LTD
MCDONALD'S
(*Suby of* BEATTY FOODS LTD)
374 Queen St E, Acton, ON, L7J 2Y5
(519) 853-9128
Emp Here 80
SIC 5812 Eating places
Jennifer Boysen

D-U-N-S 24-850-0873   (SL)
CANADIAN ASSOCIATION OF TOKEN COLLECTORS
273 Mill St E, Acton, ON, L7J 1J7
(519) 853-3812
Emp Here 230   *Sales* 20,630,080
SIC 7699 Repair services, nec
Scott Douglas

D-U-N-S 25-606-3066   (BR)
CLUBLINK CORPORATION ULC
BLUE SPRINGS GOLF CLUB
(*Suby of* TWC ENTERPRISES LIMITED)
13448 Dublin Line Suite 1, Acton, ON, L7J 2L7
(519) 853-0904
Emp Here 80
SIC 7992 Public golf courses
Greg Pacenti

D-U-N-S 20-031-6941   (SL)
DENNY BUS LINES LTD
5414 Erin Fourth Line, Acton, ON, L7J 2L8
(519) 833-9117
Emp Here 120   *Sales* 9,032,640
SIC 4151 School buses
Joyce Denny-Marshall
Vera Denny
Raymond Denny

D-U-N-S 24-421-0902   (SL)
GALVCAST MANUFACTURING INC
49 Commerce Cres, Acton, ON, L7J 2X2
(519) 853-3540
Emp Here 110   *Sales* 26,755,410
SIC 3479 Metal coating and allied services
Steven Christopher
Wilfred Christopher
Kenneth Christopher
Leonard Christopher
Randall Christopher

D-U-N-S 20-292-1065   (BR)
HALTON DISTRICT SCHOOL BOARD
MCKENZIE-SMITH BENNETT SCHOOL
(*Suby of* HALTON DISTRICT SCHOOL BOARD)
69 Acton Blvd, Acton, ON, L7J 2H4
(519) 853-3800
Emp Here 79
SIC 8211 Elementary and secondary schools
Kimberley Phillips

D-U-N-S 24-304-2868   (HQ)
HALTON HILLS HYDRO INC
43 Alice St, Acton, ON, L7J 2A9
(519) 853-3700
Sales 27,571,016
SIC 4911 Electric services
Art Skidmore
Gary Ebersberger
Kurt Durski

D-U-N-S 20-390-1918   (BR)
KAYCAN LTEE
KAYCAN LTEE
(*Suby of* KAYCAN LTEE)
323 Main St N, Acton, ON, L7J 2L9
(519) 853-1230
Emp Here 97
SIC 5031 Lumber, plywood, and millwork
Mike Phelan

D-U-N-S 24-359-7817   (HQ)
KP BUILDING PRODUCTS LTD

323 Main St N Suite 3, Acton, ON, L7J 2L9
(519) 853-1230
Sales 149,363,500
SIC 5051 Metals service centers and offices
Tami Dubrofsky
Lionel Dubrofsky

D-U-N-S 24-370-3787   (HQ)
PURITY LIFE HEALTH PRODUCTS LP
(*Suby of* BANYAN CAPITAL PARTNERS)
6 Commerce Cres, Acton, ON, L7J 2X3
(519) 853-3511
Sales 53,666,730
SIC 5122 Drugs, proprietaries, and sundries
Matthew James
Susan Cornwell
Brian Zabel
Michele Albrecht

D-U-N-S 24-543-8379   (SL)
RAPID FORMING INC
5 Mansewood Crt, Acton, ON, L7J 0A1

Emp Here 100   *Sales* 24,618,600
SIC 1799 Special trade contractors, nec
A Mungo
D Savarino

D-U-N-S 25-787-2606   (SL)
RE/MAX BLUE SPRING REALTY (HALTON) CORP
2 Mill St E, Acton, ON, L7J 1G9
(519) 853-2086
Emp Here 75   *Sales* 20,381,700
SIC 6531 Real estate agents and managers
Allan Chabassol
Phyllis Follett

D-U-N-S 20-031-7550   (HQ)
SUPERIOR GLOVE WORKS LIMITED
36 Vimy St, Acton, ON, L7J 1S1
(519) 853-1920
Emp Here 110   *Sales* 89,929,560
SIC 2381 Fabric dress and work gloves
Anthony Geng
Joseph Geng
Frank Geng

Ailsa Craig, ON N0M

D-U-N-S 24-212-0756   (SL)
CRAIGWIEL GARDENS
CRAIG HOLME NURSING HOME
221 Ailsa Craig Main St, Ailsa Craig, ON, N0M 1A0
(519) 293-3215
Emp Here 105   *Sales* 14,246,085
SIC 6513 Apartment building operators
Gerri Picken

D-U-N-S 20-125-8394   (BR)
CRAIGWOOD YOUTH SERVICES
(*Suby of* CRAIGWOOD YOUTH SERVICES)
26996 New Ontario Rd, Ailsa Craig, ON, N0M 1A0
(519) 232-4301
Emp Here 100
SIC 8322 Individual and family services
Lothar Liehmann

D-U-N-S 24-060-5691   (SL)
GREAT CANADIAN BEAN COMPANY INC, THE
26831 New Ontario Rd, Ailsa Craig, ON, N0M 1A0
(519) 232-4449
Emp Here 16   *Sales* 19,366,352
SIC 5153 Grain and field beans
William Mclean
Anne Marie Strybosch

Ajax, ON L1S

D-U-N-S 25-283-2340   (HQ)
1001943 ONTARIO LIMITED
EXCELL COMMUNICATIONS
725 Westney Rd S Unit 1, Ajax, ON, L1S 7J7
(905) 686-1212
Emp Here 9   *Sales* 11,396,000
SIC 5999 Miscellaneous retail stores, nec
Hassan Suleman

D-U-N-S 25-402-4458   (SL)
1055307 ONTARIO INC
403 Clements Rd W, Ajax, ON, L1S 6N3
(905) 428-2002
Emp Here 60   *Sales* 15,693,180
SIC 6712 Bank holding companies
Stephen Baker
Richard Baker

D-U-N-S 24-371-8793   (SL)
2072223 ONTARIO LIMITED
TUBE TECHNOLOGIES
274 Mackenzie Ave Suite 2, Ajax, ON, L1S 2E9
(905) 686-7000
Emp Here 130   *Sales* 20,061,860
SIC 2542 Partitions and fixtures, except wood
William A. Malisch

D-U-N-S 20-397-6717   (SL)
2179267 ONTARIO LTD
BRITMAN PACKAGING SERVICES
655 Finley Ave Suite 1, Ajax, ON, L1S 3V3
(905) 619-1477
Emp Here 70   *Sales* 31,445,330
SIC 7389 Business services, nec
Farhat Buchh
Peter Gabriel

D-U-N-S 20-301-7459   (SL)
949043 ONTARIO INC
AJAX NISSAN
500 Bayly St W, Ajax, ON, L1S 4G6
(905) 686-0555
Emp Here 30   *Sales* 14,942,340
SIC 5511 New and used car dealers
Nial Boatswain

D-U-N-S 25-667-7154   (SL)
AFFORDABLE PACKAGING LTD
225 Monarch Ave, Ajax, ON, L1S 7M3

Emp Here 30   *Sales* 13,304,700
SIC 7389 Business services, nec
Joe Sannella
Murray Thorimbert

D-U-N-S 20-583-6286   (SL)
AJAX SALES & SERVICE INC
AJAX MAZDA
301 Bayly St W, Ajax, ON, L1S 6M2
(905) 428-0088
Emp Here 33   *Sales* 16,436,574
SIC 5511 New and used car dealers
Roger Jugdeo

D-U-N-S 20-032-0265   (SL)
AJAX TEXTILE CORPORATION
170 Commercial Ave, Ajax, ON, L1S 2H5
(905) 683-6800
Emp Here 83   *Sales* 15,289,347
SIC 2257 Weft knit fabric mills
Terry Serra
Gordon Kerr

D-U-N-S 24-330-1921   (SL)
AUDI CANADA INC
(*Suby of* VOLKSWAGEN AG)
777 Bayly St W, Ajax, ON, L1S 7G7
(905) 428-4826
Emp Here 100   *Sales* 62,928,000
SIC 5511 New and used car dealers
Daniel Weissland
Peter S.H. Cho
Maria Stenstroem
Lori-Ann Roxburgh

D-U-N-S 20-323-0420   (HQ)

AXALTA COATING SYSTEMS CANADA COMPANY
(*Suby of* AXALTA COATING SYSTEMS LTD.)
408 Fairall St, Ajax, ON, L1S 1R6
(905) 683-5500
Emp Here 25   *Sales* 111,599,268
SIC 5013 Motor vehicle supplies and new parts
Robert Bryant
Charles Shaver
Sean Lannon
Imelda Darin

D-U-N-S 20-877-2558   (SL)
BALLYCLIFFE LODGE LIMITED
70 Station St, Ajax, ON, L1S 1R9
(905) 683-7321
Emp Here 120   *Sales* 8,227,920
SIC 8051 Skilled nursing care facilities
Ivan Irwin
Michael Bausch

D-U-N-S 24-751-0837   (SL)
CORPORATE CONTRACTING SERVICES LTD
CCSL
575 Westney Rd S, Ajax, ON, L1S 4N7
(416) 291-8644
Emp Here 35   *Sales* 16,475,585
SIC 1542 Nonresidential construction, nec
Daniel Moore
Gary Thistle
Christopher Rich

D-U-N-S 24-345-5305   (BR)
CORPORATION OF THE TOWN OF AJAX, THE
AJAX FIRE AND EMERGENCY SERVICES
(*Suby of* CORPORATION OF THE TOWN OF AJAX, THE)
435 Monarch Ave, Ajax, ON, L1S 2G7
(905) 683-3050
Emp Here 99
SIC 7389 Business services, nec
Randall Wilson

D-U-N-S 25-338-0067   (SL)
D & S MEAT PRODUCTS LTD
THE ELITE MEAT COMPANY
220 Clements Rd W Unit 1, Ajax, ON, L1S 3K5
(905) 427-9229
Emp Here 34   *Sales* 28,409,618
SIC 5147 Meats and meat products
Dejan Milanovic
Sasha Milanovic

D-U-N-S 24-859-4103   (SL)
DECOR GRATES INCORPORATED
4 Chisholm Crt, Ajax, ON, L1S 4N8
(647) 777-3544
Emp Here 60   *Sales* 11,525,100
SIC 3446 Architectural Metalwork
Ralph Oosterhuis
Tiki Oosterhuis
Owen Carroll

D-U-N-S 25-709-3344   (HQ)
DIE-MAX TOOL AND DIE LTD
23 Barr Rd, Ajax, ON, L1S 3Y1
(905) 619-6554
Emp Here 3   *Sales* 22,200,100
SIC 3544 Special dies, tools, jigs, and fixtures
Brian Stephen
David Rivett

D-U-N-S 24-420-9883   (SL)
DIEMAX MANUFACTURING LTD
729 Finley Ave, Ajax, ON, L1S 3T1
(905) 619-9380
Emp Here 55   *Sales* 12,838,925
SIC 3325 Steel foundries, nec
Brian Stephen

D-U-N-S 24-937-3580   (SL)
DISTICOR DIRECT RETAILER SERVICES INC
(*Suby of* MICROVITE INVESTMENTS LIM-

ITED)
695 Westney Rd S Unit 14, Ajax, ON, L1S
6M9
(905) 619-6565
Emp Here 20   *Sales* 14,850,400
SIC 5192 Books, periodicals, and newspapers
  Mark Lafranier
  John Lafranier

D-U-N-S 25-481-5913   (BR)
DOMINION COLOUR CORPORATION
(*Suby of* HIG CAPITAL MANAGEMENT, INC.)
445 Finley Ave, Ajax, ON, L1S 2E2
(905) 683-0231
Emp Here 90
SIC 2816 Inorganic pigments
  Bob Ralph

D-U-N-S 25-265-1807   (BR)
**DURHAM CATHOLIC DISTRICT SCHOOL
BOARD**
*ARCHBISHOP   DENIS   O'CONNOR
CATHOLIC HIGH SCHOOL*
(*Suby of* DURHAM CATHOLIC DISTRICT
SCHOOL BOARD)
80 Mandrake St, Ajax, ON, L1S 5H4
(905) 427-6667
Emp Here 90
SIC 8211 Elementary and secondary schools
  Donna Chambers

D-U-N-S 25-300-8056   (BR)
DURHAM DISTRICT SCHOOL BOARD
AJAX HIGH SCHOOL
(*Suby of* DURHAM DISTRICT SCHOOL
BOARD)
105 Bayly St E, Ajax, ON, L1S 1P2
(905) 683-1610
Emp Here 100
SIC 8211 Elementary and secondary schools
  Andrea Pemberton

D-U-N-S 24-197-3346   (SL)
DWIGHT CRANE LTD
131 Dowty Rd, Ajax, ON, L1S 2G3
(905) 686-3333
Emp Here 40   *Sales* 11,686,760
SIC 7353 Heavy construction equipment
rental
  Brian Dwight
  Debbie Dwight

D-U-N-S 20-965-3815   (HQ)
GANTREX CANADA INC
(*Suby of* HF HOLDING)
12 Barr Rd, Ajax, ON, L1S 3X9
(905) 686-0560
Sales 13,415,220
SIC 5051 Metals service centers and offices
  Lal Ajwani

D-U-N-S 25-513-5873   (HQ)
GCP CANADA INC
(*Suby of* W. R. GRACE & CO.)
294 Clements Rd W, Ajax, ON, L1S 3C6
(905) 683-8561
Emp Here 200   *Sales* 140,063,175
SIC 2819 Industrial inorganic chemicals, nec
  Paul M Palmisano
  Salim Hasham
  Michael B Cohan
  John A Mcfarland
  Mark A Shelnitz
  Robert Sorrentino
  W Brian Mcgowan
  Steven Boss
  Paul Dupuis
  Hudson La Force Iii

D-U-N-S 24-602-8005   (SL)
GIRLS INCORPORATED OF DURHAM
398 Bayly St W Suite 1a, Ajax, ON, L1S 1P1
(905) 428-8111
Emp Here 49   *Sales* 11,114,817
SIC 8399 Social services, nec
  Shawna Martin

D-U-N-S 20-032-1073   (SL)
IDEAL INDUSTRIES (CANADA), CORP
TUFF-TOTE
(*Suby of* IDEAL INDUSTRIES, INC.)
33 Fuller Rd, Ajax, ON, L1S 2E1
(905) 683-3400
Emp Here 70   *Sales* 13,330,940
SIC 3699 Electrical equipment and supplies,
nec
  Nick Shkordoff
  Robert Ackford
  Dave Juday

D-U-N-S 24-060-5477   (HQ)
**INDUSTRIAL, PETROLEUM AND MINING
SUPPLIES LIMITED**
I P M HOSE & FITTINGS
395 Westney Rd S, Ajax, ON, L1S 6M6
(905) 686-4071
Emp Here 40   *Sales* 23,751,300
SIC 5085 Industrial supplies
  Mark Forget
  Jeff Byer
  Sharon Forget
  Loma Stone

D-U-N-S 24-779-9950   (SL)
J & F WASTE SYSTEMS INC
610 Finley Ave, Ajax, ON, L1S 2E3
(905) 427-8064
Emp Here 100   *Sales* 25,713,100
SIC 4953 Refuse systems
  Lenny Campitelli

D-U-N-S 20-032-1107   (HQ)
J.& F. TRUCKING CORPORATION
610 Finley Ave, Ajax, ON, L1S 2E3
(905) 683-7111
Sales 15,427,950
SIC 4213 Trucking, except local
  Anthony Campitelli
  Bruno Campitelli
  Patricia Ricciuti

D-U-N-S 25-372-4827   (BR)
LATHAM POOL PRODUCTS INC
(*Suby of* LATHAM POOL PRODUCTS INC)
430 Finley Ave, Ajax, ON, L1S 2E3
(905) 428-6990
Emp Here 150
SIC 3949 Sporting and athletic goods, nec
  Micheal St John

D-U-N-S 24-210-5799   (SL)
LENNOX DRUM LIMITED
233 Fuller Rd, Ajax, ON, L1S 2E1
(905) 427-1441
Emp Here 60   *Sales* 28,501,560
SIC 5085 Industrial supplies
  Gerald Lennox

D-U-N-S 25-409-7405   (SL)
MACK SALES & SERVICE OF DURHAM INC
*DURHAM TRUCK & EQUIPMENT SALES &
SERVICE*
610 Finley Ave Unit 9, Ajax, ON, L1S 2E3
(905) 426-6225
Emp Here 45   *Sales* 22,413,510
SIC 5511 New and used car dealers
  John Campitelli
  Fred Campitelli
  Bruno Campitelli
  Emily Paterson

D-U-N-S 20-823-9509   (HQ)
MALPACK LTD
MALPACK POLYBAG, DIV OF
510 Finley Ave, Ajax, ON, L1S 2E3
(905) 428-3751
Sales 38,953,600
SIC 2673 Bags: plastic, laminated, and
coated
  Joe Galea
  Emanuel Dipietro

D-U-N-S 20-188-2292   (BR)
MALPACK LTD

(*Suby of* MALPACK LTD)
120 Fuller Rd, Ajax, ON, L1S 3R2
(888) 678-0707
Emp Here 75
SIC 2673 Bags: plastic, laminated, and
coated
  Lee Haydeman

D-U-N-S 24-652-9945   (SL)
MANU FORTI CORPORATION LTD
MCDONALDS RESTAURANT
222 Bayly St W, Ajax, ON, L1S 3V4
(905) 686-2133
Emp Here 100   *Sales* 4,551,900
SIC 5812 Eating places
  Doug Mckay

D-U-N-S 24-357-9302   (BR)
**MARTINREA   AUTOMOTIVE   SYSTEMS
CANADA LTD**
*MARTINREA   AUTOMOTIVE   SYSTEMS
CANADA (AJAX)*
(*Suby of* MARTINREA INTERNATIONAL INC)
650 Finley Ave, Ajax, ON, L1S 6N1
(905) 428-3737
Emp Here 95
SIC 3711 Motor vehicles and car bodies
  Joseph Pitaro

D-U-N-S 24-335-0522   (BR)
METRO ONTARIO INC
FOOD BASICS
(*Suby of* METRO INC)
280 Harwood Ave S, Ajax, ON, L1S 2J1
(905) 683-6951
Emp Here 75
SIC 5411 Grocery stores
  Bill Potter

D-U-N-S 20-559-1647   (HQ)
MONDO PRODUCTS COMPANY LIMITED
695 Westney Rd S Unit 1, Ajax, ON, L1S 6M9
(800) 465-5676
Emp Here 27   *Sales* 10,789,740
SIC 2842 Polishes and sanitation goods
  Stephen Boston
  Brad Boston

D-U-N-S 24-121-4485   (SL)
**MYERS, BOB CHEVROLET OLDSMOBILE
LTD**
BOB MYERS CHEVROLET OLDS
(*Suby of* R.F.M. HOLDINGS INC)
425 Bayly St W, Ajax, ON, L1S 6M3
(905) 427-2500
Emp Here 58   *Sales* 36,498,240
SIC 5511 New and used car dealers
  Bob Myers
  Barbara Myers

D-U-N-S 24-631-7077   (SL)
**NEWTON-TRELAWNEY PROPERTY MAN-
AGEMENT SERVICES INC**
253 Lake Driveway W, Ajax, ON, L1S 5B5
(905) 619-2886
Emp Here 33   *Sales* 10,795,191
SIC 6531 Real estate agents and managers
  Colin Sinclair
  Juliana Sinclair

D-U-N-S 20-785-2542   (SL)
**O'DONNELL   SPECIALTY   ADVERTISING
LTD**
487 Westney Rd S Unit 16, Ajax, ON, L1S
6W8
(905) 427-8818
Emp Here 60   *Sales* 44,551,200
SIC 5199 Nondurable goods, nec
  Frank Pollard

D-U-N-S 20-705-1699   (SL)
**OLYMPIC WHOLESALE COMPANY LIM-
ITED**
OLYMPIC WHOLESALE CO
75 Green Crt, Ajax, ON, L1S 6W9
(905) 426-5188
Emp Here 65   *Sales* 52,770,448

SIC 5149 Groceries and related products, nec
  Constantine Peroff
  Donna Peroff

D-U-N-S 20-878-3253   (HQ)
PERFORMANCE ORTHOTICS INC
291 Clements Rd W, Ajax, ON, L1S 3W7
(905) 428-2692
Emp Here 30   *Sales* 12,828,100
SIC 3842 Surgical appliances and supplies
  Glenn Copelend

D-U-N-S 24-077-3465   (BR)
PITNEY BOWES OF CANADA LTD
(*Suby of* PITNEY BOWES INC.)
314 Harwood Ave S Suite 200, Ajax, ON, L1S
2J1
(905) 619-7700
Emp Here 185
SIC 7389 Business services, nec
  Jackie Adams

D-U-N-S 24-844-6205   (HQ)
PRO-BEL ENTERPRISES LIMITED
PR-BEL GROUP OF COMPANIES
765 Westney Rd S, Ajax, ON, L1S 6W1
(905) 427-0616
Emp Here 79   *Sales* 97,546,000
SIC 5084 Industrial machinery and equipment
  David Street

D-U-N-S 20-842-4767   (SL)
PRO-BEL THE SAFETY ROOF ANCHOR CO
765 Westney Rd S, Ajax, ON, L1S 6W1
(905) 427-0616
Emp Here 80   *Sales* 22,389,140
SIC 2842 Polishes and sanitation goods
  Trish Parro

D-U-N-S 25-483-3718   (SL)
R.A.F. HOLDINGS LTD
TIM HORTONS
1 Harwood Ave S, Ajax, ON, L1S 2C1
(905) 683-6497
Emp Here 200   *Sales* 9,103,800
SIC 5812 Eating places
  Ryan Shoychet
  Frank Shoychet
  Allan Shoychet

D-U-N-S 25-637-8555   (HQ)
ROCKBRUNE BROTHERS LIMITED
ALL STAR MOVING IN NEW MARKET
725 Finley Ave, Ajax, ON, L1S 3T1
(905) 683-4321
Emp Here 22   *Sales* 18,513,540
SIC 4214 Local trucking with storage
  William Rockbrune
  Robert Rockbrune
  Joseph Rockbrune

D-U-N-S 20-032-0695   (HQ)
**SAFRAN LANDING SYSTEMS CANADA
INC**
(*Suby of* SAFRAN)
574 Monarch Ave, Ajax, ON, L1S 2G8
(905) 683-3100
Emp Here 600   *Sales* 232,680,000
SIC 3728 Aircraft parts and equipment, nec
  Bryan Teed
  Gordon Hofkirchner
  Helene Seguinotte
  Crystian Darveau
  Gilles Bouctot

D-U-N-S 20-042-7763   (SL)
SANDRA TEA & COFFEE LIMITED
(*Suby of* MOTHER PARKER'S TEA & COF-
FEE INC)
144 Mills Rd, Ajax, ON, L1S 2H1
(905) 683-5080
Emp Here 100   *Sales* 34,569,000
SIC 2099 Food preparations, nec
  Paul Higgins, Jr
  Michael Higgins
  Mark Hamilton

D-U-N-S 25-137-8105   (BR)

SCARBOROUGH AND ROUGE HOSPITAL
NUTRITION & FOOD SERVICES
(*Suby of* SCARBOROUGH AND ROUGE HOSPITAL)
580 Harwood Ave S Suite 199, Ajax, ON, L1S 2J4
(905) 683-2320
Emp Here 100
SIC 6324 Hospital and medical service plans
Bruce Cliff

D-U-N-S 24-345-4621   (HQ)
TRISCAP CANADA, INC
ATX NETWORKS
(*Suby of* TRIVEST PARTNERS, L.P.)
501 Clements Rd W Suite 1, Ajax, ON, L1S 7H4
(905) 428-0982
Sales 13,069,740
SIC 1731 Electrical work
Mark Beggs

D-U-N-S 24-485-3099   (SL)
UTILITY INTERNATIONAL INC
610 Finley Ave Suite 6, Ajax, ON, L1S 2E3
(905) 686-3512
Emp Here 35   *Sales* 18,198,845
SIC 4731 Freight transportation arrangement
Robert Ricciuti
John Campitelli

D-U-N-S 24-008-3998   (SL)
VILLAGE CHRYSLER DODGE JEEP LTD
201 Bayly St W, Ajax, ON, L1S 3K3
(905) 683-5429
Emp Here 55   *Sales* 34,610,400
SIC 5511 New and used car dealers
Edward T Williamson

D-U-N-S 20-152-4170   (HQ)
VOLKSWAGEN GROUP CANADA INC
VOLKSWAGEN
(*Suby of* VOLKSWAGEN AG)
777 Bayly St W, Ajax, ON, L1S 7G7
(905) 428-6700
Emp Here 140   *Sales* 92,230,800
SIC 5012 Automobiles and other motor vehicles
John White
Lorie-Ann Roxburgh
Arthur Bode
Axel Strobek
Peter Schwarzenbauer
Christian Klingler
Arno Antlitz

D-U-N-S 20-400-5276   (HQ)
WESTROCK PACKAGING SYSTEMS LP
(*Suby of* WESTROCK COMPANY)
281 Fairall St, Ajax, ON, L1S 1R7
(905) 683-2330
Sales 84,556,510
SIC 2657 Folding paperboard boxes
John Luke
Doug Mcmillan

Ajax, ON L1T

D-U-N-S 20-711-3775   (BR)
DURHAM CATHOLIC DISTRICT SCHOOL BOARD
NOTREDAME CATHOLIC SECONDARY SCHOOL
(*Suby of* DURHAM CATHOLIC DISTRICT SCHOOL BOARD)
1375 Harwood Ave N, Ajax, ON, L1T 4G8
(905) 686-4300
Emp Here 100
SIC 8211 Elementary and secondary schools
Mitch Lepage

D-U-N-S 24-329-6832   (BR)
LOBLAWS INC
REAL CANADIAN SUPERSTORE

(*Suby of* LOBLAW COMPANIES LIMITED)
30 Kingston Rd W Suite 1012, Ajax, ON, L1T 4K8
(905) 683-2272
Emp Here 200
SIC 5411 Grocery stores
Terry Bahen

D-U-N-S 20-732-1170   (BR)
LOBLAWS SUPERMARKETS LIMITED
REAL CANADIAN SUPERSTORE
(*Suby of* LOBLAW COMPANIES LIMITED)
30 Kingston Rd W Suite 1012, Ajax, ON, L1T 4K8
(905) 683-5573
Emp Here 150
SIC 5411 Grocery stores
Terry Bahen

D-U-N-S 20-290-7502   (BR)
REVERA LONG TERM CARE INC
WINBOURNE PARK
(*Suby of* GOVERNMENT OF CANADA)
1020 Westney Rd N, Ajax, ON, L1T 4K6
(905) 426-6296
Emp Here 120
SIC 8059 Nursing and personal care, nec
Kaitlyn Buck

D-U-N-S 20-793-0798   (BR)
SOBEYS CAPITAL INCORPORATED
SOBEYS
(*Suby of* EMPIRE COMPANY LIMITED)
260 Kingston Rd W, Ajax, ON, L1T 4E4
(905) 426-7144
Emp Here 100
SIC 5411 Grocery stores
Graham Foster

D-U-N-S 24-326-6215   (SL)
SPINA, JOHN DRUGS LTD
SHOPPERS DRUG MART
15 Westney Rd N Suite 2, Ajax, ON, L1T 1P5
(905) 426-3355
Emp Here 70   *Sales* 17,102,960
SIC 5912 Drug stores and proprietary stores
John Spina

D-U-N-S 25-116-8803   (HQ)
VERIDIAN CONNECTIONS INC
(*Suby of* VERIDIAN CORPORATION)
55 Taunton Rd E, Ajax, ON, L1T 3V3
(905) 427-9870
Emp Here 110   *Sales* 129,855,934
SIC 4911 Electric services
Michael Angemeer
Axel Starck
Glenn Rainbird

D-U-N-S 25-686-5676   (HQ)
VERIDIAN CORPORATION
55 Taunton Rd E, Ajax, ON, L1T 3V3
(905) 427-9870
Emp Here 35   *Sales* 103,340,848
SIC 4911 Electric services
John Wiersma
Michael Angemeer

D-U-N-S 25-111-2736   (SL)
VR MECHANICAL SOLUTIONS INC
464 Kingston Rd W, Ajax, ON, L1T 3A3
(905) 426-7551
Emp Here 100   *Sales* 23,306,500
SIC 1711 Plumbing, heating, air-conditioning
Victor Rankine
John Stewart

Ajax, ON L1Z

D-U-N-S 24-423-2794   (SL)
2176069 ONTARIO LIMITED
ENDRAS BMW DURHAM
100 Achilles Rd, Ajax, ON, L1Z 0C5
(905) 619-5522
Emp Here 40   *Sales* 19,923,120

SIC 5511 New and used car dealers
Christopher Endras

D-U-N-S 25-221-8532   (SL)
BRYSON & ASSOCIATES INSURANCE BROKERS LTD
541 Bayly St E, Ajax, ON, L1Z 1W7
(905) 426-8787
Emp Here 29   *Sales* 16,817,796
SIC 6411 Insurance agents, brokers, and service
Richard H Bryson

D-U-N-S 24-873-5276   (SL)
COMPUTER ROOM SERVICES CORPORATION
75 Chambers Dr Unit 6, Ajax, ON, L1Z 1E1
(905) 686-4000
Emp Here 28   *Sales* 29,751,748
SIC 1731 Electrical work
Greg Eaton
Craig Oldman

D-U-N-S 25-287-6016   (BR)
COSTCO WHOLESALE CANADA LTD
COSTCO
(*Suby of* COSTCO WHOLESALE CORPORATION)
150 Kingston Rd E, Ajax, ON, L1Z 1E5
(905) 619-6677
Emp Here 178
SIC 5099 Durable goods, nec
Thomas Ken

D-U-N-S 25-273-7820   (HQ)
HAZMASTERS INC
(*Suby of* WESCO INTERNATIONAL, INC.)
651 Harwood Ave N Unit 4, Ajax, ON, L1Z 0K4
(905) 231-0011
Emp Here 41   *Sales* 139,060,000
SIC 5099 Durable goods, nec
Roger James

D-U-N-S 25-080-7187   (BR)
HOME DEPOT OF CANADA INC
HOME DEPOT
(*Suby of* THE HOME DEPOT INC)
260 Kingston Rd E, Ajax, ON, L1Z 1G1
(905) 428-7939
Emp Here 200
SIC 5211 Lumber and other building materials
Tony Cocomelo

D-U-N-S 24-651-9854   (SL)
IMMEDIATE DELIVERY & COURIER SERVICE INC
255 Salem Rd N Suite D2, Ajax, ON, L1Z 0B1
(905) 427-7733
Emp Here 50   *Sales* 22,174,500
SIC 7389 Business services, nec
Carol Traill

D-U-N-S 25-146-3782   (SL)
LOGISTICS IN MOTION INC
500 Bayly St E, Ajax, ON, L1Z 0B2
(905) 427-5880
Emp Here 1,200   *Sales* 800,270,400
SIC 4731 Freight transportation arrangement
Domenico Mancini
Jacques Foisy
Hanif Nanji

D-U-N-S 24-183-1341   (SL)
PICOV DOWNS INC
AJAX DOWN SIMULCAST
380 Kingston Rd E, Ajax, ON, L1Z 1W4
(905) 686-8001
Emp Here 50   *Sales* 21,186,500
SIC 7948 Racing, including track operation
Norman Picov

D-U-N-S 24-210-1772   (HQ)
POWER BATTERY SALES LTD
EAST PENN CANADA
(*Suby of* EAST PENN MANUFACTURING CO.)
165 Harwood Ave N, Ajax, ON, L1Z 1L9

(905) 427-2718
Emp Here 228   *Sales* 186,306,216
SIC 5013 Motor vehicle supplies and new parts
James Bouchard
Chris Pruitt
Mike Bouchard
Michael Wells
Dan Langdon

D-U-N-S 25-092-7956   (BR)
POWER BATTERY SALES LTD
EAST PENN CANADA
(*Suby of* EAST PENN MANUFACTURING CO.)
165 Harwood Ave N, Ajax, ON, L1Z 1L9
(905) 427-3035
Emp Here 150
SIC 5013 Motor vehicle supplies and new parts
Luc Theriault

D-U-N-S 24-285-6482   (SL)
VANDERMEER NURSERY LTD
588 Lake Ridge Rd S Suite 1, Ajax, ON, L1Z 1X3
(905) 427-2525
Emp Here 50   *Sales* 12,652,950
SIC 5261 Retail nurseries and garden stores
Adrien Vandermeer
John Vandermeer
Mary Anne Vandermeer
Peter Vandermeer
Jane Kirsten

D-U-N-S 25-297-7814   (BR)
WAL-MART CANADA CORP
(*Suby of* WALMART INC.)
270 Kingston Rd E, Ajax, ON, L1Z 1G1
(905) 426-6160
Emp Here 300
SIC 5311 Department stores
Bob Cutler

Akwesasne, ON K6H

D-U-N-S 25-858-7963   (SL)
AHKWESAHSNE MOHAWK BOARD OF EDUCATION
169 Akwesasne International Rd, Akwesasne, ON, K6H 0G5
(613) 933-0409
Emp Here 160   *Sales* 15,859,040
SIC 8211 Elementary and secondary schools
Donna Lahache

D-U-N-S 25-124-4737   (BR)
MOHAWK COUNCIL OF AKWESASNE
AHKWESAHSNE MOHAWK BOARD OF EDUCATION
(*Suby of* MOHAWK COUNCIL OF AKWESASNE)
169 Akwesasne International Rd, Akwesasne, ON, K6H 0G5
(613) 933-0409
Emp Here 150
SIC 8211 Elementary and secondary schools
Barry Montur

D-U-N-S 24-860-6543   (SL)
SEAWAY INTERNATIONAL BRIDGE CORPORATION LTD, THE
(*Suby of* GOVERNMENT OF CANADA)
200 Akwesasne International Rd, Akwesasne, ON, K6H 5R7
(613) 932-6601
Emp Here 20   *Sales* 10,399,340
SIC 4785 Inspection and fixed facilities

Alban, ON P0M

D-U-N-S 20-258-4769   (SL)

RDH MINING EQUIPMENT LTD
904 Hwy 64, Alban, ON, P0M 1A0
(705) 857-2154
Emp Here 63   *Sales* 14,358,336
SIC 3532 Mining machinery
Gustavo Portalier
Neil Edward

Alexandria, ON K0C

D-U-N-S 24-383-2250   (SL)
GLENGARRY BUS LINE INC
104 Viau St, Alexandria, ON, K0C 1A0
(613) 525-1443
Emp Here 100   *Sales* 5,487,200
SIC 4151 School buses
Daryl Macrae
Georges Villeneuve

D-U-N-S 20-890-6313   (SL)
GLENGARRY MEMORIAL HOSPITAL
20260 County Road 43 Rr 3, Alexandria, ON,
K0C 1A0
(613) 525-2222
Emp Here 135   *Sales* 14,995,800
SIC 8062 General medical and surgical hospitals
Linda Morrow

D-U-N-S 20-032-2725   (SL)
GLENGARRY NEWS LIMITED, THE
3 Main St S, Alexandria, ON, K0C 1A0
(613) 525-2020
Emp Here 24   *Sales* 10,643,760
SIC 7389 Business services, nec
Kevin Macdonald

D-U-N-S 20-188-3084   (HQ)
HUBERT SABOURIN HOLDINGS LTD
135 Sandfield Ave, Alexandria, ON, K0C 1A0
(613) 525-1032
Emp Here 1   *Sales* 22,358,700
SIC 5051 Metals service centers and offices
Josee Sabourin

D-U-N-S 20-032-2501   (HQ)
LANTHIER BAKERY LTD
(*Suby of* CIE DE GESTION LANTHIER LTEE)
58 Dominion St, Alexandria, ON, K0C 1A0
(613) 525-2435
Emp Here 75   *Sales* 19,459,700
SIC 2051 Bread, cake, and related products
Marc Lanthier

D-U-N-S 20-032-2196   (HQ)
MOULURE ALEXANDRIA MOULDING INC
20352 Power Dam Rd, Alexandria, ON, K0C
1A0
(613) 525-2784
Emp Here 450   *Sales* 334,068,000
SIC 2431 Millwork
Andre Cholette

D-U-N-S 24-991-9093   (SL)
TALLON, DENNIS M. & ASSOCIATES INC
CANADIAN TIRE
400 Main St S, Alexandria, ON, K0C 1A0
(613) 525-2383
Emp Here 40   *Sales* 19,923,120
SIC 5531 Auto and home supply stores
Dennis Tallon

Alfred, ON K0B

D-U-N-S 20-032-3137   (SL)
139464 CANADA LIMITED
ALFRED HOME HARDWARE
4920 County Road 17, Alfred, ON, K0B 1A0
(613) 679-2252
Emp Here 42   *Sales* 10,628,478
SIC 5211 Lumber and other building materials
Marc Boucher

Pierre Paul Lalande

Alliston, ON L9R

D-U-N-S 20-508-7968   (BR)
BAXTER CORPORATION
(*Suby of* BAXTER INTERNATIONAL INC.)
89 Centre St S, Alliston, ON, L9R 1J4
(705) 435-6261
Emp Here 430
SIC 5122 Drugs, proprietaries, and sundries
John Eley

D-U-N-S 20-400-5300   (HQ)
CABLE BRIDGE ENTERPRISES LIMITED
NOTTAWASAGA INN, DIV OF
6015 Highway 89, Alliston, ON, L9R 1A4
(705) 435-5501
Sales 28,700,400
SIC 7011 Hotels and motels
Luigi Biffis
Peter Biffis
Dino Biffis
Sylvia Biffis
Rocco Lombardi

D-U-N-S 25-040-9930   (SL)
**ERNIE DEAN CHEVROLET BUICK GMC
LTD**
4906 Concession Rd 7, Alliston, ON, L9R 1V3
(705) 435-4318
Emp Here 30   *Sales* 14,942,340
SIC 5511 New and used car dealers
Frank Dean

D-U-N-S 24-951-3920   (BR)
HONDA CANADA INC
HONDA OF CANADA MFG DIV
(*Suby of* HONDA MOTOR CO., LTD.)
4700 Tottenham Rd, Alliston, ON, L9R 1A2
(705) 435-5561
Emp Here 2,000
SIC 3711 Motor vehicles and car bodies
Mark D'aliesio

D-U-N-S 24-977-9299   (SL)
HONDA TRADING CANADA INC
(*Suby of* HONDA MOTOR CO., LTD.)
4700 Industrial Pkwy, Alliston, ON, L9R 1W7
(705) 435-0172
Emp Here 40   *Sales* 17,886,960
SIC 5051 Metals service centers and offices
Kazunari Tsuruhigashi

D-U-N-S 24-784-7080   (SL)
LEADEC (CA) CORP
(*Suby of* LEADEC LUXCO SARL)
4700 Industrial Pky, Alliston, ON, L9R 1A2
(705) 435-5077
Emp Here 80   *Sales* 2,557,440
SIC 7349 Building maintenance services, nec
Joel Roger
Peggy Ortiz

D-U-N-S 20-792-4965   (SL)
MACKINNON RESTAURANTS INC
MCDONALD'S RESTAURANT 25004
137 Yonge St W, Alliston, ON, L9R 1V1
(705) 434-0003
Emp Here 100   *Sales* 4,551,900
SIC 5812 Eating places
Rory Mackinnon

D-U-N-S 20-768-6317   (SL)
MIEDEMA'S MOTOR SALES LTD
PROPER FORD LINCOLN
1 Addison Rd, Alliston, ON, L9R 1V2
(705) 435-7609
Emp Here 26   *Sales* 12,950,028
SIC 5511 New and used car dealers
Jack Van Tspyker

D-U-N-S 25-256-0057   (SL)
**NATIONAL   FOCUS   DISTRIBU-
TION/LOGISTICS INC**

151 Church St S, Alliston, ON, L9R 1E5
(705) 434-9995
Emp Here 34   *Sales* 17,124,372
SIC 5112 Stationery and office supplies
Jim Richardson

D-U-N-S 20-145-6522   (SL)
OETIKER LIMITED
(*Suby of* HANS OETIKER HOLDING AG)
203 Dufferin St S, Alliston, ON, L9R 1E9
(705) 435-4394
Emp Here 150   *Sales* 28,812,750
SIC 3429 Hardware, nec
Grant Mcleod

D-U-N-S 24-121-2885   (HQ)
**ONTARIO POTATO DIST. (ALLISTON) INC.
1991**
C & V FARMS
Gd Stn Main, Alliston, ON, L9R 1T8
(705) 435-6902
Emp Here 100   *Sales* 78,838,760
SIC 5148 Fresh fruits and vegetables
Gordon Cappuccitti
Danny Cappuccitti
Larry Cappuccitti

D-U-N-S 25-487-3714   (SL)
ROYAL LEPAGE COMPLETE REALTY
7 Victoria St W, Alliston, ON, L9R 1S9
(705) 435-3000
Emp Here 40   *Sales* 10,870,240
SIC 6531 Real estate agents and managers
Brent Bailey

D-U-N-S 20-655-1447   (BR)
**SIMCOE COUNTY DISTRICT SCHOOL
BOARD, THE**
BANTING MEMORIAL HIGH SCHOOL
(*Suby of* SIMCOE COUNTY DISTRICT
SCHOOL BOARD, THE)
203 Victoria St E, Alliston, ON, L9R 1G5
(705) 435-6288
Emp Here 150
SIC 8211 Elementary and secondary schools
Lynne Kelman

D-U-N-S 24-784-0267   (SL)
SIMCOE PARTS SERVICE INC
6795 Industrial Pky, Alliston, ON, L9R 1V4
(705) 435-7814
Emp Here 500   *Sales* 230,577,000
SIC 5013 Motor vehicle supplies and new
parts
Nobuo Sujioka

D-U-N-S 20-806-2484   (BR)
SOBEYS CAPITAL INCORPORATED
FRESHCO
(*Suby of* EMPIRE COMPANY LIMITED)
161 Young St, Alliston, ON, L9R 2A9
(705) 434-9512
Emp Here 100
SIC 5411 Grocery stores
Mike Thorn

D-U-N-S 24-559-4429   (SL)
STEVENSON MEMORIAL HOSPITAL, THE
200 Fletcher Cres, Alliston, ON, L9R 1M1
(705) 435-6281
Emp Here 250   *Sales* 27,770,000
SIC 8062 General medical and surgical hospitals
Gary Ryan

D-U-N-S 25-213-8672   (SL)
THOMSON, PETER & SONS INC
256 Victoria St W, Alliston, ON, L9R 1L9

Emp Here 35   *Sales* 15,651,090
SIC 5031 Lumber, plywood, and millwork
Robert Bewell
John Melnick

D-U-N-S 24-660-2262   (SL)
TRAILWOOD TRANSPORT LTD
4925 C.W. Leach Rd, Alliston, ON, L9R 2B1

(705) 435-4362
Emp Here 100   *Sales* 14,819,200
SIC 4213 Trucking, except local
Mark Beckstead
Rick Beckstead
Stacey Capson

D-U-N-S 20-968-6328   (HQ)
TRILLIUM FORD LINCOLN LTD
1 Addison Rd Hwy 89 E, Alliston, ON, L9R
1W1
(705) 435-7609
Emp Here 25   *Sales* 17,432,730
SIC 5511 New and used car dealers
Jack Van Spyker

D-U-N-S 25-399-1996   (HQ)
**VANDER ZAAG, H. J. FARM EQUIPMENT
LTD**
HJV EQUIPMENT
5900 County Rd 10 Suite 2, Alliston, ON, L9R
1V2
(705) 435-3226
Emp Here 28   *Sales* 23,751,300
SIC 5083 Farm and garden machinery
Dave Vander Zaag
Janet Vander Zaag
Colleen Vander Zaag

D-U-N-S 20-032-4101   (SL)
WARREN GIBSON LIMITED
GIBSON TRANSPORT
206 Church St S, Alliston, ON, L9R 2B7
(705) 435-4342
Emp Here 700   *Sales* 143,994,200
SIC 4213 Trucking, except local
Brian J. Gibson
Leonard Gibson
Michael Gibson

Alma, ON N0B

D-U-N-S 20-105-7127   (SL)
CONESTOGO AGRI SYSTEMS INC
7506 Wellington Road 11, Alma, ON, N0B 1A0
(519) 638-3022
Emp Here 27   *Sales* 12,825,702
SIC 5083 Farm and garden machinery
Richard Struyk

D-U-N-S 24-422-5699   (HQ)
**POST FARM STRUCTURES INCORPO-
RATED**
80 Peel St, Alma, ON, N0B 1A0
(519) 846-5988
Emp Here 3   *Sales* 20,712,164
SIC 1542 Nonresidential construction, nec
Herman Post
John Post Jr
Joshua Post
Daniel Post

Almonte, ON K0A

D-U-N-S 20-389-2161   (HQ)
3 SIXTY RISK SOLUTIONS LTD
3 SIXTY
83 Little Bridge St Suite 12, Almonte, ON, K0A
1A0
(866) 360-3360
Sales 79,135,600
SIC 7381 Detective and armored car services
Thomas Gerstenecker
Gaetan Lussier
David Hyde
Senator Vernon White
Thomas Gerstenecker
Igor Gimelshtein
Nancy Croitoru
Neil Weaver
Craig Bromell
Carlo Rigillo

D-U-N-S 24-269-9858   (HQ)
ALMONTE GENERAL HOSPITAL
75 Spring St Ss 1, Almonte, ON, K0A 1A0
(613) 256-2500
Sales 24,437,600
SIC 8062 General medical and surgical hospitals
 Mary Wilson Trider
 Kimberley Harbord
 Randy Shaw

D-U-N-S 20-032-4952   (SL)
PATRICE INDEPENDENT GROCER INC
401 Ottawa St, Almonte, ON, K0A 1A0
(613) 256-2080
Emp Here 100   *Sales* 29,347,700
SIC 5411 Grocery stores
 Guido Patrice

Alton, ON L7K

D-U-N-S 24-040-5733   (SL)
OSPREY VALLEY RESORTS INC
TPC TORONTO
18821 Main St Suite 2, Alton, ON, L7K 1R1
(519) 927-0586
Emp Here 75   *Sales* 5,729,775
SIC 7992 Public golf courses
 Brad Pinnell
 Dave Hunter
 Scott Brook
 Mike Hunter

Alvinston, ON N0N

D-U-N-S 20-032-5736   (HQ)
KUCERA FARM SUPPLY LIMITED
KUCERA CONSTRUCTION EQUIPMENT
3212 Nauvoo Rd, Alvinston, ON, N0N 1A0
(519) 898-2961
Sales 11,875,650
SIC 5083 Farm and garden machinery
 Daniel Kucera
 Kenneth Kucera
 Dave Kucera
 Ryan Kucera

Amherstburg, ON N0R

D-U-N-S 24-265-5111   (SL)
AMEX FREIGHT INC
7066 Smith Industrial Dr, Amherstburg, ON,
N0R 1J0
(519) 726-4444
Emp Here 75   *Sales* 38,997,525
SIC 4731 Freight transportation arrangement
 Harpreet Multani

D-U-N-S 24-862-6772   (SL)
TIMBERWOLF FOREST PRODUCTS INC
7781 Howard Ave, Amherstburg, ON, N0R 1J0
(519) 726-9653
Emp Here 27   *Sales* 12,825,702
SIC 5085 Industrial supplies
 Thomas Manherz
 Susan Manherz

Amherstburg, ON N9V

D-U-N-S 25-254-2279   (SL)
1144257 ONTARIO LIMITED
MELOCHE'S NO FRILLS
181 Sandwich St S, Amherstburg, ON, N9V
1Z9

(519) 736-7378
Emp Here 60   *Sales* 17,608,620
SIC 5411 Grocery stores
 Christopher Meloche

D-U-N-S 24-078-2763   (SL)
BARRON POULTRY LIMITED
7470 County Road 18, Amherstburg, ON, N9V
2Y7
(519) 726-5250
Emp Here 49   *Sales* 11,017,895
SIC 2015 Poultry slaughtering and processing
 Richard Barron
 Sharon Barron

D-U-N-S 24-763-0366   (SL)
BELWOOD POULTRY LIMITED
4272 4th Conc N, Amherstburg, ON, N9V 2Y9
(519) 736-2236
Emp Here 40   *Sales* 33,423,080
SIC 5144 Poultry and poultry products
 Dave Maxwell

D-U-N-S 20-515-1363   (BR)
DIAGEO CANADA INC
(*Suby of* DIAGEO PLC)
110 St. Arnaud St, Amherstburg, ON, N9V
2N8
(519) 736-2161
Emp Here 200
SIC 2085 Distilled and blended liquors
 Wayne Gilbert

D-U-N-S 20-981-2036   (BR)
SOBEYS CAPITAL INCORPORATED
(*Suby of* EMPIRE COMPANY LIMITED)
83 Sandwich St S, Amherstburg, ON, N9V 1Z5
(519) 736-4520
Emp Here 170
SIC 5411 Grocery stores
 Rene Rota

D-U-N-S 20-873-1278   (SL)
THRASHER SALES & LEASING LTD
251 Simcoe St, Amherstburg, ON, N9V 1M5
(519) 736-6481
Emp Here 32   *Sales* 15,938,496
SIC 5511 New and used car dealers
 Kenneth Thrasher

D-U-N-S 24-098-6120   (BR)
UNIFOR
CAW CANADA
(*Suby of* UNIFOR)
110 St. Arnaud St, Amherstburg, ON, N9V
2N8
(519) 730-0099
Emp Here 384
SIC 8631 Labor organizations
 Adam Hutchins

D-U-N-S 20-902-2177   (BR)
WINDSOR MOLD INC
PRECISION PLASTICS, DIV OF
(*Suby of* 873740 ONTARIO INC)
95 Victoria St N, Amherstburg, ON, N9V 3L1
(519) 736-5466
Emp Here 100
SIC 3089 Plastics products, nec
 Foreshaw Lorraine

D-U-N-S 25-146-8872   (SL)
WOLFF, MARY ANN DRUGS LTD
SHOPPERS DRUG MART
199 Sandwich St S, Amherstburg, ON, N9V
1Z9
(519) 736-5435
Emp Here 50   *Sales* 12,647,700
SIC 5912 Drug stores and proprietary stores
 Mary Ann Wolff

Amherstview, ON K7N

D-U-N-S 25-666-1414   (SL)
976736 ONTARIO LIMITED
AMHERSTVIEW FOODLAND

7 Manitou Cres W, Amherstview, ON, K7N
1B7
(613) 389-4184
Emp Here 60   *Sales* 17,608,620
SIC 5411 Grocery stores
 Ted Posadowski

D-U-N-S 20-124-7306   (SL)
GIBSON HOLDINGS (ONTARIO) LTD
HELEN HENDERSON CARE CENTRE
343 Amherst Dr Suite 133, Amherstview, ON,
K7N 1X3
(613) 384-4585
Emp Here 100   *Sales* 27,433,200
SIC 8741 Management services
 Lisa Gibson
 Angela Gibson

Ancaster, ON L9G

D-U-N-S 24-621-3016   (HQ)
2158124 ONTARIO INC
STONERIDGE INSURANCE BROKERS
1336 Sandhill Dr Unit 3, Ancaster, ON, L9G
4V5
(905) 648-6767
Emp Here 40   *Sales* 42,403,000
SIC 6411 Insurance agents, brokers, and service
 Donald Coones
 Veronica Giles

D-U-N-S 20-269-5318   (HQ)
2428391 ONTARIO INC
SUNRISE RECORDS
1430 Cormorant Rd, Ancaster, ON, L9G 4V5
(905) 304-1010
Emp Here 20   *Sales* 186,692,100
SIC 5736 Musical instrument stores
 Douglas Putman

D-U-N-S 24-340-3800   (HQ)
ANCASTER OLD MILL INC
548 Old Dundas Rd, Ancaster, ON, L9G 3J4
(905) 648-1828
Sales 19,134,500
SIC 6712 Bank holding companies
 Aaron Ciancone

D-U-N-S 24-508-7338   (SL)
ANCASTER TOYOTA INC
30 Mason Dr, Ancaster, ON, L9G 3K9
(905) 648-9910
Emp Here 40   *Sales* 19,923,120
SIC 5511 New and used car dealers
 Frank Van Der Veen

D-U-N-S 25-254-5116   (SL)
AUDCOMP GROUP INC
AUDCOMP
611 Tradewind Dr Suite 100, Ancaster, ON,
L9G 4V5
(905) 304-1775
Emp Here 46   *Sales* 10,595,640
SIC 5734 Computer and software stores
 Gary Sohal

D-U-N-S 20-647-2149   (SL)
BAKER, WALTER & CHANTAL SALES LTD
CANADIAN TIRE
1060 Wilson St W, Ancaster, ON, L9G 3K9
(905) 304-0000
Emp Here 85   *Sales* 53,488,800
SIC 5531 Auto and home supply stores
 Walter Baker
 Chantal Baker

D-U-N-S 24-197-9665   (SL)
CICCARELLI, OTTAVIO & SON CONTRACTING LTD
CICCARELLI GROUP
807 Garner Rd E Suite 1, Ancaster, ON, L9G
3K9
(905) 648-5178
Emp Here 50   *Sales* 15,057,100

SIC 4959 Sanitary services, nec
 Ottavio Ciccarelli
 John Ciccarelli

D-U-N-S 20-874-8962   (HQ)
DAVEY TREE EXPERT CO. OF CANADA, LIMITED
DAVEY TREE SERVICES DIV
(*Suby of* THE DAVEY TREE EXPERT COMPANY)
611 Tradewind Dr Suite 500, Ancaster, ON,
L9G 4V5
(905) 333-1034
Emp Here 10   *Sales* 43,350,000
SIC 7999 Amusement and recreation, nec
 Karl Warnke
 Rod Soderstrom
 Blaire Sayers
 David Adante

D-U-N-S 24-826-2115   (BR)
FIRSTCANADA ULC
FIRST STUDENT
(*Suby of* FIRSTGROUP PLC)
1185 Smith Rd, Ancaster, ON, L9G 3L1
(905) 648-1386
Emp Here 300
SIC 4151 School buses
 Angela Asher

D-U-N-S 20-710-8148   (BR)
HAMILTON-WENTWORTH DISTRICT SCHOOL BOARD, THE
ANCASTER HIGH SCHOOL
(*Suby of* HAMILTON-WENTWORTH DISTRICT SCHOOL BOARD, THE)
374 Jerseyville Rd W, Ancaster, ON, L9G 3K8
(905) 648-4468
Emp Here 75
SIC 8211 Elementary and secondary schools
 Judy Langsner

D-U-N-S 25-107-7137   (SL)
HIGHGATE RETIREMENT HOMES INC
HIGHGATE RETIREMENT RESIDENCE
325 Fiddler'S Green Rd Suite 215, Ancaster,
ON, L9G 1W9
(905) 648-8399
Emp Here 32   *Sales* 14,309,568
SIC 5047 Medical and hospital equipment
 Clare Bryja

D-U-N-S 24-143-4968   (HQ)
INCOM MANUFACTURING GROUP LTD
1259 Sandhill Dr Suite 76, Ancaster, ON, L9G
4V5
(905) 648-0774
Sales 14,250,780
SIC 5085 Industrial supplies
 Cyril W Dicks Jr
 Brian Donnelly

D-U-N-S 24-470-8418   (SL)
KNOLLWOOD GOLF LIMITED
KNOLLWOOD GOLF CLUB
1276 Shaver Rd, Ancaster, ON, L9G 3L1
(905) 648-6687
Emp Here 80   *Sales* 6,111,760
SIC 7992 Public golf courses
 Jim Harris

D-U-N-S 25-841-8136   (BR)
PIONEER FOOD SERVICES LIMITED
TIM HORTONS
(*Suby of* PIONEER FOOD SERVICES LIMITED)
1180 2 Hwy Suite 2, Ancaster, ON, L9G 3K9
(905) 648-5222
Emp Here 75
SIC 5812 Eating places
 Alan Banting

D-U-N-S 20-575-6633   (SL)
RENNSTADD PHARMA INC
SHOPPERS DRUG MART
47 Wilson St W, Ancaster, ON, L9G 1N1
(905) 648-4493
Emp Here 55   *Sales* 13,438,040

SIC 5912 Drug stores and proprietary stores
Nikola Mrksic

D-U-N-S 20-290-3592   (BR)
REVERA INC
MEADOWS LONG TERM CARE CENTRE, THE
(*Suby of* GOVERNMENT OF CANADA)
12 Tranquility Ave Suite 1, Ancaster, ON, L9G 5C2
(905) 304-1993
Emp Here 150
SIC 8322 Individual and family services
Tina Padovani

D-U-N-S 20-055-3691   (HQ)
ROBERTSON BUILDING SYSTEMS LIMITED
(*Suby of* CORNERSTONE BUILDING BRANDS, INC.)
1343 Sandhill Dr, Ancaster, ON, L9G 4V5
(905) 304-1111
Sales 24,971,050
SIC 3448 Prefabricated Metal buildings and components
Marion Alley
J.R. Husband

D-U-N-S 20-299-9348   (HQ)
STACKPOLE INTERNATIONAL ENGINEERED PRODUCTS, LTD
STACKPOLE INTERNATIONAL
(*Suby of* JOHNSON ELECTRIC HOLDINGS LIMITED)
1325 Cormorant Rd, Ancaster, ON, L9G 4V5
(905) 304-9455
Emp Here 2   *Sales* 184,461,600
SIC 5013 Motor vehicle supplies and new parts
Peter Ballantyne

D-U-N-S 25-369-9128   (BR)
STACKPOLE INTERNATIONAL ENGINEERED PRODUCTS, LTD
STACKPOLE
(*Suby of* JOHNSON ELECTRIC HOLDINGS LIMITED)
1310 Cormorant Rd, Ancaster, ON, L9G 4V5
(905) 304-8533
Emp Here 298
SIC 5013 Motor vehicle supplies and new parts
Ken Myers

D-U-N-S 20-296-0662   (HQ)
STACKPOLE INTERNATIONAL POWDER METAL, LTD.
(*Suby of* JOHNSON ELECTRIC HOLDINGS LIMITED)
1325 Cormorant Rd 2nd Fl, Ancaster, ON, L9G 4V5
(905) 304-9455
Emp Here 42   *Sales* 363,562,500
SIC 3714 Motor vehicle parts and accessories
Peter Ballantyne
Rahim Suleman

D-U-N-S 20-296-0704   (BR)
STACKPOLE INTERNATIONAL POWDER METAL, LTD.
STACKPOLE INTERNATIONAL POWDER METAL, LTD
(*Suby of* JOHNSON ELECTRIC HOLDINGS LIMITED)
1325 Cormorant Rd 1st Fl, Ancaster, ON, L9G 4V5
(905) 304-9455
Emp Here 300
SIC 3714 Motor vehicle parts and accessories
Kanti Patel

D-U-N-S 20-296-0654   (HQ)
STACKPOLE INTERNATIONAL ULC
(*Suby of* JOHNSON ELECTRIC HOLDINGS LIMITED)
1325 Cormorant Rd Fl 2, Ancaster, ON, L9G 4V5

(905) 304-9455
Emp Here 50   *Sales* 727,125,000
SIC 3714 Motor vehicle parts and accessories
Chris Hasson
Ken Myers
Doug Grodeck

D-U-N-S 24-395-3838   (BR)
STATE REALTY LIMITED
ROYAL LEPAGE
(*Suby of* STATE REALTY LIMITED)
1122 Wilson St W, Ancaster, ON, L9G 3K9
(905) 648-4451
Emp Here 103
SIC 6531 Real estate agents and managers
Barney Gordon

D-U-N-S 24-204-2252   (HQ)
SUEZ TREATMENT SOLUTIONS CANADA L.P.
(*Suby of* SUEZ)
1295 Cormorant Rd Suite 200, Ancaster, ON, L9G 4V5
(289) 346-1000
Sales 19,980,090
SIC 3589 Service industry machinery, nec
Maximilien Pellegrini
Cesare Angeretti
Stephan Jutz

D-U-N-S 20-343-0723   (HQ)
VULCRAFT CANADA, INC
(*Suby of* NUCOR CORPORATION)
1362 Osprey Dr, Ancaster, ON, L9G 4V5
(289) 443-2000
Emp Here 45   *Sales* 11,790,220
SIC 3312 Blast furnaces and steel mills
Mike Fernie
Creg Wellings

D-U-N-S 24-316-9088   (BR)
WAL-MART CANADA CORP
WALMART SUPERCENTRE
(*Suby of* WALMART INC.)
1051 Garner Rd W Suite 3127, Ancaster, ON, L9G 3K9
(905) 648-9980
Emp Here 520
SIC 5311 Department stores
Clint Lawrence

Ancaster, ON L9K

D-U-N-S 20-977-2917   (SL)
1457271 ONTARIO LIMITED
WILLOWGROVE, THE
1217 Old Mohawk Rd, Ancaster, ON, L9K 1P6
(905) 304-6781
Emp Here 188   *Sales* 12,890,408
SIC 8051 Skilled nursing care facilities
Natasha Murray

D-U-N-S 25-543-0167   (BR)
COSTCO WHOLESALE CANADA LTD
(*Suby of* COSTCO WHOLESALE CORPORATION)
100 Legend Crt Suite 1105, Ancaster, ON, L9K 1J3
(905) 304-0344
Emp Here 151
SIC 5099 Durable goods, nec
Roberto Felice

D-U-N-S 20-640-6949   (HQ)
DALTON TIMMIS INSURANCE GROUP INC
(*Suby of* NFP INTERMEDIATE HOLDINGS B CORP.)
35 Stone Church Rd, Ancaster, ON, L9K 1S5
(905) 648-3922
Emp Here 80   *Sales* 341,914,880
SIC 6331 Fire, marine, and casualty insurance
Gregory J Padovani
Domenico Tesone
Brian E Timmis Jr
Michelle Deanes

D-U-N-S 25-079-1167   (BR)
HOME DEPOT OF CANADA INC
HOME DEPOT
(*Suby of* THE HOME DEPOT INC)
122 Martindale Cres, Ancaster, ON, L9K 1J9
(905) 304-5900
Emp Here 250
SIC 5211 Lumber and other building materials
Ken Wilson

D-U-N-S 20-770-5190   (BR)
HOME DEPOT OF CANADA INC
(*Suby of* THE HOME DEPOT INC)
122 Martindale Cres, Ancaster, ON, L9K 1J9
(905) 304-6826
Emp Here 300
SIC 5211 Lumber and other building materials
Stephen Jordan

D-U-N-S 24-783-5911   (SL)
LANDMART BUILDING CORP
911 Golf Links Rd Suite 307, Ancaster, ON, L9K 1H9
(905) 304-6459
Emp Here 33   *Sales* 10,522,677
SIC 1521 Single-family housing construction
Mario Rouke

D-U-N-S 20-511-8933   (SL)
LOYALIST INSURANCE BROKERS LIMITED
911 Golf Links Rd Suite 111, Ancaster, ON, L9K 1H9
(905) 648-6767
Emp Here 25   *Sales* 21,201,500
SIC 6411 Insurance agents, brokers, and service
Donald W. Coons
James D. Coons
W. Edward Scheetz

D-U-N-S 24-363-0832   (BR)
RGIS CANADA ULC
(*Suby of* THE BLACKSTONE GROUP L P)
911 Golf Links Rd, Ancaster, ON, L9K 1H9
(905) 304-9700
Emp Here 100
SIC 7389 Business services, nec
Jd Bouchard

D-U-N-S 20-614-4003   (BR)
SIR CORP
JACK ASTOR'S BAR & GRILL
(*Suby of* SIR CORP)
839 Golf Links Rd, Ancaster, ON, L9K 1L5
(905) 304-1721
Emp Here 100
SIC 5812 Eating places
Adrian Cloutier

D-U-N-S 25-911-7554   (BR)
SOBEYS CAPITAL INCORPORATED
SOBEYS FOOD VILLAGE
(*Suby of* EMPIRE COMPANY LIMITED)
977 Golf Links Rd, Ancaster, ON, L9K 1K1
(905) 648-3534
Emp Here 150
SIC 5411 Grocery stores
John Slandja

Angus, ON L0M

D-U-N-S 25-077-9860   (SL)
JUSTIN & STACEY'S NO FRILLS
285 Mill St, Angus, ON, L0M 1B4
(705) 424-7090
Emp Here 49   *Sales* 13,433,448
SIC 5411 Grocery stores
Justin Oliver

D-U-N-S 20-702-4220   (BR)
SOBEYS CAPITAL INCORPORATED
SOBEY'S
(*Suby of* EMPIRE COMPANY LIMITED)
247 Mill St, Angus, ON, L0M 1B2

(705) 424-1588
Emp Here 125
SIC 5411 Grocery stores
Matt Derouin

Ariss, ON N0B

D-U-N-S 24-708-5236   (BR)
LINAMAR CORPORATION
ARISS MANUFACTURING
(*Suby of* LINAMAR CORPORATION)
Gd, Ariss, ON, N0B 1B0
(519) 822-4080
Emp Here 230
SIC 3531 Construction machinery
Pat Sartori

Arkona, ON N0M

D-U-N-S 20-256-2638   (HQ)
ST. FRANCIS ADVOCATES FOR THE AUTISTIC & DEVELOPMENTALLY DISABLED (SARNIA) INC
7346 Arkona Rd, Arkona, ON, N0M 1B0
(519) 828-3399
Emp Here 13   *Sales* 19,733,120
SIC 7699 Repair services, nec
Arden Magill

Arnprior, ON K7S

D-U-N-S 25-884-8985   (SL)
ANTRIM TRUCK CENTER LTD
ANTRIM WESTERN STAR
580 White Lake Rd, Arnprior, ON, K7S 3G9
(613) 623-9618
Emp Here 60   *Sales* 21,852,900
SIC 5012 Automobiles and other motor vehicles
Jack Cameron
Gail Cameron

D-U-N-S 25-366-2076   (HQ)
ARNPRIOR AEROSPACE INC
107 Baskin Dr, Arnprior, ON, K7S 3M1
(613) 623-4267
Sales 116,340,000
SIC 3728 Aircraft parts and equipment, nec
John Wilbur
George Rick
Debbie Bernard

D-U-N-S 20-789-4031   (HQ)
ARNPRIOR CHRYSLER LTD
205 Madawaska Blvd, Arnprior, ON, K7S 1S6
(613) 623-4256
Sales 10,957,716
SIC 5511 New and used car dealers
Michael Mulder
Wilma Mulder
Michael Mulder

D-U-N-S 25-165-2699   (SL)
ARNPRIOR OTTAWA AUTO PARTS LTD
5445 Madawaska Blvd, Arnprior, ON, K7S 3H4
(613) 623-7361
Emp Here 35   *Sales* 17,432,730
SIC 5531 Auto and home supply stores
Henry Aumont

D-U-N-S 20-890-4177   (HQ)
ARNPRIOR REGIONAL HEALTH
350 John St N, Arnprior, ON, K7S 2P6
(613) 623-7962
Sales 37,211,800
SIC 8062 General medical and surgical hospitals
Barbara Darlow

▲ Public Company   ■ Public Company Family Member   **HQ** Headquarters   **BR** Branch   **SL** Single Location

Chris Havey
Eric Hanna

D-U-N-S 20-026-2987   (SL)
COMPETITION COMPOSITES INC
251 Fifth Ave, Arnprior, ON, K7S 3M3
(613) 599-6951
Emp Here 15   Sales 14,789,372
SIC 2655 Fiber cans, drums, and similar products
Phil Locker
John Rae
Craig Cooper

D-U-N-S 20-033-0595   (HQ)
M. SULLIVAN & SON LIMITED
ARNPRIOR BUILDERS SUPPLIES, DIV OF
236 Madawaska Blvd Suite 100, Arnprior, ON, K7S 0A3
(613) 623-6584
Emp Here 55   Sales 25,364,220
SIC 1541 Industrial buildings and warehouses
Robert J. Ball
Kerry G. Hisko
Tim Pruner
Marty Smith
P. Gregory Sullivan

D-U-N-S 20-555-6512   (BR)
METRO ONTARIO INC
METRO
(Suby of METRO INC)
375 Daniel St S, Arnprior, ON, K7S 3K6
(613) 623-6273
Emp Here 100
SIC 5411 Grocery stores
Rick Horne

D-U-N-S 20-548-5514   (SL)
NYLENE CANADA INC
(Suby of POLYMERIC RESOURCES CORP.)
200 Mcnab St, Arnprior, ON, K7S 2C7
(613) 623-3191
Emp Here 150   Sales 42,603,150
SIC 2824 Organic fibers, noncellulosic
Don Nicholas

D-U-N-S 24-578-9284   (HQ)
PACIFIC SAFETY PRODUCTS INC
PACIFIC EMERGENCY PRODUCTS
(Suby of MAUI ACQUISITION CORP.)
124 Fourth Ave, Arnprior, ON, K7S 0A9
(613) 623-6001
Emp Here 75   Sales 38,411,800
SIC 3842 Surgical appliances and supplies
Terry Vaudry
Sherrie Dontigny
Derek Mcdorman
Jen Murch
Fraser Campbell
Ken Hight

D-U-N-S 24-390-4344   (SL)
PILLAR5 PHARMA INC
365 Madawaska Blvd, Arnprior, ON, K7S 0C9
(613) 623-4221
Emp Here 100   Sales 28,402,100
SIC 2834 Pharmaceutical preparations
Dwight Gorham
Jamie Moore
Kevin Rampton
Vince Cozzi

D-U-N-S 20-506-5113   (SL)
ROWMONT HOLDINGS LIMITED
A & O AUTO PARTS
5445 Madawaska Blvd, Arnprior, ON, K7S 3H4
(613) 623-7361
Emp Here 32   Sales 11,789,866
SIC 5013 Motor vehicle supplies and new parts
Henry Aumont
Alvin Aumont
Norah Aumont
Alan Aumont

D-U-N-S 25-627-4226   (SL)
ROXSON ENTERPRISES LIMITED
VALLEY CATERERS
80 Mcgonigal St W, Arnprior, ON, K7S 1M3

Emp Here 75   Sales 3,413,925
SIC 5812 Eating places
Russ Linton

D-U-N-S 24-268-2953   (BR)
ROYAL CANADIAN LEGION, THE
ARNPRIOR LEGION BRANCH 174
(Suby of ROYAL CANADIAN LEGION, THE)
49 Daniel St N, Arnprior, ON, K7S 2K6
(613) 623-4722
Emp Here 450
SIC 8641 Civic and social associations
Harry Hereford

D-U-N-S 24-846-5312   (BR)
SANDVIK CANADA, INC
SANDVIK MATERIALS TECHNOLOGY CANADA
(Suby of SANDVIK AB)
425 Mccartney, Arnprior, ON, K7S 3P3
(613) 623-6501
Emp Here 230
SIC 3312 Blast furnaces and steel mills
Tom Moylan

D-U-N-S 20-033-0553   (SL)
SMITHS CONSTRUCTION COMPANY ARNPRIOR LIMITED
(Suby of MILLER GROUP INC)
276 Madawaska Blvd, Arnprior, ON, K7S 3H4
(613) 623-3144
Emp Here 50   Sales 12,622,100
SIC 1611 Highway and street construction
Leo Mcarthur

D-U-N-S 25-977-8426   (SL)
TRIODETIC LTD
(Suby of PLAINTREE SYSTEMS INC)
10 Didak Dr, Arnprior, ON, K7S 0C3
(613) 623-3434
Emp Here 30   Sales 11,940,225
SIC 3441 Fabricated structural Metal
David Watson
Ron Tayler

Arthur, ON N0G

D-U-N-S 24-182-5579   (SL)
441861 ONTARIO LTD
IVAN ARMSTRONG TRUCKING
8035 Line 2 W, Arthur, ON, N0G 1A0
(519) 848-2575
Emp Here 69   Sales 10,225,248
SIC 4213 Trucking, except local
John Raftis
Amy Van Ankum

D-U-N-S 20-702-8259   (SL)
ALL TREAT FARMS LIMITED
RED RIBBON PRODUCTS
7963 Wellington Road 109 Rr 4, Arthur, ON, N0G 1A0
(519) 848-3145
Emp Here 70   Sales 24,198,300
SIC 2048 Prepared feeds, nec
George White
Lynda White
Freda White
Paul Smith

D-U-N-S 20-943-7698   (SL)
ARTHUR CHRYSLER DODGE JEEP LIMITED
165 Catherine St W, Arthur, ON, N0G 1A0
(519) 848-2016
Emp Here 30   Sales 14,942,340
SIC 5511 New and used car dealers
Ronald Rooney
Wayne Rooney

Robert Rooney

D-U-N-S 24-784-7858   (SL)
GOLDEN VALLEY FARMS INC
GOLDEN VALLEY
50 Wells St W, Arthur, ON, N0G 1A0
(519) 848-3110
Emp Here 100   Sales 26,230,900
SIC 0191 General farms, primarily crop
Wilhem Huber Sr

D-U-N-S 25-502-1560   (HQ)
MUSASHI AUTO PARTS CANADA INC
(Suby of MUSASHI SEIMITSU INDUSTRY CO., LTD.)
333 Domville St, Arthur, ON, N0G 1A0
(519) 848-2800
Emp Here 230   Sales 95,980,500
SIC 3714 Motor vehicle parts and accessories
Haru Ohtsuka

D-U-N-S 24-422-8628   (BR)
MUSASHI AUTO PARTS CANADA INC
(Suby of MUSASHI SEIMITSU INDUSTRY CO., LTD.)
500 Domville St, Arthur, ON, N0G 1A0
(519) 848-2800
Emp Here 100
SIC 3714 Motor vehicle parts and accessories
Ken Morris

Arva, ON N0M

D-U-N-S 20-041-4241   (HQ)
MURPHY, J & T LIMITED
MURPHY BUS LINES
21588 Richmond St, Arva, ON, N0M 1C0
(519) 660-8200
Emp Here 150   Sales 33,872,400
SIC 4151 School buses
Michael Murphy
Paul Murphy

D-U-N-S 20-200-6263   (SL)
SPECIAL ABILITY RIDING INSTITUTE
SARI THERAPEUTIC RIDING
12659 Medway Rd, Arva, ON, N0M 1C0
(519) 666-1123
Emp Here 27   Sales 10,730,178
SIC 8699 Membership organizations, nec
Diane Blackal

D-U-N-S 25-249-1055   (BR)
THAMES VALLEY DISTRICT SCHOOL BOARD
MEDWAY HIGH SCHOOL
(Suby of THAMES VALLEY DISTRICT SCHOOL BOARD)
14405 Medway Rd, Arva, ON, N0M 1C0
(519) 660-8418
Emp Here 90
SIC 8211 Elementary and secondary schools
James Copeland

Ashburn, ON L0B

D-U-N-S 20-904-2233   (SL)
DAGMAR RESORT LIMITED
DAGMAR SKI RESORT
1220 Lakeridge Rd Rr 1, Ashburn, ON, L0B 1A0
(905) 649-2002
Emp Here 270   Sales 25,830,360
SIC 7011 Hotels and motels
Alex Nagy

D-U-N-S 24-515-0685   (SL)
GREENWOOD MUSHROOM FARM
9760 Heron Rd, Ashburn, ON, L0B 1A0
(905) 655-3373
Emp Here 200   Sales 33,805,000
SIC 0182 Food crops grown under cover

Don Van Dusen
Clay Taylor
Brent Taylor
Nick Van Halteren

Ashton, ON K0A

D-U-N-S 20-442-0251   (HQ)
THOMAS CAVANAGH CONSTRUCTION LIMITED
(Suby of CAVANAGH, THOMAS HOLDINGS LIMITED)
9094a Cavanagh Rd, Ashton, ON, K0A 1B0
(613) 257-2918
Sales 37,866,300
SIC 1611 Highway and street construction
Thomas Cavanagh
Kathleen Cavanagh

Athens, ON K0E

D-U-N-S 20-577-8087   (SL)
HOWARD, R. A. BUS SERVICE LIMITED
31 Henry St, Athens, ON, K0E 1B0
(613) 924-2720
Emp Here 75   Sales 4,115,400
SIC 4151 School buses
Ronald A Howard
Dale Howard

D-U-N-S 20-033-1783   (HQ)
TACKABERRY, G & SONS CONSTRUCTION COMPANY LIMITED
SWEET SAND & GRAVEL
109 Washburn Rd, Athens, ON, K0E 1B0
(613) 924-2634
Emp Here 20   Sales 12,622,100
SIC 1611 Highway and street construction
George Tackaberry
June Knapp

D-U-N-S 20-889-8486   (BR)
UNITED COUNTIES OF LEEDS AND GRENVILLE
MAPLE VIEW LODGE
(Suby of UNITED COUNTIES OF LEEDS AND GRENVILLE)
746 County Rd 42, Athens, ON, K0E 1B0
(613) 924-2696
Emp Here 85
SIC 8361 Residential care
Robin Hoy

Atikokan, ON P0T

D-U-N-S 25-144-8775   (SL)
ATIKOKAN GENERAL HOSPITAL
120 Dorothy St, Atikokan, ON, P0T 1C1
(807) 597-4215
Emp Here 110   Sales 12,218,800
SIC 8062 General medical and surgical hospitals
Vic Prokopchuk

Aurora, ON L4G

D-U-N-S 25-508-1457   (SL)
1254561 ONTARIO INC
MAPLE UTILITY
67 Industrial Pky N Unit 1, Aurora, ON, L4G 4C4
(905) 726-9404
Emp Here 45   Sales 10,839,780
SIC 1623 Water, sewer, and utility lines
Kimberly Evans

Kevin Tokarski
Derek Tokarski

D-U-N-S 20-380-0545   (HQ)
1959612 ONTARIO INC
GIBSON BUILDING SUPPLIES
194 Earl Stewart Dr, Aurora, ON, L4G 6V7
(905) 726-4933
Emp Here 20   *Sales* 16,594,424
SIC 5211 Lumber and other building materials
Lucian Chouinard
Catherine Chouinard

D-U-N-S 24-986-2723   (HQ)
853569 ONTARIO LIMITED
HOLTEN IMPEX INTERNATIONAL
33 Eric T Smith Way, Aurora, ON, L4G 0Z6
(905) 726-9669
Sales 18,334,134
SIC 5032 Brick, stone, and related material
Antonius Holten
Gerda Holten

D-U-N-S 20-027-2912   (BR)
A & B RAIL SERVICES LTD
(*Suby of* UNIVERSAL RAIL SYSTEMS INC)
325 Industrial Pky S, Aurora, ON, L4G 3V8

Emp Here 100
SIC 1629 Heavy construction, nec
Dave Wilfong

D-U-N-S 24-693-6355   (SL)
AB COX AUTOMOTIVE LTD
305 Wellington St E, Aurora, ON, L4G 6C3
(905) 841-2121
Emp Here 42   *Sales* 20,919,276
SIC 5511 New and used car dealers
Ab Cox
David Darch

D-U-N-S 25-530-4537   (SL)
ALPEN HOUSE ULC, THE
ADENA SPRINGS NORTH
14875 Bayview Ave, Aurora, ON, L4G 0K8
(905) 841-0336
Emp Here 75   *Sales* 10,256,925
SIC 0272 Horses and other equines
Andrew Stronach
Mike Rogers

D-U-N-S 20-549-9643   (SL)
ANDREWS MAILING SERVICE LTD
226 Industrial Pky N Unit 7, Aurora, ON, L4G
4C3
(905) 503-1700
Emp Here 50   *Sales* 10,586,200
SIC 7331 Direct mail advertising services
Stacey Campbell
Sheila Copeland
John Campbell
Cliff Copeland

D-U-N-S 24-538-2486   (SL)
AUTO GROUP AURORA INC
AURORA TOYOTA
669 Wellington St E, Aurora, ON, L4G 0C9
(905) 727-1948
Emp Here 30   *Sales* 14,942,340
SIC 5511 New and used car dealers
John Chapman
Savinder Gill

D-U-N-S 24-829-8275   (SL)
**AVANT IMAGING & INTEGRATED MEDIA
INC**
THE AIIM GROUP
205 Industrial Pky N Unit 1, Aurora, ON, L4G
4C4
(905) 841-6444
Emp Here 90   *Sales* 14,762,430
SIC 2752 Commercial printing, lithographic
Mario Giorgio
Frank Giorgio

D-U-N-S 24-389-6537   (SL)
AXEL KRAFT INTERNATIONAL LIMITED
99 Engelhard Dr, Aurora, ON, L4G 3V1

(905) 841-6840
Emp Here 40   *Sales* 44,213,800
SIC 5122 Drugs, proprietaries, and sundries
Axel Kraft

D-U-N-S 25-107-6451   (HQ)
AXIOM GROUP INC
115 Mary St, Aurora, ON, L4G 1G3
(905) 727-2878
Sales 31,080,140
SIC 3541 Machine tools, Metal cutting type
Perry Rizzo

D-U-N-S 25-989-8559   (SL)
AXIOM PLASTICS INC
(*Suby of* AXIOM GROUP INC)
115 Mary St, Aurora, ON, L4G 1G3
(905) 727-2878
Emp Here 185   *Sales* 21,026,914
SIC 3089 Plastics products, nec
Perry Rizzo
Rocco Di Serio
Herb Jahn

D-U-N-S 24-872-8867   (SL)
**BARFITT BROS. HARDWARE (AURORA)
LTD**
*AURORA HOME HARDWARE & BUILDING
CENTRE*
289 Wellington St E, Aurora, ON, L4G 6H6
(905) 727-4751
Emp Here 50   *Sales* 12,652,950
SIC 5251 Hardware stores
Russ Barfitt
Rob Barfitt
Randy Barfitt

D-U-N-S 24-826-8315   (SL)
BIONX INTERNATIONAL CORPORATION
BIONX CANADA
(*Suby of* STRONACH GROUP INC, THE)
455 Magna Dr, Aurora, ON, L4G 7A9
(905) 726-9105
Emp Here 100   *Sales* 19,044,200
SIC 3625 Relays and industrial controls
Manfred Gingl

D-U-N-S 24-411-7990   (HQ)
BULK BARN FOODS LIMITED
(*Suby of* OFIELD, CRAIG GROUP LTD)
320 Don Hillock Dr, Aurora, ON, L4G 0G9
(905) 726-5000
Sales 83,557,700
SIC 5141 Groceries, general line
Craig Ofield

D-U-N-S 20-784-7989   (SL)
**BUNN-O-MATIC   CORPORATION   OF
CANADA**
(*Suby of* BUNN-O-MATIC CORPORATION)
280 Industrial Pky S, Aurora, ON, L4G 3T9
(905) 841-2866
Emp Here 100   *Sales* 22,200,100
SIC 3589 Service industry machinery, nec
Ross Morrison
Stephane Lauzon
Ken Cox
Gene Wilken
Arthur H Bunn

D-U-N-S 20-918-9013   (SL)
CANADIAN LAWYER MAGAZINE INC
240 Edward St, Aurora, ON, L4G 3S9
(905) 841-6480
Emp Here 40   *Sales* 29,700,800
SIC 5192 Books, periodicals, and newspapers
Stewart Morrison

D-U-N-S 24-790-5438   (SL)
**CANADIAN WIRELESS COMMUNICATIONS
INC**
CANADIAN WIRELESS
10-91 First Commerce Dr, Aurora, ON, L4G
0G2
(905) 726-2652
Emp Here 49   *Sales* 15,954,400
SIC 5999 Miscellaneous retail stores, nec
Mike Harris

D-U-N-S 24-993-0009   (SL)
CARCONE'S AUTO RECYCLING LIMITED
1030 Bloomington Rd Suite 2, Aurora, ON,
L4G 0L7
(905) 773-5778
Emp Here 50   *Sales* 18,210,750
SIC 5013 Motor vehicle supplies and new
parts
Michael Carcone
Lloydean Carcone
Paula Badaly
Lisa Russo

D-U-N-S 24-345-7152   (BR)
CHARTWELL RETIREMENT RESIDENCES
(*Suby of* CHARTWELL RETIREMENT RESI-
DENCES)
32 Mill St, Aurora, ON, L4G 2R9
(905) 727-1939
Emp Here 260
SIC 8051 Skilled nursing care facilities
Edith Schultz

D-U-N-S 25-517-4633   (SL)
CHEVALIER CHRYSLER INC
AURORA CHRYSLER
14535 Yonge St, Aurora, ON, L4G 6L1
(905) 841-1233
Emp Here 30   *Sales* 14,942,340
SIC 5511 New and used car dealers
Frank Chan
Philip So

D-U-N-S 20-115-4577   (HQ)
CLB MEDIA INC
240 Edward St Suite 1, Aurora, ON, L4G 3S9

Sales 16,402,700
SIC 2721 Periodicals
Stuart Morrison
Kent Milford

D-U-N-S 24-855-9853   (SL)
**CLEANRIVER RECYCLING SOLUTIONS
INC**
189 Earl Stewart Dr Unit 1, Aurora, ON, L4G
6V5
(905) 717-4984
Emp Here 40   *Sales* 12,045,680
SIC 4953 Refuse systems
Bruce Buchan

D-U-N-S 20-848-3339   (HQ)
**COMPASS FOOD SALES COMPANY LIM-
ITED**
260 Industrial Pky N, Aurora, ON, L4G 4C3
(905) 713-0167
Sales 20,889,425
SIC 5141 Groceries, general line
Barbara Fenwick
Ronald C Fenwick
Sean P Fenwick
Michelle Adamo

D-U-N-S 25-280-0636   (BR)
COUTTS, WILLIAM E. COMPANY, LIMITED
HALLMARK CARDS
(*Suby of* HALLMARK CARDS, INCORPO-
RATED)
100 Vandorf Sideroad, Aurora, ON, L4G 3G9

Emp Here 100
SIC 5947 Gift, novelty, and souvenir shop
Bob Darlow

D-U-N-S 25-806-7875   (SL)
CSH PARK PLACE MANOR INC
*CHARTWELL PARK PLACE RETIREMENT
RESIDENCE*
(*Suby of* CHARTWELL MASTER CARE LP)
15055 Yonge St, Aurora, ON, L4G 6T4
(905) 727-2952
Emp Here 70   *Sales* 15,460,970
SIC 6513 Apartment building operators
Stephen Suske
John Jeffs

D-U-N-S 20-260-6604   (SL)

CUBE PACKAGING SOLUTIONS INC
200 Industrial Pky N, Aurora, ON, L4G 4C3
(905) 750-2823
Emp Here 100   *Sales* 15,885,800
SIC 3089 Plastics products, nec
Souren Agemian Jr
Len Chopin
John Alexanian
Kim Camilleri

D-U-N-S 20-649-2949   (HQ)
**EQUIPMENT LEASING COMPANY LTD,
THE**
ISLAND INKJET
106 Brookeview Dr, Aurora, ON, L4G 6R5
(905) 629-3210
Emp Here 10   *Sales* 23,751,300
SIC 5085 Industrial supplies
Alex Schulz

D-U-N-S 24-859-9318   (HQ)
FEATHERLITE INDUSTRIES LIMITED
100 Engelhard Dr, Aurora, ON, L4G 3V2
(905) 727-0031
Emp Here 75   *Sales* 16,327,225
SIC 3499 Fabricated Metal products, nec
Andrew Gucciardi

D-U-N-S 25-498-6961   (HQ)
GEOTECH LTD
245 Industrial Pky N, Aurora, ON, L4G 4C4
(905) 841-5004
Sales 42,460,700
SIC 8999 Services, nec
Edward Morrison
Yin Yi

D-U-N-S 25-354-3524   (BR)
**GREAT PACIFIC ENTERPRISES LIMITED
PARTNERSHIP**
GENPAK DIV OF
(*Suby of* GREAT PACIFIC ENTERPRISES
LIMITED PARTNERSHIP)
325 Industrial Pky S, Aurora, ON, L4G 3V8
(905) 727-0121
Emp Here 200
SIC 3081 Unsupported plastics film and sheet
Andy Valy

D-U-N-S 24-858-7201   (HQ)
**GREAT PACIFIC ENTERPRISES LIMITED
PARTNERSHIP**
GENPAK FLEXIBLE
(*Suby of* PATTISON, JIM GROUP INC)
285 Industrial Pky S, Aurora, ON, L4G 3V8
(905) 727-0121
Sales 38,953,600
SIC 2671 Paper; coated and laminated pack-
aging
Salman Mohammad

D-U-N-S 25-255-6840   (SL)
GREYFIELD CONSTRUCTION CO LTD
15185 Yonge St Suite 200, Aurora, ON, L4G
1L8
(905) 713-0999
Emp Here 50   *Sales* 23,536,550
SIC 1542 Nonresidential construction, nec
Peter Hillar

D-U-N-S 20-532-6739   (SL)
HIGHLAND CHEVROLET CADILLAC LTD
HIGHLAND NATIONAL LEASING, DIV OF
(*Suby of* ARMADALE CO. LIMITED)
15783 Yonge St, Aurora, ON, L4G 1P4
(905) 727-1900
Emp Here 80   *Sales* 50,342,400
SIC 5511 New and used car dealers
Clifford Sifton
Ron Vandebeek

D-U-N-S 20-402-0317   (SL)
HOLLISTER LIMITED
(*Suby of* HOLLISTER INCORPORATED)
95 Mary St, Aurora, ON, L4G 1G3
(905) 727-4344
Emp Here 40   *Sales* 17,886,960

SIC 5047 Medical and hospital equipment
Carol Robinson

D-U-N-S 24-685-9094   (SL)
HOLTZMAN, JACK DRUGS LIMITED
SHOPPERS DRUG MART
14729 Yonge St Suite 970, Aurora, ON, L4G
1N1
(905) 727-4275
Emp Here 40   *Sales* 10,118,160
SIC 5912 Drug stores and proprietary stores
Jack Holtzman

D-U-N-S 20-514-3386   (BR)
HOME DEPOT OF CANADA INC
HOME DEPOT
(*Suby of* THE HOME DEPOT INC)
15360 Bayview Ave, Aurora, ON, L4G 7J1
(905) 726-4500
Emp Here 180
SIC 5251 Hardware stores
Carlos Veloso

D-U-N-S 20-312-2577   (BR)
IMPRIMERIES TRANSCONTINENTAL INC
TRANSCONTINENTAL PRINTING INC
(*Suby of* TRANSCONTINENTAL INC)
275 Wellington St E, Aurora, ON, L4G 6J9
(905) 841-4400
Emp Here 600
SIC 2752 Commercial printing, lithographic
Terry Barrett

D-U-N-S 24-421-9432   (SL)
JBG MANAGEMENT INC
28 Mill St, Aurora, ON, L4G 2R9

Emp Here 110   *Sales* 7,669,111
SIC 8051 Skilled nursing care facilities
Brent Binions
Greg Binions
Janice Jeffs

D-U-N-S 24-708-9337   (SL)
JOHNSON PATERSON INC
360 Industrial Pky S Suite 7, Aurora, ON, L4G
3V7
(905) 727-0084
Emp Here 25   *Sales* 11,179,350
SIC 5074 Plumbing and heating equipment
and supplies (hydronics)
Kerry Johnson
Richard Manuel

D-U-N-S 24-610-2362   (SL)
K.P. BRONZE LIMITED
16 Allaura Blvd Suite 20, Aurora, ON, L4G 3S5
(905) 727-8706
Emp Here 40   *Sales* 17,886,960
SIC 5051 Metals service centers and offices
Kiro Pecenkovski
Daisy Pecenkovski

D-U-N-S 25-033-8597   (HQ)
KERRY'S PLACE AUTISM SERVICES
34 Berczy St Unit 190, Aurora, ON, L4G 1W9
(905) 841-6611
Emp Here 600   *Sales* 207,068,000
SIC 8399 Social services, nec
Sue Vandevelde-Coke
Deborah Compton

D-U-N-S 24-764-6565   (HQ)
KTI LIMITED
33 Isaacson Cres, Aurora, ON, L4G 0A4
(905) 727-8807
Emp Here 25   *Sales* 13,300,728
SIC 5085 Industrial supplies
Dean Iwai
Darryl Iwai
Steven Lovitsotto

D-U-N-S 20-269-2299   (SL)
LOUISVILLE LADDER CORP
LOUISVILLE
100 Engelhard Dr, Aurora, ON, L4G 3V2
(905) 727-0031
Emp Here 85   *Sales* 16,327,225

SIC 3499 Fabricated Metal products, nec
Daniel Medina
Eugenio Rangel
Joe Demelo
Humberto Garcia
Edgardo Garza

D-U-N-S 25-357-3182   (SL)
M. & A. WRIGHT CO. LIMITED
CANADIAN TIRE
14700 Yonge St Suite 189, Aurora, ON, L4G
7H8
(905) 727-9484
Emp Here 120   *Sales* 55,338,480
SIC 5014 Tires and tubes
Michael Wright

D-U-N-S 20-151-6002   (HQ)
MAGNA INTERNATIONAL INC
DECOMA INTERNATIONAL, DIV OF
337 Magna Dr, Aurora, ON, L4G 7K1
(905) 726-2462
Emp Here 300   *Sales* 40,827,000,000
SIC 3714 Motor vehicle parts and accessories
Donald J. Walker
Vincent J. Galifi
Tommy J. Skudutis
Seetarama Swamy Kotagiri
Francis C. Seguin
Riccardo C. Trecroce
Aaron D. Mccarthy
Patrick W.D. Mccann
Scott E. Paradise
Paul M. Bellack

D-U-N-S 25-357-5757   (BR)
MAGNA POWERTRAIN INC
UNIMOTION GEAR
(*Suby of* MAGNA INTERNATIONAL INC)
245 Edward St, Aurora, ON, L4G 3M7
(905) 713-0746
Emp Here 260
SIC 3714 Motor vehicle parts and accessories
Kai Jacobsen

D-U-N-S 20-016-8115   (HQ)
MAGNA SEATING INC
INTEGRAM-WINDSOR, DIV OF
(*Suby of* MAGNA INTERNATIONAL INC)
337 Magna Dr, Aurora, ON, L4G 7K1
(905) 726-2462
Emp Here 100   *Sales* 7,009,485,000
SIC 3714 Motor vehicle parts and accessories
Patrick Mccann
Siegfried Wolf

D-U-N-S 24-578-6517   (SL)
MATHESON CONSTRUCTORS LIMITED
MOORE MATHESON CONSTRUCTION
(*Suby of* MATHESON GROUP INC)
205 Industrial Pkwy N Unit 5, Aurora, ON, L4G
4C4
(905) 669-7999
Emp Here 87   *Sales* 49,619,406
SIC 1542 Nonresidential construction, nec
Allan Youmans
Shahin Saleem
Neil Banerjee
Mike Brown

D-U-N-S 20-873-2631   (SL)
MCALPINE FORD LINCOLN SALES LTD
15815 Yonge St, Aurora, ON, L4G 1P4
(905) 841-2424
Emp Here 50   *Sales* 24,903,900
SIC 5511 New and used car dealers
James Mcalpine
Randy Windstone

D-U-N-S 25-058-4398   (BR)
METRO ONTARIO INC
METRO 767
(*Suby of* METRO INC)
1 Henderson Dr Unit 1, Aurora, ON, L4G 4J7
(905) 727-0185
Emp Here 140
SIC 5411 Grocery stores

Laura Saullo

D-U-N-S 24-603-7048   (BR)
METROLAND MEDIA GROUP LTD
ERA BANNER NEWSPAPER, THE
(*Suby of* TORSTAR CORPORATION)
250 Industrial Pky N, Aurora, ON, L4G 4C3

Emp Here 100
SIC 5963 Direct selling establishments
Barry Black

D-U-N-S 25-321-5206   (HQ)
MILLER, P.G. ENTERPRISES LIMITED
MCDONALD'S #5260
2 Allaura Blvd, Aurora, ON, L4G 3S5
(905) 713-1850
Sales 27,983,400
SIC 5812 Eating places
Peter Miller

D-U-N-S 25-033-8761   (BR)
OMNI HEALTH CARE LTD
WILLOWS ESTATE NURSING HOME, THE
(*Suby of* OMNI HEALTH INVESTMENTS INC)
13837 Yonge St, Aurora, ON, L4G 0N9
(905) 727-0128
Emp Here 84
SIC 8051 Skilled nursing care facilities
Linda Burr

D-U-N-S 24-413-3364   (HQ)
PIRAMAL HEALTHCARE (CANADA) LIMITED
(*Suby of* PIRAMAL ENTERPRISES LIMITED)
110 Industrial Pky N, Aurora, ON, L4G 4C3
(905) 727-9417
Sales 41,183,045
SIC 2899 Chemical preparations, nec
Wen Lung Yeh
Mark Cherutti
Yobesh Shah
Swati Piramal

D-U-N-S 20-558-5289   (SL)
PROLLENIUM MEDICAL TECHNOLOGIES INC
(*Suby of* 7054921 CANADA INC)
138 Industrial Pky N, Aurora, ON, L4G 4C3
(905) 508-1469
Emp Here 70   *Sales* 15,910,230
SIC 3841 Surgical and medical instruments
Ario Khoshbin
Khasha Ighanian

D-U-N-S 24-565-8091   (SL)
RE/MAX YORK GROUP REALTY INC
15004 Yonge St, Aurora, ON, L4G 1M6
(905) 727-1941
Emp Here 40   *Sales* 13,085,080
SIC 6531 Real estate agents and managers
William Jenkins

D-U-N-S 25-702-7854   (SL)
RICOH DOCUMENT MANAGEMENT LIMITED PARTNERSHIP
R. D. M.
205 Industrial Pky N Unit 2, Aurora, ON, L4G
4C4
(905) 841-8433
Emp Here 70   *Sales* 11,481,890
SIC 2731 Book publishing
Craig Fisk

D-U-N-S 20-306-0546   (SL)
RSCOM LTD
238 Wellington St E Suite 210, Aurora, ON,
L4G 1J5
(647) 989-8603
Emp Here 20   *Sales* 45,252,812
SIC 4899 Communication services, nec
Vitaly Potapov
Alex Skaalerud
Viktor Kokhan

D-U-N-S 24-319-5773   (SL)
RUTHERFORD CONTRACTING LTD
224 Earl Stewart Dr, Aurora, ON, L4G 6V7

(905) 726-4888
Emp Here 65   *Sales* 37,071,970
SIC 1542 Nonresidential construction, nec
Blair Chalmers
Christine Rutherford

D-U-N-S 25-484-2396   (SL)
SAN MIGUEL FOODS LTD
SWISS CHALET HARVEY'S
1 Henderson Dr Unit 4, Aurora, ON, L4G 4J7
(905) 727-7918
Emp Here 250   *Sales* 11,659,750
SIC 5812 Eating places
Joe Anselmo Sr
Mario Medeios
Joe Anselmo Jr

D-U-N-S 20-875-4317   (HQ)
SF INSURANCE PLACEMENT CORPORATION OF CANADA
STATE FARM INSURANCE
(*Suby of* STATE FARM MUTUAL AUTOMOBILE INSURANCE COMPANY)
333 First Commerce Dr, Aurora, ON, L4G 8A4
(905) 750-4100
Emp Here 30   *Sales* 2,564,361,600
SIC 6331 Fire, marine, and casualty insurance
Robert Cooke
David Hill
Barbara Kirchgasler
Stan Ommen
Dale Egeberg
Russell Schopp

D-U-N-S 20-405-6808   (HQ)
SINCLAIR TECHNOLOGIES INC
(*Suby of* HYTERA COMMUNICATIONS CORPORATION LIMITED)
85 Mary St, Aurora, ON, L4G 6X5
(905) 727-0165
Sales 19,044,200
SIC 3663 Radio and t.v. communications
equipment
Amiee Chan
Calven Iwata
Andrea Sinclair

D-U-N-S 25-911-8685   (BR)
SOBEYS CAPITAL INCORPORATED
SOBEYS
(*Suby of* EMPIRE COMPANY LIMITED)
15500 Bayview Ave, Aurora, ON, L4G 7J1
(905) 726-2530
Emp Here 150
SIC 5411 Grocery stores
Darrell Pringle

D-U-N-S 20-977-0627   (SL)
SOUTHDOWN INSTITUTE, THE
1335 St. John'S Sideroad Suite 2, Aurora, ON,
L4G 0P8
(905) 727-4214
Emp Here 85   *Sales* 9,156,795
SIC 8661 Religious organizations
Miriam D Ukeritis
Samuel Mikail

D-U-N-S 24-748-9995   (SL)
SPACESAVER SOLUTIONS INC
115 Engelhard Dr, Aurora, ON, L4G 3V1
(905) 726-3933
Emp Here 32   *Sales* 15,200,832
SIC 5085 Industrial supplies
Michael Thompson
Robert J Jones

D-U-N-S 20-179-8936   (SL)
SPECIFIED CONSTRUCTION MANAGEMENT INC
SPECIFIED FLOORING CONTRACTORS
2 Vata Crt Unit 4, Aurora, ON, L4G 4B6
(905) 726-2902
Emp Here 25   *Sales* 11,768,275
SIC 1542 Nonresidential construction, nec
Andrew Fairweather
Scott Lucas

D-U-N-S 20-964-4996   (SL)

ST. ANDREW'S COLLEGE
15800 Yonge St, Aurora, ON, L4G 3H7
(905) 727-3178
Emp Here 180   *Sales* 17,841,420
SIC 8211 Elementary and secondary schools
Kevin Mchenry

D-U-N-S 20-079-1130   (HQ)
STATE FARM INSURANCE
STATE FARM FINANCE
333 First Commerce Dr, Aurora, ON, L4G 8A4
(905) 750-4100
Sales 5,220,714,400
SIC 6411 Insurance agents, brokers, and service
Robert J. Cooke
Barbara Bellissimo
Karen Mican

D-U-N-S 24-666-8313   (SL)
STERNE MOTORS LTD
STERNE ACURA
625 St. John'S Sideroad E, Aurora, ON, L4G 0Z7
(905) 841-1400
Emp Here 35   *Sales* 17,432,730
SIC 5511 New and used car dealers
Robert Sterne

D-U-N-S 20-581-4804   (SL)
SUMMIT VETERINARY PHARMACY INC
25 Furbacher Lane Suite 1, Aurora, ON, L4G 6W3
(905) 713-2040
Emp Here 75   *Sales* 20,749,500
SIC 2834 Pharmaceutical preparations
Stephen Organ
Donald Organ

D-U-N-S 20-808-9073   (BR)
SUNRISE NORTH SENIOR LIVING LTD
SUNRISE OF AURORA
(*Suby of* WELLTOWER INC.)
3 Golf Links Dr Suite 2, Aurora, ON, L4G 7Y4
(905) 841-0022
Emp Here 100
SIC 8361 Residential care
Anna Stier

D-U-N-S 20-967-1213   (SL)
THERMOGENICS INC
6 Scanlon Crt, Aurora, ON, L4G 7B2
(905) 727-1901
Emp Here 100   *Sales* 23,306,500
SIC 1711 Plumbing, heating, air-conditioning
Ross Garland
Bryan Heppell
Andrew Mitchell

D-U-N-S 24-417-8328   (SL)
ULLMAN, KEN ENTERPRISES INC
KUE PERSONAL CARE PRODUCTS
92 Kennedy St W, Aurora, ON, L4G 2L7
(905) 727-5677
Emp Here 100   *Sales* 27,666,000
SIC 2841 Soap and other detergents
Ken Ullman

D-U-N-S 24-359-1489   (BR)
WAL-MART CANADA CORP
(*Suby of* WALMART INC.)
135 First Commerce Dr, Aurora, ON, L4G 0G2
(905) 841-0300
Emp Here 75
SIC 5311 Department stores

D-U-N-S 24-847-7895   (SL)
WHITEHOTS INC
205 Industrial Pky N Unit 3, Aurora, ON, L4G 4C4
(905) 727-9188
Emp Here 25   *Sales* 18,563,000
SIC 5192 Books, periodicals, and newspapers
Russ Culver
Sharon Culver

D-U-N-S 25-134-0691   (BR)
YORK CATHOLIC DISTRICT SCHOOL

BOARD
CARDINAL CARTER CATHOLIC HIGH SCHOOL
(*Suby of* YORK CATHOLIC DISTRICT SCHOOL BOARD)
210 Bloomington Rd Suite Side, Aurora, ON, L4G 0P9
(905) 727-2455
Emp Here 145
SIC 8211 Elementary and secondary schools
Richard Maurice

D-U-N-S 25-221-9415   (HQ)
YORK CATHOLIC DISTRICT SCHOOL BOARD
320 Bloomington Rd, Aurora, ON, L4G 0M1
(905) 713-1211
Emp Here 200   *Sales* 396,476,000
SIC 8211 Elementary and secondary schools
John Sabo
Dominic Mazzotta
Maria Marchese
Elizabeth Crowe
Theresa Mcnicol
Carol Cotton
James Ecker
Rose Cantisano
Dino Giuliani
Jennifer Wigston

D-U-N-S 20-939-9526   (HQ)
YORK REGION DISTRICT SCHOOL BOARD
60 Wellington St W, Aurora, ON, L4G 3H2
(905) 727-3141
Emp Here 200   *Sales* 530,936,140
SIC 8211 Elementary and secondary schools
Loralea Carruthers
Corrie Mcbain
Kathi Wallace
Juanita Nathan
Susan Geller
Billy Pang
Allan Tam
Martin Van Beek
Peter Adams-Luchowski
Carol Chan

Aylmer, ON N5H

D-U-N-S 20-086-7955   (SL)
1214288 ONTARIO LIMITED
AYLMER VALU-MART
125 John St N, Aylmer, ON, N5H 2A7
(519) 773-9219
Emp Here 46   *Sales* 12,610,992
SIC 5411 Grocery stores
Jeff Regier

D-U-N-S 25-311-9820   (SL)
BROWNSVILLE HOLDINGS INC
Gd Lcd Main, Aylmer, ON, N5H 2R7
(519) 866-3446
Emp Here 50   *Sales* 20,967,750
SIC 6712 Bank holding companies
Patricia Perovich

D-U-N-S 20-350-6845   (SL)
CAN-AM PEPPER COMPANY LTD
(*Suby of* 2131876 ONTARIO LIMITED)
52999 John Wise Line, Aylmer, ON, N5H 2R5
(519) 773-3250
Emp Here 600   *Sales* 112,721,400
SIC 0161 Vegetables and melons
Jammie Underhill
Chad Underhill
Daniel O'byrne
Angie Chambers

D-U-N-S 24-703-1164   (BR)
CORPORATION OF THE COUNTY OF ELGIN
TERRACE LODGE HOME FOR THE AGED
(*Suby of* CORPORATION OF THE COUNTY OF ELGIN)

475 Talbot St E, Aylmer, ON, N5H 3A5
(519) 773-9205
Emp Here 100
SIC 8361 Residential care
Rhonda Roberts

D-U-N-S 20-033-5081   (SL)
ETBO TOOL & DIE
7288 Richmond Rd, Aylmer, ON, N5H 2R5
(519) 773-5117
Emp Here 105   *Sales* 23,310,105
SIC 3541 Machine tools, Metal cutting type
Etienne Borm Jr
Heather Borm
Etienne Borm Sr

D-U-N-S 20-878-6152   (HQ)
HAMILTON WARD AND CATHERS INSURANCE SERVICE LIMITED
HWC INSURANCE
75 Talbot St E, Aylmer, ON, N5H 1H3
(519) 773-8471
Emp Here 14   *Sales* 23,745,680
SIC 6411 Insurance agents, brokers, and service
Todd Sprague

D-U-N-S 20-697-9358   (BR)
LOBLAWS SUPERMARKETS LIMITED
NO FRILLS
(*Suby of* LOBLAW COMPANIES LIMITED)
657 John St N, Aylmer, ON, N5H 2R2
(519) 765-2811
Emp Here 100
SIC 5411 Grocery stores
Ryan Barrett

D-U-N-S 24-991-9705   (SL)
MARTIN, LOUIS MERCHANDISING LTD
CANADIAN TIRE
605 John St N, Aylmer, ON, N5H 2B6
(519) 773-8424
Emp Here 42   *Sales* 20,919,276
SIC 5531 Auto and home supply stores
Louis Martin

D-U-N-S 24-770-4877   (SL)
ONTARIO POLICE COLLEGE
10716 Hacienda Rd, Aylmer, ON, N5H 2T2
(519) 773-5361
Emp Here 150   *Sales* 22,408,650
SIC 8221 Colleges and universities
Rudy Gheysen
Glen Cook

D-U-N-S 20-691-5527   (SL)
PRECISION FAB INC
259 Elm St, Aylmer, ON, N5H 3H3
(519) 773-5244
Emp Here 50   *Sales* 10,141,500
SIC 3499 Fabricated Metal products, nec
Isaak Wall
Albert Wiebe

D-U-N-S 20-128-5780   (SL)
TECUMSEH PRODUCTS OF CANADA, LIMITED
(*Suby of* TECUMSEH PRODUCTS HOLDINGS LLC)
200 Elm St, Aylmer, ON, N5H 2M8
(519) 765-1556
Emp Here 45   *Sales* 21,376,170
SIC 5084 Industrial machinery and equipment
James Connor

D-U-N-S 20-554-0425   (BR)
THAMES VALLEY DISTRICT SCHOOL BOARD
EAST ELGIN SECONDARY SCHOOL
(*Suby of* THAMES VALLEY DISTRICT SCHOOL BOARD)
362 Talbot St W, Aylmer, ON, N5H 1K6
(519) 773-3174
Emp Here 100
SIC 8211 Elementary and secondary schools
Tom Mcleod

D-U-N-S 24-267-3289   (SL)
UNION GAS
9924 Springer Hill Rd, Aylmer, ON, N5H 2R3
(519) 765-1487
Emp Here 5   *Sales* 15,790,468
SIC 4923 Gas transmission and distribution

D-U-N-S 24-344-5322   (SL)
WALKER DAIRY INC
50828 Talbot St E, Aylmer, ON, N5H 2R1
(519) 765-2406
Emp Here 12   *Sales* 14,524,764
SIC 5154 Livestock
John Walker

D-U-N-S 24-007-5002   (SL)
WHITE, GLEN INDUSTRIES LTD
STEELWAY BUILDING SYSTEMS
(*Suby of* WHITE, GLEN INVESTMENTS LTD)
7825 Springwater Rd, Aylmer, ON, N5H 2R4
(519) 765-2244
Emp Here 180   *Sales* 34,575,300
SIC 3441 Fabricated structural Metal
Patricia White

D-U-N-S 24-364-3962   (HQ)
WHITE, GLEN INVESTMENTS LTD
7825 Springwater Rd Rr 5, Aylmer, ON, N5H 2R4
(519) 765-2244
Emp Here 1   *Sales* 47,016,200
SIC 6712 Bank holding companies
Patricia White

Ayr, ON N0B

D-U-N-S 25-793-0131   (HQ)
1077947 ONTARIO LTD
105 Guthrie St Ss 1, Ayr, ON, N0B 1E0
(519) 632-9052
Sales 16,401,000
SIC 6712 Bank holding companies
Steven Lowe

D-U-N-S 25-190-1625   (BR)
ADESA AUCTIONS CANADA CORPORATION
ADESA KITCHENER
(*Suby of* KAR AUCTION SERVICES, INC.)
55 Waydom Dr Suite 1, Ayr, ON, N0B 1E0
(519) 622-9500
Emp Here 100
SIC 5012 Automobiles and other motor vehicles
Terry Fowler

D-U-N-S 24-985-1510   (HQ)
AEVITAS INC
75 Wanless Crt, Ayr, ON, N0B 1E0
(519) 740-1333
Emp Here 57   *Sales* 54,214,700
SIC 4953 Refuse systems
Byron T Day
Thomas M Maxwell

D-U-N-S 20-555-4426   (SL)
ALPINE INT'L TRANSPORTATION INC
(*Suby of* TFI INTERNATIONAL INC)
480 Waydom Dr, Ayr, ON, N0B 1E0
(519) 624-6776
Emp Here 40   *Sales* 20,798,680
SIC 4731 Freight transportation arrangement
Alex Millar

D-U-N-S 24-305-5936   (SL)
AYR FARMERS' MUTUAL INSURANCE COMPANY
1400 Northumberland St Rr 1, Ayr, ON, N0B 1E0
(519) 632-7413
Emp Here 26   *Sales* 19,723,939
SIC 6331 Fire, marine, and casualty insurance
Donald Davidson
David Paterson

Robert Gurney
Mike Murdoch
Gordon Forth
Les Leck
Gerry Pullin
Brian Sayles

D-U-N-S 25-397-3051   (HQ)
AYRLINE LEASING INC
2558 Cedar Creek Rd Ss 2, Ayr, ON, N0B 1E0
(519) 740-8209
Emp Here 1   *Sales* 10,462,120
SIC 6712 Bank holding companies
Mike Taylor

D-U-N-S 25-193-8593   (BR)
BEND ALL AUTOMOTIVE ULC
PLANT NO. 4
(Suby of ARDIAN HOLDING*)*
115 Wanless Crt, Ayr, ON, N0B 1E0
(519) 623-2003
Emp Here 100
SIC 3671 Electron tubes
Eli Crann

D-U-N-S 25-673-4286   (BR)
BEND ALL AUTOMOTIVE ULC
BEND ALL MANUFACTURING
(Suby of ARDIAN HOLDING*)*
655 Waydom Dr, Ayr, ON, N0B 1E0
(519) 623-2002
Emp Here 300
SIC 5015 Motor vehicle parts, used
Eli Crann

D-U-N-S 24-845-6030   (HQ)
BEND ALL AUTOMOTIVE ULC
(Suby of ARDIAN HOLDING*)*
575 Waydom Dr, Ayr, ON, N0B 1E0
(519) 623-2001
Emp Here 350   *Sales* 170,261,700
SIC 3499 Fabricated Metal products, nec
Alfred Napolitano
Udo Petersen
Marco Riva
Walter Zonta

D-U-N-S 24-823-3397   (SL)
CMP AUTOMATION INC
C M P
229 Boida Ave Suite 1, Ayr, ON, N0B 1E0
(519) 740-6035
Emp Here 55   *Sales* 12,210,055
SIC 3599 Industrial machinery, nec
Daniel Weinhardt
Henry Weinhardt
Rob Shwery

D-U-N-S 24-719-1950   (HQ)
DSM NUTRITIONAL PRODUCTS CANADA INC
(Suby of KONINKLIJKE DSM N.V.*)*
395 Waydom Dr Suite 2, Ayr, ON, N0B 1E0
(519) 622-2200
Emp Here 20   *Sales* 27,633,625
SIC 5122 Drugs, proprietaries, and sundries
Harald Scherf
Hugh Welsh

D-U-N-S 20-405-7731   (HQ)
EQUIPMENT EXPRESS INC
60 Wanless Crt, Ayr, ON, N0B 1E0
(519) 740-8008
Sales 13,370,890
SIC 4213 Trucking, except local
John Fitzpatrick

D-U-N-S 25-320-4218   (BR)
FARROW, RUSSELL A. LIMITED
RUSSELL A. FARROW LIMITED
(Suby of FARROW GROUP INC*)*
106 Earl Thompson Rd, Ayr, ON, N0B 1E0
(519) 740-9866
Emp Here 125
SIC 4731 Freight transportation arrangement
Peggy Unger

D-U-N-S 25-503-2781   (HQ)
HALL TRANSPORTATION GROUP LIMITED
552 Piper St, Ayr, ON, N0B 1E0
(519) 632-7429
Sales 33,348,700
SIC 6712 Bank holding companies
Jeff Hall
Lynn D'aguilar
Andrew Hall

D-U-N-S 25-280-7789   (HQ)
HERITAGE TRUCK LINES INC
(Suby of 1077947 ONTARIO LTD*)*
105 Guthrie St, Ayr, ON, N0B 1E0
(519) 632-9052
Sales 12,342,360
SIC 4213 Trucking, except local
Steven Lowe

D-U-N-S 25-081-1676   (SL)
HIGHWAY STERLING WESTERN STAR INC
1021 Industrial Rd, Ayr, ON, N0B 1E0
(519) 740-2405
Emp Here 45   *Sales* 22,413,510
SIC 5511 New and used car dealers
Jeff Cassidy
Dale Hallman
Kenneth Blast
Leslie Stollory

D-U-N-S 24-947-2937   (HQ)
J. & R. HALL TRANSPORT INC
(Suby of HALL TRANSPORTATION GROUP LIMITED*)*
552 Piper St, Ayr, ON, N0B 1E0
(519) 632-7429
Emp Here 116   *Sales* 28,798,840
SIC 4213 Trucking, except local
Jeffrey Hall
Andrew Hall
Lynn D'aguilar
Robert Hall

D-U-N-S 20-120-9504   (SL)
JBT TRANSPORT INC
235 Waydom Dr Suite 1, Ayr, ON, N0B 1E0
(519) 622-3604
Emp Here 85   *Sales* 12,596,320
SIC 4213 Trucking, except local
Denis Medeiros

D-U-N-S 24-508-3969   (SL)
LIBERTY LINEHAUL INC
(Suby of 715273 ONTARIO INC*)*
214 Boida Ave Ss 2, Ayr, ON, N0B 1E0
(519) 740-8181
Emp Here 140   *Sales* 28,798,840
SIC 4213 Trucking, except local
Brian Taylor
Christopher Gerber
Gary Higgins

D-U-N-S 20-697-9572   (HQ)
LIFTSAFE ENGINEERING AND SERVICE GROUP INC.
306 Darrell Dr, Ayr, ON, N0B 1E0
(519) 896-2430
Sales 21,562,512
SIC 7389 Business services, nec
Dirk Kerbs
Robert Barrett

D-U-N-S 20-879-4123   (HQ)
MANN+HUMMEL FILTRATION TECHNOLOGY CANADA ULC
GROUPE MANN+HUMMEL
1035 Industrial Rd, Ayr, ON, N0B 1E0
(519) 622-4545
Sales 138,346,200
SIC 5013 Motor vehicle supplies and new parts
Westley D. Haine
Timothy Ciurlik
Anja Kahle

D-U-N-S 24-336-6627   (HQ)
MILL CREEK MOTOR FREIGHT L.P.

101 Earl Thompson Rd Ss 2, Ayr, ON, N0B 1E0
(519) 623-6632
Sales 15,427,950
SIC 4213 Trucking, except local
Stuart Lowe
Renada Hargreaves

D-U-N-S 24-761-3859   (SL)
MILL CREEK MOTOR FREIGHT LTD
(Suby of KRISKA TRANSPORTATION GROUP LIMITED*)*
101 Earl Thompson Rd, Ayr, ON, N0B 1E0
(519) 623-6632
Emp Here 100
SIC 4731 Freight transportation arrangement
Renate Hargreaves

D-U-N-S 25-317-1649   (SL)
NEW AGE ROBOTICS AND CONTROLS INC
515 Waydom Dr, Ayr, ON, N0B 1E0
(519) 621-3333
Emp Here 25   *Sales* 11,875,650
SIC 5084 Industrial machinery and equipment
Cornel Cosma

D-U-N-S 25-369-6272   (SL)
PRIMEMAX ENERGY INC
2558 Cedar Creek Rd Suite 1, Ayr, ON, N0B 1E0
(519) 740-8209
Emp Here 75   *Sales* 18,324,600
SIC 5984 Liquefied petroleum gas dealers
Michael Taylor

D-U-N-S 25-554-3274   (SL)
PRIORITY MECHANICAL SERVICES LTD
3160 Alps Rd, Ayr, ON, N0B 1E0
(519) 632-7116
Emp Here 60   *Sales* 13,983,900
SIC 1711 Plumbing, heating, air-conditioning
David Kubassek

D-U-N-S 25-413-3978   (SL)
PROVIDER TRANSPORTATION & LOGISTICS INC
3184 Alps Rd, Ayr, ON, N0B 1E0

Emp Here 21   *Sales* 10,919,307
SIC 4731 Freight transportation arrangement
Norman Casarin

D-U-N-S 25-353-2170   (SL)
RESOURCE INDUSTRIAL GROUP INC
RIG
295 Waydom Dr Suite 2, Ayr, ON, N0B 1E0
(519) 622-5266
Emp Here 80   *Sales* 19,694,880
SIC 1796 Installing building equipment
Leo Henhoeffer
Brenda Henhoeffer

D-U-N-S 25-252-3209   (BR)
SEMPLE-GOODER ROOFING CORPORATION
(Suby of SEMPLE GOODER ROOFING CORPORATION*)*
309 Darrell Dr, Ayr, ON, N0B 1E0
(519) 623-3300
Emp Here 200
SIC 1761 Roofing, siding, and sheetMetal work
Bryce Mccandless

D-U-N-S 25-246-5224   (SL)
T.E.A.M. LOGISTICS SYSTEMS INC
118 Earl Thompson Rd, Ayr, ON, N0B 1E0
(519) 622-2473
Emp Here 80   *Sales* 11,855,360
SIC 4213 Trucking, except local
Robert Gordon
Michael Tate

D-U-N-S 20-940-9093   (HQ)
TRANSFRT MCNAMARA INC
1126 Industrial Rd, Ayr, ON, N0B 1E0
(519) 740-6500
Sales 28,798,840

SIC 4231 Trucking terminal facilities
Ward Tregoning
Gregory Palmer

D-U-N-S 24-756-9429   (SL)
VIKING TRUCK SALES INC
EXPRESSWAY TRUCKS WATERLOO
2943 Cedar Creek Rd Suite 1187, Ayr, ON, N0B 1E0
(519) 740-1656
Emp Here 45   *Sales* 22,413,510
SIC 5511 New and used car dealers
Scott Lawson
Gerrie Molenaar

Ayton, ON N0G

D-U-N-S 24-689-0586   (SL)
DOMM CONSTRUCTION LTD
563 Louisa St, Ayton, ON, N0G 1C0
(519) 665-7848
Emp Here 30   *Sales* 14,121,930
SIC 1542 Nonresidential construction, nec
Allan Domm
Frank Domm

Azilda, ON P0M

D-U-N-S 20-125-9991   (HQ)
DAY, WILLIAM CONSTRUCTION LIMITED
DAY TRANSPORT
2500 Elm St, Azilda, ON, P0M 1B0
(705) 682-1555
Emp Here 225   *Sales* 78,327,600
SIC 7359 Equipment rental and leasing, nec
William Day
Bart Day
Darren Day
Everrett Day
Anthony Day

Baden, ON N3A

D-U-N-S 24-684-8824   (HQ)
1936100 ONTARIO INC
SYSTEMS PLUS
1457 Gingerich Rd, Baden, ON, N3A 3J7
(519) 634-5708
Emp Here 2   *Sales* 11,179,350
SIC 5049 Professional equipment, nec
Garry Ruttan
Sheila Hannon
Denny Shiwpershad
Chris Morton

D-U-N-S 20-009-8648   (SL)
ARCADIAN PROJECTS INC
1439 Gingerich Rd Unit 2, Baden, ON, N3A 3J7
(519) 804-9697
Emp Here 50   *Sales* 12,652,950
SIC 5211 Lumber and other building materials
Luke Shantz
Dave Sowden
Dan Hesch
Cory Philips
Jerry Arai
Fraser Martin
Todd Lorentz

D-U-N-S 25-255-8218   (SL)
K-DAC ENTERPRISES INC
K-DAC EXPEDITE
3025 Sandhills Rd, Baden, ON, N3A 3B8
(519) 634-8223
Emp Here 105   *Sales* 21,599,130
SIC 4213 Trucking, except local
Bruce Schumm

Larry Leis

D-U-N-S 25-228-1647   (BR)
WATERLOO REGION DISTRICT SCHOOL BOARD
WATERLOO OXFORD DISTRICT SEC-ONDARY SCHOOL
(*Suby of* WATERLOO REGION DISTRICT SCHOOL BOARD)
1206 Snyder'S Rd W, Baden, ON, N3A 1A4
(519) 634-5441
Emp Here 90
SIC 8211 Elementary and secondary schools
Best Bodkin

Bailieboro, ON K0L

D-U-N-S 20-141-0958   (SL)
BUCKHAM TRANSPORT LIMITED
(*Suby of* WILLIAM A. F. BUCKHAM HOLD-INGS LIMITED)
Hwy 28, Bailieboro, ON, K0L 1B0
(705) 939-6311
Emp Here 65   *Sales* 13,370,890
SIC 4213 Trucking, except local
Cathrine Buckham
Jason Hedges
Leanore Buckham

Balmertown, ON P0V

D-U-N-S 20-026-4120   (SL)
1327187 ONTARIO INC
LUNDY FOOD
2 7 St, Balmertown, ON, P0V 1C0
(807) 735-2132
Emp Here 42   *Sales* 11,514,384
SIC 5411 Grocery stores
Brent Lundy

Bancroft, ON K0L

D-U-N-S 24-544-7677   (SL)
BANCROFT MOTORS LTD
29668 Hwy 62 North Rr 2, Bancroft, ON, K0L 1C0
(613) 332-3437
Emp Here 25   *Sales* 12,451,950
SIC 5511 New and used car dealers
Vaughn Lloyd

D-U-N-S 20-629-4535   (SL)
EAGLE'S NEST COFFEE AND BAKED GOODS INC
TIM HORTONS
234 Hastings St N, Bancroft, ON, K0L 1C0
(613) 332-0299
Emp Here 80   *Sales* 3,429,840
SIC 5812 Eating places
Glen Keating
Nancy Keating

D-U-N-S 25-265-3274   (BR)
HASTINGS AND PRINCE EDWARD DIS-TRICT SCHOOL BOARD
NORTH HASTINGS HIGH SCHOOL
16 Monck St Suite 14, Bancroft, ON, K0L 1C0
(613) 332-1220
Emp Here 75
SIC 8211 Elementary and secondary schools
Ken Dostaler

D-U-N-S 20-861-3120   (BR)
QUINTE HEALTHCARE CORPORATION
NORTH HASTINGS
(*Suby of* QUINTE HEALTHCARE CORPORA-TION)
1h Manor Lane, Bancroft, ON, K0L 1C0

(613) 332-2825
Emp Here 200
SIC 8069 Specialty hospitals, except psychi-atric
Donna Robinson

D-U-N-S 24-991-9663   (SL)
SUNSTRUM, GARRY W. SALES LIMITED
CANADIAN TIRE 005
341 Hastings St N Rr 2 Suite 130, Bancroft, ON, K0L 1C0
(613) 332-0145
Emp Here 80   *Sales* 50,342,400
SIC 5531 Auto and home supply stores
Garry Sunstrum
Lenora Sunstrum

Barrie, ON L4M

D-U-N-S 25-359-4105   (SL)
1500451 ONTARIO LIMITED
JOE'S NO FRILLS
165 Wellington St E, Barrie, ON, L4M 2C7
(705) 737-0389
Emp Here 170   *Sales* 49,891,090
SIC 5411 Grocery stores

D-U-N-S 25-246-0139   (SL)
ALLEN & ASSOCIATES INC
60 Collier St Unit 217, Barrie, ON, L4M 1G8

Emp Here 2   *Sales* 438,058,500
SIC 8748 Business consulting, nec
Don Allen

D-U-N-S 25-134-7316   (SL)
BARRIE NATIONAL PINES GOLF & COUN-TRY CLUB
Gd Stn Main, Barrie, ON, L4M 4S8
(705) 431-7000
Emp Here 75   *Sales* 5,729,775
SIC 7997 Membership sports and recreation clubs
Dianne Calder

D-U-N-S 25-398-7457   (SL)
CARRIAGE HILLS RESORT CORPORA-TION
(*Suby of* WYNDHAM DESTINATIONS, INC.)
1101 Horseshoe Valley Rd W, Barrie, ON, L4M 4Y8
(705) 835-0087
Emp Here 150   *Sales* 14,350,200
SIC 7011 Hotels and motels
Craig Goldstein
Sheldon Ginsburg
Kevin House

D-U-N-S 24-764-1541   (HQ)
CENTURY 21 B J ROTH REALTY LTD
CENTURY 21
355 Bayfield St Suite 5, Barrie, ON, L4M 3C3
(705) 721-9111
Emp Here 65   *Sales* 41,888,900
SIC 6531 Real estate agents and managers
Bernard Roth

D-U-N-S 20-755-0765   (SL)
DOUGLAS FORD LINCOLN SALES LTD
379 Bayfield St, Barrie, ON, L4M 3C5
(705) 728-5558
Emp Here 80   *Sales* 50,342,400
SIC 5511 New and used car dealers
Angelo Vilardo

D-U-N-S 20-772-7306   (HQ)
GEORGIAN COLLEGE OF APPLIED ARTS AND TECHNOLOGY, THE
1 Georgian Dr, Barrie, ON, L4M 3X9
(705) 728-1968
Emp Here 550   *Sales* 149,017,381
SIC 8222 Junior colleges
Marylynn West-Moynes
Tom Mcbride
Jim Bertram

Brian Davenport
Lisa Banks
Catherine Drea
Angela Lockridge
Kevin Weaver
Peter Craig

D-U-N-S 25-317-4544   (HQ)
GEORGIAN INTERNATIONAL LIMITED
85 Bayfield St Suite 500, Barrie, ON, L4M 3A7
(705) 730-5900
Sales 190,493,160
SIC 5511 New and used car dealers
James Massie
Dan Revell

D-U-N-S 20-772-2224   (SL)
GROVE PARK HOME FOR SENIOR CITI-ZENS
GROVE PARK HOME
234 Cook St Suite 1274, Barrie, ON, L4M 4H5
(705) 726-1003
Emp Here 200   *Sales* 13,665,200
SIC 8051 Skilled nursing care facilities
Marvin A Johnson
Barb Turnbull
Paul Taylor

D-U-N-S 24-667-2104   (HQ)
HOCK SHOP INC
400 Bayfield St, Barrie, ON, L4M 5A1
(705) 728-2274
Emp Here 45   *Sales* 15,792,000
SIC 6099 Functions related to deposit banking
Jeffrey Hockley

D-U-N-S 20-033-9778   (SL)
HODGKINSON A & G SALES LTD
CANADIAN TIRE
320 Bayfield St Suite M103, Barrie, ON, L4M 3C1
(705) 726-2861
Emp Here 200   *Sales* 125,856,000
SIC 5531 Auto and home supply stores
Alan Hodgkinson

D-U-N-S 20-533-0020   (SL)
HORSESHOE RESORT CORPORATION
HORSESHOE RESORT
1101 Horseshoe Valley Rd W, Barrie, ON, L4M 4Y8
(705) 835-2790
Emp Here 600   *Sales* 57,400,800
SIC 7011 Hotels and motels
Richard Andrews
Martin Kimball
John Boville

D-U-N-S 24-826-6074   (SL)
HORSESHOE VALLEY LIMITED PARTNER-SHIP
1101 Horseshoe Valley Rd W, Barrie, ON, L4M 4Y8
(705) 835-2790
Emp Here 280   *Sales* 26,787,040
SIC 7011 Hotels and motels
Derek Carmichael
Martin Kimble

D-U-N-S 20-034-1253   (HQ)
IRVINE, G. ERNEST LIMITED
IRVINE CARPET ONE & DECORATING CEN-TRE
514 Bayfield St, Barrie, ON, L4M 5A2
(705) 728-5566
Sales 18,318,816
SIC 5023 Homefurnishings
Olga Irvine
Chris Irvine

D-U-N-S 24-208-0163   (SL)
LAST CLASS, THE
1 Georgian Dr, Barrie, ON, L4M 3X9
(705) 722-1526
Emp Here 150   *Sales* 6,995,850
SIC 5812 Eating places
Mick Kingston

D-U-N-S 24-326-2990   (SL)
MARTEL, DAN PHARMACY LIMITED
SHOPPERS DRUG MART
524 Bayfield St Suite 650, Barrie, ON, L4M 5A2
(705) 722-6300
Emp Here 48   *Sales* 12,141,792
SIC 5912 Drug stores and proprietary stores
Daniel (Dan) Martel

D-U-N-S 25-300-0558   (BR)
METRO ONTARIO INC
METRO
(*Suby of* METRO INC)
400 Bayfield St Suite 1, Barrie, ON, L4M 5A1
(705) 722-8284
Emp Here 120
SIC 5411 Grocery stores

D-U-N-S 24-154-0579   (SL)
MOXIE'S CLASSIC GRILL
509 Bayfield St, Barrie, ON, L4M 4Z8
(705) 733-5252
Emp Here 145   *Sales* 6,762,655
SIC 5812 Eating places
Scott Sinclair

D-U-N-S 24-559-4460   (HQ)
NAPOLEON SYSTEMS & DEVELOPMENTS LTD
NAPOLEON
24 Napoleon Rd, Barrie, ON, L4M 0G8
(705) 721-1212
Emp Here 300   *Sales* 109,453,950
SIC 3433 Heating equipment, except electric
Wolfgang Schroeter
Ingrid Schroeter

D-U-N-S 24-773-2253   (SL)
NEIGHBOURHOOD DOMINION LENDING CENTRES
39 Collier St Suite 300, Barrie, ON, L4M 1G5
(705) 720-1001
Emp Here 49   *Sales* 11,012,456
SIC 6162 Mortgage bankers and loan corre-spondents
Gary Meger

D-U-N-S 24-125-8979   (HQ)
NEWMAN'S VALVE LIMITED
92 Davidson St, Barrie, ON, L4M 3R8
(705) 737-4216
Emp Here 10   *Sales* 11,875,650
SIC 5085 Industrial supplies
Robert Scroffel

D-U-N-S 24-471-0539   (BR)
RECIPE UNLIMITED CORPORATION
SWISS CHALET
(*Suby of* RECIPE UNLIMITED CORPORA-TION)
397 Bayfield St, Barrie, ON, L4M 3C5
(705) 737-5272
Emp Here 80
SIC 5812 Eating places
Steve Smith

D-U-N-S 25-156-3896   (BR)
RED LOBSTER HOSPITALITY LLC
RED LOBSTER RESTAURANTS
319 Bayfield St, Barrie, ON, L4M 3C2
(705) 728-2401
Emp Here 75
SIC 5812 Eating places
Valerie Lampman

D-U-N-S 20-253-5709   (SL)
ROBERT'S NO FRILLS
319 Blake St, Barrie, ON, L4M 1K7
(705) 725-8607
Emp Here 49   *Sales* 13,433,448
SIC 5411 Grocery stores
Robert Decaria

D-U-N-S 24-485-6548   (SL)
SADLON, PAUL MOTORS INCORPORATED
(*Suby of* SADLON, PAUL MOTORS (1982) INC)

550 Bayfield St, Barrie, ON, L4M 5A2
(705) 721-7733
Emp Here 62   *Sales* 39,015,360
SIC 5511 New and used car dealers
  Paul Sadlon
  Terry Garrow

D-U-N-S 25-446-9125   (BR)
SECURITAS CANADA LIMITED
SECURITAS CANADA
(*Suby of* SECURITAS AB)
400 Bayfield St Suite 215, Barrie, ON, L4M 5A1
(705) 728-7777
Emp Here 96
SIC 7381 Detective and armored car services
  David Cahoon

D-U-N-S 20-020-6477   (BR)
SIMCOE COUNTY DISTRICT SCHOOL BOARD, THE
EASTVIEW SECONDARY SCHOOL
(*Suby of* SIMCOE COUNTY DISTRICT SCHOOL BOARD, THE)
421 Grove St E, Barrie, ON, L4M 5S1
(705) 728-1321
Emp Here 150
SIC 8211 Elementary and secondary schools
  Jane Seymour

D-U-N-S 25-297-6428   (BR)
SIMCOE COUNTY DISTRICT SCHOOL BOARD, THE
BARRIE NORTH COLLEGIATE
(*Suby of* SIMCOE COUNTY DISTRICT SCHOOL BOARD, THE)
110 Grove St E, Barrie, ON, L4M 2P3
(705) 726-6541
Emp Here 130
SIC 8211 Elementary and secondary schools
  Diana Barakauskas

D-U-N-S 25-293-5564   (BR)
SIMCOE MUSKOKA CATHOLIC DISTRICT SCHOOL BOARD
ST JOSEPHS HIGH SCHOOL
(*Suby of* SIMCOE MUSKOKA CATHOLIC DISTRICT SCHOOL BOARD)
243 Cundles Rd E, Barrie, ON, L4M 6L1
(705) 728-3120
Emp Here 80
SIC 8211 Elementary and secondary schools
  Andrew Sendzik

D-U-N-S 24-918-6743   (HQ)
SIMCOE MUSKOKA CATHOLIC DISTRICT SCHOOL BOARD
46 Alliance Blvd, Barrie, ON, L4M 5K3
(705) 722-3555
Emp Here 100   *Sales* 297,357,000
SIC 8211 Elementary and secondary schools
  Michael O'keefe
  Peter Derochie

D-U-N-S 24-246-0628   (SL)
SIMCOE MUSKOKA CHILD, YOUTH AND FAMILY SERVICES
SIMCOE MUSKOKA FAMILY CONNEXIONS
60 Bell Farm Rd Suite 7, Barrie, ON, L4M 5G6
(800) 461-4236
Emp Here 400   *Sales* 39,800,750
SIC 8699 Membership organizations, nec
  Geraldine Dooley-Philips
  Gordon Hill

D-U-N-S 24-030-4910   (HQ)
SIMCOE MUSKOKA DISTRICT HEALTH UNIT
15 Sperling Dr, Barrie, ON, L4M 6K9
(705) 721-7520
Sales 16,064,600
SIC 8011 Offices and clinics of medical doctors
  Charles Gardner
  Susan Surry
  Colin Lee

D-U-N-S 25-309-1284   (BR)

SOBEYS CAPITAL INCORPORATED
SOBEYS 634
(*Suby of* EMPIRE COMPANY LIMITED)
409 Bayfield St Suite C1, Barrie, ON, L4M 6E5
(705) 739-1100
Emp Here 120
SIC 5411 Grocery stores
  Colin Mcintosh

D-U-N-S 24-383-2826   (HQ)
SOURCE (BELL) ELECTRONICS INC, THE
SOURCE, THE
(*Suby of* BCE INC)
279 Bayview Dr, Barrie, ON, L4M 4W5
(705) 728-2262
Emp Here 372   *Sales* 853,449,600
SIC 5731 Radio, television, and electronic stores
  Charles Brown
  Steven Boyack
  Wade Oosterman
  Siim Vanaselja
  Michael Cole
  George Cope
  Kevin Crull
  David Wells

D-U-N-S 24-684-8147   (SL)
SOUTHMEDIC INCORPORATED
50 Alliance Blvd, Barrie, ON, L4M 5K3
(705) 726-9383
Emp Here 100   *Sales* 22,728,900
SIC 3841 Surgical and medical instruments
  Lisette Mcdonald

D-U-N-S 20-852-3779   (HQ)
UNITED LUMBER AND BUILDING SUPPLIES COMPANY LIMITED
HOME HARDWARE
520 Bayfield St, Barrie, ON, L4M 5A2
(705) 726-8132
Emp Here 40   *Sales* 22,750,420
SIC 5211 Lumber and other building materials
  Vic Debiasio

D-U-N-S 25-166-6582   (BR)
WAL-MART CANADA CORP
(*Suby of* WALMART INC.)
450 Bayfield St, Barrie, ON, L4M 5A2
(705) 728-2833
Emp Here 200
SIC 5311 Department stores
  Linklater Bryan

D-U-N-S 20-552-7497   (BR)
WOLF STEEL LTD
NAPOLEON FIREPLACES
(*Suby of* NAPOLEON SYSTEMS & DEVELOPMENTS LTD)
9 Napoleon Rd, Barrie, ON, L4M 0G8
(705) 721-1212
Emp Here 350
SIC 3433 Heating equipment, except electric
  Roger Gripton

D-U-N-S 24-139-5680   (HQ)
WOLF STEEL LTD
NAPOLEON FIREPLACES
(*Suby of* NAPOLEON SYSTEMS & DEVELOPMENTS LTD)
24 Napoleon Rd, Barrie, ON, L4M 0G8
(705) 721-1212
Emp Here 4   *Sales* 97,292,400
SIC 3433 Heating equipment, except electric
  Wolfgang Schroeter
  Ron Mcarthur

Barrie, ON L4N

D-U-N-S 25-214-7202   (SL)
1073849 ONTARIO LIMITED
TOLLOS
(*Suby of* AURORA CAPITAL PARTNERS, L.P.)

75 Dyment Rd, Barrie, ON, L4N 3H6
(705) 733-0022
Emp Here 55   *Sales* 12,500,895
SIC 3841 Surgical and medical instruments
  Jonathan Winer
  Jim Fugitt
  Bruce Sholk
  William Shock
  Randy Smith

D-U-N-S 25-689-3769   (SL)
1235052 ONTARIO LIMITED
311 Bryne Dr, Barrie, ON, L4N 8V4
(705) 728-5322
Emp Here 28   *Sales* 11,741,940
SIC 6712 Bank holding companies
  Bruce J. Insley
  Catherine Insley

D-U-N-S 25-542-0960   (SL)
1235054 ONTARIO LIMITED
BARRIE HARLEY-DAVIDSON
311 Bryne Dr, Barrie, ON, L4N 8V4
(705) 728-5322
Emp Here 34   *Sales* 16,934,652
SIC 5571 Motorcycle dealers
  Bruce Insley
  Catherine Insley

D-U-N-S 20-106-3984   (HQ)
1342205 ONTARIO LIMITED
SURPLUS FREIGHT OF CANADA
90 Anne Street S, Barrie, ON, L4N 2E3
(613) 247-3300
Emp Here 50   *Sales* 40,005,450
SIC 5712 Furniture stores
  Alf Tarzia
  Strat Karanastasis
  Richard I.R. Winter
  David A. Belford
  Sean P. Byrne
  Christina Kline

D-U-N-S 25-194-2520   (SL)
1422718 ONTARIO INC
ACURA OF BARRIE
125 Mapleview Dr W, Barrie, ON, L4N 9H7
(705) 727-0000
Emp Here 25   *Sales* 12,451,950
SIC 5511 New and used car dealers
  Bazil Policaro
  Paul Policaro
  Anthony Policaro

D-U-N-S 20-011-9233   (SL)
1430819 ONTARIO LIMITED
OMS EXPRESS
112 Saunders Rd Unit 11, Barrie, ON, L4N 9A8
(705) 721-9809
Emp Here 45   *Sales* 20,214,855
SIC 7389 Business services, nec
  Tamas Eisner
  Melanie Jacobs
  Ronald Thompson

D-U-N-S 24-863-3245   (SL)
1569243 ONTARIO INC
ROCK SOLID SUPPLY
316 Bayview Dr, Barrie, ON, L4N 8X9
(705) 719-4870
Emp Here 45   *Sales* 10,365,300
SIC 5712 Furniture stores
  Mike Brunelle

D-U-N-S 24-177-3188   (SL)
1630389 ONTARIO LTD
KLEEN AIR SOLUTIONS
11 King St Unit 4, Barrie, ON, L4N 6B5
(705) 721-1600
Emp Here 25   *Sales* 11,179,350
SIC 5075 Warm air heating and air conditioning
  Souleiman Moussa

D-U-N-S 24-952-1675   (SL)
1637136 ONTARIO INC

CENTRAL ONTARIO WEB
(*Suby of* TORSTAR CORPORATION)
82 Welham Rd, Barrie, ON, L4N 8Y4
(705) 733-1349
Emp Here 76   *Sales* 12,466,052
SIC 2752 Commercial printing, lithographic
  George Grigaitis

D-U-N-S 20-606-9486   (SL)
1894359 ONTARIO INC
(*Suby of* DCSR INVESTMENT CORP)
455 Welham Rd, Barrie, ON, L4N 8Z6
(705) 726-5841
Emp Here 125   *Sales* 27,750,125
SIC 3569 General industrial machinery, nec
  Saprapalli Ravalli
  David Crook
  Mauro Mozzato

D-U-N-S 20-352-0697   (SL)
2437090 ONTARIO LTD
TOLLOS MANUFACTURING
75 Dyment Rd, Barrie, ON, L4N 3H6
(705) 733-0022
Emp Here 40   *Sales* 10,262,480
SIC 3841 Surgical and medical instruments
  Shawn Murray
  Joseph Bailey

D-U-N-S 24-315-8755   (SL)
477281 ONTARIO LTD
COLEMAN CARE CENTRE
140 Cundles Rd W, Barrie, ON, L4N 9X8

Emp Here 125   *Sales* 8,570,750
SIC 8051 Skilled nursing care facilities
  Pauline Dell'oso

D-U-N-S 24-419-1656   (SL)
532551 ONTARIO LIMITED
39 Anne St S, Barrie, ON, L4N 2C7
(705) 726-1444
Emp Here 45   *Sales* 73,101,800
SIC 6712 Bank holding companies
  Brian Smith
  Ross Higginson
  Garry Greenside
  Jim Sheardown

D-U-N-S 24-726-9160   (HQ)
621189 ONTARIO INC
LARWAY TRAFFIC SYSTEMS
85 Ellis Dr, Barrie, ON, L4N 8Z3
(705) 739-1551
Emp Here 1   *Sales* 12,342,360
SIC 4213 Trucking, except local
  Larry Labatt
  Stuart Pound
  Catherine Labatt

D-U-N-S 25-033-9512   (SL)
650124 ONTARIO LIMITED
MOFFATTS NORTHWOOD MAZDA
261 Mapleview Dr W, Barrie, ON, L4N 9E8
(705) 737-3440
Emp Here 38   *Sales* 18,926,964
SIC 5511 New and used car dealers
  David Wood
  Bryan Moffatt

D-U-N-S 24-337-5362   (SL)
ACTIVE OPTICAL SUPPLY
125 Anne St S Suite 207, Barrie, ON, L4N 7B6
(705) 812-2602
Emp Here 47   *Sales* 21,017,178
SIC 5049 Professional equipment, nec
  Greg Coombs

D-U-N-S 24-709-4170   (HQ)
ADVANCED MOTION & CONTROLS LTD
26 Saunders Rd, Barrie, ON, L4N 9A8
(705) 726-2260
Emp Here 35   *Sales* 18,334,134
SIC 5065 Electronic parts and equipment, nec
  Mark Schick
  David Lawson

D-U-N-S 24-991-1074   (SL)

AIRDEX CORP
230 Saunders Rd, Barrie, ON, L4N 9A2

Emp Here 40   *Sales* 19,001,040
SIC 5084 Industrial machinery and equipment
Peter Rae

D-U-N-S 25-726-1750   (HQ)
ALBARRIE CANADA LIMITED
85 Morrow Rd, Barrie, ON, L4N 3V7
(705) 737-0551
Sales 18,340,300
SIC 2297 Nonwoven fabrics
Reginald Driscoll
Peter Koetsier

D-U-N-S 20-391-6858   (SL)
ALBARRIE GEOCOMPOSITES LIMITED
85 Morrow Rd, Barrie, ON, L4N 3V7
(705) 737-0551
Emp Here 110   *Sales* 73,994,690
SIC 1389 Oil and gas field services, nec
Reginald Driscoll

D-U-N-S 24-684-6778   (SL)
ALLANDALE SCHOOL TRANSIT LIMITED
SIMCOE COUNTY AIRPORT SERVICES
137 Brock St, Barrie, ON, L4N 2M3
(705) 728-1100
Emp Here 130   *Sales* 9,785,360
SIC 4151 School buses
Leslie Martin
George Martin
Jody Martin

D-U-N-S 24-023-4869   (SL)
ALTERNATIVE BENEFIT SOLUTIONS INC
556 Bryne Dr Unit 19 & 20, Barrie, ON, L4N 9P6
(705) 726-6100
Emp Here 20   *Sales* 20,697,620
SIC 6324 Hospital and medical service plans
Matt Houghton

D-U-N-S 24-181-8244   (SL)
B & I TRUCK PARTS INC
COMPLETE SPRING & TRAILER SERVICE
480 Dunlop St W, Barrie, ON, L4N 9W5
(705) 737-3201
Emp Here 46   *Sales* 22,911,588
SIC 5531 Auto and home supply stores

D-U-N-S 25-063-9358   (SL)
BARRETT HIDES INC
75 Welham Rd, Barrie, ON, L4N 8Y3
(705) 734-9905
Emp Here 34   *Sales* 49,901,528
SIC 5159 Farm-product raw materials, nec
Jim Barrett

D-U-N-S 20-055-7341   (SL)
BARRIE AUTO AUCTION LTD
434 Tiffin St, Barrie, ON, L4N 9W8
(705) 725-8183
Emp Here 30   *Sales* 10,926,450
SIC 5012 Automobiles and other motor vehicles
Noel Robertson
Elsie Franssen

D-U-N-S 24-046-0576   (SL)
BARRIE FORD
55 Mapleview Dr W, Barrie, ON, L4N 9H7
(705) 737-2310
Emp Here 78   *Sales* 49,083,840
SIC 5511 New and used car dealers
Michael Stollery
Gary Edmonds
Peter Panagakis

D-U-N-S 20-985-2289   (SL)
BARRIE MINOR BASEBALL ASSOCIATION
14 Broadmoor Ave, Barrie, ON, L4N 3M9
(705) 726-1441
Emp Here 49   *Sales* 19,473,286
SIC 8699 Membership organizations, nec
Susan Charters

D-U-N-S 25-178-0540   (SL)
BARRIE RECREATION LTD
ST. ONGE RECREATION
65 Hart Dr, Barrie, ON, L4N 5M3
(705) 733-2280
Emp Here 40   *Sales* 19,923,120
SIC 5551 Boat dealers
Steven St Onge

D-U-N-S 20-822-9252   (HQ)
BARRIE WELDING & MACHINE (1974) LIMITED
BWM INDUSTRIAL AUTOMATION DIV
39 Anne St S, Barrie, ON, L4N 2C7
(705) 726-1444
Sales 67,410,480
SIC 3599 Industrial machinery, nec
Brian Smith
Ross Higginson
Gary Greenside
James Sheardown

D-U-N-S 25-978-5939   (SL)
BERTRAM CONSTRUCTION & DESIGN LTD
25 George St Unit E, Barrie, ON, L4N 2G5
(705) 726-0254
Emp Here 32   *Sales* 10,666,656
SIC 1541 Industrial buildings and warehouses
Edward Bertram
Lisa Bertram
Donald Eagles

D-U-N-S 24-408-4398   (HQ)
BETA-TECH INC
318 Saunders Rd, Barrie, ON, L4N 9Y2
(705) 797-0119
Emp Here 62   *Sales* 15,096,068
SIC 3544 Special dies, tools, jigs, and fixtures
Walter Kunjah
Warren Schurman
Tanya Shields

D-U-N-S 24-975-5018   (HQ)
BOWMAN FUELS LTD
PETRO-CANADA
265 Burton Ave, Barrie, ON, L4N 2R9
(705) 726-6071
Emp Here 5   *Sales* 10,328,080
SIC 5172 Petroleum products, nec
Daryl Bowman
Peggie Bowman
Steve Bowman

D-U-N-S 24-598-7581   (HQ)
BRS CANADA ACQUISITION INC
INLAND/PACIFIC DISTRIBUTORS
(*Suby of* PEAK GLOBAL HOLDINGS, LLC)
92 Caplan Ave Suite 108, Barrie, ON, L4N 9J2
(705) 719-7922
Emp Here 7   *Sales* 52,054,200
SIC 5091 Sporting and recreation goods
Steve Dorey
Mark Harrison
Ed Small

D-U-N-S 24-389-9655   (SL)
CAN-SAVE SUPPLY AND DISTRIBUTION
411 Bayview Dr, Barrie, ON, L4N 8Y2
(705) 722-7283
Emp Here 90   *Sales* 40,245,660
SIC 5039 Construction materials, nec
Cully Koza
Larry Koza

D-U-N-S 25-604-9727   (BR)
CANADIAN LINEN AND UNIFORM SERVICE CO
QUEBEC LINGE
(*Suby of* ARAMARK)
116 Victoria St, Barrie, ON, L4N 2J1
(705) 739-0573
Emp Here 100
SIC 7213 Linen supply
Naiem Nairaz

D-U-N-S 25-301-6075   (HQ)
CANADIAN MENTAL HEALTH ASSOCIA-

TION, SIMCOE COUNTY BRANCH
CMHA
15 Bradford St, Barrie, ON, L4N 1W2
(705) 726-5033
Sales 16,064,600
SIC 8011 Offices and clinics of medical doctors
Nancy Roxborough

D-U-N-S 20-101-3018   (HQ)
CANPLAS INDUSTRIES LTD
(*Suby of* ALIAXIS)
500 Veterans Dr, Barrie, ON, L4N 9J5
(705) 726-3361
Emp Here 200   *Sales* 78,347,700
SIC 3088 Plastics plumbing fixtures
Ron Marsden
Steve Thompson
Randy Winter

D-U-N-S 24-915-8796   (SL)
CASCADES CANADA ULC
CASCADES CONTAINERBOARD PACKAGING - JELLCO
35 Fraser Crt, Barrie, ON, L4N 5J5
(705) 737-0470
Emp Here 40   *Sales* 13,024,000
SIC 5999 Miscellaneous retail stores, nec
Allan Hogg

D-U-N-S 24-032-6921   (SL)
CAW LOCAL 542
26 Lorena St, Barrie, ON, L4N 4P4
(705) 739-3532
Emp Here 56   *Sales* 14,482,440
SIC 8611 Business associations
George King

D-U-N-S 24-411-7065   (SL)
CLASSIC DODGE CHRYSLER INC
145 Bradford St, Barrie, ON, L4N 3B2
(705) 795-1431
Emp Here 35   *Sales* 17,432,730
SIC 5511 New and used car dealers
Tran Larue
Gordon Coates
Alan Waters

D-U-N-S 24-369-9191   (BR)
COSTCO WHOLESALE CANADA LTD
COSTCO
(*Suby of* COSTCO WHOLESALE CORPORATION)
41 Mapleview Dr E, Barrie, ON, L4N 9A9
(705) 728-2350
Emp Here 250
SIC 5099 Durable goods, nec
Ron Rewakoski

D-U-N-S 24-603-7949   (SL)
COWDEN-WOODS DESIGN BUILDERS LTD
249 Saunders Rd Unit 1, Barrie, ON, L4N 9A3
(705) 721-8422
Emp Here 24   *Sales* 11,297,544
SIC 1542 Nonresidential construction, nec
Anita Stacey
Mike Cowden

D-U-N-S 24-350-1959   (SL)
CSR COSMETIC SOLUTIONS INC
149 Victoria St, Barrie, ON, L4N 2J6
(705) 728-5917
Emp Here 160   *Sales* 45,443,360
SIC 2844 Toilet preparations
Stephen Blanchet

D-U-N-S 20-641-6224   (HQ)
CULLIGAN WATER CONDITIONING (BARRIE) LIMITED
15 Morrow Rd, Barrie, ON, L4N 3V7
(705) 728-4782
Sales 22,358,700
SIC 5074 Plumbing and heating equipment and supplies (hydronics)
Randy Clayton
Ralph Clayton

D-U-N-S 20-901-6302   (SL)

D. G. BEVAN INSURANCE BROKERS LTD
166 Saunders Rd Unit 6, Barrie, ON, L4N 9A4
(705) 726-3381
Emp Here 27   *Sales* 15,657,948
SIC 6411 Insurance agents, brokers, and service
Douglas Bevan

D-U-N-S 25-852-3463   (BR)
DANA CANADA CORPORATION
(*Suby of* DANA INCORPORATED)
120 Welham Rd, Barrie, ON, L4N 8Y4
(705) 737-2300
Emp Here 300
SIC 3714 Motor vehicle parts and accessories
Jim Westover

D-U-N-S 25-320-8243   (HQ)
DCSR INVESTMENT CORP
PRODOMAX
455 Welham Rd, Barrie, ON, L4N 8Z6
(705) 726-5841
Emp Here 5   *Sales* 74,432,405
SIC 3569 General industrial machinery, nec
Sebastian Ravalli
David Crook

D-U-N-S 20-205-4115   (SL)
DERBYSHIRE, D MERCHANDISING LTD
CANADIAN TIRE ASSOCIATE STORE #444
75 Mapleview Dr W, Barrie, ON, L4N 9H7
(705) 792-0920
Emp Here 150   *Sales* 94,392,000
SIC 5531 Auto and home supply stores
Dale Derbyshire

D-U-N-S 20-388-5009   (SL)
DTS COMM INC
324 Saunders Rd Unit 6, Barrie, ON, L4N 9Y2
(647) 428-8838
Emp Here 67   *Sales* 12,381,466
SIC 4841 Cable and other pay television services
Harry Blackwood
Jacinthe Doucet
Arie Rogenstein
Rene Noel

D-U-N-S 24-886-4324   (SL)
DUNCOR ENTERPRISES INC
101 Big Bay Point Rd, Barrie, ON, L4N 8M5
(705) 730-1999
Emp Here 40   *Sales* 11,340,960
SIC 1611 Highway and street construction
Bruce Duncan

D-U-N-S 25-509-4096   (SL)
DV SYSTEMS INC
490 Welham Rd, Barrie, ON, L4N 8Z4
(705) 728-5657
Emp Here 52   *Sales* 11,544,052
SIC 3563 Air and gas compressors
Bogdan Harrison
Garth Greenough

D-U-N-S 24-204-9547   (SL)
EURAMAX CANADA, INC
(*Suby of* OMNIMAX HOLDINGS, INC.)
26 Lorena St, Barrie, ON, L4N 4P4
(705) 728-7141
Emp Here 80   *Sales* 22,721,680
SIC 2821 Plastics materials and resins
Dudley Rowe
Gord Mccusker

D-U-N-S 24-026-5678   (SL)
F. K. MACHINERY LIMITED
(*Suby of* 1701451 ONTARIO LIMITED)
475 Welham Rd, Barrie, ON, L4N 8Z6
(705) 721-4200
Emp Here 30   *Sales* 14,250,780
SIC 5085 Industrial supplies
John Byles
John Scott Byles

D-U-N-S 20-110-9996   (SL)
FARIS TEAM CORP, THE
ROYAL LEPAGE FIRST CONTACT REALTY

431 Bayview Dr Unit 14, Barrie, ON, L4N 8Y2
(705) 797-8485
Emp Here 46   *Sales* 15,047,842
SIC 6531 Real estate agents and managers
Mark Faris

D-U-N-S 20-647-7445   (HQ)
FIRST CONTACT REALTY LTD
ROYAL LEPAGE FIRST CONTACT REALTY
299 Lakeshore Dr Suite 100, Barrie, ON, L4N
7Y9
(705) 728-4067
Emp Here 1   *Sales* 29,322,230
SIC 6531 Real estate agents and managers
Larry Dewilde

D-U-N-S 20-205-3836   (HQ)
FLAT FEE REALTY INC
21 Patterson Rd Unit 28, Barrie, ON, L4N 7W6

Emp Here 15   *Sales* 29,322,230
SIC 6531 Real estate agents and managers
Aron Cadeau
Zygmunt Hancyk

D-U-N-S 24-784-5605   (SL)
FRESH MIX LIMITED
FRESH - A FARE
530 Welham Rd, Barrie, ON, L4N 8Z7
(705) 734-1580
Emp Here 50   *Sales* 11,242,750
SIC 2099 Food preparations, nec
Ester Sattler
Michael Witherspoon
Karin Wotherspoon

D-U-N-S 24-977-4704   (HQ)
GEEP CANADA INC
(*Suby of* MG HOLDINGS INC)
220 John St, Barrie, ON, L4N 2L2
(705) 725-1919
Emp Here 190   *Sales* 99,345,210
SIC 4953 Refuse systems
Jeffrey Jermyn
Lew Coffin
Bill King
Wallace Mackay
Bob Campling

D-U-N-S 24-394-2161   (HQ)
GEEP HOLDINGS INC
(*Suby of* MG HOLDINGS INC)
220 John St, Barrie, ON, L4N 2L2
(705) 725-1919
Emp Here 1   *Sales* 148,031,145
SIC 6712 Bank holding companies
Jefferey Jermyn
Joe Caruso
Nelson Costa
Wallace Mackay
David Guest

D-U-N-S 20-644-7521   (BR)
GOLDEN ARCH FOOD SERVICES LTD
MCDONALDS
80 Barrie View Dr, Barrie, ON, L4N 8V4
(705) 735-1700
Emp Here 100
SIC 5812 Eating places
Peter Snell

D-U-N-S 24-617-0596   (SL)
**GREY-SIMCOE SPORTS MEDICINE AND
REHABILITATION CENTRES INC.**
GREY SIMCOE SPORTS MED
480 Huronia Rd Unit 104, Barrie, ON, L4N
6M2
(705) 734-1588
Emp Here 40   *Sales* 14,449,480
SIC 8041 Offices and clinics of chiropractors
Rick Schaly

D-U-N-S 20-101-7873   (BR)
**GREYHOUND CANADA TRANSPORTA-
TION ULC**
PMCL
(*Suby of* FIRSTGROUP PLC)
24 Maple Ave Unit 205, Barrie, ON, L4N 7W4

Emp Here 100
SIC 4131 Intercity and rural bus transportation
Munoz Edgar

D-U-N-S 24-544-1001   (SL)
GYM-CON LTD
93 Rawson Ave, Barrie, ON, L4N 6E5
(705) 728-2222
Emp Here 25   *Sales* 11,179,350
SIC 5039 Construction materials, nec
Timothy Klementti
Joe Wilson

D-U-N-S 25-174-8703   (HQ)
HB SEALING PRODUCTS LTD
*HERCULES BULLDOG SEALING PROD-
UCTS*
(*Suby of* DIPLOMA PLC)
30 Saunders Rd Suite 1, Barrie, ON, L4N 9A8
(705) 739-6735
Sales 18,526,014
SIC 5085 Industrial supplies
Russ Petrie

D-U-N-S 25-408-3843   (SL)
HEALTH4ALL PRODUCTS LIMITED
GLOBAL BOTANICAL
545 Welham Rd, Barrie, ON, L4N 8Z6
(705) 733-2117
Emp Here 20   *Sales* 10,702,480
SIC 5149 Groceries and related products, nec

D-U-N-S 25-079-2314   (BR)
HOME DEPOT OF CANADA INC
HOME DEPOT
(*Suby of* THE HOME DEPOT INC)
10 Barrie View Dr, Barrie, ON, L4N 8V4
(705) 733-2800
Emp Here 300
SIC 5251 Hardware stores
Salonin Andrew

D-U-N-S 25-407-6227   (SL)
**HOMELIFE/KEMPENFELT/KELLY REALTY
LTD**
284 Dunlop St W, Barrie, ON, L4N 1B9
(705) 725-0000
Emp Here 75   *Sales* 20,381,700
SIC 6531 Real estate agents and managers
Lou Kelly

D-U-N-S 24-843-8152   (SL)
INNOVATIVE AUTOMATION INC
625 Welham Rd, Barrie, ON, L4N 0B7
(705) 733-0555
Emp Here 113   *Sales* 25,086,113
SIC 3569 General industrial machinery, nec
Stephen Loftus
Matthew Setterington
Michael Lalonde

D-U-N-S 20-904-8060   (HQ)
INVESTIGATIVE RESEARCH GROUP INC
49 Truman Rd Suite 102, Barrie, ON, L4N 8Y7
(705) 739-4800
Emp Here 35   *Sales* 18,992,544
SIC 7381 Detective and armored car services
Brian Sartorelli

D-U-N-S 24-801-4565   (HQ)
IOOF SENIORS HOMES INC
ODD FELLOWS & REBEKAH HOMES
10 Brooks St, Barrie, ON, L4N 5L3
(705) 728-2389
Emp Here 190   *Sales* 32,562,480
SIC 6513 Apartment building operators
Doreen Saunders
Dan Delisle
David Steel

D-U-N-S 24-379-6419   (SL)
JEBCO INDUSTRIES INC
111 Ellis Dr, Barrie, ON, L4N 8Z3
(705) 797-8888
Emp Here 95   *Sales* 18,248,075
SIC 3499 Fabricated Metal products, nec
Brett Murray

D-U-N-S 24-396-0528   (SL)
JOHN SK LTD
PETRO CANADA
151 Mapleview Dr W, Barrie, ON, L4N 9E8
(705) 734-0819
Emp Here 25   *Sales* 12,451,950
SIC 5541 Gasoline service stations
Atis Morkos

D-U-N-S 20-406-0339   (SL)
JOHNSTON, KERV MOTORS (1996) LTD
BARRIE HONDA AUTO SALES
80 Mapleview Dr W, Barrie, ON, L4N 9H6
(705) 733-2100
Emp Here 70   *Sales* 44,049,600
SIC 5511 New and used car dealers
Greg Johnston

D-U-N-S 25-818-6873   (BR)
KINARK CHILD AND FAMILY SERVICES
(*Suby of* KINARK CHILD AND FAMILY SER-
VICES)
34 Simcoe St Suite 3, Barrie, ON, L4N 6T4
(888) 454-6275
Emp Here 100
SIC 8322 Individual and family services
Jacquie Brown

D-U-N-S 25-088-6873   (BR)
LEON'S FURNITURE LIMITED
(*Suby of* LEON'S FURNITURE LIMITED)
81 Bryne Dr, Barrie, ON, L4N 8V8
(705) 730-1777
Emp Here 80
SIC 5712 Furniture stores
William Gadsby

D-U-N-S 20-042-0479   (HQ)
LEWIS MOTOR SALES INC
76 Mapleview Dr W, Barrie, ON, L4N 9H6
(705) 728-3026
Sales 75,513,600
SIC 5511 New and used car dealers
Dale Lewis

D-U-N-S 24-392-3666   (SL)
LINEAR TRANSFER AUTOMATION INC
61 Rawson Ave, Barrie, ON, L4N 6E5
(705) 735-0000
Emp Here 80   *Sales* 17,760,080
SIC 3569 General industrial machinery, nec
Rama Jayaweera

D-U-N-S 20-819-0525   (BR)
LINK-LINE CONSTRUCTION LTD
(*Suby of* LINK-LINE CONSTRUCTION LTD)
10 Churchill Dr, Barrie, ON, L4N 8Z5
(705) 721-9284
Emp Here 100
SIC 1521 Single-family housing construction
Michael Carnival

D-U-N-S 24-858-2186   (BR)
LOWE'S COMPANIES CANADA, ULC
(*Suby of* LOWE'S COMPANIES, INC.)
71 Bryne Dr, Barrie, ON, L4N 8V8
(905) 952-2950
Emp Here 150
SIC 5211 Lumber and other building materials
Kate Coleman

D-U-N-S 20-595-9505   (HQ)
MAYES-MARTIN LIMITED
150 Vespra St, Barrie, ON, L4N 2G9
(705) 728-5027
Emp Here 16   *Sales* 20,656,160
SIC 5172 Petroleum products, nec
Shawn Fullan

D-U-N-S 24-826-9102   (BR)
**MCDONALD'S RESTAURANTS OF
CANADA LIMITED**
MCDONALD'S
(*Suby of* MCDONALD'S CORPORATION)
201 Fairview Rd, Barrie, ON, L4N 9B1
(905) 823-8500
Emp Here 100
SIC 5812 Eating places

Sharon Labadie

D-U-N-S 20-792-5301   (BR)
**MCDONALD'S RESTAURANTS OF
CANADA LIMITED**
MCDONALD'S
(*Suby of* MCDONALD'S CORPORATION)
85 Dunlop St W, Barrie, ON, L4N 1A5
(705) 726-6500
Emp Here 80
SIC 5812 Eating places
Adam Thornhill

D-U-N-S 25-220-1918   (HQ)
MID-ONTARIO DIESEL LIMITED
MID-ONTARIO MACK
400 Dunlop St W, Barrie, ON, L4N 1C2
(705) 722-1122
Sales 22,413,510
SIC 5511 New and used car dealers
John Costa
Guido Lecce

D-U-N-S 20-171-0654   (HQ)
MODERN SALES CO-OP
AUTOSENSE AUTO PARTS
87 Caplan Ave, Barrie, ON, L4N 9J3
(705) 733-1771
Emp Here 53   *Sales* 27,316,125
SIC 5013 Motor vehicle supplies and new
parts
Donald Skuce
Reid Ferguson

D-U-N-S 24-189-9710   (SL)
MONTANA'S COOKHOUSE SALOON
66 Barrie View Dr, Barrie, ON, L4N 8V4
(705) 726-3375
Emp Here 75   *Sales* 3,413,925
SIC 5812 Eating places
Mike Legge

D-U-N-S 24-099-5373   (HQ)
MOORE PACKAGING CORPORATION
(*Suby of* PBM HOLDINGS INC)
191 John St, Barrie, ON, L4N 2L4
(705) 737-1023
Sales 82,718,325
SIC 2653 Corrugated and solid fiber boxes
Peter Moore
Daniel D Faber

D-U-N-S 24-874-4385   (BR)
MOORE PACKAGING CORPORATION
(*Suby of* PBM HOLDINGS INC)
191 John St Suite 12, Barrie, ON, L4N 2L4
(705) 737-1023
Emp Here 200
SIC 4783 Packing and crating
Dan Faber

D-U-N-S 25-170-8046   (HQ)
MUELLER CANADA LTD
MUELLER FLOW CONTROL, DIV OF
(*Suby of* MUELLER WATER PRODUCTS,
INC.)
82 Hooper Rd, Barrie, ON, L4N 8Z9
(705) 719-9965
Emp Here 60   *Sales* 195,092,000
SIC 5085 Industrial supplies
Greg Rogowski
Frederick Welsh

D-U-N-S 24-993-3748   (SL)
NEAR NORTH CUSTOMS BROKERS INC
20 Elliott Ave, Barrie, ON, L4N 4V7
(705) 739-0024
Emp Here 28   *Sales* 14,559,076
SIC 4731 Freight transportation arrangement
Myles Macleod
Jeffrey Smith
Christiana Jupp
David Jupp

D-U-N-S 24-327-9556   (SL)
NUTRAFARMS INC
261 King St, Barrie, ON, L4N 6B5

(705) 739-0669
Emp Here 100   *Sales* 83,557,700
SIC 5149 Groceries and related products, nec
  Maureen Urbanoski
  Russell Urbanoski

D-U-N-S 20-817-5398   (SL)
OUGH FIRE SYSTEMS LTD
OFS
16 Lennox Dr, Barrie, ON, L4N 9V8
(705) 720-0570
Emp Here 25   *Sales* 11,875,650
SIC 5087 Service establishment equipment
  Jeff Ough

D-U-N-S 24-357-4683   (HQ)
PARTNERS REAL ESTATE INVESTMENT TRUST
249 Saunders Rd Unit 3, Barrie, ON, L4N 9A3
(705) 725-6020
Sales 37,019,541
SIC 6798 Real estate investment trusts
  Ian Ross
  Derrick West
  Grant Anthony
  Michael Woollcombe
  Colin Chapin

D-U-N-S 25-135-9456   (SL)
PEGGY HILL & ASSOCIATES REALTY INC
PEGGY HILL TEAM
11 Victoria St Unit B3, Barrie, ON, L4N 6T3
(705) 739-4455
Emp Here 40   *Sales* 13,085,080
SIC 6531 Real estate agents and managers
  Peggy Hill

D-U-N-S 20-178-8945   (SL)
POWDER TECH LIMITED
699 Bayview Dr, Barrie, ON, L4N 9A5
(705) 726-4580
Emp Here 50   *Sales* 10,141,500
SIC 3479 Metal coating and allied services
  Edward Rozalowsky

D-U-N-S 24-276-7283   (SL)
PROVINCIAL TIRE DISTRIBUTORS INC
466 Welham Rd, Barrie, ON, L4N 8Z4
(705) 726-5510
Emp Here 40   *Sales* 14,568,600
SIC 5014 Tires and tubes
  Peter Labrecque

D-U-N-S 20-807-2756   (SL)
PRYCON CUSTOM BUILDING & RENOVATIONS INC
36 Morrow Rd Suite 100, Barrie, ON, L4N 3V8
(705) 739-0023
Emp Here 50   *Sales* 16,666,650
SIC 1541 Industrial buildings and warehouses
  Stephen Pryce

D-U-N-S 20-788-8228   (BR)
RECIPE UNLIMITED CORPORATION
HARVEY'S SWISS CHALET
(*Suby of* RECIPE UNLIMITED CORPORATION)
85 Barrie View Dr, Barrie, ON, L4N 8V4
(705) 733-0791
Emp Here 85
SIC 5812 Eating places
  Peter Metelsji

D-U-N-S 24-132-4008   (SL)
REGAL GIFTS CORPORATION
360 Saunders Rd, Barrie, ON, L4N 9Y2
(800) 565-3130
Emp Here 40   *Sales* 26,258,560
SIC 5961 Catalog and mail-order houses
  Greg Neath
  Larry Cole
  William Taggart

D-U-N-S 20-583-8944   (SL)
REID'S FURNITURE OF BARRIE LIMITED
LA-Z-BOY FURNITURE GALLERIES
491 Bryne Dr, Barrie, ON, L4N 9P7
(705) 735-3337
Emp Here 18   *Sales* 11,816,352

SIC 5963 Direct selling establishments
  Shawn Reid

D-U-N-S 20-809-7910   (SL)
ROBERTA PLACE
503 Essa Rd, Barrie, ON, L4N 9E4
(705) 733-3231
Emp Here 120   *Sales* 14,973,120
SIC 8741 Management services
  Carolyn Wright

D-U-N-S 24-389-5914   (SL)
ROYAL IRAQI HEAVY EQUIPMENT CORPORATION, THE
THERADIOMAN
55 Browning Trail, Barrie, ON, L4N 5A5
(705) 241-0082
Emp Here 45   *Sales* 13,147,605
SIC 7353 Heavy construction equipment rental
  Dale Lawson

D-U-N-S 25-283-5343   (SL)
RUSSELL SECURITY SERVICES INC
80 Bradford St Suite 826, Barrie, ON, L4N 6S7
(705) 721-1480
Emp Here 200   *Sales* 116,049,400
SIC 5065 Electronic parts and equipment, nec
  Mark Kramer

D-U-N-S 20-609-2561   (HQ)
SARJEANT COMPANY LIMITED, THE
CUSTOM CONCRETE NORTHERN, DIV OF
15 Sarjeant Dr, Barrie, ON, L4N 4V9
(705) 728-2460
Emp Here 75   *Sales* 26,882,850
SIC 3273 Ready-mixed concrete
  Scott Elliott
  Brandon Elliott
  Patrick Robbenhaar

D-U-N-S 20-607-2043   (HQ)
SIMCOE BLOCK (1979) LIMITED
SIMCOE BUILDING CENTRE
140 Ferndale Dr N, Barrie, ON, L4N 9W1
(705) 728-1773
Emp Here 20   *Sales* 23,343,500
SIC 3271 Concrete block and brick
  Ray Gariepy
  Matt Gariepy

D-U-N-S 24-822-1665   (SL)
SIMCOE COUNTY CLEANING LIMITED
SERVICE MASTER
49 Morrow Rd Unit 14, Barrie, ON, L4N 3V7
(705) 722-7203
Emp Here 75   *Sales* 3,015,675
SIC 7349 Building maintenance services, nec
  Jim Mccaskill

D-U-N-S 25-297-6584   (BR)
SIMCOE COUNTY DISTRICT SCHOOL BOARD, THE
BARRIE CENTRAL COLLEGIATE INSTITUTE
(*Suby of* SIMCOE COUNTY DISTRICT SCHOOL BOARD, THE)
125 Dunlop St W, Barrie, ON, L4N 1A9

Emp Here 100
SIC 8211 Elementary and secondary schools
  Greg Brucker

D-U-N-S 20-026-1209   (BR)
SIMCOE MUSKOKA CATHOLIC DISTRICT SCHOOL BOARD
ST. PETER'S SECONDARY SCHOOL
(*Suby of* SIMCOE MUSKOKA CATHOLIC DISTRICT SCHOOL BOARD)
201 Ashford Dr, Barrie, ON, L4N 6A3
(705) 734-0168
Emp Here 100
SIC 8211 Elementary and secondary schools
  Heinrich Bebie

D-U-N-S 20-793-8965   (BR)
SOBEYS CAPITAL INCORPORATED
(*Suby of* EMPIRE COMPANY LIMITED)

37 Mapleview Dr W, Barrie, ON, L4N 9H5
(705) 728-9858
Emp Here 150
SIC 5411 Grocery stores
  Rob Trevisan

D-U-N-S 20-653-8162   (SL)
ST. JOAN OF ARC CATHOLIC HIGH SCHOOL
SIMCOE MUSKOKA CATHOLIC DISTRICT SCHOOL BOARD SECONDARY SCHOOLS
ST JOAN OF ARC
460 Mapleton Ave, Barrie, ON, L4N 9C2
(705) 721-0398
Emp Here 100   *Sales* 9,282,600
SIC 8211 Elementary and secondary schools
  Joe Timmins

D-U-N-S 25-399-2564   (HQ)
STEWART FOODSERVICE INC
201 Saunders Rd, Barrie, ON, L4N 9A3
(705) 728-3051
Sales 80,313,216
SIC 5141 Groceries, general line
  Aubrey Macmillan
  Mike Macmillan
  Dennis Hrytzak
  Bob Blumel

D-U-N-S 24-678-0139   (HQ)
STUDENT TRANSPORTATION INC
160 Saunders Rd Unit 6, Barrie, ON, L4N 9A4
(705) 721-2626
Emp Here 185   *Sales* 637,317,000
SIC 4151 School buses
  Denis J. Gallagher
  Patrick J. Walker
  John Dimaiolo
  Paula Alteiri
  Thomas Kominsky
  Keith Engelbert

D-U-N-S 24-063-3755   (HQ)
STUDENT TRANSPORTATION OF CANADA INC
(*Suby of* STUDENT TRANSPORTATION OF AMERICA, INC.)
160 Saunders Rd Unit 6, Barrie, ON, L4N 9A4
(705) 721-2626
Emp Here 50   *Sales* 22,485,600
SIC 4151 School buses
  D Edward Wilson
  Chris Harwood
  Denis J Gallagher

D-U-N-S 20-020-6493   (HQ)
SUTTON GROUP INCENTIVE REALTY INC
241 Minet'S Point Rd, Barrie, ON, L4N 4C4
(705) 739-1300
Emp Here 1   *Sales* 12,500,776
SIC 6531 Real estate agents and managers
  Bill Kindou

D-U-N-S 20-755-5228   (HQ)
SUZUKI CANADA INC.
(*Suby of* SUZUKI MOTOR CORPORATION)
360 Saunders Rd, Barrie, ON, L4N 9Y2
(705) 999-8600
Sales 35,693,070
SIC 5012 Automobiles and other motor vehicles
  William Porter
  Piero Caleca

D-U-N-S 20-823-3098   (SL)
T.R.Y. JACKSON BROTHERS LIMITED
JACKSONS TOYOTA
181 Mapleview Dr W, Barrie, ON, L4N 9E8
(705) 726-0288
Emp Here 55   *Sales* 34,610,400
SIC 5511 New and used car dealers
  Robert B Jackson
  Heather Jackson

D-U-N-S 20-034-3192   (HQ)
THETA INDUSTRIES LIMITED
8 Truman Rd, Barrie, ON, L4N 8Y8

(705) 726-2620
Sales 34,575,300
SIC 3469 Metal stampings, nec
  Frank Gauder
  Glenn Gauder
  Irene Gauder

D-U-N-S 25-150-8958   (HQ)
THETA TTS INC
(*Suby of* THETA INDUSTRIES LIMITED)
8 Truman Rd, Barrie, ON, L4N 8Y8
(705) 726-2620
Sales 38,417,000
SIC 3469 Metal stampings, nec
  Glenn Gauder
  Irene Gauder
  Frank Gauder

D-U-N-S 20-804-0589   (SL)
TNR INDUSTRIAL DOORS INC
TNR INDUSTRIES
200 Fairview Rd Unit 2, Barrie, ON, L4N 8X8
(705) 792-9968
Emp Here 50   *Sales* 10,141,500
SIC 3442 Metal doors, sash, and trim
  Cathy Buckingham
  Warren Skromeda

D-U-N-S 20-123-7832   (SL)
ULTIMATE CONSTRUCTION INC
39 Churchill Dr Suite 1, Barrie, ON, L4N 8Z5
(705) 726-2300
Emp Here 110   *Sales* 29,803,620
SIC 1521 Single-family housing construction
  Michael Babineau

D-U-N-S 20-922-6203   (SL)
VICTORIA VILLAGE INC
VICTORIA VILLAGE MANOR
78 Ross St, Barrie, ON, L4N 1G3
(705) 728-3456
Emp Here 140   *Sales* 9,565,640
SIC 8051 Skilled nursing care facilities
  Olivia Schmitz

D-U-N-S 25-294-8575   (BR)
WAL-MART CANADA CORP
(*Suby of* WALMART INC.)
35 Mapleview Dr W, Barrie, ON, L4N 9H5
(705) 728-9122
Emp Here 175
SIC 5311 Department stores
  Vincent Vinarra

D-U-N-S 20-034-3416   (SL)
WALLWIN ELECTRIC SERVICES LIMITED
WALLWIN ELECTRIC
50 Innisfil St, Barrie, ON, L4N 4K5
(705) 726-1859
Emp Here 100   *Sales* 21,782,900
SIC 1731 Electrical work
  Craig Wallwin
  Timothy Southorn
  John Holloway
  Christopher Dixon

D-U-N-S 20-121-1930   (SL)
WELDCO-BEALES MFG. ONTARIO LTD
515 Welham Rd Suite 1, Barrie, ON, L4N 8Z6
(705) 733-2668
Emp Here 60   *Sales* 13,320,060
SIC 3531 Construction machinery
  Doug Schindel
  Jamie Lindsay
  Wayne Gordon
  Peter Tatty

D-U-N-S 24-214-5175   (SL)
WESTERN MECHANICAL ELECTRICAL MILLWRIGHT SERVICES LTD
160 Brock St, Barrie, ON, L4N 2M4
(705) 737-4135
Emp Here 190   *Sales* 46,775,340
SIC 1796 Installing building equipment
  Peter Duivenvoorden
  Larry Eisses
  Brian Smith

D-U-N-S 20-811-1091   (SL)
WIERSEMA, TRACY PHARMACY LTD
SHOPPERS DRUG MART - YONGE & BIG BAY
649 Yonge St, Barrie, ON, L4N 4E7
(705) 792-4388
Emp Here 55   *Sales* 13,438,040
SIC 5912 Drug stores and proprietary stores
Tracy Wiersema

D-U-N-S 25-812-8230   (HQ)
WILLIAMS, JIM LEASING LIMITED
THRIFTY CAR RENTAL
191 Mapleview Dr W, Barrie, ON, L4N 9E8
(705) 734-1200
Emp Here 35   *Sales* 37,756,800
SIC 5511 New and used car dealers
Jim Williams

D-U-N-S 24-377-2402   (SL)
WIRECOMM SYSTEMS (2008), INC
(*Suby of* UNITEK GLOBAL SERVICES, INC.)
122 Saunders Rd Suite 10, Barrie, ON, L4N 9A8
(905) 405-8018
Emp Here 167   *Sales* 38,154,824
SIC 4899 Communication services, nec
Christopher Scott Hisey
Daniel Hopkin
Peter Brodsky
Dean Macdonald

D-U-N-S 25-034-0189   (SL)
YANCH HEATING AND AIR CONDITIONING (BARRIE) LIMITED
89 Rawson Ave, Barrie, ON, L4N 6E5
(705) 728-5406
Emp Here 70   *Sales* 16,314,550
SIC 1711 Plumbing, heating, air-conditioning
Christopher Yanch

D-U-N-S 20-809-7894   (BR)
YMCA OF GREATER TORONTO
(*Suby of* YMCA OF GREATER TORONTO)
22 Grove St W, Barrie, ON, L4N 1M7
(705) 726-6421
Emp Here 200
SIC 8699 Membership organizations, nec
Medhat Mahdy

D-U-N-S 25-911-8651   (BR)
ZEHRMART INC
ZEHRS MARKETS
(*Suby of* LOBLAW COMPANIES LIMITED)
620 Yonge St, Barrie, ON, L4N 4E6
(705) 735-2390
Emp Here 200
SIC 5411 Grocery stores
Lisa Brown

Barrie, ON L9J

D-U-N-S 25-159-9825   (HQ)
1124965 ONTARIO LTD
SECURE STORE
800 Essa Rd, Barrie, ON, L9J 0A8
(705) 728-9211
Emp Here 15   *Sales* 10,450,572
SIC 5084 Industrial machinery and equipment
Elgin Bolton

Barrys Bay, ON K0J

D-U-N-S 24-382-5775   (HQ)
BARRY'S BAY CUSTOM WOODWORKING AND BUILDERS' SUPPLY LTD
BARRY'S BAY HOME HARDWARE BUILD-ING CENTRE
306 John St, Barrys Bay, ON, K0J 1B0
(613) 756-2794
Emp Here 25   *Sales* 12,652,950

SIC 5211 Lumber and other building materials
Susan Zurakowski

D-U-N-S 20-507-7092   (SL)
BARRY'S BAY DAIRY LTD
15 Dunn St, Barrys Bay, ON, K0J 1B0
(613) 756-2018
Emp Here 26   *Sales* 21,725,002
SIC 5143 Dairy products, except dried or canned
Anthony Yantha
Syl Yantha
Edward Yantha

D-U-N-S 25-264-3978   (SL)
BARRY'S BAY METRO
28 Bay St, Barrys Bay, ON, K0J 1B0
(613) 756-7097
Emp Here 45   *Sales* 12,336,840
SIC 5411 Grocery stores
Gerard O'malley
Neil O'reilly

D-U-N-S 24-828-9175   (BR)
PLAINTREE SYSTEMS INC
MADAWASKA DOORS
(*Suby of* PLAINTREE SYSTEMS INC)
14 Conway St, Barrys Bay, ON, K0J 1B0
(613) 756-7066
Emp Here 120
SIC 2431 Millwork

D-U-N-S 20-891-5744   (SL)
ST. FRANCIS MEMORIAL HOSPITAL AS-SOCIATION
7 St Francis Memorial Dr, Barrys Bay, ON, K0J 1B0
(613) 756-3044
Emp Here 120   *Sales* 13,329,600
SIC 8062 General medical and surgical hospi-tals
Randy Penney
Stephanie Graham

D-U-N-S 24-101-6062   (SL)
VALLEY MANOR INC
88 Mintha St, Barrys Bay, ON, K0J 1B0
(613) 756-2643
Emp Here 130   *Sales* 8,882,380
SIC 8051 Skilled nursing care facilities
Trisha Sammon
Lori Jessup
Kathryn Marion

D-U-N-S 20-325-0485   (SL)
YUILL'S VALU-MART
19625 Opeongo St, Barrys Bay, ON, K0J 1B0
(613) 756-2023
Emp Here 45   *Sales* 37,600,965
SIC 5141 Groceries, general line
Derek Yuill

Bath, ON K0H

D-U-N-S 25-364-7754   (BR)
INVISTA (CANADA) COMPANY
(*Suby of* KOSA US INVESTMENTS SARL)
Gd, Bath, ON, K0H 1G0
(613) 634-5124
Emp Here 100
SIC 2299 Textile goods, nec
Kevin Karasiuk

D-U-N-S 25-999-5124   (BR)
ONTARIO POWER GENERATION INC
(*Suby of* GOVERNMENT OF ONTARIO)
7263 Hwy 33, Bath, ON, K0H 1G0
(613) 352-3525
Emp Here 163
SIC 4911 Electric services
John Hefford

Beachburg, ON K0J

D-U-N-S 24-268-9172   (SL)
OTTAWA RIVER WHITE WATER RAFTING LIMITED
RIVER RUN
1260 Grant Settlement Rd, Beachburg, ON, K0J 1C0
(613) 646-2501
Emp Here 75   *Sales* 10,502,175
SIC 7999 Amusement and recreation, nec
Margaret Maloney
Larry Broome

Beamsville, ON L0R

D-U-N-S 20-802-2025   (BR)
ALBRIGHT GARDENS HOMES INCORPO-RATED
5050 Hillside Dr, Beamsville, ON, L0R 1B2
(905) 563-8252
Emp Here 300
SIC 8322 Individual and family services
John Buma

D-U-N-S 24-685-5381   (SL)
CEDARWAY FLORAL INC
4665 Bartlett Rd, Beamsville, ON, L0R 1B1
(905) 563-4338
Emp Here 22   *Sales* 16,335,440
SIC 5193 Flowers and florists supplies
Ken Westerhoff
Elizabeth Westerhoff

D-U-N-S 20-034-5213   (SL)
CHRISTIE'S DAIRY LIMITED
4819 Union Rd, Beamsville, ON, L0R 1B4
(905) 563-8841
Emp Here 20   *Sales* 10,702,480
SIC 5143 Dairy products, except dried or canned
Robert Christie
William Jr Christie

D-U-N-S 24-484-8768   (SL)
COMMUNITY LIVING-GRIMSBY, LINCOLN AND WEST LINCOLN
5041 King St, Beamsville, ON, L0R 1B0
(905) 563-4115
Emp Here 165   *Sales* 12,670,680
SIC 8322 Individual and family services
Sarina Labonte

D-U-N-S 24-736-3604   (SL)
COURT HOLDINGS LIMITED
5071 King St, Beamsville, ON, L0R 1B0
(905) 563-0782
Emp Here 375   *Sales* 106,093,125
SIC 3694 Engine electrical equipment
Philip D. Court
Michael C. Court
Suzanne W. Court
Tracy Murray

D-U-N-S 25-088-8831   (SL)
CULP, J. E. TRANSPORT LTD
4815 Merritt Rd, Beamsville, ON, L0R 1B1
(905) 563-5055
Emp Here 70   *Sales* 10,373,440
SIC 4212 Local trucking, without storage
James Culp
Helen Culp

D-U-N-S 24-060-9982   (BR)
DANA CANADA CORPORATION
SERVICE PARTS DIVISION
(*Suby of* DANA INCORPORATED)
5095 South Service Rd, Beamsville, ON, L0R 1B0

Emp Here 96
SIC 5013 Motor vehicle supplies and new parts
John Balasak

D-U-N-S 24-917-9219   (SL)
DORKEN SYSTEMS INC
COSELLA-DORKEN
(*Suby of* EWALD DORKEN AG)
4655 Delta Way, Beamsville, ON, L0R 1B4
(905) 563-3255
Emp Here 55   *Sales* 31,329,540
SIC 5039 Construction materials, nec
Ingo Quent
Tom Fallon
Steve White
Marcus Jadlonka

D-U-N-S 20-185-2316   (HQ)
FERGUSON-NEUDORF GLASS INC
4275 North Service Rd, Beamsville, ON, L0R 1B1
(905) 563-1394
Emp Here 70   *Sales* 46,722,720
SIC 1793 Glass and glazing work
Jeff Neudorf
John Neudorf
Danny Neudorf
Doug Lilja

D-U-N-S 20-034-5320   (SL)
FLEMING CHICKS LIMITED
(*Suby of* MAPLE LODGE HOLDING CORPO-RATION)
4412 Ontario St, Beamsville, ON, L0R 1B0
(905) 563-4914
Emp Here 60   *Sales* 12,397,020
SIC 0254 Poultry hatcheries
Michael Burrows
Jack May
Jean May
Elizabeth May
Robert May
David May
Larry May
Kathy Wienhold
Wendy Robson
Debi Kee

D-U-N-S 25-902-1806   (SL)
FOLIERA INC
4655 Bartlett Rd, Beamsville, ON, L0R 1B1
(905) 563-1066
Emp Here 28   *Sales* 20,790,560
SIC 5193 Flowers and florists supplies
John Kouwenberg

D-U-N-S 24-097-6407   (SL)
HENDRIKS, ANDREW & SONS GREEN-HOUSES INC
5095 North Service Rd, Beamsville, ON, L0R 1B3
(905) 563-8132
Emp Here 50   *Sales* 17,123,350
SIC 0181 Ornamental nursery products
Andrew C Hendriks
Richard Hendriks
Helen Mary Hendriks
Andrew J. Hendriks

D-U-N-S 24-889-1541   (SL)
J-LINE TRANSPORT LIMITED
4751 Christie Dr, Beamsville, ON, L0R 1B4
(905) 945-3122
Emp Here 45   *Sales* 10,109,311
SIC 4213 Trucking, except local
Margaret M Townsley

D-U-N-S 20-627-0688   (SL)
JADEE MEAT PRODUCTS LIMITED
4710 Bartlett Rd, Beamsville, ON, L0R 1B1
(905) 563-5381
Emp Here 50   *Sales* 11,242,750
SIC 2011 Meat packing plants
Daniel Snajdman

D-U-N-S 24-876-7436   (HQ)
JANSEN INTERNATIONAL CANADA LTD
LIVINGSTONE TERRASSO
4700 South Service Rd, Beamsville, ON, L0R 1B1
(905) 563-1822
Sales 12,212,544

SIC 5021 Furniture
Frederick Janssen

D-U-N-S 24-560-0218   (SL)
MANORCORE CONSTRUCTION INC
4707 Christie Dr, Beamsville, ON, L0R 1B4
(905) 563-8888
Emp Here 25   Sales 11,768,275
SIC 1542 Nonresidential construction, nec
Leonard Papineau

D-U-N-S 20-051-2072   (SL)
MANORCORE GROUP INC
4707 Christie Dr, Beamsville, ON, L0R 1B4
(905) 563-8888
Emp Here 24   Sales 11,297,544
SIC 1542 Nonresidential construction, nec
Leonard Papineau

D-U-N-S 20-034-5080   (HQ)
N. M. BARTLETT INC
4509 Bartlett Rd, Beamsville, ON, L0R 1B1
(905) 563-8261
Sales 29,700,800
SIC 5191 Farm supplies
Craig Bartlett
James C Bartlett
Donald Peters
David Bartlett

D-U-N-S 24-987-6673   (HQ)
NIAGARA PISTON INC
MAPLE MANUFACTURING, DIV OF
4708 Ontario St, Beamsville, ON, L0R 1B4
(905) 563-4981
Emp Here 53   Sales 23,727,358
SIC 3714 Motor vehicle parts and accessories
Michael Court
Suzanne Court
Philip Court

D-U-N-S 24-912-0072   (SL)
OPPLAST INC
4743 Christie Dr, Beamsville, ON, L0R 1B4
(905) 563-1462
Emp Here 55   Sales 11,104,335
SIC 3089 Plastics products, nec
Heiner Ophardt
Tony Knortleve-Snider
Sylvia Theroux

D-U-N-S 20-552-1110   (BR)
PARKER HANNIFIN CANADA
FLUID CONNECTORS DIV.
(Suby of PARKER-HANNIFIN CORPORA-
TION)
4635 Durham Rd Rr 3, Beamsville, ON, L0R
1B3

Emp Here 100
SIC 3714 Motor vehicle parts and accessories
Rich Braun

D-U-N-S 25-094-6738   (SL)
**PENINSULA RIDGE ESTATES WINERY LIM-
ITED**
5600 King St Rr 3, Beamsville, ON, L0R 1B3
(905) 563-0900
Emp Here 20   Sales 10,006,500
SIC 5182 Wine and distilled beverages
Norman Beal
Nancy Mcnally

D-U-N-S 20-793-0806   (BR)
SOBEYS CAPITAL INCORPORATED
(Suby of EMPIRE COMPANY LIMITED)
4610 Ontario St, Beamsville, ON, L0R 1B3
(905) 563-1088
Emp Here 110
SIC 5411 Grocery stores
Nikki Unrau

D-U-N-S 24-685-1778   (HQ)
WESTBROOK FLORAL LTD
(Suby of FLORAL GROUP LTD, THE)
4994 North Service Rd, Beamsville, ON, L0R
1B3

(905) 945-9611
Emp Here 150   Sales 45,728,220
SIC 5193 Flowers and florists supplies
Peter John Vermeer
David Vermeer
William Vermeer
Ian Vermeer
Arthur Vermeer
Charles Vermeer

D-U-N-S 20-051-4537   (HQ)
WESTBROOK GREENHOUSES LIMITED
(Suby of FLORAL GROUP LTD, THE)
4994 North Service Rd, Beamsville, ON, L0R
1B3
(289) 432-1199
Emp Here 60   Sales 20,984,720
SIC 0181 Ornamental nursery products
Ian Vermeer
Charles Vermeer

Beeton, ON L0G

D-U-N-S 20-747-7055   (SL)
BOND HEAD GOLF RESORT INC
CLUB AT BOND HEAD, THE
(Suby of GIAMPAOLO INVESTMENTS LIM-
ITED)
4805 7th Line Rr 1, Beeton, ON, L0G 1A0
(905) 778-9400
Emp Here 120   Sales 9,425,400
SIC 7992 Public golf courses
Joe Caruso

D-U-N-S 20-034-6930   (SL)
**BORDEN METAL PRODUCTS (CANADA)
LIMITED**
50 Dayfoot St, Beeton, ON, L0G 1A0
(905) 729-2229
Emp Here 55   Sales 10,564,675
SIC 3446 Architectural Metalwork
James Sealy

D-U-N-S 20-535-5048   (BR)
GOVERNMENT OF ONTARIO
D.A.R.E. (DRUG ABUSE RESISTANCE EDU-
CATION) ONTARIO
(Suby of GOVERNMENT OF ONTARIO)
29 Main St W, Beeton, ON, L0G 1A0
(905) 729-4004
Emp Here 75
SIC 8069 Specialty hospitals, except psychi-
atric

D-U-N-S 25-312-6478   (SL)
PROTOTIER-1 INC
3690 Adjala-Tecumseth Townline Suite 2,
Beeton, ON, L0G 1A0
(705) 434-0457
Emp Here 31   Sales 14,725,806
SIC 5084 Industrial machinery and equipment
Wieslaw Koziorowski
Shawn Murray

D-U-N-S 24-047-5772   (SL)
SIMCOE MANOR HOME FOR THE AGED
(Suby of CORPORATION OF THE COUNTY
OF SIMCOE)
5988 8th Line, Beeton, ON, L0G 1A0
(905) 729-2267
Emp Here 160   Sales 10,285,120
SIC 8361 Residential care
Fagan Fagan

Belle River, ON N0R

D-U-N-S 24-624-4479   (SL)
822188 ONTARIO INC
LA CHAUMIERE RETIREMENT RESIDENCE
1023 County Rd 22, Belle River, ON, N0R 1A0
(519) 727-5506
Emp Here 50   Sales 11,323,700

SIC 6513 Apartment building operators
Greg Goutis
Catherine Vankoughnett

D-U-N-S 25-249-1832   (BR)
**GREATER ESSEX COUNTY DISTRICT
SCHOOL BOARD**
BELLE RIVER DISTRICT HIGH SCHOOL
(Suby of GREATER ESSEX COUNTY DIS-
TRICT SCHOOL BOARD)
333 South St, Belle River, ON, N0R 1A0
(519) 728-1212
Emp Here 80
SIC 8211 Elementary and secondary schools
Larry Ash

D-U-N-S 20-800-6507   (SL)
KNIGHTS OF COLUMBUS
COLUMBUS CLUB
1303 County Rd 22, Belle River, ON, N0R 1A0

Emp Here 40   Sales 15,896,560
SIC 8699 Membership organizations, nec
John Chenier

D-U-N-S 24-770-7250   (HQ)
LEKTER INDUSTRIAL SERVICES INC
500 Harvard Dr Rr 1, Belle River, ON, N0R
1A0
(519) 727-3713
Sales 11,653,250
SIC 1711 Plumbing, heating, air-conditioning
David Holek
Paul Mastronardi
Debra Holek
Pam Mastronardi
John Kennedy
Brad Fahringer

D-U-N-S 25-717-0340   (SL)
WILF'S DRUG STORE LTD
SHOPPERS DRUG MART
330 Notre Dame St, Belle River, ON, N0R 1A0
(519) 728-1610
Emp Here 40   Sales 10,118,160
SIC 5912 Drug stores and proprietary stores
Wilf Fortowsky

Belleville, ON K8N

D-U-N-S 25-685-2328   (SL)
1203130 ONTARIO INC
MILL-FAB
391 College St E, Belleville, ON, K8N 5S7
(613) 962-9003
Emp Here 65   Sales 16,002,090
SIC 1796 Installing building equipment
Andy Vos
Adam Vos

D-U-N-S 24-396-2425   (HQ)
1211084 ONTARIO LTD
PETRO CANADA
6521 Hwy 62, Belleville, ON, K8N 4Z5
(613) 968-6811
Emp Here 10   Sales 24,903,900
SIC 5541 Gasoline service stations
Ash Fadil

D-U-N-S 24-764-0204   (SL)
1607408 ONTARIO INC
CLUTE, BOB SATURN
720 Dundas St W, Belleville, ON, K8N 4Z2
(613) 969-1166
Emp Here 21   Sales 10,459,638
SIC 5511 New and used car dealers
Bob Clute

D-U-N-S 24-198-9821   (SL)
381611 ONTARIO LTD
LOYALIST PROTECTION SERVICE
60 Dundas St E, Belleville, ON, K8N 1B8

Emp Here 25   Sales 11,179,350

SIC 5063 Electrical apparatus and equipment
Deryk Mcgrath

D-U-N-S 24-559-5269   (SL)
621509 ONTARIO INC
BELLEVILLE CHRYSLER DODGE JEEP
658 Dundas St W, Belleville, ON, K8N 4Z2
(613) 966-9936
Emp Here 50   Sales 24,903,900
SIC 5511 New and used car dealers
Ralph Neale

D-U-N-S 25-455-6814   (SL)
995451 ONTARIO INC
QUALITY MECHANICAL
1806 Casey Rd Suite 6, Belleville, ON, K8N
4Z6
(613) 969-7403
Emp Here 80   Sales 18,645,200
SIC 1711 Plumbing, heating, air-conditioning
Roger Chartrand

D-U-N-S 20-073-0872   (HQ)
**ACCESS CENTRE FOR HASTINGS AND
PRINCE EDWARD COUNTIES, THE**
470 Dundas St E, Belleville, ON, K8N 1G1
(613) 962-7272
Emp Here 1   Sales 19,321,200
SIC 8621 Professional organizations
Jackie Redmond

D-U-N-S 25-237-7965   (BR)
**ALGONQUIN & LAKESHORE CATHOLIC
DISTRICT SCHOOL BOARD**
NICHOLSON CATHOLIC COLLEGE
301 Church St, Belleville, ON, K8N 3C7
(613) 967-0404
Emp Here 80
SIC 8211 Elementary and secondary schools
Janet Demaiter

D-U-N-S 20-536-1694   (HQ)
BARDON SUPPLIES LIMITED
(Suby of ENTREPRISES MIRCA INC, LES)
405 College St E, Belleville, ON, K8N 4Z6
(613) 966-5643
Emp Here 60   Sales 115,931,088
SIC 5074 Plumbing and heating equipment
and supplies (hydronics)
Barry Raycroft

D-U-N-S 25-246-8285   (SL)
BELLEVILLE METAL SALES LIMITED
222 University Ave, Belleville, ON, K8N 5S5
(613) 968-2188
Emp Here 10   Sales 10,003,390
SIC 5051 Metals service centers and offices
Edwin (Ted) Zurrer
Melanie Mckee

D-U-N-S 25-073-3888   (SL)
BELLEVUE FABRICATING LTD
525 Bellevue Dr, Belleville, ON, K8N 4Z5
(613) 968-6721
Emp Here 80   Sales 15,366,800
SIC 3441 Fabricated structural Metal
Peter Lammers

D-U-N-S 20-034-8944   (HQ)
**CAMPBELL MONUMENT COMPANY LIM-
ITED**
LINDSAY MONUMENTS, DIV OF
712 Dundas St W, Belleville, ON, K8N 4Z2
(613) 966-5154
Emp Here 22   Sales 10,419,200
SIC 5999 Miscellaneous retail stores, nec
Gary Foster

D-U-N-S 24-346-4430   (BR)
**CANADIAN CORPS OF COMMISSION-
AIRES NATIONAL OFFICE, THE**
CANADIAN CORPS OF COMMISSION-
AIRES BELLEVILLE DETACHMENT QUINTE
AREA
(Suby of CANADIAN CORPS OF COMMIS-
SIONAIRES NATIONAL OFFICE, THE)
314 Pinnacle St Unit 2, Belleville, ON, K8N
3B4

(613) 962-6500
Emp Here 100
SIC 6289 Security and commodity service
Hue Brennen

D-U-N-S 25-687-0247   (HQ)
CENTURY 21 LANTHORN REAL ESTATE LTD
266 Front St Unit 202, Belleville, ON, K8N 2Z2
(613) 967-2100
Emp Here 25   *Sales* 37,700,010
SIC 6531 Real estate agents and managers
William Rorabeck
James Alexander

D-U-N-S 25-182-7002   (SL)
CLUTE, BOB PONTIAC BUICK GMC LTD
CLUTE, BOB GM
6692 Hwy 62, Belleville, ON, K8N 4Z5
(613) 962-4584
Emp Here 60   *Sales* 37,756,800
SIC 5511 New and used car dealers
Bob Clute
Cindy Jones

D-U-N-S 20-321-9886   (BR)
COCO PAVING INC
(*Suby of* COCO PAVING INC)
6520 Hwy 62, Belleville, ON, K8N 4Z5
(613) 962-3461
Emp Here 90
SIC 1611 Highway and street construction

D-U-N-S 20-210-1999   (HQ)
COMMUNITY LIVING BELLEVILLE AND AREA
91 Millennium Pky, Belleville, ON, K8N 4Z5
(613) 969-7407
Emp Here 1   *Sales* 13,665,200
SIC 8059 Nursing and personal care, nec
John Klassen

D-U-N-S 20-573-2659   (BR)
COMPAGNIE DES CHEMINS DE FER NATIONAUX DU CANADA
(*Suby of* COMPAGNIE DES CHEMINS DE FER NATIONAUX DU CANADA)
257 Airport Pky, Belleville, ON, K8N 4Z6
(613) 969-2247
Emp Here 200
SIC 4011 Railroads, line-haul operating
Ricardo Romero

D-U-N-S 24-408-3853   (SL)
COONEY BULK SALES LIMITED
(*Suby of* COONEY GROUP INC)
77 Bellevue Dr, Belleville, ON, K8N 4Z5
(613) 962-6666
Emp Here 150   *Sales* 30,855,900
SIC 4212 Local trucking, without storage
Gary Cooney

D-U-N-S 24-321-7945   (HQ)
COONEY GROUP INC
77 Bellevue Dr, Belleville, ON, K8N 4Z5
(613) 962-6666
Sales 41,002,500
SIC 6712 Bank holding companies
Gary Cooney

D-U-N-S 20-178-9641   (HQ)
COONEY TRANSPORT LTD
77 Bellevue Dr, Belleville, ON, K8N 4Z5
(613) 962-6666
Emp Here 75   *Sales* 55,314,300
SIC 4213 Trucking, except local
Gary T Cooney
Wendy Meraw

D-U-N-S 24-756-8546   (HQ)
CORNERSTONE BUILDERS LTD
195 Bellevue Dr, Belleville, ON, K8N 4Z5
(613) 968-3501
Emp Here 45   *Sales* 34,220,280
SIC 1542 Nonresidential construction, nec
Marko Turcotte
Dan Lucas

D-U-N-S 24-101-9512   (HQ)

DCB BUSINESS SYSTEMS GROUP INC
OT GROUP
175 Lahr Dr, Belleville, ON, K8N 5S2
(613) 966-6315
Sales 16,280,000
SIC 5999 Miscellaneous retail stores, nec
Douglas Bell

D-U-N-S 20-902-1245   (SL)
ELECTROLAB LIMITED
ELECTROLAB TRAINING SYSTEMS
631 College St E, Belleville, ON, K8N 0A3
(613) 962-9577
Emp Here 85   *Sales* 21,546,650
SIC 8748 Business consulting, nec
Lawrence Wilson
Donald Wilson
Barbara Tait
Norman Wilson
Carolyn Wilson

D-U-N-S 24-848-3067   (SL)
EMS-TECH INC
699 Dundas St W, Belleville, ON, K8N 4Z2
(613) 966-6611
Emp Here 70   *Sales* 12,317,060
SIC 8711 Engineering services
Peter Sorensen
Brian Stafford

D-U-N-S 24-960-7644   (SL)
EXIT REALTY GROUP BROKERAGE
5503 62 Hwy, Belleville, ON, K8N 4Z7
(613) 966-9400
Emp Here 40   *Sales* 10,870,240
SIC 6531 Real estate agents and managers
Sharon Short

D-U-N-S 25-347-8317   (SL)
FRONTIER DISCOUNT HOBBIES LTD
FRONTIER SECURITY SERVICES
277 Front St, Belleville, ON, K8N 2Z6
(613) 967-2845
Emp Here 30   *Sales* 15,936,210
SIC 6211 Security brokers and dealers
Bernie Boudreau

D-U-N-S 20-034-9868   (HQ)
GEEN'S PRESCRIPTION PHARMACY LIMITED
PHARMASAVE
276 Front St, Belleville, ON, K8N 2Z8
(613) 962-4579
Sales 12,647,700
SIC 5912 Drug stores and proprietary stores

D-U-N-S 24-388-0171   (HQ)
GLYNSKAR ENTERPRISES LTD
260 Adam St, Belleville, ON, K8N 5S4
(613) 962-5100
Emp Here 50   *Sales* 18,479,800
SIC 4899 Communication services, nec
Kristin Crow

D-U-N-S 20-613-9565   (HQ)
HANLEY CORPORATION
TIM HORTONS,DIVISION OF
289 Front St, Belleville, ON, K8N 2Z6
(613) 967-1771
Sales 16,141,235
SIC 5461 Retail bakeries
Mark Hanley
Mary Hanley

D-U-N-S 24-079-0402   (SL)
HANNAFIN, E.J. ENTERPRISES LIMITED
10 ACRE TRUCK STOP
(*Suby of* BELSHIELD CORPORATE GROUP LIMITED)
57 Cannifton Rd, Belleville, ON, K8N 4V1
(613) 966-7017
Emp Here 80
SIC 5541 Gasoline service stations
J. Roland Belanger
John Belanger

D-U-N-S 25-413-9595   (HQ)
HANON SYSTEMS CANADA INC

HANON SYSTEMS CANADA PLANT 2
(*Suby of* HAHN & CO. AUTO HOLDINGS CO., LTD.)
360 University Ave Suite 2, Belleville, ON, K8N 5T6
(613) 969-1460
Emp Here 460   *Sales* 139,608,000
SIC 3714 Motor vehicle parts and accessories
Rene Veillette
Shane Lumley

D-U-N-S 24-426-2635   (SL)
INTEGRICO INC
AUNTIE ANNE'S PRETZELS
199 Front St Suite 215, Belleville, ON, K8N 5H5
(613) 966-6466
Emp Here 40   *Sales* 27,872,400
SIC 6794 Patent owners and lessors
Maurice Rollins
Mark Rollins

D-U-N-S 24-964-4915   (HQ)
INTERNATIONAL TRUCKLOAD SERVICES INC
(*Suby of* ITS HOLDINGS INC)
107 Bellevue Dr, Belleville, ON, K8N 4Z5
(613) 961-5144
Emp Here 250   *Sales* 65,691,696
SIC 4213 Trucking, except local
Max Haggarty
Robert Haggarty
Fred La Brash
Catherine Melanson
Pamela Haggarty

D-U-N-S 20-035-0569   (SL)
KELLY, PAUL (1993) LIMITED
KELLY'S HOME HEALTH CARE
411 Bridge St E, Belleville, ON, K8N 1P7
(613) 962-5387
Emp Here 60   *Sales* 14,659,680
SIC 5912 Drug stores and proprietary stores
Paul Joseph Kelly

D-U-N-S 24-868-9770   (SL)
KENNAMETAL STELLITE, INC
(*Suby of* KENNAMETAL INC.)
471 Dundas St E, Belleville, ON, K8N 1G2
(613) 968-3481
Emp Here 136   *Sales* 24,668,768
SIC 3369 Nonferrous foundries, nec
Don Williams

D-U-N-S 24-802-2733   (SL)
L.M.B TRANSPORT LIMITED
209 Puttman Industrial Rd, Belleville, ON, K8N 4Z6
(613) 968-7541
Emp Here 75   *Sales* 21,247,500
SIC 7532 Top and body repair and paint shops
Larry Brown
Gail Brown

D-U-N-S 24-946-6087   (HQ)
MAXWELL PAPER CANADA INC
MAXWELL MEDIA PRODUCTS
270 Front St, Belleville, ON, K8N 2Z2
(613) 962-7846
Emp Here 75   *Sales* 69,595,760
SIC 5044 Office equipment
Adrian Hilmi
Colette Hilmi

D-U-N-S 20-878-7713   (HQ)
MCDOUGALL INSURANCE BROKERS LIMITED
199 Front St Suite 401, Belleville, ON, K8N 5H5
(613) 966-7001
Emp Here 35   *Sales* 181,078,716
SIC 6411 Insurance agents, brokers, and service
Ross Mcdougall
Donald Stanton

D-U-N-S 20-823-4963   (HQ)
MEYERS TRANSPORT LIMITED

(*Suby of* MOSAIC LOGISTICS LIMITED)
53 Grills Rd, Belleville, ON, K8N 4Z5
(613) 967-8440
Emp Here 50   *Sales* 87,580,975
SIC 4213 Trucking, except local
Larry Meyers
Evan Meyers
David Joyce
Mireille Meyers

D-U-N-S 20-938-7471   (SL)
MID-WAY MOTORS (QUINTE) LIMITED
BELLEVILLE TOYOTA
48 Millennium Pky, Belleville, ON, K8N 4Z5
(613) 968-4538
Emp Here 25   *Sales* 12,451,950
SIC 5511 New and used car dealers
Gino Caletti
Mary Caletti

D-U-N-S 25-858-1743   (SL)
PATHWAYS TO INDEPENDENCE
289 Pinnacle St, Belleville, ON, K8N 3B3
(613) 962-2541
Emp Here 315   *Sales* 65,226,420
SIC 8399 Social services, nec
Lorrie Heffernan

D-U-N-S 25-586-0348   (HQ)
PROALLIANCE REALTY CORPORATION
ROYAL LEPAGE PROALLIANCE REALTY
357 Front St, Belleville, ON, K8N 2Z9
(613) 966-6060
Emp Here 25   *Sales* 36,862,232
SIC 6531 Real estate agents and managers
Mark Rashotte

D-U-N-S 24-316-1911   (BR)
PROCTER & GAMBLE INC
(*Suby of* THE PROCTER & GAMBLE COMPANY)
355 University Ave, Belleville, ON, K8N 5T8
(613) 966-5130
Emp Here 400
SIC 2676 Sanitary paper products
Can Akcadag

D-U-N-S 24-418-5161   (SL)
QUEST-TECH PRECISION INC
193 Jamieson Bone Rd, Belleville, ON, K8N 5T4
(613) 966-7551
Emp Here 55   *Sales* 10,564,675
SIC 3444 Sheet Metalwork
Ahmad Khodkar
Steve Evans

D-U-N-S 20-035-1724   (HQ)
QUINTE BROADCASTING COMPANY LIMITED
CJBQ RADIO
10 South Front St, Belleville, ON, K8N 2Y3
(613) 969-5555
Emp Here 55   *Sales* 13,022,904
SIC 4832 Radio broadcasting stations
William Morton
Virginia Morton
Cynthia Thorne
Joyce Mulock
Stephen Morton

D-U-N-S 25-675-0175   (HQ)
QUINTE HEALTHCARE CORPORATION
QHC
265 Dundas St E, Belleville, ON, K8N 5A9
(613) 969-7400
Emp Here 1,400   *Sales* 194,390,000
SIC 8062 General medical and surgical hospitals
Mary Claire Egberts
Carol Smith Romeril
Brad Harrington
Jeff Hohenkerk
Karen Baker
Paul Mcauley
Susan Rowe
Douglas Mcgregor

Stuart Wright
Dick Zoutman

D-U-N-S 24-344-5124   (BR)
SERVICES FINANCIERS NCO, INC
(*Suby of* GATESTONE & CO. INC)
610 Dundas St E, Belleville, ON, K8N 1G7

Emp Here 500
SIC 7322 Adjustment and collection services

D-U-N-S 25-639-3299   (SL)
SMITH, PETER CHEVROLET CADILLAC LTD
42 Towncentre Rd, Belleville, ON, K8N 4Z5
(613) 968-6767
Emp Here 40   Sales 19,923,120
SIC 5511 New and used car dealers
Peter Smith

D-U-N-S 20-414-5197   (SL)
SPRAGUE FOODS LIMITED
,
385 College St E, Belleville, ON, K8N 5S7
(613) 966-1200
Emp Here 45   Sales 10,118,475
SIC 2032 Canned specialties
Richard Sprague
Dana Sprague
Kelly Himberg-Larsen

D-U-N-S 20-035-2425   (SL)
STEGG LIMITED
294 University Ave, Belleville, ON, K8N 5S6
(613) 966-4000
Emp Here 100   Sales 26,765,200
SIC 5251 Hardware stores
Bob Stokes
Dave Smart

D-U-N-S 20-325-0238   (SL)
STREAMLINE FOODS INC.
(*Suby of* FANJUL CORP.)
315 University Ave, Belleville, ON, K8N 5T7
(613) 961-1265
Emp Here 80   Sales 27,655,200
SIC 2061 Raw cane sugar
Jonathan Bamberger

D-U-N-S 24-345-7145   (BR)
TRENTWAY-WAGAR INC
COACH CANADA
(*Suby of* COACH USA ADMINISTRATION, INC.)
75 Bridge St E, Belleville, ON, K8N 1L9
(613) 962-2163
Emp Here 265
SIC 5963 Direct selling establishments
Pam Richardson

D-U-N-S 24-022-2351   (SL)
ULTIMATE POWER SPORTS INC
1037 Wallbridge Rd, Belleville, ON, K8N 4Z5

Emp Here 22   Sales 10,957,716
SIC 5571 Motorcycle dealers
Ralph Neale

D-U-N-S 25-725-3278   (BR)
WAL-MART CANADA CORP
(*Suby of* WALMART INC.)
274 Millennium Pky, Belleville, ON, K8N 4Z5
(613) 966-9466
Emp Here 200
SIC 5311 Department stores
Richard Everitt

Belleville, ON K8P

D-U-N-S 25-203-3816   (SL)
959009 ONTARIO INC
EAST SIDE MARIO'S
390 North Front St, Belleville, ON, K8P 3E1
(613) 962-8440
Emp Here 200   Sales 9,103,800

SIC 5812 Eating places
Todd Fletcher

D-U-N-S 20-928-3253   (BR)
BEAUTYROCK HOLDINGS INC
3 Applewood Dr Suite 3, Belleville, ON, K8P 4E3
(613) 932-2525
Emp Here 200
SIC 7389 Business services, nec
Stan Body

D-U-N-S 20-785-7822   (SL)
BELCREST NURSING HOMES LIMITED
BELMONT LONG TERM CARE FACILITY
250 Bridge St W Suite 241, Belleville, ON, K8P 5N3
(613) 968-4434
Emp Here 160   Sales 10,970,560
SIC 8051 Skilled nursing care facilities
J David Clegg

D-U-N-S 24-794-7497   (SL)
BLUE STAR NUTRACEUTICALS INC
180 North Front St Unit 6, Belleville, ON, K8P 3B9
(613) 968-2278
Emp Here 23   Sales 19,218,271
SIC 5149 Groceries and related products, nec
Adam Cloet

D-U-N-S 20-708-2087   (SL)
BUTLER BUILDINGS CANADA
5 Harvest Cres, Belleville, ON, K8P 4M2

Emp Here 60   Sales 25,364,220
SIC 1541 Industrial buildings and warehouses
Chris Ripley

D-U-N-S 24-774-1437   (BR)
CBI LIMITED
(*Suby of* CBI LIMITED)
11 Bay Bridge Rd, Belleville, ON, K8P 3P6
(613) 962-3426
Emp Here 100
SIC 8741 Management services

D-U-N-S 25-585-9696   (BR)
CROWN RIDGE HEALTH CARE SERVICES INC
WESTGATE LODGE
(*Suby of* CROWN RIDGE HEALTH CARE SERVICES INC)
37 Wilkie St, Belleville, ON, K8P 4E4
(613) 966-1323
Emp Here 85
SIC 8051 Skilled nursing care facilities
Leslie Morrow

D-U-N-S 20-734-5927   (SL)
FRY, BENTON FORD SALES LTD
321 North Front St, Belleville, ON, K8P 3C6
(613) 962-9141
Emp Here 40   Sales 19,923,120
SIC 5511 New and used car dealers
Benton Fry

D-U-N-S 20-034-9330   (HQ)
GOOD WATER COMPANY LTD, THE
CULLIGAN OF BELLEVILLE
163 College St W, Belleville, ON, K8P 2G7
(613) 707-8400
Emp Here 20   Sales 29,199,235
SIC 7389 Business services, nec
Paul Moorman
Ronald Moorman
Robert (Bob) Leslie
Stephen Buchanan

D-U-N-S 25-237-7882   (BR)
HASTINGS AND PRINCE EDWARD DISTRICT SCHOOL BOARD
WILLIAM R KIRK SCHOOL
224 Palmer Rd, Belleville, ON, K8P 4E1
(613) 962-2516
Emp Here 86
SIC 8211 Elementary and secondary schools
Ronald Moffatt

D-U-N-S 25-237-8120   (BR)
HASTINGS AND PRINCE EDWARD DISTRICT SCHOOL BOARD
QUINTE SECONDARY SCHOOL
45 College St W, Belleville, ON, K8P 2G3
(613) 962-9295
Emp Here 90
SIC 8211 Elementary and secondary schools
Liane Woodley

D-U-N-S 25-237-8096   (BR)
HASTINGS AND PRINCE EDWARD DISTRICT SCHOOL BOARD
CENTENNIAL SECONDARY SCHOOL
160 Palmer Rd, Belleville, ON, K8P 4E1
(613) 962-9233
Emp Here 75
SIC 8211 Elementary and secondary schools
Kim Sampson

D-U-N-S 20-939-1333   (HQ)
HASTINGS PRINCE EDWARD PUBLIC HEALTH
HASTINGS & PRINCE EDWARD COUNTIES HEALTH UNIT
179 North Park St, Belleville, ON, K8P 4P1
(613) 966-5500
Emp Here 90   Sales 24,726,910
SIC 8011 Offices and clinics of medical doctors
Dale Jackson
Richard Schabas

D-U-N-S 25-777-2004   (HQ)
HIGHLAND SHORES CHILDREN'S AID SOCIETY
363 Dundas St W, Belleville, ON, K8P 1B3
(613) 962-9291
Emp Here 100   Sales 47,126,347
SIC 8322 Individual and family services
Mark Kartusch

D-U-N-S 25-174-2011   (BR)
HOME DEPOT OF CANADA INC
(*Suby of* THE HOME DEPOT INC)
210 Bell Blvd, Belleville, ON, K8P 5L8
(613) 961-5340
Emp Here 150
SIC 5251 Hardware stores
Bry Love

D-U-N-S 20-035-0460   (SL)
MCCULLOUGH, D.E. ENTERPRISES LTD
CANADIAN TIRE STORE
101 Bell Blvd, Belleville, ON, K8P 4V2
(613) 968-6701
Emp Here 83   Sales 52,230,240
SIC 5531 Auto and home supply stores
Dennis Mccoullough

D-U-N-S 20-555-6553   (BR)
METRO ONTARIO INC
METRO
(*Suby of* METRO INC)
110 North Front St, Belleville, ON, K8P 5J8
(613) 962-0056
Emp Here 110
SIC 5411 Grocery stores
Sarah Mccauley

D-U-N-S 24-796-1613   (HQ)
METSO MINERALS CANADA INC
MINERAUX METSO (CANADA)
(*Suby of* METSO OYJ)
161 Bridge St W Unit 6, Belleville, ON, K8P 1K2
(613) 962-3411
Emp Here 60   Sales 70,219,250
SIC 3569 General industrial machinery, nec
Robert M. Wissing
Todd A. Dillmann
Kim Clark

D-U-N-S 25-486-7633   (BR)
NORTEL NETWORKS LIMITED
(*Suby of* NORTEL NETWORKS LIMITED)
250 Sidney St, Belleville, ON, K8P 3Z3

Emp Here 1,000
SIC 4899 Communication services, nec

D-U-N-S 24-007-9525   (HQ)
NORTH FRONT MOTORS INC
BELLVILLE VOLKSWAGON
239 North Front St, Belleville, ON, K8P 3C3
(613) 966-3333
Emp Here 20   Sales 10,459,638
SIC 5511 New and used car dealers
Michael Bandler

D-U-N-S 20-976-1423   (SL)
NORTH FRONT PRICE CHOPPER
305 North Front St Suite 5, Belleville, ON, K8P 3C3
(613) 966-0270
Emp Here 55   Sales 16,141,235
SIC 5411 Grocery stores
Bill Mcmillan

D-U-N-S 20-920-8131   (SL)
PARKHURST, AL TRANSPORTATION LTD
125 College St E, Belleville, ON, K8P 5A2
(613) 969-0606
Emp Here 80   Sales 4,389,760
SIC 4151 School buses
Alvin Parkhurst
John James (Jim) Parkhurst

D-U-N-S 20-203-5429   (HQ)
RE MAX QUINTE LTD
308 North Front St, Belleville, ON, K8P 3C4
(613) 969-9907
Emp Here 21   Sales 10,054,972
SIC 6531 Real estate agents and managers
Mary Jane Mills

D-U-N-S 20-400-6274   (HQ)
REID'S DAIRY COMPANY LIMITED, THE
222 Bell Blvd, Belleville, ON, K8P 5L7
(613) 967-1970
Sales 17,630,190
SIC 2024 Ice cream and frozen deserts
Stephen Quickert
Armin Quickert
Marilyn Quickert
David Quickert

D-U-N-S 25-278-8096   (SL)
SIR JAMES WHITNEY SCHOOL FOR THE DEAF
350 Dundas St W, Belleville, ON, K8P 1B2
(613) 967-2823
Emp Here 100   Sales 9,282,600
SIC 8211 Elementary and secondary schools
Linda Ritchey

D-U-N-S 24-326-5944   (HQ)
SULLIVAN, EVAN PHARMACY LIMITED
SHOPPERS DRUG MART
150 Sidney St Suite 1, Belleville, ON, K8P 5E2
(613) 962-3406
Emp Here 8   Sales 16,614,304
SIC 5912 Drug stores and proprietary stores
Evan Sullivan

D-U-N-S 24-229-0323   (SL)
TAYLOR HILL DEVELOPMENTS
106 North Front St, Belleville, ON, K8P 3B4
(613) 969-9907
Emp Here 4   Sales 12,788,200
SIC 1382 Oil and gas exploration services
Sean Mckinney

D-U-N-S 20-613-9870   (SL)
TIM HORTONS
165 College St W, Belleville, ON, K8P 2G7
(613) 967-2197
Emp Here 50   Sales 13,707,600
SIC 5461 Retail bakeries
Jamie Sine

D-U-N-S 20-641-7383   (BR)
UNIFOR
CAW LOCAL 1839
(*Suby of* UNIFOR)
160 Catharine St, Belleville, ON, K8P 1M8

▲ Public Company   ■ Public Company Family Member   **HQ** Headquarters   **BR** Branch   **SL** Single Location

(613) 962-8122
Emp Here 85
SIC 8631 Labor organizations
Peter Duffey

Belmont, ON N0L

D-U-N-S 25-633-4467   (SL)
WESTMINSTER MUTUAL INSURANCE COMPANY
14122 Belmont Rd, Belmont, ON, N0L 1B0
(519) 644-1663
Emp Here 22   *Sales* 27,179,196
SIC 6331 Fire, marine, and casualty insurance

Big Trout Lake, ON P0V

D-U-N-S 24-032-1286   (SL)
BIG TROUT LAKE BAND PERSONNEL OFFICE
Gd, Big Trout Lake, ON, P0V 1G0

Emp Here 200   *Sales* 287,720,200
SIC 8699 Membership organizations, nec
Donny Morris

Binbrook, ON L0R

D-U-N-S 24-676-4984   (BR)
HAMILTON-WENTWORTH   CATHOLIC SCHOOL BOARD
ST MATTHEW CATHOLIC ELEMENTARY SCHOOL
(*Suby of* HAMILTON-WENTWORTH CATHOLIC SCHOOL BOARD)
200 Windwood Dr, Binbrook, ON, L0R 1C0
(905) 523-2316
Emp Here 80
SIC 8211 Elementary and secondary schools
Flora Nordoff

D-U-N-S 20-702-7236   (SL)
O'NEIL'S FARM EQUIPMENT (1971) LIMITED
2461 Hwy 56, Binbrook, ON, L0R 1C0
(905) 572-6714
Emp Here 26   *Sales* 12,350,676
SIC 5083 Farm and garden machinery
Larry Smith
Craig Smith
Carolyn Smith

Blackstock, ON L0B

D-U-N-S 25-115-8622   (SL)
SWEDA FARMS LTD
3880 Edgerton Rd Ss 101, Blackstock, ON, L0B 1B0
(905) 986-5747
Emp Here 50   *Sales* 19,275,950
SIC 0252 Chicken eggs
Svante Lind

Blenheim, ON N0P

D-U-N-S 20-969-4020   (SL)
1520202 ONTARIO LTD
RON'S NO FRILLS
286 Chatham St N Rr 5, Blenheim, ON, N0P 1A0
(519) 676-0353
Emp Here 56   *Sales* 16,434,712

SIC 5411 Grocery stores
Ron Roy

D-U-N-S 25-372-8604   (SL)
2027844 ONTARIO INC
SINTERIS
(*Suby of* CHARTER OAK EQUITY, LP)
325 Chatham St N, Blenheim, ON, N0P 1A0
(519) 676-8161
Emp Here 83   *Sales* 11,675,820
SIC 3714 Motor vehicle parts and accessories
Phil Goodwin
Rick Armstrong
Betty Ann Kelly
Brandy Minnie

D-U-N-S 20-188-6145   (SL)
932072 ONTARIO LIMITED
25 Graham St, Blenheim, ON, N0P 1A0
(519) 676-5198
Emp Here 75   *Sales* 19,616,475
SIC 6712 Bank holding companies
Wendie Stafford

D-U-N-S 20-793-0731   (SL)
BLENHEIM SOBEY'S
20210 Communication Rd, Blenheim, ON, N0P 1A0
(519) 676-9044
Emp Here 125   *Sales* 36,684,625
SIC 5411 Grocery stores
Tim Flanagan

D-U-N-S 24-373-4592   (SL)
HOPKINS CANADA, INC
(*Suby of* HOPKINS MANUFACTURING CORPORATION)
281 Chatham St S, Blenheim, ON, N0P 1A0
(519) 676-5441
Emp Here 150   *Sales* 43,627,500
SIC 3714 Motor vehicle parts and accessories
Bradley Kraft
Louis Douramakos
Mike Williams
James Daniel

D-U-N-S 24-512-1512   (SL)
KONAL ENGINEERING AND EQUIPMENT INC
1 Graham St, Blenheim, ON, N0P 1A0
(519) 676-8133
Emp Here 70   *Sales* 15,540,070
SIC 3599 Industrial machinery, nec
Douglas Lammon
Brian Pougnet

D-U-N-S 20-462-4659   (SL)
PAT POLLOCK FARM
10972 Talbot Trail, Blenheim, ON, N0P 1A0
(519) 380-5940
Emp Here 31   *Sales* 10,616,477
SIC 0132 Tobacco
Pat Pollock

D-U-N-S 20-379-6248   (SL)
PLATINUM PRODUCE COMPANY
21037 Communication Rd, Blenheim, ON, N0P 1A0
(519) 676-1772
Emp Here 100   *Sales* 26,230,900
SIC 0182 Food crops grown under cover
Gerard Verbeek
Timothy Verbeek
Patrick Verbeek

D-U-N-S 24-487-7734   (BR)
REVERA LONG TERM CARE INC
BLENHEIM COMMUNITY VILLAGE RETIREMENT RESIDENCE
(*Suby of* GOVERNMENT OF CANADA)
10 Mary St, Blenheim, ON, N0P 1A0
(519) 676-8119
Emp Here 100
SIC 8051 Skilled nursing care facilities
Barb Ferren

D-U-N-S 24-218-1758   (HQ)
RM CLASSIC CARS INC

COLLECTOR CARS
1 Classic Car Dr Rr 5, Blenheim, ON, N0P 1A0
(519) 352-4575
Sales 24,760,835
SIC 7532 Top and body repair and paint shops
Robert Myers
Michael Fairbairn
Dan Warrener
Dan Spendick

D-U-N-S 20-327-6910   (SL)
RM SOTHEBY'S
1 Classic Car Dr, Blenheim, ON, N0P 1A0
(519) 352-4575
Emp Here 125   *Sales* 57,644,250
SIC 5012 Automobiles and other motor vehicles
Rob Myers

D-U-N-S 24-123-4327   (HQ)
ROL-LAND FARMS MUSHROOMS INC
19002 Communication Rd Rr 4, Blenheim, ON, N0P 1A0
(519) 676-8125
Sales 22,296,265
SIC 0182 Food crops grown under cover
Hendrik Vander Pol

D-U-N-S 25-974-4720   (SL)
SM FREIGHT INC
25 Graham St, Blenheim, ON, N0P 1A0
(519) 676-5198
Emp Here 75   *Sales* 11,114,400
SIC 4213 Trucking, except local
Wendie Stafford
Steve Hibbert

D-U-N-S 20-035-6111   (HQ)
THOMPSONS LIMITED
2 Hyland Dr, Blenheim, ON, N0P 1A0
(519) 676-5411
Emp Here 80   *Sales* 503,683,675
SIC 5153 Grain and field beans
Dawn Betancourt
Dave Wellington
Darcy Oliphant
Brian Harris
Gord Hyndman
Paul Johnston

Blind River, ON P0R

D-U-N-S 20-035-6699   (SL)
MILLTOWN MOTORS LIMITED
237 Causley St, Blind River, ON, P0R 1B0
(705) 356-2207
Emp Here 74   *Sales* 13,448,106
SIC 5511 New and used car dealers
Donald Lees Jr
Donald Lees

D-U-N-S 24-550-1775   (SL)
NORTH SHORE HEALTH NETWORK
NSHN
525 Causley St, Blind River, ON, P0R 1B0
(705) 356-1220
Emp Here 200   *Sales* 13,716,346
SIC 8062 General medical and surgical hospitals
Lisa High
Connie Lee
Dan Lewis
Lenka Snajdrova
Jennifer Stanton Smith
Donna Latulippe
John Frederick
Alex Solomon
Jack Cruikshank
Sharon Mackinnon

Bloomfield, ON K0K

D-U-N-S 25-590-9061   (BR)
HIGHLINE PRODUCE LIMITED
WELLINGTON MUSHROOM FARM
(*Suby of* SUMMIT FRESH PRODUCE LIMITED)
339 Conley Rd, Bloomfield, ON, K0K 1G0
(613) 399-3121
Emp Here 350
SIC 0182 Food crops grown under cover
Garry Lajoie

Blue Mountains, ON L9Y

D-U-N-S 24-024-9107   (BR)
INTRAWEST ULC
WESTIN TRILLIUM HOUSE BLUE MOUNTAIN, THE
(*Suby of* HAWK HOLDING COMPANY, LLC)
220 Gord Canning Dr, Blue Mountains, ON, L9Y 0V9
(705) 443-8080
Emp Here 80
SIC 7011 Hotels and motels
James Henry

D-U-N-S 20-262-5919   (BR)
INTRAWEST ULC
BLUE MOUNTAIN RESORT
(*Suby of* HAWK HOLDING COMPANY, LLC)
108 Jozo Weider Blvd, Blue Mountains, ON, L9Y 3Z2
(705) 445-0231
Emp Here 400
SIC 7011 Hotels and motels

Blyth, ON N0M

D-U-N-S 20-629-8622   (SL)
HOWSON & HOWSON LIMITED
HOWSON MILLS
232 Westmoreland St, Blyth, ON, N0M 1H0
(519) 523-4241
Emp Here 50   *Sales* 11,242,750
SIC 2041 Flour and other grain mill products
James Howson
Bruce Howson
Douglas Howson
William Howson
Steven Howson
Jeffrey Howson
William Frederick (Rick) Howson
Christopher Howson

D-U-N-S 20-716-5978   (HQ)
SPARLING'S PROPANE CO. LIMITED
(*Suby of* PARKLAND FUEL CORPORATION)
82948 London Rd, Blyth, ON, N0M 1H0
(519) 523-4256
Emp Here 30   *Sales* 10,261,776
SIC 5984 Liquefied petroleum gas dealers
Robert Espey
Jane Savage
Donna Strating
Allan Willms
Michael Lambert
Andrew Cruickshank
Mike Mcmillan
Robert Fink
Peter Kilty
William Rouse

Bobcaygeon, ON K0M

D-U-N-S 25-823-5753   (SL)
1179131 ONTARIO LIMITED
STRANG'S VALU-MART

▲ Public Company   ■ Public Company Family Member   **HQ** Headquarters   **BR** Branch   **SL** Single Location

101 East St S Suite 7, Bobcaygeon, ON, K0M 1A0
(705) 738-9811
Emp Here 50   *Sales* 13,707,600
SIC 5411 Grocery stores
  Fred Strang

D-U-N-S 20-405-5842   (SL)
BRITISH EMPIRE FUELS INC
41 Country Rd Suite 36, Bobcaygeon, ON, K0M 1A0
(705) 738-2121
Emp Here 27   *Sales* 12,663,135
SIC 5983 Fuel oil dealers
  Robert Whyte
  Gregory Whyte
  Madeline Whyte

D-U-N-S 20-904-0542   (SL)
CASE MANOR
28 Boyd St, Bobcaygeon, ON, K0M 1A0
(705) 738-2374
Emp Here 75   *Sales* 5,142,450
SIC 8051 Skilled nursing care facilities
  Maureen Rea

D-U-N-S 20-035-7903   (HQ)
KAWARTHA DAIRY LIMITED
3332 County Rd 36 S, Bobcaygeon, ON, K0M 1A0
(705) 738-5123
Emp Here 60   *Sales* 83,557,700
SIC 5143 Dairy products, except dried or canned
  Jeff Crowe
  Donald Crowe
  Blake Frazer

D-U-N-S 24-036-7347   (SL)
SPECIALTY CARE CASE MANOR INC
18 Boyd St, Bobcaygeon, ON, K0M 1A0
(705) 738-2374
Emp Here 100   *Sales* 6,873,300
SIC 8051 Skilled nursing care facilities
  Cindy Mcgregor

Bolton, ON L7E

D-U-N-S 24-360-1619   (SL)
1421239 ONTARIO INC
124 Commercial Rd, Bolton, ON, L7E 1K4
(905) 951-6800
Emp Here 125   *Sales* 34,168,750
SIC 6712 Bank holding companies
  Robert J Murray
  Michael Mccarron

D-U-N-S 25-197-2147   (SL)
429400 ONTARIO LTD
HIGH HILL COURIERS
6 Queen St N Suite 207, Bolton, ON, L7E 1C8
(905) 857-6949
Emp Here 27   *Sales* 11,974,230
SIC 7389 Business services, nec
  Rolland Williams

D-U-N-S 24-317-9897   (SL)
ADVANCED PRECAST INC
6 Nixon Rd, Bolton, ON, L7E 1K3
(905) 857-6111
Emp Here 60   *Sales* 11,671,750
SIC 3272 Concrete products, nec
  Mauro Brancaleoni
  Andy Bakhtiari

D-U-N-S 20-903-7779   (HQ)
AFA FOREST PRODUCTS INC
244 Ellwood Dr W, Bolton, ON, L7E 4W4
(905) 857-6423
Emp Here 35   *Sales* 96,836,760
SIC 5039 Construction materials, nec
  Murray Finkbiner
  Tracy James
  Grant Yegavian

D-U-N-S 20-183-8849   (SL)
AGROCROP EXPORTS LTD
100 Agrocrop Rd, Bolton, ON, L7E 4K4
(905) 458-4551
Emp Here 40   *Sales* 17,968,760
SIC 7389 Business services, nec
  Yash Karia
  Nirupama Karia

D-U-N-S 20-762-1629   (SL)
ALIMENTS SARDO INC., LES
SARDO FOODS
99 Pillsworth Rd, Bolton, ON, L7E 4E4
(905) 951-9096
Emp Here 50   *Sales* 11,242,750
SIC 2079 Edible fats and oils
  Mario Sardo

D-U-N-S 24-662-6316   (HQ)
ALLIANCE AGRI-TURF INC
8112 King St, Bolton, ON, L7E 0T8
(905) 857-2000
Emp Here 1   *Sales* 14,430,065
SIC 3523 Farm machinery and equipment
  David Moore

D-U-N-S 20-560-9113   (SL)
ALLIANCE FORMING LTD
(Suby of VERDI INC)
91 Parr Blvd, Bolton, ON, L7E 4E3
(416) 749-5030
Emp Here 150   *Sales* 49,217,250
SIC 1623 Water, sewer, and utility lines
  Denis Fulan
  Joseph Boner
  Dario Favot

D-U-N-S 24-195-8529   (HQ)
ALUMA SYSTEMS INC
(Suby of BRAND INDUSTRIAL SERVICES, INC.)
2 Manchester Crt, Bolton, ON, L7E 2J3
(905) 669-5282
Emp Here 150   *Sales* 156,655,200
SIC 7353 Heavy construction equipment rental
  Paul Wood
  Rick Moran
  Nikolai Mondi
  Stephen Tisdall
  Dave Witsken
  Sandy Cestra

D-U-N-S 24-750-7460   (SL)
AUTOLINX EXPRESS INC
12673 Coleraine Dr, Bolton, ON, L7E 3B5
(905) 951-1900
Emp Here 25   *Sales* 11,907,576
SIC 4212 Local trucking, without storage
  Hazoora Dhaliwal
  Satnam Dhaliwal

D-U-N-S 24-308-8630   (SL)
BOLTON STEEL TUBE CO. LTD
455a Piercey Rd, Bolton, ON, L7E 5B8
(905) 857-6830
Emp Here 65   *Sales* 11,790,220
SIC 3312 Blast furnaces and steel mills
  Winston Penny
  Virginia Koury
  Henry Koury
  Marie Penny
  Meyer Keslassy

D-U-N-S 24-793-3260   (HQ)
C. S. BACHLY BUILDERS LIMITED
BACHLY CONSTRUCTION
27 Nixon Rd, Bolton, ON, L7E 1J7
(905) 951-3100
Emp Here 45   *Sales* 14,986,843
SIC 1521 Single-family housing construction
  Andrew Bachly
  Cameron Snoddon

D-U-N-S 25-459-7545   (HQ)
CALEDON PROPANE INC
1 Betomat Crt, Bolton, ON, L7E 2V9

(905) 857-1448
Emp Here 1   *Sales* 13,438,040
SIC 5984 Liquefied petroleum gas dealers
  Hugh Sutherland Sr

D-U-N-S 24-381-7470   (SL)
CAMBRIA FABSHOP-TORONTO INC
41 Simpson Rd, Bolton, ON, L7E 2R6
(905) 951-1011
Emp Here 750   *Sales* 166,998,750
SIC 2541 Wood partitions and fixtures
  John Murray
  Martin E Davis
  Matthew L Davis
  Sanda A Solecki
  Mark E Davis

D-U-N-S 24-802-3967   (SL)
CANADIAN TIRE
99 Mcewan Dr E Suite 2, Bolton, ON, L7E 2Z7
(905) 857-5425
Emp Here 45   *Sales* 11,387,655
SIC 5251 Hardware stores
  Eric Neate

D-U-N-S 25-512-6104   (HQ)
CANAM PLASTICS 2000 INC
30 Holland Dr, Bolton, ON, L7E 1G6
(905) 951-6166
Emp Here 1   *Sales* 21,301,575
SIC 2821 Plastics materials and resins
  Gurdeep Toor
  Peter Mclaughlin

D-U-N-S 25-156-2583   (SL)
CAST-STONE PRECAST INC
487 Piercey Rd, Bolton, ON, L7E 5B8
(905) 857-6111
Emp Here 55   *Sales* 12,838,925
SIC 3272 Concrete products, nec
  Mauro Brancaleoni
  Nasrin Bakhtiari
  Evan N. Kenley

D-U-N-S 24-184-7102   (HQ)
CAVALIER TRANSPORTATION SERVICES INC
(Suby of TFI INTERNATIONAL INC)
14091 Humber Station Rd, Bolton, ON, L7E 0Z9
(905) 857-6981
Emp Here 20   *Sales* 10,399,340
SIC 4731 Freight transportation arrangement
  Josiane-Melanie Langlois
  Chantal Martel
  George A. Ledson
  Brian Ledson

D-U-N-S 24-318-2933   (BR)
CLUBLINK CORPORATION ULC
CALDON WOODS GOLFS CLUB
(Suby of TWC ENTERPRISES LIMITED)
15608 Regional Road 50, Bolton, ON, L7E 3E5
(905) 880-1400
Emp Here 80
SIC 7992 Public golf courses
  David Belletrutti

D-U-N-S 24-597-2377   (SL)
COOLTECH AIR SYSTEMS LTD
37 Nixon Rd, Bolton, ON, L7E 1K1
(905) 951-0885
Emp Here 60   *Sales* 13,983,900
SIC 1711 Plumbing, heating, air-conditioning
  Bruno Fantin
  Len Fantin

D-U-N-S 24-024-6462   (SL)
D. & R. ELECTRONICS CO. LTD
8820 George Bolton Pky, Bolton, ON, L7E 2Y4
(905) 951-9997
Emp Here 68   *Sales* 12,950,056
SIC 3669 Communications equipment, nec
  Rinaldo Darolfi
  Rita Darolfi
  Massimo Tari
  Alfredo Darolfi

D-U-N-S 20-279-7577   (SL)
DAYTONA FREIGHT SYSTEMS INC
124 Commercial Rd, Bolton, ON, L7E 1K4
(416) 744-2020
Emp Here 95   *Sales* 6,010,292
SIC 4213 Trucking, except local
  Jasbinder Matharu
  Inderpal Kahlon
  Tejinder Dhot
  Gagan Sidhu
  Sukhwinder Singh Gill

D-U-N-S 25-057-4639   (SL)
DELGANT CONSTRUCTION LIMITED
DELGANT (CIVILS)
7 Marconi Crt, Bolton, ON, L7E 1H3
(905) 857-7858
Emp Here 75   *Sales* 42,775,350
SIC 1542 Nonresidential construction, nec
  Carlo Delle Donne

D-U-N-S 20-752-6377   (HQ)
DIBCO UNDERGROUND LIMITED
135 Commercial Rd, Bolton, ON, L7E 1R6
(905) 857-0458
Sales 20,195,360
SIC 1622 Bridge, tunnel, and elevated highway construction
  Edward Dimillo

D-U-N-S 20-035-8455   (HQ)
DICK, JAMES CONSTRUCTION LIMITED
(Suby of DICK, JAMES HOLDINGS LIMITED)
14442 Regional Road 50, Bolton, ON, L7E 3E2
(905) 857-3500
Emp Here 100   *Sales* 170,888,400
SIC 5032 Brick, stone, and related material
  James Dick
  Anne Dick

D-U-N-S 20-013-2178   (HQ)
DICK, JAMES HOLDINGS LIMITED
14442 Regional Rd 50, Bolton, ON, L7E 3E2
(905) 857-3500
Sales 127,928,150
SIC 6712 Bank holding companies
  James Dick

D-U-N-S 25-273-8711   (HQ)
ENERSYS CANADA INC
(Suby of ENERSYS)
61 Parr Blvd Unit 3, Bolton, ON, L7E 4E3
(905) 951-2228
Emp Here 40   *Sales* 61,557,868
SIC 5063 Electrical apparatus and equipment
  Jim Arshad
  Robert Bryan

D-U-N-S 24-687-7146   (SL)
FINES FORD LINCOLN SALES & SERVICE LTD
12435 50 Hwy, Bolton, ON, L7E 1M3
(905) 857-1252
Emp Here 33   *Sales* 16,436,574
SIC 5511 New and used car dealers
  Robert Fines

D-U-N-S 24-545-6181   (SL)
FINES FORD LINCOLN SALES&SERVICE LTD
10 Simona Dr, Bolton, ON, L7E 4C7
(905) 857-1252
Emp Here 35   *Sales* 17,432,730
SIC 5511 New and used car dealers
  Carlos Martins

D-U-N-S 20-023-9540   (SL)
FREIGHTCOM INC
77 Pillsworth Rd Unit 1, Bolton, ON, L7E 4G4
(877) 335-8740
Emp Here 46   *Sales* 15,567,760
SIC 4213 Trucking, except local
  Zulfikar Kermally
  Turab Kermally

D-U-N-S 20-716-8220   (SL)
GARDEN FOODS - BOLTON LTD

501 Queen St S, Bolton, ON, L7E 1A1
(905) 857-1227
Emp Here 70   *Sales* 20,543,390
SIC 5411 Grocery stores
Piero Carbone
Rose Carbone

D-U-N-S 24-391-7908   (SL)
HEARTSAFE EMS INC
159 Victoria St, Bolton, ON, L7E 3G9
(416) 410-4911
Emp Here 65   *Sales* 15,228,720
SIC 8748 Business consulting, nec
Glenn Burke

D-U-N-S 20-525-4485   (HQ)
HUSKY INJECTION MOLDING SYSTEMS LTD
500 Queen St S, Bolton, ON, L7E 5S5
(905) 951-5000
Emp Here 500   *Sales* 1,073,134,424
SIC 6712 Bank holding companies

D-U-N-S 24-337-4881   (SL)
KEENA TRUCK LEASING AND TRANSPORT LIMITED
27 Simpson Rd, Bolton, ON, L7E 1E4
(905) 857-1189
Emp Here 70   *Sales* 10,373,440
SIC 4213 Trucking, except local
Frank Merola
Mary Merola

D-U-N-S 24-006-6985   (SL)
KING NURSING HOME LIMITED
49 Sterne St, Bolton, ON, L7E 1B9
(905) 857-4117
Emp Here 75   *Sales* 5,154,975
SIC 8051 Skilled nursing care facilities
Janice King
Hilda King
Archie King

D-U-N-S 24-326-0572   (HQ)
KINGSPAN INSULATED PANELS LTD
(*Suby of* KINGSPAN GROUP PUBLIC LIMITED COMPANY)
12557 Coleraine Dr, Bolton, ON, L7E 3B5
(905) 951-5600
Emp Here 100   *Sales* 38,417,000
SIC 3448 Prefabricated Metal buildings and components
Russell Shiels
Donald Casey

D-U-N-S 24-422-2691   (HQ)
MAPLE TERRAZZO MARBLE & TILE INCORPORATED
STONEWORX MARBLE & GRANITE
16 Nixon Rd, Bolton, ON, L7E 1K3
(905) 850-3006
Sales 35,843,800
SIC 3281 Cut stone and stone products
Fred Rossi

D-U-N-S 20-127-1597   (SL)
MAR-SAN EXCAVATING & GRADING LTD
21 Holland Dr, Bolton, ON, L7E 4J6
(905) 857-1616
Emp Here 60   *Sales* 14,771,160
SIC 1794 Excavation work
Gino Rotondi
Carmen Rotondi

D-U-N-S 20-307-0115   (BR)
MARS CANADA INC
(*Suby of* MARS, INCORPORATED)
12315 Coleraine Dr, Bolton, ON, L7E 3B4
(905) 857-5620
Emp Here 300
SIC 2064 Candy and other confectionery products
Rena Crumplen

D-U-N-S 20-878-1070   (HQ)
MARS CANADA INC
MASTERFOODS, DIV OF
(*Suby of* MARS, INCORPORATED)

37 Holland Dr, Bolton, ON, L7E 5S4
(905) 857-5700
Emp Here 300   *Sales* 341,169,500
SIC 2064 Candy and other confectionery products
Rena Crumplen
Mary Jane Dowling
Tami Majer
Ellen Kollar
Roy Benin

D-U-N-S 20-821-7778   (HQ)
NESEL FAST FREIGHT INCORPORATED
20 Holland Dr, Bolton, ON, L7E 1G6
(905) 951-7770
Emp Here 190   *Sales* 46,095,250
SIC 4213 Trucking, except local
Katherine Mcwilliams
Richard Muir

D-U-N-S 24-122-5416   (SL)
NORLITE INC
5 Simpson Rd, Bolton, ON, L7E 1E4
(905) 857-5955
Emp Here 28   *Sales* 12,520,872
SIC 5063 Electrical apparatus and equipment
Tim Harris
Brett Harris

D-U-N-S 25-976-7648   (SL)
NORTH WOOD CARPET & TILE COMPANY LTD
16 Nixon Rd, Bolton, ON, L7E 1K3
(905) 790-0085
Emp Here 90   *Sales* 45,797,040
SIC 5023 Homefurnishings
Joseph Paolini

D-U-N-S 24-189-3507   (SL)
NORTHTOWN STRUCTURAL LTD
18 Simpson Rd, Bolton, ON, L7E 1G9
(905) 951-6317
Emp Here 49   *Sales* 23,453,758
SIC 1542 Nonresidential construction, nec
Mark Delorenzo

D-U-N-S 24-451-0178   (SL)
OLIVER OLIVES INC
SARDO FOODS
99 Pillsworth Rd, Bolton, ON, L7E 4E4
(905) 951-9096
Emp Here 67   *Sales* 23,161,230
SIC 2033 Canned fruits and specialties
Mario Sardo
Joan Sardo

D-U-N-S 20-722-5579   (SL)
PARAMOUNT STRUCTURES LTD
46 Nixon Rd, Bolton, ON, L7E 1W2
(905) 951-7528
Emp Here 130   *Sales* 32,004,180
SIC 1799 Special trade contractors, nec
Mario Sena

D-U-N-S 25-998-6644   (HQ)
PERI FORMWORK SYSTEMS INC
(*Suby of* PERI-WERK ARTUR SCHWORER GMBH & CO. KG)
45 Nixon Rd, Bolton, ON, L7E 1K1
(905) 951-5400
Emp Here 99   *Sales* 51,637,940
SIC 7353 Heavy construction equipment rental
Stephen Jones
Carl Heathcote
Alexander Schwoerer

D-U-N-S 20-226-5331   (SL)
PERKINELMER HEALTH SCIENCES CANADA, INC
(*Suby of* PERKINELMER, INC.)
32 Nixon Rd Unit 1, Bolton, ON, L7E 1W2
(905) 857-5665
Emp Here 54   *Sales* 12,273,606
SIC 3826 Analytical instruments
Reza Javahery
Dragan Vuckovic

D-U-N-S 24-588-5819   (SL)
PIONEER ELECTRONICS OF CANADA, INC
(*Suby of* PIONEER CORPORATION)
2 Marconi Crt Unit 15, Bolton, ON, L7E 1E5
(905) 479-4411
Emp Here 70   *Sales* 40,617,290
SIC 5064 Electrical appliances, television and radio
Nobuyoshi Fukazawa
John D'silva
Tony Verni
Bruce Schepers
Richard E Clark
Daisuke Takekawa
David Welsh
Masao Kawabata

D-U-N-S 25-690-6892   (SL)
POWERSONIC INDUSTRIES INC
POWERSONIC CONNECT
13 Simpson Rd, Bolton, ON, L7E 1E4
(905) 951-6399
Emp Here 81   *Sales* 18,952,550
SIC 3679 Electronic components, nec
Jason Rampersaud
Romeena Rampersaud
Zane Rampersaud
Toni Atallah

D-U-N-S 25-605-7548   (SL)
RAFAT GENERAL CONTRACTOR INC
8850 George Bolton Pky, Bolton, ON, L7E 2Y4
(905) 951-1063
Emp Here 300   *Sales* 30,485,480
SIC 1794 Excavation work
Carlo Salim

D-U-N-S 20-785-8994   (SL)
ROMA FENCE LIMITED
10 Holland Dr, Bolton, ON, L7E 1G6
(905) 951-9063
Emp Here 50   *Sales* 22,358,700
SIC 5039 Construction materials, nec
Tony Marra

D-U-N-S 20-936-8083   (HQ)
SARDO, MARIO SALES INC
LES ALIMENTS SARDO
99 Pillsworth Rd, Bolton, ON, L7E 4E4
(905) 951-9096
Emp Here 50   *Sales* 48,463,466
SIC 5141 Groceries, general line
Mario Sardo
Joan Sardo

D-U-N-S 24-394-7780   (BR)
SCHENKER OF CANADA LIMITED
(*Suby of* BUNDESREPUBLIK DEUTSCHLAND)
12315 Coleraine Dr, Bolton, ON, L7E 3B4
(905) 857-5620
Emp Here 100
SIC 4731 Freight transportation arrangement
Rob Brace

D-U-N-S 25-989-3717   (SL)
SILCOTECH NORTH AMERICA INC
54 Nixon Rd, Bolton, ON, L7E 1W2
(905) 857-9998
Emp Here 75   *Sales* 21,301,575
SIC 2821 Plastics materials and resins
Michael Maloney
Isolde Boettger
Udo Lange
Holger Lange
Yogesh Chauhan
Virendra Aggarwal

D-U-N-S 24-220-7475   (SL)
SUMMIT DODGE CHRYSLER JEEP LIMITED
10 Simona Dr, Bolton, ON, L7E 4C7

Emp Here 26   *Sales* 12,950,028
SIC 5511 New and used car dealers
Scott Vickers
Brian Vickers

Steve Hughes

D-U-N-S 24-986-2590   (SL)
SYNTEC PROCESS EQUIPMENT LTD
77 Pillsworth Rd Unit 12, Bolton, ON, L7E 4G4
(905) 951-8000
Emp Here 23   *Sales* 10,925,598
SIC 5084 Industrial machinery and equipment
Roger Sinclair
Roland Barbazza

D-U-N-S 24-703-4887   (SL)
TEK-MOR INCORPORATED
20 Simpson Rd, Bolton, ON, L7E 1G9
(905) 857-6415
Emp Here 35   *Sales* 14,927,039
SIC 1761 Roofing, siding, and sheetMetal work
Nick Morganelli
Antonio Morganelli
Connie Sanita

D-U-N-S 20-266-7007   (SL)
TITANIUM LOGISTICS INC
(*Suby of* TITANIUM TRANSPORTATION GROUP INC)
32 Simpson Rd, Bolton, ON, L7E 1G9
(905) 851-1688
Emp Here 75   *Sales* 50,016,900
SIC 4731 Freight transportation arrangement
Theodore Daniel
Doug Billau
Kasia Malz

D-U-N-S 20-272-7996   (HQ)
TITANIUM TRANSPORTATION GROUP INC
32 Simpson Rd, Bolton, ON, L7E 1G9
(905) 851-1688
Emp Here 20   *Sales* 140,111,122
SIC 4231 Trucking terminal facilities
Theodore Daniel
Lu Galosso
William (Bill) Chyfetz
David Bradley

D-U-N-S 24-330-6474   (SL)
TITANIUM TRUCKING SERVICES INC
(*Suby of* TITANIUM TRANSPORTATION GROUP INC)
32 Simpson Rd, Bolton, ON, L7E 1G9
(905) 851-1688
Emp Here 200   *Sales* 41,141,200
SIC 4213 Trucking, except local
Ted Daniel
Marilyn Daniel
Patricia O'hara
Cesar Silva

D-U-N-S 24-622-2236   (SL)
TOPAC ENTERPRISES INC
TOPAC EXPRESS
9 Simpson Rd, Bolton, ON, L7E 1E4
(905) 857-2209
Emp Here 65   *Sales* 13,370,890
SIC 4212 Local trucking, without storage
Verne Camplin

D-U-N-S 20-682-5549   (SL)
VACUUM TRUCKS OF CANADA ULC
JACK DOHENY COMPANIES
(*Suby of* JACK DOHENY COMPANIES, INC.)
180 Healey Rd, Bolton, ON, L7E 5B1
(905) 857-7474
Emp Here 15   *Sales* 13,645,836
SIC 4212 Local trucking, without storage
Kay Doheny
Steve Shafer
Susan Simpson
Christian Bush

D-U-N-S 24-795-9711   (SL)
VERSATILE SPRAY PAINTING LTD
102 Healey Rd, Bolton, ON, L7E 5A7
(905) 857-4915
Emp Here 60   *Sales* 11,525,100
SIC 3479 Metal coating and allied services
Dave Gogo

▲ Public Company   ■ Public Company Family Member   HQ Headquarters   BR Branch   SL Single Location

Christopher Heslin

D-U-N-S 24-322-1533   (SL)
WANDEROSA WOOD PRODUCTS LIMITED PARTNERSHIP
150 Parr Blvd, Bolton, ON, L7E 4E6
(905) 857-6227
Emp Here 70   *Sales* 31,302,180
SIC 5031 Lumber, plywood, and millwork
Mark Yusishen
Marcello Repole
Gwen Gleave

D-U-N-S 24-953-1377   (SL)
WHITE OAK CUSTOM WOODWORKING LTD
10 Browning Crt, Bolton, ON, L7E 1G8
(905) 669-0919
Emp Here 50   *Sales* 11,517,000
SIC 5712 Furniture stores
Angela Scarimbolo
Anthony Scarimbolo

D-U-N-S 25-050-8512   (SL)
WINDMULLER, MONICA & KLAUS
1 Warbrick Lane, Bolton, ON, L7E 1G3
(905) 857-0882
Emp Here 55   *Sales* 13,664,052
SIC 5999 Miscellaneous retail stores, nec
Monica Windmuller

D-U-N-S 24-330-6433   (HQ)
WORLD WIDE CARRIERS LTD
124 Commercial Rd, Bolton, ON, L7E 1K4
(416) 213-1334
Sales 14,010,984
SIC 4213 Trucking, except local
Sukhi Dhaliwal

D-U-N-S 24-784-8112   (HQ)
WSI SIGN SYSTEMS LTD
KING ARCHITECTURAL PRODUCTS, DIV OF
(*Suby of* SUCCESSION CAPITAL CORPORATION)
31 Simpson Rd, Bolton, ON, L7E 2R6
(905) 857-8044
Sales 24,460,200
SIC 3993 Signs and advertising specialties
Peter Weber

D-U-N-S 25-297-8622   (BR)
ZEHRMART INC
ZEHRS MARKETS 58
(*Suby of* LOBLAW COMPANIES LIMITED)
487 Queen St S, Bolton, ON, L7E 2B4
(905) 951-7505
Emp Here 220
SIC 5411 Grocery stores
Sebastian Geraci

Bornholm, ON N0K

D-U-N-S 24-422-8276   (SL)
BAR-B-DEE FARMS LTD
Gd, Bornholm, ON, N0K 1A0
(519) 347-2966
Emp Here 10   *Sales* 12,103,970
SIC 5153 Grain and field beans
Henry Deblock
Timothy Deblock
Randy Deblock
Barbara Deblock

Bothwell, ON N0P

D-U-N-S 20-035-9552   (HQ)
MARCUS, HAROLD LIMITED
(*Suby of* MARCUS, HAROLD HOLDINGS LIMITED)
15124 Longwoods Rd Suite 2, Bothwell, ON,

N0P 1C0
(519) 695-3734
Sales 23,656,190
SIC 4213 Trucking, except local
Harold Marcus
Dennis Marcus

D-U-N-S 24-209-9724   (SL)
PARKS BLUEBERRIES & COUNTRY STORE LTD
14815 Longwoods Rd, Bothwell, ON, N0P 1C0
(519) 692-5373
Emp Here 49   *Sales* 16,780,883
SIC 0191 General farms, primarily crop
Diane Parks

Bowmanville, ON L1C

D-U-N-S 25-835-8183   (SL)
1429634 ONTARIO LIMITED
PHOENIX TRANSPORTATION
51 Port Darlington Rd Suite 1, Bowmanville, ON, L1C 3K3
(905) 697-0503
Emp Here 89   *Sales* 4,883,608
SIC 4151 School buses
Archie Groth
Susan Groth

D-U-N-S 25-365-4602   (HQ)
1435207 ONTARIO INC
PETRO CANADA
2305 Highway 2, Bowmanville, ON, L1C 3K7
(905) 623-8521
Emp Here 5   *Sales* 24,903,900
SIC 5541 Gasoline service stations
Rej Jeyakumar

D-U-N-S 24-773-2642   (SL)
BOWMANVILLE FOOD LAND
225 King St E, Bowmanville, ON, L1C 1P8
(905) 697-7256
Emp Here 49   *Sales* 14,380,373
SIC 5411 Grocery stores

D-U-N-S 24-371-3869   (SL)
CLAYTON AUTOMOTIVE GROUP INC
CLARINGTON HONDA AUTO POWERHOUSE
29 Spicer Sq, Bowmanville, ON, L1C 5M2
(905) 697-2333
Emp Here 25   *Sales* 12,451,950
SIC 5511 New and used car dealers
Charles Clayton

D-U-N-S 25-092-3898   (BR)
COCO PAVING LTD
(*Suby of* COCO PAVING INC)
3075 Maple Grove Rd, Bowmanville, ON, L1C 6N2
(905) 697-0400
Emp Here 100
SIC 1611 Highway and street construction
Yves Mageau

D-U-N-S 20-526-4625   (SL)
COWAN BUICK GMC LTD
166 King St E, Bowmanville, ON, L1C 1N8
(905) 623-3396
Emp Here 43   *Sales* 21,417,354
SIC 5511 New and used car dealers
Thomas Cowan
Vivian Cowan

D-U-N-S 24-783-9202   (SL)
DETOX ENVIRONMENTAL LTD
322 Bennett Rd, Bowmanville, ON, L1C 3Z2
(905) 623-1367
Emp Here 60   *Sales* 19,134,600
SIC 4953 Refuse systems
Brian Ritchie
Randall Duffy
Beate Ritchie

D-U-N-S 20-699-6683   (BR)
EXTENDICARE INC
STRATHHAVEN LIFECARE CENTRE
(*Suby of* EXTENDICARE INC)
264 King St E Suite 306, Bowmanville, ON, L1C 1P9
(905) 623-2553
Emp Here 100
SIC 8051 Skilled nursing care facilities
Patrick Brown

D-U-N-S 25-193-7173   (HQ)
GREELEY CONTAINMENT AND REWORK INC
200 Baseline Rd E, Bowmanville, ON, L1C 1A2
(905) 623-5678
Sales 17,939,200
SIC 7549 Automotive services, nec
Neil Clark
Brenda Kelly
Ashley Hartwick
Ed Van Oostenbrugge
Sophie Spencer

D-U-N-S 20-086-6510   (HQ)
IVAN B. WALLACE ONTARIO LAND SURVEYOR LTD
71 Mearns Crt Unit 16, Bowmanville, ON, L1C 4N4
(905) 623-2205
Sales 11,437,270
SIC 8713 Surveying services
Crystal Cranch

D-U-N-S 24-191-7934   (BR)
KAWARTHA PINE RIDGE DISTRICT SCHOOL BOARD
CLARINGTON CENTRAL SECONDARY SCHOOL
200 Clarington Blvd, Bowmanville, ON, L1C 5N8
(905) 697-9857
Emp Here 150
SIC 8211 Elementary and secondary schools
John Ford

D-U-N-S 25-528-8532   (BR)
LAKERIDGE HEALTH
LAKERIDGE HEALTH BOWANVILLE
(*Suby of* LAKERIDGE HEALTH)
47 Liberty St S, Bowmanville, ON, L1C 2N4
(905) 623-3331
Emp Here 400
SIC 6324 Hospital and medical service plans
Kevin Empy

D-U-N-S 25-076-3588   (SL)
LANGLEY UTILITIES CONTRACTING LTD
71 Mearns Crt Unit 1, Bowmanville, ON, L1C 4N4
(905) 623-5798
Emp Here 48   *Sales* 24,943,440
SIC 4911 Electric services
Ken Rerrie
Anthony Rerrie

D-U-N-S 25-504-7375   (SL)
MATTCO SERVICES LIMITED
TIM HORTONS
350 Waverley Rd, Bowmanville, ON, L1C 4Y4
(905) 623-0175
Emp Here 52   *Sales* 15,260,804
SIC 5461 Retail bakeries
Lilly Tsampalerios-Henton

D-U-N-S 20-349-7045   (BR)
PETERBOROUGH VICTORIA NORTHUMBERLAND AND CLARINGTON CATHOLIC DISTRICT SCHOOL BOARD
ST. STEPHEN CATHOLIC SECONDARY SCHOOL
(*Suby of* PETERBOROUGH VICTORIA NORTHUMBERLAND AND CLARINGTON CATHOLIC DISTRICT SCHOOL BOARD)
300 Scugog St, Bowmanville, ON, L1C 6Y8
(905) 623-3990
Emp Here 80

SIC 8211 Elementary and secondary schools
Mark Joly

D-U-N-S 24-919-5199   (SL)
PHOENIX A.M.D. INTERNATIONAL INC
41 Butler Crt, Bowmanville, ON, L1C 4P8
(905) 427-7440
Emp Here 30   *Sales* 15,265,680
SIC 5023 Homefurnishings
Albert Marrache
Dawn Rowe
Brad Definney

D-U-N-S 20-734-6177   (BR)
ST. MARYS CEMENT INC. (CANADA)
CBM CANADA BUILDING MATERIALS
(*Suby of* HEJOASSU ADMINISTRACAO S/A)
400 Bowmanville Ave, Bowmanville, ON, L1C 7B5
(905) 623-3341
Emp Here 200
SIC 3241 Cement, hydraulic
Fabio Cesconetto

Bracebridge, ON P1L

D-U-N-S 24-420-0572   (SL)
547121 ONTARIO LTD
MUSKOKA CHRYSLER SALES
380 Ecclestone Dr, Bracebridge, ON, P1L 1R1
(705) 645-8763
Emp Here 28   *Sales* 13,946,184
SIC 5511 New and used car dealers
Ross Miller
Douglas Winnington-Ingram

D-U-N-S 20-922-7800   (HQ)
CAVALCADE FORD LTD
420 Ecclestone Dr, Bracebridge, ON, P1L 1R1
(705) 645-8731
Sales 21,417,354
SIC 5511 New and used car dealers
Lawrence Miller

D-U-N-S 20-068-1497   (BR)
DISTRICT MUNICIPALITY OF MUSKOKA, THE
PINES LONG TERM CARE RESIDENCE
(*Suby of* DISTRICT MUNICIPALITY OF MUSKOKA, THE)
98 Pine St Suite 610, Bracebridge, ON, P1L 1N5
(705) 645-4488
Emp Here 225
SIC 8051 Skilled nursing care facilities
Cathryn Rannie

D-U-N-S 24-892-5125   (SL)
DOTY, RONALD T. LIMITED
CANADIAN TIRE
Hwy 118 W, Bracebridge, ON, P1L 1V4
(705) 645-5261
Emp Here 58   *Sales* 11,909,894
SIC 5311 Department stores
Ronald Doty
Mary Doty

D-U-N-S 20-699-6725   (BR)
EXTENDICARE INC
PINES LONG-TERM CARE RESIDENCE
(*Suby of* EXTENDICARE INC)
98 Pine St Suite 610, Bracebridge, ON, P1L 1N5
(705) 645-4488
Emp Here 250
SIC 8051 Skilled nursing care facilities
Jayne Dacosta

D-U-N-S 25-504-5221   (SL)
FENNER DUNLOP (BRACEBRIDGE), INC
(*Suby of* FENNER GROUP HOLDINGS LIMITED)
700 Ecclestone Dr, Bracebridge, ON, P1L 1W1

(705) 645-4431
Emp Here 90   *Sales* 43,895,700
SIC 5085 Industrial supplies
Stefan Perkic

D-U-N-S 25-318-8999   (BR)
FIRSTCANADA ULC
LAIDLAW EDUCATIONAL SERVICES
(*Suby of* FIRSTGROUP PLC)
23 Gray Rd, Bracebridge, ON, P1L 1P8

Emp Here 100
SIC 4151 School buses
Gary Darlington

D-U-N-S 20-717-4129   (HQ)
FOWLER CONSTRUCTION COMPANY LIMITED
1218 Rosewarne Dr, Bracebridge, ON, P1L 0A1
(705) 645-2214
Sales 82,028,750
SIC 1611 Highway and street construction
John Mcbride
Jeff Ivanko

D-U-N-S 20-965-4797   (SL)
GREAVETTE CHEVROLET PONTIAC BUICK CADILLAC GMC LTD
375 Ecclestone Dr, Bracebridge, ON, P1L 1T6
(705) 645-2241
Emp Here 40   *Sales* 19,923,120
SIC 5511 New and used car dealers
Glenn Greavette

D-U-N-S 20-036-1871   (HQ)
HAMMOND TRANSPORTATION LIMITED
450 Ecclestone Dr, Bracebridge, ON, P1L 1R1
(705) 645-5431
Emp Here 4   *Sales* 12,796,240
SIC 4151 School buses
Orvil Hammond
Greg Hammond
James Hammond

D-U-N-S 20-176-6990   (BR)
HOME DEPOT OF CANADA INC
HOME DEPOT
(*Suby of* THE HOME DEPOT INC)
20 Depot Dr, Bracebridge, ON, P1L 0A1
(705) 646-5600
Emp Here 150
SIC 5251 Hardware stores
Al Hilger

D-U-N-S 24-333-1704   (BR)
METRO ONTARIO INC
METRO
(*Suby of* METRO INC)
505 Muskoka Rd Hwy Suite 118, Bracebridge, ON, P1L 1T3
(705) 645-8751
Emp Here 107
SIC 5411 Grocery stores
Chris Kenney

D-U-N-S 24-818-0309   (HQ)
MUSKOKA DELIVERY SERVICES INC
581 Ecclestone Dr, Bracebridge, ON, P1L 1R2
(705) 645-1258
Emp Here 40   *Sales* 24,684,720
SIC 4212 Local trucking, without storage
Rick Irons

D-U-N-S 24-320-2747   (SL)
MUSKOKA GROWN LIMITED
50 Keith Rd Unit A, Bracebridge, ON, P1L 0A1
(705) 645-2295
Emp Here 50   *Sales* 16,367,200
SIC 2833 Medicinals and botanicals
David Grand

D-U-N-S 24-468-0018   (SL)
MUSKOKA TIMBER MILLS LTD
2152 Manitoba St, Bracebridge, ON, P1L 1X4
(705) 645-7757
Emp Here 25   *Sales* 13,013,550
SIC 5099 Durable goods, nec

Ric Singor

D-U-N-S 20-814-2013   (BR)
MUSKOKA TRANSPORT LIMITED
(*Suby of* TITANIUM TRANSPORTATION GROUP INC)
456 Ecclestone Dr, Bracebridge, ON, P1L 1R1
(705) 645-4481
Emp Here 180
SIC 4213 Trucking, except local
Darcy Hammond

D-U-N-S 20-703-8316   (HQ)
MUSKOKA TRANSPORT LIMITED
(*Suby of* TITANIUM TRANSPORTATION GROUP INC)
456 Ecclestone Dr, Bracebridge, ON, P1L 1R1
(705) 645-4481
Emp Here 125   *Sales* 35,998,550
SIC 4213 Trucking, except local
Paul G Hammond
D'arcy Hammond

D-U-N-S 25-001-6011   (SL)
PINES LONG TERM CARE RESIDENCE, THE
(*Suby of* DISTRICT MUNICIPALITY OF MUSKOKA, THE)
98 Pine St Suite 610, Bracebridge, ON, P1L 1N5
(705) 645-4488
Emp Here 200   *Sales* 12,856,400
SIC 8361 Residential care
Charmaine Kaye
Janice Fox

D-U-N-S 20-036-1442   (HQ)
PRIDE OF MUSKOKA MARINE LIMITED
1785 Beaumont Dr Rr 4, Bracebridge, ON, P1L 1X2
(705) 645-9151
Emp Here 1   *Sales* 56,635,200
SIC 5551 Boat dealers
Paul Nickel
Karen Nickel

D-U-N-S 20-298-3156   (BR)
WASTE CONNECTIONS OF CANADA INC
BFI CANADA
(*Suby of* WASTE CONNECTIONS, INC)
580 Ecclestone Dr, Bracebridge, ON, P1L 1R2
(705) 645-4453
Emp Here 80
SIC 4953 Refuse systems
Paul Wills

Bradford, ON L3Z

D-U-N-S 24-096-7398   (SL)
435682 ONTARIO LIMITED
BROADWAY AUTO SALES
19990 11 Hwy S, Bradford, ON, L3Z 2B6
(905) 775-6497
Emp Here 18   *Sales* 17,007,900
SIC 5521 Used car dealers
Antonio Tangreda
Angela Tangreda
John Peter Tangreda

D-U-N-S 25-525-1621   (SL)
AGC AUTOMOTIVE CANADA, INC
(*Suby of* AGC INC.)
120 Artesian Industrial Pky, Bradford, ON, L3Z 3G3
(905) 778-8224
Emp Here 70   *Sales* 12,545,330
SIC 3231 Products of purchased glass
Yukiharu Ohya
Alberto Trevino
George Urban
Hideki Takahashi

D-U-N-S 24-822-6672   (SL)
BRADFORD & DISTRICT PRODUCE LTD
(*Suby of* BRADFORD CO-OPERATIVE

STORAGE LIMITED)
355 Dissette St, Bradford, ON, L3Z 3H1
(905) 775-9633
Emp Here 30   *Sales* 25,067,310
SIC 5148 Fresh fruits and vegetables
Luc Fournier
Kathleen Henning

D-U-N-S 20-036-2697   (HQ)
BRADFORD CO-OPERATIVE STORAGE LIMITED
61 Bridge St, Bradford, ON, L3Z 3H3
(905) 775-3317
Sales 12,535,632
SIC 0723 Crop preparation services for market
Anthony Moro

D-U-N-S 24-036-7388   (BR)
BRADFORD GREENHOUSES LIMITED
BRADFORD GREENHOUSES GARDEN GALLERY
(*Suby of* BRADFORD GREENHOUSES LIMITED)
2433 12th Conc, Bradford, ON, L3Z 2B2
(905) 775-4769
Emp Here 80
SIC 5191 Farm supplies
Kevin Johnson

D-U-N-S 20-305-3665   (BR)
FRESHOUSE FOODS LTD
(*Suby of* FRESHOUSE FOODS LTD)
65 Reagen'S Industrial Pky, Bradford, ON, L3Z 0Z9
(905) 775-8880
Emp Here 100
SIC 5149 Groceries and related products, nec
Larry Major

D-U-N-S 20-337-7734   (SL)
GALATA CHEMICALS (CANADA) INC
(*Suby of* ARTEK SURFIN CHEMICALS LIMITED)
10 Reagen'S Industrial Pky, Bradford, ON, L3Z 0Z8
(905) 775-5000
Emp Here 70   *Sales* 47,054,840
SIC 5169 Chemicals and allied products, nec
Steven Mckeown
Matthew Yopchick
Joseph Salsbury

D-U-N-S 20-036-3182   (SL)
HILLSIDE GARDENS LIMITED
1383 River Rd, Bradford, ON, L3Z 4A6
(905) 775-3356
Emp Here 20   *Sales* 10,702,480
SIC 5148 Fresh fruits and vegetables
Susan Verkaik

D-U-N-S 24-986-9637   (SL)
HKH OPPORTUNITIES INC
TIM HORTONS
118 Holland St W, Bradford, ON, L3Z 2B4
(905) 775-0282
Emp Here 55   *Sales* 16,141,235
SIC 5461 Retail bakeries
Jack Thornton

D-U-N-S 24-361-7185   (BR)
HOME DEPOT OF CANADA INC
HOME DEPOT
(*Suby of* THE HOME DEPOT INC)
470 Holland St W, Bradford, ON, L3Z 0A2
(905) 778-2100
Emp Here 100
SIC 5251 Hardware stores
Arthur Blank

D-U-N-S 25-524-4592   (SL)
KUMI CANADA CORPORATION
(*Suby of* KUMI KASEI CO., LTD.)
55 Reagen'S Industrial Pky, Bradford, ON, L3Z 0Z9
(905) 778-1464
Emp Here 170   *Sales* 27,005,860
SIC 3089 Plastics products, nec

Kevin Chase
T Edward Scott

D-U-N-S 20-772-6308   (HQ)
MITEK CANADA, INC
(*Suby of* BERKSHIRE HATHAWAY INC.)
100 Industrial Rd, Bradford, ON, L3Z 3G7
(905) 952-2900
Emp Here 80   *Sales* 23,050,200
SIC 3448 Prefabricated Metal buildings and components
David Cattapan
Ronald Blackburn
Michael Sandbrook
Tom Manenti

D-U-N-S 24-245-0344   (SL)
PACIFIC NORTHERN RAIL CONTRACTORS CORP
251 Holland Street W, Bradford, ON, L3Z 1H9
(905) 775-6564
Emp Here 5   *Sales* 15,529,285
SIC 4923 Gas transmission and distribution

D-U-N-S 25-292-4469   (BR)
SIMCOE COUNTY DISTRICT SCHOOL BOARD, THE
BRADFORD DISTRICT HIGH SCHOOL
(*Suby of* SIMCOE COUNTY DISTRICT SCHOOL BOARD, THE)
70 Professor Day Dr, Bradford, ON, L3Z 3B9
(905) 775-2262
Emp Here 85
SIC 8211 Elementary and secondary schools
John Playford

D-U-N-S 25-214-3664   (SL)
SIMCOE ENERGY & TECHNICAL SERVICES INC
285 Dissette St, Bradford, ON, L3Z 3G9
(905) 778-8105
Emp Here 22   *Sales* 10,318,110
SIC 5984 Liquefied petroleum gas dealers
Hank Frederiks

D-U-N-S 24-175-5961   (HQ)
SIMSAK CORPORATION
PETRO CANADA
133 Holland St E, Bradford, ON, L3Z 2A8
(905) 778-9600
Emp Here 5   *Sales* 24,903,900
SIC 5541 Gasoline service stations
Kumud Joshi

D-U-N-S 20-628-9493   (BR)
SPECIALTY CARE INC
SPECIALTY CARE BRADFORD VALLEY
(*Suby of* SPECIALTY CARE INC)
2656 Line 6, Bradford, ON, L3Z 2A1
(905) 952-2270
Emp Here 200
SIC 8059 Nursing and personal care, nec
Kim Handfield

D-U-N-S 24-360-1577   (HQ)
SPECTRA ALUMINUM PRODUCTS LTD
95 Reagen'S Industrial Pky, Bradford, ON, L3Z 0Z9
(905) 778-8093
Sales 32,649,840
SIC 3354 Aluminum extruded products
David Hudson
Scott Chapman
Archie Proper

D-U-N-S 25-090-7870   (SL)
SURE FRESH FOODS INC
CERICOLA FARMS
3855 Line 4, Bradford, ON, L3Z 0Z1
(905) 939-2962
Emp Here 45   *Sales* 37,600,965
SIC 5144 Poultry and poultry products
Anthony Cericola

D-U-N-S 20-812-0928   (SL)
TEN BUSS LIMITED
CANADIAN TIRE
430 Holland St W Suite 446, Bradford, ON,

L3Z 0G1
(905) 778-4330
Emp Here 40   *Sales* 13,024,000
SIC 5999 Miscellaneous retail stores, nec
Tenn Buss

D-U-N-S 25-529-6519   (BR)
VENTRA GROUP CO
FLEX-N-GATE BRADFORD
(*Suby of* FLEX-N-GATE LLC)
75 Reagen'S Industrial Pky, Bradford, ON,
L3Z 0Z9
(705) 778-7900
Emp Here 310
SIC 3465 Automotive stampings
Gary Linton

D-U-N-S 24-024-4228   (SL)
VINS PLASTICS LTD
12 Industrial Crt, Bradford, ON, L3Z 3G6
(905) 775-7901
Emp Here 50   *Sales* 10,094,850
SIC 3081 Unsupported plastics film and sheet
Sajun Vins

D-U-N-S 24-126-3854   (SL)
**WINTERGREEN LEARNING MATERIALS
LIMITED**
3075 Line 8, Bradford, ON, L3Z 3R5
(905) 778-8584
Emp Here 56   *Sales* 11,752,155
SIC 5049 Professional equipment, nec
Michael Hayward
Joe Hayward
Brent Espinet
Hugh Moreland

Brampton, ON L6P

D-U-N-S 24-474-9037   (SL)
CASATI NATURAL GAS
7 Adriatic Cres, Brampton, ON, L6P 1W7
(905) 460-4023
Emp Here 4   *Sales* 12,423,428
SIC 4924 Natural gas distribution
Joe Casati

D-U-N-S 20-717-9466   (SL)
FERNVIEW CONSTRUCTION LIMITED
10605 Coleraine Dr, Brampton, ON, L6P 0V6
(905) 794-0132
Emp Here 56   *Sales* 14,136,752
SIC 1623 Water, sewer, and utility lines
Fernando Velocci
Vincenzo Velocci
Giovanni Seppieri

D-U-N-S 25-948-1104   (SL)
TERRAPAVE CONSTRUCTION LTD
12 Cadetta Rd Unit 1, Brampton, ON, L6P 0X4
(905) 761-2865
Emp Here 40   *Sales* 12,754,760
SIC 1521 Single-family housing construction
Sebastian Failla
Nadia Gallo-Pascazi

Brampton, ON L6R

D-U-N-S 20-368-9372   (SL)
1911661 ONTARIO INC
POLICARO BMW
5 Coachworks Cres, Brampton, ON, L6R 3Y2
(416) 981-9400
Emp Here 75   *Sales* 47,196,000
SIC 5511 New and used car dealers
Francesco Policaro Sr

D-U-N-S 24-320-3832   (SL)
1957444 ONTARIO INC
BAP TRUCKING
40 Marbleseed Cres, Brampton, ON, L6R 2J7

(905) 795-1101
Emp Here 5   *Sales* 27,421,695
SIC 4213 Trucking, except local
Barbara Planter
Lloyd Francis

D-U-N-S 20-709-2623   (BR)
2063414 ONTARIO LIMITED
LEISUREWORLD CAREGIVING CENTRE
215 Sunny Meadow Blvd, Brampton, ON, L6R 3B5
(905) 458-7604
Emp Here 100
SIC 8059 Nursing and personal care, nec
Steve Keery

D-U-N-S 20-553-3206   (SL)
FALCON MOTOR XPRESS LTD
8 Wallaby Way Bldg 8, Brampton, ON, L6R 3C7
(866) 383-9100
Emp Here 200   *Sales* 41,141,200
SIC 4212 Local trucking, without storage
Arandeep Grewal
Jarnial Sidhu

D-U-N-S 25-080-7237   (BR)
HOME DEPOT OF CANADA INC
HOME DEPOT
(*Suby of* THE HOME DEPOT INC)
60 Great Lakes Dr, Brampton, ON, L6R 2K7
(905) 792-5430
Emp Here 150
SIC 5251 Hardware stores
Jalal Hamad

D-U-N-S 25-170-9259   (SL)
I & D MCEWEN LTD
CANADIAN TIRE
10 Great Lakes Dr, Brampton, ON, L6R 2K7
(905) 793-4800
Emp Here 140   *Sales* 88,099,200
SIC 5531 Auto and home supply stores
Ian Mcewen

D-U-N-S 24-232-1649   (SL)
MAPLE GROVE CARE COMMUNITY
215 Sunny Meadow Blvd, Brampton, ON, L6R 3B5
(905) 458-7604
Emp Here 140   *Sales* 8,294,580
SIC 8361 Residential care
Michelle Mackenzie

D-U-N-S 25-091-7606   (BR)
**MCDONALD'S   RESTAURANTS   OF
CANADA LIMITED**
MCDONALD'S
(*Suby of* MCDONALD'S CORPORATION)
45 Mountainash Rd, Brampton, ON, L6R 1W4
(905) 458-7488
Emp Here 100
SIC 5812 Eating places

D-U-N-S 25-087-6687   (BR)
METRO ONTARIO INC
A AND P FOOD STORES 083
(*Suby of* METRO INC)
20 Great Lakes Dr, Brampton, ON, L6R 2K7
(905) 789-6161
Emp Here 180
SIC 5411 Grocery stores
George Lefave

D-U-N-S 20-591-3879   (BR)
PEEL DISTRICT SCHOOL BOARD
FERNFOREST PUBLIC SCHOOL
(*Suby of* PEEL DISTRICT SCHOOL BOARD)
275 Fernforest Dr, Brampton, ON, L6R 1L9
(905) 793-6157
Emp Here 80
SIC 8211 Elementary and secondary schools
Susan Whaley

D-U-N-S 20-365-7770   (SL)
POSCOR METAL RECOVERY CORP
POSCOR METAL GROUP
10095 Bramalea Rd Suite 201, Brampton, ON,

L6R 0K1
(647) 641-3928
Emp Here 31   *Sales* 23,906,066
SIC 5093 Scrap and waste materials
James Joshani

D-U-N-S 20-544-7282   (SL)
SEHDEV PHARMACY INC
SHOPPERS DRUG MART
51 Mountainash Rd Suite 1, Brampton, ON,
L6R 1W4
(905) 458-5526
Emp Here 40   *Sales* 10,118,160
SIC 5912 Drug stores and proprietary stores
Naresh Sehdev
Shelley Sehdev

D-U-N-S 20-865-1831   (HQ)
TAKBRO ENTERPRISES LIMITED
PETRO CANADA
10115 Bramalea Rd, Brampton, ON, L6R 1W6
(905) 789-0753
Emp Here 10   *Sales* 24,903,900
SIC 5541 Gasoline service stations
Guljinder Tak

D-U-N-S 25-686-9629   (HQ)
WILLIAM OSLER HEALTH SYSTEM
BRAMPTON CIVIC HOSPITAL
2100 Bovaird Dr E, Brampton, ON, L6R 3J7
(905) 494-2120
Emp Here 2,500   *Sales* 460,982,000
SIC 8062 General medical and surgical hospitals

D-U-N-S 24-352-6220   (BR)
WILLIAM OSLER HEALTH SYSTEM
BRAMPTON CIVIC HOSPITAL
(*Suby of* WILLIAM OSLER HEALTH SYSTEM)
2100 Bovaird Dr E, Brampton, ON, L6R 3J7
(905) 494-2120
Emp Here 100
SIC 8062 General medical and surgical hospitals

Brampton, ON L6S

D-U-N-S 24-688-2070   (SL)
1166709 ONTARIO LIMITED
ACURA 2000
2250 Queen St E Suite 2000, Brampton, ON,
L6S 5X9
(905) 458-7100
Emp Here 45   *Sales* 22,413,510
SIC 5511 New and used car dealers
Bazil Policaro
Paul Policaro
Anthony (Tony) Policaro

D-U-N-S 20-022-4868   (HQ)
1192901 ONTARIO LTD
NEWTRON GROUP
14 Automatic Rd Suite 38, Brampton, ON, L6S
5N5
(905) 458-1400
Emp Here 10   *Sales* 26,289,860
SIC 6411 Insurance agents, brokers, and service
Danny Fung
Robert Baldassarra
Michael Baldassarra

D-U-N-S 20-106-3018   (SL)
1470754 ONTARIO INC
NORTHWEST LEXUS
2280 Queen St E, Brampton, ON, L6S 5X9
(905) 494-1000
Emp Here 25   *Sales* 12,451,950
SIC 5511 New and used car dealers
Tony Policaro

D-U-N-S 24-381-7918   (SL)
1579901 ONTARIO INC
ASL GLOBAL LOGISTICS

27 Automatic Rd, Brampton, ON, L6S 5N8
(416) 741-5454
Emp Here 75   *Sales* 38,997,525
SIC 4731 Freight transportation arrangement
Sukhvinder Bassi

D-U-N-S 24-483-1959   (SL)
575636 ONTARIO LIMITED
GLOBAL DISTRIBUTION AND WAREHOUSING
1 Lascelles Blvd, Brampton, ON, L6S 3T1

Emp Here 43   *Sales* 16,570,480
SIC 4731 Freight transportation arrangement
John Cosgrostove

D-U-N-S 20-181-8978   (SL)
AIR-KING LIMITED
(*Suby of* LASKO GROUP, INC.)
8 Edvac Dr, Brampton, ON, L6S 5P2
(905) 456-2033
Emp Here 23   *Sales* 10,285,002
SIC 5064 Electrical appliances, television and radio
John Fox
Jeffrey Kenkelen

D-U-N-S 25-321-4688   (BR)
ALLIED SYSTEMS (CANADA) COMPANY
(*Suby of* ALLIED SYSTEMS HOLDINGS, INC.)
2000 Williams Pky, Brampton, ON, L6S 6B3
(905) 458-0900
Emp Here 100
SIC 4213 Trucking, except local
Harry Porquet

D-U-N-S 24-203-3871   (SL)
ALPATECH VINYL INC
(*Suby of* ALPA LUMBER INC)
100 Exchange Dr, Brampton, ON, L6S 0C8
(905) 678-4695
Emp Here 15   *Sales* 10,955,175
SIC 5162 Plastics materials and basic shapes
John Dipoce
Rene Condo

D-U-N-S 24-304-1175   (SL)
ANDROID - BRAMPTON, L.L.C.
ANDROID INDUSTRIES - BRAMPTON
14 Precidio Crt, Brampton, ON, L6S 6E3
(905) 458-4774
Emp Here 49   *Sales* 10,028,977
SIC 3694 Engine electrical equipment
Gregory Nichols

D-U-N-S 25-504-4760   (HQ)
APEX MOTOR EXPRESS LTD
60 Ward Rd, Brampton, ON, L6S 4L5
(905) 789-5000
Emp Here 100   *Sales* 46,095,250
SIC 4213 Trucking, except local
Don Reimer
Tom Santaguida
Anne Reimer

D-U-N-S 25-179-5290   (SL)
AUSTIN STEEL GROUP INC
GENSTEEL
39 Progress Crt, Brampton, ON, L6S 5X2
(905) 799-3324
Emp Here 55   *Sales* 12,838,925
SIC 3312 Blast furnaces and steel mills
Joe Henriques
Annie Henriques

D-U-N-S 24-101-1761   (BR)
BEST BUY CANADA LTD
(*Suby of* BEST BUY CO., INC.)
9200 Airport Rd, Brampton, ON, L6S 6G6
(905) 494-7000
Emp Here 700
SIC 5065 Electronic parts and equipment, nec
David Falconer

D-U-N-S 20-181-9125   (HQ)
CARBON STEEL PROFILES LIMITED

2190 Williams Pky, Brampton, ON, L6S 5X7
(905) 799-2427
Emp Here 125   *Sales* 86,958,040
SIC 7389 Business services, nec
 James Mcnair
 Darren Mcnair
 Linda Mcnair
 Tony Rocchetti

D-U-N-S 20-165-1416   (SL)
CARPE DIEM RESIDENTIAL TREATMENT
HOMES FOR CHILDREN INC
CARPE DIEM
9355 Dixie Rd, Brampton, ON, L6S 1J7
(905) 799-2947
Emp Here 100   *Sales* 5,924,700
SIC 8361 Residential care
 Kathy Lewis

D-U-N-S 24-214-8401   (HQ)
CEVA LOGISTICS CANADA, ULC
CEVA LOGISTICS
(*Suby of* MERIT CORPORATION SAL)
2600 North Park Dr, Brampton, ON, L6S 6E2
(905) 789-2904
Emp Here 90   *Sales* 20,570,600
SIC 4212 Local trucking, without storage
 Jonathan Gardner
 Bruce Rodgers
 Michael Todt

D-U-N-S 25-153-0960   (SL)
CHENG SHIN RUBBER CANADA, INC
MAXXIS INTERNATIONAL-CANADA
(*Suby of* CHENG SHIN RUBBER IND. CO.,
LTD.)
400 Chrysler Dr Unit C, Brampton, ON, L6S
5Z5
(905) 789-0882
Emp Here 25   *Sales* 11,875,650
SIC 5085 Industrial supplies
 Peter Chang
 John Lee

D-U-N-S 20-256-2047   (HQ)
CID BISSETT FASTENERS LIMITED
(*Suby of* BISSETT FASTENERS LIMITED)
175 Sun Pac Blvd Unit 2a, Brampton, ON, L6S
5Z6
(905) 595-0411
Emp Here 15   *Sales* 28,522,728
SIC 5072 Hardware
 Matthew Suader
 Larry John
 John Fulton
 Gary John
 Daniel Mckenna

D-U-N-S 24-180-6835   (HQ)
DATA COMMUNICATIONS MANAGEMENT
CORP
DATA GROUP OF COMPANIES, THE
9195 Torbram Rd, Brampton, ON, L6S 6H2
(905) 791-3151
Emp Here 500   *Sales* 244,691,824
SIC 2761 Manifold business forms
 Gregory J. Cochrane
 Mike Cote
 James Lorimer
 J.R. Kingsley Ward
 Mike Sifton
 William Albino
 James J. Murray
 Derek J. Watchorn
 Merri L. Jones

D-U-N-S 20-266-9243   (SL)
DAVROC TESTING LABORATORIES INC
2051 Williams Pky Unit 21, Brampton, ON,
L6S 5T3
(905) 792-7792
Emp Here 45   *Sales* 10,561,320
SIC 8734 Testing laboratories
 David Cousins
 Rocco Liscio
 Sal Fasullo

D-U-N-S 24-804-2249   (SL)
DEBRO INC.
11 Automatic Rd, Brampton, ON, L6S 4K6
(905) 799-8200
Emp Here 31   *Sales* 22,640,695
SIC 5169 Chemicals and allied products, nec
 Brian C. Imrie
 William Heise

D-U-N-S 20-026-7909   (BR)
DUFFERIN-PEEL CATHOLIC DISTRICT
SCHOOL BOARD
ST ANTHONY ELEMENTARY SCHOOL
(*Suby of* DUFFERIN-PEEL CATHOLIC DIS-
TRICT SCHOOL BOARD)
950 North Park Dr, Brampton, ON, L6S 3L5
(905) 792-2282
Emp Here 500
SIC 8211 Elementary and secondary schools
 Virginia Elizondo

D-U-N-S 25-117-1799   (BR)
DUFFERIN-PEEL CATHOLIC DISTRICT
SCHOOL BOARD
*ST THOMAS AQUINAS SECONDARY
SCHOOL*
(*Suby of* DUFFERIN-PEEL CATHOLIC DIS-
TRICT SCHOOL BOARD)
25 Corporation Dr, Brampton, ON, L6S 6A2
(905) 791-1195
Emp Here 160
SIC 8211 Elementary and secondary schools
 Casey Homick

D-U-N-S 24-985-8754   (SL)
ELITE SWEETS BRANDS INC
ELITE SWEETS
9 Edvac Dr, Brampton, ON, L6S 5X8
(905) 790-9428
Emp Here 50   *Sales* 11,242,750
SIC 2052 Cookies and crackers
 Alberto Tari
 Giovanna Dilallo

D-U-N-S 24-823-4601   (BR)
FCA CANADA INC
*FIAT CHRYSLER BRAMPTON ASSEMBLY
PLANT*
(*Suby of* FIAT CHRYSLER AUTOMOBILES
N.V.)
2000 Williams Pky, Brampton, ON, L6S 6B3
(905) 458-2800
Emp Here 100
SIC 1541 Industrial buildings and warehouses
 Jim Vo

D-U-N-S 24-425-4129   (SL)
FUTURE STEEL BUILDINGS INTL. CORP
(*Suby of* FUTURE STEEL HOLDINGS LTD)
220 Chrysler Dr, Brampton, ON, L6S 6B6
(905) 790-8500
Emp Here 50   *Sales* 10,141,500
SIC 3448 Prefabricated Metal buildings and
components
 Lui Turi

D-U-N-S 20-977-0379   (HQ)
HOLMES FREIGHT LINES INC
70 Ward Rd, Brampton, ON, L6S 4L5
(905) 458-1155
Sales 20,570,600
SIC 4213 Trucking, except local
 Esly Holmes
 Jeff Holmes
 Kevin Holmes

D-U-N-S 25-764-2327   (SL)
HOMELIFE EXPERTS REALTY LTD
50 Cottrelle Blvd Suite 29, Brampton, ON, L6S
0E1

Emp Here 35   *Sales* 11,449,445
SIC 6531 Real estate agents and managers
 Harjinder Dhillon

D-U-N-S 25-508-1101   (HQ)
HOPEWELL LOGISTICS INC

255 Chrysler Dr Suite 3a, Brampton, ON, L6S
6C8
(905) 458-8860
Sales 52,455,030
SIC 4225 General warehousing and storage
 Pat Macginnis
 Robert De Ryk
 Kelly Hillyard

D-U-N-S 24-308-3610   (BR)
HOPEWELL LOGISTICS INC
(*Suby of* HOPEWELL LOGISTICS INC)
9050 Airport Rd Suite 201, Brampton, ON,
L6S 6G6
(905) 458-1041
Emp Here 90
SIC 4225 General warehousing and storage
 Kevin Emeree

D-U-N-S 24-415-1031   (SL)
JAY CEE ENTERPRISES LIMITED
CAPS 'N PLUGS
(*Suby of* HARMAN CORPORATION)
165 Sun Pac Blvd Unit 4, Brampton, ON, L6S
5Z6
(905) 791-1303
Emp Here 15   *Sales* 10,955,175
SIC 5162 Plastics materials and basic shapes
 Paul Hamilton

D-U-N-S 25-148-3822   (SL)
JOBAL INDUSTRIES LIMITED
2 Edvac Dr, Brampton, ON, L6S 5P2
(905) 799-8555
Emp Here 70   *Sales* 18,735,640
SIC 5251 Hardware stores
 John Matharu

D-U-N-S 25-372-3142   (HQ)
MACDONALD, DETTWILER AND ASSO-
CIATES INC
MDA
(*Suby of* MAXAR TECHNOLOGIES INC.)
9445 Airport Rd Suite 100, Brampton, ON,
L6S 4J3
(905) 790-2800
Emp Here 480   *Sales* 144,843,300
SIC 3769 Space vehicle equipment, nec
 Daniel Friedmann
 Magued Iskander
 Hiten Makim
 Anil Wirasekara

D-U-N-S 24-889-5625   (BR)
MARITIME-ONTARIO FREIGHT LINES LIM-
ITED
MARITIME-ONTARIO PARCEL, DIV OF
(*Suby of* MARITIME-ONTARIO FREIGHT
LINES LIMITED)
1 Maritime Ontario Blvd Suite 100, Brampton,
ON, L6S 6G4
(905) 792-6100
Emp Here 80
SIC 4212 Local trucking, without storage
 Derek Kinsela

D-U-N-S 20-170-1067   (HQ)
MARITIME-ONTARIO FREIGHT LINES LIM-
ITED
FREIGHTWORKS
1 Maritime Ontario Blvd, Brampton, ON, L6S
6G4
(905) 792-6101
Emp Here 100   *Sales* 71,997,100
SIC 4213 Trucking, except local
 Doug Munro
 Chris Walker
 Paul Harper

D-U-N-S 25-318-2125   (BR)
MCDONALD'S RESTAURANTS OF
CANADA LIMITED
DEMRELL
(*Suby of* MCDONALD'S CORPORATION)
2450 Queen St E, Brampton, ON, L6S 5X9
(905) 793-5295
Emp Here 100
SIC 5812 Eating places

D-U-N-S 20-114-4388   (HQ)
MENASHA PACKAGING CANADA L.P.
(*Suby of* MENASHA CORPORATION)
35 Precidio Crt, Brampton, ON, L6S 6B7
(905) 792-7092
Emp Here 140   *Sales* 88,232,880
SIC 2653 Corrugated and solid fiber boxes
 Christopher Pearce
 Warren Pearce
 Edward Pearce
 Sherry Pearce

D-U-N-S 25-351-6900   (SL)
METRIC CONTRACTING SERVICES COR-
PORATION
(*Suby of* METRIC GROUP LIMITED)
34 Bramtree Crt, Brampton, ON, L6S 5Z7
(905) 793-4100
Emp Here 125   *Sales* 41,014,375
SIC 1611 Highway and street construction
 Ennio Liorti
 Frank Liorti
 Anna Liorti

D-U-N-S 24-333-8204   (HQ)
MODSPACE FINANCIAL SERVICES
CANADA, LTD
(*Suby of* MODULAR SPACE CORPORA-
TION)
2300 North Park Dr, Brampton, ON, L6S 6C6
(905) 794-3900
Emp Here 12   *Sales* 17,847,900
SIC 7519 Utility trailer rental
 Charles Paquin
 Mark Boily

D-U-N-S 20-251-3842   (SL)
NOLAN LOGISTICS GROUP INC
9150 Airport Rd Unit 10, Brampton, ON, L6S
6G1
(800) 387-5148
Emp Here 35   *Sales* 13,487,600
SIC 4731 Freight transportation arrangement
 Dan Nolan

D-U-N-S 25-148-9704   (SL)
NORTH AMERICAN PAPER INCORPO-
RATED
NAPP
16 Automatic Rd, Brampton, ON, L6S 5N3
(905) 793-8202
Emp Here 48   *Sales* 11,204,880
SIC 2679 Converted paper products, nec
 Joseph Fierro
 Arnaldo Fierro Sr

D-U-N-S 25-801-8761   (HQ)
OVER THE RAINBOW PACKAGING SER-
VICE INC
2165 Williams Pky, Brampton, ON, L6S 6B8

Emp Here 18   *Sales* 11,087,250
SIC 7389 Business services, nec
 Peter Taman
 Inderjit Gill

D-U-N-S 25-297-1171   (BR)
PEEL DISTRICT SCHOOL BOARD
NORTH PARK SECONDARY SCHOOL
(*Suby of* PEEL DISTRICT SCHOOL BOARD)
10 North Park Dr, Brampton, ON, L6S 3M1
(905) 456-1906
Emp Here 120
SIC 8211 Elementary and secondary schools
 Pradeep Rajah

D-U-N-S 25-297-1866   (BR)
PEEL DISTRICT SCHOOL BOARD
JUDITH NYMAN SECONDARY SCHOOL
(*Suby of* PEEL DISTRICT SCHOOL BOARD)
1305 Williams Pky, Brampton, ON, L6S 3J8
(905) 791-6770
Emp Here 90
SIC 8211 Elementary and secondary schools
 D. Ablett

D-U-N-S 24-721-2418   (BR)

PEEL DISTRICT SCHOOL BOARD
CHINGUACOUSY SECONDARY SCHOOL
(*Suby of* PEEL DISTRICT SCHOOL BOARD)
1370 Williams Pky, Brampton, ON, L6S 1V3
(905) 791-2400
Emp Here 100
SIC 8211 Elementary and secondary schools
Sao Mork-Gerra

D-U-N-S 24-540-1252   (SL)
POLICARO INVESTMENTS LIMITED
BRAMALEA TOYOTA
2 Maritime Ontario Blvd, Brampton, ON, L6S 0C2
(905) 791-3500
Emp Here 35   *Sales* 17,432,730
SIC 5511 New and used car dealers
Bazil Policaro
Anthony Policaro
Paul Policaro

D-U-N-S 20-358-3232   (HQ)
POLYMERSHAPES   DISTRIBUTION CANADA INC
(*Suby of* POLYMERSHAPES LLC)
9150 Airport Rd, Brampton, ON, L6S 6G1
(905) 789-3111
Emp Here 10   *Sales* 36,517,250
SIC 5162 Plastics materials and basic shapes
Kevin Short

D-U-N-S 24-077-3507   (SL)
R B & W CORPORATION OF CANADA
(*Suby of* PARK-OHIO HOLDINGS CORP.)
10 Sun Pac Blvd, Brampton, ON, L6S 4R5
(905) 595-9700
Emp Here 115   *Sales* 22,089,775
SIC 3452 Bolts, nuts, rivets, and washers
Dennis Bolden
Craig Cowan

D-U-N-S 24-991-9549   (SL)
R. B. BELL (SUPPLIES) LIMITED
CANADIAN TIRE #305
2850 Queen St E, Brampton, ON, L6S 6E8
(905) 792-9301
Emp Here 150   *Sales* 40,147,800
SIC 5251 Hardware stores
Robert Bell

D-U-N-S 24-060-6368   (SL)
RECTOR FOODS LIMITED
KERRY INGREDIENTS AND FLAVORS
(*Suby of* KERRY GROUP PUBLIC LIMITED COMPANY)
2280 North Park Dr, Brampton, ON, L6S 6C6
(905) 789-9691
Emp Here 50   *Sales* 17,284,500
SIC 2099 Food preparations, nec
Eoin O'connell

D-U-N-S 24-451-5706   (SL)
ROVA PRODUCTS CANADA INC
30 Automatic Rd, Brampton, ON, L6S 5N8
(905) 793-1955
Emp Here 50   *Sales* 22,358,700
SIC 5065 Electronic parts and equipment, nec

D-U-N-S 20-316-2581   (SL)
SKJODT-BARRETT CONTRACT PACKAGING INC
5 Precidio Crt, Brampton, ON, L6S 6B7
(905) 671-2884
Emp Here 172   *Sales* 72,710,764
SIC 1541 Industrial buildings and warehouses
Dan Skjodt

D-U-N-S 24-625-4668   (SL)
SKJODT-BARRETT FOODS INC
5 Precidio Crt, Brampton, ON, L6S 6B7
(905) 671-2884
Emp Here 200   *Sales* 69,138,000
SIC 2033 Canned fruits and specialties
Dan Skjodt
Pal Shah
Mike Durham
Chris Mifflin

Doug Mcinnis

D-U-N-S 25-988-2272   (BR)
SOBEYS CAPITAL INCORPORATED
SOBEY'S
(*Suby of* EMPIRE COMPANY LIMITED)
930 North Park Dr, Brampton, ON, L6S 3Y5
(905) 458-7673
Emp Here 200
SIC 5411 Grocery stores
Bonnie Kornberger

D-U-N-S 24-509-2796   (HQ)
SONEPAR CANADA INC
LUMEN
(*Suby of* SOCIETE DE NEGOCE ET DE PARTICIPATION)
250 Chrysler Dr Unit 4, Brampton, ON, L6S 6B6
(905) 696-2838
Emp Here 150   *Sales* 986,419,900
SIC 5063 Electrical apparatus and equipment
David Gabriel
Francois Anquetil
Paul Trudel
Olivier Verley
Francois Poncet
Philippe De Moustier
Franck Bruel

D-U-N-S 24-917-6306   (SL)
STRUCT-CON CONSTRUCTION LTD
2051 Williams Pky Unit 14, Brampton, ON, L6S 5T3
(905) 791-5445
Emp Here 40   *Sales* 22,813,520
SIC 1542 Nonresidential construction, nec
Mohammad Shariati
James Strickland

D-U-N-S 20-213-3828   (BR)
SUN RICH FRESH FOODS INC
(*Suby of* SUN RICH FRESH FOODS INC)
35 Bramtree Crt Unit 1, Brampton, ON, L6S 6G2
(905) 789-0200
Emp Here 310
SIC 2033 Canned fruits and specialties

D-U-N-S 20-118-5498   (SL)
TEAM CID INC
175 Sun Pac Blvd Suite 2a, Brampton, ON, L6S 5Z6
(905) 595-0411
Emp Here 75   *Sales* 33,538,050
SIC 5072 Hardware
Gary John
Larry John
John Fulton
Dan Mckenna
Charles Mccoll

D-U-N-S 25-477-7089   (SL)
TELEXPRESS COURIER INC
5 Edvac Dr Unit 10, Brampton, ON, L6S 5P3
(905) 792-2222
Emp Here 25   *Sales* 11,087,250
SIC 7389 Business services, nec
Martha Di Biase

D-U-N-S 24-952-3838   (HQ)
TRAILCON LEASING INC
(*Suby of* WILSON TRANSPORTATION AND LEASING GROUP INC)
15 Spar Dr, Brampton, ON, L6S 6E1
(905) 670-9061
Emp Here 50   *Sales* 45,019,700
SIC 7519 Utility trailer rental
Alan Boughton
Mike Krell
Darryl Hartman
Jim Cockburn
Don Andrews

D-U-N-S 20-968-4992   (SL)
TRIPLE J PHARMACY LTD
SHOPPERS DRUG MART
980 Central Park Dr, Brampton, ON, L6S 3L7

(905) 791-1797
Emp Here 40   *Sales* 10,118,160
SIC 5912 Drug stores and proprietary stores
James Hernane
Angela Hernane

D-U-N-S 25-027-8728   (SL)
VODDEN FOODLAND
456 Vodden St E, Brampton, ON, L6S 5Y7
(905) 453-3100
Emp Here 55   *Sales* 16,141,235
SIC 5411 Grocery stores
David Miceli

D-U-N-S 24-243-2677   (HQ)
WG PRO-MANUFACTURING INC
2110 Williams Pky Suite 6, Brampton, ON, L6S 5X6
(905) 790-3377
Sales 83,613,500
SIC 7389 Business services, nec
Karl Wirtz
Sanjay Gandhi

Brampton, ON L6T

D-U-N-S 20-050-6967   (SL)
1373744 ONTARIO INC
ONE SOURCE METAL
155 Hedgedale Rd, Brampton, ON, L6T 5P3
(905) 672-1300
Emp Here 12   *Sales* 12,004,068
SIC 5051 Metals service centers and offices
Ben Mair
William (Bill) Mair

D-U-N-S 24-451-3560   (SL)
1627880 ONTARIO INC
PRODIGY GRAPHICS GROUP
100 Parkshore Dr, Brampton, ON, L6T 5M1

Emp Here 100
SIC 2752 Commercial printing, lithographic

D-U-N-S 20-003-8060   (BR)
1939243 ONTARIO INC
TI GROUP AUTOMOTIVE OF CANADA
(*Suby of* 1939243 ONTARIO INC)
316 Orenda Rd, Brampton, ON, L6T 1G3
(905) 793-7100
Emp Here 100
SIC 3089 Plastics products, nec
Marg Wheeler

D-U-N-S 24-335-6248   (HQ)
446987 ONTARIO INC
BOMBAY COMPANY, THE
(*Suby of* BENIX & CO. INC)
3389 Steeles Ave E, Brampton, ON, L6T 5W4
(905) 494-1118
Emp Here 200   *Sales* 172,023,435
SIC 5712 Furniture stores
David Stewart

D-U-N-S 24-847-3266   (SL)
821373 ONTARIO LTD
MASTER CRAFTSMAN
3 Brewster Rd Suite 5, Brampton, ON, L6T 5G9
(905) 794-2074
Emp Here 40   *Sales* 19,001,040
SIC 5087 Service establishment equipment
Bill Mcbride

D-U-N-S 20-527-8489   (SL)
A. D. WELDING & FABRICATION INC
21 Melanie Dr, Brampton, ON, L6T 4K8
(905) 791-2914
Emp Here 24   *Sales* 10,732,176
SIC 5046 Commercial equipment, nec
Jack Bhogal
Cal Bhogal

D-U-N-S 24-704-8754   (SL)
A.B.M. TOOL & DIE CO. LTD

80 Walker Dr, Brampton, ON, L6T 4H6
(905) 458-2203
Emp Here 140   *Sales* 31,080,140
SIC 3544 Special dies, tools, jigs, and fixtures
Terry Blagonic
Doriana Blagonic

D-U-N-S 24-251-0142   (SL)
AACE FINANCIAL SERVICES LTD
5 Melanie Dr Unit 10, Brampton, ON, L6T 4K8
(905) 799-8004
Emp Here 40   *Sales* 41,395,240
SIC 6311 Life insurance
Manjinder Singh

D-U-N-S 25-140-8761   (BR)
ABB INC
(*Suby of* ABB LTD)
201 Westcreek Blvd, Brampton, ON, L6T 0G8
(905) 460-3000
Emp Here 250
SIC 5065 Electronic parts and equipment, nec
Roger Costa

D-U-N-S 24-752-4416   (BR)
ABC TECHNOLOGIES INC
ABC GROUP PRODUCT DEVELOPMENT, DIV. OF
(*Suby of* CERBERUS CAPITAL MANAGEMENT, L.P.)
303 Orenda Rd Suite B, Brampton, ON, L6T 5C3
(905) 450-3600
Emp Here 300
SIC 3089 Plastics products, nec
Rishi Sehjpal

D-U-N-S 24-950-4861   (HQ)
AC FINAL MILE INC
(*Suby of* TFI INTERNATIONAL INC)
107 Alfred Kuehne Blvd, Brampton, ON, L6T 4K3
(905) 362-2999
Emp Here 10   *Sales* 35,937,520
SIC 7389 Business services, nec
Kal Atwal
Louis Gagnon
Saskia Wijnja

D-U-N-S 24-875-8120   (SL)
ADENAT INC
3 Brewster Rd Unit 1, Brampton, ON, L6T 5G9
(905) 794-2808
Emp Here 22   *Sales* 24,317,590
SIC 5122 Drugs, proprietaries, and sundries
Israel Schwartz

D-U-N-S 25-359-6126   (BR)
ADESA AUCTIONS CANADA CORPORATION
ADESA TORONTO
(*Suby of* KAR AUCTION SERVICES, INC.)
55 Auction Lane, Brampton, ON, L6T 5P4
(905) 790-7653
Emp Here 200
SIC 5012 Automobiles and other motor vehicles
Darrel Maidment

D-U-N-S 25-173-7615   (HQ)
ADESA AUCTIONS CANADA CORPORATION
ADESA CANADA
(*Suby of* KAR AUCTION SERVICES, INC.)
55 Auction Lane 2nd Floor, Brampton, ON, L6T 5P4
(905) 790-7653
Emp Here 35   *Sales* 922,308,000
SIC 5012 Automobiles and other motor vehicles
Stephane St-Hilaire
Sheryl Watson
Trevor Henderson
Eric Loughmiller

D-U-N-S 20-120-8365   (SL)
AFA SYSTEMS LTD
AFA NORDALE PACKAGING SYSTEMS

(Suby of PJR HOLDINGS INC)
8 Tilbury Crt, Brampton, ON, L6T 3T4
(905) 456-8700
Emp Here 50   Sales 14,223,402
SIC 3565 Packaging machinery
 Paul Langen
 Ronald Langen
 Jack Langen

D-U-N-S 24-743-9193   (SL)
AIR-SERV CANADA INC.
AIR-SERVICE CANADA
(Suby of AIR SERV INTERNATIONAL, INC.)
80 Devon Rd Unit 4, Brampton, ON, L6T 5B3

Emp Here 31   Sales 14,725,806
SIC 5084 Industrial machinery and equipment
 Frank Merrill
 Bradford Merrill

D-U-N-S 20-557-5434   (SL)
AIRCRAFT APPLIANCES AND EQUIP-MENT LIMITED
REPAIR & OVERHAUL DIV OF
(Suby of OCTOPUS INDUSTRIES, INC.)
150 East Dr, Brampton, ON, L6T 1C1
(905) 791-1666
Emp Here 55   Sales 10,474,310
SIC 3677 Electronic coils and transformers
 Andrew Willnecker
 Natalia Achova

D-U-N-S 24-408-8712   (SL)
AIREX INC
5 Sandhill Crt Unit C, Brampton, ON, L6T 5J5
(905) 790-8667
Emp Here 50   Sales 22,358,700
SIC 5075 Warm air heating and air condition-ing
 Enzo Iantorno
 Mary Iantorno

D-U-N-S 24-565-4546   (HQ)
AIRPORT STEEL & TUBING LTD
155 Hedgedale Rd, Brampton, ON, L6T 5P3

Emp Here 30   Sales 17,886,960
SIC 5051 Metals service centers and offices
 Steve Crawford
 Greg Smith

D-U-N-S 25-274-1624   (SL)
ALGONQUIN POWER ENERGY FROM WASTE INC
7656 Bramalea Rd, Brampton, ON, L6T 5M5
(905) 791-2777
Emp Here 150   Sales 47,836,500
SIC 4953 Refuse systems
 Ian Robertson
 Luisa Paniconi
 Vito Ciciretto
 Chris Jarratt
 Dave Kerr

D-U-N-S 20-158-6567   (HQ)
ALMAG ALUMINUM INC
22 Finley Rd, Brampton, ON, L6T 1A9
(905) 457-9000
Sales 122,152,200
SIC 3354 Aluminum extruded products
 Joseph Jackman
 Deborah Peacock
 Rory Fitzpatrick
 Robert Peacock

D-U-N-S 24-849-3280   (SL)
ALPHA POLY CORPORATION
296 Walker Dr, Brampton, ON, L6T 4B3
(905) 789-6770
Emp Here 50   Sales 11,671,750
SIC 2673 Bags: plastic, laminated, and coated
 Patrick Kerrigan
 Paul Kerrigan
 Matthew Kerrigan
 Carole Kerrigan
 Martin Boeykens

D-U-N-S 20-719-0174   (HQ)
ALUMINART PRODUCTS LIMITED
1 Summerlea Rd, Brampton, ON, L6T 4V2
(905) 791-7521
Emp Here 150   Sales 60,807,750
SIC 3442 Metal doors, sash, and trim
 Frank Raponi

D-U-N-S 24-859-3196   (SL)
APETITO CANADA LIMITED
(Suby of APETITO AG)
12 Indell Lane, Brampton, ON, L6T 3Y3
(905) 799-1022
Emp Here 70   Sales 24,198,300
SIC 2038 Frozen specialties, nec
 Jack E Book

D-U-N-S 24-659-7868   (HQ)
AQUICON CONSTRUCTION CO. LTD
131 Delta Park Blvd Suite 1, Brampton, ON, L6T 5M8
(905) 458-1313
Sales 21,182,895
SIC 1542 Nonresidential construction, nec
 Mariano Aquino
 Daniel Aquino
 Alessandra Aquino

D-U-N-S 20-769-1692   (SL)
ARTCRAFT ELECTRIC LIMITED
8050 Torbram Rd, Brampton, ON, L6T 3T2
(905) 791-1551
Emp Here 50   Sales 10,233,650
SIC 3645 Residential lighting fixtures
 Albert Cohen
 Howard Bernstein
 Steve Cohen
 Clide Cohen

D-U-N-S 20-868-9534   (SL)
ATLAS BEARINGS CORPORATION
TRUE HARDWARE
8043 Dixie Rd, Brampton, ON, L6T 3V1
(905) 790-0283
Emp Here 87   Sales 41,327,262
SIC 5085 Industrial supplies
 Val Scorcia

D-U-N-S 20-941-3202   (SL)
ATLAS HOLDINGS COMPANY LIMITED
TRUTH HARDWARE
(Suby of TYMAN PLC)
8043 Dixie Rd, Brampton, ON, L6T 3V1
(905) 791-3888
Emp Here 60   Sales 11,525,100
SIC 3429 Hardware, nec
 Val Scorcaa

D-U-N-S 25-220-0647   (SL)
AZIMUTH THREE ENTERPRISES INC
AZIMUTH THREE COMMUNICATIONS
127 Delta Park Blvd, Brampton, ON, L6T 5M8
(437) 370-7160
Emp Here 65   Sales 14,158,885
SIC 1731 Electrical work
 Pino Tarabelli
 Jean Diab

D-U-N-S 20-272-8267   (SL)
BHI INSTALLATIONS INC
278 Orenda Rd, Brampton, ON, L6T 4X6
(905) 791-2850
Emp Here 50   Sales 11,500,827
SIC 1751 Carpentry work
 John Nolet
 Michael Nolet

D-U-N-S 24-784-6033   (HQ)
BMP METALS INC
18 Chelsea Lane, Brampton, ON, L6T 3Y4
(905) 799-2002
Emp Here 170   Sales 33,614,875
SIC 3499 Fabricated Metal products, nec
 Robert Bedard Sr
 Lorraine Bedard

D-U-N-S 20-771-6614   (HQ)
BRAMPTON ENGINEERING INC

BE
8031 Dixie Rd, Brampton, ON, L6T 3V1
(905) 793-3000
Emp Here 121   Sales 27,750,125
SIC 3559 Special industry machinery, nec
 Gary Hughes

D-U-N-S 24-355-6326   (HQ)
BRIGHTON-BEST INTERNATIONAL, (CANADA) INC
(Suby of BRIGHTON-BEST INTERNATIONAL (TAIWAN) INC.)
7900 Goreway Dr Suite 1, Brampton, ON, L6T 5W6
(905) 791-2000
Emp Here 13   Sales 16,150,884
SIC 5085 Industrial supplies
 Robert Shieh
 Shu Mei Lin

D-U-N-S 25-204-0787   (SL)
C.P. VEGETABLE OIL INC
10 Carson Crt Unit 2, Brampton, ON, L6T 4P8
(905) 792-2309
Emp Here 19   Sales 10,167,356
SIC 5149 Groceries and related products, nec
 Nigel Gonsalves

D-U-N-S 24-795-5677   (HQ)
CAN ART ALUMINUM EXTRUSION INC
85 Parkshore Dr, Brampton, ON, L6T 5M1
(905) 791-1464
Emp Here 120   Sales 114,008,720
SIC 3354 Aluminum extruded products
 Robert Saroli

D-U-N-S 25-997-4863   (SL)
CANADA WORLDWIDE SERVICES INC
ESHIPPER
9 Van Der Graaf Crt, Brampton, ON, L6T 5E5
(905) 671-1771
Emp Here 25   Sales 11,230,475
SIC 7389 Business services, nec
 Rizwan Kermalli

D-U-N-S 24-953-5568   (HQ)
CANPAR TRANSPORT L.P.
CANPAR COURIER
201 Westcreek Blvd Suite 102, Brampton, ON, L6T 0G8
(905) 499-2699
Emp Here 120   Sales 488,129,600
SIC 7389 Business services, nec
 Jim Houston

D-U-N-S 24-576-3263   (SL)
CAPITAL DRYWALL SYSTEMS LTD
396 Deerhurst Dr, Brampton, ON, L6T 5H9
(905) 458-1112
Emp Here 120   Sales 19,485,720
SIC 1742 Plastering, drywall, and insulation
 John Criscione
 Concetta Panaia
 Lucia Criscione
 Francesco Panaia

D-U-N-S 20-042-3903   (HQ)
CARDINAL MEAT SPECIALISTS LIMITED
155 Hedgedale Rd, Brampton, ON, L6T 5P3
(905) 459-4436
Sales 34,569,000
SIC 2013 Sausages and other prepared meats
 Ralph Cator
 Brent Cator

D-U-N-S 25-687-2433   (SL)
CARETEK INTEGRATED BUSINESS SOLU-TIONS INC
CARETEK IT SOLUTIONS
(Suby of 2173945 ONTARIO INC)
1900 Clark Blvd Unit 8, Brampton, ON, L6T 0E9
(416) 630-9555
Emp Here 16   Sales 11,852,835
SIC 5734 Computer and software stores
 Bikram Bajwa
 Gulwant Bajwa

D-U-N-S 24-965-2892   (HQ)
CARTIER KITCHENS INC
8 Chelsea Lane, Brampton, ON, L6T 3Y4
(905) 793-0063
Sales 23,084,400
SIC 2434 Wood kitchen cabinets
 Frank Converso
 Walter Wilowski

D-U-N-S 24-588-1255   (HQ)
CATHOLIC FAMILY SERVICES OF PEEL-DUFFERIN
60 West Dr Suite 201, Brampton, ON, L6T 3T6
(905) 450-1608
Emp Here 1   Sales 19,473,286
SIC 8699 Membership organizations, nec
 Sharon Mayne Divine
 Lyne Eaves

D-U-N-S 24-373-2786   (SL)
CHARGER LOGISTICS INC
25 Production Rd, Brampton, ON, L6T 4N8
(905) 793-3525
Emp Here 96   Sales 14,226,432
SIC 4212 Local trucking, without storage
 Andy Khera

D-U-N-S 20-036-7514   (HQ)
CHEMETALL CANADA, LIMITED
(Suby of BASF SE)
1 Kenview Blvd Suite 110, Brampton, ON, L6T 5E6
(905) 791-1628
Sales 21,180,005
SIC 5169 Chemicals and allied products, nec
 Kris Piekarz

D-U-N-S 20-408-9916   (HQ)
CHEMROY CANADA INC
(Suby of CHEMROY CHEMICALS LIMITED)
106 Summerlea Rd, Brampton, ON, L6T 4X3
(905) 789-0701
Emp Here 6   Sales 26,292,420
SIC 5169 Chemicals and allied products, nec
 William Graham
 John Graham
 Scott Harvey

D-U-N-S 24-828-3582   (SL)
CHEMROY CHEMICALS LIMITED
CHEMROY CANADA
106 Summerlea Rd, Brampton, ON, L6T 4X3
(905) 789-0701
Emp Here 2   Sales 21,180,005
SIC 5169 Chemicals and allied products, nec
 William R Graham
 Joe A Bernardi

D-U-N-S 20-693-1565   (HQ)
CLARKE TRANSPORT INC
(Suby of TFI INTERNATIONAL INC)
201 Westcreek Blvd Suite 200, Brampton, ON, L6T 5S6
(905) 291-3000
Emp Here 75   Sales 98,859,500
SIC 4731 Freight transportation arrangement
 Joseph Flinn
 Josiane Melanie Langlois
 Chantal Martel
 Rocco Biase

D-U-N-S 20-413-8861   (SL)
CLIPPER CONSTRUCTION LIMITED
COREYDALE CONTRACTING CO
16 Melanie Dr Suite 200, Brampton, ON, L6T 4K9
(905) 790-2333
Emp Here 80   Sales 19,694,880
SIC 1794 Excavation work
 Danny Sanita

D-U-N-S 20-178-8846   (BR)
COCA-COLA CANADA BOTTLING LIMITED
(Suby of COCA-COLA CANADA BOTTLING LIMITED)
15 Westcreek Blvd, Brampton, ON, L6T 5T4
(905) 874-7202
Emp Here 1,200

SIC 2086 Bottled and canned soft drinks
Patrick Odorothy

D-U-N-S 24-314-8848   (SL)
COLORTECH INC
8027 Dixie Rd, Brampton, ON, L6T 3V1
(888) 257-8324
Emp Here 60   *Sales* 16,599,600
SIC 2865 Cyclic crudes and intermediates
Alex Rom-Roginski

D-U-N-S 20-629-5016   (SL)
COMMERCIAL ROLL FORMED PRODUCTS LIMITED
225 Parkhurst Sq, Brampton, ON, L6T 5H5
(905) 790-5665
Emp Here 50   *Sales* 10,206,500
SIC 3316 Cold finishing of steel shapes
Armin Schabel
Kevin Schabel

D-U-N-S 20-298-9021   (SL)
COMPES INTERNATIONAL LIMITED
25 Devon Rd, Brampton, ON, L6T 5B6
(905) 458-5994
Emp Here 250   *Sales* 70,219,250
SIC 3544 Special dies, tools, jigs, and fixtures
Salvatore Adamo

D-U-N-S 24-745-4234   (SL)
COSMA INTERNATIONAL (CANADA) INC
2550 Steeles Ave, Brampton, ON, L6T 5R3

Emp Here 200
SIC 3714 Motor vehicle parts and accessories

D-U-N-S 20-693-0161   (SL)
COSMOS FURNITURE LTD
1055 Clark Blvd, Brampton, ON, L6T 3W4
(905) 790-2676
Emp Here 25   *Sales* 11,068,395
SIC 5021 Furniture
Avjit Kumar
Sushmita Paul

D-U-N-S 20-162-7346   (SL)
COX, FRANK J SALES LIMITED
CANADIAN CENTRAL GUAGE LABORATORY, THE DIV OF
40 West Dr, Brampton, ON, L6T 3T6
(905) 457-9190
Emp Here 30   *Sales* 13,415,220
SIC 5049 Professional equipment, nec

D-U-N-S 20-276-7596   (BR)
CRAWFORD PACKAGING INC
CRAWFORD PROVINCIAL
(*Suby of* CRAWFORD PACKAGING INC)
115 Walker Dr Unit A, Brampton, ON, L6T 5P5
(800) 265-4993
Emp Here 115
SIC 5084 Industrial machinery and equipment

D-U-N-S 24-686-0423   (HQ)
CROWNHILL PACKAGING LTD
8905 Goreway Dr, Brampton, ON, L6T 0B7
(905) 494-1191
Emp Here 80   *Sales* 66,826,800
SIC 5199 Nondurable goods, nec
John Ponzo
Ken Wong
Rodney Taylor

D-U-N-S 20-523-1132   (SL)
CULLIGAN WEST TORONTO
8985 Airport Rd, Brampton, ON, L6T 5T2
(416) 798-7670
Emp Here 40   *Sales* 26,562,684
SIC 5963 Direct selling establishments
Rob Istead

D-U-N-S 24-380-0153   (SL)
CWI CLIMATEWORX INTERNATIONAL INC
18 Chelsea Lane, Brampton, ON, L6T 3Y4
(905) 405-0800
Emp Here 25   *Sales* 11,179,350
SIC 5075 Warm air heating and air conditioning

Izabela Bedard
Lori Holjevac

D-U-N-S 24-794-2204   (HQ)
DASCO STORAGE SOLUTIONS LTD
(*Suby of* VAST INDUSTRIAL CORP)
346 Orenda Rd, Brampton, ON, L6T 1G1
(905) 792-7080
Emp Here 18   *Sales* 11,179,350
SIC 5044 Office equipment
Mark Heifz
Stephen Moulton

D-U-N-S 20-053-2641   (HQ)
DAWN FOOD PRODUCTS (CANADA), LTD
(*Suby of* DAWN FOODS, INC.)
275 Steelwell Rd, Brampton, ON, L6T 0C8
(289) 505-4640
Emp Here 70   *Sales* 62,800,089
SIC 5149 Groceries and related products, nec
Carrie Barber
Ronald Jones
Glenn Anderson
Stuart Smith
David Knowlton

D-U-N-S 20-145-3859   (HQ)
DAYBAR INDUSTRIES LIMITED
50 West Dr, Brampton, ON, L6T 2J4
(905) 625-8000
Emp Here 100   *Sales* 21,129,350
SIC 3442 Metal doors, sash, and trim
Stanley Dodson
Mark Dodson

D-U-N-S 24-917-9979   (HQ)
DEL INDUSTRIAL METALS INC
DEL METALS
7653 Bramalea Rd, Brampton, ON, L6T 5V3
(905) 595-1222
Emp Here 70   *Sales* 40,245,660
SIC 5051 Metals service centers and offices
Camille Jobin
Ric Hill

D-U-N-S 24-132-8400   (HQ)
DHL EXPRESS (CANADA) LTD
(*Suby of* DEUTSCHE POST AG)
18 Parkshore Dr, Brampton, ON, L6T 0G7
(905) 861-3400
Emp Here 150   *Sales* 719,971,000
SIC 4212 Local trucking, without storage
Andrew Williams
Gregory Hewitt
David Duncan

D-U-N-S 20-690-4869   (HQ)
DIAMO ENTERPRISES INC
CANADIAN TIRE GAS BAR
1795 Steeles Ave E, Brampton, ON, L6T 4L5
(905) 792-7108
Emp Here 11   *Sales* 10,957,716
SIC 5541 Gasoline service stations
Mohamad Hassani

D-U-N-S 24-632-8181   (SL)
DIXIE PLYMOUTH CHRYSLER LTD
8050 Dixie Rd, Brampton, ON, L6T 4W6
(905) 452-1000
Emp Here 50   *Sales* 24,903,900
SIC 5511 New and used car dealers
Mark Brennan
Hugh Brennan
Joe Cyr

D-U-N-S 24-830-3281   (SL)
DOLLKEN WOODTAPE
SURTECO
230 Orenda Rd, Brampton, ON, L6T 1E9
(905) 673-5156
Emp Here 100   *Sales* 20,189,700
SIC 3089 Plastics products, nec
Thomas Rieke

D-U-N-S 20-353-7055   (HQ)
DOT FOODS CANADA, INC
(*Suby of* DOT FOODS, INC.)

12 Barton Crt, Brampton, ON, L6T 5H6

Emp Here 10   *Sales* 10,702,480
SIC 5141 Groceries, general line
John Tracy
Bill Metzinger
Richard Tracy

D-U-N-S 25-291-1573   (SL)
DOWNSVIEW HEATING & AIR CONDITIONING LTD
4299 Queen St E, Brampton, ON, L6T 5V4
(905) 794-1489
Emp Here 70   *Sales* 16,314,550
SIC 1711 Plumbing, heating, air-conditioning
James Quattrociocchi
Frank Quattrociocchi

D-U-N-S 20-625-3072   (SL)
DOWNSVIEW PLUMBING LIMITED
4299 Queen St E Unit 1, Brampton, ON, L6T 5V4
(416) 675-6215
Emp Here 90   *Sales* 20,975,850
SIC 1711 Plumbing, heating, air-conditioning
Frank Quattrociocchi

D-U-N-S 24-784-8997   (HQ)
DRYTAC CANADA INC
105 Nuggett Crt, Brampton, ON, L6T 5A9
(905) 660-1748
Emp Here 12   *Sales* 36,517,250
SIC 5169 Chemicals and allied products, nec
Richard L. Kelley
Hayden Kelley
Darren Speizer
Jerry Hill

D-U-N-S 24-408-8134   (HQ)
DSV AIR & SEA INC
(*Suby of* DSV A/S)
70 Driver Rd Unit 4, Brampton, ON, L6T 5V2
(905) 629-0055
Emp Here 26   *Sales* 34,678,384
SIC 4731 Freight transportation arrangement
Carsten Trolle
Pamla Bronn
Saeed Dashtban

D-U-N-S 24-685-0239   (HQ)
DSV SOLUTIONS INC
VDI HEALTHCARE LOGISTICS
(*Suby of* DSV A/S)
8590 Airport Rd, Brampton, ON, L6T 0C3
(905) 789-6211
Sales 13,077,650
SIC 6712 Bank holding companies
Stephen Savarese
Steven Mcclure

D-U-N-S 20-403-0381   (HQ)
DUNDAS JAFINE INC
80 West Dr, Brampton, ON, L6T 3T6
(905) 450-7200
Sales 15,366,800
SIC 3433 Heating equipment, except electric
Murray Jafine
Paul Jafine
David Jafine

D-U-N-S 20-129-2414   (SL)
DURABLE RELEASE COATERS LIMITED
4 Finley Rd, Brampton, ON, L6T 1A9
(905) 457-2000
Emp Here 120   *Sales* 23,050,200
SIC 3479 Metal coating and allied services
Diane S Lund

D-U-N-S 24-425-5352   (SL)
DURO-COTE COMPANY LIMITED
(*Suby of* A & A COATINGS & PACKAGING LTD)
29 Melanie Dr, Brampton, ON, L6T 4K8

Emp Here 80   *Sales* 15,366,800
SIC 3479 Metal coating and allied services
Andrew W J Davidson

Bill Moist

D-U-N-S 24-953-5170   (HQ)
DYNACARE-GAMMA LABORATORY PARTNERSHIP
DYNACARE WORKPLACE
(*Suby of* LABORATORY CORPORATION OF AMERICA HOLDINGS)
115 Midair Crt, Brampton, ON, L6T 5M3
(905) 790-3515
Emp Here 700   *Sales* 977,913,000
SIC 8071 Medical laboratories
Naseem Somani

D-U-N-S 25-220-9762   (HQ)
ELECTRONICS BOUTIQUE CANADA INC
EB GAMES
(*Suby of* GAMESTOP CORP.)
8995 Airport Rd Suite 512, Brampton, ON, L6T 5T2
(905) 790-9262
Emp Here 100   *Sales* 533,406,000
SIC 5734 Computer and software stores
Jim Tyo

D-U-N-S 20-555-1393   (HQ)
EM PLASTIC & ELECTRIC PRODUCTS LIMITED
14 Brewster Rd, Brampton, ON, L6T 5B7
(905) 913-3000
Emp Here 35   *Sales* 44,717,400
SIC 5063 Electrical apparatus and equipment
Ralph J. Zarboni
Rae Townsend
Michael Gondosch

D-U-N-S 24-728-9705   (SL)
EMBASSY INGREDIENTS LTD
5 Intermodal Dr Unit 1, Brampton, ON, L6T 5V9
(905) 789-3200
Emp Here 46   *Sales* 10,343,330
SIC 2087 Flavoring extracts and syrups, nec
Martino Brambilla

D-U-N-S 25-173-2517   (HQ)
ENTERTAINMENT ONE GP LIMITED
CD PLUS GROUP OF STORES
(*Suby of* 4384768 CANADA INC)
70 Driver Rd Unit 1, Brampton, ON, L6T 5V2
(905) 624-7337
Emp Here 300   *Sales* 695,300,000
SIC 5099 Durable goods, nec
Darren Throop
Joseph Sparacio

D-U-N-S 20-807-6328   (SL)
ESSAG CANADA INC
HOLIDAY INN TORONTO BRAMPTON HOTEL & CONFERENCE CENTRE
30 Peel Centre Dr, Brampton, ON, L6T 4G3

Emp Here 80   *Sales* 7,591,920
SIC 7011 Hotels and motels
Eshri Singh
Amit Talreja
Khurram Shahid

D-U-N-S 20-562-7826   (BR)
EXP SERVICES INC
(*Suby of* EXP GLOBAL INC)
1595 Clark Blvd, Brampton, ON, L6T 4V1
(905) 793-9800
Emp Here 200
SIC 8711 Engineering services
John Mckee

D-U-N-S 25-320-2634   (HQ)
EXPORT PACKERS COMPANY INCORPORATED
107 Walker Dr, Brampton, ON, L6T 5K5
(905) 792-9700
Emp Here 150   *Sales* 157,677,520
SIC 5142 Packaged frozen goods
Jeffrey Rubenstein
Daniel Leblanc
Werter Mior

Brian Lampert

D-U-N-S 20-164-7948   (HQ)
EXPORT PACKERS COMPANY LIMITED
(*Suby of* EXPORT PACKERS COMPANY IN-
CORPORATED)
107 Walker Dr, Brampton, ON, L6T 5K5
(905) 792-9700
Emp Here 160   *Sales* 125,425,300
SIC 5142 Packaged frozen goods
Jeffrey Rubenstein
Daniel Leblanc
Werter Mior
Ralph Gobbi
Peter Kwong
Brian Lampert
Max Rubenstein

D-U-N-S 24-853-5978   (SL)
**FAURECIA EMISSIONS CONTROL TECH-
NOLOGIES CANADA, LTD**
(*Suby of* FAURECIA)
40 Summerlea Rd, Brampton, ON, L6T 4X3
(905) 595-5668
Emp Here 100   *Sales* 22,384,300
SIC 3714 Motor vehicle parts and accessories
Mark Stidham

D-U-N-S 24-527-4043   (SL)
FEATURE FOODS INTERNATIONAL INC
30 Finley Rd, Brampton, ON, L6T 1A9
(905) 452-7741
Emp Here 45   *Sales* 10,118,475
SIC 2035 Pickles, sauces, and salad dress-
ings
Lorne Krongold

D-U-N-S 24-048-7272   (HQ)
FLAME-TAMER FIRE & SAFETY LTD
8058 Torbram Rd, Brampton, ON, L6T 3T2
(905) 791-3102
Emp Here 19   *Sales* 13,013,550
SIC 5099 Durable goods, nec
Bruce Michon
Margaret Michon

D-U-N-S 20-596-0107   (BR)
**FORD MOTOR COMPANY OF CANADA,
LIMITED**
*BRAMALEA SALES PARTS DISTRIBUTION
CENTRE*
(*Suby of* FORD MOTOR COMPANY)
8000 Dixie Rd, Brampton, ON, L6T 2J7
(905) 459-2210
Emp Here 300
SIC 5013 Motor vehicle supplies and new
parts
David Goodman

D-U-N-S 24-966-1849   (SL)
FOUR SEASONS SITE DEVELOPMENT LTD
42 Wentworth Crt Unit 1, Brampton, ON, L6T
5K6
(905) 670-7655
Emp Here 49   *Sales* 13,892,676
SIC 1611 Highway and street construction
Rohit Bansal

D-U-N-S 24-744-6776   (SL)
FREEWAY TRANSPORTATION INC
15 Strathearn Ave, Brampton, ON, L6T 4P1
(905) 790-0446
Emp Here 40   *Sales* 20,798,680
SIC 4731 Freight transportation arrangement
Stewart Crawford

D-U-N-S 24-181-6693   (SL)
FYBON INDUSTRIES LIMITED
5 Tilbury Crt, Brampton, ON, L6T 3T4
(905) 291-1090
Emp Here 70   *Sales* 12,838,210
SIC 2297 Nonwoven fabrics
Steven Knapp
Joshua Ronn
Andrew Tylman

D-U-N-S 25-318-8684   (BR)
GAP (CANADA) INC

GAP
(*Suby of* THE GAP INC)
89 Walker Dr, Brampton, ON, L6T 5K5
(905) 793-8888
Emp Here 150
SIC 5651 Family clothing stores
Michele Murphy

D-U-N-S 24-180-8252   (SL)
GATEWAY CHEVROLET INC
2 Gateway Blvd, Brampton, ON, L6T 4A7
(905) 791-7111
Emp Here 60   *Sales* 37,756,800
SIC 5511 New and used car dealers
William Wallace

D-U-N-S 25-092-0972   (SL)
GATEWAY CHEVROLET OLDSMOBILE INC
GENERAL MOTORS
2 Gateway Blvd, Brampton, ON, L6T 4A7
(905) 791-7111
Emp Here 70   *Sales* 44,559,778
SIC 5511 New and used car dealers
William Wallash

D-U-N-S 25-997-1141   (HQ)
GENERAL CABLE COMPANY LTD
(*Suby of* PRYSMIAN SPA)
156 Parkshore Dr, Brampton, ON, L6T 5M1
(905) 791-6886
Emp Here 60   *Sales* 111,972,850
SIC 3315 Steel wire and related products
Massimo Battino
Sean Fagin
Emerson Moser
Jeffrey Whelan
Ramon Ceron
Charles Reagh

D-U-N-S 24-365-3003   (HQ)
**GENERAL KINETICS ENGINEERING COR-
PORATION**
110 East Dr, Brampton, ON, L6T 1C1
(905) 458-0888
Sales 15,669,010
SIC 3714 Motor vehicle parts and accessories
Charles Williamson
Robert Cathcart
Dan Marshall
Scott Griffin

D-U-N-S 20-182-7854   (HQ)
GESCO INDUSTRIES INC
(*Suby of* 2082732 ONTARIO INC)
50 Kenview Blvd, Brampton, ON, L6T 5S8
(905) 789-3755
Emp Here 20   *Sales* 69,044,160
SIC 5023 Homefurnishings
Edward Dudomaine
Sean Ward
Charles Chaikin
William Lloyd
Neil Sethi
Michael Devon

D-U-N-S 24-327-9549   (HQ)
GESCO LIMITED PARTNERSHIP
SHNIER
50 Kenview Blvd, Brampton, ON, L6T 5S8
(905) 789-3755
Emp Here 145   *Sales* 115,073,600
SIC 5023 Homefurnishings
Alan Sellery

D-U-N-S 25-365-0634   (HQ)
GIAMPAOLO INVESTMENTS LIMITED
471 Intermodal Dr, Brampton, ON, L6T 5G4
(905) 790-3095
Emp Here 2   *Sales* 32,802,000
SIC 6719 Holding companies, nec
Mike Giampaolo
Antonio Giampaolo
Lionel Perstaud

D-U-N-S 24-301-9684   (SL)
**GOLDEN FLEECE FOOD DISTRIBUTORS
AND WHOLESALERS LTD**

16 Baker Rd, Brampton, ON, L6T 4E3
(905) 458-1101
Emp Here 29   *Sales* 24,231,733
SIC 5142 Packaged frozen goods
Spiro Mikroyiannakis
Nick Mikroyiannakis
Jim Mikroyiannakis
George Mikroyiannakis
John Mikroyiannakis
Maria Mikroyiannakis

D-U-N-S 20-822-2518   (SL)
GONTE CONSTRUCTION LTD
190 Clark Blvd, Brampton, ON, L6T 4A8
(905) 456-6488
Emp Here 40   *Sales* 12,902,485
SIC 1521 Single-family housing construction
Sinduja Jeyakumar

D-U-N-S 24-378-5966   (SL)
GOREWAY STATION PARTNERSHIP
8600 Goreway Dr, Brampton, ON, L6T 0A8
(905) 595-4700
Emp Here 40   *Sales* 25,064,560
SIC 4911 Electric services
Keith Peddle

D-U-N-S 20-166-2855   (HQ)
GRAY HAND TOOL SALES LIMITED
299 Orenda Rd, Brampton, ON, L6T 1E8
(905) 457-3014
Emp Here 2   *Sales* 29,066,310
SIC 5072 Hardware
Alex Gray

D-U-N-S 25-192-3751   (SL)
GRAY TOOLS CANADA INC
(*Suby of* GRAY HAND TOOL SALES LIM-
ITED)
299 Orenda Rd, Brampton, ON, L6T 1E8
(800) 567-0518
Emp Here 62   *Sales* 11,909,270
SIC 3423 Hand and edge tools, nec
Alex Gray
Michael Wilson

D-U-N-S 24-321-1070   (HQ)
GREENFIELD GLOBAL QUEBEC INC
COMMERCIAL ALCOHOL
(*Suby of* GREENFIELD GLOBAL, INC)
2 Chelsea Ln, Brampton, ON, L6T 3Y4
(905) 790-7500
Emp Here 30   *Sales* 11,619,720
SIC 2869 Industrial organic chemicals, nec
Robert Gallant
Kenneth Field
Marty Cormier
Stewart Davidson
Gary McInerney
David Meadows
David Salt
Brian Keith
Barry Wortzman
Douglas Dias

D-U-N-S 24-337-9419   (SL)
GRENHALL INDUSTRIES INC
1 Imperial Crt, Brampton, ON, L6T 4X4
(905) 458-8549
Emp Here 25   *Sales* 18,258,625
SIC 5169 Chemicals and allied products, nec
Lou Halpern

D-U-N-S 25-099-0348   (HQ)
GUNNEBO CANADA INC
(*Suby of* GUNNEBO AB)
9 Van Der Graaf Crt, Brampton, ON, L6T 5E5
(905) 595-4140
Emp Here 75   *Sales* 87,037,050
SIC 5065 Electronic parts and equipment, nec
John Haining
Eric Schneider

D-U-N-S 20-935-2483   (SL)
**HARRCO DESIGN AND MANUFACTURING
LIMITED**
METRIC STORAGE SYSTEMS

50 Devon Rd, Brampton, ON, L6T 5B5
(905) 564-0577
Emp Here 50   *Sales* 22,358,700
SIC 5046 Commercial equipment, nec
Douglas Baxter
Jason Baxter
Jim Lawrence

D-U-N-S 20-166-7896   (HQ)
**HARWELL ELECTRIC SUPPLY CO. LIM-
ITED**
2 Wilkinson Rd, Brampton, ON, L6T 4M3
(905) 848-0060
Emp Here 15   *Sales* 17,886,960
SIC 5063 Electrical apparatus and equipment
Joseph Vassallo

D-U-N-S 20-809-1731   (SL)
HOME TEXTILES INC
35 Coventry Rd, Brampton, ON, L6T 4V7
(905) 792-1551
Emp Here 25   *Sales* 12,721,400
SIC 5023 Homefurnishings
Liliana Macreanu
Lidio Godino

D-U-N-S 20-069-5976   (SL)
**HOMELIFE SUPERSTARS REAL ESTATE
LIMITED**
2565 Steeles Ave E Unit 11, Brampton, ON,
L6T 4L6
(905) 792-7800
Emp Here 100   *Sales* 27,175,600
SIC 6531 Real estate agents and managers
Bhupinder Pal Randhawa

D-U-N-S 20-167-3159   (SL)
**HUBBERT'S PROCESSING AND SALES
LIMITED**
HUBBERTS INDUSTRIES
109 East Dr, Brampton, ON, L6T 1B6
(905) 791-0101
Emp Here 83   *Sales* 28,692,270
SIC 2079 Edible fats and oils
Kenneth Hubbert
Craig Simpkins
Mike Flammia

D-U-N-S 20-009-1189   (HQ)
HUDSON'S BAY COMPANY
SAKS FIFTH AVENUE OFF 5TH CANADA
8925 Torbram Rd, Brampton, ON, L6T 4G1
(905) 792-4400
Emp Here 600   *Sales* 7,054,530,528
SIC 5311 Department stores
Robert Baker
Richard Baker
Helena Foulkes
Ian Putnam
David J. Schwartz
Andrew Blecher
Stephen J. Gold
Bari Harlam
Janis Leigh
Kerry Mader

D-U-N-S 24-803-2265   (BR)
HUDSON'S BAY COMPANY
SAKS FIFTH AVENUE
(*Suby of* HUDSON'S BAY TRADING COM-
PANY LP)
8925 Torbram Rd, Brampton, ON, L6T 4G1
(905) 792-4400
Emp Here 80
SIC 5311 Department stores

D-U-N-S 25-092-7423   (BR)
HUDSON'S BAY COMPANY
BAY, THE
(*Suby of* HUDSON'S BAY COMPANY)
25 Peel Centre Dr Suite 3, Brampton, ON, L6T
3R5
(905) 793-5100
Emp Here 300
SIC 5311 Department stores
Timothy Ellis

D-U-N-S 24-320-1881   (SL)
IKON OFFICE SOLUTIONS, ULC
100 Westcreek Blvd, Brampton, ON, L6T 5V7

Emp Here 24   Sales 10,732,176
SIC 5044 Office equipment
Tony Martino

D-U-N-S 20-403-8012   (HQ)
IMCD CANADA LIMITED
(Suby of IMCD N.V.)
99 Summerlea Rd, Brampton, ON, L6T 4V2
(800) 575-3382
Emp Here 125   Sales 188,219,360
SIC 5169 Chemicals and allied products, nec
Kevin Russell
Spence Morris
Devin Chan
Michael Foxwell
Ross G. Clark

D-U-N-S 20-112-6468   (BR)
INDIGO BOOKS & MUSIC INC
CHAPTERS DISTRIBUTION
(Suby of INDIGO BOOKS & MUSIC INC)
100 Alfred Kuehne Blvd, Brampton, ON, L6T 4K4
(905) 789-1234
Emp Here 200
SIC 5192 Books, periodicals, and newspapers

D-U-N-S 24-765-2241   (SL)
INOX INDUSTRIES INC
60 Summerlea Rd, Brampton, ON, L6T 4X3
(905) 799-9996
Emp Here 55   Sales 12,838,925
SIC 3312 Blast furnaces and steel mills
Pat Tremamunno
Mimma Tremamunno

D-U-N-S 20-626-4749   (SL)
INTERNATIONAL PLAYING CARD COMPANY LIMITED
JARDEN
(Suby of NEWELL BRANDS INC.)
845 Intermodal Dr Unit 1, Brampton, ON, L6T 0C6
(905) 488-7102
Emp Here 25   Sales 13,013,550
SIC 5092 Toys and hobby goods and supplies
Jim Rotz

D-U-N-S 25-105-9499   (HQ)
IRON MOUNTAIN CANADA OPERATIONS ULC
ARCHIVES IRON MOUNTAIN
(Suby of IRON MOUNTAIN INCORPORATED)
195 Summerlea Rd, Brampton, ON, L6T 4P6
(905) 792-7099
Emp Here 15   Sales 239,695,300
SIC 4226 Special warehousing and storage, nec
Bob Brennan
John P. Lawrence
Ernest Cloutier

D-U-N-S 25-150-4478   (HQ)
ISG TRANSPORTATION INC
7965 Goreway Dr Suite 2, Brampton, ON, L6T 5T5
(905) 799-1300
Sales 75,099,800
SIC 4731 Freight transportation arrangement
Vincent Roti
Vito Ierullo
Spencer Mckone

D-U-N-S 25-367-8650   (BR)
ITALPASTA LIMITED
(Suby of ITALPASTA LIMITED)
199 Summerlea Rd, Brampton, ON, L6T 4E5
(905) 792-9928
Emp Here 200
SIC 2098 Macaroni and spaghetti
Vito Marchese

D-U-N-S 24-538-4698   (HQ)

ITALPASTA LIMITED
116 Nuggett Crt, Brampton, ON, L6T 5A9
(416) 798-7154
Sales 116,972,400
SIC 2098 Macaroni and spaghetti
Joseph Vitale
Frank Dimichino

D-U-N-S 25-397-5361   (SL)
JAMBO KITMEER LTD
1810 Steeles Ave E, Brampton, ON, L6T 1A7
(905) 792-3009
Emp Here 85   Sales 42,357,370
SIC 5136 Men's and boy's clothing
Ahmed Bhimji

D-U-N-S 24-665-6029   (SL)
JAY ELECTRIC LIMITED
21 Kenview Blvd Unit 2, Brampton, ON, L6T 5G7
(905) 793-4000
Emp Here 100   Sales 21,782,900
SIC 1731 Electrical work
Frank Malisani

D-U-N-S 24-369-7187   (BR)
JONES PACKAGING INC
JONES CONTRACT PACKAGING SERVICES, DIV OF
(Suby of JONES PACKAGING INC)
55 Walker Dr, Brampton, ON, L6T 5K5
(800) 387-1188
Emp Here 150
SIC 7389 Business services, nec
Robert Radich

D-U-N-S 24-337-6345   (HQ)
JORDAHL CANADA INC
CONTINENTAL DECON
35 Devon Rd, Brampton, ON, L6T 5B6
(905) 458-5855
Emp Here 1   Sales 22,200,100
SIC 3548 Welding apparatus
Thomas Karjama
Steve Logan
Martin Davies

D-U-N-S 20-085-2460   (SL)
JUST ON TIME FREIGHT SYSTEMS INC
J.O.T. FREIGHT SYSTEMS
95 Hedgedale Rd Unit 3-4, Brampton, ON, L6T 5P3
(905) 846-9552
Emp Here 45   Sales 23,398,515
SIC 4731 Freight transportation arrangement
Chandrekant Doulat
Kulwinder Nijjar

D-U-N-S 25-213-9381   (SL)
KATHDEN SERVICES INC
239 Advance Blvd, Brampton, ON, L6T 4J2

Emp Here 23   Sales 10,285,002
SIC 5074 Plumbing and heating equipment and supplies (hydronics)
Kathy Mclaughlin
Denis Dubuc
Bill Craig

D-U-N-S 25-274-9122   (HQ)
KLEEN-FLO HOLDINGS INC
75 Advance Blvd, Brampton, ON, L6T 4N1
(905) 793-4311
Emp Here 1   Sales 16,401,000
SIC 6712 Bank holding companies
Keith Osborne

D-U-N-S 20-555-1856   (HQ)
KLEEN-FLO TUMBLER INDUSTRIES LIMITED
UNIVERSAL POWER CANADA, DIV OF
(Suby of KLEEN-FLO HOLDINGS INC)
75 Advance Blvd, Brampton, ON, L6T 4N1
(905) 793-4311
Emp Here 60   Sales 28,205,172
SIC 2992 Lubricating oils and greases
Keith Osborne

Edrei Sills

D-U-N-S 20-337-8588   (BR)
KONICA MINOLTA BUSINESS SOLUTIONS (CANADA) LTD
IT WEAPONS DIV.
(Suby of KONICA MINOLTA, INC.)
7965 Goreway Dr Unit 1, Brampton, ON, L6T 5T5
(905) 494-1040
Emp Here 100
SIC 7379 Computer related services, nec
Mike Dabner

D-U-N-S 24-312-5296   (BR)
KRUGER INC
(Suby of KRUGER INC)
10 Pedigree Crt, Brampton, ON, L6T 5T8
(905) 759-1012
Emp Here 195
SIC 2653 Corrugated and solid fiber boxes
Murray Hulley

D-U-N-S 25-913-4864   (SL)
KUTCO INTERNATIONAL INC
275 Walker Dr, Brampton, ON, L6T 3W5

Emp Here 50   Sales 11,242,750
SIC 2015 Poultry slaughtering and processing
Karen Vanstone

D-U-N-S 25-255-2484   (HQ)
LEGACY TRANSPORTATION SOLUTIONS INC
(Suby of TFI INTERNATIONAL INC)
1 Kenview Blvd Unit 210, Brampton, ON, L6T 5E6
(416) 798-4940
Emp Here 15   Sales 36,679,060
SIC 4731 Freight transportation arrangement
Tony Trichilo
Gord Kipfer

D-U-N-S 24-349-8537   (BR)
MAPEI INC
(Suby of EMME ESSE VI SRL)
95 Walker Dr, Brampton, ON, L6T 5K5
(905) 799-2663
Emp Here 80
SIC 2891 Adhesives and sealants
Bob Welsh

D-U-N-S 25-531-0104   (BR)
MAPLEHURST BAKERIES INC
MAPLEHURST BAKERIES, DIV OF
(Suby of GEORGE WESTON LIMITED)
379 Orenda Rd, Brampton, ON, L6T 1G6
(905) 791-7400
Emp Here 200
SIC 2051 Bread, cake, and related products
Erik Riswik

D-U-N-S 24-317-2892   (HQ)
MATALCO INC
(Suby of TRIPLE M METAL LP)
850 Intermodal Dr, Brampton, ON, L6T 0B5
(905) 790-2511
Sales 10,753,140
SIC 3291 Abrasive products
Michael Giampaolo
Armand Sanguigni
Tito Giampaolo
Lino Persaud

D-U-N-S 20-296-0605   (HQ)
MATSU MANUFACTURING INC
MATCOR
7657 Bramalea Rd, Brampton, ON, L6T 5V3
(905) 291-5000
Emp Here 15   Sales 97,292,400
SIC 3465 Automotive stampings
Daniel Tiberini
Galliano Tiberini

D-U-N-S 25-227-6485   (SL)
MAXPRO MANAGEMENT SERVICES LTD
170 Wilkinson Rd Unit 3, Brampton, ON, L6T 4Z5

(905) 452-9669
Emp Here 12   Sales 19,060,320
SIC 8742 Management consulting services
Inderpal Kahlon
Gagan Sidhu
Tejinder Dhot

D-U-N-S 24-627-1381   (SL)
MDF MECHANICAL LIMITED
2100 Steeles Ave E, Brampton, ON, L6T 1A7
(905) 789-9944
Emp Here 140   Sales 32,629,100
SIC 1711 Plumbing, heating, air-conditioning
Angelo Triano
Vincent Triano

D-U-N-S 24-421-1439   (SL)
METEX HEAT TREATING LTD
(Suby of S & B BAWA HOLDCO LTD)
225 Wilkinson Rd, Brampton, ON, L6T 4M2
(905) 453-9700
Emp Here 45   Sales 10,504,575
SIC 3398 Metal heat treating
Surjit Bawa
Baljit Bawa

D-U-N-S 25-473-5491   (SL)
METRO WIDE PERSONNEL INC
11 Blair Dr, Brampton, ON, L6T 2H4

Emp Here 49   Sales 11,611,530
SIC 7361 Employment agencies
Tom Linton

D-U-N-S 24-195-8933   (BR)
MIDLAND TRANSPORT LIMITED
TRANSPORT DIVISION
(Suby of IRVING, J. D. LIMITED)
102 Glidden Rd, Brampton, ON, L6T 5N4
(905) 456-5555
Emp Here 200
SIC 4213 Trucking, except local
Vince White

D-U-N-S 20-270-1330   (BR)
MIDLAND TRANSPORT LIMITED
MIDLAND LOGISTICS & FREIGHT BROKERAGE, DIV OF
(Suby of IRVING, J. D. LIMITED)
102 Glidden Rd, Brampton, ON, L6T 5N4
(905) 456-5555
Emp Here 100
SIC 4212 Local trucking, without storage
Matthew Bourque

D-U-N-S 25-724-1414   (SL)
MIELE ENTERPRISES INC
87 Wentworth Crt, Brampton, ON, L6T 5L4
(416) 740-1096
Emp Here 22   Sales 10,356,082
SIC 1542 Nonresidential construction, nec
Maurizo Miele
Sandy Miele

D-U-N-S 24-204-6972   (SL)
MIXOLOGY CANADA INC
45 Armthorpe Rd, Brampton, ON, L6T 5M4
(905) 793-9100
Emp Here 25   Sales 20,889,425
SIC 5149 Groceries and related products, nec
Scott Megit
Janet Chantry
Joanne Megit
Murray Megit

D-U-N-S 25-192-3330   (SL)
MORGAN CANADA CORPORATION
12 Chelsea Lane, Brampton, ON, L6T 3Y4
(905) 791-8130
Emp Here 145   Sales 32,457,235
SIC 3713 Truck and bus bodies
Norb Markert

D-U-N-S 20-065-6408   (HQ)
MULTI-GLASS INSULATION LTD
3925 Steeles Ave E Unit 1 & 2, Brampton, ON, L6T 5W5

(416) 798-3900
Emp Here 38   Sales 20,122,830
SIC 5033 Roofing, siding, and insulation
Robert Fellows
Keith F Eaman

D-U-N-S 24-199-7006   (SL)
NAHANNI STEEL PRODUCTS INC
JANCOX STAMPINGS
38 Deerhurst Dr, Brampton, ON, L6T 5R8
(905) 791-2100
Emp Here 60   Sales 11,525,100
SIC 3469 Metal stampings, nec
Paul Janza
Vlado Zupanec

D-U-N-S 20-285-7496   (HQ)
NATIONAL RECYCLING INC
5 Copper Rd, Brampton, ON, L6T 4W5
(905) 790-2828
Sales 16,427,440
SIC 5399 Miscellaneous general merchandise
Syed Rahman
Pawel Konieczny
Saif Shah
Sarah Couto

D-U-N-S 24-078-1922   (SL)
NATURE'S SUNSHINE PRODUCTS OF
CANADA LTD
(Suby of NATURES SUNSHINE PRODUCTS,
INC.)
44 Peel Centre Dr Unit 402, Brampton, ON,
L6T 4B5
(905) 458-6100
Emp Here 28   Sales 23,396,156
SIC 5149 Groceries and related products, nec
Garry Ford
Bryant Yates

D-U-N-S 20-036-7472   (HQ)
NCH CANADA INC
LUBEMASTER CONSTRUCTION
(Suby of NCH CORPORATION)
247 Orenda Rd, Brampton, ON, L6T 1E6
(905) 457-5220
Emp Here 40   Sales 114,276,040
SIC 5169 Chemicals and allied products, nec
Irvin Levy
Russ Price
Lester Levy
Milton Levy
Carlos A. Cerqueira

D-U-N-S 20-171-5620   (HQ)
NEFF KITCHEN MANUFACTURERS LIM-
ITED
151 East Dr, Brampton, ON, L6T 1B5
(905) 791-7770
Sales 33,664,750
SIC 2434 Wood kitchen cabinets
Paul J. Neff
Paul Gardner

D-U-N-S 20-696-4418   (HQ)
NEXCYCLE CANADA LTD
235 Wilkinson Rd, Brampton, ON, L6T 4M2
(905) 454-2666
Emp Here 100   Sales 63,463,090
SIC 4953 Refuse systems
Keith Harradence

D-U-N-S 24-477-2315   (HQ)
NEXCYCLE PLASTICS INC
NPI
235 Wilkinson Rd, Brampton, ON, L6T 4M2
(905) 454-2666
Emp Here 77   Sales 55,809,250
SIC 4953 Refuse systems
Laurie Borg
Christopher Turney

D-U-N-S 25-352-6651   (BR)
NEXCYCLE PLASTICS INC
NU PLAST
(Suby of NEXCYCLE PLASTICS INC)
235 Wilkinson Rd, Brampton, ON, L6T 4M2

(905) 454-2666
Emp Here 100
SIC 4953 Refuse systems

D-U-N-S 25-818-7806   (SL)
NORTH-EAST TUBES INC
29 Nuggett Crt, Brampton, ON, L6T 5A9
(905) 792-1200
Emp Here 12   Sales 12,004,068
SIC 5051 Metals service centers and offices
Robert Zimmerman

D-U-N-S 24-869-1222   (HQ)
NORWALL GROUP INC
150 Delta Park Blvd, Brampton, ON, L6T 5T6
(905) 791-2700
Sales 34,155,920
SIC 5198 Paints, varnishes, and supplies
James J. Patton
Bruce Mitchel

D-U-N-S 20-650-2093   (HQ)
NOVA COLD LOGISTICS ULC
(Suby of BROOKFIELD ASSET MANAGE-
MENT INC)
745 Intermodal Dr, Brampton, ON, L6T 5W2
(905) 791-8585
Sales 16,456,480
SIC 4222 Refrigerated warehousing and stor-
age
Ken Maclean

D-U-N-S 24-859-1609   (SL)
O-I CANADA CORP
O-I
(Suby of OWENS-ILLINOIS, INC.)
100 West Dr, Brampton, ON, L6T 2J5
(905) 457-2423
Emp Here 380   Sales 97,162,200
SIC 3221 Glass containers
Al Strouck
Anindya Ghosh
Ed White
Jim Baehren
Ed Snyder
Carol Fleck

D-U-N-S 20-299-0727   (HQ)
OAKEN HOLDINGS INC
BOBCAT OF TORONTO
241 Deerhurst Dr, Brampton, ON, L6T 5K3
(416) 679-4172
Emp Here 24   Sales 13,300,728
SIC 5082 Construction and mining machinery
Hugo Sorensen
Kai Sorensen
Matt Dewitt

D-U-N-S 25-333-1227   (BR)
OLYMEL S.E.C.
(Suby of OLYMEL S.E.C.)
318 Orenda Rd, Brampton, ON, L6T 1G1
(905) 793-5757
Emp Here 400
SIC 2015 Poultry slaughtering and processing
Mark Cerbu

D-U-N-S 20-255-6130   (BR)
OLYMEL S.E.C.
(Suby of OLYMEL S.E.C.)
14 Westwyn Crt, Brampton, ON, L6T 4T5
(905) 796-6947
Emp Here 200
SIC 2011 Meat packing plants

D-U-N-S 20-757-5304   (HQ)
OSIRIS INC
SHOWCASE
1 Wilkinson Rd, Brampton, ON, L6T 4M6
(905) 452-0392
Emp Here 25   Sales 76,054,000
SIC 5399 Miscellaneous general merchandise
Balaji Jagadison

D-U-N-S 24-524-1344   (SL)
PACKALL CONSULTANTS (1981) LIMITED
2 Shaftsbury Lane, Brampton, ON, L6T 3X7

(905) 793-0177
Emp Here 120   Sales 19,062,960
SIC 3081 Unsupported plastics film and sheet
Henry Ciszewski

D-U-N-S 24-796-2384   (HQ)
PACKALL PACKAGING INC
2 Shaftsbury Lane, Brampton, ON, L6T 3X7
(905) 793-0177
Sales 28,594,440
SIC 3081 Unsupported plastics film and sheet
Henry Ciszewski

D-U-N-S 24-803-1247   (BR)
PARMALAT CANADA INC
(Suby of PARMALAT SPA)
16 Shaftsbury Lane, Brampton, ON, L6T 4G7
(905) 791-6100
Emp Here 250
SIC 2026 Fluid milk
Brad Beaudoin

D-U-N-S 25-297-1981   (BR)
PEEL DISTRICT SCHOOL BOARD
MAYFIELD SECONDARY SCHOOL
(Suby of PEEL DISTRICT SCHOOL BOARD)
5000 Mayfield Rd Rr 4, Brampton, ON, L6T
3S1
(905) 846-6060
Emp Here 130
SIC 8211 Elementary and secondary schools
Kent Armstrong

D-U-N-S 25-283-1409   (BR)
PEEL DISTRICT SCHOOL BOARD
NORTH FIELD OFFICE
(Suby of PEEL DISTRICT SCHOOL BOARD)
215 Orenda Rd, Brampton, ON, L6T 5L1
(905) 451-2862
Emp Here 140
SIC 8211 Elementary and secondary schools
Sonya Rubio

D-U-N-S 20-300-2704   (SL)
PLEXXIS SOFTWARE INC
PLEXXIS SOFTWARE
14 Abacus Rd, Brampton, ON, L6T 5B7
(905) 889-8979
Emp Here 60   Sales 12,831,060
SIC 7372 Prepackaged software
Christopher Loranger

D-U-N-S 20-609-9558   (SL)
POCZO MANUFACTURING COMPANY LIM-
ITED
215 Wilkinson Rd, Brampton, ON, L6T 4M2
(905) 452-0567
Emp Here 50   Sales 11,100,050
SIC 3599 Industrial machinery, nec
Rose Poczo
Edith Mcmahon

D-U-N-S 25-311-7923   (HQ)
POWERSMITHS INTERNATIONAL CORP
8985 Airport Rd, Brampton, ON, L6T 5T2
(905) 791-1493
Emp Here 1   Sales 10,233,650
SIC 3677 Electronic coils and transformers
Cyril Eldridge
Philip Ling

D-U-N-S 24-207-9791   (BR)
PRAXAIR CANADA INC
(Suby of LINDE PUBLIC LIMITED COM-
PANY)
80 Westcreek Blvd Unit 1, Brampton, ON, L6T
0B8
(905) 595-3788
Emp Here 100
SIC 2813 Industrial gases
Joe Lacharity

D-U-N-S 20-150-1943   (SL)
PREMIER EVENT TENT RENTALS INC
10 Carson Crt, Brampton, ON, L6T 4P8
(416) 225-7500
Emp Here 25   Sales 11,087,250
SIC 7389 Business services, nec

Andrew Ussher
Rachel Ussher

D-U-N-S 24-848-6420   (SL)
PREMIUM LINE TRANSPORT INC
11 West Dr, Brampton, ON, L6T 4T2
(905) 454-2222
Emp Here 34   Sales 11,278,200
SIC 4731 Freight transportation arrangement
Uwe Petroschke
Roger Cloutier
Philip Petroschke

D-U-N-S 24-699-7733   (SL)
PRIVATE RECIPES LIMITED
12 Indell Lane, Brampton, ON, L6T 3Y3
(905) 799-1022
Emp Here 49   Sales 11,203,202
SIC 2038 Frozen specialties, nec
John Morrell

D-U-N-S 24-978-0164   (SL)
PRO-PLY CUSTOM PLYWOOD INC
1195 Clark Blvd Suite 905, Brampton, ON,
L6T 3W4
(905) 564-2327
Emp Here 55   Sales 17,757,696
SIC 2435 Hardwood veneer and plywood
Vaughn Lavigne

D-U-N-S 20-181-4220   (HQ)
QUAD LOGISTIX INC
5 Paget Rd, Brampton, ON, L6T 5S2
(905) 789-6225
Emp Here 50   Sales 12,596,320
SIC 4225 General warehousing and storage
Nick Cianci

D-U-N-S 24-092-7160   (SL)
QUEST BRANDS INC
1 Van Der Graaf Crt, Brampton, ON, L6T 5E5
(905) 789-6868
Emp Here 45   Sales 11,387,655
SIC 5211 Lumber and other building materials
David Webb
Leeanne Murray

D-U-N-S 24-423-5388   (SL)
QUIET HARMONY INC
CALIFORNIA CLEANING
30 Intermodal Dr Unit 43, Brampton, ON, L6T
5K1
(905) 794-0622
Emp Here 125   Sales 3,996,000
SIC 7349 Building maintenance services, nec
Charlie Camilleri

D-U-N-S 20-556-9668   (SL)
R.M. FERGUSON & COMPANY INC
FERGUSON CHEMICAL INNOVATION, DIV
OF
(Suby of AZELIS US HOLDING, INC.)
235 Advance Blvd Suite 1, Brampton, ON, L6T
4J2
(905) 458-5553
Emp Here 25   Sales 18,258,625
SIC 5169 Chemicals and allied products, nec
David Jackson

D-U-N-S 24-124-1363   (SL)
RELAMPING SERVICES CANADA LIMITED
48 West Dr, Brampton, ON, L6T 3T6
(905) 457-1815
Emp Here 80   Sales 25,775,468
SIC 7349 Building maintenance services, nec
David Searle

D-U-N-S 24-349-8719   (HQ)
RENIN CANADA CORP
J. J. HOME PRODUCTS, DIV OF
(Suby of BBX CAPITAL CORPORATION)
110 Walker Dr, Brampton, ON, L6T 4H6
(905) 791-7930
Sales 69,597,500
SIC 2431 Millwork
Kevin Campbell
Joe Ruffo
Bob Armstrong

David Murray
Aziz Hirji

D-U-N-S 24-891-8062   (SL)
ROYAL CANADIAN STEEL INC
70 Titan Rd, Brampton, ON, L6T 4A3
(905) 454-7274
Emp Here 35   *Sales* 48,951,097
SIC 5051 Metals service centers and offices
Feroz Ali Jessani
Karim Jessani
Anwar Jessani

D-U-N-S 24-199-2502   (HQ)
ROYAL CONTAINERS LTD
80 Midair Crt, Brampton, ON, L6T 5V1
(905) 789-8787
Sales 51,289,371
SIC 2653 Corrugated and solid fiber boxes
Kim Nelson
Bill Routledge

D-U-N-S 24-244-3831   (BR)
RYDER TRUCK RENTAL CANADA LTD
(*Suby of* RYDER SYSTEM, INC.)
30 Pedigree Crt Suite 1, Brampton, ON, L6T 5T8
(905) 759-2000
Emp Here 200
SIC 8721 Accounting, auditing, and bookkeeping
Mark Greenslade

D-U-N-S 20-280-5040   (SL)
SARATOGA POTATO CHIP COMPANY INC
OLDE YORK POTATO CHIPS
230 Deerhurst Dr, Brampton, ON, L6T 5R8
(905) 458-4100
Emp Here 100   *Sales* 34,569,000
SIC 2096 Potato chips and similar snacks
Julie Forkan
Peter Margie
Janet Margie

D-U-N-S 24-544-9095   (HQ)
SAVARIA CONCORD LIFTS INC
(*Suby of* CORPORATION SAVARIA)
2 Walker Dr, Brampton, ON, L6T 5E1
(905) 791-5555
Sales 33,300,150
SIC 3534 Elevators and moving stairways
Marcel Bourassa
Sebastien Bourassa
Helene Bernier
Jean-Marie Bourassa

D-U-N-S 20-526-6794   (HQ)
SCHAEFER SYSTEM INTERNATIONAL LIMITED
(*Suby of* FRITZ SCHAFER GMBH & CO KG, EINRICHTUNGSSYSTEME)
140 Nuggett Crt, Brampton, ON, L6T 5H4
(905) 458-5399
Sales 14,054,634
SIC 5093 Scrap and waste materials
Rudolph Keller
Wolfgang Pazulla
Carmen Noori

D-U-N-S 24-926-9341   (HQ)
SENSORMATIC CANADA INCORPORATED
ADT RETAIL
(*Suby of* JOHNSON CONTROLS INTERNATIONAL PUBLIC LIMITED COMPANY)
7 Paget Rd, Brampton, ON, L6T 5S2
(905) 792-2858
Emp Here 15   *Sales* 34,132,895
SIC 7382 Security systems services
Robert Miller

D-U-N-S 20-881-5985   (HQ)
SEW-EURODRIVE COMPANY OF CANADA LTD
210 Walker Dr, Brampton, ON, L6T 3W1
(905) 791-1553
Emp Here 100   *Sales* 38,850,175
SIC 3566 Speed changers, drives, and gears

Anthony Peluso
Audrey Gallop

D-U-N-S 24-526-1326   (HQ)
SIEGWERK CANADA INC
SIEGWERK INK PACKAGING
40 Westwyn Crt, Brampton, ON, L6T 4T5

Emp Here 1   *Sales* 28,402,100
SIC 2893 Printing ink
Steven Abbott

D-U-N-S 24-850-0071   (SL)
SIERRA CUSTOM FOODS INC
275 Walker Dr, Brampton, ON, L6T 3W5
(905) 595-2260
Emp Here 30   *Sales* 11,565,570
SIC 0254 Poultry hatcheries
Luis Ramirez

D-U-N-S 25-510-6239   (HQ)
SIGAN INDUSTRIES INC
296 Orenda Rd, Brampton, ON, L6T 4X6
(905) 456-8888
Sales 21,301,575
SIC 2844 Toilet preparations
Dean Gangbar
Manjit Singh

D-U-N-S 20-403-0563   (HQ)
SIMPSON STRONG-TIE CANADA LIMITED
SST
(*Suby of* SIMPSON MANUFACTURING CO., INC.)
5 Kenview Blvd, Brampton, ON, L6T 5G5
(800) 999-5099
Sales 23,050,200
SIC 3452 Bolts, nuts, rivets, and washers
Mike Petrovic

D-U-N-S 25-796-2431   (BR)
SIR CORP
JACK ASTORS RESTAURANTS
(*Suby of* SIR CORP)
154 West Dr, Brampton, ON, L6T 5P1
(905) 457-5200
Emp Here 100
SIC 5812 Eating places
Greg Mccormick

D-U-N-S 24-420-1070   (SL)
SITHE GLOBAL CANADIAN POWER SERVICES LTD
8600 Goreway Dr, Brampton, ON, L6T 0A8
(905) 595-4700
Emp Here 25   *Sales* 12,991,375
SIC 4911 Electric services
Ron Sigur

D-U-N-S 20-337-5035   (HQ)
SLEEP COUNTRY CANADA HOLDINGS INC
7920 Airport Rd, Brampton, ON, L6T 4N8
(289) 748-0206
Emp Here 13   *Sales* 472,280,110
SIC 5712 Furniture stores
David Friesema
Stewart Schaefer
Sieg Will
Eric Solomon
Robert Masson
David Howcroft
Christine Magee
J. Douglas Bradley
John Cassaday
Andrew Moor

D-U-N-S 20-371-7306   (HQ)
SLEEP COUNTRY CANADA INC
(*Suby of* SLEEP COUNTRY CANADA HOLDINGS INC)
7920 Airport Rd, Brampton, ON, L6T 4N8
(289) 748-0206
Emp Here 175   *Sales* 293,373,300
SIC 5712 Furniture stores
David Friesema
David Shaw

Stephen Gunn

D-U-N-S 20-315-9264   (SL)
SLM-LOGISTICS CORPORATION
15 Bramalea Rd Suite 101, Brampton, ON, L6T 2W4
(416) 743-8866
Emp Here 40   *Sales* 10,285,240
SIC 4953 Refuse systems
Vito Buffone

D-U-N-S 24-624-4305   (SL)
SMART ENTERPRISES CORPORATION
SMART LASER GRAFIX
7956 Torbram Rd Unit 25, Brampton, ON, L6T 5A2
(416) 798-0168
Emp Here 65   *Sales* 10,661,755
SIC 2759 Commercial printing, nec
Phillip Hall
Maureen Roberts
Malcolm Gillingham
Craig Hall
Geaytan Spiteri

D-U-N-S 20-554-7750   (HQ)
SOLUTIONS 2 GO INC
15 Production Dr, Brampton, ON, L6T 4N8
(905) 564-1140
Emp Here 120   *Sales* 73,607,040
SIC 5072 Hardware
Gabrielle Chevalier
Oliver Bock
Mark Smith
Danielle Smith
Jason Gonsalves
Sherri Simoneau

D-U-N-S 20-257-1303   (SL)
SOLUTIONS 2 GO LATAM INC
15 Production Rd, Brampton, ON, L6T 4N8
(905) 564-1140
Emp Here 50   *Sales* 26,027,100
SIC 5092 Toys and hobby goods and supplies
Grabrielle Chevalier
Oliver Bock
Luis San Martin

D-U-N-S 25-148-5645   (SL)
STACKTECK SYSTEMS LIMITED
STACKTECK
1 Paget Rd, Brampton, ON, L6T 5S2
(416) 749-0880
Emp Here 195   *Sales* 43,290,195
SIC 3544 Special dies, tools, jigs, and fixtures
Randy Yakimishyn

D-U-N-S 24-060-4256   (HQ)
STELFAST INC
5 Parkshore Dr, Brampton, ON, L6T 5M1
(905) 670-9400
Emp Here 30   *Sales* 18,050,988
SIC 5085 Industrial supplies
Surinder Sakhuja

D-U-N-S 24-422-9782   (BR)
STERICYCLE ULC
STERICYCLE, ULC
(*Suby of* STERICYCLE, INC.)
95 Deerhurst Dr Suite 1, Brampton, ON, L6T 5R7
(905) 789-6660
Emp Here 100
SIC 4953 Refuse systems
Morris Melanson

D-U-N-S 25-412-2856   (HQ)
STERICYCLE ULC
(*Suby of* STERICYCLE, INC.)
19 Armthorpe Rd, Brampton, ON, L6T 5M4
(905) 595-2651
Emp Here 35   *Sales* 97,716,600
SIC 4953 Refuse systems
Charles A. Alutto
Paul Saabas
Ron Waine
Daniel V. Ginnetti
Felix Reney

Diane Knight

D-U-N-S 24-214-6439   (HQ)
STERLING PACKERS LIMITED
CONFEDERATION FREEZERS
250 Summerlea Rd, Brampton, ON, L6T 3V6
(905) 595-4300
Emp Here 1   *Sales* 41,141,200
SIC 4213 Trucking, except local
Allan Greenspan

D-U-N-S 24-131-0320   (SL)
SUMMIT INDUSTRIAL INCOME REIT
75 Summerlea Rd Unit B, Brampton, ON, L6T 4V2
(905) 791-1181
Emp Here 5   *Sales* 69,859,099
SIC 6722 Management investment, open-end
Paul Dykeman
Lou Maroun
Kimberley Hill
Jon Robbins
Ross Drake

D-U-N-S 20-165-7848   (HQ)
SUN CHEMICAL LIMITED
(*Suby of* DIC CORPORATION)
10 West Dr, Brampton, ON, L6T 4Y4
(905) 796-2222
Emp Here 150   *Sales* 200,090,250
SIC 2893 Printing ink
Brian Collict
Greg Main

D-U-N-S 20-573-4528   (HQ)
SURTECO CANADA LTD
DOELLKEN-WOODTAPE
(*Suby of* SURTECO GROUP SE)
230 Orenda Rd, Brampton, ON, L6T 1E9
(905) 759-1074
Sales 20,174,330
SIC 2295 Coated fabrics, not rubberized
Thomas Rieke
Jurgen Krupp

D-U-N-S 24-355-3893   (HQ)
SWISSPLAS LIMITED
735 Intermodal Dr, Brampton, ON, L6T 5W2
(905) 789-9300
Emp Here 3   *Sales* 14,132,790
SIC 3089 Plastics products, nec
Rory Godinho
Rui Francis Pinto
Hemang Mehta

D-U-N-S 20-410-7643   (SL)
T. A. BRANNON STEEL LIMITED
14 Tilbury Crt, Brampton, ON, L6T 3T4
(905) 453-4730
Emp Here 175   *Sales* 31,742,900
SIC 3398 Metal heat treating
Allan Brannon
Greg Kallies
Kirk Brannon
Kevin Brannon

D-U-N-S 24-877-0984   (SL)
TALL PINES SCHOOL INC
8525 Torbram Rd, Brampton, ON, L6T 5K4
(905) 458-6770
Emp Here 90   *Sales* 9,049,320
SIC 8211 Elementary and secondary schools
Elaine Flett
William Flett
Sheri Gilliard

D-U-N-S 20-626-3295   (SL)
TARO PHARMACEUTICALS INC
TAROPHARMA
(*Suby of* TARO PHARMACEUTICAL INDUSTRIES LTD.)
130 East Dr, Brampton, ON, L6T 1C1
(905) 791-8276
Emp Here 500   *Sales* 165,797,000
SIC 2834 Pharmaceutical preparations
Uday Baldota
Sunil Mehta

Andreas Wegner
Angela Moi
Elizabeth Ivey
Jayesh Shah
Stephen Manzano
Harshad Tarekh
Sudhir Valia
James Kedrowski

D-U-N-S 25-274-1012 (SL)
TAURUS CRACO MACHINERY INC
282 Orenda Rd, Brampton, ON, L6T 4X6
(905) 451-8430
Emp Here 25 *Sales* 11,875,650
SIC 5084 Industrial machinery and equipment
Peter Feindel

D-U-N-S 20-819-3656 (HQ)
TAYLOR FREEZERS INC
T F I
52 Armthorpe Rd, Brampton, ON, L6T 5M4
(905) 790-2211
Emp Here 59 *Sales* 28,619,136
SIC 5046 Commercial equipment, nec
Thomas Kappus
Gerald Kappus

D-U-N-S 24-424-1386 (HQ)
TENCORR PACKAGING INC
6 Shaftsbury Lane, Brampton, ON, L6T 3X7
(905) 799-9955
Emp Here 85 *Sales* 24,346,000
SIC 2679 Converted paper products, nec
Christopher Bartlett
Andrew Dutkiewicz
David Smallhorn

D-U-N-S 25-368-3445 (SL)
TERRAPROBE INC
11 Indell Lane, Brampton, ON, L6T 3Y3
(905) 796-2650
Emp Here 60 *Sales* 10,557,480
SIC 8711 Engineering services
Michael Tanos

D-U-N-S 25-206-3839 (HQ)
TFORCE FINAL MILE CANADA INC
(*Suby of* TFI INTERNATIONAL INC)
107 Alfred Kuehne Blvd, Brampton, ON, L6T 4K3
(905) 494-7600
Emp Here 75 *Sales* 217,395,100
SIC 7389 Business services, nec
Kal Atwal
Saskia Wijnja

D-U-N-S 24-350-1009 (HQ)
TI AUTOMOTIVE CANADA INC
(*Suby of* TI AUTOMOTIVE INC.)
316 Orenda Rd, Brampton, ON, L6T 1G3
(905) 793-7100
Emp Here 90 *Sales* 34,575,300
SIC 3465 Automotive stampings
William Kozyra
Joachim Eurkhardt
Michael Drover
Timothy Guerriero

D-U-N-S 24-926-1413 (SL)
TILWOOD DIRECT MARKETING INC
TILWOOD PUBLISHING SERVICES
300 Orenda Rd, Brampton, ON, L6T 1G2
(905) 793-8225
Emp Here 75 *Sales* 55,689,000
SIC 5192 Books, periodicals, and newspapers
Costa Menegakis
Peggy Kelcher
Francis Galea

D-U-N-S 25-422-7531 (SL)
TILWOOD PUBLISHING SERVICES INC
300 Orenda Rd, Brampton, ON, L6T 1G2
(905) 793-8225
Emp Here 75 *Sales* 55,689,000
SIC 5192 Books, periodicals, and newspapers
Costa Menegakis
Steve Manegakis

D-U-N-S 20-145-8346 (HQ)
TIPCO INC
1 Coventry Rd, Brampton, ON, L6T 4B1
(905) 791-9811
Emp Here 70 *Sales* 22,200,100
SIC 3544 Special dies, tools, jigs, and fixtures
Jack Tickins
John Ferrone

D-U-N-S 20-191-6835 (BR)
TNT FOODS INTERNATIONAL INC
(*Suby of* TNT FOODS INTERNATIONAL INC)
20 Westwyn Crt, Brampton, ON, L6T 4T5
(905) 672-1787
Emp Here 80
SIC 5144 Poultry and poultry products
Mark Cachia

D-U-N-S 24-860-2930 (HQ)
TNT FOODS INTERNATIONAL INC
20 Westwyn Crt, Brampton, ON, L6T 4T5
(905) 672-1787
Emp Here 7 *Sales* 23,161,230
SIC 2015 Poultry slaughtering and processing
Kristi Cachia
Tony Cachia

D-U-N-S 20-514-0812 (SL)
TOOLBOX SOLUTIONS INC
TOOLBOXSOLUTIONS.COM
126 Devon Rd Suite 2, Brampton, ON, L6T 5B3
(905) 458-9262
Emp Here 92 *Sales* 15,130,967
SIC 7379 Computer related services, nec
Marenos Papadopoulos
Mark Shepherd

D-U-N-S 24-330-7878 (SL)
TRANSNET FREIGHT LTD
247 Summerlea Rd, Brampton, ON, L6T 4E1
(647) 868-2762
Emp Here 27 *Sales* 14,039,109
SIC 4731 Freight transportation arrangement
Imran Mohammad

D-U-N-S 24-356-9493 (HQ)
TRIPLE M METAL LP
471 Intermodal Dr, Brampton, ON, L6T 5G4
(905) 793-7083
Emp Here 100 *Sales* 244,304,400
SIC 3341 Secondary nonferrous Metals
Oscar Moniz
Michael Barichello
Steven Leddy
Nelson Costa
Mike Commisso
Teresa Senisi

D-U-N-S 20-778-2371 (BR)
UNI-SELECT INC
(*Suby of* UNI-SELECT INC)
145 Walker Dr Suite 1, Brampton, ON, L6T 5P5
(905) 789-0115
Emp Here 100
SIC 5013 Motor vehicle supplies and new parts
Brendan O'brian

D-U-N-S 20-981-5450 (BR)
UNIFOR
CAW LOCAL 973
(*Suby of* UNIFOR)
15 Westcreek Blvd Suite 1, Brampton, ON, L6T 5T4
(905) 874-4026
Emp Here 700
SIC 8631 Labor organizations
Nick Singh

D-U-N-S 24-665-2895 (HQ)
UTI, CANADA, INC
(*Suby of* DSV A/S)
70 Driver Rd Unit 4, Brampton, ON, L6T 5V2
(905) 790-1616
Emp Here 35 *Sales* 100,033,800
SIC 4731 Freight transportation arrangement

Chris Penley
Judy Carvajal

D-U-N-S 24-545-1299 (HQ)
VAN DER GRAAF INC
2 Van Der Graaf Crt Unit 1, Brampton, ON, L6T 5R6
(905) 793-8100
Sales 32,449,475
SIC 3568 Power transmission equipment, nec
Alexander Kanaris
Henk Dekker
Pinder Saini

D-U-N-S 24-326-4707 (SL)
VAST-AUTO DISTRIBUTION ONTARIO LTD
10 Driver Rd, Brampton, ON, L6T 5V2
(905) 595-2886
Emp Here 40 *Sales* 14,568,600
SIC 5013 Motor vehicle supplies and new parts
John Delvasto
Tony Delvasto

D-U-N-S 20-036-4487 (SL)
VELCRO CANADA INC
114 East Dr, Brampton, ON, L6T 1C1
(905) 791-1630
Emp Here 175 *Sales* 57,073,800
SIC 3965 Fasteners, buttons, needles, and pins

D-U-N-S 25-315-0312 (BR)
VERSACOLD GROUP LIMITED PARTNERSHIP
VERSACOLD LOGISTICS SERVICES
107 Walker Dr, Brampton, ON, L6T 5K5
(905) 793-2653
Emp Here 100
SIC 4222 Refrigerated warehousing and storage
Victor Tschupikow

D-U-N-S 25-347-4902 (HQ)
VISION TRANSPORTATION SYSTEMS INC
VISION
7659 Bramalea Rd, Brampton, ON, L6T 5V3
(905) 858-7333
Emp Here 22 *Sales* 12,479,208
SIC 4731 Freight transportation arrangement
Tony D'attoma
Jason Georgie

D-U-N-S 25-498-3109 (BR)
WAL-MART CANADA CORP
(*Suby of* WALMART INC.)
30 Coventry Rd, Brampton, ON, L6T 5P9
(905) 793-1983
Emp Here 200
SIC 5311 Department stores
Brad Marchand

D-U-N-S 20-027-5126 (BR)
WASTE MANAGEMENT OF CANADA CORPORATION
(*Suby of* WASTE MANAGEMENT, INC.)
117 Wentworth Crt, Brampton, ON, L6T 5L4
(905) 595-3360
Emp Here 2,185
SIC 4953 Refuse systems
David Vollick

D-U-N-S 25-195-7882 (SL)
WESTCON TERMINALS (ONTARIO) LIMITED
30 Midair Crt, Brampton, ON, L6T 5V1
(905) 494-0880
Emp Here 37 *Sales* 14,258,320
SIC 4731 Freight transportation arrangement
Cheryl Pye-Finch

D-U-N-S 20-693-9881 (SL)
WESTON WOOD SOLUTIONS INC
300 Orenda Rd, Brampton, ON, L6T 1G2
(905) 677-9120
Emp Here 50 *Sales* 22,358,700
SIC 5031 Lumber, plywood, and millwork
Alan Lechem

Howard Kumer
Michael Bowman
David Gambell
Rick Ekstein
Peter Ekstein

D-U-N-S 24-977-6675 (BR)
WINNERS MERCHANTS INTERNATIONAL L.P.
WINNERS DISTRIBUTON CENTRE
(*Suby of* THE TJX COMPANIES INC)
55 West Dr, Brampton, ON, L6T 4A1
(905) 451-7200
Emp Here 500
SIC 5651 Family clothing stores
Richard Thompson

D-U-N-S 24-544-0037 (SL)
WOODLORE INTERNATIONAL INC
160 Delta Park Blvd, Brampton, ON, L6T 5T6
(905) 791-9555
Emp Here 200 *Sales* 30,864,400
SIC 2521 Wood office furniture
William J Phillips
Debbie Young
Barbara Phillips
William Phillips

D-U-N-S 24-338-9892 (HQ)
XPEDX CANADA, INC
XPEDX STORE
(*Suby of* INTERNATIONAL PAPER COMPANY)
156 Parkshore Dr, Brampton, ON, L6T 5M1
(905) 595-4351
Emp Here 36 *Sales* 50,365,800
SIC 5111 Printing and writing paper
Arthur J Douville
Walter R Klein
Michael Kearney

D-U-N-S 24-764-8801 (HQ)
YUSEN LOGISTICS (CANADA) INC
(*Suby of* NIPPON YUSEN KABUSHIKI KAISHA)
261 Parkhurst Sq, Brampton, ON, L6T 5H5
(905) 458-9622
Emp Here 36 *Sales* 23,398,515
SIC 4731 Freight transportation arrangement
T. Furusawa
Kenneth Mitchell
Brian Macalpine

D-U-N-S 25-530-3570 (SL)
ZADI FOODS LIMITED
CASA ITALIA
65 Deerhurst Dr, Brampton, ON, L6T 5R7
(905) 799-6666
Emp Here 45 *Sales* 10,118,475
SIC 2013 Sausages and other prepared meats
Vince Dibattista

D-U-N-S 20-286-9475 (SL)
ZGEMI INC
100 Wilkinson Rd Unit 18, Brampton, ON, L6T 4Y9
(905) 454-0111
Emp Here 111 *Sales* 30,074,562
SIC 1521 Single-family housing construction
Yusuf Yenilmaz
Metin Yenilmaz
Fevzi Temiz

D-U-N-S 20-371-4530 (SL)
ZOCHEM ULC
(*Suby of* ZOCHEM LLC)
1 Tilbury Crt, Brampton, ON, L6T 3T4
(905) 453-4100
Emp Here 45 *Sales* 12,449,700
SIC 2816 Inorganic pigments
Ron Crittendon
Barry Harms

Brampton, ON L6V

D-U-N-S 24-891-3899   (BR)
ALGOMA UNIVERSITY
(*Suby of* ALGOMA UNIVERSITY)
24 Queen St E Suite 102, Brampton, ON, L6V
1A3
(905) 451-0100
Emp Here 140
SIC 8221 Colleges and universities
Martha Brant

D-U-N-S 20-800-9865   (BR)
BEATTY FOODS LTD
MCDONALDS 10731
(*Suby of* BEATTY FOODS LTD)
372 Main St N, Brampton, ON, L6V 1P8
(905) 455-2841
Emp Here 90
SIC 5812 Eating places
Steve Cabral

D-U-N-S 24-138-5798   (HQ)
BRAMGATE AUTOMOTIVE INC
BRAMGATE VOLKSWAGEN
(*Suby of* BRAMGATE LEASING INC)
268 Queen St E, Brampton, ON, L6V 1B9
(905) 459-6040
Emp Here 20   *Sales* 40,903,200
SIC 5511 New and used car dealers
William Johnston Sr
William A Johnston
Bradley Johnston
Gary Turner

D-U-N-S 24-784-4103   (HQ)
BRAMGATE LEASING INC
268 Queen St E, Brampton, ON, L6V 1B9
(905) 459-6040
Sales 33,981,120
SIC 5511 New and used car dealers
William Johnston Sr
Margaret Johnston

D-U-N-S 20-750-2105   (SL)
COLONY FORD LINCOLN SALES INC
300 Queen St E, Brampton, ON, L6V 1C2
(905) 451-4094
Emp Here 70   *Sales* 44,049,600
SIC 5511 New and used car dealers
Keith T Coulter
David Kerr

D-U-N-S 25-796-0617   (BR)
CORPORATION OF THE CITY OF BRAMP-TON, THE
CENTURY GARDENS RECREATION CEN-TRE
(*Suby of* CORPORATION OF THE CITY OF
BRAMPTON, THE)
340 Vodden St E, Brampton, ON, L6V 2N2
(905) 874-2814
Emp Here 100
SIC 7999 Amusement and recreation, nec
Valma Fairgrieve

D-U-N-S 20-517-1999   (SL)
ELIZABETH FRY SOCIETY OF PEEL - HAL-TON
24 Queen St E Suite Lo1, Brampton, ON, L6V
1A3

Emp Here 49   *Sales* 11,114,817
SIC 8399 Social services, nec
Joan Winchell

D-U-N-S 20-289-8719   (SL)
EXIT REALTY HARE PEEL
134 Queen St E Suite 100, Brampton, ON,
L6V 1B2
(905) 451-2390
Emp Here 49   *Sales* 13,316,044
SIC 6531 Real estate agents and managers
Daryl Ruff

D-U-N-S 24-393-2527   (HQ)
EXP GLOBAL INC
56 Queen St E Suite 301, Brampton, ON, L6V

4M8
(855) 225-5397
Emp Here 45   *Sales* 559,852,040
SIC 8711 Engineering services
Vlad Stritesky
Richard Snith
Ivan John Dvorak
Deborah Walters
Mark Dvorak
Sean Mcmahon
Vincent Latendresse
Dominique Nadeau
Eric Charron
Michel Houle

D-U-N-S 24-760-2563   (HQ)
EXP SERVICES INC
(*Suby of* EXP GLOBAL INC)
56 Queen St E Suite 301, Brampton, ON, L6V
4M8
(905) 796-3200
Emp Here 45   *Sales* 394,262,000
SIC 8711 Engineering services
Vladimir Stritesky
Stan Gonsalves
Bryce English
Prescilla Ahn

D-U-N-S 25-050-7654   (BR)
FORTINOS SUPERMARKET LTD
(*Suby of* LOBLAW COMPANIES LIMITED)
60 Quarry Edge Dr, Brampton, ON, L6V 4K2
(905) 453-3600
Emp Here 100
SIC 5411 Grocery stores
Vicki Reddin-Gauthier

D-U-N-S 24-288-6018   (SL)
**GOODISON INSURANCE & FINANCIAL
SERVICES LTD**
36 Queen St E Suite 200, Brampton, ON, L6V
1A2
(905) 451-1236
Emp Here 25   *Sales* 14,498,100
SIC 6411 Insurance agents, brokers, and ser-vice
Scott Goodison
Brad Goodison

D-U-N-S 24-424-5163   (SL)
K R T CHRISTIAN SCHOOLS
K R T KIDDIES KOLLEGE
141 Kennedy Rd N, Brampton, ON, L6V 1X9
(905) 459-2300
Emp Here 75   *Sales* 6,961,950
SIC 8211 Elementary and secondary schools
Steven Green
Jamie Stewart

D-U-N-S 20-610-7989   (BR)
**MCDONALD'S   RESTAURANTS   OF
CANADA LIMITED**
MCDONALD'S
(*Suby of* MCDONALD'S CORPORATION)
344 Queen St E, Brampton, ON, L6V 1C3
(905) 459-8800
Emp Here 112
SIC 5812 Eating places
Salman Ali

D-U-N-S 25-801-6054   (BR)
METRO ONTARIO INC
FOOD BASICS
(*Suby of* METRO INC)
227 Vodden St E, Brampton, ON, L6V 1N2
(905) 451-7842
Emp Here 105
SIC 5411 Grocery stores
Graham Wright

D-U-N-S 24-175-6548   (HQ)
ORION SECURITY INCORPORATED
*ORION SECURITY AND INVESTIGATION
SERVICES*
284 Queen St E Unit 229, Brampton, ON, L6V
1C2
(905) 840-0400
Emp Here 3   *Sales* 27,697,460

SIC 7381 Detective and armored car services
James Zia
Sabrina Zia

D-U-N-S 25-413-0453   (SL)
PARKINSON COACH LINES 2000 INC
10 Kennedy Rd N, Brampton, ON, L6V 1X4
(416) 451-4776
Emp Here 90   *Sales* 4,938,480
SIC 4151 School buses
James Murray
Allan Welters

D-U-N-S 25-237-9763   (BR)
PEEL DISTRICT SCHOOL BOARD
CENTRAL PEEL SECONDARY SCHOOL
(*Suby of* PEEL DISTRICT SCHOOL BOARD)
32 Kennedy Rd N, Brampton, ON, L6V 1X4
(905) 451-0432
Emp Here 112
SIC 8211 Elementary and secondary schools

D-U-N-S 24-190-4916   (SL)
TIM HORTONS
15 Bovaird Dr E, Brampton, ON, L6V 0A2
(905) 456-0263
Emp Here 20   *Sales* 13,350,098
SIC 5963 Direct selling establishments
Sue Turpin

D-U-N-S 25-294-8815   (BR)
WAL-MART CANADA CORP
BRAMPTON NORTH SUPERCENTRE
(*Suby of* WALMART INC.)
50 Quarry Edge Dr, Brampton, ON, L6V 4K2
(905) 874-0112
Emp Here 350
SIC 5311 Department stores
Shelley Broader

Brampton, ON L6W

D-U-N-S 20-123-1771   (SL)
1519950 ONTARIO INC
NEW MILLENIUM TIRE CENTRE
25 Clark Blvd, Brampton, ON, L6W 1X4
(905) 452-0111
Emp Here 30   *Sales* 15,669,540
SIC 5531 Auto and home supply stores
Inderjit Dhugga
Kala Dhugga
Veerpal Dhugga

D-U-N-S 25-617-2250   (SL)
2326236 ONTARIO INC
EAGLE FREIGHT SYSTEM
31 Selby Rd, Brampton, ON, L6W 1K5
(905) 455-9100
Emp Here 30   *Sales* 11,560,800
SIC 4731 Freight transportation arrangement
Harry Brar

D-U-N-S 20-536-6149   (SL)
389259 ONTARIO LIMITED
HANSEN AUTOMOTIVE & TOWING
236 Rutherford Rd S, Brampton, ON, L6W 3J6
(905) 451-6470
Emp Here 43   *Sales* 15,661,245
SIC 5013 Motor vehicle supplies and new
parts
Hans Hansen
Carolyn Hansen

D-U-N-S 24-028-8282   (SL)
ALL-LIFT LTD
320 Clarence St Suite 7-10, Brampton, ON,
L6W 1T5
(905) 459-5348
Emp Here 46   *Sales* 21,851,196
SIC 5084 Industrial machinery and equipment
Allan Bennett
Gregory Bennett
Jeffrey Bennett

D-U-N-S 24-422-5889   (HQ)

AMCOR PACKAGING CANADA, INC
EMBALLAGES ALCAN LACHINE
(*Suby of* ORORA LIMITED)
95 Biscayne Cres, Brampton, ON, L6W 4R2
(905) 450-5579
Emp Here 1   *Sales* 19,476,800
SIC 2657 Folding paperboard boxes
David Andison
Gary Hoeppner
Terry Warren

D-U-N-S 20-769-1171   (BR)
AMCOR RIGID PLASTICS ATLANTIC, INC
AMCOR RIGID PLASTICS - BRAMPTON
(*Suby of* AMCOR LTD)
95 Biscayne Cres, Brampton, ON, L6W 4R2
(905) 450-5579
Emp Here 100
SIC 3089 Plastics products, nec
Chris Marshall

D-U-N-S 20-168-0808   (HQ)
ASAHI REFINING CANADA LTD
(*Suby of* ASAHI HOLDINGS, INC.)
130 Glidden Rd, Brampton, ON, L6W 3M8
(905) 453-6120
Emp Here 56   *Sales* 31,017,348
SIC 3339 Primary nonferrous Metals, nec
Keith Neureuther
Keitaro Shigemasa
Kazuo Kawabata

D-U-N-S 24-238-1013   (SL)
AUTOMANN HEAVY DUTY CANADA ULC
(*Suby of* AUTOMANN INC.)
350 First Gulf Blvd, Brampton, ON, L6W 4T5
(905) 654-6500
Emp Here 30   *Sales* 15,567,760
SIC 5013 Motor vehicle supplies and new
parts
Harjeev Khanduja
John Younger
Jim Herd
Heather Letts
Trevor Morgan

D-U-N-S 20-387-8249   (SL)
B.S.D. LOGISTICS INC
350 Rutherford Rd S Suite 202, Brampton,
ON, L6W 3M2
(289) 801-4045
Emp Here 88   *Sales* 13,040,896
SIC 4213 Trucking, except local
Andrew Shim
Sam Chandi

D-U-N-S 20-036-4164   (SL)
BLUE GIANT EQUIPMENT CORPORATION
ROL LIFT
85 Heart Lake Rd, Brampton, ON, L6W 3K2
(905) 457-3900
Emp Here 180   *Sales* 39,960,180
SIC 3569 General industrial machinery, nec
William Kostenko
Andrew Morrow

D-U-N-S 20-901-5320   (HQ)
**BRAMPTON PUBLIC LIBRARY BOARD,
THE**
BRAMPTON LIBRARY
65 Queen St E, Brampton, ON, L6W 3L6
(905) 793-4636
Emp Here 45   *Sales* 13,078,395
SIC 8231 Libraries
Adele Kostiak

D-U-N-S 24-308-1184   (BR)
BREWERS RETAIL INC
BEER STORE DISTRIBUTION CENTRE
(*Suby of* BREWERS RETAIL INC)
69 First Gulf Blvd, Brampton, ON, L6W 4T8
(905) 450-2799
Emp Here 300
SIC 5181 Beer and ale
Ronald David

D-U-N-S 24-386-9992   (SL)

BRITA CANADA CORPORATION
(*Suby of* THE CLOROX COMPANY)
150 Biscayne Cres, Brampton, ON, L6W 4V3
(905) 789-2465
Emp Here 50   *Sales* 22,358,700
SIC 5074 Plumbing and heating equipment
and supplies (hydronics)
Mark S. Malo
Faroek Hanif
Lawrence S. Peiros

      D-U-N-S 24-885-3744   (SL)
**CENTRAL WEST COMMUNITY CARE AC-
CESS CENTRE**
CCAC
199 County Court Blvd, Brampton, ON, L6W
4P3
(905) 796-0040
Emp Here 20   *Sales* 90,601,440
SIC 8049 Offices of health practitioner

      D-U-N-S 20-290-5019   (SL)
CENTURY 21 MILLENNIUM INC
350 Rutherford Rd S Suite 10, Brampton, ON,
L6W 4N6
(905) 450-8300
Emp Here 100   *Sales* 27,175,600
SIC 6531 Real estate agents and managers
Joanne Evans

      D-U-N-S 20-811-7726   (SL)
CHAUHAN PHARMACY SERVICES LTD
SHOPPERS DRUG MART
160 Main St S Suite 2, Brampton, ON, L6W
2E1
(905) 451-0111
Emp Here 65   *Sales* 15,881,320
SIC 5912 Drug stores and proprietary stores
Kalpesh Chauhan

      D-U-N-S 20-733-6728   (HQ)
**CLOROX COMPANY OF CANADA, LTD,
THE**
BRITA
(*Suby of* THE CLOROX COMPANY)
150 Biscayne Cres, Brampton, ON, L6W 4V3
(905) 595-8200
Emp Here 80   *Sales* 80,665,440
SIC 5169 Chemicals and allied products, nec
Benno Dorer
Jon Balousek
Kevin Jacobsen

      D-U-N-S 24-587-7899   (SL)
CONVERTER CORE INC
155 Orenda Rd Unit 1, Brampton, ON, L6W
1W3
(905) 459-6566
Emp Here 65   *Sales* 32,737,770
SIC 5113 Industrial and personal service paper
Philip Early

      D-U-N-S 20-718-3729   (BR)
**CORPORATION OF THE CITY OF BRAMP-
TON, THE**
*BRAMPTON FIRE & EMERGENCY SER-
VICES*
(*Suby of* CORPORATION OF THE CITY OF
BRAMPTON, THE)
8 Rutherford Rd S, Brampton, ON, L6W 3J1
(905) 874-2700
Emp Here 400
SIC 7389 Business services, nec
Michael Clark

      D-U-N-S 25-287-5737   (BR)
COSTCO WHOLESALE CANADA LTD
COSTCO
(*Suby of* COSTCO WHOLESALE CORPO-
RATION)
100 Biscayne Cres, Brampton, ON, L6W 4S1
(905) 450-2092
Emp Here 200
SIC 5099 Durable goods, nec
Andrew Nowitsky

      D-U-N-S 20-036-6433   (HQ)

D & W FORWARDERS INC
81 Orenda Rd, Brampton, ON, L6W 1V7
(905) 459-3560
Emp Here 180   *Sales* 37,982,486
SIC 4213 Trucking, except local
Bruce Peeter
Hennie Boersma

      D-U-N-S 24-161-1883   (SL)
**DANIELS SHARPSMART CANADA LIM-
ITED**
52 Bramsteele Rd Suite 8, Brampton, ON,
L6W 3M5
(905) 793-2966
Emp Here 34   *Sales* 15,203,916
SIC 5047 Medical and hospital equipment
Daniel Kennedy

      D-U-N-S 20-936-4496   (SL)
DEPENDABLE TRUCK AND TANK LIMITED
275 Clarence St, Brampton, ON, L6W 3R3
(905) 453-6724
Emp Here 50   *Sales* 10,141,500
SIC 3443 Fabricated plate work (boiler shop)
Santo Natale
Salvatore Natale
Nuncio Natale
Naz Natale

      D-U-N-S 24-418-1509   (BR)
**DIVERSICARE CANADA MANAGEMENT
SERVICES CO., INC**
TULLAMORE NURSING HOME
(*Suby of* DCMS HOLDINGS INC)
133 Kennedy Rd S, Brampton, ON, L6W 3G3
(905) 459-2324
Emp Here 160
SIC 8051 Skilled nursing care facilities
Robert Campbell

      D-U-N-S 24-772-3653   (SL)
FORBES HEWLETT TRANSPORT INC
TRANSMOUNT TRANSPORT
156 Glidden Rd, Brampton, ON, L6W 3L2
(905) 455-2211
Emp Here 125   *Sales* 25,713,250
SIC 4213 Trucking, except local
George Stott
Nicola Moschella

      D-U-N-S 24-632-5757   (SL)
G.R.T. GENESIS INC
173 Glidden Rd Suite 1, Brampton, ON, L6W
3L9
(905) 452-0552
Emp Here 33   *Sales* 24,101,385
SIC 5162 Plastics materials and basic shapes
Bruno Timpano
Bill Gaska

      D-U-N-S 20-036-6045   (SL)
**GRAHAM BROS. CONSTRUCTION LIM-
ITED**
297 Rutherford Rd S, Brampton, ON, L6W 3J8
(905) 453-1200
Emp Here 100   *Sales* 25,244,200
SIC 1611 Highway and street construction
William Graham
Alfredo Maggio
Mark Thompson
Ken Richardson
Frank Steblaj

      D-U-N-S 20-381-8893   (SL)
HBC TRANSPORTATION INC
100 Kennedy Rd S, Brampton, ON, L6W 3E7
(416) 639-6764
Emp Here 100   *Sales* 14,819,200
SIC 4213 Trucking, except local
Bhajanpreet Chahal
Harpreet Malhi

      D-U-N-S 25-213-7815   (BR)
HOME DEPOT OF CANADA INC
HOME DEPOT
(*Suby of* THE HOME DEPOT INC)
49 First Gulf Blvd, Brampton, ON, L6W 4R8

(905) 457-1800
Emp Here 220
SIC 5211 Lumber and other building materials
Navjit Singh

      D-U-N-S 24-849-4544   (HQ)
**HUNTER DOUGLAS CANADA HOLDINGS
INC**
HUNTER DOUGLAS WINDOW FASHIONS
132 First Gulf Blvd, Brampton, ON, L6W 4T7
(905) 796-7883
Emp Here 150   *Sales* 172,610,400
SIC 5023 Homefurnishings
Randy Liken
Christine Mikler

      D-U-N-S 25-149-6238   (SL)
I-L SUCCESSOR CORP
31 Hansen Rd S, Brampton, ON, L6W 3H7

Emp Here 140   *Sales* 93,647,120
SIC 7389 Business services, nec
Brian Munro

      D-U-N-S 20-766-7437   (HQ)
I.G. MACHINE & FIBERS LTD
I.G. MACHINE
(*Suby of* GOLDIS ENTERPRISES, INC.)
87 Orenda Rd, Brampton, ON, L6W 1V8
(905) 457-0745
Emp Here 35   *Sales* 19,208,500
SIC 3444 Sheet Metalwork
David Koschitzky
David Laven

      D-U-N-S 20-830-0095   (HQ)
IKO INDUSTRIES LTD
ARMOROOF DIV OF
(*Suby of* GOLDIS ENTERPRISES, INC.)
80 Stafford Dr, Brampton, ON, L6W 1L4
(905) 457-2880
Emp Here 200   *Sales* 1,172,762,500
SIC 2952 Asphalt felts and coatings
Henry Koschitzky
David Koschitzky
Saul Koschitzky
Corbet Elder
Shel Laven

      D-U-N-S 25-315-9024   (BR)
**INVESTORS GROUP FINANCIAL SER-
VICES INC**
(*Suby of* POWER CORPORATION DU
CANADA)
208 County Court Blvd, Brampton, ON, L6W
4S9
(905) 450-1500
Emp Here 100
SIC 8741 Management services
Douglas Maclachlin

      D-U-N-S 20-187-9918   (SL)
JRL HVAC INC
278 Rutherford Rd S, Brampton, ON, L6W
3K7
(905) 457-6900
Emp Here 53   *Sales* 12,352,445
SIC 1711 Plumbing, heating, air-conditioning
Robin Jones

      D-U-N-S 20-671-0035   (SL)
KOTYCK BROS. LIMITED
80 Hale Rd Suite 7, Brampton, ON, L6W 3N9
(905) 595-1127
Emp Here 18   *Sales* 18,006,102
SIC 5051 Metals service centers and offices
Michael Kotyck

      D-U-N-S 20-405-4480   (HQ)
LAIRD PLASTICS (CANADA) INC
(*Suby of* LAIRD PLASTICS, INC.)
155 Orenda Rd Unit 4, Brampton, ON, L6W
1W3
(905) 595-4800
Emp Here 25   *Sales* 268,884,800
SIC 5162 Plastics materials and basic shapes
Mark W. Kramer
Mark F. Whtley

Wilfredo Figueras

      D-U-N-S 20-732-3080   (SL)
**LOGAN, JOHN CHEVROLET OLDSMOBILE
INC**
241 Queen St E, Brampton, ON, L6W 2B5
(905) 451-2030
Emp Here 106   *Sales* 38,606,790
SIC 5012 Automobiles and other motor vehi-
cles
John Logan
David Logan

      D-U-N-S 24-565-3688   (HQ)
**MAGNUM INTEGRATED TECHNOLOGIES
INC**
ANKER-HOLTH, DIV OF
(*Suby of* MAGNUM GROUP INTERNA-
TIONAL CORP)
200 First Gulf Blvd, Brampton, ON, L6W 4T5
(905) 595-1998
Emp Here 48   *Sales* 12,876,058
SIC 3593 Fluid power cylinders and actuators
Andre Nazarian

      D-U-N-S 24-364-6023   (HQ)
METRO COMPACTOR SERVICE INC
145 Heart Lake Rd S, Brampton, ON, L6W
3K3
(416) 743-8484
Emp Here 35   *Sales* 13,863,942
SIC 7699 Repair services, nec
Danny Mauti

      D-U-N-S 24-896-5238   (BR)
METRO ONTARIO INC
METRO STORES
(*Suby of* METRO INC)
156 Main St S, Brampton, ON, L6W 2C9
(905) 459-6212
Emp Here 90
SIC 5411 Grocery stores
Rene Bal

      D-U-N-S 25-686-5510   (HQ)
MICHAELS OF CANADA, ULC
MICHAELS ARTS & CRAFTS STORE
(*Suby of* THE MICHAELS COMPANIES INC)
547 Steeles Ave E Unit 3, Brampton, ON, L6W
4S2
(905) 874-9640
Sales 36,707,400
SIC 5945 Hobby, toy, and game shops
Brian C. Cornell
Thomas A. Melito
Janet S. Morehouse
Thomas J. Making
Lisa K. Klinger
Michael J. Veitenheimer
Elaine D. Crowley
Todd Vogensen
Teri J. Williams
Shelley G. Broader

      D-U-N-S 25-486-5603   (BR)
MILLS GROUP INC, THE
BURGER KING
(*Suby of* MILLS GROUP INC, THE)
285 Queen St E, Brampton, ON, L6W 2C2
(905) 453-5818
Emp Here 75
SIC 5812 Eating places
Lynette Houlden

      D-U-N-S 24-422-8524   (SL)
NATIONAL EXHAUST SYSTEMS INC
38 Hansen Rd S, Brampton, ON, L6W 3H4
(905) 453-4111
Emp Here 45   *Sales* 16,389,675
SIC 5013 Motor vehicle supplies and new
parts
Thomas Baker

      D-U-N-S 24-851-0435   (SL)
OZBURN-HESSEY LOGISTICS
300 Kennedy Rd S Unit B, Brampton, ON,
L6W 4V2

(905) 450-1151
Emp Here 60   *Sales* 31,198,020
SIC 4731 Freight transportation arrangement
Shahzad Dad

D-U-N-S 20-711-1761   (BR)
PEEL DISTRICT SCHOOL BOARD
TURNER FENTON SECONDARY SCHOOL
(*Suby of* PEEL DISTRICT SCHOOL BOARD)
7935 Kennedy Rd, Brampton, ON, L6W 0A2
(905) 453-9220
Emp Here 150
SIC 8211 Elementary and secondary schools
Michelle Stubbings

D-U-N-S 25-196-0571   (HQ)
PEEL HOUSING CORPORATION
PEEL LIVING
(*Suby of* REGIONAL MUNICIPALITY OF PEEL, THE)
5 Wellington St E, Brampton, ON, L6W 1Y1
(905) 453-1300
Sales 58,644,460
SIC 6531 Real estate agents and managers
Ray Applebaum

D-U-N-S 24-139-5805   (SL)
PEEL PLASTIC PRODUCTS LIMITED
(*Suby of* 536892 ONTARIO LIMITED)
49 Rutherford Rd S, Brampton, ON, L6W 3J3
(905) 456-3660
Emp Here 460   *Sales* 132,325,960
SIC 2673 Bags: plastic, laminated, and coated
William Troost
David Troost

D-U-N-S 20-703-6646   (BR)
PEPSICO CANADA ULC
FRITO-LAY CANADA
(*Suby of* PEPSICO, INC.)
12 Clipper Crt, Brampton, ON, L6W 4T9
(905) 460-2400
Emp Here 500
SIC 5145 Confectionery
Jack Nadeau

D-U-N-S 20-107-2092   (HQ)
PINPOINT CAREERS INC
ARMOR PERSONNEL
181 Queen St E, Brampton, ON, L6W 2B3
(905) 454-1144
Emp Here 20   *Sales* 11,204,100
SIC 7361 Employment agencies
Lou Duggan

D-U-N-S 24-340-8452   (BR)
PRAXAIR CANADA INC
(*Suby of* LINDE PUBLIC LIMITED COMPANY)
165 Biscayne Cres, Brampton, ON, L6W 4R3
(905) 450-9353
Emp Here 100
SIC 5169 Chemicals and allied products, nec
Kevin Byford

D-U-N-S 25-643-0745   (HQ)
PRE-CON INC
(*Suby of* TREVLUC HOLDINGS LTD)
35 Rutherford Rd S, Brampton, ON, L6W 3J4
(905) 457-4140
Emp Here 150   *Sales* 102,276,000
SIC 3272 Concrete products, nec
Peter R Quail

D-U-N-S 25-354-4845   (SL)
PUREWOOD INCORPORATED
341 Heart Lake Rd, Brampton, ON, L6W 3K8
(905) 874-9797
Emp Here 100   *Sales* 19,636,100
SIC 1751 Carpentry work
Mark Bozek

D-U-N-S 24-911-5981   (SL)
QBD COOLING SYSTEMS INC
31 Bramsteele Rd, Brampton, ON, L6W 3K6
(905) 459-0709
Emp Here 250   *Sales* 67,712,000

SIC 1711 Plumbing, heating, air-conditioning
Zulfikar Jaffer

D-U-N-S 24-419-9139   (SL)
QBD MODULAR SYSTEMS INC
31 Bramsteele Rd, Brampton, ON, L6W 3K6
(905) 459-0709
Emp Here 55   *Sales* 12,818,575
SIC 1711 Plumbing, heating, air-conditioning
Zulfikar Jaffer

D-U-N-S 20-921-0132   (BR)
RE/MAX REAL ESTATE CENTRE INC
(*Suby of* RE/MAX REAL ESTATE CENTRE INC)
2 County Court Blvd Suite 150, Brampton, ON, L6W 3W8
(905) 456-1177
Emp Here 80
SIC 6531 Real estate agents and managers
George Burns

D-U-N-S 24-306-9796   (HQ)
RE/MAX REALTY SERVICES INC
295 Queen St E Suite 3, Brampton, ON, L6W 3R1
(905) 456-1000
Sales 54,874,459
SIC 6531 Real estate agents and managers
Ken Mcclenaghan

D-U-N-S 25-978-4775   (SL)
REAL ICE SPORTS FACILITY MANAGEMENT SERVICES LTD
POWERADE CENTRE
7575 Kennedy Rd, Brampton, ON, L6W 4T2
(905) 459-9340
Emp Here 100   *Sales* 14,002,900
SIC 7999 Amusement and recreation, nec
Jonas Jacob Prince
Geoffrey Wayne Squibb

D-U-N-S 20-056-3604   (HQ)
RICE DEVELOPMENT COMPANY INC
7735 Kennedy Rd, Brampton, ON, L6W 0B9
(905) 796-3630
Emp Here 1   *Sales* 34,168,750
SIC 6712 Bank holding companies
Roderick Rice
David Rice
Jeffrey Rice

D-U-N-S 20-790-2284   (SL)
ROB'S NO FRILLS
295 Queen St E, Brampton, ON, L6W 3R1
(905) 452-9200
Emp Here 174   *Sales* 51,064,998
SIC 5411 Grocery stores
Robert Klemente

D-U-N-S 20-036-8132   (HQ)
ROBERTS COMPANY CANADA LIMITED
(*Suby of* Q.E.P. CO., INC.)
34 Hansen Rd S, Brampton, ON, L6W 3H4
(905) 791-4444
Emp Here 10   *Sales* 15,053,113
SIC 2891 Adhesives and sealants
Peter Sharko
Ken Barwell

D-U-N-S 20-347-9030   (HQ)
ROMANO, DOMENIC PHARMACY INC
SHOPPERS DRUG MART
1 Kennedy Rd S Unit 1, Brampton, ON, L6W 3C9
(905) 454-4464
Emp Here 67   *Sales* 17,102,960
SIC 5912 Drug stores and proprietary stores
Domenic Romano

D-U-N-S 20-750-1743   (HQ)
ROOFMART HOLDINGS LIMITED
305 Rutherford Rd S, Brampton, ON, L6W 3R5
(905) 453-9689
Emp Here 50   *Sales* 44,717,400
SIC 5033 Roofing, siding, and insulation
Henry Koschitzky

Mira Koschitzky

D-U-N-S 24-644-2255   (SL)
SAKO MATERIALS LIMITED
71 Orenda Rd, Brampton, ON, L6W 1V8
(905) 457-5321
Emp Here 54   *Sales* 24,147,396
SIC 5033 Roofing, siding, and insulation
Saul Koschitzky

D-U-N-S 24-393-3319   (HQ)
SPEEDY TRANSPORT GROUP INC
SPEEDY TRANSPORT
265 Rutherford Rd S, Brampton, ON, L6W 1V9
(416) 510-2035
Emp Here 235   *Sales* 56,909,346
SIC 4212 Local trucking, without storage
Jared Martin
Funlola Smith
Debra L. Martin
Andre Poirier
Peter Murphy
Jamie Temple
Martin Granger

D-U-N-S 24-074-4938   (SL)
TAYLOR MANUFACTURING INDUSTRIES INC
TAYLOR GROUP, THE
(*Suby of* 874849 ONTARIO LIMITED)
255 Biscayne Cres, Brampton, ON, L6W 4R2
(905) 451-5800
Emp Here 130   *Sales* 34,393,840
SIC 3993 Signs and advertising specialties
Robert Wands
Dean Marks
Alphonse Laydon
Ross Hallam
Len Pencininni

D-U-N-S 24-685-5014   (HQ)
TEDI TRANSLOGIC EXPRESS DEDICATED INC
241 Clarence St Unit 21-24, Brampton, ON, L6W 4P2
(905) 451-3033
Emp Here 20   *Sales* 41,141,200
SIC 4212 Local trucking, without storage
Kevin Devine
Hugh Sanders

D-U-N-S 24-096-2472   (HQ)
TERRAPROBE LIMITED
10 Bram Crt, Brampton, ON, L6W 3R6
(905) 796-2650
Emp Here 40   *Sales* 21,085,920
SIC 8748 Business consulting, nec
Michael Tanos

D-U-N-S 24-859-9755   (HQ)
TIREMASTER LIMITED
145 Orenda Rd, Brampton, ON, L6W 1W3
(905) 453-4300
Emp Here 35   *Sales* 18,210,750
SIC 5014 Tires and tubes
Ronald Cherry

D-U-N-S 24-658-9493   (HQ)
TRAVELERS TRANSPORTATION SERVICES INC
195 Heart Lake Rd, Brampton, ON, L6W 3N6
(905) 457-8789
Emp Here 100   *Sales* 67,299,065
SIC 4213 Trucking, except local
Jim Hicks

Brampton, ON L6X

D-U-N-S 20-803-3311   (SL)
1408939 ONTARIO LIMITED
SAM'S NO FRILLS
345 Main St N, Brampton, ON, L6X 1N6
(905) 452-9122
Emp Here 130   *Sales* 38,152,010

SIC 5411 Grocery stores
Sam Scire

D-U-N-S 20-528-7944   (SL)
1512804 ONTARIO INC
BRAMPTON MITSUBISHI
47 Bovaird Dr W, Brampton, ON, L6X 0G9
(905) 459-2600
Emp Here 25   *Sales* 12,451,950
SIC 5511 New and used car dealers
Sam Alizadeh

D-U-N-S 24-310-3624   (BR)
ARCELORMITTAL TUBULAR PRODUCTS CANADA G.P.
SONCO STEEL TUBE DIVISION
(*Suby of* ARCELORMITTAL)
14 Holtby Ave, Brampton, ON, L6X 2M3
(905) 451-2400
Emp Here 100
SIC 3714 Motor vehicle parts and accessories
Bhikam Agarwal

D-U-N-S 24-122-2637   (HQ)
BRAMPTON CALEDON COMMUNITY LIVING
34 Church St W, Brampton, ON, L6X 1H3
(905) 453-8841
Emp Here 30   *Sales* 19,369,175
SIC 8322 Individual and family services
Kathy Bell
Bill Dowell
Mesfin Hagos
Jim Triantafilou
Dely Farrace
Alexandra Whittaker
Ron Sanderson
Crystal Jakovics

D-U-N-S 25-802-1997   (SL)
CCV INSURANCE & FINANCIAL SERVICES INC
32 Queen St W, Brampton, ON, L6X 1A1
(905) 459-6066
Emp Here 40   *Sales* 23,196,960
SIC 6411 Insurance agents, brokers, and service
Robert Lewis
Brian Evans

D-U-N-S 24-318-0168   (SL)
EVERLAST GROUP LTD
40 Holtby Ave Suite 1, Brampton, ON, L6X 2M1
(905) 846-9944
Emp Here 27   *Sales* 10,404,720
SIC 4731 Freight transportation arrangement
Victor Boutin

D-U-N-S 24-206-9602   (BR)
GAP (CANADA) INC
(*Suby of* THE GAP INC)
9500 Mclaughlin Rd, Brampton, ON, L6X 0B8
(905) 460-2060
Emp Here 100
SIC 5651 Family clothing stores
Luis Valdovinos

D-U-N-S 20-264-4944   (BR)
HOME DEPOT OF CANADA INC
(*Suby of* THE HOME DEPOT INC)
9515 Mississauga Rd, Brampton, ON, L6X 0Z8
(905) 453-3900
Emp Here 150
SIC 5251 Hardware stores
Melissa Carbis

D-U-N-S 20-264-6423   (SL)
INTERNATIONAL COMPUTER BROKERS INC
INTERNATIONAL COMPUTER BROKERS
9052 Creditview Rd, Brampton, ON, L6X 0E3
(905) 459-2100
Emp Here 35   *Sales* 15,651,090
SIC 5045 Computers, peripherals, and software

Walter Grdevich

D-U-N-S 24-452-2561 (BR)
KEG RESTAURANTS LTD
KEG STEAKHOUSE & BAR, THE
(*Suby of* RECIPE UNLIMITED CORPORA-
TION)
70 Gillingham Dr, Brampton, ON, L6X 4X7
(905) 456-3733
Emp Here 75
SIC 5812 Eating places
James Mozes

D-U-N-S 20-165-6014 (HQ)
MERITOR AFTERMARKET CANADA INC
(*Suby of* MERITOR, INC.)
60 Gillingham Dr Suite 501, Brampton, ON,
L6X 0Z9
(905) 454-7070
Emp Here 40 *Sales* 130,882,500
SIC 3714 Motor vehicle parts and accessories
Charles Mcclure

Brampton, ON L6Y

D-U-N-S 20-517-8200 (SL)
1388688 ONTARIO LIMITED
SHOPPERS WORLD BRAMPTON
(*Suby of* RIOCAN REAL ESTATE INVEST-
MENT TRUST)
499 Main St S Suite 56, Brampton, ON, L6Y
1N7
(905) 459-1337
Emp Here 53 *Sales* 11,706,163
SIC 6512 Nonresidential building operators
Dan Free

D-U-N-S 24-224-6598 (HQ)
2124964 ONTARIO INC
PETRO CANADA
471 Main St S, Brampton, ON, L6Y 1N6
(905) 451-6489
Emp Here 5 *Sales* 24,903,900
SIC 5541 Gasoline service stations
Laji Jacob Thomas

D-U-N-S 20-339-5806 (SL)
2320610 ONTARIO INC
ACTIVE SECURITY ENTERPRISE
7900 Hurontario St Suite 303, Brampton, ON,
L6Y 0P6
(905) 782-4700
Emp Here 100 *Sales* 40,026,071
SIC 7381 Detective and armored car services
Dodick Rahn

D-U-N-S 24-198-3209 (SL)
351658 ONTARIO LIMITED
LIONHEAD GOLF & COUNTRY CLUB
(*Suby of* KANEFF PROPERTIES LIMITED)
8525 Mississauga Rd, Brampton, ON, L6Y
0C1
(905) 455-8400
Emp Here 100 *Sales* 7,854,500
SIC 7992 Public golf courses
Ignat Kaneff
Gabriella Favero
Eric Mcknight

D-U-N-S 24-953-6798 (SL)
728567 ONTARIO LIMITED
*SOUTHBROOK RETIREMENT COMMU-
NITY*
400 Ray Lawson Blvd, Brampton, ON, L6Y
4G4
(905) 456-3334
Emp Here 65 *Sales* 15,139,215
SIC 6513 Apartment building operators
Jeffrey Rice

D-U-N-S 25-991-5817 (HQ)
765865 ONTARIO INC
DRYDEN AIR SERVICES
8501 Mississauga Rd Suite 302, Brampton,
ON, L6Y 5G8

(905) 497-4114
Emp Here 1 *Sales* 32,475,400
SIC 4581 Airports, flying fields, and services
Diane Beasent
Mark Beasent

D-U-N-S 20-438-6081 (SL)
9306609 CANADA INC
YAYAA BUILDING MATERIALS
2 Berkwood Hollow, Brampton, ON, L6Y 0X6
(647) 993-1968
Emp Here 5 *Sales* 27,421,695
SIC 5012 Automobiles and other motor vehicles
Sohaib Al-Sammarraie

D-U-N-S 25-813-5375 (HQ)
ASIA PULP & PAPER (CANADA) LTD
APP CANADA
20 Hereford St Suite 15, Brampton, ON, L6Y
0M1
(905) 450-2100
Emp Here 50 *Sales* 30,219,480
SIC 5113 Industrial and personal service pa-
per
David Chin-Bing
Siu-Kwan Leung

D-U-N-S 20-275-0618 (HQ)
ASIG CANADA LTD
8501 Mississauga Rd Suite 302, Brampton,
ON, L6Y 5G8
(905) 497-4114
Sales 8,867,047,500
SIC 5172 Petroleum products, nec
Tony R Lefebvre
Constance L Alden
Joseph I Goldstein
Barbara Bresnan
Richard D Rector
Daniel Marcinik
Jeffrey T Bankowitz
Benjamin A Weaver
Mark Johnstone
Thomas A Fenton

D-U-N-S 25-357-7985 (HQ)
**CANADIAN MENTAL HEALTH ASSOCIA-
TION/PEEL BRANCH**
CMHA PEEL DUFFERIN
7700 Hurontario St Suite 314, Brampton, ON,
L6Y 4M3
(905) 451-1718
Emp Here 3 *Sales* 16,064,600
SIC 8011 Offices and clinics of medical doc-
tors
Sandy Milakovic

D-U-N-S 25-301-6067 (BR)
**CANADIAN MENTAL HEALTH ASSOCIA-
TION/PEEL BRANCH**
CMHA RESSOURCE CENTRE
(*Suby of* CANADIAN MENTAL HEALTH AS-
SOCIATION/PEEL BRANCH)
7700 Hurontario St Suite 601, Brampton, ON,
L6Y 4M3
(905) 451-2123
Emp Here 100
SIC 8621 Professional organizations
Sandy Milkovic

D-U-N-S 20-770-1541 (HQ)
CANON CANADA INC
PPSG DIVISION
(*Suby of* CANON INC.)
8000 Mississauga Rd, Brampton, ON, L6Y
5Z7
(905) 863-8000
Emp Here 300 *Sales* 642,422,400
SIC 5044 Office equipment
Nobuhiko Kitajima
Yoroku Adachi
Tony Valenti
Maria Tesla

D-U-N-S 25-182-3188 (SL)
CARTER
72 Links Lane, Brampton, ON, L6Y 5H1

(416) 574-3770
Emp Here 49 *Sales* 25,478,383
SIC 4724 Travel agencies
Sylvie Villard

D-U-N-S 24-333-7024 (SL)
D & H CANADA ULC
(*Suby of* D & H DISTRIBUTING COMPANY)
7975 Heritage Rd Suite 20, Brampton, ON,
L6Y 5X5
(905) 796-0030
Emp Here 60 *Sales* 34,814,820
SIC 5065 Electronic parts and equipment, nec
Israel Schwab
Dan Schwab
Michael J Schwab
Greg Tobin

D-U-N-S 25-352-3427 (HQ)
G&W CANADA CORPORATION
7965 Heritage Rd, Brampton, ON, L6Y 5X5
(905) 542-2000
Sales 17,520,664
SIC 3613 Switchgear and switchboard appa-
ratus
Stephen Mueller
Dan Dyaks
Rupjinder Dhami

D-U-N-S 24-414-0257 (SL)
HOLLAND CHRISTIAN HOMES INC
7900 Mclaughlin Rd, Brampton, ON, L6Y 5A7
(905) 463-7002
Emp Here 200 *Sales* 13,665,200
SIC 8051 Skilled nursing care facilities
Peter Schaafsma
John Kalverda
Fred Van Laare

D-U-N-S 25-112-6848 (SL)
JAKKS PACIFIC (CANADA), INC
(*Suby of* JAKKS PACIFIC, INC.)
125 Edgeware Rd Suite 15, Brampton, ON,
L6Y 0P5
(905) 452-6279
Emp Here 12 *Sales* 810,060,000
SIC 3944 Games, toys, and children's vehicles

D-U-N-S 20-042-5940 (HQ)
KANEFF PROPERTIES LIMITED
KANEFF GROUP OF PROPERTIES
8501 Mississauga Rd Suite 200, Brampton,
ON, L6Y 5G8
(905) 454-0221
Emp Here 5 *Sales* 65,156,350
SIC 6553 Cemetery subdividers and develop-
ers
Ignat Kaneff (Hon)
Anna Maria Kaneff

D-U-N-S 20-413-7475 (HQ)
LOBLAW COMPANIES LIMITED
DOMINION
1 Presidents Choice Cir, Brampton, ON, L6Y
5S5
(905) 459-2500
Emp Here 80 *Sales* 35,398,056,686
SIC 5411 Grocery stores
Galen G Weston
Sarah R Davis
Gordon A. M Currie
Greg Ramier
Mark Wilson
Robert Chant
Barry K.Columb
Jocyanne Bourdeau
Jeff Leger
Ian Freedman

D-U-N-S 24-538-4359 (HQ)
LOBLAW PROPERTIES LIMITED
(*Suby of* LOBLAW COMPANIES LIMITED)
1 Presidents Choice Cir, Brampton, ON, L6Y
5S5
(905) 459-2500
Emp Here 22 *Sales* 17,669,680
SIC 6512 Nonresidential building operators
Robert Balcom

S. Jane Marshall
Jeremy Roberts
Sarah Davis

D-U-N-S 24-383-8930 (BR)
LOBLAWS INC
REAL CANADIAN SUPERSTORE
(*Suby of* LOBLAW COMPANIES LIMITED)
85 Steeles Ave W, Brampton, ON, L6Y 0K3
(905) 451-0917
Emp Here 150
SIC 5411 Grocery stores
Shawn Tulk

D-U-N-S 20-169-4494 (HQ)
LOBLAWS INC
A PLEIN GAZ
(*Suby of* LOBLAW COMPANIES LIMITED)
1 Presidents Choice Cir, Brampton, ON, L6Y
5S5
(905) 459-2500
Emp Here 2,300 *Sales* 97,473,376,000
SIC 5141 Groceries, general line
Galen G. Weston
Robert A Balcom

D-U-N-S 24-719-1679 (HQ)
LOBLAWS SUPERMARKETS LIMITED
ST CLAIR MARKET
(*Suby of* LOBLAW COMPANIES LIMITED)
1 Presidents Choice Cir, Brampton, ON, L6Y
5S5
(905) 459-2500
Emp Here 300 *Sales* 3,079,424,000
SIC 5411 Grocery stores
Galen Weston

D-U-N-S 25-796-1276 (BR)
LONGO BROTHERS FRUIT MARKETS INC
LONGO'S FRUIT MARKET
(*Suby of* LONGO BROTHERS FRUIT MAR-
KETS INC)
7700 Hurontario St Suite 202, Brampton, ON,
L6Y 4M3
(905) 455-3135
Emp Here 300
SIC 5431 Fruit and vegetable markets
Tony Indovia

D-U-N-S 20-555-9172 (HQ)
MAPLE LODGE FARMS LTD
MAPLE LODGE PET FOOD, DIV OF
(*Suby of* MAPLE LODGE HOLDING CORPO-
RATION)
8301 Winston Churchill Blvd, Brampton, ON,
L6Y 0A2
(905) 455-8340
Emp Here 1,900 *Sales* 1,413,416,500
SIC 2015 Poultry slaughtering and processing
Michael Burrows
Robert Cathcart
Vanessa White
John Troscolan

D-U-N-S 25-104-6108 (HQ)
MAPLE LODGE HOLDING CORPORATION
8301 Winston Churchill Blvd, Brampton, ON,
L6Y 0A2
(905) 455-8340
Emp Here 1,000 *Sales* 475,161,700
SIC 6712 Bank holding companies
David May
Michael Burrows
Greg Scott
Bob May
Jack May
Beth May
Jean May
Larry May
Wendy Robson
Debi Kee

D-U-N-S 20-285-1044 (BR)
MATRIX LOGISTICS SERVICES LIMITED
(*Suby of* MATRIX LOGISTICS SERVICES
LIMITED)
2675 Steeles Ave W, Brampton, ON, L6Y 5X3

---

(905) 451-6792
Emp Here 800
SIC 4225 General warehousing and storage

D-U-N-S 20-628-6130   (HQ)
MEDTRONIC OF CANADA LTD
99 Hereford St, Brampton, ON, L6Y 0R3
(905) 460-3800
Emp Here 50   *Sales* 28,638,414
SIC 3845 Electromedical equipment
Neil Fraser
Laura Cameron-Brookbank

D-U-N-S 25-297-1908   (BR)
PEEL DISTRICT SCHOOL BOARD
*BRAMPTON CENTENNIAL SECONDARY
SCHOOL*
(*Suby of* PEEL DISTRICT SCHOOL BOARD)
251 Mcmurchy Ave S, Brampton, ON, L6Y 1Z4
(905) 451-2860
Emp Here 101
SIC 8211 Elementary and secondary schools
Terry Whitmell

D-U-N-S 20-923-4319   (HQ)
PEEL MUTUAL INSURANCE COMPANY
103 Queen St W, Brampton, ON, L6Y 1M3
(905) 451-2386
Sales 49,859,793
SIC 6331 Fire, marine, and casualty insurance
Brain Bessey
Bill Morley
Brian Bessie
Karen Byrne
Ronald Orr
Harry Brander
Harold Parker
George Wood

D-U-N-S 20-554-3171   (SL)
POWERBEV INC
60 Hereford St, Brampton, ON, L6Y 0N3
(905) 453-2855
Emp Here 60   *Sales* 50,134,620
SIC 5149 Groceries and related products, nec
Frank Devries
Thomas Bitove
Daniel Sullivan

D-U-N-S 20-624-5466   (SL)
RHEEM CANADA LTD
(*Suby of* PALOMA CO.,LTD.)
125 Edgeware Rd Unit 1, Brampton, ON, L6Y 0P5
(905) 450-4460
Emp Here 150   *Sales* 69,006,600
SIC 5074 Plumbing and heating equipment
and supplies (hydronics)
Gary L. Tapella
Dave Mcpherson

D-U-N-S 24-327-2577   (SL)
SCRIPTECH MEDS INC
SHOPPERS DRUG MART
8965 Chinguacousy Rd Suite 1092, Brampton, ON, L6Y 0J2
(905) 454-1620
Emp Here 45   *Sales* 11,382,930
SIC 5912 Drug stores and proprietary stores
Shayan Bajwa

D-U-N-S 24-483-9106   (BR)
SHERIDAN COLLEGE INSTITUTE OF TECHNOLOGY AND ADVANCED LEARNING
DAVIS CAMPUS
(*Suby of* SHERIDAN COLLEGE INSTITUTE OF TECHNOLOGY AND ADVANCED LEARNING)
7899 Mclaughlin Rd, Brampton, ON, L6Y 5H9
(647) 309-6634
Emp Here 257
SIC 8222 Junior colleges
Dan Sibly

D-U-N-S 20-793-0723   (BR)
SOBEYS CAPITAL INCORPORATED
(*Suby of* EMPIRE COMPANY LIMITED)

8975 Chinguacousy Rd, Brampton, ON, L6Y 0J2
(905) 796-1517
Emp Here 200
SIC 5411 Grocery stores
Graeme Oglivie

D-U-N-S 20-176-3042   (SL)
SUNBEAM CORPORATION (CANADA) LIMITED
JARDEN CONSUMER SOLUTIONS
(*Suby of* NEWELL BRANDS INC.)
20 Hereford St Suite B, Brampton, ON, L6Y 0M1
(905) 593-6255
Emp Here 109   *Sales* 63,246,923
SIC 5064 Electrical appliances, television and radio
Dave Simmons
Mike Ricci

D-U-N-S 24-524-9693   (SL)
SUNFRESH LIMITED
(*Suby of* LOBLAW COMPANIES LIMITED)
1 Presidents Choice Cir, Brampton, ON, L6Y 5S5
(905) 459-2500
Emp Here 400
SIC 5141 Groceries, general line
Mark Foote
Robert Balcom
Sarah Davis
Grant Froese
Jeremy Roberts

D-U-N-S 25-462-1097   (SL)
VENDEX REALTY INC
4 Mclaughlin Rd S Unit 10, Brampton, ON, L6Y 3B2
(905) 452-7272
Emp Here 35   *Sales* 11,449,445
SIC 6531 Real estate agents and managers
Mario Hermenegild

D-U-N-S 24-418-6594   (HQ)
WADLAND PHARMACY LIMITED
DRUGSTORE PHARMACY
(*Suby of* LOBLAW COMPANIES LIMITED)
1 Presidents Choice Cir, Brampton, ON, L6Y 5S5
(905) 459-2500
Emp Here 7   *Sales* 36,707,400
SIC 5912 Drug stores and proprietary stores
Robert A. Balcom
Karl E. Frank
David Gore
Michael Lovsin
Bobbi Reinholdt
Robert Vaux

D-U-N-S 20-174-9181   (HQ)
ZEHRMART INC
ZEHRS MARKETS
(*Suby of* LOBLAW COMPANIES LIMITED)
1 Presidents Choice Cir, Brampton, ON, L6Y 5S5
(905) 459-2500
Emp Here 150   *Sales* 2,213,336,000
SIC 5411 Grocery stores
Galen Weston
John A. Lederer
Carmen Fortino
Mila Cruz
Ken Code
Glen Gonder
David Bragg

Brampton, ON L6Z

D-U-N-S 25-321-6048   (HQ)
BEATTY FOODS LTD
MCDONALDS #10305
160 Sandalwood Pky E, Brampton, ON, L6Z 1Y5

(905) 840-0700
Emp Here 3   *Sales* 27,190,537
SIC 5812 Eating places
Scott Tim

D-U-N-S 24-396-7366   (SL)
C & E EXPRESS INC
1b Conestoga Dr Suite 101, Brampton, ON, L6Z 4N5
(905) 495-7934
Emp Here 35   *Sales* 13,487,600
SIC 4789 Transportation services, nec
Louis Duffenail

D-U-N-S 25-598-0567   (HQ)
DP ENVIRONMENTAL SERVICE INC
39 Shadywood Rd, Brampton, ON, L6Z 4M1
(905) 840-4480
Emp Here 26   *Sales* 12,856,550
SIC 4959 Sanitary services, nec
Peter Wyssen
Sandra Wyssen

D-U-N-S 20-302-5411   (BR)
DUFFERIN-PEEL CATHOLIC DISTRICT SCHOOL BOARD
NOTRE DAME SECONDARY SCHOOL
(*Suby of* DUFFERIN-PEEL CATHOLIC DISTRICT SCHOOL BOARD)
2 Notre Dame Ave, Brampton, ON, L6Z 4L5
(905) 840-2802
Emp Here 140
SIC 8211 Elementary and secondary schools
John Lezon

D-U-N-S 20-694-7751   (SL)
JEG ENTERPRISES
57 Cheviot Cres, Brampton, ON, L6Z 4G8

Emp Here 20   *Sales* 16,711,540
SIC 5149 Groceries and related products, nec
Bankole Awoliyi

D-U-N-S 24-353-6658   (BR)
LOWE'S COMPANIES CANADA, ULC
LOWE'S OF NORTH BRAMPTON
(*Suby of* LOWE'S COMPANIES, INC.)
10111 Heart Lake Rd, Brampton, ON, L6Z 0E4
(905) 840-2351
Emp Here 200
SIC 5211 Lumber and other building materials

D-U-N-S 24-333-1688   (BR)
METRO ONTARIO INC
METRO
(*Suby of* METRO INC)
180 Sandalwood Pky E, Brampton, ON, L6Z 1Y4
(905) 846-2222
Emp Here 170
SIC 5411 Grocery stores
Bob Smith

D-U-N-S 20-034-2041   (BR)
PEEL DISTRICT SCHOOL BOARD
HEART LAKE SECONDARY SCHOOL
(*Suby of* PEEL DISTRICT SCHOOL BOARD)
296 Conestoga Dr, Brampton, ON, L6Z 3M1
(905) 840-2328
Emp Here 95
SIC 8211 Elementary and secondary schools
Peter Koehnen

D-U-N-S 20-614-5836   (SL)
SABRITIN HOSPITALITY INC
SWISS CHALET
370 Bovaird Dr E, Brampton, ON, L6Z 2S8
(905) 846-3321
Emp Here 80   *Sales* 3,641,520
SIC 5812 Eating places
Ralph Nobel

D-U-N-S 20-625-0136   (SL)
SILVA, MANUEL J DRUGS LTD
SHOPPERS DRUG MART - HEART LAKE TOWN CENTRE
180 Sandalwood Pky E, Brampton, ON, L6Z

1Y4
(905) 846-4700
Emp Here 60   *Sales* 14,659,680
SIC 5912 Drug stores and proprietary stores
Manuel Silva

D-U-N-S 25-840-0878   (BR)
SOBEYS CAPITAL INCORPORATED
FRESHCO
(*Suby of* EMPIRE COMPANY LIMITED)
380 Bovaird Dr E Suite 29, Brampton, ON, L6Z 2S8
(905) 840-0770
Emp Here 110
SIC 5411 Grocery stores
Terry Field

D-U-N-S 20-643-2010   (BR)
SOBEYS CAPITAL INCORPORATED
SOBEYS
(*Suby of* EMPIRE COMPANY LIMITED)
11965 Hurontario St, Brampton, ON, L6Z 4P7
(905) 846-5658
Emp Here 100
SIC 5411 Grocery stores
Dave Alexander

D-U-N-S 24-347-4645   (BR)
SPECIALTY CARE INC
SPECIALTY CARE WOODHALL PARK
(*Suby of* SPECIALTY CARE INC)
10260 Kennedy Rd, Brampton, ON, L6Z 4N7
(905) 495-4695
Emp Here 1,000
SIC 8059 Nursing and personal care, nec
Shelley Sazackerley

D-U-N-S 24-796-1147   (HQ)
WOODHALL PARK HOLDING CORP
10250 Kennedy Rd Suite Unit, Brampton, ON, L6Z 4N7
(905) 846-1441
Sales 10,191,330
SIC 6513 Apartment building operators
Andrew Post
Albert Post

Brampton, ON L7A

D-U-N-S 20-036-8140   (SL)
1035312 ONTARIO LIMITED
BRAMPTON CHRYSLER DODGE JEEP
190 Canam Cres, Brampton, ON, L7A 1A9
(905) 459-1810
Emp Here 70   *Sales* 44,049,600
SIC 5511 New and used car dealers
Edward Lewis
William Lewis
Eleanor Lewis
Linda Lewis

D-U-N-S 25-940-9514   (SL)
1042735 ONTARIO INC
MAZDA OF BRAMPTON
15 Van Kirk Dr, Brampton, ON, L7A 1W4
(905) 459-0290
Emp Here 40   *Sales* 19,923,120
SIC 5511 New and used car dealers
Sam Alizdeh

D-U-N-S 24-985-4407   (SL)
985178 ONTARIO INC
CLASSIC HONDA
30 Van Kirk Dr, Brampton, ON, L7A 2Y4
(905) 454-1434
Emp Here 103   *Sales* 64,815,840
SIC 5511 New and used car dealers
Sohrab Alizadeh
Mansour Akahaven

D-U-N-S 24-198-0036   (SL)
A. BERGER PRECISION LTD
(*Suby of* BERGER HOLDING INTERNATIONAL GMBH)
28 Regan Rd Suite 1, Brampton, ON, L7A 1A7

---

(905) 840-4207
Emp Here 120   *Sales* 29,187,720
SIC 3451 Screw machine products
Alois Berger
Alexander Berger
Baz Kutter
Kamran Khan

D-U-N-S 20-036-6128   (SL)
ATTRELL AUTO HOLDINGS LIMITED
ATTRELL TOYOTA
110 Canam Cres, Brampton, ON, L7A 1A9
(905) 451-7235
Emp Here 44   *Sales* 21,915,432
SIC 5511 New and used car dealers
John Attrell

D-U-N-S 25-467-0144   (SL)
ATTRELL MOTOR CORPORATION
ATTRELL HYUNDAI
100 Canam Cres, Brampton, ON, L7A 1A9
(905) 451-1699
Emp Here 36   *Sales* 17,930,808
SIC 5511 New and used car dealers
Robert B Attrell

D-U-N-S 20-036-4404   (HQ)
BRAMPTON BRICK LIMITED
OAKS CONCRETE PRODUCTS
225 Wanless Dr, Brampton, ON, L7A 1E9
(905) 840-1011
Emp Here 100   *Sales* 121,209,138
SIC 3251 Brick and structural clay tile
Jeffrey Kerbel
George Housh
Antonio Neves
Judy Pryma
Trevor Sandler
Brad Cobbledick
Christopher Rudolph Bratty
Jim De Gasperis
P. David Grant
Howard Kerbel

D-U-N-S 24-317-8022   (SL)
BRAMPTON NORTH NISSAN
195 Canam Cres, Brampton, ON, L7A 1G1
(905) 459-1600
Emp Here 30   *Sales* 14,942,340
SIC 5511 New and used car dealers
Oscar Molu

D-U-N-S 20-163-2676   (BR)
DAY & ROSS INC
(*Suby of* MCCAIN FOODS GROUP INC)
170 Van Kirk Dr, Brampton, ON, L7A 1K9
(905) 846-6300
Emp Here 200
SIC 4213 Trucking, except local
Jason Kirk

D-U-N-S 24-419-3611   (SL)
EXACTA TOOL 2010 ULC
WILSON TOOL CANADA
(*Suby of* WILSON TOOL INTERNATIONAL INC.)
120 Van Kirk Dr, Brampton, ON, L7A 1B1
(905) 840-2240
Emp Here 25   *Sales* 11,875,650
SIC 5084 Industrial machinery and equipment
Brian E. Robinson

D-U-N-S 20-027-7783   (SL)
EXEL CANADA LTD
100 Sandalwood Pky W, Brampton, ON, L7A 1A8
(905) 840-7540
Emp Here 25   *Sales* 45,910,869
SIC 4225 General warehousing and storage

D-U-N-S 24-005-7133   (SL)
FROST CHEVROLET BUICK GMC CADILLAC LTD
FROST CHEVROLET
150 Bovaird Dr W, Brampton, ON, L7A 0H3
(905) 459-0126
Emp Here 70   *Sales* 44,049,600
SIC 5511 New and used car dealers

Robert Johnston
Al Warkentin

D-U-N-S 25-402-8707   (SL)
GROSNOR DISTRIBUTION INC
4 Lowry Dr, Brampton, ON, L7A 1C4
(416) 744-3344
Emp Here 28   *Sales* 14,575,176
SIC 5092 Toys and hobby goods and supplies
David Yeates
Lisa Yeates

D-U-N-S 20-821-6499   (SL)
ITWAL LIMITED
440 Railside Dr, Brampton, ON, L7A 1L1
(905) 840-9400
Emp Here 60   *Sales* 50,134,620
SIC 5145 Confectionery
Ross Robertson
Glenn Stevens
Suzanne Walker
Peter Allen

D-U-N-S 24-795-8861   (HQ)
JASWALL INC
70 Van Kirk Dr, Brampton, ON, L7A 1B1
(905) 846-3177
Emp Here 80   *Sales* 72,969,300
SIC 3449 Miscellaneous Metalwork
Juan Speck

D-U-N-S 20-773-3155   (SL)
L. N. REYNOLDS CO. LIMITED
10160 Hurontario St Suite 1, Brampton, ON, L7A 0E4
(905) 840-3700
Emp Here 22   *Sales* 18,382,694
SIC 5141 Groceries, general line
Bruce Reynolds

D-U-N-S 25-991-5791   (SL)
LEVEL-RITE SYSTEMS COMPANY
(*Suby of* RITE-HITE HOLDING CORPORATION)
29 Regan Rd, Brampton, ON, L7A 1B2

Emp Here 35   *Sales* 11,414,760
SIC 3999 Manufacturing industries, nec
Steve Leachman

D-U-N-S 20-535-8096   (SL)
M & P TOOL PRODUCTS INC
SPACE AID MANUFACTURING
43 Regan Rd, Brampton, ON, L7A 1B2
(905) 840-5550
Emp Here 85   *Sales* 13,117,370
SIC 2542 Partitions and fixtures, except wood
Martin Prufer
Linda Prufer

D-U-N-S 24-189-4737   (BR)
MCDONALD'S RESTAURANTS OF CANADA LIMITED
MCDONALD'S RESTAURANTS
(*Suby of* MCDONALD'S CORPORATION)
30 Brisdale Dr, Brampton, ON, L7A 3G1
(905) 495-1122
Emp Here 80
SIC 5812 Eating places
Steve Cabral

D-U-N-S 24-333-1621   (BR)
METRO ONTARIO INC
METRO
(*Suby of* METRO INC)
10088 Mclaughlin Rd Suite 1, Brampton, ON, L7A 2X6

Emp Here 300
SIC 5411 Grocery stores
Lee Zwolman

D-U-N-S 24-664-9578   (SL)
OPTIMAX EYEWEAR INCORPORATED
55 Regan Rd Unit 2, Brampton, ON, L7A 1B2
(905) 846-6103
Emp Here 28   *Sales* 14,575,176
SIC 5099 Durable goods, nec

Tanya Bottomley
Lesley Lobao
Sid Kraitberg

D-U-N-S 25-263-7566   (BR)
PEEL DISTRICT SCHOOL BOARD
PARKHOLME SCHOOL
(*Suby of* PEEL DISTRICT SCHOOL BOARD)
10750 Chinguacousy Rd, Brampton, ON, L7A 2Z7
(905) 451-1263
Emp Here 150
SIC 8211 Elementary and secondary schools
Suzanne Bennett

D-U-N-S 24-525-4227   (BR)
PEEL DISTRICT SCHOOL BOARD
BRISDALE PUBLIC SCHOOL
(*Suby of* PEEL DISTRICT SCHOOL BOARD)
370 Brisdale Dr, Brampton, ON, L7A 3K7
(905) 840-2135
Emp Here 85
SIC 8211 Elementary and secondary schools
David Blanch

D-U-N-S 24-120-9639   (BR)
PEEL DISTRICT SCHOOL BOARD
FLETCHER'S MEADOW SECONDARY SCHOOL
(*Suby of* PEEL DISTRICT SCHOOL BOARD)
10750 Chinguacousy Rd, Brampton, ON, L7A 2Z7
(905) 495-2675
Emp Here 120
SIC 8211 Elementary and secondary schools
Jan Coomber

D-U-N-S 20-129-3164   (HQ)
PEELLE COMPANY LIMITED, THE
(*Suby of* THE PEELLE COMPANY)
195 Sandalwood Pky W, Brampton, ON, L7A 1J6
(905) 846-4545
Sales 42,722,100
SIC 5031 Lumber, plywood, and millwork
Henry Peelle
Herman Reis
Alex Stobo

D-U-N-S 24-660-6586   (HQ)
PET SCIENCE LTD
14 Regan Rd Unit 1, Brampton, ON, L7A 1B9
(905) 840-1300
Sales 16,711,540
SIC 5149 Groceries and related products, nec
John Lagerquist
Edward Lagerquist

D-U-N-S 24-008-8013   (HQ)
POLYNT COMPOSITES CANADA INC
29 Regan Rd, Brampton, ON, L7A 1B2
(905) 495-0606
Sales 10,325,770
SIC 3087 Custom compound purchased resins
Yves Gosselin
Brent Stevens

D-U-N-S 20-176-1046   (HQ)
STEVENS COMPANY LIMITED, THE
425 Railside Dr, Brampton, ON, L7A 0N8
(905) 791-8600
Emp Here 60   *Sales* 160,605,600
SIC 5047 Medical and hospital equipment
Peter Stevens
Scott Baker
Helen Nasato
Jay Stevens
David Donnelly
Robert Brabers

D-U-N-S 25-508-1127   (SL)
V.S.I. INC
VISTA SECURITY AND INVESTIGATIONS
18 Regan Rd Unit 31, Brampton, ON, L7A 1C2

Emp Here 100   *Sales* 39,567,800
SIC 7381 Detective and armored car services

Robert Mcknight
Domenic Todaro

D-U-N-S 24-991-8293   (SL)
VULSAY INDUSTRIES LTD
(*Suby of* CLEAN HARBORS, INC.)
35 Regan Rd, Brampton, ON, L7A 1B2
(905) 846-2200
Emp Here 63   *Sales* 42,141,204
SIC 7389 Business services, nec
Geoff Kilburn

D-U-N-S 24-137-9684   (SL)
WOODSTREAM CANADA CORPORATION
(*Suby of* BROCKWAY MORAN & PARTNERS, INC.)
4 Lowry Dr, Brampton, ON, L7A 1C4
(905) 840-2640
Emp Here 18   *Sales* 13,365,360
SIC 5191 Farm supplies
Harry Whaley

Brantford, ON N3P

D-U-N-S 24-194-2465   (HQ)
CANADIAN BABBITT BEARINGS LTD
CBB
64 Dalkeith Dr, Brantford, ON, N3P 1N6
(519) 752-5471
Sales 19,001,040
SIC 5085 Industrial supplies
Garth Wheldon

D-U-N-S 24-829-7079   (HQ)
KOOLATRON CORPORATION
139 Copernicus Blvd, Brantford, ON, N3P 1N4
(519) 756-3950
Emp Here 70   *Sales* 19,407,011
SIC 3086 Plastics foam products
Arun Kulkarni
Raj Chandaria
Pulin Chandaria

D-U-N-S 20-136-6528   (SL)
LION RAMPANT IMPORTS LTD
36 Easton Rd, Brantford, ON, N3P 1J5
(905) 572-6446
Emp Here 43   *Sales* 22,565,466
SIC 5092 Toys and hobby goods and supplies
Ross Fleming
Rose Kriedemann
Frank Boerboom

D-U-N-S 20-280-8671   (HQ)
PAN-GLO CANADA PAN COATINGS INC
84 Easton Rd, Brantford, ON, N3P 1J5
(519) 756-2800
Emp Here 37   *Sales* 12,501,320
SIC 7699 Repair services, nec
Robert Bundy

D-U-N-S 25-410-5810   (HQ)
SOLIS FOODS CORPORATION INC
79 Easton Rd, Brantford, ON, N3P 1J4
(519) 349-2020
Emp Here 30   *Sales* 41,917,535
SIC 2052 Cookies and crackers
Andy Vivian
Florain Meyer
Brad Beaudoin

Brantford, ON N3R

D-U-N-S 24-183-7942   (SL)
1277487 ONTARIO LIMITED
ACUREX HEALTH CARE MANUFACTURING
20 Sage Crt, Brantford, ON, N3R 7T4
(519) 752-4937
Emp Here 49   *Sales* 40,943,273
SIC 5149 Groceries and related products, nec
Kenya Reading

D-U-N-S 20-790-1344   (SL)
2030413 ONTARIO LIMITED
BRANTFORD HOME HARDWARE
10 King George Rd, Brantford, ON, N3R 5J7
(519) 751-3333
Emp Here 40   *Sales* 10,122,360
SIC 5251 Hardware stores
David Liesemer
Ronald Cicuttini

D-U-N-S 24-625-9006   (BR)
2063414 ONTARIO LIMITED
LEISUREWORLD CAREGIVING CENTER
389 West St, Brantford, ON, N3R 3V9
(519) 759-4666
Emp Here 120
SIC 8051 Skilled nursing care facilities
Jim Eagleton

D-U-N-S 24-763-7655   (HQ)
991909 ONTARIO INC
TOOTSIES FACTORY SHOE MARKET
(*Suby of* TABOH HOLDINGS INC)
595 West St Unit 5, Brantford, ON, N3R 7C5
(519) 754-4775
Emp Here 10   *Sales* 21,886,312
SIC 5661 Shoe stores
Greg Taylor
Claude Bohemier

D-U-N-S 24-938-2466   (SL)
**BEACON INTERNATIONAL WAREHOUS-
ING LTD**
325 West St Suite B110, Brantford, ON, N3R
3V6

Emp Here 30   *Sales* 11,560,800
SIC 4731 Freight transportation arrangement
Rolf Von Fintel

D-U-N-S 24-425-7093   (HQ)
**BRANT HALDIMAND NORFOLK CATHOLIC
DISTRICT SCHOOL BOARD**
322 Fairview Dr, Brantford, ON, N3R 2X6
(519) 756-6369
Emp Here 30   *Sales* 118,942,800
SIC 8211 Elementary and secondary schools
Wally Easton
Cathy Horgan
Patricia Kings
William Chopp

D-U-N-S 24-397-1470   (BR)
**BRANT HALDIMAND NORFOLK CATHOLIC
DISTRICT SCHOOL BOARD**
*ST JOHNS COLLEGE SECONDARY
SCHOOL*
(*Suby of* BRANT HALDIMAND NORFOLK
CATHOLIC DISTRICT SCHOOL BOARD)
80 Paris Rd, Brantford, ON, N3R 1H9
(519) 759-2318
Emp Here 93
SIC 8211 Elementary and secondary schools
Rob Campbell

D-U-N-S 24-539-4408   (SL)
BRANT MUTUAL INSURANCE COMPANY
20 Holiday Dr, Brantford, ON, N3R 7J4
(519) 752-0088
Emp Here 14   *Sales* 10,156,146
SIC 6311 Life insurance
Jason Cybulski
William Emmott
Robert Chambers

D-U-N-S 20-524-4882   (SL)
**BRANTFORD CHRYSLER DODGE JEEP
LTD**
180 Lynden Rd, Brantford, ON, N3R 8A3
(519) 753-7331
Emp Here 48   *Sales* 23,907,744
SIC 5511 New and used car dealers
Marlene Johnston
Allyson Teodoridis

D-U-N-S 25-166-9594   (SL)
BRANTFORD NISSAN INC

338 King George Rd, Brantford, ON, N3R 5M1
(519) 756-9240
Emp Here 35   *Sales* 17,432,730
SIC 5511 New and used car dealers
John Lecluse
Lou D'amato

D-U-N-S 20-845-0973   (SL)
BRANTMAC MANAGEMENT LIMITED
MACDONALD'S RESTAURANT
73 King George Rd, Brantford, ON, N3R 5K2
(519) 756-7350
Emp Here 75   *Sales* 3,413,925
SIC 5812 Eating places
Bruce Graham

D-U-N-S 24-861-2145   (SL)
BRODART CANADA COMPANY
BRO-DART LIBRARY SUPPLIES
109 Roy Blvd, Brantford, ON, N3R 7K1

Emp Here 200   *Sales* 30,864,400
SIC 2531 Public building and related furniture
Randall Mackenzie

D-U-N-S 20-091-5937   (SL)
CANADIAN TIRE
30 Lynden Rd, Brantford, ON, N3R 8A4
(519) 751-2878
Emp Here 30   *Sales* 14,942,340
SIC 5531 Auto and home supply stores
Danny Richer

D-U-N-S 24-828-8813   (BR)
CARRIER TRUCK CENTER INC
CARRIER EMERGENCY
(*Suby of* ROYALEX INCORPORATED)
6 Edmondson St, Brantford, ON, N3R 7J3
(519) 752-5431
Emp Here 100
SIC 5511 New and used car dealers
Marvin Long

D-U-N-S 24-953-9883   (SL)
CENTURY 21 PROFESSIONAL GROUP INC
32 Charing Cross St, Brantford, ON, N3R 2H2
(519) 756-3900
Emp Here 40   *Sales* 13,085,080
SIC 6531 Real estate agents and managers
Shawn Brians
Norma Hamilton
Mark Bennett

D-U-N-S 20-610-6635   (HQ)
DOMCLEAN LIMITED
*DOMINION EQUIPMENT & CHEMICAL, DIV
OF*
29 Craig St, Brantford, ON, N3R 7H8
(519) 752-3725
Emp Here 20   *Sales* 10,389,600
SIC 7349 Building maintenance services, nec
Ross Buzek

D-U-N-S 25-469-0167   (SL)
**DORSEY GROUP INSURANCE PLANNERS
INC, THE**
THE DORSEY GROUP
330 West St Unit 7, Brantford, ON, N3R 7V5
(519) 759-0033
Emp Here 25   *Sales* 26,096,580
SIC 6411 Insurance agents, brokers, and ser-
vice
Paula Dorsey
Noreen Novak
Gary Dorsey

D-U-N-S 20-052-7539   (SL)
**DRAKA ELEVATOR PRODUCTS INCORPO-
RATED**
17 Woodyatt Dr Unit 13, Brantford, ON, N3R
7K3
(519) 758-0605
Emp Here 10   *Sales* 10,003,390
SIC 5051 Metals service centers and offices
Christine Mudge
John Moore
Jim Goodbrand

D-U-N-S 24-461-9094   (HQ)
DURE FOODS LIMITED
120 Roy Blvd, Brantford, ON, N3R 7K2
(519) 753-5504
Emp Here 15   *Sales* 13,476,570
SIC 7389 Business services, nec
Scott Malcolm

D-U-N-S 20-923-1211   (BR)
EXTENDICARE (CANADA) INC
PARAMED HOME HEALTH CARE
(*Suby of* EXTENDICARE INC)
325 West St Unit 201, Brantford, ON, N3R 3V6
(519) 756-4606
Emp Here 91
SIC 7363 Help supply services
Maya Ramdhanie

D-U-N-S 20-037-2670   (SL)
FORBES BROS. INC
21 Lynden Rd Suite 19, Brantford, ON, N3R
8B8
(519) 759-8220
Emp Here 45   *Sales* 22,413,510
SIC 5511 New and used car dealers
James Forbes
Robert Forbes

D-U-N-S 20-037-3298   (HQ)
GUNTHER MELE LIMITED
30 Craig St, Brantford, ON, N3R 7J1
(519) 756-4330
Sales 14,607,600
SIC 2657 Folding paperboard boxes
Darrell King

D-U-N-S 20-269-6902   (HQ)
**HC CANADA OPERATING COMPANY, LTD,
THE**
KORD
325 West St Unit B200, Brantford, ON, N3R
3V6
(519) 753-2666
Sales 11,438,315
SIC 2671 Paper; coated and laminated pack-
aging
Christopher Koscho
Jim Bennett

D-U-N-S 20-901-0800   (SL)
HOGEWONING MOTORS LTD
BRANTFORD TOYOTA
5 Woodyatt Dr, Brantford, ON, N3R 7K3
(519) 752-5010
Emp Here 25   *Sales* 12,451,950
SIC 5511 New and used car dealers
Paul Hogewoning
Pauline Hogewoning

D-U-N-S 24-075-2022   (HQ)
**HOLSTEIN ASSOCIATION OF CANADA,
THE**
HOLSTEIN CANADA
20 Corporate Pl, Brantford, ON, N3R 8A6
(519) 756-8300
Emp Here 1   *Sales* 25,861,500
SIC 8611 Business associations

D-U-N-S 20-003-8870   (BR)
HOME DEPOT OF CANADA INC
HOME DEPOT
(*Suby of* THE HOME DEPOT INC)
25 Holiday Dr, Brantford, ON, N3R 7J4
(519) 757-3534
Emp Here 150
SIC 5251 Hardware stores
Lee Hazelwood

D-U-N-S 25-928-4156   (SL)
HOMEFRONT REALTY INC
*COLDWELL BANKER HOMEFRONT RE-
ALTY*
245 King George Rd, Brantford, ON, N3R 7N7
(519) 756-8120
Emp Here 40   *Sales* 13,085,080
SIC 6531 Real estate agents and managers
Michelle Amuy

D-U-N-S 20-037-1276   (SL)
HT INDUSTRIAL LTD
CHIL-CON PRODUCTS, DIV OF
(*Suby of* HENDRICKS HOLDING COMPANY,
INC.)
36 Craig St, Brantford, ON, N3R 7J1
(519) 759-3010
Emp Here 100   *Sales* 19,208,500
SIC 3443 Fabricated plate work (boiler shop)
Alex Barclay
Darc Mcfadden
Nancy Wieland
Rachel Latulippe
Jennifer Church
Ross Hainer

D-U-N-S 24-537-9029   (HQ)
KURIYAMA CANADA, INC
(*Suby of* KURIYAMA HOLDINGS CORPORA-
TION)
140 Roy Blvd, Brantford, ON, N3R 7K2
(519) 753-6717
Sales 10,484,628
SIC 3052 Rubber and plastics hose and belt-
ings
Tsutomu Hitomi
Walt Vogt
Donna Thompson
Tsunetaka Yoneuchi

D-U-N-S 24-333-1761   (BR)
METRO ONTARIO INC
METRO
(*Suby of* METRO INC)
371 St Paul Ave, Brantford, ON, N3R 4N5
(519) 758-0300
Emp Here 150
SIC 5411 Grocery stores
Guido Madrusan

D-U-N-S 20-281-5452   (SL)
MOVATI ATHLETIC (BRANTFORD) INC.
595 West St, Brantford, ON, N3R 7C5
(519) 756-0123
Emp Here 75   *Sales* 5,729,775
SIC 7991 Physical fitness facilities
Chuck Kelly
Dan Pompilii

D-U-N-S 20-290-4905   (BR)
MOVATI ATHLETIC (LONDON SOUTH) INC.
MOVATI ATHLETIC
(*Suby of* MOVATI ATHLETIC (LONDON
SOUTH) INC.)
595 West St, Brantford, ON, N3R 7C5
(519) 756-0123
Emp Here 75
SIC 7991 Physical fitness facilities
Mike Nolan

D-U-N-S 24-844-2543   (HQ)
**NATIONAL REFRIGERATION & AIR CONDI-
TIONING CANADA CORP**
KEEPRITE REFRIGERATION
(*Suby of* NATIONAL REFRIGERATION & AIR
CONDITIONING PRODUCTS, INC.)
159 Roy Blvd, Brantford, ON, N3R 7K1
(519) 751-0444
Sales 64,601,710
SIC 3585 Refrigeration and heating equip-
ment
David Teeter
Ronald Blacker

D-U-N-S 24-925-4004   (SL)
NETCHEM INC
(*Suby of* PEEKAY HOLDINGS LTD)
35 Roy Blvd, Brantford, ON, N3R 7K1
(519) 751-4700
Emp Here 14   *Sales* 10,224,830
SIC 5169 Chemicals and allied products, nec
Paul Khurana

D-U-N-S 24-351-7880   (HQ)
NEZIOL INSURANCE BROKERS LTD
NEZIOL GROUP, THE
53 Charing Cross St Suite 1, Brantford, ON,

N3R 7K9
(519) 759-2110
Emp Here 22   *Sales* 42,403,000
SIC 6411 Insurance agents, brokers, and service
Paul Neziol
Bernard Neziol

D-U-N-S 20-058-4170   (BR)
NORMERICA INC
(*Suby of* NORMERICA CAPITAL CORPORATION)
46 Morton Ave E, Brantford, ON, N3R 7J7
(519) 756-8414
Emp Here 75
SIC 3999 Manufacturing industries, nec
Andrew Reko

D-U-N-S 24-793-3807   (BR)
PMT INDUSTRIES LIMITED
PURE METAL GALVANIZING, DIV OF
(*Suby of* PMT INDUSTRIES LIMITED)
32 Bodine Dr, Brantford, ON, N3R 7M4
(519) 758-5505
Emp Here 85
SIC 3479 Metal coating and allied services
Marc Kearns

D-U-N-S 24-376-4730   (HQ)
RAMKEY COMMUNICATIONS INC
20 Roy Blvd Unit 2, Brantford, ON, N3R 7K2
(519) 759-0643
Emp Here 20   *Sales* 27,416,640
SIC 4899 Communication services, nec
Richer Mcconkey

D-U-N-S 24-342-8096   (BR)
RECIPE UNLIMITED CORPORATION
SWISS CHALET
(*Suby of* RECIPE UNLIMITED CORPORATION)
84 Lynden Rd Suite 1771, Brantford, ON, N3R 6B8
(519) 759-6990
Emp Here 75
SIC 5812 Eating places
Fernando Soares

D-U-N-S 20-005-2194   (BR)
RED LOBSTER HOSPITALITY LLC
RED LOBSTER RESTAURANTS
67 King George Rd, Brantford, ON, N3R 5K2
(519) 759-7121
Emp Here 75
SIC 5812 Eating places
Danielle Robinson

D-U-N-S 24-077-2756   (BR)
REVERA LONG TERM CARE INC
VERSA-CARE CENTRE OF BRANTFORD
(*Suby of* GOVERNMENT OF CANADA)
425 Park Rd N, Brantford, ON, N3R 7G5
(519) 759-1040
Emp Here 150
SIC 8051 Skilled nursing care facilities
Debbie Bonney

D-U-N-S 20-694-5920   (SL)
SLACAN INDUSTRIES INC
145 Roy Blvd, Brantford, ON, N3R 7K1
(519) 758-8888
Emp Here 130   *Sales* 24,757,460
SIC 3644 Noncurrent-carrying wiring devices
Ron Jee
Laurie Leinster
Jeffrey Gugick

D-U-N-S 20-921-7038   (SL)
SMITTY'S KIP IMPORTS
80 Morton Ave E Suite A, Brantford, ON, N3R 7J7

Emp Here 25   *Sales* 11,230,475
SIC 7389 Business services, nec
Kyle Smith

D-U-N-S 20-104-5379   (BR)
TIGERCAT INDUSTRIES INC

(*Suby of* TIGERCAT INTERNATIONAL INC)
54 Morton Ave E, Brantford, ON, N3R 7J7
(519) 753-2000
Emp Here 120
SIC 3531 Construction machinery
Jason Iles

D-U-N-S 20-285-8817   (BR)
TIGERCAT INDUSTRIES INC
(*Suby of* TIGERCAT INTERNATIONAL INC)
54 Morton Ave E, Brantford, ON, N3R 7J7
(519) 753-2000
Emp Here 150
SIC 3531 Construction machinery

D-U-N-S 24-953-6970   (HQ)
TIGERCAT INDUSTRIES INC
(*Suby of* TIGERCAT INTERNATIONAL INC)
54 Morton Ave E, Brantford, ON, N3R 7J7
(519) 753-2000
Emp Here 1   *Sales* 266,833,150
SIC 3531 Construction machinery
Kenneth Macdonald
Anthony Iarocci

D-U-N-S 25-680-2372   (HQ)
UNITED RENTALS OF CANADA, INC
(*Suby of* UNITED RENTALS, INC.)
150 Roy Blvd, Brantford, ON, N3R 7K2
(519) 756-0700
Emp Here 14   *Sales* 24,684,660
SIC 8741 Management services
Erik Olsson
Michael J. Kneeland
Scott Fisher
David Guernsey

D-U-N-S 20-738-7353   (BR)
WAL-MART CANADA CORP
(*Suby of* WALMART INC.)
300 King George Rd Suite 1, Brantford, ON, N3R 5L7
(519) 759-3450
Emp Here 200
SIC 5311 Department stores
David Cheesewright

D-U-N-S 20-774-5600   (SL)
WAY, G RESTAURANTS SERVICES LTD
BOSTON PIZZA
299 Wayne Gretzky Pky, Brantford, ON, N3R 8A5
(519) 751-2304
Emp Here 75   *Sales* 3,413,925
SIC 5812 Eating places
Tony Mullally

D-U-N-S 24-816-4824   (SL)
WILLIAMSON GROUP INC, THE
(*Suby of* COWAN INSURANCE GROUP LTD)
225 King George Rd, Brantford, ON, N3R 7N7
(519) 756-9560
Emp Here 78   *Sales* 144,123,876
SIC 6411 Insurance agents, brokers, and service
Paul Williamson
Donald Williamson
Dufferin Williamson

D-U-N-S 25-297-8093   (BR)
ZEHRMART INC
ZEHRS MARKETS
(*Suby of* LOBLAW COMPANIES LIMITED)
410 Fairview Dr Suite 1, Brantford, ON, N3R 7V7
(519) 754-4932
Emp Here 150
SIC 5411 Grocery stores
Ralph Von Herrath

Brantford, ON N3S

D-U-N-S 20-512-9740   (HQ)
1589711 ONTARIO INC
IZON INDUSTRIES, DIV OF

156 Adams Blvd, Brantford, ON, N3S 7V5
(905) 643-9044
Emp Here 2   *Sales* 70,219,250
SIC 3544 Special dies, tools, jigs, and fixtures
Walter Kuskowski

D-U-N-S 24-048-6423   (SL)
ABCOTT CONSTRUCTION LTD
124 Garden Ave, Brantford, ON, N3S 7W4
(519) 756-4350
Emp Here 25   *Sales* 11,768,275
SIC 1542 Nonresidential construction, nec
Patrick Hayes
Darryl Lawrie

D-U-N-S 24-610-4632   (SL)
ACIC PHARMACEUTICALS INC
(*Suby of* POLAR PHARMACEUTICALS INC)
81 Sinclair Blvd, Brantford, ON, N3S 7X6
(519) 751-3668
Emp Here 50   *Sales* 55,267,250
SIC 5122 Drugs, proprietaries, and sundries
Luciano Calenti
Chris Rayfield
Christopher H. Calenti

D-U-N-S 25-862-2042   (SL)
ACTION REALTY LTD
ROYAL LEPAGE ACTION REALTY
766 Colborne St, Brantford, ON, N3S 3S1
(519) 753-7311
Emp Here 39   *Sales* 12,757,953
SIC 6531 Real estate agents and managers
Danny Dedominicis

D-U-N-S 25-353-3053   (HQ)
APC FILTRATION INC
10c Abbott Crt Unit 303, Brantford, ON, N3S 0E7
(888) 689-1235
Emp Here 10   *Sales* 15,581,440
SIC 2674 Bags: uncoated paper and multiwall
Russell Kelly

D-U-N-S 24-389-3174   (HQ)
ARYZTA CANADA CO
(*Suby of* ARYZTA AG)
115 Sinclair Blvd Suite 1, Brantford, ON, N3S 7X6
(519) 720-2000
Emp Here 300   *Sales* 247,267,020
SIC 5145 Confectionery
Hilliard Lombard
Deborah Cochrane
Culbert Lu
Pat Morrissey
John Yamin
Steve Ricks
Ronan Minahan
Noel Herterich

D-U-N-S 24-952-5254   (HQ)
ATLAS HYDRAULICS INC
(*Suby of* GATES INDUSTRIAL CORPORATION PLC)
369 Elgin St, Brantford, ON, N3S 7P5
(519) 756-8210
Emp Here 345   *Sales* 50,926,005
SIC 3492 Fluid power valves and hose fittings
Ignacio Villalobos
Francois Godin
Ralitsa Arafin

D-U-N-S 24-044-6005   (SL)
BML MULTI TRADES GROUP LTD
32 Ryan Pl, Brantford, ON, N3S 7S1
(905) 777-7879
Emp Here 50   *Sales* 11,046,700
SIC 1711 Plumbing, heating, air-conditioning
James Dinovo
James Thomson

D-U-N-S 20-269-0046   (BR)
BRANT INSTORE CORPORATION
BRANT SCREEN CRAFT
(*Suby of* BRANT INSTORE CORPORATION)
254 Henry St, Brantford, ON, N3S 7R5

(800) 265-8480
Emp Here 175
SIC 2759 Commercial printing, nec
Trevor Mcdole

D-U-N-S 24-029-0155   (SL)
BRANTFORD ENGINEERING AND CONSTRUCTION LIMITED
(*Suby of* RICH, D.T. HOLDINGS LIMITED)
54 Ewart Ave, Brantford, ON, N3S 0H4
(519) 759-1160
Emp Here 50   *Sales* 12,622,100
SIC 1623 Water, sewer, and utility lines
David Rich
Matthew Rich
Maureen O'donoghue Rich

D-U-N-S 25-093-2675   (BR)
CASCADES CANADA ULC
CASCADES RECOVERY+
(*Suby of* CASCADES INC)
434 Henry St, Brantford, ON, N3S 7W1
(519) 756-5264
Emp Here 100
SIC 4953 Refuse systems
Scott Lumber

D-U-N-S 20-291-7084   (HQ)
CHANNEL CONTROL MERCHANTS CORPORATION
(*Suby of* CHANNEL CONTROL MERCHANTS, LLC)
225 Henry St Unit 5b, Brantford, ON, N3S 7R4
(519) 770-3403
Sales 44,551,200
SIC 5199 Nondurable goods, nec
Rob Roberts

D-U-N-S 20-964-6405   (HQ)
COMMUNITY LIVING BRANT
DUNN ENTERPRISES
366 Dalhousie St, Brantford, ON, N3S 3W2
(519) 756-2662
Emp Here 30   *Sales* 16,340,400
SIC 8322 Individual and family services
Joan Macqueen
Katherine Dubicki
Sheila Hofman
June Szeman
Janet Reansbury

D-U-N-S 25-544-0208   (SL)
DAVID CORDINGLEY TRANSPORT CORP
148 Mohawk St, Brantford, ON, N3S 7G5
(519) 752-7810
Emp Here 80   *Sales* 11,855,360
SIC 4212 Local trucking, without storage
David Cordingley

D-U-N-S 25-991-2202   (BR)
ECONO-RACK GROUP (2015) INC, THE
ENRACK-SYSTEMS DIV OF
(*Suby of* TOYOTA INDUSTRIES CORPORATION)
132 Adams Blvd, Brantford, ON, N3S 7V2
(519) 753-2227
Emp Here 150
SIC 2542 Partitions and fixtures, except wood
Mike Sennema

D-U-N-S 20-037-2878   (HQ)
GATES CANADA INC
(*Suby of* GATES INDUSTRIAL CORPORATION PLC)
225 Henry St Bldg 8, Brantford, ON, N3S 7R4
(519) 759-4141
Emp Here 163   *Sales* 324,828,180
SIC 5085 Industrial supplies
Francois Godin

D-U-N-S 20-037-2373   (SL)
GENOR RECYCLING SERVICES LIMITED
LAKESHORE RECYCLING
434 Henry St, Brantford, ON, N3S 7W1
(519) 756-5264
Emp Here 50   *Sales* 26,328,544
SIC 5093 Scrap and waste materials
Norman Haac

Louise Haac

D-U-N-S 25-238-9457   (BR)
GRAND ERIE DISTRICT SCHOOL BOARD
JOHNSON, PAULINE COLLEGIATE VOCA-
TIONAL SCHOOL
(*Suby of* GRAND ERIE DISTRICT SCHOOL BOARD)
627 Colborne St, Brantford, ON, N3S 3M8
(519) 756-1320
Emp Here 110
SIC 8211 Elementary and secondary schools
Sandy Hess

D-U-N-S 24-059-4788   (HQ)
GRAND ERIE DISTRICT SCHOOL BOARD
349 Erie Ave, Brantford, ON, N3S 2H7
(519) 756-6301
Emp Here 600   *Sales* 266,828,348
SIC 8211 Elementary and secondary schools
John Forbeck
Jamie Gunn
Rita Collver
Bill Johnston
Don Werden
Jane Angus
Shari Cann
Carol Ann Sloat
Arlene Everets
Michael Hurley

D-U-N-S 24-784-9826   (SL)
HEMATITE MANUFACTURING INC
46 Plant Farm Blvd, Brantford, ON, N3S 7W3
(519) 752-8402
Emp Here 120   *Sales* 38,269,200
SIC 4953 Refuse systems
John Pavamel

D-U-N-S 25-113-5505   (SL)
ITML HOLDINGS INC
75 Plant Farm Blvd, Brantford, ON, N3S 7W2
(519) 753-2666
Emp Here 200   *Sales* 54,670,000
SIC 6712 Bank holding companies
Kees Hensen
Kleis Hensen

D-U-N-S 25-603-7412   (BR)
LATHAM POOL PRODUCTS INC
(*Suby of* LATHAM POOL PRODUCTS INC)
383 Elgin St, Brantford, ON, N3S 7P5
(800) 638-7422
Emp Here 100
SIC 3949 Sporting and athletic goods, nec

D-U-N-S 24-419-9068   (HQ)
LIBERTY TIRE RECYCLING CANADA LTD
(*Suby of* LAUREL MOUNTAIN PARTNERS LLC)
300 Henry St, Brantford, ON, N3S 7R5
(519) 752-7696
Sales 10,285,240
SIC 4953 Refuse systems
Jeffrey D Kendall
H Dale Van Steenberg
Jonathan Walker

D-U-N-S 25-352-6222   (HQ)
METHAPHARM INC
(*Suby of* POLAR PHARMACEUTICALS INC)
81 Sinclair Blvd, Brantford, ON, N3S 7X6
(519) 751-3602
Sales 22,106,900
SIC 5122 Drugs, proprietaries, and sundries
Luciano Calenti
Christopher Calenti
Craig Williamson

D-U-N-S 20-121-0945   (HQ)
MITTEN INC
MITTEN VINYL
(*Suby of* CORNERSTONE BUILDING BRANDS, INC.)
225 Henry St Unit 5a, Brantford, ON, N3S 7R4
(519) 805-4701
Emp Here 150   *Sales* 77,613,900

SIC 3089 Plastics products, nec
Douglas Mitten
Gary Ball
Andrew Vann

D-U-N-S 20-346-0688   (HQ)
NEXXSOURCE RECYCLING INC
300 Henry St, Brantford, ON, N3S 7R5
(519) 752-7696
Sales 49,521,670
SIC 7534 Tire retreading and repair shops
William J Bethune

D-U-N-S 24-665-6987   (HQ)
PATRIOT FORGE CO.
280 Henry St, Brantford, ON, N3S 7R5
(519) 758-8100
Emp Here 200   *Sales* 51,078,510
SIC 3499 Fabricated Metal products, nec
Frank Carchidi

D-U-N-S 25-267-3657   (SL)
SAMUEL METAL BLANKING
NAMASCO BLANKING CENTER
546 Elgin St, Brantford, ON, N3S 7P8
(519) 758-1125
Emp Here 49   *Sales* 12,063,114
SIC 1791 Structural steel erection

D-U-N-S 24-027-2047   (BR)
SAMUEL, SON & CO., LIMITED
SAMUEL METAL BLANKING
(*Suby of* SAMUEL, SON & CO., LIMITED)
546 Elgin St, Brantford, ON, N3S 7P8
(519) 758-2710
Emp Here 85
SIC 5051 Metals service centers and offices
Sergio Cipriani

D-U-N-S 20-965-4305   (HQ)
SCP DISTRIBUTORS CANADA INC
(*Suby of* POOL CORPORATION)
373 Elgin St, Brantford, ON, N3S 7P5
(519) 720-9219
Emp Here 20   *Sales* 69,530,000
SIC 5091 Sporting and recreation goods
Brent Milburn
John Bliszczuk
Ken Humprey

D-U-N-S 24-074-8426   (BR)
SERVICES FINANCIERS NCO, INC
NCO GROUP
(*Suby of* GATESTONE & CO. INC)
33 Sinclair Blvd Unit 4, Brantford, ON, N3S 7X6
(519) 750-6000
Emp Here 700
SIC 7322 Adjustment and collection services
Carolyn Symes

D-U-N-S 20-119-7394   (HQ)
SONOCO CANADA CORPORATION
ROLL PACKAGING TECHNOLOGY
(*Suby of* SONOCO PRODUCTS COMPANY)
33 Park Ave E, Brantford, ON, N3S 7R9
(905) 823-7910
Emp Here 84   *Sales* 367,637,000
SIC 2655 Fiber cans, drums, and similar products
David Baxter
Jack Sanders

D-U-N-S 25-116-6997   (HQ)
SONOCO FLEXIBLE PACKAGING CANADA CORPORATION
(*Suby of* SONOCO PRODUCTS COMPANY)
33 Park Ave E, Brantford, ON, N3S 7R9
(519) 752-6591
Emp Here 5   *Sales* 119,406,000
SIC 3086 Plastics foam products
Marc Bannister
David Baxter
John Colyer

D-U-N-S 20-071-0312   (SL)
ST. JOSEPH'S LIFECARE CENTRE,
BRANTFORD

99 Wayne Gretzky Pky, Brantford, ON, N3S 6T6
(519) 751-7096
Emp Here 200   *Sales* 13,665,200
SIC 8051 Skilled nursing care facilities
Shawn Gadsby

D-U-N-S 24-183-0488   (HQ)
ST. LEONARD'S COMMUNITY SERVICES
BRANT ALCOVE REHABILITATION SER-
VICES
133 Elgin St, Brantford, ON, N3S 5A4
(519) 759-8830
Emp Here 11   *Sales* 10,156,556
SIC 8361 Residential care
Bill Sanderson

D-U-N-S 24-860-3110   (SL)
STELLARC PRECISION BAR INC
101 Wayne Gretzky Pky, Brantford, ON, N3S 7N9

Emp Here 85   *Sales* 19,841,975
SIC 3316 Cold finishing of steel shapes
Larry Thompson
Steve Thompson

D-U-N-S 25-283-8909   (SL)
STONE STRAW LIMITED
72 Plant Farm Blvd, Brantford, ON, N3S 7W3
(519) 756-1974
Emp Here 60   *Sales* 14,006,100
SIC 2656 Sanitary food containers
Walter Kuskowski
Pierre Doig

D-U-N-S 20-982-6775   (SL)
TEKSIGN INC
86 Plant Farm Blvd, Brantford, ON, N3S 7W3
(519) 756-1089
Emp Here 70   *Sales* 22,829,520
SIC 3993 Signs and advertising specialties
Daniel Mullin
George Brown
Dorothy Mullin

D-U-N-S 24-411-2298   (SL)
TULSAR CANADA LTD
TULSAR CUSTOMS CONTROL
15 Worthington Dr, Brantford, ON, N3S 0H4
(519) 748-5055
Emp Here 85   *Sales* 16,187,570
SIC 3625 Relays and industrial controls
George Micevski

D-U-N-S 20-920-1917   (SL)
WENTWORTH MOLD LTD
BLOW MOLD GROUP
156 Adams Blvd, Brantford, ON, N3S 7V5
(519) 754-5400
Emp Here 95   *Sales* 26,282,700
SIC 2821 Plastics materials and resins
Walter T Kuskowski
Jeffrey Barclay

D-U-N-S 24-860-2646   (HQ)
WENTWORTH TECH INC
156 Adams Blvd, Brantford, ON, N3S 7V5
(519) 754-5400
Emp Here 5   *Sales* 267,563,200
SIC 7389 Business services, nec
Walter Kuskowski
Jeffrey Barclay

Brantford, ON N3T

D-U-N-S 24-850-1897   (BR)
APOTEX PHARMACHEM INC
11 Spalding Dr, Brantford, ON, N3T 6B7
(519) 756-8942
Emp Here 440
SIC 2834 Pharmaceutical preparations
Jason Fisher

D-U-N-S 20-984-0537   (HQ)

APOTEX PHARMACHEM INC
34 Spalding Dr, Brantford, ON, N3T 6B8
(519) 756-8942
Emp Here 385   *Sales* 530,550,400
SIC 2834 Pharmaceutical preparations
Pere Paton
Andrew Sabuneti
Darren Hall
Jason Fischer
Jim Berhalter

D-U-N-S 25-042-1153   (SL)
BANNESTER, DR LESLIE R
AVENUE MEDICAL CENTRE
221 Brant Ave Suite 1, Brantford, ON, N3T 3J2
(519) 753-8666
Emp Here 80   *Sales* 12,851,680
SIC 8011 Offices and clinics of medical doctors
Leslie R Bannister

D-U-N-S 20-878-3381   (SL)
BELL CITY AUTO CENTRE INC
100 Old Onondaga Rd E, Brantford, ON, N3T 5L4
(800) 265-8498
Emp Here 30   *Sales* 14,942,340
SIC 5511 New and used car dealers
Peter Martyniuk
Sophia Martyniuk
Mike Martyniuk
Walter Martyniuk

D-U-N-S 24-418-2507   (HQ)
BLASTCO CORPORATION
(*Suby of* T.F. WARREN GROUP INC)
57 Old Onondaga Rd W Ss 13, Brantford, ON, N3T 5M1
(519) 756-9050
Sales 29,618,225
SIC 1721 Painting and paper hanging
Terry Warren
Al Toner

D-U-N-S 25-843-4083   (SL)
BOVE DRUGS LIMITED
SHOPPERS DRUG MART
320 Colborne St W Suite 1152, Brantford, ON, N3T 1M2
(519) 759-8133
Emp Here 55   *Sales* 13,438,040
SIC 5912 Drug stores and proprietary stores
Bruno Bove

D-U-N-S 24-304-2330   (SL)
BRANT FOOD CENTER LTD
94 Grey St, Brantford, ON, N3T 2T5
(519) 756-8002
Emp Here 50   *Sales* 13,707,600
SIC 5431 Fruit and vegetable markets
Stellio Di Pietro

D-U-N-S 24-227-7833   (BR)
BRANT HALDIMAND NORFOLK CATHOLIC DISTRICT SCHOOL BOARD
ASSUMPTION COLLEGE SCHOOL
(*Suby of* BRANT HALDIMAND NORFOLK CATHOLIC DISTRICT SCHOOL BOARD)
257 Shellard'S Lane, Brantford, ON, N3T 5L5
(519) 751-2030
Emp Here 135
SIC 8211 Elementary and secondary schools
Greg Picone

D-U-N-S 20-291-6610   (BR)
BRANT HALDIMAND NORFOLK CATHOLIC DISTRICT SCHOOL BOARD
ASSUMPTION COLLAGE SCHOOL
(*Suby of* BRANT HALDIMAND NORFOLK CATHOLIC DISTRICT SCHOOL BOARD)
257 Shellard'S Lane, Brantford, ON, N3T 5L5
(519) 751-2030
Emp Here 115
SIC 8211 Elementary and secondary schools
Lanz Patricia

D-U-N-S 20-037-5699   (HQ)
BRANT INSTORE CORPORATION

555 Greenwich St, Brantford, ON, N3T 5T3
(519) 759-4361
Emp Here 50   *Sales* 58,132,200
SIC 2759 Commercial printing, nec
John Paul Deboer
Trevor Mcdole
Jim Deboer
Heather Nicholls
Eugene Piekosz
Steve Donnell
Lance Pritchard
Eric Bethune
Curtis Farrish

D-U-N-S 24-663-6856   (SL)
BRANTFORD FINE CARS LIMITED
BRANTFORD HONDA
378 King George Rd Suite 6, Brantford, ON,
N3T 5L8
(519) 753-3168
Emp Here 46   *Sales* 22,911,588
SIC 5511 New and used car dealers
John Purkiss
John Lecluse

D-U-N-S 24-335-3703   (SL)
BRANTWOOD RESIDENTIAL DEVELOPMENT CENTRE
BRANTWOOD CENTRE
25 Bell Lane, Brantford, ON, N3T 1E1
(519) 753-2658
Emp Here 200   *Sales* 12,856,400
SIC 8361 Residential care
Dianne Belliveau
Gerry Nelson

D-U-N-S 24-779-4134   (SL)
CAMBRIDGE PRO FAB INC
84 Shaver Rd, Brantford, ON, N3T 5M1
(519) 751-4351
Emp Here 120   *Sales* 22,853,040
SIC 3621 Motors and generators
Tony Bairos
George Figueiredo

D-U-N-S 25-053-2066   (SL)
CANADIAN DEAFBLIND ASSOCIATION ONTARIO CHAPTER
54 Brant Ave Fl 3, Brantford, ON, N3T 3G8

Emp Here 160   *Sales* 33,130,880
SIC 8399 Social services, nec
Ted Isard

D-U-N-S 20-406-2582   (SL)
CITY CAB (BRANTFORD-DARLING STREET) LIMITED
CITY TAXI
40 Dalhousie St, Brantford, ON, N3T 2H8
(519) 759-7800
Emp Here 75   *Sales* 4,115,400
SIC 4121 Taxicabs
Ronald Edward Sayle
Frederick Norman Sayle

D-U-N-S 24-888-6566   (HQ)
CONCEPT PLASTICS LIMITED
(*Suby of* INDUS LIMITED)
27 Catharine Ave, Brantford, ON, N3T 1X5
(519) 759-1900
Emp Here 40   *Sales* 12,708,640
SIC 3089 Plastics products, nec
Kiran Kulkarni

D-U-N-S 25-407-8876   (SL)
CORNELL CONSTRUCTION LIMITED
410 Hardy Rd, Brantford, ON, N3T 5L8
(519) 753-3125
Emp Here 40   *Sales* 11,340,960
SIC 1611 Highway and street construction
John Mcallister
Jeff Mcallister

D-U-N-S 25-524-9724   (SL)
CRAVO EQUIPMENT LTD
(*Suby of* VOLCO INC)
30 White Swan Rd, Brantford, ON, N3T 5L4

(519) 759-8226
Emp Here 90   *Sales* 17,287,650
SIC 3448 Prefabricated Metal buildings and components
Richard Vollebregt
Paul Vollebregt

D-U-N-S 25-170-6966   (HQ)
CURTISS-WRIGHT FLOW CONTROL COMPANY CANADA
CURTISS-WRIGHT NUCLEAR CANADA
(*Suby of* CURTISS-WRIGHT CORPORATION)
15 Shaver Rd, Brantford, ON, N3T 5M1
(519) 756-4400
Sales 19,208,500
SIC 3494 Valves and pipe fittings, nec
David Linton
Michael Denton
Glenn Tynan
Martin Benante

D-U-N-S 25-195-9789   (SL)
DIVERSICARE CANADA MANAGEMENT SERVICES CO. INC
HARDY TERRACE LONG-TERM CARE FACILITY
612 Mount Pleasant Rd, Brantford, ON, N3T 5L5
(519) 484-2431
Emp Here 109   *Sales* 7,473,694
SIC 8059 Nursing and personal care, nec
Millie Christie

D-U-N-S 20-272-9513   (BR)
DIVERSICARE CANADA MANAGEMENT SERVICES CO., INC
HARDY TERRACE LONG-TERM CARE FACILITY
(*Suby of* DCMS HOLDINGS INC)
612 Mount Pleasant Rd, Brantford, ON, N3T 5L5
(519) 484-2431
Emp Here 100
SIC 8051 Skilled nursing care facilities

D-U-N-S 24-241-9732   (BR)
DIVERSICARE CANADA MANAGEMENT SERVICES CO., INC
HARDY TERRACE LTC
(*Suby of* DCMS HOLDINGS INC)
612 Mount Pleasant Rd, Brantford, ON, N3T 5L5
(519) 484-2500
Emp Here 130
SIC 8051 Skilled nursing care facilities
Paul Rooyakkers

D-U-N-S 20-270-0910   (BR)
EMERSON ELECTRIC CANADA LIMITED
ASCO NUMATICS
(*Suby of* EMERSON ELECTRIC CO.)
17 Airport Rd, Brantford, ON, N3T 5M8
(519) 758-2700
Emp Here 105
SIC 3492 Fluid power valves and hose fittings
Sean Hazelton

D-U-N-S 20-624-9419   (HQ)
EXTEND COMMUNICATIONS INC
YOUR TELEPHONE SECRETARY
49 Charlotte St, Brantford, ON, N3T 2W4
(416) 534-0477
Emp Here 24   *Sales* 29,199,235
SIC 7389 Business services, nec
Scott Lyons
Todd Lyons
Eleanor Lyons
Hilton F Lyons

D-U-N-S 24-984-7617   (SL)
FLEETWAY TRANSPORT INC
31 Garnet Rd, Brantford, ON, N3T 5M1
(519) 753-5223
Emp Here 75   *Sales* 15,427,950
SIC 4213 Trucking, except local
Allan Rees
David Rees

D-U-N-S 20-641-2512   (SL)
GERMIPHENE CORPORATION
(*Suby of* DRAKE, LESLIE MANAGEMENT INC)
1379 Colborne St E, Brantford, ON, N3T 5M1
(519) 759-7100
Emp Here 80   *Sales* 18,183,120
SIC 3843 Dental equipment and supplies
Leslie Drake
John Cady

D-U-N-S 25-496-2459   (BR)
GRAND ERIE DISTRICT SCHOOL BOARD
BRANTFORD COLLEGIATE & VOCATIONAL INSTITUTE
(*Suby of* GRAND ERIE DISTRICT SCHOOL BOARD)
120 Brant Ave, Brantford, ON, N3T 3H3
(519) 759-3210
Emp Here 100
SIC 8222 Junior colleges
Ann Myhal

D-U-N-S 20-175-4590   (SL)
HARTMANN CANADA INC
(*Suby of* THORNICO HOLDING A/S)
58 Frank St, Brantford, ON, N3T 5E2
(519) 756-8500
Emp Here 300   *Sales* 110,291,100
SIC 2675 Die-cut paper and board
Ash Sahi
Karyn Bradley
Tom Wrensted
Peter Arndrup Poulsen
Daniel Hayhurst

D-U-N-S 20-180-7711   (SL)
HARTMANN DOMINION INC
HARTMANN NORTH AMERICA
(*Suby of* THORNICO HOLDING A/S)
58 Frank St, Brantford, ON, N3T 5E2
(519) 756-8500
Emp Here 257   *Sales* 61,374,684
SIC 3086 Plastics foam products
Ash Sahi
Per Vinge Frederiksen
Michael Hedegaard Lyng

D-U-N-S 24-873-8627   (HQ)
HGC MANAGEMENT INC
50 Shaver St, Brantford, ON, N3T 5M1
(519) 754-4732
Emp Here 3   *Sales* 31,891,000
SIC 4953 Refuse systems
Herb Lambacher

D-U-N-S 25-375-2596   (BR)
INGENIA POLYMERS CORP
(*Suby of* INGENIA POLYMERS CORP)
565 Greenwich St, Brantford, ON, N3T 5M2
(519) 758-8941
Emp Here 100
SIC 2821 Plastics materials and resins
Bogdan Olejarz

D-U-N-S 25-542-6314   (SL)
INNOVATIVE STEEL GROUP INC
85 Morrell St, Brantford, ON, N3T 4J6
(519) 720-9797
Emp Here 11   *Sales* 11,003,729
SIC 5051 Metals service centers and offices
Barb Charest

D-U-N-S 25-238-9176   (SL)
LANSDOWNE CHILDREN'S CENTRE
39 Mount Pleasant St, Brantford, ON, N3T 1S7
(519) 753-3153
Emp Here 250   *Sales* 18,943,250
SIC 8093 Specialty outpatient clinics, nec
Kathy Kirby

D-U-N-S 20-903-2085   (SL)
LIFTWAY LIMITED
Gd Lcd Main, Brantford, ON, N3T 5M2
(519) 759-5590
Emp Here 42   *Sales* 19,951,092
SIC 5084 Industrial machinery and equipment

Barrie Schram
Ross Cochrane

D-U-N-S 24-874-1873   (SL)
METRO FREIGHTLINER BRANTFORD
31 Garnet Rd, Brantford, ON, N3T 5M1
(519) 750-0055
Emp Here 25   *Sales* 12,999,175
SIC 4731 Freight transportation arrangement
Jim Need

D-U-N-S 20-818-2303   (HQ)
MILLARD, ROUSE & ROSEBRUGH LLP
96 Nelson St, Brantford, ON, N3T 2N1
(519) 759-3511
Emp Here 65   *Sales* 20,768,500
SIC 8721 Accounting, auditing, and bookkeeping
Martin Dixon
Michael Terdik

D-U-N-S 20-037-5582   (HQ)
MOTT MANUFACTURING LIMITED
MOTT
452 Hardy Rd, Brantford, ON, N3T 5L8
(519) 752-7825
Emp Here 11   *Sales* 69,511,320
SIC 6712 Bank holding companies
Edward Seegmiller
Mario Di Fonte

D-U-N-S 24-783-4646   (SL)
NAVACON CONSTRUCTION INC
415 Hardy Rd, Brantford, ON, N3T 5L8
(519) 754-4646
Emp Here 42   *Sales* 10,117,128
SIC 1623 Water, sewer, and utility lines
Ernesto Constantino

D-U-N-S 20-037-5814   (HQ)
NORTHWAY FORD LINCOLN LTD
NORTHWAY FORD LINCOLN
388 King George Rd, Brantford, ON, N3T 5L8
(519) 753-8691
Emp Here 3   *Sales* 26,429,760
SIC 5511 New and used car dealers
Rick Paletta

D-U-N-S 20-552-6242   (BR)
OC CANADA HOLDINGS COMPANY
OWENS CORNING SOLUTIONS GROUP
(*Suby of* OWENS CORNING)
11 Spalding Dr, Brantford, ON, N3T 6B7
(519) 752-5436
Emp Here 75
SIC 3296 Mineral wool
Dale Murphy

D-U-N-S 20-921-0835   (BR)
OSPREY MEDIA PUBLISHING INC
BRANTFORD EXPOSITOR
(*Suby of* QUEBECOR MEDIA INC)
53 Dalhousie St Suite 306, Brantford, ON, N3T 2H9
(519) 756-2020
Emp Here 100
SIC 2711 Newspapers
Michael Pearpe

D-U-N-S 24-336-4622   (HQ)
REMBOS INC
(*Suby of* BOSCUS CANADA INC)
60 Old Onondaga Rd E, Brantford, ON, N3T 5L4
(519) 770-1207
Emp Here 2   *Sales* 17,886,960
SIC 5031 Lumber, plywood, and millwork
Dary Laflamme
Raymond Landry

D-U-N-S 20-037-4171   (HQ)
S.C. JOHNSON AND SON, LIMITED
(*Suby of* S.C. JOHNSON NETHERLANDS COOPERATIEF U.A.)
1 Webster St, Brantford, ON, N3T 5A3
(519) 756-7900
Emp Here 350   *Sales* 186,750,900
SIC 2842 Polishes and sanitation goods

Chris Moeller
Dominic Leung
Stephen L. Rose
Jay E Gueldner

D-U-N-S 20-550-2958   (HQ)
SC JOHNSON PROFESSIONAL CA INC
DEB CANADIAN HYGIENE
(*Suby of* S.C. JOHNSON NETHERLANDS II
COOPERATIEF U.A.)
1 Webster St, Brantford, ON, N3T 5R1
(519) 443-8697
Emp Here 20   *Sales* 17,041,260
SIC 2841 Soap and other detergents
Didier Bouton
Russell Baker
Nick Matterson

D-U-N-S 20-595-2682   (HQ)
SHARP BUS LINES LIMITED
(*Suby of* 608705 ONTARIO LIMITED)
567 Oak Park Rd, Brantford, ON, N3T 5L8
(519) 751-3434
Emp Here 150   *Sales* 56,214,000
SIC 4151 School buses
John Sharp
William Sharp
Donald Sharp
Mary Sharp

D-U-N-S 24-025-0741   (HQ)
T.F. WARREN GROUP INC
57 Old Onondaga Rd W, Brantford, ON, N3T
5M1
(519) 756-8222
Sales 109,652,700
SIC 6712 Bank holding companies
Terry Warren

D-U-N-S 20-304-6263   (BR)
T.F. WARREN GROUP INC
BLASTECH
(*Suby of* T.F. WARREN GROUP INC)
57 Old Onondaga Rd W, Brantford, ON, N3T
5M1
(519) 756-8222
Emp Here 75
SIC 5169 Chemicals and allied products, nec
Terry Warren

D-U-N-S 24-862-9529   (HQ)
WENDCORP HOLDINGS INC
WENDY'S OLD FASHIONED HAMBURGERS
202 Grand River Ave Suite 1, Brantford, ON,
N3T 4X9
(519) 756-8431
Emp Here 3   *Sales* 11,193,360
SIC 5812 Eating places
Dean N Braund

Brantford, ON N3V

D-U-N-S 20-967-7970   (HQ)
MARCO CORPORATION, THE
470 Hardy Rd, Brantford, ON, N3V 6T1
(519) 751-2227
Emp Here 80   *Sales* 33,571,080
SIC 8743 Public relations services
Robert Martin
Mary Kerr-Martin
Josie Bethune's

D-U-N-S 20-186-9328   (HQ)
WESCAST INDUSTRIES INC
(*Suby of* MIANYANG SCIENCE TECHNOL-
OGY CITY DEVELOPMENT INVESTMENT
(GROUP) CO., LTD.)
150 Savannah Oaks Dr, Brantford, ON, N3V
1E7
(519) 750-0000
Emp Here 100   *Sales* 443,837,100
SIC 3714 Motor vehicle parts and accessories
John Macdonald

D-U-N-S 20-565-8565   (SL)

WESTERN WAFFLES CORP
WESTERN WAFFLES
(*Suby of* TREEHOUSE FOODS, INC.)
175 Savannah Oaks Dr, Brantford, ON, N3V
1E8
(519) 759-2025
Emp Here 400   *Sales* 194,954,000
SIC 2038 Frozen specialties, nec
Steve Hunt

Brantford, ON N4G

D-U-N-S 25-920-0793   (SL)
HARVEST RETIREMENT
HARVEST CROSSING
15 Harvest Ave, Brantford, ON, N4G 0E2
(519) 688-0448
Emp Here 30   *Sales* 25,441,800
SIC 6411 Insurance agents, brokers, and ser-
vice
Subryan Bandaru

Breslau, ON N0B

D-U-N-S 24-627-1118   (SL)
BRIAN KURTZ TRUCKING LTD
6960 Speedvale Rd W Rr 2, Breslau, ON, N0B
1M0
(519) 836-5821
Emp Here 100   *Sales* 14,819,200
SIC 4213 Trucking, except local
Brian Kurtz
Trevor Kurtz

D-U-N-S 24-845-5482   (SL)
C2 GROUP INC
350 Woolwich St S, Breslau, ON, N0B 1M0
(519) 648-3118
Emp Here 49   *Sales* 14,140,567
SIC 1522 Residential construction, nec
Murray Gamble

D-U-N-S 24-424-2418   (HQ)
CONESTOGA MEAT PACKERS LTD
CONESTOGA MEATS
313 Menno St, Breslau, ON, N0B 1M0
(519) 648-2506
Emp Here 807   *Sales* 628,559,932
SIC 5147 Meats and meat products
Arnold Drung
Tony Millington

D-U-N-S 25-554-9081   (SL)
FLITE LINE SERVICES (KITCHENER) INC
HERTZ CANADA
4881 Fountain St N Suite 4, Breslau, ON, N0B
1M0
(519) 648-3404
Emp Here 15   *Sales* 15,492,120
SIC 5172 Petroleum products, nec
Richard Hammond
R Bruce Graham

D-U-N-S 20-037-8925   (HQ)
GEORGE AND ASMUSSEN LIMITED
G A MASONRY
5093 Fountain St N, Breslau, ON, N0B 1M0
(519) 648-2285
Emp Here 75   *Sales* 23,545,245
SIC 1741 Masonry and other stonework
Patrick George
Ian Letford

D-U-N-S 20-849-9376   (SL)
GROBE NURSERY LIMITED
*DESIGN BUILDING LANDSCAPE CON-
TRACTORS*
1787 Greenhouse Rd, Breslau, ON, N0B 1M0
(519) 648-2247
Emp Here 30   *Sales* 22,275,600
SIC 5193 Flowers and florists supplies

Peter Grobe
Perry Grobe

D-U-N-S 24-285-2895   (HQ)
KITCHENER AERO AVIONICS LIMITED
MID-CANADA MOD CENTER
4881 Fountain St N Suite 6, Breslau, ON, N0B
1M0
(519) 648-2921
Emp Here 50   *Sales* 15,386,240
SIC 7629 Electrical repair shops
Barry Aylward

D-U-N-S 25-398-6657   (HQ)
NATIONAL ENGINEERED FASTENERS INC
1747 Greenhouse Rd, Breslau, ON, N0B 1M0
(519) 886-0919
Sales 11,875,650
SIC 5085 Industrial supplies
Janet Steffens
Peter Steffens

D-U-N-S 24-752-8946   (SL)
NEDLAW ROOFING LIMITED
232 Woolwich St S, Breslau, ON, N0B 1M0
(519) 648-2218
Emp Here 70   *Sales* 15,248,030
SIC 1761 Roofing, siding, and sheetMetal
work
Randy Walden

D-U-N-S 20-751-2666   (HQ)
SAFETY-KLEEN CANADA INC
(*Suby of* CLEAN HARBORS, INC.)
300 Woolwich St S, Breslau, ON, N0B 1M0
(519) 648-2291
Emp Here 100   *Sales* 670,150,000
SIC 2992 Lubricating oils and greases
Dale Macintyre

D-U-N-S 20-823-2314   (SL)
WATERLOO FLOWERS LIMITED
1001 Kramp Rd, Breslau, ON, N0B 1M0

Emp Here 25   *Sales* 18,563,000
SIC 5193 Flowers and florists supplies
Mark Miziolek

D-U-N-S 20-113-4447   (SL)
XDG CONSTRUCTION LIMITED
250 Woolwich St S, Breslau, ON, N0B 1M0
(519) 648-2121
Emp Here 30   *Sales* 14,285,489
SIC 1542 Nonresidential construction, nec
Carl Harris
John G. Gunn
John A. Gunn

Brigden, ON N0N

D-U-N-S 24-376-4789   (SL)
ST. CLAIR MECHANICAL INC
2963 Brigden Rd Suite 1, Brigden, ON, N0N
1B0
(519) 864-0927
Emp Here 50   *Sales* 11,675,820
SIC 3498 Fabricated pipe and fittings
John Dawson
Tracy Dawson

Bright, ON N0J

D-U-N-S 24-284-5360   (SL)
**NORTH BLENHEIM MUTUAL INSURANCE
COMPANY**
11 Baird St N, Bright, ON, N0J 1B0
(519) 454-8661
Emp Here 28   *Sales* 51,706,452
SIC 6331 Fire, marine, and casualty insurance
Don Pruss
Jack Hamilton
Doug Murray

Terry Knight
Elmer Bretz
Terry Ross

Brighton, ON K0K

D-U-N-S 25-654-2697   (SL)
1151377 ONTARIO INC
BRIGHTON SOBEYS
14 Main St, Brighton, ON, K0K 1H0
(613) 475-0200
Emp Here 130   *Sales* 38,152,010
SIC 5411 Grocery stores
Rod Begbie

D-U-N-S 20-038-0152   (SL)
ARCHER'S POULTRY FARM LIMITED
15738 County Road 2, Brighton, ON, K0K 1H0
(613) 475-0820
Emp Here 26   *Sales* 19,305,520
SIC 5191 Farm supplies
Stuart Archer
Douglas Archer
Iris Archer

D-U-N-S 25-237-9516   (BR)
**KAWARTHA   PINE   RIDGE   DISTRICT
SCHOOL BOARD**
*EAST NORTHUMBERLAND SECONDARY
SCHOOL*
71 Dundas St, Brighton, ON, K0K 1H0
(613) 475-0540
Emp Here 120
SIC 8211 Elementary and secondary schools
Jeff Kawzenuk

D-U-N-S 24-393-1727   (HQ)
WIND WORKS POWER CORP
14 Lakecrest Cir, Brighton, ON, K0K 1H0
(613) 226-7883
Sales 54,079,859
SIC 3621 Motors and generators
Ingo Stuckmann
J.C. Pennie
Erich Bachmeyer
Dan Albano
Glen Macmullin
Greg Wilson
Henrik Woehlk

Brockville, ON K6V

D-U-N-S 25-977-7571   (BR)
1032451 B.C. LTD
RECORDER AND TIMES, THE
(*Suby of* QUEBECOR MEDIA INC)
1600 California Ave, Brockville, ON, K6V 5T6
(613) 342-4441
Emp Here 80
SIC 2711 Newspapers
Bob Pearce

D-U-N-S 25-540-8692   (BR)
3M CANADA COMPANY
(*Suby of* 3M COMPANY)
1360 California Ave, Brockville, ON, K6V 5V8
(613) 345-0111
Emp Here 100
SIC 2891 Adhesives and sealants
Simon Smith

D-U-N-S 20-267-9416   (BR)
3M CANADA COMPANY
(*Suby of* 3M COMPANY)
60 California Ave, Brockville, ON, K6V 7N5
(613) 498-5900
Emp Here 180
SIC 2672 Paper; coated and laminated, nec
Wayne Chislett

D-U-N-S 24-105-9567   (SL)

▲ Public Company   ■ Public Company Family Member   **HQ** Headquarters   **BR** Branch   **SL** Single Location

734393 ONTARIO LIMITED
1000 ISLANDS TOYOTA
555 Stewart Blvd, Brockville, ON, K6V 7H2
(613) 342-9111
Emp Here 24   *Sales* 11,953,872
SIC 5511 New and used car dealers
Richard Walker
Fran Walker

D-U-N-S 24-677-3571   (SL)
AXENS CANADA SPECIALTY ALUMINAS INC
(*Suby of* IFP ENERGIES NOUVELLES)
4000 Development Dr, Brockville, ON, K6V 5V5
(613) 342-7462
Emp Here 60   *Sales* 17,041,260
SIC 2819 Industrial inorganic chemicals, nec
Patrick Sarrazin

D-U-N-S 24-784-1398   (BR)
BLACK & DECKER CANADA INC
STANLEY BLACK & DECKER CANADA
(*Suby of* STANLEY BLACK & DECKER, INC.)
100 Central Ave W, Brockville, ON, K6V 4N8
(613) 342-6641
Emp Here 180
SIC 5084 Industrial machinery and equipment
Steve Blake

D-U-N-S 25-718-6890   (SL)
BROCKVILLE & AREA COMMUNITY LIV-ING ASSOCIATION
6 Glenn Wood Pl Suite 100, Brockville, ON, K6V 2T3
(613) 342-2953
Emp Here 85   *Sales* 5,815,870
SIC 8322 Individual and family services
Micheal Humes

D-U-N-S 20-771-3384   (BR)
BROCKVILLE AREA CENTRE FOR DEVEL-OPMENTALLY HANDICAPPED PERSONS INC
DEVELOPMENTAL SERVICES OF LEEDS AND GRENVILLE
(*Suby of* BROCKVILLE AREA CENTRE FOR DEVELOPMENTALLY HANDICAPPED PER-SONS INC)
61 King St E, Brockville, ON, K6V 1B2

Emp Here 80
SIC 8322 Individual and family services
Tom Turner

D-U-N-S 24-104-1441   (HQ)
BROCKVILLE GENERAL HOSPITAL
75 Charles St, Brockville, ON, K6V 1S8
(613) 345-5645
Emp Here 480   *Sales* 120,132,800
SIC 8062 General medical and surgical hospi-tals
Nick Vlacholias
Charlotte Patterson
Heather Quesnelle
Steven Read
Cameron Mclennan
Matthew Armstrong

D-U-N-S 20-286-2470   (BR)
BROCKVILLE GENERAL HOSPITAL
(*Suby of* BROCKVILLE GENERAL HOSPI-TAL)
42 Garden St, Brockville, ON, K6V 2C3
(613) 345-5649
Emp Here 350
SIC 8062 General medical and surgical hospi-tals
Kevin Empey

D-U-N-S 24-379-2384   (SL)
BROCKVILLE HARDWARE ENTERPRISES INC
BROCKVILLE HOME HARDWARE
584 Stewart Blvd, Brockville, ON, K6V 7H2
(613) 342-4421
Emp Here 49   *Sales* 12,399,891

SIC 5251 Hardware stores
Paul Blakney

D-U-N-S 24-355-1426   (SL)
BROCKVILLE MOTOR SALES LIMITED
1240 Stewart Blvd, Brockville, ON, K6V 7H2
(613) 342-5244
Emp Here 36   *Sales* 17,930,808
SIC 5511 New and used car dealers
Keith Bean

D-U-N-S 25-921-0433   (SL)
BROCKVILLE POLICE ASSOCIATION
2269 Parkedale Ave W, Brockville, ON, K6V 3G9
(613) 342-0127
Emp Here 75   *Sales* 29,433,750
SIC 8631 Labor organizations
Tom Nappo

D-U-N-S 25-527-3948   (SL)
CAMALOR MFG. INC
100 Central Ave W, Brockville, ON, K6V 4N8
(613) 342-2259
Emp Here 58   *Sales* 11,140,930
SIC 3499 Fabricated Metal products, nec
Marc Fortin
Wayne Gill

D-U-N-S 20-077-7777   (SL)
CANADIAN MILK MANUFACTURING INC
CMM
198 Pearl St E, Brockville, ON, K6V 1R4
(613) 970-5566
Emp Here 50   *Sales* 11,242,750
SIC 2023 Dry, condensed and evaporated dairy products
Eaton Chen
Zhidong Yang

D-U-N-S 24-393-2253   (SL)
CANADIAN TIRE
2360 Parkedale Ave, Brockville, ON, K6V 7J5
(613) 342-5841
Emp Here 49   *Sales* 24,405,822
SIC 5531 Auto and home supply stores
William Deplaedt

D-U-N-S 20-506-2391   (HQ)
CANARM LTD
2157 Parkedale Ave, Brockville, ON, K6V 0B4
(613) 342-5424
Emp Here 105   *Sales* 174,074,100
SIC 5063 Electrical apparatus and equipment
David E Beatty
James A Cooper
Steve Read
Ken Law

D-U-N-S 20-913-5586   (BR)
CATHOLIC DISTRICT SCHOOL BOARD OF EASTERN ONTARIO
ST MARY CATHOLIC HIGH SCHOOL
40 Central Ave W, Brockville, ON, K6V 4N5
(613) 342-4911
Emp Here 90
SIC 8211 Elementary and secondary schools
Jp Elliott

D-U-N-S 24-120-5991   (SL)
CHEVRON CONSTRUCTION SERVICES LTD
4475 County 15 Rd, Brockville, ON, K6V 5T2
(613) 926-0690
Emp Here 35   *Sales* 11,666,655
SIC 1541 Industrial buildings and warehouses
David Vaughan
James Annable
Darren Ross

D-U-N-S 25-976-1450   (SL)
CHROMATOGRAPHIC SPECIALTIES INC
300 Laurier Blvd, Brockville, ON, K6V 5W1
(613) 342-4678
Emp Here 42   *Sales* 18,781,308
SIC 5049 Professional equipment, nec
Michael Mckend
Tracey Jonkman

D-U-N-S 24-355-4313   (SL)
COMMUNITY & PRIMARY HEALTH CARE-LANARK, LEEDS & GRENVILLE
CPHC
2235 Parkedale Ave, Brockville, ON, K6V 6B2
(613) 342-1747
Emp Here 102   *Sales* 21,120,936
SIC 8399 Social services, nec
Ruth Kitson
John Ker
Linda Bisonette

D-U-N-S 24-270-4047   (HQ)
CORPORATION LEEDS GRENVILLE & LA-NARK DISTRICT HEALTH UNIT, THE
458 Laurier Blvd Suite 200, Brockville, ON, K6V 7K5
(613) 345-5685
Sales 22,777,480
SIC 8399 Social services, nec
William Widenmaier
Joanne Pearce
Charles Gardner

D-U-N-S 20-043-9743   (HQ)
DELHI INDUSTRIES INC
2157 Parkedale Ave, Brockville, ON, K6V 0B4
(613) 342-5424
Emp Here 80
SIC 3564 Blowers and fans
David Beatty
James Cooper

D-U-N-S 24-104-1417   (HQ)
DLK INSURANCE BROKERS LTD
35 King St W, Brockville, ON, K6V 3P7
(613) 342-8663
Sales 18,657,320
SIC 6411 Insurance agents, brokers, and ser-vice
Brian Davies
Brenda Duffy
Joanne Spero

D-U-N-S 20-788-6938   (HQ)
EASTERN INDEPENDENT TELECOMMUNI-CATIONS LTD
100 Strowger Blvd Suite 112, Brockville, ON, K6V 5J9
(613) 342-9652
Emp Here 25   *Sales* 11,179,350
SIC 5065 Electronic parts and equipment, nec
Clifton T White
Ian Officer

D-U-N-S 20-038-1580   (HQ)
EASTERN ONTARIO WATER TECHNOL-OGY LTD
CULLIGAN DU SUD-OUEST QUEBEC
240 Waltham Rd, Brockville, ON, K6V 7K3
(613) 498-2830
Emp Here 17   *Sales* 21,256,536
SIC 5999 Miscellaneous retail stores, nec
Hugo Grout
Margaret Grout

D-U-N-S 24-102-9792   (HQ)
HANSLER INDUSTRIES LTD
1385 California Ave, Brockville, ON, K6V 5V5
(613) 342-4408
Emp Here 15   *Sales* 11,417,364
SIC 7699 Repair services, nec
Daniel Smith
Peter Charlabois
Kathleen Smith
Richard Miller

D-U-N-S 20-441-6523   (HQ)
HANSLER SMITH LIMITED
1385 California Ave, Brockville, ON, K6V 5V5
(613) 342-4408
Emp Here 20   *Sales* 33,251,820
SIC 5085 Industrial supplies
Allan Smith
Brian Boucher
Steven Smith
Jon Brinkworth

D-U-N-S 20-879-9002   (SL)
KETCHUM MANUFACTURING INC
1245 California Ave, Brockville, ON, K6V 7N5
(613) 342-8455
Emp Here 50   *Sales* 10,941,200
SIC 3999 Manufacturing industries, nec
Claude Lalonde

D-U-N-S 24-121-0397   (BR)
LOBLAWS INC
REAL CANADIAN SUPERSTORE
(*Suby of* LOBLAW COMPANIES LIMITED)
1972 Parkedale Ave Suite 1017, Brockville, ON, K6V 7N4
(613) 498-0994
Emp Here 220
SIC 5411 Grocery stores
Hiet Trieu

D-U-N-S 20-544-4644   (SL)
MARK S. LESLIE APATHECARY LTD
SHOPPERS DRUG MART
2399 Parkedale Ave Suite 27, Brockville, ON, K6V 3G9
(613) 342-6701
Emp Here 40   *Sales* 10,118,160
SIC 5912 Drug stores and proprietary stores
Mark S. Leslie

D-U-N-S 25-311-0076   (BR)
MCDONALD'S RESTAURANTS OF CANADA LIMITED
MCDONALD'S #8386
(*Suby of* MCDONALD'S CORPORATION)
2454 Parkedale Ave, Brockville, ON, K6V 3G8
(613) 342-5551
Emp Here 80
SIC 5812 Eating places

D-U-N-S 25-980-8087   (BR)
METRO INC
LOEB
(*Suby of* METRO INC)
237 King St W, Brockville, ON, K6V 3S2
(613) 345-4260
Emp Here 85
SIC 5411 Grocery stores
Dave Crotty

D-U-N-S 20-227-9279   (SL)
MOTOR COILS MFG. LTD
1879 Parkedale Ave E, Brockville, ON, K6V 5T2
(613) 345-3580
Emp Here 90   *Sales* 17,139,780
SIC 3621 Motors and generators
James Mcdonald
Robert Kercher

D-U-N-S 24-325-0961   (HQ)
NEWTERRA GROUP LTD
1291 California Ave, Brockville, ON, K6V 7N5
(613) 498-1876
Emp Here 5   *Sales* 82,239,525
SIC 6712 Bank holding companies
Bruce Lounsbury
Robert Kulhawy
James Iglesias

D-U-N-S 25-108-5957   (HQ)
NEWTERRA LTD
(*Suby of* NEWTERRA GROUP LTD)
1291 California Ave, Brockville, ON, K6V 7N5
(613) 498-1876
Emp Here 50   *Sales* 32,300,855
SIC 3589 Service industry machinery, nec
Bruce Lounsbury
Robert Kennedy
Ben Fash
Tom Pokorsky
David Henderson
Daniel Weiss
James Iglesias
Robert Kulhawy
Samuel Saintonge

D-U-N-S 25-401-0796   (HQ)
NORTHERN CABLES INC

50 California Ave, Brockville, ON, K6V 6E6
(613) 345-1594
Emp Here 3   *Sales* 36,277,600
SIC 3357 Nonferrous wiredrawing and insulating
Shelley J Bacon
Todd Stafford
Hugh F Grightmire
Richard K Trapp

D-U-N-S 24-104-4726   (BR)
PROCTER & GAMBLE INC
(*Suby of* THE PROCTER & GAMBLE COMPANY)
1475 California Ave, Brockville, ON, K6V 6K4
(613) 342-9592
Emp Here 900
SIC 2841 Soap and other detergents
Rhiannon Iles

D-U-N-S 20-279-7598   (BR)
PROCTER & GAMBLE INVESTMENT CORPORATION
(*Suby of* THE PROCTER & GAMBLE COMPANY)
1475 California Ave, Brockville, ON, K6V 6K4
(613) 342-9592
Emp Here 400
SIC 2841 Soap and other detergents
Tim Penner

D-U-N-S 20-038-1226   (SL)
RIVER SIDE FORD SALES LIMITED
25 Eleanor St, Brockville, ON, K6V 4H9
(613) 342-0234
Emp Here 25   *Sales* 12,451,950
SIC 5511 New and used car dealers
Ted Hudson

D-U-N-S 20-190-5614   (BR)
SELKIRK CANADA CORPORATION
(*Suby of* SELKIRK AMERICAS, L.P.)
1400 California Ave, Brockville, ON, K6V 5V3
(888) 693-9563
Emp Here 118
SIC 3259 Structural clay products, nec
Robert Mcarthur

D-U-N-S 24-392-0605   (BR)
SHELL CANADA LIMITED
(*Suby of* ROYAL DUTCH SHELL PLC)
250 Laurier Blvd, Brockville, ON, K6V 5V7
(613) 498-5700
Emp Here 75
SIC 5541 Gasoline service stations
Mark Cimolai

D-U-N-S 20-891-7245   (HQ)
ST. LAWRENCE COLLEGE OF APPLIED ARTS AND TECHNOLOGY, THE
2288 Parkedale Ave, Brockville, ON, K6V 5X3
(613) 345-0660
Emp Here 80   *Sales* 86,089,068
SIC 8222 Junior colleges
Glenn Vollebregt
Michael Adamcryck
Kathy Obrien
Bruce Tessier
Lorraine Carter
Gordon Macdougall
Gary Earles
Patricia Kerth
Lynn Bowering
Bill Chafe

D-U-N-S 20-890-8459   (SL)
ST. LAWRENCE LODGE
(*Suby of* CORPORATION OF THE CITY OF BROCKVILLE)
1803 Highway 2 E, Brockville, ON, K6V 5T1
(613) 345-0255
Emp Here 250   *Sales* 18,156,000
SIC 8361 Residential care
Tom Harrington
Bob Jurkewycz
Bradley Morton
Tracey Davidson

Kim Cleroux

D-U-N-S 25-542-6306   (HQ)
TRILLIUM HEALTH CARE PRODUCTS INC
(*Suby of* RICHARDSON, JAMES & SONS, LIMITED)
2337 Parkdale Ave E, Brockville, ON, K6V 5W5
(613) 342-4436
Emp Here 280   *Sales* 92,846,320
SIC 2834 Pharmaceutical preparations
Peter Plows
Jay Webb

D-U-N-S 20-208-5408   (BR)
UNITED COUNTIES OF LEEDS AND GRENVILLE
(*Suby of* UNITED COUNTIES OF LEEDS AND GRENVILLE)
25 Central Ave W Suite 100, Brockville, ON, K6V 4N6
(613) 342-3840
Emp Here 100
SIC 4119 Local passenger transportation, nec
Stephen Fournier

D-U-N-S 25-486-5074   (BR)
UPPER CANADA DISTRICT SCHOOL BOARD, THE
THOUSAND ISLANDS SECONDARY SCHOOL
(*Suby of* UPPER CANADA DISTRICT SCHOOL BOARD, THE)
2510 Parkedale Ave, Brockville, ON, K6V 3H1
(613) 342-1100
Emp Here 120
SIC 8211 Elementary and secondary schools
Randy Ruttan

D-U-N-S 25-542-7957   (HQ)
UPPER CANADA DISTRICT SCHOOL BOARD, THE
225 Central Ave W, Brockville, ON, K6V 5X1
(613) 342-0371
Emp Here 100   *Sales* 269,624,299
SIC 8211 Elementary and secondary schools
Stephen Silwa
Valerie Allen
David Coombs
Susan Edwards
Tim Mills
Nancy Mccaslin-Barkley
Jeff Mcmillan
Caroll Carkner
David Mcdonald
Donald Cram

D-U-N-S 24-318-0770   (BR)
WAL-MART CANADA CORP
WALMART
(*Suby of* WALMART INC.)
1942 Parkedale Ave Suite 3006, Brockville, ON, K6V 7N4
(613) 342-9293
Emp Here 150
SIC 5311 Department stores
Doug Scott

D-U-N-S 20-894-6418   (SL)
YMCA-YWCA OF BROCKVILLE AND AREA
345 Park St, Brockville, ON, K6V 5Y7
(613) 342-7961
Emp Here 74   *Sales* 10,573,046
SIC 8641 Civic and social associations
Sueling Ching
Maribeth Graham

Brougham, ON L0H

D-U-N-S 20-844-4695   (SL)
DUTCHMASTER NURSERIES LIMITED
3735 Sideline 16, Brougham, ON, L0H 1A0
(905) 683-8211
Emp Here 100   *Sales* 74,252,000

SIC 5193 Flowers and florists supplies
Henry Tillaart
Frances Tillaart

Bruce Mines, ON P0R

D-U-N-S 20-536-0498   (HQ)
COPPER BAY HOLDINGS INC
COPPER BAY SHELL/ NUGGET FOOD STORE
9 Bennett St, Bruce Mines, ON, P0R 1C0
(705) 785-3506
Emp Here 21   *Sales* 17,432,730
SIC 5541 Gasoline service stations
Beverly Bordeleau

Brucefield, ON N0M

D-U-N-S 20-280-0553   (SL)
SUN COUNTRY HIGHWAY LTD
76000 London Rd Rr 1, Brucefield, ON, N0M 1J0
(866) 467-6920
Emp Here 25   *Sales* 12,596,167
SIC 5531 Auto and home supply stores
Kent Rathwell

Brunner, ON N0K

D-U-N-S 20-773-2959   (SL)
BOXBERG HOLDING LTD
COUNTRY MEADOWS RETIREMENT RESIDENCE
6124 Anna St, Brunner, ON, N0K 1C0
(519) 595-8903
Emp Here 24   *Sales* 13,918,176
SIC 6411 Insurance agents, brokers, and service
Margaret Morley

Burford, ON N0E

D-U-N-S 20-037-1813   (HQ)
DAVIS FUEL COMPANY LIMITED
FLYING M TRUCK STOP
22 King St, Burford, ON, N0E 1A0
(519) 449-2417
Emp Here 25   *Sales* 94,290,075
SIC 5172 Petroleum products, nec
Roger Davis
Donald Kersey
Edith Davis
Brenda Kersey
Gerome Davis
Floyd Davis

D-U-N-S 20-629-9083   (SL)
HALL, KEITH & SONS TRANSPORT LIMITED
297 Bishopsgate Rd, Burford, ON, N0E 1A0
(519) 449-2401
Emp Here 75   *Sales* 11,114,400
SIC 4213 Trucking, except local
Brian Hall
Kevin Hall
Christopher Hall

Burgessville, ON N0J

D-U-N-S 24-338-5478   (HQ)
BARNIM HOLDINGS INC
AL'S TIRE SERVICE

593771 Hwy 59, Burgessville, ON, N0J 1C0
(519) 424-9865
Emp Here 4   *Sales* 12,747,525
SIC 5014 Tires and tubes
Allan Barnim
Bruce Barnim
Brad Barnim
Sheila Barnim

Burks Falls, ON P0A

D-U-N-S 20-699-1270   (SL)
BRAWO BRASSWORKING LIMITED
LOFTHOUSE MANUFACTURING, DIV OF
(*Suby of* HOLDING UMBERTO GNUTTI SPA)
500 Ontario St N, Burks Falls, ON, P0A 1C0
(705) 382-3637
Emp Here 150   *Sales* 61,076,100
SIC 3351 Copper rolling and drawing
Gabriele Gnutti
Francesco Musig
David Overbaugh
Dan Smith
Darwin Dunn

Burlington, ON L7L

D-U-N-S 24-992-5819   (SL)
1032002 ONTARIO INC
MARILU'S MARKET
4025 New St, Burlington, ON, L7L 1S8
(905) 639-0319
Emp Here 80   *Sales* 23,478,160
SIC 5411 Grocery stores
Luigi Nudo
Mario Antico

D-U-N-S 20-582-9534   (SL)
1542053 ONTARIO LIMITED
ARBELL DISTRIBUTION PRODUCTS
(*Suby of* ELECTRONIQUES ARBELL INC)
1175 Corporate Dr Unit 8, Burlington, ON, L7L 5V5
(905) 332-7755
Emp Here 36   *Sales* 16,098,264
SIC 5065 Electronic parts and equipment, nec
Lee Wise
Paul Santoro
Kit Allen

D-U-N-S 24-337-1622   (SL)
805658 ONTARIO INC
HALTON HONDA
(*Suby of* 226138 ONTARIO INC)
4100 Harvester Rd Suite 1, Burlington, ON, L7L 0C1
(905) 632-5371
Emp Here 75   *Sales* 47,196,000
SIC 5511 New and used car dealers
Peter Bellm
Richard Bellm

D-U-N-S 24-484-8248   (SL)
864773 ONTARIO INC
TENDER CHOICE FOODS
4480 Paletta Crt, Burlington, ON, L7L 5R2
(905) 825-1856
Emp Here 250   *Sales* 121,846,250
SIC 2011 Meat packing plants

D-U-N-S 20-390-9551   (SL)
ALIGNED CAPITAL PARTNERS INC
ACPI
1001 Champlain Avenue, Suite 300, Burlington, ON, L7L 5Z4

Emp Here 45   *Sales* 12,748,185
SIC 8741 Management services
Chris Enright

D-U-N-S 24-779-4290   (HQ)

AMICO CANADA INC
AMICO-ISG
(*Suby of* GIBRALTAR INDUSTRIES, INC.)
1080 Corporate Dr, Burlington, ON, L7L 5R6
(905) 335-4474
Emp Here 56   *Sales* 14,598,460
SIC 3499 Fabricated Metal products, nec
Henning Kornbrekke
Timothy F Murphy
Jamie L. Peritore
Mackay Glenn
Frank G. Heard

    D-U-N-S 24-805-8096   (HQ)
ANAERGIA INC
4210 South Service Rd, Burlington, ON, L7L 4X5
(905) 766-3333
Emp Here 10   *Sales* 39,762,940
SIC 2869 Industrial organic chemicals, nec
Andrew Benedek
Hani El-Kaissi

    D-U-N-S 24-195-9402   (SL)
ARZON LIMITED
4485 Mainway, Burlington, ON, L7L 7P3
(905) 332-5600
Emp Here 44   *Sales* 19,503,045
SIC 3353 Aluminum sheet, plate, and foil
Jeffrey Carubba
Leigh Hammond
Peter Janack
Daviid Dries
Martin Baschiera

    D-U-N-S 24-105-7074   (HQ)
ASBURY WILKINSON INC
(*Suby of* ASBURY CARBONS, INC.)
1115 Sutton Dr, Burlington, ON, L7L 5Z8
(905) 332-0862
Emp Here 9   *Sales* 12,480,736
SIC 5051 Metals service centers and offices
Stephen Riddle
Noah Nicholson
Lynn Townsend
Nick Iacono

    D-U-N-S 25-240-7853   (HQ)
ASSOCIATED MATERIALS CANADA LIMITED
(*Suby of* ASSOCIATED MATERIALS GROUP, INC.)
1001 Corporate Dr, Burlington, ON, L7L 5V5
(905) 319-5561
Emp Here 200   *Sales* 145,938,600
SIC 3444 Sheet Metalwork
Robert Hastings

    D-U-N-S 20-610-3186   (HQ)
ASSOCIATED PAVING & MATERIALS LTD
BRYTE P MANAGEMENT
5365 Munro Crt, Burlington, ON, L7L 5M7
(905) 637-1966
Sales 23,880,450
SIC 1611 Highway and street construction
Stanley Capobianco
Kieu Duong

    D-U-N-S 24-007-1480   (HQ)
ATTRIDGE TRANSPORTATION INCORPORATED
5439 Harvester Rd, Burlington, ON, L7L 5J7
(905) 333-4047
Emp Here 299   *Sales* 48,851,528
SIC 4151 School buses
James Attridge
Glenn Attridge

    D-U-N-S 24-319-4094   (HQ)
AXYZ INTERNATIONAL INC
5330 South Service Rd, Burlington, ON, L7L 5L1
(905) 634-4940
Emp Here 5   *Sales* 25,530,115
SIC 3553 Woodworking machinery
Alf Zeuner
Gary Harvey

    D-U-N-S 24-353-9405   (HQ)
BAILEY METAL PROCESSING LIMITED
(*Suby of* BAILEY-HUNT LIMITED)
1211 Heritage Rd, Burlington, ON, L7L 4Y1
(905) 336-5111
Emp Here 16   *Sales* 14,375,008
SIC 7389 Business services, nec
Stuart Hunt

    D-U-N-S 20-154-2057   (SL)
BATTLEFIELD GRAPHICS INC
BATTLEFIELD PRESS
5355 Harvester Rd, Burlington, ON, L7L 5K4
(905) 333-4114
Emp Here 65   *Sales* 10,661,755
SIC 2752 Commercial printing, lithographic
Jerry Theoret

    D-U-N-S 20-051-7683   (SL)
BAYCOMP COMPANY
(*Suby of* PERFORMANCE MATERIALS CORPORATION)
5035 North Service Rd, Burlington, ON, L7L 5V2
(905) 332-0991
Emp Here 22   *Sales* 16,067,590
SIC 5162 Plastics materials and basic shapes
Mark Lang
Thomas W Smith
Julie A Maturo

    D-U-N-S 20-314-6063   (SL)
BELLWYCK PACKAGING INC
BELLWYCK PACKAGING SOLUTIONS
977 Century Dr, Burlington, ON, L7L 5J8
(905) 631-4475
Emp Here 25   *Sales* 11,087,250
SIC 7389 Business services, nec
Terry Dixon

    D-U-N-S 25-496-1360   (SL)
BERICAP INC
BERICAP NORTH AMERICA
835 Syscon Crt, Burlington, ON, L7L 6C5
(905) 634-2248
Emp Here 140   *Sales* 68,282,200
SIC 5085 Industrial supplies
Gunter Kroautkramer
Scott Ambrose

    D-U-N-S 20-736-9992   (HQ)
BOEHRINGER INGELHEIM (CANADA) LTD
ANIMAL HEALTH, DIV OF
(*Suby of* C.H. BOEHRINGER SOHN AG & CO. KG)
5180 South Service Rd, Burlington, ON, L7L 5H4
(905) 639-0333
Emp Here 250   *Sales* 293,102,910
SIC 5122 Drugs, proprietaries, and sundries
Richard Mole

    D-U-N-S 25-092-1835   (SL)
BOESE FOODS INTERNATIONAL INC
4145 North Service Rd 2nd Fl, Burlington, ON, L7L 6A3
(289) 288-5304
Emp Here 4   *Sales* 11,581,279
SIC 5141 Groceries, general line
Mark Boese
Sandra Boese

    D-U-N-S 20-016-3215   (SL)
BRANTHAVEN HOMES 2000 INC
(*Suby of* STIPSITS HOLDINGS CORP)
720 Oval Crt, Burlington, ON, L7L 6A9
(905) 333-8364
Emp Here 60   *Sales* 16,256,520
SIC 1521 Single-family housing construction
Steven Stipsits

    D-U-N-S 25-057-9414   (SL)
BURKERT CONTROMATIC INC
BURKERT FLUID CONTROL SYSTEMS
(*Suby of* VINCI)
5002 South Service Rd, Burlington, ON, L7L 5Y7

(905) 632-3033
Emp Here 24   *Sales* 11,400,624
SIC 5085 Industrial supplies
David Kelly

    D-U-N-S 25-187-5795   (SL)
BURLINGTON CONVENTION CENTRE
1120 Burloak Dr, Burlington, ON, L7L 6P8
(905) 319-0319
Emp Here 33   *Sales* 14,635,170
SIC 7389 Business services, nec
Jack Moreira

    D-U-N-S 24-094-3340   (SL)
BURLINGTON-FAIRVIEW NISSAN LTD
4111 North Service Rd, Burlington, ON, L7L 4X6
(905) 681-2162
Emp Here 35   *Sales* 17,432,730
SIC 5521 Used car dealers
Edward Scherle

    D-U-N-S 20-314-4035   (SL)
CANADIAN TEXTILE RECYCLING LIMITED
5385 Munro Crt, Burlington, ON, L7L 5M7
(905) 632-1464
Emp Here 50   *Sales* 26,027,100
SIC 5093 Scrap and waste materials
Paul Dekort

    D-U-N-S 25-473-6598   (SL)
CANADIAN UNIVERSITIES RECIPROCAL INSURANCE EXCHANGE
CURIE
5500 North Service Rd Suite 901, Burlington, ON, L7L 6W6
(905) 336-3366
Emp Here 14   *Sales* 17,182,677
SIC 6321 Accident and health insurance
Keith Shakespere
Brian Jessop
Dave Button
Ian Nason
Nathalie Laporte
Julia Shin Doi
Philip Stack
Jane Obrien
Jackie Podger
Steve Pottle

    D-U-N-S 20-038-8486   (SL)
CAPO INDUSTRIES LIMITED
1200 Corporate Dr, Burlington, ON, L7L 5R6
(905) 332-6626
Emp Here 45   *Sales* 12,449,700
SIC 2899 Chemical preparations, nec
Douglas Ridpath
Donald Ridpath

    D-U-N-S 24-877-3749   (BR)
CCTF CORPORATION
EMCO
(*Suby of* CANADIAN MASTER DISTRIBUTION CORPORATION)
4151 North Service Rd Unit 2, Burlington, ON, L7L 4X6
(905) 335-5320
Emp Here 100
SIC 8721 Accounting, auditing, and bookkeeping
Burck Jaap

    D-U-N-S 24-392-8822   (SL)
CEDARLANE CORPORATION
CEDARLANE LABORATORIES
4410 Paletta Crt, Burlington, ON, L7L 5R2
(289) 288-0001
Emp Here 80   *Sales* 22,132,800
SIC 2836 Biological products, except diagnostic
Cynthia Greer
John Course

    D-U-N-S 25-237-3600   (SL)
CENTRE FOR SKILLS DEVELOPMENT & TRAINING, THE
5151 New St, Burlington, ON, L7L 1V3

(905) 637-3393
Emp Here 100   *Sales* 12,012,900
SIC 8299 Schools and educational services, nec
Aldo Cianfrini

    D-U-N-S 24-347-8166   (SL)
CHEMSYNERGY INC
1100 Burloak Dr Suite 101, Burlington, ON, L7L 6B2
(905) 827-4900
Emp Here 12   *Sales* 19,900,375
SIC 5169 Chemicals and allied products, nec
Mehernosh Bhesania
Niloufer Bhesania

    D-U-N-S 24-986-2780   (SL)
CHILDREN'S AID SOCIETY OF THE REGIONAL MUNICIPALITY OF HALTON
HALTON'S CHILDREN'S AID SOCIETY
1445 Norjohn Crt, Burlington, ON, L7L 0E6
(905) 333-4441
Emp Here 78   *Sales* 5,336,916
SIC 8322 Individual and family services
Nancy Macgillivray

    D-U-N-S 24-720-1304   (HQ)
CIMTEK INC
(*Suby of* CIRCUIT CHECK HOLDINGS, INC.)
5328 John Lucas Dr, Burlington, ON, L7L 6A6
(905) 331-6338
Sales 17,684,240
SIC 7373 Computer integrated systems design
Stanford Smith
Paul P. Mizzi
James Noschese
Adrian King

    D-U-N-S 25-404-3730   (HQ)
CLASSIC CARE PHARMACY CORPORATION
1320 Heine Crt, Burlington, ON, L7L 6L9
(905) 631-9027
Emp Here 95   *Sales* 29,319,360
SIC 5999 Miscellaneous retail stores, nec
Moe Green
Girish Bansal

    D-U-N-S 25-406-7168   (SL)
CLASSIC TILE CONTRACTORS LIMITED
1175 Appleby Line Unit B2, Burlington, ON, L7L 5H9
(905) 335-1700
Emp Here 4   *Sales* 13,390,866
SIC 1752 Floor laying and floor work, nec
Ehab Shaheen

    D-U-N-S 24-181-7840   (HQ)
CLYDE UNION CANADA LIMITED
SPX CLYDE UNION CANADA
(*Suby of* SPX FLOW, INC.)
4151 North Service Rd Unit 1, Burlington, ON, L7L 4X6
(905) 315-3800
Emp Here 110   *Sales* 39,322,780
SIC 3561 Pumps and pumping equipment
Kevin Lilly
Michael Reilly
Jeremy Smeltser
Robert Harvey
John Gibson

    D-U-N-S 25-083-1054   (SL)
COMTEK ADVANCED STRUCTURES LTD
(*Suby of* AVCORP INDUSTRIES INC)
1360 Artisans Crt, Burlington, ON, L7L 5Y2
(905) 331-8121
Emp Here 100   *Sales* 48,773,000
SIC 5088 Transportation equipment and supplies
Brent Collver
Dennis Cicci

    D-U-N-S 24-151-0697   (SL)
CORPA HOLDINGS INC
2000 Appleby Line Suite G3, Burlington, ON, L7L 7H7

(905) 331-1333
Emp Here 49　　　*Sales* 13,881,357
SIC 8741 Management services
　Darrell Bryan Corpa

D-U-N-S 20-177-5137　　　(HQ)
CPC PUMPS INTERNATIONAL INC
5200 Mainway, Burlington, ON, L7L 5Z1
(289) 288-4753
Sales 43,589,728
SIC 3561 Pumps and pumping equipment
　Hani Fayeth
　Paul Gallo
　Steve Aubrey
　Zheng Li
　John Weitner

D-U-N-S 20-903-2648　　　(HQ)
CROWN WORLDWIDE LTD
CROWN RELOCATIONS
(*Suby of* JENJET INC)
1375 Artisans Crt, Burlington, ON, L7L 5Y2
(905) 827-4899
Emp Here 27　　　*Sales* 15,599,010
SIC 4783 Packing and crating
　Robert Hannon
　Dean Hefford

D-U-N-S 20-514-8260　　　(SL)
DETAIL K2 INC
DK2
1080 Clay Ave Unit 2, Burlington, ON, L7L 0A1
(905) 335-2152
Emp Here 37　　　*Sales* 11,264,970
SIC 5199 Nondurable goods, nec
　Steve Malizia
　Thomas Malizia

D-U-N-S 20-602-6957　　　(SL)
DOMINION NICKEL INVESTMENTS LTD
834 Appleby Line Suite 1, Burlington, ON, L7L 2Y7
(905) 639-9939
Emp Here 25　　　*Sales* 13,013,550
SIC 5093 Scrap and waste materials
　Frank Fleisher
　Howie Fleisher
　Danny Fleisher
　Allan Fleisher
　Sarah Fleisher

D-U-N-S 20-271-5116　　　(HQ)
EARTHFRESH FARMS INC
EARTHFRESH
1095 Clay Ave, Burlington, ON, L7L 0A1
(416) 251-2271
Sales 83,557,700
SIC 5148 Fresh fruits and vegetables
　Thomas Hughes

D-U-N-S 24-830-6102　　　(SL)
EARTHFRESH FOODS CORP
MACKAY & HUGHES
1095 Clay Ave, Burlington, ON, L7L 0A1
(416) 251-2271
Emp Here 80　　　*Sales* 66,846,160
SIC 5148 Fresh fruits and vegetables
　Tom Hughes

D-U-N-S 24-078-4561　　　(HQ)
EATON INDUSTRIES (CANADA) COMPANY
EATON ELECTRICAL, CANADIAN OPERA-TIONS DIV OF
(*Suby of* EATON CORPORATION PUBLIC LIMITED COMPANY)
5050 Mainway, Burlington, ON, L7L 5Z1
(905) 333-6442
Emp Here 50　　　*Sales* 435,185,250
SIC 5065 Electronic parts and equipment, nec
　Craig Arnold

D-U-N-S 20-561-4662　　　(HQ)
ECODYNE LIMITED
(*Suby of* BERKSHIRE HATHAWAY INC.)
4475 Corporate Dr, Burlington, ON, L7L 5T9
(905) 332-1404
Sales 15,984,072
SIC 3589 Service industry machinery, nec

Paul Holmes
Gregory Allemano
John J. Goody

D-U-N-S 24-845-4043　　　(HQ)
ENDRESS + HAUSER CANADA LTD
(*Suby of* ENDRESS+HAUSER AG)
1075 Sutton Dr, Burlington, ON, L7L 5Z8
(905) 681-9292
Emp Here 90　　　*Sales* 66,819,010
SIC 5084 Industrial machinery and equipment
　Anthony Varga

D-U-N-S 25-354-6089　　　(HQ)
ENERGY ADVANTAGE INC
5515 North Service Rd Unit 303, Burlington, ON, L7L 6G4
(905) 319-1717
Emp Here 50　　　*Sales* 11,714,400
SIC 8748 Business consulting, nec
　Robert Kirkby

D-U-N-S 25-517-7461　　　(HQ)
ESSLINGER FOODS LTD
5035 North Service Rd, Burlington, ON, L7L 5V2
(905) 332-3777
Sales 23,396,156
SIC 5141 Groceries, general line
　William Esslinger
　Robert Redmond

D-U-N-S 20-164-6742　　　(HQ)
ETHYL CANADA INC
(*Suby of* NEWMARKET CORPORATION)
5045 South Service Rd Suite 101, Burlington, ON, L7L 5Y7
(905) 631-5470
Emp Here 7　　　*Sales* 13,833,000
SIC 2819 Industrial inorganic chemicals, nec
　Sandra Duffy-Brodie
　Rudy West
　Daniel Hawkins
　David Fiorenza

D-U-N-S 20-408-9890　　　(HQ)
EVERTZ MICROSYSTEMS LTD
(*Suby of* EVERTZ TECHNOLOGIES LIMITED)
5292 John Lucas Dr, Burlington, ON, L7L 5Z9
(905) 335-3700
Emp Here 380　　　*Sales* 107,507,700
SIC 3663 Radio and t.v. communications equipment
　Romolo Magarelli
　Douglas Deburin
　Anthony Gridley

D-U-N-S 24-204-7251　　　(HQ)
EVERTZ TECHNOLOGIES LIMITED
5292 John Lucas Dr, Burlington, ON, L7L 5Z9
(905) 335-3700
Sales 288,634,237
SIC 3669 Communications equipment, nec
　Romolo Magarelli
　Douglas Debruin
　Brian Campbell
　Rakesh Patel
　Anthony Gridley
　Christopher Colclough
　Ian Mcwalter
　Thomas Pistor

D-U-N-S 20-647-1773　　　(HQ)
FIRSTCANADA ULC
FIRST STUDENT CANADA
(*Suby of* FIRSTGROUP PLC)
1111 International Blvd, Burlington, ON, L7L 6W1
(289) 288-4359
Emp Here 50　　　*Sales* 618,354,000
SIC 4151 School buses
　Dennis Maple
　Darryl Hill
　Claire Miller
　Tom Secrest
　Dean Suhre

Paul Osland

D-U-N-S 20-030-5568　　　(SL)
FORTINO'S (NEW STREET) LTD
5111 New St Suite 50, Burlington, ON, L7L 1V2
(905) 631-7227
Emp Here 50　　　*Sales* 13,707,600
SIC 5411 Grocery stores
　Charlie Alfano

D-U-N-S 24-339-4124　　　(SL)
GEMALTO CANADA INC
(*Suby of* THALES)
5347 John Lucas Dr, Burlington, ON, L7L 6A8
(905) 335-9681
Emp Here 200　　　*Sales* 133,781,600
SIC 7389 Business services, nec
　Philippe Vallee
　Philippe Amar

D-U-N-S 20-134-2623　　　(HQ)
GERRIE ELECTRIC WHOLESALE LIMITED
GERRIE SUPPLY CHAIN SERVICES
4104 South Service Rd, Burlington, ON, L7L 4X5
(905) 681-3660
Emp Here 80　　　*Sales* 145,061,750
SIC 5063 Electrical apparatus and equipment

D-U-N-S 25-145-9335　　　(BR)
GOODRICH AEROSPACE CANADA LTD
GOODRICH LANDING GEAR SERVICES
(*Suby of* UNITED TECHNOLOGIES CORPORATION)
5415 North Service Rd, Burlington, ON, L7L 5H7
(905) 319-3006
Emp Here 150
SIC 7699 Repair services, nec
　Steve King

D-U-N-S 25-967-5671　　　(SL)
GRAKON HAMSAR HOLDINGS LTD
HAMSAR DIVERSCO
5320 Downey St, Burlington, ON, L7L 6M2
(905) 332-4094
Emp Here 120　　　*Sales* 22,853,040
SIC 3679 Electronic components, nec
　Don Bartlett

D-U-N-S 24-317-3010　　　(HQ)
GRANTEK SYSTEMS INTEGRATION INC
GRANTEK CONTROL SYSTEMS
4480 Harvester Rd, Burlington, ON, L7L 4X2
(905) 634-0844
Emp Here 1　　　*Sales* 16,421,080
SIC 7373 Computer integrated systems design
　David Patterson

D-U-N-S 24-452-3528　　　(SL)
HADRIAN MANUFACTURING INC
965 Syscon Rd, Burlington, ON, L7L 5S3
(905) 333-0300
Emp Here 140　　　*Sales* 21,605,080
SIC 2542 Partitions and fixtures, except wood
　Rob Snyder
　Gary Greenway
　Jeff Bell

D-U-N-S 24-418-5799　　　(SL)
HAEFELE CANADA INC
HAFELE
(*Suby of* HAFELE GMBH & CO KG)
5323 John Lucas Dr, Burlington, ON, L7L 6A8
(905) 336-6608
Emp Here 51　　　*Sales* 23,462,244
SIC 5072 Hardware
　Barry Piercy
　Ursula Hafele

D-U-N-S 20-025-1895　　　(BR)
HALTON DISTRICT SCHOOL BOARD
NELSON SECONDARY SCHOOL
(*Suby of* HALTON DISTRICT SCHOOL BOARD)
4181 New St, Burlington, ON, L7L 1T3

(905) 637-3825
Emp Here 100
SIC 8211 Elementary and secondary schools
　Karen Hartman

D-U-N-S 20-025-2315　　　(BR)
HALTON DISTRICT SCHOOL BOARD
ROBERT BATEMAN HIGH SCHOOL
(*Suby of* HALTON DISTRICT SCHOOL BOARD)
5151 New St, Burlington, ON, L7L 1V3
(905) 632-5151
Emp Here 78
SIC 8211 Elementary and secondary schools
　Mark Duley

D-U-N-S 24-719-1547　　　(BR)
HARRIS STEEL ULC
LAUREL STEEL
(*Suby of* NUCOR CORPORATION)
5400 Harvester Rd, Burlington, ON, L7L 5N5
(905) 681-6811
Emp Here 200
SIC 3312 Blast furnaces and steel mills
　John Harris

D-U-N-S 24-794-3616　　　(BR)
HARRIS STEEL ULC
FISHER & LUDLOW, DIV OF
(*Suby of* NUCOR CORPORATION)
750 Appleby Line, Burlington, ON, L7L 2Y7
(905) 632-2121
Emp Here 140
SIC 3446 Architectural Metalwork
　Brian Rutter

D-U-N-S 24-850-2929　　　(BR)
HATCH CORPORATION
(*Suby of* HATCH CORPORATION)
5035 South Service Rd, Burlington, ON, L7L 6M9
(905) 315-3500
Emp Here 80
SIC 8711 Engineering services

D-U-N-S 25-405-0347　　　(SL)
HEARTLAND FIREPLACES LIMITED
5450 Mainway, Burlington, ON, L7L 6A4
(905) 319-0474
Emp Here 22　　　*Sales* 11,194,832
SIC 5023 Homefurnishings
　Jane Mancini
　Victor Mancini

D-U-N-S 20-134-5410　　　(SL)
HENNIGES AUTOMOTIVE SCHLEGEL CANADA INC
(*Suby of* LJ/HAH HOLDINGS CORPORATION)
4445 Fairview St, Burlington, ON, L7L 2A4
(289) 636-4461
Emp Here 258　　　*Sales* 62,753,598
SIC 3465 Automotive stampings
　Mario Daddio

D-U-N-S 20-875-1198　　　(BR)
HERCULES SLR INC
UNALLOY-IWRC, DIV OF
(*Suby of* HERCULES SLR INC)
737 Oval Crt, Burlington, ON, L7L 6A9

Emp Here 100
SIC 5051 Metals service centers and offices
　Ciony Datique

D-U-N-S 20-039-0193　　　(SL)
HIGGINSON EQUIPMENT INC
1175 Corporate Dr Unit 1, Burlington, ON, L7L 5V5
(905) 335-2211
Emp Here 24　　　*Sales* 11,400,624
SIC 5085 Industrial supplies
　James Eames
　Bill Allan

D-U-N-S 24-407-1015　　　(HQ)
HUNTER AMENITIES INTERNATIONAL LTD
1205 Corporate Dr, Burlington, ON, L7L 5V5

(905) 331-2855
Sales 111,161,250
SIC 2844 Toilet preparations
John Hunter
Paul Niedermayr
Tom Rudland

D-U-N-S 20-548-8542 (SL)
IMPACT STEEL CANADA COMPANY
1100 Burloak Dr Suite 300, Burlington, ON,
L7L 6B2
(905) 336-8939
Emp Here 10 *Sales* 10,171,635
SIC 5051 Metals service centers and offices
Darryl Waugh
Michael Easlick
Robert Feldman
Jeffrey Jaye

D-U-N-S 20-393-7255 (SL)
**INTERNATIONAL CORROSION CONTROL
INC**
ICC
930 Sheldon Crt, Burlington, ON, L7L 5K6
(905) 634-7751
Emp Here 34 *Sales* 24,831,730
SIC 5169 Chemicals and allied products, nec
William Russell

D-U-N-S 20-192-0746 (SL)
KELTOUR CONTROLS INC
4375 Mainway, Burlington, ON, L7L 5N9
(905) 335-6000
Emp Here 50 *Sales* 11,122,590
SIC 3613 Switchgear and switchboard apparatus
David Jakob

D-U-N-S 25-372-9750 (BR)
KONECRANES CANADA INC
(*Suby of* KONECRANES ABP)
5300 Mainway, Burlington, ON, L7L 6A4
(905) 332-9494
Emp Here 90
SIC 7699 Repair services, nec
Keith King

D-U-N-S 20-418-1978 (HQ)
KONECRANES CANADA INC
KCICRANE PRO SERVICES
(*Suby of* KONECRANES ABP)
5300 Mainway, Burlington, ON, L7L 6A4
(905) 332-9494
Emp Here 60 *Sales* 22,603,392
SIC 7699 Repair services, nec
Sadi Arbid
Guy Shumaker
Eric Blinkhorn
Todd Robenson
Thomas Sothard
Sandra Mancouso

D-U-N-S 20-337-8492 (HQ)
LBC CAPITAL INC
BLC CAPITAL
(*Suby of* BANQUE LAURENTIENNE DU
CANADA)
5035 South Service Rd, Burlington, ON, L7L
6M9
(905) 633-2400
Emp Here 10 *Sales* 84,587,200
SIC 6159 Miscellaneous business credit institutions
Michel C. Trudeau
Francois Desjardins
Francois Laurin
Stephane Therrien
Susan Kudzman
Deborah Rose

D-U-N-S 24-371-7944 (SL)
LCL CANADA LIMITED
LYMAN CONTAINER LINE
(*Suby of* MERIT CORPORATION SAL)
1016b Sutton Dr Unit 205, Burlington, ON, L7L
6B8
(416) 639-1889
Emp Here 12 *Sales* 14,446,700

SIC 4731 Freight transportation arrangement
Unni Nair

D-U-N-S 20-845-8984 (HQ)
LIEBHERR-CANADA LTD
LIEBHERR-AEROSPACE CANADA
(*Suby of* LIEBHERR-INTERNATIONAL S.A.)
1015 Sutton Dr, Burlington, ON, L7L 5Z8
(905) 319-9222
Sales 16,625,910
SIC 5082 Construction and mining machinery
Paul Robson

D-U-N-S 24-335-3737 (SL)
LOCKWOOD INDUSTRIES INC
1100 Corporate Dr, Burlington, ON, L7L 5R6
(905) 336-0300
Emp Here 80 *Sales* 15,235,360
SIC 3699 Electrical equipment and supplies,
nec
Edward Milic

D-U-N-S 24-772-0550 (SL)
MAGNUM STEEL & TUBE INC
4380 Corporate Dr, Burlington, ON, L7L 5R3
(905) 319-8852
Emp Here 18 *Sales* 18,006,102
SIC 5051 Metals service centers and offices
Paul Mcnicol
Graeme Clark

D-U-N-S 20-315-3432 (SL)
MAINSTREAM METALS INC
(*Suby of* COMPAGNIE AMERICAINE DE FER
& METAUX INC, LA)
4350 Harvester Rd, Burlington, ON, L7L 5S4
(905) 631-5945
Emp Here 15 *Sales* 19,586,925
SIC 5093 Scrap and waste materials
Ronald Black
Herbert Black

D-U-N-S 25-486-9415 (BR)
MAPLE LEAF FOODS INC
MAPLE LEAF DISTRIBUTION CENTRE
(*Suby of* MAPLE LEAF FOODS INC)
5100 Harvester Rd, Burlington, ON, L7L 4X4
(905) 681-5050
Emp Here 80
SIC 5147 Meats and meat products
Tim Mccabe

D-U-N-S 24-991-9028 (HQ)
MARMON/KEYSTONE CANADA INC
SPECIALTY STEELS
(*Suby of* BERKSHIRE HATHAWAY INC.)
1220 Heritage Rd, Burlington, ON, L7L 4X9
(905) 319-4646
Emp Here 22 *Sales* 60,940,308
SIC 5051 Metals service centers and offices
Lou Germano

D-U-N-S 20-917-8396 (SL)
MARSH INSTRUMENTATION LTD
MARSH CONTROL & AUTOMATION PRODUCTS
1016c Sutton Dr Unit 1, Burlington, ON, L7L
6B8
(905) 332-1172
Emp Here 45 *Sales* 11,545,290
SIC 3829 Measuring and controlling devices,
nec
Ronald Bake

D-U-N-S 24-827-1830 (HQ)
MC COMMERCIAL INC
(*Suby of* CONTROLADORA MABE, S.A. DE
C.V.)
5420 North Service Rd Suite 300, Burlington,
ON, L7L 6C7
(905) 315-2300
Emp Here 75 *Sales* 145,061,750
SIC 5064 Electrical appliances, television and
radio
Mike Mccrea
Jennifer Caldwell
James Fleck

Luis Berrondo
Francisco Berrondo

D-U-N-S 20-560-4994 (SL)
MCKEIL MARINE LIMITED
1001 Champlain Ave Suite 401, Burlington,
ON, L7L 5Z4
(905) 528-4780
Emp Here 300 *Sales* 104,208,300
SIC 4499 Water transportation services,
Steve Fletcher
Blair Mckeil
Jim Merwin
Olous Boag
Patrick Bourke
Patrick Bourke

D-U-N-S 24-391-8534 (SL)
MERZ PHARMA CANADA LTD
(*Suby of* MERZ HOLDING GMBH & CO. KG)
5515 North Service Rd Suite 202, Burlington,
ON, L7L 6G4
(905) 315-1193
Emp Here 60 *Sales* 66,320,700
SIC 5122 Drugs, proprietaries, and sundries
Robert Bennett
Karsten Schlemm

D-U-N-S 25-513-2797 (HQ)
METRICAN STAMPING CO. INC
1380 Artisans Crt, Burlington, ON, L7L 5Y2
(905) 332-3200
Emp Here 150 *Sales* 42,565,425
SIC 3469 Metal stampings, nec
Francesco Bosco
Remo Gigliotti
Joseph Bosco
Carrie Gervais
Anna Sanchez

D-U-N-S 25-300-0137 (BR)
METRO ONTARIO INC
FOOD BASIC
(*Suby of* METRO INC)
5353 Lakeshore Rd, Burlington, ON, L7L 1C8
(905) 634-1804
Emp Here 100
SIC 5411 Grocery stores
Dave Leeney

D-U-N-S 24-335-0555 (BR)
METRO ONTARIO INC
METRO
(*Suby of* METRO INC)
2010 Appleby Line, Burlington, ON, L7L 6M6
(905) 331-7900
Emp Here 300
SIC 5411 Grocery stores
Susan Zybura-Finck

D-U-N-S 24-986-7763 (BR)
METROLAND MEDIA GROUP LTD
BURLINGTON POST, THE
(*Suby of* TORSTAR CORPORATION)
5046 Mainway Unit 2, Burlington, ON, L7L 5Z1
(905) 632-4444
Emp Here 80
SIC 2711 Newspapers
David Harvey

D-U-N-S 24-394-3987 (HQ)
MILACRON CANADA CORP
CIMCOOL METAL WORKING FLUIDS
(*Suby of* MILACRON HOLDINGS CORP.)
1175 Appleby Line Unit B1, Burlington, ON,
L7L 5H9
(905) 319-1919
Sales 13,146,210
SIC 5169 Chemicals and allied products, nec
Gerrit Jue

D-U-N-S 25-495-4969 (HQ)
MOTTLAB INC
(*Suby of* MOTT MANUFACTURING LIMITED)
5230 South Service Rd, Burlington, ON, L7L
5K2
(905) 331-1877
Emp Here 21 *Sales* 10,285,002

SIC 5049 Professional equipment, nec
Robert Vansickle
Edward Seegmiller

D-U-N-S 25-034-1427 (SL)
NATIONAL 4WD CENTRE INC
5379 Harvester Rd, Burlington, ON, L7L 5K4
(905) 634-0001
Emp Here 26 *Sales* 12,950,028
SIC 5531 Auto and home supply stores
Terrance (Terry) Harvey

D-U-N-S 24-353-8761 (HQ)
NATIONAL TIRE DISTRIBUTORS INC
(*Suby of* ATD CORPORATION)
5035 South Service Rd 4th Fl, Burlington, ON,
L7L 6M9
(877) 676-0007
Emp Here 40 *Sales* 290,527,020
SIC 5014 Tires and tubes
George Mcclean
Danny Bharat
Chris Pedersen
Mary Ellen Gilhooly

D-U-N-S 20-410-2982 (HQ)
O'BRIEN LIFTING SOLUTIONS INC
4435 Corporate Dr, Burlington, ON, L7L 5T9
(905) 336-8245
Emp Here 60 *Sales* 22,200,100
SIC 3536 Hoists, cranes, and monorails
Hubert O'brien
Wayne Davis

D-U-N-S 24-364-9779 (HQ)
**O.C. TANNER RECOGNITION COMPANY
LIMITED**
(*Suby of* O. C. TANNER COMPANY)
4200 Fairview St, Burlington, ON, L7L 4Y8
(905) 632-7255
Emp Here 80 *Sales* 32,613,600
SIC 3911 Jewelry, precious Metal
Dave Petersen
Carolyn Tanner Irish
Scott Archibald
Scott Sperry

D-U-N-S 20-350-1650 (BR)
**O.C. TANNER RECOGNITION COMPANY
LIMITED**
(*Suby of* O. C. TANNER COMPANY)
4200 Fairview St, Burlington, ON, L7L 4Y8
(905) 632-7255
Emp Here 80
SIC 6351 Surety insurance
Jennifer Gates

D-U-N-S 20-229-8118 (SL)
ODYSSEY HEALTH SERVICES
1100 Burloak Dr Suite 603, Burlington, ON,
L7L 6B2
(905) 319-0202
Emp Here 30 *Sales* 31,046,430
SIC 6321 Accident and health insurance
Richard Marlin
Janet Marlin

D-U-N-S 20-114-5711 (SL)
ORANGE JULIUS CANADA LIMITED
(*Suby of* DAIRY QUEEN CANADA INC)
5045 South Service Rd Suite 3000, Burlington, ON, L7L 5Y7
(905) 639-1492
Emp Here 50 *Sales* 34,840,500
SIC 6794 Patent owners and lessors
Jean Champagne

D-U-N-S 20-982-7604 (SL)
ORGANIZATIONAL SOLUTIONS INC
OSI
5360 South Service Rd, Burlington, ON, L7L
5L1
(905) 315-7179
Emp Here 71 *Sales* 19,477,572
SIC 8741 Management services
Liz Scott
Mickey Sanghera

▲ Public Company   ■ Public Company Family Member   **HQ** Headquarters   **BR** Branch   **SL** Single Location

D-U-N-S 20-055-0069   (HQ)
OTIS CANADA, INC
(*Suby of* UNITED TECHNOLOGIES CORPORATION)
4475 North Service Rd Suite 200, Burlington, ON, L7L 4X7
(905) 332-9919
Emp Here 11   *Sales* 62,787,200
SIC 7699 Repair services, nec
  Tony Grilli
  Robert L Shirrif

D-U-N-S 20-750-9670   (HQ)
OUTOTEC (CANADA) LTD
(*Suby of* OUTOTEC OYJ)
1551 Corporate Dr, Burlington, ON, L7L 6M3
(905) 335-0002
Emp Here 98   *Sales* 23,088,104
SIC 3569 General industrial machinery, nec
  Seppo Rantakari
  Paul Merlin

D-U-N-S 25-948-4350   (BR)
PATHEON INC
(*Suby of* THERMO FISHER SCIENTIFIC INC.)
977 Century Dr, Burlington, ON, L7L 5J8
(905) 639-5254
Emp Here 120
SIC 2834 Pharmaceutical preparations
  Sanjay Sibal

D-U-N-S 25-312-2667   (HQ)
PELP LIMITED PARTNERSHIP
PIONEER PETROLEUMS
1122 International Blvd Suite 700, Burlington, ON, L7L 6Z8
(905) 639-2060
Emp Here 48   *Sales* 37,756,800
SIC 5541 Gasoline service stations
  Timothy W Hogarth
  Murray E Hogarth
  James Flindall
  Harvey Dyck
  Jack Theriault
  Victor E Holdsworth
  David Macfarlane
  Brian Kitchen
  Guy Desrochiers

D-U-N-S 20-599-4213   (SL)
PENSION PLAN - F & L
NUCORGRATING
750 Appleby Line, Burlington, ON, L7L 2Y7
(905) 632-2121
Emp Here 49   *Sales* 13,892,676
SIC 1611 Highway and street construction
  Pat Mcsadden

D-U-N-S 24-829-7889   (SL)
PHQ GLOBAL INC
1175 Appleby Line Unit C2, Burlington, ON, L7L 5H9
(905) 332-3271
Emp Here 13   *Sales* 10,944,519
SIC 5082 Construction and mining machinery
  William Quesnel
  Alan Marsden
  Larry Meyer
  Robert Lee

D-U-N-S 25-514-2408   (SL)
PINK ELEPHANT INC
PINKONLINE
(*Suby of* PINK ELEPHANT GROUP INC)
5575 North Service Rd Suite 200, Burlington, ON, L7L 6M1
(905) 331-5060
Emp Here 90   *Sales* 11,229,840
SIC 8741 Management services
  David Ratcliffe
  Rick Giel
  Lou Cino

D-U-N-S 20-147-3428   (HQ)
PINTY'S DELICIOUS FOODS INC
(*Suby of* OLYMEL S.E.C.)

5063 North Service Rd Suite 101, Burlington, ON, L7L 5H6
(905) 835-8575
Sales 243,692,500
SIC 2015 Poultry slaughtering and processing
  Jack Vanderlaan

D-U-N-S 24-985-8770   (HQ)
PIONEER FOOD SERVICES LIMITED
KFC
5100 South Service Rd Suite 1, Burlington, ON, L7L 6A5
(905) 333-9887
Sales 58,695,400
SIC 5461 Retail bakeries

D-U-N-S 20-702-5784   (SL)
PRESVAC SYSTEMS (BURLINGTON) LIMITED
(*Suby of* 919686 ONTARIO INC)
4131 Morris Dr, Burlington, ON, L7L 5L5
(905) 637-2353
Emp Here 90   *Sales* 17,287,650
SIC 3443 Fabricated plate work (boiler shop)
  Louis Sipkema

D-U-N-S 20-938-6627   (SL)
RAMPF COMPOSITE SOLUTIONS INC
5322 John Lucas Dr, Burlington, ON, L7L 6A6
(905) 331-8042
Emp Here 80   *Sales* 17,907,440
SIC 3728 Aircraft parts and equipment, nec
  Gerry Kavanaugh
  Robert Armstrong
  Kevin Mcallister

D-U-N-S 24-525-4037   (HQ)
RCAP LEASING INC
(*Suby of* ROYAL BANK OF CANADA)
5575 North Service Rd Suite 300, Burlington, ON, L7L 6M1
(905) 639-3995
Emp Here 150   *Sales* 79,300,500
SIC 6159 Miscellaneous business credit institutions
  Eugene Basolini
  Dave Markel
  Lucy Forte-Morelli
  Carl Crechiolo
  Kevin Archibald
  Robin Morrison
  Michael Segatti

D-U-N-S 20-268-5301   (SL)
RELIANCE TRADE BROKERS INC
4145 North Service Rd, Burlington, ON, L7L 6A3
(289) 201-7841
Emp Here 31   *Sales* 10,140,937
SIC 6531 Real estate agents and managers
  Michael Stewart

D-U-N-S 24-923-9161   (HQ)
RETAIL DIMENSIONS INCORPORATED
R D I
4335 Mainway, Burlington, ON, L7L 5N9

Emp Here 50   *Sales* 74,853,000
SIC 5651 Family clothing stores
  Sam Baio
  Maureen Fowler

D-U-N-S 20-268-9360   (SL)
REVOLUTION ENVIRONMENTAL SOLUTIONS ACQUISITION GP INC
TERRAPURE ENVIRONMENTAL
1100 Burloak Dr Unit 500, Burlington, ON, L7L 6B2
(800) 263-8602
Emp Here 900   *Sales* 287,019,000
SIC 4953 Refuse systems
  Todd Moser

D-U-N-S 20-268-5178   (HQ)
REVOLUTION ENVIRONMENTAL SOLUTIONS LP
TERRAPURE ENVIRONMENTAL
1100 Burloak Dr Suite 500, Burlington, ON,

L7L 6B2
(800) 263-8602
Emp Here 25   *Sales* 651,444,000
SIC 4959 Sanitary services, nec
  Todd Moser
  Ryan Reid
  Stephen Fletcher
  Glen Sivac

D-U-N-S 24-371-6722   (BR)
REVOLUTION ENVIRONMENTAL SOLUTIONS LP
TERRAPURE ENVIRONMENTAL
(*Suby of* REVOLUTION ENVIRONMENTAL SOLUTIONS LP)
1100 Burloak Dr Suite 500, Burlington, ON, L7L 6B2
(905) 315-6300
Emp Here 75
SIC 4953 Refuse systems
  Lisa Decosta

D-U-N-S 20-269-7835   (SL)
REVOLUTION LANDFILL LP
1100 Burloak Dr, Burlington, ON, L7L 6B2
(905) 315-6304
Emp Here 1,000   *Sales* 444,645,000
SIC 2844 Toilet preparations
  Margaret Dodds

D-U-N-S 20-267-4263   (SL)
REVOLUTION VSC ACQUISITION GP INC
1100 Burloak Dr Suite 200, Burlington, ON, L7L 6B2
(905) 315-6300
Emp Here 150   *Sales* 16,393,350
SIC 0721 Crop planting and protection
  Todd Moser
  Benoit Deschenes

D-U-N-S 20-042-8506   (HQ)
REVOLUTION VSC LP
TONOLLI CANADA
(*Suby of* REVOLUTION ENVIRONMENTAL SOLUTIONS LP)
1100 Burloak Dr Suite 500, Burlington, ON, L7L 6B2
(905) 279-9555
Emp Here 5   *Sales* 12,697,160
SIC 3341 Secondary nonferrous Metals
  Ross Atkinson
  Edward Camilleri
  Steve Stack

D-U-N-S 20-173-1841   (HQ)
RHI CANADA INC
4355 Fairview St, Burlington, ON, L7L 2A4
(905) 633-4500
Emp Here 130   *Sales* 81,820,800
SIC 3297 Nonclay refractories
  Hans Joerg Junger
  Dan Masson
  Lee Stratton

D-U-N-S 24-869-0679   (HQ)
ROBERTSON INC
(*Suby of* BERKSHIRE HATHAWAY INC.)
1185 Corporate Dr Suite 1, Burlington, ON, L7L 5V5
(905) 332-7776
Emp Here 17   *Sales* 11,774,441
SIC 5085 Industrial supplies

D-U-N-S 20-513-0433   (HQ)
ROMCO CORPORATION
5575 North Service Rd Suite 401, Burlington, ON, L7L 6M1
(905) 339-3555
Sales 10,483,875
SIC 6712 Bank holding companies
  Robert Mccallister
  Frank H. Coleman

D-U-N-S 25-115-1288   (SL)
ROY, SPEED & ROSS LTD
5500 North Service Rd Suite 300, Burlington, ON, L7L 6W6

(905) 331-3113
Emp Here 25   *Sales* 25,872,025
SIC 6331 Fire, marine, and casualty insurance
  Karey Davidson

D-U-N-S 24-524-4306   (HQ)
RYERSON CANADA, INC
(*Suby of* RYERSON HOLDING CORPORATION)
1219 Corporate Dr Suite 2, Burlington, ON, L7L 5V5
(416) 622-3100
Emp Here 40   *Sales* 179,236,200
SIC 5051 Metals service centers and offices
  Michael Burbach
  David Hallett
  Michael Hamilton

D-U-N-S 20-703-1431   (BR)
SANDVIK CANADA, INC
E J C
(*Suby of* SANDVIK AB)
4445 Fairview St, Burlington, ON, L7L 2A4

Emp Here 175
SIC 3532 Mining machinery
  Matti Heinio

D-U-N-S 20-366-1566   (HQ)
SEMTECH CANADA CORPORATION
4281 Harvester Rd, Burlington, ON, L7L 5M4
(905) 632-2996
Emp Here 350   *Sales* 113,166,000
SIC 3679 Electronic components, nec
  Emeka Chukwu
  Charles B. Ammann
  Gary Beauchamp
  James Lindstrom
  James Burra

D-U-N-S 24-776-9016   (BR)
SEMTECH CANADA CORPORATION
GENNUM
(*Suby of* SEMTECH CANADA CORPORATION)
4281 Harvester Rd, Burlington, ON, L7L 5M4
(905) 632-2996
Emp Here 150
SIC 3679 Electronic components, nec
  Bharat Tailor

D-U-N-S 24-910-0199   (HQ)
SHEEHAN'S TRUCK CENTRE INC
4320 Harvester Rd, Burlington, ON, L7L 5S4
(905) 632-0300
Sales 37,756,800
SIC 5511 New and used car dealers
  Kelly Sheehan
  Dennis Sheehan

D-U-N-S 24-196-0848   (SL)
SHIPWAY STAIRS LIMITED
1820 Ironstone Dr, Burlington, ON, L7L 5V3
(905) 336-1296
Emp Here 150   *Sales* 28,855,500
SIC 2431 Millwork
  Larry Shipway
  Dale Shipway
  Sarah Shipway

D-U-N-S 20-547-4690   (SL)
SHOPLOGIX INC
5100 South Service Rd Suite 39, Burlington, ON, L7L 6A5
(905) 469-9994
Emp Here 60   *Sales* 10,638,660
SIC 7371 Custom computer programming services
  Kevin Dwyer
  Steve Celestini
  Derek Smyth
  Tracy E Mainman

D-U-N-S 20-117-8618   (BR)
SIEMENS CANADA LIMITED
(*Suby of* SIEMENS AG)
1550 Appleby Line, Burlington, ON, L7L 6X7

(905) 319-3600
Emp Here 200
SIC 3625 Relays and industrial controls
Roy Chidgey

D-U-N-S 24-377-0141   (SL)
SIEMENS FINANCIAL LTD
(*Suby of* SIEMENS AG)
1550 Appleby Line, Burlington, ON, L7L 6X7
(905) 315-6868
Emp Here 50   *Sales* 11,237,200
SIC 6153 Short-term business credit institutions, except agricultural
Maria Ferraro
Roland Charlons-Browne
Matthias Grossmann

D-U-N-S 20-174-9954   (HQ)
SIR CORP
JACK ASTOR'S BAR AND GRILL
5360 South Service Rd Suite 200, Burlington, ON, L7L 5L1
(905) 681-2997
Emp Here 10   *Sales* 163,236,500
SIC 5812 Eating places
Peter Fowler
Grey Sisson

D-U-N-S 20-698-5694   (SL)
SIR ROYALTY INCOME FUND
5360 South Service Rd Suite 200, Burlington, ON, L7L 5L1
(905) 681-2997
Emp Here 5,500   *Sales* 8,710,424
SIC 6726 Investment offices, nec
Peter Fowler
John J. Mclaughlin
Paul J. Bognar
Peter Luit
Kim Van Nieuwkoop
William Rogers

D-U-N-S 24-686-3294   (HQ)
SODEXO CANADA LTD
SODEXO
(*Suby of* SODEXO)
5420 North Service Rd Suite 501, Burlington, ON, L7L 6C7
(905) 632-8592
Emp Here 60   *Sales* 513,029,000
SIC 5812 Eating places
Barry Telford
Dean Johnson
Jerome Vos

D-U-N-S 24-714-3188   (SL)
SOUND DESIGN TECHNOLOGIES LTD
ON SEMICONDUCTOR
(*Suby of* ON SEMICONDUCTOR CORPORATION)
970 Fraser Dr, Burlington, ON, L7L 5P5
(905) 635-0800
Emp Here 140   *Sales* 31,820,460
SIC 3842 Surgical appliances and supplies
Robert Tong
Keith Jackson
Donald Colvin

D-U-N-S 20-271-7187   (BR)
STATE FARM INSURANCE
(*Suby of* STATE FARM INSURANCE)
5420 North Service Rd Suite 400, Burlington, ON, L7L 6C7
(905) 315-3900
Emp Here 175
SIC 6411 Insurance agents, brokers, and service
Peter Robinson

D-U-N-S 24-389-2655   (HQ)
STIPSITS HOLDINGS CORP
720 Oval Crt, Burlington, ON, L7L 6A9
(905) 333-8364
Sales 15,943,450
SIC 1521 Single-family housing construction
Steven Stipsits

D-U-N-S 20-526-6849   (BR)

SUNRISE NORTH SENIOR LIVING LTD
SUNRISE SENIOR LIVING OF BURLINGTON
(*Suby of* WELLTOWER INC.)
5401 Lakeshore Rd, Burlington, ON, L7L 6S5
(905) 333-9969
Emp Here 80
SIC 8361 Residential care
Deborah Nelson

D-U-N-S 24-964-5474   (SL)
SURE FLOW EQUIPMENT INC
5010 North Service Rd, Burlington, ON, L7L 5R5
(905) 335-1350
Emp Here 60   *Sales* 11,525,100
SIC 3494 Valves and pipe fittings, nec
John Wordsworth

D-U-N-S 20-343-7058   (SL)
TECH-CON AUTOMATION ULC
SHAPE PROCESS AUTOMATION
(*Suby of* SHAPE TECHNOLOGIES GROUP PARENT HOLDINGS INC)
1219 Corporate Dr, Burlington, ON, L7L 5V5
(905) 639-4989
Emp Here 84   *Sales* 18,648,084
SIC 3599 Industrial machinery, nec
Nino Laduca
Steven Harris

D-U-N-S 24-815-9725   (HQ)
TELECOM COMPUTER INC
5245 Harvester Rd, Burlington, ON, L7L 5L4
(905) 333-9621
Sales 26,830,440
SIC 5045 Computers, peripherals, and software
Phil Davidson

D-U-N-S 25-344-4939   (SL)
TEMPEL CANADA COMPANY
(*Suby of* TEMPEL HOLDINGS, INC.)
5045 North Service Rd, Burlington, ON, L7L 5H6
(905) 335-2530
Emp Here 380   *Sales* 92,427,780
SIC 3469 Metal stampings, nec
Vincent Buonanno
Cliff Nastas

D-U-N-S 20-375-0948   (HQ)
TERRAPURE ENVIRONMENTAL LTD
(*Suby of* REVOLUTION ENVIRONMENTAL SOLUTIONS LP)
1100 Burloak Dr Suite 500, Burlington, ON, L7L 6B2
(800) 263-8602
Sales 651,444,000
SIC 4959 Sanitary services, nec
Todd Moser

D-U-N-S 24-340-4790   (SL)
THAMES RIVER CHEMICAL CORP
5230 Harvester Rd, Burlington, ON, L7L 4X4
(905) 681-5353
Emp Here 43   *Sales* 31,404,835
SIC 5169 Chemicals and allied products, nec
Daniel Wiggins
Ann Wiggins

D-U-N-S 24-577-5465   (HQ)
THERMO CRS LTD
THERMO FISHER SCIENTIFIC
(*Suby of* THERMO FISHER SCIENTIFIC INC.)
5250 Mainway, Burlington, ON, L7L 5Z1
(905) 332-2000
Sales 11,190,360
SIC 8742 Management consulting services
Marc N Casper
Hansjoerg Haas

D-U-N-S 20-397-9927   (SL)
THI CANADA INC
BACKRACK
(*Suby of* TRUCK HOLDINGS INC.)
5230 Harvester Rd Unit 3, Burlington, ON, L7L

4X4
(905) 849-3633
Emp Here 50   *Sales* 10,141,500
SIC 3465 Automotive stampings
William Reminder
Michael Cunningham

D-U-N-S 24-367-3493   (SL)
THOMSON METALS AND DISPOSAL LP
(*Suby of* TUCKAMORE CAPITAL)
961 Zelco Dr, Burlington, ON, L7L 4Y2
(905) 681-8832
Emp Here 50   *Sales* 12,856,550
SIC 4953 Refuse systems
Jay Berman
Robin Gresham

D-U-N-S 25-366-8834   (SL)
THOMSON, G. CAPITAL LIMITED
961 Zelco Dr, Burlington, ON, L7L 4Y2
(905) 681-8832
Emp Here 63   *Sales* 16,477,839
SIC 6712 Bank holding companies
Gary W Thomson

D-U-N-S 25-144-9427   (HQ)
TWD TECHNOLOGIES LTD
905 Century Dr, Burlington, ON, L7L 5J8
(905) 634-3324
Sales 15,836,220
SIC 8711 Engineering services
Milton Tsiapalis
Scott Wilson

D-U-N-S 25-997-5225   (SL)
UMICORE AUTOCAT CANADA CORP
(*Suby of* UMICORE)
4261 Mainway, Burlington, ON, L7L 5N9
(905) 336-3424
Emp Here 130   *Sales* 36,922,730
SIC 2819 Industrial inorganic chemicals, nec
Bill Powell
Bazil Cheeseman

D-U-N-S 24-201-4293   (BR)
UPS SCS INC
UPS SCS, INC
(*Suby of* UNITED PARCEL SERVICE, INC.)
4156 Mainway, Burlington, ON, L7L 0A7
(905) 315-5500
Emp Here 600
SIC 4731 Freight transportation arrangement
Reg Sheen

D-U-N-S 25-530-4925   (HQ)
UPS SCS INC
UPS SUPPLY CHAIN SOLUTION
(*Suby of* UNITED PARCEL SERVICE, INC.)
4156 Mainway, Burlington, ON, L7L 0A7
(905) 315-5500
Emp Here 300   *Sales* 368,762,000
SIC 4212 Local trucking, without storage
William Hook
Reg Sheen
Brad Mitchell

D-U-N-S 20-134-1617   (HQ)
VAC AERO INTERNATIONAL INC
5420 North Service Rd Suite 205, Burlington, ON, L7L 6C7
(905) 827-4171
Emp Here 50   *Sales* 35,390,502
SIC 3567 Industrial furnaces and ovens
Jeffrey Pritchard
Mike Favalaro
Scot Rush
Louis Gosselin
William H. Reil
Ross Pritchard

D-U-N-S 24-130-8472   (HQ)
VICWEST INC
VICWEST BUILDING PRODUCTS
200-5050 South Service Rd, Burlington, ON, L7L 5Y7
(905) 825-2252
Emp Here 50   *Sales* 98,751,786

SIC 3444 Sheet Metalwork
Paul Lobb
Ronan Dowling
Jason Fortuna
Russell Shiels

D-U-N-S 20-703-2736   (BR)
VOESTALPINE ROTEC SUMMO CORP
SUMMO MANUFACTURING, DIV OF
(*Suby of* VOESTALPINE AG)
1200 Burloak Dr, Burlington, ON, L7L 6B4
(905) 336-0014
Emp Here 160
SIC 5051 Metals service centers and offices
Kevork Sevadjian

D-U-N-S 24-213-0839   (HQ)
VOESTALPINE ROTEC SUMMO CORP
(*Suby of* VOESTALPINE AG)
4041 North Service Rd, Burlington, ON, L7L 4X6
(905) 336-0014
Sales 26,861,160
SIC 3714 Motor vehicle parts and accessories
Kevork Sevadjian

D-U-N-S 20-039-3239   (SL)
VOORTMAN COOKIES LIMITED
4475 North Service Rd Suite 600, Burlington, ON, L7L 4X7
(905) 335-9500
Emp Here 450   *Sales* 219,323,250
SIC 2052 Cookies and crackers
Douglas Macfarland

D-U-N-S 20-182-9447   (HQ)
WATTS   WATER   TECHNOLOGIES (CANADA) INC
(*Suby of* WATTS WATER TECHNOLOGIES, INC.)
5435 North Service Rd, Burlington, ON, L7L 5H7
(905) 332-4090
Emp Here 130   *Sales* 72,671,770
SIC 5085 Industrial supplies
Daniel Bowes

D-U-N-S 20-921-7368   (HQ)
WAXMAN INDUSTRIAL SERVICES CORP
4350 Harvester Rd, Burlington, ON, L7L 5S4
(905) 639-1111
Emp Here 30   *Sales* 20,821,680
SIC 5093 Scrap and waste materials
Aaron D Waxman
Jeremy Waxman

D-U-N-S 20-134-3118   (SL)
WIDEX CANADA LTD
(*Suby of* AURIS LUXEMBOURG I)
5041 Mainway Suite 1, Burlington, ON, L7L 5H9
(905) 315-8303
Emp Here 65   *Sales* 14,773,785
SIC 3842 Surgical appliances and supplies
Jake Haycock
Anders Westermann
Tom Westermann

D-U-N-S 20-879-9143   (HQ)
WILLARD MANUFACTURING INC
5295 John Lucas Dr Suite 1, Burlington, ON, L7L 6A8
(905) 633-6905
Emp Here 25   *Sales* 13,833,000
SIC 2844 Toilet preparations
Jeremy Willard

D-U-N-S 24-857-2013   (SL)
ZETON INC
(*Suby of* ZETON INTERNATIONAL INC)
740 Oval Crt, Burlington, ON, L7L 6A9
(905) 632-3123
Emp Here 130   *Sales* 28,860,130
SIC 3569 General industrial machinery, nec
David Beckman

D-U-N-S 24-632-2804   (HQ)
ZETON INTERNATIONAL INC

740 Oval Crt, Burlington, ON, L7L 6A9
(905) 632-3123
Sales 10,462,120
SIC 6712 Bank holding companies
Archie Bennett
David Beckman

D-U-N-S 24-425-2821　　(SL)
ZIP SIGNS LTD
5040 North Service Rd, Burlington, ON, L7L 5R5
(905) 332-8332
Emp Here 80　　*Sales* 26,090,880
SIC 3993 Signs and advertising specialties
Alfred Bennink

D-U-N-S 24-746-6084　　(SL)
ZOOK CANADA INC
4400 South Service Rd, Burlington, ON, L7L 5R8
(905) 681-2885
Emp Here 47　　*Sales* 13,003,020
SIC 2892 Explosives
Scott Muddiman

Burlington, ON L7M

D-U-N-S 20-560-1128　　(SL)
1540886 ONTARIO INC
ZARKY'S FINE FOODS
(*Suby of* ZARCONE HOLDINGS LIMITED)
2180 Itabashi Way Suite 1a, Burlington, ON, L7M 5A5
(905) 319-7272
Emp Here 200　　*Sales* 58,695,400
SIC 5411 Grocery stores
Anthony Zarcone

D-U-N-S 24-816-2364　　(SL)
602667 ONTARIO LTD
BOS. & CO.
4551 Palladium Way, Burlington, ON, L7M 0W9
(905) 335-9951
Emp Here 30　　*Sales* 14,949,660
SIC 5139 Footwear
Jim Bosco

D-U-N-S 25-249-5072　　(SL)
APEX RESULTS REALTY INC
SUTTON GROUP
2465 Walker'S Line, Burlington, ON, L7M 4K4
(905) 332-4111
Emp Here 72　　*Sales* 19,566,432
SIC 6531 Real estate agents and managers
Wim Van De Vrande
Robert (Bob) Van De Vrande

D-U-N-S 25-157-9546　　(SL)
BRULE FOODS LTD
TIM HORTONS
4000 Mainway Suite 3, Burlington, ON, L7M 4B9
(905) 319-2663
Emp Here 43　　*Sales* 11,788,536
SIC 5461 Retail bakeries
Arch Jollymore

D-U-N-S 24-223-2254　　(SL)
BURLOAK TOOL & DIE LTD
3121 Mainway, Burlington, ON, L7M 1A4
(905) 331-6838
Emp Here 65　　*Sales* 11,437,270
SIC 8711 Engineering services
Les Rackham
Arnold Rackham

D-U-N-S 25-193-4758　　(SL)
CB INDUSTRIAL PART NETWORK
2100 Clipper Cres, Burlington, ON, L7M 2P5
(905) 639-1907
Emp Here 49　　*Sales* 23,276,274
SIC 5084 Industrial machinery and equipment
Roland Bissoon

D-U-N-S 24-790-6428　　(BR)
CENTRAL WEST SPECIALIZED DEVELOP-MENTAL SERVICES
STAR LANE
(*Suby of* CENTRAL WEST SPECIALIZED DEVELOPMENTAL SERVICES)
3782 Star Lane, Burlington, ON, L7M 5A0
(905) 336-4248
Emp Here 250
SIC 8322 Individual and family services
Kelly Kocken

D-U-N-S 25-487-8069　　(SL)
COMMUNITY LIVING BURLINGTON
ARC INDUSTRIES
3057 Mainway, Burlington, ON, L7M 1A1
(905) 335-6711
Emp Here 150　　*Sales* 11,518,300
SIC 8322 Individual and family services
Judy Pryde

D-U-N-S 24-763-5407　　(SL)
ECOSYNTHETIX INC
3365 Mainway Suite 1, Burlington, ON, L7M 1A6
(905) 335-5669
Emp Here 40　　*Sales* 22,799,329
SIC 2822 Synthetic rubber
Jeff Macdonald
Robert Haire
Ted Van Egdóm
Ralph De Jong
Paul Lucas
Susan Allen
Martin Hubbes
Jeffrey Nodland

D-U-N-S 20-774-4640　　(HQ)
EII LIMITED
GO RESILIENT CANADA
(*Suby of* ENTERPRISES INTERNATIONAL INC)
1124 Northside Rd, Burlington, ON, L7M 1H4
(905) 635-3111
Emp Here 16　　*Sales* 26,830,440
SIC 5051 Metals service centers and offices
David Lamb

D-U-N-S 25-105-1025　　(SL)
ENVIRO MUSHROOM FARM INC
5200 Britannia Rd, Burlington, ON, L7M 0S3
(905) 331-8030
Emp Here 44　　*Sales* 15,068,548
SIC 0182 Food crops grown under cover
Yun Joon (Ben) Park

D-U-N-S 24-721-1527　　(BR)
FIRSTCANADA ULC
BURLINGTON LAIDLAW
(*Suby of* FIRSTGROUP PLC)
5401 Dundas St, Burlington, ON, L7M 0Y8
(905) 335-7010
Emp Here 200
SIC 4151 School buses
Karen Omera

D-U-N-S 24-751-9812　　(BR)
GENERAL ELECTRIC CANADA COMPANY
GE ENERGY SERVICES
(*Suby of* GENERAL ELECTRIC COMPANY)
1150 Walker'S Line, Burlington, ON, L7M 1V2
(905) 335-6301
Emp Here 75
SIC 3625 Relays and industrial controls
John Moelker

D-U-N-S 20-025-2331　　(BR)
HALTON CATHOLIC DISTRICT SCHOOL BOARD
NOTRE DAME ROMAN CATHOLIC SEC-ONDARY SCHOOL
(*Suby of* HALTON CATHOLIC DISTRICT SCHOOL BOARD)
2333 Headon Forest Dr, Burlington, ON, L7M 3X6
(905) 335-1544
Emp Here 100

SIC 8211 Elementary and secondary schools
Tom Dunn

D-U-N-S 20-024-9907　　(BR)
HALTON DISTRICT SCHOOL BOARD
LESTER B PEARSON HIGH SCHOOL
(*Suby of* HALTON DISTRICT SCHOOL BOARD)
1433 Headon Rd, Burlington, ON, L7M 1V7
(905) 335-0961
Emp Here 80
SIC 8211 Elementary and secondary schools
Loraine Fedurco

D-U-N-S 25-974-2190　　(BR)
HALTON DISTRICT SCHOOL BOARD
ALTON VILLAGE PUBLIC SCHOOL
(*Suby of* HALTON DISTRICT SCHOOL BOARD)
3290 Steeplechase Dr, Burlington, ON, L7M 0W1
(905) 332-4206
Emp Here 90
SIC 8211 Elementary and secondary schools
David Purcell

D-U-N-S 25-483-8634　　(HQ)
HALTON RECYCLING LTD
EMTERRA ENVIRONMENTAL
1122 Pioneer Rd Suite 1, Burlington, ON, L7M 1K4
(905) 336-9084
Emp Here 160　　*Sales* 211,719,300
SIC 4953 Refuse systems
Emmie Leung

D-U-N-S 25-514-2937　　(BR)
HOME DEPOT OF CANADA INC
HOME DEPOT
(*Suby of* THE HOME DEPOT INC)
3050 Davidson Crt, Burlington, ON, L7M 4M9
(905) 331-1700
Emp Here 250
SIC 5211 Lumber and other building materials
Ted Flegg

D-U-N-S 25-246-5240　　(SL)
LANDMARK ONTARIO LTD
LANDMARK STRUCTURES COMPANY
3091 Harrison Crt, Burlington, ON, L7M 0W4
(905) 319-7700
Emp Here 55　　*Sales* 10,564,675
SIC 3443 Fabricated plate work (boiler shop)
Douglas Lamon

D-U-N-S 25-921-4328　　(BR)
LONGO BROTHERS FRUIT MARKETS INC
LONGO'S FRUIT MARKET
(*Suby of* LONGO BROTHERS FRUIT MAR-KETS INC)
2900 Walker'S Line, Burlington, ON, L7M 4M8
(905) 331-1645
Emp Here 150
SIC 5148 Fresh fruits and vegetables
Laurianne Correa

D-U-N-S 24-779-5792　　(SL)
MARCOR AUTOMOTIVE INC
1164 Walker'S Line, Burlington, ON, L7M 1V2
(905) 549-6445
Emp Here 50　　*Sales* 18,210,750
SIC 5013 Motor vehicle supplies and new parts
Dan Moscardini

D-U-N-S 25-220-6255　　(SL)
MATRIX NORTH AMERICAN CONSTRUC-TION LTD
MATRIX NAC
(*Suby of* MATRIX SERVICE COMPANY)
3196 Mainway Suite 1, Burlington, ON, L7M 1A5
(289) 313-1600
Emp Here 300　　*Sales* 98,434,500
SIC 1629 Heavy construction, nec
Terry Stewart

D-U-N-S 20-562-3890　　(SL)

MAUSER CANADA LTD
(*Suby of* STONE CANYON INDUSTRIES LLC)
1121 Pioneer Rd, Burlington, ON, L7M 1K5
(905) 332-4800
Emp Here 60　　*Sales* 11,525,100
SIC 3412 Metal barrels, drums, and pails
Ronald Litchkowski
Clemens Willee

D-U-N-S 20-039-1332　　(HQ)
NEELANDS GROUP LIMITED
4131 Palladium Way, Burlington, ON, L7M 0V9
(905) 332-4555
Sales 67,712,000
SIC 1711 Plumbing, heating, air-conditioning
Noel Neelands

D-U-N-S 24-211-8057　　(HQ)
NICHOLSON AND CATES LIMITED
WESONT LUMBER, DIV OF
3060 Mainway Suite 300, Burlington, ON, L7M 1A3
(905) 335-3366
Emp Here 20　　*Sales* 45,570,240
SIC 5031 Lumber, plywood, and millwork
James Livermore
Lammert Jagt
Peter Livermore
David Livermore
Ricker Mcquin

D-U-N-S 25-320-9274　　(BR)
PUROLATOR INC
PUROLATOR COURIER
(*Suby of* GOVERNMENT OF CANADA)
3455 Mainway, Burlington, ON, L7M 1A9
(905) 336-3230
Emp Here 140
SIC 4731 Freight transportation arrangement

D-U-N-S 24-350-2197　　(HQ)
S.B. SIMPSON HOLDINGS LIMITED
3210 Mainway, Burlington, ON, L7M 1A5
(905) 335-6575
Emp Here 3　　*Sales* 24,601,500
SIC 6712 Bank holding companies
Scott W Simpson
Michelle Simpson Olmstead
Diana Simpson

D-U-N-S 20-134-5402　　(SL)
SANDTRON AUTOMATION LIMITED
1221 Dillon Rd, Burlington, ON, L7M 1K6
(905) 827-8230
Emp Here 32　　*Sales* 14,309,568
SIC 5065 Electronic parts and equipment, nec
Robert Hooper

D-U-N-S 20-039-2348　　(HQ)
SIMPSON, S. B. GROUP INC
JACKSON ROBSON INDUSTRIAL SUPPLY
(*Suby of* S.B. SIMPSON HOLDINGS LIM-ITED)
3210 Mainway, Burlington, ON, L7M 1A5
(905) 335-6575
Emp Here 40　　*Sales* 26,765,200
SIC 5251 Hardware stores
Craig Simpson
Scott Simpson

D-U-N-S 24-923-6159　　(HQ)
THOMSON-GORDON GROUP INC
3225 Mainway, Burlington, ON, L7M 1A6
(905) 335-1440
Sales 34,168,750
SIC 6712 Bank holding companies
George Thomson

D-U-N-S 24-876-3336　　(SL)
THORDON BEARINGS INC
THORFLEX
(*Suby of* THOMSON-GORDON GROUP INC)
3225 Mainway, Burlington, ON, L7M 1A6
(905) 335-1440
Emp Here 110　　*Sales* 53,650,300
SIC 5085 Industrial supplies

▲ Public Company　　■ Public Company Family Member　　**HQ** Headquarters　　**BR** Branch　　**SL** Single Location

Terry Mcgowan
George Thomson

D-U-N-S 20-832-0015 (SL)
UTTER-MORRIS INSURANCE BROKERS LIMITED
3070 Mainway Unit 5, Burlington, ON, L7M 3X1
(905) 332-7877
Emp Here 20 *Sales* 11,598,480
SIC 6411 Insurance agents, brokers, and service
John Thorpe
Robert Thorpe

D-U-N-S 24-329-8671 (BR)
WAL-MART CANADA CORP
(*Suby of* WALMART INC.)
4515 Dundas St Suite 1, Burlington, ON, L7M 5B4
(905) 331-0027
Emp Here 200
SIC 5311 Department stores
Mario Pilozzi

D-U-N-S 24-101-6877 (SL)
WESTLAKE & ASSOCIATES HOLDINGS INC
1149 Northside Rd, Burlington, ON, L7M 1H5
(905) 336-5200
Emp Here 90 *Sales* 24,601,500
SIC 6712 Bank holding companies
Richard Westlake
Norman Harrison
Catherine Carlson
J Czarny
Nancy Tarzwell

D-U-N-S 25-977-2291 (HQ)
WILLIS SUPPLY COMPANY LIMITED, THE
1149 Pioneer Rd, Burlington, ON, L7M 1K5
(905) 639-8584
Sales 17,886,960
SIC 5039 Construction materials, nec
Michael Hetherman
Steve Jones

Burlington, ON L7N

D-U-N-S 20-355-3748 (SL)
1087338 ONTARIO LIMITED
TNG CANADA
3320 South Service Rd Suite 200, Burlington, ON, L7N 3M6
(905) 681-1113
Emp Here 200 *Sales* 50,698,000
SIC 8748 Business consulting, nec
Peter Olson

D-U-N-S 25-998-6156 (SL)
1343929 ONTARIO LIMITED
(*Suby of* MOOTER MEDIA LIMITED)
880 Laurentian Dr Suite 1, Burlington, ON, L7N 3V6
(905) 632-0864
Emp Here 84
SIC 7371 Custom computer programming services
Brian Currie
G Colin Rayner

D-U-N-S 20-935-2181 (SL)
1428427 ONTARIO LTD
WAGGWARE
3410 South Service Rd Suite 203, Burlington, ON, L7N 3T2
(905) 331-7207
Emp Here 70 *Sales* 10,485,790
SIC 7373 Computer integrated systems design
Gary Wagstaffe

D-U-N-S 20-401-0102 (SL)
1959197 ONTARIO INC
(*Suby of* DATA COMMUNICATIONS MAN-

AGEMENT CORP)
875 Laurentian Dr Suite 12, Burlington, ON, L7N 3W7
(905) 634-1900
Emp Here 100 *Sales* 16,402,700
SIC 2752 Commercial printing, lithographic
Ralph Misale
Grant Malcolm

D-U-N-S 20-151-7641 (BR)
ABB INC
(*Suby of* ABB LTD)
3450 Harvester Rd, Burlington, ON, L7N 3W5
(905) 639-8840
Emp Here 300
SIC 3823 Process control instruments
Guy Dionne

D-U-N-S 24-139-3156 (HQ)
ABELSOFT INC
3310 South Service Rd Suite 101, Burlington, ON, L7N 3M6
(905) 333-3200
Emp Here 60 *Sales* 10,638,660
SIC 7371 Custom computer programming services
Arun Rele
Bina Rele

D-U-N-S 25-182-5345 (SL)
ALTERNATE CHOICE INC
ALTERNATE CHOICING
3325 North Service Rd Unit 1, Burlington, ON, L7N 3G2
(905) 336-8818
Emp Here 28 *Sales* 14,247,968
SIC 5021 Furniture
Gary Kirkwood

D-U-N-S 25-965-0919 (BR)
BANK OF MONTREAL
BMO
(*Suby of* BANK OF MONTREAL)
865 Harrington Crt, Burlington, ON, L7N 3P3

Emp Here 77
SIC 6021 National commercial banks
Elizabeth Swick

D-U-N-S 24-714-3584 (BR)
BDO CANADA LIMITED
BDO DUNWOODY
(*Suby of* BDO CANADA LIMITED)
3115 Harvester Rd Suite 400, Burlington, ON, L7N 3N8
(905) 639-9500
Emp Here 100
SIC 8111 Legal services
Tony Tartaglia

D-U-N-S 25-922-2214 (BR)
BDO CANADA LLP
BURLINGTON ACCOUNTING
(*Suby of* BDO CANADA LLP)
3115 Harvester Rd Suite 400, Burlington, ON, L7N 3N8
(905) 639-9500
Emp Here 120
SIC 8721 Accounting, auditing, and book-keeping
Michael Banks

D-U-N-S 24-193-7408 (HQ)
BRANT TELEPHONE INC
BRANTTEL NETWORKS
3190 Harvester Rd Suite 101, Burlington, ON, L7N 3T1
(905) 632-2000
Emp Here 40 *Sales* 12,216,400
SIC 5999 Miscellaneous retail stores, nec
Paul Falco
David J Falco
Paul J Falco
Mark J Falco

D-U-N-S 20-755-5707 (HQ)
BUNZL CANADA INC
BUNZL DISTRIBUTION

(*Suby of* BUNZL PUBLIC LIMITED COMPANY)
3150 Harvester Rd Suite 100, Burlington, ON, L7N 3W8
(289) 289-1200
Emp Here 72 *Sales* 205,195,585
SIC 5113 Industrial and personal service paper
Patrick Larmon
Dan Deambrosio
John Howlett
Daniel Lett
Jim Mccool
Barry Hentz

D-U-N-S 25-185-3248 (SL)
BURLINGTON MAZDA
805 Walker'S Line, Burlington, ON, L7N 2G1
(905) 333-1790
Emp Here 30 *Sales* 14,942,340
SIC 5511 New and used car dealers
Scott Leggat

D-U-N-S 20-773-1303 (SL)
BURLINGTON MERCHANDISING & FIXTURES INC
BMF
3100 Harvester Rd Unit 8, Burlington, ON, L7N 3W8
(905) 332-6652
Emp Here 28 *Sales* 12,578,132
SIC 7389 Business services, nec
Robert Wilbrink

D-U-N-S 20-922-9111 (SL)
CEDAR SPRINGS TENNIS LIMITED
CEDAR SPRINGS HEALTH RACQUET & SPORTS CLUB
960 Cumberland Ave, Burlington, ON, L7N 3J6
(905) 632-9758
Emp Here 125 *Sales* 9,818,125
SIC 7997 Membership sports and recreation clubs
Jack Dennison

D-U-N-S 24-506-0322 (SL)
CELADON IMPORTS INC
CELADON
3345 North Service Rd Unit 107, Burlington, ON, L7N 3G2
(905) 335-6444
Emp Here 25 *Sales* 12,721,400
SIC 5023 Homefurnishings
Neil C Maclennan
John Tynan

D-U-N-S 24-413-0464 (SL)
COGENT POWER INC
(*Suby of* TATA STEEL LIMITED)
845 Laurentian Dr, Burlington, ON, L7N 3W7
(905) 637-3033
Emp Here 310 *Sales* 260,628,160
SIC 4911 Electric services
Ronald Harper
Matthew Stimac

D-U-N-S 24-585-8816 (BR)
COMMONWEALTH HOSPITALITY LTD
HOLIDAY INN
(*Suby of* WXI/WWH PARALLEL AMALCO (ONTARIO) LTD)
3063 South Service Rd, Burlington, ON, L7N 3E9
(905) 639-4443
Emp Here 200
SIC 7011 Hotels and motels
Gordon Langford

D-U-N-S 20-070-0073 (BR)
CORPORATION OF THE CITY OF BURLINGTON
CITY OF BURLINGTON ROAD & PARK MAINTENANCE
(*Suby of* CORPORATION OF THE CITY OF BURLINGTON)
3330 Harvester Rd, Burlington, ON, L7N 3M8

(905) 333-6166
Emp Here 90
SIC 7349 Building maintenance services, nec
Dave Hickerson

D-U-N-S 25-932-4564 (SL)
DUKE MARINE TECHNICAL SERVICES CANADA INC
3425 Harvester Rd Suite 213, Burlington, ON, L7N 3N1
(800) 252-6027
Emp Here 90 *Sales* 13,983,390
SIC 7361 Employment agencies
John Logue
Sonia Logue

D-U-N-S 24-802-4379 (SL)
ECS COFFEE INC
ECS VENDING
3100 Harvester Rd Unit 6, Burlington, ON, L7N 3W8
(905) 631-1524
Emp Here 60 *Sales* 17,608,620
SIC 5499 Miscellaneous food stores
Neil Madden

D-U-N-S 24-093-9975 (HQ)
EVONIK CANADA INC
EVONIK
(*Suby of* RAG-STIFTUNG)
3380 South Service Rd Suite 5, Burlington, ON, L7N 3J5
(905) 336-3423
Emp Here 13 *Sales* 184,569,710
SIC 5169 Chemicals and allied products, nec
Douglas Woods
Greg Mulligan
John Rolando
Soumendra Saharoy

D-U-N-S 25-990-9299 (HQ)
FENGATE PROPERTY MANAGEMENT LTD
(*Suby of* FENGATE CORPORATION)
3425 Harvester Rd Unit 105, Burlington, ON, L7N 3N1
(289) 288-3822
Sales 16,565,325
SIC 6512 Nonresidential building operators
Louis Serafini Jr
Louis Serafini Sr

D-U-N-S 24-978-3668 (SL)
FLEXTRONICS (CANADA) INC
(*Suby of* FLEX LTD.)
3430 South Service Rd Suite 101, Burlington, ON, L7N 3T9
(905) 592-1443
Emp Here 100 *Sales* 14,418,200
SIC 7371 Custom computer programming services
Michael Mcnamara
Yvan Girard
Paul Read
Scott Willcocks

D-U-N-S 24-920-0528 (HQ)
FORMING TECHNOLOGIES INCORPORATED
FTI
(*Suby of* HEXAGON AB)
3370 South Service Rd Suite 203, Burlington, ON, L7N 3M6
(905) 340-3370
Emp Here 55 *Sales* 11,679,290
SIC 7372 Prepackaged software
Medhat Karima
Kenneth Harbottle

D-U-N-S 20-250-5293 (HQ)
GLOBAL CITRUS GROUP, INC
3410 South Service Rd Suite G3, Burlington, ON, L7N 3T2
(289) 895-8302
Emp Here 5 *Sales* 19,086,875
SIC 0723 Crop preparation services for market
Hugh Bowman

D-U-N-S 24-940-2459   (SL)
GOLD LINE SOLUTIONS
3228 South Service Rd Suite 102, Burlington, ON, L7N 3H8
(905) 633-3835
Emp Here 49   *Sales* 10,454,542
SIC 8732 Commercial nonphysical research

D-U-N-S 20-364-1936   (HQ)
HITACHI CAPITAL CANADA CORP
(*Suby of* HITACHI, LTD.)
3390 South Service Rd Suite 301, Burlington, ON, L7N 3J5
(866) 241-9021
Sales 13,716,600
SIC 8741 Management services
Ryan Collison
Francois Nantel
Akihiko Sugawara

D-U-N-S 20-364-0248   (SL)
INNOMOTIVE SOLUTIONS GROUP INC
(*Suby of* WHITING GROUP OF CANADA INC)
3435 South Service Rd, Burlington, ON, L7N 3W6
(877) 845-3816
Emp Here 90   *Sales* 17,287,650
SIC 3442 Metal doors, sash, and trim
Bruce Whitehouse

D-U-N-S 20-201-8169   (SL)
ISOTOPE MUSIC INC
3375 North Service Rd Unit B9-B11, Burlington, ON, L7N 3G2
(905) 333-3001
Emp Here 30   *Sales* 15,162,040
SIC 7389 Business services, nec
Gerald Mcghee

D-U-N-S 20-373-1294   (SL)
M-HEALTH SOLUTIONS INC
3190 Harvester Rd Suite 203, Burlington, ON, L7N 3T1
(289) 636-0102
Emp Here 50   *Sales* 22,358,700
SIC 5047 Medical and hospital equipment
Sandra Schwenger
Monica Gray

D-U-N-S 25-650-7310   (SL)
M.C.P. MCCAUGHEY CONSUMER PRODUCTS MANAGEMENT INC
TRILOGY BRAND MANAGEMENT, DIV OF
3365 Harvester Rd Suite 204, Burlington, ON, L7N 3N2
(905) 319-2246
Emp Here 24   *Sales* 26,528,280
SIC 5122 Drugs, proprietaries, and sundries
Gregory Mccaughey
Robert Mccaughey
Richard Gazzola

D-U-N-S 25-373-6623   (SL)
MAINWAY HANDLING SYSTEMS INC
3345 North Service Rd Unit 101, Burlington, ON, L7N 3G2
(905) 335-0133
Emp Here 17   *Sales* 10,717,182
SIC 5084 Industrial machinery and equipment
Donald Mangham

D-U-N-S 24-896-3886   (BR)
METRO ONTARIO INC
METRO
(*Suby of* METRO INC)
3365 Fairview St, Burlington, ON, L7N 3N9
(905) 634-1896
Emp Here 160
SIC 5411 Grocery stores
Dave Dinning

D-U-N-S 20-939-4493   (HQ)
SHAKLEE CANADA INC
(*Suby of* SHAKLEE INTERNATIONAL, INC)
3100 Harvester Rd Unit 7, Burlington, ON, L7N 3W8

(905) 681-1422
Emp Here 25   *Sales* 30,949,660
SIC 5122 Drugs, proprietaries, and sundries
Christina Jablonski
Jodi Muraca

D-U-N-S 20-292-0109   (SL)
SITA INFORMATION NETWORKING COMPUTING CANADA INC
SITA AIRPORT AND DESKTOP SERVICES TORONTO
777 Walker'S Line, Burlington, ON, L7N 2G1
(905) 681-6200
Emp Here 2,000   *Sales* 288,364,000
SIC 7371 Custom computer programming services
Al Leroux
Ghasson Solomon

D-U-N-S 20-388-1743   (SL)
STILMAS AMERICAS INC
(*Suby of* RAG-STIFTUNG)
3250 Harvester Rd Unit 6, Burlington, ON, L7N 3W9
(905) 639-7025
Emp Here 34   *Sales* 11,371,530
SIC 3589 Service industry machinery, nec
Benjamin Roczniak
Luca Borella

D-U-N-S 20-584-7846   (HQ)
STITCH IT CANADA'S TAILOR INC
3221 North Service Rd Suite 101, Burlington, ON, L7N 3G2
(905) 335-0922
Emp Here 15   *Sales* 44,848,000
SIC 7219 Laundry and garment services, nec
Alain Baird
Jennifer Baird
Roy Ferrari

D-U-N-S 24-953-6350   (SL)
STORCHEM INC
855 Harrington Crt, Burlington, ON, L7N 3P3
(905) 639-9700
Emp Here 10   *Sales* 13,218,570
SIC 5169 Chemicals and allied products, nec
Vadym Korsh
Mark Korsh
Robert Gillies
Joe Jurcic
Edwin Van Der Wolf

D-U-N-S 20-039-1480   (HQ)
STRESS-CRETE LIMITED
840 Walker'S Line Suite 7, Burlington, ON, L7N 2G2
(905) 827-6901
Sales 13,441,425
SIC 3272 Concrete products, nec
Michael Schwenger
Greg Button
Garry Bradford

D-U-N-S 24-539-3822   (HQ)
SYLVITE AGRI-SERVICES LTD
SYLVITE TRANSPORTATION GROUP, DIV OF
(*Suby of* SYLVITE HOLDINGS INC)
3221 North Service Rd Suite 200, Burlington, ON, L7N 3G2
(519) 485-5770
Emp Here 40   *Sales* 58,915,900
SIC 5191 Farm supplies
Hugh Loomans
Cassandra Loomans
Bob Mcnaughton
Jim Thomson
Brad Culp
Stephane St-Jacques

D-U-N-S 20-115-3298   (HQ)
SYLVITE HOLDINGS INC
SYLVITE SALES, DIV OF
3221 North Service Rd Suite 200, Burlington, ON, L7N 3G2
(905) 331-8365
Sales 64,807,490

SIC 5191 Farm supplies
Hugh Loomans
Bob Mcnaughton
Brad Culp
Ted Heggart
Jim Thomson
Melanie Warr

D-U-N-S 20-339-2266   (SL)
TAGGEL AUTOMOBILE INC
BURLINGTON MAZDA
805 Walker'S Line, Burlington, ON, L7N 2G1
(905) 333-0595
Emp Here 40   *Sales* 15,896,560
SIC 8699 Membership organizations, nec
Scott Leggat

D-U-N-S 24-926-6388   (SL)
TAMARACK LUMBER INC
(*Suby of* ALPA LUMBER INC)
3255 Service Rd North, Burlington, ON, L7N 3G2
(905) 335-1115
Emp Here 150   *Sales* 42,157,500
SIC 5211 Lumber and other building materials
John Di Poce
Giovanni Guglietti
Carmen Guglietti
Donald Maciver

D-U-N-S 20-039-2751   (SL)
TERRACE FORD LINCOLN SALES INC
900 Walker'S Line, Burlington, ON, L7N 2G2
(905) 632-6252
Emp Here 60   *Sales* 37,756,800
SIC 5511 New and used car dealers
Rick Solwicki

D-U-N-S 24-680-7767   (BR)
TRANS UNION OF CANADA, INC
(*Suby of* TRANSUNION)
3115 Harvester Rd Suite 201, Burlington, ON, L7N 3N8
(800) 663-9980
Emp Here 160
SIC 7323 Credit reporting services
Cathy Wheat

D-U-N-S 24-893-6916   (HQ)
TRANS UNION OF CANADA, INC
(*Suby of* TRANSUNION)
3115 Harvester Rd Suite 201, Burlington, ON, L7N 3N8
(800) 663-9980
Emp Here 18   *Sales* 40,074,200
SIC 7323 Credit reporting services
Ken Porter
Karen Grant
Mark Merritt
Sharon Thompson
Derrick Breau
John Blenke
Todd Skinner

D-U-N-S 25-131-9760   (HQ)
TURTLE JACK'S RESTAURANT INC
3370 South Service Rd Suite 102, Burlington, ON, L7N 3M6
(905) 332-6833
Emp Here 32   *Sales* 46,639,000
SIC 5812 Eating places
Jim Lishman

D-U-N-S 25-311-9879   (SL)
UNIQUE CHRYSLER DODGE JEEP LTD
CHRYSLER DODGE JEEP
915 Walker'S Line, Burlington, ON, L7N 3V8
(905) 631-8100
Emp Here 40   *Sales* 19,923,120
SIC 5511 New and used car dealers
John A Calder
Richard Paletta

D-U-N-S 20-641-6273   (SL)
UNIQUE MOTORS LTD
UNIQUE CHRYSLER
915 Walker'S Line, Burlington, ON, L7N 3V8

(905) 631-8100
Emp Here 43   *Sales* 21,417,354
SIC 5511 New and used car dealers
John A (Sandy) Calder
Paula A Roe
Patrick Hart

D-U-N-S 20-626-0069   (SL)
WHITING DOOR MANUFACTURING LIMITED
(*Suby of* WHITING GROUP OF CANADA INC)
3435 South Service Rd, Burlington, ON, L7N 3W6
(905) 333-6745
Emp Here 52   *Sales* 13,917,904
SIC 5211 Lumber and other building materials
Bruce Whitehouse
Ravi Tyrronne

D-U-N-S 24-390-4989   (HQ)
WHITING GROUP OF CANADA INC
3435 South Service Rd, Burlington, ON, L7N 3W6
(905) 333-6745
Sales 11,140,930
SIC 3442 Metal doors, sash, and trim
Bruce Whitehouse
Ravi Tyronne

D-U-N-S 25-195-3881   (HQ)
WOLSELEY CANADA INC
CRONKITE, DIV OF
(*Suby of* FERGUSON PLC)
880 Laurentian Dr Suite 1, Burlington, ON, L7N 3V6
(905) 335-7373
Emp Here 200   *Sales* 1,242,118,800
SIC 5074 Plumbing and heating equipment and supplies (hydronics)
Simon Oakland
Kevin Fancey
Peter Jirasek

D-U-N-S 20-010-7261   (HQ)
WOLSELEY HOLDINGS CANADA INC
(*Suby of* FERGUSON PLC)
880 Laurentian Dr Suite 1, Burlington, ON, L7N 3V6
(905) 335-7373
Emp Here 8   *Sales* 917,793,099
SIC 6712 Bank holding companies
Simon Oakland
Kevin Fancey
Peter Jirasek

D-U-N-S 20-301-8239   (BR)
WOOD CANADA LIMITED
AMEC FOSTER WHEELER
(*Suby of* JOHN WOOD GROUP P.L.C.)
3215 North Service Rd, Burlington, ON, L7N 3G2
(905) 335-2353
Emp Here 85
SIC 8711 Engineering services
Ben Hunter

Burlington, ON L7P

D-U-N-S 20-639-5410   (SL)
1028918 ONTARIO INC
BURLINGTON TOYOTA
1249 Guelph Line, Burlington, ON, L7P 2T1
(905) 335-0223
Emp Here 60   *Sales* 37,756,800
SIC 5511 New and used car dealers
Rosemond Scherle
David Scherle

D-U-N-S 25-497-2730   (HQ)
1126194 ONTARIO LIMITED
PETRO CANADA
1150 Guelph Line, Burlington, ON, L7P 2S8
(905) 335-5595
Emp Here 5   *Sales* 37,127,520

SIC 5541 Gasoline service stations
Joseph Kendrick

D-U-N-S 25-250-5656   (HQ)
AIC GLOBAL HOLDINGS INC
1375 Kerns Rd Suite 100, Burlington, ON, L7P 4V7
(905) 331-4242
Emp Here 50   *Sales* 13,077,650
SIC 6712 Bank holding companies
Michael Lee-Chin

D-U-N-S 24-130-2988   (SL)
AIC RSP AMERICAN FOCUSED FUND
PORTLAND INVESTMENT COUNCIL
1375 Kerns Rd Suite 100, Burlington, ON, L7P 4V7
(905) 331-4250
Emp Here 49   *Sales* 41,243,261
SIC 6722 Management investment, open-end
James Cole

D-U-N-S 20-055-3725   (HQ)
ALBERICI CONSTRUCTORS, LTD
(*Suby of* ALBERICI CORPORATION)
1005 Skyview Dr Suite 300, Burlington, ON, L7P 5B1
(905) 315-3000
Emp Here 53   *Sales* 30,798,252
SIC 1542 Nonresidential construction, nec
Greg Brokenshire
John Alberici
Sherman Ladner

D-U-N-S 20-406-2715   (SL)
ALDERSHOT LANDSCAPE CONTRACTORS LP
166 Flatt Rd, Burlington, ON, L7P 0T3
(905) 689-7321
Emp Here 180   *Sales* 24,908,416
SIC 0781 Landscape counseling and planning
William De Luca
Jason Spence
Renato Campagnolo
Mike Peister
Ian Souper
Justin Deluca

D-U-N-S 25-371-6468   (BR)
BEST BUY CANADA LTD
BEST BUY
(*Suby of* BEST BUY CO., INC.)
1200 Brant St Unit 1, Burlington, ON, L7P 5C6
(905) 332-4758
Emp Here 100
SIC 5731 Radio, television, and electronic stores

D-U-N-S 25-459-4302   (SL)
CAMA WOODLANDS NURSING HOME
159 Panin Rd, Burlington, ON, L7P 5A6
(905) 681-6441
Emp Here 80   *Sales* 5,485,280
SIC 8051 Skilled nursing care facilities
Arlene Lawlor
Ron Bonar
John Peneycad

D-U-N-S 24-566-0394   (BR)
CANADIAN REFORMED SOCIETY FOR A HOME FOR THE AGED INC
MOUNT NEMO CHRISTIAN NURSING HOME
4486 Guelph Line, Burlington, ON, L7P 0N2
(905) 335-3636
Emp Here 75
SIC 8051 Skilled nursing care facilities
Lynette Royepper

D-U-N-S 20-519-0270   (BR)
COSTCO WHOLESALE CANADA LTD
(*Suby of* COSTCO WHOLESALE CORPORATION)
1225 Brant St, Burlington, ON, L7P 1X7
(905) 336-6714
Emp Here 168
SIC 5099 Durable goods, nec

D-U-N-S 25-301-4021   (BR)
DELOITTE LLP
(*Suby of* DELOITTE LLP)
1005 Skyview Dr Suite 202, Burlington, ON, L7P 5B1
(905) 315-6770
Emp Here 100
SIC 8721 Accounting, auditing, and bookkeeping
Steve Irvine

D-U-N-S 25-220-5836   (HQ)
GYPSUM TECHNOLOGIES INC
GYPTECH
578 King Forest Crt, Burlington, ON, L7P 5C1
(905) 567-2000
Emp Here 80   *Sales* 33,300,150
SIC 3599 Industrial machinery, nec
Gary Murray
Jeremy Mckellar

D-U-N-S 20-229-8670   (BR)
HALTON DISTRICT SCHOOL BOARD
M.M. ROBINSON HIGH SCHOOL
(*Suby of* HALTON DISTRICT SCHOOL BOARD)
2425 Upper Middle Rd, Burlington, ON, L7P 3N9
(905) 335-5588
Emp Here 80
SIC 8211 Elementary and secondary schools
Claire Proteau

D-U-N-S 20-913-6881   (BR)
HALTON DISTRICT SCHOOL BOARD
CLARKSDALE PUBLIC SCHOOL
(*Suby of* HALTON DISTRICT SCHOOL BOARD)
2399 Mountainside Dr, Burlington, ON, L7P 1C6
(905) 335-5605
Emp Here 84
SIC 8211 Elementary and secondary schools
Janet Reesor

D-U-N-S 20-976-3853   (HQ)
HALTON DISTRICT SCHOOL BOARD
2050 Guelph Line, Burlington, ON, L7P 5A8
(905) 335-3663
Emp Here 4,000   *Sales* 415,308,610
SIC 8211 Elementary and secondary schools
Kelly Amos
Kim Graves
Stuart Miller

D-U-N-S 20-113-8017   (HQ)
INSIDEOUT BURLINGTON LTD
1515 North Service Rd, Burlington, ON, L7P 0A2
(905) 681-7173
Emp Here 10   *Sales* 11,517,000
SIC 5712 Furniture stores
Mildred Rymaszewski
Grzegorz Rymaszewksi

D-U-N-S 20-054-1308   (SL)
IPPOLITO FRUIT AND PRODUCE LIMITED
201 North Service Rd, Burlington, ON, L7P 5C4
(905) 631-7700
Emp Here 75   *Sales* 62,668,275
SIC 5148 Fresh fruits and vegetables
David Ippolito
Joel Ippolito

D-U-N-S 24-421-5294   (HQ)
IPPOLITO GROUP INC, THE
201 North Service Rd, Burlington, ON, L7P 5C4
(905) 639-1174
Emp Here 1   *Sales* 27,335,000
SIC 6712 Bank holding companies
Joel Ippolito

D-U-N-S 20-690-1733   (HQ)
IPPOLITO TRANSPORTATION INC
(*Suby of* IPPOLITO GROUP INC, THE)
201 North Service Rd Suite 1, Burlington, ON,
L7P 5C4
(905) 639-7700
Sales 20,570,600
SIC 4213 Trucking, except local
Joel Ippolito
David Ippolito

D-U-N-S 20-107-2084   (SL)
JAN KELLEY MARKETING
1005 Skyview Dr Suite 322, Burlington, ON, L7P 5B1
(905) 631-7934
Emp Here 60   *Sales* 13,708,320
SIC 4899 Communication services, nec

D-U-N-S 24-407-9307   (HQ)
NELSON AGGREGATE CO
2433 No 2 Side Rd, Burlington, ON, L7P 0G8
(905) 335-5250
Emp Here 45   *Sales* 17,507,625
SIC 1442 Construction sand and gravel
Quinn Moyer
Bruce Hustins

D-U-N-S 20-450-7615   (SL)
PIPETEK INFRASTRUCTURE SERVICES INC
2250 Industrial St, Burlington, ON, L7P 1A1
(905) 319-0500
Emp Here 50   *Sales* 22,174,500
SIC 7389 Business services, nec
Robert Lodge
Louise Lodge

D-U-N-S 24-767-0776   (SL)
PORTLAND INVESTMENT COUNSEL INC
(*Suby of* AIC GLOBAL HOLDINGS INC)
1375 Kerns Rd Suite 100, Burlington, ON, L7P 4V7
(905) 331-4242
Emp Here 55   *Sales* 51,654,735
SIC 6282 Investment advice
Michael Lee-Chin

D-U-N-S 24-796-7198   (SL)
QUANTUM AUTOMOTIVE GROUP INCORPORATED
MERCEDES-BENZ BURLINGTON
441 North Service Rd, Burlington, ON, L7P 0A3
(905) 632-4222
Emp Here 150   *Sales* 94,392,000
SIC 5511 New and used car dealers
Ken Szekely

D-U-N-S 24-610-4590   (SL)
REISER (CANADA) CO.
REISER CANADA
(*Suby of* ROBERT REISER & CO., INC.)
1549 Yorkton Crt Unit 4, Burlington, ON, L7P 5B7
(905) 631-6611
Emp Here 25   *Sales* 11,875,650
SIC 5084 Industrial machinery and equipment
Peter Taylor

D-U-N-S 20-039-1969   (SL)
RICE TOOL & MANUFACTURING INC
2247 Harold Rd, Burlington, ON, L7P 2J7
(905) 335-0181
Emp Here 50   *Sales* 16,666,650
SIC 1541 Industrial buildings and warehouses
Neil Teange
Ted Rosts

D-U-N-S 20-039-2587   (SL)
SUNSHINE BUILDING MAINTENANCE INC
2500 Industrial St, Burlington, ON, L7P 1A5
(905) 335-2020
Emp Here 100   *Sales* 4,020,900
SIC 7349 Building maintenance services, nec
John Brouwers
Ted Brouwers

D-U-N-S 25-353-0414   (SL)
WESCAM INC.
L-3 TECHNOLOGIES
(*Suby of* L3HARRIS TECHNOLOGIES, INC.)
649 North Service Rd, Burlington, ON, L7P 5B9
(905) 633-4000
Emp Here 600   *Sales* 169,749,000
SIC 3663 Radio and t.v. communications equipment
Matt Richi
Bruce Latimer
Pat Mckay

D-U-N-S 25-282-8942   (HQ)
WOODVIEW CHILDREN'S CENTRE
69 Flatt Rd, Burlington, ON, L7P 0T3
(905) 689-4727
Emp Here 1   *Sales* 12,218,800
SIC 8069 Specialty hospitals, except psychiatric
Cindy I'anson

Burlington, ON L7R

D-U-N-S 25-113-5232   (HQ)
226138 ONTARIO INC
HALTON HONDA
2300 Fairview St, Burlington, ON, L7R 2E4
(905) 681-2200
Sales 10,723,673
SIC 6712 Bank holding companies
John Bellm

D-U-N-S 20-649-7526   (SL)
2853167 CANADA INC
BURLINGTON HYUNDAI
2016 Plains Rd E, Burlington, ON, L7R 5B3
(905) 633-8811
Emp Here 25   *Sales* 12,451,950
SIC 5511 New and used car dealers
Vince Jones
Tony Lefebre

D-U-N-S 25-156-9364   (SL)
975445 ONTARIO INC
EMMA'S BACKPORCH
2084 Old Lakeshore Rd, Burlington, ON, L7R 1A3
(905) 634-2084
Emp Here 80   *Sales* 3,641,520
SIC 5812 Eating places
Craig Kowalchuk

D-U-N-S 25-095-0706   (SL)
A.S.P. INCORPORATED
ACCESS SECURITY PROFESSIONALS
460 Brant St Suite 212, Burlington, ON, L7R 4B6
(905) 333-4242
Emp Here 432   *Sales* 11,340,000
SIC 7381 Detective and armored car services
Dean Lovric
John Jacob Michalski
Tim Thomas

D-U-N-S 24-346-4315   (HQ)
ACTIVE ENERGY CORP
ACTIVE ENERGY
390 Brant St Suite 402, Burlington, ON, L7R 4J4
(416) 238-5540
Sales 46,222,600
SIC 4924 Natural gas distribution
John Klarer
Michael Stedman

D-U-N-S 20-790-2235   (SL)
BOB'S NO FRILLS
571 Brant St, Burlington, ON, L7R 2G6
(866) 987-6453
Emp Here 98   *Sales* 28,760,746
SIC 5411 Grocery stores
Robert Nedelko

D-U-N-S 20-038-7629   (SL)
BULL MOOSE TUBE LIMITED
2170 Queensway Dr, Burlington, ON, L7R 3T1

(905) 637-8261
Emp Here 60   *Sales* 14,006,100
SIC 3312 Blast furnaces and steel mills
 Suraj Paul

D-U-N-S 24-679-6481   (SL)
BURLINGTON BUSINESS FORMS INC
BURLINGTON BUISNESS FORMS
2289 Fairview St Unit 208, Burlington, ON,
L7R 2E3
(905) 632-4611
Emp Here 80   *Sales* 18,743,040
SIC 8743 Public relations services
 Rick Tonkovich
 Steve Hinrichs

D-U-N-S 25-841-9639   (HQ)
BURLINGTON HYDRO ELECTRIC INC
(*Suby of* CORPORATION OF THE CITY OF
BURLINGTON)
1340 Brant St, Burlington, ON, L7R 3Z7
(905) 332-1851
Emp Here 2   *Sales* 67,987,400
SIC 4911 Electric services
 David Collie
 Michael Kysley
 Richard Johnston
 Gord Forstner
 Archie Bennett
 Tim Dobbie
 Cam Jackson
 Gary Graham
 Michael Schwehger

D-U-N-S 24-215-6628   (SL)
BURLINGTON HYDRO INC
(*Suby of* CORPORATION OF THE CITY OF
BURLINGTON)
1340 Brant St, Burlington, ON, L7R 3Z7
(905) 332-1851
Emp Here 89   *Sales* 60,508,786
SIC 4911 Electric services
 Gerry Smallegange
 Gary D. Graham
 Cam Jackson
 Michael Schwenger
 Archie Bennett
 Roman Martiuk
 Phil Nanavati
 Darla Youldon

D-U-N-S 20-175-4350   (HQ)
COURT GROUP OF COMPANIES LTD, THE
490 Elizabeth St, Burlington, ON, L7R 2M2
(905) 333-5002
Emp Here 6   *Sales* 43,736,000
SIC 6712 Bank holding companies
 Bill Court

D-U-N-S 20-881-5472   (HQ)
**CROSSROADS CHRISTIAN COMMUNICA-
TIONS INCORPORATED**
CROSSROADS FAMILY OF MINISTRIES
1295 North Service Rd, Burlington, ON, L7R
4M2
(905) 845-5100
Emp Here 95   *Sales* 29,701,360
SIC 4833 Television broadcasting stations
 Ron Mainse
 Byron Winsor
 Diane Seymour

D-U-N-S 24-659-4907   (SL)
CUMIS GENERAL INSURANCE COMPANY
(*Suby of* CUMIS GROUP LIMITED, THE)
151 North Service Rd, Burlington, ON, L7R
4C2
(905) 632-1221
Emp Here 90   *Sales* 111,187,620
SIC 6331 Fire, marine, and casualty insurance
 Kathy Bardswick
 Kevin Daniel

D-U-N-S 24-925-3410   (HQ)
CUMIS GROUP LIMITED, THE
151 North Service Rd, Burlington, ON, L7R
4C2

(800) 263-9120
Emp Here 300   *Sales* 1,068,484,000
SIC 6311 Life insurance
 Kenneth W. Lalonde
 Ken Bolton
 Craig Marshall
 Russ Fast
 Scott Kennedy

D-U-N-S 24-058-7170   (HQ)
CUMIS LIFE INSURANCE COMPANY
(*Suby of* CUMIS GROUP LIMITED, THE)
151 North Service Rd, Burlington, ON, L7R
4C2
(905) 632-1221
Emp Here 100   *Sales* 320,545,200
SIC 6311 Life insurance
 Kevin Daniel
 Alexandra Wilson
 Bill Kiss
 Rob Wesseling
 Gilles Colbert
 John Harvie
 Jim Laverick
 Reba Plummer
 Phil Baudin
 Hazel Corcoran

D-U-N-S 24-665-7097   (HQ)
DAIRY QUEEN CANADA INC
I D Q
1111 International Blvd, Burlington, ON, L7R
3Y3
(905) 639-1492
Emp Here 10   *Sales* 48,244,000
SIC 8742 Management consulting services
 Jean Champagne
 Mark Vinton
 Peter White
 Shelly O'callaghan
 Troy Bader

D-U-N-S 25-172-8200   (SL)
**DISCOVERY FORD SALES BURLINGTON
LIMITED**
850 Brant St, Burlington, ON, L7R 2J5
(905) 632-8696
Emp Here 100   *Sales* 62,928,000
SIC 5511 New and used car dealers
 Allan Pearson

D-U-N-S 20-248-9407   (SL)
ELTHERM CANADA INC
(*Suby of* INDUS HOLDING AG)
1440 Grahams Ln Unit 5, Burlington, ON, L7R
2J2
(289) 812-6631
Emp Here 51   *Sales* 11,322,051
SIC 3567 Industrial furnaces and ovens
 Daniel Potter

D-U-N-S 24-822-5604   (SL)
GREAT WEST LIFE ASSURANCE
360 Torrance St, Burlington, ON, L7R 2R9
(905) 637-6561
Emp Here 26   *Sales* 26,906,906
SIC 6311 Life insurance
 Allen Loney

D-U-N-S 24-285-4990   (HQ)
**HALTON CATHOLIC DISTRICT SCHOOL
BOARD**
802 Drury Lane, Burlington, ON, L7R 2Y2
(905) 632-6300
Emp Here 120   *Sales* 306,522,596
SIC 8211 Elementary and secondary schools
 Diane Rabenda
 Paul Marai
 Arlene Iantomasi
 Jane Michael
 Susan Trites
 John Mark Rowe
 Anthony Danko
 Helena Karabela
 Anthony Quinn

D-U-N-S 20-714-7294   (SL)
HAMILTON NIAGARA HALDIMAND BRANT

COMMUNITY CARE ACCESS CENTRE
HNHB CCAC
440 Elizabeth St, Burlington, ON, L7R 2M1
(905) 639-5228
Emp Here 100   *Sales* 6,856,600
SIC 8059 Nursing and personal care, nec
 Carmen Harby

D-U-N-S 24-302-3223   (HQ)
HOOD PACKAGING CORPORATION
(*Suby of* HOOD FLEXIBLE PACKAGING
CORPORATION)
2380 Mcdowell Rd, Burlington, ON, L7R 4A1
(905) 637-5611
Emp Here 25   *Sales* 698,510,300
SIC 2674 Bags: uncoated paper and multiwall
 Warren A. Hood Jr
 Robert Morris
 Todd D.G. Eby
 John Johnson
 John A. Burnam

D-U-N-S 24-909-5936   (BR)
HUDSON'S BAY COMPANY
BAY, THE
(*Suby of* HUDSON'S BAY COMPANY)
777 Guelph Line Unit 8, Burlington, ON, L7R
3N2
(905) 634-8866
Emp Here 180
SIC 5311 Department stores
 Malvina Shust

D-U-N-S 25-903-0443   (BR)
MCBURL CORP
MCDONALD'S RESTAURANTS
(*Suby of* MCBURL CORP)
689 Guelph Line, Burlington, ON, L7R 3M7
(905) 639-1661
Emp Here 75
SIC 5812 Eating places
 Dave Rogers

D-U-N-S 20-175-3360   (BR)
MERIDIAN BRICK CANADA LTD
CANADA BRICK, THE REAL MC COY
(*Suby of* MERIDIAN BRICK CANADA LTD)
5155 Dundas St Rr 1, Burlington, ON, L7R
3X4
(800) 263-6229
Emp Here 120
SIC 3251 Brick and structural clay tile
 Robert Campolo

D-U-N-S 25-098-8508   (HQ)
MERIDIAN BRICK CANADA LTD
5155 Dundas St W, Burlington, ON, L7R 3Y2
(905) 335-3401
Emp Here 43   *Sales* 53,765,700
SIC 3251 Brick and structural clay tile
 Alfred Borm
 Ros Ng
 Michael P. Kane
 Chris Wilbeck
 Chad Suss

D-U-N-S 20-104-0263   (BR)
NALCO CANADA CO.
(*Suby of* ECOLAB INC.)
1055 Truman St, Burlington, ON, L7R 3V7
(905) 632-8791
Emp Here 100
SIC 5074 Plumbing and heating equipment
and supplies (hydronics)
 Dave Gingrich

D-U-N-S 20-038-7124   (HQ)
NALCO CANADA CO.
COMPAGNIE NALCO CANADA
(*Suby of* ECOLAB INC.)
1055 Truman St, Burlington, ON, L7R 3V7
(905) 633-1000
Sales 137,839,950
SIC 2819 Industrial inorganic chemicals, nec
 Erik Fyrwald

D-U-N-S 20-394-0866   (SL)

OCP COMMUNICATIONS INC
DEPENDABLEHOMETECH
2319 Fairview St Unit 601, Burlington, ON,
L7R 2E3
(289) 337-5994
Emp Here 340   *Sales* 80,073,060
SIC 1731 Electrical work
 Catherine Lewis

D-U-N-S 25-976-8570   (SL)
**SECOND NATURE BATH AND BODY PROD-
UCTS INC**
385 Smith Ave, Burlington, ON, L7R 2T9

Emp Here 32   *Sales* 21,006,848
SIC 5963 Direct selling establishments
 Ellen Solondz
 Brian Mclaughlin

D-U-N-S 24-737-3327   (SL)
TRIUS AUTOMOBILE INC
ACURA ON BRANT
629 Brant St, Burlington, ON, L7R 2H1
(905) 333-4144
Emp Here 40   *Sales* 19,923,120
SIC 5511 New and used car dealers
 Brian Leggat
 Arnold Serzysko

D-U-N-S 24-374-3973   (BR)
WAL-MART CANADA CORP
WALMART SUPERCENTRE
(*Suby of* WALMART INC.)
2065 Fairview St, Burlington, ON, L7R 0B4
(905) 637-3100
Emp Here 200
SIC 5999 Miscellaneous retail stores, nec
 Paul Anthraper

D-U-N-S 24-828-0687   (BR)
**YMCA   OF   HAMIL-
TON/BURLINGTON/BRANTFORD**
RON EDWARDS FAMILY YMCA
(*Suby   of*   YMCA   OF   HAMIL-
TON/BURLINGTON/BRANTFORD)
500 Drury Lane, Burlington, ON, L7R 2X2
(905) 632-5000
Emp Here 500
SIC 7997 Membership sports and recreation
clubs
 Cindy Webster

Burlington, ON L7S

D-U-N-S 24-506-7012   (SL)
465439 ONTARIO INC
TAYLOR MOVING AND STORAGE
1200 Plains Rd E, Burlington, ON, L7S 1W6
(905) 632-8010
Emp Here 70   *Sales* 10,373,440
SIC 4214 Local trucking with storage
 Russ Taylor

D-U-N-S 24-831-0773   (SL)
882547 ONTARIO INC
MANDARIN RESTAURANT
1235 Fairview St Suite 1, Burlington, ON, L7S
2H9
(905) 632-6000
Emp Here 80   *Sales* 3,429,840
SIC 5812 Eating places
 Patrick Feng
 Johnnie Chau

D-U-N-S 24-665-2473   (SL)
DALLOV HOLDINGS LIMITED
MAPLE VILLA LONG TERM CARE CENTRE
441 Maple Ave, Burlington, ON, L7S 1L8
(905) 639-2264
Emp Here 105   *Sales* 7,199,430
SIC 8051 Skilled nursing care facilities
 Alfred Thibodeau

D-U-N-S 24-737-0315   (HQ)

ELLIOTT TURBOMACHINERY CANADA INC
(*Suby of* EBARA CORPORATION)
955 Maple Ave, Burlington, ON, L7S 2J4
(905) 333-4101
Emp Here 26   *Sales* 11,539,680
SIC 7699 Repair services, nec
Antonio Casillo
Ralph Dickie
Gregory M. Frenette
William Keith Cox
Charles T. Steinmetz
Eugene J. O'sullivan

D-U-N-S 20-357-9490   (HQ)
FREW ENERGY LIMITED
1380 Grahams Lane, Burlington, ON, L7S 1W3
(905) 637-0033
Sales 46,587,855
SIC 4925 Gas production and/or distribution
Mark Frew

D-U-N-S 20-038-9120   (HQ)
G. C. DUKE EQUIPMENT LTD
1184 Plains Rd E, Burlington, ON, L7S 1W6
(905) 637-5216
Sales 19,001,040
SIC 5083 Farm and garden machinery
Nolan Duke
Oleh R. Onufryk
Neil Beach

D-U-N-S 24-891-4033   (SL)
GLOBAL FUELS INC
1463 Ontario St Suite C, Burlington, ON, L7S 1G6
(289) 288-0433
Emp Here 10   *Sales* 10,328,080
SIC 5172 Petroleum products, nec
Daniel Poirier
Terry Simpson
Anthony Simanavicius
Christian Payette
Danny Maslen

D-U-N-S 20-789-5314   (BR)
HUDSON'S BAY COMPANY
(*Suby of* HUDSON'S BAY COMPANY)
900 Maple Ave, Burlington, ON, L7S 2J8
(905) 681-0030
Emp Here 100
SIC 5311 Department stores
Patrick Dickinson

D-U-N-S 24-888-9784   (SL)
IBRAHIM, YASSER PHARMACY LIMITED
SHOPPERS DRUG MART
900 Maple Ave Suite 747, Burlington, ON, L7S 2J8
(905) 681-1277
Emp Here 50   *Sales* 12,647,700
SIC 5912 Drug stores and proprietary stores
Yasser Ibrahim

D-U-N-S 25-295-2536   (SL)
IVANHOE CAMBRIDGE II INC.
MAPLEVIEW SHOPPING CENTRE
900 Maple Ave, Burlington, ON, L7S 2J8
(905) 681-2900
Emp Here 300   *Sales* 40,703,100
SIC 6512 Nonresidential building operators
Lescia Valentini

D-U-N-S 20-974-4168   (HQ)
JOSEPH BRANT HOSPITAL
1245 Lakeshore Rd, Burlington, ON, L7S 0A2
(905) 632-3730
Emp Here 1,380   *Sales* 10,846,667
SIC 8062 General medical and surgical hospitals
Eric J. Vandewall
Lana Lyons
Peter Vankessel
Susan Busby

D-U-N-S 24-720-6352   (BR)
LONGO BROTHERS FRUIT MARKETS INC

LONGO'S FRUIT MARKET
(*Suby of* LONGO BROTHERS FRUIT MARKETS INC)
1225 Fairview St, Burlington, ON, L7S 1Y3
(905) 637-3804
Emp Here 135
SIC 5431 Fruit and vegetable markets
Jason Poloniato

D-U-N-S 20-179-2343   (HQ)
NUCOR CANADA INC
(*Suby of* NUCOR CORPORATION)
1455 Lakeshore Rd Suite 204n, Burlington, ON, L7S 2J1
(905) 634-6868
Sales 78,347,700
SIC 5051 Metals service centers and offices
Orlando Tesolin
Rick Blume
Evan Rohr

D-U-N-S 20-039-2728   (SL)
TAYLOR MOVING & STORAGE LIMITED
TAYLOR INTERNATIONAL
1200 Plains Rd E, Burlington, ON, L7S 1W6
(905) 632-8010
Emp Here 70   *Sales* 10,373,440
SIC 4214 Local trucking with storage
Russell (Russ) Taylor
Richard (Rick) Taylor

Burlington, ON L7T

D-U-N-S 24-986-0974   (SL)
849432 ONTARIO LIMITED
TIM HORTONS
29 Plains Rd W Unit 1, Burlington, ON, L7T 1E8
(905) 634-2669
Emp Here 40   *Sales* 10,966,080
SIC 5461 Retail bakeries
Judy A Robins
P Kennedy Robins

D-U-N-S 20-716-8725   (HQ)
ALDERSHOT GREENHOUSES LIMITED
1135 Gallagher Rd, Burlington, ON, L7T 2M7
(905) 632-9272
Emp Here 55   *Sales* 17,747,625
SIC 0181 Ornamental nursery products
Leonard Vander Lugt

D-U-N-S 20-783-2593   (SL)
BURLINGTON GOLF AND COUNTRY CLUB LIMITED
422 North Shore Blvd E, Burlington, ON, L7T 1W9
(905) 634-7726
Emp Here 80   *Sales* 6,111,760
SIC 7997 Membership sports and recreation clubs
David Desaverio

D-U-N-S 25-745-5402   (HQ)
CATHOLIC CEMETERIES OF THE DIOCESE OF HAMILTON
600 Spring Gardens Rd, Burlington, ON, L7T 1J1
(905) 522-7727
Sales 12,772,532
SIC 6531 Real estate agents and managers
John O'brien

D-U-N-S 25-283-2548   (SL)
COUGAR SHOES INC
CHECKERS, DIV OF
2 Masonry Crt, Burlington, ON, L7T 4A8
(905) 639-0100
Emp Here 25   *Sales* 12,458,050
SIC 5139 Footwear
Stephen Sedlbauer
Ronald Sedlbauer

D-U-N-S 24-316-4865   (SL)
ETRATECH ENTERPRISES INC

(*Suby of* GENTHERM INCORPORATED)
1047 Cooke Blvd, Burlington, ON, L7T 4A8
(905) 681-7544
Emp Here 400   *Sales* 113,166,000
SIC 3625 Relays and industrial controls
Michael Desnoyers
Michael Lamontagne

D-U-N-S 20-799-6831   (BR)
HYDRO ONE INC
(*Suby of* HYDRO ONE LIMITED)
1225 King Rd, Burlington, ON, L7T 0B7
(905) 681-0421
Emp Here 100
SIC 4911 Electric services
Mike Furgeson

D-U-N-S 24-641-8966   (HQ)
IKEA CANADA LIMITED PARTNERSHIP
IKEA CANADA
(*Suby of* QINGDAO HONGYISEN CONSTRUCTION ENGINEERING SERVICE CO., LTD.*)
1065 Plains Rd E, Burlington, ON, L7T 4K1
(905) 637-9440
Emp Here 569   *Sales* 1,180,427,478
SIC 5712 Furniture stores
Kerri Molinaro
Andres Bjurud

D-U-N-S 25-321-6006   (HQ)
MCBURL CORP
MCDONALD'S #40122 PLAINS RD
623 Plains Rd E, Burlington, ON, L7T 2E8
(905) 632-0072
Emp Here 9   *Sales* 23,319,500
SIC 5812 Eating places
Ralph Sgro

D-U-N-S 24-624-4297   (SL)
MOSLIM, M. PHARMACY LTD
SHOPPERS DRUG MART
484 Plains Rd E, Burlington, ON, L7T 2E1
(905) 632-3365
Emp Here 40   *Sales* 10,118,160
SIC 5912 Drug stores and proprietary stores
Michelle Moslim

D-U-N-S 20-753-9537   (HQ)
POLLARD WINDOWS INC
1217 King Rd, Burlington, ON, L7T 0B7
(905) 634-2365
Emp Here 225   *Sales* 69,597,500
SIC 2431 Millwork
Karen Pollard-Josling
Reginald Pollard
Carol Pollard
Gary Pollard

D-U-N-S 20-531-2200   (HQ)
POWER & TELEPHONE SUPPLY OF CANADA LTD
(*Suby of* POWER & TELEPHONE SUPPLY COMPANY)
1141 King Rd Unit 1, Burlington, ON, L7T 0B4
(289) 288-3260
Sales 18,781,308
SIC 5065 Electronic parts and equipment, nec
Jim Pentecost
Jean Desrosiers
Mark Kaman

D-U-N-S 20-652-8791   (SL)
ROYAL CITY SOCCER CLUB
336 Plains Rd E Suite 2, Burlington, ON, L7T 2C8
(905) 639-4178
Emp Here 200   *Sales* 16,679,000
SIC 7941 Sports clubs, managers, and promoters
Jeffrey Bryer
David Bryer

D-U-N-S 20-229-8969   (HQ)
UNGER NURSING HOMES LIMITED
HAMPTON TERRACE CARE CENTRE
75 Plains Rd W Suite 214, Burlington, ON,

L7T 1E8
(905) 631-0700
Emp Here 100   *Sales* 6,856,600
SIC 8051 Skilled nursing care facilities
Trudy Vos

D-U-N-S 24-652-2353   (BR)
VIA RAIL CANADA INC
(*Suby of* GOVERNMENT OF CANADA)
1199 Waterdown Rd, Burlington, ON, L7T 4A8

Emp Here 400
SIC 4111 Local and suburban transit
Bernard Leblanc

Caledon, ON L7C

D-U-N-S 25-089-1876   (SL)
3394603 CANADA INC
THE HARMAN TRANSPORT
34 Perdue Crt, Caledon, ON, L7C 3M6
(905) 840-4300
Emp Here 214   *Sales* 44,021,084
SIC 4213 Trucking, except local
Jasvinder Shoker
Kiram Shoker

D-U-N-S 24-034-7067   (SL)
CHEEMA CLEANING SERVICES LTD
12366 Airport Rd, Caledon, ON, L7C 2W1
(905) 951-7156
Emp Here 100   *Sales* 4,020,900
SIC 7349 Building maintenance services, nec
Jassi Cheema

D-U-N-S 24-222-6165   (HQ)
CITY ELECTRIC SUPPLY CORPORATION
T E S
10 Perdue Crt Unit 6, Caledon, ON, L7C 3M6
(905) 495-0535
Emp Here 44   *Sales* 38,009,790
SIC 5063 Electrical apparatus and equipment
Thomas Mackie
Andrew Dawes
Phil Flaherty

D-U-N-S 25-239-0950   (HQ)
GRO-BARK (ONTARIO) LTD
816 Mayfield Rd, Caledon, ON, L7C 0Y6
(905) 846-1515
Emp Here 7   *Sales* 17,041,260
SIC 2875 Fertilizers, mixing only
Neil Mckeown

D-U-N-S 24-407-3326   (SL)
PETRELLA TRANSPORT LIMITED
12404 Airport Rd, Caledon, ON, L7C 2W1
(905) 951-0584
Emp Here 70   *Sales* 10,373,440
SIC 4212 Local trucking, without storage
Antonio Petrella
Joseph Petrella

Caledon, ON L7K

D-U-N-S 24-860-3362   (HQ)
HORSESHOE HILL CONSTRUCTION INC
18859 Horseshoe Hill Rd, Caledon, ON, L7K 2B9
(905) 857-7400
Sales 38,984,400
SIC 1622 Bridge, tunnel, and elevated highway construction
Gordon Tozer

Caledon East, ON L7C

D-U-N-S 24-773-2055   (SL)
CALEDON EAST FOODLAND

▲ Public Company   ■ Public Company Family Member   **HQ** Headquarters   **BR** Branch   **SL** Single Location

15771 Airport Rd Suite 4a, Caledon East, ON, L7C 1K2
(905) 584-9677
Emp Here 49   *Sales* 13,433,448
SIC 5411 Grocery stores
Kurt Geiser

D-U-N-S 20-026-3395   (BR)
DUFFERIN-PEEL CATHOLIC DISTRICT SCHOOL BOARD
ROBERT S FRANK HALL
(*Suby of* DUFFERIN-PEEL CATHOLIC DISTRICT SCHOOL BOARD)
6500 Old Church Rd, Caledon East, ON, L7C 0H3
(905) 584-1670
Emp Here 120
SIC 8211 Elementary and secondary schools
Joe Galea

Caledon Village, ON L7K

D-U-N-S 24-750-3548   (SL)
CALEDON CREEK MECHANICAL LIMITED
18023 Horseshoe Hill Rd, Caledon Village, ON, L7K 2B8
(519) 927-0190
Emp Here 61   *Sales* 14,216,965
SIC 1711 Plumbing, heating, air-conditioning
Robert Olma

Caledonia, ON N3W

D-U-N-S 25-305-7327   (SL)
374872 ONTARIO LIMITED
TRANSPORT SALES & SERVICE
21 Industrial Dr Suite 6, Caledonia, ON, N3W 1H8
(905) 765-5424
Emp Here 110   *Sales* 22,627,660
SIC 4213 Trucking, except local
Randy Slack

D-U-N-S 20-246-9537   (HQ)
ASRJ COMMUNICATIONS INC
179 Morrison Dr, Caledonia, ON, N3W 1A8

Emp Here 40   *Sales* 12,935,860
SIC 4899 Communication services, nec
Andrew Jenner

D-U-N-S 20-039-4591   (SL)
CLARK AG SYSTEMS LTD
CLARK COMPANIES
186 Greens Rd, Caledonia, ON, N3W 1X2
(905) 765-4401
Emp Here 30   *Sales* 14,250,780
SIC 5083 Farm and garden machinery
Jason Clark
Brad Mandryk
Barb Thibert

D-U-N-S 25-034-3332   (SL)
HALDIMAND COUNTY HYDRO INC
(*Suby of* CORPORATION OF HALDIMAND COUNTY, THE)
1 Greendale Dr Suite 1, Caledonia, ON, N3W 2J3
(905) 765-5211
Emp Here 50   *Sales* 31,330,700
SIC 4911 Electric services
Jane Albert

D-U-N-S 24-338-1543   (SL)
L.A. DALTON SYSTEMS LP
1435 Highway 56, Caledonia, ON, N3W 1T1

Emp Here 55   *Sales* 15,034,250
SIC 6712 Bank holding companies
Greg Rumble

D-U-N-S 20-505-7334   (SL)

SEARLES, DENNIS CHEVROLET LIMITED
(*Suby of* 648885 ONTARIO LIMITED)
160 Argyle St S, Caledonia, ON, N3W 1K7
(905) 765-4424
Emp Here 23   *Sales* 11,455,794
SIC 5511 New and used car dealers
Dennis Searles
Linda Searles

D-U-N-S 20-039-5093   (SL)
WINEGARD MOTORS LIMITED
140 Argyle St S, Caledonia, ON, N3W 1E5
(905) 765-4444
Emp Here 32   *Sales* 20,136,960
SIC 5511 New and used car dealers
John L Winegard
Jerry Winegard
Ronald Winegard

Callander, ON P0H

D-U-N-S 25-203-1398   (HQ)
COMSATEC INC
61 High St N, Callander, ON, P0H 1H0
(705) 752-4342
Sales 62,117,140
SIC 4924 Natural gas distribution
Paul Waque Sr

D-U-N-S 24-141-5124   (SL)
NIPISSING GAME FARM INC
367 Birchgrove Dr W, Callander, ON, P0H 1H0
(705) 752-2226
Emp Here 30   *Sales* 11,565,570
SIC 0259 Poultry and eggs, nec
Scot Ryckman

Calstock, ON P0L

D-U-N-S 20-039-5390   (SL)
LECOURS LUMBER CO. LIMITED
Hwy 663 N, Calstock, ON, P0L 1B0
(705) 362-4368
Emp Here 200   *Sales* 38,474,000
SIC 2421 Sawmills and planing mills, general
Benoit Lecours
Roger Lecours
Sylvette Lecours

Cambridge, ON N1P

D-U-N-S 25-228-2108   (BR)
WATERLOO CATHOLIC DISTRICT SCHOOL BOARD
ST BENEDICT CATHOLIC SECONDARY SCHOOL
50 Saginaw Pky, Cambridge, ON, N1P 1A1
(519) 621-4050
Emp Here 140
SIC 8211 Elementary and secondary schools
Tom Forestell

Cambridge, ON N1R

D-U-N-S 25-965-6270   (SL)
405 AUTO SALES INC
CAMBRIDGE CENTRE HONDA
227 Hespeler Rd, Cambridge, ON, N1R 3H8
(519) 623-5991
Emp Here 50   *Sales* 24,903,900
SIC 5511 New and used car dealers
George Morin
Wendy Morin

D-U-N-S 24-704-9489   (BR)

A.G. SIMPSON AUTOMOTIVE INC
A G S AUTOMOTIVE
(*Suby of* J2 MANAGEMENT CORP)
560 Conestoga Blvd, Cambridge, ON, N1R 7P7
(519) 621-7953
Emp Here 150
SIC 3465 Automotive stampings
Leon Joe

D-U-N-S 20-824-2487   (HQ)
AFRICAN LION SAFARI & GAME FARM LTD
1386 Cooper Rd Rr 1, Cambridge, ON, N1R 5S2
(519) 623-2620
Sales 23,842,500
SIC 7999 Amusement and recreation, nec
James Dailley
Mike Takacs

D-U-N-S 24-823-0448   (SL)
ALLTRADE INDUSTRIAL CONTRACTORS INC
1477 Bishop St N, Cambridge, ON, N1R 7J4
(519) 740-1090
Emp Here 200   *Sales* 43,565,800
SIC 1731 Electrical work
Bob Ritzmann
Kevin Ritzmann
Mark Nokes
Duane Burley

D-U-N-S 24-488-5026   (SL)
ARC INDUSTRIES
CAMBRIDGE WOODEN TOY CO
466 Franklin Blvd, Cambridge, ON, N1R 8G6
(519) 621-0680
Emp Here 114   *Sales* 5,501,982
SIC 8331 Job training and related services
Ron Macpherson
Michael Mullen

D-U-N-S 25-496-5247   (SL)
BANBRICO LIMITED
NORTHSTAR INDUSTRIES
480 Collier Macmillan Dr, Cambridge, ON, N1R 6R5
(905) 668-9174
Emp Here 11   *Sales* 11,003,729
SIC 5051 Metals service centers and offices
Brian Pollock

D-U-N-S 20-049-6131   (SL)
BENNETT CHEVROLET CADILLAC LTD
445 Hespeler Rd, Cambridge, ON, N1R 6J2
(519) 621-1250
Emp Here 65   *Sales* 40,903,200
SIC 5511 New and used car dealers
David Bennett

D-U-N-S 24-391-7965   (SL)
BODNAR, KEN ENTERPRISES INC
CANADIAN TIRE
75 Dundas St, Cambridge, ON, N1R 6G5
(519) 621-8180
Emp Here 45   *Sales* 22,413,510
SIC 5531 Auto and home supply stores
Ken Bodnar

D-U-N-S 20-049-6255   (HQ)
BOLT AND NUT SUPPLY LIMITED
384 Franklin Blvd, Cambridge, ON, N1R 8G5
(519) 623-0370
Emp Here 26   *Sales* 15,200,832
SIC 5085 Industrial supplies
Douglas Hill
Fran Hill
Maureen Boyce

D-U-N-S 20-434-1999   (SL)
BUILT BY ENGINEERS CONSTRUCTION INC
520 Collier Macmillan Dr Suite 8, Cambridge, ON, N1R 6R6
(519) 620-8886
Emp Here 32   *Sales* 15,567,760
SIC 8711 Engineering services
Brian Collier

D-U-N-S 24-991-9838   (SL)
BUTORAC, DON LIMITED
CANADIAN TIRE
90 Pinebush Rd, Cambridge, ON, N1R 8J8
(519) 623-3360
Emp Here 49   *Sales* 24,405,822
SIC 5531 Auto and home supply stores
Don Butorac

D-U-N-S 20-038-9005   (HQ)
BWXT CANADA LTD
(*Suby of* BWX TECHNOLOGIES, INC.)
581 Coronation Blvd, Cambridge, ON, N1R 3E9
(519) 621-2130
Emp Here 900   *Sales* 604,589,355
SIC 3621 Motors and generators
Rex Geveden
John Fees
John Macquarrie
David Black
James Canafax
Regina Carter
Jason Kerr
Richard Loving
M. Alan Nethery
William Russell

D-U-N-S 24-308-1135   (BR)
BWXT CANADA LTD
(*Suby of* BWX TECHNOLOGIES, INC.)
581 Coronation Blvd, Cambridge, ON, N1R 5V3
(519) 621-2130
Emp Here 300
SIC 3621 Motors and generators
Trudy Koebel

D-U-N-S 20-378-0416   (HQ)
BWXT ITG CANADA, INC
BWXT ISOTOPE TECHNOLOGIES
(*Suby of* BWX TECHNOLOGIES, INC.)
581 Coronation Blvd, Cambridge, ON, N1R 5V3
(613) 592-3400
Emp Here 10   *Sales* 49,703,675
SIC 2834 Pharmaceutical preparations
Thomas Burnett

D-U-N-S 24-509-6425   (HQ)
CAMBRIDGE AND NORTH DUMFRIES ENERGY PLUS INC
(*Suby of* CORPORATION OF THE CITY OF CAMBRIDGE, THE)
1500 Bishop St N, Cambridge, ON, N1R 7N6
(519) 621-3530
Sales 147,539,855
SIC 4911 Electric services
Ian Miles
Steven Mccartney
Charles Cipolla
Peter Ferraro
Derek Hamilton
Doug Craig
Susan Foxton
Anita Davis
John Keating

D-U-N-S 24-078-5030   (HQ)
CAMBRIDGE MEMORIAL HOSPITAL
700 Coronation Blvd, Cambridge, ON, N1R 3G2
(519) 621-2330
Sales 133,296,000
SIC 8062 General medical and surgical hospitals
Patrick Gaskin
Ian Miles
David Pyper
Joseph Kane
Tim Edworthy
Tom Dean
Bill Deley
Elaine Habicher
Katie Hamilton
Nicola Melchers

D-U-N-S 24-876-7725   (SL)
CAMBRIDGE VOLKSWAGEN INC
275 Hespeler Rd, Cambridge, ON, N1R 3H8
(519) 621-8989
Emp Here 21   *Sales* 10,459,638
SIC 5511 New and used car dealers
  Michael Alkier

D-U-N-S 20-049-6495   (HQ)
CANADIAN GENERAL-TOWER LIMITED
CGT
52 Middleton St, Cambridge, ON, N1R 5T6
(519) 623-1633
Sales 202,990,200
SIC 3081 Unsupported plastics film and sheet
  Craig Richardson
  Winston Chong
  Jennifer Fallows

D-U-N-S 24-192-9843   (SL)
CANUCK COMPOUNDERS INC
180 Sheldon Dr Unit 12, Cambridge, ON, N1R 6V1
(519) 621-6521
Emp Here 38   *Sales* 10,513,080
SIC 2821 Plastics materials and resins
  William (Bill) Dickson
  Melita Bucek

D-U-N-S 24-046-3831   (HQ)
CASH 4 YOU CORP
250 Dundas St S Unit 10, Cambridge, ON, N1R 8A8
(519) 620-1900
Emp Here 10   *Sales* 15,792,000
SIC 6099 Functions related to deposit banking
  Amir Mahmouzadeh

D-U-N-S 20-851-8605   (SL)
CELLO PRODUCTS INC
210 Avenue Rd, Cambridge, ON, N1R 8H5
(519) 623-9150
Emp Here 70   *Sales* 13,445,950
SIC 3432 Plumbing fixture fittings and trim
  Terrance Aurini

D-U-N-S 24-985-2781   (HQ)
CENTRAL AUTOMOTIVE SERVICES LIMITED
CAMBRIDGE MACK
1220 Franklin Blvd, Cambridge, ON, N1R 8B7
(519) 653-7161
Emp Here 60   *Sales* 50,342,400
SIC 5511 New and used car dealers
  John Slotegraaf
  Steve Bremton

D-U-N-S 24-736-5646   (SL)
CHAVES GAS BARS LIMITED
CHAVES ESSO
31 Dundas St S, Cambridge, ON, N1R 8N9
(519) 622-1301
Emp Here 32   *Sales* 15,938,496
SIC 5541 Gasoline service stations
  Fernando Chaves

D-U-N-S 24-364-8628   (SL)
CHILL FRESH PRODUCE INC
1170 Franklin Blvd Unit B, Cambridge, ON, N1R 7J2
(519) 896-0124
Emp Here 50   *Sales* 41,778,850
SIC 5148 Fresh fruits and vegetables
  Brian Arrigo
  Darren Jolley

D-U-N-S 25-627-3848   (HQ)
CINNAGARD INC
CINNABON
120 Main St Unit 3, Cambridge, ON, N1R 1V7
(519) 622-3188
Sales 46,668,150
SIC 2051 Bread, cake, and related products
  Mona Benson

D-U-N-S 20-042-4034   (HQ)
COLSON GROUP CANADA, INC
CAN-AM CASTERS & WHEELS, DIV OF

(*Suby of* COLSON ASSOCIATES, INC.)
1600 Bishop St N Suite 300, Cambridge, ON, N1R 7N6
(519) 623-9420
Sales 12,485,525
SIC 3499 Fabricated Metal products, nec
  Mike Titizian

D-U-N-S 25-293-3759   (HQ)
COM DEV INTERNATIONAL LTD
(*Suby of* HONEYWELL INTERNATIONAL INC.)
155 Sheldon Dr, Cambridge, ON, N1R 7H6
(519) 622-2300
Emp Here 950   *Sales* 341,195,490
SIC 3669 Communications equipment, nec
  Marty Sheber
  Sean Burke

D-U-N-S 20-543-9433   (HQ)
COM DEV LTD
COM DEV SPACE
(*Suby of* HONEYWELL INTERNATIONAL INC.)
155 Sheldon Dr, Cambridge, ON, N1R 7H6
(519) 622-2300
Emp Here 700   *Sales* 206,527,950
SIC 3669 Communications equipment, nec
  Michael Pley
  Terry Reidel
  Mike Williams
  Paul Dyck
  Gary Calhoun

D-U-N-S 24-345-4670   (BR)
COMMUNITY LIVING CAMBRIDGE
ARC INDUSTRIES
466 Franklin Blvd, Cambridge, ON, N1R 8G6
(519) 621-0680
Emp Here 90
SIC 8331 Job training and related services
  Winston Reid

D-U-N-S 24-333-3627   (BR)
CORPORATION OF THE CITY OF CAMBRIDGE, THE
CAMBRIDGE FIRE DEPARTMENT
(*Suby of* CORPORATION OF THE CITY OF CAMBRIDGE, THE)
1625 Bishop St N, Cambridge, ON, N1R 7J4
(519) 621-6001
Emp Here 138
SIC 7389 Business services, nec
  Terry Allen

D-U-N-S 20-980-3451   (BR)
DANA CANADA CORPORATION
LONG MANUFACTURING LTD
(*Suby of* DANA INCORPORATED)
401 Franklin Blvd, Cambridge, ON, N1R 8G8
(519) 621-1303
Emp Here 200
SIC 3714 Motor vehicle parts and accessories
  John Kichinko

D-U-N-S 24-533-7808   (SL)
DAOUST, JACQUES COATINGS MANAGEMENT INC
JDCMI
32 Mckenzie St, Cambridge, ON, N1R 4E1
(519) 624-1515
Emp Here 50   *Sales* 10,141,500
SIC 3471 Plating and polishing
  Debbie Daoust
  Jacques Daoust

D-U-N-S 24-920-1112   (HQ)
DAVID & CLAUDE HOLDINGS CANADA INC
30 Cowansview Rd, Cambridge, ON, N1R 7N3
(519) 622-2320
Sales 28,501,560
SIC 5085 Industrial supplies
  David Van Wely
  Claude Dandurand

D-U-N-S 25-463-7606   (SL)

DIPIETRO FRESH MEAT & DELICATESSEN LTD
DIPIETRO
30 Glamis Rd, Cambridge, ON, N1R 7H5
(519) 622-3222
Emp Here 60   *Sales* 17,608,620
SIC 5411 Grocery stores
  Bruno Dipietro
  Peter Dipietro

D-U-N-S 24-632-5682   (HQ)
DIVERSCO SUPPLY INC
495 Conestoga Blvd, Cambridge, ON, N1R 7P4
(519) 740-1210
Emp Here 35   *Sales* 26,995,459
SIC 5085 Industrial supplies
  Robert Statham
  Jon Huddle

D-U-N-S 25-213-4804   (SL)
DREW-SMITH COMPANY LIMITED, THE
REID CANDY & NUT SHOP
42 Ainslie St N, Cambridge, ON, N1R 3J5
(519) 621-6988
Emp Here 25   *Sales* 10,483,875
SIC 6719 Holding companies, nec
  Tom Drew-Smith
  Kathryn Drew-Smith

D-U-N-S 24-140-6040   (SL)
EKUM-SEKUM INCORPORATED
BRANTCO CONSTRUCTION
1555 Bishop St N Unit 1, Cambridge, ON, N1R 7J4
(519) 622-1600
Emp Here 90   *Sales* 22,273,470
SIC 1771 Concrete work
  Joseph Graci

D-U-N-S 25-687-5170   (HQ)
FORTERRA PIPE & PRECAST, LTD
2099 Roseville Rd Suite 2, Cambridge, ON, N1R 5S3
(519) 622-7574
Emp Here 100   *Sales* 34,947,705
SIC 3272 Concrete products, nec
  Plamen Jordanoff
  Leo Steffler

D-U-N-S 24-668-0511   (SL)
GOLDEN TRIANGLE RESTORATION INC
2302 Dumfries Rd, Cambridge, ON, N1R 5S3
(519) 624-4487
Emp Here 11   *Sales* 11,383,691
SIC 6331 Fire, marine, and casualty insurance
  Wally Wood
  Charles Stewart
  Adam Wood

D-U-N-S 20-878-6277   (HQ)
GORE MUTUAL INSURANCE COMPANY
252 Dundas St S, Cambridge, ON, N1R 8A8
(519) 623-1910
Sales 448,763,280
SIC 6331 Fire, marine, and casualty insurance
  Heidi Sevcik
  Catherine Leclair
  Anna Mccrindell
  Paul Jackson
  Neil Weir
  Jamie Mcdougall
  Lorne Motton
  Sean Christie
  Andy Taylor
  Sonya Stark

D-U-N-S 24-770-6732   (HQ)
GRAND VALLEY DISTRIBUTORS INC
BREWERS CAR PARTS PLUS
1595 Bishop St N, Cambridge, ON, N1R 7J4
(519) 621-2260
Emp Here 52   *Sales* 31,686,705
SIC 5013 Motor vehicle supplies and new parts
  John Brewer

D-U-N-S 20-606-8835   (SL)

GRAND VALLEY FORTIFIERS LIMITED
486 Main St, Cambridge, ON, N1R 5S7
(519) 621-5204
Emp Here 90   *Sales* 31,112,100
SIC 2048 Prepared feeds, nec
  Ian Ross
  James Ross
  Peter Faus
  Elaine Ross

D-U-N-S 25-221-0976   (SL)
GREENTEC INTERNATIONAL INC
(*Suby of* PERROTTA & PEREIRA HOLDINGS INC)
95 Struck Crt, Cambridge, ON, N1R 8L2
(519) 624-3300
Emp Here 90   *Sales* 9,907,781
SIC 4953 Refuse systems
  Antonio Perrotta
  Betty Pereria
  Jeff Neeb

D-U-N-S 25-108-7763   (SL)
GULFSTREAM INC
145 Sheldon Dr, Cambridge, ON, N1R 5X5
(519) 622-0950
Emp Here 45   *Sales* 23,424,390
SIC 5091 Sporting and recreation goods
  Sang Tram

D-U-N-S 20-553-6399   (BR)
HOME DEPOT OF CANADA INC
HOME DEPOT
(*Suby of* THE HOME DEPOT INC)
35 Pinebush Rd, Cambridge, ON, N1R 8E2
(519) 624-2700
Emp Here 100
SIC 5211 Lumber and other building materials
  Mark Mckee

D-U-N-S 25-143-2241   (BR)
HUDSON'S BAY COMPANY
BAY, THE
(*Suby of* HUDSON'S BAY COMPANY)
355 Hespeler Rd Unit 1, Cambridge, ON, N1R 6B3
(519) 622-4919
Emp Here 100
SIC 5311 Department stores
  Annette Becker

D-U-N-S 20-324-5899   (SL)
IMPRES PHARMA INC
1165 Franklin Blvd Suite J, Cambridge, ON, N1R 8E1
(866) 781-0491
Emp Here 200   *Sales* 82,564,200
SIC 5122 Drugs, proprietaries, and sundries
  Robert Tomas

D-U-N-S 24-347-8257   (SL)
INNOVATIVE STEAM TECHNOLOGIES INC
INNOVATIVE STEAM TECHNOLOGIES
(*Suby of* FULCRUM CAPITAL PARTNERS INC)
549 Conestoga Blvd, Cambridge, ON, N1R 7P5
(519) 740-0036
Emp Here 54   *Sales* 11,988,054
SIC 3569 General industrial machinery, nec
  Slobo Andan

D-U-N-S 24-991-8988   (HQ)
JAMESWAY INCUBATOR COMPANY INC
(*Suby of* TBG AG)
30 High Ridge Crt, Cambridge, ON, N1R 7L3
(519) 624-4646
Emp Here 88   *Sales* 22,200,100
SIC 3523 Farm machinery and equipment
  Christopher Omiecinski

D-U-N-S 25-952-6259   (BR)
JMP ENGINEERING INC
(*Suby of* JMP ENGINEERING INC)
1425 Bishop St N Unit 8, Cambridge, ON, N1R 6J9
(519) 622-2505
Emp Here 100

SIC 8711 Engineering services
Mark Parker

D-U-N-S 20-292-3582   (BR)
K. A. S. PERSONNEL SERVICES INC
(*Suby of* K. A. S. PERSONNEL SERVICES INC)
534 Hespeler Rd Suite A2, Cambridge, ON, N1R 6J7
(519) 622-7788
Emp Here 100
SIC 7361 Employment agencies
Debra Heisler

D-U-N-S 20-403-1785   (HQ)
KROMET INTERNATIONAL INC
200 Sheldon Dr, Cambridge, ON, N1R 7K1
(519) 623-2511
Emp Here 150   *Sales* 60,807,750
SIC 3469 Metal stampings, nec
Mike Owens
Dan Fudge
Pat Drohan

D-U-N-S 24-143-3739   (HQ)
LATEM INDUSTRIES LIMITED
PLASTICO INDUSTRIES, DIV OF
90 Struck Crt, Cambridge, ON, N1R 8L2
(519) 740-0292
Emp Here 80   *Sales* 21,129,350
SIC 3471 Plating and polishing
Liam Nother

D-U-N-S 20-144-6648   (HQ)
MACDONALD STEEL LIMITED
(*Suby of* TIGERCAT INTERNATIONAL INC)
200 Avenue Rd, Cambridge, ON, N1R 8H5
(519) 620-0400
Sales 58,375,440
SIC 3499 Fabricated Metal products, nec
Kenneth Macdonald
James Goad

D-U-N-S 25-110-0707   (HQ)
MALTACOURT (CANADA) LTD
MALTACOURT GLOBAL LOGISTICS
150 Water St S Suite 201, Cambridge, ON, N1R 3E2
(519) 756-6463
Emp Here 7   *Sales* 24,958,416
SIC 4731 Freight transportation arrangement
Gary Debrusk
Ronda Debrusk
Troy Cowen
Ian Kurt

D-U-N-S 25-318-1374   (BR)
MCDONALD'S RESTAURANTS OF CANADA LIMITED
MCDONALD'S
(*Suby of* MCDONALD'S CORPORATION)
Gd Stn Galt, Cambridge, ON, N1R 5S8

Emp Here 100
SIC 5812 Eating places
Craig Acker

D-U-N-S 20-937-8397   (HQ)
MCGLINCHEY ENTERPRISES LIMITED
TIM HORTONS
275 Water St N, Cambridge, ON, N1R 3B9
(519) 621-2360
Emp Here 1   *Sales* 13,433,448
SIC 5461 Retail bakeries
Dwayne Mcglinchey

D-U-N-S 20-576-4728   (SL)
MEDI-SHARE INC
1986 Cedar Creek Rd, Cambridge, ON, N1R 5S5
(519) 740-3336
Emp Here 140   *Sales* 32,165,560
SIC 8731 Commercial physical research
Richard Matiasz
Lucia Matiasz

D-U-N-S 20-290-7481   (BR)
METRO ONTARIO INC

FOOD BASICS
(*Suby of* METRO INC)
95 Water St N, Cambridge, ON, N1R 3B5
(519) 623-3652
Emp Here 125
SIC 5141 Groceries, general line
Tom Mcarthur

D-U-N-S 20-227-7877   (HQ)
MW CANADA LTD
291 Elgin St N, Cambridge, ON, N1R 7H9
(519) 621-5460
Emp Here 2   *Sales* 11,574,150
SIC 2591 Drapery hardware and window blinds and shades
Robert Berger
Howard Bornstein
Dwayne Schmidt

D-U-N-S 24-751-3633   (SL)
NEMCOR INC
501 Franklin Blvd, Cambridge, ON, N1R 8G9
(519) 740-0595
Emp Here 46   *Sales* 22,922,812
SIC 5131 Piece goods and notions
Tim Mcintyre
Donald E Mcintyre
Judith Graham

D-U-N-S 20-558-4027   (SL)
NEW WORLD FRICTION CORP
(*Suby of* MOMENTUM USA, INC.)
539 Collier Macmillan Dr Unit B, Cambridge, ON, N1R 7P3
(519) 623-0011
Emp Here 130   *Sales* 29,099,590
SIC 3714 Motor vehicle parts and accessories
John Amalfe
Anil Sharma

D-U-N-S 20-171-9960   (HQ)
NOVOCOL PHARMACEUTICAL OF CANADA, INC
SEPTODONT
25 Wolseley Crt, Cambridge, ON, N1R 6X3
(519) 623-4800
Emp Here 150   *Sales* 99,478,200
SIC 2834 Pharmaceutical preparations
Kent Chiu
Eric Penrose

D-U-N-S 24-827-0654   (SL)
OL ' GRANDAD'S SNACKS (1992) INC
1680 Bishop St N, Cambridge, ON, N1R 7J3
(519) 624-9992
Emp Here 80   *Sales* 27,655,200
SIC 2096 Potato chips and similar snacks
Sam Silvestro
Michael Silvestro

D-U-N-S 24-213-9319   (HQ)
OMNIFLEX HOSE & EQUIPMENT LTD
78 Cowansview Rd Suite 3, Cambridge, ON, N1R 7N3
(519) 622-0261
Emp Here 20   *Sales* 12,350,676
SIC 5084 Industrial machinery and equipment
Dave Avery
Lou Laskas

D-U-N-S 24-334-4897   (HQ)
OXFORD MILLS HOME FASHION FACTORY OUTLET INC, THE
(*Suby of* LITERIES UNIVERSELLES PAGA INC)
425 Hespeler Rd Unit 1c, Cambridge, ON, N1R 6J2
(519) 342-3026
Emp Here 6   *Sales* 11,620,150
SIC 5719 Miscellaneous homefurnishings
Paul Nassar

D-U-N-S 25-610-1494   (SL)
PERFORMANCE POLYMERS INC
PPI
36 Raglin Pl, Cambridge, ON, N1R 7J2
(519) 622-1792
Emp Here 25   *Sales* 11,875,650

SIC 5085 Industrial supplies
Gordon Steele
Bill Chien

D-U-N-S 24-792-8062   (HQ)
PGI HOLDINGS INC
PROCESS GROUP
555 Conestoga Blvd, Cambridge, ON, N1R 7P5
(519) 622-5520
Sales 27,161,260
SIC 1796 Installing building equipment
Clifford Snyder
Jeff Snyder

D-U-N-S 24-745-4788   (HQ)
PROCESS GROUP INC
(*Suby of* PGI HOLDINGS INC)
555 Conestoga Blvd, Cambridge, ON, N1R 7P5
(519) 622-5520
Emp Here 75   *Sales* 47,784,600
SIC 1796 Installing building equipment
Cliff Snyder
Jeff Snyder
Peter Fitton
Brent Heard

D-U-N-S 20-709-3415   (SL)
QUEEN'S SCHOOL OF BUSINESS
355 Hespeler Rd, Cambridge, ON, N1R 6B3
(613) 533-2330
Emp Here 200   *Sales* 29,878,200
SIC 8221 Colleges and universities
David Saunders

D-U-N-S 25-137-2020   (BR)
RANDSTAD INTERIM INC
RANDSTAD CANADA
(*Suby of* RANDSTAD N.V.)
1315 Bishop St N, Cambridge, ON, N1R 6Z2
(519) 740-6944
Emp Here 80
SIC 7361 Employment agencies
Chris Welsh

D-U-N-S 20-353-8454   (SL)
RATHI, KANU PRIYA PHARMACY INC
SHOPPERS DRUG MART
499 Hespeler Rd, Cambridge, ON, N1R 6J2
(519) 623-6770
Emp Here 45   *Sales* 11,382,930
SIC 5912 Drug stores and proprietary stores
Satya Rathi

D-U-N-S 25-169-5425   (BR)
REVERA INC
(*Suby of* GOVERNMENT OF CANADA)
614 Coronation Blvd Suite 200, Cambridge, ON, N1R 3E8
(519) 622-1840
Emp Here 100
SIC 8051 Skilled nursing care facilities
Mike Case

D-U-N-S 25-028-5236   (BR)
REVERA LONG TERM CARE INC
RIVERBEND PLACE CAMBRIDGE
(*Suby of* GOVERNMENT OF CANADA)
650 Coronation Blvd, Cambridge, ON, N1R 7S6
(519) 740-3820
Emp Here 90
SIC 8051 Skilled nursing care facilities
Roy Feltz

D-U-N-S 20-535-3675   (SL)
RIDGEHILL FORD SALES (1980) LIMITED
217 Hespeler Rd Suite 637, Cambridge, ON, N1R 3H8
(519) 621-0720
Emp Here 45   *Sales* 22,413,510
SIC 5511 New and used car dealers
Drew Tilson
Kevin Zimic

D-U-N-S 20-019-8153   (HQ)
ROCKWELL AUTOMATION CANADA CON-

TROL SYSTEMS
(*Suby of* ROCKWELL AUTOMATION, INC.)
135 Dundas St, Cambridge, ON, N1R 5N9
(519) 623-1810
Emp Here 650   *Sales* 339,498,000
SIC 3625 Relays and industrial controls
Charles Cipoloa

D-U-N-S 24-117-5798   (BR)
ROCKWELL AUTOMATION CANADA CONTROL SYSTEMS
(*Suby of* ROCKWELL AUTOMATION, INC.)
12 Raglin Pl, Cambridge, ON, N1R 7J2
(519) 740-5500
Emp Here 100
SIC 3613 Switchgear and switchboard apparatus
Karen Beech

D-U-N-S 20-049-5935   (HQ)
ROCKWELL AUTOMATION CANADA INC
ALLEN-BRADLEY
(*Suby of* ROCKWELL AUTOMATION, INC.)
135 Dundas St N, Cambridge, ON, N1R 5X1
(519) 623-1810
Sales 282,915,000
SIC 3625 Relays and industrial controls
Blake Moret

D-U-N-S 25-574-2025   (SL)
ROYAL LEPAGE CROWN REALTY SERVICES INC
471 Hespeler Rd Unit 4, Cambridge, ON, N1R 6J2
(519) 740-6400
Emp Here 70   *Sales* 19,022,920
SIC 6531 Real estate agents and managers
Angela Asadoorian

D-U-N-S 24-794-3566   (BR)
SECURITAS CANADA LIMITED
(*Suby of* SECURITAS AB)
1425 Bishop St N Suite 14, Cambridge, ON, N1R 6J9
(519) 620-9864
Emp Here 300
SIC 7381 Detective and armored car services
Atik Taraboulsi

D-U-N-S 24-795-3102   (HQ)
SELECT FINANCIAL SERVICES INC
193 Pinebush Rd Suite 200, Cambridge, ON, N1R 7H8
(519) 622-9613
Emp Here 6   *Sales* 14,342,589
SIC 6282 Investment advice
Deryl Drysdale
Shirley Davis
Pat Murray
Terry Davis

D-U-N-S 20-610-7567   (SL)
SHIRLON PLASTIC COMPANY INC
100 Pinebush Rd, Cambridge, ON, N1R 8J8
(519) 620-1333
Emp Here 60   *Sales* 12,113,820
SIC 3089 Plastics products, nec
Alby Algranti
Selim (Sol) Algranti

D-U-N-S 25-188-1355   (BR)
SOBEYS CAPITAL INCORPORATED
FRESCHO
(*Suby of* EMPIRE COMPANY LIMITED)
75 Dundas St, Cambridge, ON, N1R 6G5
(519) 620-9022
Emp Here 130
SIC 5411 Grocery stores
Steve Aiston

D-U-N-S 20-158-1068   (SL)
TAKHAR INVESTMENTS INC
TAKHAR FINANCIAL INSTITUTE
202 Beverly St, Cambridge, ON, N1R 3Z8
(519) 622-3130
Emp Here 58   *Sales* 15,854,300
SIC 6712 Bank holding companies

Hardy Takhar
Suki Takhar

D-U-N-S 24-923-5474   (HQ)
TIGERCAT INTERNATIONAL INC
200 Avenue Rd, Cambridge, ON, N1R 8H5
(519) 620-0500
Sales 402,059,900
SIC 6712 Bank holding companies
Kenneth Macdonald
Kathy Billings

D-U-N-S 24-365-3490   (SL)
TROUNCY INC
SOUTH CAMBRIDGE HOME HARDWARE BUILDING CENTRE
200 Franklin Blvd Suite 16a, Cambridge, ON, N1R 8N8
(519) 623-2361
Emp Here 45   *Sales* 11,387,655
SIC 5251 Hardware stores
Len Greig

D-U-N-S 24-829-5438   (SL)
VON WEISE OF CANADA COMPANY
505 Conestoga Blvd, Cambridge, ON, N1R 7P4

Emp Here 225   *Sales* 63,655,875
SIC 3621 Motors and generators
Alice Mainland
Kevin Hein

D-U-N-S 25-340-8959   (SL)
W.S. NICHOLLS CONSTRUCTION INC
(*Suby of* SOUTHWEST GAS HOLDINGS, INC.)
48 Cowansview Rd, Cambridge, ON, N1R 7N3
(519) 740-3757
Emp Here 50   *Sales* 10,891,450
SIC 1731 Electrical work
Richard Delaney
William Charles Nicholls
Derek Van Patter
Bob Stillman
Terry Budd
James P. Kane
Kevin Neill

D-U-N-S 25-498-2622   (BR)
WAL-MART CANADA CORP
WAL MART
(*Suby of* WALMART INC.)
22 Pinebush Rd, Cambridge, ON, N1R 8K5
(519) 624-7467
Emp Here 300
SIC 5311 Department stores

D-U-N-S 20-982-8458   (BR)
WATERLOO   CATHOLIC   DISTRICT SCHOOL BOARD
MONSIGNOR DOYLE
185 Myers Rd, Cambridge, ON, N1R 7H2
(519) 622-1290
Emp Here 80
SIC 8211 Elementary and secondary schools
Price Wendy

D-U-N-S 25-228-1555   (BR)
WATERLOO REGION DISTRICT SCHOOL BOARD
GALT COLLEGIATE INST & VOCATIONAL
(*Suby of* WATERLOO REGION DISTRICT SCHOOL BOARD)
200 Water St N, Cambridge, ON, N1R 6V2
(519) 623-3600
Emp Here 120
SIC 8211 Elementary and secondary schools
Beverly Wood

D-U-N-S 25-228-1514   (BR)
WATERLOO REGION DISTRICT SCHOOL BOARD
GLENVIEW PARK SECONDARY SCHOOL
(*Suby of* WATERLOO REGION DISTRICT SCHOOL BOARD)
55 Mckay St, Cambridge, ON, N1R 4G6

(519) 621-9510
Emp Here 110
SIC 8211 Elementary and secondary schools
Kelly Kempel

D-U-N-S 24-046-8280   (HQ)
YOUNG MEN'S CHRISTIAN ASSOCIATION OF CAMBRIDGE
250 Hespeler Rd, Cambridge, ON, N1R 3H3
(519) 623-9622
Emp Here 150   *Sales* 26,303,000
SIC 8641 Civic and social associations
Rob Armstrong
Lynn Woeller
Jim Harding

D-U-N-S 24-327-4615   (BR)
ZEHRMART INC
ZEHRS MARKETS
(*Suby of* LOBLAW COMPANIES LIMITED)
400 Conestoga Blvd, Cambridge, ON, N1R 7L7
(519) 620-1376
Emp Here 300
SIC 5411 Grocery stores
Jesse Reeve

Cambridge, ON N1S

D-U-N-S 20-944-1070   (HQ)
CAMBRIDGE PUBLIC LIBRARY BOARD, THE
1 North Square, Cambridge, ON, N1S 2K6
(519) 621-0460
Emp Here 100   *Sales* 11,096,820
SIC 8231 Libraries
Greg Hayton
Robert Oswald

D-U-N-S 20-018-5479   (SL)
DRAYTON ENTERTAINMENT INC
46 Grand Ave S, Cambridge, ON, N1S 2L8
(519) 621-8000
Emp Here 130   *Sales* 11,591,190
SIC 7832 Motion picture theaters, except drive-in
Alex Mustakas

D-U-N-S 20-291-3047   (BR)
REVERA LONG TERM CARE INC
STIRLING HEIGHTS
(*Suby of* GOVERNMENT OF CANADA)
200 Stirling Macgregor Dr, Cambridge, ON, N1S 5B7
(519) 622-3434
Emp Here 75
SIC 8051 Skilled nursing care facilities
Shannon Dian

D-U-N-S 25-309-1003   (BR)
SOBEYS CAPITAL INCORPORATED
SOBEYS 678
(*Suby of* EMPIRE COMPANY LIMITED)
130 Cedar St, Cambridge, ON, N1S 1W4
(519) 622-8906
Emp Here 115
SIC 5411 Grocery stores
Russ King

D-U-N-S 20-302-3135   (SL)
SOUTHWORKS OUTLET MALL INC
64 Grand Ave S, Cambridge, ON, N1S 2L8
(519) 740-0380
Emp Here 225   *Sales* 30,527,325
SIC 6512 Nonresidential building operators
John Wright

D-U-N-S 25-228-1548   (BR)
WATERLOO REGION DISTRICT SCHOOL BOARD
SOUTHWOOD SECONDARY SCHOOL
(*Suby of* WATERLOO REGION DISTRICT SCHOOL BOARD)
30 Southwood Dr, Cambridge, ON, N1S 4K3

(519) 621-5920
Emp Here 150
SIC 8211 Elementary and secondary schools
Hugh Lambert

Cambridge, ON N1T

D-U-N-S 25-593-9373   (SL)
1148290 ONTARIO INC
TIM HORTONS
95 Saginaw Pky Suite A, Cambridge, ON, N1T 1W2
(519) 623-1856
Emp Here 45   *Sales* 12,336,840
SIC 5499 Miscellaneous food stores
Peter Skropolis

D-U-N-S 24-330-6946   (HQ)
1625443 ONTARIO INC
TVM
(*Suby of* T.V. MINORITY COMPANY, INC.)
75 Lingard Rd, Cambridge, ON, N1T 2A8
(519) 624-9914
Emp Here 65   *Sales* 70,023,660
SIC 4731 Freight transportation arrangement
Theodore Vance
Lynn West

D-U-N-S 20-379-1020   (HQ)
2136284 ONTARIO INC
WELLINGTON MOTOR FREIGHT
55 Fleming Dr Unit 2, Cambridge, ON, N1T 2A9
(905) 696-1977
Emp Here 40   *Sales* 13,388,585
SIC 4731 Freight transportation arrangement
Derek Koza
Peter Koza
Mahir Touma
Celso Mata

D-U-N-S 24-977-6022   (SL)
742906 ONTARIO INC
ACCUCAM MACHINING
300 Sheldon Dr, Cambridge, ON, N1T 1A8
(519) 740-7797
Emp Here 60   *Sales* 13,320,060
SIC 3599 Industrial machinery, nec
Nicholas (Nick) Eelhart
Steven (Steve) Gallant

D-U-N-S 25-993-1629   (SL)
ARISE TECHNOLOGIES CORP
150 Werlich Dr Suite 5, Cambridge, ON, N1T 1N6

Emp Here 135   *Sales* 36,740,733
SIC 5211 Lumber and other building materials
Daniel Shea
Peter Harder
Marilyn Wolfe

D-U-N-S 20-695-6174   (SL)
AXIOM MILLWRIGHTING & FABRICATION INC
55 Savage Dr, Cambridge, ON, N1T 1S5
(519) 620-2000
Emp Here 100   *Sales* 24,618,600
SIC 1796 Installing building equipment
Joe Sferraza

D-U-N-S 24-720-6006   (HQ)
BARTELSE HOLDINGS LIMITED
GROBER
162 Savage Dr, Cambridge, ON, N1T 1S4
(519) 622-2500
Emp Here 20   *Sales* 69,138,000
SIC 2048 Prepared feeds, nec
Jerry Bartelse
Ari Nuys
Mike Fortuna

D-U-N-S 20-341-7266   (BR)
BEND ALL AUTOMOTIVE ULC
(*Suby of* ARDIAN HOLDING)

445 Dobbie Dr, Cambridge, ON, N1T 1S9
(519) 623-2001
Emp Here 115
SIC 3499 Fabricated Metal products, nec
Alfred Napoleon

D-U-N-S 24-310-3947   (SL)
CAMBRIDGE BRASS, INC
(*Suby of* A. Y. MCDONALD INDUSTRIES, INC.)
140 Orion Pl, Cambridge, ON, N1T 1R9
(519) 621-5520
Emp Here 110   *Sales* 21,129,350
SIC 3432 Plumbing fixture fittings and trim
Ed Hesselink
Janet Greidanus

D-U-N-S 24-418-8975   (SL)
CANADIAN THREADALL LIMITED
CANADIAN THREADALL
130 Turnbull Crt, Cambridge, ON, N1T 1J2
(519) 576-3360
Emp Here 25   *Sales* 11,875,650
SIC 5085 Industrial supplies
Byron Nelson

D-U-N-S 24-364-6473   (HQ)
CLARION MEDICAL TECHNOLOGIES INC
125 Fleming Dr, Cambridge, ON, N1T 2B8
(519) 620-3900
Sales 69,595,760
SIC 5047 Medical and hospital equipment
Samson Ling
Dan Webb
Tom Mcpherson

D-U-N-S 20-650-7907   (HQ)
DARLING INTERNATIONAL CANADA INC
ROTHSAY
(*Suby of* DARLING INGREDIENTS INC.)
485 Pinebush Rd, Cambridge, ON, N1T 0A6
(519) 780-3342
Emp Here 50   *Sales* 162,861,000
SIC 4953 Refuse systems
Randall Stuewe
Jim Long

D-U-N-S 20-551-1020   (SL)
DELFT BLUE VEAL INC
(*Suby of* BARTELSE HOLDINGS LIMITED)
162 Savage Dr, Cambridge, ON, N1T 1S4
(519) 622-2500
Emp Here 50   *Sales* 11,242,750
SIC 2011 Meat packing plants
Jerry Bartelse

D-U-N-S 24-668-0487   (HQ)
DESCH CANADA LTD
240 Shearson Cres, Cambridge, ON, N1T 1J6
(519) 621-4560
Sales 30,876,690
SIC 5084 Industrial machinery and equipment
Hendrick Desch
Cathy Bromdacher
Stephen Pack

D-U-N-S 25-302-4293   (HQ)
DOMINO'S PIZZA NS CO
DOMINO'S PIZZA
(*Suby of* DOMINO'S PIZZA, INC.)
490 Pinebush Rd Unit 2, Cambridge, ON, N1T 0A5
(519) 748-1330
Emp Here 36   *Sales* 83,557,700
SIC 5149 Groceries and related products, nec
Cliff Stooner

D-U-N-S 24-773-1362   (HQ)
ECLIPSE AUTOMATION INC
130 Thompson Dr, Cambridge, ON, N1T 2E5
(519) 620-1906
Emp Here 80   *Sales* 22,200,100
SIC 3599 Industrial machinery, nec
Steven Mai
Todd Ronald
Richard Bula
Eric Woerner

D-U-N-S 24-079-0832　　(SL)
EGAR TOOL AND DIE LTD
336 Pinebush Rd, Cambridge, ON, N1T 1Z6
(519) 623-3023
Emp Here 190　　*Sales* 36,496,150
SIC 3469 Metal stampings, nec
　Peter Diiorio
　Frank Lenzi

D-U-N-S 20-114-5625　　(HQ)
ENDRIES INTERNATIONAL CANADA INC
(*Suby of* FERGUSON PLC)
255 Pinebush Rd Unit A, Cambridge, ON, N1T 1B9
(519) 740-3523
Emp Here 52　　*Sales* 48,773,000
SIC 5085 Industrial supplies
　Keith Vandervennet
　Frank Wemyss Roach
　Gilles Petrin
　Sheldon Brewster
　Matthew Vechart

D-U-N-S 20-049-7196　　(SL)
ENGINEERED ELECTRIC CONTROLS LIMITED
230 Sheldon Dr, Cambridge, ON, N1T 1A8
(519) 621-5370
Emp Here 16　　*Sales* 10,233,650
SIC 3613 Switchgear and switchboard apparatus
　Wayne Fischer
　John Fischer

D-U-N-S 20-175-5084　　(HQ)
ESENTIRE, INC
278 Pinebush Rd Suite 101, Cambridge, ON, N1T 1Z6
(519) 651-2200
Sales 11,962,426
SIC 7372 Prepackaged software
　Jay Paul Haynes
　Eldon Spickerhoff
　John Harrif

D-U-N-S 20-941-8821　　(SL)
FARM MUTUAL REINSURANCE PLAN INC
350 Pinebush Rd, Cambridge, ON, N1T 1Z6
(519) 740-6415
Emp Here 46　　*Sales* 98,644,641
SIC 6331 Fire, marine, and casualty insurance
　Steve Smith
　Robert Forsythe
　Tom Smith
　Brian Bessey
　Bruce Williams
　John Leeson

D-U-N-S 20-210-5297　　(SL)
FREEDOM PET SUPPLIES INC
480 Thompson Dr, Cambridge, ON, N1T 2K8
(519) 624-8069
Emp Here 72　　*Sales* 60,161,544
SIC 5149 Groceries and related products, nec
　John Ayres
　Kelly Ayres

D-U-N-S 24-662-7178　　(HQ)
FUCHS LUBRICANTS CANADA LTD
(*Suby of* FUCHS PETROLUB SE)
405 Dobbie Dr, Cambridge, ON, N1T 1S8
(519) 622-2040
Emp Here 25　　*Sales* 59,088,447
SIC 5172 Petroleum products, nec
　L Frank Kleinman
　Derek Scott
　Daniel Woo
　Ronald Gelens
　John Jedlinski

D-U-N-S 25-403-7666　　(BR)
G&K SERVICES CANADA INC
(*Suby of* CINTAS CORPORATION)
205 Turnbull Crt, Cambridge, ON, N1T 1W1
(519) 623-7703
Emp Here 130
SIC 7216 Drycleaning plants, except rugs

　John Bond

D-U-N-S 20-703-2389　　(BR)
GERDAU AMERISTEEL CORPORATION
(*Suby of* METALURGICA GERDAU S/A.)
160 Orion Pl, Cambridge, ON, N1T 1R9
(519) 740-2488
Emp Here 295
SIC 3312 Blast furnaces and steel mills
　Glen Beeby

D-U-N-S 24-379-4521　　(BR)
GROBER INC
DELFT BLUE, DIV OF
(*Suby of* BARTELSE HOLDINGS LIMITED)
425 Dobbie Dr, Cambridge, ON, N1T 1S9
(519) 622-2500
Emp Here 100
SIC 5147 Meats and meat products
　Daphne Nuis-Hall

D-U-N-S 20-975-3565　　(HQ)
GROBER INC
DELFT BLUE, DIV OF
(*Suby of* BARTELSE HOLDINGS LIMITED)
162 Savage Dr, Cambridge, ON, N1T 1S4
(519) 622-2500
Emp Here 200　　*Sales* 157,425,355
SIC 2048 Prepared feeds, nec
　Jerry Bartelse
　Jurian Bartelse

D-U-N-S 25-953-1473　　(BR)
GROBER INC
DELFT BLUE
(*Suby of* BARTELSE HOLDINGS LIMITED)
425 Dobbie Dr, Cambridge, ON, N1T 1S9
(519) 622-2500
Emp Here 200
SIC 2011 Meat packing plants
　Brandon Anger

D-U-N-S 20-648-1298　　(SL)
GROBER NUTRITION INC
GROBER
415 Dobbie Dr, Cambridge, ON, N1T 1S8
(519) 622-2500
Emp Here 249　　*Sales* 146,700,591
SIC 5191 Farm supplies
　Jerry Bartelse

D-U-N-S 25-688-4131　　(SL)
HALDEX LIMITED
(*Suby of* HALDEX AB)
500 Pinebush Rd Unit 1, Cambridge, ON, N1T 0A5
(519) 621-6722
Emp Here 24　　*Sales* 15,102,720
SIC 5531 Auto and home supply stores
　Mark Weber

D-U-N-S 20-695-3080　　(SL)
HUTTON FOREST PRODUCTS INC
320 Pinebush Road Unit 8, Cambridge, ON, N1T 1Z6
(519) 620-4374
Emp Here 17　　*Sales* 41,576,452
SIC 5031 Lumber, plywood, and millwork
　James Hutton
　Sharon Hutton

D-U-N-S 20-180-6189　　(SL)
KOCH TRANSPORT INC
151 Savage Dr Unit B, Cambridge, ON, N1T 1S6

Emp Here 110　　*Sales* 22,627,660
SIC 4213 Trucking, except local
　William Lindley

D-U-N-S 24-359-5126　　(HQ)
KODIAK GROUP HOLDINGS CO
TERRA FOOTWEAR
(*Suby of* V.F. CORPORATION)
415 Thompson Dr, Cambridge, ON, N1T 2K7
(519) 620-4000
Emp Here 5　　*Sales* 182,754,500
SIC 6719 Holding companies, nec

　Philip Williamson
　Kevin Huckle
　Stephen Webb
　David Mccarthy

D-U-N-S 24-077-6968　　(SL)
LOGIKOR INC
290 Pinebush Rd, Cambridge, ON, N1T 1Z6
(519) 622-8400
Emp Here 60　　*Sales* 38,275,650
SIC 4731 Freight transportation arrangement
　Darryl King
　Paul Silk

D-U-N-S 25-149-9141　　(SL)
LOGISENSE CORPORATION
278 Pinebush Rd Suite 102, Cambridge, ON, N1T 1Z6
(519) 249-0508
Emp Here 75　　*Sales* 3,866,259
SIC 7371 Custom computer programming services
　Flavio Gomes
　Ryan Susanna
　Tom Gros
　Christine Portwood
　Rich Kozub
　Adam Howatson
　Sunny Wu
　Rick Brock
　Mark Longo
　Christopher Brown

D-U-N-S 25-245-1351　　(HQ)
LONE WOLF REAL ESTATE TECHNOLOGIES INC
(*Suby of* VISTA EQUITY PARTNERS MANAGEMENT, LLC)
231 Shearson Cres Suite 310, Cambridge, ON, N1T 1J5
(866) 279-9653
Emp Here 150　　*Sales* 64,473,000
SIC 7372 Prepackaged software
　Patrick Arkeveld
　Brian Jamieson
　Don Harkness
　Lorne Wallace

D-U-N-S 24-345-9448　　(BR)
MATTAMY HOMES LIMITED
(*Suby of* MATTAMY HOMES LIMITED)
605 Sheldon Dr, Cambridge, ON, N1T 2K1

Emp Here 100
SIC 1522 Residential construction, nec

D-U-N-S 25-531-3967　　(SL)
METOKOTE CANADA LIMITED
(*Suby of* PPG INDUSTRIES, INC.)
50 Raglin Rd, Cambridge, ON, N1T 1Z5
(519) 621-2884
Emp Here 140　　*Sales* 26,891,900
SIC 3479 Metal coating and allied services
　Brian Somerville

D-U-N-S 24-868-5299　　(SL)
MIRION TECHNOLOGIES (IST CANADA) INC
IMAGING AND SENSING TECHNOLOGY
(*Suby of* MIRION TECHNOLOGIES (TOPCO), LTD)
465 Dobbie Dr, Cambridge, ON, N1T 1T1
(519) 623-4880
Emp Here 54　　*Sales* 21,314,762
SIC 3829 Measuring and controlling devices, nec
　Iain Wilson
　Thomas Logan

D-U-N-S 20-259-6631　　(BR)
NUTRABLEND FOODS INC
(*Suby of* BARTELSE HOLDINGS LIMITED)
415 Dobbie Dr, Cambridge, ON, N1T 1S8
(519) 622-4178
Emp Here 100
SIC 3556 Food products machinery
　Mark Lavine

D-U-N-S 24-525-0469　　(HQ)
PREFORMED LINE PRODUCTS (CANADA) LIMITED
PLP
(*Suby of* PREFORMED LINE PRODUCTS COMPANY)
1711 Bishop St N, Cambridge, ON, N1T 1N5
(519) 740-6666
Sales 10,233,650
SIC 3644 Noncurrent-carrying wiring devices
　Phil Jones
　Robert Ruhlman

D-U-N-S 24-397-2317　　(SL)
PRIDE SIGNS LIMITED
255 Pinebush Rd Unit I, Cambridge, ON, N1T 1B9
(519) 622-4040
Emp Here 120　　*Sales* 39,136,320
SIC 3993 Signs and advertising specialties
　Donald Bradley (Brad) Hillis
　Richard Beedham

D-U-N-S 25-511-8887　　(SL)
Q-PHARM INC
(*Suby of* ATLAS R & D INC)
180 Werlich Dr, Cambridge, ON, N1T 1N6
(519) 650-9850
Emp Here 35　　*Sales* 15,722,665
SIC 7389 Business services, nec
　Thomas Molloy
　Geulbang Giro Jebenian

D-U-N-S 24-757-7687　　(HQ)
REGIONAL HOSE & EQUIPMENT LTD
REGIONAL HOSE & HYDROLICS
175 Turnbull Crt, Cambridge, ON, N1T 1C6
(519) 740-1662
Emp Here 26　　*Sales* 28,501,560
SIC 5084 Industrial machinery and equipment
　Darwin T Booth
　Janna L Booth

D-U-N-S 20-369-8092　　(SL)
RICARDA'S INC
(*Suby of* DESCH CANADA LTD)
240 Shearson Cres, Cambridge, ON, N1T 1J6
(416) 304-9134
Emp Here 80　　*Sales* 3,641,520
SIC 5812 Eating places
　Hendrik Desch
　Cathy Brombacher
　Chris Glaessel

D-U-N-S 20-050-0056　　(HQ)
ROYCE-AYR CUTTING TOOLS INC
405 Sheldon Dr, Cambridge, ON, N1T 2B7
(519) 623-0580
Emp Here 10　　*Sales* 16,650,075
SIC 3541 Machine tools, Metal cutting type
　Gene Veening
　Stanley Puklicz
　Corrie Veening
　Joanne Puklicz

D-U-N-S 25-167-9437　　(HQ)
SHRED-TECH CORPORATION
295 Pinebush Rd, Cambridge, ON, N1T 1B2
(519) 621-3560
Emp Here 80　　*Sales* 19,980,090
SIC 3589 Service industry machinery, nec
　Robert Glass
　Robert Dibenedetto
　Carol Glass
　Peter Gottsegen
　Dale Tingley

D-U-N-S 25-413-2046　　(SL)
SUNOX INDUSTRIAL GASES INC
440 Sheldon Dr, Cambridge, ON, N1T 2C1
(519) 624-4413
Emp Here 22　　*Sales* 10,450,572
SIC 5085 Industrial supplies
　Claude Chabot

D-U-N-S 20-698-1727　　(SL)
SUPERFREIGHT TRANSPORTATION INC

445 Dobbie Dr, Cambridge, ON, N1T 1S9
(519) 650-5555
Emp Here 48   *Sales* 18,497,280
SIC 4731 Freight transportation arrangement
  Vasile Pop
  Joseph Gurrieri

D-U-N-S 24-394-1601   (SL)
SUTHERLAND-SCHULTZ LTD
SSL
(*Suby of* VOLLMER INC)
140 Turnbull Crt, Cambridge, ON, N1T 1J2
(519) 653-4123
Emp Here 225   *Sales* 52,989,525
SIC 1731 Electrical work
  Bradley G Vollmer

D-U-N-S 20-125-1840   (HQ)
TRAUGOTT BUILDING CONTRACTORS INC
95 Thompson Dr, Cambridge, ON, N1T 2E4
(519) 740-9444
Emp Here 60   *Sales* 57,033,800
SIC 1542 Nonresidential construction, nec
  Dan Flaminio

D-U-N-S 25-484-1190   (SL)
TRUSTWAVE CANADA, INC
231 Shearson Cres Suite 205, Cambridge, ON, N1T 1J5
(519) 620-7227
Emp Here 85   *Sales* 12,255,470
SIC 7371 Custom computer programming services
  Randall K Davis
  Kevin Karr
  Pamela Casale
  Sunil Bhargava
  Tom Wallace
  Terry Low
  Robert B Edwards Jr

D-U-N-S 24-235-5910   (SL)
WARM WITH CORN INC
HEAT BY DESIGN
55 Fleming Dr Unit 6, Cambridge, ON, N1T 2A9
(519) 624-5974
Emp Here 25   *Sales* 77,646,425
SIC 4925 Gas production and/or distribution
  Alan Brown

D-U-N-S 25-503-3177   (HQ)
WILLIAMSON-DICKIE CANADA COMPANY
(*Suby of* V.F. CORPORATION)
415 Thompson Dr, Cambridge, ON, N1T 2K7
(888) 664-6636
Emp Here 15   *Sales* 37,146,900
SIC 2326 Men's and boy's work clothing
  Mike Binnie
  Tobin Clark
  Philip Williamson
  Randy Teuber
  Philip Williamson

Cambridge, ON N3C

D-U-N-S 24-686-0639   (SL)
963488 ONTARIO LIMITED
MANCHESTER PRODUCTS
255 Holiday Inn Dr Suite 312, Cambridge, ON, N3C 3T2
(519) 220-1151
Emp Here 25   *Sales* 18,563,000
SIC 5191 Farm supplies
  Anko Scholtens
  Ralph Scholtens
  Francis Gouthor

D-U-N-S 25-882-4143   (SL)
AUTOMATED SOLUTIONS INTERNATIONAL INC
ASI
25 Milling Rd Suite 204, Cambridge, ON, N3C

1C3
(519) 220-0071
Emp Here 20   *Sales* 13,129,280
SIC 5962 Merchandising machine operators
  Peter Krotky

D-U-N-S 24-684-7370   (HQ)
BARRDAY, INC
BARRDAY PROTECTIVE SOLUTIONS
260 Holiday Inn Dr, Cambridge, ON, N3C 4E8
(519) 621-3620
Emp Here 50   *Sales* 18,340,300
SIC 2299 Textile goods, nec
  Michael Buckstein
  Tony Siorenzini
  Anne Verstraete
  Andrew Galbraith

D-U-N-S 25-623-2216   (SL)
BIMEDA-MTC ANIMAL HEALTH INC
(*Suby of* CROSS VETPHARM GROUP LIMITED)
420 Beaverdale Rd, Cambridge, ON, N3C 2W4
(519) 654-8000
Emp Here 100   *Sales* 28,402,100
SIC 2834 Pharmaceutical preparations
  Vincent Mcnally
  Carla Keenan

D-U-N-S 20-315-9298   (BR)
BUNZL CANADA INC
MCCORDICK GLOVE & SAFETY
(*Suby of* BUNZL PUBLIC LIMITED COMPANY)
400 Jamieson Pky, Cambridge, ON, N3C 4N3
(519) 651-2233
Emp Here 100
SIC 5084 Industrial machinery and equipment
  Philip Huck

D-U-N-S 20-588-4179   (HQ)
COLLABORATIVE STRUCTURES LIMITED
6683 Ellis Rd, Cambridge, ON, N3C 2V4
(519) 658-2750
Sales 18,829,240
SIC 1542 Nonresidential construction, nec
  David Timlock

D-U-N-S 20-121-0465   (SL)
CROWE FOUNDRY LIMITED
95 Sheffield St, Cambridge, ON, N3C 1C4

Emp Here 150   *Sales* 27,208,200
SIC 3321 Gray and ductile iron foundries
  Mike Promoli
  Dave Crowe

D-U-N-S 24-426-7097   (SL)
EXACTEARTH LTD
260 Holiday Inn Dr Unit 30, Cambridge, ON, N3C 4E8
(519) 622-4445
Emp Here 49   *Sales* 10,005,768
SIC 4899 Communication services, nec
  Peter Mabson
  David Martin
  Peter Dorcas
  Sean Maybee
  Eric J. Zahler
  Miguel Angel Panduro Panadero
  Miguel Angel Garcia Primo
  Lee Matheson
  Harvey B. Rein

D-U-N-S 24-422-9571   (SL)
FIVES MACHINING SYSTEMS CANADA INC
FIVES GLOBAL SERVICES
(*Suby of* FIVES ORSAY)
70 Cooper St, Cambridge, ON, N3C 2N4
(905) 673-7007
Emp Here 24   *Sales* 11,400,624
SIC 5084 Industrial machinery and equipment
  Bradley Blackburn
  Gary Finney

D-U-N-S 24-765-6655   (HQ)
IN-HOUSE SOLUTIONS INC

240 Holiday Inn Dr Unit A, Cambridge, ON, N3C 3X4
(519) 658-1471
Sales 22,805,874
SIC 5045 Computers, peripherals, and software
  Edward House
  Claire House

D-U-N-S 24-728-1470   (SL)
MAZAK CORPORATION CANADA
(*Suby of* YAMAZAKI MAZAK TRADING CORPORATION)
50 Commerce Crt, Cambridge, ON, N3C 4P7
(519) 658-2021
Emp Here 50   *Sales* 23,751,300
SIC 5084 Industrial machinery and equipment
  Brian Papke
  Ray Buxton

D-U-N-S 25-310-9771   (BR)
MCDONALD'S RESTAURANTS OF CANADA LIMITED
MCDONALD'S
(*Suby of* MCDONALD'S CORPORATION)
401 Westbound Hwy, Cambridge, ON, N3C 4B1

Emp Here 135
SIC 5812 Eating places
  Dave Kent

D-U-N-S 20-192-4292   (BR)
METRO ONTARIO INC
FOOD BASICS
(*Suby of* METRO INC)
100 Jamieson Pky, Cambridge, ON, N3C 4B3
(519) 658-1150
Emp Here 80
SIC 5411 Grocery stores
  Stephen Anderson

D-U-N-S 20-143-8322   (HQ)
NORFOLK KNITTERS LIMITED
LENS MILL STORE
50 Groh Ave, Cambridge, ON, N3C 1Y9
(519) 743-4672
Emp Here 15   *Sales* 43,979,040
SIC 5949 Sewing, needlework, and piece goods
  Peter Menary

D-U-N-S 24-214-4939   (HQ)
REID'S HERITAGE HOMES LTD
6783 Wellington Road 34, Cambridge, ON, N3C 2V4
(519) 658-6656
Emp Here 55   *Sales* 139,132,800
SIC 1521 Single-family housing construction
  Timothy Blevins

D-U-N-S 25-156-3235   (HQ)
REVERA LONG TERM CARE INC
HILLSIDE MANOR
(*Suby of* GOVERNMENT OF CANADA)
600 Jamieson Pky, Cambridge, ON, N3C 0A6
(519) 622-1840
Emp Here 85   *Sales* 290,385,500
SIC 8051 Skilled nursing care facilities
  Donna Kingelin

D-U-N-S 24-850-6672   (SL)
RHC DESIGN-BUILD
REID'S HERITAGE CONSTRUCTION
(*Suby of* REID'S HERITAGE HOMES LTD)
6783 Wellington Road 34, Cambridge, ON, N3C 2V4
(519) 249-0758
Emp Here 25   *Sales* 14,258,450
SIC 1542 Nonresidential construction, nec
  Eric Smith

D-U-N-S 24-561-0456   (SL)
SAINT LUKE'S PLACE
1624 Franklin Blvd, Cambridge, ON, N3C 3P4
(519) 658-5183
Emp Here 160   *Sales* 10,932,160
SIC 8051 Skilled nursing care facilities

Brian Swainson
Staci Bartlett
Tanya Wilson
Bruce Fraser
Paul Okrafka
Neil Brennan
Anne Tinker
David Bowyer
Tina Coleman
Barbara Fiddler

D-U-N-S 20-741-6384   (BR)
SAMUEL, SON & CO., LIMITED
BOTHWELL
(*Suby of* SAMUEL, SON & CO., LIMITED)
133 Troh Ave, Cambridge, ON, N3C 4B1
(416) 777-9554
Emp Here 100
SIC 1791 Structural steel erection
  Sandy Cabral

D-U-N-S 24-708-6721   (SL)
SCAN-TECH INSPECTION SERVICES LTD
HOIST MASTER
(*Suby of* SLING-CHOKER MFG. (HAMILTON) LTD)
221 Holiday Inn Dr, Cambridge, ON, N3C 3T2
(519) 651-1656
Emp Here 50   *Sales* 22,460,950
SIC 7389 Business services, nec
  Kane Butcher

D-U-N-S 24-423-1460   (SL)
SCHIEDEL CONSTRUCTION INCORPORATED
405 Queen St W, Cambridge, ON, N3C 1G6
(519) 658-9317
Emp Here 35   *Sales* 11,666,655
SIC 1541 Industrial buildings and warehouses
  Fred Schiedel
  Philip Schiedel

D-U-N-S 24-252-6734   (SL)
SKYLARK LOGISTICS INC
7295 Mason Rd, Cambridge, ON, N3C 2V4
(519) 821-7999
Emp Here 80   *Sales* 11,855,360
SIC 4212 Local trucking, without storage
  Sam Mann

D-U-N-S 20-121-0986   (HQ)
STRITE INDUSTRIES LIMITED
SPEED SYSTEM ORTHODONTIC SUPPLIES & PRECISION MACHINING
298 Shepherd Ave, Cambridge, ON, N3C 1V1
(519) 658-9361
Sales 45,457,800
SIC 3843 Dental equipment and supplies
  Richard Strite
  Neil Chester
  Judith Strite

D-U-N-S 25-137-3874   (BR)
WATERLOO REGION DISTRICT SCHOOL BOARD
JACOB HESPELER SECONDARY SCHOOL
(*Suby of* WATERLOO REGION DISTRICT SCHOOL BOARD)
355 Holiday Inn Dr, Cambridge, ON, N3C 1Z2
(519) 658-4910
Emp Here 120
SIC 8211 Elementary and secondary schools
  Jay Lavell

Cambridge, ON N3E

D-U-N-S 20-187-1378   (SL)
ALLCARD LIMITED
765 Boxwood Dr Suite 650, Cambridge, ON, N3E 1A4
(519) 650-9515
Emp Here 120   *Sales* 19,062,960
SIC 3089 Plastics products, nec
  Mark Brown

D-U-N-S 24-543-8247　　　(SL)
BASICS OFFICE PRODUCTS LTD
1040 Fountain St N Suite 1, Cambridge, ON,
N3E 1A3
(519) 653-8984
Emp Here 25　　*Sales* 28,527,419
SIC 5044 Office equipment
Sean Macey
Ted Hoxie
Brian Mikuliak

D-U-N-S 20-108-8098　　(HQ)
CHALLENGER INVESTMENTS INC
300 Maple Grove Rd, Cambridge, ON, N3E
1B7
(519) 653-6226
Emp Here 50　　*Sales* 28,798,840
SIC 4213 Trucking, except local
Dan Eiswecher
Doug Blair

D-U-N-S 25-075-1224　　(SL)
CHALLENGER LOGISTICS INC
(*Suby of* CHALLENGER INVESTMENTS II
INC)
300 Maple Grove Rd, Cambridge, ON, N3E
1B7
(519) 653-6226
Emp Here 32　　*Sales* 10,119,044
SIC 4731 Freight transportation arrangement
Daniel Einwechter
Eugene Moser

D-U-N-S 24-585-6935　　(HQ)
CHALLENGER MOTOR FREIGHT INC
(*Suby of* CHALLENGER INVESTMENTS II
INC)
300 Maple Grove Rd, Cambridge, ON, N3E
1B7
(519) 653-6226
Emp Here 1,200　*Sales* 168,141,160
SIC 4213 Trucking, except local
Daniel Einwechter
Eugene Moser
James Peeples

D-U-N-S 20-027-8973　　(SL)
CHEER SPORT SHARKS LIMITED
600 Boxwood Dr, Cambridge, ON, N3E 1A5
(519) 653-1221
Emp Here 70　　*Sales* 27,818,980
SIC 8699 Membership organizations, nec
Ali Moffatt
Alana Potter

D-U-N-S 20-140-4535　　(SL)
CLASS 1 INCORPORATED
CLASS 1
(*Suby of* ATLAS COPCO AB)
565 Boxwood Dr, Cambridge, ON, N3E 1A5
(519) 650-2355
Emp Here 79　　*Sales* 14,911,448
SIC 3841 Surgical and medical instruments
Dan Van Hove
Chris Over
Marian Boyer
Michael Sue
Ruben Rumero

D-U-N-S 24-363-3091　　(SL)
FIBERNETICS CORPORATION
WORLDLINE;295.CA
605 Boxwood Dr Suite 2972, Cambridge, ON,
N3E 1A5
(519) 489-6700
Emp Here 160　　*Sales* 36,555,520
SIC 4899 Communication services, nec
Jody Schnarr
John Stix

D-U-N-S 24-822-3364　　(SL)
GLENGARRY INDUSTRIES LTD
1040 Fountain St N Suite 6, Cambridge, ON,
N3E 1A3
(519) 653-1098
Emp Here 190　　*Sales* 36,183,980
SIC 3634 Electric housewares and fans
Leonard L Quinn

Don Mckenzie

D-U-N-S 24-325-8469　　(BR)
GRAND RIVER FOODS LTD
(*Suby of* GRAND RIVER FOODS LTD)
685 Boxwood Dr, Cambridge, ON, N3E 1B4
(519) 653-3577
Emp Here 300
SIC 2015 Poultry slaughtering and processing
John Mann

D-U-N-S 20-689-2809　　(HQ)
GRAND RIVER FOODS LTD
190 Vondrau Dr, Cambridge, ON, N3E 1B8
(519) 653-3577
Emp Here 50　　*Sales* 194,954,000
SIC 2015 Poultry slaughtering and processing
Dean Cebulski
John Mann
Steve Hanson
John Wendell
Tony Leone
Chris Malleck
Jason Hunter

D-U-N-S 24-305-6637　　(SL)
GRAND RIVER POULTRY LTD
GRAND RIVER FOODS
190 Vondrau Dr, Cambridge, ON, N3E 1B8
(519) 653-3577
Emp Here 75　　*Sales* 25,926,750
SIC 2015 Poultry slaughtering and processing
Craig Richarson

D-U-N-S 24-826-0986　　(SL)
MCC INDUSTRIAL SERVICES LTD
(*Suby of* MITSUI & CO., LTD.)
125 Vondrau Dr Suite 1, Cambridge, ON, N3E
1A8
(519) 650-9886
Emp Here 48　　*Sales* 11,245,824
SIC 8748 Business consulting, nec
Yujiug Asaoka

D-U-N-S 20-179-0289　　(HQ)
TOYOTA TSUSHO CANADA INC
TTCI
(*Suby of* TOYOTA TSUSHO CORPORATION)
1080 Fountain St N Unit 2, Cambridge, ON,
N3E 1A3
(519) 653-6600
Emp Here 40　　*Sales* 64,561,560
SIC 5013 Motor vehicle supplies and new
parts
Takashi Hasegawa
William Weiner
George A Pierce
Yasumasa Noguchi
Ali Tharia
Atsushi Shimizu

D-U-N-S 25-542-9938　　(HQ)
TRADE-MARK INDUSTRIAL INC
250 Royal Oak Rd, Cambridge, ON, N3E 0A4
(519) 650-7444
Emp Here 20　　*Sales* 38,227,680
SIC 1796 Installing building equipment
Russ Straus
Linda Straus
Mark Depass
Terry Moore
David Straus
Tom Straus
Dan Straus
Connie Workman

D-U-N-S 24-892-2630　　(BR)
UAP INC
UPA PIECES D'AUTO
(*Suby of* GENUINE PARTS COMPANY)
525 Boxwood Dr, Cambridge, ON, N3E 1A5
(519) 650-4444
Emp Here 150
SIC 5015 Motor vehicle parts, used
Jean Douville

Cambridge, ON N3H

D-U-N-S 24-358-9251　　(SL)
AIM INDUSTRIAL INC
29 Cherry Blossom Rd, Cambridge, ON, N3H
4R7
(519) 747-2255
Emp Here 130　　*Sales* 32,004,180
SIC 1796 Installing building equipment
Scott Henrich
Charles Asmussen
Steven Skrypec

D-U-N-S 24-407-5420　　(HQ)
ARNO HOLDINGS LTD
201b Preston Pky, Cambridge, ON, N3H 5E8
(519) 653-3171
Emp Here 3　　*Sales* 109,652,700
SIC 6712 Bank holding companies
Jamie Arnold
John Arnold
Sharon Sampson

D-U-N-S 24-326-8849　　(HQ)
ARRISCRAFT CANADA INC
(*Suby of* WIENERBERGER AG)
875 Speedsville Rd, Cambridge, ON, N3H
4R6
(519) 653-3275
Emp Here 300　　*Sales* 127,845,000
SIC 3281 Cut stone and stone products
Peter Schmidt

D-U-N-S 24-091-9712　　(HQ)
**ATS AUTOMATION TOOLING SYSTEMS
INC**
ATS ADVANCE MANUFACTURING, DIV OF
730 Fountain St Suite 2b, Cambridge, ON,
N3H 4R7
(519) 653-6500
Emp Here 100　　*Sales* 947,897,920
SIC 3569 General industrial machinery, nec
Andrew Hider
David Mcausland
Neil D. Arnold
Joanne S. Ferstman
Kirsten Lange
Michael Martino
Philip B. Whitehead
Maria Perrella

D-U-N-S 24-359-8757　　(SL)
BAUMEIER CORPORATION
1050 Fountain St N, Cambridge, ON, N3H
4R7
(519) 650-5553
Emp Here 80　　*Sales* 17,760,080
SIC 3599 Industrial machinery, nec
George Sr. Henry

D-U-N-S 24-348-4719　　(SL)
BIOMATIK CORPORATION
140 Mcgovern Dr Unit 9, Cambridge, ON, N3H
4R7
(519) 489-7195
Emp Here 10　　*Sales* 11,053,450
SIC 5122 Drugs, proprietaries, and sundries
Michael He

D-U-N-S 20-264-5925　　(SL)
BLENDTEK FINE INGREDIENTS INC
32 Cherry Blossom Rd, Cambridge, ON, N3H
4R7
(519) 279-4401
Emp Here 26　　*Sales* 18,988,970
SIC 5169 Chemicals and allied products, nec
William Zinger
Steven Zinger
Robert Bianchin
Kristie Santos

D-U-N-S 20-526-4633　　(SL)
BOCK NORTH AMERICA LTD
BOCK
(*Suby of* BOCK 1 GMBH & CO. KG)
18 Cherry Blossom Rd, Cambridge, ON, N3H

4R7
(519) 653-3334
Emp Here 100　　*Sales* 15,885,800
SIC 3089 Plastics products, nec
Hermann Bock

D-U-N-S 24-850-0014　　(HQ)
CAISSEN WATER TECHNOLOGIES INC
CULLIGAN WATER
265 Industrial Rd, Cambridge, ON, N3H 4R7
(800) 265-7841
Emp Here 60　　*Sales* 24,432,800
SIC 5963 Direct selling establishments
Robert Caissie

D-U-N-S 25-463-7986　　(BR)
**CARESSANT-CARE NURSING AND RE-
TIREMENT HOMES LIMITED**
CAMBRIDGE COUNTRY MANOR
(*Suby of* CARESSANT-CARE NURSING AND
RETIREMENT HOMES LIMITED)
3680 Speedsville Rd Suite 3, Cambridge, ON,
N3H 4R6
(519) 650-0100
Emp Here 80
SIC 8051 Skilled nursing care facilities
Tracy Richardson

D-U-N-S 20-850-2393　　(HQ)
CENTRA INDUSTRIES INC
24 Cherry Blossom Rd, Cambridge, ON, N3H
4R7
(519) 650-2828
Emp Here 265　　*Sales* 114,008,720
SIC 3369 Nonferrous foundries, nec
Larry Fritzgerald

D-U-N-S 25-911-2290　　(BR)
COMMUNITY LIVING CAMBRIDGE
VALENTINE GROUP HOME
1124 Valentine Dr, Cambridge, ON, N3H 2N8
(519) 650-5091
Emp Here 200
SIC 8361 Residential care
Mike Mullen

D-U-N-S 24-007-4138　　(HQ)
COWAN INSURANCE GROUP LTD
705 Fountain St N, Cambridge, ON, N3H 4R7
(519) 650-6360
Emp Here 50　　*Sales* 295,638,720
SIC 6411 Insurance agents, brokers, and ser-
vice
Heather Mclachlin
Lionel Beauchamp

D-U-N-S 20-124-3961　　(HQ)
DARE FOODS LIMITED
25 Cherry Blossom Rd, Cambridge, ON, N3H
4R7
(519) 893-5500
Emp Here 550　　*Sales* 682,339,000
SIC 2051 Bread, cake, and related products
Peter Luik
Bryan Dare
William Farrell
Ingrid Bett
Graham Dare

D-U-N-S 24-666-5350　　(SL)
DIETER'S METAL FABRICATING LIMITED
275 Industrial Rd, Cambridge, ON, N3H 4R7
(519) 884-8555
Emp Here 70　　*Sales* 13,445,950
SIC 3499 Fabricated Metal products, nec
Dieter Hohendorn
Edith Hohendorn
Peter Hohendorn

D-U-N-S 24-965-2256　　(HQ)
**DIMPLEX NORTH AMERICA HOLDINGS
LIMITED**
(*Suby of* GLEN DIMPLEX UNLIMITED COM-
PANY)
1367 Industrial Rd, Cambridge, ON, N3H 4W3
(519) 650-3630
Emp Here 1　　*Sales* 91,377,250
SIC 6712 Bank holding companies

Martyn Champ
Carmen Salvatore

D-U-N-S 20-730-0682 (SL)
EAGLE NORTH HOLDINGS INC
CAMBRIDGE TOYOTA
2400 Eagle St N, Cambridge, ON, N3H 4R7
(519) 653-7030
Emp Here 45   *Sales* 22,413,510
SIC 5511 New and used car dealers

D-U-N-S 24-011-5626 (SL)
FAIRVIEW MENNONITE HOMES
515 Langs Dr Suite D, Cambridge, ON, N3H
5E4
(519) 653-2222
Emp Here 160   *Sales* 10,285,120
SIC 8361 Residential care
Brenda Hagey
Tim Kennel
Brent Martin

D-U-N-S 20-533-6571 (SL)
GALT CHRYSLER DODGE LTD
2440 Eagle St N, Cambridge, ON, N3H 4R7
(519) 650-2440
Emp Here 45   *Sales* 22,413,510
SIC 5511 New and used car dealers
Gordon Nimeck
Reg Nimeck

D-U-N-S 24-784-1646 (SL)
GILLIES LUMBER INC
GILLIES STAIRCASE & MILLWORK
(*Suby of* ALPA LUMBER INC)
777 Industrial Rd, Cambridge, ON, N3H 4W2
(519) 653-3219
Emp Here 50   *Sales* 22,358,700
SIC 5031 Lumber, plywood, and millwork
John Di Poce
George Frankfort

D-U-N-S 24-390-0719 (HQ)
GLEN DIMPLEX AMERICAS LIMITED
(*Suby of* GLEN DIMPLEX UNLIMITED COMPANY)
1367 Industrial Rd Suite 768, Cambridge, ON,
N3H 4W3
(519) 650-3630
Sales 86,305,200
SIC 5023 Homefurnishings
Robert Bartucci
Carmen Salvatore

D-U-N-S 20-942-4233 (SL)
GOLDEN YEARS NURSING HOMES (CAMBRIDGE) INC
*GOLDEN YEARS NURSING & ASSISTED
LIVING CENTRE*
704 Eagle St N, Cambridge, ON, N3H 1C3
(519) 653-5493
Emp Here 125   *Sales* 8,570,750
SIC 8051 Skilled nursing care facilities
Anthony Langford

D-U-N-S 20-037-3801 (HQ)
HUSSMANN CANADA INC
HUSSMANN STORE EQUIPMENT
5 Cherry Blossom Rd Suite 3, Cambridge, ON,
N3H 4R7
(519) 653-9980
Emp Here 31   *Sales* 69,006,600
SIC 5078 Refrigeration equipment and supplies
Mark Dennison

D-U-N-S 24-830-2341 (SL)
LANGDON HALL LIMITED
*LANGDON HALL COUNTRY HOUSE HOTEL
& SPA*
1 Langdon Dr Suite 33, Cambridge, ON, N3H
4R8
(519) 740-2100
Emp Here 130   *Sales* 12,049,700
SIC 7011 Hotels and motels
William Bennett
Mary Beaton

D-U-N-S 20-641-0565 (HQ)
LITTLE SHORT STOP STORES LIMITED
(*Suby of* ARNO HOLDINGS LTD)
201b Preston Pky, Cambridge, ON, N3H 5E8
(519) 653-3171
Emp Here 15   *Sales* 48,116,000
SIC 5411 Grocery stores
Anne Arnold
Michael Arnold
Jamie Arnold
Larry Vasey

D-U-N-S 20-299-3080 (BR)
PEPSICO CANADA ULC
FRITO LAY CANADA
(*Suby of* PEPSICO, INC.)
1001 Bishop St N, Cambridge, ON, N3H 4V8
(519) 653-5721
Emp Here 500
SIC 2096 Potato chips and similar snacks
Carlos Lozana

D-U-N-S 24-626-1234 (SL)
PRECISION RESOURCE CANADA LTD
(*Suby of* PRECISION RESOURCE, INC.)
4 Cherry Blossom Rd, Cambridge, ON, N3H
4R7
(519) 653-7777
Emp Here 200   *Sales* 38,417,000
SIC 3469 Metal stampings, nec
Peter Wolcott
Kaveh Vafaei
John Weiland

D-U-N-S 20-702-3008 (BR)
RE/MAX REAL ESTATE CENTRE INC
(*Suby of* RE/MAX REAL ESTATE CENTRE
INC)
766 Hespeler Rd Suite 202, Cambridge, ON,
N3H 5L8
(519) 623-6200
Emp Here 115
SIC 6531 Real estate agents and managers
Steven Andrade

D-U-N-S 24-783-3338 (HQ)
RE/MAX REAL ESTATE CENTRE INC
766 Hespeler Rd Suite 202, Cambridge, ON,
N3H 5L8
(519) 740-0001
Emp Here 50   *Sales* 135,225,600
SIC 6531 Real estate agents and managers
Louis Klarke
Delio Olivira

D-U-N-S 20-292-6150 (HQ)
SOUTHBRIDGE HEALTH CARE LP
766 Hespeler Rd Suite 301, Cambridge, ON,
N3H 5L8
(519) 621-8886
Sales 68,670,927
SIC 8741 Management services
Keith Mcintosh
Mark Maxwell
Redge Peterson
Ryan Bell
Richard Franzke
Susan Motkalk
Reg Peterson

D-U-N-S 24-357-0590 (HQ)
STC STEEL TECHNOLOGIES CANADA LTD
(*Suby of* NUMIT LLC)
16 Cherry Blossom Rd, Cambridge, ON, N3H
4R7
(519) 653-2880
Emp Here 30   *Sales* 22,011,731
SIC 7389 Business services, nec
Stuart Ray
Mark Gemin
Michael Anderson
Hideki Takahara

D-U-N-S 24-726-7594 (HQ)
TOYOTA MOTOR MANUFACTURING CANADA INC
TMMC
(*Suby of* TOYOTA MOTOR CORPORATION)

1055 Fountain St N, Cambridge, ON, N3H
4R7
(519) 653-1111
Sales 2,326,800,000
SIC 3711 Motor vehicles and car bodies
Fred Volf
Brian Krinock
Takahiro Fujioka
Tetsuo Agata

D-U-N-S 20-527-5188 (SL)
VANN, GREG NISSAN INC
GREG VANN NISSAN
2386 Eagle St N, Cambridge, ON, N3H 4R7
(519) 650-9200
Emp Here 25   *Sales* 12,451,950
SIC 5511 New and used car dealers
Gregory Vann

D-U-N-S 24-559-3723 (SL)
VISTA CONTRACTING LTD.
1316 Dickie Settlement Rd, Cambridge, ON,
N3H 4R8
(519) 650-3481
Emp Here 40   *Sales* 11,340,960
SIC 1611 Highway and street construction
Kevin Norton

D-U-N-S 20-710-7090 (BR)
**WATERLOO REGION DISTRICT SCHOOL
BOARD**
PRESTON HIGH SCHOOL
(*Suby of* WATERLOO REGION DISTRICT
SCHOOL BOARD)
550 Rose St, Cambridge, ON, N3H 2E6
(519) 653-2367
Emp Here 100
SIC 8211 Elementary and secondary schools
Joe Bell

Cameron, ON K0M

D-U-N-S 25-684-7682 (SL)
1254711 ONTARIO LIMITED
ROCKWOOD FOREST NURSERIES
437 Mark Rd Suite 1, Cameron, ON, K0M 1G0
(705) 374-4700
Emp Here 40   *Sales* 29,700,800
SIC 5193 Flowers and florists supplies
Marc Ouellet

Campbellford, ON K0L

D-U-N-S 20-039-6901 (SL)
3059714 NOVA SCOTIA COMPANY
*WORLD'S FINEST CHOCOLATE CANADA
COMPANY*
(*Suby of* WORLD'S FINEST CHOCOLATE,
INC.)
103 Second St, Campbellford, ON, K0L 1L0
(705) 653-3590
Emp Here 18   *Sales* 15,040,386
SIC 5149 Groceries and related products, nec
Edmond Opler
Ken Tully

D-U-N-S 24-894-0629 (HQ)
BENNETT'S HOME FURNISHINGS LIMITED
13 Front St S, Campbellford, ON, K0L 1L0
(705) 653-1188
Emp Here 20   *Sales* 17,397,380
SIC 5211 Lumber and other building materials
Eric Bennett
Marlaine Bennett

D-U-N-S 24-351-5694 (SL)
**BLOMMER CHOCOLATE COMPANY OF
CANADA INC**
(*Suby of* FUJI OIL HOLDINGS INC.)
103 Second Ave, Campbellford, ON, K0L 1L0

(705) 653-5821
Emp Here 50   *Sales* 17,284,500
SIC 2066 Chocolate and cocoa products
Richard J Blommer
Peter W Blommer
Jack S Larsen
Doug Harper
Mike Smith

D-U-N-S 25-347-4571 (SL)
CAMPBELLFORD MEMORIAL HOSPITAL
146 Oliver Rd, Campbellford, ON, K0L 1L0
(705) 653-1140
Emp Here 112   *Sales* 14,011,149
SIC 8062 General medical and surgical hospitals
Varouj Eskedjian
Tim Chennette
Rosemarie Peikes
Karen Macginnis
Craig Hitchman
David Pollack
Ann Anderson
Paul Nichols
Cathy Vosper
Kevin Huestis

D-U-N-S 20-821-1524 (SL)
**CAMPBELLFORD WHOLESALE COMPANY
LTD**
11 Industrial Dr Suite 1, Campbellford, ON,
K0L 1L0
(705) 653-3640
Emp Here 15   *Sales* 11,137,800
SIC 5194 Tobacco and tobacco products
John Locke
David Locke
Marie Locke

D-U-N-S 25-371-6674 (SL)
DRUMMOND, SCOTT MOTORS LTD
501 Grand Rd Rr 1, Campbellford, ON, K0L
1L0
(705) 653-2020
Emp Here 33   *Sales* 16,436,574
SIC 5511 New and used car dealers
Scott Drummond
Kim Dafoe

D-U-N-S 20-039-6091 (SL)
**EMPIRE CHEESE & BUTTER CO-
OPERATIVE**
1120 County Rd 8, Campbellford, ON, K0L
1L0
(705) 653-3187
Emp Here 23   *Sales* 12,307,852
SIC 5143 Dairy products, except dried or
canned
Clair Petherick

D-U-N-S 20-790-2292 (SL)
FISHER'S NO FRILLS
15 Canrobert St, Campbellford, ON, K0L 1L0
(866) 987-6453
Emp Here 40   *Sales* 10,966,080
SIC 5411 Grocery stores
William Watkin

D-U-N-S 25-237-8385 (BR)
**KAWARTHA PINE RIDGE DISTRICT
SCHOOL BOARD**
CAMPBELLFORD DISTRICT HIGH SCHOOL
119 Ranney St N Unit 960, Campbellford, ON,
K0L 1L0
(705) 653-3060
Emp Here 105
SIC 8211 Elementary and secondary schools
Douglas Birch

D-U-N-S 25-487-3268 (HQ)
**NEWMAN, OLIVER & MCCARTEN INSUR-
ANCE BROKERS LTD**
35 Front St N, Campbellford, ON, K0L 1L0

Emp Here 14   *Sales* 41,554,940
SIC 6411 Insurance agents, brokers, and service
Calvin Newman

Gary Newman
Janet Newman-Philips
Gwen Bush

D-U-N-S 25-944-5617   (SL)
SHARPE FOODS LTD
SHARPE'S IGA
85 Front St N, Campbellford, ON, K0L 1L0
(705) 653-2326
Emp Here 80   *Sales* 23,478,160
SIC 5411 Grocery stores
Steven D Sharpe
Thomas G Sharpe
John C Sharpe
Marian M Morton

D-U-N-S 24-387-6294   (HQ)
TEAM EAGLE LTD
EAGLE AIRFIELD
10 Trent Dr, Campbellford, ON, K0L 1L0
(705) 653-2956
Sales 19,001,040
SIC 5084 Industrial machinery and equipment
Steven Mckeown
Paul Cudmore

Campbellville, ON L0P

D-U-N-S 20-172-1255   (SL)
3235 ONTARIO INC
OLIVER LUMBER COMPANY OF TORONTO
9184 Twiss Rd Rr 2, Campbellville, ON, L0P 1B0
(416) 233-1227
Emp Here 40   *Sales* 17,886,960
SIC 5031 Lumber, plywood, and millwork
Ian Smart

D-U-N-S 24-217-9869   (BR)
GOODFELLOW INC
OLIVER LUMBER
(*Suby of* GOODFELLOW INC)
9184 Twiss Rd, Campbellville, ON, L0P 1B0
(416) 233-1227
Emp Here 170
SIC 5031 Lumber, plywood, and millwork
Marry Lohmus

D-U-N-S 24-685-7692   (SL)
MERITCO INDUSTRIES LTD
RIDLEY WINDOWS & DOORS
2675 Reid Side Rd, Campbellville, ON, L0P 1B0
(905) 854-2228
Emp Here 23   *Sales* 10,285,002
SIC 5031 Lumber, plywood, and millwork
Paul Merritt

D-U-N-S 24-688-1544   (SL)
MOFFATT SCRAP IRON & METAL INC
9620 Guelph Line, Campbellville, ON, L0P 1B0
(905) 854-2792
Emp Here 45   *Sales* 23,424,390
SIC 5093 Scrap and waste materials
Clarence Stephen Moffatt

D-U-N-S 24-389-8561   (SL)
MONAGHAN MUSHROOMS LTD
(*Suby of* MONAGHAN MUSHROOMS IRELAND UNLIMITED COMPANY)
7345 Guelph Line, Campbellville, ON, L0P 1B0
(905) 878-9375
Emp Here 329   *Sales* 25,912,658
SIC 0182 Food crops grown under cover
Ronald Wilson
George Graham
John Stanley
Paul Wilson

D-U-N-S 20-551-4495   (HQ)
PALLET MANAGEMENT GROUP INC
9148 Twiss Rd, Campbellville, ON, L0P 1B0

(905) 857-7939
Sales 27,184,200
SIC 7699 Repair services, nec
Timothy John Mcgillion

Cannifton, ON K0K

D-U-N-S 24-846-8936   (SL)
L.M.B. TRANSPORT INC
209 Putman Industrial Rd, Cannifton, ON, K0K 1K0
(613) 968-7524
Emp Here 80   *Sales* 11,855,360
SIC 4212 Local trucking, without storage
Larry Brown

Cannington, ON L0E

D-U-N-S 24-098-6265   (HQ)
COUNTRY DRUG STORES LTD
BENS PHARMACY
6 Cameron St E, Cannington, ON, L0E 1E0
(705) 432-2644
Emp Here 10   *Sales* 19,546,240
SIC 5912 Drug stores and proprietary stores
Ben Smith
Donna Smith

D-U-N-S 20-987-8631   (SL)
SUTTON GROUP HERITAGE REALTY INC
26 Cameron St W, Cannington, ON, L0E 1E0

Emp Here 200   *Sales* 83,777,800
SIC 6531 Real estate agents and managers
Rosalind Menary

Capreol, ON P0M

D-U-N-S 24-335-7394   (BR)
ACROBAT RESEARCH LTD
ACROBAT RESULT MARKETING
(*Suby of* ACROBAT RESEARCH LTD)
Gd, Capreol, ON, P0M 1H0
(705) 858-4343
Emp Here 100
SIC 8732 Commercial nonphysical research
Roland Klassen

D-U-N-S 24-389-3414   (SL)
LAYNE CHRISTENSEN CANADA LIMITED
(*Suby of* GRANITE CONSTRUCTION INCORPORATED)
9 Regional Rd 84 Unit 84, Capreol, ON, P0M 1H0

Emp Here 78
SIC 1499 Miscellaneous nonMetallic minerals, except fuels
George R Demers
Eric R Despain
Andrew B Schmitt

Carleton Place, ON K7C

D-U-N-S 20-272-0228   (BR)
ALMONTE GENERAL HOSPITAL
LANARK COUNTY PARAMEDIC SERVICE
(*Suby of* ALMONTE GENERAL HOSPITAL)
37 Neelin St, Carleton Place, ON, K7C 2J6
(613) 205-1021
Emp Here 85
SIC 4119 Local passenger transportation, nec
Edward Mcpearson

D-U-N-S 25-280-0792   (SL)
CARLETON PLACE & DISTRICT MEMO-

RIAL HOSPITAL
211 Lake Ave E, Carleton Place, ON, K7C 1J4
(613) 257-2200
Emp Here 150   *Sales* 16,662,000
SIC 8069 Specialty hospitals, except psychiatric
Malcolm Robinson

D-U-N-S 20-893-3424   (HQ)
CARLETON PLACE DRUG MART INC
CARLETON PLACE IDA DRUG MART
47 Lansdowne Ave, Carleton Place, ON, K7C 3S9
(613) 257-1414
Emp Here 52   *Sales* 20,767,880
SIC 5912 Drug stores and proprietary stores
Aziz Dhalla
Esmail Merani

D-U-N-S 24-595-9366   (SL)
DICA ELECTRONICS LTD
160 Industrial Ave, Carleton Place, ON, K7C 3T2
(613) 257-5379
Emp Here 65   *Sales* 12,378,730
SIC 3672 Printed circuit boards
Spencer Grabe

D-U-N-S 24-361-7201   (BR)
HOME DEPOT OF CANADA INC
HOME DEPOT
(*Suby of* THE HOME DEPOT INC)
570 Mcneely Ave, Carleton Place, ON, K7C 0A7
(613) 253-3870
Emp Here 100
SIC 5251 Hardware stores
Louis Dimarco

D-U-N-S 20-286-2397   (SL)
KEYESBURY DISTRIBUTORS LIMITED
APPLIANCE ADVANTAGE
99 Bruce Cres, Carleton Place, ON, K7C 3T3
(613) 257-8100
Emp Here 24   *Sales* 10,732,176
SIC 5064 Electrical appliances, television and radio
Ian Frederick Morrison
Joanne Morrison

D-U-N-S 25-685-0959   (SL)
KINGSWAY ARMS MANAGEMENT (AT CARLETON PLACE) INC
6 Arthur St, Carleton Place, ON, K7C 4S4
(613) 253-7360
Emp Here 55   *Sales* 12,810,105
SIC 6513 Apartment building operators
Pat Bryne

D-U-N-S 25-028-5251   (BR)
REVERA LONG TERM CARE INC
STONERIDGE MANOR
(*Suby of* GOVERNMENT OF CANADA)
256 High St, Carleton Place, ON, K7C 1X1
(613) 257-4355
Emp Here 75
SIC 8051 Skilled nursing care facilities
Michelle Ferguson

D-U-N-S 24-163-4174   (SL)
SHOPPERS DRUG MART
315 Mcneely Ave, Carleton Place, ON, K7C 4S6
(613) 253-5595
Emp Here 50   *Sales* 12,647,700
SIC 5912 Drug stores and proprietary stores
Ghada Gabr

Carlsbad Springs, ON K0A

D-U-N-S 20-378-0858   (SL)
4452241 CANADA LTD
RJP TRAILERS
6019 Russell Rd Unit 2, Carlsbad Springs, ON, K0A 1K0

(613) 816-9917
Emp Here 50   *Sales* 10,301,848
SIC 7519 Utility trailer rental
Kevin Lacombe

Carp, ON K0A

D-U-N-S 20-336-4898   (SL)
1649338 ONTARIO INC
ITALFOODS
266 Westbrook Rd, Carp, ON, K0A 1L0
(613) 831-4446
Emp Here 36   *Sales* 30,080,772
SIC 5149 Groceries and related products, nec
Franco Adamo

D-U-N-S 24-382-7433   (SL)
ABSOPULSE ELECTRONICS LTD
A B S PRODUCTS & DESIGN
110 Walgreen Rd, Carp, ON, K0A 1L0
(613) 836-3511
Emp Here 125   *Sales* 23,805,250
SIC 3679 Electronic components, nec
Antal Szullo

D-U-N-S 24-685-8070   (HQ)
BLUMETRIC ENVIRONMENTAL INC
WESA
3108 Carp Rd, Carp, ON, K0A 1L0
(613) 839-3053
Emp Here 70   *Sales* 24,685,181
SIC 1623 Water, sewer, and utility lines
Scott A. Macfabe
Dan L. Scroggins
Vivian Karaiskos
Lydia Renton
Jane Pagel
Ron Donaldson
Hubert (Hu) L. Fleming
Vijay Jog
Geoff Simonett

D-U-N-S 20-442-5664   (SL)
C&M ELECTRIC LTD
3038 Carp Rd, Carp, ON, K0A 1L0
(613) 839-3232
Emp Here 55   *Sales* 11,980,595
SIC 1731 Electrical work
Kenneth Wayne Crawford
Jean Crawford
Lawrence Crawford
Deborah Craig

D-U-N-S 20-690-4620   (HQ)
CHARLAMARA HOLDINGS INC
NAUTICAL LANDS GROUP
2962 Carp Rd, Carp, ON, K0A 1L0
(613) 831-9039
Sales 16,256,520
SIC 1522 Residential construction, nec
Kirk Hoppner

D-U-N-S 24-875-9763   (SL)
EXEL CONTRACTING INC
135 Walgreen Rd, Carp, ON, K0A 1L0
(613) 831-3935
Emp Here 50   *Sales* 11,677,563
SIC 0781 Landscape counseling and planning
Ian Rowbotham
Tracey Rowbotham

D-U-N-S 25-813-1366   (SL)
G.A.L. POWER SYSTEMS INC
2558 Carp Rd, Carp, ON, K0A 1L0
(613) 831-3188
Emp Here 30   *Sales* 13,415,220
SIC 5063 Electrical apparatus and equipment
Guy Lapierre
Dal Bath
Sylvia Gruzas-Lapierre

D-U-N-S 25-306-2186   (SL)
HARDING MECHANICAL CONTRACTORS INC
HARDING HEATING AND AIR CONDITION-

ING
2210 Cavanmore Rd Rr 2, Carp, ON, K0A 1L0
(613) 831-2257
Emp Here 100   *Sales* 23,306,500
SIC 1711 Plumbing, heating, air-conditioning
Richard Harding
Kim Harding

D-U-N-S 20-553-0785   (HQ)
HELICOPTER TRANSPORT SERVICES (CANADA) INC
(*Suby of* J. & L. AIRCRAFT LEASING CO. LTD)
5 Huisson Rd, Carp, ON, K0A 1L0
(613) 839-5868
Emp Here 40   *Sales* 20,023,350
SIC 4522 Air transportation, nonscheduled
Luc Pilon
Gary Connolly
Denis Pilon

D-U-N-S 24-795-9984   (SL)
M-CON PRODUCTS INC
2150 Richardson Side Rd Rr 3, Carp, ON, K0A 1L0
(613) 831-1736
Emp Here 67   *Sales* 15,640,145
SIC 3272 Concrete products, nec
Rudy Mion
John Mion
Gustavo Mion

D-U-N-S 20-831-2244   (HQ)
MCINTOSH PERRY CONSULTING ENGINEERS LTD
115 Walgreen Rd Rr 3, Carp, ON, K0A 1L0
(613) 836-2184
Emp Here 5   *Sales* 22,342,375
SIC 8711 Engineering services
Todd Perry

D-U-N-S 20-700-2205   (SL)
MEYKNECHT-LISCHER CONTRACTORS LTD
145 Walgreen Rd, Carp, ON, K0A 1L0

Emp Here 50   *Sales* 15,943,450
SIC 1521 Single-family housing construction
Teja Lischer

D-U-N-S 20-397-4340   (SL)
MORLEY HOPPER LIMITED
1818 Bradley Side Rd, Carp, ON, K0A 1L0
(613) 831-5490
Emp Here 60   *Sales* 72,723,735
SIC 1522 Residential construction, nec
Kenneth Hoppner
Brian Morley

D-U-N-S 24-269-8272   (HQ)
SENSTAR CORPORATION
(*Suby of* MAGAL SECURITY SYSTEMS LTD.)
119 John Cavanaugh Dr, Carp, ON, K0A 1L0
(613) 839-5572
Sales 16,378,012
SIC 3699 Electrical equipment and supplies, nec
Brian Rich
Eleanor Hodgson
Jeremy Weese

D-U-N-S 25-123-2971   (SL)
SPRATT AGGREGATES LTD
2300 Carp Rd, Carp, ON, K0A 1L0
(613) 831-0717
Emp Here 40   *Sales* 10,122,360
SIC 5211 Lumber and other building materials
Bill Karson

D-U-N-S 24-764-7647   (BR)
WASTE MANAGEMENT OF CANADA CORPORATION
WASTE MANAGEMENT
(*Suby of* WASTE MANAGEMENT, INC.)
254 Westbrook Rd, Carp, ON, K0A 1L0
(613) 831-1281
Emp Here 150

SIC 4953 Refuse systems
Kevin Cinq Mark

D-U-N-S 25-407-8025   (HQ)
WEST CARLETON SAND & GRAVEL INC
KARSON AGGREGATES
(*Suby of* AECON GROUP INC)
3232 Carp Rd, Carp, ON, K0A 1L0
(613) 839-2816
Emp Here 25   *Sales* 47,101,800
SIC 1771 Concrete work
William Karson
Peter Geick
John Adshead

D-U-N-S 25-344-9060   (SL)
X-L-AIR ENERGY SERVICES LTD
141 Wescar Lane, Carp, ON, K0A 1L0
(613) 836-5002
Emp Here 63   *Sales* 14,683,095
SIC 1711 Plumbing, heating, air-conditioning
Nick Haitas
Gord Downes
Mary Haitas
Todd Bethune

Casselman, ON K0A

D-U-N-S 20-894-2300   (HQ)
417 BUS LINE LIMITED
50 Industrial St, Casselman, ON, K0A 1M0
(613) 764-2192
Emp Here 95   *Sales* 9,785,360
SIC 4151 School buses
Yvon Laplante
Mario Laplante
Marc Laplante
Gilles Laplante

D-U-N-S 20-040-0562   (SL)
DUPUIS, FORD LINCOLN INC
603 Rue St Isidore, Casselman, ON, K0A 1M0
(613) 764-2994
Emp Here 27   *Sales* 13,448,106
SIC 5511 New and used car dealers
Donald Dupuis
Michel Cardinal
Michel Dupuis
Diane Dupuis Laviolette

D-U-N-S 25-282-3380   (SL)
GESTION FSTG INC
CANADIAN TIRE
95 Lafleche Blvd, Casselman, ON, K0A 1M0
(613) 764-0401
Emp Here 50   *Sales* 18,210,750
SIC 5014 Tires and tubes
Francois St-Germain

D-U-N-S 24-101-9322   (SL)
LAPLANTE CHEVROLET PONTIAC BUICK GMC LTD
632 Principale St, Casselman, ON, K0A 1M0
(613) 764-2846
Emp Here 40   *Sales* 19,923,120
SIC 5511 New and used car dealers
Jacques Laplante

Cathcart, ON N0E

D-U-N-S 25-220-3104   (SL)
WILSON, DAVID W. MANUFACTURING LTD
193 Hwy 53, Cathcart, ON, N0E 1B0
(519) 458-8911
Emp Here 64   *Sales* 11,525,100
SIC 3499 Fabricated Metal products, nec
David W Wilson

Cayuga, ON N0A

D-U-N-S 25-367-3255   (SL)
1233481 ONTARIO INC
TORONTO MOTORSPORTS PARK
1040 Kohler Rd, Cayuga, ON, N0A 1E0
(905) 772-0303
Emp Here 100   *Sales* 8,712,800
SIC 7948 Racing, including track operation
Uli Bieri

D-U-N-S 24-514-2476   (SL)
CAYUGA DISPLAYS INC
88 Talbot St E, Cayuga, ON, N0A 1E0
(905) 772-5214
Emp Here 70   *Sales* 10,802,540
SIC 2541 Wood partitions and fixtures
Jan Vanreenen
Richard (Rick) Schotsman
John Devries
Chris Schotsman
Kirk Bessey
Ryan Schotsman
Jennifer Zuidema

D-U-N-S 20-555-0296   (HQ)
CAYUGA MATERIALS & CONSTRUCTION CO. LIMITED
HOLCIM CANADA
4219 Highway 3 Rr 4, Cayuga, ON, N0A 1E0
(905) 772-3331
Emp Here 1   *Sales* 18,674,800
SIC 1422 Crushed and broken limestone
George Miller
Lionel St. Martin
Stuart Scott

D-U-N-S 20-136-7385   (SL)
CAYUGA MUTUAL INSURANCE COMPANY
23 King St, Cayuga, ON, N0A 1E0
(905) 772-5498
Emp Here 24   *Sales* 13,918,176
SIC 6411 Insurance agents, brokers, and service
Stephen Quinn

D-U-N-S 24-456-3115   (SL)
COMMUNITY LIVING HALDIMAND
2256 River Rd E, Cayuga, ON, N0A 1E0
(905) 772-3344
Emp Here 120   *Sales* 8,210,640
SIC 8322 Individual and family services
Susan Wavell

D-U-N-S 20-789-7294   (BR)
GRAND RIVER CONSERVATION AUTHORITY
TAQUANYAH CONSERVATION AREA
(*Suby of* GRAND RIVER CONSERVATION AUTHORITY)
Gd, Cayuga, ON, N0A 1E0
(905) 768-3288
Emp Here 200
SIC 8641 Civic and social associations
Paul Emerson

D-U-N-S 24-602-9854   (SL)
HALDIMAND MOTORS LTD
42 Talbot St E, Cayuga, ON, N0A 1E0
(905) 772-3511
Emp Here 82   *Sales* 51,600,960
SIC 5521 Used car dealers
John Edelman
Arda Edelman

D-U-N-S 25-116-9512   (SL)
RIVERVIEW POULTRY LIMITED
1560 Kohler Rd, Cayuga, ON, N0A 1E0
(905) 957-0300
Emp Here 72   *Sales* 16,189,560
SIC 2015 Poultry slaughtering and processing
John Georgakakos
Louis Vassilakos

D-U-N-S 20-035-4520   (SL)
TRICAN PACKAGING INC
1078 Kohler Rd, Cayuga, ON, N0A 1E0

(905) 772-0711
Emp Here 25   *Sales* 11,875,650
SIC 5085 Industrial supplies
Carl Ahlsten

Centralia, ON N0M

D-U-N-S 20-043-8927   (SL)
DASHWOOD INDUSTRIES INC
69323 Richmond St, Centralia, ON, N0M 1K0
(519) 228-6624
Emp Here 80   *Sales* 21,412,160
SIC 5211 Lumber and other building materials
Dennis Foran
Dough Latta
Scott Sallows

D-U-N-S 24-418-6847   (SL)
KENPAL FARM PRODUCTS INC
(*Suby of* 2035033 ONTARIO INC)
69819 London Rd Suite 1, Centralia, ON, N0M 1K0
(519) 228-6444
Emp Here 65   *Sales* 22,469,850
SIC 2048 Prepared feeds, nec
Kenneth Palen
Sally Palen

Chalk River, ON K0J

D-U-N-S 20-615-7968   (HQ)
ATOMIC ENERGY OF CANADA LIMITED
AECL
(*Suby of* GOVERNMENT OF CANADA)
286 Plant Rd Stn 508a, Chalk River, ON, K0J 1J0
(613) 584-3311
Emp Here 1,500   *Sales* 684,882,574
SIC 4911 Electric services
Richard Sexton
Shannon Quin
David Smith
James Burpee
Philip Jennings
Carmen Abela
Nancy Chaput

D-U-N-S 20-281-5064   (HQ)
CANADIAN NUCLEAR LABORATORIES LTD
CNL
(*Suby of* GOVERNMENT OF CANADA)
286 Plant Rd, Chalk River, ON, K0J 1J0
(613) 584-3311
Emp Here 3,000   *Sales* 1,445,096,250
SIC 2819 Industrial inorganic chemicals, nec
Mark Lesinski
Monica Steedman
Esther Zdolec

Chapleau, ON P0M

D-U-N-S 25-449-5930   (SL)
1260261 ONTARIO INC
TRUE NORTH TIMBER
Gd, Chapleau, ON, P0M 1K0
(705) 864-1974
Emp Here 80   *Sales* 12,469,040
SIC 2411 Logging
Albert Guillemette

D-U-N-S 24-308-1031   (HQ)
BIGNUCOLO INCORPORATED
13 Beech St, Chapleau, ON, P0M 1K0
(705) 864-0774
Emp Here 45   *Sales* 16,141,235
SIC 5411 Grocery stores
Richard Bignucolo

Lucy Bignucolo

D-U-N-S 20-379-1053   (BR)
RAYONIER A.M. CANADA G.P.
RAYONIER AM CANADA ENTERPRISES INC
(*Suby of* RAYONIER A.M. CANADA G.P.)
175 Planer Rd, Chapleau, ON, P0M 1K0
(705) 864-1060
Emp Here 150
SIC 2611 Pulp mills

D-U-N-S 20-971-6922   (BR)
TEMBEC INC
(*Suby of* RAYONIER A.M. GLOBAL HOLDINGS LUXEMBOURG SCS)
175 Planer Rd, Chapleau, ON, P0M 1K0
(705) 864-3014
Emp Here 169
SIC 2421 Sawmills and planing mills, general
Ron Martel

Charing Cross, ON N0P

D-U-N-S 24-367-0312   (SL)
PEETERS, WIET FARM PRODUCTS LIMITED
PEETERS' MUSHROOM FARM
Lot 11 Conc 23, Charing Cross, ON, N0P 1G0
(519) 351-1945
Emp Here 52   *Sales* 13,640,068
SIC 0182 Food crops grown under cover

Chatham, ON N7L

D-U-N-S 20-708-7094   (BR)
BAYSHORE HEALTHCARE LTD.
BAYSHORE HEALTHCARE LTD
(*Suby of* BAYSHORE HEALTHCARE LTD.)
857 Grand Ave W Suite 206, Chatham, ON, N7L 4T1
(519) 354-2019
Emp Here 160
SIC 8059 Nursing and personal care, nec
Carolanne Gillam

D-U-N-S 24-008-7809   (HQ)
CHATHAM KENT FAMILY YOUNG MEN'S CHRISTIAN ASSOCIATION, THE
CHATHAM KENT FAMILY YMCA
101 Courthouse Lane, Chatham, ON, N7L 0B5

Emp Here 20   *Sales* 10,287,288
SIC 8641 Civic and social associations
Jim Janzen
Jim Loyer
Kim Bentley- Macdonald

D-U-N-S 20-521-7404   (SL)
CHATHAM-KENT CHILDREN'S SERVICES
495 Grand Ave W, Chatham, ON, N7L 1C5
(519) 352-0440
Emp Here 230   *Sales* 17,662,160
SIC 8322 Individual and family services
Teri Thomas-Vanos

D-U-N-S 20-995-7443   (BR)
COMPASS GROUP CANADA LTD
CHARTWELL STUDENT DINING SERVICES
(*Suby of* COMPASS GROUP PLC)
285 Mcnaughton Ave E, Chatham, ON, N7L 2G7
(519) 358-7111
Emp Here 1,184
SIC 5812 Eating places
Diane Meyerink

D-U-N-S 25-185-7173   (SL)
FALOM INC
THAMES TOWER'S APARTMENTS
600 Grand Ave W Suite 10012, Chatham, ON,

N7L 4E3
(519) 354-5842
Emp Here 50   *Sales* 11,323,700
SIC 6513 Apartment building operators
Carlo Corsini

D-U-N-S 24-952-0164   (SL)
HEUVELMANS CHEVROLET BUICK GMC CADILLAC LIMITED
755 Grand Ave E, Chatham, ON, N7L 1X5
(519) 352-9200
Emp Here 47   *Sales* 23,409,666
SIC 5511 New and used car dealers
Scott Heuvelman

D-U-N-S 20-188-2490   (BR)
JARLETTE LTD
MEADOW PARK CHATHAM
110 Sandys St, Chatham, ON, N7L 4X3
(519) 351-1330
Emp Here 110   *Sales* 588,616
SIC 8051 Skilled nursing care facilities
Alex Jarlette

D-U-N-S 20-650-9932   (BR)
LAMBTON KENT DISTRICT SCHOOL BOARD
CHATHAM-KENT SECONDARY SCHOOL
(*Suby of* LAMBTON KENT DISTRICT SCHOOL BOARD)
285 Mcnaughton Ave E, Chatham, ON, N7L 2G7
(519) 352-2870
Emp Here 100
SIC 8211 Elementary and secondary schools
Mary Mancini

D-U-N-S 24-345-7111   (BR)
LOBLAWS INC
REAL CANADIAN SUPERSTORE
(*Suby of* LOBLAW COMPANIES LIMITED)
791 St Clair St, Chatham, ON, N7L 0E9
(519) 352-4982
Emp Here 150
SIC 5411 Grocery stores
Tim Birse

D-U-N-S 25-158-8893   (SL)
PILON, RAYMOND J. ENTERPRISES LTD
CANADIAN TIRE
575 Grand Ave W, Chatham, ON, N7L 1C5
(519) 351-9510
Emp Here 100   *Sales* 20,534,300
SIC 5311 Department stores
Raymond J. Pilon

D-U-N-S 20-902-0882   (SL)
PUBLIC GENERAL HOSPITAL SOCIETY OF CHATHAM, THE
CHATHAM-KENT HEALTH ALLIANCE
80 Grand Ave W Suite 301, Chatham, ON, N7L 1B7
(519) 352-6400
Emp Here 160   *Sales* 17,772,800
SIC 8062 General medical and surgical hospitals
Lori Marshall

D-U-N-S 24-813-6678   (SL)
SHOL DICE INSURANCE
300 Grand Ave W, Chatham, ON, N7L 1C1
(519) 352-9016
Emp Here 30   *Sales* 25,441,800
SIC 6411 Insurance agents, brokers, and service
Rick Orr

D-U-N-S 25-263-7079   (BR)
ST. CLAIR CATHOLIC DISTRICT SCHOOL BOARD
URSULINE COLLEGE (THE PINES)
(*Suby of* ST. CLAIR CATHOLIC DISTRICT SCHOOL BOARD)
85 Grand Ave W, Chatham, ON, N7L 1B6
(519) 351-2987
Emp Here 160
SIC 8221 Colleges and universities
Mike Grant

D-U-N-S 25-297-7269   (BR)
WAL-MART CANADA CORP
(*Suby of* WALMART INC.)
881 St Clair St, Chatham, ON, N7L 0E9
(519) 352-1142
Emp Here 200
SIC 5311 Department stores
Peck Ann

D-U-N-S 20-040-8375   (HQ)
WESTERN EQUIPMENT LIMITED
97 St Clair St, Chatham, ON, N7L 3J2
(519) 352-0530
Sales 15,203,916
SIC 5063 Electrical apparatus and equipment
John D Meko
Mark Meko
Harvey Bondy

Chatham, ON N7M

D-U-N-S 24-684-0784   (SL)
2210961 ONTARIO LIMITED
GREAT LAKES FISH COMPANY
135 Bothwell St, Chatham, ON, N7M 5K5
(519) 354-4600
Emp Here 20   *Sales* 10,702,480
SIC 5146 Fish and seafoods
John Neate

D-U-N-S 20-371-8981   (SL)
2595385 ONTARIO INC
ENVIROSHAKE
650 Riverview Dr, Chatham, ON, N7M 0N2
(519) 380-9265
Emp Here 30   *Sales* 10,755,115
SIC 2952 Asphalt felts and coatings
Dennis Hewko
Patrick Smith

D-U-N-S 24-087-1900   (HQ)
AGRIS CO-OPERATIVE LTD
835 Park Ave W, Chatham, ON, N7M 0N1
(519) 354-7178
Emp Here 14   *Sales* 26,876,080
SIC 5999 Miscellaneous retail stores, nec
Jim Campbell

D-U-N-S 24-559-8545   (SL)
ARENS, MIKE BUILDING MATERIALS LTD
CHATHAM KENT HOME HARDWARE BUILDING CENTRE
124 Keil Dr S Suite 1719, Chatham, ON, N7M 3H1
(519) 354-0700
Emp Here 40   *Sales* 10,122,360
SIC 5211 Lumber and other building materials
Mike Arens
Wayne Jee
Jennifer Rosszell

D-U-N-S 20-040-2964   (HQ)
BRAD-LEA MEADOWS LIMITED
BEST WESTERN WHEELS INN
(*Suby of* FIRST CHATHAM CORPORATION LTD)
615 Richmond St, Chatham, ON, N7M 1R2
(519) 436-5506
Emp Here 400
SIC 7011 Hotels and motels

D-U-N-S 20-552-6531   (HQ)
BRR LOGISTICS LIMITED
24 Mcgregor Pl, Chatham, ON, N7M 5J4
(519) 352-4120
Sales 33,423,080
SIC 5143 Dairy products, except dried or canned

D-U-N-S 20-040-3152   (SL)
CAMPBELL, BOB MOTORS LTD
CAMPBELL TOYOTA
296 Richmond St, Chatham, ON, N7M 1P6
(519) 352-4740
Emp Here 21   *Sales* 10,459,638

SIC 5511 New and used car dealers
Kim Campbell
Kerri Brewer

D-U-N-S 20-920-4759   (SL)
CHAPPLE FUELS LIMITED
175 Bothwell St, Chatham, ON, N7M 5J5
(519) 351-7194
Emp Here 90   *Sales* 13,337,280
SIC 4212 Local trucking, without storage
Wayne Chapple
Darrell Chapple
Karen Chapple

D-U-N-S 20-040-3400   (SL)
CHARRON TRANSPORT LIMITED
123 Byng Ave, Chatham, ON, N7M 6C6
(519) 352-8970
Emp Here 65   *Sales* 13,370,890
SIC 4212 Local trucking, without storage
William (Bill) Charron
Murray Charron
Patricia (Patsy) Fowers
Timothy (Tim) Charron
Lawrence Charron

D-U-N-S 20-350-7173   (BR)
CONTINENTAL TIRE CANADA, INC
CONTINENTAL AUTOMOTIVE CANADA
(*Suby of* CONTINENTAL AG)
700 Park Avenue E, Chatham, ON, N7M 5M7
(519) 352-6700
Emp Here 140
SIC 5014 Tires and tubes
Bill Gillier

D-U-N-S 25-410-6735   (SL)
COPPER TERRACE LIMITED
COPPER TERRACE LONG TERM CARE
(*Suby of* APANS INC)
91 Tecumseh Rd, Chatham, ON, N7M 1B3
(519) 354-5442
Emp Here 120   *Sales* 8,199,120
SIC 8051 Skilled nursing care facilities
Susan Petahtegoose

D-U-N-S 24-425-4236   (SL)
DAJCOR ALUMINUM LTD
155 Irwin St, Chatham, ON, N7M 0N5
(519) 351-2424
Emp Here 200   *Sales* 36,277,600
SIC 3354 Aluminum extruded products
Michael Kilby

D-U-N-S 20-104-8894   (BR)
DANA CANADA CORPORATION
SEALING PRODUCTS
(*Suby of* DANA INCORPORATED)
1010 Richmond St, Chatham, ON, N7M 5J5
(519) 351-1221
Emp Here 100
SIC 2298 Cordage and twine
Jim Westover

D-U-N-S 20-790-2227   (SL)
DEAN MILLS NO FRILLS
DEAN AND BARB NO FRILLS
100 William St S, Chatham, ON, N7M 4S4
(519) 351-0355
Emp Here 49   *Sales* 13,433,448
SIC 5411 Grocery stores
Dean Mills

D-U-N-S 20-040-4218   (HQ)
DUTCH MARKET LIMITED, THE
80 William St S, Chatham, ON, N7M 4S3
(519) 352-2831
Emp Here 1   *Sales* 31,751,926
SIC 5141 Groceries, general line
Charles Huls

D-U-N-S 24-329-6568   (HQ)
ENTEGRUS INC
(*Suby of* CORPORATION OF THE MUNICIPALITY OF CHATHAM-KENT, THE)
320 Queen St, Chatham, ON, N7M 2H6
(519) 352-6300
Sales 14,656,598

SIC 8711 Engineering services
Raymond Payne
Jim Hogan

D-U-N-S 20-200-5091   (SL)
ERIE & MAIN CONSULTING INC
COLLINS BUREAU
62 Keil Dr S, Chatham, ON, N7M 3G8
(519) 351-2024
Emp Here 25   *Sales* 10,483,875
SIC 6712 Bank holding companies
John Aitken
Michael Pestowka

D-U-N-S 25-921-6679   (SL)
ERIE ST. CLAIR COMMUNITY CARE AC-CESS CENTRE
712 Richmond St, Chatham, ON, N7M 5J5
(519) 436-2222
Emp Here 75   *Sales* 17,571,600
SIC 8742 Management consulting services
Betty Kuchta
Lori Marshall

D-U-N-S 24-452-2090   (HQ)
FIRST CHATHAM CORPORATION LTD
615 Richmond St, Chatham, ON, N7M 1R2
(519) 436-5506
Sales 182,754,500
SIC 6712 Bank holding companies
John Bradley

D-U-N-S 24-788-5879   (BR)
FIRSTCANADA ULC
FIRST STUDENT CANADA
(*Suby of* FIRSTGROUP PLC)
100 Currie St, Chatham, ON, N7M 6L9
(519) 352-1920
Emp Here 100
SIC 4151 School buses
Bruce Grand

D-U-N-S 24-334-4983   (SL)
GIBBONS, JOHN AUTOMOTIVE GROUP 2010 LTD
725 Richmond St, Chatham, ON, N7M 5J5
(519) 352-6200
Emp Here 35   *Sales* 17,432,730
SIC 5511 New and used car dealers
John Gibbons
Kate Bardoel

D-U-N-S 20-040-4721   (SL)
GOLD, A. & SONS LTD
7659 Queens Line, Chatham, ON, N7M 5J5
(519) 352-0360
Emp Here 45   *Sales* 13,013,550
SIC 5093 Scrap and waste materials
Bradley A. Gold
Howard Gold
Alex Gold

D-U-N-S 25-392-3494   (SL)
HEYINK, HENRY CONSTRUCTION LTD
275 Colborne St, Chatham, ON, N7M 3M3
(519) 354-4593
Emp Here 55   *Sales* 13,884,310
SIC 1623 Water, sewer, and utility lines
Henry Heyink
Rob Hoekstra
Peter Gourlay

D-U-N-S 24-086-5340   (BR)
HOME DEPOT OF CANADA INC
(*Suby of* THE HOME DEPOT INC)
8582 Pioneer Line, Chatham, ON, N7M 5J1
(519) 380-2040
Emp Here 100
SIC 5211 Lumber and other building materials
Kelly Beckett

D-U-N-S 24-094-3092   (SL)
HONEY ELECTRIC LIMITED
400 Park Ave W, Chatham, ON, N7M 1W9
(519) 351-0484
Emp Here 60   *Sales* 13,069,740
SIC 1731 Electrical work
Reginald Macdonald

Katherine Macdonald

D-U-N-S 20-773-1055   (SL)
HURON CONSTRUCTION CO LIMITED
10785 Pinehurst Line, Chatham, ON, N7M 5J3
(519) 354-0170
Emp Here 43   *Sales* 12,191,532
SIC 1611 Highway and street construction
Peter Watson

D-U-N-S 25-958-7744   (SL)
JMHI INSURANCE GROUP INC
550 Richmond St, Chatham, ON, N7M 1R3
(226) 312-2020
Emp Here 18   *Sales* 10,438,632
SIC 6411 Insurance agents, brokers, and service
Eric Gaudrault

D-U-N-S 24-974-3204   (SL)
KENT & ESSEX MUTUAL INSURANCE COMPANY
10 Creek Rd, Chatham, ON, N7M 5J3

Emp Here 33   *Sales* 34,151,073
SIC 6331 Fire, marine, and casualty insurance
Joanne Vansevenant
Jeff Stokes
John T Jarecsni

D-U-N-S 24-413-2254   (HQ)
KENT PETROLEUM LIMITED
WADDICK FUELS
280 Richmond St, Chatham, ON, N7M 1P6
(519) 623-7411
Emp Here 20   *Sales* 49,030,839
SIC 5172 Petroleum products, nec
Mark Waddick
Thomas Waddick

D-U-N-S 20-129-1327   (SL)
LALLY KIA
725 Richmond St, Chatham, ON, N7M 5J5
(519) 352-6200
Emp Here 22   *Sales* 10,957,716
SIC 5511 New and used car dealers
Mike Weber

D-U-N-S 25-263-7475   (BR)
LAMBTON KENT DISTRICT SCHOOL BOARD
JOHN MCGREGOR SECONDARY SCHOOL
(*Suby of* LAMBTON KENT DISTRICT SCHOOL BOARD)
300 Cecile Ave, Chatham, ON, N7M 2C6
(519) 354-1740
Emp Here 75
SIC 8211 Elementary and secondary schools
John Zondag

D-U-N-S 20-040-5546   (SL)
MAPLE CITY OFFICE EQUIPMENT LTD
170 Queen St, Chatham, ON, N7M 2G8
(519) 352-2940
Emp Here 45   *Sales* 14,652,000
SIC 5999 Miscellaneous retail stores, nec
Keith Koke
Edward Koke

D-U-N-S 24-392-0514   (HQ)
MSSC CANADA INC
(*Suby of* MITSUBISHI STEEL MFG. CO., LTD.)
201 Park Ave E, Chatham, ON, N7M 3V7
(905) 878-2395
Emp Here 50   *Sales* 75,888,072
SIC 3492 Fluid power valves and hose fittings
John Trapp
Tom Marayuma
Charles Weisbaum

D-U-N-S 20-703-2962   (BR)
MSSC CANADA INC
(*Suby of* MITSUBISHI STEEL MFG. CO., LTD.)
105 St George St, Chatham, ON, N7M 4P3

(519) 354-1100
Emp Here 270
SIC 3493 Steel springs, except wire
John Trapp

D-U-N-S 20-311-4103   (SL)
ONBELAY AUTOMOTIVE INC
540 Park Ave E, Chatham, ON, N7M 5J4
(519) 354-6515
Emp Here 90   *Sales* 17,287,650
SIC 3479 Metal coating and allied services
Aly Rahemtulla

D-U-N-S 20-706-9217   (SL)
ONE WORLD LOGISTICS OF AMERICA INC
O W L
400 National Rd, Chatham, ON, N7M 5J5
(519) 380-0800
Emp Here 155   *Sales* 31,884,430
SIC 4213 Trucking, except local
Paul Cox

D-U-N-S 24-923-5144   (HQ)
PIONEER HI-BRED PRODUCTION LTD
(*Suby of* DUPONT DE NEMOURS, INC.)
7399 County Rd 2 W, Chatham, ON, N7M 5L1
(519) 352-2700
Emp Here 80   *Sales* 22,649,350
SIC 0181 Ornamental nursery products
Manuel Alves
David Charne
Robert Wichmann

D-U-N-S 25-975-9769   (SL)
PUBLIC UTILITIES COMMISSION FOR THE MUNICIPALITY OF CHATHAM-KENT
CHATHAM-KENT PUC
320 Queen St, Chatham, ON, N7M 2H6
(519) 352-6300
Emp Here 90   *Sales* 56,395,260
SIC 4911 Electric services
Scott Gawley
Ray Payne

D-U-N-S 24-631-7598   (SL)
RIVERVIEW SERVICE CENTRE LIMITED
CRAWFORD CHRYSLER JEEP DODGE
351 Richmond St, Chatham, ON, N7M 1P5
(519) 352-4937
Emp Here 30   *Sales* 14,942,340
SIC 5511 New and used car dealers
Dan Crawford
Judy Crawford

D-U-N-S 20-040-7252   (SL)
RUSSELL TOOL & DIE LIMITED
NARMCO GROUP
381 Park Ave W, Chatham, ON, N7M 1W6
(519) 352-8168
Emp Here 60   *Sales* 13,320,060
SIC 3544 Special dies, tools, jigs, and fixtures
Donald Rodzik

D-U-N-S 20-040-7468   (HQ)
SIMPSON'S FENCE LTD
1030 Richmond St, Chatham, ON, N7M 5J5
(519) 354-0540
Sales 11,179,350
SIC 5039 Construction materials, nec
William E Simpson

D-U-N-S 24-125-2055   (BR)
SONOCO CANADA CORPORATION
(*Suby of* SONOCO PRODUCTS COMPANY)
674 Richmond St, Chatham, ON, N7M 5K4
(519) 352-8201
Emp Here 75
SIC 2655 Fiber cans, drums, and similar products
Marina Iannitelli

D-U-N-S 25-173-7078   (HQ)
SOUTH WEST AG PARTNERS INC
40 Centre St Suite 200, Chatham, ON, N7M 5W3
(519) 380-0002
Emp Here 10   *Sales* 146,769,200
SIC 5153 Grain and field beans

Paul Hazzard

D-U-N-S 24-772-3745   (HQ)
TATRO EQUIPMENT SALES LTD
7744 Seventh Line E, Chatham, ON, N7M 5J6
(519) 354-4352
Sales 14,250,780
SIC 5084 Industrial machinery and equipment
Don Tetrault

D-U-N-S 20-178-2062   (SL)
TATRO TRUCKS LTD
7744 Seventh Line E, Chatham, ON, N7M 5J6
(519) 354-4352
Emp Here 30   *Sales* 10,926,450
SIC 5012 Automobiles and other motor vehicles
Donald Tetrault

D-U-N-S 25-908-7393   (HQ)
TEKSAVVY SOLUTIONS INC
800 Richmond St, Chatham, ON, N7M 5J5
(519) 360-1575
Emp Here 430   *Sales* 107,381,840
SIC 4813 Telephone communication, except radio
Marc Gaudrault

D-U-N-S 20-940-8624   (HQ)
TRANSIT TRAILER LIMITED
(*Suby of* M. J. CAMPBELL HOLDINGS LIMITED)
22217 Bloomfield Rd Suite 3, Chatham, ON, N7M 5J3
(519) 354-9944
Emp Here 20   *Sales* 16,389,675
SIC 5012 Automobiles and other motor vehicles
Murray Campbell

D-U-N-S 24-395-2491   (SL)
VICTORY FORD LINCOLN SALES LTD
301 Richmond St, Chatham, ON, N7M 1P5
(519) 436-1430
Emp Here 40   *Sales* 14,568,600
SIC 5013 Motor vehicle supplies and new parts
Warren Rychel

D-U-N-S 20-689-6248   (SL)
WALLACEBURG PREFERRED PARTNERS CORP
WPP
203 Keil Dr S, Chatham, ON, N7M 6J5
(519) 351-5558
Emp Here 150   *Sales* 33,576,450
SIC 3711 Motor vehicles and car bodies
Dan Brown

Chelmsford, ON P0M

D-U-N-S 24-414-2501   (HQ)
BELANGER CONSTRUCTION (1981) INC
100 Radisson Ave, Chelmsford, ON, P0M 1L0
(705) 855-4555
Sales 37,866,300
SIC 1611 Highway and street construction
Ronald Belanger

D-U-N-S 20-607-3645   (SL)
BELANGER FORD LINCOLN CENTRE LTD, THE
(*Suby of* BELANGER, G. A. INC)
204 Michael St, Chelmsford, ON, P0M 1L0
(705) 855-4504
Emp Here 50   *Sales* 31,464,000
SIC 5511 New and used car dealers
Michael Guilbault
Robert Giroux
Laura Belanger

D-U-N-S 20-040-8839   (HQ)
BELANGER, R.M. LIMITED
BELANGER CONSTRUCTION
(*Suby of* BELANGER CONSTRUCTION

(1981) INC)
100 Radisson Ave, Chelmsford, ON, P0M 1L0
(705) 855-4555
Sales 39,923,660
SIC 1542 Nonresidential construction, nec
  Ronald Belanger

D-U-N-S 24-848-5492   (SL)
CHARTRAND'S INDEPENDENT INC
4764 Regional Road 15 Rr 4, Chelmsford, ON, P0M 1L0
(705) 855-4588
Emp Here 70   *Sales* 20,543,390
SIC 5411 Grocery stores
  Michelle Chartrand

D-U-N-S 24-333-9111   (SL)
MABOU MINING INC
3493 Errington Ave, Chelmsford, ON, P0M 1L0
(705) 855-0796
Emp Here 100   *Sales* 25,244,200
SIC 1629 Heavy construction, nec
  David Macneil
  Darlene Macneil

D-U-N-S 24-220-4662   (SL)
MAGASIN RENE VEILLEUX INC
CANADIAN TIRE
3595 144 Hwy, Chelmsford, ON, P0M 1L0
(705) 855-9011
Emp Here 100   *Sales* 36,421,500
SIC 5014 Tires and tubes
  Rene Veilleux

Cheltenham, ON L7C

D-U-N-S 24-966-4111   (SL)
BRAMPTON FLYING CLUB
BRAMPTON CESSNA
13691 Mclaughlin Rd, Cheltenham, ON, L7C 2B2
(416) 798-7928
Emp Here 75   *Sales* 9,009,675
SIC 8299 Schools and educational services, nec
  Allan Paige
  Neil Kruiswyck
  Donald Hersey
  Chris Pulley
  Irvine Young
  Geoff Foster
  David Fisher
  Sergei Gluhushkin
  Dick Pulley

Chesley, ON N0G

D-U-N-S 20-998-0007   (SL)
MAXWELL FARM ELEVATOR
604 Concession 2, Chesley, ON, N0G 1L0
(519) 363-3423
Emp Here 10   *Sales* 12,103,970
SIC 5153 Grain and field beans
  George Maxwell

D-U-N-S 20-406-1600   (HQ)
ROBERT'S FARM EQUIPMENT SALES INC
14945 County Rd 10, Chesley, ON, N0G 1L0
(519) 363-3192
Emp Here 15   *Sales* 14,250,780
SIC 5083 Farm and garden machinery
  Brian Osterndorff
  Bruce Osterndorff

Chesterville, ON K0C

D-U-N-S 20-041-0397   (HQ)

MIKE DEAN BUTCHER LIMITED
MIKE DEAN'S SUPER FOOD STORES
19 King St, Chesterville, ON, K0C 1H0
(613) 448-2822
Emp Here 60   *Sales* 38,152,010
SIC 5411 Grocery stores
  Michael Dean
  Gordon Dean
  Nancy Dean
  Julie Dean

D-U-N-S 20-041-0504   (BR)
NESTLE CANADA INC
(*Suby of* NESTLE S.A.)
171 Main St N, Chesterville, ON, K0C 1H0
(613) 448-2338
Emp Here 300
SIC 2095 Roasted coffee
  Marsha Dion

Clarence Creek, ON K0A

D-U-N-S 20-891-1289   (SL)
CENTRE D'ACCUEIL ROGER SEGUIN
435 Lemay St Rr 1, Clarence Creek, ON, K0A 1N0
(613) 488-2053
Emp Here 135   *Sales* 8,678,070
SIC 8361 Residential care
  Lynne Joly Crichton

D-U-N-S 20-893-0180   (SL)
LAFLEUR SCHOOL TRANSPORTATION LTD
1546 Baseline Rd, Clarence Creek, ON, K0A 1N0
(613) 488-2337
Emp Here 85   *Sales* 4,664,120
SIC 4151 School buses
  Nicholas Mcrea

Clarksburg, ON N0H

D-U-N-S 25-543-4045   (SL)
BAY GROWERS INC
828114 Grey Road 40, Clarksburg, ON, N0H 1J0
(519) 599-7568
Emp Here 48   *Sales* 15,628,800
SIC 5992 Florists
  John Hewgill

Clifford, ON N0G

D-U-N-S 24-365-8460   (HQ)
DIAMOND PLUS
DIAMOND PLUS SPECIALIZED
56 Allan St W, Clifford, ON, N0G 1M0
(519) 327-4567
Sales 17,070,322
SIC 7389 Business services, nec
  Mark Freiburger

D-U-N-S 24-048-1465   (SL)
PIKE LAKE GOLF CENTRE LIMITED
Gd, Clifford, ON, N0G 1M0
(519) 338-3010
Emp Here 100   *Sales* 9,489,900
SIC 7011 Hotels and motels
  Irwin Cowen

Clinton, ON N0M

D-U-N-S 20-184-1769   (SL)
CAPPRODUCTS, LTD

(*Suby of* PHOENIX FORGING COMPANY, INC.)
25 Winnipeg Rd Rr 5, Clinton, ON, N0M 1L0
(519) 482-5000
Emp Here 120   *Sales* 23,050,200
SIC 3499 Fabricated Metal products, nec
  John E. Rodgers
  Thomas Costello

D-U-N-S 20-041-3839   (SL)
FLEMING FEED MILL LIMITED
60 Irwin St, Clinton, ON, N0M 1L0
(519) 482-3438
Emp Here 30   *Sales* 22,275,600
SIC 5191 Farm supplies
  William Fleming
  Margaret Fleming
  Richard Mcglynn

D-U-N-S 24-752-4655   (SL)
HURON COMMODITIES INC
75 Wellington St, Clinton, ON, N0M 1L0
(519) 482-8400
Emp Here 20   *Sales* 49,538,905
SIC 6799 Investors, nec
  Martin Vanderloo
  Ellen Vanderloo
  Alicia Oesch

D-U-N-S 24-683-7079   (BR)
HURON PERTH HEALTHCARE ALLIANCE
CLINTON PUBLIC HOSPITAL, THE
(*Suby of* HURON PERTH HEALTHCARE ALLIANCE)
98 Shipley St, Clinton, ON, N0M 1L0
(519) 482-3447
Emp Here 140
SIC 8062 General medical and surgical hospitals
  Bonnie Royal

D-U-N-S 20-880-7578   (SL)
HURONVIEW HOME FOR THE AGED
77722a London Rd Rr 5, Clinton, ON, N0M 1L0
(519) 482-3451
Emp Here 235   *Sales* 16,056,610
SIC 8051 Skilled nursing care facilities
  Barbara Springall
  David Carey

D-U-N-S 25-479-2989   (HQ)
RADAR AUTO PARTS INC
RADAR AUTO PARTS
20 King St, Clinton, ON, N0M 1L0
(519) 482-3445
Emp Here 2   *Sales* 10,957,716
SIC 5531 Auto and home supply stores
  Gord Lavis

D-U-N-S 20-717-7874   (SL)
SCRUTON-EDWARD CORP
EDWARD FUELS
268 Albert St, Clinton, ON, N0M 1L0
(519) 482-7381
Emp Here 15   *Sales* 15,492,120
SIC 5172 Petroleum products, nec
  Linda Edward

Cobden, ON K0J

D-U-N-S 20-892-2989   (SL)
CARESSANT CARE NURSING HOME COBDEN
12 Wren Dr, Cobden, ON, K0J 1K0
(613) 646-2109
Emp Here 75   *Sales* 5,154,975
SIC 8051 Skilled nursing care facilities
  James Leval
  Marjorie Vernon

D-U-N-S 20-301-0462   (SL)
COBDEN AGRICULTURAL SOCIETY
43 Astrolabe Rd, Cobden, ON, K0J 1K0

(613) 646-2426
Emp Here 49   *Sales* 11,909,401
SIC 6519 Real property lessors, nec
  Grace Mick

Coboconk, ON K0M

D-U-N-S 20-041-5461   (SL)
BARBOUR'S FOOD MARKET LIMITED
COBOCONK IGA
6708 35 Hwy Rr 1, Coboconk, ON, K0M 1K0
(705) 454-1414
Emp Here 40   *Sales* 10,966,080
SIC 5411 Grocery stores
  Thomas Robert Barbour

Cobourg, ON K9A

D-U-N-S 20-785-7715   (HQ)
348461 ONTARIO LIMITED
RENT-ALL CENTRE
30 Elgin St W, Cobourg, ON, K9A 5T4
(905) 372-6131
Emp Here 15   *Sales* 11,686,760
SIC 7353 Heavy construction equipment rental
  Joan Wheatley
  Brian Wheatley

D-U-N-S 20-272-0447   (SL)
ACTIVATION PRODUCTS (CAN) INC
975a Elgin St W Suite 357, Cobourg, ON, K9A 5J3
(416) 702-2962
Emp Here 35   *Sales* 25,562,075
SIC 5169 Chemicals and allied products, nec
  Ian Clark

D-U-N-S 25-529-8184   (HQ)
ARCLIN CANADA LTD
(*Suby of* ARCLIN CAYMAN HOLDINGS LTD)
56 Willmott St, Cobourg, ON, K9A 4S3
(905) 372-1896
Emp Here 50   *Sales* 333,483,750
SIC 2821 Plastics materials and resins
  Russell C Taylor
  David Morris
  Ralf D Yobp

D-U-N-S 20-041-5768   (SL)
BEHAN CONSTRUCTION LIMITED
Gd Lcd Main, Cobourg, ON, K9A 4K1
(905) 372-9862
Emp Here 50   *Sales* 12,044,200
SIC 1623 Water, sewer, and utility lines
  Thomas Edward Behan
  Alice Behan
  Thomas Michael Behan

D-U-N-S 25-192-1540   (SL)
BRANCH 133 LEGION VILLAGE INC
LEGION VILLAGE
111 Hibernia St Suite 220, Cobourg, ON, K9A 4Y7
(905) 372-8705
Emp Here 45   *Sales* 10,191,330
SIC 6513 Apartment building operators
  Cynthia Blower
  James Keeler

D-U-N-S 20-649-4481   (SL)
CAMECO FUEL MANUFACTURING INC
(*Suby of* CAMECO CORPORATION)
2c St Northam Industrial Pk, Cobourg, ON, K9A 4K5
(905) 372-0147
Emp Here 140   *Sales* 31,080,140
SIC 3545 Machine tool accessories
  Lisanne Hill
  Lloyd Jones
  Brian Walker

D-U-N-S 24-952-6724   (SL)
CANADA PALLET CORP
CPS WOOD PRODUCTS
755 Division St, Cobourg, ON, K9A 3T1
(905) 373-0761
Emp Here 125   *Sales* 24,046,250
SIC 2448 Wood pallets and skids
 Thomas Haar
 Daniel Dunkley
 Shawn Hicks

D-U-N-S 24-024-0036   (SL)
COBOURG NISSAN LTD
831 Division St, Cobourg, ON, K9A 5R9
(905) 372-3963
Emp Here 28   *Sales* 13,946,184
SIC 5511 New and used car dealers
 Colin Conroy
 Tyler Campbell

D-U-N-S 24-421-5260   (BR)
CORPORATION OF THE COUNTY OF NORTHUMBERLAND
GOLDEN PLOUGH LODGE
(*Suby of* CORPORATION OF THE COUNTY OF NORTHUMBERLAND)
983 Burnham St Suite 1321, Cobourg, ON, K9A 5J6
(905) 372-8759
Emp Here 175
SIC 8361 Residential care
 Cathie Ritchie

D-U-N-S 20-041-6188   (SL)
CUSTOM PLASTICS INTERNATIONAL LIMITED
887 D'Arcy St, Cobourg, ON, K9A 4B4
(905) 372-2281
Emp Here 80   *Sales* 16,151,760
SIC 3089 Plastics products, nec
 Peter Harrison
 Richard B. Gadd

D-U-N-S 25-410-7907   (HQ)
DALREN LIMITED
8781 Dale Rd, Cobourg, ON, K9A 4J9
(905) 377-1080
Sales 11,768,275
SIC 1542 Nonresidential construction, nec
 Matt James

D-U-N-S 20-289-6374   (BR)
EXTENDICARE INC
EXTENDICARE COBOURG
(*Suby of* EXTENDICARE INC)
130 New Densmore Rd, Cobourg, ON, K9A 5W2
(905) 372-0377
Emp Here 100
SIC 8051 Skilled nursing care facilities
 Lynda Davlut

D-U-N-S 20-343-3644   (SL)
GRAPHIC PACKAGING INTERNATIONAL CANADA ULC
(*Suby of* GRAPHIC PACKAGING HOLDING COMPANY)
740 Division St, Cobourg, ON, K9A 0H6
(905) 372-5199
Emp Here 140   *Sales* 27,267,520
SIC 2631 Paperboard mills
 Alain Levac

D-U-N-S 24-485-5557   (HQ)
HAMILTON TOWNSHIP MUTUAL INSURANCE COMPANY
HTM INSURANCE
1185 Elgin St W, Cobourg, ON, K9A 4K5
(905) 372-0186
Sales 14,804,362
SIC 6411 Insurance agents, brokers, and service
 Alec Harmer

D-U-N-S 24-361-7219   (BR)
HOME DEPOT OF CANADA INC
HOME DEPOT

(*Suby of* THE HOME DEPOT INC)
1050 Depalma Dr, Cobourg, ON, K9A 0A8
(905) 377-7600
Emp Here 100
SIC 5251 Hardware stores
 Mark Blackwell

D-U-N-S 24-363-9999   (SL)
HORIZON PLASTICS INTERNATIONAL INC
(*Suby of* CORE MOLDING TECHNOLOGIES, INC.)
Bldg 3 Northam Industrial Park, Cobourg, ON, K9A 4L1
(905) 372-2291
Emp Here 250   *Sales* 59,703,000
SIC 3089 Plastics products, nec
 Brian Read

D-U-N-S 25-238-0282   (BR)
KAWARTHA PINE RIDGE DISTRICT SCHOOL BOARD
COBOURG DISTRICT COLLEGIATE INSTITUTE EAST
335 King St E, Cobourg, ON, K9A 1M2
(905) 372-2271
Emp Here 110
SIC 8211 Elementary and secondary schools
 Laina Andrews

D-U-N-S 20-943-1204   (HQ)
KRAN MANAGEMENT SERVICES LIMITED
MCDONALD'S RESTAURANT
805 William St, Cobourg, ON, K9A 3A8
(905) 372-6335
Emp Here 89   *Sales* 8,395,020
SIC 5812 Eating places
 Leslie Andrews

D-U-N-S 20-245-3374   (SL)
LAKELAND MULTI-TRADE INC
566 D'Arcy St, Cobourg, ON, K9A 4A9
(905) 372-7413
Emp Here 100   *Sales* 22,200,100
SIC 3599 Industrial machinery, nec
 Stan Jarvis

D-U-N-S 20-846-2945   (HQ)
LIMPACT INTERNATIONAL LIMITED
569 D'Arcy St, Cobourg, ON, K9A 4B1
(905) 373-4100
Emp Here 45   *Sales* 14,010,984
SIC 3499 Fabricated Metal products, nec
 Steve Fredericks

D-U-N-S 20-209-2909   (SL)
MOULTON, RALPH HOLDINGS LTD
CANADIAN TIRE
1125 Elgin St W, Cobourg, ON, K9A 5T9
(905) 372-8781
Emp Here 100   *Sales* 62,928,000
SIC 5541 Gasoline service stations
 Cliff Ernst

D-U-N-S 25-659-2650   (SL)
NORTHUMBERLAND HILLS HOSPITAL
1000 Depalma Dr, Cobourg, ON, K9A 5W6
(905) 372-6811
Emp Here 600   *Sales* 52,065,365
SIC 8062 General medical and surgical hospitals
 Linda Davis
 Elizabeth Selby
 Lynda Kay
 Susan Walsh

D-U-N-S 20-388-2555   (SL)
ONTARIO LINE CLEARING & TREE EXPERTS INC
7790 Telephone Rd, Cobourg, ON, K9A 4J7
(905) 372-6706
Emp Here 120   *Sales* 20,868,600
SIC 0783 Ornamental shrub and tree services
 Matthew Wharram

D-U-N-S 24-330-6599   (SL)
PALLETSOURCE INC
(*Suby of* PALLET SOURCE, INC.)
755 Division St, Cobourg, ON, K9A 3T1

(905) 373-0761
Emp Here 100   *Sales* 19,237,000
SIC 2448 Wood pallets and skids
 Thomas Haar

D-U-N-S 25-137-3585   (BR)
PETERBOROUGH VICTORIA NORTHUMBERLAND AND CLARINGTON CATHOLIC DISTRICT SCHOOL BOARD
ST. MARY'S SECONDARY SCHOOL
(*Suby of* PETERBOROUGH VICTORIA NORTHUMBERLAND AND CLARINGTON CATHOLIC DISTRICT SCHOOL BOARD)
1050 Birchwood Trail, Cobourg, ON, K9A 5S9
(905) 372-4339
Emp Here 90
SIC 8211 Elementary and secondary schools
 Robert Majdel

D-U-N-S 24-316-1619   (SL)
PROTOPLAST INC
210 Willmott St Unit 2, Cobourg, ON, K9A 0E9
(905) 372-6451
Emp Here 80   *Sales* 12,708,640
SIC 3089 Plastics products, nec
 Douglas Spittal
 Andrew Stittal

D-U-N-S 25-170-7261   (SL)
ROYAL LEPAGE PROALLIANCE REALTY
1111 Elgin St W, Cobourg, ON, K9A 5H7
(905) 377-8888
Emp Here 42   *Sales* 11,413,752
SIC 6531 Real estate agents and managers
 Mark Rashotte

D-U-N-S 24-379-7763   (SL)
SABIC INNOVATIVE PLASTICS CANADA INC
(*Suby of* GOVERNMENT OF SAUDI ARABIA)
44 Normar Rd, Cobourg, ON, K9A 4L7
(905) 372-6801
Emp Here 190   *Sales* 127,720,280
SIC 5162 Plastics materials and basic shapes
 Paul Van Laren
 Niyazi Demir

D-U-N-S 24-402-5289   (SL)
SAYERS & ASSOCIATES LTD.
1000 Depalma Dr, Cobourg, ON, K9A 5W6

Emp Here 49   *Sales* 10,825,766
SIC 1711 Plumbing, heating, air-conditioning
 Neil Robinson

D-U-N-S 20-041-6600   (SL)
SPENCER, BILL CHEVROLET OLDSMOBILE LTD
1090 Elgin St W Suite 12, Cobourg, ON, K9A 5V5
(905) 372-8773
Emp Here 21   *Sales* 10,459,638
SIC 5511 New and used car dealers
 William (Bill) Spencer

D-U-N-S 20-041-7343   (SL)
THOMAS PONTIAC BUICK GMC LTD
100 University Ave E, Cobourg, ON, K9A 1C8
(905) 372-5447
Emp Here 30   *Sales* 14,942,340
SIC 5511 New and used car dealers
 Bill Campbell
 Rick Thomas

D-U-N-S 24-321-8851   (SL)
TONA, ALAN PHARMACY LIMITED
SHOPPERS DRUG MART
270 Spring St, Cobourg, ON, K9A 3K2
(905) 372-3333
Emp Here 42   *Sales* 10,624,068
SIC 5912 Drug stores and proprietary stores
 Alan Tona

D-U-N-S 24-329-8663   (BR)
WAL-MART CANADA CORP
(*Suby of* WALMART INC.)
73 Strathy Rd, Cobourg, ON, K9A 5W8

(905) 373-1239
Emp Here 200
SIC 5311 Department stores
 Robson Walton

D-U-N-S 20-551-1173   (SL)
WEETABIX OF CANADA LIMITED
(*Suby of* WESTMINSTER ACQUISITION LIMITED)
751 D'Arcy St, Cobourg, ON, K9A 4B1
(905) 372-5441
Emp Here 260   *Sales* 126,720,100
SIC 2043 Cereal breakfast foods
 Jeff Bakker
 David W Burn
 A.T. Connell

Cochrane, ON P0L

D-U-N-S 24-827-7394   (HQ)
106203 CANADA LTD
158 Second Ave, Cochrane, ON, P0L 1C0
(705) 272-4305
Sales 41,778,850
SIC 5149 Groceries and related products, nec
 Raymond Fortier

D-U-N-S 20-282-2219   (SL)
1835755 ONTARIO LIMITED
NORTH ROCK CONSTRUCTION PROJECTS
227 Hwy 11 S, Cochrane, ON, P0L 1C0
(705) 272-2090
Emp Here 75   *Sales* 18,933,150
SIC 1611 Highway and street construction
 Carl Swanson
 David Lanther

D-U-N-S 24-384-5302   (SL)
CGV BUILDERS INC
56 Connaught Ave, Cochrane, ON, P0L 1C0
(705) 272-5404
Emp Here 30   *Sales* 14,121,930
SIC 1542 Nonresidential construction, nec
 Daniel Vezeau
 Michel Vezeau

D-U-N-S 20-689-4318   (HQ)
EXPEDITION HELICOPTERS INC
EXPEDITION HELICOPTER INTERNATIONAL
190 Hwy 11 W, Cochrane, ON, P0L 1C0
(705) 272-5755
Sales 16,237,700
SIC 4522 Air transportation, nonscheduled
 Todd Calaiezzi

D-U-N-S 20-041-7939   (HQ)
FORTIER BEVERAGES LIMITED
AQUA-NOR DIV
(*Suby of* 106203 CANADA LTD)
158 Second Ave, Cochrane, ON, P0L 1C0
(705) 272-4305
Emp Here 38   *Sales* 41,778,850
SIC 5149 Groceries and related products, nec
 Raymond Fortier
 Sylvie Gravelle
 Germaine Fortier

D-U-N-S 20-041-8051   (SL)
LABELLE, M. J. CO. LTD
109 Highway 11 W, Cochrane, ON, P0L 1C0
(705) 272-4201
Emp Here 70   *Sales* 17,233,020
SIC 1794 Excavation work
 Marcel Labelle
 Peter Osmar
 Jacques Demers
 Frances Labelle

D-U-N-S 20-769-4191   (SL)
LADY MINTO HOSPITAL AT COCHRANE, THE
241 Eighth St, Cochrane, ON, P0L 1C0

(705) 272-7200
Emp Here 200   *Sales* 22,216,000
SIC 8062 General medical and surgical hospitals
Dan O'mara
Maureen Konopelky
Leo Gregoire

D-U-N-S 24-483-9221   (BR)
NORBORD INDUSTRIES INC
ROCKSHIELD ENGINEERED WOOD PRODUCTS
(*Suby of* NORBORD INC.)
4 Boisvert Cres, Cochrane, ON, P0L 1C0
(705) 272-4210
Emp Here 250
SIC 2435 Hardwood veneer and plywood
Rodney Hoogenhoud

D-U-N-S 20-260-9645   (HQ)
ONTARIO ASSOCIATION OF CHILDREN'S AID SOCIETIES
SERVICES FAMILIAUX JEANNE SAUVE FAMILY SERVICES
187 2nd Ave, Cochrane, ON, P0L 1C0
(705) 272-2449
Emp Here 1   *Sales* 10,206,274
SIC 8699 Membership organizations, nec
Marilyn Dumaresq
Marilyn Ballantyne

D-U-N-S 25-407-5831   (BR)
RAYONIER A.M. CANADA G.P.
TEMBEC
(*Suby of* RAYONIER A.M. CANADA G.P.)
70 17th Ave, Cochrane, ON, P0L 1C0
(705) 272-4321
Emp Here 170
SIC 2421 Sawmills and planing mills, general
Paulo Gignac

Colborne, ON K0K

D-U-N-S 20-036-4479   (HQ)
ANIXTER POWER SOLUTIONS CANADA INC
(*Suby of* ANIXTER INTERNATIONAL INC.)
188 Purdy Rd, Colborne, ON, K0K 1S0
(905) 355-2474
Emp Here 100   *Sales* 390,184,000
SIC 5085 Industrial supplies
Vasken Altounian

D-U-N-S 20-699-4357   (HQ)
BOWEN MANUFACTURING LIMITED
188 King St E Rr 2, Colborne, ON, K0K 1S0
(905) 355-3757
Emp Here 1   *Sales* 21,868,000
SIC 6712 Bank holding companies
Patrick J. Bowen
Lance Alton
Gregory Bowen
Scott Larsen
Alessandro Strazzari

D-U-N-S 20-955-6054   (SL)
C.M. BRAKE INC
118 County Road 31, Colborne, ON, K0K 1S0
(905) 265-0265
Emp Here 50   *Sales* 10,094,850
SIC 3069 Fabricated rubber products, nec
Michael Beri
Brian Roffey
Spencer Roffey
Brice Roffey

D-U-N-S 25-255-9489   (HQ)
CAM TRAN CO. LTD
203 Purdy Rd, Colborne, ON, K0K 1S0
(905) 355-3224
Emp Here 175   *Sales* 70,728,750
SIC 3612 Transformers, except electric
Kyle Campbell
Scott Campbell

Bryn Campbell

D-U-N-S 20-041-6618   (SL)
JEBCO MANUFACTURING INC
(*Suby of* BOWEN MANUFACTURING LIMITED)
188 King St E Rr 2, Colborne, ON, K0K 1S0
(905) 355-3757
Emp Here 70   *Sales* 15,540,070
SIC 3599 Industrial machinery, nec
Lance Alton
Scott Larson
Gregory Bowen

D-U-N-S 20-552-1735   (SL)
KNIGHT'S APPLEDEN FRUIT LIMITED
11687 County Road 2 Rr 3, Colborne, ON, K0K 1S0
(905) 349-2521
Emp Here 35   *Sales* 29,245,195
SIC 5148 Fresh fruits and vegetables
Roger Knight
Ronald Knight

D-U-N-S 24-936-4605   (SL)
PEAK ENGINEERING & CONSTRUCTION LTD
13580 County Road 2, Colborne, ON, K0K 1S0
(905) 355-1500
Emp Here 60   *Sales* 15,146,520
SIC 1629 Heavy construction, nec
Theo Brunsting
Phil Smith
Bruce Voskamp
Mark Clancy

Coldwater, ON L0K

D-U-N-S 25-483-0482   (SL)
COLDWATER FOODLAND
77 Coldwater Rd, Coldwater, ON, L0K 1E0
(705) 686-7700
Emp Here 49   *Sales* 13,433,448
SIC 5411 Grocery stores
Melanie Sauve

D-U-N-S 24-358-5176   (HQ)
NOVANNI STAINLESS INC
2978 Southorn Rd, Coldwater, ON, L0K 1E0
(705) 686-3301
Sales 14,406,375
SIC 3469 Metal stampings, nec
Ronald A Smith
Frank Brazda

Collingwood, ON L9Y

D-U-N-S 20-558-3818   (HQ)
AINLEY & ASSOCIATES LIMITED
280 Pretty River Pky N, Collingwood, ON, L9Y 4J5
(705) 445-3451
Emp Here 55   *Sales* 14,299,120
SIC 8711 Engineering services
Joseph Mullan
Simon Ainley
Mike Ainley
Mike Neumann
Tammy Kalimootoo
P. William Ainley

D-U-N-S 20-934-6725   (SL)
BAY HAVEN NURSING HOME INC
BAY HAVEN SENIOR CARE COMMUNITY
499 Hume St Suite 18, Collingwood, ON, L9Y 4H8
(705) 445-6501
Emp Here 85   *Sales* 5,828,110
SIC 8051 Skilled nursing care facilities
Dawn Strandholt

Scott Strandholt

D-U-N-S 20-041-9612   (SL)
BLUE MOUNTAIN CHRYSLER LTD
9950 26 Hwy, Collingwood, ON, L9Y 3Z1
(705) 445-2740
Emp Here 53   *Sales* 33,351,840
SIC 5511 New and used car dealers
Kip Brown

D-U-N-S 25-353-3996   (SL)
CANADIAN BASE OPERATORS INC
101 Pretty River Pky S Suite 6, Collingwood, ON, L9Y 4M8
(705) 446-9019
Emp Here 50   *Sales* 10,131,450
SIC 7538 General automotive repair shops
John Mcdonald
John Zimantas
John Keating

D-U-N-S 20-702-8036   (SL)
CANADIAN MIST DISTILLERS LIMITED
(*Suby of* BROWN-FORMAN CORPORATION)
202 Macdonald Rd, Collingwood, ON, L9Y 4J2
(705) 445-4690
Emp Here 35   *Sales* 12,099,150
SIC 2085 Distilled and blended liquors
James Chiles
Harold Ferguson
Pat Sullivan

D-U-N-S 24-653-0612   (SL)
COLLINGWOOD CARS INC
COLLINGWOOD TOYOTA
10230 26 Hwy, Collingwood, ON, L9Y 0A5
(705) 444-1414
Emp Here 26   *Sales* 12,950,028
SIC 5511 New and used car dealers
Krista Walcroft
Dean Lockhart

D-U-N-S 20-849-0748   (SL)
COLLINGWOOD GENERAL AND MARINE HOSPITAL, THE
459 Hume St, Collingwood, ON, L9Y 1W9
(705) 445-2550
Emp Here 400   *Sales* 42,971,717
SIC 8062 General medical and surgical hospitals
Norah Holder
Julia Scott
Michael Lacroix
Jory Pritchard-Kerr

D-U-N-S 24-425-9185   (SL)
COLLUS POWERSTREAM CORP
43 Stewart Rd, Collingwood, ON, L9Y 4M7
(705) 445-1800
Emp Here 24   *Sales* 15,038,736
SIC 4911 Electric services
Stewart Lee

D-U-N-S 24-205-9033   (SL)
DANIEL S. WEBSTER HOLDINGS LIMITED
CANADIAN TIRE
89 Balsam St, Collingwood, ON, L9Y 3Y6
(705) 445-4169
Emp Here 100   *Sales* 62,928,000
SIC 5531 Auto and home supply stores
Daniel Webster

D-U-N-S 24-829-9612   (HQ)
E3 (EDUCATE, ENABLE, EMPOWER) COMMUNITY SERVICES INC
E3 COMMUNITY SERVICES
100 Pretty River Pky N, Collingwood, ON, L9Y 4X2
(705) 445-6351
Emp Here 40   *Sales* 18,156,000
SIC 8351 Child day care services
Gordon Anton
Matthew Wells
Brian Saunderson
Derek Munch

Farel Anderson
Karen Burland
Richard Edwards
Peggy Baley-Guilford
Jason Green
Don Mcnally

D-U-N-S 24-193-5738   (SL)
GEORGIAN MANOR RESORT & COUNTRY CLUB INC, THE
GEORGIAN BAY HOTEL & CONFERENCE CENTRE
10 Vacation Inn Dr, Collingwood, ON, L9Y 5G4
(800) 696-5487
Emp Here 80   *Sales* 6,111,760
SIC 7997 Membership sports and recreation clubs
Russell Brown

D-U-N-S 20-042-0206   (SL)
HAMILTON CONSTRUCTION LTD
7645 Poplar, Collingwood, ON, L9Y 3Y9
(705) 445-3220
Emp Here 65   *Sales* 16,002,090
SIC 1794 Excavation work
William Hamilton
Virginia Hamilton

D-U-N-S 24-364-9055   (SL)
INTERNATIONAL GENETICS LIMITED
Gd Stn Main, Collingwood, ON, L9Y 3Z3
(705) 445-2734
Emp Here 10   *Sales* 12,103,970
SIC 5154 Livestock
Bill Young

D-U-N-S 24-023-6554   (SL)
JOHN SANFILIPPO AND CO. LTD
(*Suby of* DON'S PRODUCE INC)
333 Peel St, Collingwood, ON, L9Y 3W3
(705) 445-4200
Emp Here 20   *Sales* 16,711,540
SIC 5148 Fresh fruits and vegetables
Gerry Blake
Domenic Sanfilippo

D-U-N-S 24-609-0674   (HQ)
LAW CRANBERRY RESORT LIMITED
CRANBERRY GOLF RESORT
19 Keith Ave, Collingwood, ON, L9Y 4T9
(705) 445-6600
Sales 23,917,000
SIC 7011 Hotels and motels
Larry Law

D-U-N-S 25-902-0188   (BR)
LOBLAWS SUPERMARKETS LIMITED
LOBLAWS
(*Suby of* LOBLAW COMPANIES LIMITED)
12 Hurontario St, Collingwood, ON, L9Y 2L6
(705) 445-0461
Emp Here 170
SIC 5411 Grocery stores
Olga Karniol

D-U-N-S 24-324-6878   (SL)
LORAC COMMUNICATIONS INC
LCI
115 First St Suite 107, Collingwood, ON, L9Y 4W3
(905) 457-5350
Emp Here 500   *Sales* 114,236,000
SIC 4899 Communication services, nec
Tony Marchand

D-U-N-S 24-876-3625   (HQ)
MATTHEWS, MARK PHARMACY LTD
SHOPPERS DRUG MART
119 Hurontario St, Collingwood, ON, L9Y 2L9
(705) 444-6055
Emp Here 28   *Sales* 14,171,024
SIC 5912 Drug stores and proprietary stores
Mark Matthews

D-U-N-S 24-333-1654   (BR)
METRO ONTARIO INC
METRO
(*Suby of* METRO INC.)

---

640 First St, Collingwood, ON, L9Y 4Y7
(705) 444-5252
Emp Here 200
SIC 5411 Grocery stores
Frank Stevens

D-U-N-S 20-042-0503   (SL)
MICHAEL JACKSON MOTOR SALES LIM-ITED
MIKE JACKSON GM
480 Hume St, Collingwood, ON, L9Y 1W6
(705) 445-2222
Emp Here 30   *Sales* 14,942,340
SIC 5511 New and used car dealers
Michael Jackson
Patti Callahan

D-U-N-S 20-402-8658   (HQ)
PILKINGTON GLASS OF CANADA LTD
NSG
(*Suby of* NIPPON SHEET GLASS COM-PANY,LIMITED)
1000 26 Hwy, Collingwood, ON, L9Y 4V8
(705) 445-4780
Emp Here 240   *Sales* 76,707,000
SIC 3231 Products of purchased glass
Brian Hammond

D-U-N-S 24-048-7926   (HQ)
S.K.S. NOVELTY COMPANY LTD
30 Sandford Fleming Rd, Collingwood, ON, L9Y 4V7
(705) 444-5653
Emp Here 20   *Sales* 19,305,520
SIC 5199 Nondurable goods, nec
Donald Mcculloch

D-U-N-S 20-042-0917   (HQ)
SAUNDERS OFFICE AND SCHOOL SUP-PLIES LIMITED
SAUNDERS BOOK COMPANY
29 Stewart Rd, Collingwood, ON, L9Y 4M7
(705) 444-1696
Emp Here 55   *Sales* 41,535,760
SIC 5942 Book stores
John Saunders

D-U-N-S 25-292-5029   (BR)
SIMCOE COUNTY DISTRICT SCHOOL BOARD, THE
COLLINGWOOD COLLEGIATE INSTITUTE
(*Suby of* SIMCOE COUNTY DISTRICT SCHOOL BOARD, THE)
6 Cameron St, Collingwood, ON, L9Y 2J2
(705) 445-3161
Emp Here 100
SIC 8211 Elementary and secondary schools
Peter Stone

D-U-N-S 25-409-8924   (HQ)
TATHAM, C.C. & ASSOCIATES LTD
115 Sandford Fleming Rd Suite 200, Collingwood, ON, L9Y 5A6
(705) 444-2565
Emp Here 55   *Sales* 13,196,850
SIC 8711 Engineering services
Charles Tatham
Rex Meadley

D-U-N-S 20-026-8220   (BR)
UNITED STEELWORKERS OF AMERICA
LOCAL 252
(*Suby of* UNITED STEELWORKERS)
1000 26 Hwy, Collingwood, ON, L9Y 4V8

Emp Here 300
SIC 8631 Labor organizations
William Del Piro

D-U-N-S 25-351-7973   (SL)
VOA CANADA INC
(*Suby of* AUTOLIV, INC.)
190 Macdonald Rd, Collingwood, ON, L9Y 4N6
(705) 444-2561
Emp Here 120   *Sales* 30,015,787
SIC 2241 Narrow fabric mills

David Helm
Michael S Anderson
Steve Fredin

D-U-N-S 24-319-5091   (BR)
WAL-MART CANADA CORP
WALMART
(*Suby of* WALMART INC.)
10 Cambridge, Collingwood, ON, L9Y 0A1
(705) 445-9262
Emp Here 170
SIC 5311 Department stores
Susan Dykstra

D-U-N-S 20-745-7008   (HQ)
WN BIRD FINANCIAL GROUP INC
WAYNE BIRD FUELS
387 Raglan St, Collingwood, ON, L9Y 3Z1
(705) 445-4501
Emp Here 8   *Sales* 27,658,422
SIC 5172 Petroleum products, nec
Wayne Bird
Mary Ellen Bird

Comber, ON N0P

D-U-N-S 24-368-1744   (SL)
MCGRAIL FARM EQUIPMENT LIMITED PARTNERSHIP
8705 County Rd 46 Rr 1, Comber, ON, N0P 1J0
(519) 687-6662
Emp Here 46   *Sales* 14,977,600
SIC 5999 Miscellaneous retail stores, nec
Paul Mcgrail

Combermere, ON K0J

D-U-N-S 24-270-8964   (SL)
PASTWAY PLANING LIMITED
(*Suby of* CANWEL BUILDING MATERIALS GROUP LTD)
2916 Rockingham Rd, Combermere, ON, K0J 1L0
(613) 756-2742
Emp Here 70   *Sales* 13,465,900
SIC 2421 Sawmills and planing mills, general
Raphael Pastway

Concord, ON L4K

D-U-N-S 20-393-9967   (SL)
11108204 CANADA INC
235 Rayette Rd Unit 1a, Concord, ON, L4K 2G1
(437) 218-3702
Emp Here 22   *Sales* 18,382,694
SIC 5146 Fish and seafoods
Walid Samara
Janis Reinikovs

D-U-N-S 24-684-7578   (HQ)
1132694 ONTARIO INC
SPRAY-PAK INDUSTRIES
(*Suby of* PLZ AEROSCIENCE CORPORA-TION)
8001 Keele St, Concord, ON, L4K 1Y8
(905) 669-9855
Emp Here 10   *Sales* 40,134,480
SIC 7389 Business services, nec
Lee Paige
Wayne Houston
David Bowker
Stan Capobianco
David Porcellato

D-U-N-S 20-551-7050   (SL)
1249762 ONTARIO INC

MEGA CITY TILING
390 Edgeley Blvd Unit 8, Concord, ON, L4K 3Z6
(905) 761-9009
Emp Here 110   *Sales* 17,861,910
SIC 1743 Terrazzo, tile, marble and mossaic work
Anthony Marano

D-U-N-S 24-579-3513   (HQ)
1249932 ONTARIO INC
PETRO CANADA
1514 Steeles Ave W, Concord, ON, L4K 2P7
(905) 738-0338
Emp Here 5   *Sales* 24,903,900
SIC 5541 Gasoline service stations
Ali Razavi

D-U-N-S 25-099-2393   (SL)
1360548 ONTARIO LIMITED
PRIME PASTRIES
370 North Rivermede Rd Unit 1, Concord, ON, L4K 3N2
(905) 669-5883
Emp Here 50   *Sales* 13,707,600
SIC 5461 Retail bakeries
Steven Muchinik
Ashley Berman

D-U-N-S 24-340-8320   (HQ)
1392167 ONTARIO LIMITED
248 Bowes Rd, Concord, ON, L4K 1J9
(905) 660-5021
Sales 13,077,650
SIC 6712 Bank holding companies
John Martini
Frank Greco
Jacques Charlebois

D-U-N-S 20-955-8290   (SL)
1406284 ONTARIO INC
HILTON GARDEN INN HOTEL AND CON-FERENCE CENTRE
3201 Highway 7, Concord, ON, L4K 5Z7
(905) 660-4700
Emp Here 75   *Sales* 7,117,425
SIC 7011 Hotels and motels
Steve Gupta
Tom Copeland

D-U-N-S 20-113-1989   (SL)
1422545 ONTARIO INC
BASIC FASHION SERVICE
74 Edilcan Dr Unit 1, Concord, ON, L4K 3S5
(905) 660-3357
Emp Here 24   *Sales* 11,959,728
SIC 5137 Women's and children's clothing
Loretta Serrani
Marianne Serrani

D-U-N-S 20-210-2179   (HQ)
1428508 ONTARIO LIMITED
FORMA-CON CONSTRUCTION
407 Basaltic Rd, Concord, ON, L4K 4W8
(905) 303-8010
Sales 106,668,480
SIC 1521 Single-family housing construction
Domenic Dipede

D-U-N-S 24-593-9603   (HQ)
1475541 ONTARIO LTD
PETRO CANADA
2651 Rutherford Rd, Concord, ON, L4K 2N6
(905) 856-0662
Sales 24,903,900
SIC 5541 Gasoline service stations
Patrick Trotman
Apolinar Cadiente
Paul Cadiente

D-U-N-S 25-192-3264   (HQ)
1509611 ONTARIO INC
WADE-TECH CAD & GRAPHICS
577 Edgeley Blvd Suite 1, Concord, ON, L4K 4B2
(905) 660-4200
Emp Here 15   *Sales* 14,250,780
SIC 5084 Industrial machinery and equipment

John Walker
Les Wojcianiec
David Newton

D-U-N-S 20-822-4832   (HQ)
1642852 ONTARIO LTD
INTERNATIONAL TELE-FILM
(*Suby of* GLOBAL EAGLE ENTERTAINMENT INC.)
30 Macintosh Blvd Unit 7, Concord, ON, L4K 4P1
(416) 252-5907
Emp Here 26   *Sales* 13,415,220
SIC 5065 Electronic parts and equipment, nec
John Fisher
Allan Cohen

D-U-N-S 20-295-6744   (SL)
1719108 ONTARIO INC
ZOREN INDUSTRIES
368 Four Valley Dr, Concord, ON, L4K 5Z1
(416) 749-5665
Emp Here 27   *Sales* 34,538,693
SIC 5039 Construction materials, nec
Dan Mayer
James Hal
Marc Halioua

D-U-N-S 20-388-3624   (SL)
1923921 ONTARIO INC
CORSTEEL HYDRAULICS
200 Spinnaker Way, Concord, ON, L4K 5E5
(905) 738-3682
Emp Here 40   *Sales* 15,162,040
SIC 3542 Machine tools, Metal forming type
Tiziano Tersigni

D-U-N-S 20-554-7982   (HQ)
2014767 ONTARIO LIMITED
MCLEISH CONTAINERS
96 Planchet Rd, Concord, ON, L4K 2C7
(905) 738-0583
Emp Here 45   *Sales* 31,162,880
SIC 2653 Corrugated and solid fiber boxes
John D. Coyle
Robert Wilcox
Robyn Nolte

D-U-N-S 24-380-1086   (SL)
2088847 ONTARIO INC
TRANSPORTATION SERVICES.CA
155 Drumlin Cir Unit 2, Concord, ON, L4K 3E7
(905) 761-9999
Emp Here 50   *Sales* 19,268,000
SIC 4731 Freight transportation arrangement
Ronen Gil

D-U-N-S 20-382-5385   (SL)
2119485 ALBERTA LTD
DELLCOM AEROSPACE
301 Millway Ave, Concord, ON, L4K 4T3
(905) 761-0808
Emp Here 75   *Sales* 14,406,375
SIC 3429 Hardware, nec
Ian Harrison
Chris Heffernan
Mark Bathurst

D-U-N-S 20-301-3735   (HQ)
2172004 ONTARIO INC
QRX TECHNOLOGY GROUP
200 Connie Cres Unit 4, Concord, ON, L4K 1M1
(905) 738-1688
Sales 12,591,450
SIC 5112 Stationery and office supplies
Grace Martin

D-U-N-S 20-262-5935   (HQ)
2319793 ONTARIO INC
FRESH SELECTIONS
350 Creditstone Rd Unit 103, Concord, ON, L4K 3Z2
(905) 760-0000
Sales 31,112,100
SIC 2098 Macaroni and spaghetti
Michael Whitcombe

▲ Public Company   ■ Public Company Family Member   **HQ** Headquarters   **BR** Branch   **SL** Single Location

D-U-N-S 25-691-6545   (SL)
24 HOUR THERMAL GLASS INSULATION LTD
250 Bowes Rd, Concord, ON, L4K 1J9
(905) 738-7585
Emp Here 40   *Sales* 17,886,960
SIC 5039 Construction materials, nec
Galo Narvaez

D-U-N-S 20-983-8770   (SL)
340532 ONTARIO LIMITED
S & F FOOD IMPORTERS
565 Edgeley Blvd, Concord, ON, L4K 4G4
(905) 669-9930
Emp Here 40   *Sales* 33,423,080
SIC 5149 Groceries and related products, nec
Sol Zeidman

D-U-N-S 25-214-3771   (SL)
370271 ONTARIO LIMITED
1600 Steeles Ave W Suite 426, Concord, ON, L4K 4M2
(905) 660-4006
Emp Here 40   *Sales* 23,196,960
SIC 6411 Insurance agents, brokers, and service
Angelo Grossi
Marisa Grossi

D-U-N-S 24-365-1494   (SL)
372103 ONTARIO LTD
PT INDUSTRIAL ELECTRIC CO
33 Corstate Ave, Concord, ON, L4K 4Y2
(905) 669-5712
Emp Here 60   *Sales* 13,069,740
SIC 1731 Electrical work
Nicola (Sr) Palozzi

D-U-N-S 24-185-3100   (SL)
375645 ONTARIO LIMITED
VICTOR TRAVEL AGENCY
8800 Dufferin St Unit 101, Concord, ON, L4K 0C5
(416) 736-6010
Emp Here 30   *Sales* 11,560,800
SIC 4724 Travel agencies
Cecilia Rossos

D-U-N-S 25-294-1141   (SL)
3GMETALWORX INC
90 Snow Blvd Unit 2, Concord, ON, L4K 4A2
(905) 738-7973
Emp Here 55   *Sales* 10,474,310
SIC 3679 Electronic components, nec
Manuel Gomez

D-U-N-S 24-477-0046   (SL)
464290 ONTARIO LIMITED
AIRFLIGHT SERVICES
3300 Steeles Ave W Suite 202, Concord, ON, L4K 2Y4
(416) 445-1999
Emp Here 268   *Sales* 20,172,896
SIC 4111 Local and suburban transit
Gurinder Virk
Lakhwinder Singh
Baldev Singh

D-U-N-S 24-302-0658   (SL)
473464 ONTARIO LIMITED
TOPAX PROTEKTIVEPACKAGING
380 Spinnaker Way, Concord, ON, L4K 4W1
(905) 669-6464
Emp Here 31   *Sales* 16,118,977
SIC 4783 Packing and crating
Simon Trillwood
Bernice Trillwood
Jo-Lynn Hoffmann

D-U-N-S 20-109-2520   (SL)
6131646 CANADA INC
DAVE & BUSTERS OF CANADA
(*Suby of* DAVE & BUSTER'S ENTERTAINMENT, INC.)
120 Interchange Way, Concord, ON, L4K 5C3
(905) 760-7600
Emp Here 167   *Sales* 7,788,713
SIC 5812 Eating places

Brian Light

D-U-N-S 20-982-5736   (SL)
838116 ONTARIO INC
DONUT TIME
35 Adesso Dr Suite 18, Concord, ON, L4K 3C7
(905) 760-0850
Emp Here 70   *Sales* 24,198,300
SIC 2051 Bread, cake, and related products
Steve Tsilker
Eddie Sabba

D-U-N-S 20-924-2759   (SL)
A & D PRECISION LIMITED
289 Bradwick Dr, Concord, ON, L4K 1K5
(905) 669-5888
Emp Here 50   *Sales* 10,185,800
SIC 7699 Repair services, nec
Anthony Derbedrosian

D-U-N-S 20-014-8802   (SL)
A.R.G GROUP INC
(*Suby of* STELLARBRIDGE MANAGEMENT INC)
111 Creditstone Rd, Concord, ON, L4K 1N3
(905) 669-4133
Emp Here 50   *Sales* 21,136,850
SIC 1541 Industrial buildings and warehouses
Galiano Tiberini

D-U-N-S 25-150-9436   (SL)
ABILITY FABRICATORS INC
187 Romina Dr, Concord, ON, L4K 4V3
(905) 761-1401
Emp Here 45   *Sales* 10,504,575
SIC 3312 Blast furnaces and steel mills
Ramnauth Persaud
Haim Persaud

D-U-N-S 24-783-4109   (SL)
ACCEL CONSTRUCTION MANAGEMENT INC
50 Viceroy Rd Unit 11, Concord, ON, L4K 3A7
(905) 660-6690
Emp Here 25   *Sales* 11,087,250
SIC 7389 Business services, nec
Anthony Corsetti
Laura Corsetti

D-U-N-S 24-868-8418   (SL)
ACCORD PLASTICS CORP
60 Courtland Ave, Concord, ON, L4K 5B3

Emp Here 50   *Sales* 10,094,850
SIC 3089 Plastics products, nec
Robert Ciancio

D-U-N-S 24-363-3203   (HQ)
ACCUCUT PROFILE & GRINDING LIMITED
300 Connie Cres, Concord, ON, L4K 5W6
(416) 798-7716
Sales 29,513,484
SIC 5051 Metals service centers and offices
Luigi Corso
Adriana Corso

D-U-N-S 24-046-2978   (HQ)
ACCURATE FASTENERS LTD
ACCURATE GROUP OF COMPANIES, THE
550 Applewood Cres Suite 1, Concord, ON, L4K 4B4
(416) 798-7887
Emp Here 50   *Sales* 23,751,300
SIC 5085 Industrial supplies
Gerry Sohl
Richard Wagman

D-U-N-S 24-453-6314   (SL)
ACRYLIC FABRICATORS LIMITED
AFL DISPLAY GROUP
89a Connie Cres Unit 4, Concord, ON, L4K 1L3
(905) 660-6666
Emp Here 70   *Sales* 10,802,540
SIC 2542 Partitions and fixtures, except wood
Brian Mandelker

D-U-N-S 20-158-2889   (SL)

ACTIVE GEAR COMPANY OF CANADA LIMITED
201r Snidercroft Rd Suite 1, Concord, ON, L4K 2J9
(905) 669-2292
Emp Here 29   *Sales* 10,562,235
SIC 5013 Motor vehicle supplies and new parts
Anthony M Mainelli
David R Lieberman

D-U-N-S 25-167-9544   (SL)
ACTUS MANAGEMENT (VAUGHAN) INC
7501 Keele St, Concord, ON, L4K 1Y2
(905) 760-2700
Emp Here 75   *Sales* 20,574,900
SIC 8741 Management services
Michael N Durisin
Herbert L. Wisebrod
Stephen J Marano

D-U-N-S 24-096-4429   (SL)
AIR CAB LIMOUSINE (1985) LIMITED
7733 Keele St, Concord, ON, L4K 1Y5
(416) 225-1555
Emp Here 100   *Sales* 5,487,200
SIC 4119 Local passenger transportation, nec
Y Zahavy

D-U-N-S 25-500-3527   (HQ)
ALBERO RIDGE HOMES LTD
ASPEN RIDGE HOMES
29 Floral Pkwy, Concord, ON, L4K 5C5
(905) 669-9292
Sales 33,867,750
SIC 1521 Single-family housing construction
Andrew De Gasperis

D-U-N-S 20-143-9470   (SL)
ALEAFIA HEALTH INC
CANABO
8810 Jane St 2nd Fl, Concord, ON, L4K 2M9
(416) 860-5665
Emp Here 187   *Sales* 2,524,421
SIC 5122 Drugs, proprietaries, and sundries
Geoffrey M. Benic
Keith White
Bob Santos
Dave Shepherd
Nicholas Bergamini
Benjamin Ferdinand
Trevor J. Newell
Julian Fantino
Raf Souccar
William Stewart

D-U-N-S 24-666-6473   (SL)
ALENDEL FABRICS LIMITED
274 Edgeley Blvd, Concord, ON, L4K 3Y4
(905) 669-1998
Emp Here 21   *Sales* 10,464,762
SIC 5131 Piece goods and notions
Peter Locurto
Mary Anne Locurto

D-U-N-S 25-745-2917   (SL)
ALEXION PHARMA CANADA CORP
3100 Rutherford Rd, Concord, ON, L4K 0G6
(866) 393-1188
Emp Here 25   *Sales* 27,633,625
SIC 5122 Drugs, proprietaries, and sundries
Daniel Palmqvist
Michael V. Greco
Jeffrey M. Fryer

D-U-N-S 20-982-4101   (SL)
ANGELO'S GARDEN CENTRE LIMITED
1801 Highway 7, Concord, ON, L4K 1V4
(905) 669-9220
Emp Here 52   *Sales* 13,917,904
SIC 5261 Retail nurseries and garden stores
Carlo Ammendolia
Dominic Ammendolia

D-U-N-S 20-255-2733   (HQ)
AP INFRASTRUCTURE SOLUTIONS LP
AQUA Q

(*Suby of* TREVLUC HOLDINGS LTD)
3300 Highway 7 Suite 500, Concord, ON, L4K 4M3
(647) 795-9250
Emp Here 50   *Sales* 570,043,600
SIC 3312 Blast furnaces and steel mills
Mark Anderson
Malcolm Buxton-Forman
Dennis Lattimore
Dan Lyons
Kelly Cotton

D-U-N-S 25-093-1599   (SL)
APEX BRANDED SOLUTIONS INC
21 Graniteridge Rd Suite 1, Concord, ON, L4K 5M9
(905) 760-9946
Emp Here 30   *Sales* 33,160,350
SIC 5122 Drugs, proprietaries, and sundries
Carlo Livolsi
Laura Valvalo

D-U-N-S 24-779-1320   (HQ)
ARCELORMITTAL TAILORED BLANKS AMERICAS LIMITED
ARCELORMITTAL TAILORED BLANKS MERELBEKE
(*Suby of* ARCELORMITTAL FINANCE AND SERVICES BELGIUM)
55 Confederation Pky, Concord, ON, L4K 4Y7
(905) 761-1525
Sales 22,200,100
SIC 3542 Machine tools, Metal forming type
Todd Baker
Jagtar Taggar

D-U-N-S 24-666-9964   (SL)
ARCHITECTURAL ORNAMENT INC
55 Bradwick Dr, Concord, ON, L4K 1K5

Emp Here 60   *Sales* 16,599,600
SIC 2821 Plastics materials and resins
Murat Demirli

D-U-N-S 20-555-3498   (HQ)
ARLA FOODS INC
NATIONAL CHEESE COMPANY
(*Suby of* ARLA FOODS A.M.B.A)
675 Rivermede Rd, Concord, ON, L4K 2G9
(905) 669-9393
Sales 53,120,064
SIC 5451 Dairy products stores
Douglas Smith
Peder Tuborgh
Hans Sommer
Daniel Kastelman

D-U-N-S 20-530-3910   (SL)
ARTCRAFT COMPANY INC
ESQUIRE PROMOTIONS, DIV OF
309 Pennsylvania Ave, Concord, ON, L4K 5R9
(905) 660-1919
Emp Here 50   *Sales* 24,916,100
SIC 5131 Piece goods and notions
Moishe Bergman
Saul Randinowitz

D-U-N-S 20-106-5625   (SL)
ARTEX SYSTEMS INC
523 Bowes Rd, Concord, ON, L4K 1J5
(905) 669-1425
Emp Here 80   *Sales* 35,773,920
SIC 5032 Brick, stone, and related material
Jim Farwell

D-U-N-S 20-529-3640   (SL)
ASHLAND PAVING LTD
ASHLAND CONSTRUCTION
340 Bowes Rd, Concord, ON, L4K 1K1
(905) 660-3060
Emp Here 44   *Sales* 12,475,056
SIC 1611 Highway and street construction
Frank Tarquini

D-U-N-S 24-860-8101   (HQ)
ASSA ABLOY OF CANADA LTD
(*Suby of* ASSA ABLOY AB)
160 Four Valley Dr, Concord, ON, L4K 4T9

(905) 738-2466
Emp Here 35   *Sales* 69,006,600
SIC 5072 Hardware
Greg Erwin
Andre Gougeon

D-U-N-S 24-632-6060   (SL)
ATLAS CORPORATION, THE
111 Ortona Crt, Concord, ON, L4K 3M3
(905) 669-6825
Emp Here 50   *Sales* 23,536,550
SIC 1542 Nonresidential construction, nec
Andrew Famiglietti

D-U-N-S 25-732-2156   (SL)
AURIUM PHARMA INC
7941 Jane St Suite 105, Concord, ON, L4K 4L6
(905) 669-9057
Emp Here 40   *Sales* 10,118,160
SIC 5912 Drug stores and proprietary stores
Roman Foreys
Jacques Cousineau

D-U-N-S 25-353-7229   (HQ)
AVRON FOODS LIMITED
277 Basaltic Rd, Concord, ON, L4K 4W8
(800) 997-9752
Sales 33,423,080
SIC 5141 Groceries, general line
Avi Mezuman
Talia Mezuman

D-U-N-S 20-184-9317   (HQ)
AZTEC ELECTRICAL SUPPLY INC
25 North Rivermede Rd Unit 4-10, Concord, ON, L4K 5V4
(905) 761-7762
Emp Here 1   *Sales* 32,682,279
SIC 5063 Electrical apparatus and equipment
George Mackinnon
Kevin Borg
Frank Dennis

D-U-N-S 25-353-7039   (HQ)
B.B. BARGOON'S (1996) CORP
8201 Keele St Unit 1, Concord, ON, L4K 1Z4
(905) 761-5065
Emp Here 15   *Sales* 18,592,240
SIC 5712 Furniture stores
Lisa Nicholl
Bonnie Bickel

D-U-N-S 20-159-4959   (HQ)
BAILEY METAL PRODUCTS LIMITED
(*Suby of* BAILEY-HUNT LIMITED)
1 Caldari Rd, Concord, ON, L4K 3Z9
(905) 738-9267
Emp Here 204   *Sales* 128,076,627
SIC 3312 Blast furnaces and steel mills
David Hunt
Angelo Sarracini
Stuart Hunt
Mark Griffioen
Malcolm Nobbs
Susan Schalburg
Paul Chan
Fraser Howell

D-U-N-S 24-388-7481   (HQ)
BAILEY WEST PROCESSING INC
1 Caldari Rd, Concord, ON, L4K 3Z9
(905) 738-9267
Emp Here 10   *Sales* 20,006,780
SIC 5051 Metals service centers and offices
Dave Hunt

D-U-N-S 24-180-7502   (HQ)
BAILEY-HUNT LIMITED
1 Caldari Rd, Concord, ON, L4K 3Z9
(905) 738-9267
Sales 154,726,120
SIC 3312 Blast furnaces and steel mills
David Hunt
Paul Chan

D-U-N-S 25-148-5876   (SL)
BASE LINE DRAFTING SERVICES INC

30 Pennsylvania Ave Unit 3b, Concord, ON, L4K 4A5
(905) 660-7017
Emp Here 27   *Sales* 12,128,913
SIC 7389 Business services, nec
Walter Bezuhly
Frank Sacco
Henry Nielsen

D-U-N-S 20-560-5863   (HQ)
BASS PRO SHOPS CANADA INC
(*Suby of* BASS PRO GROUP, LLC)
1 Bass Pro Mills Dr, Concord, ON, L4K 5W4
(905) 761-4000
Emp Here 25   *Sales* 62,586,117
SIC 5941 Sporting goods and bicycle shops
Shawn Hewitt

D-U-N-S 24-633-0112   (SL)
BELROCK CONSTRUCTION GENERAL CONTRACTOR LIMITED
185 Adesso Dr, Concord, ON, L4K 3C4
(905) 669-9481
Emp Here 45   *Sales* 21,182,895
SIC 1542 Nonresidential construction, nec
Gabriel Grossi
John Ciampa
Filomina Ciera

D-U-N-S 24-919-0398   (HQ)
BLUE STREAK ELECTRONICS INC
30 Moyal Crt, Concord, ON, L4K 4R8
(905) 669-4812
Sales 11,426,520
SIC 3694 Engine electrical equipment
Aron Regev

D-U-N-S 20-935-1667   (HQ)
BONDFIELD CONSTRUCTION COMPANY LIMITED
407 Basaltic Rd, Concord, ON, L4K 4W8
(416) 667-8422
Sales 85,550,700
SIC 1542 Nonresidential construction, nec
Ralph Aquino
Steven Aquino
Ana Debortoli
John Aquino

D-U-N-S 20-696-3592   (HQ)
BOOMCO DECOR INC
LA-ZY-BOY FURNITURE GALLERIES
255 Bass Pro Mills Dr Suite, Concord, ON, L4K 0A2
(905) 660-0677
Emp Here 15   *Sales* 11,517,000
SIC 5712 Furniture stores
Paul W. Hogeboom
Heather Hogeboom

D-U-N-S 24-892-8723   (SL)
BRADLEY AIR-CONDITIONING LIMITED
150 Connie Cres Suite 14, Concord, ON, L4K 1L9
(905) 660-5400
Emp Here 50   *Sales* 11,046,700
SIC 1711 Plumbing, heating, air-conditioning
Teresa Connors

D-U-N-S 24-664-7598   (SL)
BRATTYS LLP
7501 Keele St Suite 200, Concord, ON, L4K 1Y2
(905) 760-2600
Emp Here 150   *Sales* 16,632,300
SIC 8111 Legal services
Rudolph Bratty
Mel Morassutti
Joseph Chiappetta
Herb Wisebrod
Steve Marano
Joe Fried
Gary Goldfarb
Span Rose
Micheal Cohen

D-U-N-S 25-273-8984   (SL)
BRENTWOOD CLASSICS LIMITED

57 Adesso Dr, Concord, ON, L4K 3C7
(905) 761-0195
Emp Here 27   *Sales* 10,802,540
SIC 2512 Upholstered household furniture
John Armando Colalillo

D-U-N-S 20-299-3374   (SL)
BRIDGEPOINT LOGISTICS INC
20 Barnes Crt Unit 2, Concord, ON, L4K 4L4
(416) 307-2100
Emp Here 30   *Sales* 11,094,675
SIC 4731 Freight transportation arrangement
Anurag Arun
Anurag Arunis

D-U-N-S 24-985-0124   (HQ)
BROKERS TRUST INSURANCE GROUP INC
2780 Highway 7 Suite 201, Concord, ON, L4K 3R9
(416) 427-5251
Emp Here 1   *Sales* 42,403,000
SIC 6411 Insurance agents, brokers, and service
Bruno Bertolin
Franco Cavaliere
Fred Giansange
Charles Bokor
Larry Scenna

D-U-N-S 24-507-4182   (SL)
BROWN WINDOW CORPORATION
185 Snow Blvd Suite 2, Concord, ON, L4K 4N9
(905) 738-6045
Emp Here 70   *Sales* 18,735,640
SIC 5211 Lumber and other building materials
Eros Gerardi
Pino Marinelli

D-U-N-S 25-510-7161   (SL)
BURNCO MANUFACTURING INC
40 Citron Crt, Concord, ON, L4K 2P5
(905) 761-6155
Emp Here 200   *Sales* 44,400,200
SIC 3569 General industrial machinery, nec
Homer Sayyad
Irvin Stal

D-U-N-S 20-964-6645   (SL)
BURRELL OVERHEAD DOOR CO. LIMITED
1853 Highway 7, Concord, ON, L4K 1V4
(905) 669-1711
Emp Here 45   *Sales* 18,870,975
SIC 6712 Bank holding companies
Kenneth W Burrell

D-U-N-S 24-579-5091   (HQ)
BUSY BEE MACHINE TOOLS LTD
130 Great Gulf Dr, Concord, ON, L4K 5W1
(905) 738-5115
Emp Here 35   *Sales* 13,382,600
SIC 5251 Hardware stores
Anil Balolia

D-U-N-S 25-529-3367   (HQ)
BUTTCON HOLDINGS LIMITED
8000 Jane St Suite 401, Concord, ON, L4K 5B8
(905) 907-4242
Sales 31,705,275
SIC 1541 Industrial buildings and warehouses
Michael Butt
Robert Booth
Barrie Fordham
Peter Digaetano
John Evenden

D-U-N-S 24-098-5119   (HQ)
BUTTCON LIMITED
(*Suby of* BUTTCON HOLDINGS LIMITED)
8000 Jane St, Concord, ON, L4K 5B8
(905) 907-4242
Sales 21,136,850
SIC 1541 Industrial buildings and warehouses
Michael A Butt
Peter S Digaetano
Mark Rowlands

Pina Massara

D-U-N-S 24-373-6688   (HQ)
BYNG GROUP LTD, THE
511 Edgeley Blvd Unit 2, Concord, ON, L4K 4G4
(905) 660-5454
Sales 334,454,000
SIC 7389 Business services, nec
Frank Settino
Robert Settino
Rose Settino
Sandra Settino

D-U-N-S 20-940-4185   (SL)
BYNG PLASTERING AND TILE LIMITED
511 Edgeley Blvd Unit 2, Concord, ON, L4K 4G4
(905) 660-5454
Emp Here 80   *Sales* 12,990,480
SIC 1742 Plastering, drywall, and insulation
Frank Settino

D-U-N-S 20-528-2937   (HQ)
C.H. ROBINSON COMPANY (CANADA) LTD
FRESH 1 MARKETING
(*Suby of* C.H. ROBINSON INVESTMENTS SARL)
610 Applewood Cres Unit 601, Concord, ON, L4K 0E3
(905) 851-8865
Emp Here 1   *Sales* 106,702,720
SIC 4731 Freight transportation arrangement
Mark Hong
John P. Wiehoff
Ben G. Campbell
Chris O'brien
Kelly Adam Maccormack
Christopher John Raynor
Alexander Linetsky
Nathan Zietlow

D-U-N-S 24-336-4361   (HQ)
C.R. LAURENCE OF CANADA LIMITED
(*Suby of* CRH PUBLIC LIMITED COMPANY)
65 Tigi Crt, Concord, ON, L4K 5E4
(905) 303-7966
Emp Here 45   *Sales* 11,438,315
SIC 3211 Flat glass
Gavin Brin
Don Friese

D-U-N-S 24-644-6769   (SL)
CALIBRE SALES INC
8162 Keele St, Concord, ON, L4K 2A5
(905) 660-3603
Emp Here 23   *Sales* 11,584,134
SIC 5113 Industrial and personal service paper
Mansur Kanchwala

D-U-N-S 24-802-4536   (SL)
CALLOWAY REIT (CARLETON) INC
700 Applewood Cres Suite 200, Concord, ON, L4K 5X3
(905) 326-6400
Emp Here 100   *Sales* 69,681,000
SIC 6798 Real estate investment trusts
Huw Thomas
Rudy Gobin
Mario Calabrese

D-U-N-S 20-269-1135   (SL)
CALLOWAY REIT (SOUTH KEYS) INC
700 Applewood Cres Suite 20, Concord, ON, L4K 5X3
(905) 326-6400
Emp Here 50   *Sales* 34,840,500
SIC 6798 Real estate investment trusts
Al Mawani
Rudy Gobin
Bart Munn
Mario Calabrese
David Calnan
J Michael Storey
Huw Thomas

D-U-N-S 24-992-4861   (HQ)

CALSPER DEVELOPMENTS INC
REMINGTON HOMES
7501 Keele St Suite 100, Concord, ON, L4K 1Y2
(905) 761-8200
Sales 15,943,450
SIC 1521 Single-family housing construction
Matthew Bratty

D-U-N-S 25-192-3702   (BR)
CAMFIL CANADA INC
CAMFIL FARR FILTERS
(*Suby of* CAMFIL AB)
2700 Steeles Ave W, Concord, ON, L4K 3C8
(905) 660-0688
Emp Here 91
SIC 3569 General industrial machinery, nec
Michael Dobbs

D-U-N-S 20-161-0722   (SL)
CAMPBELL AND KENNEDY ELECTRIC (1996) LIMITED
242 Applewood Cres Suite 11, Concord, ON, L4K 4E5
(905) 761-8550
Emp Here 55   *Sales* 11,980,595
SIC 1731 Electrical work
Arthur Van Halteren
John Roman
Robert Richer

D-U-N-S 25-310-2594   (SL)
CAN-PET DISTRIBUTORS INC
GLOBAL PET FOODS
84 Doney Cres Suite C, Concord, ON, L4K 3A8
(905) 738-3663
Emp Here 35   *Sales* 25,988,200
SIC 5199 Nondurable goods, nec
Morris Manna
Shelley Manna

D-U-N-S 25-995-2216   (BR)
CANADA BREAD COMPANY, LIMITED
CANADA DOUGH DELIGHT
(*Suby of* GRUPO BIMBO, S.A.B. DE C.V.)
711 Rivermede Rd, Concord, ON, L4K 2G9
(905) 660-3034
Emp Here 300
SIC 2051 Bread, cake, and related products
Anthony Scire

D-U-N-S 24-451-0525   (SL)
CANADIAN BRASS & COPPER CO
CBC SPECIALTY METALS
225 Doney Cres Suite 1, Concord, ON, L4K 1P6
(416) 736-0797
Emp Here 35   *Sales* 15,651,090
SIC 5051 Metals service centers and offices
Randy Coupland

D-U-N-S 20-145-3099   (SL)
CANADIAN HOBBYCRAFT LIMITED
HOBBYCRAFT CANADA
445 Edgeley Blvd Unit 1, Concord, ON, L4K 4G1
(905) 738-6556
Emp Here 25   *Sales* 13,013,550
SIC 5092 Toys and hobby goods and supplies
Jerome David Altbaum

D-U-N-S 24-891-1596   (HQ)
CANADIAN PAPER CONNECTION INC
200 Viceroy Rd Unit 1, Concord, ON, L4K 3N8
(905) 669-2222
Sales 20,146,320
SIC 5113 Industrial and personal service paper
Stewart Fleming
Romeo Pallisco
George Vronces
Michael Puopolo

D-U-N-S 24-259-7136   (SL)
CAPITAL TOOL & DESIGN LTD.
UTIL GROUP
270 Spinnaker Way Suite 13, Concord, ON,

L4K 4W1
(905) 760-8088
Emp Here 250   *Sales* 45,347,000
SIC 3312 Blast furnaces and steel mills
Francesco Rangoni

D-U-N-S 20-421-9471   (HQ)
CARA OPERATIONS QUEBEC LTD
(*Suby of* RECIPE UNLIMITED CORPORATION)
199 Four Valley Dr, Concord, ON, L4K 0B8
(905) 760-2244
Emp Here 240   *Sales* 121,261,400
SIC 5812 Eating places
Michael Forsayeth
Ian C Wilkie
Amir Adjani
David Barlow
James B Williams
Fred Cress
Steven Tsambalieros

D-U-N-S 24-423-5235   (HQ)
CARDINAL HEALTH CANADA INC
DISMED
(*Suby of* CARDINAL HEALTH, INC.)
1000 Tesma Way, Concord, ON, L4K 5R8
(905) 417-2900
Emp Here 50   *Sales* 374,746,400
SIC 5047 Medical and hospital equipment
David H Lees
David Murphy
Samer Abdul-Samad
Fernando Pica
Rylan O Rawlins

D-U-N-S 24-310-7138   (SL)
CARESTREAM HEALTH CANADA COMPANY
(*Suby of* ONEX CORPORATION)
8800 Dufferin St Suite 201, Concord, ON, L4K 0C5
(905) 532-0877
Emp Here 100   *Sales* 22,728,900
SIC 3843 Dental equipment and supplies
Kevin J. Hobert
Joseph F. Ruh
Barry Canipe

D-U-N-S 20-121-1013   (SL)
CARIBBEAN INTERNATIONAL SUPPLY LIMITED
160 Applewood Cres Suite 21, Concord, ON, L4K 4H2

Emp Here 40   *Sales* 17,886,960
SIC 5046 Commercial equipment, nec
Raffi Tokmakjan
Emil Toma
Allen Tome

D-U-N-S 20-178-4949   (HQ)
CARILLION CANADA INC
CARILLION CONSTRUCTION
(*Suby of* CARILLION GB LIMITED)
7077 Keele St, Concord, ON, L4K 0B6
(905) 532-5200
Sales 695,603,800
SIC 1611 Highway and street construction
Andy Jones
Nigel Franklin
Fleur Kitchingman
John Maccuish
Edmund Mahabir
Emma Mercer
Tim Parsons
Steve Thompson
Stephen Watson
Liz Reynolds

D-U-N-S 24-381-4394   (SL)
CARILLION CONSTRUCTION INC
VANBOTS
7077 Keele St, Concord, ON, L4K 0B6
(905) 532-5200
Emp Here 600   *Sales* 67,321,800
SIC 8741 Management services

Graham Brown
Nick Down
Matthew Ainley
David Rosenberg
Kirsty Vlemmiks

D-U-N-S 20-010-0886   (BR)
CASCADES CANADA ULC
NORAMPAC- VAUGHAN
(*Suby of* CASCADES INC)
655 Creditstone Rd Suite 41, Concord, ON, L4K 5P9
(905) 760-3900
Emp Here 250
SIC 2653 Corrugated and solid fiber boxes
Maria Procopi

D-U-N-S 20-694-3420   (HQ)
CCT GLOBAL SOURCING INC
SIMPLI HOME
40 Bradwick Dr Unit 5, Concord, ON, L4K 1K9
(905) 326-8452
Sales 18,218,970
SIC 5099 Durable goods, nec
Erez Weinreich
Yoram Weinreich
Steve Hall

D-U-N-S 24-783-1746   (SL)
CENTRAL CANADIAN GLASS LTD
60 Snow Blvd Unit 1, Concord, ON, L4K 4B3
(905) 660-1676
Emp Here 35   *Sales* 15,651,090
SIC 5039 Construction materials, nec
Gary Macdonald
Dan Mccormick
Dennis Collins

D-U-N-S 20-349-3523   (SL)
CENTRAL IRRIGATION SUPPLY OF CANADA INC
272 Bradwick Dr, Concord, ON, L4K 1K8
(905) 532-0977
Emp Here 20   *Sales* 10,115,819
SIC 5083 Farm and garden machinery
Bernardo Luciano
Nick Conte

D-U-N-S 25-875-2096   (SL)
CENTRAL LUMBER LIMITED
CENTRAL FAIRBANK LUMBER
(*Suby of* ALPA LUMBER INC)
1900 Steeles Ave W, Concord, ON, L4K 1A1
(416) 736-6263
Emp Here 139   *Sales* 79,178,292
SIC 5031 Lumber, plywood, and millwork
Marc Dipoce
John Dipoce
Giovanni Guglietti
Carmen Guglietti
George Frankfort
Donald Maciver

D-U-N-S 24-335-1751   (SL)
CFN PRECISION LTD
(*Suby of* SPP CANADA AIRCRAFT, INC)
1000 Creditstone Rd, Concord, ON, L4K 4P8
(905) 669-8191
Emp Here 85   *Sales* 19,319,565
SIC 3812 Search and navigation equipment
Eli Brigler
Andrew Morrow
Mike Onishi
Nicholas Simon
Luigi Mattia

D-U-N-S 24-846-6237   (SL)
CHERISON ENTERPRISES INC
53 Courtland Ave Suite 1, Concord, ON, L4K 3T2
(905) 882-6168
Emp Here 50   *Sales* 37,126,000
SIC 5199 Nondurable goods, nec
Clement Chan
Rita Chan

D-U-N-S 24-425-7049   (SL)
CIF LAB CASEWORK SOLUTIONS INC

56 Edilcan Dr, Concord, ON, L4K 3S6
(905) 738-5821
Emp Here 70   *Sales* 15,910,230
SIC 3821 Laboratory apparatus and furniture
Eric Anderson
David Ross

D-U-N-S 20-325-3471   (SL)
CIF LAE SOLUTIONS LP
53 Courtland Ave Suite 1, Concord, ON, L4K 3T2
(905) 738-5821
Emp Here 80   *Sales* 18,183,120
SIC 3821 Laboratory apparatus and furniture
Thomas O'riley
Jonathan Last

D-U-N-S 20-922-2660   (BR)
CLARKE TRANSPORT INC
CLARKE TRANSPORT
(*Suby of* TFI INTERNATIONAL INC)
751 Bowes Rd Suite 2, Concord, ON, L4K 5C9
(416) 665-5585
Emp Here 250
SIC 4213 Trucking, except local
Calvin Roberts

D-U-N-S 24-947-9676   (HQ)
CLEARWAY CONSTRUCTION INC
(*Suby of* CLEARWAY GROUP INC)
379 Bowes Rd, Concord, ON, L4K 1J1
(905) 761-6955
Sales 20,195,360
SIC 1623 Water, sewer, and utility lines
Nick Di Battista

D-U-N-S 24-452-4302   (SL)
CLEVELAND RANGE LTD
(*Suby of* WELBILT, INC.)
8251 Keele St, Concord, ON, L4K 1Z1
(905) 660-4747
Emp Here 200   *Sales* 44,400,200
SIC 3589 Service industry machinery, nec
Tony Cariati

D-U-N-S 24-664-8901   (SL)
CLOVER TOOL MANUFACTURING LTD
8271 Keele St Suite 3, Concord, ON, L4K 1Z1
(905) 669-1999
Emp Here 175   *Sales* 33,614,875
SIC 3469 Metal stampings, nec
Frank Zeni

D-U-N-S 25-660-2095   (SL)
CLUB PRO ADULT ENTERTAINMENT INC
CLUB PRO
170 Doughton Rd, Concord, ON, L4K 1R4
(905) 669-6422
Emp Here 200   *Sales* 9,103,800
SIC 5813 Drinking places
Domenic Marciano

D-U-N-S 25-273-5642   (SL)
CMI COSMETIC MANUFACTURERS INC
90 Moyal Crt, Concord, ON, L4K 4R8
(905) 879-1999
Emp Here 47   *Sales* 51,951,215
SIC 5122 Drugs, proprietaries, and sundries
Hamid Vanaki

D-U-N-S 25-468-1323   (SL)
COM-TEL MARKETING INC
163 Buttermill Ave Suite 1, Concord, ON, L4K 3X8
(905) 738-1494
Emp Here 80   *Sales* 19,546,240
SIC 5963 Direct selling establishments
Anthony Crisanti

D-U-N-S 20-581-4903   (BR)
COMPAGNIE DES CHEMINS DE FER NATIONAUX DU CANADA
CN RAIL
(*Suby of* COMPAGNIE DES CHEMINS DE FER NATIONAUX DU CANADA)
73 Diesel Dr Unit 1b, Concord, ON, L4K 1B9

Emp Here 355

SIC 4011 Railroads, line-haul operating
Jan Paul Buchard

D-U-N-S 24-123-1617   (BR)
**COMPAGNIE DES CHEMINS DE FER NA-
TIONAUX DU CANADA**
CN NORTH AMERICA
(*Suby of* COMPAGNIE DES CHEMINS DE
FER NATIONAUX DU CANADA)
Gd, Concord, ON, L4K 1B9
(905) 669-3302
Emp Here 600
SIC 4011 Railroads, line-haul operating

D-U-N-S 25-194-9004   (BR)
**COMPAGNIE DES CHEMINS DE FER NA-
TIONAUX DU CANADA**
(*Suby of* COMPAGNIE DES CHEMINS DE
FER NATIONAUX DU CANADA)
Gd, Concord, ON, L4K 1B9
(905) 669-3009
Emp Here 115
SIC 4789 Transportation services, nec
Marc Ethier

D-U-N-S 25-904-8309   (HQ)
COMSALE COMPUTER INC
COMPUTER PARTS 2000
111 Snidercroft Rd, Concord, ON, L4K 2J8
(905) 761-6466
Emp Here 55   *Sales* 36,668,268
SIC 5045 Computers, peripherals, and soft-
ware
Neil Shaul

D-U-N-S 24-513-8797   (SL)
CON-DRAIN COMPANY (1983) LIMITED
30 Floral Pky Suite 100, Concord, ON, L4K
4R1
(905) 669-5400
Emp Here 85   *Sales* 21,457,570
SIC 1623 Water, sewer, and utility lines
Alfredo De Gasperis
Angelo De Gasperis
Antonio De Gasperis

D-U-N-S 20-162-4384   (HQ)
CON-DRAIN COMPANY LIMITED
CONDRAIN GROUP
30 Floral Pky Suite 100, Concord, ON, L4K
4R1
(416) 798-7153
Sales 164,057,500
SIC 1623 Water, sewer, and utility lines
Alfredo Degasperis
Angelo Degasperis
Antonio Degasperis

D-U-N-S 24-057-5969   (SL)
CON-ELCO LTD
FIBER CON
200 Bradwick Dr, Concord, ON, L4K 1K8
(905) 669-4942
Emp Here 250   *Sales* 82,028,750
SIC 1623 Water, sewer, and utility lines
Fiore Melatti
Fred De Gasperis

D-U-N-S 24-463-3582   (HQ)
CON-STRADA CONSTRUCTION INC
30 Floral Pky, Concord, ON, L4K 4R1
(905) 660-6000
Sales 14,176,200
SIC 1611 Highway and street construction
Alfredo De Gasperis
Angelo De Gasperis
Antonio De Gasperis
Jim De Gasperis

D-U-N-S 24-770-7375   (SL)
CONBORA FORMING INC
109 Edilcan Dr, Concord, ON, L4K 3S6
(905) 738-7979
Emp Here 55   *Sales* 13,611,565
SIC 1771 Concrete work
Irving Teper

D-U-N-S 24-452-7321   (SL)

CONCORD CONCRETE & DRAIN LTD
109 Edilcan Dr, Concord, ON, L4K 3S6
(416) 736-0277
Emp Here 75   *Sales* 18,561,225
SIC 1771 Concrete work
Irving Teper

D-U-N-S 20-348-2427   (SL)
CONCORD CONCRETE GROUP INC
CCG
125 Edilcan Dr, Concord, ON, L4K 3S6
(905) 738-7979
Emp Here 1,500   *Sales* 308,559,000
SIC 4213 Trucking, except local
Irving Teper
Frank Borges

D-U-N-S 24-525-4701   (HQ)
CONCORD METAL MANUFACTURING INC
121 Spinnaker Way, Concord, ON, L4K 2T2
(905) 738-2127
Emp Here 60   *Sales* 10,030,930
SIC 2542 Partitions and fixtures, except wood
Ermanno Torelli
Marie Pagliaroli

D-U-N-S 24-977-1023   (HQ)
CONCORD PREMIUM MEATS LTD
MARCANGELO
125 Edilcan Dr, Concord, ON, L4K 3S6
(905) 738-7979
Emp Here 90   *Sales* 250,850,600
SIC 5147 Meats and meat products
Joseph Mannara
Irving Teper

D-U-N-S 24-044-6075   (SL)
CONDOR PROPERTIES LTD
CONDOR PROPERTIES
1500 Highway 7, Concord, ON, L4K 5Y4
(905) 907-1500
Emp Here 35   *Sales* 11,449,445
SIC 6531 Real estate agents and managers
Sam Balsamo
Nancy Degasperis
Angelo De Gasperis

D-U-N-S 20-976-8753   (HQ)
CONTINENTAL COSMETICS LTD
390 Millway Ave, Concord, ON, L4K 3V8
(905) 660-0622
Emp Here 14   *Sales* 21,001,555
SIC 5122 Drugs, proprietaries, and sundries

D-U-N-S 20-820-6508   (HQ)
CORMA INC
10 Mccleary Crt, Concord, ON, L4K 2Z3
(905) 669-9397
Emp Here 150   *Sales* 35,964,162
SIC 3559 Special industry machinery, nec
Manfred Lupke
Stefan Lupke
Annette Lupke-Kovalik
Renata Lupke

D-U-N-S 24-333-6729   (BR)
CORPORATION SENZA, LA
LA SENZA CORPORATION
(*Suby of* REGENT, LP)
8960 Jane St, Concord, ON, L4K 2M9

Emp Here 87
SIC 5632 Women's accessory and specialty
stores
Elizabeth Fernandes

D-U-N-S 24-912-1518   (SL)
**CORRADO CARPENTER CONTRACTOR
LIMITED**
445 Edgeley Blvd Suite 20, Concord, ON, L4K
4G1
(905) 660-4411
Emp Here 50   *Sales* 11,369,150
SIC 1751 Carpentry work
Corrado Scivoletto
Anthony Scivoletto

D-U-N-S 24-231-8405   (SL)

COUNTRYWIDE HOMES LTD
1500 Highway 7, Concord, ON, L4K 5Y4
(905) 907-1500
Emp Here 70   *Sales* 18,965,940
SIC 1522 Residential construction, nec
Angelo Degasperif
Mary Morello

D-U-N-S 25-991-9074   (SL)
CPI CARD GROUP-CANADA INC
(*Suby of* CPI CARD GROUP INC.)
460 Applewood Cres, Concord, ON, L4K 4Z3
(905) 761-8222
Emp Here 105   *Sales* 38,601,885
SIC 2675 Die-cut paper and board
Anna Rossetti
Docia Myer
Mary Martinez
Diane Jackson
Jerry Dreiling
Steve Montross

D-U-N-S 20-503-8722   (HQ)
CRH CANADA GROUP INC
DUFFERIN CONCRETE
(*Suby of* CRH PUBLIC LIMITED COMPANY)
2300 Steeles Ave W Suite 400, Concord, ON,
L4K 5X6
(905) 532-3000
Emp Here 120   *Sales* 842,631,000
SIC 3531 Construction machinery
Baudouin Nizet
Germaine Gibara
Baudouin Nizet
Paul Ostrander
Dean J Bergmame
Denzil Cotera
Gaetan Jacques
David Loomes
Patrick Dolberg
Benoit H Koch

D-U-N-S 24-631-2789   (SL)
CRYSTAL FOUNTAINS HOLDINGS INC
DECORATIVE FOUNTAIN CO, DIV OF
60 Snow Blvd Suite 3, Concord, ON, L4K 4B3
(905) 660-6674
Emp Here 60   *Sales* 11,525,100
SIC 3499 Fabricated Metal products, nec
Paul L'heureux
David L'heureux

D-U-N-S 20-188-1641   (HQ)
CTG BRANDS INC
123 Great Gulf Dr, Concord, ON, L4K 5V1
(905) 761-3330
Emp Here 1   *Sales* 20,821,680
SIC 5092 Toys and hobby goods and supplies
Grant Pittam

D-U-N-S 20-371-9898   (SL)
CUSTOM ALUMINUM, INC
40 Romina Dr Unit 2, Concord, ON, L4K 4Z7
(905) 669-8459
Emp Here 70   *Sales* 31,445,330
SIC 7389 Business services, nec
Faruk Begovic

D-U-N-S 24-796-8043   (SL)
**D.J. INDUSTRIAL SALES AND MANUFAC-
TURING INC**
(*Suby of* STS OPERATING, INC.)
25 North Rivermede Rd Unit 1, Concord, ON,
L4K 5V4
(416) 798-7575
Emp Here 25   *Sales* 11,875,650
SIC 5084 Industrial machinery and equipment
Christopher Brown

D-U-N-S 25-961-1916   (SL)
DAISY INTELLIGENCE CORPORATION
2300 Steeles Ave W Ste 250, Concord, ON,
L4K 5X6
(905) 642-2629
Emp Here 50   *Sales* 10,692,550
SIC 7372 Prepackaged software
Gary Saarenvirta

Maurizio Milani
Gorg Macdonald
John Madigan
Pat Finerty
Gary Saarernvirta

D-U-N-S 24-964-0384   (HQ)
DAL-TILE OF CANADA ULC
(*Suby of* MOHAWK INDUSTRIES, INC.)
40 Graniteridge Rd Unit 1, Concord, ON, L4K
5M8
(905) 738-2099
Emp Here 35   *Sales* 38,009,790
SIC 5032 Brick, stone, and related material
Harold Turk
Estelle Davis

D-U-N-S 25-093-2118   (SL)
DALEX CANADA INC
157 Adesso Dr, Concord, ON, L4K 3C3
(905) 738-2070
Emp Here 28   *Sales* 13,300,728
SIC 5087 Service establishment equipment
D'arcy Mcconvey
Alex Pasut

D-U-N-S 20-977-0812   (SL)
DAN-D FOODS (TORONTO) LTD
(*Suby of* DAN-D FOODS LTD)
45 Basaltic Rd Unit 5, Concord, ON, L4K 1G5
(905) 889-7807
Emp Here 20   *Sales* 16,711,540
SIC 5141 Groceries, general line
Daniel Ting

D-U-N-S 24-726-6505   (HQ)
DCL INTERNATIONAL INC
241 Bradwick Dr, Concord, ON, L4K 1K5
(905) 660-6450
Sales 15,669,010
SIC 3714 Motor vehicle parts and accessories
George Swiatek
Eva Swiatek

D-U-N-S 20-878-5923   (BR)
DEELEY, FRED IMPORTS LTD.
DEELEY HARLEY DAVIDSON
(*Suby of* FRED DEELEY LIMITED)
830 Edgeley Blvd, Concord, ON, L4K 4X1
(905) 660-3500
Emp Here 100
SIC 5012 Automobiles and other motor vehi-
cles
Buzz Green

D-U-N-S 20-841-0691   (SL)
DELUXE ALARMS INC
9000 Keele St Unit 12, Concord, ON, L4K 0B3
(416) 410-3020
Emp Here 55   *Sales* 10,474,310
SIC 3699 Electrical equipment and supplies,
nec
Stefan Tuzi

D-U-N-S 24-848-7738   (SL)
DICRETE CONSTRUCTION LTD
71 Creditstone Rd, Concord, ON, L4K 1N3
(905) 669-9595
Emp Here 50   *Sales* 14,176,200
SIC 1611 Highway and street construction
Joe Di Grevino
Angelo Di Grevino

D-U-N-S 24-333-3051   (HQ)
DIGI CANADA INCORPORATED
(*Suby of* TERAOKA SEIKO CO., LTD.)
87 Moyal Crt, Concord, ON, L4K 4R8
(905) 879-0833
Emp Here 35   *Sales* 40,245,660
SIC 5046 Commercial equipment, nec
Prashant Parekh

D-U-N-S 24-410-2828   (SL)
DISHON LIMITED
40 Citation Dr, Concord, ON, L4K 2W9
(416) 638-8900
Emp Here 70   *Sales* 15,540,070
SIC 3545 Machine tool accessories

▲ Public Company   ■ Public Company Family Member   **HQ** Headquarters   **BR** Branch   **SL** Single Location

Ilan Dishy
Valerie Wilson
Dan Dishy

D-U-N-S 20-606-3620 (HQ)
DIXIE ELECTRIC LTD
(*Suby of* MOTORCAR PARTS OF AMERICA INC)
517 Basaltic Rd, Concord, ON, L4K 4W8
(905) 879-0533
Emp Here 200 *Sales* 44,848,000
SIC 7539 Automotive repair shops, nec
Angelo Bucciol
Celesta Bucciol

D-U-N-S 25-354-0033 (SL)
DOWNING STREET PROPERTY MANAGEMENT INC
668 Millway Ave Unit 7, Concord, ON, L4K 3V2
(905) 851-1717
Emp Here 40 *Sales* 11,539,960
SIC 6512 Nonresidential building operators
Fred Ceolin

D-U-N-S 24-079-3612 (SL)
DOWNSVIEW DRYWALL CONTRACTING
160 Bass Pro Mills Dr Suite 200, Concord, ON, L4K 0A7
(905) 660-0048
Emp Here 150 *Sales* 27,478,650
SIC 1742 Plastering, drywall, and insulation
Sam Sgotto

D-U-N-S 25-253-2460 (SL)
DSI UPHOLSTERY INC
DESIGN SOURCE INTERNATIONAL
452 Millway Ave, Concord, ON, L4K 3V7
(905) 669-1357
Emp Here 150 *Sales* 23,148,300
SIC 2521 Wood office furniture
David Shamir

D-U-N-S 20-410-7460 (SL)
DVI LIGHTING INC
120 Great Gulf Dr, Concord, ON, L4K 5W1
(905) 660-2381
Emp Here 69 *Sales* 30,855,006
SIC 5063 Electrical apparatus and equipment
Robert Borg
Samuel Wineberg
David Elman

D-U-N-S 24-660-7360 (SL)
E-M AIR SYSTEMS INC
69 Romina Dr, Concord, ON, L4K 4Z9
(905) 738-0450
Emp Here 90 *Sales* 20,975,850
SIC 1711 Plumbing, heating, air-conditioning
Enzo Colosimo
Marisa Colosimo

D-U-N-S 20-328-9017 (SL)
E-TECH ELECTRICAL SERVICES INC
30 Pennsylvania Ave, Concord, ON, L4K 4A5
(905) 669-4062
Emp Here 65 *Sales* 14,158,885
SIC 1731 Electrical work
John Vigna
Claudio Fotlia

D-U-N-S 25-112-1638 (SL)
E.C.S. ENGINEERING & CONSTRUCTION LIMITED
51 Ritin Lane Unit 1, Concord, ON, L4K 4E1
(905) 761-7009
Emp Here 50 *Sales* 12,044,200
SIC 1623 Water, sewer, and utility lines
Jason Chidiac
Amel Zaag

D-U-N-S 24-319-4086 (HQ)
EARTHCO SOIL MIXTURES INC
401 Bowes Rd Suite 1, Concord, ON, L4K 1J4
(905) 761-6599
Sales 11,137,800
SIC 5191 Farm supplies
Pasquale Lamanna

Guiseppe Lamanna
Antonio Pellegrini
Robert Zanetti

D-U-N-S 24-181-3286 (SL)
EASY PLASTIC CONTAINERS CORPORATION
101 Jardin Dr Unit 10, Concord, ON, L4K 1X6
(905) 669-4466
Emp Here 125 *Sales* 19,857,250
SIC 3089 Plastics products, nec

D-U-N-S 20-117-4864 (SL)
EBERSPAECHER VECTURE INC.
(*Suby of* EBERSPACHER GRUPPE GMBH & CO. KG)
8900 Keele Street Unit 3, Concord, ON, L4K 2N2
(905) 761-0331
Emp Here 100 *Sales* 19,044,200
SIC 3691 Storage batteries
Frank Baldesarra
Angelo Catenaro
Ken Chisholm

D-U-N-S 20-349-6153 (SL)
ECMI LP
EMPIRE COMMUNITIES
125 Villarboit Cres, Concord, ON, L4K 4K2
(905) 307-8102
Emp Here 49 *Sales* 13,276,158
SIC 1521 Single-family housing construction
Daniel Guizzetti
Andrew Guizzetti
Paul Golini

D-U-N-S 20-762-7808 (SL)
EFP DESIGNS INC
50 Viceroy Rd Suite 23, Concord, ON, L4K 3A7
(905) 669-0368
Emp Here 50 *Sales* 12,652,950
SIC 5211 Lumber and other building materials
Massoud Karbakahs

D-U-N-S 20-045-0872 (SL)
EL-EN PACKAGING COMPANY LIMITED
200 Great Gulf Dr, Concord, ON, L4K 5W1
(905) 761-5975
Emp Here 30 *Sales* 15,109,740
SIC 5113 Industrial and personal service paper
Fela Lichtblau
Mark Lichtblau

D-U-N-S 24-770-7730 (HQ)
ELITE CONSTRUCTION INC
35 Romina Dr Suite 100, Concord, ON, L4K 4Z9
(905) 660-1663
Emp Here 42 *Sales* 12,619,272
SIC 8741 Management services
Enrico Lisi

D-U-N-S 20-708-4778 (SL)
EMPIRE (THE CONTINENTAL) LIMITED PARTNERSHIP
125 Villarboit Cres, Concord, ON, L4K 4K2
(905) 307-8102
Emp Here 100 *Sales* 27,094,200
SIC 1521 Single-family housing construction
Daniel Guizzetti

D-U-N-S 25-995-5029 (SL)
EMPIRE CONTINENTAL MANAGEMENT INC
COLTA HOLDINGS
125 Villarboit Cres, Concord, ON, L4K 4K2
(905) 307-8102
Emp Here 100 *Sales* 27,094,200
SIC 1521 Single-family housing construction
Daniel Guizzetti

D-U-N-S 25-319-1659 (SL)
ENCORE REPAIR SERVICES CANADA, ULC
(*Suby of* ENCORE REPAIR SERVICES, LLC)
40 North Rivermede Rd Unit 10, Concord, ON,

L4K 2H3
(905) 597-5972
Emp Here 26 *Sales* 11,094,675
SIC 7629 Electrical repair shops
Tony Graffia Jr.

D-U-N-S 20-773-3234 (SL)
ENERPOWER UTILITIES INC
585 Applewood Cres, Concord, ON, L4K 5V7

Emp Here 150 *Sales* 37,866,300
SIC 1623 Water, sewer, and utility lines
Frank Mongillo
Simon Degasperis

D-U-N-S 20-245-5791 (SL)
ENTABLATURE FRIEZE & PILLARS INC
50 Viceroy Rd Unit 23, Concord, ON, L4K 3A7
(905) 669-0368
Emp Here 50 *Sales* 12,799,495
SIC 5211 Lumber and other building materials
Massoud Karbakhsh

D-U-N-S 24-736-6859 (SL)
EXAGON MARKETING INC
A 1 SHIPPING SUPPLIES, A DIV OF
300 Confederation Pky Unit 4, Concord, ON, L4K 4T8
(905) 669-9627
Emp Here 26 *Sales* 19,305,520
SIC 5199 Nondurable goods, nec
Peter Malevris
John Malevris

D-U-N-S 24-214-8625 (HQ)
EXECUTIVE WOODWORK LTD
330 Spinnaker Way, Concord, ON, L4K 4W1
(905) 669-6429
Emp Here 30 *Sales* 29,199,235
SIC 7389 Business services, nec
Tina Siniscalco
Vince Siniscalco

D-U-N-S 25-253-1330 (HQ)
EXPERT MANUFACTURING INC
180 Viceroy Rd, Concord, ON, L4K 2L8
(905) 738-7575
Emp Here 120 *Sales* 18,518,640
SIC 2522 Office furniture, except wood
Saul Feldberg
Joe Allul

D-U-N-S 20-733-9768 (BR)
FAIRSTONE FINANCIERE INC
FAIRSTONE FINANCIAL INC
(*Suby of* FAIRSTONE FINANCIERE INC)
1750 Steeles Ave W, Concord, ON, L4K 2L7
(905) 761-4538
Emp Here 150
SIC 8742 Management consulting services
Lisa Friedenberg

D-U-N-S 24-610-3949 (HQ)
FASTENING HOUSE INC
160 Bass Pro Mills Dr, Concord, ON, L4K 0A7
(905) 669-7448
Emp Here 30 *Sales* 27,551,508
SIC 5085 Industrial supplies
Kenneth Moore
Keith Moore

D-U-N-S 24-664-6541 (SL)
FAVA INVESTMENTS INC
25 Interchange Way, Concord, ON, L4K 5W3
(905) 660-4111
Emp Here 34 *Sales* 15,203,916
SIC 5063 Electrical apparatus and equipment

D-U-N-S 20-695-2595 (SL)
FERNBROOK HOMES (LAKE OF DREAMS) LIMITED
2220 Highway 7 Unit 5, Concord, ON, L4K 1W7
(416) 667-0447
Emp Here 50 *Sales* 14,429,150
SIC 1522 Residential construction, nec
Daniel Salvatore

D-U-N-S 20-313-5355 (SL)
FERNBROOK HOMES (WILSON) LTD
FERNBROOK HOMES
2220 Highway 7 Unit 5, Concord, ON, L4K 1W7
(416) 667-0447
Emp Here 140 *Sales* 37,931,880
SIC 1522 Residential construction, nec
Danny Salvatore
Joe Salvatore
Howard Steinberg
Dave Bubersky

D-U-N-S 24-463-6551 (HQ)
FERNBROOK HOMES LIMITED
(*Suby of* OXVILLE HOMES LTD)
2220 Highway 7 Unit 5, Concord, ON, L4K 1W7
(416) 667-0447
Sales 29,803,620
SIC 1522 Residential construction, nec
Daniel Salvatore
Nick Cortellucci
Gino Di Genova

D-U-N-S 24-683-8002 (SL)
FHE GROUP INC, THE
260 Spinnaker Way Units 2-5, Concord, ON, L4K 4P9
(416) 749-1505
Emp Here 16 *Sales* 15,037,600
SIC 5023 Homefurnishings
Jonathan Levy
Adam Schachter
Albert Levy

D-U-N-S 20-045-0856 (SL)
FIVE SEASONS COMFORT LIMITED
ELECTRO AIR CANADA
351 North Rivermede Rd, Concord, ON, L4K 3N2
(905) 669-5620
Emp Here 75 *Sales* 16,650,075
SIC 3564 Blowers and fans
Beverley David
Caroline David

D-U-N-S 24-411-4781 (SL)
FLINT PACKAGING PRODUCTS LTD
311 Caldari Rd, Concord, ON, L4K 4S9
(905) 738-7205
Emp Here 55 *Sales* 12,838,925
SIC 2653 Corrugated and solid fiber boxes
Timo Mattila

D-U-N-S 24-752-0513 (SL)
FOAMCO INDUSTRIES CORPORATION
(*Suby of* IVADAR CANADA CORPORATION)
8400 Keele St Unit 2, Concord, ON, L4K 2A6
(416) 784-9777
Emp Here 80 *Sales* 12,708,640
SIC 3086 Plastics foam products
Mahendra Shah

D-U-N-S 24-951-4746 (HQ)
FOOD SUPPLIES DISTRIBUTING COMPANY INC
FOOD SUPPLIES COMPANY
355 Rayette Rd Unit 10, Concord, ON, L4K 2G2

Emp Here 19 *Sales* 23,396,156
SIC 5149 Groceries and related products, nec
Steven Clark

D-U-N-S 24-703-4671 (SL)
FOODFEST INTERNATIONAL 2000 INC
361 Connie Cres, Concord, ON, L4K 5R2
(905) 709-4775
Emp Here 20 *Sales* 10,702,480
SIC 5149 Groceries and related products, nec
Henry Ender
Fred Farnden

D-U-N-S 20-314-6691 (SL)
FOREST LABORATORIES CANADA INC
(*Suby of* TEVA PHARMACEUTICAL INDUSTRIES LIMITED)

610 Applewood Cres Unit 302, Concord, ON,
L4K 0E3
(289) 695-4700
Emp Here 10   *Sales* 11,053,450
SIC 5122 Drugs, proprietaries, and sundries
Ralph Kleinman
Francis Perier Jr
David Solomon
Howard Solomon

D-U-N-S 24-709-2000   (SL)
**FOUR VALLEYS EXCAVATING & GRADING
LIMITED**
(*Suby of* CORTELLI CONSTRUCTION LIM-
ITED)
137 Bowes Rd, Concord, ON, L4K 1H3
(905) 669-1588
Emp Here 90   *Sales* 22,156,740
SIC 1794 Excavation work
Nick Cortellucci

D-U-N-S 25-283-2522   (SL)
FOX RUN CANADA CORP
FOX RUN CRAFTSMEN
(*Suby of* FOX RUN HOLDINGS, INC)
460 Applewood Cres Suite 2, Concord, ON,
L4K 4Z3
(905) 669-4145
Emp Here 20   *Sales* 10,177,120
SIC 5023 Homefurnishings
Sean Leonard

D-U-N-S 24-221-7685   (HQ)
FRANCOTYP-POSTALIA CANADA INC
FP MAILING SOLUTIONS
(*Suby of* FRANCOTYP-POSTALIA HOLDING
AG)
82 Corstate Ave Suite 2000, Concord, ON,
L4K 4X2
(905) 761-6554
Emp Here 33   *Sales* 18,334,134
SIC 5044 Office equipment
Taby Briones
James Lister
James Rogerson

D-U-N-S 20-387-8608   (SL)
**FUNCTIONABILITY REHABILITATION SER-
VICES LP**
9135 Keele St Unit B5, Concord, ON, L4K 0J4
(905) 764-2340
Emp Here 250   *Sales* 22,315,500
SIC 8049 Offices of health practitioner
Nick Gurevich

D-U-N-S 25-953-7496   (HQ)
FUNDEX INVESTMENTS INC
(*Suby of* INDUSTRIELLE ALLIANCE, AS-
SURANCE ET SERVICES FINANCIERS INC)
400 Applewood Cres, Concord, ON, L4K 0C3
(905) 305-1651
Sales 6,261,807,200
SIC 6211 Security brokers and dealers
David Chapman
Karine Hebert
Bruno Michaud
Paul Grimes
Normand Pepin
Andre Dubuc
Gerald Bouwers
Carl Mustos

D-U-N-S 24-538-5786   (SL)
G & G GENERAL SUPPLY LTD
511 Millway Ave, Concord, ON, L4K 3V4
(905) 669-9556
Emp Here 35   *Sales* 15,651,090
SIC 5074 Plumbing and heating equipment
and supplies (hydronics)
Gaspar Galati
Salvatore Galati

D-U-N-S 24-350-3708   (HQ)
G & L GROUP LTD
401 Bowes Rd, Concord, ON, L4K 1J4
(416) 798-7050
Sales 80,411,980

SIC 6712 Bank holding companies
Alex Diomin

D-U-N-S 24-253-2062   (BR)
GAP (CANADA) INC
GAP OUTLET
(*Suby of* THE GAP INC)
1 Bass Pro Mills Dr, Concord, ON, L4K 5W4
(905) 761-7577
Emp Here 85
SIC 5651 Family clothing stores
Kashif Qamar

D-U-N-S 24-684-4757   (SL)
GEM-SEN HOLDINGS CORP
GEM-SEN DISTRIBUTION
266 Applewood Cres, Concord, ON, L4K 4B4
(905) 660-3110
Emp Here 48   *Sales* 35,640,960
SIC 5199 Nondurable goods, nec
Sal Riina
Nadia Riina
Belle Collins

D-U-N-S 24-126-3821   (SL)
**GERRITY CORRUGATED PAPER PROD-
UCTS LTD**
75 Doney Cres Suite 1, Concord, ON, L4K
1P6
(416) 798-7758
Emp Here 180   *Sales* 35,058,240
SIC 2653 Corrugated and solid fiber boxes
Thomas Gerrity
Blaine Gerrity
Scott Gerrity
Jean Gerrity

D-U-N-S 25-512-3606   (SL)
GLOBAL FILE INC
7939 Keele St, Concord, ON, L4K 1Y6
(905) 761-3284
Emp Here 190   *Sales* 29,321,180
SIC 2522 Office furniture, except wood
Sol Feldberg
Irving Stahl

D-U-N-S 24-417-8716   (SL)
GLOBAL PLAS INC
120 Spinnaker Way, Concord, ON, L4K 2P6
(905) 760-2800
Emp Here 64   *Sales* 12,921,408
SIC 3089 Plastics products, nec
Balbir Hunjan
Inderpal Sagoo
Jiandi Lu

D-U-N-S 20-248-3780   (SL)
GOLDEN FOOD & MANUFACTURE LTD
MR. GOUDAS
241 Snidercroft Rd, Concord, ON, L4K 2J8
(905) 660-3233
Emp Here 40   *Sales* 17,739,600
SIC 7389 Business services, nec
Jeevarajah Ponnampalam
Ramesh Jegarajah
Vairamuthu Sarweswaran

D-U-N-S 24-652-8962   (SL)
GOLDFARB SHULMAN PATEL & CO LLP
400 Bradwick Dr Suite 100, Concord, ON, L4K
5V9
(416) 226-6800
Emp Here 90   *Sales* 18,817,650
SIC 8721 Accounting, auditing, and book-
keeping
Lawrence Shulman
Jag Patel

D-U-N-S 20-345-4152   (HQ)
GOLF TOWN LIMITED
610 Applewood Cres Unit 302, Concord, ON,
L4K 0E3
(905) 479-0343
Emp Here 50   *Sales* 275,305,500
SIC 5941 Sporting goods and bicycle shops
Bill Gregson
Chad Mckinnon
John Varnell

D-U-N-S 20-333-0527   (HQ)
**GOLF TOWN OPERATING LIMITED PART-
NERSHIP**
GOLF TOWN
610 Applewood Cres Unit 302, Concord, ON,
L4K 0E3
(905) 479-0343
Sales 24,432,800
SIC 5941 Sporting goods and bicycle shops
Chad Mckinnon

D-U-N-S 25-173-4620   (HQ)
GOODMAN COMPANY CANADA
(*Suby of* DAIKIN INDUSTRIES, LTD.)
8305 Jane St Unit 3, Concord, ON, L4K 5Y3
(905) 760-2737
Emp Here 8   *Sales* 19,228,482
SIC 5075 Warm air heating and air condition-
ing
Chuck Caroll
Steve Saunders

D-U-N-S 24-487-0143   (SL)
GOTTARDO CONSTRUCTION LIMITED
277 Pennsylvania Ave, Concord, ON, L4K 5R9
(905) 761-7007
Emp Here 50   *Sales* 14,424,950
SIC 6512 Nonresidential building operators
Marianne Gottardo

D-U-N-S 20-844-8928   (SL)
**GOUDAS FOOD PRODUCTS AND INVEST-
MENTS LIMITED**
241 Snidercroft Rd, Concord, ON, L4K 2J8

Emp Here 200
SIC 5141 Groceries, general line

D-U-N-S 20-551-5856   (SL)
GOUDAS FOOD PRODUCTS CO. LTD
241 Snidercroft Rd, Concord, ON, L4K 2J8
(905) 660-3233
Emp Here 50   *Sales* 42,262,729
SIC 5141 Groceries, general line
Peter Goudas
Spyridon Goudas

D-U-N-S 24-256-1103   (SL)
GRAND ALARMS LTD
9000 Keele St Unit 12, Concord, ON, L4K 0B3
(416) 657-2100
Emp Here 50   *Sales* 22,358,700
SIC 5065 Electronic parts and equipment, nec
Stefan Tuzi

D-U-N-S 20-773-2368   (SL)
GTA ADANAC CUSTOM SYSTEMS INC
467 Edgeley Blvd Suite 4, Concord, ON, L4K
4E9

Emp Here 24   *Sales* 10,912,678
SIC 5065 Electronic parts and equipment, nec
Tony Rulli

D-U-N-S 25-754-0914   (SL)
GTA SECURITY GUARD SERVICES INC
150 Spinnaker Way Unit 12, Concord, ON,
L4K 4M1
(905) 760-0838
Emp Here 49   *Sales* 19,388,222
SIC 7381 Detective and armored car services
Niuma Alter

D-U-N-S 20-345-0171   (SL)
GUIDELITE FINANCIAL NETWORKS LTD
1600 Steeles Ave W Suite 231, Concord, ON,
L4K 4M2

Emp Here 52   *Sales* 12,182,976
SIC 8748 Business consulting, nec
Sosia Barabash

D-U-N-S 20-167-2474   (HQ)
H & K CANADA INC
50 Mccleary Crt, Concord, ON, L4K 3L5
(905) 695-0440
Sales 10,285,002
SIC 5046 Commercial equipment, nec

David Spain

D-U-N-S 24-096-6031   (SL)
H & M HENNES & MAURITZ INC
H & M
1 Bass Pro Mills Dr, Concord, ON, L4K 5W4
(905) 760-1769
Emp Here 60   *Sales* 10,763,760
SIC 5651 Family clothing stores
Araba Gentles

D-U-N-S 25-202-7065   (SL)
H & S BUILDING SUPPLIES LIMITED
96 Maplecrete Rd Unit 4 5, Concord, ON, L4K
2B5
(905) 738-6003
Emp Here 30   *Sales* 13,415,220
SIC 5039 Construction materials, nec
Jitendra Shanghavi
Mukesh Shanghavi
Pramod Shanghavi

D-U-N-S 20-555-4157   (SL)
H.J. SUTTON INDUSTRIES LIMITED
QUALITY HOME PRODUCTS
(*Suby of* SUTTON, H. J. HOLDINGS LIM-
ITED)
8701 Jane St Unit C, Concord, ON, L4K 2M6
(905) 660-4311
Emp Here 28   *Sales* 12,520,872
SIC 5064 Electrical appliances, television and
radio
Derek Sutton
Derek Sutton
David Sutton
Denis Cecchimi

D-U-N-S 24-342-9474   (SL)
HANAHREUM MART INC
H-MART
193 Jardin Dr, Concord, ON, L4K 1X5
(416) 792-1131
Emp Here 80   *Sales* 23,478,160
SIC 5411 Grocery stores
Joong Gab Kwon

D-U-N-S 24-977-4100   (SL)
HANDLING TECHNOLOGIES INC
HTI
21 Corrine Crt, Concord, ON, L4K 4W2
(905) 739-1350
Emp Here 25   *Sales* 11,875,650
SIC 5084 Industrial machinery and equipment
John Dalla Rosa

D-U-N-S 20-390-3377   (SL)
HANON SYSTEMS EFP CANADA LTD
(*Suby of* HAHN & CO. AUTO HOLDINGS CO.,
LTD.)
800 Tesma Way, Concord, ON, L4K 5C2
(905) 303-1689
Emp Here 600   *Sales* 174,510,000
SIC 3714 Motor vehicle parts and accessories
Michael Adams
Rene Veillette

D-U-N-S 20-182-3275   (SL)
HARBRIDGE & CROSS LIMITED
350 Creditstone Rd Suite 202, Concord, ON,
L4K 3Z2
(905) 738-0051
Emp Here 50   *Sales* 23,536,550
SIC 1542 Nonresidential construction, nec
Sam Kumar
William Waters
Colin Shear

D-U-N-S 20-629-2849   (SL)
**HAREMAR PLASTIC MANUFACTURING
LIMITED**
200 Great Gulf Dr, Concord, ON, L4K 5W1
(905) 761-7552
Emp Here 100   *Sales* 20,189,700
SIC 3081 Unsupported plastics film and sheet
Fela Lichtblau
Mark Lichtblau
Cheryl Babcock

D-U-N-S 24-199-2122 (SL)
HARKEL OFFICE FURNITURE LIMITED
1743 Creditstone Rd, Concord, ON, L4K 5X7
(905) 417-5335
Emp Here 38 *Sales* 19,336,528
SIC 5021 Furniture
Howard Klerer
Kay Klerer
Carol Klerer

D-U-N-S 24-666-1730 (SL)
HAYHOE EQUIPMENT AND SUPPLY LTD
CEDAR SPRING BOTTLED WATER
45 Villarboit Cres Suite 2, Concord, ON, L4K 4R2
(905) 669-5118
Emp Here 50 *Sales* 41,778,850
SIC 5149 Groceries and related products, nec
David Hayhoe

D-U-N-S 20-013-0248 (HQ)
HEWITT MATERIAL HANDLING INC
HEWITT MATERIAL HANDLING SYSTEMS
425 Millway Ave, Concord, ON, L4K 3V8
(905) 669-6590
Emp Here 80 *Sales* 83,401,830
SIC 5084 Industrial machinery and equipment
James William Hewitt
Roni Farah
Suzanne Bergeron
Marie Diamond

D-U-N-S 24-338-2087 (SL)
HIGHLIGHT MOTOR FREIGHT INC
391 Creditstone Rd, Concord, ON, L4K 1N8
(905) 761-1400
Emp Here 450 *Sales* 92,567,700
SIC 4213 Trucking, except local
Kirill Kalinitchenko

D-U-N-S 24-986-0495 (HQ)
HIGHRISE WINDOW TECHNOLOGIES INC
131 Caldari Rd Unit 1, Concord, ON, L4K 3Z9
(905) 738-8600
Sales 23,050,200
SIC 3442 Metal doors, sash, and trim
Stephen Miller
Percy Fink

D-U-N-S 24-488-5265 (SL)
HOLIDAY HOME FASHIONS INC
HOLIDAY FABRICS
2740 Steeles Ave W Suite 2, Concord, ON, L4K 4T4

Emp Here 100 *Sales* 18,340,300
SIC 2221 Broadwoven fabric mills, manmade
Albert Levy
Nick Grieco

D-U-N-S 24-849-7042 (SL)
HOME GAME INC, THE
114b Fernstaff Crt, Concord, ON, L4K 3L9

Emp Here 30 *Sales* 14,949,660
SIC 5136 Men's and boy's clothing
Laurin Saltzman
Mark Saltzman

D-U-N-S 25-917-7210 (HQ)
HOMELIFE/METROPARK REALTY INC
8700a Dufferin St, Concord, ON, L4K 4S6
(416) 798-7705
Emp Here 20 *Sales* 33,511,120
SIC 6531 Real estate agents and managers
Marino Farano

D-U-N-S 25-101-7943 (HQ)
HOWELL DATA SYSTEMS INC
160 Pennsylvania Ave Unit 4, Concord, ON, L4K 4A9
(905) 761-1712
Emp Here 8 *Sales* 11,179,350
SIC 5044 Office equipment
Paul Howell

D-U-N-S 24-953-4181 (HQ)
HUGO BOSS CANADA INC

(Suby of HUGO BOSS AG*)*
2600 Steeles Ave W Suite 2, Concord, ON, L4K 3C8
(905) 739-2677
Emp Here 50 *Sales* 125,629,950
SIC 5136 Men's and boy's clothing
Leslie Minion
Bernard Resnick

D-U-N-S 24-287-6426 (SL)
HVE HEALTHCARE ASSESSMENTS INC
260 Edgeley Blvd Unit 22, Concord, ON, L4K 3Y4
(905) 264-2020
Emp Here 80 *Sales* 14,433,200
SIC 8731 Commercial physical research
Doris Bernon
Brian Ledrew

D-U-N-S 20-528-3372 (HQ)
I & S WAREHOUSING INC
21 Staffern Dr, Concord, ON, L4K 2X2
(905) 761-0250
Sales 13,370,890
SIC 4225 General warehousing and storage
Shlomi Bohbot

D-U-N-S 24-325-8444 (HQ)
IAC AUTOMOTIVE COMPONENTS AL-BERTA ULC
IAC
375 Basaltic Rd, Concord, ON, L4K 4W8
(905) 879-0292
Emp Here 250 *Sales* 95,524,800
SIC 3089 Plastics products, nec
Bob Cook
William Mclaughlin
Daniel Ninvaggi

D-U-N-S 20-374-8199 (SL)
INOYAN LABORATORIES INC
INNOVITE HEALTH
(Suby of QIANJIANG YONGAN PHARMA-CEUTICAL CO., LTD.*)*
97 Saramia Cres Unit 1, Concord, ON, L4K 4P7
(905) 267-0721
Emp Here 15 *Sales* 16,580,175
SIC 5122 Drugs, proprietaries, and sundries
James Zhang
Clement Ching
Ron Hurst

D-U-N-S 24-856-6663 (SL)
INSURANCE SUPERMARKET INC
A101-8000 Jane St, Concord, ON, L4K 5B8
(888) 818-1963
Emp Here 80 *Sales* 67,844,800
SIC 6411 Insurance agents, brokers, and service
Alexandr Dudarev
Ray Mckenzie

D-U-N-S 20-935-2640 (HQ)
INTERCITY REALTY INC
163 Buttermill Ave Suite 15, Concord, ON, L4K 3X8
(905) 738-6644
Sales 35,605,565
SIC 6531 Real estate agents and managers
Victor Grossi

D-U-N-S 20-181-4345 (BR)
IRON MOUNTAIN CANADA OPERATIONS ULC
ARCHIVES IRON MOUNTAIN
(Suby of IRON MOUNTAIN INCORPO-RATED*)*
70 Talman Crt Suite 415, Concord, ON, L4K 4L5
(905) 695-0564
Emp Here 200
SIC 4226 Special warehousing and storage, nec
Darryl Westman

D-U-N-S 24-417-8018 (SL)
JEMS COATING LIMITED

210 Jacob Keffer Pky, Concord, ON, L4K 4W3
(905) 303-7433
Emp Here 200 *Sales* 38,417,000
SIC 3479 Metal coating and allied services
Robert German
Anh Ngo

D-U-N-S 24-322-2192 (HQ)
JONES APPAREL CANADA GROUP, LP
JONES GROUP, THE
388 Applewood Cres, Concord, ON, L4K 4B4
(888) 880-8730
Sales 100,503,960
SIC 5137 Women's and children's clothing
Carrie Kirkman

D-U-N-S 24-602-6447 (SL)
JONES APPAREL GROUP CANADA ULC
(Suby of JASPER PARENT, LLC*)*
388 Applewood Cres, Concord, ON, L4K 4B4
(905) 760-6000
Emp Here 400
SIC 2339 Women's and misses' outerwear, nec
Mary Ann Curran

D-U-N-S 24-891-6165 (HQ)
K-G SPRAY-PAK INC
ASSURED PACKAGING DIVISION
(Suby of PLZ AEROSCIENCE CORPORA-TION*)*
8001 Keele St, Concord, ON, L4K 1Y8
(905) 669-9855
Emp Here 50 *Sales* 133,838,145
SIC 2813 Industrial gases
Wayne Houston
Walter Drozdowsky
Kent Horne
Eva Morris

D-U-N-S 24-803-0694 (HQ)
KEAL COMPUTER SERVICES INC
KEAL TECHNOLOGIES
55 Administration Rd Unit 21, Concord, ON, L4K 4G9
(905) 738-2112
Emp Here 1 *Sales* 11,170,593
SIC 7371 Custom computer programming services
Patrick Durepos

D-U-N-S 20-112-2715 (SL)
KEELE HOLDINGS INC
8001 Keele St, Concord, ON, L4K 1Y8
(905) 669-9855
Emp Here 150 *Sales* 100,336,200
SIC 7389 Business services, nec
Wayne Houston
David Porcellato
Nick Ferring
Stan Capobianco

D-U-N-S 25-403-1719 (HQ)
KELSEY'S RESTAURANTS INC
MONTANA'S
(Suby of RECIPE UNLIMITED CORPORA-TION*)*
199 Four Valley Dr, Concord, ON, L4K 0B8
(905) 760-2244
Emp Here 40 *Sales* 699,585,000
SIC 5812 Eating places
Don Robinson
Nils Kravis
Leslie Buist

D-U-N-S 24-211-3595 (HQ)
KENWORTH TORONTO LTD
KENWORTH LONDON
(Suby of TAROLA ENTERPRISES INC*)*
500 Creditstone Rd, Concord, ON, L4K 3Z3
(905) 695-0740
Emp Here 75 *Sales* 138,346,200
SIC 5012 Automobiles and other motor vehicles
Vince Tarola
Armida Tarola

D-U-N-S 24-815-8065 (HQ)
KIDDE CANADA INC
(Suby of UNITED TECHNOLOGIES CORPO-RATION*)*
340 Four Valley Dr, Concord, ON, L4K 5Z1
(905) 695-6060
Sales 19,260,054
SIC 5099 Durable goods, nec
Guiseppe Difilippo

D-U-N-S 25-406-2136 (HQ)
KIK HOLDCO COMPANY INC
KIK CUSTOM PRODUCTS
(Suby of KIK CUSTOM PRODUCTS INC*)*
101 Macintosh Blvd, Concord, ON, L4K 4R5
(905) 660-0444
Emp Here 850 *Sales* 365,509,000
SIC 6719 Holding companies, nec
Jeffrey Nodland
Alay Shah
Ben Kaak

D-U-N-S 24-946-7077 (SL)
KIMMEL SALES LIMITED
126 Edilcan Dr Unit 1, Concord, ON, L4K 3S5
(905) 669-2083
Emp Here 20 *Sales* 10,702,480
SIC 5141 Groceries, general line
Gary Kimmel

D-U-N-S 24-780-0014 (SL)
KING KOATING ROOFING INC
(Suby of KING KOATING HOLDINGS INC*)*
41 Peelar Rd, Concord, ON, L4K 1A3
(905) 669-1771
Emp Here 50 *Sales* 10,891,450
SIC 1761 Roofing, siding, and sheetMetal work
Kevin Mcconnell

D-U-N-S 20-168-6532 (HQ)
KOHL & FRISCH LIMITED
7622 Keele St, Concord, ON, L4K 2R5
(905) 660-7622
Emp Here 250 *Sales* 350,897,850
SIC 5122 Drugs, proprietaries, and sundries
Ronald Frisch
Lance Fielding
Paul Magro
Matthew Frisch
Antoinette Russell
Sharon Fligel

D-U-N-S 24-984-9522 (SL)
KORHANI OF CANADA INC
KORHANI MANUFACTURE
7500 Keele St, Concord, ON, L4K 1Z9
(905) 660-0863
Emp Here 150 *Sales* 27,510,450
SIC 2273 Carpets and rugs
Mojtaba Korhani
Hessam Korhani

D-U-N-S 20-511-6051 (BR)
KPMG INC
(Suby of KPMG INC*)*
100 New Park Pl Suite 1400, Concord, ON, L4K 0J3
(905) 265-5900
Emp Here 490
SIC 8721 Accounting, auditing, and bookkeeping
Joyce Richards

D-U-N-S 20-624-4147 (HQ)
KRINOS FOODS CANADA LTD
251 Doney Cres, Concord, ON, L4K 1P6
(905) 669-4414
Emp Here 45 *Sales* 77,708,661
SIC 5143 Dairy products, except dried or canned
Alexander Georgiadis
Alexander Alexakis

D-U-N-S 24-363-4458 (HQ)
KRISTOFOAM INDUSTRIES INC
160 Planchet Rd, Concord, ON, L4K 2C7

(905) 669-6616
Emp Here 70   *Sales* 11,596,634
SIC 3086 Plastics foam products
Frederick (Fred) Dalakis
Michael (Mike) Dalakis
Harini Wanda

D-U-N-S 24-342-6868   (BR)
KRISTOFOAM INDUSTRIES INC
(*Suby of* KRISTOFOAM INDUSTRIES INC)
120 Planchet Rd, Concord, ON, L4K 2C7
(905) 669-6616
Emp Here 75
SIC 3086 Plastics foam products
Mike Dalakis

D-U-N-S 20-161-0979   (BR)
LAFARGE CANADA INC
(*Suby of* LAFARGEHOLCIM LTD)
7880 Keele St Unit 5, Concord, ON, L4K 4G7
(905) 738-7070
Emp Here 150
SIC 5032 Brick, stone, and related material
Barry Martin

D-U-N-S 25-365-1897   (HQ)
LAFARGE PAVING & CONSTRUCTION (EASTERN) LIMITED
(*Suby of* LAFARGEHOLCIM LTD)
7880 Keele St Unit 5, Concord, ON, L4K 4G7
(905) 738-7070
Emp Here 250   *Sales* 164,057,500
SIC 1611 Highway and street construction
Greg Sheardown
Jean Marc Bissonnette
Alain Fredette
Kenneth R. Cathcart
David Guptill

D-U-N-S 20-548-3162   (SL)
LANCORP CONSTRUCTION CO. LTD
138 Creditstone Rd, Concord, ON, L4K 1P2
(905) 660-0778
Emp Here 50   *Sales* 12,044,200
SIC 1623 Water, sewer, and utility lines
Eliseo Lancione

D-U-N-S 20-104-1287   (SL)
LIFESTYLES NETWORK SERVICES INC
LIFESTYLES GLOBAL NETWORK
8100 Keele St, Concord, ON, L4K 2A3
(905) 761-9342
Emp Here 40   *Sales* 44,213,800
SIC 5122 Drugs, proprietaries, and sundries
David Debora

D-U-N-S 24-631-4389   (SL)
M.B. PRODUCT RESEARCH DISTRIBUTING INC
INTER-CANADA FISHERIES, DIV OF
270 Pennsylvania Ave Unit 11-13, Concord, ON, L4K 3Z7
(905) 660-1421
Emp Here 28   *Sales* 23,396,156
SIC 5146 Fish and seafoods
Marc Benhaim

D-U-N-S 24-651-8278   (HQ)
MAGIC MAINTENANCE INC
25 Edilcan Dr Unit 3, Concord, ON, L4K 3S4

Sales 12,787,200
SIC 7349 Building maintenance services, nec
Michael Giammarco

D-U-N-S 20-699-6873   (HQ)
MAGNA EXTERIORS INC
(*Suby of* MAGNA INTERNATIONAL INC)
50 Casmir Crt, Concord, ON, L4K 4J5
(905) 669-2888
Emp Here 1,000   *Sales* 872,550,000
SIC 3714 Motor vehicle parts and accessories
Joseph Pittel
Michael Mccarthy
Francis Seguin
Jeffrey Palmer
Vincent Galifi
Tom Skudutis

D-U-N-S 24-320-2695   (BR)
MAGNA INTERNATIONAL INC
ROLLSTAMP MANUFACTURING, DIV OF
(*Suby of* MAGNA INTERNATIONAL INC)
90 Snidercroft Rd, Concord, ON, L4K 2K1
(905) 738-3700
Emp Here 350
SIC 3714 Motor vehicle parts and accessories
Tony Wulle

D-U-N-S 20-389-9323   (SL)
MAGNA POWERTRAIN FPC LIMITED PARTNERSHIP
(*Suby of* MAGNA INTERNATIONAL INC)
800 Tesma Way, Concord, ON, L4K 5C2
(905) 303-1689
Emp Here 532
SIC 5085 Industrial supplies
Bill Drury
Larry Cheney

D-U-N-S 24-764-5765   (HQ)
MAGNA POWERTRAIN INC
ROTO FORM, DIV OF
(*Suby of* MAGNA INTERNATIONAL INC)
50 Casmir Crt, Concord, ON, L4K 4J5
(905) 532-2100
Emp Here 25   *Sales* 1,366,995,000
SIC 3714 Motor vehicle parts and accessories

D-U-N-S 20-709-1070   (SL)
MAPLE LEAF BREAD LTD
MAPLE LEAF BREAD
144 Viceroy Rd, Concord, ON, L4K 2L8
(905) 738-1242
Emp Here 50   *Sales* 11,242,750
SIC 2041 Flour and other grain mill products
Anne Manrique

D-U-N-S 20-708-8118   (BR)
MAPLE TERRAZZO MARBLE & TILE INCORPORATED
(*Suby of* MAPLE TERRAZZO MARBLE & TILE INCORPORATED)
200 Edgeley Blvd Unit 9, Concord, ON, L4K 3Y8
(905) 760-1776
Emp Here 700
SIC 8631 Labor organizations
Joe Tersigni

D-U-N-S 20-770-0571   (SL)
MAR DEVELOPMENTS INC
VAUGHAN AUTOMOTIVE SUPPLIES
237 Romina Dr Unit 1, Concord, ON, L4K 4V3
(905) 738-2255
Emp Here 25   *Sales* 10,483,875
SIC 6712 Bank holding companies
Rocco Dantonio

D-U-N-S 25-373-8660   (HQ)
MARC ANTHONY COSMETICS LTD
(*Suby of* MAV BEAUTY BRANDS INC)
190 Pippin Rd, Concord, ON, L4K 4X9
(905) 530-2500
Sales 48,575,574
SIC 5122 Drugs, proprietaries, and sundries
Marc Anthony Venere

D-U-N-S 20-849-5457   (SL)
MARESCO LIMITED
171 Basaltic Rd Unit 2, Concord, ON, L4K 1G4
(905) 669-5700
Emp Here 30   *Sales* 17,110,140
SIC 1542 Nonresidential construction, nec
Mark Lesniak

D-U-N-S 24-738-2906   (SL)
MARTINO CONTRACTORS LTD
150 Connie Cres Unit 16, Concord, ON, L4K 1L9
(905) 760-9894
Emp Here 50   *Sales* 11,046,700
SIC 1711 Plumbing, heating, air-conditioning
Michael Martino

D-U-N-S 20-876-6758   (HQ)

MASTERS INSURANCE LIMITED
7501 Keele St Suite 400, Concord, ON, L4K 1Y2
(905) 738-4164
Emp Here 20   *Sales* 166,296,780
SIC 6411 Insurance agents, brokers, and service
Frank Ciccolini
Max Ciccolini
Gary Corby
Sam Ciccolini

D-U-N-S 20-831-9207   (SL)
MASTERS LIFE INSURANCE AGENTS LIMITED
7501 Keele St Suite 400, Concord, ON, L4K 1Y2

Emp Here 55   *Sales* 47,427,784
SIC 6411 Insurance agents, brokers, and service

D-U-N-S 24-858-2277   (SL)
MATCOM INDUSTRIAL INSTALLATIONS INC
1531 Creditstone Rd, Concord, ON, L4K 5V6
(416) 667-0463
Emp Here 70   *Sales* 13,394,780
SIC 7359 Equipment rental and leasing, nec
Matthew O'dwyer
Kathryn O'dwyer
Scott Stobo

D-U-N-S 24-817-8089   (SL)
MATICAIR SUPPLY AND MANUFACTURING (1996) LTD
99 Mccleary Crt, Concord, ON, L4K 3Z1
(905) 738-5888
Emp Here 65   *Sales* 12,485,525
SIC 3444 Sheet Metalwork
Joseph Cho
Charles Cho

D-U-N-S 24-320-3869   (HQ)
MAV BEAUTY BRANDS INC
190 Pippin Rd, Concord, ON, L4K 4X9
(905) 530-2500
Sales 20,501,250
SIC 6712 Bank holding companies
Marc Anthony Venere
Christopher Doyle
Chris Elshaw
Jeffrey Barber
Thomas Ennis
Jessica Gilligan
Stephen Smith

D-U-N-S 20-289-0971   (SL)
MAXGUARD ALARM AND SECURITY COMPANY LTD
8700 Dufferin St Unit 17, Concord, ON, L4K 4S2
(416) 893-9082
Emp Here 32   *Sales* 13,360,192
SIC 7382 Security systems services
Stefan Tuzi
Emilio Pacitto

D-U-N-S 20-348-2208   (SL)
MAXUM DRYWALL INC
1681 Langstaff Rd Unit 18, Concord, ON, L4K 5T3
(905) 856-4108
Emp Here 130   *Sales* 21,109,530
SIC 1742 Plastering, drywall, and insulation
Dino Martelli

D-U-N-S 25-507-7240   (HQ)
MAZIN FURNITURE INDUSTRIES LIMITED
8080 Keele St, Concord, ON, L4K 2A3
(905) 761-1594
Emp Here 30   *Sales* 25,442,800
SIC 5023 Homefurnishings
Michael Mazin

D-U-N-S 20-784-8540   (HQ)
MCINTOSH PERRY LIMITED
(*Suby of* SIGNAL HILL EQUITY PARTNERS

INC)
7900 Keele St Suite 200, Concord, ON, L4K 2A3
(905) 856-5200
Emp Here 100   *Sales* 27,975,900
SIC 8742 Management consulting services
Marc Sinopolio

D-U-N-S 24-368-1504   (HQ)
MERCOR LIGHTING GROUP INC, THE
MERCURY LIGHTING
71 Ortona Crt Unit 1, Concord, ON, L4K 3M2
(905) 738-6161
Sales 20,122,830
SIC 5063 Electrical apparatus and equipment
Michael Rabinowitz
Eric Tordjman

D-U-N-S 25-353-4689   (SL)
MERCURY LIGHTING LIMITED
MERCOR LIGHTING
(*Suby of* MERCOR LIGHTING GROUP INC, THE)
71 Ortona Crt Unit 1, Concord, ON, L4K 3M2
(905) 738-6161
Emp Here 41   *Sales* 18,334,134
SIC 5063 Electrical apparatus and equipment
Michael Rabinowitz
Eric Tordjman

D-U-N-S 20-261-1323   (SL)
MERLIN ENTERTAINMENTS (CANADA) INC
LEGOLAND DISCOVERY CENTRE TORONTO
1 Bass Pro Mills Dr, Concord, ON, L4K 5W4
(905) 761-7066
Emp Here 100   *Sales* 14,002,900
SIC 7999 Amusement and recreation, nec
Rene Gurter
Donald Glenn Earlam
John Ussher
David Diaz

D-U-N-S 24-660-5323   (SL)
METCON SALES AND ENGINEERING LIMITED
(*Suby of* SMITH CAMERON PUMP SOLUTIONS INC)
15 Connie Cres Unit 3, Concord, ON, L4K 1L3
(905) 738-2355
Emp Here 45   *Sales* 21,376,170
SIC 5084 Industrial machinery and equipment
Lawrence Rosen

D-U-N-S 20-690-5734   (HQ)
METRO ACQUISITION 2004, INC
METRO WALLCOVERINGS
2600 Steeles Ave W, Concord, ON, L4K 3C8
(905) 738-5177
Emp Here 38   *Sales* 37,126,000
SIC 5198 Paints, varnishes, and supplies
Victor Paul

D-U-N-S 24-047-4122   (HQ)
METRUS PROPERTIES LIMITED
30 Floral Pky Suite 200, Concord, ON, L4K 4R1
(416) 798-7173
Sales 14,356,615
SIC 6512 Nonresidential building operators
Robert De Gasperis
Antonio De Gasperis
Angelo De Gasperis
Ennio Zuccon

D-U-N-S 20-280-8085   (SL)
MGC SYSTEMS INTERNATIONAL LTD
(*Suby of* MIRCOM GROUP HOLDINGS INC)
25 Interchange Way, Concord, ON, L4K 5W3
(905) 660-4655
Emp Here 20   *Sales* 15,242,740
SIC 3669 Communications equipment, nec
Mark Falbo
Tony Falbo
Frank Vanelli

D-U-N-S 25-253-8504   (SL)
MIDOME CONSTRUCTION SERVICES LTD

▲ Public Company   ■ Public Company Family Member   **HQ** Headquarters   **BR** Branch   **SL** Single Location

665 Millway Ave Suite 65, Concord, ON, L4K 3T8
(905) 738-2211
Emp Here 50   *Sales* 23,536,550
SIC 1542 Nonresidential construction, nec
  Michael Lamanna
  Peter Lenis
  Tina Lamanna

D-U-N-S 24-816-8700   (HQ)
MIELE LIMITED
(*Suby of* MIELE & CIE. KG)
161 Four Valley Dr, Concord, ON, L4K 4V8
(905) 532-2270
Sales 44,717,400
SIC 5064 Electrical appliances, television and radio
  John Tsianakos

D-U-N-S 20-347-8461   (SL)
MILLENIUM PRINTING INC
MPI PRINT
139 Basaltic Rd, Concord, ON, L4K 1G4
(905) 760-5522
Emp Here 70   *Sales* 12,535,632
SIC 2752 Commercial printing, lithographic
  Rajinderpal Dhanju
  Ravi Iyer
  Gurinder Dhanju

D-U-N-S 20-175-4314   (SL)
MILOMA INVESTMENTS LTD
SILVERT'S STORE
3280 Steeles Ave W Unit 18, Concord, ON, L4K 2Y2
(905) 738-4545
Emp Here 50   *Sales* 32,823,200
SIC 5961 Catalog and mail-order houses
  Jeffrey Alter

D-U-N-S 20-763-0208   (SL)
MIMI FOOD PRODUCTS INC
1260 Creditstone Rd Unit 2-3, Concord, ON, L4K 5T7
(905) 660-0010
Emp Here 30   *Sales* 25,067,310
SIC 5142 Packaged frozen goods
  Mike Primucci
  Domenic Primucci

D-U-N-S 24-377-4390   (HQ)
MIRCOM GROUP HOLDINGS INC
25 Interchange Way, Concord, ON, L4K 5W3
(905) 660-4655
Emp Here 1   *Sales* 113,166,000
SIC 3669 Communications equipment, nec
  Mark Falbo
  Tony Falbo
  Rick Falbo
  Victor Sebben
  Alan Taaffe
  Edoardo Mattei

D-U-N-S 24-910-9471   (HQ)
MIRCOM TECHNOLOGIES LTD
(*Suby of* MIRCOM GROUP HOLDINGS INC)
25 Interchange Way Unit 1, Concord, ON, L4K 5W3
(905) 660-4655
Emp Here 100   *Sales* 113,166,000
SIC 3669 Communications equipment, nec
  Tony Falbo
  Mark Falbo
  Frank Vanelli

D-U-N-S 20-818-4770   (HQ)
MISTER CHEMICAL LTD
101 Jacob Keffer Pky, Concord, ON, L4K 5N8
(905) 761-9995
Emp Here 28   *Sales* 19,001,040
SIC 5087 Service establishment equipment
  Michael Jacobs

D-U-N-S 25-274-8777   (SL)
MOBILE CLIMATE CONTROL, INC
(*Suby of* VBG GROUP AB (PUBL))
7540 Jane St, Concord, ON, L4K 0A6

(905) 482-2750
Emp Here 300   *Sales* 87,255,000
SIC 3714 Motor vehicle parts and accessories
  Robert Kuzminski
  Chris Kutter
  Eric Weiss
  Maurizio Caranfa
  Tim Hested

D-U-N-S 25-204-6289   (HQ)
MOOD MEDIA ENTERTAINMENT LTD
AVALON MUSIC
99 Sante Dr Suite B, Concord, ON, L4K 3C4
(905) 761-4300
Emp Here 50   *Sales* 66,890,800
SIC 7389 Business services, nec
  Andy Burgess
  Robert Meier
  Ed Bonner
  Gordon Gibson

D-U-N-S 20-171-1769   (HQ)
MOORE, BENJAMIN & CO., LIMITED
(*Suby of* BERKSHIRE HATHAWAY INC.)
8775 Keele St, Concord, ON, L4K 2N1
(905) 761-4800
Emp Here 100   *Sales* 56,804,200
SIC 2851 Paints and allied products
  Brian Palardy

D-U-N-S 20-227-8826   (HQ)
MORRIS NATIONAL INC
100 Jacob Keffer Pky, Concord, ON, L4K 4W3
(905) 879-7777
Emp Here 20   *Sales* 143,343,200
SIC 5145 Confectionery
  Gerry Morris Zubatoff
  Abe Morris Zubatoff
  Jean-Pierre Lefebvre

D-U-N-S 20-976-2590   (SL)
MOSCONE TILE LTD
8830 Jane St Suite 1, Concord, ON, L4K 2M9
(905) 761-5722
Emp Here 60   *Sales* 16,059,120
SIC 5211 Lumber and other building materials
  Benedetto Moscone
  Argentina Moscone

D-U-N-S 25-354-4993   (SL)
MULLER MARTINI CANADA INC
SADDLE STITCHING SYSTEMS, A DIV
(*Suby of* GRAPHA-HOLDING AG)
20 Caldari Rd Suite 2, Concord, ON, L4K 4N8
(905) 660-9595
Emp Here 28   *Sales* 13,300,728
SIC 5085 Industrial supplies
  Gary Hughes

D-U-N-S 24-454-5943   (BR)
MULTIMATIC INC
MULTIMATIC MANUFACTURING
(*Suby of* MULTIMATIC HOLDINGS INC)
301 Jacob Keffer Pky, Concord, ON, L4K 4V6
(905) 879-0200
Emp Here 350
SIC 3465 Automotive stampings
  Scott Warden

D-U-N-S 25-403-9282   (BR)
MULTIMATIC INC
ANTON MANUFACTURING
(*Suby of* MULTIMATIC HOLDINGS INC)
300 Basaltic Rd Suite 1, Concord, ON, L4K 4Y9
(905) 879-0500
Emp Here 350
SIC 3429 Hardware, nec
  Mike Kuhn

D-U-N-S 24-756-9189   (SL)
MULTIRIM INC
226 Jardin Dr Suite 7, Concord, ON, L4K 1Y1
(905) 669-3566
Emp Here 50   *Sales* 13,833,000
SIC 2822 Synthetic rubber
  Ronald J. Pascucci
  George Ward

D-U-N-S 24-370-8299   (HQ)
MULTY HOME LP
7900 Keele St Unit 100, Concord, ON, L4K 2A3
(905) 760-3737
Emp Here 100   *Sales* 86,305,200
SIC 5023 Homefurnishings
  Derek Erdman

D-U-N-S 20-171-3955   (SL)
MUZZO BROTHERS GROUP INC
MAREL CONTRACTORS
50 Confederation Pky, Concord, ON, L4K 4T8
(905) 326-4000
Emp Here 200   *Sales* 32,476,200
SIC 1742 Plastering, drywall, and insulation
  Marco Muzzo
  Alex Muzzo

D-U-N-S 20-851-3515   (HQ)
NATIONAL FIRE EQUIPMENT LIMITED
40 Edilcan Dr, Concord, ON, L4K 3S6
(905) 761-6355
Emp Here 14   *Sales* 40,377,210
SIC 5087 Service establishment equipment
  Dan Webster
  Keith Webster
  Robert Cuthbert

D-U-N-S 20-377-2272   (SL)
NAVELLI DWELLINGS INC
1681 Langstaff Rd Unit 1, Concord, ON, L4K 5T3
(416) 987-5500
Emp Here 40   *Sales* 19,069,680
SIC 1531 Operative builders
  Carlo Baldassarra
  Nicholas Fidei
  Bruno Baldassarra
  Armando Baldassarra
  Claudio Aversa

D-U-N-S 24-386-8242   (HQ)
ND GRAPHICS INC
55 Interchange Way Unit 1, Concord, ON, L4K 5W3
(416) 663-6416
Emp Here 50   *Sales* 47,502,600
SIC 5084 Industrial machinery and equipment
  Mark West
  Fred Elkins

D-U-N-S 25-402-9465   (SL)
NEBB FORMING LTD
41 Ritin Lane, Concord, ON, L4K 4W6
(905) 761-6100
Emp Here 65   *Sales* 16,002,090
SIC 1799 Special trade contractors, nec
  David Krznaric
  Larry Gurizzan

D-U-N-S 25-068-2028   (SL)
NETWORK MECHANICAL INC
73 Corstate Ave Unit 1, Concord, ON, L4K 4Y2
(905) 761-1417
Emp Here 50   *Sales* 11,046,700
SIC 1711 Plumbing, heating, air-conditioning
  John Agozzino

D-U-N-S 25-352-2940   (SL)
NOLRAD INTERNATIONAL INC
1380 Creditstone Rd Unit 5, Concord, ON, L4K 0J1
(905) 738-4646
Emp Here 12   *Sales* 12,004,068
SIC 5051 Metals service centers and offices
  Nick Grbic

D-U-N-S 25-974-1791   (HQ)
NORTHCOTT SILK INC
LACE GOODS CANADA, DIV OF
101 Courtland Ave, Concord, ON, L4K 3T5
(905) 760-0072
Sales 17,820,480
SIC 5199 Nondurable goods, nec
  Brian O'rourke
  Tahseen Syed
  Paul O'rourke

  Peter Kantor
  Paul Norton

D-U-N-S 20-548-6462   (HQ)
NORTHEASTERN SWIMMING POOL DISTRIBUTORS INC
282 North Rivermede Rd, Concord, ON, L4K 3N6
(905) 761-7946
Emp Here 8   *Sales* 11,451,924
SIC 5091 Sporting and recreation goods
  Tom Dovgala

D-U-N-S 24-264-0864   (SL)
NORTHERN FORCE SECURITY
1750 Steeles Ave W, Concord, ON, L4K 2L7
(647) 982-1385
Emp Here 26   *Sales* 10,287,628
SIC 7381 Detective and armored car services

D-U-N-S 24-551-0805   (SL)
NUMAGE TRADING INC
894 Edgeley Blvd, Concord, ON, L4K 4V4
(905) 660-4172
Emp Here 20   *Sales* 10,702,480
SIC 5149 Groceries and related products, nec
  Gesualdo Mastruzzo

D-U-N-S 24-195-3804   (SL)
NUVIA CANADA INC
222 Snidercroft Rd, Concord, ON, L4K 2K1
(647) 800-1319
Emp Here 35   *Sales* 10,691,800
SIC 8999 Services, nec
  Mike Parker

D-U-N-S 25-991-6385   (SL)
OFIS SYSTEMS INC
452 Millway Ave Suite 2, Concord, ON, L4K 3V7

Emp Here 175   *Sales* 27,006,350
SIC 2521 Wood office furniture
  David Shamir

D-U-N-S 25-504-4075   (HQ)
OLDCASTLE   BUILDINGENVELOPE CANADA INC
(*Suby of* CRH PUBLIC LIMITED COMPANY)
210 Great Gulf Dr, Concord, ON, L4K 5W1
(905) 660-4520
Emp Here 350   *Sales* 153,414,000
SIC 3211 Flat glass
  Edwin Hathaway
  Mary Carol Whitry

D-U-N-S 24-215-4094   (SL)
OLYMPIC MATERIAL HANDLING LTD
300 Bradwick Dr, Concord, ON, L4K 1K8
(416) 661-4609
Emp Here 25   *Sales* 11,875,650
SIC 5084 Industrial machinery and equipment
  Silvio Marsili
  Jesse Coppola

D-U-N-S 24-783-8238   (SL)
ONTARIO POWER CONTRACTING LIMITED
340 Bowes Rd, Concord, ON, L4K 1K1

Emp Here 90   *Sales* 22,719,780
SIC 1623 Water, sewer, and utility lines
  Joseph Alfano

D-U-N-S 24-205-8514   (SL)
ONTARIO REGIONAL COMMON GROUND ALLIANCE
102-545 North Rivermede Rd, Concord, ON, L4K 4H1
(905) 532-9836
Emp Here 27   *Sales* 12,128,913
SIC 7389 Business services, nec
  Jim Douglas

D-U-N-S 20-982-7112   (SL)
OPTIQ LTD
344 North Rivermede Rd Unit 2, Concord, ON, L4K 3N2
(905) 669-6251
Emp Here 30   *Sales* 13,415,220

SIC 5049 Professional equipment, nec
Joseph Nadler
Peter Mandic
Leon Nadler

D-U-N-S 25-314-1563   (SL)
ORACLE INSURANCE RISK MANAGE-MENT SERVICES INC
100 Drumlin Circle, Concord, ON, L4K 3E6
(905) 660-9740
Emp Here 38   *Sales* 22,037,112
SIC 6411 Insurance agents, brokers, and service
Mike Dinardo

D-U-N-S 25-405-5312   (SL)
OSTACO 2000 WINDOORS INC
OSTACO WINDOWS
(*Suby of* 1392167 ONTARIO LIMITED)
248 Bowes Rd, Concord, ON, L4K 1J9
(905) 660-5021
Emp Here 112   *Sales* 12,194,192
SIC 3089 Plastics products, nec
Frank Greco
Jacques Charlebois

D-U-N-S 24-770-8548   (HQ)
OXVILLE HOMES LTD
FERNBROOK HOMES
2220 Highway 7 Unit 5, Concord, ON, L4K 1W7
(416) 667-0447
Sales 29,803,620
SIC 1522 Residential construction, nec
Danny Salvatore
Gino Digenova
Nick Cortellucci

D-U-N-S 20-938-8313   (HQ)
OZZ ELECTRIC
DIAL ONE WOLFEDALE ELECTRIC
20 Floral Pky Suite A, Concord, ON, L4K 4R1
(416) 637-7237
Emp Here 108
SIC 1731 Electrical work
Jacqueline Strachan
Jim Graham

D-U-N-S 24-876-4441   (HQ)
OZZ ELECTRIC INC
20 Floral Pky Suite A, Concord, ON, L4K 4R1
(416) 637-7237
Sales 188,407,200
SIC 1731 Electrical work
Steven Muzzo
Gerry Deluca
Jason Aspros
Doug Skrepnek

D-U-N-S 24-828-3541   (HQ)
PACE SAVINGS & CREDIT UNION LIMITED
8111 Jane St Unit 1, Concord, ON, L4K 4L7
(905) 738-8900
Emp Here 35   *Sales* 22,615,656
SIC 6062 State credit unions
Larry Smith
Kim Colacicco
Mary Benincasa
Gerry Robin
Philip Smith
Dan Coldwell

D-U-N-S 24-936-6931   (SL)
PACKAGING TECHNOLOGIES INC
PTI
310a Courtland Ave, Concord, ON, L4K 4Y6
(905) 738-8226
Emp Here 70   *Sales* 16,340,450
SIC 2653 Corrugated and solid fiber boxes
Tim Boissinot
Barbara Wolfe
Neville Wolf

D-U-N-S 25-863-8279   (HQ)
PARSEC INTERMODAL OF CANADA LIMITED
(*Suby of* PARSEC INC.)
751 Bowes Rd Suite 2, Concord, ON, L4K 5C9

(905) 669-7901
Emp Here 20   *Sales* 50,488,400
SIC 1629 Heavy construction, nec
Otto Pudig
Al Peroddin

D-U-N-S 24-325-2694   (SL)
PASTA KITCHEN LP
350 Creditstone Rd Unit 103, Concord, ON, L4K 3Z2
(905) 760-0000
Emp Here 90   *Sales* 31,112,100
SIC 2098 Macaroni and spaghetti
Michael Smith

D-U-N-S 20-057-5616   (HQ)
PENN ENGINEERED FASTENERS CORPORATION
(*Suby of* TINICUM CAPITAL PARTNERS II, L.P)
590 Basaltic Rd, Concord, ON, L4K 5A2
(905) 879-0433
Emp Here 40   *Sales* 27,551,508
SIC 5085 Industrial supplies
Neil Whitesell
Peter Kapogines

D-U-N-S 25-852-5989   (HQ)
PERMICOM PERMITS SERVICES INC
161 Pennsylvania Ave Unit 5, Concord, ON, L4K 1C3

Emp Here 40   *Sales* 43,347,980
SIC 4731 Freight transportation arrangement
Larry Babins

D-U-N-S 20-253-7176   (SL)
PERRI'S LEATHERS LTD
45 Casmir Crt Unit 11 & 15, Concord, ON, L4K 4H5
(905) 761-8549
Emp Here 50   *Sales* 11,671,750
SIC 3199 Leather goods, nec
Anthony Perri

D-U-N-S 24-308-0764   (SL)
PFAFF AUTOMOTIVE PARTNERS INC
9088 Jane St, Concord, ON, L4K 2M9
(905) 907-2834
Emp Here 30   *Sales* 14,942,340
SIC 5511 New and used car dealers
Christopher Pfaff
Michael Talmage
Mark Fisher

D-U-N-S 20-132-1197   (HQ)
PFAFF MOTORS INC
PFAFF LEASING
220 Caldari Rd, Concord, ON, L4K 4L1
(905) 761-7890
Emp Here 80   *Sales* 125,856,000
SIC 5511 New and used car dealers
Christopher Pfaff
Ruth Pfaff

D-U-N-S 20-551-0790   (SL)
PHILLIPS ENGINEERING TECHNOLOGIES CORP
385 Connie Cres, Concord, ON, L4K 5R2

Emp Here 65   *Sales* 14,430,065
SIC 3569 General industrial machinery, nec
Levkis Kishlyansky

D-U-N-S 25-726-7872   (HQ)
PHOENIX PERFORMANCE PRODUCTS INC
100 Bass Pro Mills Dr Unit 32, Concord, ON, L4K 5X1
(905) 539-0370
Sales 10,503,552
SIC 3949 Sporting and athletic goods, nec
David Anderson

D-U-N-S 25-375-6217   (HQ)
PLAN GROUP INC
(*Suby of* BOUYGUES)
2740 Steeles Ave W, Concord, ON, L4K 4T4

(416) 635-9040
Emp Here 250   *Sales* 471,018,000
SIC 1731 Electrical work
William Kurtin
Paul Sheridan
Frank Loewen
John Slattery

D-U-N-S 20-182-6559   (SL)
PLANET PAPER BOX INC
2841 Langstaff Rd Unit 1, Concord, ON, L4K 4W7
(905) 669-9363
Emp Here 90   *Sales* 21,009,150
SIC 2653 Corrugated and solid fiber boxes
Jason Berns

D-U-N-S 20-266-7734   (SL)
PLATINUM ELECTRICAL CONTRACTORS INC
270 Drumlin Cir Unit 5, Concord, ON, L4K 3E2
(905) 761-7647
Emp Here 65   *Sales* 14,158,885
SIC 1731 Electrical work
Adam Wachtel

D-U-N-S 20-550-5048   (SL)
POLYCOTE INC
8120 Keele St, Concord, ON, L4K 2A3
(905) 660-7552
Emp Here 58   *Sales* 11,140,930
SIC 3479 Metal coating and allied services
Surjit Bawa
Baljit Bawa
Sandeep Bawa
Anoop Bawa

D-U-N-S 20-161-3296   (HQ)
PPG CANADA INC
COATINGS & RELATED PRODUCTS
(*Suby of* PPG INDUSTRIES, INC.)
8200 Keele St, Concord, ON, L4K 2A5
(905) 669-1020
Emp Here 50   *Sales* 978,219,000
SIC 2851 Paints and allied products
Charles Bunch

D-U-N-S 25-436-4776   (SL)
PRACTICAL ELECTRIC CONTRACTING INC.
527 Edgeley Blvd Unit 12, Concord, ON, L4K 4G6
(416) 663-1500
Emp Here 70   *Sales* 15,248,030
SIC 1731 Electrical work
Andy Nicolaidis

D-U-N-S 25-862-6431   (BR)
PRIMERICA FINANCIAL SERVICES LTD
PRIMERICA FINANCIAL
(*Suby of* PRIMERICA, INC.)
8555 Jane St Suite 101, Concord, ON, L4K 5N9
(416) 495-0200
Emp Here 80
SIC 6411 Insurance agents, brokers, and service
Bobby Gocool

D-U-N-S 25-529-7632   (HQ)
PRISM MEDICAL LTD
485 Millway Ave Unit 2, Concord, ON, L4K 3V4
(416) 260-2145
Sales 43,572,454
SIC 6712 Bank holding companies
Charley Wallace
Steven Clark
Jeffrey A Matthews
Jeremy Bespalko
Kevin Klipfel

D-U-N-S 24-848-7134   (SL)
PRISM POWDER COATINGS LTD
321 Edgeley Blvd, Concord, ON, L4K 3Y2
(905) 660-5361
Emp Here 75   *Sales* 20,749,500
SIC 2851 Paints and allied products

Alex Ashour
Yogesh Patel
Livio Agnoletto

D-U-N-S 24-816-8163   (HQ)
PROCESS PRODUCTS LIMITED
50 Locke St Unit 1, Concord, ON, L4K 5R4
(416) 781-3399
Emp Here 40   *Sales* 28,501,560
SIC 5085 Industrial supplies
Samuel Stupp
Sydney Stupp

D-U-N-S 24-287-4733   (SL)
PROMEX DATA PUBLISHING INC
37 Staffern Dr, Concord, ON, L4K 2X2
(905) 738-0288
Emp Here 35   *Sales* 17,628,030
SIC 5112 Stationery and office supplies
Josh Lapsker

D-U-N-S 25-250-4001   (SL)
PROTEKITE
380 Spinnaker Way, Concord, ON, L4K 4W1
(905) 738-1221
Emp Here 40   *Sales* 17,968,760
SIC 7389 Business services, nec
Simon Trillwood

D-U-N-S 20-558-2120   (HQ)
PROTEMP GLASS INC
360 Applewood Cres, Concord, ON, L4K 4V2
(905) 760-0701
Emp Here 100   *Sales* 19,714,090
SIC 3211 Flat glass
Gianfranco Dimarco
Guissipina Dimarco

D-U-N-S 20-734-7998   (SL)
PROVINCIAL INDUSTRIAL ROOFING AND SHEET METAL COMPANY LIMITED
166 Bowes Rd, Concord, ON, L4K 1J6
(905) 669-2569
Emp Here 58   *Sales* 12,634,082
SIC 1761 Roofing, siding, and sheetMetal work
David Uglow

D-U-N-S 20-770-0175   (BR)
PUROLATOR INC
(*Suby of* GOVERNMENT OF CANADA)
1550 Creditstone Rd, Concord, ON, L4K 5N1
(905) 660-6007
Emp Here 100
SIC 7389 Business services, nec
Alan Wells

D-U-N-S 24-525-0621   (SL)
QRX TECHNOLOGY GROUP INC
(*Suby of* 2172004 ONTARIO INC)
200 Connie Cres Unit 4, Concord, ON, L4K 1M1
(905) 738-1688
Emp Here 25   *Sales* 16,004,877
SIC 5112 Stationery and office supplies
Grace Martin

D-U-N-S 20-785-8812   (SL)
QUADRANT INDUSTRIES INC
1800 Steeles Ave W, Concord, ON, L4K 2P3
(905) 761-9110
Emp Here 60   *Sales* 11,525,100
SIC 3499 Fabricated Metal products, nec
Sol Feldberg

D-U-N-S 24-776-4066   (SL)
QUALITY & COMPANY INC
67 Jacob Keffer Pky, Concord, ON, L4K 5N8
(905) 660-6996
Emp Here 130   *Sales* 20,061,860
SIC 2599 Furniture and fixtures, nec
Frank Caruso
Rinaldo Caruso

D-U-N-S 20-161-4732   (HQ)
RECIPE UNLIMITED CORPORATION
199 Four Valley Dr, Concord, ON, L4K 0B8
(905) 760-2244
Emp Here 250   *Sales* 903,606,033

SIC 5812 Eating places
Frank Hennessey
Bill Gregson
Julie Denton
Kenneth Grondin
David Aisenstat
Stephen Gunn
Christopher Hodgson
Michael Norris
John Rothschild
Sean Regan

D-U-N-S 24-420-9110   (SL)
REGAL ALUMINUM (1993) INC
177 Drumlin Cir Suite 1, Concord, ON, L4K 3E7
(905) 738-4375
Emp Here 55   *Sales* 14,720,860
SIC 5211 Lumber and other building materials
Abraham Balilty
Ilana Balilty

D-U-N-S 24-925-2487   (SL)
REGIONAL HOSE TORONTO LTD
15 Connie Cres Unit 2223, Concord, ON, L4K 1L3
(905) 660-5560
Emp Here 47   *Sales* 22,326,222
SIC 5084 Industrial machinery and equipment
Darwin T Booth
Logan Booth
Paul Pearson

D-U-N-S 20-173-9364   (SL)
RELCO INC
7700 Keele St Unit 10, Concord, ON, L4K 2A1
(416) 740-8632
Emp Here 26   *Sales* 12,350,676
SIC 5084 Industrial machinery and equipment
Dani Cohen

D-U-N-S 24-508-3555   (SL)
REPROMATIC SYSTEMS INC
SHELLX COURIER
60 Pippin Rd Suite 34, Concord, ON, L4K 4M8
(905) 669-2900
Emp Here 25   *Sales* 11,087,250
SIC 7389 Business services, nec
Peter Shell
Miriam Shell

D-U-N-S 24-058-7162   (SL)
RI-GO LIFT TRUCK LIMITED
175 Courtland Ave, Concord, ON, L4K 4T2
(416) 213-7277
Emp Here 82   *Sales* 38,952,132
SIC 5084 Industrial machinery and equipment
Pat Diberto

D-U-N-S 24-013-7153   (HQ)
RIVERSIDE NATURAL FOODS LTD
2720 Steeles Ave W, Concord, ON, L4K 4S3
(416) 360-8200
Emp Here 30   *Sales* 69,138,000
SIC 2032 Canned specialties
Nima Fotovat
Sahba Fotovat
Salma Fotovat

D-U-N-S 24-418-0399   (SL)
RIVIERA PARQUE, BANQUET & CONVENTION CENTRE INC
2800 Highway 7 Suite 301, Concord, ON, L4K 1W8
(905) 669-4933
Emp Here 150   *Sales* 16,017,300
SIC 7299 Miscellaneous personal service
Danny Boni

D-U-N-S 20-219-0950   (HQ)
RLOGISTICS LIMITED PARTNERSHIP
FACTORY DIRECT COMPUTERS
501 Applewood Cres, Concord, ON, L4K 4J3
(905) 660-5030
Emp Here 50   *Sales* 58,674,660
SIC 5734 Computer and software stores
Jodie O'toole

D-U-N-S 24-793-0845   (SL)
ROBELY TRADING INC
20 Barnes Crt Suite H, Concord, ON, L4K 4L4
(905) 881-2222
Emp Here 24   *Sales* 12,212,544
SIC 5023 Homefurnishings
Robert Gabay
Ely Gabay

D-U-N-S 25-756-8170   (SL)
RONCO DISPOSABLE PRODUCTS LTD
RONCO PROTECTIVE PRODUCTS
70 Planchet Rd, Concord, ON, L4K 2C7
(905) 660-6700
Emp Here 62   *Sales* 32,273,604
SIC 5099 Durable goods, nec
Ron Pecchioli
Ivor Chan
Rami Mor
Mark Ray
Vani Kshattriya

D-U-N-S 24-783-9046   (SL)
ROSENBERG SMITH & PARTNERS LLP
2000 Steeles Ave W Unit 200, Concord, ON, L4K 3E9
(905) 660-3800
Emp Here 70   *Sales* 14,537,950
SIC 8721 Accounting, auditing, and bookkeeping
Norman Rosenberg
Perry Smith
David Colodny
Stephen Rosenberg
Henry Icyk
Ron Jenkins

D-U-N-S 24-796-2061   (HQ)
ROYAL ENVELOPE LTD
ROYAL DIGITAL
111 Jacob Keffer Pky, Concord, ON, L4K 4V1
(905) 879-0000
Emp Here 136   *Sales* 22,101,973
SIC 2677 Envelopes
Peter Bowles
Lucio Tucci

D-U-N-S 20-016-3637   (SL)
S & F FOOD IMPORTERS INC
565 Edgeley Blvd, Concord, ON, L4K 4G4
(416) 410-9091
Emp Here 40   *Sales* 33,423,080
SIC 5141 Groceries, general line
Sol Zeidman

D-U-N-S 24-688-9638   (SL)
SABRINA WHOLESALE FOODS INC
SABRINA FOODS
1950 Highway 7 Unit 18, Concord, ON, L4K 3P2
(416) 665-1533
Emp Here 21   *Sales* 17,547,117
SIC 5141 Groceries, general line
Philip Di Giammarino
Sabrina Critelli

D-U-N-S 20-056-3455   (SL)
SARTREX POWER CONTROL SYSTEMS INC
222 Snidercroft Rd Suite 2, Concord, ON, L4K 2K1
(905) 669-2278
Emp Here 49   *Sales* 12,571,538
SIC 3829 Measuring and controlling devices, nec
Jaidev Sarkar
Jessie Jimeno
Sharon Mcnelles

D-U-N-S 24-316-9059   (SL)
SAWILL LTD
J 2 PRODUCTS
54 Audia Crt Unit 2, Concord, ON, L4K 3N4
(905) 669-0341
Emp Here 104   *Sales* 61,272,536
SIC 5198 Paints, varnishes, and supplies
James Fernandopulle

Nanthini Fernandopulle

D-U-N-S 24-752-6692   (SL)
SCHAEFFER & ASSOCIATES LTD
SHAEFFERS CONSULTING ENGINEERS
6 Ronrose Dr Suite 100, Concord, ON, L4K 4R3
Emp Here 110   *Sales* 20,515,660
SIC 8742 Management consulting services
Allan Steedman
Zaven Sarkissian

D-U-N-S 24-556-9165   (SL)
SCHURE SPORTS INC
345 Connie Cres, Concord, ON, L4K 5R2
(905) 669-6021
Emp Here 21   *Sales* 10,464,762
SIC 5136 Men's and boy's clothing
Michael Schure
Hugh Schure

D-U-N-S 20-045-7067   (HQ)
SCINTREX LIMITED
222 Snidercroft Rd Suite 2, Concord, ON, L4K 2K1
(905) 669-2280
Sales 11,819,028
SIC 3829 Measuring and controlling devices, nec
Chris Nind
Fred Li

D-U-N-S 25-192-3645   (HQ)
SEASON TECHNOLOGY INC
PATRICK PLASTICS
18 Basaltic Rd Suite 1, Concord, ON, L4K 1G6
(905) 660-9066
Emp Here 4   *Sales* 12,828,100
SIC 3829 Measuring and controlling devices, nec
Anne Hung

D-U-N-S 24-991-4185   (SL)
SEENERGY FOODS LIMITED
475 North Rivermede Rd, Concord, ON, L4K 3N1
(905) 660-0041
Emp Here 80   *Sales* 27,655,200
SIC 2035 Pickles, sauces, and salad dressings
Shreyas Ajmera

D-U-N-S 24-891-4350   (HQ)
SELBA INDUSTRIES INC
3231 Langstaff Rd, Concord, ON, L4K 4L2
(905) 660-1614
Sales 17,313,300
SIC 2434 Wood kitchen cabinets
Marco Selvaggi
Danny Selvaggi
Marco Selvaggi
Allan Goldman
Carmen Franceschetti

D-U-N-S 25-731-0300   (HQ)
SERVICE EMPLOYEES INTERNATIONAL UNION LOCAL 204
ORGANIZING UNION LOCAL 204
2180 Steeles Ave W Suite 200, Concord, ON, L4K 2Z5
(905) 660-1800
Emp Here 30   *Sales* 23,154,550
SIC 8631 Labor organizations
Brad Philp
Allen Ferens

D-U-N-S 24-181-8459   (SL)
SEVEN VIEW PLYMOUTH CHRYSLER LTD
SEVEN VIEW CHRYSLER DODGE JEEP
2685 Highway 7, Concord, ON, L4K 1V8
(905) 669-5051
Emp Here 40   *Sales* 19,923,120
SIC 5511 New and used car dealers
Pasquale Magarelli
Domenic Matera

D-U-N-S 24-744-5752   (SL)

D-U-N-S 24-752-6692   (SL)
SHERLOCK RESOURCES INC
289 Bradwick Dr, Concord, ON, L4K 1K5
(905) 669-5888
Emp Here 50   *Sales* 20,967,750
SIC 6712 Bank holding companies
Anthony Derbedrosian

D-U-N-S 24-076-3409   (HQ)
SHERWOOD ELECTROMOTION INC
20 Barnes Crt Unit A-E, Concord, ON, L4K 4L4
(289) 695-5555
Sales 21,925,392
SIC 7694 Armature rewinding shops
George Gavrilidis

D-U-N-S 20-280-9745   (BR)
SIEMENS CANADA LIMITED
RUGGEDCOM SIEMENS
(*Suby of* SIEMENS AG)
300 Applewood Cres Suite 1, Concord, ON, L4K 5C7
(905) 856-5288
Emp Here 100
SIC 3625 Relays and industrial controls

D-U-N-S 24-325-4146   (HQ)
SKOR FOOD SERVICE LTD
COLABOR SKOR DISTRIBUTION
10 Ronrose Dr, Concord, ON, L4K 4R3
(905) 660-1212
Emp Here 1   *Sales* 93,173,080
SIC 5142 Packaged frozen goods
Gilles Lachance
Steven Corvese
Bryan Knebel

D-U-N-S 25-372-0361   (HQ)
SMARTCENTRES MANAGEMENT SERVICES INC
SMARTCENTRES REIT
(*Suby of* SMART MANAGEMENT LIMITED PARTNERSHIP II)
3200 Highway 7, Concord, ON, L4K 5Z5
(905) 326-6400
Emp Here 275   *Sales* 379,051,000
SIC 6512 Nonresidential building operators

D-U-N-S 20-175-6111   (HQ)
SMITH, J.D. & SONS LIMITED
180 Basaltic Rd, Concord, ON, L4K 1G6
(905) 669-8980
Emp Here 150   *Sales* 49,369,440
SIC 4225 General warehousing and storage
Scott Smith
Brian Smith
Brian Death

D-U-N-S 24-451-0558   (HQ)
SPECIALTY CARE INC
CEDARVALE LODGE/SWEETBRIAR LODGE
400 Applewood Cres Suite 110, Concord, ON, L4K 0C3
Emp Here 8   *Sales* 68,326,000
SIC 8051 Skilled nursing care facilities
Paula Jourdain
Antoine Jourdain
Raymond Jourdain

D-U-N-S 24-462-8061   (HQ)
SPIRAX SARCO CANADA LIMITED
SPIRAX SARCO
(*Suby of* SPIRAX-SARCO ENGINEERING PLC)
383 Applewood Cres, Concord, ON, L4K 4J3
(905) 660-5510
Emp Here 29   *Sales* 23,253,048
SIC 5075 Warm air heating and air conditioning
Mike Gillick
Andy Stewart
Gino Lepore

D-U-N-S 24-874-6281   (HQ)
ST. JOSEPH CORPORATION
50 Macintosh Blvd, Concord, ON, L4K 4P3

(905) 660-3111
Emp Here 450   *Sales* 387,548,000
SIC 2752 Commercial printing, lithographic
Anthony Gagliano
Frank Gagliano
Gaetano Gagliano
Rudy Desiago
Karen Hacker
Tom Weber

D-U-N-S 20-174-7169   (HQ)
ST. JOSEPH PRINTING LIMITED
ST JOSEPH COMMUNICATIONS
(*Suby of* ST. JOSEPH CORPORATION)
50 Macintosh Blvd, Concord, ON, L4K 4P3
(905) 660-3111
Emp Here 450   *Sales* 387,548,000
SIC 2752 Commercial printing, lithographic
Anthony Gagliano
Frank Gagliano
Mary Jane Deiana
Frances Colacci
Phil Van Schijndel
Kin-Man Lee
Michael Chase

D-U-N-S 24-392-1983   (HQ)
STAPLES PROMOTIONAL PRODUCTS CANADA, LTD
STAPLES PROMOTIONAL PRODUCTS
(*Suby of* SYCAMORE PARTNERS MANAGEMENT, L.P.)
55 Interchange Way Unit 4, Concord, ON, L4K 5W3
(905) 660-0685
Sales 13,987,950
SIC 8743 Public relations services
Jim Doris

D-U-N-S 24-162-0017   (SL)
STORECHECK -CONCORD
2180 Steeles Ave W, Concord, ON, L4K 2Z5
(905) 660-1334
Emp Here 20   *Sales* 13,806,833
SIC 6289 Security and commodity service
Joshua Gibbons

D-U-N-S 20-114-2903   (HQ)
STRADA AGGREGATES INC
30 Floral Pky Suite 400, Concord, ON, L4K 4R1
(905) 738-2200
Sales 11,179,350
SIC 5032 Brick, stone, and related material
Jim Degasperis

D-U-N-S 20-357-0952   (SL)
STRADA CRUSH LIMITED
STRADA CRUSH AGGREGATE PROCESSING
69 Connie Cres Suite 1, Concord, ON, L4K 1L3
(905) 303-6200
Emp Here 35   *Sales* 15,651,090
SIC 5032 Brick, stone, and related material
Jim Degasperis

D-U-N-S 25-360-3104   (BR)
SUNOPTA INC
SUNOPTA FOOD DISTRIBUTION GROUP
(*Suby of* SUNOPTA INC)
8755 Keele St, Concord, ON, L4K 2N1
(905) 738-4304
Emp Here 130
SIC 5149 Groceries and related products, nec
Don Rees

D-U-N-S 20-551-6503   (HQ)
SUNRISE MEDICAL CANADA INC
(*Suby of* V.S.M. INVESTORS, LLC)
237 Romina Dr Unit 3, Concord, ON, L4K 4V3
(905) 660-2459
Emp Here 41   *Sales* 27,302,952
SIC 5047 Medical and hospital equipment
Miachel Longo

D-U-N-S 20-291-5799   (BR)
SUPERIOR SEATING HOSPITALITY INC

(*Suby of* SUPERIOR SEATING HOSPITALITY INC)
9000 Keele St Unit 11, Concord, ON, L4K 0B3
(905) 738-7900
Emp Here 100
SIC 2599 Furniture and fixtures, nec
Frank Astone

D-U-N-S 20-291-5724   (HQ)
SUPERIOR SEATING HOSPITALITY INC
SUPERIOR FRAMES
9000 Keele St Unit 11, Concord, ON, L4K 0B3
(905) 738-7900
Emp Here 70   *Sales* 13,888,980
SIC 2599 Furniture and fixtures, nec
Enzo Astone
Frank Astone

D-U-N-S 20-700-7241   (BR)
SYSCO CANADA, INC
SYSCO FINE MEATS OF TORONTO
(*Suby of* SYSCO CORPORATION)
1400 Creditstone Rd Suite B, Concord, ON, L4K 0E2
(905) 760-7200
Emp Here 75
SIC 2011 Meat packing plants

D-U-N-S 25-978-4940   (SL)
T.A.C. CONTROLS & AUTOMATION INC
259 Edgeley Blvd Unit 5, Concord, ON, L4K 3Y5
(905) 660-0878
Emp Here 35   *Sales* 22,976,240
SIC 5962 Merchandising machine operators
Steven Martin
Timothy Scheepstra

D-U-N-S 20-943-3416   (SL)
TARGET INVESTIGATION & SECURITY LTD
2900 Langstaff Rd Unit 3, Concord, ON, L4K 4R9
(905) 760-9090
Emp Here 85   *Sales* 33,632,630
SIC 7381 Detective and armored car services
John Domonkos
Elizabeth Domonkos

D-U-N-S 24-915-2526   (SL)
TARGET VACATIONS
3175 Rutherford Rd Unit 55, Concord, ON, L4K 5Y6
(416) 687-5925
Emp Here 25   *Sales* 12,999,175
SIC 4724 Travel agencies
Jason Sarracini

D-U-N-S 20-304-7634   (SL)
TAS AVIATION INC
30 Moyal Crt, Concord, ON, L4K 4R8
(905) 669-4812
Emp Here 30   *Sales* 11,052,999
SIC 5013 Motor vehicle supplies and new parts
Aron Regev

D-U-N-S 24-924-0748   (HQ)
TECMOTIV CORPORATION
131 Saramia Cres 2nd Fl, Concord, ON, L4K 4P7
(905) 669-5911
Sales 14,894,654
SIC 3795 Tanks and tank components
Arthur Hayden
Sally Look Yan

D-U-N-S 24-126-5706   (BR)
TEKNION LIMITED
TEKNION FORM
(*Suby of* GLOBAL UPHOLSTERY CO LIMITED)
1400 Alness St Unit 12, Concord, ON, L4K 2W6
(905) 669-2035
Emp Here 120
SIC 2522 Office furniture, except wood
Mario Casullo

D-U-N-S 20-066-9492   (SL)

TESTON PIPELINES LIMITED
CLEARWAY GROUP
379 Bowes Rd, Concord, ON, L4K 1J1
(905) 761-6955
Emp Here 50   *Sales* 12,044,200
SIC 1623 Water, sewer, and utility lines
Laura Di Battista

D-U-N-S 24-977-2922   (SL)
THOMPSON, ROACH & HUGHES CONSULTING INC
T R H GROUP, THE
261 Millway Ave Unit 1, Concord, ON, L4K 4K9
(905) 669-9517
Emp Here 39   *Sales* 11,048,427
SIC 8741 Management services
Mark Hughes
Mark Hughes

D-U-N-S 20-755-6135   (SL)
THORNCRETE CONSTRUCTION LIMITED
381 Spinnaker Way, Concord, ON, L4K 4N4
(905) 669-6510
Emp Here 200   *Sales* 49,496,600
SIC 1771 Concrete work
Giavonni Ruscica
John Ruscica
Ross Ruscica

D-U-N-S 20-145-4311   (HQ)
THYSSENKRUPP MATERIALS CA, LTD
THYSSENKRUPP MATERIALS NA
(*Suby of* THYSSENKRUPP AG)
2821 Langstaff Rd, Concord, ON, L4K 5C6
(905) 669-0247
Emp Here 300   *Sales* 587,755,994
SIC 6221 Commodity contracts brokers, dealers
James Tatsakos
Norbert Goertz

D-U-N-S 20-983-6352   (HQ)
TOKMAKJIAN INC
CAN-AR COACH, DIV OF
(*Suby of* CAN-AR HOLDINGS CORP)
221 Caldari Rd, Concord, ON, L4K 3Z9
(905) 669-2850
Emp Here 100   *Sales* 19,674,900
SIC 4142 Bus charter service, except local
Cy Tokmakjian
Robert Duni
Ajay Mehra

D-U-N-S 24-017-7233   (SL)
TOLIN ENTERPRISES LTD
400 Creditstone Rd, Concord, ON, L4K 3Z3
(905) 669-2711
Emp Here 20   *Sales* 11,027,790
SIC 1522 Residential construction, nec
Anthony Gargaro

D-U-N-S 24-390-6992   (BR)
TOOTSIE ROLL OF CANADA ULC
CONCORD CONFECTIONS
(*Suby of* TOOTSIE ROLL INDUSTRIES, INC.)
519 North Rivermede Rd, Concord, ON, L4K 3N1
(905) 738-9108
Emp Here 300
SIC 2064 Candy and other confectionery products
Ljubo Stankovic

D-U-N-S 20-610-2923   (HQ)
TOOTSIE ROLL OF CANADA ULC
(*Suby of* TOOTSIE ROLL INDUSTRIES, INC.)
345 Courtland Ave, Concord, ON, L4K 5A6
(905) 660-8989
Emp Here 2   *Sales* 215,014,800
SIC 5145 Confectionery
Ellen Gordon
Joe Zerafa
Melvin Gordon

D-U-N-S 24-953-0759   (SL)
TORBRIDGE CONSTRUCTION LTD
3300 Highway 7 Suite 803, Concord, ON, L4K

4M3
Emp Here 50   *Sales* 14,414,626
SIC 1611 Highway and street construction
Carmine Giardino
Daniel Giardino

D-U-N-S 20-311-7452   (SL)
TORCAN LIFT EQUIPMENT LTD
166 Bowes Rd, Concord, ON, L4K 1J6
(905) 760-1582
Emp Here 30   *Sales* 14,250,780
SIC 5084 Industrial machinery and equipment
Joe Picao

D-U-N-S 25-531-4320   (SL)
TORO ALUMINUM
330 Applewood Cres, Concord, ON, L4K 4V2
(905) 738-5220
Emp Here 300   *Sales* 72,969,300
SIC 3442 Metal doors, sash, and trim
Gianfranco Di Marco

D-U-N-S 25-989-4004   (HQ)
TOROMONT ENERGY LTD
(*Suby of* TOROMONT INDUSTRIES LTD)
3131 Highway 7 Suite A, Concord, ON, L4K 5E1
(416) 667-5758
Emp Here 24   *Sales* 15,665,350
SIC 4911 Electric services
Robert M Ogilvie

D-U-N-S 25-317-4056   (BR)
TOROMONT INDUSTRIES LTD
TOROMONT REMAN
(*Suby of* TOROMONT INDUSTRIES LTD)
548 Edgeley Blvd, Concord, ON, L4K 4G4
(416) 667-5900
Emp Here 150
SIC 5082 Construction and mining machinery
Joel Couture

D-U-N-S 20-408-3877   (HQ)
TOROMONT INDUSTRIES LTD
TOROMONT CAT, DIV OF
3131 Highway 7 Suite A, Concord, ON, L4K 5E1
(416) 667-5511
Emp Here 850   *Sales* 2,656,568,320
SIC 5082 Construction and mining machinery
Scott J. Medhurst
Paul Jewer
Michael Cuddy
Jennifer Cochrane
Lynn M. Korbak
Robert Ogilvie
Wayne Hill
Robert Franklin
Jeffrey Chisholm
Cathryn Cranston

D-U-N-S 24-537-7122   (HQ)
TORONTO REDI MIX LIMITED
(*Suby of* G & L GROUP LTD)
401 Bowes Rd, Concord, ON, L4K 1J4
(416) 798-7060
Sales 17,507,625
SIC 3273 Ready-mixed concrete
Joe Lamana

D-U-N-S 25-991-5924   (SL)
TORONTO SKY AVIATION INC
30 Rayette Rd, Concord, ON, L4K 2G3
(905) 760-0731
Emp Here 43   *Sales* 13,964,422
SIC 4581 Airports, flying fields, and services
Mike Cean

D-U-N-S 20-045-8370   (SL)
TORONTO ZENITH CONTRACTING LIMITED
226 Bradwick Dr Unit 1, Concord, ON, L4K 1K8
(905) 738-1500
Emp Here 50   *Sales* 12,044,200
SIC 1622 Bridge, tunnel, and elevated highway construction

Aldo Paganelli

D-U-N-S 20-302-2785 (SL)
TORQUE BUILDERS INC
TORQUE
72 Corstate Ave, Concord, ON, L4K 4X2
(905) 660-3334
Emp Here 24 *Sales* 11,297,544
SIC 1542 Nonresidential construction, nec
Danny Battista

D-U-N-S 24-387-0511 (SL)
TOTAL RETURN SOLUTIONS CORP
51 Graniteridge Rd, Concord, ON, L4K 5M9
(905) 761-6835
Emp Here 50 *Sales* 25,998,350
SIC 4731 Freight transportation arrangement
Ernesto Falbo
Dave Falbo

D-U-N-S 25-687-0858 (HQ)
TOTALLY ONE COMMUNICATIONS INC
BELL MOBILITY
60 Saramia Cres Suite 3, Concord, ON, L4K 4J7
(905) 761-1331
Emp Here 8 *Sales* 11,070,400
SIC 5999 Miscellaneous retail stores, nec
Dina Arduini

D-U-N-S 24-450-8503 (HQ)
TOYS 'R' US (CANADA) LTD
(*Suby of* FAIRFAX FINANCIAL HOLDINGS LIMITED)
2777 Langstaff Rd, Concord, ON, L4K 4M5
(905) 660-2000
Emp Here 192 *Sales* 688,447,287
SIC 5945 Hobby, toy, and game shops
Melanie Teed-Murch
Robert Zara
Pasquale Naccarato

D-U-N-S 24-000-6473 (SL)
TRADEMARK TOOLS INC
21 Staffern Dr, Concord, ON, L4K 2X2
(905) 532-0442
Emp Here 40 *Sales* 17,886,960
SIC 5072 Hardware
Shlomo Bohbot

D-U-N-S 24-888-6327 (SL)
TRANS POWER UTILITY CONTRACTORS INC
TRANS POWER
(*Suby of* TACC CONSTRUCTION CO. LTD)
585 Applewood Cres, Concord, ON, L4K 5V7
(905) 660-9764
Emp Here 140 *Sales* 45,936,100
SIC 1623 Water, sewer, and utility lines
Frank Mongillo
Simone Degasperis

D-U-N-S 24-195-0054 (SL)
TRANS-ONTARIO CEILING & WALL SYSTEMS INC
231 Millway Ave Unit 11, Concord, ON, L4K 3W7
(905) 669-0666
Emp Here 100 *Sales* 16,238,100
SIC 1742 Plastering, drywall, and insulation
Robert Arbour

D-U-N-S 24-309-0532 (SL)
TRANSAM CARRIERS INC
205 Doney Cres, Concord, ON, L4K 1P6
(416) 907-8101
Emp Here 150 *Sales* 30,855,900
SIC 4213 Trucking, except local
Dimitri Protas

D-U-N-S 20-555-2466 (SL)
TRANSFACTOR INDUSTRIES INC
REX POWER MAGNETICS
65 Basaltic Rd, Concord, ON, L4K 1G4
(905) 695-8844
Emp Here 280 *Sales* 46,244,618
SIC 3612 Transformers, except electric
Anneliese Viveiros

Levon Hasserjian
Simon Hasserjian

D-U-N-S 20-211-1501 (HQ)
TRILLIANT ENERGY SERVICES INC
(*Suby of* TRILLIANT NETWORKS INC.)
20 Floral Pky, Concord, ON, L4K 4R1
(905) 669-6223
Emp Here 30 *Sales* 82,311,000
SIC 3825 Instruments to measure electricity
William Vogel
Susanna Kass

D-U-N-S 25-104-5514 (HQ)
TRILLIANT HOLDINGS (ONTARIO) INC
(*Suby of* TRILLIANT NETWORKS INC.)
20 Floral Pky, Concord, ON, L4K 4R1
(905) 669-6223
Emp Here 1 *Sales* 137,185,000
SIC 3825 Instruments to measure electricity
William Vogel

D-U-N-S 20-052-6361 (HQ)
TWD ROADS MANAGEMENT INC
(*Suby of* CARILLION GB LIMITED)
7077 Keele St Suite 100, Concord, ON, L4K 0B6
(905) 532-5200
Emp Here 10 *Sales* 131,246,000
SIC 1611 Highway and street construction
Paul Quinless

D-U-N-S 24-486-8758 (HQ)
TYCO SAFETY PRODUCTS CANADA LTD
DIGITAL SECURITY CONTROLS
(*Suby of* JOHNSON CONTROLS INTERNATIONAL PLC)
3301 Langstaff Rd, Concord, ON, L4K 4L2
(905) 760-3000
Emp Here 300 *Sales* 367,789,500
SIC 3699 Electrical equipment and supplies, nec
Miguel Gutierrez

D-U-N-S 24-575-8909 (HQ)
U-BUY DISCOUNT FOODS LIMITED
WORLDWIDE DISTRIBUTORS
8811 Keele St, Concord, ON, L4K 2N1
(905) 669-8002
Emp Here 296 *Sales* 62,495,234
SIC 5141 Groceries, general line
Marshall Usher
Lauren Alto
Leonard Usher
Joel Usher
David Reid

D-U-N-S 24-422-5855 (HQ)
UNFI CANADA, INC
AUX MILLE ET UNE SAISONS
(*Suby of* UNITED NATURAL FOODS, INC.)
8755 Keele St, Concord, ON, L4K 2N1
(905) 738-4204
Emp Here 1 *Sales* 21,725,002
SIC 5149 Groceries and related products, nec
Peter Brennan
Joseph J. Traficanti
Michael Zechmeister
Michael Shirley
Eric A. Dorne

D-U-N-S 25-361-3467 (BR)
UNFI CANADA, INC
UNFI CANADA GROCERY CENTRAL
(*Suby of* UNITED NATURAL FOODS, INC.)
8755 Keele St, Concord, ON, L4K 2N1
(905) 738-4204
Emp Here 105
SIC 5149 Groceries and related products, nec
Don Rees

D-U-N-S 24-889-7811 (SL)
UNICO INC
(*Suby of* SUN-BRITE FOODS INC)
8000 Keele St, Concord, ON, L4K 2A4
(905) 669-9633
Emp Here 60 *Sales* 43,002,960

SIC 5141 Groceries, general line
John Iacobelli
Henry Iacobelli
John Porco

D-U-N-S 20-514-5431 (SL)
UNIQUE BROADBAND SYSTEMS LTD
400 Spinnaker Way Suite 1, Concord, ON, L4K 5Y9
(905) 669-8533
Emp Here 85 *Sales* 19,420,120
SIC 4813 Telephone communication, except radio
David Dane
Arthur Markaryan
Karen Safaryan
Anatoly Oxrud
Eric Rouah

D-U-N-S 24-424-1261 (SL)
UNIQUE STORE FIXTURES LTD
SIGNATURE SHOWCASE DIV
554 Millway Ave, Concord, ON, L4K 3V5
(905) 738-6588
Emp Here 65 *Sales* 10,030,930
SIC 2541 Wood partitions and fixtures
Ferruccio Corrente
Marlene Corrente

D-U-N-S 20-719-2670 (SL)
UNITEC WELDING ALLOYS
61 Villarboit Cres, Concord, ON, L4K 4R2
(905) 669-4249
Emp Here 70 *Sales* 33,251,820
SIC 5084 Industrial machinery and equipment
Steve Hertzog

D-U-N-S 24-924-7255 (BR)
UNITED PARCEL SERVICE CANADA LTD
UPS CANADA
(*Suby of* UNITED PARCEL SERVICE, INC.)
2900 Steeles Ave W, Concord, ON, L4K 3S2
(800) 742-5877
Emp Here 120
SIC 4212 Local trucking, without storage
Michael Chabot

D-U-N-S 20-734-3539 (BR)
UPS SCS INC
UPS SCS, INC
(*Suby of* UNITED PARCEL SERVICE, INC.)
777 Creditstone Rd, Concord, ON, L4K 5R5
(905) 660-6040
Emp Here 100
SIC 7389 Business services, nec
William Hook

D-U-N-S 24-220-1044 (HQ)
UTIL CANADA LIMITED
(*Suby of* B&D HOLDING SPA)
270 Spinnaker Way Suite 13, Concord, ON, L4K 4W1
(905) 760-8088
Sales 85,130,850
SIC 3469 Metal stampings, nec
Franco Degennaro
Christopher Dohle
Rod Engeland

D-U-N-S 20-191-6371 (SL)
VASTLON INVESTMENTS INC
291 Edgeley Blvd, Concord, ON, L4K 3Z4
(905) 660-9900
Emp Here 30 *Sales* 12,580,650
SIC 6712 Bank holding companies
Irene Pantalone
Charles Lee

D-U-N-S 24-827-7493 (SL)
VAUGHAN MASONRY INC
111 Ortona Crt, Concord, ON, L4K 3M3
(905) 669-6825
Emp Here 100 *Sales* 16,238,100
SIC 1741 Masonry and other stonework
Pia Famiglietti

D-U-N-S 24-849-5921 (SL)
VAUGHAN PAVING LTD

(*Suby of* VAUGHAN PAVING HOLDINGS CO. LTD)
220 Basaltic Rd, Concord, ON, L4K 1G6
(905) 669-9579
Emp Here 56 *Sales* 14,136,752
SIC 1611 Highway and street construction
Lorenzo Antonini

D-U-N-S 20-105-0882 (SL)
VEGEWAX CANDLEWORX LTD
SCENTS ALIVE
300 North Rivermede Rd, Concord, ON, L4K 3N6
(905) 760-7944
Emp Here 60 *Sales* 13,833,000
SIC 2844 Toilet preparations
Ravi Shah
Suvil Parikh
Laura Sinclair

D-U-N-S 24-846-0214 (SL)
VELANOFF, JACK HOLDINGS LIMITED
CANADIAN TIRE
3200 Rutherford Rd Suite 653, Concord, ON, L4K 5R3
(905) 303-9148
Emp Here 150 *Sales* 40,147,800
SIC 5251 Hardware stores
Jack Velanoff

D-U-N-S 20-716-8915 (SL)
VICTOR CUSTOM QUALITY MEATS LTD
VICTOR MEATS
101 Citation Dr Unit 14, Concord, ON, L4K 2S4

Emp Here 51 *Sales* 42,614,427
SIC 5142 Packaged frozen goods
Ross Macleod
Richard Forrest

D-U-N-S 25-341-7455 (SL)
VILLA DI MANNO BAKERY LTD
22 Buttermill Ave, Concord, ON, L4K 3X4
(905) 761-9191
Emp Here 67 *Sales* 23,161,230
SIC 2051 Bread, cake, and related products
Joe Di Manno

D-U-N-S 25-094-6808 (BR)
VINNIE ZUCCHINI'S CORPORATION
9100 Jane St Bldg G Unit 48, Concord, ON, L4K 0A4
(905) 761-1361
Emp Here 120
SIC 5812 Eating places
Mark Zawistowski

D-U-N-S 20-808-8422 (SL)
VINYLBILT GROUP INC
VINYLBILT WINDOWS
3333 Langstaff Rd Suite 1, Concord, ON, L4K 5A8
(905) 669-1200
Emp Here 180 *Sales* 34,626,600
SIC 2431 Millwork
Antonio Colalillo

D-U-N-S 20-713-7472 (HQ)
VITRAN EXPRESS CANADA INC
(*Suby of* TFI INTERNATIONAL INC)
1201 Creditstone Rd, Concord, ON, L4K 0C2
(416) 798-4965
Emp Here 200 *Sales* 136,257,559
SIC 4213 Trucking, except local
Tony Trichilo
Kelvin Kwan

D-U-N-S 24-024-7890 (SL)
VITULLO BROS. PLUMBING CO. LTD
121 Bradwick Dr Unit 3, Concord, ON, L4K 1K5
(905) 669-2843
Emp Here 70 *Sales* 16,314,550
SIC 1711 Plumbing, heating, air-conditioning
Goffredo Vitullo
Vincent Vitullo

D-U-N-S 20-117-8832 (HQ)

VLR FOOD CORPORATION
TRANSCONTINENTAL GOURMET FOODS
575 Oster Lane, Concord, ON, L4K 2B9
(905) 669-0700
Emp Here 220
SIC 2038 Frozen specialties, nec
 Rhys Quin
 Carl Bauernfreund

D-U-N-S 25-498-2507   (BR)
WAL-MART CANADA CORP
(*Suby of* WALMART INC.)
101 Edgeley Blvd Suite 3145, Concord, ON,
L4K 4Z4
(905) 761-7945
Emp Here 400
SIC 5311 Department stores
 Leonardo Lewis

D-U-N-S 20-296-5349   (SL)
WARE MALCOMB INC
80 Bass Pro Mills Dr Unit 1, Concord, ON, L4K
5W9
(905) 760-1221
Emp Here 49   *Sales* 21,731,010
SIC 7389 Business services, nec
 Deidre Small

D-U-N-S 20-329-5626   (SL)
WARREN AUTOMOTIVE DE MEXICO
401 Spinnaker Way, Concord, ON, L4K 4N4

Emp Here 100   *Sales* 36,421,500
SIC 5015 Motor vehicle parts, used
 Ian Higgins

D-U-N-S 24-859-5720   (HQ)
WARREN INDUSTRIES LTD
401 Spinnaker Way, Concord, ON, L4K 4N4
(905) 669-1260
Sales 121,615,500
SIC 3465 Automotive stampings
 David Freedman

D-U-N-S 20-260-5689   (HQ)
WASTE CONNECTIONS OF CANADA INC
BFI CANADA
(*Suby of* WASTE CONNECTIONS, INC.)
610 Applewood Cres, Concord, ON, L4K 0E3
(905) 532-7510
Emp Here 70   *Sales* 869,677,740
SIC 4953 Refuse systems
 Domenico Pio
 Steven F. Bouck
 Patrick J. Shea
 Ronald J. Mittelstaedt
 Worthing F. Jackman

D-U-N-S 25-362-8093   (BR)
**WASTE MANAGEMENT OF CANADA COR-
PORATION**
(*Suby of* WASTE MANAGEMENT, INC.)
550 Bowes Rd, Concord, ON, L4K 1K2
(905) 669-7196
Emp Here 80
SIC 4953 Refuse systems
 John Murray

D-U-N-S 20-179-3713   (BR)
WELDED TUBE OF CANADA CORP
(*Suby of* WELDED TUBE OF CANADA
CORP)
541 Bowes Rd, Concord, ON, L4K 1J5
(905) 669-1111
Emp Here 150
SIC 3317 Steel pipe and tubes
 Robert Pike

D-U-N-S 20-629-0827   (HQ)
WELDED TUBE OF CANADA CORP
111 Rayette Rd, Concord, ON, L4K 2E9
(905) 669-1111
Emp Here 350   *Sales* 244,304,400
SIC 3312 Blast furnaces and steel mills
 Barry Sonshine
 Robert Mandel
 Robert Pike
 Joseph Alexandre

 Donna Frost

D-U-N-S 24-968-1297   (HQ)
WESTERN CANADA EXPRESS INC
62 Administration Rd, Concord, ON, L4K 2R7
(905) 738-2106
Emp Here 17   *Sales* 53,351,360
SIC 4731 Freight transportation arrangement
 Elmer Schwarz
 Donald S. Reimer

D-U-N-S 24-450-8453   (SL)
WESTON CONSULTING GROUP INC
WESTON CONSULTING
201 Millway Ave Unit 19, Concord, ON, L4K
5K8
(905) 738-8080
Emp Here 45   *Sales* 10,705,545
SIC 8742 Management consulting services
 Peter Weston
 Mark Emery

D-U-N-S 20-811-1620   (SL)
WHOLESALE TIRE DISTRIBUTORS INC
(*Suby of* ATD CORPORATION)
35 Citron Crt, Concord, ON, L4K 2S7
(905) 882-6797
Emp Here 32   *Sales* 11,654,880
SIC 5014 Tires and tubes
 Allan Bishop

D-U-N-S 20-391-8404   (BR)
WHOLESOME HARVEST BAKING LTD
(*Suby of* WHOLESOME HARVEST BAKING
LTD)
144 Viceroy Rd, Concord, ON, L4K 2L8
(905) 738-1242
Emp Here 200
SIC 2051 Bread, cake, and related products
 Sharon Mcnamara

D-U-N-S 20-184-3414   (SL)
WIETZES MOTORS LIMITED
WIETZES TOYOTA
7080 Dufferin St, Concord, ON, L4K 0A1
(905) 761-5133
Emp Here 65   *Sales* 40,903,200
SIC 5511 New and used car dealers
 Albert Wietzes
 Egbert Wietzes

D-U-N-S 20-129-4691   (HQ)
**WIKOFF   COLOR   CORPORATION -
CANADA INC**
(*Suby of* WIKOFF COLOR CORPORATION)
475 Bowes Rd, Concord, ON, L4K 1J5
(905) 669-1311
Sales 21,301,575
SIC 2893 Printing ink
 Geoffrey A Peters
 Martin Roberts Hambrock
 Marione B Rorie

D-U-N-S 25-934-5023   (HQ)
WINDSPEC INC
1310 Creditstone Rd, Concord, ON, L4K 5T7
(905) 738-8311
Sales 10,141,500
SIC 3444 Sheet Metalwork
 John Anava

D-U-N-S 24-987-1559   (HQ)
WORLD AVIATION CORP
45 Corstate Ave, Concord, ON, L4K 4Y2
(905) 660-4462
Sales 10,001,056
SIC 7694 Armature rewinding shops

D-U-N-S 20-158-2723   (SL)
WORLD FAMOUS SALES OF CANADA INC
333 Confederation Pky Suite 1, Concord, ON,
L4K 4S1
(905) 738-4777
Emp Here 35   *Sales* 18,218,970
SIC 5091 Sporting and recreation goods
 Efram Mucher
 Michael Mucher
 Ian Mucher

D-U-N-S 20-412-9035   (SL)
YORK DISPOSAL SERVICE LIMITED
650 Creditstone Rd, Concord, ON, L4K 5C8
(905) 669-1900
Emp Here 60   *Sales* 15,427,860
SIC 4953 Refuse systems
 Armando Lecce
 Vincent Lecce

D-U-N-S 20-281-3069   (SL)
YUKON COR CORPORATION
30 Pennsylvania Ave Unit 17a, Concord, ON,
L4K 4A5

Emp Here 120   *Sales* 29,697,960
SIC 1771 Concrete work
 Oreste Perruzza
 Gabriele Cortellucci

D-U-N-S 24-514-3631   (SL)
ZAVIDA COFFEE COMPANY INC
70 Connie Cres Unit 12, Concord, ON, L4K
1L6
(905) 738-0103
Emp Here 50   *Sales* 41,778,850
SIC 5149 Groceries and related products, nec
 Charles Litterst

D-U-N-S 24-199-1645   (SL)
ZENTIL, D. MECHANICAL INC
633 Edgeley Blvd, Concord, ON, L4K 4H6
(905) 738-0569
Emp Here 75   *Sales* 17,479,875
SIC 1711 Plumbing, heating, air-conditioning
 Valerio Nonis
 Richard Zentil
 Mark Zentil
 Michael Zentil

Coniston, ON P0M

D-U-N-S 20-979-9485   (SL)
LOPES LIMITED
LOPES MECHANICAL & ELECTRICAL
84 Smelter Rd, Coniston, ON, P0M 1M0
(705) 694-4713
Emp Here 110   *Sales* 25,637,150
SIC 1711 Plumbing, heating, air-conditioning
 Felix Jr Lopes
 Noella Guy

Cookstown, ON L0L

D-U-N-S 24-735-9672   (SL)
COOKSTOWN AUTO CENTRE LTD
5046 5th, Cookstown, ON, L0L 1L0
(416) 364-0743
Emp Here 29   *Sales* 15,095,718
SIC 5093 Scrap and waste materials

D-U-N-S 25-318-1895   (BR)
**MCDONALD'S   RESTAURANTS   OF
CANADA LIMITED**
MCDONALD'S
(*Suby of* MCDONALD'S CORPORATION)
3464 County Rd 89, Cookstown, ON, L0L 1L0

Emp Here 100
SIC 5812 Eating places

D-U-N-S 25-457-7240   (SL)
RESFORM CONSTRUCTION LTD
3761 County Rd 89, Cookstown, ON, L0L 1L0
(705) 458-0600
Emp Here 300   *Sales* 70,652,700
SIC 1771 Concrete work
 Paul Gorrie

D-U-N-S 24-951-9729   (SL)
WHITE VEAL MEAT PACKERS LTD
5136 9th Line, Cookstown, ON, L0L 1L0

(416) 745-7448
Emp Here 25   *Sales* 20,889,425
SIC 5147 Meats and meat products
 Robert Tomassetti

Corbeil, ON P0H

D-U-N-S 20-880-0375   (SL)
913096 ONTARIO LIMITED
NIPISSING MANOR
1202 94 Hwy, Corbeil, ON, P0H 1K0
(705) 752-1100
Emp Here 110   *Sales* 7,542,260
SIC 8051 Skilled nursing care facilities
 Wayne Graham
 Carrol Graham

Cornwall, ON K6H

D-U-N-S 25-138-5266   (SL)
1808963 ONTARIO INC
1495 Gerald St, Cornwall, ON, K6H 7G8
(613) 932-5326
Emp Here 91   *Sales* 3,659,019
SIC 7349 Building maintenance services, nec
 Jean Cardinal
 Alain Gerald Vachon

D-U-N-S 24-802-3582   (SL)
837705 ONTARIO LTD
JEAN COUTU
5 Ninth St E, Cornwall, ON, K6H 6R3
(613) 938-7339
Emp Here 50   *Sales* 12,647,700
SIC 5912 Drug stores and proprietary stores
 Paul Trottier

D-U-N-S 20-420-8755   (SL)
AMSTERDAM PRODUCTS LTD
(*Suby of* TAYLOR CORPORATION)
2 Montreal Rd, Cornwall, ON, K6H 6L4
(613) 933-7393
Emp Here 80   *Sales* 53,512,640
SIC 7389 Business services, nec
 Travis Seward
 Kim Broadhead

D-U-N-S 20-544-4875   (SL)
BAXTROM INDEPENDENT GROCERY
31 Ninth St E, Cornwall, ON, K6H 6R3
(613) 938-8040
Emp Here 49   *Sales* 13,433,448
SIC 5411 Grocery stores
 Jorde Hess

D-U-N-S 24-100-2245   (HQ)
BENSON GROUP INC
AUTO-PAK
700 Education Rd, Cornwall, ON, K6H 6B8
(613) 933-1700
Emp Here 50   *Sales* 415,038,600
SIC 5013 Motor vehicle supplies and new
parts
 Martin Benson
 James Benson
 Gerald Benson
 Denis Mathieu
 Gary O'connor

D-U-N-S 25-957-8862   (BR)
**CANADIAN CORPS OF COMMISSION-
AIRES NATIONAL OFFICE, THE**
COMMISSIONAIRES, THE
(*Suby of* CANADIAN CORPS OF COMMIS-
SIONAIRES NATIONAL OFFICE, THE)
14 Third St E, Cornwall, ON, K6H 2C7
(613) 932-2594
Emp Here 110
SIC 7381 Detective and armored car services
 Francico Aroz

D-U-N-S 20-557-9951   (BR)

▲ Public Company   ■ Public Company Family Member   **HQ** Headquarters   **BR** Branch   **SL** Single Location

CANADIAN RED CROSS SOCIETY, THE
(*Suby of* CANADIAN RED CROSS SOCIETY, THE)
165 Montreal Rd, Cornwall, ON, K6H 1B2

Emp Here 95
SIC 8059 Nursing and personal care, nec
Marilyn Stewart

D-U-N-S 24-270-3171   (SL)
CHILDRENS AID SOCIETY UNITED COUNTIES STORMONT, DUNDAS & GLENGARRY
150 Boundary Rd, Cornwall, ON, K6H 6J5
(613) 933-2292
Emp Here 150   *Sales* 11,518,800
SIC 8322 Individual and family services
Rachel Daignault
Ronald Samson

D-U-N-S 24-975-3088   (BR)
CONSEIL SCOLAIRE DE DISTRICT CATHOLIQUE DE L'EST ONTARIEN
ECOLE SECONDAIRE CATHOLIQUE LA CITADELLE
(*Suby of* CONSEIL SCOLAIRE DE DISTRICT CATHOLIQUE DE L'EST ONTARIEN)
510 Mcconnell Ave, Cornwall, ON, K6H 4M1
(613) 933-0172
Emp Here 90
SIC 8211 Elementary and secondary schools
Tim Charron

D-U-N-S 20-650-8868   (HQ)
CORNWALL COMMUNITY HOSPITAL
840 Mcconnell Ave, Cornwall, ON, K6H 5S5
(613) 938-4240
Sales 150,166,000
SIC 8062 General medical and surgical hospitals
Helen Periard
Thomas Baitz
Dany Tombler
Louis Tremblay
Michael Turcotte
Nicholas Vlachollas
Jennifer Burke
Jean Dugay
Lorna Grant
Thomas Heard

D-U-N-S 20-043-0940   (SL)
CORNWALL FRUIT SUPPLY LIMITED
CORNWALL FRUIT
1424 Lascelle Ave, Cornwall, ON, K6H 3L2

Emp Here 20   *Sales* 10,702,480
SIC 5141 Groceries, general line
Gerald Desjardins
Charles Desjardins

D-U-N-S 20-043-1096   (SL)
CORNWALL STREET RAILWAY LIGHT AND POWER COMPANY LIMITED
CORNWALL ELECTRIC
(*Suby of* FORTIS INC)
1001 Sydney St, Cornwall, ON, K6H 3K1
(613) 932-0123
Emp Here 66   *Sales* 44,871,684
SIC 4911 Electric services
Mardon Erbland
Timothy Curtis
Fred O'brien

D-U-N-S 24-986-2418   (HQ)
DYER ROAD LEASING LTD
VILLENEUVE TANK LINES
850 Education Rd, Cornwall, ON, K6H 6B8
(613) 932-8038
Emp Here 52   *Sales* 16,867,892
SIC 4212 Local trucking, without storage
George Villeneuve

D-U-N-S 20-043-1682   (SL)
EMARD BROS. LUMBER CO. LTD
840 Tenth St E, Cornwall, ON, K6H 7S2
(613) 932-5660
Emp Here 50   *Sales* 12,652,950

SIC 5211 Lumber and other building materials
Maurice Emard
Chris Emard
Andrew Emard

D-U-N-S 25-767-9514   (BR)
FARM BOY COMPANY INC
FARM BOY FRESH MARKETS
814 Sydney St, Cornwall, ON, K6H 3J8
(613) 938-8566
Emp Here 109
SIC 5431 Fruit and vegetable markets
Marc Renaud

D-U-N-S 20-890-6560   (SL)
GLEN STOR DUN LODGE FOUNDATION
1900 Montreal Rd, Cornwall, ON, K6H 7L1
(613) 933-3384
Emp Here 155   *Sales* 9,963,710
SIC 8361 Residential care
Norm Quenneville

D-U-N-S 25-357-3539   (BR)
INDUSTRIES DOREL INC, LES
DOREL INDUSTRIES INC
(*Suby of* INDUSTRIES DOREL INC, LES)
3305 Loyalist St, Cornwall, ON, K6H 6W6
(613) 937-0711
Emp Here 350
SIC 2511 Wood household furniture
Barry Blidner

D-U-N-S 20-893-8456   (HQ)
K.F.S. LIMITED
MOE'S MENS WEAR
27 First St E, Cornwall, ON, K6H 1K5
(613) 933-7110
Emp Here 14   *Sales* 38,027,000
SIC 5311 Department stores
Kenny Langburt

D-U-N-S 24-760-6689   (SL)
M.P.I.Q.C. INC
550 Campbell St, Cornwall, ON, K6H 6T7
(613) 936-2000
Emp Here 61   *Sales* 11,616,962
SIC 3679 Electronic components, nec
Manuel Gelerman
Claude Girard

D-U-N-S 25-672-3248   (BR)
METRO ONTARIO INC
METRO
(*Suby of* METRO INC)
1315 Second St E, Cornwall, ON, K6H 7C4
(613) 932-0514
Emp Here 80
SIC 5411 Grocery stores
Pat Rennick

D-U-N-S 20-002-9549   (SL)
MISTEREL INC
CANADIAN TIRE ASSOCIATE STORE, DIV OF
201 Ninth St E, Cornwall, ON, K6H 2V1
(613) 933-0592
Emp Here 50   *Sales* 12,652,950
SIC 5251 Hardware stores
James Lavigne

D-U-N-S 20-507-2614   (HQ)
MORBERN INC
INTERNATIONAL KNITTING MILLS, DIV OF
80 Boundary Rd, Cornwall, ON, K6H 6M1
(613) 932-8811
Emp Here 325   *Sales* 94,601,200
SIC 2295 Coated fabrics, not rubberized
David Bloomfield
Eric Lamontagne
Jean-Claude Chabut
Mark Bloomfield

D-U-N-S 20-441-3520   (HQ)
NATHAR LIMITED
KASTNERS, DIV OF
27 First St E, Cornwall, ON, K6H 1K5
(613) 932-8854
Emp Here 20   *Sales* 17,939,600

SIC 5611 Men's and boys' clothing stores
Michael Langburt
Kenny Langburt
Glen Langburt
Ahron Langburt

D-U-N-S 25-971-6280   (BR)
NAV CANADA
NAV CENTRE
(*Suby of* NAV CANADA)
1950 Montreal Rd, Cornwall, ON, K6H 6L2
(613) 936-5050
Emp Here 210
SIC 8249 Vocational schools, nec
Cynthia Marino

D-U-N-S 20-746-6467   (SL)
NORBRO HOLDINGS LTD
BEST WESTERN PARKWAY INN
1515 Vincent Massey Dr, Cornwall, ON, K6H 5R6
(613) 932-0451
Emp Here 95   *Sales* 9,015,405
SIC 7011 Hotels and motels
Paul Lefebvre
Florien Couture

D-U-N-S 20-114-3984   (SL)
NOTMAN MOTOR SALES LTD
NOTMAN CHRYSLER DODGE JEEP
2205 Vincent Massey Dr, Cornwall, ON, K6H 5R6
(613) 938-0934
Emp Here 27   *Sales* 13,448,106
SIC 5511 New and used car dealers
John Notman

D-U-N-S 24-852-8007   (BR)
OTTAWA-CARLETON ASSOCIATION FOR PERSONS WITH DEVELOPMENTAL DISABILITIES
OPEN HANDS
(*Suby of* OTTAWA-CARLETON ASSOCIATION FOR PERSONS WITH DEVELOPMENTAL DISABILITIES)
1141 Sydney St Unit 1, Cornwall, ON, K6H 7C2
(613) 933-9520
Emp Here 100
SIC 8322 Individual and family services
Reg Bonvie

D-U-N-S 24-588-9860   (SL)
ROSE MECHANICAL LTD
18060 Glen Rd, Cornwall, ON, K6H 5T1
(613) 938-9867
Emp Here 100   *Sales* 23,306,500
SIC 1711 Plumbing, heating, air-conditioning
Gerard Rose
Raymond Lalonde

D-U-N-S 24-848-4628   (SL)
SEAWAY YARNS LIMITED
3320 Loyalist St, Cornwall, ON, K6H 6C8
(613) 933-2770
Emp Here 70   *Sales* 12,838,210
SIC 2299 Textile goods, nec
Joseph Ariagno
Mae Ariagno
Robert Ariagno
Donald Ariagno

D-U-N-S 25-976-4736   (SL)
SIGMAPOINT TECHNOLOGIES INC
2880 Marleau Ave, Cornwall, ON, K6H 6B5
(613) 937-4462
Emp Here 290   *Sales* 82,045,350
SIC 3672 Printed circuit boards
Dan Bergeron
Tom Kaneb
Stephane Debreuil
Steve Blouin
Gizanne Lafrance-Allaire
Paula Fontaine

D-U-N-S 24-987-2441   (BR)
SIGNIFY CANADA LTD
CANADIAN FLUORESCENT INDUSTRIES

(*Suby of* KONINKLIJKE PHILIPS N.V.)
525 Education Rd, Cornwall, ON, K6H 6C7

Emp Here 120
SIC 3641 Electric lamps
Steven Mauri

D-U-N-S 25-282-7142   (BR)
SODEXO CANADA LTD
(*Suby of* SODEXO)
1950 Montreal Rd, Cornwall, ON, K6H 6L2
(613) 936-5800
Emp Here 150
SIC 5812 Eating places
Kim Coe-Turner

D-U-N-S 25-464-3828   (BR)
ST. LAWRENCE COLLEGE OF APPLIED ARTS AND TECHNOLOGY, THE
ST LAWRENCE COLLEGE/ ONT SKILL
(*Suby of* ST. LAWRENCE COLLEGE OF APPLIED ARTS AND TECHNOLOGY, THE)
2 St Lawrence Dr, Cornwall, ON, K6H 4Z1
(613) 933-6080
Emp Here 600
SIC 8221 Colleges and universities
Volker Thomson

D-U-N-S 24-868-9085   (HQ)
TRANSPORT EXPRESS MINIMAX INC
605 Education Rd, Cornwall, ON, K6H 6C7
(613) 936-0660
Emp Here 109   *Sales* 16,767,014
SIC 4212 Local trucking, without storage
Paul Poirier
Yves Poirier
Marc Poirier
Lucy Hyde

D-U-N-S 20-552-0492   (BR)
VALSPAR INC
1915 Second St W, Cornwall, ON, K6H 5R6
(613) 932-8960
Emp Here 130   *Sales* 982,032
SIC 2821 Plastics materials and resins
Mike Sullivan

D-U-N-S 24-347-2516   (BR)
WAL-MART CANADA CORP
(*Suby of* WALMART INC.)
6227 Boundary Rd, Cornwall, ON, K6H 5R5
(613) 932-7879
Emp Here 75
SIC 4212 Local trucking, without storage
Jennifer Langlois

Cornwall, ON K6J

D-U-N-S 20-216-1860   (SL)
1497665 ONTARIO INC
CORNWALL NISSAN
1107 Brookdale Ave, Cornwall, ON, K6J 4P6
(613) 933-7555
Emp Here 30   *Sales* 14,942,340
SIC 5511 New and used car dealers
Ayman (Gaby) Gabriel

D-U-N-S 25-487-3540   (BR)
BAYSHORE HEALTHCARE LTD.
BAYSHORE HEALTHCARE LTD
(*Suby of* BAYSHORE HEALTHCARE LTD.)
112 Second St W, Cornwall, ON, K6J 1G5
(613) 938-1691
Emp Here 100
SIC 8082 Home health care services
Diane Pederson

D-U-N-S 25-370-3102   (BR)
CAPITAL SECURITY & INVESTIGATIONS
504 Pitt St, Cornwall, ON, K6J 3R5
(613) 937-4111
Emp Here 120
SIC 7381 Detective and armored car services
Norm Garce

D-U-N-S 25-137-3726   (BR)
CATHOLIC DISTRICT SCHOOL BOARD OF EASTERN ONTARIO
ST JOSEPH'S SECONDARY SCHOOL
1500a Cumberland St, Cornwall, ON, K6J 5V9
(613) 932-0349
Emp Here 100
SIC 8211 Elementary and secondary schools
John Cameron

D-U-N-S 25-227-3370   (SL)
COMMUNITY LIVING-STORMONT COUNTY
280 Ninth St W, Cornwall, ON, K6J 3A6
(613) 938-9550
Emp Here 100   *Sales* 6,856,600
SIC 8059 Nursing and personal care, nec
Linda Lister

D-U-N-S 20-043-5246   (BR)
COMPAGNIE CANADIAN TECHNICAL TAPE LTEE
CANTECH
(*Suby of* GROUPE INTERTAPE POLYMER INC, LE)
1400 Rosemount Ave, Cornwall, ON, K6J 3E6
(613) 932-3105
Emp Here 80
SIC 2672 Paper; coated and laminated, nec
Michael Montpetit

D-U-N-S 20-043-0965   (HQ)
CORNWALL GRAVEL COMPANY LTD
390 Eleventh St W, Cornwall, ON, K6J 3B2
(613) 932-6571
Sales 22,719,780
SIC 1611 Highway and street construction
Lionel Grant
David Grant
Peter Grant
Catherine Grant

D-U-N-S 24-373-3438   (HQ)
EASTERN ONTARIO HEALTH UNIT
1000 Pitt St, Cornwall, ON, K6J 5T1
(613) 933-1375
Emp Here 200   *Sales* 70,233,300
SIC 8621 Professional organizations
Tod Lalonde

D-U-N-S 25-918-2830   (BR)
EXTENDICARE (CANADA) INC
PARAMED HOME HEALTH CARE
(*Suby of* EXTENDICARE INC)
812 Pitt St Suite 16, Cornwall, ON, K6J 5R1
(613) 932-4661
Emp Here 265
SIC 8051 Skilled nursing care facilities
Michael Rasenberg

D-U-N-S 25-292-2182   (HQ)
FITNESS DEPOT INC
700 Wallrich Ave, Cornwall, ON, K6J 5X4
(613) 938-8196
Emp Here 30   *Sales* 208,590,000
SIC 5091 Sporting and recreation goods
Edwin Cameron
Scott Essery
Gus Christopoulos
Chris Busch
Mary Gault

D-U-N-S 20-894-3464   (SL)
GREAT LAKES PILOTAGE AUTHORITY
(*Suby of* GOVERNMENT OF CANADA)
202 Pitt St 2nd Fl, Cornwall, ON, K6J 3P7
(613) 933-2991
Emp Here 80   *Sales* 31,497,920
SIC 4499 Water transportation services,
Robert Lemire
Rejean Menard
Daniel Trottier

D-U-N-S 24-382-9496   (HQ)
GUINDON GLENOCO LIMITED
GUINDON ESSO
1310 Pitt St, Cornwall, ON, K6J 3T6
(613) 933-5120
Emp Here 17   *Sales* 16,415,175

SIC 5983 Fuel oil dealers
Claire-Marie Guindon
Jean-Francois Guindon

D-U-N-S 20-553-6282   (BR)
HOME DEPOT OF CANADA INC
HOME DEPOT
(*Suby of* THE HOME DEPOT INC)
1825 Brookdale Ave, Cornwall, ON, K6J 5X7
(613) 930-4470
Emp Here 100
SIC 5211 Lumber and other building materials
Mukesh Desai

D-U-N-S 25-527-4771   (SL)
JIGGERNAUT TACKLE INC
1235 Cumberland St, Cornwall, ON, K6J 4K6
(613) 932-3474
Emp Here 30   *Sales* 15,616,260
SIC 5091 Sporting and recreation goods
William Dennis
Claudette Dennis

D-U-N-S 25-843-9959   (SL)
METROPOLITAN LIFE INSURANCE COMPANY OF CANADA
55 Water St W Suite 100, Cornwall, ON, K6J 1A1

Emp Here 18   *Sales* 10,438,632
SIC 6411 Insurance agents, brokers, and service
Frank Porica

D-U-N-S 20-578-3434   (SL)
MILLER-HUGHES FORD SALES LIMITED
ALEXANDRIA FORD SALES
711 Pitt St, Cornwall, ON, K6J 3S1
(613) 932-2584
Emp Here 27   *Sales* 13,448,106
SIC 5511 New and used car dealers
Shawn Maloney
Melinda Maloney

D-U-N-S 24-728-7386   (HQ)
NORTHERN LIGHTS FITNESS PRODUCTS INCORPORATED
700 Wallrich Ave, Cornwall, ON, K6J 5X4
(613) 938-8196
Sales 26,090,880
SIC 3949 Sporting and athletic goods, nec
Edwin Cameron

D-U-N-S 25-086-1747   (SL)
NUMED CANADA INC
45 Second St W, Cornwall, ON, K6J 1G3
(613) 936-2592
Emp Here 40   *Sales* 10,262,480
SIC 3841 Surgical and medical instruments

D-U-N-S 20-809-7886   (BR)
RECIPE UNLIMITED CORPORATION
KELSEY'S RESTAURANT
(*Suby of* RECIPE UNLIMITED CORPORATION)
960 Brookdale Ave Suite 18, Cornwall, ON, K6J 4P5
(416) 852-4714
Emp Here 75
SIC 5812 Eating places
Kevin Hargraves

D-U-N-S 24-391-8930   (SL)
SEAWAY CHEVROLET CADILLAC BUICK GMC LTD
2695 Brookdale Ave, Cornwall, ON, K6J 5X9
(613) 933-3000
Emp Here 50   *Sales* 24,903,900
SIC 5511 New and used car dealers
Andre Lapointe

D-U-N-S 25-542-3956   (HQ)
ST. LAWRENCE SEAWAY MANAGEMENT CORPORATION, THE
202 Pitt St, Cornwall, ON, K6J 3P7
(613) 932-5170
Emp Here 60   *Sales* 64,197,814
SIC 4449 Water transportation of freight

Terence Bowles
Jean Aubry-Morin
Stephen Kwok
Karen Dumoulin
Tim Dool
Robert Armstrong
Gerald Carter
David Muir
Georges Robichon
Patrick Bushby

D-U-N-S 25-074-6567   (BR)
WAL-MART CANADA CORP
(*Suby of* WALMART INC.)
950 Brookdale Ave, Cornwall, ON, K6J 4P5
(613) 933-8366
Emp Here 150
SIC 5311 Department stores
Chasse Pierre

Cornwall, ON K6K

D-U-N-S 20-183-1372   (SL)
CORNWALL IRVING 24 & MAINWAY CENTRE
MAC'S CONVENIENCE
3250 Brookdale Ave, Cornwall, ON, K6K 1W3
(613) 933-5668
Emp Here 40   *Sales* 18,760,200
SIC 5983 Fuel oil dealers
Mike Belair

Corunna, ON N0N

D-U-N-S 24-831-3025   (SL)
BLUE WATER IGA
420 Lyndoch St, Corunna, ON, N0N 1G0
(519) 862-5213
Emp Here 125   *Sales* 36,684,625
SIC 5411 Grocery stores
Roy Juschka
Cindy Juschka

D-U-N-S 24-211-4486   (SL)
CHEMFAB INDUSTRIES INC
466 Polymoore Dr, Corunna, ON, N0N 1G0
(519) 862-1433
Emp Here 300   *Sales* 81,254,400
SIC 1711 Plumbing, heating, air-conditioning
Jess Devlugt

D-U-N-S 24-333-3747   (HQ)
CLEAN HARBORS CANADA INC
(*Suby of* CLEAN HARBORS, INC.)
4090 Telfer Rd, Corunna, ON, N0N 1G0
(519) 864-1021
Emp Here 135   *Sales* 146,574,900
SIC 4953 Refuse systems
Dino Giudice

D-U-N-S 24-608-9812   (SL)
FOODLAND
420 Lyndoch St, Corunna, ON, N0N 1G0
(519) 862-5213
Emp Here 49   *Sales* 13,433,448
SIC 5411 Grocery stores
Jenai Wall

D-U-N-S 24-175-2802   (SL)
INVISTA COMPANY CANADA
291 Albert St, Corunna, ON, N0N 1G0
(519) 862-6881
Emp Here 72   *Sales* 19,919,520
SIC 2822 Synthetic rubber
Grant Barclay

D-U-N-S 25-999-1578   (BR)
NOVA CHEMICALS (CANADA) LTD
(*Suby of* GOVERNMENT OF ABU DHABI)
785 Petrolia Line Rr 2, Corunna, ON, N0N 1G0

(519) 862-2911
Emp Here 500
SIC 2821 Plastics materials and resins
Todd Karran

D-U-N-S 20-043-5741   (BR)
NOVA CHEMICALS CORPORATION
(*Suby of* GOVERNMENT OF ABU DHABI)
285 Albert St, Corunna, ON, N0N 1G0
(519) 862-1445
Emp Here 250
SIC 3089 Plastics products, nec
Tom Thompson

D-U-N-S 24-714-7510   (BR)
PERFORMANCE SCIENCE MATERIALS COMPANY
(*Suby of* DUPONT DE NEMOURS, INC.)
291 Albert St, Corunna, ON, N0N 1G0
(519) 862-5700
Emp Here 75
SIC 2821 Plastics materials and resins

D-U-N-S 24-125-9790   (BR)
SHELL CANADA LIMITED
(*Suby of* ROYAL DUTCH SHELL PLC)
339 Lasalle Line Rr 1, Corunna, ON, N0N 1G0
(519) 481-1369
Emp Here 300
SIC 2992 Lubricating oils and greases
Hank Bonnet

D-U-N-S 25-306-0362   (BR)
SHELL CANADA LIMITED
(*Suby of* ROYAL DUTCH SHELL PLC)
150 St Clair Pky, Corunna, ON, N0N 1G0
(519) 481-1245
Emp Here 300
SIC 2911 Petroleum refining
Kerry Margetts

Courtice, ON L1E

D-U-N-S 24-198-1914   (SL)
1262510 ONTARIO LIMITED
KING & TOWNLINE FRESHCO
1414 Highway 2 Unit 8, Courtice, ON, L1E 3B4
(905) 433-7735
Emp Here 40   *Sales* 10,966,080
SIC 5411 Grocery stores
Rick Field

D-U-N-S 25-638-7762   (SL)
884262 ONTARIO INC
B & G TRUCK & TRAILER REPAIRS
(*Suby of* 2123973 ONTARIO LTD)
1612 Baseline Rd, Courtice, ON, L1E 2S5
(905) 435-1166
Emp Here 40   *Sales* 11,332,000
SIC 7538 General automotive repair shops
William Wright

D-U-N-S 20-405-7772   (SL)
BUNNY'S FOOD SERVICE LIMITED
1540 Highway 2, Courtice, ON, L1E 2R6
(905) 434-2444
Emp Here 30   *Sales* 19,693,920
SIC 5962 Merchandising machine operators
John Oortwyn
Ted Oortwyn
Nancy Oortwyn
Anita Oortwyn

D-U-N-S 25-663-7760   (SL)
DOM'S AUTO PARTS CO LIMITED
1604 Baseline Rd, Courtice, ON, L1E 2S5
(905) 434-4566
Emp Here 23   *Sales* 11,455,794
SIC 5531 Auto and home supply stores
Dominic Vetere
Nancy Vetere

D-U-N-S 25-106-5447   (BR)
KAWARTHA PINE RIDGE DISTRICT SCHOOL BOARD

CURTICE SECONDARY SCHOOL
1717 Nash Rd, Courtice, ON, L1E 2L8
(905) 436-2074
Emp Here 120
SIC 8211 Elementary and secondary schools
Pamela Pryjma

D-U-N-S 20-043-6277   (SL)
NICHOLS, ROY MOTORS LIMITED
2728 Courtice Rd, Courtice, ON, L1E 2M7
(905) 436-2228
Emp Here 70   *Sales* 44,049,600
SIC 5511 New and used car dealers
Robert Owen

D-U-N-S 24-719-4103   (SL)
OMNIPLAN DESIGN GROUP LIMITED
OMNIPLAN PROJECT SERVICES
1748 Baseline Rd Suite 200d, Courtice, ON,
L1E 2T1
(905) 421-9129
Emp Here 25   *Sales* 11,087,250
SIC 7389 Business services, nec
Chester Niziol

D-U-N-S 20-568-0510   (BR)
PETERBOROUGH VICTORIA NORTHUM-BERLAND AND CLARINGTON CATHOLIC DISTRICT SCHOOL BOARD
HOLY TRINITY CATHOLIC SECONDARY SCHOOL
(*Suby of* PETERBOROUGH VICTORIA NORTHUMBERLAND AND CLARINGTON CATHOLIC DISTRICT SCHOOL BOARD)
2260 Courtice Rd, Courtice, ON, L1E 2M8
(905) 404-9349
Emp Here 100
SIC 8211 Elementary and secondary schools
Lisa Cole

Courtland, ON N0J

D-U-N-S 20-934-7749   (HQ)
AGRATURF EQUIPMENT SERVICES INC
170 County Road 13, Courtland, ON, N0J 1E0
(519) 688-1011
Emp Here 30   *Sales* 20,189,070
SIC 5999 Miscellaneous retail stores, nec

D-U-N-S 24-199-0662   (SL)
REID & DELEYE CONTRACTORS LTD
4926 Highway 59, Courtland, ON, N0J 1E0
(519) 688-2600
Emp Here 40   *Sales* 13,333,320
SIC 1541 Industrial buildings and warehouses
Greg Deleye
Gregory Paul Eyre

D-U-N-S 20-550-4285   (SL)
TRACKLESS VEHICLES LIMITED
55 Thunderbird Dr, Courtland, ON, N0J 1E0
(519) 688-0370
Emp Here 90   *Sales* 20,145,870
SIC 3711 Motor vehicles and car bodies
Douglas Cadman

Courtright, ON N0N

D-U-N-S 25-543-2981   (HQ)
TERRA INTERNATIONAL (CANADA) INC
TERRA ENVIRONMENTAL TECHNOLOGIES
(*Suby of* CF INDUSTRIES HOLDINGS, INC.)
161 Bickford Line, Courtright, ON, N0N 1H0
(519) 867-2739
Sales 41,183,045
SIC 2819 Industrial inorganic chemicals, nec
Mike Bennett

Creemore, ON L0M

D-U-N-S 24-343-2718   (BR)
2063412 INVESTMENT LP
LEISUREWORLD CAREGIVING CENTRE - CREEDAN VALLEY
143 Mary St, Creemore, ON, L0M 1G0
(705) 466-3437
Emp Here 80
SIC 8051 Skilled nursing care facilities
Paula Rentner

D-U-N-S 25-860-5435   (BR)
2063414 ONTARIO LIMITED
LEISUREWORLD CAREGIVING CENTRE
143 Mary St, Creemore, ON, L0M 1G0
(705) 466-3437
Emp Here 75
SIC 8051 Skilled nursing care facilities
Paula Rentner

D-U-N-S 24-664-3480   (HQ)
CREEMORE SPRINGS BREWERY LIMITED
(*Suby of* MOLSON COORS BREWING COM-PANY)
139 Mill St Suite 369, Creemore, ON, L0M 1G0
(705) 466-2240
Emp Here 59   *Sales* 31,112,100
SIC 2082 Malt beverages
Ian Freedman
Gordon Fuller

Cumberland, ON K4C

D-U-N-S 20-052-6155   (SL)
1329481 ONTARIO INC
C AND C ENTERPRISES
2930 French Hill Rd, Cumberland, ON, K4C 1K7
(613) 833-1917
Emp Here 90   *Sales* 13,337,280
SIC 4212 Local trucking, without storage
Robert Cousins
Frank Chenier

Curve Lake, ON K0L

D-U-N-S 20-291-4011   (BR)
UNION OF ONTARIO INDIANS
ANISHINABEK NATION
1024 Mississauga Rd, Curve Lake, ON, K0L 1R0
(705) 657-9383
Emp Here 100
SIC 8399 Social services, nec
Crystal Cummings

Dashwood, ON N0M

D-U-N-S 24-826-2818   (SL)
HAYTER'S TURKEY PRODUCTS INC
HAYTER'S FARM
37451 Dashwood Rd, Dashwood, ON, N0M 1N0
(519) 237-3561
Emp Here 65   *Sales* 22,469,850
SIC 2015 Poultry slaughtering and processing
Joanne Maguire
Elaine Hayter
Sean Maguire

D-U-N-S 24-387-6018   (HQ)
MCCANN REDI-MIX INC
69478 Bronson Line, Dashwood, ON, N0M 1N0
(519) 237-3647
Emp Here 85   *Sales* 22,273,470

SIC 1771 Concrete work
James Mccann
William A. Mccann
Paul Mccann
Lawrence Mccann
Jerimiah Mccann
Brian Mccann

Deep River, ON K0J

D-U-N-S 24-843-7311   (SL)
779173 ONTARIO LIMITED
FLEURY'S VALU MART
75 Deep River Road, Deep River, ON, K0J 1P0
(613) 584-3893
Emp Here 75   *Sales* 22,010,775
SIC 5411 Grocery stores
Bert Fleury

D-U-N-S 24-483-2887   (SL)
DEEP RIVER AND DISTRICT HOSPITAL CORPORATION
117 Banting Dr, Deep River, ON, K0J 1P0
(613) 584-2484
Emp Here 140   *Sales* 15,551,200
SIC 8062 General medical and surgical hospitals
Joyce Colton

D-U-N-S 24-390-8998   (SL)
H.S. PIKE HOLDINGS INC
CANADIAN TIRE
366 Burkes Rd Rr 1, Deep River, ON, K0J 1P0
(613) 584-3337
Emp Here 45   *Sales* 22,413,510
SIC 5531 Auto and home supply stores
Stephen Pike

D-U-N-S 24-046-2189   (SL)
PEMBROKE OLD TIME FIDDLING ASSOCI-ATION INCORPORATED
Gd, Deep River, ON, K0J 1P0
(613) 635-7200
Emp Here 100   *Sales* 70,921,200
SIC 8699 Membership organizations, nec
Diane Hickey
Laurie Serran
Brian Adams
Romeo Levesseur
Richard Jones
Dan Schyrer
Don Rosien
Ian Hamilton

Delaware, ON N0L

D-U-N-S 25-629-1345   (HQ)
1068827 ONTARIO INC
GRACE MOTORS
11211 Longwoods Rd Rr 1, Delaware, ON, N0L 1E0
(519) 652-9766
Emp Here 1   *Sales* 22,413,510
SIC 5521 Used car dealers
John Vink

D-U-N-S 24-892-3310   (HQ)
TRY RECYCLING INC
11110 Longwoods Rd, Delaware, ON, N0L 1E0
(519) 858-2199
Emp Here 7   *Sales* 14,913,598
SIC 4953 Refuse systems
James Graham

Delhi, ON N4B

D-U-N-S 20-043-9685   (SL)
DALTON WHITE FARMS & SUPPLIES LIM-ITED
802 James St, Delhi, ON, N4B 2E1
(519) 582-2864
Emp Here 30   *Sales* 10,274,010
SIC 0132 Tobacco
Ed Dehooghe

D-U-N-S 20-871-7400   (SL)
DELHI IGA
227 Main Street Of Delhi, Delhi, ON, N4B 2M4
(519) 582-0990
Emp Here 44   *Sales* 12,202,397
SIC 5411 Grocery stores
Ron Ruel

D-U-N-S 24-315-3350   (SL)
DELHI NURSING HOME LIMITED
DELHI LONG TERM CARE CENTER
750 Gibralter St, Delhi, ON, N4B 3B3
(519) 582-3400
Emp Here 80   *Sales* 5,498,640
SIC 8051 Skilled nursing care facilities
William Gheysen

D-U-N-S 20-043-9925   (SL)
FERNLEA FLOWERS LIMITED
1211 Highway 3, Delhi, ON, N4B 2W6
(519) 582-3060
Emp Here 200   *Sales* 33,805,000
SIC 0181 Ornamental nursery products
Joseph Howe
Jeffrey Howe
Virginia Howe
Joseph Howe Jr
Keri-Lynn Howe
Jim Macdonald

D-U-N-S 24-626-6373   (SL)
GEORGE BRAUN & SONS FARMS LIMITED
Gd Lcd Main, Delhi, ON, N4B 2W7
(519) 582-1239
Emp Here 40   *Sales* 13,698,680
SIC 0191 General farms, primarily crop
Lonnie Duwyn
Cherie Duwyn

D-U-N-S 24-219-3886   (HQ)
TITAN TRAILERS INC
1129 Highway 3, Delhi, ON, N4B 2W6
(519) 688-4826
Emp Here 1   *Sales* 61,142,240
SIC 3715 Truck trailers
Mike Kloepfer

D-U-N-S 20-044-0600   (HQ)
VANDEN BUSSCHE IRRIGATION & EQUIP-MENT LIMITED
2515 Pinegrove Rd, Delhi, ON, N4B 2E5
(519) 582-2380
Emp Here 34   *Sales* 25,176,378
SIC 5083 Farm and garden machinery
Marc Vanden Bussche
Mary Vanden Bussche

Denfield, ON N0M

D-U-N-S 20-941-4648   (SL)
DENFIELD LIVESTOCK SALES LTD
12952 Sixteen Mile Rd, Denfield, ON, N0M 1P0
(519) 666-1140
Emp Here 17   *Sales* 20,576,749
SIC 5154 Livestock
Bruce Coulter
Gwen Coulter

Deseronto, ON K0K

D-U-N-S 24-737-3079   (HQ)

FIRST NATIONS TECHNICAL INSTITUTE
3 Old York Rd, Deseronto, ON, K0K 1X0
(613) 396-2122
Sales 10,864,840
SIC 8244 Business and secretarial schools
Tim Thompson
Terry Bernhardt

D-U-N-S 25-248-6774   (HQ)
MOHAWK IMPERIAL SALES
MIRACLE MART
406 Hwy 2 & Hwy Suite 49, Deseronto, ON,
K0K 1X0
(613) 396-3700
Emp Here 30   Sales 18,782,528
SIC 5411 Grocery stores
Andrew Clifford Miracle, Jr
Yolanda Miracle

D-U-N-S 25-368-1969   (SL)
WINCHESTER AUBURN MILLS INC
CORTAGE SOURCE, THE
70 Dundas St, Deseronto, ON, K0K 1X0
(877) 224-2673
Emp Here 120   Sales 22,008,360
SIC 2298 Cordage and twine
Keith Bridges

Dorchester, ON N0L

D-U-N-S 20-104-1451   (SL)
ARMATEC SURVIVABILITY CORP
1 Newton Ave, Dorchester, ON, N0L 1G4
(519) 268-2999
Emp Here 60   Sales 13,430,580
SIC 3795 Tanks and tank components
Karl Pfister

D-U-N-S 25-878-5450   (SL)
BOS INNOVATIONS INC
500 Hudson Dr, Dorchester, ON, N0L 1G5
(519) 268-8563
Emp Here 85   Sales 18,870,085
SIC 3569 General industrial machinery, nec
Ben Huigenbos
Joan Huigenbos

D-U-N-S 25-759-1271   (SL)
SPRINT-PIONEERS MINISTRIES INC
PIONEERS CANADA
51 Byron Ave Ss 2, Dorchester, ON, N0L 1G2
(519) 268-8778
Emp Here 100   Sales 10,772,700
SIC 8661 Religious organizations
James Kim
Todd Coile

D-U-N-S 20-514-8153   (HQ)
UNITED AGRI PRODUCTS CANADA INC
UAP
(Suby of NUTRIEN LTD)
789 Donnybrook Dr Suite 2, Dorchester, ON,
N0L 1G5
(519) 268-5900
Emp Here 20   Sales 29,700,800
SIC 5191 Farm supplies
Murray Pickel

D-U-N-S 25-770-7240   (SL)
WEAVERCROFT INTERNATIONAL
3038 Hamilton Rd Suite 119, Dorchester, ON,
N0L 1G5
(519) 868-0330
Emp Here 7   Sales 10,273,844
SIC 5154 Livestock
Jim Weaver

Dowling, ON P0M

D-U-N-S 25-397-4018   (HQ)
HLS HARD-LINE SOLUTIONS INC
HARD-LINE SOLUTIONS

53 Main St W, Dowling, ON, P0M 1R0
(705) 855-1310
Sales 19,044,200
SIC 3663 Radio and t.v. communications
equipment
Walter Siggelkow
Jamie Lachapelle

Drayton, ON N0G

D-U-N-S 24-918-7535   (SL)
MAR-SPAN TRUSS INC
MAR-SPAN HOME HARDWARE BUILDING
CENTRE
7873 Wellington Rd 8, Drayton, ON, N0G 1P0
(519) 638-3086
Emp Here 40   Sales 10,122,360
SIC 5211 Lumber and other building materials
Murray Martin
Fern Martin

D-U-N-S 24-478-0284   (HQ)
NIEUWLAND FEED & SUPPLY LIMITED
(Suby of 868229 ONTARIO LIMITED)
96 Wellington St, Drayton, ON, N0G 1P0
(519) 638-3008
Emp Here 52   Sales 72,599,621
SIC 5191 Farm supplies
Arthur Nieuwland
Scott Nieuwland

D-U-N-S 24-315-3962   (HQ)
NORWELL DAIRY SYSTEMS LTD
37 Drayton Industrial Dr, Drayton, ON, N0G
1P0
(519) 638-3535
Sales 21,376,170
SIC 5083 Farm and garden machinery
Hilco Stevens
Jack Bosman

Dresden, ON N0P

D-U-N-S 24-325-8626   (BR)
CONAGRA FOODS CANADA INC
(Suby of LAMB WESTON HOLDINGS INC)
759 Wellington St, Dresden, ON, N0P 1M0
(519) 683-4422
Emp Here 150
SIC 2032 Canned specialties
Don Roberts

D-U-N-S 25-092-0555   (BR)
DEL MONTE CANADA INC
(Suby of CONAGRA BRANDS, INC.)
Gd, Dresden, ON, N0P 1M0
(519) 683-4422
Emp Here 200
SIC 2032 Canned specialties
Karl Evans

D-U-N-S 24-182-4143   (SL)
DENNIS JACKSON SEED SERVICE LTD
1315 Jackson St, Dresden, ON, N0P 1M0
(519) 683-4413
Emp Here 10   Sales 12,103,970
SIC 5153 Grain and field beans
Dennis Jackson

D-U-N-S 24-337-6662   (SL)
DRESDEN AGRICULTURAL SOCIETY
DRESDEN RACEWAY
255 Park St Rr 5, Dresden, ON, N0P 1M0
(519) 683-1116
Emp Here 25   Sales 10,593,250
SIC 7948 Racing, including track operation
Lois Vandenbogaerde

Dryden, ON P8N

D-U-N-S 24-933-1158   (SL)
2699001 CANADA LIMITED
B TAYLOR HOME HARDWARE BUILDING
CENTRE
509 Government St, Dryden, ON, P8N 2P6
(807) 223-3381
Emp Here 42   Sales 10,628,478
SIC 5211 Lumber and other building materials
Bruce Taylor
Susan Taylor

D-U-N-S 20-835-5362   (HQ)
ANDRE TARDIFF AGENCY LIMITED
140 Colonisation Ave N, Dryden, ON, P8N
2Z5
(807) 223-4324
Sales 19,623,352
SIC 5171 Petroleum bulk stations and terminals
Bryan Tardiff

D-U-N-S 25-957-9407   (SL)
CANADIAN TIRE ASSOCIATE STORE
409 Government St, Dryden, ON, P8N 2P4
(807) 223-6644
Emp Here 50   Sales 24,903,900
SIC 5531 Auto and home supply stores
Don Viera

D-U-N-S 24-344-5090   (BR)
DOMTAR INC
(Suby of DOMTAR LUXEMBOURG INVEST-
MENTS SARL)
1 Duke St, Dryden, ON, P8N 2Z7
(807) 223-2323
Emp Here 500
SIC 2421 Sawmills and planing mills, general

D-U-N-S 25-238-0837   (BR)
DRYDEN BOARD OF EDUCATION
DRYDEN HIGH SCHOOL
79 Casimir Ave, Dryden, ON, P8N 2H4
(807) 223-2316
Emp Here 100
SIC 8211 Elementary and secondary schools
Deanna Pacheco

D-U-N-S 24-852-0231   (SL)
DRYDEN CHEVROLET BUICK GMC LTD
489 Government St, Dryden, ON, P8N 2P6
(807) 223-7123
Emp Here 43   Sales 21,417,354
SIC 5511 New and used car dealers
Nicholas Beyak

D-U-N-S 20-837-3753   (SL)
DRYDEN REGIONAL HEALTH CENTRE
58 Goodall St, Dryden, ON, P8N 1V8
(807) 223-8200
Emp Here 200   Sales 22,216,000
SIC 8062 General medical and surgical hospi-
tals
Wade Petranik

D-U-N-S 25-543-0043   (SL)
DRYDEN TRUCK STOP INC
HUSKY CAR TRUCK STOP
Gd Lcd Main, Dryden, ON, P8N 2Y6
(807) 223-2085
Emp Here 40   Sales 19,923,120
SIC 5541 Gasoline service stations
Ken Hallson

D-U-N-S 24-191-2224   (BR)
EXTENDICARE (CANADA) INC
PARAMED HOME HEALTH CARE
(Suby of EXTENDICARE INC)
40 Goodall St, Dryden, ON, P8N 1V8
(807) 223-5337
Emp Here 100
SIC 8049 Offices of health practitioner
Jody Farmer

D-U-N-S 20-522-4905   (HQ)
KENORA DISTRICT SERVICES BOARD
211 Princess St Suite 2, Dryden, ON, P8N 3L5

(807) 223-2100
Emp Here 22   Sales 37,828,500
SIC 8611 Business associations
Henry Wall

D-U-N-S 25-615-2786   (HQ)
MAG AEROSPACE CANADA CORP
MAG CANADA
(Suby of CLAIRVEST GROUP INC)
1012 Hwy 601 Unit 10, Dryden, ON, P8N 0A2
(807) 937-5544
Emp Here 35   Sales 10,256,925
SIC 0851 Forestry services
Kennedy Rotman
Mark Hill

D-U-N-S 20-046-1267   (HQ)
MCKINSTRY, WILLIAM LIMITED
MCKINSTRY'S
176 Government St, Dryden, ON, P8N 2N9
(807) 223-4214
Sales 12,950,028
SIC 5511 New and used car dealers
William (Bill) Mckinstry
Luana Mckinstry
James Mckinstry

D-U-N-S 24-112-0732   (HQ)
MILLER NORTHWEST LIMITED
351 Kennedy Rd, Dryden, ON, P8N 2Z2
(807) 223-2844
Sales 11,340,960
SIC 1611 Highway and street construction
Blair Mcarthur

D-U-N-S 25-272-0016   (BR)
SOBEYS WEST INC
SAFEWAY
(Suby of EMPIRE COMPANY LIMITED)
75 Whyte Ave, Dryden, ON, P8N 3E6
(807) 223-3276
Emp Here 120
SIC 5411 Grocery stores
Dave Mcbride

D-U-N-S 20-796-1603   (BR)
UNIFOR
CAW LOCAL 105
(Suby of UNIFOR)
34 Queen St, Dryden, ON, P8N 1A3
(807) 223-8146
Emp Here 350
SIC 8631 Labor organizations
Bruce Heal

D-U-N-S 20-548-3276   (SL)
UNION GAS
Po Box 280 Stn Main, Dryden, ON, P8N 2Y8

Emp Here 5   Sales 15,529,285
SIC 4923 Gas transmission and distribution

D-U-N-S 25-146-3816   (SL)
VANDERVAART SALES & SERVICE LTD
CANADIAN TIRE
409 Government St, Dryden, ON, P8N 2P4
(807) 223-4026
Emp Here 49   Sales 24,405,822
SIC 5531 Auto and home supply stores
Craig Murray

D-U-N-S 25-294-7577   (BR)
WAL-MART CANADA CORP
(Suby of WALMART INC.)
Hwy 17 E, Dryden, ON, P8N 2Y6
(807) 223-7190
Emp Here 250
SIC 5311 Department stores
Harry Vanderkuyl

D-U-N-S 24-111-9882   (HQ)
WILSON, ROY V (1984) LTD
WILSON'S BUSINESS SOLUTIONS
32 King St, Dryden, ON, P8N 1B3
(807) 223-3316
Emp Here 40   Sales 19,546,240
SIC 5943 Stationery stores
Greg Wilson

Dublin, ON N0K

D-U-N-S 24-183-0496   (HQ)
HURON PERTH CATHOLIC DISTRICT SCHOOL BOARD
87 Mill St, Dublin, ON, N0K 1E0
(519) 345-2440
Emp Here 250   *Sales* 51,046,285
SIC 8211 Elementary and secondary schools
Bernard Murray
Gerry Thuss

D-U-N-S 25-674-8872   (HQ)
LOOBY GROUP INCORPORATED
10 Matilda St, Dublin, ON, N0K 1E0
(519) 345-2800
Sales 10,483,875
SIC 6712 Bank holding companies
Stan Connelly
Joseph Looby

Dundalk, ON N0C

D-U-N-S 24-387-4005   (HQ)
ALUMI-BUNK CORPORATION
5 Keppel St, Dundalk, ON, N0C 1B0
(800) 700-2865
Emp Here 32   *Sales* 14,102,109
SIC 3713 Truck and bus bodies
Sulekh C Jain
Eric Jain

Dundas, ON L9H

D-U-N-S 25-167-6326   (SL)
1426420 ONTARIO INC
POULTRY HUT, THE
161 Hwy 8, Dundas, ON, L9H 5E1
(905) 627-2228
Emp Here 22   *Sales* 18,382,694
SIC 5144 Poultry and poultry products
Donna Warring
Allan Warring

D-U-N-S 24-347-2482   (SL)
6648215 CANADA LTD
H.D.D. WHOLESALE DECKING
(*Suby of* 2695341 CANADA LTD)
115 5 Hwy W, Dundas, ON, L9H 7L6
(905) 689-4774
Emp Here 50   *Sales* 22,358,700
SIC 5051 Metals service centers and offices
Thomas Jacques

D-U-N-S 25-098-5603   (SL)
ADVENTEC MANUFACTURING INC
(*Suby of* INFINITY VISTA INC)
55 Innovation Dr, Dundas, ON, L9H 7L8
(289) 895-7909
Emp Here 104   *Sales* 16,521,232
SIC 3089 Plastics products, nec
James Campbell

D-U-N-S 20-046-2356   (SL)
AERLOC INDUSTRIES LTD
64 Head St, Dundas, ON, L9H 3H7
(905) 628-6061
Emp Here 50   *Sales* 12,652,950
SIC 5211 Lumber and other building materials
Peter Dendekker

D-U-N-S 20-974-5488   (HQ)
AIRWAYS TRANSIT SERVICE LIMITED
35 5 Hwy W, Dundas, ON, L9H 7L5
(905) 333-3113
Emp Here 100   *Sales* 18,818,000
SIC 4131 Intercity and rural bus transportation
Michael Chalmers
Doug Badder

D-U-N-S 24-286-1938   (HQ)
BEVERLY GROUP INC, THE
BENSON BEVERLY TIRE
525 6 Hwy, Dundas, ON, L9H 7K1
(905) 525-9240
Emp Here 30   *Sales* 116,416,800
SIC 5531 Auto and home supply stores
William Streeter
Gail Cameron

D-U-N-S 20-513-7784   (HQ)
BURLINGTON AUTOMATION CORPORATION
(*Suby of* LINCOLN ELECTRIC HOLDINGS, INC.)
63 Innovation Dr, Dundas, ON, L9H 7L8
(905) 689-7771
Sales 12,876,058
SIC 3541 Machine tools, Metal cutting type
Justin Cercio

D-U-N-S 20-119-4672   (HQ)
CLAYBAR CONTRACTING INC
424 Macnab St, Dundas, ON, L9H 2L3
(905) 627-8000
Emp Here 80   *Sales* 27,080,460
SIC 1799 Special trade contractors, nec
Lou Cerruti

D-U-N-S 20-920-9618   (HQ)
CORESLAB STRUCTURES (ONT) INC
(*Suby of* CORESLAB INTERNATIONAL INC)
205 Coreslab Dr, Dundas, ON, L9H 0B3
(905) 689-3993
Emp Here 25   *Sales* 17,921,900
SIC 3272 Concrete products, nec
Mario Franciosa
Sidney Speigel
Domenic Franciosa
Douglas Harman
Frank Franciosa

D-U-N-S 24-505-3756   (HQ)
CURLCO INDUSTRIES INC
HAIRCRAFTERS
85 Little John Rd Suite 1585, Dundas, ON, L9H 4H1
(905) 628-4287
Emp Here 172   *Sales* 18,567,072
SIC 7231 Beauty shops
Murray Nicholson
David Nicholson

D-U-N-S 24-926-3096   (BR)
DARLING INTERNATIONAL CANADA INC
ROTHSAY
(*Suby of* DARLING INGREDIENTS INC.)
880 5 Hwy W, Dundas, ON, L9H 5E2
(905) 628-2258
Emp Here 120
SIC 4953 Refuse systems
Jim Long

D-U-N-S 24-826-5829   (SL)
EL-MET-PARTS INC
47 Head St, Dundas, ON, L9H 3H6
(905) 628-6366
Emp Here 120   *Sales* 23,050,200
SIC 3469 Metal stampings, nec
John Papakyriakou
Alex Papakyriakou
David Roser

D-U-N-S 20-876-3631   (SL)
FLAMBORO DOWNS HOLDINGS LIMITED
FLAMBORO DOWNS RACEWAY
(*Suby of* GREAT CANADIAN GAMING CORPORATION)
967 5 Hwy W, Dundas, ON, L9H 5E2
(905) 627-3561
Emp Here 270   *Sales* 22,279,590
SIC 7948 Racing, including track operation
Bruce Barbour
William Howarth

D-U-N-S 20-879-0233   (SL)
GO BEE INDUSTRIES INC

1-334 A Hatt St, Dundas, ON, L9H 2H9
(289) 238-8829
Emp Here 1,000   *Sales* 200,371,000
SIC 7319 Advertising, nec
Stephen Deighton

D-U-N-S 20-139-9818   (BR)
HAMILTON-WENTWORTH   DISTRICT SCHOOL BOARD, THE
HIGHLAND SECONDARY SCHOOL
(*Suby of* HAMILTON-WENTWORTH DISTRICT SCHOOL BOARD, THE)
310 Governors Rd, Dundas, ON, L9H 5P8
(905) 628-2203
Emp Here 80
SIC 8211 Elementary and secondary schools
Gail Cipriani

D-U-N-S 24-505-5371   (SL)
HARSTER GREENHOUSES INC
250 8 Hwy, Dundas, ON, L9H 5E1
(905) 628-2430
Emp Here 50   *Sales* 17,123,350
SIC 0181 Ornamental nursery products
Andre Harster

D-U-N-S 24-396-7762   (SL)
LEE, RON CONSTRUCTION INC
439 8 Hwy, Dundas, ON, L9H 5E1
(905) 628-4148
Emp Here 47   *Sales* 10,347,896
SIC 1794 Excavation work
Kevin Lee

D-U-N-S 24-308-6043   (HQ)
LIBURDI AUTOMATION INC
(*Suby of* LIBURDI ENGINEERING LIMITED)
400 6 Hwy, Dundas, ON, L9H 7K4
(905) 689-0734
Emp Here 50   *Sales* 13,320,060
SIC 3548 Welding apparatus
Joseph Liburdi

D-U-N-S 24-220-3461   (HQ)
LIBURDI ENGINEERING LIMITED
400 6 Hwy, Dundas, ON, L9H 7K4
(905) 689-0734
Emp Here 120   *Sales* 70,219,250
SIC 3511 Turbines and turbine generator sets
Joseph Liburdi

D-U-N-S 20-566-5768   (HQ)
LIBURDI TURBINE SERVICES INC
(*Suby of* LIBURDI ENGINEERING LIMITED)
400 6 Hwy, Dundas, ON, L9H 7K4
(905) 689-0734
Sales 46,721,150
SIC 4581 Airports, flying fields, and services
Joseph Liburdi
Andrew Mclean

D-U-N-S 24-946-5717   (SL)
LITZEN, T. SPORTS LIMITED
433 Ofield Rd S, Dundas, ON, L9H 5E2
(905) 628-3344
Emp Here 50   *Sales* 26,027,100
SIC 5091 Sporting and recreation goods
Terry Litzen
Amy Litzen

D-U-N-S 24-391-7981   (SL)
LOMBARDI, ALDO SALES INC
CANADIAN TIRE
50 Cootes Dr, Dundas, ON, L9H 1B6
(905) 627-3534
Emp Here 49   *Sales* 24,405,822
SIC 5531 Auto and home supply stores
Aldo Lombardi

D-U-N-S 20-594-8326   (SL)
M. VERNESCU DRUGS LTD
SHOPPERS DRUG MART
101 Osler Dr Suite 102, Dundas, ON, L9H 4H4
(905) 628-2251
Emp Here 70   *Sales* 17,102,960
SIC 5912 Drug stores and proprietary stores
Mariana Vernescu

D-U-N-S 24-896-3571   (BR)
METRO ONTARIO INC
(*Suby of* METRO INC)
119 Osler Dr, Dundas, ON, L9H 6X4
(905) 628-0177
Emp Here 250
SIC 5411 Grocery stores
Pano Tournidis

D-U-N-S 25-300-0467   (BR)
METRO ONTARIO INC
METRO
(*Suby of* METRO INC)
15 Governors Rd, Dundas, ON, L9H 6L9
(905) 627-4791
Emp Here 130
SIC 5411 Grocery stores
Bill Macintosh

D-U-N-S 25-484-1000   (SL)
NEIL VANDER KRUK HOLDINGS INC
CONNON NURSERIES
1155 Hwy 5, Dundas, ON, L9H 5E2
(905) 628-0112
Emp Here 190   *Sales* 111,940,210
SIC 5193 Flowers and florists supplies
Mark Vanderkruk
Case Vanderkruk
Brent Vanderkruk

D-U-N-S 25-739-2373   (HQ)
OPTUMINSIGHT (CANADA) INC
OPTUM
4 Innovation Dr, Dundas, ON, L9H 7P3
(905) 689-3980
Emp Here 97   *Sales* 23,428,800
SIC 8748 Business consulting, nec
Patricia Anderson
Mary Speagle

D-U-N-S 20-640-3433   (SL)
PICCIONI BROS MUSHROOM FARM LIMITED
355 Rock Chapel Rd, Dundas, ON, L9H 5E2
(905) 628-3090
Emp Here 80   *Sales* 20,984,720
SIC 0182 Food crops grown under cover
Battista Piccioni

D-U-N-S 24-419-9977   (BR)
RONA INC
RONA HOME & GARDEN
(*Suby of* LOWE'S COMPANIES, INC.)
52 Dundas St E, Dundas, ON, L9H 0C2
(905) 689-8700
Emp Here 120
SIC 5072 Hardware
Vasco Aguiar

D-U-N-S 20-107-0815   (HQ)
S-A-S PETROLEUM TECHNOLOGIES INC
432 Macnab St, Dundas, ON, L9H 2L3
(905) 627-5451
Emp Here 39   *Sales* 15,263,532
SIC 1799 Special trade contractors, nec
Lance Mullett

D-U-N-S 24-074-5018   (SL)
SISTERS OF ST. JOSEPHS OF HAMILTON
ST JOSEPH'S CONVENT
574 Northcliffe Ave, Dundas, ON, L9H 7L9
(905) 528-0138
Emp Here 100   *Sales* 10,772,700
SIC 8661 Religious organizations
Sister Anne Karges

D-U-N-S 20-818-6817   (SL)
ST. JOSEPH'S VILLA FOUNDATION, DUNDAS
ST JOSEPH'S VILLA, DUNDAS
56 Governors Rd, Dundas, ON, L9H 5G7
(905) 627-3541
Emp Here 550   *Sales* 37,579,300
SIC 8051 Skilled nursing care facilities
Brian Guest
David Bakker
Tony Valeri

D-U-N-S 20-181-6113   (SL)
WILLIAM DAM SEEDS LIMITED
279 Hwy 8, Dundas, ON, L9H 5E1
(905) 628-6641
Emp Here 19   *Sales* 12,472,816
SIC 5961 Catalog and mail-order houses
Rene Dam
William Dam
Annette Dam

Dungannon, ON N0M

D-U-N-S 20-941-0844   (SL)
BRINDLEY AUCTION SERVICE LTD
37110 Dungannon Rd, Dungannon, ON, N0M 1R0
(519) 529-7625
Emp Here 25   *Sales* 11,875,650
SIC 5083 Farm and garden machinery
Gordon Brindley
Angus Brindley

D-U-N-S 24-305-4186   (SL)
WEST WAWANOSH MUTUAL INSURANCE COMPANY, THE
81 Southampton St Suite 1, Dungannon, ON, N0M 1R0
(519) 529-7921
Emp Here 24   *Sales* 29,650,032
SIC 6331 Fire, marine, and casualty insurance
Ken Farrell
Cathie Simpson
Brad Vanstone
Lloyd Mcgillivray
Lloyd Morrison

Dunnville, ON N1A

D-U-N-S 24-951-6642   (SL)
566735 ONTARIO INC
HUNTER'S DRESSED MEATS
Gd Lcd Main, Dunnville, ON, N1A 2W9
(905) 774-5900
Emp Here 20   *Sales* 10,702,480
SIC 5147 Meats and meat products
Roy Hunter

D-U-N-S 25-542-5670   (SL)
BJ TAKE INC
220 Ramsey Dr, Dunnville, ON, N1A 0A7
(905) 774-5988
Emp Here 50   *Sales* 10,233,650
SIC 3646 Commercial lighting fixtures
Edward Buma

D-U-N-S 24-007-3049   (BR)
CORPORATION OF HALDIMAND COUNTY, THE
GRANDVIEW LODGE
(*Suby of* CORPORATION OF HALDIMAND COUNTY, THE)
657 Lock St W Suite A, Dunnville, ON, N1A 1V9
(800) 265-2818
Emp Here 140
SIC 8361 Residential care
Joanne Jackson

D-U-N-S 24-350-1298   (SL)
EDGEWATER GARDENS LONG-TERM CARE CENTRE
428 Broad St W, Dunnville, ON, N1A 1T3
(905) 774-2503
Emp Here 100   *Sales* 6,856,600
SIC 8051 Skilled nursing care facilities
Greg Allen

D-U-N-S 24-477-8718   (SL)
HALDIMAND WAR MEMORIAL HOSPITAL
206 John St Suite 101, Dunnville, ON, N1A 2P7

(905) 774-7431
Emp Here 150   *Sales* 16,662,000
SIC 8062 General medical and surgical hospitals
David Montgomery
John Clarke
Gord Minor
Elizabeth Hooke

D-U-N-S 20-039-7263   (HQ)
MINOR BROS. FARM SUPPLY LTD
MINOR BROS. FARM & COUNTRY
9 Mill Ave, Dunnville, ON, N1A 2W1
(905) 774-7591
Emp Here 15   *Sales* 14,659,680
SIC 5999 Miscellaneous retail stores, nec
Tim Minor
Dan Minor
Lynden Minor
Karen Minor-Tilstra

D-U-N-S 20-556-1934   (SL)
ROSA FLORA GROWERS LIMITED
Gd Lcd Main, Dunnville, ON, N1A 2W9
(905) 774-8044
Emp Here 153   *Sales* 37,382,184
SIC 5992 Florists

D-U-N-S 24-422-2311   (SL)
ROSA FLORA LIMITED
717 Diltz Rd Suite 2, Dunnville, ON, N1A 2W2
(905) 774-8044
Emp Here 65   *Sales* 17,050,085
SIC 0181 Ornamental nursery products
Otto Bulk
Corine Bulk

D-U-N-S 24-326-2560   (SL)
RYAN, D.C. SALES INC
CANADIAN TIRE
1002 Broad St E, Dunnville, ON, N1A 2Z2
(905) 774-2545
Emp Here 25   *Sales* 12,451,950
SIC 5531 Auto and home supply stores
Dan Ryan

Dunrobin, ON K0A

D-U-N-S 24-372-1458   (BR)
CLUBLINK CORPORATION ULC
EAGLE CREEK GOLF CLUB
(*Suby of* TWC ENTERPRISES LIMITED)
109 Royal Troon Lane, Dunrobin, ON, K0A 1T0
(613) 832-3804
Emp Here 100
SIC 7992 Public golf courses
Jean Leduc

D-U-N-S 20-025-3156   (BR)
OTTAWA-CARLETON DISTRICT SCHOOL BOARD
WEST CARLETON SECONDARY SCHOOL
(*Suby of* OTTAWA-CARLETON DISTRICT SCHOOL BOARD)
3088 Dunrobin Rd, Dunrobin, ON, K0A 1T0
(613) 832-0126
Emp Here 75
SIC 8211 Elementary and secondary schools
Jean Cory

Durham, ON N0G

D-U-N-S 25-705-3173   (BR)
CORPORATION OF THE COUNTY OF GREY
ROCKWOOD TERRACE
(*Suby of* CORPORATION OF THE COUNTY OF GREY)
575 Saddler St, Durham, ON, N0G 1R0
(519) 369-6035
Emp Here 130

SIC 8051 Skilled nursing care facilities
Karen Kraus

D-U-N-S 20-752-3549   (HQ)
DANZER CANADA INC
402725 Hwy 4, Durham, ON, N0G 1R0
(519) 369-3310
Emp Here 50   *Sales* 274,370,000
SIC 3861 Photographic equipment and supplies
Greg Lottes
Karl Danzer

D-U-N-S 24-923-8981   (SL)
DURHAM FURNITURE INC
450 Lambton St W, Durham, ON, N0G 1R0
(519) 369-2345
Emp Here 200   *Sales* 30,864,400
SIC 2511 Wood household furniture
Gordon Dilworth
John Rose
Ronald Simmons
Wendy Zettler

Dutton, ON N0L

D-U-N-S 20-046-7439   (SL)
COTRAC FORD LINCOLN SALES INC
204 Currie Rd, Dutton, ON, N0L 1J0
(519) 762-3536
Emp Here 19   *Sales* 14,544,660
SIC 5511 New and used car dealers
Philip Corneil
James Corneil

Eabamet Lake, ON P0T

D-U-N-S 24-052-8526   (SL)
EABAMETOONG EDUCATION AUTHORITY
Gd, Eabamet Lake, ON, P0T 1L0
(807) 242-1305
Emp Here 61   *Sales* 14,732,415
SIC 8621 Professional organizations
Nancy Waswa

Earlton, ON P0J

D-U-N-S 24-010-3028   (HQ)
462673 ONTARIO INC
NOR ARC STEEL FABRICATORS
3315 67 Hwy, Earlton, ON, P0J 1E0
(705) 563-2656
Emp Here 120   *Sales* 25,931,475
SIC 3441 Fabricated structural Metal
Mario Leveille
Yves Leveille

D-U-N-S 24-771-5907   (SL)
KOCH FARMS/AGRI-SALES INC
Lot 5 Concession 3, Earlton, ON, P0J 1E0
(705) 563-8325
Emp Here 25   *Sales* 11,768,275
SIC 1542 Nonresidential construction, nec
Norman R. Koch

East Gwillimbury, ON L9N

D-U-N-S 25-371-6302   (BR)
BEST BUY CANADA LTD
BEST BUY
(*Suby of* BEST BUY CO., INC.)
175 Green Lane E, East Gwillimbury, ON, L9N 0C9
(905) 954-1262
Emp Here 100

SIC 5731 Radio, television, and electronic stores
Jeff Mcclure

D-U-N-S 20-789-9787   (BR)
COSTCO WHOLESALE CANADA LTD
(*Suby of* COSTCO WHOLESALE CORPORATION)
18182 Yonge St, East Gwillimbury, ON, L9N 0J3
(905) 954-4733
Emp Here 220
SIC 5311 Department stores
Patrick Hillier

D-U-N-S 25-363-9819   (BR)
MULTIMATIC INC
DYNAMIC SUSPENSIONS, DIV OF
(*Suby of* MULTIMATIC HOLDINGS INC)
125 Corcoran Crt, East Gwillimbury, ON, L9N 0M8
(905) 853-8820
Emp Here 200
SIC 3429 Hardware, nec
Jonathan Vinden

East York, ON M4H

D-U-N-S 25-084-4420   (SL)
IQBAL HALAL FOODS INC
2 Thorncliffe Park Dr Unit 7-15, East York, ON, M4H 1H2
(416) 467-0177
Emp Here 50   *Sales* 41,778,850
SIC 5149 Groceries and related products, nec
Iqbal Malek
Nazimuddin Tajjuddin
Anwar All Tejani

Eden, ON N0J

D-U-N-S 24-990-8617   (HQ)
PHIL MAUER & ASSOCIATES INC
56954 Eden Line, Eden, ON, N0J 1H0
(519) 866-5677
Emp Here 6   *Sales* 14,652,066
SIC 3569 General industrial machinery, nec
Philip E Mauer
Leigh Mauer

Edwards, ON K0A

D-U-N-S 25-821-2737   (SL)
103190 ONTARIO INC
STANLEY'S OLDE MAPLE LANE FARM
2452 Yorks Corners Rd, Edwards, ON, K0A 1V0
(613) 821-2751
Emp Here 50   *Sales* 10,580,650
SIC 0831 Forest products
Earl Stanley

Eganville, ON K0J

D-U-N-S 20-615-4643   (HQ)
G & L WILCOX LIMITED
GEORGE'S MARINE & SPORTS
698 Sno-Drifters Rd, Eganville, ON, K0J 1T0
(613) 628-2424
Emp Here 18   *Sales* 18,926,964
SIC 5551 Boat dealers
Jeffrey Wilcox
Joan Marie Wilcox

▲ Public Company   ■ Public Company Family Member   **HQ** Headquarters   **BR** Branch   **SL** Single Location

Elgin, ON K0G

D-U-N-S 24-102-2656 (HQ)
LEEDS TRANSIT INC
AMERICAN BUS PRODUCTS
542 Main St, Elgin, ON, K0G 1E0
(613) 359-5344
Emp Here 32   *Sales* 27,316,125
SIC 5012 Automobiles and other motor vehicles
Kelly Backholm
Ronald Stenzl

Elizabethtown, ON K6T

D-U-N-S 20-268-1560 (SL)
TRS HEATING & COOLING LTD
3520 Coon'S Rd, Elizabethtown, ON, K6T 1A6
(613) 342-9733
Emp Here 110   *Sales* 25,637,150
SIC 1711 Plumbing, heating, air-conditioning
Mike Ford

Elliot Lake, ON P5A

D-U-N-S 24-752-7054 (SL)
749416 ONTARIO INC
ELLIOT LAKE FOODLAND
40 Hillside Dr S, Elliot Lake, ON, P5A 1M7
(705) 848-9790
Emp Here 50   *Sales* 13,707,600
SIC 5411 Grocery stores
Pierre Vaillancourt

D-U-N-S 20-046-9757 (HQ)
A.J. BUS LINES LIMITED
(*Suby of* 535616 ONTARIO INC)
2 Charles Walk, Elliot Lake, ON, P5A 2A3
(705) 848-3013
Emp Here 50   *Sales* 36,649,200
SIC 5943 Stationery stores
Tom Shamas
John Shamas

D-U-N-S 25-158-5279 (SL)
AR-LINE SECURITY AND INVESTIGATION LTD
34 Birch Rd, Elliot Lake, ON, P5A 2E2

Emp Here 48   *Sales* 32,588,304
SIC 6211 Security brokers and dealers
Arline Cardy

D-U-N-S 24-075-3699 (SL)
CHEMNORTH SYSTEMS AND SERVICES COMPANY LTD
QUEST ENTERPRISES, DIV
30 Timber Rd Suite 2, Elliot Lake, ON, P5A 2T1
(705) 461-9821
Emp Here 35   *Sales* 16,625,910
SIC 5087 Service establishment equipment
Robert Stirling

D-U-N-S 24-019-7926 (SL)
ELLIOT LAKE FIRE DEPARTMENT
55 Hillside Dr N, Elliot Lake, ON, P5A 1X5
(705) 848-3232
Emp Here 30   *Sales* 13,476,570
SIC 7389 Business services, nec
Paul Officer

D-U-N-S 24-393-9175 (SL)
PORTENGEN, R. HOME AND AUTO INC
CANADIAN TIRE
50 Hillside Dr S, Elliot Lake, ON, P5A 1M7
(705) 848-3663
Emp Here 30   *Sales* 14,942,340
SIC 5531 Auto and home supply stores

Robert Portengen

D-U-N-S 20-823-5085 (HQ)
ST. JOSEPH'S GENERAL HOSPITAL ELLIOT LAKE
70 Spine Rd, Elliot Lake, ON, P5A 1X2
(705) 848-7181
Sales 27,214,600
SIC 8062 General medical and surgical hospitals
Pierre Ozolinn

Elmira, ON N3B

D-U-N-S 20-533-0983 (BR)
2063414 ONTARIO LIMITED
LEISUREWORLD CAREGIVING CENTRE
120 Barnswallow Dr, Elmira, ON, N3B 2Y9
(519) 669-5777
Emp Here 100
SIC 8051 Skilled nursing care facilities
Cathy Holland

D-U-N-S 20-410-2362 (HQ)
APPLETON GROUP CANADA, LTD
APPLETON ELECTRIC
(*Suby of* EMERSON ELECTRIC CO.)
99 Union St, Elmira, ON, N3B 3L7
(519) 669-9222
Sales 19,044,200
SIC 3644 Noncurrent-carrying wiring devices
Russell Kerstetter
John Sperino
Curt Eslinger
Ryan Garrah
Dane Dreher

D-U-N-S 20-697-1868 (HQ)
ELMIRA PET PRODUCTS LTD
35 Martin'S Lane, Elmira, ON, N3B 2Z5
(519) 669-3330
Sales 30,075,030
SIC 2048 Prepared feeds, nec
Bryan Cook
Tim Bowman
Elliott Knox

D-U-N-S 20-178-5581 (HQ)
LANXESS CANADA CO./CIE
ANDEROL CANADA
(*Suby of* LANXESS AG)
25 Erb St, Elmira, ON, N3B 3A3
(519) 669-1671
Emp Here 218   *Sales* 586,381,250
SIC 2992 Lubricating oils and greases
Dalip Puri
Arthur Fullerton
Nancy Bissommette
Billie Flaherty
Noel Blake
Stephen Forsyth
Dimitri Makres

D-U-N-S 20-047-0979 (HQ)
MARBRO CAPITAL LIMITED
35 Earl Martin Dr, Elmira, ON, N3B 3L4
(519) 669-5171
Emp Here 4   *Sales* 11,242,750
SIC 2048 Prepared feeds, nec
D. Charles Martin
Timothy Martin
Dennis Martin

D-U-N-S 25-146-0424 (HQ)
PREMIER EQUIPMENT LTD.
275 Church St W, Elmira, ON, N3B 1N3
(519) 669-5453
Emp Here 55   *Sales* 47,719,620
SIC 5999 Miscellaneous retail stores, nec

D-U-N-S 24-488-0738 (HQ)
PROGRAMMED INSURANCE BROKERS INC
P I B

49 Industrial Dr, Elmira, ON, N3B 3B1
(519) 669-1631
Emp Here 79   *Sales* 169,992,264
SIC 6411 Insurance agents, brokers, and service
Bruce Burnham
Charles Wood
Robert Burnham
James A Mcdonough

D-U-N-S 24-965-2785 (SL)
ROLAN INC
63 Union St, Elmira, ON, N3B 2Y3
(519) 669-1842
Emp Here 30   *Sales* 13,415,220
SIC 5063 Electrical apparatus and equipment
Duane Martin
Carol Martin

D-U-N-S 24-771-5402 (SL)
RWAM INSURANCE ADMINISTRATORS INC
49 Industrial Dr, Elmira, ON, N3B 3B1
(519) 669-1632
Emp Here 118   *Sales* 14,723,568
SIC 8741 Management services
Bruce Burnham
Carole Yari
Dan Galloway
Dianne Mctavish
Paul Straus

D-U-N-S 24-389-6800 (SL)
SANYO CANADIAN MACHINE WORKS INCORPORATED
(*Suby of* SANYO CO.,LTD.)
33 Industrial Dr, Elmira, ON, N3B 3B1
(519) 669-1591
Emp Here 55   *Sales* 12,210,055
SIC 3569 General industrial machinery, nec
Masatake Horiba
Katsumi Tanno
David Mcfadden
Stephen Crew

D-U-N-S 24-848-2713 (SL)
STOLTZ SALES & SERVICE (ELMIRA) LTD
STOLTZ SALES & SERVICE
Gd Lcd Main, Elmira, ON, N3B 2Z4
(519) 669-1561
Emp Here 70   *Sales* 33,251,820
SIC 5083 Farm and garden machinery
Marlin Stoltz

D-U-N-S 24-375-1059 (BR)
TOYOTA BOSHOKU CANADA, INC
(*Suby of* TOYOTA BOSHOKU CORPORATION)
45 South Field Dr Suite 1, Elmira, ON, N3B 3L6
(519) 669-8883
Emp Here 315
SIC 3089 Plastics products, nec
Gloria Chisholm

D-U-N-S 24-544-8212 (SL)
TRI-MACH GROUP INC
23 Donway Crt, Elmira, ON, N3B 0B1
(519) 744-6565
Emp Here 80   *Sales* 13,232,596
SIC 3541 Machine tools, Metal cutting type
Krystal Darling
Michael Hahn
Ryan Martin

D-U-N-S 24-636-3451 (HQ)
TRYLON TSF INC
21 South Field Dr, Elmira, ON, N3B 0A6
(519) 669-5421
Emp Here 200   *Sales* 117,754,500
SIC 1731 Electrical work
Jeff More
Micheal Stevens
William Spurgeon
Rick Peister

D-U-N-S 20-734-7217 (SL)
TUBE-LINE MANUFACTURING LTD

6455 Reid Woods Dr Suite 4, Elmira, ON, N3B 2Z3
(519) 669-9488
Emp Here 70   *Sales* 15,540,070
SIC 3523 Farm machinery and equipment
Oscar Frey
Paul Horst

D-U-N-S 24-576-6738 (SL)
W.D. PACKAGING INC
(*Suby of* HOME HARDWARE STORES LIMITED)
49 Industrial Dr, Elmira, ON, N3B 3B1
(519) 669-5486
Emp Here 25   *Sales* 11,230,475
SIC 7389 Business services, nec
Terry Davis

D-U-N-S 20-750-0216 (HQ)
WALCO EQUIPMENT LTD
20 Arthur St N, Elmira, ON, N3B 1Z9
(519) 669-4025
Emp Here 30   *Sales* 16,625,910
SIC 5083 Farm and garden machinery
Laverne Martin

D-U-N-S 24-974-4582 (BR)
WATERLOO REGION DISTRICT SCHOOL BOARD
ELMIRA DISTRICT SECONDARY SCHOOL
(*Suby of* WATERLOO REGION DISTRICT SCHOOL BOARD)
4 University Ave W, Elmira, ON, N3B 1K2
(519) 669-5414
Emp Here 110
SIC 8211 Elementary and secondary schools
Paul Morgan

Elmvale, ON L0L

D-U-N-S 25-916-0760 (SL)
1084408 ONTARIO INC
SUPERIOR CLEANING SYSTEMS
8 Yonge St S Unit A, Elmvale, ON, L0L 1P0
(705) 737-0480
Emp Here 300   *Sales* 9,590,400
SIC 7349 Building maintenance services, nec
Leone Hesch
Tim Hesch

D-U-N-S 20-812-6099 (SL)
1459564 ONTARIO LTD
TIM HORTONS
68 Yonge St S, Elmvale, ON, L0L 1P0
(705) 322-5504
Emp Here 38   *Sales* 10,417,776
SIC 5461 Retail bakeries
Mary Langnan

D-U-N-S 24-785-0761 (SL)
GLUECKLER METAL INC
G.M.I.
13 William St, Elmvale, ON, L0L 1P0
(705) 737-9486
Emp Here 115   *Sales* 22,089,775
SIC 3499 Fabricated Metal products, nec
Anthony Glueckler
Carl Christensen
Warren Collier

D-U-N-S 24-021-3053 (SL)
HIRE HUSBAND
200 Queen St W, Elmvale, ON, L0L 1P0
(705) 733-6355
Emp Here 49   *Sales* 14,140,567
SIC 1522 Residential construction, nec
Jennifer Shute

D-U-N-S 20-257-6005 (SL)
R & P PETROLEUM INC
R & P FUELS
2236 County Road 92, Elmvale, ON, L0L 1P0
(705) 429-5179
Emp Here 5   *Sales* 60,851,602

SIC 5172 Petroleum products, nec
Rajnikant Patel
Prafulaben Patel

Elora, ON N0B

D-U-N-S 24-162-1502   (SL)
HFH INC
6006 Hwy 6, Elora, ON, N0B 1S0
(519) 821-2040
Emp Here 54   Sales 30,798,252
SIC 1542 Nonresidential construction, nec
John Martin

D-U-N-S 24-023-0065   (BR)
HUNTER AMENITIES INTERNATIONAL LTD
(Suby of HUNTER AMENITIES INTERNA-
TIONAL LTD)
37 York St E, Elora, ON, N0B 1S0
(519) 846-2489
Emp Here 100
SIC 2841 Soap and other detergents
Paul Niedermayr

D-U-N-S 25-507-6713   (SL)
JEFFERSON ELORA CORPORATION
(Suby of G-TEKT CORPORATION)
60 1st Line, Elora, ON, N0B 1S0
(519) 846-2728
Emp Here 520   Sales 126,480,120
SIC 3465 Automotive stampings
Masaaki Iwai

D-U-N-S 20-048-0853   (HQ)
L & M FOOD MARKET (ONTARIO) LIMITED
KROPF'S IGA
181 Geddes St, Elora, ON, N0B 1S0
(519) 846-1188
Emp Here 50   Sales 53,889,920
SIC 5411 Grocery stores
J Merlen Kropf
Dale Kropf
Doreen Kropf
Debra Ramage
Len Haslam

D-U-N-S 24-120-0075   (BR)
**ONTARIO LOTTERY AND GAMING CORPO-
RATION**
ELEMENTS CASINO GRAND RIVER
(Suby of GOVERNMENT OF ONTARIO)
7445 Wellington Rd 21, Elora, ON, N0B 1S0
(519) 846-2022
Emp Here 160
SIC 7999 Amusement and recreation, nec
Greg Tremble

D-U-N-S 20-508-9779   (BR)
POLYCORP LTD
(Suby of POLYCORP LTD)
33 York St W, Elora, ON, N0B 1S0
(519) 846-2075
Emp Here 150
SIC 3069 Fabricated rubber products, nec
Andrew Haber

D-U-N-S 20-921-3867   (SL)
WOOLWICH AGRICULTURAL SOCIETY
ELMIRA COUNTRY FAIR, THE
7445 Wellington Rd 21, Elora, ON, N0B 1S0
(519) 846-5455
Emp Here 130   Sales 10,727,210
SIC 7948 Racing, including track operation
Don Jewitt
Rick Charunski
Jim Mcleod
Don Taylor
Jack Hansford
Melissa Snyder

Embro, ON N0J

D-U-N-S 20-995-9683   (HQ)
FEDERAL WHITE CEMENT LTD
355151 35th Line, Embro, ON, N0J 1J0
(519) 485-5410
Emp Here 90   Sales 17,921,900
SIC 3241 Cement, hydraulic
George Doumet

Embrun, ON K0A

D-U-N-S 24-621-8226   (SL)
561861 ONTARIO LTD
ROBERT EXCAVATING, DIV OF
1482 St Jacques Rd, Embrun, ON, K0A 1W0
(613) 443-2311
Emp Here 70   Sales 17,233,020
SIC 1794 Excavation work
Robert Bourdeau

D-U-N-S 20-780-9745   (BR)
**COOPERATIVE AGRICOLE D'EMBRUN
LIMITED, LA**
(Suby of COOPERATIVE AGRICOLE
D'EMBRUN LIMITED, LA)
Gd, Embrun, ON, K0A 1W0
(613) 443-2892
Emp Here 100
SIC 5411 Grocery stores
Michel Chenier

D-U-N-S 20-047-2884   (HQ)
**COOPERATIVE AGRICOLE D'EMBRUN
LIMITED, LA**
EMBRUN ELEVATORS, DIV OF
926 Notre Dame St, Embrun, ON, K0A 1W0
(613) 443-2892
Sales 148,504,000
SIC 5191 Farm supplies
Michel Chenier
Robert Gratton

D-U-N-S 24-384-0832   (SL)
EMBRUN FORD SALES LTD
608 Notre Dame St, Embrun, ON, K0A 1W0
(613) 443-2985
Emp Here 45   Sales 22,413,510
SIC 5511 New and used car dealers
Charlene Brunet

Emeryville, ON N0R

D-U-N-S 20-731-8262   (SL)
STEVENSON, G & L TRANSPORT LIMITED
1244 County Road 22, Emeryville, ON, N0R
1C0
(519) 727-3478
Emp Here 115   Sales 8,656,280
SIC 4151 School buses
Lee Stevenson
Sandra Stevenson

Emo, ON P0W

D-U-N-S 20-047-3114   (SL)
CLOVERLEAF GROCERY (EMO) LIMITED
CLOVERLEAF GROCERY
5970 Hwy 11, Emo, ON, P0W 1E0
(807) 482-2793
Emp Here 40   Sales 10,966,080
SIC 5411 Grocery stores
Mark Loney
David Loney
Daniel Loney
Brendon Loney

Englehart, ON P0J

D-U-N-S 20-349-8787   (BR)
**ONTARIO NORTHLAND TRANSPORTA-
TION COMMISSION**
ONTARIO NORTHLANC
(Suby of GOVERNMENT OF ONTARIO)
3rd St, Englehart, ON, P0J 1H0
(705) 544-2292
Emp Here 80
SIC 4111 Local and suburban transit
Jonathan Corley

Ennismore, ON K0L

D-U-N-S 20-093-9200   (SL)
SESHA ONTARIO INC
ENNISMORE FOODLAND
476 Robinson Rd, Ennismore, ON, K0L 1T0
(705) 292-6719
Emp Here 30   Sales 25,067,310
SIC 5141 Groceries, general line
Raj Patel

Erin, ON N0B

D-U-N-S 25-388-1254   (HQ)
**GUARDIAN BUILDING PRODUCTS DISTRI-
BUTION CANADA, INC**
300 Main St Ss 1, Erin, ON, N0B 1T0
(519) 833-9645
Emp Here 40   Sales 113,925,600
SIC 5039 Construction materials, nec
Ron Van Pelt
Duane H. Faulkner
David Love

D-U-N-S 25-790-3989   (SL)
STEWART'S NEW HOLLAND LTD
9410 Wellington Rd 124, Erin, ON, N0B 1T0
(519) 833-9384
Emp Here 30   Sales 14,250,780
SIC 5083 Farm and garden machinery
Ed Stewart

D-U-N-S 20-535-4814   (SL)
**STEWART'S, ED GARAGE & EQUIPMENT
LTD**
9410 Wellington Rd 124 Rr 2, Erin, ON, N0B
1T0
(519) 833-9616
Emp Here 40   Sales 13,024,000
SIC 5999 Miscellaneous retail stores, nec
John Stewart
Jeffrey Stewart
Randy Stewart

D-U-N-S 24-926-9713   (SL)
T.S. SIMMS & CO
300 Main St, Erin, ON, N0B 1T0
(905) 362-1470
Emp Here 60   Sales 19,568,160
SIC 3991 Brooms and brushes
Phillip Iozzo

Espanola, ON P5E

D-U-N-S 20-697-9150   (SL)
1148956 ONTARIO LTD
WINKLES INDEPENDANT GROCER
745 Centre St, Espanola, ON, P5E 1S8
(705) 869-0284
Emp Here 120   Sales 35,217,240
SIC 5411 Grocery stores
Frank Winkel

D-U-N-S 20-272-9864   (BR)

DOMTAR INC
(Suby of DOMTAR LUXEMBOURG INVEST-
MENTS SARL)
1 Station Rd, Espanola, ON, P5E 1R6
(705) 869-2020
Emp Here 800
SIC 2611 Pulp mills
Michel Deshaies

D-U-N-S 24-180-7676   (SL)
ESPANOLA GENERAL HOSPITAL
825 Mckinnon Dr Suite 705, Espanola, ON,
P5E 1R4
(705) 869-1420
Emp Here 125   Sales 13,885,000
SIC 8062 General medical and surgical hospi-
tals
Paul Davies

D-U-N-S 20-965-2937   (SL)
ESPANOLA REGIONAL HYDRO
598 Second Ave, Espanola, ON, P5E 1C4
(705) 869-2771
Emp Here 20   Sales 10,393,100
SIC 4911 Electric services
Nancy Hembruff

D-U-N-S 25-784-6980   (SL)
**MCKECHNIE, ANDY BUILDING MATERI-
ALS LTD**
ESPANOLA HOME HARDWARE
830 Centre St, Espanola, ON, P5E 1J1
(705) 869-2130
Emp Here 50   Sales 12,652,950
SIC 5211 Lumber and other building materials
Andrew Mckechnie
Ann Mckechnie

D-U-N-S 20-002-6602   (SL)
**MCMASTER, PAT & MARLEEN ENTER-
PRISES LTD**
CANADIAN TIRE
801 Centre St, Espanola, ON, P5E 1N2
(705) 869-3807
Emp Here 50   Sales 24,903,900
SIC 5531 Auto and home supply stores
Pat Mcmaster
Marleen Macmaster

D-U-N-S 20-873-3399   (HQ)
MCQUARRIE MOTOR PRODUCTS INC
228 Centre St, Espanola, ON, P5E 1G1
(705) 869-1351
Emp Here 1   Sales 10,459,638
SIC 5511 New and used car dealers
Donald Mcquarrie
Arthur Madore

D-U-N-S 24-019-8320   (BR)
OUR CHILDREN, OUR FUTURE
(Suby of OUR CHILDREN, OUR FUTURE)
273 Mead Blvd, Espanola, ON, P5E 1B3
(705) 869-5545
Emp Here 100
SIC 8351 Child day care services
Tyler Campbell

Essex, ON N8M

D-U-N-S 20-750-4960   (SL)
**COUNTRYSIDE CHRYSLER DODGE LIM-
ITED**
458 Talbot St N, Essex, ON, N8M 2W6
(519) 776-5287
Emp Here 48   Sales 23,907,744
SIC 5511 New and used car dealers
Gregory Markham
Peggy Hicks

D-U-N-S 20-015-8363   (SL)
E.L.K. ENERGY INC
172 Forest Ave, Essex, ON, N8M 3E4
(519) 776-5291
Emp Here 20   Sales 10,393,100

SIC 4911 Electric services
Michael Audet
Bob Croft
Al Fazio
Joan Flood
Gord Queen
Peter Timmins
Brian Sanger
Pat O'neil
Sandra Slater
Wilber Brett

D-U-N-S 24-378-0520   (HQ)
ESSEX POWER CORPORATION
360 Fairview Ave W Suite 218, Essex, ON,
N8M 3G4
(519) 946-2002
Emp Here 3   *Sales* 67,987,400
SIC 4911 Electric services
Raymond Tracey
Richard Dimmel
Gary A. Mcnamara
Robert Bailey
John Paling
William Varga
Marie A. Campagna
John Adams
Frank C. Ricci
Luc Gagnon

D-U-N-S 25-250-2935   (SL)
ESSEX POWERLINES CORPORATION
(*Suby of* ESSEX POWER CORPORATION)
360 Fairview Ave W Suite 218, Essex, ON,
N8M 3G4

Emp Here 50   *Sales* 31,330,700
SIC 4911 Electric services
Richard Dimmel

D-U-N-S 20-047-5879   (HQ)
ESSEX TOPCROP SALES LIMITED
TOPCROP
904 County Rd 8, Essex, ON, N8M 2Y1
(519) 776-6411
Emp Here 10   *Sales* 13,481,910
SIC 2048 Prepared feeds, nec
Darryl Brummell
Craig Brummell
Sara Brummell-Orlando
Diane Brummell
Debbie Brummell

D-U-N-S 24-418-1066   (HQ)
ESSEX WELD SOLUTIONS LTD
340 Allen Ave, Essex, ON, N8M 3G6
(519) 776-9153
Sales 19,208,500
SIC 3499 Fabricated Metal products, nec
John Friesen
Abraham Freisen

D-U-N-S 20-515-9341   (HQ)
ESSEX WINDSOR SOLID WASTE AUTHOR-ITY
360 Fairview Ave W Suite 211, Essex, ON,
N8M 3G4
(519) 776-6441
Emp Here 10   *Sales* 16,839,000
SIC 4953 Refuse systems
Ilija Maodus
Michelle Bishop

D-U-N-S 20-050-7700   (HQ)
EWS INC
ESSEX WELD SOLUTIONS
(*Suby of* ESSEX WELD SOLUTIONS LTD)
340 Allen Ave, Essex, ON, N8M 3G6
(519) 776-9153
Sales 19,208,500
SIC 3499 Fabricated Metal products, nec
John Friesen
Ave Friesen

D-U-N-S 24-196-4568   (SL)
FYNBO, IB HARDWARE LTD
ESSEX HOME HARDWARE

47 Wilson Ave, Essex, ON, N8M 2L9
(519) 776-4646
Emp Here 45   *Sales* 11,387,655
SIC 5251 Hardware stores
Philip Fynbo
Ib Fynbo

D-U-N-S 24-545-4624   (HQ)
IVES INSURANCE BROKERS LTD
YOUR 50 PLUS INSURANCE BROKERS
347 Maidstone Ave E, Essex, ON, N8M 2K1
(519) 776-7371
Emp Here 40   *Sales* 36,466,580
SIC 6411 Insurance agents, brokers, and ser-vice
Jerry Ives
Jeffrey Ives

D-U-N-S 24-609-7161   (SL)
JEFF'S NO FRILLS
53 Arthur Ave, Essex, ON, N8M 2N1
(519) 776-4944
Emp Here 49   *Sales* 13,433,448
SIC 5411 Grocery stores
Jeff Nacthee

D-U-N-S 20-185-6390   (SL)
KNAPP, KEN FORD SALES LTD
390 Talbot St N, Essex, ON, N8M 2W4
(519) 776-6447
Emp Here 50   *Sales* 24,903,900
SIC 5511 New and used car dealers
Kenneth Knapp

D-U-N-S 24-388-9214   (SL)
MAL WHITLOCK ENTERPRISES LTD
CANADIAN TIRE
300 Maidstone Ave W, Essex, ON, N8M 2X6
(519) 776-5224
Emp Here 46   *Sales* 22,911,588
SIC 5531 Auto and home supply stores
Mal Whitlock

D-U-N-S 25-001-3968   (BR)
REVERA INC
ILER LODGE RETIREMENT HOME
(*Suby of* GOVERNMENT OF CANADA)
111 Iler Ave Suite 1, Essex, ON, N8M 1T6
(519) 776-5243
Emp Here 85
SIC 8051 Skilled nursing care facilities
Cheryl Labute

Etobicoke, ON M8V

D-U-N-S 20-596-5499   (SL)
1416720 ONTARIO LIMITED
TRIWASTE SERVICES (2002)
260 New Toronto St, Etobicoke, ON, M8V 2E8
(416) 243-7000
Emp Here 40   *Sales* 12,045,680
SIC 4953 Refuse systems
Wilf Goldlust

D-U-N-S 24-801-7378   (SL)
671061 ONTARIO LIMITED
EXCLUSIVE CARE SERVICES
2913 Lake Shore Blvd W Suite A, Etobicoke,
ON, M8V 1J3
(416) 599-7232
Emp Here 150   *Sales* 11,204,100
SIC 7361 Employment agencies
Gloria Osborne
Wayne Osborne

D-U-N-S 25-116-3671   (SL)
A & A MERCHANDISING LTD
3250 Lake Shore Blvd W, Etobicoke, ON, M8V
1M1
(416) 503-3343
Emp Here 200   *Sales* 43,988,600
SIC 8732 Commercial nonphysical research
Andrij Brygidyr

D-U-N-S 24-793-3872   (SL)

A B C COMPANY LIMITED
CANADIAN STORES
123 Fourth St, Etobicoke, ON, M8V 2Y6
(905) 812-5941
Emp Here 200   *Sales* 35,170,120
SIC 5311 Department stores

D-U-N-S 25-510-1537   (SL)
BDA INC
12 Drummond St Suite 1, Etobicoke, ON, M8V
1Y8
(416) 251-1757
Emp Here 50   *Sales* 23,536,550
SIC 1542 Nonresidential construction, nec
Brad Daniels
Toccar Brown

D-U-N-S 24-815-9949   (HQ)
BPSR CORPORATION
BPSR NOVELTIES
123 Fourth St, Etobicoke, ON, M8V 2Y6
(905) 999-9999
Emp Here 100   *Sales* 18,045,376
SIC 5311 Department stores

D-U-N-S 24-366-0623   (HQ)
C4MEDIA INC
2267 Lake Shore Blvd W, Etobicoke, ON, M8V
3X2
(647) 917-4470
Sales 14,057,280
SIC 8748 Business consulting, nec
Floyd Marinescu

D-U-N-S 20-161-0771   (HQ)
CAMPBELL COMPANY OF CANADA
(*Suby of* CAMPBELL SOUP COMPANY)
60 Birmingham St, Etobicoke, ON, M8V 2B8
(416) 251-1131
Emp Here 700   *Sales* 731,077,500
SIC 2032 Canned specialties
Phillip E Donne
Greg Smith
Earl Ellis

D-U-N-S 24-101-9236   (HQ)
CANADIAN TEST CASE 174
VANILLA
123 Fourth St, Etobicoke, ON, M8V 2Y6
(905) 812-5920
Sales 18,797,000
SIC 7389 Business services, nec

D-U-N-S 24-693-2313   (BR)
CANPAR TRANSPORT L.P.
(*Suby of* CANPAR TRANSPORT L.P.)
205 New Toronto St, Etobicoke, ON, M8V 0A1
(416) 869-1332
Emp Here 600
SIC 4213 Trucking, except local
Ed Stringer

D-U-N-S 25-936-0758   (SL)
DODD DRIVER PERSONNEL INC
2977e Lake Shore Blvd W Suite L, Etobicoke,
ON, M8V 1J8

Emp Here 49   *Sales* 11,611,530
SIC 7363 Help supply services
Mike Briant

D-U-N-S 24-987-6517   (BR)
DOMINION COLOUR CORPORATION
(*Suby of* HIG CAPITAL MANAGEMENT, INC.)
199 New Toronto St, Etobicoke, ON, M8V 3X4
(416) 253-4260
Emp Here 80
SIC 2816 Inorganic pigments
David Campbell

D-U-N-S 24-849-0369   (HQ)
EASTERN POWER LIMITED
2275 Lake Shore Blvd W Suite 401, Etobi-coke, ON, M8V 3Y3
(416) 234-1301
Emp Here 15   *Sales* 31,330,700
SIC 4911 Electric services
Greg Vogt

D-U-N-S 24-773-4143   (BR)
GOVERNING COUNCIL OF THE UNIVER-SITY OF TORONTO, THE
FACULTY OF LAW
(*Suby of* GOVERNING COUNCIL OF THE
UNIVERSITY OF TORONTO, THE)
78 Queens Ave, Etobicoke, ON, M8V 2N3
(416) 978-0210
Emp Here 156
SIC 8221 Colleges and universities
Edward Iacobucci

D-U-N-S 20-153-1253   (BR)
GOVERNING COUNCIL OF THE UNIVER-SITY OF TORONTO, THE
GOVERNING COUNCIL OF THE UNIVER-SITY OF TORONTO
(*Suby of* GOVERNING COUNCIL OF THE
UNIVERSITY OF TORONTO, THE)
84 Queens Ave, Etobicoke, ON, M8V 2N3
(416) 978-8789
Emp Here 100
SIC 8221 Colleges and universities
Kathy Tam

D-U-N-S 20-153-1097   (BR)
GOVERNING COUNCIL OF THE UNIVER-SITY OF TORONTO, THE
FACULTY OF MUSIC
(*Suby of* GOVERNING COUNCIL OF THE
UNIVERSITY OF TORONTO, THE)
80 Queens Ave, Etobicoke, ON, M8V 2N3
(416) 978-0414
Emp Here 80
SIC 8221 Colleges and universities
Don Mclean

D-U-N-S 24-984-6809   (BR)
HUMBER COLLEGE INSTITUTE OF TECH-NOLOGY AND ADVANCE LEARNING, THE
(*Suby of* HUMBER COLLEGE INSTITUTE OF
TECHNOLOGY AND ADVANCE LEARNING,
THE)
3199 Lake Shore Blvd W, Etobicoke, ON, M8V
1K8
(416) 675-6622
Emp Here 250
SIC 8221 Colleges and universities
Pat Ferbyack

D-U-N-S 24-827-4862   (HQ)
IMAGES 2000 INC
33 Drummond St, Etobicoke, ON, M8V 1Y7
(416) 252-9693
Sales 17,313,300
SIC 2499 Wood products, nec
Sam Oskooei
Fariba Jafari

D-U-N-S 24-728-3864   (BR)
KRAFT HEINZ CANADA ULC
(*Suby of* THE KRAFT HEINZ COMPANY)
2150 Lake Shore Blvd W, Etobicoke, ON, M8V
1A3
(416) 506-6000
Emp Here 895
SIC 2051 Bread, cake, and related products
Harold Why

D-U-N-S 20-269-4170   (SL)
LANYAP TRADE
88 Palace Pier Crt Suite 603, Etobicoke, ON,
M8V 4C2
(647) 808-2186
Emp Here 50   *Sales* 11,237,200
SIC 6111 Federal and federally sponsored
credit agencies
Abhas Rahim

D-U-N-S 25-458-8940   (HQ)
MAIN ST. GROUP INC
2275 Lake Shore Blvd W Suite 318, Etobi-coke, ON, M8V 3Y3
(519) 537-3513
Emp Here 10   *Sales* 13,304,700
SIC 7389 Business services, nec
Ralph Mooney Jr

▲ Public Company   ■ Public Company Family Member   **HQ** Headquarters   **BR** Branch   **SL** Single Location

Robert Mooney

D-U-N-S 24-254-0230   (SL)
PRO IT PLUS INC.
CHEFS WITHOUT LIMITS
16 Brookers Lane Suite 2908, Etobicoke, ON,
M8V 0A5
(905) 977-8168
Emp Here 25   *Sales* 11,179,350
SIC 5045 Computers, peripherals, and software
Michael Loomans

D-U-N-S 25-419-4533   (SL)
STOREFRONT HUMBER INCORPORATED
2445 Lake Shore Blvd W, Etobicoke, ON, M8V
1C5
(416) 259-4207
Emp Here 150   *Sales* 20,018,850
SIC 8399 Social services, nec
Mary Hansen

D-U-N-S 24-093-7755   (SL)
TRICLO INC
241 Birmingham St, Etobicoke, ON, M8V 2C7
(416) 252-4777
Emp Here 20   *Sales* 10,006,500
SIC 5162 Plastics materials and basic shapes
James Dowe
Vivian Dowe

D-U-N-S 24-621-4647   (SL)
WEINGARTEN, ALAN DRUGS LTD
SHOPPERS DRUG MART
2850 Lake Shore Blvd W, Etobicoke, ON, M8V
1H9
(416) 255-2397
Emp Here 55   *Sales* 13,438,040
SIC 5912 Drug stores and proprietary stores
Alan Weingarten
Ava Weingarten

D-U-N-S 24-097-4246   (SL)
**YORK CONDOMINIUM CORPORATION NO
382**
PALACE PIER
2045 Lake Shore Blvd W, Etobicoke, ON, M8V
2Z6
(416) 252-7701
Emp Here 50   *Sales* 16,356,350
SIC 6531 Real estate agents and managers
Bruce Conley
Juleen Marchant
Tim Sargeant

Etobicoke, ON M8W

D-U-N-S 25-176-4932   (HQ)
669779 ONTARIO LTD
CSA TRANSPORTATION
355 Horner Ave Suite 416, Etobicoke, ON,
M8W 1Z7
(416) 754-0999
Emp Here 40   *Sales* 30,855,900
SIC 4213 Trucking, except local
Herman Fallick

D-U-N-S 25-202-6265   (HQ)
966850 ONTARIO INC
CHRISTIE LITES
100 Carson St Unit A, Etobicoke, ON, M8W
3R9
(416) 259-0282
Sales 41,140,008
SIC 5049 Professional equipment, nec
Huntly C R Christie

D-U-N-S 24-868-8012   (HQ)
ACTIVE TIRE & AUTO CENTRE INC
ACTIVE GREEN + ROSS
580 Evans Ave, Etobicoke, ON, M8W 2W1
(416) 255-5581
Emp Here 18   *Sales* 19,923,120
SIC 5531 Auto and home supply stores
Ralph Chiodo

Rose Chiodo

D-U-N-S 24-876-1546   (SL)
AVANTGARD INVESTMENTS INC
LAKESHORE HONDA
3526 Lake Shore Blvd W, Etobicoke, ON,
M8W 1N6
(416) 252-0066
Emp Here 52   *Sales* 32,722,560
SIC 5511 New and used car dealers
Oscar Terenzio
Sarjit (Serge) Mundi
Marino D'alessandro

D-U-N-S 20-160-5953   (BR)
BRINK'S CANADA LIMITED
BRINKS TORONTO
(*Suby of* THE BRINK'S COMPANY)
95 Browns Line, Etobicoke, ON, M8W 3S2
(416) 461-0261
Emp Here 300
SIC 7381 Detective and armored car services
Carmel Kutschke

D-U-N-S 25-419-6983   (BR)
CASCADES CANADA ULC
CASCADES CONTAINERBOARD PACKAGING - ART & DIE
(*Suby of* CASCADES INC)
450 Evans Ave, Etobicoke, ON, M8W 2T5
(416) 255-8541
Emp Here 157
SIC 2657 Folding paperboard boxes
Luce Ayotte

D-U-N-S 24-686-1488   (HQ)
CHRISTIE LITES TORONTO LTD
(*Suby of* 966850 ONTARIO INC)
100 Carson St Unit A, Etobicoke, ON, M8W
3R9
(416) 644-1010
Emp Here 10   *Sales* 34,797,880
SIC 5049 Professional equipment, nec
Huntly C. R. Christie
Claudia Pfaffinger
Paul Dhingra
Dan Souwand
Michael Rawson

D-U-N-S 20-902-8893   (SL)
CONVENIENCE GROUP INC
10 Butterick Rd, Etobicoke, ON, M8W 3Z8
(416) 233-6900
Emp Here 30   *Sales* 13,415,220
SIC 5031 Lumber, plywood, and millwork
George Turjanica
Maryann Turjanica
Robert (Bob) Alsit

D-U-N-S 24-850-4446   (SL)
CT CONSTRUCTION LTD
55 Browns Line, Etobicoke, ON, M8W 3S2
(416) 588-8707
Emp Here 50   *Sales* 12,044,200
SIC 1622 Bridge, tunnel, and elevated highway construction
Rui Neves

D-U-N-S 20-754-2093   (HQ)
D'ALESSANDRO INVESTMENTS LIMITED
MARINO'S FINE CARS
3526 Lake Shore Blvd W, Etobicoke, ON,
M8W 1N6
(416) 252-2277
Sales 17,432,730
SIC 5511 New and used car dealers
Marino D'alessandro
Lucy D'alessandro

D-U-N-S 20-163-1629   (HQ)
DARCOR LIMITED
DARCOR CASTERS
7 Staffordshire Pl, Etobicoke, ON, M8W 1T1
(416) 255-8563
Sales 13,320,060
SIC 3562 Ball and roller bearings
Jeffrey Albaum

D-U-N-S 20-016-9634   (SL)
EVENT SCAPE INC
4 Bestobell Rd, Etobicoke, ON, M8W 4H3
(416) 231-8855
Emp Here 60   *Sales* 26,953,140
SIC 7389 Business services, nec
Gareth Brennan

D-U-N-S 20-169-3967   (HQ)
F.G. LISTER & CO., LIMITED
475 Horner Ave, Etobicoke, ON, M8W 4X7
(416) 259-7621
Emp Here 90   *Sales* 86,005,920
SIC 5148 Fresh fruits and vegetables
Anthony Arrigo Sr
Michael Arrigo
Anthony Arrigo Jr

D-U-N-S 24-198-7551   (HQ)
FLEXTILE LTD
WINDSOR CERAMICS, DIV OF
(*Suby of* OLYMPIA TILE INTERNATIONAL
INC)
121 Thirtieth St, Etobicoke, ON, M8W 3C1
(416) 255-1111
Sales 22,402,375
SIC 3253 Ceramic wall and floor tile
Mike Boldt

D-U-N-S 24-685-5811   (SL)
HIGGINS RENT-ALL LTD
389 Horner Ave, Etobicoke, ON, M8W 2A2
(416) 252-4050
Emp Here 50   *Sales* 14,608,450
SIC 7359 Equipment rental and leasing, nec
John Higgins

D-U-N-S 24-049-9608   (SL)
HILITE FINE FOODS INC
415 Horner Ave Unit 4, Etobicoke, ON, M8W
4W3
(416) 503-0499
Emp Here 25   *Sales* 20,889,425
SIC 5148 Fresh fruits and vegetables
Joseph Siegal
Brian Siegal

D-U-N-S 20-473-7571   (SL)
LUMENIX CORPORATION
LUMENIX
15 Akron Rd, Etobicoke, ON, M8W 1T3
(855) 586-3649
Emp Here 200   *Sales* 38,088,400
SIC 3674 Semiconductors and related devices
Bryant Tse
Scott Delaney
Derek Thomas
Liam Ellis
Robert Richards
Joseph Clark
George Brookman
Andrew Wilkes

D-U-N-S 20-264-2153   (HQ)
MERSEN CANADA DN LTD
(*Suby of* MERSEN)
496 Evans Ave, Etobicoke, ON, M8W 2T7
(416) 251-2334
Emp Here 60   *Sales* 19,044,200
SIC 3624 Carbon and graphite products
Marc Charlebois
Michel Lanctot

D-U-N-S 24-885-8995   (HQ)
METROPOLITAN TEA COMPANY LTD, THE
41 Butterick Rd, Etobicoke, ON, M8W 4W4
(416) 588-0089
Sales 29,245,195
SIC 5149 Groceries and related products, nec

D-U-N-S 20-115-1979   (HQ)
MURRAY DEMOLITION CORP
MRA ABATEMENT, DIV OF
345 Horner Ave Suite 300, Etobicoke, ON,
M8W 1Z6
(416) 253-6000
Sales 84,950,400
SIC 1795 Wrecking and demolition work

Shawn Murray
Antonio Cicconi
Kareem El Khatib
Dave Fusek
Joe Batista

D-U-N-S 24-986-4893   (HQ)
NANOWAVE TECHNOLOGIES INC
(*Suby of* EUROMILL EQUIHOLD INC)
425 Horner Ave Suite 1, Etobicoke, ON, M8W
4W3
(416) 252-5602
Sales 45,457,800
SIC 3812 Search and navigation equipment
Justin Miller
Ola Ore

D-U-N-S 24-354-3829   (HQ)
OUTFRONT MEDIA CANADA LP
CBS OUTDOOR CANADA
377 Horner Ave, Etobicoke, ON, M8W 1Z6
(416) 255-1392
Emp Here 50   *Sales* 10,586,200
SIC 7312 Outdoor advertising services
Nick Arakgi

D-U-N-S 24-096-2969   (HQ)
SAM KOTZER LIMITED
SAMKO SALES
77 Fima Cres, Etobicoke, ON, M8W 3R1
(416) 532-1114
Emp Here 40   *Sales* 10,880,650
SIC 5945 Hobby, toy, and game shops
Sam Kotzer
Sheryl Kotzer

D-U-N-S 20-940-6743   (SL)
SOMORICH MARKETING CORPORATION
SMARTDM
324 Horner Ave Unit A, Etobicoke, ON, M8W
1Z3
(416) 461-9271
Emp Here 170   *Sales* 34,063,070
SIC 7331 Direct mail advertising services
Bob Tier
David Dunnett
Jack Ledrew

D-U-N-S 24-216-4432   (SL)
TOOLQUIP AGENCY LTD
270 Browns Line, Etobicoke, ON, M8W 3T5

Emp Here 55   *Sales* 20,031,825
SIC 5013 Motor vehicle supplies and new
parts
John Ross

D-U-N-S 25-366-4312   (HQ)
WAKEFIELD CANADA INC
3620 Lake Shore Blvd W, Etobicoke, ON,
M8W 1N6
(416) 252-5511
Emp Here 187   *Sales* 226,996,416
SIC 5172 Petroleum products, nec
Robert Mcdonald
Robert Saurette
Kent Rennie

Etobicoke, ON M8X

D-U-N-S 24-195-0203   (HQ)
ADP CANADA CO
(*Suby of* AUTOMATIC DATA PROCESSING,
INC.)
3250 Bloor St W 6th Fl Suite 1600, Etobicoke,
ON, M8X 2X9
(416) 207-2900
Emp Here 700   *Sales* 369,706,000
SIC 8721 Accounting, auditing, and bookkeeping
Holger Kormann
Liane Lagroix
Bob Buckley
Heather Haslam

Russell Wong
Sooky Lee

D-U-N-S 24-829-0918   (HQ)
BACARDI CANADA INC
(*Suby of* BACARDI LIMITED)
3250 Bloor St W Suite 1050, Etobicoke, ON, M8X 2X9
(905) 451-6100
Emp Here 90   *Sales* 34,569,000
SIC 2085 Distilled and blended liquors
Richard Andrews
Lisa Smith
John P Esposito

D-U-N-S 24-687-8938   (SL)
BARRY PHILLIPS DRUGS LIMITED
SHOPPERS DRUG MART
3010 Bloor St W, Etobicoke, ON, M8X 1C2
(416) 234-0136
Emp Here 60   *Sales* 14,659,680
SIC 5912 Drug stores and proprietary stores
Barry Phillips

D-U-N-S 24-574-8512   (HQ)
BEAM CANADA INC
MAXXIUM CANADA
(*Suby of* MAXXIUM NEDERLAND B.V.)
3280 Bloor St W Unit 510, Etobicoke, ON, M8X 2X3
(416) 849-7300
Emp Here 63   *Sales* 134,005,280
SIC 5182 Wine and distilled beverages
William Newlands
Robert Probst

D-U-N-S 24-729-0042   (SL)
BRUNO'S FINE FOODS (ETOBICOKE) LTD
BRUNO'S FINE FOODS
4242 Dundas St W Suite 15, Etobicoke, ON, M8X 1Y6
(416) 234-1106
Emp Here 50   *Sales* 13,707,600
SIC 5411 Grocery stores
Bruno Fattore

D-U-N-S 24-463-0604   (HQ)
CBI LIMITED
CBI HEALTH
3300 Bloor St W Suite 900, Etobicoke, ON, M8X 2X2
(800) 463-2225
Emp Here 50   *Sales* 419,531,400
SIC 8049 Offices of health practitioner

D-U-N-S 25-301-2298   (BR)
EXTENDICARE (CANADA) INC
PARAMED HOME HEALTH CARE
(*Suby of* EXTENDICARE INC)
56 Aberfoyle Cres, Etobicoke, ON, M8X 2W4
(416) 236-1061
Emp Here 300
SIC 8051 Skilled nursing care facilities
Jim Topping

D-U-N-S 24-664-5670   (SL)
FLIPP CORPORATION
3250 Bloor St W Suite 1200, Etobicoke, ON, M8X 2X9
(416) 626-7092
Emp Here 160   *Sales* 23,069,120
SIC 7371 Custom computer programming services
Wehuns Tan
Charmaine D'silva

D-U-N-S 25-109-4413   (BR)
MARKET PROBE CANADA COMPANY
(*Suby of* MARKET PROBE, INCORPORATED)
1243 Islington Ave Suite 200, Etobicoke, ON, M8X 1Y9
(416) 233-1555
Emp Here 140
SIC 8732 Commercial nonphysical research
Maria Pimentel

D-U-N-S 24-181-6144   (BR)

MERIDIAN CREDIT UNION LIMITED
(*Suby of* MERIDIAN CREDIT UNION LIMITED)
3280 Bloor St W, Etobicoke, ON, M8X 2X3
(416) 597-4400
Emp Here 160
SIC 6062 State credit unions
Sean Jackson

D-U-N-S 24-859-1278   (HQ)
MONDELEZ CANADA INC
MONDELEZ INTERNATIONAL
(*Suby of* MONDELEZ INTERNATIONAL, INC.)
3300 Bloor St W Suite 1801, Etobicoke, ON, M8X 2X2

Emp Here 3,200   *Sales* 1,754,586,000
SIC 2032 Canned specialties
Dan Magliocco
Brendan Flynn
Craig Murray

D-U-N-S 20-011-9159   (HQ)
MONERIS SOLUTIONS CORPORATION
3300 Bloor St W 10th Flr, Etobicoke, ON, M8X 2X2
(416) 734-1000
Emp Here 1,100   *Sales* 396,605,300
SIC 7389 Business services, nec
Angela Brown
Jeffrey (Jeff) Guthrie
Malcolm Fowler
Amer Matar
Brian Prentice

D-U-N-S 20-257-8761   (SL)
OMT HOSPITALITY INC
OLD MILL TORONTO HOTEL
21 Old Mill Rd, Etobicoke, ON, M8X 1G5
(416) 236-2641
Emp Here 150   *Sales* 13,903,500
SIC 7011 Hotels and motels
Irene Hryniuk

D-U-N-S 25-510-4028   (SL)
REAL ESTATE COUNCIL OF ONTARIO
RECO
3300 Bloor St W Unit 1200, Etobicoke, ON, M8X 2X2
(416) 207-4800
Emp Here 119   *Sales* 15,650,285
SIC 8641 Civic and social associations

D-U-N-S 20-325-2036   (BR)
ROYAL BANK OF CANADA
RBC AUTOMOTIVE FINANCE
(*Suby of* ROYAL BANK OF CANADA)
3250 Bloor St W Suite 800, Etobicoke, ON, M8X 2X9

Emp Here 100
SIC 6159 Miscellaneous business credit institutions
Tarini Sharma

D-U-N-S 24-829-9836   (BR)
ROYAL LEPAGE LIMITED
(*Suby of* BROOKFIELD ASSET MANAGEMENT INC)
3031 Bloor St W, Etobicoke, ON, M8X 1C5
(416) 236-1871
Emp Here 120
SIC 6531 Real estate agents and managers
Carolyn Curtis

D-U-N-S 20-268-3744   (SL)
SOUTHERN GLAZER'S WINE AND SPIRITS OF CANADA, LLC
(*Suby of* SOUTHERN GLAZER'S WINE AND SPIRITS, LLC)
3250 Bloor St W Suite 901, Etobicoke, ON, M8X 2X9
(647) 347-7711
Emp Here 15   *Sales* 12,533,655
SIC 5149 Groceries and related products, nec
Wayne Chaplin
Douglas Wieland

Harvey Chaplin
Shelly Stein
Steven R. Becker
Thomas Greenlee
Lee F. Hager

D-U-N-S 20-324-7473   (SL)
STARLIGHT INVESTMENTS
(*Suby of* NORTHVIEW APARTMENT REAL ESTATE INVESTMENT TRUST)
3280 Bloor St W Unit 1400, Etobicoke, ON, M8X 2X3
(416) 234-8444
Emp Here 100   *Sales* 41,888,900
SIC 6531 Real estate agents and managers
Daniel Drimmer
Leslie Veiner

D-U-N-S 20-285-4196   (SL)
STARLIGHT INVESTMENTS LTD
3280 Bloor St W Unit 1400, Etobicoke, ON, M8X 2X3
(416) 234-8444
Emp Here 120   *Sales* 123,893,280
SIC 6799 Investors, nec
Daniel Drimmer
Glen Hirsh
Tracy Sherren

D-U-N-S 25-419-8765   (SL)
SUTTON GROUP OLD MILL REALTY INC
4237 Dundas St W, Etobicoke, ON, M8X 1Y3
(416) 234-2424
Emp Here 49   *Sales* 16,029,223
SIC 6531 Real estate agents and managers
Ann Hannah

D-U-N-S 20-608-3693   (HQ)
UNITED CHURCH OF CANADA, THE
3250 Bloor St W Suite 300, Etobicoke, ON, M8X 2Y4
(416) 231-5931
Emp Here 200   *Sales* 29,844,373
SIC 8661 Religious organizations
Nora Saunders
Fannie Hudson
Mary-Beth Moriarity
Shirley Cleave
Paul Reed
Tressa Brotsky
Sam Hou

D-U-N-S 24-818-9391   (HQ)
WE CARE HEALTH SERVICES INC
WE CARE HOME HEALTH SERVICES
3300 Bloor St W Suite 900, Etobicoke, ON, M8X 2X2
(416) 922-7601
Emp Here 48   *Sales* 7,594,967,016
SIC 6794 Patent owners and lessors
David Chapman
Robin Cakrabarti

Etobicoke, ON M8Y

D-U-N-S 20-161-2496   (HQ)
CANADIAN FRUIT & PRODUCE COMPANY INC
165 The Queensway Suite 306, Etobicoke, ON, M8Y 1H8
(416) 259-5007
Emp Here 1   *Sales* 56,310,525
SIC 5148 Fresh fruits and vegetables
Steven Weinstein
Robert Piccone
Randy Weinstein

D-U-N-S 20-694-9609   (SL)
FRESH ADVANCEMENTS INC
(*Suby of* BAMFORD PRODUCE COMPANY LIMITED)
165 The Queensway Suite 333, Etobicoke, ON, M8Y 1H8
(416) 259-5400
Emp Here 40   *Sales* 33,423,080

SIC 5148 Fresh fruits and vegetables
Stephen Bamford
Nick Nasturzio

D-U-N-S 20-178-5326   (HQ)
FRESH TASTE PRODUCE LIMITED
165 The Queensway Suite 343, Etobicoke, ON, M8Y 1H8
(416) 255-0157
Sales 83,557,700
SIC 5148 Fresh fruits and vegetables
Sal Sarraino
Ron Doucet

D-U-N-S 24-794-5652   (HQ)
GAMBLES ONTARIO PRODUCE INC
(*Suby of* TOTAL PRODUCE PUBLIC LIMITED COMPANY)
165 The Queensway Suite 240, Etobicoke, ON, M8Y 1H8
(416) 259-6391
Sales 143,343,200
SIC 5148 Fresh fruits and vegetables
Jeffrey Hughes
Robert Giles

D-U-N-S 25-957-4148   (SL)
GET A BETTER MORTGAGE
642 The Queensway, Etobicoke, ON, M8Y 1K5
(416) 252-9000
Emp Here 49   *Sales* 11,012,456
SIC 6162 Mortgage bankers and loan correspondents
Robert Distefano

D-U-N-S 20-559-9483   (SL)
ITALIAN PRODUCE CO. LIMITED
165 The Queensway Rm 314, Etobicoke, ON, M8Y 1H8
(416) 259-7641
Emp Here 26   *Sales* 21,725,002
SIC 5148 Fresh fruits and vegetables
Vito Fortunato
Joe Fortunato
Andy Lentile
Vince Bruno

D-U-N-S 25-976-4066   (HQ)
KOORNNEEF PRODUCE LTD
165 The Queensway Suite 151, Etobicoke, ON, M8Y 1H8
(416) 255-5188
Emp Here 1   *Sales* 16,711,540
SIC 5148 Fresh fruits and vegetables
Frederick Koornneef
Adrian Koornneef

D-U-N-S 20-171-8806   (SL)
NORTH AMERICAN PRODUCE BUYERS LIMITED
165 The Queensway Suite 336, Etobicoke, ON, M8Y 1H8
(416) 255-5544
Emp Here 25   *Sales* 20,889,425
SIC 5148 Fresh fruits and vegetables
Howard Davidson
Heather Davidson
Larry Davidson
Steven Davidson

D-U-N-S 20-584-7101   (SL)
PREFERRED POLYMER COATINGS LTD
APPLIED INDUSTRIAL FLOORING CANADA
31 Portland St, Etobicoke, ON, M8Y 1A6
(416) 201-9003
Emp Here 50   *Sales* 23,751,300
SIC 5085 Industrial supplies
Mark Mcleod

D-U-N-S 25-418-6000   (HQ)
PROVINCIAL FRUIT CO. LIMITED
(*Suby of* BURNAC CORPORATION)
165 The Queensway, Etobicoke, ON, M8Y 1H8
(416) 259-5001
Sales 43,002,960
SIC 5148 Fresh fruits and vegetables

Joseph Burnett
Theodore Burnett
Frank Defrancesco
Joseph Manserra

D-U-N-S 20-550-6769   (SL)
RITE-PAK PRODUCE CO. LIMITED
(*Suby of* BURNAC CORPORATION)
165 The Queensway, Etobicoke, ON, M8Y
1H8
(416) 252-3121
Emp Here 46   *Sales* 38,436,542
SIC 5148 Fresh fruits and vegetables
Domenic Raso
Joseph Burnett
Joseph Manserra
Theodore Burnett

D-U-N-S 25-818-7467   (SL)
RUSSELL, J.E. PRODUCE LTD
165 The Queensway Suite 332, Etobicoke,
ON, M8Y 1H8
(416) 252-7838
Emp Here 40   *Sales* 33,423,080
SIC 5148 Fresh fruits and vegetables

D-U-N-S 20-806-2617   (BR)
SOBEYS CAPITAL INCORPORATED
SOBEYS STORE 7383
(*Suby of* EMPIRE COMPANY LIMITED)
125 The Queensway, Etobicoke, ON, M8Y
1H6
(416) 259-1758
Emp Here 100
SIC 5411 Grocery stores
Gus Gucci

D-U-N-S 24-025-0498   (SL)
STRONACH & SONS INC
165 The Queensway Suite 318, Etobicoke,
ON, M8Y 1H8
(416) 259-5009
Emp Here 22   *Sales* 18,382,694
SIC 5148 Fresh fruits and vegetables
Ted Maxwell Kurtz
Barry Fogle

D-U-N-S 25-419-9540   (BR)
**TORONTO CATHOLIC DISTRICT SCHOOL
BOARD**
BISHOP ALLEN ACADEMY
(*Suby of* TORONTO CATHOLIC DISTRICT
SCHOOL BOARD)
721 Royal York Rd, Etobicoke, ON, M8Y 2T3
(416) 393-5549
Emp Here 115
SIC 8211 Elementary and secondary schools
Stephen Carey

D-U-N-S 25-991-0263   (BR)
TORONTO DISTRICT SCHOOL BOARD
ETOBICOKE SCHOOL OF THE ARTS
(*Suby of* TORONTO DISTRICT SCHOOL
BOARD)
675 Royal York Rd, Etobicoke, ON, M8Y 2T1
(416) 394-6910
Emp Here 100
SIC 8211 Elementary and secondary schools
Peggy Aitchison

D-U-N-S 20-177-6861   (HQ)
VEG-PAK PRODUCE LIMITED
165 The Queensway Rm 249, Etobicoke, ON,
M8Y 1H8
(416) 259-4686
Emp Here 30   *Sales* 50,134,620
SIC 5148 Fresh fruits and vegetables
Victor Carnevale
Rick Carnevale

D-U-N-S 20-051-9440   (SL)
WARRIAN, KAREN PHARMACY
SHOPPERS DRUG MART
125 The Queensway, Etobicoke, ON, M8Y
1H6
(416) 766-6196
Emp Here 40   *Sales* 10,118,160
SIC 5912 Drug stores and proprietary stores

Karen Warrian

Etobicoke, ON M8Z

D-U-N-S 24-987-1856   (SL)
1045761 ONTARIO LIMITED
*CANADIAN PHOENIX STEEL PRODUCTS,
DIV OF*
289 Horner Ave, Etobicoke, ON, M8Z 4Y4
(416) 259-1113
Emp Here 55   *Sales* 12,838,925
SIC 3312 Blast furnaces and steel mills
Jack Dym
Joseph Lamarch

D-U-N-S 24-333-8506   (HQ)
1325931 CANADA INC
INQUIRY MANAGEMENT SYSTEMS
55 Horner Ave Unit 1, Etobicoke, ON, M8Z
4X6
(416) 620-1965
Sales 20,037,100
SIC 7311 Advertising agencies
Martin Hochstein
Jim Panousis
Gina Palmer

D-U-N-S 24-616-8426   (SL)
1570707 ONTARIO INC
I.M.S.
55 Horner Ave Unit 1, Etobicoke, ON, M8Z
4X6
(416) 620-1965
Emp Here 200   *Sales* 40,074,200
SIC 7311 Advertising agencies
Martin Hochstein

D-U-N-S 20-178-2448   (HQ)
2104225 ONTARIO LTD
WESTON'S OUTLET STORE
(*Suby of* GEORGE WESTON LIMITED)
1425 The Queensway, Etobicoke, ON, M8Z
1T3
(416) 252-7323
Emp Here 200   *Sales* 962,585,375
SIC 2051 Bread, cake, and related products
Ralph Robinson
Maria Liang
Geoffrey H. Wilson
Jeremy Robert

D-U-N-S 24-335-4214   (SL)
427 AUTO COLLISION LIMITED
395 Evans Ave, Etobicoke, ON, M8Z 1K8
(416) 259-6344
Emp Here 50   *Sales* 10,131,450
SIC 7532 Top and body repair and paint shops
Ralph D'alessandro

D-U-N-S 24-476-4544   (SL)
573349 ONTARIO LIMITED
BUTCHER SHOPPE, THE
121 Shorncliffe Rd, Etobicoke, ON, M8Z 5K7
(416) 234-2290
Emp Here 95   *Sales* 79,379,815
SIC 5147 Meats and meat products
Allan Weisberg

D-U-N-S 24-859-4041   (SL)
8008655 CANADA INC.
VINTAGE HARDWOOD FLOORING
409 Evans Ave, Etobicoke, ON, M8Z 1K8
(416) 521-6100
Emp Here 75   *Sales* 11,689,725
SIC 2426 Hardwood dimension and flooring
mills
Pierre Thabet
Kenton Martin
Emanuelle Machado

D-U-N-S 24-877-3509   (SL)
822099 ONTARIO LIMITED
OK TIRE ETOBICOKE
12 Lockport Ave, Etobicoke, ON, M8Z 2R7

(416) 236-1277
Emp Here 24   *Sales* 11,953,872
SIC 5531 Auto and home supply stores
Patrick Croft
Louise Croft

D-U-N-S 24-343-6461   (HQ)
ADP DIRECT POULTRY LTD
DIRECT POULTRY
34 Vansco Rd, Etobicoke, ON, M8Z 5J4
(416) 658-0911
Sales 25,067,310
SIC 5144 Poultry and poultry products
Augusto Pinho

D-U-N-S 24-485-4980   (HQ)
ALLSEAS FISHERIES INC
MIKE'S FISH MARKET
55 Vansco Rd, Etobicoke, ON, M8Z 5Z8
(416) 255-3474
Emp Here 20   *Sales* 41,778,850
SIC 5146 Fish and seafoods
Harry Gorman
Danny Soberano
Ralph Soberano

D-U-N-S 25-409-5847   (SL)
ALLWOOD INDUSTRIES LTD
ALLWOOD CARPENTRY MANUFACTURING
33 Atomic Ave Unit 1, Etobicoke, ON, M8Z
5K8
(416) 398-1460
Emp Here 80   *Sales* 12,469,040
SIC 2431 Millwork
Jose Rocha

D-U-N-S 20-554-4117   (SL)
ANDORRA BUILDING MAINTENANCE LTD
46 Chauncey Ave, Etobicoke, ON, M8Z 2Z4
(416) 537-7772
Emp Here 160   *Sales* 5,114,880
SIC 7349 Building maintenance services, nec
Anthony Vella

D-U-N-S 20-177-7208   (HQ)
ARAMARK CANADA LTD.
ARAMARK MANAGED SERVICES
(*Suby of* ARAMARK)
811 Islington Ave, Etobicoke, ON, M8Z 5W8
(416) 255-1331
Emp Here 200   *Sales* 722,904,500
SIC 5812 Eating places
Karen Wetselaar
Lynn Ervin

D-U-N-S 20-893-3924   (SL)
ASBURY BUILDING SERVICES INC
323 Evans Ave, Etobicoke, ON, M8Z 1K2

Emp Here 450   *Sales* 1,499,400
SIC 7349 Building maintenance services, nec
Kevin Daly

D-U-N-S 24-919-7484   (HQ)
BEST BAKING INC
DUFFLET PASTRIES, A DIV OF
166 Norseman St, Etobicoke, ON, M8Z 2R4
(416) 536-1330
Emp Here 55   *Sales* 54,312,505
SIC 5149 Groceries and related products, nec
Dufflet Rosenberg

D-U-N-S 20-160-3453   (SL)
BOHNE SPRING INDUSTRIES LIMITED
60 Coronet Rd, Etobicoke, ON, M8Z 2M1
(416) 231-9000
Emp Here 60   *Sales* 28,501,560
SIC 5085 Industrial supplies
Christopher Wharin
Jeff Wharin

D-U-N-S 24-123-1802   (HQ)
BONCHEFF GREENHOUSES INC
BONCHEFF HERBS
382 Olivewood Rd, Etobicoke, ON, M8Z 2Z9
(416) 233-1800
Sales 12,533,655
SIC 5148 Fresh fruits and vegetables

George Boncheff
Tommy Boncheff

D-U-N-S 20-256-9760   (SL)
BOXES NEXT DAY INC
(*Suby of* 1220774 ONTARIO LIMITED)
54 Atomic Ave, Etobicoke, ON, M8Z 5L1
(416) 253-7350
Emp Here 65   *Sales* 12,659,920
SIC 2653 Corrugated and solid fiber boxes
Richard Ciupak
Ted Ciupak

D-U-N-S 24-846-5247   (HQ)
BRENNTAG CANADA INC
BRENNTAG TORONTO
(*Suby of* BRENNTAG AG)
43 Jutland Rd, Etobicoke, ON, M8Z 2G6
(416) 259-8231
Emp Here 80   *Sales* 336,106,000
SIC 5169 Chemicals and allied products, nec
Mike Staley

D-U-N-S 20-286-3841   (SL)
BURRITO BOYZ DISTRIBUTION INC
21 Jutland Rd, Etobicoke, ON, M8Z 2G6
(416) 251-8536
Emp Here 500   *Sales* 358,358,000
SIC 5149 Groceries and related products, nec
Joseph Michael Vassallo

D-U-N-S 24-771-6764   (SL)
CANA IMPORT EXPORT LTD
1589 The Queensway Unit 1, Etobicoke, ON,
M8Z 5W9
(416) 252-8652
Emp Here 22   *Sales* 16,335,440
SIC 5199 Nondurable goods, nec
Saleem Khan
Laiqua Khan

D-U-N-S 24-664-4280   (SL)
CANA-DATUM MOULDS LTD
DATUM GROUP
55 Goldthorne Ave, Etobicoke, ON, M8Z 5S7
(416) 252-1212
Emp Here 140   *Sales* 31,080,140
SIC 3544 Special dies, tools, jigs, and fixtures
Ignacio Musalem
Colleen Musalem

D-U-N-S 24-817-1167   (SL)
CANADA FOOD EQUIPMENT LTD
45 Vansco Rd, Etobicoke, ON, M8Z 5Z8
(416) 253-5100
Emp Here 41   *Sales* 19,476,066
SIC 5084 Industrial machinery and equipment
David Nava
Ezra Nava

D-U-N-S 20-251-3461   (SL)
CANADA UKRAINE FOUNDATION
CUF
145 Evans Ave Unit 300, Etobicoke, ON, M8Z
5X8
(416) 966-9700
Emp Here 37   *Sales* 14,704,318
SIC 8699 Membership organizations, nec
Victor Hetmanczuk

D-U-N-S 24-426-5331   (HQ)
**CANADIAN LINEN AND UNIFORM SER-
VICE CO**
QUEBEC LINGE
(*Suby of* ARAMARK)
20 Atomic Ave, Etobicoke, ON, M8Z 5L1
(416) 354-3100
Emp Here 2   *Sales* 107,635,200
SIC 7213 Linen supply
Naiem Nairaz

D-U-N-S 20-810-5853   (BR)
CARA OPERATIONS QUEBEC LTD
MILESTONE GRILL AND BAR
(*Suby of* RECIPE UNLIMITED CORPORA-
TION)
1001 The Queensway, Etobicoke, ON, M8Z
6C7

(416) 255-0464
Emp Here 80
SIC 5812 Eating places
  Joan Keyworth

D-U-N-S 20-337-8810   (BR)
CASCADES CANADA ULC
CASCADES RECOVERY+ - TORONTO
(*Suby of* CASCADES INC)
66 Shorncliffe Rd, Etobicoke, ON, M8Z 5K1
(416) 231-2525
Emp Here 362
SIC 2611 Pulp mills

D-U-N-S 25-936-9890   (SL)
CCFGLM ONTARIO LIMITED
MANDARIN RESTAURANT
1255 The Queensway, Etobicoke, ON, M8Z
1S1
(416) 252-5000
Emp Here 90   *Sales* 3,858,570
SIC 5812 Eating places
  Cheryl Guo
  Peter Leung

D-U-N-S 25-514-1137   (SL)
CENTRE ISLAND FOOD SERVICES LTD
CI FOODS
(*Suby of* BEASLEY, WILLIAM ENTERPRISES
LIMITED)
84 Advance Rd, Etobicoke, ON, M8Z 2T7
(416) 234-2345
Emp Here 80   *Sales* 3,641,520
SIC 5812 Eating places
  William Beasley

D-U-N-S 20-161-9517   (HQ)
CHIOVITTI BANANA COMPANY LIMITED
26 Magnificent Rd, Etobicoke, ON, M8Z 4T3
(416) 251-3774
Emp Here 20   *Sales* 33,423,080
SIC 5148 Fresh fruits and vegetables
  Ronald Chiovitti
  Sandra Chiovitti
  Richard Chisholme

D-U-N-S 20-044-9585   (SL)
COLEMAN CONTAINERS LIMITED
54 Atomic Ave, Etobicoke, ON, M8Z 5L1
(416) 253-7441
Emp Here 56   *Sales* 13,072,360
SIC 2653 Corrugated and solid fiber boxes
  Frank Ciupak
  Richard Ciupak
  Ted Ciupak

D-U-N-S 25-528-6353   (BR)
COMMUNITY LIVING TORONTO
(*Suby of* COMMUNITY LIVING TORONTO)
288 Judson St Unit 17, Etobicoke, ON, M8Z
5T6
(416) 252-1171
Emp Here 200
SIC 7389 Business services, nec
  Harold Tomlinson

D-U-N-S 20-573-3376   (BR)
**COMPAGNIE DES CHEMINS DE FER NA-
TIONAUX DU CANADA**
(*Suby of* COMPAGNIE DES CHEMINS DE
FER NATIONAUX DU CANADA)
123 Judson St, Etobicoke, ON, M8Z 1A4
(416) 253-6395
Emp Here 100
SIC 4011 Railroads, line-haul operating
  Don Mitchell

D-U-N-S 25-710-9611   (SL)
**COOL BEER BREWING CO. INCORPO-
RATED**
164 Evans Ave, Etobicoke, ON, M8Z 1J4
(416) 255-7100
Emp Here 24   *Sales* 14,109,984
SIC 5181 Beer and ale
  Bob Crecouzos

D-U-N-S 20-697-8590   (BR)
COSTCO WHOLESALE CANADA LTD
COSTCO

(*Suby of* COSTCO WHOLESALE CORPO-
RATION)
50 Queen Elizabeth Blvd Suite 524, Etobi-
coke, ON, M8Z 1M1
(416) 251-2832
Emp Here 200
SIC 5399 Miscellaneous general merchandise
  Carry Stockford

D-U-N-S 20-409-0625   (SL)
COURTESY CHEVROLET LTD.
1635 The Queensway, Etobicoke, ON, M8Z
1T8

Emp Here 75   *Sales* 47,196,000
SIC 5511 New and used car dealers
  Donald Polyschuk
  Joanne Werstroh

D-U-N-S 25-405-4596   (HQ)
COUTURE PARFUMS & COSMETICS LTD
997 The Queensway, Etobicoke, ON, M8Z 1P3
(416) 597-3232
Emp Here 1   *Sales* 14,652,000
SIC 5999 Miscellaneous retail stores, nec
  Steven Orrett
  Shawn James Orrett

D-U-N-S 20-163-3971   (SL)
DEL'S PASTRY LIMITED
344 Bering Ave, Etobicoke, ON, M8Z 3A7
(416) 231-4383
Emp Here 170   *Sales* 58,767,300
SIC 2051 Bread, cake, and related products
  Benno Mattes
  Tom Mattes

D-U-N-S 20-410-9680   (HQ)
DIMPFLMEIER BAKERY LIMITED
VIKING BAKERY
26 Advance Rd, Etobicoke, ON, M8Z 2T4
(416) 236-2701
Emp Here 150   *Sales* 57,038,850
SIC 2051 Bread, cake, and related products
  Alfons Dimpflmeier
  Elfriede Schoen
  Christel Dimpflmeier

D-U-N-S 24-389-2858   (SL)
DOWBICO SUPPLIES LIMITED
DRY ICE & GASES CO DIV
50 Titan Rd, Etobicoke, ON, M8Z 2J8
(416) 252-7137
Emp Here 25   *Sales* 18,258,625
SIC 5169 Chemicals and allied products, nec
  Peter William Dowbiggin

D-U-N-S 24-059-7583   (BR)
ESSILOR GROUPE CANADA INC
ESSILOR
(*Suby of* ESSILORLUXOTTICA)
347 Evans Ave, Etobicoke, ON, M8Z 1K2
(416) 252-5458
Emp Here 150
SIC 5049 Professional equipment, nec
  Harsh Ghandi

D-U-N-S 20-195-0990   (SL)
ETOBICOKE HUMANE SOCIETY
67 Six Point Rd, Etobicoke, ON, M8Z 2X3
(416) 249-6100
Emp Here 30   *Sales* 11,922,420
SIC 8699 Membership organizations, nec
  Pia Lauretti

D-U-N-S 20-924-2502   (HQ)
**ETOBICOKE MEDICAL CENTRE FAMILY
HEALTH TEAM**
85 The East Mall, Etobicoke, ON, M8Z 5W4
(416) 621-2220
Sales 12,851,680
SIC 8011 Offices and clinics of medical doc-
tors
  Hariclia Johnston
  Stuart Egier
  Matthew Ng
  Laura Fisch

D-U-N-S 20-164-9654   (SL)
FASTER LINEN SERVICE LIMITED
89 Torlake Cres, Etobicoke, ON, M8Z 1B4
(416) 252-2030
Emp Here 160   *Sales* 17,085,120
SIC 7213 Linen supply
  Mark Halberstadt

D-U-N-S 20-165-0975   (SL)
**FINCHAM AUTOMOTIVE SUPPLIES LIM-
ITED**
70 Advance Rd Suite 2484, Etobicoke, ON,
M8Z 2T7
(416) 233-5896
Emp Here 23   *Sales* 11,455,794
SIC 5511 New and used car dealers
  Tony Racioppo

D-U-N-S 24-794-3996   (SL)
FIRST AVENUE CLEARING CORPORATION
FIRST AVENUE MEDIA ONE
47 Jutland Rd, Etobicoke, ON, M8Z 2G6
(416) 259-3600
Emp Here 100   *Sales* 21,335,800
SIC 8732 Commercial nonphysical research
  Jim Higginson

D-U-N-S 25-530-5682   (HQ)
FIRST MEDIA GROUP INC
536 Kipling Ave, Etobicoke, ON, M8Z 5E3
(416) 252-2424
Sales 58,488,720
SIC 8999 Services, nec
  Grant Hood

D-U-N-S 20-308-5530   (HQ)
FLATIRON BUILDING GROUP INC
FLAT IRON
37 Advance Rd Unit 101, Etobicoke, ON, M8Z
2S6
(416) 749-3957
Sales 18,019,971
SIC 1542 Nonresidential construction, nec
  Daniel De Monte

D-U-N-S 20-994-7030   (SL)
FURNITURE BANK
25 Connell Crt Unit 1, Etobicoke, ON, M8Z
1E8
(416) 934-1229
Emp Here 29   *Sales* 20,567,148
SIC 8699 Membership organizations, nec
  Andrew Chung
  Nevine Sedki
  Anne Schenck
  John Visser
  Jennifer Russell
  Sugithan Kumaresan
  Betty Fiksel
  John Wallis
  Bob Waterworth
  Dan Kershaw

D-U-N-S 20-165-5735   (HQ)
FUTURE BAKERY LIMITED
106 North Queen St, Etobicoke, ON, M8Z 2E2
(416) 231-1491
Emp Here 65   *Sales* 24,198,300
SIC 2051 Bread, cake, and related products
  Borys Jaroszewski

D-U-N-S 20-165-7558   (SL)
**GENERAL CARTAGE & EXPRESS COM-
PANY LIMITED**
48 North Queen St, Etobicoke, ON, M8Z 2C4
(416) 236-2460
Emp Here 70   *Sales* 10,373,440
SIC 4212 Local trucking, without storage
  David Moore

D-U-N-S 20-163-7220   (HQ)
GLOBAL EGG CORPORATION
283 Horner Ave, Etobicoke, ON, M8Z 4Y4
(416) 231-2309
Emp Here 40   *Sales* 24,198,300
SIC 2015 Poultry slaughtering and processing
  Aaron B. Kwinter
  William H. Gray

  Alan R. Heimbecker
  Michael James Walsh
  David Kwinter
  William S. Parrish

D-U-N-S 20-166-1493   (HQ)
GOODYEAR CANADA INC
(*Suby of* THE GOODYEAR TIRE & RUBBER
COMPANY)
450 Kipling Ave, Etobicoke, ON, M8Z 5E1
(416) 201-4300
Emp Here 200   *Sales* 1,074,654,000
SIC 3011 Tires and inner tubes
  Samuel M. Pillow
  Paul C. Christou
  Stephen R. Mcclellan
  Oliver Gloe

D-U-N-S 24-010-9652   (SL)
HIGHLAND EQUIPMENT INC
136 The East Mall, Etobicoke, ON, M8Z 5V5
(416) 236-9610
Emp Here 74   *Sales* 14,214,290
SIC 3499 Fabricated Metal products, nec

D-U-N-S 20-785-9166   (SL)
HOMELIFE CHOLKAN REALTY CORP
109 Judge Rd, Etobicoke, ON, M8Z 5B5
(416) 236-7711
Emp Here 140   *Sales* 59,323,675
SIC 6531 Real estate agents and managers
  Ernst Grenke

D-U-N-S 20-784-5298   (SL)
HYMOPACK LTD
(*Suby of* GESTIONS ROPAL-ROJAK INC)
41 Medulla Ave, Etobicoke, ON, M8Z 5L6
(416) 232-1733
Emp Here 175   *Sales* 34,084,400
SIC 2673 Bags: plastic, laminated, and
coated

D-U-N-S 25-421-2731   (SL)
**I.M.S. INQUIRY MANAGEMENT SYSTEMS
LTD**
55 Horner Ave Unit 1, Etobicoke, ON, M8Z
4X6
(416) 620-1965
Emp Here 200   *Sales* 40,074,200
SIC 7311 Advertising agencies
  Martin Hochstein

D-U-N-S 20-181-2109   (BR)
IKEA CANADA LIMITED PARTNERSHIP
IKEA ETOBICOKE
(*Suby of* QINGDAO HONGYISEN CON-
STRUCTION ENGINEERING SERVICE CO.,
LTD.)
1475 The Queensway, Etobicoke, ON, M8Z
1T3
(866) 866-4532
Emp Here 150
SIC 5712 Furniture stores
  Mike Baker

D-U-N-S 25-405-0404   (SL)
IMPACT CLEANING SERVICES LTD
21 Goodrich Rd Suite 8, Etobicoke, ON, M8Z
6A3
(416) 253-1234
Emp Here 249   *Sales* 7,960,032
SIC 7349 Building maintenance services, nec
  Christos Boutsalis

D-U-N-S 24-172-1971   (SL)
IN STORE FOCUS
50 Queen Elizabeth Blvd, Etobicoke, ON, M8Z
1M1

Emp Here 33   *Sales* 14,824,227
SIC 7389 Business services, nec
  Allison Kursko

D-U-N-S 25-406-4611   (BR)
**INFORMATION COMMUNICATION SER-
VICES (ICS) INC**
ICS COURIER SERVICES
(*Suby of* TFI INTERNATIONAL INC)

288 Judson St Suite 1, Etobicoke, ON, M8Z 5T6

Emp Here 200
SIC 7389 Business services, nec
Mike O""neal

D-U-N-S 20-195-0982   (SL)
INSURANCE SYSTEMS INC
170 Evans Ave, Etobicoke, ON, M8Z 1J7
(416) 249-2260
Emp Here 130   *Sales* 18,960,747
SIC 7371 Custom computer programming services
Terrance Neilson

D-U-N-S 24-008-2404   (SL)
ISLINGTON NURSERIES LIMITED
ISLINGTON FLORIST & GARDEN CENTRE
1000 Islington Ave Suite 5, Etobicoke, ON, M8Z 4P8
(416) 231-8416
Emp Here 55   *Sales* 13,438,040
SIC 5992 Florists
Anthony Badali
Lena Badali

D-U-N-S 25-419-5415   (SL)
JEAN TWEED TREATMENT CENTER, THE
215 Evans Ave, Etobicoke, ON, M8Z 1J5
(416) 255-7359
Emp Here 50   *Sales* 11,341,650
SIC 8399 Social services, nec
Nancy Bradley

D-U-N-S 20-168-4305   (HQ)
KERR BROS. LIMITED
KERRS
956 Islington Ave, Etobicoke, ON, M8Z 4P6
(416) 252-7341
Emp Here 97   *Sales* 34,569,000
SIC 2064 Candy and other confectionery products
Fayez Zakaria
Laura Lu
Ryan Martic

D-U-N-S 20-918-6688   (SL)
KILIAN CANADA ULC
(*Suby of* ALTRA INDUSTRIAL MOTION CORP.)
75 Torlake Cres, Etobicoke, ON, M8Z 1B7
(416) 252-5936
Emp Here 50   *Sales* 23,751,300
SIC 5085 Industrial supplies
Patrick Kelly

D-U-N-S 25-094-9708   (HQ)
KINECTRICS INC
800 Kipling Ave Suite 2, Etobicoke, ON, M8Z 5G5
(416) 207-6000
Emp Here 357   *Sales* 109,888,131
SIC 3612 Transformers, except electric
David Harris
Shahrokh Zangeneh
Lawrence Gibbons
John D'angelo
Nancy Macdonald Exel

D-U-N-S 25-999-9084   (BR)
KOREX CANADA COMPANY
(*Suby of* PENSLER CAPITAL CORP.)
104 Jutland Rd, Etobicoke, ON, M8Z 2H1
(416) 259-9214
Emp Here 80
SIC 2842 Polishes and sanitation goods
Ed Johnson

D-U-N-S 25-510-6924   (HQ)
KOREX CANADA COMPANY
(*Suby of* PENSLER CAPITAL CORP.)
78 Titan Rd, Etobicoke, ON, M8Z 2J8
(416) 231-7800
Emp Here 10   *Sales* 25,561,890
SIC 2841 Soap and other detergents
John Koehler
Raymond Fernandes

Ed Johnson
Robin Simpson

D-U-N-S 24-172-6582   (BR)
LUCAS & MARCO INC
MCDONALD'S
(*Suby of* LUCAS & MARCO INC)
1000 Islington Ave, Etobicoke, ON, M8Z 4P8
(416) 255-4152
Emp Here 80
SIC 5812 Eating places
Tony Tinto

D-U-N-S 20-122-9452   (BR)
MAPLE LEAF FOODS INC
SCHNEIDER FOODS
(*Suby of* MAPLE LEAF FOODS INC)
550 Kipling Ave, Etobicoke, ON, M8Z 5E9

Emp Here 120
SIC 2011 Meat packing plants
Laura Kowan

D-U-N-S 25-530-4636   (SL)
MARTIN AIR HEATING & AIR CONDITIONING SERVICES LIMITED
DIRECT ENERGY
30 Fieldway Rd, Etobicoke, ON, M8Z 0E3
(416) 247-1777
Emp Here 4   *Sales* 11,046,700
SIC 1711 Plumbing, heating, air-conditioning
Martin Donnelly

D-U-N-S 25-177-5151   (HQ)
MEEST CORPORATION INC
97 Six Point Rd, Etobicoke, ON, M8Z 2X3
(416) 236-2032
Sales 12,999,175
SIC 4731 Freight transportation arrangement
Rostyslav Kisil

D-U-N-S 24-425-8591   (SL)
MILLER & SMITH FOODS INC
33 Connell Crt, Etobicoke, ON, M8Z 1E8
(416) 253-2000
Emp Here 21   *Sales* 17,547,117
SIC 5141 Groceries, general line

D-U-N-S 20-400-3867   (HQ)
MILLER & SMITH FOODS INCORPORATED
33 Connell Crt, Etobicoke, ON, M8Z 1E8
(416) 253-2000
Sales 53,067,140
SIC 5142 Packaged frozen goods
Rennie Asada
Terry Stina
Arif Khan

D-U-N-S 24-138-2415   (HQ)
MIROLIN INDUSTRIES CORP
(*Suby of* MASCO CORPORATION)
60 Shorncliffe Rd, Etobicoke, ON, M8Z 5K1
(416) 231-5790
Emp Here 30   *Sales* 71,643,600
SIC 3089 Plastics products, nec
Domenic Primucci

D-U-N-S 25-511-5099   (BR)
MIROLIN INDUSTRIES CORP
(*Suby of* MASCO CORPORATION)
200 Norseman St, Etobicoke, ON, M8Z 2R4
(416) 231-9030
Emp Here 270
SIC 3431 Metal sanitary ware
Mauro Coluccio

D-U-N-S 20-380-1662   (SL)
MISTER PRODUCE LTD
50 Jutland Rd, Etobicoke, ON, M8Z 2H1
(416) 252-9191
Emp Here 65   *Sales* 54,312,505
SIC 5148 Fresh fruits and vegetables
Mark Goodman
Ernie Goodman

D-U-N-S 20-171-5851   (SL)
MMG CANADA LIMITED
(*Suby of* DELTA MAGNETS LIMITED)

Emp Here 100   *Sales* 49,832,200

10 Vansco Rd, Etobicoke, ON, M8Z 5J4
(416) 251-2831
Emp Here 45   *Sales* 10,994,760
SIC 5995 Optical goods stores
Paul Marques
Alan Lloyd

D-U-N-S 24-485-5003   (HQ)
MYLAN PHARMACEUTICALS ULC
85 Advance Rd, Etobicoke, ON, M8Z 2S6
(416) 236-2631
Emp Here 200   *Sales* 198,956,400
SIC 2834 Pharmaceutical preparations
Richard Guest

D-U-N-S 24-206-6798   (BR)
MYLEX LIMITED
(*Suby of* MYLEX LIMITED)
1460 The Queensway, Etobicoke, ON, M8Z 1S7
(416) 259-5595
Emp Here 200
SIC 2517 Wood television and radio cabinets
Mike Burger

D-U-N-S 25-403-1982   (SL)
NATIONAL PRODUCE MARKETING INC
55 Plywood Pl Unit 102, Etobicoke, ON, M8Z 5J3
(416) 259-0833
Emp Here 14   *Sales* 22,743,060
SIC 5148 Fresh fruits and vegetables
Anthony Formusa

D-U-N-S 20-171-5265   (HQ)
NATIONAL SILICATES PARTNERSHIP
NATIONAL SILICATES
429 Kipling Ave, Etobicoke, ON, M8Z 5C7
(416) 255-7771
Emp Here 30   *Sales* 23,289,722
SIC 2819 Industrial inorganic chemicals, nec
Wig Wigaeswaran

D-U-N-S 24-192-7748   (SL)
NEKISON ENGINEERING & CONTRACTORS LIMITED
17 Saint Lawrence Ave, Etobicoke, ON, M8Z 5T8
(416) 259-4631
Emp Here 55   *Sales* 12,818,575
SIC 1711 Plumbing, heating, air-conditioning
Ramesh Jain
Asha Jain

D-U-N-S 25-172-4985   (HQ)
NEW HORIZON SYSTEM SOLUTIONS INC
(*Suby of* CAPGEMINI)
800 Kipling Ave Suite 8, Etobicoke, ON, M8Z 5G5
(416) 207-6800
Emp Here 200   *Sales* 68,626,800
SIC 8741 Management services
Jane Diercks
Gert Kollenhoven

D-U-N-S 20-257-6203   (HQ)
NORTHSTAR SCAFFOLD SERVICES INC
362 Olivewood Rd, Etobicoke, ON, M8Z 2Z7
(416) 231-1610
Emp Here 2   *Sales* 53,094,000
SIC 1799 Special trade contractors, nec
Jonathan Mccain
Brad Westoby

D-U-N-S 20-259-5331   (SL)
O.B.N. CONSULTANTS INC
O.B.N. SECURITY & INVESTIGATIONS
78 Queen Elizabeth Blvd, Etobicoke, ON, M8Z 1M3
(416) 253-7416
Emp Here 100   *Sales* 23,428,800
SIC 8748 Business consulting, nec
William Henderson

D-U-N-S 25-064-9050   (SL)
OMNITEX INC
120 The East Mall, Etobicoke, ON, M8Z 5V5

SIC 5136 Men's and boy's clothing
Firoz Somani

D-U-N-S 24-194-5641   (SL)
PANACHE ROTISSEURS (1990) INC
ST HUBERT BAR-B-Q
1633 The Queensway, Etobicoke, ON, M8Z 1T8
(416) 251-3129
Emp Here 250   *Sales* 11,659,750
SIC 5812 Eating places
James Demeroutis
Nick Yioldassis
Albert Wiltshire

D-U-N-S 24-097-3909   (SL)
PEOPLE PLAYERS INC
FAMOUS PEOPLE PLAYERS
343 Evans Ave, Etobicoke, ON, M8Z 1K2
(416) 532-1137
Emp Here 34   *Sales* 13,512,076
SIC 8699 Membership organizations, nec
Dianne Lynn Dupey

D-U-N-S 20-171-7329   (HQ)
PERFORMANCE IMPROVEMENTS SPEED SHOPS LIMITED
87 Advance Rd, Etobicoke, ON, M8Z 2S6
(416) 259-9656
Emp Here 10   *Sales* 16,361,280
SIC 5531 Auto and home supply stores
Robert Mcjannett
Andy Mcjannett
Paul Dickie

D-U-N-S 20-554-3838   (HQ)
PIZZA PIZZA LIMITED
500 Kipling Ave, Etobicoke, ON, M8Z 5E5
(416) 967-1010
Emp Here 130   *Sales* 224,384,546
SIC 5812 Eating places
Paul Goddard
Curtis Feltner
Paul Methot
Sebastian Fuschini

D-U-N-S 24-130-8381   (SL)
PIZZA PIZZA ROYALTY CORP
500 Kipling Ave, Etobicoke, ON, M8Z 5E5
(416) 967-1010
Emp Here 10   *Sales* 431,795,329
SIC 6722 Management investment, open-end
Paul Goddard
Curt Feltner
Paul Methot
Sebastian Fuschini
Richard Mccor
Edward Nash
Michelle Savoy
Jay Swartz
Kathy Welsh

D-U-N-S 25-421-8183   (SL)
PLANWAY POULTRY INC
26 Canmotor Ave, Etobicoke, ON, M8Z 4E5
(416) 252-7676
Emp Here 90   *Sales* 75,201,930
SIC 5144 Poultry and poultry products
King Lam

D-U-N-S 25-353-2774   (SL)
POINTONE GRAPHICS INC
14 Vansco Rd, Etobicoke, ON, M8Z 5J4
(416) 255-8202
Emp Here 100   *Sales* 16,402,700
SIC 2752 Commercial printing, lithographic
Dennis Low

D-U-N-S 20-402-6249   (HQ)
POLYTAINERS INC
197 Norseman St, Etobicoke, ON, M8Z 2R5
(416) 239-7311
Sales 167,168,400
SIC 3089 Plastics products, nec
Robert Barrett

D-U-N-S 24-818-0374   (SL)
PRO-SHIELD CORPORATION

(Suby of ULTRA SHIELD INC)
33 Coronet Rd, Etobicoke, ON, M8Z 2L8
(800) 561-4272
Emp Here 30   *Sales* 21,910,350
SIC 5169 Chemicals and allied products, nec
  Melvin Mandel

D-U-N-S 20-173-6014   (SL)
**QUEENSWAY MACHINE PRODUCTS LIM-
ITED, THE**
8 Rangemore Rd, Etobicoke, ON, M8Z 5H7
(416) 259-4261
Emp Here 52   *Sales* 11,544,052
SIC 3599 Industrial machinery, nec
  John Saksun Jr
  Mary Saksun

D-U-N-S 20-754-1178   (SL)
QUEENSWAY VOLKSWAGEN INC
QUEENSWAY VOLKSWAGEN AUDI
1306 The Queensway, Etobicoke, ON, M8Z
1S4
(416) 259-7656
Emp Here 71   *Sales* 31,963,987
SIC 7538 General automotive repair shops
  Robert Green
  David H Green

D-U-N-S 24-768-5048   (SL)
REGIONAL HOSE TORONTO LTD
236 Norseman St, Etobicoke, ON, M8Z 2R4
(416) 239-9555
Emp Here 47   *Sales* 22,326,222
SIC 5085 Industrial supplies
  Darwin Booth

D-U-N-S 20-170-3790   (HQ)
RJM56 INVESTMENTS INC
R.J. MCCARTHY
360 Evans Ave, Etobicoke, ON, M8Z 1K5
(416) 593-6900
Emp Here 50   *Sales* 18,298,392
SIC 5699 Miscellaneous apparel and acces-
sory stores
  Kathleen Mccarthy
  Martin Mccarthy

D-U-N-S 20-174-2129   (SL)
ROBERTSON PYROTECHEM LIMITED
ROBERTSON FIRE EQUIPMENT
50 Chauncey Ave, Etobicoke, ON, M8Z 2Z4
(416) 233-3934
Emp Here 32   *Sales* 15,200,832
SIC 5087 Service establishment equipment
  Kent Berry
  Jim Steele

D-U-N-S 25-459-5085   (SL)
ROLTEK INTERNATIONAL INC
305 Evans Ave, Etobicoke, ON, M8Z 1K2
(416) 252-1101
Emp Here 30   *Sales* 13,304,700
SIC 7389 Business services, nec
  James Theaker

D-U-N-S 24-873-0400   (HQ)
SEA MERCHANTS INC
(Suby of ALLSEAS FISHERIES INC)
55 Vansco Rd, Etobicoke, ON, M8Z 5Z8
(416) 255-2700
Emp Here 22   *Sales* 20,889,425
SIC 5146 Fish and seafoods
  Harry Gorman
  Andre Chabot

D-U-N-S 20-716-7255   (HQ)
SIRCO MACHINERY COMPANY LIMITED
40 Jutland Rd, Etobicoke, ON, M8Z 2G9
(416) 255-1321
Emp Here 27   *Sales* 15,675,858
SIC 5084 Industrial machinery and equipment
  Victor Ferko
  Danny Ferko
  Tammy Vertkas

D-U-N-S 24-993-2534   (HQ)
**SOUTHERN GRAPHIC SYSTEMS-CANADA
LTD**

5CROWD
(Suby of LOGO HOLDINGS I CORPORA-
TION)
2 Dorchester Ave, Etobicoke, ON, M8Z 4W3
(416) 252-9331
Emp Here 99   *Sales* 22,200,100
SIC 3555 Printing trades machinery
  David Corsin
  Rick Degendorfor

D-U-N-S 20-258-7879   (HQ)
**SOUTHERN   GRAPHICS   SYSTEMS-
CANADA, CO.**
2 Dorchester Ave, Etobicoke, ON, M8Z 4W3
(416) 252-9331
Sales 13,762,060
SIC 7336 Commercial art and graphic design
  Aidan Tracey

D-U-N-S 24-385-7125   (SL)
SPORTS INTERNATIONAL CSTS INC
SPORTSPHERE
(Suby of CANADIAN TIRE CORPORATION,
LIMITED)
221 Evans Ave, Etobicoke, ON, M8Z 1J5
(416) 251-2132
Emp Here 130   *Sales* 34,493,550
SIC 2329 Men's and boy's clothing, nec
  Douglas Nathanson
  Gregory Graig
  Michael Medline
  Jeffrey Stephen

D-U-N-S 24-798-1959   (SL)
STUCCOCONTRACTORS.CA
2 Fieldway Rd, Etobicoke, ON, M8Z 0B9
(416) 900-8715
Emp Here 49   *Sales* 23,453,758
SIC 1542 Nonresidential construction, nec
  Joseph Posladek

D-U-N-S 20-876-1940   (HQ)
**SWEET GALLERY EXCLUSIVE PASTRY
LIMITED**
*SWEET GALLERY EXCLUSIVE PASTRY &
CAFE*
350 Bering Ave, Etobicoke, ON, M8Z 3A9
(416) 232-1539
Emp Here 17   *Sales* 11,240,232
SIC 5461 Retail bakeries
  Radenko Jelenic
  Lydia Jelenic

D-U-N-S 24-417-1877   (SL)
TALKA ENTERPRISES LTD
CANADIAN TIRE
1608 The Queensway, Etobicoke, ON, M8Z
1V1
(416) 255-5531
Emp Here 150   *Sales* 94,392,000
SIC 5531 Auto and home supply stores
  Edmond (Ted) Mangnall

D-U-N-S 20-718-9762   (SL)
THORNCREST SHERWAY INC
SHERWAY FORD TRUCK SALES
1575 The Queensway, Etobicoke, ON, M8Z
1T9
(416) 521-7000
Emp Here 120   *Sales* 75,513,600
SIC 5511 New and used car dealers
  Delano Bedard

D-U-N-S 20-597-6046   (SL)
TORCAD LIMITED
(Suby of COURT GROUP OF COMPANIES
LTD, THE)
275 Norseman St, Etobicoke, ON, M8Z 2R5
(416) 239-3928
Emp Here 65   *Sales* 12,485,525
SIC 3471 Plating and polishing
  William Court

D-U-N-S 20-922-8220   (SL)
TORONTO SUN WAH TRADING INC
18 Canmotor Ave, Etobicoke, ON, M8Z 4E5
(416) 252-7757
Emp Here 100   *Sales* 50,365,800

SIC 5113 Industrial and personal service pa-
per
  Ricky Luk
  John Lee
  Alfred Tang

D-U-N-S 20-012-4787   (SL)
TRADE SECRET PRINTING INC
40 Horner Ave, Etobicoke, ON, M8Z 4X3
(416) 231-9660
Emp Here 130   *Sales* 21,323,510
SIC 2752 Commercial printing, lithographic
  Bashir Harv

D-U-N-S 20-556-8249   (HQ)
**TRAILERMASTER FREIGHT CARRIERS
LTD**
ATRIPCO DELIVERY SERVICE
34 Canmotor Ave, Etobicoke, ON, M8Z 4E5
(416) 252-7725
Emp Here 160   *Sales* 51,426,500
SIC 4212 Local trucking, without storage
  J Ivan Service
  Greg Service
  Lloyd Service

D-U-N-S 24-384-0837   (SL)
TRINITY COMMUNICATION SERVICES LTD
86 Torlake Cres, Etobicoke, ON, M8Z 1B8
(416) 503-9796
Emp Here 100   *Sales* 21,782,900
SIC 1731 Electrical work
  Joseph Lo Giudice
  Wendy Andrews

D-U-N-S 24-126-4332   (HQ)
UNIBEL COMPANY LTD
FERMA IMPORT & EXPORT
44 Atomic Ave, Etobicoke, ON, M8Z 5L1
(416) 533-3591
Sales 37,600,965
SIC 5141 Groceries, general line
  Antonio B Belas

D-U-N-S 24-581-7890   (SL)
**URBAN   ENVIRONMENT   CENTRE
(TORONTO), THE**
GREENSAVER
74 Six Point Rd, Etobicoke, ON, M8Z 2X2
(416) 203-3106
Emp Here 60   *Sales* 15,209,400
SIC 8748 Business consulting, nec
  Vladan M. Veljovic
  Peter D'uva
  Tyler Moore
  Tim Stoate
  Jens Lohmueller
  David House
  Dusanka Filipovic
  Hazel Mccallion

D-U-N-S 24-408-7904   (SL)
WEST STAR PRINTING LIMITED
10 North Queen St, Etobicoke, ON, M8Z 2C4
(416) 201-0881
Emp Here 160   *Sales* 26,244,320
SIC 2752 Commercial printing, lithographic
  Gulamabibas Jaffer

D-U-N-S 24-327-8186   (HQ)
WESTON FOODS (CANADA) INC
(Suby of GEORGE WESTON LIMITED)
1425 The Queensway, Etobicoke, ON, M8Z
1T3
(416) 252-7323
Sales 7,993,114,000
SIC 2051 Bread, cake, and related products
  W Galen Weston

D-U-N-S 20-645-3586   (BR)
WESTROCK COMPANY OF CANADA CORP
*ROCKTENN   MERCHANDISING   DISPLAY,
DIV OF*
(Suby of WESTROCK COMPANY)
730 Islington Ave, Etobicoke, ON, M8Z 4N8
(416) 259-8421
Emp Here 200
SIC 2653 Corrugated and solid fiber boxes

  James Sampson

D-U-N-S 20-550-0176   (HQ)
WHITE, WILLIAM F. INTERNATIONAL INC
800 Islington Ave, Etobicoke, ON, M8Z 6A1
(416) 239-5050
Emp Here 100   *Sales* 20,630,080
SIC 7819 Services allied to motion pictures
  Paul A. Bronfman
  Munir Noorbhai
  Paul Roscorla
  Michael Yee
  Allison Spicer

Etobicoke, ON M9A

D-U-N-S 20-302-2413   (HQ)
386338 ONTARIO LIMITED
39 Poplar Heights Dr, Etobicoke, ON, M9A
5A1
(416) 247-2354
Emp Here 25   *Sales* 11,322,585
SIC 6712 Bank holding companies
  Walter Szwez
  Margaret Szwez

D-U-N-S 24-511-5196   (BR)
**BENEFIT PLAN ADMINISTRATORS LIM-
ITED**
(Suby of BENEFIT PLAN ADMINISTRATORS
LIMITED)
90 Burnhamthorpe Rd, Etobicoke, ON, M9A
1H2
(905) 275-6466
Emp Here 180
SIC 8742 Management consulting services
  Stephen Houston

D-U-N-S 24-670-1457   (SL)
ETOBICOKE CAMERA CLUB
76 Anglesey Blvd, Etobicoke, ON, M9A 3C1
(416) 234-2014
Emp Here 30   *Sales* 12,122,941
SIC 8699 Membership organizations, nec

D-U-N-S 20-823-6638   (SL)
ISLINGTON GOLF CLUB, LIMITED
45 Riverbank Dr, Etobicoke, ON, M9A 5B8
(416) 231-1114
Emp Here 130   *Sales* 10,210,850
SIC 7997 Membership sports and recreation
clubs
  David Fox

D-U-N-S 20-355-9039   (SL)
LABDARA LITHUANIAN NURSING HOME
5 Resurrection Rd, Etobicoke, ON, M9A 5G1
(416) 232-2112
Emp Here 100   *Sales* 6,856,600
SIC 8051 Skilled nursing care facilities
  Vida Proctor

D-U-N-S 20-048-1658   (BR)
LOBLAWS SUPERMARKETS LIMITED
LOBLAWS
(Suby of LOBLAW COMPANIES LIMITED)
270 The Kingsway, Etobicoke, ON, M9A 3T7
(416) 231-0931
Emp Here 97
SIC 5411 Grocery stores
  Mike Zammit

D-U-N-S 20-125-2009   (SL)
ORXESTRA INC
5 Heathrow Crt, Etobicoke, ON, M9A 3A2
(416) 233-9318
Emp Here 49   *Sales* 13,668,351
SIC 8741 Management services
  John Burdett

D-U-N-S 24-991-4896   (BR)
RE/MAX PROFESSIONALS INC
RE MAX PROFESSIONALS
(Suby of RE/MAX PROFESSIONALS INC)
270 The Kingsway Suite 200, Etobicoke, ON,

▲ Public Company   ■ Public Company Family Member   **HQ** Headquarters   **BR** Branch   **SL** Single Location

M9A 3T7
(416) 236-1241
Emp Here 80
SIC 6531 Real estate agents and managers
Leah Andler

D-U-N-S 25-577-7393   (SL)
ST DEMETRIUS (UKRAINIAN CATHOLIC) DEVELOPMENT CORPORATION, THE
UKRAINIAN CANADIAN CARE CENTRE, THE
60 Richview Rd, Etobicoke, ON, M9A 5E4
(416) 243-7653
Emp Here 120   *Sales* 8,227,920
SIC 8051 Skilled nursing care facilities
Irena Dounets

D-U-N-S 20-877-9660   (SL)
ST. GEORGE'S GOLF AND COUNTRY CLUB
1668 Islington Ave, Etobicoke, ON, M9A 3M9
(416) 231-3393
Emp Here 80   *Sales* 6,111,760
SIC 7997 Membership sports and recreation clubs
Joseph Murphy
Karen Stacey

D-U-N-S 20-698-7468   (BR)
TORONTO DISTRICT SCHOOL BOARD
ETOBICOKE COLLEGIATE INSTITUTE
(*Suby of* TORONTO DISTRICT SCHOOL BOARD)
86 Montgomery Rd, Etobicoke, ON, M9A 3N5
(416) 394-7840
Emp Here 120
SIC 8211 Elementary and secondary schools
Caroline Rath

Etobicoke, ON M9B

D-U-N-S 24-347-1583   (HQ)
1690651 ONTARIO INC
FOOD BASICS
5559 Dundas St W, Etobicoke, ON, M9B 1B9
(416) 239-7171
Emp Here 1   *Sales* 29,347,700
SIC 5411 Grocery stores
Paul Denommee
Simon Rivet

D-U-N-S 24-343-6164   (HQ)
1726837 ONTARIO INC
PARAMOUNT FINE FOODS
10 Four Seasons Pl Suite 601, Etobicoke, ON, M9B 6H7
(416) 695-8900
Sales 11,242,750
SIC 2051 Bread, cake, and related products
Mohamad Fakih
Michael Nadeau
Kim Clarke
Mohammad Rizk

D-U-N-S 20-650-4529   (HQ)
ASSOCIATED ENGINEERING (ONT.) LTD
(*Suby of* ASHCO SHAREHOLDERS INC)
304 The East Mall Suite 800, Etobicoke, ON, M9B 6E2
(416) 622-9502
Emp Here 35   *Sales* 11,437,270
SIC 8711 Engineering services
Kerry Rudd
Bill Deangelis

D-U-N-S 20-115-6770   (SL)
AUSTCO MARKETING & SERVICE (CANADA) LIMITED
AUSTCO COMMUNICATION SYSTEMS
940 The East Mall Suite 101, Etobicoke, ON, M9B 6J7
(888) 670-9997
Emp Here 26   *Sales* 11,626,524
SIC 5065 Electronic parts and equipment, nec

Robert Edward Grey
Clayton Astles

D-U-N-S 24-751-8590   (HQ)
BAKA COMMUNICATIONS, INC
BAKA
630 The East Mall, Etobicoke, ON, M9B 4B1
(416) 641-2800
Emp Here 30   *Sales* 17,591,616
SIC 5999 Miscellaneous retail stores, nec
John Marion

D-U-N-S 24-390-4302   (SL)
BENEVITO FOODS INC
17 Vickers Rd, Etobicoke, ON, M9B 1C1

Emp Here 210   *Sales* 102,350,850
SIC 2051 Bread, cake, and related products
Michael Topolinski
Loreen Mitchell
David Martin

D-U-N-S 20-161-0912   (HQ)
CANADA BREAD COMPANY, LIMITED
DEMPSTER BREAD, DIV OF
(*Suby of* GRUPO BIMBO, S.A.B. DE C.V.)
10 Four Seasons Pl Suite 1200, Etobicoke, ON, M9B 6H7
(416) 622-2040
Emp Here 200   *Sales* 2,059,201,625
SIC 2051 Bread, cake, and related products
Dan Curtis
Ian Macpherson
Glen Sivec
Darrell Miller

D-U-N-S 24-410-8668   (SL)
COACHMAN INSURANCE COMPANY
(*Suby of* SGI CANADA INSURANCE SERVICES LTD)
10 Four Seasons Pl Suite 200, Etobicoke, ON, M9B 6H7
(416) 255-3417
Emp Here 32   *Sales* 59,093,088
SIC 6331 Fire, marine, and casualty insurance
Andrew Cartmell
John Espinelli
William Breckles

D-U-N-S 24-848-6961   (HQ)
COVIA CANADA LTD
(*Suby of* SCR - SIBELCO)
10 Four Seasons Pl Suite 600, Etobicoke, ON, M9B 6H7
(416) 626-1500
Emp Here 8   *Sales* 103,277,250
SIC 1459 Clay and related minerals, nec
Luke C Anderson

D-U-N-S 25-366-8677   (HQ)
EVANOV RADIO GROUP INC
5312 Dundas St W, Etobicoke, ON, M9B 1B3
(416) 213-1035
Sales 16,401,000
SIC 6712 Bank holding companies
Bill Evanov
Paul Evanov

D-U-N-S 20-699-6287   (BR)
EXTENDICARE INC
HIGHBOURNE LIFECARE CENTRE
(*Suby of* EXTENDICARE INC)
420 The East Mall, Etobicoke, ON, M9B 3Z9
(416) 621-8000
Emp Here 300
SIC 8051 Skilled nursing care facilities
Mike Boyle

D-U-N-S 25-945-3751   (SL)
H R ASSOCIATES
302 The East Mall Suite 600, Etobicoke, ON, M9B 6C7
(416) 237-1500
Emp Here 200   *Sales* 14,938,800
SIC 7361 Employment agencies
Susan Walton

D-U-N-S 25-397-3028   (HQ)

HCR PERSONNEL SOLUTIONS INC
HCR
19 Four Seasons Pl 2nd Fl, Etobicoke, ON, M9B 6E7
(416) 622-1427
Emp Here 350   *Sales* 59,755,200
SIC 7361 Employment agencies
Peter Raback

D-U-N-S 20-729-9751   (SL)
HOT OVEN BAKERY LTD, THE
250 The East Mall Suite 285, Etobicoke, ON, M9B 3Y8
(416) 233-6771
Emp Here 43   *Sales* 11,788,536
SIC 5461 Retail bakeries
Rob Wheeler

D-U-N-S 24-783-2652   (SL)
I.R.A.S. PHARMACY LTD
SHOPPERS DRUG MART
5230 Dundas St W, Etobicoke, ON, M9B 1A8
(416) 233-3269
Emp Here 70   *Sales* 17,102,960
SIC 5912 Drug stores and proprietary stores
Ian Stewart

D-U-N-S 20-121-9391   (SL)
ISLINGTON CHRYSLER PLYMOUTH (1963) LTD
5476 Dundas St W, Etobicoke, ON, M9B 1B6
(416) 239-3541
Emp Here 65   *Sales* 40,903,200
SIC 5511 New and used car dealers
Al Rams
Kristopher Rams

D-U-N-S 20-969-2552   (BR)
K-BRO LINEN SYSTEMS INC
(*Suby of* K-BRO LINEN INC)
15 Shorncliffe Rd, Etobicoke, ON, M9B 3S4
(416) 233-5555
Emp Here 150
SIC 7219 Laundry and garment services, nec
Linda Mccurdy

D-U-N-S 25-088-1612   (BR)
LOBLAWS SUPERMARKETS LIMITED
LOBLAWS 1066
(*Suby of* LOBLAW COMPANIES LIMITED)
380 The East Mall, Etobicoke, ON, M9B 6L5
(416) 695-8990
Emp Here 300
SIC 5411 Grocery stores
Brian Trevail

D-U-N-S 24-726-5903   (HQ)
MANION WILKINS & ASSOCIATES LTD
21 Four Seasons Pl Suite 500, Etobicoke, ON, M9B 0A5
(416) 234-5044
Emp Here 90   *Sales* 21,085,920
SIC 8748 Business consulting, nec
Gordon J Manion
Michael Neheli
Howard Cadesky

D-U-N-S 24-191-7962   (HQ)
MCCALL'S SCHOOL OF CAKE DECORATION (1987) INC
3810 Bloor St W, Etobicoke, ON, M9B 6C2
(416) 231-8040
Emp Here 7   *Sales* 12,073,698
SIC 5046 Commercial equipment, nec
Nicholas Mccall

D-U-N-S 25-672-2455   (BR)
METRO ONTARIO INC
METRO
(*Suby of* METRO INC)
201 Lloyd Manor Rd, Etobicoke, ON, M9B 6H6
(416) 236-3217
Emp Here 300
SIC 5411 Grocery stores
Janice Lane

D-U-N-S 25-988-9293   (BR)
METRO ONTARIO INC

(*Suby of* METRO INC)
250 The East Mall, Etobicoke, ON, M9B 3Y8
(416) 233-4149
Emp Here 200
SIC 5411 Grocery stores
Wayne Hardwick

D-U-N-S 24-327-1553   (HQ)
METRO ONTARIO INC
METRO
(*Suby of* METRO INC)
5559 Dundas St W, Etobicoke, ON, M9B 1B9
(416) 239-7171
Emp Here 500   *Sales* 4,619,136,000
SIC 5411 Grocery stores
Eric R. La Fleche
Real Raymond
Joe Fusco
Maryse Bertrand
Francois J. Coutu
Michel Coutu
Stephanie Coyles
Marc Deserres
Claude Dussault
Russell Goodman

D-U-N-S 24-335-0498   (BR)
METRO ONTARIO INC
METRO
(*Suby of* METRO INC)
25 Vickers Rd, Etobicoke, ON, M9B 1C1
(416) 234-6590
Emp Here 400
SIC 5141 Groceries, general line
Shawn Lacey

D-U-N-S 20-943-7060   (HQ)
METRO ONTARIO PHARMACIES LIMITED
PHARMACY AND DRUG BASICS
(*Suby of* METRO INC)
5559 Dundas St W, Etobicoke, ON, M9B 1B9
(416) 239-7171
Emp Here 13   *Sales* 45,884,250
SIC 5912 Drug stores and proprietary stores
Lyman Kwok
Johanne Choiniere
Emil Laswardi

D-U-N-S 24-391-3725   (SL)
NEW ZEALAND AND AUSTRALIAN LAMB COMPANY LIMITED, THE
LAMB COMPANY, THE
10 Shorncliffe Rd Unit 1, Etobicoke, ON, M9B 3S3
(416) 231-5262
Emp Here 16   *Sales* 13,369,232
SIC 5147 Meats and meat products
Geoffrey Owen Poole
Anthony A Ruffo
John P Dolan
Gary Castricum
Gerardus A Janssen
Keith T Cooper
Coll Macrury
Mark E Clarkson
Neville Newton

D-U-N-S 24-802-8586   (SL)
NOCO CANADA COMPANY
(*Suby of* NOCO INCORPORATED)
5468 Dundas St W Suite 401, Etobicoke, ON, M9B 6E3
(416) 232-6626
Emp Here 50   *Sales* 62,860,050
SIC 5172 Petroleum products, nec
Philippa Sutcliffe
Michael Bradley
Michael Newman

D-U-N-S 20-052-1768   (HQ)
NORTHERN REFLECTIONS LTD
(*Suby of* NORTHERN ACQUISITION HOLDINGS CORP)
21 Four Seasons Pl 2nd Flr, Etobicoke, ON, M9B 6J8
(416) 626-2500
Emp Here 108   *Sales* 255,747,750

▲ Public Company   ■ Public Company Family Member   **HQ** Headquarters   **BR** Branch   **SL** Single Location

SIC 5621 Women's clothing stores
Lalonnie Biggar
Karen Lynn
Colleen Elliott
Mario Chiofolo

D-U-N-S 25-237-1018   (HQ)
PACE LAW FIRM PROFESSIONAL CORPORATION
300 The East Mall Unit 500, Etobicoke, ON, M9B 6B7
(416) 236-3060
Emp Here 120   *Sales* 15,523,480
SIC 8111 Legal services
Al S Pace

D-U-N-S 25-419-4244   (HQ)
POLYCULTURAL IMMIGRANT AND COMMUNITY SERVICES
17 Four Seasons Pl Suite 102, Etobicoke, ON, M9B 6E6
(416) 233-1655
Emp Here 15   *Sales* 14,466,650
SIC 8641 Civic and social associations
Marwan Ismail

D-U-N-S 20-174-1865   (SL)
ROBERT MOTORS (1980) LIMITED
5450 Dundas St W, Etobicoke, ON, M9B 1B4
(416) 231-1984
Emp Here 30   *Sales* 14,942,340
SIC 5511 New and used car dealers
Anthony Scott Fisher
Kevin Mcgillivray

D-U-N-S 25-221-4382   (SL)
SANTEK INVESTMENTS (1991) INC
VALHALLA INN TORONTO
1 Valhalla Inn Rd, Etobicoke, ON, M9B 1S9
(416) 233-5554
Emp Here 100   *Sales* 9,489,900
SIC 7011 Hotels and motels
George Kalmar
Blain K Parsons

D-U-N-S 25-144-2273   (SL)
SCOTT-FISHER ENTERPRISES INC
ROBERT MOTORS JAGUAR
5507 Dundas St W, Etobicoke, ON, M9B 1B8
(416) 207-0565
Emp Here 30   *Sales* 14,942,340
SIC 5511 New and used car dealers
Tony Scott-Fisher

D-U-N-S 20-527-9560   (SL)
SHERWAY NISSAN (2000) LIMITED
SHERWAY NISSAN
5448 Dundas St W, Etobicoke, ON, M9B 1B4
(416) 239-1217
Emp Here 36   *Sales* 17,930,808
SIC 5511 New and used car dealers
Kenneth Yoo

D-U-N-S 24-344-0810   (BR)
SUPERIOR PLUS LP
ERCO WORLDWIDE
(*Suby of* SUPERIOR PLUS CORP)
302 The East Mall Suite 200, Etobicoke, ON, M9B 6C7
(416) 239-7111
Emp Here 95
SIC 2819 Industrial inorganic chemicals, nec
Paul Timmons

D-U-N-S 20-118-0101   (HQ)
SYSCO CANADA, INC
SYSCO CANADA
(*Suby of* SYSCO CORPORATION)
21 Four Seasons Pl Suite 400, Etobicoke, ON, M9B 6J8
(416) 234-2666
Emp Here 115   *Sales* 3,225,222,000
SIC 5141 Groceries, general line
Joseph Flinn
Joel T. Grade
Russell T. Libby
Curtis Cusinato

D-U-N-S 24-830-5138   (SL)
TEACHERS LIFE INSURANCE SOCIETY (FRATERNAL)
TEACHERS LIFE
916 The East Mall Suite C, Etobicoke, ON, M9B 6K1
(416) 620-1140
Emp Here 17   *Sales* 17,592,977
SIC 6311 Life insurance
Mark Cummings

D-U-N-S 20-033-0376   (SL)
TELEPARTNERS CALL CENTRE INC
ANSWERNET
(*Suby of* ANSWERNET, INC.)
5429 Dundas St W, Etobicoke, ON, M9B 1B5
(416) 231-0520
Emp Here 60   *Sales* 40,134,480
SIC 7389 Business services, nec
Gary Pudles
Fletcher Keating

D-U-N-S 20-698-7484   (BR)
TORONTO DISTRICT SCHOOL BOARD
MARTINGROVE COLLEGIATE INSTITUTE
(*Suby of* TORONTO DISTRICT SCHOOL BOARD)
50 Winterton Dr, Etobicoke, ON, M9B 3G7
(416) 394-7110
Emp Here 100
SIC 8211 Elementary and secondary schools
Randy Palermo

D-U-N-S 25-264-2079   (SL)
VACHON, ENRIGHT & PETER INSURANCE LTD
5468 Dundas St W Unit 200, Etobicoke, ON, M9B 6E3
(416) 239-3373
Emp Here 21   *Sales* 12,178,404
SIC 6411 Insurance agents, brokers, and service
Conrad Vachon
Bernice Vachon
Todd Peter

D-U-N-S 24-248-5568   (SL)
WAKEHAM TAYLOR HOLDINGS INC
CANADIAN TIRE
5363 Dundas St W, Etobicoke, ON, M9B 1B1

Emp Here 60   *Sales* 37,756,800
SIC 5531 Auto and home supply stores
Mary Taylor

D-U-N-S 24-222-2941   (SL)
WESTOWNE MOTORS (1983) LIMITED
WESTOWNE MAZDA
5511 Dundas St W, Etobicoke, ON, M9B 1B8
(416) 232-2011
Emp Here 38   *Sales* 18,926,964
SIC 5511 New and used car dealers
Dominic Figliano

Etobicoke, ON M9C

D-U-N-S 20-790-2342   (SL)
1057362 ONTARIO LTD
CHRIS' NO FRILLS
460 Renforth Dr Suite 1, Etobicoke, ON, M9C 2N2
(416) 622-1840
Emp Here 60   *Sales* 17,608,620
SIC 5411 Grocery stores
Chris Vaughan

D-U-N-S 24-687-6585   (SL)
2486535 ONTARIO LTD
ACURA SHERWAY
2000 The Queensway, Etobicoke, ON, M9C 5H5
(416) 913-5780
Emp Here 28   *Sales* 13,946,184
SIC 5511 New and used car dealers
David Obront

D-U-N-S 20-779-4723   (SL)
3499481 CANADA INC
PJ'S PET CENTRE
25 The West Mall, Etobicoke, ON, M9C 1B8
(905) 593-3179
Emp Here 31   *Sales* 10,093,600
SIC 5999 Miscellaneous retail stores, nec
Gary Sims

D-U-N-S 24-792-9565   (HQ)
APPLEONE SERVICES LTD
APPLE ONE EMPLOYMENT SERVICES
50 Paxman Rd Suite 6, Etobicoke, ON, M9C 1B7
(416) 622-0100
Emp Here 12   *Sales* 11,204,100
SIC 7361 Employment agencies
Gary Gregg
Steven Gregg

D-U-N-S 24-314-1400   (HQ)
ARCTURUS REALTY CORPORATION
(*Suby of* BGIS GLOBAL INTEGRATED SOLUTIONS CANADA LP)
191 The West Mall Suite 400, Etobicoke, ON, M9C 5K8
(905) 943-4100
Emp Here 100   *Sales* 118,322,400
SIC 6531 Real estate agents and managers
Laurel Arnott
Robert Last

D-U-N-S 24-334-2763   (SL)
BAKER STREET BAKERY INC
130 The West Mall, Etobicoke, ON, M9C 1B9
(416) 785-9666
Emp Here 32   *Sales* 26,738,464
SIC 5149 Groceries and related products, nec
Mary Somerton
Esther Kravice

D-U-N-S 24-319-8194   (SL)
BIOTRONIK CANADA INC
(*Suby of* MS HOLDING II SE)
185 The West Mall Suite 1000, Etobicoke, ON, M9C 5L5
(416) 620-0069
Emp Here 29   *Sales* 12,968,046
SIC 5047 Medical and hospital equipment
Dean Wood
Dan Nguyen

D-U-N-S 20-181-3008   (HQ)
CAMPUS LIVING CENTRES INC
RESIDENCE AND CONFERENCE CENTRE
(*Suby of* LONDON PROPERTY CORP)
5405 Eglinton Ave W Suite 214, Etobicoke, ON, M9C 5K6
(416) 620-0635
Emp Here 7   *Sales* 279,356,800
SIC 1531 Operative builders
Michael Paul
Brian Freeman
Hal Gould
Raymond Stanton

D-U-N-S 24-196-9914   (BR)
CANADA BREAD COMPANY, LIMITED
(*Suby of* GRUPO BIMBO, S.A.B. DE C.V.)
35 Rakely Crt Suite 1, Etobicoke, ON, M9C 5A5
(416) 622-2040
Emp Here 200
SIC 2051 Bread, cake, and related products
Luc Maselle

D-U-N-S 20-051-1975   (HQ)
CATELLI FOODS CORPORATION
CATELLI
(*Suby of* EBRO FOODS, SA)
401 The West Mall Suite 11, Etobicoke, ON, M9C 5J5
(416) 626-3500
Emp Here 60   *Sales* 173,021,675
SIC 2099 Food preparations, nec
Douglas M Watt
Elizabeth B. Woodard
Gregory Richardson

Antonio Hernandez Callejas

D-U-N-S 24-345-7186   (BR)
CHARTWELL RETIREMENT RESIDENCES
(*Suby of* CHARTWELL RETIREMENT RESIDENCES)
495 The West Mall, Etobicoke, ON, M9C 5S3
(416) 622-7094
Emp Here 210
SIC 8059 Nursing and personal care, nec
Nelson Ribeiro

D-U-N-S 20-248-8813   (SL)
CLARIANT PLASTICS & COATINGS CANADA INC
(*Suby of* CLARIANT AG)
2 Lone Oak Crt, Etobicoke, ON, M9C 5R9
(416) 847-7000
Emp Here 55   *Sales* 36,971,660
SIC 5169 Chemicals and allied products, nec
Kenneth Golder

D-U-N-S 25-367-5631   (BR)
CORPORATION OF THE CITY OF TORONTO
WESBURN MANOR
(*Suby of* CORPORATION OF THE CITY OF TORONTO)
400 The West Mall, Etobicoke, ON, M9C 5S1
(416) 394-3600
Emp Here 200
SIC 8051 Skilled nursing care facilities
Susan Schendel

D-U-N-S 24-953-7861   (SL)
EMERAUD CANADA LIMITED
SAN-O-PHONE HEALTH CARE DIV.
145 The West Mall, Etobicoke, ON, M9C 5P5
(416) 767-4200
Emp Here 72   *Sales* 79,584,840
SIC 5122 Drugs, proprietaries, and sundries

D-U-N-S 20-708-3580   (BR)
EXTENDICARE INC
MCCALL CENTRE FOR CONTINUING CARE
(*Suby of* EXTENDICARE INC)
140 Sherway Dr, Etobicoke, ON, M9C 1A4
(416) 259-2573
Emp Here 190
SIC 8051 Skilled nursing care facilities
Barbara Stark

D-U-N-S 20-824-0119   (HQ)
G4S SECURE SOLUTIONS (CANADA) LTD
G4S CANADA
(*Suby of* G4S PLC)
703 Evans Ave Unit 103, Etobicoke, ON, M9C 5E9
(416) 620-0762
Emp Here 50   *Sales* 2,745,729,000
SIC 7381 Detective and armored car services
Peter Panaritis
Peter Loughlin

D-U-N-S 24-685-9842   (HQ)
GALLAGHER, ARTHUR J (CANADA) GROUP
(*Suby of* ARTHUR J. GALLAGHER & CO.)
185 The West Mall Suite 1710, Etobicoke, ON, M9C 5L5
(416) 620-8030
Emp Here 10   *Sales* 21,201,500
SIC 6411 Insurance agents, brokers, and service
Glen Walker

D-U-N-S 24-355-2341   (SL)
GLOBETROTTER LOGISTICS INC
35 Rakely Crt, Etobicoke, ON, M9C 5A5
(416) 742-2232
Emp Here 110   *Sales* 73,358,120
SIC 4731 Freight transportation arrangement
Anca Nediu
Adrian Nediu

D-U-N-S 25-633-6892   (SL)
GOLDENLIFE FINANCIAL CORP

---

555 Burnhamthorpe Rd Suite 305, Etobicoke, ON, M9C 2Y3
(416) 620-0615
Emp Here 30   *Sales* 15,936,210
SIC 6282 Investment advice
Marek Protrowicz

D-U-N-S 20-108-5599   (BR)
HOME DEPOT OF CANADA INC
HOME DEPOT
(*Suby of* THE HOME DEPOT INC)
193 North Queen St, Etobicoke, ON, M9C 1A7
(416) 626-9800
Emp Here 350
SIC 5251 Hardware stores
Lou Severin

D-U-N-S 24-977-3847   (BR)
HUDSON'S BAY COMPANY
THE BAY
(*Suby of* HUDSON'S BAY COMPANY)
25 The West Mall, Etobicoke, ON, M9C 1B8
(416) 626-4711
Emp Here 200
SIC 5311 Department stores
Betty Maxwell

D-U-N-S 24-010-5080   (BR)
INVESTORS GROUP FINANCIAL SERVICES INC
INVESTORS GROUP
(*Suby of* POWER CORPORATION DU CANADA)
295 The West Mall Suite 700, Etobicoke, ON, M9C 4Z4
(416) 695-8600
Emp Here 80
SIC 8742 Management consulting services
Ken Beck

D-U-N-S 24-316-2208   (BR)
J.F. & L. RESTAURANTS LIMITED
PICKLE BARREL, THE
(*Suby of* J.F. & L. RESTAURANTS LIMITED)
25 The West Mall Suite 1019, Etobicoke, ON, M9C 1B8
(416) 621-4465
Emp Here 120
SIC 5812 Eating places
Shane Vermeire

D-U-N-S 25-400-4492   (HQ)
JONVIEW CANADA INC
VACANCES TOURBEC
(*Suby of* H.I.S. CO., LTD.)
191 The West Mall Suite 800, Etobicoke, ON, M9C 5K8
(416) 323-9090
Emp Here 50   *Sales* 60,020,280
SIC 4725 Tour operators
Lise Gagnon
Bernard Bussieres
David Mounteer
Michel Bellefeuille

D-U-N-S 25-196-6446   (SL)
JONVIEW CANADA TRANSAT
800-191 The West Mall, Etobicoke, ON, M9C 5K8
(416) 323-9090
Emp Here 49   *Sales* 25,478,383
SIC 4724 Travel agencies
Lise Gagnon

D-U-N-S 24-693-0333   (HQ)
JUNIOR ACHIEVEMENT OF CANADA
JA CANADA
1 Eva Rd Suite 218, Etobicoke, ON, M9C 4Z5
(416) 622-4602
Emp Here 14   *Sales* 12,012,900
SIC 8299 Schools and educational services, nec
Stephen Ashworth
Claudia Bishop

D-U-N-S 20-047-7370   (HQ)
LENNOX INDUSTRIES (CANADA) LTD
(*Suby of* LENNOX INTERNATIONAL INC.)

400 Norris Glen Rd, Etobicoke, ON, M9C 1H5
(416) 621-9302
Emp Here 350   *Sales* 148,530,375
SIC 3634 Electric housewares and fans
Kenneth C. Fernandez
Timothy G. Inch

D-U-N-S 20-295-1786   (HQ)
LIVINGSTON INTERNATIONAL INC
405 The West Mall Suite 400, Etobicoke, ON, M9C 5K7
(416) 626-2800
Emp Here 300   *Sales* 1,265,401,600
SIC 4731 Freight transportation arrangement
Daniel J. Mchugh
Tom Cronin
Roy G. Coburn
Michael Meierkort
David Rish

D-U-N-S 24-019-9062   (SL)
MARSHALL & WOODWARK INSURANCE BROKERS LTD
320 North Queen St Suite 132, Etobicoke, ON, M9C 5K4
(416) 626-7831
Emp Here 30   *Sales* 17,397,720
SIC 6411 Insurance agents, brokers, and service
Bill Woodwark
Charlie Woowark
Paul Flewwelling
Robert Flewwelling

D-U-N-S 25-092-6185   (BR)
METRO ONTARIO INC
(*Suby of* METRO INC)
170 The West Mall, Etobicoke, ON, M9C 5L6
(416) 626-4910
Emp Here 400
SIC 4225 General warehousing and storage
Frank Jurisevic

D-U-N-S 25-753-3745   (SL)
MISSISSAUGA HALTON COMMUNITY CARE ACCESS CENTRE
MISSISSAUGA HALTON CCAC
401 The West Mall Suite 1001, Etobicoke, ON, M9C 5J5
(905) 855-9090
Emp Here 100   *Sales* 16,064,600
SIC 8011 Offices and clinics of medical doctors
Astrid Lakats
Kelly Bottone
Anne Ptolemy
Bruce Mccuaig
Melody Miles
Brigitte Tuekam
Sivram Viniyagamoorthy
Bob Cooke
Barbara Burton

D-U-N-S 24-122-5572   (SL)
MSCM LLP
701 Evans Ave Suite 800, Etobicoke, ON, M9C 1A3
(416) 626-6000
Emp Here 60   *Sales* 12,461,100
SIC 8721 Accounting, auditing, and bookkeeping
Jack Cooper
Brian Hochman
James Molyneux
Alex Makuz
David Thorman
Rosario Suppa
James Glover
Sandra Solecki
Patricia Kajda
David Danzinger

D-U-N-S 24-094-5873   (HQ)
NOCO CANADA INC
NOCO PETROLEUM DIV
133 The West Mall Unit 11, Etobicoke, ON, M9C 1C2

(416) 232-6626
Sales 62,928,000
SIC 5541 Gasoline service stations
Jeremy Hinchcliffe
Robert Newman
Arlene Hitchcliffe
Philippa Sutcliffe

D-U-N-S 20-347-9548   (BR)
NORDSTROM CANADA RETAIL, INC
NORDSTROM SHERWAY GARDENS
(*Suby of* NORDSTROM, INC.)
25 The West Mall Unit 1150a, Etobicoke, ON, M9C 1B8
(647) 798-4200
Emp Here 80
SIC 5311 Department stores
Jennifer Gross

D-U-N-S 24-633-0880   (HQ)
OOCL (CANADA) INC
(*Suby of* ORIENT OVERSEAS (INTERNATIONAL) LIMITED)
703 Evans Ave Suite 300, Etobicoke, ON, M9C 5E9
(416) 620-4040
Emp Here 11   *Sales* 50,016,900
SIC 4731 Freight transportation arrangement
Ellaine Fan
Philip Chow
Erxin Yao

D-U-N-S 24-339-9479   (HQ)
PANDORA JEWELRY LTD
5535 Eglinton Ave W Suite 234, Etobicoke, ON, M9C 5K5
(416) 626-1211
Sales 10,410,840
SIC 5094 Jewelry and precious stones
John White
Michael Lund
Mikkel Vendelin Olesen
Nazir Noormohamed

D-U-N-S 20-594-2167   (HQ)
PARMALAT CANADA INC
ALIMENTS AULT
(*Suby of* PARMALAT SPA)
405 The West Mall 10th Fl, Etobicoke, ON, M9C 5J1
(416) 626-1973
Emp Here 100   *Sales* 487,385,000
SIC 2023 Dry, condensed and evaporated dairy products
Mark Taylor
Louis Frenette
Pierluigi Bonavita
Ed Perugini

D-U-N-S 24-326-9896   (BR)
PARMALAT CANADA INC
(*Suby of* PARMALAT SPA)
405 The West Mall, Etobicoke, ON, M9C 5J1
(416) 626-1973
Emp Here 80
SIC 2023 Dry, condensed and evaporated dairy products
David Poirier

D-U-N-S 20-892-1759   (SL)
PARMALAT DAIRY & BAKERY INC
405 The West Mall 10th Fl, Etobicoke, ON, M9C 5J1

Emp Here 2,800
SIC 2026 Fluid milk

D-U-N-S 25-402-9432   (SL)
PARMALAT HOLDINGS LIMITED
405 The West Mall 10th Floor, Etobicoke, ON, M9C 5J1
(416) 626-1973
Emp Here 3,000   *Sales* 1,710,000,000
SIC 2026 Fluid milk

D-U-N-S 20-047-7412   (SL)
PARTROSE DRUGS LIMITED
PHARMASAVE
666 Burnhamthorpe Rd, Etobicoke, ON, M9C

2Z4
(416) 621-2330
Emp Here 180   *Sales* 43,979,040
SIC 5912 Drug stores and proprietary stores

D-U-N-S 25-406-1641   (HQ)
PAYLESS SHOESOURCE CANADA INC
(*Suby of* WBG-PSS HOLDINGS LLC)
191 The West Mall Suite 1100, Etobicoke, ON, M9C 5K8
(416) 626-3666
Emp Here 10   *Sales* 149,706,000
SIC 5661 Shoe stores
Lorelei Lane

D-U-N-S 25-350-5762   (HQ)
PERENNIAL INC
15 Waulron St, Etobicoke, ON, M9C 1B4
(416) 251-2180
Emp Here 78   *Sales* 16,029,680
SIC 7336 Commercial art and graphic design
Christopher Lund
Joseph P Jackman
Cameron Whitworth

D-U-N-S 20-531-2994   (HQ)
PROTOS SHIPPING LTD
701 Evans Ave Suite 700, Etobicoke, ON, M9C 1A3
(416) 621-4381
Emp Here 15   *Sales* 20,798,680
SIC 4731 Freight transportation arrangement
Andre Neuendorff
Leslie Coburn
Thriti Bamji

D-U-N-S 25-122-0877   (BR)
RED LOBSTER HOSPITALITY LLC
RED LOBSTER RESTAURANTS
1790 The Queensway, Etobicoke, ON, M9C 5H5
(416) 620-9990
Emp Here 80
SIC 5812 Eating places
Ron Evans

D-U-N-S 20-977-4074   (HQ)
REDBERRY FRANCHISING CORP
BURGER KING
(*Suby of* RESTAURANT BRANDS INTERNATIONAL INC)
401 The West Mall Suite 700, Etobicoke, ON, M9C 5J4
(416) 626-6464
Emp Here 55   *Sales* 17,387,745,000
SIC 6794 Patent owners and lessors
Grant Sutherland
Barbara Lee

D-U-N-S 25-738-6417   (SL)
SHAW MANAGEMENT CONSULTANTS INC
145 The West Mall, Etobicoke, ON, M9C 5P5
(416) 767-4200
Emp Here 78   *Sales* 21,397,896
SIC 8741 Management services

D-U-N-S 20-202-6089   (SL)
SHERWAY FINE CARS LTD
2000 The Queensway, Etobicoke, ON, M9C 5H5
(416) 620-1987
Emp Here 45   *Sales* 22,790,478
SIC 5521 Used car dealers
Ameer Khan

D-U-N-S 20-175-4801   (HQ)
SINCERE TRADING OF K.B.A. CO-OPERATIVE LTD
169 The West Mall, Etobicoke, ON, M9C 1C2
(416) 789-7544
Emp Here 20   *Sales* 25,067,310
SIC 5145 Confectionery
Julia Bae

D-U-N-S 24-170-2088   (BR)
SIR CORP
JACK ASTOR'S BAR AND GRILL
(*Suby of* SIR CORP)
1900 The Queensway, Etobicoke, ON, M9C

5H5
(416) 626-2700
Emp Here 100
SIC 5813 Drinking places
Alex Gibbs

D-U-N-S 25-455-9099   (SL)
SLOVENIAN LINDEN FOUNDATION
DOM LIPA NURSING HOME
52 Neilson Dr, Etobicoke, ON, M9C 1V7
(416) 621-3820
Emp Here 85   *Sales* 5,828,110
SIC 8051 Skilled nursing care facilities
Theresa Macdermid
Anthony Klemencic

D-U-N-S 20-048-8026   (BR)
SNC-LAVALIN INC
(Suby of GROUPE SNC-LAVALIN INC)
195 The West Mall, Etobicoke, ON, M9C 5K1
(416) 252-5315
Emp Here 640
SIC 8711 Engineering services
Robert Marzetti

D-U-N-S 25-221-3319   (HQ)
SNC-LAVALIN OPERATIONS & MAINTE-NANCE INC
ADRESSE BARS SYMPHONIQUE, L'
(Suby of GROUPE SNC-LAVALIN INC)
195 The West Mall, Etobicoke, ON, M9C 5K8
(416) 207-4700
Emp Here 50   *Sales* 270,451,200
SIC 6531 Real estate agents and managers
Dale Clarke
Narsain Jaipersaud
Christina Costy
Genevieve Simard

D-U-N-S 20-821-5061   (SL)
SOUTH WESTERN INSURANCE GROUP LIMITED
SWG CANADA
401 The West Mall Suite 700, Etobicoke, ON, M9C 5J4
(416) 620-6604
Emp Here 70   *Sales* 59,364,200
SIC 6411 Insurance agents, brokers, and service
John A. Barclay

D-U-N-S 25-905-6372   (BR)
SPORTING LIFE INC
SPORTING LIFE SHERWAY GARDENS
(Suby of FAIRFAX FINANCIAL HOLDINGS LIMITED)
25 The West Mall Suite 7, Etobicoke, ON, M9C 1B8
(416) 620-7002
Emp Here 200
SIC 5941 Sporting goods and bicycle shops
Jacques Martins

D-U-N-S 20-639-2573   (SL)
STAFFORD TEXTILES LIMITED
STAFTEX
1 Eva Rd Suite 101, Etobicoke, ON, M9C 4Z5
(416) 252-3133
Emp Here 35   *Sales* 30,324,080
SIC 5131 Piece goods and notions
Malcolm Stafford
David Schwartz

D-U-N-S 24-027-8606   (SL)
TAYCO PANELINK LTD
400 Norris Glen Rd, Etobicoke, ON, M9C 1H5
(416) 252-8000
Emp Here 250   *Sales* 55,666,250
SIC 2521 Wood office furniture
Kevin Philips
Phil Philips
Nicole Chapman

D-U-N-S 20-942-9463   (HQ)
TRADER CORPORATION
AUTO TRADER
(Suby of APAX PARTNERS LLP)
405 The West Mall Suite 110, Etobicoke, ON,

M9C 5J1
(416) 784-5200
Emp Here 400   *Sales* 116,264,400
SIC 2721 Periodicals
Sebastian Baldwin
Mitch Truitt
Irina Hemmers
Marcelo Gigliani
Sebastien Baldwin
John King
Lawrence S Chernin
Norman Theberge
David Mcminn
Gerry O'reilly

D-U-N-S 20-804-3153   (BR)
TRANSAT DISTRIBUTION CANADA INC
TRAVELPLUS
(Suby of TRANSAT A.T. INC)
191 The West Mall Suite 700, Etobicoke, ON, M9C 5K8

Emp Here 90
SIC 4724 Travel agencies
Dennise Heffron

D-U-N-S 24-047-7778   (HQ)
UNILOCK LTD
401 The West Mall Suite 610, Etobicoke, ON, M9C 5J5
(416) 646-5180
Emp Here 50   *Sales* 127,845,000
SIC 3272 Concrete products, nec
Andrew Bryant
Edward Bryant
Tony Hooper

D-U-N-S 25-297-7707   (BR)
WAL-MART CANADA CORP
(Suby of WALMART INC.)
165 North Queen St Suite 3031, Etobicoke, ON, M9C 1A7
(416) 239-7090
Emp Here 150
SIC 5311 Department stores

D-U-N-S 20-371-9844   (SL)
WILSON'S TRUCK LINES INC
111 The West Mall, Etobicoke, ON, M9C 1C1
(416) 621-9020
Emp Here 400   *Sales* 83,235,387
SIC 4212 Local trucking, without storage
Marc Mousseau

D-U-N-S 20-178-4840   (HQ)
WILSON'S TRUCK LINES LIMITED
111 The West Mall, Etobicoke, ON, M9C 1C1
(416) 621-9020
Emp Here 220   *Sales* 82,239,525
SIC 6712 Bank holding companies
James Wilson
Marc Mousseau
Greg Biles
Douglas Wilson

Etobicoke, ON M9P

D-U-N-S 25-597-8942   (HQ)
GLOBAL WIRELESS SOLUTIONS INC
22 Dixon Rd Suite 2, Etobicoke, ON, M9P 2L1
(416) 246-1656
Emp Here 1   *Sales* 14,000,800
SIC 5999 Miscellaneous retail stores, nec
Derek Seelochan

D-U-N-S 25-791-6502   (SL)
SUTTON WEST REALTY INC
6 Dixon Rd, Etobicoke, ON, M9P 2L1
(416) 240-1000
Emp Here 50   *Sales* 16,356,350
SIC 6531 Real estate agents and managers
Tirdad Gharachorloo

Etobicoke, ON M9R

D-U-N-S 25-921-4898   (SL)
CARPET CARE SYSTEMS
34 Ashmount Cres, Etobicoke, ON, M9R 1C7
(416) 247-7311
Emp Here 80   *Sales* 38,002,080
SIC 5087 Service establishment equipment
Andrew Kosmachuk

D-U-N-S 20-411-0860   (SL)
FOUZIA AKHTAR DRUGS LTD
SHOPPERS DRUG MART
415 The Westway Suite 1, Etobicoke, ON, M9R 1H5
(416) 249-8344
Emp Here 49   *Sales* 12,394,746
SIC 5912 Drug stores and proprietary stores
Fouzia Akhtar

D-U-N-S 20-816-3915   (SL)
STATE BUILDING MAINTENANCE LIMITED
34 Ashmount Cres, Etobicoke, ON, M9R 1C7
(416) 247-1290
Emp Here 90   *Sales* 3,660,723
SIC 7349 Building maintenance services, nec
Andrew Kosmachuk

D-U-N-S 20-809-4651   (SL)
VISTA PROPERTY MANAGEMENT INC
380 Dixon Rd Suite 100, Etobicoke, ON, M9R 1T3
(416) 241-9171
Emp Here 31   *Sales* 10,140,937
SIC 6531 Real estate agents and managers
Sandra Elder

Etobicoke, ON M9V

D-U-N-S 25-074-2660   (SL)
1794318 ONTARIO INC
BESTCO FOOD MART
1701 Martin Grove Rd Suite 1, Etobicoke, ON, M9V 4N4
(416) 742-8688
Emp Here 45   *Sales* 12,336,840
SIC 5411 Grocery stores
Hou Zhong Yu

D-U-N-S 24-326-9391   (SL)
BAJAJ DRUGS LIMITED
SHOPPERS DRUG MART
1530 Albion Rd Suite 925, Etobicoke, ON, M9V 1B4
(416) 741-7711
Emp Here 50   *Sales* 12,647,700
SIC 5912 Drug stores and proprietary stores
Jaspreet Bajaj

D-U-N-S 20-162-1059   (SL)
CLARK, KENNEDY COMPANY, LIMITED
15 Leading Rd, Etobicoke, ON, M9V 4B7
(416) 743-5911
Emp Here 23   *Sales* 10,925,598
SIC 5084 Industrial machinery and equipment
Beverly Lewis
Mildred Lewis

D-U-N-S 25-100-1210   (SL)
ETOBICOKE HOSPITAL VOLUNTEER AS-SOCIATION GIFT SHOP
101 Humber College Blvd, Etobicoke, ON, M9V 1R8
(416) 747-3400
Emp Here 50   *Sales* 10,880,650
SIC 5947 Gift, novelty, and souvenir shop
Helen Istrati

D-U-N-S 20-015-1400   (HQ)
FORBO FLOORING SYSTEMS
(Suby of FORBO HOLDING AG)
111 Westmore Dr, Etobicoke, ON, M9V 3Y6
(416) 745-4200
Emp Here 40   *Sales* 23,407,376

SIC 5023 Homefurnishings
Dennis Darragh

D-U-N-S 24-991-9721   (SL)
G. C. LOH MERCHANDISING LTD
CANADIAN TIRE 294
1530 Albion Rd, Etobicoke, ON, M9V 1B4
(416) 745-9070
Emp Here 150   *Sales* 94,392,000
SIC 5531 Auto and home supply stores
Christie Loh

D-U-N-S 24-826-1005   (BR)
GOVERNMENT OF ONTARIO
MINISTRY OF HEALTH
(Suby of GOVERNMENT OF ONTARIO)
101 Humber College Blvd, Etobicoke, ON, M9V 1R8
(416) 747-3400
Emp Here 100
SIC 8062 General medical and surgical hospitals
Ericka Coobs

D-U-N-S 25-025-6740   (SL)
HOMELIFE/MIRACLE REALTY LTD
5010 Steeles Ave W Suite 11a, Etobicoke, ON, M9V 5C6
(416) 747-9777
Emp Here 60   *Sales* 16,305,360
SIC 6531 Real estate agents and managers
Ajay Shah

D-U-N-S 20-293-0871   (SL)
INSIGHT TECHNOLOGIES CONSTRUC-TION CORP
6817 Steeles Ave W, Etobicoke, ON, M9V 4R9
(416) 745-8228
Emp Here 70   *Sales* 39,923,660
SIC 1542 Nonresidential construction, nec
Christopher Rypkema
Mila Bejatovic

D-U-N-S 25-089-5836   (HQ)
KHANNA TRANSPORT INC
100 Westmore Dr Suite 12b, Etobicoke, ON, M9V 5C3
(416) 675-9388
Sales 11,313,830
SIC 4213 Trucking, except local
Sukhdeep Gill

D-U-N-S 20-171-8293   (SL)
NORBEL METAL SERVICE LIMITED
100 Guided Crt, Etobicoke, ON, M9V 4K6
(416) 744-9988
Emp Here 62   *Sales* 27,851,578
SIC 7389 Business services, nec
Nico Guglielmin
Paul Guglielmin
Bruno Guglielmin

D-U-N-S 24-392-0704   (SL)
ORBIS CANADA LIMITED
(Suby of MENASHA CORPORATION)
39 Westmore Dr, Etobicoke, ON, M9V 3Y6
(416) 745-6980
Emp Here 29   *Sales* 59,703,000
SIC 3089 Plastics products, nec
James M Kotek
James Sarosiek

D-U-N-S 25-240-7986   (SL)
PHOENIX FLOOR & WALL PRODUCTS INC
111 Westmore Dr, Etobicoke, ON, M9V 3Y6
(416) 745-4200
Emp Here 44   *Sales* 22,389,664
SIC 5023 Homefurnishings
Andy Richia
Michael Georgopoulos

D-U-N-S 20-405-2922   (SL)
SUMMIT FORD SALES (1982) LIMITED
12 Carrier Dr, Etobicoke, ON, M9V 2C1
(416) 741-6221
Emp Here 79   *Sales* 49,713,120
SIC 5511 New and used car dealers
Scott Vickers

Brian Vickers

D-U-N-S 20-025-1952   (BR)
TORONTO DISTRICT SCHOOL BOARD
NORTH ALBION COLLEGIATE INSTITUTE
(*Suby of* TORONTO DISTRICT SCHOOL BOARD)
2580 Kipling Ave, Etobicoke, ON, M9V 3B2
(416) 394-7550
Emp Here 75
SIC 8211 Elementary and secondary schools
Faz Khan

D-U-N-S 25-000-6749   (BR)
TORONTO DISTRICT SCHOOL BOARD
WEST HUMBER COLLEGIATE INSTITUTE
(*Suby of* TORONTO DISTRICT SCHOOL BOARD)
1675 Martin Grove Rd, Etobicoke, ON, M9V 3S3
(416) 394-7570
Emp Here 100
SIC 8211 Elementary and secondary schools
Dilawar Alvi

D-U-N-S 24-123-6066   (SL)
ULTRA-FORM MFG. CO. LTD
73 Baywood Rd, Etobicoke, ON, M9V 3Y8
(416) 749-9323
Emp Here 90   *Sales* 19,980,090
SIC 3545 Machine tool accessories
Mo Shahid
Morley Brodie

D-U-N-S 25-687-3019   (BR)
WILLIAM OSLER HEALTH SYSTEM
ETOBICOKE GENERAL HOSPITAL
(*Suby of* WILLIAM OSLER HEALTH SYSTEM)
101 Humber College Blvd, Etobicoke, ON, M9V 1R8
(416) 494-2120
Emp Here 1,000
SIC 8062 General medical and surgical hospitals
Ruth Beck

Etobicoke, ON M9W

D-U-N-S 25-974-8655   (SL)
1112308 ONTARIO INC
246 Attwell Dr, Etobicoke, ON, M9W 5B4
(416) 675-1635
Emp Here 210   *Sales* 6,713,280
SIC 7342 Disinfecting and pest control services

D-U-N-S 24-688-9232   (HQ)
1125151 ONTARIO LIMITED
SI VOUS PLAY SPORTS
6931 Steeles Ave W, Etobicoke, ON, M9W 6K7
(416) 675-9235
Emp Here 100   *Sales* 37,426,500
SIC 5661 Shoe stores
Frank Colarassi

D-U-N-S 20-803-0093   (SL)
1199893 ONTARIO INC
SAMOSA AND SWEET FACTORY
1850 Albion Rd Unit 6, Etobicoke, ON, M9W 6J9
(416) 213-1165
Emp Here 45   *Sales* 12,336,840
SIC 5441 Candy, nut, and confectionery stores
Harminder Sandhu
Harpal Sandhu

D-U-N-S 24-953-6996   (SL)
1265534 ONTARIO INC
SHERATON TORONTO AIRPORT HOTEL AND CONFERENCE CENTRE
(*Suby of* LARCO INVESTMENTS LTD)
801 Dixon Rd, Etobicoke, ON, M9W 1J5

(416) 675-6100
Emp Here 150   *Sales* 13,903,500
SIC 7011 Hotels and motels
Anupis Rani

D-U-N-S 20-096-0313   (HQ)
1442503 ONTARIO INC
REXDALE BRICK
18 Namco Rd, Etobicoke, ON, M9W 1M5
(416) 741-4498
Emp Here 1   *Sales* 12,545,330
SIC 3251 Brick and structural clay tile
Joseph Zamparo

D-U-N-S 20-809-0089   (HQ)
1531011 ONTARIO INC
JDS WHOLESALES & DISTRIBUTION
185 Carlingview Dr Suite 1, Etobicoke, ON, M9W 5E8
(416) 285-0041
Emp Here 8   *Sales* 14,850,400
SIC 5199 Nondurable goods, nec
Darshan Gill

D-U-N-S 24-966-1570   (BR)
1561716 ONTARIO LTD
LONE STAR CAFE
(*Suby of* 1561716 ONTARIO LTD)
930 Dixon Rd, Etobicoke, ON, M9W 1J9
(416) 674-7777
Emp Here 80
SIC 5812 Eating places
Tom Pappin

D-U-N-S 20-057-6051   (HQ)
2016099 ONTARIO INC
31 Constellation Crt, Etobicoke, ON, M9W 1K4
(905) 673-2000
Emp Here 60   *Sales* 15,879,300
SIC 7334 Photocopying and duplicating services
Andy Chiodo
Shaun Mccartney

D-U-N-S 20-293-5177   (SL)
2076631 ONTARIO LIMITED
THE SHOE CLUB
151 Carlingview Dr Unit 6, Etobicoke, ON, M9W 5S4
(416) 679-8884
Emp Here 60   *Sales* 10,763,760
SIC 5661 Shoe stores
Vincent Gil
Guan Gil

D-U-N-S 24-738-0926   (SL)
2154781 CANADA LTD
ROBERT POSITANO'S WOODBINE PONTIAC BUICK GMC
25 Vice Regent Blvd, Etobicoke, ON, M9W 6N2
(416) 748-2900
Emp Here 65   *Sales* 40,903,200
SIC 5511 New and used car dealers
Robert Positano
Mario Cammerota

D-U-N-S 24-917-6850   (HQ)
3618358 CANADA INC
96 Disco Rd, Etobicoke, ON, M9W 0A3
(416) 679-7979
Emp Here 200   *Sales* 300,101,400
SIC 4731 Freight transportation arrangement
Michael Andlauer
Bob Brogan

D-U-N-S 25-369-7940   (SL)
6232698 CANADA INC
DIRECT FIRE PROTECTION SYSTEMS
397 Humberline Dr Unit 1, Etobicoke, ON, M9W 5T5
(416) 213-0088
Emp Here 27   *Sales* 11,974,230
SIC 7389 Business services, nec

D-U-N-S 25-332-9890   (SL)
875578 ONTARIO LIMITED
CUSTOM WOOD

31 Racine Rd, Etobicoke, ON, M9W 2Z4

Emp Here 40   *Sales* 17,056,322
SIC 6719 Holding companies, nec
Sam Milstein

D-U-N-S 24-938-1468   (SL)
939927 ONTARIO LIMITED
MANDARIN RESTAURANT
200 Queen'S Plate Dr, Etobicoke, ON, M9W 6Y9
(416) 746-6000
Emp Here 80   *Sales* 3,641,520
SIC 5812 Eating places
Alan Low

D-U-N-S 20-554-1399   (BR)
A. LASSONDE INC
LASSONDE BEVERAGES CANADA, DIV OF
(*Suby of* 3346625 CANADA INC)
95 Vulcan St, Etobicoke, ON, M9W 1L4
(416) 244-4224
Emp Here 200
SIC 2086 Bottled and canned soft drinks
Adam Olds

D-U-N-S 25-222-0694   (HQ)
ABC AIR MANAGEMENT SYSTEMS INC
(*Suby of* CERBERUS CAPITAL MANAGEMENT, L.P.)
110 Ronson Dr, Etobicoke, ON, M9W 1B6
(416) 744-3113
Emp Here 75
SIC 3089 Plastics products, nec
Mike Schmidt

D-U-N-S 25-214-7277   (HQ)
ABC CLIMATE CONTROL SYSTEMS INC
(*Suby of* CERBERUS CAPITAL MANAGEMENT, L.P.)
54 Bethridge Rd, Etobicoke, ON, M9W 1N1
(416) 744-3113
Sales 76,419,840
SIC 3089 Plastics products, nec
Helga Schmidt

D-U-N-S 20-559-5858   (HQ)
ABC INOAC EXTERIOR SYSTEMS INC
220 Brockport Dr, Etobicoke, ON, M9W 5S1
(416) 675-7480
Emp Here 350   *Sales* 83,584,200
SIC 3089 Plastics products, nec
Hisao Tsuge
Angelo Cesta

D-U-N-S 25-373-7779   (SL)
ABC INTERIOR SYSTEMS INC
MSB PLASTICS MANUFACTURING (PLANT 2)
(*Suby of* CERBERUS CAPITAL MANAGEMENT, L.P.)
10 Disco Rd, Etobicoke, ON, M9W 1L7
(416) 675-2220
Emp Here 300   *Sales* 71,643,600
SIC 3089 Plastics products, nec
Helga Schmidt
Tim Schmidt

D-U-N-S 24-318-6546   (BR)
ABC TECHNOLOGIES INC
ABC PLASTICS MOULDING, A DIV OF
(*Suby of* CERBERUS CAPITAL MANAGEMENT, L.P.)
20 Brydon Dr, Etobicoke, ON, M9W 5R6

Emp Here 200
SIC 3089 Plastics products, nec
Mike Schmidt

D-U-N-S 20-300-7794   (SL)
ABCOR FILTERS INC
(*Suby of* CERBERUS CAPITAL MANAGEMENT, L.P.)
41 City View Dr, Etobicoke, ON, M9W 5A5
(416) 245-6886
Emp Here 45   *Sales* 10,072,935
SIC 3714 Motor vehicle parts and accessories

Helga Schmidt
Stefano Namari
Tommaso Cornaglia
Pier Antonio Cornaglia
Robert Kunihiro
Mark Poynton

D-U-N-S 20-527-6835   (HQ)
ABELL PEST CONTROL INC
246 Attwell Dr, Etobicoke, ON, M9W 5B4
(416) 675-1635
Emp Here 30   *Sales* 20,258,910
SIC 7342 Disinfecting and pest control services
Ralph Abell
John Abell
Robert Mcanally

D-U-N-S 24-583-6783   (HQ)
ACCESS CASH GENERAL PARTNERSHIP
191 Attwell Dr Unit 4, Etobicoke, ON, M9W 5Z2
(416) 247-0200
Sales 19,740,000
SIC 6099 Functions related to deposit banking
Chris Chandler

D-U-N-S 24-977-4464   (HQ)
AECON CONSTRUCTION AND MATERIALS LIMITED
(*Suby of* AECON GROUP INC)
20 Carlson Crt Suite 800, Etobicoke, ON, M9W 7K6
(905) 454-1078
Emp Here 500   *Sales* 164,057,500
SIC 1629 Heavy construction, nec
John Beck
Scott C Balfour

D-U-N-S 20-230-7898   (HQ)
AECON GROUP INC
AECON MINING, DIV OF
20 Carlson Crt Suite 800, Etobicoke, ON, M9W 7K6
(416) 297-2600
Emp Here 200   *Sales* 2,476,181,740
SIC 1541 Industrial buildings and warehouses
Jean-Louis Servranckx
David Smales
Yonni Fushman
John Almeida
Adam Borgatti
Blair Brandon
Michael Derksen
Marty Harris
Mathew Kattapuram
Alistair Maccallum

D-U-N-S 25-274-9650   (HQ)
AECON MATERIALS ENGINEERING CORP
(*Suby of* AECON GROUP INC)
20 Carlson Crt Suite 800, Etobicoke, ON, M9W 7K6
(416) 293-7004
Sales 11,671,750
SIC 1481 NonMetallic mineral services
John M Beck

D-U-N-S 20-158-4273   (HQ)
AHEARN & SOPER INC
100 Woodbine Downs Blvd, Etobicoke, ON, M9W 5S6
(416) 675-3999
Emp Here 75   *Sales* 44,717,400
SIC 5044 Office equipment
John Paul
Paul Pope

D-U-N-S 25-535-2726   (HQ)
AIOLOS INC
135 Queen'S Plate Dr Suite 300, Etobicoke, ON, M9W 6V1
(416) 674-3017
Sales 11,133,164
SIC 8711 Engineering services
Sergio Raimondo
Dobrilo Vucicevic
Steven Hills

▲ Public Company   ■ Public Company Family Member   **HQ** Headquarters   **BR** Branch   **SL** Single Location

Jc Irani

D-U-N-S 20-404-2774 (HQ)
AKZO NOBEL COATINGS LTD
(*Suby of* AKZO NOBEL N.V.)
110 Woodbine Downs Blvd Unit 4, Etobicoke,
ON, M9W 5S6
(416) 674-6633
Emp Here 20   *Sales* 28,402,100
SIC 2851 Paints and allied products
David Smith
Clara Chin

D-U-N-S 25-203-7312 (HQ)
**ALCOHOL COUNTERMEASURE SYSTEMS
CORP**
GUARDIAN INTERLOCK SERVICES, DIV OF
60 International Blvd, Etobicoke, ON, M9W
6J2
(416) 619-3500
Emp Here 200   *Sales* 51,775,150
SIC 3829 Measuring and controlling devices,
nec
Felix Je Comeau

D-U-N-S 20-145-2216 (SL)
ALL PARTS AUTOMOTIVE LIMITED
GENERAL AUTO PARTS
66 Ronson Dr, Etobicoke, ON, M9W 1B6
(416) 743-1200
Emp Here 45   *Sales* 16,389,675
SIC 5013 Motor vehicle supplies and new
parts
Harold Baker

D-U-N-S 20-213-5315 (HQ)
ALLEGION CANADA INC
SECURITY AND SAFETY, DIV OF
(*Suby of* ALLEGION PUBLIC LIMITED COM-
PANY)
51 Worcester Rd, Etobicoke, ON, M9W 4K2
(800) 900-1434
Emp Here 40   *Sales* 136,564,400
SIC 5084 Industrial machinery and equipment
Mark Wilson
Shawn White
Janice Telfer

D-U-N-S 25-620-0163 (SL)
ALMON ENVIRONMENTAL LTD
45 Racine Rd, Etobicoke, ON, M9W 2Z4
(416) 743-1364
Emp Here 50   *Sales* 14,176,200
SIC 1611 Highway and street construction
Jake Ally

D-U-N-S 24-506-3797 (SL)
ALMON EQUIPMENT LTD
45 Racine Rd, Etobicoke, ON, M9W 2Z4
(416) 743-1771
Emp Here 50   *Sales* 14,176,200
SIC 1611 Highway and street construction
Jake Ally

D-U-N-S 24-764-0121 (SL)
ALTE-REGO CORPORATION
36 Tidemore Ave, Etobicoke, ON, M9W 5H4
(416) 740-3397
Emp Here 90   *Sales* 24,899,400
SIC 2821 Plastics materials and resins
Devin Sidhu
Mohan Sidhu

D-U-N-S 24-124-9879 (HQ)
ALTERNA SAVINGS
165 Attwell Dr, Etobicoke, ON, M9W 5Y5
(416) 213-7900
Emp Here 100   *Sales* 102,480,600
SIC 6062 State credit unions
Robert Paterson

D-U-N-S 24-624-2606 (SL)
ALUMICOR INTERNATIONAL INC
290 Humberline Dr, Etobicoke, ON, M9W 5S2
(416) 745-4222
Emp Here 300   *Sales* 57,625,500
SIC 3479 Metal coating and allied services
Amy Cole

D-U-N-S 20-150-2937 (HQ)
ALUMICOR LIMITED
(*Suby of* APOGEE ENTERPRISES, INC.)
290 Humberline Dr Suite 1, Etobicoke, ON,
M9W 5S2
(416) 745-4222
Emp Here 1   *Sales* 72,969,300
SIC 3479 Metal coating and allied services
Paul Antoniadis

D-U-N-S 20-557-6023 (BR)
APOTEX INC
50 Steinway Blvd Suite 3, Etobicoke, ON,
M9W 6Y3
(416) 675-0338
Emp Here 900
SIC 2834 Pharmaceutical preparations

D-U-N-S 25-353-7583 (SL)
ASL ENTERPRISES INC
ASL CONSULTING
155 Rexdale Blvd Suite 800, Etobicoke, ON,
M9W 5Z8
(416) 740-6996
Emp Here 40   *Sales* 10,973,280
SIC 8741 Management services
Anthony Latchoo
Cecil Latchoo
Colin Harrison
Samantha Noort
Norman R Williams

D-U-N-S 20-413-4746 (HQ)
ATLAS-APEX ROOFING INC
65 Disco Rd, Etobicoke, ON, M9W 1M2
(416) 421-6244
Emp Here 72   *Sales* 32,674,350
SIC 1761 Roofing, siding, and sheetMetal
work
John Petrachek
Brenda Dickson
Frank Alwaro

D-U-N-S 20-016-6143 (BR)
ATLIFIC INC
*COURTYARD BY MARRIOTT - TORONTO-
AIRPORT*
231 Carlingview Dr, Etobicoke, ON, M9W 5E8
(416) 675-0411
Emp Here 100
SIC 7011 Hotels and motels
Kelly Anne Yeaman

D-U-N-S 25-118-0253 (SL)
**AUTOMATED STEEL DETAILING ASSO-
CIATES LTD**
A S D A
(*Suby of* ASDA HOLDINGS LTD)
77 Belfield Rd Unit 100, Etobicoke, ON, M9W
1G6
(416) 241-6967
Emp Here 25   *Sales* 11,230,475
SIC 7389 Business services, nec
Larry Davis
Barry King

D-U-N-S 24-853-0516 (SL)
AUTOTEK ELECTROPLATING LTD
20 Huddersfield Rd, Etobicoke, ON, M9W 5Z6
(416) 674-0063
Emp Here 50   *Sales* 10,141,500
SIC 3471 Plating and polishing
Robert E. Edwards
David Edwards
Robert P. Edwards
Edward Astrauskas

D-U-N-S 20-210-7801 (HQ)
AVISCAR INC
(*Suby of* AVIS BUDGET GROUP, INC.)
1 Convair Dr, Etobicoke, ON, M9W 6Z9
(416) 213-8400
Emp Here 400   *Sales* 238,142,880
SIC 7514 Passenger car rental
Larry De Shon
David B. Wyshner
Jean-Marie Sera
Jon Zuber

D-U-N-S 20-388-4853 (SL)
AVOKERIE HEALTHCARE INC
10 Humberline Dr Unit 301, Etobicoke, ON,
M9W 6J5
(416) 628-7151
Emp Here 532   *Sales* 36,349,432
SIC 8059 Nursing and personal care, nec
Luke Hudson
Patience Anthony
Oliver Howe
Nick Smith
Ella Davis

D-U-N-S 25-190-9776 (BR)
BBA INC
(*Suby of* GROUPE BBA INC)
10 Carlson Crt Suite 420, Etobicoke, ON,
M9W 6L2
(416) 585-2115
Emp Here 700
SIC 8711 Engineering services
Andre Allaire

D-U-N-S 20-056-3935 (SL)
BDP CANADA, ULC
BDP INTERNATIONAL
(*Suby of* BDP INTERNATIONAL, INC.)
10 Carlson Crt Suite 801, Etobicoke, ON,
M9W 6L2
(905) 602-0200
Emp Here 21   *Sales* 10,919,307
SIC 4731 Freight transportation arrangement
Richard J Bolte, Jr
John Bolte
Barry Murphy
Robert Bolte

D-U-N-S 24-144-2818 (BR)
**BENTALLGREENOAK (CANADA) LIMITED
PARTNERSHIP**
(*Suby of* BENTALLGREENOAK (CANADA)
LIMITED PARTNERSHIP)
10 Carlson Crt Suite 500, Etobicoke, ON,
M9W 6L2
(416) 674-7707
Emp Here 80
SIC 6531 Real estate agents and managers
Katherine Weiss

D-U-N-S 24-679-6549 (SL)
BERETTA FARMS INC
(*Suby of* SPROTT RESOURCE HOLDINGS
INC)
80 Galaxy Blvd Unit 1, Etobicoke, ON, M9W
4Y8
(416) 674-5609
Emp Here 50   *Sales* 13,115,450
SIC 0119 Cash grains, nec
Stephen Yuzpe
Andrew Stronach
Blaine Favel
Jason Gould
Kevin Mccredie
Michael Beretta
Michelle Tessaro

D-U-N-S 20-211-7438 (SL)
BERTOZZI, ADRIANO IMPORTING INC
2070 Codlin Cres Unit 2, Etobicoke, ON, M9W
7J2
(416) 213-0075
Emp Here 20   *Sales* 16,711,540
SIC 5141 Groceries, general line
Elvira Bertozzi
Patricia Bertozzi

D-U-N-S 25-283-0971 (SL)
BIK HYDRAULICS LTD
41 Claireville Dr Unit A, Etobicoke, ON, M9W
5Z7
(416) 679-3838
Emp Here 24   *Sales* 11,400,624
SIC 5084 Industrial machinery and equipment
Elemer Ivan

D-U-N-S 24-329-7389 (SL)
BIOSYENT INC
170 Attwell Dr Suite 520, Etobicoke, ON, M9W

5Z5
(905) 206-0013
Emp Here 20   *Sales* 16,319,683
SIC 2834 Pharmaceutical preparations
Rene C Goehrum
Alfred D'souza
Kevin Wilson
Peter Weiler
Navid Ashrafi
Ramesh Moothan
Sharan Raghubir
Tom Carson
Larry Andrews
Sara Elford

D-U-N-S 20-273-2426 (SL)
BRAMWOOD FOREST INC
(*Suby of* WESTON FOREST PRODUCTS
INC)
38 Taber Rd, Etobicoke, ON, M9W 3A8
(416) 747-7244
Emp Here 50   *Sales* 22,358,700
SIC 5031 Lumber, plywood, and millwork
Steve Rhone
Nir Mitzer

D-U-N-S 20-878-1328 (SL)
BRAZILIAN CANADIAN COFFEE CO. LTD
BRAZILIAN COFFEE
1260 Martin Grove Rd, Etobicoke, ON, M9W
4X3
(416) 749-2000
Emp Here 45   *Sales* 37,600,965
SIC 5149 Groceries and related products, nec
Bryan Caskie

D-U-N-S 20-116-3099 (HQ)
BRENLO LTD
(*Suby of* LBS GROUP LIMITED)
41 Racine Rd, Etobicoke, ON, M9W 2Z4
(416) 749-6857
Emp Here 100   *Sales* 23,084,400
SIC 2431 Millwork
John W F Kitchen
James Maxwell
S Jill Kitchen

D-U-N-S 24-425-6152 (HQ)
BROKERHOUSE DISTRIBUTORS INC
108 Woodbine Downs Blvd Unit 4, Etobicoke,
ON, M9W 5S6
(416) 798-3537
Emp Here 25   *Sales* 18,324,600
SIC 5962 Merchandising machine operators
Jeff Suitor

D-U-N-S 20-120-4216 (HQ)
BROOK CROMPTON LTD
(*Suby of* WOLONG ELECTRIC GROUP CO.,
LTD.)
264 Attwell Dr, Etobicoke, ON, M9W 5B2
(416) 675-3844
Emp Here 50   *Sales* 30,753,091
SIC 5063 Electrical apparatus and equipment
Wolfgang Kloser
Simon Chung
Giovanni Bindoni
Graham David Harries
Neil Anthony Stewardson
Leo A. Mcguire

D-U-N-S 25-108-4695 (SL)
BROOK RESTORATION LTD
11 Kelfield St, Etobicoke, ON, M9W 5A1
(416) 663-7976
Emp Here 30   *Sales* 14,121,930
SIC 1542 Nonresidential construction, nec
Geoff Grist

D-U-N-S 25-726-6437 (HQ)
BSM TECHNOLOGIES INC
(*Suby of* GEOTAB INC)
75 International Blvd Suite 100, Etobicoke,
ON, M9W 6L9
(866) 768-4771
Emp Here 150   *Sales* 52,422,040
SIC 7379 Computer related services, nec

Louis De Jong
Stephen De Bolster
Andrew Gutman
Frank Maw
Leonard Metcalfe
Gregory Monahan
David D. Sgro
Kelly Edmison

D-U-N-S 25-370-0223   (HQ)
BSM TECHNOLOGIES LTD
(*Suby of* GEOTAB INC)
75 International Blvd Suite 100, Etobicoke, ON, M9W 6L9
(416) 675-1201
Emp Here 69   *Sales* 34,279,560
SIC 3699 Electrical equipment and supplies, nec
Louis De Jong
Amber D'aguiar
Stephen De Bolster
Mike Morrissey

D-U-N-S 20-924-0241   (HQ)
BUDGETAUTO INC
A-BUDGET CAR AND TRUCK RENTALS
(*Suby of* AVIS BUDGET GROUP, INC.)
1 Convair Dr, Etobicoke, ON, M9W 6Z9
(416) 213-8400
Emp Here 31   *Sales* 53,817,600
SIC 7514 Passenger car rental
David B. Wyshner
Jon Zuber
Larry De Shon

D-U-N-S 24-311-1684   (SL)
CAD TEK INC
321 Humberline Dr, Etobicoke, ON, M9W 5T6
(416) 679-9780
Emp Here 15   *Sales* 15,005,085
SIC 5051 Metals service centers and offices
Michael Mccannell
Richard Dick

D-U-N-S 25-102-8999   (SL)
CAN MAR CONTRACTING LIMITED
169 City View Dr, Etobicoke, ON, M9W 5B1
(416) 674-8791
Emp Here 30   *Sales* 14,121,930
SIC 1542 Nonresidential construction, nec
Mark Lecce

D-U-N-S 20-287-5829   (SL)
CANADA WATERWORKS INC
35 Shaft Rd, Etobicoke, ON, M9W 4M3
(416) 244-4848
Emp Here 11   *Sales* 11,752,155
SIC 5039 Construction materials, nec
Guenther Koehler
Paul Quattrociocchi
Anthony Quattrociocchi
Bruno Tozzo

D-U-N-S 20-289-8230   (SL)
CANADIAN INTERNATIONAL FREIGHT FORWARDERS ASSOCIATION INC
CIFFA
170 Attwell Dr Unit 480, Etobicoke, ON, M9W 5Z5
(416) 234-5100
Emp Here 50   *Sales* 25,998,350
SIC 4731 Freight transportation arrangement
Gary Vince
Bruce Rodgers
Paul Lobas
Arnon Melo
Garry Mooney
Paul Hughes
Paul Courtney
Angelo Loffredi
William Gottlieb
Jeff Cullen

D-U-N-S 20-846-0014   (HQ)
CANADIAN KENNEL CLUB, THE
200 Ronson Dr Suite 400, Etobicoke, ON, M9W 5Z9

(416) 675-5511
Sales 16,181,505
SIC 8621 Professional organizations
Joe Mouro

D-U-N-S 24-096-3041   (SL)
CANADIAN N D E TECHNOLOGY LTD
CANDET
124 Skyway Ave, Etobicoke, ON, M9W 4Y9
(416) 213-8000
Emp Here 23   *Sales* 10,925,598
SIC 5084 Industrial machinery and equipment
Antonia Dewalle

D-U-N-S 20-547-2389   (HQ)
CANADIAN SPECIALTY METALS ULC
A.S.A. ALLOYS, DIV OF
81 Steinway Blvd, Etobicoke, ON, M9W 6H6
(416) 213-0000
Emp Here 26   *Sales* 101,567,180
SIC 5051 Metals service centers and offices
Gregg Cousins
Thomas J. Dagenback

D-U-N-S 25-306-1725   (BR)
CANADIAN STANDARDS ASSOCIATION
C.S.A GROUP
(*Suby of* CANADIAN STANDARDS ASSOCIATION)
178 Rexdale Blvd, Etobicoke, ON, M9W 1R3
(416) 747-4000
Emp Here 300
SIC 8734 Testing laboratories
John Romano

D-U-N-S 20-772-7462   (HQ)
CANADIAN STANDARDS ASSOCIATION
CSA GROUP
178 Rexdale Blvd, Etobicoke, ON, M9W 1R3
(416) 747-4000
Emp Here 800   *Sales* 253,613,986
SIC 8734 Testing laboratories
Paul Keane
Esteban De Bernardis
Robert J Falconi
Frances Pegeot
John Harrickey
Roland Hosein
David Fung
Gregory Thomas
Greg Weeres
Malcolm O'hagan

D-U-N-S 25-420-9802   (SL)
CANADIAN UNION OF BREWERY AND GENERAL WORKERS LOCAL 325
1 Carlingview Dr, Etobicoke, ON, M9W 5E5
(416) 675-2648
Emp Here 49   *Sales* 19,166,742
SIC 8631 Labor organizations
Glenn Hamilton

D-U-N-S 24-937-0230   (BR)
CARGILL LIMITED
CARGILL FOODS
(*Suby of* CARGILL, INCORPORATED)
71 Rexdale Blvd, Etobicoke, ON, M9W 1P1

Emp Here 800
SIC 2011 Meat packing plants
Leonard Penner

D-U-N-S 20-706-1029   (HQ)
CARQUEST CANADA LTD
(*Suby of* ADVANCE AUTO PARTS, INC.)
35 Worcester Rd Suite 1, Etobicoke, ON, M9W 1K9
(416) 679-3045
Emp Here 200   *Sales* 295,009,600
SIC 4225 General warehousing and storage
Steve Gushie
Magella Boutin
Rob Scott
Doug Gilbert

D-U-N-S 24-787-7512   (SL)
CGTA GIFT SHOW
42 Voyager Crt S, Etobicoke, ON, M9W 5M7

(416) 679-0170
Emp Here 35   *Sales* 15,722,665
SIC 7389 Business services, nec
Peter Moore

D-U-N-S 24-475-6784   (SL)
CHELL GROUP CORPORATION
14 Meteor Dr, Etobicoke, ON, M9W 1A4
(416) 675-3536
Emp Here 125   *Sales* 18,022,750
SIC 7371 Custom computer programming services
David Bolink
Don Pagnutti
Adrian Towing
Stephen Mcdermott

D-U-N-S 24-364-9105   (SL)
CITILOGISTICS INC
22 Huddersfield Rd, Etobicoke, ON, M9W 5Z6
(416) 251-5545
Emp Here 167   *Sales* 111,707,636
SIC 7389 Business services, nec
Nechtario Mavromihelakis
Danny Charlesworth
Kimberly Bungay

D-U-N-S 20-784-7393   (BR)
CKF INC
(*Suby of* SCOTIA INVESTMENTS LIMITED)
30 Iron St, Etobicoke, ON, M9W 5E1
(416) 249-2207
Emp Here 150
SIC 2679 Converted paper products, nec
Robert Millar

D-U-N-S 20-708-2327   (BR)
CKF INC
(*Suby of* SCOTIA INVESTMENTS LIMITED)
218 Belfield Rd, Etobicoke, ON, M9W 1H3
(416) 249-4612
Emp Here 200
SIC 3086 Plastics foam products
Phil Harrison

D-U-N-S 24-334-5159   (SL)
CLUB COFFEE L.P.
55 Carrier Dr Suite 1, Etobicoke, ON, M9W 5V9
(416) 675-1300
Emp Here 150   *Sales* 107,507,400
SIC 5149 Groceries and related products, nec
John Pigott
Alan Halter
Wes Douglas

D-U-N-S 20-206-7125   (SL)
CO-PAK PACKAGING CORP
1231 Martin Grove Rd, Etobicoke, ON, M9W 4X2
(905) 799-0092
Emp Here 80   *Sales* 35,937,520
SIC 7389 Business services, nec
Roy Whiston

D-U-N-S 24-704-8549   (HQ)
CONCORD TRANSPORTATION INC
(*Suby of* TFI INTERNATIONAL INC)
96 Disco Rd, Etobicoke, ON, M9W 0A3
(416) 679-7400
Emp Here 30   *Sales* 30,855,900
SIC 4213 Trucking, except local
Josiane-M Langlois
Chantal Martel

D-U-N-S 24-077-0677   (SL)
CONSTRUCTION SAFETY ASSOCIATION OF ONTARIO
21 Voyager Crt S, Etobicoke, ON, M9W 5M7

Emp Here 103   *Sales* 16,166,606
SIC 8611 Business associations

D-U-N-S 20-145-3537   (SL)
CONTINUOUS COLOUR COAT LIMITED
(*Suby of* MATERIAL SCIENCES CORPORATION)
1430 Martin Grove Rd, Etobicoke, ON, M9W 4Y1

(416) 743-7980
Emp Here 110   *Sales* 21,129,350
SIC 3479 Metal coating and allied services
Kevin Mccallum

D-U-N-S 20-219-6171   (SL)
COPPER CORE LIMITED
275 Carrier Dr, Etobicoke, ON, M9W 5Y8
(416) 675-1177
Emp Here 60   *Sales* 11,525,100
SIC 3433 Heating equipment, except electric
Daniel V Pawlick

D-U-N-S 20-162-6470   (HQ)
CORONET WALLPAPERS (ONTARIO) LIMITED
CROWN WALLPAPER + FABRICS
88 Ronson Dr, Etobicoke, ON, M9W 1B9
(416) 245-2900
Emp Here 59   *Sales* 49,006,320
SIC 5198 Paints, varnishes, and supplies
Gilbert Goodman
Mark Goodman
Bonnie Goodman-Bloom

D-U-N-S 24-860-1304   (SL)
COVERTECH FABRICATING INC
COVERTECH FLEXIBLE PACKAGING
279 Humberline Dr Suite 1, Etobicoke, ON, M9W 5T6
(416) 798-1340
Emp Here 75   *Sales* 15,142,275
SIC 3089 Plastics products, nec
Furio Orologio
John Starr
Julie D'alessandro

D-U-N-S 20-750-0968   (SL)
CWH DISTRIBUTION SERVICES INC
HENDERSON, CW DISTRIBUTION
1245 Martin Grove Rd, Etobicoke, ON, M9W 4X2
(416) 674-5826
Emp Here 120   *Sales* 24,684,720
SIC 4212 Local trucking, without storage
Derm Holwell

D-U-N-S 20-209-4632   (SL)
D C SECURITY INC
22 Goodmark Pl Unit 20, Etobicoke, ON, M9W 6R2
(416) 213-1995
Emp Here 100   *Sales* 53,120,700
SIC 6211 Security brokers and dealers
Farisha Mohammed

D-U-N-S 20-292-7950   (HQ)
DECO ADHESIVE PRODUCTS (1985) LIMITED
DECO LABELS & FLEXIBLE PACKAGING
28 Greensboro Dr, Etobicoke, ON, M9W 1E1
(416) 247-7878
Emp Here 32   *Sales* 10,586,200
SIC 7336 Commercial art and graphic design
Randy Ford

D-U-N-S 20-163-5885   (HQ)
DINEEN CONSTRUCTION CORPORATION
70 Disco Rd Suite 300, Etobicoke, ON, M9W 1L9
(416) 675-7676
Sales 25,364,220
SIC 1541 Industrial buildings and warehouses
Peter J. Clarke
William E. Love
Eric R. Wight
Joseph Tomaino
Dennis Trevisiol
Paul Clarke

D-U-N-S 20-609-5460   (SL)
DIRCAM ELECTRIC LIMITED
42 Steinway Blvd Suite 10, Etobicoke, ON, M9W 6Y6
(416) 798-1115
Emp Here 80   *Sales* 17,426,320
SIC 1731 Electrical work
Anthony Dirienzo

D-U-N-S 24-210-9017   (HQ)
DISTINCT INFRASTRUCTURE GROUP INC
77 Belfield Rd Unit 102, Etobicoke, ON, M9W
1G6
(416) 675-6485
Emp Here 1   *Sales* 55,065,116
SIC 1623 Water, sewer, and utility lines
Alex Agius
Joe Lanni
Micheal Mifsud
William Nurnberger
Manny Bettencourt
Doug Horner
Micheal Newman
Robert Normandeau

D-U-N-S 20-536-6156   (SL)
DONALD CONSTRUCTION LIMITED
333 Humberline Dr, Etobicoke, ON, M9W 5X3
(416) 675-4134
Emp Here 60   *Sales* 14,848,980
SIC 1771 Concrete work
Rina Manarin
Sergio Manarin

D-U-N-S 24-923-9377   (HQ)
DOUBLE DOUBLE PIZZA CHICKEN LTD
DOUBLE DOUBLE FOOD GROUP
1 Greensboro Dr Suite 28, Etobicoke, ON,
M9W 1C8
(416) 241-0088
Emp Here 10   *Sales* 34,840,500
SIC 6794 Patent owners and lessors
Arman Jalili
Fred Rayman

D-U-N-S 20-036-5468   (SL)
DRANCO CONSTRUCTION LIMITED
1919 Albion Rd, Etobicoke, ON, M9W 5S8
(416) 675-2682
Emp Here 200   *Sales* 49,496,600
SIC 1771 Concrete work
John Simone

D-U-N-S 25-369-4533   (SL)
DYNEVOR EXPRESS LTD
24 Bethridge Rd, Etobicoke, ON, M9W 1N1
(416) 749-2010
Emp Here 120   *Sales* 24,684,720
SIC 4213 Trucking, except local
Alagaratnam Uthayakumar

D-U-N-S 20-335-3263   (BR)
EATON INDUSTRIES (CANADA) COMPANY
(*Suby of* EATON CORPORATION PUBLIC
LIMITED COMPANY)
380 Carlingview Dr, Etobicoke, ON, M9W 5X9
(416) 798-0112
Emp Here 80
SIC 3679 Electronic components, nec
Rob Woolner

D-U-N-S 25-204-5687   (HQ)
EFI CONCEPTS
315 Humberline Dr Suite A, Etobicoke, ON,
M9W 5T6
(416) 674-6744
Emp Here 25   *Sales* 19,053,425
SIC 5075 Warm air heating and air condition-
ing
Robert Batelli

D-U-N-S 24-366-7164   (SL)
ELEVENTH FLOOR APPAREL LTD
(*Suby of* ELGNER, ROGER HOLDINGS LTD)
100 Ronson Dr, Etobicoke, ON, M9W 1B6
(416) 696-2818
Emp Here 50   *Sales* 24,916,100
SIC 5137 Women's and children's clothing
Roger Elgner
John Kehl

D-U-N-S 20-145-4287   (HQ)
EQUIPMENT SALES & SERVICE LIMITED
1030 Martin Grove Rd, Etobicoke, ON, M9W
4W3
(416) 249-8141
Emp Here 50   *Sales* 73,159,500

SIC 5082 Construction and mining machinery
Michael Willis
Peter Willis
Mark Finkelstein

D-U-N-S 25-408-3827   (HQ)
**EXPERTECH NETWORK INSTALLATION
INC**
(*Suby of* BCE INC)
240 Attwell Dr, Etobicoke, ON, M9W 5B2
(866) 553-5539
Emp Here 100   *Sales* 618,824,890
SIC 1623 Water, sewer, and utility lines
Marylynne Campbell
Bernard Le Duc
Mary Ann Turcke
Sylvie Couture

D-U-N-S 20-042-4679   (SL)
EXTRUDE-A-TRIM INC
ALUMINUM WAREHOUSE
360 Carlingview Dr, Etobicoke, ON, M9W 5X9
(416) 798-1277
Emp Here 20   *Sales* 20,006,780
SIC 5051 Metals service centers and offices
William R Benson
Tony Schoeppich

D-U-N-S 20-773-7516   (SL)
FELCOR CANADA CO
HOLIDAY INN - TORONTO AIRPORT
(*Suby of* RLJ LODGING TRUST)
970 Dixon Rd, Etobicoke, ON, M9W 1J9
(416) 675-7611
Emp Here 200   *Sales* 19,133,600
SIC 7011 Hotels and motels
Thomas Corcoran

D-U-N-S 20-596-3473   (SL)
FERMAR ASPHALT LIMITED
1921 Albion Rd, Etobicoke, ON, M9W 5S8
(416) 675-3550
Emp Here 100   *Sales* 23,343,500
SIC 2951 Asphalt paving mixtures and blocks
Ashton Martin
Malcolm Martin
Christine Macri

D-U-N-S 20-532-3132   (HQ)
FERMAR PAVING LIMITED
1921 Albion Rd, Etobicoke, ON, M9W 5S8
(416) 675-3550
Sales 37,866,300
SIC 1611 Highway and street construction
Ashton Martin

D-U-N-S 24-476-4288   (SL)
**FIRST INTERNATIONAL COURIER SYS-
TEMS INC**
33 International Blvd, Etobicoke, ON, M9W
6H3
(416) 968-2000
Emp Here 25   *Sales* 11,087,250
SIC 7389 Business services, nec
Adrienne Rosen
Helen Mills

D-U-N-S 24-595-6839   (SL)
FIRST NATIONAL FOOD BROKERAGE
26 Claireville Dr, Etobicoke, ON, M9W 5T9
(416) 679-0833
Emp Here 30   *Sales* 25,067,310
SIC 5141 Groceries, general line
Leo Myer

D-U-N-S 24-469-0244   (SL)
FITCH SECURITY INTEGRATION INC
14 Meteor Dr, Etobicoke, ON, M9W 1A4
(416) 235-1818
Emp Here 40   *Sales* 13,024,000
SIC 5999 Miscellaneous retail stores, nec

D-U-N-S 24-978-2137   (SL)
FORMNET INC
(*Suby of* COURT GROUP OF COMPANIES
LTD, THE)
326 Humber College Blvd, Etobicoke, ON,
M9W 5P4

(416) 675-3404
Emp Here 70   *Sales* 13,445,950
SIC 3444 Sheet Metalwork
Lawrence Buganto
William Court

D-U-N-S 24-788-6380   (SL)
FORTIGO FREIGHT INC
50 Belfield Rd Suite 5, Etobicoke, ON, M9W
1G1
(416) 367-8446
Emp Here 49   *Sales* 18,882,640
SIC 4731 Freight transportation arrangement
Elias Demangos

D-U-N-S 20-299-6708   (SL)
FORTIGO FREIGHT SERVICES INC
50 Belfield Rd Suite 4, Etobicoke, ON, M9W
1G1
(416) 367-8446
Emp Here 55   *Sales* 28,598,185
SIC 4731 Freight transportation arrangement
Elias Demangos
Andy Rocha
Peter Karells

D-U-N-S 24-822-4602   (HQ)
GARLAND CANADA INC
(*Suby of* GARLAND INDUSTRIES, INC.)
209 Carrier Dr, Etobicoke, ON, M9W 5Y8
(416) 747-7995
Sales 22,189,350
SIC 5211 Lumber and other building materials
Charbel Boulos

D-U-N-S 24-478-2751   (HQ)
GATSTEEL INDUSTRIES INC
361 Attwell Dr, Etobicoke, ON, M9W 5C2
(416) 675-2370
Emp Here 46   *Sales* 21,464,352
SIC 5051 Metals service centers and offices
Toros Assadourian
John Davis

D-U-N-S 20-182-2863   (HQ)
GAZZOLA PAVING LIMITED
529 Carlingview Dr, Etobicoke, ON, M9W 5H2
(416) 675-7007
Emp Here 80   *Sales* 25,244,200
SIC 1611 Highway and street construction
Mark Gazzola
Antoinette Lawson
Vern Gazzola

D-U-N-S 20-181-0822   (HQ)
GDI SERVICES (CANADA) LP
(*Suby of* GDI SERVICES AUX IMMEUBLES
INC)
60 Worcester Rd, Etobicoke, ON, M9W 5X2
(416) 736-1144
Emp Here 50   *Sales* 1,929,420,000
SIC 7349 Building maintenance services, nec
Daniel Sklivas

D-U-N-S 24-803-3391   (HQ)
GIFFELS CORPORATION
(*Suby of* INGENIUM GROUP INC)
2 International Blvd, Etobicoke, ON, M9W 1A2
(416) 798-5500
Sales 24,955,200
SIC 8741 Management services
Victor Smith
Marc Turcotte

D-U-N-S 24-846-5551   (HQ)
GIVE AND GO PREPARED FOODS CORP
CREATE-A-TREAT
(*Suby of* THOMAS H. LEE ADVISORS II, L.P.)
15 Marmac Dr Unit 200, Etobicoke, ON, M9W
1E7
(416) 675-0114
Emp Here 125   *Sales* 592,660,160
SIC 2051 Bread, cake, and related products
Joel Flatt

D-U-N-S 25-362-8622   (HQ)
GLASSCELL ISOFAB INC
(*Suby of* 518162 ALBERTA INC)
1000 Martin Grove Rd Suite 1, Etobicoke, ON,

M9W 4V8
(416) 241-8663
Emp Here 45   *Sales* 82,596,060
SIC 5033 Roofing, siding, and insulation
John Rudyk
Ross Wilson
George Gilley

D-U-N-S 20-182-3036   (HQ)
GRAFF COMPANY ULC, THE
(*Suby of* CENTERBRIDGE PARTNERS, L.P.)
35 Precision Rd, Etobicoke, ON, M9W 5H3
(905) 457-8120
Sales 32,172,790
SIC 1771 Concrete work
C. George Bush
Bruce Lux
David S. Neal

D-U-N-S 24-687-9985   (SL)
GRASCAN CONSTRUCTION LTD
61 Steinway Blvd, Etobicoke, ON, M9W 6H6
(416) 644-8858
Emp Here 60   *Sales* 15,146,520
SIC 1629 Heavy construction, nec
Angelo Grassa
John Balazic

D-U-N-S 20-166-4232   (SL)
GROSNOR INDUSTRIES INC
PRODESIGN SOLUTIONS
375 Rexdale Blvd, Etobicoke, ON, M9W 1R9
(416) 744-2011
Emp Here 150   *Sales* 24,604,050
SIC 2782 Blankbooks and looseleaf binders
Richard Wilkinson
George Schnarr

D-U-N-S 24-920-3019   (BR)
GUARDIAN INDUSTRIES CANADA CORP
(*Suby of* KOCH INDUSTRIES, INC.)
355 Attwell Dr, Etobicoke, ON, M9W 5C2
(416) 674-6945
Emp Here 100
SIC 3211 Flat glass
Steve Patience

D-U-N-S 24-614-0552   (HQ)
HAIN-CELESTIAL CANADA, ULC
(*Suby of* THE HAIN CELESTIAL GROUP
INC)
180 Attwell Dr Suite 410, Etobicoke, ON, M9W
6A9
(416) 849-6210
Emp Here 50   *Sales* 62,569,890
SIC 2075 Soybean oil mills
Beena Goldenberg
Jeff Scott

D-U-N-S 20-984-1196   (HQ)
**HALLMARK HOUSEKEEPING SERVICES
INC**
34 Racine Rd, Etobicoke, ON, M9W 2Z3
(416) 748-0330
Emp Here 1,120   *Sales* 76,723,200
SIC 7349 Building maintenance services, nec
Manuel (Manny) Clementino

D-U-N-S 20-166-6401   (SL)
HANDY & HARMAN OF CANADA, LIMITED
(*Suby of* STEEL PARTNERS HOLDINGS L.P.)
290 Carlingview Dr, Etobicoke, ON, M9W 5G1
(416) 675-1860
Emp Here 55   *Sales* 10,564,675
SIC 3499 Fabricated Metal products, nec
Keith Mctaggart
Pat Merrin

D-U-N-S 20-145-4790   (SL)
HANFORD LUMBER LIMITED
45 Bethridge Rd Suite 1, Etobicoke, ON, M9W
1M9
(416) 743-5384
Emp Here 30   *Sales* 13,415,220
SIC 5031 Lumber, plywood, and millwork
Wendy Rigby
Mary Jane Price
George Barlas

D-U-N-S 20-699-1395   (BR)
HAWORTH, LTD
(*Suby of* HAWORTH INTERNATIONAL, LTD.)
110 Carrier Dr, Etobicoke, ON, M9W 5R1

Emp Here 180
SIC 2542 Partitions and fixtures, except wood

D-U-N-S 24-028-4810   (SL)
HERNICK, J. LIMITED
63 Galaxy Blvd Suite 5, Etobicoke, ON, M9W 5R7
(416) 213-9913
Emp Here 40   *Sales* 14,568,600
SIC 5013 Motor vehicle supplies and new parts
Jack Hernick

D-U-N-S 20-875-6072   (HQ)
HERTZ CANADA LIMITED
HERTZ
(*Suby of* HERTZ GLOBAL HOLDINGS, INC.)
2 Convair Dr, Etobicoke, ON, M9W 7A1
(416) 674-2020
Emp Here 5   *Sales* 22,872,480
SIC 7514 Passenger car rental
Scott Sider
Simon Ellis
Jeffrey Zimmerman
David Parkoff
Scott Massengill
Paul Dorian
Jeff Pitz

D-U-N-S 20-259-2663   (HQ)
HLS THERAPEUTICS INC
10 Carlson Crt Unit 701, Etobicoke, ON, M9W 6L2
(647) 495-9000
Emp Here 40   *Sales* 61,415,000
SIC 2834 Pharmaceutical preparations
Gregory Gubitz
Bill Wells
Gilbert Godin
Tim Hendrickson
Jason A Gross
Carmel Daughtery
J. Spencer Lanthier
Yvon Bastien
Laura A. Brege
Don Degolyer

D-U-N-S 20-145-3024   (SL)
HOLIDAY INN TORONTO AIRPORT EAST
600 Dixon Rd, Etobicoke, ON, M9W 1J1
(416) 240-7511
Emp Here 100   *Sales* 9,489,900
SIC 7011 Hotels and motels
Sohail Saeed

D-U-N-S 25-080-7203   (BR)
HOME DEPOT OF CANADA INC
HOME DEPOT
(*Suby of* THE HOME DEPOT INC)
1983 Kipling Ave, Etobicoke, ON, M9W 4J4
(416) 746-1357
Emp Here 167
SIC 5251 Hardware stores

D-U-N-S 20-175-8554   (HQ)
HS SPRING OF CANADA INC
25 Worcester Rd, Etobicoke, ON, M9W 1K9
(416) 675-9072
Sales 19,208,500
SIC 3493 Steel springs, except wire
Steve Aretakis
Paul Cairoli

D-U-N-S 24-006-4311   (BR)
HUDSON'S BAY COMPANY
HBC LOGISTICS
(*Suby of* HUDSON'S BAY COMPANY)
145 Carrier Dr, Etobicoke, ON, M9W 5N5
(416) 798-5755
Emp Here 530
SIC 5099 Durable goods, nec
Ted Medaglia

D-U-N-S 25-118-1871   (BR)
HUDSON'S BAY COMPANY
BAY, THE
(*Suby of* HUDSON'S BAY COMPANY)
500 Rexdale Blvd, Etobicoke, ON, M9W 6K5
(416) 674-6000
Emp Here 200
SIC 5311 Department stores
Alan Cannon

D-U-N-S 20-845-5394   (HQ)
HUMBER COLLEGE INSTITUTE OF TECH-NOLOGY AND ADVANCE LEARNING, THE
205 Humber College Blvd, Etobicoke, ON, M9W 5L7
(416) 675-3111
Emp Here 800   *Sales* 346,648,446
SIC 8222 Junior colleges
Chris Whitaker
Rani K. Dhaliwal
John Mason
Lori A.Diduch
Sanjay Puri

D-U-N-S 24-761-1317   (SL)
HYPHEN TRANSPORTATION MANAGE-MENT INC
(*Suby of* TFI INTERNATIONAL INC)
96 Disco Rd, Etobicoke, ON, M9W 0A3
(877) 549-7436
Emp Here 20   *Sales* 10,399,340
SIC 4731 Freight transportation arrangement
Steve Crossman
Richard Tremblay

D-U-N-S 25-722-4832   (SL)
I-CAR CANADA
110 Woodbine Downs Blvd Unit 4, Etobicoke, ON, M9W 5S6

Emp Here 90   *Sales* 21,440,560
SIC 8742 Management consulting services
Jackie Schalwtz

D-U-N-S 25-165-1063   (SL)
IMEX SYSTEMS INC
34 Greensboro Dr 2nd Fl, Etobicoke, ON, M9W 1E1
(647) 352-7520
Emp Here 80   *Sales* 1,777,206
SIC 7372 Prepackaged software
Rob Klein
Kris Parthiban
Aldis Levalds
Kizito Serumaga
Andrew Lindzon
Issa Nakhleh
Shibu Abraham

D-U-N-S 24-379-9819   (SL)
INDEPENDENT MECHANICAL SUPPLY INC
310 Carlingview Dr, Etobicoke, ON, M9W 5G1
(416) 679-1048
Emp Here 68   *Sales* 30,407,832
SIC 5074 Plumbing and heating equipment and supplies (hydronics)
Greg Tester
Paul Blaik
David Walker

D-U-N-S 20-167-5337   (HQ)
INDUSTRIAL ELECTRICAL CONTRAC-TORS LIMITED
INDUSTRIAL ELECTRIC
7 Vulcan St, Etobicoke, ON, M9W 1L3
(416) 749-9782
Emp Here 35   *Sales* 25,199,463
SIC 1731 Electrical work
Keith Rundle
Steve Warrian
William Reeves
Rick Emuss
Ronald Gray
Robert Boisvert
Daniel Bradley
Deepak Arora
Bruce Maltby

D-U-N-S 25-333-1144   (HQ)
INFORMATION COMMUNICATION SER-VICES (ICS) INC
ICS COURIER SERVICES
(*Suby of* TFI INTERNATIONAL INC)
96 Disco Rd, Etobicoke, ON, M9W 0A3
(416) 642-2477
Emp Here 80   *Sales* 267,417,800
SIC 4212 Local trucking, without storage
Chantal Martel
Josiane-Melanie Langlois

D-U-N-S 25-192-3850   (HQ)
INGENIUM GROUP INC
2 International Blvd, Etobicoke, ON, M9W 1A2
(416) 675-5950
Sales 197,131,000
SIC 8712 Architectural services
Victor Smith
Marc Turcotte
John Mckellar

D-U-N-S 24-875-3717   (SL)
INLINE FIBERGLASS LTD
30 Constellation Crt, Etobicoke, ON, M9W 1K1
(416) 679-1171
Emp Here 200   *Sales* 35,843,800
SIC 3299 NonMetallic mineral products,
Marianna Rokicki

D-U-N-S 24-105-8916   (HQ)
INTEL OF CANADA, LTD
(*Suby of* INTEL CORPORATION)
200 Ronson Dr Suite 201, Etobicoke, ON, M9W 5Z9
(647) 259-0101
Emp Here 50   *Sales* 44,717,400
SIC 5045 Computers, peripherals, and soft-ware
Doug Cooper

D-U-N-S 20-817-1611   (HQ)
INTER-VARSITY CHRISTIAN FELLOWSHIP OF CANADA
PIONEER CAMP
1 International Blvd, Etobicoke, ON, M9W 6H3
(416) 443-1170
Emp Here 137   *Sales* 20,824,600
SIC 8661 Religious organizations
Geri Rodmen
T.V. Thomas

D-U-N-S 20-278-9111   (SL)
IPS OF CANADA, U.L.C.
INTELISPEND
170 Attwell Dr Unit 550, Etobicoke, ON, M9W 5Z5
(800) 293-1136
Emp Here 51   *Sales* 11,420,991
SIC 6153 Short-term business credit institu-tions, except agricultural
W. Stephen Maritz
Holly Francois
Chris Carril
Richard T. Ramos
Steven M. Gallant
Jeffrey R. Blucher

D-U-N-S 24-950-5090   (SL)
ITALIAN HOME BAKERY LIMITED
SUPERIOR BREAD
271 Attwell Dr, Etobicoke, ON, M9W 5B9
(416) 674-4555
Emp Here 100   *Sales* 22,485,500
SIC 2051 Bread, cake, and related products
Dennis Rossetti
John Rossetti

D-U-N-S 24-804-8717   (SL)
JDC #10 LIMITED
MCLEISH CORR-A-BOX PACKAGING & DE-SIGN
274 Humberline Dr, Etobicoke, ON, M9W 5S2
(416) 675-1123
Emp Here 130   *Sales* 25,319,840
SIC 2653 Corrugated and solid fiber boxes

John Coyle
Robert Wilcox

D-U-N-S 20-272-2021   (SL)
JM (RETAIL) INC
110 Ronson Dr, Etobicoke, ON, M9W 1B6
(416) 674-7433
Emp Here 150   *Sales* 27,361,984
SIC 5621 Women's clothing stores
Ilaria Varoli
Roger Elgner
Michael Sourial

D-U-N-S 25-272-8738   (BR)
KEG RESTAURANTS LTD
KEG STEAK HOUSE & BAR, THE
(*Suby of* RECIPE UNLIMITED CORPORA-TION)
927 Dixon Rd, Etobicoke, ON, M9W 1J8
(416) 675-2311
Emp Here 100
SIC 5812 Eating places
Steve Carroll

D-U-N-S 24-354-7333   (BR)
KIK HOLDCO COMPANY INC
KIK CUSTOM PRODUCTS
(*Suby of* KIK CUSTOM PRODUCTS INC)
13 Bethridge Rd, Etobicoke, ON, M9W 1M6
(416) 740-7400
Emp Here 600
SIC 2842 Polishes and sanitation goods
Hal Donly

D-U-N-S 25-361-0042   (BR)
KIK HOLDCO COMPANY INC
KIK CUSTOM PRODUCTS
(*Suby of* KIK CUSTOM PRODUCTS INC)
2000 Kipling Ave, Etobicoke, ON, M9W 4J6
(416) 743-6255
Emp Here 900
SIC 2842 Polishes and sanitation goods

D-U-N-S 24-976-6882   (SL)
KSD ENTERPRISES LTD
DELTA TORONTO AIRPORT HOTEL
655 Dixon Rd Suite 1, Etobicoke, ON, M9W 1J3
(416) 244-1711
Emp Here 220   *Sales* 21,046,960
SIC 7011 Hotels and motels
Peter Wong

D-U-N-S 25-283-1979   (SL)
LAMBTON LUMBER INC
TRIM CARPENTERS SUPPLY
170 Brockport Dr Unit 14, Etobicoke, ON, M9W 5C8
(416) 798-1994
Emp Here 25   *Sales* 11,179,350
SIC 5031 Lumber, plywood, and millwork
Tim Vanwart
John Mcgregor
Jerry Vanwart
Paul Mcgregor

D-U-N-S 20-984-0396   (SL)
LAMWOOD PRODUCTS (1990) LIMITED
KRONOPOL MARKETING
44 Woodbine Downs Blvd, Etobicoke, ON, M9W 5R2

Emp Here 25   *Sales* 12,721,400
SIC 5023 Homefurnishings
Levana Schwartz

D-U-N-S 25-318-4121   (SL)
LEGGAT CHEVROLET BUICK GMC LTD
360 Rexdale Blvd, Etobicoke, ON, M9W 1R7
(416) 743-1810
Emp Here 80   *Sales* 29,137,200
SIC 5012 Automobiles and other motor vehi-cles
Douglas Leggat

D-U-N-S 20-383-1151   (SL)
LIFELABS INC
100 International Blvd, Etobicoke, ON, M9W

6J6
(416) 675-4530
Emp Here 500   *Sales* 162,985,500
SIC 8071 Medical laboratories
  Charles Brown

D-U-N-S 20-407-8471   (HQ)
LINEMAN'S TESTING LABORATORIES OF CANADA LIMITED
46 Meridian Rd, Etobicoke, ON, M9W 4Z7
(416) 742-6911
Emp Here 50   *Sales* 25,577,360
SIC 8734 Testing laboratories
  Robert Burgess

D-U-N-S 24-704-4654   (HQ)
LISI MECHANICAL CONTRACTORS LTD
LISI SERVICES
160 Disco Rd, Etobicoke, ON, M9W 1M4
(416) 674-8333
Emp Here 200   *Sales* 74,483,200
SIC 1711 Plumbing, heating, air-conditioning
  Bruno Lisi
  Robert Lisi

D-U-N-S 24-645-5562   (SL)
LOGITEK DATA SCIENCES LTD
QLOGITEK
155 Rexdale Blvd Suite 801, Etobicoke, ON, M9W 5Z8
(416) 741-1595
Emp Here 100   *Sales* 17,731,100
SIC 7371 Custom computer programming services
  Latiq Qureshi
  John Magalhaes
  Fatima Qureshi

D-U-N-S 20-559-6588   (SL)
MCCLUSKEY TRANSPORTATION SERVICES LIMITED
514 Carlingview Dr Unit 200, Etobicoke, ON, M9W 5R3
(416) 246-1422
Emp Here 90   *Sales* 4,938,480
SIC 4151 School buses
  Lorraine Mccluskey
  John Mccluskey

D-U-N-S 20-191-4913   (SL)
MCRAE INTEGRATION LTD
34 Meridian Rd, Etobicoke, ON, M9W 4Z7
(416) 252-8833
Emp Here 60   *Sales* 14,057,280
SIC 8742 Management consulting services
  Andy Bentley

D-U-N-S 24-862-5493   (SL)
MEDI GROUP MASONRY LIMITED
56 Brockport Dr Suite 3, Etobicoke, ON, M9W 5N1
(416) 747-5170
Emp Here 100   *Sales* 16,238,100
SIC 1741 Masonry and other stonework
  Joe Panettieri

D-U-N-S 24-797-8612   (HQ)
MENZIES AVIATION FUELING CANADA LIMITED
10 Carlson Ct Unit 301, Etobicoke, ON, M9W 6A2
(647) 798-3890
Emp Here 17   *Sales* 709,363,800
SIC 5172 Petroleum products, nec
  David C Matthew

D-U-N-S 25-896-1960   (HQ)
METRO CHUTE SERVICE INC
23 Racine Rd, Etobicoke, ON, M9W 2Z4
(416) 746-5547
Sales 10,578,040
SIC 7699 Repair services, nec
  Carlo Mauti
  Nello Dicarli
  Danny Mauti

D-U-N-S 24-425-0965   (SL)
MIDLAND FOOD PRODUCTS INC

195 Rexdale Blvd, Etobicoke, ON, M9W 1P7
(416) 741-0123
Emp Here 45   *Sales* 37,600,965
SIC 5146 Fish and seafoods
  Yau-Wai Lai

D-U-N-S 20-306-5339   (HQ)
MILLENNIUM PROCESS GROUP, INC
MILLENNIUM 1 SOLUTIONS
251 Attwell Dr, Etobicoke, ON, M9W 7G2
(416) 503-1800
Sales 157,084,200
SIC 8741 Management services
  Patricia Yim
  Victor Otley
  Ross Fuller
  Michael Tian
  Michael Eblin

D-U-N-S 20-227-2043   (SL)
MILLIPORE (CANADA) LTD
(*Suby of* MERCK KG AUF AKTIEN)
109 Woodbine Downs Blvd Unit 5, Etobicoke, ON, M9W 6Y1
(416) 675-1598
Emp Here 100   *Sales* 22,975,400
SIC 8731 Commercial physical research
  J Edward Lary
  Klaus Bischoff
  Laura Knuckle
  Anthony Mattacchione

D-U-N-S 20-162-9664   (SL)
MILTEX CONSTRUCTION LIMITED
CUSTOM WOOD FABRICATING COMPANY
31 Racine Rd Suite 416, Etobicoke, ON, M9W 2Z4

Emp Here 50   *Sales* 23,751,300
SIC 5084 Industrial machinery and equipment
  Harold Milstein

D-U-N-S 20-227-4718   (HQ)
MOLSON BREWERIES OF CANADA LIMITED
MOLSON COORS BREWING COMPANY
(*Suby of* MOLSON COORS BREWING COMPANY)
33 Carlingview Dr, Etobicoke, ON, M9W 5E4
(416) 679-1786
Emp Here 2,500   *Sales* 2,512,599,000
SIC 5181 Beer and ale
  Kelly Brown
  Lori Ball

D-U-N-S 24-010-9298   (BR)
MOLSON CANADA 2005
(*Suby of* MOLSON COORS BREWING COMPANY)
1 Carlingview Dr, Etobicoke, ON, M9W 5E5
(416) 675-1786
Emp Here 1,000
SIC 2082 Malt beverages
  Andrew Molson

D-U-N-S 24-803-1205   (HQ)
MOLSON CANADA 2005
MOLSON CANADA
(*Suby of* MOLSON COORS BREWING COMPANY)
33 Carlingview Dr Suite 2005, Etobicoke, ON, M9W 5E4
(416) 679-1786
Emp Here 250   *Sales* 1,608,370,500
SIC 2082 Malt beverages
  Fred Landtmeters

D-U-N-S 25-512-6187   (HQ)
MOLSON COORS CANADA INC
(*Suby of* MOLSON COORS BREWING COMPANY)
33 Carlingview Dr, Etobicoke, ON, M9W 5E4
(416) 679-1786
Emp Here 100   *Sales* 11,002,800,000
SIC 2082 Malt beverages
  Frederic Landtmeters
  Peter H. Coors

Geoffrey E. Molson
Mark R. Hunter
Peter J. Coors
Andrew T. Molson
Betty K. Devita
Charles M. Herington
Douglas D. Tough
Franklin W. Hobbs

D-U-N-S 24-212-1416   (HQ)
MOORES THE SUIT PEOPLE INC
MOORES CLOTHING FOR MEN
(*Suby of* TAILORED BRANDS, INC.)
129 Carlingview Dr, Etobicoke, ON, M9W 5E7
(416) 675-1900
Emp Here 80   *Sales* 224,559,000
SIC 5611 Men's and boys' clothing stores
  Richard Bull
  Denis Button
  Daniel Paramsook
  Michael Macfarland

D-U-N-S 20-753-9198   (HQ)
MSO CONSTRUCTION LIMITED
(*Suby of* MILLER GROUP INC)
175 Bethridge Rd, Etobicoke, ON, M9W 1N4
(416) 743-3224
Sales 76,778,910
SIC 1611 Highway and street construction
  Blair Mcarthur

D-U-N-S 20-352-0481   (SL)
MYANT INC
(*Suby of* MYANT CAPITAL PARTNERS INC)
100 Ronson Dr, Etobicoke, ON, M9W 1B6
(416) 423-7906
Emp Here 50   *Sales* 11,100,050
SIC 3552 Textile machinery
  Tony Chahine
  Ilaria Varoli
  Aiman Dally

D-U-N-S 20-703-5346   (HQ)
MYLEX LIMITED
37 Bethridge Rd, Etobicoke, ON, M9W 1M8
(416) 745-1733
Sales 23,148,300
SIC 2517 Wood television and radio cabinets
  Michael Burger
  Dave Burger

D-U-N-S 24-783-4591   (SL)
NAKA SALES LIMITED
NAKA HERBS & VITAMINS
252 Brockport Dr, Etobicoke, ON, M9W 5S1
(416) 748-3073
Emp Here 22   *Sales* 18,382,694
SIC 5149 Groceries and related products, nec
  Michael Nacachian
  Raffi Nacachian

D-U-N-S 20-768-4833   (HQ)
NATIONAL CONCRETE ACCESSORIES COMPANY INC
(*Suby of* COOPERATIE NOVA ARGENT U.A.)
172 Bethridge Rd, Etobicoke, ON, M9W 1N3
(416) 245-4720
Emp Here 50   *Sales* 11,671,750
SIC 3272 Concrete products, nec
  Mike Hardman
  Marvin Ramsay
  Christopher Ruhland
  Ray Billings
  Neil Hastie
  Kevin Smith
  Mike Wilson
  Anna Maria Campoli
  Anne Donavan
  Derek Dass

D-U-N-S 24-645-7741   (BR)
NESTLE CANADA INC
NESTLE FOOD SERVICES, DIV OF
(*Suby of* NESTLE S.A.)
65 Carrier Dr, Etobicoke, ON, M9W 5V9
(416) 675-1300
Emp Here 100

SIC 5149 Groceries and related products, nec
  Oscar Rutishauser

D-U-N-S 25-693-5073   (BR)
NEWGEN RESTAURANT SERVICES INC
TUCKER'S MARKETPLACE
(*Suby of* NEWGEN RESTAURANT SERVICES INC)
15 Carlson Crt, Etobicoke, ON, M9W 6A2
(416) 675-8818
Emp Here 75
SIC 5812 Eating places
  Darlene Moran

D-U-N-S 24-877-1958   (HQ)
NFI DOMINION CANADA, ULC
1920 Albion Rd, Etobicoke, ON, M9W 5T2
(416) 744-2438
Emp Here 120   *Sales* 22,864,110
SIC 4225 General warehousing and storage
  Sid Brown

D-U-N-S 24-886-4233   (SL)
NORTEX ROOFING LTD
40 Bethridge Rd, Etobicoke, ON, M9W 1N1
(416) 236-6090
Emp Here 125   *Sales* 27,228,625
SIC 1761 Roofing, siding, and sheetMetal work
  Joe Dovale
  Augustino Oliviera

D-U-N-S 24-688-7970   (HQ)
NORTH AMERICAN FUR AUCTIONS INC
(*Suby of* NORTH AMERICAN FUR PRODUCERS INC)
65 Skyway Ave, Etobicoke, ON, M9W 6C7
(416) 675-9320
Emp Here 44   *Sales* 113,557,774
SIC 5159 Farm-product raw materials, nec
  Michael Mengar
  James Bogus
  John Lang
  Laurie Wood
  Christopher Macisaac
  Bill Evans
  Stan Smith
  Mark Dawber
  Brad Wiebensohn
  Don Boyd

D-U-N-S 20-016-3298   (HQ)
NORTH AMERICAN FUR PRODUCERS INC
NORTH AMERICAN FUR AUCTIONS
65 Skyway Ave, Etobicoke, ON, M9W 6C7
(416) 675-9320
Emp Here 64   *Sales* 18,041,100
SIC 6712 Bank holding companies
  Herman Jansen
  Douglas Fizzell
  Michael Mengar

D-U-N-S 24-247-3697   (SL)
ONTARIO RACING COMMISSION
10 Carlson Crt Suite 400, Etobicoke, ON, M9W 6L2

Emp Here 80   *Sales* 6,671,600
SIC 7948 Racing, including track operation
  Rod Seiling
  Pam Frostad
  John Macdonald
  Dan Nixon
  Anne Walker
  Brenda Walker

D-U-N-S 25-403-2386   (HQ)
ONTARIO REDIMIX LTD
21 Goodmark Pl Unit 3, Etobicoke, ON, M9W 6P9
(416) 674-8237
Sales 11,204,880
SIC 3271 Concrete block and brick
  Laura Sciacca

D-U-N-S 25-099-9406   (HQ)
ONYX-FIRE PROTECTION SERVICES INC
42 Shaft Rd, Etobicoke, ON, M9W 4M2

(416) 674-5633
Sales 23,740,680
SIC 7382 Security systems services
Mark Freeman
George Lyons

D-U-N-S 24-394-2914   (SL)
ORFORD SALES LTD
CANADIAN TIRE
2025 Kipling Ave, Etobicoke, ON, M9W 4J8
(416) 743-6950
Emp Here 30   *Sales* 14,942,340
SIC 5531 Auto and home supply stores
Randy Orford

D-U-N-S 20-345-8674   (HQ)
PARAMOUNT PALLET LP
1330 Martin Grove Rd, Etobicoke, ON, M9W 4X3
(416) 742-6006
Sales 69,597,500
SIC 2448 Wood pallets and skids
Mark Sura
Rob Lolande

D-U-N-S 25-795-7886   (SL)
PATROLMAN SECURITY SERVICES INC
680 Rexdale Blvd Suite 205, Etobicoke, ON, M9W 0B5
(416) 748-3202
Emp Here 175   *Sales* 4,593,750
SIC 7381 Detective and armored car services
Joseph Nawaz

D-U-N-S 24-539-1131   (SL)
PEPES MEXICAN FOODS INC
(*Suby of* GEORGE WESTON LIMITED)
122 Carrier Dr, Etobicoke, ON, M9W 5R1
(416) 674-0882
Emp Here 110   *Sales* 38,025,900
SIC 2099 Food preparations, nec
Ronaldo Sardelitti
Ralph Robinson

D-U-N-S 25-511-2385   (HQ)
PERCON CONSTRUCTION INC
20 Airview Rd, Etobicoke, ON, M9W 4P2
(416) 744-9967
Sales 16,475,585
SIC 1542 Nonresidential construction, nec
Frank Perricone
Janine De Rosnay

D-U-N-S 24-708-6564   (SL)
PETER THE CHEF FINE FOOD LIMITED
401 Humberline Dr Suite 4, Etobicoke, ON, M9W 6Y4
(416) 674-5800
Emp Here 120   *Sales* 41,482,800
SIC 2038 Frozen specialties, nec
Peter Rugiano
Eliana Mariglia
Betty Bozzi

D-U-N-S 20-912-3756   (BR)
PLASTIPAK INDUSTRIES INC
(*Suby of* GROUPE HAMRO INC)
260 Rexdale Blvd, Etobicoke, ON, M9W 1R2
(416) 744-4220
Emp Here 130
SIC 3089 Plastics products, nec
Normand Tanguay

D-U-N-S 24-008-3667   (HQ)
PMT INDUSTRIES LIMITED
PURE METAL GALVANIZING, DIV OF
369 Attwell Dr, Etobicoke, ON, M9W 5C2
(416) 675-3352
Emp Here 20   *Sales* 28,812,750
SIC 3479 Metal coating and allied services
Bruce Phillips
Douglas Phillips
Jeffrey Howe
Jeffrey Phillips

D-U-N-S 25-819-1295   (HQ)
PRECISION PROPERTY MANAGEMENT INC
22 Goodmark Pl Unit 22, Etobicoke, ON, M9W

6R2
(416) 675-2223
Emp Here 1   *Sales* 10,870,240
SIC 6531 Real estate agents and managers
Arthur Eram

D-U-N-S 24-363-7998   (SL)
PREMIUM BEER COMPANY INC, THE
NIAGARA BREWING COMPANY
275 Belfield Rd, Etobicoke, ON, M9W 7H9
(905) 855-7743
Emp Here 45   *Sales* 26,456,220
SIC 5181 Beer and ale
Matthew Oland
Derek Oland
Paul Mcgraw

D-U-N-S 20-300-5681   (SL)
PRO PAK PACKAGING LIMITED
BURNAC PRODUCE
51 Kelfield St, Etobicoke, ON, M9W 5A3
(416) 246-0550
Emp Here 40   *Sales* 17,739,600
SIC 7389 Business services, nec
John Courtman

D-U-N-S 20-316-6020   (SL)
PRODESIGN LIMITED
375 Rexdale Blvd, Etobicoke, ON, M9W 1R9
(416) 744-2011
Emp Here 167   *Sales* 27,392,509
SIC 2782 Blankbooks and looseleaf binders
George Schnarr

D-U-N-S 24-850-3559   (HQ)
PRUDENT BENEFITS ADMINISTRATION SERVICES INC
PBAS
61 International Blvd Suite 110, Etobicoke, ON, M9W 6K4
(416) 674-8581
Emp Here 60   *Sales* 32,953,700
SIC 8748 Business consulting, nec

D-U-N-S 24-816-9096   (BR)
PUROLATOR INC
(*Suby of* GOVERNMENT OF CANADA)
62 Vulcan St, Etobicoke, ON, M9W 1L2
(416) 241-4496
Emp Here 1,500
SIC 4731 Freight transportation arrangement
Sherry Singh

D-U-N-S 24-345-5065   (BR)
PUROLATOR INC
PUROLATOR FREIGHT
(*Suby of* GOVERNMENT OF CANADA)
1151 Martin Grove Rd Suite 7, Etobicoke, ON, M9W 0C1
(416) 614-0300
Emp Here 150
SIC 4731 Freight transportation arrangement
Rob Tetryszyn

D-U-N-S 25-684-1271   (HQ)
QPS EVALUATION SERVICES INC
QPS
81 Kelfield St Unit 8, Etobicoke, ON, M9W 5A3
(416) 241-8857
Emp Here 45   *Sales* 51,505,916
SIC 7389 Business services, nec
John Gulino

D-U-N-S 20-526-7099   (SL)
QUALIFIED METAL FABRICATORS LTD
55 Steinway Blvd, Etobicoke, ON, M9W 6H6
(416) 675-7777
Emp Here 95   *Sales* 18,248,075
SIC 3444 Sheet Metalwork
Bryan Haryott

D-U-N-S 24-543-5342   (HQ)
QUALIFIRST FOODS LTD
GOURMET TRADING
89 Carlingview Dr, Etobicoke, ON, M9W 5E4
(416) 244-1177
Emp Here 20   *Sales* 25,067,310
SIC 5141 Groceries, general line

Yves Farges

D-U-N-S 25-398-6012   (SL)
R.F.G. CANADA INC
RICCI FOOD GROUP CANADA
(*Suby of* 1077792 ONTARIO INC)
50a Claireport Cres, Etobicoke, ON, M9W 6P4
(416) 798-9900
Emp Here 50   *Sales* 17,284,500
SIC 2038 Frozen specialties, nec
Michele Ricci
Joe Ricci
Maria Ricci

D-U-N-S 20-716-8311   (SL)
RACEWAY PLYMOUTH CHRYSLER LTD
RACEWAY CHRYSLER DODGE JEEP
150 Rexdale Blvd, Etobicoke, ON, M9W 1P6
(416) 743-9900
Emp Here 85   *Sales* 53,488,800
SIC 5511 New and used car dealers
Reg Nimeck
Gordon Nimeck
Shozo Yoshihara

D-U-N-S 24-364-7588   (SL)
RAVAGO CANADA CO
MUEHLSTEIN CANADA, DIV OF
(*Suby of* RAVAGO)
180 Attwell Dr Suite 260, Etobicoke, ON, M9W 6A9
(416) 977-5456
Emp Here 50   *Sales* 36,517,250
SIC 5162 Plastics materials and basic shapes
David Skoczen
Ronald Nardozzi
John Provost

D-U-N-S 25-214-4761   (HQ)
RAYNA PEARL INVESTMENT LTD
19 Shaft Rd, Etobicoke, ON, M9W 4M3
(416) 241-1521
Emp Here 155   *Sales* 29,600,340
SIC 5621 Women's clothing stores
Saul Greenspan

D-U-N-S 24-197-3569   (HQ)
RE/MAX WEST REALTY INC
96 Rexdale Blvd Suite 1, Etobicoke, ON, M9W 1N7
(416) 745-2300
Emp Here 96   *Sales* 169,032,000
SIC 6531 Real estate agents and managers
Frank Colatosti

D-U-N-S 24-312-6401   (SL)
REAL DEALS ENTERPRISES INC
RD ENTERPRISES
18 Huddersfield Rd Suite 1, Etobicoke, ON, M9W 5Z6
(416) 248-2020
Emp Here 35   *Sales* 17,809,960
SIC 5023 Homefurnishings
Joel Claridge

D-U-N-S 20-565-5637   (SL)
RESEARCH AND MANAGEMENT CORPORATION
WSI INTERNET CONSULTING & EDUCATION
(*Suby of* WORLD TECHNOLOGY GROUP INC)
20 Carlson Crt Suite 10, Etobicoke, ON, M9W 7K6
(905) 678-7588
Emp Here 140   *Sales* 486,856,860
SIC 6794 Patent owners and lessors
Louis Zalany

D-U-N-S 25-213-4721   (SL)
RICMAR ENTERPRISES LTD
PAT & MARIO'S RESTAURANT
925 Dixon Rd, Etobicoke, ON, M9W 1J8
(416) 674-3031
Emp Here 75   *Sales* 3,413,925
SIC 5812 Eating places
John Rothschild

D-U-N-S 20-793-5024   (HQ)
ROYAL ADHESIVES & SEALANTS CANADA LTD
CHEMQUE
(*Suby of* H.B. FULLER COMPANY)
266 Humberline Dr, Etobicoke, ON, M9W 5X1
(416) 679-5676
Sales 28,402,100
SIC 2899 Chemical preparations, nec

D-U-N-S 25-798-8675   (BR)
ROYAL HOST INC
TRAVELODGE TORONTO AIRPORT
(*Suby of* HOLLOWAY LODGING CORPORATION)
925 Dixon Rd, Etobicoke, ON, M9W 1J8
(416) 674-2222
Emp Here 150
SIC 7011 Hotels and motels
Brian Wallace

D-U-N-S 24-666-2878   (HQ)
ROYAL LASER MFG INC
(*Suby of* 1836826 ONTARIO INC)
25 Claireville Dr, Etobicoke, ON, M9W 5Z7
(416) 679-9474
Emp Here 50   *Sales* 19,208,500
SIC 3499 Fabricated Metal products, nec
John Cheung
William Iannaci
Samir Dalal

D-U-N-S 24-139-1044   (HQ)
SAAND INC
SAAND DISTRIBUTION
250 Brockport Dr Suite 3, Etobicoke, ON, M9W 5S1
(416) 798-2345
Emp Here 120   *Sales* 199,369,800
SIC 5039 Construction materials, nec
Mark Franklin

D-U-N-S 20-337-4632   (BR)
SAAND INC
SAAND DISTRIBUTION
(*Suby of* SAAND INC)
355 Attwell Dr, Etobicoke, ON, M9W 5C2
(416) 674-6945
Emp Here 91
SIC 5039 Construction materials, nec

D-U-N-S 24-844-1693   (SL)
SAAND TORONTO INC
250 Brockport Dr Suite 3, Etobicoke, ON, M9W 5S1
(416) 798-2345
Emp Here 106   *Sales* 18,997,214
SIC 3231 Products of purchased glass
Mark Franklin
Hilton Berger

D-U-N-S 25-155-8318   (BR)
SAFWAY SERVICES CANADA, ULC
(*Suby of* BRAND INDUSTRIAL SERVICES, INC.)
503 Carlingview Dr, Etobicoke, ON, M9W 5H2
(416) 675-2449
Emp Here 100
SIC 1799 Special trade contractors, nec

D-U-N-S 24-805-4996   (SL)
SAI GLOBAL INC
20 Carlson Crt Suite 200, Etobicoke, ON, M9W 7K6
(416) 401-8700
Emp Here 45   *Sales* 10,705,545
SIC 8742 Management consulting services
Chris Jouppi

D-U-N-S 20-699-2245   (BR)
SCHENKER OF CANADA LIMITED
SCHENKER LOGISTICS
(*Suby of* BUNDESREPUBLIK DEUTSCHLAND)
1920 Albion Rd, Etobicoke, ON, M9W 5T2
(416) 798-8070
Emp Here 100
SIC 4226 Special warehousing and storage,

nec
Jamie Mclauglan

D-U-N-S 25-397-5254   (HQ)
SCI GROUP INC
(Suby of GOVERNMENT OF CANADA)
180 Attwell Dr Suite 600, Etobicoke, ON, M9W
6A9
(416) 401-3011
Emp Here 300   Sales 110,628,600
SIC 4213 Trucking, except local
John Ferguson
Roger Rees
Paul Ragan

D-U-N-S 24-848-4698   (HQ)
SCI LOGISTICS LTD
(Suby of GOVERNMENT OF CANADA)
180 Attwell Dr Suite 600, Etobicoke, ON, M9W
6A9
(416) 401-3011
Emp Here 200   Sales 109,686,780
SIC 4225 General warehousing and storage
Chris Galindo
Liz Galloway

D-U-N-S 20-116-8999   (HQ)
SEAGULL COMPANY INCORPORATED,
THE
20 Voyager Crt S Suite A, Etobicoke, ON,
M9W 5M7
(416) 847-4612
Emp Here 20   Sales 44,551,200
SIC 5199 Nondurable goods, nec
Chin Yoon Wong
Poh Kon Yong

D-U-N-S 20-187-3317   (HQ)
SECOND DIMENSION INTERNATIONAL
LIMITED
SDI MARKETING
175 Galaxy Blvd Unit 202, Etobicoke, ON,
M9W 0C9
(416) 674-9010
Emp Here 70   Sales 94,665,000
SIC 8743 Public relations services
Roy Roedger
Andy Harkness
Geoff Comnant
Clyde Lendurm

D-U-N-S 20-551-5604   (HQ)
SHAWCOR LTD
GUARDIAN, DIV OF
25 Bethridge Rd, Etobicoke, ON, M9W 1M7
(416) 743-7111
Emp Here 78   Sales 1,602,684,162
SIC 3533 Oil and gas field machinery
S.M. Orr
P.G Robinson
G.A. Tano
D.R. Ewert
J.T. Baldwin
D.S. Blackwood
J.W. Derrick
K.J. Forbes
M.S. Hanley
P.S. Pierce

D-U-N-S 25-077-5681   (SL)
SHERWOOD INNOVATIONS INC
125 Bethridge Rd, Etobicoke, ON, M9W 1N4
(416) 740-2777
Emp Here 80   Sales 29,137,200
SIC 5013 Motor vehicle supplies and new
parts
Caesar (Chris) Cosentino

D-U-N-S 20-369-8808   (SL)
SILVER CROSS AUTOMOTIVE INC
(Suby of CORPORATION SAVARIA)
14 Goodmark Pl, Etobicoke, ON, M9W 6R1
(905) 799-5533
Emp Here 30   Sales 18,878,400
SIC 5511 New and used car dealers
Marcel Bourassa

D-U-N-S 20-077-8111   (HQ)

SIMERRA PROPERTY MANAGEMENT INC
89 Skyway Ave Suite 200, Etobicoke, ON,
M9W 6R4
(416) 293-5900
Emp Here 65   Sales 16,220,880
SIC 8741 Management services
Tasso Eracles
Janice Pynn

D-U-N-S 24-253-3383   (BR)
SIR CORP
JACK ASTOR'S BAR AND GRILL
(Suby of SIR CORP)
25 Carlson Crt, Etobicoke, ON, M9W 6A2
(416) 213-1688
Emp Here 80
SIC 5812 Eating places
Steve Brennan

D-U-N-S 25-976-5832   (HQ)
SKYWAY CANADA LIMITED
170 Claireville Dr, Etobicoke, ON, M9W 5Y3
(416) 744-6000
Emp Here 50   Sales 51,211,650
SIC 5082 Construction and mining machinery
Robert Chafee

D-U-N-S 24-910-4035   (SL)
SPEC FURNITURE INC
(Suby of SAUDER WOODWORKING CO.)
165 City View Dr, Etobicoke, ON, M9W 5B1
(416) 246-5550
Emp Here 90   Sales 13,888,980
SIC 2522 Office furniture, except wood
Donald Taylor

D-U-N-S 24-757-3678   (SL)
SPRINT MECHANICAL INC
50 Woodbine Downs Blvd, Etobicoke, ON,
M9W 5R2
(416) 747-6059
Emp Here 100   Sales 23,306,500
SIC 1711 Plumbing, heating, air-conditioning
Albert Salvatore
Christopher Rapkyma
Ross Caruso
John Bottos

D-U-N-S 24-666-5038   (HQ)
STARPLEX SCIENTIFIC INC
STARPLEX
50a Steinway Blvd, Etobicoke, ON, M9W 6Y3
(416) 674-7474
Sales 25,472,480
SIC 3841 Surgical and medical instruments
Fred Panini
Ann Mccarley

D-U-N-S 25-173-0271   (SL)
STIR STICKS & PICKS INTERNATIONAL
INC
50 Fasken Dr Unit 9, Etobicoke, ON, M9W 1K5
(416) 675-2064
Emp Here 25   Sales 12,591,450
SIC 5113 Industrial and personal service pa-
per
Richard Griffiths

D-U-N-S 25-591-6561   (BR)
STOCK TRANSPORTATION LTD
STOCK ON THE JOURNEY OF LEARNING
(Suby of NATIONAL EXPRESS GROUP PLC)
60 Mcculloch Ave, Etobicoke, ON, M9W 4M6
(416) 244-5341
Emp Here 280
SIC 4151 School buses
Allan Peck

D-U-N-S 20-733-6397   (HQ)
STURDELL INDUSTRIES INC
(Suby of VOESTALPINE AG)
1907 Albion Rd, Etobicoke, ON, M9W 5S8
(416) 675-2025
Sales 53,512,640
SIC 7389 Business services, nec
Nick Laird

D-U-N-S 24-362-3324   (SL)

SUNWING AIRLINES INC
(Suby of SUNWING TRAVEL GROUP INC)
27 Fasken Dr, Etobicoke, ON, M9W 1K6
(416) 620-4955
Emp Here 200   Sales 53,395,600
SIC 4522 Air transportation, nonscheduled
Mark Williams
Colin Hunter

D-U-N-S 20-803-7924   (SL)
SUNWING CANADA INC
(Suby of SUNWING TRAVEL GROUP INC)
27 Fasken Dr, Etobicoke, ON, M9W 1K6
(416) 695-0500
Emp Here 500   Sales 158,676,000
SIC 4522 Air transportation, nonscheduled
Colin Hunter
Paul Chan
Ross Woods
Stephen Hunter

D-U-N-S 24-351-5793   (HQ)
SUNWING TRAVEL GROUP INC
27 Fasken Dr, Etobicoke, ON, M9W 1K6
(416) 620-4955
Emp Here 50   Sales 316,350,400
SIC 4724 Travel agencies
Colin Hunter
Stephen Hunter
Paul Chan

D-U-N-S 24-689-1204   (HQ)
SUNWING VACATIONS INC
SIGNATURE VACATIONS
(Suby of SUNWING TRAVEL GROUP INC)
27 Fasken Dr, Etobicoke, ON, M9W 1K6
(416) 620-5999
Sales 66,689,200
SIC 4725 Tour operators
Colin Hunter

D-U-N-S 25-320-1404   (BR)
SUPREMEX INC
(Suby of SUPREMEX INC)
400 Humberline Dr, Etobicoke, ON, M9W 5T3
(416) 675-9370
Emp Here 160
SIC 2677 Envelopes
Marguerit Oneil

D-U-N-S 24-290-1619   (HQ)
SYNNEX CANADA LIMITED
EMJ DATA SYSTEMS, DIV OF
(Suby of SYNNEX CORPORATION)
200 Ronson Dr Suite 104, Etobicoke, ON,
M9W 5Z9
(416) 240-7012
Emp Here 300   Sales 374,746,400
SIC 5045 Computers, peripherals, and soft-
ware
Mitchell Martin
Dave Dukowski
Diane Maefs

D-U-N-S 24-947-2853   (SL)
TAC MECHANICAL INC
215 Carlingview Dr Suite 311, Etobicoke, ON,
M9W 5X8
(416) 798-8400
Emp Here 50   Sales 11,046,700
SIC 1711 Plumbing, heating, air-conditioning
Dennis Chedli
Patrick Carbone

D-U-N-S 24-898-4387   (SL)
TATA GLOBAL BEVERAGES CANADA INC
(Suby of TATA GLOBAL BEVERAGES
GROUP LIMITED)
10 Carlson Crt Suite 700, Etobicoke, ON,
M9W 6L2
(416) 798-1224
Emp Here 14   Sales 11,698,078
SIC 5149 Groceries and related products, nec
Abhijit Lahiri
Lakshmanan Krishnakumar

D-U-N-S 24-307-4630   (SL)
TECHNAKORD CHEMICAL INDUSTRIES

INC
5 Mclachlan Dr, Etobicoke, ON, M9W 1E3
(416) 798-9898
Emp Here 100   Sales 27,666,000
SIC 2819 Industrial inorganic chemicals, nec
Michael Baran

D-U-N-S 20-289-6929   (SL)
TECHNICAL STANDARDS AND SAFETY
AUTHORITY
TSSA
345 Carlingview Dr, Etobicoke, ON, M9W 6N9
(416) 734-3300
Emp Here 350   Sales 54,411,244
SIC 8733 Noncommercial research organiza-
tions
Bonnie Rose
Nancy Webb
David Scriven
Peter Wong
Tom Ayres
Kyoko Kobayashi
Georgina Kossivas
Norman Inkster
Douglas Harrison
Lynda Bowles

D-U-N-S 20-059-9269   (HQ)
TEMPCO HEATING & SHEET METAL INC
180 Belfield Rd, Etobicoke, ON, M9W 1H1
(416) 766-1237
Emp Here 50   Sales 22,358,700
SIC 5051 Metals service centers and offices
Ramzi Handal
Rami Handal

D-U-N-S 25-996-4195   (SL)
TETI BAKERY INC
27 Signal Hill Ave Suite 3, Etobicoke, ON,
M9W 6V8
(416) 798-8777
Emp Here 50   Sales 13,707,600
SIC 5461 Retail bakeries
Franko Teti

D-U-N-S 24-525-0936   (HQ)
TFI TRANSPORT 17 LP
TFORCE INTEGRATED SOLUTIONS
96 Disco Rd, Etobicoke, ON, M9W 0A3
(416) 679-7979
Sales 25,998,350
SIC 4731 Freight transportation arrangement
Maggie Smith

D-U-N-S 24-965-3734   (BR)
THOMSON TERMINALS LIMITED
(Suby of THOMSON TERMINALS LIMITED)
55 City View Dr, Etobicoke, ON, M9W 5A5
(416) 240-0897
Emp Here 100
SIC 4225 General warehousing and storage
Gary Rodrigue

D-U-N-S 24-728-2445   (HQ)
THOMSON TERMINALS LIMITED
102 Iron St, Etobicoke, ON, M9W 5L9
(416) 240-0897
Emp Here 30   Sales 92,190,500
SIC 4213 Trucking, except local
Jim Thomson
Sally Thomson

D-U-N-S 24-827-1467   (SL)
THUNDER TOOL & MANUFACTURING LTD
975 Martin Grove Rd, Etobicoke, ON, M9W
4V6
(416) 742-1936
Emp Here 75   Sales 14,406,375
SIC 3469 Metal stampings, nec
Bhupinder Singh Hansra
Rakesh Choudhary
Louie Paonessa

D-U-N-S 24-367-3261   (SL)
TIFFANY GATE FOODS INC
195 Steinway Blvd, Etobicoke, ON, M9W 6H6
(416) 213-9720
Emp Here 250   Sales 179,179,000

SIC 5149 Groceries and related products, nec
Rich Rotzang
Sharon Rotzang

D-U-N-S 20-273-4224   (SL)
TMG NORTH AMERICA INC
155 Rexdale Blvd Suite 207, Etobicoke, ON,
M9W 5Z8
(416) 303-3504
Emp Here 25   *Sales* 11,875,650
SIC 5084 Industrial machinery and equipment
Brent Stucke

D-U-N-S 24-597-9443   (SL)
TORBRIDGE CONSTRUCTION LTD
61 Steinway Blvd, Etobicoke, ON, M9W 6H6
(905) 669-3909
Emp Here 60   *Sales* 15,146,520
SIC 1622 Bridge, tunnel, and elevated high-
way construction
Carmen Giardino

D-U-N-S 25-100-0733   (SL)
**TORONTO AIRPORT CHRISTIAN FELLOW-
SHIP**
TACF
272 Attwell Dr, Etobicoke, ON, M9W 6M3
(416) 674-8463
Emp Here 135   *Sales* 14,056,605
SIC 8661 Religious organizations
John Arnott

D-U-N-S 24-926-5273   (SL)
TORONTO AIRPORT MARRIOTT LTD, THE
(*Suby of* MARRIOTT INTERNATIONAL, INC.)
901 Dixon Rd, Etobicoke, ON, M9W 1J5
(416) 674-9400
Emp Here 250   *Sales* 23,917,000
SIC 7011 Hotels and motels
J.W. Marriott Jr
Arne Sorenson
Carl Berquist

D-U-N-S 25-274-6441   (SL)
TORONTO CONGRESS CENTRE LTD
650 Dixon Rd, Etobicoke, ON, M9W 1J1
(416) 245-5000
Emp Here 30   *Sales* 13,304,700
SIC 7389 Business services, nec
Alain Sutton

D-U-N-S 25-092-8764   (SL)
TOWER EVENTS & SEATING RENTALS INC
365 Attwell Dr, Etobicoke, ON, M9W 5C2
(416) 213-1666
Emp Here 100   *Sales* 44,921,900
SIC 7389 Business services, nec
John Farano

D-U-N-S 25-927-4397   (SL)
TRISTAR INDUSTRIES LTD
160 Bethridge Rd, Etobicoke, ON, M9W 1N3
(416) 747-5767
Emp Here 70   *Sales* 36,437,940
SIC 5093 Scrap and waste materials
Shabbair Rahemtula

D-U-N-S 20-182-9074   (SL)
TURK, ROY INDUSTRIAL SALES LIMITED
106 Vulcan St, Etobicoke, ON, M9W 1L2
(416) 742-2777
Emp Here 42   *Sales* 19,951,092
SIC 5085 Industrial supplies
Roy Turk
Eileen Turk
Andrew Turk
Debbie Mantis
Tony Cavacece

D-U-N-S 25-819-1642   (HQ)
TWI FOODS INC
40 Shaft Rd Suite 20, Etobicoke, ON, M9W
4M2
(647) 775-1400
Emp Here 150   *Sales* 19,916,778
SIC 2051 Bread, cake, and related products
Ali Kizilbash
Yuhana Kizilbash

D-U-N-S 20-534-4109   (SL)
U-PAK DISPOSALS (1989) LTD
15 Tidemore Ave, Etobicoke, ON, M9W 7E9
(416) 675-3700
Emp Here 90   *Sales* 23,141,790
SIC 4953 Refuse systems
Mary Molony

D-U-N-S 25-283-7109   (HQ)
UCC GROUP INC
262 Galaxy Blvd, Etobicoke, ON, M9W 5R8
(416) 675-7455
Emp Here 75   *Sales* 32,172,790
SIC 1771 Concrete work
Pat Dipaolo
Domenic Evangelista

D-U-N-S 25-097-2825   (BR)
UNILEVER CANADA INC
(*Suby of* UNILEVER PLC)
195 Belfield Rd, Etobicoke, ON, M9W 1G8
(416) 246-1650
Emp Here 100
SIC 2099 Food preparations, nec
Stan Reid

D-U-N-S 20-846-9262   (HQ)
**UNITED FOOD AND COMMERCIAL WORK-
ERS CANADA UNION**
UFCW CANADA
(*Suby of* UNITED FOOD AND COMMERCIAL
WORKERS INTERNATIONAL UNION)
61 International Blvd Unit 300, Etobicoke, ON,
M9W 6K4
(416) 675-1104
Emp Here 10   *Sales* 19,557,900
SIC 8631 Labor organizations
Harold Meinema

D-U-N-S 25-248-5230   (SL)
URBAN MECHANICAL CONTRACTING LTD
254 Attwell Dr, Etobicoke, ON, M9W 5B2
(416) 240-8830
Emp Here 125   *Sales* 29,133,125
SIC 1711 Plumbing, heating, air-conditioning
Edward J Winter
Alan Lipszyc

D-U-N-S 25-089-4227   (SL)
URSUS TRANSPORT INC
85 Vulcan St, Etobicoke, ON, M9W 1L4
(416) 243-8780
Emp Here 20   *Sales* 17,385,282
SIC 4213 Trucking, except local
John Poreba

D-U-N-S 20-095-9505   (SL)
VANDEGRIFT CANADA ULC
63 Galaxy Blvd Unit 1-2, Etobicoke, ON, M9W
5R7
(416) 213-9093
Emp Here 30   *Sales* 15,599,010
SIC 4731 Freight transportation arrangement
Tom Roberts

D-U-N-S 25-990-3581   (HQ)
**VENDING PRODUCTS OF CANADA LIM-
ITED**
*DISTRIBUTION VENDING PRODUCT DU
CANADA*
(*Suby of* BROKERHOUSE DISTRIBUTORS
INC)
108 Woodbine Downs Blvd Unit 1, Etobicoke,
ON, M9W 5S6
(416) 213-8363
Emp Here 12   *Sales* 41,778,850
SIC 5145 Confectionery
Sam Neill
Jeff Allan Suitor
Gregory James Suitor

D-U-N-S 25-359-7892   (HQ)
VENTURE STEEL INC
GATSTEEL
(*Suby of* TRIPLE M METAL LP)
60 Disco Rd, Etobicoke, ON, M9W 1L8
(416) 798-9396
Sales 128,452,610

SIC 5051 Metals service centers and offices
Tony Kafato
Gary Fisher

D-U-N-S 25-807-6926   (SL)
VICOR MECHANICAL LTD
11 Haas Rd, Etobicoke, ON, M9W 3A1
(416)
Emp Here 50   *Sales* 11,046,700
SIC 1711 Plumbing, heating, air-conditioning
Armando Orefice

D-U-N-S 24-330-0485   (BR)
WAL-MART CANADA CORP
(*Suby of* WALMART INC.)
2245 Islington Ave Suite 3740, Etobicoke, ON,
M9W 3W6
(416) 747-6499
Emp Here 200
SIC 5311 Department stores
Marco Costa

D-U-N-S 20-596-2558   (SL)
WALLCROWN LIMITED
88 Ronson Dr, Etobicoke, ON, M9W 1B9
(416) 245-2900
Emp Here 73   *Sales* 17,238,119
SIC 2679 Converted paper products, nec
Gilbert Goodman
Bonnie Goodman-Bloom

D-U-N-S 20-292-5046   (SL)
WESCO AIRCRAFT EUROPE, LTD
(*Suby of* WESCO AIRCRAFT HOLDINGS,
INC.)
22 Worcester Rd, Etobicoke, ON, M9W 5X2
(416) 674-0770
Emp Here 100
SIC 5085 Industrial supplies
Randy Snyder

D-U-N-S 25-722-6662   (BR)
**WESTMONT HOSPITALITY MANAGEMENT
LIMITED**
HOLIDAY INN
(*Suby of* WESTMONT HOSPITALITY MAN-
AGEMENT LIMITED)
600 Dixon Rd, Etobicoke, ON, M9W 1J1
(416) 240-7511
Emp Here 80
SIC 7011 Hotels and motels
Sohail Saeed

D-U-N-S 25-276-2323   (SL)
WILTON INDUSTRIES CANADA COMPANY
(*Suby of* WILTON BRANDS LLC)
98 Carrier Dr, Etobicoke, ON, M9W 5R1
(416) 679-0790
Emp Here 40   *Sales* 20,354,240
SIC 5023 Homefurnishings
Vincent Naccarato
Jeff Mclaughlin
Steven Fraser
Mary Merfield

D-U-N-S 24-964-2372   (HQ)
WINPAK PORTION PACKAGING LTD
(*Suby of* WINPAK LTD)
26 Tidemore Ave, Etobicoke, ON, M9W 7A7
(416) 741-6182
Sales 28,435,582
SIC 3089 Plastics products, nec
Christopher Crooks
Tom Herlihy

D-U-N-S 24-385-4205   (SL)
WORLD AUTO PARTS (CANADA) LTD
WORLD AUTOMOTIVE WAREHOUSE
(*Suby of* GROUPE MONACO AUTOMOTIVE
INC)
355 Carlingview Dr Unit 1, Etobicoke, ON,
M9W 5G8
(416) 675-6750
Emp Here 40   *Sales* 25,171,200
SIC 5511 New and used car dealers
Dominic Monaco

D-U-N-S 20-968-1113   (SL)

WORLD WIDE IOZZA LTD
240 Humberline Dr Suite D, Etobicoke, ON,
M9W 5X1
(416) 675-1930
Emp Here 25   *Sales* 12,458,050
SIC 5131 Piece goods and notions
Roberto D'arolfi
Alba D'arolfi
Mario Cavelli

D-U-N-S 24-745-0216   (HQ)
XTL TRANSPORT INC
(*Suby of* SERGA HOLDING INC)
75 Rexdale Blvd, Etobicoke, ON, M9W 1P1
(416) 742-0610
Emp Here 80   *Sales* 114,070,286
SIC 4213 Trucking, except local
Serge Gagnon
Genevieve Gagnon
Andre Leroux

Exeter, ON N0M

D-U-N-S 20-014-0460   (HQ)
1476399 ONTARIO LIMITED
DELTA POWER EQUIPMENT
71301 London Rd, Exeter, ON, N0M 1S3
(519) 235-2121
Sales 14,214,200
SIC 6712 Bank holding companies
Cameron Currie
Michael Macko
Mark Macko
Jerry Beernink
Greg Sanders
Mark Sanders
Bert Sanders

D-U-N-S 20-047-8329   (SL)
533438 ONTARIO LIMITED
NORTHLANDER INDUSTRIES
(*Suby of* 875174 ONTARIO LIMITED)
165 Thames Rd W Ss 3 Suite 83, Exeter, ON,
N0M 1S3
(519) 235-1530
Emp Here 170   *Sales* 16,198,000
SIC 2451 Mobile homes
Robert Hamather

D-U-N-S 25-800-9067   (BR)
**AVON MAITLAND DISTRICT SCHOOL
BOARD**
SOUTH HURON DISTRICT HIGH SCHOOL
92 Gidley E, Exeter, ON, N0M 1S0
(519) 235-0880
Emp Here 75
SIC 8211 Elementary and secondary schools
Kevin Mills

D-U-N-S 20-772-0983   (HQ)
DAVE MOORE FUELS LTD
315 Main St N Suite 3, Exeter, ON, N0M 1S3
(519) 235-0853
Emp Here 1   *Sales* 27,658,422
SIC 5172 Petroleum products, nec
David Moore

D-U-N-S 20-075-5077   (HQ)
DELTA POWER EQUIPMENT
(*Suby of* 1476399 ONTARIO LIMITED)
71301 London Rd, Exeter, ON, N0M 1S3
(519) 235-2121
Emp Here 29   *Sales* 12,460,728
SIC 5999 Miscellaneous retail stores, nec
Cameron Currie

D-U-N-S 24-411-6133   (HQ)
ELLISON TRAVEL & TOURS LTD
CARLSON WAGONLIT TRAVEL
311 Main St N, Exeter, ON, N0M 1S3
(519) 235-2000
Emp Here 50   *Sales* 40,013,520
SIC 4725 Tour operators
Doug Ellison

Frances Ellison
Cathy Pfaff

D-U-N-S 20-047-8485　　(HQ)
EXETER PRODUCE AND STORAGE COMPANY, LIMITED
215 Thames Rd W Ss 3, Exeter, ON, N0M 1S3
(519) 235-0141
Sales 41,778,850
SIC 5148 Fresh fruits and vegetables
Leonard Veri
Noel Veri
Michael Veri
Jim Veri

D-U-N-S 20-405-4191　　(SL)
HURON MOTOR PRODUCTS LIMITED
70704 London Rd, Exeter, ON, N0M 1S1
(514) 700-0180
Emp Here 60　　*Sales* 37,756,800
SIC 5511 New and used car dealers
Robert Hamather
Donna Hamather
Timothy Hamather

D-U-N-S 20-537-2816　　(HQ)
HURON PRODUCE LIMITED
40534 Thames Rd, Exeter, ON, N0M 1S5
(519) 235-2650
Emp Here 19　　*Sales* 29,245,195
SIC 5148 Fresh fruits and vegetables
Jeffrey Kints

D-U-N-S 25-362-2997　　(HQ)
HURON TRACTOR LTD
39995 Harvest Rd, Exeter, ON, N0M 1S3
(519) 235-1115
Emp Here 55　　*Sales* 101,447,840
SIC 5083 Farm and garden machinery
Henry Winters
Paul Van Off

D-U-N-S 24-196-5961　　(SL)
J.M.R. ELECTRIC LTD
301 Thames Rd, Exeter, ON, N0M 1S3
(519) 235-1516
Emp Here 380　　*Sales* 89,493,420
SIC 1731 Electrical work
John Rasenberg
Steven J. Rasenberg

D-U-N-S 24-679-8578　　(SL)
K & J FAMILY HOLDINGS LTD
CANADIAN TIRE
100 Thames Rd W Ss 3 Suite 3, Exeter, ON, N0M 1S3
(519) 235-0160
Emp Here 45　　*Sales* 22,413,510
SIC 5531 Auto and home supply stores
Alan Webster

D-U-N-S 24-020-0621　　(BR)
MCCANN REDI-MIX INC
(*Suby of* MCCANN REDI-MIX INC)
140 Thames Rd W Ss 3, Exeter, ON, N0M 1S3
(519) 235-0338
Emp Here 113
SIC 3273 Ready-mixed concrete
Adam Mccann

D-U-N-S 25-107-6477　　(SL)
MILLER BROS. ROOFING & SHEET METAL CO LIMITED
206 Victoria St W, Exeter, ON, N0M 1S2
(519) 235-3643
Emp Here 54　　*Sales* 11,762,766
SIC 1761 Roofing, siding, and sheetMetal work
Jeffrey Keller

D-U-N-S 25-278-1703　　(SL)
SOUTH HURON HOSPITAL ASSOCIATION
24 Huron St W, Exeter, ON, N0M 1S2
(519) 235-2700
Emp Here 119　　*Sales* 13,218,520
SIC 8062 General medical and surgical hospitals
Bruce Quigley

D-U-N-S 25-401-7783　　(SL)
SUNTASTIC HOTHOUSE INC
40534 Thames Rd E, Exeter, ON, N0M 1S5
(519) 235-3357
Emp Here 80　　*Sales* 20,984,720
SIC 0182 Food crops grown under cover
Burkhard Metzger
Jeff Kints

Falconbridge, ON P0M

D-U-N-S 20-716-6356　　(SL)
JEWELL, E & R CONTRACTING LIMITED
6 Chesser St, Falconbridge, ON, P0M 1S0
(705) 693-3761
Emp Here 44　　*Sales* 10,598,896
SIC 1629 Heavy construction, nec
Russell Jewell
Marlene Jewell

Fenelon Falls, ON K0M

D-U-N-S 25-139-3120　　(HQ)
1759800 ONTARIO INC
B TOWN GROUP
804 County Road 8, Fenelon Falls, ON, K0M 1N0
(705) 887-9458
Sales 10,285,002
SIC 5032 Brick, stone, and related material
Bill Sisson

D-U-N-S 20-528-5823　　(SL)
FENELON COURT LONG TERM CARE CENTRE
44 Wychwood Cres, Fenelon Falls, ON, K0M 1N0
(705) 887-2100
Emp Here 80　　*Sales* 5,485,280
SIC 8051 Skilled nursing care facilities
Derek Watchorn

D-U-N-S 20-790-2391　　(BR)
SOBEYS CAPITAL INCORPORATED
SOBEYS FENELON FALLS
(*Suby of* EMPIRE COMPANY LIMITED)
15 Lindsay St, Fenelon Falls, ON, K0M 1N0
(705) 887-3611
Emp Here 100
SIC 5411 Grocery stores
Mark Knoester

D-U-N-S 25-061-5010　　(BR)
TRILLIUM LAKELANDS DISTRICT SCHOOL BOARD
FENELON FALLS SECONDARY SCHOOL
(*Suby of* TRILLIUM LAKELANDS DISTRICT SCHOOL BOARD)
66 Lindsay St, Fenelon Falls, ON, K0M 1N0
(705) 887-2018
Emp Here 100
SIC 8211 Elementary and secondary schools
Ray Este

Fenwick, ON L0S

D-U-N-S 24-987-5428　　(SL)
968502 ONTARIO INC
UNITED FLORAL DISTRIBUTORS
1050 Canboro Rd, Fenwick, ON, L0S 1C0
(905) 892-4766
Emp Here 65　　*Sales* 48,263,800
SIC 5193 Flowers and florists supplies
Debbie Boverhof
Albert Elmers

D-U-N-S 20-336-5742　　(SL)
BERRY FRESH FARMS

1760 Balfour St, Fenwick, ON, L0S 1C0
(905) 892-8231
Emp Here 30　　*Sales* 10,274,010
SIC 0171 Berry crops
David Klyn Hsselink

D-U-N-S 20-048-0077　　(HQ)
CLARE'S CYCLE & SPORTS LTD
799 Hwy 20, Fenwick, ON, L0S 1C0
(905) 892-2664
Emp Here 20　　*Sales* 25,171,200
SIC 5571 Motorcycle dealers
John F Clare
Irene Clare
Randy Clare
Robin Primerano

D-U-N-S 25-863-7891　　(SL)
MUTUAL SUPPORT SYSTEMS OF THE NIAGARA REGION
MUTUAL SUPPORT SYSTEMS
792 Canboro Rd, Fenwick, ON, L0S 1C0
(905) 892-4332
Emp Here 40　　*Sales* 15,896,560
SIC 8699 Membership organizations, nec
Dave Schulz

D-U-N-S 24-507-7615　　(SL)
WILLOWBROOK NURSERIES INC
935 Victoria Ave, Fenwick, ON, L0S 1C0
(905) 892-5350
Emp Here 50　　*Sales* 17,123,350
SIC 0181 Ornamental nursery products
John Langendoen
Jocelyn Langendoen

Fergus, ON N1M

D-U-N-S 20-165-7897　　(HQ)
A.O. SMITH ENTERPRISES LTD
A.O. SMITH GSW WATER HEATING
(*Suby of* A. O. SMITH CORPORATION)
599 Hill St W, Fergus, ON, N1M 2X1
(519) 843-1610
Emp Here 10　　*Sales* 19,044,200
SIC 3639 Household appliances, nec
David Hammond
Geoffrey Holloway
John Weiler

D-U-N-S 24-327-2650　　(SL)
DREVER, S. PHARMACY LIMITED
SHOPPERS DRUG MART
710 Tower St S, Fergus, ON, N1M 2R3
(519) 843-3160
Emp Here 50　　*Sales* 12,647,700
SIC 5912 Drug stores and proprietary stores
Shirley Drever

D-U-N-S 25-626-6636　　(SL)
ELLIOTT COACH LINES (FERGUS) LTD
680 Glen Garry Cres, Fergus, ON, N1M 2W8

Emp Here 85　　*Sales* 4,664,120
SIC 4151 School buses
Allan Mckay
Micheline Mckay

D-U-N-S 25-952-5590　　(BR)
GRANDI COMPANY LIMITED
MCDONALDS RESTAURANT
(*Suby of* GRANDI COMPANY LIMITED)
870 Tower St S, Fergus, ON, N1M 3N7
(519) 787-5125
Emp Here 80
SIC 5812 Eating places
Michae Grandi

D-U-N-S 24-181-5133　　(SL)
GROVES MEMORIAL COMMUNITY HOSPITAL
235 Union St E, Fergus, ON, N1M 1W3
(519) 843-2010
Emp Here 230　　*Sales* 25,548,400

SIC 8062 General medical and surgical hospitals
Dana Seiling

D-U-N-S 20-048-0929　　(BR)
MOORE CANADA CORPORATION
R.R. DONNELLEY
(*Suby of* R. R. DONNELLEY & SONS COMPANY)
650 Victoria Terr, Fergus, ON, N1M 1G7
(519) 843-2510
Emp Here 150
SIC 2761 Manifold business forms
Gerry Shanahan

D-U-N-S 24-986-6765　　(BR)
NEXANS CANADA INC
(*Suby of* NEXANS)
670 Gzowski St, Fergus, ON, N1M 2W9
(519) 843-3000
Emp Here 250
SIC 3312 Blast furnaces and steel mills
Cameron Matthew

D-U-N-S 24-764-1210　　(SL)
ONTARIO NUTRI LAB INC
6589 First Line Suite 3, Fergus, ON, N1M 2W4
(519) 843-5669
Emp Here 50　　*Sales* 11,734,800
SIC 8734 Testing laboratories
Christine Stec
Brian K Ausman

D-U-N-S 24-688-7723　　(HQ)
OSTIC INSURANCE BROKERS LIMITED
OSTIC GROUP
210 St Patrick St W, Fergus, ON, N1M 1L7
(519) 843-2540
Emp Here 19　　*Sales* 29,682,100
SIC 6411 Insurance agents, brokers, and service
James Ostic
Jeffrey T Ostic
Thomas Waind
Hugh Waind
Ivan R Ostic

D-U-N-S 25-481-4155　　(SL)
ROYAL LEPAGE ROYAL CITY REALTY LTD
840 Tower St S, Fergus, ON, N1M 2R3
(519) 843-1365
Emp Here 40　　*Sales* 13,085,080
SIC 6531 Real estate agents and managers
Robb Atkinson

D-U-N-S 24-827-1058　　(SL)
VANDERMAREL TRUCKING LIMITED
655 Dickson Dr, Fergus, ON, N1M 2W7
(519) 787-1563
Emp Here 85　　*Sales* 12,596,320
SIC 4213 Trucking, except local
Antonie Vandermarel
Mary Vandermarel

D-U-N-S 25-297-8051　　(BR)
ZEHRMART INC
ZEHRS MARKETS
(*Suby of* LOBLAW COMPANIES LIMITED)
800 Tower St S, Fergus, ON, N1M 2R3
(519) 843-5500
Emp Here 150
SIC 5411 Grocery stores
Jeremy Hewitt

Flesherton, ON N0C

D-U-N-S 24-020-0894　　(SL)
CROFT, MICHAEL SAND & GRAVEL INC
400421 Grey Rd Suite 4, Flesherton, ON, N0C 1E0
(519) 924-2429
Emp Here 40　　*Sales* 11,340,960
SIC 1611 Highway and street construction
Mike Croft

▲ Public Company　　■ Public Company Family Member　　**HQ** Headquarters　　**BR** Branch　　**SL** Single Location

D-U-N-S 24-286-3413   (HQ)
FLESHERTON CONCRETE PRODUCTS INC
FLESHCON
Gd, Flesherton, ON, N0C 1E0
(519) 924-2429
Sales 11,671,750
SIC 3273 Ready-mixed concrete
Michael Croft
John Croft

Flinton, ON K0H

D-U-N-S 24-423-2880   (SL)
FLINTSHIRE FARMS INC
79 Pheasant Farm Rd, Flinton, ON, K0H 1P0
(613) 336-8552
Emp Here 35   *Sales* 29,245,195
SIC 5144 Poultry and poultry products
Chuck Drost
Annette Drost

Floradale, ON N0B

D-U-N-S 20-048-2289   (SL)
FLORADALE FEED MILL LIMITED
2131 Floradale Rd, Floradale, ON, N0B 1V0
(519) 669-5478
Emp Here 104   *Sales* 21,393,424
SIC 4213 Trucking, except local
Craig Schwindt
Kathy Schwindt

Fonthill, ON L0S

D-U-N-S 20-146-3296   (SL)
CENTRAL MOTORS (PELHAM) LTD
AUTO PRO NIAGARA
227 Hwy 20, Fonthill, ON, L0S 1E6
(905) 892-2653
Emp Here 40   *Sales* 19,923,120
SIC 5511 New and used car dealers
Gary Riley

D-U-N-S 24-972-9393   (BR)
DISTRICT SCHOOL BOARD OF NIAGARA
E L CROSSLEY SECONDARY SCHOOL
350 Hwy 20 W, Fonthill, ON, L0S 1E0
(905) 892-5308
Emp Here 85
SIC 8211 Elementary and secondary schools
Karen Simpson

D-U-N-S 20-372-3841   (SL)
DULIBAN INSURANCE BROKERS LIMITED
165 Hwy 20 Suite 7, Fonthill, ON, L0S 1E5
(905) 892-5723
Emp Here 43   *Sales* 24,936,732
SIC 6411 Insurance agents, brokers, and service
Adam Duliban
Jason Duliban

D-U-N-S 20-923-8471   (SL)
ROWENDA INVESTMENTS LTD
MCDONALD'S RESTAURANTS
124 Hwy 20 E, Fonthill, ON, L0S 1E6
(905) 892-7906
Emp Here 187   *Sales* 8,512,053
SIC 5812 Eating places
Ronald Perry
Wendy Perry

D-U-N-S 20-806-2492   (BR)
SOBEYS CAPITAL INCORPORATED
SOBEYS STORE# 7329
(*Suby of* EMPIRE COMPANY LIMITED)
110 20 Hwy E, Fonthill, ON, L0S 1E0

(905) 892-2570
Emp Here 125
SIC 5411 Grocery stores
Cindy Cameron

Forest, ON N0N

D-U-N-S 20-547-2090   (BR)
CORPORATION OF THE COUNTY OF LAMBTON
NORTH LAMBTON LODGE
(*Suby of* CORPORATION OF THE COUNTY OF LAMBTON)
39 Morris St, Forest, ON, N0N 1J0
(519) 786-2151
Emp Here 100
SIC 8059 Nursing and personal care, nec
Jane Joris

D-U-N-S 20-048-3782   (HQ)
LAKESIDE GRAIN & FEED LIMITED
7858 Rawlings Rd Suite 1, Forest, ON, N0N 1J0
(519) 786-2106
Sales 20,048,040
SIC 5191 Farm supplies
Ian Shipley
Ron Shipley
Kevin Shipley
Eric Bosveld
Donald Henderson

Fort Albany, ON P0L

D-U-N-S 24-286-3280   (BR)
JAMES BAY GENERAL HOSPITAL
FORT ALBANY WING
(*Suby of* JAMES BAY GENERAL HOSPITAL)
Gd, Fort Albany, ON, P0L 1H0
(705) 278-3330
Emp Here 75
SIC 8062 General medical and surgical hospitals
Andrew Poonae

Fort Erie, ON L2A

D-U-N-S 25-215-1949   (SL)
1083211 ONTARIO LTD
BORDER CITY CASTINGS
19 Warren St, Fort Erie, ON, L2A 2N4
(905) 994-0800
Emp Here 14   *Sales* 14,004,746
SIC 5051 Metals service centers and offices
Robert Nadeau
Daniel Lint
Shirley Nadeau
Laura Lint

D-U-N-S 24-340-6225   (SL)
2097738 ONTARIO INC
FORT ERIE TRUCK STOP & SERVICE CENTRE
1637 Pettit Rd, Fort Erie, ON, L2A 5M4

Emp Here 30   *Sales* 15,193,652
SIC 5541 Gasoline service stations
Carl Cotton

D-U-N-S 24-422-6619   (HQ)
531442 ONTARIO INC
FRONTIER DISTRIBUTING
1031 Helena St, Fort Erie, ON, L2A 4K3
(905) 871-3358
Sales 40,013,520
SIC 4731 Freight transportation arrangement
John Hamilton

D-U-N-S 24-424-8969   (HQ)

AIRBUS HELICOPTERS CANADA LIMITED
AIRBUS
(*Suby of* AIRBUS SE)
1100 Gilmore Rd, Fort Erie, ON, L2A 5M4
(905) 871-7772
Emp Here 161   *Sales* 36,710,252
SIC 3721 Aircraft
Romain Trapp
Dwayne Charette

D-U-N-S 25-530-1244   (SL)
BUFFALO AND FORT ERIE PUBLIC BRIDGE COMPANY
PEACE BRIDGE AUTHORITY
100 Queen St, Fort Erie, ON, L2A 3S6
(905) 871-1608
Emp Here 68   *Sales* 31,072,000
SIC 4785 Inspection and fixed facilities
Ron Rienas

D-U-N-S 24-348-0915   (HQ)
CANADIAN NIAGARA POWER INC
(*Suby of* FORTIS INC)
1130 Bertie St, Fort Erie, ON, L2A 5Y2
(905) 871-0330
Sales 18,798,420
SIC 4911 Electric services
William Daley

D-U-N-S 24-318-5717   (HQ)
CENTURY 21 TODAY REALTY LTD
225 Garrison Rd, Fort Erie, ON, L2A 1M8
(905) 871-2121
Sales 29,322,230
SIC 6531 Real estate agents and managers
Eugene Pilato
Roy Zanatta
Anita Zanatta

D-U-N-S 24-485-7819   (SL)
COMMUNITY LIVING - FORT ERIE
615 Industrial Dr, Fort Erie, ON, L2A 5M4
(905) 871-6770
Emp Here 85   *Sales* 5,815,870
SIC 8322 Individual and family services
Maureen Brown

D-U-N-S 20-292-3202   (BR)
CONMED DEVELOPMENTS INC
CRESCENT PARK LODGE
(*Suby of* CONMED DEVELOPMENTS INC)
4 Hagey Ave, Fort Erie, ON, L2A 1W3
(905) 871-8330
Emp Here 100
SIC 8051 Skilled nursing care facilities
Rose Turner

D-U-N-S 25-282-8918   (SL)
CRESCENT PARK LODGE
CONMED
(*Suby of* CONMED DEVELOPMENTS INC)
4 Hagey Ave, Fort Erie, ON, L2A 1W3
(905) 871-8330
Emp Here 75   *Sales* 5,142,450
SIC 8051 Skilled nursing care facilities
Rose Turner

D-U-N-S 20-014-4736   (SL)
DUREZ CANADA COMPANY LTD
SBHPP
(*Suby of* SUMITOMO BAKELITE COMPANY LIMITED)
100 Dunlop St, Fort Erie, ON, L2A 5M6
(905) 346-8700
Emp Here 100   *Sales* 28,732,978
SIC 2821 Plastics materials and resins
Seiji Suzuki
Robert Hunt

D-U-N-S 24-318-6561   (SL)
FLEET CANADA INC
1011 Gilmore Rd, Fort Erie, ON, L2A 5M4
(905) 871-2100
Emp Here 145   *Sales* 32,457,235
SIC 3728 Aircraft parts and equipment, nec
Glenn Stansfield
Paul Williams

Mark Maybank

D-U-N-S 24-560-2248   (SL)
FORT ERIE NATIVE CULTURAL CENTRE INC
FORT ERIE NATIVE FRIENDSHIP CENTRE
796 Buffalo Rd, Fort Erie, ON, L2A 5H2
(905) 871-6592
Emp Here 100   *Sales* 6,842,200
SIC 8322 Individual and family services
Jackie Poulin

D-U-N-S 20-531-6508   (HQ)
FORTISONTARIO INC
(*Suby of* FORTIS INC)
1130 Bertie St, Fort Erie, ON, L2A 5Y2
(905) 871-0330
Emp Here 55   *Sales* 88,383,620
SIC 4911 Electric services
Scott Hawkes
Glen King
Jie Han
Tim Lavoie

D-U-N-S 20-803-7650   (SL)
JESSE & KELLY'S NO FRILLS
1135 Thompson Rd, Fort Erie, ON, L2A 6T7
(866) 987-6453
Emp Here 40   *Sales* 10,966,080
SIC 5411 Grocery stores
Jesse Edmondson

D-U-N-S 24-359-0416   (BR)
LIVINGSTON INTERNATIONAL INC
LIVINGSTON CUSTOM BROKERAGE
(*Suby of* LIVINGSTON INTERNATIONAL INC)
36 Queen St, Fort Erie, ON, L2A 0B5
(905) 871-6500
Emp Here 230
SIC 4731 Freight transportation arrangement
Jody Faraday

D-U-N-S 25-300-2901   (SL)
MILLER'S AUTO RECYCLING (1992) LTD
1557 Bowen Rd, Fort Erie, ON, L2A 5M4
(800) 263-8104
Emp Here 65   *Sales* 15,881,320
SIC 5932 Used merchandise stores
James Miller
William Miller

D-U-N-S 25-828-1583   (SL)
MILLER'S COLLISION & CAR SALES
1557 Bowen Rd, Fort Erie, ON, L2A 5M4
(905) 871-5105
Emp Here 60   *Sales* 37,756,800
SIC 5521 Used car dealers
Joanne Godin
William Miller

D-U-N-S 25-176-3058   (SL)
MILLS-ROY ENTERPRISES LIMITED
CANADIAN TIRE
240 Garrison Rd, Fort Erie, ON, L2A 1M7
(905) 871-8081
Emp Here 65   *Sales* 17,397,380
SIC 5251 Hardware stores
Patti Mills-Roy

D-U-N-S 24-987-3092   (HQ)
NATIONAL COMMITTEE FOR THE NATIONAL PILGRIM VIRGIN OF CANADA, THE
NATIONAL PILGRIM
452 Kraft Rd, Fort Erie, ON, L2A 4M7
(905) 871-7607
Emp Here 185   *Sales* 31,657,211
SIC 2721 Periodicals
Nicholas Gruner
Coralie Graham

D-U-N-S 20-934-6246   (HQ)
NORMA DONUTS LIMITED
TIM HORTONS
141 Garrison Rd, Fort Erie, ON, L2A 1M3
(905) 871-1743
Emp Here 80   *Sales* 9,327,800

▲ Public Company   ■ Public Company Family Member   **HQ** Headquarters   **BR** Branch   **SL** Single Location

SIC 5812 Eating places
Helmut Strom
Wilma Strom

D-U-N-S 24-662-9836   (SL)
PEACE BRIDGE DUTY FREE INC
1 Peace Bridge Plaza, Fort Erie, ON, L2A 5N1
(905) 871-5400
Emp Here 75   *Sales* 15,400,725
SIC 5399 Miscellaneous general merchandise
George Slipp
Alec Rossman
John Marsh
Charles Loewen
Jim Pearce

D-U-N-S 20-982-7435   (SL)
PENINSULA PLASTICS LIMITED
PEN PLAST
620 Industrial Dr, Fort Erie, ON, L2A 5M4
(905) 871-4766
Emp Here 100   *Sales* 14,040,828
SIC 3089 Plastics products, nec
Craig Bolton
Colleen Bredin
Jake Bolton

D-U-N-S 20-048-5951   (SL)
RICH PRODUCTS OF CANADA LIMITED
(*Suby of* RICH PRODUCTS CORPORATION)
12 Hagey Ave, Fort Erie, ON, L2A 1W3
(905) 871-2605
Emp Here 200   *Sales* 97,477,000
SIC 2053 Frozen bakery products, except bread
William G Gisel Jr.
Robert E Rich
Melinda Rich
Richard Ferranti
James Deuschle
Maureen Hurley
Kevin Malchoff

D-U-N-S 25-524-8916   (HQ)
RMC INTERNATIONAL INC
505 Central Ave, Fort Erie, ON, L2A 3T9
(905) 991-0431
Sales 13,182,762
SIC 3825 Instruments to measure electricity
Anestos Stefanidis
John Stefanidis
Stamatia Vassou

D-U-N-S 25-541-4138   (BR)
SHERWIN-WILLIAMS CANADA INC
(*Suby of* THE SHERWIN-WILLIAMS COMPANY)
224 Catherine St, Fort Erie, ON, L2A 0B1
(905) 871-2724
Emp Here 80
SIC 2851 Paints and allied products
Paul Sidillotti

D-U-N-S 24-329-8655   (BR)
WAL-MART CANADA CORP
(*Suby of* WALMART INC.)
750 Garrison Rd, Fort Erie, ON, L2A 1N7
(905) 991-9971
Emp Here 200
SIC 5311 Department stores
Danielle Brigantino

D-U-N-S 25-312-7138   (BR)
WEYERHAEUSER COMPANY LIMITED
GREEN FOREST LUMBER DIV OF
(*Suby of* WEYERHAEUSER COMPANY)
40 Dunlop St, Fort Erie, ON, L2A 4H8

Emp Here 117
SIC 5031 Lumber, plywood, and millwork
John Sereny

Fort Frances, ON P9A

D-U-N-S 20-945-8405   (HQ)
GILLONS' INSURANCE BROKERS LTD
326 Church St, Fort Frances, ON, P9A 1E1
(807) 274-7716
Emp Here 22   *Sales* 27,137,920
SIC 6411 Insurance agents, brokers, and service
Myron Romaniuk

D-U-N-S 20-434-7702   (HQ)
MACDONALD, JIM MOTORS LTD
MACDONALD CHEVROLET
1324 King'S Hwy, Fort Frances, ON, P9A 2X6
(807) 274-5321
Sales 12,950,028
SIC 5511 New and used car dealers
James Macdonald
Linda Macdonald
Fern Pochailo

D-U-N-S 24-040-2479   (HQ)
NORTHWEST CATHOLIC DISTRICT SCHOOL BOARD, THE
555 Flinders Ave, Fort Frances, ON, P9A 3L2
(807) 274-2931
Emp Here 15   *Sales* 19,099,282
SIC 8211 Elementary and secondary schools
Brendan Hyatt
Jackie Robinson

D-U-N-S 25-275-2696   (BR)
PF RESOLU CANADA INC
(*Suby of* RESOLUTE FOREST PRODUCTS INC)
427 Mowat Ave, Fort Frances, ON, P9A 1Y8
(807) 274-5311
Emp Here 427
SIC 2611 Pulp mills
Ryan Ellard

D-U-N-S 24-236-6599   (HQ)
RIVERSIDE HEALTH CARE FACILITIES INC
LAVERENDRYE GENERAL HOSPITAL
110 Victoria Ave, Fort Frances, ON, P9A 2B7
(807) 274-3266
Emp Here 250   *Sales* 67,574,700
SIC 8062 General medical and surgical hospitals
Allan Katz
Michelle Marinaro
Douglas Robinson
Craig Sanders
Shanna Weir
Phillip Whatley
Norma Elliott
Lori Maki
Meghan Cox
Janice Beazley

D-U-N-S 20-009-9682   (BR)
SHAW CABLESYSTEMS G.P.
(*Suby of* SHAW COMMUNICATIONS INC)
1037 First St E, Fort Frances, ON, P9A 1L8
(807) 274-5522
Emp Here 200
SIC 4841 Cable and other pay television services
Chuck Croker

D-U-N-S 20-481-4353   (SL)
SPECTRA ENERGY
410 Mowat Ave, Fort Frances, ON, P9A 1Y7
(807) 274-3924
Emp Here 5   *Sales* 15,529,285
SIC 4924 Natural gas distribution

D-U-N-S 24-317-1951   (BR)
WAL-MART CANADA CORP
WALMART
(*Suby of* WALMART INC.)
1250 King'S Hwy, Fort Frances, ON, P9A 2X6
(807) 274-1373
Emp Here 150
SIC 5311 Department stores

D-U-N-S 20-048-7817   (SL)
WEBB, J.N. & SONS LIMITED

930 Fifth St W, Fort Frances, ON, P9A 3C7
(807) 274-5613
Emp Here 19   *Sales* 15,875,963
SIC 5141 Groceries, general line
Larry Webb
Alan Webb
Jay Webb

D-U-N-S 25-282-4917   (SL)
WEECHI - IT - TE - WIN FAMILY SERVICES INC
1450 Idylwyld Dr, Fort Frances, ON, P9A 3M3
(807) 274-3201
Emp Here 60   *Sales* 13,609,980
SIC 8399 Social services, nec
Laurie Rose

D-U-N-S 20-048-7825   (SL)
WEST END MOTORS (FORT FRANCES) INCORPORATED
(*Suby of* 65176 ONTARIO INC)
600 King'S Hwy, Fort Frances, ON, P9A 2W9
(807) 274-7751
Emp Here 31   *Sales* 15,440,418
SIC 5511 New and used car dealers
Roy Avis
Barbara Avis

Fort William First Nation, ON P7J

D-U-N-S 25-487-4662   (HQ)
DILICO ANISHINABEK FAMILY CARE
200 Anemki Pl Suite 1, Fort William First Nation, ON, P7J 1L6
(807) 623-8511
Emp Here 300   *Sales* 62,120,400
SIC 8399 Social services, nec
Donald (Dan) Auger

D-U-N-S 20-635-7365   (HQ)
WASAYA AIRWAYS LIMITED PARTNERSHIP
300 Anemki Pl Unit B, Fort William First Nation, ON, P7J 1H9
(807) 473-1200
Emp Here 90   *Sales* 95,205,600
SIC 4512 Air transportation, scheduled
Michael Rodyniuk
Nick Purich

Foxboro, ON K0K

D-U-N-S 25-393-1257   (SL)
PARLIAMENT, ART FOODS LIMITED
FOODLAND
54 Frankford Rd, Foxboro, ON, K0K 2B0
(613) 968-5721
Emp Here 38   *Sales* 10,417,776
SIC 5411 Grocery stores
Art Parliament

Fraserville, ON K0L

D-U-N-S 20-939-3875   (SL)
KAWARTHA DOWNS LTD
KAWARTHA DOWNS & SPEEDWAY
1382 County Road 28, Fraserville, ON, K0L 1V0
(705) 939-6316
Emp Here 200   *Sales* 16,679,000
SIC 7948 Racing, including track operation
Harvey Ambrose

Freelton, ON L8B

D-U-N-S 24-718-9616   (HQ)
FANCHEM LTD
PVS CHEMICALS
(*Suby of* PRESSURE VESSEL SERVICE, INC.)
1012 Gore Rd, Freelton, ON, L8B 0Z5
(905) 659-3351
Sales 11,685,520
SIC 5169 Chemicals and allied products, nec
Jess Inkes
Allan Schlumberger
Timothy Nicholson
Jeffrey Inkes
David Nicholson

Gananoque, ON K7G

D-U-N-S 25-353-3020   (SL)
1000 ISLANDS R.V. CENTRE INC
1000 ISLAND R.V., POWER SPORTS AND MARINE
409 County Road 2 E, Gananoque, ON, K7G 2V4
(613) 382-4400
Emp Here 22   *Sales* 10,957,716
SIC 5561 Recreational vehicle dealers
Paul Preston
Henry Boer

D-U-N-S 24-858-1670   (SL)
2417821 CANADA INC
210 James A. Brennan Rd, Gananoque, ON, K7G 1N7
(613) 549-3221
Emp Here 45   *Sales* 12,449,700
SIC 2865 Cyclic crudes and intermediates
Brian Cosgrove
Nancy Cosgrove
David Barrett
Wayne Nicholson

D-U-N-S 24-325-9491   (SL)
AJRAM'S, ANNY PHARMACY LTD
SHOPPERS DRUG MART
615 King St E, Gananoque, ON, K7G 1H4
(613) 382-2303
Emp Here 45   *Sales* 11,382,930
SIC 5912 Drug stores and proprietary stores
Anny Ajram

D-U-N-S 20-788-0261   (SL)
CARVETH NURSING HOME LIMITED
CARVETH CARE CENTRE
375 James St, Gananoque, ON, K7G 2Z1
(613) 382-4752
Emp Here 100   *Sales* 6,873,300
SIC 8051 Skilled nursing care facilities
Brett Gibson

D-U-N-S 20-293-8528   (SL)
FRONTLINE SYSTEMS INC
210 James A. Brennan Rd, Gananoque, ON, K7G 1N7
(613) 463-9575
Emp Here 9   *Sales* 20,653,913
SIC 5084 Industrial machinery and equipment
James Barber
Phoebe Barber

D-U-N-S 20-649-8669   (HQ)
GANANOQUE BOAT LINE LIMITED
280 Main St, Gananoque, ON, K7G 2M2
(613) 382-2144
Emp Here 57   *Sales* 16,172,940
SIC 4489 Water passenger transportation
Christopher Mccarney
Harry Clarke

D-U-N-S 20-892-8184   (SL)
GANANOQUE MOTORS LTD
GANANOQUE CHEV CADILLAC
439 King St E, Gananoque, ON, K7G 1G9
(613) 382-2168
Emp Here 55   *Sales* 34,610,400

SIC 5511 New and used car dealers
Dwight Hall
Sharon Hall

D-U-N-S 20-050-1575   (SL)
**LUDLOW   TECHNICAL   PRODUCTS
CANADA, LTD**
215 Herbert St, Gananoque, ON, K7G 2Y7
(613) 382-4733
Emp Here 450   *Sales* 123,466,500
SIC 3845 Electromedical equipment
Brent Eamon

D-U-N-S 25-300-0368   (BR)
METRO ONTARIO INC
METRO
(*Suby of* METRO INC)
333 King St E, Gananoque, ON, K7G 1G6
(613) 382-7090
Emp Here 100
SIC 5411 Grocery stores
Dale Plumley

Garson, ON P3L

D-U-N-S 24-340-3677   (SL)
CASTONGUAY G.P.
640 Garson Coniston Rd, Garson, ON, P3L
1R3
(705) 693-3887
Emp Here 249   *Sales* 81,700,635
SIC 1629 Heavy construction, nec
Gilles Trudel

D-U-N-S 25-537-7608   (SL)
GARSON PIPE CONTRACTORS LIMITED
1191 O'Neil Dr W, Garson, ON, P3L 1L5
(705) 693-1242
Emp Here 60   *Sales* 15,146,520
SIC 1623 Water, sewer, and utility lines
Thomas Lafreniere
John Van Druenen

Georgetown, ON L7G

D-U-N-S 24-720-1791   (SL)
942599 ONTARIO LIMITED
GEORGETOWN HONDA
316 Guelph St, Georgetown, ON, L7G 4B5
(905) 873-1818
Emp Here 26   *Sales* 12,950,028
SIC 5511 New and used car dealers
Peter Herman
Tim Hoogaars

D-U-N-S 25-647-4201   (SL)
**AERODROME INTERNATIONAL MAINTE-
NANCE INC**
A.I.M
330 Guelph St Unit 4, Georgetown, ON, L7G
4B5
(905) 873-8777
Emp Here 103   *Sales* 457,039
SIC 4212 Local trucking, without storage
Craig Seifried
Willy Pontes

D-U-N-S 24-375-6249   (BR)
ALIMENTS SAPUTO LIMITEE
SAPUTO FOODS
(*Suby of* JOLINA CAPITAL INC)
279 Guelph St, Georgetown, ON, L7G 4B3
(905) 702-7200
Emp Here 250
SIC 2026 Fluid milk
Emmanuelle Saputo

D-U-N-S 24-708-5699   (SL)
APPLIED WIRING (GEORGETOWN) INC.
2 Rosetta St, Georgetown, ON, L7G 3P2
(905) 873-1717
Emp Here 60   *Sales* 11,426,520

SIC 3644 Noncurrent-carrying wiring devices
Grant Turner
Paul Tessier

D-U-N-S 24-285-1632   (SL)
APPLIED WIRING ASSEMBLIES INC
2 Rosetta St, Georgetown, ON, L7G 3P2
(905) 873-1717
Emp Here 90   *Sales* 66,826,800
SIC 5191 Farm supplies
Grant Turner

D-U-N-S 24-685-1740   (SL)
BFG CANADA LTD
(*Suby of* TREEHOUSE FOODS, INC.)
88 Todd Rd, Georgetown, ON, L7G 4R7
(905) 873-8744
Emp Here 50   *Sales* 11,242,750
SIC 2099 Food preparations, nec
Trent Hillbert

D-U-N-S 20-158-4042   (SL)
BRADFORD WHITE - CANADA INC
(*Suby of* BRADFORD WHITE CORPORA-
TION)
9 Brigden Gate, Georgetown, ON, L7G 0A3
(905) 203-0600
Emp Here 35   *Sales* 15,651,090
SIC 5064 Electrical appliances, television and
radio
Nicholas Giuffre
Paul Mcdonald

D-U-N-S 20-009-9716   (BR)
CLUBLINK CORPORATION ULC
EAGLE RIDGE GOLF CLUB
(*Suby of* TWC ENTERPRISES LIMITED)
11742 Tenth Line Suite 4, Georgetown, ON,
L7G 4S7
(905) 877-8468
Emp Here 100
SIC 7992 Public golf courses
Andrew Vento

D-U-N-S 20-314-4092   (HQ)
**COMMUNICATIONS & POWER INDUS-
TRIES CANADA INC**
CPI CANADA
(*Suby of* VERITAS CAPITAL MANAGEMENT
LLC)
45 River Dr Upper Level, Georgetown, ON,
L7G 2J4
(905) 877-0161
Sales 99,020,250
SIC 3663 Radio and t.v.   communications
equipment
Joe Caldarelli
Robert J. Kemp
John R. Beighley

D-U-N-S 20-288-7311   (BR)
**COMMUNICATIONS & POWER INDUS-
TRIES CANADA INC**
SATCOM DIV.
(*Suby of* VERITAS CAPITAL MANAGEMENT
LLC)
Lower Level 45 River Dr, Georgetown, ON,
L7G 2J4
(905) 877-0161
Emp Here 150
SIC 3663 Radio and t.v.   communications
equipment
Andy Tafler

D-U-N-S 20-287-2032   (BR)
**COOPER-STANDARD   AUTOMOTIVE
CANADA LIMITED**
SEALING SYSTEMS GROUP
(*Suby of* COOPER-STANDARD HOLDINGS
INC.)
346 Guelph St, Georgetown, ON, L7G 4B5
(905) 873-6921
Emp Here 357
SIC 2891 Adhesives and sealants
Glenn Guerten

D-U-N-S 20-133-9033   (SL)
DIE-MOLD TOOL LIMITED

82 Todd Rd, Georgetown, ON, L7G 4R7
(905) 877-3071
Emp Here 39   *Sales* 10,789,740
SIC 2821 Plastics materials and resins
Natalie Mckenzie

D-U-N-S 20-732-2249   (HQ)
EFCO CANADA CO
EFCO
(*Suby of* WILIAN HOLDING COMPANY)
30 Todd Rd, Georgetown, ON, L7G 4R7
(905) 877-6957
Emp Here 73   *Sales* 21,705,605
SIC 3444 Sheet Metalwork

D-U-N-S 24-412-2537   (HQ)
ERRION GROUP INC
OLON INDUSTRIES
42 Armstrong Ave, Georgetown, ON, L7G 4R9
(905) 877-7300
Emp Here 100   *Sales* 38,474,000
SIC 2426 Hardwood dimension and flooring
mills
Ernie Saveriano

D-U-N-S 24-538-2536   (SL)
**FERN BROOK SPRINGS BOTTLED WATER
COMPANY LIMITED**
10 Brigden Gate, Georgetown, ON, L7G 0A3

Emp Here 50   *Sales* 41,778,850
SIC 5149 Groceries and related products, nec
Bob Elliott

D-U-N-S 24-406-9035   (HQ)
FLO-DRAULIC CONTROLS LTD
45 Sinclair Ave, Georgetown, ON, L7G 4X4
(905) 702-9456
Emp Here 31   *Sales* 22,801,248
SIC 5084 Industrial machinery and equipment
Lou Laskis

D-U-N-S 24-793-7274   (HQ)
FRESHOUSE FOODS LTD
71 Todd Rd, Georgetown, ON, L7G 4R8
(905) 671-0220
Sales 41,778,850
SIC 5147 Meats and meat products
Adriano Belli

D-U-N-S 20-691-6822   (SL)
**GEORGETOWN CHEVROLET BUICK GMC
LTD**
33 Mountainview Rd N, Georgetown, ON, L7G
4J7
(905) 877-6944
Emp Here 33   *Sales* 16,436,574
SIC 5511 New and used car dealers
Ryan Finch
Mike Stollery

D-U-N-S 20-050-3191   (SL)
**GEORGETOWN TERMINAL WAREHOUSES
LIMITED**
34 Armstrong Ave, Georgetown, ON, L7G 4R9
(905) 873-2750
Emp Here 80   *Sales* 16,456,480
SIC 4226 Special warehousing and storage,
nec
Brenda Sisnett
Larry Sisnett

D-U-N-S 24-395-7672   (SL)
GRAYWOOD ELECTRIC LIMITED
10783 Sixth Line, Georgetown, ON, L7G 4S6
(905) 877-6070
Emp Here 60   *Sales* 13,069,740
SIC 1731 Electrical work
Gilbert Zylstra

D-U-N-S 20-711-0896   (BR)
**HALTON CATHOLIC DISTRICT SCHOOL
BOARD**
CHRIST THE KING SECONDARY
(*Suby of* HALTON CATHOLIC DISTRICT
SCHOOL BOARD)
161 Guelph St, Georgetown, ON, L7G 4A1

(905) 702-8838
Emp Here 130
SIC 8211 Elementary and secondary schools
Niojle Citonis

D-U-N-S 24-391-0911   (BR)
**HALTON CATHOLIC DISTRICT SCHOOL
BOARD**
GEORGETOWN DISTRICT HIGH SCHOOL
(*Suby of* HALTON CATHOLIC DISTRICT
SCHOOL BOARD)
70 Guelph St, Georgetown, ON, L7G 3Z5
(905) 877-6966
Emp Here 110
SIC 8211 Elementary and secondary schools
Marie Jacobs

D-U-N-S 20-568-2912   (BR)
HALTON DISTRICT SCHOOL BOARD
SILVER CREEK PUBLIC SCHOOL
(*Suby of* HALTON DISTRICT SCHOOL
BOARD)
170 Eaton St, Georgetown, ON, L7G 5V6
(905) 877-0151
Emp Here 80
SIC 8211 Elementary and secondary schools
Brenda Pearce

D-U-N-S 20-129-2661   (HQ)
HAYWARD GORDON ULC
5 Brigden Gate, Georgetown, ON, L7G 0A3
(905) 693-8595
Emp Here 73   *Sales* 41,944,780
SIC 5084 Industrial machinery and equipment
Bill Dube
John Hayward
Ed Rogers
Graham Hicks
Brent Mcconomy
Jim Pompos
Matthew Keogh
John Pascual
Mohamed Fouda

D-U-N-S 24-220-6969   (HQ)
**HOWELL PLUMBING SUPPLIES DASCO
LIMITED**
HOWELL PIPE & SUPPLY, DIV OF
11 Armstrong Ave, Georgetown, ON, L7G 4S1
(905) 877-2293
Emp Here 44   *Sales* 23,751,300
SIC 5085 Industrial supplies
Duncan Stacey
Martin Glaude
Lene Fisker
Wayne Singer

D-U-N-S 24-126-5003   (HQ)
HOWMET CANADA COMPANY
HOWMET GEORGETOWN CASTING
93 Mountainview Rd N, Georgetown, ON, L7G
4J6
(905) 877-6936
Sales 18,138,800
SIC 3365 Aluminum foundries
Alain Taillefer

D-U-N-S 20-162-5340   (SL)
I.S.P.A. WOODWORKING LIMITED
I.S.P.A. GROUP
114 Armstrong Ave, Georgetown, ON, L7G
4S2
(905) 702-2727
Emp Here 70   *Sales* 10,802,540
SIC 2541 Wood partitions and fixtures
Douglas Soules

D-U-N-S 24-383-7122   (BR)
LOBLAWS INC
REAL CANADIAN SUPERSTORE
(*Suby of* LOBLAW COMPANIES LIMITED)
171 Guelph St Suite 2811, Georgetown, ON,
L7G 4A1
(905) 877-7005
Emp Here 300
SIC 5411 Grocery stores
Manal Kalada

D-U-N-S 25-797-7637   (BR)
LOBLAWS SUPERMARKETS LIMITED
(*Suby of* LOBLAW COMPANIES LIMITED)
300 Guelph St, Georgetown, ON, L7G 4B1
(905) 877-4711
Emp Here 275
SIC 5411 Grocery stores
Lucia Mann

D-U-N-S 20-011-8870   (BR)
MATSU MANUFACTURING INC
MATCOR METAL FABRICATION, DIV OF
(*Suby of* MATSU MANUFACTURING INC)
71 Todd Rd, Georgetown, ON, L7G 4R8

Emp Here 150
SIC 8711 Engineering services
Pete Sok

D-U-N-S 25-274-5401   (SL)
MINUS FORTY TECHNOLOGIES CORP
30 Armstrong Ave, Georgetown, ON, L7G 4R9
(905) 702-1441
Emp Here 150   *Sales* 33,300,150
SIC 3585 Refrigeration and heating equipment
Julian Attree
Chris Strong
Marinko Tepic
Aaron Reid
Debra Mccullagh

D-U-N-S 20-699-1700   (HQ)
MOLD-MASTERS (2007) LIMITED
(*Suby of* MILACRON HOLDINGS CORP.)
233 Armstrong Ave, Georgetown, ON, L7G 4X5
(905) 877-0185
Sales 157,291,120
SIC 3559 Special industry machinery, nec
Ronald Krisanta
Larry Hogan
Hugh O'donnell
Thomas Goeke
John Francy

D-U-N-S 20-594-8230   (SL)
MOUNTAINVIEW RESIDENCE
222 Mountainview Rd N Suite 233, Georgetown, ON, L7G 3R2
(905) 877-1800
Emp Here 45   *Sales* 10,191,330
SIC 6513 Apartment building operators
Christoph Summer

D-U-N-S 20-550-5639   (HQ)
PATLON AIRCRAFT & INDUSTRIES LIMITED
8130 Fifth Line, Georgetown, ON, L7G 0B8
(905) 864-8706
Emp Here 35   *Sales* 19,001,040
SIC 5088 Transportation equipment and supplies
Patrick Mann
Stephen Mann

D-U-N-S 24-017-3646   (SL)
QRC LOGISTICS (1978) LTD
8020 Fifth Line, Georgetown, ON, L7G 0B8
(905) 791-9000
Emp Here 120   *Sales* 80,268,960
SIC 7389 Business services, nec
Rick Mutiger

D-U-N-S 25-796-6820   (SL)
RADICALS CAR CLUB INC
14 Todd Rd, Georgetown, ON, L7G 4R7
(905) 877-9937
Emp Here 35   *Sales* 13,909,490
SIC 8699 Membership organizations, nec
Bill Mavel

D-U-N-S 20-047-7743   (HQ)
SHERIDAN NURSERIES LIMITED
12302 Tenth Line, Georgetown, ON, L7G 4S7
(905) 873-0522
Emp Here 50   *Sales* 98,367,500

SIC 5261 Retail nurseries and garden stores
Karl Stensson
William Stensson
Rick Friesen
Manuel Sobrinho
Pieter Joubert
Valerie Stensson
Art Vanden Enden
Rob Naraj

D-U-N-S 24-224-6838   (SL)
SIX PILLARS LTD
PETRO CANADA
375 Mountainview Rd S, Georgetown, ON, L7G 5X3
(905) 873-9982
Emp Here 30   *Sales* 14,942,340
SIC 5541 Gasoline service stations
Yasir Suliman

D-U-N-S 20-936-0593   (SL)
SOLINST CANADA LTD
35 Todd Rd, Georgetown, ON, L7G 4R8
(905) 873-2255
Emp Here 65   *Sales* 14,773,785
SIC 3823 Process control instruments
Sarah Belshaw

D-U-N-S 25-122-7575   (SL)
STARSHIP LOGISTICS INC
STARSHIP FREIGHT
36 Armstrong Ave Suite 200, Georgetown, ON, L7G 4R9
(905) 702-1800
Emp Here 21   *Sales* 10,919,307
SIC 4731 Freight transportation arrangement
Michael Mcdonald
Maria Mcdonald

D-U-N-S 24-602-5654   (SL)
TERRA COTTA FOODS LTD
36 Armstrong Ave Unit 9, Georgetown, ON, L7G 4R9
(905) 877-4216
Emp Here 50   *Sales* 11,242,750
SIC 2052 Cookies and crackers
Jason Brass

D-U-N-S 20-769-6246   (HQ)
WATCH TOWER BIBLE AND TRACT SOCIETY OF CANADA
13893 Highway 7, Georgetown, ON, L7G 4S4
(905) 873-4100
Sales 38,733,756
SIC 8661 Religious organizations
Kenneth Little
Andre F Ramseyer

D-U-N-S 20-050-4330   (HQ)
YOUNGS PHARMACY LIMITED
YOUNGS PHARMACY & HOMECARE
47 Main St S, Georgetown, ON, L7G 3G2
(905) 877-2711
Emp Here 47   *Sales* 12,647,700
SIC 5912 Drug stores and proprietary stores
Neil Young

Georgian Bluffs, ON N0H

D-U-N-S 24-964-9377   (SL)
911803 ONTARIO INC
SOLWAY'S IGA
370 William St, Georgian Bluffs, ON, N0H 2T0
(519) 534-0760
Emp Here 45   *Sales* 12,336,840
SIC 5411 Grocery stores
Mike Solway
Dave Delchiaro

D-U-N-S 20-642-4660   (SL)
ASHCROFT & ASSOCIATES NATURAL STONE LTD
A & A NATURAL STONE
381297 Concession 17, Georgian Bluffs, ON,

N0H 2T0
(519) 534-5966
Emp Here 50   *Sales* 11,671,750
SIC 1411 Dimension stone
Tony Forbes
Dawn Forbes

D-U-N-S 20-183-3878   (SL)
CAFRAMO LIMITED
501273 Grey Road 1, Georgian Bluffs, ON, N0H 2T0
(519) 534-1080
Emp Here 55   *Sales* 12,210,055
SIC 3564 Blowers and fans
Anthony (Tony) Solecki

Geraldton, ON P0T

D-U-N-S 24-266-7434   (HQ)
GERALDTON DISTRICT HOSPITAL
500 Hogarth St, Geraldton, ON, P0T 1M0
(807) 854-1862
Emp Here 115   *Sales* 13,329,600
SIC 8062 General medical and surgical hospitals
Kurt Pristanski

Glenburnie, ON K0H

D-U-N-S 20-891-5868   (SL)
FAIRMOUNT HOME FOR THE AGED
2069 Battersea Rd, Glenburnie, ON, K0H 1S0
(613) 548-9400
Emp Here 100   *Sales* 5,924,700
SIC 8361 Residential care
Elizabeth Folton
Bill Macdonald

Glencoe, ON N0L

D-U-N-S 20-293-4782   (SL)
1777621 ONTARIO INC
PENTA TILLAGE
73 Main St, Glencoe, ON, N0L 1M0
(519) 913-5420
Emp Here 104   *Sales* 50,723,920
SIC 5083 Farm and garden machinery
Glenn Buurma

D-U-N-S 24-720-2815   (BR)
COOPER-STANDARD   AUTOMOTIVE CANADA LIMITED
FLUID HANDLING SYSTEMS DIV
(*Suby of* COOPER-STANDARD HOLDINGS INC.)
268 Appin Rd Rr 4, Glencoe, ON, N0L 1M0
(519) 287-2450
Emp Here 400
SIC 3714 Motor vehicle parts and accessories
Rita Betts

D-U-N-S 20-050-5774   (SL)
FULLINE FARM & GARDEN EQUIPMENT LTD
21911 Simpson Rd, Glencoe, ON, N0L 1M0
(519) 287-2840
Emp Here 20   *Sales* 10,000,000
SIC 5083 Farm and garden machinery
Rick Podolinsky
Paul Vanbilson
Joe Neto

D-U-N-S 25-593-0034   (SL)
GLENCOE AGRICULTURAL SOCIETY
268 Currie St, Glencoe, ON, N0L 1M0
(519) 287-2836
Emp Here 101   *Sales* 23,645,211
SIC 8621 Professional organizations

David May

D-U-N-S 24-616-8822   (SL)
GLENCOE FOODLAND
195 Main St, Glencoe, ON, N0L 1M0
(519) 287-2776
Emp Here 40   *Sales* 10,966,080
SIC 5411 Grocery stores
Fred Bork

Gloucester, ON K1B

D-U-N-S 25-393-0325   (SL)
1248671 ONTARIO INC
MACARTNEY FARMS
1481 Michael St Unit C, Gloucester, ON, K1B 3R5
(613) 742-9999
Emp Here 100   *Sales* 83,557,700
SIC 5148 Fresh fruits and vegetables

D-U-N-S 20-788-8103   (SL)
417 COLLISION CENTER
1599 Star Top Rd, Gloucester, ON, K1B 5P5
(613) 749-8382
Emp Here 75   *Sales* 47,742,619
SIC 5511 New and used car dealers
Paul Giacomin

D-U-N-S 20-507-6045   (SL)
417 INFINITI NISSAN LTD
1599 Star Top Rd, Gloucester, ON, K1B 5P5
(613) 749-9417
Emp Here 50   *Sales* 24,903,900
SIC 5511 New and used car dealers
Fred Mckinley
Brent Mckinley
Paul Giacomin

D-U-N-S 20-376-6290   (HQ)
7902476 CANADA INC
LA-Z-BOY FURNITURE GALLERIES OF OTTAWA/KINGSTON
1750 Cyrville Rd, Gloucester, ON, K1B 3L8
(613) 749-0001
Sales 10,365,300
SIC 5712 Furniture stores
David Maxwell
James Maxwell

D-U-N-S 24-338-5403   (SL)
99702 CANADA LTEE
1750 Cyrville Rd, Gloucester, ON, K1B 3L8
(613) 749-0001
Emp Here 45   *Sales* 10,365,300
SIC 5712 Furniture stores
Paul J Raymond

D-U-N-S 24-365-8890   (BR)
AMICA MATURE LIFESTYLES INC
AMICA AT BEARBROOK
(*Suby of* AMICA SENIOR LIFESTYLES INC)
2645 Innes Rd Suite 342, Gloucester, ON, K1B 3J7
(613) 837-8720
Emp Here 75
SIC 8361 Residential care
Luke Goulette

D-U-N-S 24-726-4922   (HQ)
BOONE PLUMBING AND HEATING SUPPLY INC
DESROSIERS DISTRIBUTEURS
(*Suby of* ENTREPRISES MIRCA INC, LES)
1282 Algoma Rd Suite 613, Gloucester, ON, K1B 3W8
(613) 746-8560
Emp Here 107   *Sales* 64,406,160
SIC 5074 Plumbing and heating equipment and supplies (hydronics)
Jacques Deschenes
Francois Deschenes
Martin Deschenes
Marc Lapierre

D-U-N-S 24-369-9217   (BR)
COSTCO WHOLESALE CANADA LTD
COSTCO
(*Suby of* COSTCO WHOLESALE CORPORATION)
1900 Cyrville Rd, Gloucester, ON, K1B 1A5
(613) 748-9966
Emp Here 280
SIC 5199 Nondurable goods, nec
Darren Dudyricki

D-U-N-S 24-104-6259   (SL)
DILFO MECHANICAL LIMITED
1481 Cyrville Rd, Gloucester, ON, K1B 3L7
(613) 741-7731
Emp Here 50   *Sales* 11,046,700
SIC 1711 Plumbing, heating, air-conditioning
Paul Dillon

D-U-N-S 24-102-1252   (BR)
G4S CASH SOLUTIONS (CANADA) LTD
(*Suby of* G4S PLC)
1303 Michael St, Gloucester, ON, K1B 3M9

Emp Here 150
SIC 4212 Local trucking, without storage
Peter Mian

D-U-N-S 20-973-3224   (SL)
GUARANTEE CO OF NORTH AMERICA, (THE)
36 Parkridge Cres, Gloucester, ON, K1B 3E7

Emp Here 50   *Sales* 28,996,200
SIC 6411 Insurance agents, brokers, and service
Robert A Dempsey

D-U-N-S 25-749-2595   (BR)
HOME DEPOT OF CANADA INC
HOME DEPOT
(*Suby of* THE HOME DEPOT INC)
1616 Cyrville Rd, Gloucester, ON, K1B 3L8
(613) 744-1700
Emp Here 250
SIC 5251 Hardware stores
Cory Kennedy

D-U-N-S 20-892-3656   (HQ)
HOSIE & BROWN AUTO ELECTRIC LTD
1352 Gosset St, Gloucester, ON, K1B 3P7
(613) 741-8112
Emp Here 40   *Sales* 18,574,965
SIC 5013 Motor vehicle supplies and new parts
Rodd Brown

D-U-N-S 20-138-5127   (HQ)
LOEB PACKAGING LTD
1475 Star Top Rd Suite 8, Gloucester, ON, K1B 3W5
(613) 746-8171
Emp Here 35   *Sales* 14,006,100
SIC 2653 Corrugated and solid fiber boxes
David Loeb
Kenneth Loeb

D-U-N-S 20-138-1738   (SL)
MARCHAND ELECTRICAL COMPANY LIMITED
1283 Algoma Rd, Gloucester, ON, K1B 3W7
(613) 749-2279
Emp Here 50   *Sales* 22,358,700
SIC 5063 Electrical apparatus and equipment
Jacques Marchand

D-U-N-S 25-509-7180   (HQ)
MBNA CANADA BANK
(*Suby of* TORONTO-DOMINION BANK, THE)
1600 James Naismith Dr Suite 800, Gloucester, ON, K1B 5N8
(613) 907-4800
Emp Here 1,250   *Sales* 337,500,014
SIC 6021 National commercial banks
Joe Desantis

D-U-N-S 20-336-4427   (SL)
NORTH HOUSE FOODS LTD

NATURAL GOURMET
1169 Parisien St, Gloucester, ON, K1B 4W4
(613) 746-6662
Emp Here 42   *Sales* 35,094,234
SIC 5148 Fresh fruits and vegetables
Paul Gorman
Darcy Rivard

D-U-N-S 25-398-4363   (SL)
ON PATH BUSINESS SOLUTIONS INC
(*Suby of* CONNECTEL COMMUNICATIONS CORPORATION)
1165 Kenaston St, Gloucester, ON, K1B 3N9
(613) 564-6565
Emp Here 60   *Sales* 13,708,320
SIC 4899 Communication services, nec
Dan Scheunert

D-U-N-S 20-393-0792   (SL)
ONTARIO MEDICAL SUPPLY INC
(*Suby of* MEDICAL PHARMACIES GROUP LIMITED)
1100 Algoma Rd, Gloucester, ON, K1B 0A3
(613) 244-8620
Emp Here 300   *Sales* 160,605,600
SIC 5047 Medical and hospital equipment
John Leader
Richard Sevazlian
Greg Hunter

D-U-N-S 20-298-3206   (SL)
OTTAWA FOOD BANK, THE
1317 Michael St, Gloucester, ON, K1B 3M9
(613) 745-7001
Emp Here 15   *Sales* 10,260,493
SIC 8399 Social services, nec
David K. Law
Greg Strahl
Sarah Tremblay
Irene Cameron
Barbara Carroll
Erin Crowe
Ivan Gedz

D-U-N-S 25-754-4148   (SL)
OTWA N MOTORS LTD
417 NISSAN INFINITI
(*Suby of* AUTOCANADA INC)
1599 Star Top Rd Suite 417, Gloucester, ON, K1B 5P5
(613) 749-9417
Emp Here 49   *Sales* 30,834,720
SIC 5511 New and used car dealers
Jean Malouin

D-U-N-S 20-997-6547   (HQ)
PROULX, GRATIEN BUILDING MATERIALS LTD
1499 Star Top Rd Suite A, Gloucester, ON, K1B 3W5
(613) 749-3344
Sales 29,066,310
SIC 5039 Construction materials, nec
Gratien Proulx

D-U-N-S 20-747-3711   (HQ)
REGIONAL CRANE RENTALS LTD
1409 Cyrville Rd, Gloucester, ON, K1B 3L7
(613) 748-7922
Emp Here 42   *Sales* 12,271,098
SIC 7353 Heavy construction equipment rental
Rosaire Burelle
Fay Burelle

D-U-N-S 24-382-0883   (HQ)
RITCHIE FEED & SEED INC
1390 Windmill Lane, Gloucester, ON, K1B 4V5
(613) 741-4430
Emp Here 75   *Sales* 26,765,200
SIC 5261 Retail nurseries and garden stores
Douglas Ritchie

D-U-N-S 24-936-3862   (HQ)
ST JOSEPH PRINT GROUP INC
ST JOSEPH PRINT GROUP OTTAWA, DIV OF

(*Suby of* ST. JOSEPH CORPORATION)
1165 Kenaston St, Gloucester, ON, K1B 3N9
(613) 729-4303
Sales 116,264,400
SIC 2752 Commercial printing, lithographic
John Gagliano
Murray Skinner
Andre Aubrey
Pierre Ness
David Parslow

D-U-N-S 20-136-3181   (HQ)
SWISS PASTRIES & DELICATESSEN OF OTTAWA LIMITED
1423 Star Top Rd, Gloucester, ON, K1B 3W5

Emp Here 26   *Sales* 19,662,959
SIC 5461 Retail bakeries
Connie Zuberbuehler
Hans Zuberbuehler

D-U-N-S 24-309-9665   (BR)
WASTE CONNECTIONS OF CANADA INC
BFI CANADA
(*Suby of* WASTE CONNECTIONS, INC)
1152 Kenaston St, Gloucester, ON, K1B 3P5
(613) 749-8000
Emp Here 300
SIC 4953 Refuse systems
Robert Ross

Gloucester, ON K1G

D-U-N-S 20-702-3503   (BR)
FLYNN CANADA LTD
(*Suby of* FLYNN CANADA LTD)
5661 Power Rd, Gloucester, ON, K1G 3N4

Emp Here 100
SIC 1761 Roofing, siding, and sheetMetal work
Robert Quesnel

D-U-N-S 24-874-4724   (HQ)
GREELY CONSTRUCTION INC
5689 Power Rd, Gloucester, ON, K1G 3N4
(613) 822-0500
Sales 17,670,940
SIC 1623 Water, sewer, and utility lines
John Fernandes
John Lourenco
Trac Ngo

D-U-N-S 24-438-4863   (SL)
MCDONALD, GRANT P. HOLDINGS INC
SCHOONER TRANSPORT
2680 Overton Dr, Gloucester, ON, K1G 6T8
(613) 225-9588
Emp Here 50   *Sales* 10,131,450
SIC 7538 General automotive repair shops
Grant Mcdonald
Steen Mcdonald

D-U-N-S 24-911-3713   (BR)
OFI L.P.
OTTAWA FIBRE
(*Suby of* OFI L.P.)
3985 Belgreen Dr, Gloucester, ON, K1G 3N2
(613) 736-1215
Emp Here 100
SIC 3296 Mineral wool
Joseph Skarzenski

D-U-N-S 24-365-9120   (BR)
VEOLIA ES CANADA SERVICES INDUSTRIELS INC
(*Suby of* VEOLIA ENVIRONNEMENT)
4140 Belgreen Dr, Gloucester, ON, K1G 3N2
(613) 739-1150
Emp Here 98
SIC 7389 Business services, nec
Lance Evraire

Gloucester, ON K1J

D-U-N-S 25-349-7036   (SL)
3705391 CANADA LIMITED
PREMIERE VAN LINES
5370 Canotek Rd Unit 1, Gloucester, ON, K1J 9E6
(613) 742-7555
Emp Here 70   *Sales* 10,373,440
SIC 4214 Local trucking with storage
James Doucet Sr
Judy Doucet

D-U-N-S 24-910-7400   (SL)
A.S.G. INC
APPLICATION SYSTEMS GROUP
1010 Polytek St Suite 8, Gloucester, ON, K1J 9H8
(613) 749-8353
Emp Here 85   *Sales* 13,819,640
SIC 7379 Computer related services, nec
Pierre Dupuis

D-U-N-S 24-872-6093   (SL)
ACCREDITATION CANADA
1150 Cyrville Rd Suite 759, Gloucester, ON, K1J 7S9
(613) 738-3800
Emp Here 125   *Sales* 19,781,706
SIC 8399 Social services, nec
George Weber
Karima Velji
Wendy Nicklin
Luc Boileau
Gavin Brown
Bonnie Cham
Joe Gallagher
Mary Marshall
Aldea Landry
John Maxted

D-U-N-S 25-145-4278   (BR)
ALSTOM CANADA INC
(*Suby of* GE RENEWABLE HOLDING B.V.)
1430 Blair Pl Suite 600, Gloucester, ON, K1J 9N2
(613) 747-5222
Emp Here 96
SIC 7699 Repair services, nec
Richard Lake

D-U-N-S 20-043-8125   (SL)
AMBICO LIMITED
1120 Cummings Ave, Gloucester, ON, K1J 7R8
(613) 746-4663
Emp Here 62   *Sales* 11,909,270
SIC 3442 Metal doors, sash, and trim
Jack Shinder
Judah Silverman
Yvonne Gardner

D-U-N-S 24-595-8186   (SL)
AMTEK ENGINEERING SERVICES LTD
(*Suby of* CALIAN GROUP LTD)
1900 City Park Dr Suite 510, Gloucester, ON, K1J 1A3
(613) 749-3990
Emp Here 85
SIC 8711 Engineering services
Lester Sellars
Scott Fincham

D-U-N-S 20-039-5460   (SL)
B M W ELITE AUTOMOBILES INC
1040 Ogilvie Rd, Gloucester, ON, K1J 8G9
(613) 749-7700
Emp Here 40   *Sales* 19,923,120
SIC 5511 New and used car dealers
Armie Mierns

D-U-N-S 24-919-6684   (BR)
BELL MOBILITE INC
(*Suby of* BCE INC)
1420 Blair Pl Suite 700, Gloucester, ON, K1J 9L8

Emp Here 120
SIC 5063 Electrical apparatus and equipment

D-U-N-S 20-793-1754   (BR)
BEST BUY CANADA LTD
FUTURE SHOP
(*Suby of* BEST BUY CO., INC.)
1525 City Park Dr, Gloucester, ON, K1J 1H3
(613) 747-7636
Emp Here 100
SIC 5731 Radio, television, and electronic stores
Andre Lapensee

D-U-N-S 20-288-8715   (HQ)
BRUNET-GOULARD AGENCIES INC
BG DISTRIBUTION
5370 Canotek Rd Unit 21, Gloucester, ON, K1J 9E8
(613) 748-7377
Emp Here 12   Sales 17,439,786
SIC 5065 Electronic parts and equipment, nec
Marcel Goulard
Francine Goulard

D-U-N-S 24-436-8742   (HQ)
CAISSE POPULAIRE TRILLIUM INC
1173 Cyrville Rd, Gloucester, ON, K1J 7S6
(613) 745-2123
Emp Here 20   Sales 14,430,034
SIC 6062 State credit unions
Ronald Tourigny
Thomas Blais

D-U-N-S 20-050-5677   (SL)
CHAMPLAIN LHIN
1900 City Park Dr Suite 204, Gloucester, ON, K1J 1A3
(613) 747-6784
Emp Here 18   Sales 18,627,858
SIC 6324 Hospital and medical service plans

D-U-N-S 20-245-3176   (BR)
CINEPLEX ODEON CORPORATION
SILVERCITY GLOUCESTER
(*Suby of* CINEPLEX INC)
2385 City Park Dr, Gloucester, ON, K1J 1G1
(613) 749-5861
Emp Here 200
SIC 7832 Motion picture theaters, except drive-in
Gary Findley

D-U-N-S 24-848-7290   (HQ)
CONSEIL DES ECOLES CATHOLIQUES DE LANGUE FRANCAISE DU CENTRE-EST
4000 Labelle St, Gloucester, ON, K1J 1A1
(613) 744-2555
Emp Here 60   Sales 118,942,800
SIC 8211 Elementary and secondary schools
Reajan Sirois
Kristen Crisson

D-U-N-S 25-265-2763   (BR)
CONSEIL DES ECOLES CATHOLIQUES DE LANGUE FRANCAISE DU CENTRE-EST
CECCE
(*Suby of* CONSEIL DES ECOLES CATHOLIQUES DE LANGUE FRANCAISE DU CENTRE-EST)
4000 Labelle St, Gloucester, ON, K1J 1A1
(613) 744-2555
Emp Here 200
SIC 8211 Elementary and secondary schools
Bernard Roy

D-U-N-S 24-324-2570   (BR)
CONSEILLERS EN GESTION ET INFORMATIQUE CGI INC
CGI
(*Suby of* CGI INC)
1410 Blair Pl, Gloucester, ON, K1J 9B9
(613) 740-5900
Emp Here 200
SIC 7379 Computer related services, nec

D-U-N-S 25-526-2487   (HQ)

DAOUST, PAUL CONSTRUCTION GROUP INC
5424 Canotek Rd, Gloucester, ON, K1J 1E9
(613) 590-1694
Emp Here 2   Sales 19,961,830
SIC 1542 Nonresidential construction, nec
Jean Daoust
Jane Daoust

D-U-N-S 24-844-4945   (HQ)
ELECTRONIC WARFARE ASSOCIATES - CANADA, LTD
EWA-CANADA
(*Suby of* INTERTEK GROUP PLC)
1223 Michael St N Suite 200, Gloucester, ON, K1J 7T2
(613) 230-6067
Emp Here 34   Sales 16,305,567
SIC 8734 Testing laboratories
Mark Kuske
William Joey Keating
Ron Starman
Carlos Diaz Lopez
Ken Armstrong
Paul Zatychec

D-U-N-S 24-846-2558   (HQ)
ENCON GROUP INC
PRIVATE CLIENT SERVICES, DIV OF
(*Suby of* MARSH & MCLENNAN COMPANIES, INC.)
1400 Blair Pl Suite 50, Gloucester, ON, K1J 9B8
(613) 786-2000
Sales 1,566,214,320
SIC 6411 Insurance agents, brokers, and service
Jean F. Laurin
Edward Pimentel
Marilyn Reddigan
Michel Yip

D-U-N-S 20-699-6360   (BR)
EXTENDICARE INC
EXTENDICARE LAURIER MANOR
(*Suby of* EXTENDICARE INC)
1715 Montreal Rd, Gloucester, ON, K1J 6N4
(613) 741-5122
Emp Here 250
SIC 8051 Skilled nursing care facilities
Pamela Nisdet

D-U-N-S 24-105-2349   (HQ)
GASTOPS LTD
1011 Polytek St, Gloucester, ON, K1J 9J3
(613) 744-3530
Emp Here 95   Sales 20,733,724
SIC 8711 Engineering services
David Muir
Bernard Macisaac
Grant Blanchard

D-U-N-S 25-771-5102   (SL)
GLOBAL HEALTH CARE SERVICES INC
5450 Canotek Rd, Gloucester, ON, K1J 9G7
(613) 230-4104
Emp Here 150   Sales 20,018,850
SIC 8399 Social services, nec
Guylain Page

D-U-N-S 24-118-6316   (BR)
LOBLAWS SUPERMARKETS LIMITED
LOBLAWS
(*Suby of* LOBLAW COMPANIES LIMITED)
1980 Ogilvie Rd, Gloucester, ON, K1J 9L3
(613) 746-5724
Emp Here 250
SIC 5411 Grocery stores
Yves St Jean

D-U-N-S 25-303-9549   (BR)
LONDON LIFE, COMPAGNIE D'ASSURANCE-VIE
LONDON LIFE INSURANCE COMPANY
(*Suby of* POWER CORPORATION DU CANADA)
1223 Michael St N Suite 300, Gloucester, ON,

K1J 7T2
(613) 748-3455
Emp Here 160
SIC 6311 Life insurance
Brad Powe

D-U-N-S 25-779-0451   (BR)
LONE STAR GROUP OF COMPANIES LIMITED
LONESTAR TEXAS GRILL
(*Suby of* LONE STAR GROUP OF COMPANIES LIMITED)
1211 Lemieux St, Gloucester, ON, K1J 1A2
(613) 742-9378
Emp Here 150
SIC 5812 Eating places
Brad Adams

D-U-N-S 25-285-9483   (SL)
MARCIL LAVALLEE
1420 Blair Pl Suite 400, Gloucester, ON, K1J 9L8
(613) 745-8387
Emp Here 60   Sales 12,545,100
SIC 8721 Accounting, auditing, and bookkeeping
Michel Coulombe
Lionel Nolet
Gilles Berger

D-U-N-S 24-344-4994   (BR)
METRO ONTARIO INC
(*Suby of* METRO INC)
1930 Montreal Rd, Gloucester, ON, K1J 6N2
(613) 744-2961
Emp Here 115
SIC 5411 Grocery stores
Luc Monfils

D-U-N-S 20-718-7944   (SL)
MINI OTTAWA EAST (6125)
1020 Ogilvie Rd, Gloucester, ON, K1J 8G9
(613) 728-8888
Emp Here 25   Sales 12,451,950
SIC 5511 New and used car dealers
Steve Simard

D-U-N-S 24-482-8992   (HQ)
NORTAK SOFTWARE LTD
1105 Cadboro Rd, Gloucester, ON, K1J 7T8
(613) 234-7212
Emp Here 50   Sales 10,010,820
SIC 7379 Computer related services, nec
Norio Takemura
Gus Rodriguez
Mike O'neil

D-U-N-S 20-700-7378   (SL)
OGILVIE MOTORS LTD
1020 Ogilvie Rd, Gloucester, ON, K1J 8G9
(613) 745-9191
Emp Here 50   Sales 24,903,900
SIC 5511 New and used car dealers
Colleen Mierins
Arnis Mierins

D-U-N-S 25-033-4190   (BR)
OTTAWA CATHOLIC DISTRICT SCHOOL BOARD
PEARSON, LESTER B CATHOLIC HIGH SCHOOL
(*Suby of* OTTAWA CATHOLIC DISTRICT SCHOOL BOARD)
2072 Jasmine Cres, Gloucester, ON, K1J 8M5
(613) 741-4525
Emp Here 100
SIC 8211 Elementary and secondary schools
Nano Seguin

D-U-N-S 25-318-8890   (BR)
OTTAWA-CARLETON DISTRICT SCHOOL BOARD
GLOUCESTER HIGH SCHOOL
(*Suby of* OTTAWA-CARLETON DISTRICT SCHOOL BOARD)
2060 Ogilvie Rd, Gloucester, ON, K1J 7N8
(613) 745-7176
Emp Here 150

SIC 8211 Elementary and secondary schools
Jennifer Perry

D-U-N-S 25-777-9991   (BR)
PRIMERICA FINANCIAL SERVICES LTD
(*Suby of* PRIMERICA, INC.)
839 Shefford Rd Suite 200, Gloucester, ON, K1J 9K8
(613) 742-0768
Emp Here 300
SIC 6282 Investment advice
Robert Giroux

D-U-N-S 24-078-5183   (SL)
ROCHEBANYAN
5310 Canotek Rd Suite 10, Gloucester, ON, K1J 9N5
(613) 749-5027
Emp Here 49   Sales 41,554,940
SIC 6411 Insurance agents, brokers, and service
Malcolm Fletcher

D-U-N-S 24-320-4444   (SL)
S&S/BOLTON ELECTRIC INC
5411 Canotek Rd, Gloucester, ON, K1J 9M3
(613) 748-0432
Emp Here 140   Sales 30,496,060
SIC 1731 Electrical work
Brian Doxtator
Yves Frechette

D-U-N-S 24-849-3855   (SL)
SENSE INC
2339 Ogilvie Rd Suite 46095, Gloucester, ON, K1J 8M6
(877) 556-5268
Emp Here 150   Sales 80,302,800
SIC 5047 Medical and hospital equipment
Maihan Baktash

D-U-N-S 20-139-2503   (BR)
SHEFFIELD MOVING AND STORAGE INC
TIPPET-RICHARDSON LIMITED
(*Suby of* SHEFFIELD MOVING AND STORAGE INC)
5499 Canotek Rd, Gloucester, ON, K1J 9J5
(613) 741-3015
Emp Here 120
SIC 4214 Local trucking with storage
Gord Smith

D-U-N-S 24-482-8729   (SL)
STERLING FORD SALES (OTTAWA) INC
1425 Ogilvie Rd, Gloucester, ON, K1J 7P3
(613) 741-3720
Emp Here 45   Sales 22,413,510
SIC 5511 New and used car dealers
Claude Soucy
John Marshall

D-U-N-S 25-784-6196   (SL)
STUDY BREAK LIMITED
BYTOWN CATERING
5480 Canotek Rd Suite 20, Gloucester, ON, K1J 9H7
(613) 745-6389
Emp Here 90   Sales 4,096,710
SIC 5812 Eating places
Steve Lachance

D-U-N-S 24-891-7619   (SL)
TREVOR J LOWE INC
CANADIAN TIRE
2010 Ogilvie Rd, Gloucester, ON, K1J 8X3
(613) 748-0637
Emp Here 70   Sales 18,735,640
SIC 5251 Hardware stores
William Rupert
Trevor Lowe

Gloucester, ON K1T

D-U-N-S 25-498-4099   (SL)
1019884 ONTARIO INC

SOLE PRODUCE
1913 Kingsdale Ave, Gloucester, ON, K1T 1H9

Emp Here 35   Sales 11,986,345
SIC 0139 Field crops, except cash grain
Pierre Abboud
Michel Abboud
Charbel Abboud

D-U-N-S 24-612-0419   (HQ)
1197767 ONTARIO LTD
PETRO CANADA
2536 Bank St, Gloucester, ON, K1T 1M9
(613) 260-7331
Emp Here 5   Sales 24,903,900
SIC 5541 Gasoline service stations
Natale Busa

D-U-N-S 20-810-5747   (SL)
1364279 ONTARIO INC
BANK STREET KIA
2559 Bank St, Gloucester, ON, K1T 1M8
(613) 736-7022
Emp Here 30   Sales 14,942,340
SIC 5511 New and used car dealers

D-U-N-S 24-320-8415   (HQ)
1686943 ONTARIO LIMITED
4726 Bank St, Gloucester, ON, K1T 3W7
(613) 822-7400
Emp Here 2   Sales 47,836,250
SIC 6712 Bank holding companies
David Stinson
Eric Stinson

D-U-N-S 24-709-1226   (HQ)
724412 ONTARIO LIMITED
HUNT CLUB HONDA
2555 Bank St, Gloucester, ON, K1T 1M8
(613) 526-5202
Sales 44,049,600
SIC 5511 New and used car dealers
Carl Sytema

D-U-N-S 24-784-5548   (SL)
AECON UTILITIES INC
PREMIERE CABLE CONSTRUCTION
2495 Del Zotto Ave, Gloucester, ON, K1T 3V6
(613) 822-6193
Emp Here 50   Sales 27,768,620
SIC 1623 Water, sewer, and utility lines
Paul Mease

D-U-N-S 20-043-8190   (HQ)
BYTOWN LUMBER INC
BONHOMME
(Suby of ENTREPRISES P. BONHOMME LTEE, LES)
1740 Queensdale Ave, Gloucester, ON, K1T 1J6
(613) 733-9303
Emp Here 7   Sales 13,382,600
SIC 5211 Lumber and other building materials
Paul Bonhomme
Michel Charest
Donald Marcil
Robert Bonhomme

D-U-N-S 20-136-6754   (SL)
CAM-TAG INDUSTRIES INC
2783 Fenton Rd, Gloucester, ON, K1T 3T8
(613) 822-1921
Emp Here 46   Sales 10,738,010
SIC 3365 Aluminum foundries
Gilles Demers
Stephanie Barrett

D-U-N-S 24-444-3040   (SL)
CANADIAN TIRE
4792 Bank St, Gloucester, ON, K1T 3W7
(613) 822-2163
Emp Here 30   Sales 10,926,450
SIC 5014 Tires and tubes
Dave Frasier
Jody Reid

D-U-N-S 20-789-0542   (SL)

COLAUTTI CONSTRUCTION LTD
COLAUTTI GROUP
2562 Del Zotto Ave, Gloucester, ON, K1T 3V7
(613) 822-1440
Emp Here 100   Sales 25,244,200
SIC 1623 Water, sewer, and utility lines
Alister Miller
Stephen R Weiss
Ronald D Colautti
Dennis Colautti

D-U-N-S 20-789-7414   (SL)
CONDAIR HUMIDITY LTD
(Suby of MEIER TOBLER GROUP AG)
2740 Fenton Rd, Gloucester, ON, K1T 3T7
(613) 822-0335
Emp Here 90   Sales 19,980,090
SIC 3585 Refrigeration and heating equipment
Urs Schenk
Anthony Mcglynn

D-U-N-S 25-103-7271   (SL)
D.W.S. ROOFING AND WATERPROOFING SERVICES INC
2562 Del Zotto Ave, Gloucester, ON, K1T 3V7
(613) 260-7700
Emp Here 60   Sales 13,069,740
SIC 1761 Roofing, siding, and sheetMetal work
Douglas Stalker

D-U-N-S 20-919-4260   (SL)
DIRECT MOTOR COMPANY LTD
BANK STREET MAZDA
2575 Bank St, Gloucester, ON, K1T 1M8
(613) 739-3088
Emp Here 75   Sales 47,196,000
SIC 5511 New and used car dealers
Shiv Dilawri
Ken Holmes

D-U-N-S 25-464-3455   (SL)
HUNT CLUB MOTORS LIMITED
HUNT CLUB VOLKSWAGEN
2655 Bank St, Gloucester, ON, K1T 1N1
(613) 521-2300
Emp Here 40   Sales 19,923,120
SIC 5511 New and used car dealers
Allyson Bell

D-U-N-S 24-824-0934   (SL)
ONEIL MOTORS INC
1493 Sieveright Rd, Gloucester, ON, K1T 1M5

Emp Here 49   Sales 10,095,811
SIC 7515 Passenger car leasing
Dick O'neill

D-U-N-S 24-103-8355   (SL)
PRYOR METALS LIMITED
2683 Fenton Rd, Gloucester, ON, K1T 3T8
(613) 822-0953
Emp Here 150   Sales 28,812,750
SIC 3469 Metal stampings, nec
Claude Pryor
Michael Chinkiwsky

D-U-N-S 24-466-4442   (HQ)
W.O. STINSON & SON LIMITED
(Suby of 1686943 ONTARIO LIMITED)
4726 Bank St, Gloucester, ON, K1T 3W7
(613) 822-7400
Emp Here 100   Sales 144,313,000
SIC 5541 Gasoline service stations
David Stinson
Eric Stinson

Gloucester, ON K1V

D-U-N-S 20-123-0955   (BR)
AVISCAR INC
AVIS
(Suby of AVIS BUDGET GROUP, INC.)

180 Paul Benoit Dr, Gloucester, ON, K1V 2E5
(613) 521-7541
Emp Here 100
SIC 7514 Passenger car rental
Shaun Slater

D-U-N-S 25-983-5700   (SL)
HYLANDS GOLF CLUB
2101 Alert Rd, Gloucester, ON, K1V 1J9
(613) 521-1842
Emp Here 80   Sales 6,111,760
SIC 7997 Membership sports and recreation clubs
Cody Barbeau

D-U-N-S 20-175-0440   (BR)
NAV CANADA
(Suby of NAV CANADA)
1600 Tom Roberts Ave, Gloucester, ON, K1V 1E6
(800) 876-4693
Emp Here 212
SIC 4899 Communication services, nec
Patrick Landrigan

D-U-N-S 25-996-9681   (HQ)
UNIVEX MANAGEMENT LIMITED
303 River Rd Suite 3, Gloucester, ON, K1V 1H2
(613) 526-1500
Sales 13,716,600
SIC 8741 Management services
Michael Caletti

Gloucester, ON K1X

D-U-N-S 24-270-1092   (SL)
GRANDOR LUMBER INC
GRANDOR GROUP
(Suby of ALPA LUMBER INC)
5224 Bank St, Gloucester, ON, K1X 1H2
(613) 822-3390
Emp Here 100   Sales 26,765,200
SIC 5211 Lumber and other building materials
John Dipoce
Victor Farr Jr

D-U-N-S 20-393-4401   (SL)
HR OTTAWA, L.P.
RIDEAU CARLTON RACEWAY CASINO
4837 Albion Rd, Gloucester, ON, K1X 1A3
(613) 822-8668
Emp Here 750   Sales 71,751,000
SIC 7011 Hotels and motels
Richard Gardner

Goderich, ON N7A

D-U-N-S 24-506-0595   (HQ)
BLUEWATER OFFICE EQUIPMENT LTD
MICROAGE BASICS
223 Huron Rd, Goderich, ON, N7A 2Z8
(519) 524-9863
Emp Here 31   Sales 15,203,916
SIC 5045 Computers, peripherals, and software
John Peet
Harold Peet
Maureen Peet

D-U-N-S 25-721-7521   (SL)
CAMP KINTAIL
CAMP KINTAIL SUMMER OFFICE
85153 Bluewater Hwy, Goderich, ON, N7A 3X9
(519) 529-7317
Emp Here 45   Sales 17,883,630
SIC 8699 Membership organizations, nec
Jonathan Lee

D-U-N-S 24-286-9592   (BR)
COMPASS MINERALS CANADA CORP

COMPASS MINERAL
(Suby of COMPASS MINERALS INTERNATIONAL, INC.)
300 North Harbour Rd W, Goderich, ON, N7A 3Y9
(519) 524-8351
Emp Here 325
SIC 1481 NonMetallic mineral services
Rowland Howe

D-U-N-S 24-097-2653   (BR)
COMPASS MINERALS CANADA CORP
SIFTO SALT, DIV OF
(Suby of COMPASS MINERALS INTERNATIONAL, INC.)
245 Regent St, Goderich, ON, N7A 3Y5
(519) 524-8351
Emp Here 100
SIC 2899 Chemical preparations, nec
Dan Loebach

D-U-N-S 24-023-4534   (HQ)
EDWARD FUELS LIMITED
263 Huron Rd, Goderich, ON, N7A 2Z8
(519) 524-8386
Emp Here 42   Sales 124,138,665
SIC 5172 Petroleum products, nec
Donald Edward
Robert Jeffrey

D-U-N-S 24-451-0780   (HQ)
HURONIA/MED-E-OX LTD
MEDICHAIR, DIV OF
282 Suncoast Dr E, Goderich, ON, N7A 4K4
(519) 524-5363
Emp Here 35   Sales 29,213,800
SIC 5169 Chemicals and allied products, nec
Douglas (Doug) Fines
Margo Fines

D-U-N-S 20-268-8966   (SL)
K2 WIND ONTARIO LIMITED PARTNERSHIP
46 Victoria St N, Goderich, ON, N7A 2R6
(519) 441-1067
Emp Here 50   Sales 31,330,700
SIC 4911 Electric services
Stuart Lee

D-U-N-S 20-576-0841   (SL)
KECHNIE CHEVROLET OLDSMOBILE LTD
74 Kingston St, Goderich, ON, N7A 3K4

Emp Here 22   Sales 10,957,716
SIC 5511 New and used car dealers
Mary Ann Kechnie

D-U-N-S 20-050-7481   (SL)
MCGEE MOTORS LTD
MCGEE PONTIAC BUICK CADILLAC GMC
180 Suncoast Dr E, Goderich, ON, N7A 4N4
(519) 524-8391
Emp Here 22   Sales 10,957,716
SIC 5511 New and used car dealers
Martin Mcgee

D-U-N-S 25-543-1488   (BR)
REVERA INC
MAITLAND MANOR
(Suby of GOVERNMENT OF CANADA)
290 South St, Goderich, ON, N7A 4G6
(519) 524-7324
Emp Here 100
SIC 8361 Residential care
Amanda Beddow

D-U-N-S 24-391-8054   (SL)
RUBIN, MARILYN D. SALES & SERVICE INC
CANADIAN TIRE
35430 Huron Rd Rr 2 Suite 2, Goderich, ON, N7A 3X8
(519) 524-2121
Emp Here 45   Sales 22,413,510
SIC 5531 Auto and home supply stores
Marilynn Rubin

D-U-N-S 25-294-8690   (BR)
WAL-MART CANADA CORP

WALMART STORE 3126
(Suby of WALMART INC.)
35400 Huron Rd, Goderich, ON, N7A 3X8
(519) 524-5060
Emp Here 180
SIC 5311 Department stores

D-U-N-S 24-194-9051   (BR)
ZEHRMART INC
ZEHRS MARKETS
(Suby of LOBLAW COMPANIES LIMITED)
Hwy 8 S, Goderich, ON, N7A 4C6
(519) 524-2229
Emp Here 180
SIC 5411 Grocery stores
  Steve Hewitt

Golden Lake, ON K0J

D-U-N-S 20-122-7741   (SL)
HOKUM, BEN AND SON LIMITED
206 Black Point Rd, Golden Lake, ON, K0J
1X0
(613) 757-2399
Emp Here 110   *Sales* 21,160,700
SIC 2421 Sawmills and planing mills, general
  Benjamin F. Hokum Jr
  Dean S. Felhaber
  Valerie Wojtowicz
  Lois Hokum

Gore Bay, ON P0P

D-U-N-S 24-193-0676   (SL)
CARNBRO LTD
Hwy 540 B, Gore Bay, ON, P0P 1H0
(705) 282-2723
Emp Here 35   *Sales* 13,487,600
SIC 4731 Freight transportation arrangement
  Joan Prior

D-U-N-S 24-976-9159   (HQ)
JET TRANSPORT LTD
MANITOULIN TRANSPORT
(Suby of NORTH CHANNEL OF GEORGIAN
BAY HOLDINGS LTD)
154 540b Hwy Rr 1, Gore Bay, ON, P0P 1H0
(705) 282-2640
Emp Here 1   *Sales* 14,399,420
SIC 4213 Trucking, except local
  Gordon Smith

D-U-N-S 20-050-8745   (HQ)
MANITOULIN TRANSPORT INC
(Suby of NORTH CHANNEL OF GEORGIAN
BAY HOLDINGS LTD)
154 540b Hwy, Gore Bay, ON, P0P 1H0
(705) 282-2640
Emp Here 5   *Sales* 28,579,055
SIC 4213 Trucking, except local
  Gordon Smith
  Douglas Smith
  Donald Goodwill
  Myles Macleod
  Jeffrey Smith
  Rolando Meo
  Steven Forgie

Gormley, ON L0H

D-U-N-S 20-154-4665   (SL)
ANDERSON, DON HAULAGE LIMITED
36 Gordon Collins Dr, Gormley, ON, L0H 1G0
(416) 798-7737
Emp Here 80   *Sales* 16,456,480
SIC 4213 Trucking, except local
  Michael Anderson
  Maris Anderson

D-U-N-S 24-505-3624   (HQ)
BENCH PRESS LTD, THE
CREATIVE OUTDOOR ADVERTISING
2402 Stouffville Rd Rr 1, Gormley, ON, L0H
1G0
(905) 887-3043
Sales 10,586,200
SIC 7312 Outdoor advertising services
  David Gray
  Gordon Gray
  Elizabeth Grayford

D-U-N-S 20-707-8770   (BR)
CLUBLINK CORPORATION ULC
STATION CREEK GOLF CLUB
(Suby of TWC ENTERPRISES LIMITED)
12657 Woodbine Ave S, Gormley, ON, L0H
1G0
(905) 888-1219
Emp Here 90
SIC 7992 Public golf courses
  Brad Sewards

D-U-N-S 24-663-0524   (SL)
INFRASOURCE SERVICES
21 Cardico Dr, Gormley, ON, L0H 1G0

Emp Here 4   *Sales* 12,632,375
SIC 4922 Natural gas transmission

D-U-N-S 20-360-1526   (SL)
PGC SERVICES INC
180 Ram Forest Rd, Gormley, ON, L0H 1G0
(905) 900-0010
Emp Here 500   *Sales* 44,848,000
SIC 7699 Repair services, nec
  Bill Powell

D-U-N-S 24-207-1913   (SL)
RABCON CONTRACTORS LTD
9 Gormley Industrial Ave, Gormley, ON, L0H
1G0
(905) 888-6281
Emp Here 60   *Sales* 15,146,520
SIC 1623 Water, sewer, and utility lines
  Vincent Rabito
  Gaegano Rabito

D-U-N-S 20-941-3061   (SL)
RAM FOREST PRODUCTS INC
1 Ram Forest Rd, Gormley, ON, L0H 1G0

Emp Here 100
SIC 2491 Wood preserving

D-U-N-S 25-246-9747   (SL)
ROUGE RIVER FARMS INC
24 Gormley Industrial Ave, Gormley, ON, L0H
1G0
(800) 773-9216
Emp Here 150   *Sales* 25,353,750
SIC 0161 Vegetables and melons
  Richard Reesor
  Robert Reesor

D-U-N-S 24-419-9915   (SL)
STRUCTFORM INTERNATIONAL LIMITED
(Suby of STRUCTURAL FLOOR FINISHING
LIMITED)
29 Gormley Industrial Ave Unit 6, Gormley,
ON, L0H 1G0
(416) 291-7576
Emp Here 100   *Sales* 57,033,800
SIC 1542 Nonresidential construction, nec
  Edward Ziraldo
  Louis Bernardi
  James Creig
  Edward Paul Ziraldo
  Adamo Lecce
  Anita Shum

D-U-N-S 24-513-8888   (SL)
STRUCTURAL CONTRACTING LTD
29 Gormley Industrial Ave Unit 6, Gormley,
ON, L0H 1G0
(416) 291-7576
Emp Here 150   *Sales* 36,927,900
SIC 1791 Structural steel erection

  Adam Lecce

D-U-N-S 20-718-4524   (HQ)
STRUCTURAL FLOOR FINISHING LIMITED
29 Gormley Industrial Rd, Gormley, ON, L0H
1G0
(416) 291-7576
Sales 24,748,300
SIC 1771 Concrete work
  Adam Lecce
  Edward Ziraldo

Gormley, ON L4A

D-U-N-S 20-627-3716   (HQ)
TAM-KAL LIMITED
34 Cardico Dr Unit 2, Gormley, ON, L4A 2G5
(905) 888-9200
Sales 13,069,740
SIC 1761 Roofing, siding, and sheetMetal
work
  Michael Tamburro
  Lorraine Tamburro

Grafton, ON K0K

D-U-N-S 25-543-5455   (HQ)
926715 ONTARIO INC
STE ANNE'S COUNTRY INN & SPA
1009 Massey Rd, Grafton, ON, K0K 2G0
(905) 349-2493
Sales 11,781,750
SIC 7991 Physical fitness facilities
  James Corcoran
  Russet Preston

D-U-N-S 20-070-0099   (BR)
926715 ONTARIO INC
HALIDIMAND HILLS SPAS VILLAGE, THE
(Suby of 926715 ONTARIO INC)
384 Academy Hill Rd, Grafton, ON, K0K 2G0
(905) 349-2493
Emp Here 185
SIC 7991 Physical fitness facilities
  Jim Corcoran

Grand Bend, ON N0M

D-U-N-S 24-560-2495   (SL)
**OKE WOODSMITH BUILDING SYSTEMS
INC**
LITE FORM ONTARIO, DIVISION OF
70964 Bluewater Hwy Suite 9, Grand Bend,
ON, N0M 1T0
(519) 238-8893
Emp Here 43   *Sales* 13,711,367
SIC 1521 Single-family housing construction
  Randall Oke
  Wayne Oke
  Kevin Oke
  Bradley Oke

D-U-N-S 20-806-2500   (BR)
SOBEYS CAPITAL INCORPORATED
SOBEYS STORE 6722
(Suby of EMPIRE COMPANY LIMITED)
55 Main St E, Grand Bend, ON, N0M 1T0
(519) 238-8944
Emp Here 80
SIC 5411 Grocery stores
  Bob Green

Grand Valley, ON L9W

D-U-N-S 24-887-7743   (SL)

KEMBER HARDWOOD FLOORING INC
KEMBER INTERIORS
246022 County Rd 16, Grand Valley, ON, L9W
6K2
(289) 804-0032
Emp Here 50   *Sales* 11,369,150
SIC 1752 Floor laying and floor work, nec
  Peter Kember

Granton, ON N0M

D-U-N-S 24-353-1477   (SL)
**PENNER FARM SERVICES (AVONBANK)
LTD**
PENNER FARM SERVICES
15456 Elginfield Rd Rr 3, Granton, ON, N0M
1V0
(519) 225-2507
Emp Here 63   *Sales* 29,926,638
SIC 5083 Farm and garden machinery
  Frank Hogervorster
  Jerry Martens
  Darrel Penner
  Reg Penner

Gravenhurst, ON P1P

D-U-N-S 25-332-6854   (SL)
1127919 ONTARIO LIMITED
TERRY'S INDEPENDENT GROCERY
290 First St N, Gravenhurst, ON, P1P 1H3
(705) 687-0554
Emp Here 140   *Sales* 41,086,780
SIC 5411 Grocery stores
  Darlene Atkinson
  Tal Atkinson

D-U-N-S 25-604-8729   (BR)
2063414 ONTARIO LIMITED
LEISUREWORLD CAREGIVING CENTRE
200 Kelly Dr, Gravenhurst, ON, P1P 1P3
(705) 687-3444
Emp Here 180
SIC 8051 Skilled nursing care facilities
  Angela Coupts

D-U-N-S 24-180-9458   (SL)
DUNN HOLDINGS INC
WALKERS POINT MARINA
1035 Marina Rd, Gravenhurst, ON, P1P 1R2
(705) 687-7793
Emp Here 25   *Sales* 12,451,950
SIC 5551 Boat dealers
  Earl Dunn
  Sharon Dunn
  John Dunn

D-U-N-S 20-358-4990   (SL)
MUSKOKA BAY GOLF CORPORATION
MUSKOKA BAY RESORT
1217 North Muldrew Lake Rd, Gravenhurst,
ON, P1P 1T9
(705) 687-4900
Emp Here 75   *Sales* 5,729,775
SIC 7992 Public golf courses
  Peter Freed
  Chuck Macdougall

D-U-N-S 25-780-1672   (SL)
**MUSKOKA SPRINGS NATURAL SPRING
WATER INC**
MUSKOKA SPRINGS
220 Bay St, Gravenhurst, ON, P1P 1H1
(705) 687-8852
Emp Here 30   *Sales* 25,067,310
SIC 5149 Groceries and related products, nec
  Mike Billinghurst
  Terry Galbraith

D-U-N-S 25-605-9148   (BR)
REMAX NORTH COUNTRY REALTY INC

REMAX
405 Muskoka Rd S Unit B, Gravenhurst, ON,
P1P 1T1
(705) 687-2243
Emp Here 90
SIC 6531 Real estate agents and managers
Ray Jarvis

Greely, ON K4P

D-U-N-S 24-764-1769   (SL)
1633936 ONTARIO INC
1349 Meadow Dr, Greely, ON, K4P 1N3
(613) 821-3016
Emp Here 49   Sales 13,659,382
SIC 5411 Grocery stores
Blair Mackinnon

D-U-N-S 24-727-8450   (SL)
727849 ONTARIO LIMITED
VISCOUNT GLASS & ALUMINUM
1357 Barfield Rd, Greely, ON, K4P 1A1
(613) 821-0166
Emp Here 45   Sales 11,387,655
SIC 5211 Lumber and other building materials
John Kaczmarek

D-U-N-S 25-087-1753   (HQ)
D&G LANDSCAPING INC
1341 Coker St, Greely, ON, K4P 1A1
(613) 821-4444
Sales 18,933,150
SIC 1611 Highway and street construction
Gregory Clunie
Douglas Clunie

D-U-N-S 24-382-0487   (SL)
GREELY SAND & GRAVEL INC
1971 Old Prescott Rd, Greely, ON, K4P 1L3
(613) 821-3003
Emp Here 42   Sales 10,628,478
SIC 5211 Lumber and other building materials
Brent Pyper
Donna Pyper

D-U-N-S 20-441-3934   (SL)
LEO'S LIVESTOCK EXCHANGE LIMITED
OTTAWA LIVESTOCK EXCHANGE
(Suby of SPRATT W A & SONS LIMITED)
1643 Sale Barn Rd, Greely, ON, K4P 1N6
(613) 821-2634
Emp Here 20   Sales 29,353,840
SIC 5154 Livestock
Leo Menard
Steve Spratt

D-U-N-S 20-120-9702   (HQ)
MARATHON DRILLING CORPORATION
6847 Hiram Dr, Greely, ON, K4P 1A2
(613) 821-4800
Emp Here 24   Sales 19,694,880
SIC 1799 Special trade contractors, nec
David Mcphedran

D-U-N-S 24-268-8729   (HQ)
**MARATHON UNDERGROUND CONSTRUC-
TOR CORPORATION**
*(Suby of MARATHON DRILLING CORPORA-
TION)*
6847 Hiram Dr, Greely, ON, K4P 1A2
(613) 821-4800
Sales 43,724,135
SIC 1381 Drilling oil and gas wells
David Mcphedran

D-U-N-S 25-685-0918   (SL)
PMU OVL INC
1491 Manotick Station Rd, Greely, ON, K4P
1P6
(613) 821-2233
Emp Here 80   Sales 18,632,880
SIC 6513 Apartment building operators
Joe Princiotta

Green Valley, ON K0C

D-U-N-S 24-382-5601   (BR)
COCO PAVING INC
CRUICKSHANK-GLENGARRY DIVISION
(Suby of COCO PAVING INC)
4139 Hwy 34, Green Valley, ON, K0C 1L0
(613) 525-1750
Emp Here 80
SIC 1611 Highway and street construction
Jp Chardonneau

D-U-N-S 20-051-2747   (SL)
ROY'S CHEVROLET BUICK GMC INC
4000 County Rd 34, Green Valley, ON, K0C
1L0
(613) 525-2300
Emp Here 30   Sales 14,942,340
SIC 5511 New and used car dealers
Sylvianne Labonte
Gerald Labonte

Greenwood, ON L0H

D-U-N-S 24-320-5643   (SL)
KLEENZONE LTD
2489 Sixth Concession Rd, Greenwood, ON,
L0H 1H0
(905) 686-6500
Emp Here 130   Sales 4,155,840
SIC 7349 Building maintenance services, nec
Peter Dellaportas

Grimsby, ON L3M

D-U-N-S 24-337-0959   (HQ)
ALLIED TRACK SERVICES INC
169a South Service Rd, Grimsby, ON, L3M
4H6
(905) 769-1317
Emp Here 35   Sales 25,244,200
SIC 1629 Heavy construction, nec
Dave Malay
Andy Jones
Steve Spear
Attal Ibrahimi
Rick Middaugh
Mike Firmin

D-U-N-S 25-929-0856   (BR)
ANDREW PELLER LIMITED
VINEYARD ESTATE WINES
(Suby of ANDREW PELLER LIMITED)
697 South Service Rd, Grimsby, ON, L3M 4E8
(905) 643-4131
Emp Here 400
SIC 2084 Wines, brandy, and brandy spirits
Peter Patchet

D-U-N-S 20-534-5754   (HQ)
ANDREW PELLER LIMITED
GLOBAL VINTNERS
697 South Service Rd, Grimsby, ON, L3M 4E8
(905) 643-4131
Emp Here 150   Sales 289,667,470
SIC 2084 Wines, brandy, and brandy spirits
John E. Peller
Randy A. Powell
Gregory J. Berti
Shawn Macleod
James H. Cole
Sara Presutto
J. Gavin Hawthorne
Erin L. Rooney
Craig D. Mcdonald
Brendan Wall

D-U-N-S 24-450-9535   (SL)
CIMCORP AUTOMATION LTD

(Suby of MURATA MACHINERY,LTD.)
635 South Service Rd, Grimsby, ON, L3M 4E8
(905) 643-9700
Emp Here 55   Sales 12,210,055
SIC 3569 General industrial machinery, nec
Douglas Pickard
Rick Trigatti
Marjo Rimpela

D-U-N-S 20-025-1903   (BR)
DISTRICT SCHOOL BOARD OF NIAGARA
GRIMSBY HIGH SECONDARY SCHOOL
5 Boulton Ave, Grimsby, ON, L3M 1H6
(905) 945-5416
Emp Here 90
SIC 8211 Elementary and secondary schools
Mike Jenken

D-U-N-S 20-535-4269   (SL)
EMPIRE TRANSPORTATION LTD
263 South Service Rd, Grimsby, ON, L3M 1Y6
(905) 945-9654
Emp Here 100   Sales 24,618,600
SIC 1799 Special trade contractors, nec
John Kingma
Paul Kingma

D-U-N-S 20-702-9638   (HQ)
FORTY CREEK DISTILLERY LTD
CAMPARI CANADA
(Suby of LAGFIN)
297 South Service Rd, Grimsby, ON, L3M 1Y6
(905) 945-9225
Sales 29,383,650
SIC 2085 Distilled and blended liquors
Massimo Mottura
Tim Burrows
Bill Ashburn
Beth Warner

D-U-N-S 20-873-1955   (SL)
GRIMSBY CHRYSLER DODGE JEEP LTD.
421 South Service Rd, Grimsby, ON, L3M 4E8
(905) 945-9606
Emp Here 21   Sales 10,459,638
SIC 5511 New and used car dealers
Gen Brady

D-U-N-S 24-891-1054   (SL)
GRIMSBY UTILITY CONSTRUCTION INC
GUCI
211 Roberts Rd, Grimsby, ON, L3M 4E8
(905) 945-8878
Emp Here 80   Sales 20,195,360
SIC 1623 Water, sewer, and utility lines
Jeffrey Brown

D-U-N-S 20-166-6369   (HQ)
**HANDLING SPECIALTY MANUFACTURING
LIMITED**
HANDLING SPECIALTY
(Suby of G. K. ENTERPRISES, INC.)
219 South Service Rd, Grimsby, ON, L3M 1Y6
(905) 945-9661
Sales 12,654,057
SIC 3599 Industrial machinery, nec
Thomas Beach
Martin Sear
H. Rudi Kroeker
Jeffrey Kahn
Nick Sestili

D-U-N-S 20-053-2661   (HQ)
JOHN DEERE CANADA ULC
JOHN DEERE
(Suby of DEERE & COMPANY)
295 Hunter Rd, Grimsby, ON, L3M 4H5
(905) 945-9281
Emp Here 200   Sales 256,440,701
SIC 3523 Farm machinery and equipment
Debra Harrison
James E Temperley
Gail E. Mccombs
David A. Kirk
Margaret A. Curry

D-U-N-S 20-876-6451   (SL)

LAKE FOUNDRY LTD
(Suby of LAKE HOLDINGS INC)
287 South Service Rd, Grimsby, ON, L3M 1Y6
(905) 643-1248
Emp Here 48   Sales 11,204,880
SIC 3321 Gray and ductile iron foundries
Frank Verdinsek
Theresa Verdinsek
Debbie Plute

D-U-N-S 25-537-5263   (SL)
LEISURE MANUFACTURING INC
SUNRISE WHIRLPOOL SPAS
317 South Service Rd Suite 2, Grimsby, ON,
L3M 4E8
(905) 309-1800
Emp Here 50   Sales 16,280,000
SIC 5999 Miscellaneous retail stores, nec
Jack Layfield

D-U-N-S 24-383-7130   (BR)
LOBLAWS INC
REAL CANADIAN SUPERSTORE
(Suby of LOBLAW COMPANIES LIMITED)
361 South Service Rd Suite 2806, Grimsby,
ON, L3M 4E8
(905) 309-3911
Emp Here 300
SIC 5411 Grocery stores
John Farrington

D-U-N-S 24-418-9692   (HQ)
NRB INC
MODULAR BUILDING SYSTEMS
183 South Service Rd Bureau 1, Grimsby, ON,
L3M 4H6
(905) 945-9622
Emp Here 55   Sales 28,812,750
SIC 3448 Prefabricated Metal buildings and
components
Robert J Mcneil
Bob Mcneil

D-U-N-S 24-191-4787   (SL)
PHELPS HOMES LTD
166 Main St W, Grimsby, ON, L3M 1S3
(905) 945-5451
Emp Here 53   Sales 14,359,926
SIC 1521 Single-family housing construction
Paul Phelps
Wendy Phelps

D-U-N-S 24-963-4361   (SL)
R J J HOLDINGS LTD
CANADIAN TIRE STORE 40
44 Livingston Ave Suite 40, Grimsby, ON, L3M
1L1
(905) 945-5441
Emp Here 48   Sales 23,907,744
SIC 5531 Auto and home supply stores
Ron Jaskula

D-U-N-S 25-792-8945   (SL)
REALTY NETWORK 100 INC
263 Main St E, Grimsby, ON, L3M 1P7
(905) 945-4555
Emp Here 70   Sales 19,022,920
SIC 6531 Real estate agents and managers
Greg Knapman

D-U-N-S 20-055-2966   (HQ)
RED-D-ARC LIMITED
RED-D-ARC WELDER RENTALS
*(Suby of L'AIR LIQUIDE SOCI-
ETE ANONYME POUR L'ETUDE ET
L'EXPLOITATION DES PROCEDES
GEORGES CLAUDE)*
667 South Service Rd, Grimsby, ON, L3M 4E8
(905) 643-4212
Emp Here 37   Sales 32,981,652
SIC 7359 Equipment rental and leasing, nec
Mitchel Imielinski
Donald S Darroch

D-U-N-S 20-652-1093   (BR)
REVERA INC
*MAPLECREST VILLAGE RETIREMENT
RESIDENCE*

(Suby of GOVERNMENT OF CANADA)
85 Main St E, Grimsby, ON, L3M 1N6
(905) 945-7044
Emp Here 75
SIC 6513 Apartment building operators
Greg Fortier

D-U-N-S 25-517-5606   (SL)
RJ'S FRUGAL MARKETS INC
RAY'S FOOD BASICS
63 Main St W, Grimsby, ON, L3M 4H1
(905) 945-3323
Emp Here 45   *Sales* 12,336,840
SIC 5411 Grocery stores
Ray Wong

D-U-N-S 25-021-5894   (SL)
**SHALOM MANOR LONG TERM CARE
HOME**
12 Bartlett Ave, Grimsby, ON, L3M 0A2
(905) 945-9631
Emp Here 230   *Sales* 15,714,980
SIC 8051 Skilled nursing care facilities
Konnie Peet
Hilda Roukema
Art Dreyer
Doug Stuive

D-U-N-S 20-189-1822   (BR)
SHERWIN-WILLIAMS CANADA INC
*DURACOAT POWDER MANUFACTURING
DIV*
(Suby of THE SHERWIN-WILLIAMS COM-
PANY)
13 Iroquois Trail, Grimsby, ON, L3M 5E6
(905) 945-3802
Emp Here 80
SIC 2851 Paints and allied products
Mauro Finocchi

D-U-N-S 20-606-3257   (SL)
SLESSOR AUTO WORLD
NAPA AUTOPRO
569 Main St W, Grimsby, ON, L3M 1V1
(905) 643-1221
Emp Here 45   *Sales* 22,413,510
SIC 5511 New and used car dealers
Robert Slessor
Donald Heidman

D-U-N-S 25-309-1839   (BR)
SOBEYS CAPITAL INCORPORATED
SOBEYS
(Suby of EMPIRE COMPANY LIMITED)
44 Livingston Ave, Grimsby, ON, L3M 1L1
(905) 945-9973
Emp Here 75
SIC 5411 Grocery stores
Debbie Farr

D-U-N-S 20-207-0970   (SL)
VTR FEEDER SOLUTIONS INC
VTR
623 South Service Rd Unit 6, Grimsby, ON,
L3M 4E8
(905) 643-7300
Emp Here 56   *Sales* 12,432,056
SIC 3559 Special industry machinery, nec
Tom Davies

D-U-N-S 24-792-7528   (HQ)
**WIDE RANGE TRANSPORTATION SER-
VICES INC**
WIDE RANGE TRANSPORTATION GROUP
689 South Service Rd, Grimsby, ON, L3M 4E8
(905) 643-5100
Sales 18,198,845
SIC 4731 Freight transportation arrangement
Robert Dell

D-U-N-S 20-528-3182   (SL)
WILLS CHEVROLET LTD
337 Main St E, Grimsby, ON, L3M 5N9
(905) 309-3356
Emp Here 35   *Sales* 17,432,730
SIC 5511 New and used car dealers
Thomas (Tom) Wills

Guelph, ON N1C

D-U-N-S 20-158-8881   (SL)
1266304 ONTARIO INC
FUSION HOMES
500 Hanlon Creek Blvd, Guelph, ON, N1C
0A1
(519) 826-6700
Emp Here 75   *Sales* 20,320,650
SIC 1521 Single-family housing construction
Lee Piccoli

D-U-N-S 24-860-0954   (SL)
7093373 CANADA INC
VAS
4 Foxwood Cres, Guelph, ON, N1C 1A6
(519) 400-9587
Emp Here 40   *Sales* 11,331,720
SIC 8741 Management services
Peter Schultz
Chris Murphy

D-U-N-S 25-554-8703   (SL)
**BELCHIM CROP PROTECTION CANADA
INC**
(Suby of BELCHIM MANAGEMENT)
104 Cooper Dr Unit 3, Guelph, ON, N1C 0A4
(519) 826-7878
Emp Here 30   *Sales* 22,275,600
SIC 5191 Farm supplies
Ray Chyc

D-U-N-S 20-724-9665   (HQ)
WURTH CANADA LIMITED
(Suby of ADOLF WURTH GMBH & CO. KG)
345 Hanlon Creek Blvd, Guelph, ON, N1C
0A1
(905) 564-6225
Emp Here 100   *Sales* 250,693,220
SIC 5085 Industrial supplies
Ernest Sweeney

Guelph, ON N1E

D-U-N-S 24-124-0456   (SL)
CAMERON INDUSTRIES INC
INDEPENDENT PAPER CONVERTERS
309 Elizabeth St, Guelph, ON, N1E 2X8
(519) 824-3561
Emp Here 50   *Sales* 11,671,750
SIC 2672 Paper; coated and laminated, nec
Brian Rowell
Janine Rowell
Bernardine Cameron

D-U-N-S 24-425-8575   (BR)
CARGILL LIMITED
*BETTER BEEF-CARGILL MEAT SOLU-
TIONS, DIV OF*
(Suby of CARGILL, INCORPORATED)
781 York Rd, Guelph, ON, N1E 6N1
(519) 823-5200
Emp Here 1,540
SIC 2011 Meat packing plants
Julian Hatherell

D-U-N-S 20-051-6367   (HQ)
DUROSE MANUFACTURING LIMITED
460 Elizabeth St, Guelph, ON, N1E 6C1
(519) 822-5251
Emp Here 1   *Sales* 18,248,075
SIC 3446 Architectural Metalwork
Angelo Maggiolo

D-U-N-S 20-037-0583   (HQ)
ELLIS PACKAGING WEST INC
136 Victoria Rd S, Guelph, ON, N1E 5P6
(519) 822-7060
Sales 12,659,920
SIC 2657 Folding paperboard boxes
Sharon Ellis

D-U-N-S 24-122-0615   (SL)
GMA COVER CORP
965 York Rd, Guelph, ON, N1E 6Y9

Emp Here 220   *Sales* 63,987,000
SIC 3714 Motor vehicle parts and accessories
Glenn Verkindt
Robert Murison

D-U-N-S 20-973-4334   (HQ)
GUELPH GENERAL HOSPITAL
115 Delhi St, Guelph, ON, N1E 4J4
(519) 822-5350
Sales 126,619,473
SIC 8062 General medical and surgical hospi-
tals
Marianne Walker
Dale Mills
Kathy Wilkie
Christine Bevan-Stewart
Bob Carter
Jennifer Caspers
Brian Cowan
Fraser Edward
David Forestall
Rena Hubers

D-U-N-S 24-215-5328   (SL)
GUELPH SERVICES FOR THE AUTISTIC
BRIDGES-OVER-BARRIERS
16 Caribou Cres, Guelph, ON, N1E 1C9
(519) 823-9232
Emp Here 30   *Sales* 11,922,420
SIC 8699 Membership organizations, nec
Elizabeth Bloomfield

D-U-N-S 24-947-4156   (HQ)
HOMEWOOD HEALTH CENTRE INC
(Suby of RBJ SCHLEGEL HOLDINGS INC)
150 Delhi St, Guelph, ON, N1E 6K9
(519) 824-1010
Sales 51,927,850
SIC 8063 Psychiatric hospitals
Jagoda Pike
Ronald Schelegel
Kim Mirotta
James Schlegel
Rob Schlegel
Brad Schlegel

D-U-N-S 20-269-5201   (HQ)
HOMEWOOD HEALTH INC
49 Emma St Suite 100, Guelph, ON, N1E 6X1
(519) 821-9258
Emp Here 500   *Sales* 340,978,500
SIC 8093 Specialty outpatient clinics, nec
Robbie R. Shlegel
James M. Shlegel

D-U-N-S 25-237-7387   (SL)
J. P. ABBOTT DISTRIBUTION SERVICE LTD
534 Speedvale Ave E, Guelph, ON, N1E 1P6
(519) 821-3206
Emp Here 200   *Sales* 40,074,200
SIC 7319 Advertising, nec
Clyde Abbott
Joan Abbott

D-U-N-S 24-471-1354   (BR)
**LAPOINTE-FISHER NURSING HOME, LIM-
ITED**
(Suby of LAPOINTE-FISHER NURSING
HOME, LIMITED)
271 Metcalfe St, Guelph, ON, N1E 4Y8
(519) 821-9030
Emp Here 100
SIC 8051 Skilled nursing care facilities
Danny Bailey

D-U-N-S 24-607-8351   (BR)
METRO ONTARIO INC
FOOD BASIC
(Suby of METRO INC)
380 Eramosa Rd, Guelph, ON, N1E 6R2
(519) 824-8700
Emp Here 160
SIC 5411 Grocery stores

Norm Kassian

D-U-N-S 20-727-2886   (SL)
**PESTALTO ENVIRONMENTAL HEALTH
SERVICES INC**
400 Elizabeth St Unit I, Guelph, ON, N1E 2Y1

Emp Here 75   *Sales* 19,284,825
SIC 4959 Sanitary services, nec
Barry Tyler

D-U-N-S 24-189-3242   (HQ)
PLANET BEAN INC
PLANET BEAN
(Suby of SUMAC COMMUNITY WORKER
CO-OPERATIVE INC)
259 Grange Rd Unit 2, Guelph, ON, N1E 6R5
(519) 837-1040
Emp Here 14   *Sales* 17,547,117
SIC 5149 Groceries and related products, nec
Byron Cunningham
William Barrett
John Brouwer
Peter Cameron

D-U-N-S 24-923-9989   (HQ)
POLYMER DISTRIBUTION INC
PDI
256 Victoria Rd S, Guelph, ON, N1E 5R1
(519) 837-4535
Emp Here 28   *Sales* 30,855,900
SIC 4225 General warehousing and storage
Richard Standish
Bruce Bottomley

D-U-N-S 24-327-2676   (SL)
R.C. PHARMACY LTD
SHOPPERS DRUG MART
380 Eramosa Rd, Guelph, ON, N1E 6R2
(519) 822-2480
Emp Here 83   *Sales* 20,279,224
SIC 5912 Drug stores and proprietary stores
Robert Chin

D-U-N-S 25-407-5666   (SL)
RED CAR SERVICE INC
RED CAR AIRPORT SERVICE
530 Elizabeth St, Guelph, ON, N1E 6C3
(519) 824-9344
Emp Here 80   *Sales* 4,389,760
SIC 4131 Intercity and rural bus transportation
Neil Wilson

D-U-N-S 20-923-5076   (SL)
SUTHERLAND, JOHN & SONS LIMITED
SUTHERLAND INSURANCE
240 Victoria Rd N, Guelph, ON, N1E 6L8
(519) 822-0160
Emp Here 34   *Sales* 19,717,416
SIC 6411 Insurance agents, brokers, and ser-
vice
Jeffrey Sutherland

D-U-N-S 20-939-3941   (HQ)
**UPPER GRAND DISTRICT SCHOOL
BOARD, THE**
COLLEGE HEIGHTS S.S.
500 Victoria Rd N, Guelph, ON, N1E 6K2
(519) 822-4420
Emp Here 80   *Sales* 346,916,500
SIC 8211 Elementary and secondary schools
Linda Busuttil
Martha Rogers
Glen Regier

D-U-N-S 20-730-4536   (SL)
**VANDERGRIFT WHOLESALE FLORIST
LTD**
353 Elizabeth St, Guelph, ON, N1E 2X9
(519) 822-8097
Emp Here 25   *Sales* 18,563,000
SIC 5193 Flowers and florists supplies
Chris Vandergrift

D-U-N-S 20-024-9543   (BR)
**WELLINGTON CATHOLIC DISTRICT
SCHOOL BOARD**

ST. JAMES CATHOLIC HIGH SCHOOL
57 Victoria Rd N, Guelph, ON, N1E 5G9
(519) 822-4290
Emp Here 125
SIC 8211 Elementary and secondary schools
Peter Ingram

D-U-N-S 20-874-1848   (SL)
WILSON'S, MARK BETTER USED CAR LIMITED
700 York Rd, Guelph, ON, N1E 6A5
(519) 836-2900
Emp Here 60   *Sales* 37,756,800
SIC 5521 Used car dealers
Mark Mcmullen

D-U-N-S 25-297-8010   (BR)
ZEHRMART INC
ZEHRS MARKETS
(*Suby of* LOBLAW COMPANIES LIMITED)
297 Eramosa Rd, Guelph, ON, N1E 2M7
(519) 763-4550
Emp Here 150
SIC 5411 Grocery stores
Peter Marchant

Guelph, ON N1G

D-U-N-S 25-531-4015   (HQ)
AGRICORP
(*Suby of* GOVERNMENT OF ONTARIO)
1 Stone Rd W, Guelph, ON, N1G 4Y2
(888) 247-4999
Emp Here 420   *Sales* 146,236,622
SIC 6331 Fire, marine, and casualty insurance
Douglas Larose
Erich Beifuss
Murray Porteous
Maria Van Bommel
Anna Bragg
John Core
Carolyn Fuerth
Sheryl King
Patricia Lorenz
James Rickard

D-U-N-S 20-006-4249   (SL)
ALAM DRUGS LIMITED
SHOPPERS DRUG MART #1089
615 Scottsdale Dr Suite 1089, Guelph, ON, N1G 3P4
(519) 823-8000
Emp Here 65   *Sales* 15,881,320
SIC 5912 Drug stores and proprietary stores
Tayab Alam

D-U-N-S 24-986-4786   (HQ)
ALLTECH CANADA INC
(*Suby of* ALLTECH, INC.)
20 Cutten Pl, Guelph, ON, N1G 4Z7
(519) 763-3331
Sales 22,275,600
SIC 5191 Farm supplies
Ty Yeast
Anthony Ford
Thomas Pearce Lyons
Nathan Hohman

D-U-N-S 20-118-5613   (SL)
BARBER GROUP INVESTMENTS INC
485 Southgate Dr, Guelph, ON, N1G 3W6

Emp Here 110   *Sales* 62,659,080
SIC 5039 Construction materials, nec
John Barber

D-U-N-S 24-817-6703   (SL)
CLARKE ROLLER & RUBBER LIMITED
485 Southgate Dr, Guelph, ON, N1G 3W6
(519) 763-7655
Emp Here 49   *Sales* 35,786,905
SIC 5169 Chemicals and allied products, nec
Robert Wolstenholme

D-U-N-S 20-846-8512   (SL)
COLDWELL BANKER NEUMANN HERB REAL ESTATE LTD
COLDWELL BANKER NEUMANN REAL ESTATE
824 Gordon St Suite 201, Guelph, ON, N1G 1Y7
(519) 821-3600
Emp Here 35   *Sales* 11,582,051
SIC 6531 Real estate agents and managers
Herbert Neumann

D-U-N-S 20-267-0308   (SL)
COLDWELL BANKER NEUMANN REAL ESTATE
824 Gordon St Unit 201, Guelph, ON, N1G 1Y7
(519) 821-3600
Emp Here 50   *Sales* 13,587,800
SIC 6531 Real estate agents and managers
Jeff Neumann

D-U-N-S 20-784-0919   (SL)
D. L. PAGANI LIMITED
RAMADA HOTEL & CONFERENCE CENTRE
716 Gordon St, Guelph, ON, N1G 1Y6
(519) 836-1240
Emp Here 80   *Sales* 7,591,920
SIC 7011 Hotels and motels
Richard Pagani

D-U-N-S 20-201-1412   (SL)
GEOSYNTEC CONSULTANTS INTERNATIONAL INC
(*Suby of* GEOSYNTEC CONSULTANTS, INC.)
130 Stone Rd W, Guelph, ON, N1G 3Z2
(519) 822-2230
Emp Here 55   *Sales* 13,941,950
SIC 8748 Business consulting, nec
Rudolph Bonaparte
Thomas Krug

D-U-N-S 25-952-1532   (BR)
GRANDI COMPANY LIMITED
MCDONALD'S RESTAURANTS
(*Suby of* GRANDI COMPANY LIMITED)
372 Stone Rd W, Guelph, ON, N1G 4T8
(519) 763-8842
Emp Here 75
SIC 5812 Eating places
Tracy Montin

D-U-N-S 20-327-8577   (SL)
GUELPH HYDRO ELECTRIC SYSTEMS INC
395 Southgate Dr, Guelph, ON, N1G 4Y1
(519) 822-3010
Emp Here 100   *Sales* 62,661,400
SIC 4911 Electric services
Bud Smith

D-U-N-S 25-149-2658   (HQ)
HAMMOND POWER SOLUTIONS INC
HPS
595 Southgate Dr, Guelph, ON, N1G 3W6
(519) 822-2441
Emp Here 800   *Sales* 238,106,192
SIC 3612 Transformers, except electric

D-U-N-S 24-963-4205   (SL)
HOMELIFE REALTY (GUELPH) LIMITED
1027 Gordon St, Guelph, ON, N1G 4X1
(519) 836-1072
Emp Here 38   *Sales* 12,430,826
SIC 6531 Real estate agents and managers
Gasper Russo

D-U-N-S 24-624-2903   (SL)
MACKINNON TRANSPORT INC
405 Laird Rd, Guelph, ON, N1G 4P7
(519) 821-2311
Emp Here 100
SIC 4213 Trucking, except local
Evan Mackinnon
Alex Mackinnon
Richard Sharpe

D-U-N-S 20-057-5533   (HQ)

MANDEL SCIENTIFIC COMPANY INC
(*Suby of* MANSCI TECHNOLOGIES INC)
2 Admiral Pl, Guelph, ON, N1G 4N4
(888) 883-3636
Sales 48,181,680
SIC 5049 Professional equipment, nec
Michael Cauley

D-U-N-S 24-850-5708   (SL)
MANTECH INC.
2 Admiral Pl, Guelph, ON, N1G 4N4
(519) 763-4245
Emp Here 75   *Sales* 12,828,100
SIC 3821 Laboratory apparatus and furniture
Robert Menegotto

D-U-N-S 24-384-3067   (HQ)
MCKELLAR STRUCTURED SETTLEMENTS INC
MCKELLAR GROUP
649 Scottsdale Dr Suite 100, Guelph, ON, N1G 4T7
(519) 836-1672
Sales 14,873,796
SIC 6282 Investment advice
Ralph Fenik
John Rousseau
Gordon Hornsfeld

D-U-N-S 25-466-6381   (SL)
MDM INSURANCE SERVICES INC
834 Gordon St, Guelph, ON, N1G 1Y7
(519) 837-1531
Emp Here 25   *Sales* 14,498,100
SIC 6411 Insurance agents, brokers, and service
Michael D. Mckay

D-U-N-S 25-361-5751   (HQ)
METALUMEN HOLDINGS INC
(*Suby of* SMAEA HOLDINGS INC)
570 Southgate Dr, Guelph, ON, N1G 4P6
(519) 822-4381
Emp Here 1   *Sales* 18,091,990
SIC 3648 Lighting equipment, nec
Martin Stocker
Sandra Stocker

D-U-N-S 24-123-5159   (SL)
METALUMEN MANUFACTURING INC
(*Suby of* SMAEA HOLDINGS INC)
570 Southgate Dr, Guelph, ON, N1G 4P6
(519) 822-4381
Emp Here 100   *Sales* 19,044,200
SIC 3646 Commercial lighting fixtures
Martin Stocker

D-U-N-S 24-335-0399   (BR)
METRO ONTARIO INC
METRO
(*Suby of* METRO INC)
500 Edinburgh Rd S, Guelph, ON, N1G 4Z1
(519) 763-3552
Emp Here 300
SIC 5411 Grocery stores
Wayne Harewick

D-U-N-S 25-494-9688   (SL)
NSF CANADA
NSF INTERNATIONAL
(*Suby of* NSF INTERNATIONAL)
125 Chancellors Way, Guelph, ON, N1G 0E7
(519) 821-1246
Emp Here 54   *Sales* 11,487,700
SIC 8731 Commercial physical research
Kevan Lawlor
Michael Walsh
Tom Chestnut

D-U-N-S 25-361-9282   (HQ)
ORGANIC MEADOW INC
335 Laird Rd Unit 1, Guelph, ON, N1G 4P7
(519) 767-9694
Sales 36,218,760
SIC 5149 Groceries and related products, nec
Donald Rees
Paul Van Weelie

D-U-N-S 20-354-5871   (SL)
ORGANIC MEADOW LIMITED PARTNERSHIP
335 Laird Rd Unit 1, Guelph, ON, N1G 4P7
(519) 767-9694
Emp Here 47   *Sales* 39,272,119
SIC 5143 Dairy products, except dried or canned
Donald Rees

D-U-N-S 25-392-6455   (SL)
POLY-NOVA TECHNOLOGIES INC
(*Suby of* 1V2T INC)
125 Southgate Dr, Guelph, ON, N1G 3M5
(519) 822-2109
Emp Here 90   *Sales* 14,297,220
SIC 3069 Fabricated rubber products, nec
Richard Valeriote

D-U-N-S 24-761-4535   (SL)
POLY-NOVA TECHNOLOGIES LIMITED PARTNERSHIP
(*Suby of* BETA BERATUNGS- UND BETEILIGUNGS-GMBH)
125 Southgate Dr, Guelph, ON, N1G 3M5
(519) 822-2109
Emp Here 120   *Sales* 19,062,960
SIC 3069 Fabricated rubber products, nec
John Timmerman

D-U-N-S 25-560-0561   (SL)
PRIME RESTAURANTS
EAST SIDE MARIO'S
370 Stone Rd W Suite Side, Guelph, ON, N1G 4V9
(519) 763-7861
Emp Here 80   *Sales* 3,641,520
SIC 5812 Eating places
Sue Auger

D-U-N-S 24-033-3583   (HQ)
PROMINENT FLUID CONTROLS LTD
(*Suby of* PROMINENT GMBH)
490 Southgate Dr, Guelph, ON, N1G 4P5
(519) 836-5692
Emp Here 42   *Sales* 22,358,700
SIC 5074 Plumbing and heating equipment and supplies (hydronics)
Garth Debruyn
Victor Dulger

D-U-N-S 24-659-9971   (HQ)
ROWAN WILLIAMS DAVIES & IRWIN INC
RWDI
(*Suby of* RWDI GROUP INC)
600 Southgate Dr, Guelph, ON, N1G 4P6
(519) 823-1311
Sales 59,139,300
SIC 8711 Engineering services
Michael Soligo
Peter Irwin
Ray Sincorair
Scott Gamble
Frank Kriksic
Mark Vanderheyden
Anton Davies

D-U-N-S 20-175-3493   (HQ)
RWDI AIR INC
(*Suby of* RWDI GROUP INC)
600 Southgate Dr, Guelph, ON, N1G 4P6
(519) 823-1311
Emp Here 200   *Sales* 78,852,400
SIC 8711 Engineering services
Michael Soligo
Aimee Smith
Mark Jackson
Frank Kriksic
John Alberico
Christopher Wren
Peter Irwin

D-U-N-S 20-055-7481   (HQ)
RWDI GROUP INC
600 Southgate Dr, Guelph, ON, N1G 4P6
(519) 823-1311
Sales 59,139,300

SIC 8711 Engineering services
Michael Soligo
Rob Tonin
David Chadder
Mike Soligo
Gord Dunn
Anton Davies
Ray Sinclair

D-U-N-S 20-269-6225   (SL)
SHEARER'S FOODS CANADA, INC
745 Southgate Dr, Guelph, ON, N1G 3R3
(519) 746-0045
Emp Here 225   *Sales* 77,780,250
SIC 2096 Potato chips and similar snacks
Cj Fraleigh

D-U-N-S 24-737-5322   (HQ)
SLEEMAN BREWERIES LTD
OKANAGAN SPRING BREWERY
(*Suby of* SAPPORO HOLDINGS LIMITED)
505 Southgate Dr, Guelph, ON, N1G 3W6
(519) 822-1834
Emp Here 200   *Sales* 365,538,750
SIC 2082 Malt beverages
John W Sleeman
Yasuhiro Hanazawa
Masashi Minami
Yosuke Nakamura
Hirofumi Kishi

D-U-N-S 25-360-3005   (HQ)
SMAEA HOLDINGS INC
570 Southgate Dr, Guelph, ON, N1G 4P6
(519) 822-4381
Emp Here 1   *Sales* 18,091,990
SIC 3648 Lighting equipment, nec
Martin Stocker

D-U-N-S 24-002-3226   (HQ)
SYNGENTA CANADA INC
(*Suby of* CHINA NATIONAL CHEMICAL
CORPORATION LIMITED)
140 Research Lane, Guelph, ON, N1G 4Z3
(519) 836-5665
Emp Here 90   *Sales* 164,964,520
SIC 5191 Farm supplies
Trevor Heck
Mark Patrick

D-U-N-S 24-888-4058   (SL)
TIGER DRYLAC CANADA INC
(*Suby of* IKBE PRIVATSTIFTUNG)
110 Southgate Dr, Guelph, ON, N1G 4P5
(519) 766-4781
Emp Here 118   *Sales* 33,514,478
SIC 2851 Paints and allied products
Larry Mcneely
Dejan Simovic
Rosemary Lemieux

D-U-N-S 24-357-6837   (HQ)
TROUW NUTRITION CANADA INC
SHUR-GAIN
150 Research Lane Suite 200, Guelph, ON,
N1G 4T2
(519) 823-7000
Emp Here 35   *Sales* 584,862,000
SIC 2048 Prepared feeds, nec
Jerry Vergeer
Eduardo Perugini
Jacques Leclerc
Michiel Heringa
Cees Van Rijn

D-U-N-S 20-847-2209   (HQ)
UNIVERSITY OF GUELPH
50 Stone Rd E, Guelph, ON, N1G 2W1
(519) 824-4120
Emp Here 3,000   *Sales* 630,799,140
SIC 8221 Colleges and universities
Charlotte Yates
Don O'leary
Daniel Atlin
Malcolm Campbell
Daniel Atlin

D-U-N-S 20-113-7556   (BR)
UNIVERSITY OF GUELPH
LABORATORY SERVICES
(*Suby of* UNIVERSITY OF GUELPH)
95 Stone Rd W, Guelph, ON, N1G 2Z4
(519) 767-6299
Emp Here 250
SIC 8221 Colleges and universities
John Melichercik

D-U-N-S 24-550-7736   (BR)
**WESTMONT HOSPITALITY MANAGEMENT
LIMITED**
HOLIDAY INN GUELPH
(*Suby of* WESTMONT HOSPITALITY MAN-
AGEMENT LIMITED)
601 Scottsdale Dr, Guelph, ON, N1G 3E7
(519) 836-0231
Emp Here 150
SIC 7011 Hotels and motels
Bennie Devasa

Guelph, ON N1H

D-U-N-S 20-182-8469   (SL)
1511905 ONTARIO INC
GUELPH VOLKSWAGEN
359 Woodlawn Rd W, Guelph, ON, N1H 7K9
(519) 824-9150
Emp Here 25   *Sales* 12,451,950
SIC 5511 New and used car dealers
Jason Chow
Jeffery Taylor

D-U-N-S 24-778-2311   (HQ)
2421593 CANADA INC
(*Suby of* CO-OPERATORS GROUP LIMITED,
THE)
130 Macdonell St, Guelph, ON, N1H 2Z6
(519) 824-4400
Emp Here 10   *Sales* 151,514,844
SIC 6411 Insurance agents, brokers, and ser-
vice
John Asher
Andrew Carlyle
Paul Mlodzik
George Hardy

D-U-N-S 24-736-6243   (SL)
7013990 CANADA INC
TRANS 99 LOGISTICS
367 Speedvale Ave W, Guelph, ON, N1H 1C7
(519) 265-5161
Emp Here 25   *Sales* 18,803,448
SIC 4213 Trucking, except local
Harpreet Garcha
Balwinder Sekhon
Gurpreet Garcha
Karam Singh

D-U-N-S 24-415-1171   (SL)
775757 ONTARIO INC
TWO WHEEL MOTORSPORT
55473 Highway 6 N, Guelph, ON, N1H 6J2
(519) 836-1957
Emp Here 26   *Sales* 12,950,028
SIC 5571 Motorcycle dealers
Jens Christensen

D-U-N-S 20-117-3452   (SL)
AG ENERGY CO-OPERATIVE LTD
FIREFLY ENERGY
45 Speedvale Ave E Suite 2, Guelph, ON, N1H
1J2
(519) 763-3026
Emp Here 11   *Sales* 34,164,427
SIC 4924 Natural gas distribution
William Ravensbergen
Mike Slaman
Arjan Vos
Anthony Lanni
Jamie Van Spronsen
Jan Van Zanten
Roman Golovchenko

Jim Grey

D-U-N-S 24-318-5167   (SL)
AOC RESINS AND COATINGS COMPANY
(*Suby of* COMPOSITE RESINS HOLDING
B.V.)
38 Royal Rd, Guelph, ON, N1H 1G3
(519) 821-5180
Emp Here 95   *Sales* 26,981,995
SIC 2821 Plastics materials and resins
Myron Dzulynsky
Randall Weghorst
James Griffith
Frederick Norman
Reagan Stephens

D-U-N-S 20-563-2271   (HQ)
ARMTEC HOLDINGS LIMITED
370 Speedvale Ave W Suite 101, Guelph, ON,
N1H 7M7
(519) 822-0210
Sales 89,491,500
SIC 3272 Concrete products, nec
Charles Phillips
James Newell

D-U-N-S 20-311-3816   (SL)
AXIS SORTING INC
300 Willow Rd Unit 102b, Guelph, ON, N1H
7C6
(519) 212-4990
Emp Here 75   *Sales* 21,247,500
SIC 7549 Automotive services, nec
Lynn Gmelin

D-U-N-S 20-051-9189   (SL)
BLOUNT CANADA LTD
(*Suby of* AMERICAN SECURITIES LLC)
505 Edinburgh Rd N, Guelph, ON, N1H 6L4
(519) 822-6870
Emp Here 700   *Sales* 196,613,900
SIC 3568 Power transmission equipment, nec
Josh Collins
Nick Galouich

D-U-N-S 20-605-3332   (HQ)
BLOUNT HOLDINGS LTD
(*Suby of* AMERICAN SECURITIES LLC)
505 Edinburgh Rd N, Guelph, ON, N1H 6L4
(519) 822-6870
Emp Here 3   *Sales* 194,584,800
SIC 3425 Saw blades and handsaws
Josh Collins

D-U-N-S 20-847-3546   (SL)
BOOKSHELF OF GUELPH LIMITED
41 Quebec St, Guelph, ON, N1H 2T1
(519) 821-3311
Emp Here 70   *Sales* 17,102,960
SIC 5942 Book stores
Douglas Minett
Barbara Minett

D-U-N-S 24-513-5017   (SL)
C.J.W. PHARMACY INCORPORATED
SHOPPERS DRUG MART
104 Silvercreek Pky N, Guelph, ON, N1H 7B4
(519) 821-5080
Emp Here 50   *Sales* 12,647,700
SIC 5912 Drug stores and proprietary stores
Charles Wambeke

D-U-N-S 20-852-7507   (HQ)
**CO-OPERATORS GENERAL INSURANCE
COMPANY**
130 Macdonell St, Guelph, ON, N1H 2Z6
(519) 824-4400
Emp Here 500   *Sales* 2,007,265,873
SIC 6411 Insurance agents, brokers, and ser-
vice
Rob Wesseling
Alec Blundell
Kevin Daniel
Emmie Fukuchi
Lisa Guglietti
Paul Hanna
Steve Phillips

Carol Poulsen
Karen Higgins
John Harvie

D-U-N-S 20-784-7880   (HQ)
CO-OPERATORS GROUP LIMITED, THE
CO-OPERATORS, THE
130 Macdonell St, Guelph, ON, N1H 2Z6
(519) 824-4400
Emp Here 500   *Sales* 9,759,532,856
SIC 6331 Fire, marine, and casualty insurance
Kathy Bardswick
John Harvie
Kevin Daniel
Rick Mccombie
Carol Poulsen
Rob Wesseling
P. Bruce West

D-U-N-S 24-610-3360   (HQ)
**COMMUNITY LIVING GUELPH WELLING-
TON**
VOCATION SERVICES
8 Royal Rd, Guelph, ON, N1H 1G3
(519) 824-2480
Emp Here 135   *Sales* 54,264,000
SIC 8299 Schools and educational services,
nec
Robert Butella
Bernie Mitchell
Kim Uhrig
Malcolm Mackenzie

D-U-N-S 24-704-8796   (BR)
**COMMUNITY LIVING GUELPH WELLING-
TON**
ARC INDUSTRIES
(*Suby of* COMMUNITY LIVING GUELPH
WELLINGTON)
8 Royal Rd, Guelph, ON, N1H 1G3
(519) 824-2480
Emp Here 120
SIC 8322 Individual and family services
Clark Chris

D-U-N-S 20-051-5997   (SL)
COX CONSTRUCTION LIMITED
965 York Rd, Guelph, ON, N1H 6K5
(519) 824-6570
Emp Here 50   *Sales* 14,176,200
SIC 1611 Highway and street construction
Russel Cox
Regan Cox

D-U-N-S 24-336-9576   (HQ)
DANBY PRODUCTS LIMITED
DANBY
(*Suby of* COLDPOINT HOLDINGS LIMITED)
5070 Whitelaw Rd, Guelph, ON, N1H 6Z9
(519) 837-0920
Emp Here 50   *Sales* 78,333,345
SIC 5064 Electrical appliances, television and
radio
James Estill
Andrew Raymond

D-U-N-S 20-784-7153   (SL)
EDEN HOUSE CARE FACILITY INC
5016 Wellington Road 29, Guelph, ON, N1H
6H8
(519) 856-4622
Emp Here 78   *Sales* 5,361,174
SIC 8051 Skilled nursing care facilities
John Bouwmeester
Gail Bouwmeester

D-U-N-S 24-334-4061   (SL)
ETSM TECHNICAL SERVICES LTD
407 Silvercreek Pky N, Guelph, ON, N1H 8G8
(519) 827-1500
Emp Here 52   *Sales* 11,544,052
SIC 3599 Industrial machinery, nec
Kenneth Lennox
Karolyn Lennox
Christine Hayden

D-U-N-S 20-691-9537   (SL)

FILSINGER, W. & SONS LIMITED
RONA CASHWAY BUILDING CENTRE
55 Dawson Rd Suite 1, Guelph, ON, N1H 1B1
(519) 821-5744
Emp Here 55   *Sales* 13,942,266
SIC 5211 Lumber and other building materials
 Wayne Filsinger
 Brian Salo

    D-U-N-S 24-925-4558   (SL)
FLOCHEM LTD
6986 Wellington Road 124, Guelph, ON, N1H 6J4
(519) 763-5441
Emp Here 40   *Sales* 29,213,800
SIC 5169 Chemicals and allied products, nec
 Terrence Tucker

    D-U-N-S 24-951-9398   (HQ)
FLOWSERVE CANADA CORP
FLOWSERVE PUMP, DIV OF
(*Suby of* FLOWSERVE CORPORATION)
225 Speedvale Ave W, Guelph, ON, N1H 1C5
(519) 824-4600
Emp Here 124   *Sales* 105,890,629
SIC 3561 Pumps and pumping equipment
 Lewis M Kling
 Matthew Irwin

    D-U-N-S 20-595-8812   (HQ)
GAMSBY AND MANNEROW LIMITED
255 Woodlawn Rd W Suite 210, Guelph, ON, N1H 8J1
(519) 824-8150
Emp Here 45   *Sales* 11,437,270
SIC 8711 Engineering services
 Dave Heicknell

    D-U-N-S 20-771-2928   (BR)
GAY LEA FOODS CO-OPERATIVE LIMITED
GAY LEA FOODS
(*Suby of* GAY LEA FOODS CO-OPERATIVE LIMITED)
21 Speedvale Ave W, Guelph, ON, N1H 1J5
(519) 822-5530
Emp Here 75
SIC 2021 Creamery butter
 Deanne Reilly

    D-U-N-S 25-626-6750   (BR)
GRANDI COMPANY LIMITED
MCDONALD'S RESTAURANT
(*Suby of* GRANDI COMPANY LIMITED)
243 Woodlawn Rd S, Guelph, ON, N1H 8J1
(519) 826-0507
Emp Here 85
SIC 5812 Eating places
 Nelissa Wilson

    D-U-N-S 20-732-8092   (SL)
GUELPH COMMUNITY HEALTH CENTRE
176 Wyndham St N Suite 1, Guelph, ON, N1H 8N9
(519) 821-6638
Emp Here 106   *Sales* 24,815,766
SIC 8621 Professional organizations
 Bruce Ryan
 Stacey Armstrong
 Jim Bonk
 Jennifer Maddock
 Michael Nightingale
 Marg Hedley
 Charles Davidson
 Mitra Salarvand
 Joan Todd
 Sylvain Painchaud

    D-U-N-S 20-051-7894   (HQ)
GUELPH MANUFACTURING GROUP INC
39 Royal Rd, Guelph, ON, N1H 1G2
(519) 822-5401
Emp Here 200   *Sales* 218,907,900
SIC 3465 Automotive stampings
 Robert Ireland

    D-U-N-S 20-005-7284   (BR)
GUELPH MANUFACTURING GROUP INC
(*Suby of* GUELPH MANUFACTURING

GROUP INC)
20 Massey Rd, Guelph, ON, N1H 7X8
(519) 822-5401
Emp Here 150
SIC 3465 Automotive stampings
 Mike Huisman

    D-U-N-S 24-121-4183   (SL)
GUELPH PROFESSIONAL FIRE FIGHTERS ASSOCIATION
50 Wyndham St S, Guelph, ON, N1H 4E1

Emp Here 133   *Sales* 88,964,764
SIC 7389 Business services, nec
 Collen Hunter

    D-U-N-S 24-336-5306   (BR)
GUELPH, CITY OF
COMMUNITY SERVICES
(*Suby of* GUELPH, CITY OF)
19 Northumberland St, Guelph, ON, N1H 3A6
(519) 837-5618
Emp Here 200
SIC 8611 Business associations
 Rob Mackay

    D-U-N-S 24-060-2144   (BR)
GUELPH, CITY OF
GUELPH PUBLIC LIBRARY
(*Suby of* GUELPH, CITY OF)
100 Norfolk St, Guelph, ON, N1H 4J6
(519) 824-6220
Emp Here 80
SIC 8231 Libraries
 Norman Mcleod

    D-U-N-S 24-336-1321   (BR)
GUELPH, CITY OF
GUELPH FIRE DEPARTMENT
(*Suby of* GUELPH, CITY OF)
50 Wyndham St S, Guelph, ON, N1H 4E1
(519) 824-6590
Emp Here 149
SIC 7389 Business services, nec
 Shawn Armstrong

    D-U-N-S 24-693-7437   (SL)
H.L.O. HEALTH SERVICES INC
341 Woolwich St, Guelph, ON, N1H 3W4
(519) 823-2784
Emp Here 120   *Sales* 19,277,520
SIC 8011 Offices and clinics of medical doctors
 Helen Oates
 F Lauren Henry

    D-U-N-S 25-525-9681   (HQ)
HALTON INVESTMENTS INC
PROJOY SPORTSWEAR (DIV)
(*Suby of* EDGEHILL PROPERTIES LIMITED)
166 Woolwich St, Guelph, ON, N1H 3V3
(519) 763-8024
Emp Here 1   *Sales* 10,723,673
SIC 6719 Holding companies, nec
 Randee Whites
 David Hastings

    D-U-N-S 20-051-7514   (HQ)
HAMMOND MANUFACTURING COMPANY LIMITED
394 Edinburgh Rd N, Guelph, ON, N1H 1E5
(519) 822-2960
Emp Here 300   *Sales* 110,381,167
SIC 3469 Metal stampings, nec
 Robert Hammond
 Ray Shatzel
 Ross N Hammond
 Alexander Stirling
 Edward Sehl
 Paul Quigley
 Sheila Hammond
 Michael Fricker
 William Wiener
 Sarah Hansen

    D-U-N-S 24-211-6143   (HQ)
HI-TECH GEARS CANADA INC, THE

(*Suby of* THE HI-TECH GEARS LIMITED)
361 Speedvale Ave W Suite 29, Guelph, ON, N1H 1C7
(519) 836-3180
Emp Here 120   *Sales* 33,432,630
SIC 3499 Fabricated Metal products, nec
 Deep Kapuria
 Pranav Kapuria
 Nirav Joshi

    D-U-N-S 24-125-2535   (SL)
HITACHI CONSTRUCTION TRUCK MANUFACTURING LTD
(*Suby of* HITACHI, LTD.)
200 Woodlawn Rd W, Guelph, ON, N1H 1B6
(519) 823-2000
Emp Here 320   *Sales* 89,880,640
SIC 3532 Mining machinery
 Bruce Murray
 Mounir Marcus
 Nobuhiko Kuwahara

    D-U-N-S 24-000-2969   (BR)
HOME DEPOT OF CANADA INC
(*Suby of* THE HOME DEPOT INC)
63 Woodlawn Rd W, Guelph, ON, N1H 1G8
(519) 780-3400
Emp Here 150
SIC 5251 Hardware stores
 Jake Mccarthy

    D-U-N-S 24-057-6553   (BR)
IMPERIAL TOBACCO COMPAGNIE LIMITEE
(*Suby of* IMPERIAL TOBACCO CANADA LIMITEE)
107 Woodlawn Rd W, Guelph, ON, N1H 1B4

Emp Here 600
SIC 2111 Cigarettes
 Patrick Hodgins

    D-U-N-S 20-107-4031   (SL)
INBOX MARKETER CORPORATION
(*Suby of* SUNNYHOLME INC)
2 Wyndham St N, Guelph, ON, N1H 4E3
(519) 824-6664
Emp Here 80   *Sales* 7,980,210
SIC 4899 Communication services, nec
 Geoffrey Linton
 Colleen Preisner
 Kelly Cleghorn
 Peter Sieunarine
 Kim Mcdonald
 Philip Thomson
 Matthew Anstett

    D-U-N-S 25-953-1887   (SL)
J. D. MASONRY
5954 Wellington Road 7, Guelph, ON, N1H 6J2
(519) 836-4311
Emp Here 70   *Sales* 11,366,670
SIC 1741 Masonry and other stonework
 Dave Gorgi
 Carol Gorgi

    D-U-N-S 24-632-1491   (SL)
J.L. BELISLE BUILDING MATERIALS LTD
389 Speedvale Ave W, Guelph, ON, N1H 1C7
(519) 822-8230
Emp Here 50   *Sales* 12,652,950
SIC 5211 Lumber and other building materials
 Jl Belisle
 Andre Belisle

    D-U-N-S 20-414-8084   (SL)
KORZITE COATINGS INC
7134 Wellington Rd W, Guelph, ON, N1H 6J3
(519) 821-1250
Emp Here 40   *Sales* 11,066,400
SIC 2851 Paints and allied products
 Stephen Cooke
 Lloyd Lum

    D-U-N-S 20-109-5747   (BR)
LINAMAR CORPORATION

TRAXLE MANUFACTURING
(*Suby of* LINAMAR CORPORATION)
280 Speedvale Ave W, Guelph, ON, N1H 1C4
(519) 824-8899
Emp Here 228
SIC 3714 Motor vehicle parts and accessories
 John Graham

    D-U-N-S 25-306-1931   (BR)
LINAMAR CORPORATION
VEHCOM MANUFACTURING
(*Suby of* LINAMAR CORPORATION)
74 Campbell Rd, Guelph, ON, N1H 1C1
(519) 821-1650
Emp Here 482
SIC 3714 Motor vehicle parts and accessories
 Thomas Horvat

    D-U-N-S 20-983-1544   (HQ)
LINAMAR CORPORATION
ESTON MANUFACTURING, DIV OF
287 Speedvale Ave W, Guelph, ON, N1H 1C5
(519) 836-7550
Emp Here 11,736   *Sales* 5,777,178,455
SIC 3714 Motor vehicle parts and accessories
 Linda Hasenfratz
 Jim Jarrell
 Roger Fulton
 Mark Stoddart
 Dale Schneider
 Frank Hasenfratz
 Terry Reidel
 William Harrison
 Dennis Grimm

    D-U-N-S 25-105-7402   (BR)
LINAMAR CORPORATION
COMTECH MANUFACTURING
(*Suby of* LINAMAR CORPORATION)
355 Silvercreek Pky N, Guelph, ON, N1H 1E6
(519) 821-7576
Emp Here 230
SIC 3714 Motor vehicle parts and accessories
 Zlatko Cado

    D-U-N-S 25-116-2343   (BR)
LINAMAR CORPORATION
ESTON MANUFACTURING
(*Suby of* LINAMAR CORPORATION)
277 Silvercreek Pky N, Guelph, ON, N1H 1E6
(519) 763-0063
Emp Here 200
SIC 3714 Motor vehicle parts and accessories
 Sean Congdon

    D-U-N-S 24-494-3838   (BR)
LINAMAR CORPORATION
LPP MANUFACTURING
(*Suby of* LINAMAR CORPORATION)
347 Silvercreek Pky N, Guelph, ON, N1H 1E6
(519) 837-3055
Emp Here 100
SIC 3714 Motor vehicle parts and accessories
 David Buehlow

    D-U-N-S 20-553-4667   (SL)
LINAMAR HOLDINGS INC.
INVAR MANUFACTURING DIV
(*Suby of* LINAMAR CORPORATION)
287 Speedvale Ave W, Guelph, ON, N1H 1C5
(519) 836-7550
Emp Here 1,800   *Sales* 523,530,000
SIC 3714 Motor vehicle parts and accessories
 Linda Hasenfratz
 Jim Jarrell
 Mark Stoddard
 Michael Annable
 Roger Fulton
 Frank Hasenfratz

    D-U-N-S 24-356-1425   (SL)
LINERGY MANUFACTURING INC
(*Suby of* LINAMAR CORPORATION)
87 Campbell Rd, Guelph, ON, N1H 1B9
(519) 341-5996
Emp Here 250   *Sales* 70,219,250
SIC 3569 General industrial machinery, nec

Francis Gobbi

D-U-N-S 24-098-9673   (SL)
MADDOCKS ENGINEERING LTD
84 Royal Rd, Guelph, ON, N1H 1G3
(519) 823-1092
Emp Here 55   *Sales* 12,311,365
SIC 3714 Motor vehicle parts and accessories
Gerald Maddocks

D-U-N-S 20-279-6710   (SL)
MAMMOET CRANE (ASSETS) INC
7504 Mclean Rd E, Guelph, ON, N1H 6H9
(519) 740-0550
Emp Here 100
SIC 3537 Industrial trucks and tractors

D-U-N-S 25-526-6959   (SL)
MEADOWVILLE GARDEN CENTRE INC
7767 Wellington Road 124, Guelph, ON, N1H 6H7
(519) 822-0840
Emp Here 40   *Sales* 13,698,680
SIC 0181 Ornamental nursery products
Joanne Saliba
Joseph Saliba

D-U-N-S 25-131-5529   (SL)
MELITRON CORPORATION
(*Suby of* 2051611 ONTARIO INC)
404 Silvercreek Pkwy N, Guelph, ON, N1H 1E8
(519) 763-6660
Emp Here 160   *Sales* 30,733,600
SIC 3499 Fabricated Metal products, nec
Michael Turner

D-U-N-S 20-051-9064   (SL)
NATIONAL-STANDARD COMPANY OF CANADA, LTD
20 Campbell Rd, Guelph, ON, N1H 1C1

Emp Here 95   *Sales* 14,392,714
SIC 3496 Miscellaneous fabricated wire products

D-U-N-S 25-193-7363   (SL)
NEWTON GROUP LTD
41 Massey Rd, Guelph, ON, N1H 7M6
(519) 822-5281
Emp Here 35   *Sales* 14,795,795
SIC 1541 Industrial buildings and warehouses
Edwin Newton

D-U-N-S 24-917-8450   (SL)
ONTARIO SCHOOL BOARDS' INSURANCE EXCHANGE
OSBIE
91 Westmount Rd, Guelph, ON, N1H 5J2
(519) 767-2182
Emp Here 21   *Sales* 37,330,801
SIC 6411 Insurance agents, brokers, and service
Jim H. Sami
Fran Fournier
Cathy Modesto
Bob Kaye
Peter Derochie
Chris Howarth
Jim Mckenzie
Lynn Schaule
Michael Carson
Brian Oburn

D-U-N-S 24-346-6278   (SL)
ORION FOUNDRY (CANADA), ULC
MOXY MEDIA
503 Imperial Rd N, Guelph, ON, N1H 6T9
(519) 827-1999
Emp Here 70   *Sales* 12,411,770
SIC 7374 Data processing and preparation
Ted Hastings
Brandon Nussey
Miles Arnone
Greg Pogue

D-U-N-S 24-394-5800   (SL)
PMD RETAIL SALES INC

CANADIAN TIRE
10 Woodlawn Rd E Suite 260, Guelph, ON, N1H 1G7
(519) 821-2244
Emp Here 49   *Sales* 24,405,822
SIC 5531 Auto and home supply stores
Peter Davies

D-U-N-S 24-793-7063   (HQ)
PURESOURCE INC
GENESIS FOODS
(*Suby of* NOW HEALTH GROUP, INC.)
5068 Whitelaw Rd Unit 5, Guelph, ON, N1H 6J3
(519) 837-2140
Emp Here 100   *Sales* 107,507,400
SIC 5149 Groceries and related products, nec
Mark Chilvers
Albert Powers
Sharon Wong

D-U-N-S 24-153-8532   (SL)
QUALITY SERVICES INC
497 Woolwich St Unit 2, Guelph, ON, N1H 3X9
(519) 827-1147
Emp Here 64   *Sales* 14,994,432
SIC 8742 Management consulting services
Jeffrey Fisher

D-U-N-S 24-062-1862   (HQ)
RLB LLP
15 Lewis Rd Suite 1, Guelph, ON, N1H 1E9
(519) 822-9933
Emp Here 43   *Sales* 11,422,675
SIC 8721 Accounting, auditing, and bookkeeping
Dave Mcellistrum
Alan Riddell

D-U-N-S 24-336-4424   (HQ)
SANIMAX LTD
(*Suby of* JO-AL DISTRIBUTING LTD)
5068 Whitelaw Rd Suite 6, Guelph, ON, N1H 6J3
(519) 824-2381
Emp Here 56   *Sales* 20,729,150
SIC 4953 Refuse systems
Martin Couture

D-U-N-S 24-346-5379   (BR)
SCHLEGEL VILLAGES INC
THE VILLAGE OF RIVERSIDE GLEN
60 Woodlawn Rd E, Guelph, ON, N1H 8M8
(519) 822-5272
Emp Here 130
SIC 6513 Apartment building operators
Paul Brown

D-U-N-S 24-587-7949   (HQ)
SKYJACK INC
LINAMAR CONSUMER PRODUCTS
(*Suby of* LINAMAR CORPORATION)
55 Campbell Rd Suite 1, Guelph, ON, N1H 1B9
(519) 837-0888
Emp Here 50   *Sales* 252,789,300
SIC 3531 Construction machinery
Linda Hasenfratz
Brad Boehler
David Stewart
Frank Hasenfratz
James Jarrell

D-U-N-S 24-468-0398   (BR)
SKYJACK INC
PLANT 1
(*Suby of* LINAMAR CORPORATION)
55 Campbell Rd, Guelph, ON, N1H 1B9
(519) 837-0888
Emp Here 100
SIC 3531 Construction machinery
James Hacking

D-U-N-S 20-699-6238   (SL)
SNOWBEAR LIMITED
SNOWBEAR TRAILERS
155 Dawson Rd, Guelph, ON, N1H 1A4

Emp Here 80   *Sales* 17,760,080
SIC 3523 Farm machinery and equipment
Andre Sa Machado
Tim French
George So
Newton Glassman

D-U-N-S 24-429-6778   (BR)
SOCIETE XYLEM CANADA
XYLEM APPLIED WATER SYSTEMS
(*Suby of* SOCIETE XYLEM CANADA)
55 Royal Rd, Guelph, ON, N1H 1T1
(519) 821-1900
Emp Here 90
SIC 5084 Industrial machinery and equipment
Jason Lake

D-U-N-S 24-508-4678   (SL)
SODROX CHEMICALS LTD
7040 Wellington Road 124, Guelph, ON, N1H 6J3
(519) 837-2330
Emp Here 32   *Sales* 23,371,040
SIC 5169 Chemicals and allied products, nec
H Thomas Jarvis
David Ballantyne
Bart Jarvis

D-U-N-S 20-523-4136   (SL)
ST JOSEPH'S HEALTH CENTRE (GUELPH)
100 Westmount Rd, Guelph, ON, N1H 5H8
(519) 824-6000
Emp Here 500   *Sales* 34,163,000
SIC 8051 Skilled nursing care facilities
David Wormald

D-U-N-S 20-371-6311   (HQ)
SUNNYHOLME INC
2 Wyndham St N, Guelph, ON, N1H 4E3
(519) 824-6664
Sales 21,868,000
SIC 6712 Bank holding companies
Geoffrey Linton

D-U-N-S 24-344-0760   (BR)
SUPERIOR PLUS LP
SUPERIOR PROPANE
(*Suby of* SUPERIOR PLUS CORP)
7022 Wellington Rd, Guelph, ON, N1H 6H8
(807) 223-2980
Emp Here 170
SIC 5984 Liquefied petroleum gas dealers
Ronald Shoemaker

D-U-N-S 24-318-6736   (BR)
SYNNEX CANADA LIMITED
EMJ DATA SYSTEMS DIV OF
(*Suby of* SYNNEX CORPORATION)
107 Woodlawn Rd W, Guelph, ON, N1H 1B4
(519) 837-2444
Emp Here 140
SIC 5045 Computers, peripherals, and software
Mark Tanner

D-U-N-S 24-078-5378   (HQ)
TC INDUSTRIES OF CANADA COMPANY
249 Speedvale Ave W, Guelph, ON, N1H 1C5
(519) 836-7100
Sales 33,424,363
SIC 3531 Construction machinery
Thomas Hayward
George Berry Iv
Bill Mitchell
Jeff Quarrie
Robert F Berry
John C Nelson
Kathleen M Martinez
Frank O Brewster
David I Wakely

D-U-N-S 24-210-1496   (SL)
TIM HORTONS LTD
1 Nicholas Beaver Rd, Guelph, ON, N1H 6H9
(519) 822-4748
Emp Here 50   *Sales* 13,707,600
SIC 5461 Retail bakeries

Sandy Lane

D-U-N-S 24-773-7906   (SL)
TRANSIT PETROLEUM
516 Imperial Rd N, Guelph, ON, N1H 1G4
(519) 571-1220
Emp Here 40   *Sales* 50,288,040
SIC 5172 Petroleum products, nec
Trevor Chambers

D-U-N-S 25-997-4723   (SL)
TRANSPORT N SERVICE INC
5075 Whitelaw Rd, Guelph, ON, N1H 6J4
(519) 821-0400
Emp Here 80   *Sales* 11,855,360
SIC 4213 Trucking, except local
Earl Allen
Trina Allen
Kevin Allen

D-U-N-S 24-919-4952   (HQ)
UPI INC
UPI ENERGY
105 Silvercreek Pky N Suite 200, Guelph, ON, N1H 8M1
(519) 821-2667
Sales 100,684,800
SIC 5541 Gasoline service stations
Robert P Sicard
Robert Mcintosh
Robert Peden
Don Petrella

D-U-N-S 20-025-4139   (BR)
UPPER GRAND DISTRICT SCHOOL BOARD, THE
GUELPH COLLEGIATE & VOCATIONAL INSTITUTE
(*Suby of* UPPER GRAND DISTRICT SCHOOL BOARD, THE)
155 Paisley St Suite Upper, Guelph, ON, N1H 2P3
(519) 824-9800
Emp Here 100
SIC 8211 Elementary and secondary schools
Julie Prendergast

D-U-N-S 24-539-8193   (SL)
VANTAGE REALTY LTD
ROYAL LEPAGE VANTAGE REALTY
214 Speedvale Ave W Suite 1, Guelph, ON, N1H 1C4
(519) 822-7842
Emp Here 60   *Sales* 16,305,360
SIC 6531 Real estate agents and managers
Robert Atkinson

D-U-N-S 24-329-8515   (BR)
WAL-MART CANADA CORP
(*Suby of* WALMART INC.)
11 Woodlawn Rd W, Guelph, ON, N1H 1G8
(519) 767-1600
Emp Here 200
SIC 5311 Department stores
Ted Wynhoffen

D-U-N-S 20-052-0856   (HQ)
WALINGA INC
ULTRAVAC
5656 Highway 6, Guelph, ON, N1H 6J2
(519) 824-8520
Emp Here 180   *Sales* 45,059,880
SIC 3713 Truck and bus bodies
Cor Lodder
Cornilius Medemblik
Terrance Medemblik
Clarence Wvaing
John Medemblik
Paul Broekema
Theo Flach

D-U-N-S 24-343-2692   (BR)
WATERLOO WELLINGTON LOCAL HEALTH INTEGRATION NETWORK
WATERLOO WELLINGTON CCAC
(*Suby of* WATERLOO WELLINGTON LOCAL HEALTH INTEGRATION NETWORK)
450 Speedvale Ave W Suite 201, Guelph, ON.

▲ Public Company   ■ Public Company Family Member   **HQ** Headquarters   **BR** Branch   **SL** Single Location

N1H 7G7
(519) 823-2550
Emp Here 150
SIC 8082 Home health care services
Ross Kirkconnell

D-U-N-S 20-024-9519   (BR)
**WELLINGTON CATHOLIC DISTRICT
SCHOOL BOARD**
*OUR LADY OF LOURDES CATHOLIC HIGH
SCHOOL*
54 Westmount Rd, Guelph, ON, N1H 5H7
(519) 836-2170
Emp Here 75
SIC 8211 Elementary and secondary schools
John Candiotto

D-U-N-S 24-306-4391   (BR)
WESTROCK COMPANY OF CANADA CORP
(*Suby of* WESTROCK COMPANY)
390 Woodlawn Rd W, Guelph, ON, N1H 7K3
(519) 821-4930
Emp Here 350
SIC 2653 Corrugated and solid fiber boxes
Carolyn Mcdermott

D-U-N-S 24-488-5570   (SL)
WOODRILL LTD
7861 7 Hwy, Guelph, ON, N1H 6H8
(519) 821-1018
Emp Here 20   *Sales* 24,207,940
SIC 5153 Grain and field beans
Peter Hannam
Jim Timmings

Guelph, ON N1K

D-U-N-S 24-625-8602   (SL)
699215 ONTARIO LIMITED
GUELPH CITY MAZDA
949 Woodlawn Rd W, Guelph, ON, N1K 1C9
(519) 837-3020
Emp Here 23   *Sales* 14,473,440
SIC 5511 New and used car dealers
Frank Spencer

D-U-N-S 24-817-0847   (SL)
798826 ONTARIO INC
TRI-CITY HAULAGE
91 Monarch Rd, Guelph, ON, N1K 1S4
(519) 767-9628
Emp Here 50   *Sales* 14,176,200
SIC 1611 Highway and street construction
Rosemary Armishaw
Jeff Armishaw

D-U-N-S 24-008-9110   (SL)
ACCUFLEX INDUSTRIAL HOSE LTD
(*Suby of* KURIYAMA HOLDINGS CORPORA-
TION)
760 Imperial Rd N, Guelph, ON, N1K 1Z3
(519) 836-5460
Emp Here 65   *Sales* 10,325,770
SIC 3052 Rubber and plastics hose and belt-
ings
Donna Thompson
Greg Eston
Tony Jameson

D-U-N-S 25-672-1044   (SL)
ALLIANCE ROOFING & SHEET METAL LTD
25 Cope Crt, Guelph, ON, N1K 0A4
(519) 763-1442
Emp Here 65   *Sales* 14,158,885
SIC 1761 Roofing, siding, and sheetMetal
work
Glenn Schwantz

D-U-N-S 20-281-5379   (SL)
AWC MANUFACTURING LP
(*Suby of* HIDDEN HARBOR CAPITAL PART-
NERS, LLC)
163 Curtis Dr, Guelph, ON, N1K 1S9
(519) 822-0577
Emp Here 80   *Sales* 15,366,800

SIC 3499 Fabricated Metal products, nec
Michael Hayton
Sharon Baines

D-U-N-S 20-774-5415   (SL)
BREWIS, CHARLES LIMITED
OLYMPIC HONDA
995 Woodlawn Rd W, Guelph, ON, N1K 1C9
(519) 836-0645
Emp Here 30   *Sales* 14,942,340
SIC 5511 New and used car dealers
Charles Brewis
David Brewis

D-U-N-S 20-786-4831   (SL)
BUSINESS IMPROVEMENT GROUP INC
400 Michener Rd Suite 3, Guelph, ON, N1K
1E4
(519) 823-1110
Emp Here 50   *Sales* 10,619,850
SIC 8748 Business consulting, nec
Mark Curtis

D-U-N-S 20-058-7264   (HQ)
CANADIAN SOLAR INC
SOLAR MODULE MANUFACTURING
545 Speedvale Ave W, Guelph, ON, N1K 1E6
(519) 837-1881
Emp Here 10   *Sales* 3,744,512,000
SIC 3312 Blast furnaces and steel mills
Shawn Qu
Huifeng Chang
Arthur Chien
Guoqiang Xing
Guangchun Zhang
Jianyi Zhang
Yan Zhuang
Lars-Eric Johansson
Robert Mcdermott
Harry E. Ruda

D-U-N-S 24-047-2498   (SL)
CGL MANUFACTURING INC
151 Arrow Rd, Guelph, ON, N1K 1S8
(519) 836-0322
Emp Here 175   *Sales* 38,850,175
SIC 3599 Industrial machinery, nec
Michael Ritchie

D-U-N-S 20-536-1215   (SL)
**CULLEN, BARRY CHEVROLET CADILLAC
LTD**
905 Woodlawn Rd W, Guelph, ON, N1K 1B7
(519) 824-0210
Emp Here 70   *Sales* 44,049,600
SIC 5511 New and used car dealers
Barry Cullen

D-U-N-S 20-174-7446   (SL)
ENERGY SOURCE CANADA INC
ENERGY SOURCE NATURAL GAS
415 Michener Rd, Guelph, ON, N1K 1E8
(519) 826-0777
Emp Here 7   *Sales* 21,740,999
SIC 4924 Natural gas distribution
Dave Cornies

D-U-N-S 24-390-4179   (SL)
ENERGY SOURCE NATURAL GAS INC
415 Michener Rd Unit 1, Guelph, ON, N1K
1E8
(519) 826-0777
Emp Here 10   *Sales* 31,058,570
SIC 4924 Natural gas distribution
David Cornies

D-U-N-S 20-256-7350   (SL)
GHP GROUP ULC
(*Suby of* GHP GROUP, INC.)
271 Massey Rd, Guelph, ON, N1K 1B2
(519) 837-9724
Emp Here 35   *Sales* 15,651,090
SIC 5074 Plumbing and heating equipment
and supplies (hydronics)
Gus Haramaras
Steve Haramaras
Rasik Patel

Ronald Calvert

D-U-N-S 24-141-2329   (SL)
GUELPH NISSAN INFINITI INC
805 Woodlawn Rd W, Guelph, ON, N1K 1E9
(519) 822-9200
Emp Here 40   *Sales* 25,171,200
SIC 5511 New and used car dealers
Goen Yates

D-U-N-S 20-051-4693   (HQ)
HAYTON GROUP INC
163 Curtis Dr, Guelph, ON, N1K 1S9
(519) 822-0577
Emp Here 95   *Sales* 23,050,200
SIC 3499 Fabricated Metal products, nec
Michael Hayton
Sharon Baines

D-U-N-S 24-386-8374   (BR)
JOHNSON & JOHNSON INC
*MCNEIL CONSUMER HEALTH CARE DIV
OF*
(*Suby of* JOHNSON & JOHNSON)
890 Woodlawn Rd W, Guelph, ON, N1K 1A5
(519) 826-6226
Emp Here 300
SIC 2834 Pharmaceutical preparations
Chris Lebrun

D-U-N-S 24-077-2764   (BR)
JOHNSON & JOHNSON INC
MCNEIL CONSUMER HEALTHCARE
890 Woodlawn Rd W, Guelph, ON, N1K 1A5

Emp Here 370
SIC 2834 Pharmaceutical preparations

D-U-N-S 25-595-5999   (BR)
JONES PACKAGING INC
(*Suby of* JONES PACKAGING INC)
271 Massey Rd, Guelph, ON, N1K 1B2

Emp Here 100
SIC 2657 Folding paperboard boxes
James Lee

D-U-N-S 20-176-3070   (BR)
LINAMAR CORPORATION
CAMTAC MANUFACTURING
(*Suby of* LINAMAR CORPORATION)
148 Arrow Rd, Guelph, ON, N1K 1T4
(519) 780-2270
Emp Here 425
SIC 3714 Motor vehicle parts and accessories
Andy Scapinello

D-U-N-S 25-362-6592   (BR)
LINAMAR CORPORATION
HASTECH MANUFACTURING
(*Suby of* LINAMAR CORPORATION)
301 Massey Rd, Guelph, ON, N1K 1B2
(519) 767-9711
Emp Here 275
SIC 3714 Motor vehicle parts and accessories
Frank Carpino

D-U-N-S 24-341-0565   (BR)
LINAMAR CORPORATION
CEMTOL MANUFACTURING
(*Suby of* LINAMAR CORPORATION)
150 Arrow Rd, Guelph, ON, N1K 1T4
(519) 822-6627
Emp Here 250
SIC 3714 Motor vehicle parts and accessories
Waheed Osman

D-U-N-S 25-192-2977   (BR)
LINAMAR CORPORATION
ROCTEL MANUFACTURING
(*Suby of* LINAMAR CORPORATION)
415 Elmira Rd N, Guelph, ON, N1K 1H3
(519) 763-5369
Emp Here 250
SIC 3714 Motor vehicle parts and accessories
Steve Norris

D-U-N-S 24-000-6077   (BR)

LINAMAR CORPORATION
LINAMAR GEAR
(*Suby of* LINAMAR CORPORATION)
32 Independence Pl, Guelph, ON, N1K 1H8
(519) 827-9423
Emp Here 80
SIC 3714 Motor vehicle parts and accessories
Ray Iravani

D-U-N-S 25-687-4405   (BR)
LINAMAR CORPORATION
LINAMAR PERFORMANCE CENTRE
(*Suby of* LINAMAR CORPORATION)
30 Minto Rd, Guelph, ON, N1K 1H5
(519) 821-1429
Emp Here 400
SIC 3714 Motor vehicle parts and accessories
Scott Bradshaw

D-U-N-S 24-926-6941   (BR)
LINAMAR CORPORATION
AUTOCOM MANUFACTURING
(*Suby of* LINAMAR CORPORATION)
375 Massey Rd, Guelph, ON, N1K 1B2
(519) 822-9008
Emp Here 380
SIC 3714 Motor vehicle parts and accessories
Helen Robson

D-U-N-S 24-858-3648   (BR)
LINAMAR CORPORATION
HASTECH MFG. PLANT 2
(*Suby of* LINAMAR CORPORATION)
381 Massey Rd, Guelph, ON, N1K 1B2
(519) 767-9711
Emp Here 100
SIC 3714 Motor vehicle parts and accessories
Nandor Novak

D-U-N-S 25-542-4285   (BR)
LINAMAR CORPORATION
CORVEX MANUFACTURING
(*Suby of* LINAMAR CORPORATION)
12 Independence Pl, Guelph, ON, N1K 1H8
(519) 827-9423
Emp Here 250
SIC 3714 Motor vehicle parts and accessories
David Deneski

D-U-N-S 24-844-0059   (BR)
LINAMAR CORPORATION
QUADRAD MANUFACTURING
(*Suby of* LINAMAR CORPORATION)
30 Malcolm Rd, Guelph, ON, N1K 1A9
(519) 767-0219
Emp Here 400
SIC 3714 Motor vehicle parts and accessories
Ray Iravani

D-U-N-S 20-104-0677   (BR)
LINAMAR CORPORATION
SPINIC MANUFACTURING
(*Suby of* LINAMAR CORPORATION)
285 Massey Rd, Guelph, ON, N1K 1B2
(519) 763-0704
Emp Here 170
SIC 3714 Motor vehicle parts and accessories
Fred Brunnmeier

D-U-N-S 20-109-5663   (BR)
LINAMAR CORPORATION
LINEX MANUFACTURING
(*Suby of* LINAMAR CORPORATION)
355 Massey Rd, Guelph, ON, N1K 1B2
(519) 837-0880
Emp Here 490
SIC 3714 Motor vehicle parts and accessories
Tim Feil

D-U-N-S 25-354-9091   (SL)
LINAMAR TRANSPORTATION INC
(*Suby of* LINAMAR CORPORATION)
32 Independence Pl, Guelph, ON, N1K 1H8
(519) 837-2056
Emp Here 160   *Sales* 32,912,960
SIC 4213 Trucking, except local
Linda Hasenfratz

▲ Public Company   ■ Public Company Family Member   **HQ** Headquarters   **BR** Branch   **SL** Single Location

Jim Garrell
Frank Hasenfratz

D-U-N-S 24-868-0126   (BR)
MAGNA INTERNATIONAL INC
POLYCON INDUSTRIES
(*Suby of* MAGNA INTERNATIONAL INC)
65 Independence Pl, Guelph, ON, N1K 1H8
(519) 763-6042
Emp Here 1,300
SIC 3714 Motor vehicle parts and accessories
David Gray

D-U-N-S 24-760-4767   (HQ)
MAILLETTE HOLDINGS INC
PETRO CANADA
80 Imperial Rd S, Guelph, ON, N1K 2A1
(519) 822-2175
Emp Here 5   *Sales* 24,903,900
SIC 5541 Gasoline service stations
Jeff Maillette

D-U-N-S 25-627-3061   (SL)
MARBLE ELECTRONICS INC
650 Woodlawn Rd W Suite 16a, Guelph, ON,
N1K 1B8
(519) 767-2863
Emp Here 50   *Sales* 10,233,650
SIC 3647 Vehicular lighting equipment
George Gill

D-U-N-S 20-025-2091   (SL)
MCNEIL PDI INC
MCNEIL CONSUMER HEALTH CARE
890 Woodlawn Rd W, Guelph, ON, N1K 1A5

Emp Here 300
SIC 2834 Pharmaceutical preparations

D-U-N-S 24-424-0040   (SL)
MERIT GLASS LTD
61 Arrow Rd, Guelph, ON, N1K 1S8
(519) 822-7470
Emp Here 100   *Sales* 24,618,600
SIC 1793 Glass and glazing work
Rick Busato

D-U-N-S 24-288-9103   (HQ)
**ONTARIO DAIRY HERD IMPROVEMENT
CORPORATION**
CANWEST DHI
660 Speedvale Ave W Suite 101, Guelph, ON,
N1K 1E5
(519) 824-2320
Sales 49,177,050
SIC 8611 Business associations
Neil Petreny

D-U-N-S 20-124-9612   (HQ)
PATENE BUILDING SUPPLIES LTD
641 Speedvale Ave W, Guelph, ON, N1K 1E6
(519) 824-4030
Emp Here 55   *Sales* 91,140,480
SIC 5039 Construction materials, nec
Patrick George

D-U-N-S 20-877-2293   (HQ)
PAVACO PLASTICS INC
HEMATITE MANUFACTURING, DIV OF
659 Speedvale Ave W, Guelph, ON, N1K 1E6
(519) 823-1383
Sales 72,712,500
SIC 3714 Motor vehicle parts and accessories
John Pavanel

D-U-N-S 25-609-7767   (SL)
PITMAN, WAYNE FORD LINCOLN INC
895 Woodlawn Rd W, Guelph, ON, N1K 1B7
(519) 824-6400
Emp Here 77   *Sales* 48,454,560
SIC 5511 New and used car dealers
Wayne Pitman
Wayne Bricknell

D-U-N-S 25-458-0137   (SL)
PROSON UTILITY SOLUTIONS INC
355 Elmira Rd N Unit 138, Guelph, ON, N1K
1S5

(519) 767-2843
Emp Here 90   *Sales* 42,752,340
SIC 5084 Industrial machinery and equipment
Patrick Della Croce

D-U-N-S 25-320-9043   (BR)
PUROLATOR INC
(*Suby of* GOVERNMENT OF CANADA)
147 Massey Rd, Guelph, ON, N1K 1B2
(905) 660-6007
Emp Here 200
SIC 4731 Freight transportation arrangement
Mark Connallen

D-U-N-S 20-051-9817   (SL)
ROBINSON BUICK GMC LTD
875 Woodlawn Rd W, Guelph, ON, N1K 1B7
(519) 821-0520
Emp Here 45   *Sales* 22,413,510
SIC 5511 New and used car dealers
Cynthia Robinson

D-U-N-S 24-079-6409   (SL)
ROBINSON LEASING AND SALES LIMITED
875 Woodlawn Rd W, Guelph, ON, N1K 1B7
(519) 821-0520
Emp Here 40   *Sales* 19,923,120
SIC 5511 New and used car dealers
Howard Robinson

D-U-N-S 25-477-9135   (SL)
ROYAL CITY AMBULANCE SERVICE LTD
355 Elmira Rd N Suite 134, Guelph, ON, N1K
1S5
(519) 824-1510
Emp Here 95   *Sales* 5,212,840
SIC 4119 Local passenger transportation, nec
Harold (Harry) Hitchon
Leonard Steele

D-U-N-S 24-991-0928   (SL)
ROYAL CITY MOTORS LTD
GUELPH TOYOTA
635 Woodlawn Rd W, Guelph, ON, N1K 1E9
(519) 837-3431
Emp Here 74   *Sales* 46,566,720
SIC 5511 New and used car dealers
Barry Dohms
Jacques La Point

D-U-N-S 25-213-1271   (HQ)
ROYAL J & M DISTRIBUTING INC
ROYAL DISTRIBUTING
925 Woodlawn Rd W, Guelph, ON, N1K 1B7
(519) 822-7081
Emp Here 85   *Sales* 14,970,600
SIC 5699 Miscellaneous apparel and acces-
sory stores
Scott Stark
Mark Fries
John Mochrie
Marion Mochrie
Paul Messier

D-U-N-S 24-816-9922   (SL)
STOCKADE INVESTMENTS LTD
STOCKADE WOOD & CRAFT SUPPLIES
785 Imperial Rd N, Guelph, ON, N1K 1X4
(519) 763-1050
Emp Here 18   *Sales* 11,816,352
SIC 5961 Catalog and mail-order houses
Ross Pinniger
Colleen Pinniger

D-U-N-S 20-735-7898   (SL)
SUNSTAR AMERICAS, INC
(*Suby of* SUNSTAR INC.)
515 Governors Rd, Guelph, ON, N1K 1C7
(519) 837-2500
Emp Here 60   *Sales* 32,121,120
SIC 5047 Medical and hospital equipment
Thomas Studney
Daniel Descary
Hubert Diks

D-U-N-S 20-881-1778   (HQ)
TRIMASTER MANUFACTURING INC
(*Suby of* GENNX360 CAPITAL PARTNERS,

L.P.)
95 Curtis Dr, Guelph, ON, N1K 1E1
(519) 823-2661
Sales 38,417,000
SIC 3444 Sheet Metalwork
Howard Singleton
Bonnie Fagan

D-U-N-S 20-943-8308   (HQ)
TRIUMPH TOOL LTD
91 Arrow Rd, Guelph, ON, N1K 1S8
(519) 836-4811
Emp Here 23   *Sales* 15,675,858
SIC 5084 Industrial machinery and equipment
Ernest Duffy
John Duffy
Patrick Duffy
Leslie Duffy

D-U-N-S 24-665-6532   (SL)
WELLINGTON COUNTY BREWERY INC
WELLINGTON BREWERY
950 Woodlawn Rd W, Guelph, ON, N1K 1G2
(519) 837-2337
Emp Here 45   *Sales* 10,118,475
SIC 2082 Malt beverages
Brent Davies

D-U-N-S 20-052-0963   (SL)
WELLINGTON MOTORS LIMITED
(*Suby of* WILSON WOODS LTD)
935 Woodlawn Rd W, Guelph, ON, N1K 1B7
(519) 651-2422
Emp Here 52   *Sales* 32,722,560
SIC 5511 New and used car dealers
Edward Woods
Michael Woods
Joan Woods
Marthese Doerner

Guelph, ON N1L

D-U-N-S 25-104-9128   (HQ)
ABS FRICTION INC
55 Taggart St, Guelph, ON, N1L 1M6
(519) 763-9000
Sales 33,576,450
SIC 3714 Motor vehicle parts and accessories
Rick Jamieson

D-U-N-S 20-406-9504   (HQ)
BARZOTTI WOODWORKING LIMITED
2 Watson Rd S, Guelph, ON, N1L 1E2
(519) 821-3670
Emp Here 113   *Sales* 30,779,980
SIC 5211 Lumber and other building materials
Vincent Barzotti
Bruna Barzotti

D-U-N-S 20-735-4200   (SL)
DENSO MANUFACTURING CANADA, INC
(*Suby of* DENSO CORPORATION)
900 Southgate Dr, Guelph, ON, N1L 1K1
(519) 837-6600
Emp Here 625   *Sales* 288,221,250
SIC 5013 Motor vehicle supplies and new
parts
Rich Vanoorschot
Shigeki Aoyama

D-U-N-S 24-555-0645   (HQ)
ELECTRO-WIND SUPPLY INC
ELECTRO-WIND EIFCO
2 Taggart St, Guelph, ON, N1L 1M5
(519) 836-2280
Sales 12,520,872
SIC 5051 Metals service centers and offices
Elio B Tedesco
Michelle A Tedesco

D-U-N-S 20-556-6235   (SL)
ELLIOTT, FRED COACH LINES LIMITED
ELMIRA BUS LINES, A DIV OF
(*Suby of* STUDENT TRANSPORTATION OF

AMERICA, INC.)
760 Victoria Rd S, Guelph, ON, N1L 1C6
(519) 822-5225
Emp Here 85   *Sales* 6,398,120
SIC 4151 School buses
Martha Jakowlew
Victor Jakowlew
Allan Mckay

D-U-N-S 24-326-6207   (SL)
GARY DANIELS PHARMACIES LTD
SHOPPERS DRUG MART
7 Clair Rd W Suite 1213, Guelph, ON, N1L
0A6
(519) 763-3431
Emp Here 45   *Sales* 11,382,930
SIC 5912 Drug stores and proprietary stores
Gary Daniels

D-U-N-S 24-802-1909   (SL)
GUNN METAL STAMPINGS COMPANY
32 Airpark Pl, Guelph, ON, N1L 1B2

Emp Here 100   *Sales* 19,208,500
SIC 3429 Hardware, nec
Robert Bosco
James Robinson
Daniel M Dickinson
Gordon Plan
Scott Gibaratz
Richard Snell

D-U-N-S 25-954-0953   (SL)
JAYCEE HERB TRADERS LTD
21 Airpark Pl, Guelph, ON, N1L 1B2
(519) 829-3535
Emp Here 45   *Sales* 12,336,840
SIC 5499 Miscellaneous food stores
Wolfgang Breisser

D-U-N-S 24-662-9745   (SL)
NOVA-LINK LIMITED
NL NOVALINK
935a Southgate Dr Unit 5, Guelph, ON, N1L
0B9
(905) 858-3500
Emp Here 75   *Sales* 11,574,150
SIC 2522 Office furniture, except wood
Antonius Vander Park
Maria Vander Park

D-U-N-S 20-754-3414   (HQ)
RALSTON METAL PRODUCTS LIMITED
50 Watson Rd S, Guelph, ON, N1L 1E2
(519) 836-2968
Sales 19,208,500
SIC 3469 Metal stampings, nec
Inglis Berry
Paul Berry
Stephen Berry
Ian Berry
Pat Berry

D-U-N-S 24-341-0755   (HQ)
SAPPORO CANADA INC
SLEEMAN BREWERY
(*Suby of* SAPPORO HOLDINGS LIMITED)
551 Clair Rd W, Guelph, ON, N1L 1E9
(519) 822-1834
Sales 27,335,000
SIC 6712 Bank holding companies
John W. Sleeman
Nobuhiro Hashiba
Yoshiyuki Mochida

D-U-N-S 20-104-2533   (SL)
**SLEEMAN BREWING & MALTING COM-
PANY LTD, THE**
(*Suby of* SAPPORO HOLDINGS LIMITED)
551 Clair Rd W, Guelph, ON, N1L 1E9
(519) 822-1834
Emp Here 750   *Sales* 365,538,750
SIC 2082 Malt beverages
John Sleeman
Shige Yokoi
Mike Minami
Pierre Ferland

D-U-N-S 24-319-8525   (BR)
TDL GROUP CORP, THE
TIM HORTON REGIONAL OFFICE
(*Suby of* RESTAURANT BRANDS INTERNA-
TIONAL INC)
950 Southgate Dr, Guelph, ON, N1L 1S7
(519) 824-1304
Emp Here 100
SIC 5812 Eating places
Ken Haire

D-U-N-S 20-861-1959   (BR)
**UPPER GRAND DISTRICT SCHOOL
BOARD, THE**
*WELLINGTON CENTRE FOR CONTINUING
EDUCATION*
(*Suby of* UPPER GRAND DISTRICT
SCHOOL BOARD, THE)
1428 Gordon St, Guelph, ON, N1L 1C8
(519) 836-7280
Emp Here 250
SIC 8211 Elementary and secondary schools

D-U-N-S 24-391-3634   (SL)
VIQUA HOLDINGS
425 Clair Rd W, Guelph, ON, N1L 1R1
(519) 763-1032
Emp Here 50   *Sales* 13,833,000
SIC 2899 Chemical preparations, nec
Frank Profiti

D-U-N-S 20-524-3335   (BR)
**WELLINGTON CATHOLIC DISTRICT
SCHOOL BOARD**
*BISHOP MACDONELL CATHOLIC HIGH
SCHOOL*
200 Clair Rd W, Guelph, ON, N1L 1G1
(519) 822-8502
Emp Here 700
SIC 8211 Elementary and secondary schools
Richard Olson

Hagersville, ON N0A

D-U-N-S 20-965-6102   (SL)
987112 ONTARIO INC
HAGERSVILLE FOODLAND
32 King St E, Hagersville, ON, N0A 1H0
(905) 768-3571
Emp Here 50   *Sales* 13,707,600
SIC 5411 Grocery stores
Bessie Johnson
Cameron Johnston
Gail Weatherston
Cathy Winger

D-U-N-S 24-793-3344   (HQ)
ARMSTRONG MILLING CO. LTD
1021 Haldimand Rd Unit 20, Hagersville, ON,
N0A 1H0
(905) 779-2473
Sales 10,118,475
SIC 2048 Prepared feeds, nec
Kenneth Zantingh
Douglas Murphy
Larry Murphy

D-U-N-S 24-720-2245   (BR)
CGC INC
(*Suby of* USG NETHERLANDS GLOBAL
HOLDINGS B.V.)
55 Third Line Rd, Hagersville, ON, N0A 1H0
(905) 768-3331
Emp Here 340
SIC 3275 Gypsum products
Bruce Clarice

D-U-N-S 24-338-1519   (HQ)
CONTRANS FLATBED GROUP GP INC
(*Suby of* TFI INTERNATIONAL INC)
80 Third Line Rd, Hagersville, ON, N0A 1H0
(905) 768-3375
Sales 46,095,250
SIC 4213 Trucking, except local

Allain Bedard
Greg Rumble

D-U-N-S 20-291-6693   (BR)
GRAND ERIE DISTRICT SCHOOL BOARD
HAGERSVILLE SECONDARY SCHOOL
(*Suby of* GRAND ERIE DISTRICT SCHOOL
BOARD)
70 Parkview Rd, Hagersville, ON, N0A 1H0
(905) 768-3318
Emp Here 80
SIC 8211 Elementary and secondary schools
Shaun Mcmahon

D-U-N-S 24-211-9642   (HQ)
HARWIL FARMS MOBILE FEEDS LTD
4410 Highway 6 Rr 6, Hagersville, ON, N0A
1H0
(905) 768-1118
Sales 15,592,920
SIC 5191 Farm supplies
Lea Metcalfe
Wendy Metcalfe

D-U-N-S 20-052-1763   (SL)
HEASLIP FORD SALES LTD
18 Main St S, Hagersville, ON, N0A 1H0
(905) 768-3393
Emp Here 28   *Sales* 13,946,184
SIC 5511 New and used car dealers
Kenneth Heaslip

D-U-N-S 20-052-1771   (HQ)
HEWITT'S DAIRY LIMITED
(*Suby of* GAY LEA FOODS CO-OPERATIVE
LIMITED)
128 King St E, Hagersville, ON, N0A 1H0
(905) 768-3524
Emp Here 44   *Sales* 43,719,676
SIC 5143 Dairy products, except dried or
canned
Michael Barrett
Ove Hansen
Steve Dolson
John Rebry
Mark Hamel
Roger Harrop
Paul Vickers

D-U-N-S 20-552-0096   (HQ)
LAIDLAW CARRIERS FLATBED LP
11 6 Hwy N, Hagersville, ON, N0A 1H0
(905) 768-3375
Sales 16,456,480
SIC 4213 Trucking, except local
Steve Brookshaw

D-U-N-S 25-075-4793   (SL)
ONTARIO TIRE RECOVERY INC
2985 Concession 12 Walpole, Hagersville,
ON, N0A 1H0

Emp Here 40   *Sales* 19,923,120
SIC 5531 Auto and home supply stores
Lynda Moffatt

D-U-N-S 24-047-3348   (SL)
WEST HALDIMAND GENERAL HOSPITAL
75 Parkview Rd, Hagersville, ON, N0A 1H0
(905) 768-3311
Emp Here 150   *Sales* 16,662,000
SIC 8062 General medical and surgical hospi-
tals
Tom Thompson
Ernest Sersen

Haileybury, ON P0J

D-U-N-S 25-591-3139   (BR)
JARLETTE LTD
TEMISKAMING LODGE
100 Bruce St, Haileybury, ON, P0J 1K0
(705) 672-2123
Emp Here 80   *Sales* 588,616

SIC 8051 Skilled nursing care facilities
Francine Gosselin

D-U-N-S 20-938-9196   (SL)
MIKE'S ONE STOP INC
SUBWAY
229 Rorke Ave S, Haileybury, ON, P0J 1K0
(705) 672-3667
Emp Here 24   *Sales* 11,953,872
SIC 5541 Gasoline service stations
Michel Bouffard

Haley Station, ON K0J

D-U-N-S 20-193-6494   (BR)
MAGELLAN AEROSPACE LIMITED
HALEY INDUSTRIES
(*Suby of* MAGELLAN AEROSPACE CORPO-
RATION)
634 Magnesium Rd, Haley Station, ON, K0J
1Y0
(613) 432-8841
Emp Here 500
SIC 3365 Aluminum foundries
James Lemonchick

Haliburton, ON K0M

D-U-N-S 20-052-3132   (SL)
CURRY MOTORS LIMITED
5065 County Rd 21 Rr 3, Haliburton, ON, K0M
1S0
(705) 457-2765
Emp Here 36   *Sales* 18,138,481
SIC 5511 New and used car dealers
Don Popple
Michael Iles

D-U-N-S 20-052-3199   (HQ)
EMMERSON LUMBER LIMITED
EMMERSON LUMBER
63 Maple Ave, Haliburton, ON, K0M 1S0
(705) 457-1550
Emp Here 38   *Sales* 12,652,950
SIC 5211 Lumber and other building materials
Kim Emmerson

D-U-N-S 25-646-2342   (BR)
**HALIBURTON HIGHLANDS HEALTH SER-
VICES CORPORATION**
HALIBURTON HOSPITAL
(*Suby of* HALIBURTON HIGHLANDS
HEALTH SERVICES CORPORATION)
7199 Gelert Rd, Haliburton, ON, K0M 1S0
(705) 457-1392
Emp Here 210
SIC 8062 General medical and surgical hospi-
tals
Jeff Gollob

D-U-N-S 25-500-5878   (HQ)
**HALIBURTON HIGHLANDS HEALTH SER-
VICES CORPORATION**
HHHS
7199 Gelert Rd Rr 3, Haliburton, ON, K0M
1S0
(705) 457-1392
Emp Here 90   *Sales* 20,152,241
SIC 8062 General medical and surgical hospi-
tals
Carolyn Plummer
Kathy Newton
Stephanie Maclaren
Beth Archibald
Michelle Douglas
April De Carlo
Kris Baird

D-U-N-S 20-408-6706   (SL)
**HALIBURTON LUMBER & ENTERPRISES
LIMITED**

Gd, Haliburton, ON, K0M 1S0
(705) 457-2510
Emp Here 35   *Sales* 15,651,090
SIC 5039 Construction materials, nec
John Wilson
Greg Scheffee

D-U-N-S 24-184-9244   (SL)
HIGHLANDS SUMMER FESTIVAL, THE
5358 County Rd 21, Haliburton, ON, K0M 1S0
(705) 457-9933
Emp Here 27   *Sales* 10,730,178
SIC 8699 Membership organizations, nec
Jack Brezina

D-U-N-S 25-069-1888   (SL)
PATIENT NEWS PUBLISHING LTD
5152 County Rd 121, Haliburton, ON, K0M
1S0
(705) 457-4030
Emp Here 70   *Sales* 11,481,890
SIC 2741 Miscellaneous publishing
Wayne Lavery
Karen Galley

D-U-N-S 24-199-4685   (SL)
PINESTONE REGIONAL SALES OFFICE
4252 County Rd 21, Haliburton, ON, K0M 1S0

Emp Here 25   *Sales* 11,230,475
SIC 7389 Business services, nec
Matthew Phillips

D-U-N-S 24-120-2741   (SL)
TODD'S YIG 803 LTD
5121 County Rd 21 Rr 3, Haliburton, ON, K0M
1S0
(705) 455-9775
Emp Here 70   *Sales* 20,543,390
SIC 5411 Grocery stores
Steve Todd

D-U-N-S 24-124-5476   (BR)
**YMCA OF HAMIL-
TON/BURLINGTON/BRANTFORD**
YMCA WANAKITA
(*Suby of* YMCA OF HAMIL-
TON/BURLINGTON/BRANTFORD)
1883 Koshlong Lake Rd, Haliburton, ON, K0M
1S0
(705) 457-2132
Emp Here 100
SIC 7999 Amusement and recreation, nec
Marc Clare

Hamilton, ON L8E

D-U-N-S 20-052-6291   (SL)
BAYCOAT LIMITED
244 Lanark St, Hamilton, ON, L8E 4B3
(905) 561-0965
Emp Here 200   *Sales* 38,417,000
SIC 3479 Metal coating and allied services
Lionel Motl
Gary W. Grishkewich
Bob W. Nuttall
Sean Patrick Donnelly
Grant Allan Davidson
William C. Harrison
Thomas J. O'toole
Kevin Wong

D-U-N-S 20-574-2252   (SL)
BODYLINE INC
BODYLINE AUTO RECYCLERS
185 Bancroft St, Hamilton, ON, L8E 4L4
(905) 573-7000
Emp Here 33   *Sales* 16,436,574
SIC 5511 New and used car dealers
James Mcdonald
David Mcdonald

D-U-N-S 24-466-3709   (BR)
CATELLI FOODS CORPORATION
OLIVIERI FOODS DIV

▲ Public Company   ■ Public Company Family Member   **HQ** Headquarters   **BR** Branch   **SL** Single Location

(Suby of EBRO FOODS, SA)
80 Brockley Dr, Hamilton, ON, L8E 3C5
(905) 560-6200
Emp Here 75
SIC 2098 Macaroni and spaghetti
Allison Hussey

D-U-N-S 24-693-1286   (BR)
CBI LIMITED
CBI HOME HEALTH
(Suby of CBI LIMITED)
45 Goderich Rd, Hamilton, ON, L8E 4W8
(905) 777-1255
Emp Here 100
SIC 8741 Management services

D-U-N-S 20-645-3396   (SL)
CHILDREN'S AID SOCIETY OF HAMILTON, THE
26 Arrowsmith Rd, Hamilton, ON, L8E 4H8
(905) 522-1121
Emp Here 325   *Sales* 24,957,400
SIC 8322 Individual and family services

D-U-N-S 24-993-1577   (SL)
DEEP CLEAN AUTOMATIC CLEANING & RESTORATION INC
26 Burford Rd Unit 200, Hamilton, ON, L8E 3C7
(905) 578-3445
Emp Here 33   *Sales* 10,522,677
SIC 1521 Single-family housing construction
Jay Lozecki
John Gardener

D-U-N-S 20-053-5318   (HQ)
FELLFAB LIMITED
FELLFAB
2343 Barton St E, Hamilton, ON, L8E 5V8
(905) 560-9230
Emp Here 5   *Sales* 34,493,550
SIC 2399 Fabricated textile products, nec
Nick Efthimiadis
John Smith
Saif Mir
Brenda Mackay
Shannon Mcgee

D-U-N-S 25-318-9583   (BR)
FIRSTCANADA ULC
FIRST STUDENT
(Suby of FIRSTGROUP PLC)
50 Covington St, Hamilton, ON, L8E 2Y5
(905) 522-3232
Emp Here 250
SIC 4151 School buses
Philip Kuckyt

D-U-N-S 24-745-5306   (SL)
FOX 40 INTERNATIONAL INC
340 Grays Rd, Hamilton, ON, L8E 2Z2
(905) 561-4040
Emp Here 50   *Sales* 10,941,200
SIC 3949 Sporting and athletic goods, nec
Ronald Foxcroft
David Foxcroft
Mark Groleau

D-U-N-S 20-038-3193   (SL)
HAMILTON ARTS & CRAFTS
303 Highridge Ave, Hamilton, ON, L8E 3W1
(905) 578-0750
Emp Here 40   *Sales* 19,932,880
SIC 5131 Piece goods and notions
Nael Nebout

D-U-N-S 20-185-0612   (BR)
HAMILTON REGION CONSERVATION AUTHORITY
WILD WATERWORKS
(Suby of HAMILTON REGION CONSERVATION AUTHORITY)
585 Van Wagners Beach Rd, Hamilton, ON, L8E 3L8
(905) 561-2292
Emp Here 103
SIC 7996 Amusement parks
Rob Howe

D-U-N-S 25-514-3133   (BR)
HOME DEPOT OF CANADA INC
HOME DEPOT
(Suby of THE HOME DEPOT INC)
350 Centennial Pky N, Hamilton, ON, L8E 2X4
(905) 561-9755
Emp Here 250
SIC 5251 Hardware stores
Kelly Ritossa

D-U-N-S 24-469-3339   (SL)
IMAGE AUTOMOBILES INC
IMAGE HONDA
(Suby of SETAY HOLDINGS LIMITED)
155 Centennial Pky N, Hamilton, ON, L8E 1H8
(905) 561-4100
Emp Here 35   *Sales* 22,024,800
SIC 5511 New and used car dealers
Terry Yates
Brenda Yates
Randy Young

D-U-N-S 24-324-0004   (BR)
KROMET INTERNATIONAL INC
ALUMABRITE ANODIZING, DIV
(Suby of KROMET INTERNATIONAL INC)
20 Milburn Rd, Hamilton, ON, L8E 3L9
(905) 561-7773
Emp Here 75
SIC 3469 Metal stampings, nec
Mike Morgason

D-U-N-S 25-484-2503   (BR)
MAPLE LEAF FOODS INC
(Suby of MAPLE LEAF FOODS INC)
21 Brockley Dr, Hamilton, ON, L8E 3C3
(800) 268-3708
Emp Here 350
SIC 2011 Meat packing plants
Roderick Compton

D-U-N-S 24-099-9649   (SL)
MATTINA MECHANICAL LIMITED
211 Lanark St Unit A, Hamilton, ON, L8E 2Z9
(905) 544-6380
Emp Here 57   *Sales* 13,284,705
SIC 1711 Plumbing, heating, air-conditioning
Dominic Mattina
Sammy Mattina

D-U-N-S 24-853-4252   (BR)
METRO ONTARIO INC
FOOD BASICS
(Suby of METRO INC)
2500 Barton St E, Hamilton, ON, L8E 4A2
(905) 578-5454
Emp Here 120
SIC 5411 Grocery stores
Jerry Seward

D-U-N-S 20-070-6294   (SL)
MY INSURANCE BROKER HAMILTON CORP
163 Centennial Pky N Suite 2, Hamilton, ON, L8E 1H8
(905) 528-2886
Emp Here 21   *Sales* 12,178,404
SIC 6411 Insurance agents, brokers, and service
Doug Speirs

D-U-N-S 24-946-8406   (SL)
NELLA CUTLERY (HAMILTON) INC
2775 Barton St E, Hamilton, ON, L8E 2J8
(905) 561-3456
Emp Here 20   *Sales* 10,177,120
SIC 5023 Homefurnishings
Augusto Nella
Bernardo Nella
Bruno Nella
Stefano Nella

D-U-N-S 20-730-5553   (SL)
NUTECH FIRE PROTECTION CO. LTD
2814 Barton St E, Hamilton, ON, L8E 2J9
(905) 662-9991
Emp Here 25   *Sales* 11,087,250

SIC 7389 Business services, nec
Jean Gajthier

D-U-N-S 20-974-8854   (BR)
PEPSI BOTTLING GROUP (CANADA), ULC, THE
PEPSICO BEVERAGES CANADA
(Suby of PBG INVESTMENT (LUXEMBOURG) SARL)
2799 Barton St E, Hamilton, ON, L8E 2J8
(905) 560-7774
Emp Here 100
SIC 2086 Bottled and canned soft drinks
Jason Lemaich

D-U-N-S 24-470-5166   (HQ)
PIONEER BALLOON CANADA LIMITED
(Suby of CONTINENTAL AMERICAN CORPORATION)
333 Kenora Ave, Hamilton, ON, L8E 2W3
(905) 560-6534
Sales 31,771,600
SIC 3069 Fabricated rubber products, nec

D-U-N-S 20-902-2334   (BR)
PUROLATOR INC
(Suby of GOVERNMENT OF CANADA)
21 Warrington St, Hamilton, ON, L8E 3L1
(888) 744-7123
Emp Here 100
SIC 7389 Business services, nec
Garnett Mcdonald

D-U-N-S 25-155-4457   (SL)
QUEENSTON CHEVROLET INC
282 Centennial Pky N, Hamilton, ON, L8E 2X4
(905) 560-2020
Emp Here 50   *Sales* 24,903,900
SIC 5511 New and used car dealers
Terry Yates

D-U-N-S 20-303-3147   (BR)
RECIPE UNLIMITED CORPORATION
KELSEY'S
(Suby of RECIPE UNLIMITED CORPORATION)
200 Centennial Pky N, Hamilton, ON, L8E 4A1
(416) 599-4133
Emp Here 90
SIC 5812 Eating places
James Williams

D-U-N-S 24-864-4622   (SL)
RED HILL TOYOTA
PARKWAY MOTORS
2333 Barton St E, Hamilton, ON, L8E 2W8
(905) 561-1202
Emp Here 80   *Sales* 50,342,400
SIC 5511 New and used car dealers
Ilya Pinassi

D-U-N-S 20-594-8680   (HQ)
RONDAR INC
333 Centennial Pky N, Hamilton, ON, L8E 2X6
(905) 561-2808
Emp Here 20   *Sales* 34,296,165
SIC 7629 Electrical repair shops
Jason Sparaga
Andrew Clark
Eric Waxman

D-U-N-S 24-078-6343   (SL)
RYCOTT WHOLESALE FOODS INC
RYCOTT FOODSERVICE
(Suby of RYCOTT HOLDINGS INC)
504 Kenora Ave, Hamilton, ON, L8E 3X8
(905) 560-2424
Emp Here 44   *Sales* 36,765,388
SIC 5146 Fish and seafoods
Charles Ricottone Jr
Henry Szwarz
Mike Speth
John Ricottone

D-U-N-S 20-154-3774   (SL)
SCHREIBER BROTHERS LIMITED
SCHREIBER ROOFING
50 Brockley Dr, Hamilton, ON, L8E 3P1

(905) 561-7780
Emp Here 60   *Sales* 13,069,740
SIC 1761 Roofing, siding, and sheetMetal work
Marinos Barlas

D-U-N-S 25-504-5874   (SL)
SETAY MOTORS INC
QUEENSTON LEASING
282 Centennial Pky N, Hamilton, ON, L8E 2X4
(905) 549-4656
Emp Here 30   *Sales* 14,942,340
SIC 5511 New and used car dealers
Terry Yates
Randy Young

D-U-N-S 25-859-6386   (SL)
SEVEN STAR EXPRESS LINE LTD
36 Covington St, Hamilton, ON, L8E 2Y5

Emp Here 100   *Sales* 14,819,200
SIC 4213 Trucking, except local
Stephen Jurcic
Mijo Jurcic
Marinko Jurcic

D-U-N-S 24-736-0993   (SL)
SOBOTEC LTD
67 Burford Rd, Hamilton, ON, L8E 3C6
(905) 578-1278
Emp Here 175   *Sales* 33,614,875
SIC 3499 Fabricated Metal products, nec
Vladimir Sobot
Chedo Sobot

D-U-N-S 24-708-3702   (SL)
TASUS CANADA CORPORATION
(Suby of TSUCHIYA HC.LTD.)
41a Brockley Dr Unit 1, Hamilton, ON, L8E 3C3
(905) 560-1337
Emp Here 68   *Sales* 11,153,836
SIC 2759 Commercial printing, nec
Melanie Hart
David Bosher
Kevin Mills

D-U-N-S 24-919-5264   (SL)
TAYLOR CHRYSLER DODGE INC
(Suby of TAYLOR STEEL INC)
260 Centennial Pky N, Hamilton, ON, L8E 2X4
(905) 561-0333
Emp Here 50   *Sales* 28,316,641
SIC 5511 New and used car dealers
Micheal W Taylor
Michael Coughlan
David Grosvenor

D-U-N-S 20-039-3114   (HQ)
U-HAUL CO. (CANADA) LTD
(Suby of AMERCO)
526 Grays Rd, Hamilton, ON, L8E 2Z4
(905) 560-0014
Emp Here 13   *Sales* 80,726,400
SIC 7519 Utility trailer rental
Jake Stelic
Gary B. Horton
Jennifer Settles

D-U-N-S 25-403-8086   (BR)
UNITED PARCEL SERVICE CANADA LTD
UPS
(Suby of UNITED PARCEL SERVICE, INC.)
456 Grays Rd, Hamilton, ON, L8E 2Z4
(905) 578-2699
Emp Here 100
SIC 7389 Business services, nec
Bevin Flett

Hamilton, ON L8G

D-U-N-S 24-395-3796   (SL)
AND 07 CONSULTING
674 Queenston Rd, Hamilton, ON, L8G 1A3

▲ Public Company   ■ Public Company Family Member   **HQ** Headquarters   **BR** Branch   **SL** Single Location

(905) 561-8960
Emp Here 45   *Sales* 10,542,960
SIC 8748 Business consulting, nec
 Glen Steeves

D-U-N-S 24-556-7495   (BR)
SOBEYS CAPITAL INCORPORATED
FRESHCO
(*Suby of* EMPIRE COMPANY LIMITED)
700 Queenston Rd Unit A, Hamilton, ON, L8G 1A3
(905) 560-8111
Emp Here 110
SIC 5411 Grocery stores
 Nick Alfieri

D-U-N-S 20-703-6042   (BR)
ST. JOSEPH'S HEALTHCARE FOUNDA-TION, HAMILTON
ST JOSEPH HEALTHCARE CENTRE FOR AMBULATORY
(*Suby of* ST. JOSEPH'S HEALTH SYSTEM)
2757 King St E, Hamilton, ON, L8G 5E4
(905) 573-7777
Emp Here 300
SIC 8093 Specialty outpatient clinics, nec
 Julie Holmes

Hamilton, ON L8H

D-U-N-S 24-544-3627   (SL)
600956 ONTARIO LTD
PLASTICS PLUS
469 Woodward Ave, Hamilton, ON, L8H 6N6
(905) 549-4572
Emp Here 70   *Sales* 14,132,790
SIC 3089 Plastics products, nec
 Laurent Mermuys

D-U-N-S 25-687-3100   (SL)
A. RAYMOND TINNERMAN MANUFACTUR-ING HAMILTON, INC
(*Suby of* A RAYMOND ET COMPAGNIE)
686 Parkdale Ave N, Hamilton, ON, L8H 5Z4
(905) 549-4661
Emp Here 193   *Sales* 37,072,405
SIC 3429 Hardware, nec
 Daniel J Dolan
 Antoine Raymond
 Matthew Mcdonald

D-U-N-S 25-459-4633   (SL)
AGE LINK PERSONNEL SERVICES INC
SENIORS FOR SENIORS
400 Parkdale Ave N Unit 2a, Hamilton, ON, L8H 5Y2
(905) 572-6162
Emp Here 75   *Sales* 6,949,875
SIC 8322 Individual and family services
 Ross Auckland

D-U-N-S 24-374-4054   (BR)
AMERICAN IRON & METAL LP
AIM RECYCLING HAMILTON
75 Steel City Crt, Hamilton, ON, L8H 3Y2
(905) 547-5533
Emp Here 80   *Sales* 1,204,568
SIC 4953 Refuse systems
 Stephen Mangotich

D-U-N-S 20-215-1346   (SL)
BIRLA CARBON CANADA LTD
BIRLA CARBON
(*Suby of* INDIGOLD CARBON COOPER-ATIEF U.A.)
755 Parkdale Ave N, Hamilton, ON, L8H 7N5
(905) 544-3343
Emp Here 103   *Sales* 29,254,163
SIC 2895 Carbon black
 John Loudermilk
 Jeff Hanson
 George Zolis

D-U-N-S 25-975-3275   (HQ)
C.F.F. HOLDINGS INC

1840 Burlington St E, Hamilton, ON, L8H 3L4
(905) 549-2603
Emp Here 1   *Sales* 77,669,020
SIC 5051 Metals service centers and offices
 Brian Mccomb

D-U-N-S 24-451-9211   (HQ)
C.F.F. STAINLESS STEELS INC
(*Suby of* C.F.F. HOLDINGS INC)
1840 Burlington St E, Hamilton, ON, L8H 3L4
(905) 549-2603
Emp Here 113   *Sales* 71,694,480
SIC 5051 Metals service centers and offices
 Brian Mccomb
 Harriet Thomas

D-U-N-S 20-769-4329   (SL)
CLOW CANADA INC
1757 Burlington St E, Hamilton, ON, L8H 3L5
(905) 548-9604
Emp Here 30   *Sales* 14,250,780
SIC 5085 Industrial supplies
 Rick Benoit

D-U-N-S 20-552-6622   (BR)
COCA-COLA REFRESHMENTS CANADA COMPANY
(*Suby of* THE COCA-COLA COMPANY)
1575 Barton St E, Hamilton, ON, L8H 7K6
(905) 548-3206
Emp Here 100
SIC 2086 Bottled and canned soft drinks
 Darren Carey

D-U-N-S 24-561-2650   (SL)
COLE CARRIERS CORP
89 Glow Ave, Hamilton, ON, L8H 3V7
(905) 548-0979
Emp Here 150   *Sales* 30,855,900
SIC 4212 Local trucking, without storage
 Philip Farcassi

D-U-N-S 20-053-4246   (SL)
EAST HAMILTON RADIO LIMITED
EHR
1325 Barton St E, Hamilton, ON, L8H 2W2
(905) 549-3581
Emp Here 47   *Sales* 15,303,200
SIC 5999 Miscellaneous retail stores, nec
 Ronald Taillon
 Margaret Taillon

D-U-N-S 20-403-3153   (HQ)
EASTGATE FORD SALES & SERVICE (82) COMPANY INC
350 Parkdale Ave N, Hamilton, ON, L8H 5Y3
(905) 547-2521
Emp Here 95   *Sales* 75,513,600
SIC 5511 New and used car dealers
 Lorne Richter
 Ronald Richter
 Lowell Richter

D-U-N-S 24-991-0043   (HQ)
ELECTROMART (ONTARIO) INC
ELECTROMART LIGHTING & ELECTRICAL SUPPLY
1701 Brampton St, Hamilton, ON, L8H 3S2
(905) 524-1555
Emp Here 40   *Sales* 17,886,960
SIC 5051 Metals service centers and offices
 Murray Orgel

D-U-N-S 20-261-7346   (BR)
FIRSTONTARIO CREDIT UNION LIMITED
(*Suby of* FIRSTONTARIO CREDIT UNION LIMITED)
1299 Barton St E, Hamilton, ON, L8H 2V4
(800) 616-8878
Emp Here 400
SIC 6062 State credit unions
 Terry Zytaruk

D-U-N-S 20-267-8025   (BR)
GAY LEA FOODS CO-OPERATIVE LIMITED
(*Suby of* GAY LEA FOODS CO-OPERATIVE LIMITED)
20 Morley St, Hamilton, ON, L8H 3R7

(905) 544-6281
Emp Here 1,000
SIC 2021 Creamery butter
 Brad Beaudoin

D-U-N-S 25-684-3392   (BR)
GDI SERVICES (CANADA) LP
GDI INTEGRATED FACILITY SVC
(*Suby of* GDI SERVICES AUX IMMEUBLES INC)
39 Dunbar Ave, Hamilton, ON, L8H 3E3

Emp Here 120
SIC 7349 Building maintenance services, nec
 Daniel Somera

D-U-N-S 20-053-7900   (SL)
GROVES, WM. LIMITED
800 Rennie St, Hamilton, ON, L8H 3R2
(905) 545-1117
Emp Here 45   *Sales* 10,839,780
SIC 1623 Water, sewer, and utility lines
 Robert J Groves
 Nancy Groves

D-U-N-S 24-010-0255   (SL)
HAMILTON EAST KIWANIS BOYS & GIRLS CLUB INCORPORATED
BOYS & GIRLS CLUBS OF HAMILTON
45 Ellis Ave, Hamilton, ON, L8H 4L8
(905) 543-9994
Emp Here 100   *Sales* 7,854,500
SIC 7997 Membership sports and recreation clubs
 Heather Geddes
 Glenn Harkness
 Roberta Morris

D-U-N-S 20-384-3086   (SL)
HAMILTON-WENTWORTH   CATHOLIC CHILD CARE CENTRES INC
785 Britannia Ave, Hamilton, ON, L8H 2B6
(905) 523-2349
Emp Here 400   *Sales* 575,440,400
SIC 8699 Membership organizations, nec
 Carrie Horn

D-U-N-S 20-718-3745   (SL)
HC-TECH INC
665 Parkdale Ave N, Hamilton, ON, L8H 5Z1
(905) 547-5693
Emp Here 20   *Sales* 10,006,500
SIC 5169 Chemicals and allied products, nec
 Peter Tam

D-U-N-S 24-217-9323   (HQ)
HT PRODUCTIONS INC
WHITEBIRD
690 Rennie St, Hamilton, ON, L8H 3R2
(905) 544-7575
Sales 22,275,600
SIC 5199 Nondurable goods, nec
 Henry Heikoop
 Jack Tamminga

D-U-N-S 20-054-2611   (SL)
KEMP, JAMES CONSTRUCTION LIMITED
121 Vansitmart Ave, Hamilton, ON, L8H 3A6
(905) 547-7715
Emp Here 75   *Sales* 31,705,275
SIC 1541 Industrial buildings and warehouses
 Thomas Kemp
 Ronald Kemp
 Douglas Kemp
 John Kemp

D-U-N-S 25-320-3343   (SL)
MADDOCKS ENGINEERED MACHINERY INC
MADDOCKS INDUSTRIAL FILTER DIV
663 Woodward Ave, Hamilton, ON, L8H 6P3
(905) 549-9626
Emp Here 30   *Sales* 14,250,780
SIC 5085 Industrial supplies
 Jonathan Maddocks

D-U-N-S 20-318-5137   (SL)
MCASPHALT MARINE TRANSPORTATION

LTD
(*Suby of* BOUYGUES)
180 Pier 24 Gateway, Hamilton, ON, L8H 0A3
(905) 549-9408
Emp Here 60   *Sales* 23,623,440
SIC 4412 Deep sea foreign transportation of freight
 John Carrick
 Kelly Carrick
 Craig Smith

D-U-N-S 20-054-6885   (HQ)
MCNALLY CONSTRUCTION INC
MCNALLY MARINE, DIV OF
(*Suby of* WEEKS MARINE, INC.)
1855 Barton St E Suite 4, Hamilton, ON, L8H 2Y7
(905) 549-6561
Emp Here 50   *Sales* 12,622,100
SIC 1629 Heavy construction, nec
 Murray Malott
 David Stanyar
 Greg Burke
 Corrie Prince
 Arthur Smeding
 Matthew Reece

D-U-N-S 25-542-2628   (HQ)
MCNALLY INTERNATIONAL INC
(*Suby of* WEEKS MARINE, INC.)
1855 Barton St E, Hamilton, ON, L8H 2Y7
(905) 549-6561
Emp Here 2   *Sales* 65,623,000
SIC 1629 Heavy construction, nec
 Patrick Mcnally

D-U-N-S 20-055-9367   (HQ)
ORLICK INDUSTRIES LIMITED
411 Parkdale Ave N, Hamilton, ON, L8H 5Y4
(905) 544-1997
Emp Here 165   *Sales* 305,380,500
SIC 3365 Aluminum foundries
 David Braley
 Al Brown

D-U-N-S 24-009-9978   (SL)
POSNER METALS LIMITED
610 Beach Rd, Hamilton, ON, L8H 3L1
(905) 544-1881
Emp Here 40   *Sales* 20,821,680
SIC 5093 Scrap and waste materials
 Fred Posner
 Michael Kam

D-U-N-S 24-708-0864   (SL)
RUETGERS CANADA INC
(*Suby of* RAIN INDUSTRIES LIMITED)
725 Strathearne Ave, Hamilton, ON, L8H 5L3
(905) 544-2891
Emp Here 69   *Sales* 19,597,449
SIC 2865 Cyclic crudes and intermediates
 Henri Steinmetz
 Max Padberg
 Robert Gittus
 Nelu Spiratos
 Kris Vanherbergen
 Joachim Eilert
 Thomas Doestch

D-U-N-S 20-055-4723   (SL)
SALERNO DAIRY PRODUCTS LIMITED
20 Morley St, Hamilton, ON, L8H 3R7
(905) 544-6281
Emp Here 170   *Sales* 58,767,300
SIC 2022 Cheese; natural and processed
 Angelo Fidanza
 Marianna Marzaro
 Barbara Cortina
 Anna Fidanza
 Eugenio Marzaro
 Eugene Mazurkiewicz
 Angelo Fidanza Sr

D-U-N-S 25-542-6918   (BR)
SAMUEL, SON & CO., LIMITED
SAMUEL   FLAT   ROLLED   PROCESSING GROUP

(*Suby of* SAMUEL, SON & CO., LIMITED)
410 Nash Rd N, Hamilton, ON, L8H 7R9
(800) 263-6553
Emp Here 135
SIC 5051 Metals service centers and offices

D-U-N-S 24-693-9300   (HQ)
SLING-CHOKER MFG. (HAMILTON) LTD
WIRE ROPE INDUSTRIES
605 Rennie St, Hamilton, ON, L8H 3P8
(905) 545-5025
Emp Here 36   *Sales* 11,682,090
SIC 3536 Hoists, cranes, and monorails
Paul Villgren
Kane Butcher

D-U-N-S 20-639-5634   (SL)
SPRINGER'S MEATS INC
544 Parkdale Ave N, Hamilton, ON, L8H 5Y7
(905) 544-0782
Emp Here 70   *Sales* 58,490,390
SIC 5147 Meats and meat products
Walter Mueller Sr
Lina Mueller
Walter Mueller Jr
Manuella Mueller

D-U-N-S 24-318-3506   (HQ)
TERRATEC ENVIRONMENTAL LTD
(*Suby of* AMERICAN WATER ENTER-
PRISES, LLC)
200 Eastport Blvd, Hamilton, ON, L8H 7S4
(905) 544-0444
Emp Here 35   *Sales* 33,485,550
SIC 4953 Refuse systems
Dan Goldhawk

D-U-N-S 20-596-4088   (SL)
TIM HORTONS
136 Kenilworth Ave N Suite 130, Hamilton,
ON, L8H 4R8
(905) 543-1811
Emp Here 40   *Sales* 10,966,080
SIC 5461 Retail bakeries
Maureen Sauve
David Suave

D-U-N-S 25-291-1094   (HQ)
TRIPLE CROWN ENTERPRISES LTD
(*Suby of* 1438771 ONTARIO INC)
665 Parkdale Ave N, Hamilton, ON, L8H 5Z1
(905) 540-1630
Sales 42,273,700
SIC 1541 Industrial buildings and warehouses
John Ng

D-U-N-S 25-975-2129   (BR)
TRIPLE M METAL LP
(*Suby of* TRIPLE M METAL LP)
1640 Brampton St, Hamilton, ON, L8H 3S1
(905) 545-7083
Emp Here 75
SIC 5093 Scrap and waste materials
Mike Giampaolo

D-U-N-S 24-964-7637   (SL)
UNION DRAWN STEEL II LIMITED
1350 Burlington St E, Hamilton, ON, L8H 3L3
(905) 547-4480
Emp Here 100   *Sales* 23,343,500
SIC 3316 Cold finishing of steel shapes
Michael Pitterich
Gregory Frenette

D-U-N-S 24-329-5081   (SL)
**UNION DRAWN STEEL II LIMITED PART-
NERSHIP**
1350 Burlington St E, Hamilton, ON, L8H 3L3
(905) 547-4480
Emp Here 64   *Sales* 11,608,832
SIC 3316 Cold finishing of steel shapes
Michael Pitterich
George Bereziuk

D-U-N-S 20-056-0894   (SL)
**WEBB, JERVIS B. COMPANY OF CANADA,
LTD**
(*Suby of* DAIFUKU CO., LTD.)

1647 Burlington St E, Hamilton, ON, L8H 3L2
(905) 547-0411
Emp Here 230   *Sales* 64,601,710
SIC 3535 Conveyors and conveying equip-
ment
John Doychich
Robert Meijer
Brian Stewart
Tim Veeser

Hamilton, ON L8K

D-U-N-S 25-149-1478   (SL)
1389773 ONTARIO INC
D'ALESIO'S FOOD MARKET
399 Greenhill Ave, Hamilton, ON, L8K 6N5
(905) 561-2221
Emp Here 50   *Sales* 13,707,600
SIC 5411 Grocery stores
Guy D'alesio
Paul Parente

D-U-N-S 20-273-4620   (SL)
1906351 ONTARIO INC
KELLER WILLIAMS COMPLETE REALTY
1821 King St E, Hamilton, ON, L8K 1V8
(905) 308-8333
Emp Here 49   *Sales* 16,029,223
SIC 6531 Real estate agents and managers
Dan Corcoran

D-U-N-S 24-912-0247   (SL)
COAST TO COAST DEALER SERVICES INC
COAST TO COAST WARRANTY
1945 King St E Suite 100, Hamilton, ON, L8K
1W2
(905) 578-7477
Emp Here 52   *Sales* 64,241,736
SIC 6399 Insurance carriers, nec
William N. Wereha

D-U-N-S 20-053-2968   (SL)
DEWILDT CAR SALES LIMITED
DEWILDT CHRYSLER DODGE JEEP
1600 Main St E, Hamilton, ON, L8K 1E7
(905) 312-0404
Emp Here 47   *Sales* 23,409,666
SIC 5511 New and used car dealers
Johanna (Jane) Dewildt
Richard Dewildt
Miriam Dewildt
Ken Dewildt

D-U-N-S 24-095-6102   (SL)
GSS SECURITY LTD
1219 Main St E, Hamilton, ON, L8K 1A5
(905) 547-5552
Emp Here 175   *Sales* 4,593,750
SIC 7381 Detective and armored car services
Brian Glynn

D-U-N-S 24-092-2117   (SL)
LIVE DIFFERENT
1429 Main St E Suite 111, Hamilton, ON, L8K
1C2
(905) 777-1662
Emp Here 31   *Sales* 21,985,572
SIC 8699 Membership organizations, nec
Kerry Brandt
Charles Roberts
Alison Willis
Jenn Digiandomenico
Ryan Wood
Ashley Smart
Derek Boyce
Heather Gingras
Bill Rawlins
Kim Mcintyre-Leighton

D-U-N-S 24-569-9033   (BR)
METRO ONTARIO INC
METRO SUPERMARKETS
(*Suby of* METRO INC)
1900 King St E, Hamilton, ON, L8K 1W1

(905) 545-5929
Emp Here 100
SIC 5411 Grocery stores
Robert Hall

D-U-N-S 25-254-9683   (SL)
RGIS INVENTORY SERVICES LLC
1889 King St E, Hamilton, ON, L8K 1V9
(905) 527-8383
Emp Here 30   *Sales* 13,703,230
SIC 7389 Business services, nec

D-U-N-S 20-716-6794   (HQ)
SETAY HOLDINGS LIMITED
78 Queenston Rd, Hamilton, ON, L8K 6R6
(905) 549-4656
Emp Here 7   *Sales* 45,102,750
SIC 6712 Bank holding companies
Terry Yates
Brenda Yates
Randy Young

Hamilton, ON L8L

D-U-N-S 20-800-6010   (SL)
1290685 ONTARIO INC
FOOD BASIC
135 Barton St E, Hamilton, ON, L8L 8A8
(905) 523-0641
Emp Here 49   *Sales* 13,433,448
SIC 5411 Grocery stores
David Anderson

D-U-N-S 24-309-7040   (SL)
1650473 ONTARIO INC
SCRAPMEN
10 Hillyard St, Hamilton, ON, L8L 8J9

Emp Here 100   *Sales* 52,054,200
SIC 5093 Scrap and waste materials
Seema Boparai
Randy Boparai

D-U-N-S 24-196-3123   (SL)
AATEL COMMUNICATIONS INC
413 Victoria Ave N, Hamilton, ON, L8L 8G4
(905) 523-5451
Emp Here 55   *Sales* 11,980,595
SIC 1731 Electrical work
Gordon Chaput
Mike Moore
Darren Croucher

D-U-N-S 20-052-6093   (HQ)
BARTON AUTO PARTS LIMITED
367 Cannon St E Unit 361, Hamilton, ON, L8L
2C3
(905) 522-5124
Emp Here 50   *Sales* 21,852,900
SIC 5013 Motor vehicle supplies and new
parts
Stephen Krieger
Robin Krieger

D-U-N-S 24-718-9251   (HQ)
BARTONAIR FABRICATIONS INC
PLATINUM RAIL
394 Sherman Ave N, Hamilton, ON, L8L 6P1
(905) 524-2234
Sales 11,671,750
SIC 3291 Abrasive products
Bruno Schirripa
Yvonna Di Cristofaro

D-U-N-S 20-733-0903   (SL)
BELL & MACKENZIE CO. LTD
500 Sherman Ave N, Hamilton, ON, L8L 8J6
(905) 527-6000
Emp Here 16   *Sales* 13,319,109
SIC 5032 Brick, stone, and related material

D-U-N-S 20-304-5950   (SL)
**BERMINGHAM FOUNDATION SOLUTIONS
LIMITED**
BERMINGHAM CONSTRUCTION

(*Suby of* VINCI)
600 Ferguson Ave N, Hamilton, ON, L8L 4Z9
(905) 528-7924
Emp Here 140
SIC 1629 Heavy construction, nec

D-U-N-S 25-310-7767   (BR)
BRINK'S CANADA LIMITED
BRINK'S HAMILTON
(*Suby of* THE BRINK'S COMPANY)
75 Lansdowne Ave, Hamilton, ON, L8L 8A3
(905) 549-5997
Emp Here 100
SIC 7381 Detective and armored car services
Bruce Martin

D-U-N-S 24-925-1356   (BR)
BUNGE OF CANADA LTD
(*Suby of* BUNGE LIMITED)
515 Victoria Ave N, Hamilton, ON, L8L 8G7
(905) 527-9121
Emp Here 130
SIC 2076 Vegetable oil mills, nec
Robert Farr

D-U-N-S 24-985-5933   (SL)
**CANADIAN LIQUIDS PROCESSORS LIM-
ITED**
(*Suby of* HALTON RECYCLING LTD)
15 Biggar Ave, Hamilton, ON, L8L 3Z3
(888) 312-1000
Emp Here 85   *Sales* 27,107,350
SIC 4953 Refuse systems
Lori Dupont Freill
Sean O'neill
Erica Seibert

D-U-N-S 24-938-0445   (SL)
CITY CHEVROLET GEO OLDSMOBILE LTD
155 Cannon St E, Hamilton, ON, L8L 2A6

Emp Here 42   *Sales* 20,919,276
SIC 5511 New and used car dealers
Paul Burroughs

D-U-N-S 20-053-3818   (SL)
DUKE ELECTRIC (1977) LIMITED
986 Barton St E, Hamilton, ON, L8L 3C7
(905) 547-9171
Emp Here 40   *Sales* 17,886,960
SIC 5063 Electrical apparatus and equipment
Eric D. Raab
David Raab

D-U-N-S 24-008-5365   (HQ)
FIBRE LAMINATIONS LTD
CANUCK INDUSTRIES
651 Burlington St E, Hamilton, ON, L8L 4J5
(905) 312-9152
Sales 11,649,235
SIC 3299 NonMetallic mineral products,
Gordon Cormick

D-U-N-S 20-053-5722   (SL)
FLUKE TRANSPORT LIMITED
FLUKE TRANSPORTATION GROUP
(*Suby of* FOXCROFT CAPITAL CORP)
450 Sherman Ave N 2nd Fl, Hamilton, ON,
L8L 8J6
(905) 578-0677
Emp Here 200   *Sales* 41,141,200
SIC 4214 Local trucking with storage
Ron Foxcroft
Mark Groleau
Kevin Hagen
Steven Foxcroft

D-U-N-S 24-911-4844   (SL)
HEDDLE MARINE SERVICE INC
208 Hillyard St, Hamilton, ON, L8L 6B6
(905) 528-2635
Emp Here 60   *Sales* 13,430,580
SIC 3731 Shipbuilding and repairing
Richard W Heddle

D-U-N-S 20-054-0664   (HQ)
HOTZ AND SONS COMPANY INC
239 Lottridge St, Hamilton, ON, L8L 6W1

▲ Public Company   ■ Public Company Family Member   **HQ** Headquarters   **BR** Branch   **SL** Single Location

(905) 545-2665
Sales 52,054,200
SIC 5093 Scrap and waste materials
Martin Hotz

D-U-N-S 20-646-3684   (SL)
INTERINFORMA INC
701 GOLD BOOK
400 Wellington St N Unit 1, Hamilton, ON, L8L 5B1
(905) 526-0701
Emp Here 100   *Sales* 13,538,600
SIC 2731 Book publishing
David Turkstera
Greg Turkstera

D-U-N-S 24-208-0887   (SL)
J C INDOOR CLEAN AIR SERVICES INC
18 Linden St, Hamilton, ON, L8L 3H6
(905) 383-7855
Emp Here 25   *Sales* 10,380,725
SIC 4961 Steam and air-conditioning supply

D-U-N-S 24-183-5292   (BR)
JNE CONSULTING LTD
121 Shaw St, Hamilton, ON, L8L 3P6
(905) 529-5122
Emp Here 350
SIC 8711 Engineering services
Joe Ng

D-U-N-S 25-214-6824   (HQ)
JNE CONSULTING LTD
176 Shaw St, Hamilton, ON, L8L 3P7
(905) 529-5122
Emp Here 100   *Sales* 49,282,750
SIC 8711 Engineering services
Joe Ng
Winnie Ng

D-U-N-S 24-367-6314   (SL)
KARMA CANDY INC
356 Emerald St N, Hamilton, ON, L8L 8K6
(905) 527-6222
Emp Here 400   *Sales* 194,954,000
SIC 2064 Candy and other confectionery products
Aditya Jha
Vasu Chanchlani

D-U-N-S 25-185-4105   (BR)
LIUNA GARDENS LIMITED
LIUNA STATION
360 James St N Suite 201, Hamilton, ON, L8L 1H5
(905) 525-2410
Emp Here 75
SIC 7299 Miscellaneous personal service
Rosatone Vico

D-U-N-S 24-803-0111   (SL)
MAX AICHER (NORTH AMERICA) LIMITED
MANA STEEL
(*Suby of* MAX AICHER STIFTUNG)
855 Industrial Dr, Hamilton, ON, L8L 0B2
(289) 426-5670
Emp Here 100   *Sales* 18,138,800
SIC 3312 Blast furnaces and steel mills
Thomas Fetzer
Max Aicher

D-U-N-S 24-676-5833   (SL)
MAX AICHER (NORTH AMERICA) REALTY INC
(*Suby of* MAX AICHER STIFTUNG)
855 Industrial Dr, Hamilton, ON, L8L 0B2
(289) 426-5670
Emp Here 125   *Sales* 50,896,750
SIC 3312 Blast furnaces and steel mills
Thomas Fetzer
Jim Etzl
Dave Cameron
Max Aicher
Gerhard Weichenhain

D-U-N-S 24-009-3518   (HQ)
MISSION SERVICES OF HAMILTON, INC
196 Wentworth St N, Hamilton, ON, L8L 5V7

(905) 528-4211
Emp Here 17   *Sales* 12,011,310
SIC 8399 Social services, nec
Edward Raddatz

D-U-N-S 20-346-3542   (HQ)
NATT TOOLS GROUP INC
INGERSOL TILLAGE GROUP
460 Sherman Ave N, Hamilton, ON, L8L 8J6
(905) 549-7433
Sales 26,994,824
SIC 3523 Farm machinery and equipment
Stephen Garrette
Roger Murdock

D-U-N-S 24-320-0883   (HQ)
NORTH HAMILTON COMMUNITY HEALTH CENTRE
438 Hughson St N, Hamilton, ON, L8L 4N5
(905) 523-1184
Emp Here 1   *Sales* 12,851,680
SIC 8011 Offices and clinics of medical doctors
Elizabeth Beader

D-U-N-S 20-964-8880   (SL)
PEEPERS INTERNATIONAL LTD
360 Wentworth St N, Hamilton, ON, L8L 5W3

Emp Here 20   *Sales* 10,174,797
SIC 5137 Women's and children's clothing
Ralph Orman

D-U-N-S 20-184-8566   (HQ)
POINTE-CLAIRE STEEL INC
(*Suby of* POINTE-CLAIRE/GREEN VALLEY STEEL GROUP INC)
408 Wentworth St N, Hamilton, ON, L8L 5W3
(905) 544-5604
Sales 23,253,048
SIC 5051 Metals service centers and offices
James Edger
Soheil Monzavi

D-U-N-S 20-337-4285   (HQ)
POINTE-CLAIRE/GREEN VALLEY STEEL GROUP INC
408 Wentworth St N, Hamilton, ON, L8L 5W3
(905) 544-5604
Emp Here 4   *Sales* 19,675,656
SIC 5051 Metals service centers and offices
Michel Blais
Soheil Monzavi
Robert Dube

D-U-N-S 20-369-2041   (HQ)
STELCO HOLDINGS INC
(*Suby of* BEDROCK INDUSTRIES)
386 Wilcox St, Hamilton, ON, L8L 8K5
(905) 528-2511
Sales 1,020,087,054
SIC 6712 Bank holding companies
Alan Kestenbaum
Don P. Newman
Sujit Sanyal
David Cheney
Peter Bowie
Jeffrey B. Bunder
Michael W. Dees
Brian Michael Levitt
Alan Goldberg
Indira V. Samarasekera

D-U-N-S 20-361-2536   (HQ)
STELCO INC
(*Suby of* BEDROCK INDUSTRIES)
386 Wilcox St, Hamilton, ON, L8L 8K5
(905) 528-2511
Sales 1,254,346,677
SIC 3312 Blast furnaces and steel mills
Alan Kestenbaum
David Cheney
Michael Mcquade
Sujit Sanyal
Don Newman

D-U-N-S 20-547-8741   (HQ)
TRAVALE TIRE & SERVICE INC

340 Wentworth St N, Hamilton, ON, L8L 5W3
(905) 777-8473
Emp Here 5   *Sales* 12,451,950
SIC 5531 Auto and home supply stores
John Travale
Michael Travale

D-U-N-S 24-926-2585   (BR)
VICTORIAN ORDER OF NURSES FOR CANADA
VON HAMILTON DISTRICT
(*Suby of* VICTORIAN ORDER OF NURSES FOR CANADA)
414 Victoria Ave N Suite M2, Hamilton, ON, L8L 5G8
(905) 529-0700
Emp Here 200
SIC 8082 Home health care services
Lucy Trigiani

D-U-N-S 25-365-4990   (BR)
VON CANADA FOUNDATION
VON HAMILTON
414 Victoria Ave N Suite 568, Hamilton, ON, L8L 5G8
(905) 529-0700
Emp Here 143
SIC 8399 Social services, nec
Janis North

Hamilton, ON L8M

D-U-N-S 25-747-8826   (SL)
CATHOLIC CHILDREN'S AID SOCIETY OF HAMILTON-WENTWORTH
CCAS HAMILTON
735 King St E, Hamilton, ON, L8M 1A1
(905) 525-2012
Emp Here 180   *Sales* 13,822,560
SIC 8322 Individual and family services
Jamie Anderson
Dan Hinsperger
Giulia Gambacorta
Joe Spotts
Ersilia Dinardo
Vito Colella
Christine Hendrie

D-U-N-S 24-567-4432   (SL)
ELIZABETH FRY SOC. OF HAMILTON
85 Holton Ave S, Hamilton, ON, L8M 2L4
(905) 527-3097
Emp Here 28   *Sales* 11,127,592
SIC 8699 Membership organizations, nec
Elaine Bright

Hamilton, ON L8N

D-U-N-S 20-822-2299   (SL)
386140 ONTARIO LIMITED
TRAYNOR BAKERY WHOLESALE
191 Victoria Ave S, Hamilton, ON, L8N 0A4
(905) 522-2730
Emp Here 25   *Sales* 20,889,425
SIC 5149 Groceries and related products, nec
Mike Traynor
John Traynor

D-U-N-S 25-069-2365   (SL)
717940 ONTARIO LIMITED
DANNY'S NO FRILLS
435 Main St E, Hamilton, ON, L8N 1K1
(905) 528-5493
Emp Here 56   *Sales* 16,434,712
SIC 5411 Grocery stores
Danny Nedelko

D-U-N-S 20-053-3354   (HQ)
ARCELORMITTAL DOFASCO G.P.
(*Suby of* ARCELORMITTAL)
1330 Burlington St E, Hamilton, ON, L8N 3J5

(905) 548-7200
Sales 2,432,310,000
SIC 3479 Metal coating and allied services
Sean Donnelly
Andrew Connor
Vasudha Seth
Tony Valeri
Roger Tang-Poy
Katrina Mcfadden
Lisa Marcuzzi
Scott Maki
Angela Pappin
Brad Davey

D-U-N-S 20-734-6532   (HQ)
BEHAVIOUR INSTITUTE
57 Young St, Hamilton, ON, L8N 1V1
(905) 570-0777
Emp Here 25   *Sales* 20,805,743
SIC 8999 Services, nec
Nicole Walton-Allen

D-U-N-S 24-525-7217   (SL)
BLUE LINE TRANSPORTATION LTD
BLUE LINE TAXI
160 John St S, Hamilton, ON, L8N 2C4
(905) 525-2583
Emp Here 75   *Sales* 5,645,400
SIC 4121 Taxicabs
Anthony F Rizzuto
Anthony R Rizzuto
Luke Hayes
Josephine Rizzuto
James Milligan

D-U-N-S 20-968-6674   (SL)
CITYHOUSING FIRST PLACE HAMILTON
350 King St E Suite 300, Hamilton, ON, L8N 3Y3
(905) 525-9800
Emp Here 60   *Sales* 25,133,340
SIC 6531 Real estate agents and managers
Gary Quart
Ralph Pawson

D-U-N-S 20-817-5281   (HQ)
CUNNINGHAM LINDSEY CANADA LIMITED
ENVIROMENTAL SOLUTIONS
(*Suby of* FAIRFAX FINANCIAL HOLDINGS LIMITED)
46 Jackson St E, Hamilton, ON, L8N 1L1
(905) 528-1481
Emp Here 20   *Sales* 2,083,539,656
SIC 6411 Insurance agents, brokers, and service
Rob Seal
Gary Dalton
Claudine Davoodi

D-U-N-S 20-053-2893   (HQ)
DENNINGER, R. LIMITED
DENNINGER'S FOODS OF THE WORLD
284 King St E, Hamilton, ON, L8N 1B7
(905) 528-8468
Emp Here 150   *Sales* 146,215,500
SIC 2013 Sausages and other prepared meats
Curtis Murray
Gabriella Frank
Mary Aduckiewicz

D-U-N-S 24-947-5807   (HQ)
EFFORT CORPORATION
242 Main St E Suite 240, Hamilton, ON, L8N 1H5
(905) 528-8956
Sales 27,335,000
SIC 6719 Holding companies, nec
Thomas J Weisz

D-U-N-S 20-848-2638   (HQ)
EFFORT TRUST COMPANY, THE
(*Suby of* EFFORT CORPORATION)
240 Main St E, Hamilton, ON, L8N 1H5
(905) 528-8956
Emp Here 84   *Sales* 19,137,465
SIC 6021 National commercial banks
Thomas J Weisz

Arthur Weisz

D-U-N-S 25-743-1452 (HQ)
GOOD SHEPHERD CENTRE HAMILTON, THE
143 Wentworth St S Suite 302, Hamilton, ON, L8N 2Z1
(905) 528-5877
Emp Here 30   *Sales* 12,194,192
SIC 8322 Individual and family services
Richard Macphee
Justin Houson
Edward Lynch

D-U-N-S 20-645-6324 (BR)
HAMILTON HEALTH SCIENCES CORPORATION
HHS VOLUNTEER ASSOCIATION
(*Suby of* HAMILTON HEALTH SCIENCES CORPORATION)
1200 Main St W Rm 2, Hamilton, ON, L8N 3Z5
(905) 521-2100
Emp Here 100
SIC 8699 Membership organizations, nec
Mark Rizzo

D-U-N-S 25-846-6093 (BR)
IMARKETING SOLUTIONS GROUP INC
(*Suby of* IMARKETING SOLUTIONS GROUP INC)
4 Hughson St S Suite P400, Hamilton, ON, L8N 3Z1
(905) 529-7896
Emp Here 100
SIC 8399 Social services, nec
Andrew Langhorne

D-U-N-S 20-364-3841 (SL)
LOTLINX INC
8 Main St E Suite 200, Hamilton, ON, L8N 1E8

Emp Here 84   *Sales* 53,748,553
SIC 5511 New and used car dealers
Len Short

D-U-N-S 25-283-2118 (BR)
MCMASTER UNIVERSITY
(*Suby of* MCMASTER UNIVERSITY)
Gd, Hamilton, ON, L8N 3Z5
(905) 521-2100
Emp Here 2,182
SIC 8221 Colleges and universities
Bonnie Hugill

D-U-N-S 20-875-5363 (BR)
METROLAND MEDIA GROUP LTD
HAMILTON SPECTATOR, THE
(*Suby of* TORSTAR CORPORATION)
44 Frid St, Hamilton, ON, L8N 3G3
(905) 526-3333
Emp Here 400
SIC 2711 Newspapers
Neil Oliver

D-U-N-S 25-526-5118 (SL)
MOHAWK STUDENT'S ASSOCIATION
MSA
135 Fennel Ave W Rm G109, Hamilton, ON, L8N 3T2
(905) 575-2393
Emp Here 90   *Sales* 12,011,310
SIC 8399 Social services, nec
Kathy Inman

D-U-N-S 20-054-8923 (SL)
NATIONAL STEEL CAR LIMITED
600 Kenilworth Ave N, Hamilton, ON, L8N 3J4
(905) 544-3311
Emp Here 1,000   *Sales* 290,850,000
SIC 3743 Railroad equipment
Gregory J. Aziz
Peter Scott
Todd Pafford
Vince De Luca
Lorraine Johnson

D-U-N-S 20-974-6734 (SL)
PASWORD COMMUNICATIONS INC

122 Hughson St S, Hamilton, ON, L8N 2B2
(905) 974-1683
Emp Here 75   *Sales* 33,691,425
SIC 7389 Business services, nec
Paul Lloyd

D-U-N-S 24-364-7281 (SL)
PASWORD GROUP INC, THE
ANSWER PLUS
122 Hughson St S, Hamilton, ON, L8N 2B2
(905) 645-1162
Emp Here 100   *Sales* 44,921,900
SIC 7389 Business services, nec
Paul Lloyd

D-U-N-S 25-248-9976 (BR)
REVERA LONG TERM CARE INC
VERSA-CARE CENTRE HAMILTON
(*Suby of* GOVERNMENT OF CANADA)
330 Main St E, Hamilton, ON, L8N 3T9
(905) 523-1604
Emp Here 260
SIC 8051 Skilled nursing care facilities
Janet Cornier

D-U-N-S 24-010-1246 (SL)
RIZZUTO BROS. LIMITED
160 John St S, Hamilton, ON, L8N 2C4
(905) 522-2525
Emp Here 90   *Sales* 4,938,480
SIC 4121 Taxicabs
Anthony F. Rizzuto

D-U-N-S 24-923-6431 (SL)
ROTSAERT DENTAL LABORATORY SERVICES INC
71 Emerald St S, Hamilton, ON, L8N 2V4
(905) 527-1422
Emp Here 90   *Sales* 7,024,320
SIC 8072 Dental laboratories
Paul Rotsaert
Nicole Rotsaert
Eric Rotsaert
Peter Rotsaert
Mark Rotsaert

D-U-N-S 24-231-0675 (HQ)
ST. JOSEPH'S HEALTH SYSTEM
50 Charlton Ave E, Hamilton, ON, L8N 4A6
(905) 522-4941
Emp Here 2,000   *Sales* 7,049,144,900
SIC 8699 Membership organizations, nec
Anne Anderson
Anthony Tonnos
Allan Beaupre
Brian Guest
Margaret Kane
Patricia Valeriote
Anne Mcloughlin
Isobel Gallotti
Gerard Bergie
Peter Sullivan

D-U-N-S 20-750-8896 (HQ)
TAYLOR, LEIBOW LLP
105 Main St E Suite 700, Hamilton, ON, L8N 1G6
(905) 523-0003
Emp Here 45   *Sales* 13,499,525
SIC 8721 Accounting, auditing, and bookkeeping
Harold Pomerantz
Stephen Wiseman
Michael Moore

D-U-N-S 24-849-3137 (HQ)
WENTWORTH-HALTON X-RAY AND ULTRASOUND INC
(*Suby of* 1389851 ONTARIO LIMITED)
1 Young St Suite 218, Hamilton, ON, L8N 1T8
(905) 522-2344
Emp Here 10   *Sales* 55,415,070
SIC 8071 Medical laboratories
Micheal Romeo

Hamilton, ON L8P

D-U-N-S 20-787-0424 (BR)
AIESEC CANADA INC
A.I.E.S.E.C. CANADA INC
(*Suby of* AIESEC CANADA INC)
116 King St W, Hamilton, ON, L8P 4V3
(905) 529-5515
Emp Here 200
SIC 6513 Apartment building operators
Syed Gardezi

D-U-N-S 20-889-5602 (SL)
ALERT BEST NURSING INCORPORATED
290 Caroline St S Suite 4, Hamilton, ON, L8P 3L9
(905) 524-5990
Emp Here 75   *Sales* 4,842,000
SIC 8059 Nursing and personal care, nec
Yvonne Griggs

D-U-N-S 25-353-3061 (HQ)
ALEXANIAN FLOORING LIMITED
ALEXANIAN CARPET & FLOORING
601 Main St W, Hamilton, ON, L8P 1K9
(905) 527-2857
Emp Here 10   *Sales* 23,240,300
SIC 5713 Floor covering stores
Andrew Alexanian
Edward Gian Colla
Albert Alexanian

D-U-N-S 24-060-3886 (BR)
AVIVA INSURANCE COMPANY OF CANADA
(*Suby of* GENERAL ACCIDENT PLC)
1 King St W Suite 600, Hamilton, ON, L8P 1A4
(289) 391-2600
Emp Here 130
SIC 6331 Fire, marine, and casualty insurance
John Alaimo

D-U-N-S 20-158-9699 (HQ)
BURGEONVEST BICK SECURITIES LIMITED
21 King St W Suite 1100, Hamilton, ON, L8P 4W7
(905) 528-6505
Emp Here 5   *Sales* 16,467,417
SIC 6211 Security brokers and dealers
Mario Frankovich

D-U-N-S 25-508-5268 (HQ)
CANCABLE INC
DEPENDABLE HOMETECH
100 King St W Unit 700, Hamilton, ON, L8P 1A2
(905) 769-9705
Emp Here 50   *Sales* 235,509,000
SIC 1731 Electrical work
Ross Jepson
Mark Thompson

D-U-N-S 24-850-3687 (SL)
CHCH TV
CHCH HAMILTON
163 Jackson St W, Hamilton, ON, L8P 0A8
(905) 522-1101
Emp Here 170   *Sales* 38,840,240
SIC 4833 Television broadcasting stations
John Mc Laughlin

D-U-N-S 25-294-6447 (BR)
CUNNINGHAM LINDSEY CANADA LIMITED
(*Suby of* FAIRFAX FINANCIAL HOLDINGS LIMITED)
25 Main St W Suite 1810, Hamilton, ON, L8P 1H1
(905) 528-1481
Emp Here 150
SIC 6411 Insurance agents, brokers, and service
Doug Hopkins

D-U-N-S 24-316-7587 (SL)
DIRECT TRAFFIC MANAGEMENT INC
70 Frid St Suite 8, Hamilton, ON, L8P 4M4

(905) 529-7000
Emp Here 90   *Sales* 40,429,710
SIC 7389 Business services, nec
Peter Wehmeyer

D-U-N-S 24-107-6301 (SL)
DURAND NEIGHBOURHOOD INVESTMENTS INC
15 Bold St, Hamilton, ON, L8P 1T3

Emp Here 30   *Sales* 15,163,770
SIC 6733 Trusts, nec
Cathy Gordino

D-U-N-S 20-554-5957 (SL)
DURISOL MATERIALS LIMITED
67 Frid St, Hamilton, ON, L8P 4M3
(905) 521-0999
Emp Here 125   *Sales* 34,168,750
SIC 6712 Bank holding companies
Hans Rerup

D-U-N-S 20-981-7261 (BR)
ECONOMICAL MUTUAL INSURANCE COMPANY
ECONOMICAL INSURANCE
(*Suby of* ECONOMICAL MUTUAL INSURANCE COMPANY)
120 King St W Suite 750, Hamilton, ON, L8P 4V2
(519) 570-8200
Emp Here 100
SIC 6331 Fire, marine, and casualty insurance
Julian Manazone

D-U-N-S 24-358-1308 (BR)
FIRST REAL PROPERTIES LIMITED
JACKSON SQUARE
(*Suby of* IMMEUBLES YALE LIMITEE, LES)
100 King St W Suite 200, Hamilton, ON, L8P 1A2
(905) 522-3501
Emp Here 75
SIC 6512 Nonresidential building operators
Vivien Johnson

D-U-N-S 25-274-6664 (SL)
FORTINOS (DUNDURN) LTD
FORTINOS
50 Dundurn St S, Hamilton, ON, L8P 4W3
(905) 529-4290
Emp Here 300   *Sales* 57,739,200
SIC 5411 Grocery stores
Taner Yalchin
Russel Rankin
John Raycraft

D-U-N-S 20-188-4330 (BR)
G-WLG LP
(*Suby of* G-WLG LP)
1 Main St W, Hamilton, ON, L8P 4Z5
(905) 540-8208
Emp Here 140
SIC 8111 Legal services
Mark Easden

D-U-N-S 25-311-8244 (BR)
GOWLING WLG (CANADA) LLP
(*Suby of* GOWLING WLG (CANADA) LLP)
1 Main St W, Hamilton, ON, L8P 4Z5
(905) 540-8208
Emp Here 135
SIC 8111 Legal services
Mark Tammanga

D-U-N-S 20-328-5051 (SL)
HAMILTON ENTERTAINMENT AND CONVENTION FACILITIES INC, THE
1 Summers Ln, Hamilton, ON, L8P 4Y2
(905) 546-3000
Emp Here 49   *Sales* 22,011,731
SIC 7389 Business services, nec
Brad Calder

D-U-N-S 20-751-0322 (HQ)
HAMILTON HEALTH SCIENCES CORPORATION
100 King St W Suite 2300, Hamilton, ON, L8P 1A2

▲ Public Company   ■ Public Company Family Member   **HQ** Headquarters   **BR** Branch   **SL** Single Location

(905) 521-2100
Emp Here 300   *Sales* 1,212,884,075
SIC 8062 General medical and surgical hospitals
  Rob Macisaac
  David Mccaig
  Wes Stephen
  Michael Stacy
  Anna Ventresca
  Kirsten Krull
  Ted Scott
  Rebecca Repa
  Sharon Pierson
  Teresa Smith

D-U-N-S 24-389-0761   (HQ)
HAMILTON YOUNG WOMEN'S CHRISTIAN ASSOCIATION, THE
YWCA
75 Macnab St S, Hamilton, ON, L8P 3C1
(905) 522-9922
Sales 26,303,000
SIC 8641 Civic and social associations
  Charlotte Yates
  Mia Laister Peck
  Sue Bennison
  Medora Uppal
  Winnie Linker
  Janet Arsenault
  Sarah Ernest
  Mylene Vincent
  Denise Doyle

D-U-N-S 24-911-0651   (HQ)
HANBALI, JEFF DRUGS LTD
SHOPPERS DRUG MART
620 King St W Suite 1458, Hamilton, ON, L8P 1C2
(905) 522-0599
Emp Here 40   *Sales* 24,432,800
SIC 5912 Drug stores and proprietary stores
  Jeff Hanbali

D-U-N-S 20-943-5510   (BR)
KPMG LLP
(*Suby of* KPMG LLP)
21 King St W Suite 700, Hamilton, ON, L8P 4W7
(905) 523-2259
Emp Here 100
SIC 8721 Accounting, auditing, and bookkeeping
  Barry Frieday

D-U-N-S 24-709-0454   (SL)
MABEL'S LABELS INC
150 Chatham St Unit 1, Hamilton, ON, L8P 2B6
(905) 667-0306
Emp Here 44   *Sales* 10,271,140
SIC 2679 Converted paper products, nec
  Julie Ellis
  Julie Cole
  Tricia Mumby
  Cynthia Esp
  Karma Bryan-Ingle

D-U-N-S 20-279-1711   (BR)
NATURAL RESOURCES CANADA
CANMET MATERIALS
(*Suby of* GOVERNMENT OF CANADA)
183 Longwood Rd S, Hamilton, ON, L8P 0A5
(905) 645-0683
Emp Here 100
SIC 2861 Gum and wood chemicals
  Hitech Jain

D-U-N-S 24-182-1644   (SL)
OLD REPUBLIC INSURANCE COMPANY OF CANADA
(*Suby of* OLD REPUBLIC INTERNATIONAL CORPORATION)
100 King St W Unit 1100, Hamilton, ON, L8P 1A2
(905) 523-5936
Emp Here 28   *Sales* 34,591,704
SIC 6331 Fire, marine, and casualty insurance
  Paul Field

D-U-N-S 20-153-8951   (SL)
PARKVIEW HEALTH CARE PARTNERSHIP
PARKVIEW NURSING CENTRE
545 King St W Suite 412, Hamilton, ON, L8P 1C1
(905) 525-5903
Emp Here 150   *Sales* 10,248,900
SIC 8051 Skilled nursing care facilities
  Michael Busch

D-U-N-S 20-641-0255   (SL)
PIPEFLO CONTRACTING CORP
111 Frid St, Hamilton, ON, L8P 4M3
(905) 572-7767
Emp Here 50   *Sales* 22,358,700
SIC 5032 Brick, stone, and related material
  Bruce Noble
  Darlene Noble

D-U-N-S 24-213-5119   (BR)
PRICEWATERHOUSECOOPERS LLP
(*Suby of* PRICEWATERHOUSECOOPERS LLP)
21 King St W Suite 100, Hamilton, ON, L8P 4W7

Emp Here 76
SIC 8721 Accounting, auditing, and bookkeeping
  Sean Casey

D-U-N-S 20-256-6360   (HQ)
PT HEALTHCARE SOLUTIONS CORP
PT HEALTH
70 Frid St Unit 2, Hamilton, ON, L8P 4M4
(877) 734-9887
Emp Here 1,001   *Sales* 89,351,262
SIC 8049 Offices of health practitioner
  Mark Cho
  Peter Ruttan
  Paulette Gardiner Millar

D-U-N-S 20-900-2856   (SL)
RELIABLE LIFE INSURANCE COMPANY
(*Suby of* OLD REPUBLIC INTERNATIONAL CORPORATION)
100 King St W, Hamilton, ON, L8P 1A2
(905) 525-5031
Emp Here 120   *Sales* 256,436,160
SIC 6311 Life insurance
  Paul Field
  Aldo Zucaro
  Brian Reeve
  J W Nevil Thomas
  Thomas A Hickey
  Spencer Leroy
  Gary E Lewis

D-U-N-S 20-552-1508   (SL)
REPUBLIC CANADIAN DRAWN, INC
(*Suby of* INDUSTRIAS CH, S.A.B. DE C.V.)
155 Chatham St, Hamilton, ON, L8P 2B7
(905) 546-5656
Emp Here 65   *Sales* 11,790,220
SIC 3316 Cold finishing of steel shapes
  Rico Gambale
  Mary Anne Gill

D-U-N-S 24-976-3533   (HQ)
SECOND REAL PROPERTIES LIMITED
(*Suby of* IMMEUBLES YALE LIMITEE, LES)
100 King St W, Hamilton, ON, L8P 1A2
(905) 522-3501
Emp Here 25   *Sales* 20,351,550
SIC 6512 Nonresidential building operators
  Emile Mashaal
  Jacques Phaneuf
  Edward Quigg
  Victor Mashaal
  Elise Bourret
  Kevin Powers
  Ingrid Gendreau
  Peter Hill
  Michael Mashaal
  Ronald Mashaal

D-U-N-S 24-425-8971   (BR)

D-U-N-S **SP DATA CAPITAL ULC**
(*Suby of* SP DATA CAPITAL ULC)
110 King St W Suite 500, Hamilton, ON, L8P 4S6
(905) 645-5610
Emp Here 400
SIC 7389 Business services, nec
  Cheryl Tost

D-U-N-S 20-270-0357   (HQ)
TANDIA FINANCIAL CREDIT UNION LIMITED
75 James St S, Hamilton, ON, L8P 2Y9
(800) 598-2891
Emp Here 200   *Sales* 68,320,400
SIC 6062 State credit unions
  Richard Davies

D-U-N-S 20-002-6867   (HQ)
TEACHERS CREDIT UNION LIMITED
75 James St S, Hamilton, ON, L8P 2Y9
(905) 525-8131
Emp Here 70   *Sales* 15,351,100
SIC 6062 State credit unions
  Beryl Roberto
  Betty Gruba

D-U-N-S 25-930-7999   (SL)
TEXTURES FINE CRAFTS
236 Locke St S, Hamilton, ON, L8P 4B7
(905) 523-0636
Emp Here 55   *Sales* 12,853,225
SIC 8621 Professional organizations
  Sharon Beasley

D-U-N-S 20-773-1311   (HQ)
VRANCOR PROPERTY MANAGEMENT INC
VRANCOR GROUP OF COMPANIES
366 King St W, Hamilton, ON, L8P 1B3
(905) 540-4800
Emp Here 5   *Sales* 15,817,200
SIC 6553 Cemetery subdividers and developers
  Darko Vranich

D-U-N-S 24-868-9093   (BR)
WORKPLACE SAFETY & INSURANCE BOARD, THE
WSIB
(*Suby of* WORKPLACE SAFETY & INSURANCE BOARD, THE)
120 King St W, Hamilton, ON, L8P 4V2
(800) 387-0750
Emp Here 400
SIC 6331 Fire, marine, and casualty insurance
  Dave Whitney

D-U-N-S 25-873-6149   (SL)
WORLDWIDE EVANGELIZATION FOR CHRIST
WEC INTERNATIONAL
37 Aberdeen Ave, Hamilton, ON, L8P 2N6
(905) 529-0166
Emp Here 72   *Sales* 48,161,376
SIC 7389 Business services, nec
  Henry Bell

D-U-N-S 24-079-3984   (HQ)
YMCA   OF   HAMILTON/BURLINGTON/BRANTFORD
79 James St S, Hamilton, ON, L8P 2Z1
(905) 529-7102
Emp Here 1,000   *Sales* 36,493,511
SIC 7997 Membership sports and recreation clubs
  Jim Commerford
  Brenda Flaherty
  Brian Heagle
  Bruce Pearson
  Jean A. Byrnes

Hamilton, ON L8R

D-U-N-S 20-349-9728   (HQ)
ALECTRA UTILITIES CORPORATION

HORIZON UTILITIES
(*Suby of* ALECTRA INC)
55 John St N, Hamilton, ON, L8R 3M8
(905) 522-9200
Emp Here 345   *Sales* 1,201,411,744
SIC 4911 Electric services
  Brian Bentz
  Max Cananzi
  Peter Gregg
  Dennis Nolan
  Lawrence Wilde
  John Basilio
  Jamie Gribbon

D-U-N-S 20-119-8152   (SL)
ALECTRA UTILITIES CORPORATION
HORIZON UTILITIES
(*Suby of* CORPORATION OF THE CITY OF MISSISSAUGA)
55 John St N, Hamilton, ON, L8R 3M8
(905) 522-6611
Emp Here 500   *Sales* 420,368,000
SIC 4911 Electric services
  Max Canazi
  John Basilio
  Brian Bentz
  Peter Gregg
  James Macumber
  Kathy Lerette
  Eileen Campbell
  Robert Hull
  Dennis Nolan

D-U-N-S 20-704-7239   (HQ)
AMITY GOODWILL INDUSTRIES
225 King William St, Hamilton, ON, L8R 1B1
(905) 526-8482
Emp Here 1   *Sales* 63,829,080
SIC 8699 Membership organizations, nec
  Paul Chapin

D-U-N-S 24-323-4411   (SL)
AVL MANUFACTURING INC
243 Queen St N, Hamilton, ON, L8R 3N6
(905) 545-7660
Emp Here 50   *Sales* 35,395,896
SIC 8711 Engineering services
  Vince Di Cristofaro
  Lisa Di Cristofaro
  Mike Paletta

D-U-N-S 20-316-9362   (SL)
COPPLEY LTD
56 York Blvd, Hamilton, ON, L8R 0A2
(905) 529-1112
Emp Here 250   *Sales* 209,383,250
SIC 5136 Men's and boy's clothing
  Richard Sexton
  Warwick Jones

D-U-N-S 25-501-6768   (SL)
FUELS INC
136 Cannon St W, Hamilton, ON, L8R 2B9
(905) 528-0241
Emp Here 11   *Sales* 11,360,888
SIC 5172 Petroleum products, nec
  Michael Borisuk
  Peter Ewen

D-U-N-S 20-056-0803   (SL)
G.S. WARK LIMITED
370 York Blvd Suite 101, Hamilton, ON, L8R 3L1
(905) 529-4717
Emp Here 20   *Sales* 25,407,393
SIC 1542 Nonresidential construction, nec
  George W Wark
  Craig Hambly
  John Wark
  Scott Fearnside

D-U-N-S 25-149-6915   (SL)
HAMILTON HEALTH SCIENCES FOUNDATION
40 Wellington St N Suite 203, Hamilton, ON, L8R 1M8
(905) 522-3863
Emp Here 36   *Sales* 26,166,296

SIC 7389 Business services, nec
  Pearl Veenema

D-U-N-S 20-944-1559   (HQ)
HAMILTON PUBLIC LIBRARY BOARD, THE
55 York Blvd, Hamilton, ON, L8R 3K1
(905) 546-3200
Emp Here 250   *Sales* 21,414,816
SIC 8231 Libraries
  Paul Takala
  Karen Anderson
  Lisa Dupelle
  Sherry Fahim
  Tony Del Monaco

D-U-N-S 25-099-9950   (SL)
HAMILTON UTILITIES CORPORATION
(*Suby of* CITY OF HAMILTON, THE)
55 John St N, Hamilton, ON, L8R 3M8
(905) 317-4595
Emp Here 333   *Sales* 279,965,088
SIC 4911 Electric services
  Art Leitch
  John G Basillio
  Marjorie Richards
  Max Cananzi
  Ian Collins
  Robert Desnoyers
  Charles Hantho
  Robert Dolan
  Owens Shewfelt
  Gary Graham

D-U-N-S 20-941-4812   (HQ)
**HAMILTON-WENTWORTH   CATHOLIC
SCHOOL BOARD**
90 Mulberry St, Hamilton, ON, L8R 2C8
(905) 525-2930
Emp Here 60   *Sales* 396,476,000
SIC 8211 Elementary and secondary schools
  Patricia Amos

D-U-N-S 20-590-7426   (BR)
**HAMILTON-WENTWORTH   CATHOLIC
SCHOOL BOARD**
(*Suby of* HAMILTON-WENTWORTH
CATHOLIC SCHOOL BOARD)
90 Mulberry St, Hamilton, ON, L8R 2C8

Emp Here 100
SIC 8211 Elementary and secondary schools
  Marcel Castura

D-U-N-S 25-823-1398   (BR)
**HAMILTON-WENTWORTH   DISTRICT
SCHOOL BOARD, THE**
*SIR JOHN A MACDONALD SECONDARY
SCHOOL*
(*Suby of* HAMILTON-WENTWORTH DIS-
TRICT SCHOOL BOARD, THE)
130 York Blvd, Hamilton, ON, L8R 1Y5
(905) 528-8363
Emp Here 120
SIC 8211 Elementary and secondary schools
  D Pent

D-U-N-S 25-093-1748   (BR)
HARSCO CANADA CORPORATION
MULTISERV
(*Suby of* HARSCO CORPORATION)
151 York Blvd, Hamilton, ON, L8R 3M2
(905) 522-8123
Emp Here 215
SIC 3295 Minerals, ground or treated
  Ian Kirk

D-U-N-S 25-624-3429   (SL)
MARTINO NURSING CENTRES LIMITED
TOWNSVIEW LIFECARE CENTRE
39 Mary St, Hamilton, ON, L8R 3L8
(905) 523-6427
Emp Here 230   *Sales* 15,714,980
SIC 8051 Skilled nursing care facilities
  Walter Sguazzin

D-U-N-S 20-522-2107   (HQ)
TRAVEL SUPERSTORE INC

TRIPCENTRAL.CA
(*Suby of* TRANSAT A.T. INC)
77 James St N Suite 230, Hamilton, ON, L8R
2K3
(905) 570-9999
Emp Here 20   *Sales* 33,277,888
SIC 4724 Travel agencies
  Richard Vanderlubbe
  Sean Furlong

D-U-N-S 24-302-0518   (SL)
VICTORIA PARK COMMUNITY HOMES INC
155 Queen St N, Hamilton, ON, L8R 2V6
(905) 527-0221
Emp Here 60   *Sales* 13,252,260
SIC 6514 Dwelling operators, except apart-
ments
  Colin Gage
  David Martin
  David Lowden
  Mac Carson
  Grant Martin
  Debra Russon
  Gary Elliott
  Steve Naylor
  Patrick Woolley
  David Reid

Hamilton, ON L8S

D-U-N-S 25-751-9629   (SL)
CANADIAN ASSOCIATION OF CLERGY
114 Arkell St, Hamilton, ON, L8S 1N7
(905) 522-3775
Emp Here 49   *Sales* 11,643,648
SIC 8621 Professional organizations
  Tony J Ouwehand

D-U-N-S 20-348-2401   (SL)
**CANADIAN RESEARCH DATA CENTER
NETWORK**
1280 Main St W, Hamilton, ON, L8S 4M1
(905) 525-9140
Emp Here 49   *Sales* 10,630,375
SIC 8732 Commercial nonphysical research
  S Martin Taylor

D-U-N-S 24-846-8175   (SL)
**COLUMBIA   PRIVATE   SECONDARY
SCHOOL INC**
COLUMBIA INTERNATIONAL COLLEGE
1003 Main St W Suite 163, Hamilton, ON, L8S
4P3
(905) 572-7883
Emp Here 190   *Sales* 17,636,940
SIC 8211 Elementary and secondary schools
  Bill Ironside

D-U-N-S 25-465-1953   (SL)
HAMILTON JEWISH HOME FOR THE AGED
SHALOM VILLAGE
70 Macklin St N, Hamilton, ON, L8S 3S1
(905) 528-5377
Emp Here 250   *Sales* 16,070,500
SIC 8361 Residential care
  Renee Guder

D-U-N-S 25-292-6670   (BR)
**HAMILTON-WENTWORTH   CATHOLIC
SCHOOL BOARD**
*ST. MARY'S CATHOLIC SECONDARY
SCHOOL*
(*Suby   of   HAMILTON-WENTWORTH
CATHOLIC SCHOOL BOARD*)
200 Whitney Ave, Hamilton, ON, L8S 2G7
(905) 528-0214
Emp Here 100
SIC 8211 Elementary and secondary schools
  Michael Gravina

D-U-N-S 20-301-6717   (BR)
**HAMILTON-WENTWORTH   DISTRICT
SCHOOL BOARD, THE**
WESTDALE SECONDARY SCHOOL

(*Suby of* HAMILTON-WENTWORTH DIS-
TRICT SCHOOL BOARD, THE)
700 Main St W, Hamilton, ON, L8S 1A5
(905) 522-1387
Emp Here 150
SIC 8211 Elementary and secondary schools
  Timothy Powell-Mcbride

D-U-N-S 24-329-2245   (SL)
**MCMASTER STUDENTS UNION INCORPO-
RATED**
1280 Main St W Rm 1, Hamilton, ON, L8S 4K1
(905) 525-9140
Emp Here 700   *Sales* 199,361,400
SIC 8631 Labor organizations
  John Popham

D-U-N-S 20-751-0108   (HQ)
MCMASTER UNIVERSITY
1280 Main St W Gh209, Hamilton, ON, L8S
4L8
(905) 525-9140
Sales 848,003,126
SIC 8221 Colleges and universities
  Patrick Deane
  Roger Couldrey
  David Wilkinson
  Mohamed Elbestawi
  John Kelton
  Mary Williams
  Nancy Gray
  Suzanne Labarge

D-U-N-S 25-292-3974   (BR)
METRO ONTARIO INC
METRO
(*Suby of* METRO INC)
845 King St W, Hamilton, ON, L8S 1K4
(905) 523-5044
Emp Here 180
SIC 5411 Grocery stores
  Michael Lavell

D-U-N-S 20-255-7575   (BR)
MONDELEZ CANADA INC
MONDELEZ INTERNATIONAL CANADA
(*Suby of MONDELEZ INTERNATIONAL,
INC.*)
45 Ewen Rd, Hamilton, ON, L8S 3C3
(905) 526-7212
Emp Here 300
SIC 2032 Canned specialties
  Andres Ruiz

Hamilton, ON L8T

D-U-N-S 24-391-0986   (BR)
**HAMILTON-WENTWORTH   DISTRICT
SCHOOL BOARD, THE**
BARTON SECONDARY SCHOOL
(*Suby of* HAMILTON-WENTWORTH DIS-
TRICT SCHOOL BOARD, THE)
75 Palmer Rd, Hamilton, ON, L8T 3G1
(905) 389-2234
Emp Here 85
SIC 8211 Elementary and secondary schools
  B Lennox

D-U-N-S 24-326-5589   (SL)
J.R. GIUDICE PHARMACY INC
SHOPPERS DRUG MART
902 Mohawk Rd E, Hamilton, ON, L8T 2R8
(905) 387-2300
Emp Here 50   *Sales* 12,647,700
SIC 5912 Drug stores and proprietary stores
  Joe Giudice

D-U-N-S 20-812-8582   (BR)
METRO RICHELIEU INC
BARN, THE
(*Suby of* METRO INC)
967 Fennell Ave E, Hamilton, ON, L8T 1R1
(905) 318-7777
Emp Here 85

SIC 5411 Grocery stores
  Lance Farrise

Hamilton, ON L8V

D-U-N-S 20-013-6633   (HQ)
BANYAN COMMUNITY SERVICES INC
ARRELL YOUTH CENTRE
688 Queensdale Ave E Unit 2b, Hamilton, ON,
L8V 1M1
(905) 545-0133
Emp Here 20   *Sales* 287,720,200
SIC 8699 Membership organizations, nec
  Kim Ciavarella
  Jacqueline Barrett
  Glenn Cooke
  Jill Mckenzie
  Michael Spencer
  D'arcy Wilson
  Donna Zan
  Maria Zegarac

D-U-N-S 25-642-2825   (BR)
BAYSHORE HEALTHCARE LTD.
BAYSHORE HEALTHCARE LTD
(*Suby of* BAYSHORE HEALTHCARE LTD.)
755 Concession St Suite 100, Hamilton, ON,
L8V 1C4
(905) 523-5999
Emp Here 315
SIC 8082 Home health care services
  Luanne Ellison

D-U-N-S 25-094-2273   (HQ)
**CATHOLIC FAMILY SERVICES OF HAMIL-
TON**
CFS
2b-688 Queensdale Ave E, Hamilton, ON, L8V
1M1
(905) 527-3823
Sales 10,943,638
SIC 8399 Social services, nec
  Linda Dayler

D-U-N-S 25-867-2153   (SL)
FORTINOS (MALL 1994) LTD
FORTINO'S SUPERMARKET
65 Mall Rd, Hamilton, ON, L8V 5B8
(905) 387-7673
Emp Here 260   *Sales* 50,040,640
SIC 5411 Grocery stores
  Carmine Gallo

D-U-N-S 20-025-4444   (BR)
**HAMILTON HEALTH SCIENCES CORPO-
RATION**
HENDERSON HOSPITAL
(*Suby of* HAMILTON HEALTH SCIENCES
CORPORATION)
711 Concession St Suite 201, Hamilton, ON,
L8V 1C3
(905) 389-4411
Emp Here 1,345
SIC 8062 General medical and surgical hospi-
tals
  Ari Collerman

D-U-N-S 24-365-7616   (BR)
**HAMILTON HEALTH SCIENCES CORPO-
RATION**
JURAVINSKI CANCER CENTRE
(*Suby of* HAMILTON HEALTH SCIENCES
CORPORATION)
699 Concession St, Hamilton, ON, L8V 5C2
(905) 387-9495
Emp Here 400
SIC 8093 Specialty outpatient clinics, nec
  Ralph Meyer

D-U-N-S 24-336-8479   (HQ)
ROMARAH INCORPORATED
GOODNESS ME NATURAL FOOD MARKET
1000 Upper Gage Ave Suite 14, Hamilton, ON,
L8V 4R5

(905) 388-8400
Sales 10,966,080
SIC 5499 Miscellaneous food stores
  Scott Jacks
  Janet Jacks

Hamilton, ON L8W

D-U-N-S 20-366-4784   (HQ)
1716871 ONTARIO INC
CARSTAR AUTOMOTIVE CANADA
1460 Stone Church Rd E, Hamilton, ON, L8W 3V3
(905) 388-2264
Emp Here 45   *Sales* 1,043,264,700
SIC 6794 Patent owners and lessors
  Samuel Mercanti

D-U-N-S 24-868-7089   (HQ)
BAR HYDRAULICS INC
1632 Upper Ottawa St, Hamilton, ON, L8W 3P2
(905) 385-2257
Sales 17,100,936
SIC 5084 Industrial machinery and equipment
  Peter Bardoel
  Doreen Bardoel
  Peter W Bardoel

D-U-N-S 20-038-2070   (BR)
CANADA BREAD COMPANY, LIMITED
DEMPSTER BREAD, DIV OF
(*Suby of* GRUPO BIMBO, S.A.B. DE C.V.)
155 Nebo Rd Suite 1, Hamilton, ON, L8W 2E1
(905) 387-3935
Emp Here 100
SIC 5149 Groceries and related products, nec
  Mike Slammia

D-U-N-S 20-402-5498   (SL)
CENTURA (HAMILTON) LIMITED
CENTURA FLOOR & WALL TILE
(*Suby of* CENTURA LIMITED)
140 Nebo Rd, Hamilton, ON, L8W 2E4
(905) 383-5100
Emp Here 33   *Sales* 16,792,248
SIC 5023 Homefurnishings
  Brian Cowie
  Peter Donath
  Bob Sheehan

D-U-N-S 20-558-9794   (SL)
DIVAL DEVELOPMENTS LTD
NU-WALL
90 Trinity Church Rd, Hamilton, ON, L8W 3S2
(905) 387-8214
Emp Here 50   *Sales* 11,008,400
SIC 1794 Excavation work
  Jason Pacenza
  Tony Pacenza

D-U-N-S 20-052-5918   (HQ)
DRIVE STAR SHUTTLE SYSTEMS LTD
(*Suby of* DRIVE STAR INTERNATIONAL INC)
1625 Stone Church Rd E, Hamilton, ON, L8W 3Y5
(866) 378-7827
Sales 24,684,720
SIC 4213 Trucking, except local
  Andrew Priest
  Doug Billyard
  Gary Ward

D-U-N-S 20-505-6021   (SL)
EDSON PACKAGING MACHINERY LIMITED
215 Hempstead Dr, Hamilton, ON, L8W 2E6
(905) 385-3201
Emp Here 70   *Sales* 15,540,070
SIC 3565 Packaging machinery
  Gary Evans
  Tony Bozelli

D-U-N-S 25-370-6394   (HQ)
FEATURE WALTERS INC
(*Suby of* WALTER'S GROUP INC)

1318 Rymal Rd E, Hamilton, ON, L8W 3N1
(905) 388-7111
Sales 11,618,035
SIC 8712 Architectural services
  Julian Bowron
  Walt Koppelaar
  Patrick Desarzens

D-U-N-S 20-639-5261   (HQ)
FERRELL BUILDERS SUPPLY LIMITED
FERRELL CONTRACT - HARDWARE, DIV OF
1549 Rymal Rd E, Hamilton, ON, L8W 3N2
(905) 387-1948
Emp Here 34   *Sales* 26,765,200
SIC 5211 Lumber and other building materials
  Peter Cicchi

D-U-N-S 24-991-3005   (SL)
FINE ANALYSIS LABORATORIES LTD
236 Pritchard Rd, Hamilton, ON, L8W 3P7

Emp Here 86
SIC 8734 Testing laboratories

D-U-N-S 20-940-1132   (HQ)
FORTINOS SUPERMARKET LTD
(*Suby of* LOBLAW COMPANIES LIMITED)
1275 Rymal Rd E Suite 2, Hamilton, ON, L8W 3N1
(905) 318-4532
Emp Here 80   *Sales* 129,008,880
SIC 5141 Groceries, general line
  Vince Scornaienchi
  Elaine Martin

D-U-N-S 20-626-4996   (HQ)
G. T. FRENCH PAPER LIMITED
90 Glover Rd, Hamilton, ON, L8W 3T7
(905) 574-0275
Emp Here 84   *Sales* 47,343,852
SIC 5113 Industrial and personal service paper
  Paul Martin

D-U-N-S 25-292-6621   (BR)
HAMILTON-WENTWORTH   CATHOLIC SCHOOL BOARD
ST JEAN DE BREBEUF SCHOOL
(*Suby of* HAMILTON-WENTWORTH CATHOLIC SCHOOL BOARD)
200 Acadia Dr, Hamilton, ON, L8W 1B8
(905) 388-7020
Emp Here 135
SIC 8211 Elementary and secondary schools
  Margarita Lawlor

D-U-N-S 20-054-3767   (HQ)
LANCASTER GROUP INC
195 Hempstead Dr, Hamilton, ON, L8W 2E6
(905) 388-3800
Emp Here 60   *Sales* 13,983,900
SIC 1711 Plumbing, heating, air-conditioning
  Blair Hubber
  Elizabeth Hubber

D-U-N-S 20-793-1853   (BR)
METRO ONTARIO INC
FOOD BASICS
(*Suby of* METRO INC)
505 Rymal Rd E Suite 3, Hamilton, ON, L8W 3X1
(905) 574-5298
Emp Here 210
SIC 5411 Grocery stores
  Joe Mastriani

D-U-N-S 25-292-3933   (BR)
METRO ONTARIO INC
(*Suby of* METRO INC)
1070 Stone Church Rd E, Hamilton, ON, L8W 3K8

Emp Here 100
SIC 5411 Grocery stores
  Robert Hall

D-U-N-S 20-696-1018   (HQ)

NIKOLAOS FINE FOODS INC.
225 Nebo Rd Unit 5, Hamilton, ON, L8W 2E1
(905) 388-8074
Sales 25,067,310
SIC 5144 Poultry and poultry products
  Aristi Varsakis

D-U-N-S 20-505-8621   (SL)
P.J. DALY CONTRACTING LIMITED
1320 Stone Church Rd E, Hamilton, ON, L8W 2C8
(905) 575-1525
Emp Here 300   *Sales* 54,957,300
SIC 1742 Plastering, drywall, and insulation
  Daniel J. Daly
  Matthew Daly

D-U-N-S 20-605-7424   (SL)
PARSONS PRECAST INC
PARSONS UNIT STEP
1315 Rymal Rd E, Hamilton, ON, L8W 3N1
(905) 387-0810
Emp Here 40   *Sales* 17,886,960
SIC 5032 Brick, stone, and related material
  Ted Acton

D-U-N-S 24-563-7202   (HQ)
PAUL'S RESTORATIONS INC
1640 Upper Ottawa St, Hamilton, ON, L8W 3P2
(905) 388-7285
Emp Here 30   *Sales* 15,943,450
SIC 1521 Single-family housing construction
  Paul Giardini
  Mark Sebastianutti
  David Sebastianutti

D-U-N-S 20-140-1481   (SL)
SCOTT STEEL ERECTORS INC
SCOTT STEEL
58 Bigwin Rd, Hamilton, ON, L8W 3R4
(905) 631-8708
Emp Here 160   *Sales* 67,637,920
SIC 1541 Industrial buildings and warehouses
  Daniel Scott

D-U-N-S 25-138-3089   (BR)
SOBEYS CAPITAL INCORPORATED
FRESHCO
(*Suby of* EMPIRE COMPANY LIMITED)
905 Rymal Rd E, Hamilton, ON, L8W 3M2
(905) 383-9930
Emp Here 150
SIC 5411 Grocery stores
  Ryan Bribgeman

D-U-N-S 20-025-5409   (BR)
STATE REALTY LIMITED
(*Suby of* STATE REALTY LIMITED)
987 Rymal Rd E, Hamilton, ON, L8W 3M2
(905) 574-4600
Emp Here 100
SIC 6531 Real estate agents and managers
  Doug Punis

D-U-N-S 24-183-7210   (SL)
TARESCO LTD
QSI
175a Nebo Rd, Hamilton, ON, L8W 2E1
(905) 575-8078
Emp Here 50   *Sales* 11,369,150
SIC 1751 Carpentry work
  Tares Bobiak

D-U-N-S 25-157-1055   (SL)
TERRA   RESTORATION   STEAMATIC HAMILTON
115 Hempstead Dr Suite 5, Hamilton, ON, L8W 2Y6
(905) 387-0662
Emp Here 14   *Sales* 10,156,146
SIC 6331 Fire, marine, and casualty insurance
  Dave Thompson

D-U-N-S 20-338-4276   (SL)
TURPOL TECH INDUSTRIES INC
100 Lancing Dr Unit 3, Hamilton, ON, L8W 3L6

(905) 512-9881
Emp Here 49   *Sales* 10,002,370
SIC 3325 Steel foundries, nec
  Ugur Kavalcilar
  Agata Grotek

D-U-N-S 24-318-0473   (HQ)
WALTER'S GROUP INC
1318 Rymal Rd E, Hamilton, ON, L8W 3N1
(905) 388-7111
Emp Here 1   *Sales* 65,672,370
SIC 3499 Fabricated Metal products, nec
  Walter Koppelaar
  Peter Kranendonk
  Tim Verhey

D-U-N-S 20-056-0688   (HQ)
WALTER'S INC
(*Suby of* WALTER'S GROUP INC)
1318 Rymal Rd E, Hamilton, ON, L8W 3N1
(905) 388-7111
Emp Here 100   *Sales* 87,563,160
SIC 3499 Fabricated Metal products, nec
  Walter Koppelaar
  Peter J Kranendonk
  Walt Koppelaar
  Edward Lacroix
  Mark Koppelaar
  Wally Verhey
  Tim Verhey

D-U-N-S 24-744-4631   (HQ)
ZARCONE BROTHERS LTD
ZARKY'S FINE FOODS
(*Suby of* ZARCONE HOLDINGS LIMITED)
20 Hempstead Dr, Hamilton, ON, L8W 2E7
(905) 574-1500
Sales 83,557,700
SIC 5149 Groceries and related products, nec
  Jerry Zarcone
  Anthony Zarcone

Hamilton, ON L9A

D-U-N-S 20-178-0348   (SL)
1555965 ONTARIO INC
TIM HORTONS
473 Concession St, Hamilton, ON, L9A 1C1
(905) 383-7160
Emp Here 70   *Sales* 20,543,390
SIC 5461 Retail bakeries
  Andrew Grigg
  Grace Grigg

D-U-N-S 25-865-7659   (SL)
BARTON RETIREMENT INC
WELLINGTON, THE
1430 Upper Wellington St, Hamilton, ON, L9A 5H3
(905) 385-2111
Emp Here 165   *Sales* 36,443,715
SIC 6513 Apartment building operators
  Daniel Scully

D-U-N-S 25-301-2405   (BR)
EXTENDICARE (CANADA) INC
PARAMED HOME HEALTH CARE
(*Suby of* EXTENDICARE INC)
883 Upper Wentworth St Suite 301, Hamilton, ON, L9A 4Y6
(905) 318-8522
Emp Here 200
SIC 8051 Skilled nursing care facilities
  Lijoy Ulahannan

D-U-N-S 24-560-1745   (HQ)
HAMILTON BUILDERS' SUPPLY INC
164 Limeridge Rd E, Hamilton, ON, L9A 2S3
(905) 388-2352
Emp Here 15   *Sales* 10,122,360
SIC 5211 Lumber and other building materials
  Ross Head

D-U-N-S 25-292-6019   (BR)
HAMILTON-WENTWORTH   CATHOLIC

SCHOOL BOARD
SAINT CHARLES ADULT EDUCATION CON-TINUING EDUCATION
(*Suby of* HAMILTON-WENTWORTH CATHOLIC SCHOOL BOARD)
150 East 5th St, Hamilton, ON, L9A 2Z8
(905) 575-5202
Emp Here 150
SIC 8211 Elementary and secondary schools
Michael Silvestro

D-U-N-S 20-024-9253   (BR)
HAMILTON-WENTWORTH   DISTRICT SCHOOL BOARD, THE
HILL PARK SCHOOL
(*Suby of* HAMILTON-WENTWORTH DIS-TRICT SCHOOL BOARD, THE)
465 East 16th St, Hamilton, ON, L9A 4K6
(905) 318-1291
Emp Here 125
SIC 8211 Elementary and secondary schools
Dean Shareski

D-U-N-S 25-502-4002   (HQ)
HAMILTON-WENTWORTH   DISTRICT SCHOOL BOARD, THE
20 Education Crt, Hamilton, ON, L9A 0B9
(905) 527-5092
Emp Here 400   *Sales* 594,714,000
SIC 8211 Elementary and secondary schools
Donald Grant

D-U-N-S 24-416-8477   (SL)
HANBALI, JEFF DRUGS LTD
SHOPPERS DRUG MART
999 Upper Wentworth St Suite 200, Hamilton, ON, L9A 4X5
(905) 388-8450
Emp Here 40   *Sales* 10,118,160
SIC 5912 Drug stores and proprietary stores
Jeff Hanbali

D-U-N-S 25-301-2090   (BR)
HUDSON'S BAY COMPANY
THE BAY LIMERIDGE
(*Suby of* HUDSON'S BAY COMPANY)
999 Upper Wentworth St, Hamilton, ON, L9A 4X5
(905) 318-8008
Emp Here 200
SIC 5311 Department stores
Helen Clark

D-U-N-S 20-559-4125   (HQ)
TURKSTRA INDUSTRIES INC
TURKSTRA MILL
(*Suby of* TURKSTRA LUMBER COMPANY LIMITED)
1050 Upper Wellington St, Hamilton, ON, L9A 3S6
(905) 388-8220
Emp Here 100   *Sales* 23,084,400
SIC 2431 Millwork
Carl Turkstra

D-U-N-S 20-055-9383   (HQ)
TURKSTRA LUMBER COMPANY LIMITED
TURKSTRA WINDOWS
1050 Upper Wellington St, Hamilton, ON, L9A 3S6
(905) 388-8220
Emp Here 11   *Sales* 71,539,053
SIC 5211 Lumber and other building materials
Peter Turkstra
Jon Wagner

Hamilton, ON L9B

D-U-N-S 24-484-3793   (SL)
1053038 ONTARIO LIMITED
STERLING HONDA
1495 Upper James St, Hamilton, ON, L9B 1K2
(905) 574-8200
Emp Here 49   *Sales* 24,405,822

SIC 5511 New and used car dealers
John Lecluse

D-U-N-S 20-161-6153   (SL)
1527 UPPER JAMES ST.,HAMILTON, IN-CORPORATED
1527 Upper James St, Hamilton, ON, L9B 1K2
(905) 385-1523
Emp Here 75   *Sales* 14,348,279
SIC 8641 Civic and social associations
Peter Murray

D-U-N-S 25-088-2735   (SL)
651233 ONTARIO INC
SWEET PARADISE BAKERY
630 Stone Church Rd W, Hamilton, ON, L9B 1A7
(905) 389-3487
Emp Here 55   *Sales* 16,141,235
SIC 5461 Retail bakeries
Pietro Mancini
Pat Mancini
Dino Mancini
Lidio Mancini

D-U-N-S 24-477-1374   (SL)
AIRPORT FORD LINCOLN SALES LIMITED
49 Rymal Rd E, Hamilton, ON, L9B 1B9
(905) 388-6665
Emp Here 43   *Sales* 21,417,354
SIC 5511 New and used car dealers
Anthony Kajah

D-U-N-S 25-292-6522   (BR)
HAMILTON-WENTWORTH   CATHOLIC SCHOOL BOARD
ST THOMAS MORE CATHOLIC SEC-ONDARY SCHOOL
(*Suby of* HAMILTON-WENTWORTH CATHOLIC SCHOOL BOARD)
1045 Upper Paradise Rd, Hamilton, ON, L9B 2N4
(905) 388-1178
Emp Here 180
SIC 8211 Elementary and secondary schools
John Valvasori

D-U-N-S 24-309-1787   (BR)
INCH FOODS INC
MCDONALD'S RESTAURANTS
(*Suby of* INCH FOODS INC)
20 Rymal Rd E, Hamilton, ON, L9B 1T7
(905) 387-9282
Emp Here 110
SIC 5812 Eating places
Diana Paul

D-U-N-S 20-056-6508   (SL)
MAR-HAM AUTOMOTIVE INC
HAMILTON VOLVO
57 Rymal Rd W, Hamilton, ON, L9B 1B5
(905) 389-7111
Emp Here 24   *Sales* 11,953,872
SIC 5511 New and used car dealers
John Martins

D-U-N-S 20-291-5935   (SL)
MITCHELL & ABBOTT GROUP INSUR-ANCE BROKERS LIMITED,
2000 Garth St Suite 101, Hamilton, ON, L9B 0C1
(905) 385-6383
Emp Here 40   *Sales* 23,196,960
SIC 6411 Insurance agents, brokers, and ser-vice
Wayne Abbott

D-U-N-S 24-685-2396   (SL)
PLAZA NISSAN LIMITED
1545 Upper James St, Hamilton, ON, L9B 1K2
(905) 389-3588
Emp Here 24   *Sales* 11,953,872
SIC 5511 New and used car dealers
Mike Wojtowicz

D-U-N-S 20-195-9322   (BR)
PRIME RESTAURANTS INC
EAST SIDE MARIO'S

(*Suby of* RECIPE UNLIMITED CORPORA-TION)
1389 Upper James St Suite Side, Hamilton, ON, L9B 1K2
(905) 574-3890
Emp Here 75
SIC 5812 Eating places
Brett Lierch

D-U-N-S 20-290-5480   (HQ)
RE/MAX ESCARPMENT REALTY INC
(*Suby of* CREARE HOLDINGS INC)
1595 Upper James St Unit 101, Hamilton, ON, L9B 0H7
(905) 575-5478
Emp Here 100   *Sales* 81,135,360
SIC 6531 Real estate agents and managers
Anne Zurini

D-U-N-S 24-047-5335   (SL)
RYGIEL SUPPORTS FOR COMMUNITY LIV-ING
930 Upper Paradise Rd Unit 11, Hamilton, ON, L9B 2N1
(905) 525-4311
Emp Here 250   *Sales* 16,070,500
SIC 8361 Residential care
Donna Marcaccio
John Baxter
Susan Mcclure

D-U-N-S 20-518-0685   (BR)
SCHLEGEL VILLAGES INC
THE VILLAGE OF WENTWORTH HEIGHTS
1620 Upper Wentworth St, Hamilton, ON, L9B 2W3
(905) 575-4735
Emp Here 200
SIC 8051 Skilled nursing care facilities

D-U-N-S 24-203-3608   (SL)
ST. JOSEPH'S HOME CARE
1550 Upper James St Suite 201, Hamilton, ON, L9B 2L6
(905) 522-6887
Emp Here 200   *Sales* 15,340,200
SIC 8082 Home health care services
Carolyn Gosse
Lori Lawson
Sonny Monzavi
Adriaan Korstanje
Peter Tice
Lynn Mcneil
Leo Perri
David Tonin
Barbara Beaudoin
Lee Clayton

D-U-N-S 25-987-3735   (SL)
UPPER JAMES 2004 LTD
FORTINO'S
1550 Upper James St, Hamilton, ON, L9B 2L6
(905) 383-9700
Emp Here 170   *Sales* 49,891,090
SIC 5411 Grocery stores
Jason Zelinski

Hamilton, ON L9C

D-U-N-S 24-875-0606   (SL)
1145678 ONTARIO LIMITED
HAMILTON VOLKSWAGEN AUDI
1221 Upper James St, Hamilton, ON, L9C 3B2
(905) 574-8989
Emp Here 30   *Sales* 14,942,340
SIC 5511 New and used car dealers
Robert Wright

D-U-N-S 25-145-3981   (SL)
718695 ONTARIO INC
KEG STEAKHOUSE & BAR, THE
1170 Upper James St, Hamilton, ON, L9C 3B1
(905) 574-7880
Emp Here 83   *Sales* 3,778,077

SIC 5812 Eating places
Jim Drury

D-U-N-S 20-275-9668   (SL)
7868774 CANADA INC
STRATICS NETWORKS
762 Upper James St Unit 287, Hamilton, ON, L9C 3A2
(866) 635-6918
Emp Here 52   *Sales* 28,379,155
SIC 4899 Communication services, nec

D-U-N-S 20-292-3111   (HQ)
AIRE ONE HEATING AND COOLING INC
1065 Upper James St, Hamilton, ON, L9C 3A6
(905) 385-2800
Emp Here 20   *Sales* 11,046,700
SIC 1711 Plumbing, heating, air-conditioning

D-U-N-S 20-639-5253   (SL)
BEAR, JOHN PONTIAC BUICK CADILLAC LTD
(*Suby of* BEAR, JOHN C. HOLDINGS LTD)
1200 Upper James St, Hamilton, ON, L9C 3B1
(905) 575-9400
Emp Here 100   *Sales* 62,928,000
SIC 5511 New and used car dealers
John Bear
Jamie Lalande

D-U-N-S 20-552-0146   (BR)
EXTENDICARE (CANADA) INC
EXTENDICARE HAMILTON
(*Suby of* EXTENDICARE INC)
90 Chedmac Dr Suite 2317, Hamilton, ON, L9C 7W1
(905) 318-4472
Emp Here 100
SIC 8051 Skilled nursing care facilities
Patti Green

D-U-N-S 20-056-6227   (SL)
HAMILTON COMMUNITY CARE ACCESS CENTRE
310 Limeridge Rd W, Hamilton, ON, L9C 2V2
(905) 523-8600
Emp Here 250   *Sales* 18,889,774
SIC 7363 Help supply services
Susan Johnstone

D-U-N-S 24-086-0341   (SL)
HAMILTON HORNETS RUGBY FOOTBALL CLUB INC
1300 Garth St, Hamilton, ON, L9C 4L7
(905) 575-3133
Emp Here 140   *Sales* 11,675,300
SIC 7941 Sports clubs, managers, and pro-moters
Tom Edwards
Daniel Croskerry
Tim Gainfort

D-U-N-S 24-059-5954   (SL)
HAMILTON TECH DRIVE INC
1030 Upper James St Suite 308, Hamilton, ON, L9C 6X6
(888) 723-3183
Emp Here 25   *Sales* 16,973,075
SIC 6289 Security and commodity service
Carmen Talarco

D-U-N-S 24-830-6185   (BR)
HAMILTON-WENTWORTH   DISTRICT SCHOOL BOARD, THE
WESTMOUNT SECONDARY SCHOOL
(*Suby of* HAMILTON-WENTWORTH DIS-TRICT SCHOOL BOARD, THE)
39 Montcalm Dr, Hamilton, ON, L9C 4B1
(905) 385-5395
Emp Here 85
SIC 8211 Elementary and secondary schools
Angela Ferguson

D-U-N-S 20-286-9215   (BR)
HAMILTON-WENTWORTH   DISTRICT SCHOOL BOARD, THE
SIR ALLAN MACNAB
(*Suby of* HAMILTON-WENTWORTH DIS-

TRICT SCHOOL BOARD, THE)
145 Magnolia Dr, Hamilton, ON, L9C 5P4
(905) 383-3337
Emp Here 90
SIC 8211 Elementary and secondary schools
　Theodore Cozner

D-U-N-S 20-847-5657　　(SL)
HILLFIELD-STRATHALLAN COLLEGE
299 Fennell Ave W, Hamilton, ON, L9C 1G3
(905) 389-1367
Emp Here 200　　*Sales* 19,823,800
SIC 8211 Elementary and secondary schools
　Thomas Matthews
　Darcy Wallace

D-U-N-S 24-141-1974　　(SL)
IDLEWYLD MANOR
449 Sanatorium Rd, Hamilton, ON, L9C 2A7
(905) 574-2000
Emp Here 285　　*Sales* 18,320,370
SIC 8361 Residential care
　Elizabeth Manganelli
　Anthony Tirone
　Susan Tkachuk
　Robert Luckhart
　Guy Dixon
　Jane Lemke
　Ted Capstick

D-U-N-S 20-054-2017　　(SL)
JOHNSTON MOTOR SALES CO. LIMITED
JOHNSTON CHRYSLER DODGE JEEP
1350 Upper James St, Hamilton, ON, L9C 3B4
(905) 388-5502
Emp Here 60　　*Sales* 37,756,800
SIC 5511 New and used car dealers
　James A (Jim) Johnston
　Allyson Teodoridis

D-U-N-S 24-335-0415　　(BR)
METRO ONTARIO INC
METRO
(*Suby of* METRO INC)
751 Upper James St, Hamilton, ON, L9C 3A1
(905) 575-5545
Emp Here 175
SIC 5411 Grocery stores
　Robert Hall

D-U-N-S 25-221-2915　　(BR)
MOHAWK COLLEGE OF APPLIED ARTS AND TECHNOLOGY, THE
(*Suby of* MOHAWK COLLEGE OF APPLIED ARTS AND TECHNOLOGY, THE)
135 Fennell Ave W, Hamilton, ON, L9C 0E5
(905) 575-1212
Emp Here 1,650
SIC 8222 Junior colleges
　Maureen Monaghan

D-U-N-S 20-819-5289　　(HQ)
MOHAWK COLLEGE OF APPLIED ARTS AND TECHNOLOGY, THE
135 Fennell Ave W, Hamilton, ON, L9C 0E5
(905) 575-1212
Emp Here 100　　*Sales* 148,901,693
SIC 8222 Junior colleges
　Ron Mckerlie
　Paul Armstrong
　Katie Burrows
　Hillary Dawson
　Tom Ferns
　Alison Horton

D-U-N-S 20-505-2996　　(SL)
MOHAWK FORD SALES LIMITED
930 Upper James St, Hamilton, ON, L9C 3A5
(905) 388-1711
Emp Here 46　　*Sales* 22,911,588
SIC 5511 New and used car dealers
　Lloyd Ferguson
　Mark Jewiss

D-U-N-S 20-920-0026　　(SL)
SON'S OF ITALY CHARITABLE CORPORATION

VILLA ITALIA RETIREMENT RESIDENCE
530 Upper Paradise Rd, Hamilton, ON, L9C 7W2
(905) 388-4552
Emp Here 49　　*Sales* 19,473,286
SIC 8699 Membership organizations, nec
　Patrick Mostacci

D-U-N-S 20-956-3134　　(BR)
ST. JOSEPH'S HEALTHCARE FOUNDATION, HAMILTON
(*Suby of* ST. JOSEPH'S HEALTH SYSTEM)
100 West 5th St, Hamilton, ON, L9C 0E3
(905) 388-2511
Emp Here 300
SIC 8063 Psychiatric hospitals

D-U-N-S 20-790-2201　　(SL)
TONY'S NO FRILLS LTD
770 Upper James St Suite 723, Hamilton, ON, L9C 3A2
(905) 574-2069
Emp Here 80　　*Sales* 23,478,160
SIC 5411 Grocery stores
　Tony Dippolito

D-U-N-S 20-299-5817　　(SL)
UMBRELLA FAMILY AND CHILD CENTRES OF HAMILTON
310 Limeridge Rd W Unit 9, Hamilton, ON, L9C 2V2
(905) 312-9836
Emp Here 209　　*Sales* 13,036,166
SIC 8351 Child day care services
　Patricia Houlton

D-U-N-S 25-077-5541　　(BR)
WAL-MART CANADA CORP
(*Suby of* WALMART INC.)
675 Upper James St, Hamilton, ON, L9C 2Z5
(905) 389-6333
Emp Here 250
SIC 5311 Department stores
　Donna Cardinal

Hampton, ON L0B

D-U-N-S 20-801-4774　　(SL)
KNIGHTS OF COLUMBUS INSURANCE
26 Davis Crt, Hampton, ON, L0B 1J0
(905) 263-4212
Emp Here 16　　*Sales* 16,558,096
SIC 6311 Life insurance
　Raymond Richer

D-U-N-S 25-821-2240　　(SL)
PINGLE'S FARM MARKET
1805 Taunton Rd, Hampton, ON, L0B 1J0
(905) 725-6089
Emp Here 40　　*Sales* 10,492,360
SIC 0191 General farms, primarily crop
　Colleen Pingle

Hannon, ON L0R

D-U-N-S 24-101-0706　　(SL)
4259891 CANADA LTD
QUEENSTON ON THE MOUNTAIN-BUICK-CHEVROLET-GMC
2260 Rymal Rd E, Hannon, ON, L0R 1P0
(905) 528-7001
Emp Here 40　　*Sales* 19,923,120
SIC 5511 New and used car dealers
　Perry Yates
　Michael Dubois
　Amy Cochren

D-U-N-S 24-302-1771　　(SL)
944622 ONTARIO LIMITED
CALEDONIA TRANSPORTATION CO
175 Swayze Rd, Hannon, ON, L0R 1P0

(905) 692-4488
Emp Here 110　　*Sales* 8,279,920
SIC 4151 School buses
　Tim Towle

D-U-N-S 24-985-9414　　(SL)
DR. DONUT INC
TIM HORTONS
2200 Rymal Rd E, Hannon, ON, L0R 1P0
(905) 692-3556
Emp Here 47　　*Sales* 12,885,144
SIC 5461 Retail bakeries
　Steven Kennish

D-U-N-S 25-255-3607　　(BR)
HAMILTON-WENTWORTH CATHOLIC SCHOOL BOARD
BISHOP RYAN CATHOLIC SECONDARY SCHOOL
(*Suby of* HAMILTON-WENTWORTH CATHOLIC SCHOOL BOARD)
1824 Rymal Rd, Hannon, ON, L0R 1P0
(905) 573-2151
Emp Here 100
SIC 8211 Elementary and secondary schools
　Emidio Piccioni

D-U-N-S 24-127-5002　　(SL)
REIMAR CONSTRUCTION CORPORATION
REIMAR FORMING & CONSTRUCTION
328 Trinity Church Rd, Hannon, ON, L0R 1P0
(905) 692-9900
Emp Here 80　　*Sales* 19,694,880
SIC 1799 Special trade contractors, nec
　Miguel Martins
　Carlos Reis
　Shari Hamilton

D-U-N-S 24-319-5125　　(BR)
WAL-MART CANADA CORP
WALMART
(*Suby of* WALMART INC.)
2190 Rymal Rd E Suite 1042, Hannon, ON, L0R 1P0
(905) 692-7000
Emp Here 120
SIC 5311 Department stores
　Mario Pilozzi

Hanover, ON N4N

D-U-N-S 20-056-4136　　(SL)
1020012 ONTARIO INC
HANOVER HOME HARDWARE BUILDING CENTRE
580 24th Ave Suite 1, Hanover, ON, N4N 3B8
(519) 364-3410
Emp Here 40　　*Sales* 10,122,360
SIC 5211 Lumber and other building materials
　David Gross
　Kimberley (Kim) Gross
　Douglas Gross

D-U-N-S 24-373-7801　　(SL)
2145150 ONTARIO INC
HANOVER HONDA
150 7th Ave, Hanover, ON, N4N 2G9
(519) 364-1010
Emp Here 35　　*Sales* 17,432,730
SIC 5511 New and used car dealers
　Larry Lantz

D-U-N-S 25-033-4786　　(SL)
784704 ONTARIO LTD
GRANT'S INDEPENDENT
832 10th St, Hanover, ON, N4N 1S3
(519) 364-4661
Emp Here 100　　*Sales* 29,347,700
SIC 5411 Grocery stores
　John Grant

D-U-N-S 25-238-9523　　(HQ)
BRUCE-GREY CATHOLIC DISTRICT SCHOOL BOARD
799 16th Ave, Hanover, ON, N4N 3A1

(519) 364-5820
Emp Here 35　　*Sales* 59,471,400
SIC 8211 Elementary and secondary schools
　Bruce Macpherson

D-U-N-S 24-391-0697　　(SL)
CANADIAN TIRE
896 10th St, Hanover, ON, N4N 3P2
(519) 364-2870
Emp Here 40　　*Sales* 19,923,120
SIC 5531 Auto and home supply stores
　Dale Cousins

D-U-N-S 25-649-9609　　(HQ)
CRAIG MCDONALD REDDON INSURANCE BROKERS LTD
467 10th St Suite 200, Hanover, ON, N4N 1R3
(519) 364-3540
Emp Here 13　　*Sales* 70,173,042
SIC 6311 Life insurance
　Daniel T Craig
　Bruce Mcdonald
　William Reddon
　James (Jim) Diemert

D-U-N-S 20-705-3000　　(SL)
ELECTRICAL CONTACTS LIMITED
519 22nd Ave, Hanover, ON, N4N 3T6
(519) 364-1878
Emp Here 120　　*Sales* 22,853,040
SIC 3643 Current-carrying wiring devices
　Peter Allen
　Allan Cs Wong

D-U-N-S 25-761-1728　　(HQ)
EXCELDOR FOODS LTD
BUTTERBALL
(*Suby of* EXCELDOR COOPERATIVE)
478 14th St, Hanover, ON, N4N 1Z9
(519) 364-1770
Emp Here 350　　*Sales* 170,584,750
SIC 2015 Poultry slaughtering and processing
　+Ene Proulx
　Anthony Tavares
　Christian Jacques

D-U-N-S 24-412-7684　　(SL)
HANOVER AND DISTRICT HOSPITAL
90 7th Ave Suite 1, Hanover, ON, N4N 1N1
(519) 364-2340
Emp Here 200　　*Sales* 13,946,996,136
SIC 8062 General medical and surgical hospitals
　Katrina Wilson
　Dave Cardwell
　Brandon Koebel
　Marnie Ferguson
　Stacy Hogg
　Dana Howes
　Lynda Mallinos
　Barbara Hicks
　Susan Boron
　Christopher Barfoot

D-U-N-S 24-316-8143　　(SL)
HANOVER, BENTINCK & BRANT AGRICULTURAL SOCIETY
HANOVER RACEWAY
265 5th St, Hanover, ON, N4N 3X3
(519) 364-2860
Emp Here 104　　*Sales* 8,673,080
SIC 7948 Racing, including track operation
　Randy Rier
　Gord Dougan

D-U-N-S 24-124-7493　　(SL)
KUNKEL BUS LINES LTD
KUNKEL LIMOSINE SERVICES
301205 Knapville Rd, Hanover, ON, N4N 3T1
(519) 364-2530
Emp Here 180　　*Sales* 13,548,960
SIC 4111 Local and suburban transit
　Stephen J Kunkel
　Michael J Kunkel

D-U-N-S 25-411-7674　　(BR)
MAPLE LEAF FOODS INC
HORIZON POULTRY

▲ Public Company　　■ Public Company Family Member　　**HQ** Headquarters　　**BR** Branch　　**SL** Single Location

(*Suby of* MAPLE LEAF FOODS INC)
90 10th Ave, Hanover, ON, N4N 3B8
(519) 364-3200
Emp Here 150
SIC 5144 Poultry and poultry products
Sheryl Firby

D-U-N-S 20-039-7698   (BR)
REVERA INC
VILLAGE SENIORS COMMUNITY, THE
(*Suby of* GOVERNMENT OF CANADA)
101 10th St Suite 2006, Hanover, ON, N4N
1M9
(519) 364-4320
Emp Here 100
SIC 6513 Apartment building operators
Shirley Person

D-U-N-S 25-462-6146   (SL)
SELECT FARM & EXPORT SERVICES INC
Gd Lcd Main, Hanover, ON, N4N 3C2
(519) 369-6000
Emp Here 12   *Sales* 14,524,764
SIC 5154 Livestock
Harold Wright

D-U-N-S 20-056-4383   (HQ)
SMITTY'S SHOPPING CENTRE LIMITED
SMITTY'S FINE FURNITURE
170 3rd St, Hanover, ON, N4N 1B2
(519) 364-3800
Emp Here 50   *Sales* 13,944,180
SIC 5712 Furniture stores
Lloyd Schmidt
Robert (Bob) Gray
Elmer Schmidt

D-U-N-S 24-727-4004   (BR)
SOBEYS CAPITAL INCORPORATED
IGA
(*Suby of* EMPIRE COMPANY LIMITED)
236 10th St, Hanover, ON, N4N 1N9
(519) 364-2891
Emp Here 80
SIC 5411 Grocery stores
Rob Haron

D-U-N-S 24-062-6960   (BR)
TELESAT CANADA
OPERATIONS NETWORK CENTRE
(*Suby of* RED ISLE PRIVATE INVESTMENTS
INC)
Gd, Hanover, ON, N4N 3C2
(519) 364-1221
Emp Here 100
SIC 4899 Communication services, nec
Daniel Goldberg

D-U-N-S 20-738-6454   (BR)
WAL-MART CANADA CORP
(*Suby of* WALMART INC.)
1100 10th St, Hanover, ON, N4N 3B8
(519) 364-0867
Emp Here 100
SIC 5311 Department stores
Michel Soucy

D-U-N-S 24-977-4142   (SL)
WEST FURNITURE CO INC
WEST BROS FURNITURE
582 14th St, Hanover, ON, N4N 2A1
(519) 364-7770
Emp Here 70   *Sales* 10,802,540
SIC 2511 Wood household furniture
Paul West

Harley, ON N0E

D-U-N-S 20-693-1508   (SL)
STUBBE'S PRECAST COMMERCIAL INC
44 Muir Line, Harley, ON, N0E 1E0
(519) 424-2183
Emp Here 250   *Sales* 53,094,000
SIC 1791 Structural steel erection
Andy Stubbe

D-U-N-S 20-267-2254   (SL)
STUBBE'S REDI-MIX INC
STUBBE'S PRECAST
30 Muir Line, Harley, ON, N0E 1E0
(519) 424-2183
Emp Here 200   *Sales* 35,843,800
SIC 3272 Concrete products, nec
Andy Stubbe

Harriston, ON N0G

D-U-N-S 20-817-5349   (BR)
**CARESSANT-CARE NURSING AND RE-
TIREMENT HOMES LIMITED**
(*Suby of* CARESSANT-CARE NURSING AND
RETIREMENT HOMES LIMITED)
24 Louise St, Harriston, ON, N0G 1Z0
(519) 338-3700
Emp Here 100
SIC 8051 Skilled nursing care facilities
Lynn Jamieson

D-U-N-S 20-056-5240   (SL)
DON MCPHAIL MOTORS LTD
MCPHAIL'S OF HARRISTON
6332 Wellington Rd, Harriston, ON, N0G 1Z0
(519) 338-3422
Emp Here 25   *Sales* 12,451,950
SIC 5561 Recreational vehicle dealers
Donald Mcphail
Paul Mcphail
Lorna Mcphail
Phillip Sanderson

D-U-N-S 20-980-4657   (HQ)
HARKNESS, JIM EQUIPMENT LTD
HARCO AG EQUIPMENT
5808 Highway 9 Rr 4, Harriston, ON, N0G 1Z0
(519) 338-3946
Emp Here 18   *Sales* 11,400,624
SIC 5083 Farm and garden machinery
Jim Harkness
Doreen Harkness

D-U-N-S 20-056-5224   (HQ)
LESLIE MOTORS LTD
73 Elora St, Harriston, ON, N0G 1Z0
(519) 338-2310
Emp Here 15   *Sales* 22,413,510
SIC 5511 New and used car dealers
Ronald Leslie
Mark Leslie
Donald Leslie
Lisa Leslie

D-U-N-S 24-261-8506   (SL)
MINTO TRUCK CENTRE LIMITED
5196 Hwy 23 N, Harriston, ON, N0G 2P0
(519) 510-2120
Emp Here 100   *Sales* 14,819,200
SIC 4212 Local trucking, without storage
Amanda Van Stee

D-U-N-S 24-060-2060   (HQ)
**NORTH WELLINGTON CO-OPERATIVE
SERVICES**
56 Margaret St, Harriston, ON, N0G 1Z0
(519) 338-2331
Emp Here 47   *Sales* 66,826,800
SIC 5191 Farm supplies
Gord South
Michael Oberle
Kelly Boyle

D-U-N-S 20-629-8457   (SL)
SPEARE SEEDS
99 John St N, Harriston, ON, N0G 1Z0
(519) 338-3840
Emp Here 20   *Sales* 14,850,400
SIC 5191 Farm supplies
Richard Elliott

Harrow, ON N0R

D-U-N-S 25-221-3780   (SL)
452056 ONTARIO LTD
ROBINSON TRANSPORT & WAREHOUSE
3191 County Road 11, Harrow, ON, N0R 1G0
(519) 738-6885
Emp Here 70   *Sales* 10,373,440
SIC 4213 Trucking, except local
Robert Robinson
Patricia Robinson

D-U-N-S 24-506-6857   (HQ)
ATLAS TUBE CANADA ULC
(*Suby of* ZEKELMAN INDUSTRIES, INC.)
200 Clark St, Harrow, ON, N0R 1G0
(519) 738-5000
Emp Here 160   *Sales* 244,304,400
SIC 3317 Steel pipe and tubes
Barry Zekelman
Michael Mcnamara
Frank Riddick

D-U-N-S 24-859-2032   (SL)
DELTA WIRE & MFG
29 Delta Dr, Harrow, ON, N0R 1G0
(519) 738-3514
Emp Here 60   *Sales* 13,320,060
SIC 3535 Conveyors and conveying equip-
ment
Tom Smith
Howard Campbell Jr

D-U-N-S 24-048-3396   (HQ)
RENAUD, LARRY FORD & RV SALES
175 King St W, Harrow, ON, N0R 1G0
(519) 738-6767
Emp Here 1   *Sales* 15,102,720
SIC 5511 New and used car dealers
Larry Renaud

D-U-N-S 20-524-8438   (SL)
SELLICK EQUIPMENT LIMITED
(*Suby of* AVIS INDUSTRIAL CORPORATION)
2131 Roseborough Rd, Harrow, ON, N0R 1G0
(519) 738-2255
Emp Here 75   *Sales* 16,650,075
SIC 3537 Industrial trucks and tractors
Leland Boren
Howard Sellick
David Sellick
Collin Sellick

Hartington, ON K0H

D-U-N-S 20-893-8803   (HQ)
BMP (1985) LIMITED
ATKINSON HOME BUILDING CENTRE
5276 Hinchinbrooke Rd, Hartington, ON, K0H
1W0
(613) 372-2838
Emp Here 45   *Sales* 20,073,900
SIC 5211 Lumber and other building materials
Darlene Atkinson
Roy (Tal) Atkinson

Hastings, ON K0L

D-U-N-S 25-823-2842   (HQ)
2037247 ONTARIO LIMITED
LUZZI'S VALU-MART
52 Bridge St, Hastings, ON, K0L 1Y0
(705) 696-3504
Emp Here 1   *Sales* 11,514,384
SIC 5411 Grocery stores
Chris Luzzi

Hawkesbury, ON K6A

D-U-N-S 25-990-0116   (SL)
1055551 ONTARIO INC
HAWKESBURY TOYOTA
341 Tupper St, Hawkesbury, ON, K6A 3T6
(613) 632-6598
Emp Here 24   *Sales* 11,953,872
SIC 5511 New and used car dealers
Jacques Parisien
Wayne Assley
Sandra Sauve

D-U-N-S 25-970-7859   (SL)
1129822 ONTARIO INC
TIM HORTONS
1000 Mcgill St, Hawkesbury, ON, K6A 1R6
(613) 632-8278
Emp Here 45   *Sales* 12,336,840
SIC 5461 Retail bakeries
Marc Gatien
Nicole Gatien

D-U-N-S 24-330-1558   (SL)
1443635 ONTARIO INC
PETROLE CAMPBELL PETROLEUM 2001
3235 Front Rd, Hawkesbury, ON, K6A 2R2
(613) 632-6256
Emp Here 16   *Sales* 16,524,928
SIC 5172 Petroleum products, nec
Norman Campbell

D-U-N-S 20-268-9519   (SL)
1476482 ONTARIO INC
LIQUID PARTNERS
323 Front Rd, Hawkesbury, ON, K6A 2T1
(613) 632-1816
Emp Here 30   *Sales* 16,005,120
SIC 4731 Freight transportation arrangement
Jeffrey Hopkins
Scott Hopkins

D-U-N-S 24-092-2877   (SL)
2004104 ONTARIO LIMITED
PRICE CHOPPER
857 Cecile Blvd, Hawkesbury, ON, K6A 1P4
(613) 632-5994
Emp Here 95   *Sales* 27,880,315
SIC 5411 Grocery stores
Nancy Leduc

D-U-N-S 24-145-8012   (SL)
2058658 ONTARIO INC
JEAN COUTU GROUP
(*Suby of* METRO INC)
1275 Tupper St, Hawkesbury, ON, K6A 3T5
(613) 675-1515
Emp Here 75   *Sales* 18,324,600
SIC 5912 Drug stores and proprietary stores
Trever Cook

D-U-N-S 24-366-4617   (SL)
4475518 CANADA INC
HAWKESBURY HONDA
455 County Rd 17, Hawkesbury, ON, K6A 3R4
(613) 632-5222
Emp Here 21   *Sales* 10,459,638
SIC 5511 New and used car dealers
Jean Gagne
Alexandre Gagne
Claudie Gagne

D-U-N-S 24-575-0765   (SL)
845453 ONTARIO LTD
HAWKESBURY MAZDA
959 Mcgill St, Hawkesbury, ON, K6A 3K8
(613) 632-4125
Emp Here 28   *Sales* 13,946,184
SIC 5511 New and used car dealers
Christian Joanisse
Pierre Sauve

D-U-N-S 20-220-1203   (SL)
ALIMENTS MATRIX INC, LES
896 Cecile Blvd, Hawkesbury, ON, K6A 3R5
(613) 632-8623
Emp Here 36   *Sales* 30,080,772

▲ Public Company   ■ Public Company Family Member   **HQ** Headquarters   **BR** Branch   **SL** Single Location

SIC 5143 Dairy products, except dried or canned
Denis Guindon
Melanie Guindon

D-U-N-S 24-752-3384   (HQ)
ASCO CONSTRUCTION LTD
1125 Tupper St Unit 1, Hawkesbury, ON, K6A 3T5
(613) 632-0121
Emp Here 5   *Sales* 10,826,813
SIC 1542 Nonresidential construction, nec
Anthony Assaly
Jason Assaly

D-U-N-S 24-268-9057   (HQ)
COMPAGNIE D'EDITION ANDRE PAQUE-TTE INC, LA
IMPRIMERIE PRESCOTT & RUSSELL
1100 Aberdeen St, Hawkesbury, ON, K6A 1K7
(613) 632-4155
Emp Here 54   *Sales* 12,302,025
SIC 2711 Newspapers
Bertrand Castonguay
Roger Duplantie

D-U-N-S 25-137-3114   (BR)
CONSEIL SCOLAIRE DE DISTRICT CATHOLIQUE DE L'EST ONTARIEN
ECOLE SECONDAIRE REGIONAL DE HAWKESBURY
(*Suby of* CONSEIL SCOLAIRE DE DISTRICT CATHOLIQUE DE L'EST ONTARIEN)
572 Kitchener St Suite 8e, Hawkesbury, ON, K6A 2P3
(613) 632-7055
Emp Here 80
SIC 8211 Elementary and secondary schools
Jean Villeneuve

D-U-N-S 25-510-4796   (HQ)
DART AEROSPACE LTD
(*Suby of* ERA GROUP INC.)
1270 Aberdeen St, Hawkesbury, ON, K6A 1K7
(613) 632-5200
Sales 14,250,780
SIC 5088 Transportation equipment and supplies
Michael O'reilly

D-U-N-S 20-507-5062   (HQ)
GRAY HAWK (1991) CO. LTD
(*Suby of* 760568 ONTARIO LTD)
772 Main St E, Hawkesbury, ON, K6A 1B4
(613) 632-0921
Sales 13,983,900
SIC 1711 Plumbing, heating, air-conditioning
Jacques Labelle

D-U-N-S 20-056-7733   (SL)
HAWKESBURY LUMBER SUPPLY COMPANY LIMITED
HOME HARDWARE BUILDING CENTRE
900 Alexander Siversky St, Hawkesbury, ON, K6A 3N4
(613) 632-4663
Emp Here 44   *Sales* 11,134,596
SIC 5211 Lumber and other building materials
Jean-Francois Bertrand
Benoit Bertrand

D-U-N-S 24-313-0338   (HQ)
HEARX HEARING INC
HELIX HEARING CARE
290 Mcgill St Suite A, Hawkesbury, ON, K6A 1P8
(877) 268-1045
Emp Here 25   *Sales* 29,319,360
SIC 5999 Miscellaneous retail stores, nec
Debbie Zelisko

D-U-N-S 20-010-1959   (SL)
HOPITAL GENERAL DE HAWKESBURY & DISTRICT GENERAL HOSPITAL INC
1111 Ghislain St, Hawkesbury, ON, K6A 3G5
(613) 632-1111
Emp Here 700   *Sales* 77,756,000
SIC 8062 General medical and surgical hospi-

tals
Marc Leboutillier
Sebastien Racine
Jacques Parisien
Marcel Leclair
Don Hay
Denis Desaulniers
Joanne Gratton
Nathalie Ladouceur
Daniel Lalonde
Lorraine Lariviere

D-U-N-S 24-482-6962   (SL)
HOTTE AUTOMOBILE INC
HOTTE FORD
640 Main St W, Hawkesbury, ON, K6A 2J3
(613) 632-1159
Emp Here 24   *Sales* 11,953,872
SIC 5511 New and used car dealers
Alan Cote
Stephan Hollander

D-U-N-S 20-891-3749   (BR)
IKO INDUSTRIES LTD
ARMOROOF DIV OF
(*Suby of* GOLDIS ENTERPRISES, INC.)
1451 Spence Ave, Hawkesbury, ON, K6A 3T4
(613) 632-8581
Emp Here 80
SIC 2952 Asphalt felts and coatings
Michael Horner

D-U-N-S 24-419-7898   (SL)
LEGER, D L SALES INC
CANADIAN TIRE
1525 Cameron St, Hawkesbury, ON, K6A 3R3
(613) 632-3399
Emp Here 80   *Sales* 21,412,160
SIC 5251 Hardware stores
Denis Leger

D-U-N-S 20-774-5949   (BR)
LOBLAWS SUPERMARKETS LIMITED
LAURIN YOUR INDEPENDENT GROCER
(*Suby of* LOBLAW COMPANIES LIMITED)
1560 Cameron St Suite 820, Hawkesbury, ON, K6A 3S5
(613) 632-9215
Emp Here 120
SIC 5411 Grocery stores
Rheal Laurin

D-U-N-S 20-548-0812   (SL)
MAYLAN CONSTRUCTION SERVICES INC
CIBS CONSTRUCTION
(*Suby of* 760568 ONTARIO LTD)
372 Bertha St, Hawkesbury, ON, K6A 2A8
(613) 632-5553
Emp Here 25   *Sales* 14,258,450
SIC 1542 Nonresidential construction, nec
Daniel Landry

D-U-N-S 25-350-8121   (SL)
PHARMACIE SYRHAK PHARMACY INC
PHARMACIE JEAN COUTU # 159
80 Main St E Suite 159, Hawkesbury, ON, K6A 1A3
(613) 632-2743
Emp Here 55   *Sales* 13,438,040
SIC 5912 Drug stores and proprietary stores
Sylvie Robillard

D-U-N-S 24-801-5950   (SL)
PRESCOTT & RUSSEL RESIDENCE
1020 Cartier Blvd, Hawkesbury, ON, K6A 1W7
(613) 632-2755
Emp Here 120   *Sales* 7,109,640
SIC 8361 Residential care
Louise Lalonde

D-U-N-S 24-926-8624   (HQ)
TULMAR SAFETY SYSTEMS INC
TULMAR TECHNICAL SERVICES
1123 Cameron St, Hawkesbury, ON, K6A 2B8
(613) 632-1282
Sales 14,297,220
SIC 3069 Fabricated rubber products, nec

Barney E Bangs

D-U-N-S 20-055-2032   (SL)
VOITH CANADA INC
VOITH PAPER FABRIC & ROLL SYSTEMS
(*Suby of* VOITH FAMILIEN VERWALTUNG GMBH)
925 Tupper St, Hawkesbury, ON, K6A 3T5
(613) 632-4163
Emp Here 64   *Sales* 12,916,600
SIC 2221 Broadwoven fabric mills, manmade
Bernard Chaine

Hawkestone, ON L0L

D-U-N-S 24-366-9947   (HQ)
PARKVIEW TRANSIT INC
5 Small Cres, Hawkestone, ON, L0L 1T0
(705) 327-7100
Sales 22,581,600
SIC 4151 School buses
Jon Knowles

Hawkesville, ON N0B

D-U-N-S 20-533-5185   (SL)
FREY BROTHERS LIMITED
FREY BUILDING CONTRACTORS
3435 Broadway St, Hawkesville, ON, N0B 1X0
(519) 699-4641
Emp Here 60   *Sales* 34,220,280
SIC 1542 Nonresidential construction, nec
Albert Frey
Mahlon Frey
Nyle Bauman
Ryan Martin

Hearst, ON P0L

D-U-N-S 20-937-8186   (SL)
1535477 ONTARIO LIMITED
HEARST HUSKY RESTAURANT & TRUCK STOP
Gd, Hearst, ON, P0L 1N0
(705) 362-4085
Emp Here 30   *Sales* 14,942,340
SIC 5541 Gasoline service stations
Carmen Plourde
Marc Plourde

D-U-N-S 20-056-9101   (SL)
ARMAND H. COUTURE LTD
1226 Front St, Hearst, ON, P0L 1N0
(705) 362-4941
Emp Here 20   *Sales* 20,656,160
SIC 5171 Petroleum bulk stations and terminals
Gilles Boucher
Miguel Lachance

D-U-N-S 24-393-9027   (SL)
CRONIER, J.P. ENTERPRISES INC
CANADIAN TIRE
1330 Front St, Hearst, ON, P0L 1N0
(705) 362-5822
Emp Here 40   *Sales* 19,923,120
SIC 5531 Auto and home supply stores
Jean-Pierre Cronier

D-U-N-S 24-089-0525   (SL)
EXPERT CHEVROLET BUICK GMC LTD
500 Hwy 11 E, Hearst, ON, P0L 1N0
(705) 362-8001
Emp Here 22   *Sales* 10,957,716
SIC 5511 New and used car dealers
Alain Mitron

D-U-N-S 20-773-4690   (HQ)

EXPERT GARAGE LIMITED
TIMMINS GARAGE
420 Hwy 11 E, Hearst, ON, P0L 1N0
(705) 362-4301
Emp Here 21   *Sales* 25,800,480
SIC 5511 New and used car dealers
Pierre Delage
Alain Mitron
Jean-Paul Albert
Regean Joulet

D-U-N-S 20-056-9713   (HQ)
LECOURS, JEAN PAUL LIMITED
LECOURS MOTOR SALES
733 Front St, Hearst, ON, P0L 1N0
(705) 362-4011
Emp Here 13   *Sales* 10,957,716
SIC 5511 New and used car dealers
Jean Paul Lecours Jr
Patrick Lacours

D-U-N-S 20-056-9762   (HQ)
LEVESQUE PLYWOOD LIMITED
COLUMBIA FOREST PRODUCTS, DIV
(*Suby of* COLUMBIA FOREST PRODUCTS, INC.)
225 Prince St, Hearst, ON, P0L 1N0
(705) 362-4242
Sales 75,165,300
SIC 2435 Hardwood veneer and plywood
Bradley Thompson
Gills Levesque

D-U-N-S 24-660-8681   (HQ)
PEPCO CORP
25 Gaspesie Rd, Hearst, ON, P0L 1N0
(844) 362-4523
Emp Here 10   *Sales* 44,002,035
SIC 5172 Petroleum products, nec
Jean-Guy Pepin
Nicole Pepin

D-U-N-S 20-249-6451   (SL)
PEPCO ENERGY CORP
25 Ch. Gaspesie Rd, Hearst, ON, P0L 1N0
(844) 362-4523
Emp Here 10   *Sales* 10,328,080
SIC 5172 Petroleum products, nec
Jean-Guy Pepin

D-U-N-S 20-289-1250   (SL)
PHARMACIE BRUNET-CANTIN INC
PHARMACIE NOVENA
4 Ninth St, Hearst, ON, P0L 1N0
(705) 372-1212
Emp Here 45   *Sales* 11,382,930
SIC 5912 Drug stores and proprietary stores
Theresa Brunet
Denis Cantin
Luc Vashon

D-U-N-S 24-308-9455   (SL)
VILLENEUVE, C. CONSTRUCTION CO. LTD
1533 Hwy 11 W, Hearst, ON, P0L 1N0
(705) 372-1838
Emp Here 80   *Sales* 20,195,360
SIC 1611 Highway and street construction
Claude Villeneuve
Ghislain Lacroix

Heidelberg, ON N0B

D-U-N-S 24-588-0349   (SL)
STEMMLER MEATS & CHEESE (HEIDELBERG) INCORPORATED
STEMMLER MEATS & CHEESE
3031 Lobsinger Line, Heidelberg, ON, N0B 2M1
(519) 699-4590
Emp Here 45   *Sales* 12,336,840
SIC 5421 Meat and fish markets
Terry Stemmler
Kevin Stemmler
Shawn Stemmler

▲ Public Company   ■ Public Company Family Member   **HQ** Headquarters   **BR** Branch   **SL** Single Location

Hensall, ON N0M

D-U-N-S 20-749-5474   (SL)
CITAIR, INC
GENERAL COACH CANADA
(*Suby of* THOR INDUSTRIES, INC.)
73 Mill Rd, Hensall, ON, N0M 1X0
(519) 262-2600
Emp Here 140   *Sales* 31,338,020
SIC 3792 Travel trailers and campers
  Roger Faulkner
  Chris Faulkner

D-U-N-S 20-057-0505   (HQ)
HENSALL DISTRICT CO-OPERATIVE, IN-
CORPORATED
DIVISION 2
1 Davidson Dr, Hensall, ON, N0M 1X0
(519) 262-3002
Emp Here 250   *Sales* 549,473,100
SIC 5153 Grain and field beans
  Earl Wagner
  Ross Mcintosh
  Gerald Hayter
  Bill Wallace
  Buddy Richardson
  Robert Cornelis
  Gerhard Eilers
  Jorg Genoch
  Grant Mccomb
  Greg Kerrigan

D-U-N-S 25-615-2216   (SL)
ICECULTURE INC
81 Brock St, Hensall, ON, N0M 1X0
(519) 262-3500
Emp Here 50   *Sales* 11,242,750
SIC 2097 Manufactured ice
  Heidi Bayley
  Julian Bayley

D-U-N-S 20-818-4101   (SL)
PROVINCIAL LONG TERM CARE INC
QUEENSWAY NURSING & RETIREMENT
HOME
100 Queen St E, Hensall, ON, N0M 1X0
(519) 262-2830
Emp Here 85   *Sales* 5,842,305
SIC 8051 Skilled nursing care facilities
  Edward Ozimek
  Carolyn Ozimek

Hillsburgh, ON N0B

D-U-N-S 24-149-4900   (SL)
STATION 50
2 Station, Hillsburgh, ON, N0B 1Z0

Emp Here 30   *Sales* 13,703,230
SIC 7389 Business services, nec
  Jim Peagoy

Holland Landing, ON L9N

D-U-N-S 24-373-6266   (SL)
1758691 ONTARIO INC
ATV FARMS
21360 Bathurst St, Holland Landing, ON, L9N
1P6
(905) 830-0333
Emp Here 16   *Sales* 13,369,232
SIC 5148 Fresh fruits and vegetables
  Anthony Agresti
  Mary Agresti
  Viviano Agresti
  Travis Agresti

D-U-N-S 24-721-2905   (HQ)
CARLING PROPANE INC

PANDA PROPANE-REPAIR CO DIV OF
19752 Holland Landing Rd Unit 201, Holland
Landing, ON, L9N 0A1
(905) 952-0146
Emp Here 12   *Sales* 12,451,950
SIC 5541 Gasoline service stations
  Alex Goerk

D-U-N-S 20-966-4085   (HQ)
INSCAPE CORPORATION
OFFICE SPECIALTY
67 Toll Rd, Holland Landing, ON, L9N 1H2
(905) 836-7676
Emp Here 6   *Sales* 71,793,218
SIC 2522 Office furniture, except wood
  Brian Mirsky
  David Parshad
  Cecilia Nugent
  David Gerson
  John Gols
  Aziz Hirji
  Dennis Dyke

D-U-N-S 24-790-5966   (SL)
SOUTHDOWN INSTITUTE, THE
18798 Old Yonge St, Holland Landing, ON,
L9N 0L1
(905) 727-4214
Emp Here 40   *Sales* 15,896,560
SIC 8699 Membership organizations, nec
  Dorothy Heiderscheit

Honey Harbour, ON P0E

D-U-N-S 25-401-7999   (SL)
1212360 ONTARIO LIMITED
DELAWANA INN & RESORT
42 Delawana Rd, Honey Harbour, ON, P0E
1E0
(705) 756-2424
Emp Here 160   *Sales* 14,830,400
SIC 7011 Hotels and motels
  Vivian Jacques
  Morris Fischtein
  Will Fischtein

Hornby, ON L0P

D-U-N-S 20-636-5152   (SL)
ANGUS GEOSOLUTIONS INC
AGSI
13029 Steeles Ave, Hornby, ON, L0P 1E0
(905) 876-0700
Emp Here 75   *Sales* 17,571,600
SIC 8748 Business consulting, nec
  Christopher Cameron

D-U-N-S 24-078-4652   (SL)
PUTZER, M. HORNBY LIMITED
M PUTZER HORNSBY NURSERIES
7314 Sixth Line, Hornby, ON, L0P 1E0
(905) 878-7226
Emp Here 70   *Sales* 18,361,630
SIC 0181 Ornamental nursery products
  Bill Putzer

D-U-N-S 20-529-5629   (SL)
VAN DONGEN LANDSCAPING & NURS-
ERIES LTD
VAN DONGEN TREE FARM
6750 Trafalgar Rd Suite 1, Hornby, ON, L0P
1E0
(905) 878-1105
Emp Here 40   *Sales* 10,122,360
SIC 5261 Retail nurseries and garden stores
  Adrian Van Dongen

Huntsville, ON P1H

D-U-N-S 20-915-4819   (SL)
2043665 ONTARIO LIMITED
ROBINSON'S INDEPENDENT GROCER
131 Howland Dr, Huntsville, ON, P1H 2P7
(705) 789-6972
Emp Here 100   *Sales* 29,347,700
SIC 5411 Grocery stores
  Randall P Robinson
  Tracy L Robinson

D-U-N-S 24-214-1596   (HQ)
CAVALCADE COLOUR LAB INC
34 King William St, Huntsville, ON, P1H 1G5
(705) 789-9603
Emp Here 75   *Sales* 10,437,650
SIC 7384 Photofinish laboratories
  William Spring
  Donald Spring

D-U-N-S 20-699-9331   (BR)
DELTA HOTELS LIMITED
DELTA GRANDVIEW RESORT (MUSKOKA)
(*Suby of* GOVERNMENT OF THE
PROVINCE OF BRITISH COLUMBIA)
939 60 Hwy, Huntsville, ON, P1H 1B2
(705) 789-4417
Emp Here 100
SIC 8741 Management services
  Esa Paltanen

D-U-N-S 20-735-6726   (SL)
EDMONDS CHEVROLET PONTIAC BUICK
GMC LTD
138 Hanes Rd, Huntsville, ON, P1H 1M4
(705) 789-5507
Emp Here 25   *Sales* 12,451,950
SIC 5511 New and used car dealers
  Ward Edmonds
  Allan Holder

D-U-N-S 24-991-6875   (HQ)
FANOTECH ENVIRO INC
220 Old North Rd, Huntsville, ON, P1H 2J4
(705) 788-3046
Sales 17,907,440
SIC 3713 Truck and bus bodies
  Gabriel Tomassoni

D-U-N-S 25-615-3552   (SL)
HUNTSVILLE DISTRICT NURSING HOME
INC
FAIRVERN NURSING HOME
14 Mill St Suite 101, Huntsville, ON, P1H 2A4
(705) 789-4476
Emp Here 90   *Sales* 6,170,940
SIC 8051 Skilled nursing care facilities
  Barry Monaghan

D-U-N-S 20-290-7148   (BR)
JARLETTE LTD
MUSKOKA LANDING CARE CENTRE
65 Rogers Cove Dr, Huntsville, ON, P1H 2L9
(705) 788-7713
Emp Here 100   *Sales* 588,616
SIC 8051 Skilled nursing care facilities
  Erin Cunningham

D-U-N-S 20-753-0023   (BR)
KIMBERLY-CLARK INC
(*Suby of* KIMBERLY-CLARK CORPORA-
TION)
570 Ravenscliffe Rd, Huntsville, ON, P1H 2A1
(705) 788-5200
Emp Here 220
SIC 2621 Paper mills
  Tim Foster

D-U-N-S 25-051-0427   (SL)
M.B.R.P. INC
315 Old Ferguson Rd Suite 1, Huntsville, ON,
P1H 2J2
(705) 788-2845
Emp Here 100   *Sales* 22,384,300
SIC 3714 Motor vehicle parts and accessories
  Martin Barkey
  Ginger Barkey

D-U-N-S 20-555-6397   (BR)
METRO ONTARIO INC
METRO
(*Suby of* METRO INC)
70 King William St Suite 5a, Huntsville, ON,
P1H 2A5
(705) 789-9619
Emp Here 100
SIC 5411 Grocery stores
  Andrew Purvis

D-U-N-S 24-684-2970   (SL)
MILFORA DAIRY SUPPLIES INC
743 Skyhills Rd, Huntsville, ON, P1H 2N5
(705) 789-4557
Emp Here 3   *Sales* 13,604,352
SIC 5149 Groceries and related products, nec
  Marcel Rast
  Tracey Rast

D-U-N-S 20-900-9646   (SL)
MOSER, K.G. LIMITED
CANADIAN TIRE
77 King William St, Huntsville, ON, P1H 1E5
(705) 789-5569
Emp Here 100   *Sales* 62,928,000
SIC 5531 Auto and home supply stores
  Kenneth Moser
  Gail Moser

D-U-N-S 25-646-7291   (BR)
MUSKOKA ALGONQUIN HEALTHCARE
COMMUNITY CARE ACCESS CENTRE
(*Suby of* MUSKOKA ALGONQUIN HEALTH-
CARE)
8 Crescent Rd, Huntsville, ON, P1H 0B3
(705) 789-6451
Emp Here 150
SIC 8099 Health and allied services, nec
  Vaughn Adamson

D-U-N-S 20-973-4888   (HQ)
MUSKOKA ALGONQUIN HEALTHCARE
HUNTSVILLE DISTRICT MEMORIAL HOSPI-
TAL
100 Frank Miller Dr, Huntsville, ON, P1H 1H7
(705) 789-2311
Emp Here 450   *Sales* 57,978,784
SIC 8062 General medical and surgical hospi-
tals
  Natalie Bubela
  Charles Forret
  Evelyn Brown
  Gregg Evans
  Ross Maund
  Donna Denny
  Cameron Renwick
  Phil Matthews
  Dave Wilkin
  Brenda Gefucia

D-U-N-S 20-121-3980   (HQ)
MUSKOKA AUTO PARTS LIMITED
DENNIS LOU AUTOMOTIVE & MARINE
11 King William St, Huntsville, ON, P1H 1G6
(705) 789-2321
Sales 44,049,600
SIC 5531 Auto and home supply stores
  Paul Dennis
  David Dennis

D-U-N-S 20-056-6201   (SL)
MUSKOKA MINERALS & MINING INC
HUTCHESON SAND & GRAVEL
1265 Aspdin Rd, Huntsville, ON, P1H 2J2
(705) 789-4457
Emp Here 55   *Sales* 12,838,925
SIC 1442 Construction sand and gravel
  Bruce Smith
  Peter D. Smuk
  Kimberly Garner

D-U-N-S 20-180-1516   (SL)
NORTH ATLANTIC INTERNATIONAL LO-
GISTICS INC
22 Dairy Lane Suite 291, Huntsville, ON, P1H
1T4

▲ Public Company   ■ Public Company Family Member   **HQ** Headquarters   **BR** Branch   **SL** Single Location

(416) 291-2688
Emp Here 21   *Sales* 10,919,307
SIC 4731 Freight transportation arrangement
Robert Birch
Anthony Mestroni

D-U-N-S 24-199-6599   (SL)
ONE KID'S PLACE
100 Frank Miller Dr Suite 2, Huntsville, ON,
P1H 1H7
(705) 789-9985
Emp Here 100   *Sales* 6,842,200
SIC 8322 Individual and family services
Judy Sharpe

D-U-N-S 24-314-2093   (SL)
PANOLAM INDUSTRIES LTD
61 Domtar Rd, Huntsville, ON, P1H 2J7
(705) 789-9683
Emp Here 220   *Sales* 42,321,400
SIC 2436 Softwood veneer and plywood
Al Stobbeart

D-U-N-S 20-358-9804   (SL)
PEERLESS SECURITY INC
21 High St, Huntsville, ON, P1H 1N9
(705) 789-6253
Emp Here 60   *Sales* 26,830,440
SIC 5065 Electronic parts and equipment, nec
Douglas Stiller

D-U-N-S 24-826-4467   (SL)
**ROB ROLSTON BUILDING MATERIALS
LTD**
ROLSTON HOME BUILDING CENTRE
35 Crescent Rd, Huntsville, ON, P1H 1Y3
(705) 789-4111
Emp Here 50   *Sales* 12,652,950
SIC 5211 Lumber and other building materials
Robert Rolston
Rosemary Rolston

D-U-N-S 25-631-8056   (SL)
SKYLINE DEERHURST RESORT INC
DEERHURST RESORT
1235 Deerhurst Dr, Huntsville, ON, P1H 2E8
(705) 789-6411
Emp Here 450   *Sales* 43,050,600
SIC 7011 Hotels and motels
Michael Sneyd
Vadim Shub

D-U-N-S 24-829-4837   (BR)
UPONOR INFRA LTD
37 Centre St N, Huntsville, ON, P1H 1X4
(705) 789-2396
Emp Here 85   *Sales* 463,590
SIC 3088 Plastics plumbing fixtures
Chris Stilwell

D-U-N-S 24-318-0804   (BR)
WAL-MART CANADA CORP
WALMART
(*Suby of* WALMART INC.)
111 Howland Dr Unit 10, Huntsville, ON, P1H
2P4
(705) 787-1137
Emp Here 150
SIC 5311 Department stores
Carl Frechette

Huron Park, ON N0M

D-U-N-S 25-255-9596   (SL)
BLUEWATER RECYCLING ASSOCIATION
415 Canada Ave, Huron Park, ON, N0M 1Y0
(519) 228-6678
Emp Here 65   *Sales* 20,729,150
SIC 4953 Refuse systems
Francis Veilleux

D-U-N-S 24-764-7191   (SL)
GNUTTI CARLO CANADA LTD
(*Suby of* GNUTTI CARLO SPA)
404 Canada Ave, Huron Park, ON, N0M 1Y0

(519) 228-6685
Emp Here 212   *Sales* 60,327,729
SIC 3714 Motor vehicle parts and accessories
Paul Buchanan
Kevin Siroen
Rick Hope

D-U-N-S 20-325-7092   (SL)
NEW UNITED GODERICH INC
403 Canada Ave, Huron Park, ON, N0M 1Y0
(519) 228-6052
Emp Here 125   *Sales* 33,372,250
SIC 4581 Airports, flying fields, and services
Blaine Field
Cathy Forsyth

D-U-N-S 24-704-1429   (SL)
SAF-T-CAB, INC
(*Suby of* SAF-T-CAB, INC.)
7 Canada Ave, Huron Park, ON, N0M 1Y0
(519) 228-6538
Emp Here 60   *Sales* 13,320,060
SIC 3531 Construction machinery
Dave Bryson

Ignace, ON P0T

D-U-N-S 24-378-4365   (SL)
1383791 ONTARIO INC
RALEIGH FALLS TIMBER
(*Suby of* 777603 ONTARIO INC)
952 Humphrey Rd, Ignace, ON, P0T 1T0
(807) 934-6500
Emp Here 200   *Sales* 38,474,000
SIC 2411 Logging
Louie Ricci

D-U-N-S 24-852-8861   (HQ)
777603 ONTARIO INC
RICCI'S TRUCKING
952 Humphrey Rd, Ignace, ON, P0T 1T0
(807) 934-6500
Emp Here 3   *Sales* 24,684,720
SIC 4212 Local trucking, without storage
Louie Ricci

Ilderton, ON N0M

D-U-N-S 24-843-7873   (SL)
COLDSTREAM CONCRETE LIMITED
402 Quaker Lane, Ilderton, ON, N0M 2A0
(519) 666-0604
Emp Here 45   *Sales* 10,350,855
SIC 3272 Concrete products, nec
Robert S Brown
Amy Koteles
Patricia Brown

D-U-N-S 20-128-4700   (SL)
SPENCER STEEL LIMITED
200 King St, Ilderton, ON, N0M 2A0
(519) 471-6888
Emp Here 75
SIC 1791 Structural steel erection
Richard Spencer Sr
Richard Spencer Jr

Ingersoll, ON N5C

D-U-N-S 20-705-3869   (SL)
AL BARNIM INC
AL'S TIRE CRAFT
(*Suby of* BARNIM HOLDINGS INC)
90 Samnah Cres, Ingersoll, ON, N5C 3J7
(519) 424-3402
Emp Here 35   *Sales* 12,747,525
SIC 5014 Tires and tubes
Brad Barnim

Bruce Barnim
Sheila Barnim

D-U-N-S 24-121-1242   (SL)
ALEXANDRA HOSPITAL INGERSOLL, THE
29 Noxon St, Ingersoll, ON, N5C 1B8
(519) 485-1700
Emp Here 150   *Sales* 16,662,000
SIC 8062 General medical and surgical hospitals

D-U-N-S 24-831-3033   (BR)
ATLANTIC PACKAGING PRODUCTS LTD
(*Suby of* ATLANTIC PACKAGING PRODUCTS LTD)
45 Chisholm Dr, Ingersoll, ON, N5C 2C7
(800) 268-5620
Emp Here 120
SIC 2653 Corrugated and solid fiber boxes
Mike Burnett

D-U-N-S 20-753-7481   (SL)
BELL-CAMP MANUFACTURING INC
543925 Clarke Rd E, Ingersoll, ON, N5C 3J8
(519) 485-3120
Emp Here 54   *Sales* 10,372,590
SIC 3499 Fabricated Metal products, nec
Bradley Stuebe

D-U-N-S 25-362-5032   (BR)
BONDUELLE CANADA INC
(*Suby of* BONDUELLE)
583278 Hamilton Rd, Ingersoll, ON, N5C 3J7
(519) 485-0282
Emp Here 150
SIC 5142 Packaged frozen goods
Rob Anderson

D-U-N-S 20-388-2324   (BR)
**BUTCHER ENGINEERING ENTERPRISES
LIMITED, THE**
(*Suby of* BUTCHER ENGINEERING ENTERPRISES LIMITED, THE)
17 Underwood Rd, Ingersoll, ON, N5C 3K1
(519) 425-0999
Emp Here 450
SIC 7538 General automotive repair shops
Gord Cukieski

D-U-N-S 25-361-7187   (HQ)
CARMEUSE LIME (CANADA) LIMITED
CARMEUSE NATURAL CHEMICALS
374681 County Rd 6, Ingersoll, ON, N5C 3K5
(519) 423-6283
Emp Here 175   *Sales* 67,757,850
SIC 3274 Lime
Yves Willems
Jonathan Bright
Jeff Bittner
Melissa Croll
Jack Fahler

D-U-N-S 20-181-4063   (SL)
COILPLUS CANADA INC
COILPLUS
(*Suby of* MITSUBISHI CORPORATION)
18 Underwood Rd, Ingersoll, ON, N5C 3V6
(519) 485-6393
Emp Here 65   *Sales* 38,834,510
SIC 5051 Metals service centers and offices
Douglas Thompson
Tatsuya Naoki

D-U-N-S 25-355-4380   (BR)
**DIVERSICARE CANADA MANAGEMENT
SERVICES CO., INC**
OXFORD REGIONAL NURSING HOME
(*Suby of* DCMS HOLDINGS INC)
263 Wonham St S, Ingersoll, ON, N5C 3P6
(519) 485-3920
Emp Here 100
SIC 8051 Skilled nursing care facilities
Leslie Hancock

D-U-N-S 25-742-4622   (SL)
ELM HURST INN
415 Harris St, Ingersoll, ON, N5C 3J8

(519) 485-5321
Emp Here 80   *Sales* 7,591,920
SIC 7011 Hotels and motels
Pat Frey

D-U-N-S 24-826-4397   (SL)
ERTH (HOLDINGS) INC
COULTER WATER METER SERVICE
180 Whiting St, Ingersoll, ON, N5C 3B5
(519) 485-6038
Emp Here 50   *Sales* 13,592,100
SIC 7629 Electrical repair shops
Chris White

D-U-N-S 24-977-5466   (SL)
FIELD GATE ORGANICS INC
194338 19th Line, Ingersoll, ON, N5C 3J6
(519) 425-8799
Emp Here 40   *Sales* 33,423,080
SIC 5149 Groceries and related products, nec
Mark Soudant

D-U-N-S 24-484-1193   (HQ)
**FURST-MCNESS COMPANY OF CANADA
LIMITED**
FURST-MCMIRACLE FEEDS
(*Suby of* FURST-MCNESS COMPANY)
30 Wilson St, Ingersoll, ON, N5C 4E8
(519) 485-5600
Emp Here 12   *Sales* 13,365,360
SIC 5191 Farm supplies
Shelley Martin
Frank E Furst

D-U-N-S 24-680-6199   (BR)
GENERAL MOTORS OF CANADA COMPANY
CAMI ASSEMBLY
(*Suby of* GENERAL MOTORS COMPANY)
300 Ingersoll St, Ingersoll, ON, N5C 3J7
(519) 485-6400
Emp Here 2,600
SIC 3711 Motor vehicles and car bodies
Gary Duff

D-U-N-S 20-121-5530   (SL)
GLASSFORD MOTORS LIMITED
30 Samnah Cres Suite 4, Ingersoll, ON, N5C
3J7
(519) 485-0940
Emp Here 23   *Sales* 11,455,794
SIC 5511 New and used car dealers
John M. Glassford

D-U-N-S 24-049-4799   (SL)
HURLEY FOODS LTD
HURLEY'S INDEPENDENT GROCER
273 King St W, Ingersoll, ON, N5C 2K9
(519) 425-4406
Emp Here 180   *Sales* 52,825,860
SIC 5411 Grocery stores
Dale Hurley
Berdine Hurley

D-U-N-S 25-303-9879   (SL)
HYDRA DYNE TECHNOLOGY INC
55 Samnah Cres, Ingersoll, ON, N5C 3J7
(519) 485-2200
Emp Here 60   *Sales* 13,320,060
SIC 3593 Fluid power cylinders and actuators
Stephan Bohner
William Csinos

D-U-N-S 20-121-5795   (SL)
INGERSOLL PAPER BOX CO. LIMITED
327 King St W, Ingersoll, ON, N5C 2K9
(519) 485-1830
Emp Here 75   *Sales* 17,507,625
SIC 2657 Folding paperboard boxes
David Skinner

D-U-N-S 24-363-6610   (SL)
INGERSOLL SUPPORT SERVICES INC
148 Thames St S, Ingersoll, ON, N5C 2T4
(519) 425-0005
Emp Here 85   *Sales* 5,531,375
SIC 8361 Residential care
Jayden Nancekivell

▲ Public Company   ■ Public Company Family Member   **HQ** Headquarters   **BR** Branch   **SL** Single Location

D-U-N-S 25-214-9265   (SL)
MCCLAY GROUP LTD
132 Ingersoll St S, Ingersoll, ON, N5C 3K1
(519) 485-3088
Emp Here 200   *Sales* 41,141,200
SIC 4212 Local trucking, without storage
Troy Mcclay
Ryan Mcclay

D-U-N-S 20-039-8398   (SL)
NATIONAL TIRE DISTRIBUTORS
311 Ingersoll St S, Ingersoll, ON, N5C 3J7
(519) 425-1228
Emp Here 25   *Sales* 15,732,000
SIC 5531 Auto and home supply stores

D-U-N-S 24-918-8079   (SL)
NIFAST CANADA CORPORATION
NICA
(*Suby of* MITSUBISHI CORPORATION)
12 Underwood Rd, Ingersoll, ON, N5C 3J9
(519) 485-1050
Emp Here 27   *Sales* 12,825,702
SIC 5085 Industrial supplies
Nancy Bryers
Dave Groh
Ian Hunt
Pita Allard

D-U-N-S 24-044-7797   (BR)
R. BRUCE GRAHAM LIMITED
GRAHAM ENERGY
203 Bell St, Ingersoll, ON, N5C 2P2

Emp Here 100
SIC 5172 Petroleum products, nec

D-U-N-S 20-731-6191   (SL)
SCOTT-DOUGLAS PLASTICS LIMITED
50 Janes Rd, Ingersoll, ON, N5C 0A9
(519) 485-1943
Emp Here 55   *Sales* 11,104,335
SIC 3089 Plastics products, nec
Donald Douglas
Thomas Douglas

D-U-N-S 24-380-1854   (BR)
SIVACO WIRE GROUP 2004 L.P.
SIVACO ONTARIO
(*Suby of* SIVACO WIRE GROUP 2004 L.P.)
330 Thomas St, Ingersoll, ON, N5C 3K5
(800) 265-0418
Emp Here 80
SIC 3496 Miscellaneous fabricated wire products
Lawrence Pye

D-U-N-S 25-249-1543   (BR)
THAMES VALLEY DISTRICT SCHOOL BOARD
INGERSOLL DISTRICT COLLEGIATE INSTITUTE
(*Suby of* THAMES VALLEY DISTRICT SCHOOL BOARD)
37 Alma St, Ingersoll, ON, N5C 1N1
(519) 485-1200
Emp Here 90
SIC 8211 Elementary and secondary schools
Kyle Blyde

D-U-N-S 20-044-0634   (SL)
VERSPEETEN CARTAGE LIMITED
(*Suby of* 1207719 ONTARIO LIMITED)
274129 Wallace Line Rr 4, Ingersoll, ON, N5C 3J7
(519) 425-7881
Emp Here 350   *Sales* 64,533,350
SIC 4213 Trucking, except local
Ronald Verspeeten
Robert Gyenes
Archie Verspeeten

Ingleside, ON K0C

D-U-N-S 25-975-7334   (SL)
3635112 CANADA INC
M & L SUPPLY FIRE & SAFETY
14935 County Rd 2, Ingleside, ON, K0C 1M0
(613) 537-9559
Emp Here 25   *Sales* 11,875,650
SIC 5087 Service establishment equipment
Mark Prendergast
Lori Prendergast

D-U-N-S 25-282-5294   (SL)
FINES HOME HARDWARE & BUILDING CENTRE
HOME HARDWARE
9 Thorold Ln, Ingleside, ON, K0C 1M0
(613) 537-2233
Emp Here 40   *Sales* 10,122,360
SIC 5251 Hardware stores
Murray Fines

D-U-N-S 24-159-7025   (BR)
KELLY SERVICES (CANADA), LTD
KELLY SERVICES
(*Suby of* KELLY SERVICES, INC.)
70 Dickinson Dr, Ingleside, ON, K0C 1M0
(613) 537-8491
Emp Here 80
SIC 7361 Employment agencies
Carl T. Camden

D-U-N-S 24-268-1682   (BR)
KRAFT HEINZ CANADA ULC
KRAFT HEINZ
(*Suby of* THE KRAFT HEINZ COMPANY)
70 Dickinson Dr, Ingleside, ON, K0C 1M0
(613) 537-2226
Emp Here 390
SIC 2022 Cheese; natural and processed
Glenda O'brian

Inglewood, ON L7C

D-U-N-S 24-065-3902   (HQ)
CRAILIN LOGISTICS SERVICES INC
CSI LOGISTICS
(*Suby of* ITS HOLDINGS INC)
14722 Heart Lake Rd, Inglewood, ON, L7C 2J7
(905) 838-3215
Emp Here 100   *Sales* 73,358,120
SIC 4731 Freight transportation arrangement
Craig Cottrell
Linda Cottrell

D-U-N-S 25-051-4973   (SL)
S.H.A.R.E. AGRICULTURE FOUNDATION
S.H.A.R.E
14110 Kennedy Rd, Inglewood, ON, L7C 2G3
(905) 838-0897
Emp Here 45   *Sales* 20,214,855
SIC 7389 Business services, nec
Joe Gray

Inkerman, ON K0E

D-U-N-S 24-850-6615   (HQ)
SEVITA INTERNATIONAL CORPORATION
11451 Cameron Rd, Inkerman, ON, K0E 1J0
(613) 989-3000
Emp Here 30   *Sales* 92,464,596
SIC 5153 Grain and field beans
David Hendrick
Bob Hart
Michael Staedler
Don Rees

Innerkip, ON N0J

D-U-N-S 24-779-4621   (HQ)
GREATARIO INDUSTRIAL STORAGE SYSTEMS LTD
GREATARIO ENGINEERED STORAGE SYSTEMS
715647 County Rd 4, Innerkip, ON, N0J 1M0
(519) 469-8169
Sales 12,309,300
SIC 1791 Structural steel erection
Glen Gregory
Scott Burn
Peter Pressey

D-U-N-S 25-214-3193   (SL)
ONTARIO HARVESTORE SYSTEMS SERVICES INC
ONTARIO HARVESTORE SYSTEMS
715647 County Rd Nw Suite 4, Innerkip, ON, N0J 1M0
(519) 469-8200
Emp Here 35   *Sales* 14,795,795
SIC 1541 Industrial buildings and warehouses
Glen Gregory
Peter Pressey

D-U-N-S 20-531-4461   (BR)
SHARP BUS LINES LIMITED
(*Suby of* 608705 ONTARIO LIMITED)
6 Scott St, Innerkip, ON, N0J 1M0

Emp Here 75
SIC 4151 School buses
Rob Reeves

Innisfil, ON L9S

D-U-N-S 24-320-2010   (SL)
2311390 ONTARIO INC
AUDI BARRIE
2484 Doral Dr, Innisfil, ON, L9S 0A3
(705) 431-9393
Emp Here 32   *Sales* 15,938,496
SIC 5511 New and used car dealers
Kapil Dilawri
Omar Khan

D-U-N-S 25-361-8789   (BR)
CANADIAN AUTOMOTIVE INSTITUTE, THE
KEMPENFELT CONFERENCE CENTRE, THE
(*Suby of* CANADIAN AUTOMOTIVE INSTITUTE, THE)
3722 Fairway Rd, Innisfil, ON, L9S 1A5

Emp Here 100
SIC 7299 Miscellaneous personal service
Wes Shedler

D-U-N-S 25-088-7528   (SL)
CHANTLER TRANSPORT INC
3235 Clifford Crt, Innisfil, ON, L9S 3V8
(705) 431-4022
Emp Here 107   *Sales* 22,010,542
SIC 4213 Trucking, except local
Steve Chantler
Ron Gosselin

D-U-N-S 20-770-8269   (BR)
CLUBLINK CORPORATION ULC
NATIONAL PINES GOLF CLUB
(*Suby of* TWC ENTERPRISES LIMITED)
8165 10 Sideroad Suite 11, Innisfil, ON, L9S 4T3
(705) 431-7000
Emp Here 200
SIC 7992 Public golf courses
Kevin Bailie

D-U-N-S 20-851-4356   (SL)
COMET CHEMICAL COMPANY LTD
COLT CHEMICAL, DIV OF
3463 Thomas St, Innisfil, ON, L9S 3W4
(705) 436-5580
Emp Here 20   *Sales* 14,606,900

SIC 5169 Chemicals and allied products, nec
James Stewart
Jeffrey Stewart

D-U-N-S 24-751-7303   (HQ)
DE RIGUEUR INC
JOE JOHNSON EQUIPMENT
(*Suby of* FEDERAL SIGNAL CORPORATION)
2521 Bowman St, Innisfil, ON, L9S 0E9
(705) 733-7700
Emp Here 50   *Sales* 31,702,450
SIC 5082 Construction and mining machinery
Joseph Johnson Jr
Jamie Johnson
Ted Hui
Jeff Johnson
Teresa Johnson

D-U-N-S 24-214-1638   (SL)
HOMELIFE-KEMPENFELT KELLY REAL ESTATE LTD
7886 Yonge St, Innisfil, ON, L9S 1L4
(705) 436-5111
Emp Here 75   *Sales* 20,381,700
SIC 6531 Real estate agents and managers
Lou Kelly

D-U-N-S 20-258-6715   (SL)
INNISFIL ENERGY SERVICES LIMITED
7251 Yonge St, Innisfil, ON, L9S 0J3
(705) 431-4321
Emp Here 20   *Sales* 10,393,100
SIC 4911 Electric services
Wade Morris

D-U-N-S 25-597-8710   (SL)
INNPOWER CORPORATION
7251 Yonge St, Innisfil, ON, L9S 0J3
(705) 431-4321
Emp Here 41   *Sales* 21,305,855
SIC 4911 Electric services
Wade Morris

D-U-N-S 25-371-8829   (SL)
NORTHERN AUTO AUCTIONS OF CANADA INC
NORTH TORONTO AUCTION
3230 Thomas St, Innisfil, ON, L9S 3W5
(705) 436-4111
Emp Here 75   *Sales* 33,691,425
SIC 7389 Business services, nec
Frank Panza
Stuart Ralph
Matthew Rispin

D-U-N-S 24-946-5303   (HQ)
RES PRECAST INC
3450 Thomas St, Innisfil, ON, L9S 3W6
(705) 436-7383
Emp Here 30   *Sales* 14,006,100
SIC 3272 Concrete products, nec
Joseph Di leo
Paul Gorrie

D-U-N-S 24-597-3391   (SL)
TARPIN LUMBER INCORPORATED
2267 Bowman St, Innisfil, ON, L9S 3V5
(705) 436-5373
Emp Here 40   *Sales* 10,122,360
SIC 5211 Lumber and other building materials
David J. Pratt
Donald G. Pratt

D-U-N-S 20-316-5787   (SL)
TEMPO FLEXO LTD
2237 Industrial Park Rd, Innisfil, ON, L9S 3V9
(705) 436-4442
Emp Here 130   *Sales* 25,319,840
SIC 2671 Paper; coated and laminated packaging
Michael Mencarelli
Richard Hardwick

D-U-N-S 20-364-1977   (SL)
TIREKICKER INSPECTIONS INC
3230 Thomas St, Innisfil, ON, L9S 3W5

---

(705) 436-4111
Emp Here 100   *Sales* 36,421,500
SIC 5012 Automobiles and other motor vehicles
Matt Rispin

Iroquois, ON K0E

D-U-N-S 24-104-8461   (HQ)
CRAIG PACKAGING LIMITED
REPUBLIC PACKAGING OF CANADA
(*Suby of* REPUBLIC PACKAGING CORP.)
5911 Carmen Rd S, Iroquois, ON, K0E 1K0
(613) 652-4856
Emp Here 33   *Sales* 11,671,750
SIC 2653 Corrugated and solid fiber boxes
Charles Wood

D-U-N-S 20-859-4010   (HQ)
ROSS VIDEO LIMITED
8 John St, Iroquois, ON, K0E 1K0
(613) 652-4886
Emp Here 50   *Sales* 198,040,500
SIC 3663 Radio and t.v. communications equipment

D-U-N-S 20-073-3273   (SL)
TRANSCANADA PIPELINES LTD
11235 Zeron Rd, Iroquois, ON, K0E 1K0
(613) 652-4287
Emp Here 5   *Sales* 15,529,285
SIC 4922 Natural gas transmission

Iroquois Falls, ON P0K

D-U-N-S 24-617-0356   (SL)
IROQUOIS FALLS FOODLAND
171 Ambridge Dr, Iroquois Falls, ON, P0K 1G0
(705) 232-4071
Emp Here 45   *Sales* 12,336,840
SIC 5411 Grocery stores
Yvan Leveille

Jacksons Point, ON L0E

D-U-N-S 20-629-8101   (SL)
BRIARS ESTATES LIMITED
BRIARS INN & COUNTRY CLUB
(*Suby of* 625631 ONTARIO INC)
55 Hedge Rd Rr 1, Jacksons Point, ON, L0E 1L0
(800) 465-2376
Emp Here 100   *Sales* 9,269,000
SIC 7011 Hotels and motels
John D Sibbald
Barbara Sibbald

D-U-N-S 20-720-8237   (SL)
TIM HORTONS
20945 Dalton Rd, Jacksons Point, ON, L0E 1R0
(905) 722-7762
Emp Here 45   *Sales* 12,336,840
SIC 5461 Retail bakeries
Jesse Woodrow

Jarvis, ON N0A

D-U-N-S 25-407-5302   (HQ)
D & W GROUP INC
DOUGHTY & WILLIAMSON, DIV OF
2173 Highway 3, Jarvis, ON, N0A 1J0
(519) 587-2273
Emp Here 2   *Sales* 22,478,176
SIC 5999 Miscellaneous retail stores, nec
Drew Williamson

Don Muirhead

D-U-N-S 24-561-0696   (SL)
WABISA MUTUAL INSURANCE COMPANY
35 Talbot St W, Jarvis, ON, N0A 1J0
(519) 587-4454
Emp Here 19   *Sales* 13,783,341
SIC 6331 Fire, marine, and casualty insurance
Gary Whitwell
Kenneth Marshall

Johnstown, ON K0E

D-U-N-S 24-978-0409   (HQ)
SYSTEMES ET CABLES PRYSMIAN CANADA LTEE
(*Suby of* PRYSMIAN SPA)
137 Commerce Pl, Johnstown, ON, K0E 1T1
(613) 925-6008
Emp Here 150   *Sales* 65,623,000
SIC 1623 Water, sewer, and utility lines
Hakan Ozmen
Fabio Bocchio
Christina Trainor
Fabio Romeo

Jordan Station, ON L0R

D-U-N-S 20-606-4487   (HQ)
AVONDALE STORES LIMITED
DONUT DINER
4520 Jordan Rd, Jordan Station, ON, L0R 1S0
(905) 562-4173
Emp Here 40   *Sales* 153,971,200
SIC 5411 Grocery stores
Robert Stewart
Frank Stewart
Paul Stewart
Barbara Stewart
Robert Ruttan
Larry Stewart
James Moretti

D-U-N-S 24-848-7308   (HQ)
BAYVIEW FLOWERS (JORDAN STATION) LTD
3764 Jordan Rd, Jordan Station, ON, L0R 1S0
(905) 562-7321
Sales 63,114,200
SIC 5193 Flowers and florists supplies
Stewart Van Staalduinen
Clarence Van Staalduinen

D-U-N-S 24-763-8166   (HQ)
CAVE SPRING CELLARS LTD
CAVE SPRING VINEYARDS
3836 Main St Rr 1, Jordan Station, ON, L0R 1S0
(905) 562-3581
Emp Here 1   *Sales* 20,577,060
SIC 5182 Wine and distilled beverages
Len Pennachetti
John W Pennachetti

D-U-N-S 24-581-2313   (SL)
FLOWER GROUP OPERATING LP
ONE FLORAL GROUP
2350 4th Ave, Jordan Station, ON, L0R 1S0
(905) 562-4118
Emp Here 596   *Sales* 100,738,900
SIC 0181 Ornamental nursery products
Bob Clamp
John Sprowl

D-U-N-S 25-638-6541   (SL)
INN ON THE TWENTY LTD
3836 Main St, Jordan Station, ON, L0R 1S0
(905) 562-7313
Emp Here 100   *Sales* 4,551,900
SIC 5812 Eating places
Don Dyson

D-U-N-S 20-595-8408   (HQ)
LAKESHORE INC
2350 Fourth Ave Rr 1, Jordan Station, ON, L0R 1S0
(905) 562-4118
Sales 103,804,556
SIC 6712 Bank holding companies
Jim Dertinger
James Olsthoorn

D-U-N-S 20-122-1678   (SL)
MOYER DIEBEL LIMITED
CHAMPION MOYER DIEBEL
(*Suby of* THE BIG SKY TRUST)
2674 North Service Rd, Jordan Station, ON, L0R 1S0
(905) 562-4195
Emp Here 75   *Sales* 16,650,075
SIC 3589 Service industry machinery, nec
Eric Nommsen
Christa Miller
Elaine Maude

D-U-N-S 24-524-3035   (HQ)
STUCOR CONSTRUCTION LTD
2540 South Service Rd, Jordan Station, ON, L0R 1S0
(905) 562-1118
Emp Here 90   *Sales* 57,033,800
SIC 1542 Nonresidential construction, nec
Brian Gill

D-U-N-S 20-179-6851   (HQ)
VINELAND GROWERS CO-OPERATIVE LIMITED
4150 Jordan Rd Suite 700, Jordan Station, ON, L0R 1S0
(905) 562-4133
Emp Here 15   *Sales* 25,067,310
SIC 5148 Fresh fruits and vegetables
George Mitges
Chris Andrews
Philip Tregunno
George Lepp
Thomas Platts Jr
Micheal Honsberger
Scott Macsween
Trevor Falk
Jamie Warner
David Wall

Joyceville, ON K0H

D-U-N-S 20-823-7537   (SL)
1085453 ONTARIO LTD
KINGSTON HUSKY CAR & TRUCK STOP
2054 Joyceville Rd, Joyceville, ON, K0H 1Y0
(613) 546-5025
Emp Here 30   *Sales* 14,942,340
SIC 5541 Gasoline service stations
Gregory Mcdougall

Kanata, ON K2K

D-U-N-S 25-100-5351   (HQ)
3517667 CANADA INC
411 Legget Dr Suite 600, Kanata, ON, K2K 3C9
(613) 599-9991
Emp Here 130   *Sales* 43,916,000
SIC 7371 Custom computer programming services
Peter Allen
Greg Friesen
Alan Soleheim
Tom Mclellan
Russell James Frederick
David Farrar
Erik Boch
Barry Dahan
Cesar Cesaratto

Claude Carman Haw

D-U-N-S 24-855-3526   (SL)
A HUNDRED ANSWERS INC
340 March Rd Suite 500, Kanata, ON, K2K 2E4
(613) 271-3700
Emp Here 47   *Sales* 11,181,347
SIC 8742 Management consulting services
Sean Murphy
Tracy Murphy

D-U-N-S 20-188-7895   (SL)
ALCATEL HOLDINGS CANADA CORP
(*Suby of* NOKIA OYJ)
600 March Rd, Kanata, ON, K2K 2T6
(613) 591-3600
Emp Here 125   *Sales* 45,688,625
SIC 6712 Bank holding companies
Hubert Pesquidoux
David Wilson

D-U-N-S 25-361-9134   (BR)
ASTENJOHNSON, INC
ASTENJOHNSON DRYER FABRIC
(*Suby of* ASTENJOHNSON, INC.)
48 Richardson Side Rd, Kanata, ON, K2K 1X2
(613) 592-5851
Emp Here 115
SIC 2221 Broadwoven fabric mills, manmade
Dan Cappell

D-U-N-S 20-222-4267   (HQ)
ASTENJOHNSON, INC
AUTOVAC
(*Suby of* ASTENJOHNSON, INC.)
1243 Teron Rd, Kanata, ON, K2K 1X2
(613) 592-5851
Emp Here 36   *Sales* 94,601,200
SIC 2299 Textile goods, nec
Daniel D Cappell
William A. Finn
Graham Jackson
Thomas Durkin

D-U-N-S 24-965-6906   (SL)
BELAIR NETWORKS INC
ERICSSON
(*Suby of* TELEFON AB LM ERICSSON)
603 March Rd, Kanata, ON, K2K 2M5
(613) 254-7070
Emp Here 51   *Sales* 11,652,072
SIC 4813 Telephone communication, except radio
Bernard Herscovich
Peter Rose
Pat Dipietro
Adam Chowaniec
Chris Albinson
David Ziberman
Larry Lang
Stephen G. Rayment

D-U-N-S 24-360-6832   (HQ)
BEST THERATRONICS LTD
413 March Rd Suite 25, Kanata, ON, K2K 0E4
(613) 591-2100
Emp Here 95   *Sales* 27,274,680
SIC 3841 Surgical and medical instruments
Krishnan Suthanthiran
David Choo
Chandrakanth Arya

D-U-N-S 20-857-6686   (HQ)
BMT CANADA LTD
(*Suby of* BMT GROUP LIMITED)
311 Legget Dr, Kanata, ON, K2K 1Z8
(613) 592-2830
Emp Here 67   *Sales* 17,067,926
SIC 8711 Engineering services
Darcy Byrtus
Chris Tokarchuk

D-U-N-S 20-180-6861   (SL)
BROOKSTREET HOTEL CORPORATION
(*Suby of* WESLEY CLOVER CORPORATION)
525 Legget Dr, Kanata, ON, K2K 2W2

(613) 271-3582
Emp Here 138   *Sales* 13,202,184
SIC 7011 Hotels and motels
Nyle Kelly
Troy Hughes
Mark Nisbett

D-U-N-S 24-886-6162   (HQ)
COMPUTER SCIENCES CANADA INC
CSC
(*Suby of* DXC TECHNOLOGY COMPANY)
555 Legget Dr, Kanata, ON, K2K 2X3
(613) 591-1810
Emp Here 150   *Sales* 353,684,800
SIC 7373 Computer integrated systems design
Charles A. Whelen
William L. Deckelman

D-U-N-S 24-428-6659   (HQ)
DYNEX POWER INC
(*Suby of* CRRC GROUP CO., LTD.)
515 Legget Dr Suite 800, Kanata, ON, K2K 3G4
(613) 822-2500
Sales 194,382,745
SIC 5065 Electronic parts and equipment, nec
Clive Vacher
Alan Lyons
Liu Ke'an
Debbie Weinstein
David Banks
Richard Wu
George Guo
Gary Liu

D-U-N-S 25-411-6577   (SL)
ENTRUST DATACARD LIMITED
(*Suby of* ENTRUST DATACARD CORPORATION)
1000 Innovation Dr, Kanata, ON, K2K 3E7
(613) 270-3400
Emp Here 200   *Sales* 28,836,400
SIC 7371 Custom computer programming services
Todd Wilkinson
Tony Ball
Chris Pelletier
Phil Kasper
Jeff Smolinski
Kurt Ishaug
Karen Kaukol
Beth Klehr

D-U-N-S 25-401-8302   (BR)
ESIT CANADA ENTERPRISE SERVICES CO
COMPAQ
(*Suby of* DXC TECHNOLOGY COMPANY)
100 Herzberg Rd, Kanata, ON, K2K 3B7
(613) 592-5111
Emp Here 325
SIC 5045 Computers, peripherals, and software
Tim Dooley

D-U-N-S 20-576-9805   (HQ)
FILTRAN LIMITED
API TECHNOLOGIES, DIV OF
(*Suby of* API TECHNOLOGIES CORP.)
360 Terry Fox Dr Suite 100, Kanata, ON, K2K 2P5
(613) 270-9009
Sales 28,566,300
SIC 3677 Electronic coils and transformers
Phillip Dezwirek
Jason Dezwirek
Claudio Mannarino

D-U-N-S 20-694-7793   (SL)
FLEXTRONICS CANADA DESIGN SERVICES INC
(*Suby of* FLEX LTD.)
1280 Teron Rd, Kanata, ON, K2K 2C1
(613) 895-2050
Emp Here 200   *Sales* 35,747,800
SIC 8711 Engineering services
Francisco Ledda

Michael Mcnamarc

D-U-N-S 25-673-6828   (HQ)
GILMORE GLOBAL LOGISTICS SERVICES INC
(*Suby of* GILMORE, R. E. INVESTMENTS CORP)
120 Herzberg Rd, Kanata, ON, K2K 3B7
(613) 599-6065
Sales 24,955,200
SIC 8741 Management services
Robert Gilmore
Richard Weedmark
Paul Brennan

D-U-N-S 20-891-8581   (SL)
GILMORE PRINTING SERVICES INC
(*Suby of* GILMORE, R. E. INVESTMENTS CORP)
110 Herzberg Rd, Kanata, ON, K2K 3B7
(613) 599-3776
Emp Here 85   *Sales* 13,942,295
SIC 2752 Commercial printing, lithographic
Robert Gilmore

D-U-N-S 24-437-2942   (HQ)
GILMORE, R. E. INVESTMENTS CORP
GILMORE REPRODUCTIONS
120 Herzberg Rd, Kanata, ON, K2K 3B7
(613) 592-2944
Emp Here 465   *Sales* 96,887,000
SIC 2759 Commercial printing, nec
Robert Gilmore

D-U-N-S 24-708-7377   (BR)
HERJAVEC GROUP INC, THE
(*Suby of* HERJAVEC GROUP INC, THE)
555 Legget Dr Suite 530, Kanata, ON, K2K 2X3
(613) 271-2400
Emp Here 160
SIC 5045 Computers, peripherals, and software
Robert Herjavec

D-U-N-S 24-802-5558   (HQ)
INSTANT BRANDS INC
INSTANT POT COMPANY
495 March Rd Suite 200, Kanata, ON, K2K 3G1
(800) 828-7280
Emp Here 29   *Sales* 14,756,742
SIC 5065 Electronic parts and equipment, nec
Robert J. Wang
Dongjun Wang
Yi Qin
Christopher Larocque

D-U-N-S 24-719-9284   (HQ)
INTERNATIONAL DATACASTING CORPORATION
(*Suby of* NOVRA TECHNOLOGIES INC)
10 Brewer Hunt Way, Kanata, ON, K2K 2B5
(613) 596-4120
Emp Here 10   *Sales* 19,615,526
SIC 3669 Communications equipment, nec
Chris Van Staveren
David Smith
Eric Apps
Glenn Mcdougall

D-U-N-S 24-923-8346   (HQ)
INTOUCH INSIGHT INC
(*Suby of* INTOUCH INSIGHT LTD)
400 March Rd, Kanata, ON, K2K 3H4
(613) 270-7900
Emp Here 35   *Sales* 13,196,580
SIC 8732 Commercial nonphysical research
Michael Gaffney
Neil Milton
Rainer Paduch

D-U-N-S 20-344-9350   (HQ)
INTOUCH INSIGHT LTD
400 March Rd, Kanata, ON, K2K 3H4
(613) 270-7916
Emp Here 45   *Sales* 11,286,964

SIC 7376 Computer facilities management
Cameron Watt
Ravi Puvan
Robin Sutherland
David Newby
George Pretli
Michael Gaffney
Eric Beutel
W. David Oliver
Rainer Paduch

D-U-N-S 20-180-4882   (SL)
IRDETO CANADA CORPORATION
IRDETO
(*Suby of* MULTICHOICE GROUP HOLDINGS B.V.)
2500 Solandt Rd Suite 300, Kanata, ON, K2K 3G5
(613) 271-9446
Emp Here 110   *Sales* 15,860,020
SIC 7371 Custom computer programming services
Pierre Fauvel
Martin Sendyk

D-U-N-S 24-845-9166   (HQ)
J-SQUARED TECHNOLOGIES INC
(*Suby of* MAZIN INVESTMENTS LTD)
4015 Carling Ave Suite 101, Kanata, ON, K2K 2A3
(613) 592-9540
Emp Here 11   *Sales* 10,285,002
SIC 5065 Electronic parts and equipment, nec
Jeffrey Gibson
Alison Gibson

D-U-N-S 20-177-8177   (HQ)
JUNIPER NETWORKS CANADA INC
(*Suby of* JUNIPER NETWORKS, INC.)
340 Terry Fox Dr, Kanata, ON, K2K 3A2
(613) 591-2700
Emp Here 47   *Sales* 21,476,368
SIC 4899 Communication services, nec
Rahim Pagerami

D-U-N-S 24-308-3321   (SL)
KONGSBERG GEOSPATIAL LTD
(*Suby of* KONGSBERG GRUPPEN ASA)
411 Legget Dr Suite 400, Kanata, ON, K2K 3C9
(613) 271-5500
Emp Here 60   *Sales* 10,010,820
SIC 7372 Prepackaged software
Ranald Mcgillis

D-U-N-S 25-097-6107   (SL)
LPI LEVEL PLATFORMS INC
LEVEL PLATFORMS
309 Legget Dr Suite 300, Kanata, ON, K2K 3A3
(613) 232-1000
Emp Here 127   *Sales* 18,311,114
SIC 7371 Custom computer programming services
Peter Sandiford
Barry Mckibbon
Patrick Smith
Larry Moore
Jim Ambrose

D-U-N-S 24-703-5264   (HQ)
MARCH NETWORKS CORPORATION
(*Suby of* INFINOVA INTERNATIONAL LIMITED)
303 Terry Fox Dr Suite 200, Kanata, ON, K2K 3J1
(613) 591-8181
Emp Here 153   *Sales* 74,972,475
SIC 3699 Electrical equipment and supplies, nec
Peter G. Strom
Jeff Range
Jeffery Z Liu
Net Payne

D-U-N-S 20-512-5334   (HQ)
MAZIN INVESTMENTS LTD
4015 Carling Ave Suite 102, Kanata, ON, K2K

2A3
(613) 831-9943
Emp Here 2   *Sales* 22,358,700
SIC 5065 Electronic parts and equipment, nec
Jeff Gibson
Alison Gibson

D-U-N-S 24-191-2166   (SL)
MEAD JOHNSON NUTRITION (CANADA) CO
(*Suby of* RECKITT BENCKISER GROUP PLC)
535 Legget Dr Suite 900, Kanata, ON, K2K 3B8
(613) 595-4700
Emp Here 110   *Sales* 78,838,760
SIC 5149 Groceries and related products, nec
Stephen Golsby
William P Pool
Stanley Burhans

D-U-N-S 20-747-5054   (HQ)
MICROSEMI SEMICONDUCTOR ULC
(*Suby of* MICROCHIP TECHNOLOGY INC)
400 March Rd, Kanata, ON, K2K 3H4
(613) 592-0200
Emp Here 5   *Sales* 247,550,625
SIC 3674 Semiconductors and related devices
Kirk K Mandy
Henry Simon
Adam Chowaniec
Hubert Lacroix
J. Spencer Lanthier
Jules Meunier
Dennis Roberson
Oleg Khaykin

D-U-N-S 25-168-0708   (HQ)
MITEL NETWORKS CORPORATION
INTER-TEL
350 Legget Dr, Kanata, ON, K2K 2W7
(613) 592-2122
Emp Here 200   *Sales* 1,059,100,000
SIC 3661 Telephone and telegraph apparatus
Richard Mcbee
Steven Spooner
Bob Agnes
Todd Abbott
Graham Bevington
Terence Matthews
John Mchugh
Peter Charbonneau
Benjamin Ball
David Williams

D-U-N-S 24-340-9484   (SL)
MOTION MICRO SOLUTIONS INC
300 March Rd Suite 400, Kanata, ON, K2K 2E2
(613) 667-9157
Emp Here 25   *Sales* 16,973,075
SIC 6211 Security brokers and dealers
Tony El-Khoury
Jeffrey Gibson

D-U-N-S 25-685-6139   (SL)
N-ABLE TECHNOLOGIES INTERNATIONAL INC
450 March Rd, Kanata, ON, K2K 3K2
(613) 592-6676
Emp Here 120   *Sales* 20,021,640
SIC 7372 Prepackaged software
Gavin Garbutt

D-U-N-S 24-662-3821   (HQ)
NANOMETRICS INC
250 Herzberg Rd, Kanata, ON, K2K 2A1
(613) 592-6776
Emp Here 100   *Sales* 32,924,400
SIC 3829 Measuring and controlling devices, nec
Neil Spriggs
Tim Hayman
Ian Talbot
Bruce Townsend
David Shorey
Mark Hayman

D-U-N-S 24-978-0784 (HQ)
NEPTEC DESIGN GROUP LTD
(*Suby of* MAXAR TECHNOLOGIES INC.)
302 Legget Dr Unit 202, Kanata, ON, K2K 1Y5
(613) 599-7602
Sales 13,405,425
SIC 8711 Engineering services
Michael Greenley

D-U-N-S 20-111-2088 (HQ)
NORDION (CANADA) INC
NORDION
447 March Rd, Kanata, ON, K2K 1X8
(613) 592-2790
Sales 533,574,000
SIC 2819 Industrial inorganic chemicals, nec
John Mayberry
Douglas S Prince
Les Hockey
Leslee Tape
David Nichols
Debi King
Peter Dans
Peter Brent
Mark Witkowski
Glen Ibbott

D-U-N-S 24-926-7162 (SL)
NUVO NETWORK MANAGEMENT INC
400 March Rd Suite 190, Kanata, ON, K2K
3H4

Emp Here 115 *Sales* 19,187,405
SIC 7376 Computer facilities management
Phil Weaver
Richard Anderson
Terry Hall
Peter Sommerer
Barry Gekiere

D-U-N-S 20-290-6256 (BR)
OMNI HEALTH CARE LTD
FOREST HILL
(*Suby of* OMNI HEALTH INVESTMENTS INC)
6501 Campeau Dr Suite 353, Kanata, ON,
K2K 3E9
(613) 599-1991
Emp Here 200
SIC 8051 Skilled nursing care facilities
Susan Bell

D-U-N-S 20-583-5668 (HQ)
**OPTELIAN ACCESS NETWORKS CORPO-
RATION**
OPTELIAN
1 Brewer Hunt Way, Kanata, ON, K2K 2B5
(613) 287-2000
Sales 14,309,568
SIC 5049 Professional equipment, nec
David Weymouth
Brenda Snarr
Scott Agnew
Bryan Hall

D-U-N-S 20-288-8512 (BR)
**OTTAWA CATHOLIC DISTRICT SCHOOL
BOARD**
ALL SAINTS HIGH SCHOOL
(*Suby of* OTTAWA CATHOLIC DISTRICT
SCHOOL BOARD)
5115 Kanata Ave, Kanata, ON, K2K 3K5
(613) 271-4254
Emp Here 80
SIC 8211 Elementary and secondary schools
Sean Kelly

D-U-N-S 25-263-5883 (BR)
**OTTAWA-CARLETON DISTRICT SCHOOL
BOARD**
EARL OF MARCH SECONDARY SCHOOL
(*Suby of* OTTAWA-CARLETON DISTRICT
SCHOOL BOARD)
4 Parkway The, Kanata, ON, K2K 1Y4
(613) 592-3361
Emp Here 90
SIC 8211 Elementary and secondary schools
Jon Harris

D-U-N-S 24-436-2604 (HQ)
QNX SOFTWARE SYSTEMS LIMITED
(*Suby of* BLACKBERRY LIMITED)
1001 Farrar Rd, Kanata, ON, K2K 0B3
(613) 591-0931
Emp Here 222 *Sales* 73,241,328
SIC 7372 Prepackaged software
Dan Dodge
Derek Kuhn
John Wall

D-U-N-S 24-333-2942 (BR)
QUEST SOFTWARE CANADA INC
QUEST SOFTWARE
(*Suby of* FRANCISCO PARTNERS MANAGE-
MENT, L.P.)
515 Legget Dr Suite 1001, Kanata, ON, K2K
3G4
(613) 270-1500
Emp Here 150
SIC 7371 Custom computer programming ser-
vices
Harold Dyck

D-U-N-S 25-283-4601 (HQ)
SABA SOFTWARE (CANADA) INC
495 March Rd Suite 100, Kanata, ON, K2K
3G1
(613) 270-1011
Emp Here 389 *Sales* 116,051,400
SIC 7372 Prepackaged software
Phil Saunders
Pete Low
Karen Williams
Srini Ogireddy
John Hiraoka
Debbie Shotwell

D-U-N-S 24-843-8426 (SL)
SCI BROCKVILLE CORP
SANMINA-SCI NPI
(*Suby of* SANMINA CORPORATION)
500 March Rd, Kanata, ON, K2K 0J9
(613) 886-6148
Emp Here 125 *Sales* 23,805,250
SIC 3661 Telephone and telegraph apparatus
Jack Alexander
Ann Markle
Steven Jackman

D-U-N-S 24-481-1873 (HQ)
SCIEMETRIC INSTRUMENTS INC
359 Terry Fox Dr Suite 100, Kanata, ON, K2K
2E7
(613) 254-7054
Emp Here 40 *Sales* 23,638,056
SIC 3823 Process control instruments
Nathan Sheaff
Joe Ventimiglio
Don Silverman
Richard Brine

D-U-N-S 24-770-9967 (HQ)
SHAPIRO COHEN LLP
555 Legget Dr Suite 830, Kanata, ON, K2K
2X3
(613) 232-5300
Sales 36,135,540
SIC 6794 Patent owners and lessors
Chantal Bertosa
Victoria Carrington

D-U-N-S 20-692-5724 (SL)
SIDENSE CORP
84 Hines Rd Suite 260, Kanata, ON, K2K 3G3
(613) 287-0292
Emp Here 60 *Sales* 11,426,520
SIC 3674 Semiconductors and related devices
Xerxes Wania
Richard J. Shorkey

D-U-N-S 20-691-0593 (HQ)
SOLACE CORPORATION
535 Legget Dr Fl 3, Kanata, ON, K2K 3B8
(613) 271-1010
Sales 55,148,370
SIC 3825 Instruments to measure electricity
Craig Betts

Randolph Cowen
Steve Pusey

D-U-N-S 24-378-1023 (SL)
TELEPIN SOFTWARE CORPORATION
411 Legget Dr Suite 100, Kanata, ON, K2K
3C9
(613) 366-1910
Emp Here 75 *Sales* 13,298,325
SIC 7371 Custom computer programming services
Vincent Kadar

D-U-N-S 20-146-2009 (HQ)
TEXAS INSTRUMENTS CANADA LIMITED
(*Suby of* TEXAS INSTRUMENTS INCORPO-
RATED)
505 March Rd Suite 200, Kanata, ON, K2K
3A4
(613) 271-8649
Emp Here 8 *Sales* 34,879,572
SIC 5065 Electronic parts and equipment, nec

D-U-N-S 24-381-6514 (SL)
THINKWRAP SOLUTIONS INC
450 March Rd Suite 500, Kanata, ON, K2K
3K2
(613) 751-4441
Emp Here 90 *Sales* 15,957,990
SIC 7371 Custom computer programming ser-
vices
Stephen Byrne
Marc Lamoureux
Christopher Lamoureux
Peter Lui-Hing

D-U-N-S 25-733-8871 (SL)
WATCHFIRE CORPORATION
1 Hines Rd, Kanata, ON, K2K 3C7

Emp Here 170 *Sales* 28,363,990
SIC 7372 Prepackaged software
Micheal Weider
Peter C Mckay
Kenneth Macaskill
James C Mccartney
John J. Gannon

D-U-N-S 25-689-4734 (HQ)
WESLEY CLOVER CORPORATION
390 March Rd Suite 110, Kanata, ON, K2K
0G7
(613) 271-6305
Emp Here 30 *Sales* 56,784,420
SIC 6799 Investors, nec
Sir Terence H. Matthews
Paul Chiarelli

D-U-N-S 25-678-5890 (SL)
XMARK CORPORATION
STANLEY HEALTHCARE SOLUTIONS
(*Suby of* STANLEY BLACK & DECKER, INC.)
309 Legget Dr Suite 100, Kanata, ON, K2K
3A3
(613) 592-6997
Emp Here 100 *Sales* 19,044,200
SIC 3679 Electronic components, nec
Andrew Brazier
Joe Diilio
Michael Bartone
Erin Mora

D-U-N-S 20-307-0081 (SL)
YOU I LABS INC
YOU.I TV
307 Legget Dr, Kanata, ON, K2K 3C8
(613) 228-9107
Emp Here 150 *Sales* 21,627,300
SIC 7371 Custom computer programming ser-
vices
Jason Flick
Andrew Emmons
Rob White
Don Liberty

Kanata, ON K2L

D-U-N-S 25-770-0385 (SL)
1172413 ONTARIO INC
EAST SIDE MARIO'S
651 Terry Fox Dr Suite Side, Kanata, ON, K2L
4E7
(613) 836-3680
Emp Here 80 *Sales* 3,641,520
SIC 5812 Eating places
Ali Chahrour

D-U-N-S 20-892-0843 (SL)
CENTURY 21-JOHN DEVRIES LTD
444 Hazeldean Rd, Kanata, ON, K2L 1V2
(613) 836-2570
Emp Here 56 *Sales* 15,218,336
SIC 6531 Real estate agents and managers
John Devries

D-U-N-S 24-536-3622 (BR)
OMNI HEALTH CARE LTD
GARDEN TERRACE
(*Suby of* OMNI HEALTH INVESTMENTS INC)
100 Aird Pl, Kanata, ON, K2L 4H8
(613) 254-9702
Emp Here 200
SIC 8051 Skilled nursing care facilities
Carolyn Della Foresta

D-U-N-S 25-224-8844 (BR)
**OTTAWA-CARLETON DISTRICT SCHOOL
BOARD**
A.Y. JACKSON SECONDARY SCHOOL
(*Suby of* OTTAWA-CARLETON DISTRICT
SCHOOL BOARD)
150 Abbeyhill Dr, Kanata, ON, K2L 1H7
(613) 836-2527
Emp Here 75
SIC 8211 Elementary and secondary schools
Sandra Blakely

D-U-N-S 20-026-6497 (SL)
ROYAL LEPAGE TEAM
484 Hazeldean Rd Suite 1, Kanata, ON, K2L
1V4
(613) 867-2508
Emp Here 45 *Sales* 12,229,020
SIC 6531 Real estate agents and managers
Randy Oickle

D-U-N-S 20-278-0610 (BR)
TOROMONT INDUSTRIES LTD
TOROMONT CAT
(*Suby of* TOROMONT INDUSTRIES LTD)
5 Edgewater St, Kanata, ON, K2L 1V7
(613) 836-5171
Emp Here 80
SIC 5082 Construction and mining machinery
Dan Rouleau

Kanata, ON K2M

D-U-N-S 20-182-2538 (SL)
1514505 ONTARIO INC
VCL CONSTRUCTION
240 Terence Matthews Cres Suite 101,
Kanata, ON, K2M 2C4
(613) 592-1114
Emp Here 22 *Sales* 10,356,082
SIC 1542 Nonresidential construction, nec
Mark Dalton
Michelle Brown

D-U-N-S 24-876-7311 (HQ)
1737868 ONTARIO INC.
CCR
200 Terence Matthews Cres, Kanata, ON,
K2M 2C6
(613) 591-0044
Emp Here 24 *Sales* 27,633,625
SIC 5122 Drugs, proprietaries, and sundries
Christopher Simpson

D-U-N-S 20-393-5254 (SL)

2551194 ONTARIO INC
74 Osprey Cres, Kanata, ON, K2M 2Z8
(613) 567-7100
Emp Here 175   *Sales* 51,358,475
SIC 5461 Retail bakeries
Craig Buckley

D-U-N-S 20-649-8040   (HQ)
BRADLEY AIR SERVICES LIMITED
FIRST AIR
(*Suby of* SOCIETE MAKIVIK)
20 Cope Dr, Kanata, ON, K2M 2V8
(613) 254-6200
Emp Here 200   *Sales* 317,352,000
SIC 4522 Air transportation, nonscheduled
Chris Avery
Alexandra Pontbriand
Johnny Adams
Jobie Epoo
Kim Trang Hoang
Charlie Watt (Jr.)
Allan John Baydala
Patricia Mcleod

D-U-N-S 20-789-5517   (SL)
CANADIAN WILDLIFE FEDERATION
350 Michael Cowpland Dr, Kanata, ON, K2M 2W1
(613) 599-9594
Emp Here 49   *Sales* 15,998,442
SIC 8999 Services, nec

D-U-N-S 24-269-4172   (HQ)
JATOM SYSTEMS INC
JSI TELECOM
99 Michael Cowpland Dr, Kanata, ON, K2M 1X3
(613) 591-5910
Emp Here 200   *Sales* 48,911,845
SIC 7371 Custom computer programming services
Greg Brown
Tom Skinner
Paul Singh

D-U-N-S 24-569-6419   (SL)
LAURA'S YOUR INDEPENDENT GROCERY
300 Eagleson Rd, Kanata, ON, K2M 1C9
(613) 592-3850
Emp Here 49   *Sales* 13,433,448
SIC 5411 Grocery stores
Laura Pubois

D-U-N-S 24-383-8914   (BR)
LOBLAWS INC
REAL CANADIAN SUPERSTORE
(*Suby of* LOBLAW COMPANIES LIMITED)
760 Eagleson Rd, Kanata, ON, K2M 0A7
(613) 254-6050
Emp Here 150
SIC 5411 Grocery stores
Jason Euverman

D-U-N-S 20-145-7710   (HQ)
MODERN NIAGARA DESIGN SERVICES INC
(*Suby of* MODERN/NIAGARA GROUP INC)
85 Denzil Doyle Court, Kanata, ON, K2M 2G8
(613) 591-7505
Sales 189,593,600
SIC 1711 Plumbing, heating, air-conditioning
Tony Sottile
David Campbell

D-U-N-S 24-270-8345   (HQ)
MODERN NIAGARA HVAC SERVICES INC
(*Suby of* MODERN/NIAGARA GROUP INC)
85 Denzil Doyle Crt, Kanata, ON, K2M 2G8
(613) 591-7505
Emp Here 20   *Sales* 22,141,175
SIC 1711 Plumbing, heating, air-conditioning
Rick Bracken
Brad Mcaninch

D-U-N-S 24-784-1471   (HQ)
MODERN NIAGARA OTTAWA INC
(*Suby of* MODERN/NIAGARA GROUP INC)

85 Denzil Doyle Crt, Kanata, ON, K2M 2G8
(613) 591-7505
Sales 13,983,900
SIC 1711 Plumbing, heating, air-conditioning
Terry Dunlop
Brad Mcaninch

D-U-N-S 24-366-7177   (SL)
NOVATECH ENGINEERING CONSULTANTS LTD
240 Michael Cowpland Dr Suite 200, Kanata, ON, K2M 1P6
(613) 254-9643
Emp Here 100   *Sales* 17,595,800
SIC 8711 Engineering services
John Riddell

D-U-N-S 20-203-1938   (SL)
OTTAWA NETWORK FOR BORDERLINE PERSONALITY DISORDER
412 Rosingdale St, Kanata, ON, K2M 0L8

Emp Here 150   *Sales* 16,662,000
SIC 8062 General medical and surgical hospitals

D-U-N-S 24-763-7635   (SL)
THINKING IN PICTURES EDUCATIONAL SERVICE
160 Terence Matthews Cres Suite B2, Kanata, ON, K2M 0B2
(613) 592-8800
Emp Here 26   *Sales* 10,332,764
SIC 8699 Membership organizations, nec
Jennifer Wyatt
Deborah Wyatt

Kanata, ON K2T

D-U-N-S 24-139-5321   (BR)
BEST BUY CANADA LTD
FUTUE SHOP
(*Suby of* BEST BUY CO., INC.)
255 Kanata Ave Unit D1, Kanata, ON, K2T 1K5

Emp Here 120
SIC 5999 Miscellaneous retail stores, nec
Patrick Digby

D-U-N-S 24-363-5708   (BR)
BEST BUY CANADA LTD
BEST BUY
(*Suby of* BEST BUY CO., INC.)
745 Kanata Ave Suite Gg1, Kanata, ON, K2T 1H9
(613) 287-3912
Emp Here 100
SIC 5731 Radio, television, and electronic stores
Christopher Askew

D-U-N-S 24-370-7317   (SL)
ELISSA GROUP CO
4 Maricona Way, Kanata, ON, K2T 1H1
(613) 799-6473
Emp Here 12   *Sales* 10,026,924
SIC 5148 Fresh fruits and vegetables
Ali El-Husseini

D-U-N-S 25-080-6874   (SL)
INNVEST HOTELS GP VIII LTD
HOLIDAY INN & SUITES SELECT OTTAWA WEST (KANATA)
101 Kanata Ave, Kanata, ON, K2T 1E6
(613) 271-3057
Emp Here 100   *Sales* 9,489,900
SIC 7011 Hotels and motels
Kristine Dempster

D-U-N-S 24-773-9514   (SL)
LOBLAWS
200 Earl Grey Dr, Kanata, ON, K2T 1B6
(613) 599-9934
Emp Here 40   *Sales* 13,024,000

SIC 5992 Florists
Walter Klien

D-U-N-S 24-252-5454   (SL)
MON 3047 INC
MONTANA'S COOK HOUSE
140 Earl Grey Dr, Kanata, ON, K2T 1B6
(613) 270-0518
Emp Here 110   *Sales* 5,130,290
SIC 5812 Eating places
Matt Davidson

D-U-N-S 20-642-4868   (BR)
SIR CORP
JACK ASTOR'S BAR & GRILL
(*Suby of* SIR CORP)
125 Roland Michener Dr Suite B1, Kanata, ON, K2T 1G7
(613) 271-1041
Emp Here 85
SIC 5813 Drinking places
Andrew Smith

D-U-N-S 25-769-7375   (SL)
UNITED MALWOOD MERCHANTS INC
CANADIAN TIRE
8181 Campeau Dr Suite 457, Kanata, ON, K2T 1B7
(613) 599-5105
Emp Here 145   *Sales* 91,245,600
SIC 5531 Auto and home supply stores
David Malcomson
P.J. Malcomson

D-U-N-S 25-498-3141   (BR)
WAL-MART CANADA CORP
(*Suby of* WALMART INC.)
500 Earl Grey Dr, Kanata, ON, K2T 1B6
(613) 599-6765
Emp Here 150
SIC 5311 Department stores
Neil Campbell

Kanata, ON K2V

D-U-N-S 20-703-0516   (HQ)
ARAMARK ENTERTAINMENT SERVICES (CANADA) INC
(*Suby of* ARAMARK)
1000 Palladium Dr Suite 107, Kanata, ON, K2V 1A4
(613) 599-0230
Sales 219,144,550
SIC 8742 Management consulting services
Doug Weatherbee
Brian Pressler

D-U-N-S 20-181-0665   (SL)
CAPITAL DODGE CHRYSLER JEEP LIMITED
2500 Palladium Dr Suite 1200, Kanata, ON, K2V 1E2
(613) 271-7114
Emp Here 60   *Sales* 37,756,800
SIC 5511 New and used car dealers
Jim Durrell

D-U-N-S 25-501-1439   (SL)
DRS TECHNOLOGIES CANADA LTD
(*Suby of* LEONARDO SPA)
700 Palladium Dr, Kanata, ON, K2V 1C6
(613) 591-6000
Emp Here 150
SIC 3674 Semiconductors and related devices

D-U-N-S 20-010-9564   (SL)
DRS TECHNOLOGIES CANADA LTD
(*Suby of* LEONARDO SPA)
500 Palladium Dr Suite 1100, Kanata, ON, K2V 1C2
(613) 591-5800
Emp Here 270   *Sales* 76,387,050
SIC 3674 Semiconductors and related devices
Martin Munro
Chris Tymofichuk

D-U-N-S 24-104-1862   (HQ)
DY 4 SYSTEMS INC
CURTISS WRIGHT CONTROLS EMBEDDED COMPUTING
(*Suby of* CURTISS-WRIGHT CORPORATION)
333 Palladium Dr, Kanata, ON, K2V 1A6
(613) 599-9199
Emp Here 348   *Sales* 100,434,825
SIC 3672 Printed circuit boards
David Adams
Andrew Thomson
Darren Frey

D-U-N-S 20-889-6076   (HQ)
EMS TECHNOLOGIES CANADA, LTD
EMS AVIATION
(*Suby of* HONEYWELL INTERNATIONAL INC.)
400 Maple Grove Rd, Kanata, ON, K2V 1B8
(613) 591-6040
Sales 82,311,000
SIC 3812 Search and navigation equipment
Joanne Walker
Victor Miller
Carl Esposito
Deborah Van Damme
Robert Topolski

D-U-N-S 25-831-9995   (BR)
HOME DEPOT OF CANADA INC
HOME DEPOT
(*Suby of* THE HOME DEPOT INC)
10 Frank Nighbor Pl Suite Frnt, Kanata, ON, K2V 1B9
(613) 271-7577
Emp Here 200
SIC 5251 Hardware stores
Rob Forgie

D-U-N-S 25-412-9653   (BR)
IBM CANADA LIMITED
IBM RATIONAL SOFTWARE
(*Suby of* INTERNATIONAL BUSINESS MACHINES CORPORATION)
770 Palladium Dr, Kanata, ON, K2V 1C8

Emp Here 170
SIC 7371 Custom computer programming services

D-U-N-S 24-482-3555   (SL)
KANATA HYDRO ELECTRIC COMMISSION
100 Maple Grove Rd, Kanata, ON, K2V 1B8

Emp Here 43   *Sales* 25,301,518
SIC 4911 Electric services

D-U-N-S 24-482-1732   (HQ)
KINAXIS INC
700 Silver Seven Rd Suite 500, Kanata, ON, K2V 1C3
(613) 592-5780
Emp Here 45   *Sales* 150,727,000
SIC 7371 Custom computer programming services
John Sicard
Richard Monkman
Michael Mauger
Megan Paterson
Jay Muelhoefer
Paul Carreiro
Anne G. Robinson
Andrew Mcdonald
John (Ian) Giffen
Angel Mendez

D-U-N-S 24-102-5063   (SL)
MYERS KANATA CHEV BUICK GMC INC
2500 Palladium Dr Suite 200, Kanata, ON, K2V 1E2
(613) 592-9221
Emp Here 70   *Sales* 44,049,600
SIC 5511 New and used car dealers
John Stanton

D-U-N-S 24-965-9137   (SL)

MYERS VOLKSWAGEN
2500 Palladium Dr Suite 501, Kanata, ON, K2V 1E2
(613) 592-8484
Emp Here 27   *Sales* 13,448,106
SIC 5511 New and used car dealers
  Dean Burton

D-U-N-S 25-500-9680   (HQ)
SKYWAVE MOBILE COMMUNICATIONS INC
ORBCOMM
(*Suby of* ORBCOMM INC.)
750 Palladium Dr Suite 368, Kanata, ON, K2V 1C7
(613) 836-4844
Sales 34,814,820
SIC 5065 Electronic parts and equipment, nec
  Sherife Elkholy

D-U-N-S 24-244-9705   (BR)
SMART TECHNOLOGIES ULC
(*Suby of* HON HAI PRECISION INDUSTRY CO., LTD.)
501 Palladium Dr, Kanata, ON, K2V 0A2
(403) 245-0333
Emp Here 500
SIC 3674 Semiconductors and related devices
  David Jackson

D-U-N-S 25-404-4837   (SL)
SPIRENT COMMUNICATIONS OF OTTAWA LTD
DLS, DIV OF
(*Suby of* SPIRENT COMMUNICATIONS PLC)
750 Palladium Dr Unit 310, Kanata, ON, K2V 1C7
(613) 592-2661
Emp Here 65   *Sales* 12,378,730
SIC 3669 Communications equipment, nec
  Jaynie Coulterman

D-U-N-S 24-023-5064   (SL)
TONY GRAHAM KANATA LIMITED
KANATA TOYOTA
2500 Palladium Dr Suite 600, Kanata, ON, K2V 1E2
(613) 271-8200
Emp Here 35   *Sales* 17,432,730
SIC 5511 New and used car dealers
  Patrick Graham

D-U-N-S 24-338-5320   (HQ)
TURPIN GROUP LTD
TURPIN PONTIAC BUICK GMC
2500 Palladium Dr Unit 200, Kanata, ON, K2V 1E2
Emp Here 70   *Sales* 62,928,000
SIC 5511 New and used car dealers
  Fernand Turpin Jr

D-U-N-S 25-775-3483   (SL)
TURPIN SATURN SAAB ISUZU LIMITED
2500 Palladium Dr Unit 400, Kanata, ON, K2V 1E2
Emp Here 40   *Sales* 20,258,202
SIC 5511 New and used car dealers
  Yves Laberge

Kanata, ON K2W

D-U-N-S 25-183-4458   (BR)
SOBEYS CAPITAL INCORPORATED
(*Suby of* EMPIRE COMPANY LIMITED)
840 March Rd, Kanata, ON, K2W 0C9
(613) 599-8965
Emp Here 150
SIC 5411 Grocery stores
  Dennis Hansen

Kapuskasing, ON P5N

D-U-N-S 25-406-8513   (SL)
AECOM CANADIAN OPERATIONS LTD
(*Suby of* AECOM)
Gd Lcd Main, Kapuskasing, ON, P5N 2X9
(705) 335-3800
Emp Here 200
SIC 1475 Phosphate rock
  Allan Tarasuk
  Randolph Hill

D-U-N-S 20-291-6065   (SL)
ASSURANCES ROBICHAUD INSURANCE BROKERS INC
37 Riverside Dr, Kapuskasing, ON, P5N 1A7
(705) 335-2371
Emp Here 21   *Sales* 12,178,404
SIC 6411 Insurance agents, brokers, and service
  Guy Robichaud
  Kevin Robichaud

D-U-N-S 20-289-9543   (BR)
CONSEIL SCOLAIRE CATHOLIQUE DE DISTRICT DES GRANDES RIVIERES, LE
(*Suby of* CONSEIL SCOLAIRE CATHOLIQUE DE DISTRICT DES GRANDES RIVIERES, LE)
75 Queen St, Kapuskasing, ON, P5N 1H5
(705) 335-6091
Emp Here 1,000
SIC 8211 Elementary and secondary schools
  Jeremie Letage

D-U-N-S 20-050-3147   (SL)
EASTVIEW CHEVROLET BUICK GMC LTD
KAP COLLISION & AUTOGLASS
222 Government Rd, Kapuskasing, ON, P5N 2X2
(705) 335-6187
Emp Here 57   *Sales* 35,868,960
SIC 5511 New and used car dealers
  Robert Guertin
  Maurice Guertin
  Paul Lavoie

D-U-N-S 24-418-4326   (SL)
GESTION DOMINIC PAQUETTE INC
CANADIAN TIRE
25 Brunetville Rd Suite 30, Kapuskasing, ON, P5N 2E9
(705) 335-6066
Emp Here 40   *Sales* 19,923,120
SIC 5531 Auto and home supply stores
  Dominic Paquette

D-U-N-S 25-033-5387   (SL)
NORTH CENTENNIAL MANOR INC
2 Kimberly Dr, Kapuskasing, ON, P5N 1L5
(705) 335-6125
Emp Here 88   *Sales* 6,033,808
SIC 8051 Skilled nursing care facilities
  Joanne Chiasson
  Andre Filion
  Laurier Bourgeois

D-U-N-S 20-816-1109   (SL)
SENSENBRENNER HOSPITAL
101 Progress Cres, Kapuskasing, ON, P5N 3H5
(705) 337-6111
Emp Here 215   *Sales* 23,882,200
SIC 8062 General medical and surgical hospitals
  Al Yarush
  Keith Landriault
  Denise Kennedy
  Frank Empey

D-U-N-S 24-892-5042   (HQ)
SPRUCE FALLS ACQUISITION CORP
(*Suby of* RAYONIER A.M. GLOBAL HOLDINGS LUXEMBOURG SCS)
1 Government Rd, Kapuskasing, ON, P5N 2Y2
(705) 337-1311
Sales 182,754,500

SIC 6712 Bank holding companies
  James Lopez

D-U-N-S 24-324-3560   (BR)
TEMBEC INC
(*Suby of* RAYONIER A.M. GLOBAL HOLDINGS LUXEMBOURG SCS)
1 Government Rd W, Kapuskasing, ON, P5N 2X8
(705) 337-9784
Emp Here 1,000
SIC 2621 Paper mills
  Mike Shusterman

D-U-N-S 20-704-4447   (SL)
VAL ALBERT MOTORS LIMITED
392 Government Rd E Rr 1, Kapuskasing, ON, P5N 2X7
(705) 335-5000
Emp Here 30   *Sales* 14,942,340
SIC 5511 New and used car dealers
  Gilbert Mondoux
  Marc Rancourt

D-U-N-S 25-297-6154   (BR)
WAL-MART CANADA CORP
(*Suby of* WALMART INC.)
350 Government Rd E, Kapuskasing, ON, P5N 2X7
(705) 335-6111
Emp Here 120
SIC 5311 Department stores

Kashechewan, ON P0L

D-U-N-S 24-912-2458   (SL)
HISHKOONIKUN EDUCATION AUTHORITY
ST ANDREWS SCHOOL
Gd, Kashechewan, ON, P0L 1S0
(705) 275-4111
Emp Here 84   *Sales* 21,293,160
SIC 8748 Business consulting, nec
  Alice Sutherland

Keene, ON K9J

D-U-N-S 25-251-0763   (SL)
B.R.T. DISTRIBUTING LTD
B.R.T. PET FOODS, DIV OF
(*Suby of* BURRETT CAPITAL CORPORATION)
1368 Highway 7, Keene, ON, K9J 0G6
(705) 295-6832
Emp Here 18   *Sales* 13,365,360
SIC 5199 Nondurable goods, nec
  Phil Burrett

D-U-N-S 24-850-2762   (HQ)
KONRAD GROUP, INC
1726 Henderson Line, Keene, ON, K9J 6X8
(416) 551-3684
Emp Here 100   *Sales* 33,369,400
SIC 7374 Data processing and preparation
  George Konrad
  Bill Konrad
  Hooman Bahador

D-U-N-S 24-947-1467   (HQ)
MCCLOSKEY INTERNATIONAL LIMITED
1 Mccloskey Rd, Keene, ON, K9J 0G6
(705) 295-4925
Sales 109,872,055
SIC 3531 Construction machinery
  Paschal Mccloskey
  Wayne Harding

Kemble, ON N0H

D-U-N-S 20-607-8719   (HQ)

SUTHERLAND, HAROLD CONSTRUCTION LTD
323545 E Linton W, Kemble, ON, N0H 1S0
(519) 376-5698
Sales 22,358,700
SIC 5032 Brick, stone, and related material
  Harold Sutherland
  Chayle Sutherland
  Jennifer Sutherland-Prentice
  Michael Sutherland

Kemptville, ON K0G

D-U-N-S 24-224-4866   (SL)
JAMIE D. TEMPLE PHARMACY LTD
SHOPPERS DRUG MART
2727 Hwy 43, Kemptville, ON, K0G 1J0
(613) 258-2557
Emp Here 50   *Sales* 12,647,700
SIC 5912 Drug stores and proprietary stores
  Jamie Temple

D-U-N-S 20-889-0962   (HQ)
KEMPTVILLE BUILDING CENTRE LTD
KEMPTVILLE HOME FURNITURE, DIV OF
2540 Hwy 43, Kemptville, ON, K0G 1J0
(613) 258-6000
Sales 12,652,950
SIC 5211 Lumber and other building materials
  Eric Norenberg
  Christa Norenberg

D-U-N-S 20-891-2220   (SL)
KEMPTVILLE DISTRICT HOSPITAL
2675 Concession Rd, Kemptville, ON, K0G 1J0
(613) 258-3435
Emp Here 140   *Sales* 15,551,200
SIC 8062 General medical and surgical hospitals
  Colin Goodfellow

D-U-N-S 24-481-1675   (SL)
MYERS KEMPTVILLE CHEVROLET BUICK GMC INC
104 Elvira St E, Kemptville, ON, K0G 1J0
(613) 258-3403
Emp Here 33   *Sales* 16,436,574
SIC 5511 New and used car dealers
  Bob Mczgith

D-U-N-S 24-634-1408   (BR)
NAVISTAR CANADA, INC
KEMPTVILLE TRUCK CENTRE
(*Suby of* NAVISTAR INTERNATIONAL CORPORATION)
405 Van Buren St, Kemptville, ON, K0G 1J0
(613) 258-1126
Emp Here 240
SIC 3711 Motor vehicles and car bodies
  Gerald Tallman

D-U-N-S 20-153-3077   (SL)
SELECT SIRES CANADA INC
2 Industrial Rd, Kemptville, ON, K0G 1J0
(613) 258-3800
Emp Here 40   *Sales* 58,707,680
SIC 5159 Farm-product raw materials, nec
  Brenda Sheppard

D-U-N-S 24-355-3067   (BR)
UNIVERSITY OF GUELPH
KEMPTVILLE COLLEGE CAMPUS
(*Suby of* UNIVERSITY OF GUELPH)
830 Prescott St, Kemptville, ON, K0G 1J0
(613) 258-8336
Emp Here 80
SIC 8221 Colleges and universities
  Michael Goss

D-U-N-S 20-022-2011   (SL)
VALLEY BUS LINES LTD
782 Van Buren St, Kemptville, ON, K0G 1J0
(613) 258-4022
Emp Here 75   *Sales* 4,115,400

▲ Public Company   ■ Public Company Family Member   **HQ** Headquarters   **BR** Branch   **SL** Single Location

SIC 4111 Local and suburban transit
Michael (Mike) Healey

D-U-N-S 20-789-1669   (SL)
W O STINSON & SON LTD
2955 Hwy 43, Kemptville, ON, K0G 1J0
(613) 258-1826
Emp Here 40   *Sales* 50,288,040
SIC 5172 Petroleum products, nec
Jean Marc Nadon

Kenilworth, ON N0G

D-U-N-S 24-704-5842   (HQ)
QUALITY ENGINEERED HOMES LTD
7307 Hwy 6, Kenilworth, ON, N0G 2E0
(519) 323-4208
Emp Here 160   *Sales* 33,664,750
SIC 2452 Prefabricated wood buildings
Bryan Bougher

Kenora, ON P9N

D-U-N-S 24-418-4334   (SL)
1146490 ONTARIO INC
CANADIAN TIRE
1229 Highway 17 E Suite 1, Kenora, ON, P9N
1L9
(807) 468-3014
Emp Here 60   *Sales* 37,756,800
SIC 5531 Auto and home supply stores
Mike Major

D-U-N-S 24-427-7265   (HQ)
DEROUARD MOTOR PRODUCTS LTD
1405 Railway St, Kenora, ON, P9N 0B3
(807) 467-4450
Sales 17,432,730
SIC 5511 New and used car dealers
Wilfred Derouard
Paul Derouard
Allan Derouard
Leonard Derouard

D-U-N-S 20-569-2577   (HQ)
DINGWALL FORD SALES LTD
927 Highway 17 E, Kenora, ON, P9N 1L9
(807) 468-6443
Emp Here 30   *Sales* 44,049,600
SIC 5511 New and used car dealers
William Dingwall
Jeffrey Dingwall

D-U-N-S 20-832-6967   (HQ)
GCT REPRESENTITIVE SERVICES
GRAND COUNCIL TREATY #3
237 Airport Rd, Kenora, ON, P9N 0A2
(807) 548-4214
Emp Here 1   *Sales* 11,217,360
SIC 8621 Professional organizations
Mervin Gryschuk

D-U-N-S 25-868-8456   (SL)
JERITRISH COMPANY LTD
MCDONALD'S RESTAURANTS
900 Highway 17 E, Kenora, ON, P9N 1L9
(807) 468-3018
Emp Here 75   *Sales* 3,413,925
SIC 5812 Eating places
Steve Ford

D-U-N-S 20-122-5398   (SL)
KANTOLA MOTORS LIMITED
200 Lakeview Dr, Kenora, ON, P9N 0H2
(807) 468-8984
Emp Here 30   *Sales* 14,942,340
SIC 5511 New and used car dealers
Richard Kantola

D-U-N-S 25-238-0555   (BR)
**KEEWATIN PATRICIA DISTRICT SCHOOL
BOARD**

BEAVER BRAE SECONDARY SCHOOL
(*Suby of* KEEWATIN PATRICIA DISTRICT
SCHOOL BOARD)
1400 Ninth St N, Kenora, ON, P9N 2T7
(807) 468-6401
Emp Here 100
SIC 8211 Elementary and secondary schools
Tracey Benoit

D-U-N-S 24-428-5003   (HQ)
**KEEWATIN PATRICIA DISTRICT SCHOOL
BOARD**
240 Veterans Dr 4th Fl, Kenora, ON, P9N 3Y5
(807) 468-5571
Emp Here 20   *Sales* 79,295,200
SIC 8211 Elementary and secondary schools
David Penny
Richard Findlay

D-U-N-S 25-399-1350   (BR)
KENORA FOREST PRODUCTS LTD
(*Suby of* PRENDIVILLE CORPORATION)
1060 Lakeview Dr, Kenora, ON, P9N 3X8
(807) 468-1550
Emp Here 120
SIC 2421 Sawmills and planing mills, general
Bob Smith

D-U-N-S 20-329-4954   (HQ)
**KENORA-RAINY RIVER DISTRICTS CHILD
AND FAMILY SERVICES**
820 Lakeview Dr, Kenora, ON, P9N 3P7
(807) 467-5437
Emp Here 100   *Sales* 251,755,175
SIC 8699 Membership organizations, nec
William Leonard
Carmen Marginet

D-U-N-S 20-838-3422   (HQ)
**LAKE OF THE WOODS DISTRICT HOSPI-
TAL**
21 Sylvan St, Kenora, ON, P9N 3W7
(807) 468-9861
Sales 55,540,000
SIC 8062 General medical and surgical hospi-
tals
Mark Balcaen
John Reid

D-U-N-S 25-971-6074   (BR)
LOBLAWS INC
EXTRA FOODS
(*Suby of* LOBLAW COMPANIES LIMITED)
538 Park St, Kenora, ON, P9N 1A1
(807) 468-1868
Emp Here 80
SIC 5411 Grocery stores
Joel Maccullam

D-U-N-S 25-957-1131   (BR)
REVERA INC
*RETIREMENT RESIDENCES REAL ESTATE
INVESTMENT TRUST*
(*Suby of* GOVERNMENT OF CANADA)
237 Lakeview Dr, Kenora, ON, P9N 4J7
(807) 468-9532
Emp Here 100
SIC 8051 Skilled nursing care facilities
Wendy Sarfi

D-U-N-S 25-272-6112   (BR)
SOBEYS WEST INC
KENORA SAFEWAY
(*Suby of* EMPIRE COMPANY LIMITED)
400 First Ave S, Kenora, ON, P9N 1W4
(807) 468-5868
Emp Here 130
SIC 5411 Grocery stores

D-U-N-S 20-834-9316   (HQ)
**STANDARD INSURANCE BROKERS LTD,
THE**
319 Second St S, Kenora, ON, P9N 1G3
(807) 468-3333
Emp Here 34   *Sales* 140,428,392
SIC 6411 Insurance agents, brokers, and ser-
vice

Brian Ingo
Glenn Alcock

D-U-N-S 25-083-7218   (SL)
SYLVAN LEARNING CENTRE INC
205 Second St S, Kenora, ON, P9N 1G1
(807) 467-8374
Emp Here 70   *Sales* 11,229,820
SIC 8299 Schools and educational services,
nec
Darrell Landry

D-U-N-S 24-329-8689   (BR)
WAL-MART CANADA CORP
(*Suby of* WALMART INC.)
24 Miikana Way Unit 1, Kenora, ON, P9N 4J1
(807) 468-6379
Emp Here 200
SIC 5311 Department stores
Jeff Robb

D-U-N-S 20-555-9540   (BR)
WEYERHAEUSER COMPANY LIMITED
I LEVEL BY WEYERHAUSER
(*Suby of* WEYERHAEUSER COMPANY)
1000 Jones Rd, Kenora, ON, P9N 3X8
(807) 548-8000
Emp Here 150
SIC 2439 Structural wood members, nec
William Candline

Kerwood, ON N0M

D-U-N-S 25-117-1039   (SL)
MIDDLESEX CONCRETE FORMING LTD
(*Suby of* VANBREE, J HOLDINGS LTD)
9644 Townsend Line Suite 3, Kerwood, ON,
N0M 2B0
(519) 247-3752
Emp Here 45   *Sales* 11,136,735
SIC 1771 Concrete work
Joe Van Bree

D-U-N-S 25-400-5564   (HQ)
VANBREE, J HOLDINGS LTD
9644 Townsend Line, Kerwood, ON, N0M 2B0
(519) 247-3752
Sales 12,031,438
SIC 6712 Bank holding companies
Joseph Vanbree

Keswick, ON L4P

D-U-N-S 20-778-3593   (SL)
2144011 ONTARIO INC
KESWICK PRICE CHOPPER
443 The Queensway S Suite 26, Keswick, ON,
L4P 3J4
(905) 476-7773
Emp Here 53   *Sales* 15,554,281
SIC 5411 Grocery stores
John Taylor

D-U-N-S 25-175-7266   (BR)
JOB SKILLS
GEORGINA JOB SKILLS
(*Suby of* JOB SKILLS)
155 Riverglen Dr Suite 7, Keswick, ON, L4P
3M3
(905) 476-8088
Emp Here 120
SIC 7361 Employment agencies
Catherine Turner

D-U-N-S 25-204-5828   (HQ)
KESMAC INC
BROUWER TURF
23324 Woodbine Ave, Keswick, ON, L4P 3E9
(888) 341-5113
Emp Here 60   *Sales* 13,320,060
SIC 3523 Farm machinery and equipment
Gerald J Brouwer

Eric Brouwer

D-U-N-S 20-820-4651   (SL)
S & B KESWICK MOTORS LIMITED
(*Suby of* 924891 ONTARIO INC)
475 The Queensway S, Keswick, ON, L4P 2E2
(905) 476-3111
Emp Here 27   *Sales* 13,448,106
SIC 5511 New and used car dealers
Edward Baiden
Beth Baiden

D-U-N-S 25-469-1025   (BR)
SPECIALTY CARE INC
CEDARVALE LODGE
(*Suby of* SPECIALTY CARE INC)
121 Morton Ave Suite 308, Keswick, ON, L4P
3T5
(905) 476-2656
Emp Here 120
SIC 8051 Skilled nursing care facilities
Donna Taylor

D-U-N-S 20-122-7469   (SL)
WELLER, W.M. TREE SERVICE LTD
18 Circle Ridge Dr, Keswick, ON, L4P 2G9
(905) 476-4593
Emp Here 150   *Sales* 26,085,750
SIC 0783 Ornamental shrub and tree services
Wilf Weller

D-U-N-S 25-106-9803   (BR)
**YORK CATHOLIC DISTRICT SCHOOL
BOARD**
*OUR LADY OF THE LAKE CATHOLIC COL-
LEGE SCHOOL*
(*Suby of* YORK CATHOLIC DISTRICT
SCHOOL BOARD)
185 Glenwoods Ave, Keswick, ON, L4P 2W6
(905) 656-9140
Emp Here 75
SIC 8211 Elementary and secondary schools
Fran Fraser

D-U-N-S 20-292-3459   (BR)
YORK REGION DISTRICT SCHOOL BOARD
KESWICK HIGH SCHOOL
(*Suby of* YORK REGION DISTRICT SCHOOL
BOARD)
100 Biscayne Blvd, Keswick, ON, L4P 3S2
(905) 476-0933
Emp Here 120
SIC 8211 Elementary and secondary schools
Doug Case

Kimberley, ON N0C

D-U-N-S 20-818-0695   (SL)
TALISMAN MOUNTAIN RESORT LTD
150 Talisman Blvd, Kimberley, ON, N0C 1G0

Emp Here 100   *Sales* 9,489,900
SIC 7011 Hotels and motels
Michael Wagner

Kinburn, ON K0A

D-U-N-S 24-826-3894   (SL)
PAROUSIA INVESTMETS LTD
OTTAWA ARGO SALES AND SERVICE
3152 Donald B Munro Dr, Kinburn, ON, K0A
2H0
(613) 254-6599
Emp Here 15   *Sales* 10,183,845
SIC 6282 Investment advice
Glenn Lucas

Kincardine, ON N2Z

D-U-N-S 20-349-6229   (SL)
1797509 ALBERTA ULC
SUPERHEAT
1463 Highway 21, Kincardine, ON, N2Z 2X3
(519) 396-1324
Emp Here 336   *Sales* 99,194,694
SIC 6712 Bank holding companies
David Norman Macarthur
Sundip Bajaj

D-U-N-S 20-734-3273   (SL)
CANADIAN TIRE KINCARDINE
811 Durham St, Kincardine, ON, N2Z 3B8
(519) 395-2886
Emp Here 40   *Sales* 19,923,120
SIC 5531 Auto and home supply stores
John Sikorska

D-U-N-S 24-991-9457   (SL)
CANADIANTIRE
CANADIAN TIRE
811 Durham St, Kincardine, ON, N2Z 3B8
(519) 395-2886
Emp Here 25   *Sales* 12,451,950
SIC 5531 Auto and home supply stores
John Satosek

D-U-N-S 20-955-0198   (HQ)
DOIDGE BUILDING CENTRES LTD
NORTHERN BUILDALL TIMBER MART
(*Suby of* DOIDGE HOLDINGS LTD)
1768 Highway 21, Kincardine, ON, N2Z 2Y6
(705) 645-8284
Emp Here 20   *Sales* 11,387,655
SIC 5211 Lumber and other building materials
Dennis Doidge
Edward Minty

D-U-N-S 20-703-8469   (SL)
EMC POWER CANADA LTD
2091 Highway 21, Kincardine, ON, N2Z 2X4
(844) 644-3627
Emp Here 100   *Sales* 21,782,900
SIC 1731 Electrical work
Lou Camara
Darryl Goodal

D-U-N-S 25-019-8678   (HQ)
MILLER INSURANCE BROKERS INC
1115 Sutton St, Kincardine, ON, N2Z 2C5

Emp Here 11   *Sales* 16,113,140
SIC 6411 Insurance agents, brokers, and service
Donald J Turcotte
Douglas Storrey
Mark Rosner
Keith Hopkins
David Young

D-U-N-S 25-028-5244   (BR)
REVERA LONG TERM CARE INC
TRILLIUM COURT SENIORS COMMUNITY
(*Suby of* GOVERNMENT OF CANADA)
550 Philip Pl, Kincardine, ON, N2Z 3A6
(519) 396-4400
Emp Here 95
SIC 8051 Skilled nursing care facilities
Vida Proctor

D-U-N-S 25-142-0584   (BR)
SOBEYS CAPITAL INCORPORATED
KINCARDINE SOBEYS
(*Suby of* EMPIRE COMPANY LIMITED)
814 Durham St, Kincardine, ON, N2Z 3B9
(519) 395-0022
Emp Here 100
SIC 5411 Grocery stores
Steve Palmer

D-U-N-S 25-362-4308   (HQ)
SUPERHEAT FGH CANADA INC
(*Suby of* SUPERTECH HOLDINGS INC.)
1463 Highway 21, Kincardine, ON, N2Z 2X3
(519) 396-1324
Emp Here 60   *Sales* 13,405,425

SIC 8711 Engineering services
Norm Macarthur
George Paul
Sandra Hofmann

D-U-N-S 24-074-3588   (SL)
SUPERHEAT FGH TECHNOLOGIES INC
(*Suby of* SUPERTECH HOLDINGS INC.)
1463 Highway 21, Kincardine, ON, N2Z 2X3
(519) 396-1324
Emp Here 100   *Sales* 19,208,500
SIC 3498 Fabricated pipe and fittings
Norm Macarthur

King City, ON L7B

D-U-N-S 20-595-7731   (SL)
CASEY TRANSPORTATION COMPANY LIMITED
1312 Wellington St W Suite 1, King City, ON, L7B 1K5

Emp Here 77   *Sales* 4,225,144
SIC 4151 School buses
Denis Casey
Charles Casey

D-U-N-S 25-306-2467   (SL)
CEC SERVICES LIMITED (AURORA)
16188 Bathurst St, King City, ON, L7B 1K5
(905) 713-3711
Emp Here 80   *Sales* 17,426,320
SIC 1731 Electrical work
Kevin Beswick
David Beswick

D-U-N-S 20-153-9298   (BR)
CLUBLINK CORPORATION ULC
KING'S RIDING GOLD CLUB
(*Suby of* TWC ENTERPRISES LIMITED)
14700 Bathurst St, King City, ON, L7B 1K5
(905) 713-6875
Emp Here 100
SIC 7992 Public golf courses
Andrew George

D-U-N-S 24-991-4284   (HQ)
CLUBLINK CORPORATION ULC
EMERALD HILLS GOLF AND COUNTRY CLUB
(*Suby of* TWC ENTERPRISES LIMITED)
15675 Dufferin St, King City, ON, L7B 1K5
(905) 841-3730
Emp Here 140   *Sales* 37,622,500
SIC 7992 Public golf courses
K. (Rai) Sahi
Edge M. Caravaggio
Neil E. Osborne
Charles F. Lorimer
Scott A Davidson
Robert Visentin
Bruce S. Simmonds
Jack D Winberg
Patrick S. Brigham
Donald W. Turple

D-U-N-S 25-224-9396   (SL)
COUNTRY DAY SCHOOL, THE
13415 Dufferin St, King City, ON, L7B 1K5
(905) 833-5366
Emp Here 120   *Sales* 11,894,280
SIC 8211 Elementary and secondary schools
Paul Duckett

D-U-N-S 24-953-9578   (SL)
CROSSFIELD ENVIRONMENTAL CONSULTANTS OF CANADA LIMITED
CROSSFIELD PLANT INTERIOR
242 Burns Blvd, King City, ON, L7B 1E1
(905) 833-2108
Emp Here 28   *Sales* 12,417,720
SIC 7389 Business services, nec
Rhea Crossfield

D-U-N-S 20-156-9837   (HQ)
K.J BEAMISH CONSTRUCTION CO. LTD
3300 King Vaughan Rd, King City, ON, L7B 1B2
(905) 833-4666
Emp Here 50   *Sales* 164,057,500
SIC 1611 Highway and street construction
Robin Beamish
Robert E Graham
Douglas Leslie

D-U-N-S 24-337-2257   (HQ)
K.J. BEAMISH HOLDINGS LIMITED
3300 King Vaughan Rd, King City, ON, L7B 1B2
(905) 833-4666
Sales 15,233,615
SIC 3281 Cut stone and stone products
Robert Graham
Mike Henstock
Kingston J. Beamish
Linda Arthur
Robin Beamish

D-U-N-S 20-153-9520   (SL)
KCLC PROPERTIES ULC
KINGBRIDGE CENTRE, THE
12750 Jane St, King City, ON, L7B 1A3
(905) 833-3086
Emp Here 150   *Sales* 100,336,200
SIC 7389 Business services, nec
John Abele

D-U-N-S 20-770-1111   (HQ)
LGL LIMITED
22 Fisher St, King City, ON, L7B 1G3
(905) 833-1244
Emp Here 43   *Sales* 21,085,920
SIC 8748 Business consulting, nec
Bob Bocking
Constance Agnew

D-U-N-S 25-275-7406   (HQ)
PRIESTLY DEMOLITION INC
3200 Lloydtown-Aurora Rd, King City, ON, L7B 0G3
(905) 841-3735
Sales 57,341,520
SIC 1795 Wrecking and demolition work
Ryan Priestly

D-U-N-S 24-383-5456   (SL)
SOMERVILLE, ROBERT B. CO., LIMITED
13176 Dufferin St, King City, ON, L7B 1K5
(905) 833-3100
Emp Here 250   *Sales* 82,028,750
SIC 1623 Water, sewer, and utility lines
Nicolas De Koning
Paul Mease
Rob Mitchell
Sean Bell
Gord Butson

D-U-N-S 24-097-1650   (SL)
TEMA CONTER MEMORIAL TRUST, THE
175 Patricia Dr, King City, ON, L7B 1H3

Emp Here 50   *Sales* 34,840,500
SIC 6732 Trusts: educational, religious, etc.
Vince Savoia

D-U-N-S 25-150-7901   (HQ)
TWC ENTERPRISES LIMITED
CLUBLINK ONE MEMBERSHIP MORE GOLF
15675 Dufferin St, King City, ON, L7B 1K5
(905) 841-5372
Sales 422,930,000
SIC 7999 Amusement and recreation, nec
K. Rai Sahi
Robert Visentin
Robert Wright
Jamie King
Brent Miller
Fraser Berrill
Patrick S. Brigham
Paul Campbell

John Lokker
Samuel J.B. Pollock

D-U-N-S 25-293-6422   (BR)
YORK REGION DISTRICT SCHOOL BOARD
KING CITY SECONDARY SCHOOL
(*Suby of* YORK REGION DISTRICT SCHOOL BOARD)
2001 King Rd, King City, ON, L7B 1K2
(905) 833-5332
Emp Here 90
SIC 8211 Elementary and secondary schools
Catherine Mcginley

Kingston, ON K7K

D-U-N-S 24-435-9949   (SL)
127897 CANADA LTD
MOTOSPORT PLUS
295 Dalton Ave, Kingston, ON, K7K 6Z1
(613) 544-4600
Emp Here 30   *Sales* 14,942,340
SIC 5571 Motorcycle dealers
Stephen Bray
Norman Levitt

D-U-N-S 20-123-7336   (BR)
2104225 ONTARIO LTD
WESTON BAKERIES LIMITED
(*Suby of* GEORGE WESTON LIMITED)
83 Railway St, Kingston, ON, K7K 2L7
(613) 548-4434
Emp Here 100
SIC 2051 Bread, cake, and related products
Shane Mallen

D-U-N-S 20-528-2226   (SL)
401 AUTO DEALERS EXCHANGE
60 Rigney St, Kingston, ON, K7K 6Z2
(613) 536-0401
Emp Here 50   *Sales* 18,210,750
SIC 5012 Automobiles and other motor vehicles
Terry Simmons

D-U-N-S 20-711-4914   (BR)
ALGONQUIN & LAKESHORE CATHOLIC DISTRICT SCHOOL BOARD
REGIOPOLIS-NOTRE DAME CATHOLIC HIGH SCHOOL
130 Russell St, Kingston, ON, K7K 2E9
(613) 545-1902
Emp Here 120
SIC 8211 Elementary and secondary schools
Terri Daniel

D-U-N-S 20-122-9911   (SL)
ANDRE, T. A. & SONS (ONTARIO) LIMITED
30 Rigney St, Kingston, ON, K7K 6Z2
(613) 549-8060
Emp Here 25   *Sales* 11,768,275
SIC 1542 Nonresidential construction, nec
Roderick Pollock
Douglas Pollock
Michael Pollock

D-U-N-S 25-365-3539   (SL)
B & G KERR SALES LTD
CANADIAN TIRE
1040 Division St Suite 694, Kingston, ON, K7K 0C3
(613) 546-1922
Emp Here 30   *Sales* 14,942,340
SIC 5531 Auto and home supply stores
Brad Kerr

D-U-N-S 24-482-0817   (HQ)
BRAEBURY HOMES CORPORATION
BRAEBURY
(*Suby of* 1059810 ONTARIO LTD)
366 King St E Suite 400, Kingston, ON, K7K 6Y3
(613) 546-3400
Sales 14,986,843

SIC 1521 Single-family housing construction

D-U-N-S 20-891-2618   (HQ)
BROWN'S FINE FOOD SERVICES INC
BROWN'S FINE FOODS SERVICES
844 Division St, Kingston, ON, K7K 4C3
(613) 546-3246
Emp Here 200   *Sales* 12,032,862
SIC 5812 Eating places
James D Brown
Phillip Brown

D-U-N-S 20-117-9095   (BR)
**CORPORATION   OF   THE   CITY   OF
KINGSTON, THE**
RIDEAUCREST HOME FOR THE AGED
(*Suby of* CORPORATION OF THE CITY OF
KINGSTON, THE)
175 Rideau St Suite 416, Kingston, ON, K7K
3H6
(613) 530-2818
Emp Here 243
SIC 8361 Residential care
Linda Peever

D-U-N-S 20-894-2367   (HQ)
DALTCO ELECTRIC & SUPPLY (1979) LTD
26 Lappans Lane, Kingston, ON, K7K 6Z4
(613) 546-3677
Emp Here 14   *Sales* 15,203,916
SIC 5065 Electronic parts and equipment, nec
Peter Dalton

D-U-N-S 25-215-1196   (HQ)
**ENGINEERING   SEISMOLOGY   GROUP
CANADA INC**
ESG SOLUTIONS
(*Suby of* SPECTRIS PLC)
20 Hyperion Crt, Kingston, ON, K7K 7K2
(613) 548-8287
Emp Here 96   *Sales* 67,267,900
SIC 1382 Oil and gas exploration services
Ken Arnold

D-U-N-S 25-422-4405   (SL)
**EXCALIBUR LEARNING RESOURCE CEN-
TRE, CANADA CORP**
25 Markland St, Kingston, ON, K7K 1S2

Emp Here 100   *Sales* 17,660,100
SIC 8249 Vocational schools, nec
Robin Quantick
Laurie Davey-Quandick

D-U-N-S 24-829-3599   (HQ)
GEORGE A. WRIGHT & SON LIMITED
146 Hickson Ave, Kingston, ON, K7K 2N9
(613) 542-4913
Sales 15,540,070
SIC 3599 Industrial machinery, nec
John Wright
Steve Wright

D-U-N-S 25-090-7250   (SL)
**GORDON'S STATE SERVICES LTD., BRO-
KERAGE**
ESTATE SETTLER
490 Discovery Ave Unit 7, Kingston, ON, K7K
7E9
(613) 542-0963
Emp Here 40   *Sales* 13,085,080
SIC 6531 Real estate agents and managers
Barry Gordon

D-U-N-S 24-595-7704   (SL)
HARLEY DAVIDSON OF KINGSTON
295 Dalton Ave, Kingston, ON, K7K 6Z1
(613) 544-4600
Emp Here 30   *Sales* 15,193,652
SIC 5571 Motorcycle dealers
Steve Bray

D-U-N-S 20-114-5716   (HQ)
INSURANCE CENTRE INC, THE
THOMSON, JEMMETT, VOGELZANG
321 Concession St, Kingston, ON, K7K 2B9
(613) 544-5313
Emp Here 43   *Sales* 97,930,326

SIC 6411 Insurance agents, brokers, and ser-
vice
Gord Crothers
Blair Shaw

D-U-N-S 20-123-3798   (HQ)
LEVAC SUPPLY LIMITED
25 Railway St, Kingston, ON, K7K 2L7
(613) 546-6663
Emp Here 5   *Sales* 11,875,650
SIC 5085 Industrial supplies
Mark Levac
Roger Levac

D-U-N-S 20-289-6945   (BR)
LIMESTONE DISTRICT SCHOOL BOARD
QUEEN ELIZABETH COLLEGIATE
145 Kirkpatrick St, Kingston, ON, K7K 2P4

Emp Here 90
SIC 8211 Elementary and secondary schools
Carol Butler

D-U-N-S 20-123-4531   (SL)
MCRAE, W. R. COMPANY LIMITED
549 Montreal St, Kingston, ON, K7K 3J1
(613) 544-6611
Emp Here 19   *Sales* 10,167,356
SIC 5141 Groceries, general line
Ian Buchanan

D-U-N-S 24-763-8737   (HQ)
METAL CRAFT MARINE INCORPORATED
METALCRAFT FASTSHIPS
347 Wellington St, Kingston, ON, K7K 6N7
(613) 549-7747
Emp Here 60   *Sales* 13,430,580
SIC 3732 Boatbuilding and repairing
Michael Chapmann
Lyman Smith
Deborah Berry
Ron Peddle
Robert Clark

D-U-N-S 25-639-5765   (BR)
OSPREY MEDIA PUBLISHING INC
KINGSTON WHIG STANDARD, THE
(*Suby of* QUEBECOR MEDIA INC)
6 Cataraqui St Suite 427, Kingston, ON, K7K
1Z7
(613) 544-5000
Emp Here 190
SIC 2711 Newspapers
Fred Laflamme

D-U-N-S 20-123-6783   (HQ)
**TACKABERRY HEATING SUPPLIES LIM-
ITED**
*TACKABERRY HEATING & REFRIGERA-
TION SUPPLIES*
60 Dalton Ave, Kingston, ON, K7K 6C3
(613) 549-3320
Emp Here 35   *Sales* 13,944,180
SIC 5722 Household appliance stores
Frances Tackaberry
Paul Tackaberry

D-U-N-S 24-269-4180   (HQ)
TANDET EASTERN LIMITED
TANDET KENWORTH, DIV OF
(*Suby of* TANDET MANAGEMENT INC)
191 Dalton Ave, Kingston, ON, K7K 6C2
(613) 544-1212
Emp Here 17   *Sales* 24,903,900
SIC 5511 New and used car dealers
John Tilley
Jeff Cockshutt

D-U-N-S 20-203-4877   (BR)
**UNION OF NATIONAL DEFENCE EMPLOY-
EES**
U N D E LOCAL 641
17 Princess Mary, Kingston, ON, K7K 7B4

Emp Here 800
SIC 8631 Labor organizations

D-U-N-S 20-890-0514   (HQ)

**VANZUYLEN'S ALIGNMENT SERVICE LIM-
ITED**
213 Concession St, Kingston, ON, K7K 2B6
(613) 548-7444
Emp Here 17   *Sales* 22,413,510
SIC 5531 Auto and home supply stores
Henry Vanzuylen Sr
Guy Vanzuylen
Henry Vanzuylen Jr

D-U-N-S 25-690-1919   (HQ)
ZYCOM TECHNOLOGY INC
271 Concession St, Kingston, ON, K7K 2B7
(613) 549-6558
Sales 21,017,178
SIC 5045 Computers, peripherals, and soft-
ware
Timothy R. Allen
Michael D. Lucas

Kingston, ON K7L

D-U-N-S 24-326-6090   (HQ)
ADAMS PHARMACY LTD
SHOPPERS DRUG MART
797 Princess St, Kingston, ON, K7L 1G1
(613) 544-2500
Emp Here 4   *Sales* 14,415,352
SIC 5912 Drug stores and proprietary stores
Brian Adams

D-U-N-S 20-891-5512   (SL)
**ALMA MATER SOCIETY OF QUEEN'S UNI-
VERSITY INCORPORATED**
AMS
99 University Ave, Kingston, ON, K7L 3N5
(613) 533-2725
Emp Here 750   *Sales* 144,732,000
SIC 8742 Management consulting services
Liam Pharp

D-U-N-S 20-506-0106   (SL)
ANCHOR CONCRETE PRODUCTS LIMITED
1645 Sydenham Rd, Kingston, ON, K7L 4V4
(613) 546-6683
Emp Here 100   *Sales* 17,921,900
SIC 3272 Concrete products, nec
Jeffrey R Bradfield
Barbara Bradfield
Roy Baron
John Tait

D-U-N-S 24-653-2642   (SL)
ASSANTE FINANCIAL MANAGEMENT
264 King St E, Kingston, ON, K7L 3A9
(613) 549-8602
Emp Here 24   *Sales* 16,294,152
SIC 6282 Investment advice
Walter Fenlon

D-U-N-S 24-382-1089   (BR)
CANCER CARE ONTARIO
KINGSTON REGIONAL CANCER CENTR
(*Suby of* CANCER CARE ONTARIO)
25 King St W, Kingston, ON, K7L 5P9
(613) 544-2630
Emp Here 200
SIC 8069 Specialty hospitals, except psychi-
atric
Joe De Mora

D-U-N-S 24-438-2495   (SL)
CANCOIL THERMAL CORPORATION
991 John F. Scott Rd, Kingston, ON, K7L 4V3
(613) 541-1235
Emp Here 130   *Sales* 28,860,130
SIC 3585 Refrigeration and heating equip-
ment
Chander Datta
Margrit Datta
Joti Datta

D-U-N-S 25-639-7761   (BR)
CHEZ PIGGY RESTAURANT LIMITED

PAN CHANCHO BAKERY
(*Suby of* CHEZ PIGGY RESTAURANT LIM-
ITED)
44 Princess St, Kingston, ON, K7L 1A4
(613) 544-7790
Emp Here 80
SIC 5461 Retail bakeries
Nick Waterfield

D-U-N-S 24-102-7572   (HQ)
CHEZ PIGGY RESTAURANT LIMITED
68r Princess St, Kingston, ON, K7L 1A5
(613) 549-7673
Emp Here 30   *Sales* 51,853,500
SIC 2051 Bread, cake, and related products
Zoe Yanovsky
Nick Waterfield

D-U-N-S 20-123-0257   (SL)
DJD DEVELOPMENT CORPORATION
BENNETT'S VALUE MART
235 Gore Rd Suite 1, Kingston, ON, K7L 0C3
(613) 542-3406
Emp Here 60   *Sales* 17,608,620
SIC 5411 Grocery stores
David Bennett

D-U-N-S 20-788-1079   (HQ)
EMPIRE LIFE INSURANCE COMPANY, THE
EMPIRE LIFE
(*Suby of* E-L FINANCIAL CORPORATION
LIMITED)
259 King St E, Kingston, ON, K7L 3A8
(613) 548-1881
Emp Here 450   *Sales* 1,389,029,200
SIC 6311 Life insurance
Mark Sylvia
Duncan N R Jackman
Ian Hardacre
Richard Cleaver
Edward Gibson
Sean Kilburn
Ron Friesen
Steve S. Pong
John Brierley
Edward Iacobucci

D-U-N-S 25-967-2496   (SL)
EMPIRE LIFE INVESTMENTS INC
(*Suby of* E-L FINANCIAL CORPORATION
LIMITED)
259 King St E, Kingston, ON, K7L 3A8
(613) 548-1881
Emp Here 30   *Sales* 24,833,310
SIC 6722 Management investment, open-end
Mark Sylvia
Ian Hardacre
Richard Carty
Scott Ewert

D-U-N-S 25-459-0532   (SL)
GRIZZLY GRILL INC, THE
GRIZZLY GRILL, THE
395 Princess St, Kingston, ON, K7L 1B9
(613) 544-7566
Emp Here 85   *Sales* 3,869,115
SIC 5812 Eating places
Ross Grieves

D-U-N-S 20-614-8371   (HQ)
HOMESTEAD LAND HOLDINGS LIMITED
80 Johnson St, Kingston, ON, K7L 1X7
(613) 546-3146
Emp Here 100   *Sales* 39,074,976
SIC 6513 Apartment building operators
A Britton Smith
Francine Moore
Britton C Smith
Alexander Smith

D-U-N-S 20-553-7355   (HQ)
INVISTA (CANADA) COMPANY
(*Suby of* KOSA US INVESTMENTS SARL)
455 Front Rd, Kingston, ON, K7L 4Z6
(613) 544-6000
Emp Here 10   *Sales* 260,153,300
SIC 2299 Textile goods, nec

B Warren Primeaux
Anne Watson
Nancy Kowalski
Norman Leblanc
Peter Kraus
Craig Munson
Chris Chessmore

D-U-N-S 24-242-0268   (SL)
KINGSTON AND THE ISLANDS POLITICAL PARTY
LIBERAL PARTY OF ONTARIO
15 Alamein Dr, Kingston, ON, K7L 4R5
(613) 546-6081
Emp Here 200   *Sales* 62,414,800
SIC 8651 Political organizations
Catherine M Milks

D-U-N-S 20-788-1103   (HQ)
KINGSTON GENERAL HOSPITAL
76 Stuart St, Kingston, ON, K7L 2V7
(613) 548-3232
Sales 269,591,160
SIC 8062 General medical and surgical hospitals
David Pichora
Michael Fitzpatrick
Elizabeth Bardon
Sandra Carlton
Amit Bansal

D-U-N-S 20-377-9244   (SL)
KINGSTON HEALTH SCIENCES CENTRE
KINGSTON GENERAL HOSPITAL
76 Stuart St, Kingston, ON, K7L 2V7
(613) 549-6666
Emp Here 4,000   *Sales* 444,320,000
SIC 8062 General medical and surgical hospitals
David Pichora
David O'toole
Silvie Crawford
Troy Jones
Mike Mcdonald
Jneene Coghlan
Brenda Carter
Elizabeth Bardon
Sandra Carlton
Roger Deeley

D-U-N-S 25-305-5362   (BR)
LIMESTONE DISTRICT SCHOOL BOARD
LA SALLE SECONDARY SCHOOL
773 Highway 15, Kingston, ON, K7L 5H6
(613) 546-1737
Emp Here 75
SIC 8211 Elementary and secondary schools
Lynn Sadlowski

D-U-N-S 25-974-4282   (SL)
MELO, J.S. INC
FOUR POINTS BY SHERATON KINGSTON, THE
285 King St E, Kingston, ON, K7L 3B1
(613) 544-4434
Emp Here 100   *Sales* 9,269,000
SIC 7011 Hotels and motels
Maria Melo
Susan Freitas
Robert Melo
Fatima Rebelo
Elisabeth Sullivan

D-U-N-S 25-676-1982   (BR)
METRO ONTARIO INC
METRO
(*Suby of* METRO INC)
310 Barrie St, Kingston, ON, K7L 5L4
(613) 542-5795
Emp Here 200
SIC 5411 Grocery stores
Paul Gilbert

D-U-N-S 25-195-1299   (SL)
NCIC CLINICAL TRIALS GROUP
10 Stuart St, Kingston, ON, K7L 2V5

(613) 533-6430
Emp Here 140   *Sales* 70,943,040
SIC 8733 Noncommercial research organizations
Joe Pater
Elizabeth Eisenhauer

D-U-N-S 24-103-8215   (HQ)
PROVIDENCE CARE CENTRE
ST MARYS OF THE LAKE HOSPITAL
340 Union St, Kingston, ON, K7L 5A2
(613) 548-7222
Emp Here 50   *Sales* 122,986,800
SIC 8051 Skilled nursing care facilities
Cathy Szabo
Brian Devlin
David Berg
Josee Theriault
David Walker
Tony Button
Jennifer Fisher
Chris Frank
Felicia Iftene
Sheila Langton

D-U-N-S 20-706-2030   (BR)
PROVIDENCE CARE CENTRE
(*Suby of* PROVIDENCE CARE CENTRE)
752 King St W, Kingston, ON, K7L 4X3
(613) 548-5567
Emp Here 500
SIC 8063 Psychiatric hospitals
Dan Coghlan

D-U-N-S 24-342-2263   (BR)
QUEEN'S UNIVERSITY AT KINGSTON
PHYSICAL PLANT SERVICES
(*Suby of* QUEEN'S UNIVERSITY AT KINGSTON)
207 Stuart St, Kingston, ON, K7L 2V9
(613) 533-6075
Emp Here 200
SIC 7349 Building maintenance services, nec
David Clark

D-U-N-S 20-788-4032   (HQ)
QUEEN'S UNIVERSITY AT KINGSTON
QUEEN'S UNIVERSITY
99 University Ave, Kingston, ON, K7L 3N5
(613) 533-2000
Emp Here 6,534   *Sales* 938,300,502
SIC 8221 Colleges and universities
William L Young
Daniel Woolf
William Bryck
Donna Janiec
Heather Woermke

D-U-N-S 25-983-8639   (BR)
QUEEN'S UNIVERSITY AT KINGSTON
QUEEN'S HOUSING & ANCILLARY SERVICES
(*Suby of* QUEEN'S UNIVERSITY AT KINGSTON)
75 Bader Lane Rm D015, Kingston, ON, K7L 3N8
(613) 533-2529
Emp Here 150
SIC 8221 Colleges and universities
Bruce Griffiths

D-U-N-S 25-146-7460   (BR)
QUEEN'S UNIVERSITY AT KINGSTON
SCHOOL OF COMPUTING
(*Suby of* QUEEN'S UNIVERSITY AT KINGSTON)
25 Union St, Kingston, ON, K7L 3N5
(613) 533-6050
Emp Here 100
SIC 8221 Colleges and universities
Dean Mckeown

D-U-N-S 24-850-2630   (SL)
REGION 9 REGIONAL TOURISM ORGANIZATION
GREAT WATERWAY, THE
945 Princess St Suite 202, Kingston, ON, K7L

5L9
(613) 344-2095
Emp Here 50   *Sales* 46,958,850
SIC 6282 Investment advice
Richard Johnston
Gary Brett
Catherine Christensen
Anne Marie Forcier
Heather Ford
Bryan Mercer

D-U-N-S 20-891-1685   (HQ)
RELIGIOUS HOSPITALLERS OF SAINT JOSEPH OF THE HOTEL DIEU OF KINGSTON
HOTEL DIEU HOSPITAL
166 Brock St Suite 262d, Kingston, ON, K7L 5G2
(613) 544-3310
Sales 120,132,800
SIC 8062 General medical and surgical hospitals
David Pichora
Steve Miller
Sherri Mccullough
Eric Bennett
Robert Boucher
Peter Candlish
George Caron
Alan Cosford
Michael J. Hickey
Joan Kalchbrenner

D-U-N-S 20-889-5172   (BR)
RELIGIOUS HOSPITALLERS OF SAINT JOSEPH OF THE HOTEL DIEU OF KINGSTON
(*Suby of* RELIGIOUS HOSPITALLERS OF SAINT JOSEPH OF THE HOTEL DIEU OF KINGSTON)
166 Brock St, Kingston, ON, K7L 5G2
(613) 549-2680
Emp Here 900
SIC 8069 Specialty hospitals, except psychiatric
Sherri Mccullough

D-U-N-S 20-892-2476   (SL)
SHAREAN DRUGS LTD
SHOPPERS DRUG MART
445 Princess St, Kingston, ON, K7L 1C3
(613) 546-3696
Emp Here 80   *Sales* 19,546,240
SIC 5912 Drug stores and proprietary stores
Ashok (Art) Acharya

D-U-N-S 24-344-5116   (BR)
SODEXO CANADA LTD
(*Suby of* SODEXO)
75 Bader Lane, Kingston, ON, K7L 3N8
(613) 533-2953
Emp Here 500
SIC 5812 Eating places
Phil Sparks

D-U-N-S 25-651-2708   (SL)
THOUSAND ISLANDS INSURANCE & FINANCIAL GROUP LIMITED
1996 Highway 15, Kingston, ON, K7L 4V3
(613) 542-4440
Emp Here 100   *Sales* 84,806,000
SIC 6411 Insurance agents, brokers, and service
Carl Holmberg

D-U-N-S 20-057-4874   (BR)
TWD ROADS MANAGEMENT INC
(*Suby of* CARILLION GB LIMITED)
1010 Middle Rd, Kingston, ON, K7L 4V3

Emp Here 120
SIC 5082 Construction and mining machinery
Tim Mccullough

Kingston, ON K7M

D-U-N-S 25-280-4885   (SL)
1034250 ONTARIO LTD
KINGSTON HYUNDAI
401 Bath Rd, Kingston, ON, K7M 7C9
(613) 634-4000
Emp Here 32   *Sales* 15,938,496
SIC 5511 New and used car dealers
Scott Sly

D-U-N-S 20-559-4836   (SL)
1132145 ONTARIO LIMITED
GORD & KIM'S NO FRILLS
1030 Coverdale Dr, Kingston, ON, K7M 9E1
(613) 389-0090
Emp Here 100   *Sales* 29,347,700
SIC 5411 Grocery stores
Gord Mcgregor
Kim Mcgregor

D-U-N-S 20-063-1354   (SL)
2445120 ONTARIO INC
BMW KINGSTON
1412 Bath Rd, Kingston, ON, K7M 4X6
(613) 817-1808
Emp Here 25   *Sales* 12,451,950
SIC 5511 New and used car dealers
Scott Douglas

D-U-N-S 24-103-9320   (SL)
421342 ONTARIO LIMITED
KINGSTON NISSAN
775 Gardiners Rd, Kingston, ON, K7M 7H8
(613) 384-2531
Emp Here 35   *Sales* 17,432,730
SIC 5511 New and used car dealers
Ronald Cotton

D-U-N-S 24-437-5622   (HQ)
548050 ONTARIO INC
1388 Bath Rd, Kingston, ON, K7M 4X6
(613) 546-2211
Emp Here 2   *Sales* 37,756,800
SIC 5511 New and used car dealers
Steven Petrie

D-U-N-S 25-248-8200   (SL)
995547 ONTARIO LTD
KINGSTON VOLKSWAGEN
1670 Bath Rd, Kingston, ON, K7M 4X9
(613) 384-1000
Emp Here 24   *Sales* 10,064,520
SIC 6719 Holding companies, nec
Mark Durant

D-U-N-S 24-719-5357   (HQ)
AGNEW, J. E. FOOD SERVICES LTD
TIM HORTONS
83 Terry Fox Dr Suite A, Kingston, ON, K7M 8N4
(613) 544-9400
Emp Here 15   *Sales* 20,054,770
SIC 5812 Eating places
Jeff Agnew
Sherri Agnew

D-U-N-S 24-099-1737   (SL)
ANDOLA FIBRES LTD
(*Suby of* ANDOLA FIBRES LIMITED)
740 Progress Ave, Kingston, ON, K7M 4W9
(613) 389-1261
Emp Here 45   *Sales* 22,424,490
SIC 5131 Piece goods and notions
Jim Walker

D-U-N-S 24-911-1675   (BR)
BOMBARDIER INC
(*Suby of* BOMBARDIER INC)
1059 Taylor-Kidd Blvd, Kingston, ON, K7M 6J9
(613) 384-3100
Emp Here 300
SIC 2754 Commercial printing, gravure
Ziad Raza

D-U-N-S 20-390-7501   (SL)
COMMUNITY LIVING KINGSTON AND DIS-

TRICT
541 Days Rd Unit 6, Kingston, ON, K7M 3R8
(613) 546-6613
Emp Here 300   *Sales* 23,037,600
SIC 8322 Individual and family services
 Peter Sproul

D-U-N-S 24-207-1038   (BR)
CORPORATION OF THE CITY OF
KINGSTON, THE
NORMAN ROGERS AIRPORT
(*Suby of* CORPORATION OF THE CITY OF
KINGSTON, THE)
1114 Len Birchall Way, Kingston, ON, K7M
9A1
(613) 389-6404
Emp Here 237
SIC 4581 Airports, flying fields, and services
 Shirley De Silva

D-U-N-S 20-123-1511   (SL)
DEODATO, TONY & SONS LIMITED
100 Binnington Crt, Kingston, ON, K7M 8N1
(613) 548-3073
Emp Here 50   *Sales* 41,778,850
SIC 5148 Fresh fruits and vegetables
 Anthony Deodato
 Anthony Deodato Jr
 Michael Deodato
 Joseph Deodato
 Theodore Deodato

D-U-N-S 20-194-3912   (SL)
EPSILON INDUSTRIES INC
751 Dalton Ave, Kingston, ON, K7M 8N6
(613) 544-1133
Emp Here 80   *Sales* 17,760,080
SIC 3585 Refrigeration and heating equip-
ment
 Chris Wiederick

D-U-N-S 25-941-2740   (BR)
EXTENDICARE (CANADA) INC
EXTENDICARE KINGSTON
(*Suby of* EXTENDICARE INC)
309 Queen Mary Rd, Kingston, ON, K7M 6P4
(613) 549-5010
Emp Here 100
SIC 8051 Skilled nursing care facilities
 Marilyn Benn

D-U-N-S 20-889-2208   (BR)
EXTENDICARE INC
EXTENDICARE KINGSTON
(*Suby of* EXTENDICARE INC)
309 Queen Mary Rd, Kingston, ON, K7M 6P4
(613) 549-5010
Emp Here 96
SIC 8051 Skilled nursing care facilities

D-U-N-S 24-610-6538   (SL)
FINDLAY FOODS (KINGSTON) LTD
675 Progress Ave, Kingston, ON, K7M 0C7
(613) 384-5331
Emp Here 70   *Sales* 58,490,390
SIC 5141 Groceries, general line
 Stewart Findlay

D-U-N-S 24-089-9950   (BR)
G4S SECURE SOLUTIONS (CANADA) LTD
(*Suby of* G4S PLC)
2437 Princess St Suite 204, Kingston, ON,
K7M 3G1
(613) 389-1744
Emp Here 100
SIC 7381 Detective and armored car services
 Scott Jupp

D-U-N-S 25-671-4395   (BR)
HOME DEPOT OF CANADA INC
(*Suby of* THE HOME DEPOT INC)
606 Gardiners Rd, Kingston, ON, K7M 3X9
(613) 384-3511
Emp Here 200
SIC 5251 Hardware stores
 Brian Marshal

D-U-N-S 25-301-2470   (BR)

HUDSON'S BAY COMPANY
BAY, THE
(*Suby of* HUDSON'S BAY COMPANY)
945 Gardiners Rd, Kingston, ON, K7M 7H4
(613) 384-3888
Emp Here 100
SIC 5311 Department stores
 Norman St Goddard

D-U-N-S 20-894-6442   (HQ)
JACK FRENCH LIMITED
ALLIANCE COMMUNICATION
200 Binnington Crt, Kingston, ON, K7M 8R6
(613) 547-6666
Sales 30,512,328
SIC 5211 Lumber and other building materials
 Jack French
 Bradley French
 Marie French

D-U-N-S 24-436-3834   (SL)
KIN LEM DRUGS LIMITED
SHOPPERS DRUG MART
1875 Bath Rd, Kingston, ON, K7M 4Y3
(613) 384-6990
Emp Here 40   *Sales* 10,118,160
SIC 5912 Drug stores and proprietary stores
 Kin Lem

D-U-N-S 24-267-9223   (SL)
KINGSTON DODGE CHRYSLER (1980) LTD
1429 Princess St, Kingston, ON, K7M 3E9
(613) 549-8900
Emp Here 53   *Sales* 33,351,840
SIC 5511 New and used car dealers
 Michael Laframboise
 Elteena Laframboise

D-U-N-S 20-219-8672   (SL)
KINGSTON DODGE JEEP EAGLE LTD
PARTS DEPARTMENT
1429 Princess St, Kingston, ON, K7M 3E9
(613) 549-8900
Emp Here 49   *Sales* 24,405,822
SIC 5511 New and used car dealers
 Michael Laframboist

D-U-N-S 24-104-9154   (SL)
KINGSTON INDEPENDENT NYLON WORK-
ERS UNION OFFICE & RECREATION CEN-
TRE
725 Arlington Park Pl, Kingston, ON, K7M 7E4
(613) 389-5255
Emp Here 40   *Sales* 41,395,240
SIC 6371 Pension, health, and welfare funds
 Bruce Bridger

D-U-N-S 20-711-4765   (BR)
LIMESTONE DISTRICT SCHOOL BOARD
FRONTENAC SECONDARY SCHOOL
1789 Bath Rd, Kingston, ON, K7M 4Y3
(613) 389-2130
Emp Here 80
SIC 8211 Elementary and secondary schools
 Diane Sackfield

D-U-N-S 25-305-5115   (BR)
LIMESTONE DISTRICT SCHOOL BOARD
EDUCATIONAL SERVICES
153 Van Order Dr, Kingston, ON, K7M 1B9
(613) 542-9871
Emp Here 100
SIC 8211 Elementary and secondary schools
 Darlene Scarlett

D-U-N-S 25-265-3928   (BR)
LIMESTONE DISTRICT SCHOOL BOARD
BAYRIDGE SECONDARY SCHOOL
1059 Taylor-Kidd Blvd, Kingston, ON, K7M
6J9
(613) 389-8932
Emp Here 80
SIC 8211 Elementary and secondary schools
 Caroline Worthy

D-U-N-S 25-305-5404   (BR)
LIMESTONE DISTRICT SCHOOL BOARD
LOYALIST COLLEGIATE & VOCATIONAL IN-

STITUTE
153 Van Order Dr, Kingston, ON, K7M 1B9
(613) 546-5575
Emp Here 80
SIC 8211 Elementary and secondary schools
 Roxanne Saunders

D-U-N-S 20-789-4866   (SL)
MARTIN, BOB CONSTRUCTION CO LTD
1473 John Counter Blvd Suite 400, Kingston,
ON, K7M 8Z6
(613) 548-7136
Emp Here 40   *Sales* 12,754,760
SIC 1521 Single-family housing construction
 Robert Martin
 Jean Martin

D-U-N-S 20-123-4481   (SL)
MCKEOWN MOTORS LIMITED
THOMPSON PLYMOUTH CHRYSLER
805 Gardiners Rd, Kingston, ON, K7M 7E6
(613) 389-4426
Emp Here 30   *Sales* 14,942,340
SIC 5511 New and used car dealers
 James Thompson

D-U-N-S 24-852-7561   (BR)
METRO ONTARIO INC
FOOD BASICS
(*Suby of* METRO INC)
1300 Bath Rd, Kingston, ON, K7M 4X4
(613) 544-9317
Emp Here 75
SIC 5411 Grocery stores
 Michael Raposo

D-U-N-S 24-335-0506   (BR)
METRO ONTARIO INC
METRO
(*Suby of* METRO INC)
466 Gardiners Rd, Kingston, ON, K7M 7W8
(613) 384-6334
Emp Here 130
SIC 5411 Grocery stores
 Sid Marsten

D-U-N-S 20-747-3133   (HQ)
ONGWANADA HOSPITAL
191 Portsmouth Ave, Kingston, ON, K7M 8A6
(613) 548-4417
Emp Here 80   *Sales* 32,898,672
SIC 8361 Residential care
 Allan Twohey
 Jack Thompson
 Roy Smith
 Wade Durling
 Thomas Collard

D-U-N-S 24-102-6640   (HQ)
PETRIE FORD SALES (KINGSTON) LTD
(*Suby of* 548050 ONTARIO INC)
1388 Bath Rd, Kingston, ON, K7M 4X6
(613) 544-6203
Sales 56,005,920
SIC 5511 New and used car dealers
 Stephen Petrie
 David Petrie

D-U-N-S 25-980-9945   (BR)
PROVIGO DISTRIBUTION INC
LOEB #8094
(*Suby of* LOBLAW COMPANIES LIMITED)
1225 Princess St, Kingston, ON, K7M 3E1
(613) 544-8202
Emp Here 130
SIC 5411 Grocery stores
 Clarke Kevin

D-U-N-S 20-555-4269   (BR)
RONA INC
(*Suby of* LOWE'S COMPANIES, INC.)
2342 Princess St, Kingston, ON, K7M 3G4
(613) 531-6225
Emp Here 100
SIC 5072 Hardware
 Al Melanson

D-U-N-S 20-916-2036   (HQ)
SOUTH EAST COMMUNITY CARE ACCESS
CENTRE
1471 John Counter Blvd Suite 200, Kingston,
ON, K7M 8S8
(613) 544-7090
Sales 89,164,069
SIC 8011 Offices and clinics of medical doc-
tors
 Janet Balson
 Karen Gilroy

D-U-N-S 25-140-5155   (SL)
SPECIALTY CARE EAST INC
TRILLIUM CENTRE
800 Edgar St Suite 114, Kingston, ON, K7M
8S4
(613) 547-0040
Emp Here 120   *Sales* 8,227,920
SIC 8051 Skilled nursing care facilities
 Paula Jourdain
 Ray Jourdain

D-U-N-S 20-614-6953   (HQ)
ST LAWRENCE POOLS (1995) LIMITED
525 Days Rd, Kingston, ON, K7M 3R8
(613) 389-5510
Emp Here 47   *Sales* 15,263,532
SIC 1799 Special trade contractors, nec
 Chuck Dickison

D-U-N-S 24-366-7359   (BR)
ST. LAWRENCE COLLEGE OF APPLIED
ARTS AND TECHNOLOGY, THE
(*Suby of* ST. LAWRENCE COLLEGE OF AP-
PLIED ARTS AND TECHNOLOGY, THE)
100 Portsmouth Ave, Kingston, ON, K7M 1G2
(613) 544-5400
Emp Here 400
SIC 8221 Colleges and universities
 Volker Thomson

D-U-N-S 20-426-7835   (SL)
SUBARU OF KINGSTON
399 Bath Rd, Kingston, ON, K7M 7C9
(613) 546-7000
Emp Here 39   *Sales* 19,425,042
SIC 5511 New and used car dealers
 Dave Tidman

D-U-N-S 20-578-5090   (SL)
TAYLOR, JEROME D CHEVROLET CADIL-
LAC LIMITED
TAYLOR AUTOMALL
2440 Princess St, Kingston, ON, K7M 3G4
(613) 549-1311
Emp Here 90   *Sales* 56,635,200
SIC 5511 New and used car dealers
 Marilyn Taylor
 Brian Smith

D-U-N-S 25-158-9693   (BR)
UNIFOR
CAW LOCAL 31
(*Suby of* UNIFOR)
728 Arlington Park Pl, Kingston, ON, K7M 8H9
(613) 542-7368
Emp Here 220
SIC 8631 Labor organizations
 Kevin Pond

Kingston, ON K7P

D-U-N-S 24-606-3148   (SL)
1195149 ONTARIO LIMITED
PETRO CANADA
1586 Centennial Dr, Kingston, ON, K7P 0C7
(613) 389-8010
Emp Here 70   *Sales* 20,543,390
SIC 5411 Grocery stores
 Mark Snider

D-U-N-S 20-575-8886   (BR)
ALGONQUIN & LAKESHORE CATHOLIC

DISTRICT SCHOOL BOARD
HOLY CROSS CATHOLIC SECONDARY SCHOOL
1085 Woodbine Rd, Kingston, ON, K7P 2V9
(613) 384-1919
Emp Here 110
SIC 8211 Elementary and secondary schools
Paul Walsh

D-U-N-S 20-861-6156   (SL)
CANADIAN TIRE
640 Cataraqui Woods Dr, Kingston, ON, K7P 2Y5
(613) 384-1766
Emp Here 30   *Sales* 14,942,340
SIC 5531 Auto and home supply stores
Randy Casford

D-U-N-S 24-977-1486   (SL)
CARDINAL MOVERS KINGSTON INC
CARDINAL
921 Woodbine Rd, Kingston, ON, K7P 2X4
(289) 395-0003
Emp Here 216   *Sales* 44,432,496
SIC 4212 Local trucking, without storage
Carl Pope
Kendy Vendone

D-U-N-S 25-097-2023   (BR)
COSTCO WHOLESALE CANADA LTD
COSTCO
(*Suby of* COSTCO WHOLESALE CORPORATION)
1015 Centennial Dr, Kingston, ON, K7P 3B7
(613) 549-2527
Emp Here 210
SIC 5141 Groceries, general line
Kelly Flegel

D-U-N-S 24-850-1835   (SL)
DERBYSHIRE E.D. & SONS LIMITED
CANADIAN TIRE ASSOCIATE STORE
2560 Princess St Suite 417, Kingston, ON, K7P 2S8
(613) 384-4414
Emp Here 250   *Sales* 144,313,000
SIC 5531 Auto and home supply stores
Elwin D Derbyshire
Beverly T Derbyshire

D-U-N-S 25-301-2488   (BR)
EXTENDICARE (CANADA) INC
PARAMED HOME HEALTH CARE
(*Suby of* EXTENDICARE INC)
786 Blackburn Mews, Kingston, ON, K7P 2N7
(613) 549-0112
Emp Here 200
SIC 8051 Skilled nursing care facilities
Vera Rabadi

D-U-N-S 25-651-2856   (SL)
FORD'S, SCOTT PHARMACY LTD
SHOPPERS DRUG MART
775 Strand Blvd Suite 11, Kingston, ON, K7P 2S7
(613) 384-7477
Emp Here 70   *Sales* 17,102,960
SIC 5912 Drug stores and proprietary stores
Scott Ford

D-U-N-S 25-986-2741   (SL)
FRULACT CANADA INC
(*Suby of* FRULACT - SOCIEDADE GESTORA DE PARTICIPACOES SOCIAIS, S.A.)
1295 Centennial Dr, Kingston, ON, K7P 0R6
(613) 507-7500
Emp Here 30   *Sales* 25,067,310
SIC 5143 Dairy products, except dried or canned
Benoit Keppenne
Andre Miguel Cachada Pinto Da Rocha
Duarte Nuno Da Silva Almeida Faria
Joao Evangelista Sousa Miranda

D-U-N-S 20-717-5659   (HQ)
LIMESTONE ADVISORY FOR CHILD CARE PROGRAMS
930 Woodbine Rd, Kingston, ON, K7P 2X4

(613) 384-5188
Emp Here 1   *Sales* 19,870,700
SIC 8699 Membership organizations, nec
Karen Stevenson

D-U-N-S 25-649-7975   (BR)
LOBLAWS SUPERMARKETS LIMITED
LOBLAWS
(*Suby of* LOBLAW COMPANIES LIMITED)
1048 Midland Ave, Kingston, ON, K7P 2X9
(613) 389-4119
Emp Here 250
SIC 5411 Grocery stores
Jeff Brierley

D-U-N-S 24-179-7286   (SL)
MCCOY TOURS
566 Cataraqui Woods Dr, Kingston, ON, K7P 2Y5
(613) 384-0347
Emp Here 49   *Sales* 18,882,640
SIC 4724 Travel agencies
Shawn Gary

D-U-N-S 24-860-2336   (SL)
MCKERCHER HOLDINGS LIMITED
2730 Princess St, Kingston, ON, K7P 2W6
(613) 384-2418
Emp Here 50   *Sales* 20,967,750
SIC 6719 Holding companies, nec
Gil Mckercher

D-U-N-S 24-437-5408   (SL)
MCKERCHER KINGSTON LIMITED
LEON'S FURNITURE & APPLIANCES
2730 Princess St, Kingston, ON, K7P 2W6
(613) 384-2418
Emp Here 60   *Sales* 13,944,180
SIC 5712 Furniture stores
Mark Mckercher
Peter Jr Mckercher
Paul Mckercher

D-U-N-S 24-344-4861   (BR)
METRO ONTARIO INC
(*Suby of* METRO INC)
775 Bayridge Dr, Kingston, ON, K7P 2P1
(613) 384-8800
Emp Here 120
SIC 5411 Grocery stores
Cindy Mckenna

D-U-N-S 25-462-8258   (HQ)
PROFESSIONAL   INVESTMENTS (KINGSTON) INC
PROFESSIONAL INSURANCE
1180 Clyde Crt, Kingston, ON, K7P 2E4
(613) 384-7511
Emp Here 20   *Sales* 65,742,390
SIC 6211 Security brokers and dealers
D Oswald (Ossie) Fisher
Paul Fisher

D-U-N-S 25-482-4857   (BR)
PROVIGO DISTRIBUTION INC
LOEB BAYRIDGE
(*Suby of* LOBLAW COMPANIES LIMITED)
775 Bayridge Dr, Kingston, ON, K7P 2P1
(613) 384-8800
Emp Here 80
SIC 5141 Groceries, general line
Cindy Mckennis

D-U-N-S 24-317-2868   (HQ)
ROBINSON SOLUTIONS (CANADA) INC
(*Suby of* 2082486 ONTARIO INC)
1456 Centennial Dr, Kingston, ON, K7P 0K4
(613) 389-7611
Emp Here 3   *Sales* 438,610,800
SIC 6712 Bank holding companies
Bernard (Bernie) Robinson
Micheal Robinson
Brad Detlor

D-U-N-S 20-561-1291   (SL)
ROBINSON SOLUTIONS (KINGSTON) INC
ROBINSON PRE-WEIGH SERVICES
(*Suby of* 1524990 ONTARIO INC)

1456 Centennial Dr, Kingston, ON, K7P 0K4
(613) 634-7552
Emp Here 120   *Sales* 80,268,960
SIC 7389 Business services, nec
Bernie Robinson
Michael Robinson
David Amelotte

D-U-N-S 24-764-8926   (HQ)
SLH TRANSPORT INC
(*Suby of* HOLDING CANADIAN AMERICAN TRANSPORTATION C.A.T. INC)
1585 Centennial Dr, Kingston, ON, K7P 0K4
(613) 384-9515
Emp Here 120   *Sales* 92,190,500
SIC 4213 Trucking, except local
Paul Cooper
Brent Fowler
Evelyn Dodd
Daniel Goyette

D-U-N-S 24-595-9671   (BR)
SYSCO CANADA, INC
SYSCO KINGSTON
(*Suby of* SYSCO CORPORATION)
650 Cataraqui Woods Dr, Kingston, ON, K7P 2Y4
(613) 384-6666
Emp Here 170
SIC 5141 Groceries, general line
Rod Stroud

D-U-N-S 25-404-0231   (HQ)
TRANSFORMIX ENGINEERING INC
1150 Gardiners Rd, Kingston, ON, K7P 1R7
(613) 544-5970
Emp Here 40   *Sales* 17,760,080
SIC 3569 General industrial machinery, nec
Peng-Sang Cau
Martin Smith
Kenneth Nicholson

D-U-N-S 25-145-2470   (HQ)
UNIVERSAL INDUSTRIAL SUPPLY GROUP INC
NAPA AUTO PARTS
505 O'Connor Dr, Kingston, ON, K7P 1J9
(613) 634-6272
Emp Here 33   *Sales* 32,415,135
SIC 5013 Motor vehicle supplies and new parts
Tom Mondoux
Peter Penfold

D-U-N-S 25-297-6196   (BR)
WAL-MART CANADA CORP
KINGSTON SUPERCENTRE STORE- #3043
(*Suby of* WALMART INC.)
1130 Midland Ave, Kingston, ON, K7P 2X9
(613) 384-9071
Emp Here 175
SIC 5311 Department stores
Jonathan Carroll

Kingsville, ON N9Y

D-U-N-S 20-869-8147   (HQ)
1068409 ONTARIO INC
DOUBLE DIAMOND SALES
2237 County Rd 31, Kingsville, ON, N9Y 2E5
(519) 326-5919
Emp Here 30   *Sales* 41,778,850
SIC 5148 Fresh fruits and vegetables
Nick D Mastronardi

D-U-N-S 25-974-9901   (SL)
1362385 ONTARIO LIMITED
SPECIAL EDITION MARKETING
1932 Setterington Dr, Kingsville, ON, N9Y 2E5

Emp Here 20   *Sales* 10,702,480
SIC 5148 Fresh fruits and vegetables
Ronald Lapos
James Dinenna

D-U-N-S 20-697-1967   (SL)
1627198 ONTARIO INC
UNIVERSAL FABRICATING
1956 Setterington Dr, Kingsville, ON, N9Y 2E5
(519) 326-1333
Emp Here 59   *Sales* 10,701,892
SIC 3312 Blast furnaces and steel mills
Abram Wiebe
Abram Harms
Peter Neufeld
Neil Harms

D-U-N-S 24-654-6837   (SL)
658612 ONTARIO LTD
215 Industry Rd, Kingsville, ON, N9Y 1K9
(519) 733-9100
Emp Here 45   *Sales* 37,600,965
SIC 5146 Fish and seafoods
Antonio Giacalone

D-U-N-S 24-829-3102   (SL)
A.M.A. HOLICULTURE INC
2011 Spinks Dr, Kingsville, ON, N9Y 2E5
(519) 322-1397
Emp Here 18   *Sales* 13,365,360
SIC 5193 Flowers and florists supplies
Allen Monsma
Cornellia Bradt
Richard Bradt
Shirley Monsma

D-U-N-S 24-303-2752   (SL)
CORNIES FARMS LTD
1545 Kratz Rd, Kingsville, ON, N9Y 3K4
(519) 733-5416
Emp Here 40   *Sales* 13,698,680
SIC 0191 General farms, primarily crop
James Cornies
Robert Cornies
Louise Cornies

D-U-N-S 20-772-8036   (SL)
CSH ROYAL OAK LTC INC
ROYAL OAK LONG TERM CARE CENTER
1750 Division Rd N Suite 415, Kingsville, ON, N9Y 4G7
(519) 733-9303
Emp Here 150   *Sales* 10,404,019
SIC 8059 Nursing and personal care, nec
Brent Binions
Vlad Volodarski

D-U-N-S 25-502-7542   (SL)
DEL SOL GREENHOUSES INC
1665 Graham, Kingsville, ON, N9Y 2E4
(519) 733-8373
Emp Here 27   *Sales* 22,560,579
SIC 5148 Fresh fruits and vegetables
Dave Delellis

D-U-N-S 24-560-6538   (HQ)
DOUBLE DIAMOND ACRES LIMITED
2024 Spinks Dr, Kingsville, ON, N9Y 2E5
(519) 326-1000
Emp Here 100   *Sales* 17,578,600
SIC 0182 Food crops grown under cover
Benjamin Mastronardi
Christopher Mastronardi

D-U-N-S 25-838-0955   (SL)
ERIEVIEW ACRES INC
1930 Seacliff Dr, Kingsville, ON, N9Y 2N1
(519) 326-3013
Emp Here 69   *Sales* 101,270,748
SIC 5159 Farm-product raw materials, nec
Robert Hansen

D-U-N-S 20-697-1900   (HQ)
EXCALIBUR PLASTICS LTD
1397 Road 3 E, Kingsville, ON, N9Y 2E5
(519) 326-6000
Emp Here 10   *Sales* 12,037,155
SIC 5162 Plastics materials and basic shapes
Richard Colasanti

D-U-N-S 20-902-8612   (HQ)
GOLDEN ACRE FARMS INC
1451 Road 2 E, Kingsville, ON, N9Y 2E4

Emp Here 35   *Sales* 17,050,085
SIC 0182 Food crops grown under cover
Louis Chibante
Lynne Chibante

D-U-N-S 25-536-9019   (SL)
GREAT NORTHERN HYDROPONICS
1507 Road 3 E, Kingsville, ON, N9Y 2E5
(519) 322-2000
Emp Here 250   *Sales* 18,952,550
SIC 0182 Food crops grown under cover
Guido Van Het Hof

D-U-N-S 25-033-6021   (SL)
J-D MARKETING (LEAMINGTON) INC
2400 Graham, Kingsville, ON, N9Y 2E5
(519) 733-3663
Emp Here 60   *Sales* 50,134,620
SIC 5148 Fresh fruits and vegetables
James M Dimenna

D-U-N-S 20-565-2329   (HQ)
JEM D INTERNATIONAL PARTNERS LP
RED SUN FARMS
2400 Graham, Kingsville, ON, N9Y 2E5
(519) 733-3663
Emp Here 75   *Sales* 57,337,280
SIC 5148 Fresh fruits and vegetables
James Dimenna
Jamie Mastronardi
Steve Macchio
Carlos Visconti

D-U-N-S 24-987-3993   (SL)
KINGSVILLE STAMPING LIMITED
1931 Setterington Dr, Kingsville, ON, N9Y 2E5
(519) 326-6331
Emp Here 130   *Sales* 24,971,050
SIC 3469 Metal stampings, nec
Peter Dyck
Gerhard Dyck
Aganetha Dyck
Jamie Dyck

D-U-N-S 24-664-0882   (SL)
LA NASSA FOODS INC
LA NASSA FOODS
215 Industry Rd, Kingsville, ON, N9Y 1K9
(519) 733-9100
Emp Here 50   *Sales* 41,778,850
SIC 5146 Fish and seafoods
Antonio (Tony) Giacalone
Claudio Adragna
Vito Figliomeni
Vito O. Figliomeni
Doreen Shulick

D-U-N-S 24-626-4618   (HQ)
LIQUI-FORCE SERVICES (ONTARIO) INC
2015 Spinks Dr Suite 2, Kingsville, ON, N9Y 2E5
(519) 322-4600
Sales 12,232,890
SIC 7699 Repair services, nec
Kim Lewis Sr
Jeff Lewis
Kim Lewis Jr
Chris Lewis

D-U-N-S 20-125-8472   (HQ)
MASTRONARDI PRODUCE LIMITED
SUNSET
2100 Road 4 E, Kingsville, ON, N9Y 2E5
(519) 326-3218
Emp Here 460   *Sales* 946,065,120
SIC 5148 Fresh fruits and vegetables
Donald Mastronardi
Paul Mastronardi
Kevin Safrance
Kathy Mastronardi
Marne Safrance
Frank Mastronardi

D-U-N-S 25-656-8528   (SL)
MUCCI FARMS LTD
1876 Seacliff Dr, Kingsville, ON, N9Y 2N1

(519) 326-8881
Emp Here 30   *Sales* 10,274,010
SIC 0182 Food crops grown under cover
Antonino Mucci
Gino Mucci

D-U-N-S 24-412-8906   (HQ)
PELEE ISLAND WINERY & VINEYARDS INC
455 Seacliff Dr, Kingsville, ON, N9Y 2K5
(519) 733-6551
Sales 22,469,850
SIC 2084 Wines, brandy, and brandy spirits
Walter Schmoranz

D-U-N-S 24-373-0434   (SL)
PETERSON SPRING OF CANADA LIMITED
(*Suby of* PETERSON AMERICAN CORPO-
RATION)
208 Wigle Ave, Kingsville, ON, N9Y 2J9
(519) 733-2358
Emp Here 60   *Sales* 11,525,100
SIC 3492 Fluid power valves and hose fittings
Craig Gray
Rick Sbrocca

D-U-N-S 20-272-1072   (SL)
RED SUN FARMS CANADA INC
2400 Graham Siderd, Kingsville, ON, N9Y 2E5
(519) 733-3663
Emp Here 120   *Sales* 190,534,250
SIC 6712 Bank holding companies
Steve Macchio
Carlos Visconti
Roberto Saldana

D-U-N-S 25-094-7017   (SL)
TWIN PEAKS HYDROPONICS INC
2237 County Rd 31, Kingsville, ON, N9Y 2E5
(519) 326-1000
Emp Here 65   *Sales* 17,050,085
SIC 0182 Food crops grown under cover
Nick Mastronardi

Kintore, ON N0M

D-U-N-S 24-668-6906   (BR)
THAMES VALLEY PROCESSORS LTD
COLD SPRINGS FARM
15 Line 155390, Kintore, ON, N0M 2C0

Emp Here 100
SIC 2015 Poultry slaughtering and processing
Darrell Dobbie

Kirkland Lake, ON P2N

D-U-N-S 24-078-9198   (SL)
**ALEX MACINTYRE & ASSOCIATES LIM-
ITED**
1390 Government Rd W, Kirkland Lake, ON, P2N 3J5
(705) 567-3266
Emp Here 150   *Sales* 358,132,350
SIC 1081 Metal mining services
Sydney Mcdougall
James Mcdougall
Glen Whyte

D-U-N-S 24-686-4391   (SL)
CABO DRILLING (ONTARIO) CORP
(*Suby of* CABO DRILLING CORP)
34 Duncan Ave N, Kirkland Lake, ON, P2N 3L3
(705) 567-9311
Emp Here 150   *Sales* 31,856,400
SIC 1799 Special trade contractors, nec
John Versfelt
Grenville Whyte
Pierre Germain

D-U-N-S 24-124-5047   (HQ)

COMMUNITY LIVING KIRKLAND LAKE
CLKL
51 Government Rd W, Kirkland Lake, ON, P2N 2E5
(705) 567-9331
Emp Here 1   *Sales* 16,565,440
SIC 8399 Social services, nec
Heather Topliss
Janet Duchene
Debbie Orth
Lauri Lambert
Traci Fong

D-U-N-S 20-260-7250   (HQ)
**DISTRICT OF TIMISKAMING SOCIAL SER-
VICES ADMINISTRATION BOARD**
DTSSAB
(*Suby of* GOVERNMENT OF ONTARIO)
29 Duncan Ave S, Kirkland Lake, ON, P2N 1X5
(705) 567-9366
Emp Here 101   *Sales* 38,792,250
SIC 8611 Business associations
Don Studholme
Doug Jelly

D-U-N-S 25-228-0656   (BR)
**DISTRICT SCHOOL BOARD ONTARIO
NORTH EAST**
*KIRKLAND LAKE DISTRICT COMPOSITE
SCHOOL*
(*Suby of* DISTRICT SCHOOL BOARD ON-
TARIO NORTH EAST)
Gd, Kirkland Lake, ON, P2N 3P4
(705) 567-4981
Emp Here 75
SIC 8211 Elementary and secondary schools
,Alison Fantin

D-U-N-S 20-638-3085   (HQ)
EPC CANADA EXPLOSIVES LTD
EPC NORDEX
(*Suby of* FINANCECOM)
22 Government Rd E, Kirkland Lake, ON, P2N 1A3
(705) 642-3265
Sales 12,411,736
SIC 2892 Explosives
Jim Taylor
Ferdinand Bodenan

D-U-N-S 20-343-1721   (BR)
KIRKLAND LAKE GOLD LTD
(*Suby of* KIRKLAND LAKE GOLD LTD)
1350 Government Rd W, Kirkland Lake, ON, P2N 3J1
(705) 567-5208
Emp Here 800
SIC 1081 Metal mining services
Robert Macdonald

D-U-N-S 25-504-1204   (SL)
KIRKLAND LAKE POWER CORP
505 Archer Dr, Kirkland Lake, ON, P2N 3M7
(705) 567-9501
Emp Here 30   *Sales* 15,589,650
SIC 4911 Electric services
James Temerty

D-U-N-S 24-802-8081   (SL)
MEDEIROS, PAUL ENTERPRISES LIMITED
CANADIAN TIRE
146 Government Rd W, Kirkland Lake, ON, P2N 2E9
(705) 567-9281
Emp Here 50   *Sales* 24,903,900
SIC 5531 Auto and home supply stores
Paul Medeiros

D-U-N-S 24-184-1253   (BR)
**NORTHERN COLLEGE OF APPLIED ARTS
& TECHNOLOGY**
140 Government Rd W, Kirkland Lake, ON, P2N 2E9
(705) 567-9291
Emp Here 80
SIC 8221 Colleges and universities
Peter Mac Lean

D-U-N-S 20-124-1189   (SL)
TECK NEWS AGENCY (1977) LIMITED
5 Kirkland St E, Kirkland Lake, ON, P2N 1N9

Emp Here 21   *Sales* 15,592,920
SIC 5192 Books, periodicals, and newspapers
Cliff Connelly

Kitchener, ON N2A

D-U-N-S 25-927-2623   (SL)
BETTER WELLNESS JMC LTD
SHOPPERS DRUG MART
1221 Weber St E Suite 1086, Kitchener, ON, N2A 1C2
(519) 748-2430
Emp Here 40   *Sales* 10,118,160
SIC 5912 Drug stores and proprietary stores
Todd Spedder

D-U-N-S 20-124-3326   (SL)
CHARCOAL STEAK HOUSE INC
2980 King St E, Kitchener, ON, N2A 1A9
(519) 893-6570
Emp Here 150   *Sales* 6,827,850
SIC 5812 Eating places
Tim Wideman
Tom Wideman

D-U-N-S 20-015-6953   (HQ)
FOCUS ASSESSMENTS INC
1601 River Rd E Unit 10, Kitchener, ON, N2A 3Y4
(519) 893-5972
Emp Here 6   *Sales* 20,313,249
SIC 6321 Accident and health insurance
Mircea Bogden
Toi Chong Fong
Douglas Friars
James Friars
Diane Squires

D-U-N-S 20-942-0710   (SL)
GRAHAM, L.G. HOLDINGS INC
TIM HORTONS
1020 Ottawa St N Suite 510, Kitchener, ON, N2A 3Z3
(519) 894-1499
Emp Here 44   *Sales* 12,062,688
SIC 5461 Retail bakeries
Leonard Graham

D-U-N-S 20-124-6006   (SL)
HEFFNER MOTORS LIMITED
HEFFNER LEXUS TOYOTA
3121 King St E, Kitchener, ON, N2A 1B1
(519) 748-9666
Emp Here 150   *Sales* 94,392,000
SIC 5511 New and used car dealers
John Heffner Jr
William (Willy) Heffner

D-U-N-S 24-779-5206   (HQ)
PENSKE LOGISTICS CANADA LTD
(*Suby of* PENSKE TRUCK LEASING CO.,
L.P.)
3065 King St E, Kitchener, ON, N2A 1B1
(519) 650-0123
Emp Here 100   *Sales* 73,752,400
SIC 4213 Trucking, except local
Marc Althen
Dennis Abruzzi
David Battisti
Jeffrey Bullard
Joseph Carlier
Brian Hard
Joel Rose

D-U-N-S 20-346-1504   (SL)
SAVIC HOMES LTD
26 Idle Ridge Crt, Kitchener, ON, N2A 3W3
(519) 954-0370
Emp Here 40   *Sales* 12,754,760
SIC 1521 Single-family housing construction

Bob Savic

D-U-N-S 25-297-8705 (BR)
ZEHRMART INC
ZEHRS MARKETS
(*Suby of* LOBLAW COMPANIES LIMITED)
1375 Weber St E, Kitchener, ON, N2A 3Y7
(519) 748-4570
Emp Here 150
SIC 5411 Grocery stores
Ryan Brook

Kitchener, ON N2B

D-U-N-S 24-466-0168 (SL)
2142242 ONTARIO INC
BMW GRAND RIVER
1800 Victoria St N, Kitchener, ON, N2B 3E5
(519) 747-0269
Emp Here 82   *Sales* 51,600,960
SIC 5511 New and used car dealers
Reg Quinn
Jordan Domelle

D-U-N-S 24-359-8781 (SL)
ACAPULCO POOLS LIMITED
1550 Victoria St N, Kitchener, ON, N2B 3E2
(519) 743-6357
Emp Here 150   *Sales* 104,295,000
SIC 5091 Sporting and recreation goods
Bernhard Gall

D-U-N-S 20-113-4488 (SL)
ACL STEEL LTD
2255 Shirley Dr, Kitchener, ON, N2B 3X4
(519) 568-8822
Emp Here 55   *Sales* 10,564,675
SIC 3441 Fabricated structural Metal
Paul Seibel

D-U-N-S 24-318-0275 (HQ)
BALL CONSTRUCTION (CANADA) INC
5 Shirley Ave, Kitchener, ON, N2B 2E6
(519) 742-5851
Sales 21,868,000
SIC 6712 Bank holding companies
Jason Ball
Cameron Ball
Gary Hauck

D-U-N-S 25-597-0592 (SL)
BALL CONSTRUCTION INC
(*Suby of* BALL CONSTRUCTION (CANADA) INC)
5 Shirley Ave, Kitchener, ON, N2B 2E6
(519) 742-5851
Emp Here 60   *Sales* 34,220,280
SIC 1542 Nonresidential construction, nec
Jason Ball
Cameron Ball
Gary Hauck
Gregg King

D-U-N-S 20-819-2430 (SL)
BALL CONSTRUCTION LTD
(*Suby of* BALL CONSTRUCTION (CANADA) INC)
5 Shirley Ave, Kitchener, ON, N2B 2E6
(519) 742-5851
Emp Here 60   *Sales* 16,256,520
SIC 1521 Single-family housing construction
Jason Ball
Cameron Ball
Gregg King

D-U-N-S 25-975-3804 (HQ)
BINGEMANS INC
425 Bingemans Centre Dr, Kitchener, ON, N2B 3X7
(519) 744-1555
Emp Here 440   *Sales* 23,319,500
SIC 5812 Eating places
Lawrence Bingeman
Esther Gascho

D-U-N-S 20-536-9325 (SL)
BRODA ENTERPRISES INC
BRODA SEATING
(*Suby of* M L E HOLDINGS, INC.)
560 Bingemans Centre Dr, Kitchener, ON, N2B 3X9
(519) 746-8080
Emp Here 65   *Sales* 14,773,785
SIC 3842 Surgical appliances and supplies
David Heap

D-U-N-S 24-393-8979 (SL)
CARKAE ENGLISH SALES LTD
CANADIAN TIRE
1080 Victoria St N Suite 139, Kitchener, ON, N2B 3C4
(519) 744-1153
Emp Here 30   *Sales* 14,942,340
SIC 5531 Auto and home supply stores
Scott English

D-U-N-S 25-977-6453 (SL)
CROSBY AUDI INC
AUDI KITCHENER-WATERLOO
2350 Shirley Dr, Kitchener, ON, N2B 3X5
(519) 514-0100
Emp Here 31   *Sales* 19,507,680
SIC 5511 New and used car dealers
Michael Crosby
Margaret Crosby
Kathleen Marton

D-U-N-S 20-703-7805 (SL)
CUSTOM LEATHER CANADA LIMITED
GRIZZLY FITNESS ACCESSORIES
460 Bingemans Centre Dr, Kitchener, ON, N2B 3X9
(519) 741-2070
Emp Here 97   *Sales* 16,660,949
SIC 2387 Apparel belts
Frank Kastelic
Mike Hallett

D-U-N-S 24-729-1503 (SL)
ERB AND ERB INSURANCE BROKERS LTD
(*Suby of* LACKNER MCLENNAN INSURANCE LTD)
818 Victoria St N, Kitchener, ON, N2B 3C1
(519) 579-4270
Emp Here 60   *Sales* 74,125,080
SIC 6331 Fire, marine, and casualty insurance
David Westfall
James Chmiel
William J Kirkwood
Jim Kibble

D-U-N-S 24-709-2125 (SL)
FAIRVIEW IMPORT MOTORS INC
SCHLUETER ACURA OF KITCHENER
2385 Shirley Dr, Kitchener, ON, N2B 3X4
(519) 893-9000
Emp Here 30   *Sales* 14,942,340
SIC 5511 New and used car dealers
Harold Schlueter

D-U-N-S 20-361-0076 (HQ)
FRESHSTONE BRANDS INC
KEYBRAND FOODS
1326 Victoria St N, Kitchener, ON, N2B 3E2
(519) 578-2940
Emp Here 130   *Sales* 28,869,600
SIC 5411 Grocery stores
Steven Diakowsky
Mike Swan
Rod Senft
Trevor Johnstone
Derek Senft
Richard Harris

D-U-N-S 24-926-8749 (SL)
GALL CONSTRUCTION LIMITED
(*Suby of* GALL, BERNHARD HOLDINGS LIMITED)
1550 Victoria St N, Kitchener, ON, N2B 3E2
(519) 743-6357
Emp Here 200   *Sales* 27,135,400
SIC 6519 Real property lessors, nec

Bernhard Gall

D-U-N-S 20-556-9759 (SL)
H. L. STAEBLER COMPANY LIMITED
STAEBLER INSURANCE
871 Victoria St N Suite 7b, Kitchener, ON, N2B 3S4
(519) 743-5221
Emp Here 59   *Sales* 109,016,778
SIC 6411 Insurance agents, brokers, and service
Stephen Philpott
Kim Philpott

D-U-N-S 24-977-2539 (SL)
KITCHENER NISSAN (2009) INC
KITCHENER NISSAN
1450 Victoria St N, Kitchener, ON, N2B 3E2
(519) 744-1188
Emp Here 25   *Sales* 12,451,950
SIC 5511 New and used car dealers
Michael Alkier

D-U-N-S 25-472-8744 (SL)
KITCHENER-WATERLOO AND NORTH WATERLOO HUMANE SOCIETY
250 Riverbend Dr, Kitchener, ON, N2B 2E9
(519) 745-5615
Emp Here 33   *Sales* 13,114,662
SIC 8699 Membership organizations, nec
Jack Kinch

D-U-N-S 24-515-0198 (SL)
KNELL INVESTMENTS INC
2090 Shirley Dr, Kitchener, ON, N2B 0A3
(519) 578-1000
Emp Here 50   *Sales* 22,358,700
SIC 5072 Hardware
Robert Dippell
Judith Scheifele
Frances Wiseman

D-U-N-S 20-124-7723 (HQ)
KNELL, WILLIAM AND COMPANY LIMITED
KNELL DOOR & HARDWARE
2090 Shirley Dr, Kitchener, ON, N2B 0A3
(519) 578-1000
Sales 20,570,004
SIC 5072 Hardware
Robert Dipple
Judith Scheifele
Frances Wiseman

D-U-N-S 25-034-5287 (HQ)
LACKNER MCLENNAN INSURANCE LTD
818 Victoria St N, Kitchener, ON, N2B 3C1
(519) 579-3330
Sales 138,580,650
SIC 6411 Insurance agents, brokers, and service
David Stark
Cameron Yule
Cynthia Roth
Stephen Bleizeffer

D-U-N-S 20-606-3075 (HQ)
M & T INSTA-PRINT LIMITED
907 Frederick St Suite 4, Kitchener, ON, N2B 2B9
(519) 571-0101
Emp Here 1   *Sales* 16,402,700
SIC 2752 Commercial printing, lithographic
Donald Froome

D-U-N-S 24-859-8856 (HQ)
MACNAUGHTON HERMSEN BRITTON CLARKSON PLANNING LIMITED
540 Bingemans Centre Dr Suite 200, Kitchener, ON, N2B 3X9
(519) 576-3650
Emp Here 40   *Sales* 11,714,400
SIC 8742 Management consulting services
Ian Macnaughton
Bernie Hermsen
Paul Britton
Brent Clarkson
James Parkin
Carol Wiebe

D-U-N-S 20-124-8879 (SL)
MONARCH OIL (KITCHENER) LIMITED
(*Suby of* 1163291 ONTARIO LTD)
808 Victoria St N, Kitchener, ON, N2B 3C1
(519) 743-8241
Emp Here 15   *Sales* 18,858,015
SIC 5172 Petroleum products, nec
Jerome Berberich
Don Ripley
Keith Brighton

D-U-N-S 25-857-6370 (HQ)
MTE CONSULTANTS INC
SZE STRAKA ENGINEERS, DIV OF
520 Bingemans Centre Dr, Kitchener, ON, N2B 3X9
(519) 743-6500
Emp Here 140   *Sales* 44,684,750
SIC 8711 Engineering services
Ted Rowe
Jeff Martens
Douglas Winger
Steve Cooper

D-U-N-S 20-364-9298 (SL)
O'CONNOR ELECTRIC LTD
9 Centennial Rd Unit 2, Kitchener, ON, N2B 3E9
(519) 745-8886
Emp Here 260   *Sales* 61,232,340
SIC 1731 Electrical work
Paul Morell
Matthew Morell

D-U-N-S 20-118-6850 (SL)
ONWARD CLUTHE HARDWARE PRODUCTS INC
(*Suby of* ONWARD MULTI-CORP INC)
10 Centennial Rd, Kitchener, ON, N2B 3G1
(519) 742-8446
Emp Here 60   *Sales* 16,059,120
SIC 5251 Hardware stores
Rick Sellner
James Sellner

D-U-N-S 24-218-6369 (HQ)
RE/MAX TWIN CITY REALTY INC
842 Victoria St N Suite 1, Kitchener, ON, N2B 3C1
(519) 579-4110
Emp Here 1   *Sales* 24,295,562
SIC 6531 Real estate agents and managers
Peter Degroot

D-U-N-S 25-401-8906 (HQ)
S.T.O.P. RESTAURANT SUPPLY LTD
206 Centennial Crt, Kitchener, ON, N2B 3X2
(519) 749-2710
Emp Here 18   *Sales* 14,309,568
SIC 5046 Commercial equipment, nec
Boyd Blackwell
Richard Beeksma

D-U-N-S 20-125-1246 (SL)
SPAENAUR INC
815 Victoria St N, Kitchener, ON, N2B 3C3
(519) 578-0381
Emp Here 97   *Sales* 46,077,522
SIC 5085 Industrial supplies
Jonathan Spaetzel
Pauline Spaetzel
Elizabeth Milas
Elizabeth Blakely

D-U-N-S 25-678-2004 (HQ)
STEVENSON INSULATION INC
260 Shirley Ave, Kitchener, ON, N2B 2E1
(519) 743-2857
Emp Here 1   *Sales* 12,178,575
SIC 1742 Plastering, drywall, and insulation
Darryl Stevenson

D-U-N-S 20-955-6476 (HQ)
TYCORRA INVESTMENTS INC
WABASH CANADA
10 Forwell Rd, Kitchener, ON, N2B 3E7
(519) 576-9290
Emp Here 55   *Sales* 87,705,310

SIC 5012 Automobiles and other motor vehicles
Brent Larson
Rob Smiley
Shawn Lacey

D-U-N-S 25-081-9398   (SL)
VICTORIA STAR MOTORS INC
125 Centennial Rd, Kitchener, ON, N2B 3E9
(519) 579-4460
Emp Here 35   *Sales* 17,432,730
SIC 5511 New and used car dealers
Michael Alkier

D-U-N-S 24-484-4148   (HQ)
WATERLOO BREWING LTD
FORMOSA SPRINGS BREWERY
400 Bingemans Centre Dr, Kitchener, ON, N2B 3X9
(519) 742-2732
Emp Here 50   *Sales* 37,407,254
SIC 5921 Liquor stores

D-U-N-S 25-034-6236   (SL)
WESTMOUNT STOREFRONT SYSTEMS LTD
20 Riverview Pl, Kitchener, ON, N2B 3X8
(519) 570-2850
Emp Here 60   *Sales* 14,771,160
SIC 1793 Glass and glazing work
Timothy Mitchell

D-U-N-S 24-224-8321   (HQ)
WOLLE REALTY INC
ROYAL LEPAGE WOLLE REALTY
842 Victoria St N Suite 15, Kitchener, ON, N2B 3C1
(519) 578-7300
Sales 24,714,451
SIC 6531 Real estate agents and managers
Mark Wolle

Kitchener, ON N2C

D-U-N-S 24-986-9843   (SL)
940734 ONTARIO LIMITED
TIM HORTONS
670 Fairway Rd S, Kitchener, ON, N2C 1X3
(519) 894-0811
Emp Here 80   *Sales* 3,641,520
SIC 5812 Eating places
Ernie J Davies

D-U-N-S 20-977-6152   (HQ)
AMPACET CANADA COMPANY
(*Suby of* AMPACET CORPORATION)
101 Sasaga Dr, Kitchener, ON, N2C 2G8
(519) 748-5576
Sales 19,881,470
SIC 2816 Inorganic pigments
Alvaro Mendoza
Yves Carette
Terry Elliott
Nick Dunne
Michael Gaudio
Robert Oakes
Andrew Mcclellan

D-U-N-S 25-626-6289   (SL)
ANSWER PRECISION TOOL INC
146 Otonabee Dr, Kitchener, ON, N2C 1L6
(519) 748-0079
Emp Here 50   *Sales* 18,210,750
SIC 5013 Motor vehicle supplies and new parts
David Henning
Michelle Henning

D-U-N-S 25-857-7642   (SL)
BAST, PAUL & ASSOCIATES
PRIMERICA FINANCIAL SERVICES
625 Wabanaki Dr Unit 4, Kitchener, ON, N2C 2G3
(519) 893-3500
Emp Here 40   *Sales* 10,973,280

SIC 8741 Management services
Paul Bast

D-U-N-S 24-011-8609   (BR)
BEST BUY CANADA LTD
BEST BUY
(*Suby of* BEST BUY CO., INC.)
215 Fairway Rd S, Kitchener, ON, N2C 1X2
(519) 783-0333
Emp Here 80
SIC 5731 Radio, television, and electronic stores
Adam Doan

D-U-N-S 25-362-8101   (HQ)
BROCK SOLUTIONS HOLDINGS INC
88 Ardelt Ave, Kitchener, ON, N2C 2C9
(519) 571-1522
Sales 80,777,489
SIC 6712 Bank holding companies
Vivienne Ojala

D-U-N-S 24-678-7746   (BR)
BROCK SOLUTIONS INC
(*Suby of* BROCK SOLUTIONS HOLDINGS INC)
90 Ardelt Ave, Kitchener, ON, N2C 2C9
(519) 571-1522
Emp Here 250
SIC 3491 Industrial valves
Rick Brock

D-U-N-S 20-168-3922   (HQ)
BROCK SOLUTIONS INC
(*Suby of* BROCK SOLUTIONS HOLDINGS INC)
88 Ardelt Ave, Kitchener, ON, N2C 2C9
(519) 571-1522
Emp Here 250   *Sales* 94,820,400
SIC 8748 Business consulting, nec
Vivienne Ojala
Richard Brock

D-U-N-S 20-294-5440   (BR)
CHILDREN'S AID SOCIETY OF THE REGIONAL MUNICIPALITY OF WATERLOO, THE
FAMILY AND CHILDREN'S SERVICES OF THE REGIONAL MUNICIPALITY OF WATERLOO
(*Suby of* CHILDREN'S AID SOCIETY OF THE REGIONAL MUNICIPALITY OF WATERLOO, THE)
200 Ardelt Ave, Kitchener, ON, N2C 2L9
(519) 576-0540
Emp Here 80
SIC 8322 Individual and family services
Cameron Dearlove

D-U-N-S 24-364-2501   (HQ)
CHILDREN'S AID SOCIETY OF THE REGIONAL MUNICIPALITY OF WATERLOO, THE
FAMILY AND CHILDREN'S SERVICES OF THE REGIONAL MUNICIPALITY OF WATERLOO
200 Ardelt Ave, Kitchener, ON, N2C 2L9
(519) 576-0540
Emp Here 140   *Sales* 38,396,000
SIC 8322 Individual and family services
Alison Scott
Brenda Hagey
Earl Rayner
Peter Ringrose

D-U-N-S 25-367-3479   (SL)
COLT CANADA CORPORATION
(*Suby of* COLT DEFENSE HOLDING LLC)
1036 Wilson Ave, Kitchener, ON, N2C 1J3
(519) 893-6840
Emp Here 105   *Sales* 20,168,925
SIC 3484 Small arms
Gerald Dinkel

D-U-N-S 20-125-0479   (SL)
DURON PLASTICS LIMITED
965 Wilson Ave, Kitchener, ON, N2C 1J1

(519) 884-8011
Emp Here 50   *Sales* 10,094,850
SIC 3089 Plastics products, nec
Gary Cluthe

D-U-N-S 20-206-6108   (SL)
FASTENAL CANADA LTD
900 Wabanaki Dr, Kitchener, ON, N2C 0B7
(519) 748-6566
Emp Here 300   *Sales* 146,319,000
SIC 5085 Industrial supplies
Jason Powers

D-U-N-S 25-626-1371   (HQ)
FASTENAL CANADA, LTEE
(*Suby of* FASTENAL COMPANY)
900 Wabanaki Dr, Kitchener, ON, N2C 0B7
(519) 748-6566
Emp Here 100   *Sales* 243,865,000
SIC 5085 Industrial supplies
Jeffery Watts
Maximilian Bezner
Darrell Cooper

D-U-N-S 24-049-1522   (HQ)
FLANAGAN FOODSERVICE INC
145 Otonabee Dr, Kitchener, ON, N2C 1L7
(519) 748-6878
Emp Here 223   *Sales* 230,065,836
SIC 5141 Groceries, general line
Dee Flanagan
Ryan Kirk
Trevor R. Austin
Barry Reid
Paul Blackwell
Murray Flanagan

D-U-N-S 20-124-5313   (SL)
GEMINI MOTORS LIMITED
26 Manitou Dr, Kitchener, ON, N2C 1L1
(519) 894-2050
Emp Here 33   *Sales* 16,436,574
SIC 5511 New and used car dealers
Larry Mcknight

D-U-N-S 20-565-2345   (SL)
GREAT CANADIAN COACHES INC
353 Manitou Dr, Kitchener, ON, N2C 1L5
(519) 896-8687
Emp Here 90   *Sales* 4,938,480
SIC 4142 Bus charter service, except local
Larry Hundt

D-U-N-S 24-977-5362   (SL)
GREAT CANADIAN HOLIDAYS INC
353 Manitou Dr, Kitchener, ON, N2C 1L5
(519) 896-8687
Emp Here 43   *Sales* 16,570,480
SIC 4725 Tour operators
Lorna Hundt

D-U-N-S 25-407-5864   (HQ)
HERCULES TIRE INTERNATIONAL INC
HERCULES INTERNATIONAL
(*Suby of* ATD CORPORATION)
155 Ardelt Ave, Kitchener, ON, N2C 2E1
(519) 885-3100
Emp Here 20   *Sales* 69,173,100
SIC 5014 Tires and tubes
Robert Keller

D-U-N-S 24-400-3104   (SL)
HERITAGE DESIGN
227 Manitou Dr Suite 4, Kitchener, ON, N2C 1L4

Emp Here 34   *Sales* 10,841,546
SIC 1521 Single-family housing construction
Ken Smith

D-U-N-S 25-131-7624   (HQ)
IMT PARTNERSHIP
INGERSOLL AXLES
530 Manitou Dr, Kitchener, ON, N2C 1L3
(519) 748-0848
Sales 72,969,300
SIC 3444 Sheet Metalwork
James Hacking
Greg Edmonds

D-U-N-S 24-423-7889   (SL)
J. C. VENDING (ONTARIO) LIMITED
625 Wabanaki Dr Unit 6, Kitchener, ON, N2C 2G3

Emp Here 60   *Sales* 14,659,680
SIC 5962 Merchandising machine operators
Tom Gutoski
Jerry Gutoski

D-U-N-S 24-008-1877   (HQ)
KIRBY INTERNATIONAL TRUCKS LTD
ALTRUCK INTERNATIONAL TRUCK CENTRES, DIV OF
48 Ardelt Ave, Kitchener, ON, N2C 2C9
(519) 578-6680
Emp Here 38   *Sales* 94,392,000
SIC 5511 New and used car dealers
Ryan Kirby
Jeff Kirby

D-U-N-S 20-124-7350   (HQ)
KISSNER MILLING COMPANY LIMITED
KISSNER SALTS & CHEMICALS
(*Suby of* KISSNER GROUP HOLDINGS LP)
148 Manitou Dr Suite 301, Kitchener, ON, N2C 1L3
(519) 279-4860
Emp Here 50   *Sales* 100,831,800
SIC 5169 Chemicals and allied products, nec
David Safran
Bill Zinger

D-U-N-S 25-147-6669   (SL)
KRUG INC
KRUG FURNITURE
421 Manitou Dr, Kitchener, ON, N2C 1L5
(519) 748-5100
Emp Here 425   *Sales* 78,347,700
SIC 2521 Wood office furniture
Leonard Ruby
Matthew Ruby
Mark Fisher

D-U-N-S 20-026-1625   (SL)
KRUG INC
KRUG FURNITURE
421 Manitou Dr, Kitchener, ON, N2C 1L5
(519) 748-5100
Emp Here 425   *Sales* 94,632,625
SIC 2522 Office furniture, except wood
Leonard Ruby

D-U-N-S 20-124-7954   (SL)
KUNTZ ELECTROPLATING INC
851 Wilson Ave, Kitchener, ON, N2C 1J1
(519) 893-7680
Emp Here 850   *Sales* 206,746,350
SIC 3471 Plating and polishing
Paul Kuntz
Robert Kuntz Sr
Terry Reidel
Dave Kuntz
Robert Kuntz Jr
Michael Director

D-U-N-S 24-378-5909   (SL)
LABSTAT INTERNATIONAL INC
262 Manitou Dr, Kitchener, ON, N2C 1L3
(519) 748-5409
Emp Here 348   *Sales* 111,261,516
SIC 8734 Testing laboratories
Martin Oughton
Kimberly Stevenson Chow

D-U-N-S 25-588-2474   (SL)
LUTHERAN HOMES KITCHENER-WATERLOO
TRINITY VILLAGE CARE CENTRE
2727 Kingsway Dr Suite 227, Kitchener, ON, N2C 1A7
(519) 893-6320
Emp Here 200   *Sales* 13,713,200
SIC 8051 Skilled nursing care facilities
William (Bill) Smith
Caroline Verleyen
Jeanne Jackson

D-U-N-S 24-043-7587   (BR)
METRO ONTARIO INC
FOOD BASICS
(*Suby of* METRO INC)
655 Fairway Rd S, Kitchener, ON, N2C 1X4
(519) 896-5100
Emp Here 100
SIC 5411 Grocery stores
   Mark Thaves

D-U-N-S 20-124-9539   (SL)
PANO CAP (CANADA) LIMITED
(*Suby of* MAGNACAP INC)
55 Webster Rd, Kitchener, ON, N2C 2E7
(519) 893-6055
Emp Here 80   *Sales* 12,708,640
SIC 3089 Plastics products, nec
   Jan Eberhardt
   Denis Laderoute

D-U-N-S 24-060-2326   (SL)
PERFEXIA INC
111 Bleams Rd, Kitchener, ON, N2C 2G2
(519) 884-8650
Emp Here 27   *Sales* 12,825,702
SIC 5084 Industrial machinery and equipment
   David Jones

D-U-N-S 24-678-2812   (SL)
ROBERTS ONSITE INC
(*Suby of* BLACK & MCDONALD GROUP LIMITED)
209 Manitou Dr, Kitchener, ON, N2C 1L4
(519) 578-2230
Emp Here 350   *Sales* 82,428,150
SIC 1731 Electrical work
   Dan Moore
   Michael Birmingham

D-U-N-S 20-125-0529   (HQ)
RUBBERLINE PRODUCTS LIMITED
81 Bleams Rd, Kitchener, ON, N2C 2G2
(519) 894-0400
Emp Here 15   *Sales* 20,426,118
SIC 5085 Industrial supplies
   Robert Luelo
   William Ferguson
   Gerry Glaves
   Gary Linkert

D-U-N-S 24-477-5318   (SL)
SCHERER, STEVE PONTIAC BUICK GMC LTD
1225 Courtland Ave E, Kitchener, ON, N2C 2N8
(519) 893-8888
Emp Here 82   *Sales* 23,230,600
SIC 7538 General automotive repair shops
   Steve Scherer
   John Scherer

D-U-N-S 20-974-7831   (SL)
SCHLUETER CHEVROLET OLDSMOBILE LIMITED
2685 Kingsway Dr, Kitchener, ON, N2C 1A7
(519) 884-9000
Emp Here 72   *Sales* 45,308,160
SIC 5511 New and used car dealers
   Dennis Schlueter
   Harold Schlueter

D-U-N-S 20-117-2603   (HQ)
SOWA HOLDINGS LTD
SOWA TOOL & MACHINE COMPANY
500 Manitou Dr, Kitchener, ON, N2C 1L3
(519) 748-5750
Emp Here 75   *Sales* 20,501,250
SIC 6712 Bank holding companies
   Gerhard Sowa Sr

D-U-N-S 20-125-1238   (SL)
SOWA TOOL AND MACHINE COMPANY LIMITED
(*Suby of* SOWA HOLDINGS LTD)
500 Manitou Dr, Kitchener, ON, N2C 1L3
(519) 748-5750
Emp Here 75   *Sales* 40,151,400
SIC 5049 Professional equipment, nec

   Gerhard Sowa Sr
   Gerhard Sowa Jr

D-U-N-S 24-353-6518   (SL)
STANCE HEALTHCARE INC
45 Goodrich Dr, Kitchener, ON, N2C 0B8
(519) 896-2400
Emp Here 50   *Sales* 14,010,984
SIC 5047 Medical and hospital equipment
   Bruce Kennedy
   Carl Kennedy
   Brian Kennedy

D-U-N-S 25-967-7599   (BR)
SUNBEAM CENTRE
SUNBEAM RESIDENTIAL GROUP HOME
595 Greenfield Ave Suite 43, Kitchener, ON, N2C 2N7
(519) 894-2098
Emp Here 300
SIC 8059 Nursing and personal care, nec

D-U-N-S 25-592-3468   (BR)
UNIFOR
CANADIAN AUTO WORKERS
(*Suby of* UNIFOR)
1111 Homer Watson Blvd, Kitchener, ON, N2C 2P7

Emp Here 2,000
SIC 8631 Labor organizations
   Ray Wintermeyer

D-U-N-S 25-297-6279   (BR)
WAL-MART CANADA CORP
(*Suby of* WALMART INC.)
2960 Kingsway Dr Suite 3045, Kitchener, ON, N2C 1X1
(519) 894-6600
Emp Here 200
SIC 5311 Department stores
   Reck Qushair

D-U-N-S 20-710-7322   (BR)
WATERLOO CATHOLIC DISTRICT SCHOOL BOARD
ST MARY'S HIGH SCHOOL
1500 Block Line Rd, Kitchener, ON, N2C 2S2
(519) 745-6891
Emp Here 200
SIC 8211 Elementary and secondary schools
   Theresa Horan

D-U-N-S 24-182-0505   (HQ)
WATERLOO REGION DISTRICT SCHOOL BOARD
51 Ardelt Ave, Kitchener, ON, N2C 2R5
(519) 570-0300
Emp Here 200   *Sales* 693,833,000
SIC 8211 Elementary and secondary schools
   Linda Fabi
   Matthew Gerard
   Ian Gaudet
   Nick Landry

D-U-N-S 20-125-2624   (SL)
WENDELL MOTOR SALES LTD
549 Fairway Rd S, Kitchener, ON, N2C 1X4
(519) 893-1501
Emp Here 55   *Sales* 34,610,400
SIC 5511 New and used car dealers
   Craig Hendry
   William Hendry

Kitchener, ON N2E

D-U-N-S 24-545-0101   (HQ)
506165 ONTARIO LIMITED
TRILLIUM METAL STAMPINGS
50 Steckle Pl, Kitchener, ON, N2E 2C3
(519) 748-5295
Sales 10,564,675
SIC 3469 Metal stampings, nec
   Carol Ann Zettel
   Andrew Zettel

   Dan Zettel
   Dave Zettel
   Kevin Zettel

D-U-N-S 25-246-3757   (SL)
982875 ONTARIO LIMITED
KITCHENER HYUNDAI
44 Alpine Rd, Kitchener, ON, N2E 1A1
(519) 749-1314
Emp Here 30   *Sales* 14,942,340
SIC 5511 New and used car dealers
   Vince Palladino

D-U-N-S 25-399-0667   (SL)
AMT ELECTROSURGERY INC
20 Steckle Pl Unit 16, Kitchener, ON, N2E 2C3
(519) 895-0452
Emp Here 40   *Sales* 17,886,960
SIC 5047 Medical and hospital equipment
   Chris Mcnamara

D-U-N-S 24-322-2697   (HQ)
BOEHMER BOX LP
120 Trillium Dr, Kitchener, ON, N2E 2C4
(519) 576-2480
Sales 110,291,100
SIC 2652 Setup paperboard boxes
   Terry Macleod
   Karl Broderick
   Mike Hobbs
   Katie Morrison

D-U-N-S 20-179-4406   (BR)
CANADA POST CORPORATION
KITCHENER MAIL PROCESSING PLANT
(*Suby of* GOVERNMENT OF CANADA)
70 Trillium Dr, Kitchener, ON, N2E 0E2
(519) 748-3056
Emp Here 250
SIC 4311 U.s. postal service
   Chris Ashley

D-U-N-S 20-923-7481   (SL)
CAVCO FOOD SERVICES LTD
MCDONALDS RESTAURANTS
715 Ottawa St S, Kitchener, ON, N2E 3H5
(519) 569-7224
Emp Here 85   *Sales* 3,869,115
SIC 5812 Eating places
   Rick Cavanagh

D-U-N-S 25-034-6244   (SL)
COLLINS RANKIN INSURANCE BROKERS
645 Westmount Rd E, Kitchener, ON, N2E 3S3

Emp Here 18   *Sales* 10,438,632
SIC 6411 Insurance agents, brokers, and service
   Larry Collins

D-U-N-S 20-323-7821   (HQ)
CONESTOGA COLD STORAGE LIMITED
299 Trillium Dr, Kitchener, ON, N2E 1W9
(519) 748-5415
Emp Here 11   *Sales* 16,456,480
SIC 4222 Refrigerated warehousing and storage
   Larry Laurin
   Greg Laurin
   Denise St Croix

D-U-N-S 20-200-6636   (HQ)
CORNERSTONE COURIER INC
219 Shoemaker St, Kitchener, ON, N2E 3B3
(519) 741-0446
Emp Here 50   *Sales* 24,257,826
SIC 7389 Business services, nec
   Kevin Harding
   Sharon Harding

D-U-N-S 20-877-3614   (SL)
CUSTOM FOAM SYSTEMS LTD
360 Trillium Dr, Kitchener, ON, N2E 2K6
(519) 748-1700
Emp Here 100   *Sales* 20,189,700
SIC 3086 Plastics foam products
   Bob Germann

   Thomas Germann Jr

D-U-N-S 24-097-1572   (SL)
EXUS PHARMACEUTICALS LTD
SHOPPERS DRUG MART
700 Strasburg Rd, Kitchener, ON, N2E 2M2
(519) 576-8340
Emp Here 50   *Sales* 12,647,700
SIC 5912 Drug stores and proprietary stores
   John Snow

D-U-N-S 24-334-4470   (HQ)
GATEMAN-MILLOY INC
270 Shoemaker St, Kitchener, ON, N2E 3E1
(519) 748-6500
Sales 10,928,900
SIC 0781 Landscape counseling and planning
   Michael Milloy
   Peter Hersics
   Shawn Milloy
   Rui Pedro

D-U-N-S 20-553-6084   (BR)
HOME DEPOT OF CANADA INC
(*Suby of* THE HOME DEPOT INC)
1400 Ottawa St S, Kitchener, ON, N2E 4E2
(519) 569-4300
Emp Here 100
SIC 5211 Lumber and other building materials
   Bill Masson

D-U-N-S 24-564-1535   (SL)
LIBRARY SERVICES CENTRE
131 Shoemaker St, Kitchener, ON, N2E 3B5
(519) 746-4420
Emp Here 145   *Sales* 85,428,055
SIC 5192 Books, periodicals, and newspapers
   Michael Monahan

D-U-N-S 20-017-3404   (HQ)
MEIKLE AUTOMATION INC
975 Bleams Rd Unit 5-10, Kitchener, ON, N2E 3Z5
(519) 896-0800
Emp Here 40   *Sales* 42,131,550
SIC 3599 Industrial machinery, nec
   Andrew Meikle
   Andrew Stribling
   Jeff Hoffman
   Tom Giger
   Wade Sanderson

D-U-N-S 24-320-2080   (BR)
NATIONAL HEARING SERVICES INC
UNITRON HEARING DIVISION
(*Suby of* SONOVA HOLDING AG)
20 Beasley Dr, Kitchener, ON, N2E 1Y6
(519) 895-0100
Emp Here 150
SIC 8731 Commercial physical research
   Ara Talaslian

D-U-N-S 24-602-0275   (SL)
NMT MACHINING GROUP INC
290 Shoemaker St, Kitchener, ON, N2E 3E1
(519) 748-5459
Emp Here 60   *Sales* 12,169,800
SIC 3499 Fabricated Metal products, nec
   Nirmal Chatha
   Gord Chatha

D-U-N-S 24-478-4096   (HQ)
PENTAIR CANADA, INC
(*Suby of* PENTAIR PUBLIC LIMITED COMPANY)
269 Trillium Dr, Kitchener, ON, N2E 1W9
(519) 748-5470
Emp Here 21   *Sales* 16,625,910
SIC 5084 Industrial machinery and equipment
   Alan W. Noble
   Ian S Mackinnon

D-U-N-S 25-778-4223   (SL)
POLLOCK, PAUL S. ENTERPRISES LTD
CANADIAN TIRE
1400 Ottawa St S, Kitchener, ON, N2E 4E2
(519) 743-1113
Emp Here 250   *Sales* 144,313,000

SIC 5531 Auto and home supply stores
Paul S. Pollock

D-U-N-S 24-134-0426   (BR)
REGIONAL MUNICIPALITY OF WATERLOO, THE
GRAND RIVER TRANSIT
(*Suby of* REGIONAL MUNICIPALITY OF WATERLOO, THE)
250 Strasburg Rd, Kitchener, ON, N2E 3M6
(519) 585-7597
Emp Here 80
SIC 4173 Bus terminal and service facilities
Kent Seiling

D-U-N-S 20-806-2534   (BR)
SOBEYS CAPITAL INCORPORATED
SOBEYS STORE 852
(*Suby of* EMPIRE COMPANY LIMITED)
1187 Fischer Hallman Rd Suite 852, Kitchener, ON, N2E 4H9
(519) 576-1280
Emp Here 200
SIC 5411 Grocery stores
Chris Mcdonald

D-U-N-S 25-140-4976   (BR)
UNITED PARCEL SERVICE CANADA LTD
UPS
(*Suby of* UNITED PARCEL SERVICE, INC.)
65 Trillium Park Pl, Kitchener, ON, N2E 1X1
(800) 742-5877
Emp Here 110
SIC 7389 Business services, nec

D-U-N-S 24-683-9240   (SL)
VANTAGE ENDOSCOPY INC
(*Suby of* DIPLOMA PLC)
20 Steckle Pl Unit 16, Kitchener, ON, N2E 2C3
(866) 677-4121
Emp Here 30   *Sales* 13,415,220
SIC 5047 Medical and hospital equipment
Kevin Blackburn
Daniel Brown
Craig Gardiner

D-U-N-S 24-319-5042   (BR)
WAL-MART CANADA CORP
WALMART
(*Suby of* WALMART INC.)
1400 Ottawa St S Unit E, Kitchener, ON, N2E 4E2
(519) 576-0921
Emp Here 120
SIC 5311 Department stores
Rick Qushair

D-U-N-S 20-656-2733   (BR)
WATERLOO REGION DISTRICT SCHOOL BOARD
W T TOWNSHEND PUBLIC SCHOOL
(*Suby of* WATERLOO REGION DISTRICT SCHOOL BOARD)
245 Activa Ave, Kitchener, ON, N2E 4A3
(519) 579-1160
Emp Here 75
SIC 8211 Elementary and secondary schools
Barb Brown

D-U-N-S 20-849-6919   (SL)
WINSTON HALL NURSING HOME LTD
VILLAGE OF WINSTON PARK, THE
695 Block Line Rd, Kitchener, ON, N2E 3K1
(519) 576-2430
Emp Here 200   *Sales* 13,713,200
SIC 8051 Skilled nursing care facilities
Ronald Schlegel

Kitchener, ON N2G

D-U-N-S 24-826-7817   (SL)
ABLE-ONE SYSTEMS INC
127 Victoria St S Suite 101, Kitchener, ON, N2G 2B4

(519) 570-9100
Emp Here 45   *Sales* 20,122,830
SIC 5045 Computers, peripherals, and software
Peter Paleczny
Andre Kula

D-U-N-S 25-094-6829   (BR)
AIRBOSS OF AMERICA CORP
AIRBOSS RUBBER COMPOUNDING
(*Suby of* AIRBOSS OF AMERICA CORP)
101 Glasgow St, Kitchener, ON, N2G 4X8
(519) 576-5565
Emp Here 300
SIC 3069 Fabricated rubber products, nec
Robert Dodd

D-U-N-S 20-292-1107   (BR)
BELL MEDIA INC
(*Suby of* BCE INC)
864 King St W, Kitchener, ON, N2G 1E8
(519) 578-1313
Emp Here 105
SIC 4833 Television broadcasting stations
Dennis Watson

D-U-N-S 20-124-3235   (SL)
CENTRAL MEAT MARKET (KITCHENER) LIMITED
CENTRAL FRESH MARKET
760 King St W, Kitchener, ON, N2G 1E6
(519) 576-9400
Emp Here 100   *Sales* 29,347,700
SIC 5411 Grocery stores
Ben Pino
Mike Williamson

D-U-N-S 25-512-1824   (HQ)
CHRISTIE DIGITAL SYSTEMS CANADA INC
CHRISTIE
(*Suby of* USHIO INC.)
809 Wellington St N, Kitchener, ON, N2G 4Y7
(519) 744-8005
Emp Here 600   *Sales* 197,546,400
SIC 3861 Photographic equipment and supplies
Jack Kline
Greg Shepherd
Takeshi Suzuki
Ihor Stech

D-U-N-S 20-802-5234   (HQ)
COMMUNITECH CORPORATION
151 Charles St W Suite 100, Kitchener, ON, N2G 1H6
(519) 888-9944
Emp Here 2   *Sales* 24,568,425
SIC 8611 Business associations
Iain Klugman
Avvey Peters

D-U-N-S 24-011-0619   (HQ)
CONESTOGA COLLEGE COMMUNICATIONS CORPORATION
(*Suby of* CONESTOGA COLLEGE INSTITUTE OF TECHNOLOGY AND ADVANCED LEARNING)
299 Doon Valley Dr, Kitchener, ON, N2G 4M4
(519) 748-5220
Emp Here 500   *Sales* 59,471,400
SIC 8222 Junior colleges
John Tibbits
Kevin Mullan

D-U-N-S 20-294-4237   (HQ)
CONESTOGA COLLEGE INSTITUTE OF TECHNOLOGY AND ADVANCED LEARNING
299 Doon Valley Dr, Kitchener, ON, N2G 4M4
(519) 748-5220
Sales 69,383,300
SIC 8222 Junior colleges
John Tibbits

D-U-N-S 25-696-9080   (SL)
CONESTOGA STUDENTS INCORPORATED
CSI
299 Doon Valley Dr, Kitchener, ON, N2G 4M4

(519) 748-5131
Emp Here 100   *Sales* 14,287,900
SIC 8641 Civic and social associations
Sheena Sonser

D-U-N-S 20-068-0283   (BR)
CORPORATION OF THE CITY OF KITCHENER
(*Suby of* CORPORATION OF THE CITY OF KITCHENER)
200 King St W, Kitchener, ON, N2G 4V6
(519) 741-2345
Emp Here 100
SIC 1611 Highway and street construction
Greg Hummel

D-U-N-S 24-936-5164   (BR)
CTV SPECIALTY TELEVISION INC
AFFILIATED: BELL CANADA
(*Suby of* BCE INC)
864 King St W, Kitchener, ON, N2G 1E8

Emp Here 130
SIC 4833 Television broadcasting stations
Dennis Watson

D-U-N-S 20-201-8573   (HQ)
D2L CORPORATION
151 Charles St W Suite 400, Kitchener, ON, N2G 1H6
(519) 772-0325
Emp Here 1   *Sales* 180,984,800
SIC 7373 Computer integrated systems design
John Baker
Yvonne Bell
April Oman
Anna Forgione
Cheryl Ainoa
Puneet Arora
Jeremy Auger
Melissa Howatson
Nick Oddson

D-U-N-S 20-778-8659   (BR)
DELOITTE LLP
(*Suby of* DELOITTE LLP)
195 Joseph St, Kitchener, ON, N2G 1J6
(519) 650-7600
Emp Here 170
SIC 8721 Accounting, auditing, and bookkeeping
Adam Burke

D-U-N-S 20-414-2939   (HQ)
DELTA ELEVATOR COMPANY LIMITED
509 Mill St, Kitchener, ON, N2G 2Y5
(519) 745-5789
Sales 16,310,520
SIC 7699 Repair services, nec
Andrew Friedel
Walter Guderian
Evelyn Guderian

D-U-N-S 24-089-9216   (BR)
DELTA HOTELS LIMITED
(*Suby of* GOVERNMENT OF THE PROVINCE OF BRITISH COLUMBIA)
105 King St E, Kitchener, ON, N2G 2K8
(519) 569-4588
Emp Here 150
SIC 8741 Management services
Zubair Siddiqi

D-U-N-S 25-561-1550   (BR)
G4S SECURE SOLUTIONS (CANADA) LTD
(*Suby of* G4S PLC)
1448 King St E, Kitchener, ON, N2G 2N7

Emp Here 200
SIC 7381 Detective and armored car services

D-U-N-S 24-009-1413   (HQ)
GRAND RIVER HOSPITAL CORPORATION
835 King St W, Kitchener, ON, N2G 1G3
(519) 742-3611
Emp Here 1,900   *Sales* 289,807,720
SIC 8062 General medical and surgical hospi-

tals
Malcolm Maxwell
Tracy Elop
Jeff Evans
Ted Bleaney
D'arcy Delamere
Pamela Maki
Ashok Sharma
William Weiler
David Uffelmann
Barry Cheal

D-U-N-S 20-775-3067   (HQ)
HOUSE OF FRIENDSHIP
51 Charles St E, Kitchener, ON, N2G 2P3
(519) 742-8327
Emp Here 10   *Sales* 179,825,125
SIC 8699 Membership organizations, nec
Elizabeth Mcnair
Keith Cressman
Brian Knight
Lester Kehl
Trent Bauman

D-U-N-S 24-664-8372   (HQ)
K-W HABILITATION SERVICES
99 Ottawa St S, Kitchener, ON, N2G 3S8
(519) 744-6307
Emp Here 100   *Sales* 32,141,000
SIC 8361 Residential care
Jeff Collins
Ann Bilodeau

D-U-N-S 20-557-0229   (SL)
KITCHENER-WILMOT HYDRO INC
301 Victoria St S, Kitchener, ON, N2G 4L2
(519) 745-4771
Emp Here 170   *Sales* 115,578,580
SIC 4911 Electric services
Jerry Van Ooteghem
Margaret Nanninga

D-U-N-S 24-365-0103   (HQ)
MIOVISION TECHNOLOGIES INCORPORATED
137 Glasgow St Suite 110, Kitchener, ON, N2G 4X8
(519) 513-2407
Sales 10,092,740
SIC 7371 Custom computer programming services
Kurtis Mcbride
Anthony Brijpaul
Kevin Madill

D-U-N-S 20-943-0123   (HQ)
MTD PRODUCTS LIMITED
LES DISTRIBUTION R.V.I, DIR OF
(*Suby of* MTD HOLDINGS INC.)
97 Kent Ave, Kitchener, ON, N2G 3R2
(519) 579-5500
Emp Here 173   *Sales* 97,546,000
SIC 5083 Farm and garden machinery
Robert Moll
John Walter Norman
Edward Henderson
Jean Hlay

D-U-N-S 25-204-5281   (BR)
MTD PRODUCTS LIMITED
MODERN POWER PRODUCTS, DIV OF
(*Suby of* MTD HOLDINGS INC.)
97 Kant Ave, Kitchener, ON, N2G 4J1
(519) 579-5500
Emp Here 100
SIC 5083 Farm and garden machinery
John Norman

D-U-N-S 25-095-3965   (BR)
NORDIA INC
(*Suby of* PLATINUM EQUITY, LLC)
160 King St E Suite 400, Kitchener, ON, N2G 4L3
(519) 579-8906
Emp Here 400
SIC 4899 Communication services, nec
Robillard Daniel

D-U-N-S 20-316-0809   (SL)
NORTH INC
27 Gaukel St, Kitchener, ON, N2G 1Y6
(888) 777-2546
Emp Here 200   *Sales* 28,836,400
SIC 7371 Custom computer programming services
Stephen Lake
Matthew Bailey
Aaron Grant
Mike Galbraith

D-U-N-S 20-180-6775   (HQ)
ONTARIO SEED CO LIMITED
77 Wellington St S, Kitchener, ON, N2G 2E6
(519) 886-0557
Emp Here 25   *Sales* 37,126,000
SIC 5191 Farm supplies
Scott Uffelman

D-U-N-S 20-117-9988   (HQ)
PEER GROUP HOLDINGS INC
72 Victoria St S Suite 400, Kitchener, ON, N2G 4Y9
(519) 749-9554
Sales 27,335,000
SIC 6712 Bank holding companies
Michael Kropp
Robert P Harris

D-U-N-S 24-918-0647   (HQ)
PEER GROUP INC, THE
(*Suby of* PEER GROUP HOLDINGS INC)
72 Victoria St S Suite 400, Kitchener, ON, N2G 4Y9
(519) 749-9554
Sales 15,845,466
SIC 7372 Prepackaged software
Michael Kropp
Robert P Harris

D-U-N-S 20-124-2245   (SL)
SWANSON, JIM LUMBER LTD
HOME BUILDING CENTRE
166 Park St, Kitchener, ON, N2G 1M8
(519) 743-1404
Emp Here 49   *Sales* 12,399,891
SIC 5211 Lumber and other building materials
Brad Swanson

D-U-N-S 24-889-0980   (BR)
TORSTAR CORPORATION
RECORD, THE
(*Suby of* TORSTAR CORPORATION)
160 King St E, Kitchener, ON, N2G 4E5
(519) 821-2022
Emp Here 375
SIC 2711 Newspapers
Dana Robbins

D-U-N-S 20-125-2087   (HQ)
UNITRON HEARING LTD
UNITRON CONNECT
(*Suby of* SONOVA HOLDING AG)
20 Beasley Dr, Kitchener, ON, N2G 4X1
(519) 895-0100
Sales 40,912,020
SIC 3842 Surgical appliances and supplies
Cameron Hay
Bruce Brown
Jim Nafziger
Darren Farry

D-U-N-S 24-736-8962   (SL)
WALPER TERRACE HOTEL INC
1 King St W, Kitchener, ON, N2G 1A1
(519) 745-4321
Emp Here 100   *Sales* 9,489,900
SIC 7011 Hotels and motels
Brad Lacey

D-U-N-S 25-228-1597   (BR)
WATERLOO REGION DISTRICT SCHOOL BOARD
CAMERON HEIGHTS COLLEGIATE INSTITUTE
(*Suby of* WATERLOO REGION DISTRICT

SCHOOL BOARD)
301 Charles St E, Kitchener, ON, N2G 2P8
(519) 578-8330
Emp Here 140
SIC 8211 Elementary and secondary schools
Ray Teed

D-U-N-S 25-525-6513   (SL)
WOODHOUSE INVESTMENTS INC
207 Madison Ave S Suite 2, Kitchener, ON, N2G 3M7
(519) 749-3790
Emp Here 73   *Sales* 19,093,369
SIC 6712 Bank holding companies
Ken Woodhouse
Doug Woodhouse

D-U-N-S 25-300-6902   (BR)
WORKPLACE SAFETY & INSURANCE BOARD, THE
(*Suby of* WORKPLACE SAFETY & INSURANCE BOARD, THE)
55 King St W Suite 502, Kitchener, ON, N2G 4W1
(800) 387-0750
Emp Here 100
SIC 6331 Fire, marine, and casualty insurance

Kitchener, ON N2H

D-U-N-S 24-563-4605   (SL)
798983 ONTARIO INC
SUZUKI K/W
663 Victoria St N, Kitchener, ON, N2H 5G3

Emp Here 26   *Sales* 12,950,028
SIC 5511 New and used car dealers
Ray Kraishnik
Ron Kraishnik
Ned Kraishnik

D-U-N-S 24-313-2870   (HQ)
ATRIA NETWORKS LP
301 Victoria St N, Kitchener, ON, N2H 5E1
(888) 623-0623
Emp Here 23   *Sales* 22,847,200
SIC 4899 Communication services, nec
Brenda Tithecott

D-U-N-S 20-745-1209   (SL)
BELFIORE'S VALUMART
385 Frederick St, Kitchener, ON, N2H 2P2
(519) 571-7248
Emp Here 60   *Sales* 17,608,620
SIC 5411 Grocery stores
Tony Belfiore

D-U-N-S 24-851-6051   (SL)
BUILDSCALE, INC
VIDYARD
8 Queen St N Unit 1, Kitchener, ON, N2H 2G8
(800) 530-3878
Emp Here 50   *Sales* 10,692,550
SIC 7372 Prepackaged software
Michael Litt
Devon Galloway
Matthew Hodgson
Tyler Lessard

D-U-N-S 25-999-4747   (HQ)
COREWORX INC
22 Frederick St Suite 800, Kitchener, ON, N2H 6M6
(519) 772-3181
Sales 30,515,064
SIC 5045 Computers, peripherals, and software
John K. Gillberry
Allen Boudreaux
Tom Gosling
Erik Vander Ahe
Paul Sunderland
Peter Walker
Dawn Fiander-Mccann

Baxter Mcelroy
Keith Wettlaufer
Steven Airey

D-U-N-S 24-885-6650   (SL)
CORNERSTONE STRUCTRUAL RESTORATION INC
85 Edwin St, Kitchener, ON, N2H 4N7
(519) 745-8121
Emp Here 35   *Sales* 16,475,585
SIC 1542 Nonresidential construction, nec
Dave Romagnoli
Rod Smith

D-U-N-S 20-068-0333   (BR)
CORPORATION OF THE CITY OF KITCHENER
BREITHAUPT COMMUNITY CENTRE
(*Suby of* CORPORATION OF THE CITY OF KITCHENER)
350 Margaret Ave, Kitchener, ON, N2H 4J8
(519) 741-2502
Emp Here 120
SIC 8322 Individual and family services
Denise Keelen

D-U-N-S 20-788-3575   (SL)
CROSSROADS ESSO
DEROS
593 Victoria St N, Kitchener, ON, N2H 5E9
(519) 741-0424
Emp Here 25   *Sales* 12,451,950
SIC 5541 Gasoline service stations
Debbie Despres

D-U-N-S 20-125-0925   (HQ)
E. & E. SEEGMILLER LIMITED
AUTOMATIC WELDING MACHINE SUPPLY CO
305 Arnold St, Kitchener, ON, N2H 6G1
(519) 579-6460
Emp Here 30   *Sales* 11,864,774
SIC 1611 Highway and street construction
Harold Seegmiller
Timothy Seegmiller
William Seegmiller

D-U-N-S 20-816-5522   (SL)
EARLY BIRD COMMUNICATORS INC
111 Water St N, Kitchener, ON, N2H 5B1

Emp Here 175
SIC 7334 Photocopying and duplicating services

D-U-N-S 24-470-7865   (HQ)
FACTORY SHOE (KITCHENER) LTD
FACTORY SHOE
686 Victoria St N, Kitchener, ON, N2H 5G1
(519) 743-2021
Emp Here 15   *Sales* 10,763,760
SIC 5661 Shoe stores
David Sloan

D-U-N-S 20-280-8655   (HQ)
FINANCIAL HORIZONS INCORPORATED
FORCE FINANCIERE EXCEL
(*Suby of* FINANCIAL HORIZONS GROUP INC)
22 Frederick St Suite 112, Kitchener, ON, N2H 6M6
(519) 742-4474
Sales 10,348,810
SIC 6311 Life insurance
John Hamilton
Will Chang
Bertrand Fortier
Marc Lantaigne
James Mcmahon
Duncan Smith
Murray Wallace

D-U-N-S 25-143-5835   (BR)
G4S CASH SOLUTIONS (CANADA) LTD
(*Suby of* G4S PLC)
108 Ahrens St W, Kitchener, ON, N2H 4C3

Emp Here 150

SIC 7381 Detective and armored car services
Will Torrez

D-U-N-S 24-367-0499   (BR)
GDI SERVICES (CANADA) LP
(*Suby of* GDI SERVICES AUX IMMEUBLES INC)
100 Campbell Ave Suite 12, Kitchener, ON, N2H 4X8

Emp Here 100
SIC 7349 Building maintenance services, nec
Peter Horst

D-U-N-S 20-124-5446   (HQ)
GOLDEN WINDOWS LIMITED
888 Guelph St, Kitchener, ON, N2H 5Z6
(519) 579-3810
Emp Here 75   *Sales* 27,291,672
SIC 3089 Plastics products, nec
Paul Kreutner
Tammy Lindner

D-U-N-S 24-194-0571   (BR)
GOWLING WLG (CANADA) LLP
(*Suby of* GOWLING WLG (CANADA) LLP)
50 Queen St N Unit 1020, Kitchener, ON, N2H 6P4
(519) 576-6910
Emp Here 110
SIC 8111 Legal services
Brenda Ashton

D-U-N-S 20-057-0492   (BR)
GOWLING WLG (CANADA) LLP
GOWLINGS
(*Suby of* GOWLING WLG (CANADA) LLP)
50 Queen St N Suite 1020, Kitchener, ON, N2H 6P4
(519) 576-6910
Emp Here 84
SIC 8111 Legal services
John S Doherty

D-U-N-S 24-176-1316   (BR)
GOWLING WLG (CANADA) LLP
(*Suby of* GOWLING WLG (CANADA) LLP)
50 Queen St N Suite 1020, Kitchener, ON, N2H 6P4
(519) 575-7506
Emp Here 108
SIC 8111 Legal services
Michelle Mccallum

D-U-N-S 24-184-0904   (BR)
GOWLING WLG (CANADA) LLP
GOWLING LAFLEUR AND HENDERSON
(*Suby of* GOWLING WLG (CANADA) LLP)
50 Queen St N Suite 1020, Kitchener, ON, N2H 6P4
(519) 576-6910
Emp Here 100
SIC 8111 Legal services
Robert Snyder

D-U-N-S 20-124-5917   (HQ)
HARMAN HEAVY VEHICLE SPECIALISTS LTD
8 Sereda Rd, Kitchener, ON, N2H 4X7
(519) 743-4378
Emp Here 30   *Sales* 15,661,245
SIC 5013 Motor vehicle supplies and new parts
Jay Johnston
Robert Everett

D-U-N-S 25-361-2261   (SL)
HAROLD E. SEEGMILLER HOLDINGS LIMITED
305 Arnold St, Kitchener, ON, N2H 6G1
(519) 579-6460
Emp Here 35   *Sales* 14,677,425
SIC 6712 Bank holding companies
Harold Seegmiller

D-U-N-S 20-719-5694   (HQ)
HOGG FUEL & SUPPLY LIMITED
ECOHOME TECHNOLOGIES

---

5 Hill St, Kitchener, ON, N2H 5T4
(519) 579-5330
Sales 19,546,240
SIC 5983 Fuel oil dealers
Harold Seegmiller
William Seegmiller
John Heeley

D-U-N-S 20-124-6824   (HQ)
JOSEPH & COMPANY INC
REGIONAL WASTE
257 Victoria St N, Kitchener, ON, N2H 5C9
(519) 743-0205
Emp Here 15   *Sales* 10,410,840
SIC 5093 Scrap and waste materials
Max Norris
David Tsarfati

D-U-N-S 24-007-9947   (HQ)
KITCHENER PUBLIC LIBRARY BOARD
85 Queen St N, Kitchener, ON, N2H 2H1
(519) 743-0271
Emp Here 125   *Sales* 13,078,395
SIC 8231 Libraries
Dan Carli
Elizabeth Esenbergs
Lynn Gazzola
Bruce Macneil
Brian Burnley
Berry Vrbanovic

D-U-N-S 24-181-9838   (HQ)
**KITCHENER WATERLOO YOUNG MENS
CHRISTIAN ASSOCIATION, THE**
YMCA OF KITCHENER WATERLOO
460 Frederick St Suite 203, Kitchener, ON,
N2H 2P5
(519) 584-7479
Emp Here 10   *Sales* 359,650,250
SIC 8699 Membership organizations, nec
John Haddock

D-U-N-S 25-239-5231   (HQ)
KITCHENER-WATERLOO YWCA
84 Frederick St, Kitchener, ON, N2H 2L7
(519) 576-8856
Emp Here 90   *Sales* 8,447,120
SIC 8322 Individual and family services
Doris M'timkulu
Vanessa Kuntz

D-U-N-S 20-124-8432   (HQ)
MARKS SUPPLY INC
300 Arnold St, Kitchener, ON, N2H 6E9
(519) 578-5560
Emp Here 30   *Sales* 31,302,180
SIC 5074 Plumbing and heating equipment
and supplies (hydronics)
Robin Todd

D-U-N-S 20-553-6951   (SL)
MAX CANADA INSURANCE COMPANY
(*Suby of* CHELSEA AVONDALE HOLDINGS
(CANADA) INC)
50 Queen St N Unit 710, Kitchener, ON, N2H
6P4
(519) 634-5267
Emp Here 18   *Sales* 18,627,858
SIC 6331 Fire, marine, and casualty insurance
David Wine

D-U-N-S 24-326-9870   (BR)
MCAP SERVICE CORPORATION
(*Suby of* MCAP SERVICE CORPORATION)
101 Frederick St Suite 600, Kitchener, ON,
N2H 6R2
(519) 743-7800
Emp Here 305
SIC 6162 Mortgage bankers and loan corre-
spondents
Steve Maker

D-U-N-S 20-379-2358   (SL)
NATIONAL HEARING SERVICES
50 Queen St N, Kitchener, ON, N2H 6M2

Emp Here 50   *Sales* 16,553,809
SIC 5999 Miscellaneous retail stores, nec

D-U-N-S 25-361-7294   (BR)
NCR CANADA CORP
NCR WATERLOO
(*Suby of* NCR CORPORATION)
580 Weber St E, Kitchener, ON, N2H 1G8

Emp Here 650
SIC 3578 Calculating and accounting equip-
ment
Tim Willowshby

D-U-N-S 20-124-9067   (SL)
NELCO MECHANICAL LIMITED
77 Edwin St, Kitchener, ON, N2H 4N7
(519) 744-6511
Emp Here 75   *Sales* 17,479,875
SIC 1711 Plumbing, heating, air-conditioning

D-U-N-S 24-865-6808   (SL)
ONTARIO ECONOMIC DEVELOPMENT
30 Duke St W Suite 906, Kitchener, ON, N2H
3W5
(519) 571-6074
Emp Here 24   *Sales* 12,748,968
SIC 6211 Security brokers and dealers
Peter Hui

D-U-N-S 25-606-4932   (HQ)
**PARENTS FOR COMMUNITY LIVING
KITCHENER WATERLOO INC**
82 Weber St E, Kitchener, ON, N2H 1C7
(519) 742-5849
Emp Here 40   *Sales* 10,676,720
SIC 8399 Social services, nec
Kathy Loveys

D-U-N-S 20-360-0577   (SL)
QUARTERHILL INC
30 Duke St W Suite 604, Kitchener, ON, N2H
3W5
(613) 688-1693
Emp Here 361   *Sales* 77,401,000
SIC 4899 Communication services, nec
Douglas Parker
Prashant Watchmaker
Russ Stuebing
Neil Urquuhart
Shaun Mcewan
John Gillberry
James Skippen
Paul Mccarten
Richard Shorkey
Roxanne Anderson

D-U-N-S 20-116-0749   (SL)
ROME SALES INC
100 Campbell Ave Unit 2, Kitchener, ON, N2H
4X8
(519) 883-4105
Emp Here 70   *Sales* 31,445,330
SIC 7389 Business services, nec
Julia Olsen

D-U-N-S 20-266-6835   (HQ)
ROME TRANSPORTATION INC
ROME LOGISTICS
100 Campbell Ave Unit 2, Kitchener, ON, N2H
4X8
(519) 883-4105
Emp Here 16   *Sales* 44,681,764
SIC 4731 Freight transportation arrangement
Erik Olsen
Derrick Stroebel
Melissa Schaefer

D-U-N-S 24-803-5086   (HQ)
SARONA ASSET MANAGEMENT INC
55 Victoria St N Unit K, Kitchener, ON, N2H
5B7
(519) 883-7557
Sales 14,899,986
SIC 6726 Investment offices, nec
Gerhard Pries
Serge Levert-Chiasson
Vivina Berla
Menno Derks
Alex Hartzler

D-U-N-S 25-214-6972   (SL)
STOCKIE, GARY CHEVROLET LIMITED
20 Ottawa St N, Kitchener, ON, N2H 0A4

Emp Here 44   *Sales* 21,915,432
SIC 5511 New and used car dealers
Gary Stockie
Robert Stockie
Margot Stockie

D-U-N-S 20-790-1823   (SL)
VICTORIA ST GAS BAR LTD
DEROS ESSO
593 Victoria St N, Kitchener, ON, N2H 5E9
(519) 741-0424
Emp Here 25   *Sales* 12,451,950
SIC 5541 Gasoline service stations
Deborah Despres

D-U-N-S 24-329-5461   (BR)
**WATERLOO   CATHOLIC   DISTRICT
SCHOOL BOARD**
CATHOLIC EDUCATION CENTER
35a Weber St W, Kitchener, ON, N2H 3Z1
(519) 578-3660
Emp Here 100
SIC 8211 Elementary and secondary schools
Lorita Notten

D-U-N-S 25-228-1472   (BR)
**WATERLOO REGION DISTRICT SCHOOL
BOARD**
EASTWOOD COLLEGIATE INSTITUTE
(*Suby of* WATERLOO REGION DISTRICT
SCHOOL BOARD)
760 Weber St E, Kitchener, ON, N2H 1H6
(519) 742-1848
Emp Here 125
SIC 8211 Elementary and secondary schools
Jeff Klinck

Kitchener, ON N2J

D-U-N-S 20-180-5348   (SL)
FORBES MOTORS INC
165 Weber St S, Kitchener, ON, N2J 4A6
(519) 742-4463
Emp Here 70   *Sales* 44,049,600
SIC 5511 New and used car dealers
Russell Forbes
Ralph Forbes
Jack Forbes
Mike Sweeney
Russ Jones

D-U-N-S 24-947-6888   (HQ)
MANULIFE BANK OF CANADA
(*Suby of* MANULIFE FINANCIAL CORPORA-
TION)
500 King St N Suite 500-Ma, Kitchener, ON,
N2J 4Z6
(519) 747-7000
Sales 20,144,700
SIC 6021 National commercial banks
J. Roman Fedchyshyn
Michael Novak

D-U-N-S 24-219-3084   (HQ)
MANULIFE CANADA LTD
(*Suby of* MANULIFE FINANCIAL CORPORA-
TION)
500 King St N, Kitchener, ON, N2J 4Z6
(519) 747-7000
Emp Here 255   *Sales* 747,938,800
SIC 6311 Life insurance
Marianne Harrison

Kitchener, ON N2K

D-U-N-S 24-562-8490   (SL)
553562 ONTARIO LIMITED

BELL, W S CARTAGE
7 Grand Ave, Kitchener, ON, N2K 1B2
(519) 744-3597
Emp Here 90   *Sales* 13,337,280
SIC 4213 Trucking, except local
Winston Bell
Jason Bell

D-U-N-S 20-641-3825   (SL)
CONESTOGO MECHANICAL INC
50 Dumart Pl, Kitchener, ON, N2K 3C7
(519) 579-6740
Emp Here 55   *Sales* 12,818,575
SIC 1711 Plumbing, heating, air-conditioning
Wes Quickfall
Brenda S. Forristal
Nancy Roberts

D-U-N-S 24-302-1300   (HQ)
CRAWFORD & COMPANY (CANADA) INC
(*Suby of* CRAWFORD & COMPANY)
539 Riverbend Dr, Kitchener, ON, N2K 3S3
(519) 578-5540
Emp Here 120   *Sales* 6,644,545,600
SIC 6411 Insurance agents, brokers, and ser-
vice
Pat Van Bakel
Jim Eso
Gary Gardner
Heather Matthews
Greg Smith

D-U-N-S 20-286-3106   (BR)
**ECONOMICAL MUTUAL INSURANCE COM-
PANY**
(*Suby of* ECONOMICAL MUTUAL INSUR-
ANCE COMPANY)
590 Riverbend Dr, Kitchener, ON, N2K 3S2
(519) 570-8335
Emp Here 300
SIC 6331 Fire, marine, and casualty insurance
Terry Demmone

D-U-N-S 25-297-1288   (BR)
ERNST & YOUNG INC
(*Suby of* ERNST & YOUNG INC)
515 Riverbend Dr, Kitchener, ON, N2K 3S3
(519) 744-1171
Emp Here 100
SIC 8721 Accounting, auditing, and book-
keeping
Greg Mccauley

D-U-N-S 24-360-6543   (HQ)
HENDRIX GENETICS LIMITED
ISA NORTH AMERICA, DIV OF
(*Suby of* HENDRIX GENETICS B.V.)
650 Riverbend Dr Unit C, Kitchener, ON, N2K
3S2
(519) 578-2740
Emp Here 27   *Sales* 43,209,870
SIC 0259 Poultry and eggs, nec
David Libertini

D-U-N-S 24-890-9947   (HQ)
IMPCO ECOTRANS TECHNOLOIGES, INC
100 Hollinger Cres, Kitchener, ON, N2K 2Z3
(519) 576-4270
Emp Here 1   *Sales* 16,401,000
SIC 6712 Bank holding companies
Kam Mofid

D-U-N-S 24-720-5834   (SL)
PETER BENNINGER REALTY LTD
*COLDWELL BANKER PETER BENNIGER
REALTY*
508 Riverbend Dr Suite 352, Kitchener, ON,
N2K 3S2
(519) 743-5211
Emp Here 120   *Sales* 50,266,680
SIC 6531 Real estate agents and managers
Peter Benninger

D-U-N-S 20-322-1767   (HQ)
WESTPORT POWER INC
(*Suby of* WESTPORT FUEL SYSTEMS INC)
100 Hollinger Cres, Kitchener, ON, N2K 2Z3

---

(519) 576-4270
Emp Here 150　　*Sales* 36,934,095
SIC 3714 Motor vehicle parts and accessories
Mark Haskins
Richard Nielsen
Peter Chase

Kitchener, ON N2M

D-U-N-S 25-318-1291　　(BR)
CAVCO FOOD SERVICES LTD
MCDONALD'S
(*Suby of* CAVCO FOOD SERVICES LTD)
431 Highland Rd W, Kitchener, ON, N2M 3C6
(519) 578-8630
Emp Here 100
SIC 5812 Eating places
Brenda Mcnaughton

D-U-N-S 20-532-0398　　(SL)
GLOGOWSKI EURO FOOD LTD
403 Highland Rd W, Kitchener, ON, N2M 3C6
(519) 584-7190
Emp Here 50　　*Sales* 13,707,600
SIC 5411 Grocery stores
Jan Glogowski
Tomasz Chudyk
Bogdan Pelczar

D-U-N-S 25-199-7602　　(SL)
GRAND VALLEY REALTY INC
ROYAL LEPAGE GRAND VALLEY REALTY
370 Highland Rd W, Kitchener, ON, N2M 5J9
(519) 745-7000
Emp Here 45　　*Sales* 12,434,697
SIC 6531 Real estate agents and managers
Keith Church

D-U-N-S 20-124-5990　　(HQ)
HEER'S DECORATING AND DESIGN CENTRES INC
HEER'S DECORATING
428 Gage Ave Unit 4, Kitchener, ON, N2M 5C9
(519) 578-5330
Emp Here 45　　*Sales* 24,503,160
SIC 5198 Paints, varnishes, and supplies
Robert Heer

D-U-N-S 24-335-0456　　(BR)
METRO ONTARIO INC
FOOD BASICS
(*Suby of* METRO INC)
370 Highland Rd W Suite 1, Kitchener, ON, N2M 5J9
(519) 744-4100
Emp Here 120
SIC 5411 Grocery stores
Dave Decoppel

D-U-N-S 20-622-6859　　(BR)
METRO ONTARIO INC
FOOD BASICS
(*Suby of* METRO INC)
851 Fischer Hallman Rd, Kitchener, ON, N2M 5N8
(519) 570-2500
Emp Here 80
SIC 5411 Grocery stores
Dennis Vanderburgh

D-U-N-S 25-996-1019　　(SL)
NEXT CYCLE INC
275 Gage Ave, Kitchener, ON, N2M 2C9
(519) 747-7776
Emp Here 55　　*Sales* 27,407,710
SIC 5136 Men's and boy's clothing
Mahjoub Banafunzi
Amina Banafunzi

D-U-N-S 20-260-9108　　(SL)
OUR PLACE FAMILY RESOURCE AND EARLY YEARS CENTRE
154 Gatewood Rd, Kitchener, ON, N2M 4E4

(519) 571-1626
Emp Here 30　　*Sales* 11,922,420
SIC 8699 Membership organizations, nec
Tracey Weiler

D-U-N-S 25-524-0723　　(BR)
SOBEYS CAPITAL INCORPORATED
SOBEYS
(*Suby of* EMPIRE COMPANY LIMITED)
274 Highland Rd W, Kitchener, ON, N2M 3C5
(519) 744-6561
Emp Here 120
SIC 5411 Grocery stores
Debbie Gouthro

D-U-N-S 24-721-1589　　(HQ)
ST. MARY'S GENERAL HOSPITAL
911 Queens Blvd Suite 453, Kitchener, ON, N2M 1B2
(519) 744-3311
Sales 110,674,282
SIC 8011 Offices and clinics of medical doctors
Don Shilton
Angela Stanley
Blair Egerdie
Gary Higgs
Peter Potts
Dieter Kays
Tom Motz
Stan Nahrgang
Christine Henhoeffer
Viona Duncan

D-U-N-S 20-104-3234　　(SL)
W.F.M.H. ENGINEERING LIMITED
546 Belmont Ave W, Kitchener, ON, N2M 5E3

Emp Here 130　　*Sales* 23,236,070
SIC 8711 Engineering services
Ed Fowler
Tom Polzin

D-U-N-S 20-638-0487　　(HQ)
WALTER FEDY PARTNERSHIP, THE
675 Queen St S Suite 111, Kitchener, ON, N2M 1A1
(519) 576-2150
Emp Here 120　　*Sales* 23,236,070
SIC 8711 Engineering services
Allan Hayes
David Buck
Paul Reitzel

D-U-N-S 25-228-1506　　(BR)
WATERLOO REGION DISTRICT SCHOOL BOARD
FOREST HEIGHTS COLLEGIATE INSTITUTE
(*Suby of* WATERLOO REGION DISTRICT SCHOOL BOARD)
255 Fischer Hallman Rd, Kitchener, ON, N2M 4X8
(519) 744-6567
Emp Here 160
SIC 8211 Elementary and secondary schools
Nelson Cuthbert

D-U-N-S 20-704-3324　　(SL)
WESTMOUNT GOLF AND COUNTRY CLUB LIMITED
WESTMOUNT GOLF & COUNTRY CLUB
50 Inverness Dr, Kitchener, ON, N2M 4Z9
(519) 742-2323
Emp Here 80　　*Sales* 6,283,600
SIC 7997 Membership sports and recreation clubs

Kitchener, ON N2N

D-U-N-S 24-333-1209　　(BR)
DEVTEK AEROSPACE INC
DEVTEK AEROSPACE INC.
(*Suby of* HEROUX-DEVTEK INC)
1665 Highland Rd W, Kitchener, ON, N2N 3K5

(519) 576-8910
Emp Here 170
SIC 3728 Aircraft parts and equipment, nec

D-U-N-S 24-804-7990　　(HQ)
DEVTEK AEROSPACE INC
AEROSPATIALE HOCHELAGA
(*Suby of* HEROUX-DEVTEK INC)
1665 Highland Rd W, Kitchener, ON, N2N 3K5
(519) 576-8910
Emp Here 179　　*Sales* 155,313,900
SIC 3728 Aircraft parts and equipment, nec
Gilles Labbe
Real Belanger
Martin Brassard
Stephane Arsenault
Jean Gravel
Rui Furtado

D-U-N-S 24-382-2207　　(BR)
LOBLAWS INC
REAL CANADIAN SUPERSTORE
(*Suby of* LOBLAW COMPANIES LIMITED)
875 Highland Rd W Suite 178, Kitchener, ON, N2N 2Y2
(519) 745-4781
Emp Here 240
SIC 5411 Grocery stores
Jeff Rettinger

D-U-N-S 25-321-4290　　(BR)
REVERA LONG TERM CARE INC
FOREST HEIGHTS LONG TERM CARE CENTER
(*Suby of* GOVERNMENT OF CANADA)
60 Westheights Dr, Kitchener, ON, N2N 2A8
(519) 576-3320
Emp Here 250
SIC 8051 Skilled nursing care facilities
Thomas Wellner

D-U-N-S 20-710-7421　　(BR)
WATERLOO CATHOLIC DISTRICT SCHOOL BOARD
RESURRECION CATHOLIC SECONDARY SCHOOL
455 University Ave W, Kitchener, ON, N2N 3B9
(519) 741-1990
Emp Here 160
SIC 8211 Elementary and secondary schools
Dan Witt

Kitchener, ON N2P

D-U-N-S 20-344-3200　　(BR)
AECOM CANADA LTD
ARCHITECTURAL DIVISION
(*Suby of* AECOM)
50 Sportsworld Crossing Rd Suite 290, Kitchener, ON, N2P 0A4
(519) 650-5313
Emp Here 90
SIC 8742 Management consulting services
Ray Tufgar

D-U-N-S 20-789-8136　　(SL)
AZGA INSURANCE AGENCY CANADA LTD
(*Suby of* ALLIANZ SE)
4273 King St E, Kitchener, ON, N2P 2E9
(519) 742-2800
Emp Here 200　　*Sales* 949,220,800
SIC 6411 Insurance agents, brokers, and service
Stacey Rous

D-U-N-S 24-888-6137　　(SL)
AZGA SERVICE CANADA INC
ALLIANZ GLOBAL ASSISTANCE
(*Suby of* ALLIANZ SE)
4273 King St E, Kitchener, ON, N2P 2E9
(519) 742-2800
Emp Here 200　　*Sales* 18,156,000
SIC 8322 Individual and family services
Phil Hibbert

Gino Riola
Richard Ollier
Teresa Straatsma
Markus Mueller

D-U-N-S 24-995-8711　　(BR)
BEST BUY CANADA LTD
FUTURE SHOP
(*Suby of* BEST BUY CO., INC.)
50 Gateway Park Dr, Kitchener, ON, N2P 2J4

Emp Here 95
SIC 5731 Radio, television, and electronic stores
Sharolyn Mathieu Vettese

D-U-N-S 24-197-5879　　(HQ)
CHRISTIAN HORIZONS
4278 King St E, Kitchener, ON, N2P 2G5
(519) 650-0966
Emp Here 50　　*Sales* 186,417,800
SIC 8361 Residential care
Janet Nolan
Beth Woof
Angelica Mckay

D-U-N-S 24-886-0132　　(BR)
COSTCO WHOLESALE CANADA LTD
COSTCO
(*Suby of* COSTCO WHOLESALE CORPORATION)
4438 King St E Suite 512, Kitchener, ON, N2P 2G4
(519) 650-3662
Emp Here 180
SIC 5399 Miscellaneous general merchandise
Ken Shantz

D-U-N-S 24-991-4771　　(BR)
HOME DEPOT OF CANADA INC
(*Suby of* THE HOME DEPOT INC)
100 Gateway Park Dr, Kitchener, ON, N2P 2J4
(519) 650-3900
Emp Here 200
SIC 5251 Hardware stores
Craig Ingram

D-U-N-S 24-060-2904　　(SL)
KIESWETTER MOTORS INC
4202 King St E, Kitchener, ON, N2P 2G5
(519) 653-2540
Emp Here 50　　*Sales* 24,903,900
SIC 5521 Used car dealers
Malcolm Kieswetter Jr
Robert Kieswetter

D-U-N-S 24-744-9176　　(SL)
PAULTOM MOTORS LIMITED
KITCHENER HONDA
3800 King St E, Kitchener, ON, N2P 2G5
(519) 744-4119
Emp Here 25　　*Sales* 12,451,950
SIC 5511 New and used car dealers
Paul Leung

D-U-N-S 24-423-7046　　(SL)
RESTAURANT INNOVATIONS INC
MOOSE WINOOSKI'S
20 Heldmann Rd, Kitchener, ON, N2P 0A6
(519) 653-9660
Emp Here 80　　*Sales* 3,641,520
SIC 5812 Eating places
Thomas (Tom) Wideman

D-U-N-S 20-710-7447　　(BR)
WATERLOO CATHOLIC DISTRICT SCHOOL BOARD
BLESSED KATERI SCHOOL
560 Pioneer Dr, Kitchener, ON, N2P 1P2
(519) 895-1716
Emp Here 331
SIC 8211 Elementary and secondary schools
Bill Haber

D-U-N-S 24-058-9259　　(HQ)
YOUR NEIGHBOURHOOD CREDIT UNION LIMITED
38 Executive Pl, Kitchener, ON, N2P 2N4

---

(519) 804-9190
Emp Here 10   *Sales* 14,276,523
SIC 6062 State credit unions
  Rmoew Gallant
  Jim Conlin

Kitchener, ON N2R

D-U-N-S 20-416-4982   (HQ)
8262900 CANADA INC
CAREPARTNERS
139 Washburn Dr, Kitchener, ON, N2R 1S1
(519) 748-5002
Sales 504,913,500
SIC 8741 Management services
  Linda Knight
  Roy Cramp
  Cathy Walker
  Dwight Winfield
  Linda Deans
  Karen Macneil
  Jeff Bond

D-U-N-S 20-293-5003   (SL)
BARBARIAN SPORTSWEAR INC
575 Trillium Dr, Kitchener, ON, N2R 1J9
(519) 895-1932
Emp Here 100   *Sales* 13,667,400
SIC 2329 Men's and boy's clothing, nec
  Steve Wagner

D-U-N-S 20-100-4541   (SL)
BLM DECK DIVISION INC
120 Mcbrine Dr, Kitchener, ON, N2R 1E7
(519) 894-0008
Emp Here 30   *Sales* 15,599,010
SIC 4731 Freight transportation arrangement
  James Mcconnell

D-U-N-S 25-246-5026   (SL)
BLM GROUP INC, THE
BLM TRANSPORTATION GROUP
120 Mcbrine Dr, Kitchener, ON, N2R 1E7
(519) 748-9880
Emp Here 200   *Sales* 41,141,200
SIC 4213 Trucking, except local
  James Mcconnell

D-U-N-S 24-322-2366   (BR)
BOEHMER BOX LP
(*Suby of* BOEHMER BOX LP)
1560 Battler Rd, Kitchener, ON, N2R 1J6
(519) 576-2480
Emp Here 300
SIC 2652 Setup paperboard boxes
  Terry Macleod

D-U-N-S 20-255-6762   (HQ)
CAREPARTNERS INC
139 Washburn Dr, Kitchener, ON, N2R 1S1
(519) 748-5002
Sales 114,124,200
SIC 8011 Offices and clinics of medical doctors
  Linda Knight

D-U-N-S 24-426-0399   (SL)
CLEARPATH ROBOTICS INC
1425 Strasburg Rd Unit 2a, Kitchener, ON, N2R 1H2
(519) 513-2416
Emp Here 170   *Sales* 31,706,020
SIC 8742 Management consulting services
  Matthew Rendall
  Bryan Webb
  Ryan Gariepy

D-U-N-S 20-124-3482   (HQ)
COBER PRINTING LIMITED
COBER
1351 Strasburg Rd, Kitchener, ON, N2R 1H2
(519) 745-7136
Emp Here 160   *Sales* 20,234,151
SIC 2752 Commercial printing, lithographic
  Peter Cober

Todd Cober

D-U-N-S 20-765-1758   (SL)
DIVA INTERNATIONAL INC
222 Mcintyre Dr, Kitchener, ON, N2R 1E8
(519) 896-9103
Emp Here 31   *Sales* 13,243,859
SIC 5122 Drugs, proprietaries, and sundries
  Francine Chambers
  Carinne Chambers

D-U-N-S 24-652-5356   (BR)
FIRSTCANADA ULC
(*Suby of* FIRSTGROUP PLC)
40 Mcbrine Dr, Kitchener, ON, N2R 1E7
(519) 748-4777
Emp Here 100
SIC 4151 School buses

D-U-N-S 20-158-3585   (SL)
GROWER'S CHOICE LANDSCAPE PRODUCTS INC
LANDSCAPE SUPPLY DEPOT
1720 Huron Rd, Kitchener, ON, N2R 1R6
(519) 748-6551
Emp Here 100   *Sales* 24,432,800
SIC 5992 Florists
  Michael Milloy
  Blaire Gateman

D-U-N-S 24-924-9749   (HQ)
MCINTYRE GROUP OFFICE SERVICES INC
825 Trillium Dr, Kitchener, ON, N2R 1J9
(519) 740-7636
Sales 36,927,900
SIC 1799 Special trade contractors, nec
  Dean Mcintyre

D-U-N-S 20-629-6576   (HQ)
PACA INDUSTRIAL DISTRIBUTION LTD
WHD CANADA
84 Mcbrine Pl, Kitchener, ON, N2R 1H3
(519) 748-5650
Emp Here 24   *Sales* 11,400,624
SIC 5084 Industrial machinery and equipment
  Richard Hodgson
  Carolyn Hodgson

D-U-N-S 20-278-9228   (SL)
PRINTERON INC
(*Suby of* HP INC.)
221 Mcintyre Dr, Kitchener, ON, N2R 1G1
(519) 748-2848
Emp Here 200   *Sales* 38,754,800
SIC 2711 Newspapers
  Angus Cunningham
  Kenneth Noreikis
  Kwang Seuk Kim
  Michael Park
  Holly Snider

D-U-N-S 20-414-4737   (SL)
PWO CANADA INCORPORATED
(*Suby of* PROGRESS-WERK OBERKIRCH AG)
255 Mcbrine Dr, Kitchener, ON, N2R 1G7
(519) 893-6880
Emp Here 150   *Sales* 36,484,650
SIC 3469 Metal stampings, nec
  Volker Simon
  Karl Schreyer
  Bernd Bartmann
  Johannes Obrecht

D-U-N-S 24-079-2341   (SL)
RAPID PRECISION MACHINING & GEARING LTD
RAPID GEAR
1596 Strasburg Rd, Kitchener, ON, N2R 1E9
(519) 748-4828
Emp Here 69   *Sales* 15,318,069
SIC 3566 Speed changers, drives, and gears
  Julian Sabados
  Ana Sabados

D-U-N-S 24-094-5001   (SL)
SANI-GEAR INC
SANI-GEAR FIRE

545 Trillium Dr Unit 4, Kitchener, ON, N2R 1J4
(519) 893-1235
Emp Here 25   *Sales* 11,230,475
SIC 7389 Business services, nec
  Inge Pudelek

D-U-N-S 24-220-6738   (HQ)
THINGS ENGRAVED INC
THINGS ENGRAVED
(*Suby of* UCH,INC.)
61 Mcbrine Pl, Kitchener, ON, N2R 1H5
(519) 748-2211
Emp Here 40   *Sales* 91,768,500
SIC 5947 Gift, novelty, and souvenir shop
  Michael Serruya
  Michael Serruya
  Joseph Cabral
  Jordan Schwartz
  Simon Serruya
  Aaron Serruya

D-U-N-S 25-330-4554   (HQ)
ULTRA MANUFACTURING LIMITED
MITCHELL PLASTIC, DIV OF
60 Washburn Dr, Kitchener, ON, N2R 1S2
(519) 893-3831
Emp Here 370   *Sales* 181,497,120
SIC 3089 Plastics products, nec
  Joe D'angelo

D-U-N-S 25-671-4759   (BR)
VENTRA GROUP CO
VENTRA PLASTIC KITCHENER
(*Suby of* FLEX-N-GATE LLC)
675 Trillium Dr, Kitchener, ON, N2R 1G6
(519) 895-0290
Emp Here 150
SIC 3714 Motor vehicle parts and accessories
  Allan Wood

D-U-N-S 20-605-7176   (SL)
WATERLOO BEDDING COMPANY, LIMITED
WATERLOO BEDDING
(*Suby of* STRYKER CORPORATION)
825 Trillium Dr, Kitchener, ON, N2R 1J9

Emp Here 105
SIC 2515 Mattresses and bedsprings
  A. Leigh Harrington
  George Eydt
  Thomas Steward
  Habib Gorgi
  Frank Lumbar
  Russell Banks

D-U-N-S 20-125-2483   (HQ)
WEBER SUPPLY COMPANY INC
CENTRAL DISTRIBUTION CENTRE
1830 Strasburg Rd, Kitchener, ON, N2R 1E9
(519) 888-4200
Emp Here 112   *Sales* 86,328,210
SIC 5085 Industrial supplies
  David Kent Weber
  Jane Weber
  Rob Sutherland

Kleinburg, ON L0J

D-U-N-S 24-133-6473   (SL)
BEST CHOICE OCEAN CONTAINER TERMINAL INC
11339 Albion Vaughan Rd, Kleinburg, ON, L0J 1C0

Emp Here 100   *Sales* 14,819,200
SIC 4214 Local trucking with storage
  Parker Chan
  Mimi Chan

D-U-N-S 24-138-2076   (SL)
BULK TRANSFER SYSTEMS INC
11339 Albion Vaughan Rd, Kleinburg, ON, L0J 1C0
(905) 893-2626
Emp Here 150   *Sales* 30,855,900

SIC 4212 Local trucking, without storage
  Dario Muscillo

D-U-N-S 25-319-1050   (SL)
C. VALLEY PAVING LTD
10535 Hwy 50, Kleinburg, ON, L0J 1C0
(416) 736-4220
Emp Here 40   *Sales* 11,340,960
SIC 1611 Highway and street construction
  Vince Borzenllino

D-U-N-S 20-288-3299   (SL)
COPPER CREEK LIMITED PARTNERSHIP
COPPER CREEK GOLF CLUB
11191 Hwy 27, Kleinburg, ON, L0J 1C0
(905) 893-3370
Emp Here 150   *Sales* 11,781,750
SIC 7992 Public golf courses
  Chris Neale

D-U-N-S 20-010-1726   (SL)
GOLD FREIGHT
11339 Albion Vaughan Line, Kleinburg, ON, L0J 1C0
(905) 893-0700
Emp Here 20   *Sales* 10,399,340
SIC 4731 Freight transportation arrangement

D-U-N-S 20-643-6482   (SL)
GUSGO TRANSPORT LP
(*Suby of* CLEARSTREAM ENERGY SERVICES INC)
7050 Major Mackenzie Dr, Kleinburg, ON, L0J 1C0
(905) 893-9930
Emp Here 80   *Sales* 16,456,480
SIC 4213 Trucking, except local
  Gus Gougoulias

D-U-N-S 20-879-7399   (SL)
MCMICHAEL CANADIAN ART COLLECTION
10365 Islington Ave, Kleinburg, ON, L0J 1C0
(905) 893-1121
Emp Here 100   *Sales* 9,136,900
SIC 8412 Museums and art galleries
  Mary Benvenuto
  Alexander Meadu
  Ian A. C. Dejardin

D-U-N-S 20-515-2486   (BR)
PARSEC INTERMODAL OF CANADA LIMITED
VAUGHN YARD, THE
(*Suby of* PARSEC INC.)
6830 Rutherford Rd, Kleinburg, ON, L0J 1C0
(888) 333-8111
Emp Here 85
SIC 1629 Heavy construction, nec
  Derrick Dibbons

D-U-N-S 24-057-2636   (SL)
SANT, GEORGE & SONS LTD
11831 Cold Creek Rd Suite 1, Kleinburg, ON, L0J 1C0
(905) 893-1592
Emp Here 40   *Sales* 15,451,720
SIC 1531 Operative builders
  Daniel Sant
  Ronald Sant
  Richard Sant

D-U-N-S 20-129-5045   (HQ)
TANK TRUCK TRANSPORT INC
11339 Albion Vaughan Rd, Kleinburg, ON, L0J 1C0
(905) 893-3447
Emp Here 30   *Sales* 20,570,600
SIC 4213 Trucking, except local
  John Lynde

D-U-N-S 25-999-1425   (SL)
VILLA COLOMBO VAUGHAN
10443 Hwy 27, Kleinburg, ON, L0J 1C0
(289) 202-2222
Emp Here 49   *Sales* 11,412,639
SIC 6513 Apartment building operators
  Valeria De Simone

Komoka, ON N0L

D-U-N-S 24-539-0265　　(SL)
C & C INSURANCE CONSULTANTS LTD
22425 Jefferies Rd Unit 6, Komoka, ON, N0L
1R0
(519) 657-1446
Emp Here 21　　*Sales* 12,178,404
SIC 6411 Insurance agents, brokers, and ser-
vice
Jeffrey Ische
William Alex Campbell

D-U-N-S 25-104-0507　　(SL)
JPW SYSTEMS INC
30 Doan Dr, Komoka, ON, N0L 1R0
(519) 474-9797
Emp Here 25　　*Sales* 11,179,350
SIC 5072 Hardware
Paul Wraith
Jo-Anne Wraith

D-U-N-S 24-744-1652　　(SL)
MELCHERS CONSTRUCTION LIMITED
22662 Komoka Rd, Komoka, ON, N0L 1R0
(519) 473-4149
Emp Here 36　　*Sales* 11,479,284
SIC 1521 Single-family housing construction
Ted Melchers

D-U-N-S 24-355-3208　　(SL)
**OMNI HEALTH COUNTRY TERRACE NURS-
ING HOME**
COUNTRY TERRACE
10072 Oxbow Dr, Komoka, ON, N0L 1R0
(519) 657-2955
Emp Here 120　　*Sales* 8,227,920
SIC 8051 Skilled nursing care facilities
Karen Dann

L'Orignal, ON K0B

D-U-N-S 25-503-9828　　(HQ)
**CONSEIL SCOLAIRE DE DISTRICT
CATHOLIQUE DE L'EST ONTARIEN**
CSDCEO
875 County Road 17, L'Orignal, ON, K0B 1K0
(613) 675-4691
Emp Here 100　　*Sales* 138,766,600
SIC 8211 Elementary and secondary schools

D-U-N-S 24-102-6889　　(SL)
IVACO ROLLING MILLS 2004 L.P.
IVACO ROLLING MILLS
1040 Hwy 17, L'Orignal, ON, K0B 1K0
(613) 675-4671
Emp Here 500　　*Sales* 90,694,000
SIC 3312 Blast furnaces and steel mills
Luc Lachapelle
Joseph Olenick

La Salette, ON N0E

D-U-N-S 24-556-5601　　(SL)
B. & C. NIGHTINGALE FARMS LTD
1931 Windham Rd 19 Rr 1, La Salette, ON,
N0E 1H0
(519) 582-2461
Emp Here 65　　*Sales* 17,050,085
SIC 0191 General farms, primarily crop
William Nightingale Sr

D-U-N-S 25-366-7570　　(SL)
NIGHTINGALE FARMS LIMITED
1492 Windham Rd 19, La Salette, ON, N0E
1H0
(519) 582-2461
Emp Here 250　　*Sales* 42,256,250
SIC 0191 General farms, primarily crop

William G. Nightingale

Lakefield, ON K0L

D-U-N-S 20-026-2371　　(SL)
BLETSOE ENTERPRISES INC
LAKEFIELD IGA SUPERMARKET
1 Queen St, Lakefield, ON, K0L 2H0
(705) 652-3202
Emp Here 80　　*Sales* 23,478,160
SIC 5411 Grocery stores
Ross Bletsoe
Carol Bletsoe

D-U-N-S 20-292-0158　　(BR)
EXTENDICARE INC
EXTENDICARE LAKEFIELD
(*Suby of* EXTENDICARE INC)
19 Fraser St, Lakefield, ON, K0L 2H0
(705) 652-7112
Emp Here 120
SIC 8051 Skilled nursing care facilities
John Gray

D-U-N-S 20-628-9076　　(SL)
HAMILTON, ELLWOOD ENTERPRISES LTD
HAMILTON ELLWOOD BUS LINES
1325 Old Young'S Point Rd, Lakefield, ON,
K0L 2H0
(705) 652-6090
Emp Here 75　　*Sales* 1,824,018
SIC 4151 School buses
Lisa Howie

D-U-N-S 20-125-3937　　(HQ)
KINGDON LUMBER LIMITED
KINGDON TIM-BR MART
34 Deyncourt St, Lakefield, ON, K0L 2H0
(705) 652-3361
Emp Here 30　　*Sales* 16,059,120
SIC 5211 Lumber and other building materials
Donald Dyck

D-U-N-S 20-537-2857　　(SL)
SAVAGE ARMS (CANADA) INC
(*Suby of* CALIBER COMPANY)
248 Water St, Lakefield, ON, K0L 2H0
(705) 652-8000
Emp Here 120　　*Sales* 23,050,200
SIC 3484 Small arms
Al Kasper

D-U-N-S 24-426-6016　　(BR)
SGS CANADA INC
3347 Lakefield Rd Rr 3, Lakefield, ON, K0L
2H0
(705) 652-2000
Emp Here 350
SIC 8734 Testing laboratories
Chris Bates

Lakeside, ON N0M

D-U-N-S 20-179-2793　　(HQ)
HUTTON TRANSPORT LIMITED
962979 19th Line, Lakeside, ON, N0M 2G0
(519) 349-2233
Emp Here 80　　*Sales* 1,580,378
SIC 4212 Local trucking, without storage
Bradley Grant

Lancaster, ON K0C

D-U-N-S 24-270-1530　　(SL)
MUNRO AGROMART LTD
6011 34 Hwy, Lancaster, ON, K0C 1N0
(613) 347-3063
Emp Here 9　　*Sales* 10,893,573
SIC 5153 Grain and field beans

Bruce Munro
Rhona Munro
Edward Oke

D-U-N-S 24-435-7463　　(HQ)
ROZON INSURANCE BROKERS LTD
150 Main St N, Lancaster, ON, K0C 1N0
(613) 347-7600
Emp Here 25　　*Sales* 30,530,160
SIC 6411 Insurance agents, brokers, and ser-
vice
Todd Rozon

Langton, ON N0E

D-U-N-S 20-287-3881　　(SL)
SCHONBERGER FAMILY FARMS LIMITED
1412 Concession 1 Rd Enr, Langton, ON, N0E
1G0
(519) 875-2988
Emp Here 30　　*Sales* 10,274,010
SIC 0161 Vegetables and melons

Lansdowne, ON K0E

D-U-N-S 25-144-8148　　(SL)
**FRIENDS OF CHARLESTON LAKE PARK,
THE**
CHARLES LAKE PROVINCIAL PK
148 Woodvale Rd, Lansdowne, ON, K0E 1L0
(613) 659-2065
Emp Here 12　　*Sales* 12,418,572
SIC 6311 Life insurance
Claudette Weststrate

D-U-N-S 20-652-4717　　(SL)
THOUSAND ISLANDS BRIDGE CO
THOUSAND ISLANDS BRIDGE AUTHOITY
379 Hwy 137, Lansdowne, ON, K0E 1L0
(613) 659-2308
Emp Here 150　　*Sales* 100,033,800
SIC 4785 Inspection and fixed facilities
Robert Horr

Lasalle, ON N9H

D-U-N-S 24-560-7549　　(BR)
**WINDSOR-ESSEX CATHOLIC DISTRICT
SCHOOL BOARD, THE**
HOLY CROSS ELEMENTARY SCHOOL
(*Suby of* WINDSOR-ESSEX CATHOLIC DIS-
TRICT SCHOOL BOARD, THE)
2555 Sandwich West Pky, Lasalle, ON, N9H
2P7
(519) 972-6050
Emp Here 80
SIC 8211 Elementary and secondary schools
Steve Bellaire

D-U-N-S 25-033-3986　　(BR)
ZEHRMART INC
ZEHRS MARKETS
(*Suby of* LOBLAW COMPANIES LIMITED)
5890 Malden Rd, Lasalle, ON, N9H 1S4
(519) 966-6030
Emp Here 400
SIC 5411 Grocery stores
Dave Bowden

Lasalle, ON N9J

D-U-N-S 25-357-4594　　(BR)
CENTERLINE (WINDSOR) LIMITED
(*Suby of* CENTERLINE (WINDSOR) LIM-
ITED)

655 Morton Dr, Lasalle, ON, N9J 3T9
(519) 734-8330
Emp Here 150
SIC 3548 Welding apparatus
Michael Beneteau

D-U-N-S 24-977-6766　　(BR)
CENTERLINE (WINDSOR) LIMITED
(*Suby of* CENTERLINE (WINDSOR) LIM-
ITED)
595 Morton Dr, Lasalle, ON, N9J 3T8
(519) 734-6886
Emp Here 100
SIC 3548 Welding apparatus
David Beneteau

D-U-N-S 20-555-0085　　(BR)
**PAPP PLASTICS AND DISTRIBUTING LIM-
ITED**
(*Suby of* PAPP PLASTICS AND DISTRIBUT-
ING LIMITED)
6110 Morton Industrial Pky, Lasalle, ON, N9J
3W3
(519) 734-0700
Emp Here 75
SIC 3089 Plastics products, nec
Michael Papp

Leamington, ON N8H

D-U-N-S 25-531-9956　　(SL)
1196977 ONTARIO LTD
HUY, HOWARD GREENHOUSES
1002 Mersea Road 7, Leamington, ON, N8H
3V8
(519) 324-0631
Emp Here 30　　*Sales* 10,274,010
SIC 0182 Food crops grown under cover
Howard Huy
Zora Huy

D-U-N-S 20-560-1060　　(SL)
1266093 ONTARIO LIMITED
ENNS PLANT FARM
614 Highway 77, Leamington, ON, N8H 3V8
(519) 326-9878
Emp Here 35　　*Sales* 11,986,345
SIC 0182 Food crops grown under cover
Kenneth Enns
Rita Enns
Steve Enns
Shelly Enns

D-U-N-S 20-176-6891　　(SL)
1443190 ONTARIO INC
UE ENCLOSURES
605 County Rd 18, Leamington, ON, N8H 3V5
(519) 322-2264
Emp Here 70　　*Sales* 13,445,950
SIC 3469 Metal stampings, nec
George Bergen

D-U-N-S 24-021-3533　　(SL)
1544982 ONTARIO INC
EWS LEAMINGTON
(*Suby of* ESSEX WELD SOLUTIONS LTD)
50 Victoria Ave N, Leamington, ON, N8H 2W1
(519) 776-9153
Emp Here 50　　*Sales* 10,141,500
SIC 3471 Plating and polishing
John Friesen

D-U-N-S 25-541-3361　　(SL)
745926 ONTARIO LIMITED
T G & G MASTRONARDI
159 Fraser Rd, Leamington, ON, N8H 4E6
(519) 322-2769
Emp Here 52　　*Sales* 14,088,984
SIC 1521 Single-family housing construction
Antonio Mastronardi
Gerry Mastronardi
Gregery Mastronardi

D-U-N-S 24-923-9849　　(SL)

944743 ONTARIO INC
UNI-FAB
477 Highway 77, Leamington, ON, N8H 3V6
(519) 325-1005
Emp Here 109   *Sales* 23,743,361
SIC 1761 Roofing, siding, and sheetMetal work
Abe Fehr

D-U-N-S 25-161-0614   (HQ)
ALL TEMP FOODS LTD
15 Industrial Rd, Leamington, ON, N8H 4W4
(519) 326-8611
Emp Here 40   *Sales* 34,258,657
SIC 5146 Fish and seafoods
Vito Peralta

D-U-N-S 25-203-9961   (SL)
AMCO FARMS INC
523 Wilkinson Dr, Leamington, ON, N8H 1A6
(519) 326-9095
Emp Here 225   *Sales* 38,030,625
SIC 0191 General farms, primarily crop
Fausto Amicone

D-U-N-S 25-203-9052   (SL)
AMCO PRODUCE INC
523 Wilkinson Dr, Leamington, ON, N8H 3V5
(519) 326-9095
Emp Here 250   *Sales* 179,179,000
SIC 5148 Fresh fruits and vegetables
Fausto Amicone
Pasquale Amicone

D-U-N-S 20-559-0842   (SL)
ARMSTRONG TOP PACK LTD
500 County Rd 18, Leamington, ON, N8H 3V5
(519) 326-3273
Emp Here 200   *Sales* 133,781,600
SIC 7389 Business services, nec
Tony Mastronardi
Donald Mastronardi
Dominic Mastronardi
Michael Mastronardi
David Mastronardi
Robert Mastronardi

D-U-N-S 25-524-7876   (HQ)
CAXTON MARK INC
10 Iroquois Rd, Leamington, ON, N8H 3V7
(519) 322-1002
Emp Here 20   *Sales* 17,886,960
SIC 5044 Office equipment
Nicholas Poole

D-U-N-S 25-361-9118   (BR)
CORPORATION OF THE COUNTY OF ESSEX, THE
SUN PARLOR HOMES
(*Suby of* CORPORATION OF THE COUNTY OF ESSEX, THE)
175 Talbot St E, Leamington, ON, N8H 1L9
(519) 326-5731
Emp Here 250
SIC 8361 Residential care
Bill Macdonald

D-U-N-S 20-525-5235   (SL)
DI CIOCCO FARMS INCORPORATED
DI CIOCCO FARMS EASTSIDE
308 Talbot Rd E, Leamington, ON, N8H 3V6
(519) 326-2339
Emp Here 120   *Sales* 20,283,000
SIC 0161 Vegetables and melons
Carmen Di Ciocco
Diane Di Ciocco

D-U-N-S 24-796-5841   (HQ)
ELRINGKLINGER CANADA, INC
(*Suby of* ELRINGKLINGER AG)
1 Seneca Rd Suite 4, Leamington, ON, N8H 5P2
(519) 326-6113
Sales 19,026,655
SIC 3714 Motor vehicle parts and accessories
Stefan Wolf
Thomas Bachle

Thomas Jessulat

D-U-N-S 20-175-8716   (BR)
ELRINGKLINGER CANADA, INC
(*Suby of* ELRINGKLINGER AG)
1 Seneca Rd, Leamington, ON, N8H 5P2
(519) 326-6113
Emp Here 180
SIC 3053 Gaskets; packing and sealing devices

D-U-N-S 20-717-4921   (SL)
ERIE-JAMES LIMITED
102 Queens Ave, Leamington, ON, N8H 3H4
(519) 326-4417
Emp Here 40   *Sales* 33,423,080
SIC 5148 Fresh fruits and vegetables
Mark Slater
James Slater

D-U-N-S 24-848-9242   (BR)
FD ALPHA CANADA ACQUISITION INC
(*Suby of* FORT DEARBORN HOLDING COMPANY, INC.)
128 Oak St W, Leamington, ON, N8H 2B6
(519) 326-3173
Emp Here 225
SIC 2759 Commercial printing, nec
Tony Policella

D-U-N-S 24-419-6833   (SL)
GABRIELE FLOOR & HOME
55 Talbot St W, Leamington, ON, N8H 1M5
(519) 326-5786
Emp Here 45   *Sales* 11,387,655
SIC 5211 Lumber and other building materials
Shelly Gale

D-U-N-S 24-886-5735   (SL)
GREAT LAKES GREENHOUSES INC
834 Mersea Road 4, Leamington, ON, N8H 3V6
(519) 326-7589
Emp Here 300   *Sales* 31,135,520
SIC 0191 General farms, primarily crop
Paul Dyck
Susan Dyck

D-U-N-S 24-325-9350   (SL)
GRECO, ROBERTO DRUGS LTD
SHOPPERS DRUG MART
269 Erie St S Suite 1117, Leamington, ON, N8H 3C4
(519) 326-2663
Emp Here 100   *Sales* 24,432,800
SIC 5912 Drug stores and proprietary stores
Robert Greco

D-U-N-S 24-142-7111   (SL)
GROSSI, T. & SON CONSTRUCTION LTD
33 Princess St Unit 204, Leamington, ON, N8H 5C5
(519) 326-9081
Emp Here 25   *Sales* 11,768,275
SIC 1542 Nonresidential construction, nec
Carl Grossi

D-U-N-S 20-282-5303   (SL)
HIGHBURY CANCO CORPORATION
148 Erie St S, Leamington, ON, N8H 0C3
(519) 322-1288
Emp Here 515   *Sales* 178,030,350
SIC 2099 Food preparations, nec
Sam Diab
Helen Diab

D-U-N-S 20-527-1927   (HQ)
HIGHLINE PRODUCE LIMITED
WELLINGTON MUSHROOM FARM
(*Suby of* SUMMIT FRESH PRODUCE LIMITED)
506 Mersea Road 5, Leamington, ON, N8H 3V5
(519) 326-8643
Emp Here 400   *Sales* 169,082,100
SIC 0182 Food crops grown under cover
Murray O'neil
Wilhelm Zimmermann

Joyce Zimmermann
Harry Enns
Wilmer Pritchard

D-U-N-S 25-033-6013   (SL)
HOWARD HUY FARMS LTD
ULTRA FRESH
932 Mersea Road 7, Leamington, ON, N8H 3V8
(519) 324-0631
Emp Here 30   *Sales* 10,274,010
SIC 0181 Ornamental nursery products
Howard Huy
Zora Huy

D-U-N-S 20-125-9637   (SL)
KEEPSAKE PLANTS LTD
(*Suby of* ARIS HORTICULTURE, INC.)
268 Seacliff Dr W, Leamington, ON, N8H 4C8
(519) 326-6121
Emp Here 50   *Sales* 37,126,000
SIC 5191 Farm supplies
Scott Schaefer
William Rasbach
Dave Kirwin

D-U-N-S 20-753-9412   (SL)
LEAMINGTON CHRYSLER (1992) LTD
170 Oak St W, Leamington, ON, N8H 2B6
(519) 326-9052
Emp Here 26   *Sales* 12,950,028
SIC 5511 New and used car dealers
Micheal Herbert
Timothy Vida

D-U-N-S 20-934-9620   (HQ)
LEAMINGTON DISTRICT MEMORIAL HOSPITAL
ERIE SHORES HEALTHCARE
194 Talbot St W Suite 167, Leamington, ON, N8H 1N9
(519) 326-2373
Sales 31,799,862
SIC 8062 General medical and surgical hospitals
Terry Shields
C. Deter
T. Heinz
B. Colaizzi
R. Stapleton
G. Belanger
David Glass
Tyler Chadwick
Terry Shields
Michelle Boutros

D-U-N-S 24-098-0578   (BR)
LOBLAWS INC
REAL CANADIAN SUPERSTORE
(*Suby of* LOBLAW COMPANIES LIMITED)
201 Talbot St E, Leamington, ON, N8H 3X5
(519) 322-1371
Emp Here 120
SIC 5411 Grocery stores
Mike Tetreault

D-U-N-S 20-108-2919   (SL)
M & M FARMS LTD
331 Talbot St W, Leamington, ON, N8H 4H3
(519) 326-2287
Emp Here 40   *Sales* 13,698,680
SIC 0191 General farms, primarily crop
Michael Mastronardi
Connie Mastronardi

D-U-N-S 20-691-5469   (SL)
MARTENS, W. GREENHOUSES INC
1812 Mersea Road 5, Leamington, ON, N8H 3V6

Emp Here 35   *Sales* 11,986,345
SIC 0181 Ornamental nursery products
William (Bill) Martens
Katharina Martens

D-U-N-S 25-026-5212   (BR)
METRO ONTARIO INC
A & P FOOD STORES

(*Suby of* METRO INC)
288 Erie St S, Leamington, ON, N8H 3C5
(519) 322-1414
Emp Here 200
SIC 5411 Grocery stores
Bruce Mcferison

D-U-N-S 24-684-6919   (SL)
NATURA NATURALS INC
279 Talbot St W, Leamington, ON, N8H 4H3
(877) 786-6286
Emp Here 75   *Sales* 19,673,175
SIC 0182 Food crops grown under cover
Mike A Mastronardi
Claudio Mastronardi
Isolina Mastronardi

D-U-N-S 25-094-6779   (HQ)
NATURE FRESH FARMS INC
634 Mersea Road 7, Leamington, ON, N8H 3V8
(519) 326-8603
Sales 32,445,478
SIC 0182 Food crops grown under cover
Peter Quiring

D-U-N-S 24-684-8316   (SL)
NATURE FRESH FARMS SALES INC
4 Seneca Rd, Leamington, ON, N8H 5H7
(519) 326-1111
Emp Here 50   *Sales* 41,778,850
SIC 5148 Fresh fruits and vegetables
Peter Quiring

D-U-N-S 24-793-5257   (SL)
NEW CASTLE FARM LTD
414 Mersea Road 3, Leamington, ON, N8H 3V5
(519) 322-5411
Emp Here 50   *Sales* 17,123,350
SIC 0191 General farms, primarily crop
Robert Mastronardi

D-U-N-S 20-280-9737   (SL)
ORANGELINE FARMS LIMITED
627 Essex Road 14, Leamington, ON, N8H 3V8
(519) 322-0400
Emp Here 100   *Sales* 26,230,900
SIC 0161 Vegetables and melons
Dufton Richard Kniaziew
David Richard Kniaziew
Pauline Kniaziew

D-U-N-S 24-095-9648   (SL)
PIER-C PRODUCE INC
7r M C R Dr, Leamington, ON, N8H 3N2
(519) 326-8807
Emp Here 140   *Sales* 24,346,700
SIC 0722 Crop harvesting
Doug Pearce

D-U-N-S 20-125-8639   (HQ)
PLANT PRODUCTS INC
50 Hazelton St, Leamington, ON, N8H 1B8
(519) 326-9037
Emp Here 50   *Sales* 58,915,900
SIC 5191 Farm supplies
Chris Stickles
Julie Rieter
Perry Stickles

D-U-N-S 25-542-8492   (SL)
PRISM FARMS LIMITED
731 Mersea Road 6, Leamington, ON, N8H 3V8
(519) 324-9009
Emp Here 40   *Sales* 13,698,680
SIC 0191 General farms, primarily crop
Victor Tiessen
Ryan Tiessen
Michael Tiessen
Dawn Tiessen

D-U-N-S 20-548-7700   (SL)
PURE HOTHOUSE FOODS INC
459 Highway 77, Leamington, ON, N8H 3V6

(519) 326-8444
Emp Here 60   *Sales* 50,134,620
SIC 5148 Fresh fruits and vegetables
Jamie Moracci
Matthew Mastronardi
Jeffrey Moracci
Joseph Moracci

D-U-N-S 25-406-8570   (SL)
PYRAMID FARMS LIMITED
209 Erie St N, Leamington, ON, N8H 3A5
(519) 326-4989
Emp Here 40   *Sales* 13,698,680
SIC 0181 Ornamental nursery products
Dean Tiessen
Jason Tiessen
William Tiessen
Janet Tiessen

D-U-N-S 24-393-0307   (SL)
RICHARD, MARIAN ENTERPRISES LTD
CANADIAN TIRE
262 Erie St S, Leamington, ON, N8H 3C5
(519) 326-8191
Emp Here 100   *Sales* 20,534,300
SIC 5311 Department stores
Marian Richard

D-U-N-S 25-650-0125   (HQ)
SECURITY ONE ALARM SYSTEMS LTD
200 Sherk St, Leamington, ON, N8H 0A8
(519) 326-2020
Emp Here 15   *Sales* 11,179,350
SIC 5063 Electrical apparatus and equipment
Reiner Neumann

D-U-N-S 24-419-5012   (HQ)
SORENSEN GREENHOUSES INC
3 Mill St E, Leamington, ON, N8H 1R6
(519) 322-5024
Sales 19,437,875
SIC 0181 Ornamental nursery products
Claus Sorensen
Cleone Sorensen

D-U-N-S 25-149-9976   (SL)
SOUTH ESSEX FABRICATING INC
4 Seneca Rd, Leamington, ON, N8H 5H7
(519) 322-5995
Emp Here 60   *Sales* 44,551,200
SIC 5191 Farm supplies
Peter Quiring

D-U-N-S 24-382-6927   (SL)
SOUTH POINT CHEVROLET PONTIAC BUICK GMC LTD
108 Erie St N, Leamington, ON, N8H 0A9
(519) 326-3206
Emp Here 21   *Sales* 10,459,638
SIC 5511 New and used car dealers
Julie Fleischmann
John Fleischmann

D-U-N-S 20-786-2095   (SL)
SUN PARLOR HOME
175 Talbot St E, Leamington, ON, N8H 1L9
(519) 326-5731
Emp Here 250   *Sales* 16,070,500
SIC 8361 Residential care
Brian Gregg
Bill Mcdonald

D-U-N-S 24-025-4151   (HQ)
SUN PARLOUR GREENHOUSE GROWERS CO-OPERATIVE LIMITED
230 County Rd 31, Leamington, ON, N8H 3V5
(519) 326-8681
Sales 41,778,850
SIC 5148 Fresh fruits and vegetables
Rick Mastronardi
Michael Anderson
Tom Magri
Steve Enns
Albert Mastronardi
Mike Mastronardi
Dan Zaccardi
Dan Cacciavillani
Robert Magri

D-U-N-S 24-310-3756   (SL)
SUN PARLOUR GROWER SUPPLY LIMITED
(*Suby of* SUN PARLOUR GREENHOUSE GROWERS CO-OPERATIVE LIMITED)
230 County Rd 31, Leamington, ON, N8H 3W2
(519) 326-8681
Emp Here 20   *Sales* 14,850,400
SIC 5191 Farm supplies
Tom Magri
Steve Enns
Albert Mastronardi
Dan Zaccardi
Michael Anderson

D-U-N-S 25-221-3871   (SL)
TRI-B ACRES INC
132 Mersea Road 5, Leamington, ON, N8H 3V5
(519) 326-0042
Emp Here 30   *Sales* 25,067,310
SIC 5148 Fresh fruits and vegetables
Peter J Brunato

D-U-N-S 20-738-6330   (BR)
WAL-MART CANADA CORP
LEAMINGTON SUPERCENTRE STORE # 3164
(*Suby of* WALMART INC.)
304 Erie St S, Leamington, ON, N8H 3C5
(519) 326-3900
Emp Here 200
SIC 5311 Department stores

D-U-N-S 24-488-3922   (HQ)
WIEBE, J. BUILDING MATERIALS LTD
HOME BUILDING CENTRE LEAMINGTON
241 Oak St E, Leamington, ON, N8H 4W8
(519) 326-4474
Emp Here 35   *Sales* 10,881,537
SIC 5211 Lumber and other building materials
John Wiebe

D-U-N-S 24-027-3326   (HQ)
WILL INSURANCE BROKERS LTD
148 Erie St N, Leamington, ON, N8H 3A2
(519) 326-5746
Emp Here 21   *Sales* 26,289,860
SIC 6411 Insurance agents, brokers, and service
Dennis Will

Limoges, ON K0A

D-U-N-S 20-629-5383   (SL)
CAYER, JEAN-CLAUDE ENTERPRISES LTD
708 Limoges Rd, Limoges, ON, K0A 2M0
(613) 443-2293
Emp Here 27   *Sales* 12,073,698
SIC 5072 Hardware
Jean-Claude Cayer
Francine Cayer

D-U-N-S 20-888-9956   (SL)
GENESIS GARDENS INC
ST VIATEUR NURSING HOME
1003 Limoges Rd, Limoges, ON, K0A 2M0
(613) 443-5751
Emp Here 78   *Sales* 5,361,174
SIC 8051 Skilled nursing care facilities
Richard Marleau

Lindsay, ON K9V

D-U-N-S 20-790-1617   (SL)
1254613 ONTARIO LIMITED
HOME HARDWARE LINDSAY
207 Kent St W, Lindsay, ON, K9V 2Y9
(705) 324-4611
Emp Here 23   *Sales* 10,285,002

SIC 5072 Hardware
Harry Morrison

D-U-N-S 20-299-1944   (HQ)
1439037 ONTARIO LTD
HOME BUILDING CENTER
220 Lindsay St S, Lindsay, ON, K9V 2N3
(705) 324-3516
Sales 21,412,160
SIC 5251 Hardware stores
Stephen Gynane
Harry Morrison
Frank Geerlinks

D-U-N-S 24-646-0034   (SL)
1543892 ONTARIO LTD
REID'S VALU-MART
42 Russell St W, Lindsay, ON, K9V 2W9
(705) 328-0622
Emp Here 100   *Sales* 29,347,700
SIC 5411 Grocery stores
Mark Reid

D-U-N-S 20-786-6252   (SL)
381572 ONTARIO LIMITED
T S MANUFACTURING CO
2 Fleetwood Rd, Lindsay, ON, K9V 6H4
(705) 324-3762
Emp Here 75   *Sales* 16,650,075
SIC 3553 Woodworking machinery
Edward C. Smith
Evelyn Smith

D-U-N-S 20-940-7907   (SL)
ARMADA TOOLWORKS LIMITED
(*Suby of* ZYNIK CAPITAL CORPORATION)
6 Lof Dr, Lindsay, ON, K9V 4S5
(705) 328-9599
Emp Here 260   *Sales* 49,066,496
SIC 3089 Plastics products, nec
Chris Van Den Berg

D-U-N-S 24-965-2116   (SL)
CAMERON STEEL INC
52 Walsh Rd Suite 3, Lindsay, ON, K9V 4R3
(705) 878-0544
Emp Here 60   *Sales* 13,320,060
SIC 3599 Industrial machinery, nec
Jim Bogar
James Bogar
Maria Bogar

D-U-N-S 20-732-5270   (BR)
CAMPBELL, JAMES INC
MCDONALD'S
(*Suby of* CAMPBELL, JAMES INC)
333 Kent St W, Lindsay, ON, K9V 2Z7
(705) 324-6668
Emp Here 105
SIC 5812 Eating places
Todd Fournier

D-U-N-S 24-785-3349   (SL)
CANADA BUILDS COMPANY LTD
423 County Rd 36 Unit 2, Lindsay, ON, K9V 4R3
(705) 324-8777
Emp Here 32   *Sales* 10,203,808
SIC 1521 Single-family housing construction
Roy Graham

D-U-N-S 24-062-3124   (HQ)
CARDIOMED SUPPLIES INC
199 St David St, Lindsay, ON, K9V 5K7
(705) 328-2518
Sales 14,309,568
SIC 5047 Medical and hospital equipment
Christian Dube
Raphael Dube
Vera Dube

D-U-N-S 24-316-2344   (BR)
CARESSANT-CARE NURSING AND RETIREMENT HOMES LIMITED
CARESSANT CARE LINDSAY
(*Suby of* CARESSANT-CARE NURSING AND RETIREMENT HOMES LIMITED)
240 Mary St N, Lindsay, ON, K9V 5K5

(705) 324-1913
Emp Here 100
SIC 8051 Skilled nursing care facilities
Judy Sedgley

D-U-N-S 20-810-0201   (BR)
CARESSANT-CARE NURSING AND RETIREMENT HOMES LIMITED
(*Suby of* CARESSANT-CARE NURSING AND RETIREMENT HOMES LIMITED)
114 Mclaughlin Rd, Lindsay, ON, K9V 6L1
(705) 324-0300
Emp Here 110
SIC 8051 Skilled nursing care facilities
Nancy Rooney

D-U-N-S 20-296-0753   (HQ)
COMMONWELL MUTUAL INSURANCE GROUP, THE
336 Angeline St S, Lindsay, ON, K9V 0J8
(705) 324-2146
Sales 101,771,312
SIC 6331 Fire, marine, and casualty insurance
Tim Shauf
Bob Nielson
Reggie Campbell
Terry Malcolm
Kevin Mcbride
Bernard Mcdonell
Dwight Proudfoot
Randy Straeten
Jack Taylor
Anne Marie Thomas

D-U-N-S 20-272-6035   (BR)
CORPORATION OF THE CITY OF KAWARTHA LAKES, THE
CITY OF KAWARTHA LAKES FIRE RESCUE SERVICE
(*Suby of* CORPORATION OF THE CITY OF KAWARTHA LAKES, THE)
9 Cambridge St N, Lindsay, ON, K9V 4C4
(705) 324-5731
Emp Here 400
SIC 7389 Business services, nec
David Guilbauld

D-U-N-S 25-481-5152   (BR)
CORPORATION OF THE CITY OF KAWARTHA LAKES, THE
VICTORIA MANOR
(*Suby of* CORPORATION OF THE CITY OF KAWARTHA LAKES, THE)
220 Angeline St S, Lindsay, ON, K9V 0J8
(705) 324-3558
Emp Here 175
SIC 8361 Residential care
Hildy Nickel

D-U-N-S 20-126-0791   (SL)
DENURE TOURS LTD
71 Mount Hope St, Lindsay, ON, K9V 5N5
(705) 324-9161
Emp Here 45   *Sales* 17,341,200
SIC 4725 Tour operators
Raymond Scott Denure

D-U-N-S 20-270-3112   (HQ)
DLF PICKSEED CANADA INC
(*Suby of* DANSK LANDBRUGS FROSEL-SKAB A.M.B.A)
1 Greenfield Rd, Lindsay, ON, K9V 4S3
(705) 878-9240
Sales 14,850,400
SIC 5191 Farm supplies
Rob Clark
Pamela Koolhaas

D-U-N-S 24-407-1635   (SL)
ECONOMY WHEELS LTD
NATIONAL CAR RENTAL
129 Angeline St N, Lindsay, ON, K9V 4M9
(705) 324-5566
Emp Here 26   *Sales* 12,950,028
SIC 5511 New and used car dealers
Ronald Szego
John Naylor

James Naylor

D-U-N-S 20-292-1289 (BR)
EXTENDICARE (CANADA) INC
PARAMED HOME HEALTH CARE
(*Suby of* EXTENDICARE INC)
108 Angeline St S Suite 1, Lindsay, ON, K9V 3L5
(705) 328-2280
Emp Here 350
SIC 8051 Skilled nursing care facilities
Liz Hughes

D-U-N-S 20-699-6634 (BR)
EXTENDICARE INC
EXTENDICARE KAWARTHA LAKES
(*Suby of* EXTENDICARE INC)
125 Colborne St E, Lindsay, ON, K9V 6J2
(705) 878-5392
Emp Here 100
SIC 8051 Skilled nursing care facilities
Nancy Rooney

D-U-N-S 20-537-1784 (SL)
FOX, DOMINIC LIMITED
CANADIAN TIRE
377 Kent St W, Lindsay, ON, K9V 2Z7
(705) 324-8301
Emp Here 120 *Sales* 75,513,600
SIC 5531 Auto and home supply stores
Dominic Fox

D-U-N-S 25-859-1916 (BR)
HALIBURTON KAWARTHA PINE RIDGE DISTRICT HEALTH UNIT
(*Suby of* HALIBURTON KAWARTHA PINE RIDGE DISTRICT HEALTH UNIT)
108 Angeline St S, Lindsay, ON, K9V 3L5

Emp Here 140
SIC 7991 Physical fitness facilities
May Catherine Mascianrelo

D-U-N-S 25-398-8505 (SL)
HOLSAG CANADA INC
(*Suby of* M L E HOLDINGS, INC.)
164 Needham St, Lindsay, ON, K9V 5R7
(888) 745-0721
Emp Here 120 *Sales* 13,266,785
SIC 2512 Upholstered household furniture
Tony Smith

D-U-N-S 20-291-2973 (BR)
ICT CANADA MARKETING INC
(*Suby of* SYKES ENTERPRISES INCORPORATED)
370 Kent St W Unit 16, Lindsay, ON, K9V 6G8

Emp Here 250
SIC 7389 Business services, nec

D-U-N-S 24-123-6587 (SL)
LAMANTIA, J & B LTD
LAMANTIA COUNTRY MARKET
50 William St S, Lindsay, ON, K9V 3A5
(705) 324-6625
Emp Here 55 *Sales* 16,141,235
SIC 5411 Grocery stores
James Lamantia
David Lamantia

D-U-N-S 20-126-2003 (SL)
LINDSAY BUICK
150 Angeline St N Suite 484, Lindsay, ON, K9V 4N1
(705) 324-2148
Emp Here 60 *Sales* 37,756,800
SIC 5511 New and used car dealers
Paul Cross

D-U-N-S 20-846-9820 (SL)
LINDSAY SQUARE MALL
401 Kent St W Suite 20, Lindsay, ON, K9V 4Z1
(705) 324-1123
Emp Here 49 *Sales* 13,937,413
SIC 6512 Nonresidential building operators
Lois Vivian

D-U-N-S 20-105-9776 (BR)
LOBLAWS SUPERMARKETS LIMITED
LOBLAWS
(*Suby of* LOBLAW COMPANIES LIMITED)
400 Kent St W, Lindsay, ON, K9V 6K2
(705) 878-4605
Emp Here 200
SIC 5411 Grocery stores
Richard Salmonds

D-U-N-S 20-565-4960 (SL)
MARIPOSA DAIRY LTD
201 St George St, Lindsay, ON, K9V 5Z9
(705) 324-9306
Emp Here 150 *Sales* 51,853,500
SIC 2022 Cheese; natural and processed
Bruce Vandenberg
Sharon Vendenberg

D-U-N-S 24-335-0480 (BR)
METRO ONTARIO INC
(*Suby of* METRO INC)
363 Kent St W, Lindsay, ON, K9V 2Z7
(705) 878-3300
Emp Here 100
SIC 5411 Grocery stores
Jean Miljilvick

D-U-N-S 20-126-1922 (SL)
NORTHERN CASKET (1976) LIMITED
165 St Peter St, Lindsay, ON, K9V 5A7
(705) 324-6164
Emp Here 85 *Sales* 27,721,560
SIC 3995 Burial caskets
Gordon Ferguson
Caley Ferguson
Karen Ferguson

D-U-N-S 25-182-2649 (BR)
OMNI HEALTH CARE LTD
FROST MANOR
(*Suby of* OMNI HEALTH INVESTMENTS INC)
225 Mary St W, Lindsay, ON, K9V 5K3
(705) 324-8333
Emp Here 80
SIC 8361 Residential care
Connie Abram

D-U-N-S 24-060-0387 (SL)
PAYNE MACHINE COMPANY LTD
46 Mount Hope St, Lindsay, ON, K9V 5G4
(705) 324-8990
Emp Here 23 *Sales* 10,925,598
SIC 5088 Transportation equipment and supplies
W L (Tim) Payne

D-U-N-S 20-715-4576 (SL)
POLITO FORD LINCOLN SALES LTD
2 Harvest St, Lindsay, ON, K9V 4S5
(705) 328-3673
Emp Here 30 *Sales* 14,942,340
SIC 5511 New and used car dealers
Anthony Polito

D-U-N-S 20-126-2052 (SL)
QUINN'S PHARMACY LIMITED (1987)
SHOPPERS DRUG MART
74 Kent St W Suite 948, Lindsay, ON, K9V 2Y4
(705) 324-7400
Emp Here 41 *Sales* 10,371,114
SIC 5912 Drug stores and proprietary stores
David Walker

D-U-N-S 20-975-1601 (SL)
ROSS MEMORIAL HOSPITAL, THE
10 Angeline St N, Lindsay, ON, K9V 4M8
(705) 324-6111
Emp Here 800 *Sales* 88,864,000
SIC 8062 General medical and surgical hospitals
Val Harris
Wanda Percival
Dave Kimmerly
Bill Charlton
Kyle Cotton
Larry Hope

Bonnie Kennedy
Bob Nielson
Christine Norris
Ivan Reynolds

D-U-N-S 20-081-3066 (SL)
ROYAL LEPAGE KAWARTHA LAKES REALTY INC
261 Kent St W, Lindsay, ON, K9V 2Z3
(705) 878-3737
Emp Here 35 *Sales* 11,449,445
SIC 6531 Real estate agents and managers
Tracey Hennenham

D-U-N-S 24-477-7462 (HQ)
TRILLIUM LAKELANDS DISTRICT SCHOOL BOARD
300 County Rd 36, Lindsay, ON, K9V 4R4
(705) 324-6776
Emp Here 5 *Sales* 217,614,000
SIC 8211 Elementary and secondary schools
Larry Hope
Louise Clodd
Bruce Barrett
Andrea Gillespie
Katherine Maciver
Dianna Scates
Bob Kaye
Dave Golden

D-U-N-S 25-447-0503 (BR)
TRILLIUM LAKELANDS DISTRICT SCHOOL BOARD
LINDSAY COLLEGIATE AND VOCATIONAL INSTITUTE
(*Suby of* TRILLIUM LAKELANDS DISTRICT SCHOOL BOARD)
260 Kent St W, Lindsay, ON, K9V 2Z5
(705) 324-3556
Emp Here 75
SIC 8211 Elementary and secondary schools
Christopher Schweitzer

D-U-N-S 25-181-3663 (BR)
TRILLIUM LAKELANDS DISTRICT SCHOOL BOARD
I E WELDON SECONDARY SCHOOL
(*Suby of* TRILLIUM LAKELANDS DISTRICT SCHOOL BOARD)
24 Weldon Rd, Lindsay, ON, K9V 4R4
(705) 324-3585
Emp Here 160
SIC 8211 Elementary and secondary schools
Mark Cossarin

D-U-N-S 25-931-0464 (SL)
VALU-MART INC
42 Russell St W, Lindsay, ON, K9V 2W9
(705) 328-0622
Emp Here 90 *Sales* 26,412,930
SIC 5411 Grocery stores
Marc Reid

Linwood, ON N0B

D-U-N-S 25-283-8800 (SL)
J. M. LAHMAN MFG. INC
3617 Lichty Rd, Linwood, ON, N0B 2A0
(519) 698-2440
Emp Here 19 *Sales* 19,006,441
SIC 5051 Metals service centers and offices
Jesse Lahman
Hannah Lahman
Tim Zehr

D-U-N-S 20-126-2763 (HQ)
JONES FEED MILLS LIMITED
1024 Alfred St, Linwood, ON, N0B 2A0
(519) 698-2082
Emp Here 65 *Sales* 82,482,260
SIC 5191 Farm supplies
Jeffrey Jones

Listowel, ON N4W

D-U-N-S 24-325-2561 (SL)
1708828 ONTARIO LIMITED
HORST WELDING
8082 Road 129, Listowel, ON, N4W 3G8
(519) 291-4162
Emp Here 250 *Sales* 70,219,250
SIC 3523 Farm machinery and equipment
Oscar Frey
Ryan Frey
Lamar Frey

D-U-N-S 20-590-7244 (BR)
AVON MAITLAND DISTRICT SCHOOL BOARD
LISTOWEL DISTRICT SECONDARY SCHOOL
155 Maitland Ave S, Listowel, ON, N4W 2M4
(519) 291-1880
Emp Here 75
SIC 8211 Elementary and secondary schools
Petra Goetz

D-U-N-S 20-578-3272 (SL)
B.T.E. ASSEMBLY LTD
BTE TRANSPORT GROUP
801 Tremaine Ave S, Listowel, ON, N4W 3G9
(519) 291-5322
Emp Here 80 *Sales* 16,151,760
SIC 3089 Plastics products, nec
James Brooks
Michael Brooks

D-U-N-S 20-126-3159 (BR)
CAMPBELL COMPANY OF CANADA
(*Suby of* CAMPBELL SOUP COMPANY)
1400 Mitchell Rd S, Listowel, ON, N4W 3G7

Emp Here 625
SIC 5142 Packaged frozen goods
Kim Wolf

D-U-N-S 20-791-9767 (SL)
CASSIE CO ENTERPRISES LTD
CANADIAN TIRE 57
500 Mitchell Rd S, Listowel, ON, N4W 3G7
(519) 291-1960
Emp Here 50 *Sales* 12,652,950
SIC 5251 Hardware stores
Julie Caissie

D-U-N-S 24-181-9184 (HQ)
DAVID CARSON FARMS & AUCTION SERVICES LTD
CARSON FEED & SUPPLY, DIV OF
5531 Perth Line 86, Listowel, ON, N4W 3G8
(519) 291-2049
Emp Here 18 *Sales* 29,353,840
SIC 5154 Livestock
David Carson

D-U-N-S 24-311-0181 (SL)
EAGLE, JAMES R. HOLDINGS LIMITED
TRIEAGLE MARKETING
172 Main St W, Listowel, ON, N4W 1A1
(519) 291-1011
Emp Here 45 *Sales* 33,413,400
SIC 5199 Nondurable goods, nec
James (Jim) Eagle

D-U-N-S 24-011-0932 (HQ)
ELMA STEEL & EQUIPMENT LTD
515 Tremaine Ave S, Listowel, ON, N4W 3G9
(519) 291-1388
Emp Here 15 *Sales* 20,006,780
SIC 5051 Metals service centers and offices
John Schildroth
Jacquie Espensen

D-U-N-S 20-317-2044 (BR)
ERIE MEAT PRODUCTS LIMITED
LISTOWEL COLD STORAGE
1400 Mitchell Rd S, Listowel, ON, N4W 3G7
(519) 291-6593
Emp Here 175

SIC 2011 Meat packing plants
Robert Goodhope

D-U-N-S 20-730-4007 (BR)
GRAY, L. H. & SON LIMITED
GRAY EGGS
(*Suby of* GRAY RIDGE INVESTMENTS LIMITED)
955 Tremaine Ave S, Listowel, ON, N4W 3G9
(519) 291-5150
Emp Here 80
SIC 5995 Optical goods stores
Rich Baechler

D-U-N-S 24-024-6140 (SL)
HUDSON, LARRY PONTIAC BUICK GMC (1995) INC
1000 Wallace Ave N, Listowel, ON, N4W 1M5
(519) 291-3791
Emp Here 49 *Sales* 24,405,822
SIC 5511 New and used car dealers
Larry Hudson

D-U-N-S 20-126-3571 (HQ)
IDEAL SUPPLY INC
1045 Wallace Ave N Suite Ph519, Listowel, ON, N4W 1M6
(519) 291-1060
Emp Here 100 *Sales* 232,679,047
SIC 5063 Electrical apparatus and equipment
Timothy Macdonald
John Macdonald
Steve Smith
John P Macdonald
Joan Waecther
Colleen Macdonald
Stephen Smith

D-U-N-S 20-126-3712 (SL)
KROTZ, HARVEY LIMITED
KROTZ, HARVEY FORD SALES
1199 Wallace Ave N, Listowel, ON, N4W 1M6
(519) 291-3520
Emp Here 30 *Sales* 14,942,340
SIC 5511 New and used car dealers
Douglas Johnston
Sharon Johnston

D-U-N-S 24-028-2830 (HQ)
LISTOWEL MEMORIAL HOSPITAL, THE
255 Elizabeth St E, Listowel, ON, N4W 2P5
(519) 291-3120
Sales 15,297,383
SIC 8062 General medical and surgical hospitals
Karl Ellis

D-U-N-S 25-407-9668 (SL)
LISTOWEL TECHNOLOGY INC
(*Suby of* MORIROKU HOLDINGS COMPANY, LTD.)
1700 Mitchell Rd S, Listowel, ON, N4W 3H4
(519) 291-9900
Emp Here 400 *Sales* 100,479,588
SIC 3089 Plastics products, nec
Mitsuru Sakuma
Don Zilliax
Manabue Tori
Nick Nigishi

D-U-N-S 20-126-3902 (SL)
MOLESWORTH FARM SUPPLY LTD
44743 Perth Line 86, Listowel, ON, N4W 3G6
(519) 291-3740
Emp Here 60 *Sales* 44,551,200
SIC 5191 Farm supplies
Ronald Coghlin
Andrew Coghlin

D-U-N-S 25-366-8149 (SL)
SPINRITE CORP
320 Livingstone Ave S, Listowel, ON, N4W 0C9
(519) 291-3780
Emp Here 450 *Sales* 106,426,350
SIC 2281 Yarn spinning mills
Ryan Newell
Jeffrey Mccuaig

D-U-N-S 20-126-4173 (HQ)
SPINRITE LIMITED PARTNERSHIP
SPINRITE
(*Suby of* SPINRITE ACQUISITION CORP)
320 Livingstone Ave S, Listowel, ON, N4W 3H3
(519) 291-3780
Emp Here 400 *Sales* 106,426,350
SIC 2281 Yarn spinning mills
Ryan Newell
Jeffrey Mccuaig

D-U-N-S 24-826-2107 (SL)
STOP 23 AUTO SALES LTD
910 Wallace Ave N, Listowel, ON, N4W 1M5
(519) 291-5757
Emp Here 20 *Sales* 42,614,042
SIC 5511 New and used car dealers
Scott Davidson

D-U-N-S 20-773-0404 (SL)
STOP 23 SERVICE LIMITED
910 Wallace Ave N, Listowel, ON, N4W 1M5
(519) 291-3628
Emp Here 30 *Sales* 14,942,340
SIC 5521 Used car dealers
Scott Davidson

D-U-N-S 24-086-2404 (SL)
SYNERGY SERVICES INC
515 Maitland Ave S, Listowel, ON, N4W 2M7
(519) 291-4638
Emp Here 20 *Sales* 24,207,940
SIC 5154 Livestock
Cathy Templeton

D-U-N-S 20-832-1641 (HQ)
TRILLIUM MUTUAL INSURANCE COMPANY
495 Mitchell Rd S, Listowel, ON, N4W 0C8
(519) 291-9300
Sales 33,357,226
SIC 6411 Insurance agents, brokers, and service
Joseph Dietrich
Ron Wilson
George Heiz
Scott Cumming
Ben Rier
Ross Stone
Ken Schaus
Ross Lamont

Little Current, ON P0P

D-U-N-S 24-221-3775 (HQ)
MANITOULIN HEALTH CENTRE
11 Merideth St, Little Current, ON, P0P 1K0
(705) 368-2300
Emp Here 100 *Sales* 16,662,000
SIC 8062 General medical and surgical hospitals
Derek Graham
Karen King

D-U-N-S 24-385-5132 (SL)
ORR'S LITTLE CURRENT VALUE MART
40 Meredith, Little Current, ON, P0P 1K0
(705) 368-0617
Emp Here 37 *Sales* 10,143,624
SIC 5411 Grocery stores
Mike Stevens

Lively, ON P3Y

D-U-N-S 25-332-7423 (SL)
1144259 ONTARIO LIMITED
BATTISTELLIS'
65 Regional Rd 24, Lively, ON, P3Y 1H3
(705) 692-3514
Emp Here 80 *Sales* 23,478,160

SIC 5411 Grocery stores
Brent Battistelli
Frank Battistelli

D-U-N-S 25-071-0357 (HQ)
1168170 ONTARIO LTD
ALL NORTH TRUCK CENTRE
10 Duhamel Rd, Lively, ON, P3Y 1L4
(705) 692-4746
Emp Here 20 *Sales* 24,903,900
SIC 5511 New and used car dealers
Joe Veilleux
Marc Levesque
Robert Lecours
Donald Lecours

D-U-N-S 20-308-6145 (SL)
1468792 ONTARIO INC
GDB CONSTRUCTEURS
206 Fielding Rd, Lively, ON, P3Y 1L6
(705) 682-4471
Emp Here 65 *Sales* 16,408,730
SIC 1611 Highway and street construction
Glenn Daniel Bot

D-U-N-S 20-278-2145 (SL)
ABS MANUFACTURING AND DISTRIBUTING LIMITED
ABS GROUP OF COMPANIES
185 Magill St, Lively, ON, P3Y 1K6
(705) 692-5445
Emp Here 90 *Sales* 19,980,090
SIC 3569 General industrial machinery, nec
John Bradley
Kyle Bradley

D-U-N-S 24-849-6945 (HQ)
ANMAR MECHANICAL AND ELECTRICAL CONTRACTORS LTD
199 Mumford Rd, Lively, ON, P3Y 0A4
(705) 692-0888
Sales 94,796,800
SIC 1711 Plumbing, heating, air-conditioning
Giulio Grossi
Gianni Grossi
Frank Grossi
Anthony Grossi

D-U-N-S 24-374-1837 (BR)
ATLAS COPCO CANADA INC
ATLAS COPCO CONSTRUCTION AND MINING CANADA, DIV OF
(*Suby of* ATLAS COPCO AB)
200 Mumford Rd Suite A, Lively, ON, P3Y 1L2
(705) 673-6711
Emp Here 150
SIC 5082 Construction and mining machinery
Marcy Visockas

D-U-N-S 20-406-5650 (HQ)
CARRIERE INDUSTRIAL SUPPLY LIMITED
190 Magill St, Lively, ON, P3Y 1K7
(705) 692-4784
Emp Here 120 *Sales* 31,920,840
SIC 5082 Construction and mining machinery
Michael Carriere

D-U-N-S 20-153-9418 (SL)
COMMERCIAL TRANSPORT (NORTHERN) LIMITED
70 Magill St, Lively, ON, P3Y 1K7
(705) 692-4727
Emp Here 100 *Sales* 14,819,200
SIC 4213 Trucking, except local
Dougald Munro
Carol Munro

D-U-N-S 24-011-1211 (SL)
HURLEY MINING EQUIPMENT & SERVICES INC
10 Nelson Rd, Lively, ON, P3Y 1M1
(705) 682-0681
Emp Here 25 *Sales* 11,875,650
SIC 5082 Construction and mining machinery
Daniel Hurley
Marie-Ange Hurley
Bartley Hurley

D-U-N-S 25-116-1865 (SL)
INDUSTRIAL FABRICATION INC
MINECAT
240 Fielding Rd, Lively, ON, P3Y 1L6
(705) 523-1621
Emp Here 52 *Sales* 11,544,052
SIC 3532 Mining machinery
Paul Villgren
Peter Villgren
Daryl Rautiainen

D-U-N-S 25-252-9524 (SL)
MORAN MINING & TUNNELLING LTD
159 Fielding Rd, Lively, ON, P3Y 1L7
(705) 682-4070
Emp Here 65 *Sales* 17,566,640
SIC 1241 Coal mining services
John Moran

D-U-N-S 24-662-0306 (HQ)
RCR INDUSTRIAL INC
MTI
(*Suby of* KOMATSU LTD.)
145 Magill St, Lively, ON, P3Y 1K6
(705) 692-3661
Emp Here 50 *Sales* 72,747,143
SIC 3532 Mining machinery
Robert S Lipic
Peter Snucins

D-U-N-S 20-595-3318 (SL)
RINTALA CONSTRUCTION COMPANY LIMITED
377 Black Lake Rd, Lively, ON, P3Y 1H8
(705) 692-3648
Emp Here 24 *Sales* 10,732,176
SIC 5032 Brick, stone, and related material
Voitto Rintala
Richard Rintala
Esme Rintala
Catherine Rintala
Robert Rintala
Ronald Rintala

D-U-N-S 24-826-0890 (BR)
SANDVIK CANADA, INC
SANDVIK MINING AND CONSTRUCTION
(*Suby of* SANDVIK AB)
100 Magill St, Lively, ON, P3Y 1K7
(705) 692-5881
Emp Here 100
SIC 5051 Metals service centers and offices
Bill Martin

D-U-N-S 24-765-3327 (SL)
SUDBURY NEUTRINO OBSERVATORY
SNOLAB
1039 Regional Rd 24, Lively, ON, P3Y 1N2
(705) 692-7000
Emp Here 100 *Sales* 28,474,700
SIC 8733 Noncommercial research organizations
Nigel Smith

D-U-N-S 20-139-9180 (SL)
TECHNICA GROUP INC
TECHNICA MINING
225 Fielding Rd, Lively, ON, P3Y 1L8
(705) 692-2204
Emp Here 50 *Sales* 10,206,500
SIC 1499 Miscellaneous nonMetallic minerals, except fuels
Mario Grossi

D-U-N-S 25-304-9175 (BR)
TOROMONT INDUSTRIES LTD
(*Suby of* TOROMONT INDUSTRIES LTD)
25 Mumford Rd, Lively, ON, P3Y 1K9
(705) 692-4764
Emp Here 75
SIC 5082 Construction and mining machinery
Scott Medhurst

Lombardy, ON K0G

▲ Public Company ■ Public Company Family Member **HQ** Headquarters **BR** Branch **SL** Single Location

D-U-N-S 20-398-2488   (SL)
QCE CANADA (ONTARIO) LTD
56 R2, Lombardy, ON, K0G 1L0
(905) 424-4403
Emp Here 100   *Sales* 23,306,500
SIC 1711 Plumbing, heating, air-conditioning
 Robert Scoffield

London, ON N5V

D-U-N-S 20-700-5534   (HQ)
1142024 ONTARIO INC
SLE-CO
1425 Creamery Rd, London, ON, N5V 5B3
(519) 451-3748
Sales 11,769,885
SIC 6712 Bank holding companies
 Jeffrey Sleegers

D-U-N-S 24-524-6772   (SL)
1312983 ONTARIO INC
TIMBERFIELD ROOF TRUSS
2016 Oxford St E, London, ON, N5V 2Z8
(519) 659-2711
Emp Here 100   *Sales* 15,586,300
SIC 2439 Structural wood members, nec
 Murray Dietz

D-U-N-S 20-809-9932   (SL)
1498882 ONTARIO INC
EAST SIDE MARIO'S
1915 Dundas St Suite Side, London, ON, N5V
5J9
(519) 451-5737
Emp Here 85   *Sales* 3,869,115
SIC 5812 Eating places
 Peter Tatrallyay

D-U-N-S 24-802-4759   (SL)
1827212 ONTARIO LIMITED
ADRIAN'S NO FRILLS
1925 Dundas St Suite 3453, London, ON, N5V
1P7
(519) 453-8226
Emp Here 85   *Sales* 24,945,545
SIC 5411 Grocery stores
 Adrian J Newland
 Gillian Newland

D-U-N-S 20-127-9676   (HQ)
3M CANADA COMPANY
(*Suby of* 3M COMPANY)
300 Tartan Dr, London, ON, N5V 4M9
(519) 451-2500
Emp Here 1,200   *Sales* 889,290,000
SIC 2891 Adhesives and sealants
 Inge G. Thulin
 George W Buckley
 Lars Hanseid
 Patrick Campbell
 Linda G Alvarado
 Vance Coffman
 Michael Eskew
 W. James Farrell

D-U-N-S 24-192-5387   (SL)
469006 ONTARIO INC
METROPOLITAN MAINTENANCE
163 Stronach Cres, London, ON, N5V 3G5
(519) 679-8810
Emp Here 140   *Sales* 4,475,520
SIC 7349 Building maintenance services, nec
 Michael Malerba
 Joanne Malerba
 Mark Malerba

D-U-N-S 24-684-3940   (SL)
680061 ONTARIO LIMITED
VARCO INDUSTRIAL SALES
44 Belleisle Crt, London, ON, N5V 4L2
(519) 659-2696
Emp Here 25   *Sales* 11,875,650
SIC 5085 Industrial supplies

Phil Faulkner
Jon Varey

D-U-N-S 24-215-6776   (HQ)
947465 ONTARIO LTD
VOYAGEUR TRANSPORTATION SERVICES
573 Admiral Crt, London, ON, N5V 4L3
(519) 455-1390
Emp Here 580   *Sales* 45,915,920
SIC 4151 School buses
 Perry Ferguson
 Corey Jarvis

D-U-N-S 20-059-4252   (SL)
ADJ HOLDINGS INC
AMT
2068 Piper Lane, London, ON, N5V 3N6
(519) 455-4065
Emp Here 50   *Sales* 13,592,100
SIC 7692 Welding repair
 Andrew Charabin

D-U-N-S 25-967-6653   (SL)
ADJ INDUSTRIES INC
COORSTEK ENGINEERED METALS
2068 Piper Lane, London, ON, N5V 3N6
(519) 455-4065
Emp Here 75   *Sales* 14,406,375
SIC 3441 Fabricated structural Metal
 Andrew Charabin

D-U-N-S 24-794-2485   (HQ)
ALLIED COFFEE CORP
MARITIME COFFEE SERVICE
775 Industrial Rd Unit 2, London, ON, N5V
3N5
(519) 451-8220
Emp Here 16   *Sales* 17,968,760
SIC 7389 Business services, nec
 David Mcintosh
 Sam Tedford
 Dwayne Storey

D-U-N-S 24-910-7863   (SL)
ARCON ELECTRIC LTD
1065 Clarke Rd, London, ON, N5V 3B3
(519) 451-6699
Emp Here 55   *Sales* 11,980,595
SIC 1731 Electrical work
 Mark Przewieda

D-U-N-S 24-362-4314   (HQ)
ARGO CANADA HOLDING ULC
3020 Gore Rd, London, ON, N5V 4T7
(519) 457-3400
Sales 124,273,060
SIC 6712 Bank holding companies
 Marvin Devries
 Cristian Williamson
 Jeffrey Kafka
 Kathy Davis
 Peter Martensson
 Ted Mao
 Trevor Noye
 Wesley From

D-U-N-S 24-378-8796   (BR)
AUTONEUM CANADA LTD
RIETER AUTOMOTIVE CANADA CARPET
1800 Huron St, London, ON, N5V 3A6
(519) 659-0560
Emp Here 300
SIC 2299 Textile goods, nec
 Jeff Miller

D-U-N-S 24-784-1166   (SL)
BLUE-CON INC
BLUE-CON CONSTRUCTION
1915 Crumlin, London, ON, N5V 3B8
(519) 659-2400
Emp Here 55   *Sales* 13,884,310
SIC 1623 Water, sewer, and utility lines
 Michael Turek
 Joe Haasen

D-U-N-S 20-127-7316   (HQ)
BOUTETTE & BARNETT INC
BOUTETTE & BARNETT TRADE DISTRIBU-

TION CENTRE
1950 Oxford St E, London, ON, N5V 2Z8
(519) 679-1770
Emp Here 48   *Sales* 36,294,288
SIC 5075 Warm air heating and air condition-
ing
 Thomas Boutette
 Lorraine Boutette

D-U-N-S 20-126-7556   (BR)
BRINK'S CANADA LIMITED
BRINK'S
(*Suby of* THE BRINK'S COMPANY)
1495 Spanner St, London, ON, N5V 1Z1
(519) 659-3457
Emp Here 100
SIC 7381 Detective and armored car services
 Don Flynn

D-U-N-S 25-312-6593   (HQ)
CANADA STEEL SERVICE CENTRE INC
25 Cuddy Blvd, London, ON, N5V 3Y3
(519) 453-5600
Emp Here 18   *Sales* 26,830,440
SIC 5051 Metals service centers and offices
 John Anderson

D-U-N-S 20-057-7000   (BR)
CARGILL LIMITED
CARGILL VALUE ADDED MEATS
(*Suby of* CARGILL, INCORPORATED)
10 Cuddy Blvd, London, ON, N5V 5E3
(519) 453-4996
Emp Here 900
SIC 2015 Poultry slaughtering and processing
 Sean Merpaw

D-U-N-S 20-699-9539   (HQ)
CCTF CORPORATION
CCTF
(*Suby of* CANADIAN MASTER DISTRIBU-
TION CORPORATION)
2124 Oxford St E, London, ON, N5V 0B7
(519) 453-3488
Emp Here 6   *Sales* 41,327,262
SIC 5084 Industrial machinery and equipment
 Richard Klau
 Mark Whitley
 Bradford Latner

D-U-N-S 24-365-6592   (HQ)
CENTENNIAL WINDOWS LTD
CENTENNIAL WINDOWS KITCHENER
687 Sovereign Rd, London, ON, N5V 4K8
(519) 451-0508
Emp Here 62   *Sales* 25,526,930
SIC 1751 Carpentry work
 Terry Lee
 Rick Reddam
 John Saunders

D-U-N-S 25-358-4007   (BR)
CEVA LOGISTICS CANADA, ULC
(*Suby of* MERIT CORPORATION SAL)
15745 Robin'S Hill Rd, London, ON, N5V 0A5
(519) 659-2382
Emp Here 230
SIC 4731 Freight transportation arrangement
 Rick Evans

D-U-N-S 20-127-3109   (HQ)
CIE MCCORMICK CANADA CO., LA
INDUSTRIAL, DIV OF
(*Suby of* MCCORMICK & COMPANY INCOR-
PORATED)
600 Clarke Rd, London, ON, N5V 3K5
(519) 432-7311
Emp Here 415   *Sales* 237,356,495
SIC 2099 Food preparations, nec
 Angela Francolini
 Frank Snyder
 Fred Fretz
 David Grimshaw
 Brian E. Rainey
 Dennis R. Luc
 Carman Hamilton
 Keith Gibbons

David Smith
Beverley Tschirhart

D-U-N-S 20-699-1817   (BR)
COLABOR LIMITED PARTNERSHIP
SUMMIT FOOD SERVICE, A DIVISION OF
COLABOR
(*Suby of* GROUPE COLABOR INC)
580 Industrial Rd, London, ON, N5V 1V1
(519) 453-3410
Emp Here 150
SIC 5141 Groceries, general line
 Jack Battersby

D-U-N-S 24-323-5608   (HQ)
COLABOR LIMITED PARTNERSHIP
SUMMIT FOOD SERVICE DISTRIBUTORS,
DIV OF
(*Suby of* GROUPE COLABOR INC)
580 Industrial Rd, London, ON, N5V 1V1
(800) 265-9267
Emp Here 500   *Sales* 645,044,400
SIC 5141 Groceries, general line
 Claude Gariepy

D-U-N-S 24-876-8202   (HQ)
COLEMAN, DOUG TRUCKING LTD
540 First St, London, ON, N5V 1Z3
(519) 451-4349
Emp Here 70   *Sales* 47,312,380
SIC 4212 Local trucking, without storage
 Doug Coleman

D-U-N-S 20-754-9338   (SL)
**CONTINENTAL CABINET COMPANY IN-
CORPORATED**
(*Suby of* VOLK HOLDINGS INC)
547 Clarke Rd, London, ON, N5V 2E1
(519) 455-3830
Emp Here 58   *Sales* 11,157,460
SIC 2431 Millwork
 Wilhelm Volk
 Peter Volk
 Ilona Volk

D-U-N-S 20-126-9883   (HQ)
**COURTNEY   WHOLESALE   CONFEC-
TIONERY LIMITED**
600 Third St, London, ON, N5V 2C2
(519) 451-7440
Emp Here 89   *Sales* 80,215,392
SIC 5145 Confectionery
 Michael Courtney
 Lloyd Courtney

D-U-N-S 24-985-9356   (HQ)
CRAIG EVAN CORPORATION, THE
FLIGHTEXEC
2480 Huron St Unit 3, London, ON, N5V 0B1
(519) 455-6760
Emp Here 25   *Sales* 15,993,040
SIC 4899 Communication services, nec
 Nick Erb
 Michel Boucher

D-U-N-S 20-126-9933   (HQ)
CRAWFORD PACKAGING INC
CRAWFORD PACKAGING EQUIPMENT
3036 Page St, London, ON, N5V 4P2
(519) 659-0507
Emp Here 78   *Sales* 54,791,787
SIC 5199 Nondurable goods, nec
 Clarence Covey
 John Ashby
 Martin Schieck
 Jessica Covey
 Andy Craig

D-U-N-S 20-119-9093   (SL)
DAVIS & MCCAULEY FUELS LTD
660 Clarke Rd, London, ON, N5V 3A9
(519) 453-6960
Emp Here 16   *Sales* 16,524,928
SIC 5172 Petroleum products, nec
 Michael Mccauley
 David Davis

D-U-N-S 24-420-4921   (HQ)

DEETAG LTD
649 Third St, London, ON, N5V 2C1
(519) 659-4673
Emp Here 25   *Sales* 14,725,806
SIC 5085 Industrial supplies
Dean Gordon
Heather Mansi

D-U-N-S 24-965-9145   (SL)
DIAMOND AIRCRAFT INDUSTRIES INC
(*Suby of* WANFENG AUTO HOLDING GROUP CO., LTD.)
1560 Crumlin, London, ON, N5V 1S2
(519) 457-4000
Emp Here 230   *Sales* 66,895,500
SIC 3721 Aircraft
Peter Maurer

D-U-N-S 20-013-5569   (HQ)
DOCK PRODUCTS CANADA INC
(*Suby of* ASSA ABLOY AB)
639 Sovereign Rd, London, ON, N5V 4K8
(519) 457-7155
Emp Here 20   *Sales* 14,771,160
SIC 1799 Special trade contractors, nec
Kelly Esquimaux
Steven Flear
Keith Moore
Paul Venesky

D-U-N-S 25-496-5528   (SL)
EDPRO ENERGY GROUP INC
5 Cuddy Blvd, London, ON, N5V 3Y3
(519) 690-0000
Emp Here 40   *Sales* 18,760,200
SIC 5984 Liquefied petroleum gas dealers
Donald Edwards
Joe Erskine
Doug Montgomery
Peter Sleegers

D-U-N-S 20-127-1475   (HQ)
ELLISDON CONSTRUCTION LTD
(*Suby of* ELLISDON HOLDINGS INC)
2045 Oxford St E, London, ON, N5V 2Z7
(519) 455-6770
Emp Here 120   *Sales* 838,070,400
SIC 1541 Industrial buildings and warehouses
Geoffrey Smith
Jim King
John Bernhardt

D-U-N-S 24-016-3048   (HQ)
ELLISDON CONSTRUCTION SERVICES INC
(*Suby of* ELLISDON HOLDINGS INC)
2045 Oxford St E, London, ON, N5V 2Z7
(519) 455-6770
Sales 677,440,240
SIC 1542 Nonresidential construction, nec
Geoff Smith
Stephen Damp
John Bernhardt

D-U-N-S 20-115-7158   (HQ)
ELLISDON CORPORATION
(*Suby of* ELLISDON HOLDINGS INC)
2045 Oxford St E, London, ON, N5V 2Z7
(519) 455-6770
Sales 977,748,800
SIC 1542 Nonresidential construction, nec

D-U-N-S 20-122-8017   (SL)
ELLISDON FORMING LTD
(*Suby of* ELLISDON HOLDINGS INC)
2045 Oxford St E, London, ON, N5V 2Z7
(519) 455-6770
Emp Here 100
SIC 1542 Nonresidential construction, nec
John Bernhartt

D-U-N-S 24-368-5778   (HQ)
ELLISDON HOLDINGS INC
2045 Oxford St E, London, ON, N5V 2Z7
(519) 455-6770
Sales 907,909,600
SIC 1542 Nonresidential construction, nec

Geoffrey Smith
Michael Smith
J. Spencer Lanthier
George Schott

D-U-N-S 25-688-2945   (HQ)
ELLISDON RESIDENTIAL INC
(*Suby of* ELLISDON HOLDINGS INC)
2045 Oxford St E, London, ON, N5V 2Z7
(519) 455-6770
Sales 14,429,150
SIC 1522 Residential construction, nec
Geoffrey Smith

D-U-N-S 20-127-1541   (HQ)
EMCO CORPORATION
BATIMAT
(*Suby of* HAJOCA CORPORATION)
2124 Oxford St E, London, ON, N5V 0B7
(519) 453-9600
Emp Here 45   *Sales* 1,042,459,704
SIC 5074 Plumbing and heating equipment and supplies (hydronics)
Richard J Fantham
Mark F Whitley
Christopher Pappo
Keith W Colburn
Richard Klau

D-U-N-S 24-484-1250   (HQ)
FARM BUSINESS CONSULTANTS INC
FBC
(*Suby of* FARM BUSINESS CONSULTANTS LTD)
2109 Oxford St E, London, ON, N5V 2Z9
(519) 453-5040
Emp Here 50   *Sales* 16,017,300
SIC 7291 Tax return preparation services
James Ibbotson

D-U-N-S 25-393-3790   (HQ)
FPH GROUP INC
570 Industrial Rd, London, ON, N5V 1V1
(519) 686-9965
Sales 36,577,002
SIC 5084 Industrial machinery and equipment
Barry Gilmour
Manoj Mehta
John Cabral

D-U-N-S 20-175-6876   (HQ)
GENERAL DYNAMICS LAND SYSTEMS - CANADA CORPORATION
GDLS-C
(*Suby of* GENERAL DYNAMICS CORPORATION)
1991 Oxford St E Bldg 15, London, ON, N5V 2Z7
(519) 964-5900
Emp Here 2,000   *Sales* 639,870,000
SIC 3711 Motor vehicles and car bodies
Danny Deep
Charles M. Hall
Michael J. Mancuso
David A. Savner
Arthur J. Veitch

D-U-N-S 24-312-1717   (BR)
GENERAL DYNAMICS LAND SYSTEMS - CANADA CORPORATION
(*Suby of* GENERAL DYNAMICS CORPORATION)
2035 Oxford St E, London, ON, N5V 2Z7
(519) 964-5900
Emp Here 350
SIC 3711 Motor vehicles and car bodies
Larry Kish

D-U-N-S 20-416-8108   (HQ)
GREAT LAKES COPPER LTD
(*Suby of* MUELLER INDUSTRIES, INC.)
1010 Clarke Rd, London, ON, N5V 3B2
(519) 455-0770
Sales 105,865,240
SIC 3351 Copper rolling and drawing
Jean B. Noelting
Frank J. Sullivan

Donald K. Wellington
Bozena Sazon
Gari Gordon

D-U-N-S 24-102-0379   (SL)
HCL LOGISTICS INC
2021 Oxford St E, London, ON, N5V 2Z7
(519) 681-4254
Emp Here 160   *Sales* 32,912,960
SIC 4225 General warehousing and storage
Tim Van Holst
Franco Barbon

D-U-N-S 20-281-1691   (SL)
HEALTHCARE MATERIALS MANAGEMENT SERVICES
HMMS
188 Stronach Cres Suite 519, London, ON, N5V 3A1
(519) 453-7888
Emp Here 130   *Sales* 30,457,440
SIC 8742 Management consulting services
Pat Klein
Pauline Bessegato
Carolina Rappos

D-U-N-S 25-035-0238   (SL)
HICKMAN MOUNT RECONSTRUCTION INC
562 Sovereign Rd Unit 5, London, ON, N5V 4K6
(519) 457-1970
Emp Here 20   *Sales* 14,508,780
SIC 6331 Fire, marine, and casualty insurance
Michael Hickman
Nancy Hickman

D-U-N-S 20-400-9450   (SL)
INTERNATIONAL NAME PLATE SUPPLIES LIMITED
1420 Crumlin, London, ON, N5V 1S1
(519) 455-7647
Emp Here 80   *Sales* 26,090,880
SIC 3993 Signs and advertising specialties
Werner Humann
Pamela Humann
David Humann

D-U-N-S 24-408-4588   (HQ)
J-AAR EXCAVATING LIMITED
AAROC EQUIPMENT
3003 Page St, London, ON, N5V 4J1
(519) 652-2104
Emp Here 60   *Sales* 16,002,090
SIC 1794 Excavation work
Matt Falls

D-U-N-S 20-127-5583   (HQ)
JONES PACKAGING INC
3000 Page St Suite 1, London, ON, N5V 5H3
(519) 451-2100
Sales 220,582,200
SIC 2657 Folding paperboard boxes
Ronald Harris
Christine Harris Jones
Rick Jankura

D-U-N-S 20-589-7473   (SL)
KAISER ALUMINUM CANADA LIMITED
KAISER ALUMINUM
(*Suby of* KAISER ALUMINUM CORPORATION)
3021 Gore Rd, London, ON, N5V 5A9
(519) 457-3610
Emp Here 200   *Sales* 36,277,600
SIC 3354 Aluminum extruded products
Jack Hockema
Carl Heaman
Mike Oakes

D-U-N-S 20-180-2639   (HQ)
LASER SALES INC
CUTTERS CHOICE
(*Suby of* BETHEL SALES INC)
1717 Oxford St E, London, ON, N5V 2Z5
(519) 452-0501
Sales 22,358,700
SIC 5072 Hardware
William C. Bethel

William A. Bethel
Andy Bethel

D-U-N-S 20-127-6532   (SL)
LEAVENS VOLKSWAGEN INC
2360 Auto Mall Ave, London, ON, N5V 0B4
(519) 455-2580
Emp Here 35   *Sales* 17,432,730
SIC 5511 New and used car dealers
Edward Leavens
Kenneth Giles
Kelly Leavens

D-U-N-S 20-127-4354   (HQ)
LONDON MACHINERY INC
(*Suby of* OSHKOSH CORPORATION)
15790 Robin'S Hill Rd, London, ON, N5V 0A4
(519) 963-2500
Emp Here 75   *Sales* 76,551,300
SIC 3531 Construction machinery
Brad Nelson

D-U-N-S 24-059-4820   (SL)
LUBRICO WARRANTY INC
2124 Jetstream Rd, London, ON, N5V 3P5
(519) 451-1900
Emp Here 40   *Sales* 41,395,240
SIC 6399 Insurance carriers, nec
Terence Fletcher
Sheila Fletcher

D-U-N-S 24-057-4277   (SL)
MACMASTER CHEVROLET LTD
KEN MCMASTER
1350 Driver Lane, London, ON, N5V 0B4
(519) 455-6200
Emp Here 85   *Sales* 53,488,800
SIC 5511 New and used car dealers
Kenneth Macmaster
Douglas Mclean

D-U-N-S 20-127-8967   (HQ)
MAGIL CONSTRUCTION ONTARIO INC
(*Suby of* FAYOLLE CANADA INC)
1665 Oxford St E, London, ON, N5V 2Z5
(519) 451-5270
Emp Here 125   *Sales* 87,299,000
SIC 1542 Nonresidential construction, nec
Owen Whelan

D-U-N-S 24-846-3192   (SL)
MILITEX COATINGS INC
1881 Huron St, London, ON, N5V 3A5
(519) 659-0528
Emp Here 90   *Sales* 17,287,650
SIC 3471 Plating and polishing
Andre Maas

D-U-N-S 24-985-3441   (SL)
PARNALL MAILING CORP
KEYCONTACT
555 Admiral Dr Suite 6, London, ON, N5V 4L6
(519) 452-3000
Emp Here 35   *Sales* 22,976,240
SIC 5963 Direct selling establishments
Wanda Mckay
Kenneth Fischer

D-U-N-S 24-524-6533   (SL)
PCCA CORP
744 Third St, London, ON, N5V 5J2
(519) 455-0690
Emp Here 40   *Sales* 44,213,800
SIC 5122 Drugs, proprietaries, and sundries
David Sparks
Ari Pailakian

D-U-N-S 20-974-1453   (SL)
PINTO-PACKAGING LTD
148 Stronach Cres, London, ON, N5V 3A1
(519) 455-5790
Emp Here 70   *Sales* 16,340,450
SIC 2653 Corrugated and solid fiber boxes
Peter Di Pinto

D-U-N-S 24-385-4809   (HQ)
PRORESP INC
GASPRO, DIVISION OF PRORESP INC

(Suby of TRUDELL MEDICAL LIMITED)
1909 Oxford St E Suite 1, London, ON, N5V 4L9
(519) 686-2615
Emp Here 15   *Sales* 33,314,800
SIC 7352 Medical equipment rental
Mitch Baron

D-U-N-S 24-470-0464   (SL)
RHO-CAN MACHINE & TOOL COMPANY LTD
770 Industrial Rd, London, ON, N5V 3N7
(519) 451-9100
Emp Here 90   *Sales* 19,980,090
SIC 3544 Special dies, tools, jigs, and fixtures
Alfred Marques
Cas Marques
Diamantino De Jesus

D-U-N-S 24-336-1987   (SL)
SENTON INCORPORATED
SENTON PRINTING & PACKAGING
1669 Oxford St E, London, ON, N5V 2Z5
(519) 455-5500
Emp Here 110   *Sales* 18,042,970
SIC 2752 Commercial printing, lithographic
John Thain

D-U-N-S 20-845-5220   (SL)
SHARON FARMS & ENTERPRISES LTD
KENSINGTON VILLAGE
1340 Huron St, London, ON, N5V 3R3
(519) 455-3910
Emp Here 225   *Sales* 15,373,350
SIC 8051 Skilled nursing care facilities
Peter Schlegel
Amy Schlegel

D-U-N-S 25-169-4329   (SL)
SIMPLY MOBILE LTD
VESPA SCOOTERS
1920 Dundas St, London, ON, N5V 3P1
(519) 451-5120
Emp Here 60   *Sales* 37,756,800
SIC 5571 Motorcycle dealers
Ron Hillmann

D-U-N-S 24-850-5083   (HQ)
SLE-CO PLASTICS INC
(Suby of 1142024 ONTARIO INC)
1425 Creamery Rd, London, ON, N5V 5B3
(519) 451-3748
Emp Here 60   *Sales* 16,925,435
SIC 3089 Plastics products, nec
Jeffrey Sleegers

D-U-N-S 20-127-7324   (HQ)
SLEEGERS ENGINEERED PRODUCTS INC.
5 Cuddy Blvd, London, ON, N5V 3Y3
(519) 451-5480
Sales 10,141,500
SIC 3441 Fabricated structural Metal
Joseph L. Adams
Andy Bite

D-U-N-S 25-528-2428   (SL)
SPECIALIZED PACKAGING (LONDON) COMPANY ULC
(Suby of SUN CAPITAL PARTNERS, INC.)
5 Cuddy Blvd, London, ON, N5V 3Y3
(519) 659-7011
Emp Here 200
SIC 2679 Converted paper products, nec
Carlton Highsmith

D-U-N-S 24-708-2076   (HQ)
STARTECH.COM LTD
45 Artisans Cres, London, ON, N5V 5E9
(800) 265-1844
Sales 128,484,480
SIC 5045 Computers, peripherals, and software
Lynn Smurthwaite Murphy
Paul Seed

D-U-N-S 25-396-8648   (SL)
STAX PACKAGING SERVICES INC

575 Industrial Rd, London, ON, N5V 1V2
(519) 455-0119
Emp Here 25   *Sales* 11,087,250
SIC 7389 Business services, nec
D. Thomas Hodgins
Donna Hodgins

D-U-N-S 25-729-2466   (BR)
TFORCE FINAL MILE CANADA INC
SAMEDAY COURIER
(Suby of TFI INTERNATIONAL INC)
2515 Blair Blvd Suite B, London, ON, N5V 3Z9
(519) 659-8224
Emp Here 80
SIC 7389 Business services, nec
Quinn Feunekes

D-U-N-S 24-556-0297   (SL)
TOP SHOP INC, THE
502 First St, London, ON, N5V 1Z3
(519) 455-9400
Emp Here 50   *Sales* 12,652,950
SIC 5211 Lumber and other building materials
David Dean
Magdalena Dean
John Biemans

D-U-N-S 24-329-0298   (SL)
TRIBE MEDICAL GROUP INC
TRIBE MEDICAL GROUP
580 Sovereign Rd, London, ON, N5V 4K7
(519) 680-0707
Emp Here 55   *Sales* 24,594,570
SIC 5047 Medical and hospital equipment
Gord Mcarthur

D-U-N-S 20-293-7363   (HQ)
TROJAN TECHNOLOGIES GROUP ULC
(Suby of DANAHER CORPORATION)
3020 Gore Rd, London, ON, N5V 4T7
(519) 457-3400
Sales 95,498,180
SIC 3589 Service industry machinery, nec
Marvin R. Devries
Trevor J.L. Noye
Thomas J. Walkosak
Christian Williamson
Kathy Davis
Wesley D. From
Ted Mao
Andrew Mcleland
Jennifer Muller
Jeffrey S. Kafka

D-U-N-S 20-329-8203   (SL)
TRUDELL MEDICAL INTERNATIONAL
725 Baransway Dr, London, ON, N5V 5G4
(519) 455-7060
Emp Here 100   *Sales* 22,728,900
SIC 3841 Surgical and medical instruments
Bill Paterson

D-U-N-S 20-553-0657   (SL)
TRUDELL MEDICAL INTERNATIONAL EUROPE LIMITED
(Suby of TRUDELL MEDICAL LIMITED)
725 Baransway Dr, London, ON, N5V 5G4
(519) 455-7060
Emp Here 30   *Sales* 13,415,220
SIC 5047 Medical and hospital equipment
Mitchell Baran
Mark Pickard

D-U-N-S 24-860-9042   (HQ)
TRUDELL MEDICAL MARKETING LIMITED
(Suby of TRUDELL MEDICAL LIMITED)
758 Baransway Dr, London, ON, N5V 5J7
(519) 685-8800
Sales 43,375,878
SIC 5047 Medical and hospital equipment
Gerald Slemko

D-U-N-S 24-333-8667   (HQ)
TSC STORES L.P.
(Suby of PEAVEY INDUSTRIES LIMITED)
1000 Clarke Rd, London, ON, N5V 3A9
(519) 453-5270
Emp Here 300   *Sales* 337,260,000

SIC 5251 Hardware stores
Derryl Jenkins

D-U-N-S 20-939-8028   (SL)
VAN HOUTTE COFFEE SERVICE
775 Industrial Rd Unit 1, London, ON, N5V 3N5

Emp Here 25   *Sales* 20,889,425
SIC 5149 Groceries and related products, nec
David Mcintosh

D-U-N-S 24-624-0522   (HQ)
VOYAGEUR PATIENT TRANSFER SERVICES INC
573 Admiral Crt, London, ON, N5V 4L3
(519) 455-4579
Emp Here 75   *Sales* 26,345,200
SIC 4111 Local and suburban transit
Perry Ferguson

D-U-N-S 20-090-7827   (SL)
WEATHERTECH RESTORATION SERVICES INC
553 Clarke Rd, London, ON, N5V 2E1
(519) 258-0535
Emp Here 55   *Sales* 13,611,565
SIC 1771 Concrete work
Glen Bogart

D-U-N-S 24-849-4247   (HQ)
WILSON, J C CHEMICALS LTD
WILSON HOT TUB AND POOLS
1900 Huron St Unit 2, London, ON, N5V 4A3

Emp Here 6   *Sales* 10,955,175
SIC 5169 Chemicals and allied products, nec
John C Wilson

London, ON N5W

D-U-N-S 20-345-5423   (SL)
2518879 ONTARIO INC
JUST COZY
1712 Dundas St, London, ON, N5W 3C9
(519) 659-8725
Emp Here 60   *Sales* 10,763,760
SIC 5621 Women's clothing stores
Michael Vaughan

D-U-N-S 24-150-9020   (SL)
5 STAR DEALERS INC
5 STAR DEALERS
1500 Dundas St, London, ON, N5W 3B9
(519) 455-4227
Emp Here 30   *Sales* 14,942,340
SIC 5521 Used car dealers
Larry Weir

D-U-N-S 24-627-3569   (SL)
ACCURIDE CANADA INC
(Suby of ARMOR PARENT CORP.)
31 Firestone Blvd, London, ON, N5W 6E6
(519) 453-0880
Emp Here 171   *Sales* 38,277,153
SIC 3714 Motor vehicle parts and accessories
Richard F. Dauch
Gregory A. Risch
John Christopher Cain

D-U-N-S 24-379-7169   (HQ)
AIRIA LEASING INC
511 Mccormick Blvd, London, ON, N5W 4C8
(519) 457-1904
Emp Here 2   *Sales* 21,868,000
SIC 6712 Bank holding companies
John Franklin
Rainer Blomster

D-U-N-S 24-424-2462   (SL)
AIRIA RESIDENTIAL SYSTEMS INC
(Suby of AIRIA LEASING INC)
511 Mccormick Blvd, London, ON, N5W 4C8
(519) 457-1904
Emp Here 80   *Sales* 38,002,080

SIC 5084 Industrial machinery and equipment
John Franklin

D-U-N-S 24-859-5621   (HQ)
AMPRO ELECTRIC LTD
406 First St, London, ON, N5W 4N1
(519) 439-9748
Sales 11,070,400
SIC 5999 Miscellaneous retail stores, nec
Gerhard (Gerry) Siemon

D-U-N-S 24-524-7291   (SL)
ASSOCIATED AUCTIONEERS INC
MCKENZIE ASSOCIATED AUCTIONEERS
1881 Scanlan St, London, ON, N5W 6C3
(519) 453-7182
Emp Here 25   *Sales* 11,087,250
SIC 7389 Business services, nec
John Mckenzie

D-U-N-S 24-304-8139   (HQ)
CANUSA AUTOMOTIVE WAREHOUSING INC
AUTO PARTS CENTRES
2290 Scanlan St, London, ON, N5W 6G7
(519) 268-7070
Emp Here 55   *Sales* 113,270,400
SIC 5511 New and used car dealers
Robert Jones
Ivor Jones
Stephen Drake

D-U-N-S 20-184-8595   (HQ)
CENTRAL BEAUTY SUPPLY LIMITED
300 Ashland Ave, London, ON, N5W 4E4
(519) 453-4590
Emp Here 16   *Sales* 13,300,728
SIC 5087 Service establishment equipment
Michael Murphy
Annette Murphy

D-U-N-S 25-075-4335   (SL)
CHROME DATA SOLUTIONS, LP
345 Saskatoon St, London, ON, N5W 4R4
(519) 451-2323
Emp Here 240   *Sales* 44,297,520
SIC 7371 Custom computer programming services
Gregory Perrier

D-U-N-S 20-190-1266   (BR)
CINTAS CANADA LIMITED
(Suby of CINTAS CORPORATION)
30 Charterhouse Cres, London, ON, N5W 5V5
(519) 453-5010
Emp Here 130
SIC 7218 Industrial launderers
Carmin Garofalo

D-U-N-S 25-403-7484   (BR)
COMPAGNIE DES CHEMINS DE FER NATIONAUX DU CANADA
(Suby of COMPAGNIE DES CHEMINS DE FER NATIONAUX DU CANADA)
363 Egerton St, London, ON, N5W 6B1

Emp Here 150
SIC 7699 Repair services, nec

D-U-N-S 25-169-5532   (HQ)
CORPORATE INVESTIGATIVE SERVICES LTD
CIS
544 Egerton St, London, ON, N5W 3Z8
(519) 652-2163
Sales 19,783,900
SIC 7381 Detective and armored car services
Guy Parent

D-U-N-S 24-666-4239   (SL)
FOREST CITY SURPLUS (1986) LIMITED
FOREST CITY SURPLUS CANADA
1712 Dundas St, London, ON, N5W 3C9
(519) 451-0246
Emp Here 29   *Sales* 19,037,456
SIC 5961 Catalog and mail-order houses
Robert Reave
Bryan Wildman

D-U-N-S 20-939-5227   (HQ)
FORM & BUILD SUPPLY INC
(Suby of F & B ROSS HOLDINGS INC)
1175 Frances St, London, ON, N5W 2L9
(519) 453-4300
Emp Here 15   *Sales* 13,415,220
SIC 5039 Construction materials, nec
 William Ross

D-U-N-S 20-391-9894   (HQ)
G-TEL ENGINEERING INC
(Suby of OAKVILLE HYDRO ELECTRICITY DISTRIBUTION INC)
1150 Frances St 2nd Fl, London, ON, N5W 5N5
(519) 439-0763
Emp Here 20   *Sales* 10,619,850
SIC 8748 Business consulting, nec
 Kenneth Ritchie
 Paul Laham

D-U-N-S 24-602-1406   (BR)
GOVERNING COUNCIL OF THE SALVA-TION ARMY IN CANADA, THE
(Suby of GOVERNING COUNCIL OF THE SALVATION ARMY IN CANADA, THE)
1340 Dundas St, London, ON, N5W 3B6
(519) 455-4810
Emp Here 75
SIC 8351 Child day care services
 Beverly Hamilton

D-U-N-S 20-128-2324   (SL)
HIGHBURY FORD SALES LIMITED
1365 Dundas St, London, ON, N5W 3B5
(519) 455-1800
Emp Here 70   *Sales* 44,049,600
SIC 5511 New and used car dealers
 Robert Vitali
 Rex Kelly

D-U-N-S 24-315-7356   (BR)
HOME DEPOT OF CANADA INC
HOME DEPOT
(Suby of THE HOME DEPOT INC)
448 Clarke Rd, London, ON, N5W 6H1
(519) 457-5800
Emp Here 100
SIC 5251 Hardware stores
 James Vanderweyst

D-U-N-S 20-126-5717   (SL)
HOMEWAY COMPANY LIMITED
ALUMINUM ASSOCIATES
1801 Trafalgar St, London, ON, N5W 1X7
(519) 453-6400
Emp Here 49   *Sales* 12,399,891
SIC 5211 Lumber and other building materials

D-U-N-S 20-128-4007   (SL)
LKQ SHAW AUTO RECYCLERS INC
SHAW AUTO RECYCLERS
(Suby of LKQ CORPORATION)
1765 Pension Lane, London, ON, N5W 6C7
(519) 455-1200
Emp Here 35   *Sales* 22,024,800
SIC 5531 Auto and home supply stores
 Patrick Devincenzo

D-U-N-S 25-868-7631   (HQ)
LONDON INTERCOMMUNITY HEALTH CENTRE
659 Dundas St, London, ON, N5W 2Z1
(519) 660-0874
Emp Here 14   *Sales* 11,341,650
SIC 8399 Social services, nec
 Michelle Hurtubise

D-U-N-S 20-530-5246   (SL)
LONDON TRANSIT COMMISSION, THE
450 Highbury Ave N, London, ON, N5W 5L2
(519) 451-1340
Emp Here 450   *Sales* 25,296,300
SIC 4111 Local and suburban transit
 Larry Ducharme
 Gary Williams

D-U-N-S 24-885-3988   (SL)

LOR-DON LIMITED
485 Mccormick Blvd, London, ON, N5W 5N1
(519) 679-2322
Emp Here 80   *Sales* 15,366,800
SIC 3441 Fabricated structural Metal
 George Gallant
 Victoria Gallant

D-U-N-S 24-335-0548   (BR)
METRO ONTARIO INC
METRO
(Suby of METRO INC)
155 Clarke Rd, London, ON, N5W 5C9
(519) 455-5604
Emp Here 100
SIC 5411 Grocery stores
 Joe Hall

D-U-N-S 24-743-8500   (HQ)
MISTEELCO INC
KITCHENER STEEL SERVICE CENTRE
850 Dundas St, London, ON, N5W 2Z7
(519) 679-1939
Emp Here 25   *Sales* 44,717,400
SIC 5051 Metals service centers and offices
 Robert Richardson
 William Milliken

D-U-N-S 24-406-5793   (SL)
PICCOLI, N. CONSTRUCTION LTD
1933 Gore Rd Suite 2, London, ON, N5W 6B9
(519) 473-9665
Emp Here 55   *Sales* 13,884,310
SIC 1611 Highway and street construction
 Nicola Piccoli
 Guntis Glinavs

D-U-N-S 20-774-3477   (HQ)
RAMSDEN INDUSTRIES LIMITED
128 Oakland Ave, London, ON, N5W 4H6
(519) 451-6720
Sales 15,310,260
SIC 3365 Aluminum foundries
 Robert Ramsden
 Andrew Ramsden

D-U-N-S 25-743-3516   (SL)
SAAND LONDON INC
14 Firestone Blvd, London, ON, N5W 5L4
(519) 659-0819
Emp Here 70   *Sales* 16,340,450
SIC 3231 Products of purchased glass
 Mark Franklin
 Hilton Berger

D-U-N-S 20-292-6218   (HQ)
SALMON CAPITAL CORPORATION
DREXEL INDUSTRIES
100 Kellogg Lane, London, ON, N5W 0B4
(519) 266-3400
Sales 22,358,700
SIC 5065 Electronic parts and equipment, nec
 Jason Salmon
 Tara Salmon

D-U-N-S 20-209-4350   (SL)
SENTINEL POLYMERS CANADA INC
1105 Frances St, London, ON, N5W 2L9
(519) 451-7677
Emp Here 20   *Sales* 10,006,500
SIC 5162 Plastics materials and basic shapes
 Todd Gruden

D-U-N-S 25-170-7865   (SL)
TEAHEN & TEAHEN BUILDING SUPPLIES LTD
HOME HARDWARE BUILDING CENTRE LONDON EAST
1780 Dundas St, London, ON, N5W 3E5
(519) 455-0660
Emp Here 40   *Sales* 10,122,360
SIC 5211 Lumber and other building materials
 Frank Teahen
 Joan Teahen

D-U-N-S 25-528-1545   (HQ)
THAMES VALLEY DISTRICT SCHOOL BOARD

1250 Dundas St, London, ON, N5W 5P2
(519) 452-2000
Emp Here 250   *Sales* 659,125,527
SIC 8211 Elementary and secondary schools
 Matt Reid
 Arlene Morell
 Joyce Bennett
 Rob Campbell
 Chris Goodall
 Graham Hart
 Phil Schulyer
 Peter Jaffe
 Bill Mckinnon
 Sheri Polhill

D-U-N-S 24-410-6472   (HQ)
VAUGHN CUSTOM SPORTS CANADA LTD
VAUGHN SPORTS
455 Highbury Ave N, London, ON, N5W 5K7
(519) 453-4229
Emp Here 1   *Sales* 22,829,520
SIC 3949 Sporting and athletic goods, nec
 Scott Carter
 Michael Vaughn
 Kevin Collins
 Eric Carlson

D-U-N-S 20-783-4664   (BR)
VICTORIAN ORDER OF NURSES FOR CANADA
VON MIDDLESEX-ELGIN MAIN OFFICE
(Suby of VICTORIAN ORDER OF NURSES FOR CANADA)
1151 Florence St Suite 100, London, ON, N5W 2M7
(519) 659-2273
Emp Here 500
SIC 8082 Home health care services
 Lynne Leclair

D-U-N-S 25-297-6394   (BR)
WAL-MART CANADA CORP
(Suby of WALMART INC.)
330 Clarke Rd, London, ON, N5W 6G4
(519) 455-8910
Emp Here 200
SIC 5311 Department stores

D-U-N-S 24-602-8526   (HQ)
WAYS MENTAL HEALTH SUPPORT
714 York St, London, ON, N5W 2S8
(519) 432-2209
Sales 12,856,400
SIC 8361 Residential care
 Brenda Hall

D-U-N-S 20-128-8420   (SL)
ZUBICK, JOHN LIMITED
(Suby of ZUBICK INVESTMENTS LIMITED)
105 Clarke Rd, London, ON, N5W 5C9
(519) 451-5470
Emp Here 70   *Sales* 48,671,000
SIC 5093 Scrap and waste materials
 George Zubick
 Bruce Zubick
 Doris England

London, ON N5X

D-U-N-S 24-737-1888   (HQ)
1319691 ONTARIO INCORPORATED
PETRO CANADA
1845 Adelaide St N, London, ON, N5X 0E3
(519) 660-1205
Emp Here 5   *Sales* 24,903,900
SIC 5541 Gasoline service stations
 Brent Bergeron

D-U-N-S 20-070-1931   (BR)
BEST BUY CANADA LTD
FUTURE SHOP
(Suby of BEST BUY CO., INC.)
1735 Richmond St Suite 111, London, ON, N5X 3Y2

(519) 640-2900
Emp Here 100
SIC 5731 Radio, television, and electronic stores
 Nick Demelo

D-U-N-S 20-126-9495   (SL)
COMPETITION TOYOTA LTD
1515 Rob Panzer Rd, London, ON, N5X 0M7
(519) 451-3880
Emp Here 31   *Sales* 15,440,418
SIC 5511 New and used car dealers
 William Comstock

D-U-N-S 25-057-7574   (SL)
IVEY BUSINESS SCHOOL FOUNDATION
551 Windermere Rd, London, ON, N5X 2T1
(519) 679-4546
Emp Here 75   *Sales* 50,168,100
SIC 7389 Business services, nec
 John Irwin

D-U-N-S 20-200-6149   (SL)
R. GREEN SUPERMARKETS INC
SOBEYS
1595 Adelaide St N, London, ON, N5X 4E8
(519) 645-8868
Emp Here 45   *Sales* 12,336,840
SIC 5411 Grocery stores
 Robert Green

D-U-N-S 25-525-0805   (HQ)
ROBUCK CONTRACTING (1986) LIMITED
2326 Fanshawe Park Rd E, London, ON, N5X 4A2
(519) 455-1108
Emp Here 2   *Sales* 20,967,750
SIC 6712 Bank holding companies
 Robert Buckland
 Jerry Fassaert

D-U-N-S 25-239-9043   (BR)
THAMES VALLEY DISTRICT SCHOOL BOARD
A. B. LUCAS SECONDARY SCHOOL
(Suby of THAMES VALLEY DISTRICT SCHOOL BOARD)
656 Tennent Ave, London, ON, N5X 1L8
(519) 452-2600
Emp Here 100
SIC 8211 Elementary and secondary schools
 Paul Snyder

D-U-N-S 24-207-5542   (BR)
TRILAND REALTY LTD
ROYAL LEPAGE TRILAND REALTY
(Suby of TRILAND REALTY LTD)
235 North Centre Rd Suite 1, London, ON, N5X 4E7
(519) 661-0380
Emp Here 90
SIC 6531 Real estate agents and managers
 Peter Hoffman

London, ON N5Y

D-U-N-S 24-214-3253   (HQ)
ARNSBY, M. F. PROPERTY MANAGEMENT LTD
924 Oxford St E, London, ON, N5Y 3J9
(519) 455-6080
Emp Here 50   *Sales* 62,833,350
SIC 6531 Real estate agents and managers
 Michael Arnsby

D-U-N-S 20-128-4288   (SL)
DOWNIE, DALE NISSAN INC
1111 Oxford St E, London, ON, N5Y 3L7
(519) 451-4560
Emp Here 80   *Sales* 50,342,400
SIC 5511 New and used car dealers
 Dale Downie

D-U-N-S 20-127-1319   (HQ)
EDUCATOR SUPPLIES LIMITED
SCHOLAR'S CHOICE

▲ Public Company   ■ Public Company Family Member   **HQ** Headquarters   **BR** Branch   **SL** Single Location

2323 Trafalgar St, London, ON, N5Y 5S7
(519) 453-7470
Emp Here 80   *Sales* 176,666,160
SIC 5049 Professional equipment, nec
  Scott Webster
  Cindy Webster

  D-U-N-S 20-783-3864   (HQ)
**FANSHAWE COLLEGE OF APPLIED ARTS
AND TECHNOLOGY, T**
FANSHAWE COLLEGE
1001 Boul Fanshawe College, London, ON,
N5Y 5R6
(519) 452-4277
Emp Here 550   *Sales* 63,039,684
SIC 8222 Junior colleges
  John Leitch
  Peter Devlin

  D-U-N-S 20-005-1154   (SL)
FESUK, ROBERT S. PHARMACY LTD
SHOPPERS DRUG MART
759 Adelaide St N, London, ON, N5Y 2L7
(519) 679-4567
Emp Here 45   *Sales* 11,382,930
SIC 5912 Drug stores and proprietary stores
  Robert S Fesuk

  D-U-N-S 20-327-1598   (SL)
**LONDON & MIDDLESEX HOUSING COR-
PORATION**
(Suby of CORPORATION OF THE CITY OF
LONDON, THE)
1299 Oxford St E Unit 5c5, London, ON, N5Y
4W5
(519) 434-2765
Emp Here 68   *Sales* 28,484,452
SIC 6531 Real estate agents and managers
  Josh Brown

  D-U-N-S 25-310-9797   (BR)
**MCDONALD'S   RESTAURANTS   OF
CANADA LIMITED**
MCDONALD'S
(Suby of MCDONALD'S CORPORATION)
1159 Highbury Ave N, London, ON, N5Y 1A6
(519) 451-6830
Emp Here 89
SIC 5812 Eating places
  Pat Yake

  D-U-N-S 25-300-0194   (BR)
METRO ONTARIO INC
METRO
(Suby of METRO INC)
1030 Adelaide St N, London, ON, N5Y 2M9
(519) 672-8994
Emp Here 200
SIC 5411 Grocery stores
  Terry Duque

  D-U-N-S 24-964-9179   (BR)
METRO ONTARIO INC
FOOD BASICS
(Suby of METRO INC)
1299 Oxford St E, London, ON, N5Y 4W5
(519) 453-8510
Emp Here 80
SIC 5411 Grocery stores
  Gord Fisher

  D-U-N-S 25-483-6752   (HQ)
RE/MAX CENTRE CITY REALTY INC
RE/MAX CENTRE CITY
675 Adelaide St N, London, ON, N5Y 2L4
(519) 667-1800
Sales 50,266,680
SIC 6531 Real estate agents and managers
  Carl Vandergoot

  D-U-N-S 24-227-0143   (BR)
RECIPE UNLIMITED CORPORATION
HARVEY'S
(Suby of RECIPE UNLIMITED CORPORA-
TION)
1141 Highbury Ave N, London, ON, N5Y 1A5
(519) 453-8100
Emp Here 214

SIC 5812 Eating places
  Chuck Hillls

  D-U-N-S 24-568-6592   (SL)
ROYAL LEPAGE FACILITY
955 Highbury Ave N, London, ON, N5Y 1A3
(519) 659-9058
Emp Here 49   *Sales* 13,668,351
SIC 8741 Management services
  Iqbal Bhangu

  D-U-N-S 20-010-0209   (BR)
ST. JOSEPH'S HEALTH CARE, LONDON
*REGIONAL MENTAL HEALTH CARE, LON-
DON*
(Suby of ST. JOSEPH'S HEALTH CARE,
LONDON)
850 Highbury Ave N, London, ON, N5Y 1A4
(519) 455-5110
Emp Here 786
SIC 8093 Specialty outpatient clinics, nec
  Sandra Sisma

  D-U-N-S 25-239-9464   (BR)
**THAMES   VALLEY   DISTRICT   SCHOOL
BOARD**
MONTCALM SECONDARY SCHOOL
(Suby of THAMES VALLEY DISTRICT
SCHOOL BOARD)
1350 Highbury Ave N, London, ON, N5Y 1B5
(519) 452-2730
Emp Here 100
SIC 8211 Elementary and secondary schools
  Margaret Sullivan

  D-U-N-S 20-122-6201   (SL)
TORA LONDON LIMITED
GIANT TIGER
1251 Huron St, London, ON, N5Y 4V1
(613) 521-8222
Emp Here 65   *Sales* 13,347,295
SIC 5399 Miscellaneous general merchandise
  Sam Sanfillipio

  D-U-N-S 20-771-7315   (HQ)
Z REALTY COMPANY LIMITED
Z GROUP
1135 Adelaide St N Suite 300, London, ON,
N5Y 5K7
(519) 673-1730
Sales 11,645,550
SIC 6513 Apartment building operators
  Bernie Zaifman

London, ON N5Z

  D-U-N-S 25-498-5286   (HQ)
1212551 ONTARIO INC
TIM HORTONS
95 Pond Mills Rd, London, ON, N5Z 3X3
(519) 645-1917
Emp Here 90   *Sales* 4,096,710
SIC 5812 Eating places
  Doug Mccurdy

  D-U-N-S 24-737-6101   (HQ)
1553690 ONTARIO INC
PETRO CANADA
277 Highbury Ave N, London, ON, N5Z 2W8
(519) 455-0329
Emp Here 5   *Sales* 24,903,900
SIC 5541 Gasoline service stations
  Terry M. Futher

  D-U-N-S 20-126-8406   (BR)
**CANADIAN LINEN AND UNIFORM SER-
VICE CO**
(Suby of ARAMARK)
155 Adelaide St S, London, ON, N5Z 3K8
(519) 686-5000
Emp Here 150
SIC 7213 Linen supply
  Doug Larocque

  D-U-N-S 20-771-7703   (HQ)

COMMUNITY LIVING LONDON INC
OPP ART
190 Adelaide St S, London, ON, N5Z 3L1
(519) 686-3000
Emp Here 30   *Sales* 23,037,600
SIC 8322 Individual and family services
  Michelle Palmer
  Brian Sim-Little

  D-U-N-S 25-481-5285   (BR)
COMMUNITY LIVING LONDON INC
OPPORTUNITY PLASTIC PACKAGING
(Suby of COMMUNITY LIVING LONDON
INC)
180 Adelaide St S Suite 4, London, ON, N5Z
3L1
(519) 686-3000
Emp Here 88
SIC 8322 Individual and family services

  D-U-N-S 20-704-8745   (BR)
COMSTOCK CANADA LTD
1200 Trafalgar St, London, ON, N5Z 1H5

Emp Here 300   *Sales* 662,802
SIC 1711 Plumbing, heating, air-conditioning
  Tim White

  D-U-N-S 20-507-9544   (HQ)
CUDDY INTERNATIONAL CORPORATION
CUDDY FARMS
(Suby of CUDDY GROUP LIMITED)
1226 Trafalgar St, London, ON, N5Z 1H5
(800) 265-1061
Emp Here 180   *Sales* 405,504,320
SIC 2015 Poultry slaughtering and processing
  Gerald Slemko
  Chris Palmer

  D-U-N-S 24-524-7580   (HQ)
FOREST CITY FIRE PROTECTION LTD
*FOREST CITY FIRE PROTECTION & SECU-
RITY*
160 Adelaide St S Unit A, London, ON, N5Z
3L1
(519) 668-0010
Emp Here 105   *Sales* 54,169,600
SIC 1711 Plumbing, heating, air-conditioning
  Daniel Bird
  Randy Bird
  Mike Caskanette
  John Allen

  D-U-N-S 24-143-6351   (BR)
GDI SERVICES (CANADA) LP
(Suby of GDI SERVICES AUX IMMEUBLES
INC)
931 Leathorne St Unit E, London, ON, N5Z
3M7
(519) 681-3330
Emp Here 600
SIC 7349 Building maintenance services, nec
  Angelo Masciotra

  D-U-N-S 20-127-7506   (SL)
**LONDON SALVAGE AND TRADING COM-
PANY LIMITED**
333 Egerton St, London, ON, N5Z 2H3
(519) 451-0680
Emp Here 30   *Sales* 15,616,260
SIC 5093 Scrap and waste materials
  Terry Kummer
  Larry Kummer
  Wayne Kummer

  D-U-N-S 20-522-3121   (SL)
LOVER (1996) LTD
LOVERS ATWORK OFFICE FURNITURE
200 Adelaide St S, London, ON, N5Z 3L1
(519) 681-2254
Emp Here 32   *Sales* 16,283,392
SIC 5021 Furniture
  Robert Dale Lover

  D-U-N-S 24-048-9443   (SL)
MADAME VANIER CHILDREN'S SERVICES
VANIER CHILDREN'S SERVICES
871 Trafalgar St, London, ON, N5Z 1E6

(519) 433-3101
Emp Here 135   *Sales* 10,229,355
SIC 8093 Specialty outpatient clinics, nec
  Joanne Sherin
  Chris Churney
  Jan Derose
  Silence Genti
  Loretta Hillier
  Diana Lloyd
  Jillian Marshman
  Pat Moloney
  Robbie Osman
  Nancy Miller

  D-U-N-S 20-822-1895   (HQ)
MISSION SERVICES OF LONDON
415 Hamilton Rd, London, ON, N5Z 1S1
(519) 433-2807
Emp Here 9   *Sales* 35,822,764
SIC 8399 Social services, nec
  Deb Miller
  Allen Page
  Jennifer Morse

  D-U-N-S 24-845-5743   (SL)
NORTHERN MARKETING & SALES INC
11 Buchanan Crt, London, ON, N5Z 4P9
(519) 680-0385
Emp Here 24   *Sales* 10,732,176
SIC 5063 Electrical apparatus and equipment
  Frank Meyer
  Larry Dawdy

  D-U-N-S 24-301-8132   (HQ)
PETERBILT OF ONTARIO INC
PETERBILT OF LONDON
31 Buchanan Crt, London, ON, N5Z 4P9
(519) 686-1000
Sales 115,158,240
SIC 5511 New and used car dealers
  David Climie

  D-U-N-S 24-382-1027   (HQ)
SCS SUPPLY GROUP INC
APPLIED INDUSTRIAL TECHNOLOGIES
(Suby of APPLIED INDUSTRIAL TECH-
NOLOGIES, INC.)
145 Adelaide St S, London, ON, N5Z 3K7
(519) 686-2650
Sales 10,925,598
SIC 5085 Industrial supplies
  John Shore
  Robert Sharpe

  D-U-N-S 20-068-0838   (BR)
**THAMES   VALLEY   DISTRICT   SCHOOL
BOARD**
FACILITY SERVICES DEPARTMENT
(Suby of THAMES VALLEY DISTRICT
SCHOOL BOARD)
951 Leathorne St Suite 1, London, ON, N5Z
3M7
(519) 452-2444
Emp Here 100
SIC 8211 Elementary and secondary schools
  Kevin Buschll

London, ON N6A

  D-U-N-S 24-783-2223   (SL)
11292580 ONTARIO LIMITED
ARCHIES SURF SHOP
649 Richmond St, London, ON, N6A 3G7
(519) 238-2720
Emp Here 30   *Sales* 14,949,660
SIC 5136 Men's and boy's clothing
  James Archibald

  D-U-N-S 24-737-2279   (SL)
2018775 ONTARIO LIMITED
OXFORD STREET VALUE-MART
234 Oxford St E, London, ON, N6A 1T7
(519) 432-1127
Emp Here 65   *Sales* 19,076,005
SIC 5411 Grocery stores

▲ Public Company   ■ Public Company Family Member   **HQ** Headquarters   **BR** Branch   **SL** Single Location

Drew Brundritt

D-U-N-S 24-576-6167   (SL)
300322 ONTARIO LIMITED
150 Dufferin Ave Suite 100, London, ON, N6A
5N6
(519) 672-5272
Emp Here 90   *Sales* 23,539,770
SIC 6719 Holding companies, nec
Colin Cockburn
Brian Foster

D-U-N-S 20-811-3253   (SL)
3823202 CANADA INC
CARPROOF.COM
130 Dufferin Ave Suite 204, London, ON, N6A
5R2
(519) 675-1415
Emp Here 21   *Sales* 17,809,260
SIC 6411 Insurance agents, brokers, and ser-
vice
Paul Antony
Holden Rhodes
Richard Mclaren

D-U-N-S 24-231-8232   (SL)
AMG LONDON INC
230 Victoria St, London, ON, N6A 2C2
(519) 667-0660
Emp Here 120   *Sales* 148,250,160
SIC 6324 Hospital and medical service plans
Garth Mann

D-U-N-S 20-027-8412   (SL)
ARCANE DIGITAL INC
ARCANE
304 Talbot St, London, ON, N6A 2R4
(226) 289-2445
Emp Here 71   *Sales* 15,032,404
SIC 7311 Advertising agencies
Eric Vardon

D-U-N-S 24-976-9001   (SL)
AUTODATA SOLUTIONS COMPANY
CHROME SOLUTIONS
(*Suby of* INTERNET BRANDS, INC.)
100 Dundas St Suite 500, London, ON, N6A
5B6
(519) 451-2323
Emp Here 230   *Sales* 42,451,790
SIC 7371 Custom computer programming ser-
vices
Gregory Perrier
Tom Trowsdale
Chris Wedermann
Neal James
Maureen Morton
Hans Otten
Keten Ramji

D-U-N-S 20-979-9857   (BR)
**AVIVA INSURANCE COMPANY OF
CANADA**
(*Suby of* GENERAL ACCIDENT PLC)
255 Queens Ave Suite 1500, London, ON,
N6A 5R8
(519) 672-2880
Emp Here 75
SIC 6331 Fire, marine, and casualty insurance
Haji Nazir

D-U-N-S 25-367-9641   (SL)
BBO SERVICES LIMITED PARTNERSHIP
380 Wellington St Suite 1600, London, ON,
N6A 5B5
(519) 679-0450
Emp Here 49   *Sales* 22,011,731
SIC 7389 Business services, nec
Bob Sandhu

D-U-N-S 20-918-2034   (SL)
BIG BLUE BUBBLE INC
220 Dundas St Suite 900, London, ON, N6A
1H3
(519) 649-0071
Emp Here 47   *Sales* 10,825,980
SIC 5734 Computer and software stores
Damir Slogar

D-U-N-S 20-400-8742   (HQ)
BLACKBURN RADIO INC
CKNX AM
700 Richmond St Unit 102, London, ON, N6A
5C7
(519) 679-8680
Emp Here 4   *Sales* 47,979,120
SIC 4832 Radio broadcasting stations
Ron Dann
Jim Knowles
Richard Brock

D-U-N-S 20-294-5481   (SL)
CARPROOF CORPORATION
CARPROOF
(*Suby of* IHS MARKIT LTD)
130 Dufferin Ave Suite 1101, London, ON,
N6A 5R2
(866) 835-8612
Emp Here 60   *Sales* 110,864,520
SIC 6411 Insurance agents, brokers, and ser-
vice
Paul W. Antony
Mark Rousseau
Holden J. Rhodes
Joe Varkey
Karim Hemani
Greg Beckman
Shawn Vording
Drew Forret

D-U-N-S 20-514-8658   (BR)
**CIBC MELLON GLOBAL SECURITIES SER-
VICES COMPANY**
(*Suby of* CIBC MELLON GLOBAL SECURI-
TIES SERVICES COMPANY)
150 Dufferin Ave 5th Fl, London, ON, N6A 5N6
(519) 873-2218
Emp Here 90
SIC 6091 Nondeposit trust facilities
Wendy Tiede

D-U-N-S 25-134-8058   (SL)
**CLINICAL RESEARCH DENTAL SUPPLIES
& SERVICES INC**
167 Central Ave Suite 200, London, ON, N6A
1M6
(519) 641-3066
Emp Here 33   *Sales* 14,756,742
SIC 5047 Medical and hospital equipment
Peter Jordan

D-U-N-S 20-703-7219   (SL)
**CO-FO CONCRETE FORMING CONSTRUC-
TION LIMITED**
MOBILE MIX CONCRETE
72 Ann St, London, ON, N6A 1P9
(519) 432-2391
Emp Here 65   *Sales* 15,173,275
SIC 3273 Ready-mixed concrete
Aniela Dziadura
Edward Koza
Elaine Mckenzie

D-U-N-S 24-126-0660   (HQ)
COPP BUILDING MATERIALS LIMITED
COPP'S BUILDALL
(*Suby of* COPP LIMITED)
45 York St, London, ON, N6A 1A4
(519) 679-9000
Emp Here 611   *Sales* 96,836,760
SIC 5039 Construction materials, nec
Steven S Copp
T Brayl Copp

D-U-N-S 20-126-9974   (HQ)
**CRICH HOLDINGS AND BUILDINGS LIM-
ITED**
560 Wellington St, London, ON, N6A 3R4
(519) 434-1808
Sales 13,077,650
SIC 6719 Holding companies, nec
Donald Crich

D-U-N-S 25-743-6725   (SL)
**D G DUNBAR INSURANCE BROKER LIM-
ITED**

255 Queens Ave Suite 1050, London, ON,
N6A 5R8
(519) 642-0858
Emp Here 22   *Sales* 12,758,328
SIC 6411 Insurance agents, brokers, and ser-
vice
Ian Mccowan

D-U-N-S 24-756-8140   (BR)
DILLON CONSULTING LIMITED
DILLON CONSULTING MANAGEMENT
(*Suby of* DILLON CONSULTING LIMITED)
130 Dufferin Ave Suite 1400, London, ON,
N6A 5R2
(519) 438-6192
Emp Here 100
SIC 8711 Engineering services
Rob Kell

D-U-N-S 24-142-8234   (BR)
**ECONOMICAL MUTUAL INSURANCE COM-
PANY**
(*Suby of* ECONOMICAL MUTUAL INSUR-
ANCE COMPANY)
148 Fullarton St Suite 1200, London, ON, N6A
5P3
(800) 265-4441
Emp Here 110
SIC 6331 Fire, marine, and casualty insurance

D-U-N-S 20-849-2546   (SL)
EMBERS SERVICES LIMITED
80 Dufferin Ave, London, ON, N6A 1K4
(519) 672-4510
Emp Here 200   *Sales* 44,174,200
SIC 6512 Nonresidential building operators
Earl Cherniak
Robert Moses
Janet Stewart

D-U-N-S 25-297-1684   (BR)
ERNST & YOUNG INC
(*Suby of* ERNST & YOUNG INC)
255 Queens Ave Suite 1800, London, ON,
N6A 5R8
(519) 672-6100
Emp Here 100
SIC 8721 Accounting, auditing, and book-
keeping
Moira Burke

D-U-N-S 24-845-6212   (BR)
ERNST & YOUNG LLP
(*Suby of* ERNST & YOUNG LLP)
1800-255 Queens Ave, London, ON, N6A 5S8
(519) 744-1171
Emp Here 140
SIC 8721 Accounting, auditing, and book-
keeping
West Garry

D-U-N-S 24-337-0405   (BR)
EXTENDICARE INC
EXTENDICARE LONDON
(*Suby of* EXTENDICARE INC)
860 Waterloo St, London, ON, N6A 3W6
(519) 433-6658
Emp Here 160
SIC 8051 Skilled nursing care facilities
Abe Moharram

D-U-N-S 24-057-3873   (SL)
**FOSTER, TOWNSEND, GRAHAM & ASSO-
CIATES LLP**
150 Dufferin Ave Suite 900, London, ON, N6A
5N6
(519) 672-5272
Emp Here 84   *Sales* 9,314,088
SIC 8111 Legal services
James R Townsend
John F Graham
Larry Abey
Evelyn Ten Cate
Thomas Lacerte
Christopher Prince

D-U-N-S 25-281-5006   (BR)
G4S SECURE SOLUTIONS (CANADA) LTD

(*Suby of* G4S PLC)
383 Richmond St Suite 503, London, ON, N6A
3C4
(647) 678-5111
Emp Here 225
SIC 7381 Detective and armored car services
Terry Pimlatt

D-U-N-S 20-403-7212   (SL)
**GEDDES ENTERPRISES OF LONDON LIM-
ITED**
ROGER'S COMMUNICATIONS
140 Fullarton St Suite 604, London, ON, N6A
5P2

Emp Here 100   *Sales* 24,432,800
SIC 5994 News dealers and newsstands
James Geddes
Glady Geddes
Graham Price

D-U-N-S 24-968-5181   (SL)
GLC ASSET MANAGEMENT GROUP LTD
(*Suby of* POWER CORPORATION DU
CANADA)
255 Dufferin Ave, London, ON, N6A 4K1
(519) 432-7229
Emp Here 30   *Sales* 28,175,310
SIC 6211 Security brokers and dealers
Brian R. Allison
Ruth Ann Mcconkey
Geoffrey P. Calllaghan
Helen Kasdorf
W. Paul Finkbeiner
Robert J. Ritchie

D-U-N-S 25-590-0917   (SL)
GOVIRAL INC
383 Richmond St Unit 1010, London, ON, N6A
3C4
(519) 850-1991
Emp Here 85   *Sales* 15,071,435
SIC 7371 Custom computer programming services
Taylor Ablitt

D-U-N-S 25-144-6035   (SL)
HARRISON PENSA LLP
450 Talbot St, London, ON, N6A 5J6
(519) 679-9660
Emp Here 150   *Sales* 16,632,300
SIC 8111 Legal services
Dave Williams
Maurice Pellerin

D-U-N-S 20-127-3943   (HQ)
**HAYMAN, JOHN AND SONS COMPANY,
LIMITED, THE**
HAYMAN CONSTRUCTION
636 Wellington St, London, ON, N6A 3R9
(519) 433-3966
Sales 11,999,988
SIC 1541 Industrial buildings and warehouses
Peter Hayman
Brian Hayman
Michael Hayman

D-U-N-S 24-253-9075   (SL)
HRDOWNLOADS INC
195 Dufferin Ave Suite 500, London, ON, N6A
1K7
(519) 438-9763
Emp Here 60   *Sales* 25,476,420
SIC 8999 Services, nec
Matthew Telford
Anthony Boyle

D-U-N-S 24-393-0901   (HQ)
ICORR HOLDINGS INC
700 Richmond St Suite 100, London, ON, N6A
5C7
(519) 432-0120
Emp Here 1   *Sales* 21,868,000
SIC 6712 Bank holding companies
Ron Wolf

D-U-N-S 25-282-2051   (HQ)
ICORR PROPERTIES MANAGEMENT INC

ICORR PROPERTIES INTERNATIONAL
(*Suby of* ICORR HOLDINGS INC)
700 Richmond St Suite 100, London, ON, N6A 5C7
(519) 432-1888
Emp Here 25   *Sales* 17,669,680
SIC 6513 Apartment building operators
Ron Wolf
Joan Hall

D-U-N-S 25-406-2714   (HQ)
INFO-TECH RESEARCH GROUP INC
345 Ridout St N, London, ON, N6A 2N8
(519) 432-3550
Emp Here 150   *Sales* 23,320,960
SIC 7299 Miscellaneous personal service
Joel Mclean
Marcel Van Hulle
Jennifer Rozon
Gina Bowen
Ashley Jongsma

D-U-N-S 20-259-4490   (SL)
INNOVATIVE SECURITY MANAGEMENT (1998) INC
ISM SECURITY
148 York St Suite 309, London, ON, N6A 1A9
(519) 858-4100
Emp Here 150   *Sales* 3,937,500
SIC 7381 Detective and armored car services
Gordon Fisher
Michael Weyers

D-U-N-S 25-830-1019   (BR)
INTACT INSURANCE COMPANY
ING HALIFAX
(*Suby of* INTACT FINANCIAL CORPORATION)
255 Queens Ave Suite 900, London, ON, N6A 5R8
(519) 432-6721
Emp Here 172
SIC 6331 Fire, marine, and casualty insurance
Alan Blair

D-U-N-S 24-026-5327   (SL)
JACKS
539 Richmond St, London, ON, N6A 3E9
(519) 438-1876
Emp Here 140   *Sales* 6,529,460
SIC 5813 Drinking places
Darryl Moore

D-U-N-S 24-451-6787   (SL)
JOE KOOL'S RESTAURANTS LIMITED
JOE KOOL'S
(*Suby of* IS THIS ANY WAY TO RUN A RESTAURANT LIMITED)
595 Richmond St, London, ON, N6A 3G2
(519) 663-5665
Emp Here 120   *Sales* 5,596,680
SIC 5812 Eating places
Michael Smith

D-U-N-S 24-992-9597   (SL)
JOHN LABATT LIMITED
LABATT BREWERY
(*Suby of* ANHEUSER-BUSCH INBEV)
150 Simcoe St, London, ON, N6A 8M3
(519) 663-5050
Emp Here 200   *Sales* 69,138,000
SIC 2082 Malt beverages
Sophie Landry

D-U-N-S 25-104-9425   (SL)
KING'S UNIVERSITY COLLEGE AT THE UNIVERSITY OF WESTERN ONTARIO
266 Epworth Ave, London, ON, N6A 2M3
(519) 433-3491
Emp Here 325   *Sales* 36,862,171
SIC 8221 Colleges and universities
Craig Minielly
Dan Mathieson
Jeff Major
Kelly Regan
Lynne Cram
Pio Beorchia

Sauro Camiletti
Vic Cote
David Ducharme
Samira El-Hindi

D-U-N-S 20-976-5239   (HQ)
LAMPLIGHTER INNS (LONDON) LIMITED
BEST WESTERN LAMPLIGHTER INN & CONFERENCE CENTRE
100 Piccadilly St, London, ON, N6A 1R8
(519) 681-7151
Emp Here 9   *Sales* 26,213,032
SIC 7011 Hotels and motels
Sheldon Aaron

D-U-N-S 20-403-7378   (SL)
LEO'S DISTRIBUTING COMPANY CANADA LIMITED
E B FOODS
149 Piccadilly St, London, ON, N6A 1R9
(519) 439-2730
Emp Here 35   *Sales* 29,245,195
SIC 5141 Groceries, general line
Tony Buragina

D-U-N-S 24-861-0354   (HQ)
LERNERS LLP
80 Dufferin Ave, London, ON, N6A 1K4
(519) 672-4510
Emp Here 312   *Sales* 63,680,568
SIC 8111 Legal services
Graham Porter
Lisa Munro
Christina Weir
Sylvia Davis
David Desumma
Kirsten Parker
Orna Dobner
Robert Moses
Michelle Medel

D-U-N-S 20-937-4479   (HQ)
LIBRO CREDIT UNION LIMITED
LIBRO FINANCIAL GROUP
217 York St Suite 100, London, ON, N6A 5P9
(519) 672-0124
Sales 48,165,882
SIC 6062 State credit unions
Stephen Bolton
Tony Strybosch
Julian Dentandt
Rick Hoevenaars
Mary Catharine Kusch
Kathleen Grogan
Ken Meinzinger
Rick Joyal
Beth Dinardo
Tony Sleegers

D-U-N-S 20-179-1303   (SL)
LONDON CIVIC CENTRE CORPORATION
JOHN LABATT CENTRE, THE
99 Dundas St, London, ON, N6A 6K1
(519) 667-5700
Emp Here 300   *Sales* 24,755,100
SIC 7941 Sports clubs, managers, and promoters
Brian Ohl

D-U-N-S 24-375-5860   (BR)
LONDON HEALTH SCIENCES CENTRE
SOUTH STREET HOSPITAL
(*Suby of* LONDON HEALTH SCIENCES CENTRE)
375 South St, London, ON, N6A 4G5
(519) 685-8500
Emp Here 500
SIC 8062 General medical and surgical hospitals
Peter Johnson

D-U-N-S 25-038-7909   (BR)
LONDON HEALTH SCIENCES CENTRE
LONDON HEALTH SCIENCE CENTER UNIVERSITY HOSPITAL
(*Suby of* LONDON HEALTH SCIENCES CENTRE)

339 Windermere Rd, London, ON, N6A 5A5
(519) 685-8500
Emp Here 500
SIC 8011 Offices and clinics of medical doctors

D-U-N-S 25-401-0648   (HQ)
LONDON HEALTH SCIENCES CENTRE
LONDON HEALTH SCIENCE CENTER UNIVERSITY HOSPITAL
800 Commissioners Rd E, London, ON, N6A 5W9
(519) 685-8500
Emp Here 4,000   *Sales* 857,946,895
SIC 8062 General medical and surgical hospitals
Murray Glendining
Ruth Anne Conyngham
Tom Gergely
Vaness Burkoski
Tony Larocca
Steve Coulahan
David Hill
Robin Walker
Neil Johnson
Laurie Gould

D-U-N-S 24-626-1911   (HQ)
LONDON INSURANCE GROUP INC
(*Suby of* POWER CORPORATION DU CANADA)
255 Dufferin Ave Suite 540, London, ON, N6A 4K1
(519) 432-5281
Emp Here 2,600   *Sales* 15,920,411,600
SIC 6311 Life insurance
Paul Desmarais Jr
Garry Macnicholas
Stefan Kristjanson
Arshil Jamal

D-U-N-S 20-769-1783   (HQ)
LONDON LIFE, COMPAGNIE D'ASSURANCE-VIE
(*Suby of* POWER CORPORATION DU CANADA)
255 Dufferin Ave Suite 273, London, ON, N6A 4K1
(519) 432-5281
Sales 534,242,000
SIC 6311 Life insurance
R. Jeffrey Orr
Paul A. Mahon
Laurie A. Speers
Andre Desmarais
Paul Jr. Desmarais
Marcel R. Coutu
Chaviva M. Hosek
Gregory D. Tretiak
Jerome J. Selitto
J. David A. Jackson

D-U-N-S 24-992-7492   (HQ)
LONDON REINSURANCE GROUP INC
(*Suby of* POWER CORPORATION DU CANADA)
255 Dufferin Ave Suite 540, London, ON, N6A 4K1
(519) 432-2000
Emp Here 5   *Sales* 27,335,000
SIC 6712 Bank holding companies
Vincent Cleary
John Occleshaw
Glenn Hickling
Arshil Jamal

D-U-N-S 20-880-2686   (HQ)
MAY-MCCONVILLE-OMNI INSURANCE BROKERS LIMITED
685 Richmond St Suite 300, London, ON, N6A 5M1
(519) 673-0880
Sales 73,866,360
SIC 6311 Life insurance
Peter Mcconville

D-U-N-S 25-976-8927   (SL)

MIDDLESEX LONDON HEALTH UNIT
50 King St Suite 101, London, ON, N6A 5L7
(519) 663-5317
Emp Here 300   *Sales* 97,791,300
SIC 8071 Medical laboratories
Trish Fulton
Ian Peer
Jesse Helmer
Maureen Cassidy
Trevor Hunter
Tino Kasi
Marcel Meyer
Michael Clarke
Kurtis Smith
Joanne Vanderheyden

D-U-N-S 25-328-0457   (SL)
NORLON BUILDERS LONDON LIMITED
151 York St, London, ON, N6A 1A8
(519) 672-7590
Emp Here 25   *Sales* 11,768,275
SIC 1542 Nonresidential construction, nec
Maurice Demaiter
Jeremy Valeriote

D-U-N-S 24-745-6940   (HQ)
OLD OAK PROPERTIES INC
465 Richmond St Suite 600, London, ON, N6A 5P4
(519) 661-0215
Sales 15,460,970
SIC 6512 Nonresidential building operators
Greg Bierbaum
Ewald Bierbaum
Carol Scott

D-U-N-S 25-459-5119   (HQ)
OMNI INSURANCE BROKERS
560 Wellington St, London, ON, N6A 3R4
(519) 667-1100
Emp Here 10   *Sales* 33,922,400
SIC 6411 Insurance agents, brokers, and service
Gerry Cox
Steve Cox

D-U-N-S 24-916-6497   (SL)
PACIFIC & WESTERN PUBLIC SECTOR FINANCING CORP
140 Fullarton St, London, ON, N6A 5P2
(519) 645-1919
Emp Here 116   *Sales* 26,201,097
SIC 6159 Miscellaneous business credit institutions
David Taylor

D-U-N-S 25-542-0291   (SL)
PEARL RIVER HOLDINGS LIMITED
383 Richmond St Suite 502, London, ON, N6A 3C4
(519) 679-1200
Emp Here 500   *Sales* 39,128,877
SIC 3089 Plastics products, nec
George W. Lunick
Jorge Enrique Autrique Ruiz
Jim Filer
Rod Bell
Anne Dang

D-U-N-S 24-653-4580   (SL)
PENSA AND ASSOCIATES
450 Talbot St, London, ON, N6A 5J6
(519) 679-9660
Emp Here 75   *Sales* 8,456,017
SIC 8111 Legal services
C M Pensa
David Williams
G D Wilson
A J Campbell
David W Lewis
Paul Ledroit
D B Williams
J R Adams

D-U-N-S 25-096-9136   (SL)
PORTFOLIO MANAGEMENT SOLUTIONS INC

200 Queens Ave Suite 700, London, ON, N6A 1J3
(519) 432-0075
Emp Here 119   *Sales* 23,844,149
SIC 7322 Adjustment and collection services
 R Gerald Coffin

D-U-N-S 20-547-5093   (BR)
PRICEWATERHOUSECOOPERS LLP
PWC
(*Suby of* PRICEWATERHOUSECOOPERS LLP)
465 Richmond St Suite 300, London, ON, N6A 5P4
(519) 640-8000
Emp Here 75
SIC 8721 Accounting, auditing, and bookkeeping
 Chirag Shah

D-U-N-S 20-696-0085   (HQ)
QUADRAS INVESTMENT SERVICES LTD
(*Suby of* POWER CORPORATION DU CANADA)
255 Dufferin Ave, London, ON, N6A 4K1
(519) 435-4826
Sales 170,776,560
SIC 6282 Investment advice
 Michael Campbell
 Geoffrey P Heyland
 Nicholas L. Pszeniczny
 Cheryl A. Munro-Sharpe
 Stefan Kristjanson
 Gerry Hasset
 Ruth Ann Mcconkey
 Lesley Duffy

D-U-N-S 20-085-9705   (SL)
ROBERTSON INSURANCE AND FINANCIAL SERVICES INC
ROBERTSON HALL INSURANCE
431 Richmond St Suite 300, London, ON, N6A 6E2
(519) 680-3111
Emp Here 28   *Sales* 16,237,872
SIC 6411 Insurance agents, brokers, and service
 William Robertson
 Kenneth Hall
 James Robertson

D-U-N-S 24-632-6557   (HQ)
ROMAN CATHOLIC EPISCOPAL CORPORATION OF THE DIOCESE OF LONDON IN ONTARIO, THE
DIOCESE OF LONDON
1070 Waterloo St, London, ON, N6A 3Y2
(519) 433-0658
Emp Here 25   *Sales* 88,504,550
SIC 8661 Religious organizations
 Ronald Peter Fabbro
 David Savel

D-U-N-S 20-524-2519   (SL)
SHEFFAR, POTTER, MUCHAN INC
SHEFFAR PLANNING AND REFERRAL SERVICES
362 Oxford St E, London, ON, N6A 1V7
(519) 432-6199
Emp Here 14   *Sales* 11,872,840
SIC 6411 Insurance agents, brokers, and service
 Michael Sheffar
 Tim Potter
 Keith Muchan
 Matt Churchill
 Tim Faught

D-U-N-S 20-975-5206   (HQ)
SISKINDS LLP
SISKINDS, THE LAW FIRM
680 Waterloo St, London, ON, N6A 0B3
(519) 672-2121
Emp Here 210   *Sales* 47,008,620
SIC 8111 Legal services
 James J. Mays
 Catherine R. Bruni

Fred G. Rose

D-U-N-S 24-407-9646   (SL)
ST JOSEPH'S HEALTH CENTRE AUXILARY
ST JOSEPH HOSPITAL AUXILARY GIFT SHOP
268 Grosvenor St, London, ON, N6A 4L6
(519) 646-6000
Emp Here 250   *Sales* 45,884,250
SIC 5947 Gift, novelty, and souvenir shop
 Margaret Herbert
 John Mockler

D-U-N-S 20-188-2441   (BR)
ST. JOSEPH'S HEALTH CARE, LONDON
REGIONAL MENTAL HEALTH CARE, LONDON
(*Suby of* ST. JOSEPH'S HEALTH CARE, LONDON)
268 Grosvenor St, London, ON, N6A 4V2
(519) 646-6100
Emp Here 1,500
SIC 8093 Specialty outpatient clinics, nec
 Sherry Rohekar

D-U-N-S 20-900-4548   (HQ)
ST. JOSEPH'S HEALTH CARE, LONDON
MOUNT HOPE CENTRE FOR LONG-TERM CARE
268 Grosvenor St, London, ON, N6A 4V2
(519) 646-6100
Emp Here 1,500   *Sales* 352,779,616
SIC 8361 Residential care
 Cliff Nordal
 Gerald Killan
 James Flett
 Sandra Letton
 Larry Walls
 Gillian Kernaghan

D-U-N-S 20-010-0159   (BR)
ST. JOSEPH'S HEALTH CARE, LONDON
MOUNT HOPE CENTRE FOR LONG TERM CARE
(*Suby of* ST. JOSEPH'S HEALTH CARE, LONDON)
268 Grosvenor St, London, ON, N6A 4V2
(519) 646-6100
Emp Here 418
SIC 8361 Residential care
 Cliff Nordal

D-U-N-S 24-358-2764   (BR)
STANTEC CONSULTING LTD
(*Suby of* STANTEC INC)
171 Queens Ave 6th Floor, London, ON, N6A 5J7
(519) 645-2007
Emp Here 126
SIC 8711 Engineering services
 Jeff Paul

D-U-N-S 25-204-3443   (HQ)
SYKES ASSISTANCE SERVICES CORPORATION
(*Suby of* SYKES ENTERPRISES INCORPORATED)
248 Pall Mall St, London, ON, N6A 5P6
(519) 434-3221
Emp Here 640   *Sales* 125,574,400
SIC 7549 Automotive services, nec
 Bruce Woods

D-U-N-S 25-685-6048   (HQ)
THINQ TECHNOLOGIES LTD
DIRECT DIAL.COM
572 Wellington St, London, ON, N6A 3R3
(519) 659-4900
Emp Here 30   *Sales* 15,651,090
SIC 5045 Computers, peripherals, and software
 Greg Bruzas

D-U-N-S 24-317-2769   (BR)
UNIVERSITY OF WESTERN ONTARIO, THE
RICHARD IVEY SCHOOL OF BUSINESS, THE
(*Suby of* UNIVERSITY OF WESTERN ON-

TARIO, THE)
1151 Richmond St Suite 3140, London, ON, N6A 3K7
(519) 661-2111
Emp Here 300
SIC 8748 Business consulting, nec
 Jacquie Davison

D-U-N-S 20-846-9452   (HQ)
UNIVERSITY OF WESTERN ONTARIO, THE
WESTERN UNIVERSITY
1151 Richmond St Suite 2, London, ON, N6A 5B8
(519) 661-2111
Emp Here 3,000   *Sales* 958,199,021
SIC 8221 Colleges and universities
 Amit Chakma
 Andrew N Hyrmak
 John Capone
 Lynn Logan

D-U-N-S 24-336-7732   (BR)
UNIVERSITY OF WESTERN ONTARIO, THE
DIVISION OF HOUSING AND ANCILLARY SERVICES
(*Suby of* UNIVERSITY OF WESTERN ONTARIO, THE)
1151 Richmond St Suite 3, London, ON, N6A 5B9
(519) 661-2111
Emp Here 200
SIC 6531 Real estate agents and managers
 Amit Chakma

D-U-N-S 20-788-0415   (BR)
UNIVERSITY OF WESTERN ONTARIO, THE
SCHULICH SCHOOL OF MEDICINE AND DENTISTRY
(*Suby of* UNIVERSITY OF WESTERN ONTARIO, THE)
1151 Richmond St Rm 4, London, ON, N6A 5C1
(519) 661-2111
Emp Here 250
SIC 8062 General medical and surgical hospitals
 Sharon Rasul

D-U-N-S 24-266-2245   (SL)
VERSABANK
140 Fullarton St Suite 2002, London, ON, N6A 5P2
(519) 645-1919
Emp Here 50   *Sales* 57,926,412
SIC 6021 National commercial banks
 David R. Taylor
 Jean-Paul Beker
 Michael Dixon
 Ross Duggan
 Nick Kristo
 Jonathan F.P. Taylor
 Steve Creery
 Wooi Koay
 Aly Lalani
 Andy Min

D-U-N-S 25-300-6704   (BR)
WORKPLACE SAFETY & INSURANCE BOARD, THE
WSIB
(*Suby of* WORKPLACE SAFETY & INSURANCE BOARD, THE)
148 Fullarton St Suite 402, London, ON, N6A 5P3
(800) 387-0750
Emp Here 200
SIC 6331 Fire, marine, and casualty insurance
 Pat Lamanna

London, ON N6B

D-U-N-S 25-675-0233   (BR)
1032451 B.C. LTD
LONDON FREE PRESS

(*Suby of* QUEBECOR MEDIA INC)
369 York St Suite 2a, London, ON, N6B 3R4
(519) 679-1111
Emp Here 335
SIC 2711 Newspapers
 Susan Muszak

D-U-N-S 20-934-5342   (SL)
ALICE SADDY ASSOCIATION
111 Waterloo St Suite 401, London, ON, N6B 2M4
(519) 433-2801
Emp Here 100   *Sales* 70,921,200
SIC 8699 Membership organizations, nec
 Ken Maclellan

D-U-N-S 25-030-5927   (SL)
ANOVA: A FUTURE WITHOUT VIOLENCE
ANOVA
255 Horton St E Fl 3, London, ON, N6B 1L1
(519) 642-3003
Emp Here 95   *Sales* 67,375,140
SIC 8699 Membership organizations, nec
 Kate Wiggins

D-U-N-S 20-287-6678   (HQ)
CANADIAN MENTAL HEALTH ASSOCIATION, MIDDLESEX
CMHA
534 Queens Ave, London, ON, N6B 1Y6
(519) 668-0624
Sales 70,233,300
SIC 8621 Professional organizations
 Heather Bishop
 Lorri Lowe

D-U-N-S 25-463-8430   (HQ)
CENTURY 21 FIRST CANADIAN CORP
420 York St Suite 21, London, ON, N6B 1R1
(519) 673-3390
Emp Here 147   *Sales* 62,833,350
SIC 6531 Real estate agents and managers
 Vito Campanale

D-U-N-S 20-699-9414   (BR)
DELTA HOTELS LIMITED
(*Suby of* GOVERNMENT OF THE PROVINCE OF BRITISH COLUMBIA)
325 Dundas St, London, ON, N6B 1T9
(519) 679-6111
Emp Here 200
SIC 8741 Management services
 Gerry Champagne

D-U-N-S 24-765-4403   (SL)
GLOBAL WARRANTY CORPORATION
471 Waterloo St, London, ON, N6B 2P4
(519) 672-9356
Emp Here 30   *Sales* 31,046,430
SIC 6399 Insurance carriers, nec

D-U-N-S 20-096-6401   (BR)
GOODWILL INDUSTRIES, ONTARIO GREAT LAKES
GOODWILL CAREER CENTRE, THE
(*Suby of* GOODWILL INDUSTRIES, ONTARIO GREAT LAKES)
390 King St, London, ON, N6B 1S3
(519) 850-9675
Emp Here 200
SIC 8331 Job training and related services
 Lisa Bowden

D-U-N-S 20-771-8446   (HQ)
GOODWILL INDUSTRIES, ONTARIO GREAT LAKES
255 Horton St E, London, ON, N6B 1L1
(519) 645-1455
Emp Here 8   *Sales* 42,213,510
SIC 5932 Used merchandise stores
 Michelle Quintyn
 Scott Louch
 Jason Livingstone
 Melanie Mclagan
 Yvonne Bell
 Brad N Macdougall
 Terry Off

D-U-N-S 24-336-6023 (BR)
IBM CANADA LIMITED
(*Suby of* INTERNATIONAL BUSINESS MA-CHINES CORPORATION)
275 Dundas St, London, ON, N6B 3L1

Emp Here 120
SIC 7379 Computer related services, nec
Christina Dodge

D-U-N-S 24-757-6671 (SL)
INNVEST HOTELS (LONDON) LTD
DELTA LONDON ARMOURIES HOTEL
325 Dundas St, London, ON, N6B 1T9
(519) 679-6111
Emp Here 150   *Sales* 13,903,500
SIC 7011 Hotels and motels
Gery Champagne

D-U-N-S 24-394-2286 (SL)
LATTANVILLE HOLDINGS CORPORATION
CANADIAN TIRE
378 Horton St E Suite 494, London, ON, N6B 1L7
(519) 642-7142
Emp Here 38   *Sales* 18,926,964
SIC 5531 Auto and home supply stores
Craig Lattanville

D-U-N-S 24-953-1112 (SL)
LONDON (KING ST.) PURCHASECO INC
HILTON LONDON
(*Suby of* HOLLOWAY LODGING CORPORA-TION)
300 King St, London, ON, N6B 1S2
(519) 439-1661
Emp Here 150   *Sales* 14,350,200
SIC 7011 Hotels and motels
Joe Drummond

D-U-N-S 25-280-5155 (SL)
LONDON CONVENTION CENTRE CORPO-RATION, THE
300 York St, London, ON, N6B 1P8
(519) 661-6200
Emp Here 115   *Sales* 76,924,420
SIC 7389 Business services, nec
Lori Dasliva
Betty Holme

D-U-N-S 20-771-7497 (SL)
LONDON HOSPITAL LINEN SERVICE IN-CORPORATED
11 Maitland St, London, ON, N6B 3K7
(519) 438-2925
Emp Here 225   *Sales* 20,181,600
SIC 7213 Linen supply
Gary Koreen
Jack Brooks
Manning Macrae
John Cronin
Lloyd Stevens
Brendan O'neill
William Wood
Tom Logan
John Sealey

D-U-N-S 24-049-0318 (SL)
LONDON HYDRO INC
(*Suby of* CORPORATION OF THE CITY OF LONDON, THE)
111 Horton St E, London, ON, N6B 3N9
(519) 661-5503
Emp Here 250   *Sales* 210,184,000
SIC 4911 Electric services
Vinay Sharma
Hans Schreff
Elizabeth Carswell

D-U-N-S 20-934-0017 (HQ)
LONDON X-RAY ASSOCIATES
450 Central Ave Unit 104, London, ON, N6B 2E8
(519) 672-7900
Sales 19,558,260
SIC 8071 Medical laboratories
Stephen Eakins

Roman Kozak
Donald Taves
John Bennett
William Dawson
Walter Romano
Gregory Garvin
Justin Amann
Barry Hobbs

D-U-N-S 25-816-5703 (HQ)
MCFARLAN   ROWLANDS   INSURANCE BROKERS INC
503 York St, London, ON, N6B 1R4
(519) 679-5440
Emp Here 1   *Sales* 221,729,040
SIC 6411 Insurance agents, brokers, and ser-vice
Rodney Hancock

D-U-N-S 24-826-8997 (SL)
PARTICIPATION HOUSE SUPPORT SER-VICES - LONDON AND AREA
633 Colborne St Suite 101, London, ON, N6B 2V3
(519) 660-6635
Emp Here 145   *Sales* 30,024,860
SIC 8399 Social services, nec
Elizabeth Leighton
Debra Jazey
Patricia James
Leroy Innanen

D-U-N-S 20-128-4445 (SL)
SMITH, L & H FRUIT COMPANY LIMITED
22 Maitland St, London, ON, N6B 3L2
(519) 433-4004
Emp Here 30   *Sales* 25,067,310
SIC 5148 Fresh fruits and vegetables
Daniel Smith
Lynne Hevey

D-U-N-S 24-564-2467 (HQ)
SPECTRUM COMMUNICATIONS INTERNA-TIONAL INC
79 Wellington St, London, ON, N6B 2K4
(519) 663-2109
Emp Here 35   *Sales* 13,438,040
SIC 5999 Miscellaneous retail stores, nec
Gordon Mayhew
Derek Dixon
Roger Ruby
Jeffrey Balicki

D-U-N-S 20-347-4825 (HQ)
SPECTRUM COMMUNICATIONS LTD
79 Wellington St, London, ON, N6B 2K4
(519) 663-2109
Sales 22,358,700
SIC 5065 Electronic parts and equipment, nec
Gordon Mayhew

D-U-N-S 25-160-0441 (HQ)
THAMES EMERGENCY MEDICAL SER-VICES INC
340 Waterloo St, London, ON, N6B 2N6
(519) 679-5466
Emp Here 1   *Sales* 12,419,880
SIC 4119 Local passenger transportation, nec
Mac Gilpin

D-U-N-S 25-239-9290 (BR)
THAMES VALLEY DISTRICT SCHOOL BOARD
LONDON CENTRAL SECONDARY SCHOOL
(*Suby of* THAMES VALLEY DISTRICT SCHOOL BOARD)
509 Waterloo St, London, ON, N6B 2P8
(519) 452-2620
Emp Here 100
SIC 8211 Elementary and secondary schools
Don Scanlon

D-U-N-S 25-481-2472 (HQ)
TRILAND REALTY LTD
ROYAL LEPAGE TRILAND REALTY
240 Waterloo St Unit 103, London, ON, N6B 2N4

(519) 672-9880
Emp Here 100   *Sales* 62,833,350
SIC 6531 Real estate agents and managers
Peter Hoffman
Robert Breuer

D-U-N-S 20-364-4067 (SL)
WINDLEY ELY LEGAL SERVICES PROFES-SIONAL CORPORATION
275 Colborne St, London, ON, N6B 2S7
(519) 657-4242
Emp Here 75   *Sales* 17,571,600
SIC 8742 Management consulting services
Michael Arblaster

London, ON N6C

D-U-N-S 20-316-5543 (SL)
2275510 ONTARIO LTD
MERCEDES-BENZ LONDON
(*Suby of* FINCH AUTO GROUP LTD)
35 Southdale Rd E, London, ON, N6C 4X5
(519) 668-0600
Emp Here 38   *Sales* 18,926,964
SIC 5511 New and used car dealers
Ryan Finch
Rob Stockie

D-U-N-S 24-874-5036 (SL)
570230 ONTARIO INC
EAST SIDE MARIO'S
387 Wellington Rd, London, ON, N6C 4P9
(519) 680-1830
Emp Here 80   *Sales* 3,429,840
SIC 5812 Eating places
Peter Tatrallyay
Kathy Tatrallyay

D-U-N-S 25-406-3928 (HQ)
COMCARE (CANADA) LIMITED
COMCARE HEALTH SERVICES
339 Wellington Rd Suite 200, London, ON, N6C 5Z9
(800) 663-5775
Emp Here 70   *Sales* 357,048,000
SIC 8049 Offices of health practitioner
Peter Tanaka
Greg More
Wendy Theis
Jeff Bond

D-U-N-S 20-917-8909 (BR)
COMMUNITY LIFECARE INC
GRAND WOOD PARK APARTMENTS AND RESIDENCE
81 Grand Ave, London, ON, N6C 1M2
(519) 432-1162
Emp Here 85
SIC 6513 Apartment building operators
Rose Mary Rowley

D-U-N-S 24-794-9779 (SL)
FINCH HYUNDAI
(*Suby of* 3070964 CANADA LTD)
300 Southdale Rd E, London, ON, N6C 5Y7
(519) 649-7779
Emp Here 100   *Sales* 45,019,700
SIC 7515 Passenger car leasing
Ryan Finch

D-U-N-S 24-009-1744 (BR)
LAMPLIGHTER INNS (LONDON) LIMITED
BEST WESTERN LAMPLIGHTER INN
(*Suby of* LAMPLIGHTER INNS (LONDON) LIMITED)
591 Wellington Rd, London, ON, N6C 4R3
(519) 681-7151
Emp Here 100
SIC 7011 Hotels and motels
Wendy Longe

D-U-N-S 24-383-6561 (SL)
LAWSON RESEARCH INSTITUTE
LAWSON HEALTH RESEARCH INSTITUTE
750 Base Line Rd E Suite 300, London, ON,

N6C 5Z2
(519) 646-6100
Emp Here 50   *Sales* 14,237,350
SIC 8733 Noncommercial research organiza-tions
David Hill
Stacey Larizza

D-U-N-S 24-333-1613 (BR)
METRO ONTARIO INC
METRO
(*Suby of* METRO INC)
395 Wellington Rd, London, ON, N6C 5Z6
(519) 680-2317
Emp Here 100
SIC 5411 Grocery stores
Tanya Morrison

D-U-N-S 24-803-3219 (BR)
NORDION (CANADA) INC
MDS LABORATORIES
(*Suby of* NORDION (CANADA) INC)
746 Base Line Rd E Suite 11, London, ON, N6C 5Z2
(877) 849-3637
Emp Here 75
SIC 8071 Medical laboratories
Sharon Kousineau

D-U-N-S 25-672-8908 (BR)
RED LOBSTER HOSPITALITY LLC
RED LOBSTER RESTAURANTS
667 Wellington Rd, London, ON, N6C 4R4
(519) 668-0220
Emp Here 100
SIC 5812 Eating places
Betty Sanford

D-U-N-S 24-470-0167 (HQ)
THAMES VALLEY CHILDREN'S CENTRE
TVCC
779 Base Line Rd E, London, ON, N6C 5Y6
(519) 685-8680
Sales 27,877,684
SIC 8093 Specialty outpatient clinics, nec
Van Simpson
Eileen Aiello
Jackie Bond
Jaap Burck
Chris Cunneen
Linda Eligh
Laurie Gould
Ernie Gross
Mary Herlick
Neal James

D-U-N-S 25-239-9084 (BR)
THAMES   VALLEY   DISTRICT   SCHOOL BOARD
SIR   WILFRID   LAURIER   SECONDARY SCHOOL
(*Suby of* THAMES VALLEY DISTRICT SCHOOL BOARD)
450 Millbank Dr, London, ON, N6C 4W7
(519) 452-2840
Emp Here 100
SIC 8211 Elementary and secondary schools
Frank Galizia

D-U-N-S 20-590-6006 (BR)
THAMES   VALLEY   DISTRICT   SCHOOL BOARD
LONDON SOUTH SECONDARY SCHOOL
(*Suby of* THAMES VALLEY DISTRICT SCHOOL BOARD)
371 Tecumseh Ave E, London, ON, N6C 1T4
(519) 452-2860
Emp Here 75
SIC 8211 Elementary and secondary schools
Larry Schneider

D-U-N-S 25-838-5657 (BR)
WE CARE HEALTH SERVICES INC
(*Suby of* WE CARE HEALTH SERVICES INC)
190 Wortley Rd Suite 100f, London, ON, N6C 4Y7
(519) 642-1208
Emp Here 75

SIC 8322 Individual and family services
Brian Mihon

London, ON N6E

D-U-N-S 25-365-5708   (SL)
1767388 ONTARIO INC
STRYKER MEDICAL LONDON
(*Suby of* STRYKER CORPORATION)
1020 Adelaide St S, London, ON, N6E 1R6
(519) 963-4010
Emp Here 100   *Sales* 44,717,400
SIC 5047 Medical and hospital equipment
Archie Leach

D-U-N-S 20-004-9976   (SL)
1ST LONDON REAL ESTATE SERVICES INC
COLDWELL BANKER 1ST LONDON REAL ESTATE
1069 Wellington Rd, London, ON, N6E 2H6

Emp Here 70   *Sales* 19,022,920
SIC 6531 Real estate agents and managers
Jim Holody

D-U-N-S 20-299-0537   (SL)
2365927 ONTARIO LIMITED
90 Bessemer Rd Unit 2, London, ON, N6E 1R1
(519) 668-7331
Emp Here 30   *Sales* 13,415,220
SIC 5031 Lumber, plywood, and millwork
Chris Hamilton

D-U-N-S 20-126-5758   (HQ)
AMWAY CANADA CORPORATION
AMWAY GLOBAL
(*Suby of* ALTICOR GLOBAL HOLDINGS INC.)
375 Exeter Rd, London, ON, N6E 2Z3
(519) 685-7700
Sales 44,213,800
SIC 5122 Drugs, proprietaries, and sundries
Lydia Ayora

D-U-N-S 20-852-5303   (SL)
ARCHIBALD, GRAY & MCKAY LTD
AGM SURVEYING ENGINEERING
3514 White Oak Rd, London, ON, N6E 2Z9
(519) 685-5300
Emp Here 37   *Sales* 12,047,200
SIC 5995 Optical goods stores
Bruce Baker
Richard Dykstra
Jason Wilband

D-U-N-S 24-824-8502   (SL)
BELLA FLOR CANADA
444 Newbold St, London, ON, N6E 1K3
(800) 667-1902
Emp Here 24   *Sales* 12,087,792
SIC 5112 Stationery and office supplies
Sarah Picard

D-U-N-S 20-267-7951   (SL)
CASE 'N DRUM OIL INC
3462 White Oak Rd, London, ON, N6E 2Z9
(519) 681-3772
Emp Here 20   *Sales* 20,656,160
SIC 5172 Petroleum products, nec
Pierre Crevier
Mathieu St-Louis
Jean-Francois Crevier
Louis-Philippe Crevier

D-U-N-S 25-369-4665   (BR)
COMMISSIONAIRES (GREAT LAKES)
COMMISSIONAIRES GREAT LAKES
(*Suby of* COMMISSIONAIRES (GREAT LAKES))
1112 Dearness Dr Unit 14, London, ON, N6E 1N9
(519) 433-6763
Emp Here 200

SIC 7381 Detective and armored car services
Kevin Armstrong

D-U-N-S 24-513-4416   (SL)
CON-WALL CONCRETE INC
525 Exeter Rd, London, ON, N6E 2Z3
(519) 681-6910
Emp Here 100   *Sales* 24,748,300
SIC 1771 Concrete work
Joseph Liberatore
Victor Liberatore

D-U-N-S 24-893-6890   (SL)
CONKRISDA HOLDINGS LIMITED
FOUR POINTS BY SHERATON
1150 Wellington Rd, London, ON, N6E 1M3
(519) 681-0600
Emp Here 100   *Sales* 9,489,900
SIC 7011 Hotels and motels
Friedrich Kristinus

D-U-N-S 20-652-1747   (BR)
COSTCO WHOLESALE CANADA LTD
COSTCO
(*Suby of* COSTCO WHOLESALE CORPORATION)
4313 Wellington Rd S, London, ON, N6E 2Z8
(519) 680-1027
Emp Here 200
SIC 5141 Groceries, general line
Raied Shatara

D-U-N-S 24-305-3324   (SL)
DAVID'S VACATION CLUB RENTALS
(*Suby of* CAPITOL TECHNOLOGIES)
4-1106 Dearness Dr, London, ON, N6E 1N9
(519) 686-7694
Emp Here 40   *Sales* 20,798,680
SIC 4724 Travel agencies
David Mullett

D-U-N-S 20-179-9009   (SL)
EAGLE SURVEILLANCE GROUP LTD
EAGLE INVESTIGATIONS
1069 Wellington Rd Suite 229, London, ON, N6E 2H6
(519) 680-3269
Emp Here 30   *Sales* 11,870,340
SIC 7381 Detective and armored car services
Walter Baker

D-U-N-S 24-308-4340   (HQ)
HERITAGE COFFEE CO. LTD
97 Bessemer Rd Unit 8, London, ON, N6E 1P9
(519) 686-3620
Emp Here 45   *Sales* 46,792,312
SIC 5149 Groceries and related products, nec
Kevin Daw
Brian Martell
John Noble
Satish Tatel

D-U-N-S 25-301-1498   (BR)
HUDSON'S BAY COMPANY
BAY, THE
(*Suby of* HUDSON'S BAY COMPANY)
1105 Wellington Rd Suite 5, London, ON, N6E 1V4
(519) 685-4100
Emp Here 250
SIC 5311 Department stores
Stacey Salonin

D-U-N-S 25-094-5524   (BR)
HYDRO ONE NETWORKS INC
(*Suby of* HYDRO ONE LIMITED)
727 Exeter Rd, London, ON, N6E 1L3
(519) 668-5800
Emp Here 80
SIC 4911 Electric services
Lori Lickman

D-U-N-S 24-327-2635   (SL)
KNAUER, CLAIRE PHARMACY LTD
SHOPPERS DRUG MART
395 Southdale Rd E Suite 1, London, ON, N6E 1A2

---

(519) 685-1160
Emp Here 40   *Sales* 10,118,160
SIC 5912 Drug stores and proprietary stores
Claire Knauer
Paul Knauer

D-U-N-S 24-078-0288   (SL)
LAMKO TOOL & MOLD INCORPORATED
105 Towerline Pl, London, ON, N6E 2T3
(519) 686-2643
Emp Here 130   *Sales* 28,860,130
SIC 3544 Special dies, tools, jigs, and fixtures
Kan Yuk Lam
Nina Chen

D-U-N-S 25-743-3797   (BR)
LOBLAWS SUPERMARKETS LIMITED
LOBLAWS WHITE OAKS
(*Suby of* LOBLAW COMPANIES LIMITED)
635 Southdale Rd E, London, ON, N6E 3W6
(519) 686-8007
Emp Here 250
SIC 5411 Grocery stores
Rob Osbalbeston

D-U-N-S 20-581-1552   (BR)
LONDON DISTRICT CATHOLIC SCHOOL BOARD
REGINA MUNDI CATHOLIC COLLEGE
5250 Wellington Rd S, London, ON, N6E 3X8
(519) 663-2088
Emp Here 84
SIC 8221 Colleges and universities
James Martin

D-U-N-S 24-909-4277   (HQ)
MASTERFEEDS INC
(*Suby of* ALLTECH, INC.)
1020 Hargrieve Rd Suite 9, London, ON, N6E 1P5
(519) 685-4300
Sales 85,894,615
SIC 6712 Bank holding companies
Robert Flack
Bill Kittmer

D-U-N-S 20-320-1595   (HQ)
MASTERFEEDS INC
ALLTECH, DIV OF
(*Suby of* ALLTECH, INC.)
1020 Hargrieve Rd Suite 1, London, ON, N6E 1P5
(519) 685-4300
Emp Here 50   *Sales* 243,692,500
SIC 2048 Prepared feeds, nec
Robert Flack

D-U-N-S 20-641-9231   (BR)
MCDONALD'S RESTAURANTS OF CANADA LIMITED
MCDONALD'S RESTAURANTS
(*Suby of* MCDONALD'S CORPORATION)
1074 Wellington Rd, London, ON, N6E 1M2
(519) 691-1042
Emp Here 106
SIC 5812 Eating places
Shannon Smith

D-U-N-S 24-827-5562   (SL)
MEADOW PARK (LONDON) INC
1210 Southdale Rd E Suite 9, London, ON, N6E 1B4
(519) 686-0484
Emp Here 130   *Sales* 8,913,580
SIC 8051 Skilled nursing care facilities
Alex Jarlette
David Jarlette

D-U-N-S 24-735-9193   (HQ)
MUFFLERMAN INC, THE
3480 White Oak Rd, London, ON, N6E 2Z9
(519) 685-0002
Emp Here 8   *Sales* 42,768,715
SIC 7533 Auto exhaust system repair shops
John Brouwer Jr
William Karelsen
Peter Brouwer
Edward Brouwer

Anthony Brouwer

D-U-N-S 20-322-9088   (SL)
NORCARD ENTERPRISES LTD
444 Newbold St, London, ON, N6E 1K3
(519) 690-1717
Emp Here 30   *Sales* 13,304,700
SIC 7389 Business services, nec
Greg Picard

D-U-N-S 25-753-9387   (SL)
ONTARIO WEST INSURANCE BROKERS
1069 Wellington Rd Suite 208, London, ON, N6E 2H6
(519) 657-1400
Emp Here 20   *Sales* 11,598,480
SIC 6411 Insurance agents, brokers, and service
William Boland

D-U-N-S 20-515-6032   (SL)
PRC BOOKS OF LONDON LIMITED
1112 Dearness Dr Unit 15, London, ON, N6E 1N9

Emp Here 120   *Sales* 80,268,960
SIC 7389 Business services, nec

D-U-N-S 20-818-9191   (HQ)
RAM DISTRIBUTORS LIMITED
CENTURA LONDON
993 Adelaide St S, London, ON, N6E 1R5
(519) 681-1961
Emp Here 40   *Sales* 23,407,376
SIC 5023 Homefurnishings
Douglas Del Net

D-U-N-S 24-385-3673   (SL)
RUNDLES NO FRILLS
635 Southdale Rd E, London, ON, N6E 3W6
(866) 987-6453
Emp Here 45   *Sales* 12,336,840
SIC 5411 Grocery stores
Robert Rundle
Marj Rundle

D-U-N-S 20-810-6521   (SL)
SANDY MCTYRE RETAIL LTD
CANADIAN TIRE ASSOCIATE STORE
1125 Wellington Rd, London, ON, N6E 1M1
(519) 681-2655
Emp Here 24   *Sales* 14,942,340
SIC 5531 Auto and home supply stores
Chris Shearer

D-U-N-S 25-487-1726   (HQ)
SAVARIA SALES INSTALLATION AND SERVICES INC
85 Bessemer Rd, London, ON, N6E 1P9
(519) 681-3311
Sales 12,309,300
SIC 1796 Installing building equipment
Marcel Bourassa
William Williams
Christopher Rastin
Eric Bishum

D-U-N-S 25-743-0744   (BR)
SIR CORP
JACK ASTOR'S BAR & GRILL
(*Suby of* SIR CORP)
1070 Wellington Rd Suite 1, London, ON, N6E 3V8
(519) 680-3800
Emp Here 100
SIC 5812 Eating places
Richard Gere

D-U-N-S 25-093-1623   (SL)
STAR-TECH ENTERPRISES INC
25 Invicta Crt, London, ON, N6E 2T4
(519) 681-8672
Emp Here 157   *Sales* 34,854,157
SIC 3544 Special dies, tools, jigs, and fixtures

D-U-N-S 25-239-9126   (BR)
THAMES VALLEY DISTRICT SCHOOL BOARD
WHITE OAKS PUBLIC SCHOOL

(*Suby of* THAMES VALLEY DISTRICT SCHOOL BOARD)
565 Bradley Ave, London, ON, N6E 3Z8
(519) 452-8680
Emp Here 100
SIC 8211 Elementary and secondary schools
Rick Lee

D-U-N-S 24-380-8016   (SL)
UPI OIL LP
3462 White Oak Rd, London, ON, N6E 2Z9
(519) 681-3772
Emp Here 38   *Sales* 47,773,638
SIC 5172 Petroleum products, nec
Robert Sicard

D-U-N-S 24-155-4190   (SL)
VUPOINT SYSTEMS LTD
1025 Hargrieve Rd Unit 8, London, ON, N6E 1P7
(519) 690-0865
Emp Here 52   *Sales* 14,088,984
SIC 1521 Single-family housing construction
Peter Enwright

D-U-N-S 24-329-6725   (BR)
WAL-MART CANADA CORP
(*Suby of* WALMART INC.)
1105 Wellington Rd Suite 3051, London, ON, N6E 1V4
(519) 681-7500
Emp Here 200
SIC 5311 Department stores
Natalie Holder

D-U-N-S 20-559-3411   (HQ)
WIRCO PRODUCTS LIMITED
1011 Adelaide St S, London, ON, N6E 1R4
(519) 681-2100
Sales 11,525,100
SIC 3496 Miscellaneous fabricated wire products
Ronald Scafe

London, ON N6G

D-U-N-S 25-174-1443   (SL)
DHAMI, TEJI DRUGS LTD
SHOPPERS DRUG MART
1680 Richmond St Suite 764, London, ON, N6G 3Y9
(519) 663-9370
Emp Here 52   *Sales* 12,705,056
SIC 5912 Drug stores and proprietary stores
Teji Dhami

D-U-N-S 20-304-6409   (BR)
HUDSON'S BAY COMPANY
BAY, THE
(*Suby of* HUDSON'S BAY COMPANY)
1680 Richmond St, London, ON, N6G 3Y9
(519) 675-0080
Emp Here 110
SIC 5311 Department stores
Elaine Slack-Smith

D-U-N-S 24-099-4525   (SL)
HURON UNIVERSITY COLLEGE
1349 Western Rd, London, ON, N6G 1H3
(519) 679-7905
Emp Here 95   *Sales* 10,700,420
SIC 8221 Colleges and universities
Ramona Lumpkin
Neil Carruthers

D-U-N-S 25-300-0038   (BR)
METRO ONTARIO INC
METRO
(*Suby of* METRO INC)
1225 Wonderland Rd N, London, ON, N6G 2V9
(519) 472-5601
Emp Here 130
SIC 5411 Grocery stores
Tanya Morrison

D-U-N-S 20-182-9558   (HQ)
RETIREMENT LIVING CENTRES INC
EMPIRE LIVING CENTRE
1673 Richmond St Suite 147, London, ON, N6G 2N3
(519) 858-9889
Sales 34,442,100
SIC 6712 Bank holding companies
Rodney Mitchell

D-U-N-S 20-047-7201   (BR)
REVERA INC
MCGARREL PLACE
(*Suby of* GOVERNMENT OF CANADA)
355 Mcgarrell Dr, London, ON, N6G 0B1
(519) 672-0500
Emp Here 170
SIC 8322 Individual and family services
Lynn Mellows

D-U-N-S 20-590-4746   (BR)
THAMES VALLEY DISTRICT SCHOOL BOARD
WILFRID JURY PUBLIC SCHOOL
(*Suby of* THAMES VALLEY DISTRICT SCHOOL BOARD)
950 Lawson Rd, London, ON, N6G 3M2
(519) 452-8690
Emp Here 80
SIC 8211 Elementary and secondary schools
Michael Tamasi

D-U-N-S 25-955-9847   (BR)
UNIVERSITY OF WESTERN ONTARIO, THE
FACULTY OF EDUCATION
(*Suby of* UNIVERSITY OF WESTERN ONTARIO, THE)
1137 Western Rd Suite 1118, London, ON, N6G 1G7
(519) 661-3182
Emp Here 120
SIC 8221 Colleges and universities
Allen Pearson

D-U-N-S 24-411-3049   (BR)
URSULINE RELIGIOUS OF THE DIOCESE OF LONDON IN ONTARIO
BRESCIA UNIVERSITY COLLEGE
(*Suby of* URSULINE RELIGIOUS OF THE DIOCESE OF LONDON IN ONTARIO)
1285 Western Rd, London, ON, N6G 1H2
(519) 432-8353
Emp Here 100
SIC 8221 Colleges and universities
Theresa Topic Md

London, ON N6H

D-U-N-S 24-388-3670   (SL)
1279028 ONTARIO LIMITED
ANGELO'S BAKERY AND DELI
755 Wonderland Rd N, London, ON, N6H 4L1
(519) 777-7772
Emp Here 120   *Sales* 35,217,240
SIC 5461 Retail bakeries
Theresa Ferraro

D-U-N-S 24-093-1068   (SL)
1594058 ONTARIO LTD
REMARK FRESH MARKETS
1190 Oxford St W, London, ON, N6H 4N2
(519) 474-2561
Emp Here 180   *Sales* 52,825,860
SIC 5411 Grocery stores
John Harding
Clifford Remark
Gerry Remark

D-U-N-S 20-625-6885   (SL)
242747 ONTARIO LIMITED
WESTGATE HONDA
680 Oxford St W, London, ON, N6H 1T9
(519) 472-4890
Emp Here 50   *Sales* 24,903,900

SIC 5511 New and used car dealers
Richard Wilson Jr
Penny Wilson
Joseph Haslinger

D-U-N-S 24-632-5245   (SL)
657720 ONTARIO LTD
BELLAMERE WINERY AND EVENTS CENTRE
1260 Gainsborough Rd, London, ON, N6H 5K8
(519) 473-2273
Emp Here 40   *Sales* 10,966,080
SIC 5431 Fruit and vegetable markets
Dan Mader
David Mader
Maureen Thuss
Ross King

D-U-N-S 24-200-5101   (SL)
ABRAHAM, R.J. DRUGS LTD
SHOPPERS DRUG MART
1186 Oxford St W, London, ON, N6H 4N2
(519) 471-7151
Emp Here 40   *Sales* 10,118,160
SIC 5912 Drug stores and proprietary stores
Raison Abraham

D-U-N-S 20-792-3975   (SL)
BARNETT, WINNIFRED MARY KAY CONSULTANT
185 Hunt Club Dr, London, ON, N6H 3Y8
(519) 471-7227
Emp Here 25   *Sales* 16,411,600
SIC 5961 Catalog and mail-order houses
Winnifred Barnett

D-U-N-S 20-635-7357   (SL)
CADILLAC HUMMER OF LONDON
600 Oxford St W, London, ON, N6H 1T9
(519) 472-1199
Emp Here 35   *Sales* 17,634,634
SIC 5511 New and used car dealers
Sarah Mcmaster

D-U-N-S 20-623-5207   (SL)
CHELSEY PARK RETIREMENT COMMUNITY
312 Oxford St W, London, ON, N6H 4N7
(519) 434-3164
Emp Here 49   *Sales* 11,412,639
SIC 6513 Apartment building operators
Sandra Gormandy

D-U-N-S 24-098-3515   (BR)
COSTCO WHOLESALE CANADA LTD
COSTCO
(*Suby of* COSTCO WHOLESALE CORPORATION)
693 Wonderland Rd N Suite 530, London, ON, N6H 4L1
(519) 474-5301
Emp Here 150
SIC 5099 Durable goods, nec
Siamak Nassori

D-U-N-S 24-484-0740   (BR)
DIVERSICARE CANADA MANAGEMENT SERVICES CO., INC
CHELSEY PARK RETIREMENT COMMUNITY
(*Suby of* DCMS HOLDINGS INC)
312 Oxford St W, London, ON, N6H 4N7
(519) 432-1855
Emp Here 300
SIC 8051 Skilled nursing care facilities
Suzi Mcarthur

D-U-N-S 20-127-1665   (HQ)
ESAM CONSTRUCTION LIMITED
ESAM GROUP
301 Oxford St W, London, ON, N6H 1S6
(519) 433-7291
Emp Here 15   *Sales* 22,087,100
SIC 6513 Apartment building operators
Howard Katz
Harvey Katz
Helen Barris

Martin Karp
Gilda Whyne
Priscilla Gerofski

D-U-N-S 24-393-6148   (SL)
FINCH CHEVROLET CADILLAC BUICK GMC LTD
(*Suby of* FINCH AUTO GROUP LTD)
640 Wonderland Rd N, London, ON, N6H 3E5
(519) 657-9411
Emp Here 90   *Sales* 56,635,200
SIC 5511 New and used car dealers
Ryan Finch

D-U-N-S 24-992-5702   (HQ)
FORWARD VISION GROUP INC.
I VISION
1828 Blue Heron Dr Suite 37, London, ON, N6H 0B7
(519) 471-6665
Sales 14,659,680
SIC 5995 Optical goods stores
Scott Catton
Jeanette Pink
Penny Simpson

D-U-N-S 24-728-3484   (HQ)
GOODLIFE FITNESS CENTRES INC
GOODLIFE FITNESS CLUBS
710 Proudfoot Lane, London, ON, N6H 5G5
(519) 661-0190
Emp Here 80   *Sales* 174,568,400
SIC 7991 Physical fitness facilities
David Patchell-Evans
Dan Sawa
Jane Riddell
Pat Davidson

D-U-N-S 25-864-0747   (SL)
JUST VACATIONS INC
VALENTINE TRAVEL
101 Cherryhill Blvd, London, ON, N6H 4S4
(519) 472-2700
Emp Here 25   *Sales* 12,999,175
SIC 4724 Travel agencies
Michael Dawson

D-U-N-S 24-383-8948   (BR)
LOBLAWS INC
REAL CANADIAN SUPERSTORE
(*Suby of* LOBLAW COMPANIES LIMITED)
1205 Oxford St W, London, ON, N6H 1V9
(519) 641-3653
Emp Here 150
SIC 5411 Grocery stores
Richard Masse

D-U-N-S 24-524-5766   (HQ)
LONDON AGRICULTURAL COMMODITIES INC
LAC
(*Suby of* MICHIGAN AGRICULTURAL COMMODITIES, INC.)
1615 North Routledge Pk Unit 43, London, ON, N6H 5L6
(519) 473-9333
Emp Here 27   *Sales* 390,107,000
SIC 6799 Investors, nec
Richard Smibert
Chris Mcmichael

D-U-N-S 24-964-9252   (BR)
METRO ONTARIO INC
METRO
(*Suby of* METRO INC)
301 Oxford St W, London, ON, N6H 1S6
(519) 433-1708
Emp Here 110
SIC 5411 Grocery stores
Ralph Hildebrand

D-U-N-S 20-404-0802   (HQ)
MOFFATT & POWELL LIMITED
MOFFATT & POWELL RONA
1282 Hyde Park Rd, London, ON, N6H 5K5
(519) 472-2000
Emp Here 30   *Sales* 37,146,998
SIC 5211 Lumber and other building materials

Keith Moffatt
Nancy Powell
David Powell
Darcey Quinn

D-U-N-S 25-743-8440   (SL)
MOVATI ATHLETIC (LONDON NORTH) INC.
755 Wonderland Rd N, London, ON, N6H 4L1
(519) 471-7181
Emp Here 100   *Sales* 7,639,700
SIC 7991 Physical fitness facilities
Chuck Kelly

D-U-N-S 24-567-6304   (HQ)
NRZ INVESTMENTS INC
491 Oxford St W, London, ON, N6H 1T2
(519) 472-5410
Emp Here 5   *Sales* 24,903,900
SIC 5541 Gasoline service stations
Nazmin Charania

D-U-N-S 20-851-0792   (SL)
OAKRIDGE FORD SALES (1981) LIMITED
601 Oxford St W, London, ON, N6H 1T8
(519) 472-0944
Emp Here 80   *Sales* 50,342,400
SIC 5511 New and used car dealers
Amain Kadrie

D-U-N-S 24-057-3808   (SL)
OXFORD DODGE CHRYSLER (1992) LTD
1249 Hyde Park Rd, London, ON, N6H 5K6
(519) 473-1010
Emp Here 100   *Sales* 62,928,000
SIC 5511 New and used car dealers
James Bennet

D-U-N-S 20-004-6883   (SL)
PRAXAIR
1435 Hyde Park Rd, London, ON, N6H 0B5
(519) 473-7834
Emp Here 25   *Sales* 18,258,625
SIC 5169 Chemicals and allied products, nec
Lisa Esneault

D-U-N-S 20-179-3333   (BR)
RONA INC
RONA HOME & GARDEN LONDON NORTH
(Suby of LOWE'S COMPANIES, INC.)
820 Blythwood Rd, London, ON, N6H 5T8
(519) 471-6621
Emp Here 110
SIC 5072 Hardware
Nick Ramundo

D-U-N-S 24-373-3412   (HQ)
SOUTH WEST LOCAL HEALTH INTEGRA-TION NETWORK
356 Oxford St W, London, ON, N6H 1T3
(519) 672-0445
Emp Here 20   *Sales* 10,516,275
SIC 8621 Professional organizations
Ron Sapsford

D-U-N-S 24-451-3057   (SL)
SOUTHSIDE CONSTRUCTION (LONDON) LIMITED
SOUTHSIDE GROUP OF COMPANIES
75 Blackfriars St, London, ON, N6H 1K8
(519) 433-0634
Emp Here 40   *Sales* 18,829,240
SIC 1542 Nonresidential construction, nec
Vito Frijia

D-U-N-S 20-128-5020   (HQ)
STERLING MARKING PRODUCTS INC
CANADA STAMP
1147 Gainsborough Rd, London, ON, N6H 5L5
(519) 434-5785
Emp Here 110   *Sales* 42,397,680
SIC 3953 Marking devices
Robert Schram

D-U-N-S 20-590-5735   (BR)
THAMES VALLEY DISTRICT SCHOOL BOARD
OAKRIDGE SECONDARY SCHOOL

(Suby of THAMES VALLEY DISTRICT SCHOOL BOARD)
1040 Oxford St W, London, ON, N6H 1V4
(519) 452-2750
Emp Here 80
SIC 8211 Elementary and secondary schools
Tracy Langelaan

D-U-N-S 25-353-1883   (SL)
UNGER FARM MARKET INC
1010 Gainsborough Rd, London, ON, N6H 5L4
(519) 472-8126
Emp Here 40   *Sales* 10,966,080
SIC 5461 Retail bakeries
Chris Unger
Greg Unger
Kevin Unger

London, ON N6J

D-U-N-S 25-333-5509   (HQ)
1025091 ONTARIO LIMITED
GODFATHER PIZZA
585 Springbank Dr Suite 204, London, ON, N6J 1H3
(519) 641-1178
Emp Here 11   *Sales* 12,825,725
SIC 5812 Eating places
Allan Macdonald

D-U-N-S 25-157-0867   (SL)
990550 ONTARIO INC
GRAND TOURING CARS
766 Wharncliffe Rd S, London, ON, N6J 2N4
(519) 685-2277
Emp Here 30   *Sales* 14,942,340
SIC 5511 New and used car dealers
William Duffield Sr
William Duffield Jr

D-U-N-S 20-547-5929   (BR)
BELL MEDIA INC
NEW PL, THE
(Suby of BCE INC)
1 Communications Rd, London, ON, N6J 4Z1
(519) 686-8810
Emp Here 175
SIC 4832 Radio broadcasting stations
Don Munford

D-U-N-S 20-288-7238   (SL)
BOOMCO DECOR INC
LA-Z-BOY FURNITURE GALLERIES
760 Wharncliffe Rd S, London, ON, N6J 2N4
(519) 686-1441
Emp Here 185   *Sales* 42,994,555
SIC 5712 Furniture stores
Paul Hogeboom
Gregory Hogeboom
Sarah Hewgill

D-U-N-S 24-408-4885   (SL)
COURTESY FORD LINCOLN SALES LIM-ITED
684 Wharncliffe Rd S, London, ON, N6J 2N4
(519) 680-1200
Emp Here 67   *Sales* 42,161,760
SIC 5511 New and used car dealers
William Eansor

D-U-N-S 24-009-4292   (SL)
CULLEN, RAY CHEVROLET LTD
730 Wharncliffe Rd S, London, ON, N6J 2N4
(519) 686-2875
Emp Here 68   *Sales* 42,791,040
SIC 5511 New and used car dealers
Raymond Cullen
Paul Glew

D-U-N-S 20-127-0154   (SL)
DALMAR MOTORS LIMITED
DALMAR VOLKSWAGEN AUDI
475 Wharncliffe Rd S, London, ON, N6J 2N1

(519) 433-3181
Emp Here 37   *Sales* 18,428,886
SIC 5511 New and used car dealers
Michael Dalglish
Marianna Dalglish

D-U-N-S 20-344-8654   (SL)
DAVIS MARTINDALE PROFESSIONAL CORPORATION
373 Commissioners Rd W, London, ON, N6J 1Y4
(519) 673-3141
Emp Here 90   *Sales* 21,085,920
SIC 8748 Business consulting, nec
Brenda Walton

D-U-N-S 20-627-0290   (HQ)
EAST LONDON SPORTS LIMITED
BOARDSHOP, THE
406 Wharncliffe Rd S, London, ON, N6J 2M4
(519) 673-3810
Emp Here 60   *Sales* 15,636,992
SIC 5941 Sporting goods and bicycle shops
Colin Hopper
Frank Wheatley
Jerry Henry

D-U-N-S 25-149-0652   (HQ)
HOGEBOOM, PAUL W. HOLDINGS LTD
LA-Z-BOY FURNITURE GALLERIES
760 Wharncliffe Rd S, London, ON, N6J 2N4
(519) 686-1441
Emp Here 22   *Sales* 11,517,000
SIC 5712 Furniture stores
Paul Hogeboom
Heather Hogeboom

D-U-N-S 24-685-5662   (HQ)
LARLYN PROPERTY MANAGEMENT LIM-ITED
540 Wharncliffe Rd S Suite 200, London, ON, N6J 2N4
(519) 690-0600
Emp Here 40   *Sales* 54,270,800
SIC 6514 Dwelling operators, except apart-ments
Michael Holmes
Larry Holmes
Lynn Holmes

D-U-N-S 25-100-0048   (SL)
LONDON FINE CARS LTD
LONDON HONDA CAR SALES
560 Wharncliffe Rd S, London, ON, N6J 2N4
(519) 649-0889
Emp Here 50   *Sales* 24,903,900
SIC 5511 New and used car dealers
Peter Johnson

D-U-N-S 25-310-9698   (BR)
MCDONALD'S RESTAURANTS OF CANADA LIMITED
MCDONALD'S
(Suby of MCDONALD'S CORPORATION)
462 Wharncliffe Rd S, London, ON, N6J 2M9
(519) 673-0680
Emp Here 75
SIC 5812 Eating places
Cory Mclean

D-U-N-S 24-539-4978   (SL)
MENDRINOS, B. DRUGS LTD
SHOPPERS DRUG MART
467 Wharncliffe Rd S, London, ON, N6J 2M8
(519) 672-4970
Emp Here 50   *Sales* 12,647,700
SIC 5912 Drug stores and proprietary stores
Bertha Mendrinos
George Mendrinos

D-U-N-S 25-743-6089   (BR)
METRO ONTARIO INC
FOOD BASICS
(Suby of METRO INC)
509 Commissioners Rd W, London, ON, N6J 1Y5
(519) 473-2857
Emp Here 150

SIC 5411 Grocery stores
Tim Beclaok

D-U-N-S 25-487-1577   (SL)
OLIVER & ASSOCIATES REAL ESTATE BROKERAGE INC
99 Horton St W, London, ON, N6J 4Y6
(519) 657-2020
Emp Here 75   *Sales* 20,381,700
SIC 6531 Real estate agents and managers
Dennis Oliver

D-U-N-S 24-823-5871   (HQ)
PREFERRED INSURANCE GROUP LIM-ITED
778 Wharncliffe Rd S, London, ON, N6J 2N4
(519) 661-0200
Emp Here 13   *Sales* 19,505,380
SIC 6411 Insurance agents, brokers, and ser-vice
Arthur Lenehan
James Mckellar
Peter Carr

D-U-N-S 20-403-7121   (HQ)
PROBART MOTORS LIMITED
PROBART MAZDA
652 Wharncliffe Rd S, London, ON, N6J 2N4
(519) 649-1440
Emp Here 40   *Sales* 23,409,666
SIC 5511 New and used car dealers
Josef Prossler
Anneliese Prossler
Jeff Prossler

D-U-N-S 25-028-5293   (BR)
REVERA LONG TERM CARE INC
ELMWOOD PLACE
(Suby of GOVERNMENT OF CANADA)
46 Elmwood Pl, London, ON, N6J 1J2
(519) 433-7259
Emp Here 80
SIC 8051 Skilled nursing care facilities
Donna Mccloud

D-U-N-S 25-177-8387   (HQ)
ROBERT Q'S AIRBUS INC
ROBERT Q AIRBUS
105 Wharncliffe Rd S, London, ON, N6J 2K2
(519) 673-6804
Sales 13,548,960
SIC 4131 Intercity and rural bus transportation
Nancy Woodworth

D-U-N-S 20-849-1548   (HQ)
ROBERT Q'S TRAVEL MART INC
105 Wharncliffe Rd S, London, ON, N6J 2K2
(519) 672-9020
Emp Here 1   *Sales* 131,377,724
SIC 4724 Travel agencies
Nancy Woodworth
Pat Collins

D-U-N-S 20-127-6300   (SL)
SOUTH WEST CHRYSLER DODGE INC
658 Wharncliffe Rd S, London, ON, N6J 2N4
(519) 649-2121
Emp Here 33   *Sales* 16,436,574
SIC 5511 New and used car dealers

D-U-N-S 24-070-1081   (SL)
SUDANESE CANADIAN COMMUNITY AS-SOCIATION OF LONDON
360 Springbank Dr Suite 9, London, ON, N6J 1G5
(519) 681-6719
Emp Here 25   *Sales* 10,102,450
SIC 8699 Membership organizations, nec
Nader Abdelmajed
Salh Saidahmed

D-U-N-S 25-239-9209   (BR)
THAMES VALLEY DISTRICT SCHOOL BOARD
WESTMINSTER SECONDARY SCHOOL
(Suby of THAMES VALLEY DISTRICT SCHOOL BOARD)
230 Base Line Rd W, London, ON, N6J 1W1

(519) 452-2900
Emp Here 85
SIC 8211 Elementary and secondary schools
Todd Woollings

D-U-N-S 20-538-4321   (SL)
UNION GAS LIMITED
109 Commissioners Rd W, London, ON, N6J 1X7
(519) 667-4100
Emp Here 5   *Sales* 15,529,285
SIC 4923 Gas transmission and distribution
Ian Ross

London, ON N6K

D-U-N-S 24-418-5042   (BR)
CINEPLEX ODEON CORPORATION
CINEPLEX CINEMAS WESTMOUNT & VIP
(*Suby of* CINEPLEX INC)
755 Wonderland Rd S, London, ON, N6K 1M6
(519) 474-2152
Emp Here 131
SIC 7832 Motion picture theaters, except drive-in
Jeremy Snow

D-U-N-S 20-627-1660   (SL)
COULTER'S PHARMACY (LONDON) LTD
SHOPPERS DRUG MART
1051 Wonderland Rd S, London, ON, N6K 3X4
(519) 472-2222
Emp Here 40   *Sales* 10,118,160
SIC 5912 Drug stores and proprietary stores
Carolee Coulter

D-U-N-S 20-730-0992   (SL)
DIAMOND SECURITY
377 Grand View Ave, London, ON, N6K 2T1
(519) 471-8095
Emp Here 80   *Sales* 31,654,240
SIC 7381 Detective and armored car services
Barry Wilcox

D-U-N-S 20-771-7331   (SL)
DONALD F. JOHNSTON HOLDINGS LTD
CANADIAN TIRE ASSOCIATE STORE
1020 Wonderland Rd S, London, ON, N6K 3S4
(519) 680-1770
Emp Here 180   *Sales* 113,270,400
SIC 5531 Auto and home supply stores
Donald F. Johnston

D-U-N-S 20-051-6891   (SL)
K.G. ENTERPRISES INC
2126 Jack Nash Dr, London, ON, N6K 5R1
(519) 473-4111
Emp Here 226   *Sales* 54,970,206
SIC 3479 Metal coating and allied services
Ken Giles
Sally Giles
Peter Giles

D-U-N-S 25-752-5444   (HQ)
LONDON CHILDREN'S CONNECTION INC
346 Wonderland Rd S, London, ON, N6K 1L3
(519) 471-4300
Sales 18,712,200
SIC 8351 Child day care services
Marion Dunleavy

D-U-N-S 24-877-0877   (BR)
LONDON HEALTH SCIENCES CENTRE
LONDON REGIONAL CANCER CENTRE
(*Suby of* LONDON HEALTH SCIENCES CENTRE)
790 Commissioners Rd W, London, ON, N6K 1C2
(519) 685-8300
Emp Here 365
SIC 8011 Offices and clinics of medical doctors
Robert Bartha

D-U-N-S 25-500-6686   (SL)
MUTUAL CONCEPT COMPUTER GROUP INC
MCCG
785 Wonderland Rd S Suite 253, London, ON, N6K 1M6
(519) 432-8553
Emp Here 55   *Sales* 11,761,805
SIC 7372 Prepackaged software
Frank Barretto
Dave Patterson
Rob Mckinlay
Don Davidson
James House
Wayne Paling
Gord Smith
Ernie Koehler

D-U-N-S 20-181-6928   (BR)
PALASAD BILLIARDS LIMITED
(*Suby of* PALASAD BILLIARDS LIMITED)
141 Pine Valley Blvd, London, ON, N6K 3T6
(519) 685-1390
Emp Here 100
SIC 5044 Office equipment
Bennett Glenn

D-U-N-S 20-508-0617   (HQ)
SIFTON PROPERTIES LIMITED
1295 Riverbend Rd Suite 300, London, ON, N6K 0G2
(519) 434-1000
Emp Here 40   *Sales* 191,745,830
SIC 6553 Cemetery subdividers and developers
Glen Sifton
Richard M. Sifton
Wayne Reid
Martha Wainright
William M. Sifton
Brayl Copp
Donald N Stevens
Ian Wallace
James Harrison
Terri-Lynn Green

D-U-N-S 20-291-3252   (BR)
SIFTON PROPERTIES LIMITED
LONGWORTH RETIREMENT VILLAGE
600 Longworth Rd Suite 118, London, ON, N6K 4X9
(519) 472-1115
Emp Here 75
SIC 6513 Apartment building operators
Mary Jane Mcarthur

D-U-N-S 24-059-6333   (SL)
STIRIS RESEARCH INC
1650 Birchwood Pl, London, ON, N6K 4X3
(519) 471-6211
Emp Here 60   *Sales* 14,057,280
SIC 8742 Management consulting services
Shantal Feltham

D-U-N-S 25-025-4760   (BR)
THAMES VALLEY DISTRICT SCHOOL BOARD
SAUNDERS SECONDARY SCHOOL
(*Suby of* THAMES VALLEY DISTRICT SCHOOL BOARD)
941 Viscount Rd, London, ON, N6K 1H5
(519) 452-2770
Emp Here 150
SIC 8211 Elementary and secondary schools
Brendon White

D-U-N-S 24-784-1083   (SL)
WOMEN'S CHRISTIAN ASSOCIATION OF LONDON
MCCORMICK HOME
2022 Kains Rd Suite 2105, London, ON, N6K 0A8
(519) 432-2648
Emp Here 190   *Sales* 12,213,580
SIC 8361 Residential care
Steve Crawford
Terri Guzyk

London, ON N6L

D-U-N-S 25-747-4353   (SL)
ATCHISON, S. W. PLUMBING & HEATING LTD
4186 Raney Cres Unit 4, London, ON, N6L 1C3
(519) 652-0673
Emp Here 46   *Sales* 10,162,964
SIC 1711 Plumbing, heating, air-conditioning
Scott Atchison
Brenda Atchison

D-U-N-S 20-922-0995   (SL)
BELISLE, G. HOLDINGS (LONDON) LIMITED
4231 Blakie Rd, London, ON, N6L 1B8
(519) 652-5183
Emp Here 100   *Sales* 23,306,500
SIC 1711 Plumbing, heating, air-conditioning
Guy Belisle

D-U-N-S 20-508-6119   (SL)
CANADIAN PREMIER AUTOMOTIVE LTD
TOYOTATOWN
1065 Wharncliffe Rd S, London, ON, N6L 1J9
(519) 680-1800
Emp Here 100   *Sales* 28,330,000
SIC 7515 Passenger car leasing
Emaine Kadri
Walt Darwich
Mark Eisan

D-U-N-S 24-453-0879   (SL)
CANDUCT INDUSTRIES LIMITED
4575 Blakie Rd, London, ON, N6L 1P8
(519) 652-9014
Emp Here 70   *Sales* 16,340,450
SIC 2655 Fiber cans, drums, and similar products
Mark Greaves

D-U-N-S 20-126-8562   (SL)
CARDINAL FINE CABINETRY CORPORATION
165 Exeter Rd, London, ON, N6L 1A4
(519) 652-3295
Emp Here 47   *Sales* 10,825,980
SIC 5712 Furniture stores
Paul Bilyea

D-U-N-S 20-292-5558   (SL)
COLLINS FAMILY CARS INC
LONDON MITSUBISHI
1035 Wharncliffe Rd S, London, ON, N6L 1J9
(519) 690-1600
Emp Here 48   *Sales* 23,907,744
SIC 5511 New and used car dealers
Randy Collins
Gord Colins
Steve Mckeown

D-U-N-S 24-390-8972   (SL)
DODSON, JIM SALES LTD
CANADIAN TIRE
3100 Wonderland Rd S, London, ON, N6L 1A6
(519) 680-2277
Emp Here 45   *Sales* 22,413,510
SIC 5531 Auto and home supply stores
Jim Dodson

D-U-N-S 24-688-1296   (SL)
GERRY'S TRUCK CENTRE LTD
4049 Eastgate Cres, London, ON, N6L 1B7
(519) 652-2100
Emp Here 42   *Sales* 20,919,276
SIC 5511 New and used car dealers
Gerald Wardle
Susan Wardle

D-U-N-S 20-870-1982   (BR)
HOME DEPOT OF CANADA INC
HOME DEPOT
(*Suby of* THE HOME DEPOT INC)
3035 Wonderland Rd S, London, ON, N6L 1R4
(519) 691-1400
Emp Here 200
SIC 5251 Hardware stores
Fraser Rae

D-U-N-S 24-771-5311   (SL)
HULLY GULLY AUTOMOBILES INC
ALTIMATE AUTOMOBILES
940 Wharncliffe Rd S, London, ON, N6L 1K3
(519) 686-3754
Emp Here 35   *Sales* 17,432,730
SIC 5511 New and used car dealers
Randy Collins
Audrey Collins

D-U-N-S 24-947-9916   (HQ)
JMP ENGINEERING INC
4026 Meadowbrook Dr Unit 143, London, ON, N6L 1C9
(519) 652-2741
Sales 16,086,510
SIC 8711 Engineering services
Scott Shawyer

D-U-N-S 20-127-5542   (SL)
JOHNSTONE, T. W. COMPANY LIMITED
JOHNSTONE, T. W.
284 Exeter Rd, London, ON, N6L 1A3
(519) 652-9581
Emp Here 80   *Sales* 20,195,360
SIC 1623 Water, sewer, and utility lines
David Johnstone

D-U-N-S 25-674-7056   (HQ)
LINK + CORPORATION
LINK + CUSTOM BROKERS
4151 Perkins Rd, London, ON, N6L 1G8
(519) 681-4002
Emp Here 30   *Sales* 39,346,628
SIC 4731 Freight transportation arrangement
Brad Leison
John Paczkowski
Charles Kloetstra

D-U-N-S 24-801-4557   (HQ)
MOHWAK MEDBUY CORPORATION
4056 Meadowbrook Dr Unit 135, London, ON, N6L 1E4
(519) 652-1688
Sales 14,375,008
SIC 7389 Business services, nec
Kent Nicholson
Ron Mckerrow
Allan Mongraw
Paul Faguy

D-U-N-S 24-213-8485   (HQ)
OES INC
4056 Blakie Rd, London, ON, N6L 1P7
(519) 652-5833
Sales 10,028,977
SIC 3625 Relays and industrial controls
Linda Russell
Carl Thompson
Michael Reeve

D-U-N-S 20-339-4569   (SL)
PHAETON AUTOMOTIVE GROUP INC
1065 Wharncliffe Rd S, London, ON, N6L 1J9
(519) 680-1800
Emp Here 1   *Sales* 63,656,826
SIC 5511 New and used car dealers
Mohan Janakiraman

D-U-N-S 24-926-0282   (SL)
SIMCONA ELECTRONICS OF CANADA INC
3422 Wonderland Rd S, London, ON, N6L 1A7
(519) 652-1130
Emp Here 25   *Sales* 11,179,350
SIC 5065 Electronic parts and equipment, nec
Carl Candler
Angelo Casciani
Marc Iacona
Blanche Fenster

D-U-N-S 25-156-2138   (SL)

SOUTH LONDON INFINITI-NISSAN INC
1055 Wharncliffe Rd S, London, ON, N6L 1J9
(519) 685-5497
Emp Here 49   *Sales* 24,405,822
SIC 5511 New and used car dealers
John Purkiss
Mark Mccarville

D-U-N-S 20-668-1827   (SL)
SOUTHSIDE CONSTRUCTION LONDON
3089 Wonderland Rd S, London, ON, N6L
1R4
(519) 657-6583
Emp Here 49   *Sales* 15,887,368
SIC 1521 Single-family housing construction
Vito Frijia

D-U-N-S 20-508-0880   (HQ)
SPIVAK, N-J LIMITED
3334 Wonderland Rd S Suite 2, London, ON,
N6L 1A6
(519) 652-3276
Sales 11,905,185
SIC 3273 Ready-mixed concrete
Nick Spivak

D-U-N-S 24-364-8164   (BR)
TEPPERMAN, N. LIMITED
TEPPERMAN'S
(*Suby of* TEPPERMAN, N. LIMITED)
1150 Wharncliffe Rd S, London, ON, N6L 1K3
(519) 433-5353
Emp Here 200
SIC 5712 Furniture stores
Alan Withers

D-U-N-S 25-065-4225   (HQ)
TORNADO INSULATION LTD
4231 Blakie Rd, London, ON, N6L 1B8
(519) 652-5183
Emp Here 20   *Sales* 23,306,500
SIC 1711 Plumbing, heating, air-conditioning
Guy Belisle

D-U-N-S 20-127-7878   (HQ)
TT GROUP LIMITED
LULLABIES OF LONDON DIV OF
1806 Wharncliffe Rd S, London, ON, N6L 1K1
(519) 652-0080
Emp Here 30   *Sales* 142,380,610
SIC 5139 Footwear
James Perivolaris
Andrew Fediw

D-U-N-S 25-140-3002   (SL)
V J L R H LONDON INC
VOLVO OF LONDON
1035 Wharncliffe Rd S, London, ON, N6L 1J9
(519) 681-9400
Emp Here 60   *Sales* 37,756,800
SIC 5511 New and used car dealers
William Duffield

D-U-N-S 25-689-0419   (HQ)
**VANDERWESTEN & RUTHERFORD ASSO-
CIATES, INC**
7242 Colonel Talbot Rd, London, ON, N6L
1H8
(519) 652-5047
Emp Here 40   *Sales* 10,724,340
SIC 8711 Engineering services
Peter Vanderwesten
Bill Rutherford
Robert W Clifford

D-U-N-S 20-582-0546   (SL)
VOSKAMP GREENHOUSES INC
6867 Wellington Rd S, London, ON, N6L 1M3
(519) 686-0303
Emp Here 27   *Sales* 12,709,737
SIC 1542 Nonresidential construction, nec
Ice Bougenstein

London, ON N6M

D-U-N-S 24-424-4740   (BR)
0429746 B.C. LTD
THE ORIGINAL CAKERIE
2825 Innovation Dr, London, ON, N6M 0B6
(519) 937-7777
Emp Here 80
SIC 5142 Packaged frozen goods
Lindsay Jones

D-U-N-S 24-368-5760   (SL)
1376302 ONTARIO INC
DISTINCTIVE HOMES
329 Sovereign Rd, London, ON, N6M 1A6
(519) 859-5056
Emp Here 80   *Sales* 12,469,040
SIC 2434 Wood kitchen cabinets
Michael Juma
Terry Juma

D-U-N-S 25-168-5905   (HQ)
AFFINITY FOOD GROUP INC
WENDY'S RESTAURANT
480 Sovereign Rd Unit 3, London, ON, N6M
1A4
(519) 453-6873
Emp Here 5   *Sales* 18,655,600
SIC 5812 Eating places
Linda Chiarelli
Susan Allison

D-U-N-S 24-006-9310   (SL)
AGO INDUSTRIES INC
500 Sovereign Rd, London, ON, N6M 1A4
(519) 452-3780
Emp Here 100   *Sales* 22,728,900
SIC 3842 Surgical appliances and supplies
Clay Grandy

D-U-N-S 20-844-0289   (BR)
BREWERS RETAIL INC
BEER STORE, THE
(*Suby of* BREWERS RETAIL INC)
280 Sovereign Rd, London, ON, N6M 1B3
(519) 451-3699
Emp Here 200
SIC 5921 Liquor stores
Steve Nangle

D-U-N-S 20-773-0552   (SL)
CANADA TUBEFORM INC
2879 Innovation Dr, London, ON, N6M 0B6
(519) 451-9995
Emp Here 58   *Sales* 11,140,930
SIC 3465 Automotive stampings
Christopher Campbell
David Hewitt
Mark Hamacher

D-U-N-S 24-364-5988   (SL)
CS AUTOMOTIVE TUBING INC
2400 Innovation Dr, London, ON, N6M 0C5
(519) 453-0123
Emp Here 72   *Sales* 16,807,320
SIC 3317 Steel pipe and tubes
Dave Inman

D-U-N-S 20-156-7245   (HQ)
ELGIE BUS LINES LIMITED
400 Sovereign Rd, London, ON, N6M 1A5
(519) 451-4440
Emp Here 12   *Sales* 13,548,960
SIC 4111 Local and suburban transit
Ray Delegard

D-U-N-S 25-398-1690   (HQ)
GIVENS ENGINEERING INC
327 Sovereign Rd, London, ON, N6M 1A6
(519) 453-9008
Sales 11,544,052
SIC 3599 Industrial machinery, nec
Raymond Givens

D-U-N-S 24-346-4448   (BR)
M & T INSTA-PRINT LIMITED
(*Suby of* M & T INSTA-PRINT LIMITED)
318 Neptune Cres Suite 1, London, ON, N6M
1A1

(519) 455-6667
Emp Here 100
SIC 2752 Commercial printing, lithographic
Don Froome

D-U-N-S 24-795-2799   (HQ)
**MCCABE PROMOTIONAL ADVERTISING
INC**
384 Sovereign Rd, London, ON, N6M 1A5
(519) 455-7009
Emp Here 30   *Sales* 26,730,720
SIC 5199 Nondurable goods, nec
James Mccabe
Sandy Mccabe

D-U-N-S 20-750-2774   (SL)
PRO ELECTRIC INC
347 Sovereign Rd, London, ON, N6M 1A6
(519) 451-8740
Emp Here 105   *Sales* 17,516,825
SIC 1731 Electrical work
Richard Krygsman
Darlene Van Der Velde
William William
Tim Beerda
Justin Pennings

D-U-N-S 25-373-4453   (SL)
TALBOT MARKETING INC
NOVAKS UNIFORMS SOLUTIONS
383 Sovereign Rd, London, ON, N6M 1A3
(519) 659-5862
Emp Here 36   *Sales* 14,480,603
SIC 5199 Nondurable goods, nec
Steve Levschuk

London, ON N6N

D-U-N-S 20-554-0409   (SL)
BROSE CANADA INC
(*Suby of* BROSE FAHRZEUGTEILE GMBH &
CO. KG, COBURG)
1500 Max Brose Dr, London, ON, N6N 1P7
(519) 644-5200
Emp Here 950   *Sales* 268,769,250
SIC 3679 Electronic components, nec
Kurt Sauernheimer

D-U-N-S 20-148-4128   (HQ)
CAMPBELL BROS. MOVERS LIMITED
*CAMPBELL'S AUTOMATED RECORDS
MANAGEMENT*
55 Midpark Cres, London, ON, N6N 1A9
(519) 681-5710
Emp Here 50   *Sales* 64,533,350
SIC 4214 Local trucking with storage
Donald Campbell
Neil Campbell
Vickie Campbell

D-U-N-S 20-911-0225   (HQ)
CASSENS TRANSPORT LTD
(*Suby of* CASSENS CORP.)
1237 Green Valley Rd, London, ON, N6N 1E4
(519) 690-2603
Sales 36,409,962
SIC 4212 Local trucking, without storage
Richard Suhre
James Walker
Al Ricard

D-U-N-S 20-059-6067   (BR)
COCA-COLA CANADA BOTTLING LIMITED
(*Suby of* COCA-COLA CANADA BOTTLING
LIMITED)
950 Green Valley Rd, London, ON, N6N 1E3
(800) 241-2653
Emp Here 160
SIC 2086 Bottled and canned soft drinks
Bill Pickering

D-U-N-S 24-121-7108   (HQ)
**COLUMBIA SPORTSWEAR CANADA LIM-
ITED**
(*Suby of* COLUMBIA SPORTSWEAR COM-

PANY)
1425 Max Brose Dr Suite 1, London, ON, N6N
0A2
(519) 644-5000
Sales 50,251,980
SIC 5136 Men's and boy's clothing
Tim Boyle

D-U-N-S 24-737-7604   (SL)
COLUMBIA SPORTSWEAR CANADA LP
(*Suby of* COLUMBIA SPORTSWEAR COM-
PANY)
1425 Max Brose Dr Suite 1, London, ON, N6N
0A2
(519) 644-5000
Emp Here 300   *Sales* 251,259,900
SIC 5136 Men's and boy's clothing
David Brule

D-U-N-S 24-576-5458   (SL)
DIELCO INDUSTRIAL CONTRACTORS LTD
80 Enterprise Dr S, London, ON, N6N 1C2
(519) 685-2224
Emp Here 70   *Sales* 17,233,020
SIC 1796 Installing building equipment
Case Dieleman
Jason Dieleman
Grace Dieleman

D-U-N-S 25-524-3487   (SL)
ELGIN MOTOR FREIGHT INC
(*Suby of* CHALLENGER INVESTMENTS
INC)
1497 Wilton Grove Rd, London, ON, N6N 1M3
(519) 644-9090
Emp Here 170   *Sales* 34,970,020
SIC 4213 Trucking, except local
Daniel Einwechter
Eugene Moser

D-U-N-S 20-126-6079   (SL)
FOREST CITY GRAPHICS LIMITED
982 Hubrey Rd, London, ON, N6N 1B5
(519) 668-2191
Emp Here 100   *Sales* 16,402,700
SIC 2771 Greeting cards
Dan Robson

D-U-N-S 24-009-4342   (SL)
GORDON, AL ELECTRIC LIMITED
1099 Progress Dr, London, ON, N6N 1B7
(519) 672-1273
Emp Here 65   *Sales* 14,158,885
SIC 1731 Electrical work
Allan Gordon
Margaret Gordon

D-U-N-S 20-085-9697   (BR)
IPEX INC
MULTI FITTINGS
(*Suby of* ALIAXIS)
1055 Wilton Grove Rd, London, ON, N6N 1C9
(519) 681-2140
Emp Here 115
SIC 3089 Plastics products, nec
Derek Reeves

D-U-N-S 20-400-9732   (HQ)
LAFLECHE ROOFING (1992) LIMITED
1100 Progress Dr, London, ON, N6N 1B8
(519) 681-7610
Emp Here 29   *Sales* 11,980,595
SIC 1761 Roofing, siding, and sheetMetal
work
Christopher Lafleche
Mark Lafleche
Mark Garland

D-U-N-S 24-357-9245   (SL)
**LONDON AUTOMOTIVE & MANUFACTUR-
ING LTD**
LA&M
(*Suby of* BEAR DIVERSIFIED, INC.)
1477 Sise Rd, London, ON, N6N 1E1
(519) 686-0489
Emp Here 47   *Sales* 29,576,160
SIC 5511 New and used car dealers
Gregory Ducharme

Craig Hodgins
Miriam Ducharme

D-U-N-S 20-346-3740   (BR)
MAGNA SEATING INC
QUALTECH SEATING SYSTEMS DIV OF
(*Suby of* MAGNA INTERNATIONAL INC)
3915 Commerce Rd, London, ON, N6N 1P4
(519) 808-9035
Emp Here 350
SIC 3714 Motor vehicle parts and accessories
Kurt Windibank

D-U-N-S 20-177-9829   (HQ)
MARTINREA AUTOMOTIVE SYSTEMS CANADA LTD
MARTINREA AUTOMOTIVE SYSTEMS CANADA (LONDON)
(*Suby of* MARTINREA INTERNATIONAL INC)
3820 Commerce Rd, London, ON, N6N 1P6
(519) 644-1567
Emp Here 100   *Sales* 22,384,300
SIC 3711 Motor vehicles and car bodies
Rocco Marinaccio

D-U-N-S 25-220-8087   (SL)
MEDICAL TECHNOLOGY (W.B.) INC
MEDTECH
1015 Green Valley Rd, London, ON, N6N 1E4
(519) 686-0028
Emp Here 220   *Sales* 58,204,960
SIC 3999 Manufacturing industries, nec
Ranjie Singh
Karen Parsan-Singh

D-U-N-S 24-763-7445   (SL)
MEDICAL TECHNOLOGY (W.B.) INC
MED TECH
1040 Wilton Grove Rd, London, ON, N6N 1C7
(519) 686-0028
Emp Here 49   *Sales* 10,722,376
SIC 3999 Manufacturing industries, nec
Ranjie Singh

D-U-N-S 20-311-4392   (SL)
NATRA CHOCOLATE AMERICA INC
(*Suby of* NATRA SOCIEDAD ANONIMA)
2800 Roxburgh Rd, London, ON, N6N 1K9
(519) 681-9494
Emp Here 54   *Sales* 32,289,567
SIC 5149 Groceries and related products, nec
Pedro Betancor

D-U-N-S 25-999-9035   (BR)
NESTLE CANADA INC
(*Suby of* NESTLE S.A.)
980 Wilton Grove Rd, London, ON, N6N 1C7
(519) 686-0182
Emp Here 500
SIC 2023 Dry, condensed and evaporated dairy products
Jamie Music

D-U-N-S 24-846-4950   (BR)
PEPSI BOTTLING GROUP (CANADA), ULC, THE
PEPSICO BEVERAGES CANADA
(*Suby of* PBG INVESTMENT (LUXEMBOURG) SARL)
40 Enterprise Dr Suite 1, London, ON, N6N 1A7
(519) 681-0030
Emp Here 103
SIC 5149 Groceries and related products, nec
Todd Squarek

D-U-N-S 24-345-9968   (BR)
PEPSICO CANADA ULC
FRITO LAY CANADA
(*Suby of* PEPSICO, INC.)
40 Enterprise Dr Suite 2, London, ON, N6N 1A7
(519) 668-4004
Emp Here 150
SIC 5145 Confectionery
Terry Long

D-U-N-S 25-352-3377   (SL)

PERMANENT SASH & DOOR COMPANY LTD
1040 Wilton Grove Rd, London, ON, N6N 1C7
(519) 686-6020
Emp Here 60   *Sales* 15,693,180
SIC 6712 Bank holding companies
Robert A Hunt
Douglas Langford

D-U-N-S 24-059-5157   (SL)
RIVERSIDE MILLWORK GROUP INC
1275 Hubrey Rd Suite 7, London, ON, N6N 1E2
(519) 686-7573
Emp Here 75   *Sales* 33,538,050
SIC 5031 Lumber, plywood, and millwork
Denis Crane
Wayne Dunn
Catherine Crane
Diane Dunn

D-U-N-S 25-147-4698   (SL)
ROCKY'S HARLEY DAVIDSON LTD
ROCKY'S HARLEY DAVIDSON
900 Wilton Grove Rd, London, ON, N6N 1C7
(519) 438-1450
Emp Here 25   *Sales* 12,451,950
SIC 5571 Motorcycle dealers
Jeffri Duncan
Dominick Gaudino
Brian Duncan

D-U-N-S 24-425-9045   (BR)
RYDER TRUCK RENTAL CANADA LTD
RYDER CANADA
(*Suby of* RYDER SYSTEM, INC.)
2724 Roxburgh Rd Suite 7, London, ON, N6N 1K9

Emp Here 200
SIC 7513 Truck rental and leasing, no drivers
Mark Edds

D-U-N-S 24-336-4551   (HQ)
STIHL LIMITED
(*Suby of* STIHL HOLDING AG & CO. KG.)
1515 Sise Rd Suite 5666, London, ON, N6N 1E1
(519) 681-3000
Emp Here 60   *Sales* 40,969,320
SIC 5084 Industrial machinery and equipment
Gregory Quigg
Angelo Dethomasis
Elizabeth Evanski
Jack Jones
Hans Peter Stihl

D-U-N-S 20-943-8852   (HQ)
TEAM TRUCK CENTRES LIMITED
795 Wilton Grove Rd, London, ON, N6N 1N7
(519) 681-6868
Emp Here 40   *Sales* 94,392,000
SIC 5511 New and used car dealers
Robert O'dowda Sr
Robert O'dowda Jr

D-U-N-S 24-924-5911   (BR)
TEAM TRUCK CENTRES LIMITED
(*Suby of* TEAM TRUCK CENTRES LIMITED)
1040 Wilton Grove Rd, London, ON, N6N 1C7
(519) 453-2970
Emp Here 160
SIC 5511 New and used car dealers
Kathee Johnson

D-U-N-S 24-079-9312   (SL)
TONDA CONSTRUCTION LIMITED
1085 Wilton Grove Rd, London, ON, N6N 1C9
(519) 686-5200
Emp Here 32   *Sales* 15,063,392
SIC 1542 Nonresidential construction, nec
Thomas Weller
Darrin Weller
Tracey Poels
Dorothy Weller

D-U-N-S 24-763-8125   (SL)
TRAC RAIL INC

ZTR CONTROL SYSTEMS CANADA
955 Green Valley Rd, London, ON, N6N 1E4
(519) 452-1233
Emp Here 70   *Sales* 13,330,940
SIC 3625 Relays and industrial controls
Sam Hassan
Tod Warner
Aldo Liberatore
Derek Shipley

D-U-N-S 20-555-4145   (SL)
TRANSFORM AUTOMOTIVE CANADA LIMITED
(*Suby of* AMSTED INDUSTRIES INCORPORATED)
3745 Commerce Rd, London, ON, N6N 1R1
(519) 644-2434
Emp Here 100   *Sales* 22,384,300
SIC 3714 Motor vehicle parts and accessories
D William Shaw
Denis Hartman

D-U-N-S 20-375-5726   (SL)
UNION GAS
1151 Green Valley Rd, London, ON, N6N 1E4

Emp Here 5   *Sales* 15,529,285
SIC 4923 Gas transmission and distribution

D-U-N-S 25-403-8128   (BR)
UNITED PARCEL SERVICE CANADA LTD
UPS
(*Suby of* UNITED PARCEL SERVICE, INC.)
60 Midpark Rd, London, ON, N6N 1B3
(519) 686-8200
Emp Here 112
SIC 4513 Air courier services
Carlos Toth

D-U-N-S 24-985-2617   (SL)
WILTON GROVE TRUCK SALES & SERVICES LIMITED
LONDON MACK
(*Suby of* CENTRAL AUTOMOTIVE SERVICES LIMITED)
1445 Sise Rd Suite 1, London, ON, N6N 1E1
(519) 649-1771
Emp Here 24   *Sales* 11,953,872
SIC 5511 New and used car dealers
John Slotegraaf
Barbara Slotegraaf

London, ON N6P

D-U-N-S 25-743-4183   (BR)
ALLIED SYSTEMS (CANADA) COMPANY
(*Suby of* ALLIED SYSTEMS HOLDINGS, INC.)
6151 Colonel Talbot Rd, London, ON, N6P 1J2

Emp Here 400
SIC 4213 Trucking, except local
Peter Henderson

D-U-N-S 20-701-2055   (SL)
ARMO-TOOL LIMITED
(*Suby of* 552461 ONTARIO LTD)
9827 Longwoods Rd, London, ON, N6P 1P2
(519) 652-3700
Emp Here 140   *Sales* 31,080,140
SIC 3544 Special dies, tools, jigs, and fixtures
Benjamin Whitney

D-U-N-S 20-555-0320   (SL)
CAN-AM TRAILERS LIMITED
CAN-AM RV CENTRE
6068 Colonel Talbot Rd, London, ON, N6P 1J1
(519) 652-3284
Emp Here 28   *Sales* 13,946,184
SIC 5561 Recreational vehicle dealers
Andrew D. Thomson
Kirk Thomson

D-U-N-S 20-059-3304   (HQ)
CARVEST PROPERTIES LIMITED
TRICAR
(*Suby of* CARAPELLA GROUP LIMITED)
3800 Colonel Talbot Rd, London, ON, N6P 1H5
(519) 653-4124
Sales 46,915,568
SIC 6531 Real estate agents and managers
Joe Carapella

D-U-N-S 24-413-0555   (SL)
D. GRANT CONSTRUCTION LIMITED
9887 Longwoods Rd, London, ON, N6P 1P2
(519) 652-2949
Emp Here 35   *Sales* 16,475,585
SIC 1542 Nonresidential construction, nec
Michael Grant

D-U-N-S 25-361-9860   (HQ)
ENERGY FUNDAMENTALS GROUP LIMITED PARTNERSHIP
2324 Main St, London, ON, N6P 1A9
(519) 652-3196
Sales 27,952,713
SIC 4922 Natural gas transmission
J.P. Todd Karry
Joe Brophy
Greg Marchant

D-U-N-S 24-879-8725   (SL)
R V OUTFITTERS
6068 Colonel Talbot Rd, London, ON, N6P 1J1
(519) 652-3284
Emp Here 25   *Sales* 12,451,950
SIC 5561 Recreational vehicle dealers
Andrew Thompson

D-U-N-S 24-823-7034   (SL)
TRICAR DEVELOPMENTS INC
3800 Colonel Talbot Rd, London, ON, N6P 1H5
(519) 652-8900
Emp Here 50   *Sales* 14,429,150
SIC 1522 Residential construction, nec
Joe Carapella
Craig James

Long Sault, ON K0C

D-U-N-S 25-580-6192   (BR)
OMNI HEALTH CARE LTD
WOODLAND VILLA NURSING HOME
(*Suby of* OMNI HEALTH INVESTMENTS INC)
30 Mille Roches Rd Suite 388, Long Sault, ON, K0C 1P0
(613) 534-2276
Emp Here 120
SIC 8051 Skilled nursing care facilities
Michael Rasenberg

D-U-N-S 24-363-5450   (HQ)
SABIC INNOVATIVE PLASTICS CANADA INC
SABIC POLYMERSHAPES
1 Structured Product Dr, Long Sault, ON, K0C 1P0
(905) 372-6801
Sales 73,943,320
SIC 5162 Plastics materials and basic shapes
Yousef Abdullah Al-Benyan
Paul Van Laren
Sameer Singla

Longford Mills, ON L0K

D-U-N-S 24-822-8546   (HQ)
STEPAN CANADA INC
(*Suby of* STEPAN COMPANY)
3800 Longford Mills Rd, Longford Mills, ON,

L0K 1L0
(705) 326-7329
Emp Here 57   *Sales* 17,609,302
SIC 2869 Industrial organic chemicals, nec
James Hurlbutt

Longlac, ON P0T

D-U-N-S 20-279-7700   (SL)
LONGLAC LUMBER INC
101 Blueberry Rd, Longlac, ON, P0T 2A0
(807) 876-2626
Emp Here 70   *Sales* 10,910,410
SIC 2421 Sawmills and planing mills, general
Wolf Gericke

Lucknow, ON N0G

D-U-N-S 20-129-0004   (HQ)
MONTGOMERY FORD SALES LIMITED
701 Campbell St, Lucknow, ON, N0G 2H0
(519) 528-2813
Emp Here 18   *Sales* 17,930,808
SIC 5511 New and used car dealers
Ian Montgomery

D-U-N-S 24-025-9457   (HQ)
SNOBELEN FARMS LTD
323 Havelock St, Lucknow, ON, N0G 2H0
(519) 528-2092
Emp Here 8   *Sales* 29,353,840
SIC 5153 Grain and field beans
Troy Snobelen

Lyn, ON K0E

D-U-N-S 20-129-0202   (HQ)
BURNBRAE FARMS LIMITED
3356 County Road 27, Lyn, ON, K0E 1M0
(613) 345-5651
Emp Here 800   *Sales* 716,716,000
SIC 5144 Poultry and poultry products
Margaret Hudson
Donald Oddie
Joseph Edward Hudson
Joseph Hudson

D-U-N-S 25-197-1321   (HQ)
WESLEYAN CHURCH OF CANADA
3545 Centennial Rd, Lyn, ON, K0E 1M0
(613) 345-3424
Emp Here 4   *Sales* 10,828,792
SIC 8661 Religious organizations
Mark Parker

Lyndhurst, ON K0E

D-U-N-S 24-199-2663   (BR)
TOWNSHIP OF LEEDS AND THE THOU-SAND ISLANDS
F D TWO REAR OF LEEDS & LANSDOWNE
(*Suby of* TOWNSHIP OF LEEDS AND THE THOUSAND ISLANDS)
Gd, Lyndhurst, ON, K0E 1N0
(613) 928-3303
Emp Here 100
SIC 1521 Single-family housing construction
Gary Bennet

Maberly, ON K0H

D-U-N-S 20-015-0253   (HQ)

1059895 ONTARIO INC
CRAIN'S CONSTRUCTION
Gd, Maberly, ON, K0H 2B0
(613) 268-2308
Emp Here 4   *Sales* 16,401,000
SIC 6712 Bank holding companies
Wilbert Crain
Norman Crain
Thomas Crain
Archie Crain

D-U-N-S 20-893-5270   (SL)
CRAINS' CONSTRUCTION LIMITED
(*Suby of* 1059895 ONTARIO INC)
1800 Mayberly 2 Elphin Rd, Maberly, ON, K0H 2B0
(613) 268-2308
Emp Here 55   *Sales* 13,540,230
SIC 1794 Excavation work
Wilbert Crain
Norman Crain
Tom Crain
Archie Crain

Mactier, ON P0C

D-U-N-S 20-716-2298   (SL)
GORDON BAY MARINE LTD
55a Hatherley Rd Suite 1, Mactier, ON, P0C 1H0
(705) 375-2623
Emp Here 40   *Sales* 19,923,120
SIC 5551 Boat dealers
Bruce Hatherley
Benjamin Hatherley

Madawaska, ON K0J

D-U-N-S 20-034-4034   (HQ)
MURRAY BROS. LUMBER COMPANY LIM-ITED
24749 Hwy 60, Madawaska, ON, K0J 2C0
(613) 637-2840
Emp Here 1   *Sales* 15,446,960
SIC 2421 Sawmills and planing mills, general
Dowdall Murray
Terrence Murray
Edward Murray
Rita Murray
Robert Murray

Madoc, ON K0K

D-U-N-S 24-315-5228   (BR)
IKO INDUSTRIES LTD
ARMOROOF DIV OF
(*Suby of* GOLDIS ENTERPRISES, INC.)
105084 Hwy 7, Madoc, ON, K0K 2K0
(613) 473-0430
Emp Here 110
SIC 2952 Asphalt felts and coatings
Paul Paszt

D-U-N-S 20-122-0753   (SL)
IVANHOE CHEESE INC
(*Suby of* GAY LEA FOODS CO-OPERATIVE LIMITED)
11301 Hwy 62, Madoc, ON, K0K 2K0
(613) 473-4269
Emp Here 80   *Sales* 27,655,200
SIC 2022 Cheese; natural and processed
Michael Barrett

Magnetawan, ON P0A

D-U-N-S 24-176-1217   (SL)
DAVIS INDUSTRIES
4855 520 Hwy, Magnetawan, ON, P0A 1P0

Emp Here 46   *Sales* 13,274,818
SIC 1522 Residential construction, nec
Rob Davis

Maidstone, ON N0R

D-U-N-S 24-197-2199   (SL)
401 TRUCKSOURCE INC
401 MACK
4293 County Rd 46, Maidstone, ON, N0R 1K0
(519) 737-6956
Emp Here 53   *Sales* 33,351,840
SIC 5511 New and used car dealers
Frank Kemski
Erwin Pare
Michel (Mike) Billette
Susan Cassidy
Willy Janca

D-U-N-S 24-889-6649   (SL)
905364 ONTARIO LIMITED
EXPRESSWAY TRUCKS WINDSOR
3817 County Rd 46 Rr 3, Maidstone, ON, N0R 1K0
(519) 737-2630
Emp Here 26   *Sales* 12,950,028
SIC 5531 Auto and home supply stores
Scott Lawson
Harold Paquette

Maitland, ON K0E

D-U-N-S 20-563-2362   (BR)
INVISTA (CANADA) COMPANY
(*Suby of* KOSA US INVESTMENTS SARL)
1400 County Rd 2, Maitland, ON, K0E 1P0
(613) 348-4204
Emp Here 80
SIC 5169 Chemicals and allied products, nec
Joe Hendricks

Mallorytown, ON K0E

D-U-N-S 25-105-6008   (SL)
SERSA TOTAL TRACK LTD
(*Suby of* RHOMBERG SERSA RAIL HOLD-ING GMBH)
68 County Rd 5, Mallorytown, ON, K0E 1R0
(613) 923-5702
Emp Here 54   *Sales* 13,294,044
SIC 1799 Special trade contractors, nec
Marko Pohlmann

Manitouwadge, ON P0T

D-U-N-S 25-248-8424   (SL)
MANROC DEVELOPMENTS INC
7 Black Rd, Manitouwadge, ON, P0T 2C0
(807) 826-4564
Emp Here 100   *Sales* 25,244,200
SIC 1629 Heavy construction, nec
Don Simoneau

Manotick, ON K4M

D-U-N-S 25-501-2817   (HQ)
ALSCOTT AIR SYSTEMS LIMITED
1127 River Rd, Manotick, ON, K4M 1B4

---

(613) 692-9517
Emp Here 1   *Sales* 11,653,250
SIC 1711 Plumbing, heating, air-conditioning
Alan Wyllie
Keith Carlaw

D-U-N-S 25-458-2703   (HQ)
ARMSTRONG & QUAILE ASSOCIATES INC
5858 Rideau Valley Dr N, Manotick, ON, K4M 1B3
(613) 692-0751
Emp Here 4   *Sales* 21,248,280
SIC 6211 Security brokers and dealers
Kenneth Armstrong

D-U-N-S 25-353-9993   (HQ)
CARCANADA CORPORATION
5791 Regional Road 73, Manotick, ON, K4M 1A5
(613) 489-1212
Emp Here 45   *Sales* 37,756,800
SIC 5511 New and used car dealers
Patrick Butler

D-U-N-S 25-350-2496   (SL)
HURST MARINA LTD
2726 River Rd, Manotick, ON, K4M 1B4
(613) 692-1234
Emp Here 40   *Sales* 19,923,120
SIC 5551 Boat dealers
Peter Hurst
Barb Gour

D-U-N-S 24-633-7968   (SL)
MURPHY, DAN FORD SALES LTD
1346 Bankfield Rd, Manotick, ON, K4M 1A7
(613) 692-3594
Emp Here 37   *Sales* 18,428,886
SIC 5511 New and used car dealers
Charlene Brunet
Jonathon Donaldson

D-U-N-S 24-312-2087   (BR)
OTTAWA CATHOLIC DISTRICT SCHOOL BOARD
ST. MARK CATHOLIC HIGH SCHOOL
(*Suby of* OTTAWA CATHOLIC DISTRICT SCHOOL BOARD)
1040 Dozois Rd, Manotick, ON, K4M 1B2
(613) 692-2551
Emp Here 130
SIC 8211 Elementary and secondary schools
Andre Potvin

D-U-N-S 24-851-0294   (HQ)
RIDEAU VALLEY CONSERVATION AU-THORITY
3889 Rideau Valley Dr, Manotick, ON, K4M 1A5
(613) 692-3571
Emp Here 70   *Sales* 14,076,640
SIC 8713 Surveying services
Sommer Casgrain

D-U-N-S 24-093-7867   (SL)
ROBINSON'S YOUR INDEPENDENT GRO-CER
1160 Beaverwood Dr, Manotick, ON, K4M 1A5
(613) 692-2828
Emp Here 75   *Sales* 22,010,775
SIC 5411 Grocery stores
Jaime Robinson

D-U-N-S 20-203-0461   (SL)
ROYAL LEPAGE GALE REAL ESTATE
5510 Manotick Main St, Manotick, ON, K4M 0A1
(613) 692-2555
Emp Here 45   *Sales* 12,229,020
SIC 6531 Real estate agents and managers
Kim Aiello

Maple, ON L4A

D-U-N-S 25-499-8602   (HQ)
VAUGHAN PUBLIC LIBRARIES

BATHURST CLARK RESOURCE LIBRARY
2191 Major Mackenzie Dr, Maple, ON, L4A 4W2
(905) 653-7323
Emp Here 80   *Sales* 20,608,380
SIC 8231 Libraries
Margie Singleton

Maple, ON L6A

D-U-N-S 20-823-3577   (HQ)
ALPA ROOF TRUSSES INC
ALPA ROOF TRUSSES
(*Suby of* ALPA LUMBER INC)
10311 Keele St, Maple, ON, L6A 3Y9
(905) 832-2250
Sales 28,855,500
SIC 2439 Structural wood members, nec
Brandon Frankfort

D-U-N-S 20-181-9281   (HQ)
ANCO CHEMICALS INC
85 Malmo Crt, Maple, ON, L6A 1R4
(905) 832-2276
Emp Here 15   *Sales* 14,606,900
SIC 5169 Chemicals and allied products, nec
Anthony Roehrig
John Evans
Tony Roehrig

D-U-N-S 25-074-1373   (SL)
ANNE & MAX TANENBAUM COMMUNITY HEBREW ACADEMY OF TORONTO
9600 Bathurst St, Maple, ON, L6A 3Z8

Emp Here 100   *Sales* 9,282,600
SIC 8211 Elementary and secondary schools
Ellen Chaikof
Sara Dobner
Sidney Eisen
Gary Elman
Judy Engel
Michelle Factor
Percy Fink
Melvyn Finkelstein
Stephen Freedhoof
Brenlee Gales

D-U-N-S 20-596-2517   (SL)
ARGO LUMBER INC
ARGO LUMBER
(*Suby of* ALPA LUMBER INC)
10275 Keele St, Maple, ON, L6A 3Y9
(905) 832-2251
Emp Here 60   *Sales* 34,177,680
SIC 5031 Lumber, plywood, and millwork
John Di Poce
Giovanni Guglietti
George Frankforth
Carmen Guglietti
Donald A. Maciver

D-U-N-S 20-182-0180   (SL)
BLAIR BUILDING MATERIALS INC
10445 Keele St, Maple, ON, L6A 3Y9
(416) 798-4996
Emp Here 50   *Sales* 12,652,950
SIC 5211 Lumber and other building materials
Martin Lieberman
Dante Digiovanni

D-U-N-S 20-383-7286   (BR)
COMSALE COMPUTER INC
(*Suby of* COMSALE COMPUTER INC)
158 Wallenberg Dr, Maple, ON, L6A 4M2
(647) 648-2323
Emp Here 100
SIC 5045 Computers, peripherals, and software
Jack Hayes

D-U-N-S 20-734-6540   (SL)
DALIMONTE, M. PHARMACY LTD
SHOPPERS DRUG MART

2943 Major Mackenzie Dr Suite 1, Maple, ON, L6A 3N9
(905) 832-9954
Emp Here 40   *Sales* 10,118,160
SIC 5912 Drug stores and proprietary stores
Marcello Dalimonte

D-U-N-S 20-189-8454   (SL)
EAGLES NEST GOLF CLUB INC
(*Suby of* YORK MAJOR HOLDINGS INC)
10000 Dufferin St, Maple, ON, L6A 1S3
(905) 417-2300
Emp Here 80   *Sales* 20,195,360
SIC 1629 Heavy construction, nec
Duane Aubie

D-U-N-S 24-175-9526   (SL)
EASTERN POWER DEVELOPERS
7 Eaglet Crt, Maple, ON, L6A 4E2

Emp Here 80   *Sales* 50,129,120
SIC 4911 Electric services
Todd Brillinger

D-U-N-S 24-945-6229   (HQ)
FABCO PLASTIQUES INC
(*Suby of* FABCO PLASTICS WHOLESALE (ONTARIO) LIMITED)
2175 Teston Rd Po Box 2175 Stn Main, Maple, ON, L6A 1T3
(905) 832-0600
Emp Here 45   *Sales* 38,708,285
SIC 5162 Plastics materials and basic shapes
William Kehren
Gary Davidson

D-U-N-S 20-145-4352   (HQ)
FABRICATED PLASTICS LIMITED
(*Suby of* DENALI INCORPORATED)
2175 Teston Rd, Maple, ON, L6A 1R3
(905) 832-8161
Sales 16,488,148
SIC 3299 NonMetallic mineral products,
Greg Landry
Peter Young

D-U-N-S 25-213-2097   (SL)
GLOBAL PRECAST INC
(*Suby of* MAVONE HOLDINGS LIMITED)
2101 Teston Rd, Maple, ON, L6A 1R3
(905) 832-4307
Emp Here 110   *Sales* 19,714,090
SIC 3272 Concrete products, nec
Vito Cannone

D-U-N-S 24-329-6857   (BR)
LOBLAWS INC
FORTINOS
(*Suby of* LOBLAW COMPANIES LIMITED)
2911 Major Mackenzie Dr Suite 80, Maple, ON, L6A 3N9
(905) 417-0490
Emp Here 250
SIC 5411 Grocery stores
Anita Williams

D-U-N-S 24-353-8159   (BR)
LOWE'S COMPANIES CANADA, ULC
LOWE'S OF MAPLE
(*Suby of* LOWE'S COMPANIES, INC.)
200 Mcnaughton Rd E, Maple, ON, L6A 4E2
(905) 879-2450
Emp Here 100
SIC 5211 Lumber and other building materials
Derek Briggs

D-U-N-S 25-107-9380   (SL)
LT CUSTOM FURNISHINGS INC
10899 Keele St, Maple, ON, L6A 0K6
(905) 303-0005
Emp Here 180   *Sales* 27,777,960
SIC 2541 Wood partitions and fixtures
Frank Polsinelli
Nghi Nguyen
Brian Moreland

D-U-N-S 24-823-2261   (SL)
MAPLE ACURA

111 Auto Vaughan Dr, Maple, ON, L6A 4A1
(289) 342-0185
Emp Here 25   *Sales* 12,451,950
SIC 5511 New and used car dealers
Anthony Scigliano

D-U-N-S 25-962-9116   (SL)
MAPLE VOLKSWAGEN
260 Sweetriver Blvd, Maple, ON, L6A 4V3
(905) 832-5711
Emp Here 30   *Sales* 14,942,340
SIC 5511 New and used car dealers
Jim Garofalo

D-U-N-S 20-550-1877   (HQ)
MODULAR & CUSTOM CABINETS LIMITED
MCC
10721 Keele St, Maple, ON, L6A 3Y9
(905) 832-8311
Sales 12,500,895
SIC 3843 Dental equipment and supplies
John Cocciardi
Wayne Lebeau
Jim Michel

D-U-N-S 24-305-7668   (SL)
NORTHERN TRANSFORMER CORPORATION
245 Mcnaughton Rd E, Maple, ON, L6A 4P5
(905) 669-1853
Emp Here 80   *Sales* 15,235,360
SIC 3612 Transformers, except electric
Alexei Miecznikowski
Giovanni Marcelli
Justin Emmanuel

D-U-N-S 24-096-3905   (SL)
SHERWOOD COURT LONG TERM CARE CENTRE
300 Ravineview Dr Suite 1, Maple, ON, L6A 3P8
(905) 303-3565
Emp Here 76   *Sales* 4,575,048
SIC 8052 Intermediate care facilities
Gary Bowers

D-U-N-S 24-624-4982   (SL)
SOLID WALL CONCRETE FORMING LTD
45 Rodinea Rd Suite 8, Maple, ON, L6A 1R3
(905) 832-4311
Emp Here 80   *Sales* 19,798,640
SIC 1771 Concrete work
Helio Dias
Marco Desimone

D-U-N-S 25-139-0241   (SL)
ST. PHILLIPS FOODS LIMITED
ST. PHILLIPS BAKERY
2563 Major Mackenzie Dr Suite 8, Maple, ON, L6A 2E8
(905) 832-5688
Emp Here 100   *Sales* 83,557,700
SIC 5141 Groceries, general line
Robert Bozzo

D-U-N-S 25-966-7470   (SL)
SUBARU OF MAPLE
250 Sweetriver Blvd, Maple, ON, L6A 4V3
(289) 342-7800
Emp Here 30   *Sales* 14,942,340
SIC 5521 Used car dealers
Remo Ferri

D-U-N-S 25-392-6232   (SL)
TECTONIC INFRASTRUCTURE INC
120 Rodinea Rd Unit 1, Maple, ON, L6A 1R5
(416) 637-6073
Emp Here 75   *Sales* 18,933,150
SIC 1629 Heavy construction, nec
Galliano Tiberini
Anthony Tiberini
Louie Frustaglio

D-U-N-S 25-107-0264   (BR)
YORK CATHOLIC DISTRICT SCHOOL BOARD
HOLY JUBILEE
(*Suby of* YORK CATHOLIC DISTRICT

SCHOOL BOARD)
400 St. Joan Of Arc Ave, Maple, ON, L6A 2S8
(905) 303-6121
Emp Here 80
SIC 8211 Elementary and secondary schools
Susie Quadrini-Ferguson

D-U-N-S 20-189-7597   (HQ)
YORK MAJOR HOLDINGS INC
10000 Dufferin St, Maple, ON, L6A 1S3
(905) 417-2300
Emp Here 5   *Sales* 13,444,620
SIC 6552 Subdividers and developers, nec
Jim Degasperis
Marco Muzzo
Jeff Kerbel
Duane Aubie

D-U-N-S 20-591-2608   (BR)
YORK REGION DISTRICT SCHOOL BOARD
MAPLE HIGH SCHOOL
(*Suby of* YORK REGION DISTRICT SCHOOL BOARD)
50 Springside Rd, Maple, ON, L6A 2W5
(905) 417-9444
Emp Here 130
SIC 8211 Elementary and secondary schools
Lois Agard

D-U-N-S 20-352-7791   (BR)
YUMMY MARKET INC
(*Suby of* YUMMY MARKET INC)
1390 Major Mackenzie Dr, Maple, ON, L6A 4H6
(905) 417-4117
Emp Here 230
SIC 5411 Grocery stores

Marathon, ON P0T

D-U-N-S 20-758-5357   (HQ)
SUPERIOR GREENSTONE DISTRICT SCHOOL BOARD
12 Hemlo Dr Bag A, Marathon, ON, P0T 2E0
(807) 229-0436
Emp Here 20   *Sales* 39,647,600
SIC 8211 Elementary and secondary schools
Bruce Rousseau
David Tamblyn

D-U-N-S 24-852-9760   (SL)
WILLIAMS OPERATING CORPORATION
WILLIAMS MINE
Hwy 17, Marathon, ON, P0T 2E0
(807) 238-1100
Emp Here 600   *Sales* 1,432,529,400
SIC 1041 Gold ores
Mike Lipkewich
Greg Lang

D-U-N-S 24-851-9068   (SL)
WILSON MEMORIAL GENERAL HOSPITAL
26 Peninsula Rd, Marathon, ON, P0T 2E0
(807) 229-1740
Emp Here 80   *Sales* 8,170,640
SIC 8062 General medical and surgical hospitals
Paul Paradis

Markdale, ON N0C

D-U-N-S 20-298-9492   (SL)
1124029 ONTARIO INC
MARKDALE FOODLAND
217 Toronto St S, Markdale, ON, N0C 1H0
(519) 986-3683
Emp Here 50   *Sales* 13,707,600
SIC 5411 Grocery stores
Douglas Crawford
Margaret Crawford

D-U-N-S 20-823-8576   (HQ)
CHAPMAN'S, DAVID ICE CREAM LIMITED
CHAPMAN'S ICE CREAM
100 Chapman'S Cres, Markdale, ON, N0C 1H0
(519) 986-3131
Emp Here 256   *Sales* 341,169,500
SIC 2024 Ice cream and frozen deserts
David Chapman
Penny Chapman

D-U-N-S 25-477-8145   (SL)
GREY GABLES
(*Suby of* CORPORATION OF THE COUNTY OF GREY)
206 Toronto St S, Markdale, ON, N0C 1H0
(519) 986-3010
Emp Here 83   *Sales* 5,671,058
SIC 8051 Skilled nursing care facilities
Jennifer Cornell

D-U-N-S 20-271-8235   (SL)
MEDIKE BRANDING SOLUTIONS INC
216 Main St W, Markdale, ON, N0C 1H0
(519) 986-2072
Emp Here 100   *Sales* 15,389,520
SIC 3199 Leather goods, nec
Jonathan Harris

D-U-N-S 25-500-2552   (HQ)
SECURE INSURANCE SOLUTIONS GROUP INC
181 Toronto St, Markdale, ON, N0C 1H0
(519) 986-3250
Emp Here 27   *Sales* 25,441,800
SIC 6411 Insurance agents, brokers, and service
Gary Hawkins

Markham, ON L3P

D-U-N-S 20-289-8693   (BR)
AMICA MATURE LIFESTYLES INC
AMICA AT SWAN LAKE
(*Suby of* AMICA SENIOR LIFESTYLES INC)
6360 16th Ave Suite 336, Markham, ON, L3P 7Y9
(905) 201-6058
Emp Here 100
SIC 8361 Residential care

D-U-N-S 25-458-5607   (SL)
CANWELL INSURANCE AND FINANCIAL SERVICES INC
121 Robinson St, Markham, ON, L3P 1P2

Emp Here 21   *Sales* 12,383,230
SIC 6411 Insurance agents, brokers, and service

D-U-N-S 24-771-1187   (SL)
CARSON & WEEKS INSURANCE BROKERS LIMITED
59 Main St N, Markham, ON, L3P 1X7
(905) 294-0722
Emp Here 24   *Sales* 13,918,176
SIC 6411 Insurance agents, brokers, and service
Frederick Ast
R Gregory Weeks
Rod Beaton

D-U-N-S 24-572-8394   (SL)
CORAL ENERGY
30 Avondale Cres, Markham, ON, L3P 2K1

Emp Here 4   *Sales* 12,423,428
SIC 4925 Gas production and/or distribution
Donald Rae

D-U-N-S 20-644-6507   (SL)
DON VALLEY NORTH TOYOTA LIMITED
MARKVILLE TOYOTA
5362 Highway 7 E, Markham, ON, L3P 1B9

(905) 294-8100
Emp Here 49   *Sales* 24,405,822
SIC 5521 Used car dealers
Hag Ampagoumian

D-U-N-S 25-097-2791   (SL)
INTEK COMMUNICATIONS INC
9 Heritage Rd, Markham, ON, L3P 1M3
(905) 294-0400
Emp Here 210   *Sales* 47,979,120
SIC 4899 Communication services, nec
Andrew Wray
Christopher Robinson

D-U-N-S 20-216-5457   (SL)
JAYFER   AUTOMOTIVE   GROUP (MARKHAM) INC
MARKHAM MAZDA
5426 Highway 7 E, Markham, ON, L3P 1B7
(905) 294-1210
Emp Here 50   *Sales* 10,131,450
SIC 7538 General automotive repair shops
Kenneth Yoo
Gin Siow
Nick Sgro

D-U-N-S 24-452-5622   (HQ)
MARKHAM STOUFFVILLE HOSPITAL
381 Church St, Markham, ON, L3P 7P3
(905) 472-7000
Emp Here 1,600   *Sales* 188,836,000
SIC 8062 General medical and surgical hospitals
Janet Beed
Robert Bull
Neil Walker
David Austin

D-U-N-S 25-359-8031   (HQ)
PRIME COMMUNICATIONS CANADA INC
WIRELESS EXPRESS
9275 Highway 48 Unit 1b3, Markham, ON, L3P 3J3
(647) 848-1388
Emp Here 16   *Sales* 19,420,120
SIC 4812 Radiotelephone communication
Donna Woodbury
William Copeland
Joseph Chesham
Akbar Mohamed
Farid Virani

D-U-N-S 25-404-1924   (SL)
SITCONF LIMITED
160 Bullock Dr, Markham, ON, L3P 1W2
(905) 554-6029
Emp Here 30   *Sales* 15,265,680
SIC 5021 Furniture
Aida D'ulisse
Peter D'ulisse

D-U-N-S 20-640-6928   (SL)
SUPREME LIGHTING & ELECTRIC SUPPLY LTD
9 Laidlaw Blvd, Markham, ON, L3P 1W5
(905) 477-3113
Emp Here 25   *Sales* 11,179,350
SIC 5063 Electrical apparatus and equipment
Michael Stam
Robert Lippa

D-U-N-S 24-007-0193   (SL)
T.FLEXO CORPORATION
R.K. PACKAGING
528 Raymerville Dr, Markham, ON, L3P 6G4
(647) 477-8482
Emp Here 57   *Sales* 13,305,795
SIC 2673 Bags: plastic, laminated, and coated
Rajiv Kaushal

D-U-N-S 20-314-8085   (SL)
TRAVEL INSURANCE OFFICE INC
190 Bullock Dr Suite 2, Markham, ON, L3P 7N3
(905) 201-1571
Emp Here 15   *Sales* 10,881,585
SIC 6321 Accident and health insurance

Dan Donnelly

D-U-N-S 25-297-8895   (BR)
YORK REGION DISTRICT SCHOOL BOARD
MARKHAM DISTRICT HIGH SCHOOL
(*Suby of* YORK REGION DISTRICT SCHOOL BOARD)
89 Church St, Markham, ON, L3P 2M3
(905) 294-1886
Emp Here 130
SIC 8211 Elementary and secondary schools
Michelle Kane

Markham, ON L3R

D-U-N-S 25-075-5188   (SL)
1095141 ONTARIO LIMITED
FRANKIE TOMATTOS
7225 Woodbine Ave Suite 119, Markham, ON, L3R 1A3
(905) 940-2199
Emp Here 90   *Sales* 3,858,570
SIC 5812 Eating places
Hal Roback
Vincent Sy

D-U-N-S 20-697-3591   (HQ)
1220579 ONTARIO INC
750 Cochrane Dr, Markham, ON, L3R 8E1
(416) 293-8365
Sales 10,462,120
SIC 6712 Bank holding companies
Robert Kainz

D-U-N-S 24-795-2922   (HQ)
1371185 ONTARIO INC
SYNNEX CANADA
(*Suby of* SYNNEX CORPORATION)
4011 14th Ave, Markham, ON, L3R 0Z9
(905) 415-1166
Emp Here 125   *Sales* 117,777,440
SIC 5045 Computers, peripherals, and software
Frank Luk

D-U-N-S 25-180-4183   (SL)
1686416 ONTARIO INC
FOUR POINTS EXPRESS
10 Alden Rd Suite 6, Markham, ON, L3R 2S1
(905) 305-0071
Emp Here 101   *Sales* 67,559,708
SIC 7389 Business services, nec
Rita Maalouli

D-U-N-S 24-329-4613   (HQ)
1692246 ONTARIO INC
PALMA BRAVA
91 Esna Park Dr Unit 8, Markham, ON, L3R 2S2
(905) 845-6556
Emp Here 1   *Sales* 11,517,000
SIC 5712 Furniture stores
Susan Lee

D-U-N-S 24-333-0029   (SL)
2063414 INVESTMENT LP
LEISUREWORLD CAREGIVING CENTRES
302 Town Centre Blvd Suite 200, Markham, ON, L3R 0E8
(905) 477-4006
Emp Here 100   *Sales* 6,856,600
SIC 8051 Skilled nursing care facilities
David Cutler

D-U-N-S 24-952-3700   (SL)
2075894 ONTARIO INC
LCG FOODS DISTRIBUTION
170 Esna Park Dr Unit 14, Markham, ON, L3R 1E3
(905) 752-0460
Emp Here 20   *Sales* 10,702,480
SIC 5149 Groceries and related products, nec
Justine Yau
Paul Yip

D-U-N-S 24-320-1586   (HQ)
2384309 ONTARIO INC
(*Suby of* THE RECON GROUP INC)
7357 Woodbine Ave Suite 619, Markham, ON, L3R 6L3
(905) 944-0700
Sales 11,714,400
SIC 8742 Management consulting services
Sender Shamiss
Ravi Ramnarain
Ofir Gabriel
Chuck Johnston
Pete Carfrae

D-U-N-S 24-320-2671   (SL)
3500 STEELES AVENUE EAST LP
(*Suby of* FIERA PROPERTIES LIMITED)
3500 Steeles Ave E Unit 201, Markham, ON, L3R 0X1
(905) 754-4826
Emp Here 2   *Sales* 15,669,540
SIC 6531 Real estate agents and managers
Michael Mccormick
Michael Vilner

D-U-N-S 20-769-1051   (SL)
656706 ONTARIO INC
CREST CIRCUIT
2701 John St, Markham, ON, L3R 2W5
(905) 479-9515
Emp Here 85   *Sales* 16,187,570
SIC 3672 Printed circuit boards
Dahyabhai Patel

D-U-N-S 24-644-1455   (SL)
673927 ONTARIO INC
TORONTO LUBE SERVICE
3175 14th Ave Unit 2, Markham, ON, L3R 0H1
(905) 479-8444
Emp Here 10   *Sales* 10,328,080
SIC 5172 Petroleum products, nec
Allan Trim

D-U-N-S 24-141-3512   (SL)
679475 ONTARIO INC
DSL TRAVELLERS TOURS
4440 Steeles Ave E Unit 3, Markham, ON, L3R 0L4

Emp Here 22   *Sales* 11,439,274
SIC 4724 Travel agencies
Lilian Chan

D-U-N-S 20-312-7113   (SL)
7251246 CANADA INC
DRAPER WHITMAN
90c Centurian Dr Unit 209, Markham, ON, L3R 8C5
(416) 483-2200
Emp Here 15   *Sales* 83,835,070
SIC 7361 Employment agencies
Wayne Burgess
John Clark

D-U-N-S 24-771-7721   (SL)
788265 ONTARIO LIMITED
COMMERCIAL MARKETING
250 Shields Crt Unit 1, Markham, ON, L3R 9W7
(905) 415-8020
Emp Here 21   *Sales* 15,592,920
SIC 5199 Nondurable goods, nec
Victor Arluk
Malka Arluk

D-U-N-S 25-063-3575   (SL)
892316 ONTARIO LIMITED
THE VILLAGE GROCER
4476 16th Ave, Markham, ON, L3R 0M1
(905) 940-0655
Emp Here 100   *Sales* 29,347,700
SIC 5411 Grocery stores
Cathy Mcdonald
Evan Macdonald

D-U-N-S 24-845-4324   (SL)
901089 ONTARIO LIMITED
GENTEC

---

90 Royal Crest Crt Suite 1, Markham, ON, L3R 9X6
(905) 513-7733
Emp Here 80   *Sales* 35,773,920
SIC 5043 Photographic equipment and supplies
Joel Seigel
Margaret Adat
Brad Lloyd
Allen Top
Eddie Bozo
Dick Tuerlings
Anthony Sesel

D-U-N-S 25-156-0967   (SL)
987217 ONTARIO LIMITED
PROMOTIONAL SPECIALISTS, THE
168 Konrad Cres Unit 2, Markham, ON, L3R 9T9
(905) 474-9304
Emp Here 30   *Sales* 22,275,600
SIC 5199 Nondurable goods, nec
Aaron Moscoe
Andrew Rotenberg

D-U-N-S 25-139-5950   (HQ)
A.C. NIELSEN COMPANY OF CANADA LIMITED
(*Suby of* NIELSEN HOLDINGS PLC)
160 Mcnabb St, Markham, ON, L3R 4B8
(905) 475-3344
Emp Here 500   *Sales* 204,082,000
SIC 8732 Commercial nonphysical research
Stephen Churchill
Janice Jackson
John Mee
Mark Lewis

D-U-N-S 24-767-0750   (SL)
ABBOTT MEDICAL OPTICAL INC
80 Whitehall Dr, Markham, ON, L3R 0P3
(905) 305-3305
Emp Here 35   *Sales* 11,396,000
SIC 5995 Optical goods stores
Chris Baker

D-U-N-S 25-248-7905   (SL)
ACCULOGIC INC
175 Riviera Dr Suite 1, Markham, ON, L3R 5J6
(905) 475-5907
Emp Here 75   *Sales* 13,298,325
SIC 7371 Custom computer programming services
Saeed Taheri

D-U-N-S 24-857-9760   (BR)
AECOM CANADA LTD
(*Suby of* AECOM)
300 Town Centre Blvd Suite 300, Markham, ON, L3R 5Z6

Emp Here 150
SIC 8742 Management consulting services
Tracy Cannizzaro

D-U-N-S 20-344-3049   (HQ)
AGF - REBAR INC
(*Suby of* GROUPE AGF INC)
2800 14th Ave Suite 204, Markham, ON, L3R 0E4
(416) 862-5015
Sales 10,141,500
SIC 3449 Miscellaneous Metalwork
Maxime Gendron
Serge Gendron
Mark Clarke

D-U-N-S 20-179-1550   (SL)
ALCO ELECTRONICS INC
(*Suby of* ALCO ELECTRONICS LIMITED)
725 Denison St, Markham, ON, L3R 1B8
(905) 477-7878
Emp Here 22   *Sales* 11,451,924
SIC 5099 Durable goods, nec
Ryan Leung

D-U-N-S 24-947-7092   (HQ)

ALL GOLD IMPORTS INC
4255 14th Ave, Markham, ON, L3R 0J2
(416) 740-4653
Sales 14,204,809
SIC 5149 Groceries and related products, nec
Gary Pillemer
Jason Berman
Louis Pillemer

D-U-N-S 20-769-1544   (HQ)
ALLSTATE INSURANCE COMPANY OF CANADA
(*Suby of* THE ALLSTATE CORPORATION)
27 Allstate Pky Suite 100, Markham, ON, L3R 5P8
(905) 477-6900
Emp Here 100   *Sales* 584,589,186
SIC 6331 Fire, marine, and casualty insurance
Thomas Clarkson
Ryan Michel
Jeff Wickware
Howard A. Tanenbaum
Gerald S. Kishner
Carole Workman
Mark Richardson
Jonathan D. Adkisson
Kathy Mabe

D-U-N-S 24-911-3671   (HQ)
ALLSTATE LIFE INSURANCE COMPANY OF CANADA
(*Suby of* THE ALLSTATE CORPORATION)
27 Allstate Pky Suite 100, Markham, ON, L3R 5P8
(905) 477-6900
Emp Here 1   *Sales* 82,547,416
SIC 6722 Management investment, open-end
Thomas Clarkson
Ryan Michel
Howard A. Tanenbaum
Gerald S. Kishner
Carole Workman
Mark Richardson
Jonathan D. Adkisson
Kathy Mabe

D-U-N-S 20-355-0405   (HQ)
ALLSTREAM BUSINESS INC
ENTREPRISE ALLSTREAM
(*Suby of* ZAYO GROUP HOLDINGS, INC.)
7550 Birchmount Rd, Markham, ON, L3R 6C6
(905) 513-4600
Emp Here 192   *Sales* 43,565,800
SIC 1731 Electrical work
Kenneth Desgarennes
Daniel Caruso
Michael R. Strople

D-U-N-S 24-817-1977   (HQ)
ALPHA PRO TECH, LTD
ALPHA PRO TECH
60 Centurian Dr Suite 112, Markham, ON, L3R 9R2
(800) 749-1363
Emp Here 15   *Sales* 46,624,000
SIC 3842 Surgical appliances and supplies
Lloyd Hoffman
Chris Louisos
Bruce Hayden
Danny Montgomery
Colleen Mcdonald

D-U-N-S 24-874-6166   (SL)
ALTHON INC
140 Shields Crt, Markham, ON, L3R 9T5
(905) 513-1221
Emp Here 40   *Sales* 17,886,960
SIC 5045 Computers, peripherals, and software
Rex Tsang

D-U-N-S 24-345-7095   (BR)
AMEX CANADA INC
GLOBAL SERVICES
(*Suby of* AMERICAN EXPRESS COMPANY)
80 Micro Crt Suite 300, Markham, ON, L3R 9Z5

(905) 475-2177
Emp Here 300
SIC 6153 Short-term business credit institutions, except agricultural
Howard Grosfield

D-U-N-S 20-158-8316   (SL)
ANGLO ORIENTAL LIMITED
255 Shields Crt, Markham, ON, L3R 8V2
(905) 752-0612
Emp Here 20   *Sales* 10,177,120
SIC 5023 Homefurnishings
Robert Lindberg
Norman Welch
Sylvia Lindberg
Claudio Carlevaris

D-U-N-S 20-697-0993   (SL)
ANTELOPE HILLS CONSTRUCTION LTD
CONSERVATORY GROUP, THE
80 Tiverton Crt Suite 300, Markham, ON, L3R 0G4
(905) 477-7609
Emp Here 50   *Sales* 14,429,150
SIC 1522 Residential construction, nec
Sheldon Libfeld
Jay Libfeld

D-U-N-S 20-968-0321   (HQ)
ARAUCO CANADA LIMITED
ARAUCO NORTH AMERICA
(*Suby of* INVERSIONES ANGELINI Y COMPANIA LIMITADA)
80 Tiverton Crt Suite 701, Markham, ON, L3R 0G4
(905) 475-9686
Emp Here 20   *Sales* 367,637,000
SIC 2631 Paperboard mills
Kelly Shotbolt
Kevin Shotbolt
Robert Henry
Casuy Mccart
Jake Bleston
Michael Rosso

D-U-N-S 25-973-5488   (SL)
ARSYSTEMS INTERNATIONAL INC
SHOWCARE SOLUTIONS
2770 14th Ave Suite 101, Markham, ON, L3R 0J1
(905) 968-3096
Emp Here 79   *Sales* 35,488,301
SIC 7389 Business services, nec
Debbie Baxter
Ewa Boldok

D-U-N-S 25-536-6460   (HQ)
ASI COMPUTER TECHNOLOGIES (CANADA) CORP
(*Suby of* ASI COMPUTER TECHNOLOGIES INC)
3930 14th Ave Unit 1, Markham, ON, L3R 0A8
(905) 470-1000
Emp Here 40   *Sales* 24,594,570
SIC 5045 Computers, peripherals, and software
Christine Liang

D-U-N-S 24-926-3807   (HQ)
ASIAN TELEVISION NETWORK INTERNATIONAL LIMITED
330 Cochrane Dr, Markham, ON, L3R 8E4
(905) 948-8199
Emp Here 6   *Sales* 11,242,373
SIC 4833 Television broadcasting stations
Shan Chandrasekar
Jaya Chandrasekar
Prakash Naidoo
Kyrill Classen
J.E. Boyle
Bruce Buckley

D-U-N-S 25-101-3397   (HQ)
ASM CANADA, INC
ADVANTAGE SALES AND MARKETING CANADA
(*Suby of* ADVANTAGE SALES & MARKETING INC.)

160 Mcnabb St Suite 330, Markham, ON, L3R 4E4
(905) 475-9623
Emp Here 110   *Sales* 215,014,800
SIC 5141 Groceries, general line
Henry Gerstel

D-U-N-S 24-977-5461   (SL)
ASSOCIATED PRO-CLEANING SERVICES CORP
3400 14th Ave Suite 39, Markham, ON, L3R 0H7
(905) 477-6966
Emp Here 75   *Sales* 3,015,675
SIC 7349 Building maintenance services, nec
Jim Sidiros

D-U-N-S 24-253-6691   (SL)
ASSURANT LIFE OF CANADA MARKHAM
FAMILY SIDE PURPLE SHIELD
95 Royal Crest Crt Unit 19, Markham, ON, L3R 9X5
(905) 943-4447
Emp Here 10   *Sales* 10,348,810
SIC 6311 Life insurance

D-U-N-S 24-423-6303   (SL)
ASTELLAS PHARMA CANADA, INC
(*Suby of* ASTELLAS PHARMA INC.)
675 Cochrane Dr Suite 500, Markham, ON, L3R 0B8
(905) 470-7990
Emp Here 110   *Sales* 45,410,310
SIC 5122 Drugs, proprietaries, and sundries
Steve Sabus

D-U-N-S 25-576-9010   (SL)
ATLAS GRAPHIC SUPPLY INC
121 Whitehall Dr, Markham, ON, L3R 9T1
(905) 948-9800
Emp Here 42   *Sales* 31,185,840
SIC 5199 Nondurable goods, nec
Richard Solnick

D-U-N-S 24-382-5077   (BR)
AUTOLIV CANADA INC
(*Suby of* AUTOLIV, INC.)
7455 Birchmount Rd, Markham, ON, L3R 5C2
(905) 475-1468
Emp Here 100
SIC 2394 Canvas and related products

D-U-N-S 25-094-6449   (HQ)
AVAYA CANADA CORP
(*Suby of* AVAYA HOLDINGS CORP.)
11 Allstate Pky Suite 300, Markham, ON, L3R 9T8
(905) 474-6000
Emp Here 310   *Sales* 150,544,800
SIC 4899 Communication services, nec
Mario Belanger

D-U-N-S 25-402-5570   (SL)
AVIV INTERNATIONAL TRADE CORPORATION
31 Telson Rd Suite 2, Markham, ON, L3R 1E4
(905) 479-5047
Emp Here 40   *Sales* 19,932,880
SIC 5136 Men's and boy's clothing
Brad Nissan

D-U-N-S 20-106-0394   (SL)
B WYZE INC
B WYZE SOLUTIONS
20 Valleywood Dr Unit 100, Markham, ON, L3R 6G1
(905) 780-0444
Emp Here 150   *Sales* 27,975,900
SIC 8742 Management consulting services
John F. Towsley
Rick Beaudry

D-U-N-S 20-044-4727   (HQ)
BANCTEC (CANADA), INC
(*Suby of* EXELA TECHNOLOGIES, INC.)
100 Allstate Pky Suite 400, Markham, ON, L3R 6H3
(905) 475-6060
Emp Here 24   *Sales* 13,697,290

SIC 7371 Custom computer programming services
Malcolm Gurney

D-U-N-S 20-771-0260   (HQ)
BARNES J.D., LIMITED
140 Renfrew Dr Suite 100, Markham, ON, L3R 6B3
(905) 477-3600
Emp Here 130   *Sales* 35,747,800
SIC 8713 Surveying services
Frank Mauro
John Barber
Joe Young
Colin Bogue
Alfonso Roccaforte
John Knowles
B. Gary Kirstine
Ron Terin

D-U-N-S 20-273-5346   (HQ)
BAYLIN TECHNOLOGIES INC
60 Columbia Way Suite 205, Markham, ON, L3R 0C9
(416) 805-9127
Emp Here 50   *Sales* 103,264,106
SIC 3661 Telephone and telegraph apparatus
Randy Dewey
Cliff Gary
Jay Giblon
Daniel Kim
Linda Barabe
Kelly Myles
Helder Constantino
Michael Wolfe
Jeffrey C. Royer

D-U-N-S 24-373-1564   (SL)
BAYSHORE SPECIALTY RX LTD
(*Suby of* BAYSHORE HEALTHCARE LTD.)
233 Alden Rd, Markham, ON, L3R 3W6
(905) 474-0822
Emp Here 319   *Sales* 58,548,303
SIC 5961 Catalog and mail-order houses
Stuart J, Cottrelle

D-U-N-S 25-321-0298   (BR)
BDO CANADA LLP
BDO CANADA
(*Suby of* BDO CANADA LLP)
60 Columbia Way Suite 300, Markham, ON, L3R 0C9
(905) 946-1066
Emp Here 100
SIC 8721 Accounting, auditing, and bookkeeping
Allan Rudolph

D-U-N-S 24-815-8487   (HQ)
BEAVER VALLEY STONE LIMITED
8081 Woodbine Ave, Markham, ON, L3R 2P1
(416) 222-2424
Emp Here 20   *Sales* 22,864,110
SIC 5999 Miscellaneous retail stores, nec
Antonio Pacitto
Mark Pacitto
Tania Pacitto

D-U-N-S 25-512-7805   (SL)
BEGHELLI CANADA INC
(*Suby of* BEGHELLI SPA)
3900 14th Ave Suite 1, Markham, ON, L3R 4R3
(905) 948-9500
Emp Here 114   *Sales* 21,710,388
SIC 3646 Commercial lighting fixtures
Dania La Spada
Bruno Areito

D-U-N-S 24-885-8078   (HQ)
BELLE-PAK PACKAGING INC
7465 Birchmount Rd, Markham, ON, L3R 5X9
(905) 475-5151
Emp Here 150   *Sales* 38,953,600
SIC 2673 Bags: plastic, laminated, and coated
Peter Nanji
Yves Nahmias

D-U-N-S 20-088-4901   (HQ)
BENTO INC
BENTO SUSHI
25 Centurian Dr Suite 208, Markham, ON, L3R 5N8
(905) 513-0028
Emp Here 80   *Sales* 23,319,500
SIC 5812 Eating places
Glenn Brown
Richard Hodgson .
Edward Knighton

D-U-N-S 25-510-9480   (HQ)
BEYOND DIGITAL IMAGING INC
36 Apple Creek Blvd, Markham, ON, L3R 4Y4
(905) 415-1888
Sales 17,805,510
SIC 7384 Photofinish laboratories
Larry Chan

D-U-N-S 24-486-3684   (SL)
BGI BENCHMARK GROUP INTERNATIONAL INC
BGI
207-30 Centurian Dr, Markham, ON, L3R 8B8
(905) 305-8900
Emp Here 65   *Sales* 17,831,580
SIC 8741 Management services
David Hartnoll

D-U-N-S 25-497-7663   (HQ)
BGIS GLOBAL INTEGRATED SOLUTIONS CANADA LP
4175 14th Ave Suite 300, Markham, ON, L3R 0J2
(905) 943-4100
Sales 405,676,800
SIC 6531 Real estate agents and managers
Gordon Hicks
Mike Greinadus
Peter Papagiannis
Jim Neal

D-U-N-S 24-771-3704   (SL)
BIGGS AND NARCISO CONSTRUCTION SERVICES INC
181 Bentley St Suite 14, Markham, ON, L3R 3Y1
(905) 470-8788
Emp Here 90   *Sales* 22,156,740
SIC 1799 Special trade contractors, nec
Luis Narciso
Timothy Biggs

D-U-N-S 25-118-7266   (SL)
BIO BASIC CANADA INC
20 Konrad Cres Suite 1, Markham, ON, L3R 8T4
(905) 474-4493
Emp Here 500   *Sales* 336,106,000
SIC 5169 Chemicals and allied products, nec
Jennifer Wang
Qi-Son Wang
Tracy Wang

D-U-N-S 24-757-1698   (SL)
BIOSCRYPT INC
(*Suby of* ADVENT INTERNATIONAL CORPORATION)
50 Acadia Ave Unit 200, Markham, ON, L3R 0B3
(905) 624-7700
Emp Here 60   *Sales* 11,426,520
SIC 3663 Radio and t.v. communications equipment
Helene Seguinotte

D-U-N-S 24-985-7764   (SL)
BOILERMAKER'S NATIONAL BENEFIT PLANS
BOILERMAKER'S BENEFIT & TRUST
45 Mcintosh Dr, Markham, ON, L3R 8C7
(905) 946-2530
Emp Here 44   *Sales* 81,252,996
SIC 6371 Pension, health, and welfare funds
Susan Bird

D-U-N-S 20-294-5978   (SL)

BRAIN BUSTER INC
MIND GAMES
206 Telson Rd, Markham, ON, L3R 1E6
(905) 604-5055
Emp Here 100   *Sales* 24,432,800
SIC 5945 Hobby, toy, and game shops
Ray Razi

D-U-N-S 24-414-9795   (HQ)
BRAINS II SOLUTIONS, INC
165 Konrad Cres, Markham, ON, L3R 9T9
(905) 946-8700
Emp Here 20   *Sales* 133,838,000
SIC 5045 Computers, peripherals, and software
Charles G Hanna

D-U-N-S 20-116-2075   (SL)
BRANDVENTURE INC
335 Renfrew Dr Suite 202, Markham, ON, L3R 9S9
(888) 277-9737
Emp Here 25   *Sales* 10,702,480
SIC 5141 Groceries, general line
David Bates

D-U-N-S 20-723-4043   (HQ)
BRIARLANE RENTAL PROPERTY MANAGEMENT INC
85 Spy Crt Suite 100, Markham, ON, L3R 4Z4
(905) 944-9406
Emp Here 5   *Sales* 11,645,550
SIC 6513 Apartment building operators
Brad Smith
Susanne Maguire
Monish Comar
Pat Brawn
Andrus Kung

D-U-N-S 24-365-9377   (SL)
BRIGHOLME INC
BRIGHOLME INTERIORS GROUP
(*Suby of* LIGHTSTREET LTD)
4118 14th Ave, Markham, ON, L3R 0J3
(905) 475-0043
Emp Here 32   *Sales* 16,283,392
SIC 5021 Furniture
Joseph (Joe) Williams

D-U-N-S 24-737-5751   (HQ)
BROADRIDGE CUSTOMER COMMUNICATIONS CANADA, ULC
BROADRIDGE
(*Suby of* BROADRIDGE FINANCIAL SOLUTIONS, INC.)
2601 14th Ave, Markham, ON, L3R 0H9
(905) 470-2000
Emp Here 170   *Sales* 40,692,540
SIC 2759 Commercial printing, nec
Joseph Faria
Andrew Idzior
Robert Wylie

D-U-N-S 20-212-9508   (HQ)
BROWNE & CO
505 Apple Creek Blvd Unit 2, Markham, ON, L3R 5B1
(905) 475-6104
Sales 35,843,800
SIC 3262 Vitreous china table and kitchenware
Michael Browne
Peter Browne

D-U-N-S 25-100-5005   (SL)
BTNX INC
570 Hood Rd Unit 23, Markham, ON, L3R 4G7
(905) 944-9565
Emp Here 40   *Sales* 11,066,400
SIC 2835 Diagnostic substances
Iqbal Sunderani

D-U-N-S 20-408-7134   (SL)
BUYERS GROUP OF MISSISSAUGA INC
DIRECT BUY
205 Torbay Rd Suite 12, Markham, ON, L3R 3W4

(905) 948-1911
Emp Here 25   *Sales* 11,179,350
SIC 5072 Hardware
Justin Yoshimura
Dylan Astle
Philip Rondeau

D-U-N-S 24-386-6985   (SL)
CAMPTECH II CIRCUITS INC
81 Bentley St, Markham, ON, L3R 3L1
(905) 477-8790
Emp Here 95   *Sales* 18,091,990
SIC 3672 Printed circuit boards
Pat Campagna

D-U-N-S 24-991-3059   (SL)
CANADIAN NETWORK INSTALLATIONS LTD
CNI
1351 Rodick Rd Unit 6, Markham, ON, L3R 5K4
(905) 946-2188
Emp Here 65   *Sales* 12,011,870
SIC 4899 Communication services, nec
Dimitrios Babalis

D-U-N-S 24-816-0269   (SL)
CANCARD INC
CANADIAN CARD SYSTEMS
177 Idema Rd Suite 8, Markham, ON, L3R 1A9
(416) 449-8111
Emp Here 25   *Sales* 11,875,650
SIC 5084 Industrial machinery and equipment
John Flett
Scott Cowan

D-U-N-S 24-790-5537   (SL)
CANKOSH INC
7030 Woodbine Ave Suite 500, Markham, ON, L3R 6G2
(905) 943-7990
Emp Here 49   *Sales* 32,166,736
SIC 5963 Direct selling establishments
Parviz Almassi Gouran

D-U-N-S 20-349-5809   (SL)
CANON MEDICAL SYSTEMS CANADA LIMITED
CANON MEDICAL SYSTEMS
75 Tiverton Ct, Markham, ON, L3R 4M8
(800) 668-9729
Emp Here 130   *Sales* 29,547,570
SIC 3845 Electromedical equipment
Jens Dettmann
Ken Sam
Yoshiyuki Sakamitsu
Masatoshi Ishihara
Hiroshi Tani

D-U-N-S 20-640-2885   (HQ)
CANTOL CORP
199 Steelcase Rd W, Markham, ON, L3R 2M4
(905) 475-6141
Sales 13,833,000
SIC 2842 Polishes and sanitation goods
Elmer Snethen
Jim Gormley

D-U-N-S 25-109-5550   (HQ)
CASH NOWPLUS INC
CASH NOW
3100 Steeles Ave E Suite 906, Markham, ON, L3R 8T3
(905) 470-0084
Emp Here 15   *Sales* 10,857,000
SIC 6099 Functions related to deposit banking

D-U-N-S 24-721-2517   (HQ)
CASIO CANADA LTD
(*Suby of* CASIO COMPUTER CO., LTD.)
141 Mcpherson St, Markham, ON, L3R 3L3
(905) 248-4400
Sales 11,972,466
SIC 5099 Durable goods, nec
Michael Powers

D-U-N-S 24-848-4073   (HQ)
CATECH SYSTEMS LTD

201 Whitehall Dr Unit 4, Markham, ON, L3R
9Y3
(905) 477-0160
Emp Here 100   *Sales* 28,099,941
SIC 1731 Electrical work
Scott Forrestall

D-U-N-S 25-323-2615   (SL)
CBL DATA RECOVERY TECHNOLOGIES INC
CBL
590 Alden Rd Suite 105, Markham, ON, L3R
8N2
(905) 479-9938
Emp Here 82   *Sales* 14,539,502
SIC 7375 Information retrieval services
William Margeson

D-U-N-S 25-353-6155   (SL)
CELLAY CANADA INC
TUZY-MUZY DRIED FLOWERS
30 Royal Crest Crt Suite 8, Markham, ON,
L3R 9W8

Emp Here 25   *Sales* 18,563,000
SIC 5193 Flowers and florists supplies
John Chiu

D-U-N-S 25-230-2963   (HQ)
CENTRECORP MANAGEMENT SERVICES LIMITED
2851 John St Suite 1, Markham, ON, L3R 5R7
(905) 477-9200
Emp Here 52   *Sales* 18,774,035
SIC 6512 Nonresidential building operators
Robert S Green
John Preston

D-U-N-S 20-640-1171   (SL)
CENTRIC GROUP, THE
161 Alden Rd Unit 9, Markham, ON, L3R 3W7
(905) 415-9577
Emp Here 45   *Sales* 10,542,960
SIC 8743 Public relations services
Gabriel Constantin

D-U-N-S 25-121-4250   (SL)
CENTURY 21 KING'S QUAY REAL ESTATE INC
CENTURY 21
7300 Warden Ave Suite 401, Markham, ON,
L3R 9Z6
(905) 940-3428
Emp Here 50   *Sales* 16,356,350
SIC 6531 Real estate agents and managers
Steve Chow

D-U-N-S 25-957-1974   (BR)
CERIDIAN CANADA LTD
CERIDIAN LIFEWORKS SERVICES
(*Suby of* FOUNDATION HOLDINGS, INC.)
675 Cochrane Dr Suite 515n, Markham, ON,
L3R 0B8
(905) 947-7000
Emp Here 100
SIC 8721 Accounting, auditing, and book-keeping
Cande Dandele

D-U-N-S 20-394-4970   (SL)
CHANGFENG ENERGY INC
32 South Unionville Avenue, Markham, ON,
L3R 9S6
(647) 313-0066
Emp Here 5   *Sales* 15,529,285
SIC 4923 Gas transmission and distribution
Ann Lin

D-U-N-S 24-330-4453   (SL)
CHANGFENG ENERGY INC
32 South Unionville Ave Suite 2036-2038,
Markham, ON, L3R 9S6
(647) 313-0066
Emp Here 100   *Sales* 57,648,832
SIC 4923 Gas transmission and distribution
Huajun Lin
Ann S.Y. Lin
Ping Chen

Yan Zhao
Yan Li
Hui Cai
Dan Liu
Wencheng Zhang
Yongbiao Ding

D-U-N-S 20-719-0315   (SL)
CHESTWOOD STATIONERY LIMITED
CHESTWOOD-NEZEY DISTRIBUTION
100 Steelcase Rd E Suite 105, Markham, ON,
L3R 1E8
(905) 475-5542
Emp Here 25   *Sales* 12,591,450
SIC 5112 Stationery and office supplies
Barkat Ali
Ruhman Ali
Iqbal Ali
Mehboob Ali

D-U-N-S 20-184-8186   (SL)
CHRISTIAN CHILDREN'S FUND OF CANADA
CCFC
1200 Denison St, Markham, ON, L3R 8G6
(905) 754-1001
Emp Here 175   *Sales* 251,755,175
SIC 8699 Membership organizations, nec
Patrick Canagasingham
Dave Wilson
Tim Dsouza

D-U-N-S 24-333-2228   (SL)
CHRISTOPHER YEE DRUGS LTD
SHOPPERS DRUG MART
5000 Highway 7 E, Markham, ON, L3R 4M9
(905) 477-6320
Emp Here 40   *Sales* 10,118,160
SIC 5912 Drug stores and proprietary stores
Christopher Yee

D-U-N-S 25-180-4050   (SL)
CHUANG'S COMPANY LTD
110 Denison St Unit 8, Markham, ON, L3R
1B6
(905) 415-2812
Emp Here 20   *Sales* 10,702,480
SIC 5149 Groceries and related products, nec
Sally Chuang

D-U-N-S 24-172-3043   (SL)
CIRCUIT TECH INC
399 Denison St, Markham, ON, L3R 1B7
(905) 474-9227
Emp Here 14   *Sales* 10,233,650
SIC 3672 Printed circuit boards
Surinder Burmi
Pat Dougdeen

D-U-N-S 24-325-4278   (SL)
CLARKE, DOUGLAS K INSURANCE BROKERS LIMITED
DKC GROUP
151 Esna Park Dr Suite 26, Markham, ON,
L3R 3B1

Emp Here 26   *Sales* 26,906,906
SIC 6311 Life insurance
Kirk Mcmillan

D-U-N-S 20-936-6608   (BR)
CO-OPERATORS GROUP LIMITED, THE
CO-OPERATORS, THE
(*Suby of* CO-OPERATORS GROUP LIMITED,
THE)
7300 Warden Ave Suite 110, Markham, ON,
L3R 9Z6
(905) 470-7300
Emp Here 80
SIC 6411 Insurance agents, brokers, and service
Phil Thorpe

D-U-N-S 24-892-1413   (SL)
COCONUT GROVE PADS INC
COCONUT GROVE INTIMATES
(*Suby of* IFABRIC CORP)
525 Denison St Unit 1, Markham, ON, L3R

1B8
(905) 752-0566
Emp Here 40   *Sales* 11,147,733
SIC 2342 Bras, girdles, and allied garments
Hylton Karon
Giancarlo Beevis
Hilton Price

D-U-N-S 25-368-7594   (SL)
COLE ENGINEERING GROUP LTD
MAS ENGINEERING, DIV OF
70 Valleywood Dr, Markham, ON, L3R 4T5
(905) 940-6161
Emp Here 275   *Sales* 49,153,225
SIC 8711 Engineering services
Scott Cole

D-U-N-S 24-632-9536   (SL)
COMMERCIAL DRYWALL SUPPLY (ONTARIO) INC
CDS DOORS, DIV OF
235 Don Park Rd, Markham, ON, L3R 1C2
(905) 415-7777
Emp Here 50   *Sales* 12,652,950
SIC 5211 Lumber and other building materials
Garry O'brien
Gerard O'brien

D-U-N-S 24-424-9223   (HQ)
COMMUNICATIONS FORMEDIC INC
20 Torbay Rd, Markham, ON, L3R 1G6
(905) 415-1940
Sales 16,678,456
SIC 4899 Communication services, nec
Joseph Trager

D-U-N-S 20-920-0349   (SL)
COMPAGNIE D'ASSURANCE HABITATION ET AUTO TD
5 MILLION ADVANTAGE
(*Suby of* TORONTO-DOMINION BANK, THE)
675 Cochrane Dr Suite 100, Markham, ON,
L3R 0B8
(905) 415-8400
Emp Here 50   *Sales* 92,387,100
SIC 6411 Insurance agents, brokers, and service
Kenneth W. Lalonde
Antonietta Di Girolamo
Riaz Ahmed
Susan Ann Cummings
Philip C. Moore
John W. Thompson
John Capozzolo
Elaine Lajeunesse
John W. Pilkington

D-U-N-S 24-517-5232   (SL)
COMPUTER DATA SOURCE CANADA CORP
CDS
3780 14th Ave Unit 106, Markham, ON, L3R
9Y5
(905) 474-2100
Emp Here 47   *Sales* 10,825,980
SIC 5734 Computer and software stores
Doug Kennedy
Ronald Wollner
Joseph Massaro
Mike Mckee
Karen Mcdonald

D-U-N-S 20-690-0412   (SL)
CONCEPTS ON WHEELS INC
2600 John St Unit 224, Markham, ON, L3R
3W3
(905) 513-1595
Emp Here 30   *Sales* 14,250,780
SIC 5085 Industrial supplies
Dean Pursade

D-U-N-S 25-064-6395   (SL)
CONCORD IDEA CORP
3993 14th Ave, Markham, ON, L3R 4Z6
(905) 513-7686
Emp Here 160   *Sales* 36,555,520
SIC 4899 Communication services, nec

Lawrence Lai

D-U-N-S 24-937-1881   (SL)
CONFI-DENT INC
90 Nolan Crt Unit 14, Markham, ON, L3R 4L9
(905) 474-4444
Emp Here 30   *Sales* 13,415,220
SIC 5047 Medical and hospital equipment
David Marks
Lenny Arenson

D-U-N-S 24-373-2364   (HQ)
CONNORS BROS. CLOVER LEAF SEAFOODS COMPANY
(*Suby of* CLOVER LEAF HOLDINGS COMPANY)
80 Tiverton Crt Suite 600, Markham, ON, L3R
0G4
(905) 474-0608
Emp Here 5   *Sales* 698,798,100
SIC 5146 Fish and seafoods
Ron Schindler
Daniel Butto

D-U-N-S 24-320-9470   (SL)
CORNELL INSURANCE BROKERS LTD
275 Renfrew Dr Suite 208, Markham, ON, L3R
0C8
(905) 471-3868
Emp Here 40   *Sales* 23,196,960
SIC 6411 Insurance agents, brokers, and service
Kevin Towers
Mike Cannon

D-U-N-S 20-162-7221   (HQ)
COUTTS, WILLIAM E. COMPANY, LIMITED
HAPPY HOUR CARD'N PARTY SHOPS
(*Suby of* HALLMARK CARDS, INCORPORATED)
3762 14th Ave Unit 100, Markham, ON, L3R
0G7
(416) 492-1300
Emp Here 900   *Sales* 348,793,200
SIC 2771 Greeting cards
Michael Perry
Patrick Carr
Rodger King
Kevin Hennessy
John Debois
Michael Gibbons
Steven Hawn
Kay Homer

D-U-N-S 24-688-8184   (BR)
CRH CANADA GROUP INC
DUFFERIN CUSTOM CONCRETE
(*Suby of* CRH PUBLIC LIMITED COMPANY)
7655 Woodbine Ave, Markham, L3R 2N4
(905) 475-6631
Emp Here 100
SIC 3273 Ready-mixed concrete
Colin Brown

D-U-N-S 20-009-8916   (SL)
CUSTOMIZED DELIVERY SERVICE INC
3075 14th Ave Suite 209, Markham, ON, L3R
0G9
(905) 475-5908
Emp Here 30   *Sales* 13,304,700
SIC 7389 Business services, nec
Bernie Prusznowski

D-U-N-S 24-077-6468   (SL)
D.S.L. DIAGNOSTIC PRODUCTS INCORPORATED
INTER MEDICO
50 Valleywood Dr Suite 1, Markham, ON, L3R
6E9
(905) 470-0431
Emp Here 41   *Sales* 18,334,134
SIC 5047 Medical and hospital equipment
Daniel Lichtman
Catherine Trewin

D-U-N-S 24-876-5612   (HQ)
DAIWA DISTRIBUTION (ONTARIO) INC
(*Suby of* DAIWA HOLDINGS INC)

361 Alden Rd, Markham, ON, L3R 3L4
(905) 940-2889
Sales 15,669,540
SIC 5045 Computers, peripherals, and software
Kenneth Yuen
Herman Lau

D-U-N-S 24-452-6794 (SL)
DAVIS GROUP OF COMPANIES CORP
25 Riviera Dr Suite 7, Markham, ON, L3R 8N4
(905) 477-7440
Emp Here 100 *Sales* 16,402,700
SIC 2782 Blankbooks and looseleaf binders
Douglas Davis

D-U-N-S 20-890-3880 (SL)
DELCAN INTERNATIONAL CORPORATION
625 Cochrane Dr Suite 500, Markham, ON, L3R 9R9
(905) 943-0500
Emp Here 100
SIC 8711 Engineering services
James (Jim) Kerr
Jack Powers
W. Victor Anderson
Joseph K. Lam
Charles Orolowitz
Alan Rumsey
David Smith
W. James Corbett

D-U-N-S 20-301-5289 (BR)
DELOITTE LLP
DELOITTE
(*Suby of* DELOITTE LLP)
15 Allstate Pky Suite 400, Markham, ON, L3R 5B4

Emp Here 110
SIC 8742 Management consulting services

D-U-N-S 24-524-2490 (SL)
DELPHI SOLUTIONS CORP
7550 Birchmount Rd, Markham, ON, L3R 6C6

Emp Here 200
SIC 7622 Radio and television repair

D-U-N-S 20-635-5534 (SL)
DENTAL BRANDS FOR LESS INC
61 Amber St, Markham, ON, L3R 3J7
(905) 669-9329
Emp Here 30 *Sales* 13,415,220
SIC 5047 Medical and hospital equipment
Moti Betesh
Liat Betesh

D-U-N-S 20-844-7680 (SL)
DEPENDABLE ANODIZING LIMITED
268 Don Park Rd Suite 1, Markham, ON, L3R 1C3
(905) 475-1229
Emp Here 65 *Sales* 13,183,950
SIC 3471 Plating and polishing
Horst Stoll
Jochim Schauer
Karl Mueller

D-U-N-S 24-802-2329 (SL)
DESCOR INDUSTRIES INC
(*Suby of* GLOBAL UPHOLSTERY CO LIMITED)
15 Riviera Dr, Markham, ON, L3R 8N4
(905) 470-0010
Emp Here 120 *Sales* 18,518,640
SIC 2521 Wood office furniture
Chanoch Friedel
Mark Polak

D-U-N-S 24-736-1470 (HQ)
DEVJO INDUSTRIES INC
(*Suby of* DEVJO HOLDINGS LIMITED)
375 Steelcase Rd E, Markham, ON, L3R 1G3
(905) 477-7689
Sales 13,077,650
SIC 6712 Bank holding companies
G. Michael Devine

Cynthia J. Devine

D-U-N-S 20-515-2213 (BR)
DH CORPORATION
D+H
(*Suby of* VISTA EQUITY PARTNERS MANAGEMENT, LLC)
81 Whitehall Dr, Markham, ON, L3R 9T1
(905) 944-1231
Emp Here 300
SIC 6211 Security brokers and dealers

D-U-N-S 25-663-1854 (SL)
DIGNITY TRANSPORTATION INC
50 Mcintosh Dr Suite 110, Markham, ON, L3R 9T3
(905) 470-2399
Emp Here 80 *Sales* 4,389,760
SIC 4111 Local and suburban transit
Lloyd Pollock
Jeff Pasoff

D-U-N-S 24-985-2351 (SL)
DIRECT MULTI-PAK MAILING LTD
PROFESSIONAL TARGETED MARKETING
20 Torbay Rd, Markham, ON, L3R 1G6
(905) 415-1940
Emp Here 80 *Sales* 16,937,920
SIC 7331 Direct mail advertising services
Joe Trager

D-U-N-S 20-251-2224 (HQ)
DOXIM SOLUTIONS INC
1380 Rodick Rd Suite 102, Markham, ON, L3R 4G5
(647) 484-0467
Emp Here 94 *Sales* 64,600,550
SIC 7371 Custom computer programming services
David Christian Rasmussen

D-U-N-S 25-418-9459 (SL)
EASTON'S 28 SERVICE CENTRE LTD
3100 Steeles Ave E Suite 401, Markham, ON, L3R 8T3
(905) 940-9409
Emp Here 50 *Sales* 24,903,900
SIC 5541 Gasoline service stations
Steve Gupta

D-U-N-S 24-341-9319 (HQ)
EASTON'S GROUP OF HOTELS INC
FAIRFIELD INN & SUITESSM BY MARRIOTT TORONTO AIRPORT
3100 Steeles Ave E Suite 601, Markham, ON, L3R 8T3
(905) 940-9409
Emp Here 5 *Sales* 18,538,000
SIC 7011 Hotels and motels
Steve Gupta

D-U-N-S 20-547-8527 (SL)
EASTON'S TORONTO AIRPORT HOTEL (COROGA) LP
3100 Steeles Ave E, Markham, ON, L3R 8T3
(905) 940-9409
Emp Here 75 *Sales* 7,199,859
SIC 7011 Hotels and motels
Steve Gupta

D-U-N-S 24-317-4398 (SL)
EASTSIDE CHEVROLET BUICK GMC LTD
(*Suby of* OLD MILL PONTIAC BUICK CADILLAC LIMITED)
8435 Woodbine Ave Suite 7, Markham, ON, L3R 2P4
(905) 475-7373
Emp Here 60 *Sales* 37,756,800
SIC 5511 New and used car dealers
Lou Vavaroutsos

D-U-N-S 25-354-4134 (HQ)
ECCO SHOES CANADA INC
(*Suby of* ECCO HOLDING A/S)
10 Whitehall Dr, Markham, ON, L3R 5Z7
(905) 947-8148
Emp Here 15 *Sales* 39,865,760
SIC 5139 Footwear

Ali Jafri
Manuel Dulanto

D-U-N-S 20-052-2501 (SL)
EDJAR FOOD GROUP INC
7650 Birchmount Rd, Markham, ON, L3R 6B9
(905) 474-0710
Emp Here 70 *Sales* 18,308,710
SIC 6712 Bank holding companies
Daniel Chim
James Chim

D-U-N-S 20-145-5425 (HQ)
ELCO FINE FOODS INC
233 Alden Rd, Markham, ON, L3R 3W6
(604) 651-1551
Emp Here 1 *Sales* 78,838,760
SIC 5141 Groceries, general line
John Hearn
Maurice Cussen
Maurice Tapiero
Deborah Stevenson

D-U-N-S 25-359-5565 (HQ)
ELCO SYSTEMS INC
215 Shields Crt Unit 4-6, Markham, ON, L3R 8V2
(905) 470-0082
Sales 36,668,268
SIC 5045 Computers, peripherals, and software
Frankie Wong

D-U-N-S 20-275-4552 (HQ)
ELECTRO SONIC GROUP INC
60 Renfrew Dr Suite 110, Markham, ON, L3R 0E1
(905) 470-3015
Emp Here 5 *Sales* 13,415,220
SIC 5065 Electronic parts and equipment, nec
Jamil Nizam

D-U-N-S 20-164-4010 (HQ)
ELECTRONIC METALFORM INDUSTRIES LIMITED
435 Steelcase Rd E, Markham, ON, L3R 2M2
(905) 475-1217
Sales 13,445,950
SIC 3499 Fabricated Metal products, nec
Harry Drew
Ian Fockler
Frank Defina
W Mohamed

D-U-N-S 20-707-3086 (SL)
ELFA INSURANCE SERVICES INC
3950 14th Ave Unit 105, Markham, ON, L3R 0A9
(905) 470-1038
Emp Here 50 *Sales* 28,996,200
SIC 6411 Insurance agents, brokers, and service
Pattie Cole

D-U-N-S 20-817-2718 (SL)
EMPIRE FOODS LIMITED
205 Torbay Rd Unit 7, Markham, ON, L3R 3W4
(905) 475-9988
Emp Here 33 *Sales* 27,574,041
SIC 5141 Groceries, general line
Peter Tserpes
Jordan Giazitzidis

D-U-N-S 24-127-0052 (HQ)
ENERCARE INC
7400 Birchmount Rd, Markham, ON, L3R 5V4
(416) 649-1900
Emp Here 9 *Sales* 985,751,958
SIC 6712 Bank holding companies
Jenine Krause
John Toffoletto
Geoff Lowe
William M. Wells
John Piercy
Jim Pantelidis
Roy J. Pearce
Lisa De Wilde

Michael Rousseau
Jerry Patava

D-U-N-S 20-259-0055 (SL)
ENGAGE PEOPLE INC
1380 Rodick Rd Suite 300, Markham, ON, L3R 4G5
(416) 775-9180
Emp Here 121 *Sales* 57,569,632
SIC 7379 Computer related services, nec
Jonathan Silver
Ron Benegbi
Mario Crudo
Len Covello

D-U-N-S 24-602-4137 (HQ)
ENGHOUSE SYSTEMS LIMITED
SYNTELLECT CANADA, DIV OF
80 Tiverton Crt Suite 800, Markham, ON, L3R 0G4
(905) 946-3200
Emp Here 75 *Sales* 264,795,650
SIC 7371 Custom computer programming services
Stephen Sadler
Vince Mifsud
Doug Bryson
Sam Anidjar
Geoff Bartle
Todd May
Eric Demirian
Reid Drury
John Gibson
Pierre Lassonde

D-U-N-S 24-992-0216 (HQ)
ENTERPRISE RENT-A-CAR CANADA COMPANY
(*Suby of* THE CRAWFORD GROUP INC)
200-7390 Woodbine Ave, Markham, ON, L3R 1A5
(905) 477-1688
Emp Here 40 *Sales* 43,054,080
SIC 7514 Passenger car rental
William W. Snyder
Brian M. Oddy
Andrew C. Taylor
Pamela M. Nicholson

D-U-N-S 20-327-1184 (SL)
ENVIZION VENTURE CAPITAL CORP
3601 Highway 7 E, Markham, ON, L3R 0M3
(289) 301-4485
Emp Here 29 *Sales* 13,077,520
SIC 7389 Business services, nec
Glenn Sutton
Richard Mirseh
Anthony Lynch

D-U-N-S 20-052-5660 (SL)
EPM GLOBAL SERVICES INC
VEXOS
195 Royal Crest Crt, Markham, ON, L3R 9X6
(905) 479-6203
Emp Here 148 *Sales* 28,185,416
SIC 3679 Electronic components, nec
Paul Jona
Kaspars Fricbergs
Cyril Fernandes
Wayne Hawkins
Stanley Chen
Stephanie Martin
Roger Dunfield

D-U-N-S 24-886-1528 (HQ)
EPROM INC
100 Shields Crt, Markham, ON, L3R 9T5
(905) 944-9000
Sales 26,830,440
SIC 5045 Computers, peripherals, and software
Paul Ling

D-U-N-S 24-359-9024 (HQ)
EPSON CANADA LIMITED EPSON CANADA LIMITEE
(*Suby of* SEIKO EPSON CORPORATION)

185 Renfrew Dr, Markham, ON, L3R 6G3
(416) 498-4574
Sales 107,070,400
SIC 5045 Computers, peripherals, and software
Allan Pound

D-U-N-S 20-526-8683   (HQ)
ESBE SCIENTIFIC INDUSTRIES INC
SB SCIENTIFIC
80 Mcpherson St, Markham, ON, L3R 3V6
(905) 475-8232
Emp Here 41   *Sales* 21,464,352
SIC 5049 Professional equipment, nec
Laurel Wiseman

D-U-N-S 25-359-4964   (SL)
EURO VERVE CO. LTD
951 Denison St Unit 16, Markham, ON, L3R 3W9
(905) 513-8283
Emp Here 70   *Sales* 34,882,540
SIC 5137 Women's and children's clothing
Alice Tse

D-U-N-S 25-369-0630   (HQ)
EVEREST CLINICAL RESEARCH CORPORATION
675 Cochrane Dr Suite 408, Markham, ON, L3R 0B8
(905) 752-5222
Emp Here 65   *Sales* 28,592,590
SIC 8732 Commercial nonphysical research
Irene Zhang

D-U-N-S 20-366-3141   (SL)
EVERTRUST DEVELOPMENT GROUP CANADA INC
3100 Steeles Ave E Suite 302, Markham, ON, L3R 8T3
(647) 501-2345
Emp Here 3,000   *Sales* 2,095,176,000
SIC 1542 Nonresidential construction, nec
Jiancheng Zhou

D-U-N-S 24-422-3215   (SL)
EXCEL INSURANCE AGENCY INC
80 Acadia Ave Suite 205, Markham, ON, L3R 9V1
(905) 470-8222
Emp Here 215   *Sales* 1,020,412,360
SIC 6411 Insurance agents, brokers, and service
Margaret Cheng
Roy Cheng

D-U-N-S 25-101-1011   (BR)
EXCO TECHNOLOGIES LIMITED
EXCO EXTRUSION DIES
(*Suby of* EXCO TECHNOLOGIES LIMITED)
130 Spy Crt Unit 1, Markham, ON, L3R 5H6
(905) 477-3065
Emp Here 115
SIC 3544 Special dies, tools, jigs, and fixtures
Janet Sledmere

D-U-N-S 20-164-8052   (HQ)
EXCO TECHNOLOGIES LIMITED
EXCO ENGINEERING
130 Spy Crt, Markham, ON, L3R 5H6
(905) 477-3065
Emp Here 10   *Sales* 465,798,915
SIC 3465 Automotive stampings
William Schroers
Darren M. Kirk
Drew R. Knight
Jeff Blackburn
Nick Gnatyuk
Laurie T.F. Bennett
Edward Kernaghan
Nicole A. Kirk
Robert Magee
Philip B. Matthews

D-U-N-S 24-666-5509   (HQ)
EXTENDICARE (CANADA) INC
(*Suby of* EXTENDICARE INC)
3000 Steeles Ave E Suite 700, Markham, ON,

L3R 9W2
(905) 470-1400
Emp Here 120   *Sales* 1,229,868,000
SIC 8051 Skilled nursing care facilities
Timothy Lukenda

D-U-N-S 20-641-6851   (HQ)
EXTENDICARE INC
3000 Steeles Ave E Suite 103, Markham, ON, L3R 4T9
(905) 470-4000
Emp Here 50   *Sales* 859,733,600
SIC 8051 Skilled nursing care facilities
Michael Guerriere
Karen Scanlan
Jillian Fountain
Mark Lugowski
Gary Loder
Christina Mckey
Michael Harris
Brandon Parent
Elaine Everson
Tracey Mulcahy

D-U-N-S 24-453-1372   (SL)
FILBITRON SYSTEMS GROUP INC
FILBITRON MARKETING
178 Torbay Rd, Markham, ON, L3R 1G6
(905) 477-0450
Emp Here 30   *Sales* 13,415,220
SIC 5045 Computers, peripherals, and software
James Clark
Mario Massarella
Henry Fischler

D-U-N-S 24-826-3717   (SL)
FISKARS CANADA, INC
FISKARS BRAND
(*Suby of* FISKARS OYJ ABP)
675 Cochrane Dr, Markham, ON, L3R 0B8
(905) 940-8460
Emp Here 23   *Sales* 11,972,466
SIC 5099 Durable goods, nec
Paul Tonnesen
Kevin Murphy
David Lambrecht
Christian Steinmetz

D-U-N-S 20-151-0450   (HQ)
FITZHENRY & WHITESIDE LIMITED
195 Allstate Pky, Markham, ON, L3R 4T8
(905) 477-9700
Emp Here 37   *Sales* 31,185,840
SIC 5192 Books, periodicals, and newspapers
Sharon Fitzhenry
Robert I Fitzhenry

D-U-N-S 25-095-5580   (HQ)
FLEXTRONICS AUTOMOTIVE INC
(*Suby of* FLEX LTD.)
450 Hood Rd, Markham, ON, L3R 9Z3
(800) 668-5649
Emp Here 45   *Sales* 63,546,260
SIC 7389 Business services, nec
Greg Polityka

D-U-N-S 20-374-7048   (SL)
FLOWR CORPORATION, THE
100 Allstate Pky Suite 201, Markham, ON, L3R 6H3
(905) 940-3993
Emp Here 60   *Sales* 16,599,600
SIC 2833 Medicinals and botanicals
Jonathan Day-Reiner

D-U-N-S 20-812-0191   (SL)
FORRESTALL GROUP INC, THE
201 Whitehall Dr Unit 4, Markham, ON, L3R 9Y3

Emp Here 100   *Sales* 16,258,400
SIC 7379 Computer related services, nec
Vince Forrestall

D-U-N-S 24-885-4036   (SL)
FOUR SEASONS DRYWALL SYSTEMS & ACOUSTICS LIMITED

200 Konrad Cres, Markham, ON, L3R 8T9
(905) 474-9960
Emp Here 100   *Sales* 16,238,100
SIC 1742 Plastering, drywall, and insulation
Werner Zapfe

D-U-N-S 25-692-5355   (HQ)
FUTURE SALES CORPORATION
FUTURE STEEL BUILDINGS
1405 Denison St, Markham, ON, L3R 5V2
(905) 477-1894
Sales 14,406,375
SIC 3441 Fabricated structural Metal
Marcel Aitoro

D-U-N-S 24-707-5260   (HQ)
G.A. PAPER INTERNATIONAL INC
G.A. PAPER
327 Renfrew Dr Suite 102, Markham, ON, L3R 9S8
(905) 479-7600
Emp Here 25   *Sales* 14,575,176
SIC 5099 Durable goods, nec
Ibrahim Elgammal
Nermine Elgammal

D-U-N-S 24-830-0428   (BR)
G.N. JOHNSTON EQUIPMENT CO. LTD.
G.N. JOHNSTON EQUIPMENT CO. LTD
(*Suby of* TOYOTA INDUSTRIES CORPORATION)
181 Whitehall Dr Suite 2, Markham, ON, L3R 9T1
(416) 798-7195
Emp Here 90
SIC 3537 Industrial trucks and tractors
Frank Buis

D-U-N-S 25-300-2943   (HQ)
GARDEN BASKET FOOD MARKETS INCORPORATED, THE
GARDEN BASKET, THE
7676 Woodbine Ave Unit 1, Markham, ON, L3R 2N2
(905) 305-8220
Emp Here 4   *Sales* 49,891,090
SIC 5411 Grocery stores
Jack Comella

D-U-N-S 20-348-0223   (BR)
GENERAL MOTORS OF CANADA COMPANY
CANADIAN TECHNICAL CENTRE
(*Suby of* GENERAL MOTORS COMPANY)
101 Mcnabb St, Markham, ON, L3R 4H8
(905) 644-5000
Emp Here 130
SIC 7389 Business services, nec
Brian Tossan

D-U-N-S 25-987-7772   (SL)
GENTEC INTERNATIONAL
90 Royal Crest Crt, Markham, ON, L3R 9X6
(905) 513-7733
Emp Here 82   *Sales* 53,349,590
SIC 5099 Durable goods, nec
Joel Siegel

D-U-N-S 20-720-4525   (SL)
GENTOX LABORATORIES INC
VITA-TECH
1345 Denison St, Markham, ON, L3R 5V2
(416) 798-4988
Emp Here 300   *Sales* 97,528,275
SIC 8734 Testing laboratories
Michael Lane

D-U-N-S 24-952-4133   (SL)
GLOBAL AEROSPACE UNDERWRITING MANAGERS (CANADA) LIMITED
(*Suby of* MUNCHENER RUCKVERSICHERUNGS-GESELLSCHAFT AG IN MUNCHEN)
100 Renfrew Dr Suite 200, Markham, ON, L3R 9R6
(905) 479-2244
Emp Here 25   *Sales* 21,201,500
SIC 6411 Insurance agents, brokers, and ser-

vice
Gavin Mcmahon
Steve Hughes

D-U-N-S 20-522-3865   (HQ)
GLOBAL CREDIT & COLLECTION INC
1490 Denison St, Markham, ON, L3R 9T7
(905) 479-2222
Emp Here 80   *Sales* 20,037,100
SIC 7322 Adjustment and collection services
Martin Sugar
Daniel Elmalem
Rob Yarmo

D-U-N-S 24-150-3213   (SL)
GLOBAL LINK REALTY GROUP INC
351 Ferrier St Unit 2351, Markham, ON, L3R 2Z5
(905) 475-0028
Emp Here 40   *Sales* 13,085,080
SIC 6531 Real estate agents and managers
Dundas Kwok

D-U-N-S 24-576-3743   (SL)
GLOBAL TRAVEL COMPUTER HOLDINGS LTD
GLOBAL MATRIX
7550 Birchmount Rd, Markham, ON, L3R 6C6
(905) 479-4949
Emp Here 60   *Sales* 10,638,660
SIC 7374 Data processing and preparation
Ian Lang
James Warren
Graham Irvine

D-U-N-S 20-364-1964   (SL)
GOBA SPORTS GROUP INC
151 Whitehall Dr, Markham, ON, L3R 9T1
(888) 989-4015
Emp Here 100   *Sales* 52,929,688
SIC 5091 Sporting and recreation goods
Steven Holmes

D-U-N-S 25-333-4809   (HQ)
GOLD LINE TELEMANAGEMENT INC
GOLD LINE
300 Allstate Pky, Markham, ON, L3R 0P2
(905) 709-3570
Emp Here 220   *Sales* 100,363,200
SIC 4899 Communication services, nec
Ata Moeini
Neda Moeini
Anissa Moeini
Borna Moeini
Shala Yazdani

D-U-N-S 24-964-9195   (BR)
GRANT THORNTON LLP
CAPSERVCO
(*Suby of* GRANT THORNTON LLP)
15 Allstate Pky Suite 200, Markham, ON, L3R 5B4
(416) 607-2656
Emp Here 200
SIC 8721 Accounting, auditing, and bookkeeping
Greg Baker

D-U-N-S 25-498-6714   (SL)
GRAPE ARBOR CONSTRUCTION LTD
MAJESTIC CONDOMINIUM SALES
80 Tiverton Crt Suite 300, Markham, ON, L3R 0G4
(905) 477-7609
Emp Here 5   *Sales* 14,901,810
SIC 1522 Residential construction, nec
Sheldon Libfeld

D-U-N-S 24-538-0548   (HQ)
HAMILTON BEACH BRANDS CANADA, INC
(*Suby of* HAMILTON BEACH BRANDS HOLDING COMPANY)
7300 Warden Ave Suite 201, Markham, ON, L3R 9Z6
(905) 513-6222
Sales 11,179,350
SIC 5064 Electrical appliances, television and radio

Rick Simpson

D-U-N-S 24-859-7528   (SL)
HOLMES PLASTIC BINDINGS LTD
HOLMES THE FINISHING HOUSE
200 Ferrier St, Markham, ON, L3R 2Z5
(905) 513-6211
Emp Here 100   *Sales* 16,402,700
SIC 2789 Bookbinding and related work
Robert Holmes

D-U-N-S 25-794-3621   (BR)
HOME DEPOT OF CANADA INC
HOME DEPOT
(*Suby of* THE HOME DEPOT INC)
3155 Highway 7 E, Markham, ON, L3R 0T9
(905) 940-5900
Emp Here 200
SIC 5251 Hardware stores
Chris Rinnela

D-U-N-S 24-984-9498   (SL)
HOMELIFE/GOLDEN EAST REALTY INC
200 Town Centre Blvd Suite 206, Markham, ON, L3R 8G5
(905) 415-1331
Emp Here 40   *Sales* 10,870,240
SIC 6531 Real estate agents and managers
Jane Yuen

D-U-N-S 25-722-3222   (SL)
HOMELIFE/LEADER INC
3636 Steeles Ave E Unit 307, Markham, ON, L3R 1K9
(416) 298-6633
Emp Here 100   *Sales* 27,175,600
SIC 6531 Real estate agents and managers
Paul Lau

D-U-N-S 25-459-7800   (SL)
HONTA TRADING INTERNATIONAL INC
110a Cochrane Dr, Markham, ON, L3R 5S7
(905) 305-0688
Emp Here 30   *Sales* 15,616,260
SIC 5099 Durable goods, nec
Tommy Ho

D-U-N-S 20-044-3836   (SL)
HORTON SPICE MILLS LIMITED
256 Steelcase Rd W, Markham, ON, L3R 1B3
(905) 475-6130
Emp Here 20   *Sales* 10,702,480
SIC 5149 Groceries and related products, nec
Thomas D Horton Jr

D-U-N-S 24-092-0439   (HQ)
HOUSE OF ELECTRICAL SUPPLIES LIMITED
115 Shields Crt Unit B, Markham, ON, L3R 9T5
(905) 752-2323
Emp Here 19   *Sales* 12,968,046
SIC 5063 Electrical apparatus and equipment
Austin Brennan, Sr
Austin Brennan, Jr
Guido Colosimo

D-U-N-S 24-374-2090   (HQ)
HUAWEI TECHNOLOGIES CANADA CO., LTD
(*Suby of* HUAWEI INVESTMENT & HOLDING CO., LTD.)
19 Allstate Pky, Markham, ON, L3R 5A4
(905) 944-5000
Emp Here 50   *Sales* 102,812,400
SIC 4899 Communication services, nec
Shengli Wang
Wanzhou Meng
Shaohua Ding

D-U-N-S 24-964-9518   (BR)
HUDSON'S BAY COMPANY
BAY, THE
(*Suby of* HUDSON'S BAY COMPANY)
5000 Highway 7 E, Markham, ON, L3R 4M9
(905) 513-1770
Emp Here 100
SIC 5311 Department stores

Cheri Roberts

D-U-N-S 24-326-5373   (SL)
HUYNH, KIM DRUGS LTD
SHOPPERS DRUG MART
7060 Warden Ave, Markham, ON, L3R 5Y2
(905) 474-1414
Emp Here 60   *Sales* 14,659,680
SIC 5912 Drug stores and proprietary stores
Kim Huynh

D-U-N-S 24-420-7387   (HQ)
HYUNDAI AUTO CANADA CORP
(*Suby of* HYUNDAI MOTOR COMPANY)
75 Frontenac Dr, Markham, ON, L3R 6H2
(905) 477-0202
Sales 73,784,640
SIC 5012 Automobiles and other motor vehicles
Don Romano
David Park
Seung Jo (Scott) Lee
Ho Il Lee
Peter Kim Hyung Cheong

D-U-N-S 20-044-3976   (HQ)
IBM CANADA LIMITED
IBM GLOBAL SERVICES
(*Suby of* INTERNATIONAL BUSINESS MACHINES CORPORATION)
3600 Steeles Ave E, Markham, ON, L3R 9Z7
(905) 316-5000
Emp Here 4,000   *Sales* 4,494,032,000
SIC 3571 Electronic computers
Dino Tevisani
Xerxes Cooper
Matt Snell

D-U-N-S 25-459-8279   (HQ)
ICON DIGITAL PRODUCTIONS INC
ICON PRINT
7495 Birchmount Rd, Markham, ON, L3R 5G2
(905) 889-2800
Sales 12,022,260
SIC 7336 Commercial art and graphic design
Juan Lau
Peter Evans
Peter Yeung

D-U-N-S 24-382-3478   (SL)
ICON MEDIA COMMUNICATIONS INC
(*Suby of* ICON DIGITAL PRODUCTIONS INC)
7495 Birchmount Rd, Markham, ON, L3R 5G2
(905) 889-1944
Emp Here 50   *Sales* 26,027,100
SIC 5099 Durable goods, nec
Juan Lau
Peter Evans
Alex Christopoulos
Praveen Gupta
Shawn O'brien

D-U-N-S 24-351-2329   (HQ)
IFABRIC CORP
525 Denison St Unit 2, Markham, ON, L3R 1B8
(905) 752-0566
Emp Here 5   *Sales* 15,034,665
SIC 6799 Investors, nec
Hylton Karon
Hilton Price
Jeff Coyne
Mark Greenspan
Mark Cochran

D-U-N-S 25-938-3081   (SL)
IN-PRO CLEANING SYSTEMS LTD
570 Hood Rd Unit 24, Markham, ON, L3R 4G7
(905) 475-2020
Emp Here 185   *Sales* 5,914,080
SIC 7349 Building maintenance services, nec
Anthony Smilis
Anastasia Smilis

D-U-N-S 20-692-3018   (SL)
INFINITE CABLES INC
PHANTOM CABLES

3993 14th Ave, Markham, ON, L3R 4Z6
(905) 477-4433
Emp Here 30   *Sales* 13,415,220
SIC 5045 Computers, peripherals, and software
George Arvanitopoulos
Chris Frangos

D-U-N-S 25-190-7986   (HQ)
INNOVATIVE CONTROL SOLUTIONS INC
ICS
(*Suby of* MAC VALVES, INC.)
3115 14th Ave Suite 8, Markham, ON, L3R 0H1
(905) 709-4220
Emp Here 16   *Sales* 11,875,650
SIC 5085 Industrial supplies
James (Jim) Knudson

D-U-N-S 20-298-8978   (HQ)
INNOVISION HOLDINGS CORPORATION
55 Renfrew Dr, Markham, ON, L3R 8H3
(905) 940-2488
Sales 12,580,650
SIC 6712 Bank holding companies
Kevin Ho Tung Au-Yeung
Norman Ho Yee Au-Yeung

D-U-N-S 25-405-1204   (SL)
INTEGRATED MAINTENANCE & OPERATIONS SERVICES INC
IMOS
Gd, Markham, ON, L3R 9R8
(905) 475-6660
Emp Here 100   *Sales* 25,244,200
SIC 1611 Highway and street construction
Barrie Brayford
Doug Wipperman

D-U-N-S 20-550-0127   (HQ)
INTEGRATED TECHNOLOGY LIMITED
I T L CIRCUITS
90 Don Park Rd, Markham, ON, L3R 1C4
(905) 475-6658
Emp Here 5   *Sales* 27,614,090
SIC 3672 Printed circuit boards
Michael Campbell
Adolf Czudnochowsky

D-U-N-S 20-115-0922   (HQ)
IRIS TECHNOLOGIES INC
IRISTEL
675 Cochrane Dr Suite 6, Markham, ON, L3R 0B8
(416) 800-4747
Emp Here 40   *Sales* 27,416,640
SIC 4899 Communication services, nec
Samer Bishay
Magdi Wanis

D-U-N-S 20-625-1779   (HQ)
J.F. & L. RESTAURANTS LIMITED
PICKLE BARREL, THE
110 Denison St Unit 3, Markham, ON, L3R 1B6
(905) 479-2402
Emp Here 15   *Sales* 46,639,000
SIC 5812 Eating places
Frederick Sharf
Peter Higley

D-U-N-S 24-533-7485   (HQ)
JACCO TOURS ONTARIO INC
7828 Kennedy Rd Suite 203, Markham, ON, L3R 5P1
(905) 305-3888
Emp Here 40   *Sales* 23,398,515
SIC 4724 Travel agencies
Benny Li

D-U-N-S 24-575-6531   (HQ)
JAMAC SALES LIMITED
141 Don Park Rd, Markham, ON, L3R 1C2
(905) 947-9824
Emp Here 12   *Sales* 17,886,960
SIC 5039 Construction materials, nec
Donald Mcbride

D-U-N-S 25-283-7414   (BR)
JOHNSON & JOHNSON INC
JOHNSON & JOHNSON MEDICAL COMPANIES
(*Suby of* JOHNSON & JOHNSON)
200 Whitehall Dr, Markham, ON, L3R 0T5
(905) 946-8999
Emp Here 200
SIC 3842 Surgical appliances and supplies
Bernard Zovighian

D-U-N-S 20-222-4200   (HQ)
JOHNSON & JOHNSON INC
JOHNSON & JOHNSON MEDICAL COMPANIES
(*Suby of* JOHNSON & JOHNSON)
88 Mcnabb St, Markham, ON, L3R 5L2
(905) 968-2000
Emp Here 350   *Sales* 823,110,000
SIC 3842 Surgical appliances and supplies

D-U-N-S 24-507-8548   (SL)
K-DENTAL INC
(*Suby of* 1220579 ONTARIO INC)
750 Cochrane Dr, Markham, ON, L3R 8E1
(416) 293-8365
Emp Here 50   *Sales* 22,358,700
SIC 5047 Medical and hospital equipment
Robert Kainz

D-U-N-S 24-873-4469   (SL)
KEATING TECHNOLOGIES INC
25 Royal Crest Crt Suite 120, Markham, ON, L3R 9X4
(905) 479-0230
Emp Here 80   *Sales* 21,946,560
SIC 8741 Management services
Larry Keating

D-U-N-S 24-452-6810   (HQ)
KINARK CHILD AND FAMILY SERVICES
500 Hood Rd Suite 200, Markham, ON, L3R 9Z3
(905) 474-9595
Emp Here 20   *Sales* 53,754,400
SIC 8322 Individual and family services
Sheila Masters
Bill Clark
Kathy Newton
Mark Welch

D-U-N-S 24-728-0696   (SL)
KL FOODS INC
235 Hood Rd Unit 3, Markham, ON, L3R 4N3
(905) 479-9048
Emp Here 25   *Sales* 20,889,425
SIC 5145 Confectionery
Matt Velshi

D-U-N-S 24-708-8008   (SL)
KRIKORIAN, S.H. & CO LTD
1 Valleywood Dr Unit 4, Markham, ON, L3R 5L9
(905) 479-4080
Emp Here 14   *Sales* 15,474,830
SIC 5122 Drugs, proprietaries, and sundries
Sarkis Krikorian
Nicholas Krikorian
Natasha Krikorian
Nigel Krikorian
Leda Krikorian

D-U-N-S 24-470-3930   (HQ)
LEA CONSULTING LTD
(*Suby of* LEA GROUP HOLDINGS INC)
625 Cochrane Dr 9th Flr, Markham, ON, L3R 9R9
(905) 470-0015
Sales 24,129,765
SIC 8711 Engineering services
David Saunders
Peter Ojala
Glenn Johnson
Paul Duncan

D-U-N-S 24-797-9586   (HQ)
LEA GROUP HOLDINGS INC
625 Cochrane Dr Suite 900, Markham, ON,

L3R 9R9
(905) 470-0015
Emp Here 8   *Sales* 26,453,372
SIC 8711 Engineering services
David R. Saunders
John Farrow
Pinacki Chowdhury
Otto Steenkamp
M.P. Raju
Terry Wallace

D-U-N-S 24-108-6383   (SL)
LEDOUX, LEW & PATTERSON INSURANCE BROKERS LTD
7030 Woodbine Ave Suite 100, Markham, ON, L3R 6G2
(905) 944-1188
Emp Here 35   *Sales* 20,297,340
SIC 6411 Insurance agents, brokers, and service
Steve Hisey

D-U-N-S 24-356-4551   (HQ)
LEISUREWORLD SENIOR CARE LP
302 Town Centre Blvd Suite 200, Markham, ON, L3R 0E8
(905) 477-4006
Sales 661,312,800
SIC 8741 Management services
David Cutler
Martin Liddell

D-U-N-S 20-338-5505   (SL)
LIFEWORKS CANADA LTD
(*Suby of* MORNEAU SHEPELL INC)
675 Cochrane Dr 5th Fl, Markham, ON, L3R 0B8
(905) 947-7214
Emp Here 140   *Sales* 19,970,415
SIC 8748 Business consulting, nec
Jamie True
Jon Harris
Cande Dandele
Jack Bekhor

D-U-N-S 20-339-2316   (SL)
LINKAGE GROUP INC, THE
30 Centurian Dr Suite 200, Markham, ON, L3R 8B8
(905) 415-2300
Emp Here 400   *Sales* 74,602,400
SIC 8742 Management consulting services
Robert Proctor

D-U-N-S 24-756-7126   (SL)
LINSEY FOODS LTD
121 Mcpherson St, Markham, ON, L3R 3L3
(905) 940-3850
Emp Here 30   *Sales* 10,370,700
SIC 2099 Food preparations, nec
Douglas Woolsey
Bruce Fitzgerald

D-U-N-S 24-525-6292   (SL)
LIVING GROUP OF COMPANIES INC
7030 Woodbine Ave Suite 300, Markham, ON, L3R 6G2
(905) 474-0500
Emp Here 40   *Sales* 41,888,900
SIC 6531 Real estate agents and managers
Stephen Wong
Eric Chan

D-U-N-S 24-420-7031   (HQ)
LIVING REALTY INC
LIVING GROUPS OF COMPANIES
7030 Woodbine Ave Suite 300, Markham, ON, L3R 6G2
(905) 474-9856
Emp Here 250   *Sales* 219,741,600
SIC 6531 Real estate agents and managers
Steven Wong
Eric Chan

D-U-N-S 24-709-1218   (BR)
LONGO BROTHERS FRUIT MARKETS INC
LONGO'S FRUIT MARKET
(*Suby of* LONGO BROTHERS FRUIT MAR-

KETS INC)
3085 Highway 7 E, Markham, ON, L3R 0J5
(905) 479-8877
Emp Here 160
SIC 5411 Grocery stores
Vince Tortorici

D-U-N-S 24-924-9947   (HQ)
LONGVIEW SOLUTIONS INC
(*Suby of* PRECISE HOLDCO B.V.)
65 Allstate Pky Suite 200, Markham, ON, L3R 9X1
(905) 940-1510
Emp Here 160   *Sales* 54,157,320
SIC 7372 Prepackaged software
John Power
Gerard Chiasson
Roland Hlscher
David Hughes
Brad Smith
Wayne Stevens

D-U-N-S 20-380-5510   (SL)
LUMIFY INC
2700 John St, Markham, ON, L3R 2W4
(905) 474-0555
Emp Here 50   *Sales* 10,233,650
SIC 3648 Lighting equipment, nec
Zhenghua Luo
William Andrew
Derrick Milne

D-U-N-S 20-273-9780   (SL)
MAGNASONIC INC.
SONIGEM PRODUCTS
300 Alden Rd, Markham, ON, L3R 4C1

Emp Here 49   *Sales* 12,816,097
SIC 6712 Bank holding companies
Godfrey D'cruz

D-U-N-S 24-159-1549   (SL)
MARANTZ CANADA INC
D & M CANADA
505 Apple Creek Blvd Unit 5, Markham, ON, L3R 5B1
(905) 415-9292
Emp Here 30   *Sales* 13,415,220
SIC 5065 Electronic parts and equipment, nec
Marcel Mukerjee

D-U-N-S 20-044-4446   (SL)
MARIE, F. LIMITED
123 Denison St, Markham, ON, L3R 1B5
(905) 475-0093
Emp Here 25   *Sales* 11,875,650
SIC 5084 Industrial machinery and equipment
Sandra Marie Rundle

D-U-N-S 24-326-4665   (SL)
MARKHAM WOODBINE HOSPITALITY LTD
MARRIOTT
3100 Steeles Ave E Suite 601, Markham, ON, L3R 8T3
(905) 940-9409
Emp Here 150   *Sales* 13,903,500
SIC 7011 Hotels and motels
Steve Gupta

D-U-N-S 25-323-3183   (HQ)
MAYFAIR TENNIS COURTS LIMITED
MAYFAIR RAQUET & FITNESS CLUBS
50 Steelcase Rd E, Markham, ON, L3R 1E8
(905) 475-6668
Emp Here 15   *Sales* 18,811,250
SIC 7997 Membership sports and recreation clubs
Shirley Vedder
Garry Zentil
Jeanie Villanueva

D-U-N-S 20-163-9622   (HQ)
MCKESSON CORPORATION
GUARDIAN DRUGS
(*Suby of* MCKESSON CORPORATION)
131 Mcnabb St, Markham, ON, L3R 5V7
(905) 943-9499
Emp Here 160   *Sales* 82,564,200

SIC 5122 Drugs, proprietaries, and sundries
Andy Giancamilli
Eugene Gidaro
Peter Quintilliani
James Hutton
Terrence Connoy
N. Arthur Smith
Frank Tonon
Michael Brunelle
Peter Whitfield
Larry Latowsky

D-U-N-S 20-342-7810   (SL)
MCLEAN HALLMARK INSURANCE GROUP LTD
(*Suby of* NFP INTERMEDIATE HOLDINGS B CORP.)
10 Konrad Cres, Markham, ON, L3R 8T7
(416) 364-4000
Emp Here 20   *Sales* 16,961,200
SIC 6411 Insurance agents, brokers, and service
Daryn Mclean
Bert Long
Tracy Mclean
Chris Mildon
Gerry Olsthoorn
Pat Bastedo
Trevor Craig

D-U-N-S 24-738-1767   (HQ)
MEDICAL PHARMACIES GROUP LIMITED
300 Town Centre Blvd 4th Fl, Markham, ON, L3R 5Z6
(866) 689-3169
Emp Here 50   *Sales* 100,945,350
SIC 5912 Drug stores and proprietary stores
Richard Sevazlian
Erast R Huculak
Sydney Shrott
Stephen Pearson
Anthony Di Mito

D-U-N-S 20-883-6114   (HQ)
MELOCHE MONNEX FINANCIAL SERVICES INC
TD MELOCHE MONNEX
(*Suby of* TORONTO-DOMINION BANK, THE)
101 Mcnabb St, Markham, ON, L3R 4H8
(416) 484-1112
Emp Here 200   *Sales* 1,917,426,016
SIC 6411 Insurance agents, brokers, and service
James V. Russell
Raymond C. H. Chun
Kenneth W. Lalonde

D-U-N-S 24-487-7254   (SL)
MERIDICAN TRAVEL INC
MERIDICAN INCENTIVE CONSULTANTS
16 Esna Park Dr Suite 103, Markham, ON, L3R 5X1
(905) 477-7700
Emp Here 30   *Sales* 15,599,010
SIC 4724 Travel agencies
Anthony Byron
Terry Manion

D-U-N-S 20-378-5993   (SL)
MERITIGROUP LTD
7100 Woodbine Ave Suite 218, Markham, ON, L3R 5J2
(905) 489-8299
Emp Here 30   *Sales* 20,367,690
SIC 6211 Security brokers and dealers
Weimin Zhu

D-U-N-S 20-644-6333   (SL)
MICROLAND TECHNICAL SERVICES INC
170 Alden Rd Unit 2, Markham, ON, L3R 4C1
(905) 940-1982
Emp Here 60   *Sales* 10,638,660
SIC 7371 Custom computer programming services
Hossein Abar

D-U-N-S 24-785-1074   (SL)

MID-RANGE COMPUTER GROUP INC
MID-RANGE TECHNICAL SERVICES
85 Idema Rd, Markham, ON, L3R 1A9
(905) 940-1814
Emp Here 50   *Sales* 11,517,000
SIC 5734 Computer and software stores
Daniel Duffy
Zdy Orlinski

D-U-N-S 20-170-7791   (HQ)
MIDDLETON GROUP INC
75 Denison St Suite 6, Markham, ON, L3R 1B5
(905) 475-6556
Emp Here 80   *Sales* 18,863,105
SIC 2759 Commercial printing, nec
Robert Middleton
Herbert Riethmacher
Gina Jeronimo

D-U-N-S 24-827-3294   (BR)
MILLER THOMSON LLP
(*Suby of* MILLER THOMSON LLP)
60 Columbia Way Suite 600, Markham, ON, L3R 0C9
(905) 415-6700
Emp Here 100
SIC 8111 Legal services
Peter Mckelvey

D-U-N-S 24-829-3268   (SL)
MILLER TRANSIT LIMITED
(*Suby of* MILLER GROUP INC)
8050 Woodbine Ave, Markham, ON, L3R 2N8
(905) 475-1367
Emp Here 265   *Sales* 14,896,710
SIC 4111 Local and suburban transit
Blair Mcarthur
Barrie Brayford

D-U-N-S 20-360-0676   (SL)
MILLER WASTE SYSTEMS INC
8050 Woodbine Ave, Markham, ON, L3R 2N8
(905) 475-6356
Emp Here 1,000   *Sales* 318,910,000
SIC 4953 Refuse systems
Denis Goulet
Mike Buchanan

D-U-N-S 20-170-9003   (SL)
MILNE & NICHOLLS LIMITED
7270 Woodbine Ave Suite 200, Markham, ON, L3R 4B9
(905) 513-9700
Emp Here 80   *Sales* 45,627,040
SIC 1542 Nonresidential construction, nec
Roland Nicholls
Bradley Nicholls
Victor Catchick
Stan Hunter
L J Nicholls-Car

D-U-N-S 24-183-5610   (HQ)
MITSUBISHI ELECTRIC SALES CANADA INC
(*Suby of* MITSUBISHI ELECTRIC CORPORATION)
4299 14th Ave, Markham, ON, L3R 0J2
(905) 475-7728
Emp Here 36   *Sales* 18,334,134
SIC 5075 Warm air heating and air conditioning
Akihiko Ninomyna
Francis Chan

D-U-N-S 24-860-1270   (HQ)
MULTIMATIC INC
MULTIMATIC TECHNICAL CENTRE
(*Suby of* MULTIMATIC HOLDINGS INC)
8688 Woodbine Ave Suite 200, Markham, ON, L3R 8B9
(905) 470-9149
Emp Here 200   *Sales* 486,462,000
SIC 3429 Hardware, nec
Peter Czapka
Emily Watson
Martin Bressel

D-U-N-S 20-343-8213   (SL)
MULTIMATIC NICHE VEHICLES INC
8688 Woodbine Ave, Markham, ON, L3R 8B9
(905) 470-9149
Emp Here 50   *Sales* 10,141,500
SIC 3429 Hardware, nec
Peter Czapka
Martin Bressel

D-U-N-S 20-296-4516   (SL)
NADG U.S. CORE PLUS ACQUISITION FUND (CANADIAN) L.P.
2851 John St Suite 1, Markham, ON, L3R 5R7
(905) 477-9200
Emp Here 49   *Sales* 40,561,073
SIC 6722 Management investment, open-end
Robert Green

D-U-N-S 24-816-1432   (HQ)
NAPG EQUITIES INC
2851 John St Suite 1, Markham, ON, L3R 5R7
(905) 477-9200
Emp Here 1   *Sales* 41,888,900
SIC 6531 Real estate agents and managers
Robert S Green
John Preston

D-U-N-S 20-160-0905   (HQ)
NEOPOST CANADA LIMITED
(*Suby of* NEOPOST SA)
150 Steelcase Rd W, Markham, ON, L3R 3J9
(905) 475-3722
Emp Here 60   *Sales* 79,232,096
SIC 5044 Office equipment
Lou Gizzarelli
Grant Gillhan
Jules Kronis
Patrick Nangle

D-U-N-S 24-478-0110   (SL)
NEW CIRCUITS LIMITED
399 Denison St, Markham, ON, L3R 1B7
(905) 474-9227
Emp Here 75   *Sales* 14,283,150
SIC 3672 Printed circuit boards
Tarsam Singh Burmi

D-U-N-S 24-889-2127   (HQ)
NEXANS CANADA INC
(*Suby of* NEXANS)
140 Allstate Pky Suite 300, Markham, ON, L3R 0Z7
(905) 944-4300
Emp Here 50   *Sales* 14,511,040
SIC 3312 Blast furnaces and steel mills
Christopher Guerin
Steven Vermeulen
Georges Chodron De Courcel
Cyrille Duval
Marie-Cecile De Fougieres
Veronique Guillot-Pelpel
Colette Lewiner
Fanny Letier
Andronico Craig
Francisco Mackenna

D-U-N-S 25-369-7379   (HQ)
NEXIA HEALTH TECHNOLOGIES INC
15 Allstate Prkwy 6th Fl, Markham, ON, L3R 5B4
(905) 415-3063
Emp Here 26   *Sales* 31,008,395
SIC 7372 Prepackaged software
Sam Chebib
Nick Clemenzi
James Iglesias
Azmin Daya

D-U-N-S 24-365-5388   (SL)
NGK SPARK PLUGS CANADA LIMITED
(*Suby of* NGK SPARK PLUG CO., LTD.)
275 Renfrew Dr Suite 101, Markham, ON, L3R 0C8
(905) 477-7780
Emp Here 36   *Sales* 13,111,740
SIC 5013 Motor vehicle supplies and new parts

Toru Morimoto
Alok Saxena

D-U-N-S 25-146-6298   (HQ)
NIELSEN MEDIA RESEARCH LIMITED
NIELSEN
(*Suby of* NIELSEN HOLDINGS PLC)
160 Mcnabb St, Markham, ON, L3R 4B8
(905) 475-1131
Emp Here 150   *Sales* 102,041,000
SIC 8732 Commercial nonphysical research
Jeanne Danubio
Ralph Hosein
Harris Black
David A. Schwartz-Leeper
Michael Boland
David Berger

D-U-N-S 20-404-1230   (SL)
NITTA CASINGS (CANADA) INC
(*Suby of* NITTA CORPORATION)
57 Steelcase Rd W, Markham, ON, L3R 2M4
(905) 475-6441
Emp Here 70   *Sales* 50,170,120
SIC 5149 Groceries and related products, nec
Bernard Abenoja

D-U-N-S 20-151-7893   (HQ)
NORDSON CANADA, LIMITED
FINISHING, DIV OF
(*Suby of* NORDSON CORPORATION)
1211 Denison St, Markham, ON, L3R 4B3
(905) 475-6730
Emp Here 31   *Sales* 19,951,092
SIC 5084 Industrial machinery and equipment
Katherine Toffan

D-U-N-S 24-631-3324   (HQ)
NORSPEX LTD
290 Ferrier St Suite 1, Markham, ON, L3R 2Z5
(905) 513-8889
Emp Here 40   *Sales* 11,120,060
SIC 3089 Plastics products, nec
Albert Matsushita

D-U-N-S 24-045-1617   (SL)
NORTH AMERICAN IMPEX INCORPORATED
600 Hood Rd, Markham, ON, L3R 3K9

Emp Here 20   *Sales* 16,711,540
SIC 5149 Groceries and related products, nec
Subash Ghelani
Surendra Ghelani
Jashu Ghelani
Navin Ghelani
Bipin Ghelani

D-U-N-S 24-920-0569   (SL)
NORTHWOOD MORTGAGE LTD
7676 Woodbine Ave Suite 300, Markham, ON, L3R 2N2
(416) 969-8130
Emp Here 80   *Sales* 17,979,520
SIC 6163 Loan brokers
Art Appelberg

D-U-N-S 24-744-5513   (SL)
NORTON MCMULLEN & CO. LLP
1 Valleywood Dr Suite 200, Markham, ON, L3R 5L9
(905) 479-7001
Emp Here 50   *Sales* 10,454,250
SIC 8721 Accounting, auditing, and bookkeeping
William Mcmullen
John Karram
Rod Russell
Paul Simpson
Paul Mcmullen
Mike Mcneill

D-U-N-S 25-686-9819   (SL)
NTI INSURANCE BROKERS
800 Denison St Suite 200, Markham, ON, L3R 5M9

Emp Here 18   *Sales* 10,438,632

SIC 6411 Insurance agents, brokers, and service
Henry Kettunen
David Palermo
Gary Forrest

D-U-N-S 20-982-6684   (SL)
O'CONNELL, ANN INTERIOR DESIGN LTD
7321 Victoria Park Ave Suite 2, Markham, ON, L3R 2Z8
(905) 477-4695
Emp Here 27   *Sales* 11,974,230
SIC 7389 Business services, nec
Ann Oconnell

D-U-N-S 20-228-8916   (SL)
ORIENTEX IND. INC
155 Torbay Rd, Markham, ON, L3R 1G7
(905) 475-8540
Emp Here 40   *Sales* 19,932,880
SIC 5136 Men's and boy's clothing
Michael Chao
Anthony Chao
Emily Kwong

D-U-N-S 24-368-2932   (HQ)
OSPREY MEDIA PUBLISHING INC
(*Suby of* QUEBECOR MEDIA INC)
100 Renfrew Dr Suite 110, Markham, ON, L3R 9R6
(905) 752-1132
Emp Here 50   *Sales* 513,501,100
SIC 2711 Newspapers
Michael Sifton
Julia Kamula
Blair Mackenzie
Shannon Mcpeak
Ron Laurin
Mike Power
Dan Johnson
Paul Mccuaig
Daryl Smith
Jean-Francois Pruneau

D-U-N-S 20-151-8867   (HQ)
P&C GENERAL CONTRACTING LTD
250 Shields Crt Suite 24, Markham, ON, L3R 9W7
(905) 479-3015
Sales 14,121,930
SIC 1542 Nonresidential construction, nec
William Penny

D-U-N-S 25-410-6552   (SL)
PAJ CANADA COMPANY
(*Suby of* CANFEL INVESTMENT, INC.)
168 Konrad Cres Unit 1, Markham, ON, L3R 9T9
(905) 752-2080
Emp Here 25   *Sales* 13,013,550
SIC 5094 Jewelry and precious stones
Felix Chen

D-U-N-S 20-293-5482   (SL)
PANCAP PHARMA INC
50 Valleywood Dr Suite 6, Markham, ON, L3R 6E9
(905) 470-6844
Emp Here 40   *Sales* 11,066,400
SIC 2834 Pharmaceutical preparations
John Mikhail

D-U-N-S 20-901-4000   (HQ)
PARK PROPERTY MANAGEMENT INC
16 Esna Park Dr Suite 200, Markham, ON, L3R 5X1
(905) 940-1718
Emp Here 36   *Sales* 29,322,230
SIC 6531 Real estate agents and managers
Gerd U. Wengler
Henry Popp
Margaret Herd

D-U-N-S 20-408-9460   (HQ)
PARSONS INC
(*Suby of* THE PARSONS CORPORATION)
625 Cochrane Dr Suite 500, Markham, ON, L3R 9R9

(905) 943-0500
Emp Here 275   *Sales* 147,848,250
SIC 8711 Engineering services
James Kerr
Sylvain Montminy
Clyde E. Jr. Ellis
Peter Marrocco
Michael Johnson

D-U-N-S 24-000-4866   (HQ)
PATHER PLASTICS CANADA INC
PATHER PLASTICS INTERNATIONAL
7400 Victoria Park Ave Suite 1, Markham, ON, L3R 2V4
(905) 475-6549
Sales 378,530,500
SIC 2542 Partitions and fixtures, except wood
Nevelle Pather
Tracy Pather

D-U-N-S 24-505-9134   (SL)
PATRICK PLASTICS INC
S TECH DIV
(*Suby of* SEASON TECHNOLOGY INC)
1495 Denison St, Markham, ON, L3R 5H1
(905) 660-9066
Emp Here 50   *Sales* 11,364,450
SIC 3829 Measuring and controlling devices, nec
Anne Hung
Tony Tam
Fred Halpern

D-U-N-S 24-719-7742   (HQ)
PCI GEOMATICS ENTERPRISES INC
(*Suby of* PCI GEOMATICS GROUP INC)
90 Allstate Pky Suite 501, Markham, ON, L3R 6H3
(905) 764-0614
Emp Here 40   *Sales* 12,255,470
SIC 7371 Custom computer programming services
Robert Moses

D-U-N-S 20-845-9016   (HQ)
PEMBRIDGE INSURANCE COMPANY
27 Allstate Pkwy Suite 100, Markham, ON, L3R 5P8
(905) 513-4013
Emp Here 1   *Sales* 35,484,770
SIC 6331 Fire, marine, and casualty insurance
Michael Haskell
Stella Thompson
Casey Sylla

D-U-N-S 20-182-3163   (HQ)
PEOPLETOGO INC
201 Whitehall Dr Unit 4, Markham, ON, L3R 9Y3
(905) 940-9292
Sales 89,632,800
SIC 7363 Help supply services
Vince Forrestall
David Duncan

D-U-N-S 20-980-5365   (HQ)
PERLE SYSTEMS LIMITED
(*Suby of* PHOENIX CONTACT GMBH & CO. KG)
60 Renfrew Dr Suite 100, Markham, ON, L3R 0E1
(905) 475-8885
Emp Here 50   *Sales* 12,255,470
SIC 7371 Custom computer programming services
Joseph E Perle
John L Feeney
Derrick Barnett
Stephen Rider
Jean Noelting

D-U-N-S 24-123-9078   (HQ)
PET VALU CANADA INC
PET VALU
130 Royal Crest Crt, Markham, ON, L3R 0A1
(905) 946-1200
Emp Here 5   *Sales* 373,184,689
SIC 6712 Bank holding companies

Thomas Mcneely
Kevin Herring
Dasha Stupak

D-U-N-S 24-737-8102 (SL)
PETROFF PARTNERSHIP ARCHITECTS
260 Town Centre Blvd Suite 300, Markham,
ON, L3R 8H8
(905) 470-7000
Emp Here 160 *Sales* 28,598,240
SIC 8712 Architectural services
Andrzej Lipinski
Guela Solow-Ruda
Glen Meschino
Michaela Weiner
Mark Feldman

D-U-N-S 20-175-1237 (SL)
PHARMASYSTEMS INC
151 Telson Rd, Markham, ON, L3R 1E7
(905) 475-2500
Emp Here 36 *Sales* 39,792,420
SIC 5122 Drugs, proprietaries, and sundries
Lawrence Senders
Harry Senders
Debbie Greenspoon

D-U-N-S 24-763-9644 (SL)
PHOTON DYNAMICS CANADA INC
221 Whitehall Dr, Markham, ON, L3R 9T1

Emp Here 100
SIC 3599 Industrial machinery, nec

D-U-N-S 20-301-4907 (HQ)
PIVOT TECHNOLOGY SOLUTIONS INC
55 Renfrew Dr Suite 200, Markham, ON, L3R
8H3
(416) 360-4777
Sales 1,373,630,000
SIC 8731 Commercial physical research
Kevin Shank
Matt Girardot
Wendy Coticchia
Hunter Li
David Toews
Matt Olson
Mike Flanagan
Wade Dawe
John Anderson
Stephen Moore

D-U-N-S 24-988-1009 (SL)
PLANVIEW UTILITY SERVICES LIMITED
(*Suby of* CORPORATION OF THE TOWN OF
OAKVILLE, THE)
7270 Woodbine Ave Suite 201, Markham, ON,
L3R 4B9
(289) 800-7110
Emp Here 100 *Sales* 7,469,400
SIC 7363 Help supply services
Robert Irwin
Kris Philpott

D-U-N-S 25-177-5532 (HQ)
**PMA BRETHOUR REAL ESTATE CORPO-
RATION INC**
PMA GROUP OF COMPANIES
250 Shields Crt Unit 1, Markham, ON, L3R
9W7
(905) 415-2720
Sales 62,833,350
SIC 6531 Real estate agents and managers
Kent Wengler

D-U-N-S 20-173-3623 (HQ)
POI BUSINESS INTERIORS INC
120 Valleywood Dr, Markham, ON, L3R 6A7
(905) 479-1123
Emp Here 100 *Sales* 94,935,720
SIC 5021 Furniture
Gary Scholl
Julie Anne Smedley
Steven D'amelio

D-U-N-S 25-404-3185 (HQ)
POWERNODE COMPUTER INC
35 Riviera Dr Suite 11-12, Markham, ON, L3R

8N4
(905) 474-1040
Emp Here 15 *Sales* 12,968,046
SIC 5045 Computers, peripherals, and soft-
ware
Ken Chan

D-U-N-S 24-852-8254 (BR)
**PRODUITS MENAGERS FREUDENBERG
INC**
VILEDA PROFESSIONAL
(*Suby of* FREUDENBERG & CO. KG)
15 Allstate Pky, Markham, ON, L3R 5B4
(905) 669-9949
Emp Here 150
SIC 5199 Nondurable goods, nec
Harry Piiparinen

D-U-N-S 24-024-8815 (SL)
PROPHARM LIMITED
(*Suby of* MCKESSON CORPORATION)
131 Mcnabb St, Markham, ON, L3R 5V7
(905) 943-9736
Emp Here 98 *Sales* 14,129,836
SIC 7371 Custom computer programming ser-
vices
Larry Latowsky

D-U-N-S 25-053-0425 (SL)
PROTECT AIR CO
(*Suby of* THE PARSONS CORPORATION)
2751 John St, Markham, ON, L3R 2Y8
(905) 944-8877
Emp Here 91 *Sales* 12,879,301
SIC 8748 Business consulting, nec
Michael Butler
Gord Blair

D-U-N-S 24-938-1146 (SL)
QTA CIRCUITS LTD
DATA CIRCUITS
144 Gibson Dr, Markham, ON, L3R 2Z3
(905) 477-4400
Emp Here 50 *Sales* 10,233,650
SIC 3672 Printed circuit boards
Jaime Iturriaga
Hin Liu
Mike Mehra

D-U-N-S 25-411-8920 (SL)
QUANSER CONSULTING INC
119 Spy Crt, Markham, ON, L3R 5H6
(905) 940-3575
Emp Here 65 *Sales* 14,773,785
SIC 3821 Laboratory apparatus and furniture
Paul Gilbert
Jacob Apkarian
Pascal Helou

D-U-N-S 24-652-6750 (HQ)
RAI INSURANCE BROKERS LTD
RAI GRANT INSURANCE BROKERS
140 Renfrew Dr Suite 230, Markham, ON, L3R
6B3
(905) 475-5800
Sales 96,082,584
SIC 6411 Insurance agents, brokers, and ser-
vice
Paul Rai
Christopher Rai
Elizabeth Rai

D-U-N-S 20-369-3601 (SL)
RE/MAX IMPERIAL REALTY INC
3000 Steeles Ave E Suite 309, Markham, ON,
L3R 4T9
(905) 305-0033
Emp Here 100 *Sales* 27,490,345
SIC 6531 Real estate agents and managers
Feng Lu

D-U-N-S 24-686-0522 (HQ)
RE/MAX REALTRON REALTY INC
88 Konrad Cres Suite 1, Markham, ON, L3R
8T7
(905) 944-8800
Emp Here 1 *Sales* 270,451,200
SIC 6531 Real estate agents and managers

Alex Pilarski
Richard Pilarski

D-U-N-S 24-859-0841 (SL)
RED CARPET REAL WORLD REALTY INC
340 Ferrier St Unit 218, Markham, ON, L3R
2Z5
(905) 415-8855
Emp Here 42 *Sales* 13,739,334
SIC 6531 Real estate agents and managers
Maokun Gong
Dong Fu

D-U-N-S 24-356-8487 (HQ)
REDLINE COMMUNICATIONS GROUP INC
REDLINE INNOVATIONS GROUP
302 Town Centre Blvd 4th Fl, Markham, ON,
L3R 0E8
(905) 479-8344
Emp Here 112 *Sales* 27,103,427
SIC 4899 Communication services, nec
Stephen Sorocky
Joan Ritchie
Reno Moccia
Louis Lambert
Brad Stimpson
Abdelsalam Aldwikat
Jeff Mulvey
Nizar Jaffer Somji
Eric Demirian
John Brunette

D-U-N-S 25-530-7282 (SL)
REDLINE COMMUNICATIONS INC
(*Suby of* REDLINE COMMUNICATIONS
GROUP INC)
302 Town Centre Blvd Suite 100, Markham,
ON, L3R 0E8
(905) 479-8344
Emp Here 130 *Sales* 36,778,950
SIC 3661 Telephone and telegraph apparatus
Eric Melka
Phillipe De Gaspe Beaubien Iii
Jane Todd
Frank Di Tomaso
Rob Follows
Skuli Mogensen
Rob Soni

D-U-N-S 20-303-5605 (SL)
REMEDY HOLDINGS INC
REMEDY'S RX
675 Cochrane Dr Suite 110, Markham, ON,
L3R 0B8
(647) 794-3388
Emp Here 450 *Sales* 82,591,650
SIC 5912 Drug stores and proprietary stores
Bruce Moody
Chris Henderson
Robert Stevens
David Ku

D-U-N-S 25-311-7675 (SL)
RICHMOND HILL WHOLESALE MEAT LTD
70 Denison St Suite 8, Markham, ON, L3R
1B6
(905) 513-1817
Emp Here 34 *Sales* 28,409,618
SIC 5147 Meats and meat products
Paul Gallucci
Vinh Trung Lam

D-U-N-S 24-850-5877 (SL)
RUBIE'S COSTUME COMPANY (CANADA)
(*Suby of* RUBIE'S COSTUME COMPANY,
INC.)
2710 14th Ave, Markham, ON, L3R 0J1
(905) 470-0300
Emp Here 50 *Sales* 26,027,100
SIC 5099 Durable goods, nec
Marc Beige
Michael Maskery
Howard Beige

D-U-N-S 20-026-4443 (SL)
SAADCO EXPRESS INC
300 Steelcase Rd W Unit 9, Markham, ON,
L3R 2W2

(905) 940-1680
Emp Here 35 *Sales* 15,522,150
SIC 7389 Business services, nec
Mike Saad

D-U-N-S 24-214-3907 (SL)
SAFETY INSURANCE SERVICE (1959) LTD
8300 Woodbine Ave Suite 200, Markham, ON,
L3R 9Y7

Emp Here 27 *Sales* 15,657,948
SIC 6411 Insurance agents, brokers, and ser-
vice
Stephen Palmer

D-U-N-S 24-286-6440 (HQ)
SAINT ELIZABETH HEALTH CARE
SEHC BC
90 Allstate Pky Suite 300, Markham, ON, L3R
6H3
(905) 940-9655
Emp Here 1,800 *Sales* 176,412,300
SIC 8082 Home health care services
Shirlee Sharkey
Bill Chambers
John Stackhouse
Noreen Taylor

D-U-N-S 24-425-2862 (HQ)
SAMSON CONTROLS INC
(*Suby of* SAMSON AG)
105 Riviera Dr Unit 1, Markham, ON, L3R 5J7
(905) 474-0354
Emp Here 25 *Sales* 12,350,676
SIC 5084 Industrial machinery and equipment
Hans Grimm
Michael Espey

D-U-N-S 24-867-9664 (SL)
SAMTACK INC
SAMTACK COMPUTER
1100 Rodick Rd, Markham, ON, L3R 8C3
(905) 940-1880
Emp Here 100 *Sales* 53,535,200
SIC 5045 Computers, peripherals, and soft-
ware
Royson Ng
Sam Chiu
Robert Chin
Parag Gandhi

D-U-N-S 24-783-9061 (BR)
SAMUEL, SON & CO., LIMITED
ASSOCIATED TUBE CANADA, DIV OF
(*Suby of* SAMUEL, SON & CO., LIMITED)
7455 Woodbine Ave, Markham, ON, L3R 1A7
(905) 475-6464
Emp Here 300
SIC 5051 Metals service centers and offices

D-U-N-S 20-784-3228 (SL)
**SANDS COMMERCIAL FLOOR COVER-
INGS INC**
180 Bentley St, Markham, ON, L3R 3L2
(905) 475-6380
Emp Here 30 *Sales* 15,265,680
SIC 5023 Homefurnishings
Peter Sands
David Breen
Christine Ryan

D-U-N-S 24-544-8550 (HQ)
**SANGOMA TECHNOLOGIES CORPORA-
TION**
TECHNOLOGIES SANGOMA
100 Renfrew Dr Suite 100, Markham, ON, L3R
9R6
(905) 474-1990
Emp Here 15 *Sales* 19,997,258
SIC 7372 Prepackaged software
William J. Wignall
Frederic Dickey
Doug Vilim
David S. Moore
Tony Lewis
Nenad Corbic

D-U-N-S 24-953-7036 (SL)

SCI INTERIORS LIMITED
11 Allstate Pky Suite 204, Markham, ON, L3R 9T8
(905) 479-7007
Emp Here 38   *Sales* 19,336,528
SIC 5021 Furniture
John Stone
Simon Bolter
Bruce Young

D-U-N-S 20-152-1663   (SL)
SHIPMASTER CONTAINERS LIMITED
380 Esna Park Dr, Markham, ON, L3R 1G5
(416) 493-9193
Emp Here 60   *Sales* 14,006,100
SIC 2653 Corrugated and solid fiber boxes
Neil Fyfe
Lou Kozak
Peter Newell

D-U-N-S 24-555-4100   (SL)
SHISEIDO (CANADA) INC
(*Suby of* SHISEIDO COMPANY, LIMITED)
303 Allstate Pky, Markham, ON, L3R 5P9
(905) 763-1250
Emp Here 140   *Sales* 57,794,940
SIC 5122 Drugs, proprietaries, and sundries
Lou Anne Mcgrory
Paul Ramos
Tulsi Datt

D-U-N-S 24-393-1800   (HQ)
SIENNA SENIOR LIVING INC
302 Town Centre Blvd Suite 300, Markham, ON, L3R 0E8
(905) 477-4006
Emp Here 10   *Sales* 486,689,354
SIC 8361 Residential care
Lois Cormack
Michael Annable
Joanne Dykeman
Lisa Kachur
Cristina Alaimo
Nitin Jain
Brian Richardson
Dino Chiesa
Janet Graham
Paula Coleman

D-U-N-S 20-286-0920   (HQ)
SIGNODE PACKAGING GROUP CANADA ULC
SIGNODE CANADA
(*Suby of* CROWN HOLDINGS INC.)
241 Gough Rd, Markham, ON, L3R 5B3
(905) 479-9754
Emp Here 50   *Sales* 19,476,800
SIC 2673 Bags: plastic, laminated, and coated
Paul Cox

D-U-N-S 20-015-7969   (HQ)
SILLIKER CANADA CO
(*Suby of* COMPAGNIE MERIEUX ALLIANCE)
90 Gough Rd Unit 4, Markham, ON, L3R 5V5
(905) 479-5255
Sales 31,971,700
SIC 8734 Testing laboratories
Jocelyn Alfieri
Phillipe Sanf

D-U-N-S 25-529-3532   (BR)
SING TAO NEWSPAPERS (CANADA 1988) LIMITED
SING TAO DAILY
(*Suby of* SING TAO NEWS CORPORATION LIMITED)
221 Whitehall Dr, Markham, ON, L3R 9T1
(416) 596-8140
Emp Here 130
SIC 2711 Newspapers
Peter Li

D-U-N-S 24-369-0489   (SL)
SMARTEYES DIRECT INC
GALAXY SECURITY
7755 Warden Ave Unit 1, Markham, ON, L3R

0N3
(905) 946-8998
Emp Here 25   *Sales* 11,179,350
SIC 5043 Photographic equipment and supplies
Li Fang Chen

D-U-N-S 20-175-6228   (SL)
SMITH AND LONG LIMITED
115 Idema Rd, Markham, ON, L3R 1A9
(416) 391-0443
Emp Here 260   *Sales* 61,232,340
SIC 1731 Electrical work
Robert Riopelle
Jeff Scott

D-U-N-S 20-845-8778   (SL)
SMITHS MEDICAL CANADA LTD
(*Suby of* SMITHS GROUP PLC)
301 Gough Rd, Markham, ON, L3R 4Y8
(905) 477-2000
Emp Here 40   *Sales* 17,886,960
SIC 5047 Medical and hospital equipment
Douglas Tingey
John Bordin

D-U-N-S 25-619-5058   (HQ)
SMTC CORPORATION
7050 Woodbine Ave Suite 300, Markham, ON, L3R 4G8
(905) 479-1810
Emp Here 1,110   *Sales* 216,131,000
SIC 3672 Printed circuit boards
Edward Smith
Clarke Bailey
Josh Chien
Steve Brown
Carlos Diaz
Phil Wehrli
Terry Wegman
Bob Miller
Blair Mcinnis
Seth Choi

D-U-N-S 24-576-1267   (HQ)
SMTC MANUFACTURING CORPORATION OF CANADA
SMTC
(*Suby of* SMTC CORPORATION)
7050 Woodbine Ave Suite 300, Markham, ON, L3R 4G8
(905) 479-1810
Emp Here 10   *Sales* 70,728,750
SIC 3672 Printed circuit boards
Edward Smith
Blair McInnis
Steven M Waszak
Rich Fitzgerald
Carlos Diaz

D-U-N-S 25-685-1379   (SL)
SMTC NOVA SCOTIA COMPANY
(*Suby of* SMTC CORPORATION)
7050 Woodbine Ave Suite 300, Markham, ON, L3R 4G8
(905) 479-1810
Emp Here 2,600   *Sales* 735,579,000
SIC 3672 Printed circuit boards
John Caldwell
Wayne Mcloed
Jane Todd

D-U-N-S 20-232-5031   (HQ)
SMUCKER FOODS OF CANADA CORP
ROBIN HOOD MULTIFOODS
(*Suby of* THE J M SMUCKER COMPANY)
80 Whitehall Dr, Markham, ON, L3R 0P3
(905) 940-9600
Emp Here 200   *Sales* 131,593,950
SIC 2033 Canned fruits and specialties
Dave Lemmon
Stephen Kori
Carl Blouin
Aurelio Calabretta
Bobby Modi
Todd Campbell
Adam Zitney

George Ellinidis
Melody Crawford

D-U-N-S 24-550-2976   (SL)
SPLASH INTERNATIONAL MARKETING INC
(*Suby of* HARRIS, B. MARKETING LTD)
395 Cochrane Dr Suite 3, Markham, ON, L3R 9R5
(905) 947-4440
Emp Here 50   *Sales* 12,388,846
SIC 5199 Nondurable goods, nec
Brian Harris
Joe Harris
Geoff Mak

D-U-N-S 20-288-5448   (SL)
SPRINGFREE TRAMPOLINE INC
151 Whitehall Dr Unit 2, Markham, ON, L3R 9T1
(905) 948-0124
Emp Here 55   *Sales* 17,937,480
SIC 3949 Sporting and athletic goods, nec
Steven Holmes

D-U-N-S 20-699-6774   (HQ)
SRB EDUCATION SOLUTIONS INC
200 Town Centre Blvd Suite 400, Markham, ON, L3R 8G5
(877) 772-4685
Emp Here 155   *Sales* 23,069,120
SIC 7371 Custom computer programming services
Steve Thompson

D-U-N-S 20-107-2753   (BR)
STANTEC CONSULTING LTD
(*Suby of* STANTEC INC)
675 Cochrane Dr Suite 300 W, Markham, ON, L3R 0B8
(905) 944-7777
Emp Here 300
SIC 8711 Engineering services
Christine Caccavella

D-U-N-S 24-319-2994   (SL)
STEEL ART SIGNS CORP
37 Esna Park Dr, Markham, ON, L3R 1C9
(905) 474-1678
Emp Here 70   *Sales* 22,829,520
SIC 3993 Signs and advertising specialties
Thomas Hrivnak

D-U-N-S 24-826-5951   (SL)
STEELITE INTERNATIONAL CANADA LIMITED
(*Suby of* ST ATHENA GLOBAL HOLDINGS LIMITED)
26 Riviera Dr Unit 2, Markham, ON, L3R 5M1
(905) 752-1074
Emp Here 20   *Sales* 10,177,120
SIC 5023 Homefurnishings
Ray Perkins
George Vasil

D-U-N-S 24-860-7012   (HQ)
STERLING CENTRECORP INC
2851 John St Suite 1, Markham, ON, L3R 5R7
(905) 477-9200
Emp Here 70   *Sales* 15,817,200
SIC 6552 Subdividers and developers, nec
Robert S. Green
A. David Kosoy
John Preston
David Bloom
Peter R. Burnim
Stewart Robertson

D-U-N-S 25-702-8241   (SL)
STUART, W H HOLDINGS LIMITED
STUART, W H INSURANCE AGENCY
11 Allstate Pky Suite 410, Markham, ON, L3R 9T8
(905) 305-0880
Emp Here 30   *Sales* 20,367,690
SIC 6282 Investment advice
Howard Stuart
Dianne Stuart

D-U-N-S 24-860-0793   (HQ)
SUNNY CRUNCH FOODS HOLDINGS LTD
200 Shields Crt, Markham, ON, L3R 9T5
(905) 475-0422
Emp Here 1   *Sales* 31,112,100
SIC 2043 Cereal breakfast foods
Richard Pelzer

D-U-N-S 20-629-2054   (SL)
SUNNY CRUNCH FOODS LIMITED
(*Suby of* SUNNY CRUNCH FOODS HOLDINGS LTD)
200 Shields Crt, Markham, ON, L3R 9T5
(905) 475-0422
Emp Here 90   *Sales* 17,236,494
SIC 5149 Groceries and related products, nec
Richard Pelzer

D-U-N-S 24-192-1006   (HQ)
SWAROVSKI CANADA LIMITED
(*Suby of* D. SWAROVSKI KG)
80 Gough Rd Unit 2, Markham, ON, L3R 6E8
(905) 752-0498
Emp Here 45   *Sales* 82,591,650
SIC 5944 Jewelry stores
Paula Cavaco
Tora Perez
Susan Wolf

D-U-N-S 20-262-0423   (HQ)
SWEGON NORTH AMERICA INC
VIBRO-ACOUSTICS
(*Suby of* INVESTMENT AB LATOUR)
355 Apple Creek Blvd, Markham, ON, L3R 9X7
(416) 291-7371
Sales 19,996,410
SIC 3625 Relays and industrial controls
Jeff Bailey
Brian F Guenther
Sylvia Guenther

D-U-N-S 20-702-8783   (SL)
SYMTECH INNOVATIONS LTD
35 Riviera Dr, Markham, ON, L3R 8N4
(905) 940-8044
Emp Here 150   *Sales* 32,674,350
SIC 1731 Electrical work
Denny Jackson
Shawn Cohen
Nick Gallo
Sadek Chawdhury
Fiona Jia

D-U-N-S 20-719-2316   (SL)
TASTE OF NATURE FOODS INC
230 Ferrier St, Markham, ON, L3R 2Z5
(905) 415-8218
Emp Here 95   *Sales* 79,379,815
SIC 5149 Groceries and related products, nec
Michael Bannister

D-U-N-S 25-363-9736   (SL)
TEAMRECRUITER.COM INC
15 Allstate Pky Suite 600, Markham, ON, L3R 5B4
(905) 889-8326
Emp Here 100   *Sales* 15,537,100
SIC 7361 Employment agencies
Leonard Jean-Pierre

D-U-N-S 24-679-3629   (SL)
TECH DIGITAL MANUFACTURING LTD
350 Steelcase Rd W, Markham, ON, L3R 1B3
(905) 513-8094
Emp Here 49   *Sales* 10,028,977
SIC 3679 Electronic components, nec
Phil Teerink

D-U-N-S 24-366-2231   (HQ)
TECHTRONIC INDUSTRIES CANADA INC
TTI CANADA
7303 Warden Ave Suite 202, Markham, ON, L3R 5Y6
(905) 479-4355
Emp Here 60   *Sales* 44,717,400
SIC 5072 Hardware
Craig Baxter

Russell Laird
Horst Pudwill
Gary S. Rossiter

D-U-N-S 24-203-8714 (SL)
TELEFLEX MEDICAL CANADA INC
(*Suby of* TELEFLEX INCORPORATED)
500 Hood Rd Suite 310, Markham, ON, L3R
9Z3
(800) 387-9699
Emp Here 100   *Sales* 53,535,200
SIC 5047 Medical and hospital equipment
Daniel Price
Matthew Howald
Jake Elguicze
James Leyden
Christine Mazurk

D-U-N-S 24-336-8482 (SL)
TELEFLEX MEDICAL L.P
165 Gibson Dr Suite 1, Markham, ON, L3R
3K7
(905) 943-9000
Emp Here 35   *Sales* 15,651,090
SIC 5047 Medical and hospital equipment
Ron Steiner
David Mills

D-U-N-S 24-752-8953 (SL)
TEMPO DRAFTING SERVICES INC
260 Town Centre Blvd Suite 300, Markham,
ON, L3R 8H8
(905) 470-7000
Emp Here 70   *Sales* 31,445,330
SIC 7389 Business services, nec
Virginia Rogers

D-U-N-S 20-702-1015 (BR)
TEVA CANADA LIMITED
(*Suby of* TEVA PHARMACEUTICAL INDUS-
TRIES LIMITED)
575 Hood Rd, Markham, ON, L3R 4E1
(905) 475-3370
Emp Here 180
SIC 2834 Pharmaceutical preparations
Steve Liberty

D-U-N-S 24-764-2242 (SL)
TFB & ASSOCIATES LIMITED
7300 Warden Ave Suite 210, Markham, ON,
L3R 9Z6
(905) 940-0889
Emp Here 27   *Sales* 29,844,315
SIC 5122 Drugs, proprietaries, and sundries
Robert Riddell
Matthew Riddell
Brian Riddell

D-U-N-S 24-385-2543 (SL)
THINKUNSURE LTD
11 Allstate Pky Unit 206, Markham, ON, L3R
9T8
(905) 415-8800
Emp Here 30   *Sales* 31,046,430
SIC 6331 Fire, marine, and casualty insurance
Dean Waddell

D-U-N-S 20-044-1780 (SL)
THOMAS ALLEN & SON LIMITED
195 Allstate Pkwy, Markham, ON, L3R 4T8
(905) 475-9126
Emp Here 45   *Sales* 33,413,400
SIC 5192 Books, periodicals, and newspapers
John D Allen
Jim Allen
Dean Einarson

D-U-N-S 20-784-0018 (HQ)
THOMAS, LARGE & SINGER INC
15 Allstate Pky Suite 500, Markham, ON, L3R
5B4
(800) 268-5542
Sales 107,507,400
SIC 5141 Groceries, general line
Peter D Singer
Anthony Carter
David Singer
Peter Wagner

D-U-N-S 20-044-5930 (HQ)
TIMEX GROUP CANADA, INC
(*Suby of* TIMEX GROUP B.V.)
7300 Warden Ave 115, Markham, ON, L3R
9Z6
(905) 477-8463
Sales 86,912,500
SIC 5094 Jewelry and precious stones
Leo Fournier
Ray To
Daniel Des Cotes

D-U-N-S 20-561-1528 (HQ)
TORONTO AIRWAYS LIMITED
TORONTAIR
(*Suby of* ARMADALE CO. LIMITED)
2833 16th Ave Suite 100, Markham, ON, L3R
0P8
(905) 477-8100
Sales 24,028,020
SIC 4581 Airports, flying fields, and services
Heather Sifton
Derek Sifton
Michael Sifton Jr
Clifford Sifton

D-U-N-S 25-418-4955 (HQ)
TORRES AVIATION INCORPORATED
SKYWORDS TRAFFIC NETWORK
95 Royal Crest Crt Unit 5, Markham, ON, L3R
9X5
(905) 470-7655
Emp Here 25   *Sales* 23,740,680
SIC 7383 News syndicates
Frank Torres

D-U-N-S 20-549-7415 (HQ)
TOSHIBA OF CANADA LIMITED
OFFICE PRODUCTS GROUP, DIV OF
(*Suby of* TOSHIBA CORPORATION)
75 Tiverton Crt, Markham, ON, L3R 4M8
(905) 470-3500
Emp Here 312   *Sales* 237,901,270
SIC 5064 Electrical appliances, television and
radio
Ralph Hyatt
Phil Devor
Kiyofumi Kakudo
Osumi Masaaki
Arthur Kitamura

D-U-N-S 25-973-7781 (HQ)
**TOSHIBA TEC CANADA BUSINESS SOLU-
TIONS INC**
TOSHIBA
(*Suby of* TOSHIBA CORPORATION)
75 Tiverton Crt, Markham, ON, L3R 4M8
(905) 470-3500
Emp Here 90   *Sales* 187,373,200
SIC 5044 Office equipment
Richard Baird
Robert Assal

D-U-N-S 24-950-2782 (HQ)
TOSHIBA TEC CANADA INC
(*Suby of* TOSHIBA CORPORATION)
75 Tiverton Crt, Markham, ON, L3R 4M8
(905) 470-3500
Sales 14,309,568
SIC 5044 Office equipment
Kevin Shmizu
Donald Ashford

D-U-N-S 24-927-5389 (SL)
**TOWNE MEADOW DEVELOPMENT COR-
PORATION INC**
80 Tiverton Crt Suite 300, Markham, ON, L3R
0G4
(905) 477-7609
Emp Here 50   *Sales* 15,943,450
SIC 1521 Single-family housing construction

D-U-N-S 24-868-5323 (HQ)
TOYOTA CREDIT CANADA INC
(*Suby of* TOYOTA MOTOR CORPORATION)
80 Micro Crt Suite 200, Markham, ON, L3R
9Z5

(905) 513-8200
Emp Here 100   *Sales* 79,300,500
SIC 6141 Personal credit institutions
Lorenzo Baldesarra
Anthony Wearing
Yoichi Tomihara
Eiji Hirano
Real Tanguay

D-U-N-S 20-158-7524 (HQ)
TRANE CANADA ULC
(*Suby of* INGERSOLL-RAND PUBLIC LIM-
ITED COMPANY)
525 Cochrane Dr Suite 101, Markham, ON,
L3R 8E3
(416) 499-3600
Emp Here 120   *Sales* 140,438,500
SIC 3585 Refrigeration and heating equip-
ment
Guy Bourbonniere

D-U-N-S 24-212-3081 (BR)
TRANSCANADA PIPELINES LIMITED
(*Suby of* TC ENERGY CORPORATION)
675 Cochrane Dr Suite 701, Markham, ON,
L3R 0B8
(905) 946-7800
Emp Here 100
SIC 4922 Natural gas transmission
Ross Parker

D-U-N-S 20-699-1551 (HQ)
TRANSPORT TFI 3 L.P.
HIGHLAND TRANSPORT
2815 14th Ave, Markham, ON, L3R 0H9
(800) 268-6231
Emp Here 60   *Sales* 25,713,250
SIC 4213 Trucking, except local
Jean Dodier
Terry Gardiner

D-U-N-S 20-044-1764 (HQ)
TYCO ELECTRONICS CANADA ULC
(*Suby of* TE CONNECTIVITY LTD.)
20 Esna Park Dr, Markham, ON, L3R 1E1
(905) 475-6222
Emp Here 130   *Sales* 31,422,930
SIC 3643 Current-carrying wiring devices
Kevin Irons

D-U-N-S 20-167-4975 (HQ)
**UMICORE PRECIOUS METALS CANADA
INC**
(*Suby of* UMICORE)
451 Denison St, Markham, ON, L3R 1B7
(905) 475-9566
Sales 10,520,504
SIC 3341 Secondary nonferrous Metals
Thelma Chuakay

D-U-N-S 24-426-1389 (SL)
UNDERWRITING COMPLIANCE SERVICES
25 Valleywood Dr Suite 7, Markham, ON, L3R
5L9
(905) 754-6324
Emp Here 20   *Sales* 11,598,480
SIC 6411 Insurance agents, brokers, and service

D-U-N-S 24-215-5018 (HQ)
UNI-RAM CORPORATION
381 Bentley St Suite 117, Markham, ON, L3R
9T2
(905) 477-5911
Emp Here 36   *Sales* 18,050,988
SIC 5084 Industrial machinery and equipment
Sam Yamamoto
June Yamamoto

D-U-N-S 25-512-5734 (SL)
UNION POULTRY CANADA INC
70 Denison St Suite 2, Markham, ON, L3R
1B6
(905) 305-1913
Emp Here 66   *Sales* 55,148,082
SIC 5144 Poultry and poultry products
Frank Caravelli
Paul Gallucci

D-U-N-S 20-938-2738 (HQ)
UNIONVILLE HOME SOCIETY
HERITAGE VILLAGE, DIV OF
4300 Highway 7 E Suite 1, Markham, ON, L3R
1L8
(905) 477-2822
Emp Here 220   *Sales* 14,463,450
SIC 8361 Residential care
Debra Cooper Burger
Glenn Crosby

D-U-N-S 20-051-9739 (SL)
**UNIONVILLE HOME SOCIETY FOUNDA-
TION**
4300 Highway 7 E Suite 1, Markham, ON, L3R
1L8
(905) 477-2822
Emp Here 210   *Sales* 142,097,599
SIC 7389 Business services, nec

D-U-N-S 24-876-6057 (HQ)
**UNITED REFRIGERATION OF CANADA
LTD**
(*Suby of* UNITED REFRIGERATION, INC.)
130 Riviera Dr, Markham, ON, L3R 5M1
(905) 479-1212
Emp Here 14   *Sales* 18,334,134
SIC 5078 Refrigeration equipment and sup-
plies
Steven Mock
John Reilly
Carmen Carosella

D-U-N-S 24-685-5118 (HQ)
**UPPER CANADA SPECIALTY HARDWARE
LIMITED**
7100 Warden Ave Unit 1, Markham, ON, L3R
8B5
(905) 940-8358
Emp Here 38   *Sales* 20,122,830
SIC 5072 Hardware
Boyd Roberton
Sam Scutella
Ian Brown

D-U-N-S 20-174-0805 (HQ)
UTHANE RESEARCH LTD
RIPPLEPAK, DIV OF
140 Bentley St Unit 2, Markham, ON, L3R 3L2
(905) 940-2356
Emp Here 23   *Sales* 22,189,350
SIC 3081 Unsupported plastics film and sheet
Ragui Ghali

D-U-N-S 24-632-7795 (SL)
VENTURER ELECTRONICS INC
725 Denison St, Markham, ON, L3R 1B8
(905) 477-7878
Emp Here 29   *Sales* 13,415,220
SIC 5065 Electronic parts and equipment, nec
Manson Li

D-U-N-S 20-118-9391 (SL)
VEONEER CANADA, INC
(*Suby of* VEONEER, INC.)
7455 Birchmount Rd, Markham, ON, L3R 5C2
(905) 475-4150
Emp Here 740   *Sales* 209,357,100
SIC 3679 Electronic components, nec
Steve Rode
Paul Tucker

D-U-N-S 25-351-3964 (BR)
**VICTORIAN ORDER OF NURSES FOR
CANADA**
VON TORONTO-YORK REGION
(*Suby of* VICTORIAN ORDER OF NURSES
FOR CANADA)
7100 Woodbine Ave Suite 402, Markham, ON,
L3R 5J2
(905) 479-3201
Emp Here 300
SIC 8082 Home health care services
Susan Clarke

D-U-N-S 24-422-9464 (SL)
VIEWMARK HOMES LTD
CONSERVATORY GROUP

80 Tiverton Crt Suite 300, Markham, ON, L3R 0G4
(905) 477-7609
Emp Here 65   *Sales* 17,611,230
SIC 1521 Single-family housing construction
Sheldon Libfeld
Mark Libfeld

D-U-N-S 20-328-2363   (SL)
VOYZANT INC
7100 Woodbine Ave Unit 102, Markham, ON, L3R 5J2
(647) 783-3371
Emp Here 50   *Sales* 76,213,700
SIC 4724 Travel agencies
Tanmay Kar
Chitparan Jedathesan
Prabha Selvadurai

D-U-N-S 20-936-9248   (HQ)
W INTERCONNECTIONS CANADA INC
WEIDMULLER CANADA
(*Suby of* PETER GLASEL BETEILIGUNGS GMBH & CO. KG)
10 Spy Crt, Markham, ON, L3R 5H6
(905) 475-1507
Sales 20,122,830
SIC 5065 Electronic parts and equipment, nec
James Harding
Kathleen Donius

D-U-N-S 24-709-0186   (HQ)
W.H.B. IDENTIFICATION SOLUTIONS INC
SETON CANADA
(*Suby of* BRADY CORPORATION)
710 Cochrane Dr, Markham, ON, L3R 5N7
(905) 764-1122
Sales 41,718,000
SIC 5099 Durable goods, nec
Michael Naumann

D-U-N-S 25-204-3492   (SL)
WAH LUNG LABELS (CANADA) INC
WAH LUNG LABELS
150 Telson Rd, Markham, ON, L3R 1E5
(905) 948-8877
Emp Here 75   *Sales* 13,755,225
SIC 2241 Narrow fabric mills
Mimi Chau
Fred Kwan
Fat Chow
Shui Wah Lee

D-U-N-S 25-294-7189   (BR)
WAL-MART CANADA CORP
(*Suby of* WALMART INC.)
5000 Highway 7 E Unit Y006a, Markham, ON, L3R 4M9
(905) 477-6060
Emp Here 200
SIC 5311 Department stores
Justin Robertson

D-U-N-S 25-973-3715   (SL)
WATER PIK TECHNOLOGIES CANADA INC
(*Suby of* CHURCH & DWIGHT CO., INC.)
625 Cochrane Dr, Markham, ON, L3R 9R9

Emp Here 100
SIC 5074 Plumbing and heating equipment and supplies (hydronics)
Ernest Brock
Roger Williams
Barbara Miller
Anthony Prudhomme
Richard Bisson
Robert Rasp

D-U-N-S 25-691-0480   (SL)
WATERFORD SERVICES INC
800 Denison St Unit 7, Markham, ON, L3R 5M9
(905) 470-7766
Emp Here 400   *Sales* 12,787,200
SIC 7349 Building maintenance services, nec
Kenneth H Crystal

D-U-N-S 20-821-0146   (HQ)

WEINS CANADA INC
MARKVILLE TOYOTA
(*Suby of* YOKOHAMA TOYOPET SEIBI CO.LTD)
3120 Steeles Ave E, Markham, ON, L3R 1G9
(905) 475-0308
Emp Here 190   *Sales* 375,213,800
SIC 5511 New and used car dealers
Norio Naka
David Lalonde
Yoshinobu Niiro

D-U-N-S 24-303-0095   (HQ)
WEISDORF GROUP OF COMPANIES INC, THE
POSTCARD FACTORY, THE
2801 John St, Markham, ON, L3R 2Y8
(905) 477-9901
Sales 26,027,100
SIC 5099 Durable goods, nec
Irving Weisdorf

D-U-N-S 24-377-1808   (SL)
WEISDORF, IRVING HOLDINGS INC
2801 John St, Markham, ON, L3R 2Y8
(905) 477-9901
Emp Here 50   *Sales* 26,464,844
SIC 5099 Durable goods, nec
Irving Weisdorf

D-U-N-S 24-826-1687   (SL)
WEREK ENTERPRISES INC
EXECUTIVE MAINTENANCE SERVICES
164 Torbay Rd, Markham, ON, L3R 1G6
(905) 479-3131
Emp Here 300   *Sales* 9,590,400
SIC 7349 Building maintenance services, nec
Zeev Werek

D-U-N-S 25-371-5304   (HQ)
WESCO DISTRIBUTION CANADA LP
BRUCKNER SUPPLY CANADA
(*Suby of* WESCO INTERNATIONAL, INC.)
500 Hood Rd, Markham, ON, L3R 9Z3
(905) 475-7400
Emp Here 60   *Sales* 365,555,610
SIC 5063 Electrical apparatus and equipment
Roger Reese

D-U-N-S 24-310-5561   (BR)
WHITEHILL TECHNOLOGIES INC
(*Suby of* WHITEHILL TECHNOLOGIES INC)
19 Allstate Pky Suite 400, Markham, ON, L3R 5A4
(905) 475-2112
Emp Here 80
SIC 7371 Custom computer programming services
Christopher Smith

D-U-N-S 24-876-2312   (SL)
WILBY COMMERCIAL LTD
110 Torbay Rd Unit 3-4, Markham, ON, L3R 1G6
(905) 513-7505
Emp Here 15   *Sales* 12,533,655
SIC 5141 Groceries, general line
Hui Ben (Willie) Lao
Aloma Lao
Timoteo Soto
Jeffrey Go
Tiao Guan Uy
Lilian Co
Friea Siahiangco

D-U-N-S 25-056-4309   (SL)
WING ON CHEONG (CANADA) LIMITED
WINGS OF CANADA
235 Hood Rd Unit 2, Markham, ON, L3R 4N3

Emp Here 25   *Sales* 18,563,000
SIC 5199 Nondurable goods, nec
Michael Li
John Li

D-U-N-S 20-187-8316   (HQ)
WING ON NEW GROUP CANADA INC
CHINA'S TIME-HONORED BRAND

351 Ferrier St Suite 6, Markham, ON, L3R 5Z2
(905) 604-4677
Sales 10,271,695
SIC 5411 Grocery stores
Minguang Lu

D-U-N-S 25-221-2931   (BR)
WINNERS MERCHANTS INTERNATIONAL L.P.
WINNERS
(*Suby of* THE TJX COMPANIES INC)
5000 Highway 7 E, Markham, ON, L3R 4M9
(905) 415-1441
Emp Here 120
SIC 5651 Family clothing stores
Jennifer Moore

D-U-N-S 25-981-8045   (SL)
WOODBINE CHRYSLER LTD
WOODBINE CHRYSLER
8280 Woodbine Ave, Markham, ON, L3R 2N8
(905) 415-2260
Emp Here 35   *Sales* 17,432,730
SIC 5511 New and used car dealers
Steve Longman

D-U-N-S 24-218-2244   (HQ)
WOODBINE TOOL & DIE MANUFACTUR-ING LTD
190 Royal Crest Crt, Markham, ON, L3R 9X6
(905) 475-5223
Emp Here 65   *Sales* 17,124,536
SIC 3541 Machine tools, Metal cutting type
Tibor Urbanek

D-U-N-S 24-354-4462   (BR)
WOODBINE TOOL & DIE MANUFACTUR-ING LTD
(*Suby of* WOODBINE TOOL & DIE MANU-FACTURING LTD)
3300 14th Ave, Markham, ON, L3R 0H3
(905) 475-5223
Emp Here 75
SIC 3469 Metal stampings, nec
Dorothy Adams

D-U-N-S 24-705-0214   (HQ)
WORKERS HEALTH AND SAFETY CENTRE FEDERATION OF ONTARIO
WHSC
710-675 Cochrane Dr, Markham, ON, L3R 0B8
(416) 441-1939
Emp Here 49   *Sales* 33,951,312
SIC 8733 Noncommercial research organizations
David Killham
Gordon Wilson
Lyle Hargrove
Cliff Pilkey

D-U-N-S 25-275-6358   (HQ)
WORLDSOURCE FINANCIAL MANAGE-MENT INC
(*Suby of* GUARDIAN CAPITAL GROUP LIM-ITED)
625 Cochrane Dr Suite 700, Markham, ON, L3R 9R9
(905) 940-0044
Emp Here 47   *Sales* 55,411,443
SIC 6282 Investment advice
Paul Brown
Andy Mitchell
Trevor Line

D-U-N-S 20-345-4462   (HQ)
WORLDSOURCE SECURITIES INC
(*Suby of* GUARDIAN CAPITAL GROUP LIM-ITED)
625 Cochrane Dr Suite 700, Markham, ON, L3R 9R9
(905) 940-0094
Sales 30,418,800
SIC 8748 Business consulting, nec
John T Hunt
C Verner Christensen

D-U-N-S 20-345-4488   (SL)

WORLDSOURCE WEALTH MANAGEMENT INC
625 Cochrane Dr Suite 700, Markham, ON, L3R 9R9
(905) 940-5500
Emp Here 70   *Sales* 19,203,240
SIC 8741 Management services
Andrew (Andy) Mitchell

D-U-N-S 24-793-8731   (BR)
WSP CANADA INC
(*Suby of* AST TRUST COMPANY (CANADA))
600 Cochrane Dr Floor 5, Markham, ON, L3R 5K3
(905) 475-8727
Emp Here 300
SIC 7363 Help supply services
Brian Barber

D-U-N-S 24-874-5044   (BR)
WSP CANADA INC
GENIVAR
(*Suby of* AST TRUST COMPANY (CANADA))
600 Cochrane Dr Suite 500, Markham, ON, L3R 5K3
(905) 475-7270
Emp Here 300
SIC 8711 Engineering services

D-U-N-S 24-862-6749   (HQ)
YATSEN GROUP INC
SAKKIO JAPAN
7650 Birchmount Rd, Markham, ON, L3R 6B9
(905) 474-0710
Emp Here 90   *Sales* 46,639,000
SIC 5812 Eating places
James Chim
Daniel Chim

D-U-N-S 24-868-2320   (HQ)
YOGEN FRUZ CANADA INC
YOGEN FRUZ
210 Shields Crt Suite 1, Markham, ON, L3R 8V2
(905) 479-8762
Sales 15,329,820
SIC 6794 Patent owners and lessors
Aaron Serruya
Simon Serruya
Sarah Kulbatski

D-U-N-S 24-384-0654   (HQ)
YOUR PETSCHOICE ULC
7300 Warden Ave Suite 106, Markham, ON, L3R 9Z6
(905) 946-1200
Emp Here 1   *Sales* 41,778,850
SIC 5149 Groceries and related products, nec
Ed Casey

D-U-N-S 20-166-9140   (HQ)
ZWILLING J.A. HENCKELS CANADA LTD
INTERNATIONAL CUTLERY PRODUCTS, DIV OF
(*Suby of* WILH. WERHAHN KG)
435 Cochrane Dr Suite 4, Markham, ON, L3R 9R5
(905) 475-2555
Sales 16,792,248
SIC 5023 Homefurnishings
Mrinal Sharma
Alberto Imperio
David Hale

Markham, ON L3S

D-U-N-S 24-110-4517   (SL)
1530431 ONTARIO LIMITED
LISTRO'S NO FRILLS
7075 Markham Rd, Markham, ON, L3S 3J9
(905) 471-0089
Emp Here 120   *Sales* 35,217,240
SIC 5411 Grocery stores
John Listro

D-U-N-S 25-330-4976   (SL)
BIGTECH CLI INC
BIGTECH
5990 14th Ave, Markham, ON, L3S 4M4
(905) 695-0100
Emp Here 80   *Sales* 14,184,880
SIC 7378 Computer maintenance and repair
Aldo Cozza
Timothy Lazaris

D-U-N-S 25-220-1546   (SL)
BURMAN & FELLOWS GROUP INC
BFG ENTERPRISE SERVICES
170 Travail Rd, Markham, ON, L3S 3J1
(905) 472-1056
Emp Here 430   *Sales* 101,268,870
SIC 1731 Electrical work
Scott Andersen
Michael Bathgate

D-U-N-S 20-169-9874   (SL)
CANADIAN TIRE
7650 Markham Rd, Markham, ON, L3S 4S1
(905) 472-1638
Emp Here 30   *Sales* 18,878,400
SIC 5541 Gasoline service stations

D-U-N-S 24-218-3861   (SL)
COSMO COMMUNICATIONS CANADA INC
(*Suby of* NINGBO YINZHOU STARLIGHT
ELECTRONICS CO., LTD.)
55 Travail Rd Unit 2, Markham, ON, L3S 3J1
(905) 209-0488
Emp Here 40   *Sales* 17,886,960
SIC 5065 Electronic parts and equipment, nec
Peter Horak

D-U-N-S 24-354-8927   (BR)
COSTCO WHOLESALE CANADA LTD
COSTCO
(*Suby of* COSTCO WHOLESALE CORPO-
RATION)
65 Kirkham Dr Suite 545, Markham, ON, L3S
0A9
(905) 201-3502
Emp Here 200
SIC 5099 Durable goods, nec
Ken Kjelbgaard

D-U-N-S 24-890-0883   (SL)
DGA FULFILLMENT SERVICES INC
80 Travail Rd Unit 1, Markham, ON, L3S 3H9

Emp Here 50   *Sales* 22,174,500
SIC 7389 Business services, nec
Pauline Skinner

D-U-N-S 24-486-6620   (HQ)
GROTE INDUSTRIES CO.
GROTE ELECTRONICS, DIV OF
(*Suby of* GROTE INDUSTRIES, INC.)
230 Travail Rd, Markham, ON, L3S 3J1
(905) 209-9744
Emp Here 115   *Sales* 104,681,958
SIC 5013 Motor vehicle supplies and new
parts
Eric Morris

D-U-N-S 20-553-4329   (BR)
HOME DEPOT OF CANADA INC
HOME DEPOT
(*Suby of* THE HOME DEPOT INC)
50 Kirkham Dr, Markham, ON, L3S 4K7
(905) 201-2590
Emp Here 150
SIC 5211 Lumber and other building materials
Farhan-Syed Ahmad

D-U-N-S 24-858-6708   (HQ)
ITW CANADA INC
120 Travail Rd, Markham, ON, L3S 3J1
(905) 201-8399
Emp Here 50   *Sales* 389,194,000
SIC 5084 Industrial machinery and equipment
Mark Ristow
Mary Ann Spiegel
David Livingston

D-U-N-S 24-325-8865   (BR)
**ITW CANADA INVESTMENTS LIMITED
PARTNERSHIP**
PASLODE CANADA DIV OF
120 Travail Rd, Markham, ON, L3S 3J1
(905) 471-4250
Emp Here 150   *Sales* 999,999
SIC 1541 Industrial buildings and warehouses
Frank Heard

D-U-N-S 20-920-1276   (HQ)
KUBOTA CANADA LTD
(*Suby of* KUBOTA CORPORATION)
5900 14th Ave, Markham, ON, L3S 4K4
(905) 294-7477
Emp Here 91   *Sales* 51,699,380
SIC 5084 Industrial machinery and equipment
Robert Hickey

D-U-N-S 25-704-1111   (SL)
MAGIC NORTH AMERICA INC
110 Travail Rd, Markham, ON, L3S 3J1
(905) 471-7780
Emp Here 40   *Sales* 19,001,040
SIC 5084 Industrial machinery and equipment
Mike Merrick
Harvey Gentles

D-U-N-S 20-549-6800   (SL)
MARA TECHNOLOGIES INC
5680 14th Ave, Markham, ON, L3S 3K8
(905) 201-1787
Emp Here 100   *Sales* 19,044,200
SIC 3672 Printed circuit boards
Frank Lam
Fred Lam
Florence Yum
Kerry Mannella
Matthew Ruscica

D-U-N-S 24-307-5595   (SL)
MERANGUE INTERNATIONAL LIMITED
55 Travail Rd Unit 2, Markham, ON, L3S 3J1
(905) 209-0955
Emp Here 50   *Sales* 25,182,900
SIC 5112 Stationery and office supplies
John Moreau

D-U-N-S 20-172-6205   (SL)
PARKER PAD AND PRINTING LIMITED
208 Travail Rd, Markham, ON, L3S 3J1
(905) 294-7997
Emp Here 80   *Sales* 13,122,160
SIC 2752 Commercial printing, lithographic
Janis Parker

D-U-N-S 25-406-3886   (SL)
PC PARTS NOW INC
5990 14th Ave, Markham, ON, L3S 4M4
(905) 752-0222
Emp Here 23   *Sales* 11,584,134
SIC 5112 Stationery and office supplies
Heike Fischer

D-U-N-S 20-344-5192   (SL)
SUPER DISCOUNT STORE INC
46 Norman Ross Dr, Markham, ON, L3S 2Z1
(416) 939-5451
Emp Here 250   *Sales* 38,027,000
SIC 5311 Department stores
Aslam Badat

D-U-N-S 24-559-6887   (SL)
THAI INDOCHINE TRADING INC
TI FOODS
50 Travail Rd, Markham, ON, L3S 3J1
(416) 292-2228
Emp Here 45   *Sales* 37,600,965
SIC 5141 Groceries, general line
Samuel Sum
Rattana Sum
Teresa Takounseun
Darren Chung
Ted Takounseun

D-U-N-S 20-711-4567   (BR)
**YORK CATHOLIC DISTRICT SCHOOL
BOARD**

FR. MICHAEL MCGIVNEY CATHOLIC
ACADEMY
(*Suby of* YORK CATHOLIC DISTRICT
SCHOOL BOARD)
5300 14th Ave, Markham, ON, L3S 3K8
(905) 472-4961
Emp Here 100
SIC 8211 Elementary and secondary schools
Lou Paonessa

D-U-N-S 25-297-9760   (BR)
YORK REGION DISTRICT SCHOOL BOARD
MIDDLEFIELD COLLEGIATE INSTITUTE
(*Suby of* YORK REGION DISTRICT SCHOOL
BOARD)
525 Highglen Ave, Markham, ON, L3S 3L5
(905) 472-8900
Emp Here 150
SIC 8211 Elementary and secondary schools
Cecil Roach

Markham, ON L3T

D-U-N-S 20-166-5947   (SL)
ALLANSON INTERNATIONAL INC
83 Commerce Valley Dr E, Markham, ON, L3T
7T3
(416) 755-1191
Emp Here 70   *Sales* 15,248,030
SIC 1731 Electrical work
Richard Woodgate

D-U-N-S 24-756-6805   (HQ)
ALLANSON INTERNATIONAL INC
83 Commerce Valley Dr E, Markham, ON, L3T
7T3
(800) 668-9162
Sales 19,044,200
SIC 3612 Transformers, except electric
Richard Woodgate
Errol Lanns
Ray Morrish
Faiek Dabiet

D-U-N-S 24-610-2081   (HQ)
ATI TECHNOLOGIES ULC
(*Suby of* ADVANCED MICRO DEVICES,
INC.)
1 Commerce Valley Dr E, Markham, ON, L3T
7X6
(905) 882-2600
Sales 1,151,595,700
SIC 3577 Computer peripheral equipment,
nec

D-U-N-S 20-251-7678   (HQ)
**CANADIAN ADDICTION TREATMENT
PHARMACY LP**
CATP
175 Commerce Valley Dr W, Markham, ON,
L3T 7P6
(905) 773-3884
Emp Here 2   *Sales* 61,923,150
SIC 5122 Drugs, proprietaries, and sundries
Jeff Daiter

Markham, ON L6B

D-U-N-S 20-084-7445   (HQ)
**CEREBRAL PALSY PARENT COUNCIL OF
TORONTO**
PARTICIPATION HOUSE, MARKHAM
379 Church St Suite 402, Markham, ON, L6B
0T1
(905) 513-2756
Emp Here 14   *Sales* 31,060,200
SIC 8399 Social services, nec
Frances Dicarlo
Phil Garnett
Bill Crothers

D-U-N-S 24-357-2646   (BR)

CHARTWELL RETIREMENT RESIDENCES
WOODHAVEN, THE
(*Suby of* CHARTWELL RETIREMENT RESI-
DENCES)
380 Church St Suite 421, Markham, ON, L6B
1E1
(905) 472-3320
Emp Here 246
SIC 8059 Nursing and personal care, nec
Sonia Ryerson

D-U-N-S 20-536-9841   (SL)
CSH WOODHAVEN LTC INC
380 Church St, Markham, ON, L6B 1E1
(905) 472-3320
Emp Here 253   *Sales* 16,263,346
SIC 8361 Residential care
Michelle Stroud

D-U-N-S 20-770-6664   (HQ)
EBSCO CANADA LTD
(*Suby of* EBSCO INDUSTRIES, INC.)
110 Copper Creek Dr Suite 305, Markham,
ON, L6B 0P9
(416) 297-8282
Emp Here 37   *Sales* 21,113,293
SIC 7389 Business services, nec
Tim Collins
Cindy Dejesus Northcut
Sam Brooks

D-U-N-S 20-288-8934   (BR)
**YEE HONG CENTRE FOR GERIATRIC
CARE**
YEE HONG
(*Suby of* YEE HONG CENTRE FOR GERI-
ATRIC CARE)
2780 Bur Oak Ave, Markham, ON, L6B 1C9
(905) 471-3232
Emp Here 150
SIC 8059 Nursing and personal care, nec
Amy Go

Markham, ON L6C

D-U-N-S 24-622-3903   (HQ)
1300323 ONTARIO INC
AMJ CAMPBELL VAN LINES
(*Suby of* 2015825 ONTARIO INC)
176 Hillmount Rd, Markham, ON, L6C 1Z9
(905) 887-5557
Emp Here 300   *Sales* 110,628,600
SIC 4214 Local trucking with storage
Denis Frappier
Gilles Frappier
Joanne Lambert
Pierre Frappier
Marc Frappier
Carole Frappier

D-U-N-S 20-706-0559   (HQ)
BOSE LIMITED
(*Suby of* BOSE CORPORATION)
280 Hillmount Rd Suite 5, Markham, ON, L6C
3A1
(905) 887-5950
Sales 12,073,698
SIC 5065 Electronic parts and equipment, nec
Amar G Bose
Russ Noble

D-U-N-S 24-327-1157   (SL)
BRACKENRIG ENTERPRISES INC
CANADIAN TIRE
2900 Major Mackenzie Dr E, Markham, ON,
L6C 0G6
(416) 907-8237
Emp Here 100   *Sales* 62,928,000
SIC 5531 Auto and home supply stores
Jeff Doty

D-U-N-S 24-420-4769   (HQ)
CHUM SATELLITE SERVICES LIMITED
CHUM SATELLITE SERVICES

(*Suby of* GROUPE STINGRAY INC)
280 Hillmount Rd Unit 6, Markham, ON, L6C 3A1
(905) 475-1661
Emp Here 5   *Sales* 10,586,200
SIC 7313 Radio, television, publisher representatives
 Pascal Tremblay
 Eric Boyco
 Francois-Charles Sirious

D-U-N-S 24-947-8397   (HQ)
GE MULTILIN
GE INNOVATION CENTER
(*Suby of* GENERAL ELECTRIC COMPANY)
650 Markland St, Markham, ON, L6C 0M1
(905) 927-7070
Sales 84,874,500
SIC 3625 Relays and industrial controls
 Wuan Macius

D-U-N-S 24-802-3731   (SL)
GIESECKE+DEVRIENT MOBILE SECURITY CANADA, INC
(*Suby of* MC FAMILIENGES. MBH)
316 Markland St, Markham, ON, L6C 0C1
(905) 475-1333
Emp Here 400   *Sales* 95,524,800
SIC 3089 Plastics products, nec
 Edgar Salib
 Mandy Enriquez
 Kevin Fitzgerald

D-U-N-S 24-243-5688   (SL)
HILL, NORMAN REALTY INC
20 Cachet Woods Crt Suite 2, Markham, ON, L6C 3G1
(416) 226-5515
Emp Here 45   *Sales* 14,720,715
SIC 6531 Real estate agents and managers
 Norman Hill

D-U-N-S 24-686-2023   (HQ)
HONDA CANADA FINANCE INC
HONDA FINANCIAL SERVICES
(*Suby of* HONDA MOTOR CO., LTD.)
180 Honda Blvd Suite 200, Markham, ON, L6C 0H9
(905) 888-4188
Emp Here 132   *Sales* 118,950,750
SIC 6141 Personal credit institutions
 Hideo Tanaka
 Hideo Moroe
 Manabu Nishimae
 Jerry Chenkin
 David Sudbury
 Harald Ladewig

D-U-N-S 20-530-8034   (HQ)
HONDA CANADA INC
HONDA OF CANADA MANUFACTURING
(*Suby of* HONDA MOTOR CO., LTD.)
180 Honda Blvd Suite 200, Markham, ON, L6C 0H9
(905) 888-8110
Emp Here 600   *Sales* 1,454,250,000
SIC 3711 Motor vehicles and car bodies
 Dave Gardner
 Barry Holt
 Mickey M. Yaksich
 Tsutonu Morimoto
 Toshiaki Mikoshiba
 Soichiro Takazawa
 Sogo Nakata

D-U-N-S 24-286-7489   (SL)
JANNEX ENTERPRISES (1980) LIMITED
280 Hillmount Rd Unit 7, Markham, ON, L6C 3A1
(905) 284-8484
Emp Here 40   *Sales* 20,146,320
SIC 5112 Stationery and office supplies
 David Hes
 Ellen Bean

D-U-N-S 24-366-1431   (BR)
LIVANOVA CANADA CORP
(*Suby of* LIVANOVA PLC)

280 Hillmount Rd Unit 8, Markham, ON, L6C 3A1
(905) 284-4245
Emp Here 250
SIC 3841 Surgical and medical instruments
 R. Stewart

D-U-N-S 24-384-6730   (HQ)
MATRIX TECHNOLOGY LTD
280 Hillmount Rd Unit 6, Markham, ON, L6C 3A1
(905) 477-4442
Sales 13,415,220
SIC 5065 Electronic parts and equipment, nec
 William Dube

D-U-N-S 20-271-9621   (HQ)
MOBIS PART CANADA CORPORATION
(*Suby of* HYUNDAI MOBIS CO., LTD.)
10 Mobis Dr, Markham, ON, L6C 0Y3
(905) 927-3350
Sales 73,784,640
SIC 5012 Automobiles and other motor vehicles
 Jong Hwan
 Martin Song

D-U-N-S 24-203-9068   (SL)
NOVO PLASTICS INC
388 Markland St, Markham, ON, L6C 1Z6
(905) 887-8818
Emp Here 68   *Sales* 13,728,996
SIC 3089 Plastics products, nec
 Chahat Gulati

D-U-N-S 24-602-2040   (SL)
ORTHOTIC GROUP INC, THE
160 Markland St, Markham, ON, L6C 0C6
(800) 551-3008
Emp Here 180   *Sales* 14,792,900
SIC 3842 Surgical appliances and supplies
 Jason Kraus
 Ivan Sabel
 Andy Perz
 Gus Pergantis

D-U-N-S 20-718-8780   (HQ)
PHILIPS CANADA LTD
(*Suby of* KONINKLIJKE PHILIPS N.V.)
281 Hillmount Rd, Markham, ON, L6C 2S3
(905) 201-4100
Emp Here 3   *Sales* 512,202,000
SIC 6712 Bank holding companies
 Britta Lesaux
 Steve Hurwitz
 Danielle Lavallee
 Rahul Gupta
 Onno Van De Griend

D-U-N-S 20-172-9944   (HQ)
PHILIPS ELECTRONICS LTD
PHILIPS HEALTH CARE, DIV OF
(*Suby of* KONINKLIJKE PHILIPS N.V.)
281 Hillmount Rd, Markham, ON, L6C 2S3
(905) 201-4100
Emp Here 300   *Sales* 1,160,494,000
SIC 5064 Electrical appliances, television and radio
 Iain Burns
 Steve Hurwitz
 Danielle Lavallee
 Rahul Gupta

D-U-N-S 24-555-3248   (SL)
RAMESH ESSO
550 Bur Oak Ave, Markham, ON, L6C 0C4
(905) 927-0920
Emp Here 4   *Sales* 12,423,428
SIC 4925 Gas production and/or distribution

D-U-N-S 20-275-0571   (SL)
RYASH COFFEE CORPORATION
TIM HORTONS
9251 Woodbine Ave, Markham, ON, L6C 1Y9
(905) 887-8444
Emp Here 60   *Sales* 17,608,620
SIC 5461 Retail bakeries
 Wendy Brown

D-U-N-S 20-404-3392   (HQ)
SCHOLASTIC CANADA LTD
(*Suby of* SCHOLASTIC CORPORATION)
175 Hillmount Rd, Markham, ON, L6C 1Z7
(905) 887-7323
Emp Here 420   *Sales* 361,154,467
SIC 5192 Books, periodicals, and newspapers
 Iole Lucchese
 Anne Browne
 Nancy Pearson
 Richard Robinson

D-U-N-S 20-328-7532   (HQ)
SIGNIFY CANADA LTD
SIGNIFY
(*Suby of* KONINKLIJKE PHILIPS N.V.)
281 Hillmount Rd, Markham, ON, L6C 2S3
(905) 927-4900
Emp Here 250   *Sales* 198,040,500
SIC 3646 Commercial lighting fixtures
 David Grinstdad
 Anthony Cornacchia
 Kyle Kemper

D-U-N-S 24-426-9838   (SL)
TRADEMARK INDUSTRIES INC
380 Markland St, Markham, ON, L6C 1T6
(905) 532-0442
Emp Here 120   *Sales* 55,205,280
SIC 5072 Hardware
 Shlomo Bohbot
 Cyril Brenman

D-U-N-S 24-325-9798   (SL)
WONG, VICKY C.K. DRUGS LTD
SHOPPERS DRUG MART - CACHET CENTRE
9255 Woodbine Ave Suite 27, Markham, ON, L6C 1Y9
(905) 887-3000
Emp Here 65   *Sales* 15,881,320
SIC 5912 Drug stores and proprietary stores
 Vicky Wong

D-U-N-S 20-711-4666   (BR)
YORK CATHOLIC DISTRICT SCHOOL BOARD
ST AUGUSTINE CATHOLIC HIGH SCHOOL
(*Suby of* YORK CATHOLIC DISTRICT SCHOOL BOARD)
2188 Rodick Rd, Markham, ON, L6C 1S3
(905) 887-6171
Emp Here 100
SIC 8211 Elementary and secondary schools
 Antonella Rubino

D-U-N-S 20-288-8199   (BR)
YORK REGION DISTRICT SCHOOL BOARD
PIERRE ELLIOTT TRUDEAU HIGH SCHOOL
(*Suby of* YORK REGION DISTRICT SCHOOL BOARD)
90 Bur Oak Ave, Markham, ON, L6C 2E6
(905) 887-2216
Emp Here 100
SIC 8211 Elementary and secondary schools
 Linda Balaishis

D-U-N-S 24-006-0699   (SL)
YOUNG, PETER LIMITED
INDUSTRIAL PROPERTY SERVICES
9693 Kennedy Rd, Markham, ON, L6C 1A4
(905) 887-9122
Emp Here 65   *Sales* 16,713,515
SIC 4959 Sanitary services, nec
 Peter Young
 Alan Geddis

Markham, ON L6E

D-U-N-S 24-333-7818   (HQ)
1359470 ONTARIO INC.
STENTECH
138 Anderson Ave Unit 6, Markham, ON, L6E 1A4

(905) 472-7773
Emp Here 25   *Sales* 11,204,880
SIC 2631 Paperboard mills
 Sibthain Akbar

D-U-N-S 24-744-0241   (BR)
GARDEN BASKET FOOD MARKETS INCORPORATED, THE
GARDEN BASKET, THE
(*Suby of* GARDEN BASKET FOOD MARKETS INCORPORATED, THE)
9271 Markham Rd, Markham, ON, L6E 1A1
(905) 471-0777
Emp Here 150
SIC 5411 Grocery stores
 Tony Auciello

D-U-N-S 24-250-0010   (BR)
HOME DEPOT OF CANADA INC
(*Suby of* THE HOME DEPOT INC)
1201 Castlemore Ave, Markham, ON, L6E 0G5
(905) 201-5500
Emp Here 154
SIC 5251 Hardware stores
 Kassim Karawalli

D-U-N-S 24-843-2028   (BR)
METRO ONTARIO INC
FOOD BASICS
(*Suby of* METRO INC)
1220 Castlemore Ave, Markham, ON, L6E 0H7
(905) 209-9200
Emp Here 75
SIC 5411 Grocery stores
 Eric La Fleche

Markham, ON L6G

D-U-N-S 25-353-2949   (HQ)
8388059 CANADA INC
TRANSCONTINENTAL
(*Suby of* TRANSCONTINENTAL INC)
210 Duffield Dr, Markham, ON, L6G 1C9
(416) 848-8500
Sales 87,198,300
SIC 2752 Commercial printing, lithographic
 Brian Reed
 Francois Olivier

D-U-N-S 24-924-8485   (SL)
965046 ONTARIO INC
QUALITY ALLIED ELEVATOR
80 Citizen Crt Unit 11, Markham, ON, L6G 1A7
(905) 305-0195
Emp Here 110   *Sales* 21,156,080
SIC 7699 Repair services, nec
 Rick Sokoloff

D-U-N-S 24-920-1799   (HQ)
AVIVA CANADA INC
(*Suby of* GENERAL ACCIDENT PLC)
10 Aviva Way Suite 100, Markham, ON, L6G 0G1
(416) 288-1800
Emp Here 1,250   *Sales* 1,927,074,700
SIC 6411 Insurance agents, brokers, and service
 Greg Somerville
 Jim Falle
 Brian W. Barr
 J Charles Caty
 J. William Rowley

D-U-N-S 25-536-4457   (HQ)
BEAUTY EXPRESS CANADA INC
PURE BEAUTY
170 Duffield Dr Suite 200, Markham, ON, L6G 1B5
(905) 258-0684
Emp Here 30   *Sales* 161,452,800
SIC 7231 Beauty shops
 Brian Luborsky

D-U-N-S 20-404-9928   (SL)
BELMONT PRESS LIMITED
5 Bodrington Crt, Markham, ON, L6G 1A6
(905) 940-4900
Emp Here 67   *Sales* 30,097,673
SIC 7389 Business services, nec
Paul Schaeffer

D-U-N-S 24-744-2213   (HQ)
BRENNAN PAVING & CONSTRUCTION LTD
505 Miller Ave, Markham, ON, L6G 1B2
(905) 475-1440
Emp Here 50   *Sales* 25,244,200
SIC 1611 Highway and street construction
Leo Mcarthur
John Carrick

D-U-N-S 24-254-6039   (HQ)
BRENNAN PAVING LIMITED
505 Miller Ave, Markham, ON, L6G 1B2
(905) 475-1440
Emp Here 1   *Sales* 25,244,200
SIC 1611 Highway and street construction
Leo Anthony Mcarthur
William Barrie Brayford

D-U-N-S 20-967-3714   (SL)
CANDYM ENTERPRISES LTD
ACCENT IMPORTS
95 Clegg Rd, Markham, ON, L6G 1B9
(905) 474-1555
Emp Here 48   *Sales* 35,640,960
SIC 5199 Nondurable goods, nec
Brian Matheson
Brad Baker

D-U-N-S 24-318-1534   (HQ)
CDI COMPUTER DEALERS INC
130 South Town Centre Blvd, Markham, ON,
L6G 1B8
(905) 946-1119
Sales 220,565,024
SIC 5045 Computers, peripherals, and software
Saar Pikar
Naipaul Sheosankar
Leszek Biurkowski
Chris Bristow
Fred Hastings

D-U-N-S 20-379-6300   (HQ)
CGRIFF21 HOLDINGS INC
TEAM INDUSTRIAL SERVICES
25 Bodrington Crt, Markham, ON, L6G 1B6
(905) 940-9334
Emp Here 25   *Sales* 26,908,800
SIC 7699 Repair services, nec
Clint Griffin

D-U-N-S 20-343-5701   (HQ)
CIRBA INC
DENSIFY
179 Enterprise Blvd Unit 400, Markham, ON,
L6G 0E7
(905) 731-0090
Sales 14,418,200
SIC 7371 Custom computer programming services
Gerry Smith
Riyaz Somani
Andrew Hiller
Scott Browne
Dana Carcas

D-U-N-S 20-792-0112   (BR)
COSTCO WHOLESALE CANADA LTD
(*Suby of* COSTCO WHOLESALE CORPORATION)
1 Yorktech Dr Suite 151, Markham, ON, L6G
1A6
(905) 477-5718
Emp Here 150
SIC 5099 Durable goods, nec
Randy Martel

D-U-N-S 20-334-3293   (BR)
CREATION TECHNOLOGIES LP
(*Suby of* CREATION TECHNOLOGIES LP)

110 Clegg Rd, Markham, ON, L6G 1E1
(866) 754-5004
Emp Here 300
SIC 3679 Electronic components, nec
Duncan Reed

D-U-N-S 24-026-5090   (HQ)
HANNA PAPER FIBRES LIMITED
(*Suby of* HANNA GROUP LTD, THE)
70 Addiscott Crt, Markham, ON, L6G 1A6
(905) 475-9844
Sales 81,430,500
SIC 4953 Refuse systems
George Millar
Larry Burns
Jim Millar
George I Millar

D-U-N-S 24-514-1171   (BR)
HYDRO ONE NETWORKS INC
(*Suby of* HYDRO ONE LIMITED)
185 Clegg Rd, Markham, ON, L6G 1B7
(800) 434-1235
Emp Here 200
SIC 7299 Miscellaneous personal service
Tom Kydd

D-U-N-S 20-625-2694   (HQ)
MANCHU WOK (CANADA) INC
85 Citizen Crt Unit 9, Markham, ON, L6G 1A8
(905) 946-7200
Emp Here 25   *Sales* 18,049,293
SIC 5812 Eating places
Brian Worts

D-U-N-S 24-101-1597   (HQ)
MARKHAM SUITES HOTEL LIMITED
HILTON SUITES CONFERENCE CENTRE & SPA
8500 Warden Ave, Markham, ON, L6G 1A5
(905) 470-8500
Sales 47,834,000
SIC 7011 Hotels and motels
Herman Grad

D-U-N-S 24-423-5537   (SL)
MICROART SERVICES INC
190 Duffield Dr, Markham, ON, L6G 1B5
(905) 752-0800
Emp Here 170   *Sales* 32,375,140
SIC 3679 Electronic components, nec
Tyler Fisher
Peter Fisher

D-U-N-S 25-246-8244   (HQ)
MILLER GROUP INC
505 Miller Ave, Markham, ON, L6G 1B2
(905) 475-6660
Emp Here 150   *Sales* 721,853,000
SIC 1611 Highway and street construction
Leo Mcarthur
Barrie Bayford

D-U-N-S 20-405-7814   (HQ)
MILLER PAVING LIMITED
MILLER WASTE SYSTEMS DIV OF
(*Suby of* MILLER GROUP INC)
505 Miller Ave, Markham, ON, L6G 1B2
(905) 475-6660
Emp Here 400   *Sales* 1,115,591,000
SIC 1611 Highway and street construction
Leo Mcarthur
Blair Mcarthur
Jay Gu

D-U-N-S 20-703-3630   (HQ)
MOTOROLA SOLUTIONS CANADA INC
(*Suby of* MOTOROLA SOLUTIONS, INC.)
8133 Warden Ave, Markham, ON, L6G 1B3
(905) 948-5200
Emp Here 60   *Sales* 81,234,580
SIC 5065 Electronic parts and equipment, nec
John Wozniak
George Krausz

D-U-N-S 20-250-8057   (SL)
OWENS, R S & COMPANY INCORPORATED
271 Yorktech Dr, Markham, ON, L6G 1A6

(905) 754-3355
Emp Here 49   *Sales* 13,540,004
SIC 6531 Real estate agents and managers
Richard Fikfer

D-U-N-S 25-365-1707   (SL)
PLANTBEST, INC
TRADEX
170 Duffield Dr Unit 200, Markham, ON, L6G
1B5
(905) 470-0724
Emp Here 214   *Sales* 2,288,964
SIC 2879 Agricultural chemicals, nec
Batstiaan Matthijis Millenaar
Brian Luborsky

D-U-N-S 20-517-3847   (SL)
ST. REGIS CRYSTAL INC
271 Yorktech Dr, Markham, ON, L6G 1A6
(905) 754-3355
Emp Here 65   *Sales* 33,835,230
SIC 5099 Durable goods, nec
Richard Firkser

D-U-N-S 25-512-8779   (HQ)
**TEAM INDUSTRIAL SERVICES (CANADA)
INC**
25 Bodrington Crt, Markham, ON, L6G 1B6
(905) 940-9334
Emp Here 1   *Sales* 29,542,320
SIC 1799 Special trade contractors, nec
Steve Griffin

D-U-N-S 20-568-0700   (HQ)
**VERTEX CUSTOMER MANAGEMENT
(CANADA) LIMITED**
(*Suby of* VTX HOLDINGS LIMITED)
185 Clegg Rd, Markham, ON, L6G 1B7
(905) 944-3200
Sales 234,117,800
SIC 7389 Business services, nec
Earl Davison
Gary Cook

Marmora, ON K0K

D-U-N-S 25-705-9667   (BR)
**CARESSANT-CARE NURSING AND RE-
TIREMENT HOMES LIMITED**
CARESSANT CARE MARMORA
(*Suby of* CARESSANT-CARE NURSING AND
RETIREMENT HOMES LIMITED)
58 Bursthall St, Marmora, ON, K0K 2M0
(613) 472-3130
Emp Here 110
SIC 8051 Skilled nursing care facilities
Linda Merkley

D-U-N-S 20-641-5929   (SL)
MARMORA FOOD MARKET LIMITED
VALUE MART
42 Mathew St, Marmora, ON, K0K 2M0
(613) 472-2706
Emp Here 42   *Sales* 11,514,384
SIC 5411 Grocery stores
Kelly Welch
Dwayne L Welch
Betty Welch
Kelly-Lynne Welch

Massey, ON P0P

D-U-N-S 24-514-9414   (SL)
MASSEY WHOLESALE LTD
FARQUHAR MASSEY WHOLESALE
(*Suby of* FARQUHAR, THOMAS & SON CO.
LIMITED)
400 Carlalbert St, Massey, ON, P0P 1P0
(705) 865-2051
Emp Here 55   *Sales* 40,838,600
SIC 5194 Tobacco and tobacco products
Donald Farquhar

Aurel Rivet

Matachewan, ON P0K

D-U-N-S 20-282-4504   (BR)
ALAMOS GOLD INC
YOUNG-DAVIDSON MINE
(*Suby of* ALAMOS GOLD INC)
259 Matheson St, Matachewan, ON, P0K 1M0
(705) 565-9800
Emp Here 500
SIC 1041 Gold ores
Luc Guimonb

Matheson, ON P0K

D-U-N-S 24-858-7474   (SL)
1685300 ONTARIO INC
LPL CONTRACTING
1835 Diamond Rd, Matheson, ON, P0K 1N0
(705) 273-3219
Emp Here 70   *Sales* 17,670,940
SIC 1629 Heavy construction, nec
Larry Phibbs

D-U-N-S 20-880-2520   (SL)
BINGHAM MEMORIAL HOSPITAL
507 8th Ave, Matheson, ON, P0K 1N0
(705) 273-2424
Emp Here 80   *Sales* 8,170,640
SIC 8062 General medical and surgical hospitals
Ann Desjardins
Willogene Baragar
Robert Browne
Stephen Chiang
Gail Waghorn

D-U-N-S 24-091-9613   (SL)
**SOUTH COCHRANE CHILD AND YOUTH
SERVICE INCORPORATED**
507 Eigth Ave Suite 15, Matheson, ON, P0K
1N0
(705) 273-3041
Emp Here 45   *Sales* 10,379,163
SIC 8399 Social services, nec
Cory Van Dyk

Maxville, ON K0C

D-U-N-S 20-148-1629   (HQ)
MACEWEN AGRICENTRE INC
40 Catherine St W, Maxville, ON, K0C 1T0
(613) 527-2175
Emp Here 30   *Sales* 37,126,000
SIC 5191 Farm supplies
James Macewen

D-U-N-S 20-894-6186   (HQ)
MACEWEN PETROLEUM INC
18 Adelaide St, Maxville, ON, K0C 1T0
(613) 527-2100
Emp Here 50   *Sales* 100,576,080
SIC 5172 Petroleum products, nec
W Allan Macewen

D-U-N-S 20-789-0419   (SL)
MAXVILLE MANOR
80 Mechanic St W Suite 620, Maxville, ON,
K0C 1T0
(613) 527-2170
Emp Here 130   *Sales* 8,882,380
SIC 8051 Skilled nursing care facilities
Craig Munro

D-U-N-S 24-269-8686   (SL)
ROXBOROUGH BUS LINES LIMITED
17504 Dyer Rd, Maxville, ON, K0C 1T0

▲ Public Company   ■ Public Company Family Member   **HQ** Headquarters   **BR** Branch   **SL** Single Location

(613) 538-2461
Emp Here 140   *Sales* 10,538,080
SIC 4151 School buses
Daryl Mcrae
George Villeneuve
Jean Villeneuve

Mcdougall, ON P2A

D-U-N-S 25-606-9840   (BR)
TIM HORTON CHILDREN'S FOUNDATION, INC
TIM HORTON MEMORIAL CAMP
(*Suby of* TIM HORTON CHILDREN'S FOUNDATION, INC)
550 Lorimer Lake Rd, Mcdougall, ON, P2A 2W7
(705) 389-2773
Emp Here 85
SIC 7032 Sporting and recreational camps
Jullian Rouse

Meaford, ON N4L

D-U-N-S 20-057-0307   (SL)
EARTH POWER TRACTORS AND EQUIPMENT INC
(*Suby of* EARTH POWER INC)
206005 Hwy 26 W, Meaford, ON, N4L 1A5
(519) 538-1660
Emp Here 35   *Sales* 16,625,910
SIC 5083 Farm and garden machinery
James Kelly

D-U-N-S 20-769-8184   (SL)
MEAFORD NURSING HOME LTD
135 William St, Meaford, ON, N4L 1T4
(519) 538-1010
Emp Here 95   *Sales* 6,529,635
SIC 8051 Skilled nursing care facilities
Ronald Gingrich
Spike De Schiffert
John Fast

Melbourne, ON N0L

D-U-N-S 24-098-8568   (SL)
MELBOURNE FARM AUTOMATION LTD
6687 Longwoods Rd, Melbourne, ON, N0L 1T0
(519) 289-5256
Emp Here 25   *Sales* 11,875,650
SIC 5083 Farm and garden machinery
Garry Gilroy

Merrickville, ON K0G

D-U-N-S 24-964-7806   (SL)
RIDEAU COMMUNITY HEALTH SERVICES
354 Read St, Merrickville, ON, K0G 1N0
(613) 269-3400
Emp Here 100   *Sales* 16,064,600
SIC 8011 Offices and clinics of medical doctors
Pamela Blackstock
Anne Carter
Ainsley Charles
Christina Doglowicz
Dutton Don
Roderick Fournier

Metcalfe, ON K0A

D-U-N-S 20-700-4490   (SL)
CONTINENTAL MUSHROOM CORPORATION (1989) LTD
2545 Ninth Line Rd, Metcalfe, ON, K0A 2P0

Emp Here 260   *Sales* 48,845,940
SIC 0182 Food crops grown under cover
Lyle Whitham
Nicholas George Pora
Leanna Pora-Whitham
Casandra Pora
Virginia Pora
John Pierre Haralovich

D-U-N-S 25-263-5602   (BR)
OTTAWA-CARLETON DISTRICT SCHOOL BOARD
OSGOODE TOWNSHIP HIGH SCHOOL
(*Suby of* OTTAWA-CARLETON DISTRICT SCHOOL BOARD)
2800 8th Line Rd, Metcalfe, ON, K0A 2P0
(613) 821-2241
Emp Here 75
SIC 8211 Elementary and secondary schools
Nancy Girozan

D-U-N-S 24-625-9154   (SL)
TOWNSHIP OF OSGOODE CARE CENTRE
7650 Snake Island Rd Rr 3, Metcalfe, ON, K0A 2P0

Emp Here 115   *Sales* 4,842,007
SIC 8051 Skilled nursing care facilities
Murray Munro

Midhurst, ON L0L

D-U-N-S 20-033-0785   (HQ)
ARNOTT CONSTRUCTION LIMITED
THE EQUIPMENT SOLUTION
2 Bertram Industrial Pky Suite 1, Midhurst, ON, L0L 1X0
(705) 735-9121
Emp Here 5   *Sales* 30,293,040
SIC 1623 Water, sewer, and utility lines
Wayne Arnott
Brenda David

D-U-N-S 24-008-4442   (HQ)
SIMCOE COUNTY DISTRICT SCHOOL BOARD, THE
1170 Hwy 26, Midhurst, ON, L0L 1X0
(705) 734-6363
Emp Here 180   *Sales* 540,750,049
SIC 8211 Elementary and secondary schools
Kathi Wallace
Peter Beacock
Donna Armstrong
Debra Edward
Jodi Lloyd
Robert North
Caroline Smith
Nicole Black
Suzanne Lay
Michelle Lock

Midhurst, ON L9X

D-U-N-S 24-936-6113   (HQ)
CURRIE, DONALD TRUCKS INC
CURRIE TRUCK CENTRE
2 Currie Dr, Midhurst, ON, L9X 0N3
(705) 734-1953
Sales 31,513,790
SIC 7538 General automotive repair shops
Donald Currie

Midland, ON L4R

D-U-N-S 25-674-4962   (SL)
894812 ONTARIO INC
MIDLAND TOYOTA
806 King St, Midland, ON, L4R 0B8
(705) 526-6640
Emp Here 23   *Sales* 11,455,794
SIC 5511 New and used car dealers
James Koch
Richard Maltby

D-U-N-S 25-401-1687   (HQ)
BAYTECH PLASTICS INC
320 Elizabeth St, Midland, ON, L4R 1Y9
(705) 526-7801
Sales 31,771,600
SIC 3089 Plastics products, nec
David Webster
Paul Goyette

D-U-N-S 24-174-0518   (BR)
BAYTECH PLASTICS INC
16403 Hwy 12, Midland, ON, L4R 4L6
(705) 526-7801
Emp Here 100
SIC 3089 Plastics products, nec
Jacques Belcourt

D-U-N-S 20-130-2593   (SL)
BOURGEOIS MOTORS LIMITED
281 Cranston Cres, Midland, ON, L4R 4L1
(705) 526-2278
Emp Here 40   *Sales* 19,923,120
SIC 5511 New and used car dealers
Adam Bourgeois

D-U-N-S 25-541-4468   (HQ)
FRANKE KINDRED CANADA LIMITED
1000 Kindred Rd, Midland, ON, L4R 4K9
(705) 526-5427
Sales 19,208,500
SIC 3499 Fabricated Metal products, nec
Shaun Desroehes

D-U-N-S 20-532-8966   (BR)
GENERAL MILLS CANADA CORPORATION
(*Suby of* GENERAL MILLS, INC.)
111 Pillsbury Dr, Midland, ON, L4R 4L4
(705) 526-6311
Emp Here 200
SIC 2041 Flour and other grain mill products

D-U-N-S 24-029-9847   (SL)
GEOCALM INC
LABX
478 Bay St Suite 216, Midland, ON, L4R 1K9
(705) 528-6888
Emp Here 102   *Sales* 54,605,904
SIC 5049 Professional equipment, nec
Robert Kafato

D-U-N-S 24-010-6906   (SL)
GEORGIAN BAY GENERAL HOSPITAL
1112 St Andrews Dr, Midland, ON, L4R 4P4
(705) 526-1300
Emp Here 650   *Sales* 72,202,000
SIC 8062 General medical and surgical hospitals
Karen Mcgrath
Neal Foot
Donna Macfarlane
Jane Millar
Suzanne Beatty
Brian Scott
Dar Shepherdson
Mary Jane Deacon
Sara Lankshear
Ralph Befort

D-U-N-S 24-418-4268   (SL)
H.G. CAMPBELL ENTERPRISES LTD
CANADIAN TIRE
Hwy 93 S, Midland, ON, L4R 5K9
(705) 526-9321
Emp Here 49   *Sales* 24,405,822
SIC 5531 Auto and home supply stores

Harry Campbell

D-U-N-S 24-086-9094   (SL)
J.B. MERCHANDISE DESIGN INC
233 Whitfield Cres, Midland, ON, L4R 5E3
(705) 361-2012
Emp Here 50   *Sales* 22,174,500
SIC 7389 Business services, nec
Jon Buckland
Brad Thompson

D-U-N-S 25-061-5580   (SL)
KYSY INC
MIDLAND FOODLAND
795 Balm Beach Rd E, Midland, ON, L4R 4K4
(705) 527-4067
Emp Here 49   *Sales* 13,433,448
SIC 5411 Grocery stores
Shawn Freer

D-U-N-S 24-108-8769   (BR)
LOBLAWS INC
REAL CANADIAN SUPERSTORE, THE
(*Suby of* LOBLAW COMPANIES LIMITED)
9292 93 Hwy, Midland, ON, L4R 4K4
(705) 527-0388
Emp Here 160
SIC 5411 Grocery stores
Wendy Madden

D-U-N-S 24-875-5431   (HQ)
MCAMM ENTERPRIZES LTD
MACDONALDS
9195 Hwy 93, Midland, ON, L4R 4K4
(705) 526-4631
Emp Here 80   *Sales* 3,641,520
SIC 5812 Eating places
Mark Cruden
Carol Cruden

D-U-N-S 20-329-4046   (SL)
MIDLAND AUTOMOTIVE CORPORATION
MIDLAND HONDA
868 King St, Midland, ON, L4R 0B8
(705) 526-1344
Emp Here 28   *Sales* 13,242,012
SIC 5511 New and used car dealers
Peter Brenzel
Richard Davies
Nick Derlis

D-U-N-S 20-130-3633   (SL)
MIDLAND LUMBER & BUILDING SUPPLIES LTD
MIDLAND TIM-BR MART
200 Third St, Midland, ON, L4R 3R9
(705) 526-2264
Emp Here 40   *Sales* 10,122,360
SIC 5211 Lumber and other building materials
Robert Bray

D-U-N-S 20-273-1654   (SL)
MIDLAND POWER UTILITY CORPORATION
16984 12 Hwy, Midland, ON, L4R 4P4
(705) 526-9361
Emp Here 16   *Sales* 10,025,824
SIC 4911 Electric services
Phil Marley

D-U-N-S 20-965-8921   (HQ)
NEBS BUSINESS PRODUCTS LIMITED
NEBS
(*Suby of* DELUXE CORPORATION)
330 Cranston Cres, Midland, ON, L4R 4V9
(705) 526-4233
Emp Here 300   *Sales* 77,509,600
SIC 2761 Manifold business forms
Thom Leiper

D-U-N-S 25-195-5126   (BR)
RAYTHEON CANADA LIMITED
RAYTHEON ELCAN OPTICAL TECHNOLOGIES
(*Suby of* RAYTHEON COMPANY)
450 Leitz Rd Suite 2, Midland, ON, L4R 5B8
(705) 526-5401
Emp Here 662
SIC 3827 Optical instruments and lenses

▲ Public Company   ■ Public Company Family Member   HQ Headquarters   BR Branch   SL Single Location

Ed Kristufek

D-U-N-S 24-124-4482 (HQ)
REMAX GEORGIAN BAY REALTY LTD
833 King St, Midland, ON, L4R 0B7
(705) 526-9366
Emp Here 31   *Sales* 13,587,800
SIC 6531 Real estate agents and managers
Robert Armstrong
Bernard Mailloux
Ralph Poole

D-U-N-S 20-130-2783 (SL)
SCHOTT GEMTRON (CANADA) CORPORATION
(*Suby of* CARL-ZEISS-STIFTUNG)
125 Albert St, Midland, ON, L4R 4L3
(705) 526-3771
Emp Here 140   *Sales* 25,090,660
SIC 3231 Products of purchased glass
Mike Jones
Brian Marchand
Doug Roberts
Dianne Allmon

D-U-N-S 25-292-4659 (BR)
SIMCOE COUNTY DISTRICT SCHOOL BOARD, THE
MIDLAND SECONDARY SCHOOL
(*Suby of* SIMCOE COUNTY DISTRICT SCHOOL BOARD, THE)
865 Hugel Ave, Midland, ON, L4R 1X8
(705) 526-7817
Emp Here 95
SIC 8211 Elementary and secondary schools
Diane Fletcher

D-U-N-S 24-829-0298 (SL)
SMITH, TOM CHEVROLET LIMITED
(*Suby of* TOM SMITH CHEV OLDS LTD)
824 King St, Midland, ON, L4R 0B8
(705) 526-0193
Emp Here 42   *Sales* 26,429,760
SIC 5511 New and used car dealers
Thomas Smith
Larry Pattullo
Richard Maltby

D-U-N-S 20-732-2413 (SL)
STONELEIGH MOTORS LIMITED
9186 County Road Hwy Suite 93, Midland, ON, L4R 4K6
(705) 526-3724
Emp Here 46   *Sales* 22,911,588
SIC 5511 New and used car dealers
Michael Stone
Matthew Stone
Linda Hamelin

D-U-N-S 25-509-1977 (SL)
STREIT MANUFACTURING INC
STREIT GROUP
(*Suby of* STREIT USA ARMORING, LLC)
111 Pillsbury Dr, Midland, ON, L4R 4L4
(705) 526-6557
Emp Here 150   *Sales* 33,576,450
SIC 3711 Motor vehicles and car bodies
Guerman Goutorov
Michael Blair

D-U-N-S 24-425-0874 (SL)
TOLMIE, M. B. DRUGS LTD
SHOPPERS DRUG MART
9226 93 Hwy, Midland, ON, L4R 4K4
(705) 526-7855
Emp Here 55   *Sales* 13,438,040
SIC 5912 Drug stores and proprietary stores
Michael Tolmie
Donna Tolmie

D-U-N-S 24-317-1837 (BR)
WAL-MART CANADA CORP
WALMART STORE 3645
(*Suby of* WALMART INC.)
16845 12 Hwy, Midland, ON, L4R 0A9
(705) 526-4754
Emp Here 250

SIC 5311 Department stores
Liz Celej

D-U-N-S 20-402-3337 (HQ)
WEBER MANUFACTURING TECHNOLOGIES INC
WEBER TOOL & MOLD, DIV OF
(*Suby of* ZYNIK CAPITAL CORPORATION)
16566 Hwy 12, Midland, ON, L4R 4L1
(705) 526-7896
Emp Here 200   *Sales* 61,792,940
SIC 3541 Machine tools, Metal cutting type
Christopher Edwards

D-U-N-S 24-357-1200 (BR)
ZF AUTOMOTIVE CANADA LIMITED
(*Suby of* ZEPPELIN-STIFTUNG)
16643 Hwy 12, Midland, ON, L4R 4L5
(705) 526-8791
Emp Here 200
SIC 3544 Special dies, tools, jigs, and fixtures
Katherine Rowe-Bailey

Mildmay, ON N0G

D-U-N-S 20-344-3759 (SL)
AMERICAN POULTRY SERVICES LTD
63 Elora St, Mildmay, ON, N0G 2J0
(800) 963-3488
Emp Here 3   *Sales* 14,749,660
SIC 0751 Livestock services, except veterinary
Brent Herman

D-U-N-S 24-451-3594 (SL)
BRIANS POULTRY SERVICES LTD
Gd, Mildmay, ON, N0G 2J0
(519) 367-2675
Emp Here 150   *Sales* 26,085,750
SIC 0751 Livestock services, except veterinary
Brian Herman

Millbrook, ON L0A

D-U-N-S 20-818-9071 (SL)
1356594 ONTARIO LTD
EAGLESON CONSTRUCTION
1516 Carmel Line, Millbrook, ON, L0A 1G0
(705) 932-2996
Emp Here 40   *Sales* 12,754,760
SIC 1521 Single-family housing construction
Roger Eagleson
Tracy Eagleson
Ryan Eagleson
Jordon Eagleson

D-U-N-S 20-817-4151 (SL)
CALHOUN FOODS LAND
FOODLAND
6 Century Blvd, Millbrook, ON, L0A 1G0
(705) 932-2139
Emp Here 38   *Sales* 10,417,776
SIC 5411 Grocery stores
Diderica Calhoun

D-U-N-S 20-568-2870 (SL)
CENTENNIAL PLACE
2 Centennial Lane Rr 3, Millbrook, ON, L0A 1G0
(705) 932-4464
Emp Here 120   *Sales* 8,227,920
SIC 8051 Skilled nursing care facilities
Karen Wolf

D-U-N-S 25-529-5339 (SL)
NEXICOM COMMUNICATIONS INC
NEXICOM GROUP
5 King St E, Millbrook, ON, L0A 1G0
(888) 639-4266
Emp Here 80   *Sales* 17,426,320

SIC 1731 Electrical work
R Paul Downs
John E Downs

D-U-N-S 20-287-0775 (SL)
NEXICOM TELECOMMUNICATIONS INC
NEXICOM
9 Bank St N, Millbrook, ON, L0A 1G0
(705) 775-5394
Emp Here 55   *Sales* 10,163,890
SIC 4899 Communication services, nec
Paul Downes

Millgrove, ON L0R

D-U-N-S 20-698-8557 (SL)
BENNETT MECHANICAL INSTALLATION (2001) LTD
524 6th Concession Rd W, Millgrove, ON, L0R 1V0
(905) 689-7242
Emp Here 50   *Sales* 11,046,700
SIC 1711 Plumbing, heating, air-conditioning
Anthony Quinn
Tom Cecchetto
Dave Inrig

D-U-N-S 20-550-9719 (SL)
BENNETT MECHANICAL INSTALLATIONS (2001) LTD
524 Sixth Conc W, Millgrove, ON, L0R 1V0
(905) 689-7242
Emp Here 75   *Sales* 18,933,150
SIC 1629 Heavy construction, nec
Anthony Quinn

D-U-N-S 25-967-0995 (SL)
BENNETT MECHANICAL INSTALLATIONS LTD
524 6th Concession Rd W, Millgrove, ON, L0R 1V0

Emp Here 80   *Sales* 20,195,360
SIC 1629 Heavy construction, nec

D-U-N-S 20-564-5794 (SL)
MINE AND MILL INSTALLATIONS LTD
524 6th Concession Rd W, Millgrove, ON, L0R 1V0

Emp Here 30   *Sales* 12,580,650
SIC 6712 Bank holding companies
Colin Bennett
Anthony Quinn

Millgrove, ON L8B

D-U-N-S 20-767-6243 (SL)
FLORA-DEI
632 Safari Rd, Millgrove, ON, L8B 1S8
(905) 659-3354
Emp Here 30   *Sales* 22,275,600
SIC 5193 Flowers and florists supplies
Ryan Degelder

Milton, ON L9E

D-U-N-S 20-351-6919 (BR)
HALTON DISTRICT SCHOOL BOARD
BOYNE PUBLIC SCHOOL
(*Suby of* HALTON DISTRICT SCHOOL BOARD)
1110 Farmstead Dr, Milton, ON, L9E 0B5
(905) 864-9641
Emp Here 113
SIC 8211 Elementary and secondary schools
Peter Marshall

Milton, ON L9T

D-U-N-S 20-528-7720 (SL)
1031647 ONTARIO LTD
FOODMART
575 Ontario St S Unit 9, Milton, ON, L9T 2N2

Emp Here 100   *Sales* 29,347,700
SIC 5411 Grocery stores
Onkar Rai
Timothy Lee

D-U-N-S 20-640-1635 (SL)
1341805 ONTARIO INC
MILTON TOYOTA
1245 Steeles Ave E, Milton, ON, L9T 0K2
(905) 875-1700
Emp Here 45   *Sales* 22,413,510
SIC 5511 New and used car dealers
James Gorman
Christopher Gorman

D-U-N-S 24-360-0314 (SL)
2095008 ONTARIO INC
TEAM HONDA POWERHOUSE OF MILTON
170 Steeles Ave E, Milton, ON, L9T 2Y5
(905) 864-8588
Emp Here 35   *Sales* 17,432,730
SIC 5511 New and used car dealers
Brian Leggat
Kelly Jennings

D-U-N-S 25-110-1838 (BR)
3M CANADA COMPANY
(*Suby of* 3M COMPANY)
2751 Peddie Rd, Milton, ON, L9T 0K1
(905) 875-2568
Emp Here 100
SIC 4225 General warehousing and storage
Janette Batten

D-U-N-S 24-924-5705 (HQ)
673753 ONTARIO LIMITED
TRAFFIX
375 Wheelabrator Way Suite 1, Milton, ON, L9T 3C1
(905) 875-0708
Emp Here 100   *Sales* 242,592,640
SIC 4731 Freight transportation arrangement
Chuck Snow
Ann Mary Snow
Daniel Snow
Mark Southey

D-U-N-S 20-605-4132 (HQ)
ACTIVE TRANSPORT INC
245 Bronte St N, Milton, ON, L9T 3N7
(905) 878-8167
Emp Here 1   *Sales* 24,684,720
SIC 4212 Local trucking, without storage
Bradley Grant

D-U-N-S 24-875-5126 (HQ)
AFIMAC CANADA INC
8160 Parkhill Dr, Milton, ON, L9T 5V7
(905) 693-0746
Emp Here 26   *Sales* 76,270,250
SIC 7381 Detective and armored car services
Peter Martin
Darrell Parsons
Desmond Taljaard
Jim Rovers
Stephen Anderson
Rob Shuster

D-U-N-S 24-703-3830 (HQ)
ALTEC INDUSTRIES LTD
(*Suby of* ALTEC, INC.)
831 Nipissing Rd, Milton, ON, L9T 4Z4
(905) 875-2000
Emp Here 25   *Sales* 23,276,274
SIC 5084 Industrial machinery and equipment
Lee J Styslinger Jr
Jeff Benda
Judy Kehoe

J Donald Williams

D-U-N-S 24-736-3674   (SL)
BLUE LINE DISTRIBUTION LIMITED
8175 Lawson Rd, Milton, ON, L9T 5E5
(905) 875-4630
Emp Here 134   *Sales* 27,564,604
SIC 4213 Trucking, except local
Tom Della Maestra
Julia Della Maestra

D-U-N-S 24-473-6869   (SL)
BRUKER LTD
(*Suby of* BRUKER CORPORATION)
2800 Highpoint Dr, Milton, ON, L9T 6P4
(905) 876-4641
Emp Here 29   *Sales* 12,968,046
SIC 5049 Professional equipment, nec
Henry Stronks
Werner Maas
Robert D Lessman

D-U-N-S 20-042-3788   (HQ)
CANADIAN BUSINESS MACHINES LIMITED
CBM METAL
8750 Holgate Cres, Milton, ON, L9T 0K3
(905) 878-0648
Sales 22,089,775
SIC 3499 Fabricated Metal products, nec
John Williams

D-U-N-S 20-403-8616   (SL)
CHUDLEIGH'S APPLE FARM LTD
624 Mcgeachie Dr, Milton, ON, L9T 3Y5
(905) 878-2725
Emp Here 80   *Sales* 20,984,720
SIC 0175 Deciduous tree fruits
Thomas Chudleigh
Carol Chudleigh

D-U-N-S 25-801-4752   (HQ)
CHUDLEIGH'S LTD
8501 Chudleigh Way, Milton, ON, L9T 0L9
(905) 878-8781
Sales 35,217,240
SIC 5461 Retail bakeries
Dean Chudleigh
Scott Chudleigh

D-U-N-S 24-194-1900   (BR)
COMMUNITY LIVING NORTH HALTON
(*Suby of* COMMUNITY LIVING NORTH HALTON)
500 Valleyview Cres, Milton, ON, L9T 3L2
(905) 693-0528
Emp Here 130
SIC 8322 Individual and family services
Nancy Macniel

D-U-N-S 25-802-2466   (HQ)
COMMUNITY LIVING NORTH HALTON
HORIZON PACKAGING MILTON
917 Nipissing Rd, Milton, ON, L9T 5E3
(905) 878-2337
Emp Here 20   *Sales* 13,438,600
SIC 8322 Individual and family services
Greg Edmiston
Joel Jamieson

D-U-N-S 24-875-0432   (SL)
CONNECT CONVEYOR BELTING INC
405 Industrial Dr Unit 128, Milton, ON, L9T 5B1
(905) 878-5552
Emp Here 25   *Sales* 11,875,650
SIC 5085 Industrial supplies
Yasi Ish

D-U-N-S 20-735-4424   (BR)
CONTRANS GROUP INC
PETER HODGE TRANSPORT LIMITED
100 Market Dr, Milton, ON, L9T 3H5
(905) 693-8088
Emp Here 150   *Sales* 426,784
SIC 4449 Water transportation of freight
Dave Peddie

D-U-N-S 20-554-8571   (BR)
CRH CANADA GROUP INC
DUFFERIN AGGREGATES, DIV. OF
(*Suby of* CRH PUBLIC LIMITED COMPANY)
9410 Dublin Line, Milton, ON, L9T 2X7
(905) 878-6051
Emp Here 100
SIC 1481 NonMetallic mineral services
Mark Graves

D-U-N-S 24-160-6701   (SL)
CROATION CLUB KARLOVAC
1880 Thompson Rd S, Milton, ON, L9T 2X5
(905) 878-6185
Emp Here 200   *Sales* 63,464,542
SIC 8651 Political organizations
Branko Mikan

D-U-N-S 25-341-4478   (HQ)
CWB GROUP - INDUSTRY SERVICES CORP
QUASAR, DIV OF
8260 Parkhill Dr, Milton, ON, L9T 5V7
(905) 542-1312
Emp Here 50   *Sales* 33,946,095
SIC 8621 Professional organizations
Douglas Luciani

D-U-N-S 25-193-1130   (SL)
CWSDS PASSPORT
917 Nipissing Rd Unit 1a, Milton, ON, L9T 5E3
(905) 693-8885
Emp Here 13   *Sales* 13,453,453
SIC 6371 Pension, health, and welfare funds
Maureen Robinson

D-U-N-S 25-253-2817   (BR)
DARE FOODS LIMITED
(*Suby of* DARE FOODS LIMITED)
725 Steeles Ave E, Milton, ON, L9T 5H1
(905) 875-1223
Emp Here 80
SIC 2064 Candy and other confectionery products
Lynne Hill

D-U-N-S 24-354-6038   (HQ)
EAGLEBURGMANN CANADA INC
NOVA MAGNETICS
(*Suby of* FREUDENBERG & CO. KG)
8699 Escarpment Way Suite 9, Milton, ON, L9T 0J5
(905) 693-8782
Emp Here 20   *Sales* 14,250,780
SIC 5085 Industrial supplies
Al Marques
Sebastian Weiss

D-U-N-S 20-231-4139   (BR)
EATON INDUSTRIES (CANADA) COMPANY
EATON ELECTRICAL
(*Suby of* EATON CORPORATION PUBLIC LIMITED COMPANY)
610 Industrial Dr, Milton, ON, L9T 5C3
(905) 875-4379
Emp Here 160
SIC 3625 Relays and industrial controls
Mike Masur

D-U-N-S 20-639-3985   (HQ)
FASTENERS & FITTINGS INC
901 Steeles Ave E, Milton, ON, L9T 5H3
(905) 670-2503
Emp Here 70   *Sales* 38,002,080
SIC 5085 Industrial supplies
Ted Robinson

D-U-N-S 25-106-3368   (HQ)
FRASER DIRECT DISTRIBUTION SERVICES LTD
JAGUAR BOOK GROUP, DIV OF
8300 Lawson Rd, Milton, ON, L9T 0A4
(905) 877-4411
Emp Here 75   *Sales* 60,020,280
SIC 4731 Freight transportation arrangement
Lois Fraser
Al Fraser
Alex Fraser

Bruce White
Mary Duncan
Diane Grandy

D-U-N-S 20-389-1747   (SL)
FRESH START FOODS CANADA LTD
EATING NEW CREATIONS
(*Suby of* GORDON FOOD SERVICE, INC.)
2705 Durante Way, Milton, ON, L9T 5J1
(905) 878-9000
Emp Here 300   *Sales* 80,025,504
SIC 5148 Fresh fruits and vegetables
Richard Wolowski
Scott Lewis
Dean Noble
Jeffrey Maddox
Alisha Cieslak
Frank Geier
David Gray

D-U-N-S 20-130-6610   (SL)
GALLINGER MOTORS LIMITED
GALLINGER FORD LINCOLN
655 Main St E, Milton, ON, L9T 3J2
(905) 875-3673
Emp Here 35   *Sales* 17,432,730
SIC 5511 New and used car dealers
William Gallinger
Tom Gallinger

D-U-N-S 20-291-1681   (HQ)
GORDON FOOD SERVICE CANADA LTD
FRIGO NATIONAL
(*Suby of* GORDON FOOD SERVICE, INC.)
2999 James Snow Pky N, Milton, ON, L9T 5G4
(905) 864-3700
Emp Here 100   *Sales* 179,179,000
SIC 5141 Groceries, general line
Dean Noble
Frank Geier
Jeffrey Maddox

D-U-N-S 24-410-7264   (HQ)
GORRUD LIMITED
410 Steeles Ave E, Milton, ON, L9T 1Y4
(905) 875-2277
Sales 14,942,340
SIC 5521 Used car dealers
Phyllis Gorman
Andrew Gorman

D-U-N-S 20-216-4526   (SL)
GORRUD'S AUTO GROUP
GORRUD'S AUTO CENTRE
410 Steeles Ave E, Milton, ON, L9T 1Y4
(905) 875-2277
Emp Here 49   *Sales* 24,405,822
SIC 5521 Used car dealers
Andrew Gorman

D-U-N-S 24-228-4557   (SL)
GRANT, JAMIE & BARB SALES LTD
CANADIAN TIRE
1210 Steeles Ave E, Milton, ON, L9T 6R1
(905) 878-2349
Emp Here 105   *Sales* 66,074,400
SIC 5531 Auto and home supply stores
Douglas Grant
Barbara M Grant

D-U-N-S 24-757-3652   (HQ)
GROENEVELD LUBRICATION SOLUTIONS INC
(*Suby of* THE TIMKEN COMPANY)
8450 Lawson Rd Unit 5, Milton, ON, L9T 0J8
(905) 875-1017
Emp Here 20   *Sales* 12,309,300
SIC 1796 Installing building equipment
Tim Wynia
Graham Keltie
Johannes Van Boxtel
Henk Groeneveld

D-U-N-S 20-814-0264   (BR)
HALTON CATHOLIC DISTRICT SCHOOL BOARD
BISHOP P.F. REDING SECONDARY

(*Suby of* HALTON CATHOLIC DISTRICT SCHOOL BOARD)
1120 Main St E, Milton, ON, L9T 6H7
(905) 875-0124
Emp Here 125
SIC 8211 Elementary and secondary schools
Anthony Cordeiro

D-U-N-S 25-116-7623   (BR)
HALTON DISTRICT SCHOOL BOARD
CRAIG KIELBURGER SECONDARY SCHOOL
(*Suby of* HALTON DISTRICT SCHOOL BOARD)
1151 Ferguson Dr, Milton, ON, L9T 7V8
(905) 878-0575
Emp Here 124
SIC 8211 Elementary and secondary schools
Jacquie Pece

D-U-N-S 20-351-6976   (BR)
HALTON DISTRICT SCHOOL BOARD
TIGER JEET SINGH PUBLIC SCHOOL
(*Suby of* HALTON DISTRICT SCHOOL BOARD)
650 Yates Dr, Milton, ON, L9T 7P6
(905) 878-2255
Emp Here 104
SIC 8211 Elementary and secondary schools
Krista Benedetti

D-U-N-S 20-351-6901   (BR)
HALTON DISTRICT SCHOOL BOARD
ANNE J. MACARTHUR PS
(*Suby of* HALTON DISTRICT SCHOOL BOARD)
820 Farmstead Dr, Milton, ON, L9T 8J6
(905) 878-2076
Emp Here 84
SIC 8211 Elementary and secondary schools
Katherine Mcarthur

D-U-N-S 20-536-2853   (BR)
HALTON DISTRICT SCHOOL BOARD
MILTON DISTRICT HIGH SCHOOL
(*Suby of* HALTON DISTRICT SCHOOL BOARD)
396 Williams Ave, Milton, ON, L9T 2G4
(905) 878-2839
Emp Here 80
SIC 8211 Elementary and secondary schools
Rasa Baksys

D-U-N-S 25-816-5443   (BR)
HALTON DISTRICT SCHOOL BOARD
IRMA COULSON PUBLIC SCHOOL
(*Suby of* HALTON DISTRICT SCHOOL BOARD)
625 Sauve St, Milton, ON, L9T 8M4
(905) 693-0712
Emp Here 87
SIC 8211 Elementary and secondary schools
Brian Slemko

D-U-N-S 24-885-4598   (SL)
HALTON FORMING (1992) LTD
HALTON FORMING
593 Main St E, Milton, ON, L9T 3J2
(905) 693-4889
Emp Here 75   *Sales* 18,561,225
SIC 1771 Concrete work
Lou Rocca
Carlos Lourenco

D-U-N-S 25-092-5901   (HQ)
HELIGEAR CANADA ACQUISITION CORPORATION
NORTHSTAR AEROSPACE (MILTON)
(*Suby of* HELIGEAR ACQUISITION CO.)
180 Market Dr, Milton, ON, L9T 3H5
(905) 875-4000
Sales 44,768,600
SIC 3728 Aircraft parts and equipment, nec
David Mcconnaughey
Robert Burkhardt
David Anderson

D-U-N-S 24-101-5218   (BR)
HOME DEPOT OF CANADA INC
HOME DEPOT
(*Suby of* THE HOME DEPOT INC)
1013 Maple Ave, Milton, ON, L9T 0A5
(905) 864-1200
Emp Here 140
SIC 5251 Hardware stores
 Bonnie Boyce

D-U-N-S 24-911-9819   (SL)
HUNT CHRYSLER LTD
500 Bronte St S, Milton, ON, L9T 9H5
(905) 876-2580
Emp Here 25   *Sales* 12,451,950
SIC 5511 New and used car dealers
 Gary Hunt
 Claude Lockwood

D-U-N-S 20-973-7308   (SL)
HYDRO DISTRIBUTION INC
MILTON HYDRO
8069 Lawson Rd, Milton, ON, L9T 5C4
(905) 876-4611
Emp Here 30   *Sales* 15,589,650
SIC 4911 Electric services
 Frank Lasowski

D-U-N-S 25-883-6964   (HQ)
INSURANCE SEARCH BUREAU OF CANADA INC
ISB CANADA
8160 Parkhill Dr, Milton, ON, L9T 5V7
(905) 875-0556
Sales 16,961,200
SIC 6411 Insurance agents, brokers, and service
 Michael Thompson
 Maeve Davis
 Stephen Anderson
 Ron Hartman
 Charlie Charalambous
 Sarah Baldeo

D-U-N-S 24-150-6729   (BR)
JOHNSON CONTROLS NOVA SCOTIA U.L.C.
(*Suby of* JOHNSON CONTROLS INTERNATIONAL PUBLIC LIMITED COMPANY)
8205 Parkhill Dr, Milton, ON, L9T 5G8
(905) 875-2128
Emp Here 200
SIC 3822 Environmental controls
 Venkat Kumar

D-U-N-S 25-354-8978   (SL)
KETER CANADA INC
KIS
(*Suby of* KRONA ACQUISITION SARL)
205 Market Dr, Milton, ON, L9T 4Z7
(905) 864-6695
Emp Here 100   *Sales* 23,240,300
SIC 5712 Furniture stores
 Lucio Spadotto

D-U-N-S 24-132-0444   (HQ)
KINDERSTAR INC
KIDLOGIC
690 Auger Terr, Milton, ON, L9T 5M2
(905) 864-4420
Emp Here 1   *Sales* 27,335,000
SIC 6712 Bank holding companies
 Shahid Zahur

D-U-N-S 24-334-3365   (SL)
LIZZI, C. ENTERPRISES INC
LA ROSE ITALIAN BAKERY & DELICATESSEN
327 Bronte St S Unit 1, Milton, ON, L9T 4A4
(905) 875-0303
Emp Here 40   *Sales* 10,966,080
SIC 5411 Grocery stores
 Cosimo Lizzi

D-U-N-S 24-383-8971   (BR)
LOBLAWS INC
REAL CANADIAN SUPERSTORE

(*Suby of* LOBLAW COMPANIES LIMITED)
820 Main St E Suite 2810, Milton, ON, L9T 0J4
(905) 875-3600
Emp Here 150
SIC 5411 Grocery stores
 Richard Camera

D-U-N-S 20-113-2052   (SL)
LYNDEN CANADA CO
(*Suby of* LYNDEN INCORPORATED)
8300 Parkhill Dr Unit 3, Milton, ON, L9T 5V7
(905) 636-2970
Emp Here 35   *Sales* 18,198,845
SIC 4731 Freight transportation arrangement
 David A. Richardson

D-U-N-S 20-385-1175   (SL)
MANHAL AL HABBOBI CONSULTANTS
6541 Derry Rd, Milton, ON, L9T 7W1
(905) 491-6864
Emp Here 50   *Sales* 10,619,850
SIC 8748 Business consulting, nec
 Manhal Al-Habbobi
 Zaid Shakir
 Ali Al-Habbobi

D-U-N-S 20-876-7590   (BR)
MANHEIM AUTO AUCTIONS COMPANY
MANHEIM TORONTO
(*Suby of* COX ENTERPRISES, INC.)
8277 Lawson Rd, Milton, ON, L9T 5C7
(905) 275-3000
Emp Here 325
SIC 7389 Business services, nec
 Kenneth Morin

D-U-N-S 25-364-2995   (BR)
MATTAMY HOMES LIMITED
MATTAMY HAWTHORNE VILLAGE
(*Suby of* MATTAMY HOMES LIMITED)
1550 Derry Rd, Milton, ON, L9T 1A1
(905) 875-2692
Emp Here 100
SIC 5211 Lumber and other building materials
 Brent Carey

D-U-N-S 20-396-3975   (SL)
MCKESSON SPECIALIZED DISTRIBUTION INC
MCKESSON SPECIALIZED DISTRIBUTION
(*Suby of* MCKESSON CORPORATION)
8449 Lawson Rd Unit 102, Milton, ON, L9T 9L1
(905) 827-1300
Emp Here 54   *Sales* 11,053,450
SIC 5122 Drugs, proprietaries, and sundries
 Paula Keays
 Dimitris Polygenis
 Loris Zancan

D-U-N-S 20-558-5081   (HQ)
MEDLINE CANADA, CORPORATION
(*Suby of* MEDLINE INDUSTRIES, INC.)
8690 Escarpment Way Unit 3, Milton, ON, L9T 0M1
(905) 636-2100
Sales 336,895,110
SIC 5047 Medical and hospital equipment
 Charles N Mills
 Alex Liberman
 James Mills
 James Abrams

D-U-N-S 20-641-7586   (HQ)
MERCURY MARINE LIMITED
(*Suby of* BRUNSWICK CORPORATION)
8698 Escarpment Way, Milton, ON, L9T 0M1
(905) 567-6372
Emp Here 48   *Sales* 31,232,520
SIC 5091 Sporting and recreation goods
 Georges Jalbert
 Marsha T Vaughn
 Jim Ennis
 Judy Zelisko

D-U-N-S 20-130-7527   (SL)
MILTON CHRYSLER DODGE LIMITED
81 Ontario St N, Milton, ON, L9T 2T2

(905) 878-8877
Emp Here 30   *Sales* 14,942,340
SIC 5511 New and used car dealers
 Carl Boedecker

D-U-N-S 24-561-0712   (SL)
MILTON DISTRICT HOSPITAL AUXILIARY
MILTON DIST HOSPITAL GIFT SHOP
Gd Lcd Main, Milton, ON, L9T 2Y2
(905) 878-2383
Emp Here 200   *Sales* 41,413,600
SIC 8399 Social services, nec
 Carol Wilson

D-U-N-S 25-802-3803   (SL)
MILTON HARDWARE & BUILDING SUPPLIES LTD
MILTON HOME HARDWARE BUILDING CENTRE
385 Steeles Ave E, Milton, ON, L9T 3G6
(905) 878-9222
Emp Here 45   *Sales* 11,387,655
SIC 5251 Hardware stores
 Angelo Demedicis

D-U-N-S 24-873-5391   (SL)
MILTON HYDRO DISTRIBUTION INC
200 Chisholm Dr, Milton, ON, L9T 3G9
(905) 876-4611
Emp Here 32   *Sales* 20,051,648
SIC 4911 Electric services
 Mary-Jo Corkum

D-U-N-S 24-199-3278   (SL)
MTB TRUCK & BUS COLLISION INC
MTB TRANSIT SOLUTIONS
(*Suby of* 1057260 ONTARIO LTD)
8170 Lawson Rd, Milton, ON, L9T 5C4
(905) 876-0669
Emp Here 44   *Sales* 12,465,200
SIC 7538 General automotive repair shops
 Gara Hay
 Tom Glover
 Liam Finan
 Carlos Rapaso

D-U-N-S 24-885-4346   (SL)
NORTH AMERICAN TRANSIT SUPPLY CORPORATION
NATSCO
375 Bronte St N, Milton, ON, L9T 3N7
(905) 876-0255
Emp Here 40   *Sales* 19,001,040
SIC 5088 Transportation equipment and supplies
 David Roy
 Craig Parsley
 Mark Dubeau
 Todd Coulter
 Paul Mitchell

D-U-N-S 24-320-4821   (BR)
OLDCASTLE BUILDING PRODUCTS CANADA, INC
PERMACON GROUP
(*Suby of* CRH PUBLIC LIMITED COMPANY)
8375 No 5 Side Rd, Milton, ON, L9T 2X7
(905) 875-4215
Emp Here 100
SIC 5039 Construction materials, nec

D-U-N-S 24-846-5007   (HQ)
ONTARIO DOOR SALES LTD
ELTON MANUFACTURING
8400 Lawson Rd Unit 2, Milton, ON, L9T 0J8
(905) 876-1290
Sales 37,196,850
SIC 3089 Plastics products, nec
 Anthony Boer

D-U-N-S 25-981-9357   (SL)
ONTARIO NEW ENGLAND EXPRESS INC
ONE FOR FREIGHT
8450 Lawson Rd Unit 2, Milton, ON, L9T 0J8
(905) 876-3996
Emp Here 60   *Sales* 12,342,360
SIC 4213 Trucking, except local
 David Carruth

 Geoff Black
 Mark Carruth
 Rick Marshall

D-U-N-S 24-652-2569   (BR)
PARKER HANNIFIN CANADA
MOTION & CONTROL DIV
(*Suby of* PARKER-HANNIFIN CORPORATION)
160 Chisholm Dr Suite 1, Milton, ON, L9T 3G9
(905) 693-3000
Emp Here 180
SIC 3593 Fluid power cylinders and actuators
 Ron Dusseldorp

D-U-N-S 24-425-4439   (SL)
PHOENIX CONTACT LTD
(*Suby of* PHOENIX CONTACT GMBH & CO. KG)
8240 Parkhill Dr, Milton, ON, L9T 5V7
(905) 864-8700
Emp Here 48   *Sales* 17,886,960
SIC 5065 Electronic parts and equipment, nec
 Joe Pefetto
 Andreas Sobotta
 Klaus Eisert

D-U-N-S 24-277-4479   (BR)
RECOCHEM INC
CONSUMER DIVISION
(*Suby of* HIG CAPITAL MANAGEMENT, INC.)
8725 Holgate Cres, Milton, ON, L9T 5G7
(905) 878-5544
Emp Here 115
SIC 3221 Glass containers
 Fred Mauti

D-U-N-S 24-779-8994   (HQ)
ROXUL INC
ROCKWOOL
(*Suby of* ROCKWOOL INTERNATIONAL A/S)
8024 Esquesing Line, Milton, ON, L9T 6W3
(905) 878-8474
Emp Here 500   *Sales* 204,552,000
SIC 3296 Mineral wool
 Jens Birgersson

D-U-N-S 24-122-2413   (HQ)
SARGENT FARMS LIMITED
SARGENT, T & R
189 Mill St, Milton, ON, L9T 1S3
(905) 878-4401
Emp Here 2   *Sales* 86,005,920
SIC 5144 Poultry and poultry products
 Thomas Sargent
 Robert Sargent

D-U-N-S 25-895-6044   (SL)
SELTECH ELECTRONICS INC
342 Bronte St S Unit 5-6, Milton, ON, L9T 5B7
(905) 875-2985
Emp Here 25   *Sales* 11,179,350
SIC 5065 Electronic parts and equipment, nec
 Ron Armstrong
 Simon Dearden

D-U-N-S 20-112-6997   (HQ)
STORAGE & TRANSFER TECHNOLOGIES, INC
STT STANCO
8485 Parkhill Dr, Milton, ON, L9T 5E9
(905) 693-9301
Emp Here 30   *Sales* 17,873,900
SIC 8711 Engineering services
 Kim Law
 Ali Abbas
 John Wilby

D-U-N-S 24-395-3887   (SL)
SUBIR BAINS PHARMACY LTD
SHOPPERS DRUG MART 708
265 Main St E Unit 104, Milton, ON, L9T 1P1
(905) 878-4492
Emp Here 25   *Sales* 16,411,600
SIC 5961 Catalog and mail-order houses
 Don Bell

D-U-N-S 25-220-9002   (SL)

SYNERVEST HOLDINGS INC
490 Mcgeachie Dr, Milton, ON, L9T 3Y5

Emp Here 39   *Sales* 12,766,416
SIC 2851 Paints and allied products
Ross Mitchell

D-U-N-S 24-317-2962   (SL)
T & R SARGENT FARMS LIMITED
SARGENT FARMS
(*Suby of* SARGENT FARMS LIMITED)
189 Mill St, Milton, ON, L9T 1S3
(905) 878-4401
Emp Here 120   *Sales* 86,005,920
SIC 5144 Poultry and poultry products
Tom Sargent
Bob Sargent

D-U-N-S 25-132-6591   (SL)
TSYCCO LTD
PRO-CHECK HOME SERVICES
290 Bronte St S, Milton, ON, L9T 1Y8
(905) 625-1234
Emp Here 55   *Sales* 14,946,580
SIC 6531 Real estate agents and managers
Lyndsay Mclaughlin

D-U-N-S 25-419-3204   (SL)
TUNCER TRADE INC
PETRO CANADA
235 Steeles Ave E, Milton, ON, L9T 1Y2
(905) 878-5829
Emp Here 23   *Sales* 11,455,794
SIC 5541 Gasoline service stations
Falih Tuncer
Sirma Tuncer

D-U-N-S 24-250-1661   (HQ)
ULINE CANADA CORPORATION
ULINE SHIPPING SUPPLIES
(*Suby of* ULINE, INC.)
3333 James Snow Pky N, Milton, ON, L9T 8L1
(800) 295-5510
Sales 25,686,558
SIC 5113 Industrial and personal service paper
Karam Lal

D-U-N-S 24-121-5842   (BR)
WAL-MART CANADA CORP
(*Suby of* WALMART INC.)
1280 Steeles Ave E Suite 1000, Milton, ON, L9T 6R1
(905) 864-6027
Emp Here 150
SIC 5311 Department stores
Baria Raynd

D-U-N-S 20-155-2577   (SL)
WILCOX BODIES LIMITED
WILCOX GROUND SERVICES
550 Mcgeachie Dr, Milton, ON, L9T 3Y5
(905) 203-9995
Emp Here 60   *Sales* 13,430,580
SIC 3713 Truck and bus bodies
John Dick
David Dick
Helen Dick

Milverton, ON N0K

D-U-N-S 24-352-1304   (SL)
ADVANCED TOWER SERVICES (2007) LTD
54 Mill St W, Milverton, ON, N0K 1M0
(519) 595-3500
Emp Here 72   *Sales* 13,830,120
SIC 3441 Fabricated structural Metal
Vernon Goudy
Robert Morrison

D-U-N-S 20-043-7341   (HQ)
BOSHART INDUSTRIES INC
25 Whaley Ave, Milverton, ON, N0K 1M0
(519) 595-4444
Sales 53,124,586

SIC 5085 Industrial supplies
Gary Boshart
Julie Storey

D-U-N-S 20-821-5228   (SL)
KNOLLCREST LODGE
50 William St Suite 221, Milverton, ON, N0K 1M0
(519) 595-8121
Emp Here 80   *Sales* 5,206,000
SIC 8361 Residential care
Susan Rae

Minden, ON K0M

D-U-N-S 24-951-2963   (SL)
DOLLO BROS. FOOD MARKET LIMITED
DOLLO'S I G A
123 25 Hwy Suite 35, Minden, ON, K0M 2K0
(705) 286-1121
Emp Here 60   *Sales* 17,608,620
SIC 5411 Grocery stores
David Dollo
Diane Dollo

D-U-N-S 20-940-5976   (SL)
MINDEN HARDWARE LTD
MINDEN HOME HARDWARE & BUILDING SUPPLIES
16 Bobcaygion Rd, Minden, ON, K0M 2K0
(705) 286-1351
Emp Here 40   *Sales* 10,122,360
SIC 5251 Hardware stores
John Pentney Jr
Linda Pentney
Dave Pentney
Bonnie Pentney

Minett, ON P0B

D-U-N-S 24-802-6846   (BR)
LUXURY HOTELS INTERNATIONAL OF CANADA ULC
LUXURY HOTELS INTERNATIONAL OF CANADA, ULC
(*Suby of* MARRIOTT INTERNATIONAL, INC.)
1050 Paignton House Rd, Minett, ON, P0B 1G0
(705) 765-1900
Emp Here 200
SIC 7011 Hotels and motels
Tony Tamburro

Mississauga, ON L4T

D-U-N-S 25-155-8540   (HQ)
2116160 ONTARIO INC
PETRO-CANADA
7355 Goreway Dr, Mississauga, ON, L4T 2T8
(905) 405-0881
Emp Here 5   *Sales* 24,903,900
SIC 5541 Gasoline service stations
Selvadurai Thanarajah

D-U-N-S 20-706-4205   (HQ)
AGRICO CANADA LIMITED
AGRICO
(*Suby of* COOP FEDEREE, LA)
7420 Airport Rd Unit 202, Mississauga, ON, L4T 4E5
(905) 672-5700
Emp Here 22   *Sales* 34,171,222
SIC 5191 Farm supplies
Ghislain Gervais
Luc Forget
Jean-Francois Harel
Muriel Dubois
Gaetan Desroches

D-U-N-S 24-388-1984   (HQ)
ALL CANADA CRANE RENTAL CORP
(*Suby of* ALL ERECTION' & CRANE RENTAL CORP)
7215 Torbram Rd, Mississauga, ON, L4T 1G7
(905) 795-1090
Sales 17,221,860
SIC 7353 Heavy construction equipment rental
Mike Liptak
Larry Liptak

D-U-N-S 24-750-9008   (HQ)
ALPA LUMBER INC
7630 Airport Rd, Mississauga, ON, L4T 4G6
(905) 612-1222
Emp Here 14   *Sales* 797,479,200
SIC 5031 Lumber, plywood, and millwork
John Di Poce
George Frankford
Carmen Guglieti
Ricardo Guglieti

D-U-N-S 24-631-6772   (SL)
AVIALL (CANADA) LTD
(*Suby of* THE BOEING COMPANY)
7150 Torbram Rd Suite 15, Mississauga, ON, L4T 3Z8
(905) 676-1695
Emp Here 1   *Sales* 14,725,806
SIC 5088 Transportation equipment and supplies
Eric D. Strafel
Steve Dandridge

D-U-N-S 20-549-8012   (HQ)
BOLTS PLUS INCORPORATED
7100 Torbram Rd, Mississauga, ON, L4T 4B5
(905) 673-5554
Emp Here 6   *Sales* 13,415,220
SIC 5072 Hardware
Brian Wood

D-U-N-S 25-750-6253   (SL)
CANAMEX-CARBRA TRANSPORTATION SERVICES INC
7415 Torbram Rd, Mississauga, ON, L4T 1G8
(905) 458-5363
Emp Here 10   *Sales* 21,794,976
SIC 4213 Trucking, except local
Gurjit Hundal
Kaiz Thobani
Fraser Wray

D-U-N-S 25-105-1231   (HQ)
CASA BELLA WINDOWS INC
(*Suby of* ALPA LUMBER INC)
7630 Airport Rd, Mississauga, ON, L4T 4G6
(416) 650-1033
Sales 10,094,850
SIC 3089 Plastics products, nec
John Di Poce

D-U-N-S 24-816-8593   (SL)
CELTRADE CANADA INC
7566 Bath Rd, Mississauga, ON, L4T 1L2
(905) 678-1322
Emp Here 85   *Sales* 29,383,650
SIC 2035 Pickles, sauces, and salad dressings
David Christopher Bouchard
Ron Mcavan

D-U-N-S 25-419-1943   (HQ)
CHRISTIAN AND MISSIONARY ALLIANCE IN CANADA, THE
7560 Airport Rd Unit 1, Mississauga, ON, L4T 4H4
(416) 674-7878
Emp Here 40   *Sales* 11,407,500
SIC 8661 Religious organizations
David Hearn
Ken Pelissero

D-U-N-S 24-884-4818   (SL)
CONGLOM FUTURCHEM INC
CONGLOM

7385 Bren Rd Suite 3, Mississauga, ON, L4T 1H3

Emp Here 150   *Sales* 28,566,300
SIC 3648 Lighting equipment, nec
Amy Mccrea

D-U-N-S 24-096-3376   (SL)
CORA FRANCHISE GROUP INC, THE
2798 Thamesgate Dr Unit 1, Mississauga, ON, L4T 4E8
(905) 673-2672
Emp Here 70   *Sales* 48,776,700
SIC 6794 Patent owners and lessors
Nicholas Tsouflidis
David Polny

D-U-N-S 20-045-0583   (HQ)
DOWNSVIEW WOODWORKING LIMITED
DOWNSVIEW KITCHENS
2635 Rena Rd, Mississauga, ON, L4T 1G6
(905) 677-9354
Sales 61,245,800
SIC 2434 Wood kitchen cabinets
Michael D'uva

D-U-N-S 24-098-5098   (HQ)
E-CYCLE SOLUTIONS INC
ECYCLE SOLUTIONS
7510 Bren Rd, Mississauga, ON, L4T 4H1
(905) 671-2900
Emp Here 110   *Sales* 63,782,000
SIC 4953 Refuse systems
Sean Weir

D-U-N-S 25-815-9920   (SL)
FEDERAL SCREEN PRODUCTS INC
7524 Bath Rd, Mississauga, ON, L4T 1L2
(905) 677-4171
Emp Here 50   *Sales* 10,141,500
SIC 3496 Miscellaneous fabricated wire products
Vito Sabia
Doug James

D-U-N-S 24-317-9819   (SL)
FLEX-O-MARK INC
2633 Drew Rd, Mississauga, ON, L4T 1G1
(905) 678-7997
Emp Here 42   *Sales* 19,951,092
SIC 5084 Industrial machinery and equipment
Omesh Sharma

D-U-N-S 24-198-2701   (SL)
G.E. FORWARDERS LTD
G.E. LOGISTICS
2797 Thamesgate Dr, Mississauga, ON, L4T 1G5
(905) 676-9555
Emp Here 26   *Sales* 13,519,142
SIC 4731 Freight transportation arrangement
Sendy Leung
Linda Leung

D-U-N-S 20-895-2291   (SL)
HOPE AERO PROPELLER & COMPONENTS INC
(*Suby of* HOPE, H. HOLDINGS LTD)
7605 Bath Rd, Mississauga, ON, L4T 3T1
(905) 677-8747
Emp Here 30   *Sales* 14,250,780
SIC 5088 Transportation equipment and supplies
Terry Hope
Michael Hope
Cathy Dunn

D-U-N-S 24-333-5080   (SL)
IMPERIAL FLAVOURS INC
7550 Torbram Rd, Mississauga, ON, L4T 3L8
(905) 678-6680
Emp Here 54   *Sales* 18,667,260
SIC 2087 Flavoring extracts and syrups, nec
Val Miller

D-U-N-S 25-397-2442   (SL)
INTERNATIONAL TRANSACTION SYSTEMS (CANADA) LTD

ITS CANADA
7415 Torbram Rd, Mississauga, ON, L4T 1G8
(905) 677-2088
Emp Here 52   *Sales* 11,544,052
SIC 3578 Calculating and accounting equipment
Charles Ahern
Neil Baijnauth

D-U-N-S 25-121-0431   (SL)
JAS CANADA INC
7685 Bath Rd, Mississauga, ON, L4T 3T1
(905) 677-3497
Emp Here 60   *Sales* 31,198,020
SIC 4731 Freight transportation arrangement
John Garvey
David Waldock

D-U-N-S 25-901-8174   (BR)
LONGO BROTHERS FRUIT MARKETS INC
LONGO'S MALTON FRUIT MARKET
(*Suby of* LONGO BROTHERS FRUIT MARKETS INC)
7085 Goreway Dr, Mississauga, ON, L4T 3X6
(905) 677-3481
Emp Here 100
SIC 5411 Grocery stores
Rob Morgan

D-U-N-S 20-596-4463   (HQ)
MAGELLAN AEROSPACE CORPORATION
3160 Derry Rd E, Mississauga, ON, L4T 1A9
(905) 677-1889
Sales 732,897,383
SIC 6712 Bank holding companies
Phillip C. Underwood
N. Murray Edwards
Jim Powell
Mark Allcock
Don Boitson
Jo-Ann Ball
Karen Yoshiki-Gravelsins
Jason Addis
Haydn Martin
Larry G. Moeller

D-U-N-S 25-116-2418   (HQ)
MAGELLAN AEROSPACE LIMITED
HALEY INDUSTRIES DIV OF
(*Suby of* MAGELLAN AEROSPACE CORPORATION)
3160 Derry Rd E, Mississauga, ON, L4T 1A9
(905) 677-1889
Emp Here 25   *Sales* 290,850,000
SIC 3728 Aircraft parts and equipment, nec
Phillip Underwood
Don Boitson
Jo-Ann Ball
Larry Winegarden
Daniel Zanatta
Mark Allcock
Elena Milantoni
Jason Addis
Haydn Martin
James S. Butyniec

D-U-N-S 20-112-6203   (SL)
MAKSTEEL CORP
7615 Torbram Rd, Mississauga, ON, L4T 4A8
(905) 671-9000
Emp Here 150   *Sales* 33,300,150
SIC 3599 Industrial machinery, nec
Phillip Dobbs
Jeff Hanley
Mike Mckernan
Jerry Chopiany
Steve Rebello
Lucian Nicholas

D-U-N-S 20-917-9451   (SL)
MALTON NEIGHBOURHOOD SERVICES
3540 Morning Star Dr, Mississauga, ON, L4T 1Y2
(905) 677-6270
Emp Here 30   *Sales* 21,276,360
SIC 8699 Membership organizations, nec
Lucy Hutchinson

Aimee Gurcharn
Narda Blaauw
Vinay Nair
Jacquie Lewis
Rita Bonavota
Keshna Sood
Amir Akhtar
Bernadette Boddie
Jean Beckles

D-U-N-S 20-170-2206   (SL)
MARX METALS LIMITED
CENTRAL MACHINERY & METALS
2520 Rena Rd, Mississauga, ON, L4T 3C9

Emp Here 23   *Sales* 11,972,466
SIC 5093 Scrap and waste materials
David Marx
Robert Rakovsky
Martha James

D-U-N-S 25-310-9375   (BR)
MCDONALD'S RESTAURANTS OF CANADA LIMITED
MCDONALD'S 8108
(*Suby of* MCDONALD'S CORPORATION)
3510 Derry Rd E, Mississauga, ON, L4T 3V7
(905) 677-8711
Emp Here 100
SIC 5812 Eating places

D-U-N-S 20-391-5921   (BR)
METRO LOGISTIQUE INC
(*Suby of* GROUPE DE CHAINE D'APPROVISIONNEMENT METRO INC)
7380 Bren Rd Unit 2, Mississauga, ON, L4T 1H3
(905) 461-0006
Emp Here 80
SIC 4225 General warehousing and storage
Thomas Gewarges

D-U-N-S 24-745-5975   (SL)
NEWMAR WINDOW MANUFACTURING INC
(*Suby of* ALPA LUMBER INC)
7630 Airport Rd, Mississauga, ON, L4T 4G6
(905) 672-1233
Emp Here 175   *Sales* 27,800,150
SIC 3089 Plastics products, nec
John Di Poce
George Frankfort

D-U-N-S 25-263-7764   (BR)
PEEL DISTRICT SCHOOL BOARD
LINCOLN M. ALEXANDER SECONDARY SCHOOL
(*Suby of* PEEL DISTRICT SCHOOL BOARD)
3545 Morning Star Dr, Mississauga, ON, L4T 1Y3
(905) 676-1191
Emp Here 135
SIC 8211 Elementary and secondary schools
Peter Hill

D-U-N-S 24-076-1080   (SL)
PHARWAHA DRUGS LIMITED
SHOPPER'S DRUG MART
7205 Goreway Dr Suite B1, Mississauga, ON, L4T 2T9
(905) 677-7181
Emp Here 65   *Sales* 15,881,320
SIC 5912 Drug stores and proprietary stores
Narinder Pharwaha

D-U-N-S 20-123-4544   (SL)
POLARIS INTERNATIONAL CARRIERS INC
7099 Torbram Rd, Mississauga, ON, L4T 1G7
(905) 672-7952
Emp Here 125   *Sales* 83,361,500
SIC 4731 Freight transportation arrangement
Larry Cox

D-U-N-S 25-191-6284   (SL)
POLARIS TRANSPORT CARRIERS INC
POLARIS TRANSPORTATION GROUP
7099 Torbram Rd, Mississauga, ON, L4T 1G7
(905) 671-3100
Emp Here 120   *Sales* 80,027,040

SIC 4731 Freight transportation arrangement
Lawrence Cox
David Cox

D-U-N-S 20-528-0246   (SL)
PRO-X EXHIBIT INC
7621 Bath Rd, Mississauga, ON, L4T 3T1
(905) 696-0993
Emp Here 65   *Sales* 29,199,235
SIC 7389 Business services, nec
Claude Gautier

D-U-N-S 24-846-6401   (SL)
RANGER EXPRESS FORWARDING INC
RANGER GROUP OF COMPANIES
(*Suby of* RANGER HOUSE INC)
7685 Bath Rd, Mississauga, ON, L4T 3T1
(905) 672-3434
Emp Here 32   *Sales* 16,638,944
SIC 4731 Freight transportation arrangement
Dave Waldock
John Garvey

D-U-N-S 20-260-1860   (SL)
REAL ALLOY CANADA LTD
(*Suby of* REAL ALLOY HOLDING, LLC)
7496 Torbram Rd, Mississauga, ON, L4T 1G9
(905) 672-5569
Emp Here 85   *Sales* 15,417,980
SIC 3341 Secondary nonferrous Metals
Terrance J Hogan
Daniel F Rangal

D-U-N-S 24-720-9562   (HQ)
RUSH ELECTRONICS LTD
2738 Slough St, Mississauga, ON, L4T 1G3

Emp Here 23   *Sales* 13,415,220
SIC 5065 Electronic parts and equipment, nec
Linda Langille

D-U-N-S 20-392-5151   (HQ)
RUSH TRUCK CENTRES OF CANADA LIMITED
(*Suby of* RUSH ENTERPRISES, INC.)
7450 Torbram Rd, Mississauga, ON, L4T 1G9
(905) 671-7600
Emp Here 150   *Sales* 317,488,600
SIC 5511 New and used car dealers
Kevin Tallman
Roger Poirier

D-U-N-S 24-421-5211   (BR)
SOBEYS CAPITAL INCORPORATED
FRESHCO
(*Suby of* EMPIRE COMPANY LIMITED)
7205 Goreway Dr Unit1, Mississauga, ON, L4T 2T9
(905) 677-0239
Emp Here 80
SIC 5411 Grocery stores
Dave Goodwin

D-U-N-S 20-746-4074   (SL)
TALLMAN TRUCK CENTRE LIMITED
7450 Torbram Rd, Mississauga, ON, L4T 1G9
(905) 671-7600
Emp Here 550   *Sales* 463,408,800
SIC 5511 New and used car dealers
Kevin Tallman
Roger Poirier

D-U-N-S 20-955-5338   (HQ)
WESTON FOREST PRODUCTS INC
7600 Torbram Rd, Mississauga, ON, L4T 3L8
(905) 677-9364
Sales 44,717,400
SIC 5031 Lumber, plywood, and millwork
Rick Ekstein
Steve Rhone
Steve Ekstein
Brian Grossman

Mississauga, ON L4V

D-U-N-S 20-734-8780   (HQ)
105675 ONTARIO LIMITED
KASTNER METALS
6577 Northwest Dr, Mississauga, ON, L4V 1L1
(905) 293-9900
Emp Here 45   *Sales* 10,564,675
SIC 3471 Plating and polishing
Jason Isakis

D-U-N-S 20-380-6356   (HQ)
10647802 CANADA LIMITED
DEXTERRA
5915 Airport Rd Suite 425, Mississauga, ON, L4V 1T1
(416) 483-5152
Emp Here 10   *Sales* 13,716,600
SIC 8741 Management services
John Maccuish
Ajit Isaac
Simon Landy
Stephen Wallace
David Johnston
Paul Rivett

D-U-N-S 20-809-8462   (SL)
1453633 ONTARIO INC
MOTOR VEHICLE PERSONNEL (MVP)
6205 Airport Rd Suite 500, Mississauga, ON, L4V 1E1
(416) 622-4766
Emp Here 150   *Sales* 11,204,100
SIC 7363 Help supply services
Henry Kort

D-U-N-S 24-814-1681   (HQ)
2941881 CANADA INC
6415 Northwest Dr Unit 11, Mississauga, ON, L4V 1X1
(905) 612-1170
Emp Here 50   *Sales* 22,728,900
SIC 3841 Surgical and medical instruments
Michael Frazzette
Peter Bulla
Ian Mclean
Christine Horsman
Craig Middleton
Wilfred Woesthuis
Simona Esposito
Chris Driver
Holger Furstenberg
Kelley Martin

D-U-N-S 25-170-4771   (BR)
4513380 CANADA INC
LIVINGSTON INTERNATIONAL
(*Suby of* 4513380 CANADA INC)
6725 Airport Rd Suite 400, Mississauga, ON, L4V 1V2
(905) 676-3700
Emp Here 400
SIC 4731 Freight transportation arrangement
Orie Marshall

D-U-N-S 20-317-0493   (BR)
4513380 CANADA INC
LIVINGSTON INTERNATIONAL
(*Suby of* 4513380 CANADA INC)
6725 Airport Rd Unit 500, Mississauga, ON, L4V 1V2
(905) 676-3700
Emp Here 400
SIC 4731 Freight transportation arrangement
Tod Walton

D-U-N-S 24-320-4878   (SL)
6257 AIRPORT TORONTO HOSPITALITY INC
FOUR POINTS TORONTO AIRPORT
6257 Airport Rd, Mississauga, ON, L4V 1E4
(905) 678-1400
Emp Here 115   *Sales* 10,968,678
SIC 7011 Hotels and motels
Steve Gupta
Rashmi Gupta

D-U-N-S 24-783-9681   (SL)
722140 ONTARIO LIMITED

3160 Caravelle Dr, Mississauga, ON, L4V 1K9

Emp Here 100   *Sales* 26,155,300
SIC 6712 Bank holding companies
 Ralph Cator

D-U-N-S 25-252-8864   (HQ)
979861 ONTARIO INC
TOTAL EXPRESS, THE
3220 Caravelle Dr, Mississauga, ON, L4V 1K9
(905) 362-8877
Emp Here 30   *Sales* 25,998,350
SIC 4731 Freight transportation arrangement
 Chang Choi
 Hye Sun Choi

D-U-N-S 24-751-8780   (BR)
ABC TECHNOLOGIES INC
ABC PLASTIC MOULDING
(*Suby of* CERBERUS CAPITAL MANAGE-
MENT, L.P.)
3325 Orlando Dr, Mississauga, ON, L4V 1C5
(905) 671-0310
Emp Here 125
SIC 3089 Plastics products, nec

D-U-N-S 24-966-3139   (HQ)
ABCO INTERNATIONAL FREIGHT INC
ABCO
(*Suby of* NOMA BROKERAGE LIMITED)
5945 Airport Rd Suite 338, Mississauga, ON,
L4V 1R9
(905) 405-8088
Emp Here 25   *Sales* 20,798,680
SIC 4731 Freight transportation arrangement
 Donald Lucky
 Dominic Chan
 John Iacuone

D-U-N-S 24-991-8921   (SL)
ABF CUSTOM MFG. LTD
6750 Professional Crt, Mississauga, ON, L4V
1X6
(905) 612-0743
Emp Here 50   *Sales* 10,141,500
SIC 3469 Metal stampings, nec
 Abdul Samad Panchbhaya

D-U-N-S 24-632-2440   (SL)
ADVANCE AUTOMOTIVE INDUSTRIES INC
6520 Viscount Rd, Mississauga, ON, L4V 1H3
(905) 677-0912
Emp Here 50   *Sales* 24,903,900
SIC 5511 New and used car dealers
 John Burness

D-U-N-S 24-684-4633   (HQ)
ADVANTEX EXPRESS INC
6725 Airport Rd Suite 101, Mississauga, ON,
L4V 1V2
(905) 677-0340
Emp Here 35   *Sales* 23,918,482
SIC 4731 Freight transportation arrangement
 Gregory Richard
 Jan Nyberg
 John Vella
 Andre Leclerc

D-U-N-S 25-418-9368   (HQ)
AIR CANADA PILOTS ASSOCIATION
6299 Airport Rd Suite 205, Mississauga, ON,
L4V 1N3
(905) 678-9008
Emp Here 1   *Sales* 10,561,266
SIC 8631 Labor organizations
 Andy Wilson

D-U-N-S 20-329-7643   (SL)
AIRLINE EXPRESS SERVICES INC
CORE LOGISTICS
3133 Orlando Dr, Mississauga, ON, L4V 1C5
(905) 670-2000
Emp Here 50   *Sales* 19,268,000
SIC 4731 Freight transportation arrangement
 Brian Gomes

D-U-N-S 20-641-0636   (SL)
ALPA STAIRS & RAILINGS INC.

(*Suby of* ALPA LUMBER INC)
3770 Nashua Dr Unit 3, Mississauga, ON, L4V
1M5
(905) 694-9556
Emp Here 80   *Sales* 15,389,600
SIC 2431 Millwork
 John Dipoce
 Frank Giordano

D-U-N-S 20-548-2339   (SL)
AMI AIR MANAGEMENT INC
AMI
3223 Orlando Dr, Mississauga, ON, L4V 1C5
(905) 694-9676
Emp Here 52   *Sales* 11,819,028
SIC 3822 Environmental controls
 Abdul Panchbhaya
 Meena Hans

D-U-N-S 24-653-0141   (HQ)
**ATLAS INTERNATIONAL FREIGHT FOR-
WARDING INC**
ATLAS CARGO
6365 Northwest Dr Suite 18, Mississauga,
ON, L4V 1J8
(905) 673-5000
Sales 16,638,944
SIC 4731 Freight transportation arrangement
 Ken Singh
 Jessie Singh

D-U-N-S 24-324-3768   (SL)
BAUER PARTNERSHIP
6490 Viscount Rd, Mississauga, ON, L4V 1H3

Emp Here 100   *Sales* 26,155,300
SIC 6712 Bank holding companies
 Michael Bauer

D-U-N-S 20-626-6991   (HQ)
**BEACON INTERNATIONAL DESPATCH
LIMITED**
2-6300 Northwest Dr, Mississauga, ON, L4V
1J7
(416) 640-0434
Emp Here 9   *Sales* 15,599,010
SIC 4731 Freight transportation arrangement
 Rolf Von Fintel
 Norm Pride
 Renate Von Fintel

D-U-N-S 20-525-5052   (HQ)
BESTBUY DISTRIBUTORS LIMITED
3355 American Dr, Mississauga, ON, L4V 1Y7
(905) 673-0444
Emp Here 80   *Sales* 29,137,200
SIC 5013 Motor vehicle supplies and new
parts
 Douglas Squires
 Gary Thibault
 Robert Therrien

D-U-N-S 25-977-1855   (SL)
BLUEGENESIS.COM CORP
(*Suby of* DELUXE CORPORATION)
5915 Airport Rd Suite 800, Mississauga, ON,
L4V 1T1
(905) 673-3232
Emp Here 122
SIC 4813 Telephone communication, except
radio
 Bill Campbell
 Franc Nemanic
 John Nemanic
 Colin Campbell

D-U-N-S 24-310-6403   (SL)
BOTHWELL-ACCURATE CO. INC.
6675 Rexwood Rd, Mississauga, ON, L4V
1V1
(905) 673-0615
Emp Here 135   *Sales* 26,057,835
SIC 1761 Roofing, siding, and sheetMetal
work
 George Vassallo
 Brian Jamieson
 Mario Giraldi

 Rosemary Vassalo
 Manuel Figueiredo
 Lenny Baptista

D-U-N-S 20-114-3646   (HQ)
BSI GROUP CANADA INC
(*Suby of* BRITISH STANDARDS INSTITU-
TION)
6205b Airport Rd Suite 108, Mississauga, ON,
L4V 1E3
(416) 620-9991
Sales 13,716,600
SIC 8741 Management services
 Sarah Murphy
 Tim Adams
 Marc Rougeot
 Todd Vanderven

D-U-N-S 24-360-8015   (HQ)
CARDINAL COURIERS LTD
6600 Goreway Dr Unit D, Mississauga, ON,
L4V 1S6
(905) 507-4111
Emp Here 75   *Sales* 109,032,004
SIC 7389 Business services, nec
 Richard Cooper
 Gordon Cooper
 Marion Plante

D-U-N-S 20-347-2154   (BR)
CARDTRONICS CANADA HOLDINGS INC
DIRECTCASH PAYMENTS ULC
(*Suby of* CARDTRONICS PLC)
3269 American Dr Suite 1, Mississauga, ON,
L4V 1V4
(905) 678-7373
Emp Here 80
SIC 6099 Functions related to deposit banking
 Adel Elassal

D-U-N-S 20-295-7890   (BR)
CDW CANADA CORP
(*Suby of* CDW CORPORATION)
5925 Airport Rd Unit 800, Mississauga, ON,
L4V 1W1
(647) 259-1034
Emp Here 100
SIC 5045 Computers, peripherals, and soft-
ware
 Mike Carnovale

D-U-N-S 20-906-1667   (SL)
**CHALMERS SUSPENSION INTERNA-
TIONAL INC**
(*Suby of* K S T INDUSTRIES INC)
6400 Northam Dr, Mississauga, ON, L4V 1J1
(905) 362-6400
Emp Here 50   *Sales* 11,192,150
SIC 3715 Truck trailers
 Balwainder Takhar
 Joseph Jeyanayagan

D-U-N-S 20-547-2330   (HQ)
CNB COMPUTERS INC
6400 Northwest Dr, Mississauga, ON, L4V
1K1
(905) 501-0099
Emp Here 12   *Sales* 31,302,180
SIC 5045 Computers, peripherals, and soft-
ware
 Bony Singh
 Kelvin Castelino
 Manu Kohli

D-U-N-S 25-915-7246   (BR)
COLGATE-PALMOLIVE CANADA INC
(*Suby of* COLGATE-PALMOLIVE COMPANY)
6400 Northwest Dr, Mississauga, ON, L4V
1K1

Emp Here 100
SIC 2844 Toilet preparations
 Scott Jeffrey

D-U-N-S 20-357-6608   (BR)
**CONCENTRIX TECHNOLOGIES SERVICES
(CANADA) LIMITED**
(*Suby of* SYNNEX CORPORATION)

6725 Airport Rd 6th Fl, Mississauga, ON, L4V
1V2
(416) 380-3800
Emp Here 82
SIC 8721 Accounting, auditing, and bookkeeping
 Stephanie Glancy

D-U-N-S 20-256-2828   (SL)
CONCEPTWAVE SOFTWARE INC
(*Suby of* TELEFON AB LM ERICSSON)
5935 Airport Rd Suite 1105, Mississauga, ON,
L4V 1W5

Emp Here 214
SIC 7371 Custom computer programming ser-
vices
 Zarar Rana
 Chun Ling Woon

D-U-N-S 20-293-2554   (HQ)
**CONGO CORPORATE WOODS INCORPO-
RATED**
CCWI-CANADA
5935 Airport Rd, Mississauga, ON, L4V 1W5
(647) 388-6615
Emp Here 20   *Sales* 48,092,500
SIC 2499 Wood products, nec
 Guy Dihoulou
 Cordell Melin
 Shaka Patrong
 Edward Ndobuba

D-U-N-S 24-061-4193   (SL)
CORE LOGISTICS INTERNATIONAL INC
AES WAREHOUSE & DISTRIBUTION
3133 Orlando Dr, Mississauga, ON, L4V 1C5
(905) 670-2000
Emp Here 100   *Sales* 32,475,400
SIC 4581 Airports, flying fields, and services
 Brian Gomes

D-U-N-S 20-171-4821   (BR)
CORPORATION MCKESSON CANADA, LA
(*Suby of* MCKESSON FINANCIAL HOLD-
INGS II UNLIMITED COMPANY)
6355 Viscount Rd, Mississauga, ON, L4V
1W2
(905) 671-4586
Emp Here 200
SIC 5122 Drugs, proprietaries, and sundries
 Mike Pisani

D-U-N-S 25-641-5373   (BR)
CORPORATION SERVICES MONERIS
OPTIMAL SERVICE GROUP, THE
(*Suby of* MONERIS SOLUTIONS CORPORA-
TION)
3190 Orlando Dr, Mississauga, ON, L4V 1R5

Emp Here 110
SIC 7378 Computer maintenance and repair
 Dan Misieri

D-U-N-S 20-194-2422   (HQ)
COTT CORPORATION
COTT BEVERAGES CANADA
6525 Viscount Rd, Mississauga, ON, L4V 1H6
(905) 672-1900
Emp Here 2,446   *Sales* 2,269,700,000
SIC 2086 Bottled and canned soft drinks
 Jerry Fowden
 Marni Morgan Poe
 Jay Wells
 David T. Gibbons
 Stephen H. Halperin
 Betty Jane Hess
 Gregory Monahan
 Mario Pilozzi
 Andrew Prozes
 Graham Savage

D-U-N-S 25-120-5878   (SL)
CREE CANADA CORP
(*Suby of* CREE, INC.)
6889 Rexwood Rd Unit 3, Mississauga, ON,
L4V 1R2

(905) 671-1991
Emp Here 23   *Sales* 10,285,002
SIC 5063 Electrical apparatus and equipment
  Shirley A. Coyle

D-U-N-S 20-212-6616   (SL)
E M I MUSIC CANADA
3109 American Dr, Mississauga, ON, L4V 0A2

Emp Here 60   *Sales* 31,232,520
SIC 5099 Durable goods, nec
  Dean Cameron

D-U-N-S 24-385-2790   (SL)
ELS MARKETING LIMITED PARTNERSHIP
3133 Orlando Dr, Mississauga, ON, L4V 1C5
(905) 612-1259
Emp Here 70   *Sales* 18,688,460
SIC 4512 Air transportation, scheduled
  Manju Aneja

D-U-N-S 24-410-3490   (SL)
EXEL LOGISTICS CANADA INC
6700 Northwest Dr, Mississauga, ON, L4V
1L5

Emp Here 23   *Sales* 19,541,499
SIC 5141 Groceries, general line
  Paul Ragan

D-U-N-S 24-917-0218   (HQ)
FLYNN CANADA LTD
6435 Northwest Dr, Mississauga, ON, L4V
1K2
(905) 671-3971
Emp Here 20   *Sales* 579,063,000
SIC 1761 Roofing, siding, and sheetMetal
work
  Douglas Flynn
  Sharon Sovak
  John Mcmanus

D-U-N-S 24-560-7486   (SL)
FOUR STAR DAIRY LIMITED
3400 American Dr, Mississauga, ON, L4V 1C1
(905) 671-8100
Emp Here 40   *Sales* 15,420,760
SIC 0241 Dairy farms
  Peter Eftaxias
  John Tavaras

D-U-N-S 20-293-2745   (SL)
FRESHOUSE SALES LTD
6480 Viscount Rd Unit 2, Mississauga, ON,
L4V 1H3
(905) 671-0220
Emp Here 50   *Sales* 11,242,750
SIC 2011 Meat packing plants
  Adriano Belli

D-U-N-S 20-558-9989   (HQ)
G&K SERVICES CANADA INC
(*Suby of* CINTAS CORPORATION)
5935 Airport Rd, Mississauga, ON, L4V 1W5
(905) 677-6161
Emp Here 35   *Sales* 116,604,800
SIC 7213 Linen supply
  Douglas Milroy
  Kevin Fancey
  Jeffrey Cotter
  David Euson
  John Vegas

D-U-N-S 20-788-8236   (HQ)
G3 WORLDWIDE (CANADA) INC
SPRING GLOBAL MAIL
(*Suby of* POSTNL N.V.)
3198 Orlando Dr, Mississauga, ON, L4V 1R5
(905) 405-8900
Emp Here 40   *Sales* 10,586,200
SIC 7331 Direct mail advertising services
  Lou Lasorep

D-U-N-S 24-749-0795   (SL)
GATSBY VALET INC
6900 Airport Rd, Mississauga, ON, L4V 1E8
(416) 239-6998
Emp Here 300   *Sales* 26,908,800

SIC 7299 Miscellaneous personal service
  Daniel Grima
  Greg Rzeplinski

D-U-N-S 20-561-1903   (SL)
GENERAL MILLS RESTAURANTS INC
DARDEN RESTAURANTS INC , DIV OF
5915 Airport Rd Suite 910, Mississauga, ON,
L4V 1T1
(905) 673-7898
Emp Here 5   *Sales* 188,716,674
SIC 5812 Eating places

D-U-N-S 25-500-7312   (HQ)
GENERAL NUTRITION CENTRES COMPANY
GNC
(*Suby of* GNC HOLDINGS, INC.)
6299 Airport Rd Suite 300, Mississauga, ON,
L4V 1N3
(905) 612-1016
Emp Here 18   *Sales* 192,464,000
SIC 5499 Miscellaneous food stores
  John Castiglione

D-U-N-S 24-493-3438   (HQ)
GEODIS FF CANADA LTD
3061 Orlando Dr, Mississauga, ON, L4V 1R4
(905) 677-5266
Emp Here 42   *Sales* 39,518,580
SIC 4731 Freight transportation arrangement
  Christopher Johnston
  Brian Rusak
  Gillian M Lochhead
  John M Gallahan
  Gerhardus Bosua

D-U-N-S 24-075-2121   (SL)
GOULD FASTENERS
6209 Northwest Dr, Mississauga, ON, L4V
1P6
(905) 677-8253
Emp Here 25   *Sales* 11,875,650
SIC 5085 Industrial supplies
  Irwin Gould
  Judith Gould

D-U-N-S 20-273-3648   (SL)
GRASSHOPPER SOLAR CORPORATION
5935 Airport Rd Suite 210, Mississauga, ON,
L4V 1W5
(866) 310-1575
Emp Here 48   *Sales* 10,604,832
SIC 1711 Plumbing, heating, air-conditioning
  Azeem Qureshi

D-U-N-S 20-900-7251   (HQ)
HARTWICK O'SHEA & CARTWRIGHT LIMITED
HOC GLOBAL SOLUTIONS
3245 American Dr, Mississauga, ON, L4V 1B8
(905) 672-5100
Emp Here 40   *Sales* 56,685,820
SIC 4731 Freight transportation arrangement
  Stephen George Cartwright
  Kyle Hartwick

D-U-N-S 24-372-9931   (BR)
HILTON CANADA CO.
*HILTON TORONTO AIRPORT HOTEL &
SUITES*
(*Suby of* HILTON WORLDWIDE HOLDING
LLP)
5875 Airport Rd, Mississauga, ON, L4V 1N1
(905) 677-9900
Emp Here 220
SIC 7011 Hotels and motels
  Gordon Chow

D-U-N-S 24-679-5053   (SL)
JETRICH CANADA LIMITED
3270 Orlando Dr Suite A, Mississauga, ON,
L4V 1C6
(905) 673-3110
Emp Here 45   *Sales* 22,898,520
SIC 5023 Homefurnishings
  Malcolm Mcarthur

D-U-N-S 20-335-8069   (SL)
**KEYSTONE AUTOMOTIVE OPERATIONS
OF CANADA INC**
(*Suby of* LKQ CORPORATION)
3770 Nashua Dr Unit 4, Mississauga, ON, L4V
1M5
(905) 405-0999
Emp Here 80   *Sales* 36,892,320
SIC 5013 Motor vehicle supplies and new
parts
  Edward H Orzetti
  Ralph Ruzzi
  Don Grimes

D-U-N-S 24-684-5507   (HQ)
**KINTETSU WORLD EXPRESS (CANADA)
INC**
(*Suby of* KINTETSU WORLD EXPRESS,
INC.)
6405 Northam Dr, Mississauga, ON, L4V 1J2
(905) 677-8830
Emp Here 100   *Sales* 118,631,400
SIC 4731 Freight transportation arrangement
  Atoni Donato
  Desmond Gouveia

D-U-N-S 24-505-6924   (SL)
KRONES MACHINERY CO. LIMITED
(*Suby of* FAMILIE KRONSEDER KONSORTIUM GBR)
6285 Northam Dr Suite 108, Mississauga, ON,
L4V 1X5
(905) 364-4900
Emp Here 22   *Sales* 10,450,572
SIC 5084 Industrial machinery and equipment
  Sebastian Delgado-Schilz
  Christopher Larson

D-U-N-S 20-213-3559   (HQ)
LAFARGE CANADA INC
(*Suby of* LAFARGEHOLCIM LTD)
6509 Airport Rd, Mississauga, ON, L4V 1S7
(905) 738-7070
Emp Here 30   *Sales* 3,299,265,900
SIC 2891 Adhesives and sealants
  Rene Thibault
  Thomas Robert Cartmel
  Kenneth Cathcart
  Alain Thibault
  Stephen H Ker
  Yvon Brind'amour
  Robert Cooper
  Mark Anderson
  Alain Fredette

D-U-N-S 24-703-9548   (SL)
**LANGE TRANSPORTATION & STORAGE
LTD**
3965 Nashua Dr, Mississauga, ON, L4V 1P3
(905) 362-1290
Emp Here 40   *Sales* 17,968,760
SIC 7389 Business services, nec
  Eric Lange
  Robert George
  Mary Lange
  Dion Burt

D-U-N-S 24-953-8802   (HQ)
LASERNETWORKS INC
6300 Viscount Rd Unit 2, Mississauga, ON,
L4V 1H3
(800) 461-4879
Emp Here 70   *Sales* 37,505,640
SIC 3955 Carbon paper and inked ribbons
  Christopher Stoate

D-U-N-S 24-525-5042   (SL)
LEI TECHNOLOGY CANADA LTD
(*Suby of* LANNER ELECTRONICS INC.)
3160 Orlando Dr Unit A, Mississauga, ON,
L4V 1R5
(877) 813-2132
Emp Here 31   *Sales* 18,952,550
SIC 5045 Computers, peripherals, and software
  Geoffrey Egger
  Yi Wen Chou

Carol Li

D-U-N-S 24-488-4859   (SL)
LEXSUCO CORP
(*Suby of* PRODUITS POUR TOITURES
FRANSYL LTEE)
3275 Orlando Dr, Mississauga, ON, L4V 1C5
(905) 792-8800
Emp Here 40   *Sales* 10,706,080
SIC 5211 Lumber and other building materials
  Richard Smith

D-U-N-S 20-383-4643   (SL)
M CONSOLIDATION LINES LTD
M LINES
6300 Northwest Dr Unit 2, Mississauga, ON,
L4V 1J7
(905) 362-0249
Emp Here 40   *Sales* 20,798,680
SIC 4731 Freight transportation arrangement

D-U-N-S 24-411-5028   (SL)
MAILPORT COURIER (1986) INC
SUPERIOR DELIVERY
3405 American Dr Unit 1, Mississauga, ON,
L4V 1T6
(416) 679-1777
Emp Here 40   *Sales* 44,921,900
SIC 7389 Business services, nec
  Peter Stelcener
  Stuart Stern
  Eddy Cook

D-U-N-S 20-529-4911   (SL)
MARWICK MANUFACTURING INC
6325 Northwest Dr, Mississauga, ON, L4V
1P6
(905) 677-0677
Emp Here 90   *Sales* 14,762,430
SIC 2789 Bookbinding and related work
  Roland Leupolt

D-U-N-S 25-352-7857   (SL)
MEDISOLUTIONS INC
5935 Airport Rd Suite 500, Mississauga, ON,
L4V 1W5
(905) 673-7715
Emp Here 51   *Sales* 22,805,874
SIC 5045 Computers, peripherals, and software
  Andre Thompson
  Jacques Rancourt

D-U-N-S 20-550-6140   (SL)
MELMART DISTRIBUTORS INC
6100 Indian Line, Mississauga, ON, L4V 1G5
(905) 677-7600
Emp Here 70   *Sales* 35,619,920
SIC 5023 Homefurnishings
  Grant Heggie
  Dean Martin
  Howard Carr
  Bill Lorusso

D-U-N-S 24-362-9250   (SL)
MERGE HEALTHCARE CANADA CORP
MERGE HEALTHCARE
(*Suby of* INTERNATIONAL BUSINESS MACHINES CORPORATION)
6303 Airport Rd Suite 500, Mississauga, ON,
L4V 1R8
(905) 672-2100
Emp Here 250   *Sales* 46,143,250
SIC 7371 Custom computer programming services
  Anne Le Grand
  Alok Gupta
  Antonia Wells
  Todd Brill
  Steve Tolle
  Monica Chambers
  Nancy Stevens
  Mandy Long
  Jen Naylor

D-U-N-S 25-093-1917   (HQ)
MHI CANADA AEROSPACE INC
(*Suby of* MITSUBISHI HEAVY INDUSTRIES,

LTD.)
6390 Northwest Dr, Mississauga, ON, L4V
1S1
(905) 612-6781
Emp Here 10   *Sales* 87,255,000
SIC 3728 Aircraft parts and equipment, nec
Haruhiko Machiyama
Takashi Marukawa
Raymond C. Kong

D-U-N-S 20-166-8043   (BR)
MULTIPAK LTEE
6417 Viscount Rd, Mississauga, ON, L4V 1K8

Emp Here 100
SIC 2759 Commercial printing, nec
Robert Mclernon

D-U-N-S 24-726-6000   (SL)
NADEL ENTERPRISES INC
3320 Caroga Dr, Mississauga, ON, L4V 1L4
(416) 745-2622
Emp Here 25   *Sales* 13,013,550
SIC 5099 Durable goods, nec
Martin A Nadel

D-U-N-S 24-384-6805   (SL)
NPS ALLELIX CORP
NPS PHARMACEUTICALS
6850 Goreway Dr, Mississauga, ON, L4V 1V7
(905) 677-0831
Emp Here 60   *Sales* 14,659,680
SIC 5912 Drug stores and proprietary stores
Hunter Jackson
Francois Nader
David Clark

D-U-N-S 24-406-9001   (HQ)
NUANCE GROUP (CANADA) INC, THE
TAX AND DUTY FREE
(*Suby of* DUFRY AG)
5925 Airport Rd Suite 300, Mississauga, ON,
L4V 1W1
(905) 673-7299
Emp Here 460   *Sales* 76,054,000
SIC 5399 Miscellaneous general merchandise
Richard Rendek
John Menchella
Gary Cavanagh

D-U-N-S 20-390-0519   (SL)
OCEAN WAVE IMPORTS INC
6295 Northam Dr Unit 14, Mississauga, ON,
L4V 1W8
(905) 672-5050
Emp Here 30   *Sales* 20,904,300
SIC 6799 Investors, nec
Ashwin Lachman

D-U-N-S 20-529-5124   (HQ)
ORLANDO CORPORATION
(*Suby of* WESBAR HOLDINGS LIMITED)
6205 Airport Rd Suite 500, Mississauga, ON,
L4V 1E1
(905) 677-5480
Sales 20,622,904
SIC 6512 Nonresidential building operators
Carlo Fidani
Phil King
Blair Wolk
William O'rourke
Doug Kilner
Albert Page
Rudy Bloom
Larry Morasutti

D-U-N-S 20-182-3101   (SL)
PANTRY SHELF FOOD CORPORATION
3983 Nashua Dr Unit B, Mississauga, ON, L4V
1P3
(905) 677-7200
Emp Here 25   *Sales* 20,889,425
SIC 5141 Groceries, general line
Kanu Patel
Kantu Patel

D-U-N-S 20-170-8492   (SL)
PAPER FIBRES INC

6405 Northwest Dr, Mississauga, ON, L4V
1K2
(905) 672-7222
Emp Here 35   *Sales* 18,218,970
SIC 5093 Scrap and waste materials
Peter Benedetto
Peter Mateer
Bob Hayward

D-U-N-S 20-190-0631   (SL)
PD KANCO LP
5945 Airport Rd Suite 360, Mississauga, ON,
L4V 1R9
(416) 234-8444
Emp Here 130   *Sales* 17,842,291
SIC 6513 Apartment building operators
Daniel Drimmer
David Pullen

D-U-N-S 24-420-1104   (SL)
**PEARSON INTERNATIONAL FUEL FACILI-
TIES CORPORATION**
PIFFC
5915 Airport Rd Unit 110, Mississauga, ON,
L4V 1T1
(905) 677-1020
Emp Here 20   *Sales* 20,656,160
SIC 5172 Petroleum products, nec
James Fee

D-U-N-S 24-536-5783   (SL)
PIONEER STANDARD CANADA INC
3415 American Dr, Mississauga, ON, L4V 1T4

Emp Here 49   *Sales* 21,911,526
SIC 5065 Electronic parts and equipment, nec
Warren Saxe

D-U-N-S 24-254-6229   (HQ)
PLAYER ONE AMUSEMENT GROUP INC
6420 Viscount Rd, Mississauga, ON, L4V 1H3
(416) 251-2122
Emp Here 450   *Sales* 268,251,500
SIC 5087 Service establishment equipment
Joe Mccullagh
John Kolliniatis
Jon Brady
Jim Smiley
Tres Sprinkle
Joe Ingui
John Lemieux
Tommy Hayes
Blair Schopp
Alli Cambridge

D-U-N-S 20-966-0380   (HQ)
PNF HOLDINGS LIMITED
PARK 'N' FLY
5815 Airport Rd, Mississauga, ON, L4V 1C8
(905) 677-9143
Sales 25,497,000
SIC 7521 Automobile parking
Samuel Bresler
Ronald Bresler
Rita Bresler
Eric Bresler

D-U-N-S 20-417-5132   (SL)
**PROACTIVE SUPPLY CHAIN SOLUTIONS
INC**
3909 Nashua Drive Unit 4-9, Mississauga,
ON, L4V 1R3
(416) 798-3303
Emp Here 45   *Sales* 15,138,121
SIC 4731 Freight transportation arrangement
Salvatore Mancuso
Marcus Spilotro

D-U-N-S 20-344-3234   (SL)
PROFILE DRILLING INC
6525 Northam Dr, Mississauga, ON, L4V 1J2
(416) 650-6444
Emp Here 25   *Sales* 11,875,650
SIC 5084 Industrial machinery and equipment
Greg Douglas

D-U-N-S 20-014-4751   (SL)
QUEST WINDOW SYSTEMS INC

6811 Goreway Dr Unit 1, Mississauga, ON,
L4V 1L9
(905) 851-8588
Emp Here 50   *Sales* 10,141,500
SIC 3442 Metal doors, sash, and trim
Martin Cash
Jody Cash
Lev Bedoev

D-U-N-S 24-325-5317   (HQ)
RED APPLE STORES INC
BARGAIN SHOP, THE
(*Suby of* BLACKROCK CAPITAL INVEST-
MENT CORPORATION)
6877 Goreway Dr Suite 3, Mississauga, ON,
L4V 1L9
(905) 293-9700
Emp Here 100   *Sales* 212,951,200
SIC 5399 Miscellaneous general merchandise
Clinton Wolff
Hanspal Jando
Don Smith

D-U-N-S 20-376-9666   (HQ)
REFRESCO CANADA INC
(*Suby of* SUNSHINE EQUITY B.V.)
6525 Viscount Rd, Mississauga, ON, L4V 1H6
(905) 672-1900
Emp Here 50   *Sales* 34,569,000
SIC 2086 Bottled and canned soft drinks
Howard Drabinsky

D-U-N-S 20-819-4977   (HQ)
RUTHERFORD, WILLIAM L. LIMITED
*RUTHERFORD INTERNATIONAL FREIGHT
SERVICE*
3350 Airway Dr, Mississauga, ON, L4V 1T3
(905) 673-2222
Emp Here 30   *Sales* 125,375,696
SIC 4731 Freight transportation arrangement
Romas Krilavicius
Larry Wiseman
Gwen Krilavicius
Prans Krilavicius

D-U-N-S 20-413-2179   (HQ)
SCHENKER OF CANADA LIMITED
SCHENKER DISTRIBUTION
(*Suby of* BUNDESREPUBLIK DEUTSCH-
LAND)
5935 Airport Rd Suite 9, Mississauga, ON,
L4V 1W5
(905) 676-0676
Emp Here 120   *Sales* 474,525,600
SIC 4731 Freight transportation arrangement
Eric Dewey
Arnold Dasilva
Thomas Lieb
Heiner Murmann
James Pelliccio
Dennis Eittreim
Petra Kuester

D-U-N-S 24-121-7868   (HQ)
SECOND CUP LTD, THE
6303 Airport Rd Flr 2, Mississauga, ON, L4V
1R8
(905) 362-1827
Sales 19,493,835
SIC 5812 Eating places
Garry Macdonald
Ba Linh Le
Vanda Provato
Chris Sonnen
Ted Tai
Audra Wosik
Michael Bregman
Melinda Lee
Alton Mcewen
Alan Simpson

D-U-N-S 24-093-1407   (HQ)
SEDGWICK CMS CANADA INC
CLAIMS MANAGEMENT SERVICES
5915 Airport Rd Suite 200, Mississauga, ON,
L4V 1T1
(905) 671-7800
Emp Here 30   *Sales* 42,403,000

SIC 6411 Insurance agents, brokers, and ser-
vice
Michael Holden
Terry Dreamer
Laurie Walker

D-U-N-S 24-986-9918   (SL)
SIGMA CONVECTOR ENCLOSURE CORP
SIGMA
3325a Orlando Dr, Mississauga, ON, L4V 1C5
(905) 670-3200
Emp Here 60   *Sales* 13,320,060
SIC 3567 Industrial furnaces and ovens
David Herzstein
Anthony Gaspari

D-U-N-S 20-346-5687   (BR)
SOFINA FOODS INC
(*Suby of* SOFINA FOODS INC)
3340 Orlando Dr, Mississauga, ON, L4V 1C7
(905) 673-7145
Emp Here 100
SIC 2038 Frozen specialties, nec

D-U-N-S 24-925-5902   (SL)
STARR CULINARY DELIGHTS INC
3880 Nashua Dr, Mississauga, ON, L4V 1M5
(905) 612-1958
Emp Here 100   *Sales* 83,557,700
SIC 5149 Groceries and related products, nec
Kelly Perera

D-U-N-S 25-113-5026   (HQ)
STATE GROUP INC, THE
TCS
3206 Orlando Dr, Mississauga, ON, L4V 1R5
(905) 672-2772
Emp Here 500   *Sales* 251,632,922
SIC 1731 Electrical work
Marc Dumont
Gavin Trewern
Doug Brown
Tyler Smyrski
Bennet Grill
Michael Ranson

D-U-N-S 20-022-3709   (SL)
STERIPRO CANADA INC
6580 Northwest Dr Unit B, Mississauga, ON,
L4V 1L5
(905) 766-4051
Emp Here 120   *Sales* 22,380,720
SIC 8742 Management consulting services
Arun Jain
James Afara
Vikram Dhaddha
Anthony Lai
Ajay Jain

D-U-N-S 20-551-8322   (SL)
STRATACACHE CANADA INC
(*Suby of* STRATACACHE, INC.)
5925 Airport Rd Suite 200, Mississauga, ON,
L4V 1W1
(905) 405-6208
Emp Here 85   *Sales* 14,181,995
SIC 7372 Prepackaged software
Christopher Mellway

D-U-N-S 24-409-9925   (SL)
SUMMA ENGINEERING LIMITED
6423 Northam Dr, Mississauga, ON, L4V 1J2
(905) 678-3388
Emp Here 45   *Sales* 20,122,830
SIC 5065 Electronic parts and equipment, nec
Fernando Chua
Frank Cosentino

D-U-N-S 24-221-0805   (SL)
T.I.C.C. LIMITED
INTERNATIONAL CENTRE, THE
6900 Airport Rd Suite 120, Mississauga, ON,
L4V 1E8
(905) 677-6131
Emp Here 150   *Sales* 14,242,950
SIC 7999 Amusement and recreation, nec
Michael Prescott
Michael Rudberg

James Shenkman
Michael Shulman

D-U-N-S 20-609-9079   (HQ)
THOMPSON, AHERN & CO. LIMITED
THOMPSON AHERN INTERNATIONAL
6299 Airport Rd Suite 506, Mississauga, ON,
L4V 1N3
(905) 677-3471
Emp Here 38   *Sales* 25,998,350
SIC 4731 Freight transportation arrangement
Donald Butcher
John Decaria
Laurel Marshall

D-U-N-S 20-148-4193   (HQ)
TIMKEN CANADA LP
BEDFORD, DIV OF
(*Suby of* THE TIMKEN COMPANY)
5955 Airport Rd Suite 100, Mississauga, ON,
L4V 1R9
(905) 826-9520
Emp Here 350   *Sales* 148,864,810
SIC 3562 Ball and roller bearings
William Thompson

D-U-N-S 24-830-2093   (BR)
TOURAM LIMITED PARTNERSHIP
AIR CANADA VACATION
(*Suby of* TOURAM LIMITED PARTNERSHIP)
5925 Airport Rd Suite 700, Mississauga, ON,
L4V 1W1
(905) 615-8020
Emp Here 75
SIC 4724 Travel agencies
Zeina Gedoen

D-U-N-S 25-683-1728   (HQ)
**TRANSGLOBE PROPERTY MANAGEMENT
SERVICES LTD**
5935 Airport Rd Unit 600, Mississauga, ON,
L4V 1W5

Emp Here 250
SIC 6531 Real estate agents and managers
Kelly Hancyk
Daniel Drimmer
Michael Bolahood
Barry Kadoch

D-U-N-S 25-031-1347   (BR)
TRENTWAY-WAGAR INC
COACH CANADA
(*Suby of* COACH USA ADMINISTRATION,
INC.)
6020 Indian Line, Mississauga, ON, L4V 1G5
(905) 677-3841
Emp Here 200
SIC 4142 Bus charter service, except local
Valley Dan

D-U-N-S 25-282-1186   (HQ)
TRI-ED LTD
TRI-ED DISTRIBUTION
(*Suby of* ANIXTER INTERNATIONAL INC.)
3688 Nashua Dr Unit A-F, Mississauga, ON,
L4V 1M5
(905) 677-8664
Emp Here 50   *Sales* 87,037,050
SIC 5065 Electronic parts and equipment, nec
Steve Roth
Jason Roth

D-U-N-S 20-058-9856   (SL)
TRIPLE DELTA HOLDINGS INC
6205 Airport Rd Suite 500, Mississauga, ON,
L4V 1E1
(905) 677-5480
Emp Here 1,200   *Sales* 438,610,800
SIC 6712 Bank holding companies
Carlo Fidani

D-U-N-S 24-752-0455   (HQ)
**TRIUMPH EXPRESS SERVICE CANADA
INC**
3030 Orlando Dr Suite 509, Mississauga, ON,
L4V 1S8
(905) 673-9300
Emp Here 20   *Sales* 12,999,175

SIC 4731 Freight transportation arrangement
Harvey Rei
Edward Rei
Helen Rei

D-U-N-S 25-988-1472   (BR)
UNITED PARCEL SERVICE CANADA LTD
UPS
(*Suby of* UNITED PARCEL SERVICE, INC.)
3195 Airway Dr, Mississauga, ON, L4V 1C2
(800) 742-5877
Emp Here 100
SIC 7389 Business services, nec
Clayton Potts

D-U-N-S 25-311-9184   (BR)
UPS SCS INC
UPS SCS, INC.
(*Suby of* UNITED PARCEL SERVICE, INC.)
6655 Airport Rd, Mississauga, ON, L4V 1V8
(905) 677-6735
Emp Here 235
SIC 4731 Freight transportation arrangement
Paul Winters

D-U-N-S 20-933-8524   (SL)
USC CONSULTING GROUP (CANADA), LP
(*Suby of* USC CONSULTING GROUP, LP)
5925 Airport Rd Suite 730, Mississauga, ON,
L4V 1W1
(905) 673-2600
Emp Here 200   *Sales* 24,955,200
SIC 8741 Management services
Dave Shouldice

D-U-N-S 25-202-9806   (HQ)
VERSENT CORPORATION ULC
LASER QUEST
3415 American Dr, Mississauga, ON, L4V 1T4
(416) 613-4555
Emp Here 100   *Sales* 119,850,400
SIC 7929 Entertainers and entertainment
groups
Robert Johnston
Mike Lowry

D-U-N-S 25-360-3153   (HQ)
VIQ SOLUTIONS INC
5915 Airport Rd Suite 700, Mississauga, ON,
L4V 1T1
(905) 948-8266
Sales 11,462,804
SIC 3651 Household audio and video equip-
ment
Sebastien Pare
Larry D. Taylor
Harvey Gordon
Mike Kessel
Joseph Quarin
Malcolm Macallum
Gilles-Andre Morin
Alexie Edwards
Susan Sumner
Laura Haggard

D-U-N-S 20-770-7423   (HQ)
W.D. COLLEDGE COMPANY LIMITED
3220 Orlando Dr Unit 3, Mississauga, ON,
L4V 1R5
(905) 677-4428
Emp Here 16   *Sales* 12,073,698
SIC 5046 Commercial equipment, nec
Christopher Jeens
Neville Jeens
Robert (Bob) Morrison
Duane Gunn

D-U-N-S 25-351-8906   (SL)
WATERS LIMITED
(*Suby of* WATERS CORPORATION)
6427 Northam Dr, Mississauga, ON, L4V 1J2
(905) 678-2162
Emp Here 43   *Sales* 19,228,482
SIC 5049 Professional equipment, nec
Aaron Wolkoff

D-U-N-S 20-806-5946   (HQ)
WESTERN INVENTORY SERVICE LTD

WIS INTERNATIONAL
(*Suby of* ARES CAPITAL CORPORATION)
3770 Nashua Dr Suite 5, Mississauga, ON,
L4V 1M5
(905) 677-1947
Emp Here 50   *Sales* 762,702,500
SIC 7389 Business services, nec
Bret Bero
Thomas Compogiannis
Helen Yang
Brian Graff

D-U-N-S 20-129-3008   (HQ)
WESTROCK PACKAGING COMPANY
(*Suby of* WESTROCK COMPANY)
3270 American Dr, Mississauga, ON, L4V 1B5
(905) 677-3592
Emp Here 310   *Sales* 71,696,380
SIC 2752 Commercial printing, lithographic
Tony Sgro
Joe Gattafoni
Tom Englehart

D-U-N-S 20-515-9051   (BR)
WESTROCK PACKAGING COMPANY
(*Suby of* WESTROCK COMPANY)
3270 American Dr, Mississauga, ON, L4V 1B5
(416) 683-1270
Emp Here 150
SIC 2679 Converted paper products, nec
Robert Burton Sr

D-U-N-S 20-511-7539   (BR)
**WINNERS MERCHANTS INTERNATIONAL
L.P.**
WINNERS
(*Suby of* THE TJX COMPANIES INC)
3185 American Dr, Mississauga, ON, L4V 1B8
(905) 672-2228
Emp Here 800
SIC 5651 Family clothing stores
Greg Stalker

D-U-N-S 24-984-8458   (SL)
**WRIGHT INTERNATIONAL AIRCRAFT
MAINTENANCE SERVICES INC**
3182 Orlando Dr Suite 14, Mississauga, ON,
L4V 1R5
(905) 677-6393
Emp Here 40   *Sales* 12,990,160
SIC 4581 Airports, flying fields, and services
Mario Sturino

D-U-N-S 24-006-0806   (BR)
XEROX CANADA LTD
(*Suby of* XEROX CORPORATION)
6800 Northwest Dr, Mississauga, ON, L4V
1Z1
(905) 672-4700
Emp Here 150
SIC 5044 Office equipment
Mike Parkinson

D-U-N-S 24-986-5775   (BR)
XEROX CANADA LTD
(*Suby of* XEROX CORPORATION)
5925 Airport Rd, Mississauga, ON, L4V 1W1

Emp Here 120
SIC 5044 Office equipment
Leon Elliott

D-U-N-S 20-651-2472   (BR)
XEROX CANADA LTD
(*Suby of* XEROX CORPORATION)
6800 Northwest Dr, Mississauga, ON, L4V
1Z1
(905) 672-4709
Emp Here 100
SIC 5044 Office equipment

D-U-N-S 20-922-4554   (BR)
XEROX CANADA LTD
(*Suby of* XEROX CORPORATION)
3060 Caravelle Dr, Mississauga, ON, L4V 1L7
(905) 672-4700
Emp Here 106
SIC 7374 Data processing and preparation

D-U-N-S 25-144-9344   (SL)
YARDI SYSTEMS
(*Suby of* YARDI SYSTEMS, INC.)
5925 Airport Rd Suite 605, Mississauga, ON,
L4V 1W1
(905) 671-0315
Emp Here 200   *Sales* 33,369,400
SIC 7372 Prepackaged software
Anant Yardi
Peter Altobelli

Mississauga, ON L4W

D-U-N-S 25-991-7458   (HQ)
1348441 ONTARIO INC
*SOLUTIONS-YOUR ORGANIZED LIVING
STORE*
1775 Sismet Rd, Mississauga, ON, L4W 1P9
(905) 282-9371
Emp Here 30   *Sales* 66,675,750
SIC 5719 Miscellaneous homefurnishings
Gurmej Walia

D-U-N-S 20-191-1661   (SL)
1371500 ONTARIO INC
TIRE TERMINAL, THE
1770 Britannia Rd E, Mississauga, ON, L4W
1J3
(905) 565-8406
Emp Here 21   *Sales* 10,459,638
SIC 5531 Auto and home supply stores
David Blackwood

D-U-N-S 25-687-1906   (SL)
1389984 ONTARIO INC
41 DIXIE SUZUKI
5525 Ambler Dr, Mississauga, ON, L4W 3Z1
(905) 602-0884
Emp Here 22   *Sales* 10,957,716
SIC 5511 New and used car dealers
Rick Paletta

D-U-N-S 24-134-1473   (SL)
1426195 ONTARIO LIMITED
HINO TRUCK CENTRE
1257 Eglinton Ave E, Mississauga, ON, L4W
1K7
(905) 629-4044
Emp Here 55   *Sales* 34,610,400
SIC 5511 New and used car dealers
Andrea Napier

D-U-N-S 24-135-1340   (SL)
1437782 ONTARIO INC
CARLSON WAGONLIT TRAVEL
2810 Matheson Blvd E Suite 300, Mississauga, ON, L4W 4X7
(905) 694-2650
Emp Here 40   *Sales* 20,798,680
SIC 4724 Travel agencies
Bill Mclean

D-U-N-S 20-121-0031   (SL)
1459243 ONTARIO INC
FIRST LADY COIFFURES
2180 Matheson Blvd E Unit 1, Mississauga,
ON, L4W 5E1
(905) 206-5500
Emp Here 80   *Sales* 38,002,080
SIC 5087 Service establishment equipment
Leslie Martin

D-U-N-S 20-299-7164   (SL)
1478575 ONTARIO LIMITED
401 DIXIE KIA
5505 Ambler Dr, Mississauga, ON, L4W 3Z1
(905) 206-8886
Emp Here 30   *Sales* 14,942,340
SIC 5511 New and used car dealers
Michelle Ciampaglia

D-U-N-S 24-327-9069   (SL)
1503647 ONTARIO LIMITED
DBS
1173 Matheson Blvd E, Mississauga, ON,

L4W 1B6
(416) 255-7370
Emp Here 25   Sales 11,179,350
SIC 5075 Warm air heating and air conditioning
Paul Ruch

D-U-N-S 24-353-5163   (HQ)
2156775 ONTARIO INC
D'ANGELO BRANDS
4544 Eastgate Pky, Mississauga, ON, L4W 3W6
(905) 238-6300
Sales 34,569,000
SIC 2086 Bottled and canned soft drinks
Frank D'angelo

D-U-N-S 20-362-6143   (SL)
2224855 ONTARIO INC
5450 Explorer Dr Unit 300, Mississauga, ON, L4W 5M1
(416) 649-3939
Emp Here 900   Sales 328,958,100
SIC 6712 Bank holding companies
Frank Demarinis

D-U-N-S 24-522-5763   (SL)
2248085 ONTARIO INC
401 DIXIE VOLKSWAGEN
5500 Dixie Rd, Mississauga, ON, L4W 4N3
(905) 238-7188
Emp Here 46   Sales 22,911,588
SIC 5511 New and used car dealers
Kapil Dilawri

D-U-N-S 20-369-1969   (SL)
2350936 ONTARIO INC
SHAAN TRUCK LINES
1080 Fewster Dr Unit 10, Mississauga, ON, L4W 2T2
(905) 282-6000
Emp Here 70   Sales 10,373,440
SIC 4213 Trucking, except local
Raj Sidhu

D-U-N-S 20-388-7042   (SL)
2410147 ONTARIO INC
PFAFF BMW
4505 Dixie Rd, Mississauga, ON, L4W 5K3
(905) 625-7533
Emp Here 150   Sales 94,392,000
SIC 5511 New and used car dealers
Christopher Pfaff
Daniel Russman

D-U-N-S 24-688-2302   (BR)
3627730 CANADA INC
FREEMAN AUDIO VISUAL
(Suby of TFC NETHERLANDS COOPERATIEF U.A.)
2365 Matheson Blvd E, Mississauga, ON, L4W 5B3
(905) 366-9200
Emp Here 250
SIC 7359 Equipment rental and leasing, nec
Crick John

D-U-N-S 20-109-0227   (HQ)
3856011 CANADA INC
BLOOMSTAR BOUQUET
4800 Eastgate Pky Unit 4, Mississauga, ON, L4W 3W6
(905) 366-0800
Emp Here 15   Sales 40,838,600
SIC 5193 Flowers and florists supplies
Michael Mcadam
Tony Succar
Oscar Succar
Sam Succar

D-U-N-S 24-719-1265   (SL)
401 DIXIE NISSAN LTD
5500 Dixie Rd Unit B, Mississauga, ON, L4W 4N3
(905) 238-5500
Emp Here 65   Sales 40,903,200
SIC 5511 New and used car dealers
Sohail Iqbal

D-U-N-S 25-371-6559   (SL)
4247728 CANADA INC
DIXIE TOYOTA
1600 Toyo Circle, Mississauga, ON, L4W 0E7
(905) 238-6000
Emp Here 58   Sales 36,498,240
SIC 5511 New and used car dealers
Masayuki Mario Toyotoshi
Peter Virtue

D-U-N-S 24-738-3599   (SL)
4247744 CANADA INC
IDEAL HONDA
1700 Toyo Cir, Mississauga, ON, L4W 0E7
(905) 816-4200
Emp Here 75   Sales 47,196,000
SIC 5511 New and used car dealers
Mario Toyotoshi
Wayne Popert
Peter Virtue

D-U-N-S 25-148-1255   (SL)
4358376 CANADA INC
ITRAVEL 2000.COM
400-5450 Explorer Dr, Mississauga, ON, L4W 5N1
(905) 238-3399
Emp Here 180   Sales 120,040,560
SIC 4724 Travel agencies
Jonathan Carroll
Jeff Mackenzie
Jack Fraser
Chris Mottershead

D-U-N-S 25-353-3384   (HQ)
609574 ONTARIO LIMITED
2395 Skymark Ave, Mississauga, ON, L4W 4Y6
(905) 629-8999
Sales 21,868,000
SIC 6719 Holding companies, nec
Eric J Green
Constance Joan Green
Douglas E Green

D-U-N-S 20-337-8872   (SL)
7506406 CANADA INC
ORNGE ROTOR WING
(Suby of ORNGE)
5310 Explorer Dr, Mississauga, ON, L4W 5H8
(647) 428-2005
Emp Here 85
SIC 4522 Air transportation, nonscheduled
Andrew Mccallum
Rob Giguere
Dan Wright

D-U-N-S 25-996-7909   (HQ)
762695 ONTARIO LIMITED
2770 Matheson Blvd E, Mississauga, ON, L4W 4M5
(905) 238-3466
Emp Here 65   Sales 17,767,750
SIC 6712 Bank holding companies
Robert Gorrie

D-U-N-S 24-765-5590   (SL)
765620 ONTARIO INC
ONTARIO MAZDA
5500 Dixie Rd Unit F, Mississauga, ON, L4W 4N3
(905) 238-9888
Emp Here 35   Sales 17,432,730
SIC 5511 New and used car dealers
Swarna Dilawri

D-U-N-S 24-205-0792   (SL)
887804 ONTARIO INC
P.O.S CANADA
5580 Ambler Dr, Mississauga, ON, L4W 2K9
(905) 629-2990
Emp Here 95   Sales 42,481,530
SIC 5045 Computers, peripherals, and software
Bruce Hendersen
Phylis Hendersen

D-U-N-S 20-638-9538   (SL)

888930 ONTARIO INC
CITY WIDE CATERING
1290 Fewster Dr, Mississauga, ON, L4W 1A4
(905) 625-4447
Emp Here 32   Sales 21,006,848
SIC 5963 Direct selling establishments
Nick Basile
Jim Macri

D-U-N-S 24-526-0831   (HQ)
9517154 CANADA LTD
APPLE EXPRESS
5300 Satellite Dr, Mississauga, ON, L4W 5J2
(905) 602-1225
Sales 25,507,544
SIC 4226 Special warehousing and storage, nec
A-Nasir Syed

D-U-N-S 25-832-2486   (SL)
A.S. MAY POWELL CORPORATION
2475 Skymark Ave Unit 1, Mississauga, ON, L4W 4Y6
(905) 625-9306
Emp Here 25   Sales 20,889,425
SIC 5141 Groceries, general line
J David Cardy
Michael Marotta
Timothy Powell

D-U-N-S 24-285-6175   (SL)
ABLE INSURANCE BROKERS LTD
2560 Matheson Blvd E Suite 400, Mississauga, ON, L4W 4Y9
(905) 629-2253
Emp Here 65   Sales 55,123,900
SIC 6411 Insurance agents, brokers, and service
Rahul Chawla
Sukhwant Pandher

D-U-N-S 24-875-4699   (HQ)
ACCENTURE INC
5450 Explorer Dr Suite 400, Mississauga, ON, L4W 5N1
(416) 641-5000
Emp Here 500   Sales 586,447,200
SIC 8741 Management services
Julie Sweet

D-U-N-S 20-296-1983   (HQ)
ADT SECURITY SERVICES CANADA, INC
(Suby of ADT INC.)
2815 Matheson Blvd E, Mississauga, ON, L4W 5J8
(416) 218-1000
Sales 116,049,400
SIC 5063 Electrical apparatus and equipment
Jim Devries
Lee Jackson
Jeff Likosar

D-U-N-S 20-923-7015   (BR)
AECOM CANADA LTD
UMA ACOM
(Suby of AECOM)
5080 Commerce Blvd, Mississauga, ON, L4W 4P2
(905) 238-0007
Emp Here 150
SIC 8711 Engineering services
Tom Knight

D-U-N-S 20-697-1454   (SL)
AIRSTART INC
AIRSTART REGIONAL SPARES
2680 Skymark Ave Suite 901, Mississauga, ON, L4W 5L6
(905) 366-8730
Emp Here 25   Sales 11,875,650
SIC 5088 Transportation equipment and supplies
Robert Wills
Anne Vinet
Sam Cupelli

D-U-N-S 25-734-8185   (SL)
AJB SOFTWARE DESIGN INC

5255 Solar Dr, Mississauga, ON, L4W 5B8
(905) 282-1877
Emp Here 120   Sales 17,301,840
SIC 7371 Custom computer programming services
Naresh Bangia

D-U-N-S 20-022-5725   (SL)
AKUNA CANADA INC
5115 Satellite Dr, Mississauga, ON, L4W 5B6
(905) 290-0326
Emp Here 40   Sales 10,966,080
SIC 5499 Miscellaneous food stores
Zdenka Forst
Marston Gordon
Tomas Soural

D-U-N-S 24-141-4940   (HQ)
AKUNA INTERNATIONAL CORP
5115 Satellite Dr, Mississauga, ON, L4W 5B6
(905) 848-0428
Sales 22,106,900
SIC 5122 Drugs, proprietaries, and sundries
Zdenka Forst

D-U-N-S 25-359-3313   (HQ)
ALLSTREAM BUSINESS INC
(Suby of ZAYO GROUP HOLDINGS, INC.)
5160 Orbitor Dr, Mississauga, ON, L4W 5H2
(888) 288-2273
Emp Here 2,000   Sales 1,839,992,000
SIC 4899 Communication services, nec
Pierre Bluion
Kelvin Shepherd
Wayne Demkey

D-U-N-S 24-329-7640   (SL)
ALPHA COMMODITIES CORP
ALPHA FIELD PRODUCTS CO
5750 Timberlea Blvd Unit 17, Mississauga, ON, L4W 5N8
(416) 907-5505
Emp Here 5   Sales 14,792,900
SIC 5153 Grain and field beans
Radek Stasiewicz
Iwona Stasiewicz

D-U-N-S 24-208-4718   (HQ)
AMDOCS CANADIAN MANAGED SERVICES INC
(Suby of AMDOCS LIMITED)
1705 Tech Ave Unit 2, Mississauga, ON, L4W 0A2
(905) 614-4000
Emp Here 180   Sales 37,301,200
SIC 8742 Management consulting services
Paul Douglas Struthers
Ronen Jacob

D-U-N-S 20-158-9330   (HQ)
APPLIED ELECTRONICS LIMITED
1260 Kamato Rd, Mississauga, ON, L4W 1Y1
(905) 625-4321
Emp Here 52   Sales 70,225,300
SIC 5099 Durable goods, nec
Paul Stechly
Susan Stechly
John Stechly
John Leermakers
Mike Dalton
Dan Moulton

D-U-N-S 20-699-7319   (HQ)
AQUATERRA CORPORATION
CANADIAN SPRINGS
(Suby of COTT CORPORATION)
1200 Britannia Rd E, Mississauga, ON, L4W 4T5
(905) 795-6500
Emp Here 100   Sales 358,358,000
SIC 5149 Groceries and related products, nec
Shawn Trinier
Kevin Godwin
James Mcgill
Daniel Samuel
Storrs Mccall

D-U-N-S 25-145-4948   (HQ)
ARCADIS CANADA INC
(*Suby of* ARCADIS N.V.)
4005 Hickory Dr, Mississauga, ON, L4W 1L1
(905) 614-1978
Emp Here 275   *Sales* 44,188,103
SIC 8748 Business consulting, nec
Thomas J. Franz
John Vogan
Chris A. Ludwig
Scott Hackey
Cheryl Boswell
Jan Bouten
Joachim J. Ebert
Thomas T. Gnanayudam
Michael Paczkowski

D-U-N-S 20-115-7398   (HQ)
ARIANA HOLDINGS INC
D'ANGELO BRANDS
4544 Eastgate Pky, Mississauga, ON, L4W 3W6
(905) 238-6300
Emp Here 4   *Sales* 23,852,610
SIC 2033 Canned fruits and specialties
Frank D'angelo
Nino Stillatio

D-U-N-S 24-948-1326   (SL)
ASTRA DESIGN SYSTEMS INC
5155 Creekbank Rd, Mississauga, ON, L4W 1X2
(905) 282-9000
Emp Here 42   *Sales* 19,951,092
SIC 5084 Industrial machinery and equipment
Stesan Scheichl

D-U-N-S 25-319-8287   (BR)
ATLANTIC PACKAGING PRODUCTS LTD
(*Suby of* ATLANTIC PACKAGING PRODUCTS LTD)
5711 Atlantic Dr, Mississauga, ON, L4W 1H3
(800) 268-5620
Emp Here 100
SIC 2653 Corrugated and solid fiber boxes
Michael Barnett

D-U-N-S 25-253-8517   (SL)
AUTOTEK CAR SALES & SERVICE (1996) LTD
AUTOPRICE CANADA
1630 Matheson Blvd Suite 1, Mississauga, ON, L4W 1Y4
(905) 625-4100
Emp Here 25   *Sales* 12,451,950
SIC 5511 New and used car dealers
Ramzi Diab
Joseph Diab

D-U-N-S 25-372-0379   (SL)
AVANADE CANADA INC
(*Suby of* ACCENTURE PUBLIC LIMITED COMPANY)
5450 Explorer Dr Suite 400, Mississauga, ON, L4W 5N1
(416) 641-5111
Emp Here 140   *Sales* 20,185,480
SIC 7371 Custom computer programming services
Rick Birkenstock

D-U-N-S 25-889-2355   (SL)
AXIS DATABASE MARKETING GROUP INC
DMW & ASSOCIATES
1331 Crestlawn Dr Unit A, Mississauga, ON, L4W 2P9
(416) 503-3210
Emp Here 50   *Sales* 11,734,800
SIC 8732 Commercial nonphysical research
Michael Booth
Donna Booth

D-U-N-S 24-849-4440   (SL)
BASIC FUN, LTD
1200 Aerowood Dr Unit 27-28, Mississauga, ON, L4W 2S7
(905) 629-3836
Emp Here 52   *Sales* 49,188,559

SIC 3944 Games, toys, and children's vehicles
Brad Peterson
John Macdonald
Steve Beilman

D-U-N-S 20-145-6084   (HQ)
BAYER INC
BAYER HEALTHCARE, DIV OF
(*Suby of* BAYER AG)
2920 Matheson Blvd E Suite 1, Mississauga, ON, L4W 5R6
(416) 248-0771
Emp Here 550   *Sales* 536,667,300
SIC 5122 Drugs, proprietaries, and sundries
Christian Lauterbach
Shurjeel Choudhri
Michael Cels
Doug Grant
Gord Johnston

D-U-N-S 25-819-1097   (BR)
BAYLIS MEDICALE CIE INC
BAYLIS MEDICAL CANADA
(*Suby of* GESTION BMC-DORIAN INC)
2645 Matheson Blvd E, Mississauga, ON, L4W 5S4
(905) 602-4875
Emp Here 165
SIC 5047 Medical and hospital equipment
Krishan Shah

D-U-N-S 24-506-3961   (SL)
BELL CONFERENCING INC
(*Suby of* BCE INC)
5099 Creekbank Rd Suite B4, Mississauga, ON, L4W 5N2
(905) 602-3900
Emp Here 100   *Sales* 66,890,800
SIC 7389 Business services, nec
Franco Sciannamblo

D-U-N-S 24-375-2826   (BR)
BELL MOBILITE INC
(*Suby of* BCE INC)
5055 Satellite Dr Unit 1, Mississauga, ON, L4W 5K7

Emp Here 280
SIC 5731 Radio, television, and electronic stores

D-U-N-S 25-250-9484   (HQ)
BEVERTEC CST INC
5025 Orbitor Dr Bldg 6 Unit 400, Mississauga, ON, L4W 4Y5
(416) 695-7525
Sales 13,347,760
SIC 7379 Computer related services, nec
Barry Walsh

D-U-N-S 25-947-4344   (SL)
BI VIEW BUILDING SERVICES LTD
5004 Timberlea Blvd Unit 26-29, Mississauga, ON, L4W 5C5
(905) 712-1831
Emp Here 160   *Sales* 5,114,880
SIC 7349 Building maintenance services, nec
Jim Tran
Danny Tran

D-U-N-S 24-403-9892   (SL)
BIDCOR SALES AND MARKETING INC
2785 Skymark Ave Suite 14, Mississauga, ON, L4W 4Y3

Emp Here 40   *Sales* 33,423,080
SIC 5141 Groceries, general line
Rick Tetreault

D-U-N-S 20-007-3625   (HQ)
BIRD CONSTRUCTION COMPANY LIMITED
(*Suby of* BIRD CONSTRUCTION INC)
5700 Explorer Dr Suite 400, Mississauga, ON, L4W 0C6
(905) 602-4122
Emp Here 50   *Sales* 558,713,600
SIC 1542 Nonresidential construction, nec

D-U-N-S 24-329-4282   (HQ)
BIRD CONSTRUCTION INC
5700 Explorer Dr Suite 400, Mississauga, ON, L4W 0C6
(905) 602-4122
Emp Here 500   *Sales* 1,047,533,214
SIC 1542 Nonresidential construction, nec
Ian J Boyd
Gilles Royer
Richard Ellis-Smith
Paul Bergman
Mark Dreschel
Teri Mckibbon
Wayne Gingrich
Paul Charette
Richard Bird
Greg Doyle

D-U-N-S 20-585-7696   (BR)
BISON TRANSPORT INC
(*Suby of* JANPHER INVESTMENTS INC)
5850 Shawson Dr, Mississauga, ON, L4W 3W5
(905) 364-4401
Emp Here 250
SIC 4213 Trucking, except local
Mark Irwin

D-U-N-S 25-511-0181   (SL)
BORDER TRENDS INC
5496 Gorvan Dr, Mississauga, ON, L4W 3E8
(905) 238-1807
Emp Here 35   *Sales* 17,809,960
SIC 5023 Homefurnishings
Paul Ksiazek

D-U-N-S 20-160-5656   (HQ)
BREWERS RETAIL INC
BEER STORE, THE
5900 Explorer Dr, Mississauga, ON, L4W 5L2
(905) 361-1005
Emp Here 150   *Sales* 1,027,807,200
SIC 5921 Liquor stores
Ted Moroz

D-U-N-S 20-280-4712   (SL)
BROCCOLINI   CONSTRUCTION (TORONTO) INC
2680 Matheson Blvd E Suite 104, Mississauga, ON, L4W 0A5
(416) 242-7772
Emp Here 30   *Sales* 14,121,930
SIC 1542 Nonresidential construction, nec
John Broccolini
Paul Broccolini
Joseph Broccolini

D-U-N-S 20-160-7942   (SL)
BUCKLEY CARTAGE LIMITED
LOGISTIC FREIGHT MANAGEMENT
1905 Shawson Dr, Mississauga, ON, L4W 1T9
(905) 564-3211
Emp Here 300   *Sales* 61,711,800
SIC 4213 Trucking, except local
Bart Buckley

D-U-N-S 20-160-7967   (SL)
BUCKLEY, W. K. INVESTMENTS LIMITED
5230 Orbitor Dr, Mississauga, ON, L4W 5G7

Emp Here 30   *Sales* 12,580,650
SIC 6719 Holding companies, nec
Frank Buckley

D-U-N-S 24-385-5731   (HQ)
C. DECICCO AGENCIES INC
INTERCOSMETICS
1035 Stacey Crt, Mississauga, ON, L4W 2X7
(905) 238-1485
Emp Here 5   *Sales* 19,896,210
SIC 5122 Drugs, proprietaries, and sundries
Cristina Ramirez
Andrew Decicco
Eugenia Decicco

D-U-N-S 24-122-9889   (HQ)
C.B. POWELL LIMITED

POWELL-MAY INTERNATIONAL
2475 Skymark Ave Suite 1, Mississauga, ON, L4W 4Y6
(905) 206-7797
Emp Here 20   *Sales* 25,067,310
SIC 5141 Groceries, general line
Timothy Powell
Brian Powell
Ann Coulson

D-U-N-S 20-268-6924   (HQ)
CALEA LTD
CALEA HOMECARE, DIV OF
(*Suby of* FRESENIUS SE & CO. KGAA)
2785 Skymark Ave Unit 2, Mississauga, ON, L4W 4Y3
(905) 238-1234
Emp Here 150   *Sales* 103,205,250
SIC 5122 Drugs, proprietaries, and sundries
Matthew Rotenberg

D-U-N-S 24-323-6812   (SL)
CAMSO DISTRIBUTION CANADA INC
SOLIDEAL
(*Suby of* COMPAGNIE GENERALE DES ETABLISSEMENTS MICHELIN)
5485 Tomken Rd, Mississauga, ON, L4W 3Y3
(416) 674-5441
Emp Here 42   *Sales* 15,297,030
SIC 5014 Tires and tubes
Kent Carson
Ken W Paul
Normand Potvin

D-U-N-S 20-533-4886   (HQ)
CANLIGHT MANAGEMENT INC
5160 Explorer Dr Suite 17, Mississauga, ON, L4W 4T7
(905) 625-1522
Sales 13,077,650
SIC 6719 Holding companies, nec
Don Kason

D-U-N-S 20-529-0281   (HQ)
CARLSON WAGONLIT CANADA
CARLSON WAGONLIT TRAVEL
2425 Matheson Blvd E Suite 600, Mississauga, ON, L4W 5K4
(905) 740-3500
Emp Here 60   *Sales* 253,080,320
SIC 4724 Travel agencies
Sherry Saunder

D-U-N-S 20-161-5317   (HQ)
CARLTON CARDS LIMITED
(*Suby of* CLAYTON, DUBILIER & RICE, INC.)
1820 Matheson Blvd Unit B1, Mississauga, ON, L4W 0B3
(905) 219-6410
Emp Here 60   *Sales* 1,088,792,900
SIC 5112 Stationery and office supplies
Roderick Sturtridge

D-U-N-S 24-376-9960   (BR)
CASCADE (CANADA) LTD
(*Suby of* TOYOTA INDUSTRIES CORPORATION)
5570 Timberlea Blvd, Mississauga, ON, L4W 4M6
(905) 629-7777
Emp Here 85
SIC 3537 Industrial trucks and tractors
Chandica Harry

D-U-N-S 25-332-2770   (HQ)
CENTIMARK LTD
(*Suby of* CENTIMARK CORPORATION)
5597 Timberlea Blvd, Mississauga, ON, L4W 2S4
(905) 206-0255
Sales 22,872,045
SIC 1761 Roofing, siding, and sheetMetal work
Edward Dunlap
Timothy Dunlap
Robert Rudzik

D-U-N-S 20-407-7051   (HQ)

CENTRAL GRAPHICS AND CONTAINER GROUP LTD
CENTRAL GROUP, THE
5526 Timberlea Blvd, Mississauga, ON, L4W 2T7
(905) 238-8400
Emp Here 250   *Sales* 99,261,990
SIC 2653 Corrugated and solid fiber boxes
Rick M. Eastwood

D-U-N-S 24-836-7161   (HQ)
CENTURA BRANDS INC
1200 Aerowood Dr Unit 50, Mississauga, ON, L4W 2S7
(905) 602-1965
Emp Here 17   *Sales* 23,212,245
SIC 5122 Drugs, proprietaries, and sundries
Myles Robinson
Sam Forgione
Lawrence Laing

D-U-N-S 25-122-1503   (BR)
CERIDIAN CANADA LTD
(*Suby of* FOUNDATION HOLDINGS, INC.)
5600 Explorer Dr Suite 400, Mississauga, ON, L4W 4Y2
(905) 282-8100
Emp Here 150
SIC 8721 Accounting, auditing, and book-keeping

D-U-N-S 24-559-9279   (HQ)
CERTICOM CORP
(*Suby of* BLACKBERRY LIMITED)
4701 Tahoe Blvd, Mississauga, ON, L4W 0B5
(905) 507-4220
Emp Here 120   *Sales* 39,542,739
SIC 7372 Prepackaged software
Scott A Vanstone
Frank Cotter

D-U-N-S 25-510-5058   (HQ)
CEVA FREIGHT CANADA CORP
(*Suby of* MERIT CORPORATION SAL)
1880 Matheson Blvd E, Mississauga, ON, L4W 5N4
(905) 672-3456
Emp Here 100   *Sales* 100,033,800
SIC 4731 Freight transportation arrangement
Matthew Ryan
Mark Carlson
Marcel Brailthwaite
Sondra Sultemeier
David Souza
Burch Kenneth

D-U-N-S 24-850-5620   (SL)
CHIP REIT NO 23 OPERATIONS LIMITED PARTNERSHIP
SANDALWOOD SUITES HOTEL
5050 Orbitor Dr, Mississauga, ON, L4W 4X2
(905) 238-9600
Emp Here 100   *Sales* 9,489,900
SIC 7011 Hotels and motels
Edward Pitoniak

D-U-N-S 25-124-2566   (HQ)
CHOICE HOTELS CANADA INC
5015 Spectrum Way Suite 400, Mississauga, ON, L4W 0E4
(905) 602-2222
Emp Here 3   *Sales* 33,446,880
SIC 6794 Patent owners and lessors
Noreen Schembri
Brian Leon

D-U-N-S 20-982-4945   (SL)
CINTEX INTERNATIONAL (CANADA) LIMITED
5195 Maingate Dr, Mississauga, ON, L4W 1G4
(905) 795-8052
Emp Here 22   *Sales* 11,451,924
SIC 5091 Sporting and recreation goods
Surendra Girdhar
Sudarsharm Girdhar

D-U-N-S 24-125-2944   (BR)

CITIGROUP GLOBAL MARKETS CANADA INC
(*Suby of* CITIGROUP INC.)
2920 Matheson Blvd E, Mississauga, ON, L4W 5R6
(905) 624-9889
Emp Here 1,100
SIC 6722 Management investment, open-end
Robert Smuk

D-U-N-S 24-678-2093   (HQ)
CLAIMSPRO LP
(*Suby of* SCM INSURANCE SERVICES INC)
1550 Enterprise Rd Suite 310, Mississauga, ON, L4W 4P4
(905) 671-0185
Sales 249,445,170
SIC 6411 Insurance agents, brokers, and service
Sandra Cramb

D-U-N-S 20-817-5083   (SL)
CLOSING THE GAP HEALTHCARE GROUP INC
2810 Matheson Blvd E Suite 100, Mississauga, ON, L4W 4X7
(905) 306-0202
Emp Here 1,200   *Sales* 81,991,200
SIC 8059 Nursing and personal care, nec
Leighton Mcdonald
Connie Clerici
Kenneth Kirsh
Ronnie Saust

D-U-N-S 25-418-8618   (HQ)
COLIO ESTATE WINES INC
5900 Ambler Dr Suite 7, Mississauga, ON, L4W 2N3
(905) 949-4246
Emp Here 25   *Sales* 29,319,360
SIC 5921 Liquor stores
Enzo Deluca
Jim Clark
Kelly Elliott
John Clark

D-U-N-S 20-115-1029   (SL)
COLOURFAST SECURE CARD TECHNOLOGY INC
COLOURFAST PRINTING
5380 Timberlea Blvd, Mississauga, ON, L4W 2S6
(905) 206-9477
Emp Here 65   *Sales* 13,123,305
SIC 3089 Plastics products, nec
Andrew Mimnagh

D-U-N-S 20-400-9203   (HQ)
COMMONWEALTH HOSPITALITY LTD
HOLIDAY INN HOTELS
(*Suby of* WXI/WWH PARALLEL AMALCO (ONTARIO) LTD)
5090 Explorer Dr Suite 700, Mississauga, ON, L4W 4T9
(905) 602-6224
Emp Here 10   *Sales* 18,538,000
SIC 7011 Hotels and motels
Kenny Gibson
George Kosziwka
Fareed Mangalji

D-U-N-S 20-561-4092   (HQ)
COMPUCOM CANADA CO.
COMPUCOM SYSTEMS
(*Suby of* OFFICE DEPOT, INC.)
1830 Matheson Blvd Unit 1, Mississauga, ON, L4W 0B3
(289) 261-3000
Emp Here 350   *Sales* 321,211,200
SIC 5045 Computers, peripherals, and software
Jim Wixon
Jeffrey E Frick
Mike Simpson
Robert J Jourbran
Eva M Kalawski

D-U-N-S 24-892-0431   (SL)

COMPUTER ENHANCEMENT CORPORATION
CEC
5112 Timberlea Blvd Suite 2, Mississauga, ON, L4W 2S5
(905) 625-9100
Emp Here 24   *Sales* 10,732,176
SIC 5045 Computers, peripherals, and software
Russell Roberts

D-U-N-S 20-132-3235   (HQ)
CONAGRA FOODS CANADA INC
ALIMENTS V-H
(*Suby of* LAMB WESTON HOLDINGS INC)
5055 Satellite Dr Unit 1-2, Mississauga, ON, L4W 5K7
(416) 679-4200
Emp Here 120   *Sales* 173,021,675
SIC 2032 Canned specialties
Thomas Gunter
Brendy Sealock
Ian Roberts
Pablo Heyman
Jim Newman
Christine Raptopulos
Tanja Fratangeli

D-U-N-S 24-130-5635   (SL)
COUNSEL GROUP FUNDS
2680 Skymark Ave Suite 700, Mississauga, ON, L4W 5L6
(905) 625-9885
Emp Here 49   *Sales* 26,029,143
SIC 6211 Security brokers and dealers
Sam Febbraro

D-U-N-S 20-205-9791   (SL)
COUNSEL PORTFOLIO SERVICES INC
2680 Skymark Ave Suite 700, Mississauga, ON, L4W 5L6
(905) 625-9885
Emp Here 19   *Sales* 13,236,863
SIC 6722 Management investment, open-end
Sam Febbraro

D-U-N-S 24-131-3662   (SL)
COUNSEL SELECT SMALL CAP
2680 Skymark Ave Unit 700, Mississauga, ON, L4W 5L6
(905) 625-9885
Emp Here 49   *Sales* 40,561,073
SIC 6722 Management investment, open-end
Christopher Reynolds

D-U-N-S 24-757-0690   (HQ)
COUNTERFORCE CORPORATION
(*Suby of* UNITED TECHNOLOGIES CORPORATION)
2740 Matheson Blvd E Unit 2a, Mississauga, ON, L4W 4X3
(905) 282-6200
Emp Here 59   *Sales* 24,532,036
SIC 7382 Security systems services
Bruce Currer
George Tomko
Stephen Hopkins

D-U-N-S 20-693-6101   (HQ)
COVALON TECHNOLOGIES LTD
1660 Tech Ave Unit 5, Mississauga, ON, L4W 5S7
(905) 568-8400
Emp Here 14   *Sales* 20,457,066
SIC 8731 Commercial physical research
Brian Pedlar
Hamed Abbasian
Kim Crooks
Greg Leszczynski
Danny Brannagan
Abe Schwartz
Joseph Cordiano
Martin C. Bernholtz
Murray Miller
Jeffrey Mandel

D-U-N-S 24-885-2675   (SL)

CRITICAL PATH COURIERS LTD
1257 Kamato Rd, Mississauga, ON, L4W 2M2
(905) 212-8333
Emp Here 50   *Sales* 22,460,950
SIC 7389 Business services, nec
Greg Doff

D-U-N-S 25-197-3830   (HQ)
CROSSMARK CANADA INC
(*Suby of* CROSSMARK, INC.)
5580 Explorer Dr Suite 300, Mississauga, ON, L4W 4Y1
Emp Here 35   *Sales* 78,887,500
SIC 8743 Public relations services
Glen Wilson
Bruce Forbes
Brian Carley

D-U-N-S 24-057-6777   (BR)
CSG SECURITY CORPORATION
CHUBB SECURITY SYSTEMS
(*Suby of* UNITED TECHNOLOGIES CORPORATION)
2740 Matheson Blvd E Unit 1, Mississauga, ON, L4W 4X3
(905) 629-2600
Emp Here 300
SIC 5065 Electronic parts and equipment, nec
Gregory Painter

D-U-N-S 20-705-8629   (HQ)
CSG SECURITY CORPORATION
CHUBB SECURITY SYSTEMS, DIV OF
(*Suby of* UNITED TECHNOLOGIES CORPORATION)
5201 Explorer Dr, Mississauga, ON, L4W 4H1
(905) 629-1446
Emp Here 150   *Sales* 169,749,000
SIC 3699 Electrical equipment and supplies, nec

D-U-N-S 24-342-0325   (HQ)
DAFCO FILTRATION GROUP CORPORATION
(*Suby of* FILTRATION GROUP CORPORATION)
5390 Ambler Dr, Mississauga, ON, L4W 1G9
(905) 624-9165
Emp Here 150   *Sales* 84,263,100
SIC 3569 General industrial machinery, nec
Marc Saad
Alex Burt

D-U-N-S 20-114-0733   (SL)
DAMCO CANADA INC
(*Suby of* A.P. MOLLER OG HUSTRU CHASTINE MC-KINNEY MOLLERS FOND TIL ALMENE FORMAAL)
5700 Explorer Dr Unit 101, Mississauga, ON, L4W 0C6
(866) 361-3073
Emp Here 35   *Sales* 18,198,845
SIC 4731 Freight transportation arrangement
David Cardin
Gary Brocklesby

D-U-N-S 20-564-4888   (SL)
DAY & NIGHT CARRIERS LTD
1270 Aerowood Dr, Mississauga, ON, L4W 1B7
Emp Here 80   *Sales* 11,855,360
SIC 4213 Trucking, except local
Tasheen Sadig

D-U-N-S 24-379-2699   (HQ)
DCR STRATEGIES INC
TRUCASH
2680 Skymark Ave Suite 420, Mississauga, ON, L4W 5L6
(905) 212-9100
Sales 73,579,880
SIC 7389 Business services, nec
Huguette Masse
Diana Fletcher

D-U-N-S 24-392-9812   (HQ)

DEALERTRACK CANADA INC
(*Suby of* COX ENTERPRISES, INC.)
2700 Matheson Blvd E Suite 702, Mississauga, ON, L4W 4V9
(905) 281-6200
Emp Here 90   *Sales* 15,016,230
SIC 7372 Prepackaged software
Michael Collins

D-U-N-S 20-699-9455   (BR)
DELTA HOTELS LIMITED
DELTA TORONTO AIRPORT WEST
(*Suby of* GOVERNMENT OF THE PROVINCE OF BRITISH COLUMBIA)
5444 Dixie Rd Suite 47, Mississauga, ON, L4W 2L2
(905) 624-1144
Emp Here 160
SIC 8741 Management services
Martin Stitt

D-U-N-S 25-371-1758   (BR)
DESJARDINS GROUPE D'ASSURANCES GENERALES INC
(*Suby of* FEDERATION DES CAISSES DESJARDINS DU QUEBEC)
5070 Dixie Rd, Mississauga, ON, L4W 1C9
(905) 366-4430
Emp Here 900
SIC 6411 Insurance agents, brokers, and service
Rui Pita

D-U-N-S 24-927-0729   (HQ)
DIMERCO EXPRESS (CANADA) CORPORATION
(*Suby of* DIMERCO EXPRESS CORPORATION)
5100 Orbitor Dr Suite 201, Mississauga, ON, L4W 4Z4
(905) 282-8118
Emp Here 23   *Sales* 16,638,944
SIC 4731 Freight transportation arrangement
Roy Chen

D-U-N-S 24-454-0860   (SL)
DIVACCO LIMITED
5191 Creekbank Rd, Mississauga, ON, L4W 1R3
(905) 564-1711
Emp Here 90   *Sales* 17,287,650
SIC 3479 Metal coating and allied services
Ernest Pitman
Michael J Pitman
John Buchan

D-U-N-S 24-477-3586   (SL)
DIXIE FORD SALES LIMITED
5495 Dixie Rd, Mississauga, ON, L4W 1E6
(905) 629-1300
Emp Here 66   *Sales* 41,532,480
SIC 5511 New and used car dealers
Ainslie Hogan

D-U-N-S 20-373-6066   (SL)
DIXIE MOTORS LP
401 DIXIE HYUNDAI
(*Suby of* AUTOCANADA INC)
5515 Ambler Dr, Mississauga, ON, L4W 3Z1
(905) 238-8080
Emp Here 65   *Sales* 40,903,200
SIC 5511 New and used car dealers

D-U-N-S 20-292-6267   (SL)
DR. REDDY'S LABORATORIES CANADA INC
(*Suby of* DR REDDY'S LABORATORIES LIMITED)
2425 Matheson Blvd E 7th Fl, Mississauga, ON, L4W 5K4
(289) 201-2299
Emp Here 10   *Sales* 11,053,450
SIC 5122 Drugs, proprietaries, and sundries
Viswanatha Bonthu
Saumen Chakraborty
Satish Reddy

D-U-N-S 20-565-0604   (SL)

DRAEGER MEDICAL CANADA INC
(*Suby of* STEFAN DRAGER GMBH)
2425 Skymark Ave Unit 1, Mississauga, ON, L4W 4Y6
(905) 212-6600
Emp Here 28   *Sales* 12,520,872
SIC 5047 Medical and hospital equipment
Fred Donaldson
Botho Oppermann
Nathan Chiefetz

D-U-N-S 24-779-9281   (HQ)
DRAEGER SAFETY CANADA LIMITED
(*Suby of* STEFAN DRAGER GMBH)
2425 Skymark Ave Unit 1, Mississauga, ON, L4W 4Y6
(905) 212-6600
Emp Here 20   *Sales* 16,545,438
SIC 5049 Professional equipment, nec
Joseph Jagdeo

D-U-N-S 20-268-5921   (SL)
DRIVE COURIER XPRESS LLC. CORPORATION
2680 Matheson Blvd E, Mississauga, ON, L4W 0A5
(905) 291-0888
Emp Here 28   *Sales* 12,417,720
SIC 7389 Business services, nec
Shawn Roberts
Andrew Roberts
Igor Wilderman

D-U-N-S 24-314-4628   (HQ)
DRIVE PRODUCTS INC
1665 Shawson Dr, Mississauga, ON, L4W 1T7
(905) 564-5800
Emp Here 100   *Sales* 146,319,000
SIC 5084 Industrial machinery and equipment
Gregory Edmonds
Russell W. Bilyk

D-U-N-S 25-830-5382   (BR)
DUFFERIN-PEEL CATHOLIC DISTRICT SCHOOL BOARD
JOHN CABOT CATHOLIC SECONDARY
(*Suby of* DUFFERIN-PEEL CATHOLIC DISTRICT SCHOOL BOARD)
635 Willowbank Trail, Mississauga, ON, L4W 3L6
(905) 279-1554
Emp Here 100
SIC 8211 Elementary and secondary schools
John Minardi

D-U-N-S 25-166-6681   (BR)
DUFFERIN-PEEL CATHOLIC DISTRICT SCHOOL BOARD
ST BASIL SCHOOL
(*Suby of* DUFFERIN-PEEL CATHOLIC DISTRICT SCHOOL BOARD)
4235 Golden Orchard Dr, Mississauga, ON, L4W 3G1
(905) 624-4529
Emp Here 500
SIC 8211 Elementary and secondary schools
Marianne Tomczak

D-U-N-S 20-716-8485   (SL)
DURON ONTARIO LTD
1860 Shawson Dr, Mississauga, ON, L4W 1R7
(905) 670-1998
Emp Here 150   *Sales* 37,122,450
SIC 1771 Concrete work
John Dagonas
Geoff Kinney

D-U-N-S 24-135-9749   (SL)
E.O.E. GROUP INC
5484 Tomken Rd Unit 4, Mississauga, ON, L4W 2Z6
(905) 602-6400
Emp Here 25   *Sales* 11,179,350
SIC 5044 Office equipment
Stephen Wilson
Myrinna Szagala
Rita Kormentzas

D-U-N-S 20-259-2283   (SL)
ECHELON FINANCIAL HOLDINGS INC
ECHELON INSURANCE
2680 Matheson Blvd E Suite 300, Mississauga, ON, L4W 0A5
(905) 214-7880
Emp Here 300   *Sales* 23,804,403
SIC 6411 Insurance agents, brokers, and service
Matthew Turack
Joe Colby
Ken Coulson
Grace Kemp
Jamal Madbak
Darryll Mcdonald
Eric Millaire-Morin
Ron Pavelack
Josee Roy
Ingrid Wilson

D-U-N-S 20-700-7134   (SL)
ECHELON GENERAL INSURANCE COMPANY
(*Suby of* EGI FINANCIAL HOLDINGS INC)
2680 Matheson Blvd E Suite 300, Mississauga, ON, L4W 0A5
(905) 214-7880
Emp Here 100   *Sales* 184,774,200
SIC 6411 Insurance agents, brokers, and service
Serge Lavoie

D-U-N-S 24-388-8448   (HQ)
ECOLAB CO.
ECOLAB
(*Suby of* ECOLAB INC.)
5105 Tomken Rd Suite 1, Mississauga, ON, L4W 2X5
(905) 238-0171
Emp Here 60   *Sales* 469,933,674
SIC 2842 Polishes and sanitation goods
Joseph Ross Rae
Michael A. Hickey
Bobby Mendez
Jill Wayant
Thomas A. Mckee
David F. Duvick
Ching-Meng Chew
David J. Mitchell
Astrid Mitchell
Toni Del Vasto

D-U-N-S 20-691-9669   (HQ)
EGI FINANCIAL HOLDINGS INC
2680 Matheson Blvd E Suite 300, Mississauga, ON, L4W 0A5
(905) 214-7880
Sales 264,908,869
SIC 6411 Insurance agents, brokers, and service
Steve Dobronyi
Rob Purves
Douglas Mcintyre
Sylvain Guilbert
Ingrid Wilson
Robert Fuller
Stephen Steele
Michael Rocchi
John Czerwinski
Alvin Sharma

D-U-N-S 25-462-3549   (SL)
ELITE REALTY T. W. INC
PRUDENTIAL ELITE REALTY
5090 Explorer Dr Unit 7, Mississauga, ON, L4W 4X6
(905) 629-1515
Emp Here 50   *Sales* 16,356,350
SIC 6531 Real estate agents and managers
Vince Tersigni

D-U-N-S 25-102-1093   (SL)
ELIZABETH ARDEN (CANADA) LIMITED
(*Suby of* REVLON, INC.)
1590 South Gateway Rd, Mississauga, ON, L4W 0A8

(905) 276-4500
Emp Here 40   *Sales* 44,213,800
SIC 5122 Drugs, proprietaries, and sundries
Heide Rand
Robin Mitchell
Mary Becker
Joel B. Ronkin

D-U-N-S 20-164-5108   (SL)
ELLIS PAPER BOX INC
(*Suby of* ELLIS PACKAGING LIMITED)
2345 Matheson Blvd E, Mississauga, ON, L4W 5B3
(905) 212-9177
Emp Here 50   *Sales* 11,671,750
SIC 2657 Folding paperboard boxes
David Ellis
Cathleen Valdal

D-U-N-S 24-208-9805   (SL)
EMTERRA ENVIRONMENTAL
1611 Britannia Road E, Mississauga, ON, L4W 1S5
(289) 562-0091
Emp Here 49   *Sales* 12,599,419
SIC 4953 Refuse systems

D-U-N-S 25-483-6612   (SL)
ENGINEERED CASE MANUFACTURERS INC
ECM
5191 Creekbank Rd, Mississauga, ON, L4W 1R3
(905) 366-2273
Emp Here 52   *Sales* 12,138,620
SIC 3161 Luggage
Steve Binder

D-U-N-S 24-830-9395   (BR)
ERB TRANSPORT LIMITED
(*Suby of* ERB ENTERPRISES INC)
1889 Britannia Rd E, Mississauga, ON, L4W 1S6
(905) 670-8490
Emp Here 200
SIC 4213 Trucking, except local
Bryan Swanson

D-U-N-S 24-644-1810   (BR)
ERICSSON CANADA INC
(*Suby of* TELEFON AB LM ERICSSON)
5255 Satellite Dr, Mississauga, ON, L4W 5E3
(905) 629-6700
Emp Here 120
SIC 4899 Communication services, nec
Mark Henderson

D-U-N-S 25-144-7553   (SL)
EUROPEAN FINE FOODS CO. INC
1191 Crestlawn Dr, Mississauga, ON, L4W 1A7
(905) 206-0964
Emp Here 12   *Sales* 10,026,924
SIC 5141 Groceries, general line
Margaret Szczepanik
Barbara Szczepanik
Konrad Szczepanik
Teresa Szczepanik

D-U-N-S 24-556-1220   (SL)
EUROTRADE IMPORT-EXPORT INC
5484 Timberlea Blvd, Mississauga, ON, L4W 2T7
(905) 624-2064
Emp Here 25   *Sales* 20,889,425
SIC 5149 Groceries and related products, nec
Ekrem Altic
Adriana Altic-Pedisic

D-U-N-S 20-300-5442   (SL)
EXCEL LATIN AMERICA BOND FUND
2810 Matheson Blvd E Suite 800, Mississauga, ON, L4W 4X7

Emp Here 30   *Sales* 24,833,310
SIC 6722 Management investment, open-end
Dhim Asdhir

D-U-N-S 24-168-3598   (HQ)

FEDERAL EXPRESS CANADA CORPORATION
FEDEX
(*Suby of* FEDEX CORPORATION)
5985 Explorer Dr, Mississauga, ON, L4W 5K6
(800) 463-3339
Emp Here 250   *Sales* 2,142,126,000
SIC 4512 Air transportation, scheduled
Frederick W Smith
David J Bronczek
Lisa Lisson
Alan B Graf Jr
Mark Allen

D-U-N-S 25-843-6674   (SL)
FERRI, R AUTOMOBILES INC
BMW OF MISSISSAUGA
4505 Dixie Rd, Mississauga, ON, L4W 5K3
(905) 625-7533
Emp Here 50   *Sales* 24,903,900
SIC 5511 New and used car dealers
Remo Ferri

D-U-N-S 24-079-7662   (HQ)
FESTO INC
(*Suby of* FESTO BETEILIGUNGEN GMBH & CO. KG)
5300 Explorer Dr, Mississauga, ON, L4W 5G4
(905) 624-9000
Emp Here 100   *Sales* 58,527,600
SIC 5085 Industrial supplies
Roger Hallet
Roy Pietila

D-U-N-S 20-290-6231   (SL)
FIRST DATA CANADA LIMITED
FIRST DATA LOAN COMPANY
(*Suby of* FIRST DATA CORPORATION)
2630 Skymark Ave Suite 400, Mississauga, ON, L4W 5A4
(905) 602-3509
Emp Here 150   *Sales* 35,030,700
SIC 6099 Functions related to deposit banking
Brian Green
Boyd Whalen

D-U-N-S 25-460-6718   (HQ)
FOOD BANKS CANADA
5090 Explorer Dr Suite 203, Mississauga, ON, L4W 4T9
(905) 602-5234
Emp Here 5   *Sales* 33,590,794
SIC 8699 Membership organizations, nec

D-U-N-S 20-300-9147   (SL)
FRENCH'S FOOD COMPANY INC, THE
(*Suby of* MCCORMICK & COMPANY INCORPORATED)
1680 Tech Ave Unit 2, Mississauga, ON, L4W 5S9
(905) 283-7000
Emp Here 25   *Sales* 20,889,425
SIC 5149 Groceries and related products, nec
Elliot Penner
Stuart King
Stephen Pike

D-U-N-S 20-401-8303   (HQ)
FRENDEL KITCHENS LIMITED
1350 Shawson Dr, Mississauga, ON, L4W 1C5
(905) 670-7898
Sales 97,812,560
SIC 5021 Furniture
Tony Deltin
Carole Deltin

D-U-N-S 24-479-2446   (HQ)
FURLANI'S FOOD CORPORATION
1730 Aimco Blvd, Mississauga, ON, L4W 1V1
(905) 602-6102
Emp Here 15   *Sales* 170,584,750
SIC 2051 Bread, cake, and related products
Paul Kawaja
Andrew Anderson
Jonathan Kawaja

D-U-N-S 24-964-6308   (HQ)

G. V. INTERIOR CONTRACTORS LTD
5446 Gorvan Dr, Mississauga, ON, L4W 3E8

Sales 14,121,930
SIC 1542 Nonresidential construction, nec
Valerio Roscetti
Giacomo (Jack) Roscetti

D-U-N-S 20-276-4700   (SL)
G.T.A. WORLD CARGO LTD
2710 Britannia Rd E (Cargo 2 Tower 7), Mississauga, ON, L4W 2P7
(905) 671-4443
Emp Here 35   *Sales* 11,366,390
SIC 4581 Airports, flying fields, and services
Mario D'urso
Gary Ogden

D-U-N-S 20-165-6931   (HQ)
GARLAND COMMERCIAL RANGES LIMITED
GARLAND CANADA
(*Suby of* WELBILT, INC.)
1177 Kamato Rd, Mississauga, ON, L4W 1X4
(905) 624-0260
Sales 70,219,250
SIC 3589 Service industry machinery, nec
Jacques Seguin
David Banks

D-U-N-S 24-523-4351   (HQ)
GATE GOURMET CANADA INC
(*Suby of* RRJ MANAGEMENT (HK) LIMITED)
2498 Britannia Rd E, Mississauga, ON, L4W 2P7
(905) 405-4100
Emp Here 1,200   *Sales* 56,386,551
SIC 5812 Eating places
Kenny Colangelo
Anthony Tolliss
Justin Elyea

D-U-N-S 20-402-2289   (HQ)
GAY LEA FOODS CO-OPERATIVE LIMITED
LONGLIFE OF CANADA
5200 Orbitor Dr, Mississauga, ON, L4W 5B4
(905) 283-5300
Emp Here 80   *Sales* 200,802,620
SIC 2021 Creamery butter
Michael Barrett
Larry Hook
Amrit Leighl
Michael Eusebi
John Rebry

D-U-N-S 20-702-8820   (HQ)
GENERAL MILLS CANADA CORPORATION
(*Suby of* GENERAL MILLS, INC.)
5825 Explorer Dr, Mississauga, ON, L4W 5P6
(905) 212-4000
Emp Here 1,000   *Sales* 974,770,000
SIC 2041 Flour and other grain mill products
David Paul Homer
Gina Goetter
Tunku Pal
Douglas Mcgillivray

D-U-N-S 25-168-7877   (SL)
GENEX SERVICES OF CANADA INC
(*Suby of* KKR & CO. INC.)
2800 Skymark Ave Suite 401, Mississauga, ON, L4W 5A6

Emp Here 30   *Sales* 55,432,260
SIC 6411 Insurance agents, brokers, and service
Carol Valentic

D-U-N-S 25-852-4206   (SL)
GENZYME CANADA INC
(*Suby of* SANOFI)
2700 Matheson Blvd E Suite 800, Mississauga, ON, L4W 4V9
(905) 625-0011
Emp Here 73   *Sales* 30,135,933
SIC 5122 Drugs, proprietaries, and sundries
Marie E Lamont

Sanford D Smith
Brian Lewis
Marlene Leblanc

D-U-N-S 20-716-4075   (HQ)
GEOX CANADA INC
(*Suby of* LIR SRL)
2110 Matheson Blvd E Suite 100, Mississauga, ON, L4W 5E1
(905) 629-8500
Emp Here 20   *Sales* 43,639,055
SIC 5661 Shoe stores
Livio Libralesso

D-U-N-S 24-819-2879   (SL)
GIGG EXPRESS INC
5355 Creekbank Rd, Mississauga, ON, L4W 5L5
(905) 614-0544
Emp Here 90   *Sales* 13,337,280
SIC 4212 Local trucking, without storage
Gurjinder Singh
Jack Conley
Gurvinder Virk

D-U-N-S 20-129-2570   (SL)
GILBERT STEEL LIMITED
1650 Britannia Rd E, Mississauga, ON, L4W 1J2
(905) 670-5771
Emp Here 200   *Sales* 38,417,000
SIC 3441 Fabricated structural Metal
Gary Gilbert

D-U-N-S 25-094-3958   (SL)
GIVAUDAN CANADA CO
(*Suby of* GIVAUDAN SA)
2400 Matheson Blvd E, Mississauga, ON, L4W 5G9
(905) 282-9808
Emp Here 23   *Sales* 19,218,271
SIC 5149 Groceries and related products, nec
Magda Ghali

D-U-N-S 24-194-7050   (HQ)
GLASVAN TRAILERS INC
1201 Aimco Blvd Suite 625, Mississauga, ON, L4W 1B3
(905) 625-8441
Emp Here 70   *Sales* 50,726,940
SIC 5012 Automobiles and other motor vehicles
George M Cobham
Paul Cobham
George Jr Cobham

D-U-N-S 20-123-3488   (SL)
GLOBEWAYS CANADA INC
SARA
(*Suby of* HAKAN HOLDINGS LIMITED)
2570 Matheson Blvd E Suite 110, Mississauga, ON, L4W 4Z3
(905) 712-1010
Emp Here 12   *Sales* 17,612,304
SIC 5153 Grain and field beans
Tanvir Zaidi

D-U-N-S 20-559-1621   (SL)
GORRIE ADVERTISING MANAGEMENT LIMITED
GORRIE MARKETING SERVICES
(*Suby of* 762695 ONTARIO LIMITED)
2770 Matheson Blvd E, Mississauga, ON, L4W 4M5
(905) 238-3466
Emp Here 44   *Sales* 10,308,672
SIC 8743 Public relations services
Robert Gorrie
Katie Gorrie
David Grant
Ashley Gorrie

D-U-N-S 20-291-4461   (BR)
GOVERNMENT OF ONTARIO
SPECIAL INVESTIGATIONS UNIT
(*Suby of* GOVERNMENT OF ONTARIO)
5090 Commerce Blvd Unit 100, Mississauga, ON, L4W 5M4

(416) 622-0748
Emp Here 81
SIC 7381 Detective and armored car services

D-U-N-S 20-200-9341   (HQ)
GP WEALTH MANAGEMENT CORPORATION
5045 Orbitor Dr Suite 400 Building 11, Mississauga, ON, L4W 4Y4
(416) 622-9969
Emp Here 30   *Sales* 18,743,040
SIC 8742 Management consulting services
George Aguiar
Paula Sprentz

D-U-N-S 24-093-4245   (SL)
GRANDMOTHER'S TOUCH INC
THE GRANDMOTHER'S TOUCH
5359 Timberlea Blvd Suite 20, Mississauga, ON, L4W 4N5
(905) 361-0485
Emp Here 100   *Sales* 4,020,900
SIC 7349 Building maintenance services, nec
Lexton Bates
Edward Sendrea

D-U-N-S 24-660-9135   (SL)
GRAPHIC COMMUNICATIONS BENEFITS ADMINISTRATION COR
GCIU
5025 Orbitor Dr Suite 210, Mississauga, ON, L4W 4Y5

Emp Here 13   *Sales* 13,453,453
SIC 6371 Pension, health, and welfare funds
Randy Bruce

D-U-N-S 25-531-1342   (SL)
GRAPHIC PACKAGING INTERNATIONAL CANADA CORPORATION
(*Suby of* GRAPHIC PACKAGING HOLDING COMPANY)
1355 Aerowood Dr, Mississauga, ON, L4W 1C2
(905) 602-7877
Emp Here 50   *Sales* 11,100,050
SIC 3556 Food products machinery
David Scheible

D-U-N-S 20-918-8569   (HQ)
GREENLAWN, LTD
TRUGREEN
(*Suby of* TRUGREEN HOLDING CORPORATION)
2385 Matheson Blvd E, Mississauga, ON, L4W 5B3
(905) 290-1844
Sales 29,585,800
SIC 0782 Lawn and garden services
Gavin Dawson
Mark Furgiuele
Carol J. Pearson

D-U-N-S 24-822-4990   (SL)
GREENWORLD FOOD EXPRESS INC
5380 Maingate Dr, Mississauga, ON, L4W 1R8
(905) 212-7720
Emp Here 30   *Sales* 25,067,310
SIC 5141 Groceries, general line
Mohamad Harb

D-U-N-S 20-934-7686   (SL)
HALTON INDOOR CLIMATE SYSTEMS, LTD
(*Suby of* OY HALTON GROUP LTD)
1021 Brevik Pl, Mississauga, ON, L4W 3R7
(905) 624-0301
Emp Here 68   *Sales* 15,096,068
SIC 3564 Blowers and fans
Rick Bagwell
Rich Catan
Nick Kakarellis
Michael Ianniello

D-U-N-S 20-201-3447   (HQ)
HASBRO CANADA CORPORATION
HASBRO
(*Suby of* HASBRO, INC.)

2645 Skymark Ave Suite 200, Mississauga, ON, L4W 4H2
(905) 238-3374
Emp Here 30   *Sales* 31,232,520
SIC 5092 Toys and hobby goods and supplies
Michael Hogg
Linda Merlo
Barry Nagler
Brian Goldner

D-U-N-S 24-143-2574   (HQ)
HERSHEY CANADA INC
HERSHEY
(*Suby of* HERSHEY COMPANY)
5750 Explorer Dr Suite 400, Mississauga, ON, L4W 0A9
(905) 602-9200
Emp Here 140   *Sales* 779,816,000
SIC 2064 Candy and other confectionery products
Matthew Lindsay

D-U-N-S 20-342-4502   (SL)
HEWLETT PACKARD ENTERPRISE CANADA CO
(*Suby of* HEWLETT PACKARD ENTERPRISE COMPANY)
5150 Spectrum Way Suite 400, Mississauga, ON, L4W 5G2
(905) 206-4725
Emp Here 60,000   *Sales* 12,244,920,000
SIC 8731 Commercial physical research
Paula Hodgins
Jon Beck
Jim Vibert

D-U-N-S 24-486-9426   (SL)
HOODEX INDUSTRIES LIMITED
H W JANITORIAL SUPPLIES
5650 Tomken Rd Unit 4, Mississauga, ON, L4W 4P1
(905) 624-8668
Emp Here 320   *Sales* 10,229,760
SIC 7349 Building maintenance services, nec
Morley Hood

D-U-N-S 20-261-7478   (HQ)
HP CANADA CO
(*Suby of* HP INC.)
5150 Spectrum Way 6 Fl, Mississauga, ON, L4W 5G2
(888) 206-0289
Emp Here 430   *Sales* 91,836,900
SIC 8731 Commercial physical research
Mary Ann Yule
Lisa Le Neve
Mizuho Abe

D-U-N-S 24-093-6810   (SL)
I CHECK INC
1136 Matheson Blvd E, Mississauga, ON, L4W 2V4
(905) 625-5156
Emp Here 40   *Sales* 11,543,320
SIC 1522 Residential construction, nec
Peter Cabral

D-U-N-S 24-622-4166   (SL)
INDEPENDENT CORRUGATOR INC
ICI
1177 Aerowood Dr, Mississauga, ON, L4W 1Y6
(905) 629-2702
Emp Here 100   *Sales* 23,343,500
SIC 2653 Corrugated and solid fiber boxes
Richard F Eastwood
Richard M Eastwood
Marco Studer

D-U-N-S 20-371-5045   (HQ)
INFLAMAX RESEARCH LIMITED
CLIANTHA RESEARCH
(*Suby of* CLIANTHA RESEARCH LIMITED)
1310 Fewster Dr, Mississauga, ON, L4W 1A4
(905) 282-1808
Emp Here 154   *Sales* 53,762,436
SIC 8731 Commercial physical research
Vijay Patel

Naveen Sharma

D-U-N-S 24-394-8788   (SL)
INFRASTRUCTURE HEALTH AND SAFETY ASSOCIATION
IHSA
5110 Creekbank Rd Suite 400, Mississauga, ON, L4W 0A1
(416) 674-2726
Emp Here 110   *Sales* 23,960,492
SIC 8611 Business associations
Enzo Garritano
Mike Archambault
Joe Redshaw
Michael Frolick
Joe Pessoa
Len Poirier
Brian Macdonald
Dave Whyte
Don Schultz
Tom Lachance

D-U-N-S 24-556-1675   (HQ)
INGENICO CANADA LTD
INGENICO GROUP
5180 Orbitor Dr 2nd Fl, Mississauga, ON, L4W 5L9
(905) 212-9464
Emp Here 80   *Sales* 17,982,081
SIC 3578 Calculating and accounting equipment
Victor Young

D-U-N-S 25-880-3642   (HQ)
INSURANCELAND INC
INSURANCELAND
2585 Skymark Ave Unit 300, Mississauga, ON, L4W 4L5
(905) 238-0668
Emp Here 1   *Sales* 34,770,460
SIC 6411 Insurance agents, brokers, and service
Paul Hainer
Rick Hainer
Peter Hainer

D-U-N-S 20-214-7174   (HQ)
INTER-CONTINENTAL GEAR & BRAKE INC
1415 Shawson Dr Suite 1, Mississauga, ON, L4W 1C4
(905) 564-5633
Emp Here 17   *Sales* 10,926,450
SIC 5013 Motor vehicle supplies and new parts
Ronald Schwartz
Jordan Schwartz

D-U-N-S 24-304-7008   (HQ)
INTROTEL COMMUNICATIONS INC
5170 Timberlea Blvd Unit B, Mississauga, ON, L4W 2S5
(905) 625-8700
Emp Here 39   *Sales* 17,886,960
SIC 5065 Electronic parts and equipment, nec

D-U-N-S 24-997-0369   (HQ)
INTUIT CANADA ULC
(*Suby of* INTUIT INC.)
5100 Spectrum Way, Mississauga, ON, L4W 5S2
(888) 843-5449
Emp Here 5   *Sales* 54,789,160
SIC 7371 Custom computer programming services
Yves Millette
Jeffrey Hank

D-U-N-S 24-425-3717   (HQ)
INVESTMENT PLANNING COUNSEL INC
(*Suby of* POWER CORPORATION DU CANADA)
5015 Spectrum Way Suite 200, Mississauga, ON, L4W 0E4
(905) 212-9799
Sales 30,294,810
SIC 8741 Management services
Stephen J. Meehan
Christoher Reynolds

R. Jeffrey Orr
Murray J. Taylor
Gregory D. Tretiak
Charles R. Sims
Murray Douglas Kilfoyle

D-U-N-S 25-204-1827   (SL)
INVESTMENT PLANNING COUNSEL OF CANADA LIMITED
2680 Skymark Ave Suite 700, Mississauga, ON, L4W 5L6

Emp Here 200
SIC 8741 Management services

D-U-N-S 20-304-1959   (SL)
ISYARI CANADA INC
UNIGLOBE TOUS TRAVEL GROUP
5045 Orbitor Dr Building 12 Suite 400, Mississauga, ON, L4W 4Y4
(905) 212-2515
Emp Here 36   *Sales* 13,872,960
SIC 4724 Travel agencies
Jeffrey Verman

D-U-N-S 20-251-9690   (SL)
J & M GROUP INC
5225 Orbitor Dr Unit 8, Mississauga, ON, L4W 4Y8
(905) 766-2157
Emp Here 49   *Sales* 11,657,149
SIC 8742 Management consulting services
Magesh Yaghavan
Jatinder Banwait

D-U-N-S 20-822-4113   (SL)
J.M. DIE LIMITED
909 Pantera Dr, Mississauga, ON, L4W 2R9
(905) 625-9571
Emp Here 70   *Sales* 15,540,070
SIC 3541 Machine tools, Metal cutting type
Joseph Skof

D-U-N-S 20-772-7884   (HQ)
JFC INTERNATIONAL (CANADA) INC
(*Suby of* KIKKOMAN CORPORATION)
1025 Kamato Rd, Mississauga, ON, L4W 0C1
(905) 629-0993
Sales 16,711,540
SIC 5141 Groceries, general line
Masahiro Yamamoto

D-U-N-S 24-952-9298   (SL)
JJM MANUFACTURING LTD
5430 Timberlea Blvd Suite 2, Mississauga, ON, L4W 2T7
(905) 206-2150
Emp Here 50   *Sales* 24,916,100
SIC 5137 Women's and children's clothing
James Jolly
Stephen P O'mara
Catherine Chant

D-U-N-S 20-288-4961   (SL)
JOHN FORSYTH SHIRT COMPANY INC, THE
2645 Skymark Ave Unit 105, Mississauga, ON, L4W 4H2
(905) 362-4040
Emp Here 45   *Sales* 22,424,490
SIC 5137 Women's and children's clothing
Oliver Morante

D-U-N-S 25-226-0484   (HQ)
JONES DESLAURIERS INSURANCE MANAGEMENT INC
2375 Skymark Ave, Mississauga, ON, L4W 4Y6
(416) 259-4625
Emp Here 145   *Sales* 783,107,160
SIC 6411 Insurance agents, brokers, and service
Shawn Desantis
Mike Jack
Michael Bastone
Matt Croswell
Dina Godinho
Steve Horvath

Scott Irwin
Danny Sgro
Lucy Sousa
Kevin Stedman

D-U-N-S 20-351-3940   (SL)
KAPSCH TRAFFICCOM CANADA INC
6020 Ambler Dr, Mississauga, ON, L4W 2P1
(905) 624-3020
Emp Here 145   *Sales* 27,614,090
SIC 3669 Communications equipment, nec
Christopher F Murray

D-U-N-S 24-335-0352   (SL)
KASSEI ER FOOD PRODUCTS INC
1031 Brevik Pl, Mississauga, ON, L4W 3R7
(905) 629-2142
Emp Here 30   *Sales* 25,067,310
SIC 5141 Groceries, general line
Erich Lamshoeft Sr
Erich A Lamshoeft Jr

D-U-N-S 20-174-7367   (HQ)
KELLOGG CANADA INC
(*Suby of* KELLOGG COMPANY)
5350 Creekbank Rd, Mississauga, ON, L4W 5S1
(905) 290-5200
Emp Here 125   *Sales* 414,277,250
SIC 2043 Cereal breakfast foods
Gregory Peterson
Avinash Maharaj
Vincenzo Fiorenza
Carol Stewart

D-U-N-S 20-878-8682   (HQ)
KING-O-MATIC INDUSTRIES LIMITED
PRO-KING
(*Suby of* TRANSTAR HOLDING COMPANY)
955 Pantera Dr, Mississauga, ON, L4W 2T4
(905) 624-1956
Emp Here 5   *Sales* 69,270,240
SIC 5531 Auto and home supply stores
Greg Gyllstrom
Jeffrey Marshall
Richard Sedory
Robert Roxburgh
Rajat Duggal

D-U-N-S 24-692-0680   (SL)
KIRKWOOD & MURPHY LTD
5150 Timberlea Blvd, Mississauga, ON, L4W 2S5
(905) 602-6900
Emp Here 20   *Sales* 14,850,400
SIC 5199 Nondurable goods, nec
Michael Murphy
Paul Gallagher

D-U-N-S 20-964-5639   (HQ)
KONICA MINOLTA BUSINESS SOLUTIONS (CANADA) LTD
IT WEAPONS DIV.
(*Suby of* KONICA MINOLTA, INC.)
5875 Explorer Dr, Mississauga, ON, L4W 0E1
(905) 890-6600
Emp Here 100   *Sales* 401,514,000
SIC 5044 Office equipment
Chris Dewart
Richard Taylor

D-U-N-S 25-503-7095   (SL)
KSB PUMPS INC
(*Suby of* KSB STIFTUNG)
5205 Tomken Rd, Mississauga, ON, L4W 3N8
(905) 568-9200
Emp Here 30   *Sales* 14,250,780
SIC 5085 Industrial supplies
Michael Blundell

D-U-N-S 20-420-2352   (HQ)
LEDVANCE LTD
SYLVANIA LIGHTING SERVICES
(*Suby of* EUROLIGHT LUXEMBOURG HOLDINGS SARL)
5450 Explorer Dr Suite 100, Mississauga, ON, L4W 5N1

(905) 361-9333
Emp Here 130   *Sales* 162,959,040
SIC 3641 Electric lamps
John Preville
Lawrence Lin
Mattias Rosenthal
Tim Yun Chen
James Johnson
Erol Kirilmaz

D-U-N-S 25-361-9290   (BR)
LOBLAW COMPANIES LIMITED
MARC'S NOFRILLS
(*Suby of* LOBLAW COMPANIES LIMITED)
925 Rathburn Rd E Unit A, Mississauga, ON,
L4W 4C3
(905) 276-6560
Emp Here 96
SIC 5411 Grocery stores
Marc Borg

D-U-N-S 24-320-8035   (HQ)
LOWE'S COMPANIES CANADA, ULC
(*Suby of* LOWE'S COMPANIES, INC.)
5150 Spectrum Way, Mississauga, ON, L4W
5G2
(905) 219-1000
Emp Here 150   *Sales* 1,686,300,000
SIC 5211 Lumber and other building materials
Sylvain Prud'homme

D-U-N-S 20-331-1246   (HQ)
LOWE'S HOLDING CANADA, ULC
(*Suby of* LOWE'S COMPANIES, INC.)
5150 Spectrum Way Suite 200, Mississauga,
ON, L4W 5G2
(905) 219-1000
Sales 6,214,018,509
SIC 6712 Bank holding companies
Sylvain Prud'homme

D-U-N-S 25-998-6115   (HQ)
LOXCREEN CANADA LTD
BENGARD MANUFACTURING, DIV OF
(*Suby of* M-D BUILDING PRODUCTS, INC.)
5720 Ambler Dr, Mississauga, ON, L4W 2B1
(905) 625-3210
Emp Here 59   *Sales* 12,485,525
SIC 3442 Metal doors, sash, and trim
John W Parrish Jr
Joseph L Comitale
Charles C Rone Jr
Ronald B Rhymer

D-U-N-S 24-390-0219   (HQ)
LTS TG LTD
LONG TALL SALLY
(*Suby of* TRISMO VERWALTUNGS GMBH)
5045 Orbitor Dr Bldg 12 Suite 202, Missis-
sauga, ON, L4W 4Y4
(905) 890-2430
Emp Here 5   *Sales* 17,939,600
SIC 5621 Women's clothing stores
Maurice Bennett
Susan Smith Muccilli

D-U-N-S 25-388-0884   (HQ)
**LUXURY HOTELS INTERNATIONAL OF
CANADA ULC**
*MARRIOTT HALIFAX HARBOURFRONT HO-
TEL*
(*Suby of* MARRIOTT INTERNATIONAL, INC.)
2425 Matheson Blvd E Suite 100, Missis-
sauga, ON, L4W 5K4
(905) 366-5200
Emp Here 60   *Sales* 292,744,080
SIC 7011 Hotels and motels
Ron Harrison
Eric Deudny

D-U-N-S 24-217-1387   (HQ)
MAERSK CANADA INC
MAERSK LINE
(*Suby of* A.P. MOLLER OG HUSTRU CHAS-
TINE MC-KINNEY MOLLERS FOND TIL
ALMENE FORMAAL)
2576 Matheson Blvd E Suite 101, Missis-
sauga, ON, L4W 5H1

(905) 624-5585
Emp Here 110   *Sales* 98,859,500
SIC 4731 Freight transportation arrangement
David Cardin
John Crewson
Russell Bruner
William Woodhour

D-U-N-S 20-069-7055   (BR)
MAGIL CONSTRUCTION ONTARIO INC
(*Suby of* FAYOLLE CANADA INC)
5285 Solar Dr Unit 102, Mississauga, ON,
L4W 5B8
(905) 890-9193
Emp Here 80
SIC 1542 Nonresidential construction, nec
Sean Fitzpatrick

D-U-N-S 20-169-8917   (SL)
**MAGNETO ELECTRIC SERVICE CO. LIM-
ITED**
1150 Eglinton Ave E, Mississauga, ON, L4W
2M6
(905) 625-9450
Emp Here 80   *Sales* 10,185,800
SIC 7694 Armature rewinding shops
Michael Vassallo
Carmella Vassallo
Jim Wilson

D-U-N-S 24-414-4077   (HQ)
MAJOLI FURNITURE (1983) LIMITED
SLEEP FACTORY, THE
5510 Ambler Dr Unit 2, Mississauga, ON, L4W
2V1
(905) 542-0481
Emp Here 8   *Sales* 12,345,760
SIC 2515 Mattresses and bedsprings
Nick Barbieri

D-U-N-S 25-150-3108   (SL)
**MASON GROUP OF COMPANIES LIMITED,
THE**
1205 Britannia Rd E, Mississauga, ON, L4W
1C7
(905) 795-0122
Emp Here 40   *Sales* 10,462,120
SIC 6712 Bank holding companies
Colin Mason
Gareth Mason
Jeffery Mason
Janice Mason
Fiona Mason
Dorothy Mason

D-U-N-S 20-366-0576   (HQ)
MATCH MG CANADA INC
MATCH MARKETING GROUP
5225 Satellite Dr, Mississauga, ON, L4W 5P9
(905) 566-2824
Emp Here 50   *Sales* 23,428,800
SIC 8743 Public relations services
Michael Dill
Antoine Adams
Rob Elliott

D-U-N-S 25-255-7806   (SL)
MAVRON TRANSPORT INC
5758 Dixie Rd, Mississauga, ON, L4W 1E7
(905) 670-9455
Emp Here 110   *Sales* 22,627,660
SIC 4213 Trucking, except local
Manny Bhullar

D-U-N-S 24-918-7204   (SL)
**MAYFIELD SUITES GENERAL PARTNER
INC**
*STAGEWEST ALL SUITE HOTEL & THE-
ATRE RESTAURANT*
5400 Dixie Rd, Mississauga, ON, L4W 4T4
(905) 238-0159
Emp Here 80   *Sales* 23,917,000
SIC 7011 Hotels and motels
Howard Pechet

D-U-N-S 20-527-9268   (SL)
MEMME EXCAVATION COMPANY LIMITED
MEMME CONSTRUCTION

1315 Shawson Dr, Mississauga, ON, L4W
1C4
(905) 564-7972
Emp Here 80   *Sales* 20,195,360
SIC 1623 Water, sewer, and utility lines
Antonio Nativio

D-U-N-S 24-254-9470   (SL)
**MERCEDES-BENZ FINANCIAL SERVICES
CANADA CORPORATION**
DAIMLER TRUCK FINANCIAL
(*Suby of* DAIMLER AG)
2680 Matheson Blvd E Suite 500, Missis-
sauga, ON, L4W 0A5
(800) 532-7362
Emp Here 150   *Sales* 18,716,400
SIC 8741 Management services
Stefan Karrenbauer

D-U-N-S 24-335-0563   (BR)
METRO ONTARIO INC
FOOD BASICS
(*Suby of* METRO INC)
4141 Dixie Rd Unit 2, Mississauga, ON, L4W
1V5
(905) 238-1366
Emp Here 120
SIC 5411 Grocery stores
Nick Malfara

D-U-N-S 24-140-9200   (HQ)
MI GROUP LTD, THE
M I GROUP
2425 Matheson Blvd E, Mississauga, ON,
L4W 5K4
(905) 812-8900
Emp Here 170   *Sales* 148,289,250
SIC 4731 Freight transportation arrangement
Chris Lesiuk
Gail Reinhart
Rob Stone
Tyler Fearn
Michaelene (Mickey) Spaulding
Dwayne Waldrop
Ida Ceravolo
Mary-Ann Teal
Sarah Kenning
Marsha Mongeau

D-U-N-S 24-666-7554   (SL)
MIDNIGHT EXPRESS & CARTAGE LTD
5355 Creekbank Rd, Mississauga, ON, L4W
5L5
(905) 629-0712
Emp Here 100   *Sales* 20,570,600
SIC 4213 Trucking, except local
Gary Garrard
Glenn Garrard
Grant Garrard
Graham Garrard

D-U-N-S 20-059-5788   (SL)
**MITSUBISHI MOTOR SALES OF CANADA,
INC**
(*Suby of* MITSUBISHI MOTORS CORPORA-
TION)
2090 Matheson Blvd E, Mississauga, ON,
L4W 5P8
(905) 214-9000
Emp Here 20   *Sales* 10,399,340
SIC 4731 Freight transportation arrangement
Dan Booth
Bruce A. Chapple
Yoichi Yokozawa
Koji Soga
Tony Laframboise
Akihiko Mizumoto
Shinsaku Katayama
Kenichiro Yamamoto

D-U-N-S 24-892-6305   (SL)
MIZUNO CANADA LTD
(*Suby of* MIZUNO CORPORATION)
5206 Timberlea Blvd, Mississauga, ON, L4W
2S5
(905) 629-0500
Emp Here 28   *Sales* 14,575,176

SIC 5091 Sporting and recreation goods
John Stacey
Mark Hansen
Dave Bartlett

D-U-N-S 20-166-0164   (SL)
MM&T PACKAGING COMPANY
(*Suby of* WESTROCK COMPANY)
5485 Tomken Rd, Mississauga, ON, L4W 3Y3
(800) 651-5951
Emp Here 75   *Sales* 12,302,025
SIC 2752 Commercial printing, lithographic
Tony Sgro
Joe Gattafoni
April Burke

D-U-N-S 25-215-1295   (HQ)
MME MULTIURETHANES LTD
5245 Creekbank Rd, Mississauga, ON, L4W
1N3
(905) 564-7650
Sales 10,732,176
SIC 5039 Construction materials, nec
Peter White
Patrick Melady
Hania White

D-U-N-S 24-784-3709   (SL)
MONARCH WEALTH CORPORATION
5090 Explorer Dr Suite 200, Mississauga, ON,
L4W 4X6
(416) 640-2285
Emp Here 15   *Sales* 10,450,155
SIC 6722 Management investment, open-end
Jacqueline Boddaert

D-U-N-S 20-552-0443   (SL)
**MOSAIC SALES SOLUTIONS CANADA OP-
ERATING CO.**
MOSAIC
(*Suby of* MACQUARIE GROUP LIMITED)
2700 Matheson Blvd E Unit 101, Mississauga,
ON, L4W 4V9
(905) 238-8058
Emp Here 800   *Sales* 126,220,000
SIC 8743 Public relations services
Robert E. Hill Jr
Aidan Tracey
Jeff Rogers
Philip P. Monti
Reece B. Alford
Sean Anthony

D-U-N-S 20-052-5996   (HQ)
MSC INDUSTRIAL SUPPLY ULC
(*Suby of* MSC INDUSTRIAL DIRECT CO.,
INC.)
2595 Skymark Ave Suite 202, Mississauga,
ON, L4W 4L5
(905) 219-6300
Emp Here 240   *Sales* 195,092,000
SIC 5085 Industrial supplies
Gregory Milzcnik

D-U-N-S 20-903-9924   (SL)
MTD METRO TOOL & DIE LIMITED
(*Suby of* 1006368 ONTARIO LIMITED)
1065 Pantera Dr, Mississauga, ON, L4W 2X4
(905) 625-8464
Emp Here 160   *Sales* 32,912,960
SIC 4225 General warehousing and storage
Marcel Pantano
Edward Cooray

D-U-N-S 24-925-3857   (SL)
**MULDOON'S OWN AUTHENTIC COFFEE
CORP**
5680 Timberlea Blvd, Mississauga, ON, L4W
4M6
(905) 712-2233
Emp Here 25   *Sales* 20,889,425
SIC 5149 Groceries and related products, nec
Shaun Muldoon
James Muldoon

D-U-N-S 25-660-2640   (SL)
NADINE INTERNATIONAL INC
2325 Skymark Ave, Mississauga, ON, L4W

5A9
(905) 602-1850
Emp Here 74   *Sales* 13,121,014
SIC 7371 Custom computer programming services
Ajwad Gebara

D-U-N-S 20-708-6708   (SL)
NATIONAL INCOME PROTECTION PLAN INC
ONCIDIUM HEALTH GROUP
(*Suby of* IMPERIAL CAPITAL GROUP LTD)
2595 Skymark Ave Unit 206, Mississauga, ON, L4W 4L5
(905) 219-0096
Emp Here 144
SIC 8748 Business consulting, nec
Derrick Hamilton
Hana Ifrah
Michelle Braga

D-U-N-S 24-758-2224   (SL)
NATIONAL SAFETY ASSOCIATES OF CANADA INC / NSA CANADA INC
NSA
2785 Skymark Ave Suite 15, Mississauga, ON, L4W 4Y3
(905) 624-6368
Emp Here 12   *Sales* 10,026,924
SIC 5149 Groceries and related products, nec
Paul Stewart
Douglas Arscott
Roger Pearsall
Jacques E. Blondeau

D-U-N-S 25-318-3867   (BR)
NAV CANADA
TORONTO AREA CONTROL CENTRE
(*Suby of* NAV CANADA)
6055 Midfield Rd, Mississauga, ON, L4W 2P7
(905) 676-5045
Emp Here 400
SIC 4899 Communication services, nec
John Urban

D-U-N-S 24-413-0287   (HQ)
NEATFREAK GROUP INC
5320 Timberlea Blvd, Mississauga, ON, L4W 2S6
(905) 624-6262
Sales 10,094,850
SIC 3089 Plastics products, nec
Owen Mellon

D-U-N-S 20-054-9020   (HQ)
NELLA CUTLERY & FOOD EQUIPMENT INC
1255 Fewster Dr, Mississauga, ON, L4W 1A2
(905) 823-1110
Emp Here 3   *Sales* 18,334,134
SIC 5046 Commercial equipment, nec
Mark Nella
Robert Nella
Marisa Nella

D-U-N-S 20-917-8164   (SL)
NETSUITE INC
(*Suby of* ORACLE CORPORATION)
5800 Explorer Dr Suite 100, Mississauga, ON, L4W 5K9
(905) 219-8534
Emp Here 49   *Sales* 11,387,747
SIC 5734 Computer and software stores
Marc Huffman

D-U-N-S 20-015-0881   (SL)
NEWS-GLOBAL SOURCING COMPANY
1109 Britannia Rd E, Mississauga, ON, L4W 3X1
(905) 564-2100
Emp Here 23   *Sales* 17,077,960
SIC 5191 Farm supplies
Syed Ahmad
Durri Ahmad

D-U-N-S 24-684-8795   (HQ)
NFI IPD, LLC
NFI CANADA

(*Suby of* NFI INDUSTRIES, INC.)
2800 Skymark Ave Suite 501, Mississauga, ON, L4W 5A6
(905) 625-2300
Sales 28,598,185
SIC 4731 Freight transportation arrangement
Sidney Brown
Sandra Bell

D-U-N-S 24-320-2064   (SL)
NIIT LEARNING SOLUTIONS (CANADA) LTD
5045 Orbitor Dr Unit 100, Mississauga, ON, L4W 4Y4
(905) 572-1664
Emp Here 50   *Sales* 11,895,050
SIC 8742 Management consulting services
Sapnesh Lalla
Pr Subramanian

D-U-N-S 24-083-5355   (HQ)
NIKON CANADA INC
(*Suby of* NIKON CORPORATION)
1366 Aerowood Dr, Mississauga, ON, L4W 1C1
(905) 625-9910
Emp Here 60   *Sales* 42,481,530
SIC 5043 Photographic equipment and supplies
Michael Finch

D-U-N-S 20-114-3765   (HQ)
NISSAN CANADA INC
(*Suby of* NISSAN MOTOR CO.,LTD.)
5290 Orbitor Dr, Mississauga, ON, L4W 4Z5
(905) 602-0792
Emp Here 250   *Sales* 404,507,600
SIC 5012 Automobiles and other motor vehicles
Joni Paiva
Marie-Claude Morrissette
Christian Meunier

D-U-N-S 20-178-5040   (SL)
NORAM ENTERPRISES INC
NORAM GLASS
1325 Aimco Blvd, Mississauga, ON, L4W 1B4
(905) 238-0470
Emp Here 30   *Sales* 15,265,680
SIC 5023 Homefurnishings
Ted Redlarski

D-U-N-S 24-134-4530   (SL)
NORDIC EQUITY LIMITED
NORDIC TRAVEL GROUP
2800 Skymark Ave, Mississauga, ON, L4W 5A6
(905) 629-8530
Emp Here 85   *Sales* 44,197,195
SIC 4725 Tour operators
Michael Friisdahl

D-U-N-S 20-191-8104   (BR)
NORDION (CANADA) INC
MDS PHARMA SERVICES
(*Suby of* NORDION (CANADA) INC)
1980 Matheson Blvd E Suite 1, Mississauga, ON, L4W 5R7
(905) 206-8887
Emp Here 200
SIC 8071 Medical laboratories
Maureen Smith

D-U-N-S 20-552-3632   (HQ)
NORTHAMPTON GROUP INC
2601 Matheson Blvd E Suite 212, Mississauga, ON, L4W 5A8
(905) 629-9992
Sales 27,720,131
SIC 7011 Hotels and motels
Vinod Patel
Narendan Patel
Nagin Patel
Kantu Patel
Robert Preston
Edwin Cohen
Keith Gray

D-U-N-S 24-372-9956   (HQ)
NORTHSTAR HOSPITALITY LIMITED PARTNERSHIP
5090 Explorer Dr Suite 700, Mississauga, ON, L4W 4T9
(905) 629-3400
Sales 47,834,000
SIC 7011 Hotels and motels
Tamara Lawson

D-U-N-S 25-543-4987   (HQ)
NORTRAX CANADA INC
(*Suby of* DEERE & COMPANY)
1655 Britannia Rd E Suite 155, Mississauga, ON, L4W 1S5
(905) 670-1655
Emp Here 50   *Sales* 209,723,900
SIC 5082 Construction and mining machinery
Michael Rugeroni

D-U-N-S 24-321-4124   (HQ)
NUCLEUS DISTRIBUTION INC
FORWARD 600 PRECISION TOOLS & MACHINERY
(*Suby of* OCTAGON DISTRIBUTION COMPANY LIMITED)
5220 General Rd, Mississauga, ON, L4W 1G8
(800) 263-4283
Emp Here 20   *Sales* 19,001,040
SIC 5084 Industrial machinery and equipment
Philip Jamieson
David Campbell
Robert Jamieson
Henry Becher
Robert Bond
Cathy Rochwerg
Debra Walton-Collings
John Wilby

D-U-N-S 24-383-7247   (SL)
OAKGROUP AUTOMOTIVE CORPORATION
1035 Ronsa Crt, Mississauga, ON, L4W 2N6
(905) 614-0777
Emp Here 100   *Sales* 62,928,000
SIC 5511 New and used car dealers
Ralph Dellatroce

D-U-N-S 24-420-4819   (HQ)
OCTAGON DISTRIBUTION COMPANY LIMITED
5220 General Rd, Mississauga, ON, L4W 1G8

Sales 19,001,040
SIC 5084 Industrial machinery and equipment
Barry Dixon
Chris Irwin

D-U-N-S 25-203-4905   (SL)
OFFICE SOURCE INCORPORATED, THE
4800 Eastgate Pky Unit 1, Mississauga, ON, L4W 3W6
(905) 602-7090
Emp Here 40   *Sales* 20,354,240
SIC 5021 Furniture
Margaret Skinner
Allan Skinner

D-U-N-S 25-221-1743   (HQ)
OLSEN FASHION CANADA INC
5112 Timberlea Blvd, Mississauga, ON, L4W 2S5
(905) 290-1919
Emp Here 35   *Sales* 25,115,440
SIC 5621 Women's clothing stores
Michael Wolff
Bryan Farman
Stan Aehaide

D-U-N-S 24-876-2916   (SL)
ONTARIO CHRYSLER JEEP DODGE INC
ONTARIO CHRYSLER
5280 Dixie Rd, Mississauga, ON, L4W 2A7
(905) 625-8801
Emp Here 100   *Sales* 62,928,000
SIC 5511 New and used car dealers
Bary Gray
Linda Hillmer

D-U-N-S 25-087-0953   (SL)
OPALIS SOFTWARE INC
2680 Matheson Blvd E Suite 202, Mississauga, ON, L4W 0A5
(905) 670-8180
Emp Here 60   *Sales* 10,638,660
SIC 7371 Custom computer programming services
Todd Delaughter
Gregory Twinney

D-U-N-S 20-955-8266   (HQ)
ORNGE
ORNGE
5310 Explorer Dr, Mississauga, ON, L4W 5H8
(647) 428-2005
Emp Here 400   *Sales* 142,336,948
SIC 4522 Air transportation, nonscheduled
Andrew Mccallum
Susan Kennedy
Inna Kravitz

D-U-N-S 24-680-2651   (SL)
OSC CONSTRUCTORS ULC
5149 Bradco Blvd, Mississauga, ON, L4W 2A6
(905) 458-1005
Emp Here 100   *Sales* 24,618,600
SIC 1795 Wrecking and demolition work
Gil Nicolau
James F Williams
Jon M Williams

D-U-N-S 20-217-0890   (HQ)
P.K. DOUGLASS INC
1033 Jayson Crt, Mississauga, ON, L4W 2P4
(905) 624-3300
Emp Here 35   *Sales* 23,424,390
SIC 5099 Durable goods, nec
John Turner Sr.
Carol Turner
John P Turner
Robert P Turner
S Peter Turner
Ian Torrance

D-U-N-S 20-401-5531   (SL)
PACIFIC PAVING OF MARKHAM LIMITED
5845 Luke Rd Suite 204, Mississauga, ON, L4W 2K5
(905) 670-7730
Emp Here 35   *Sales* 14,677,425
SIC 6719 Holding companies, nec
Frank Finelli
Pino Finelli
Tony Finelli

D-U-N-S 25-322-8803   (HQ)
PAGING NETWORK OF CANADA INC
PAGENET
(*Suby of* MADISON TELECOMMUNICATIONS HOLDINGS INC)
1685 Tech Ave Suite 1, Mississauga, ON, L4W 0A7
(905) 614-3100
Emp Here 38   *Sales* 87,617,297
SIC 5065 Electronic parts and equipment, nec
Garry Fitzgerald
Al Dykstra
George Rivers

D-U-N-S 20-145-5862   (HQ)
PANASONIC CANADA INC
PANASONIC
(*Suby of* PANASONIC CORPORATION)
5770 Ambler Dr Suite 70, Mississauga, ON, L4W 2T3
(905) 624-5010
Emp Here 300   *Sales* 345,246,965
SIC 5064 Electrical appliances, television and radio
Ian Vatcher
Ken Buschlen

D-U-N-S 20-543-8414   (BR)
PANASONIC CANADA INC
(*Suby of* PANASONIC CORPORATION)

5810 Ambler Dr Unit 4, Mississauga, ON, L4W 4J5

Emp Here 400
SIC 5065 Electronic parts and equipment, nec
Fearn Lee

D-U-N-S 20-312-3674   (SL)
PANASONIC ECO SOLUTIONS CANADA INC
(Suby of PANASONIC CORPORATION)
5770 Ambler Dr Unit 70, Mississauga, ON, L4W 2T3
(905) 624-5010
Emp Here 100   Sales 22,975,400
SIC 8731 Commercial physical research
Walter Buzzelli
Dan Silver
Jeff Bloszies
Iordan Novakov
Brian Mcmullan

D-U-N-S 20-155-1359   (SL)
PATTISON OUTDOOR ADVERTISING LIMITED PARTNERSHIP
2700 Matheson Blvd E Suite 500, Mississauga, ON, L4W 4V9
(905) 282-6800
Emp Here 150   Sales 30,055,650
SIC 7312 Outdoor advertising services
Randy Otto
Barry Wild

D-U-N-S 20-642-0069   (SL)
PEEL TRUCK & TRAILER EQUIPMENT INC
1715 Britannia Rd E, Mississauga, ON, L4W 2A3
(905) 670-1780
Emp Here 68   Sales 19,264,400
SIC 7539 Automotive repair shops, nec
Kevin Thomas
Dionisio Di Franco
Dennis Di Franco Jr

D-U-N-S 25-989-4921   (HQ)
PEPSI BOTTLING GROUP (CANADA), ULC, THE
PEPSICO BEVERAGES CANADA
(Suby of PBG INVESTMENT (LUXEMBOURG) SARL)
5205 Satellite Dr, Mississauga, ON, L4W 5J7
(905) 212-7377
Emp Here 257   Sales 2,924,310,000
SIC 2086 Bottled and canned soft drinks
Richard Glover
Mary Manocchio
Corey Michael Baker

D-U-N-S 24-321-4116   (HQ)
PEPSICO CANADA ULC
FRITO LAY CANADA
(Suby of PEPSICO, INC.)
5550 Explorer Dr, Mississauga, ON, L4W 0C3
(289) 374-5000
Emp Here 80   Sales 1,949,540,000
SIC 2096 Potato chips and similar snacks
Richard Glover
Jason Mcdonell

D-U-N-S 25-106-8359   (SL)
PHILIPPE DANDURAND WINES LIMITED
VINS PHILLIPE DANDURAND WINES
(Suby of PHILDAN INC)
1660 Tech Ave Suite 3, Mississauga, ON, L4W 5S7
(416) 368-3344
Emp Here 38   Sales 22,340,808
SIC 5182 Wine and distilled beverages
Philippe Dandurand

D-U-N-S 20-173-1197   (HQ)
PITNEY BOWES OF CANADA LTD
PITNEY BOWES GLOBAL CREDIT SERVICES
(Suby of PITNEY BOWES INC.)
5500 Explorer Dr Suite 1, Mississauga, ON, L4W 5C7

(905) 219-3000
Emp Here 200   Sales 803,028,000
SIC 5044 Office equipment
Marc Lautenbach
Michael Monahan
Linda Alvarado
Roger Fradin
Anne M. Busquet
Anne Sutherland Fuchs
S Douglas Hutcheson
Marc Lautenbach
Eduardo Menasce
Michael Roth

D-U-N-S 24-675-9026   (BR)
PITNEY BOWES OF CANADA LTD
(Suby of PITNEY BOWES INC.)
5500 Explorer Dr Unit 2, Mississauga, ON, L4W 5C7
(800) 672-6937
Emp Here 200
SIC 5044 Office equipment
Karen Bell

D-U-N-S 24-425-0325   (SL)
PLATINUM HEALTH BENEFITS SOLUTIONS INC
5090 Explorer Dr Suite 501, Mississauga, ON, L4W 4T9
(905) 602-0404
Emp Here 25   Sales 25,872,025
SIC 6324 Hospital and medical service plans
Barbara Mustapha

D-U-N-S 24-393-0281   (HQ)
POINTCLICKCARE CORP
5570 Explorer Dr, Mississauga, ON, L4W 0C4
(905) 858-8885
Emp Here 17   Sales 77,367,600
SIC 7372 Prepackaged software
Mike Wessinger
Richard Guttman
David Belbeck
Terri Weckle
Travis Palmquist
Angelo Papatheodorou
Cheryl Alden
Terry Low
Nani Mcdonnell
Russ Depriest

D-U-N-S 25-312-0687   (HQ)
POINTCLICKCARE TECHNOLOGIES INC
(Suby of POINTCLICKCARE CORP)
5570 Explorer Dr, Mississauga, ON, L4W 0C4
(905) 858-8885
Emp Here 250   Sales 77,367,600
SIC 7372 Prepackaged software
Michael Wessinger
Andrew Brigant
David Wessinger
David Belveck

D-U-N-S 24-049-1845   (HQ)
POLARIS REALTY (CANADA) LIMITED
2605 Skymark Ave Suite 105, Mississauga, ON, L4W 4L5
(905) 238-8363
Emp Here 19   Sales 17,669,680
SIC 6512 Nonresidential building operators
Rainer Hackert
Nancy Brauweiler
Harold Little

D-U-N-S 25-883-3797   (HQ)
POPPA CORN CORP
(Suby of SUPER-PUFFT SNACKS CORP)
5135 Creekbank Rd Unit C, Mississauga, ON, L4W 1R3
(905) 212-9855
Emp Here 21   Sales 22,560,579
SIC 5145 Confectionery
Michel Cousineau

D-U-N-S 25-109-5279   (SL)
POWERFUL GROUP OF COMPANIES INC
POWERFUL ELECTRICAL SERVICES
5155 Spectrum Way Suite 8, Mississauga,

ON, L4W 5A1
(416) 674-8046
Emp Here 69   Sales 16,081,485
SIC 1711 Plumbing, heating, air-conditioning
Paul Docherty

D-U-N-S 20-937-2853   (HQ)
PPL AQUATIC, FITNESS & SPA GROUP INC
5170 Timberlea Blvd Unit A, Mississauga, ON, L4W 2S5
(905) 501-7210
Sales 139,060,000
SIC 5091 Sporting and recreation goods
Dale Papke
Paul Denstedt
Tim Bown
Steve Onoprijenko

D-U-N-S 25-351-5753   (SL)
PREMIER CANDLE CORP
960 Britannia Rd E, Mississauga, ON, L4W 5M7
(905) 795-8833
Emp Here 250   Sales 66,142,000
SIC 3999 Manufacturing industries, nec
Jackey Cheng
Suk-Yee Cheng
Sze Man Cheng
William Cheng
Chak-Yin Cheng

D-U-N-S 20-797-4069   (HQ)
PREMIERE VAN LINES INC
5800 Ambler Dr Unit 210, Mississauga, ON, L4W 4J4
(905) 712-8960
Emp Here 19   Sales 20,904,300
SIC 6794 Patent owners and lessors
Tim Moore
Walt Peniuk
Ricky Amponssa

D-U-N-S 20-327-4860   (HQ)
PRIMUS MANAGEMENT ULC
PRIMUS CANADA
(Suby of FUSION CONNECT, INC.)
2680 Skymark Ave Unit 100, Mississauga, ON, L4W 5L6
(416) 236-3636
Emp Here 300   Sales 117,090,400
SIC 4813 Telephone communication, except radio
Bradley Fisher
Tamara Flemington
Maureen Merkler
Jill C. Schatz

D-U-N-S 24-389-8678   (SL)
PROFOUND MEDICAL INC
2400 Skymark Ave Unit 6, Mississauga, ON, L4W 5K5
(647) 476-1350
Emp Here 64   Sales 14,704,256
SIC 8731 Commercial physical research
Arun Menawat
Rashed Dewan
Hartmut Warnken
Goldy Singh
Ron Kurtz
Aaron Davidson
Jean-Francois Pariseau
Brian Ellacott
Linda Maxwell
Kenneth Galbraith

D-U-N-S 20-166-9272   (HQ)
PROVINCIAL CAPITAL CORP
PROVINCIAL TRAILER RENTALS
1611 Britannia Rd E, Mississauga, ON, L4W 1S5
(905) 670-7077
Emp Here 40   Sales 21,247,500
SIC 7519 Utility trailer rental
Douglas Vanderspek
Steve Nash

D-U-N-S 24-823-3298   (HQ)
QUIK X TRANSPORTATION INC

QUIK X LOGISTICS
(Suby of TFI INTERNATIONAL INC)
5425 Dixie Rd Bldg B, Mississauga, ON, L4W 1E6
(905) 238-8584
Emp Here 200   Sales 175,161,950
SIC 4213 Trucking, except local
Josiane-M. Langlois
Chantal Martel
Jeffery King

D-U-N-S 20-128-9510   (SL)
R&R REAL ESTATE INVESTMENT TRUST
5090 Explorer Dr Suite 700, Mississauga, ON, L4W 4X6
(905) 206-7100
Emp Here 5   Sales 15,517,964
SIC 6798 Real estate investment trusts
Michael Klingher
Bob Choo
Majid Mangalji
Graham Blyth
Derek Dermott
Irfan Lakha

D-U-N-S 24-645-5281   (SL)
RAYNOR CANADA CORP
RICHARDS-WILCOX CANADA
(Suby of NEISEWANDER ENTERPRISES INC.)
5100 Timberlea Blvd Suite A, Mississauga, ON, L4W 2S5
(905) 625-0037
Emp Here 150   Sales 36,484,650
SIC 3442 Metal doors, sash, and trim
Raymond Friesen
Randolph Hiebert
Edward Chin
Jon Keesey

D-U-N-S 20-374-9036   (SL)
RB HEALTH (CANADA) INC
(Suby of RECKITT BENCKISER GROUP PLC)
1680 Tech Ave Unit 2, Mississauga, ON, L4W 5S9
(905) 283-7000
Emp Here 98
SIC 2833 Medicinals and botanicals
Lee Coomber
Victoria Woot
Gregory Woot

D-U-N-S 24-886-8820   (HQ)
RECKITT BENCKISER (CANADA) INC
RECKITT BENCKISER HEALTH
(Suby of RECKITT BENCKISER GROUP PLC)
1680 Tech Ave Unit 2, Mississauga, ON, L4W 5S9
(905) 283-7000
Sales 104,491,575
SIC 2842 Polishes and sanitation goods
Gregory Wood
Lee Comber
Philippe Escoffier
Stephen Pike

D-U-N-S 24-354-8125   (HQ)
RED LABEL VACATIONS INC
ITRAVEL2000
(Suby of RED LABEL HOLDINGS INC)
5450 Explorer Dr Suite 400, Mississauga, ON, L4W 5N1
(905) 283-6020
Emp Here 1   Sales 40,013,520
SIC 4724 Travel agencies
Enzo Demarinis
Frank Demarinis
Joseph Demarinis
Sandra Lombardi

D-U-N-S 20-057-3116   (SL)
REDMOND/WILLIAMS DISTRIBUTIONS INC
5605 Timberlea Blvd, Mississauga, ON, L4W 2S4

(905) 238-8208
Emp Here 40   *Sales* 17,886,960
SIC 5075 Warm air heating and air conditioning
Chris Redmond
Tony Koopman
Henry Chin

D-U-N-S 20-916-0501   (BR)
RESOLVE CORPORATION
2400 Skymark Ave Unit 6, Mississauga, ON, L4W 5K5

Emp Here 200
SIC 8742 Management consulting services
Margaret Nichols

D-U-N-S 20-109-5507   (HQ)
REVERA INC
(*Suby of* GOVERNMENT OF CANADA)
5015 Spectrum Way Suite 600, Mississauga, ON, L4W 0E4
(289) 360-1252
Emp Here 100   *Sales* 694,055,508
SIC 8051 Skilled nursing care facilities
Thomas G Wellner
Frank Cerrone
Barbara Hill
Krys Hoeg
Pat Jacobsen
Terrance Royer
Calvin R. Stiller
Marie-Josee Turmel
Gary Colter
John Valentini

D-U-N-S 24-345-7178   (BR)
REVERA INC
(*Suby of* GOVERNMENT OF CANADA)
1500 Rathburn Rd E, Mississauga, ON, L4W 4L7
(905) 238-0800
Emp Here 200
SIC 6513 Apartment building operators
Debra Rushton

D-U-N-S 20-506-0882   (HQ)
REVLON CANADA INC
(*Suby of* REVLON, INC.)
1590 South Gateway Rd, Mississauga, ON, L4W 0A8
(905) 276-4500
Sales 42,603,150
SIC 2844 Toilet preparations
Andrew Pegg
Robert Kretzman
Michael Sheehan
Timothy Ricks
Simon Worraker

D-U-N-S 24-363-0741   (HQ)
RGIS CANADA ULC
(*Suby of* THE BLACKSTONE GROUP L P)
2560 Matheson Blvd E Suite 224, Mississauga, ON, L4W 4Y9
(905) 206-1107
Emp Here 100   *Sales* 1,337,816,000
SIC 7389 Business services, nec
Nick Ford
Holly Tomilson

D-U-N-S 24-451-1143   (SL)
RICHEMONT CANADA, INC
(*Suby of* COMPAGNIE FINANCIERE RICHEMONT SA)
4610 Eastgate Pky Unit 1, Mississauga, ON, L4W 3W6
(905) 602-8532
Emp Here 30   *Sales* 15,616,260
SIC 5094 Jewelry and precious stones
Alain Viot
John Forest

D-U-N-S 24-214-0135   (HQ)
RICOH CANADA INC
(*Suby of* RICOH COMPANY,LTD.)
5560 Explorer Dr Suite 100, Mississauga, ON, L4W 5M3

(905) 795-9659
Emp Here 200   *Sales* 1,124,239,200
SIC 5044 Office equipment
Glenn Laverty
Marc Cotie
Eric Fletcher
Bob Leonhardt
Richard Perri

D-U-N-S 24-862-6582   (SL)
ROBINSON FORGIONE GROUP INC
CENTURA BRANDS
1200 Aerowood Dr Suite 50, Mississauga, ON, L4W 2S7
(905) 602-1965
Emp Here 25   *Sales* 11,875,650
SIC 5087 Service establishment equipment
Myles Robinson
Sam Forgione

D-U-N-S 20-774-0135   (SL)
ROMET LIMITED
5030 Timberlea Blvd, Mississauga, ON, L4W 2S5
(905) 624-1591
Emp Here 120   *Sales* 27,274,680
SIC 3824 Fluid meters and counting devices
Brent Collver
Wan Zhou

D-U-N-S 24-079-3364   (SL)
S.D.R. DISTRIBUTION SERVICES
COLD STORAGE
1880 Matheson Blvd E, Mississauga, ON, L4W 5N4
(905) 625-7377
Emp Here 45   *Sales* 22,424,490
SIC 5137 Women's and children's clothing
Steve Resnick

D-U-N-S 24-366-2249   (SL)
SAFESEA-AMI SHIPPING INC
1030 Kamato Rd Suite 210, Mississauga, ON, L4W 4B6

Emp Here 35   *Sales* 36,397,690
SIC 4731 Freight transportation arrangement
Adnan Khan
Vincent Hachez

D-U-N-S 20-398-3705   (SL)
SAHIB FREIGHT SERVICES INC
1665 Enterprise Rd, Mississauga, ON, L4W 4L4
(905) 696-8050
Emp Here 27   *Sales* 10,404,720
SIC 4731 Freight transportation arrangement
Sarabpreet Pangli

D-U-N-S 25-598-3694   (HQ)
SCHAWK CANADA INC
SCHAWK TRISTAR, DIV OF
(*Suby of* MATTHEWS INTERNATIONAL CORPORATION)
1620 Tech Ave Suite 3, Mississauga, ON, L4W 5P4
(905) 219-1600
Emp Here 160   *Sales* 40,074,200
SIC 7336 Commercial art and graphic design
Robert Cockerill

D-U-N-S 24-795-8762   (SL)
SENSORS & SOFTWARE INC
1040 Stacey Crt, Mississauga, ON, L4W 2X8
(905) 614-1789
Emp Here 43   *Sales* 11,032,166
SIC 3829 Measuring and controlling devices, nec
Peter Annan
Gigi Liczner

D-U-N-S 24-823-1144   (HQ)
SERVICEMASTER OF CANADA LIMITED
MERRY MAIDS
(*Suby of* SERVICEMASTER GLOBAL HOLDINGS, INC.)
5462 Timberlea Blvd, Mississauga, ON, L4W 2T7

(905) 670-0000
Sales 10,613,428
SIC 6794 Patent owners and lessors
Joel Degroat

D-U-N-S 20-423-6699   (HQ)
SGS CANADA INC
5825 Explorer Dr, Mississauga, ON, L4W 5P6
(905) 364-3757
Emp Here 100   *Sales* 18,367,380,000
SIC 8734 Testing laboratories
Frankie Ng
Samantha Elder
Gerard O'dell
Chris Lowry

D-U-N-S 20-550-9735   (HQ)
SKECHERS USA CANADA, INC
(*Suby of* SKECHERS U.S.A., INC.)
5055 Satellite Dr Unit 6, Mississauga, ON, L4W 5K7
(905) 238-7121
Sales 17,441,270
SIC 5139 Footwear
John Hartssorn

D-U-N-S 24-310-3772   (SL)
SKOR CULINARY CONCEPTS INC
1330 Crestlawn Dr, Mississauga, ON, L4W 1P8
(905) 625-4447
Emp Here 75   *Sales* 16,864,125
SIC 2099 Food preparations, nec
Vince A. Capobianco
Steve Corvese

D-U-N-S 25-832-1132   (BR)
SLH TRANSPORT INC
(*Suby of* HOLDING CANADIAN AMERICAN TRANSPORTATION C.A.T. INC)
905 Shawson Dr, Mississauga, ON, L4W 1T9
(905) 893-5170
Emp Here 200
SIC 4213 Trucking, except local
Sylvain Moffatt

D-U-N-S 20-324-7382   (HQ)
SMART EMPLOYEE BENEFITS INC
5500 Explorer Dr 4th Flr, Mississauga, ON, L4W 5C7
(888) 939-8885
Emp Here 15   *Sales* 59,310,668
SIC 7372 Prepackaged software
John Mckimm
Mario Correia
Annie Holmes
Rohan D'souza
Robert Prentice
Peter Yu
Latiq Qureshi
Stephen Peacock
John Mckimm
Christine J. Hrudka

D-U-N-S 20-316-5535   (SL)
SODASTREAM CANADA LTD
5450 Explorer Dr Suite 202, Mississauga, ON, L4W 5N1
(905) 629-4450
Emp Here 23   *Sales* 10,925,598
SIC 5084 Industrial machinery and equipment
Leon Paul
Daniel Birnbaum
Eyal Shohat

D-U-N-S 24-062-4403   (HQ)
SS&C TECHNOLOGIES CANADA CORP
(*Suby of* SS&C TECHNOLOGIES HOLDINGS, INC.)
5255 Orbitor Dr Unit 1, Mississauga, ON, L4W 5M6
(905) 629-8000
Emp Here 200   *Sales* 46,143,250
SIC 7371 Custom computer programming services
William C. Stone
Normand A. Boulanger
Patrick G. Pedonti

Stephen J. Ashbury

D-U-N-S 25-101-0914   (HQ)
STAHLSCHMIDT LTD
STAHLSCHMIDT CABLE SYSTEMS
5208 Everest Dr, Mississauga, ON, L4W 2R4
(905) 629-4568
Sales 15,366,800
SIC 3465 Automotive stampings
George Jaeggi

D-U-N-S 24-131-9354   (HQ)
STRONGCO CORPORATION
1640 Enterprise Rd, Mississauga, ON, L4W 4L4
(905) 670-5100
Emp Here 25   *Sales* 312,419,899
SIC 7353 Heavy construction equipment rental
Robert J. Beutel
J. David Wood
William J. Ostrander
Oliver Nachevski
Rick Ziegler
Steve Diloreto
Stephen George
Peter Rayner
John Anhang
Anne Brace

D-U-N-S 24-776-7788   (HQ)
STRONGCO ENGINEERED SYSTEMS INC
1640 Enterprise Rd, Mississauga, ON, L4W 4L4
(905) 670-5100
Emp Here 1   *Sales* 38,850,175
SIC 3541 Machine tools, Metal cutting type
Robin Maclean
Kevin Metcalf
Bill Van Duyn
David Navas

D-U-N-S 24-365-9013   (HQ)
STRONGCO LIMITED PARTNERSHIP
1640 Enterprise Rd, Mississauga, ON, L4W 4L4
(905) 670-5100
Emp Here 100   *Sales* 292,638,000
SIC 5082 Construction and mining machinery
Leonard Philips

D-U-N-S 25-709-6982   (BR)
SUPREMEX INC
(*Suby of* SUPREMEX INC)
5300 Tomken Rd, Mississauga, ON, L4W 1P2
(905) 624-4973
Emp Here 150
SIC 2677 Envelopes
Stacy Daily

D-U-N-S 24-575-7935   (HQ)
SYMBOL TECHNOLOGIES CANADA, ULC
5180 Orbitor Dr, Mississauga, ON, L4W 5L9
(905) 629-7226
Sales 40,245,660
SIC 5065 Electronic parts and equipment, nec
Michael Reid
David Succurro

D-U-N-S 20-112-9173   (BR)
SYMCOR INC
(*Suby of* SYMCOR INC)
1625 Tech Ave, Mississauga, ON, L4W 5P5
(289) 360-2000
Emp Here 400
SIC 2752 Commercial printing, lithographic
Glenn Ryder

D-U-N-S 20-515-4938   (HQ)
TEC BUSINESS SOLUTIONS LTD
1048 Ronsa Crt, Mississauga, ON, L4W 3Y4
(905) 828-8132
Sales 10,073,160
SIC 5112 Stationery and office supplies
Thierry Cecilia
Michael Prencipe

D-U-N-S 24-409-7200   (HQ)

▲ Public Company   ■ Public Company Family Member   **HQ** Headquarters   **BR** Branch   **SL** Single Location

TECH-TREK LTD
1015 Matheson Blvd E Suite 6, Mississauga,
ON, L4W 3A4
(905) 238-0319
Emp Here 28   *Sales* 17,886,960
SIC 5065 Electronic parts and equipment, nec
William Ford
Brian Grigor

D-U-N-S 24-744-3765   (SL)
TERDUN MATERIAL MANAGEMENT INC
5130 Creekbank Rd, Mississauga, ON, L4W
2G2
(905) 602-4567
Emp Here 50   *Sales* 11,671,750
SIC 2675 Die-cut paper and board
John Klass
Duncan Smith

D-U-N-S 24-076-6212   (HQ)
TEVELEC LIMITED
5350 Timberlea Blvd Suite 1, Mississauga,
ON, L4W 2S6
(905) 624-5241
Emp Here 40   *Sales* 22,358,700
SIC 5051 Metals service centers and offices
John White
Earl Echlin

D-U-N-S 25-486-9753   (SL)
TEXTILE PRODUCTS LTD
1581 Matheson Blvd, Mississauga, ON, L4W
1H9
(905) 361-1831
Emp Here 50   *Sales* 24,916,100
SIC 5131 Piece goods and notions
Hamida Marfatia

D-U-N-S 25-687-0684   (SL)
THANE DIRECT CANADA INC
(*Suby of* THANE INTERNATIONAL, INC.)
5255 Orbitor Dr Suite 501, Mississauga, ON,
L4W 5M6
(905) 625-3800
Emp Here 38   *Sales* 19,336,528
SIC 5023 Homefurnishings
Amir Tukulj
Patty Booth

D-U-N-S 24-205-7441   (HQ)
THANE DIRECT COMPANY
(*Suby of* THANE INTERNATIONAL, INC.)
5255 Orbitor Dr Suite 501, Mississauga, ON,
L4W 5M6
(905) 625-3800
Sales 22,389,664
SIC 5023 Homefurnishings
Amir Tukulj
Sladjana Tukulj
Patricia Booth

D-U-N-S 20-550-7726   (SL)
TOP GRADE MOLDS LTD
929 Pantera Dr, Mississauga, ON, L4W 2R9
(905) 625-9865
Emp Here 120   *Sales* 26,640,120
SIC 3544 Special dies, tools, jigs, and fixtures
Joseph Slobodnik
Vince Ciccone
Ron Stewart

D-U-N-S 20-385-4336   (BR)
TORONTO-DOMINION BANK, THE
TD CANADA TRUST
(*Suby of* TORONTO-DOMINION BANK, THE)
4880 Tahoe Blvd 5th Fl, Mississauga, ON,
L4W 5P3
(905) 293-5613
Emp Here 100
SIC 6021 National commercial banks

D-U-N-S 24-682-7096   (SL)
TRAILER WIZARDS LTD
1880 Britannia Rd E, Mississauga, ON, L4W
1J3
(905) 670-7077
Emp Here 320   *Sales* 28,702,720
SIC 7519 Utility trailer rental

Carl Vanderspek
Douglas Vanderspek

D-U-N-S 24-126-0764   (SL)
TRANS4 LOGISTICS
1575 South Gateway Rd Unit A&B, Mississauga, ON, L4W 5J1
(905) 212-9001
Emp Here 450   *Sales* 92,567,700
SIC 4213 Trucking, except local
James Houston
Larry Fuaco

D-U-N-S 25-361-5686   (BR)
TRANSPORT TFI 5, S.E.C.
KINGSWAY TRANSPORT
(*Suby of* TRANSPORT TFI 5, S.E.C.)
1100 Haultain Crt, Mississauga, ON, L4W 2T1
(905) 624-4050
Emp Here 150
SIC 4213 Trucking, except local
Tracy Mckinney

D-U-N-S 20-301-7793   (SL)
TRAPEZE SOFTWARE GROUP, INC
TRAPEZE GROUP
(*Suby of* CONSTELLATION SOFTWARE
INC)
5800 Explorer Dr Unit 500, Mississauga, ON,
L4W 5K9
(905) 629-8727
Emp Here 235   *Sales* 43,374,655
SIC 7371 Custom computer programming services
Mark Miller
John Hines
Nathan Partington
Grace Annab
Brian Beattie
Steve Cimicata

D-U-N-S 20-178-2302   (HQ)
TRAVELBRANDS INC
AGENCE DE VOYAGES SEARS
(*Suby of* RED LABEL HOLDINGS INC)
5450 Explorer Dr Unit 300, Mississauga, ON,
L4W 5M1
(416) 649-3939
Emp Here 400   *Sales* 355,894,200
SIC 4725 Tour operators
Frank Demarinis
Tony Saunders

D-U-N-S 25-372-4496   (BR)
TRIANGLE FREIGHT SERVICES LTD
CREEKBANK TRANSPORT, DIV OF
(*Suby of* EKS HOLDINGS LTD)
5355 Creekbank Rd, Mississauga, ON, L4W
5L5
(905) 624-1614
Emp Here 150
SIC 4212 Local trucking, without storage
Ian Forbes

D-U-N-S 24-370-1443   (SL)
TRUCK TRANSFER INC
5939 Shawson Dr, Mississauga, ON, L4W
3Y2
(416) 717-1000
Emp Here 27   *Sales* 14,039,109
SIC 4731 Freight transportation arrangement
Bogdan Paras
Cristina Petroiu

D-U-N-S 24-764-3034   (HQ)
TS MACHINES AND SERVICE CORP
5940 Shawson Dr, Mississauga, ON, L4W
3W5
(905) 670-5785
Emp Here 21   *Sales* 11,179,350
SIC 5072 Hardware
Anita Birk-Mueller

D-U-N-S 20-354-2753   (HQ)
TST OVERLAND EXPRESS
5200 Maingate Dr, Mississauga, ON, L4W
1G5

(905) 625-7500
Sales 11,714,400
SIC 8742 Management consulting services
Wayne Gruszka

D-U-N-S 25-306-0917   (BR)
TST SOLUTIONS L.P.
TST OVERLAND EXPRESS
(*Suby of* TST SOLUTIONS L.P.)
5200 Maingate Dr, Mississauga, ON, L4W
1G5

Emp Here 200
SIC 4111 Local and suburban transit
Robert O'reilly

D-U-N-S 20-705-0634   (HQ)
TST SOLUTIONS L.P.
TST AUTOMOTIVE SERVICES, DIV OF
5200 Maingate Dr, Mississauga, ON, L4W
1G5
(905) 625-7601
Emp Here 80   *Sales* 151,620,400
SIC 4213 Trucking, except local
Alain Bedard
Wayne Fruszka

D-U-N-S 20-788-0779   (BR)
TST SOLUTIONS L.P.
(*Suby of* TST SOLUTIONS L.P.)
5200 Maingate Dr, Mississauga, ON, L4W
1G5
(905) 624-7058
Emp Here 250
SIC 4731 Freight transportation arrangement
Faye Mcnalty

D-U-N-S 24-577-6307   (HQ)
TUBE-FAB LTD
1020 Brevik Pl Unit 11, Mississauga, ON, L4W
4N7
(905) 206-0311
Emp Here 90   *Sales* 25,931,475
SIC 3469 Metal stampings, nec
Wesley Eric Foley
Gary Edwards

D-U-N-S 20-150-8892   (HQ)
**TYCO INTEGRATED FIRE & SECURITY
CANADA, INC**
(*Suby of* JOHNSON CONTROLS INTERNATIONAL PUBLIC LIMITED COMPANY)
2400 Skymark Ave Suite 1, Mississauga, ON,
L4W 5K5
(905) 212-4400
Emp Here 200   *Sales* 306,161,700
SIC 1731 Electrical work
Tracy Long
Joe O'connell
William Bower
Heather Brown
Camelia Burtea
Caram Rai

D-U-N-S 20-851-1089   (SL)
TYNDALL NURSING HOME LIMITED
1060 Eglinton Ave E Suite 417, Mississauga,
ON, L4W 1K3
(905) 624-1511
Emp Here 120   *Sales* 8,227,920
SIC 8051 Skilled nursing care facilities
Denham Jolly

D-U-N-S 20-732-5986   (HQ)
UNIFIRST CANADA LTD
(*Suby of* UNIFIRST CORPORATION)
5250 Orbitor Dr, Mississauga, ON, L4W 5G7
(905) 624-8525
Emp Here 40   *Sales* 58,302,400
SIC 7213 Linen supply
Mike Szymanski
Tim Sullivan

D-U-N-S 25-168-6184   (HQ)
UNIQUE RESTORATION LTD
1220 Matheson Blvd E, Mississauga, ON,
L4W 1R2
(905) 629-9100
Sales 45,627,040

SIC 1542 Nonresidential construction, nec
John Kennedy
Steve Leblanc

D-U-N-S 25-367-3511   (HQ)
UTC FIRE & SECURITY CANADA INC
CHUBB EDWARDS SECURITY
(*Suby of* UNITED TECHNOLOGIES CORPORATION)
5201 Explorer Dr, Mississauga, ON, L4W 4H1
(905) 629-2600
Emp Here 100   *Sales* 226,332,000
SIC 3669 Communications equipment, nec
Tiina Zeggil
Mia Lalonde
Mohit Narang

D-U-N-S 25-635-8177   (BR)
UTI, CANADA, INC
(*Suby of* DSV A/S)
2540 Matheson Blvd E, Mississauga, ON,
L4W 4Z2

Emp Here 90
SIC 4731 Freight transportation arrangement
Anita Nelson

D-U-N-S 25-465-9014   (SL)
VENATOR ELECTRONICS SALES & SERVICE LTD
4500 Dixie Rd Unit 10, Mississauga, ON, L4W
1V7

Emp Here 33   *Sales* 14,756,742
SIC 5065 Electronic parts and equipment, nec
Theo Heuthorst
Tammy Venator

D-U-N-S 20-257-6047   (SL)
VERIDAY INC
5520 Explorer Dr Unit 400, Mississauga, ON,
L4W 5L1
(905) 273-4399
Emp Here 60   *Sales* 14,220,090
SIC 8743 Public relations services
Marc Lamoureux
Andrew Chung
Nick Quach
Chris Lamoureux
Tim Merrill
Jason Stargratt
Jonah Cohn
Tyson Kingsbury

D-U-N-S 24-966-3204   (HQ)
VERLY CONSTRUCTION GROUP INC
1650 Sismet Rd, Mississauga, ON, L4W 1R4
(905) 212-9420
Emp Here 15   *Sales* 11,768,275
SIC 1542 Nonresidential construction, nec
Paul Catania
Claire Catania

D-U-N-S 20-702-3763   (SL)
VIBRA FINISH LIMITED
5329 Maingate Dr, Mississauga, ON, L4W
1G6
(905) 625-9955
Emp Here 120   *Sales* 26,640,120
SIC 3541 Machine tools, Metal cutting type
Douglas Bradshaw
Brian Mcgillivray

D-U-N-S 24-954-0568   (SL)
VINPAC LINES (TORONTO) INC
2601 Matheson Blvd E Unit 202, Mississauga,
ON, L4W 5A8

Emp Here 35   *Sales* 18,198,845
SIC 4731 Freight transportation arrangement
Kai Koon Teng

D-U-N-S 25-120-6025   (SL)
VISIONMAX SOLUTIONS INC
2680 Skymark Ave Suite 600, Mississauga,
ON, L4W 5L6
(905) 282-0503
Emp Here 90   *Sales* 12,976,380

SIC 7371 Custom computer programming services
David Mcdougall
Jason Galletti
Robert Mcdougall
Graham Silver
Sanjay Issar
Orlando Salvador

D-U-N-S 25-322-5999   (HQ)
VOLARIS GROUP INC
TRAPEZE
(*Suby of* CONSTELLATION SOFTWARE INC)
5060 Spectrum Way Suite 110, Mississauga, ON, L4W 5N5
(905) 267-5400
Emp Here 100   *Sales* 77,520,660
SIC 7371 Custom computer programming services
Mark Miller
Rick Bacchus
Ian Keaveny
Fran Fendelet
Mark Leonard

D-U-N-S 24-587-2726   (HQ)
VOLUME TANK TRANSPORT INC
1230 Shawson Dr, Mississauga, ON, L4W 1C3
(905) 670-7090
Emp Here 45   *Sales* 14,193,714
SIC 4212 Local trucking, without storage
Peter Balan
Robert Chafee

D-U-N-S 20-563-2032   (SL)
VONAGE CANADA CORP
(*Suby of* VONAGE HOLDINGS CORP.)
2660 Matheson Blvd E Suite 301, Mississauga, ON, L4W 5M2
(416) 907-6100
Emp Here 200
SIC 4899 Communication services, nec
John Rego
Gerald Maloney
Don Leary

D-U-N-S 24-058-4144   (SL)
WATERDALE INC
1303 Aerowood Dr, Mississauga, ON, L4W 2P6
(905) 624-2600
Emp Here 31   *Sales* 23,018,120
SIC 5193 Flowers and florists supplies
Jose C. Borges
William Waters
William Jeffrey Waters

D-U-N-S 24-394-4100   (SL)
WESKO LOCKS LTD
4570 Eastgate Pky, Mississauga, ON, L4W 3W6
(905) 629-3227
Emp Here 80   *Sales* 15,366,800
SIC 3429 Hardware, nec
Gabriele Westwinkel
Sybilla Mcleod
John Maclean

D-U-N-S 25-369-8260   (BR)
WILSON, J. A. DISPLAY LTD
(*Suby of* WILSON, J. A. DISPLAY LTD)
1610 Sismet Rd, Mississauga, ON, L4W 1R4
(905) 625-6778
Emp Here 156
SIC 2542 Partitions and fixtures, except wood
John Allen

D-U-N-S 20-178-4709   (HQ)
WILSON, J. A. DISPLAY LTD
WILSON DISPLAY
1645 Aimco Blvd, Mississauga, ON, L4W 1H8
(905) 625-9200
Sales 15,432,200
SIC 2542 Partitions and fixtures, except wood
Frank Ruffolo

D-U-N-S 24-394-9968   (HQ)
WORKPLACE SAFETY & PREVENTION SERVICES
5110 Creekbank Rd Suite 300, Mississauga, ON, L4W 0A1
(905) 614-1400
Emp Here 10   *Sales* 32,225,052
SIC 8748 Business consulting, nec
Elizabeth Mills
Normand Cote
Rashpal Brar-Grewal
Pat Coursey
Kin Choi
Ryan Fabi
Ken Forth
Peter Gregg
Jamie Hansen
Jon Johnson

D-U-N-S 25-094-5938   (HQ)
WORLD TECHNOLOGY GROUP INC
WSI
1660 Tech Ave Suite 2, Mississauga, ON, L4W 5S7
(905) 678-7588
Sales 20,501,250
SIC 6712 Bank holding companies
Doug Schust

D-U-N-S 24-364-9923   (BR)
WORLEYPARSONSCORD LP
(*Suby of* WORLEYPARSONS LIMITED)
2645 Skymark Ave, Mississauga, ON, L4W 4H2
(905) 940-4774
Emp Here 270
SIC 8711 Engineering services
Fritz Venter

D-U-N-S 25-096-7841   (HQ)
WW HOTELS CORP
RADISSON HOTEL
5090 Explorer Dr Suite 700, Mississauga, ON, L4W 4T9
(905) 624-9720
Sales 19,203,240
SIC 8741 Management services
George Kozswika
Kenny Gibson
A. Majid Mangalji

D-U-N-S 24-101-7800   (SL)
XENTEX TRADING INC
AMTEX
5960 Shawson Dr, Mississauga, ON, L4W 3W5
(905) 696-9329
Emp Here 25   *Sales* 18,563,000
SIC 5199 Nondurable goods, nec
Zein Dawood

D-U-N-S 20-058-9211   (HQ)
XPO LOGISTICS FREIGHT CANADA INC
(*Suby of* XPO LOGISTICS, INC.)
5425 Dixie Rd Room 202, Mississauga, ON, L4W 1E6
(905) 602-9477
Emp Here 16   *Sales* 56,789,348
SIC 4213 Trucking, except local
Greg Lehmkuhl
John Hardig
Nurhan Aycan
Brad Reid

D-U-N-S 25-272-6997   (BR)
YRC FREIGHT CANADA COMPANY
FAST AS FLIGHT
(*Suby of* YRC WORLDWIDE INC.)
5919 Shawson Dr, Mississauga, ON, L4W 3Y2
(905) 670-9366
Emp Here 300
SIC 4213 Trucking, except local
Dave O'connor

D-U-N-S 20-549-1595   (SL)
ZEBRA PAPER CONVERTERS INC
5130 Creekbank Rd, Mississauga, ON, L4W

2G2
(905) 602-1100
Emp Here 72   *Sales* 36,263,376
SIC 5113 Industrial and personal service paper
David Klass
David Rosen
Darryn Cohen

Mississauga, ON L4X

D-U-N-S 24-204-4647   (SL)
1376371 ONTARIO INC
GOLDEN PHOENIX MEAT COMPANY
3066 Jarrow Ave, Mississauga, ON, L4X 2C7
(905) 238-9818
Emp Here 20   *Sales* 10,702,480
SIC 5147 Meats and meat products
Wai Keung Kwan
Augo Pinho

D-U-N-S 24-422-1342   (SL)
2214264 ONTARIO INC
MI5 PRINT & DIGITAL COMMUNICATIONS
1550 Caterpillar Rd, Mississauga, ON, L4X 1E7
(905) 848-1550
Emp Here 125   *Sales* 23,037,606
SIC 2752 Commercial printing, lithographic
Derek Mcgeachie

D-U-N-S 20-936-4256   (HQ)
ABS EQUIPMENT LEASING LTD
1495 Sedlescomb Dr, Mississauga, ON, L4X 1M4
(905) 625-5941
Emp Here 120   *Sales* 61,792,940
SIC 3545 Machine tool accessories

D-U-N-S 20-527-8505   (SL)
ABS MACHINING INC
(*Suby of* ABS EQUIPMENT LEASING LTD)
1495 Sedlescomb Dr, Mississauga, ON, L4X 1M4
(905) 625-5941
Emp Here 200   *Sales* 38,417,000
SIC 3499 Fabricated Metal products, nec

D-U-N-S 24-925-6058   (HQ)
AV-CANADA INC
1655 Queensway E Unit 2, Mississauga, ON, L4X 2Z5
(905) 566-5500
Sales 19,655,732
SIC 7359 Equipment rental and leasing, nec
Ralph J Strachan
Stephen Bond
Danny Dobriansky

D-U-N-S 20-012-7087   (HQ)
AYA KITCHENS AND BATHS LTD
AYA KITCHENS
1551 Caterpillar Rd, Mississauga, ON, L4X 2Z6
(905) 848-1999
Emp Here 150   *Sales* 90,476,750
SIC 2434 Wood kitchen cabinets
David Marcus
Huwh Wahad
Noel Santos
David Shanta

D-U-N-S 20-042-3622   (HQ)
BRAND FELT OF CANADA LIMITED
2559 Wharton Glen Ave, Mississauga, ON, L4X 2A8
(905) 279-6680
Emp Here 25   *Sales* 15,589,255
SIC 2231 Broadwoven fabric mills, wool
Wolfgang Kirsten
Jack Brand

D-U-N-S 20-552-6064   (HQ)
BRANDT, G. MEAT PACKERS LIMITED
BRANDT MEATS & DELICATESSEN

1878 Mattawa Ave, Mississauga, ON, L4X 1K1
(905) 279-4460
Emp Here 130   *Sales* 51,853,500
SIC 2013 Sausages and other prepared meats

D-U-N-S 24-488-1587   (BR)
BRICK WAREHOUSE LP, THE
THE BRICK
(*Suby of* BRICK WAREHOUSE LP, THE)
1607 Dundas St E, Mississauga, ON, L4X 1L5
(905) 629-2900
Emp Here 150
SIC 5712 Furniture stores
Kim Dickson

D-U-N-S 25-751-9884   (HQ)
CANADIAN EMPLOYMENT CONTRACTORS INC
CEC PERSONNEL SOLUTIONS
2077 Dundas St E Unit 101, Mississauga, ON, L4X 1M2
(905) 282-9578
Emp Here 200
SIC 7361 Employment agencies
Gerrie Schummer

D-U-N-S 20-754-0097   (HQ)
DAVIES AUTO ELECTRIC LIMITED
2571 Wharton Glen Ave, Mississauga, ON, L4X 2A8
(905) 279-6300
Emp Here 25   *Sales* 25,171,200
SIC 5511 New and used car dealers
Andrew Davies
Chris Davies
Greta Davies

D-U-N-S 25-807-4418   (SL)
DELTRO ELECTRIC LTD
1706 Mattawa Ave, Mississauga, ON, L4X 1K1
(905) 566-9816
Emp Here 90   *Sales* 19,604,610
SIC 1731 Electrical work
David Del Mastro

D-U-N-S 20-354-7927   (HQ)
ENTERTAINMENT   LIQUIDATORS   OF CANADA INC
1550 Caterpillar Rd, Mississauga, ON, L4X 1E7
(905) 629-7283
Emp Here 23   *Sales* 13,862,394
SIC 5045 Computers, peripherals, and software
Thomas Anczurouski

D-U-N-S 24-477-6464   (SL)
EPIC FOODS INC
3258 Wharton Way, Mississauga, ON, L4X 2C1

Emp Here 50   *Sales* 41,778,850
SIC 5144 Poultry and poultry products
Lee Q Shim
Li Poi Shim
James Chin

D-U-N-S 24-027-3250   (HQ)
ERIE MEAT PRODUCTS LIMITED
3240 Wharton Way, Mississauga, ON, L4X 2C1
(905) 624-3811
Emp Here 100   *Sales* 69,138,000
SIC 2011 Meat packing plants
Simon Rosen
Richard Gole

D-U-N-S 25-295-2825   (BR)
FEDERAL EXPRESS CANADA CORPORATION
FEDEX SHIP CENTRE
(*Suby of* FEDEX CORPORATION)
1450 Caterpillar Rd, Mississauga, ON, L4X 2Y1
(800) 463-3339
Emp Here 200

SIC 7389 Business services, nec

D-U-N-S 25-363-9975   (HQ)
INTEGRATED DISTRIBUTION SYSTEMS LIMITED PARTNERSHIP
(*Suby of* WAJAX CORPORATION)
3280 Wharton Way, Mississauga, ON, L4X 2C5
(905) 212-3300
Emp Here 25   *Sales* 21,376,170
SIC 5084 Industrial machinery and equipment
Mark Foote

D-U-N-S 20-321-6809   (BR)
INTEGRATED DISTRIBUTION SYSTEMS LIMITED PARTNERSHIP
WAJAX EQUIPMENT
(*Suby of* WAJAX CORPORATION)
1865 Sharlyn Rd, Mississauga, ON, L4X 1R1
(905) 624-5611
Emp Here 100
SIC 5082 Construction and mining machinery
Joe Dipede

D-U-N-S 24-422-0398   (HQ)
KUBIK INC
1680 Mattawa Ave, Mississauga, ON, L4X 3A5
(905) 272-2818
Sales 66,142,000
SIC 3993 Signs and advertising specialties
Sam Kohn
Elliot Kohn
Tom Bradfield
Larry Yunger

D-U-N-S 20-956-1781   (SL)
LEAVOY ROWE BEEF CO. LTD
3066 Jarrow Ave, Mississauga, ON, L4X 2C7
(905) 272-2330
Emp Here 25   *Sales* 20,889,425
SIC 5147 Meats and meat products
William Leavoy Jr
Rod W Rowe
Ronald Leavoy

D-U-N-S 24-057-2276   (SL)
LK PROTECTION INC
1590 Dundas St E Suite 220, Mississauga, ON, L4X 2Z2
(905) 566-7008
Emp Here 121   *Sales* 3,176,250
SIC 7381 Detective and armored car services
Leonard Labelle
Vadim Konev

D-U-N-S 20-849-1035   (SL)
MARQUIS BUILDING MAINTENANCE SUPPLIES LIMITED
1786 Mattawa Ave Unit 2, Mississauga, ON, L4X 1K1
(905) 275-0985
Emp Here 50   *Sales* 22,358,700
SIC 5039 Construction materials, nec
Rupert Mclymont

D-U-N-S 20-184-2270   (SL)
MI5 DIGITAL COMMUNICATIONS INC
1550 Caterpillar Rd, Mississauga, ON, L4X 1E7
(905) 848-1550
Emp Here 125   *Sales* 20,503,375
SIC 2752 Commercial printing, lithographic
Derek Mcgeachie
Peter Mitchos

D-U-N-S 20-943-2343   (SL)
MISSISSAUGA TOYOTA INC
2215 Dundas St E, Mississauga, ON, L4X 2X2
(905) 625-3420
Emp Here 40   *Sales* 19,923,120
SIC 5511 New and used car dealers
Rosalee Gubasta
Joseph Gubasta

D-U-N-S 25-263-7640   (BR)
PEEL DISTRICT SCHOOL BOARD
GLENFOREST SECONDARY SCHOOL

(*Suby of* PEEL DISTRICT SCHOOL BOARD)
3575 Fieldgate Dr, Mississauga, ON, L4X 2J6
(905) 625-7731
Emp Here 88
SIC 8211 Elementary and secondary schools
Cheri Riddell

D-U-N-S 20-002-6669   (BR)
PRIMERICA FINANCIAL SERVICES LTD
(*Suby of* PRIMERICA, INC.)
1425 Dundas St E Suite 207, Mississauga, ON, L4X 2W4
(905) 602-1167
Emp Here 80
SIC 6282 Investment advice
Terry Treasure

D-U-N-S 24-077-6716   (HQ)
SKIIS LTD
SKIIS & BIIKES
1945 Dundas St E Suite 210, Mississauga, ON, L4X 2T8
(905) 896-1206
Emp Here 50   *Sales* 47,719,620
SIC 5941 Sporting goods and bicycle shops
Paul Montgomery
Sharon Montgomery

D-U-N-S 24-937-4323   (SL)
SKY TECK LABS INC
3289 Lenworth Dr Suite B, Mississauga, ON, L4X 2H1
(905) 602-8007
Emp Here 20   *Sales* 10,006,500
SIC 5169 Chemicals and allied products, nec
Weston Little

D-U-N-S 20-559-7032   (SL)
STANDARD MECHANICAL SYSTEMS LIMITED
3055 Universal Dr, Mississauga, ON, L4X 2E2
(905) 625-9505
Emp Here 50   *Sales* 11,046,700
SIC 1711 Plumbing, heating, air-conditioning
Jack Mcaughey
Roger Shorey

D-U-N-S 20-696-9441   (HQ)
STARSKY FINE FOODS MISSISSAUGA INC
2040 Dundas St E Unit 2, Mississauga, ON, L4X 2X8
(905) 279-8889
Emp Here 150   *Sales* 67,362,400
SIC 5411 Grocery stores
Marek Sikorski
Piotr Zuski
Alexsander Radecki

D-U-N-S 20-409-9196   (SL)
STRONCO DESIGNS INC
STRONCO SHOW SERVICES
(*Suby of* SUNSHINE MOUNTAIN INVESTMENTS INC)
1510 Caterpillar Rd, Mississauga, ON, L4X 2Y1
(905) 270-6767
Emp Here 80   *Sales* 53,512,640
SIC 7389 Business services, nec
John Ralph Strachan
Bruce Morrison
Saira Beig

D-U-N-S 24-334-7267   (SL)
SUREWAY INTERNATIONAL ELECTRIC INC
SURELITE
3151 Wharton Way, Mississauga, ON, L4X 2B6
(905) 624-0077
Emp Here 55   *Sales* 24,594,570
SIC 5063 Electrical apparatus and equipment
Deborah May

D-U-N-S 20-042-8431   (HQ)
TECHNICAL ADHESIVES LIMITED
3035 Jarrow Ave, Mississauga, ON, L4X 2C6
(905) 625-1284
Emp Here 1   *Sales* 13,833,000

SIC 2891 Adhesives and sealants
Conrad Maziarczyk
Lou Cavallo
Armandina Maziarczyk

D-U-N-S 20-647-1344   (HQ)
UNIROPE LIMITED
(*Suby of* PAMPUS INDUSTRIEBETEILIGUNGEN GMBH & CO. KG)
3070 Universal Dr, Mississauga, ON, L4X 2C8
(905) 624-5131
Emp Here 55   *Sales* 19,806,248
SIC 5251 Hardware stores
Knut Buschmann
Thomas Critelli

D-U-N-S 24-343-9523   (SL)
UNISON INSURANCE & FINANCIAL SERVICES INC.
2077 Dundas St E Suite 103, Mississauga, ON, L4X 1M2
(905) 624-5300
Emp Here 23   *Sales* 23,802,263
SIC 6311 Life insurance
William Carser
John Collaton

D-U-N-S 20-417-9345   (HQ)
VISUAL PLANNING CORPORATION
3071 Universal Dr, Mississauga, ON, L4X 2E2
(905) 629-7397
Emp Here 4   *Sales* 33,835,230
SIC 5099 Durable goods, nec
Joseph Josephson
Helen Jean Josephson

D-U-N-S 20-614-9528   (HQ)
WAJAX CORPORATION
3280 Wharton Way, Mississauga, ON, L4X 2C5
(905) 212-3300
Sales 1,123,201,649
SIC 5084 Industrial machinery and equipment
A. Mark Foote
Stuart Auld
Steven Deck
Thomas Plain
Donna Baratto
Cristian Rodriguez
Trevor Carson
Andrew Tan
Thomas M. Alford
Edward M. Barrett

Mississauga, ON L4Y

D-U-N-S 25-256-1803   (SL)
2144205 ONTARIO INC
ELAD BUSINESS SERVICES
3415 Dixie Rd Suite 113, Mississauga, ON, L4Y 2B1
(905) 670-7677
Emp Here 24   *Sales* 15,755,136
SIC 5961 Catalog and mail-order houses
Daniel Colby

D-U-N-S 20-042-3283   (HQ)
ASTRAZENECA CANADA INC
(*Suby of* ASTRAZENECA PLC)
1004 Middlegate Rd Suite 5000, Mississauga, ON, L4Y 1M4
(905) 277-7111
Emp Here 800   *Sales* 497,391,000
SIC 2834 Pharmaceutical preparations
Elaine Campbell
Karen A. Burke
Marion Mccourt
Laura Mably
Mario Tremblay

D-U-N-S 24-195-7604   (HQ)
BAMFORD PRODUCE COMPANY LIMITED
2501 Stanfield Rd Suite A, Mississauga, ON, L4Y 1R6

(905) 615-9400
Sales 107,507,400
SIC 5148 Fresh fruits and vegetables
James Bamford
Stephen Bamford

D-U-N-S 24-987-3860   (HQ)
BURGESS, JOHN WILLIAM ENTERPRISES INC
TIM HORTONS
799 Dundas St E, Mississauga, ON, L4Y 2B7
(905) 566-4982
Emp Here 40   *Sales* 10,493,775
SIC 5812 Eating places
John William Burgess
Lesley Anne Burgess

D-U-N-S 24-684-5663   (HQ)
CORPORATION DE SECURITE GARDA CANADA
GARDA
(*Suby of* GW INTERMEDIATE HOLDCO CORPORATION)
2345 Stanfield Rd Unit 400, Mississauga, ON, L4Y 3Y3
(416) 915-9500
Emp Here 20   *Sales* 42,933,024
SIC 7349 Building maintenance services, nec
Jean-Luc Meunier
Pierre-Hubert Seguin
Patrick Prince

D-U-N-S 25-359-5201   (HQ)
D.O.T FURNITURE LIMITED
D.O.T. FURNITURE PATIO EXPERTS
3105 Dixie Rd, Mississauga, ON, L4Y 4E3
(416) 252-2228
Emp Here 30   *Sales* 19,754,255
SIC 5712 Furniture stores
Anthony Niceforo

D-U-N-S 20-260-9749   (SL)
DAHNAY LOGISTICS CANADA LTD
(*Suby of* DAHNAY LOGISTICS PRIVATE LIMITED)
2501 Stanfield Rd, Mississauga, ON, L4Y 1R6
(289) 803-1982
Emp Here 25   *Sales* 12,999,175
SIC 4731 Freight transportation arrangement
David Lyman

D-U-N-S 20-530-8869   (SL)
DEMAN CONSTRUCTION CORP
776 Dundas St E Suite 201, Mississauga, ON, L4Y 2B6
(905) 277-0363
Emp Here 70   *Sales* 39,923,660
SIC 1542 Nonresidential construction, nec
Garry Deman
Wayne Smith
Peter Deman

D-U-N-S 20-819-5128   (HQ)
ELLIS-DON CONSTRUCTION LTD
1004 Middlegate Rd Suite 1000, Mississauga, ON, L4Y 1M4
(877) 980-4821
Sales 174,598,000
SIC 1542 Nonresidential construction, nec
Geoff Smith
John Bernhardt
Stephen Damp
Kieran Hawe

D-U-N-S 25-099-0728   (SL)
FRESHLINE FOODS LTD
(*Suby of* BAMFORD PRODUCE COMPANY LIMITED)
2501 Stanfield Rd Suite A, Mississauga, ON, L4Y 1R6
(416) 253-6040
Emp Here 50   *Sales* 41,778,850
SIC 5148 Fresh fruits and vegetables
Stephen Bamford
Nick Nasturzio
Noel Brigido

D-U-N-S 24-198-2396   (SL)

J AHMAD DRUGS LTD
SHOPPERS DRUG MART
700 Burnhamthorpe Rd E, Mississauga, ON, L4Y 2X3
(905) 279-1812
Emp Here 40   *Sales* 10,118,160
SIC 5912 Drug stores and proprietary stores
Jauher Ahmad

D-U-N-S 20-724-7276   (SL)
KA DJORDJEVIC PHARMACY INC
SHOPPERS DRUG MART
1077 North Service Rd Suite 27, Mississauga, ON, L4Y 1A6
(905) 277-3661
Emp Here 50   *Sales* 12,647,700
SIC 5912 Drug stores and proprietary stores
Kathryn Djordjevic

D-U-N-S 24-320-3557   (SL)
KIM-TAM LOGISTICS INC
(*Suby of* KIM-TAM HOLDINGS INC)
2360 Dixie Rd, Mississauga, ON, L4Y 1Z7
(905) 335-9195
Emp Here 1   *Sales* 37,905,100
SIC 4212 Local trucking, without storage
Mark Samuel

D-U-N-S 24-896-5196   (BR)
METRO ONTARIO INC
DOMINION SAV-A-CENTRE
(*Suby of* METRO INC)
1077 North Service Rd Suite 41, Mississauga, ON, L4Y 1A6

Emp Here 80
SIC 5411 Grocery stores
Carol Sciaraffa

D-U-N-S 24-985-3987   (SL)
MOLINARO'S FINE ITALIAN FOODS LTD
2345 Stanfield Rd Unit 50, Mississauga, ON, L4Y 3Y3
(905) 281-0352
Emp Here 175   *Sales* 60,495,750
SIC 2038 Frozen specialties, nec
Gino Molinaro
Vince Molinaro

D-U-N-S 20-641-6729   (HQ)
MOTHER PARKER'S TEA & COFFEE INC
HIGGINS & BURKE GOURMET
2531 Stanfield Rd, Mississauga, ON, L4Y 1S4
(905) 279-9100
Emp Here 250   *Sales* 207,138,625
SIC 2095 Roasted coffee
Paul Higgins Jr
Michael Higgins

D-U-N-S 20-294-5333   (BR)
MOTHER PARKER'S TEA & COFFEE INC
(*Suby of* MOTHER PARKER'S TEA & COFFEE INC)
2530 Stanfield Rd, Mississauga, ON, L4Y 1S4
(905) 279-9100
Emp Here 145
SIC 2095 Roasted coffee
Mark Hamilton

D-U-N-S 20-206-5640   (SL)
RIVER VALLEY MASONRY GROUP LTD
2444 Haines Rd, Mississauga, ON, L4Y 1Y6
(905) 270-0599
Emp Here 35   *Sales* 13,279,182
SIC 1741 Masonry and other stonework
Rui Pereira

D-U-N-S 20-042-7748   (HQ)
SAMUEL, SON & CO., LIMITED
SAMUEL BOTHWELL, DIV OF
2360 Dixie Rd, Mississauga, ON, L4Y 1Z7
(905) 279-5460
Emp Here 400   *Sales* 1,802,690,388
SIC 6712 Bank holding companies
William T. Chisholm
Mark Chadburn Samuel
Cecile Chung

John E. Caldwell
Richard M. Balaz
Krystana Hoeg
Dezso Horvath
Matthew W. Barrett
Donald A. Pether
Kimberley E. Samuel

D-U-N-S 20-074-7025   (BR)
SUNRISE NORTH ASSISTED LIVING LTD
SUNRISE SENIOR LIVING OF MISSISSAUGA
(*Suby of* WELLTOWER INC.)
1279 Burnhamthorpe Rd E Suite 220, Mississauga, ON, L4Y 3V7
(905) 625-1344
Emp Here 75
SIC 8361 Residential care
Laura Mcsorley

D-U-N-S 24-351-9175   (SL)
TOCAN HOLDING CORP
1333 Tonolli Rd, Mississauga, ON, L4Y 4C2
(905) 279-9555
Emp Here 70   *Sales* 16,340,450
SIC 3341 Secondary nonferrous Metals
Robert D. Chafee
Robert E. Chafee

D-U-N-S 20-251-5115   (SL)
TOTAL HEALTH AND FAMILY CENTRE
1090 Dundas St E Suite 1105, Mississauga, ON, L4Y 2B8
(905) 275-4993
Emp Here 15   *Sales* 15,523,215
SIC 6321 Accident and health insurance
Virginia Nsitem

D-U-N-S 24-964-7082   (HQ)
TREBOR PERSONNEL INC
TPI PERSONNEL
1090 Dundas St E Suite 203, Mississauga, ON, L4Y 2B8
(905) 566-0922
Emp Here 120   *Sales* 37,347,000
SIC 7361 Employment agencies
Robert Bryce
Brenda Bryce

D-U-N-S 25-537-6436   (SL)
UVIEW ULTRAVIOLET SYSTEMS INC
1324 Blundell Rd, Mississauga, ON, L4Y 1M5
(905) 615-8620
Emp Here 60   *Sales* 13,430,580
SIC 3714 Motor vehicle parts and accessories
Phil Trigiani
Tony Ferraro

D-U-N-S 20-042-8852   (SL)
WEDLOCK PAPER CONVERTERS LIMITED
(*Suby of* WHI INC)
2327 Stanfield Rd, Mississauga, ON, L4Y 1R6
(905) 277-9461
Emp Here 100   *Sales* 19,476,800
SIC 2674 Bags: uncoated paper and multiwall
Sean Wedlock
Marcus Wedlock

Mississauga, ON L4Z

D-U-N-S 24-380-3272   (HQ)
1207273 ALBERTA ULC
INVACARE CANADA
(*Suby of* INVACARE CORPORATION)
570 Matheson Blvd E Unit 8, Mississauga, ON, L4Z 4G4
(905) 890-8300
Sales 44,717,400
SIC 5047 Medical and hospital equipment
Carmalita Labardo
Brian Ellacott

D-U-N-S 20-057-6101   (SL)
1335270 ONTARIO LTD

MANDARIN RESTAURANT
87 Matheson Blvd E, Mississauga, ON, L4Z 2Y5
(905) 502-8000
Emp Here 80   *Sales* 3,641,520
SIC 5812 Eating places
Elise Chan

D-U-N-S 24-378-8291   (SL)
2142064 ONTARIO INC
DVT GROUP, THE
5570 Kennedy Rd, Mississauga, ON, L4Z 2A9
(905) 238-1777
Emp Here 15   *Sales* 14,092,708
SIC 3674 Semiconductors and related devices
Michael Singh
Tim Malone

D-U-N-S 25-146-0994   (HQ)
ABLE TRANSLATIONS LTD
5749 Coopers Ave, Mississauga, ON, L4Z 1R9
(905) 502-0000
Emp Here 1   *Sales* 17,070,322
SIC 7389 Business services, nec
Wilson S Teixeira
Annabelle Teixeira

D-U-N-S 24-198-1393   (SL)
ACER AMERICA CORPORATION CANADA
5540 Mcadam Rd, Mississauga, ON, L4Z 1P1
(905) 755-5570
Emp Here 25   *Sales* 11,179,350
SIC 5065 Electronic parts and equipment, nec
Gianfranco Lanci

D-U-N-S 25-458-9146   (HQ)
ACROBAT RESEARCH LTD
ACROBAT RESULT MARKETING
170 Robert Speck Pky Suite 201, Mississauga, ON, L4Z 3G1
(416) 503-4343
Emp Here 100   *Sales* 81,632,800
SIC 8732 Commercial nonphysical research
Roland Klassen
Tim Sinke
Beth Depatie

D-U-N-S 24-251-7295   (BR)
AGAT LABORATORIES LTD
AGAT
5835 Coopers Ave, Mississauga, ON, L4Z 1Y2
(905) 712-5100
Emp Here 120
SIC 8731 Commercial physical research
Marcus Mcguire

D-U-N-S 24-310-6387   (HQ)
ALLAN CANDY COMPANY LIMITED, THE
(*Suby of* HERSHEY COMPANY)
3 Robert Speck Pky Suite 250, Mississauga, ON, L4Z 2G5
(905) 270-2221
Emp Here 150   *Sales* 268,061,750
SIC 2064 Candy and other confectionery products
Marty Thrasher
Peter James
David Plamondon
Rejean Demers

D-U-N-S 24-760-2035   (HQ)
ALSAFA FOODS CANADA LIMITED
AL SAFA HALAL
57 Village Centre Pl Suite 302, Mississauga, ON, L4Z 1V9
(800) 268-8174
Sales 16,711,540
SIC 5142 Packaged frozen goods
Abdul Munim Sheikh
Jafari Mohammad
Umar Farooqi
Sarfaraz Rehman

D-U-N-S 20-309-8942   (SL)
AMAZING KOBOTIC INDUSTRIES INC
5671 Kennedy Rd, Mississauga, ON, L4Z 3E1

(905) 712-1000
Emp Here 70   *Sales* 13,445,950
SIC 3444 Sheet Metalwork
Fred Lai
Amedeo Pellegrino
Asher Lai

D-U-N-S 20-511-3272   (SL)
AMHIL ENTERPRISES
AMDIL NORTH AMERICA
400 Traders Blvd E, Mississauga, ON, L4Z 1W7
(905) 890-5261
Emp Here 300   *Sales* 71,958,222
SIC 3089 Plastics products, nec
Jeff Barclay

D-U-N-S 20-699-1130   (HQ)
AMHIL ENTERPRISES LTD
(*Suby of* WENTWORTH TECHNOLOGIES COMPANY LIMITED)
400 Traders Blvd E, Mississauga, ON, L4Z 1W7
(905) 890-5261
Emp Here 400   *Sales* 107,465,400
SIC 3089 Plastics products, nec
Walter Kuskowski
Jeff Barclay

D-U-N-S 24-555-5685   (SL)
ANTEX DESIGNS INC
330 Britannia Rd E, Mississauga, ON, L4Z 1X9
(905) 507-8778
Emp Here 75   *Sales* 13,755,225
SIC 2211 Broadwoven fabric mills, cotton
Ajit Someshwar
Adam Mark Erlich

D-U-N-S 25-264-8282   (SL)
ATTO & ASSOCIATES INSURANCE BROKERS INC
5660 Mcadam Rd Suite A1, Mississauga, ON, L4Z 1T2
(905) 890-1412
Emp Here 35   *Sales* 20,297,340
SIC 6411 Insurance agents, brokers, and service
John Atto
Robert Pissey
Rob Atto
Barbara Hubel

D-U-N-S 24-576-0871   (SL)
AXIOMATIC TECHNOLOGIES CORPORATION
5915 Wallace St, Mississauga, ON, L4Z 1Z8
(905) 602-9270
Emp Here 50   *Sales* 10,233,650
SIC 3679 Electronic components, nec
Greville Hampson
Dale Quinn
David Laton

D-U-N-S 20-106-3141   (SL)
BARTECH TECHNICAL SERVICES OF CANADA, LTD
BARTECH GROUP, THE
(*Suby of* IMPELLAM GROUP PLC)
160 Traders Blvd E Suite 112, Mississauga, ON, L4Z 3K7
(905) 502-9914
Emp Here 125   *Sales* 9,336,750
SIC 7361 Employment agencies
Michell Mc Elliot

D-U-N-S 20-877-6468   (SL)
BASIC PACKAGING INDUSTRIES INC
5591 Mcadam Rd, Mississauga, ON, L4Z 1N4
(905) 890-0922
Emp Here 75   *Sales* 13,833,000
SIC 2842 Polishes and sanitation goods
John Ursino
Joseph Ursino

D-U-N-S 24-859-8187   (HQ)
BELIMO AIRCONTROLS (CAN.) INC
5845 Kennedy Rd, Mississauga, ON, L4Z 2G3

(905) 712-3118
Sales 12,520,872
SIC 5063 Electrical apparatus and equipment
Lars Vander Haegen
Michael Leblanc

D-U-N-S 24-794-8297   (SL)
CACEIS (CANADA) LIMITED
1 Robert Speck Pky Suite 1510, Mississauga,
ON, L4Z 3M3
(905) 281-4145
Emp Here 49   *Sales* 13,881,357
SIC 8741 Management services
Margaret Gray

D-U-N-S 24-525-0399   (SL)
CANADA GARLIC IMPORTING INC
315 Traders Blvd E Unit 2, Mississauga, ON,
L4Z 3E4
(905) 501-8868
Emp Here 20   *Sales* 10,702,480
SIC 5148 Fresh fruits and vegetables
John Wang

D-U-N-S 24-024-6868   (HQ)
**CANADIAN NATIONAL SPORTSMEN'S
SHOWS (1989) LIMITED**
PEOPLE IN MOTION
30 Village Centre Pl, Mississauga, ON, L4Z
1V9
(905) 361-2677
Sales 10,332,037
SIC 7389 Business services, nec
Peter Lockhart

D-U-N-S 20-316-7486   (SL)
CARGOJET PARTNERSHIP
350 Britannia Rd E Unit 5 6, Mississauga, ON,
L4Z 1X9
(905) 501-7373
Emp Here 250   *Sales* 79,338,000
SIC 4512 Air transportation, scheduled
Sanjeev Maini

D-U-N-S 20-052-8664   (SL)
**CENTRAL ONTARIO DAIRY DISTRIBUTING
INC**
5820 Kennedy Rd, Mississauga, ON, L4Z 2C3
(905) 501-9168
Emp Here 25   *Sales* 20,889,425
SIC 5143 Dairy products, except dried or
canned
Nicole Rabba
Jim Foster

D-U-N-S 24-108-7563   (SL)
CENTRAL ONTARIO DAIRY DISTRIBUTION
260 Brunel Rd Suite B, Mississauga, ON, L4Z
1T5
(905) 507-0084
Emp Here 40   *Sales* 33,423,080
SIC 5141 Groceries, general line
Jack Rabba

D-U-N-S 20-048-0700   (SL)
CENTURY 21 ASSOCIATES INC
5659 Mcadam Rd Unit C1, Mississauga, ON,
L4Z 1N9
(905) 279-8888
Emp Here 40   *Sales* 13,085,080
SIC 6531 Real estate agents and managers
Michael Perretta

D-U-N-S 24-708-4874   (SL)
CENTURY 21 BEST SELLERS LTD
4 Robert Speck Pky Suite 150, Mississauga,
ON, L4Z 1S1
(905) 273-4211
Emp Here 50   *Sales* 16,356,350
SIC 6531 Real estate agents and managers
Frank Menardo

D-U-N-S 25-248-5701   (SL)
**CERTAS DIRECT COMPAGNIE
D'ASSURANCE**
DESJARDINS INSURANCE
(*Suby of* FEDERATION DES CAISSES DES-
JARDINS DU QUEBEC)
3 Robert Speck Pky, Mississauga, ON, L4Z

2G5
(905) 306-3900
Emp Here 250   *Sales* 534,242,000
SIC 6331 Fire, marine, and casualty insurance
Guy Cormier
Michel Magnan
Pierre Reichert
Denis Dubois
Scott Banda
Pierre Couillard
Bernard Morency
Marie-Eve Tremblay
Helene Blackburn
Clermont Tremblay

D-U-N-S 20-369-3809   (SL)
COLLABERA CANADA INC
1 Robert Speck Pky Unit 900, Mississauga,
ON, L4Z 3M3
(416) 639-6250
Emp Here 80   *Sales* 12,429,680
SIC 7361 Employment agencies
Hiten Patel

D-U-N-S 25-412-2047   (HQ)
COMFORT SYSTEM SOLUTIONS INC
GLOMAR
150 Britannia Rd E Unit 1, Mississauga, ON,
L4Z 2A4
(905) 568-1661
Sales 17,439,786
SIC 5075 Warm air heating and air condition-
ing
William (Bill) Browne
Robert Rutherford
Pat Garon

D-U-N-S 20-823-6844   (HQ)
**COMMERCIAL SPRING AND TOOL COM-
PANY LIMITED**
CST
160 Watline Ave, Mississauga, ON, L4Z 1R1
(905) 568-3899
Sales 72,969,300
SIC 3495 Wire springs
Frank Martinitz
Gurmail Gill

D-U-N-S 25-274-0568   (SL)
COMMUNITY HOMEMAKERS LTD
COMMUNITY CARE SERVICES
160 Traders Blvd E Suite 103, Mississauga,
ON, L4Z 3K7
(905) 275-0544
Emp Here 300   *Sales* 23,010,300
SIC 8082 Home health care services
Peter Gooch

D-U-N-S 24-709-1770   (HQ)
**CPT CANADA POWER TECHNOLOGY LIM-
ITED**
161 Watline Ave, Mississauga, ON, L4Z 1P2
(905) 890-6900
Sales 16,625,910
SIC 5084 Industrial machinery and equipment
Tim Bequiri
Gavin Bequiri

D-U-N-S 20-044-9916   (HQ)
**CRAWFORD, ALLAN ASSOCIATES LIM-
ITED**
5805 Kennedy Rd, Mississauga, ON, L4Z 2G3
(905) 890-2010
Emp Here 10   *Sales* 29,066,310
SIC 5065 Electronic parts and equipment, nec
Brian Flippance
Jim Turner

D-U-N-S 20-811-2958   (SL)
**CREIGHTON & COMPANY INSURANCE
BROKERS LTD**
315 Matheson Blvd E, Mississauga, ON, L4Z
1X8
(905) 890-0090
Emp Here 33   *Sales* 19,137,492
SIC 6411 Insurance agents, brokers, and service

Melody Murray

D-U-N-S 24-876-0472   (HQ)
D & A COLLECTION CORPORATION
D & A GROUP SERVICES
75 Watline Ave Suite 142, Mississauga, ON,
L4Z 3E5
(905) 507-1147
Emp Here 140   *Sales* 40,074,200
SIC 7322 Adjustment and collection services
Philip A. Morrison
Manny Cabral

D-U-N-S 24-372-4684   (SL)
DENSO SALES CANADA, INC
(*Suby of* DENSO CORPORATION)
195 Brunel Rd, Mississauga, ON, L4Z 1X3
(905) 890-0890
Emp Here 28   *Sales* 10,198,020
SIC 5013 Motor vehicle supplies and new
parts
Hiroshi Kamiya
Kenichiro Ito

D-U-N-S 24-390-7404   (SL)
DEZINECORP INC
369 Britannia Rd E, Mississauga, ON, L4Z
2H5

Emp Here 35   *Sales* 25,988,200
SIC 5199 Nondurable goods, nec
Paul Bami
Bill Yelland

D-U-N-S 20-720-0945   (HQ)
ELECTROTEMP TECHNOLOGIES INC
406 Watline Ave, Mississauga, ON, L4Z 1X2
(905) 488-9263
Sales 16,280,000
SIC 5999 Miscellaneous retail stores, nec
Andrei Yoo
Margaret Yui
Larissa Yui

D-U-N-S 24-192-8662   (HQ)
ELEMENT FLEET MANAGEMENT INC
(*Suby of* ELEMENT FLEET MANAGEMENT
CORP)
4 Robert Speck Pky Suite 900, Mississauga,
ON, L4Z 1S1
(905) 366-8900
Emp Here 167   *Sales* 17,670,112
SIC 7515 Passenger car leasing
Jay Forbes
David Colman
Vito Culmone
Jim Halliday
Jacqui Mcgillivray
Karen Martin

D-U-N-S 20-767-8728   (SL)
FERNANDES GROUP, THE
260 Brunel Rd, Mississauga, ON, L4Z 1T5

Emp Here 28   *Sales* 51,706,452
SIC 6311 Life insurance
Sylvester Fernandes

D-U-N-S 20-208-9897   (HQ)
FLITE HOCKEY INC
FLITE
705 Matheson Blvd E, Mississauga, ON, L4Z
3X9
(905) 828-6030
Sales 82,016,080
SIC 3949 Sporting and athletic goods, nec
Gerry Mcsorley

D-U-N-S 24-548-7868   (SL)
FLUKE ELECTRONICS CANADA INC.
400 Britannia Rd E Unit 1, Mississauga, ON,
L4Z 1X9
(800) 363-5853
Emp Here 35   *Sales* 15,914,322
SIC 5063 Electrical apparatus and equipment

D-U-N-S 24-721-2806   (SL)
FLUKE ELECTRONICS CANADA LP

(*Suby of* FORTIVE CORPORATION)
400 Britannia Rd E Unit 1, Mississauga, ON,
L4Z 1X9
(905) 890-7601
Emp Here 60   *Sales* 29,263,800
SIC 5084 Industrial machinery and equipment
Barbara Hulit
Monti Ackerman
Jim Cavoretto
Daren Couture
Clement Feng
Tom Nealon

D-U-N-S 25-223-6026   (SL)
FRED C RYALL INSURANCE INC
53 Village Centre Pl, Mississauga, ON, L4Z
1V9
(416) 419-0240
Emp Here 25   *Sales* 14,498,100
SIC 6411 Insurance agents, brokers, and service
Fred Ryall

D-U-N-S 24-316-3511   (SL)
GLOBAL LUMBER RESOURCES INC
48 Village Centre Pl Unit 100, Mississauga,
ON, L4Z 1V9
(905) 306-7874
Emp Here 34   *Sales* 13,974,670
SIC 5031 Lumber, plywood, and millwork
Zulfiqar Ahmad
Saba Amjad

D-U-N-S 20-819-1460   (SL)
GLOBAL ROYALTIES LIMITED
145 Traders Blvd E Unit 1, Mississauga, ON,
L4Z 3L3
(905) 890-3000
Emp Here 25   *Sales* 13,013,550
SIC 5094 Jewelry and precious stones

D-U-N-S 20-013-3259   (SL)
GLOBAL SEA SERVICES LTD
GLOBAL CATERING
2 Robert Speck Pky Suite 750, Mississauga,
ON, L4Z 1H8
(905) 908-2141
Emp Here 1   *Sales* 23,504,310
SIC 5812 Eating places
Avinash Bhagat
Vaidehi Raut
Jayden Scott
Rumi Guard

D-U-N-S 25-275-6127   (SL)
**GOODMAN & GRIFFIN BARRISTERS & SO-
LICITORS**
44 Village Centre Pl 3rd Fl Suite 300, Missis-
sauga, ON, L4Z 1V9
(905) 276-5050
Emp Here 70   *Sales* 10,780,770
SIC 8111 Legal services
Jack Goodman
Michael J Griffin

D-U-N-S 25-477-8111   (SL)
GYMNASTICS MISSISSAUGA
5600 Rose Cherry Pl, Mississauga, ON, L4Z
4B6
(905) 270-6161
Emp Here 70   *Sales* 49,644,840
SIC 8699 Membership organizations, nec
Walter Edwards

D-U-N-S 20-151-2142   (HQ)
HARCO CO. LTD
HARDCO ATLANTIC
(*Suby of* SYLON INC)
5610 Mcadam Rd, Mississauga, ON, L4Z 1P1
(905) 890-1220
Emp Here 40   *Sales* 22,801,248
SIC 5087 Service establishment equipment
Robert C. Jackson
Robert F Stevens
Malcom Caldwell

D-U-N-S 24-327-2403   (SL)
HAUNSLA PHARMACY LTD

SHOPPERS DRUG MART
5035 Hurontario St Suite 1100, Mississauga, ON, L4Z 3X7
(905) 890-1313
Emp Here 60   *Sales* 14,659,680
SIC 5912 Drug stores and proprietary stores
Gurdeep Kithoray

D-U-N-S 20-625-8014   (HQ)
HIGHLAND FARMS INC
50 Matheson Blvd E, Mississauga, ON, L4Z 1N5
(905) 501-9545
Emp Here 25   *Sales* 72,174,000
SIC 5411 Grocery stores
Charles Coppa
John Coppa
Michael Coppa

D-U-N-S 20-921-8759   (HQ)
HOERBIGER (CANADA) LTD
(*Suby of* HOERBIGER-STIFTUNG)
330 Brunel Rd, Mississauga, ON, L4Z 2C2
(905) 568-3013
Emp Here 15   *Sales* 14,406,375
SIC 3494 Valves and pipe fittings, nec
Craig Thompson

D-U-N-S 25-799-1141   (SL)
HOMELIFE/RESPONSE REALTY INC
4312 Village Centre Crt, Mississauga, ON, L4Z 1S2
(905) 949-0070
Emp Here 130   *Sales* 54,455,570
SIC 6531 Real estate agents and managers
Thomas Turner
Anthony Damborsio

D-U-N-S 20-370-7062   (BR)
HYDRO EXTRUSION CANADA INC
SAPA EXTRUSION AMERIQUE DU NORD
(*Suby of* NORSK HYDRO ASA)
5675 Kennedy Rd, Mississauga, ON, L4Z 2H9
(905) 890-8821
Emp Here 220
SIC 3354 Aluminum extruded products

D-U-N-S 20-345-7866   (HQ)
INMARCA HOLDING INC
SELMA ALTIKUM ALISEZEN
51 Village Centre Pl Unit 7, Mississauga, L4Z 1V9
(416) 471-1914
Emp Here 15   *Sales* 13,964,997
SIC 5039 Construction materials, nec
Selma Altinkum
Ali Sezen

D-U-N-S 24-804-6901   (SL)
INVACARE CANADA L.P.
570 Matheson Blvd E Suite 8, Mississauga, ON, L4Z 4G4
(905) 890-8300
Emp Here 50   *Sales* 22,358,700
SIC 5047 Medical and hospital equipment
Carmalita Labardo

D-U-N-S 25-315-8224   (BR)
INVESTORS GROUP FINANCIAL SERVICES INC
(*Suby of* POWER CORPORATION DU CANADA)
1 Robert Speck Pkwy 10 Fl, Mississauga, ON, L4Z 3M3
(905) 306-0031
Emp Here 90
SIC 8742 Management consulting services
Andrew Mackenzie

D-U-N-S 20-225-2771   (HQ)
JTI-MACDONALD CORP
(*Suby of* JAPAN TOBACCO INC.)
1 Robert Speck Pky Suite 1601, Mississauga, ON, L4Z 0A2
(905) 804-7300
Emp Here 80   *Sales* 65,791,250
SIC 2111 Cigarettes
Michel A. Poirier

David Marshall
Martin-Ralph Frauendorfer

D-U-N-S 20-145-5292   (HQ)
KINNEAR INDUSTRIES CORPORATION LIMITED
WAYNE-DALTON COMMERCIAL DOORS
(*Suby of* HRH DOOR CORP.)
254 Matheson Blvd E, Mississauga, ON, L4Z 1P5
(905) 890-1402
Emp Here 26   *Sales* 21,911,526
SIC 5031 Lumber, plywood, and millwork
Thomas Bennett Iii

D-U-N-S 20-860-4066   (HQ)
KLENZOID CANADA INC
245 Matheson Blvd E Suite 2, Mississauga, ON, L4Z 3C9
(905) 712-4000
Emp Here 25   *Sales* 17,041,260
SIC 2899 Chemical preparations, nec
Gordon Nelson
Ed Myers

D-U-N-S 25-530-4339   (HQ)
KRG LOGISTICS INC
170 Traders Blvd E, Mississauga, ON, L4Z 1W7
(905) 501-7277
Emp Here 25   *Sales* 16,118,977
SIC 4731 Freight transportation arrangement
Kyran Bartlett

D-U-N-S 20-159-1203   (HQ)
LARSON-JUHL CANADA LTD
LARSON JUHL
(*Suby of* BERKSHIRE HATHAWAY INC.)
416 Watline Ave, Mississauga, ON, L4Z 1X2
(905) 890-1234
Emp Here 42   *Sales* 50,885,600
SIC 5023 Homefurnishings
Jeff Cohen

D-U-N-S 25-512-7920   (HQ)
LCI LASERCOM CLINICS INTERNATIONAL INC
LCI
4310 Sherwoodtowne Blvd, Mississauga, ON, L4Z 4C4
(905) 896-4000
Emp Here 10   *Sales* 21,356,400
SIC 7231 Beauty shops
Gordon West
Diane Macgillis
Douglas Coombs

D-U-N-S 25-373-6482   (BR)
LEON'S FURNITURE LIMITED
(*Suby of* LEON'S FURNITURE LIMITED)
201 Britannia Rd E, Mississauga, ON, L4Z 3X8
(905) 501-9505
Emp Here 150
SIC 5712 Furniture stores
Rob Brown

D-U-N-S 24-911-5403   (SL)
MACRO ENGINEERING & TECHNOLOGY INC
MACRO ENGINEERING
(*Suby of* HENGLI PETROCHEMICAL CO., LTD.)
199 Traders Blvd E, Mississauga, ON, L4Z 2E5
(905) 507-9000
Emp Here 135   *Sales* 29,970,135
SIC 3559 Special industry machinery, nec
Mirek Planeta

D-U-N-S 25-504-4976   (SL)
MANTRALOGIX INC
267 Matheson Blvd E Suite 5, Mississauga, ON, L4Z 1X8
(905) 629-3200
Emp Here 60   *Sales* 16,459,920
SIC 8741 Management services
Kerry Mann

D-U-N-S 24-875-7015   (HQ)
MAPLE RIDGE COMMUNITY MANAGEMENT LTD
5753 Coopers Ave Unit A, Mississauga, ON, L4Z 1R9
(905) 507-6726
Emp Here 28   *Sales* 13,587,800
SIC 6531 Real estate agents and managers
Michael Le Page
Audrey Le Page

D-U-N-S 20-695-4906   (SL)
MARKWINS CANADA CORPORATION
267 Matheson Blvd E Suite 1, Mississauga, ON, L4Z 1X8
(905) 507-4545
Emp Here 22   *Sales* 24,317,590
SIC 5122 Drugs, proprietaries, and sundries
Derek Andrulat
Eric Chen
Lina Chen

D-U-N-S 25-692-7823   (SL)
MEYER, GENE INSURANCE AGENCIES LTD
315 Oxbow Cres, Mississauga, ON, L4Z 2S4
(905) 890-0998
Emp Here 21   *Sales* 12,178,404
SIC 6411 Insurance agents, brokers, and service
Gene Meyer

D-U-N-S 24-703-7963   (HQ)
NKC OF CANADA INC
(*Suby of* NAKANISHI METAL WORKS CO., LTD.)
55 Village Centre Pl Suite 213, Mississauga, ON, L4Z 1V9
(905) 273-4011
Sales 24,701,352
SIC 5084 Industrial machinery and equipment
Kiichiro Yamamoto
John S. Gorris

D-U-N-S 20-942-8952   (HQ)
NSK CANADA INC
(*Suby of* NSK LTD.)
5585 Mcadam Rd, Mississauga, ON, L4Z 1N4
(905) 890-0740
Emp Here 40   *Sales* 47,027,574
SIC 5085 Industrial supplies
Michael St. Jacques

D-U-N-S 24-211-4192   (SL)
OH ENVIRONMENTAL INC
OHE CONSULTANTS
311 Matheson Blvd E, Mississauga, ON, L4Z 1X8
(905) 890-9000
Emp Here 50   *Sales* 10,619,850
SIC 8748 Business consulting, nec
Farid Alatrach

D-U-N-S 20-059-4435   (SL)
OUTLOOK EYEWEAR CANADA LIMITED
290 Brunel Rd, Mississauga, ON, L4Z 2C2
(905) 890-1391
Emp Here 40   *Sales* 20,821,680
SIC 5099 Durable goods, nec
Floyd Owen
Jack Owen
Jim Owen

D-U-N-S 20-878-9305   (HQ)
PERSONNELLE,   COMPAGNIE D'ASSURANCES, LA
PERSONNELLE, LA
(*Suby of* FEDERATION DES CAISSES DESJARDINS DU QUEBEC)
3 Robert Speck Pky Suite 550, Mississauga, ON, L4Z 3Z9
(905) 306-5252
Emp Here 355   *Sales* 1,025,744,640
SIC 6331 Fire, marine, and casualty insurance
Guy Cormier
Jean Royer
Helene Blackburn

Clermont Tremblay
Robert J. Boucher
Alex Johnston
Sonia Gauthier
Henry Jr. Klecan
Claude Lafleur
Michel Magnan

D-U-N-S 20-405-1858   (HQ)
PHARMA PLUS DRUGMARTS LTD
REXALL
(*Suby of* KATZ GROUP INC)
5965 Coopers Ave, Mississauga, ON, L4Z 1R9
(905) 501-7800
Emp Here 150   *Sales* 405,800,307
SIC 5912 Drug stores and proprietary stores
Andy Giancamilli
Eugene Gidaro

D-U-N-S 24-687-8672   (SL)
PHILCOS ENTERPRISER LTD
120 Brunel Rd, Mississauga, ON, L4Z 1T5
(905) 568-1823
Emp Here 30   *Sales* 14,949,660
SIC 5136 Men's and boy's clothing

D-U-N-S 20-011-8243   (SL)
PIONEER STEEL LIMITED
355 Traders Blvd E, Mississauga, ON, L4Z 2E5
(905) 890-0209
Emp Here 20   *Sales* 20,006,780
SIC 5051 Metals service centers and offices
Gulbanu Jassani
Anar Jassani
Farhaz Jassani

D-U-N-S 24-093-0586   (SL)
R.M.P. ATHLETIC LOCKER LIMITED
135 Matheson Blvd Unit 201, Mississauga, ON, L4Z 1R2
(905) 361-2390
Emp Here 50   *Sales* 24,916,100
SIC 5137 Women's and children's clothing
Mike Dyon
Jason Bonany

D-U-N-S 24-076-3177   (HQ)
RABBA, J. COMPANY LIMITED, THE
VARIETY FOOD FAIR
5820 Kennedy Rd, Mississauga, ON, L4Z 2C3
(905) 890-2436
Emp Here 10   *Sales* 13,707,600
SIC 5411 Grocery stores
Richard Rabba
Robert Loa

D-U-N-S 24-101-7586   (SL)
RADIATION SOLUTIONS INC
5875 Whittle Rd, Mississauga, ON, L4Z 2H4
(905) 890-1111
Emp Here 34   *Sales* 15,920,300
SIC 3829 Measuring and controlling devices, nec
Jens Hovgaard
Ed Mcgovern
Flavio Stanesdu
Stephen Monkhousc
Bhavini Gajaria

D-U-N-S 24-096-1743   (SL)
REMAX REALTY SPECIALISTS INC
4310 Sherwoodtowne Blvd Unit 200, Mississauga, ON, L4Z 4C4
(905) 361-4663
Emp Here 49   *Sales* 16,029,223
SIC 6531 Real estate agents and managers
Sylvia Perdue

D-U-N-S 20-354-5348   (HQ)
REXALL PHARMACY GROUP LTD
(*Suby of* MCKESSON CORPORATION)
5965 Coopers Ave, Mississauga, ON, L4Z 1R9
(905) 501-7800
Emp Here 20   *Sales* 183,537,000
SIC 5912 Drug stores and proprietary stores

Domenic Pilla
Barry Elliott
Todd Baldanzi
John Saia
Alan Champagne
Paul Thomson
Michael Martin
Al Wilkie
Ben Kachuk

D-U-N-S 20-145-7371   (HQ)
REYNOLDS AND REYNOLDS (CANADA) LIMITED
(*Suby of* UNIVERSAL COMPUTER SYS-TEMS, INC.)
3 Robert Speck Pky Unit 600, Mississauga, ON, L4Z 2G5
(905) 267-6000
Emp Here 150   *Sales* 182,019,680
SIC 5045 Computers, peripherals, and soft-ware
Ian Reilly

D-U-N-S 20-025-2554   (HQ)
RODAN ENERGY SOLUTIONS INC
165 Matheson Blvd E Suite 6, Mississauga, ON, L4Z 3K2
(905) 625-9900
Sales 14,250,780
SIC 5084 Industrial machinery and equipment
Paul Grod
Borys Chartchenko

D-U-N-S 20-052-8169   (HQ)
ROTOPRECISION INC
304 Watline Ave, Mississauga, ON, L4Z 1P4
(905) 712-3800
Emp Here 23   *Sales* 11,875,650
SIC 5085 Industrial supplies
Keith Mayo
Nigel Mayo

D-U-N-S 25-399-0915   (SL)
S.M.P SPECIALTY METAL PRODUCTS LTD
SPECIALTY METAL PRODUCTS
326 Watline Ave, Mississauga, ON, L4Z 1X2

Emp Here 10   *Sales* 10,003,390
SIC 5051 Metals service centers and offices
John Cunerty
Gary Comeau
May Anis

D-U-N-S 24-952-4385   (SL)
SEARCH REALTY CORP
50 Village Centre Pl Unit 100, Mississauga, ON, L4Z 1V9
(416) 993-7653
Emp Here 150   *Sales* 62,833,350
SIC 6531 Real estate agents and managers
Sterling Wong

D-U-N-S 24-362-2219   (BR)
SECURITAS CANADA LIMITED
(*Suby of* SECURITAS AB)
420 Britannia Rd E Suite 100, Mississauga, ON, L4Z 3L5
(905) 272-0330
Emp Here 200
SIC 7381 Detective and armored car services
Tom Fulford

D-U-N-S 20-900-3623   (HQ)
SHARP ELECTRONICS OF CANADA LTD
SHARP
(*Suby of* SHARP CORPORATION)
335 Britannia Rd E, Mississauga, ON, L4Z 1W9
(905) 890-2100
Sales 63,827,170
SIC 5064 Electrical appliances, television and radio
Keiichi Katsuta
Roger G. Doe
Arthur R. Kitamura

D-U-N-S 25-352-0803   (HQ)

SHERWIN-WILLIAMS STORE GROUP INC
SHERWIN-WILLIAMS STORES GROUP, CANADA
(*Suby of* THE SHERWIN-WILLIAMS COM-PANY)
170 Brunel Rd Unit B, Mississauga, ON, L4Z 1T5
(905) 507-0166
Emp Here 8   *Sales* 82,482,260
SIC 5198 Paints, varnishes, and supplies
John Morikes
Dave Skinner

D-U-N-S 20-717-8182   (SL)
SIGNATURE SERVICE GMAC REAL ES-TATE
186 Robert Speck Pky, Mississauga, ON, L4Z 3G1
(905) 896-4622
Emp Here 35   *Sales* 11,449,445
SIC 6531 Real estate agents and managers
Emilia Antunes

D-U-N-S 20-811-0432   (SL)
SMG CANADA ULC
5500 Rose Cherry Pl, Mississauga, ON, L4Z 4B6
(905) 502-9100
Emp Here 200   *Sales* 18,990,600
SIC 7999 Amusement and recreation, nec
Mike Hamilton

D-U-N-S 20-371-9984   (SL)
SMP SPECIALTY METAL PRODUCTS INC
326 Watline Ave, Mississauga, ON, L4Z 1X2
(905) 568-4459
Emp Here 10   *Sales* 10,003,390
SIC 5051 Metals service centers and offices
John Cunerty
May Anis
Gary Comeau

D-U-N-S 24-964-2554   (HQ)
SONOCO PLASTICS CANADA ULC
(*Suby of* SONOCO PRODUCTS COMPANY)
245 Britannia Rd E, Mississauga, ON, L4Z 4J3
(905) 624-2337
Emp Here 300   *Sales* 179,109,000
SIC 3089 Plastics products, nec
Pushminder Judge
Marion Maclean
Graeme Malloch
Audrey Lalande

D-U-N-S 20-354-7067   (SL)
SPHERE 3D CORP
240 Matheson Blvd E, Mississauga, ON, L4Z 1X1
(416) 749-5999
Emp Here 388   *Sales* 9,030,000
SIC 7371 Custom computer programming ser-vices
Eric Kelly
Joseph Odaniel
Peter Tassiopoulos
Kurt L. Kalbfleisch
Vivekanand Mahadevan
Cheemin Bo-Linn
Duncan Mcewan

D-U-N-S 24-452-4039   (HQ)
STAGEVISION INC
SET DESIGN
5915 Coopers Ave, Mississauga, ON, L4Z 1R9
(905) 890-8200
Emp Here 38   *Sales* 18,867,198
SIC 7389 Business services, nec
Roy Wasley
Hardy Sohl
Bill Armstrong

D-U-N-S 24-413-4086   (HQ)
STEEL CANADA LIMITED
355 Traders Blvd E, Mississauga, ON, L4Z 2E5
(905) 890-0209
Emp Here 21   *Sales* 13,415,220

SIC 5051 Metals service centers and offices
Feroz Ali Jassani
Anita Jassani

D-U-N-S 24-644-5191   (SL)
STERIS CANADA INC
(*Suby of* STERIS LIMITED)
375 Britannia Rd E Unit 2, Mississauga, ON, L4Z 3E2
(905) 677-0863
Emp Here 400   *Sales* 214,140,800
SIC 5047 Medical and hospital equipment

D-U-N-S 25-098-6833   (SL)
STORCK CANADA INC
WERTHER'S ORIGINAL
(*Suby of* AUGUST STORCK KG)
2 Robert Speck Pky Suite 695, Mississauga, ON, L4Z 1H8
(905) 272-4480
Emp Here 20   *Sales* 16,711,540
SIC 5149 Groceries and related products, nec
Scott Ellis

D-U-N-S 25-511-3482   (SL)
SUMAGGO COLLECTION INC
5715 Coopers Ave Suite 7, Mississauga, ON, L4Z 2C7
(905) 712-9777
Emp Here 20   *Sales* 10,006,500
SIC 5136 Men's and boy's clothing
Maggie Yeung

D-U-N-S 24-822-6573   (HQ)
SYLON INC
5610 Mcadam Rd, Mississauga, ON, L4Z 1P1
(905) 890-1220
Emp Here 35   *Sales* 19,001,040
SIC 5087 Service establishment equipment
Robert Jackson
Robert Stevens

D-U-N-S 25-531-4437   (HQ)
SYMCOR INC
1 Robert Speck Pky Suite 400, Mississauga, ON, L4Z 4E7
(905) 273-1000
Emp Here 600   *Sales* 1,039,440,000
SIC 7374 Data processing and preparation
Chameli Naraine
Silvio Silvestre
Gary Eisen
Megan Hinds
Connie Rose
John Wall
Craig Menzies
Haresh Desai

D-U-N-S 24-783-2926   (HQ)
SYSCO GUEST SUPPLY CANADA INC
(*Suby of* SYSCO CORPORATION)
570 Matheson Blvd E Suite 8, Mississauga, ON, L4Z 4G4
(905) 896-1060
Sales 17,886,960
SIC 5046 Commercial equipment, nec
Thomas Macdonald

D-U-N-S 20-318-4697   (HQ)
SYSTEMATIX TECHNOLOGY CONSUL-TANTS INC
5975 Whittle Rd Suite 120, Mississauga, ON, L4Z 3N1
(416) 650-9669
Emp Here 100   *Sales* 25,027,050
SIC 7379 Computer related services, nec
Lyle Dahl

D-U-N-S 20-878-1104   (HQ)
TEAMSTERS LOCAL UNION 938
275 Matheson Blvd E, Mississauga, ON, L4Z 1X8
(905) 502-0062
Emp Here 2   *Sales* 10,561,266
SIC 8631 Labor organizations
Larry Thomas
Larry Mcdonald

D-U-N-S 20-108-9377   (SL)
TITLE & JONES INVESTMENTS LTD
4230 Sherwoodtowne Blvd, Mississauga, ON, L4Z 2G6
(905) 281-3463
Emp Here 33   *Sales* 12,919,566
SIC 6798 Real estate investment trusts
Herbert Title
Jeffrey Jones

D-U-N-S 20-286-8683   (SL)
TMS FULFILMENT INC
5641 Mcadam Rd, Mississauga, ON, L4Z 1N9
(416) 706-9658
Emp Here 24   *Sales* 10,643,760
SIC 7389 Business services, nec
Craig Holmes
Wilfrid Michaud

D-U-N-S 25-308-2333   (HQ)
TRANSCORE LINK LOGISTICS CORPORA-TION
(*Suby of* ROPER TECHNOLOGIES, INC.)
2 Robert Speck Pky Suite 900, Mississauga, ON, L4Z 1H8
(905) 795-0580
Emp Here 25   *Sales* 73,358,120
SIC 4731 Freight transportation arrangement
Claudia Malicevic

D-U-N-S 24-859-0866   (SL)
TRANSPECT INVESTMENT INC
4 Robert Speck Pky Suite 1500, Mississauga, ON, L4Z 1S1
(905) 366-7320
Emp Here 39   *Sales* 65,028,591
SIC 4731 Freight transportation arrangement
Mahmoud Moussa

D-U-N-S 24-028-7193   (HQ)
TYSON FOODS CANADA INC
(*Suby of* TYSON FOODS, INC.)
226 Britannia Rd E, Mississauga, ON, L4Z 1S6
(905) 206-0443
Emp Here 11   *Sales* 54,312,505
SIC 5142 Packaged frozen goods
Thomas P. Hayes

D-U-N-S 20-334-8631   (SL)
VALIA TRADING CORP
4 Robert Speck Pkwy 15 Fl Suite 1530, Mis-sissauga, ON, L4Z 1S1
(647) 701-9656
Emp Here 11   *Sales* 21,545,618
SIC 5146 Fish and seafoods
Cesar Lara
Leslie Ontiveros

D-U-N-S 25-372-9339   (SL)
VILLA FORUM
175 Forum Dr, Mississauga, ON, L4Z 4E5
(905) 501-1443
Emp Here 200   *Sales* 13,713,200
SIC 8051 Skilled nursing care facilities
Maria Cherbel

D-U-N-S 20-116-7868   (HQ)
VOLT CANADA INC
VMC GAMES LABS
(*Suby of* VOLT INFORMATION SCIENCES INC)
3 Robert Speck Pky Suite 260, Mississauga, ON, L4Z 2G5
(905) 306-1920
Emp Here 500   *Sales* 76,228,000
SIC 7361 Employment agencies
Jit Dhaliwal
Howard B Weinreich
Seti Hamalian
Brahm M Gelfand

D-U-N-S 20-177-9105   (HQ)
WAINBEE LIMITED
5789 Coopers Ave, Mississauga, ON, L4Z 3S6
(905) 568-1700
Emp Here 58   *Sales* 108,763,790

SIC 5084 Industrial machinery and equipment
Ronald J. Rodger
Robert Young
Wanda Wade
Wayne Mang
Doug Pickard
Derek Sutton
Ray Thompson

D-U-N-S 24-819-1319 (BR)
WE CARE HEALTH SERVICES INC
PROHOME HEALTH SERVICES INC DIVISION
(*Suby of* WE CARE HEALTH SERVICES INC)
160 Traders Blvd E Suite 208, Mississauga, ON, L4Z 3K7
(905) 275-7250
Emp Here 600
SIC 8051 Skilled nursing care facilities
Sheron Mceachron

D-U-N-S 24-924-1324 (HQ)
WILLIAMS TELECOMMUNICATIONS CORP
5610 Kennedy Rd, Mississauga, ON, L4Z 2A9
(905) 712-4242
Sales 38,456,964
SIC 5065 Electronic parts and equipment, nec
Jim Williams

D-U-N-S 24-058-5323 (HQ)
WOODBRIDGE FOAM CORPORATION
WOODBRIDGE GROUP, THE
4240 Sherwoodtowne Blvd Suite 300, Mississauga, ON, L4Z 2G6
(905) 896-3626
Emp Here 200 *Sales* 1,910,496,000
SIC 3086 Plastics foam products
Charles Daly
T Robert Beamish
Richard J Jocsak
Marie-Claude Manseau
Joe Estriga
Heather Beamish
David Beamish
Brian Beamish
James D Chaplin
Roland J Deschamps

D-U-N-S 20-411-7592 (HQ)
ZESTA ENGINEERING LIMITED
212 Watline Ave, Mississauga, ON, L4Z 1P4
(905) 568-3112
Sales 22,358,700
SIC 5075 Warm air heating and air conditioning
G Vincent Eastman
Ruth Eastman
Greg Eastman

Mississauga, ON L5A

D-U-N-S 24-097-2443 (SL)
2059010 ONTARIO INC
ELITE GROUP TEMPORARY STAFFING, THE
2515 Hurontario St Unit 2006, Mississauga, ON, L5A 4C8
(905) 281-9175
Emp Here 75 *Sales* 11,652,825
SIC 7361 Employment agencies
Kimberly Bigelow
Brian Bigelow

D-U-N-S 24-135-0201 (SL)
783312 ONTARIO LIMITED
TIVERON FARMS
2281 Camilla Rd, Mississauga, ON, L5A 2K2
(905) 848-4840
Emp Here 70 *Sales* 20,543,390
SIC 5411 Grocery stores
Dave Tiveron

D-U-N-S 20-378-3014 (SL)
9778233 CANADA INC

MEETSU SOLUTIONS
99 Dundas St E 2nd Fl, Mississauga, ON, L5A 1W7
(905) 232-5200
Emp Here 100 *Sales* 15,717,049
SIC 7361 Employment agencies
Josefina Cheng

D-U-N-S 24-822-4735 (SL)
ACORN PACKAGING INC
563 Queensway E Unit B, Mississauga, ON, L5A 3X6
(905) 279-5256
Emp Here 135 *Sales* 22,143,645
SIC 2759 Commercial printing, nec
Elizabeth Grigonis
Moez Chatur

D-U-N-S 24-335-5765 (SL)
C.J. GRAPHICS INC
C.J. DIGITAL
560 Hensall Cir, Mississauga, ON, L5A 1Y1
(416) 588-0808
Emp Here 200 *Sales* 32,805,400
SIC 2752 Commercial printing, lithographic
Jay Mandarino
Tony Hyland

D-U-N-S 24-101-8907 (SL)
CANADIAN TEST CASE 56
5770 Hurontario St, Mississauga, ON, L5A 4G4
Emp Here 20 *Sales* 10,775,010
SIC 2421 Sawmills and planing mills, general

D-U-N-S 20-161-6588 (SL)
CATANIA, M. L. COMPANY LIMITED
CATANIA WORLDWIDE
575 Orwell St Suite 3, Mississauga, ON, L5A 2W4
(416) 236-9394
Emp Here 20 *Sales* 10,702,480
SIC 5148 Fresh fruits and vegetables
Paul Catania Jr
Paul Catania Sr

D-U-N-S 20-609-6559 (BR)
CHARTWELL RETIREMENT RESIDENCES
CAWTHRA GARDENS LONGTERM CARE
(*Suby of* CHARTWELL RETIREMENT RESIDENCES)
590 Lolita Gdns Suite 355, Mississauga, ON, L5A 4N8
(905) 306-9984
Emp Here 225
SIC 8051 Skilled nursing care facilities
Heidi Elliott

D-U-N-S 20-629-4241 (HQ)
CINCOM SYSTEMS OF CANADA LTD
(*Suby of* CINCOM SYSTEMS, INC.)
2085 Hurontario St Suite 500, Mississauga, ON, L5A 4G1
(905) 279-4220
Emp Here 5 *Sales* 13,415,220
SIC 5045 Computers, peripherals, and software
Thomas Nies

D-U-N-S 24-094-6053 (SL)
COOKSVILLE DODGE CHRYSLER INC
COOKSVILLE CHRYSLER DODGE JEEP
290 Dundas St E, Mississauga, ON, L5A 1W9
(905) 279-3031
Emp Here 60 *Sales* 37,756,800
SIC 5511 New and used car dealers
Sean Kelly
John Esplen
Stuart Esplen

D-U-N-S 20-042-4281 (HQ)
COOKSVILLE STEEL LIMITED
510 Hensall Cir, Mississauga, ON, L5A 1Y1
(905) 277-9538
Emp Here 22 *Sales* 10,756,760
SIC 3441 Fabricated structural Metal
Eric Miszczuk

Olga Miszczuk
Robert Miszczuk

D-U-N-S 24-363-7766 (HQ)
DIXON, M.J. CONSTRUCTION LIMITED
2600 Edenhurst Dr Suite 200, Mississauga, ON, L5A 3Z8
(905) 270-7770
Sales 11,768,275
SIC 1542 Nonresidential construction, nec
John Dixon

D-U-N-S 20-337-8005 (HQ)
FRISCHKORN AUDIO-VISUAL CORP
FMAV
(*Suby of* IRONBRIDGE EQUITY PARTNERS II, LP)
2360 Tedlo St, Mississauga, ON, L5A 3V3
(905) 281-9000
Emp Here 26 *Sales* 58,745,700
SIC 7359 Equipment rental and leasing, nec
William Brown
Peter Samson
Alan Gordon Sellery
Andrew Mitchell
Nancy Bugbee
Nobert Frichkorn

D-U-N-S 24-025-6578 (HQ)
HINSPERGERS POLY INDUSTRIES LTD
645 Needham Lane, Mississauga, ON, L5A 1T9
(905) 272-0144
Emp Here 50 *Sales* 10,933,920
SIC 2399 Fabricated textile products, nec
Peter Hinsperger
Mark Bedford

D-U-N-S 20-143-5294 (SL)
ILSCO OF CANADA COMPANY
(*Suby of* BARDES CORPORATION)
615 Orwell St, Mississauga, ON, L5A 2W4
(905) 274-2341
Emp Here 140 *Sales* 26,661,880
SIC 3643 Current-carrying wiring devices
James Smith
David Fitzgibbon

D-U-N-S 24-093-6125 (SL)
MAPLE COMPUTERS INC
MAPLE COMPUTERS
20 Dundas St E Unit 4, Mississauga, ON, L5A 1W2
(905) 272-1446
Emp Here 100 *Sales* 24,432,800
SIC 5932 Used merchandise stores
Khurram Khan

D-U-N-S 25-055-7162 (SL)
MEGAPOL CANADA
833 Mississauga Valley Blvd, Mississauga, ON, L5A 1Z7
(416) 346-1554
Emp Here 74 *Sales* 33,090,876
SIC 5044 Office equipment
Dan Ilowicz

D-U-N-S 25-300-2885 (BR)
METRO ONTARIO INC
METRO
(*Suby of* METRO INC)
1585 Mississauga Valley Blvd, Mississauga, ON, L5A 3W9
(905) 566-9100
Emp Here 200
SIC 5411 Grocery stores
Dan Wright

D-U-N-S 24-369-2394 (BR)
METRO ONTARIO INC
FOOD BASICS
(*Suby of* METRO INC)
377 Burnhamthorpe Rd E, Mississauga, ON, L5A 3Y1
(905) 270-2143
Emp Here 90
SIC 5411 Grocery stores
Kori Willis

D-U-N-S 24-844-0245 (HQ)
N.K.S. PHARMACY LIMITED
N K S HEALTH
130 Dundas St E Suite 500, Mississauga, ON, L5A 3V8
(905) 232-2322
Emp Here 20 *Sales* 11,714,400
SIC 8742 Management consulting services
Nancy Simonot

D-U-N-S 24-693-0093 (SL)
NUSTEF FOODS LIMITED
2440 Cawthra Rd, Mississauga, ON, L5A 2X1
(905) 896-3060
Emp Here 60 *Sales* 20,741,400
SIC 2051 Bread, cake, and related products
Emiliana Deluca

D-U-N-S 24-056-0586 (HQ)
OFC DISTRIBUTION INC
580 Orwell St, Mississauga, ON, L5A 3V7
(905) 270-2009
Emp Here 13 *Sales* 16,711,540
SIC 5141 Groceries, general line
Jack Li
Youguo Guo
Pingdi Zhang

D-U-N-S 20-055-5766 (HQ)
PADDON + YORKE INC
95 Dundas St E, Mississauga, ON, L5A 1W7
(905) 272-3204
Emp Here 18 *Sales* 93,917,700
SIC 6282 Investment advice
Clyde Yorke
John Delo
Ken Peake
Brenda Wood
Barry Peak
Don Bruce

D-U-N-S 24-800-6962 (SL)
POP ENVIRO BAGS & PRODUCTS
615 Orwell St, Mississauga, ON, L5A 2W4
(905) 272-2247
Emp Here 49 *Sales* 11,438,315
SIC 2673 Bags: plastic, laminated, and coated
Steve Mitchell

D-U-N-S 25-466-9757 (SL)
QUEENSWAY CAWTHRA HOLDINGS LTD
MISSISSAUGA KAR KARE CENTRE
655 Queensway E, Mississauga, ON, L5A 3X6
(905) 273-9357
Emp Here 25 *Sales* 10,483,875
SIC 6712 Bank holding companies
William Barber

D-U-N-S 24-966-4244 (HQ)
READY IMPORT LIMITED
READY HONDA
(*Suby of* ERIKACO INC)
230 Dundas St E, Mississauga, ON, L5A 1W9
(905) 896-3500
Sales 23,907,744
SIC 5511 New and used car dealers
Robert (Bob) Redinger

D-U-N-S 20-550-6913 (HQ)
RUOFF & COMPANY INC
2360 Tedlo St, Mississauga, ON, L5A 3V3
(905) 281-9000
Sales 33,314,800
SIC 7359 Equipment rental and leasing, nec
Bill Brown

D-U-N-S 20-166-4794 (SL)
S. GUMPERT CO. OF CANADA LTD
2500 Tedlo St, Mississauga, ON, L5A 4A9
(905) 279-2600
Emp Here 60 *Sales* 17,608,620
SIC 5461 Retail bakeries
Dan Mcpherson

D-U-N-S 20-287-1815 (SL)
SUTTON GROUP ELITE REALTY INC
SUTTON REALTY

3643 Cawthra Rd Suite 201, Mississauga, ON,
L5A 2Y4
(905) 848-9800
Emp Here 38   *Sales* 12,430,826
SIC 6531 Real estate agents and managers
 Susan Meckiffe

D-U-N-S 20-704-1229   (HQ)
WESTWAY MACHINERY LTD
2370 Cawthra Rd, Mississauga, ON, L5A 2X1
(905) 803-9999
Sales 11,875,650
SIC 5084 Industrial machinery and equipment

Mississauga, ON L5B

D-U-N-S 24-319-0447   (SL)
2539393 ONTARIO INC
ONTARIO DIAGNOSTIC CENTRES
71 King St W Suite 102, Mississauga, ON,
L5B 4A2
(905) 897-1144
Emp Here 160   *Sales* 25,703,360
SIC 8011 Offices and clinics of medical doctors
 Amit Bhardwaj
 Anmol Bhardwaj
 Raj Dhami

D-U-N-S 24-660-9150   (HQ)
ACCOR CANADA INC
NOVOTEL HOTELS
(*Suby of* ACCOR)
3670 Hurontario St, Mississauga, ON, L5B
1P3
(905) 896-1000
Emp Here 100   *Sales* 28,700,400
SIC 7011 Hotels and motels
 Georges Le Mener
 Robert Gauthier
 Olivier Poirot
 Didier Bosc
 Alan Rabinowitz
 Stephen Manthey
 Kent Howarton

D-U-N-S 20-553-6647   (HQ)
AEROTEK ULC
AEROTEK AVIATION
(*Suby of* ALLEGIS GROUP, INC.)
350 Burnhamthorpe Rd W Suite 800, Mississauga, ON, L5B 3J1
(905) 283-1200
Emp Here 50   *Sales* 37,347,000
SIC 7361 Employment agencies
 Todd Mohr
 Thomas Kelly
 Jeffrey W. Reichert

D-U-N-S 20-206-3827   (SL)
**BAKER, BERTRAND, CHASSE & GOGUEN
CLAIM SERVICES LIMITED**
BBCG
(*Suby of* HILL INTERNATIONAL, INC.)
3660 Hurontario St Suite 601, Mississauga,
ON, L5B 3C4
(905) 279-8880
Emp Here 15   *Sales* 12,720,900
SIC 6411 Insurance agents, brokers, and service
 William Edward Baker

D-U-N-S 25-808-4102   (BR)
BDO CANADA LLP
MISSISSAUGA ACCOUNTING
(*Suby of* BDO CANADA LLP)
1 City Centre Dr Suite 1700, Mississauga, ON,
L5B 1M2
(905) 270-7700
Emp Here 80
SIC 8721 Accounting, auditing, and bookkeeping
 Peter Campbell

D-U-N-S 20-844-5395   (HQ)
BENEFIT PLAN ADMINISTRATORS LIMITED
90 Burnhamthorpe Rd W Suite 300, Mississauga, ON, L5B 3C3
(905) 275-6466
Sales 11,714,400
SIC 8742 Management consulting services

D-U-N-S 20-997-5218   (HQ)
BERLITZ CANADA INC
(*Suby of* BENESSE HOLDINGS,INC.)
3660 Hurontario St Suite 302, Mississauga,
ON, L5B 3C4
(905) 896-0215
Emp Here 30   *Sales* 40,698,000
SIC 8299 Schools and educational services,
nec
 Darryl Simsovic
 Mark Harris

D-U-N-S 20-269-6811   (SL)
**BLACK DIAMOND MANAGEMENT GROUP
CORPORATION**
77 City Centre Dr, Mississauga, ON, L5B 1M5
(289) 201-7898
Emp Here 28   *Sales* 19,009,844
SIC 6211 Security brokers and dealers
 Stefan Buckheimer

D-U-N-S 25-404-4985   (SL)
BORDERWARE TECHNOLOGIES INC
(*Suby of* WATCHGUARD TECHNOLOGIES,
INC.)
50 Burnhamthorpe Rd W Suite 502, Mississauga, ON, L5B 3C2
(905) 804-1855
Emp Here 130   *Sales* 18,743,660
SIC 7371 Custom computer programming services
 David Folk

D-U-N-S 24-595-3067   (SL)
BRIDGEMARK BRANDING & DESIGN
33 City Centre Dr Suite 380, Mississauga, ON,
L5B 2N5
(905) 281-7240
Emp Here 40   *Sales* 17,968,760
SIC 7389 Business services, nec
 Aubrey Ferguson

D-U-N-S 24-423-8614   (HQ)
CGC INC
(*Suby of* USG NETHERLANDS GLOBAL
HOLDINGS B.V.)
350 Burnhamthorpe Rd W Suite 500, Mississauga, ON, L5B 3J1
(905) 803-5600
Emp Here 100   *Sales* 243,161,190
SIC 3275 Gypsum products
 Christopher Macey
 James Mcewen
 Christopher Griffin
 William Foote
 James Metcalf
 D. Rick Lowes

D-U-N-S 25-938-7157   (BR)
CHILDREN'S AID SOCIETY OF THE REGION OF PEEL, THE
(*Suby of* CHILDREN'S AID SOCIETY OF
THE REGION OF PEEL, THE)
101 Queensway W Suite 500, Mississauga,
ON, L5B 2P7

Emp Here 150
SIC 8399 Social services, nec
 Sharon Williams

D-U-N-S 20-373-8856   (BR)
CINEPLEX ODEON CORPORATION
CINEPLEX CINEMAS MISSISSAUGA
(*Suby of* CINEPLEX INC)
309 Rathburn Rd W, Mississauga, ON, L5B
4C1
(905) 275-4969
Emp Here 130

SIC 7832 Motion picture theaters, except
drive-in
 Chris Benjamin

D-U-N-S 24-421-3377   (HQ)
CLAIMSECURE INC
1 City Centre Dr Suite 620, Mississauga, ON,
L5B 1M2
(705) 673-2541
Emp Here 20   *Sales* 641,090,400
SIC 6324 Hospital and medical service plans
 Peter Craig
 Paul Hardwick
 Dave Wowchuk
 Danica Riengeutte

D-U-N-S 20-006-9227   (HQ)
CORPORATION MORGUARD
55 City Centre Dr Suite 800, Mississauga, ON,
L5B 1M3
(905) 281-3800
Emp Here 350   *Sales* 890,866,887
SIC 6531 Real estate agents and managers
 K Rai Sahi
 Beverley G. Flynn
 Angela Sahi
 Robert D. Wright
 Robert Mcfarlane
 Brian Athey
 Paul Miatello
 Bruce K. Robertson
 David A. King
 Leonard Peter Sharpe

D-U-N-S 24-379-7458   (HQ)
**CUNNINGHAM LINDSEY CANADA CLAIMS
SERVICES LTD**
ENVIRONMENTAL SOLUTIONS REMEDIATION SERVICES
50 Burnhamthorpe Rd W Suite 1102, Mississauga, ON, L5B 3C2
(905) 896-8181
Emp Here 3   *Sales* 23,428,800
SIC 8748 Business consulting, nec
 Rob Seal
 Edmund Mullen
 Mark Samis

D-U-N-S 20-784-1594   (HQ)
**DOLLAR THRIFTY AUTOMOTIVE GROUP
CANADA INC**
(*Suby of* HERTZ GLOBAL HOLDINGS, INC.)
3660 Hurontario St, Mississauga, ON, L5B
3C4
(905) 612-1881
Emp Here 40   *Sales* 44,848,000
SIC 7515 Passenger car leasing
 Gary L. Paxton

D-U-N-S 24-254-2996   (SL)
**DONATO ACADEMY OF HAIRSTYLING
AND AESTHETICS**
100 City Centre Dr, Mississauga, ON, L5B
2C9
(416) 252-8999
Emp Here 100   *Sales* 8,962,900
SIC 7231 Beauty shops
 John Donato

D-U-N-S 25-142-4008   (BR)
**DUFFERIN-PEEL CATHOLIC DISTRICT
SCHOOL BOARD**
*FATHER MICHAEL GOETZ SECONDARY
SCHOOL*
(*Suby of* DUFFERIN-PEEL CATHOLIC DISTRICT SCHOOL BOARD)
330 Central Pky W, Mississauga, ON, L5B
3K6
(905) 277-0326
Emp Here 150
SIC 8211 Elementary and secondary schools
 Susan Ruschka

D-U-N-S 24-424-0870   (HQ)
EASYFINANCIAL SERVICES INC
(*Suby of* GOEASY LTD)
33 City Centre Dr Suite 510, Mississauga, ON,
L5B 2N5

(905) 272-2788
Emp Here 57   *Sales* 153,842,970
SIC 6141 Personal credit institutions
 Sabrina Anzini

D-U-N-S 25-254-1438   (HQ)
EDWARD D. JONES & CO. CANADA HOLDING CO., INC
EDWARD JONES
(*Suby of* JONES FINANCIAL COMPANIES,
L.L.L.P.)
90 Burnhamthorpe Rd W Suite 902, Mississauga, ON, L5B 3C3
(905) 306-8600
Emp Here 1,600   *Sales* 35,578,450,000
SIC 6211 Security brokers and dealers
 Gary Reamey
 Donald J Burwell
 Kevin Bastien

D-U-N-S 20-649-5694   (SL)
FS REALTY CENTRE CORPORATION
ROYAL LEPAGE
2150 Hurontario St Unit 202e, Mississauga,
ON, L5B 1M8
(416) 253-0066
Emp Here 140   *Sales* 258,683,880
SIC 6411 Insurance agents, brokers, and service
 Phil Sbrocchi

D-U-N-S 24-308-9703   (SL)
GLENN DAVIS GROUP INC
77 City Centre Dr Unit 2, Mississauga, ON,
L5B 1M5
(905) 270-2501
Emp Here 95   *Sales* 20,113,780
SIC 7336 Commercial art and graphic design
 Glenn Davis
 Ron Davis

D-U-N-S 24-948-9758   (HQ)
GOEASY LTD
33 City Centre Dr Suite 510, Mississauga, ON,
L5B 2N5
(905) 272-2788
Emp Here 147   *Sales* 383,744,409
SIC 7359 Equipment rental and leasing, nec
 David Ingram
 Jason Mullins
 Steve Goertz
 Andrea Fiederer
 Jason Appel
 David Cooper
 Shadi Khatib
 Shane Pennell
 Steven Poole
 David Yeilding

D-U-N-S 20-315-9728   (BR)
GRANT THORNTON LLP
(*Suby of* GRANT THORNTON LLP)
201 City Centre Dr Suite 501, Mississauga,
ON, L5B 2T4
(416) 369-7076
Emp Here 80
SIC 8721 Accounting, auditing, and bookkeeping

D-U-N-S 25-403-9431   (BR)
GWL REALTY ADVISORS INC
(*Suby of* POWER CORPORATION DU
CANADA)
1 City Centre Dr Suite 300, Mississauga, ON,
L5B 1M2
(905) 275-6600
Emp Here 90
SIC 6531 Real estate agents and managers

D-U-N-S 20-369-1113   (HQ)
HCL AXON TECHNOLOGIES INC
(*Suby of* HCL TECHNOLOGIES LIMITED)
77 City Centre Dr, Mississauga, ON, L5B 1M5
(905) 603-4381
Sales 60,381,717,825
SIC 7372 Prepackaged software
 Roshni Nadar Malhotra
 Shiv Nadar

C Vijayakumar
Prateek Aggarwal
Gh Rao
Rahul Singh
Ajit Kumar
Apparao V V
Anand Birjie
Anil Ganjoo

D-U-N-S 24-356-1235   (BR)
HUDSON'S BAY COMPANY
BAY, THE
(*Suby of* HUDSON'S BAY COMPANY)
100 City Centre Dr Suite 200, Mississauga,
ON, L5B 2C9
(905) 270-7600
Emp Here 100
SIC 5311 Department stores
 Monika Riegart

D-U-N-S 24-575-3231   (HQ)
IMPACT AUTO AUCTIONS LTD
(*Suby of* KAR AUCTION SERVICES, INC.)
50 Burnhamthorpe Rd W Suite 800, Mississauga, ON, L5B 3C2
(905) 896-9727
Emp Here 25   *Sales* 107,025,280
SIC 7389 Business services, nec
 Terry Daniels

D-U-N-S 20-328-3254   (HQ)
INGREDION CANADA CORPORATION
(*Suby of* INGREDION INCORPORATED)
90 Burnhamthorpe Rd W Unit 1600, Mississauga, ON, L5B 0H9
(905) 281-7950
Emp Here 100   *Sales* 34,569,000
SIC 2046 Wet corn milling
 Robert Douglas Desmond Kee
 James P. Zallie
 Richard J. O'shanna

D-U-N-S 20-784-0281   (HQ)
KELLY SERVICES (CANADA), LTD
KELLY TEMPORARY SERVICES
(*Suby of* KELLY SERVICES, INC.)
77 City Centre Dr, Mississauga, ON, L5B 1M5
(416) 368-1058
Emp Here 40   *Sales* 45,736,800
SIC 7363 Help supply services
 Terrance E. Adderley
 Michael Curran
 Karen French

D-U-N-S 20-168-4842   (HQ)
KIMBERLY-CLARK INC
(*Suby of* KIMBERLY-CLARK CORPORATION)
50 Burnhamthorpe Rd W Suite 1402, Mississauga, ON, L5B 3C2
(905) 277-6500
Emp Here 80   *Sales* 1,102,911,000
SIC 2676 Sanitary paper products
 Tom Mielke

D-U-N-S 24-868-2924   (HQ)
KNOWLEDGE FIRST FINANCIAL INC
(*Suby of* INTERNATIONAL SCHOLARSHIP FOUNDATION, THE)
50 Burnhamthorpe Rd W Suite 1000, Mississauga, ON, L5B 4A5
(905) 270-8777
Emp Here 120   *Sales* 291,943,650
SIC 6732 Trusts: educational, religious, etc.
 George Hopkinson
 Donald Hunter
 Eric Jodoin
 Carma Lecuyer
 Suzanne Martyn-Jones
 Jacques Naud
 Peter Thompson
 Darrell Bartlett
 Stephen Rotz
 Ellen Bessner

D-U-N-S 24-364-2076   (SL)
LIFEBRIDGE HEALTH MANAGEMENT INC

90 Burnhamthorpe Rd W Suite 206, Mississauga, ON, L5B 3C3

Emp Here 20   *Sales* 21,045,729
SIC 6311 Life insurance

D-U-N-S 24-387-9418   (BR)
**LONDON   LIFE,   COMPAGNIE
D'ASSURANCE-VIE**
LONDON LIFE INSURANCE COMPANY
(*Suby of* POWER CORPORATION DU CANADA)
1 City Centre Dr Suite 1600, Mississauga, ON, L5B 1M2
(905) 276-1177
Emp Here 100
SIC 6311 Life insurance
 Art Jefferson

D-U-N-S 20-059-3601   (SL)
MARINA COMMODITIES INC
90 Burnhamthorpe Rd W Suite 1102, Mississauga, ON, L5B 3C3
(905) 828-0777
Emp Here 12   *Sales* 14,524,764
SIC 5153 Grain and field beans
 Farhan Adam
 Faheem Adam

D-U-N-S 24-859-7056   (HQ)
MORGUARD INVESTMENTS LIMITED
MISSISSAUGA CITY CENTRE OFFICE BUILDING
(*Suby of* CORPORATION MORGUARD)
55 City Centre Dr Suite 800, Mississauga, ON, L5B 1M3
(905) 281-3800
Emp Here 150   *Sales* 270,451,200
SIC 6531 Real estate agents and managers
 George Schott
 David Wyatt

D-U-N-S 20-294-2637   (BR)
MORGUARD INVESTMENTS LIMITED
(*Suby of* CORPORATION MORGUARD)
55 City Centre Dr Suite 800, Mississauga, ON, L5B 1M3
(905) 281-3800
Emp Here 300
SIC 6798 Real estate investment trusts
 Brian Athey

D-U-N-S 20-381-1083   (SL)
MORGUARD NORTH AMERICAN RESIDENTIAL REAL ESTATE INVESTMENT TRUST
55 City Centre Dr Suite 1000, Mississauga, ON, L5B 1M3
(905) 281-3800
Emp Here 6   *Sales* 177,453,623
SIC 6798 Real estate investment trusts
 K. Rai Sahi
 Paul Miatello
 John Talano
 Sanjay Rateja
 Beverley G. Flynn
 Robert D. Wright

D-U-N-S 25-531-0567   (HQ)
MORGUARD REAL ESTATE INVESTMENT TRUST
55 City Centre Dr Suite 800, Mississauga, ON, L5B 1M3
(905) 281-3800
Sales 209,594,734
SIC 6726 Investment offices, nec
 K. Rai Sahi
 Robert Wright
 Beverley G. Flynn
 Paul Miatello
 Andrew Tamlin
 Timothy J. Walker
 Paul F. Cobb
 Edward C. Kress
 Michael A.J. Catford
 Antony K. Stephens

D-U-N-S 24-093-1332   (BR)
MOXIE'S RESTAURANTS, LIMITED PARTNERSHIP
100 City Centre Dr Unit 2-730, Mississauga, ON, L5B 2C9
(905) 276-6555
Emp Here 120
SIC 5812 Eating places
 Chris Yeo

D-U-N-S 20-657-9356   (BR)
OLD NAVY (CANADA) INC
(*Suby of* THE GAP INC)
100 City Centre Dr Unit E6, Mississauga, ON, L5B 2C9
(905) 275-5155
Emp Here 100
SIC 5651 Family clothing stores
 Sam Armetta

D-U-N-S 20-288-9205   (BR)
OUTFRONT MEDIA CANADA LP
CBS CANADA HOLDINGS CO
(*Suby of* OUTFRONT MEDIA CANADA LP)
309 Rathburn Rd W, Mississauga, ON, L5B 4C1
(905) 275-4969
Emp Here 100
SIC 7832 Motion picture theaters, except drive-in

D-U-N-S 25-992-2409   (BR)
PLAYER ONE AMUSEMENT GROUP INC
(*Suby of* PLAYER ONE AMUSEMENT GROUP INC)
99 Rathburn Rd W, Mississauga, ON, L5B 4C1
(905) 273-9000
Emp Here 120
SIC 7999 Amusement and recreation, nec
 Len Keywood

D-U-N-S 24-090-1889   (HQ)
PNB REMITTANCE COMPANY (CANADA)
(*Suby of* PHILIPPINE NATIONAL BANK)
3050 Confederation Pky Unit 104, Mississauga, ON, L5B 3Z6
(905) 897-9600
Emp Here 17   *Sales* 10,264,800
SIC 6099 Functions related to deposit banking
 Manuel Arnaldo

D-U-N-S 20-177-4676   (HQ)
PRAXAIR CANADA INC
DISTRIBUTION PRAXAIR
(*Suby of* LINDE PUBLIC LIMITED COMPANY)
1 City Centre Dr Suite 1200, Mississauga, ON, L5B 1M2
(905) 803-1600
Emp Here 320   *Sales* 755,896,500
SIC 2813 Industrial gases
 James J Fuchs
 Jose R Rivero
 Edgar C Hotard
 Paul J Bilek
 Lawrence A Gibbons

D-U-N-S 24-302-3942   (SL)
PROPHIX SOFTWARE INC
350 Burnhamthorpe Rd W Suite 1000, Mississauga, ON, L5B 3J1
(905) 279-8711
Emp Here 150   *Sales* 21,627,300
SIC 7371 Custom computer programming services
 Paul Barber
 Alok Ajmera
 Geoffrey Ng
 Ken Lavoie
 Michael Tindal
 Jens Bille
 Ryan Van Hatten

D-U-N-S 25-050-6136   (SL)
QUALITY CONTINUOUS IMPROVEMENT CENTRE FOR COMMUNITY EDUCATION

AND TRAINING
CENTRE FOR EDUCATION AND TRAINING
90 Burnhamthorpe Rd W Suite 210, Mississauga, ON, L5B 3C3
(905) 949-0049
Emp Here 300   *Sales* 14,478,900
SIC 8331 Job training and related services
 Merv Hillier
 Jeff Brown
 Farhad Sethna
 Andrew Gall
 Ben Earle
 Epsit Jajal
 Pamela Wong
 Robert Murison
 Adnan Masood

D-U-N-S 20-207-6720   (SL)
RE/MAX REALTY ONE INC
50 Burnhamthorpe Rd W Suite 102, Mississauga, ON, L5B 3C2
(905) 277-0771
Emp Here 115   *Sales* 48,172,235
SIC 6531 Real estate agents and managers
 Masi Satoungar

D-U-N-S 20-529-6015   (HQ)
REVENUE PROPERTIES COMPANY LIMITED
(*Suby of* CORPORATION MORGUARD)
55 City Centre Dr Suite 1000, Mississauga, ON, L5B 1M3
(905) 281-5943
Emp Here 25   *Sales* 16,959,625
SIC 6512 Nonresidential building operators
 Antony K Stephens
 Rai Sahi
 Mark E Tanz
 Jack Winberg
 David King
 Wayne P E Mang
 Bruce Simmonds

D-U-N-S 25-236-5531   (HQ)
RTO ASSET MANAGEMENT INC
(*Suby of* GOEASY LTD)
33 City Centre Dr Suite 510, Mississauga, ON, L5B 2N5
(905) 272-2788
Emp Here 30   *Sales* 188,561,768
SIC 7359 Equipment rental and leasing, nec
 David Ingram

D-U-N-S 24-366-5247   (HQ)
SBI CANADA BANK
(*Suby of* STATE BANK OF INDIA)
77 City Centre Dr Suite 106, Mississauga, ON, L5B 1M5
(905) 896-6540
Sales 18,130,230
SIC 6021 National commercial banks
 Arun Nagarajan
 Ajay Bandon

D-U-N-S 24-318-4624   (BR)
SEPHORA BEAUTY CANADA, INC
(*Suby of* LVMH MOET HENNESSY LOUIS VUITTON)
100 City Centre Dr Unit 2-930, Mississauga, ON, L5B 2C9
(905) 279-4400
Emp Here 100
SIC 5999 Miscellaneous retail stores, nec
 Philippe Pinatel

D-U-N-S 20-364-1410   (BR)
**SHERIDAN   COLLEGE   INSTITUTE   OF
TECHNOLOGY AND ADVANCED LEARNING**
HAZEL MCCALLION CAMPUS
(*Suby of* SHERIDAN COLLEGE INSTITUTE OF TECHNOLOGY AND ADVANCED LEARNING)
4180 Duke Of York Blvd, Mississauga, ON, L5B 0G5
(905) 845-9430
Emp Here 737

SIC 8222 Junior colleges
Mary Preece

D-U-N-S 20-027-9151 (BR)
SIR CORP
CANYON CREEK STEAK & CHOPHOUSE
(*Suby of* SIR CORP)
299 Rathburn Rd W, Mississauga, ON, L5B 4C1
(905) 279-3342
Emp Here 100
SIC 5812 Eating places
Gina Hertz

D-U-N-S 25-724-4830 (BR)
SIR CORP
SCADDABUSH ITALIAN KITCHEN & BAR
(*Suby of* SIR CORP)
209 Rathburn Rd W, Mississauga, ON, L5B 4C1
(905) 281-1721
Emp Here 100
SIC 5812 Eating places
Tiffany Smrekar

D-U-N-S 25-786-2573 (BR)
SIR CORP
JACK ASTOR'S
(*Suby of* SIR CORP)
219 Rathburn Rd W, Mississauga, ON, L5B 4C1
(905) 566-4662
Emp Here 130
SIC 5812 Eating places
John Mackay

D-U-N-S 24-344-8706 (BR)
SYNERGIE HUNT INTERNATIONAL INC
HUNT PERSONNEL
(*Suby of* HB COLLECTOR SARL)
50 Burnhamthorpe Rd W Suite 204, Mississauga, ON, L5B 3C2
(905) 273-3221
Emp Here 80
SIC 7361 Employment agencies
Rona Long

D-U-N-S 20-389-1317 (HQ)
TEKSYSTEMS CANADA CORP
TEKSYSTEMS
(*Suby of* ALLEGIS GROUP, INC.)
350 Burnhamthorpe Rd W, Mississauga, ON, L5B 3J1
(905) 283-1300
Emp Here 50 *Sales* 76,228,000
SIC 7361 Employment agencies
Sean Mcgraw
Jay W Alvather
Francis Buckley

D-U-N-S 24-333-8139 (HQ)
TEMPLE HOTELS INC
55 City Centre Dr Suite 1000, Mississauga, ON, L5B 1M3
(905) 281-4800
Emp Here 5 *Sales* 129,753,193
SIC 6798 Real estate investment trusts
K. Rai. Sahi
Beverley G. Flynn
Eugene Hretzay
Patrick Seward
Sanjay Rateja
Paul Miatello
Chris Cahill
Jonathan Carnella
David J. Nunn
Brent Mclean

D-U-N-S 25-172-5446 (BR)
TOWERS WATSON CANADA INC
(*Suby of* WILLIS TOWERS WATSON PUBLIC LIMITED COMPANY)
201 City Centre Dr Suite 1000, Mississauga, ON, L5B 4E4
(905) 272-6322
Emp Here 200
SIC 6411 Insurance agents, brokers, and ser-

vice
Laura Samaroo

D-U-N-S 25-671-0398 (HQ)
TRILLIUM HEALTH PARTNERS
100 Queensway W, Mississauga, ON, L5B 1B8
(905) 848-7580
Emp Here 1,290 *Sales* 790,016,724
SIC 8062 General medical and surgical hospitals
Michelle Diemanuele
Wayne Bossert
Patti Cochrane
Kathryn Hayward-Murray
Dean Martin
Steve Hall
Karli Farrow
Leslie Starr-Hemburrow
Debra Carson
Alison Quigley

D-U-N-S 20-850-0215 (HQ)
TRILLIUM HEALTH PARTNERS VOLUNTEERS
MISSISSAUGA HOSPITAL GIFT SHOP
100 Queensway W, Mississauga, ON, L5B 1B8
(905) 848-7276
Sales 10,994,760
SIC 5947 Gift, novelty, and souvenir shop
Percey Elliott
David (Dave) Voyce
Marianne Di Lullo

D-U-N-S 24-327-4474 (BR)
WAL-MART CANADA CORP
(*Suby of* WALMART INC.)
100 City Centre Dr Suite 100, Mississauga, ON, L5B 2G7
(905) 270-9300
Emp Here 150
SIC 5311 Department stores
Jacob Kennedy

D-U-N-S 24-764-8330 (BR)
YMCA OF GREATER TORONTO
MISSISSAUGA YMCA
(*Suby of* YMCA OF GREATER TORONTO)
325 Burnhamthorpe Rd W, Mississauga, ON, L5B 3R2
(905) 897-6801
Emp Here 200
SIC 7991 Physical fitness facilities
Diana Deakin-Thomas

Mississauga, ON L5C

D-U-N-S 24-526-5616 (SL)
596042 ONTARIO LIMITED
LE BON CROISSANT
720 Burnhamthorpe Rd W Unit 28, Mississauga, ON, L5C 3G1
(905) 270-9840
Emp Here 75 *Sales* 62,668,275
SIC 5149 Groceries and related products, nec
Dokse Perklin

D-U-N-S 20-560-8730 (HQ)
APPLEWOOD AIR-CONDITIONING LIMITED
(*Suby of* GRONWALL HOLDINGS INC)
3525 Hawkestone Rd, Mississauga, ON, L5C 2V1
(905) 275-4500
Sales 13,983,900
SIC 1711 Plumbing, heating, air-conditioning
George Gronwall
John Elinesky

D-U-N-S 24-022-4808 (HQ)
ARI FINANCIAL SERVICES INC
(*Suby of* HOLMAN ENTERPRISES INC.)
1270 Central Pky W Suite 500, Mississauga,

ON, L5C 4P4
(905) 803-8000
Emp Here 85 *Sales* 24,955,200
SIC 8741 Management services
Chris Conroy
Mark Bryan
Rick Tousaw
Gernot Leinenbach
Anthony Foursha

D-U-N-S 25-306-4497 (BR)
CO-OPERATORS GENERAL INSURANCE COMPANY
(*Suby of* CO-OPERATORS GENERAL INSURANCE COMPANY)
1270 Central Pky W Suite 600, Mississauga, ON, L5C 4P4

Emp Here 90
SIC 6411 Insurance agents, brokers, and service
Hawken Jacky

D-U-N-S 20-104-7094 (SL)
EDWARDS LIFESCIENCES (CANADA) INC
(*Suby of* EDWARDS LIFESCIENCES CORP)
1290 Central Pky W Suite 300, Mississauga, ON, L5C 4R3
(905) 273-7138
Emp Here 25 *Sales* 11,179,350
SIC 5047 Medical and hospital equipment
Brian Heyland
Cathy Bernaerts

D-U-N-S 24-952-7698 (SL)
ELIK, MIKE LIMITED
CANADIAN TIRE
3050 Mavis Rd Suite 346, Mississauga, ON, L5C 1T8
(905) 270-9200
Emp Here 152 *Sales* 40,683,104
SIC 5251 Hardware stores
Mike Elik

D-U-N-S 24-077-4336 (SL)
EVEREST NURSING & COMMUINITY CARE AGENCY INC
EVEREST HOME HEALTH CARE
2341 Nikanna Rd, Mississauga, ON, L5C 2W8
(905) 270-4426
Emp Here 200 *Sales* 26,691,800
SIC 8399 Social services, nec
Esther Stewart
Evelyn Martindale
Eflyn Blair

D-U-N-S 20-042-4950 (HQ)
FIELDING CHEMICAL TECHNOLOGIES INC
3575 Mavis Rd, Mississauga, ON, L5C 1T7
(905) 279-5122
Sales 40,134,480
SIC 7389 Business services, nec
Ellen Mcgregor

D-U-N-S 20-073-5954 (BR)
FIRSTCANADA ULC
(*Suby of* FIRSTGROUP PLC)
3599 Wolfedale Rd, Mississauga, ON, L5C 1V8
(905) 270-0561
Emp Here 235
SIC 4151 School buses
Michelle Sargent

D-U-N-S 25-282-8843 (SL)
GMRI CANADA, INC
RED LOBSTER
790 Burnhamthorpe Rd W, Mississauga, ON, L5C 4G3
(905) 848-8477
Emp Here 4,000 *Sales* 186,556,000
SIC 5812 Eating places
Paul Vesquez

D-U-N-S 24-560-4194 (SL)
GRAHAM PACKAGING CANADA LIMITED
(*Suby of* PACKAGING HOLDINGS LIMITED)

3174 Mavis Rd, Mississauga, ON, L5C 1T8
(905) 277-1486
Emp Here 120 *Sales* 19,062,960
SIC 3089 Plastics products, nec
Phil Yates
Roger Prevot
John Hamilton
Paul Wannemacher

D-U-N-S 25-088-1794 (BR)
HOME DEPOT OF CANADA INC
HOME DEPOT
(*Suby of* THE HOME DEPOT INC)
3065 Mavis Rd, Mississauga, ON, L5C 1T7
(905) 281-6230
Emp Here 173
SIC 5251 Hardware stores
Michael Pedinelli

D-U-N-S 20-413-5354 (HQ)
INDAL TECHNOLOGIES INC
CURTISS-WRIGHT DEFENSE SOLUTIONS
(*Suby of* CURTISS-WRIGHT CORPORATION)
3570 Hawkestone Rd, Mississauga, ON, L5C 2V8
(905) 275-5300
Sales 35,591,037
SIC 3728 Aircraft parts and equipment, nec
Colleen Williams
Patricia Haslegrave

D-U-N-S 20-553-8353 (HQ)
INNOPHOS CANADA, INC
(*Suby of* INNOPHOS HOLDINGS, INC.)
3265 Wolfedale Rd, Mississauga, ON, L5C 1V8
(905) 270-9328
Emp Here 5 *Sales* 22,721,680
SIC 2819 Industrial inorganic chemicals, nec
Randolph Gress
Neil Salmon
Louis Calvarin

D-U-N-S 25-273-5832 (HQ)
KAL-TRADING INC
KAL-POLYMERS
3440 Wolfedale Rd, Mississauga, ON, L5C 1W4
(905) 273-7400
Sales 54,775,875
SIC 5162 Plastics materials and basic shapes
Gobi Saha

D-U-N-S 25-942-3903 (BR)
LIVING REALTY INC
(*Suby of* LIVING REALTY INC)
1177 Central Pky W Unit 32, Mississauga, ON, L5C 4P3
(905) 896-0002
Emp Here 100
SIC 6531 Real estate agents and managers
William Lui

D-U-N-S 24-329-6931 (BR)
LOBLAWS INC
REAL CANADIAN SUPERSTORE
(*Suby of* LOBLAW COMPANIES LIMITED)
3045 Mavis Rd Suite 2841, Mississauga, ON, L5C 1T7
(905) 275-6171
Emp Here 200
SIC 5411 Grocery stores
Barbara Chaulk

D-U-N-S 20-042-6252 (SL)
LYONS AUTO BODY LIMITED
1020 Burnhamthorpe Rd W, Mississauga, ON, L5C 2S4
(905) 277-1456
Emp Here 100 *Sales* 28,330,000
SIC 7532 Top and body repair and paint shops
Jack Lyons
Julia Lyons

D-U-N-S 25-755-6621 (BR)
METROLAND MEDIA GROUP LTD
MISSISSAUGA NEWS, THE

(Suby of TORSTAR CORPORATION)
3145 Wolfedale Rd, Mississauga, ON, L5C 3A9
(905) 281-5656
Emp Here 160
SIC 2711 Newspapers

D-U-N-S 20-805-8458   (BR)
METROLINX
GO TRANSIT
(Suby of METROLINX)
3500 Wolfedale Rd, Mississauga, ON, L5C 2V6

Emp Here 120
SIC 3743 Railroad equipment
Luke Togo

D-U-N-S 25-239-7864   (HQ)
MINI-SKOOL A CHILD'S PLACE INC
1100 Central Pky W Suite 17, Mississauga, ON, L5C 4E5
(905) 275-2378
Emp Here 20   Sales 15,593,500
SIC 8351 Child day care services
Gillian D'souza

D-U-N-S 25-293-7610   (BR)
PEEL DISTRICT SCHOOL BOARD
WOODLANDS SCHOOL
(Suby of PEEL DISTRICT SCHOOL BOARD)
3225 Erindale Station Rd, Mississauga, ON, L5C 1Y5
(905) 279-0575
Emp Here 135
SIC 8211 Elementary and secondary schools
Carol Suhay

D-U-N-S 25-317-5228   (SL)
PROG-DIE TOOL & STAMPING LTD
3161 Wolfedale Rd, Mississauga, ON, L5C 1V8
(905) 277-4651
Emp Here 60   Sales 13,320,060
SIC 3544 Special dies, tools, jigs, and fixtures
Santiago A. Almiron

D-U-N-S 20-983-9802   (SL)
PROVINCIAL STORE FIXTURES LTD
910 Central Pky W, Mississauga, ON, L5C 2V5
(905) 564-6700
Emp Here 130   Sales 20,877,744
SIC 2431 Millwork
Samer Joubran
Edward Joubran
Henry Joubran

D-U-N-S 25-034-0700   (HQ)
RE/MAX PERFORMANCE REALTY INC
141-1140 Burnhamthorpe Rd W, Mississauga, ON, L5C 4E9
(905) 270-2000
Emp Here 145   Sales 41,888,900
SIC 6531 Real estate agents and managers
John Bradley

D-U-N-S 20-561-9484   (BR)
RE/MAX PERFORMANCE REALTY INC
(Suby of RE/MAX PERFORMANCE REALTY INC)
1140 Burnhamthorpe Rd W Suite 141, Mississauga, ON, L5C 4E9
(905) 270-2000
Emp Here 130
SIC 6531 Real estate agents and managers
John Bradley

D-U-N-S 24-848-4255   (HQ)
RE/MAX PROFESSIONALS INC
1645 Dundas St W, Mississauga, ON, L5C 1E3
(905) 270-8840
Emp Here 35   Sales 13,587,800
SIC 6531 Real estate agents and managers
John Alexander
Pamela Alexander

D-U-N-S 20-526-7362   (SL)
SPACEMAKER LIMITED
3069 Wolfedale Rd, Mississauga, ON, L5C 1V9
(905) 279-2632
Emp Here 55   Sales 10,564,675
SIC 3448 Prefabricated Metal buildings and components
Norma Danbrook
George Smith

D-U-N-S 25-120-7262   (BR)
SPECTRUM HEALTH CARE LTD
SPECTRUM HEALTH AMBULATORY CARE CLINIC
(Suby of SPECTRUM HEALTH CARE LTD)
1290 Central Pky W Suite 302, Mississauga, ON, L5C 4R3
(905) 272-2271
Emp Here 400
SIC 8741 Management services
Anna Romain

D-U-N-S 25-803-5377   (HQ)
SUTTON GROUP REALTY SYSTEMS INC
SUTTON GROUP
1528 Dundas St W Unit 1, Mississauga, ON, L5C 1E4
(905) 896-3333
Emp Here 5   Sales 101,419,200
SIC 6531 Real estate agents and managers
Marianne Semen

D-U-N-S 25-808-8731   (SL)
SUTTON GROUP-SUMMIT REALTY INC
1100 Burnhamthorpe Rd W Unit 27, Mississauga, ON, L5C 4G4
(905) 897-9555
Emp Here 150   Sales 62,833,350
SIC 6531 Real estate agents and managers
Brian Maguire

D-U-N-S 25-135-3707   (SL)
T&R SARGENT FARMS LTD
3410 Semenyk Crt Suite 5, Mississauga, ON, L5C 4P8
(905) 896-1059
Emp Here 49   Sales 18,890,431
SIC 0251 Broiler, fryer, and roaster chickens
Robert Giguere

D-U-N-S 24-487-2412   (HQ)
TERRA NOVA STEEL & IRON (ONTARIO) INC
3595 Hawkestone Rd, Mississauga, ON, L5C 2V1
(905) 273-3872
Emp Here 22   Sales 15,651,090
SIC 5051 Metals service centers and offices
Mario Zitella

D-U-N-S 25-403-9639   (SL)
WHITEOAK FORD LINCOLN SALES LIMITED
3285 Mavis Rd, Mississauga, ON, L5C 1T7
(905) 270-8210
Emp Here 50   Sales 24,903,900
SIC 5511 New and used car dealers
Ronald Loveys
David Mcquilkin

Mississauga, ON L5E

D-U-N-S 24-418-6045   (SL)
A.J. LANZAROTTA WHOLESALE FRUIT & VEGETABLES LTD
1000 Lakeshore Rd E, Mississauga, ON, L5E 1E4
(905) 891-0510
Emp Here 85   Sales 71,024,045
SIC 5148 Fresh fruits and vegetables
Augustus Lanzarotta

D-U-N-S 20-562-8105   (BR)
ALLEGION CANADA INC

INGERSOLL RAND SECURITIES TECHNOLOGIES
(Suby of ALLEGION PUBLIC LIMITED COMPANY)
1076 Lakeshore Rd E, Mississauga, ON, L5E 1E4
(905) 403-1800
Emp Here 150
SIC 5072 Hardware
Mark Wilson

D-U-N-S 20-792-1672   (SL)
CHRIS & STACEY'S NO FRILLS
1250 South Service Rd, Mississauga, ON, L5E 1V4
(905) 891-1021
Emp Here 120   Sales 35,217,240
SIC 5411 Grocery stores
Chris Dunn

D-U-N-S 25-412-1932   (SL)
FILAMAT COMPOSITES INC
(Suby of MONTECO LTD)
880 Rangeview Rd, Mississauga, ON, L5E 1G9
(905) 891-3993
Emp Here 50   Sales 11,671,750
SIC 3299 NonMetallic mineral products,
Scott Monteith

D-U-N-S 20-165-7517   (SL)
GENCO MARINE LIMITED
1008 Rangeview Rd, Mississauga, ON, L5E 1H3
(416) 504-2891
Emp Here 22   Sales 11,451,924
SIC 5099 Durable goods, nec
Nicolo Genco
Ignazio Genco Jr

D-U-N-S 20-180-9485   (HQ)
INTERIOR MANUFACTURING GROUP INC
IMG
974 Lakeshore Rd E, Mississauga, ON, L5E 1E4
(905) 278-9510
Emp Here 100   Sales 29,321,180
SIC 2542 Partitions and fixtures, except wood
Marcus Pachul
Fritz Winkels
Charles Fu
Michael Scafetta

D-U-N-S 20-120-1410   (SL)
INTERNATIONAL SILVER DEVELOPMENT INC
1260 Lakeshore Rd E, Mississauga, ON, L5E 3B8

Emp Here 25   Sales 13,013,550
SIC 5094 Jewelry and precious stones
Ray Narine

D-U-N-S 20-700-8699   (SL)
METAGENICS CANADA, INC
(Suby of ALTICOR GLOBAL HOLDINGS INC.)
851 Rangeview Rd Suite 1, Mississauga, ON, L5E 1H1
(905) 891-1300
Emp Here 28   Sales 30,949,660
SIC 5122 Drugs, proprietaries, and sundries
Gene Dixon

D-U-N-S 20-820-6474   (SL)
NATIONAL BAIT INC
946 Lakeshore Rd E, Mississauga, ON, L5E 1E4
(905) 278-0180
Emp Here 120   Sales 70,699,080
SIC 5199 Nondurable goods, nec
Joseph Haupert

D-U-N-S 25-293-8386   (BR)
PEEL DISTRICT SCHOOL BOARD
GORDON GRAYDON MEMORIAL SECONDARY SCHOOL
(Suby of PEEL DISTRICT SCHOOL BOARD)

1490 Ogden Ave, Mississauga, ON, L5E 2H8
(905) 274-2391
Emp Here 140
SIC 8211 Elementary and secondary schools
Doreen Johnson

D-U-N-S 24-704-1437   (SL)
PLASTER FORM INC
1180 Lakeshore Rd E, Mississauga, ON, L5E 1E9
(905) 891-9500
Emp Here 125   Sales 22,402,375
SIC 3275 Gypsum products
Louis Borges

D-U-N-S 20-647-1187   (SL)
SHERIDAN FORD LINCOLN SALES LTD
1345 Lakeshore Rd E, Mississauga, ON, L5E 1G5

Emp Here 55   Sales 34,610,400
SIC 5511 New and used car dealers
William Posivy
Anne Posivy
Fred Vanderjagt
Brian Posivy

D-U-N-S 20-822-4295   (SL)
TORONTO GOLF CLUB LINKS, THE
1305 Dixie Rd, Mississauga, ON, L5E 2P5
(905) 278-5255
Emp Here 97   Sales 7,618,865
SIC 7997 Membership sports and recreation clubs
Kim Na

D-U-N-S 24-991-0498   (HQ)
WILCOX DOOR SERVICE INC
1045 Rangeview Rd, Mississauga, ON, L5E 1H2
(905) 274-5850
Emp Here 40   Sales 11,781,660
SIC 1751 Carpentry work
William D Stewart
Judy Stewart

Mississauga, ON L5G

D-U-N-S 24-523-4732   (HQ)
AMP SOLAR GROUP INC
55 Port St E Unit A, Mississauga, ON, L5G 4P3
(905) 271-7800
Sales 18,798,420
SIC 4911 Electric services
David Rogers
Paul Ezekiel
Taras Bezchlibnyk
Steve Schaefer
Roberto Ricci

D-U-N-S 20-820-3166   (HQ)
CENTRE CITY CAPITAL LIMITED
PORT CREDIT HARBOUR MARINA
1 Port St E Suite 301, Mississauga, ON, L5G 4N1
(905) 274-5212
Emp Here 60   Sales 18,980,640
SIC 6553 Cemetery subdividers and developers
William James
Astrid James
Wayne Petryk

D-U-N-S 24-392-6230   (BR)
CENTRE CITY CAPITAL LIMITED
WATERSIDE INN, THE
(Suby of CENTRE CITY CAPITAL LIMITED)
15 Stavebank Rd S Suite 804, Mississauga, ON, L5G 2T2
(905) 891-7770
Emp Here 100
SIC 7011 Hotels and motels
Diego Masciaga

D-U-N-S 25-122-3962   (SL)
FRAM BUILDING GROUP LTD
141 Lakeshore Rd E, Mississauga, ON, L5G
1E8

Emp Here 60   *Sales* 15,693,180
SIC 6719 Holding companies, nec
Frank Giannone
Grant Lorimer
Madeline Barton

D-U-N-S 24-353-5460   (HQ)
NORMERICA CAPITAL CORPORATION
1599 Hurontario St Suite 300, Mississauga,
ON, L5G 4S1
(416) 626-0556
Emp Here 1   *Sales* 121,428,528
SIC 6712 Bank holding companies
Colin Gleason
Sue Sri
John Kimmel

D-U-N-S 24-886-6675   (HQ)
NORMERICA INC
NORTHDOWN INDUSTRIES
(*Suby of* NORMERICA CAPITAL CORPORA-
TION)
1599 Hurontario St Suite 300, Mississauga,
ON, L5G 4S1
(416) 626-0556
Emp Here 50   *Sales* 89,491,500
SIC 3295 Minerals, ground or treated
John Kimmel
Colin Gleason
Sue Sri

D-U-N-S 24-963-0625   (BR)
PEEL DISTRICT SCHOOL BOARD
CAWTHRA PARK SECONDARY SCHOOL
(*Suby of* PEEL DISTRICT SCHOOL BOARD)
1305 Cawthra Rd, Mississauga, ON, L5G 4L1
(905) 274-1271
Emp Here 95
SIC 8211 Elementary and secondary schools
Wendy Lautamus

D-U-N-S 24-188-5735   (BR)
**PEEL HALTON ACQUIRED BRAIN IN-
JURIES SERVICES**
(*Suby of* PEEL HALTON ACQUIRED BRAIN
INJURIES SERVICES)
1048 Cawthra Rd, Mississauga, ON, L5G 4K2
(905) 891-8384
Emp Here 200
SIC 8093 Specialty outpatient clinics, nec
Barbara Gilchrist

D-U-N-S 25-018-5071   (BR)
ROYAL LEPAGE LIMITED
ROYAL LEPAGE REAL ESTATE SERVICES
(*Suby of* BROOKFIELD ASSET MANAGE-
MENT INC)
1654 Lakeshore Rd E, Mississauga, ON, L5G
1E2
(905) 278-5273
Emp Here 100
SIC 6531 Real estate agents and managers
Dan Levy

D-U-N-S 20-368-9638   (SL)
RSM US LLP
81 Lakeshore Road E, Mississauga, ON, L5G
4S7

Emp Here 350   *Sales* 65,786,701
SIC 8721 Accounting, auditing, and bookkeeping

D-U-N-S 25-807-3576   (SL)
SNUG HARBOUR SEAFOOD BAR & GRILL
14 Stavebank Rd S, Mississauga, ON, L5G
2T1
(905) 274-5000
Emp Here 130   *Sales* 6,063,070
SIC 5812 Eating places
Andy Clifton
Paul Clifton

Roy Clifton

D-U-N-S 24-094-0817   (SL)
STRONG, J.E. LIMITED
SERVICEMASTER CONTRACT SERVICES
19 Ann St, Mississauga, ON, L5G 3E9
(905) 274-2327
Emp Here 300   *Sales* 9,590,400
SIC 7349 Building maintenance services, nec
Jeffrey Strong
Julie Strong

Mississauga, ON L5H

D-U-N-S 20-155-1652   (SL)
EARTH BORING CO. LIMITED
1576 Ifield Rd, Mississauga, ON, L5H 3W1
(905) 277-9632
Emp Here 60   *Sales* 15,162,399
SIC 1622 Bridge, tunnel, and elevated high-
way construction
Carmen Yarley
Gene Woodbridge

D-U-N-S 25-803-5039   (BR)
LOBLAWS SUPERMARKETS LIMITED
LOBLAWS
(*Suby of* LOBLAW COMPANIES LIMITED)
250 Lakeshore Rd W, Mississauga, ON, L5H
1G6
(905) 271-9925
Emp Here 150
SIC 5411 Grocery stores
Rae-Lynn Steadwell

D-U-N-S 20-772-5334   (SL)
**MISSISSAUGUA GOLF AND COUNTRY
CLUB, THE**
*MISSISSAUGUA GOLF AND COUNTRY
CLUB*
1725 Mississauga Rd, Mississauga, ON, L5H
2K4
(905) 278-4857
Emp Here 120   *Sales* 9,425,400
SIC 7997 Membership sports and recreation
clubs
Jeff Germond
Debra O'neill
Jeff Germond

D-U-N-S 24-421-0142   (SL)
PEEL CHRYSLER PLYMOUTH (1991) INC
PEEL FIAT
212 Lakeshore Rd W, Mississauga, ON, L5H
1G6
(905) 278-6181
Emp Here 25   *Sales* 12,451,950
SIC 5511 New and used car dealers
Ralph Chiodo

D-U-N-S 24-963-0948   (BR)
PEEL DISTRICT SCHOOL BOARD
LORNE PARK SECONDARY SCHOOL
(*Suby of* PEEL DISTRICT SCHOOL BOARD)
1324 Lorne Park Rd, Mississauga, ON, L5H
3B1
(905) 278-6177
Emp Here 100
SIC 8211 Elementary and secondary schools
Peter Hill

D-U-N-S 25-174-0916   (SL)
SALAMEH DRUGS LTD
SHOPPERS DRUG MART
321 Lakeshore Rd W, Mississauga, ON, L5H
1G9
(905) 271-4581
Emp Here 40   *Sales* 10,118,160
SIC 5912 Drug stores and proprietary stores
Gus Salameh

Mississauga, ON L5J

D-U-N-S 20-012-5321   (HQ)
ASHLAND CANADA CORP
(*Suby of* ASHLAND GLOBAL HOLDINGS
INC.)
2620 Royal Windsor Dr, Mississauga, ON, L5J
4E7
(800) 274-5263
Sales 14,606,900
SIC 5169 Chemicals and allied products, nec
David A Rines

D-U-N-S 24-679-7034   (SL)
BLACKIE CONSTRUCTION INC
2133 Royal Windsor Dr Unit 22, Mississauga,
ON, L5J 1K5

Emp Here 37   *Sales* 17,417,047
SIC 1542 Nonresidential construction, nec
William Blackie

D-U-N-S 24-523-3916   (HQ)
BOART LONGYEAR CANADA
(*Suby of* BOART LONGYEAR LIMITED)
2442 South Sheridan Way, Mississauga, ON,
L5J 2M7
(905) 822-7922
Emp Here 500   *Sales* 196,023,048
SIC 1799 Special trade contractors, nec
Jeffrey Olsen
Robert Closner
Marcus Randolph
Kyle Cruz
Miguel Desdin
Denis Despres
Kari Plaster
Brendan Ryan

D-U-N-S 25-195-8070   (HQ)
**BULK PLUS LOGISTICS LIMITED PART-
NERSHIP**
452 Southdown Rd, Mississauga, ON, L5J
2Y4
(905) 403-7854
Emp Here 25   *Sales* 66,689,200
SIC 4731 Freight transportation arrangement
Terry Molkoski

D-U-N-S 24-463-1354   (SL)
C & B DISPLAY PACKAGING INC
2560 South Sheridan Way, Mississauga, ON,
L5J 2M4
(905) 823-7770
Emp Here 50   *Sales* 10,206,500
SIC 2653 Corrugated and solid fiber boxes
Larry Cooper
Geordie Brown
Pamela Cooper-Brown

D-U-N-S 24-389-4644   (SL)
COHERENT CANADA INC
1222 April Dr, Mississauga, ON, L5J 3J7
(905) 823-5808
Emp Here 100   *Sales* 19,044,200
SIC 3699 Electrical equipment and supplies,
nec
Helene Simonet
Bret Dimarco
Mitchell Mcpeek

D-U-N-S 20-041-2823   (BR)
CRH CANADA GROUP INC
ST-LAWRENCE CEMENT
(*Suby of* CRH PUBLIC LIMITED COMPANY)
2391 Lakeshore Rd W, Mississauga, ON, L5J
1K1
(905) 822-1653
Emp Here 300
SIC 3241 Cement, hydraulic
Philip Trunk

D-U-N-S 20-041-2237   (HQ)
DAHL BROTHERS (CANADA) LIMITED
2600 South Sheridan Way, Mississauga, ON,
L5J 2M4
(905) 822-2330
Sales 47,516,170
SIC 6712 Bank holding companies

Janaike Godfree
Trygve Husebye
Tara Greenwood
Aase Husebye

D-U-N-S 20-377-5549   (SL)
DAHL VALVE LIMITED
(*Suby of* DAHL BROTHERS (CANADA) LIM-
ITED)
2600 South Sheridan Way, Mississauga, ON,
L5J 2M4
(905) 822-2330
Emp Here 130   *Sales* 24,971,050
SIC 3494 Valves and pipe fittings, nec
Jannike Godfrey
Thomas D. Husebye
Tara Greenwood

D-U-N-S 25-978-0880   (SL)
DEMYSH GROUP INC
DEMYSH METAL
2568 Royal Windsor Dr, Mississauga, ON, L5J
1K7

Emp Here 100   *Sales* 19,044,200
SIC 3612 Transformers, except electric

D-U-N-S 25-097-3765   (HQ)
ENVIRO-COATINGS CANADA LTD
2359 Royal Windsor Dr Unit 10, Mississauga,
ON, L5J 4S9

Sales 28,402,100
SIC 2851 Paints and allied products
Kaie Pugi

D-U-N-S 20-212-0358   (HQ)
H.L. BLACHFORD, LTD
2323 Royal Windsor Dr, Mississauga, ON, L5J
1K5
(905) 823-3200
Sales 17,566,640
SIC 2992 Lubricating oils and greases
John Blachford
David Mccoy

D-U-N-S 20-177-5277   (HQ)
**ICS UNIVERSAL DRUM RECONDITIONING
LIMITED PARTNERSHIP**
2460 Royal Windsor Dr, Mississauga, ON, L5J
1K7
(905) 822-3280
Emp Here 70   *Sales* 48,773,000
SIC 5085 Industrial supplies
Angelo Petrucci

D-U-N-S 25-145-1613   (BR)
IPEX INC
IPEX MANAGEMENT
(*Suby of* ALIAXIS)
2441 Royal Windsor Dr, Mississauga, ON, L5J
4C7
(905) 403-8133
Emp Here 100
SIC 3494 Valves and pipe fittings, nec
Marisa Amendola

D-U-N-S 20-735-4770   (HQ)
LATOPLAST LTD
1661 Finfar Crt, Mississauga, ON, L5J 4K1
(905) 823-6150
Emp Here 25   *Sales* 20,821,680
SIC 5099 Durable goods, nec
Bruce Batler
Emanuel Batler
Anthony Batler

D-U-N-S 20-041-2518   (SL)
LIQUID CARGO LINES LIMITED
452 Southdown Rd, Mississauga, ON, L5J
2Y4

Emp Here 78   *Sales* 11,558,976
SIC 4212 Local trucking, without storage
Roy Scott
Robin Beamish

D-U-N-S 24-984-8862   (BR)
LONGYEAR CANADA, ULC

(*Suby of* BOART LONGYEAR LIMITED)
2442 South Sheridan Way, Mississauga, ON,
L5J 2M7
(905) 822-7922
Emp Here 100
SIC 3532 Mining machinery
Bret Walters

D-U-N-S 24-911-4281   (SL)
MELBURN TRUCK LINES CORP
(*Suby of* MUSKET TRANSPORT LTD, THE)
2215 Royal Windsor Dr, Mississauga, ON, L5J
1K5
(905) 823-7800
Emp Here 350   *Sales* 64,533,350
SIC 4213 Trucking, except local
Andy Balij

D-U-N-S 25-936-9049   (BR)
METRO ONTARIO INC
METRO
(*Suby of* METRO INC)
910 Southdown Rd Unit 46, Mississauga, ON,
L5J 2Y4
(905) 823-4800
Emp Here 150
SIC 5411 Grocery stores
Dominic Canonico

D-U-N-S 24-552-7390   (SL)
MISSISSAUGA AUTOMOTIVE INC
MEADOWVALE HONDA
1800 Lakeshore Rd W, Mississauga, ON, L5J
1J7
(905) 567-8881
Emp Here 25   *Sales* 12,451,950
SIC 5511 New and used car dealers
Steven Duong

D-U-N-S 20-131-9600   (SL)
MUSKET EQUIPMENT LEASING LTD
MUSKET MELBURN
2215 Royal Windsor Dr, Mississauga, ON, L5J
1K5
(905) 823-7800
Emp Here 120   *Sales* 24,684,720
SIC 4213 Trucking, except local
Andy Balij
Wojtek Swiercz

D-U-N-S 25-202-6174   (HQ)
MUSKET TRANSPORT LTD, THE
2215 Royal Windsor Dr, Mississauga, ON, L5J
1K5
(905) 823-7800
Emp Here 100   *Sales* 73,752,400
SIC 4213 Trucking, except local
Andy Balij
Wojciech Swiercz

D-U-N-S 20-181-2562   (BR)
NESTLE CANADA INC
NESTLE PURINA PET CARE DIV OF
(*Suby of* NESTLE S.A.)
2500 Royal Windsor Dr, Mississauga, ON, L5J
1K8
(905) 822-1611
Emp Here 350
SIC 2047 Dog and cat food
Kuwahara Karen

D-U-N-S 24-414-7943   (SL)
OBI PARTS INC
350 Hazelhurst Rd, Mississauga, ON, L5J 4T8
(905) 403-7800
Emp Here 35   *Sales* 12,747,525
SIC 5012 Automobiles and other motor vehicles
Jarvis Wendy

D-U-N-S 20-846-4982   (SL)
ONTARIO RACQUET SPORT ENTERPRISES LTD
884 Southdown Rd, Mississauga, ON, L5J
2Y4
(905) 822-5240
Emp Here 60   *Sales* 13,252,260
SIC 6512 Nonresidential building operators

John Bailey
Helmut Kiel
Arthur Boese
John Welton
Stan Zuk
Ken Hune
Mike Raham
Leslie Nemez

D-U-N-S 24-963-0559   (BR)
PEEL DISTRICT SCHOOL BOARD
CLARKSON SECONDARY SCHOOL
(*Suby of* PEEL DISTRICT SCHOOL BOARD)
2524 Bromsgrove Rd, Mississauga, ON, L5J
1L8
(905) 822-6700
Emp Here 90
SIC 8211 Elementary and secondary schools
Jim Kardash

D-U-N-S 24-391-7148   (HQ)
PETRO-CANADA LUBRICANTS INC
(*Suby of* HOLLYFRONTIER CORPORATION)
2310 Lakeshore Rd W, Mississauga, ON, L5J
1K2
(866) 335-3369
Emp Here 83   *Sales* 689,265,159
SIC 5172 Petroleum products, nec
Steven Williams
Denise Mcwatters
Mark Plake
Neil Hazan
Richard Voliva

D-U-N-S 20-384-6852   (BR)
PNR RAILWORKS INC
(*Suby of* WIND POINT PARTNERS, L.P.)
2380 Royal Windsor Dr Unit 11, Mississauga,
ON, L5J 1K7
(519) 515-1219
Emp Here 300
SIC 1629 Heavy construction, nec
Justin View

D-U-N-S 20-531-3356   (BR)
PPG CANADA INC
CLARKSON DIV
(*Suby of* PPG INDUSTRIES, INC.)
2301 Royal Windsor Dr, Mississauga, ON, L5J
1K5

Emp Here 350
SIC 2851 Paints and allied products
Harry Nasab

D-U-N-S 24-024-6165   (SL)
RE/MAX REALTY ENTERPRISES INC
1697 Lakeshore Rd W, Mississauga, ON, L5J
1J4
(905) 823-3400
Emp Here 105   *Sales* 43,983,345
SIC 6531 Real estate agents and managers
David Ferrari Ferrari
Gino Ferrari
William Mcquade

D-U-N-S 24-215-9812   (BR)
REGIONAL MUNICIPALITY OF PEEL, THE
SHERIDAN VILLA HOME FOR AGED
(*Suby of* REGIONAL MUNICIPALITY OF
PEEL, THE)
2460 Truscott Dr, Mississauga, ON, L5J 3Z8
(905) 791-8668
Emp Here 200
SIC 8051 Skilled nursing care facilities
Rejane Dunn

D-U-N-S 25-104-4012   (SL)
RUMBLE FOUNDATIONS (ONTARIO) LTD
580 Hazelhurst Rd, Mississauga, ON, L5J 2Z7
(905) 822-3000
Emp Here 75   *Sales* 15,669,540
SIC 1741 Masonry and other stonework
David Rumble

D-U-N-S 24-489-2782   (SL)
SHERIDAN VENTURES LTD
SHERIDAN SPECIALTIES

2222 South Sheridan Way Unit 210, Mississauga, ON, L5J 2M4
(905) 823-7780
Emp Here 30   *Sales* 25,067,310
SIC 5149 Groceries and related products, nec
William Ray Hart
Doris Hart
John Hart
Cheryl Boyle

D-U-N-S 24-873-4444   (BR)
STACKPOLE INTERNATIONAL ENGINEERED PRODUCTS, LTD
STACKPOLE INTERNATIONAL
(*Suby of* JOHNSON ELECTRIC HOLDINGS
LIMITED)
2400 Royal Windsor Dr, Mississauga, ON, L5J
1K7
(905) 403-0550
Emp Here 200
SIC 5013 Motor vehicle supplies and new
parts
Robert Mooy

D-U-N-S 25-905-6869   (SL)
STAR SECURITY INCORPORATED
2351 Royal Windsor Dr Suite 205, Mississauga, ON, L5J 4S7
(905) 855-7827
Emp Here 150   *Sales* 3,937,500
SIC 7381 Detective and armored car services

D-U-N-S 20-690-3432   (SL)
STARWOOD MANUFACTURING INC
2370 South Sheridan Way, Mississauga, ON,
L5J 2M4

Emp Here 55   *Sales* 10,580,350
SIC 2426 Hardwood dimension and flooring
mills
Peter Prytula
Aivor Khourkine
Alex Binko
Todor Batkov

D-U-N-S 25-120-1497   (SL)
SUTTON GROUP QUANTUM REALTY INC
1673 Lakeshore Rd W, Mississauga, ON, L5J
1J4
(905) 822-5000
Emp Here 65   *Sales* 17,664,140
SIC 6531 Real estate agents and managers
Tina Gardin

D-U-N-S 20-923-4830   (SL)
TAKARA COMPANY, CANADA, LTD
BELMONT
(*Suby of* TAKARA BELMONT CORPORATION)
2076 South Sheridan Way, Mississauga, ON,
L5J 2M4
(905) 822-2755
Emp Here 30   *Sales* 14,250,780
SIC 5087 Service establishment equipment
Brian Kennedy
Masahiro Ando

D-U-N-S 24-394-2948   (SL)
TREMBLAY, C.J. INVESTMENTS INC
CANADIAN TIRE
900 Southdown Rd, Mississauga, ON, L5J
2Y4
(905) 822-6234
Emp Here 45   *Sales* 22,413,510
SIC 5531 Auto and home supply stores
Chris Tremblay

Mississauga, ON L5K

D-U-N-S 20-551-5039   (HQ)
ALPHORA RESEARCH INC
2395 Speakman Dr Suite 2001, Mississauga,
ON, L5K 1B3
(905) 403-0477
Emp Here 50   *Sales* 34,463,100

SIC 8731 Commercial physical research
Isobel Ralston

D-U-N-S 25-100-8686   (SL)
**ANGELS PHARMACEUTICAL SERVICES
LTD**
WOODCHESTER I.D.A. PHARMACY
2458 Dundas St W Unit 13, Mississauga, ON,
L5K 1R8
(905) 823-7895
Emp Here 45   *Sales* 11,382,930
SIC 5912 Drug stores and proprietary stores
Karam Kamel Anton

D-U-N-S 24-182-8169   (HQ)
BAYSHORE HEALTHCARE LTD.
2101 Hadwen Rd, Mississauga, ON, L5K 2L3
(905) 822-8075
Emp Here 50   *Sales* 383,505,000
SIC 8082 Home health care services
Stuart Cottrelle
Ramy Mikhail
Scott Murray

D-U-N-S 20-117-9087   (SL)
CARGOJET AIRWAYS LTD
(*Suby of* CARGOJET HOLDINGS LIMITED
PARTNERSHIP)
2281 North Sheridan Way, Mississauga, ON,
L5K 2S3
(905) 501-7373
Emp Here 900   *Sales* 299,993,343
SIC 4512 Air transportation, scheduled
Ajay K Virmani
Jamie Porteous
Pauline Dhillon
Gord Johnston
George Sugar
Paul Rinaldo
Anju Virmani
John Kim

D-U-N-S 24-421-1806   (HQ)
CARGOJET HOLDINGS LIMITED PARTNERSHIP
2281 North Sheridan Way, Mississauga, ON,
L5K 2S3
(905) 501-7373
Emp Here 40   *Sales* 346,868,041
SIC 6712 Bank holding companies
Ajay Virmani

D-U-N-S 24-421-1798   (HQ)
CARGOJET HOLDINGS LTD
CARGOJET
(*Suby of* CARGOJET HOLDINGS LIMITED
PARTNERSHIP)
2281 North Sheridan Way, Mississauga, ON,
L5K 2S3
(905) 501-7373
Emp Here 40   *Sales* 253,362,122
SIC 4581 Airports, flying fields, and services
Ajay Virmani

D-U-N-S 24-130-8399   (HQ)
CARGOJET INC
2281 North Sheridan Way, Mississauga, ON,
L5K 2S3
(905) 501-7373
Emp Here 35   *Sales* 344,860,600
SIC 4512 Air transportation, scheduled
Ajay Virmani
Jamie B Porteous
Pauline Dhillon
Gord Johnston
George Sugar
Paul Rinaldo
John Kim
Anju Virmani
James Crane
John Webster

D-U-N-S 24-776-7119   (BR)
CHARTWELL MASTER CARE LP
*CHARTWELL WENLEIGH LONG TERM
CARE RESIDENCE*
(*Suby of* CHARTWELL MASTER CARE LP)
2065 Leanne Blvd, Mississauga, ON, L5K 2L6

(905) 822-4663
Emp Here 200
SIC 8052 Intermediate care facilities
Sheri Chateavert

D-U-N-S 20-059-9475   (HQ)
CONTACT RESOURCE SERVICES INC
CRS
2225 Erin Mills Pkwy, Mississauga, ON, L5K 2P0
(905) 855-8106
Emp Here 1   *Sales* 29,053,795
SIC 7322 Adjustment and collection services
Michael A Cornale

D-U-N-S 24-368-1538   (HQ)
ELEMENT MATERIALS TECHNOLOGY CANADA INC
(*Suby of* ELEMENTS, INC.)
2395 Speakman Dr Suite 583, Mississauga, ON, L5K 1B3
(905) 822-4111
Emp Here 600   *Sales* 607,462,300
SIC 8734 Testing laboratories
David Brash

D-U-N-S 24-873-9294   (SL)
EMD INC
EMD SERONO, DIV OF
(*Suby of* MERCK KG AUF AKTIEN)
2695 North Sheridan Way Suite 200, Mississauga, ON, L5K 2N6
(905) 919-0200
Emp Here 150   *Sales* 61,923,150
SIC 5122 Drugs, proprietaries, and sundries
Deborah Brown

D-U-N-S 24-761-1341   (SL)
EPIC DEALS INC
CANADIAN HOME SECURITY
2400 Dundas St W Suite 211, Mississauga, ON, L5K 2R8
(647) 478-9002
Emp Here 49   *Sales* 10,374,476
SIC 7311 Advertising agencies
Rameez Ul-Haq

D-U-N-S 24-767-0859   (SL)
ERINOAK KIDS CENTRE FOR TREATMENT
2655 North Sheridan Way Suite N, Mississauga, ON, L5K 2P8
(905) 855-2690
Emp Here 41   *Sales* 16,293,974
SIC 8699 Membership organizations, nec
Pamela Aasen

D-U-N-S 25-393-1224   (HQ)
HATCH CORPORATION
2800 Speakman Dr, Mississauga, ON, L5K 2R7
(905) 855-2010
Emp Here 290   *Sales* 145,876,940
SIC 8711 Engineering services
David White
Peter Wickens
Gordon Smith
Michael Blackburn
Ronald Nolan
Rob Davies

D-U-N-S 20-552-0893   (HQ)
HATCH LTD
HATCH ENERGY
(*Suby of* HATCHCOS HOLDINGS LTD)
2800 Speakman Dr, Mississauga, ON, L5K 2R7
(905) 855-7600
Emp Here 500   *Sales* 2,168,441,000
SIC 8711 Engineering services
John Bianchini
Doug Stirling
Bert O. Wasmund

D-U-N-S 24-783-8865   (HQ)
HATCHCOS HOLDINGS LTD
2800 Speakman Dr, Mississauga, ON, L5K 2R7
(905) 855-7600
Emp Here 2,100   *Sales* 887,089,500

SIC 8711 Engineering services
John P. Tummers
John D. Pearson
John Bianchini
Martin Doble
Anthony Hylton
Robert Metka
Greg Fauquier
Kurt A. Strobele
Robert Francki
Nils Voermann

D-U-N-S 20-403-1801   (HQ)
IMAX CORPORATION
IMAX EXPERIENCE, THE
2525 Speakman Dr, Mississauga, ON, L5K 1B1
(905) 403-6500
Sales 374,401,000
SIC 5049 Professional equipment, nec
Richard Gelfond
Carrie Lindzon-Jacobs
Don Savant
Greg Foster
Craig Dehmel
Bruce Markoe
Robert D. Lister
Patrick Mcclymont
Brian Bonnick
Megan Colligan

D-U-N-S 25-938-8866   (SL)
INDEPENDENT REHABILITATION SERVICES INC
IRSI
2155 Leanne Blvd Suite 240, Mississauga, ON, L5K 2K8
(905) 823-8895
Emp Here 20   *Sales* 11,598,480
SIC 6411 Insurance agents, brokers, and service
Susan Phillips

D-U-N-S 20-529-4382   (HQ)
MCCORMICK RANKIN CORPORATION
2655 North Sheridan Way Suite 300, Mississauga, ON, L5K 2P8
(905) 823-8500
Emp Here 175   *Sales* 62,558,650
SIC 8711 Engineering services
Ian Williams
Moreno Radolli

D-U-N-S 25-120-6215   (BR)
METRO ONTARIO INC
METRO
(*Suby of* METRO INC)
2225 Erin Mills Pky, Mississauga, ON, L5K 1T9
(905) 829-3737
Emp Here 250
SIC 5411 Grocery stores
Blair Wall

D-U-N-S 25-323-8042   (SL)
MITEC TECHNOLOGIES INC
2333 North Sheridan Way Suite 200, Mississauga, ON, L5K 1A7
(905) 822-8170
Emp Here 100   *Sales* 44,717,400
SIC 5065 Electronic parts and equipment, nec
Jeffrey A Mandel
Robert Boisjoli
Hubert R Marleau
David B Parkes
Noah Billick
Bruno Dumais

D-U-N-S 24-847-9727   (HQ)
NOR-SHAM HOLDINGS INC
2125 North Sheridan Way, Mississauga, ON, L5K 1A3
(905) 305-5503
Emp Here 1   *Sales* 82,239,525
SIC 6712 Bank holding companies
Noordin Charania
Farhana Charania

Ameer Ishani
Shamas Charania
Sebunisa Sunderji
Dhas Thambapillai

D-U-N-S 24-847-9644   (SL)
NOR-SHAM HOTELS INC
HOLIDAY INN
(*Suby of* NOR-SHAM HOLDINGS INC)
2125 North Sheridan Way, Mississauga, ON, L5K 1A3
(905) 855-2000
Emp Here 75   *Sales* 6,951,750
SIC 7011 Hotels and motels
Farhana Charania
Ameer Ishani
Shamas Charania
Drew Archer

D-U-N-S 25-293-7891   (BR)
PEEL DISTRICT SCHOOL BOARD
ERINDALE SECONDARY SCHOOL
(*Suby of* PEEL DISTRICT SCHOOL BOARD)
2021 Dundas St W, Mississauga, ON, L5K 1R2
(905) 828-7206
Emp Here 100
SIC 8211 Elementary and secondary schools
Sandra Trupp

D-U-N-S 24-831-0625   (BR)
ROYAL & SUN ALLIANCE INSURANCE COMPANY OF CANADA
COMMERCIAL LINES & CLAIMS
(*Suby of* RSA INSURANCE GROUP PLC)
2225 Erin Mills Pky Suite 1000, Mississauga, ON, L5K 2S9
(905) 403-2333
Emp Here 600
SIC 6331 Fire, marine, and casualty insurance
Lisa Mclellan

D-U-N-S 25-214-2153   (SL)
ROYAL LEPAGE REALTY PLUS LTD
2575 Dundas St W Suite 3, Mississauga, ON, L5K 2M6
(905) 828-6550
Emp Here 45   *Sales* 14,720,715
SIC 6531 Real estate agents and managers
Carlo Racioppo

D-U-N-S 24-288-0078   (HQ)
SHAW SATELLITE SERVICES INC
CANCOM BROADCAST SOLUTIONS
(*Suby of* SHAW COMMUNICATIONS INC)
2055 Flavelle Blvd, Mississauga, ON, L5K 1Z8
(905) 403-2020
Emp Here 100   *Sales* 367,998,400
SIC 4899 Communication services, nec
Brad Shaw
Steve Wilson
Jay Mehr

D-U-N-S 20-379-7456   (SL)
SHERIDAN RETAIL INC
2225 Erin Mills Pky, Mississauga, ON, L5K 1T9
(905) 822-0344
Emp Here 50   *Sales* 14,424,950
SIC 6512 Nonresidential building operators
Michael Dipasquale
John Zanni

D-U-N-S 20-289-5095   (BR)
SIFTON PROPERTIES LIMITED
ERIN MILLS LODGE
2132 Dundas St W, Mississauga, ON, L5K 2K7
(905) 823-7273
Emp Here 160
SIC 8059 Nursing and personal care, nec
Maurice Rouleau

D-U-N-S 20-763-4684   (HQ)
SNC-LAVALIN NUCLEAR INC
CANATOM NPM
(*Suby of* GROUPE SNC-LAVALIN INC)
2251 Speakman Dr, Mississauga, ON, L5K

1B2
(905) 829-8808
Emp Here 80   *Sales* 67,658,100
SIC 8999 Services, nec
Preston Swafford
Arden R. Furlotte
Janet Oh
Alexander S. Taylor
Joel Tache

D-U-N-S 24-632-9783   (BR)
SUNCOR ENERGY INC
PETRO-CANADA BUSINESS CENTER
(*Suby of* SUNCOR ENERGY INC)
2489 North Sheridan Way, Mississauga, ON, L5K 1A8
(905) 804-4500
Emp Here 700
SIC 1389 Oil and gas field services, nec
Gordon Mock

D-U-N-S 24-075-0695   (HQ)
SUNCOR ENERGY PRODUCTS INC
(*Suby of* SUNCOR ENERGY INC)
2489 North Sheridan Way, Mississauga, ON, L5K 1A8
(905) 804-4500
Emp Here 200   *Sales* 1,172,762,500
SIC 2911 Petroleum refining
Steven Williams
Mark Little
Alister Cowan
Arlene Strom

D-U-N-S 20-017-3032   (HQ)
SURE GOOD FOODS LTD
2333 North Sheridan Way Suite 100, Mississauga, ON, L5K 1A7
(905) 286-1619
Sales 329,170,590
SIC 5147 Meats and meat products
Troy Warren
David Forgan
Ray Mccague

D-U-N-S 25-536-0901   (SL)
WESTERN ASSURANCE COMPANY
(*Suby of* RSA INSURANCE GROUP PLC)
2225 Erin Mills Pky Suite 1000, Mississauga, ON, L5K 2S9
(905) 403-2333
Emp Here 125   *Sales* 267,121,000
SIC 6331 Fire, marine, and casualty insurance
Shelley Toyota

D-U-N-S 20-943-0453   (BR)
XEROX CANADA INC
XEROX RESEARCH CENTRE OF CDA
(*Suby of* XEROX CORPORATION)
2660 Speakman Dr, Mississauga, ON, L5K 2L1
(905) 823-7091
Emp Here 120
SIC 8731 Commercial physical research
Hadi Mahabadi

Mississauga, ON L5L

D-U-N-S 25-482-7983   (SL)
1004839 ONTARIO LIMITED
MANDARIN RESTAURANT
3105 Dundas St W Suite 101, Mississauga, ON, L5L 3R8
(905) 569-7000
Emp Here 75   *Sales* 3,413,925
SIC 5812 Eating places
Anthony (Tony) Ding

D-U-N-S 24-561-1272   (SL)
1083153 ONTARIO LTD
ERIN MILLS MAZDA (1994)
2400 Motorway Blvd, Mississauga, ON, L5L 1X3
(905) 828-0070
Emp Here 42   *Sales* 20,919,276

SIC 5511 New and used car dealers
Kap Dilwari

D-U-N-S 25-103-0714   (SL)
1234121 ONTARIO LIMITED
CAMP KODIAK
4069 Pheasant Run, Mississauga, ON, L5L
2C2
(905) 569-7595
Emp Here 100   *Sales* 9,489,900
SIC 7032 Sporting and recreational camps
David Stoch

D-U-N-S 24-736-5963   (SL)
2177761 ONTARIO INC
ERIN MILLS MITSUBISHI
2477 Motorway Blvd Suite 3, Mississauga,
ON, L5L 3R2
(905) 828-8488
Emp Here 25   *Sales* 12,451,950
SIC 5511 New and used car dealers
Andrew Chung

D-U-N-S 25-533-0219   (HQ)
3499481 CANADA INC
PJ'S PET CENTRE, DIV OF
4161 Sladeview Cres Unit 12, Mississauga,
ON, L5L 5R3
(905) 593-3177
Emp Here 25   *Sales* 168,854,040
SIC 5999 Miscellaneous retail stores, nec
Margaret Kordas

D-U-N-S 20-192-5943   (SL)
553032 ONTARIO INC
4120 Ridgeway Dr Unit 28, Mississauga, ON,
L5L 5S9
(905) 607-8200
Emp Here 141   *Sales* 38,988,744
SIC 6712 Bank holding companies

D-U-N-S 20-219-7617   (SL)
734758 ONTARIO LIMITED
HUNTINGTON TRAVEL GROUP, THE
3100 Ridgeway Dr Unit 16, Mississauga, ON,
L5L 5M5
(905) 820-2266
Emp Here 38   *Sales* 14,643,680
SIC 4724 Travel agencies
Kiran Budhdev
Bravina Budhdev

D-U-N-S 24-526-1037   (SL)
982874 ONTARIO LIMITED
MISSISSAUGA HYUNDAI
3045 Glen Erin Dr, Mississauga, ON, L5L 1J3
(905) 828-5923
Emp Here 65   *Sales* 40,903,200
SIC 5511 New and used car dealers
Navdeep Bhatia

D-U-N-S 20-698-5348   (SL)
ACA TMETRIX INC
(Suby of CRAWFORD, ALLAN ASSOCIATES
LIMITED)
3585 Laird Rd Unit 15-16, Mississauga, ON,
L5L 5Y4
(905) 890-2010
Emp Here 98   *Sales* 56,864,206
SIC 5065 Electronic parts and equipment, nec
Jim Turner
Patrick Leung
Brian Flippance

D-U-N-S 25-321-5271   (HQ)
**ADVANCED PRESENTATION PRODUCTS
INC**
APG DISPLAYS
(Suby of 3193845 CANADA INC)
4180 Sladeview Cres Unit 4, Mississauga,
ON, L5L 0A1
(905) 502-1110
Sales 12,949,384
SIC 5999 Miscellaneous retail stores, nec
David Weatherhead
John Weatherhead
Mark Mcpherson
Jordan Domey

Mark Mulford

D-U-N-S 20-155-1330   (SL)
APPLEWOOD HOLDINGS INC
*APPLEWOOD CHEVROLET OLDSMOBILE
CADILLAC*
3000 Woodchester Dr, Mississauga, ON, L5L
2R4
(905) 828-2221
Emp Here 125   *Sales* 78,660,000
SIC 5511 New and used car dealers
Paul Atkinson
Danny Blough

D-U-N-S 24-704-3375   (HQ)
**APPLIED CONSUMER & CLINICAL EVALU-
ATIONS INC**
2575b Dunwin Dr, Mississauga, ON, L5L 3N9
(905) 828-0493
Sales 16,082,780
SIC 8731 Commercial physical research
Raymond L Berta

D-U-N-S 24-063-3920   (SL)
**ASSA ABLOY ENTRANCE SYSTEM
CANADA INC**
(Suby of ASSA ABLOY AB)
4020a Sladeview Cres Suite 4, Mississauga,
ON, L5L 6B1
(905) 608-9242
Emp Here 70   *Sales* 17,233,020
SIC 1796 Installing building equipment
Per Hanson
Dennis Lamarre
Michael P. Mccaslin

D-U-N-S 24-771-4603   (HQ)
BELER HOLDINGS INC
D F X DISTRIBUTION
4050a Sladeview Cres Suite 1a, Mississauga,
ON, L5L 5Y5
(905) 569-1277
Sales 13,365,360
SIC 5199 Nondurable goods, nec
Michael Beler
Marcella Burlon

D-U-N-S 20-702-5099   (SL)
BELL LIFESTYLE PRODUCTS INC
BELL DISTRIBUTORS RGD
3164 Pepper Mill Crt Unit 1-8, Mississauga,
ON, L5L 4X4
(905) 820-7000
Emp Here 27   *Sales* 29,844,315
SIC 5122 Drugs, proprietaries, and sundries
Nick Jerch
Brigette Jerch

D-U-N-S 24-370-1427   (SL)
BODKIN FINANCIAL CORPORATION
2150 Dunwin Dr Suite 1, Mississauga, ON,
L5L 5M8
(905) 820-4550
Emp Here 50   *Sales* 11,237,200
SIC 6159 Miscellaneous business credit insti-
tutions
Donald Bodkin
Charles E. Danielson
John D. Mitchell
William Patton
Paul H. Royds
Rajakumar Singh

D-U-N-S 24-965-3783   (HQ)
BURLODGE CANADA LTD
(Suby of THE BIG SKY TRUST)
3400 Ridgeway Dr Unit 14, Mississauga, ON,
L5L 0A2
(905) 790-1881
Emp Here 13   *Sales* 16,711,540
SIC 5141 Groceries, general line
Paul Gauntley

D-U-N-S 20-269-6886   (BR)
CELESTICA INTERNATIONAL LP
(Suby of ONEX CORPORATION)
3333 Unity Dr Suite A, Mississauga, ON, L5L
3S6

(416) 448-2559
Emp Here 600
SIC 3812 Search and navigation equipment

D-U-N-S 20-689-6297   (SL)
CERVOL SERVICE GROUP INC
2295 Dunwin Dr Unit 4, Mississauga, ON, L5L
3S4
(905) 569-0557
Emp Here 50   *Sales* 11,046,700
SIC 1711 Plumbing, heating, air-conditioning
Joe Pavao
Mario Pavao

D-U-N-S 24-505-6866   (HQ)
CHEMARKETING INDUSTRIES INC
2155 Dunwin Dr Unit 15, Mississauga, ON,
L5L 4M1
(905) 607-6800
Sales 10,955,175
SIC 5169 Chemicals and allied products, nec
James Robert Fell

D-U-N-S 24-847-2870   (HQ)
CINTAS CANADA LIMITED
SALLY FOURMY & ASSOCIATES
(Suby of CINTAS CORPORATION)
4170 Sladeview Cres Unit 2, Mississauga,
ON, L5L 0A1
(416) 763-4400
Emp Here 200   *Sales* 89,696,000
SIC 7218 Industrial launderers
Richard Scott
Anna Costa

D-U-N-S 20-810-0490   (BR)
COSTCO WHOLESALE CANADA LTD
COSTCO
(Suby of COSTCO WHOLESALE CORPO-
RATION)
3180 Laird Rd, Mississauga, ON, L5L 6A5
(905) 828-3340
Emp Here 150
SIC 5099 Durable goods, nec
Adrian Smith

D-U-N-S 20-361-8038   (SL)
DDJLR ONTARIO LTD
ERIN MILLS MITSUBISHI
2477 Motorway Blvd, Mississauga, ON, L5L
3R2
(905) 828-8488
Emp Here 27   *Sales* 12,037,155
SIC 5511 New and used car dealers
Daniel Joerges
Richard Holton

D-U-N-S 20-174-1530   (HQ)
DIVERSEY CANADA, INC
(Suby of BAIN CAPITAL, LP)
3755 Laird Rd Unit 10, Mississauga, ON, L5L
0B3
(905) 829-1200
Emp Here 150   *Sales* 222,322,500
SIC 2842 Polishes and sanitation goods
Lori P. Marin
John Alexander
Jeffrey M. Haufschild
Tracey Healey

D-U-N-S 24-079-4917   (SL)
ERIN DODGE CHRYSLER LTD
2365 Motorway Blvd, Mississauga, ON, L5L
2M4
(905) 828-2004
Emp Here 75   *Sales* 47,196,000
SIC 5511 New and used car dealers
Paul Kaye
Mark Keenan

D-U-N-S 24-693-5167   (SL)
ERIN MILLS IMPORT INC
ERIN MILLS ACURA
3025 Woodchester Dr, Mississauga, ON, L5L
3V3
(905) 828-5800
Emp Here 51   *Sales* 32,093,280
SIC 5511 New and used car dealers
Joseph (Joe) Zanchin

Catherine Zanchin

D-U-N-S 20-113-1195   (SL)
ERIN PARK AUTOMOTIVE PARTNERSHIP
ERIN PARK TOYOTA
2411 Motorway Blvd, Mississauga, ON, L5L
3R2
(905) 828-7711
Emp Here 138   *Sales* 86,840,640
SIC 5511 New and used car dealers
Joel Cohen
Gino Caletti
Herb Singer

D-U-N-S 20-922-8162   (SL)
ERINDALE COLLEGE STUDENT UNION
ECSU
3359 Mississauga Rd, Mississauga, ON, L5L
1C6
(905) 828-5249
Emp Here 55   *Sales* 15,036,725
SIC 8651 Political organizations
Sean O,Connell

D-U-N-S 24-124-1025   (SL)
ERINMOTORWAY INVESTMENTS LIMITED
MISSISSAUGA HONDA
2380 Motorway Blvd, Mississauga, ON, L5L
1X3
(905) 828-1650
Emp Here 105   *Sales* 66,074,400
SIC 5511 New and used car dealers
Koji Handa
Bryndon Davies
Rick Mcgraw
Cathy Elminshawi

D-U-N-S 24-060-0718   (HQ)
**ERINOAKKIDS CENTRE FOR TREATMENT
AND DEVELOPMENT**
ERINOAK
2277 South Millway, Mississauga, ON, L5L
2M5
(905) 855-2690
Sales 62,948,665
SIC 8093 Specialty outpatient clinics, nec
Bridget Fewtrell
Danny Sirmis
Kathy Swaile
Pauline Eaton
Chris Hartley
Christina Djokoto
Karen Fitzpatrick

D-U-N-S 20-554-9009   (SL)
ERINWOOD FORD SALES LIMITED
2395 Motorway Blvd, Mississauga, ON, L5L
1V4
(905) 828-1600
Emp Here 60   *Sales* 37,756,800
SIC 5511 New and used car dealers
Sean Hallett
David Bessuille

D-U-N-S 24-720-6048   (SL)
FARMBRO ALL-TRAC LTD
4200 Sladeview Cres, Mississauga, ON, L5L
5Z2
(905) 569-0592
Emp Here 60   *Sales* 16,998,000
SIC 7549 Automotive services, nec
John Farmer
Terry Sugar

D-U-N-S 25-213-0307   (SL)
GOURMET TRADING CO. LTD
3750a Laird Rd Suite 7, Mississauga, ON, L5L
0A6
(905) 826-6800
Emp Here 20   *Sales* 10,702,480
SIC 5149 Groceries and related products, nec
Timothy Pinnington
Christopher Dohle

D-U-N-S 20-696-8468   (HQ)
**GREAT PACIFIC ENTERPRISES LIMITED
PARTNERSHIP**
GENPAK, DIV OF

3185 Pepper Mill Crt, Mississauga, ON, L5L 4X3
(905) 569-3660
Emp Here 100　　*Sales* 119,406,000
SIC 3086 Plastics foam products
　Kristine Arthurs
　Vicki Etcheverry

D-U-N-S 24-366-7529　　(SL)
GREEN IMAGING SUPPLIES INC
GIS
3330 Ridgeway Dr Unit 17, Mississauga, ON, L5L 5Z9
(905) 607-2525
Emp Here 50　　*Sales* 25,182,900
SIC 5112 Stationery and office supplies
　Mehdi Oskui

D-U-N-S 25-754-0906　　(SL)
GTA PLUMBING LTD
3995 Sladeview Cres Unit 6, Mississauga, ON, L5L 5Y1
(905) 569-7558
Emp Here 47　　*Sales* 10,383,898
SIC 1711 Plumbing, heating, air-conditioning
　Neil Munro
　Lovat Munro

D-U-N-S 24-664-9206　　(SL)
HEISSIG IMPORT & EXPORT LTD
3100 Ridgeway Dr Unit 30, Mississauga, ON, L5L 5M5

Emp Here 35　　*Sales* 12,747,525
SIC 5013 Motor vehicle supplies and new parts
　Ulrike Heissig

D-U-N-S 20-167-2029　　(HQ)
HONEYWELL LIMITED
HONEYWELL AEROSPACE TORONTO
(*Suby of* HONEYWELL INTERNATIONAL INC.)
3333 Unity Dr, Mississauga, ON, L5L 3S6
(905) 608-6000
Emp Here 100　　*Sales* 823,110,000
SIC 3822 Environmental controls
　Jim Colby
　Thomas Larkins
　Deborah Van Damme

D-U-N-S 25-405-8878　　(HQ)
HOYA LENS CANADA INC
HOYA VISION CARE, CANADA
(*Suby of* HOYA CORPORATION)
3330 Ridgeway Dr Unit 21, Mississauga, ON, L5L 5Z9
(905) 828-3477
Emp Here 55　　*Sales* 42,034,356
SIC 5049 Professional equipment, nec
　David Pietrobon

D-U-N-S 24-252-1347　　(SL)
INGENUITY DEVELOPMENT INC
INGENUITY GROUP
3800a Laird Rd Unit 1, Mississauga, ON, L5L 0B2
(905) 569-2624
Emp Here 10　　*Sales* 11,432,055
SIC 1541 Industrial buildings and warehouses
　Mario Viti
　Matthew Bucci
　Peter Viti

D-U-N-S 24-275-6765　　(HQ)
INTERMEC TECHNOLOGIES CANADA ULC
HONEYWELL
3333 Unity Dr, Mississauga, ON, L5L 3S6
(905) 608-3167
Emp Here 19　　*Sales* 11,626,524
SIC 5045 Computers, peripherals, and software
　Paul Lefebvre
　Tony Oliverio

D-U-N-S 20-273-2970　　(SL)
IT XCHANGE (ONTARIO) CORP
IT XCHANGE

3500 Ridgeway Dr Unit 4, Mississauga, ON, L5L 0B4
(888) 829-5333
Emp Here 35　　*Sales* 15,651,090
SIC 5045 Computers, peripherals, and software
　Alan Rupp

D-U-N-S 24-875-6884　　(HQ)
KRAVET FABRICS CANADA COMPANY
(*Suby of* KRAVET INC.)
3600b Laird Rd Unit 5, Mississauga, ON, L5L 6A7
(905) 607-0706
Sales 15,030,630
SIC 5131 Piece goods and notions
　Cary Kravet
　Lisa Kravet
　Brian Donovan
　Scott Kravet

D-U-N-S 24-212-1374　　(SL)
LIKRO PRECISION LIMITED
3150 Pepper Mill Crt, Mississauga, ON, L5L 4X4
(905) 828-9191
Emp Here 55　　*Sales* 12,210,055
SIC 3545 Machine tool accessories
　Josip Pavicic
　Zorica Pavicic

D-U-N-S 20-514-2222　　(BR)
LONGO BROTHERS FRUIT MARKETS INC
LONGO'S FRUIT MARKET
(*Suby of* LONGO BROTHERS FRUIT MARKETS INC)
3163 Winston Churchill Blvd, Mississauga, ON, L5L 2W1
(905) 828-0008
Emp Here 150
SIC 5411 Grocery stores

D-U-N-S 25-256-0925　　(HQ)
MARATHON FASTENERS & HARDWARE INC
4170 Sladeview Cres Unit 7, Mississauga, ON, L5L 0A1
(905) 607-8665
Sales 15,651,090
SIC 5072 Hardware
　Bruce Davies
　Jack Lin
　Bob Atkinson

D-U-N-S 25-799-5712　　(SL)
MARINDUSTRIAL ONTARIO INC
(*Suby of* ENTREPRISES ELECTRIQUES NADCO INC)
4090 Ridgeway Dr Unit 8, Mississauga, ON, L5L 5X5
(905) 607-5052
Emp Here 25　　*Sales* 11,875,650
SIC 5084 Industrial machinery and equipment
　Eric Nadeau

D-U-N-S 25-064-9563　　(SL)
MEDELA CANADA INC
(*Suby of* OLLE LARSSON HOLDING AG)
4160 Sladeview Cres Unit 8, Mississauga, ON, L5L 0A1
(905) 608-7272
Emp Here 32　　*Sales* 14,309,568
SIC 5047 Medical and hospital equipment
　Steven Mccormack

D-U-N-S 24-093-3338　　(BR)
METRO ONTARIO INC
FOOD BASICS
(*Suby of* METRO INC)
3476 Glen Erin Dr, Mississauga, ON, L5L 3R4
(905) 569-2162
Emp Here 93
SIC 5411 Grocery stores
　Doug Greenway

D-U-N-S 24-918-6057　　(HQ)
METROLAND MEDIA GROUP LTD
BRAMPTON GUARDIAN

(*Suby of* TORSTAR CORPORATION)
3715 Laird Rd Unit 6, Mississauga, ON, L5L 0A3
(905) 281-5656
Emp Here 130　　*Sales* 503,812,400
SIC 2711 Newspapers
　Ian Oliver
　Tim Whittaker
　Wayne Zubek
　Susan Wilson
　Peter Marsh

D-U-N-S 20-011-9670　　(SL)
NATIONAL CORPORATE HOUSEKEEPING SERVICES INC
NCH SERVICES
3481 Kelso Cres, Mississauga, ON, L5L 4R3
(905) 608-8004
Emp Here 100　　*Sales* 4,020,900
SIC 7349 Building maintenance services, nec
　Kenneth W Grant

D-U-N-S 25-338-3715　　(SL)
NETTLEWOODS INC
4060 Ridgeway Dr Unit 16, Mississauga, ON, L5L 5X9
(905) 608-1919
Emp Here 75　　*Sales* 20,749,500
SIC 2844 Toilet preparations
　Lori Freeman

D-U-N-S 24-830-0139　　(HQ)
NU SKIN CANADA, INC
(*Suby of* NU SKIN ENTERPRISES, INC.)
4085 Sladeview Cres, Mississauga, ON, L5L 5X3
(905) 569-5100
Emp Here 38　　*Sales* 46,424,490
SIC 5122 Drugs, proprietaries, and sundries
　Paul Hanson
　Blake M Roney
　Steven J Lund
　Walt Cottle

D-U-N-S 25-736-9066　　(SL)
OMCAN MANUFACTURING & DISTRIBUTING COMPANY INC
OMCAN
3115 Pepper Mill Crt, Mississauga, ON, L5L 4X5
(905) 828-0234
Emp Here 70　　*Sales* 33,251,820
SIC 5084 Industrial machinery and equipment

D-U-N-S 24-886-3219　　(HQ)
PALL (CANADA) ULC
(*Suby of* DANAHER CORPORATION)
3450 Ridgeway Dr Unit 6, Mississauga, ON, L5L 0A2
(905) 542-0330
Sales 26,825,150
SIC 5085 Industrial supplies
　Tom Shields

D-U-N-S 24-845-4860　　(HQ)
PSI PERIPHERAL SOLUTIONS INC
PSI ENGINEERING
3535 Laird Rd Unit 9, Mississauga, ON, L5L 5Z4
(905) 858-3600
Sales 13,415,220
SIC 5045 Computers, peripherals, and software
　John Panunto

D-U-N-S 20-337-1943　　(HQ)
QM LP
QM ENVIRONMENTAL
3580 Laird Rd Unit 1, Mississauga, ON, L5L 5Z7
(416) 253-6000
Emp Here 1　　*Sales* 148,663,200
SIC 1795 Wrecking and demolition work
　Justine Sharp
　Kevin Watson

D-U-N-S 24-064-2798　　(SL)
QX LTD

QX TECHNICAL SERVICES
(*Suby of* AECON GROUP INC)
4140 Sladeview Cres Unit 4, Mississauga, ON, L5L 6A1
(905) 828-9055
Emp Here 200　　*Sales* 139,678,400
SIC 1541 Industrial buildings and warehouses
　Mike Henderson

D-U-N-S 24-123-5050　　(HQ)
RAPID AID CORP
4120a Sladeview Cres Unit 1-4, Mississauga, ON, L5L 5Z3
(905) 820-4788
Sales 57,617,700
SIC 3842 Surgical appliances and supplies
　Jeffrey Whitely

D-U-N-S 20-180-6911　　(SL)
RDHR INVESTMENTS & HOLDINGS INC
2187 Dunwin Dr, Mississauga, ON, L5L 1X2
(905) 820-7887
Emp Here 30　　*Sales* 11,881,090
SIC 6794 Patent owners and lessors

D-U-N-S 24-663-5858　　(HQ)
SAFETY EXPRESS LTD
(*Suby of* ARAMSCO HOLDINGS, INC.)
4190 Sladeview Cres Unit 1-2, Mississauga, ON, L5L 0A1
(905) 608-0111
Emp Here 19　　*Sales* 31,232,520
SIC 5099 Durable goods, nec
　Kelly Robertson
　Eva Robertson

D-U-N-S 20-709-5865　　(HQ)
SALUMATICS INC.
3250 Ridgeway Dr Unit 10, Mississauga, ON, L5L 5Y6
(905) 362-2230
Emp Here 35　　*Sales* 17,518,935
SIC 7374 Data processing and preparation
　Allan Magnacca

D-U-N-S 20-560-4655　　(HQ)
SEALED AIR (CANADA) CO./CIE
CRYOVAC
(*Suby of* SEALED AIR CORPORATION)
3755 Laird Rd Unit 10, Mississauga, ON, L5L 0B3
(905) 829-1200
Emp Here 250　　*Sales* 95,524,800
SIC 3089 Plastics products, nec
　Kim Leung
　Andre Schmidt

D-U-N-S 25-840-2007　　(SL)
SERVICE PLUS AQUATICS INC
3600b Laird Rd Unit 7, Mississauga, ON, L5L 6A7
(905) 569-7899
Emp Here 35　　*Sales* 18,218,970
SIC 5091 Sporting and recreation goods
　Roland Guy

D-U-N-S 24-830-9122　　(SL)
SPRINGBANK MECHANICAL SYSTEMS LIMITED
3615 Laird Rd Unit 1, Mississauga, ON, L5L 5Z8
(905) 569-8990
Emp Here 65　　*Sales* 15,149,225
SIC 1711 Plumbing, heating, air-conditioning
　Gregg Little
　David Parr

D-U-N-S 24-380-1771　　(BR)
STARSKY FINE FOODS MISSISSAUGA INC
(*Suby of* STARSKY FINE FOODS MISSISSAUGA INC)
3115 Dundas St W, Mississauga, ON, L5L 3R8
(905) 363-2000
Emp Here 200
SIC 5411 Grocery stores
　Tom Podkowa

▲ Public Company　　■ Public Company Family Member　　**HQ** Headquarters　　**BR** Branch　　**SL** Single Location

D-U-N-S 20-717-4843 (BR)
SUNRISE NORTH SENIOR LIVING LTD
SUNRISE SENIOR LIVING OF ERIN MILLS
(*Suby of* WELLTOWER INC.)
4046 Erin Mills Pky, Mississauga, ON, L5L
2W7
(905) 569-0004
Emp Here 150
SIC 8322 Individual and family services
Mary Wideman

D-U-N-S 25-091-8588 (SL)
SUPER SHINE JANITORIAL SERVICES LIMITED
4161 Sladeview Cres Unit 21, Mississauga, ON, L5L 5R3
(905) 607-8200
Emp Here 140 *Sales* 4,475,520
SIC 7349 Building maintenance services, nec
Frank Novelli

D-U-N-S 20-565-9472 (SL)
TBM SERVICE GROUP INC
2450 Dunwin Dr Unit 6, Mississauga, ON, L5L 1J9
(905) 608-8989
Emp Here 850 *Sales* 27,172,800
SIC 7349 Building maintenance services, nec
Ravi Ramanand
Caroline Harduwar

D-U-N-S 25-469-0829 (HQ)
TECHSPAN INDUSTRIES INC
TECHSPAN AUTOMOTIVE
3131 Pepper Mill Crt Unit 1, Mississauga, ON, L5L 4X6
(905) 820-6150
Emp Here 66 *Sales* 13,330,940
SIC 3643 Current-carrying wiring devices
Frank Dunnigan
Mary Dunnigan

D-U-N-S 20-820-1160 (SL)
TIRCONNELL PHARMACY LIMITED
SHOPPERS DRUG MART
3163 Winston Churchill Blvd Suite 1098, Mississauga, ON, L5L 2W1
(905) 607-7871
Emp Here 53 *Sales* 12,949,384
SIC 5912 Drug stores and proprietary stores
Donna Young

D-U-N-S 25-191-6896 (SL)
TRENDS INTERNATIONAL PUBLISHING CORPORATION
3500 Laird Rd Unit 2, Mississauga, ON, L5L 5Y4
(905) 569-8500
Emp Here 125 *Sales* 20,503,375
SIC 2741 Miscellaneous publishing
Philip St. Jean

D-U-N-S 20-794-3189 (SL)
TRILLIUM THERAPEUTICS INC
2488 Dunwin Dr, Mississauga, ON, L5L 1J9
(416) 595-0627
Emp Here 60 *Sales* 19,558,260
SIC 8071 Medical laboratories
Niclas Stiernholm
Penka Petrova
James Parsons
Robert Uger
Yaping Shou
Calvin Stiller
Luke Beshar
Henry Friesen
Robert Kirkman
Michael Moore

D-U-N-S 25-094-5842 (BR)
UKRAINIAN HOME FOR THE AGED
IVAN FRANKO HOME
(*Suby of* UKRAINIAN HOME FOR THE AGED)
3058 Winston Churchill Blvd Suite 1, Mississauga, ON, L5L 3J1
(905) 820-0573
Emp Here 130

SIC 8361 Residential care
Eugenia Pasternak

D-U-N-S 25-215-1154 (BR)
UNIFIRST CANADA LTD
(*Suby of* UNIFIRST CORPORATION)
2290 Dunwin Dr, Mississauga, ON, L5L 1C7
(905) 828-9621
Emp Here 150
SIC 7213 Linen supply
Ron Risebrough

D-U-N-S 20-022-9719 (SL)
UTMC CANADA INC
(*Suby of* ESSILORLUXOTTICA)
2390 Dunwin Dr, Mississauga, ON, L5L 1J9
(905) 828-9300
Emp Here 40 *Sales* 10,262,480
SIC 3827 Optical instruments and lenses
Dan Tlante

D-U-N-S 20-350-6167 (HQ)
VERTIV CANADA ULC
3800b Laird Rd Unit 7, Mississauga, ON, L5L 0B2
(905) 569-8282
Sales 110,246,930
SIC 5063 Electrical apparatus and equipment
Mike Cousineau

D-U-N-S 24-329-7004 (BR)
WAL-MART CANADA CORP
WALMART SUPERCENTRE
(*Suby of* WALMART INC.)
2160 Burnhamthorpe Rd W, Mississauga, ON, L5L 5Z5
(905) 608-0922
Emp Here 200
SIC 5311 Department stores
Dave Commission

D-U-N-S 20-559-8308 (SL)
WOODCHESTER IMPORTS INC
WOODCHESTER KIA
3089 Woodchester Dr, Mississauga, ON, L5L 1J2
(905) 828-2289
Emp Here 25 *Sales* 12,451,950
SIC 5511 New and used car dealers
Sandy Liguori
Nick Liguori

D-U-N-S 24-927-5082 (SL)
WOODCHESTER NISSAN INC
WOODCHESTER INFINITI NISSAN
2560 Motorway Blvd, Mississauga, ON, L5L 1X3
(905) 828-7001
Emp Here 30 *Sales* 14,942,340
SIC 5511 New and used car dealers
Nicola Liguori
Sandy Liguori

D-U-N-S 25-084-0121 (SL)
WORLD MEATS INC
2255 Dunwin Dr Unit 1, Mississauga, ON, L5L 1A3
(905) 569-0559
Emp Here 30 *Sales* 25,067,310
SIC 5147 Meats and meat products
Augustino De Oliveira
Agnes De Oliveira

D-U-N-S 25-406-1237 (HQ)
YASKAWA CANADA INC
(*Suby of* YASKAWA ELECTRIC CORPORATION)
3530 Laird Rd Unit 3, Mississauga, ON, L5L 5Z7
(905) 569-6686
Emp Here 41 *Sales* 24,226,326
SIC 5084 Industrial machinery and equipment
Lianne Cutone
Trevor Jones
Steve Barhorst

Mississauga, ON L5M

D-U-N-S 24-179-1032 (HQ)
1122630 ONTARIO LIMITED
S&H HEALTH FOODS
5399 Durie Rd, Mississauga, ON, L5M 2C8
(905) 567-6457
Emp Here 5 *Sales* 13,707,600
SIC 5499 Miscellaneous food stores
Harry Sandu

D-U-N-S 24-760-2696 (SL)
1815264 ONTARIO INC
SWAD GRAIN EXPORTS
251 Queen St S Unit 252, Mississauga, ON, L5M 1L7
(905) 593-4204
Emp Here 12 *Sales* 14,524,764
SIC 5153 Grain and field beans
Tanveer Hashmi

D-U-N-S 24-389-1434 (HQ)
2041188 ONTARIO INC
PETRO CANADA
2632 Credit Valley Rd, Mississauga, ON, L5M 4J6
(647) 986-0000
Emp Here 5 *Sales* 33,351,840
SIC 5541 Gasoline service stations
Shoyaib Khan
Huma Khan

D-U-N-S 20-805-3202 (HQ)
4-HOWELL BROTHERS INC
PETRO CANADA
3030 Artesian Dr, Mississauga, ON, L5M 7P5
(905) 828-5926
Emp Here 5 *Sales* 24,903,900
SIC 5541 Gasoline service stations
Edward Howell

D-U-N-S 20-290-3394 (BR)
AMICA MATURE LIFESTYLES INC
AMICA AT ERIN MILLS
(*Suby of* AMICA SENIOR LIFESTYLES INC)
4620 Kimbermount Ave, Mississauga, ON, L5M 5W5
(905) 816-9163
Emp Here 100
SIC 8361 Residential care
Ernie Hagen

D-U-N-S 24-252-0034 (HQ)
BATH & BODY WORKS INC
5100 Erin Mills Pky, Mississauga, ON, L5M 4Z5
(905) 820-1112
Emp Here 1 *Sales* 15,106,195
SIC 5719 Miscellaneous homefurnishings
Camille Mcdonald

D-U-N-S 24-555-3792 (SL)
CENTURY 21 NEW AGE REALTY INC
5618 Tenth Line W Unit 9, Mississauga, ON, L5M 7L9
(905) 567-1411
Emp Here 49 *Sales* 16,029,223
SIC 6531 Real estate agents and managers
Chris Dormer

D-U-N-S 20-555-4582 (HQ)
CTS OF CANADA CO
(*Suby of* CTS CORPORATION)
80 Thomas St, Mississauga, ON, L5M 1Y9
(905) 826-1141
Sales 61,392,555
SIC 3679 Electronic components, nec
William Cahill
Jeffrey Gulbranson

D-U-N-S 25-398-7465 (HQ)
DAKIN NEWS SYSTEMS INC
INTERNATIONAL NEWS
238 Queen St S Suite 2, Mississauga, ON, L5M 1L5
(905) 826-0862
Emp Here 21 *Sales* 20,904,300

SIC 6794 Patent owners and lessors
Samuel Davis

D-U-N-S 20-294-6849 (BR)
DUFFERIN-PEEL CATHOLIC DISTRICT SCHOOL BOARD
ST. ALOYSIUS GONZAGA SECONDARY SCHOOL
(*Suby of* DUFFERIN-PEEL CATHOLIC DISTRICT SCHOOL BOARD)
2800 Erin Centre Blvd, Mississauga, ON, L5M 6R5
(905) 820-3900
Emp Here 100
SIC 8211 Elementary and secondary schools
Michael O'grady

D-U-N-S 24-346-8936 (BR)
DUFFERIN-PEEL CATHOLIC DISTRICT SCHOOL BOARD
ST. JOAN OF ARC CATHOLIC SECONDARY SCHOOL
(*Suby of* DUFFERIN-PEEL CATHOLIC DISTRICT SCHOOL BOARD)
3801 Thomas St, Mississauga, ON, L5M 7G2
(905) 285-0050
Emp Here 80
SIC 8211 Elementary and secondary schools
Clara Pitoscia

D-U-N-S 24-937-6708 (HQ)
HSG HEALTH SYSTEMS GROUP LIMITED
HEALTH SYSTEMS GROUP
51 Tannery St, Mississauga, ON, L5M 1V3
(905) 858-0333
Sales 47,551,750
SIC 8011 Offices and clinics of medical doctors
Douglas Cowan

D-U-N-S 25-301-1779 (BR)
HUDSON'S BAY COMPANY
BAY, THE
(*Suby of* HUDSON'S BAY COMPANY)
5100 Erin Mills Pky Unit Y001, Mississauga, ON, L5M 4Z5
(905) 820-8300
Emp Here 150
SIC 5311 Department stores
Christy Bautista

D-U-N-S 20-812-4060 (SL)
JODHA PHARMACY INC
SHOPPERS DRUG MART
128 Queen St S Suite 3, Mississauga, ON, L5M 1K8
(905) 567-0744
Emp Here 45 *Sales* 11,382,930
SIC 5912 Drug stores and proprietary stores
Jagdeep Jodha

D-U-N-S 25-372-9594 (BR)
LONGO BROTHERS FRUIT MARKETS INC
LONGO'S FRUIT MARKET
(*Suby of* LONGO BROTHERS FRUIT MARKETS INC)
5636 Glen Erin Dr Unit 1, Mississauga, ON, L5M 6B1
(905) 567-4450
Emp Here 200
SIC 5411 Grocery stores
Frank Longo

D-U-N-S 24-860-1072 (SL)
MACLAI DRUGS LIMITED
SHOPPERS DRUG MART
5100 Erin Mills Pky Suite 904, Mississauga, ON, L5M 4Z5
(905) 569-3939
Emp Here 40 *Sales* 10,118,160
SIC 5912 Drug stores and proprietary stores
Nawroza Macklai

D-U-N-S 24-373-1028 (HQ)
MAINWAY HUNTER CREIGHTON INSURANCE INC
MHC
101 Queen St S Suite 100, Mississauga, ON,

L5M 1K7
(905) 826-3215
Emp Here 5   *Sales* 11,598,480
SIC 6411 Insurance agents, brokers, and service
Melody Murray
Lynda Smith
Dominic Albanese

D-U-N-S 25-263-7723   (BR)
PEEL DISTRICT SCHOOL BOARD
STREETSVILLE SECONDARY SCHOOL
(*Suby of* PEEL DISTRICT SCHOOL BOARD)
72 Joymar Dr, Mississauga, ON, L5M 1G3
(905) 826-1195
Emp Here 90
SIC 8211 Elementary and secondary schools
Tamer Kamel

D-U-N-S 25-293-8345   (BR)
PEEL DISTRICT SCHOOL BOARD
JOHN FRASER SECONDARY SCHOOL
(*Suby of* PEEL DISTRICT SCHOOL BOARD)
2665 Erin Centre Blvd, Mississauga, ON, L5M 5H6
(905) 858-5910
Emp Here 100
SIC 8211 Elementary and secondary schools
Mary Nanavati

D-U-N-S 25-213-2279   (BR)
RE/MAX REALTY SPECIALISTS INC
RE/MAX SPECIALISTS
(*Suby of* RE/MAX REALTY SPECIALISTS INC)
2691 Credit Valley Rd Suite 101, Mississauga, ON, L5M 7A1
(905) 828-3434
Emp Here 86
SIC 6531 Real estate agents and managers
Dan Saracini

D-U-N-S 25-811-7860   (BR)
ROYAL LEPAGE LIMITED
(*Suby of* BROOKFIELD ASSET MANAGEMENT INC)
5055 Plantation Pl Unit 1, Mississauga, ON, L5M 6J3
(905) 828-1122
Emp Here 100
SIC 6531 Real estate agents and managers
Ahmed Helmi

D-U-N-S 25-292-6126   (BR)
ROYAL LEPAGE REAL ESTATE SERVICES LTD
(*Suby of* BRIDGEMARQ REAL ESTATE SERVICES INC)
5055 Plantation Pl Unit 1, Mississauga, ON, L5M 6J3
(905) 828-1122
Emp Here 100
SIC 6531 Real estate agents and managers
Linda Wheeler

D-U-N-S 20-793-0780   (BR)
SOBEYS CAPITAL INCORPORATED
(*Suby of* EMPIRE COMPANY LIMITED)
5602 Tenth Line W, Mississauga, ON, L5M 7L9
(905) 858-2899
Emp Here 110
SIC 5411 Grocery stores
David Jeffs

D-U-N-S 20-302-2231   (BR)
TRILLIUM HEALTH PARTNERS
THE CREDIT VALLEY HOSPITAL
(*Suby of* TRILLIUM HEALTH PARTNERS)
2200 Eglinton Ave W Suite 905, Mississauga, ON, L5M 2N1
(905) 813-2200
Emp Here 300
SIC 8062 General medical and surgical hospitals
Michelle Diemanuele

D-U-N-S 24-388-2735   (SL)

TROTT TRANSIT LTD
15 James St, Mississauga, ON, L5M 1R4

Emp Here 93   *Sales* 5,103,096
SIC 4142 Bus charter service, except local
Raymond Trott
Joyce Trott
Ursula Trott

Mississauga, ON L5N

D-U-N-S 24-101-4062   (SL)
1661899 ONTARIO LIMITED
6980 Creditview Rd, Mississauga, ON, L5N 8E2
(905) 812-7300
Emp Here 200   *Sales* 69,138,000
SIC 2043 Cereal breakfast foods
Paul Henry
Kevin Godwin

D-U-N-S 20-938-9089   (SL)
383565 ONTARIO INC
ROTOFLEX TOOLING, DIV OF
(*Suby of* MARK ANDY INC)
2660 Meadowvale Blvd Unit 17, Mississauga, ON, L5N 6M6
(905) 670-8700
Emp Here 116   *Sales* 32,581,732
SIC 3599 Industrial machinery, nec
Reinhard Muhs
Harold Muhs
Val Rimas
Rod Allen

D-U-N-S 20-228-6670   (HQ)
A. M. CASTLE & CO. (CANADA) INC
CASTLE METALS
(*Suby of* A.M. CASTLE & CO.)
2150 Argentia Rd, Mississauga, ON, L5N 2K7
(905) 858-3888
Emp Here 20   *Sales* 38,834,510
SIC 5051 Metals service centers and offices
Steven W. Scheinkman
Jonathan B. Mellin
G Thomas Mckane
Patrick R. Anderson
Marec E. Edgar
Ronald E. Knopp

D-U-N-S 24-446-2912   (SL)
ACCIDENT BENEFIT SOLUTION
6300 Prairie Cir, Mississauga, ON, L5N 5Y9
(905) 824-4476
Emp Here 13   *Sales* 13,453,453
SIC 6321 Accident and health insurance
Peter Hancock

D-U-N-S 25-148-9217   (SL)
ACTAVIS PHARMA COMPANY
(*Suby of* ALLERGAN PUBLIC LIMITED COMPANY)
6500 Kitimat Rd, Mississauga, ON, L5N 2B8
(905) 814-1820
Emp Here 280   *Sales* 92,846,320
SIC 2834 Pharmaceutical preparations
Jean-Guy Goulet
Henry Koziarski

D-U-N-S 20-108-0087   (SL)
ACTIVE NETWORK
TORONTO OFFICE (RESERVEAMERICA)
(*Suby of* PAPAY HOLDCO, LLC)
2480 Meadowvale Blvd Suite 1, Mississauga, ON, L5N 8M6
(905) 286-6600
Emp Here 130   *Sales* 18,743,660
SIC 7371 Custom computer programming services
Dave Alberga

D-U-N-S 24-181-5364   (SL)
ADDISON CHEVROLET BUICK GMC (WEST)

6600 Turner Valley Rd, Mississauga, ON, L5N 5Z1
(866) 980-6928
Emp Here 65   *Sales* 40,903,200
SIC 5511 New and used car dealers
Clark Addison
Steve Vieira

D-U-N-S 25-530-3182   (HQ)
AGILENT TECHNOLOGIES CANADA INC
(*Suby of* AGILENT TECHNOLOGIES, INC.)
6705 Millcreek Dr Unit 5, Mississauga, ON, L5N 5M4
(289) 290-3859
Emp Here 99   *Sales* 85,352,750
SIC 5084 Industrial machinery and equipment
Ronald Podio
Andrew Harrison

D-U-N-S 24-416-2319   (HQ)
AIR PRODUCTS CANADA LTD
(*Suby of* AIR PRODUCTS AND CHEMICALS, INC.)
2233 Argentia Rd, Mississauga, ON, L5N 2X7
(905) 816-6670
Emp Here 18   *Sales* 84,026,500
SIC 5169 Chemicals and allied products, nec
Roger Lecuyer

D-U-N-S 24-205-3143   (SL)
AKTELUX CORPORATION
2145 Meadowpine Blvd, Mississauga, ON, L5N 6R8

Emp Here 45   *Sales* 11,545,290
SIC 3812 Search and navigation equipment
Thomas Wallace
Pierre Jeanniot

D-U-N-S 20-158-5064   (SL)
ALCON CANADA INC
(*Suby of* NOVARTIS AG)
2665 Meadowvale Blvd, Mississauga, ON, L5N 8C7
(905) 826-6700
Emp Here 95   *Sales* 39,217,995
SIC 5122 Drugs, proprietaries, and sundries
Laurent Attias

D-U-N-S 20-359-9360   (HQ)
ALECTRA INC
2185 Derry Rd W, Mississauga, ON, L5N 7A6
(905) 273-7425
Sales 203,962,200
SIC 4911 Electric services
Brian Bentz

D-U-N-S 24-953-5824   (HQ)
ALLIANCE CORPORATION
(*Suby of* ALLIANCE HOLDCO INC)
2395 Meadowpine Blvd, Mississauga, ON, L5N 7W6
(905) 821-4797
Emp Here 100   *Sales* 87,037,050
SIC 5065 Electronic parts and equipment, nec
Ron Moss
Greg Hunter

D-U-N-S 24-384-2072   (SL)
AMA NSG INC
6699 Campobello Rd, Mississauga, ON, L5N 2L7
(905) 826-3922
Emp Here 50   *Sales* 10,619,850
SIC 8748 Business consulting, nec
Daniel Tin Yan Cheng
Timothy Tin Cho Wong
Sanny Siu Sing Wong

D-U-N-S 20-286-4229   (HQ)
AMAZON CANADA FULFILLMENT SERVICES INC
(*Suby of* AMAZON.COM, INC.)
6363 Millcreek Dr, Mississauga, ON, L5N 1L8
(289) 998-0300
Emp Here 10   *Sales* 14,850,400
SIC 5192 Books, periodicals, and newspapers
Thomas Szkutak

Michelle Wilson
Jason Bristow
Marc Onetto
Michael Deal
Tim Stone

D-U-N-S 24-872-9444   (HQ)
AMGEN CANADA INC
(*Suby of* AMGEN INC.)
6775 Financial Dr Suite 100, Mississauga, ON, L5N 0A4
(905) 285-3000
Sales 82,564,200
SIC 5122 Drugs, proprietaries, and sundries
Daniel Billen

D-U-N-S 24-326-4855   (SL)
APPLIED SYSTEMS CANADA ULC
(*Suby of* APPLIED SYSTEMS, INC.)
6865 Century Avenue Suite 3000, Mississauga, ON, L5N 2E2
(905) 363-6500
Emp Here 63   *Sales* 12,959,478
SIC 4213 Trucking, except local
James Kellner
Andrew Balson
Andrew Long
Colleen Mikuce

D-U-N-S 20-063-1868   (SL)
ATRENS-COUNSEL INSURANCE BROKERS INC
ATRENS-COUNSEL INSURANCE BROKERS
(*Suby of* ARTHUR J. GALLAGHER & CO.)
7111 Syntex Dr Suite 200, Mississauga, ON, L5N 8C3
(905) 567-6222
Emp Here 50   *Sales* 42,403,000
SIC 6411 Insurance agents, brokers, and service
Mark Shedden

D-U-N-S 20-001-8855   (SL)
AUDMET CANADA LTD
OTICON CANADA
(*Suby of* WILLIAM DEMANT FONDEN)
6950 Creditview Rd, Mississauga, ON, L5N 0A6
(905) 677-3231
Emp Here 150   *Sales* 41,155,500
SIC 3842 Surgical appliances and supplies
Brock Neuman
Mikael Worning
Niels Jacobsen
Michael Schmid
Svend Thomsen

D-U-N-S 24-752-7864   (SL)
AUTO CONTROL MEDICAL INC
6695 Millcreek Dr Unit 6, Mississauga, ON, L5N 5R8
(905) 814-6350
Emp Here 30   *Sales* 13,415,220
SIC 5047 Medical and hospital equipment
Robert Burgy
Vaughan Preveteet

D-U-N-S 24-380-2852   (HQ)
AVIYA TECHNOLOGIES INC
AVIYA AEROSPACE SYSTEMS
2495 Meadowpine Blvd, Mississauga, ON, L5N 6C3
(905) 812-9995
Sales 14,979,700
SIC 7373 Computer integrated systems design
John Koumoundouros
Basile Papaevangelou
Louis Brown
Joseph Sum

D-U-N-S 20-421-8804   (HQ)
AVNET INTERNATIONAL (CANADA) LTD
AVNET CANADA
(*Suby of* AVNET, INC.)
6950 Creditview Rd Unit 2, Mississauga, ON,

▲ Public Company   ■ Public Company Family Member   **HQ** Headquarters   **BR** Branch   **SL** Single Location

L5N 0A6
(905) 812-4400
Emp Here 50　　*Sales* 58,024,700
SIC 5065 Electronic parts and equipment, nec
Roy Vallee
Gavin Miller
Raymond Sadowski
David R Birk
Jun Li

D-U-N-S 20-280-0058　　(SL)
B. BRAUN OF CANADA, LTD
(*Suby of* LUDWIG G. BRAUN GMBH U. CO.
KG)
6711 Mississauga Rd Suite 504, Mississauga,
ON, L5N 2W3
(905) 363-4335
Emp Here 25　　*Sales* 11,179,350
SIC 5047 Medical and hospital equipment
Bob Comer

D-U-N-S 24-357-1911　　(SL)
**BAMBERGER POLYMERS (CANADA)
CORP**
(*Suby of* BAMBERGER POLYMERS CORP.)
2000 Argentia Rd Suite 306, Mississauga,
ON, L5N 1P7
(905) 821-9400
Emp Here 15　　*Sales* 93,903,550
SIC 5162 Plastics materials and basic shapes
Dennis Don
Steven Goldberg
Theodore M Dwyer
Paul Coco
Jeffrey Macleod

D-U-N-S 20-365-3662　　(SL)
BAUER HOCKEY LTD
6925 Century Ave Unit 600, Mississauga, ON,
L5N 7K2
(905) 363-3200
Emp Here 141　　*Sales* 45,985,176
SIC 3949 Sporting and athletic goods, nec
Ed Kinnaly
Paul Dachsteiner
Julie Zaleski
Ivars Jakobsons

D-U-N-S 20-032-3889　　(HQ)
BAXTER CORPORATION
(*Suby of* BAXTER INTERNATIONAL INC.)
7125 Mississauga Rd, Mississauga, ON, L5N
0C2
(905) 369-6000
Emp Here 444　　*Sales* 331,594,000
SIC 2834 Pharmaceutical preparations
Rehana Doobay
Mike Oliver
Michael Thuy
Stephen Thompson

D-U-N-S 20-597-0598　　(SL)
BD BIOSCIENCES
2280 Argentia Rd, Mississauga, ON, L5N 6H8

Emp Here 49　　*Sales* 21,911,526
SIC 5047 Medical and hospital equipment
Alex Adams

D-U-N-S 20-124-2229　　(HQ)
BEAUTY SYSTEMS GROUP (CANADA) INC
OBSCO BEAUTY SUPPLY
(*Suby of* SALLY BEAUTY HOLDINGS, INC.)
2345 Argentia Rd Suite 102, Mississauga,
ON, L5N 8K4
(905) 696-2600
Emp Here 80　　*Sales* 146,319,000
SIC 5087 Service establishment equipment
Julie Walton

D-U-N-S 24-524-0304　　(SL)
BECKMAN COULTER CANADA INC
(*Suby of* DANAHER CORPORATION)
7075 Financial Dr, Mississauga, ON, L5N 6V8
(905) 819-1234
Emp Here 194　　*Sales* 103,858,288
SIC 5047 Medical and hospital equipment

D-U-N-S 24-421-9882　　(SL)
BECTON DICKINSON CANADA INC
BD - CANADA
(*Suby of* BECTON, DICKINSON AND COM-
PANY)
2100 Derry Rd W Suite 100, Mississauga, ON,
L5N 0B3
(905) 288-6000
Emp Here 300　　*Sales* 160,605,600
SIC 5047 Medical and hospital equipment
Frank Florio
David G. Butler
Gary Defazio

D-U-N-S 24-023-7073　　(HQ)
BIZERBA CANADA INC
(*Suby of* BIZERBA SE & CO. KG)
2810 Argentia Rd Unit 9, Mississauga, ON,
L5N 8L2
(905) 816-0498
Emp Here 22　　*Sales* 16,625,910
SIC 5084 Industrial machinery and equipment
Robert Slykhuis

D-U-N-S 20-212-8013　　(HQ)
BRINK'S CANADA LIMITED
(*Suby of* THE BRINK'S COMPANY)
2233 Argentia Rd Suite 400, Mississauga,
ON, L5N 2X7
(905) 306-9600
Emp Here 40　　*Sales* 52,500,000
SIC 7381 Detective and armored car services
Ronald F Rokosz
Frank T Lennon

D-U-N-S 20-105-1328　　(HQ)
BUREAU VERITAS CANADA (2019) INC
BV LABS
(*Suby of* BUREAU VERITAS)
1919 Minnesota Crt Suite 500, Mississauga,
ON, L5N 0C9
(905) 288-2150
Emp Here 90　　*Sales* 448,980,400
SIC 8734 Testing laboratories
Donna Garbutt
Natalia Shuman
Steve Quon
Robert Wiebe
Margaret Bailey
Brenda Arseneault

D-U-N-S 20-015-2457　　(SL)
**C/S CONSTRUCTION SPECIALTIES COM-
PANY**
(*Suby of* CONSTRUCTION SPECIALTIES
INC.)
2240 Argentia Rd, Mississauga, ON, L5N 2K7
(905) 274-3611
Emp Here 90　　*Sales* 17,287,650
SIC 3446 Architectural Metalwork
Ronald Dadd
Daniel Chan
James Blaney

D-U-N-S 24-827-4383　　(HQ)
CALDIC CANADA INC
(*Suby of* CALDIC HOLDCO B.V.)
6980 Creditview Rd, Mississauga, ON, L5N
8E2
(905) 812-7300
Emp Here 174　　*Sales* 101,376,080
SIC 2043 Cereal breakfast foods
Olav Van Caldenborgah
Steve Owen
Jill Wuthmann
Bernard Whitt
Michael Lipinski

D-U-N-S 24-664-4454　　(SL)
**CANADIAN ANALYTICAL LABORATORIES
INC**
6733 Kitimat Rd, Mississauga, ON, L5N 1W3
(416) 286-3332
Emp Here 50　　*Sales* 11,016,400
SIC 8734 Testing laboratories
Christian Sood
Manohar Sood

Angelina Sood

D-U-N-S 24-631-4538　　(SL)
**CANADIAN MEASUREMENT-METROLOGY
INC**
C M M
2433 Meadowvale Blvd, Mississauga, ON,
L5N 5S2
(905) 819-7878
Emp Here 40　　*Sales* 19,001,040
SIC 5085 Industrial supplies
Elliott Foster
Margot Wax

D-U-N-S 24-096-6309　　(HQ)
**CANADIAN MINI-WAREHOUSE PROPER-
TIES COMPANY**
PUBLIC STORAGE
1740 Argentia Rd, Mississauga, ON, L5N 3K3
(905) 677-0363
Emp Here 6　　*Sales* 28,798,840
SIC 4225 General warehousing and storage
David Singelyn

D-U-N-S 24-332-2588　　(SL)
CANADIAN TEST CASE 120-TEST
6750 Century Ave Suite 305, Mississauga,
ON, L5N 0B7
(905) 812-5920
Emp Here 20　　*Sales* 10,000,000
SIC 5083 Farm and garden machinery

D-U-N-S 24-101-9046　　(SL)
CANADIAN TEST CASE 16
6750 Century Ave Suite 305, Mississauga,
ON, L5N 2V8
(905) 812-5920
Emp Here 1　　*Sales* 26,283,510
SIC 7389 Business services, nec

D-U-N-S 24-101-8808　　(SL)
CANADIAN TEST CASE 172
6750 Century Ave Suite 305, Mississauga,
ON, L5N 0B7

Emp Here 100
SIC 5311 Department stores

D-U-N-S 24-101-9566　　(SL)
CANADIAN TEST CASE 173
(*Suby of* CANADIAN TEST CASE 8)
6750 Century Ave, Suite 305, Mississauga,
ON, L5N 0B7
(905) 812-5920
Emp Here 230　　*Sales* 66,895,500
SIC 3732 Boatbuilding and repairing

D-U-N-S 20-320-1871　　(SL)
CANADIAN TEST CASE 176
(*Suby of* CANADIAN TEST CASE 170)
6750 Century Ave Suite 305, Mississauga,
ON, L5N 2V8
(905) 812-5920
Emp Here 7　　*Sales* 85,576,480
SIC 5812 Eating places

D-U-N-S 20-320-1876　　(SL)
CANADIAN TEST CASE 177 CORP
6750 Century Ave Suite 305, Mississauga,
ON, L5N 2V8
(905) 812-5920
Emp Here 500　　*Sales* 26,557,153,480
SIC 5812 Eating places

D-U-N-S 24-101-8766　　(HQ)
CANADIAN TEST CASE 185
6750 Century Ave Suite 300, Mississauga,
ON, L5N 0B7
(905) 812-5920
Emp Here 300　　*Sales* 25,186,611,516
SIC 3714 Motor vehicle parts and accessories

D-U-N-S 24-101-9053　　(SL)
CANADIAN TEST CASE 187
6750 Century Ave Suite 305, Mississauga,
ON, L5N 2V8
(905) 812-5920
Emp Here 10　　*Sales* 17,708,400

SIC 5812 Eating places

D-U-N-S 24-101-9244　　(HQ)
CANADIAN TEST CASE 20
6750 Century Ave Suite 305, Mississauga,
ON, L5N 0B7
(905) 812-5920
Sales 24,689,880
SIC 8741 Management services

D-U-N-S 24-101-9285　　(SL)
CANADIAN TEST CASE 21
(*Suby of* CANADIAN TEST CASE 55)
6750 Century Ave Suite 305, Mississauga,
ON, L5N 2V8
(905) 812-5920
Emp Here 101　　*Sales* 241,142,449
SIC 1044 Silver ores

D-U-N-S 24-331-2084　　(SL)
CANADIAN TEST CASE 29-B
6750 Century Ave Suite 305, Mississauga,
ON, L5N 2V8
(905) 812-5922
Emp Here 50　　*Sales* 92,332,950
SIC 6324 Hospital and medical service plans

D-U-N-S 24-101-8774　　(SL)
CANADIAN TEST CASE 31 LTD
6750 Century Ave Suite 305, Mississauga,
ON, L5N 2V8
(905) 812-5920
Emp Here 50　　*Sales* 37,126,000
SIC 5199 Nondurable goods, nec

D-U-N-S 24-101-8972　　(SL)
CANADIAN TEST CASE 36 LIMITED
6750 Century Ave Suite 305, Mississauga,
ON, L5N 2V8

Emp Here 70　　*Sales* 14,374,010
SIC 5331 Variety stores

D-U-N-S 24-101-9533　　(SL)
CANADIAN TEST CASE 49 LTD
6750 Century Ave Suite 305, Mississauga,
ON, L5N 2V8
(905) 812-5920
Emp Here 60　　*Sales* 74,125,080
SIC 6311 Life insurance

D-U-N-S 24-101-9186　　(SL)
CANADIAN TEST CASE 62
6750 Century Ave Suite 305, Mississauga,
ON, L5N 2V8
(437) 999-9999
Emp Here 100　　*Sales* 23,428,800
SIC 8748 Business consulting, nec

D-U-N-S 24-101-9301　　(SL)
CANADIAN TEST CASE 65
6750 Century Ave Suite 305, Mississauga,
ON, L5N 2V8
(905) 812-5920
Emp Here 70　　*Sales* 16,340,450
SIC 1011 Iron ores

D-U-N-S 24-101-9319　　(SL)
CANADIAN TEST CASE 87
6750 Century Ave Suite 305, Mississauga,
ON, L5N 2V8
(905) 812-5920
Emp Here 120　　*Sales* 29,319,360
SIC 5932 Used merchandise stores

D-U-N-S 20-232-6518　　(HQ)
CASCADES GROUPE PAPIERS FINS INC
(*Suby of* CASCADES INC)
7280 West Credit Ave, Mississauga, ON, L5N
5N1
(905) 813-9400
Sales 202,200,350
SIC 2621 Paper mills

D-U-N-S 24-174-1300　　(BR)
CDSL CANADA LIMITED
CGI
(*Suby of* CGI INC)
2480 Meadowvale Blvd Suite 100, Missis-

sauga, ON, L5N 8M6
(905) 858-7100
Emp Here 2,000
SIC 7379 Computer related services, nec
  Serge Godin

D-U-N-S 24-394-6196   (SL)
CELGENE CANADA INC
(*Suby of* CELGENE CORPORATION)
6755 Mississauga Rd Suite 600, Mississauga,
ON, L5N 7Y2
(289) 291-0200
Emp Here 70   *Sales* 77,374,150
SIC 5122 Drugs, proprietaries, and sundries
  Ken Harris
  Kevin Leshuk

D-U-N-S 20-272-8812   (SL)
CHEMOURS CANADA COMPANY, THE
(*Suby of* THE CHEMOURS COMPANY)
2233 Argentia Rd Unit 402, Mississauga, ON,
L5N 2X7
(905) 816-2310
Emp Here 72   *Sales* 20,449,512
SIC 2816 Inorganic pigments
  Nevil Whitty
  Brian Morrissey
  Sacha Debleds

D-U-N-S 24-208-8060   (HQ)
CHEP CANADA INC
(*Suby of* BRAMBLES LIMITED)
7400 East Danbro Cres, Mississauga, ON,
L5N 8C6
(905) 790-2437
Emp Here 140   *Sales* 179,899,920
SIC 7359 Equipment rental and leasing, nec
  Laura Nador
  Paola Floris

D-U-N-S 24-219-0502   (HQ)
**CHILDREN'S AID SOCIETY OF THE RE-
GION OF PEEL, THE**
PEEL CAS
6860 Century Ave, Mississauga, ON, L5N
2W5
(905) 363-6131
Emp Here 450   *Sales* 39,931,840
SIC 8322 Individual and family services
  Rav Bains
  Solomon Owoo

D-U-N-S 24-396-8745   (SL)
CHIVA AUTO GOUP INC
DIRECT NISSAN
2290 Battleford Rd, Mississauga, ON, L5N
3K6
(905) 812-8882
Emp Here 23   *Sales* 11,455,794
SIC 5511 New and used car dealers
  Peter Pickering

D-U-N-S 24-314-7501   (HQ)
**CHRISTIAN LABOUR ASSOCIATION OF
CANADA**
CLAC
2335 Argentia Rd, Mississauga, ON, L5N 0A3
(905) 812-2855
Emp Here 10   *Sales* 35,320,500
SIC 8631 Labor organizations
  Dick Heinen
  Hank Beekhuis
  Susan Salvati

D-U-N-S 24-375-0366   (BR)
CIBA VISION CANADA INC
CIBA VISION DIV.
(*Suby of* NOVARTIS AG)
7 Rimini Mews, Mississauga, ON, L5N 4K1

Emp Here 300
SIC 5048 Ophthalmic goods
  Joseph Foos

D-U-N-S 20-959-7140   (SL)
CLDH MEADOWVALE INC
*DELTA MEADOWVALE RESORT & CONFER-
ENCE CENTRE*

(*Suby of* HOST HOTELS & RESORTS, INC.)
6750 Mississauga Rd, Mississauga, ON, L5N
2L3
(905) 826-0940
Emp Here 400   *Sales* 38,267,200
SIC 7011 Hotels and motels
  Martin Stitt
  W. Edward Walter
  Gregory J. Larson
  Ernest Mcnee
  David L. Buckley

D-U-N-S 20-698-7120   (BR)
**COMPAGNIE DE TELEPHONE BELL DU
CANADA OU BELL CANADA, LA**
BELL CANADA
(*Suby of* BCE INC)
7111 Syntex Dr, Mississauga, ON, L5N 8C3

Emp Here 230
SIC 4899 Communication services, nec

D-U-N-S 24-375-5217   (HQ)
COMPASS MINERALS CANADA CORP
(*Suby of* COMPASS MINERALS INTERNA-
TIONAL, INC.)
6700 Century Ave Suite 202, Mississauga,
ON, L5N 6A4
(905) 567-0231
Emp Here 30   *Sales* 247,865,400
SIC 1479 Chemical and fertilizer mining
  Angelo Brisimitzakis
  Rodney Underdown
  Jerry Smith
  Dennis Bergeson
  Victoria Heider
  Gerald Bucan
  Keith Clark

D-U-N-S 24-317-5119   (HQ)
CONTITECH CANADA, INC
GRANFORD
(*Suby of* CONTINENTAL AG)
6711 Mississauga Rd Suite 01, Mississauga,
ON, L5N 2W3
(905) 366-2010
Emp Here 30   *Sales* 238,812,000
SIC 3069 Fabricated rubber products, nec
  James T. Hill
  Guy Enta

D-U-N-S 24-876-1249   (HQ)
**CONTRACT PHARMACEUTICALS LIMITED
CANADA**
CPL
7600 East Danbro Cres, Mississauga, ON,
L5N 6L6
(905) 821-7600
Emp Here 245   *Sales* 99,478,200
SIC 2834 Pharmaceutical preparations
  Peter Wege Ii
  Ken Paige
  Jan Sahai

D-U-N-S 20-273-3655   (BR)
**CONTRACT PHARMACEUTICALS LIMITED
CANADA**
CPL
(*Suby of* CONTRACT PHARMACEUTICALS
LIMITED CANADA)
2145 Meadowpine Blvd 1st Fl, Mississauga,
ON, L5N 6R8
(905) 821-7600
Emp Here 90
SIC 2834 Pharmaceutical preparations
  Ildiko Riss

D-U-N-S 25-203-9755   (HQ)
COTTON CANDY INC
2600 Argentia Rd, Mississauga, ON, L5N 5V4
(905) 858-2600
Emp Here 55   *Sales* 55,689,000
SIC 5199 Nondurable goods, nec
  John Houlding
  Jody Bilous
  David Houlding
  Kerry Houlding

D-U-N-S 25-529-7970   (BR)
CREATION TECHNOLOGIES LP
(*Suby of* CREATION TECHNOLOGIES LP)
6820 Creditview Rd, Mississauga, ON, L5N
0A9
(877) 812-4212
Emp Here 250
SIC 3679 Electronic components, nec
  Mark Krzyczkowski

D-U-N-S 20-336-5788   (HQ)
CRESCITA THERAPEUTICS INC
6733 Mississauga Rd Suite 610, Mississauga,
ON, L5N 6J5
(905) 673-4295
Sales 12,605,720
SIC 8731 Commercial physical research
  Serge Verreault
  Daniel N. Chicoine
  Wade Hull
  Jean Colas
  Alain Dugal
  Isabelle Villeneuve
  David A. Copeland
  Jean-Francois Tremblay
  Samira Sakhia
  Anthony E. Dobranowski

D-U-N-S 20-143-4180   (SL)
**CRONE GEOPHYSICS & EXPLORATION
LTD**
2135 Meadowpine Blvd, Mississauga, ON,
L5N 6L5
(905) 814-0100
Emp Here 50   *Sales* 12,828,100
SIC 3829 Measuring and controlling devices,
nec
  Bill Ravenhurst

D-U-N-S 20-162-9805   (HQ)
**CYCLONE MANUFACTURING INCORPO-
RATED**
(*Suby of* SOCHAJ INVESTMENTS LTD)
7300 Rapistan Crt, Mississauga, ON, L5N
5S1
(905) 567-5601
Emp Here 200   *Sales* 78,137,458
SIC 3728 Aircraft parts and equipment, nec
  Andrew Sochaj
  Robert Sochaj
  Daniel Dobrjanski

D-U-N-S 20-554-9371   (HQ)
D&B COMPANIES OF CANADA ULC, THE
DUN & BRADSTREET
(*Suby of* STAR PARENT, LP)
6750 Century Ave Suite 305, Mississauga,
ON, L5N 2V8

Emp Here 45   *Sales* 13,825,599
SIC 7323 Credit reporting services

D-U-N-S 20-877-7110   (HQ)
DAIRY FARMERS OF ONTARIO
6780 Campobello Rd, Mississauga, ON, L5N
2L8
(905) 821-8970
Emp Here 60   *Sales* 17,500,983
SIC 8611 Business associations
  William Emmott
  David Murray
  Ian Harrop
  Patrick Hop Hing
  Peter Gould

D-U-N-S 24-357-2435   (SL)
DAY & ROSS DEDICATED LOGISTICS
6711 Mississauga Rd Suite 410, Mississauga,
ON, L5N 2W3
(905) 285-2355
Emp Here 900   *Sales* 185,135,400
SIC 4212 Local trucking, without storage
  William Dougherty

D-U-N-S 24-627-4229   (BR)
DELTA HOTELS LIMITED
*TORONTO DELTA MEADOWVALE RESORT
& CONFERENCE CENTRE, THE*

(*Suby of* GOVERNMENT OF THE
PROVINCE OF BRITISH COLUMBIA)
6750 Mississauga Rd, Mississauga, ON, L5N
2L3
(905) 821-1981
Emp Here 400
SIC 8741 Management services
  Rob Housez

D-U-N-S 20-145-7132   (HQ)
DEMATIC LIMITED
(*Suby of* KION GROUP AG)
6750 Century Ave Suite 302, Mississauga,
ON, L5N 2V8
(877) 567-7300
Emp Here 47   *Sales* 48,773,000
SIC 5084 Industrial machinery and equipment
  Hasan Dandashly
  Jeff Moss
  Frank Herzog
  Scott Watts
  Jan Vercammen
  Bernard Biolchini
  Stuart Stables
  Glen Borg

D-U-N-S 20-044-4214   (HQ)
**DIEBOLD COMPANY OF CANADA LIM-
ITED, THE**
(*Suby of* DIEBOLD NIXDORF, INCORPO-
RATED)
6630 Campobello Rd, Mississauga, ON, L5N
2L8
(905) 817-7600
Emp Here 145   *Sales* 67,461,009
SIC 1731 Electrical work
  Bruce Pearce
  Rakesh Malhotra

D-U-N-S 24-213-1399   (HQ)
**DIVERSICARE CANADA MANAGEMENT
SERVICES CO., INC**
TILBURY MANOR NURSING HOME
(*Suby of* DCMS HOLDINGS INC)
2121 Argentia Rd Suite 301, Mississauga,
ON, L5N 2X4
(905) 821-1161
Sales 136,652,000
SIC 8051 Skilled nursing care facilities
  John Carnella
  Dennis Boschetto
  Millie Christie
  Elroy Jespersen
  David Bird
  Denise Achonu
  Paige Chan
  Karen Kotanko

D-U-N-S 20-040-6759   (HQ)
DUPONT PIONEER
(*Suby of* DUPONT DE NEMOURS, INC.)
1919 Minnesota Crt, Mississauga, ON, L5N
0C9
(519) 352-6350
Sales 73,644,875
SIC 5191 Farm supplies
  Ian Grant
  Jeff Austin
  Rosalie Bertino
  Dean Oestreich

D-U-N-S 20-274-0374   (SL)
DYNABLAST INC
2625 Meadowpine Blvd, Mississauga, ON,
L5N 7K5
(888) 881-6667
Emp Here 200   *Sales* 44,400,200
SIC 3589 Service industry machinery, nec
  Peter Smith

D-U-N-S 24-727-2107   (HQ)
DYNAMIC PAINT PRODUCTS INC
PAINT SUNDRY PRODUCTS
(*Suby of* THE MERIT DISTRIBUTION
GROUP LLC)
7040 Financial Dr, Mississauga, ON, L5N 7H5

(905) 812-9319
Emp Here 75   *Sales* 74,252,000
SIC 5198 Paints, varnishes, and supplies
James Mumby, Jr

D-U-N-S 25-285-0367   (HQ)
E. & J. GALLO WINERY CANADA, LTD
(*Suby of* E. & J. GALLO WINERY)
6711 Mississauga Rd Suite 202, Mississauga,
ON, L5N 2W3
(905) 819-9600
Emp Here 25   *Sales* 46,682,440
SIC 4731 Freight transportation arrangement
Armand G. Skol
Joseph E. Gallo

D-U-N-S 20-266-8653   (HQ)
**EDGEWELL PERSONAL CARE CANADA
ULC**
EDGEWELL (TM)
6733 Mississauga Rd Suite 700, Mississauga,
ON, L5N 6J5
(905) 363-2720
Emp Here 350   *Sales* 25,263,600
SIC 8052 Intermediate care facilities
David P Hatfield
Rod R Little
John Hill

D-U-N-S 25-149-2435   (HQ)
ENERGIZER CANADA INC
(*Suby of* ENERGIZER HOLDINGS, INC.)
6733 Mississauga Rd Suite 800, Mississauga,
ON, L5N 6J5
(800) 383-7323
Emp Here 20   *Sales* 22,853,040
SIC 3691 Storage batteries
Edmond Maclellan
Krystine Jankowski
Alan Hoskins
Craig Dunaway
James Macintosh

D-U-N-S 24-025-7659   (HQ)
ENERSOURCE CORPORATION
(*Suby of* CORPORATION OF THE CITY OF
MISSISSAUGA)
2185 Derry Rd W, Mississauga, ON, L5N 7A6
(905) 273-9050
Emp Here 121   *Sales* 277,442,880
SIC 4911 Electric services
Peter Greg
Dan Pastoric
Norm Wolff
Kimberly Boyle
James Macumber
Chris Hudson
Norman Loberg
Gerald E. Beasley
Robert Maccallum
Bonnie Crombie

D-U-N-S 24-060-5048   (HQ)
ENGIE MULTITECH LTD
(*Suby of* ENGIE SERVICES INC)
2025 Meadowvale Blvd Unit 2, Mississauga,
ON, L5N 5N1
(905) 812-7900
Emp Here 244   *Sales* 67,712,000
SIC 1711 Plumbing, heating, air-conditioning
Luc Duguay

D-U-N-S 24-339-0460   (HQ)
ENGINEERED ASSEMBLIES INC
6535 Millcreek Dr Unit 75, Mississauga, ON,
L5N 2M2
(905) 816-2218
Sales 11,179,350
SIC 5039 Construction materials, nec
John Kubassek
Blair Davies

D-U-N-S 20-278-5465   (SL)
ENTERRA HOLDINGS LTD
6925 Century Ave Suite 100, Mississauga,
ON, L5N 7K2
(905) 567-4444
Emp Here 8,000   *Sales* 607,602,100

SIC 7363 Help supply services

D-U-N-S 24-587-4110   (SL)
EPPENDORF CANADA LTD
(*Suby of* ACEG BETEILIGUNGSGES. MBH)
2810 Argentia Rd Unit 2, Mississauga, ON,
L5N 8L2
(905) 826-5525
Emp Here 30   *Sales* 13,415,220
SIC 5049 Professional equipment, nec
Joseph Crowley
Christoph Asschenfeldt
David Roy

D-U-N-S 24-644-0275   (HQ)
**EXIDE TECHNOLOGIES CANADA CORPO-
RATION**
(*Suby of* EXIDE TECHNOLOGIES)
6950 Creditview Rd Suite 3, Mississauga, ON,
L5N 0A6
(905) 817-1773
Emp Here 65   *Sales* 87,037,050
SIC 5063 Electrical apparatus and equipment
Ron Nicolson
Way Sin Chan

D-U-N-S 20-194-6329   (HQ)
EXIT REALTY CORP. INTERNATIONAL
2345 Argentia Rd Suite 200, Mississauga,
ON, L5N 8K4
(905) 363-4050
Emp Here 50   *Sales* 31,416,675
SIC 6531 Real estate agents and managers
Steve Morris
Joyce Paron
Tami Bonnell
Maria Orzakovski

D-U-N-S 24-631-9347   (HQ)
FANUC CANADA, LTD
(*Suby of* FANUC CORPORATION)
6774 Financial Dr, Mississauga, ON, L5N 7J6
(905) 812-2300
Emp Here 50   *Sales* 23,751,300
SIC 5084 Industrial machinery and equipment
Peter Fitzgerald

D-U-N-S 20-164-9951   (SL)
FEDERAL-MOGUL CANADA LIMITED
FEDERAL-MOGUL WINDSOR, DIV OF
(*Suby of* ICAHN ENTERPRISES L.P.)
6860 Century Ave, Mississauga, ON, L5N
2W5
(905) 761-5400
Emp Here 100
SIC 3714 Motor vehicle parts and accessories
Chip Mcclare
Mike Holland

D-U-N-S 24-196-8767   (HQ)
FIRST CHOICE HAIRCUTTERS LTD
REGIS CANADA
(*Suby of* REGIS CORPORATION)
6400 Millcreek Dr, Mississauga, ON, L5N 3E7
(905) 858-8100
Emp Here 20   *Sales* 9,737,137,200
SIC 6794 Patent owners and lessors
John Fraser

D-U-N-S 25-406-9826   (SL)
FIRST GULF GROUP INC
(*Suby of* FIRST GULF DEVELOPMENT
CORPORATION)
6860 Century Ave Suite 1000, Mississauga,
ON, L5N 2W5
(905) 812-8030
Emp Here 100   *Sales* 12,477,600
SIC 8741 Management services
David Gibson
Norman Reisman

D-U-N-S 25-122-1859   (SL)
FIRST LINK LOGISTICS LTD
7467 Ninth Line, Mississauga, ON, L5N 7C3
(905) 565-1459
Emp Here 70   *Sales* 10,875,970
SIC 7361 Employment agencies
Robert Leon

D-U-N-S 25-990-8291   (HQ)
FNF CANADA COMPANY
(*Suby of* FIDELITY NATIONAL FINANCIAL,
INC.)
2700 Argentia Rd, Mississauga, ON, L5N 5V4
(905) 813-7174
Emp Here 220   *Sales* 641,090,400
SIC 6361 Title insurance
Reta Coburn
Marian Poon

D-U-N-S 20-609-6273   (SL)
FOOD SERVICE SOLUTIONS INC
6599 Kitimat Rd Unit 2, Mississauga, ON, L5N
4J4
(905) 363-0309
Emp Here 24   *Sales* 10,309,158
SIC 5046 Commercial equipment, nec
Chris Koehler
Farhad Oseyn
Megan Koehler
Miles Chesher
Jim Greenwood
Jill Koehler

D-U-N-S 20-329-7585   (HQ)
FUGRO CANADA CORP
FUGRO ROADWARE, A DIVISION OF
(*Suby of* STICHTING ADMINISTRATIEKAN-
TOOR FUGRO)
2505 Meadowvale Blvd, Mississauga, ON,
L5N 5S2
(905) 567-2870
Sales 18,650,600
SIC 8742 Management consulting services
Mark Heine
Paul Verhagen
Brice Bouffard

D-U-N-S 24-000-5475   (SL)
FUSEPOINT INC
6800 Millcreek Dr, Mississauga, ON, L5N 4J9
(905) 363-3737
Emp Here 130   *Sales* 16,220,880
SIC 8741 Management services
George Kerns

D-U-N-S 24-341-9244   (SL)
GAP WIRELESS INC
GWI TELECOM
2880 Argentia Rd Unit 8-9, Mississauga, ON,
L5N 7X8
(905) 826-3781
Emp Here 60   *Sales* 26,830,440
SIC 5065 Electronic parts and equipment, nec
Marc Bouvrette
Glenn Poulos

D-U-N-S 20-163-2924   (HQ)
GE BETZDEARBORN CANADA COMPANY
GE BETZ CANADA
(*Suby of* SUEZ)
2300 Meadowvale Blvd, Mississauga, ON,
L5N 5P9
(905) 465-3030
Sales 13,120,800
SIC 6712 Bank holding companies
George Oliver
Kent Roy
Peter Donovan
David Brennan

D-U-N-S 20-174-5465   (SL)
GE VFS CANADA LIMITED PARTNERSHIP
2300 Meadowvale Blvd Suite 200, Mississauga, ON, L5N 5P9
(905) 858-5100
Emp Here 50   *Sales* 11,237,200
SIC 6153 Short-term business credit institutions, except agricultural
Richard Hirsch

D-U-N-S 20-161-2512   (HQ)
GENERAL ELECTRIC CANADA COMPANY
GE ENERGY
(*Suby of* GENERAL ELECTRIC COMPANY)
1919 Minnesota Crt, Mississauga, ON, L5N

0C9
(905) 858-5100
Emp Here 500   *Sales* 2,829,150,000
SIC 3625 Relays and industrial controls

D-U-N-S 24-946-9818   (SL)
**GENERAL ELECTRIC CANADA INTERNA-
TIONAL INC**
(*Suby of* GENERAL ELECTRIC COMPANY)
2300 Meadowvale Blvd Suite 100, Missis-
sauga, ON, L5N 5P9
(905) 858-5100
Emp Here 150   *Sales* 26,810,850
SIC 8711 Engineering services
Lyne Girard
Bruce N. Futterer
Manjit K Sharma

D-U-N-S 20-559-6679   (HQ)
GENERAL ELECTRIC CAPITAL CANADA
*TRANSPORTATION AND INDUSTRIAL
FUNDING*
(*Suby of* GENERAL ELECTRIC COMPANY)
2300 Meadowvale Blvd, Mississauga, ON,
L5N 5P9
(905) 858-5100
Emp Here 250   *Sales* 478,612,800
SIC 6153 Short-term business credit institu-
tions, except agricultural
Elyse Allan
Robert Weese
David Daubaras
Peter Donovan
David Brennan
Kenneth Pizer

D-U-N-S 25-102-4845   (SL)
GHD INC
6705 Millcreek Dr Suite 1, Mississauga, ON,
L5N 5M4
(416) 213-7121
Emp Here 70   *Sales* 12,317,060
SIC 8711 Engineering services
Chrisann Boucher

D-U-N-S 20-349-3598   (SL)
**GLASSHOUSE PHARMACEUTICALS LIM-
ITED CANADA**
2145 Meadowpine Blvd, Mississauga, ON,
L5N 6R8
(905) 821-7600
Emp Here 12   *Sales* 13,264,140
SIC 5122 Drugs, proprietaries, and sundries
Kenneth Paige
Rajiv Mathur
Marcel Vieno
Jan Sahai
Erika Derango
Colin Watson
Faye Vandervooren

D-U-N-S 25-402-4656   (SL)
**GLAXOSMITHKLINE CONSUMER HEALTH-
CARE INC**
THE BUCKLEY'S COMPANY
(*Suby of* GLAXOSMITHKLINE PLC)
7333 Mississauga Rd, Mississauga, ON, L5N
6L4
(905) 819-3000
Emp Here 70   *Sales* 77,374,150
SIC 5122 Drugs, proprietaries, and sundries
David Linsenmeier
Ian Khan
Lynette Miranda

D-U-N-S 20-555-6368   (HQ)
GLAXOSMITHKLINE INC
GSK
(*Suby of* GLAXOSMITHKLINE PLC)
7333 Mississauga Rd, Mississauga, ON, L5N
6L4
(905) 819-3000
Emp Here 900   *Sales* 596,869,200
SIC 2834 Pharmaceutical preparations
Hal Barron
Josee Gravelle

D-U-N-S 20-191-4681   (BR)

GLAXOSMITHKLINE INC
(*Suby of* GLAXOSMITHKLINE PLC)
7333 Mississauga Rd, Mississauga, ON, L5N
6L4
(905) 819-3000
Emp Here 100
SIC 2834 Pharmaceutical preparations
 Paul Lucas

D-U-N-S 24-853-4203   (SL)
GLOBAL COMMODITIES TRADERS INC
2430 Meadowpine Blvd Suite 103, Mississauga, ON, L5N 6S2
(905) 908-0092
Emp Here 5   *Sales* 17,936,974
SIC 5159 Farm-product raw materials, nec
 Noor Un Faridi
 Faisal Usmani
 Hasan Talsar
 Muhammad Aftab Ghouri

D-U-N-S 20-279-6470   (SL)
GO SMOOTH TRANSPORT LTD
7 Rimini Mews, Mississauga, ON, L5N 4K1
(905) 696-7023
Emp Here 1   *Sales* 16,219,308
SIC 4212 Local trucking, without storage
 Bob Richardson
 Eric Carusi
 Brad Crowther
 Matthew Crowther
 Gordon Crowther

D-U-N-S 24-794-8797   (HQ)
GOLDER ASSOCIATES CORPORATION
6925 Century Ave Suite 100, Mississauga,
ON, L5N 7K2
(905) 567-4444
Sales 752,669,929
SIC 8711 Engineering services
 B H Conlin
 Mike Moran

D-U-N-S 24-665-1244   (HQ)
GOLDER ASSOCIATES LTD
(*Suby of* GOLDER ASSOCIATES CORPORATION)
6925 Century Ave, Mississauga, ON, L5N 0E3
(905) 567-4444
Emp Here 300   *Sales* 469,368,911
SIC 8711 Engineering services
 Mark Brightman
 Tony Linardi
 Jill Lepage

D-U-N-S 24-829-6139   (HQ)
HARRIS CANADA SYSTEMS, INC
(*Suby of* L3HARRIS TECHNOLOGIES, INC.)
2895 Argentia Rd Unit 5, Mississauga, ON,
L5N 8G6
(905) 817-8300
Emp Here 300   *Sales* 237,648,600
SIC 3679 Electronic components, nec
 Daniel P E Fournier
 Eugene S Cavallucci
 Charles J Greene
 Ken Morrison

D-U-N-S 25-100-2689   (HQ)
HENKEL CANADA CORPORATION
HENKEL LOCTITE
(*Suby of* HENKEL AG & CO. KGAA)
2515 Meadowpine Blvd Unit 1, Mississauga,
ON, L5N 6C3
(905) 814-6511
Emp Here 100   *Sales* 341,595,972
SIC 5169 Chemicals and allied products, nec
 Robert Bertok
 Carolyn Newson
 Hans Van Bylen

D-U-N-S 25-360-2049   (HQ)
HILL-ROM CANADA LTD
BATESVILLE CASKET CANADA, DIV OF
(*Suby of* HILL-ROM HOLDINGS, INC.)
6950 Creditview Rd Unit 4, Mississauga, ON,
L5N 0A6

(905) 206-1355
Sales 31,302,180
SIC 5047 Medical and hospital equipment
 Wayne Flynn
 Peter Soderberg

D-U-N-S 20-806-3024   (HQ)
HINO MOTORS CANADA, LTD
(*Suby of* TOYOTA MOTOR CORPORATION)
6975 Creditview Rd Unit 2, Mississauga, ON,
L5N 8E9
(905) 670-3352
Sales 25,495,050
SIC 5012 Automobiles and other motor vehicles
 Yumiko Kawamura
 Shavak Madon
 Takashi Ono
 Yoshiniro Noguchi

D-U-N-S 20-221-3096   (HQ)
HOFFMANN-LA ROCHE LIMITED
ROCHE CANADA
(*Suby of* ROCHE HOLDING AG)
7070 Mississauga Rd, Mississauga, ON, L5N
5M8
(800) 561-1759
Emp Here 458   *Sales* 243,389,996
SIC 2834 Pharmaceutical preparations
 Ronald Miller

D-U-N-S 24-317-1779   (BR)
HOME DEPOT OF CANADA INC
HOME DEPOT
(*Suby of* THE HOME DEPOT INC)
2920 Argentia Rd, Mississauga, ON, L5N 8C5
(905) 814-3860
Emp Here 183
SIC 5251 Hardware stores

D-U-N-S 24-142-9968   (HQ)
HOMESTARTS INCORPORATED
6537 Mississauga Rd Unit B, Mississauga,
ON, L5N 1A6
(905) 858-1110
Sales 17,744,300
SIC 8748 Business consulting, nec
 Diane Kurt

D-U-N-S 24-589-2950   (SL)
**HUB PARKING TECHNOLOGY CANADA
LTD**
HUB CANADA
(*Suby of* ENTE ARCIDIOCESI DI BOLOGNA)
2900 Argentia Rd Suite 1, Mississauga, ON,
L5N 7X9
(905) 813-1966
Emp Here 23   *Sales* 10,285,002
SIC 5065 Electronic parts and equipment, nec
 John Lovell

D-U-N-S 24-659-6910   (HQ)
ICYNENE INC
(*Suby of* FFL PARTNERS, LLC)
6747 Campobello Rd, Mississauga, ON, L5N
2L7
(905) 363-4040
Sales 12,708,640
SIC 3086 Plastics foam products
 Mark Sarvary
 Randy Scott
 Scott Campbell
 Sheila Cipriani
 Larry Genyn
 Sheila Cipriani

D-U-N-S 25-102-6530   (HQ)
**INDUSTRIAL ROOF CONSULTANTS (IRC)
GROUP INC**
2121 Argentia Rd Suite 401, Mississauga,
ON, L5N 2X4
(905) 607-7244
Emp Here 35   *Sales* 22,342,375
SIC 8711 Engineering services
 Albert Duwyn

D-U-N-S 20-385-2152   (HQ)
INFRA PIPE SOLUTIONS LTD

(*Suby of* WYNNCHURCH CAPITAL, LLC)
6507 Mississauga Rd Unit A, Mississauga,
ON, L5N 1A6
(905) 858-0206
Sales 33,614,875
SIC 3498 Fabricated pipe and fittings
 Sandeep Dhillon

D-U-N-S 24-829-8978   (SL)
INGLIS, D.W. LIMITED
CANADIAN TIRE 169
6670 Meadowvale Town Centre Cir, Mississauga, ON, L5N 4B7
(905) 821-1087
Emp Here 172   *Sales* 108,236,160
SIC 5531 Auto and home supply stores
 Douglas Inglis
 Karen Inglis

D-U-N-S 20-011-4572   (BR)
INTACT INSURANCE COMPANY
(*Suby of* INTACT FINANCIAL CORPORATION)
6925 Century Ave Suite 900, Mississauga,
ON, L5N 0E3
(905) 858-1070
Emp Here 85
SIC 6331 Fire, marine, and casualty insurance
 Roberta Ray

D-U-N-S 24-564-7701   (HQ)
INTERLINE BRANDS INC
SEXAUER LTD
6990 Creditview Rd Suite 4, Mississauga, ON,
L5N 8R9
(905) 821-8292
Emp Here 15   *Sales* 22,358,700
SIC 5074 Plumbing and heating equipment
and supplies (hydronics)
 Jim Davy

D-U-N-S 24-692-5036   (HQ)
INTERTEK HEALTH SCIENCES INC.
*INTERTEK SCIENTIFIC AND REGULATORY
CONSULTING SERVICES*
(*Suby of* INTERTEK GROUP PLC)
2233 Argentia Rd Suite 201, Mississauga,
ON, L5N 2X7
(905) 542-2900
Sales 29,151,350
SIC 8748 Business consulting, nec
 Matthew Allen

D-U-N-S 24-883-3720   (SL)
IRC BUILDING SCIENCES GROUP
LE GROUPE IRC
2121 Argentia Rd Suite 401, Mississauga,
ON, L5N 2X4
(905) 607-7244
Emp Here 70   *Sales* 12,317,060
SIC 8711 Engineering services
 Albert Duwyn

D-U-N-S 25-213-4739   (SL)
JACOX HARLEY-DAVIDSON INC
2815 Argentia Rd, Mississauga, ON, L5N 8G6
(905) 858-0966
Emp Here 25   *Sales* 12,451,950
SIC 5571 Motorcycle dealers
 Pat Jacox
 Marshall Horner

D-U-N-S 20-928-1153   (HQ)
JOHN BROOKS COMPANY LIMITED
2625 Meadowpine Blvd, Mississauga, ON,
L5N 7K5
(905) 624-4200
Emp Here 50   *Sales* 63,404,900
SIC 5084 Industrial machinery and equipment
 Gord Bell
 Peter Smith
 Roger Minkhorst
 Keith Minkhorst

D-U-N-S 20-222-4226   (HQ)
JOHNSON-ROSE INC
7300 East Danbro Cres, Mississauga, ON,
L5N 6C2

(905) 817-1470
Emp Here 28   *Sales* 16,625,910
SIC 5087 Service establishment equipment
 Ernest Berman
 Elliott Berman
 Saul Berman
 Barry Berman
 Hilda Berman

D-U-N-S 24-896-5787   (SL)
KARL STORZ ENDOSCOPY CANADA LTD
7171 Millcreek Dr, Mississauga, ON, L5N 3R3
(905) 816-8100
Emp Here 45   *Sales* 11,545,290
SIC 3845 Electromedical equipment
 Karl Storz

D-U-N-S 25-370-1940   (HQ)
KEYENCE CANADA INC
(*Suby of* KEYENCE CORPORATION)
6775 Financial Dr Suite 202, Mississauga,
ON, L5N 0A4
(905) 366-7655
Sales 19,951,092
SIC 5085 Industrial supplies
 Yyul King

D-U-N-S 20-171-1546   (HQ)
KONE INC
ASCENSEURS RE-NO
(*Suby of* KONE OYJ)
6696 Financial Dr Suite 2, Mississauga, ON,
L5N 7J6
(905) 858-8383
Emp Here 35   *Sales* 43,592,256
SIC 7699 Repair services, nec
 Henrik Ehrnrooth
 Ralf Heitz

D-U-N-S 24-394-3615   (HQ)
KRUGER PRODUCTS L.P.
(*Suby of* KRUGER INC)
1900 Minnesota Crt Suite 200, Mississauga,
ON, L5N 5R5
(905) 812-6900
Emp Here 100   *Sales* 908,207,137
SIC 2621 Paper mills
 Mario Gosselin

D-U-N-S 20-176-6610   (SL)
KTS TRADING INC
3744 Trelawny Cir, Mississauga, ON, L5N 5J7
(905) 824-5679
Emp Here 50   *Sales* 19,575,100
SIC 6799 Investors, nec
 Kamal Saridar
 Majda Yousif

D-U-N-S 20-264-3094   (BR)
KUEHNE + NAGEL LTD
(*Suby of* KUHNE HOLDING AG)
2300 Hogan Dr, Mississauga, ON, L5N 0C8
(905) 567-4168
Emp Here 500
SIC 4731 Freight transportation arrangement
 Tony Joe Hull

D-U-N-S 20-158-1691   (BR)
LABORATOIRES ABBOTT, LIMITEE
ABBOTT DIAGNOSTICS, DIV OF
(*Suby of* ABBOTT LABORATORIES)
7115 Millcreek Dr, Mississauga, ON, L5N 3R3
(905) 858-2450
Emp Here 100
SIC 2834 Pharmaceutical preparations
 Dan Harma

D-U-N-S 24-061-7829   (HQ)
LAKESIDE PROCESS CONTROLS LTD
2475 Hogan Dr, Mississauga, ON, L5N 0E9
(905) 412-0500
Emp Here 105   *Sales* 68,282,200
SIC 5084 Industrial machinery and equipment
 Gregory Houston
 Gregory Robertson
 Scott James

D-U-N-S 25-509-3130   (SL)

LANGEN PACKAGING INC
MPAC LANGEN
(*Suby of* MPAC GROUP PLC)
6500 Kitimat Rd Unit 1, Mississauga, ON, L5N
2B8
(905) 670-7200
Emp Here 100   *Sales* 48,773,000
SIC 5084 Industrial machinery and equipment
  Jose Cornejo
  Alan Makins
  William Wilkins
  Mohammad Attal Ibrahimi
  Baljit Virdee
  Daniel Jackson

    D-U-N-S 24-543-9294   (HQ)
LAWSON PRODUCTS INC. (ONTARIO)
PREMIER FASTENERS (DIV OF)
(*Suby of* LAWSON PRODUCTS, INC.)
7315 Rapistan Crt, Mississauga, ON, L5N 5Z4
(905) 567-0089
Sales 19,001,040
SIC 5085 Industrial supplies
  Scott Aimers

    D-U-N-S 24-884-4453   (SL)
LEESWOOD DESIGN BUILD LTD
LEESWOOD CONSTRUCTION
7200 West Credit Ave, Mississauga, ON, L5N
5N1
(416) 309-4482
Emp Here 38   *Sales* 17,887,778
SIC 1542 Nonresidential construction, nec
  Michael Clark
  Bradley Woodbine
  Patrick Spanjers

    D-U-N-S 25-510-6387   (SL)
LINVATEC CANADA ULC
CONMED LINVATEC
(*Suby of* CONMED CORPORATION)
2330 Millrace Crt Unit 5, Mississauga, ON,
L5N 1W2
(905) 814-8900
Emp Here 45   *Sales* 20,122,830
SIC 5047 Medical and hospital equipment
  Richard Mckillop

    D-U-N-S 24-677-0668   (SL)
LUMEN DYNAMICS GROUP INC
LUMEN DYNAMICS
(*Suby of* EXCELITAS TECHNOLOGIES
HOLDINGS LLC)
2260 Argentia Rd, Mississauga, ON, L5N 6H7
(905) 821-2600
Emp Here 90   *Sales* 20,456,010
SIC 3827 Optical instruments and lenses
  David Nislick
  Daniel Colbert
  John Nestor
  Sola Kuk
  Tony Lastoria
  Sylvia Peat

    D-U-N-S 24-751-5638   (HQ)
LUXOTTICA CANADA INC
LENSCRAFTERS
(*Suby of* DELFIN SARL)
2000 Argentia Rd Suite 2, Mississauga, ON,
L5N 1P7
(905) 858-0008
Emp Here 15   *Sales* 275,305,500
SIC 5995 Optical goods stores
  Dominic Guglielmi

    D-U-N-S 24-371-9023   (HQ)
LUXOTTICA RETAIL CANADA INC
PEARLE VISION
(*Suby of* DELFIN SARL)
2000 Argentia Rd Unit 2, Mississauga, ON,
L5N 1P7
(905) 858-0008
Emp Here 15   *Sales* 367,074,000
SIC 5995 Optical goods stores
  Michael A. Boxer
  Kerry Bradley

    D-U-N-S 24-341-0714   (SL)

LYNCH DYNAMICS INC
1799 Argentia Rd, Mississauga, ON, L5N 3A2
(905) 363-2400
Emp Here 62   *Sales* 14,091,918
SIC 3812 Search and navigation equipment
  Ernest Lynch
  Angela Lynch

    D-U-N-S 24-719-1885   (HQ)
LYNCH FLUID CONTROLS INC
1799 Argentia Rd, Mississauga, ON, L5N 3A2
(905) 363-2400
Sales 16,327,225
SIC 3492 Fluid power valves and hose fittings

    D-U-N-S 24-308-7541   (HQ)
M & M MEAT SHOPS LTD
M&M FOOD MARKET
2240 Argentia Rd Suite 100, Mississauga,
ON, L5N 2K7
(905) 465-6325
Emp Here 100   *Sales* 38,152,010
SIC 5411 Grocery stores
  Andy O' Brian

    D-U-N-S 24-204-7624   (SL)
M K IMPEX CANADA
6382 Lisgar Dr, Mississauga, ON, L5N 6X1
(416) 509-4462
Emp Here 20   *Sales* 25,144,020
SIC 5172 Petroleum products, nec
  Ketan Ketakia

    D-U-N-S 24-329-9786   (HQ)
MA PMGI BROKERAGE INC
6505 Mississauga Rd Unit A, Mississauga,
ON, L5N 1A6
(905) 542-9100
Emp Here 10   *Sales* 11,237,200
SIC 6163 Loan brokers
  Bob Ord
  Alice Chan

    D-U-N-S 20-161-1308   (HQ)
MAPLE LEAF FOODS INC
MAPLE LEAF
6985 Financial Dr, Mississauga, ON, L5N 0A1
(905) 285-5000
Emp Here 665   *Sales* 2,649,959,945
SIC 2011 Meat packing plants
  Michael H. Mccain
  Curtis Frank
  Ben Brooks
  Rocco Cappuccitti
  Chris Compton
  Adam Grogan
  Ian Henry
  Lynda Kuhn
  Josh Kuehnbaum
  Rory Mcalpine

    D-U-N-S 20-409-5640   (BR)
MAPLE LEAF FOODS INC
MAPLE LEAF POULTRY
(*Suby of* MAPLE LEAF FOODS INC)
2626 Argentia Rd, Mississauga, ON, L5N 5N2
(905) 890-0053
Emp Here 110
SIC 2015 Poultry slaughtering and processing
  Ben Brooks

    D-U-N-S 24-317-5200   (BR)
MAPLE LEAF FOODS INC
(*Suby of* MAPLE LEAF FOODS INC)
6985 Financial Dr, Mississauga, ON, L5N 0A1
(905) 285-5000
Emp Here 600
SIC 2011 Meat packing plants
  Adam Grogan

    D-U-N-S 20-145-5730   (HQ)
MAPLE REINDERS CONSTRUCTORS LTD
MAPLE CDB CENTRAL JV
(*Suby of* REINDERS GROUP LTD)
2660 Argentia Rd, Mississauga, ON, L5N 5V4
(905) 821-4844
Sales 14,076,640

SIC 8711 Engineering services
  Frederick J Reinders
  Michael Reinders
  John Haanstra

    D-U-N-S 20-513-5440   (HQ)
MAPLE REINDERS GROUP LTD
(*Suby of* REINDERS GROUP LTD)
2660 Argentia Rd, Mississauga, ON, L5N 5V4
(905) 821-4844
Emp Here 50   *Sales* 91,377,250
SIC 6712 Bank holding companies
  Harold Reinders
  Robert Zen
  Paul Gibson
  Ken Kamminga
  Eric Van Ginkel

    D-U-N-S 24-905-3273   (HQ)
MAPLE-REINDERS INC
(*Suby of* REINDERS GROUP LTD)
2660 Argentia Rd, Mississauga, ON, L5N 5V4
(905) 821-4844
Emp Here 4   *Sales* 14,258,450
SIC 1542 Nonresidential construction, nec
  Michael Reinders
  Joe Zwaagstra
  Eric Van Ginkel

    D-U-N-S 24-875-9771   (HQ)
MAPLEHURST BAKERIES INC
CATALOG SALES, DIV OF
(*Suby of* GEORGE WESTON LIMITED)
2095 Meadowvale Blvd, Mississauga, ON,
L5N 5N1
(905) 567-0660
Emp Here 150   *Sales* 414,277,250
SIC 2053 Frozen bakery products, except
bread
  Ralph Robinson

    D-U-N-S 24-217-5578   (HQ)
MARTIN-BROWER OF CANADA CO
MARTIN-BROWER
(*Suby of* REYES HOLDINGS, L.L.C.)
6985 Financial Dr 3rd Fl, Mississauga, ON,
L5N 0G3
(905) 363-7000
Emp Here 55   *Sales* 502,519,800
SIC 5113 Industrial and personal service pa-
per
  Peter Hobbes
  Roochita Patel

    D-U-N-S 20-295-5951   (SL)
MARWAL INVESTMENTS INC
2875 Argentia Rd Unit 2, Mississauga, ON,
L5N 8G6
(905) 813-3005
Emp Here 90   *Sales* 37,846
SIC 6719 Holding companies, nec
  Marlene Budgell
  Wally Budgell

    D-U-N-S 24-138-5574   (HQ)
MARY KAY COSMETICS LTD
(*Suby of* MARY KAY HOLDING CORPORA-
TION)
2020 Meadowvale Blvd, Mississauga, ON,
L5N 6Y2
(905) 858-0020
Emp Here 108   *Sales* 45,410,310
SIC 5122 Drugs, proprietaries, and sundries
  Ray Patrick
  Linda Rose

    D-U-N-S 25-513-9677   (BR)
MATCOR AUTOMOTIVE INC
7299 East Danbro Cres, Mississauga, ON,
L5N 6P8
(905) 819-9900
Emp Here 130
SIC 3465 Automotive stampings

    D-U-N-S 24-421-9833   (HQ)
MATCOR METAL FABRICATION INC
7275 East Danbro Cres, Mississauga, ON,
L5N 6P8

(905) 814-7479
Emp Here 250   *Sales* 113,166,000
SIC 3699 Electrical equipment and supplies,
nec
  John Dogoje
  Manfred Kretschmer
  Enrico Depasquale

    D-U-N-S 24-062-6791   (SL)
MAUI JIM CANADA ULC
MAUI JIM SUNGLASSES
2830 Argentia Rd Unit 3, Mississauga, ON,
L5N 8G4
(905) 286-9714
Emp Here 25   *Sales* 13,013,550
SIC 5099 Durable goods, nec
  Michael W. Dalton

    D-U-N-S 24-992-6189   (SL)
**MEADOWVALE FORD SALES AND SER-
VICE LIMITED**
2230 Battleford Rd, Mississauga, ON, L5N
3K6
(905) 542-3673
Emp Here 55   *Sales* 34,610,400
SIC 5511 New and used car dealers
  Jay Gandhi

    D-U-N-S 24-812-1675   (SL)
MEDICALE ABBOTT CANADA, INC
(*Suby of* ABBOTT LABORATORIES)
6975 Creditview Rd Unit 1, Mississauga, ON,
L5N 8E9
(905) 812-8600
Emp Here 140   *Sales* 74,949,280
SIC 5047 Medical and hospital equipment
  Brian B. Yoor
  Benedetta D'elia
  Rina Mercuri
  Jorge Sacco

    D-U-N-S 20-122-7589   (SL)
MENU FOODS INCOME FUND
(*Suby of* SIMMONS PET FOOD ON, INC)
8 Falconer Dr Unit 1, Mississauga, ON, L5N
1B1
(905) 826-3870
Emp Here 721   *Sales* 396,544,953
SIC 6722 Management investment, open-end
  Mark A. Wiens
  C. Ian Ross
  Alexander Aird
  L. Gale Prince
  Eric Demirian
  Thomas Di Giacomo

    D-U-N-S 20-555-6439   (BR)
METRO ONTARIO INC
METRO
(*Suby of* METRO INC)
3221 Derry Rd W Suite 16, Mississauga, ON,
L5N 7L7
(905) 785-1844
Emp Here 150
SIC 5411 Grocery stores
  Bob Leier

    D-U-N-S 24-953-0205   (BR)
METRO ONTARIO INC
DOMINION STORES
(*Suby of* METRO INC)
6677 Meadowvale Town Centre Cir, Missis-
sauga, ON, L5N 2R5
(905) 826-2717
Emp Here 200
SIC 5411 Grocery stores
  Bob Dudegon

    D-U-N-S 24-545-5076   (HQ)
MICROSOFT CANADA INC
MICROSOFT
(*Suby of* MICROSOFT CORPORATION)
1950 Meadowvale Blvd, Mississauga, ON,
L5N 8L9
(905) 568-0434
Emp Here 400   *Sales* 347,978,800
SIC 5045 Computers, peripherals, and soft-
ware

Keith Dolliver
Eric Gales
Benjamin Orndorff

D-U-N-S 24-977-1346   (SL)
MIQ LOGISTICS, LLC
(*Suby of* MIQ HOLDINGS, INC.)
6580 Millcreek Dr Suite 905, Mississauga,
ON, L5N 8B3
(905) 542-7525
Emp Here 75   *Sales* 15,427,950
SIC 4213 Trucking, except local
David Griffith

D-U-N-S 20-132-8080   (SL)
MISSISSAUGA CRUISE SHIP CENTRE
EXPEDIA CRUISE SHIP CENTRE
6465 Millcreek Dr Suite 170, Mississauga,
ON, L5N 5R3
(905) 821-7447
Emp Here 22   *Sales* 11,439,274
SIC 4724 Travel agencies
Doug Edmonds

D-U-N-S 20-791-6180   (HQ)
MITUTOYO CANADA INC
(*Suby of* MITUTOYO CORPORATION)
2121 Meadowvale Blvd, Mississauga, ON,
L5N 5N1
(905) 821-1261
Emp Here 50   *Sales* 28,501,560
SIC 5084 Industrial machinery and equipment

D-U-N-S 24-685-6541   (SL)
MSI STONE ULC
(*Suby of* M S INTERNATIONAL, INC.)
2140 Meadowpine Blvd, Mississauga, ON,
L5N 6H6
(905) 812-6100
Emp Here 30   *Sales* 13,718,466
SIC 5032 Brick, stone, and related material
Manahar Shah
Rajesh Shah
Chandrika Shah
Rupesh Shah
Raman Mangat

D-U-N-S 20-327-1770   (SL)
NATCO PHARMA (CANADA) INC
(*Suby of* NATCO PHARMA LIMITED)
2000 Argetia Rd Plaza 1 Suite 200, Missis-
sauga, ON, L5N 1P7
(905) 997-3353
Emp Here 16   *Sales* 25,472,480
SIC 5122 Drugs, proprietaries, and sundries
Madhusudhan Ventakatachari

D-U-N-S 20-302-1204   (HQ)
**NEPTUNE TECHNOLOGY GROUP
(CANADA) LIMITED**
(*Suby of* ROPER TECHNOLOGIES, INC.)
7275 West Credit Ave, Mississauga, ON, L5N
5M9
(905) 858-4211
Sales 11,364,450
SIC 3824 Fluid meters and counting devices
David Stoddart

D-U-N-S 25-099-3060   (HQ)
NITROCHEM CORP
6733 Mississauga Rd Suite 306, Mississauga,
ON, L5N 6J5
(905) 814-6665
Sales 42,603,150
SIC 2899 Chemical preparations, nec
Eric Brooks
Cathy Mcphail

D-U-N-S 20-011-2535   (HQ)
NOVARTIS ANIMAL HEALTH CANADA INC
(*Suby of* ELI LILLY AND COMPANY)
2000 Argentia Rd Suite 400, Mississauga,
ON, L5N 1P7
(905) 814-0840
Sales 99,481,050
SIC 5122 Drugs, proprietaries, and sundries
Paul Leger
Pauline Chan

Jason Drake
Noami Potts
Stefan Kundert
Robert Pelzer
Susan Andrew
Jyoti Singh
Steve Myette
France Gagne

D-U-N-S 20-188-6756   (BR)
NOVARTIS PHARMA CANADA INC
CIBA VISION CANADA DIV
(*Suby of* NOVARTIS AG)
2150 Torquay Mews, Mississauga, ON, L5N
2M6

Emp Here 280
SIC 5048 Ophthalmic goods
Paul Smyth

D-U-N-S 24-692-1373   (SL)
NOVO NORDISK CANADA INC
(*Suby of* NOVO NORDISK FONDEN)
2476 Argentia Rd Unit 101, Mississauga, ON,
L5N 6M1
(905) 629-4222
Emp Here 95   *Sales* 39,217,995
SIC 5122 Drugs, proprietaries, and sundries
Claus Eilerson
Sean Weir

D-U-N-S 24-388-2417   (BR)
NPL CANADA LTD
(*Suby of* SOUTHWEST GAS HOLDINGS,
INC.)
7505 Danbro Cres, Mississauga, ON, L5N
6P9
(905) 821-8383
Emp Here 100
SIC 1623 Water, sewer, and utility lines
Randy Taylor

D-U-N-S 24-886-5156   (BR)
**NTN BEARING CORPORATION OF
CANADA LIMITED**
NTN BEARING MANUFACTURING CANADA
(*Suby of* NTN CORPORATION)
6740 Kitimat Rd, Mississauga, ON, L5N 1M6
(905) 826-5500
Emp Here 115
SIC 3562 Ball and roller bearings

D-U-N-S 24-393-0414   (SL)
NULOGX INC
*NULOGX MANAGE TRANSPORTATION SO-
LUTIONS*
2233 Argentia Rd Suite 202, Mississauga,
ON, L5N 2X7
(905) 486-1162
Emp Here 50   *Sales* 11,895,050
SIC 8742 Management consulting services
Robert Drassinower
Doug Payne

D-U-N-S 24-923-5631   (HQ)
NUVO PHARMACEUTICALS INC
NUVO PHARMACEUTICALS
6733 Mississauga Rd Unit 610, Mississauga,
ON, L5N 6J5
(905) 673-6980
Emp Here 42   *Sales* 15,160,524
SIC 2834 Pharmaceutical preparations
Jesse Ledger
Tina Loucaides
Mary-Jane Burkett
Cally Lunetta
Robert Harris
John London
Daniel Chicoine
Anthony Dobranowski
Jacques Messier
David Copeland

D-U-N-S 25-749-1902   (HQ)
OBSIDIAN GROUP INC
CRABBY JOES BAR
1770 Argentia Rd, Mississauga, ON, L5N 3S7

(905) 814-8030
Emp Here 10   *Sales* 27,872,400
SIC 6794 Patent owners and lessors
Gus Karamountzos

D-U-N-S 20-187-4018   (HQ)
ONTARIO CONSERVATORY OF MUSIC INC
2915 Argentia Rd Unit 3, Mississauga, ON,
L5N 8G6
(905) 286-1133
Emp Here 12   *Sales* 27,132,000
SIC 8299 Schools and educational services,
nec
Frank Zolnai Sr
Bernie Lawler
Frank Zolnai Jr

D-U-N-S 24-095-6797   (SL)
OPAL OPTICAL LTD
10 Falconer Dr Unit 11, Mississauga, ON, L5N
3L8

Emp Here 27   *Sales* 12,073,698
SIC 5049 Professional equipment, nec
Jack Greenwood
Kelly Jarmain

D-U-N-S 25-997-3915   (HQ)
OPTIVA CANADA INC
(*Suby of* OPTIVA INC)
2233 Argentia Rd Suite 302, Mississauga,
ON, L5N 2X7
(905) 625-2622
Emp Here 5   *Sales* 184,573,000
SIC 7371 Custom computer programming ser-
vices
Danielle Royston
Scott Brighton
Anin Basu
Jozsef Czapovics
Erez Sverdlov
Demetrios Anaipakos
Chris Helling
Christy Jones
Andrew Price
Robert Stabile

D-U-N-S 24-368-6461   (HQ)
OPTIVA INC
2233 Argentia Rd Suite 302, Mississauga,
ON, L5N 2X7
(905) 625-2622
Emp Here 113   *Sales* 137,923,734
SIC 7371 Custom computer programming ser-
vices
Danielle Royston
Jozsef Czapovics
Erez Sverdlov
Anin Basu
Mo Jamal
Matthew Rhoden
Scott Brighton
Demetrios Anaipakos
Chris Helling
Christy Jones

D-U-N-S 20-866-4524   (HQ)
PACCAR OF CANADA LTD
CANADIAN KENWORTH COMPANY
(*Suby of* PACCAR INC)
6711 Mississauga Rd Suite 500, Mississauga,
ON, L5N 4J8
(905) 858-7000
Emp Here 30   *Sales* 46,115,400
SIC 5012 Automobiles and other motor vehi-
cles
Mark C Piggott
Thomas E. Plimpton
James S. Medwid
D. D. Sobic

D-U-N-S 25-213-2923   (SL)
PARKWAY PLYMOUTH CHRYSLER LTD
2260 Battleford Rd, Mississauga, ON, L5N
3K6
(905) 567-1700
Emp Here 50   *Sales* 24,903,900
SIC 5511 New and used car dealers

Mike Karim

D-U-N-S 24-076-9596   (HQ)
PATHEON INC
(*Suby of* THERMO FISHER SCIENTIFIC
INC.)
2100 Syntex Crt, Mississauga, ON, L5N 7K9
(905) 821-4001
Emp Here 900   *Sales* 2,155,361,000
SIC 2834 Pharmaceutical preparations
Michel Lagarde
James Mullen
Stuart Grant
Michael Lytton
Michael E Lytton
Francisco Negron
Harry Gill
Rebecca Holland
Ray Guidotti
Eric Sherbet

D-U-N-S 25-293-8147   (BR)
PEEL DISTRICT SCHOOL BOARD
WEST CREDIT SECONDARY SCHOOL
(*Suby of* PEEL DISTRICT SCHOOL BOARD)
6325 Montevideo Rd, Mississauga, ON, L5N
4G7
(905) 858-3087
Emp Here 80
SIC 8211 Elementary and secondary schools
Marcel Giraldi

D-U-N-S 24-963-1391   (BR)
PEEL DISTRICT SCHOOL BOARD
MEADOWVALE SECONDARY SCHOOL
(*Suby of* PEEL DISTRICT SCHOOL BOARD)
6700 Edenwood Dr, Mississauga, ON, L5N
3B2
(905) 824-1790
Emp Here 130
SIC 8211 Elementary and secondary schools
Brent Coakwell

D-U-N-S 25-312-6395   (HQ)
PENSKE TRUCK LEASING CANADA INC
(*Suby of* PENSKE TRUCK LEASING CO.,
L.P.)
7405 East Danbro Cres, Mississauga, ON,
L5N 6P8
(905) 819-7900
Emp Here 15   *Sales* 62,787,200
SIC 7513 Truck rental and leasing, no drivers
Brian Hard

D-U-N-S 20-113-8997   (HQ)
PENTAX CANADA INC
PENTAX MEDICAL
(*Suby of* HOYA CORPORATION)
6715 Millcreek Dr Unit 1, Mississauga, ON,
L5N 5V2
(905) 286-5570
Sales 22,358,700
SIC 5043 Photographic equipment and sup-
plies
David Harrison

D-U-N-S 20-172-8318   (HQ)
**PENTECOSTAL ASSEMBLIES OF
CANADA, THE**
2450 Milltower Crt, Mississauga, ON, L5N 5Z6
(905) 542-7400
Emp Here 70   *Sales* 114,535,300
SIC 8661 Religious organizations
David Wells
David Hazzard
Murray Cornelius

D-U-N-S 24-452-4625   (HQ)
PINCHIN LTD
2470 Milltower Crt, Mississauga, ON, L5N
7W5
(905) 363-0678
Emp Here 250   *Sales* 87,708,870
SIC 8748 Business consulting, nec
Jeff Grossi
Larry Backman
Vico Paloschi
Greg Rusling

Chris Burke
Mike Agostinelli
Terence Gang

D-U-N-S 20-217-3621 (HQ)
PIONEER HI-BRED LIMITED
TONA LOGISTICS
(*Suby of* DUPONT DE NEMOURS, INC.)
1919 Minnesota Crt, Mississauga, ON, L5N 0C9
(905) 821-3300
Emp Here 300   *Sales* 889,290,000
SIC 2824 Organic fibers, noncellulosic
Bryce Eger

D-U-N-S 24-348-7407 (HQ)
PREMIER TECH HOME & GARDEN INC
(*Suby of* GESTION BELANGER, BERNARD LTEE)
1900 Minnesota Crt Suite 125, Mississauga, ON, L5N 3C9
(905) 812-8556
Emp Here 30   *Sales* 74,252,000
SIC 5199 Nondurable goods, nec
Jean Belanger
Rene Mondugo
Martin Noel

D-U-N-S 24-688-9471 (SL)
PRIDE PAK CANADA LTD
6768 Financial Dr, Mississauga, ON, L5N 7J6
(905) 828-8280
Emp Here 200   *Sales* 34,781,000
SIC 0723 Crop preparation services for market
Steven Karr

D-U-N-S 24-918-8012 (HQ)
PRIMERICA LIFE INSURANCE COMPANY OF CANADA
PRIMERICA
(*Suby of* PRIMERICA, INC.)
2000 Argentia Rd Suite 5, Mississauga, ON, L5N 1P7
(905) 812-3520
Emp Here 170   *Sales* 416,708,760
SIC 6311 Life insurance
John Adams
Jeffrey Dumanski
Guy Sauve
Richard Williams
Robert Mcdowell
John Addison
Frederick S Mallett

D-U-N-S 24-784-3816 (HQ)
QUINTERRA PROPERTY MAINTENANCE INC
6535 Millcreek Dr Unit 63, Mississauga, ON, L5N 2M2
(905) 821-7171
Emp Here 19   *Sales* 147,052,800
SIC 7349 Building maintenance services, nec
Ray Quinn
David Weakley
Frank Fini

D-U-N-S 25-117-0767 (HQ)
RBC GENERAL INSURANCE COMPANY
(*Suby of* ROYAL BANK OF CANADA)
6880 Financial Dr Suite 200, Mississauga, ON, L5N 7Y5
(905) 816-5400
Emp Here 410   *Sales* 993,690,120
SIC 6331 Fire, marine, and casualty insurance

D-U-N-S 20-817-0142 (HQ)
RBC INSURANCE COMPANY OF CANADA
(*Suby of* ROYAL BANK OF CANADA)
6880 Financial Dr Suite 200, Mississauga, ON, L5N 7Y5
(905) 949-3663
Emp Here 120   *Sales* 1,091,603,920
SIC 6411 Insurance agents, brokers, and service
David Lafayette
John D Mckenna

Stan Seggie
Rosemary Troiani
Richard Burton

D-U-N-S 25-115-2104 (SL)
RBC INSURANCE SERVICES INC
6880 Financial Dr West Tower, Mississauga, ON, L5N 7Y5
(905) 949-3663
Emp Here 20   *Sales* 14,508,780
SIC 6311 Life insurance
John Carinci
Cathy Preston

D-U-N-S 20-750-8573 (HQ)
RBC LIFE INSURANCE COMPANY
(*Suby of* ROYAL BANK OF CANADA)
6880 Financial Dr Suite 1000, Mississauga, ON, L5N 8E8
(905) 816-2746
Emp Here 400   *Sales* 3,397,779,120
SIC 6311 Life insurance
John Young
Neil Skelding

D-U-N-S 24-316-2369 (HQ)
RE/MAX REALTY SPECIALISTS INC
6850 Millcreek Dr Unit 200, Mississauga, ON, L5N 4J9
(905) 858-3434
Emp Here 150   *Sales* 169,032,000
SIC 6531 Real estate agents and managers
Greg Gilmour

D-U-N-S 24-378-8937 (HQ)
REDISHRED CAPITAL CORP
PROSHRED
6505 Mississauga Rd Suite A, Mississauga, ON, L5N 1A6
(416) 490-8600
Emp Here 10   *Sales* 11,114,028
SIC 7389 Business services, nec
Jeffrey I. Hasham
Kasia Pawluk
Ron Gable
Francesco Marascia
Robert M. Crozier
Brad E. Foster
Philip H. Gaunce
James C. Lawley
Mark J. Macmillan
Robert G. Richardson

D-U-N-S 25-510-6932 (HQ)
REGIONAL POWER INC
(*Suby of* MANULIFE FINANCIAL CORPORATION)
6755 Mississauga Rd Suite 308, Mississauga, ON, L5N 7Y2
(905) 363-4200
Sales 15,665,350
SIC 4911 Electric services
Chris Lambeck
Matt O'brien
Ryan Lapointe

D-U-N-S 24-684-3002 (SL)
REGIONAL POWER OPCO INC
(*Suby of* MANULIFE FINANCIAL CORPORATION)
6755 Mississauga Rd Suite 308, Mississauga, ON, L5N 7Y2
(905) 363-4200
Emp Here 19   *Sales* 11,905,666
SIC 4911 Electric services
Colin C. Coolican
J. Alex F. Mcdonald
William Eeuwes

D-U-N-S 24-376-5448 (HQ)
REINDERS GROUP LTD
2660 Argentia Rd, Mississauga, ON, L5N 5V4
(905) 821-4844
Emp Here 6   *Sales* 49,282,750
SIC 8711 Engineering services
Harold Reinders
Paul Gibson

Gerald Hessels
Harold Reinders
Simon Kouwenhoven
Jac G. Vanooro
Jeremy Olthuis
Eric Van Ginkel
Ken Kamminga
Keith Zorn

D-U-N-S 24-796-8241 (SL)
RESERVEAMERICA ON INC
RESERVEAMERICA
(*Suby of* PAPAY HOLDCO, LLC)
2480 Meadowvale Blvd Suite 1, Mississauga, ON, L5N 8M6
(905) 286-6600
Emp Here 130
SIC 7371 Custom computer programming services
Terry Barnes
Seth Rosenberg
Sharon Deaver-Fisher

D-U-N-S 24-337-5870 (SL)
RIELLO CANADA, INC
(*Suby of* UNITED TECHNOLOGIES CORPORATION)
2165 Meadowpine Blvd, Mississauga, ON, L5N 6H6
(905) 542-0303
Emp Here 58   *Sales* 25,150,521
SIC 3433 Heating equipment, except electric
Keith Farrell
Fausto Cacciapuoti

D-U-N-S 20-174-1139 (HQ)
RINGBALL CORPORATION
2160 Meadowpine Blvd, Mississauga, ON, L5N 6H6
(905) 826-1100
Emp Here 85   *Sales* 102,423,300
SIC 5085 Industrial supplies
Gary Scheichl

D-U-N-S 24-581-2177 (HQ)
ROBERT ALLEN FABRICS (CANADA) LTD
ROBERT ALLEN GROUP, THE
(*Suby of* DECOR HOLDINGS, INC.)
2880 Argentia Rd Unit 11, Mississauga, ON, L5N 7X8
(905) 826-7750
Emp Here 13   *Sales* 14,949,660
SIC 5131 Piece goods and notions
Brian Richards
Ronald Cordover
Saima Jafry
Jeffrey Cordover

D-U-N-S 20-160-4352 (HQ)
ROBERT BOSCH INC
SKIL BOSCH POWER TOOL, DIV OF
(*Suby of* R O B E R T B O S C H S T I F T U N G GESELLSCHAFT MIT BESCHRANKTER HAFTUNG)
6955 Creditview Rd, Mississauga, ON, L5N 1R1
(905) 826-6060
Sales 116,758,200
SIC 5085 Industrial supplies
Michael Langstaff
John Scinocca

D-U-N-S 20-042-7557 (HQ)
ROBERTSON BRIGHT INC
2875 Argentia Rd Unit 1, Mississauga, ON, L5N 8G6
(905) 813-3005
Emp Here 50   *Sales* 18,515,465
SIC 1731 Electrical work
Wally Budgell
Kirk Hochrein

D-U-N-S 25-255-0009 (HQ)
ROLLED ALLOYS-CANADA, INC
7111 Syntex Dr Suite 120, Mississauga, ON, L5N 8C3
(905) 363-0277
Emp Here 10   *Sales* 37,905,100

SIC 5051 Metals service centers and offices
Bernie Saunders
Heather Salvati

D-U-N-S 20-412-6395 (HQ)
ROTORK CONTROLS (CANADA) LTD
(*Suby of* ROTORK P.L.C.)
6705 Millcreek Dr Unit 3, Mississauga, ON, L5N 5M4
(905) 363-0313
Emp Here 23   *Sales* 35,626,950
SIC 5085 Industrial supplies
Kevin Hostetler
Jonathan Davis
Kathy Callaghan

D-U-N-S 20-008-4853 (HQ)
RUSSEL METALS INC
ACIER LEROUX
6600 Financial Dr, Mississauga, ON, L5N 7J6
(905) 819-7777
Emp Here 150   *Sales* 3,157,494,830
SIC 5051 Metals service centers and offices
John G. Reid
Marion E. Britton
John F. Maclean
Lesley Coleman
David Halcrow
Maureen A. Kelly
Ryan W. Macdermid
James F. Dinning
Alain Benedetti
Brian R. Hedges

D-U-N-S 24-889-7407 (BR)
RUSSEL METALS INC
(*Suby of* RUSSEL METALS INC)
1900 Minnesota Crt Suite 210, Mississauga, ON, L5N 3C9
(905) 567-8500
Emp Here 100
SIC 5051 Metals service centers and offices
Brian Hedges

D-U-N-S 24-343-0241 (HQ)
RYAN ULC
(*Suby of* RYAN, LLC)
6775 Financial Dr Suite 102, Mississauga, ON, L5N 0A4
(905) 567-7926
Emp Here 50   *Sales* 22,380,720
SIC 8742 Management consulting services
Garry Round
Jim Day
Michel Ducharme
Louis Galvo
Mark Joyce
Sandra Smith
Clyde Seymour
Richard Mckeown
Danny Ladouceur
Walter Gardisch

D-U-N-S 20-174-6146 (HQ)
RYDER TRUCK RENTAL CANADA LTD
RYDER CANADA
(*Suby of* RYDER SYSTEM, INC.)
6755 Mississauga Rd Suite 201, Mississauga, ON, L5N 7Y2
(905) 826-8777
Emp Here 60   *Sales* 117,950,240
SIC 7513 Truck rental and leasing, no drivers
Todd Skiles
John Deris
Marc Thibeau
Alex Madrinkian
Delores Lail
Dan Mchugh
Michael R. Thompson
Mark Edds
Robert E. Sanchez

D-U-N-S 24-386-0046 (HQ)
SAMSUNG ELECTRONICS CANADA INC
(*Suby of* SAMSUNG ELECTRONICS CO., LTD.)
2050 Derry Rd W Suite 1, Mississauga, ON,

L5N 0B9
(905) 542-3535
Emp Here 182   *Sales* 354,530,917
SIC 5064 Electrical appliances, television and radio
Seo Gy
Michael Sangwhun Park

D-U-N-S 24-676-9793   (SL)
SAMSUNG RENEWABLE ENERGY INC
(*Suby of* SAMSUNG C&T CORPORATION)
2050 Derry Rd W 2fl, Mississauga, ON, L5N 0B9
(905) 501-4934
Emp Here 28   *Sales* 17,545,192
SIC 4911 Electric services
Jeong Tack Lee
Heung-Do Kim
Youngjin Cho

D-U-N-S 20-233-6053   (HQ)
SANDVIK CANADA, INC
DORMER
(*Suby of* SANDVIK AB)
2550 Meadowvale Blvd Unit 3, Mississauga, ON, L5N 8C2
(905) 826-8900
Emp Here 60   *Sales* 341,411,000
SIC 5084 Industrial machinery and equipment
Peter Corcoran
Richard Askin
Manny Maloney
Jacqueline Richter
Claudia Stanic

D-U-N-S 20-719-5871   (BR)
SANDVIK CANADA, INC
SANDVIK MINING
(*Suby of* SANDVIK AB)
2550 Meadowvale Blvd Unit 3, Mississauga, ON, L5N 8C2
(905) 826-8900
Emp Here 200
SIC 3312 Blast furnaces and steel mills
David Thompson

D-U-N-S 20-118-6488   (HQ)
SAVVIS COMMUNICATIONS CANADA, INC
(*Suby of* CENTURYLINK, INC.)
6800 Millcreek Dr, Mississauga, ON, L5N 4J9
(905) 363-3737
Emp Here 100   *Sales* 16,220,880
SIC 8741 Management services
William D Fathers

D-U-N-S 25-990-2252   (HQ)
SCOTTS CANADA LTD
(*Suby of* THE SCOTTS MIRACLE-GRO COMPANY)
2000 Argentia Rd Suite 300, Mississauga, ON, L5N 1P7
(905) 814-7425
Emp Here 50   *Sales* 46,036,240
SIC 5199 Nondurable goods, nec
John Warren

D-U-N-S 24-377-5041   (HQ)
SEPRACOR CANADA, INC
6790 Century Ave Suite 100, Mississauga, ON, L5N 2V8
(905) 814-9145
Emp Here 1   *Sales* 16,401,000
SIC 6712 Bank holding companies
Douglas Reynolds

D-U-N-S 24-537-9631   (HQ)
SEXAUER LTD
(*Suby of* THE HOME DEPOT INC)
6990 Creditview Rd Unit 3, Mississauga, ON, L5N 8R9
(905) 821-8292
Emp Here 22   *Sales* 24,594,570
SIC 5074 Plumbing and heating equipment and supplies (hydronics)
Howard Richards

D-U-N-S 25-531-7349   (SL)
SILVER HOTEL (AMBLER) INC

FOUR POINTS BY SHERATON MISSISSAUGA MEDOWVALE
2501 Argentia Rd, Mississauga, ON, L5N 4G8
(905) 858-2424
Emp Here 100   *Sales* 9,489,900
SIC 7011 Hotels and motels
Melissa French

D-U-N-S 20-627-8798   (HQ)
SIMMONS PET FOOD ON, INC
8 Falconer Dr, Mississauga, ON, L5N 1B1
(905) 826-3870
Sales 116,972,400
SIC 2047 Dog and cat food
Mike Defrias
Paul Henderson
Todd Simmons
Mark Simmons
Mark Wiens

D-U-N-S 25-409-7181   (HQ)
SKYLINK EXPRESS INC
2000 Argentia Rd Plaza 4 Suite 101, Mississauga, ON, L5N 1W1
(416) 925-4530
Emp Here 1   *Sales* 20,023,350
SIC 4512 Air transportation, scheduled
Surjit Babra
Daniel Rocheleau
Walter Arbib
Richard Mcdole

D-U-N-S 20-529-5751   (SL)
SMITHS DETECTION MONTREAL INC
(*Suby of* SMITHS GROUP PLC)
6865 Century Ave Suite 3002, Mississauga, ON, L5N 7K2
(905) 817-5990
Emp Here 205   *Sales* 56,245,850
SIC 3812 Search and navigation equipment
Franko Cerantola

D-U-N-S 25-156-3581   (SL)
SNAP-ON TOOLS OF CANADA LTD
WHEELTRONIC
(*Suby of* SNAP-ON INCORPORATED)
6500a Millcreek Dr, Mississauga, ON, L5N 2W6
(905) 826-8600
Emp Here 160   *Sales* 35,520,160
SIC 3536 Hoists, cranes, and monorails
Brian Ross

D-U-N-S 20-349-6000   (SL)
SPECIALTY SALES & MARKETING INC
6725 Millcreek Dr Unit 5, Mississauga, ON, L5N 5V3
(905) 816-0011
Emp Here 31   *Sales* 11,290,665
SIC 5013 Motor vehicle supplies and new parts
Kenneth Coulter
Sherri Langfield

D-U-N-S 20-323-2756   (HQ)
SPP CANADA AIRCRAFT, INC
2025 Meadowvale Blvd Unit 1, Mississauga, ON, L5N 5N1
(905) 821-9339
Sales 28,893,400
SIC 3728 Aircraft parts and equipment, nec
Eli Brigler
Tetsuichiro Shibazaki
Andrew Morrow

D-U-N-S 24-632-3653   (SL)
STANDARDBRED CANADA
2150 Meadowvale Blvd Suite 1, Mississauga, ON, L5N 6R6
(905) 858-3060
Emp Here 90   *Sales* 21,487,500
SIC 8611 Business associations
Ted Smith
Rosenna So
Heather Reid

D-U-N-S 24-097-4881   (HQ)
STANLEY BLACK & DECKER CANADA

CORPORATION
STANLEY HARDWARE
(*Suby of* STANLEY BLACK & DECKER, INC.)
6275 Millcreek Dr, Mississauga, ON, L5N 7K6
(289) 290-4638
Emp Here 60   *Sales* 206,746,350
SIC 3429 Hardware, nec
James M Loree
Donald Allan Jr

D-U-N-S 24-285-8843   (SL)
STARKEY LABS-CANADA CO
2476 Argentia Rd Suite 301, Mississauga, ON, L5N 6M1
(905) 542-7555
Emp Here 155   *Sales* 35,229,795
SIC 3842 Surgical appliances and supplies
Jason Toone
William F. Austin
Jerome Ruzicka

D-U-N-S 25-214-2237   (SL)
STARWOOD HOTEL
(*Suby of* WESTMONT HOSPITALITY MANAGEMENT LIMITED)
2501 Argentia Rd, Mississauga, ON, L5N 4G8
(905) 858-2424
Emp Here 100
SIC 7011 Hotels and motels
Imran Meghani
Majid Mangalji

D-U-N-S 20-024-7492   (SL)
STORESUPPORT CANADA INC
STORE SUPPORT
2000 Argentia Rd Suite 440, Mississauga, ON, L5N 1P7
(905) 847-6513
Emp Here 200   *Sales* 32,805,400
SIC 2789 Bookbinding and related work
Sara Clarkson
Christer Lihammer
Cecelia Lihammer

D-U-N-S 20-955-9876   (SL)
STRABAG INC
(*Suby of* STRABAG SE)
6790 Century Ave Suite 401, Mississauga, ON, L5N 2V8
(905) 353-5500
Emp Here 280   *Sales* 195,549,760
SIC 1541 Industrial buildings and warehouses
Lloyd Furguson
Robert Raddlinger

D-U-N-S 25-136-1528   (SL)
STREETSVILLE HYUNDAI
6225 Mississauga Rd, Mississauga, ON, L5N 1A4
(905) 812-5401
Emp Here 30   *Sales* 14,942,340
SIC 5511 New and used car dealers
Jerry Hussar

D-U-N-S 20-789-9667   (HQ)
SUNOPTA INC
2233 Argentia Rd Suite 401, Mississauga, ON, L5N 2X7
(905) 821-9669
Emp Here 100   *Sales* 1,260,852,000
SIC 5149 Groceries and related products, nec
Joseph D. Ennen
Robert Mckeracher
Gerard Versteegh
James Gratzek
Jeff Gough
Rob Duchscher
Jill Barnett
Dean Hollis
Al Bolles
Katrina Houde

D-U-N-S 20-050-5381   (HQ)
SUNOVION PHARMACEUTICALS CANADA INC
(*Suby of* SUMITOMO CHEMICAL COMPANY, LIMITED)

6790 Century Ave Suite 100, Mississauga, ON, L5N 2V8
(905) 814-9145
Sales 11,066,400
SIC 2834 Pharmaceutical preparations
Doug Reynolds
Peter Saunders
William Neeson

D-U-N-S 20-785-1395   (SL)
TAILOR DRUGS LIMITED
SHOPPERS DRUG MART
6975 Meadowvale Town Centre Cir, Mississauga, ON, L5N 2V7
(905) 826-7112
Emp Here 70   *Sales* 17,102,960
SIC 5912 Drug stores and proprietary stores
Jayesh Tailor

D-U-N-S 25-122-9944   (SL)
TEAM FUTURES SCHOOL OF GYMNASTICS INC
6991 Millcreek Dr, Mississauga, ON, L5N 6B9

Emp Here 150   *Sales* 108,171,013
SIC 8699 Membership organizations, nec
Sharon Treleaven

D-U-N-S 24-549-3283   (HQ)
TECH DATA CANADA CORPORATION
(*Suby of* TECH DATA CORPORATION)
6911 Creditview Rd, Mississauga, ON, L5N 8G1
(905) 286-6800
Sales 267,676,000
SIC 5045 Computers, peripherals, and software
Rich Hume
Robert M. (Bob) Dutkowsky
Charles E. Adair
Harry J. Harczak , Jr
Charles V. Dannewitz

D-U-N-S 24-373-7843   (HQ)
TENOVA GOODFELLOW INC
(*Suby of* AROTEC INVESTMENTS B.V.)
6711 Mississauga Rd Suite 200, Mississauga, ON, L5N 2W3
(905) 567-3030
Sales 11,801,852
SIC 3823 Process control instruments
Howard Goodfellow
Marcello Pozzi
Maurizio Parodi
Mauro Bianchi Ferri

D-U-N-S 20-350-7058   (HQ)
TETRA TECH CANADA INC
(*Suby of* TETRA TECH, INC.)
6835 Century Ave Unit A, Mississauga, ON, L5N 7K2
(905) 369-3000
Emp Here 100   *Sales* 625,586,500
SIC 8711 Engineering services
William R. Brownlie
Robert J. Sumsion
Richard A. Lemmon

D-U-N-S 24-366-9426   (SL)
THERAPURE BIOPHARMA INC
2585 Meadowpine Blvd, Mississauga, ON, L5N 8H9
(905) 286-6200
Emp Here 310   *Sales* 102,794,140
SIC 2834 Pharmaceutical preparations
Nicholas Green
Paul Stojanovski
David N. Bell
Safa'a Al-Rais
Dina Iezzi
Dirk Alkema
David Long

D-U-N-S 20-311-7783   (SL)
THERMI GROUP
6745 Financial Dr, Mississauga, ON, L5N 7J7
(905) 813-9600
Emp Here 49   *Sales* 22,011,731

SIC 7389 Business services, nec
Bryan Bennett

D-U-N-S 24-631-7960   (HQ)
THERMO FISHER SCIENTIFIC (MISSIS-SAUGA) INC
(*Suby of* THERMO FISHER SCIENTIFIC INC.)
2845 Argentia Rd Unit 4, Mississauga, ON, L5N 8G6
(905) 890-1034
Sales 17,886,960
SIC 5049 Professional equipment, nec
Luc Dionne

D-U-N-S 24-180-2219   (SL)
THIARA SUPERMARKET LTD.
3899 Trelawny Cir Suite 1, Mississauga, ON, L5N 6S3
(905) 824-8960
Emp Here 60   *Sales* 17,904,776
SIC 5411 Grocery stores
Avater Thiara

D-U-N-S 25-147-4417   (HQ)
TRIOS CORPORATION
6755 Mississauga Rd Suite 103, Mississauga, ON, L5N 7Y2
(905) 814-7212
Sales 49,559,500
SIC 8211 Elementary and secondary schools
Frank Gerencser
Stuart Bentley

D-U-N-S 24-576-4212   (HQ)
U.S. TRAFFIC LIMITED
6645 Kitimat Rd Suite 18, Mississauga, ON, L5N 6J3
(905) 858-2222
Emp Here 20   *Sales* 11,439,274
SIC 4731 Freight transportation arrangement
John Mcdonald
James Jardine

D-U-N-S 24-977-0132   (HQ)
UNITED FOOD & COMMERCIAL WORKER CANADA
UFCW
2200 Argentia Rd Suite 175, Mississauga, ON, L5N 2K7
(905) 821-8329
Emp Here 1   *Sales* 37,024,260
SIC 8631 Labor organizations
Shawn Haggerty

D-U-N-S 20-549-5695   (SL)
UPPER CANADA - SIERRA GROUP SERVICE
7088 Financial Dr, Mississauga, ON, L5N 7H5
(905) 814-8800
Emp Here 50   *Sales* 22,358,700
SIC 5031 Lumber, plywood, and millwork
Warren Spitz
Maureen Spitz
Andrea Moore

D-U-N-S 24-632-9932   (HQ)
UPPER CANADA FOREST PRODUCTS LTD
UCS FOREST GROUP
7088 Financial Dr, Mississauga, ON, L5N 7H5
(905) 814-8000
Emp Here 50   *Sales* 79,747,920
SIC 5031 Lumber, plywood, and millwork
Warren Spitz
Maureen Spitz

D-U-N-S 20-177-6440   (HQ)
VANGUARD STEEL LTD
(*Suby of* ETABLISSEMENT TRICAN SA)
2160 Meadowpine Blvd, Mississauga, ON, L5N 6H6
(905) 821-1100
Emp Here 70   *Sales* 125,465,340
SIC 5051 Metals service centers and offices
Gary Scheichl
Craig Spence
Heino Knoop
Louis Kalchhauser

D-U-N-S 24-005-9790   (SL)
VARTEGEZ SIMONIAN PHARMACY LTD
SHOPPERS DRUG MART - GLEN ERIN PLAZA
6040 Glen Erin Dr Suite 1, Mississauga, ON, L5N 3M4
(905) 821-8020
Emp Here 43   *Sales* 10,877,022
SIC 5912 Drug stores and proprietary stores
Vartegez Simonian

D-U-N-S 25-992-6756   (HQ)
VITALAIRE CANADA INC
VITALAIRE HEALTHCARE/SANTE
(*Suby of* L'AIR LIQUIDE SOCIETE ANONYME POUR L'ETUDE ET L'EXPLOITATION DES PROCEDES GEORGES CLAUDE)
6990 Creditview Rd Unit 6, Mississauga, ON, L5N 8R9
(905) 855-0414
Emp Here 70   *Sales* 473,237,248
SIC 5169 Chemicals and allied products, nec
Paul Ostrowski
Jean-Pierre Girouard
Jean-Marc De Royere
Pierre Dufour
Oliver Petit
Scott Krapf

D-U-N-S 20-402-9300   (HQ)
VOESTALPINE HIGH PERFORMANCE METALS LTD
(*Suby of* VOESTALPINE AG)
2595 Meadowvale Blvd, Mississauga, ON, L5N 7Y3
(905) 812-9440
Emp Here 45   *Sales* 42,481,530
SIC 5051 Metals service centers and offices
Paul Cavanagh

D-U-N-S 24-845-8069   (HQ)
VWR INTERNATIONAL CO.
(*Suby of* AVANTOR, INC.)
2360 Argentia Rd, Mississauga, ON, L5N 5Z7
(905) 813-7377
Emp Here 200   *Sales* 107,070,400
SIC 5049 Professional equipment, nec
Nav Arora
Gregory Blakely
Richard Tymczyszyn

D-U-N-S 20-562-7313   (HQ)
WAJAX LIMITED
INDUSTRIES WAJAX
(*Suby of* WAJAX CORPORATION)
2250 Argentia Rd, Mississauga, ON, L5N 6A5
(905) 212-3300
Emp Here 25   *Sales* 58,527,600
SIC 5084 Industrial machinery and equipment
Mark Foote
Darren Yaworsky

D-U-N-S 20-042-8773   (BR)
WAL-MART CANADA CORP
WAL-MART SPORTS CENTER-KITIMAT
(*Suby of* WALMART INC.)
6600 Kitimat Rd, Mississauga, ON, L5N 1L9
(905) 817-1824
Emp Here 150
SIC 5311 Department stores
Cordell Benrnard

D-U-N-S 24-976-3145   (HQ)
WAL-MART CANADA CORP
(*Suby of* WALMART INC.)
1940 Argentia Rd, Mississauga, ON, L5N 1P9
(905) 821-2111
Emp Here 1,000   *Sales* 13,689,720,000
SIC 5311 Department stores
Lee John Tappenden
John Bayliss
Trudy M. N. Fahie
Rhonda Maines-Corrado
Kirsten Evans
Susan Muigai
David Criscione

Luigina Pick
Xavier Dominique Piesvaux
Benoit Nachtergael

D-U-N-S 25-294-7346   (BR)
WAL-MART CANADA CORP
(*Suby of* WALMART INC.)
3155 Argentia Rd, Mississauga, ON, L5N 8E1
(905) 821-8150
Emp Here 300
SIC 5311 Department stores
Peter Kirkwood

D-U-N-S 25-294-7304   (BR)
WAL-MART CANADA CORP
(*Suby of* WALMART INC.)
1940 Argentia Rd, Mississauga, ON, L5N 1P9
(800) 328-0402
Emp Here 400
SIC 5311 Department stores
Dominic Vitalie

D-U-N-S 24-376-5828   (BR)
WEIR CANADA, INC
WEIR MINERALS
(*Suby of* WEIR GROUP PLC(THE))
2360 Millrace Crt, Mississauga, ON, L5N 1W2
(905) 812-7100
Emp Here 100
SIC 3569 General industrial machinery, nec
Matt Goodbrand

D-U-N-S 20-229-5846   (HQ)
WEIR CANADA, INC
OIL AND GAS
(*Suby of* WEIR GROUP PLC(THE))
2360 Millrace Crt, Mississauga, ON, L5N 1W2
(905) 812-7100
Emp Here 110   *Sales* 331,656,400
SIC 5084 Industrial machinery and equipment
Serge Lamirande
Ian Dundee

D-U-N-S 20-167-5634   (HQ)
WHIRLPOOL CANADA LP
(*Suby of* WHIRLPOOL CORPORATION)
6750 Century Ave Unit 200, Mississauga, ON, L5N 0B7
(905) 821-6400
Emp Here 220   *Sales* 84,874,500
SIC 3633 Household laundry equipment
Joe Sanguinetti

D-U-N-S 24-236-7683   (SL)
WILLIAMS, KELLER REALTY
KELLER WILLIAMS REAL ESTATE ASSOCIATES
7145 West Credit Ave Bldg 1 Suite 201, Mississauga, ON, L5N 6J7
(905) 812-8123
Emp Here 49   *Sales* 13,316,044
SIC 6531 Real estate agents and managers

D-U-N-S 20-537-4010   (HQ)
WILLSON INTERNATIONAL LIMITED
2345 Argentia Rd Suite 201, Mississauga, ON, L5N 8K4
(905) 363-1133
Emp Here 160   *Sales* 98,859,500
SIC 4731 Freight transportation arrangement
Peter Willson
Jim Mckinnon

D-U-N-S 24-814-9601   (HQ)
WOLVERINE WORLD WIDE CANADA ULC
HUSH PUPPIES
(*Suby of* WOLVERINE WORLD WIDE, INC.)
6225 Millcreek Dr, Mississauga, ON, L5N 0G2
(905) 285-9560
Emp Here 50   *Sales* 92,128,630
SIC 5139 Footwear
Bruke W Kruger
Michael D Stornant
Fotini Dermatis

D-U-N-S 20-016-5897   (HQ)
ZEBRA TECHNOLGIES CANADA, ULC
PSION TEKLOGIX

(*Suby of* MOTOROLA SOLUTIONS, INC.)
2100 Meadowvale Blvd, Mississauga, ON, L5N 7J9
(905) 813-9900
Sales 113,166,000
SIC 3663 Radio and t.v. communications equipment
John Conoley
Dan Pearce
Adrian Coleman
Ronald Caines

D-U-N-S 20-145-9104   (HQ)
ZIMMER OF CANADA LIMITED
ZIMMER BIOMET
(*Suby of* ZIMMER BIOMET HOLDINGS, INC.)
2323 Argentia Rd, Mississauga, ON, L5N 5N3
(905) 858-8588
Emp Here 9   *Sales* 18,334,134
SIC 5047 Medical and hospital equipment
James Williams

Mississauga, ON L5P

D-U-N-S 25-811-2564   (SL)
1572900 ONTARIO INC
TRAVEL STORE, THE
6301 Silver Dart Dr, Mississauga, ON, L5P 1B2
(416) 776-2247
Emp Here 35   *Sales* 13,487,600
SIC 4724 Travel agencies
Bernard Drag

D-U-N-S 24-093-4062   (SL)
AIRPORT TERMINAL SERVICE INC CANADIAN
6500 Silver Dart Dr Unit 211, Mississauga, ON, L5P 1B1
(905) 405-9550
Emp Here 300   *Sales* 80,093,400
SIC 4581 Airports, flying fields, and services
Natasa Radenkoveis

D-U-N-S 20-251-6126   (BR)
ASIG CANADA LTD
ASIG
(*Suby of* ASIG CANADA LTD)
5600 Silver Dart Dr, Mississauga, ON, L5P 1C4
(905) 694-2846
Emp Here 200
SIC 5172 Petroleum products, nec
Jules Molinari

D-U-N-S 20-935-6856   (SL)
ATLANTIS TRANSPORTATION SERVICES INC
(*Suby of* THORFAM CORP)
6500 Silver Dart Dr, Mississauga, ON, L5P 1C4
(905) 672-5171
Emp Here 88   *Sales* 18,102,128
SIC 4213 Trucking, except local
Robert A. Thorndyke
Theodore Daniel
Mel Ureten

D-U-N-S 24-744-4227   (BR)
CLS CATERING SERVICES LTD
CLS CATERING
(*Suby of* DEUTSCHE LUFTHANSA AG)
2950 Convair Dr, Mississauga, ON, L5P 1A2
(905) 676-3218
Emp Here 150
SIC 5812 Eating places
Rick Bushell

D-U-N-S 20-182-9798   (SL)
CONSOLIDATED AVIATION FUELING OF TORONTO, ULC
(*Suby of* ALLIED AVIATION LLC.)
5600 Silver Dart Dr, Mississauga, ON, L5P 1A2

▲ **Public Company**   ■ **Public Company Family Member**   **HQ** Headquarters   **BR** Branch   **SL** Single Location

(905) 694-2846
Emp Here 270   *Sales* 319,213,710
SIC 5172 Petroleum products, nec
John Muirhead
Robert L Rose

D-U-N-S 25-075-5600   (HQ)
GREATER TORONTO AIRPORTS AUTHORITY
TORONTO PEARSON INTERNATIONAL AIRPORT
3111 Convair Dr, Mississauga, ON, L5P 1B2
(416) 776-3000
Sales 1,073,552,308
SIC 4581 Airports, flying fields, and services
Howard Eng
Ian Clarke
Howard Bohan
Nicole Desloges
Brian Gabel
Scott Collier
Toby Lennox
Patrick Neville
Selma M. Lussenburg
Douglas Allingham

D-U-N-S 24-000-2894   (BR)
HACHETTE DISTRIBUTION SERVICES (CANADA) INC
LS TRAVEL RETAIL NORTH AMERICA
(*Suby of* LAGARDERE SCA)
Gd, Mississauga, ON, L5P 1B2
(905) 694-9696
Emp Here 250
SIC 5994 News dealers and newsstands

D-U-N-S 20-313-4374   (SL)
NAVSTAR AVIATION INC
(*Suby of* WGA-AVCON ENTERPRISES INC)
6500 Silver Dart Dr Suite 205, Mississauga, ON, L5P 1A5
(905) 673-7827
Emp Here 110   *Sales* 29,367,580
SIC 4581 Airports, flying fields, and services
Wayne Anaka
Kevin Carruthers

D-U-N-S 20-358-2069   (SL)
RBG SECURITY INC
6500 Silver Dart Dr Suite 228a, Mississauga, ON, L5P 1A2
(647) 729-2360
Emp Here 200   *Sales* 5,250,000
SIC 7381 Detective and armored car services
Ron Boyko

D-U-N-S 20-306-2872   (HQ)
SKY REGIONAL AIRLINES INC
6120 Midfield Rd, Mississauga, ON, L5P 1B1
(905) 362-5941
Emp Here 450   *Sales* 142,808,400
SIC 4512 Air transportation, scheduled
L. Russell Payson
Catherine Duff-Caron
Jacquelin Smalec

D-U-N-S 20-708-8969   (HQ)
SKY SERVICE F.B.O. INC.
6120 Midfield Rd, Mississauga, ON, L5P 1B1
(905) 677-3300
Sales 66,744,500
SIC 4581 Airports, flying fields, and services
Russell Payson
Marshall Myles

D-U-N-S 20-252-3564   (HQ)
SKYSERVICE BUSINESS AVIATION INC
(*Suby of* SKYSERVICE INVESTMENTS INC)
6120 Midfield Rd, Mississauga, ON, L5P 1B1
(905) 677-3300
Emp Here 250   *Sales* 161,849,520
SIC 4522 Air transportation, nonscheduled
Marshall Myles
Emlyn David

D-U-N-S 25-975-6484   (HQ)
SKYSERVICE INVESTMENTS INC
6120 Midfield Rd, Mississauga, ON, L5P 1B1

(905) 678-5767
Emp Here 1   *Sales* 109,652,700
SIC 6719 Holding companies, nec
Russell Payson

D-U-N-S 20-520-0285   (HQ)
SOCIETE AIR FRANCE
(*Suby of* AIR FRANCE - KLM)
6500 Silver Dart Dr Vista, Mississauga, ON, L5P 1A2
(905) 676-2782
Emp Here 16   *Sales* 10,392,128
SIC 4512 Air transportation, scheduled
Rory Burrell

D-U-N-S 24-207-0766   (HQ)
SWISSPORT CANADA HANDLING INC
(*Suby of* HAINAN JIAOGUAN HOLDING CO., LTD.)
6500 Silver Dart Dr, Mississauga, ON, L5P 1A2
(905) 676-2888
Emp Here 267   *Sales* 158,676,000
SIC 4581 Airports, flying fields, and services
Rodrigue E Levesque
Richard Van Bruygom

D-U-N-S 24-320-9124   (SL)
UNITED AIRLINES
Po Box 247 Stn Toronto Amf, Mississauga, ON, L5P 1B1

Emp Here 40   *Sales* 20,798,680
SIC 4729 Passenger transportation arrangement

D-U-N-S 24-794-8607   (SL)
VCC CARGO SERVICE INC
6500 Silver Dart Dr, Mississauga, ON, L5P 1B1
(905) 676-4047
Emp Here 54   *Sales* 17,536,716
SIC 4512 Air transportation, scheduled
John Mckinnon

Mississauga, ON L5R

D-U-N-S 24-348-1855   (SL)
1721502 ONTARIO INC
KING'S PASTRY
5880 Falbourne St, Mississauga, ON, L5R 0E6
(905) 238-8328
Emp Here 130   *Sales* 31,799,366
SIC 2051 Bread, cake, and related products
Sum Chuen Ho
Kwok Leong Tsang
Man Chor Wong

D-U-N-S 24-349-3418   (HQ)
6929818 CANADA INC
ENTREPRISES TAG, LES
10 Kingsbridge Garden Cir Suite 704, Mississauga, ON, L5R 3K6

Emp Here 100
SIC 2421 Sawmills and planing mills, general
Serge Dominique
Christopher Bellahoussof
Jean-Yves Cardinal
Eb Reinbergs

D-U-N-S 24-682-1438   (HQ)
ADVANZ PHARMA CORP
5770 Hurontario St Suite 310, Mississauga, ON, L5R 3G5
(905) 842-5150
Emp Here 20   *Sales* 183,292,524
SIC 5122 Drugs, proprietaries, and sundries
Graeme Duncan
Randy Benson
Simon Tucker
Paul Burden
Barry Fishman
Florian Hager

Robert Manzo
Frances Cloud
Maurice Chagnaud
Adeel Ahmad

D-U-N-S 25-690-6470   (HQ)
AGFA HEALTHCARE INC
(*Suby of* AGFA-GEVAERT)
5975 Falbourne St Suite 2, Mississauga, ON, L5R 3V8
(416) 241-1110
Emp Here 25   *Sales* 176,666,160
SIC 5047 Medical and hospital equipment
William Corsten
Gunther Mertens
Peter Wilkens

D-U-N-S 20-358-8983   (SL)
AGFA INC
(*Suby of* AGFA-GEVAERT)
5975 Falbourne St Suite 2, Mississauga, ON, L5R 3V8
(905) 361-6982
Emp Here 115   *Sales* 18,863,105
SIC 2752 Commercial printing, lithographic
Jared Houk
Lizabeth Franco
David Fast

D-U-N-S 20-773-4005   (HQ)
ALLIANCES DES MANUFACTURIERS ET DES EXPORTATEURS DU CANADA
CME
55 Standish Crt Suite 620, Mississauga, ON, L5R 4B2
(905) 672-3466
Emp Here 10   *Sales* 20,689,200
SIC 8611 Business associations
Dennis Darby

D-U-N-S 24-365-1288   (SL)
ALLSEATING CORPORATION
5800 Avebury Rd Unit 3, Mississauga, ON, L5R 3M3
(905) 502-7200
Emp Here 100   *Sales* 15,432,200
SIC 2522 Office furniture, except wood
Gary Neil

D-U-N-S 25-364-9529   (SL)
ANATOME INC
5800 Avebury Rd Unit 3, Mississauga, ON, L5R 3M3
(905) 502-7200
Emp Here 100   *Sales* 44,717,400
SIC 5044 Office equipment
Gary Neil

D-U-N-S 20-999-3146   (HQ)
ANIXTER CANADA INC
(*Suby of* ANIXTER INTERNATIONAL INC.)
200 Foster Cres, Mississauga, ON, L5R 3Y5
(905) 568-8999
Emp Here 450   *Sales* 426,481,545
SIC 5063 Electrical apparatus and equipment
Grant Gamble
Gary Mistak
Marcelo Fiaes
Cindy Yuan

D-U-N-S 20-371-9831   (SL)
ARCONAS CORPORATION
(*Suby of* ARCONAS HOLDINGS LTD)
5700 Keaton Cres Unit 1, Mississauga, ON, L5R 3H5
(905) 272-0727
Emp Here 66   *Sales* 10,185,252
SIC 2531 Public building and related furniture
Dan Nassbaum
Pablo Reich
Shanti Defehr
Arthur Defehr

D-U-N-S 20-372-0961   (HQ)
ARCONAS INVESTMENTS LTD
ARCONAS
(*Suby of* ARCONAS HOLDINGS LTD)
5700 Keaton Cres Unit 1, Mississauga, ON,

L5R 3H5
(905) 272-0727
Sales 26,055,643
SIC 2531 Public building and related furniture
Dan Nussbaum
Pablo Reich
Lynn Gordon
Lowell Hendricks
Shanti Defehr
Ray Vella
Arthur Defehr

D-U-N-S 20-832-9466   (SL)
ARJO CANADA INC
ARJO
(*Suby of* ARJOHUNTLEIGH MAGOG INC)
90 Matheson Blvd W Suite 350, Mississauga, ON, L5R 3R3
(905) 238-7880
Emp Here 2,015   *Sales* 73,946,860
SIC 5047 Medical and hospital equipment
Anne Sigouin
Pierre Fortier

D-U-N-S 25-183-6735   (SL)
AVERSAN INC
30 Eglinton Ave W Suite 500, Mississauga, ON, L5R 3E7
(416) 289-1554
Emp Here 200   *Sales* 35,747,800
SIC 8711 Engineering services
Ted Sherlock
Daniel Pirog
Mojdeh Toyserkani

D-U-N-S 20-105-8166   (BR)
AVOTUS CORPORATION
(*Suby of* AVOTUS CORPORATION)
110 Matheson Blvd W Suite 300, Mississauga, ON, L5R 4G7
(905) 890-9199
Emp Here 100
SIC 4899 Communication services, nec
Brian Kremer

D-U-N-S 20-572-2965   (BR)
BASF CANADA INC
(*Suby of* BASF SE)
100 Milverton Dr Floor 5, Mississauga, ON, L5R 4H1
(289) 360-1300
Emp Here 75
SIC 2821 Plastics materials and resins

D-U-N-S 20-210-8015   (HQ)
BASF CANADA INC
(*Suby of* BASF SE)
100 Milverton Dr Unit 500, Mississauga, ON, L5R 4H1
(289) 360-1300
Emp Here 140   *Sales* 311,251,500
SIC 2821 Plastics materials and resins
Marcelo Lu

D-U-N-S 20-696-1208   (SL)
BENCHMARK ATHLETIC INC
6085 Belgrave Rd, Mississauga, ON, L5R 4E6
(905) 361-2390
Emp Here 20   *Sales* 10,006,500
SIC 5137 Women's and children's clothing
Michael Dyon

D-U-N-S 24-116-1038   (BR)
BEST BUY CANADA LTD
(*Suby of* BEST BUY CO., INC.)
6075 Mavis Rd Unit 1, Mississauga, ON, L5R 4G6
(905) 361-8251
Emp Here 150
SIC 5999 Miscellaneous retail stores, nec
Analisa King

D-U-N-S 20-863-2380   (HQ)
BRIDGESTONE CANADA INC
GCR TIRE CENTRES
(*Suby of* BRIDGESTONE CORPORATION)
5770 Hurontario St Suite 400, Mississauga, ON, L5R 3G5

(877) 468-6270
Emp Here 2,100   *Sales* 1,383,462,000
SIC 5014 Tires and tubes
  Larry Magee
  Pamela Scarrow
  Yannick Amiot
  Kenneth Weaver
  Terry Lee Reedy
  Isaku Motohashi
  Fiona Gardner
  Jim Schmidt

    D-U-N-S 20-525-3912   (SL)
**BROADRIDGE INVESTOR COMMUNICA-
TIONS CORPORATION**
(*Suby of* BROADRIDGE FINANCIAL SOLU-
TIONS, INC.)
5970 Chedworth Way, Mississauga, ON, L5R
4G5
(905) 507-5100
Emp Here 129   *Sales* 32,700,210
SIC 8748 Business consulting, nec
  Patricia Rosch

    D-U-N-S 24-358-1621   (SL)
CANADA DRY MOTT'S INC
(*Suby of* KEURIG DR PEPPER INC.)
30 Eglinton Ave W Suite 600, Mississauga,
ON, L5R 3E7
(905) 712-4121
Emp Here 75   *Sales* 25,926,750
SIC 2086 Bottled and canned soft drinks
  Larry Young

    D-U-N-S 24-331-9360   (HQ)
**CANADIAN MARKETING TEST CASE 200
LIMITED**
HIGH HOOPS
5770 Hurontario St, Mississauga, ON, L5R
3G5
(800) 986-5569
Emp Here 150   *Sales* 55,443,120
SIC 3949 Sporting and athletic goods, nec

    D-U-N-S 24-331-9378   (SL)
**CANADIAN MARKETING TEST CASE 201
LIMITED**
SWIFT SWEEPING CO
5770 Hurontario St, Mississauga, ON, L5R
3G5
Emp Here 30   *Sales* 14,250,780
SIC 5087 Service establishment equipment

    D-U-N-S 24-331-9402   (SL)
**CANADIAN MARKETING TEST CASE 204
LIMITED**
DOWNHILL SKIER
5770 Hurontario St, Mississauga, ON, L5R
3G5
Emp Here 50   *Sales* 26,027,100
SIC 5091 Sporting and recreation goods

    D-U-N-S 24-331-9501   (SL)
**CANADIAN MARKETING TEST CASE 206
LIMITED**
PRINTERS TO THE WORLD
5770 Hurontario St, Mississauga, ON, L5R
3G5
(905) 555-5555
Emp Here 150   *Sales* 24,604,050
SIC 2732 Book printing

    D-U-N-S 24-331-9550   (SL)
CANADIAN MARKETING TEST CASE 217
5770 Hurontario St, Mississauga, ON, L5R
3G5
Emp Here 150   *Sales* 21,370,140
SIC 6719 Holding companies, nec

    D-U-N-S 24-101-9608   (SL)
CANADIAN TEST CASE 101 LTD
5770 Hurontario St, Mississauga, ON, L5R
3G5
Emp Here 750
SIC 2899 Chemical preparations, nec

    D-U-N-S 24-101-8840   (SL)
CANADIAN TEST CASE 11
5770 Hurontario St, Mississauga, ON, L5R
3G5
Emp Here 50   *Sales* 20,274,854
SIC 7389 Business services, nec

    D-U-N-S 24-332-2489   (SL)
CANADIAN TEST CASE 110
5770 Hurontario St, Mississauga, ON, L5R
3G5
Emp Here 1,170
SIC 3949 Sporting and athletic goods, nec

    D-U-N-S 24-332-2497   (SL)
CANADIAN TEST CASE 111
5770 Hurontario St, Mississauga, ON, L5R
3G5
Emp Here 550
SIC 3949 Sporting and athletic goods, nec

    D-U-N-S 24-332-2554   (SL)
CANADIAN TEST CASE 117
5770 Hurontario St, Mississauga, ON, L5R
3G5
Emp Here 250
SIC 5137 Women's and children's clothing

    D-U-N-S 24-332-2745   (SL)
CANADIAN TEST CASE 145
MONTGOMERY PHARMA PACKAGING
5770 Hurontario St, Mississauga, ON, L5R
3G5
Emp Here 55   *Sales* 15,216,300
SIC 2834 Pharmaceutical preparations

    D-U-N-S 24-332-3099   (SL)
CANADIAN TEST CASE 165
5770 Hurontario St, Mississauga, ON, L5R
3G5
Emp Here 200
SIC 2421 Sawmills and planing mills, general

    D-U-N-S 24-101-9202   (SL)
CANADIAN TEST CASE 167
5770 Hurontario St, Mississauga, ON, L5R
3G5
Emp Here 6   *Sales* 28,788,247,200
SIC 7389 Business services, nec

    D-U-N-S 24-332-3123   (HQ)
CANADIAN TEST CASE 168 INC.
CANADIAN TEST CASE 169 DIV
5770 Hurontario St, Mississauga, ON, L5R
3G5
Emp Here 375
SIC 3714 Motor vehicle parts and accessories

    D-U-N-S 24-332-3172   (SL)
CANADIAN TEST CASE 174
5770 Hurontario St, Mississauga, ON, L5R
3G5
Emp Here 1,000   *Sales* 19,124,700
SIC 6021 National commercial banks

    D-U-N-S 24-101-9327   (SL)
CANADIAN TEST CASE 22
5770 Hurontario St, Mississauga, ON, L5R
3G5
Emp Here 100
SIC 7389 Business services, nec

    D-U-N-S 24-101-9525   (SL)
CANADIAN TEST CASE 27 LTD
PAT'S NAME CHANGE
5770 Hurontario St, Mississauga, ON, L5R
3G5
Emp Here 106

SIC 2992 Lubricating oils and greases

    D-U-N-S 24-101-9335   (SL)
CANADIAN TEST CASE 44
5770 Hurontario St, Mississauga, ON, L5R
3G5
Emp Here 600
SIC 7389 Business services, nec

    D-U-N-S 24-101-8741   (SL)
CANADIAN TEST CASE 52
5770 Hurontario St, Mississauga, ON, L5R
3G5
Emp Here 80
SIC 3949 Sporting and athletic goods, nec

    D-U-N-S 24-101-8758   (SL)
CANADIAN TEST CASE 74
CANADIAN TEST CASE 30, DIVISION
5770 Hurontario St, Mississauga, ON, L5R
3G5
Emp Here 30   *Sales* 36,428,000
SIC 7389 Business services, nec

    D-U-N-S 24-101-9673   (SL)
CANADIAN TEST CASE 95 INC
5770 Hurontario St, Mississauga, ON, L5R
3G5
Emp Here 200   *Sales* 37,157,143
SIC 8711 Engineering services

    D-U-N-S 20-875-5223   (SL)
CASTLE BUILDING CENTRES GROUP LTD
100 Milverton Dr Suite 400, Mississauga, ON,
L5R 4H1
(905) 564-3307
Emp Here 37   *Sales* 16,409,130
SIC 7389 Business services, nec
  Ken Jenkins
  Sarina Kaluzny
  James Jones

    D-U-N-S 20-193-7609   (HQ)
CHARTWELL MASTER CARE LP
CHARTWELL RETIREMENT RESIDENCES
100 Milverton Dr Suite 700, Mississauga, ON,
L5R 4H1
(905) 501-9219
Sales 1,113,484,000
SIC 8322 Individual and family services
  Brent Bonions
  Vlad Volodarski

    D-U-N-S 20-193-7591   (HQ)
CHARTWELL RETIREMENT RESIDENCES
*CHARTWELL SENIORS HOUSING REAL
ESTATE INVESTMENT TRUST*
100 Milverton Dr Suite 700, Mississauga, ON,
L5R 4H1
(905) 501-9219
Emp Here 4,701   *Sales* 657,012,131
SIC 6719 Holding companies, nec
  Brent Binions
  Karen Sullivan
  Vlad Volodarski
  Sheri Chateauvert
  Jonatha Boulakia
  Michael Deane Harris
  Sharon Sallows
  V. Ann Davis
  Lise Bastarache
  Sidney P.H. Robinson

    D-U-N-S 20-291-1496   (HQ)
CHILDREN'S PLACE (CANADA), LP, THE
(*Suby of* THE CHILDREN'S PLACE INC)
6040 Cantay Rd, Mississauga, ON, L5R 4J2
(905) 502-0353
Emp Here 25   *Sales* 249,510,000
SIC 5641 Children's and infants' wear stores
  Lori Webber

    D-U-N-S 20-560-8693   (SL)
CITI CARDS CANADA INC
(*Suby of* CITIGROUP INC.)

5900 Hurontario St, Mississauga, ON, L5R
0B8
(905) 285-7500
Emp Here 3,000   *Sales* 1,196,532,000
SIC 6153 Short-term business credit institu-
tions, except agricultural
  Bruce Clark
  Hannah Sorsher
  John Lavigne
  Frank O'brien
  Betty Devitay
  Richard Mclaughlin
  Jeffery Newman

    D-U-N-S 24-575-3306   (HQ)
COINAMATIC CANADA INC
(*Suby of* WASH MULTIFAMILY LAUNDRY
SYSTEMS, LLC)
301 Matheson Blvd W, Mississauga, ON, L5R
3G3
(905) 755-1946
Emp Here 130   *Sales* 26,908,800
SIC 7215 Coin-operated laundries and clean-
ing
  Gord Alderdice
  Don Neufeld
  Mike Pilolli

    D-U-N-S 24-322-1467   (HQ)
COOPER INDUSTRIES (CANADA) INC
(*Suby of* EATON CORPORATION PUBLIC
LIMITED COMPANY)
5925 Mclaughlin Rd, Mississauga, ON, L5R
1B8
(905) 501-3000
Sales 127,928,150
SIC 6712 Bank holding companies
  Roger Shea
  Grant L. Gawronski
  Terrance V. Helz
  Donald C. Matheson

    D-U-N-S 24-310-7120   (HQ)
COOPER INDUSTRIES (ELECTRICAL) INC
COOPER CROUSE-HINDS
(*Suby of* EATON CORPORATION PUBLIC
LIMITED COMPANY)
5925 Mclaughlin Rd, Mississauga, ON, L5R
1B8
(905) 501-3000
Emp Here 1   *Sales* 53,530,400
SIC 5211 Lumber and other building materials
  Terrance Helz
  Donald Matheson
  Stephen Kole
  Grant Gawronski

    D-U-N-S 25-266-4255   (BR)
COOPER INDUSTRIES (ELECTRICAL) INC
COOPER LIGHTING, DIV OF
(*Suby of* EATON CORPORATION PUBLIC
LIMITED COMPANY)
5925 Mclaughlin Rd, Mississauga, ON, L5R
1B8
(905) 507-4000
Emp Here 200
SIC 4911 Electric services
  Robert Conway

    D-U-N-S 24-848-4586   (SL)
COSECO INSURANCE INC.
COSECO INSURANCE COMPANY
(*Suby of* CO-OPERATORS GENERAL IN-
SURANCE COMPANY)
5600 Cancross Crt, Mississauga, ON, L5R
3E9
(905) 507-6156
Emp Here 10   *Sales* 10,348,810
SIC 6331 Fire, marine, and casualty insurance
  G Terry Squire
  Jeff Contant

    D-U-N-S 24-312-0941   (BR)
COSTCO WHOLESALE CANADA LTD
(*Suby of* COSTCO WHOLESALE CORPO-
RATION)
5900 Rodeo Dr Suite 526, Mississauga, ON,

L5R 3S9
(905) 568-4828
Emp Here 100
SIC 5099 Durable goods, nec
Hyder Rattani

D-U-N-S 24-829-9018   (BR)
CUSHMAN & WAKEFIELD ULC
CUSHMAN & WAKEFIELD LTD
(*Suby of* CUSHMAN & WAKEFIELD PLC)
5770 Hurontario St Suite 200, Mississauga,
ON, L5R 3G5
(905) 568-9500
Emp Here 125
SIC 6531 Real estate agents and managers
Mark Stainer

D-U-N-S 24-666-1524   (SL)
DE'LONGHI CANADA INC
6150 Mclaughlin Rd Suite 2, Mississauga, ON,
L5R 4E1
(905) 362-2340
Emp Here 27   *Sales* 12,073,698
SIC 5064 Electrical appliances, television and
radio
Paul Belluz
John O'brien
George Hogan
Fabio De'longhi

D-U-N-S 24-048-9799   (HQ)
**DUFFERIN-PEEL CATHOLIC DISTRICT
SCHOOL BOARD**
40 Matheson Blvd W, Mississauga, ON, L5R
1C5
(905) 890-1221
Emp Here 100   *Sales* 792,952,000
SIC 8211 Elementary and secondary schools
Julie Cherepacha
Stephanie Strong
Brian Hester
Mathew Thomas

D-U-N-S 24-587-5075   (HQ)
ESAB GROUP CANADA INC
ESAB WELDING & CUTTING PRODUCTS
(*Suby of* COLFAX CORPORATION)
6200 Cantay Rd Unit 20, Mississauga, ON,
L5R 3Y9
(905) 670-0220
Emp Here 30   *Sales* 24,701,352
SIC 5084 Industrial machinery and equipment
Neil Armstrong

D-U-N-S 24-986-3077   (HQ)
EXEL CANADA LTD
DHL SUPPLY CHAIN (CANADA)
(*Suby of* DEUTSCHE POST AG)
90 Matheson Blvd W Suite 111, Mississauga,
ON, L5R 3R3
(905) 366-7700
Emp Here 50   *Sales* 123,423,600
SIC 4225 General warehousing and storage
Todd Yates
Nigel Mathew
Paolo Mari

D-U-N-S 24-507-6039   (HQ)
EXPEDITORS CANADA INC
(*Suby of* EXPEDITORS INTERNATIONAL OF
WASHINGTON, INC.)
55 Standish Crt Suite 1100, Mississauga, ON,
L5R 4A1
(905) 290-6000
Emp Here 135   *Sales* 150,266,440
SIC 4731 Freight transportation arrangement
Ross Hurst

D-U-N-S 25-942-3416   (SL)
FOREMOST INTERNATIONAL LTD
(*Suby of* FOREMOST GROUPS, INC.)
5970 Chedworth Way Suite B, Mississauga,
ON, L5R 4G5
(905) 507-2005
Emp Here 40   *Sales* 17,886,960
SIC 5074 Plumbing and heating equipment
and supplies (hydronics)
Liang Chou Chen

Peter J Riley
Jennifer Earl
Cuc Quech

D-U-N-S 20-771-1805   (HQ)
FORESTERS LIFE INSURANCE COMPANY
(*Suby of* INDEPENDENT ORDER OF
FORESTERS, THE)
100 Milverton Dr Suite 400, Mississauga, ON,
L5R 4H1
(905) 219-8000
Sales 40,626,498
SIC 6311 Life insurance
Anthony W Poole
Geoffrey L. Harrison
Hugh Haney
Andre St Maour
George Mohacsi
Chris Mcilvaine
David Morrison
Ross Walker

D-U-N-S 20-760-6799   (HQ)
FUJIFILM CANADA INC
(*Suby of* FUJIFILM HOLDINGS CORPORA-
TION)
600 Suffolk Crt, Mississauga, ON, L5R 4G4
(800) 461-0416
Emp Here 120   *Sales* 107,070,400
SIC 5043 Photographic equipment and sup-
plies
Shunji Saito
Brian Boulanger

D-U-N-S 20-413-5735   (HQ)
G.N. JOHNSTON EQUIPMENT CO. LTD.
JOHNSON EQUIPMENT
(*Suby of* TOYOTA INDUSTRIES CORPORA-
TION)
5990 Avebury Rd, Mississauga, ON, L5R 3R2
(905) 712-6000
Emp Here 320   *Sales* 317,024,500
SIC 5084 Industrial machinery and equipment
Michael Marcotte
Randy Thompson
Andrew Troiano
Randy Wronsberg

D-U-N-S 20-303-0288   (BR)
G.N. JOHNSTON EQUIPMENT CO. LTD.
G.N. JOHNSTON EQUIPMENT CO. LTD
(*Suby of* TOYOTA INDUSTRIES CORPORA-
TION)
5990 Avebury Rd, Mississauga, ON, L5R 3R2
(905) 712-6000
Emp Here 80
SIC 5084 Industrial machinery and equipment
Nailah Ali

D-U-N-S 24-092-3672   (HQ)
**GES EXPOSITION SERVICES (CANADA)
LIMITED**
GES CANADA
(*Suby of* VIAD CORP)
5675 Mclaughlin Rd, Mississauga, ON, L5R
3K5
(905) 283-0500
Emp Here 70   *Sales* 76,270,250
SIC 7389 Business services, nec
Steve Moster
Michael Lecour

D-U-N-S 24-728-5570   (HQ)
GETINGE CANADA LIMITED
(*Suby of* GETINGE AB)
90 Matheson Blvd W Suite 300, Mississauga,
ON, L5R 3R3
(905) 629-8777
Emp Here 33   *Sales* 20,570,004
SIC 5047 Medical and hospital equipment
Maximo Nougues
Therese Mueller
Mario Camara

D-U-N-S 25-107-9893   (HQ)
GLOBALSTAR CANADA SATELLITE CO.
(*Suby of* GLOBALSTAR LP)

115 Matheson Blvd W Unit 100, Mississauga,
ON, L5R 3L1
(905) 890-1377
Emp Here 60   *Sales* 20,916,270
SIC 5731 Radio, television, and electronic
stores
Steven Bell

D-U-N-S 24-394-2419   (HQ)
GLOVIS CANADA, INC
(*Suby of* HYUNDAI GLOVIS CO., LTD.)
5770 Hurontario St Suite 700, Mississauga,
ON, L5R 3G5
(905) 361-1642
Emp Here 4   *Sales* 158,334,665
SIC 4212 Local trucking, without storage
Edward Kim
Arnold Kingu
Jin-Kyu Roh

D-U-N-S 20-341-6367   (SL)
GP INTERNATIONAL INC
HYLEYS CANADA
796 Four Winds Way, Mississauga, ON, L5R
3W8
(416) 948-0336
Emp Here 18   *Sales* 14,403,938
SIC 6799 Investors, nec
Gaston Perera
Marina Perera

D-U-N-S 24-720-3177   (HQ)
GREENHAWK INC
*GREENHAWK HARNESS & EQUESTRIAN
SUPPLIES*
5665 Mclaughlin Rd, Mississauga, ON, L5R
3K5
(905) 238-0311
Emp Here 40   *Sales* 34,205,920
SIC 5941 Sporting goods and bicycle shops
Gordon Russell
Garry Millage
Ian Russell

D-U-N-S 24-991-7329   (HQ)
GROHE CANADA INC
(*Suby of* GROHE GROUP SARL)
5900 Avebury Rd, Mississauga, ON, L5R 3M3
(905) 271-2929
Sales 19,857,250
SIC 3088 Plastics plumbing fixtures
William Mclean
Patrick Hurley

D-U-N-S 20-349-4807   (BR)
**H.B. GROUP INSURANCE MANAGEMENT
LTD**
(*Suby of* CO-OPERATORS GROUP LIMITED,
THE)
5600 Cancross Crt, Mississauga, ON, L5R
3E9
(905) 507-6156
Emp Here 500
SIC 6331 Fire, marine, and casualty insurance
Geoffery Beechy

D-U-N-S 24-872-6804   (HQ)
**H.B. GROUP INSURANCE MANAGEMENT
LTD**
(*Suby of* CO-OPERATORS GROUP LIMITED,
THE)
5600 Cancross Crt Suite A, Mississauga, ON,
L5R 3E9
(905) 507-6156
Emp Here 325   *Sales* 2,064,555,240
SIC 6411 Insurance agents, brokers, and ser-
vice
Karen Higgins
George Hardy

D-U-N-S 25-418-7594   (SL)
**HEALTHPRO PROCUREMENT SERVICES
INC**
5770 Hurontario St Suite 902, Mississauga,
ON, L5R 3G5
(905) 568-3478
Emp Here 50   *Sales* 22,174,500
SIC 7389 Business services, nec

Cynthia Valaitiss
John Green

D-U-N-S 25-403-2931   (HQ)
HEYS INTERNATIONAL LTD
333 Foster Cres Suite 1, Mississauga, ON,
L5R 4E5
(905) 565-8100
Emp Here 3   *Sales* 10,410,840
SIC 5099 Durable goods, nec
Yahya Sheikh

D-U-N-S 25-213-7773   (BR)
HOME DEPOT OF CANADA INC
HOME DEPOT
(*Suby of* THE HOME DEPOT INC)
650 Matheson Blvd W, Mississauga, ON, L5R
3T2

Emp Here 200
SIC 5251 Hardware stores
James Meagher

D-U-N-S 24-680-5162   (HQ)
INGRAM MICRO INC
INGRAM MICRO CANADA
(*Suby of* HNA TECHNOLOGY CO., LTD.)
55 Standish Crt Suite 1, Mississauga, ON,
L5R 4A1
(905) 755-5000
Emp Here 800   *Sales* 535,352,000
SIC 5045 Computers, peripherals, and soft-
ware
Mark Snider

D-U-N-S 25-671-6150   (HQ)
INTRIA ITEMS INC
(*Suby of* CANADIAN IMPERIAL BANK OF
COMMERCE)
5705 Cancross Ct, Mississauga, ON, L5R 3E9
(905) 755-2400
Emp Here 100   *Sales* 400,432,800
SIC 7374 Data processing and preparation
Robert Bouey

D-U-N-S 20-160-1098   (HQ)
INVIS INC
INVIS CANADA'S MORTGAGES EXPERTS
5770 Hurontario St Suite 600, Mississauga,
ON, L5R 3G5
(905) 283-3300
Emp Here 10   *Sales* 36,789,940
SIC 7389 Business services, nec
Stan Falkowski
Cameron Strong
Gary Siegle
Kelly Nueber
Scott Musselman

D-U-N-S 24-534-2857   (SL)
JOHNSTON EQUIPMENT ENGINEERED
5990 Avebury Rd, Mississauga, ON, L5R 3R2
(905) 712-6000
Emp Here 1,200   *Sales* 349,020,000
SIC 3743 Railroad equipment
Michael Marcotte

D-U-N-S 25-510-6221   (HQ)
KIA CANADA INC
KIA
(*Suby of* KIA MOTORS CORPORATION)
180 Foster Cres, Mississauga, ON, L5R 4J5
(905) 755-6250
Emp Here 121   *Sales* 64,561,560
SIC 5012 Automobiles and other motor vehi-
cles
Jay Chung
Maria Soklis
Elias El-Achhab
Harold Mun

D-U-N-S 20-567-1712   (HQ)
KUEHNE + NAGEL LTD
(*Suby of* KUHNE HOLDING AG)
77 Foster Cres, Mississauga, ON, L5R 0K1
(905) 502-7776
Emp Here 382   *Sales* 553,613,200
SIC 4731 Freight transportation arrangement

Brenda Lemieux
Brian Pedersen
Goetz Alebrand
Patrick Berner

D-U-N-S 24-477-4527   (SL)
LEDOUX, LEW & PATTERSON INSURANCE BROKERS LIMITED
115 Matheson Blvd W Suite 202, Mississauga, ON, L5R 3L1
(905) 890-1877
Emp Here 35   *Sales* 20,297,340
SIC 6411 Insurance agents, brokers, and service
Steven Hisey
Dwight Hickson

D-U-N-S 24-024-5936   (SL)
LIFT RITE INC
(*Suby of* TOYOTA INDUSTRIES CORPORATION)
5975 Falbourne St Unit 3, Mississauga, ON, L5R 3L8
(905) 456-2603
Emp Here 90
SIC 3499 Fabricated Metal products, nec

D-U-N-S 24-350-8723   (HQ)
LIXIL CANADA INC
AMERICAN STANDARD
5900 Avebury Rd, Mississauga, ON, L5R 3M3
(905) 949-4800
Sales 38,417,000
SIC 3431 Metal sanitary ware
Jay Gould
Valerie Malone
Edward Manley
Lisa Rei
Rita Danyszczuk
Maria Chiclana
Steve Delarge
Henry Johansson
Yves Dalcourt

D-U-N-S 20-337-5576   (BR)
LOWE-MARTIN COMPANY INC
(*Suby of* 746746 ONTARIO LIMITED)
5990 Falbourne St, Mississauga, ON, L5R 3S7
(905) 507-8782
Emp Here 200
SIC 2752 Commercial printing, lithographic

D-U-N-S 20-123-2126   (BR)
MAPLE LEAF FOODS INC
(*Suby of* MAPLE LEAF FOODS INC)
30 Eglinton Ave W Suite 500, Mississauga, ON, L5R 3E7
(905) 501-3076
Emp Here 200
SIC 2011 Meat packing plants
Scott Steckly

D-U-N-S 20-983-1171   (SL)
MATTEL CANADA INC
(*Suby of* MATTEL, INC.)
6155 Freemont Blvd, Mississauga, ON, L5R 3W2
(905) 501-0404
Emp Here 120   *Sales* 83,436,000
SIC 5092 Toys and hobby goods and supplies
Geoff Massingberd
Dean Ikin

D-U-N-S 24-122-6091   (HQ)
MEDICAL MART SUPPLIES LIMITED
6200 Cantay Rd, Mississauga, ON, L5R 3Y9
(905) 624-6200
Emp Here 120   *Sales* 93,686,600
SIC 5047 Medical and hospital equipment
Ernie Philip
Diane Reid
Antoinette Triumbari

D-U-N-S 20-257-9165   (BR)
MENASHA PACKAGING CANADA L.P.
PORTABLE PACKAGING
(*Suby of* MENASHA CORPORATION)

5875 Chedworth Way, Mississauga, ON, L5R 3L9
(905) 507-3042
Emp Here 100
SIC 2653 Corrugated and solid fiber boxes

D-U-N-S 20-161-3189   (HQ)
MESSER CANADA INC
5860 Chedworth Way, Mississauga, ON, L5R 0A2
(905) 501-1700
Emp Here 150   *Sales* 672,212,000
SIC 5169 Chemicals and allied products, nec
Bruce Hart
Christopher T Ebeling
Christian Lafleur
Jens Luehring
Mohammed Lakhani

D-U-N-S 20-278-3874   (BR)
MOORE CANADA CORPORATION
TOPS PRODUCTS CANADA
(*Suby of* R. R. DONNELLEY & SONS COMPANY)
333 Foster Cres Suite 2, Mississauga, ON, L5R 3Z9
(905) 890-1080
Emp Here 400
SIC 2782 Blankbooks and looseleaf binders
Jeffrey Good

D-U-N-S 25-399-2937   (HQ)
MORTGAGE INTELLIGENCE INC
5770 Hurontario St Suite 600, Mississauga, ON, L5R 3G5
(905) 283-3600
Emp Here 45   *Sales* 12,988,578
SIC 6163 Loan brokers
Karl Wondrak

D-U-N-S 24-555-5818   (HQ)
NACORA INSURANCE BROKERS LTD
(*Suby of* KUHNE HOLDING AG)
77 Foster Cres, Mississauga, ON, L5R 0K1
(905) 507-1551
Emp Here 34   *Sales* 109,016,778
SIC 6411 Insurance agents, brokers, and service
John Levin
David Schleifer
Stefan Kneubuhler

D-U-N-S 24-992-7286   (SL)
NEW VENTURES REALTY INC
20 Kingsbridge Garden Cir Suite 2004, Mississauga, ON, L5R 3K7
(905) 507-3030
Emp Here 100   *Sales* 23,291,100
SIC 6513 Apartment building operators
Kul Singh

D-U-N-S 25-823-9623   (BR)
NEWGEN RESTAURANT SERVICES INC
TUCKER'S MARKETPLACE
(*Suby of* NEWGEN RESTAURANT SERVICES INC)
5975 Mavis Rd, Mississauga, ON, L5R 3T7
(905) 502-8555
Emp Here 100
SIC 5812 Eating places
Kevin Chong

D-U-N-S 24-388-8427   (SL)
NORTHBUD DISTRIBUTORS LTD
6030 Freemont Blvd, Mississauga, ON, L5R 3X4

Emp Here 26   *Sales* 21,725,002
SIC 5147 Meats and meat products

D-U-N-S 24-096-6861   (SL)
ONTARIO NATURAL FOOD COMPANY INC
5800 Keaton Cres, Mississauga, ON, L5R 3K2
(905) 507-2021
Emp Here 53   *Sales* 44,285,581
SIC 5149 Groceries and related products, nec
Randy Whitteker

D-U-N-S 20-294-2140   (HQ)
ORACLE CANADA ULC
(*Suby of* ORACLE CORPORATION)
100 Milverton Dr Suite 100, Mississauga, ON, L5R 4H1
(905) 890-8100
Sales 184,573,000
SIC 7371 Custom computer programming services
Larry Ellison

D-U-N-S 24-575-2043   (SL)
ORACLE CORPORATION CANADA INC
100 Milverton Dr Suite 100, Mississauga, ON, L5R 4H1

Emp Here 400
SIC 7372 Prepackaged software

D-U-N-S 25-366-7919   (HQ)
ORKIN CANADA CORPORATION
ORKIN PCO SERVICES
(*Suby of* ROLLINS, INC.)
5840 Falbourne St, Mississauga, ON, L5R 4B5
(905) 502-9700
Emp Here 60   *Sales* 53,059,050
SIC 7342 Disinfecting and pest control services
Gary Muldoon

D-U-N-S 20-561-6006   (HQ)
PANALPINA INC
(*Suby of* PANALPINA WELTTRANSPORT (HOLDING) AG)
6350 Cantay Rd, Mississauga, ON, L5R 4E2
(905) 755-4500
Emp Here 250   *Sales* 118,631,400
SIC 4731 Freight transportation arrangement
Tony Jaques
Paul Dalla Torre

D-U-N-S 24-079-5344   (HQ)
PEEL DISTRICT SCHOOL BOARD
5650 Hurontario St Suite 106, Mississauga, ON, L5R 1C6
(905) 890-1099
Emp Here 550   *Sales* 1,448,930
SIC 8211 Elementary and secondary schools
Tony Pontes
Janet Mcdougald
Suzanne Nurse
David Green
Brad Macdonald
Rick Williams
Stan Cameron
Sue Lawton
Kathy Mcdonald
Carrie Andrews

D-U-N-S 24-990-6009   (BR)
PEPSI BOTTLING GROUP (CANADA), ULC, THE
PEPSICO BEVERAGES CANADA
(*Suby of* PBG INVESTMENT (LUXEMBOURG) SARL)
5900 Falbourne St, Mississauga, ON, L5R 3M2
(905) 568-8787
Emp Here 400
SIC 2086 Bottled and canned soft drinks
Patricia Shea

D-U-N-S 20-609-4203   (BR)
PEPSICO CANADA ULC
HOSTESS FRITO LAY CANADA, DIV OF
(*Suby of* PEPSICO, INC.)
55 Standish Crt Suite 700, Mississauga, ON, L5R 4B2

Emp Here 150
SIC 2096 Potato chips and similar snacks
Marc Guay

D-U-N-S 20-383-4283   (SL)
PF CONSUMER HEALTHCARE CANADA ULC
PFIZER CONSUMER HEALTHCARE

CANADA
(*Suby of* PFIZER INC.)
55 Standish Crt Suite 450, Mississauga, ON, L5R 4B2
(905) 507-7000
Emp Here 710   *Sales* 235,431,740
SIC 2834 Pharmaceutical preparations
Camilo Tedde

D-U-N-S 20-700-0675   (HQ)
PHARMA MEDICA RESEARCH INC
(*Suby of* 2065424 ONTARIO LIMITED)
6100 Belgrave Rd, Mississauga, ON, L5R 0B7
(905) 624-9115
Emp Here 112   *Sales* 76,530,750
SIC 8731 Commercial physical research
Latifa Yamlahi
Mohammed Bouhajib
Michael Panayi

D-U-N-S 24-334-1018   (HQ)
PRIME RESTAURANTS INC
EAST SIDE MARIO'S
(*Suby of* RECIPE UNLIMITED CORPORATION)
10 Kingsbridge Garden Cir Suite 600, Mississauga, ON, L5R 3K6
(905) 568-0000
Emp Here 93   *Sales* 37,311,200
SIC 5812 Eating places
Nicholas M. Perpick
H. Ross R. Bain
Grant Cobb
Rob Carmichael
William Grady
Andrew Berzins
Brian Elliot
John Verdon
Jack Gardner
Nalini Barma

D-U-N-S 24-719-1877   (HQ)
PUROLATOR HOLDINGS LTD
(*Suby of* GOVERNMENT OF CANADA)
5995 Avebury Rd Suite 100, Mississauga, ON, L5R 3T8
(905) 712-1251
Emp Here 1,300   *Sales* 4,942,975,000
SIC 4731 Freight transportation arrangement
Robert C Johnson
Sheldon Bell
Jim Mcdade
Brian Meagher
Stephen Gould
William Henderson

D-U-N-S 20-177-2506   (HQ)
PUROLATOR INC
PUROLATOR LOGISTICS
(*Suby of* GOVERNMENT OF CANADA)
5995 Avebury Rd, Mississauga, ON, L5R 3P9
(905) 712-1084
Emp Here 350   *Sales* 4,547,537,000
SIC 4731 Freight transportation arrangement
Patrick Nangle

D-U-N-S 20-563-2396   (SL)
QUALITY STORES LTD
5770 Hurontario St, Mississauga, ON, L5R 3G5

Emp Here 100
SIC 5311 Department stores

D-U-N-S 24-805-1000   (SL)
RESOLVE RECRUIT INC
30 Eglinton Ave W Suite 812, Mississauga, ON, L5R 3E7
(905) 568-8828
Emp Here 100   *Sales* 15,537,100
SIC 7361 Employment agencies
Kim Muir
Andre Muir
Vanessa Yapp

D-U-N-S 24-745-7526   (BR)
REXEL CANADA ELECTRICAL INC

NEDCO
(*Suby of* REXEL)
5600 Keaton Cres, Mississauga, ON, L5R
3G3
(905) 712-4004
Emp Here 175
SIC 5063 Electrical apparatus and equipment

D-U-N-S 25-150-2381   (HQ)
REXEL CANADA ELECTRICAL INC
NEDCO, DIV OF
(*Suby of* REXEL)
5600 Keaton Cres, Mississauga, ON, L5R
3G3
(905) 712-4004
Emp Here 181   *Sales* 1,160,494,000
SIC 5063 Electrical apparatus and equipment
Roger Little
Rene Merat
Rashid Maqsood
Adrian Trotman
Robert Blague
Pat Foley

D-U-N-S 20-175-8646   (HQ)
SCHNEIDER ELECTRIC CANADA INC
SCHNEIDER ELECTRIC
(*Suby of* SCHNEIDER ELECTRIC SE)
5985 Mclaughlin Rd, Mississauga, ON, L5R
1B8
(905) 366-3999
Sales 70,728,750
SIC 3699 Electrical equipment and supplies,
nec
Gary Abrams
George Powers
Jeaneyes Moullet

D-U-N-S 20-325-4669   (SL)
SFE ENERGY MARYLAND, INC
100 Milverton Dr Suite 608, Mississauga, ON,
L5R 4H1
(905) 366-7037
Emp Here 40   *Sales* 25,064,560
SIC 4911 Electric services
Shelley Lewis

D-U-N-S 24-079-0779   (HQ)
SOTI INC
(*Suby of* RODRIGUEZ HOLDING CORP)
5770 Hurontario St Suite 1100, Mississauga,
ON, L5R 3G5
(905) 624-9828
Emp Here 205   *Sales* 40,052,341
SIC 7371 Custom computer programming ser-
vices
Carl Rodrigues
Lynette Rodrigues
Rob Auld

D-U-N-S 24-204-0728   (HQ)
SOUTHWIRE CANADA COMPANY
(*Suby of* SOUTHWIRE COMPANY, LLC)
5705 Cancross Crt Suite 100, Mississauga,
ON, L5R 3E9
(800) 668-0303
Emp Here 100   *Sales* 27,208,200
SIC 3357 Nonferrous wiredrawing and insulat-
ing
Rich Stinson
J. Guyton Cochrane
Floyd Smith
Jeff Herrin

D-U-N-S 24-925-0820   (HQ)
SPRINGS CANADA, INC
(*Suby of* KEECO, LLC)
110 Matheson Blvd W Suite 200, Mississauga,
ON, L5R 3T4
(905) 890-4994
Emp Here 30   *Sales* 24,916,100
SIC 5131 Piece goods and notions
Catherine Callaghan

D-U-N-S 24-561-5641   (SL)
STRACHAN, ALASTAIR
5770 Hurontario St Suite 200, Mississauga,
ON, L5R 3G5

(905) 568-9500
Emp Here 40   *Sales* 10,870,240
SIC 6531 Real estate agents and managers
Clynn Miranda

D-U-N-S 20-994-2630   (HQ)
SUBARU CANADA, INC
(*Suby of* SUBARU CORPORATION)
560 Suffolk Crt, Mississauga, ON, L5R 4J7
(905) 568-4959
Emp Here 20   *Sales* 18,210,750
SIC 5012 Automobiles and other motor vehi-
cles
Norio Osakabe
Brian Hawkins

D-U-N-S 24-000-3637   (SL)
SUMMITT ENERGY MANAGEMENT INC
100 Milverton Dr Suite 608, Mississauga, ON,
L5R 4H1
(905) 366-7000
Emp Here 30   *Sales* 18,798,420
SIC 4911 Electric services
Gerald M Haggarty
Gaetana Girardi
William E Thomson
John Yarnell

D-U-N-S 25-321-0488   (BR)
TORONTO-DOMINION BANK, THE
TD BANK
(*Suby of* TORONTO-DOMINION BANK, THE)
20 Milverton Dr Suite 10, Mississauga, ON,
L5R 3G2
(905) 568-3600
Emp Here 75
SIC 6021 National commercial banks
Joni Timbers

D-U-N-S 20-013-3580   (HQ)
TREE OF LIFE CANADA ULC
(*Suby of* KEHE DISTRIBUTORS, LLC)
6185 Mclaughlin Rd, Mississauga, ON, L5R
3W7
(905) 507-6161
Emp Here 140   *Sales* 286,686,400
SIC 5141 Groceries, general line
James Moody
Bill Ivany
Chris Powell
Peter Clarke
Gordon E. Walker
Helen Morrison
Barry Sheldrick
Howard Chong
Sheila Farah
Leeola Zanetti

D-U-N-S 24-135-9798   (SL)
UNIPETRO DIXIE INC
HUSKY TRUCK STOP
6035 Mclaughlin Rd, Mississauga, ON, L5R
1B9
(905) 712-8800
Emp Here 50   *Sales* 24,903,900
SIC 5541 Gasoline service stations
Judith Blake

D-U-N-S 20-702-4667   (HQ)
UPPER CANADA SOAP & CANDLE MAK-
ERS CORPORATION
5875 Chedworth Way, Mississauga, ON, L5R
3L9
(905) 897-1710
Sales 44,551,200
SIC 5199 Nondurable goods, nec
Stephen G Flatt
Chantelle Tersigni

D-U-N-S 20-178-1390   (SL)
WELLA CANADA, INC
WELLA MARKET
(*Suby of* COTY INC.)
5800 Avebury Rd Unit 1, Mississauga, ON,
L5R 3M3
(905) 568-2494
Emp Here 80   *Sales* 67,002,640
SIC 5131 Piece goods and notions

David Dias
Joseph Iannuzzi
Rod Little
Reuben Carranza
Zhibiao Chen

D-U-N-S 24-874-1852   (SL)
WELLS FARGO FINANCIAL RETAIL SER-
VICES COMPANY OF CANADA
TRANS CANADA
(*Suby of* WELLS FARGO & COMPANY)
55 Standish Crt Suite 300, Mississauga, ON,
L5R 4B2
Emp Here 800   *Sales* 180,984,800
SIC 7322 Adjustment and collection services
Dan Abbott
Mike Clancy

D-U-N-S 24-850-6714   (BR)
WESCO DISTRIBUTION CANADA LP
(*Suby of* WESCO INTERNATIONAL, INC.)
6170 Belgrave Rd, Mississauga, ON, L5R 4G8
(905) 890-3344
Emp Here 85
SIC 5063 Electrical apparatus and equipment
Al Boch

D-U-N-S 20-383-8375   (SL)
WINMAGIC CORP
(*Suby of* WINMAGIC INC)
5600a Cancross Crt, Mississauga, ON, L5R
3E9
(905) 502-7000
Emp Here 130   *Sales* 18,743,660
SIC 7371 Custom computer programming ser-
vices
Thi Nguyen-Huu
Mark Hickman
Michael Inglis

D-U-N-S 25-530-6508   (HQ)
WINMAGIC INC
5600 Cancross Crt, Mississauga, ON, L5R
3E9
(905) 502-7000
Sales 17,352,088
SIC 7372 Prepackaged software
Thi Nguyen-Huu
Silvia Nguyen-Huu

D-U-N-S 20-180-5616   (HQ)
WINNERS MERCHANTS INTERNATIONAL
L.P.
HOMESENSE
(*Suby of* THE TJX COMPANIES INC)
60 Standish Crt, Mississauga, ON, L5R 0G1
(905) 405-8000
Emp Here 600   *Sales* 1,497,060,000
SIC 5651 Family clothing stores
Douglas Mizzi
Jens Cermak
Douglas Moffatt

Mississauga, ON L5S

D-U-N-S 25-370-7806   (BR)
1132694 ONTARIO INC
SPRAY-PAK INDUSTRIES
(*Suby of* PLZ AEROSCIENCE CORPORA-
TION)
7550 Kimbel St, Mississauga, ON, L5S 1A2
(905) 677-1948
Emp Here 75
SIC 7389 Business services, nec
Antonietta Mauro

D-U-N-S 25-849-6553   (HQ)
1149318 ONTARIO INC
C.C.T. LOGISTICS SERVICES
6900 Tranmere Dr, Mississauga, ON, L5S 1L9
(866) 576-4228
Sales 12,596,320
SIC 4214 Local trucking with storage

Tom Hillier

D-U-N-S 20-057-3918   (SL)
1519418 ONTARIO INC
VANGUARD DELIVERS
265 Export Blvd, Mississauga, ON, L5S 1Y4
(905) 670-9300
Emp Here 23   *Sales* 11,959,241
SIC 4731 Freight transportation arrangement
Richard Court
Edward Ayranto
Mark Bates
Joseph Pariselli
John Hunkin

D-U-N-S 20-900-6105   (SL)
333111 ONTARIO LIMITED
KOSS AEROSPACE
(*Suby of* CAJIC FAMILY HOLDINGS INC)
7805 Tranmere Dr, Mississauga, ON, L5S 1V5
(905) 364-5000
Emp Here 95   *Sales* 21,265,085
SIC 3728 Aircraft parts and equipment, nec
Drago Cajic
Alex Cajic
David Cajic
Helene Cajic

D-U-N-S 20-954-8267   (SL)
4166621 CANADA INC
FLEX PRESSION (ONTARIO)
2244 Drew Road Units 4 & 5, Mississauga,
ON, L5S 1B1
(905) 671-2244
Emp Here 80
SIC 7389 Business services, nec
Dean Bond
Edward Bergshoeff

D-U-N-S 24-347-1617   (SL)
4213424 CANADA INC
GRANT BROTHERS SALES
7885 Tranmere Dr Unit 1, Mississauga, ON,
L5S 1V8
(905) 677-7299
Emp Here 90   *Sales* 32,779,350
SIC 5013 Motor vehicle supplies and new
parts
John Grant

D-U-N-S 24-818-0671   (SL)
701466 ONTARIO LIMITED
ANTHOS ENGINEERING
7195 Tranmere Dr Suite 4, Mississauga, ON,
L5S 1N4
(905) 672-6370
Emp Here 12   *Sales* 12,004,068
SIC 5051 Metals service centers and offices
William Bletsas
Sofia Bletsas

D-U-N-S 24-205-0073   (HQ)
ACCO BRANDS CANADA INC
GBC
(*Suby of* ACCO BRANDS CORPORATION)
7381 Bramalea Rd, Mississauga, ON, L5S
1C4
(905) 364-2600
Emp Here 120   *Sales* 108,137,645
SIC 3579 Office machines, nec
Boris Elisman
Neal V Fenwick
Mark C. Anderson
Jagannath Bobji
Kathleen D. Hood

D-U-N-S 24-420-5159   (HQ)
ACCO BRANDS CANADA LP
HILROY
7381 Bramalea Rd, Mississauga, ON, L5S
1C4
(905) 364-2600
Sales 29,215,200
SIC 2678 Stationery products
Robert Hodan

D-U-N-S 25-215-2202   (HQ)
ACE BAKERY LIMITED

(Suby of GEORGE WESTON LIMITED)
580 Secretariat Crt, Mississauga, ON, L5S 2A5
(905) 565-8138
Emp Here 200   Sales 96,232,000
SIC 5461 Retail bakeries
  Roy Benin
  Daryl Hanstead
  Jason Poledano

D-U-N-S 24-094-0015   (HQ)
ACTION TRAILER SALES INC
NEWCOM MEDIA INC
2332 Drew Rd, Mississauga, ON, L5S 1B8
(905) 678-1444
Sales 29,137,200
SIC 5012 Automobiles and other motor vehicles
  Bob Ray

D-U-N-S 24-315-9878   (HQ)
AGORA MANUFACTURING INC
7770 Tranmere Dr, Mississauga, ON, L5S 1L9
(905) 362-1700
Sales 13,445,950
SIC 3499 Fabricated Metal products, nec
  Mike Simone
  Len Bozzi

D-U-N-S 25-220-8236   (HQ)
AIR GEORGIAN LIMITED
AIR CANADA EXPRESS
(Suby of GEORGIAN INTERNATIONAL LIMITED)
2450 Derry Rd E Suite 3, Mississauga, ON, L5S 1B2
(905) 676-1221
Sales 68,230,680
SIC 4522 Air transportation, nonscheduled
  James Massie Jr
  Paul Mulrooney

D-U-N-S 24-666-3082   (HQ)
ALL-CAN MEDICAL INC
7575 Kimbel St Unit 5, Mississauga, ON, L5S 1C8
(905) 677-9410
Emp Here 1   Sales 24,846,856
SIC 4925 Gas production and/or distribution
  Joe Lassaline

D-U-N-S 24-409-0577   (HQ)
AMJ CAMPBELL INC
AMJ VAN LINES
(Suby of 2015825 ONTARIO INC)
7075 Tomken Rd, Mississauga, ON, L5S 1R7
(905) 795-3785
Emp Here 50   Sales 41,141,200
SIC 4214 Local trucking with storage
  Bruce D Bowser
  Denis Frappier
  Johnny Ciampi
  Richard Smart

D-U-N-S 20-694-3859   (SL)
ASD SOLUTIONS LTD
(Suby of SOLUTIONS 2 GO INC)
190 Statesman Dr, Mississauga, ON, L5S 1X7
(519) 271-4900
Emp Here 60   Sales 32,121,120
SIC 5045 Computers, peripherals, and software
  Oliver Bock
  Gabrielle Chevalier

D-U-N-S 20-974-2337   (HQ)
AURORA IMPORTING & DISTRIBUTING LIMITED
815 Gana Crt, Mississauga, ON, L5S 1P2
(905) 670-1855
Sales 33,423,080
SIC 5149 Groceries and related products, nec
  Anthony Morello

D-U-N-S 24-076-1754   (BR)
AXXESS INTERNATIONAL COURTIERS EN DOUANES INC
1804 Alstep Dr Unit 1, Mississauga, ON, L5S

1W1
(905) 672-0270
Emp Here 112
SIC 4731 Freight transportation arrangement
  Terry Walsh

D-U-N-S 20-650-4685   (HQ)
BATESVILLE CANADA LTD
2390 Anson Dr, Mississauga, ON, L5S 1G2
(905) 673-7717
Emp Here 11   Sales 23,751,300
SIC 5087 Service establishment equipment
  Kenneth A. Camp
  John R. Zerkle
  Cindy Lucchese
  Gregpru R/ Wylie

D-U-N-S 25-246-9036   (SL)
BELVIKA TRADE & PACKAGING LTD
A-450 Export Blvd, Mississauga, ON, L5S 2A4
(905) 502-7444
Emp Here 75   Sales 33,691,425
SIC 7389 Business services, nec
  Tom Golias
  Mario Golias
  Bryan Knebel

D-U-N-S 20-878-4249   (HQ)
BRYTOR INTERNATIONAL MOVING INC
275 Export Blvd, Mississauga, ON, L5S 1Y4
(905) 564-8855
Emp Here 25   Sales 15,722,665
SIC 7389 Business services, nec
  Michael Rathbone
  Brian Jones
  Jay Ryan

D-U-N-S 24-340-8304   (SL)
CANADA CARTAGE DIVERSIFIED ULC
(Suby of CANADA CARTAGE SYSTEM LIMITED PARTNERSHIP)
1115 Cardiff Blvd, Mississauga, ON, L5S 1L8
(905) 564-2115
Emp Here 51   Sales 10,491,006
SIC 4212 Local trucking, without storage
  Jeff Lindsay

D-U-N-S 20-085-1660   (HQ)
CANADA CARTAGE SYSTEM LIMITED PARTNERSHIP
1115 Cardiff Blvd, Mississauga, ON, L5S 1L8
(905) 564-2115
Emp Here 10   Sales 25,998,350
SIC 4731 Freight transportation arrangement
  William Jeffrey Lindsay
  David Bacon
  Dave Zavitz
  Steve Sacha

D-U-N-S 24-361-5960   (HQ)
CANADIAN BEARINGS LTD
1600 Drew Rd, Mississauga, ON, L5S 1S5
(905) 670-7422
Emp Here 100   Sales 141,441,700
SIC 5085 Industrial supplies
  Farrokh Khalili

D-U-N-S 20-041-2989   (BR)
CANAM BATIMENTS ET STRUCTURES INC
CANAM BATIMENTS ET STRUCTURES INC
(Suby of CANAM LUX PARENT COMPANY SARL)
1739 Drew Rd, Mississauga, ON, L5S 1J5
(905) 671-3460
Emp Here 185
SIC 3441 Fabricated structural Metal
  Warren Fournier

D-U-N-S 24-559-4960   (SL)
CAPITAL SAFETY GROUP CANADA ULC
PROTECTA
(Suby of 3M COMPANY)
260 Export Blvd, Mississauga, ON, L5S 1Y9
(905) 795-9333
Emp Here 200   Sales 45,457,800
SIC 3842 Surgical appliances and supplies
  Frank Courtemanche

D-U-N-S 20-036-4909   (HQ)
CARRIER ENTERPRISE CANADA, L.P.
WWG TOTALLINE
195 Statesman Dr, Mississauga, ON, L5S 1X4
(905) 672-0606
Emp Here 95   Sales 159,175,224
SIC 5075 Warm air heating and air conditioning
  Paul Davignon
  Steven Boyack
  Gord Lambert
  Robert Mcdonough

D-U-N-S 20-594-9407   (BR)
CASCADES CANADA ULC
CASCADE BOXBOARD GROUP, THE
(Suby of CASCADES INC)
7830 Tranmere Dr Suite Unit, Mississauga, ON, L5S 1L9
(905) 678-8211
Emp Here 200
SIC 7389 Business services, nec
  Roland Bettesworth

D-U-N-S 24-466-4707   (BR)
CASCADES CANADA ULC
CASCADES CONTAINERBOARD PACKAGING - MISSISSAUGA
(Suby of CASCADES INC)
7447 Bramalea Rd, Mississauga, ON, L5S 1C4
(905) 671-2940
Emp Here 110
SIC 2631 Paperboard mills
  Joe Zenga

D-U-N-S 20-300-7810   (SL)
CCD LIMITED PARTNERSHIP
1115 Cardiff Blvd, Mississauga, ON, L5S 1L8
(905) 564-2115
Emp Here 75   Sales 20,501,250
SIC 6712 Bank holding companies
  William Jeffrey Lindsay
  David Bacon
  Dave Zavitz
  Steve Sacha

D-U-N-S 20-048-0273   (HQ)
CCT CANADA INC
6900 Tranmere Dr, Mississauga, ON, L5S 1L9
(905) 362-9198
Emp Here 3   Sales 49,396,865
SIC 4731 Freight transportation arrangement
  Dave Campbell

D-U-N-S 20-273-4125   (SL)
CENTURY 21 SKYLARK REAL ESTATE LTD
1510 Drew Rd Unit 6, Mississauga, ON, L5S 1W7
(905) 673-3100
Emp Here 49   Sales 16,029,223
SIC 6531 Real estate agents and managers
  Manjit Saggu

D-U-N-S 24-868-8400   (HQ)
CHARTRIGHT AIR INC
CHARTRIGHT AIR GROUP
2450 Derry Rd E, Mississauga, ON, L5S 1B2
(905) 671-4674
Emp Here 50   Sales 14,920,480
SIC 8742 Management consulting services
  Adam E Keller

D-U-N-S 25-362-0736   (HQ)
CHURCH & DWIGHT CANADA CORP
(Suby of CHURCH & DWIGHT CO., INC.)
635 Secretariat Crt, Mississauga, ON, L5S 0A5
(905) 696-6570
Sales 56,804,200
SIC 2834 Pharmaceutical preparations
  Gregory J Drohan

D-U-N-S 25-195-7932   (SL)
CONTINENTAL CARGO SYSTEMS INC
7175 Tranmere Dr Unit 1b, Mississauga, ON, L5S 1N4

(905) 405-0096
Emp Here 30   Sales 11,560,800
SIC 4731 Freight transportation arrangement
  Colin Campbell

D-U-N-S 20-047-6950   (HQ)
CREIGHTON ROCK DRILL LIMITED
2222 Drew Rd, Mississauga, ON, L5S 1B1
(905) 673-8200
Emp Here 21   Sales 20,426,118
SIC 5082 Construction and mining machinery
  Robert Creighton
  Susan Tomowich
  Alexander Creighton
  James Creighton
  Peter Creighton

D-U-N-S 24-302-0765   (HQ)
CURTIS INTERNATIONAL LTD
(Suby of CURTIS HOLDINGS INC)
7045 Beckett Dr Unit 15, Mississauga, ON, L5S 2A3
(416) 674-2123
Emp Here 37   Sales 350,723,929
SIC 5065 Electronic parts and equipment, nec
  Aaron Herzog
  Yann Penot
  Jacob Herzog
  Cameron Dickson

D-U-N-S 25-167-6599   (SL)
DATA DIRECT GROUP INC
2001 Drew Rd Unit 1, Mississauga, ON, L5S 1S4
(905) 564-0150
Emp Here 65   Sales 13,762,060
SIC 7331 Direct mail advertising services
  Ebraham Sesook
  Nam Nguyen

D-U-N-S 20-260-9970   (HQ)
DATAWIND INC
7895 Tranmere Dr Suite 207, Mississauga, ON, L5S 1V9
(905) 671-0202
Sales 43,964,387
SIC 4813 Telephone communication, except radio
  Suneet Singh Tuli
  Jonathan Brockhouse
  Jerry Tarasofsky
  Hemant Nayak
  Raja Singh Tuli

D-U-N-S 24-869-1545   (HQ)
DESCO PLUMBING AND HEATING SUPPLY INC
(Suby of ENTREPRISES MIRCA INC, LES)
7550 Tranmere Dr, Mississauga, ON, L5S 1S6
(416) 293-8219
Emp Here 41   Sales 67,626,468
SIC 5074 Plumbing and heating equipment and supplies (hydronics)
  Jacques Deschenes
  John Leeson
  Martin Deschenes
  Joe Senese
  Marc Lapierre
  Francois Deschenes

D-U-N-S 24-126-4071   (BR)
DHL GLOBAL FORWARDING (CANADA) INC
(Suby of DEUTSCHE POST AG)
1825 Alstep Dr, Mississauga, ON, L5S 1Y5

Emp Here 150
SIC 4731 Freight transportation arrangement
  John O'conner

D-U-N-S 20-007-5851   (HQ)
DIRECT LIMITED PARTNERSHIP
1115 Cardiff Blvd, Mississauga, ON, L5S 1L8
(905) 564-2115
Emp Here 30   Sales 202,819,100
SIC 4212 Local trucking, without storage
  William Jeffrey Lindsay
  Steve Sacha

D-U-N-S 20-354-5801   (SL)
DISPLAY-VU CORP
7045 Beckett Dr Unit 15, Mississauga, ON, L5S 2A3
(416) 674-2123
Emp Here 50   *Sales* 22,358,700
SIC 5065 Electronic parts and equipment, nec
Jacob Herzog
Aaron Herzog
Cameron Dickson

D-U-N-S 20-769-1494   (HQ)
DR. OETKER CANADA LTD
(*Suby of* DR. AUGUST OETKER KG)
2229 Drew Rd, Mississauga, ON, L5S 1E5
(905) 678-1311
Sales 41,482,800
SIC 2038 Frozen specialties, nec
Christian Von Twickel
Dave Spragge
Thomas Kruegar

D-U-N-S 25-396-7376   (SL)
DUBWEAR INC
DUBWEAR CLOTHING COMPANY
7880 Tranmere Dr, Mississauga, ON, L5S 1L9
(905) 362-1334
Emp Here 26   *Sales* 12,956,372
SIC 5136 Men's and boy's clothing
Paul Dub

D-U-N-S 25-105-4177   (HQ)
ECU LINE CANADA INC
1804 Alstep Dr Suite 2, Mississauga, ON, L5S 1W1
(905) 677-8334
Emp Here 1   *Sales* 14,039,109
SIC 4731 Freight transportation arrangement
Michael Mccarthy
Michael Teixeira
Elvio Lancione

D-U-N-S 20-288-5232   (HQ)
EVOQUA WATER TECHNOLOGIES LTD
GROUP ISH20TOP
(*Suby of* EVOQUA WATER TECHNOLOGIES CORP.)
2045 Drew Rd, Mississauga, ON, L5S 1S4
(905) 890-2803
Emp Here 30   *Sales* 19,980,090
SIC 3589 Service industry machinery, nec
Richard Donatelli
Ronald C. Keating
Edward May
Benedict T. Stas

D-U-N-S 20-714-7617   (BR)
FEDERAL EXPRESS CANADA CORPORATION
FEDEX SHIP CENTRE
(*Suby of* FEDEX CORPORATION)
6895 Bramalea Rd Suite 1, Mississauga, ON, L5S 1Z7
(800) 463-3339
Emp Here 300
SIC 4215 Courier services, except by air

D-U-N-S 25-120-6983   (BR)
FIELD AVIATION COMPANY INC
(*Suby of* FIELD AEROSPACE, INC.)
2450 Derry Rd E, Mississauga, ON, L5S 1B2
(905) 676-1540
Emp Here 205
SIC 4581 Airports, flying fields, and services
Charles Korozsi

D-U-N-S 25-120-0465   (SL)
FIVE STAR RAGS INC
7500 Kimbel St, Mississauga, ON, L5S 1A2
(905) 405-8365
Emp Here 90   *Sales* 21,989,520
SIC 5932 Used merchandise stores
Salim Karmali
Mohamed Karmali
Karim Karmali

D-U-N-S 20-715-7512   (SL)
FURNACE BELT COMPANY LIMITED, THE

1874 Drew Rd Unit 7, Mississauga, ON, L5S 1J6
(905) 677-5068
Emp Here 25   *Sales* 11,875,650
SIC 5084 Industrial machinery and equipment
Joseph Tatone
Mario Dicenso

D-U-N-S 24-139-4295   (SL)
GARRY MACHINE MFG INC
165 Statesman Dr, Mississauga, ON, L5S 1X4
(905) 564-5340
Emp Here 55   *Sales* 12,210,055
SIC 3569 General industrial machinery, nec
Raghbir Bhullar

D-U-N-S 24-384-5823   (HQ)
GIDDEN MORTON ASSOCIATES INC
GMA
7050a Bramalea Rd Unit 27a, Mississauga, ON, L5S 1T1
(905) 671-8111
Emp Here 16   *Sales* 15,651,090
SIC 5065 Electronic parts and equipment, nec
Larry Morton
Sterling Steeves

D-U-N-S 24-977-6162   (SL)
GLOBAL AEROSPACE CORPORATION
7075 Fir Tree Dr, Mississauga, ON, L5S 1J7
(905) 678-6311
Emp Here 33   *Sales* 10,716,882
SIC 4581 Airports, flying fields, and services
David Kersteman
Adams Scott
Sandra Kersteman

D-U-N-S 20-343-3651   (SL)
GRAPHIC PACKAGING INTERNATIONAL CANADA ULC
(*Suby of* GRAPHIC PACKAGING HOLDING COMPANY)
7830 Tranmere Dr, Mississauga, ON, L5S 1L9
(905) 678-8211
Emp Here 100   *Sales* 19,476,800
SIC 2631 Paperboard mills
Kevin Ronney

D-U-N-S 24-871-2374   (HQ)
HELLMANN WORLDWIDE LOGISTICS INC
(*Suby of* HELLMANN WORLDWIDE LOGISTICS SE & CO. KG)
1375 Cardiff Blvd Unit 1, Mississauga, ON, L5S 1R1
(905) 564-6620
Emp Here 32   *Sales* 37,345,952
SIC 4731 Freight transportation arrangement
Peter Teixeira
Benny Tom
Julian Riches

D-U-N-S 24-538-3583   (SL)
HIGH STRENGTH PLATES & PROFILES INC
HARDBOR STEELS INTERNATIONAL
7464 Tranmere Dr, Mississauga, ON, L5S 1K4
(905) 673-5770
Emp Here 50   *Sales* 11,671,750
SIC 3312 Blast furnaces and steel mills
Jason Brock

D-U-N-S 25-117-5451   (SL)
HOMETURF LTD
HOMETURF LAWN CARE SERVICES
7123 Fir Tree Dr, Mississauga, ON, L5S 1G4
(905) 791-8873
Emp Here 20   *Sales* 14,508,780
SIC 6331 Fire, marine, and casualty insurance
Bruce Haastrecht

D-U-N-S 20-167-2508   (HQ)
HUBERGROUP CANADA LIMITED
HUBERGROUP
(*Suby of* MHM HOLDING GESELLSCHAFT MIT BESCHRANKTER HAFTUNG)
2150a Drew Rd, Mississauga, ON, L5S 1B1
(905) 671-0750
Emp Here 35   *Sales* 25,071,264

SIC 2893 Printing ink
Vivy Dacosta

D-U-N-S 24-765-3108   (HQ)
IMPULSE TECHNOLOGIES LTD
920 Gana Crt, Mississauga, ON, L5S 1Z4
(905) 564-9266
Emp Here 31   *Sales* 15,651,090
SIC 5051 Metals service centers and offices
Fabrizio Vatri
Terry Robertson

D-U-N-S 24-198-7544   (SL)
INTRALEC ELECTRICAL PRODUCTS LTD
1200 Cardiff Blvd Unit 1, Mississauga, ON, L5S 1P6
(905) 670-0970
Emp Here 21   *Sales* 10,919,307
SIC 4731 Freight transportation arrangement
Ted Doherty
Murray Chamney

D-U-N-S 24-254-9108   (SL)
K.A.S. GROUP OF COMPANIES INC, THE
7895 Tranmere Dr Suite 18, Mississauga, ON, L5S 1V9
(905) 677-3368
Emp Here 45   *Sales* 10,663,650
SIC 7361 Employment agencies
Karen Siff Exkorn

D-U-N-S 20-804-2999   (BR)
L3 TECHNOLOGIES MAS INC
L-3 COMMUNICATIONS MAS (CANADA) INC
(*Suby of* L3HARRIS TECHNOLOGIES, INC.)
7785 Tranmere Dr, Mississauga, ON, L5S 1W5
(905) 671-5879
Emp Here 75
SIC 4581 Airports, flying fields, and services
Gary Sternklar

D-U-N-S 25-360-8160   (BR)
LINCOLN ELECTRIC COMPANY OF CANADA LP
INDALCO ALLOYS
(*Suby of* LINCOLN ELECTRIC HOLDINGS, INC.)
939 Gana Crt, Mississauga, ON, L5S 1N9
(905) 564-1151
Emp Here 125
SIC 3548 Welding apparatus
Belinda Carino

D-U-N-S 20-536-3245   (HQ)
MARKEM-IMAJE INC
(*Suby of* DOVER CORPORATION)
7075 Edwards Blvd Unit 2, Mississauga, ON, L5S 1Z2
(800) 267-5108
Emp Here 26   *Sales* 19,476,066
SIC 5084 Industrial machinery and equipment
Lionel Ginisty
Donald Redford

D-U-N-S 24-951-9521   (SL)
MASTERNET LTD
690 Gana Crt, Mississauga, ON, L5S 1P2
(905) 795-0005
Emp Here 50   *Sales* 10,094,850
SIC 3089 Plastics products, nec
Paul Hartman
Linda Duval
Steven Hartman

D-U-N-S 25-169-5383   (SL)
MECHANICAL SYSTEMS REMANUFAC-TURING INC
1740 Drew Rd, Mississauga, ON, L5S 1J6
(905) 673-5733
Emp Here 30   *Sales* 14,250,780
SIC 5088 Transportation equipment and supplies
Robert Mckeracher

D-U-N-S 24-918-4144   (HQ)
MESTEK CANADA INC
RBI DIVISION OF MESTEK CANADA

(*Suby of* MESTEK, INC.)
7555 Tranmere Dr, Mississauga, ON, L5S 1L4
(905) 670-5888
Emp Here 3   *Sales* 17,095,565
SIC 3433 Heating equipment, except electric
Manny Dasilva
John E. Reed
Timothy Scanlan
Stephen M. Shea

D-U-N-S 24-737-4072   (HQ)
MONTE CARLO HOTEL-MOTEL INTERNATIONAL INC
MONTE CARLO INNS
7045 Edwards Blvd Fl 5, Mississauga, ON, L5S 1X2
(905) 564-6194
Emp Here 12   *Sales* 19,901,447
SIC 7011 Hotels and motels
Dominic Meffe

D-U-N-S 20-512-3552   (SL)
MPI PACKAGING INC
7400b Bramalea Rd, Mississauga, ON, L5S 1W9
(905) 673-6447
Emp Here 60   *Sales* 12,113,820
SIC 3085 Plastics bottles
Ron O'brien

D-U-N-S 24-455-5298   (HQ)
NATIONAL ENERGY EQUIPMENT INC
NEE
1850 Derry Rd E, Mississauga, ON, L5S 1Y6
(905) 564-2422
Emp Here 90   *Sales* 226,794,450
SIC 5084 Industrial machinery and equipment
Tom Ferries
Nama Namasivayam
Joe Lynch

D-U-N-S 20-364-3890   (BR)
NCS INTERNATIONAL CO
NORAMCO WIRE & CABLE
(*Suby of* GII HOLDINGS CORP)
7635 Tranmere Dr, Mississauga, ON, L5S 1L4
(905) 673-0660
Emp Here 75
SIC 5063 Electrical apparatus and equipment

D-U-N-S 25-174-4905   (BR)
NCS INTERNATIONAL CO
(*Suby of* GII HOLDINGS CORP)
7635 Tranmere Dr, Mississauga, ON, L5S 1L4
(905) 673-0660
Emp Here 100
SIC 5063 Electrical apparatus and equipment
Dave Klarer

D-U-N-S 24-094-4017   (SL)
O-TWO SYSTEMS INTERNATIONAL INC
7575 Kimbel St Unit 5, Mississauga, ON, L5S 1C8

Emp Here 47   *Sales* 12,058,414
SIC 3842 Surgical appliances and supplies

D-U-N-S 20-007-5230   (SL)
PEACE TRANSPORTATION
7370 Bramalea Rd Suite 22, Mississauga, ON, L5S 1N6
(905) 405-1002
Emp Here 35   *Sales* 18,198,845
SIC 4731 Freight transportation arrangement

D-U-N-S 25-144-1986   (SL)
PRAIRIE FINANCIAL GROUP LTD
2355 Derry Rd E Unit 29, Mississauga, ON, L5S 1V6
(905) 612-0800
Emp Here 20   *Sales* 14,508,780
SIC 6311 Life insurance
Bishan Gill

D-U-N-S 24-077-5692   (SL)
PUDDY BROS. LIMITED
7120 Edwards Blvd, Mississauga, ON, L5S 1Z1

(289) 541-7875
Emp Here 250   *Sales* 121,846,250
SIC 2015 Poultry slaughtering and processing
Louis Mastromatteo
Morgan Mastromatteo

D-U-N-S 24-101-1704   (SL)
QWINSTAR CANADA INC
CASHTECH CURRENCY PRODUCTS
(*Suby of* QWINSTAR HOLDINGS LLC)
1040 Cardiff Blvd, Mississauga, ON, L5S 1P3
(905) 696-8102
Emp Here 60   *Sales* 15,162,040
SIC 8741 Management services
Larry Mccarter
Andrea Lombardi
Matthew Lombardi
Gino Lombardi

D-U-N-S 24-927-2345   (SL)
RDI CHEMICAL CORPORATION
KEM CANADA MANUFACTURING
1875 Drew Rd, Mississauga, ON, L5S 1J5
(905) 673-2556
Emp Here 30   *Sales* 21,910,350
SIC 5169 Chemicals and allied products, nec
James (Jim) Damianoff
Patricia (Jane) Robbins

D-U-N-S 24-419-6630   (SL)
RUNNALLS INDUSTRIES INC
1275 Cardiff Blvd, Mississauga, ON, L5S 1R1
(905) 453-4220
Emp Here 11   *Sales* 11,003,729
SIC 5051 Metals service centers and offices
Melvin Runnalls
Debbie Reid

D-U-N-S 24-850-8777   (SL)
S.A.T SOLAR & ALTERNATIVE TECHNOLOGY
1935 Drew Rd Suite 28, Mississauga, ON, L5S 1M7
(905) 673-6060
Emp Here 200   *Sales* 46,613,000
SIC 1711 Plumbing, heating, air-conditioning
Remo Bonewitz

D-U-N-S 20-401-5994   (SL)
SCARLETT HOUSE FOOD GROUP INC
7615 Kimbel St Unit 8, Mississauga, ON, L5S 1A8
(905) 672-6302
Emp Here 175   *Sales* 7,965,825
SIC 5812 Eating places
Stephen Coulighan
Paul Andersen
Beniamino Contella
Maher Ahmed

D-U-N-S 20-145-3552   (SL)
SCM GROUP CANADA INC
(*Suby of* SCM GROUP SPA)
1180 Lorimar Dr, Mississauga, ON, L5S 1M9
(905) 670-5110
Emp Here 23   *Sales* 10,925,598
SIC 5084 Industrial machinery and equipment
Richard Bluteau
Susanna Bartolomeo

D-U-N-S 20-693-4056   (SL)
SHEEN LEGEND PACKAGING CORP
BENECO PACKAGING
2280 Drew Rd Suite B, Mississauga, ON, L5S 1B8
(905) 677-2888
Emp Here 50   *Sales* 11,671,750
SIC 2657 Folding paperboard boxes
Carol Jiang

D-U-N-S 20-718-0340   (HQ)
SILGAN PLASTICS CANADA INC
(*Suby of* SILGAN HOLDINGS INC.)
1575 Drew Rd, Mississauga, ON, L5S 1S5
(905) 677-2324
Emp Here 120   *Sales* 162,392,160
SIC 3089 Plastics products, nec
Emidio Di Meo

Russell Gervais

D-U-N-S 24-965-4153   (SL)
STAINLESS PROCESS EQUIPMENT INC
1317 Cardiff Blvd, Mississauga, ON, L5S 1R1
(905) 670-1163
Emp Here 35   *Sales* 15,651,090
SIC 5046 Commercial equipment, nec
Brian Coutts
Dennis O'brien
Edward Cole

D-U-N-S 24-951-8887   (SL)
STAR PLASTICS INC
1930 Drew Rd Unit 1, Mississauga, ON, L5S 1J6
(905) 672-0298
Emp Here 125   *Sales* 19,857,250
SIC 3089 Plastics products, nec
Jas Dhami

D-U-N-S 20-176-4123   (HQ)
SUPER-PUFFT SNACKS CORP
880 Gana Crt, Mississauga, ON, L5S 1N8
(905) 564-1180
Sales 121,846,250
SIC 2096 Potato chips and similar snacks
Yousif Al Ali
Yahya Abbas
Mohammad Ali

D-U-N-S 24-760-7521   (SL)
TBS CANADA INC
(*Suby of* BERKSHIRE HATHAWAY INC.)
7090 Edwards Blvd, Mississauga, ON, L5S 1Z1
(905) 362-5206
Emp Here 150   *Sales* 38,023,500
SIC 8748 Business consulting, nec
Christopher Hanes

D-U-N-S 24-745-3798   (HQ)
TORLYS INC
1900 Derry Rd E, Mississauga, ON, L5S 1Y6
(905) 612-8772
Emp Here 40   *Sales* 35,619,920
SIC 5023 Homefurnishings
Peter Barretto
Fernando Luz
Jeff Conley
Anibal Claudino

D-U-N-S 24-736-9515   (SL)
TRESMAN STEEL INDUSTRIES LTD
(*Suby of* TRESMAN HOLDINGS LTD)
286 Statesman Dr, Mississauga, ON, L5S 1X7
(905) 795-8757
Emp Here 50   *Sales* 11,168,640
SIC 3441 Fabricated structural Metal
Guerrino Trentin
Ivano Trentin
Imre Kenedi

D-U-N-S 20-628-7633   (HQ)
TSUBAKI OF CANADA LIMITED
(*Suby of* TSUBAKIMOTO CHAIN CO.)
1630 Drew Rd, Mississauga, ON, L5S 1J6
(905) 676-0400
Emp Here 120   *Sales* 68,282,200
SIC 5085 Industrial supplies
Kevin Power
Jos Sueters
Fernando Andrade

D-U-N-S 25-194-7529   (SL)
TVH CANADA LTD
TVH
(*Suby of* TVH PARTS CO.)
1039 Cardiff Blvd, Mississauga, ON, L5S 1P4
(905) 564-0003
Emp Here 32   *Sales* 11,654,880
SIC 5013 Motor vehicle supplies and new parts
Patrick Mclaughlin

D-U-N-S 24-007-6505   (HQ)
UNITED PARCEL SERVICE CANADA LTD
UPS CANADA

(*Suby of* UNITED PARCEL SERVICE, INC.)
1930 Derry Rd E, Mississauga, ON, L5S 1E2
(800) 742-5877
Emp Here 100   *Sales* 2,396,953,000
SIC 4212 Local trucking, without storage
Alan Gershenhorn
Christoph Atz
Dominic Porporino
Paul Winters
Craig Podrebarac
Bill Fahrlender
Edwin Langdon
Amgad Shehata
Alice Lee
Daniel Shea

D-U-N-S 20-703-5259   (BR)
UPS SCS INC
UPS SCS, INC
(*Suby of* UNITED PARCEL SERVICE, INC.)
1930 Derry Rd E, Mississauga, ON, L5S 1E2
(800) 742-5877
Emp Here 170
SIC 4512 Air transportation, scheduled
Donald Hogan

D-U-N-S 24-424-8183   (SL)
WINSTON STEEL INC
7496 Tranmere Dr, Mississauga, ON, L5S 1K4
(905) 747-7579
Emp Here 60   *Sales* 26,830,440
SIC 5051 Metals service centers and offices
Ronald Kenwood
Bill Shaw
Douglas Gauthier

Mississauga, ON L5T

D-U-N-S 20-042-8589   (HQ)
1008648 ONTARIO INC
THERMO KING OF TORONTO
6243 Netherhart Rd, Mississauga, ON, L5T 1G5
(905) 564-2800
Emp Here 40   *Sales* 15,149,225
SIC 1711 Plumbing, heating, air-conditioning
Keith Petrosky
George Hasrouni

D-U-N-S 20-736-3826   (SL)
1175648 ONTARIO LIMITED
ADCO LOGISTICS
1190 Meyerside Dr, Mississauga, ON, L5T 1R7
(905) 564-8784
Emp Here 120   *Sales* 24,684,720
SIC 4213 Trucking, except local
Balayogendiran Balasingam

D-U-N-S 20-004-0520   (SL)
1327601 ONTARIO INC
BOSTON PIZZA 505
50 Courtneypark Dr E, Mississauga, ON, L5T 2Y3
(905) 565-6225
Emp Here 135   *Sales* 6,145,065
SIC 5812 Eating places
Jeff Dick

D-U-N-S 24-765-6853   (HQ)
1334869 ONTARIO LIMITED
MASCOT TRUCK PARTS
6575 Kestrel Rd, Mississauga, ON, L5T 1P4
(905) 670-9100
Sales 38,500,996
SIC 3714 Motor vehicle parts and accessories
Glenn Hanthorn

D-U-N-S 24-391-9094   (HQ)
1341611 ONTARIO INC
ITN LOGISTICS GROUP
6975 Pacific Cir Unit D, Mississauga, ON, L5T 2H3
(905) 362-1111
Sales 25,998,350

SIC 4731 Freight transportation arrangement
Ian Kennedy

D-U-N-S 24-396-8299   (SL)
1776963 ONTARIO INC
AMJ CAMPBELL INTERNATIONAL - TORONTO
1445 Courtneypark Dr E, Mississauga, ON, L5T 2E3
(905) 670-6683
Emp Here 30   *Sales* 13,304,700
SIC 7389 Business services, nec
Ole Jensen

D-U-N-S 20-271-8649   (SL)
2213802 ONTARIO INC
BUSINESS SYSTEMS
964 Westport Cres Suite 6, Mississauga, ON, L5T 1S3
(905) 696-6932
Emp Here 23   *Sales* 10,285,002
SIC 5045 Computers, peripherals, and software
Frank Waszun
Donald Mackinnon
Tito Gandhi

D-U-N-S 24-358-8410   (HQ)
3580768 CANADA INC
DST TRANSPORTATION
6505 Vipond Dr, Mississauga, ON, L5T 1J9
(905) 670-6613
Emp Here 75   *Sales* 11,262,592
SIC 4212 Local trucking, without storage
Daljit Singh
Mohinder Kaur Tatla

D-U-N-S 24-180-2081   (HQ)
4 OFFICE AUTOMATION LTD
425 Superior Blvd Unit 1, Mississauga, ON, L5T 2W5
(905) 564-0522
Emp Here 80   *Sales* 44,717,400
SIC 5044 Office equipment
William Norgate

D-U-N-S 24-092-5792   (SL)
421229 ONTARIO LIMITED
DAPHNE FLOWER IMPORTS
7255 Pacific Cir, Mississauga, ON, L5T 1V1
(905) 564-5581
Emp Here 50   *Sales* 16,280,000
SIC 5992 Florists
Daphne Wijesinha
Rohan Wijesinha

D-U-N-S 24-140-0931   (SL)
540731 ONTARIO LIMITED
PANCOR
7105 Pacific Cir, Mississauga, ON, L5T 2A8
(905) 564-5620
Emp Here 75   *Sales* 12,907,015
SIC 1721 Painting and paper hanging
Lougi Panerese

D-U-N-S 25-220-2668   (HQ)
995843 ONTARIO LTD
ALL GRAPHICS SUPPLIES
6691 Edwards Blvd Suite 1, Mississauga, ON, L5T 2H8
(905) 795-2610
Emp Here 32   *Sales* 19,476,066
SIC 5084 Industrial machinery and equipment
Cledwyn Desouza
Charles Desouza
Christopher Desouza

D-U-N-S 24-093-1589   (SL)
A-1 BAGS & SUPPLIES INC
A-1 CASH & CARRY
6400 Kennedy Rd, Mississauga, ON, L5T 2Z5
(905) 676-9950
Emp Here 28   *Sales* 13,300,728
SIC 5087 Service establishment equipment
Amjad Parvaiz
Rifat Parvaiz

D-U-N-S 25-091-7895   (SL)

A-1 PERSONNEL RESOURCES INC
6685 Tomken Rd Suite 211, Mississauga, ON, L5T 2C5
(905) 564-1040
Emp Here 200   *Sales* 14,938,800
SIC 7363 Help supply services
Gunther Wagner
Linda Chapell
Lubo Nazurkiewicz

D-U-N-S 24-626-8981   (SL)
ACCESS METAL SERVICE INC
1035 Mid-Way Blvd, Mississauga, ON, L5T 2C1
(905) 670-3151
Emp Here 11   *Sales* 11,003,729
SIC 5051 Metals service centers and offices
Fab Grant
Kenn Grant

D-U-N-S 24-712-0777   (HQ)
ACIER INOXYDABLE PINACLE INC
455 Ambassador Dr, Mississauga, ON, L5T 2J3
(905) 795-2882
Emp Here 45   *Sales* 71,694,480
SIC 5051 Metals service centers and offices
John Gough
Marc Hebert

D-U-N-S 24-684-6815   (HQ)
ADVANCE DISTRIBUTION LOGISTICS INTERNATIONAL INC
ADLI LOGISTICS
7391 Pacific Cir, Mississauga, ON, L5T 2A4
(905) 362-0548
Sales 12,999,175
SIC 4731 Freight transportation arrangement
Max Greco
Massimo Greco

D-U-N-S 20-257-7433   (SL)
ADVANCED COPPER FOIL INC
ACF
1116 Mid-Way Blvd Unit 5, Mississauga, ON, L5T 2H2
(905) 362-8404
Sales 10,003,390
SIC 5051 Metals service centers and offices
Jim Cuthbertson

D-U-N-S 20-421-2336   (HQ)
AGILITY LOGISTICS, CO
GEOLOGISTICS
(*Suby of* AGILITY PUBLIC WAREHOUSING COMPANY K.S.C.P.)
185 Courtneypark Dr E Suite B, Mississauga, ON, L5T 2T6
(905) 612-7500
Emp Here 80   *Sales* 83,832,856
SIC 4731 Freight transportation arrangement
Michael Shum
Kate Murdoch

D-U-N-S 24-631-4850   (SL)
ALL TRADE COMPUTER FORMS INC
(*Suby of* DELUXE CORPORATION)
60 Admiral Blvd, Mississauga, ON, L5T 2W1

Emp Here 75
SIC 2761 Manifold business forms
Michael Sullivan
Gary P Gregory

D-U-N-S 20-377-4492   (SL)
ALTA E-SOLUTIONS
1145 Westport Cres, Mississauga, ON, L5T 1E8
(905) 564-5539
Emp Here 32   *Sales* 14,309,568
SIC 5045 Computers, peripherals, and software
Moneer Altamimi
Sam Altamimi

D-U-N-S 20-927-9426   (HQ)
ALTERNATIVE BEAUTY SERVICES LTD
1680 Courtneypark Dr E Unit 9, Mississauga,

ON, L5T 1R4
(905) 670-0611
Emp Here 1   *Sales* 18,526,014
SIC 5087 Service establishment equipment
Tony Marinaccio
Sean Coile

D-U-N-S 24-662-9158   (HQ)
APPS CARTAGE INC
APPS INTERNATIONAL
(*Suby of* APPS TRANSPORT GROUP INC)
6495 Tomken Rd, Mississauga, ON, L5T 2X7
(905) 451-2720
Emp Here 148   *Sales* 55,314,300
SIC 4212 Local trucking, without storage
Robert M. Mcdonald
Brent T. Byers

D-U-N-S 24-374-3742   (HQ)
APPS TRANSPORT GROUP INC
6495 Tomken Rd, Mississauga, ON, L5T 2X7
(905) 451-2720
Emp Here 187   *Sales* 109,652,700
SIC 6712 Bank holding companies
Robert Mcdonald
Brent Byers
Lance Norman
Scott Casson

D-U-N-S 24-025-2890   (SL)
ARANA GARDENING SUPPLIES LIMITED
ACTION IMPORTS
6300 Kennedy Rd Unit 1, Mississauga, ON, L5T 2X5
(905) 670-8500
Emp Here 40   *Sales* 29,700,800
SIC 5193 Flowers and florists supplies
Gerry Lekkerkerker
Diana Lekkerkerker
Michelle Lekkerkerker

D-U-N-S 24-951-8218   (HQ)
ARMBRO TRANSPORT INC
6050 Dixie Rd, Mississauga, ON, L5T 1A6
(416) 213-7299
Emp Here 145   *Sales* 97,366,232
SIC 4731 Freight transportation arrangement
Peter Di Tecco

D-U-N-S 24-419-3319   (SL)
ARROW ECS CANADA LIMITED
(*Suby of* ARROW ELECTRONICS, INC.)
171 Superior Blvd Unit 2, Mississauga, ON, L5T 2L6
(905) 670-4699
Emp Here 100   *Sales* 16,684,700
SIC 7372 Prepackaged software
Robert Boulet

D-U-N-S 20-214-1586   (HQ)
ARROW ELECTRONICS CANADA LTD
ARROW/BELL COMPONENTS
(*Suby of* ARROW ELECTRONICS, INC.)
171 Superior Blvd Suite 2, Mississauga, ON, L5T 2L6
(905) 565-4405
Emp Here 100   *Sales* 87,037,050
SIC 5065 Electronic parts and equipment, nec
Michael Long
Paul Reilly
Peter Brown

D-U-N-S 20-348-2468   (HQ)
ARTERRA WINES CANADA, INC
(*Suby of* ONTARIO TEACHERS' PENSION PLAN BOARD)
441 Courtneypark Dr E, Mississauga, ON, L5T 2V3
(905) 564-6900
Emp Here 150   *Sales* 1,188,244,630
SIC 2084 Wines, brandy, and brandy spirits
Jay Wright
Don Dychuk

D-U-N-S 20-210-4550   (HQ)
ATLAS COPCO CANADA INC
ATLAS COPCO COMPRESSORS CANADA, DIV OF

(*Suby of* ATLAS COPCO AB)
1025 Tristar Dr, Mississauga, ON, L5T 1W5
(289) 562-0100
Emp Here 45   *Sales* 365,797,500
SIC 5082 Construction and mining machinery
Johan Halling
Geladi Louka
Jim Levitt

D-U-N-S 20-313-6890   (BR)
ATLAS COPCO CANADA INC
ATLAS COPCO MINING & ROCK EXCAVATION TECHNIQUE CANADA
(*Suby of* ATLAS COPCO AB)
1025 Tristar Dr, Mississauga, ON, L5T 1W5
(289) 562-0100
Emp Here 75
SIC 5082 Construction and mining machinery
Andrew Lyon

D-U-N-S 24-872-5533   (HQ)
ATLAS TIRE WHOLESALE INC
6200 Tomken Rd, Mississauga, ON, L5T 1X7
(905) 670-7354
Sales 64,561,560
SIC 5014 Tires and tubes
Peter Gregory
Deborah Gregory
Diane Tymocko

D-U-N-S 24-851-1136   (SL)
ATOS INC
(*Suby of* ATOS SE)
6375 Shawson Dr, Mississauga, ON, L5T 1S7
(905) 819-5761
Emp Here 160   *Sales* 26,695,520
SIC 7379 Computer related services, nec
Maureen Mccarthy

D-U-N-S 24-977-5537   (HQ)
ATTAR METALS INC
1856 Romani Crt, Mississauga, ON, L5T 1J1
(905) 670-1491
Emp Here 35   *Sales* 28,629,810
SIC 5093 Scrap and waste materials
Larry Attar
Alan Attar
Andy Attar

D-U-N-S 24-145-6453   (SL)
AVENIDA CARPENTRY LTD
6801 Columbus Rd, Mississauga, ON, L5T 2G9
(905) 565-0813
Emp Here 70   *Sales* 11,341,965
SIC 1751 Carpentry work
Ricardo Sousa
Rui Sousa
Steven Sousa

D-U-N-S 24-826-7978   (SL)
BACKERHAUS VEIT LTD
6745 Invader Cres, Mississauga, ON, L5T 2B6
(905) 850-9229
Emp Here 125   *Sales* 43,211,250
SIC 2053 Frozen bakery products, except bread
Sabine Veit

D-U-N-S 25-292-1572   (HQ)
BDI CANADA INC
(*Suby of* FORGE INDUSTRIES, INC.)
6235 Tomken Rd, Mississauga, ON, L5T 1K2
(905) 238-3392
Emp Here 50   *Sales* 117,055,200
SIC 5085 Industrial supplies
Theodore Chisholm
Carl James
Daniel Maisonville

D-U-N-S 20-823-9160   (SL)
BERNARDO METAL PRODUCTS LIMITED
170 Capital Crt, Mississauga, ON, L5T 2R8
(905) 362-1252
Emp Here 60   *Sales* 11,525,100
SIC 3499 Fabricated Metal products, nec
Larry Simmons

D-U-N-S 20-554-8811   (SL)
BESTWAY CARTAGE LIMITED
6505 Vipond Dr, Mississauga, ON, L5T 1J9
(905) 565-8877
Emp Here 90   *Sales* 13,337,280
SIC 4212 Local trucking, without storage
Clem D'alessandro
Peter D'alessandro

D-U-N-S 20-819-7566   (HQ)
BIO-RAD LABORATORIES (CANADA) LIMITED
LIVE SCIENCE GROUP
(*Suby of* BIO-RAD LABORATORIES, INC.)
1329 Meyerside Dr, Mississauga, ON, L5T 1C9
(905) 364-3435
Sales 29,066,310
SIC 5049 Professional equipment, nec
David Glennie

D-U-N-S 24-318-6012   (HQ)
BLUM CANADA LIMITED
(*Suby of* BLUM GROUP HOLDING GMBH)
7135 Pacific Cir, Mississauga, ON, L5T 2A8
(905) 670-7920
Emp Here 27   *Sales* 31,245,354
SIC 5072 Hardware
Kevin P Tratt

D-U-N-S 25-878-9676   (SL)
BOLTON SUPERMARKETS LTD
BONANZA GARDEN CENTRE
6790 Pacific Cir, Mississauga, ON, L5T 1N8
(905) 670-1204
Emp Here 40   *Sales* 10,966,080
SIC 5411 Grocery stores
Gene Bidinot

D-U-N-S 24-978-3007   (BR)
BOMBARDIER INC
BOMBARDIER TRANSPORT
(*Suby of* BOMBARDIER INC)
6291 Ordan Dr, Mississauga, ON, L5T 1G9
(905) 795-7869
Emp Here 80
SIC 4111 Local and suburban transit
Tony Sutton

D-U-N-S 20-811-0515   (SL)
BOSTON SCIENTIFIC LTD
(*Suby of* BOSTON SCIENTIFIC CORPORATION)
6430 Vipond Dr, Mississauga, ON, L5T 1W8
(705) 291-6900
Emp Here 45   *Sales* 11,545,290
SIC 3841 Surgical and medical instruments
Pete Nicholas

D-U-N-S 24-830-9759   (SL)
BREADKO NATIONAL BAKING LTD
BREADKO BAKERY
6310 Kestrel Rd, Mississauga, ON, L5T 1Z3
(905) 670-4949
Emp Here 100   *Sales* 29,347,700
SIC 5461 Retail bakeries

D-U-N-S 24-325-5267   (BR)
BRICK WAREHOUSE LP, THE
(*Suby of* BRICK WAREHOUSE LP, THE)
6765 Kennedy Rd, Mississauga, ON, L5T 0A2
(905) 696-3400
Emp Here 200
SIC 5712 Furniture stores
Dominic Sousa

D-U-N-S 20-302-1183   (SL)
BUILD IT BY DESIGN (2014) INC
BUILD IT
1580 Trinity Dr Unit 12, Mississauga, ON, L5T 1L6
(905) 696-0468
Emp Here 22   *Sales* 10,356,082
SIC 1542 Nonresidential construction, nec
Simon Shahin

D-U-N-S 25-202-7867   (HQ)
CANADIAN AMERICAN BOXED MEAT

CORP
CAN-AM
6905 Kenderry Gate Suite 2, Mississauga, ON, L5T 2Y8
(905) 949-8882
Sales 25,067,310
SIC 5147 Meats and meat products
David Munro
Craig Munro
Vicky Munro

D-U-N-S 24-094-1450   (SL)
CANADIAN AUTOMATION & TOOL INTER-NATIONAL INC
6811 Edwards Blvd, Mississauga, ON, L5T 2S2
(905) 795-1232
Emp Here 45   *Sales* 29,540,880
SIC 5962 Merchandising machine operators
Louis Galant
Ann Galant

D-U-N-S 25-510-6734   (SL)
CANADIAN STEEL NETWORK INC
6445 Kennedy Rd Unit A, Mississauga, ON, L5T 2W4
(905) 670-2900
Emp Here 30   *Sales* 13,415,220
SIC 5051 Metals service centers and offices
Gulzar Ali Jessani
Rozina Jessani
Amin U Jessani

D-U-N-S 25-462-6658   (SL)
CANNING CONTRACTING LIMITED
525 Abilene Dr, Mississauga, ON, L5T 2H7

Emp Here 60   *Sales* 34,220,280
SIC 1542 Nonresidential construction, nec
Oscar D'silva

D-U-N-S 25-691-4862   (BR)
CARDINAL HEALTH CANADA INC
(*Suby of* CARDINAL HEALTH, INC.)
1330 Meyerside Dr, Mississauga, ON, L5T 1C2
(905) 761-0068
Emp Here 200
SIC 5047 Medical and hospital equipment
Brian Carras

D-U-N-S 20-044-8900   (HQ)
CATLEN HOLDINGS LIMITED
BUILDERS' SUPPLIES
7361 Pacific Cir, Mississauga, ON, L5T 2A4
(905) 362-1161
Emp Here 30   *Sales* 20,122,830
SIC 5039 Construction materials, nec
James Holmes
Peter Miles

D-U-N-S 24-848-4235   (SL)
CENTRAL ROAST INC
TOASTY PISTACHIOS ROASTING & COATING
(*Suby of* GREENSPACE BRANDS INC)
6880 Columbus Rd, Mississauga, ON, L5T 2G1
(416) 661-7366
Emp Here 12   *Sales* 10,026,924
SIC 5145 Confectionery
David Reingold

D-U-N-S 20-849-0974   (BR)
CHILDREN'S EDUCATIONAL FOUNDATION OF CANADA, THE
CHILDREN'S EDUCATION FUNDS
(*Suby of* CHILDREN'S EDUCATIONAL FOUNDATION OF CANADA, THE)
6705 Tomken Rd Unit 236, Mississauga, ON, L5T 2J6

Emp Here 158
SIC 6733 Trusts, nec
Paul Dhulku

D-U-N-S 20-162-1190   (SL)
CLARKE ROLLER & RUBBER LIMITED

PERSISTA POLYURETHANE PRODUCTS DIV
6225 Kennedy Rd, Mississauga, ON, L5T 2S8
(905) 564-3215
Emp Here 50   *Sales* 10,094,850
SIC 3069 Fabricated rubber products, nec
Rob Wolstenholme

D-U-N-S 24-951-6576   (HQ)
COATINGS 85 LTD
ACADIAN GROUP
6995 Davand Dr, Mississauga, ON, L5T 1L5
(905) 564-1711
Emp Here 250   *Sales* 72,969,300
SIC 3471 Plating and polishing
Ernest Pitman
Michael Pitman
John Buchan

D-U-N-S 20-104-4182   (BR)
COLABOR LIMITED PARTNERSHIP
SUMMIT FOOD SERVICE DISTRIBUTORS
(*Suby of* GROUPE COLABOR INC)
6270 Kenway Dr, Mississauga, ON, L5T 2N3
(905) 795-2400
Emp Here 120
SIC 5142 Packaged frozen goods
Gary Englebercht

D-U-N-S 24-889-2812   (SL)
COLET SHIPPING SUPPLIES INC
COLET PACKAGING
165 Annagem Blvd, Mississauga, ON, L5T 2V1
(905) 670-4919
Emp Here 25   *Sales* 12,591,450
SIC 5113 Industrial and personal service paper
Frank Marchegiano
Mary Marchegiano

D-U-N-S 20-167-9730   (HQ)
COLLECTCENTS INC
CREDIT BUREAU OF CANADA COLLECTIONS
1450 Meyerside Dr Unit 200, Mississauga, ON, L5T 2N5
(905) 670-7575
Emp Here 140   *Sales* 46,085,330
SIC 7322 Adjustment and collection services
Jonathan Finley

D-U-N-S 20-014-1948   (SL)
COLOMER CANADA, LTD
(*Suby of* REVLON, INC.)
1055 Courtneypark Dr E Suite A, Mississauga, ON, L5T 1M7
(905) 565-7047
Emp Here 22   *Sales* 10,963,084
SIC 5131 Piece goods and notions
Jim Amos

D-U-N-S 24-859-3969   (SL)
CONXCORP LTD
VIVIX
6350 Netherhart Rd Unit 2, Mississauga, ON, L5T 1K3
(866) 815-2669
Emp Here 73   *Sales* 13,902,266
SIC 3648 Lighting equipment, nec
Jason Lightfoot

D-U-N-S 20-359-9998   (HQ)
COOPER EQUIPMENT RENTALS LIMITED
(*Suby of* SEAFORT CAPITAL INC)
6335 Edwards Blvd, Mississauga, ON, L5T 2W7
(877) 329-6531
Emp Here 30   *Sales* 130,546,000
SIC 7353 Heavy construction equipment rental
Darryl Cooper

D-U-N-S 20-700-2291   (BR)
CUMMINS EST DU CANADA SEC
(*Suby of* CUMMINS EST DU CANADA SEC)
7175 Pacific Cir, Mississauga, ON, L5T 2A8

(905) 795-0050
Emp Here 85
SIC 5084 Industrial machinery and equipment
Richard Hoyle

D-U-N-S 24-665-7282   (SL)
DAINOLITE LIMITED
1401 Courtneypark Dr E Unit 2, Mississauga, ON, L5T 2E4
(905) 564-1262
Emp Here 48   *Sales* 21,464,352
SIC 5063 Electrical apparatus and equipment
Dainis A Marsons
Elizabeth Marsons

D-U-N-S 20-708-6419   (HQ)
DAIRY PRODUCTS IN MOTION INC
6045 Edwards Blvd, Mississauga, ON, L5T 2W7
(905) 565-5210
Emp Here 60   *Sales* 52,641,351
SIC 5143 Dairy products, except dried or canned
Manny Valadao

D-U-N-S 25-293-2819   (BR)
DATA COMMUNICATIONS MANAGEMENT CORP
THE FSA GROUP
(*Suby of* DATA COMMUNICATIONS MANAGEMENT CORP)
80 Ambassador Dr, Mississauga, ON, L5T 2Y9
(905) 696-8884
Emp Here 100
SIC 2759 Commercial printing, nec
John Montpetit

D-U-N-S 24-213-0599   (SL)
DATA PARCEL EXPRESS INCORPORATED
INSTANT COURIER SERVICE
6500 Van Deemter Crt, Mississauga, ON, L5T 1S1
(905) 564-5555
Emp Here 40   *Sales* 20,798,680
SIC 4731 Freight transportation arrangement
Michael Dean

D-U-N-S 20-145-8171   (HQ)
DAYTON SUPERIOR CANADA LTD
(*Suby of* OAKTREE CAPITAL GROUP, LLC)
6650 Pacific Cir, Mississauga, ON, L5T 1V6
(416) 798-2000
Sales 10,756,760
SIC 3444 Sheet Metalwork
Brad Penn

D-U-N-S 24-008-0267   (HQ)
DBG CANADA LIMITED
DBG
(*Suby of* DBG GROUP LTD)
110 Ambassador Dr, Mississauga, ON, L5T 2X8
(905) 362-2311
Emp Here 65   *Sales* 77,833,920
SIC 3499 Fabricated Metal products, nec
Mike De Biasi
Joseph De Biasi
Attilio De Biasi
Josie De Biasi

D-U-N-S 20-188-4488   (HQ)
DBG GROUP LTD
110 Ambassador Dr, Mississauga, ON, L5T 2X8
(905) 670-1555
Emp Here 1   *Sales* 175,126,320
SIC 3499 Fabricated Metal products, nec
Mike De Biasi

D-U-N-S 24-859-8922   (SL)
DEACRO INDUSTRIES LTD
135 Capital Crt, Mississauga, ON, L5T 2R8
(905) 564-6566
Emp Here 70   *Sales* 15,540,070
SIC 3554 Paper industries machinery
Ed Deboer

D-U-N-S 24-891-9144   (SL)

DESIGN LABEL SYSTEMS INC
150 Capital Crt, Mississauga, ON, L5T 2R8
(905) 405-1121
Emp Here 60   *Sales* 14,006,100
SIC 2672 Paper; coated and laminated, nec
Zeb Faruqui
Imran Faruqui

D-U-N-S 24-359-9636   (SL)
DGN MARKETING SERVICES LTD
(*Suby of* GERRYMARSH HOLDINGS LTD)
1633 Meyerside Dr, Mississauga, ON, L5T 1B9
(905) 670-4070
Emp Here 150   *Sales* 30,855,900
SIC 4225 General warehousing and storage
Gerry Nudds
John Nudds
Doug Smith

D-U-N-S 20-568-2180   (HQ)
DHL GLOBAL FORWARDING (CANADA) INC
DGF
(*Suby of* DEUTSCHE POST AG)
6200 Edwards Blvd Suite 100, Mississauga, ON, L5T 2V7
(289) 562-6500
Emp Here 85   *Sales* 158,175,200
SIC 4731 Freight transportation arrangement
Hans Toggweiler
Allan Vickers
Donna Letterio
Nick Verrecchia

D-U-N-S 24-964-3891   (SL)
DOM-MERIDIAN CONSTRUCTION LTD
1021 Meyerside Dr Unit 10, Mississauga, ON, L5T 1J6
(905) 564-5594
Emp Here 50   *Sales* 12,044,200
SIC 1623 Water, sewer, and utility lines
Archie Iacobucci

D-U-N-S 20-818-6528   (SL)
DOMINION SURE SEAL LIMITED
6175 Danville Rd, Mississauga, ON, L5T 2H7
(905) 670-5411
Emp Here 45   *Sales* 12,449,700
SIC 2891 Adhesives and sealants
Greg Morton
Anna Morton

D-U-N-S 24-314-5190   (BR)
DOMTAR INC
ARIVA
(*Suby of* DOMTAR LUXEMBOURG INVESTMENTS SARL)
1330 Courtneypark Dr E, Mississauga, ON, L5T 1K5
(905) 670-1330
Emp Here 200
SIC 5111 Printing and writing paper
Susan Darr

D-U-N-S 24-099-2982   (HQ)
DRAFTING CLINIC CANADA LIMITED, THE
1500 Trinity Dr Suite 16, Mississauga, ON, L5T 1L6
(905) 564-1300
Emp Here 25   *Sales* 12,520,872
SIC 5049 Professional equipment, nec
Ralph Richter
Frank Jarman

D-U-N-S 20-145-4139   (SL)
EARLSCOURT METAL INDUSTRIES LTD
6660 Ordan Dr, Mississauga, ON, L5T 1J7
(905) 564-9000
Emp Here 40   *Sales* 19,001,040
SIC 5084 Industrial machinery and equipment
Stan Dodson

D-U-N-S 20-784-6395   (SL)
EBERSPAECHER CLIMATE CONTROL SYSTEMS CANADA INC
(*Suby of* EBERSPACHER GRUPPE GMBH & CO. KG)

6099a Vipond Dr, Mississauga, ON, L5T 2B2
(905) 670-0960
Emp Here 68   *Sales* 46,703,280
SIC 5013 Motor vehicle supplies and new parts
Oleg Riabtsev

D-U-N-S 25-254-8904   (HQ)
EMEC MACHINE TOOLS INC
205 Admiral Blvd, Mississauga, ON, L5T 2T3
(905) 565-3570
Emp Here 33   *Sales* 19,001,040
SIC 5084 Industrial machinery and equipment
William Mara
Tejal Mehta
Trevor Smethurst

D-U-N-S 20-161-0573   (SL)
ENESCO CANADA CORPORATION
(*Suby of* ENESCO, LLC)
989 Derry Rd E Suite 303, Mississauga, ON, L5T 2J8
(905) 673-9200
Emp Here 120   *Sales* 69,044,160
SIC 5023 Homefurnishings
Grace Kiss
Sandy Ross

D-U-N-S 25-313-9141   (SL)
ENGLISH BAY BATTER (TORONTO) INC
6925 Invader Cres, Mississauga, ON, L5T 2B7
(905) 670-1110
Emp Here 150   *Sales* 51,853,500
SIC 2052 Cookies and crackers
Constantin Trusca

D-U-N-S 20-363-1619   (HQ)
EPIROC CANADA INC
EPIROC CUSTOMER CENTRE, DIV OF
1025 Tristar Dr, Mississauga, ON, L5T 1W5
(289) 562-0100
Emp Here 70   *Sales* 219,478,500
SIC 5082 Construction and mining machinery
Jason Smith
Louka Geladi

D-U-N-S 24-859-1489   (HQ)
ERGOCENTRIC INC
ERGOCENTRIC SEATING SYSTEMS
275 Superior Blvd Unit 2, Mississauga, ON, L5T 2L6
(905) 696-6800
Emp Here 160   *Sales* 27,777,960
SIC 2522 Office furniture, except wood
Terry Cassaday

D-U-N-S 24-175-5867   (HQ)
ESSENDANT CANADA, INC
ADOX/OKI BERING
(*Suby of* EGG PARENT INC.)
6400 Ordan Dr, Mississauga, ON, L5T 2H6
(905) 670-1223
Emp Here 42   *Sales* 26,027,100
SIC 5099 Durable goods, nec
John Leclair
Michael Leclair

D-U-N-S 20-313-4903   (HQ)
ETG COMMODITIES INC
(*Suby of* ETC GROUP)
6220 Shawson Dr, Mississauga, ON, L5T 1J8
(416) 900-4148
Sales 19,510,680
SIC 6799 Investors, nec
Gaurav Kapoor
Anshul Nagar
Ketankumar Patel
Maheshkumar Patel

D-U-N-S 25-705-5020   (SL)
EVEREST STEEL LTD
6445 Kennedy Rd Unit C, Mississauga, ON, L5T 2W4
(905) 670-7373
Emp Here 15   *Sales* 15,005,085
SIC 5051 Metals service centers and offices
Aziz Jassani

D-U-N-S 20-164-7732   (SL)
EXCLUSIVE CANDY AND NOVELTY DISTRIBUTING LIMITED
EXCLUSIVE BRANDS
(*Suby of* 2032339 ONTARIO INC)
1832 Bonhill Rd, Mississauga, ON, L5T 1C4
(905) 795-8781
Emp Here 15   *Sales* 12,533,655
SIC 5145 Confectionery
James Picard
Kevin Crux
Julia Mercy
Richard Brown

D-U-N-S 20-236-3404   (HQ)
FEDEX TRADE NETWORKS TRANSPORT & BROKERAGE (CANADA), INC
(*Suby of* FEDEX CORPORATION)
7075 Ordan Dr, Mississauga, ON, L5T 1K6
(905) 677-7371
Emp Here 200   *Sales* 197,719,000
SIC 4731 Freight transportation arrangement
Lynn Wark

D-U-N-S 20-648-5547   (BR)
FEDEX TRADE NETWORKS TRANSPORT & BROKERAGE (CANADA), INC
FEDEX TRADE NETWORKS
(*Suby of* FEDEX CORPORATION)
7075 Ordan Dr, Mississauga, ON, L5T 1K6
(905) 677-7371
Emp Here 200
SIC 4231 Trucking terminal facilities
Lynn Wark

D-U-N-S 20-171-4912   (HQ)
FILTRATION GROUP CANADA CORPORATION
(*Suby of* FILTRATION GROUP LLC)
6190 Kestrel Rd, Mississauga, ON, L5T 1Z1
(905) 795-9559
Emp Here 75   *Sales* 21,090,095
SIC 3569 General industrial machinery, nec
Adrian Hanley

D-U-N-S 20-412-0661   (SL)
FINICA FOOD SPECIALTIES LIMITED
65 Superior Blvd Unit 1, Mississauga, ON, L5T 2X9
(905) 696-2770
Emp Here 24   *Sales* 10,702,480
SIC 5143 Dairy products, except dried or canned
Thomas Gellert
Paul Blake
George Gellert

D-U-N-S 20-059-0037   (SL)
FIRST CHOICE BEVERAGE INC
265 Courtneypark Dr E, Mississauga, ON, L5T 2T6
(905) 565-7288
Emp Here 50   *Sales* 11,242,750
SIC 2037 Frozen fruits and vegetables
John Borkowski
James Chin
Edward Choy
Clement Fung
Val Miller
Lee Q. Shim

D-U-N-S 24-329-8382   (HQ)
FIRST TEAM TRANSPORT INC
SCI-WHITE GLOVE SERVICES
(*Suby of* GOVERNMENT OF CANADA)
6141 Vipond Dr, Mississauga, ON, L5T 2B2
(416) 500-8541
Emp Here 10   *Sales* 14,819,200
SIC 4212 Local trucking, without storage
H James Eckler
Louis O'brien
Phil Drane

D-U-N-S 20-363-1627   (HQ)
FIRSTONSITE CANADIAN HOLDINGS, INC.
60 Admiral Blvd, Mississauga, ON, L5T 2W1

(905) 696-2900
Emp Here 2   *Sales* 292,407,200
SIC 6712 Bank holding companies
Jeff Johnson
Al Sutherland
Matthew Constantino

D-U-N-S 25-966-9872   (HQ)
FIRSTONSITE RESTORATION LIMITED
FIRSTONSITE RESTORATION
(*Suby of* FIRSTONSITE CANADIAN HOLDINGS, INC.)
60 Admiral Blvd, Mississauga, ON, L5T 2W1
(905) 696-2900
Emp Here 35   *Sales* 116,758,200
SIC 1799 Special trade contractors, nec
Dave Demos
Jeff Johnson
Al Sutherland
Andrew Schweibold
Matthew Constantino

D-U-N-S 24-060-7432   (HQ)
FLUID HOSE & COUPLING INC
6150 Dixie Rd Unit 1, Mississauga, ON, L5T 2E2
(905) 670-0955
Emp Here 10   *Sales* 16,625,910
SIC 5084 Industrial machinery and equipment
Joe Pasternak
Barbara Pasternak
Barbara Pasternak
Alison Colley

D-U-N-S 20-126-8864   (SL)
FORMCRETE (1994) LTD
7060 Pacific Cir, Mississauga, ON, L5T 2A7
(905) 669-8017
Emp Here 40   *Sales* 15,943,450
SIC 1521 Single-family housing construction
Jose Azevedo
Gabriella Brockie
Renato Minuti

D-U-N-S 20-181-9856   (SL)
FREUD CANADA, INC
(*Suby of* ROBERT BOSCH STIFTUNG GESELLSCHAFT MIT BESCHRANKTER HAFTUNG)
7450 Pacific Cir, Mississauga, ON, L5T 2A3
(905) 670-1025
Emp Here 25   *Sales* 11,875,650
SIC 5084 Industrial machinery and equipment
Tony Meznaric

D-U-N-S 20-717-4355   (SL)
G.A.L. CANADA ELEVATOR PRODUCTS CORP
(*Suby of* GOLDEN GATE CAPITAL)
6500 Gottardo Crt, Mississauga, ON, L5T 2A2
(905) 564-0838
Emp Here 38   *Sales* 26,465,192
SIC 5084 Industrial machinery and equipment
Mark Boelhouwer
Steve Husband
Angelo Messina

D-U-N-S 24-205-3986   (SL)
GALAXY HOME FURNISHING INC
455 Gibraltar Dr, Mississauga, ON, L5T 2S9
(905) 670-5555
Emp Here 37   *Sales* 18,827,672
SIC 5021 Furniture
Ranjit Guhman
Sudhir Gupta

D-U-N-S 24-371-9536   (HQ)
GCO CANADA INC
LIDS
(*Suby of* GENESCO INC.)
6300 Dixie Rd, Mississauga, ON, L5T 1A7
(905) 670-2514
Sales 35,879,200
SIC 5611 Men's and boys' clothing stores
Matthew Johnson
James S. Gulmi
Jeff Mcfater

Robert Dennis

D-U-N-S 24-715-2036   (HQ)
GENUINE PARTS HOLDINGS LTD
(*Suby of* GENUINE PARTS COMPANY)
1450 Meyerside Dr Suite 305, Mississauga, ON, L5T 2N5
(905) 696-9301
Emp Here 1   *Sales* 186,409,590
SIC 6712 Bank holding companies
Robert Susor
Peter Brushaber

D-U-N-S 25-994-0591   (SL)
GLOBAL DRIVER SERVICES INC
(*Suby of* CPC LOGISTICS INC.)
1415 Bonhill Rd Suite 16, Mississauga, ON, L5T 1R2
(905) 564-2309
Emp Here 125   *Sales* 9,336,750
SIC 7363 Help supply services
John Harrison
John Sr. Bickels

D-U-N-S 20-857-9545   (SL)
GOLDWELL COSMETICS (CANADA) LTD
KPSS GOLDWELL
1045 Tristar Dr, Mississauga, ON, L5T 1W5
(905) 670-2844
Emp Here 45   *Sales* 14,821,698
SIC 5999 Miscellaneous retail stores, nec
Brian Ahrens

D-U-N-S 24-486-3791   (SL)
GREDICO FOOTWEAR LIMITED
415 Annagem Blvd, Mississauga, ON, L5T 3A7
(866) 855-0755
Emp Here 40   *Sales* 19,932,880
SIC 5139 Footwear
Richard Diradour

D-U-N-S 20-404-5470   (SL)
GREEN BELTING INDUSTRIES LIMITED
(*Suby of* ALPHA ABMD HOLDCO B.V.)
381 Ambassador Dr, Mississauga, ON, L5T 2J3
(905) 564-6712
Emp Here 75   *Sales* 10,250,550
SIC 2399 Fabricated textile products, nec
Jim Mcfarlane

D-U-N-S 20-161-0136   (SL)
GREENGROCER INC, THE
CALEDONIA PRODUCE DISTRIBUTORS
6110 Shawson Dr, Mississauga, ON, L5T 1E6
(416) 253-9070
Emp Here 25   *Sales* 20,889,425
SIC 5148 Fresh fruits and vegetables
Joseph Polito

D-U-N-S 20-166-3994   (SL)
GRIFFIN, HAROLD T. INC
HT GRIFFIN FOOD INGREDIENTS
7491 Pacific Cir, Mississauga, ON, L5T 2A4
(905) 564-1710
Emp Here 30   *Sales* 25,067,310
SIC 5149 Groceries and related products, nec
Grant Kenney
Bernard Witte
Olav C. Van Caldenborgh
Jill Wuthmann

D-U-N-S 20-717-5712   (SL)
H.S.T. SYNTHETICS LTD
6630 Edwards Blvd, Mississauga, ON, L5T 2V6
(905) 670-3432
Emp Here 80   *Sales* 16,151,760
SIC 3089 Plastics products, nec
Julia Tiler
Thomas E. Tiler

D-U-N-S 24-627-2900   (HQ)
HARMAN INVESTMENTS LTD
HARMAN IMPORTS
310 Annagem Blvd, Mississauga, ON, L5T 2V5

(905) 670-0801
Sales 13,230,256
SIC 5023 Homefurnishings
Harry Bagga
Sudesh Bagga

D-U-N-S 25-496-9041   (HQ)
HEART LOGISTICS INC
(*Suby of* ITN TRANSBORDER SERVICES INC)
6975 Pacific Cir Unit D, Mississauga, ON, L5T 2H3
(905) 362-1100
Emp Here 6   *Sales* 11,439,274
SIC 4731 Freight transportation arrangement
Monica Kennedy

D-U-N-S 24-783-3015   (SL)
HEARTLAND SHIPPING SUPPLIES INC
6690 Innovator Dr, Mississauga, ON, L5T 2J3
(905) 564-9777
Emp Here 31   *Sales* 15,613,398
SIC 5113 Industrial and personal service paper
Paul Boyes
Bruce Chiasson

D-U-N-S 24-463-2519   (HQ)
HEIDELBERG CANADA GRAPHIC EQUIPMENT LIMITED
(*Suby of* HEIDELBERGER DRUCKMASCHINEN AG)
6265 Kenway Dr, Mississauga, ON, L5T 2L3
(905) 362-4400
Emp Here 100   *Sales* 165,828,200
SIC 5084 Industrial machinery and equipment
Niels Winther
Richard Armstrong
Jason Roth

D-U-N-S 24-370-2821   (SL)
HOFLAND, JOHN G LTD.
6695 Pacific Cir, Mississauga, ON, L5T 1V6
(905) 670-8220
Emp Here 110   *Sales* 26,876,080
SIC 5992 Florists
Glenn Hofland
Rodney Hofland

D-U-N-S 20-976-4257   (HQ)
HOMAG CANADA INC
(*Suby of* DURR AG)
5090 Edwards Blvd, Mississauga, ON, L5T 2W3
(905) 670-1700
Sales 18,050,988
SIC 5084 Industrial machinery and equipment
Christian Vollmers

D-U-N-S 24-761-5722   (SL)
HUDSON ENERGY CANADA CORP
(*Suby of* JUST ENERGY GROUP INC)
6345 Dixie Rd Suite 200, Mississauga, ON, L5T 2E6
(905) 670-4440
Emp Here 20   *Sales* 12,532,280
SIC 4911 Electric services
Kate Livesey
Beth Summers
Ken Hartwick
Rebecca Macdonald

D-U-N-S 24-423-4980   (HQ)
HYDROGENICS CORPORATION
220 Admiral Blvd, Mississauga, ON, L5T 2N6
(905) 361-3660
Emp Here 102   *Sales* 33,896,000
SIC 5063 Electrical apparatus and equipment
Daryl Wilson
Joseph Cargnelli
Wido Westbroek
Marc Beisheim
Filip Smeets
Douglas Alexander
David C Ferguson
Donald Lowry
Sara Elford
Pierre-Etienne Franc

D-U-N-S 24-393-3749   (HQ)
HYDROPOOL INC
HYDROPOOL HOT TUBS AND SWIM SPAS
(*Suby of* INVESTINDUSTRIAL VI L.P.)
335 Superior Blvd, Mississauga, ON, L5T 2L6
(800) 465-2933
Sales 27,530,550
SIC 5999 Miscellaneous retail stores, nec
David Jackson

D-U-N-S 24-911-8134   (HQ)
I.R.P. INDUSTRIAL RUBBER LTD
6300 Edwards Blvd Unit 1, Mississauga, ON, L5T 2V7
(905) 670-5700
Emp Here 50   *Sales* 26,126,430
SIC 5085 Industrial supplies
Richard Mallett
Mike Mallett
Ted Flewwelling
Sharon Heaman

D-U-N-S 25-404-2898   (HQ)
INTEGRAL TRANSPORTATION NETWORKS CORP
I T N
6975 Pacific Cir Unit D, Mississauga, ON, L5T 2H3
(905) 362-1111
Emp Here 70   *Sales* 54,685,144
SIC 4731 Freight transportation arrangement
Ian Kennedy

D-U-N-S 25-149-5842   (HQ)
ITN TRANSBORDER SERVICES INC
6975 Pacific Cir Unit D, Mississauga, ON, L5T 2H3
(905) 362-1122
Sales 23,398,515
SIC 4731 Freight transportation arrangement
Monica Kennedy

D-U-N-S 24-263-4849   (SL)
J Y S ENTERPRISE INC
1081 Meyerside Dr Unit 8, Mississauga, ON, L5T 1M4
(905) 565-1472
Emp Here 24   *Sales* 10,781,256
SIC 7389 Business services, nec

D-U-N-S 20-647-3027   (HQ)
JAN-MAR SALES LIMITED
(*Suby of* BUNZL PUBLIC LIMITED COMPANY)
6976 Columbus Rd, Mississauga, ON, L5T 2G1
(416) 255-8535
Emp Here 23   *Sales* 12,825,702
SIC 5087 Service establishment equipment
Shiraz Chatur

D-U-N-S 20-565-5207   (SL)
JASCO SALES INC
HI-LITE
1680 Bonhill Rd, Mississauga, ON, L5T 1C8
(905) 677-4032
Emp Here 26   *Sales* 12,350,676
SIC 5082 Construction and mining machinery
Dave Jackson
Barry Jackson

D-U-N-S 25-193-0624   (HQ)
JUST ENERGY GROUP INC
6345 Dixie Rd Suite 400, Mississauga, ON, L5T 2E6
(905) 670-4440
Sales 2,886,804,119
SIC 4911 Electric services
Patrick Mccullough
Rebecca Macdonald
Jonah Davids
Jim Brown
James Pickren
William Weld
John Brussa
R. Scott Gahn
Brett Perlman
Dallas Ross

D-U-N-S 20-697-7717   (HQ)
JUST ENERGY ONTARIO L.P
6345 Dixie Rd Suite 200, Mississauga, ON, L5T 2E6
(905) 670-4440
Sales 311,072,320
SIC 4911 Electric services
Brennan Mulcahy
Lisa Whittington

D-U-N-S 20-168-2887   (HQ)
KARRYS BROS., LIMITED
KARRYS WHOLESALE DISTRIBUTORS
180 Courtneypark Dr E, Mississauga, ON, L5T 2S5
(905) 565-1000
Emp Here 170   *Sales* 143,343,200
SIC 5141 Groceries, general line
Steven J Karrys
Bob Hall
Shawn Schultz

D-U-N-S 24-965-3890   (SL)
KEE TRANSPORT GROUP INC
6760 Davand Dr Suite 9, Mississauga, ON, L5T 2L9
(905) 670-0835
Emp Here 70   *Sales* 36,397,690
SIC 4731 Freight transportation arrangement
Kieran O'brian

D-U-N-S 24-380-8123   (HQ)
KO-REC-TYPE (CANADA) LTD
1100 Courtneypark Dr E Unit 4, Mississauga, ON, L5T 1L7

Emp Here 69   *Sales* 33,251,820
SIC 5084 Industrial machinery and equipment
Brian Birenbaum
Jeffery Birenbaum

D-U-N-S 24-361-0396   (BR)
KRISKA HOLDINGS LIMITED
KIRSKA TRANSPORTATION
(*Suby of* KRISKA TRANSPORTATION GROUP LIMITED)
6424a Danville Rd, Mississauga, ON, L5T 2S6
(905) 795-2770
Emp Here 170
SIC 4213 Trucking, except local
Mark Seymour

D-U-N-S 25-684-2402   (BR)
KUEHNE + NAGEL LTD
(*Suby of* KUEHNE HOLDING AG)
6335 Edwards Blvd, Mississauga, ON, L5T 2W7
(905) 670-6901
Emp Here 100
SIC 4731 Freight transportation arrangement
Brenda Lemieux

D-U-N-S 24-047-9683   (HQ)
KYOCERA DOCUMENT SOLUTIONS CANADA, LTD
(*Suby of* KYOCERA CORPORATION)
6120 Kestrel Rd, Mississauga, ON, L5T 1S8
(905) 670-4425
Emp Here 30   *Sales* 18,781,308
SIC 5044 Office equipment
Raymond Baraya

D-U-N-S 24-860-4162   (SL)
LAKESIDE PERFORMANCE GAS SERVICES LTD
6915 Dixie Rd, Mississauga, ON, L5T 2G2
(289) 562-0054
Emp Here 55   *Sales* 13,884,310
SIC 1623 Water, sewer, and utility lines
Greg Robertson

D-U-N-S 24-837-7512   (SL)
LEE LI HOLDINGS INC
299 Courtneypark Dr E, Mississauga, ON, L5T 2T6
(905) 565-5968
Emp Here 75   *Sales* 62,668,275
SIC 5149 Groceries and related products, nec

Ken Chin

D-U-N-S 20-129-2836   (HQ)
LIFTOW LIMITED
1400 Courtneypark Dr E, Mississauga, ON, L5T 1H1
(905) 677-3270
Emp Here 85   *Sales* 170,705,500
SIC 5084 Industrial machinery and equipment
Roger Sutton
Blane H Bowen
Fred Barton

D-U-N-S 24-021-5736   (SL)
MAD ELEVATOR INC
6635 Ordan Dr, Mississauga, ON, L5T 1K6
(416) 245-8500
Emp Here 180   *Sales* 28,049,774
SIC 3534 Elevators and moving stairways
Carl Strychaluk
Emanuele Emiliani

D-U-N-S 24-577-1605   (HQ)
MANITOULIN GLOBAL FORWARDING INC
(*Suby of* NORTH CHANNEL OF GEORGIAN BAY HOLDINGS LTD)
7035 Ordan, Mississauga, ON, L5T 1T1
(905) 283-1600
Emp Here 40   *Sales* 60,020,280
SIC 4731 Freight transportation arrangement
Dwayne Hihn

D-U-N-S 24-977-2781   (SL)
MAPLE LEAF WHEELCHAIR MANUFACTURING INC
6540 Tomken Rd, Mississauga, ON, L5T 2E9
(905) 564-2250
Emp Here 40   *Sales* 10,262,480
SIC 3842 Surgical appliances and supplies
Christopher Mohan
Ramkaly Mohan

D-U-N-S 24-868-6628   (HQ)
MARTIN SPROCKET & GEAR CANADA INC
(*Suby of* MARTIN SPROCKET & GEAR, INC.)
896 Meyerside Dr, Mississauga, ON, L5T 1R9
(905) 670-1991
Emp Here 40   *Sales* 35,626,950
SIC 5085 Industrial supplies
Shawn Grant
Gary Martin
Robert Dillenback
John Ball

D-U-N-S 24-684-5440   (HQ)
MARVIN WINDOWS INC
MARVIN WINDOWS & DOORS
(*Suby of* MARVIN LUMBER AND CEDAR COMPANY)
1455 Courtneypark Dr E, Mississauga, ON, L5T 2E3
(905) 670-5052
Emp Here 30   *Sales* 13,382,600
SIC 5211 Lumber and other building materials
Knut Holmsen

D-U-N-S 20-629-3276   (HQ)
MASON'S MASONRY SUPPLY LIMITED
6291 Netherhart Rd, Mississauga, ON, L5T 1A2
(905) 670-1233
Emp Here 1   *Sales* 22,358,700
SIC 5032 Brick, stone, and related material
Graham Mason
Andrew Mason
Paul Mason

D-U-N-S 24-335-9841   (HQ)
MATRIX ELECTRONICS LIMITED
(*Suby of* E.D.H. HOLDINGS CORPORATION)
1124 Mid-Way Blvd, Mississauga, ON, L5T 2C1
(905) 670-8400
Sales 15,651,090
SIC 5065 Electronic parts and equipment, nec
Kieran Healy

D-U-N-S 24-999-9947   (HQ)

MATRIX LOGISTICS SERVICES LIMITED
6941 Kennedy Rd, Mississauga, ON, L5T 2R6
(905) 795-2200
Emp Here 400   *Sales* 205,706,000
SIC 4225 General warehousing and storage
Todd Yates
Paolo Mari

D-U-N-S 24-489-0463   (HQ)
MERCER, GARRY TRUCKING INC
MERCER TRUCKING
1140 Mid-Way Blvd, Mississauga, ON, L5T 2C1
(905) 670-4721
Sales 13,370,890
SIC 4213 Trucking, except local
Garry Mercer

D-U-N-S 20-148-4300   (HQ)
MERSEN CANADA TORONTO INC
MERSEN ELECTRICAL POWER
(*Suby of* MERSEN)
6200 Kestrel Rd, Mississauga, ON, L5T 1Z1
(416) 252-9371
Emp Here 74   *Sales* 30,324,080
SIC 3679 Electronic components, nec
Bruce Brown
Dean Cousins
Daniel Beaudron
Daniel Balkus
Jeffrey Michael Hewitt

D-U-N-S 24-426-4219   (BR)
MERSEN CANADA TORONTO INC
(*Suby of* MERSEN)
6220 Kestrel Rd, Mississauga, ON, L5T 1Y9
(647) 846-8684
Emp Here 75
SIC 3679 Electronic components, nec
Ralph Wickel

D-U-N-S 24-610-5977   (HQ)
METAL SUPERMARKETS SERVICE COMPANY INC
(*Suby of* METAL SUPERMARKETS IP INC)
520 Abilene Dr 2nd Fl, Mississauga, ON, L5T 2H7
(905) 362-8226
Sales 10,732,176
SIC 5051 Metals service centers and offices
Stephen Schober
Andrew Arminem

D-U-N-S 20-145-6035   (SL)
METEOR FOUNDRY COMPANY LIMITED
1730 Bonhill Rd, Mississauga, ON, L5T 1C8
(905) 670-2890
Emp Here 43   *Sales* 10,037,705
SIC 3365 Aluminum foundries
Marcus Wittich
Brigitte Wittich
Erwin Wittich

D-U-N-S 25-534-5563   (SL)
MEX Y CAN TRADING (EAST) INC.
6799 Pacific Cir Unit 4, Mississauga, ON, L5T 1S6
(905) 670-3355
Emp Here 30   *Sales* 22,275,600
SIC 5193 Flowers and florists supplies
Michael Lasher

D-U-N-S 24-588-6973   (SL)
MEXICAN FLOWER TRADING INC
1240 Mid-Way Blvd Unit A, Mississauga, ON, L5T 2B8
(905) 670-0870
Emp Here 45   *Sales* 14,652,000
SIC 5992 Florists
Michael Smith

D-U-N-S 20-951-6819   (HQ)
MISSISSAUGA BUS, COACH & TRUCK REPAIRS INC
MISSISSAUGA BUS GROUP OF COMPANIES
6625 Kestrel Rd, Mississauga, ON, L5T 1P4

(905) 696-8328
Sales 56,060,000
SIC 7538 General automotive repair shops
Mahendra Mahadeo
Predita Mahadeo

D-U-N-S 24-537-8724   (SL)
MISSISSAUGA PAPER FIBRES LTD
1111 Tristar Dr Unit 1, Mississauga, ON, L5T 1W5
(905) 564-7260
Emp Here 40   *Sales* 20,821,680
SIC 5093 Scrap and waste materials
John Labrie
George Millar
Jim Millar

D-U-N-S 24-099-2354   (SL)
MITRI, S HAULAGE LTD
S MITRI TRANSPORT, DIV
6855 Invader Cres, Mississauga, ON, L5T 2B7
(905) 564-1200
Emp Here 82   *Sales* 12,151,744
SIC 4212 Local trucking, without storage
Theresa Maria Mitri

D-U-N-S 24-885-7518   (HQ)
MOMENTIS CANADA CORP
JUST ENERGY
6345 Dixie Rd Suite 200, Mississauga, ON, L5T 2E6
(905) 670-4440
Emp Here 100   *Sales* 345,586,200
SIC 4924 Natural gas distribution
Ken Hartwick C.A
Rebecca Macdonald
James Lewis
Darren Pritchett
Beth Summers

D-U-N-S 24-420-4793   (HQ)
MOORE CANADA CORPORATION
R.R. DONNELLEY
(*Suby of* R. R. DONNELLEY & SONS COMPANY)
6100 Vipond Dr, Mississauga, ON, L5T 2X1
(905) 362-3100
Emp Here 400   *Sales* 511,712,600
SIC 6712 Bank holding companies
Andrew Sullivan
Sean Byrne

D-U-N-S 24-093-8063   (SL)
MTI POLYFAB INC
3M CANADA
(*Suby of* 3M COMPANY)
7381 Pacific Cir, Mississauga, ON, L5T 2A4
(800) 265-1840
Emp Here 100   *Sales* 74,252,000
SIC 5199 Nondurable goods, nec
Ravi Ravishanker

D-U-N-S 25-500-7858   (SL)
MULTI-LINE FASTENER SUPPLY CO. LTD
1100 Courtneypark Dr E Unit 5, Mississauga, ON, L5T 1L7
(905) 677-5088
Emp Here 24   *Sales* 11,400,624
SIC 5085 Industrial supplies
Brenda Chu
Herbert Halsall

D-U-N-S 24-693-2057   (SL)
MULTICHAIR INC
MULTITUBE
6900 Davand Dr, Mississauga, ON, L5T 1J5

Emp Here 120   *Sales* 21,766,560
SIC 3312 Blast furnaces and steel mills
Frank Simmons
Larry Simmons
Daniel Kenneth Wootton

D-U-N-S 25-990-2104   (HQ)
NATIONAL BROKERS INSURANCE SERVICES INC
6725 Edwards Blvd, Mississauga, ON, L5T 2V9

Sales 25,441,800
SIC 6411 Insurance agents, brokers, and service
Joyce Usher-Mesiano

D-U-N-S 20-057-0278   (SL)
NEW DIRECTIONS AROMATICS INC
6781 Columbus Rd, Mississauga, ON, L5T 2G9
(905) 362-1915
Emp Here 152   *Sales* 23,583,312
SIC 5122 Drugs, proprietaries, and sundries
Alex Thomas
Annie Thomas

D-U-N-S 20-921-5722   (HQ)
NEWLY WEDS FOODS CO.
(*Suby of* NEWLY WEDS FOODS, INC.)
450 Superior Blvd, Mississauga, ON, L5T 2R9
(905) 670-7776
Emp Here 214   *Sales* 71,640,639
SIC 2099 Food preparations, nec
Charles Angell
Ased Malik
Paul Legere
Wayne Farrell

D-U-N-S 20-145-1994   (SL)
NILFISK CANADA COMPANY
(*Suby of* NILFISK HOLDING A/S)
240 Superior Blvd, Mississauga, ON, L5T 2L2
(905) 696-4840
Emp Here 42   *Sales* 19,951,092
SIC 5087 Service establishment equipment
Andy Ray
Steven Furtel

D-U-N-S 24-507-7029   (HQ)
NIPPON EXPRESS CANADA LTD
(*Suby of* NIPPON EXPRESS CO., LTD.)
6250 Edwards Blvd, Mississauga, ON, L5T 2X3
(905) 565-7525
Emp Here 100   *Sales* 116,706,100
SIC 4731 Freight transportation arrangement
Yoichi Satake
David Street
Peter Hayden
Chiemi Honma

D-U-N-S 24-830-1095   (BR)
NIPPON EXPRESS CANADA LTD
OCEAN CARGO DIVISION
(*Suby of* NIPPON EXPRESS CO., LTD.)
6250 Edwards Blvd, Mississauga, ON, L5T 2X3
(905) 565-7525
Emp Here 90
SIC 4731 Freight transportation arrangement
Hiroshi Sato

D-U-N-S 20-174-3783   (SL)
NORTHERN DOCK SYSTEMS INC
415 Ambassador Dr, Mississauga, ON, L5T 2J3
(905) 625-1758
Emp Here 50   *Sales* 23,751,300
SIC 5082 Construction and mining machinery
Kirby Moore
Chris Brady

D-U-N-S 20-358-9247   (SL)
OLAM CANADA COMPANY
1100 Mid-Way Blvd Unit 7, Mississauga, ON, L5T 1V8
(905) 795-8871
Emp Here 30   *Sales* 19,230,770
SIC 5149 Groceries and related products, nec
Saiyid Hussain

D-U-N-S 25-918-1790   (SL)
OMEGA FOOD IMPORTERS CO. LTD
395 Pendant Dr Unit 2, Mississauga, ON, L5T 2W9
(905) 212-9252
Emp Here 35   *Sales* 29,245,195
SIC 5149 Groceries and related products, nec
Peter Zuski

Marek Sikorski

D-U-N-S 24-388-9912   (SL)
OMNI FLOORCOVERINGS LTD
6310 Kestrel Rd, Mississauga, ON, L5T 1Z3

Emp Here 35   *Sales* 17,809,960
SIC 5023 Homefurnishings
John Cerisano
Susan Allen

D-U-N-S 20-846-8033   (SL)
ONTARIO FLOWER GROWERS CO-OPERATIVE LIMITED
910 Mid-Way Blvd, Mississauga, ON, L5T 1T9
(905) 670-9556
Emp Here 140   *Sales* 36,206,100
SIC 8611 Business associations
Rene Juraschka
John Newland
Jan Verbruggen
Jouke Sypkes

D-U-N-S 24-355-4180   (HQ)
ONTARIO HOSE SPECIALTIES LIMITED
7245 Pacific Cir, Mississauga, ON, L5T 1V1
(905) 670-0113
Emp Here 26   *Sales* 28,501,560
SIC 5085 Industrial supplies
Newell Kraik

D-U-N-S 24-993-3565   (SL)
ORCHARD INTERNATIONAL INC
275 Superior Blvd Unit 1, Mississauga, ON, L5T 2L6
(905) 564-9848
Emp Here 60   *Sales* 66,320,700
SIC 5122 Drugs, proprietaries, and sundries
Shelley Peters-Wishart

D-U-N-S 24-414-5751   (HQ)
PARADIGM ELECTRONICS INC
205 Annagem Blvd, Mississauga, ON, L5T 2V1
(905) 564-1994
Sales 38,088,400
SIC 3651 Household audio and video equipment
Christopher Leader
Scott Bagby
Anne Leone
John Carinci

D-U-N-S 20-640-9138   (HQ)
PAYSTATION INC
6345 Dixie Rd Unit 4, Mississauga, ON, L5T 2E6
(905) 364-0700
Emp Here 43   *Sales* 64,242,240
SIC 5044 Office equipment
Robert M Warner

D-U-N-S 24-046-5864   (SL)
PEARLON PRODUCTS INC
PEARLON BEAUTY SUPPLIES
6290 Shawson Dr, Mississauga, ON, L5T 1H5
(905) 670-1040
Emp Here 515   *Sales* 146,270,815
SIC 2844 Toilet preparations
Andy Noordeh

D-U-N-S 24-624-9825   (HQ)
PEEL CHILDREN'S CENTRE
85 Aventura Crt Unit A, Mississauga, ON, L5T 2Y6
(905) 795-3500
Emp Here 100   *Sales* 56,381,750
SIC 8999 Services, nec
Humphrey Mitchell

D-U-N-S 25-974-6980   (HQ)
PERFORMANCE EQUIPMENT LTD
P O MACK
6950 Tomken Rd, Mississauga, ON, L5T 2S3
(905) 564-8333
Emp Here 100   *Sales* 75,513,600
SIC 5511 New and used car dealers
John Slottegraaf

▲ Public Company   ■ Public Company Family Member   **HQ** Headquarters   **BR** Branch   **SL** Single Location

Steven Brenton
John Cecconi

D-U-N-S 25-511-2237 (SL)
PERFUMES ETC. LTD
(*Suby of* PREMIER BRANDS DISTRIBUTORS INC)
6880 Columbus Rd Unit 2, Mississauga, ON, L5T 2G1
(905) 850-8060
Emp Here 20 *Sales* 22,106,900
SIC 5122 Drugs, proprietaries, and sundries
Vikas Mahajan

D-U-N-S 25-194-8121 (SL)
PHILIP BUSINESS DEVELOPMENT & INVESTMENT LTD.
TONER EXPRESS
1680 Courtneypark Dr E Unit 5, Mississauga, ON, L5T 1R4
(905) 366-8999
Emp Here 25 *Sales* 11,179,350
SIC 5044 Office equipment
Philip Xu

D-U-N-S 24-327-9127 (SL)
PHOENIX/PMA INC
PHOENIX EDT
1080 Meyerside Dr, Mississauga, ON, L5T 1J4
(905) 678-9400
Emp Here 10 *Sales* 10,003,390
SIC 5051 Metals service centers and offices
Duane Astrauskas

D-U-N-S 24-193-9842 (BR)
PRATT & WHITNEY CANADA CIE
(*Suby of* PRATT AERO LIMITED PARTNERSHIP)
1801 Courtneypark Dr E, Mississauga, ON, L5T 1J3
(905) 564-7500
Emp Here 529
SIC 3519 Internal combustion engines, nec
Dave Maclennam

D-U-N-S 25-986-7351 (SL)
PREMIER TRUCK GROUP OF MISSISSAUGA
(*Suby of* PENSKE AUTOMOTIVE GROUP, INC.)
7035 Pacific Cir, Mississauga, ON, L5T 2A8
(905) 564-8270
Emp Here 50 *Sales* 31,464,000
SIC 5511 New and used car dealers
Chris Ritchie

D-U-N-S 20-145-4006 (HQ)
PRESSTEK CANADA CORP
(*Suby of* MAI HOLDINGS, INC.)
400 Ambassador Dr, Mississauga, ON, L5T 2J3
(905) 362-0610
Emp Here 40 *Sales* 39,018,400
SIC 5084 Industrial machinery and equipment
Fred Woods
Gerry Welstead
Edward Marino
Moosa Moosa
James Scafide

D-U-N-S 20-338-2671 (HQ)
PRIDE GROUP LOGISTICS LTD
6050 Dixie Rd, Mississauga, ON, L5T 1A6
(905) 564-7458
Sales 24,684,720
SIC 4212 Local trucking, without storage
Sulakhan Johal
Aman Johal

D-U-N-S 24-927-8474 (HQ)
PROVINCE ELECTRIC SUPPLY LTD
425 Superior Blvd Unit 6, Mississauga, ON, L5T 2W5
(905) 795-1795
Emp Here 25 *Sales* 31,607,560
SIC 5063 Electrical apparatus and equipment
John Mole

D-U-N-S 24-660-7345 (SL)
PURATOS CANADA INC
(*Suby of* COPREM)
520 Slate Dr, Mississauga, ON, L5T 0A1
(905) 362-3668
Emp Here 60 *Sales* 20,741,400
SIC 2052 Cookies and crackers
Benoit Keppenne
Eddy Van Belle
Bertrand Vanthournout

D-U-N-S 24-652-6842 (HQ)
PURETAP WATER DISTILLERS LTD
950 Verbena Rd, Mississauga, ON, L5T 1T6
(905) 670-7400
Sales 21,725,002
SIC 5149 Groceries and related products, nec
Mario Iorio

D-U-N-S 20-076-7445 (BR)
PUROLATOR INC
(*Suby of* GOVERNMENT OF CANADA)
6520 Kestrel Rd, Mississauga, ON, L5T 1Z6
(905) 565-9306
Emp Here 200
SIC 7389 Business services, nec
Wright Jamie

D-U-N-S 20-231-1288 (HQ)
PYLON ELECTRONICS INC
(*Suby of* ANDROCAN INC)
6355 Danville Rd Unit 10, Mississauga, ON, L5T 2L4
(905) 362-1395
Emp Here 12 *Sales* 17,309,520
SIC 7629 Electrical repair shops
Barrie Rose

D-U-N-S 24-463-6304 (SL)
QUINTAIN DEVELOPMENTS INC
6720 Columbus Rd, Mississauga, ON, L5T 2G1
(905) 670-3599
Emp Here 75 *Sales* 20,381,700
SIC 6531 Real estate agents and managers
Walter Ellison
Walter Mark Ellison

D-U-N-S 20-292-8123 (HQ)
RADIANT GLOBAL LOGISTICS (CANADA) INC
(*Suby of* RADIANT LOGISTICS, INC.)
1280 Courtneypark Dr E, Mississauga, ON, L5T 1N6
(905) 602-2700
Emp Here 140 *Sales* 93,364,880
SIC 4731 Freight transportation arrangement
Tim Boyce
Laurie Fox

D-U-N-S 24-795-9695 (HQ)
REEFER SALES & SERVICE (TORONTO) INCORPORATED
ATLANTIC CARRIER TRANSICOLD, DIV OF
425 Gibraltar Dr, Mississauga, ON, L5T 2S9
(905) 795-0234
Sales 17,309,520
SIC 7623 Refrigeration service and repair
Kenneth Henwood
Mark Nice
Larry Palko

D-U-N-S 24-121-4071 (HQ)
REGAL BELOIT CANADA
320 Superior Blvd Suite 1, Mississauga, ON, L5T 2N7
(905) 670-4770
Emp Here 45 *Sales* 58,024,700
SIC 5063 Electrical apparatus and equipment
Glen Peer

D-U-N-S 20-717-7031 (BR)
REXEL CANADA ELECTRICAL INC
WESTBURNE ONTARIO
(*Suby of* REXEL)
1180 Courtneypark Dr E, Mississauga, ON, L5T 1P2

(905) 670-2800
Emp Here 75
SIC 5063 Electrical apparatus and equipment

D-U-N-S 24-349-5459 (BR)
REXEL CANADA ELECTRICAL INC
WESTBURNE RUDDY ELECTRIC
(*Suby of* REXEL)
301 Ambassador Dr, Mississauga, ON, L5T 2J3
(905) 565-2985
Emp Here 200
SIC 5063 Electrical apparatus and equipment
Trevor Jones

D-U-N-S 20-174-0495 (HQ)
RICHARDS PACKAGING INC
REXPLAS
(*Suby of* RICHARDS PACKAGING INCOME FUND)
6095 Ordan Dr, Mississauga, ON, L5T 2M7
(905) 670-7760
Emp Here 50 *Sales* 95,628,060
SIC 3221 Glass containers
Gerry Glynn
David Prupas
Perry Watson
Howard Sandys
Wayne Mcleod
Derek Ridout
Donald Wright
Rami Younes

D-U-N-S 20-703-2868 (HQ)
RICHARDS PACKAGING INCOME FUND
6095 Ordan Dr, Mississauga, ON, L5T 2M7
(905) 670-7760
Emp Here 4 *Sales* 241,120,406
SIC 5099 Durable goods, nec
Gerry Glynn
David Prupas
Terry Edwards
Susan Allen
Enzio Gennaro
Donald Wright
Rami Younes

D-U-N-S 25-214-7244 (HQ)
RITTAL SYSTEMS LTD
(*Suby of* FRIEDHELM LOH STIFTUNG & CO. KG)
6485 Ordan Dr, Mississauga, ON, L5T 1X2
(905) 795-0777
Emp Here 32 *Sales* 22,358,700
SIC 5063 Electrical apparatus and equipment
Tim Rourke

D-U-N-S 25-354-9166 (HQ)
RODAIR INTERNATIONAL LTD
SEKO CANADA LOGISTICS
(*Suby of* RODAIR HOLDINGS LTD)
350 Pendant Dr, Mississauga, ON, L5T 2W6
(905) 671-4655
Emp Here 90 *Sales* 65,708,775
SIC 4731 Freight transportation arrangement
Jeffrey Cullen
Sarah Mcdonagh
Bryan Brooks
Chris Matthews

D-U-N-S 20-939-7470 (SL)
ROKAN LAMINATING CO LTD
PLAK-IT
1660 Trinity Dr, Mississauga, ON, L5T 1L6
(905) 564-7525
Emp Here 55 *Sales* 24,707,045
SIC 7389 Business services, nec
James A Shaw
Tim Seebach
Lonnie Shaw

D-U-N-S 24-829-3458 (SL)
ROOF TILE MANAGEMENT INC
RTM
360 Gibraltar Dr, Mississauga, ON, L5T 2P5
(905) 672-9992
Emp Here 100 *Sales* 21,782,900

SIC 1761 Roofing, siding, and sheetMetal work
Nick Mather
Pieter Chung

D-U-N-S 20-533-8767 (HQ)
ROSEDALE TRANSPORT LIMITED
THE ROSEDALE GROUP
6845 Invader Cres, Mississauga, ON, L5T 2B7
(905) 670-0057
Emp Here 210 *Sales* 65,455,255
SIC 4212 Local trucking, without storage
Rowland Uloth
Ron Uloth
Ron Picklyk
Barry Smith

D-U-N-S 25-220-9747 (SL)
ROTO FASCO CANADA INC.
(*Suby of* ROTO FRANK AG)
6625 Ordan Dr Unit 1, Mississauga, ON, L5T 1X2
(905) 670-8559
Emp Here 140 *Sales* 25,394,320
SIC 3364 Nonferrous die-castings except aluminum
James Stapleton
Mark Straub

D-U-N-S 20-174-6120 (HQ)
RYDER MATERIAL HANDLING ULC
CROWN LIFT TRUCKS
(*Suby of* CROWN EQUIPMENT CORPORATION)
210 Annagem Blvd, Mississauga, ON, L5T 2V5
(905) 565-2100
Emp Here 110 *Sales* 170,705,500
SIC 5084 Industrial machinery and equipment
Ronald Greer
Danny Fatigati

D-U-N-S 24-625-9378 (HQ)
S & S TRUCK PARTS CANADA INC
(*Suby of* S&S TRUCK PARTS, LLC)
6460 Kestrel Rd, Mississauga, ON, L5T 1Z7
(905) 564-7100
Sales 12,019,095
SIC 5013 Motor vehicle supplies and new parts
Bernard Sacks
Richard Hoffman
Stephen Danzinger

D-U-N-S 20-174-9389 (SL)
SCANTRADE INTERNATIONAL LIMITED
6685 Kennedy Rd Suite 7, Mississauga, ON, L5T 3A5
(905) 795-9380
Emp Here 36 *Sales* 37,146,488
SIC 5023 Homefurnishings
Larry Henderson Sr
Jini Henderson
Larry M Henderson Jr
Jan Henderson

D-U-N-S 20-696-6843 (SL)
SCHMOLZ + BICKENBACH CANADA, INC.
6350 Vipond Dr, Mississauga, ON, L5T 1G2
(416) 675-5941
Emp Here 54 *Sales* 32,262,516
SIC 5051 Metals service centers and offices
Tony Elfstrom
Ted Callighen

D-U-N-S 20-534-9053 (HQ)
SEA AIR INTERNATIONAL FORWARDERS LIMITED
1720 Meyerside Dr, Mississauga, ON, L5T 1A3
(905) 677-7701
Emp Here 35 *Sales* 20,798,680
SIC 4731 Freight transportation arrangement
Peter Smith
Geoffrey Robinson

D-U-N-S 24-991-6867 (SL)
SEYDACO PACKAGING CORP

215 Courtneypark Dr E, Mississauga, ON, L5T 2T6
(905) 565-8030
Emp Here 42   *Sales* 18,781,308
SIC 5045 Computers, peripherals, and software
David Seychell

D-U-N-S 20-366-8041   (BR)
SGS CANADA INC
6490 Vipond Dr, Mississauga, ON, L5T 1W8
(905) 364-3757
Emp Here 233
SIC 8734 Testing laboratories
Michael Lindsay

D-U-N-S 24-216-7385   (HQ)
SHERWAY WAREHOUSING INC
325a Annagem Blvd Suite 2, Mississauga, ON, L5T 3A7
(905) 364-3300
Emp Here 35   *Sales* 41,141,200
SIC 4225 General warehousing and storage
Paul Rockett

D-U-N-S 20-105-7408   (BR)
SIEMENS CANADA LIMITED
SIEMENS IT SOLUTIONS AND SERVICES
(Suby of SIEMENS AG*)*
6375 Shawson Dr, Mississauga, ON, L5T 1S7
(905) 212-4500
Emp Here 100
SIC 8742 Management consulting services

D-U-N-S 20-550-5386   (SL)
SILEX INNOVATIONS INC
6659 Ordan Dr, Mississauga, ON, L5T 1K6
(905) 612-4000
Emp Here 60   *Sales* 13,320,060
SIC 3567 Industrial furnaces and ovens
Todd Stephens
Calum Forsyth
John Wilson

D-U-N-S 24-678-9478   (SL)
SILFAB SOLAR INC
SILFAB ONTARIO
(Suby of GRIDCO SRL*)*
240 Courtneypark Dr E, Mississauga, ON, L5T 2S5
(905) 255-2501
Emp Here 220   *Sales* 62,241,300
SIC 3674 Semiconductors and related devices
Franco Traverso
Paolo Maccario
Hanna Ayyad
Anton Szpitalak

D-U-N-S 24-737-1701   (SL)
SLEEVER INTERNATIONAL INC
(Suby of SA SINEF*)*
6815 Columbus Rd, Mississauga, ON, L5T 2G9
(905) 565-0952
Emp Here 65   *Sales* 12,659,920
SIC 2679 Converted paper products, nec
Laurent Lamotte
Kendra Wasylyk
Jean-Charles Fresnel

D-U-N-S 24-364-6242   (HQ)
SPIRAL OF CANADA INC
6155 Tomken Rd Unit 10, Mississauga, ON, L5T 1X3
(905) 564-8990
Emp Here 75
SIC 3089 Plastics products, nec
Sarah Cordeiro
Louis Cordeiro

D-U-N-S 20-174-7144   (SL)
ST. JOHN'S TROPHIES LTD
1750 Bonhill Rd, Mississauga, ON, L5T 1C8
(905) 564-2001
Emp Here 45   *Sales* 23,424,390
SIC 5094 Jewelry and precious stones
James Stevenson Jr

D-U-N-S 24-771-0437   (SL)
ST. SHREDDIES CELLO CO. LTD
POLY-CEL PACKAGING PRODUCTS
6141 Atlantic Dr Unit 1, Mississauga, ON, L5T 1L9
(905) 670-2414
Emp Here 54   *Sales* 10,902,438
SIC 3084 Plastics pipe
Richard Radvany
Diane Lesage

D-U-N-S 24-602-7742   (SL)
STAR PACKAGING EQUIPMENT LIMITED
6935 Davand Dr, Mississauga, ON, L5T 1L5
(905) 564-0092
Emp Here 28   *Sales* 13,300,728
SIC 5084 Industrial machinery and equipment
Josephine Williamson

D-U-N-S 24-815-9204   (SL)
STATE CHEMICAL LTD
(Suby of STATE INDUSTRIAL PRODUCTS CORPORATION*)*
1745 Meyerside Dr Suite 1, Mississauga, ON, L5T 1C6
(905) 670-4669
Emp Here 65   *Sales* 47,472,425
SIC 5169 Chemicals and allied products, nec
Harold Uhrman
Paul Chatterton

D-U-N-S 20-145-8064   (HQ)
STEEL FIRE EQUIPMENT LIMITED
150 Superior Blvd, Mississauga, ON, L5T 2L2
(905) 564-1500
Sales 10,450,572
SIC 5087 Service establishment equipment
Jason Steel

D-U-N-S 20-181-4126   (HQ)
STEPHENSON'S RENTAL SERVICES INC
(Suby of GMP CAPITAL INC*)*
6895 Columbus Rd Suite 502, Mississauga, ON, L5T 2G9
(905) 507-3650
Emp Here 25   *Sales* 99,944,400
SIC 7359 Equipment rental and leasing, nec
William D Swisher
James R. Mcinnis

D-U-N-S 20-178-0418   (SL)
SUN-GLO PRODUCTS INC
6681 Excelsior Crt, Mississauga, ON, L5T 2J2
(905) 678-6456
Emp Here 30   *Sales* 22,275,600
SIC 5199 Nondurable goods, nec
Brian Barr
Pierre Comtois
Dianne Dyer
Joan Barr

D-U-N-S 24-045-6033   (SL)
SUNDINE PRODUCE INC
6075 Kestrel Rd, Mississauga, ON, L5T 1Y8
(905) 364-1600
Emp Here 20   *Sales* 10,702,480
SIC 5148 Fresh fruits and vegetables
Sreedhar Mundluru
Divya Donthi

D-U-N-S 25-513-7473   (HQ)
SYNERGEX CORPORATION
1280 Courtneypark Dr E, Mississauga, ON, L5T 1N6
(905) 565-1212
Emp Here 210   *Sales* 131,161,240
SIC 5045 Computers, peripherals, and software
David O. A. Aiello
John L. Smith
Neil E Fleshner

D-U-N-S 24-816-2752   (SL)
TARGUS (CANADA) LTD
(Suby of TARGUS INTERNATIONAL LLC*)*
6725 Edwards Blvd, Mississauga, ON, L5T 2V9

(905) 564-9300
Emp Here 35   *Sales* 18,218,970
SIC 5099 Durable goods, nec
Zeno Ricci
Michael Hoopis
Victor Streufert

D-U-N-S 24-801-9192   (HQ)
TELECOR INC
6205 Kestrel Rd, Mississauga, ON, L5T 2A1
(905) 564-0801
Sales 10,724,340
SIC 8712 Architectural services
Peter Jova

D-U-N-S 20-818-0919   (HQ)
THERMO-KINETICS COMPANY LIMITED
6740 Invader Cres, Mississauga, ON, L5T 2B6
(905) 670-2266
Emp Here 40   *Sales* 12,828,100
SIC 3829 Measuring and controlling devices, nec
Jeff Dello

D-U-N-S 24-877-0059   (SL)
TORONTO MICROELECTRONICS INC
TME
6185 Danville Rd, Mississauga, ON, L5T 2H7
(905) 362-8090
Emp Here 78   *Sales* 17,728,542
SIC 3861 Photographic equipment and supplies
Quang Nguyen
Janneth Nguyen

D-U-N-S 24-194-8298   (HQ)
TOTAL POWER LIMITED
6450 Kestrel Rd Unit 3, Mississauga, ON, L5T 1Z7
(905) 670-1535
Emp Here 73   *Sales* 19,234,642
SIC 3621 Motors and generators
Graham Clark
Andrew Rudderham
Slavka Batchvarova

D-U-N-S 20-879-3711   (SL)
TOTES ISOTONER CANADA LIMITED
TOTES
(Suby of TOTES ISOTONER HOLDINGS CORPORATION*)*
6335 Shawson Dr, Mississauga, ON, L5T 1S7
(905) 564-4798
Emp Here 23   *Sales* 11,461,406
SIC 5139 Footwear
Don Wilson
Bradford E Phillips
Doug Gernert

D-U-N-S 20-691-3548   (SL)
TRADESPAN CARGO LTD
6305 Danville Rd Unit 2, Mississauga, ON, L5T 2H7
(416) 410-1009
Emp Here 35   *Sales* 18,198,845
SIC 4731 Freight transportation arrangement
Knud Sander
Sean Sander
Celina Sander

D-U-N-S 20-646-8274   (HQ)
TRAIN TRAILER RENTALS LIMITED
(Suby of CUBE TRANSPORTATION EUROPE COOPERATIEF U.A.*)*
400 Annagem Blvd, Mississauga, ON, L5T 3A8
(905) 564-7247
Sales 15,581,500
SIC 7519 Utility trailer rental
Rick Kloepfer
Ming Zhuang

D-U-N-S 24-793-1249   (SL)
TRI-AD INTERNATIONAL FREIGHT FORWARDING LTD
375 Annagem Blvd Unit 100, Mississauga, ON, L5T 3A7

(905) 624-8214
Emp Here 30   *Sales* 15,599,010
SIC 4731 Freight transportation arrangement
Linda Collier

D-U-N-S 20-285-9120   (SL)
TRISAN GENERAL CONTRACTORS INC
6459 Netherhart Rd, Mississauga, ON, L5T 1C3

Emp Here 45   *Sales* 21,182,895
SIC 1542 Nonresidential construction, nec
Max Santos

D-U-N-S 20-401-6430   (HQ)
TROPHY FOODS INC
71 Admiral Blvd, Mississauga, ON, L5T 2T1
(905) 670-8050
Emp Here 250   *Sales* 344,023,680
SIC 5145 Confectionery
Brian Paul
Bruce Mitchell
Sunil Gandhi

D-U-N-S 24-094-1047   (SL)
TRY HARD INDUSTRIAL SUPPLY CO LTD
1411 Courtneypark Dr E, Mississauga, ON, L5T 2E3
(905) 565-8700
Emp Here 30   *Sales* 14,250,780
SIC 5085 Industrial supplies
Frank Ferko
Dario Ferko
John Ferko

D-U-N-S 24-543-7793   (SL)
ULTRA-FIT MANUFACTURING INCORPORATED
(Suby of ARVA LIMITED*)*
1840 Courtneypark Dr E, Mississauga, ON, L5T 1W1
(905) 795-0344
Emp Here 114   *Sales* 21,897,690
SIC 3498 Fabricated pipe and fittings
Michael Stevens
John Stevens
Donald Hockin

D-U-N-S 24-215-9770   (HQ)
UNISYNC GROUP LIMITED
HAMMILL
(Suby of YORK UNIFORMS HOLDINGS LIMITED*)*
6375 Dixie Rd Unit 6, Mississauga, ON, L5T 2E7
(905) 361-8989
Emp Here 30   *Sales* 42,453,600
SIC 2337 Women's and misses' suits and coats
B. James Bottoms
David Selley
Douglas Good
Richard Smith
Bruce Aunger

D-U-N-S 20-145-8577   (HQ)
UNITED VAN LINES (CANADA) LTD
MAYFLOWER CANADA
7229 Pacific Cir, Mississauga, ON, L5T 1S9
(905) 564-6400
Emp Here 100   *Sales* 23,656,190
SIC 4212 Local trucking, without storage
Anne Martin

D-U-N-S 24-924-9525   (SL)
V & L ASSOCIATES INC
6315 Danville Rd, Mississauga, ON, L5T 2H7
(905) 565-7535
Emp Here 30   *Sales* 15,616,260
SIC 5092 Toys and hobby goods and supplies
Sidney Law

D-U-N-S 25-508-2737   (BR)
VERITIV CANADA, INC
(Suby of VERITIV CORPORATION*)*
1475 Courtneypark Dr E, Mississauga, ON, L5T 2R1
(905) 795-7400
Emp Here 240

SIC 5113 Industrial and personal service paper
Sylvie Clarke

D-U-N-S 20-329-3907   (HQ)
VERSA FITTINGS INC
290 Courtneypark Dr E, Mississauga, ON, L5T 2S5
(905) 564-2600
Sales 31,302,180
SIC 5074 Plumbing and heating equipment and supplies (hydronics)
David Tomlinson

D-U-N-S 24-611-2478   (SL)
VIBRANT POWER INC
VIBRANT PERFORMANCE
310 Courtneypark Dr E, Mississauga, ON, L5T 2S5
(905) 564-8644
Emp Here 50   Sales 22,358,700
SIC 5072 Hardware
Dino Rossi Sr

D-U-N-S 25-397-7045   (HQ)
VIPOND INC
INTEGRATED PROTECTION
(Suby of API GROUP INC.)
6380 Vipond Dr, Mississauga, ON, L5T 1A1
(905) 564-7060
Emp Here 120   Sales 133,390,093
SIC 3569 General industrial machinery, nec
Russel Becker
Bernard Beliveau
Grant Neal

D-U-N-S 24-422-8230   (SL)
VORTEX FREIGHT SYSTEMS INC
6615 Ordan Dr Unit 14-15, Mississauga, ON, L5T 1X2
(905) 499-3000
Emp Here 24   Sales 12,479,208
SIC 4731 Freight transportation arrangement
Gavin Killen
Patrick Russell

D-U-N-S 25-406-9909   (HQ)
WESBELL GROUP OF COMPANIES INC, THE
WESBELL TECHNOLOGIES
(Suby of WESBELL TELECOM DESIGN SERVICES INC)
6300 Ordan Dr, Mississauga, ON, L5T 1W6
(905) 595-8000
Sales 28,559,000
SIC 4899 Communication services, nec
Nick Mazze

D-U-N-S 24-891-8190   (BR)
WHITE GLOVE TRANSPORTATION SYSTEMS LTD
(Suby of GOVERNMENT OF CANADA)
6141 Vipond Dr, Mississauga, ON, L5T 2B2
(905) 565-1053
Emp Here 150
SIC 4212 Local trucking, without storage
Justin Dodd

D-U-N-S 25-997-0432   (HQ)
WHITE GLOVE TRANSPORTATION SYSTEMS LTD
(Suby of GOVERNMENT OF CANADA)
215 Courtneypark Dr E, Mississauga, ON, L5T 2T6
(905) 565-1053
Sales 20,570,600
SIC 4212 Local trucking, without storage
Chris Galindo

D-U-N-S 20-178-3511   (SL)
WHOLESALE LETTERING AND CARVING LIMITED
6215 Netherhart Rd, Mississauga, ON, L5T 1G5

Emp Here 25   Sales 13,013,550
SIC 5099 Durable goods, nec
James Desroches

D-U-N-S 24-625-9352   (SL)
WILD FLAVORS (CANADA) INC
7315 Pacific Cir, Mississauga, ON, L5T 1V1
(905) 670-1108
Emp Here 45   Sales 10,118,475
SIC 2087 Flavoring extracts and syrups, nec
Tamara Robichaud

D-U-N-S 20-784-0075   (HQ)
WORLD VISION CANADA
1 World Dr Suite 2500, Mississauga, ON, L5T 2Y4
(905) 565-6100
Emp Here 450   Sales 37,619,232
SIC 8322 Individual and family services
Ron Mckerlie
Michael Messenger
Elizabeth Cummings
Dan Fortin
Ron Mckerlie
Serge Fontaine
Mike Gartner
Carson Pue
Kevin Jenkins
Lori Lutes

D-U-N-S 24-610-4624   (HQ)
WORLDPAC CANADA INC
(Suby of ADVANCE AUTO PARTS, INC.)
6956 Columbus Rd, Mississauga, ON, L5T 2G1
(905) 238-9390
Emp Here 16   Sales 14,932,815
SIC 5013 Motor vehicle supplies and new parts
Steven P. Gushie
Robert E. Cushing
Michael A. Norona
Darren R. Jackson

D-U-N-S 20-977-1638   (SL)
XTRUX INC
6175 Kenway Dr, Mississauga, ON, L5T 2L3
(905) 362-1277
Emp Here 106   Sales 70,690,552
SIC 4731 Freight transportation arrangement
David Oilieo

Mississauga, ON L5V

D-U-N-S 20-295-9276   (SL)
2207544 ONTARIO INC
ANDERSON CONSULTING
1250 Eglinton Ave W Suite 138, Mississauga, ON, L5V 1N3
(905) 795-7781
Emp Here 112   Sales 28,390,880
SIC 8748 Business consulting, nec
Edward Anderson
Robert Goodwin

D-U-N-S 25-483-8105   (BR)
DUFFERIN-PEEL CATHOLIC DISTRICT SCHOOL BOARD
ST JOSEPH SECONDARY SCHOOL
(Suby of DUFFERIN-PEEL CATHOLIC DISTRICT SCHOOL BOARD)
5555 Creditview Rd, Mississauga, ON, L5V 2B9
(905) 812-1376
Emp Here 150
SIC 8211 Elementary and secondary schools
Jeff Quenneville

D-U-N-S 24-337-0207   (HQ)
ELECTROLUX CANADA CORP
ELECTROLUX MAJOR APPLIANCES
(Suby of AB ELECTROLUX)
5855 Terry Fox Way, Mississauga, ON, L5V 3E4
(905) 813-7700
Emp Here 170   Sales 131,135,822
SIC 5064 Electrical appliances, television and radio

Scott Ride
Sue Stevenson
John Milani
Tony Anzivino
Marie Murphy

D-U-N-S 24-205-8811   (HQ)
HUSQVARNA CANADA CORP
(Suby of HUSQVARNA AB)
850 Matheson Blvd W Suite 4, Mississauga, ON, L5V 0B4
(905) 817-1510
Sales 19,208,500
SIC 3425 Saw blades and handsaws
Michael A Jones
Randy Legare

D-U-N-S 20-129-3024   (HQ)
MCMILLAN & SAUNDERS INC
MCMILLAN & SAUNDERS VOLVO
797 Bancroft Dr, Mississauga, ON, L5V 2Y6
(905) 858-0712
Emp Here 35   Sales 34,610,400
SIC 5511 New and used car dealers
Robert Mcmillan

D-U-N-S 20-576-9057   (BR)
PEEL DISTRICT SCHOOL BOARD
RICK HANSON SECONDARY SCHOOL
(Suby of PEEL DISTRICT SCHOOL BOARD)
1150 Dream Crest Rd, Mississauga, ON, L5V 1N6
(905) 567-4260
Emp Here 100
SIC 8211 Elementary and secondary schools
Patricia Whyte

D-U-N-S 20-700-4669   (BR)
PVH CANADA, INC
TOMMY HILFIGER
(Suby of PVH CORP.)
775 Britannia Rd W Unit 1, Mississauga, ON, L5V 2Y1
(905) 826-9645
Emp Here 80
SIC 5136 Men's and boy's clothing
Sherrie Scymore

D-U-N-S 25-153-5837   (SL)
SOMI INC
SUBARU OF MISSISSAUGA
(Suby of SUBARU CORPORATION)
6160 Mavis Rd, Mississauga, ON, L5V 2X4
(905) 569-7777
Emp Here 36   Sales 22,654,080
SIC 5511 New and used car dealers
Brian Hawkins

D-U-N-S 20-818-4721   (HQ)
STAEDTLER-MARS LIMITED
(Suby of STAEDTLER STIFTUNG)
850 Matheson Blvd W Unit 4, Mississauga, ON, L5V 0B4
(905) 501-9008
Emp Here 32   Sales 32,670,880
SIC 5199 Nondurable goods, nec
Diane Sant

D-U-N-S 20-182-6091   (SL)
TEAM CHRYSLER JEEP DODGE INC
TEAM CHRYSLER JEEP DODGE
777 Bancroft Dr, Mississauga, ON, L5V 2Y6
(905) 819-0001
Emp Here 75   Sales 47,196,000
SIC 5511 New and used car dealers
Barry Gray
Brenda Gray
Burk Boyd

Mississauga, ON L5W

D-U-N-S 25-102-1085   (HQ)
AMERICAN EAGLE OUTFITTERS CANADA CORPORATION
BRAEMAR

(Suby of AMERICAN EAGLE OUTFITTERS, INC.)
450 Courtneypark Dr W, Mississauga, ON, L5W 1Y6
(289) 562-8000
Emp Here 10   Sales 361,789,500
SIC 5651 Family clothing stores
Carm Sivers

D-U-N-S 24-195-6325   (SL)
BOND BRAND LOYALTY INC
6900 Maritz Dr, Mississauga, ON, L5W 1L8
(905) 696-9400
Emp Here 400   Sales 44,881,200
SIC 8741 Management services
Robert Macdonald
Rob Daniel
Sean Claessen
Carlo Pirillo
Mike Mcdowell
Maria Pallante
Scott Robinson
Anne Bowie
Morana Bakula
Brian Kim

D-U-N-S 20-625-0003   (HQ)
CML HEALTHCARE INC
60 Courtneypark Dr W Unit 1, Mississauga, ON, L5W 0B3
(905) 565-0043
Emp Here 700   Sales 353,457,560
SIC 8071 Medical laboratories
Patrice Merrin
Thomas Wellner
Kent Wentzell
Thomas Weber
Peter Van Der Velden
Gerry Barry
Dr. Joseph Fairbrother
Robert Fisher Jr
Stephen Wiseman

D-U-N-S 20-072-2457   (HQ)
COMPASS GROUP CANADA LTD
CHARTWELL
(Suby of COMPASS GROUP PLC)
1 Prologis Blvd Suite 400, Mississauga, ON, L5W 0G2
(905) 795-5100
Emp Here 150   Sales 1,026,058,000
SIC 5812 Eating places
Saajid Khan
Brent Mooney
Ian Baskerville

D-U-N-S 24-367-6140   (HQ)
GENUINE CANADIAN CORP, THE
BONNIE TOGS
(Suby of CARTER'S, INC.)
1 Prologis Blvd, Mississauga, ON, L5W 0G2
(519) 624-6574
Emp Here 75   Sales 837,533,000
SIC 5137 Women's and children's clothing
Michael Casey
Paul Rubinstein
Paul Ariston
Richard Westenter

D-U-N-S 24-376-4698   (SL)
GRACIOUS LIVING INNOVATIONS INC
151 Courtneypark Dr W Suite 201, Mississauga, ON, L5W 1Y5
(905) 795-5505
Emp Here 200   Sales 31,771,600
SIC 3089 Plastics products, nec
Enzo Macri
Vito Galloro

D-U-N-S 24-463-7914   (HQ)
IMAGINIT CANADA INC
IMAGINIT TECHNOLOGIES
151 Courtneypark Dr W Suite 201, Mississauga, ON, L5W 1Y5
(905) 602-8783
Emp Here 17   Sales 23,358,580
SIC 7372 Prepackaged software

Bob Heeg
Martin Cheung

D-U-N-S 20-140-9059   (HQ)
KAO CANADA INC
KAO BRANDS
(*Suby of* KAO CORPORATION)
75 Courtneypark Dr W Unit 2, Mississauga,
ON, L5W 0E3
(905) 670-7890
Emp Here 40   *Sales* 77,374,150
SIC 5122 Drugs, proprietaries, and sundries
Ronald Puistonen
Joseph B. Workman
Richard Deutsch

D-U-N-S 24-757-5798   (HQ)
KCI MEDICAL CANADA INC
(*Suby of* CHIRON GUERNSEY HOLDINGS
L.P. INC.)
75 Courtneypark Dr W Suite 2, Mississauga,
ON, L5W 0E3
(905) 565-7187
Emp Here 40   *Sales* 160,605,600
SIC 5047 Medical and hospital equipment
Carol Robinson
Rob Russell
Mike Holvey

D-U-N-S 24-078-7697   (HQ)
KENAIDAN CONTRACTING LTD
(*Suby of* OBAYASHI CORPORATION)
7080 Derrycrest Dr, Mississauga, ON, L5W
0G5
(905) 670-2660
Emp Here 100   *Sales* 49,282,750
SIC 8711 Engineering services
Aidan Flatley
John Goffredo
Ian Smith
Deborah A. Fillippe

D-U-N-S 24-978-0875   (SL)
KENAIDAN GROUP LTD
(*Suby of* OBAYASHI CORPORATION)
7080 Derrycrest Dr, Mississauga, ON, L5W
0G5
(905) 670-2660
Emp Here 500   *Sales* 164,057,500
SIC 1629 Heavy construction, nec
Aidan Flatley
Peter Sullivan
Ruth Flatley

D-U-N-S 25-204-6628   (HQ)
**LA CAPITALE FINANCIAL SECURITY IN-
SURANCE COMPANY**
7150 Derrycrest Dr Suite 1150, Mississauga,
ON, L5W 0E5
(905) 795-2300
Emp Here 180   *Sales* 427,393,600
SIC 6321 Accident and health insurance
Francois Jutras
Didier Ledeur
Rene Rouleau
Dominique Dubuc
Francois Latreille
Richard Fiset
Dominique Salvy
Patrice Forget
Steven Ross
Pierre Marc Bellavance

D-U-N-S 24-361-2624   (HQ)
**NATIONAL LOGISTICS SERVICES (2006)
INC**
NLS
150 Courtneypark Dr W, Mississauga, ON,
L5W 1Y6
(905) 364-0033
Sales 25,912,744
SIC 5137 Women's and children's clothing
Peter Reaume
Michael Andlauer

D-U-N-S 20-640-5508   (HQ)
NTN BEARING CORPORATION OF

CANADA LIMITED
(*Suby of* NTN CORPORATION)
305 Courtneypark Dr W, Mississauga, ON,
L5W 1Y4
(905) 564-2700
Emp Here 60   *Sales* 102,423,300
SIC 5085 Industrial supplies
Hiroaki Tachibana
Paul Meo

D-U-N-S 24-344-9076   (BR)
PEEL DISTRICT SCHOOL BOARD
MISSISSAUGA SECONDARY SCHOOL
(*Suby of* PEEL DISTRICT SCHOOL BOARD)
550 Courtneypark Dr W, Mississauga, ON,
L5W 1L9
(905) 564-1033
Emp Here 75
SIC 8211 Elementary and secondary schools
Giota Woods

D-U-N-S 24-752-5173   (HQ)
PLASP CHILD CARE SERVICES
60 Courtneypark Dr W Unit 5, Mississauga,
ON, L5W 0B3
(905) 890-1711
Emp Here 50   *Sales* 47,745,342
SIC 8351 Child day care services
Lynn Hiebert
Frank Andreacchi
Duncan Fletcher
Sandy Edmonds
Rani Dhaliwal
Susan Clunie
Wayne Edwards
Leslie Howard
Sherry Fodor
Paul Street

D-U-N-S 24-610-6140   (HQ)
RAND A TECHNOLOGY CORPORATION
RAND WORLDWIDE
(*Suby of* RAND WORLDWIDE, INC.)
151 Courtneypark Dr W Suite 201, Missis-
sauga, ON, L5W 1Y5
(905) 565-2929
Emp Here 140   *Sales* 50,491,350
SIC 8741 Management services
Marc Dulude

D-U-N-S 25-215-0487   (SL)
ROGUE TRANSPORTATION SERVICES INC
ROGUE SPECIALTY TRANSPORT
255 Courtneypark Dr W Unit 102, Missis-
sauga, ON, L5W 0A5
(905) 362-9401
Emp Here 55   *Sales* 11,313,830
SIC 4212 Local trucking, without storage
Richard Brown
Richard Brown
Rick Robertson
Allan Pick
Dave Furtado
Paul Guentner

D-U-N-S 20-718-7431   (SL)
SHOES FOR CREWS
199 Longside Dr, Mississauga, ON, L5W 1Z9

Emp Here 21   *Sales* 10,640,766
SIC 5139 Footwear

D-U-N-S 25-977-9148   (HQ)
SHOPPERS DRUG MART INC
(*Suby of* LOBLAW COMPANIES LIMITED)
60 Courtneypark Dr W, Mississauga, ON, L5W
0B3
(416) 493-1220
Sales 103,244,400
SIC 6794 Patent owners and lessors
Frank Pedinelli
Michael Moltz
Joanne Gould

D-U-N-S 20-250-4627   (SL)
SONOVA CANADA INC
(*Suby of* SONOVA HOLDING AG)

80 Courtneypark Dr W Suite 1, Mississauga,
ON, L5W 0B3
(905) 677-1167
Emp Here 100   *Sales* 22,728,900
SIC 3842 Surgical appliances and supplies
Jan Metzdorff
Darren Farry
Patrick Buechi
Brad Caves
Steven Mahon
Alessandra Perego
Paul Thompson
Rob Walesa

D-U-N-S 24-384-2981   (SL)
**SONY INTERACTIVE ENTERTAINMENT
CANADA INC**
(*Suby of* SONY CORPORATION)
1 Prologis Blvd Suite 103, Mississauga, ON,
L5W 0G2
(905) 795-5152
Emp Here 20   *Sales* 10,410,840
SIC 5092 Toys and hobby goods and supplies
Kazuo Hirai
Jack Tretton
James C. Bass
Stephen Turvey

D-U-N-S 24-357-2039   (SL)
SPECTRUM BRANDS CANADA, INC
RAYOVAC DIVISION
(*Suby of* SPECTRUM BRANDS HOLDINGS,
INC.)
255 Longside Dr Unit 101, Mississauga, ON,
L5W 0G7
(800) 566-7899
Emp Here 150   *Sales* 33,300,150
SIC 3524 Lawn and garden equipment
Jeff Haltrecht

D-U-N-S 20-968-3465   (SL)
UNICA INSURANCE INC
7150 Derrycrest Dr Suite 1, Mississauga, ON,
L5W 0E5
(905) 677-9777
Emp Here 45   *Sales* 46,569,645
SIC 6331 Fire, marine, and casualty insurance
Martin Delage
Shaun Jackson
Roger Wingfield
Steve Smith

D-U-N-S 20-282-4488   (HQ)
WALMART CANADA LOGISTICS ULC
(*Suby of* WALMART INC.)
6800 Maritz Dr, Mississauga, ON, L5W 1W2
(905) 670-9966
Emp Here 800   *Sales* 575,976,800
SIC 4225 General warehousing and storage
Shelley Broader
Ronald Strathdee
William Tofflemire

D-U-N-S 24-329-9521   (BR)
WALMART CANADA LOGISTICS ULC
SUPPLY CHAIN MANAGEMENT
(*Suby of* WALMART INC.)
200 Courtneypark Dr W, Mississauga, ON,
L5W 1Y6
(905) 564-1484
Emp Here 300
SIC 4225 General warehousing and storage
Frank Herceg

Mississauga, ON L9H

D-U-N-S 25-002-5681   (SL)
PHYSIO CONTROL CANADA SALES LTD
45 Innovation Dr, Mississauga, ON, L9H 7L8
(800) 895-5896
Emp Here 25   *Sales* 11,179,350
SIC 5047 Medical and hospital equipment
Bryan Webster

Mississauga, ON N5W

D-U-N-S 25-483-3841   (HQ)
PRGX CANADA CORP
(*Suby of* PRGX GLOBAL, INC.)
60 Courtney Park Dr Unit 4, Mississauga,
ON, N5W 0B3
(905) 670-7879
Emp Here 30   *Sales* 20,768,500
SIC 8721 Accounting, auditing, and book-
keeping
Jimmy How

Mitchell, ON N0K

D-U-N-S 20-609-3382   (SL)
2026798 ONTARIO LIMITED
WALKOM'S VALUE MART
120 Ontario Rd, Mitchell, ON, N0K 1N0
(519) 348-8446
Emp Here 45   *Sales* 12,336,840
SIC 5411 Grocery stores
Steve Walkom
Terry Walkom

D-U-N-S 25-251-6307   (SL)
ADVANTAGE MACHINE & TOOL INC
155 Huron Rd Ss 1, Mitchell, ON, N0K 1N0
(519) 348-4414
Emp Here 61   *Sales* 13,542,061
SIC 3541 Machine tools, Metal cutting type
Dave Mccarthy

D-U-N-S 24-207-5476   (HQ)
BIO AGRI MIX LP
11 Ellens St, Mitchell, ON, N0K 1N0
(519) 348-9865
Sales 13,833,000
SIC 2834 Pharmaceutical preparations
Paul Lake
Adam Hopper

D-U-N-S 20-130-9945   (BR)
CONTITECH CANADA, INC
(*Suby of* CONTINENTAL AG)
79 Arthur St, Mitchell, ON, N0K 1N0

Emp Here 220
SIC 3559 Special industry machinery, nec

Moorefield, ON N0G

D-U-N-S 24-887-9244   (BR)
DARLING INTERNATIONAL CANADA INC
ROTHSAY
(*Suby of* DARLING INGREDIENTS INC.)
8406 Wellington County Rr, Moorefield, ON,
N0G 2K0
(519) 638-3081
Emp Here 100
SIC 4953 Refuse systems

Mooretown, ON N0N

D-U-N-S 25-367-3297   (BR)
NOVA CHEMICALS (CANADA) LTD
(*Suby of* GOVERNMENT OF ABU DHABI)
510 Moore Line, Mooretown, ON, N0N 1M0
(519) 862-2961
Emp Here 230
SIC 2869 Industrial organic chemicals, nec
Maxine Mcbain

D-U-N-S 20-698-1438   (BR)
NOVA CHEMICALS CORPORATION
(*Suby of* GOVERNMENT OF ABU DHABI)

510 Moore Line, Mooretown, ON, N0N 1M0
(519) 862-2961
Emp Here 200
SIC 2821 Plastics materials and resins
  Tom Thompson

D-U-N-S 24-101-0722   (BR)
SUNCOR ENERGY INC
(*Suby of* SUNCOR ENERGY INC)
535 Rokeby Line Rr 1, Mooretown, ON, N0N
1M0
(519) 481-0454
Emp Here 100
SIC 2911 Petroleum refining
  Andre Boucher

Moose Creek, ON K0C

D-U-N-S 24-269-1426   (SL)
SOLS CALCO SOILS INC, LES
17354 Allaire Rd, Moose Creek, ON, K0C
1W0
(613) 538-2885
Emp Here 17   *Sales* 24,950,764
SIC 5159 Farm-product raw materials, nec
  Andre Lafleche
  Josee Lafleche
  Claudette Lafleche
  Nathalie Lafleche
  Eric Quesnell

Moose Factory, ON P0L

D-U-N-S 24-850-4466   (HQ)
**MOOSE BAND DEVELOPMENT CORPORA-
TION**
22 Jonathan Thethoo, Moose Factory, ON,
P0L 1W0
(705) 658-4335
Sales 14,121,930
SIC 1542 Nonresidential construction, nec
  Bobbie Thethoo
  Derrick Thum

D-U-N-S 25-104-0713   (HQ)
WEENEEBAYKO HEALTH AHTUSKAYWIN
WEENEEBAYKO GENERAL HOSPITAL
19 Hospital Dr, Moose Factory, ON, P0L 1W0
(705) 658-4544
Sales 25,548,400
SIC 8062 General medical and surgical hospi-
tals
  Bernie Schmidt
  John Sutherland
  George Small Jr.
  Gail Valentine

Moosonee, ON P0L

D-U-N-S 25-642-0022   (SL)
CREE-ASKI SERVICES LTD FIELD OFFICE
196 Ferguson Rd, Moosonee, ON, P0L 1Y0
(705) 336-2828
Emp Here 40   *Sales* 12,754,760
SIC 1521 Single-family housing construction
  Gary Small

D-U-N-S 24-184-3788   (HQ)
JAMES BAY GENERAL HOSPITAL
78 Furguson Rd, Moosonee, ON, P0L 1Y0
(705) 336-2947
Emp Here 40   *Sales* 16,662,000
SIC 8062 General medical and surgical hospi-
tals
  Alec Czap
  William Burnie
  Simone Hood
  Bishop Hennessey

Susan Clark

Morewood, ON K0A

D-U-N-S 24-876-7998   (SL)
GUILDCREST BUILDING CORPORATION
(*Suby of* GROUPE PRO-FAB INC)
20 Mill St, Morewood, ON, K0A 2R0
(613) 448-2349
Emp Here 135   *Sales* 25,969,950
SIC 2452 Prefabricated wood buildings
  David G Poupore
  Robert Egan
  John Coppens

Morrisburg, ON K0C

D-U-N-S 25-464-2051   (HQ)
BRISTER INSURANCE BROKERS LTD
BRISTER GROUP-MORRISBURG
83 Main St, Morrisburg, ON, K0C 1X0
(613) 543-3731
Emp Here 7   *Sales* 27,985,980
SIC 6411 Insurance agents, brokers, and ser-
vice
  Roy Brister
  William Barcley
  Robert Steele
  Douglas Bush

D-U-N-S 20-577-8103   (SL)
ECKEL INDUSTRIES OF CANADA LIMITED
35 Allison Ave, Morrisburg, ON, K0C 1X0
(613) 543-2967
Emp Here 75   *Sales* 7,581,020
SIC 3625 Relays and industrial controls
  Thomas Walton
  Stephen Mccann
  Brian Harris
  Alan Eckel
  Alex Eckel

D-U-N-S 25-374-0203   (SL)
EVONIK OIL ADDITIVES CANADA INC
(*Suby of* RAG-STIFTUNG)
12695 County Road 28, Morrisburg, ON, K0C
1X0
(613) 543-2983
Emp Here 32   *Sales* 23,371,040
SIC 5169 Chemicals and allied products, nec
  Owen Caves

D-U-N-S 20-874-8181   (SL)
PROULX, MICHEL STORE INC
CANADIAN TIRE
12329 County Rd 2, Morrisburg, ON, K0C 1X0
(613) 543-2845
Emp Here 40   *Sales* 19,923,120
SIC 5531 Auto and home supply stores
  Michel Proulx

D-U-N-S 24-425-8757   (SL)
SYBRON CANADA LP
BEAVERS DENTAL
55 Laurier Dr, Morrisburg, ON, K0C 1X0
(613) 543-3791
Emp Here 280   *Sales* 76,823,600
SIC 3843 Dental equipment and supplies
  Steve Jones
  Alli Olegario

D-U-N-S 20-700-6297   (SL)
UPPER CANADA MOTOR SALES LIMITED
12375 County Road 28, Morrisburg, ON, K0C
1X0
(613) 543-2925
Emp Here 30   *Sales* 14,942,340
SIC 5511 New and used car dealers
  Paul Goupil
  Rita Goupil

Morriston, ON N0B

D-U-N-S 25-504-4208   (SL)
LLEWELLYN SECURITY INCORPORATED
107 Queen St, Morriston, ON, N0B 2C0

Emp Here 70   *Sales* 27,697,460
SIC 7381 Detective and armored car services

D-U-N-S 24-976-6023   (HQ)
**NORTH AMERICA CONSTRUCTION (1993)
LTD**
21 Queen St, Morriston, ON, N0B 2C0
(519) 821-8000
Emp Here 100   *Sales* 196,869,000
SIC 1629 Heavy construction, nec
  Denis Gagnon
  Gordon Lindsay
  Scott Mcpherson
  Jeff Chipchase
  Louis Landry
  Jim Prytula

Mount Albert, ON L0G

D-U-N-S 24-597-1986   (SL)
**EPERNAY TASTING & PROMOTIONAL
COMPANY LTD, THE**
4 Cleverdon Blvd, Mount Albert, ON, L0G 1M0
(905) 473-5905
Emp Here 49   *Sales* 10,176,026
SIC 8743 Public relations services
  Pauline Waite

Mount Brydges, ON N0L

D-U-N-S 20-373-1182   (SL)
HILLEN NURSERY LTD
23078 Adelaide Rd, Mount Brydges, ON, N0L
1W0
(519) 264-9057
Emp Here 30   *Sales* 10,274,010
SIC 0181 Ornamental nursery products
  Mark Endicott

D-U-N-S 25-213-4366   (SL)
MT. BRYDGES FORD SALES LTD
8791 Glendon Dr, Mount Brydges, ON, N0L
1W0
(519) 264-1912
Emp Here 25   *Sales* 12,451,950
SIC 5511 New and used car dealers
  Ron Kok

Mount Elgin, ON N0J

D-U-N-S 25-220-1454   (HQ)
GREEN LEA AG CENTER INC
324055 Mount Elgin Rd, Mount Elgin, ON, N0J
1N0
(519) 485-6861
Sales 13,976,550
SIC 5083 Farm and garden machinery
  J L Scott Mclean
  Alan Mclean

Mount Forest, ON N0G

D-U-N-S 25-194-4187   (SL)
2032244 ONTARIO LIMITED
FOODLAND
121 Main St S, Mount Forest, ON, N0G 2L0

(519) 323-1390
Emp Here 60   *Sales* 17,608,620
SIC 5411 Grocery stores
  Michael Armstrong
  Carol Armstrong

D-U-N-S 25-634-6479   (BR)
**COMMUNITY LIVING GUELPH WELLING-
TON**
(*Suby of* COMMUNITY LIVING GUELPH
WELLINGTON)
135 Fergus St S, Mount Forest, ON, N0G 2L2
(519) 323-4050
Emp Here 75
SIC 8322 Individual and family services
  Janette Andersen

D-U-N-S 25-221-2147   (BR)
DANA CANADA CORPORATION
POWER TECHNOLOGIES GROUP
(*Suby of* DANA INCORPORATED)
205 Industrial Dr, Mount Forest, ON, N0G 2L1
(519) 323-9494
Emp Here 210
SIC 3443 Fabricated plate work (boiler shop)
  Acey Kaspar

D-U-N-S 20-876-9075   (SL)
**NORTH WELLINGTON HEALTH CARE
CORPORATION**
LOUISE MARSHALL HOSPITAL
630 Dublin St, Mount Forest, ON, N0G 2L3
(519) 323-2210
Emp Here 100   *Sales* 12,287,700
SIC 8062 General medical and surgical hospi-
tals
  David Craig
  Pierre Noel
  Bruce England

D-U-N-S 25-076-4164   (SL)
SAUGEEN VALLEY NURSING CENTER LTD
465 Dublin St, Mount Forest, ON, N0G 2L3
(519) 323-2140
Emp Here 85   *Sales* 5,842,305
SIC 8051 Skilled nursing care facilities
  Peter Schlegel
  Faye Moore

D-U-N-S 25-370-8556   (BR)
SOLOWAVE DESIGN INC
(*Suby of* SOLOWAVE INVESTMENTS LIM-
ITED)
375 Sligo Rd W Ss 1 Suite 1, Mount Forest,
ON, N0G 2L0
(519) 323-3833
Emp Here 96
SIC 3949 Sporting and athletic goods, nec
  Richard Boyer

D-U-N-S 24-393-2113   (SL)
TELFER, S & T MERCHANDISING LTD
CANADIAN TIRE
525 Queen St W, Mount Forest, ON, N0G 2L1
(519) 323-1080
Emp Here 40   *Sales* 14,568,600
SIC 5014 Tires and tubes
  Shaun Telfer

D-U-N-S 24-577-6026   (HQ)
VIKING-CIVES LTD
(*Suby of* CIVES CORPORATION)
42626 Grey Rd 109, Mount Forest, ON, N0G
2L0
(519) 323-4433
Sales 26,861,160
SIC 3711 Motor vehicles and car bodies
  Ray Phillips
  Bill Reeves
  John S Donovan
  John M Connor

D-U-N-S 20-191-5949   (SL)
VINTEX INC
1 Mount Forest Dr Ss 2, Mount Forest, ON,
N0G 2L2
(519) 323-0100
Emp Here 105   *Sales* 14,350,770

SIC 2399 Fabricated textile products, nec
Steven Wood
James Merrill
Donald Wallbank
Paul Helsby

Mount Hope, ON L0R

D-U-N-S 20-123-2894   (SL)
1520940 ONTARIO LTD
GREEN PIECE WIRE ART
9196 Dickenson Rd, Mount Hope, ON, L0R 1W0
(905) 679-6066
Emp Here 10   *Sales* 10,003,390
SIC 5051 Metals service centers and offices
Peter Braun

D-U-N-S 20-052-7786   (HQ)
BRAUN NURSERY LIMITED
BRAUN HORTICULTURE
2004 Glancaster Rd, Mount Hope, ON, L0R 1W0
(905) 648-1911
Sales 13,115,450
SIC 0181 Ornamental nursery products
Peter Braun
Mark Sellars
David Wylie
Kenneth Young

D-U-N-S 20-821-8321   (SL)
CANADIAN WARPLANE HERITAGE INC
CANADIAN WARPLANE HERITAGE MU-SEUM
9280 Airport Rd, Mount Hope, ON, L0R 1W0
(905) 679-4183
Emp Here 28   *Sales* 11,127,592
SIC 8699 Membership organizations, nec
Pamela Rickards

D-U-N-S 25-279-2879   (BR)
CARGOJET INC
CARGOJET
(*Suby of* CARGOJET INC)
9300 Airport Rd Suite 320, Mount Hope, ON, L0R 1W0
(905) 679-9127
Emp Here 200
SIC 4512 Air transportation, scheduled

D-U-N-S 24-756-8835   (SL)
GLANFORD AVIATION SERVICES LTD
9300 Airport Rd Suite 200, Mount Hope, ON, L0R 1W0
(905) 679-4127
Emp Here 31   *Sales* 38,973,231
SIC 5172 Petroleum products, nec
Herbert E Hallatt
Marion Hallatt

D-U-N-S 25-687-0676   (SL)
HAMILTON INTERNATIONAL AIRPORT LIMITED
JOHN MUNRO AIRPORT
(*Suby of* TRADEPORT INTERNATIONAL CORPORATION)
9300 Airport Rd Suite 2206, Mount Hope, ON, L0R 1W0
(905) 679-1999
Emp Here 53   *Sales* 14,149,834
SIC 4581 Airports, flying fields, and services
Frank Scremin
Ron Foxcroft
George Casey
Stewart Steeves

D-U-N-S 20-505-7938   (SL)
HAMILTON STREET RAILWAY COMPANY, THE
HSR
(*Suby of* CITY OF HAMILTON, THE)
2200 Upper James St, Mount Hope, ON, L0R 1W0

---

(905) 528-4200
Emp Here 600   *Sales* 33,728,400
SIC 4111 Local and suburban transit
Don Hull
Rae Blanchard

D-U-N-S 25-978-8941   (HQ)
JETPORT INC
9300 Airport Rd Suite 520, Mount Hope, ON, L0R 1W0
(905) 679-2400
Sales 10,392,128
SIC 4512 Air transportation, scheduled
Ronald Joyce

D-U-N-S 20-136-9803   (BR)
KELOWNA FLIGHTCRAFT AIR CHARTER LTD
(*Suby of* RAINMAKER INDUSTRIES INC)
9300 Airport Rd, Mount Hope, ON, L0R 1W0

Emp Here 135
SIC 4581 Airports, flying fields, and services

D-U-N-S 24-335-6628   (BR)
KELOWNA FLIGHTCRAFT LTD
(*Suby of* KELOWNA FLIGHTCRAFT LTD)
9500 Airport Rd, Mount Hope, ON, L0R 1W0
(905) 679-3313
Emp Here 145
SIC 4581 Airports, flying fields, and services
Peter Dacosta

D-U-N-S 25-662-8236   (SL)
PETRO-CANADA
4663 6 Hwy S, Mount Hope, ON, L0R 1W0
(905) 679-1445
Emp Here 6   *Sales* 18,635,142
SIC 4925 Gas production and/or distribution
Vasi Mega

D-U-N-S 24-117-4239   (BR)
PUROLATOR INC
(*Suby of* GOVERNMENT OF CANADA)
9300 Airport Rd, Mount Hope, ON, L0R 1W0
(905) 679-5722
Emp Here 149
SIC 7389 Business services, nec
Dereck Palmer

Muncey, ON N0L

D-U-N-S 24-562-3876   (SL)
MNAASGED CHILD AND FAMILY SERVICES
311 Jubilee Dr, Muncey, ON, N0L 1Y0
(519) 289-1117
Emp Here 30   *Sales* 11,922,420
SIC 8699 Membership organizations, nec
Carrie Tabobondung

Nairn Centre, ON P0M

D-U-N-S 24-138-5228   (BR)
EACOM TIMBER CORPORATION
(*Suby of* KELSO & COMPANY, L.P.)
100 Old Nairn Rd, Nairn Centre, ON, P0M 2L0
(705) 869-4020
Emp Here 90
SIC 2421 Sawmills and planing mills, general
Donald Droun

D-U-N-S 24-830-0360   (HQ)
T BELL TRANSPORT INC
231 Hwy 17, Nairn Centre, ON, P0M 2L0
(705) 869-5959
Sales 12,342,360
SIC 4213 Trucking, except local
Ted Bell
Colleen Beilhartz

Nakina, ON P0T

D-U-N-S 20-836-8290   (SL)
NAKINA OUTPOST CAMPS & AIR SERVICE LTD
NAKINA AIR SERVICE
Gd, Nakina, ON, P0T 2H0
(807) 329-5341
Emp Here 32   *Sales* 10,392,128
SIC 4512 Air transportation, scheduled
Don Bourdignon
Millie Bourdignon

Nanticoke, ON N0A

D-U-N-S 25-534-6751   (BR)
STELCO INC
LAKE ERIE
(*Suby of* BEDROCK INDUSTRIES)
2330 Haldimand Rd 3, Nanticoke, ON, N0A 1L0
(519) 587-4541
Emp Here 1,200
SIC 3312 Blast furnaces and steel mills
Brian Vaughn

Napanee, ON K7R

D-U-N-S 24-396-3266   (SL)
1652472 ONTARIO INC
NORTH KEY CONSTRUCTION
24 Advance Ave, Napanee, ON, K7R 3Y6
(613) 354-7653
Emp Here 40   *Sales* 11,340,960
SIC 1611 Highway and street construction
Andrew Isbester

D-U-N-S 20-281-2269   (SL)
ABCANN MEDICINALS INC
126 Vanluven Rd, Napanee, ON, K7R 3L2
(613) 354-6384
Emp Here 22   *Sales* 24,317,590
SIC 5122 Drugs, proprietaries, and sundries
Linda Smith
Michael Bumby

D-U-N-S 24-057-2719   (SL)
AMBURG LIMITED
GIANT TIGER STORE
13 Industrial Blvd, Napanee, ON, K7R 1M7
(613) 354-4371
Emp Here 85   *Sales* 17,454,155
SIC 5399 Miscellaneous general merchandise
Michael Lewis
Gregory Farrell

D-U-N-S 24-847-8737   (SL)
BEEBE, D LUMBER CO LTD
NAPANEE HOME HARDWARE BUILDING CENTRE
199 Jim Kimmett Blvd, Napanee, ON, K7R 3L1
(613) 354-3315
Emp Here 55   *Sales* 14,720,860
SIC 5251 Hardware stores
Dale Beebe

D-U-N-S 24-420-6561   (SL)
CONTINENTAL CONVEYOR (ONTARIO) LIMITED
100 Richmond Blvd, Napanee, ON, K7R 4A4
(613) 354-3318
Emp Here 52   *Sales* 24,701,352
SIC 5084 Industrial machinery and equipment
David Lynn
Brian Lynn
Philip Lynn
Trevor Lynn
Rene Beaudoin

D-U-N-S 25-350-3288   (BR)
COUNTY OF LENNOX & ADDINGTON
JOHN M PARROTT CENTRE
(*Suby of* COUNTY OF LENNOX & ADDING-TON)
309 Bridge St W Suite 113, Napanee, ON, K7R 2G4

Emp Here 200
SIC 8059 Nursing and personal care, nec
Brian Smith

D-U-N-S 25-185-0848   (HQ)
FLYING J CANADA INC
FLYING J TRAVEL PLAZA
(*Suby of* FJ MANAGEMENT INC.)
628 County Rd 41, Napanee, ON, K7R 3L1
(613) 354-7044
Emp Here 30   *Sales* 228,014,540
SIC 5541 Gasoline service stations
Mark Ford

D-U-N-S 20-287-8372   (BR)
G.T. MACHINING & FABRICATING LTD
(*Suby of* G.T. MACHINING & FABRICATING LTD)
7 Kellwood Cres, Napanee, ON, K7R 4A1
(613) 354-6621
Emp Here 92
SIC 3443 Fabricated plate work (boiler shop)
Gord Carter

D-U-N-S 24-077-5916   (HQ)
G.T. MACHINING & FABRICATING LTD
101 Richmond Blvd, Napanee, ON, K7R 3Z8
(613) 354-6621
Emp Here 40   *Sales* 20,424,092
SIC 3599 Industrial machinery, nec
Gordon Carter
Ted Melburn
Douglas Carter

D-U-N-S 24-889-5542   (BR)
GOODYEAR CANADA INC
GOODYEAR NAPANEE TIRE MANUFAC-TURING FACILITY
(*Suby of* THE GOODYEAR TIRE & RUBBER COMPANY)
388 Goodyear Rd, Napanee, ON, K7R 3L2
(613) 354-7411
Emp Here 500
SIC 3011 Tires and inner tubes
Lester Brooks

D-U-N-S 24-796-9269   (SL)
GREATER NAPANEE FIRE DEPARTMENT
66 Advance Ave, Napanee, ON, K7R 3Y6
(613) 354-3415
Emp Here 49   *Sales* 22,011,731
SIC 7389 Business services, nec
Terry Gervais

D-U-N-S 25-078-4055   (SL)
LENNOX AND ADDINGTON COUNTY GENERAL HOSPITAL ASSOCIATION
L & A HOSPITAL
8 Richmond Park Dr, Napanee, ON, K7R 2Z4
(613) 354-3301
Emp Here 175   *Sales* 21,711,878
SIC 8062 General medical and surgical hospitals
Wayne Coveyduck
Allan Macgregor
Deb Lowry

D-U-N-S 25-354-0645   (BR)
LIMESTONE DISTRICT SCHOOL BOARD
NAPANEE DISTRICT SECONDARY SCHOOL
245 Belleville Rd, Napanee, ON, K7R 3M7
(613) 354-3381
Emp Here 240
SIC 8211 Elementary and secondary schools
Erin Pincivero

D-U-N-S 24-009-6941   (SL)
MARTIN, C. BUS SERVICE LIMITED

MARTIN'S BUS SERVICE
106 Advance Ave, Napanee, ON, K7R 3Y6
(613) 354-7545
Emp Here 80   *Sales* 4,389,760
SIC 4151 School buses
  Sean Payne

    D-U-N-S 25-300-0566   (BR)
METRO ONTARIO INC
METRO
(*Suby of* METRO INC)
35 Alkenbrack St, Napanee, ON, K7R 4C4
(613) 354-2882
Emp Here 170
SIC 5411 Grocery stores
  Paul Gilbert

    D-U-N-S 20-968-6757   (BR)
STRATHCONA PAPER LP
(*Suby of* STRATHCONA PAPER LP)
77 County Rd 16, Napanee, ON, K7R 3L2
(613) 378-6672
Emp Here 172
SIC 2631 Paperboard mills
  Mark Sklar

    D-U-N-S 24-309-5325   (HQ)
STRATHCONA PAPER LP
77 County Rd 16, Napanee, ON, K7R 3L2
(613) 378-6676
Sales 35,058,240
SIC 2631 Paperboard mills
  Mark Sklar

    D-U-N-S 25-310-9110   (BR)
TAYLYX LTD
MCDONALD'S RESTAURANT
475 Centre St N, Napanee, ON, K7R 3S4
(613) 354-9707
Emp Here 85
SIC 5812 Eating places
  Dan Doyle

    D-U-N-S 24-688-0389   (SL)
VI-LUX BUILDING PRODUCTS INC
105 Richmond Blvd, Napanee, ON, K7R 3Z8
(613) 354-4830
Emp Here 30   *Sales* 21,910,350
SIC 5162 Plastics materials and basic shapes
  Arkadi Bykhovsky
  Eva Bykhovsky

    D-U-N-S 24-991-9978   (SL)
ZYWOT, T. HOLDINGS LIMITED
CANADIAN TIRE
476 Centre St N, Napanee, ON, K7R 1P8
(613) 354-2222
Emp Here 25   *Sales* 12,451,950
SIC 5531 Auto and home supply stores
  Thomas Zywot

Navan, ON K4B

    D-U-N-S 20-893-5312   (SL)
BEDARD, JACQUES EXCAVATION LIMITED
3006 Tenth Line Rd, Navan, ON, K4B 1H8
(613) 824-3208
Emp Here 50   *Sales* 12,309,300
SIC 1794 Excavation work
  Jacques Bedard
  Laurier Cadieux
  Celine Bedard

    D-U-N-S 25-772-1209   (BR)
CLUBLINK CORPORATION ULC
GREYHAWK GOLF CLUB
(*Suby of* TWC ENTERPRISES LIMITED)
4999 Boundary Rd, Navan, ON, K4B 1P5
(613) 822-1454
Emp Here 80
SIC 7992 Public golf courses
  Dany Lacombe

    D-U-N-S 25-361-5975   (SL)

LAVERGNE WESTERN BEEF INC
3971 Navan Rd, Navan, ON, K4B 1H9
(613) 824-8175
Emp Here 35   *Sales* 29,245,195
SIC 5147 Meats and meat products
  Mariel Ericson

    D-U-N-S 20-203-1030   (SL)
LEMIRE, ERIC ENTERPRISES INC
4815b Mcneely Rd, Navan, ON, K4B 0J3
(613) 835-4040
Emp Here 55   *Sales* 13,540,230
SIC 1791 Structural steel erection
  Eric Lemire

Nepean, ON K2B

    D-U-N-S 25-991-6682   (SL)
910259 ONTARIO INC
SPORTS EXPERTS
100 Bayshore Dr Unit 301, Nepean, ON, K2B 8C1
(613) 829-7680
Emp Here 70   *Sales* 17,102,960
SIC 5941 Sporting goods and bicycle shops
  Michael Swartzack
  Robert Kipp
  Edward Horton

    D-U-N-S 25-983-6021   (SL)
WAHA ENTERPRISES INC
MOXIE'S CLASSIC GRILL
100 Bayshore Dr, Nepean, ON, K2B 8C1
(613) 721-2918
Emp Here 80   *Sales* 3,641,520
SIC 5812 Eating places
  John Carey

    D-U-N-S 24-312-4356   (BR)
WINNERS MERCHANTS INTERNATIONAL L.P.
WINNERS
(*Suby of* THE TJX COMPANIES INC)
100 Bayshore Dr, Nepean, ON, K2B 8C1
(613) 721-6451
Emp Here 80
SIC 5651 Family clothing stores
  Jeff Clemenhagen

Nepean, ON K2C

    D-U-N-S 20-298-8648   (SL)
1702660 ONTARIO INC
LUCAS CONTRACTING
2013 Prince Of Wales Dr, Nepean, ON, K2C 3J7
(613) 913-5539
Emp Here 60   *Sales* 13,069,740
SIC 1761 Roofing, siding, and sheetMetal work
  Lucas O'connor

    D-U-N-S 20-129-4170   (SL)
MAY, JACK CHEVROLET BUICK GMC LIMITED
3788 Prince Of Wales Dr, Nepean, ON, K2C 3H1
(613) 692-3553
Emp Here 48   *Sales* 23,907,744
SIC 5511 New and used car dealers
  John May Jr
  Richmond Wilson

    D-U-N-S 20-300-7166   (BR)
STANTEC ARCHITECTURE LTD
(*Suby of* STANTEC INC)
1331 Clyde Ave Suite 400, Nepean, ON, K2C 3G4
(613) 722-4420
Emp Here 275
SIC 8712 Architectural services

John Krug

Nepean, ON K2E

    D-U-N-S 24-924-4146   (BR)
1032451 B.C. LTD
OTTAWA SUN, THE
(*Suby of* QUEBECOR MEDIA INC)
6 Antares Dr Suite 3, Nepean, ON, K2E 8A9

Emp Here 290
SIC 2711 Newspapers
  Shen Boylan

    D-U-N-S 25-144-0699   (SL)
1048536 ONTARIO LTD
UNICLEAN BUILDING MAINTENANCE
148 Colonnade Rd Suite 13, Nepean, ON, K2E 7R4
(613) 727-0413
Emp Here 160   *Sales* 5,114,880
SIC 7349 Building maintenance services, nec
  Dickson Behnke
  Yvon Henri

    D-U-N-S 20-013-1584   (SL)
1120919 ONTARIO LTD
PHOENIX HOMES
(*Suby of* 871442 ONTARIO INC)
18 Bentley Ave Suite A, Nepean, ON, K2E 6T8
(613) 723-9227
Emp Here 60   *Sales* 16,256,520
SIC 1521 Single-family housing construction
  Cuckoo Kochar

    D-U-N-S 25-078-5631   (HQ)
152610 CANADA INC
LAURIN & COMPANY
43 Auriga Dr, Nepean, ON, K2E 7Y8
(800) 565-2874
Emp Here 19   *Sales* 11,768,275
SIC 1542 Nonresidential construction, nec
  Dennis Laurin
  Jim Dark

    D-U-N-S 24-377-4317   (SL)
1770918 ONTARIO INC
COHEN & COHEN
92 Bentley Ave, Nepean, ON, K2E 6T9
(613) 225-9111
Emp Here 60   *Sales* 14,771,160
SIC 1795 Wrecking and demolition work
  Gary Colautti

    D-U-N-S 24-204-8945   (HQ)
4577 NUNAVUT INC
BAFFIN BUILDING SYSTEMS
69 Jamie Ave, Nepean, ON, K2E 7Y6

Emp Here 5   *Sales* 13,415,220
SIC 5039 Construction materials, nec
  Chris Groves
  Thomas Mattrass
  Wynn Jones
  Eleanor O'neal
  Penny O'neal
  Murray Wilson

    D-U-N-S 20-916-0709   (SL)
6074961 CANADA INC
SEI
20 Gurdwara Rd Unit 16, Nepean, ON, K2E 8B3
(613) 225-5500
Emp Here 75   *Sales* 18,463,950
SIC 1799 Special trade contractors, nec
  Peter Chatelaine
  Robert Brunet

    D-U-N-S 25-769-6716   (SL)
709226 ONTARIO LIMITED
DILAWRI JEEP DODGE CHRYSLER
370 West Hunt Club Rd, Nepean, ON, K2E 1A5

(613) 523-9951
Emp Here 65   *Sales* 40,903,200
SIC 5511 New and used car dealers
  Shiv Dilawri

    D-U-N-S 20-013-0545   (HQ)
871442 ONTARIO INC
18 Bentley Ave Suite A, Nepean, ON, K2E 6T8
(613) 723-9227
Sales 16,256,520
SIC 1521 Single-family housing construction
  Cuckoo Kochar

    D-U-N-S 25-220-5778   (SL)
974475 ONTARIO LIMITED
MCDANIEL'S Y.I.G.
200 Grant Carman Dr, Nepean, ON, K2E 7Z8
(613) 727-1672
Emp Here 140   *Sales* 41,086,780
SIC 5411 Grocery stores
  Gerald Mcdaniel
  Lisa Mcdaniel

    D-U-N-S 24-822-2648   (HQ)
ALDUS CAPITAL CORP
FRANCIS CANADA PRODUCTS
28 Concourse Gate Suite 105, Nepean, ON, K2E 7T7
(613) 723-4567
Emp Here 10   *Sales* 125,720,100
SIC 5172 Petroleum products, nec
  William John Francis
  William Brent Francis

    D-U-N-S 24-105-0921   (SL)
AMS IMAGING INC
77 Auriga Dr Unit 17, Nepean, ON, K2E 7Z7
(613) 723-1668
Emp Here 35   *Sales* 15,651,090
SIC 5044 Office equipment
  Pierre Vachon

    D-U-N-S 25-221-9282   (SL)
ASHCROFT HOMES - CENTRAL PARK INC
18 Antares Dr Unit 102, Nepean, ON, K2E 1A9
(613) 226-7266
Emp Here 100   *Sales* 27,094,200
SIC 1521 Single-family housing construction
  David Choo

    D-U-N-S 20-954-5966   (HQ)
ATS SERVICES LTD
35 Auriga Dr Suite 213, Nepean, ON, K2E 8B7
(613) 288-9139
Emp Here 10   *Sales* 34,270,800
SIC 4899 Communication services, nec
  Cameron Mason

    D-U-N-S 20-105-2854   (BR)
CANADIAN BANK NOTE COMPANY, LIMITED
(*Suby of* CANADIAN BANK NOTE COMPANY, LIMITED)
18 Auriga Dr, Nepean, ON, K2E 7T9
(613) 722-3421
Emp Here 100
SIC 2796 Platemaking services

    D-U-N-S 24-199-7654   (SL)
CANADIAN CORPS OF COMMISSIONAIRES (OTTAWA DIVISION)
24 Colonnade Rd N, Nepean, ON, K2E 7J6
(613) 228-0715
Emp Here 3,600   *Sales* 94,500,000
SIC 7381 Detective and armored car services
  Robert Dupuis

    D-U-N-S 25-281-4058   (BR)
CANADIAN CORPS OF COMMISSIONAIRES NATIONAL OFFICE, THE
(*Suby of* CANADIAN CORPS OF COMMISSIONAIRES NATIONAL OFFICE, THE)
24 Colonnade Rd N, Nepean, ON, K2E 7J6

Emp Here 2,002
SIC 7381 Detective and armored car services
  Paul Guindon

D-U-N-S 20-287-8497   (SL)
CAPITAL MORTGAGES
18 Deakin St Suite 106, Nepean, ON, K2E
8B7
(613) 228-3888
Emp Here 49   *Sales* 11,140,001
SIC 6162 Mortgage bankers and loan corre-
spondents
Stefan Krepski
Po Krepski
Richard Morgan

D-U-N-S 20-789-4734   (SL)
CAPITAL OFFICE INTERIORS LIMITED
16 Antares Dr, Nepean, ON, K2E 7Y7
(613) 723-2000
Emp Here 30   *Sales* 15,265,680
SIC 5021 Furniture
Mike Mccarthy, Jr
Neil Chadwick

D-U-N-S 20-136-8164   (SL)
CENTRAL PRECAST INC
25 Bongard Ave, Nepean, ON, K2E 6V2
(613) 225-9510
Emp Here 70   *Sales* 16,340,450
SIC 3272 Concrete products, nec
Rodolfo Mion
Giovanni Mion

D-U-N-S 24-987-7721   (HQ)
COSTCO CANADA HOLDINGS INC
(*Suby of* COSTCO WHOLESALE CORPO-
RATION)
415 West Hunt Club Rd, Nepean, ON, K2E
1C5
(613) 221-2000
Emp Here 200   *Sales* 1,408,555,500
SIC 6712 Bank holding companies
Russell Miller
Louise Wendling
Ross Hunt
Stuart Shamis
David Nickle
Pierre Riel
Craig Jelinek
Joseph Portera
James Sinegal

D-U-N-S 25-287-5349   (HQ)
COSTCO WHOLESALE CANADA LTD
(*Suby of* COSTCO WHOLESALE CORPO-
RATION)
415 West Hunt Club Rd, Nepean, ON, K2E
1C5
(613) 221-2010
Emp Here 190   *Sales* 10,081,850,000
SIC 5099 Durable goods, nec
Ross Hunt
Joseph P Portera
Andree Brien
Joel Benoliel
Richard Olin
Richard Galanti
Hubert De Suduiraut
Stuart Shamis
Louise Wendling

D-U-N-S 24-102-7515   (SL)
DALMACIJA FORMING LTD
11 Gifford St Suite 201, Nepean, ON, K2E 7S3
(613) 727-1371
Emp Here 60   *Sales* 14,848,980
SIC 1771 Concrete work
Ante Bulat

D-U-N-S 20-137-1960   (HQ)
DRUMMOND FUELS (OTTAWA) LTD
DRUMMOND'S GAS
30 Rideau Heights Dr, Nepean, ON, K2E 7A6
(613) 226-4444
Emp Here 12   *Sales* 32,722,560
SIC 5541 Gasoline service stations
Russell Drummond

D-U-N-S 20-442-4204   (SL)
DRUMMOND, GEORGE W. LIMITED

30 Rideau Heights Dr, Nepean, ON, K2E 7A6
(613) 226-4440
Emp Here 50   *Sales* 12,044,200
SIC 1629 Heavy construction, nec
E Marilynne Drummond
P Scott Drummond

D-U-N-S 25-782-5794   (HQ)
E-DJUSTER INC
28 Concourse Gate Unit 203, Nepean, ON,
K2E 7T7
(866) 779-5950
Emp Here 1   *Sales* 133,037,424
SIC 6411 Insurance agents, brokers, and ser-
vice
David Levy
Andrew Williams
David Hunter
Gary Jeffope

D-U-N-S 25-813-0731   (BR)
EXP SERVICES INC
(*Suby of* EXP GLOBAL INC)
154 Colonnade Rd S, Nepean, ON, K2E 7J5
(613) 225-9940
Emp Here 100
SIC 8711 Engineering services
Dan Mcnicoll

D-U-N-S 24-719-2180   (HQ)
FISHER SCIENTIFIC COMPANY
(*Suby of* THERMO FISHER SCIENTIFIC
INC.)
112 Colonnade Rd S, Nepean, ON, K2E 7L6
(613) 226-8874
Emp Here 180   *Sales* 208,787,280
SIC 5049 Professional equipment, nec
John Tourlas
Mike Aronson
Sue Hannah
Heidi Kornherr
Bob Thompson

D-U-N-S 20-137-4303   (HQ)
FRANCIS FUELS LTD
FRANCIS FUELS
28 Concourse Gate Suite 105, Nepean, ON,
K2E 7T7
(613) 723-4567
Emp Here 3   *Sales* 21,105,225
SIC 5983 Fuel oil dealers
William J Francis
William Brent Francis
Donald R Jacobs

D-U-N-S 24-532-1869   (SL)
HCN MOTORS LTD
HUNT CLUB NISSAN
(*Suby of* AUTOCANADA INC)
275 West Hunt Club Rd, Nepean, ON, K2E
1A6
(613) 521-6262
Emp Here 80   *Sales* 50,342,400
SIC 5511 New and used car dealers
Hussein Habbel

D-U-N-S 20-429-1951   (SL)
ICG PROPANE LTD.
71 Bongard Ave, Nepean, ON, K2E 6V2
(613) 723-5823
Emp Here 5   *Sales* 15,709,144
SIC 4924 Natural gas distribution

D-U-N-S 25-773-6405   (HQ)
**INDEPENDANT   PLANNING   GROUP
INC/GROUPE INDEPENDANT DE PLAN-
IFICATION INC**
IPG INSURANCE
35 Antares Dr, Nepean, ON, K2E 8B1
(613) 738-3388
Emp Here 18   *Sales* 12,220,614
SIC 6282 Investment advice
Vince Valenti

D-U-N-S 24-383-8679   (HQ)
INTELCAN TECHNOSYSTEMS INC
(*Suby of* WHITTVEST HOLDINGS LIMITED)
69 Auriga Dr, Nepean, ON, K2E 7Z2

(613) 228-1150
Emp Here 40   *Sales* 10,228,005
SIC 3812 Search and navigation equipment
Michael Lang
Zvi Glanz
Paulina Yee
Philip Whittall
Ron Weissberger

D-U-N-S 24-326-0044   (BR)
**INTERMAP TECHNOLOGIES CORPORA-
TION**
(*Suby of* INTERMAP TECHNOLOGIES COR-
PORATION)
2 Gurdwara Rd Suite 200, Nepean, ON, K2E
1A2
Emp Here 100
SIC 7389 Business services, nec
Mark Foerster

D-U-N-S 20-955-1436   (HQ)
IRONHORSE CORPORATION
IRONHORSE GROUP, THE
9 Capella Crt Unit 200, Nepean, ON, K2E 8A7
(613) 228-2813
Emp Here 600   *Sales* 535,126,400
SIC 7389 Business services, nec
Robin St Martin

D-U-N-S 25-978-9402   (HQ)
J2 GLOBAL CANADA, INC
MYFAX
(*Suby of* J2 GLOBAL, INC.)
2 Gurdwara Rd, Nepean, ON, K2E 1A2
(613) 733-0000
Sales 83,636,000
SIC 4899 Communication services, nec
Jeffrey Adelman
Kathleen Griggs
Richard Cheung

D-U-N-S 20-513-3544   (SL)
**LEISURE MART & RV CANADA CORPORA-
TION**
POWERSPORTS RV CANADA
2098 Prince Of Wales Dr, Nepean, ON, K2E
7A5
(613) 226-8228
Emp Here 50   *Sales* 24,903,900
SIC 5561 Recreational vehicle dealers
Lynn Norton
Patrick (Pat) Butler

D-U-N-S 25-836-0429   (BR)
LOBLAWS SUPERMARKETS LIMITED
ZIGGYS
(*Suby of* LOBLAW COMPANIES LIMITED)
1460 Merivale Rd, Nepean, ON, K2E 5P2
(613) 226-6001
Emp Here 1,500
SIC 5411 Grocery stores
Dave Harnish

D-U-N-S 20-120-7631   (SL)
LUMENERA CORPORATION
(*Suby of* TELEDYNE TECHNOLOGIES INC)
7 Capella Crt, Nepean, ON, K2E 8A7
(613) 736-4077
Emp Here 65   *Sales* 14,773,785
SIC 3861 Photographic equipment and sup-
plies
Huw Leahy
Stephen Shaw
Dany Longval
Brooks Riendeau
Doug Sanderson
Rob Sample
Christine Longpre
Nick Bulitka

D-U-N-S 24-361-5643   (SL)
MAGOR COMMUNICATIONS CORP
(*Suby of* WESLEY CLOVER CORPORA-
TION)
400-1 Antares Dr, Nepean, ON, K2E 8C4
(613) 686-1731
Emp Here 30   *Sales* 13,415,220

SIC 5065 Electronic parts and equipment, nec
Michael Pascoe
Terry Matthews
Sherwin Sim
Dan Rusheleau
Rick Miskiman
Ken Davison
Paul Chiarelli
Brian Baker

D-U-N-S 24-826-2821   (SL)
MARCAN PHARMACEUTICALS INC
(*Suby of* EMCURE PHARMACEUTICALS
LIMITED)
2 Gurdwara Rd Suite 112, Nepean, ON, K2E
1A2
(613) 228-2600
Emp Here 32   *Sales* 43,855,598
SIC 5122 Drugs, proprietaries, and sundries
Atul Aggarwal

D-U-N-S 25-963-9198   (BR)
MDA SYSTEMS LTD
(*Suby of* MAXAR TECHNOLOGIES INC.)
57 Auriga Dr Unit 201, Nepean, ON, K2E 8B2
(613) 727-1087
Emp Here 718
SIC 7373 Computer integrated systems de-
sign
Michael Greenley

D-U-N-S 20-873-3001   (SL)
MERCURY FILMWORKS EAST INC
53 Auriga Dr, Nepean, ON, K2E 8C3
(613) 482-1814
Emp Here 240   *Sales* 21,527,040
SIC 7812 Motion picture and video production
Clint Eland
Jerry Popwich

D-U-N-S 20-892-7707   (HQ)
N. HARRIS COMPUTER CORPORATION
HARRIS COMPUTER SYSTEMS
(*Suby of* CONSTELLATION SOFTWARE
INC)
1 Antares Dr Suite 400, Nepean, ON, K2E
8C4
(613) 226-5511
Emp Here 50   *Sales* 26,673,670
SIC 7371 Custom computer programming ser-
vices
Jeff Bender
Todd Richardson

D-U-N-S 24-109-0781   (SL)
NEWCAP RADIO OTTAWA
HOT 89 9 FM CIHT
6 Antares Dr Suite 100, Nepean, ON, K2E 8A9
(613) 723-8990
Emp Here 60   *Sales* 11,087,880
SIC 4832 Radio broadcasting stations
Scott Broderick

D-U-N-S 20-513-9194   (HQ)
**OTTAWA COMMUNITY HOUSING CORPO-
RATION**
39 Auriga Dr, Nepean, ON, K2E 7Y8
(613) 731-7223
Emp Here 120   *Sales* 101,419,200
SIC 6531 Real estate agents and managers
Stephane Giguere
Ven Giannantonio

D-U-N-S 20-802-5697   (BR)
**OTTAWA COMMUNITY HOUSING CORPO-
RATION**
(*Suby of* OTTAWA COMMUNITY HOUSING
CORPORATION)
39 Auriga Dr, Nepean, ON, K2E 7Y8
(613) 731-1182
Emp Here 300
SIC 6531 Real estate agents and managers
David Mccarron

D-U-N-S 20-890-2270   (SL)
OTTAWA GOODTIME CENTRE LIMITED
450 West Hunt Club Rd, Nepean, ON, K2E

1B2
(613) 731-9071
Emp Here 35   *Sales* 17,432,730
SIC 5571 Motorcycle dealers
Bryan Thoms
Zoi Thoms

D-U-N-S 24-566-1657   (SL)
OTTAWA HUMANE SOCIETY
SPA D' OTTAWA
245 West Hunt Club Rd, Nepean, ON, K2E 1A6
(613) 725-3166
Emp Here 102   *Sales* 146,737,302
SIC 8699 Membership organizations, nec
Bruce Roney

D-U-N-S 20-788-9411   (SL)
OTTAWA REGIONAL HOSPITAL LINEN SERVICES INCORPORATED
ORHLS
45 Gurdwara Rd, Nepean, ON, K2E 7X6
(613) 842-3000
Emp Here 130   *Sales* 13,881,660
SIC 7218 Industrial launderers
Rocco Romeo
Pete Rainville

D-U-N-S 20-657-2427   (BR)
PCL CONSTRUCTORS CANADA INC
(*Suby of* PCL EMPLOYEES HOLDINGS LTD)
49 Auriga Dr, Nepean, ON, K2E 8A1
(613) 225-6130
Emp Here 150
SIC 1542 Nonresidential construction, nec
Kevin Skinner

D-U-N-S 20-348-6006   (SL)
PICIS CLINICAL SOLUTIONS, INC
PICIS ENVISION
(*Suby of* CONSTELLATION SOFTWARE INC)
1 Antares Dr Suite 400, Nepean, ON, K2E 8C4
(613) 226-5511
Emp Here 200   *Sales* 28,836,400
SIC 7371 Custom computer programming services
Steve Hammond

D-U-N-S 20-394-1570   (SL)
PINE ENVIRONMENTAL CANADA, INC
159 Colonnade Rd S Units 3 And 4, Nepean, ON, K2E 7J4
(343) 882-1470
Emp Here 60   *Sales* 14,659,680
SIC 5999 Miscellaneous retail stores, nec
Graham Johnstone

D-U-N-S 24-363-1418   (SL)
POWER SPORTS CANADA INC
1 Laser St, Nepean, ON, K2E 7V1
(613) 224-7899
Emp Here 35   *Sales* 17,432,730
SIC 5571 Motorcycle dealers
Lynn Norton

D-U-N-S 25-885-0940   (BR)
PROMARK-TELECON INC
(*Suby of* CAPITAL REGIONAL ET COOPERATIF DESJARDINS)
203 Colonnade Rd S Unit 10, Nepean, ON, K2E 7K3
(613) 723-9888
Emp Here 150
SIC 1623 Water, sewer, and utility lines
Michel Legros

D-U-N-S 24-936-4696   (SL)
RANDEBAR ENTERPRISES INC
WALMAR VENTILATION PRODUCTS
24 Gurdwara Rd, Nepean, ON, K2E 8B5
(613) 225-9774
Emp Here 28   *Sales* 12,520,872
SIC 5075 Warm air heating and air conditioning
Gil Cavill
Randy Cavill

Debbie Turcotte
Thomas Mercier
Mary Cavill

D-U-N-S 20-003-8763   (BR)
ROSS VIDEO LIMITED
(*Suby of* ROSS VIDEO LIMITED)
64 Auriga Dr Suite 1, Nepean, ON, K2E 1B8
(613) 228-0688
Emp Here 200
SIC 3663 Radio and t.v. communications equipment
David Ross

D-U-N-S 25-397-4539   (SL)
SAFENET CANADA INC
RAINBOW CHRYSALIS
(*Suby of* THALES)
20 Colonnade Rd Suite 200, Nepean, ON, K2E 7M6
(613) 723-5077
Emp Here 60   *Sales* 11,426,520
SIC 3699 Electrical equipment and supplies, nec
David Longbottom
Peggy Duperron
Thomas A Seche

D-U-N-S 25-769-4885   (BR)
SAINT ELIZABETH HEALTH CARE
(*Suby of* SAINT ELIZABETH HEALTH CARE)
30 Colonnade Rd N Suite 225, Nepean, ON, K2E 7J6
(613) 738-9661
Emp Here 100
SIC 8059 Nursing and personal care, nec
Jane Williams

D-U-N-S 25-076-3497   (SL)
SCI SITECAST INTERNATIONAL INC
16 Concourse Gate Suite 200, Nepean, ON, K2E 7S8
(613) 225-8118
Emp Here 44   *Sales* 20,712,164
SIC 1542 Nonresidential construction, nec
Steve Kaminski
Shawn Hickey

D-U-N-S 25-773-7262   (HQ)
WESTBORO FLOORING & DECOR INC
195 Colonnade Rd S, Nepean, ON, K2E 7K3
(613) 226-3830
Sales 11,781,660
SIC 1752 Floor laying and floor work, nec
Steven Kimmel
Adina Libin

D-U-N-S 20-139-4491   (SL)
WHYTE, J. G. & SON LIMITED
15 Capella Crt Suite 124, Nepean, ON, K2E 7X1

Emp Here 25   *Sales* 13,013,550
SIC 5092 Toys and hobby goods and supplies
Ian Whyte
Kenneth Whyte

Nepean, ON K2G

D-U-N-S 25-130-3574   (SL)
1350950 ONTARIO LTD
NICASTRO'S BROS FOOD
1558 Merivale Rd, Nepean, ON, K2G 3J9
(613) 225-3470
Emp Here 27   *Sales* 22,560,579
SIC 5149 Groceries and related products, nec
Frank Nicastro
Joe Nicastro
Rocco Nicastro

D-U-N-S 24-889-0253   (SL)
1496201 ONTARIO INC
FREEDOM HARLEY-DAVIDSON OF OTTAWA
1963 Merivale Rd, Nepean, ON, K2G 1G1

(613) 736-8899
Emp Here 30   *Sales* 14,942,340
SIC 5571 Motorcycle dealers
Patrick Butler
John Hubbard

D-U-N-S 24-330-7258   (SL)
1716530 ONTARIO INC
PRINCE OF WALES MANOR HOME
22 Barnstone Dr, Nepean, ON, K2G 2P9
(613) 843-9887
Emp Here 50   *Sales* 11,323,700
SIC 6513 Apartment building operators
Irene Sauve

D-U-N-S 20-747-5179   (HQ)
ALGONQUIN COLLEGE OF APPLIED ARTS AND TECHNOLOGY
ATI
1385 Woodroffe Ave, Nepean, ON, K2G 1V8
(613) 727-4723
Emp Here 1,000   *Sales* 260,558,353
SIC 8222 Junior colleges
Robert Gillett
Duane Mcnair
James Robblee
William Johnson

D-U-N-S 24-104-8149   (HQ)
ARGOS CARPETS LTD
1914 Merivale Rd, Nepean, ON, K2G 1E8
(613) 226-6573
Sales 11,752,155
SIC 5023 Homefurnishings
Spiros Foustanellas
Andre Foustanellas

D-U-N-S 24-199-1566   (BR)
BELL TECHNICAL SOLUTIONS INC
(*Suby of* BCE INC)
1740 Woodroffe Ave, Nepean, ON, K2G 3R8
(613) 746-4465
Emp Here 130
SIC 4899 Communication services, nec

D-U-N-S 25-474-1796   (HQ)
COBURN REALTY LTD
COLDWELL BANKER COBURN REALTY
1415 Woodroffe Ave, Nepean, ON, K2G 1V9
(613) 226-8790
Emp Here 64   *Sales* 29,322,230
SIC 6531 Real estate agents and managers
John Coburn

D-U-N-S 25-529-6816   (BR)
COSTCO WHOLESALE CANADA LTD
(*Suby of* COSTCO WHOLESALE CORPORATION)
1849 Merivale Rd Suite 540, Nepean, ON, K2G 1E3
(613) 727-4786
Emp Here 287
SIC 5141 Groceries, general line
Daniel Parent

D-U-N-S 20-890-8210   (HQ)
FRISBY TIRE CO. (1974) LIMITED
1377 Clyde Ave, Nepean, ON, K2G 3H7
(613) 224-2200
Sales 56,635,200
SIC 5531 Auto and home supply stores
Don Frisby
Verna Hilliard

D-U-N-S 24-708-3959   (HQ)
GENERAL DYNAMICS INFORMATION TECHNOLOGY CANADA, LIMITED
VANGENT CANADA
(*Suby of* GENERAL DYNAMICS CORPORATION)
30 Camelot Dr, Nepean, ON, K2G 5X8
(613) 723-9500
Sales 17,518,935
SIC 7374 Data processing and preparation
Chris Hughes

D-U-N-S 24-268-0916   (HQ)
GRAHAM, TONY MOTORS (1980) LIMITED

AADA CAR LEASING
1855 Merivale Rd, Nepean, ON, K2G 1E3
(613) 225-1212
Sales 181,834,380
SIC 5511 New and used car dealers
Marine Graham
Elizabeth Graham

D-U-N-S 25-843-0867   (SL)
JAPAN OTTAWA TRAVEL INC
139 Craig Henry Dr, Nepean, ON, K2G 3Z8
(613) 820-8800
Emp Here 30   *Sales* 11,560,800
SIC 4725 Tour operators
Sayoko Konnoko

D-U-N-S 25-057-7061   (SL)
KRUPP, MASHA TRANSLATION GROUP LTD, THE
MKTG
1547 Merivale Rd Suite 500, Nepean, ON, K2G 4V3
(613) 820-4566
Emp Here 50   *Sales* 22,174,500
SIC 7389 Business services, nec
Masha Krupp

D-U-N-S 20-138-0771   (SL)
LOUCON METAL LIMITED
39 Grenfell Cres Suite 37, Nepean, ON, K2G 0G3
(613) 226-1102
Emp Here 16   *Sales* 16,005,424
SIC 5051 Metals service centers and offices

D-U-N-S 24-809-5085   (HQ)
NORAMTEC CONSULTANTS INC
(*Suby of* 9508384 CANADA INC)
1400 Clyde Ave Suite 217, Nepean, ON, K2G 3J2
(613) 727-3997
Emp Here 4   *Sales* 106,719,200
SIC 7361 Employment agencies
Glenn Holland

D-U-N-S 20-894-1385   (HQ)
OTTAWA CATHOLIC DISTRICT SCHOOL BOARD
OTTAWA CATHOLIC SCHOOL BOARD
570 West Hunt Club Rd, Nepean, ON, K2G 3R4
(613) 224-2222
Emp Here 300   *Sales* 380,026,500
SIC 8211 Elementary and secondary schools
Elaine Mcmahon
Joanne Macewan
John Curry
Sandra Moore
Brian Coburn
Spencer Warren
Jeremy Wittet
Mark D. Mullan
Regan Preszcator
Therese Maloney-Cousineau

D-U-N-S 25-263-6402   (BR)
OTTAWA-CARLETON DISTRICT SCHOOL BOARD
MERIVALE HIGH SCHOOL
(*Suby of* OTTAWA-CARLETON DISTRICT SCHOOL BOARD)
1755 Merivale Rd, Nepean, ON, K2G 1E2
(613) 224-1807
Emp Here 95
SIC 8211 Elementary and secondary schools
Barb Gage

D-U-N-S 25-090-9413   (HQ)
OXOID INC
OXOID COMPANY
(*Suby of* THERMO FISHER SCIENTIFIC INC.)
1926 Merivale Rd Suite 100, Nepean, ON, K2G 1E8
(613) 226-1318
Sales 24,899,400
SIC 2835 Diagnostic substances
Stephane Perreault

▲ Public Company   ■ Public Company Family Member   **HQ** Headquarters   **BR** Branch   **SL** Single Location

D-U-N-S 20-533-2880   (SL)
PRESTIGE DESIGNS & CONSTRUCTION (OTTAWA) LTD
50 Camelot Dr, Nepean, ON, K2G 5X8
(613) 224-9437
Emp Here 50   *Sales* 14,176,200
SIC 1611 Highway and street construction
Claudio Mazzarello
John Mazzarello

D-U-N-S 25-173-8852   (SL)
R.J. BONNEVILLE ENTERPRISES INC
CANADIAN TIRE
1820 Merivale Rd Door # 258, Nepean, ON, K2G 1E6
(613) 224-9330
Emp Here 140   *Sales* 28,748,020
SIC 5399 Miscellaneous general merchandise
Tom Oglivie

D-U-N-S 20-308-7986   (BR)
RECIPE UNLIMITED CORPORATION
MONTANA'S COOKHOUSE
(*Suby of* RECIPE UNLIMITED CORPORATION)
1711 Merivale Rd, Nepean, ON, K2G 3K2
(613) 288-0517
Emp Here 80
SIC 5812 Eating places
Glen Pinsonneault

D-U-N-S 25-131-3110   (BR)
RED LOBSTER HOSPITALITY LLC
RED LOBSTER RESTAURANTS
1595 Merivale Rd, Nepean, ON, K2G 3J4
(613) 727-0035
Emp Here 100
SIC 5812 Eating places
Daniel Sheehan

D-U-N-S 20-894-0221   (SL)
SENTRY PRECISION SHEET METAL LTD
20 Enterprise Ave, Nepean, ON, K2G 0A6
(613) 224-4341
Emp Here 75   *Sales* 14,406,375
SIC 3499 Fabricated Metal products, nec
David Hudson
William Reid

D-U-N-S 20-566-7582   (SL)
UPPER ROOM HOME FURNISHINGS INC, THE
545 West Hunt Club Rd, Nepean, ON, K2G 5W5
(613) 721-5873
Emp Here 30   *Sales* 10,402,827
SIC 5712 Furniture stores
Allan Nolan
Patrick Nolan

Nepean, ON K2H

D-U-N-S 20-247-7519   (SL)
8603600 CANADA INC
MONSTER HOLLOWEEN
27 Northside Rd Unit 2710, Nepean, ON, K2H 8S1
(613) 265-4095
Emp Here 50   *Sales* 10,880,650
SIC 5947 Gift, novelty, and souvenir shop
Sandra Harvey
Deborah Weinstein
Lynn Norton

D-U-N-S 24-752-9183   (SL)
ABBOTT POINT OF CARE CANADA LIMITED
185 Corkstown Rd, Nepean, ON, K2H 8V4
(613) 688-5949
Emp Here 650   *Sales* 178,340,500
SIC 3841 Surgical and medical instruments
Benedetta D'elia
Brian B. Yoor
Elizabeth Onwudiwe

Jorge Luque

D-U-N-S 20-918-9005   (SL)
COLLINS BARROW OTTAWA LLP
301 Moodie Dr Suite 400, Nepean, ON, K2H 9C4
(613) 820-8010
Emp Here 75   *Sales* 15,681,375
SIC 8721 Accounting, auditing, and bookkeeping
Bruce Brooks

D-U-N-S 24-357-9021   (SL)
DISTIL INTERACTIVE LTD
16 Fitzgerald Rd Suite 200, Nepean, ON, K2H 8R6

Emp Here 25   *Sales* 13,013,550
SIC 5092 Toys and hobby goods and supplies
Jonathan Adair

D-U-N-S 20-257-1972   (BR)
GENERAL DYNAMICS LAND SYSTEMS - CANADA CORPORATION
GENERAL DYNAMICS MISSION SYSTEMS-CANADA, DIV OF
(*Suby of* GENERAL DYNAMICS CORPORATION)
1941 Robertson Rd, Nepean, ON, K2H 5B7
(613) 596-7000
Emp Here 1,500
SIC 3711 Motor vehicles and car bodies

D-U-N-S 24-985-0561   (BR)
GOLDER ASSOCIATES LTD
(*Suby of* GOLDER ASSOCIATES CORPORATION)
1931 Robertson Rd, Nepean, ON, K2H 5B7
(613) 592-9600
Emp Here 160
SIC 8711 Engineering services
Rick Branchaud

D-U-N-S 25-091-3993   (SL)
GRAHAM AUTOMOTIVE SALES INC
GRAHAM, TONY INFINITI NISSAN
2185 Robertson Rd, Nepean, ON, K2H 5Z2
(613) 596-1515
Emp Here 100   *Sales* 62,928,000
SIC 5511 New and used car dealers
Patrick Graham

D-U-N-S 25-734-3160   (SL)
GRAHAM AUTOMOTIVE SALES LTD
TONY GRAHAM NISSAN
2195 Robertson Rd, Nepean, ON, K2H 5Z2
(613) 596-1515
Emp Here 50   *Sales* 24,903,900
SIC 5511 New and used car dealers
Dan Sproul

D-U-N-S 20-804-5372   (SL)
JONATHAN'S DONUTS LTD
TIM HORTONS
250 Greenbank Rd, Nepean, ON, K2H 8X4
(613) 829-8691
Emp Here 30   *Sales* 13,304,700
SIC 7389 Business services, nec
Gerald Hruidwarth

D-U-N-S 25-027-7852   (BR)
LOBLAWS INC
LOBLAWS
(*Suby of* LOBLAW COMPANIES LIMITED)
2065a Robertson Rd, Nepean, ON, K2H 5Y9
(613) 829-4680
Emp Here 170
SIC 5141 Groceries, general line
Doug Hatoum

D-U-N-S 24-344-4929   (BR)
METRO ONTARIO INC
(*Suby of* METRO INC)
1811 Robertson Rd, Nepean, ON, K2H 8X3
(613) 721-7028
Emp Here 100
SIC 5141 Groceries, general line
David Landers

D-U-N-S 20-369-8019   (SL)
MYERS KANATA NISSAN INC
2185 Robertson Rd, Nepean, ON, K2H 5Z2
(613) 596-1515
Emp Here 35   *Sales* 17,432,730
SIC 5511 New and used car dealers
Henry Mews
Robert Mews

D-U-N-S 25-861-3868   (HQ)
NEUTRONICS COMPONENTS LTD
245 Menten Pl Suite 301, Nepean, ON, K2H 9E8
(613) 599-1263
Emp Here 15   *Sales* 12,578,132
SIC 7389 Business services, nec
Dave Stubbs
Joe Lazzara

D-U-N-S 24-437-4591   (SL)
OTTAWA FASTENER SUPPLY LTD
(*Suby of* DESCOURS ET CABAUD SA)
2205 Robertson Rd, Nepean, ON, K2H 5Z2
(613) 828-5311
Emp Here 32   *Sales* 14,309,568
SIC 5072 Hardware
Mike Wilson

D-U-N-S 25-673-1464   (HQ)
OTTAWA-CARLETON DISTRICT SCHOOL BOARD
133 Greenbank Rd, Nepean, ON, K2H 6L3
(613) 721-1820
Emp Here 350   *Sales* 693,833,000
SIC 8211 Elementary and secondary schools
Lynn Graham
Lynn Scott
Lorne Rachlis
Mike Carson
Michael Clarke

D-U-N-S 25-263-5453   (BR)
OTTAWA-CARLETON DISTRICT SCHOOL BOARD
SIR ROBERT BORDEN HIGH SCHOOL
(*Suby of* OTTAWA-CARLETON DISTRICT SCHOOL BOARD)
131 Greenbank Rd, Nepean, ON, K2H 8R1
(613) 721-1820
Emp Here 100
SIC 8211 Elementary and secondary schools
David Mcmahon

D-U-N-S 25-263-6089   (BR)
OTTAWA-CARLETON DISTRICT SCHOOL BOARD
BELL HIGH SCHOOL
(*Suby of* OTTAWA-CARLETON DISTRICT SCHOOL BOARD)
40 Cassidy Rd, Nepean, ON, K2H 6K1
(613) 828-9101
Emp Here 80
SIC 8211 Elementary and secondary schools
Stephen Collins

D-U-N-S 20-892-5016   (HQ)
QUEENSWAY-CARLETON HOSPITAL
Queensway-Carleton Hospital, Nepean, ON, K2H 8P4
(613) 721-2000
Sales 151,837,598
SIC 8062 General medical and surgical hospitals
Thomas Schonberg
Carolyn Brennan
Peter Strum
Gerry Barker
Cathy Jordan
Elaine Mcnaughton
Andrew Falconer
Sanjay Acharya
Chris Winckel
Clare Beckton

D-U-N-S 20-105-8315   (SL)
RECOGNIA INC
301 Moodie Dr Suite 200, Nepean, ON, K2H

9C4
(613) 789-2267
Emp Here 20   *Sales* 10,624,140
SIC 6282 Investment advice
Rick Escher
Rainer Paduch
Paul Halpern
John Dill
Brian O'higgins

D-U-N-S 25-169-7926   (SL)
RIVERPARK PLACE LIMITED PARTNERSHIP
RIVERPARK PLACE RETIREMENT RESIDENCE
1 Corkstown Rd, Nepean, ON, K2H 1B6
(613) 828-8882
Emp Here 100   *Sales* 5,924,700
SIC 8361 Residential care
Miriam Gartland

D-U-N-S 24-360-5917   (SL)
SPARTAN BIOSCIENCE INC
2934 Baseline Rd Suite 500, Nepean, ON, K2H 1B2
(613) 228-7756
Emp Here 70   *Sales* 15,910,230
SIC 3826 Analytical instruments
Paul Lem
John Lem
Mark Houghting
Jamie Spiegelman
Ken Paige
Michael Stork
Paul Markell

D-U-N-S 20-058-5979   (SL)
STILLWATER CREEK LIMITED PARTNERSHIP
STILLWATER CREEK RETIREMENT COMMUNITY
2018 Robertson Rd Suite 353, Nepean, ON, K2H 1C6
(613) 828-7575
Emp Here 80   *Sales* 5,485,280
SIC 8059 Nursing and personal care, nec
Cindy Hunt

D-U-N-S 24-991-9341   (SL)
TEX-DON LTD
CANADIAN TIRE 272
2135 Robertson Rd, Nepean, ON, K2H 5Z2
(613) 829-9580
Emp Here 65   *Sales* 40,903,200
SIC 5531 Auto and home supply stores
Donald Brooks

Nepean, ON K2J

D-U-N-S 20-117-4401   (SL)
1470341 ONTARIO INC
BARRHAVEN SOBEYS
1581 Greenbank Rd Suite 16, Nepean, ON, K2J 4Y6
(613) 825-5495
Emp Here 160   *Sales* 46,956,320
SIC 5411 Grocery stores
Dana Conley
Sandra Conley

D-U-N-S 24-097-3805   (SL)
A 1 MEDICAL CENTRE INC
STRANDHERD CROSSING MEDICAL CENTER
3161 Strandherd Dr Unit 305, Nepean, ON, K2J 5N1
(613) 823-7766
Emp Here 15   *Sales* 10,881,585
SIC 6324 Hospital and medical service plans
Narinder Birgi
Melanie Mcguire

D-U-N-S 20-137-0897   (HQ)
DAVIS AGENCY OF OTTAWA LIMITED
HALLMARK

3161 Greenbank Rd Unit A7, Nepean, ON, K2J 4H9
(613) 825-0755
Emp Here 11   *Sales* 32,984,280
SIC 5947 Gift, novelty, and souvenir shop
  Robert Wild
  Gerry Henri
  Jennifer Dobson

D-U-N-S 20-324-5360   (SL)
IDEABYTES INC
142 Golflinks Dr, Nepean, ON, K2J 5N5
(613) 692-9908
Emp Here 65   *Sales* 11,525,215
SIC 7371 Custom computer programming services
  George Philip Kongalath

D-U-N-S 20-381-2453   (HQ)
KOTT INC
3228 Moodie Dr, Nepean, ON, K2J 4S8
(613) 838-2775
Emp Here 100   *Sales* 142,407,000
SIC 5031 Lumber, plywood, and millwork
  Ryan Kruyne
  Melissa Kruyne

D-U-N-S 24-828-0380   (SL)
LAREN HOLDINGS INC
3228 Moodie Dr, Nepean, ON, K2J 4S8
(613) 838-2775
Emp Here 225   *Sales* 82,239,525
SIC 6712 Bank holding companies
  Paul Kruyne

D-U-N-S 25-801-1360   (BR)
LOBLAWS SUPERMARKETS LIMITED
LOBLAWS
(*Suby of* LOBLAW COMPANIES LIMITED)
3201 Greenbank Rd Suite 1035, Nepean, ON, K2J 4H9
(613) 825-0812
Emp Here 300
SIC 5411 Grocery stores
  Jeff Mitchel

D-U-N-S 24-382-7987   (HQ)
LUMENTUM CANADA LTD
(*Suby of* LUMENTUM HOLDINGS INC.)
61 Bill Leathem Dr, Nepean, ON, K2J 0P7
(613) 843-3000
Emp Here 200   *Sales* 164,622,000
SIC 3827 Optical instruments and lenses
  Alan Lowe
  Anthony Muller
  Ken Scott

D-U-N-S 24-348-1988   (HQ)
LUMENTUM OTTAWA INC
(*Suby of* LUMENTUM HOLDINGS INC.)
61 Bill Leathem Dr, Nepean, ON, K2J 0P7
(613) 843-3000
Emp Here 45   *Sales* 10,233,650
SIC 3669 Communications equipment, nec
  Alan Lowe
  Aaron Tachibana
  Christopher S Dewees
  Adam Kubelka

D-U-N-S 25-886-2598   (BR)
MCDONALD'S   RESTAURANTS   OF CANADA LIMITED
MCDONALD'S
(*Suby of* MCDONALD'S CORPORATION)
3773 Strandherd Dr, Nepean, ON, K2J 4B1
(613) 823-7838
Emp Here 80
SIC 5812 Eating places

D-U-N-S 24-616-1322   (BR)
METRO ONTARIO INC
FOOD BASIC
(*Suby of* METRO INC)
900 Greenbank Rd, Nepean, ON, K2J 4P6
(613) 823-4458
Emp Here 75
SIC 5411 Grocery stores

Derek Turner

D-U-N-S 24-344-4853   (BR)
METRO ONTARIO INC
LOEB
(*Suby of* METRO INC)
3201 Strandherd Dr, Nepean, ON, K2J 5N1
(613) 823-8825
Emp Here 100
SIC 5411 Grocery stores
  Karen Carmondia

D-U-N-S 20-369-8022   (SL)
MYERS HY WEST INC
MYERS HYUNDAI
4115 Strandherd Dr, Nepean, ON, K2J 6H8
(613) 714-8888
Emp Here 34   *Sales* 16,934,652
SIC 5511 New and used car dealers
  Henry Mews
  Robert Mews

D-U-N-S 20-288-9346   (BR)
OTTAWA CATHOLIC DISTRICT SCHOOL BOARD
ST JOSEPH HIGH SCHOOL
(*Suby of* OTTAWA CATHOLIC DISTRICT SCHOOL BOARD)
3333 Greenbank Rd, Nepean, ON, K2J 4J1
(613) 823-4797
Emp Here 125
SIC 8211 Elementary and secondary schools
  Sue Arbour

D-U-N-S 20-026-2405   (BR)
OTTAWA CATHOLIC DISTRICT SCHOOL BOARD
MOTHER TERESA HIGH SCHOOL
(*Suby of* OTTAWA CATHOLIC DISTRICT SCHOOL BOARD)
440 Longfields Dr, Nepean, ON, K2J 4T1
(613) 823-1663
Emp Here 120
SIC 8211 Elementary and secondary schools
  Mary Donaghy

D-U-N-S 20-590-4894   (BR)
OTTAWA-CARLETON DISTRICT SCHOOL BOARD
JOHN MCCRAE SECONDARY SCHOOL
(*Suby of* OTTAWA-CARLETON DISTRICT SCHOOL BOARD)
103 Malvern Dr, Nepean, ON, K2J 4T2
(613) 823-0367
Emp Here 75
SIC 8211 Elementary and secondary schools
  Tom Schultz

D-U-N-S 24-326-9565   (SL)
PINEO, P. PHARMACEUTICALS INC
SHOPPERS DRUG MART
3151 Strandherd Dr Suite 1302, Nepean, ON, K2J 5N1
(613) 825-8717
Emp Here 50   *Sales* 12,647,700
SIC 5912 Drug stores and proprietary stores
  Paul Pineo

D-U-N-S 24-329-7012   (BR)
WAL-MART CANADA CORP
(*Suby of* WALMART INC.)
3651 Strandherd Dr, Nepean, ON, K2J 4G8
(613) 823-8714
Emp Here 200
SIC 5311 Department stores
  Marcia Mctaggard

Nepean, ON K2R

D-U-N-S 20-246-0569   (BR)
FIRSTCANADA ULC
FIRST STUDENT CANADA
(*Suby of* FIRSTGROUP PLC)
1027 Moodie Dr, Nepean, ON, K2R 1H4

Emp Here 150
SIC 4151 School buses
  Adel Jahshan

D-U-N-S 20-388-2139   (SL)
MYERS BARRHAVEN NIS INC
MYERS BARRHAVEN NISSAN
530 Motor Works Pvt, Nepean, ON, K2R 0A5
(613) 778-8893
Emp Here 28   *Sales* 13,946,184
SIC 5511 New and used car dealers
  Harry Mews
  Robert Mews

D-U-N-S 24-785-3620   (HQ)
TOMLINSON ENVIRONMENTAL SERVICES LTD
(*Suby of* TOMLINSON, R. W. LIMITED)
970 Moodie Dr, Nepean, ON, K2R 1H3
(613) 820-2332
Emp Here 5   *Sales* 19,980,090
SIC 3559 Special industry machinery, nec
  Ron Tomlinson

New Hamburg, ON N3A

D-U-N-S 20-734-0191   (SL)
ALLOY CASTING INDUSTRIES LIMITED
374 Hamilton Rd Unit 1, New Hamburg, ON, N3A 2K2
(519) 662-3111
Emp Here 75   *Sales* 17,507,625
SIC 3325 Steel foundries, nec
  Stephen Blenkhorn
  Michel Fortier

D-U-N-S 25-274-8710   (HQ)
ERB ENTERPRISES INC
290 Hamilton Rd, New Hamburg, ON, N3A 1A2
(519) 662-2710
Emp Here 62   *Sales* 438,610,800
SIC 6712 Bank holding companies
  Vernon Erb
  Victor Thiessen
  Kevin Cooper
  Viola Erb
  Wendell Erb
  Dorene Rudy-Snyder

D-U-N-S 20-348-2534   (SL)
ERB GROUP OF COMPANIES, THE
290 Hamilton Rd, New Hamburg, ON, N3A 1A2
(519) 662-2710
Emp Here 1,500   *Sales* 308,559,000
SIC 4213 Trucking, except local
  Vernon Erb

D-U-N-S 20-347-9837   (HQ)
ERB INTERNATIONAL INC
290 Hamilton Rd, New Hamburg, ON, N3A 1A2
(519) 662-2710
Sales 1,003,362,000
SIC 7389 Business services, nec
  Vernon Erb

D-U-N-S 20-181-5388   (HQ)
ERB TRANSPORT LIMITED
(*Suby of* ERB ENTERPRISES INC)
290 Hamilton Rd, New Hamburg, ON, N3A 1A2
(519) 662-2710
Emp Here 75   *Sales* 276,571,500
SIC 4212 Local trucking, without storage
  Wendell Erb
  Vernon Erb
  Vic Thiessen
  Kevin Cooper
  Dale Bauman
  Karen Erb
  Floyd Gerber
  Irene Holdbrook

David Dietrich
Greg Tuckwell

D-U-N-S 24-406-8078   (HQ)
EXPRESSWAY MOTORS LTD
EXPRESSWAY FORD LINCOLN
1554 Haysville Rd, New Hamburg, ON, N3A 1A3
(519) 662-3900
Emp Here 35   *Sales* 29,576,160
SIC 5511 New and used car dealers
  Ray Brenneman
  Neilda Brenneman
  Douglas Brenneman
  Dwight Brenneman
  Michael Brenneman

D-U-N-S 24-476-3389   (HQ)
JOSSLIN INSURANCE BROKERS LIMITED
118 Peel St, New Hamburg, ON, N3A 1E3
(519) 662-1644
Emp Here 15   *Sales* 42,403,000
SIC 6411 Insurance agents, brokers, and service
  Donald Wagler
  Scott Wagler
  Steven Wagler
  Rose Wagler

D-U-N-S 20-536-5323   (SL)
KLASSEN BRONZE LIMITED
30 Marvin St, New Hamburg, ON, N3A 4H8
(519) 662-1010
Emp Here 75   *Sales* 24,460,200
SIC 3993 Signs and advertising specialties
  Jeff Whitesell

D-U-N-S 20-180-6437   (HQ)
MAGNUSSEN HOME FURNISHINGS LTD
MAGNUSSEN HOME
66 Hincks St Suite 1, New Hamburg, ON, N3A 2A3
(519) 662-3040
Sales 57,536,800
SIC 5021 Furniture
  Jeff Cook
  Richard Magnussen
  Bruce Ballantyne
  Russ Langford
  Richard Olmeda
  Marylin Magnussen
  Nathan Cressman
  Lisa Cressman

D-U-N-S 20-706-3413   (BR)
MAPLE LEAF FOODS INC
MAPLE LEAF FOODS, DIV OF
(*Suby of* MAPLE LEAF FOODS INC)
70 Heritage Dr, New Hamburg, ON, N3A 2J4
(519) 662-1501
Emp Here 80
SIC 0254 Poultry hatcheries
  Kyle Wynette

D-U-N-S 24-333-0391   (HQ)
ONTARIO DRIVE & GEAR LIMITED
ARGO
3551 Bleams Rd, New Hamburg, ON, N3A 2J1
(519) 662-2840
Sales 87,255,000
SIC 3711 Motor vehicles and car bodies
  Brad Darling
  Michael Eckardt
  Joerg Stieber

D-U-N-S 25-050-9148   (HQ)
PESTELL MINERALS & INGREDIENTS INC
141 Hamilton Rd, New Hamburg, ON, N3A 2H1
(519) 662-2877
Sales 40,838,600
SIC 5191 Farm supplies
  Donald Pestell
  William Zinger
  Randy Coulombe
  Peter Brunelle

D-U-N-S 25-398-9735   (SL)
PESTELL SHAVINGS LIMITED
PESTELL WOOD SHAVINGS
(*Suby of* PESTELL MINERALS & INGREDI-ENTS INC)
141 Hamilton Rd Suite 794, New Hamburg, ON, N3A 2H1
(519) 662-6565
Emp Here 15   *Sales* 11,137,800
SIC 5191 Farm supplies
  Craig Pestell

D-U-N-S 20-179-9728   (SL)
PFENNING'S ORGANIC VEGETABLES INC
1209 Waterloo St, New Hamburg, ON, N3A 1T1
(519) 662-3468
Emp Here 35   *Sales* 29,245,195
SIC 5148 Fresh fruits and vegetables
  Wilham Pfenning
  Ekk Pfenning

D-U-N-S 20-144-7224   (SL)
RIVERSIDE BRASS & ALUMINUM FOUNDRY LIMITED
RIVERSIDE BRASS
(*Suby of* STEINVEST INDUSTRIES LIM-ITED)
55 Hamilton Rd, New Hamburg, ON, N3A 2H1
(800) 265-2197
Emp Here 135   *Sales* 24,487,380
SIC 3369 Nonferrous foundries, nec
  David Seyler
  Doug Steinmann
  Susan Seyler

D-U-N-S 24-597-4555   (HQ)
ZEHR INSURANCE BROKERS LIMITED
59 Huron St, New Hamburg, ON, N3A 1K1
(519) 662-1710
Emp Here 10   *Sales* 21,201,500
SIC 6411 Insurance agents, brokers, and service
  John Zehr
  John Smith

New Liskeard, ON P0J

D-U-N-S 25-418-6398   (HQ)
BOARD OF HEALTH FOR THE TIMISKAM-ING HEALTH UNIT
TIMISKAMING HEALTH UNIT
421 Shepherdson Rd, New Liskeard, ON, P0J 1P0
(705) 647-4305
Emp Here 24   *Sales* 13,289,410
SIC 8099 Health and allied services, nec
  Esther Millar

D-U-N-S 25-592-8210   (SL)
CHARTRAND, R. J. HOLDINGS LIMITED
CHARTRAND INDEPENDENT GROCER
55 Scott St, New Liskeard, ON, P0J 1P0
(705) 647-8844
Emp Here 100   *Sales* 29,347,700
SIC 5411 Grocery stores
  Roger Chartrand
  Vivianne Chartrand

D-U-N-S 20-772-7538   (SL)
DESPRES-PACEY INSURANCE BROKERS LIMITED
26 Armstrong St, New Liskeard, ON, P0J 1P0
(705) 647-6713
Emp Here 30   *Sales* 17,397,720
SIC 6411 Insurance agents, brokers, and service
  Wilfred Despres

D-U-N-S 25-238-8533   (BR)
DISTRICT SCHOOL BOARD ONTARIO NORTH EAST
TIMISKAMING DISTRICT SECONDARY SCHOOL

(*Suby of* DISTRICT SCHOOL BOARD ON-TARIO NORTH EAST)
90 Niven St, New Liskeard, ON, P0J 1P0
(705) 647-7336
Emp Here 90
SIC 8211 Elementary and secondary schools
  Cathy Beauchamp

D-U-N-S 20-754-7829   (SL)
FINDLAY'S DRUG STORE (NEW LISKEARD) LIMITED
237 Whitewood Ave Unit 25, New Liskeard, ON, P0J 1P0
(705) 647-8186
Emp Here 60   *Sales* 14,659,680
SIC 5912 Drug stores and proprietary stores
  Bruce Alexander

D-U-N-S 20-286-8535   (HQ)
GRANT FARMS CORP
863169 Uno Park Rd, New Liskeard, ON, P0J 1P0
(705) 647-3129
Sales 26,830,440
SIC 5039 Construction materials, nec
  Peter Grant

D-U-N-S 25-187-9896   (HQ)
GRANT FUELS INC.
PETRO CANADA
251 Gray Rd, New Liskeard, ON, P0J 1P0
(705) 647-6566
Emp Here 7   *Sales* 14,459,312
SIC 5171 Petroleum bulk stations and terminals
  Gordon Grant

D-U-N-S 20-047-3775   (HQ)
GRANT LUMBER BUILDING CENTRES LTD
GRANT HOME HARDWARE
Gd, New Liskeard, ON, P0J 1P0
(705) 647-9311
Emp Here 3   *Sales* 13,917,904
SIC 5211 Lumber and other building materials
  David Grant
  Julie Grant

D-U-N-S 24-505-8979   (SL)
GRANT'S TRANSPORT LIMITED
GRW TRANSPORT, DIV OF
251 Gray Rd, New Liskeard, ON, P0J 1P0
(705) 647-8171
Emp Here 120   *Sales* 24,684,720
SIC 4213 Trucking, except local
  Gordon Grant

D-U-N-S 24-991-4805   (BR)
MILLER PAVING LIMITED
MILLER PAVING NORTHERN
(*Suby of* MILLER GROUP INC)
704024 Rockley Rd, New Liskeard, ON, P0J 1P0
(705) 647-4331
Emp Here 200
SIC 1611 Highway and street construction
  Jean-Kiterre Breteon

D-U-N-S 24-964-2778   (SL)
MILLER PAVING LTD
(*Suby of* MILLER GROUP INC)
883316 Hwy 65, New Liskeard, ON, P0J 1P0
(877) 842-0543
Emp Here 50   *Sales* 12,622,100
SIC 1611 Highway and street construction
  Leo Mcarthur

D-U-N-S 20-131-9290   (SL)
PEDERSEN CONSTRUCTION INC
11 & 65 Hwy W, New Liskeard, ON, P0J 1P0
(705) 647-6223
Emp Here 100   *Sales* 25,244,200
SIC 1623 Water, sewer, and utility lines
  Karl Pedersen
  Dennis Pedersen
  Terry Pedersen
  Alec Pedersen

D-U-N-S 20-188-1773   (HQ)

PRO-AB EQUIPEMENTS 2003 INC
MEGA CENTRE KUBOTA
883304 Hwy 65, New Liskeard, ON, P0J 1P0
(705) 647-6065
Sales 11,875,650
SIC 5084 Industrial machinery and equipment
  Bernard Levesque
  Estelle Baril

D-U-N-S 20-771-6432   (SL)
THREE H FURNITURE SYSTEMS LIMITED
THREE H
156462 Clover Valley Rd, New Liskeard, ON, P0J 1P0
(705) 647-4323
Emp Here 100   *Sales* 15,432,200
SIC 2521 Wood office furniture
  Karl Dittmann
  Roy Dittmann
  Tom Cambridge
  Mark Conlin
  Brian Conlin

D-U-N-S 20-879-8566   (SL)
THREE-H MANUFACTURING LTD
156462 Clover Valley Rd, New Liskeard, ON, P0J 1P0
(705) 647-4323
Emp Here 100   *Sales* 23,240,300
SIC 5712 Furniture stores
  Roy Dittmann

D-U-N-S 24-344-8714   (BR)
TIMISKAMING CHILD AND FAMILY SER-VICES
(*Suby of* TIMISKAMING CHILD AND FAMILY SERVICES)
25 Paget St, New Liskeard, ON, P0J 1P0
(705) 647-1200
Emp Here 100
SIC 8322 Individual and family services
  John Raymond

D-U-N-S 24-953-3092   (HQ)
WABI IRON & STEEL CORP
330 Broadwood Ave, New Liskeard, ON, P0J 1P0
(705) 647-4383
Emp Here 130   *Sales* 24,124,604
SIC 3325 Steel foundries, nec
  Jeremy Birnie

D-U-N-S 20-338-5187   (SL)
WB MELBACK CORPORATION
742252 Dawson Point Rd, New Liskeard, ON, P0J 1P0
(705) 647-5879
Emp Here 50   *Sales* 11,046,700
SIC 1711 Plumbing, heating, air-conditioning
  Melvin Peddie

D-U-N-S 24-393-0323   (SL)
WHITE, BART SALES LTD
CANADIAN TIRE
997431 Hwy 11, New Liskeard, ON, P0J 1P0
(705) 647-7331
Emp Here 40   *Sales* 14,568,600
SIC 5014 Tires and tubes
  Bart White

D-U-N-S 20-534-5549   (SL)
WILSON CHEVROLET LIMITED
WILSON CHEVROLET BUICK GMC
100 Wilson St, New Liskeard, ON, P0J 1P0
(705) 647-2031
Emp Here 47   *Sales* 23,409,666
SIC 5511 New and used car dealers
  John Wilson

Newbury, ON N0L

D-U-N-S 20-783-7360   (SL)
FOUR COUNTIES HEALTH SERVICES CORPORATION, THE
1824 Concession Dr, Newbury, ON, N0L 1Z0

(519) 693-4441
Emp Here 130   *Sales* 13,277,290
SIC 8062 General medical and surgical hospitals
  Janak Jass
  John Kavallers

D-U-N-S 20-131-7054   (SL)
MCNAUGHTON AUTOMOTIVE LIMITED
MCNAUGHTON HOME HARDWARE BUILD-ING CENTRE
22789 Hagerty Rd, Newbury, ON, N0L 1Z0
(519) 693-4449
Emp Here 65   *Sales* 17,397,380
SIC 5211 Lumber and other building materials
  Micheal Mcnaughton
  Monte Mcnaughton
  Heather Mcvicar

Newcastle, ON L1B

D-U-N-S 20-576-6822   (SL)
NEWCASTLE FOODLAND INC
131 King Ave E, Newcastle, ON, L1B 1H3
(905) 987-4627
Emp Here 100   *Sales* 29,347,700
SIC 5411 Grocery stores
  Ryan Ormiston

D-U-N-S 25-664-4998   (SL)
SUNSPACE MODULAR ENCLOSURES INC
SUNSPACE SUNROOMS
300 Toronto St, Newcastle, ON, L1B 1C2
(905) 987-4111
Emp Here 50   *Sales* 10,141,500
SIC 3448 Prefabricated Metal buildings and components
  Steven Hunt
  Helen Hunt
  Paul Kok

D-U-N-S 20-641-3093   (BR)
WILSON FOODS CENTRE LTD
MCDONALD'S
1000 Regional Rd 17, Newcastle, ON, L1B 0T7
(905) 987-0505
Emp Here 76
SIC 5812 Eating places
  Steve Wilson

Newmarket, ON L3X

D-U-N-S 24-786-5264   (HQ)
AIRBOSS OF AMERICA CORP
AIRBOSS RUBBER COMPOUNDING, DIV OF
16441 Yonge St, Newmarket, ON, L3X 2G8
(905) 751-1188
Emp Here 11   *Sales* 316,603,000
SIC 3069 Fabricated rubber products, nec
  Grenville Schoch
  Lisa Swartzman
  Chris Bitsakakis
  Daniel Gagnon
  Robert Hagerman
  Mary Matthews
  Robert Mcleish
  Brian A. Robbins
  Alan J. Watson

D-U-N-S 24-862-5410   (HQ)
ALLIED INTERNATIONAL CREDIT CORP
AIC
(*Suby of* BILL GOSLING OUTSOURCING HOLDING CORP)
16635 Yonge St Suite 26, Newmarket, ON, L3X 1V6
(905) 470-8181
Emp Here 775   *Sales* 28,846,155
SIC 4899 Communication services, nec

David Rae
Kenny Johnston
David Gallagher
Tom Mccausland

D-U-N-S 20-344-9285   (SL)
ANB CANADA INC
25 Millard Ave W Unit 1, Newmarket, ON, L3X 7R5
(905) 953-9777
Emp Here 45   *Sales* 49,740,525
SIC 5122 Drugs, proprietaries, and sundries
Brent Larkan
Tim Moore
Ronald Stubbs

D-U-N-S 24-886-3045   (HQ)
BILL GOSLING OUTSOURCING HOLDING CORP
16635 Yonge St Suite 26, Newmarket, ON, L3X 1V6
(905) 470-8181
Sales 66,595,545
SIC 6712 Bank holding companies
David A Rae
Kenny Johnston
David R Gallagher
Thomas Mccausland
Joe Fanutti

D-U-N-S 24-374-8238   (SL)
BRANDS INTERNATIONAL CORPORATION
594 Newpark Blvd, Newmarket, ON, L3X 2S2
(905) 830-4404
Emp Here 50   *Sales* 13,833,000
SIC 2844 Toilet preparations
Mark Rubinoff

D-U-N-S 20-554-3762   (SL)
GLENWAY COUNTRY CLUB LIMITED
470 Crossland Gate, Newmarket, ON, L3X 1B8
(905) 235-5422
Emp Here 100   *Sales* 7,639,700
SIC 7997 Membership sports and recreation clubs
Gary Lester
Greg Seeman

D-U-N-S 24-545-6884   (HQ)
HOMEGUARD FUNDING LTD
HOMEGUARD FUNDING VERICO
83 Dawson Manor Blvd, Newmarket, ON, L3X 2H5
(905) 895-1777
Emp Here 15   *Sales* 217,107,000
SIC 6163 Loan brokers
Wayne Sudsbury
William (Bill) Eves
Sheila Sudsbury

D-U-N-S 20-116-8338   (HQ)
MAGNA CLOSURES INC
MEGA PLAS
(*Suby of* MAGNA INTERNATIONAL INC)
521 Newpark Blvd, Newmarket, ON, L3X 2S2
(905) 898-2665
Emp Here 5   *Sales* 281,303,940
SIC 5013 Motor vehicle supplies and new parts
Frank Seguin

D-U-N-S 20-317-1590   (BR)
MAGNA SEATING INC
CAM-SLIDE
(*Suby of* MAGNA INTERNATIONAL INC)
564 Newpark Blvd, Newmarket, ON, L3X 2S2
(905) 853-3604
Emp Here 600
SIC 3714 Motor vehicle parts and accessories
Phil Holjak

D-U-N-S 24-366-6240   (BR)
MAGNA SEATING INC
CAM-SLIDE
(*Suby of* MAGNA INTERNATIONAL INC)
550 Newpark Blvd, Newmarket, ON, L3X 2S2

(905) 895-4701
Emp Here 600
SIC 3714 Motor vehicle parts and accessories
Phil Holjak

D-U-N-S 20-555-6611   (BR)
METRO ONTARIO INC
METRO
(*Suby of* METRO INC)
16640 Yonge St Unit 1, Newmarket, ON, L3X 2N8
(905) 853-5100
Emp Here 200
SIC 5411 Grocery stores
Ian Searle

D-U-N-S 25-396-8911   (SL)
NATURE'S EMPORIUM BULK & HEALTH FOODS LTD
NATURE'S EMPORIUM WHOLISTIC MARKET
16655 Yonge St Suite 27, Newmarket, ON, L3X 1V6
(905) 898-1844
Emp Here 50   *Sales* 13,707,600
SIC 5499 Miscellaneous food stores
Giuseppe D'addario
Nicola Tavernese

D-U-N-S 24-827-8702   (SL)
TIANJIN AUTO PARTS INC
TJ AUTO PARTS
431 Woodspring Ave, Newmarket, ON, L3X 3H5
(647) 999-9612
Emp Here 100   *Sales* 52,871,221
SIC 4731 Freight transportation arrangement
Ben Tian

D-U-N-S 20-291-8202   (BR)
YORK REGION DISTRICT SCHOOL BOARD
SIR WILLIAM MULOCK SECONDARY SCHOOL
(*Suby of* YORK REGION DISTRICT SCHOOL BOARD)
705 Columbus Way, Newmarket, ON, L3X 2M7
(905) 967-1045
Emp Here 150
SIC 8211 Elementary and secondary schools
Joe Ravesi

D-U-N-S 20-918-8064   (SL)
YORK REGIONAL POLICE ASSOCIATION, THE
600 Stonehaven Ave, Newmarket, ON, L3X 2M4
(905) 830-4947
Emp Here 26   *Sales* 10,170,108
SIC 8631 Labor organizations
John Miskiw

Newmarket, ON L3Y

D-U-N-S 25-534-7619   (SL)
1148044 ONTARIO LTD
CAMBRIA DESIGN BUILD
1250 Journey'S End Cir Suite 1, Newmarket, ON, L3Y 0B9
(905) 830-6026
Emp Here 30   *Sales* 14,121,930
SIC 1542 Nonresidential construction, nec
Spencer Lavis

D-U-N-S 20-702-3214   (SL)
1221271 ONTARIO INC
NEW MARKET GROUP
200 Davis Dr Suite 1, Newmarket, ON, L3Y 2N4

Emp Here 47   *Sales* 11,181,347
SIC 8742 Management consulting services
Cheryl Vesanen

D-U-N-S 25-115-9513   (SL)
1246110 ONTARIO INC

YORK MEDICAL
18120 Yonge St, Newmarket, ON, L3Y 4V8

Emp Here 100   *Sales* 18,534,000
SIC 8011 Offices and clinics of medical doctors
Kenneth Lay

D-U-N-S 20-549-9580   (SL)
1340123 ONTARIO LTD
VINCE'S COUNTRY MARKET
869 Mulock Dr Suite 6, Newmarket, ON, L3Y 8S3
(905) 853-3356
Emp Here 40   *Sales* 10,966,080
SIC 5411 Grocery stores
Carmen Trimarchi
Mario Testa

D-U-N-S 24-141-0893   (SL)
87029 CANADA LTD
NEWMARKET GROUP
200 Davis Dr, Newmarket, ON, L3Y 2N4

Emp Here 50   *Sales* 22,174,500
SIC 7389 Business services, nec
William Farr
Dan Flanagan
Jack Battersby
Frank Geier

D-U-N-S 25-610-8176   (SL)
953866 ONTARIO LIMITED
NEWMARKET HYUNDAI
17735 Leslie St, Newmarket, ON, L3Y 3E3
(905) 898-2721
Emp Here 42   *Sales* 20,919,276
SIC 5511 New and used car dealers
Tonino Delgobbo

D-U-N-S 24-419-7604   (SL)
967961 ONTARIO LIMITED
DAVE WOOD MAZDA
349 Mulock Dr, Newmarket, ON, L3Y 5W2
(416) 798-7877
Emp Here 35   *Sales* 17,432,730
SIC 5511 New and used car dealers
Dave Wood
Lenora Wood

D-U-N-S 25-237-5845   (HQ)
ACUSHNET CANADA INC
TITLEIST FOOTJOY
(*Suby of* FILA KOREA LTD.)
500 Harry Walker Pky Ne, Newmarket, ON, L3Y 8T6
(905) 898-7575
Sales 52,054,200
SIC 5091 Sporting and recreation goods
Ted Manning
Chris Perkins
Shanon Grauer
Walter R Uihlein

D-U-N-S 25-212-7287   (BR)
AIRTEX MANUFACTURING PARTNERSHIP
ENGINEERED AIR
(*Suby of* RESMAN HOLDINGS LTD)
1175 Twinney Dr, Newmarket, ON, L3Y 9C8
(905) 898-1114
Emp Here 200
SIC 3585 Refrigeration and heating equipment
David Taylor

D-U-N-S 24-485-6704   (SL)
ALCOS MACHINERY INC
190 Harry Walker Pky N, Newmarket, ON, L3Y 7B4
(905) 836-6030
Emp Here 75   *Sales* 35,626,950
SIC 5084 Industrial machinery and equipment
Hasan Albulak
Gulgun Albulak

D-U-N-S 20-001-8722   (SL)
ASSURANT LIFE OF CANADA
1111 Davis Drive, Newmarket, ON, L3Y 9E5

(888) 977-3752
Emp Here 16   *Sales* 16,558,096
SIC 6311 Life insurance

D-U-N-S 25-185-3990   (SL)
AUTO GROUP NEWMARKET INC
NEWMARKET TOYOTA
1171 Davis Dr, Newmarket, ON, L3Y 8R1
(905) 953-2890
Emp Here 35   *Sales* 17,432,730
SIC 5511 New and used car dealers
Saminder Gill
John Chapman

D-U-N-S 24-987-2011   (HQ)
B & B DIXON AUTOMOTIVE INC
395 Harry Walker Pky N Unit 3, Newmarket, ON, L3Y 7B3
(905) 895-5184
Sales 12,019,095
SIC 5013 Motor vehicle supplies and new parts
Bruce Dixon
Barry Borovoy
William Dixon

D-U-N-S 24-506-2583   (SL)
BAJAR, ANTONIO GREENHOUSES LIMITED
18545 Keele St, Newmarket, ON, L3Y 4V9
(905) 775-2773
Emp Here 25   *Sales* 18,563,000
SIC 5193 Flowers and florists supplies
Antonio Bajar
Mila Bajar
David Bajar
Melanie Bajar Sheppard
Matthew Sheppard

D-U-N-S 25-914-2016   (HQ)
BALTA IMPORTS LTD
17600 Yonge St Suite 43, Newmarket, ON, L3Y 4Z1
(905) 853-5281
Emp Here 5   *Sales* 15,616,260
SIC 5099 Durable goods, nec
Robert Balta
Hanna Balta

D-U-N-S 25-997-1182   (SL)
BEAVER MACHINE CORPORATION
MACHINE-O-MATIC, DIV OF
250 Harry Walker Pky N Unit 1, Newmarket, ON, L3Y 7B4
(905) 836-4700
Emp Here 75   *Sales* 16,650,075
SIC 3581 Automatic vending machines
Bernard Schwarzli

D-U-N-S 25-482-9245   (SL)
BENSON KEARLEY & ASSOCIATES INSURANCE BROKERS LTD
BENSON KEARLEY IFG
17705 Leslie St Suite 101, Newmarket, ON, L3Y 3E3
(905) 898-3815
Emp Here 67   *Sales* 123,798,714
SIC 6411 Insurance agents, brokers, and service
Stephen Kearley
Lindsay Yaciuk
Roxanne Phillips
Mike Mcquaid
Michelle Cowell
Jeff Rodin

D-U-N-S 25-984-6368   (BR)
BEST BUY CANADA LTD
FUTURE SHOP
(*Suby of* BEST BUY CO., INC.)
17890 Yonge St, Newmarket, ON, L3Y 8S1

Emp Here 80
SIC 5999 Miscellaneous retail stores, nec
Karm Kang

D-U-N-S 25-292-3016   (SL)
BLACKBROOK CHEMICAL LTD

1245 Maple Hill Crt Suite 1, Newmarket, ON, L3Y 9E8

Emp Here 40   *Sales* 11,252,523
SIC 2899 Chemical preparations, nec
  Tom Barrow

D-U-N-S 24-062-6556   (SL)
BRAY'S FUELS LIMITED
19870 Hwy 11, Newmarket, ON, L3Y 4V9
(905) 775-3120
Emp Here 14   *Sales* 14,459,312
SIC 5172 Petroleum products, nec
  Alan Bray
  Kent Bray

D-U-N-S 24-985-9158   (SL)
BUCKLEY INSURANCE BROKERS LTD
247 Main St S, Newmarket, ON, L3Y 3Z4
(905) 836-7283
Emp Here 46   *Sales* 26,676,504
SIC 6411 Insurance agents, brokers, and service
  Robert Buckley

D-U-N-S 25-512-6369   (SL)
BURKE'S RESTORATION INC
BURKE'S RESTORATION
17705 Leslie St Unit 7, Newmarket, ON, L3Y 8C6
(905) 895-2456
Emp Here 40   *Sales* 12,754,760
SIC 1521 Single-family housing construction
  Gary Burke

D-U-N-S 20-183-6319   (SL)
C.C. MARINE DISTRIBUTORS INC
460 Harry Walker Pky S, Newmarket, ON, L3Y 8E3
(905) 830-0000
Emp Here 30   *Sales* 14,250,780
SIC 5088 Transportation equipment and supplies
  Charles C. Bulmer Jr
  Pandien Dason

D-U-N-S 20-823-3908   (SL)
CE DE CANDY COMPANY LIMITED
(*Suby of* CE DE CANDY, INC.)
150 Harry Walker Pky N, Newmarket, ON, L3Y 7B2
(905) 853-7171
Emp Here 120   *Sales* 41,482,800
SIC 2064 Candy and other confectionery products
  Cyril Wolfe
  Jonathan Dee

D-U-N-S 20-375-0906   (BR)
CELESTICA INTERNATIONAL LP
(*Suby of* ONEX CORPORATION)
213 Harry Walker Pky S, Newmarket, ON, L3Y 8T3
(416) 448-2559
Emp Here 700
SIC 3672 Printed circuit boards

D-U-N-S 24-795-6865   (HQ)
CHILDREN AND FAMILY SERVICES FOR YORK REGION
YORK REGION CHILDREN AID SOCIETY
16915 Leslie St, Newmarket, ON, L3Y 9A1
(905) 895-2318
Emp Here 100   *Sales* 16,894,240
SIC 8322 Individual and family services
  Patrick Lake
  Tammy Ward

D-U-N-S 25-501-0282   (BR)
CINTAS CANADA LIMITED
SALLY FOURMY & ASSOCIATES
(*Suby of* CINTAS CORPORATION)
255 Harry Walker Pky S Suite 1, Newmarket, ON, L3Y 8Z5
(905) 853-4409
Emp Here 150
SIC 7213 Linen supply
  Todd Willford

D-U-N-S 20-769-4407   (SL)
COLONIAL CHEVROLET LTD
18100 Yonge St, Newmarket, ON, L3Y 8V1
(905) 895-1171
Emp Here 68   *Sales* 42,791,040
SIC 5511 New and used car dealers
  Leslie Kensit
  Larry Kensit

D-U-N-S 24-047-0260   (HQ)
COMMUNITY LIVING NEWMARKET/AURORA DISTRICT
195 Harry Walker Pky N, Newmarket, ON, L3Y 7B3
(905) 773-6346
Emp Here 20   *Sales* 43,484,280
SIC 8399 Social services, nec
  Larry Palmer

D-U-N-S 24-203-3368   (SL)
CONCORD SCREEN INC
1311 Kerrisdale Blvd, Newmarket, ON, L3Y 8Z8
(905) 953-8100
Emp Here 28   *Sales* 13,300,728
SIC 5085 Industrial supplies
  Brian Mcbain
  Sean Henderson

D-U-N-S 24-868-4821   (SL)
CORRPAR INDUSTRIES LTD
17775 Leslie St, Newmarket, ON, L3Y 3E3
(905) 836-4599
Emp Here 55   *Sales* 12,838,925
SIC 2653 Corrugated and solid fiber boxes
  Norman Badat

D-U-N-S 20-163-5547   (HQ)
DIESEL EQUIPMENT LIMITED
DEL EQUIPMENT
210 Harry Walker Pky N, Newmarket, ON, L3Y 7B4
(416) 421-5851
Emp Here 5   *Sales* 61,078,500
SIC 3713 Truck and bus bodies
  Paul Martin
  Terry Quinn
  David Martin
  Roger Martin

D-U-N-S 24-044-4369   (SL)
DIRECT SUPPORT CARE INC
236 Parkview Cres, Newmarket, ON, L3Y 2C8
(905) 895-5800
Emp Here 135   *Sales* 10,536,480
SIC 8049 Offices of health practitioner
  Anne Mcdonald

D-U-N-S 20-132-0249   (HQ)
DIXON TICONDEROGA INC
(*Suby of* PENCIL SPA)
210 Pony Dr Unit 1, Newmarket, ON, L3Y 7B6
(905) 895-5122
Sales 11,995,200
SIC 5112 Stationery and office supplies
  Brian Lane
  Pam Mills

D-U-N-S 24-738-3417   (BR)
EXCO TECHNOLOGIES LIMITED
EXCO ENGINEERING
(*Suby of* EXCO TECHNOLOGIES LIMITED)
1314 Ringwell Dr, Newmarket, ON, L3Y 9C6
(905) 853-8568
Emp Here 140
SIC 3544 Special dies, tools, jigs, and fixtures
  Jan Tesar

D-U-N-S 25-301-2686   (BR)
EXTENDICARE (CANADA) INC
PARAMED HOME HEALTH CARE
(*Suby of* EXTENDICARE INC)
320 Harry Walker Pky N Suite 11, Newmarket, ON, L3Y 7B4

Emp Here 80
SIC 8051 Skilled nursing care facilities
  Debra Mancini

D-U-N-S 20-716-1886   (SL)
FORD, WAYNE SALES LIMITED
CANADIAN TIRE STORE
17750 Yonge St, Newmarket, ON, L3Y 8P4
(905) 895-4565
Emp Here 195   *Sales* 122,709,600
SIC 5531 Auto and home supply stores
  Wayne Ford

D-U-N-S 25-671-4312   (BR)
HOME DEPOT OF CANADA INC
HOME DEPOT
(*Suby of* THE HOME DEPOT INC)
17850 Yonge St, Newmarket, ON, L3Y 8S1
(905) 898-0090
Emp Here 200
SIC 5251 Hardware stores
  Erik Penno

D-U-N-S 24-789-0945   (SL)
ICD INSURANCE BROKERS LTD
569 Steven Crt Suite 5, Newmarket, ON, L3Y 6Z3
(905) 830-9000
Emp Here 23   *Sales* 13,338,252
SIC 6411 Insurance agents, brokers, and service
  Robert Zolumoff
  Giuseppe Craparotta

D-U-N-S 20-071-4603   (SL)
INSIGHTU.COM INC
INSIGHT U
350 Harry Walker Pky N Suite 14, Newmarket, ON, L3Y 8L3
(905) 883-9620
Emp Here 39   *Sales* 10,698,948
SIC 8741 Management services
  Kevin Dixon
  Dagmar Dixon
  Susan Easby
  Ron Easby
  Jack Steckel

D-U-N-S 24-409-4561   (SL)
INSTACHANGE DISPLAYS LIMITED
(*Suby of* JORDAN INDUSTRIES, INC.)
360 Harry Walker Pky S Unit 1-3, Newmarket, ON, L3Y 9E9
(289) 279-1100
Emp Here 35   *Sales* 11,414,760
SIC 3993 Signs and advertising specialties
  Howard Topping

D-U-N-S 24-664-4058   (HQ)
INTERROLL CANADA LIMITED
1201 Gorham St, Newmarket, ON, L3Y 8Y2
(905) 953-8510
Sales 18,870,085
SIC 3535 Conveyors and conveying equipment
  Tim Mcgill

D-U-N-S 24-365-7186   (SL)
JET ICE LIMITED
1091 Kerrisdale Blvd, Newmarket, ON, L3Y 8W1
(905) 853-4204
Emp Here 23   *Sales* 17,077,960
SIC 5198 Paints, varnishes, and supplies
  Deborah Wilcock

D-U-N-S 24-384-8504   (HQ)
LAKE SIMCOE REGION CONSERVATION AUTHORITY
LSRCA
120 Bayview Pky, Newmarket, ON, L3Y 3W3
(905) 895-1281
Emp Here 1   *Sales* 41,429,510
SIC 8999 Services, nec
  Virginia Hackson
  Gale Wood

D-U-N-S 24-121-1320   (BR)
LOBLAWS SUPERMARKETS LIMITED
REAL CANADIAN SUPERSTORE
(*Suby of* LOBLAW COMPANIES LIMITED)
18120 Yonge St, Newmarket, ON, L3Y 4V8

(905) 830-4072
Emp Here 250
SIC 5411 Grocery stores
  Marc Boucher

D-U-N-S 25-105-3377   (HQ)
LOTEK WIRELESS INC
(*Suby of* LOTEK GROUP INC, THE)
115 Pony Dr, Newmarket, ON, L3Y 7B5
(905) 836-5329
Sales 21,448,680
SIC 8711 Engineering services
  James Lotimer
  Ronald J Batten
  Peter L Anson
  Andrew Heinrzman
  John Vanden Elzen

D-U-N-S 24-353-4471   (BR)
LOWE'S COMPANIES CANADA, ULC
LOWE'S OF E. GWILLIMBURY
(*Suby of* LOWE'S COMPANIES, INC.)
18401 Yonge St, Newmarket, ON, L3Y 4V8
(905) 952-2950
Emp Here 200
SIC 5211 Lumber and other building materials
  Bill Gogen

D-U-N-S 20-276-0781   (SL)
M.A.R.C. MANAGEMENT & ENTERTAINMENT INC
1135 Stellar Dr, Newmarket, ON, L3Y 7B8

Emp Here 100   *Sales* 17,731,100
SIC 7374 Data processing and preparation
  Christopher Shawn Humphries

D-U-N-S 20-875-8631   (SL)
MACIVER DODGE LIMITED
MACIVER DODGE JEEP
17615 Yonge St, Newmarket, ON, L3Y 5H6
(905) 898-1900
Emp Here 54   *Sales* 33,981,120
SIC 5511 New and used car dealers
  Ian Maciver

D-U-N-S 24-037-6397   (SL)
MACIVER DODGE-JEEP LTD
17615 Yonge St, Newmarket, ON, L3Y 5H6
(905) 898-1900
Emp Here 60   *Sales* 37,756,800
SIC 5511 New and used car dealers
  Frank Caietta

D-U-N-S 24-425-7390   (SL)
MACNAMARA, SAMUEL P. ENTERPRISES LIMITED
MACNAMARA FUELS
2220 Davis Dr, Newmarket, ON, L3Y 4W1
(905) 898-5678
Emp Here 12   *Sales* 12,393,696
SIC 5172 Petroleum products, nec
  Samuel Macnamara

D-U-N-S 24-704-7889   (BR)
MARS CANADA INC
(*Suby of* MARS, INCORPORATED)
285 Harry Walker Pky N, Newmarket, ON, L3Y 7B3
(905) 853-6000
Emp Here 115
SIC 2064 Candy and other confectionery products
  Lori Rodger

D-U-N-S 25-300-0376   (BR)
METRO ONTARIO INC
(*Suby of* METRO INC)
17725 Yonge St Suite 1, Newmarket, ON, L3Y 7C1
(905) 895-9700
Emp Here 150
SIC 5411 Grocery stores
  Michael Boddy

D-U-N-S 20-555-6579   (BR)
METRO ONTARIO INC
METRO

(*Suby of* METRO INC)
1111 Davis Dr, Newmarket, ON, L3Y 9E5
(905) 853-5355
Emp Here 230
SIC 5411 Grocery stores

D-U-N-S 25-332-5617   (SL)
MICROCEL CORPORATION
1274 Ringwell Dr Unit 2, Newmarket, ON, L3Y
9C7
(905) 853-2568
Emp Here 25   *Sales* 11,179,350
SIC 5065 Electronic parts and equipment, nec
Richard Henry
Abraham Cherian
Ali Mroue
Steven Medlar

D-U-N-S 24-311-3813   (BR)
MILLER, P.G. ENTERPRISES LIMITED
MCDONALD'S
(*Suby of* MILLER, P.G. ENTERPRISES LIM-
ITED)
1100 Davis Dr, Newmarket, ON, L3Y 8W8
(905) 853-0118
Emp Here 90
SIC 5812 Eating places
Neil Mcphee

D-U-N-S 20-801-1887   (BR)
MILLER, P.G. ENTERPRISES LIMITED
MCDONALDS
(*Suby of* MILLER, P.G. ENTERPRISES LIM-
ITED)
17760 Yonge St, Newmarket, ON, L3Y 8P4
(905) 895-1222
Emp Here 80
SIC 5812 Eating places
Peter Miller

D-U-N-S 24-074-8830   (SL)
NEW MARKET INVESTMENT LIMITED
NEW MARKET HONDA
75 Mulock Dr, Newmarket, ON, L3Y 8V2
(416) 798-7854
Emp Here 34   *Sales* 16,934,652
SIC 5511 New and used car dealers
Kevin Pearson
Doug Moshoian

D-U-N-S 20-558-5987   (SL)
NEW MARKET MEAT PACKERS LTD
15452 Warden Ave, Newmarket, ON, L3Y
4W1
(905) 836-7001
Emp Here 27   *Sales* 22,560,579
SIC 5147 Meats and meat products
Nicola D'elia
Gino Plastino
Nick D'elia

D-U-N-S 20-113-1203   (SL)
NEWMARKET HYDRO HOLDINGS INC
(*Suby of* CORPORATION OF THE TOWN OF
NEWMARKET)
590 Steven Crt, Newmarket, ON, L3Y 6Z2
(905) 895-2309
Emp Here 38   *Sales* 23,811,332
SIC 4911 Electric services
Paul Ferguson

D-U-N-S 24-360-0686   (SL)
**NEWMARKET-TAY POWER DISTRIBUTION
LTD**
590 Steven Crt, Newmarket, ON, L3Y 6Z2
(905) 895-2309
Emp Here 40   *Sales* 25,064,560
SIC 4911 Electric services
Paul Ferguson
U. Phillip Daniels
Andreas (Andy) Ott
Scott Warnock
Paul H. Nelson
Tom Taylor
Tony Van Bynen

D-U-N-S 20-311-4384   (SL)
NOOELEC INC

NOOELEC
250 Harry Walker Pky N Unit 3, Newmarket,
ON, L3Y 7B4
(888) 653-3532
Emp Here 40   *Sales* 17,886,960
SIC 5065 Electronic parts and equipment, nec
Jeff Crispino
Melissa Clark

D-U-N-S 25-540-8254   (SL)
**NORTH AMERICAN METALS OF CANADA
LTD**
EUROSPEC
130 Harry Walker Pky N, Newmarket, ON, L3Y
7B2
(905) 898-2291
Emp Here 100   *Sales* 19,208,500
SIC 3469 Metal stampings, nec
Christopher Potter
Steven Potter
Kevin Botham

D-U-N-S 20-966-2555   (SL)
NUVU CORPORATION
NETVERSITY SOLUTIONS
450 Harry Walker Pky S, Newmarket, ON, L3Y
8E3
(905) 952-2288
Emp Here 10   *Sales* 10,003,390
SIC 5051 Metals service centers and offices
Michael Gauthier
Colin Padley

D-U-N-S 20-817-2460   (HQ)
**ONTARIO SOCIETY FOR THE PREVEN-
TION OF CRUELTY TO ANIMALS, THE**
ONTARIO HUMANE SOCIETY
16586 Woodbine Ave Suite 3, Newmarket,
ON, L3Y 4W1
(905) 898-7122
Emp Here 25   *Sales* 215,790,150
SIC 8699 Membership organizations, nec
Kate Macdonald
Lisa Veit

D-U-N-S 20-553-2141   (SL)
OPEN ROAD MOTORS INC
OPEN ROAD BMW
87 Mulock Dr, Newmarket, ON, L3Y 8V2
(905) 895-8700
Emp Here 25   *Sales* 12,451,950
SIC 5511 New and used car dealers
Michael Croxon

D-U-N-S 25-096-9326   (BR)
PEARSON CANADA HOLDINGS INC
(*Suby of* PEARSON PLC)
195 Harry Walker Pky N Suite A, Newmarket,
ON, L3Y 7B3
(905) 853-7888
Emp Here 200
SIC 2731 Book publishing
John Makinson

D-U-N-S 20-705-6172   (BR)
PEARSON CANADA INC
PENGUIN BOOKS CANADA
(*Suby of* PEARSON PLC)
195 Harry Walker Pky N Suite A, Newmarket,
ON, L3Y 7B3
(905) 853-7888
Emp Here 700
SIC 2731 Book publishing
Allan Reynolds

D-U-N-S 24-181-2064   (SL)
PICKERING COLLEGE
16945 Bayview Ave, Newmarket, ON, L3Y
4X2
(905) 895-1700
Emp Here 105   *Sales* 10,407,495
SIC 8211 Elementary and secondary schools
Peter Sturrup
Ian Proudfoot
Charles Beer
Gilles Cinq-Mars
Dawn Beswick

Beth Egan
Richard Geurts
Jonathan Knaul
Jennifer Mitchinson
Glenor Pitters

D-U-N-S 25-203-0341   (SL)
**PLASSEIN INTERNATIONAL OF NEWMAR-
KET INC**
175 Deerfield Rd, Newmarket, ON, L3Y 2L8
(905) 895-2308
Emp Here 184
SIC 3081 Unsupported plastics film and sheet

D-U-N-S 20-706-3517   (BR)
REGIONAL MUNICIPALITY OF YORK, THE
NEWMARKET HEALTH CENTRE, THE
(*Suby of* REGIONAL MUNICIPALITY OF
YORK, THE)
194 Eagle St Suite 3011, Newmarket, ON,
L3Y 1J6
(905) 895-2382
Emp Here 400
SIC 8051 Skilled nursing care facilities
Carol Hotchkiss

D-U-N-S 20-938-2964   (BR)
REVERA LONG TERM CARE INC
MACKENZIE PLCE
(*Suby of* GOVERNMENT OF CANADA)
52 George St, Newmarket, ON, L3Y 4V3
(905) 853-3242
Emp Here 90
SIC 8059 Nursing and personal care, nec
Sanja Freeborn

D-U-N-S 20-771-1750   (SL)
RIGA FARMS LTD
RIGA FARMS
19810 Dufferin St, Newmarket, ON, L3Y 4V9
(905) 775-4217
Emp Here 31   *Sales* 10,616,477
SIC 0161 Vegetables and melons
Rosario Riga

D-U-N-S 20-967-9526   (SL)
S I METRIC MANIFACTURING LTD
150 Pony Dr, Newmarket, ON, L3Y 7B6
(905) 898-6322
Emp Here 40   *Sales* 18,187,797
SIC 5049 Professional equipment, nec
Brian Arthurs

D-U-N-S 24-351-8300   (SL)
SHANAHAN CARRIAGE CO. LTD, THE
567 Davis Dr, Newmarket, ON, L3Y 2P5
(416) 798-4858
Emp Here 50   *Sales* 24,903,900
SIC 5511 New and used car dealers
Michael Shanahan

D-U-N-S 25-099-3029   (SL)
SHANAHAN FORD LINCOLN SALES
567 Davis Dr, Newmarket, ON, L3Y 2P5
(905) 853-5000
Emp Here 56   *Sales* 14,646,968
SIC 6719 Holding companies, nec
Michael Shanahan

D-U-N-S 25-204-7006   (SL)
**SILVER LAKES GOLF & COUNTRY CLUB
INC**
21114 Yonge St, Newmarket, ON, L3Y 4V8
(905) 836-8070
Emp Here 80   *Sales* 6,111,760
SIC 7997 Membership sports and recreation
clubs
Harold Macdonald

D-U-N-S 25-915-7543   (BR)
SNAP-ON TOOLS OF CANADA LTD
SNAP-ON TOOLS OF CANADA LTD
(*Suby of* SNAP-ON INCORPORATED)
145 Harry Walker Pky N, Newmarket, ON, L3Y
7B3
(905) 812-5774
Emp Here 250
SIC 3469 Metal stampings, nec

Larry Durst

D-U-N-S 20-045-7471   (HQ)
SNAP-ON TOOLS OF CANADA LTD
INDUSTRIAL DIVISION
(*Suby of* SNAP-ON INCORPORATED)
195 Harry Walker Pky N Unit A, Newmarket,
ON, L3Y 7B3
(905) 836-8121
Emp Here 11   *Sales* 184,461,600
SIC 5013 Motor vehicle supplies and new
parts
Brian Ross
Thomas J. Ward

D-U-N-S 20-912-2352   (HQ)
SOCIAL ENTERPRISE FOR CANADA
*ACCREDITATION ASSISTANCE ACCESS
CENTRE*
17705a Leslie St Suite 202, Newmarket, ON,
L3Y 3E3
(905) 895-0809
Sales 56,736,960
SIC 8699 Membership organizations, nec
Patricia Cousins
Judy Shawney

D-U-N-S 20-846-7324   (HQ)
SOUTHLAKE REGIONAL HEALTH CENTRE
596 Davis Dr, Newmarket, ON, L3Y 2P9
(905) 895-4521
Sales 320,800,413
SIC 8062 General medical and surgical hospi-
tals
Arden Krystal
Helena Hutton
Annette Jones
Rob Bull
Rick Gowrie

D-U-N-S 20-559-9855   (SL)
**SPECTRUM EDUCATIONAL SUPPLIES
LIMITED**
SI MANUFACTURING
(*Suby of* GENEVE HOLDINGS, INC.)
150 Pony Dr, Newmarket, ON, L3Y 7B6
(905) 898-0031
Emp Here 70   *Sales* 17,102,960
SIC 5961 Catalog and mail-order houses
Brett Caldwell
Francis Lui

D-U-N-S 24-422-7500   (HQ)
SPINNAKER INDUSTRIES INC
1171 Gorham St, Newmarket, ON, L3Y 8Y2
(416) 742-0598
Sales 28,812,750
SIC 3499 Fabricated Metal products, nec
Maurice Lattanzio
Gunther Schumacher

D-U-N-S 24-986-0461   (SL)
STAIRFAB AND RAILINGS INC
(*Suby of* ALPA LUMBER INC)
450 Kent Dr, Newmarket, ON, L3Y 4Y9
(905) 895-1050
Emp Here 70   *Sales* 13,465,900
SIC 2431 Millwork
Brandon Frankfort
Sam Salerno

D-U-N-S 24-991-3133   (SL)
TECHNICAL CONCRETE SOLUTIONS LTD
TCS CONSTRUCTION
1341 Kerrisdale Blvd, Newmarket, ON, L3Y
8W8
(905) 761-9330
Emp Here 65   *Sales* 12,438,010
SIC 7353 Heavy construction equipment
rental
Robert Giordano

D-U-N-S 24-688-3458   (HQ)
THERMOR LTD
16975 Leslie St, Newmarket, ON, L3Y 9A1
(905) 952-3737
Sales 13,415,220
SIC 5047 Medical and hospital equipment

Gary Reed
David Reed
Mark Beaton

D-U-N-S 25-529-1908   (HQ)
TORQUIN CORPORATION LIMITED
200 Pony Dr, Newmarket, ON, L3Y 7B6
(905) 836-0988
Emp Here 1   *Sales* 43,309,240
SIC 7359 Equipment rental and leasing, nec
Ronald Craig

D-U-N-S 24-765-5384   (HQ)
TS TECH CANADA INC
(*Suby of* TS TECH CO., LTD.)
17855 Leslie St, Newmarket, ON, L3Y 3E3
(905) 953-0098
Sales 89,066,000
SIC 2531 Public building and related furniture
Isao Okada

D-U-N-S 24-937-9439   (HQ)
TURF CARE PRODUCTS CANADA LIMITED
CANADIAN CART SALES, DIV OF
(*Suby of* TORQUIN CORPORATION LIM-
ITED)
200 Pony Dr, Newmarket, ON, L3Y 7B6
(905) 836-0988
Emp Here 85   *Sales* 27,750,125
SIC 3523 Farm machinery and equipment
Ronald Craig
John Jarman
Jamie Worden

D-U-N-S 25-163-6098   (HQ)
TURN KEY STAFFING SOLUTIONS INC
200 Davis Dr Suite 7, Newmarket, ON, L3Y
2N4
(905) 953-9133
Emp Here 1   *Sales* 15,537,100
SIC 7363 Help supply services
Tammy Agnew

D-U-N-S 20-967-9633   (HQ)
UNITY CONNECTED SOLUTIONS INC
UNITY
450 Harry Walker Pky S, Newmarket, ON, L3Y
8E3
(905) 952-2475
Emp Here 75   *Sales* 64,987,664
SIC 5065 Electronic parts and equipment, nec
Erin Sherry
Randy Bergeron

D-U-N-S 20-552-7182   (HQ)
VEOLIA WATER CANADA, INC
(*Suby of* VEOLIA ENVIRONNEMENT)
150 Pony Dr Unit 2, Newmarket, ON, L3Y 7B6
(905) 868-9683
Emp Here 2   *Sales* 33,483,800
SIC 4941 Water supply
Laurent Auguste
Mark Rupke
Brian J. Clarke
Mary Kamstra
Francis X. Ferrara

D-U-N-S 24-277-7928   (HQ)
VILLEROY & BOCH TABLEWARE LTD
VILLEROY & BOCH CANADA
(*Suby of* VILLEROY & BOCH AG)
1100 Gorham St Unit 22, Newmarket, ON,
L3Y 8Y8
(705) 458-0435
Emp Here 10   *Sales* 16,283,392
SIC 5023 Homefurnishings
Bernard Reuter

D-U-N-S 25-294-7502   (BR)
WAL-MART CANADA CORP
(*Suby of* WALMART INC.)
17940 Yonge St, Newmarket, ON, L3Y 8S4
(905) 853-8811
Emp Here 240
SIC 5311 Department stores
Qushair Rick

D-U-N-S 24-098-3432   (BR)

WE CARE HEALTH SERVICES INC
(*Suby of* WE CARE HEALTH SERVICES INC)
1124 Stellar Dr, Newmarket, ON, L3Y 7B7
(905) 715-7950
Emp Here 120
SIC 8082 Home health care services
Leslie Nead

D-U-N-S 20-105-3076   (HQ)
XE CORPORATION
XE.COM
1145 Nicholson Rd Suite 200, Newmarket,
ON, L3Y 9C3
(416) 214-5606
Sales 19,134,500
SIC 6712 Bank holding companies
Beric Farmer
Steven Dengler
Mina Nesiem
Susan Moreland
Magued Hanna
Leanne Christopher
Jl Verboomen

D-U-N-S 24-563-0157   (HQ)
**YOR-SUP-NET SUPPORT SERVICE NET-
WORK**
YORK SUPPORT SERVICES NETWORK
102 Main St S Unit 3, Newmarket, ON, L3Y
3Y7
(905) 898-3721
Emp Here 58   *Sales* 13,345,900
SIC 8399 Social services, nec
Mary Lauzier

D-U-N-S 25-151-0327   (BR)
**YORK CATHOLIC DISTRICT SCHOOL
BOARD**
SACRED HEART HIGH SCHOOL
(*Suby of* YORK CATHOLIC DISTRICT
SCHOOL BOARD)
1 Crusader Way, Newmarket, ON, L3Y 6R2
(905) 895-3340
Emp Here 100
SIC 8211 Elementary and secondary schools
John Heinrich

D-U-N-S 25-931-5513   (SL)
YORK COUNTY BOWMEN INC
15887 Mccowan Rd, Newmarket, ON, L3Y
4W1
Emp Here 80   *Sales* 7,723,999
SIC 7999 Amusement and recreation, nec
Willy Wakenhut

D-U-N-S 25-293-5937   (BR)
YORK REGION DISTRICT SCHOOL BOARD
NEWMARKET HIGH SCHOOL
(*Suby of* YORK REGION DISTRICT SCHOOL
BOARD)
505 Pickering Cres, Newmarket, ON, L3Y 8H1
(905) 895-5159
Emp Here 85
SIC 8211 Elementary and secondary schools
Shawn Bredin

D-U-N-S 25-293-5895   (BR)
YORK REGION DISTRICT SCHOOL BOARD
HURON HEIGHTS SECONDARY SCHOOL
(*Suby of* YORK REGION DISTRICT SCHOOL
BOARD)
40 Huron Heights Dr, Newmarket, ON, L3Y
3J9
(905) 895-2384
Emp Here 175
SIC 8211 Elementary and secondary schools
Mirella Sanwalka

D-U-N-S 25-293-5978   (BR)
YORK REGION DISTRICT SCHOOL BOARD
*DR. JOHN M. DENISON SECONDARY
SCHOOL*
(*Suby of* YORK REGION DISTRICT SCHOOL
BOARD)
135 Bristol Rd, Newmarket, ON, L3Y 8J7
(905) 836-0021
Emp Here 105

SIC 8211 Elementary and secondary schools
Janet Atkinson

D-U-N-S 24-986-2715   (HQ)
ZAHID, M. DRUGS LTD
SHOPPERS DRUG MART
1111 Davis Dr Suite 46, Newmarket, ON, L3Y
8X2
(905) 898-7771
Emp Here 60   *Sales* 26,876,080
SIC 5912 Drug stores and proprietary stores
Mohammed Zahid

Newton, ON N0K

D-U-N-S 20-899-9172   (SL)
BIMINI UNITED CHURCH CAMP
3180 113 Rd, Newton, ON, N0K 1V0
(519) 271-4129
Emp Here 85   *Sales* 7,878,650
SIC 7032 Sporting and recreational camps
Jim Drummond

Niagara Falls, ON L2E

D-U-N-S 24-538-0837   (SL)
647802 ONTARIO LIMITED
SOUVENIR CITY
4199 River Rd, Niagara Falls, ON, L2E 3E7
(905) 357-1133
Emp Here 70   *Sales* 17,102,960
SIC 5947 Gift, novelty, and souvenir shop
Joseph Dicosimo
Frank Dicosimo
Tim Geddes

D-U-N-S 24-602-3725   (SL)
828324 ONTARIO LIMITED
DESIGN ELECTRONICS
6913 Oakwood Dr, Niagara Falls, ON, L2E
6S5
(905) 646-3333
Emp Here 34   *Sales* 15,203,916
SIC 5065 Electronic parts and equipment, nec
Lorne Bjorgan
Barbara Bjorgan

D-U-N-S 25-179-3121   (SL)
A-A-A BATTERIES LTD
NIAGARA BATTERY & TIRE
5559 George St, Niagara Falls, ON, L2E 7K9
(905) 371-0666
Emp Here 25   *Sales* 12,451,950
SIC 5531 Auto and home supply stores
Jim Titul

D-U-N-S 24-362-5394   (SL)
**CAN-ENG FURNACES INTERNATIONAL
LTD**
(*Suby of* CAN-ENG PARTNERS LTD)
6800 Montrose Rd, Niagara Falls, ON, L2E
6V5
(905) 356-1327
Emp Here 85   *Sales* 18,870,085
SIC 3567 Industrial furnaces and ovens
Alan Van Geyn
John Krediet

D-U-N-S 24-378-7194   (HQ)
CAN-ENG PARTNERS LTD
6800 Montrose Rd, Niagara Falls, ON, L2E
6V5
(905) 356-1327
Sales 19,536,088
SIC 3567 Industrial furnaces and ovens
Alan Van Geyn
G. John Krediet
Gerrit Van Geyn
Chris Krediet
Rudolph Krediet

D-U-N-S 20-132-9349   (HQ)

CANADIAN NIAGARA HOTELS INC
SKYLINE SHERATON ON THE FALLS
5685 Falls Ave 3rd-5th Fl, Niagara Falls, ON,
L2E 6W7
(905) 374-4444
Sales 81,317,800
SIC 7011 Hotels and motels
Dino Dicienzo

D-U-N-S 20-272-7863   (SL)
COMPLEX SUPPLY INC
(*Suby of* CASINO NIAGARA LIMITED)
Po Box 300 Stn Main, Niagara Falls, ON, L2E
6T3
(905) 374-6928
Emp Here 100   *Sales* 9,495,300
SIC 7999 Amusement and recreation, nec
Clare Copeland
Bruce Clarke Caughill
Kevin Wilson
Art Frank

D-U-N-S 25-347-7335   (SL)
COTTON INC
COTTON READY MIX
2125 Fruitbelt Dr, Niagara Falls, ON, L2E 6S4
(905) 262-2000
Emp Here 115   *Sales* 28,311,390
SIC 1794 Excavation work
Mike Colaneri
Jack Van Beek
Gerald Penney

D-U-N-S 24-507-2814   (HQ)
**CRAWFORD SMITH & SWALLOW CHAR-
TERED ACCOUNTANTS LLP**
4741 Queen St, Niagara Falls, ON, L2E 2M2
(905) 356-4200
Emp Here 50   *Sales* 15,576,375
SIC 8721 Accounting, auditing, and book-
keeping
Robert Smith
John Swallow

D-U-N-S 24-048-0793   (SL)
DIGITAL ATTRACTIONS INC
6650 Niagara River, Niagara Falls, ON, L2E
6T2
(905) 371-2003
Emp Here 100   *Sales* 8,962,900
SIC 7221 Photographic studios, portrait
Lindsey Deluca

D-U-N-S 20-181-1262   (HQ)
E.S. FOX LIMITED
FOX CONSTRUCTORS
9127 Montrose Rd, Niagara Falls, ON, L2E
7J9
(905) 354-3700
Emp Here 150   *Sales* 270,848,000
SIC 1711 Plumbing, heating, air-conditioning
E Spencer Fox
Ernest Downes
Robert Arsenault
Denis Carrier

D-U-N-S 24-773-9878   (HQ)
FENA INSURANCE SOLUTIONS INC
4056 Dorchester Rd Unit 2, Niagara Falls, ON,
L2E 6M9
(905) 356-3362
Emp Here 10   *Sales* 11,598,480
SIC 6411 Insurance agents, brokers, and ser-
vice
Jack Muraco

D-U-N-S 24-078-9339   (HQ)
GALE'S GAS BARS LIMITED
GALE'S FUELS
4388 Portage Rd, Niagara Falls, ON, L2E 6A4
(905) 356-4820
Emp Here 9   *Sales* 56,635,200
SIC 5541 Gasoline service stations
Jessica Friesen

D-U-N-S 24-045-0817   (BR)
**GOVERNING COUNCIL OF THE SALVA-
TION ARMY IN CANADA, THE**

EVENTIDE HOME
(*Suby of* GOVERNING COUNCIL OF THE
SALVATION ARMY IN CANADA, THE)
5050 Jepson St, Niagara Falls, ON, L2E 1K5
(905) 356-1221
Emp Here 100
SIC 8051 Skilled nursing care facilities
Randy Randell

D-U-N-S 20-362-8987   (SL)
GROUP EMPORIO CONSTRUCTION INC
4025 Dorchester Rd Suite 338, Niagara Falls,
ON, L2E 7K8

Emp Here 60   *Sales* 16,256,520
SIC 1521 Single-family housing construction
Manuel Oliveira

D-U-N-S 24-119-3775   (BR)
HATCH LTD
HATCH ENERGY
(*Suby of* HATCHCOS HOLDINGS LTD)
4342 Queen St Suite 500, Niagara Falls, ON,
L2E 7J7
(905) 374-5200
Emp Here 1,000
SIC 8711 Engineering services
Robert Dawson

D-U-N-S 20-514-9367   (BR)
HOME DEPOT OF CANADA INC
HOME DEPOT
(*Suby of* THE HOME DEPOT INC)
7190 Morrison St, Niagara Falls, ON, L2E 7K5
(905) 371-7470
Emp Here 150
SIC 5211 Lumber and other building materials
Kelly Ritossa

D-U-N-S 24-048-2125   (HQ)
LOCOCO, A. WHOLESALE LTD
LOCOCO'S FRUITS & VEGTABLES
4167 Victoria Ave, Niagara Falls, ON, L2E 4B2
(905) 358-3281
Emp Here 3   *Sales* 23,478,160
SIC 5431 Fruit and vegetable markets
Daniel Lococo
Erin Lococo
Cecelia Lococo

D-U-N-S 20-310-9533   (SL)
LOOP RECYCLED PRODUCTS INC
940 Chippawa Creek Rd, Niagara Falls, ON,
L2E 6S5
(905) 353-0068
Emp Here 62   *Sales* 16,594,424
SIC 5231 Paint, glass, and wallpaper stores
Josh Wiwcharyk
James Shannon

D-U-N-S 25-835-6682   (BR)
NIAGARA PARKS COMMISSION, THE
QUEEN VICTORIA PLACE
(*Suby of* NIAGARA PARKS COMMISSION,
THE)
6345 Niagara Pkwy, Niagara Falls, ON, L2E
6T2
(905) 356-2217
Emp Here 90
SIC 5812 Eating places
Linda Boucher

D-U-N-S 20-009-8023   (BR)
NIAGARA PARKS COMMISSION, THE
TABLE ROCK RESTAURANT
(*Suby of* NIAGARA PARKS COMMISSION,
THE)
6650 Niagara Pky, Niagara Falls, ON, L2E 6T2
(877) 642-7275
Emp Here 100
SIC 5812 Eating places
Erin Muir

D-U-N-S 24-423-2203   (SL)
NIAGARA PENINSULA ENERGY INC
7447 Pin Oak Dr, Niagara Falls, ON, L2E 6S9
(905) 356-2681
Emp Here 130   *Sales* 88,383,620

SIC 4911 Electric services
Brian Wilkie
Janie Palmer
Russell Lowden
Suzanne Wilson
Daniel Sebert
Thomas Sielicki
Margaret Battista
Wayne Thomson
Carolynn Loannoni
Brian Walker

D-U-N-S 25-673-1597   (SL)
OXY VINYLS CANADA CO
(*Suby of* OCCIDENTAL PETROLEUM COR-
PORATION)
8800 Thorold Town Line, Niagara Falls, ON,
L2E 6V9
(905) 357-3131
Emp Here 163   *Sales* 46,295,423
SIC 2821 Plastics materials and resins
Rob Peterson
Angie Belcastro

D-U-N-S 20-124-5503   (HQ)
POLYONE CANADA INC
(*Suby of* POLYONE CORPORATION)
940 Chippawa Creek Rd, Niagara Falls, ON,
L2E 6S5
(905) 353-4200
Emp Here 50   *Sales* 56,804,200
SIC 2821 Plastics materials and resins
Thomas Waltermire
Michel Roy
Mario Tremblay

D-U-N-S 24-572-5200   (BR)
TRENTWAY-WAGAR INC
(*Suby of* COACH USA ADMINISTRATION,
INC.)
4555 Erie Ave, Niagara Falls, ON, L2E 7G9
(905) 358-7230
Emp Here 100
SIC 4111 Local and suburban transit
Brent Rainey

D-U-N-S 20-585-2473   (SL)
**WALKER COMMUNITY DEVELOPMENT
CORP**
2800 Thorold Town Line, Niagara Falls, ON,
L2E 6S4
(905) 227-4142
Emp Here 400   *Sales* 109,354,432
SIC 1422 Crushed and broken limestone
John Fisher

D-U-N-S 24-868-5737   (HQ)
**WALKER INDUSTRIES HOLDINGS LIM-
ITED**
2800 Thorold Town Line, Niagara Falls, ON,
L2E 6S4
(905) 227-4142
Emp Here 200   *Sales* 289,176,300
SIC 1411 Dimension stone
John Fisher
Geordie Walker

D-U-N-S 24-664-1021   (SL)
**WASHINGTON MILLS ELECTRO MINER-
ALS CORPORATION**
(*Suby of* WASHINGTON MILLS GROUP,
INC.)
7780 Stanley Ave, Niagara Falls, ON, L2E 6X8
(905) 357-5500
Emp Here 100   *Sales* 17,921,900
SIC 3291 Abrasive products
Sandro Borghesi
Michael Sproule
Ronald Campbell
Aldon Harris
Warner Fletcher
Nancy Gates

Niagara Falls, ON L2G

D-U-N-S 24-361-6039   (SL)
1712093 ONTARIO LIMITED
FALLSVIEW PLAZA HOTEL
6455 Fallsview Blvd, Niagara Falls, ON, L2G
3V9
(905) 357-5200
Emp Here 150   *Sales* 13,903,500
SIC 7011 Hotels and motels
Carman Menechella

D-U-N-S 24-316-9153   (SL)
2095527 ONTARIO LIMITED
EMBASSY SUITES HOTEL
6740 Fallsview Blvd, Niagara Falls, ON, L2G
3W6
(905) 356-3600
Emp Here 800   *Sales* 76,534,400
SIC 7011 Hotels and motels
Victor Menechella

D-U-N-S 20-379-8694   (SL)
2619473 ONTARIO INC
FACTOR FORMS NIAGARA
8481 Earl Thomas Ave, Niagara Falls, ON,
L2G 0B5
(905) 358-0699
Emp Here 70   *Sales* 10,288,850
SIC 2761 Manifold business forms
Christoph Gleis
Derek Thompson
Kimberly Cuddy

D-U-N-S 24-554-9308   (SL)
577793 ONTARIO INC
RENAISSANCE FALLSVIEW HOTEL
6455 Fallsview Blvd, Niagara Falls, ON, L2G
3V9
(905) 357-1151
Emp Here 150   *Sales* 13,903,500
SIC 7011 Hotels and motels
Robert Saks
Tom Saks

D-U-N-S 20-205-8389   (SL)
727432 ONTARIO LIMITED
RON'S NO FRILLS
6460 Lundy'S Lane, Niagara Falls, ON, L2G
1T6
(905) 357-4623
Emp Here 40   *Sales* 10,966,080
SIC 5411 Grocery stores
Ron Sairburn

D-U-N-S 24-313-6376   (BR)
ARROW GAMES CORPORATION
BAZAAR & NOVELTY
(*Suby of* ARROW INTERNATIONAL, INC.)
6199 Don Murie St, Niagara Falls, ON, L2G
0B1
(905) 354-7300
Emp Here 85
SIC 5092 Toys and hobby goods and supplies
Ian Bright

D-U-N-S 25-293-2744   (BR)
ATLIFIC INC
COMFORT INN NIAGARA FALLS
4960 Clifton Hill, Niagara Falls, ON, L2G 3N4
(905) 358-3293
Emp Here 1,000
SIC 7011 Hotels and motels
Patrick Clary

D-U-N-S 25-227-7637   (HQ)
BOYS AND GIRLS CLUB OF NIAGARA
6681 Culp St, Niagara Falls, ON, L2G 2C5
(905) 357-2444
Emp Here 65   *Sales* 10,715,925
SIC 8641 Civic and social associations
Joanne Hett

D-U-N-S 24-822-9833   (SL)
CADE HOLDING INC
BEST WESTERN CAIRN CROFT HOTEL
6400 Lundy'S Lane, Niagara Falls, ON, L2G
1T6
(905) 356-1161
Emp Here 100   *Sales* 9,489,900

SIC 7011 Hotels and motels
Frederick T Cade
Leonard Cade

D-U-N-S 20-086-9258   (BR)
CANADIAN NIAGARA HOTELS INC
SHERATON ON THE FALLS
(*Suby of* CANADIAN NIAGARA HOTELS INC)
5875 Falls Ave, Niagara Falls, ON, L2G 3K7
(905) 374-4444
Emp Here 100
SIC 7011 Hotels and motels
Sarah Vasquez

D-U-N-S 25-981-5934   (HQ)
CASINO NIAGARA LIMITED
5705 Falls Ave, Niagara Falls, ON, L2G 7M9
(905) 374-6928
Sales 320,790,000
SIC 7999 Amusement and recreation, nec
Brad Hutchings
Jay Meilstrup

D-U-N-S 25-984-9172   (BR)
CASINO NIAGARA INC
(*Suby of* CASINO NIAGARA LIMITED)
5705 Falls Ave, Niagara Falls, ON, L2G 3K6
(905) 374-3598
Emp Here 3,000
SIC 7999 Amusement and recreation, nec
Drew Chamberlain

D-U-N-S 20-124-9567   (SL)
**CHIPPAWA VOLUNTEER FIREFIGHTER
ASSOCIATION**
FIRE DEPARTMENT
8696 Banting Ave, Niagara Falls, ON, L2G 6Z8
(905) 295-4398
Emp Here 40   *Sales* 17,968,760
SIC 7389 Business services, nec
Tim Koabel

D-U-N-S 24-062-2407   (SL)
COLLINS CONCESSIONS LIMITED
8621 Earl Thomas Ave, Niagara Falls, ON,
L2G 0B5

Emp Here 100   *Sales* 34,569,000
SIC 2064 Candy and other confectionery
products
Thomas Collins

D-U-N-S 24-711-3702   (SL)
CYRO CANADA INC
6515 Barker St, Niagara Falls, ON, L2G 1Y6
(905) 677-1388
Emp Here 49   *Sales* 16,309,627
SIC 2821 Plastics materials and resins
Rene Lemay

D-U-N-S 25-525-0144   (SL)
DYACO CANADA INC
(*Suby of* DYACO INTERNATIONAL INC.)
5955 Don Murie St, Niagara Falls, ON, L2G
0A9
(905) 353-8955
Emp Here 26   *Sales* 13,534,092
SIC 5091 Sporting and recreation goods
Brian Patterson
Frank Lucia

D-U-N-S 20-312-9614   (SL)
EXCEL RETAIL LIMITED
CANADIAN TIRE
6840 Mcleod Rd, Niagara Falls, ON, L2G 3G6
(905) 358-0161
Emp Here 49   *Sales* 24,405,822
SIC 5531 Auto and home supply stores
Ray Mcdonald

D-U-N-S 20-736-3271   (SL)
**FALLSVIEW NIAGARA LODGING COM-
PANY**
RADISSON FALLSVIEW
(*Suby of* BUFFALO LODGING ASSOCIATES
LLC)
6733 Fallsview Blvd, Niagara Falls, ON, L2G
3W7

---

(905) 356-1944
Emp Here 82   *Sales* 7,600,580
SIC 7011 Hotels and motels
James Bertulli

D-U-N-S 24-097-4126   (SL)
FAMOUS COFFEE SHOP, THE
6380 Fallsview Blvd Unit R 1, Niagara Falls,
ON, L2G 7Y6
(905) 354-7775
Emp Here 80   *Sales* 3,641,520
SIC 5812 Eating places
Frank Scordino

D-U-N-S 20-132-9935   (SL)
FERGUSON, N. DRUGS LTD
SHOPPER'S DRUG MART
6565 Lundy'S Lane Suite 799, Niagara Falls,
ON, L2G 1V1
(905) 354-3845
Emp Here 40   *Sales* 10,118,160
SIC 5912 Drug stores and proprietary stores
Nina Ferguson

D-U-N-S 24-602-7072   (SL)
FOOD ROLL SALES (NIAGARA) LTD
8464 Earl Thomas Ave, Niagara Falls, ON,
L2G 0B6
(905) 358-5747
Emp Here 50   *Sales* 11,242,750
SIC 2038 Frozen specialties, nec
Henry Wong
Dominic Difranco

D-U-N-S 24-644-1372   (HQ)
GARDEN CITY CUSTOMS SERVICES INC
G C CUSTOMS BROKERS
6045 Progress St, Niagara Falls, ON, L2G 7X1
(905) 353-8735
Emp Here 14   *Sales* 11,959,241
SIC 4731 Freight transportation arrangement
Helmut Hagenberg
Karin Hagenberg

D-U-N-S 20-943-5507   (SL)
HARD ROCK CAFE
5685 Falls Ave, Niagara Falls, ON, L2G 3K6
(905) 356-7625
Emp Here 80   *Sales* 3,641,520
SIC 5812 Eating places
George Mendez

D-U-N-S 20-774-5907   (BR)
HOCO LIMITED
(*Suby of* HOCO LIMITED)
4960 Clifton Hill, Niagara Falls, ON, L2G 3N4
(905) 357-5911
Emp Here 400
SIC 5812 Eating places
Harry Oakes

D-U-N-S 20-132-5578   (HQ)
HOCO LIMITED
COMFORT INN CLIFTON HILL
4960 Clifton Hill, Niagara Falls, ON, L2G 3N4
(905) 358-3293
Emp Here 150   *Sales* 76,534,400
SIC 7011 Hotels and motels
Harry N Oakes
Philip Oakes
Earl Vandenberg
Harry P Oakes

D-U-N-S 20-132-5602   (SL)
HOLIDAY INN (NIAGARA FALLS) LIMITED
HOLIDAY INN BY THE FALLS
5339 Murray St, Niagara Falls, ON, L2G 2J3
(905) 356-1333
Emp Here 80   *Sales* 7,591,920
SIC 7011 Hotels and motels
George Yerich
Violet Yerich

D-U-N-S 20-328-9053   (SL)
HOSPITALITY FALLSVIEW HOLDINGS INC
6361 Fallsview Blvd, Niagara Falls, ON, L2G
3V9
(905) 354-7887
Emp Here 400   *Sales* 146,203,600

SIC 6712 Bank holding companies
Joseph Dicosimo
Vincent Dicosimo Jr
Frank Dicosimo

D-U-N-S 20-968-6401   (HQ)
HOSPITALITY MOTELS LIMITED
FRONTIER RESTAURANT
6361 Fallsview Blvd, Niagara Falls, ON, L2G
3V9
(905) 357-3184
Emp Here 15   *Sales* 66,967,600
SIC 7011 Hotels and motels
Vincent Dicosimo
Joe Dicosimo
Frank Dicosimo
Vince Dicosimo
Ida Dicosimo

D-U-N-S 25-095-4609   (BR)
KERRIO CORPORATION
*APPLEBEE'S NEIGHBORHOOD GRILL &
BAR*
(*Suby of* KERRIO CORPORATION)
6546 Fallsview Blvd, Niagara Falls, ON, L2G
3W2
(905) 356-6965
Emp Here 100
SIC 5812 Eating places
Peter Ennis

D-U-N-S 24-061-8058   (HQ)
MANCUSO CHEMICALS LIMITED
5725 Progress St, Niagara Falls, ON, L2G 0C1
(905) 357-3626
Sales 13,556,340
SIC 2899 Chemical preparations, nec
Antonio Mancuso

D-U-N-S 20-413-2211   (SL)
MODERN MOSAIC LIMITED
8620 Oakwood Dr, Niagara Falls, ON, L2G
0J2
(905) 356-3045
Emp Here 50   *Sales* 12,652,950
SIC 5211 Lumber and other building materials

D-U-N-S 20-132-9091   (HQ)
MYER SALIT LIMITED
SALIT STEEL
7771 Stanley Ave, Niagara Falls, ON, L2G
0C7
(905) 354-5691
Emp Here 126   *Sales* 89,618,100
SIC 5051 Metals service centers and offices
Steven Cohen
Laurence Cohen
Marlene Cohen
Joy Cohen

D-U-N-S 20-563-4210   (BR)
NIAGARA 21ST GROUP INC
*MARRIOTT NIAGARA FALLS FALLSVIEW
HOTEL & SPA*
(*Suby of* NIAGARA 21ST GROUP INC)
6740 Fallsview Blvd, Niagara Falls, ON, L2G
3W6
(905) 357-7300
Emp Here 1,500
SIC 7011 Hotels and motels
David Searel

D-U-N-S 25-984-4561   (HQ)
NIAGARA 21ST GROUP INC
5950 Victoria Ave, Niagara Falls, ON, L2G 3L7
(905) 353-4044
Emp Here 250   *Sales* 57,400,800
SIC 7011 Hotels and motels
Cosmo Menechella

D-U-N-S 20-075-3288   (BR)
**NIAGARA COLLEGE OF APPLIED ARTS &
TECHNOLOGY**
MAID OF THE MIST CAMPUS
(*Suby of* NIAGARA COLLEGE OF APPLIED
ARTS & TECHNOLOGY)
5881 Dunn St, Niagara Falls, ON, L2G 2N9

(905) 735-2211
Emp Here 600
SIC 8221 Colleges and universities
Dan Patterson

D-U-N-S 24-858-6278   (SL)
NIAGARA CONVENTION & CIVIC CENTER
SCOTIABANK CONVENTION CENTER
6815 Stanley Ave, Niagara Falls, ON, L2G 3Y9
(905) 357-6222
Emp Here 150   *Sales* 16,017,300
SIC 7299 Miscellaneous personal service
Kerry Panter

D-U-N-S 24-024-6827   (SL)
NIAGARA FALLS BRIDGE COMMISSION
RAINBOW BRIDGE
5781 River Rd, Niagara Falls, ON, L2G 3K9
(905) 354-5641
Emp Here 40   *Sales* 15,414,400
SIC 4785 Inspection and fixed facilities
Victor Montalbo

D-U-N-S 20-013-2079   (BR)
NIAGARA HEALTH SYSTEM
*THE GREATER NIAGARA GENERAL HOSPI-
TAL*
(*Suby of* NIAGARA HEALTH SYSTEM)
5546 Portage Rd, Niagara Falls, ON, L2G 5X8
(905) 378-4647
Emp Here 950
SIC 8062 General medical and surgical hospi-
tals
Sue Bolibruck

D-U-N-S 25-936-5765   (HQ)
NIAGARA HOSPITALITY HOTELS INC
DAYS INN-LUNDY'S LANE
6546 Fallsview Blvd, Niagara Falls, ON, L2G
3W2
(905) 358-4666
Emp Here 170   *Sales* 16,220,750
SIC 7011 Hotels and motels
Vincent Kerrio

D-U-N-S 24-556-5593   (HQ)
NIAGARA KANKO TOURS INC
5719 Stanley Ave, Niagara Falls, ON, L2G 3X6
(905) 356-2025
Sales 41,597,360
SIC 4725 Tour operators
Seiichiro Takizawa
Yoshiro Takizawa

D-U-N-S 20-820-2499   (HQ)
NIAGARA PARKS COMMISSION, THE
QUEENSTON HEIGHTS RESTAURANT
7400 Portage Rd, Niagara Falls, ON, L2G 0E5
(905) 356-2241
Emp Here 50   *Sales* 95,706,475
SIC 5947 Gift, novelty, and souvenir shop
David Adames
Sandie Bellows
April Jeffs
Brenda Garett
Marcelo Gruosso

D-U-N-S 25-634-1421   (SL)
OAKWOOD PARK LODGE
6747 Oakwood Dr, Niagara Falls, ON, L2G
0J3
(905) 356-8732
Emp Here 140   *Sales* 9,599,240
SIC 8051 Skilled nursing care facilities
Bob Simon
Mary Simon

D-U-N-S 24-844-7088   (HQ)
PALFINGER INC
(*Suby of* HPT HOLDING GMBH)
7942 Dorchester Rd, Niagara Falls, ON, L2G
7W7
(905) 374-3363
Sales 31,702,450
SIC 5084 Industrial machinery and equipment
Hubert Palfinger

D-U-N-S 24-379-1147   (SL)

POST FOODS CANADA INC
(*Suby of* POST HOLDINGS, INC.)
5651 Lewis Ave, Niagara Falls, ON, L2G 3R8
(905) 374-7111
Emp Here 225   *Sales* 109,661,625
SIC 2043 Cereal breakfast foods
David P Skarie
Thomas G Granneman
Kevin J Hunt
Sandy K Laux
Charles G Huber Jr
Scott Monette
Helen Varley
Lawrence M Mullen
Cynthia K Vinyard

D-U-N-S 24-485-6530   (HQ)
PUMPCRETE CORPORATION
6000 Progress St, Niagara Falls, ON, L2G 0C4
(905) 354-3855
Emp Here 12   *Sales* 17,221,860
SIC 7353 Heavy construction equipment
rental
Ken Williams Jr
Herb Magiera
Mark Williams

D-U-N-S 24-736-2122   (HQ)
RE/MAX NIAGARA REALTY LTD
5627 Main St, Niagara Falls, ON, L2G 5Z3
(905) 356-9600
Sales 33,511,120
SIC 6531 Real estate agents and managers
Angelo Muraco
Ron Joncas
Mary Muraco

D-U-N-S 20-303-2982   (BR)
RECIPE UNLIMITED CORPORATION
KELSEY'S
(*Suby of* RECIPE UNLIMITED CORPORA-
TION)
4960 Clifton Hill, Niagara Falls, ON, L2G 3N4
(905) 353-0051
Emp Here 130
SIC 5812 Eating places
Phillip Oakes

D-U-N-S 25-705-1342   (BR)
RED LOBSTER HOSPITALITY LLC
RED LOBSTER RESTAURANTS
6220 Lundy'S Lane, Niagara Falls, ON, L2G
1T6
(905) 357-1303
Emp Here 80
SIC 5812 Eating places
Justyna Sandoval

D-U-N-S 24-329-6972   (BR)
WAL-MART CANADA CORP
WALMART CANADA
(*Suby of* WALMART INC.)
7481 Oakwood Dr, Niagara Falls, ON, L2G
0J5
(905) 371-3999
Emp Here 200
SIC 5311 Department stores
Karl Frechette

Niagara Falls, ON L2H

D-U-N-S 25-092-4300   (SL)
2010162 ONTARIO LTD
ZIPPO CANADA SALES
6868 Kinsmen Crt, Niagara Falls, ON, L2H
0Y5
(905) 358-3674
Emp Here 38   *Sales* 28,215,760
SIC 5199 Nondurable goods, nec
Gary Hyde

D-U-N-S 25-179-0606   (SL)
ADVANTAGE RESTAURANT SUPPLY INC
FRONT HOUSE SEATING

4529 Kent Ave, Niagara Falls, ON, L2H 1J1
(905) 356-1152
Emp Here 50   *Sales* 22,358,700
SIC 5046 Commercial equipment, nec
Tony Angelo Vizzari
Lino Camillo Cornacchia

D-U-N-S 20-048-5464   (SL)
ALO CANADA INC
(*Suby of* FORT KNOX FORVARING AB)
8485 Montrose Rd, Niagara Falls, ON, L2H 3L7
(800) 361-7563
Emp Here 25   *Sales* 11,875,650
SIC 5082 Construction and mining machinery
Dana Hoover
Stelio Denmark
Ann-Sofie Lofvenius
Patrick Nygren
Lars-Erik Blom
Jan-Erik Forsberg
Lena Rydstom
David Pietrangelo

D-U-N-S 20-021-7581   (SL)
BIAMONTE INVESTMENTS LTD
MICK & ANGELO'S EATERY AND BAR
7600 Lundy'S Lane, Niagara Falls, ON, L2H 1H1
(905) 354-2211
Emp Here 80   *Sales* 3,641,520
SIC 5812 Eating places
Ralph Biamonte

D-U-N-S 24-097-6779   (HQ)
CIRCUS WORLD DISPLAYS LIMITED
SVAT ELECTRONICS
4080 Montrose Rd, Niagara Falls, ON, L2H 1J9
(905) 353-0732
Emp Here 86   *Sales* 19,044,200
SIC 3651 Household audio and video equipment
Ramesh C Jain
Sujata Jain
Deepak Jain
Rajesh Jain

D-U-N-S 25-278-7726   (SL)
CLUB ITALIA,NIAGARA, ORDER SONS OF ITALY OF CANADA
CLUB ITALIA LODGE NO 5
2525 Montrose Rd, Niagara Falls, ON, L2H 0T9
(905) 374-7388
Emp Here 100   *Sales* 10,678,200
SIC 7299 Miscellaneous personal service
Nick Radice

D-U-N-S 24-990-9557   (HQ)
CYTEC CANADA INC
(*Suby of* SOLVAY)
9061 Garner Rd, Niagara Falls, ON, L2H 0Y2
(905) 356-9000
Sales 42,603,150
SIC 2819 Industrial inorganic chemicals, nec
Mike Radossish
Donald Sorley

D-U-N-S 20-595-8978   (SL)
DAN'S PRODUCE LIMITED
7201 Beechwood Rd, Niagara Falls, ON, L2H 0W8
(905) 356-1560
Emp Here 25   *Sales* 20,889,425
SIC 5148 Fresh fruits and vegetables
Daniel Bouwman

D-U-N-S 20-026-3213   (BR)
DISTRICT SCHOOL BOARD OF NIAGARA
WESTLANE SECONDARY SCHOOL
5960 Pitton Rd, Niagara Falls, ON, L2H 1T5
(905) 356-2401
Emp Here 90
SIC 8211 Elementary and secondary schools
Matt Wilson

D-U-N-S 20-132-4753   (HQ)

FLEXO PRODUCTS LIMITED
4777 Kent Ave, Niagara Falls, ON, L2H 1J5
(905) 354-2723
Emp Here 40   *Sales* 35,626,950
SIC 5087 Service establishment equipment
Stephen Parker

D-U-N-S 20-833-7837   (SL)
HAMBLET'S ROOFING & SIDING INC
HAMBLET'S ROOFING SIDING WINDOWS
7130 Kinsmen Crt, Niagara Falls, ON, L2H 0Y5
(905) 988-6263
Emp Here 75   *Sales* 16,337,175
SIC 1761 Roofing, siding, and sheetMetal work
Robert Hamblet
Sean Temple

D-U-N-S 24-486-1704   (SL)
HODGSON CUSTOM ROLLING INC
5580 Kalar Rd, Niagara Falls, ON, L2H 3L1
(905) 356-8132
Emp Here 50   *Sales* 10,141,500
SIC 3449 Miscellaneous Metalwork
Christopher Hodgson
Chris Van Grieken

D-U-N-S 24-858-2178   (BR)
LOWE'S COMPANIES CANADA, ULC
(*Suby of* LOWE'S COMPANIES, INC.)
7959 Mcleod Rd, Niagara Falls, ON, L2H 0G5
(905) 374-5520
Emp Here 150
SIC 5211 Lumber and other building materials
Jim Terkalas

D-U-N-S 25-651-7368   (BR)
METRO ONTARIO INC
A & P
(*Suby of* METRO INC)
3770 Montrose Rd, Niagara Falls, ON, L2H 3C8
(905) 371-3200
Emp Here 150
SIC 5411 Grocery stores
Gregory Shannon

D-U-N-S 24-758-0947   (SL)
NIAGARA AIR BUS INC
8626 Lundy'S Lane, Niagara Falls, ON, L2H 1H4
(905) 374-8111
Emp Here 75   *Sales* 4,115,400
SIC 4111 Local and suburban transit
Tim Towle
Paul Mountain

D-U-N-S 20-591-6062   (BR)
NIAGARA CATHOLIC DISTRICT SCHOOL BOARD
ST MICHAEL CATHOLIC HIGH SCHOOL
(*Suby of* NIAGARA CATHOLIC DISTRICT SCHOOL BOARD)
8699 Mcleod Rd, Niagara Falls, ON, L2H 0Z2
(905) 356-5155
Emp Here 80
SIC 8211 Elementary and secondary schools
James Whittard

D-U-N-S 20-883-6267   (SL)
NIAGARA EMPLOYMENT AGENCY INC
NIAGARA RECYCLING
4935 Kent Ave, Niagara Falls, ON, L2H 1J5
(905) 354-4141
Emp Here 60   *Sales* 19,134,600
SIC 4953 Refuse systems
Norman Kraft

D-U-N-S 24-319-5968   (SL)
NORJOHN CONTRACTING AND PAVING LIMITED
(*Suby of* WALKER INDUSTRIES HOLDINGS LIMITED)
9101 Brown Rd, Niagara Falls, ON, L2H 0X1
(905) 371-0809
Emp Here 60   *Sales* 15,146,520

SIC 1611 Highway and street construction
John Fisher
John Blake
Greg Reiser

D-U-N-S 25-488-4802   (SL)
RATTRAY, WILLIAM HOLDINGS LTD
CANADIAN TIRE 71
3770 Montrose Rd, Niagara Falls, ON, L2H 3C8
(905) 354-3848
Emp Here 70   *Sales* 18,735,640
SIC 5251 Hardware stores
William Rattray

D-U-N-S 25-204-3518   (BR)
REGIONAL MUNICIPALITY OF NIAGARA, THE
MEADOWS DORCHESTER, THE
(*Suby of* REGIONAL MUNICIPALITY OF NIAGARA, THE)
6623 Kalar Rd Suite 312, Niagara Falls, ON, L2H 2T3
(905) 357-1911
Emp Here 116
SIC 8051 Skilled nursing care facilities
Colleen Tuff

D-U-N-S 20-132-8861   (HQ)
ROMAN CHEESE PRODUCTS LIMITED
7770 Canadian Dr, Niagara Falls, ON, L2H 0X3
(905) 356-2639
Emp Here 1   *Sales* 38,436,542
SIC 5141 Groceries, general line
Alfred Varalli
Nicholas Varalli

D-U-N-S 20-974-6163   (HQ)
SWS STAR WARNING SYSTEMS INC
7695 Blackburn Pky, Niagara Falls, ON, L2H 0A6
(905) 357-0222
Sales 11,807,404
SIC 3647 Vehicular lighting equipment
Francis Balogh
Carolyn Harris
Tom Chopp
Sherri Harris

D-U-N-S 24-487-7551   (SL)
YOUNG MENS CHRISTIAN ASSOCIATION
Y M C OF NIAGARA
7150 Montrose Rd, Niagara Falls, ON, L2H 3N3
(905) 358-9622
Emp Here 110   *Sales* 158,246,110
SIC 8699 Membership organizations, nec
Ted Mcdonald

Niagara Falls, ON L2J

D-U-N-S 24-819-1582   (SL)
1788741 ONTARIO INC
COMMISSO'S FRESH FOODS
6161 Thorold Stone Rd Suite 3, Niagara Falls, ON, L2J 1A4
(905) 357-6600
Emp Here 130   *Sales* 38,152,010
SIC 5461 Retail bakeries
Rocco Commisso
Frank Commisso
Tony Commisso

D-U-N-S 20-056-9247   (SL)
FALLS CHEVROLET CADILLAC LTD
5888 Thorold Stone Rd, Niagara Falls, ON, L2J 1A2
(905) 353-9123
Emp Here 35   *Sales* 17,432,730
SIC 5511 New and used car dealers
Brian Cullen
Brian Cullen Jr
Carrie Sherk

D-U-N-S 20-132-7293   (SL)
MARTIN, DENNIS M DRUGS INC
SHOPPERS DRUG MART
3701 Portage Rd Unit 1, Niagara Falls, ON, L2J 2K8
(905) 354-6511
Emp Here 45   *Sales* 11,382,930
SIC 5912 Drug stores and proprietary stores
Dennis M Martin

D-U-N-S 25-224-9453   (BR)
NIAGARA CATHOLIC DISTRICT SCHOOL BOARD
SAINT PAUL CATHOLIC HIGH SCHOOL
(*Suby of* NIAGARA CATHOLIC DISTRICT SCHOOL BOARD)
3834 Windermere Rd, Niagara Falls, ON, L2J 2Y5
(905) 356-4313
Emp Here 80
SIC 8211 Elementary and secondary schools
Francis Brockensharie

D-U-N-S 25-934-7441   (BR)
SOBEYS CAPITAL INCORPORATED
(*Suby of* EMPIRE COMPANY LIMITED)
3714 Portage Rd, Niagara Falls, ON, L2J 2K9
(905) 371-2270
Emp Here 160
SIC 5411 Grocery stores
Jim Albanese

D-U-N-S 20-133-0677   (SL)
ZAVITZ, G. LIMITED
5795 Thorold Stone Rd, Niagara Falls, ON, L2J 1A1
(905) 356-4945
Emp Here 95   *Sales* 14,078,240
SIC 4213 Trucking, except local
Gerald (Tim) Zavitz

Niagara On The Lake, ON L0S

D-U-N-S 24-382-5960   (SL)
2188652 ONTARIO INC
(*Suby of* SUNOPTA INC)
337 Four Mile Creek Rd, Niagara On The Lake, ON, L0S 1J0
(905) 262-8200
Emp Here 30   *Sales* 10,370,700
SIC 2034 Dried and dehydrated fruits, vegetables and soup mixes
John Boot

D-U-N-S 24-622-0834   (HQ)
465912 ONTARIO INC
AUTOMOTIVE WAREHOUSE
343 Airport Rd, Niagara On The Lake, ON, L0S 1J0
(905) 682-1711
Sales 28,317,600
SIC 5511 New and used car dealers
Fred Boychuk

D-U-N-S 25-541-5309   (HQ)
542144 ONTARIO LTD
1695 Niagara Stone Rd, Niagara On The Lake, ON, L0S 1J0
(905) 468-3217
Sales 51,976,400
SIC 5193 Flowers and florists supplies
Leno Mori

D-U-N-S 25-670-1178   (BR)
ANDREW PELLER LIMITED
TRIUS WINERY - HILLEBRAND
(*Suby of* ANDREW PELLER LIMITED)
1249 Niagara Stone Rd, Niagara On The Lake, ON, L0S 1J0
(905) 468-7123
Emp Here 120
SIC 2084 Wines, brandy, and brandy spirits
Greg Berti

D-U-N-S 25-461-0603   (BR)

CHARTWELL RETIREMENT RESIDENCES
CHATEAU GARDENS NIAGARA
(*Suby of* CHARTWELL RETIREMENT RESI-DENCES)
120 Wellington St, Niagara On The Lake, ON, L0S 1J0
(905) 468-2111
Emp Here 150
SIC 8051 Skilled nursing care facilities
 Lorraine Koop

D-U-N-S 24-197-5838   (HQ)
CN WORLDWIDE DISTRIBUTION SERVICES (CANADA) INC
CN WORLDWIDE
(*Suby of* COMPAGNIE DES CHEMINS DE FER NATIONAUX DU CANADA)
303 Townline Rd Suite 200, Niagara On The Lake, ON, L0S 1J0
(905) 641-3139
Emp Here 20   *Sales* 41,141,200
SIC 4225 General warehousing and storage
 Paul Tonsager
 Gilles B. Legault
 Bernd Beyer

D-U-N-S 20-123-1821   (HQ)
DIAMOND ESTATES WINES & SPIRITS LTD
1067 Niagara Stone Rd, Niagara On The Lake, ON, L0S 1J0
(905) 685-5673
Emp Here 30   *Sales* 47,033,280
SIC 5182 Wine and distilled beverages
 Murray Marshall
 Andrew Green

D-U-N-S 25-301-2884   (BR)
EXTENDICARE (CANADA) INC
PARAMED HOME HEALTH CARE
(*Suby of* EXTENDICARE INC)
509 Glendale Ave Suite 200, Niagara On The Lake, ON, L0S 1J0
(905) 682-6555
Emp Here 500
SIC 8051 Skilled nursing care facilities
 Hattie Hills

D-U-N-S 25-321-0389   (BR)
FIRSTCANADA ULC
LAIDLAW EDUCATIONAL SERVICES
(*Suby of* FIRSTGROUP PLC)
349 Airport Rd, Niagara On The Lake, ON, L0S 1J0
(905) 688-9600
Emp Here 160
SIC 4151 School buses
 Yvonne Sodtka

D-U-N-S 20-013-0941   (SL)
GARDEN CITY GROWERS INC
405 Concession 5 Rd, Niagara On The Lake, ON, L0S 1J0
(905) 685-1120
Emp Here 35   *Sales* 11,396,000
SIC 5992 Florists
 Ted Vanderkaay

D-U-N-S 20-147-2032   (SL)
GENAIRE LIMITED
(*Suby of* AMASER LIMITED)
468 Niagara Stone Rd Unit D, Niagara On The Lake, ON, L0S 1J0
(905) 684-1165
Emp Here 40   *Sales* 10,679,120
SIC 4581 Airports, flying fields, and services
 Lorraine Warner
 Bob Lennox
 Gerald Wooll
 Harry Picken
 Melissa Warner

D-U-N-S 24-758-1580   (SL)
HARVEST BARN OF NIAGARA LTD
1822 Niagara Stone Rd, Niagara On The Lake, ON, L0S 1J0
(905) 468-3224
Emp Here 80   *Sales* 23,478,160

SIC 5431 Fruit and vegetable markets
 Douglas Dineley

D-U-N-S 24-164-2636   (HQ)
HENRY SCHEIN CANADA, INC
(*Suby of* HENRY SCHEIN, INC.)
345 Townline Rd, Niagara On The Lake, ON, L0S 1J0
(905) 646-1711
Emp Here 260   *Sales* 508,584,400
SIC 5047 Medical and hospital equipment
 Cyril F. Elborne
 Glen Watson
 Peter D. Jugoon
 Tom Killy

D-U-N-S 24-829-8689   (HQ)
LAIS HOTEL PROPERTIES LIMITED
PRINCE OF WALES HOTEL
155 Byron St, Niagara On The Lake, ON, L0S 1J0
(905) 468-2195
Sales 23,917,000
SIC 7011 Hotels and motels
 April Brunet

D-U-N-S 20-769-2919   (SL)
LAIS HOTEL PROPERTIES LIMITED
QUEENS LANDING HOTEL AND CONFERENCE RESORT
48 John St, Niagara On The Lake, ON, L0S 1J0
(888) 669-5566
Emp Here 600   *Sales* 57,400,800
SIC 7011 Hotels and motels
 Mark Simon
 Royston Chow Tai Quen

D-U-N-S 20-183-4707   (BR)
LAIS HOTEL PROPERTIES LIMITED
PRINCE OF WALES HOTEL
(*Suby of* LAIS HOTEL PROPERTIES LIMITED)
6 Pinot Trail, Niagara On The Lake, ON, L0S 1J0
(905) 468-3246
Emp Here 160
SIC 7011 Hotels and motels
 Michelle Miller

D-U-N-S 25-638-4777   (SL)
LAKEVIEW CELLARS ESTATE WINERY LIMITED
20 BEES WINERY
1067 Niagara Stone Rd, Niagara On The Lake, ON, L0S 1J0
(905) 641-1042
Emp Here 50   *Sales* 11,242,750
SIC 2084 Wines, brandy, and brandy spirits
 Murray Marshall
 Chevonn Cook
 Tom Green
 Derek Cartlidge
 Andrew D Green

D-U-N-S 20-175-7262   (BR)
LEON'S FURNITURE LIMITED
(*Suby of* LEON'S FURNITURE LIMITED)
440 Taylor Rd, Niagara On The Lake, ON, L0S 1J0
(905) 682-8519
Emp Here 100
SIC 5712 Furniture stores
 Nelson Sampson

D-U-N-S 20-391-6882   (SL)
MEYERS FRUIT FARMS LTD
1444 Irvine Rd Rr 4, Niagara On The Lake, ON, L0S 1J0
(905) 934-3925
Emp Here 50   *Sales* 37,126,000
SIC 5193 Flowers and florists supplies
 Fred Meyers
 Elly Hoff
 Aron Hoff

D-U-N-S 20-534-2710   (HQ)
MORI NURSERIES LIMITED

MORISTAR PERRENIALS, DIV OF
(*Suby of* 542144 ONTARIO LTD)
1695 Niagara Stone Rd, Niagara On The Lake, ON, L0S 1J0
(905) 468-3217
Sales 51,976,400
SIC 5193 Flowers and florists supplies
 Leno Mori

D-U-N-S 24-926-2510   (SL)
MURDERS TASTEFULLY EXECUTED INC
128 William St, Niagara On The Lake, ON, L0S 1J0
(905) 468-0007
Emp Here 80   *Sales* 12,109,520
SIC 7922 Theatrical producers and services
 David Johnston

D-U-N-S 25-483-9178   (HQ)
NIAGARA GORGE JET BOATING LTD
WHIRLPOOL JET BOAT TOURS
61 Melville St, Niagara On The Lake, ON, L0S 1J0
(905) 468-4800
Emp Here 10   *Sales* 10,399,340
SIC 4724 Travel agencies
 John Kinney
 John Kowalski
 Joseph Kowalski
 Joanne Clifford

D-U-N-S 20-945-2247   (BR)
NIAGARA HEALTH SYSTEM
NIAGARA ON THE LAKE GENERAL HOSPITAL
(*Suby of* NIAGARA HEALTH SYSTEM)
176 Wellington St, Niagara On The Lake, ON, L0S 1J0
(905) 378-4647
Emp Here 100
SIC 8062 General medical and surgical hospitals
 Debbie Sevenpiser

D-U-N-S 25-607-2398   (SL)
PILLITTERI ESTATES WINERY INC
1696 Niagara Stone Rd, Niagara On The Lake, ON, L0S 1J0
(905) 468-3147
Emp Here 30   *Sales* 10,274,010
SIC 0172 Grapes
 Gary Pillitteri
 Connie Pillitteri

D-U-N-S 20-174-5432   (SL)
S TEAM 92 AUTOMATION TECHNOLOGY INC
STEAM-ASD
827 Line 4 Rr 2, Niagara On The Lake, ON, L0S 1J0

Emp Here 12   *Sales* 10,271,161
SIC 7373 Computer integrated systems design
 Dirk Froehlich
 Felix Winterstein

D-U-N-S 20-786-8779   (SL)
SHAW FESTIVAL THEATRE FOUNDATION CANADA
SHAW FESTIVAL THEATRE, CANADA
10 Queens Parade, Niagara On The Lake, ON, L0S 1J0
(905) 468-2172
Emp Here 120   *Sales* 21,288,507
SIC 7922 Theatrical producers and services
 Colleen Blake
 Jackie Maxwell
 Janet Mckelvey
 Hazel Claxton

D-U-N-S 24-633-0450   (HQ)
ST DAVIDS HYDROPONICS LTD
822 Concession 7 Rd Rr 4, Niagara On The Lake, ON, L0S 1J0
(905) 682-7570
Emp Here 60   *Sales* 26,230,900
SIC 0182 Food crops grown under cover

Maarten Bos
Toine Vanderknaap

D-U-N-S 24-890-2541   (SL)
THWAITES FARMS LTD
1984 Townline Rd Suite 3, Niagara On The Lake, ON, L0S 1J0
(905) 934-3880
Emp Here 44   *Sales* 15,068,548
SIC 0179 Fruits and tree nuts, nec
 Nelson Thwaites

D-U-N-S 20-904-1565   (SL)
TREGUNNO FRUIT FARMS INC
15176 Niagara River Pky, Niagara On The Lake, ON, L0S 1J0
(905) 262-4755
Emp Here 75   *Sales* 16,864,125
SIC 2037 Frozen fruits and vegetables
 Phillip Tregunno
 Lorna Tregunno

D-U-N-S 20-328-0383   (SL)
TWO SISTERS VINEYARD CORP
240 John St E, Niagara On The Lake, ON, L0S 1J0
(905) 468-0592
Emp Here 60   *Sales* 13,491,300
SIC 2084 Wines, brandy, and brandy spirits
 Angela Marotta
 Melissa Marotta-Paolicelli

D-U-N-S 20-342-9261   (SL)
UPPER CANADA GROWERS LTD
149 Read Rd, Niagara On The Lake, ON, L0S 1J0
(289) 646-0737
Emp Here 51   *Sales* 13,377,759
SIC 0191 General farms, primarily crop
 Robert Haynes
 Megan Haynes
 Megan Haynes
 Jason Haynes

D-U-N-S 24-075-4531   (SL)
WHITE OAKS TENNIS WORLD INC
WHITE OAKS CONFERENCE RESORT & SPA
253 Taylor Rd Ss 4, Niagara On The Lake, ON, L0S 1J0
(905) 688-2550
Emp Here 350   *Sales* 234,117,800
SIC 7389 Business services, nec
 George Wakil
 John Holjak
 Michael Wakil
 Jasmine Wakil-Tonnos
 Ameer Wakil
 Adelene Wakil-Booth

D-U-N-S 25-603-5403   (SL)
WIENS FAMILY FARM INC
1178 6 Rd, Niagara On The Lake, ON, L0S 1J0

Emp Here 30   *Sales* 10,274,010
SIC 0191 General farms, primarily crop
 Abram Wiens

Nipigon, ON P0T

D-U-N-S 24-497-2436   (HQ)
NIPIGON DISTRICT MEMORIAL HOSPITAL
125 Hogan Rd, Nipigon, ON, P0T 2J0
(807) 887-3026
Emp Here 1   *Sales* 12,107,720
SIC 8062 General medical and surgical hospitals
 Kurt Pristanski

D-U-N-S 20-133-2061   (SL)
ZECHNER'S LIMITED
ZECHNER'S FOOD MARKET
155 Railway St, Nipigon, ON, P0T 2J0

▲ Public Company   ■ Public Company Family Member   **HQ** Headquarters   **BR** Branch   **SL** Single Location

(807) 887-2910
Emp Here 39   *Sales* 10,691,928
SIC 5411 Grocery stores
John Zechner Sr
Carol Zechner
Lesley Zechner-Willan
Jeffery Zechner
John Zechner Jr

Nobel, ON P0G

D-U-N-S 25-604-1344   (BR)
SELKIRK CANADA CORPORATION
(*Suby of* SELKIRK AMERICAS, L.P.)
21 Woods Rd, Nobel, ON, P0G 1G0
(705) 342-5236
Emp Here 110
SIC 3259 Structural clay products, nec
James Mcquay

Nobleton, ON L0G

D-U-N-S 24-102-5795   (SL)
ATTFIELD, ROGER INC
ATTFIELD, ROGER RACING STABLE
Gd, Nobleton, ON, L0G 1N0
(416) 675-1231
Emp Here 30   *Sales* 12,711,900
SIC 7948 Racing, including track operation
Roger Attfield

D-U-N-S 24-523-2884   (HQ)
GREEN TRACTORS INC
6770 King Rd, Nobleton, ON, L0G 1N0
(905) 859-0581
Emp Here 3   *Sales* 21,989,520
SIC 5999 Miscellaneous retail stores, nec
Karl Davis
Ken Svendsen

North Bay, ON P1A

D-U-N-S 24-688-9364   (SL)
1121121 ONTARIO INC
CANARINO NISSAN
240 Lakeshore Dr, North Bay, ON, P1A 2B6
(705) 476-5100
Emp Here 25   *Sales* 12,451,950
SIC 5511 New and used car dealers
Carmine Canarino
Nicolas Canarino

D-U-N-S 20-770-4334   (SL)
1510610 ONTARIO INC
CENTRAL WELDING & IRON WORKS
1811 Seymour St, North Bay, ON, P1A 0C7
(705) 474-0350
Emp Here 50   *Sales* 10,185,800
SIC 7692 Welding repair
Stefan Thomsen

D-U-N-S 24-417-1943   (HQ)
1530460 ONTARIO INC
SOUTHLAND SHELL
390 Lakeshore Dr Suite 7, North Bay, ON, P1A 2C7
(705) 476-1230
Emp Here 10   *Sales* 11,953,872
SIC 5541 Gasoline service stations
Shawnee Johnson

D-U-N-S 24-216-9977   (BR)
2063414 ONTARIO LIMITED
WATERS EDGE CARE COMMUNITY
401 William St, North Bay, ON, P1A 1X5
(705) 476-2602
Emp Here 140
SIC 8051 Skilled nursing care facilities

Ruth Gauthier

D-U-N-S 20-773-5739   (SL)
331265 ONTARIO LIMITED
G & P WELDING & IRON WORKS
1872 Seymour St Suite 3, North Bay, ON, P1A 0E2
(705) 472-5454
Emp Here 50   *Sales* 10,141,500
SIC 3441 Fabricated structural Metal
George Popp

D-U-N-S 20-581-2423   (HQ)
611421 ONTARIO INC.
BAYWOOD ENTERPRISES
119 Progress Crt, North Bay, ON, P1A 0C1
(705) 476-4222
Emp Here 50   *Sales* 12,087,522
SIC 3799 Transportation equipment, nec
Carl Crewson
Gloria Crewson
David Crewson
Sherri Crewson

D-U-N-S 24-610-3303   (HQ)
618717 ONTARIO INC
PRONORTH EQUIPMENT
348 Birchs Rd, North Bay, ON, P1A 4A9
(705) 476-4411
Emp Here 200
SIC 4213 Trucking, except local
Brian Glass
Dale Glass

D-U-N-S 24-919-3616   (HQ)
682439 ONTARIO INC
PRONORTH TRANSPORTATION
(*Suby of* TITANIUM TRANSPORTATION GROUP INC)
348 Birchs Rd Suite 824, North Bay, ON, P1A 4A9
(705) 476-0444
Emp Here 255
SIC 4213 Trucking, except local
Brian Glass
Dale Glass
Bill Ayers

D-U-N-S 20-704-1997   (SL)
AUTOGENE INDUSTRIES NORTH BAY INC
1811 Seymour St, North Bay, ON, P1A 0C7
(705) 474-0350
Emp Here 50   *Sales* 13,592,100
SIC 7692 Welding repair
Stefan Thomsen
Gail Thomsen

D-U-N-S 20-778-8949   (BR)
CHISHOLM, R. FOOD SERVICES INC
MCDONALD'S RESTAURANTS
(*Suby of* CHISHOLM, R. FOOD SERVICES INC)
140 Lakeshore Dr, North Bay, ON, P1A 2A8
(705) 474-9770
Emp Here 100
SIC 5812 Eating places
Robert Mcgirr

D-U-N-S 20-406-5759   (SL)
FORACO CANADA LTD
1839 Seymour St, North Bay, ON, P1A 0C7
(705) 495-6363
Emp Here 230   *Sales* 48,846,480
SIC 1799 Special trade contractors, nec
Tim Bremner

D-U-N-S 24-321-1724   (HQ)
FORACO CANADA LTD
1839 Seymour St, North Bay, ON, P1A 0C7
(705) 495-6363
Emp Here 90   *Sales* 36,927,900
SIC 1799 Special trade contractors, nec
Timothy Bremner

D-U-N-S 20-405-7186   (HQ)
HASKINS INDUSTRIAL INC
1371 Franklin St, North Bay, ON, P1A 2W1

(705) 474-4420
Sales 11,875,650
SIC 5085 Industrial supplies
Brian Haskins
Brian Haskins
Sheila Haskins

D-U-N-S 24-009-6354   (SL)
INVEST REIT
BEST WESTERN NORTH BAY HOTEL AND CONFERENCE CENTRE, THE
700 Lakeshore Dr, North Bay, ON, P1A 2G4
(705) 474-5800
Emp Here 90   *Sales* 8,540,910
SIC 7011 Hotels and motels
Angela Johnson

D-U-N-S 25-742-5132   (BR)
METRO ONTARIO INC
METRO
(*Suby of* METRO INC)
390 Lakeshore Dr, North Bay, ON, P1A 2C7
(705) 840-2424
Emp Here 220
SIC 5411 Grocery stores
Charlie Lang

D-U-N-S 20-133-6575   (SL)
NORTH BAY CHRYSLER LTD
352 Lakeshore Dr, North Bay, ON, P1A 2C2
(705) 472-0820
Emp Here 40   *Sales* 19,923,120
SIC 5511 New and used car dealers
Steven Farquhar

D-U-N-S 24-093-9181   (SL)
NORTH BAY HYDRO DISTRIBUTION LIMITED
74 Commerce Cres, North Bay, ON, P1A 0B4
(705) 474-8100
Emp Here 45   *Sales* 23,384,475
SIC 4911 Electric services
Bill Walton

D-U-N-S 20-551-7758   (SL)
PILOT DIAMOND TOOLS LIMITED
1851 Seymour St, North Bay, ON, P1A 0C7
(705) 497-3715
Emp Here 60   *Sales* 13,320,060
SIC 3545 Machine tool accessories
Steve Perrin
Murray Norman

D-U-N-S 20-697-3674   (BR)
PIONEER CONSTRUCTION INC
(*Suby of* PIONEER CONSTRUCTION INC)
175 Progress Rd, North Bay, ON, P1A 0B8
(705) 472-0890
Emp Here 100
SIC 1611 Highway and street construction
Len Lanthier

D-U-N-S 24-227-5514   (BR)
STOCK TRANSPORTATION LTD
(*Suby of* NATIONAL EXPRESS GROUP PLC)
59 Commerce Cres, North Bay, ON, P1A 0B3
(705) 474-4370
Emp Here 150
SIC 4151 School buses
Lubke Storry

North Bay, ON P1B

D-U-N-S 24-208-8920   (SL)
442527 ONTARIO LIMITED
METAL FAB
40 Exeter St, North Bay, ON, P1B 8G5
(705) 474-7880
Emp Here 75   *Sales* 21,247,500
SIC 7539 Automotive repair shops, nec
James Grasser

D-U-N-S 25-743-6626   (SL)
974479 ONTARIO LIMITED
DOLLAR'S YOUR INDEPENDANT GRO-

CERY
1 Laurentian Ave, North Bay, ON, P1B 9T2
(705) 472-8866
Emp Here 200   *Sales* 58,695,400
SIC 5411 Grocery stores
Brian Dollar

D-U-N-S 20-938-3363   (HQ)
ABBEY CARDS & GIFTS LIMITED, THE
HALLMARK
126 Main St W, North Bay, ON, P1B 2T5
(705) 472-2760
Emp Here 6   *Sales* 26,143,096
SIC 5947 Gift, novelty, and souvenir shop
John J Lyle
David Lyle

D-U-N-S 25-751-8225   (SL)
AFFIRMATIVE DYNAMIC INDUSTRY INC
WOOD SHOPPE, THE
1765 Jane St, North Bay, ON, P1B 3K3
(705) 476-8809
Emp Here 35   *Sales* 25,988,200
SIC 5199 Nondurable goods, nec
Lynn Mantha

D-U-N-S 25-974-9455   (SL)
BLACK SAXON III INC
CLARION RESORT
201 Pinewood Park Dr, North Bay, ON, P1B 8Z4
(705) 472-0810
Emp Here 75   *Sales* 7,117,425
SIC 7011 Hotels and motels
Al Pace

D-U-N-S 25-852-4545   (HQ)
BLUE SKY FINANCIAL GROUP INC
128 Mcintyre St W Suite 100, North Bay, ON, P1B 2Y6
(705) 497-3723
Emp Here 5   *Sales* 21,201,500
SIC 6411 Insurance agents, brokers, and service
Hal Beatty
Chantal Trudel Falardeau

D-U-N-S 25-093-2444   (BR)
BOMBARDIER INC
BOMBARDIER A?RONAUTIQUE
(*Suby of* BOMBARDIER INC)
1500 Airport Rd, North Bay, ON, P1B 8G2

Emp Here 500
SIC 8711 Engineering services
Guy C. Hachey

D-U-N-S 20-849-8535   (HQ)
CANADORE COLLEGE OF APPLIED ARTS AND TECHNOLOGY
100 College Dr, North Bay, ON, P1B 8K9
(705) 474-7600
Emp Here 214   *Sales* 35,682,840
SIC 8222 Junior colleges
Robert Nicholls
Nancy Ann Hedican
George Burton
Richard Peters

D-U-N-S 20-849-4336   (SL)
CASSELLHOLME HOME FOR THE AGED
400 Olive St, North Bay, ON, P1B 6J4
(705) 474-4250
Emp Here 220   *Sales* 14,142,040
SIC 8361 Residential care
Cheryl Church
Ric Campbell

D-U-N-S 24-773-0943   (HQ)
CEMENTATION CANADA INC
590 Graham Dr, North Bay, ON, P1B 7S1
(705) 472-3381
Emp Here 140   *Sales* 45,943,520
SIC 1241 Coal mining services
Roy Slack
Robert Gripper
Justing Wayne Oleson

Eric Kohtakangas
David Setchell
Richard Pope
Orrie Fenn
Michael Nadon
David Meyer

D-U-N-S 25-146-9748   (HQ)
CHILDREN'S AID SOCIETY OF THE DIS-
TRICT OF NIPISSING & PARRY SOUND,
THE
433 Mcintyre St W, North Bay, ON, P1B 2Z3
(705) 472-0910
Emp Here 74   *Sales* 10,520,504
SIC 8322 Individual and family services
John Stopper
Darlene Vanderlee
Joanne Schmidt
Bonnie Barker
Gisele Hebert
Cathy Bellefeuille
Joe Rogers
Tom Stone
Barb Davis

D-U-N-S 24-044-5510   (HQ)
COMMUNITY LIVING NORTH BAY
161 Main St E, North Bay, ON, P1B 1A9
(705) 476-3288
Emp Here 1   *Sales* 14,360,104
SIC 8322 Individual and family services
Candace Barry
Robert Fetterly
Stella Curtis
Bonnie Roynon
Phil Harrison
Frank O'hagan
Yvonne Weir
Sherry Carnevale

D-U-N-S 20-965-3711   (BR)
CONSEIL SCOLAIRE DU DISTRICT DU
NORD-EST DE L'ONTARIO
ECOLE PUBLIQUE HERITAGE
(*Suby of* CONSEIL SCOLAIRE DU DISTRICT
DU NORD-EST DE L'ONTARIO)
2345 Connaught Ave, North Bay, ON, P1B
0A3
(705) 497-8700
Emp Here 350
SIC 8211 Elementary and secondary schools
Pascale Pellerin

D-U-N-S 20-072-4073   (BR)
CORPORATION OF THE CITY OF NORTH
BAY, THE
NORTH BAY FIRE DEPARTMENT, THE
(*Suby of* CORPORATION OF THE CITY OF
NORTH BAY, THE)
119 Princess St W, North Bay, ON, P1B 6C2
(705) 474-5662
Emp Here 87
SIC 7389 Business services, nec
Grant Love

D-U-N-S 25-095-7339   (HQ)
CRISIS CENTRE NORTH BAY
198 Second Ave W, North Bay, ON, P1B 3K9

Emp Here 1   *Sales* 19,280,805
SIC 8399 Social services, nec
Robert Barraclough
Carol Mcleod
Patricia Porter
Kathleen Hallett

D-U-N-S 25-497-9537   (HQ)
DISTRICT OF NIPISSING SOCIAL SER-
VICES ADMINISTRATION BOARD
DNSSAB
200 Mcintyre St E, North Bay, ON, P1B 8V6
(705) 474-2151
Emp Here 65   *Sales* 10,676,720
SIC 8399 Social services, nec
Joseph Bradbury

D-U-N-S 20-549-8624   (SL)

EMPIRE LIVING CENTRE INC
EMPIRE TERRACE SUITES
(*Suby of* RETIREMENT LIVING CENTRES
INC)
425 Fraser St Suite 505, North Bay, ON, P1B
3X1
(705) 474-9555
Emp Here 50   *Sales* 11,645,550
SIC 6513 Apartment building operators
Rod Mitchell

D-U-N-S 25-301-2728   (BR)
EXTENDICARE (CANADA) INC
PARAMED HOME HEALTH CARE
(*Suby of* EXTENDICARE INC)
222 Mcintyre St W Suite 202, North Bay, ON,
P1B 2Y8
(705) 495-4391
Emp Here 165
SIC 8051 Skilled nursing care facilities
Susan Slack

D-U-N-S 24-660-4821   (HQ)
FABRENE INC
FABRENE
(*Suby of* BERRY GLOBAL GROUP, INC.)
240 Dupont Rd, North Bay, ON, P1B 9B4
(705) 476-7057
Emp Here 220   *Sales* 54,632,193
SIC 2221 Broadwoven fabric mills, manmade
John Spencer
Eric Henderson

D-U-N-S 20-967-5180   (SL)
FELDCAMP EQUIPMENT LIMITED
FELDCAMP FLUIDPOWER
701 Graham Dr, North Bay, ON, P1B 9E6
(705) 472-5885
Emp Here 25   *Sales* 11,875,650
SIC 5084 Industrial machinery and equipment
Larry Feldcamp
Frieda Feldcamp

D-U-N-S 20-133-4760   (SL)
GAP CONSTRUCTION CO. LTD
1310 Franklin St, North Bay, ON, P1B 2M3
(705) 474-3730
Emp Here 50   *Sales* 23,536,550
SIC 1542 Nonresidential construction, nec
Ralph Priolo
Fredrick Priolo
Stanley Priolo

D-U-N-S 24-182-0000   (HQ)
GIN-COR INDUSTRIES INC
GINGRAS CORRIVEAU
255a Fisher St, North Bay, ON, P1B 2C8
(705) 744-5543
Emp Here 30   *Sales* 18,210,750
SIC 5012 Automobiles and other motor vehi-
cles
Luc Stang
Joel Long

D-U-N-S 20-553-6365   (BR)
HOME DEPOT OF CANADA INC
(*Suby of* THE HOME DEPOT INC)
1275 Seymour St, North Bay, ON, P1B 9V6
(705) 845-2300
Emp Here 100
SIC 5251 Hardware stores
Tania Marques

D-U-N-S 24-222-5969   (SL)
HOPPER AUTOMOBILES LTD
HOPPER BUICK GMC
550 Mckeown Ave, North Bay, ON, P1B 7M2
(888) 392-9178
Emp Here 50   *Sales* 17,753,750
SIC 5511 New and used car dealers

D-U-N-S 20-819-3276   (SL)
JACKMAN FLOWER SHOP LIMITED
JACKMAN'S
157 Worthington St E, North Bay, ON, P1B
1G4
(705) 494-8000
Emp Here 35   *Sales* 11,396,000

SIC 5992 Florists
Barry Pond
Marcia Pond

D-U-N-S 20-903-8694   (HQ)
KENNEDY INSURANCE BROKERS INC
414 Fraser St, North Bay, ON, P1B 3W9
(705) 472-5950
Emp Here 17   *Sales* 10,438,632
SIC 6411 Insurance agents, brokers, and ser-
vice
Tony Limina
Simon Lennie
Peter Rooney
Jamie Martyn

D-U-N-S 24-192-1790   (SL)
KNOX INSURANCE BROKERS LTD
705 Cassells St, North Bay, ON, P1B 4A3
(705) 474-4000
Emp Here 45   *Sales* 26,096,580
SIC 6411 Insurance agents, brokers, and ser-
vice
Bruce Knox
Hugh Knox

D-U-N-S 24-966-7114   (SL)
LAMONT, PAUL AUTOMOTIVE LTD
CANADIAN TIRE
890 Mckeown Ave, North Bay, ON, P1B 8M1
(705) 472-3000
Emp Here 150   *Sales* 30,801,450
SIC 5399 Miscellaneous general merchandise
William Lamont
Bernadine Lamont

D-U-N-S 20-652-9559   (SL)
LEWIS MOTOR SALES (NORTH BAY) INC
19 Hewitt Dr, North Bay, ON, P1B 8K5
(705) 472-7220
Emp Here 25   *Sales* 12,451,950
SIC 5511 New and used car dealers
Dale Lewis

D-U-N-S 20-734-0407   (SL)
LHD EQUIPMENT LIMITED
MINING TECHNOLOGIES INTERNATIONAL
(*Suby of* KOMATSU LTD.)
21 Exeter St, North Bay, ON, P1B 8G5
(705) 472-5207
Emp Here 84   *Sales* 18,648,084
SIC 3593 Fluid power cylinders and actuators
Robert S. Lipic

D-U-N-S 25-147-0761   (SL)
MIKE AND LORI'S NO FRILLS
975 Mckeown Ave, North Bay, ON, P1B 9P2
(866) 987-6453
Emp Here 49   *Sales* 13,433,448
SIC 5411 Grocery stores
Mike Sheehan

D-U-N-S 25-473-4981   (SL)
NIPISSING TRANSITION HOUSE
547 John St, North Bay, ON, P1B 2M9
(705) 476-2429
Emp Here 29   *Sales* 11,474,662
SIC 7381 Detective and armored car services
Jeannine Lafernier

D-U-N-S 24-693-7510   (SL)
NIPISSING UNIVERSITY
100 College Dr, North Bay, ON, P1B 8L7
(705) 474-3450
Emp Here 370   *Sales* 60,442,216
SIC 8221 Colleges and universities
Mike Degagne
Cheryl Sutton
Marianne Berube
Gord Durnan

D-U-N-S 20-292-7877   (HQ)
NORDIC MINESTEEL TECHNOLOGIES INC
373 Main St W Unit 1, North Bay, ON, P1B
2T9
(705) 474-2777
Sales 19,980,090
SIC 3532 Mining machinery

Ronald Elliott
Gordon Brooks

D-U-N-S 24-658-9519   (HQ)
NORTH BAY PARRY SOUND DISTRICT
HEALTH UNIT
345 Oak St W, North Bay, ON, P1B 2T2
(705) 474-1400
Emp Here 50   *Sales* 24,353,008
SIC 8621 Professional organizations
Jim Chirico

D-U-N-S 25-743-3334   (BR)
NORTH EAST COMMUNITY CARE ACCESS
CENTRE
(*Suby of* NORTH EAST COMMUNITY CARE
ACCESS CENTRE)
1164 Devonshire Ave, North Bay, ON, P1B
6X7
(705) 474-5885
Emp Here 100
SIC 8059 Nursing and personal care, nec
Doris Perron

D-U-N-S 20-133-6864   (HQ)
ONTARIO NORTHLAND TRANSPORTA-
TION COMMISSION
ONTARIO NORTHLAND RAILWAY
(*Suby of* GOVERNMENT OF ONTARIO)
555 Oak St E, North Bay, ON, P1B 8E3
(705) 472-4500
Emp Here 80   *Sales* 316,350,400
SIC 4731 Freight transportation arrangement
Corina Moore
Dennis Higgs
Grant Bailey
Chad Evans
Donna Jacques
Rebecca Mcglynn

D-U-N-S 20-133-7854   (BR)
OSPREY MEDIA PUBLISHING INC
NORTH BAY NUGGET
(*Suby of* QUEBECOR MEDIA INC)
259 Worthington St W, North Bay, ON, P1B
3B5
(705) 472-3200
Emp Here 90
SIC 2711 Newspapers
Dan Johnson

D-U-N-S 20-298-9356   (SL)
RAILINK CANADA LTD
OTTAWA VALLEY RAILWAY
(*Suby of* GENESEE & WYOMING INC.)
445 Oak St E, North Bay, ON, P1B 1A3
(705) 472-6200
Emp Here 40   *Sales* 10,781,960
SIC 4011 Railroads, line-haul operating
Mario Brault

D-U-N-S 24-846-1105   (SL)
RAN DON CRANE & LEASING LTD
3736 Highway 11 N Suite 2, North Bay, ON,
P1B 8G3
(705) 474-4374
Emp Here 6   *Sales* 14,329,735
SIC 1794 Excavation work
Randolph Ollivier
Bartley Hutson

D-U-N-S 20-415-6905   (HQ)
REDPATH CANADA LIMITED
REDPATH GROUP
(*Suby of* ATON 2 GMBH)
101 Worthington St E, North Bay, ON, P1B
1G5
(705) 474-2461
Emp Here 60   *Sales* 186,228,822
SIC 1081 Metal mining services
George Flumerfelt
Torsten Kahn
Bruce Dunlop
David C.Hansman
Lelani Robertson

D-U-N-S 24-888-9461   (HQ)
REDPATH MINING INC

(*Suby of* ATON 2 GMBH)
101 Worthington St E 3rd Fl, North Bay, ON, P1B 1G5
(705) 474-2461
Emp Here 5   *Sales* 186,228,822
SIC 1081 Metal mining services
George Flumerfelt

D-U-N-S 24-367-6207   (BR)
SANDVIK CANADA, INC
SANDVIK MINING AND CONSTRUCTION
(*Suby of* SANDVIK AB)
400 Kirkpatrick St Suite B, North Bay, ON, P1B 8G5

Emp Here 85
SIC 5082 Construction and mining machinery
Brad Searle

D-U-N-S 25-743-5875   (BR)
SOBEYS CAPITAL INCORPORATED
FRESHCO
(*Suby of* EMPIRE COMPANY LIMITED)
2555 Trout Lake Rd, North Bay, ON, P1B 7S8
(705) 495-4221
Emp Here 75
SIC 5141 Groceries, general line
Dave Russell

D-U-N-S 25-743-5883   (BR)
SOBEYS CAPITAL INCORPORATED
(*Suby of* EMPIRE COMPANY LIMITED)
1899 Algonquin Ave, North Bay, ON, P1B 4Y8
(705) 472-4001
Emp Here 200
SIC 5411 Grocery stores
Paul Belanger

D-U-N-S 24-214-1695   (SL)
ST. JOSEPH-SCOLLARD HALL CATHOLIC SECONDARY SCHOOL
675 O'Brien St, North Bay, ON, P1B 9R3
(705) 494-8600
Emp Here 85   *Sales* 7,890,210
SIC 8211 Elementary and secondary schools
Don Houle
Derek Belanger

D-U-N-S 25-184-7195   (BR)
STANTEC CONSULTING INTERNATIONAL LTD
(*Suby of* STANTEC INC)
147 Mcintyre St W Suite 200, North Bay, ON, P1B 2Y5
(705) 494-8255
Emp Here 108
SIC 8711 Engineering services
Brian Mashford

D-U-N-S 24-010-5395   (HQ)
STOCKFISH, GEORGE FORD SALES (1987) LTD
Hwy 17 E, North Bay, ON, P1B 8J5
(705) 476-1506
Emp Here 1   *Sales* 49,083,840
SIC 5511 New and used car dealers
George Stockfish
Lynne Stockfish
Ray Irwin

D-U-N-S 20-115-1631   (BR)
SYKES ASSISTANCE SERVICES CORPORATION
SYKES TELEHEALTH
(*Suby of* SYKES ENTERPRISES INCORPORATED)
555 Oak St E, North Bay, ON, P1B 8E3

Emp Here 100
SIC 8099 Health and allied services, nec
Diane Legault

D-U-N-S 24-963-3710   (SL)
TRUE NORTH CHEVROLET CADILLAC LTD
1370 Seymour St, North Bay, ON, P1B 9V6
(705) 472-1210
Emp Here 52   *Sales* 32,722,560
SIC 5511 New and used car dealers

Peter Schoen
Karen Schoen
Nick Forte

D-U-N-S 20-337-1724   (SL)
VOYAGEUR AEROTECH INC
(*Suby of* CHORUS AVIATION INC)
1500 Airport Rd, North Bay, ON, P1B 8G2
(705) 476-1750
Emp Here 85
SIC 4581 Airports, flying fields, and services
Max Shapiro
Jeff Cooke
Anil Mohan

D-U-N-S 20-532-8255   (SL)
VOYAGEUR AIRWAYS LIMITED
(*Suby of* CHORUS AVIATION INC)
1500 Airport Rd, North Bay, ON, P1B 8G2
(705) 476-1750
Emp Here 250   *Sales* 79,338,000
SIC 4512 Air transportation, scheduled
Scott Tapson
Cory Cousineau
Grant Warner

D-U-N-S 20-281-5734   (HQ)
VOYAGEUR AVIATION CORP.
(*Suby of* CHORUS AVIATION INC)
1500 Airport Rd, North Bay, ON, P1B 8G2
(705) 476-1750
Emp Here 5   *Sales* 100,514,975
SIC 6712 Bank holding companies
Max Shapiro
Scott Tapson
Duncan Sharp
Cory Cousineau
Sharon Campbell

D-U-N-S 24-329-6998   (BR)
WAL-MART CANADA CORP
(*Suby of* WALMART INC.)
1500 Fisher St Suite 102, North Bay, ON, P1B 2H3
(705) 472-1704
Emp Here 200
SIC 5311 Department stores

D-U-N-S 24-847-1927   (HQ)
WORKPLACE SAFETY NORTH
690 Mckeown Ave, North Bay, ON, P1B 7M2
(705) 474-7233
Sales 86,479,260
SIC 6331 Fire, marine, and casualty insurance
Paul Andre
Dwight Harper

D-U-N-S 24-288-7008   (HQ)
YOUNG MEN'S CHRISTIAN ASSOCIATION OF NORTH BAY AND DISTRICT
YMCA OF NORTH BAY
186 Chippewa St W, North Bay, ON, P1B 6G2
(705) 497-9622
Emp Here 100   *Sales* 26,303,000
SIC 8641 Civic and social associations
Lee Crawford
Kim Kanmacher

D-U-N-S 25-997-4413   (SL)
ZEDD CUSTOMER SOLUTIONS L P INC
180 Shirreff Ave Suite 225, North Bay, ON, P1B 7K9
(705) 495-1333
Emp Here 49   *Sales* 21,731,010
SIC 7389 Business services, nec
Jason Pichette

North Bay, ON P1C

D-U-N-S 24-488-1228   (SL)
LAURENTIAN SKI HILL SNOWBOARDING CLUB
LAURENTIAN SKI HILL
15 Janey Ave, North Bay, ON, P1C 1N1

(705) 494-7463
Emp Here 100   *Sales* 14,002,900
SIC 7999 Amusement and recreation, nec
Trish Pecore

D-U-N-S 24-011-6046   (HQ)
NEAR NORTH DISTRICT SCHOOL BOARD
963 Airport Rd, North Bay, ON, P1C 1A5
(705) 472-8170
Emp Here 40   *Sales* 135,702,501
SIC 8211 Elementary and secondary schools
Heli Vail
Elizabeth Therrien

North Bay, ON P2A

D-U-N-S 20-648-1231   (SL)
WASAUKSING FIRST NATION
1508 Lane G Parry Island, North Bay, ON, P2A 2X4
(705) 746-2531
Emp Here 45   *Sales* 10,937,205
SIC 6519 Real property lessors, nec
Shane Tabobondung

North Gower, ON K0A

D-U-N-S 25-869-2409   (HQ)
1168768 ONTARIO INC
ABC OPERATIONS
6750 Fourth Line Rd, North Gower, ON, K0A 2T0
(613) 489-0120
Sales 16,401,000
SIC 6712 Bank holding companies
Andrew Cinnamon
Dawn Cinnamon

North York, ON M1R

D-U-N-S 20-150-6714   (SL)
CITY BUICK CHEVROLET CADILLAC GMC LTD
CITY NATIONAL LEASING DIV
1900 Victoria Park Ave, North York, ON, M1R 1T6
(416) 751-5920
Emp Here 147   *Sales* 92,504,160
SIC 5511 New and used car dealers
John Carmichael Jr
John Anderson

North York, ON M2H

D-U-N-S 25-349-9909   (SL)
852515 ONTARIO LIMITED
ACTION COLLECTIONS AND RECEIVABLES MANAGEMENT
716 Gordon Baker Rd Suite 212, North York, ON, M2H 3B4
(416) 503-9633
Emp Here 50   *Sales* 12,615,550
SIC 7322 Adjustment and collection services
Paul Esteves
Susan Lockhart

D-U-N-S 20-116-5862   (SL)
A & F GALATI LIMITED
GALATI MARKET FRESH
5845 Leslie St, North York, ON, M2H 1J8
(416) 756-2000
Emp Here 120   *Sales* 35,217,240
SIC 5411 Grocery stores
Frank Galati
Robert Galati
Grace Galati

D-U-N-S 20-057-8693   (SL)
AMVIC INC
501 Mcnicoll Ave, North York, ON, M2H 2E2
(416) 410-5674
Emp Here 160   *Sales* 28,675,040
SIC 3271 Concrete block and brick
Victor Amend

D-U-N-S 20-844-5973   (SL)
BUCKLER AQUATICS LIMITED
562 Mcnicoll Ave, North York, ON, M2H 2E1
(416) 499-0151
Emp Here 93   *Sales* 13,022,697
SIC 7999 Amusement and recreation, nec
Michael Rolph
Pamela Perry

D-U-N-S 24-859-9487   (SL)
CANADA FENG TAI INTERNATIONAL INC
1100 Gordon Baker Rd, North York, ON, M2H 3B3
(416) 497-6666
Emp Here 20   *Sales* 10,702,480
SIC 5141 Groceries, general line
Chang Wi

D-U-N-S 25-146-8604   (SL)
CANADIAN MEMORIAL CHIROPRACTIC COLLEGE
CMCC
6100 Leslie St, North York, ON, M2H 3J1
(416) 482-2340
Emp Here 225   *Sales* 33,612,975
SIC 8221 Colleges and universities
David Wickes
David Gryfe
Rahim Karim
Richard Mercier

D-U-N-S 20-213-4888   (HQ)
CANERECTOR INC
1 Sparks Ave, North York, ON, M2H 2W1
(416) 225-6240
Emp Here 6   *Sales* 729,693,000
SIC 3443 Fabricated plate work (boiler shop)
Cecil Hawkins
Amanda Hawkins
Jonathan Puddy
Bill Nickel

D-U-N-S 25-991-1436   (HQ)
CANPRO KING-REED LP.
155 Gordon Baker Rd Suite 101, North York, ON, M2H 3N5
(416) 449-8677
Sales 11,769,885
SIC 6719 Holding companies, nec
Brian King

D-U-N-S 24-889-5997   (HQ)
CCL INTERNATIONAL INC
(*Suby of* CCL INDUSTRIES INC)
105 Gordon Baker Rd Suite 800, North York, ON, M2H 3P8
(416) 756-8500
Emp Here 5   *Sales* 367,637,000
SIC 2679 Converted paper products, nec
Meldon H Snider
Steven Lancaster
Bohdan Sirota

D-U-N-S 20-112-6559   (SL)
CHEMTRADE LOGISTICS (US) INC
(*Suby of* CHEMTRADE LOGISTICS INCOME FUND)
155 Gordon Baker Rd Suite 300, North York, ON, M2H 3N5
(416) 496-5856
Emp Here 450   *Sales* 302,495,400
SIC 5169 Chemicals and allied products, nec
Mark Davis
Tom Briand

D-U-N-S 25-195-1794   (HQ)
CHEMTRADE LOGISTICS INC
(*Suby of* CHEMTRADE LOGISTICS INCOME FUND)
155 Gordon Baker Rd Unit 300, North York,

ON, M2H 3N5
(416) 496-5856
Emp Here 125   *Sales* 1,026,231,238
SIC 2819 Industrial inorganic chemicals, nec
Mark Davis
Douglas Cadwell
Rohit Bhardwaj
Louis Hollander
David Gee
Lorie Waisberg
James William Leech

D-U-N-S 20-112-6716   (HQ)
CHEMTRADE LOGISTICS INCOME FUND
155 Gordon Baker Rd Suite 300, North York,
ON, M2H 3N5
(416) 496-5856
Emp Here 550   *Sales* 1,209,738,992
SIC 2819 Industrial inorganic chemicals, nec
Mark Davis
Rohit Bhardwaj
Leon Aarts
Dan Dietz
Tab Mccullough
Emily Powers
Michael St. Pierre
Tejinder Kaushik
Susan Pare
Lorie Waisberg

D-U-N-S 20-180-1102   (HQ)
**CHEMTRADE PERFORMANCE CHEMI-
CALS CANADA INC**
(*Suby of* CHEMTRADE LOGISTICS INCOME
FUND)
155 Gordon Baker Rd Suite 300, North York,
ON, M2H 3N5
(416) 496-5856
Sales 18,258,625
SIC 5169 Chemicals and allied products, nec
Mark Davis

D-U-N-S 20-180-1144   (SL)
**CHEMTRADE PERFORMANCE CHEMI-
CALS US, LLC**
(*Suby of* CHEMTRADE LOGISTICS INCOME
FUND)
155 Gordon Baker Rd Suite 300, North York,
ON, M2H 3N5
(416) 496-5856
Emp Here 75   *Sales* 50,415,900
SIC 5169 Chemicals and allied products, nec
Mark Davis
Tom Briand

D-U-N-S 24-760-2845   (HQ)
**CHEMTRADE WEST LIMITED PARTNER-
SHIP**
155 Gordon Baker Rd Suite 300, North York,
ON, M2H 3N5
(416) 496-5856
Emp Here 10   *Sales* 14,606,900
SIC 5169 Chemicals and allied products, nec
Laurie Tugman

D-U-N-S 20-708-6401   (BR)
COCA-COLA LTD
(*Suby of* THE COCA-COLA COMPANY)
3389 Steeles Ave E Suite 500, North York,
ON, M2H 3S8

Emp Here 150
SIC 5149 Groceries and related products, nec
Nikos Koumettis

D-U-N-S 25-169-2869   (SL)
**DELL FINANCIAL SERVICES CANADA LIM-
ITED**
(*Suby of* DELL TECHNOLOGIES INC.)
155 Gordon Baker Rd Suite 501, North York,
ON, M2H 3N5
(800) 864-8156
Emp Here 325   *Sales* 171,817,750
SIC 6159 Miscellaneous business credit insti-
tutions
Bruce Smith
Thomas Vallone

Janet Wright

D-U-N-S 25-531-9949   (SL)
DYADEM INTERNATIONAL LTD
(*Suby of* IHS MARKIT LTD)
155 Gordon Baker Rd Suite 401, North York,
ON, M2H 3N5
(416) 649-9200
Emp Here 105
SIC 5045 Computers, peripherals, and soft-
ware
Kevin North
Andrew Shannon
Sam Zawaideh

D-U-N-S 24-125-6663   (HQ)
ENERCARE CONNECTIONS INC
(*Suby of* ENERCARE INC)
4000 Victoria Park Ave, North York, ON, M2H
3P4
(416) 649-1900
Emp Here 1   *Sales* 31,033,800
SIC 8611 Business associations
John Macdonald
Evelyn Sutherland

D-U-N-S 25-092-1033   (SL)
FONG TAI INTERNATIONAL FOOD LIMITED
1100 Gordon Baker Rd, North York, ON, M2H
3B3
(416) 497-6666
Emp Here 20   *Sales* 10,702,480
SIC 5141 Groceries, general line
Chang Wi

D-U-N-S 25-093-6465   (SL)
GALATI MARKET FRESH INC
5845 Leslie St, North York, ON, M2H 1J8
(416) 747-1899
Emp Here 75   *Sales* 22,010,775
SIC 5411 Grocery stores
Robert Galati
Grace Galati
Frank Galati, Sr

D-U-N-S 24-162-6480   (HQ)
**GENUMARK PROMOTIONAL MERCHAN-
DISE INC**
GENUMARK
(*Suby of* MENLI ENTERPRISES INC)
707 Gordon Baker Rd, North York, ON, M2H
2S6
(416) 391-9191
Sales 54,946,480
SIC 5199 Nondurable goods, nec
Mark Freed
John Gill
David Lewenberg

D-U-N-S 25-406-3183   (SL)
**GLOBAL PAYMENT SYSTEMS OF
CANADA, LTD**
(*Suby of* GLOBAL PAYMENTS INC.)
3381 Steeles Ave E Suite 200, North York,
ON, M2H 3S7
(416) 644-5959
Emp Here 60   *Sales* 40,134,480
SIC 7389 Business services, nec
Mig H. Migirdicyan

D-U-N-S 20-044-2226   (SL)
HABCO MANUFACTURING INC
501 Gordon Baker Rd, North York, ON, M2H
2S6
(416) 491-6008
Emp Here 125   *Sales* 27,750,125
SIC 3585 Refrigeration and heating equip-
ment
George Brown
James Maynard
Scott Brown

D-U-N-S 24-852-9542   (SL)
ISECURITY INC
(*Suby of* DAPASOFT INC)
111 Gordon Baker Rd 6th Fl, North York, ON,
M2H 3R1

(416) 843-6018
Emp Here 60   *Sales* 10,010,820
SIC 7379 Computer related services, nec
Raheel Qureshi
Kees Pouw

D-U-N-S 25-794-0239   (BR)
J.F. & L. RESTAURANTS LIMITED
PICKLE BARREL RESTAURANT, THE
(*Suby of* J.F. & L. RESTAURANTS LIMITED)
5941 Leslie St, North York, ON, M2H 1J8
(416) 493-4444
Emp Here 150
SIC 5812 Eating places
Simone Nitsch

D-U-N-S 24-795-1445   (HQ)
LEXISNEXIS CANADA INC
(*Suby of* RELX PLC)
111 Gordon Baker Rd Suite 900, North York,
ON, M2H 3R1
(905) 479-2665
Emp Here 200   *Sales* 50,381,240
SIC 2731 Book publishing
Patrick Collins
Loik Amis
Linda Kee
Antoine Shiu

D-U-N-S 24-526-0039   (HQ)
MERIT INSURANCE BROKERS INC
111 Gordon Baker Rd Suite 100, North York,
ON, M2H 3R1
(416) 497-5556
Emp Here 1   *Sales* 22,049,560
SIC 6411 Insurance agents, brokers, and ser-
vice
Ronald (Ron) Barry

D-U-N-S 24-758-5250   (HQ)
MULTI-HEALTH SYSTEMS INC
MHS
3770 Victoria Park Ave, North York, ON, M2H
3M6
(416) 492-2627
Sales 21,039,670
SIC 8748 Business consulting, nec
Hazel Wheldon
Steven Stein
Gerald Fitzgerald
Martin Block
Rodeen Stein

D-U-N-S 20-784-0604   (SL)
**NATIONAL UTILITY SERVICE (CANADA)
LIMITED**
NUS CONSULTING GROUP
(*Suby of* NATIONAL UTILITY SERVICE, INC.)
111 Gordon Baker Rd Suite 500, North York,
ON, M2H 3R2
(416) 490-9922
Emp Here 50   *Sales* 11,714,400
SIC 8742 Management consulting services
Wally Khalil
Gary Soultanian
Richard Soultanian

D-U-N-S 25-291-1771   (SL)
NEWCON INTERNATIONAL LTD
NEWCON OPTIK
105 Sparks Ave, North York, ON, M2H 2S5
(416) 663-6963
Emp Here 34   *Sales* 20,239,731
SIC 5049 Professional equipment, nec
Peter Biro
Michael Beker
Alla Rudiy
Alex Rudiy

D-U-N-S 25-513-9602   (SL)
QUALICOM INNOVATIONS INC
3389 Steeles Ave E Suite 401, North York,
ON, M2H 3S8
(416) 492-3833
Emp Here 110   *Sales* 20,515,660
SIC 8742 Management consulting services
William Chan
David Mok

Richard Chan
Kwok-Ki Lam

D-U-N-S 20-014-6566   (HQ)
QUANTEC GEOSCIENCE LIMITED
146 Sparks Ave, North York, ON, M2H 2S4
(416) 306-1941
Emp Here 25   *Sales* 73,101,800
SIC 6712 Bank holding companies
Oliver Kuhn
Kevin Blackshaw
Roger Sharpe

D-U-N-S 25-333-6952   (SL)
REHO INTERNATIONAL INC
7 Equestrian Crt, North York, ON, M2H 3M9
(416) 269-2950
Emp Here 40   *Sales* 29,213,800
SIC 5169 Chemicals and allied products, nec
Shao Jun Teng

D-U-N-S 24-795-6618   (HQ)
SELECT FOOD SERVICES INC
SELECT SANDWICH CO.
155 Gordon Baker Rd Unit 214, North York,
ON, M2H 3N5
(416) 391-1244
Emp Here 6   *Sales* 28,569,210
SIC 6794 Patent owners and lessors
Brian Kahn
Carol Kahn

D-U-N-S 25-282-1137   (SL)
SLI MANUFACTURING INC
550 Mcnicoll Ave, North York, ON, M2H 2E1
(416) 493-8900
Emp Here 100   *Sales* 22,200,100
SIC 3577 Computer peripheral equipment,
nec
Andy Sin

D-U-N-S 24-764-7035   (HQ)
SYMANTEC (CANADA) CORPORATION
(*Suby of* SYMANTEC CORPORATION)
3381 Steeles Ave E, North York, ON, M2H 3S7
(416) 774-0000
Sales 28,836,400
SIC 7371 Custom computer programming ser-
vices
Chris Calisi
John Thomson

D-U-N-S 20-176-5468   (HQ)
TAB PRODUCTS OF CANADA, CO.
TAB CANADA
(*Suby of* TAB INTERNATIONAL COOPER-
ATIEF U.A.)
136 Sparks Ave, North York, ON, M2H 2S4
(416) 497-1552
Emp Here 75   *Sales* 80,302,800
SIC 5044 Office equipment
John Palmer
Janet Campbell
Ross Nepean
Jonathon Shea
Jonathan Cowie
Brad Hicks
Henry Van Pypen
Aggie Koniak Jaggers

D-U-N-S 20-295-9540   (HQ)
TANGERINE BANK
CAFE DE MONTREAL
(*Suby of* BANK OF NOVA SCOTIA, THE)
3389 Steeles Ave E, North York, ON, M2H 3S8
(416) 497-5157
Sales 249,745,320
SIC 6036 Savings institutions, except federal
Gillian Riley
Emily Tan
Steven G. Cannon
Barbara F. Mason
James I. Mcphedran
Gerald Girard
Ronald Elwood Porter
Kyle Francis Mcnamara
Kevin John Teslyk

▲ Public Company   ■ Public Company Family Member   **HQ** Headquarters   **BR** Branch   **SL** Single Location

Maria A. Theofilaktidis

D-U-N-S 20-700-2663   (BR)
TORONTO DISTRICT SCHOOL BOARD
A Y JACKSON SECONDARY SCHOOL
(*Suby of* TORONTO DISTRICT SCHOOL
BOARD)
50 Francine Dr, North York, ON, M2H 2G6
(416) 395-3140
Emp Here 75
SIC 8211 Elementary and secondary schools
Peter Paputsis

D-U-N-S 20-934-5771   (HQ)
UNIFOR
205 Placer Crt, North York, ON, M2H 3H9
(416) 497-4110
Emp Here 96   *Sales* 89,587,603
SIC 8631 Labor organizations
Jerry Dias
Bob Orr

D-U-N-S 20-597-1492   (HQ)
WARNER MUSIC CANADA CO.
(*Suby of* ACCESS INDUSTRIES, INC.)
155 Gordon Baker Rd Unit 401, North York,
ON, M2H 3N5
(416) 491-5005
Sales 19,044,200
SIC 3652 Prerecorded records and tapes
Steve Kane

D-U-N-S 20-044-6367   (HQ)
WRIGLEY CANADA INC
(*Suby of* MARS, INCORPORATED)
3389 Steeles Ave E, North York, ON, M2H 3S8
(416) 449-8600
Emp Here 500   *Sales* 292,431,000
SIC 2067 Chewing gum
Kenneth Keller
Shai Altman
Anthony Gedeller
Daniel Alvo
John Gladiator
Janis Hazlewood

D-U-N-S 24-805-6991   (HQ)
**XPERA RISK MITIGATION & INVESTIGA-
TION LP**
CKR GLOBAL
(*Suby of* SCM INSURANCE SERVICES INC)
155 Gordon Baker Rd Suite 101, North York,
ON, M2H 3N5
(416) 449-8677
Emp Here 150   *Sales* 50,491,350
SIC 8741 Management services
Robert Burns
Brian D. King
Ken M. Cahoon
Nino G. Calabrese
Royston Colbourne
Jason J Dumbreck
Matt Henschel
Tim Houghton
Paul Mcparlan

D-U-N-S 20-795-1393   (HQ)
YAMAHA MOTOR CANADA LTD
(*Suby of* YAMAHA MOTOR CO., LTD.)
480 Gordon Baker Rd, North York, ON, M2H
3B4
(416) 498-1911
Sales 111,248,000
SIC 5091 Sporting and recreation goods
Yoichiro Kojima
Steve Tanaka
Peter R Braund
William T Pashby

North York, ON M2J

D-U-N-S 24-239-8795   (SL)
2023225 ONTARIO LTD
MIDLAND METALS

259 Yorkland Rd Suite 300, North York, ON,
M2J 5B2
(416) 733-9500
Emp Here 15   *Sales* 15,005,085
SIC 5051 Metals service centers and offices
Alex Schnider
Danny Tilis

D-U-N-S 24-242-3353   (SL)
2100050 ONTARIO INC
TONE TAI SUPERMARKET
3030 Don Mills Rd Suite 26, North York, ON,
M2J 3C1
(416) 756-1668
Emp Here 50   *Sales* 13,707,600
SIC 5411 Grocery stores
Wen Qing He

D-U-N-S 20-822-7710   (HQ)
802912 ONTARIO LIMITED
FITNESS INSTITUTE, THE
(*Suby of* CAMBRIDGE GROUP OF CLUB)
2235 Sheppard Ave E Suite 901, North York,
ON, M2J 5B5
(416) 492-7611
Emp Here 200   *Sales* 37,622,500
SIC 7991 Physical fitness facilities
Clive Caldwell
Steve Roest

D-U-N-S 25-511-5867   (SL)
**ADVANCED UTILITY SYSTEMS CORPORA-
TION**
(*Suby of* CONSTELLATION SOFTWARE
INC)
2235 Sheppard Ave E Suite 1400, North York,
ON, M2J 5B5
(416) 496-0149
Emp Here 140   *Sales* 20,185,480
SIC 7371 Custom computer programming ser-
vices
Peter Sanous

D-U-N-S 20-558-9757   (HQ)
AMEX CANADA INC
AMERICAN EXPRESS
(*Suby of* AMERICAN EXPRESS COMPANY)
2225 Sheppard Ave E, North York, ON, M2J
5C2
(905) 474-8000
Emp Here 2,000   *Sales* 583,845,000
SIC 6099 Functions related to deposit banking
Rob Mcclean
Shawn Klerer
Betty Daruwala
David Barnes

D-U-N-S 20-283-4693   (HQ)
ARZ GROUP OF COMPANIES LIMITED
279 Yorkland Blvd, North York, ON, M2J 1S5
(416) 847-0350
Emp Here 15   *Sales* 21,937,356
SIC 5399 Miscellaneous general merchandise
Armand Boyadjian
Hovic Boyadjian

D-U-N-S 20-337-5191   (HQ)
**ATHLETE'S CARE SPORTS MEDICINE
CENTRES INC**
505 Consumers Rd Suite 809, North York, ON,
M2J 4V8
(416) 479-8562
Emp Here 30   *Sales* 43,176,989
SIC 8011 Offices and clinics of medical doc-
tors
Shafiq Bhanji
William Arvanitis

D-U-N-S 20-968-2624   (SL)
**BARBER STEWART MCVITTIE & WALLACE
INSURANCE BROKERS LTD**
6 Lansing Sq Suite 230, North York, ON, M2J
1T5
(416) 493-0050
Emp Here 22   *Sales* 12,758,328
SIC 6411 Insurance agents, brokers, and ser-
vice
Glenn Wallace

D-U-N-S 25-852-7183   (SL)
BEST ADVICE FINANCIAL SERVICES INC
BEST ADVICE INSURANCE
250 Consumers Rd Suite 1111, North York,
ON, M2J 4V6
(416) 490-1474
Emp Here 40   *Sales* 10,973,280
SIC 8741 Management services
Abaraham Jakarsezian

D-U-N-S 24-181-9028   (SL)
**BRITACAN FACILITIES MANAGEMENT
GROUP INC**
505 Consumers Rd Suite 1010, North York,
ON, M2J 4V8
(416) 494-2007
Emp Here 27   *Sales* 11,974,230
SIC 7389 Business services, nec
Michael Ellis
Heidi Ellis

D-U-N-S 24-424-0446   (HQ)
BROKERFORCE INSURANCE INC
200 Consumers Rd Suite 608, North York, ON,
M2J 4R4
(416) 494-2696
Emp Here 1   *Sales* 37,314,640
SIC 6411 Insurance agents, brokers, and ser-
vice
Eldon Smith
Scott Fraser
Roger Wingfield

D-U-N-S 20-605-5931   (HQ)
BROUGHTON, B. COMPANY LIMITED
BROUGHTON'S
322 Consumers Rd, North York, ON, M2J 1P8
(416) 690-4777
Sales 18,563,000
SIC 5192 Books, periodicals, and newspapers
Brian Broughton

D-U-N-S 24-850-2015   (HQ)
C.S.T. CONSULTANTS INC
(*Suby of* CANADIAN SCHOLARSHIP TRUST
FOUNDATION)
2235 Sheppard Ave E Unit 1600, North York,
ON, M2J 5B8
(416) 445-7377
Sales 126,195,435
SIC 6732 Trusts: educational, religious, etc.
John Kearns
Raymond Riley
Christine Perl
Carole Matear

D-U-N-S 25-950-9354   (HQ)
CANADIAN HEART RESEARCH CENTRE
259 Yorkland Rd Suite 200, North York, ON,
M2J 0B5
(416) 977-8010
Sales 14,934,010
SIC 8731 Commercial physical research
Anatoly Langer
Shaun Goodman

D-U-N-S 24-121-1176   (HQ)
**CANADIAN INSTITUTE OF TRAVEL COUN-
SELLORS OF ONTARIO**
C I T C
505 Consumers Rd Suite 406, North York, ON,
M2J 4V8
(416) 484-4450
Emp Here 20   *Sales* 11,684,750
SIC 8621 Professional organizations
Steve Gillick

D-U-N-S 24-787-6027   (SL)
CANADIAN PROTECTION PROVIDERS INC
251 Consumers Rd Suite 1200, North York,
ON, M2J 4R3
(647) 330-0313
Emp Here 15   *Sales* 10,183,845
SIC 6211 Security brokers and dealers
Rihana Syed

D-U-N-S 20-079-0496   (HQ)
CANADIAN SCHOLARSHIP TRUST FOUN-

DATION
2225 Sheppard Ave E Suite 600, North York,
ON, M2J 5C2
(416) 445-7377
Sales 243,286,375
SIC 6732 Trusts: educational, religious, etc.
Sherry Mcdonald
Colin Litton
Elaine Bourassa
Colin J Dodds
Gisele D Wilson
Elizabeth Wright
Rodney W J Seyffert
David Lewis
Ted Cadsby
Michelle Savoy

D-U-N-S 20-101-7816   (BR)
CBRE LIMITEE
CBRE LIMITED
(*Suby of* CBRE LIMITED PARTNERSHIP)
2001 Sheppard Ave E Suite 300, North York,
ON, M2J 4Z8
(416) 494-0600
Emp Here 100
SIC 6531 Real estate agents and managers
Adrian Lee

D-U-N-S 20-848-9518   (HQ)
CH2M HILL CANADA LIMITED
(*Suby of* JACOBS ENGINEERING GROUP
INC.)
245 Consumers Rd Suite 400, North York, ON,
M2J 1R3
(416) 499-9000
Emp Here 250   *Sales* 143,905,630
SIC 8711 Engineering services
Peter Nicol
Andrew Phillip
David Larter
Bruce Tucker
Dottie Swallow
Gary Webster
Shawn Gibbons
William T. Dohn
M. Catherine Santee
Ronald A. Campbell

D-U-N-S 24-347-0981   (HQ)
CIK TELECOM INC
282 Consumers Rd, North York, ON, M2J 1P8
(416) 800-4111
Emp Here 47   *Sales* 124,450,368
SIC 4899 Communication services, nec
Wai Yin Alice Chiu
Juxia Guo
Yang Hao
Yanqing Jin
Liu Kai

D-U-N-S 24-426-6248   (SL)
COFACE SERVICES CANADA COMPANY
COFACE CANADA
(*Suby of* COFACE SA)
251 Consumers Rd Suite 910, North York, ON,
M2J 4R3
(647) 426-4730
Emp Here 100   *Sales* 12,477,600
SIC 8741 Management services
Kerstin Braun
Christopher Short
Daniel Shultis
Friedrich Von Krusenstiern
Braun Kerstin
Michael J. Ferrante
Kenneth Moyle

D-U-N-S 20-817-2528   (HQ)
CROSSEY ENGINEERING LTD
(*Suby of* LACELA HOLDINGS CORP)
2255 Sheppard Ave E, North York, ON, M2J
4Y1
(416) 497-3111
Emp Here 134   *Sales* 25,023,460
SIC 8711 Engineering services
Wallace Eley
Clive Lacey

Andrew Pratt
Duane Waite

D-U-N-S 25-691-6198   (SL)
DBPC GROUP OF COMPANIES LTD
250 Consumers Rd Suite 605, North York, ON,
M2J 4V6
(416) 755-9198
Emp Here 180   *Sales* 13,444,920
SIC 7361 Employment agencies
Grace Santos
Bob Weir

D-U-N-S 20-046-1874   (SL)
DESTINATION TRAVEL HEALTH PLAN
211 Consumers Rd Suite 200, North York, ON,
M2J 4G8
(416) 499-6616
Emp Here 20   *Sales* 20,697,620
SIC 6321 Accident and health insurance
Ron Lewin

D-U-N-S 20-127-0626   (HQ)
DILLON CONSULTING LIMITED
235 Yorkland Blvd Suite 800, North York, ON,
M2J 4Y8
(416) 229-4646
Emp Here 77   *Sales* 137,991,700
SIC 8711 Engineering services
Sean Hanlon
Richard Fitzgerald
Jim R Balfour
Gary Komar
Jeffrey Matthews
Terry Boutilier
Flavio Forest
Andrew Wilson
Bill Ross
Dennis Heinrichs

D-U-N-S 24-862-0791   (HQ)
DOMINION COLOUR CORPORATION
DCC
(*Suby of* HIG CAPITAL MANAGEMENT, INC.)
515 Consumers Rd Unit 700, North York, ON,
M2J 4Z2
(416) 791-4200
Emp Here 25   *Sales* 133,393,500
SIC 2816 Inorganic pigments
Mark Vincent
Graham Dickie
Probyn Forbes
Peter Baggen

D-U-N-S 24-131-9420   (SL)
EDUCATOR'S FINANCIAL GROUP
2225 Sheppard Ave E Suite 1105, North York,
ON, M2J 5C2
(416) 752-9410
Emp Here 49   *Sales* 40,561,073
SIC 6722 Management investment, open-end
Chuck Hamilton

D-U-N-S 25-998-1058   (SL)
ENBRIDGE COMMERCIAL SERVICES INC
(*Suby of* ENBRIDGE INC)
500 Consumers Rd, North York, ON, M2J 1P8
(416) 492-5000
Emp Here 1,000
SIC 8741 Management services
Dwight Willett
Paul Dalglish

D-U-N-S 25-679-6798   (HQ)
ENBRIDGE ENERGY DISTRIBUTION INC
(*Suby of* ENBRIDGE INC)
500 Consumers Rd, North York, ON, M2J 1P8
(416) 492-5000
Emp Here 400   *Sales* 2,905,227,988
SIC 4924 Natural gas distribution
Al Monaco
D. Guy Jarvis
J. Richard Bird
Karen Radford
Bob Rooney
John K. Whelen
William T. Yardley
Vern Yu

D-U-N-S 24-206-9461   (SL)
EPIC REALTY PARTNERS INC
2225 Sheppard Ave E Suite 900, North York,
ON, M2J 5C2
(416) 497-9332
Emp Here 50   *Sales* 11,895,050
SIC 8742 Management consulting services
Gordon Thompson
Sandra Gay

D-U-N-S 20-938-3694   (SL)
FAIRMALL LEASEHOLDS INC
FAIRVIEW MALL
1800 Sheppard Ave E Suite 330, North York,
ON, M2J 5A7
(416) 491-0151
Emp Here 45   *Sales* 12,982,455
SIC 6512 Nonresidential building operators
Kevin Grey

D-U-N-S 24-830-4537   (HQ)
FERRING INC
FERRING PHARMACEUTICALS
200 Yorkland Blvd Suite 500, North York, ON,
M2J 5C1
(416) 490-0121
Emp Here 30   *Sales* 66,320,700
SIC 5122 Drugs, proprietaries, and sundries
Rick Jeysman
Michel Pettigrew
Michael Penman

D-U-N-S 20-072-1980   (SL)
FOOD ALLERGY CANADA
2005 Sheppard Ave E Suite 800, North York,
ON, M2J 5B4
(416) 785-5666
Emp Here 25   *Sales* 11,230,475
SIC 7389 Business services, nec
Laurie Harada

D-U-N-S 24-795-5482   (BR)
FOREVER XXI ULC
1800 Sheppard Ave E, North York, ON, M2J
5A7
(416) 494-6363
Emp Here 80
SIC 5651 Family clothing stores
Rebecca Soglia

D-U-N-S 25-696-2143   (BR)
G4S SECURE SOLUTIONS (CANADA) LTD
(*Suby of* G4S PLC)
2 Lansing Sq Suite 204, North York, ON, M2J
4P8
(416) 490-8329
Emp Here 800
SIC 7381 Detective and armored car services
Tom Doyle

D-U-N-S 20-285-0814   (SL)
**GENERAL MOTORS FINANCIAL OF
CANADA, LTD.**
GM FINANCIAL
(*Suby of* GENERAL MOTORS COMPANY)
2001 Sheppard Ave E Unit 600, North York,
ON, M2J 4Z8
(416) 753-4000
Emp Here 200   *Sales* 105,734,000
SIC 6159 Miscellaneous business credit insti-
tutions
Howard Cobham
Jennifer Hardy-Ogle

D-U-N-S 25-373-8306   (SL)
**GENERATION 5 MATHEMATICAL TECH-
NOLOGIES INC**
515 Consumers Rd Suite 600, North York, ON,
M2J 4Z2

Emp Here 49   *Sales* 10,454,542
SIC 8732 Commercial nonphysical research
Milorad Krneta

D-U-N-S 25-663-0070   (SL)
GUTHRIE INSURANCE BROKERS LTD
GUTHRIE FIANANCIAL SERVICES
505 Consumers Rd Suite 308, North York, ON,

M2J 4V8
(416) 487-5200
Emp Here 23   *Sales* 13,338,252
SIC 6411 Insurance agents, brokers, and ser-
vice
Ryan Guthrie

D-U-N-S 25-718-7617   (SL)
HEALTHSOURCE PLUS INC
SOURCE SANTE PLUS
(*Suby of* PEOPLE CORPORATION)
2225 Sheppard Ave E Suite 1400, North York,
ON, M2J 5C2

Emp Here 15   *Sales* 27,699,885
SIC 6321 Accident and health insurance
Bruce Bell
John Gullivan
Bonnie Echwartzki
Brevan Canning
Laurie Goldberg

D-U-N-S 24-138-5152   (HQ)
HERITAGE EDUCATION FUNDS INC
HERITAGE SCHOLARSHIP TRUST PLAN
2005 Sheppard Ave E Suite 700, North York,
ON, M2J 5B4
(416) 758-4400
Sales 106,269,840
SIC 6732 Trusts: educational, religious, etc.
Scott Mcindless
Onofiro Loduca
Robert Coleman
Jason R.B. Maquire
D. Bruce Elliott

D-U-N-S 24-080-0896   (SL)
**HOGG SHAIN & SCHECK PROFESSIONAL
CORPORATION**
2235 Sheppard Ave E Unit 800, North York,
ON, M2J 5B5
(416) 499-3100
Emp Here 255   *Sales* 52,959,675
SIC 8721 Accounting, auditing, and book-
keeping
Kenneth Shain
Edward Scheck

D-U-N-S 20-700-8830   (BR)
HUDSON'S BAY COMPANY
THE BAY
(*Suby of* HUDSON'S BAY COMPANY)
1800 Sheppard Ave E Suite 1, North York, ON,
M2J 5A7
(416) 491-2010
Emp Here 450
SIC 5311 Department stores
Sunil Singh

D-U-N-S 24-218-9033   (SL)
HURLSTONE HOLDINGS CORP
HERON HOMES
245 Yorkland Blvd Suite 100, North York, ON,
M2J 4W9
(416) 490-1400
Emp Here 50   *Sales* 13,547,100
SIC 1521 Single-family housing construction
Hugh Heron
T Ekulend
E Flening
E Krangle
Sheldor Alspector
Bradley Foster

D-U-N-S 24-685-2784   (HQ)
INGENIA POLYMERS CORP
200 Yorkland Blvd Suite 605, North York, ON,
M2J 5C1
(416) 920-8100
Emp Here 7   *Sales* 28,402,100
SIC 2821 Plastics materials and resins
John Lefas
Nicholas Dowd
Maria Lefas
John Sotos

D-U-N-S 24-284-4835   (BR)
INSURANCE BUREAU OF CANADA

(*Suby of* INSURANCE BUREAU OF
CANADA)
2235 Sheppard Ave E Suite 1100, North York,
ON, M2J 5B5
(416) 445-5912
Emp Here 170
SIC 6411 Insurance agents, brokers, and ser-
vice

D-U-N-S 25-315-7515   (BR)
**INVESTORS GROUP FINANCIAL SER-
VICES INC**
(*Suby of* POWER CORPORATION DU
CANADA)
200 Yorkland Blvd Suite 300, North York, ON,
M2J 5C1
(416) 491-7400
Emp Here 80
SIC 8741 Management services
Bill Jack

D-U-N-S 25-830-3312   (BR)
INVESTORS GROUP TRUST CO. LTD
INVESTORS GROUP FINANCIAL SERVICE
(*Suby of* POWER CORPORATION DU
CANADA)
200 Yorkland Blvd Unit 300, North York, ON,
M2J 5C1
(647) 456-5160
Emp Here 120
SIC 6282 Investment advice
Bill Jack

D-U-N-S 20-699-2633   (SL)
KNRV INVESTMENTS INC
515 Consumers Rd Unit 700, North York, ON,
M2J 4Z2
(416) 791-4200
Emp Here 400   *Sales* 146,203,600
SIC 6712 Bank holding companies
Michael Klein
Jack Nelligan
Mark Vincent
Robert Ralph

D-U-N-S 24-326-9318   (SL)
KOLANDJIAN, A. PHARMACY LTD
SHOPPERS DRUG MART
4865 Leslie St, North York, ON, M2J 2K8
(416) 493-2111
Emp Here 50   *Sales* 12,647,700
SIC 5912 Drug stores and proprietary stores
Ara Kolandjian

D-U-N-S 24-626-0343   (SL)
LIPTON CHARTERED ACCOUNTANTS LLP
245 Fairview Mall Dr Suite 600, North York,
ON, M2J 4T1
(416) 496-2900
Emp Here 50   *Sales* 10,454,250
SIC 8721 Accounting, auditing, and book-
keeping
Stephen Altbaum
Mel Leiderman

D-U-N-S 24-826-0622   (HQ)
M. E. T. UTILITIES MANAGEMENT LTD
2810 Victoria Park Ave Suite 105, North York,
ON, M2J 4A9
(416) 495-9448
Sales 11,230,475
SIC 7389 Business services, nec
Tim Bain

D-U-N-S 25-509-2918   (SL)
MAGINDUSTRIES CORP
235 Yorkland Blvd Unit 409, North York, ON,
M2J 4Y8
(416) 491-6088
Emp Here 300   *Sales* 122,152,200
SIC 3356 Nonferrous rolling and drawing, nec
Richie S Morrow
Stephane Rigny
William Burton
Victor Wells
Bryan Benitz

D-U-N-S 20-555-2573   (HQ)

MATTAMY (MONARCH) LIMITED
2550 Victoria Park Ave Suite 200, North York, ON, M2J 5A9
(416) 491-7440
Emp Here 80   *Sales* 22,459,680
SIC 8741 Management services
Brian K Johnston
David A George
J. Lynn Whelan

D-U-N-S 24-333-1712   (BR)
METRO ONTARIO INC
FOOD BASICS
(*Suby of* METRO INC)
2452 Sheppard Ave E, North York, ON, M2J 1X1
(416) 756-2513
Emp Here 150
SIC 5411 Grocery stores
Dave Darling

D-U-N-S 24-668-6526   (SL)
METTKO CONSTRUCTION INC
(*Suby of* METTKO GROUP INC)
200 Yorkland Blvd Suite 610, North York, ON, M2J 5C1
(416) 444-9600
Emp Here 30   *Sales* 17,110,140
SIC 1542 Nonresidential construction, nec
Mo Ettehadieh

D-U-N-S 25-409-7447   (SL)
MIDLAND METALS INTERNATIONAL INC
MIDLAND GROUP
259 Yorkland Rd Suite 300, North York, ON, M2J 5B2
(416) 733-9500
Emp Here 50   *Sales* 22,358,700
SIC 5051 Metals service centers and offices
Alex Shnaider
Aaron Zak

D-U-N-S 20-771-4627   (HQ)
MITCHELL PARTNERSHIP INC, THE
T M P CONSULTING ENGINEERS
285 Yorkland Blvd, North York, ON, M2J 1S5
(416) 499-8000
Emp Here 85   *Sales* 16,980,205
SIC 8711 Engineering services
John Lowden

D-U-N-S 20-981-6545   (SL)
NAVIGATORS INSURANCE BROKERS LTD
4 Lansing Sq Suite 100, North York, ON, M2J 5A2

Emp Here 35   *Sales* 20,297,340
SIC 6411 Insurance agents, brokers, and service
John Walters

D-U-N-S 24-927-7898   (HQ)
NORSTAN CANADA LTD
BLACK BOX NETWORK SERVICES
(*Suby of* ESSAR GLOBAL LIMITED)
2225 Sheppard Ave E Suite 1600, North York, ON, M2J 5C2
(416) 490-9500
Emp Here 61   *Sales* 42,481,530
SIC 5065 Electronic parts and equipment, nec
Brian Genderon
Dan Tyndale

D-U-N-S 20-288-5463   (SL)
OPUS ONE DESIGN BUILD & CONSTRUCTION PROJECT MANAGEMENT
6 Lansing Sq Suite 237, North York, ON, M2J 1T5

Emp Here 38   *Sales* 12,666,654
SIC 1541 Industrial buildings and warehouses
Yousof Nassar

D-U-N-S 20-629-3029   (SL)
PETER IGEL GROUP INC
PETER IGEL WINES & SPIRITS
2235 Sheppard Ave E Suite 909, North York, ON, M2J 5B5

(416) 493-8800
Emp Here 15   *Sales* 12,533,655
SIC 5141 Groceries, general line
Erik H Igel
Peter Igel
Vincent Hanna
Wendy Clemes Little

D-U-N-S 25-503-6204   (SL)
PLANDIRECT INSURANCE SERVICES INC
PDADMIN GROUP
211 Consumers Rd Suite 200, North York, ON, M2J 4G8
(416) 490-0072
Emp Here 30   *Sales* 17,397,720
SIC 6411 Insurance agents, brokers, and service
Rolph Normandin

D-U-N-S 20-876-7418   (HQ)
R. V. ANDERSON ASSOCIATES LIMITED
TOUCHIE ENGINEERING, DIV OF
2001 Sheppard Ave E Suite 400, North York, ON, M2J 4Z8
(416) 497-8600
Emp Here 150   *Sales* 35,747,800
SIC 8711 Engineering services
Kenneth Morrison
Reginald J Andres
Kenneth Campbell
Gary Farrell
T Harold Mccolm
Vaino Raun
Allan R Perks
Vincent Nazareth
Zoran Filinov

D-U-N-S 20-774-0812   (HQ)
REINHART FOODS LIMITED
REINHART FOODS
235 Yorkland Blvd Suite 1101, North York, ON, M2J 4Y8
(416) 645-4910
Emp Here 7   *Sales* 48,396,600
SIC 2099 Food preparations, nec
Thomas Singer
Louise Watt
Tony Hum
Scott Singer

D-U-N-S 24-319-4052   (HQ)
RELIANCE COMFORT LIMITED PARTNERSHIP
RELIANCE HOME COMFORT, DIV OF
2 Lansing Sq, North York, ON, M2J 4P8
(416) 499-7600
Sales 406,272,000
SIC 1711 Plumbing, heating, air-conditioning
Sean O'brien
Kevin Johnstone
Celso Mello
Catherine David Nolan
Rob Medved

D-U-N-S 24-387-6963   (HQ)
RRJ INSURANCE GROUP LIMITED
KRG INSURANCE BROKERS
2450 Victoria Park Ave Suite 700, North York, ON, M2J 4A1
(416) 636-4544
Emp Here 60   *Sales* 184,774,200
SIC 6411 Insurance agents, brokers, and service
Abraham Baboujian
Paul Martin

D-U-N-S 20-634-4970   (HQ)
SECURITAS CANADA LIMITED
(*Suby of* SECURITAS AB)
400-235 Yorkland Blvd, North York, ON, M2J 4Y8
(416) 774-2500
Emp Here 45   *Sales* 2,440,648,000
SIC 7381 Detective and armored car services
Perry Clarke
John Coletti
Tim Beaver

Lance Kelly
Trevor Thompson
Rowan Hamilton
Dustin Lambert
Kim Hunt

D-U-N-S 20-784-5645   (HQ)
SENECA COLLEGE OF APPLIED ARTS & TECHNOLOGY
1750 Finch Ave E, North York, ON, M2J 2X5
(416) 491-5050
Emp Here 600   *Sales* 99,617,818
SIC 8222 Junior colleges
Rajula Atherton
Colin Locke
Bruce Campbell
Scott Farber
David Agnew
Jeanette Diaz D'sousa
Alexander Adeyinka
Tessa Benn-Ireland
Marc Caira
Davis S Cooke

D-U-N-S 24-171-5767   (SL)
SENIORS HEALTH CENTRE OF NORTH YORK GENERAL HOSPITAL
2 Buchan Crt, North York, ON, M2J 5A3
(416) 756-1040
Emp Here 80   *Sales* 5,485,280
SIC 8051 Skilled nursing care facilities
Sara Rooney

D-U-N-S 25-991-0156   (HQ)
SHOPPERS DRUG MART CORPORATION
SHOPPERS DRUG MART
(*Suby of* LOBLAW COMPANIES LIMITED)
243 Consumers Rd, North York, ON, M2J 4W8
(416) 493-1220
Emp Here 100   *Sales* 212,902,920
SIC 5912 Drug stores and proprietary stores
Domenic Pilla
Dorian Lo
Bradley Lukow
Michael Motz
Frank Pedinelli
Mary-Alice Vuicic
James Hankinson
Sarah Raiss
Beth Pritchard
Johanna Waterous

D-U-N-S 24-422-9014   (HQ)
SHOPPERS HOME HEALTH CARE (CANADA) INC
(*Suby of* LOBLAW COMPANIES LIMITED)
243 Consumers Rd, North York, ON, M2J 4W8
(416) 493-1220
Emp Here 5   *Sales* 183,537,000
SIC 5999 Miscellaneous retail stores, nec
Michael Motz
Frank Pedinelli

D-U-N-S 20-281-5874   (SL)
SIMPLY COMFORT INC.
2225 Sheppard Ave E Suite 1501, North York, ON, M2J 5C2
(416) 477-0626
Emp Here 400   *Sales* 108,339,200
SIC 1711 Plumbing, heating, air-conditioning
Justin Coles

D-U-N-S 25-109-4223   (SL)
SO CANADA INC
2005 Sheppard Ave E Suite 100, North York, ON, M2J 5B4

Emp Here 90   *Sales* 16,237,350
SIC 8731 Commercial physical research
James Mannos
Joanne Yuen
Louie Lee

D-U-N-S 20-948-7966   (HQ)
SONY OF CANADA LTD
SONY STORES, THE
(*Suby of* SONY CORPORATION)

2235 Sheppard Ave E Suite 700, North York, ON, M2J 5B5
(416) 499-1414
Emp Here 200   *Sales* 464,197,600
SIC 5064 Electrical appliances, television and radio
Barry Hasler
Tariq Shameem
Diana Zangrilli
Susan Bean
Anil Sethi
Martin Huntington
Raj Rawana
Ravi Nookala

D-U-N-S 25-708-1729   (BR)
TERREQUITY REALTY INC
(*Suby of* TERREQUITY REALTY INC)
211 Consumers Rd Unit 105, North York, ON, M2J 4G8
(416) 496-9220
Emp Here 375
SIC 6531 Real estate agents and managers
Ray Azar

D-U-N-S 24-784-3998   (SL)
TODDGLEN MANAGEMENT LIMITED
2225 Sheppard Ave E Suite 1100, North York, ON, M2J 5C2
(416) 492-2450
Emp Here 68   *Sales* 18,654,576
SIC 8741 Management services

D-U-N-S 24-334-1158   (SL)
TODDGLEN WINDERMERE LIMITED
2225 Sheppard Ave E Suite 1100, North York, ON, M2J 5C2
(416) 492-2450
Emp Here 70   *Sales* 16,400,160
SIC 8742 Management consulting services
John Todd

D-U-N-S 24-195-7810   (HQ)
TOTAL CREDIT RECOVERY LIMITED
225 Yorkland Blvd, North York, ON, M2J 4Y7
(416) 774-4000
Emp Here 300   *Sales* 120,222,600
SIC 7322 Adjustment and collection services
George Krieser

D-U-N-S 25-813-1390   (HQ)
UNIVERSAL MUSIC CANADA INC
VIVENDI VISUAL ENTERTAINMENT
(*Suby of* VIVENDI)
2450 Victoria Park Ave Suite 1, North York, ON, M2J 5H3
(416) 718-4000
Emp Here 190   *Sales* 139,060,000
SIC 5099 Durable goods, nec
Randy Lennox
Sarah Scott
Mark Jones

D-U-N-S 20-169-6861   (HQ)
UNIVERSAL STUDIOS CANADA INC
UNIVERSAL FILMS CANADA
(*Suby of* COMCAST CORPORATION)
2450 Victoria Park Ave Suite 4, North York, ON, M2J 4A2
(416) 491-3000
Sales 11,591,190
SIC 7822 Motion picture and tape distribution
Ron Suter
Eugene Amodeo
Steve Dorman

D-U-N-S 24-545-5704   (SL)
UNIWORLD TRAVEL & TOURS INC
235 Yorkland Blvd Suite 300, North York, ON, M2J 4Y8
(416) 493-3322
Emp Here 30   *Sales* 11,560,800
SIC 4724 Travel agencies
Sidney Green
Michael Rosen
Lisa M Green

D-U-N-S 20-553-2810   (HQ)

VERANOVA PROPERTIES LIMITED
505 Consumers Rd Suite 812, North York, ON, M2J 4V8
(416) 701-9000
Sales 50,709,600
SIC 6531 Real estate agents and managers
Rob Kirby
Michael Maccormick
David Read
Colin Carroll

D-U-N-S 25-405-0735   (HQ)
VERSA SYSTEMS LTD
(*Suby of* MICROPACT HOLDINGS, LLC)
200 Yorkland Blvd Suite 200, North York, ON, M2J 5C1
(416) 493-1833
Emp Here 73   *Sales* 12,513,525
SIC 7372 Prepackaged software
Brock Philip
Brenda Riddell
Tom Gottlieb

D-U-N-S 24-668-5817   (SL)
VP PROTECTION INC
259 Yorkland Rd 3rd Fl, North York, ON, M2J 5B2
(416) 218-3226
Emp Here 400   *Sales* 10,500,000
SIC 7381 Detective and armored car services
Kevin Minard
Richard Benoit

D-U-N-S 24-347-9479   (SL)
WORK ABLE CENTRES INC
4 Lansing Sq Suite 102, North York, ON, M2J 5A2
(416) 496-6166
Emp Here 24   *Sales* 24,837,144
SIC 6321 Accident and health insurance
Brenda Rasmussen

D-U-N-S 25-099-1817   (BR)
WW HOTELS CORP
2447496 ONTARIO INC
(*Suby of* WW HOTELS CORP)
55 Hallcrown Pl, North York, ON, M2J 4R1
(416) 493-7000
Emp Here 110
SIC 7011 Hotels and motels
Satinder Dhillon

North York, ON M2K

D-U-N-S 25-118-1905   (SL)
1265768 ONTARIO LTD
VALU-MART ON BAYVIEW
3259 Bayview Ave, North York, ON, M2K 1G4
(416) 221-6702
Emp Here 78   *Sales* 22,891,206
SIC 5411 Grocery stores
Grant Wilson

D-U-N-S 24-757-2068   (SL)
711620 ONTARIO LIMITED
LITTLE REMEDY CENTRE
20 Mango Dr, North York, ON, M2K 2G1
(416) 733-8285
Emp Here 31   *Sales* 34,265,695
SIC 5122 Drugs, proprietaries, and sundries
Philip Borsook

D-U-N-S 24-789-5936   (HQ)
A. FARBER & PARTNERS INC
1220 Sheppard Ave E Suite 300, North York, ON, M2K 2S5
(416) 496-1200
Emp Here 49   *Sales* 14,973,120
SIC 8741 Management services
Alan Farber

D-U-N-S 24-320-4142   (SL)
AND AGENCY INC
(*Suby of* AND AGENCY LLC)
1220 Sheppard Ave E Suite 100, North York,

ON, M2K 2S5
(416) 493-6111
Emp Here 200   *Sales* 7,581,020
SIC 8732 Commercial nonphysical research
Adam Kamieniak
Johann Ho

D-U-N-S 25-535-2536   (SL)
CONCORD ADEX DEVELOPMENTS CORP
(*Suby of* ADEX SECURITIES INC)
1001 Sheppard Ave E, North York, ON, M2K 1C2
(416) 813-0999
Emp Here 85   *Sales* 13,444,620
SIC 6553 Cemetery subdividers and developers
Dennis Au-Yeung

D-U-N-S 20-881-9974   (SL)
CONFERENCE WORLD TOURS
1200 Sheppard Ave E Suite 201, North York, ON, M2K 2S5
(416) 221-6411
Emp Here 65   *Sales* 33,797,855
SIC 4724 Travel agencies
Brian Robertson

D-U-N-S 20-852-6897   (HQ)
DAC GROUP (HOLDINGS) LIMITED
DAC GROUP
1210 Sheppard Ave E Suite 500, North York, ON, M2K 1E3
(416) 492-4322
Emp Here 237   *Sales* 119,591,150
SIC 7311 Advertising agencies
Norman Hagarty
Jesse Waltman
Marcel Labbe
Jared Hendrickson
Mike Corak
Eli Grant

D-U-N-S 24-311-1098   (SL)
DAC GROUP/CANADA LTD
(*Suby of* DAC GROUP (HOLDINGS) LIMITED)
1210 Sheppard Ave E Suite 500, North York, ON, M2K 1E3
(416) 492-4322
Emp Here 200   *Sales* 40,074,200
SIC 7311 Advertising agencies
Norm Hagarty
Peter Kaju

D-U-N-S 25-666-9680   (BR)
EXTENDICARE (CANADA) INC
BAYVIEW VILLA NURSING HOME
(*Suby of* EXTENDICARE INC)
550 Cummer Ave, North York, ON, M2K 2M2
(416) 226-1331
Emp Here 200
SIC 8051 Skilled nursing care facilities
Sandy Hall

D-U-N-S 20-699-6519   (BR)
EXTENDICARE INC
EXTENDICARE BAYVIEW
(*Suby of* EXTENDICARE INC)
550 Cummer Ave, North York, ON, M2K 2M2
(416) 226-1331
Emp Here 300
SIC 8051 Skilled nursing care facilities
Nikolas Chandrabalan

D-U-N-S 25-664-8627   (SL)
HOMELIFE FOUNDATION REALTY INC
648 Finch Ave E Suite 12, North York, ON, M2K 2E6
(416) 229-0515
Emp Here 40   *Sales* 13,085,080
SIC 6531 Real estate agents and managers
Kin Au

D-U-N-S 24-424-4679   (SL)
INSTITUTE OF NATUROPATHIC EDUCATION AND RESEARCH
CANADIAN COLLEGE OF NATUROPATHIC MEDICINE

1255 Sheppard Ave E, North York, ON, M2K 1E2
(416) 498-1255
Emp Here 250   *Sales* 37,347,750
SIC 8221 Colleges and universities
Robert Bernhardt
Colleen Mcqarrie
Sameet Batavia

D-U-N-S 25-310-8930   (BR)
MCDONALD'S RESTAURANTS OF CANADA LIMITED
MCDONALD'S
(*Suby of* MCDONALD'S CORPORATION)
1125 Sheppard Ave E, North York, ON, M2K 1C5

Emp Here 90
SIC 5812 Eating places

D-U-N-S 20-847-7927   (HQ)
NORTH YORK GENERAL HOSPITAL
NYGH
4001 Leslie St, North York, ON, M2K 1E1
(416) 756-6000
Emp Here 1,600   *Sales* 306,546,093
SIC 8062 General medical and surgical hospitals
Joshua Tepper
Rudy Dahdal
Bessie Leung
Donna Mcritchie
Karyn Popovich

D-U-N-S 24-248-2821   (SL)
ONTARIO EAST INSURANCE AGENCY/ BFG FINANCIAL
1210 Sheppard Ave E Suite 401, North York, ON, M2K 1E3
(416) 498-1444
Emp Here 20   *Sales* 11,598,480
SIC 6411 Insurance agents, brokers, and service
Rob Berry

D-U-N-S 24-120-8714   (BR)
PITNEY BOWES OF CANADA LTD
(*Suby of* PITNEY BOWES INC.)
1200 Sheppard Ave E Suite 400, North York, ON, M2K 2S5

Emp Here 75
SIC 5044 Office equipment
Jamie Anglin

D-U-N-S 24-339-3688   (HQ)
QUARTERBACK TRANSPORTATION INC
1210 Sheppard Ave E Suite 114, North York, ON, M2K 1E3
(416) 385-2713
Emp Here 70   *Sales* 66,689,200
SIC 4731 Freight transportation arrangement
Mark Moness
Wayne Holtzman

D-U-N-S 20-184-2044   (HQ)
SCHICKEDANZ BROS. LIMITED
3311 Bayview Ave Suite 105, North York, ON, M2K 1G4
(416) 223-0710
Emp Here 25   *Sales* 11,645,550
SIC 6513 Apartment building operators
Gustav Schickedanz
Elma Schickedanz
Daniel Schickedanz
Johanna Schickedanz

D-U-N-S 24-937-0156   (SL)
SELLORS, ERIC R. HOLDINGS LIMITED
CANADIAN TIRE
1019 Sheppard Ave E Suite 4, North York, ON, M2K 1C2
(416) 226-4415
Emp Here 200   *Sales* 125,856,000
SIC 5531 Auto and home supply stores
Eric Sellors

D-U-N-S 20-773-1696   (HQ)

VISION 2000 TRAVEL MANAGEMENT INC
1200 Sheppard Ave E Suite 201, North York, ON, M2K 2S5
(416) 487-5385
Emp Here 60   *Sales* 100,033,800
SIC 4724 Travel agencies
Brian Robertson
Stephanie Anevich

D-U-N-S 20-051-5299   (HQ)
VIXS SYSTEMS INC
(*Suby of* PIXELWORKS, INC.)
1210 Sheppard Ave E Suite 800, North York, ON, M2K 1E3
(416) 646-2000
Emp Here 1   *Sales* 35,930,205
SIC 3674 Semiconductors and related devices
Sohail Khan
Charlie Glavin
Perry Chappell
Michael Economy
Andrew Shih
Donna Wong
Peter Currie
Philip Deck
Andrew Olsen
Arun Netravali

D-U-N-S 24-745-7096   (BR)
YMCA OF GREATER TORONTO
YMCA
(*Suby of* YMCA OF GREATER TORONTO)
567 Sheppard Ave E, North York, ON, M2K 1B2
(416) 225-9622
Emp Here 250
SIC 8351 Child day care services
Dan Wise

North York, ON M2L

D-U-N-S 24-462-6727   (SL)
CHIU, WALLY DRUGS LTD
SHOPPERS DRUG MART
2528 Bayview Ave, North York, ON, M2L 1A9
(416) 816-1823
Emp Here 75   *Sales* 18,324,600
SIC 5912 Drug stores and proprietary stores
Wally Chiu

D-U-N-S 24-892-4938   (SL)
HOLDBEST LTD
24 Mellowood Dr, North York, ON, M2L 2E3
(905) 831-0100
Emp Here 400   *Sales* 146,203,600
SIC 6712 Bank holding companies
Bernardo Sztabinski

D-U-N-S 25-534-9037   (BR)
METRO ONTARIO INC
DOMINION
(*Suby of* METRO INC)
291 York Mills Rd, North York, ON, M2L 1L3
(416) 444-5809
Emp Here 150
SIC 5411 Grocery stores
Paul Cughan

D-U-N-S 24-219-5824   (HQ)
ONTARIO MISSION FOR THE DEAF, THE
BOB RUMBALL CENTRE FOR THE DEAF
2395 Bayview Ave, North York, ON, M2L 1A2
(416) 449-9651
Emp Here 130   *Sales* 9,320,890
SIC 8361 Residential care
Shirley Cassel
Alistair Fraser
Derek Rumball

North York, ON M2M

D-U-N-S 20-640-5990   (SL)
1152174 ONTARIO LIMITED
A BUCK OR TWO
6464 Yonge St, North York, ON, M2M 3X4

Emp Here 35   Sales 11,396,000
SIC 5999 Miscellaneous retail stores, nec
  Namir Hamo

D-U-N-S 24-560-3022   (HQ)
A.P.I. ALARM INC
700-5775 Yonge St, North York, ON, M2M 4J1
(416) 661-5566
Emp Here 150   Sales 48,043,836
SIC 1731 Electrical work
  Howard Garr

D-U-N-S 20-561-2617   (HQ)
AHMAD, J DRUGS LTD
SHOPPERS DRUG MART
6428 Yonge St, North York, ON, M2M 3X4
(416) 223-6250
Sales 21,989,520
SIC 5912 Drug stores and proprietary stores
  Mario Paggos

D-U-N-S 25-106-7583   (HQ)
AXA INSURANCE (CANADA)
(Suby of AXA ASSURANCES INC)
5700 Yonge St Suite 1400, North York, ON, M2M 4K2
(416) 218-4175
Emp Here 200   Sales 961,635,600
SIC 6331 Fire, marine, and casualty insurance
  Jean-Denis Talon
  Jean-Francois Blais
  Mathieu Lamy
  Joseph Fung
  Carmen Crigg
  Tenny Yeung
  Paule Dore
  Francois De Meneval
  Pierre Monahan
  Gilles G Charette

D-U-N-S 24-348-6094   (SL)
CENTURY 21 YOUR NUMBER ONE REALTY INC BROKERAGE
6400 Yonge St Suite 200, North York, ON, M2M 3X4

Emp Here 100   Sales 27,175,600
SIC 6531 Real estate agents and managers
  Kevin Najafi

D-U-N-S 25-940-3418   (HQ)
CONSEIL SCOLAIRE CATHOLIQUE MON-AVENIR
110 Drewry Ave, North York, ON, M2M 1C8
(416) 397-6564
Emp Here 35   Sales 54,403,500
SIC 8211 Elementary and secondary schools
  Roland Demers
  Diane Corriveau
  Francois Rivet
  Nicole Fournier
  Stephan Poulin
  Roland Rochon

D-U-N-S 25-530-2416   (HQ)
CONSEIL SCOLAIRE DE DISTRICT CATHOLIQUE CENTRE-SUD
C.S.D.C.C.S.
110 Drewry Ave, North York, ON, M2M 1C8
(416) 250-1754
Emp Here 100   Sales 128,622,810
SIC 8211 Elementary and secondary schools
  Dereck Chin
  Bernard Lavallee
  Adrian Lamoureux
  Melinda Chartrand
  Cindy Labas
  Lucille Gauthier
  Marcel Levesque
  Dorothee Petit-Pas
  Claude Legere
  Nathalie Dufour-Seguin

D-U-N-S 25-321-8945   (BR)
ECONOMICAL MUTUAL INSURANCE COM-PANY
ECONOMICAL INSURANCE GROUP
(Suby of ECONOMICAL MUTUAL INSUR-ANCE COMPANY)
5700 Yonge St Suite 1600, North York, ON, M2M 4K2
(800) 268-8801
Emp Here 125
SIC 6331 Fire, marine, and casualty insurance
  Marc Lefebvre

D-U-N-S 24-488-0126   (HQ)
EQUIFAX CANADA CO.
INSURANCE INFORMATION SERVICES
(Suby of EQUIFAX INC.)
5700 Yonge St Suite 1700, North York, ON, M2M 4K2
(800) 278-0278
Emp Here 200   Sales 135,738,600
SIC 7323 Credit reporting services
  Carol Gray
  Robert M.A. Brabers
  Rodolfo Ploder
  Joel Heft

D-U-N-S 20-177-5124   (SL)
HALLCON CREW TRANSPORT INC
(Suby of SOUTHFIELD CAPITAL ADVISORS, LLC)
5775 Yonge St Suite 1010, North York, ON, M2M 4J1
(416) 964-9191
Emp Here 300   Sales 16,864,200
SIC 4111 Local and suburban transit
  Anton G Plut
  Brian Kirk
  Kevin A Ramsay
  Kevin Blair Melnyk
  Bradley Wayne Ashley

D-U-N-S 25-301-1696   (BR)
HUDSON'S BAY COMPANY
(Suby of HUDSON'S BAY COMPANY)
6500 Yonge St, North York, ON, M2M 3X4
(416) 226-4202
Emp Here 100
SIC 5311 Department stores
  Roch Cote

D-U-N-S 24-873-2844   (HQ)
J & B ENGINEERING INC
5734 Yonge St Suite 501, North York, ON, M2M 4E7
(416) 229-2636
Emp Here 3   Sales 10,557,480
SIC 8711 Engineering services
  James Machan
  Walter Posnikoff

D-U-N-S 20-338-7340   (SL)
KARE FOR KIDS INTERNATIONAL
7 Bishop Ave Suite 2107, North York, ON, M2M 4J4
(416) 226-4111
Emp Here 85   Sales 60,283,020
SIC 8699 Membership organizations, nec
  George Marton

D-U-N-S 20-051-1017   (SL)
MUZYK, D.J. DRUGS LTD
SHOPPERS DRUG MART
1515 Steeles Ave E, North York, ON, M2M 3Y7
(416) 226-1313
Emp Here 50   Sales 12,647,700
SIC 5912 Drug stores and proprietary stores
  Dan Muzyk

D-U-N-S 24-927-2170   (SL)
NOVEX INSURANCE COMPANY
(Suby of INTACT FINANCIAL CORPORA-TION)
5775 Yonge St Suite 600, North York, ON, M2M 4J1
(416) 228-2618
Emp Here 50   Sales 92,332,950

SIC 6331 Fire, marine, and casualty insurance
  Jack P Mccarthy

D-U-N-S 24-538-6008   (HQ)
ONTARIO TEACHERS' PENSION PLAN BOARD
OTPP
5650 Yonge St Suite 300, North York, ON, M2M 4H5
(416) 228-5900
Emp Here 800   Sales 140,086,544,065
SIC 6371 Pension, health, and welfare funds
  Ron Mock
  Bjarne Graven Larsen
  David Mcgraw
  Rosemarie Mcclean
  Jean Turmel
  Barbara Palk
  David Smith
  Daniel Sullivan
  Bill Chinery
  Patti Croft

D-U-N-S 24-377-4663   (SL)
PLAZA CONSULTING INC
QA CONSULTANTS
5700 Yonge St Suite 1400, North York, ON, M2M 4K2
(416) 238-5333
Emp Here 70   Sales 13,055,420
SIC 8742 Management consulting services
  Alex Rodov

D-U-N-S 25-996-9863   (SL)
PRUDENTIAL RELOCATION CANADA LTD
(Suby of PRUDENTIAL FINANCIAL, INC.)
5700 Yonge St Suite 1110, North York, ON, M2M 4K2

Emp Here 60   Sales 40,134,480
SIC 7389 Business services, nec
  Jennifer Sue Chuck

D-U-N-S 20-355-6555   (SL)
QUESTRADE, INC
5650 Yonge St Suite 1700, North York, ON, M2M 4G3
(416) 227-9876
Emp Here 110   Sales 156,545,180
SIC 6211 Security brokers and dealers
  Edward Kholodenko
  Inna Kholodenko
  Dean Percy
  Gary Miskin

D-U-N-S 24-027-0934   (SL)
ST JOHN'S REHABILITATION HOSPITAL
ST JOHN'S REHAB HOSPITAL
285 Cummer Ave, North York, ON, M2M 2G1
(416) 226-6780
Emp Here 400   Sales 30,309,200
SIC 8093 Specialty outpatient clinics, nec
  Malcolm Moffat
  Charles Seguin
  Sally M Horsfall

D-U-N-S 25-665-6323   (SL)
SUNDER GROUP OF COMPANIES LTD
HISTAR MANAGEMENT
5650 Yonge St, North York, ON, M2M 4G3
(416) 226-1809
Emp Here 46   Sales 13,031,478
SIC 8741 Management services
  Paul Chicholm

D-U-N-S 20-025-5425   (BR)
TORONTO CATHOLIC DISTRICT SCHOOL BOARD
ST. JOSEPH MORROW PARK CATHOLIC SECONDARY SCHOOL
(Suby of TORONTO CATHOLIC DISTRICT SCHOOL BOARD)
3379 Bayview Ave, North York, ON, M2M 3S4
(416) 393-5516
Emp Here 75
SIC 8211 Elementary and secondary schools
  Marie Deans

D-U-N-S 20-918-8437   (BR)
TORONTO CATHOLIC DISTRICT SCHOOL BOARD
BREBEUF   COLLEGE   SECONDARY SCHOOL
(Suby of TORONTO CATHOLIC DISTRICT SCHOOL BOARD)
211 Steeles Ave E, North York, ON, M2M 3Y6
(416) 393-5508
Emp Here 75
SIC 8211 Elementary and secondary schools
  John Wujek

D-U-N-S 20-025-1796   (BR)
TORONTO DISTRICT SCHOOL BOARD
NEWTONBROOK SECONDARY SCHOOL
(Suby of TORONTO DISTRICT SCHOOL BOARD)
155 Hilda Ave, North York, ON, M2M 1V6
(416) 395-3280
Emp Here 120
SIC 8211 Elementary and secondary schools
  Saverio Zupo

D-U-N-S 24-000-4817   (BR)
TORONTO HYDRO-ELECTRIC SYSTEM LIMITED
TORONTO HYDRO
(Suby of CORPORATION OF THE CITY OF TORONTO)
5800 Yonge St, North York, ON, M2M 3T3
(416) 542-3564
Emp Here 375
SIC 4911 Electric services
  David Williams

D-U-N-S 20-322-4977   (SL)
UNITY   MANAGING   UNDERWRITERS HOLDCO LIMITED
5734 Yonge St Suite 605, North York, ON, M2M 4E7
(416) 222-0676
Emp Here 30   Sales 17,397,720
SIC 6411 Insurance agents, brokers, and ser-vice
  Winkey Ngan

D-U-N-S 25-222-1072   (SL)
YORK CONSULTING INC
19 Hendon Ave, North York, ON, M2M 4G8
(416) 410-2222
Emp Here 23   Sales 10,332,037
SIC 7389 Business services, nec
  Jay Plesner

North York, ON M2N

D-U-N-S 20-116-1697   (HQ)
1484558 ONTARIO INC
(Suby of ZYLOG SYSTEMS LIMITED)
2 Sheppard Ave E Suite 700, North York, ON, M2N 5Y7
(416) 203-1800
Emp Here 25   Sales 11,951,040
SIC 7361 Employment agencies
  John Mckimm
  Robert Prentice
  Bhaktraj Singh

D-U-N-S 25-940-1800   (SL)
1529295 ONTARIO INC
EXPEDIA CRUISESHIPCENTRES WILLOW-DALE
386 Sheppard Ave E Unit 2, North York, ON, M2N 3B7
(416) 226-6667
Emp Here 30   Sales 15,599,010
SIC 4724 Travel agencies
  Elisa Goldman
  Melvyn Goldman

D-U-N-S 25-370-8705   (HQ)
4386396 CANADA INC
(Suby of ZYLOG SYSTEMS LIMITED)

2 Sheppard Ave E Suite 2000, North York, ON,
M2N 5Y7
(416) 225-9900
Emp Here 170
SIC 7361 Employment agencies
Rag Singh
Robert Prentice

D-U-N-S 20-349-1360   (SL)
7667965 CANADA INC
BELLAIR HOMES
2942 Bayview Ave, North York, ON, M2N 5K5
(416) 388-2806
Emp Here 45   *Sales* 14,349,105
SIC 1521 Single-family housing construction
Troy Coarser

D-U-N-S 24-369-1248   (HQ)
ASSURANT SERVICES CANADA INC
ASSURANT SOLUTIONS
(*Suby of* ASSURANT, INC.)
5000 Yonge St Suite 2000, North York, ON,
M2N 7E9
(416) 733-3360
Sales 20,697,620
SIC 6351 Surety insurance
Keith Demmings
Jeannie Aragon-Cruz
Steve Makins

D-U-N-S 24-222-8187   (HQ)
BARNEY RIVER INVESTMENTS LIMITED
4576 Yonge St Suite 300, North York, ON,
M2N 6N4
(416) 620-7200
Emp Here 60   *Sales* 13,473,131
SIC 6513 Apartment building operators
Salim Manji
Derik Lou
Jennifer Stubbs
Samir Manji

D-U-N-S 25-535-5059   (SL)
BRAVO PRODUCTS & EXPORTS INC
170 Sheppard Ave E Suite 303a, North York,
ON, M2N 3A4
(416) 590-9605
Emp Here 3   *Sales* 11,675,820
SIC 5142 Packaged frozen goods
Edward Zilli

D-U-N-S 24-214-1190   (SL)
CAN-CARE HEALTH SERVICES INC
45 Sheppard Ave E Suite 204, North York, ON,
M2N 5W9
(647) 725-1048
Emp Here 550
SIC 8082 Home health care services

D-U-N-S 25-690-7023   (SL)
**CANADIAN PREMIER LIFE INSURANCE
COMPANY**
25 Sheppard Ave W, North York, ON, M2N
6S6
(416) 883-6300
Emp Here 90   *Sales* 166,199,310
SIC 6311 Life insurance
Isaac Sanaes

D-U-N-S 20-522-3154   (SL)
CAPITAL ONE SERVICES (CANADA) INC
(*Suby of* CAPITAL ONE FINANCIAL CORPO-
RATION)
5140 Yonge St Suite 1900, North York, ON,
M2N 6L7
(416) 549-2500
Emp Here 68   *Sales* 15,227,988
SIC 6153 Short-term business credit institu-
tions, except agricultural
Shane Holdaway
Christopher Newkirk

D-U-N-S 24-565-2151   (HQ)
**CATHOLIC CEMETERIES-ARCHDIOCESE
OF TORONTO**
4950 Yonge St Suite 206, North York, ON,
M2N 6K1
(416) 733-8544
Emp Here 23   *Sales* 11,660,480

SIC 7261 Funeral service and crematories
Richard Hayes

D-U-N-S 25-529-4449   (SL)
**CENTRAL COMMUNITY CARE ACCESS
CENTRE**
CENTRAL CCAC
45 Sheppard Ave E Suite 700, North York, ON,
M2N 5W9
(416) 222-2241
Emp Here 200   *Sales* 38,041,400
SIC 8011 Offices and clinics of medical doc-
tors
Cathy Szabo

D-U-N-S 25-369-4541   (BR)
CENTRAL MONTESSORI SCHOOLS INC
CENTRAL MONTESSORI SCHOOL
(*Suby of* CENTRAL MONTESSORI
SCHOOLS INC)
200 Sheppard Ave E, North York, ON, M2N
3A9
(416) 222-5940
Emp Here 85
SIC 8211 Elementary and secondary schools
Minoo Mohajer

D-U-N-S 24-860-8742   (SL)
CENTURION ASSET MANAGEMENT INC
25 Sheppard Ave W Suite 710, North York,
ON, M2N 6S6
(416) 733-5600
Emp Here 100   *Sales* 27,175,600
SIC 6531 Real estate agents and managers
Greg Romundt
Wayne Tuck

D-U-N-S 24-918-9630   (SL)
CHAITON MANAGEMENT LTD
CHAITON & CHAITON
185 Sheppard Ave W, North York, ON, M2N
1M9
(416) 222-8888
Emp Here 80   *Sales* 12,320,880
SIC 8111 Legal services
David Chaiton

D-U-N-S 20-818-1164   (HQ)
CRAWFORD METAL CORPORATION
132 Sheppard Ave W Suite 200, North York,
ON, M2N 1M5
(416) 224-1515
Emp Here 20   *Sales* 104,554,450
SIC 5051 Metals service centers and offices
Gary Stern
Sidney Spiegel
Naomi Spiegel

D-U-N-S 20-335-2745   (SL)
**CROSSLINX TRANSIT SOLUTIONS CON-
STRUCTORS GP**
4711 Yonge St Unit 1500, North York, ON,
M2N 6K8
(416) 679-6116
Emp Here 300   *Sales* 55,951,800
SIC 8742 Management consulting services
John Bisanti
Bill Henry

D-U-N-S 25-509-6299   (HQ)
DAVPART INC
4576 Yonge St Unit 700, North York, ON, M2N
6N4
(416) 222-3010
Sales 12,229,020
SIC 6531 Real estate agents and managers
David Hofstedter

D-U-N-S 24-874-7503   (BR)
DELOITTE LLP
(*Suby of* DELOITTE LLP)
5140 Yonge St Suite 1700, North York, ON,
M2N 6L7
(416) 601-6150
Emp Here 327
SIC 8721 Accounting, auditing, and book-
keeping
Williams Ettie

D-U-N-S 25-529-9125   (SL)
**DEPOSIT INSURANCE CORPORATION OF
ONTARIO**
4711 Yonge St Suite 700, North York, ON,
M2N 6K8
(416) 325-9444
Emp Here 40   *Sales* 41,395,240
SIC 6399 Insurance carriers, nec
Laura Talbot
Andrew Poprawa

D-U-N-S 20-844-2913   (HQ)
**DUCA FINANCIAL SERVICES CREDIT
UNION LTD**
5290 Yonge St, North York, ON, M2N 5P9
(416) 223-8502
Emp Here 28   *Sales* 10,164,047
SIC 6062 State credit unions
Tom Vandeloo
Henry Buikema
Jeff Hogan
Marijke Kanters
Cameron Loopstra
Tony Niessen
Anne-Marie Thomas
Conrad Willemse
Martin Van Denzen

D-U-N-S 24-367-5787   (SL)
ETHOCA TECHNOLOGIES INC
(*Suby of* ETHOCA LIMITED)
100 Sheppard Ave E Suite 605, North York,
ON, M2N 6N5
(416) 849-6091
Emp Here 30   *Sales* 13,415,220
SIC 5065 Electronic parts and equipment, nec
Andre Edelbrock
Darryl Green

D-U-N-S 20-388-1870   (BR)
EXP REALTY OF CANADA, INC
(*Suby of* EXP WORLD HOLDINGS, INC.)
4711 Yonge St 10 Fl, North York, ON, M2N
6K8
(866) 530-7737
Emp Here 80
SIC 6531 Real estate agents and managers
Mary Caird

D-U-N-S 20-877-7797   (HQ)
FERRERO CANADA LIMITED
(*Suby of* FERRERO INTERNATIONAL)
100 Sheppard Ave E Suite 900, North York,
ON, M2N 6N5
(416) 590-0775
Sales 389,908,000
SIC 2064 Candy and other confectionery
products
Allan Cosman
Imma Rachiele
Vladimiro Sinatti
Irwin Cass
Steven Gray

D-U-N-S 25-248-7996   (HQ)
**FIELDGATE DEVELOPMENT AND CON-
STRUCTION LTD**
FIELDGATE HOMES
5400 Yonge St Suite 2, North York, ON, M2N
5R5
(416) 227-2220
Emp Here 80   *Sales* 15,817,200
SIC 6553 Cemetery subdividers and develop-
ers
Ezra Jakubovic

D-U-N-S 25-695-9867   (BR)
FOREST HILL REAL ESTATE INC
(*Suby of* FOREST HILL REAL ESTATE INC)
500 Sheppard Ave E Suite 201, North York,
ON, M2N 6H7
(416) 226-1987
Emp Here 200
SIC 6531 Real estate agents and managers
Mark Armstrong

D-U-N-S 24-130-7110   (SL)

**FORESTERS FINANCIAL INVESTMENT
MANAGEMENT COMPANY OF CANADA
INC**
IMAXX MONEY MARKET FUND
5000 Yonge St 8th Floor, North York, ON, M2N
7J8
(416) 883-5800
Emp Here 15   *Sales* 10,450,155
SIC 6722 Management investment, open-end
Greg Ross

D-U-N-S 20-041-1101   (HQ)
**FRANKLIN TEMPLETON INVESTMENTS
CORP**
(*Suby of* FRANKLIN RESOURCES, INC.)
5000 Yonge St Suite 900, North York, ON,
M2N 0A7
(416) 957-6000
Sales 75,134,160
SIC 6282 Investment advice
Duane Green

D-U-N-S 24-736-7667   (SL)
G.S.K. MANAGEMENT INC
40 Sheppard Ave W Suite 700, North York,
ON, M2N 6K9
(416) 225-9400
Emp Here 30   *Sales* 12,580,650
SIC 6712 Bank holding companies
Alan Goldman
Sheldon Spring
Steven Kichler

D-U-N-S 20-334-1888   (SL)
**GIBRALTAR CONSOLIDATED CORPORA-
TION**
*GIBRALTAR CONSOLIDATED EQUITY & IN-
VESTMENTS*
4936 Yonge St Suite 508, North York, ON,
M2N 6S3
(416) 819-0644
Emp Here 50   *Sales* 13,077,650
SIC 6719 Holding companies, nec
Richard Swifton
Edward Peman
Alphonse Fleming
Alejandro Garcia

D-U-N-S 25-318-8809   (SL)
**GILLILAND GOLD YOUNG CONSULTING
INC**
*SOFTWARE MAINTENANCE & DEVELOP-
MENT*
5001 Yonge St Suite 1300, North York, ON,
M2N 6P6
(416) 250-6777
Emp Here 75   *Sales* 13,298,325
SIC 7371 Custom computer programming ser-
vices
William(Bill) Young
Phil Gold
Dave Gilliland

D-U-N-S 20-762-4354   (HQ)
**GUARANTEE COMPANY OF NORTH
AMERICA, THE**
4950 Yonge St Suite 1400, North York, ON,
M2N 6K1
(416) 223-9580
Emp Here 96   *Sales* 291,472
SIC 6411 Insurance agents, brokers, and ser-
vice
Alister Campbell
Maureen Cowan
Kris Betkowski
Dean Bast
Alan Rabin
Randall Musselman
Robert Dempsey
Bruno Desjardins
Jules R. Quennville
Thomas C Macmillan

D-U-N-S 24-756-8587   (HQ)
**HEALTHCARE INSURANCE RECIPROCAL
OF CANADA**
HIROC

4711 Yonge St Suite 1600, North York, ON, M2N 6K8
(416) 733-2773
Emp Here 52   *Sales* 67,947,990
SIC 6351 Surety insurance
Cathy Szabo
Gregory King

D-U-N-S 24-303-2075   (HQ)
HEWITT ASSOCIATES CORP
(*Suby of* AON PLC)
2 Sheppard Ave E Suite 1500, North York, ON, M2N 7A4
(416) 225-5001
Emp Here 50   *Sales* 308,166,300
SIC 8748 Business consulting, nec
Anthony Gaffney
James Hubbard
Jean-Francois Chartray
Rejean Tremblay
Martin Papillion
Scott Bunker
Terri-Lynne Devonish

D-U-N-S 24-562-4601   (SL)
HIROC FOUNDATION, THE
4711 Yonge St Suite 1600, North York, ON, M2N 6K8
(416) 733-2773
Emp Here 49   *Sales* 19,473,286
SIC 8699 Membership organizations, nec
Ronald Haines

D-U-N-S 20-645-5383   (SL)
HIROC INSURANCE SERVICES LIMITED
4711 Yonge St Suite 1600, North York, ON, M2N 6K8
(416) 733-2773
Emp Here 34   *Sales* 35,185,954
SIC 6311 Life insurance
Rob Chang

D-U-N-S 24-212-4774   (HQ)
HYUNDAI CANADA INC
(*Suby of* HYUNDAI CORPORATION)
5160 Yonge St Suite 1003, North York, ON, M2N 6L9
(416) 229-6668
Sales 65,758,104
SIC 5051 Metals service centers and offices
Yong Ho Ahn

D-U-N-S 20-010-1587   (HQ)
INFOSYS LIMITED
(*Suby of* INFOSYS LIMITED)
5140 Yonge St Suite 1400, North York, ON, M2N 6L7
(416) 224-7400
Emp Here 50   *Sales* 30,032,460
SIC 7379 Computer related services, nec
Divakar Shenoy
Andrew Shnuriwsky

D-U-N-S 20-280-2443   (SL)
INNOVATIVE BIOMETRIC TECHNOLOGIES CORP
5000 Yonge St Suite 1901, North York, ON, M2N 7E9
(416) 222-5000
Emp Here 20   *Sales* 37,068,948
SIC 3663 Radio and t.v. communications equipment
Michael Burmi

D-U-N-S 20-283-4578   (SL)
INVESCO CANDA LTD
5140 Yonge St Suite 800, North York, ON, M2N 6X7
(416) 590-9855
Emp Here 49   *Sales* 40,561,073
SIC 6722 Management investment, open-end
Peter Intraligi

D-U-N-S 24-047-5434   (HQ)
IVARI CANADA ULC
IVARI
(*Suby of* WILTON RE LTD)
5000 Yonge St Unit 500, North York, ON, M2N

7J8
(416) 883-5000
Emp Here 500   *Sales* 1,068,484,000
SIC 6311 Life insurance
Todd Lawrence

D-U-N-S 20-336-6356   (SL)
KEB HANA BANK CANADA
4950 Yonge St Unit 1101, North York, ON, M2N 6K1
(416) 536-8046
Emp Here 170   *Sales* 34,245,990
SIC 6021 National commercial banks
Hyun Soo Lee

D-U-N-S 20-934-3714   (HQ)
KEB HANA BANK CANADA
(*Suby of* HANA FINANCIAL GROUP INC.)
4950 Yonge St Suite 103, North York, ON, M2N 6K1
(416) 222-5200
Emp Here 35   *Sales* 32,072,891
SIC 6021 National commercial banks
Larry Klane
Richard Wacker
Jang Myoung Kee

D-U-N-S 24-977-5834   (SL)
KIMATSU ENTERPRISES
KIMATSU INTERNATIONAL
5334 Yonge St, North York, ON, M2N 6V1

Emp Here 66   *Sales* 68,141,304
SIC 6799 Investors, nec

D-U-N-S 25-663-8198   (SL)
KRONIS, ROTSZTAIN, MARGLES, CAPPEL LLP
25 Sheppard Ave W Suite 700, North York, ON, M2N 6S6
(416) 225-8750
Emp Here 90   *Sales* 9,979,380
SIC 8111 Legal services
Jules Kronis
Bruce Cappel
Jack Rotsztain
Onofrio Ferlisi
Ajay Kapur
Grace Latini
Mark Lieberman
Andrea Margles
A. Mitchell Schachter
Allan Weiss

D-U-N-S 20-691-2607   (SL)
LAUDERVEST DEVELOPMENTS LTD
4576 Yonge St Suite 500, North York, ON, M2N 6N4
(416) 224-1200
Emp Here 50   *Sales* 14,429,150
SIC 1522 Residential construction, nec
Glenn Farber

D-U-N-S 24-803-7512   (BR)
LOWE'S COMPANIES CANADA, ULC
(*Suby of* LOWE'S COMPANIES, INC.)
5160 Yonge St Suite 2, North York, ON, M2N 6L9
(416) 730-7300
Emp Here 140
SIC 5211 Lumber and other building materials
Jason Brooks

D-U-N-S 20-875-4440   (HQ)
MANPOWER SERVICES CANADA LIMITED
MANPOWER TEMPORARY SERVICES
(*Suby of* MANPOWERGROUP INC.)
4950 Yonge St Suite 700, North York, ON, M2N 6K1
(416) 225-4455
Emp Here 40   *Sales* 38,114,000
SIC 7363 Help supply services
Nadia Clani
Richard Pett
Mike Vanhandel
Sandra Clarke
Jo-Anne Yanuziello
Stephen Walker

D-U-N-S 24-666-7885   (HQ)
MARSHALL-BARWICK INC
(*Suby of* MARSHALL-BARWICK HOLDINGS INC)
100 Sheppard Ave E Unit 930, North York, ON, M2N 6N5
(416) 225-6240
Emp Here 6   *Sales* 121,615,500
SIC 3441 Fabricated structural Metal
Stanley R Hawkins

D-U-N-S 25-989-8716   (SL)
MENKES CONSTRUCTION LIMITED
(*Suby of* MENKES HOLDINGS INC)
4711 Yonge St Suite 1400, North York, ON, M2N 7E4
(416) 491-2222
Emp Here 100
SIC 6553 Cemetery subdividers and developers
Alan Menkes
Steven Menkes
Peter Menkes

D-U-N-S 20-625-8071   (HQ)
MENKES HOLDINGS INC
MDL
4711 Yonge St Suite 1400, North York, ON, M2N 7E4
(416) 491-2222
Emp Here 80   *Sales* 23,725,800
SIC 6553 Cemetery subdividers and developers
Alan Menkes
Steven Menkes
Peter Menkes

D-U-N-S 20-194-6469   (HQ)
MENKES PROPERTY MANAGEMENT SERVICES LTD
4711 Yonge St Suite 1400, North York, ON, M2N 7E4
(416) 491-2222
Emp Here 1   *Sales* 15,817,200
SIC 6553 Cemetery subdividers and developers
Alan Menkes

D-U-N-S 20-552-8669   (BR)
METRO ONTARIO INC
METRO
(*Suby of* METRO INC)
20 Church Ave, North York, ON, M2N 0B7
(416) 229-6200
Emp Here 300
SIC 5411 Grocery stores
Bill Flipetz

D-U-N-S 20-120-6591   (HQ)
MINTO APARTMENTS LIMITED
90 Sheppard Ave E Suite 500, North York, ON, M2N 3A1
(416) 977-0777
Emp Here 500
SIC 6531 Real estate agents and managers
Roger Greenberg
Peter Goring
Alan Greenberg
Daniel Greenberg
J Eric Mckinney
Andrew Price

D-U-N-S 24-067-2167   (BR)
MOXIE'S RESTAURANTS, LIMITED PARTNERSHIP
MOXIE'S
4950 Yonge St Suite 105, North York, ON, M2N 6K1

Emp Here 100
SIC 5812 Eating places
Carlo Darao

D-U-N-S 20-381-9896   (HQ)
MPX INTERNATIONAL CORPORATION
5255 Yonge St Ste 701, North York, ON, M2N 6P4

(416) 840-6632
Sales 29,844,315
SIC 5122 Drugs, proprietaries, and sundries

D-U-N-S 20-553-8283   (HQ)
MR. SUBMARINE LIMITED
MR. SUB
(*Suby of* GROUPE D'ALIMENTATION MTY INC)
4576 Yonge St Suite 600, North York, ON, M2N 6N4
(416) 225-5545
Emp Here 26   *Sales* 20,904,300
SIC 6794 Patent owners and lessors
Jack Levinson
Barry Wilde
Earl Linzon
Bernard Levinson
Jerald Shuman
Jess Collins

D-U-N-S 24-075-4275   (HQ)
NESTLE CANADA INC
NESPRESSO
(*Suby of* NESTLE S.A.)
25 Sheppard Ave W Suite 1700, North York, ON, M2N 6S6
(416) 512-9000
Emp Here 300   *Sales* 1,705,847,500
SIC 2095 Roasted coffee
Shelley Martin
Andrew Allshire

D-U-N-S 25-274-1632   (SL)
OASIS TECHNOLOGY HOLDINGS LTD
90 Sheppard Ave E Suite 100, North York, ON, M2N 3A1
(416) 228-8000
Emp Here 170   *Sales* 24,510,940
SIC 7371 Custom computer programming services
Ashraf Dimitri
Sunny Siu

D-U-N-S 25-406-0080   (SL)
ONTARIO PODIATRIC MEDICAL ASSOCIATION
OPMA
45 Sheppard Ave E Suite 900, North York, ON, M2N 5W9
(416) 927-9111
Emp Here 57   *Sales* 13,766,355
SIC 8621 Professional organizations
James Hill

D-U-N-S 25-153-5654   (SL)
PEAK SPORTS MANAGEMENT INC
TORONTO ICE HOCKEY LEAGUE
2996 Bayview Ave, North York, ON, M2N 5K9

Emp Here 45   *Sales* 19,067,850
SIC 7941 Sports clubs, managers, and promoters
Kerry Sokalsky

D-U-N-S 20-771-1029   (SL)
PEOPLES MINISTRIES INC
PEOPLES CHURCH
374 Sheppard Ave E, North York, ON, M2N 3B6
(416) 222-3341
Emp Here 110   *Sales* 11,453,530
SIC 8661 Religious organizations
Charles Price
Lowry Chua
Gary Patriquin
Art Brooker
George Gooderham

D-U-N-S 24-327-8228   (HQ)
PLANET ENERGY CORP
5525 Yonge St Suite 1500, North York, ON, M2N 5S3

Sales 18,743,040
SIC 8748 Business consulting, nec
Paul Devries
Chris Gaffney

David Ellis

D-U-N-S 20-173-4217 (HQ)
PROCTER & GAMBLE INC
(*Suby of* THE PROCTER & GAMBLE COMPANY)
4711 Yonge St, North York, ON, M2N 6K8
(416) 730-4711
Emp Here 700 *Sales* 844,825,500
SIC 2841 Soap and other detergents
Timothy H Penner
Eric Glass

D-U-N-S 25-370-8853 (BR)
PROCTER & GAMBLE INC
(*Suby of* THE PROCTER & GAMBLE COMPANY)
4711 Yonge St, North York, ON, M2N 6K8
(416) 730-4711
Emp Here 100
SIC 5169 Chemicals and allied products, nec
Kathy Burgers

D-U-N-S 20-325-0956 (SL)
PUBLIC SERVICES HEALTH AND SAFETY ASSOCIATION
4950 Yonge St Suite 1800, North York, ON, M2N 6K1
(416) 250-2131
Emp Here 45 *Sales* 10,685,025
SIC 8099 Health and allied services, nec
Ken Williamson

D-U-N-S 20-077-4029 (BR)
RE/MAX REALTRON REALTY INC
(*Suby of* RE/MAX REALTRON REALTY INC)
183 Willowdale Ave, North York, ON, M2N 4Y9
(416) 222-8600
Emp Here 169
SIC 6531 Real estate agents and managers
Barbara Raber

D-U-N-S 24-891-5712 (SL)
S. F. PARTNERSHIP LLP
4950 Yonge St Suite 400, North York, ON, M2N 6K1
(416) 250-1212
Emp Here 65 *Sales* 13,499,525
SIC 8721 Accounting, auditing, and bookkeeping
Irving Feldman
Stanley I Rapkin
Bradley D H Waese
Jason Crystal

D-U-N-S 25-843-3713 (BR)
SECOND CUP LTD, THE
2233451 ONTARIO INC
(*Suby of* SECOND CUP LTD, THE)
5095 Yonge St, North York, ON, M2N 6Z4
(416) 227-9332
Emp Here 226
SIC 5812 Eating places
Queenie Chong

D-U-N-S 25-149-2260 (HQ)
SHENGLIN FINANCIAL INC
SHENGLIN FINANCIAL GROUP
170 Sheppard Ave E Suite 500, North York, ON, M2N 3A4
(416) 789-3691
Emp Here 1 *Sales* 63,006,318
SIC 6311 Life insurance
Shenglin Xian
Christine Xian

D-U-N-S 20-578-0455 (HQ)
SMSI TRAVEL CENTRES INC
HMS HOST
(*Suby of* EDIZIONE SRL)
45 Sheppard Ave E Suite 302, North York, ON, M2N 5W9
(416) 221-4900
Emp Here 25 *Sales* 74,622,400
SIC 5812 Eating places
Vijay Francis
Bruce Carbone
Bernard Brown

D-U-N-S 25-531-7737 (SL)
SMT DIRECT MARKETING INC
5255 Yonge St Suite 1400, North York, ON, M2N 6P4

Emp Here 120 *Sales* 26,393,160
SIC 8732 Commercial nonphysical research
Tony Nadra
Shimon Shachar

D-U-N-S 20-649-9738 (BR)
SSQ SOCIETE D'ASSURANCE-VIE INC
SSQ FINANCIAL GROUP
(*Suby of* FONDS DE SOLIDARITE DES TRAVAILLEURS DU QUEBEC (F.T.Q.))
110 Sheppard Ave E Unit 500, North York, ON, M2N 6Y8
(416) 221-3477
Emp Here 150
SIC 6351 Surety insurance
Sarah Harrison

D-U-N-S 20-192-5893 (HQ)
STARBUCKS COFFEE CANADA, INC
STARBUCKS COFFEE COMPANY
(*Suby of* STARBUCKS CORPORATION)
5140 Yonge St Suite 1205, North York, ON, M2N 6L7
(416) 228-7300
Emp Here 150 *Sales* 233,195,000
SIC 5812 Eating places
Michael Conway
Clifford Burrows
Masanori Murakami
Sophie Hager Hume
Scott Harlan Maw

D-U-N-S 24-770-7441 (HQ)
SUNDIAL HOMES LIMITED
4576 Yonge St Suite 500, North York, ON, M2N 6N4
(416) 224-1200
Sales 12,754,760
SIC 1521 Single-family housing construction
Robert Yanowski

D-U-N-S 20-980-3865 (HQ)
TARION WARRANTY CORPORATION
5160 Yonge St 12th Fl, North York, ON, M2N 6L9
(416) 229-3828
Emp Here 80 *Sales* 54,261,097
SIC 6351 Surety insurance
Howard Bogach
David Guiney
Edmond Lee
Lesley Ross
Mark Basciano
Lea Ray
Loralea Carruthers
Victor Fiume
Daniel Gabriele
Frank Giannone

D-U-N-S 25-727-7608 (SL)
THAI OCCIDENTAL LTD
5334 Yonge St Suite 907, North York, ON, M2N 6V1

Emp Here 75
SIC 2258 Lace and warp knit fabric mills

D-U-N-S 20-177-5777 (SL)
THOUGHTCORP SYSTEMS INC
(*Suby of* EPAM SYSTEMS, INC.)
4950 Yonge St Suite 1700, North York, ON, M2N 6K1
(416) 591-4004
Emp Here 100 *Sales* 16,684,700
SIC 7379 Computer related services, nec
David Bercovitch
Kirk Robinson

D-U-N-S 24-124-6941 (HQ)
TORONTO CATHOLIC DISTRICT SCHOOL BOARD
TCDSB
80 Sheppard Ave E, North York, ON, M2N 6E8

(416) 222-8282
Emp Here 302 *Sales* 901,710,547
SIC 8211 Elementary and secondary schools
Ann Andrachuk
Sandra Pessione

D-U-N-S 20-711-1670 (BR)
TORONTO CATHOLIC DISTRICT SCHOOL BOARD
SPECIAL SERVICES CATHOLIC EDUCATION CENTRE
(*Suby of* TORONTO CATHOLIC DISTRICT SCHOOL BOARD)
80 Sheppard Ave E Suite 222, North York, ON, M2N 6E8
(416) 222-8282
Emp Here 80
SIC 8211 Elementary and secondary schools
Ann Terron

D-U-N-S 20-025-1259 (BR)
TORONTO DISTRICT SCHOOL BOARD
EARL HAIG SECONDARY SCHOOL
(*Suby of* TORONTO DISTRICT SCHOOL BOARD)
100 Princess Ave, North York, ON, M2N 3R7
(416) 395-3210
Emp Here 150
SIC 8211 Elementary and secondary schools
Renata Gonsalves

D-U-N-S 24-288-9145 (HQ)
TORONTO DISTRICT SCHOOL BOARD
5050 Yonge St 5th Fl, North York, ON, M2N 5N8
(416) 397-3000
Emp Here 200 *Sales* 2,123,032,343
SIC 8211 Elementary and secondary schools
Robin Pilkey
John Malloy

D-U-N-S 24-676-7235 (BR)
VALE CANADA LIMITED
(*Suby of* VALE S/A)
5 Park Home Ave Suite 300, North York, ON, M2N 6L4

Emp Here 135
SIC 1629 Heavy construction, nec
Samantha Espley

D-U-N-S 20-983-9468 (SL)
VTRAC CONSULTING CORPORATION
4950 Yonge St Suite 1005, North York, ON, M2N 6K1
(416) 366-2600
Emp Here 100 *Sales* 23,428,800
SIC 8748 Business consulting, nec
Maryam Bekhrad
Forood Malekzadeh

D-U-N-S 20-044-2325 (HQ)
WOLTERS KLUWER CANADA LIMITED
(*Suby of* WOLTERS KLUWER N.V.)
90 Sheppard Ave E Suite 300, North York, ON, M2N 6X1
(416) 224-2224
Emp Here 200 *Sales* 87,779,622
SIC 2721 Periodicals
Frans Klaassen

D-U-N-S 25-660-1857 (HQ)
WORLD FINANCIAL GROUP INSURANCE AGENCY OF CANADA INC
WFG
(*Suby of* AEGON N.V.)
5000 Yonge St Suite 800, North York, ON, M2N 7E9

Emp Here 5 *Sales* 92,332,950
SIC 6311 Life insurance
Richard Williams
Andrew Norris
Leesa Easley

North York, ON M2P

D-U-N-S 20-693-8933 (SL)
1107078 ONTARIO INC
SHELL
4021 Yonge St, North York, ON, M2P 1N6
(416) 223-0837
Emp Here 25 *Sales* 12,451,950
SIC 5541 Gasoline service stations
Sam Kee

D-U-N-S 20-104-2806 (SL)
AFILIAS CANADA, CORP
LIBERTY REGISTRY MANAGEMENT SERVICES CO
(*Suby of* AFILIAS LIMITED)
4141 Yonge St Suite 204, North York, ON, M2P 2A8
(416) 646-3304
Emp Here 135 *Sales* 31,016,790
SIC 8731 Commercial physical research
Henry Lubsen
Ram Mohan
Steven Pack

D-U-N-S 24-947-5120 (HQ)
ARVA LIMITED
4120 Yonge St Suite 310, North York, ON, M2P 2B8
(416) 222-0842
Emp Here 4 *Sales* 21,457,570
SIC 1623 Water, sewer, and utility lines
Michael Stevens
John W Stevens
William Smith

D-U-N-S 24-424-3932 (SL)
BBS SECURITIES INC
VIRTUAL BROKERS
4100 Yonge St Suite 506, North York, ON, M2P 2B5
(416) 235-0200
Emp Here 30 *Sales* 20,367,690
SIC 6211 Security brokers and dealers
Bardya Ziaian

D-U-N-S 20-119-2494 (HQ)
BLUECAT NETWORKS, INC
(*Suby of* BLUECAT NETWORKS (USA) INC.)
4100 Yonge St Suite 300, North York, ON, M2P 2B5
(416) 646-8400
Emp Here 200 *Sales* 33,369,400
SIC 7379 Computer related services, nec
Michael Harris
Andrew Wertkin
Eric Vermillion
Jim Williams
Jeannie Cho
Cheryl Kerrigan
Michael Hyatt
Douglas C. Grissom
Matthew W. Norton
Brendan T. Barrett

D-U-N-S 24-787-4444 (SL)
BROADSTREET DATA SOLUTIONS INC
10 York Mills Rd Suite 214, North York, ON, M2P 2G4
(416) 792-2000
Emp Here 80 *Sales* 18,585,169
SIC 4899 Communication services, nec

D-U-N-S 20-787-1609 (HQ)
CANADIAN FEDERATION OF INDEPENDENT BUSINESS
C F I B
4141 Yonge St Suite 401, North York, ON, M2P 2A8
(416) 222-8022
Emp Here 90 *Sales* 75,657,000
SIC 8611 Business associations
Dan Kelly
Laura Jones

D-U-N-S 25-683-1983 (HQ)
CIRCLE OF HOME CARE SERVICES (TORONTO)
CIRCLE OF CARE

4211 Yonge St Suite 401, North York, ON, M2P 2A9
(416) 635-2860
Sales 42,143,325
SIC 8059 Nursing and personal care, nec
Carey Lucki
Allan Rudolph
Jeff Carbell
Harvey Bernstein
Michael Hollend
Brian Lass
Gary Newton
Stephen M. Pustil
Les Richmond
Bernice Royce

D-U-N-S 20-057-6796   (SL)
DOCUMENT DIRECTION LIMITED
DDL
4100 Yonge St Suite 600, North York, ON, M2P 2B5
(416) 218-4360
Emp Here 80   *Sales* 35,773,920
SIC 5044 Office equipment
Perry Edwards
Jim Schmidt

D-U-N-S 25-513-9271   (HQ)
DORCHESTER OAKS CORPORATION
COMPLEXE SOUTHWEST ONE
(*Suby of* DORCHESTER CORPORATION, THE)
120 Yonge St Suite 215, North York, ON, M2P 2B8
(416) 628-6238
Emp Here 13   *Sales* 24,388,350
SIC 6799 Investors, nec
Morris Shohet
John Quattrocchi

D-U-N-S 20-036-6453   (SL)
GALLAGHER BASSETT CANADA INC
(*Suby of* ARTHUR J. GALLAGHER & CO.)
4311 Yonge St Suite 404, North York, ON, M2P 1N6
(416) 861-8212
Emp Here 20   *Sales* 16,961,200
SIC 6411 Insurance agents, brokers, and service
Camille Alexander

D-U-N-S 20-279-0028   (HQ)
HITACHI SOLUTIONS CANADA, LTD
(*Suby of* HITACHI, LTD.)
36 York Mills Rd Suite 502, North York, ON, M2P 2E9
(416) 961-4332
Emp Here 60   *Sales* 29,198,225
SIC 7372 Prepackaged software
Masakazu Kuji
Maria Oppegard
Mike Gillis
Yoshihiro Miyoshi

D-U-N-S 24-948-1573   (SL)
HUGH WOOD CANADA LTD
4120 Yonge St Suite 201, North York, ON, M2P 2B8
(416) 229-6600
Emp Here 35   *Sales* 64,670,970
SIC 6411 Insurance agents, brokers, and service
Kyle Nichols
Doug Poole
Lionel Cohen
Sabina Taylor
Ingeborg Koch

D-U-N-S 20-153-5437   (SL)
IDEACA LIMITED
36 York Mills Rd, North York, ON, M2P 2E9
(416) 961-4332
Emp Here 38   *Sales* 10,765,134
SIC 8741 Management services
Tracy Deans
Leslie Barnes

D-U-N-S 25-345-5026   (HQ)

INFORMATION BALANCE INC
4141 Yonge St Suite 205, North York, ON, M2P 2A8
(416) 962-5235
Sales 15,016,230
SIC 7379 Computer related services, nec
Gabor Szirmak
Michael Doiron
Linda Mackiewicz

D-U-N-S 25-300-6415   (BR)
KPMG LLP
(*Suby of* KPMG LLP)
4100 Yonge St Unit 200, North York, ON, M2P 2B5
(416) 228-7000
Emp Here 170
SIC 8721 Accounting, auditing, and bookkeeping
Toni Sasso

D-U-N-S 25-367-8098   (HQ)
LENOVO (CANADA) INC
(*Suby of* LENOVO GROUP LIMITED)
10 York Mills Rd Suite 400, North York, ON, M2P 2G4
(855) 253-6686
Emp Here 500   *Sales* 154,482,350
SIC 3571 Electronic computers
Murray Wright
Verne Deneault

D-U-N-S 20-835-5623   (HQ)
MAKE-A-WISH FOUNDATION OF CANADA
4211 Yonge St Suite 520, North York, ON, M2P 2A9
(416) 224-9474
Emp Here 20   *Sales* 35,460,600
SIC 8699 Membership organizations, nec
Jennifer Ritter
Kenrick Sproul
Eileen Uyede
Christopher Pon
Daniel Bourque
Benjamin Lo
Gerry Savaria

D-U-N-S 20-708-0875   (SL)
MANULIFE SECURITIES INSURANCE
4101 Yonge St Suite 700, North York, ON, M2P 1N6
(416) 218-8707
Emp Here 40   *Sales* 33,922,400
SIC 6411 Insurance agents, brokers, and service
Dominic Scavuzzedo

D-U-N-S 25-086-5961   (BR)
MINTO GROUP INC
MINTO MANAGEMENT
(*Suby of* MINTO GROUP INC)
4101 Yonge St Unit 600, North York, ON, M2P 1N6
(416) 977-0777
Emp Here 170
SIC 1521 Single-family housing construction
Rob Pike

D-U-N-S 20-729-9327   (HQ)
NEXJ SYSTEMS INC
10 York Mills Rd Suite 700, North York, ON, M2P 2G4
(416) 222-5611
Emp Here 16   *Sales* 17,007,260
SIC 7379 Computer related services, nec
Paul O'donnell
William M. Tatham
Ken Szeto
Peter Murray
Owen Pond
Matthew Bogart
Paul Devriendt
David W. Shepherd
Rajneesh Sapra
Frank Cianciotta

D-U-N-S 25-149-8234   (HQ)
ONTARIO LOTTERY AND GAMING CORPO-

RATION
OLG
(*Suby of* GOVERNMENT OF ONTARIO)
4120 Yonge St Suite 500, North York, ON, M2P 2B8
(416) 224-1772
Emp Here 300   *Sales* 606,900,000
SIC 7999 Amusement and recreation, nec
Stephen Rigby
Paul V. Godfrey
Shirley Hoy
Dale Lastman
Anthony Melman
Thomas O'brien
William Swirsky
Ron Carinci
Jan Westcott
Charlotte Burke

D-U-N-S 24-126-2252   (HQ)
PARKINSON SOCIETY CANADA
4211 Yonge St Suite 316, North York, ON, M2P 2A9
(416) 227-9700
Emp Here 28   *Sales* 46,807,992
SIC 8699 Membership organizations, nec
Joyce Gordon

D-U-N-S 24-981-3481   (BR)
RICOH CANADA INC
DOCUMENT DIRECTION
(*Suby of* RICOH COMPANY,LTD.)
4100 Yonge St Suite 600, North York, ON, M2P 2B5
(416) 218-4360
Emp Here 130
SIC 5044 Office equipment
Jack Andrew.

D-U-N-S 24-830-1251   (HQ)
SAP CANADA INC
(*Suby of* SAP SE)
222 Bay St Suite 1800, 1900, 2000, North York, ON, M2P 2B8
(416) 229-0574
Emp Here 304   *Sales* 560,141,424
SIC 7372 Prepackaged software
Bill Mcdermott
Mark Aboud
Christian Klein
Luka Mucic
Stefan Ries

D-U-N-S 20-784-5215   (HQ)
SAVE THE CHILDREN CANADA
4141 Yonge St Suite 300, North York, ON, M2P 2A8
(416) 221-5501
Emp Here 29   *Sales* 42,317,773
SIC 8399 Social services, nec
David Morley
William Chambers
Dan Legault

D-U-N-S 24-418-6503   (HQ)
SECUREKEY TECHNOLOGIES INC
4101 Yonge St Suite 501, North York, ON, M2P 1N6
(416) 477-5625
Sales 10,233,650
SIC 3699 Electrical equipment and supplies, nec
Greg Wolfond
Jaime Shapiro
John Swainson
David House

D-U-N-S 20-412-2113   (HQ)
SMITH AND ANDERSEN CONSULTING ENGINEERING
SMITH & ANDERSEN
4211 Yonge St Suite 500, North York, ON, M2P 2A9
(416) 487-8151
Emp Here 52   *Sales* 10,724,340
SIC 8711 Engineering services
Ian Smith

Karol Goldman
Douglas Smith
Raymond Niepage
Kevin Farbridge

D-U-N-S 24-211-5983   (HQ)
SPIRE GROUP LIMITED
4110 Yonge St Suite 602, North York, ON, M2P 2B7
(416) 250-0090
Emp Here 13   *Sales* 45,688,625
SIC 6712 Bank holding companies
Patrick Gouveia
John Dobrei
Ian Macnair

D-U-N-S 25-926-9876   (HQ)
STERLING SILVER DEVELOPMENT CORPORATION
STERLING KARAMAR PROPERTY MANAGEMENT
53 The Links Rd, North York, ON, M2P 1T7
(416) 226-9400
Sales 15,817,200
SIC 6553 Cemetery subdividers and developers
Austin Phillips

D-U-N-S 25-296-1230   (BR)
SUNCOR ENERGY PRODUCTS INC
(*Suby of* SUNCOR ENERGY INC)
36 York Mills Rd Suite 110, North York, ON, M2P 2E9
(416) 498-7751
Emp Here 250
SIC 2911 Petroleum refining
Tom Ryley

D-U-N-S 24-560-3170   (HQ)
SWEDA CANADA INC
4101 Yonge St Suite 500, North York, ON, M2P 1N6
(416) 614-0199
Emp Here 45   *Sales* 10,813,650
SIC 7371 Custom computer programming services
Norman Tsui
Peter Chan
Russell Brown
James Chao
Ella Agnew
Irene Chu
Mario Emard
J. Graham Long
Rick Farmer

D-U-N-S 20-646-8709   (BR)
VOXDATA SOLUTIONS INC
VOXDATA CALL CENTER
(*Suby of* VOXDATA SOLUTIONS INC)
20 York Mills Rd Suite 201, North York, ON, M2P 2C2

Emp Here 200
SIC 4899 Communication services, nec
Nadia Desentis

D-U-N-S 24-915-5623   (BR)
WAWANESA LIFE INSURANCE COMPANY, THE
(*Suby of* WAWANESA MUTUAL INSURANCE COMPANY, THE)
4110 Yonge St Suite 100, North York, ON, M2P 2B7
(519) 886-4320
Emp Here 150
SIC 6311 Life insurance
Norman Southwood

D-U-N-S 20-934-1585   (BR)
WAWANESA MUTUAL INSURANCE COMPANY, THE
(*Suby of* WAWANESA MUTUAL INSURANCE COMPANY, THE)
4110 Yonge St Suite 100, North York, ON, M2P 2B7
(416) 250-9292
Emp Here 180

SIC 6331 Fire, marine, and casualty insurance
Tim Greer

D-U-N-S 24-047-2167   (SL)
WCC CONSTRUCTION CANADA, ULC
WALSH CANADA
(*Suby of* THE WALSH GROUP LTD)
36 York Mills Rd Suite 302, North York, ON,
M2P 2E9
(416) 849-9000
Emp Here 143   *Sales* 66,319,968
SIC 1522 Residential construction, nec
Daniel P Walsh

D-U-N-S 20-178-6993   (HQ)
XEROX CANADA INC
(*Suby of* XEROX CORPORATION)
20 York Mills Rd 5th Flr, North York, ON, M2P
2C2
(416) 229-3769
Emp Here 400   *Sales* 2,034,337,600
SIC 5044 Office equipment
Ursula M. Burns
Lynn R. Blodgett
James A. Firestone
Kathryn A. Mikells
Armando Zagalo De Lima
Don H. Liu
Thomas J. Maddison
Herve Tessler
David Amoriell
Thomas Blodgett

D-U-N-S 24-938-0049   (HQ)
XEROX CANADA LTD
(*Suby of* XEROX CORPORATION)
20 York Mills Rd Suite 500, North York, ON,
M2P 2C2
(416) 733-6501
Emp Here 350   *Sales* 825,916,500
SIC 5999 Miscellaneous retail stores, nec
Mandy Shapansky

North York, ON M2R

D-U-N-S 20-085-6255   (SL)
ADVENT HEALTH CARE CORPORATION
VALLEY VIEW
541 Finch Ave W, North York, ON, M2R 3Y3
(416) 636-5800
Emp Here 200   *Sales* 141,842,400
SIC 8699 Membership organizations, nec
Brian Fenton

D-U-N-S 20-880-8204   (HQ)
**ASSOCIATED HEBREW SCHOOLS OF
TORONTO**
252 Finch Ave W, North York, ON, M2R 1M9
(416) 494-7666
Emp Here 70   *Sales* 22,797,370
SIC 8211 Elementary and secondary schools
Elliott Brodkin
David W. Brown
Sheldon Carr

D-U-N-S 25-852-3612   (BR)
**DIVERSICARE CANADA MANAGEMENT
SERVICES CO., INC**
CHELTENHAM NURSING HOME
(*Suby of* DCMS HOLDINGS INC)
5935 Bathurst St, North York, ON, M2R 1Y8
(416) 223-4050
Emp Here 160
SIC 8051 Skilled nursing care facilities

D-U-N-S 24-411-3502   (SL)
GREEN, ESTHER DRUGS LTD
SHOPPERS DRUG MART #919
6205 Bathurst St, North York, ON, M2R 2A5
(416) 222-5464
Emp Here 60   *Sales* 14,659,680
SIC 5912 Drug stores and proprietary stores
Esther Green

D-U-N-S 20-011-3855   (SL)

**INTERNATIONAL ECONOMY SERVICES
INC**
1057 Steeles Ave W Suite 1, North York, ON,
M2R 2S9
(416) 725-1294
Emp Here 103   *Sales* 19,210,118
SIC 8742 Management consulting services

D-U-N-S 20-879-2309   (HQ)
**JEWISH FAMILY AND CHILD SERVICE OF
GREATER TORONTO**
JEWISH FAMILY & CHILD
4600 Bathurst St Suite 1, North York, ON,
M2R 3V3
(416) 638-7800
Emp Here 90   *Sales* 20,706,800
SIC 8399 Social services, nec
Richard Cummings
Zachy Lahav
Wendy Wolfman
Howard Hurwitz
Monica Auerbach

D-U-N-S 25-998-5786   (BR)
NORTH YORK GENERAL HOSPITAL
(*Suby of* NORTH YORK GENERAL HOSPI-
TAL)
555 Finch Ave W Suite 262, North York, ON,
M2R 1N5
(416) 633-9420
Emp Here 500
SIC 8062 General medical and surgical hospi-
tals
Sue Olson

D-U-N-S 20-820-6623   (HQ)
SANOFI PASTEUR LIMITED
(*Suby of* SANOFI)
1755 Steeles Ave W, North York, ON, M2R
3T4
(416) 667-2700
Emp Here 1,100   *Sales* 364,753,400
SIC 2836 Biological products, except diagnos-
tic
Sabina Steinkellner
Robin Keslassy
Tony D'amore

D-U-N-S 25-896-3883   (BR)
SOBEYS CAPITAL INCORPORATED
PRICE CHOPPER
(*Suby of* EMPIRE COMPANY LIMITED)
6201 Bathurst St, North York, ON, M2R 2A5

Emp Here 81
SIC 5411 Grocery stores
Matt Spensieri

D-U-N-S 20-874-7410   (HQ)
**UNITED JEWISH APPEAL OF GREATER
TORONTO**
4600 Bathurst St Unit 5, North York, ON, M2R
3V3
(416) 631-5716
Sales 53,134,920
SIC 6732 Trusts: educational, religious, etc.
Allan Reitzes
David Zion
Harry Goreman
Jack Rose

North York, ON M3A

D-U-N-S 20-323-0263   (SL)
2179321 ONTARIO LIMITED
NATIONAL SERVICES
27 Larabee Cres, North York, ON, M3A 3E6
(416) 219-1050
Emp Here 25   *Sales* 11,179,350
SIC 5074 Plumbing and heating equipment
and supplies (hydronics)
Joseph Del Mortal
Leo Liao

D-U-N-S 20-824-0788   (SL)

DONALDA CLUB
12 Bushbury Dr, North York, ON, M3A 2Z7
(416) 447-5575
Emp Here 100   *Sales* 7,854,500
SIC 7997 Membership sports and recreation
clubs
Charles Powell

D-U-N-S 24-976-8383   (BR)
FIRSTCANADA ULC
AIRPORTER, SERVICE, DIV OF
(*Suby of* FIRSTGROUP PLC)
103 Railside Rd, North York, ON, M3A 1B2
(905) 294-5104
Emp Here 212
SIC 4151 School buses
Ellie Camoeron

D-U-N-S 20-169-6648   (SL)
LYNCH, W. T. FOODS LIMITED
LYNCH FOOD
72 Railside Rd, North York, ON, M3A 1A3
(416) 449-5464
Emp Here 140   *Sales* 48,396,600
SIC 2099 Food preparations, nec
Walker Lynch
Scott Lynch
Douglas Roger Nowlan

D-U-N-S 24-768-7747   (BR)
METRO ONTARIO INC
FOOD BASICS
(*Suby of* METRO INC)
1277 York Mills Rd, North York, ON, M3A 1Z5
(416) 444-7921
Emp Here 75
SIC 5411 Grocery stores
Brian Miljevic

D-U-N-S 20-258-5741   (SL)
PROTECTOLITE COMPOSITES INC
84 Railside Rd, North York, ON, M3A 1A3
(416) 444-4484
Emp Here 60   *Sales* 13,320,060
SIC 3569 General industrial machinery, nec
Paul Szasz
Karl Szasz

D-U-N-S 20-703-5531   (SL)
ST. JOSEPH PRINT GROUP INC
ST. JOSEPH PRINT THORN
(*Suby of* ST. JOSEPH CORPORATION)
135 Railside Rd, North York, ON, M3A 1B7
(613) 746-4005
Emp Here 101   *Sales* 16,566,727
SIC 2752 Commercial printing, lithographic
Frank Gagliano
Anthony Gagliano
Rudy Desiato

D-U-N-S 24-972-4550   (BR)
TORONTO DISTRICT SCHOOL BOARD
VICTORIA PARK COLLEGIATE INSTITUTE
(*Suby of* TORONTO DISTRICT SCHOOL
BOARD)
15 Wallingford Rd, North York, ON, M3A 2V1
(416) 395-3310
Emp Here 100
SIC 8211 Elementary and secondary schools
Vance Scott

D-U-N-S 20-178-5458   (HQ)
WINTERS INSTRUMENTS LTD
121 Railside Rd, North York, ON, M3A 1B2
(416) 444-2345
Emp Here 30   *Sales* 10,262,480
SIC 3824 Fluid meters and counting devices
W D Jeffrey Smith
J David Hilborn

North York, ON M3B

D-U-N-S 24-401-4960   (SL)
401 PAVING LTD

1260 Don Mills Rd, North York, ON, M3B 2W6
(416) 441-0401
Emp Here 49   *Sales* 13,892,676
SIC 1611 Highway and street construction
Sam Bahadori

D-U-N-S 24-371-3976   (SL)
**ACHIEVO NETSTAR SOLUTIONS COM-
PANY**
(*Suby of* ACHIEVO CORPORATION)
220 Duncan Mill Rd Suite 505, North York,
ON, M3B 3J5
(416) 383-1818
Emp Here 80
SIC 7371 Custom computer programming ser-
vices
Nestor Cruz
Sing Cheong Chan
Jeffrey Tung
Julio Leung

D-U-N-S 20-270-4847   (SL)
ANNEX-NEWCOM LIMITED PARTNERSHIP
80 Valleybrook Dr, North York, ON, M3B 2S9
(416) 442-5600
Emp Here 300   *Sales* 58,132,200
SIC 2721 Periodicals
Alex Papanou

D-U-N-S 24-353-9488   (HQ)
AVANTE LOGIXX INC
1959 Leslie St, North York, ON, M3B 2M3
(416) 923-6984
Sales 15,908,026
SIC 1731 Electrical work
Craig Campbell
Leland Verner
Rose Baker
Raghu Sampath
Andrew Coles
Bruce Bronfman
James Joseph Leeder
Michael Pilato

D-U-N-S 25-404-7954   (SL)
AVANTE SECURITY INC
(*Suby of* AVANTE LOGIXX INC)
1959 Leslie St, North York, ON, M3B 2M3
(416) 923-2435
Emp Here 60   *Sales* 28,844,700
SIC 7382 Security systems services
Emmanuel Mounouchos

D-U-N-S 25-367-6688   (BR)
BELL EXPRESSVU INC
(*Suby of* BCE INC)
115 Scarsdale Rd, North York, ON, M3B 2R2
(416) 383-6299
Emp Here 150
SIC 4899 Communication services, nec
Bobby Zlateski

D-U-N-S 24-181-7022   (SL)
BLIZZARD COURIER SERVICE LTD
1937 Leslie St, North York, ON, M3B 2M3
(416) 444-0596
Emp Here 75   *Sales* 33,691,425
SIC 7389 Business services, nec
Behzad Khaze
Roya Golesorkhi
Leslie Bresge
Paul Bresge

D-U-N-S 24-682-1206   (SL)
BRAVADO DESIGNS LTD
(*Suby of* OLLE LARSSON HOLDING AG)
60 Scarsdale Rd Unit 100, North York, ON,
M3B 2R7
(416) 466-8652
Emp Here 30   *Sales* 14,949,660
SIC 5137 Women's and children's clothing
Philippe Eilinger
Kathryn From
Ruedi Temperli

D-U-N-S 20-850-8663   (SL)
**BUILDING INDUSTRY AND LAND DEVEL-
OPMENT ASSOCIATION**

BILD
20 Upjohn Rd Suite 100, North York, ON, M3B 2V9
(416) 391-3445
Emp Here 42   *Sales* 10,027,500
SIC 8611 Business associations
 Sam Asusa
 Stephen Dupuis

    D-U-N-S 20-178-8437   (HQ)
CARL ZEISS CANADA LIMITED
(*Suby of* CARL-ZEISS-STIFTUNG)
45 Valleybrook Dr, North York, ON, M3B 2S6
(416) 449-4660
Emp Here 143   *Sales* 36,649,200
SIC 5995 Optical goods stores
 Jim Sharp
 George C Tiviluk

    D-U-N-S 20-939-4097   (SL)
CDSPI
155 Lesmill Rd, North York, ON, M3B 2T8
(416) 296-9401
Emp Here 60   *Sales* 110,864,520
SIC 6411 Insurance agents, brokers, and service
 Susan M. Armstrong
 Ruby Zack
 Lyle R. Best
 Jeff Williams
 Ron S. Beaton
 Wayne A. Chou
 Tom C. Larder
 Robert Sullivan
 Mitch Orr

    D-U-N-S 24-577-3320   (HQ)
CENTURY 21 NEW CONCEPT LTD
1993 Leslie St, North York, ON, M3B 2M3
(416) 449-7600
Emp Here 37   *Sales* 12,500,776
SIC 6531 Real estate agents and managers
 John Cho

    D-U-N-S 24-329-7772   (HQ)
CHESSWOOD GROUP LIMITED
156 Duncan Mill Rd Suite 15, North York, ON, M3B 3N2
(416) 386-3099
Sales 83,835,468
SIC 8741 Management services
 Barry Shafran
 Lisa Stevenson
 Frederick W. Steiner
 Clare R. Copeland
 Robert J. Day
 Samuel Leeper
 David Obront

    D-U-N-S 25-064-8706   (HQ)
COLLEGA INTERNATIONAL INC
210 Lesmill Rd, North York, ON, M3B 2T5
(416) 754-1444
Sales 82,564,200
SIC 5122 Drugs, proprietaries, and sundries
 Orazio Civello
 Raffaela Caruso
 James Senyi

    D-U-N-S 20-942-9257   (HQ)
COMMUNITY LIVING ONTARIO
RECYCLING MATTERS
240 Duncan Mill Rd Suite 403, North York, ON, M3B 3S6
(416) 447-4348
Emp Here 25   *Sales* 11,518,800
SIC 8322 Individual and family services
 Keith Powell
 Ray Luxon

    D-U-N-S 25-870-9211   (SL)
COMP-TECH MFG. INC
58 Scarsdale Rd, North York, ON, M3B 2R7
(416) 510-1035
Emp Here 100   *Sales* 19,208,500
SIC 3469 Metal stampings, nec
 Carlo Gabbrielli

    D-U-N-S 24-197-0268   (HQ)
CONROS CORPORATION
FIRELOG, DIV OF
41 Lesmill Rd, North York, ON, M3B 2T3
(416) 751-4343
Emp Here 210   *Sales* 69,597,500
SIC 2499 Wood products, nec
 Navin Chandaria
 Shernee Chandaria
 Ajay Rao

    D-U-N-S 20-933-7872   (SL)
CURTIS INSURANCE LIMITED
1500 Don Mills Rd Suite 501, North York, ON, M3B 3K4
(416) 447-4499
Emp Here 26   *Sales* 15,078,024
SIC 6411 Insurance agents, brokers, and service
 John Boynton

    D-U-N-S 20-956-4587   (SL)
ENDEVOR CORPORATION
48 Lesmill Rd, North York, ON, M3B 2T5
(416) 445-5850
Emp Here 158   *Sales* 43,189,300
SIC 6712 Bank holding companies
 Gerge F Kelk
 Peter G Kelk

    D-U-N-S 20-380-2460   (SL)
ERIS INFORMATION LIMITED PARTNERSHIP
ERIS INFORMATION
38 Lesmill Rd Suite 2, North York, ON, M3B 2T5
(416) 510-5204
Emp Here 90   *Sales* 15,957,990
SIC 7375 Information retrieval services
 Carol Lenoury

    D-U-N-S 20-709-6798   (HQ)
ERSKINE GREEN LIMITED
(*Suby of* GREENWIN INC)
1 Valleybrook Dr Suite 201, North York, ON, M3B 2S7
(416) 487-3883
Emp Here 196   *Sales* 44,174,200
SIC 6519 Real property lessors, nec
 Miriam Green
 Cary Joseph Green
 Kevin Marc Green

    D-U-N-S 20-345-8898   (SL)
FIXT WIRELESS INC
FIXT WIRELESS REPAIR
1875 Leslie St Unit 4, North York, ON, M3B 2M5
(416) 441-3498
Emp Here 67   *Sales* 18,213,414
SIC 7629 Electrical repair shops
 Garry Woods
 Lyndon Jones
 Donna Custance

    D-U-N-S 25-194-6414   (SL)
FUNDATA CANADA INC
26 Lesmill Rd Suite 1b, North York, ON, M3B 2T5
(416) 445-5443
Emp Here 50   *Sales* 26,560,350
SIC 6289 Security and commodity service
 Janny Vincent

    D-U-N-S 24-091-9662   (HQ)
GATESTONE & CO. INC
180 Duncan Mill Rd Unit 300, North York, ON, M3B 1Z6
(416) 961-9622
Emp Here 302   *Sales* 140,259,700
SIC 7322 Adjustment and collection services
 J Bruce Conley
 Nicholas Wilson
 Barry Kryba
 Boris Dybenko

    D-U-N-S 20-816-2446   (HQ)
GREENWIN INC

19 Lesmill Rd Unit 100, North York, ON, M3B 2T3
(416) 487-3883
Emp Here 250   *Sales* 162,812,400
SIC 6512 Nonresidential building operators
 Kris Boyce
 Cary J Green
 Kevin Green
 Jess Faigal
 Ron Eilath
 Patrick Eratostene

    D-U-N-S 25-410-0175   (HQ)
GS1 CANADA
1500 Don Mills Rd Suite 800, North York, ON, M3B 3K4
(416) 510-8039
Emp Here 78   *Sales* 27,740,900
SIC 8611 Business associations
 N. Arthur Smith

    D-U-N-S 25-109-3068   (HQ)
HAYS SPECIALIST RECRUITMENT (CANADA) INC
HAYS PERSONNEL
(*Suby of* HAYS PLC)
1500 Don Mills Rd Suite 402, North York, ON, M3B 3K4
(416) 203-1925
Emp Here 26   *Sales* 18,152,940
SIC 7299 Miscellaneous personal service
 Rowan O'grady
 Douglas Evans

    D-U-N-S 20-515-4698   (HQ)
HERJAVEC GROUP INC, THE
180 Duncan Mill Rd Suite 700, North York, ON, M3B 1Z6
(416) 639-2193
Emp Here 197   *Sales* 55,371,900
SIC 7371 Custom computer programming services
 Robert Herjavec
 George Frempong
 John Moy
 Sean Higgins
 Jennifer Ogle

    D-U-N-S 24-644-1414   (SL)
HOLMAN EXHIBITS LIMITED
160 Lesmill Rd, North York, ON, M3B 2T5

Emp Here 70   *Sales* 22,829,520
SIC 3993 Signs and advertising specialties
 Wendy Cudney

    D-U-N-S 20-048-3183   (SL)
HOMELIFE/VISION REALTY INC
1945 Leslie St, North York, ON, M3B 2M3
(416) 383-1828
Emp Here 170   *Sales* 71,211,130
SIC 6531 Real estate agents and managers
 Kenneth Kakoullis

    D-U-N-S 20-305-0745   (SL)
ICC IMAGINE COMMUNICATIONS CANADA LTD
IMAGINE COMMUNICATIONS
(*Suby of* THE GORES GROUP LLC)
25 Dyas Rd, North York, ON, M3B 1V7
(416) 445-9640
Emp Here 402   *Sales* 113,731,830
SIC 3663 Radio and t.v. communications equipment
 Tom Cotney
 Terry Hungle
 Mark Herold

    D-U-N-S 25-849-7932   (BR)
KEG RESTAURANTS LTD
KEG STEAKHOUSE & BAR, THE
(*Suby of* RECIPE UNLIMITED CORPORATION)
1977 Leslie St, North York, ON, M3B 2M3
(416) 446-1045
Emp Here 100
SIC 5812 Eating places

Scott Wilmot

    D-U-N-S 24-374-9582   (SL)
KING-REED HOLDINGS LTD
85 Scarsdale Rd Suite 309, North York, ON, M3B 2R2
(416) 449-8677
Emp Here 120   *Sales* 32,802,000
SIC 6712 Bank holding companies
 Brian D. King

    D-U-N-S 20-165-7681   (HQ)
KRAFT HEINZ CANADA ULC
CLASSICO GOURMET
(*Suby of* THE KRAFT HEINZ COMPANY)
95 Moatfield Dr Suite 316, North York, ON, M3B 3L6
(416) 441-5000
Emp Here 350   *Sales* 2,269,264,560
SIC 2043 Cereal breakfast foods
 Av Maharaj
 Carlos Piani
 Taryn Miller

    D-U-N-S 20-531-3641   (HQ)
LCL BUILDS CORPORATION
98 Scarsdale Rd, North York, ON, M3B 2R7
(416) 492-0500
Sales 14,121,930
SIC 1542 Nonresidential construction, nec
 Mark Garland

    D-U-N-S 20-694-1879   (SL)
LEPAGES 2000 INC
GOULD PACKAGING DIV OF
41 Lesmill Rd, North York, ON, M3B 2T3
(416) 751-4343
Emp Here 50   *Sales* 10,094,850
SIC 3086 Plastics foam products
 Navin Chandaria

    D-U-N-S 20-941-1933   (SL)
MACMARMON FOUNDATION
BAYVIEW GLEN SCHOOL
275 Duncan Mill Rd, North York, ON, M3B 3H9
(416) 443-1030
Emp Here 100   *Sales* 9,269,000
SIC 7032 Sporting and recreational camps
 Audrey Elliott
 Poonam Kumar
 Mark Faiz
 Frank Mastinsek
 Terry Guest
 Robert Kane
 David Steingart
 Brendon Pooran
 Mary Beth Williamson
 Tony Colangelo

    D-U-N-S 25-497-5329   (SL)
MEDIPAC INTERNATIONAL INC
180 Lesmill Rd, North York, ON, M3B 2T5
(416) 441-7070
Emp Here 35   *Sales* 36,220,835
SIC 6321 Accident and health insurance
 Ross Quigley
 Tracey Benoit

    D-U-N-S 20-059-6935   (HQ)
MEDISYSTEM PHARMACY LIMITED
(*Suby of* LOBLAW COMPANIES LIMITED)
75 Lesmill Rd Suite 3, North York, ON, M3B 2T8
(416) 441-2293
Emp Here 250   *Sales* 185,769,450
SIC 5122 Drugs, proprietaries, and sundries
 Helen Huh
 Fred Bruns

    D-U-N-S 25-826-5867   (HQ)
MEDISYSTEM TECHNOLOGIES INC
(*Suby of* LOBLAW COMPANIES LIMITED)
75 Lesmill Rd Unit 3, North York, ON, M3B 2T8
(416) 441-2293
Emp Here 20   *Sales* 17,767,750
SIC 6712 Bank holding companies
 Helen Huh

Domenic Pilla
Paula Marchione

D-U-N-S 20-552-8511   (SL)
MFXCHANGE HOLDINGS INC
(*Suby of* FAIRFAX FINANCIAL HOLDINGS
LIMITED)
225 Duncan Mill Rd Suite 320, North York,
ON, M3B 3K9
(416) 385-4800
Emp Here 120   *Sales* 569,532,480
SIC 6411 Insurance agents, brokers, and ser-
vice
Raymond Roy
David L Mcdonough

D-U-N-S 20-333-5211   (BR)
MOORE CANADA CORPORATION
RR DONNELLEY
(*Suby of* R. R. DONNELLEY & SONS COM-
PANY)
180 Bond Ave, North York, ON, M3B 3P3
(416) 445-8800
Emp Here 200
SIC 2752 Commercial printing, lithographic

D-U-N-S 25-179-0036   (SL)
NORTHWEST-ATLANTIC (CANADA) INC
(*Suby of* JONES LANG LASALLE INCORPO-
RATED)
864 York Mills Rd, North York, ON, M3B 1Y4
(416) 391-3900
Emp Here 45   *Sales* 18,850,005
SIC 6531 Real estate agents and managers
Samuel Winberg

D-U-N-S 20-763-0815   (SL)
NPD GROUP CANADA INC, THE
(*Suby of* THE NPD GROUP INC)
1500 Don Mills Rd Suite 502, North York, ON,
M3B 3K4
(647) 723-7700
Emp Here 65   *Sales* 14,296,295
SIC 8732 Commercial nonphysical research
Keith Barber

D-U-N-S 25-938-3479   (SL)
NPD INTELECT CANADA INC
NPD GROUP
(*Suby of* THE NPD GROUP INC)
1500 Don Mills Rd Suite 502, North York, ON,
M3B 3K4
(647) 723-7700
Emp Here 75
SIC 8732 Commercial nonphysical research
Keith Barber
Jane Graham

D-U-N-S 20-817-1942   (HQ)
NUMERIS
1500 Don Mills Rd Suite 305, North York, ON,
M3B 3L7
(416) 445-9800
Emp Here 200   *Sales* 128,761,050
SIC 8621 Professional organizations
Neil Mceneaney
Anna Giagkou
Mark Reid
Jacques Gaboury

D-U-N-S 20-849-6448   (HQ)
**ONTARIO PUBLIC SERVICE EMPLOYEES
UNION**
OPSEU
100 Lesmill Rd, North York, ON, M3B 3P8
(416) 443-8888
Emp Here 140   *Sales* 79,744,560
SIC 8631 Labor organizations
Warren (Smokey) Thomas
Eduardo Almeida

D-U-N-S 20-968-5791   (SL)
ONTARIO REAL ESTATE ASSOCIATION
OREA
99 Duncan Mill Rd, North York, ON, M3B 1Z2
(416) 445-9910
Emp Here 115   *Sales* 29,001,850
SIC 8611 Business associations

Edward Barisa

D-U-N-S 24-386-5201   (SL)
**PAISLEY-MANOR INSURANCE BROKERS
INC**
PAISLEY MANOR INSURANCE GROUP
1446 Don Mills Rd Suite 110, North York, ON,
M3B 3N3
(416) 510-1177
Emp Here 50   *Sales* 28,996,200
SIC 6411 Insurance agents, brokers, and ser-
vice
Ira Kuchinsky
Michael Paisley

D-U-N-S 24-379-7300   (SL)
PAYTECH LTD
1500 Don Mills Rd Suite 400, North York, ON,
M3B 3K4
(888) 263-1938
Emp Here 151   *Sales* 33,522,151
SIC 3578 Calculating and accounting equip-
ment
Hakan Toprak
Yesim Yalcin

D-U-N-S 20-251-7918   (SL)
PHIPPS DESSERTS LTD
1875 Leslie St Unit 21, North York, ON, M3B
2M5
(416) 391-5800
Emp Here 22   *Sales* 18,382,694
SIC 5143 Dairy products, except dried or
canned
Andrew Mcnairn
Petrina Mcnairn

D-U-N-S 20-811-2297   (HQ)
POST ROAD HEALTH & DIET INC
*DR STANLEY K BERNSTEIN'S HEALTH &
DIET CLINICS*
21 Kern Rd, North York, ON, M3B 1S9
(416) 447-3438
Emp Here 16   *Sales* 22,731,900
SIC 8093 Specialty outpatient clinics, nec
Stanley Bernstein

D-U-N-S 20-820-4065   (HQ)
**PREMIER OPERATING CORPORATION
LIMITED**
PREMIER THEATRES
1262 Don Mills Rd Suite 92, North York, ON,
M3B 2W7
(416) 443-1645
Emp Here 1   *Sales* 20,982,745
SIC 6512 Nonresidential building operators
Brian Allen

D-U-N-S 20-035-5514   (SL)
**PRUDENTIAL SADIE MORANIS REALTY
LIMITED**
PRUDENTIAL SADIE MORANIS REALTY
35 Lesmill Rd, North York, ON, M3B 2T3
(416) 960-9995
Emp Here 49   *Sales* 13,316,044
SIC 6531 Real estate agents and managers
Terry Moranis

D-U-N-S 25-371-7359   (SL)
REFERRED REALTY INC
KELLER WILLIAMS REFERRED REALTY
156 Duncan Mill Rd Suite 1, North York, ON,
M3B 3N2
(416) 445-8855
Emp Here 55   *Sales* 14,946,580
SIC 6531 Real estate agents and managers
Glen Mcqueenie

D-U-N-S 24-720-9703   (SL)
REGENCY APPAREL CO LTD
255 Duncan Mill Rd Suite 303, North York,
ON, M3B 3H9

Emp Here 100   *Sales* 13,667,400
SIC 2329 Men's and boy's clothing, nec

D-U-N-S 24-097-3040   (HQ)
ROSE CORPORATION, THE

156 Duncan Mill Rd Suite 12, North York, ON,
M3B 3N2
(416) 449-3535
Emp Here 50   *Sales* 26,891,900
SIC 3443 Fabricated plate work (boiler shop)
Sam Reisman
Gary Maister
Gary Steinhart
Martin Simon

D-U-N-S 24-665-8041   (HQ)
ROTHMANS, BENSON & HEDGES INC
(*Suby of* PHILIP MORRIS INTERNATIONAL
INC.)
1500 Don Mills Rd Suite 900, North York, ON,
M3B 3L1
(416) 449-5525
Emp Here 145   *Sales* 205,795,030
SIC 2111 Cigarettes
John R Barnett
Faryl A Hausman
Robert J Carew
Brenda J Moher

D-U-N-S 24-025-0209   (SL)
SADIE MORANIS REALTY CORPORATION
35 Lesmill Rd, North York, ON, M3B 2T3
(416) 449-2020
Emp Here 150   *Sales* 62,833,350
SIC 6531 Real estate agents and managers
Sadie Moranis
Stephen Moranis
Terry Moranis

D-U-N-S 20-556-0621   (SL)
SECURE 724 LTD
AVANTE SECURITY
1959 Leslie St, North York, ON, M3B 2M3
(416) 923-6984
Emp Here 50   *Sales* 10,233,650
SIC 3699 Electrical equipment and supplies,
nec
Emmanuel Mounouchos

D-U-N-S 24-918-0522   (SL)
SENATOR HOMES INC
250 Lesmill Rd, North York, ON, M3B 2T5
(416) 445-8552
Emp Here 40   *Sales* 12,754,760
SIC 1521 Single-family housing construction
Angelo Breda
Paul Breda

D-U-N-S 24-794-4077   (BR)
SGS CANADA INC
S G S MINERALS SERVICES
1885 Leslie St, North York, ON, M3B 2M3
(416) 736-2782
Emp Here 100
SIC 8734 Testing laboratories
Bruce Robertson

D-U-N-S 20-554-0917   (HQ)
SHELLEY INDUSTRIAL AUTOMATION INC
SHELLEY AUTOMATION
41 Coldwater Rd, North York, ON, M3B 1Y8
(416) 447-6471
Emp Here 42   *Sales* 22,326,222
SIC 5084 Industrial machinery and equipment
Gardiner Shelley
Brian R. Shelley
Judie Pillsworth

D-U-N-S 24-632-8983   (SL)
SHELLEY, R G ENTERPRISES (1990) INC
41 Coldwater Rd, North York, ON, M3B 1Y8
(416) 447-6471
Emp Here 55   *Sales* 26,126,430
SIC 5084 Industrial machinery and equipment
Robert G Shelley
Peter G Shelley
Brian R Shelley

D-U-N-S 24-365-4618   (HQ)
SOCAN FOUNDATION, THE
41 Valleybrook Dr, North York, ON, M3B 2S6
(416) 445-8700
Emp Here 3   *Sales* 244,113,915

SIC 7389 Business services, nec
Eric Baptiste
Stan Meissner
Catharine Saxberg
Kit Wheeler
Janice Scott
Jennifer Brown
Mike King
Onix Belleus
Jeff King
Jean-Robert Bisaillon

D-U-N-S 20-818-6304   (HQ)
**SOCIETY OF COMPOSERS, AUTHORS
AND MUSIC PUBLISHERS OF CANADA**
SOCAN
41 Valleybrook Dr, North York, ON, M3B 2S6
(416) 445-8700
Emp Here 265   *Sales* 231,417,386
SIC 7313 Radio, television, publisher repre-
sentatives
Eric Baptiste
Catharine Saxberg
Jennifer Brown
Janice Scott
Kit Wheeler
Jeff King
David Wood
Andrew Berthoff
Michael Mccarty
Randy Wark

D-U-N-S 20-694-1556   (SL)
SOLUTION Q INC
ECLIPSE PPM
222 Lesmill Rd, North York, ON, M3B 2T5
(416) 385-0774
Emp Here 35   *Sales* 15,651,090
SIC 5045 Computers, peripherals, and soft-
ware
Craig Macinnis
Brad Robbins

D-U-N-S 20-038-9075   (HQ)
SOUND INSURANCE SERVICES INC
205 Lesmill Rd, North York, ON, M3B 2V1
(416) 756-3334
Sales 22,049,560
SIC 6411 Insurance agents, brokers, and ser-
vice
Mark Giardetti
Matthew Giardetti
Neil Mahajan
Sue Alexander

D-U-N-S 24-351-2295   (BR)
ST. JOSEPH PRINTING LIMITED
ST. JOSEPH COMMUNICATIONS
(*Suby of* ST. JOSEPH CORPORATION)
236 Lesmill Rd, North York, ON, M3B 2T5
(416) 449-4579
Emp Here 200
SIC 2711 Newspapers
Don Albin

D-U-N-S 24-311-6295   (BR)
**STERICYCLE COMMUNICATION SOLU-
TIONS, ULC**
(*Suby of* STERICYCLE COMMUNICATION
SOLUTIONS, ULC)
2 Duncan Mill Rd, North York, ON, M3B 1Z4

Emp Here 80
SIC 4899 Communication services, nec
Pamela Mullins

D-U-N-S 24-461-9177   (SL)
TECHNOR DEVELOPMENTS LIMITED
RICHMOND HILL GOLF CLUB
85 Scarsdale Rd, North York, ON, M3B 2R2
(905) 889-4653
Emp Here 100   *Sales* 7,639,700
SIC 7997 Membership sports and recreation
clubs
Morris Macarz
Phillip Macarz

D-U-N-S 20-101-5513   (HQ)
TERRAPEX ENVIRONMENTAL LTD
90 Scarsdale Rd, North York, ON, M3B 2R7
(416) 245-0011
Emp Here 20   *Sales* 10,542,960
SIC 8748 Business consulting, nec
Michael Osborne

D-U-N-S 20-192-3682   (HQ)
THALES CANADA INC
THALES CANADA, DIVISION AERONAU-TIQUE
(*Suby of* THALES)
105 Moatfield Dr Suite 100, North York, ON, M3B 0A4
(416) 742-3900
Emp Here 151   *Sales* 76,881,090
SIC 8711 Engineering services
Mark Halinaty
Michelle Forbrigger
Daniel Marion
Nina Devito
Adrian Abramovici
Siegfried Usal
Dominique Gaiardo
Jerry Mclean
Dale Potter
Michel Grenier

D-U-N-S 20-035-5043   (BR)
TORONTO DISTRICT SCHOOL BOARD
YORK MILLS COLLEGIATE INSTITUTE
(*Suby of* TORONTO DISTRICT SCHOOL BOARD)
490 York Mills Rd, North York, ON, M3B 1W6
(416) 395-3340
Emp Here 84
SIC 8211 Elementary and secondary schools
Jennifer Chan

D-U-N-S 20-881-4582   (SL)
TORONTO REAL ESTATE BOARD, THE
TREB
1400 Don Mills Rd Suite 1, North York, ON, M3B 3N1
(416) 443-8100
Emp Here 104   *Sales* 26,227,760
SIC 8611 Business associations
Don Richardson
Dolores Bragagnolo
Stuart Braund
Heather Fuller
John Jerry England
C. Anne Briscoe
William E. Johnston
Richard Silver
Garry Lander
Joseph C.W. Schum

D-U-N-S 24-192-0362   (HQ)
TOUR EAST HOLIDAYS (CANADA) INC
TEH - TFS
15 Kern Rd Suite 9, North York, ON, M3B 1S9
(416) 250-1098
Emp Here 19   *Sales* 20,798,680
SIC 4724 Travel agencies
Annie Tsu
Rita Tsang

D-U-N-S 24-760-4189   (SL)
TRAVEL CORPORATION (CANADA), THE
33 Kern Rd, North York, ON, M3B 1S9
(416) 322-8468
Emp Here 200   *Sales* 133,378,400
SIC 4725 Tour operators
Jeffery Element
Dwayne Moore

D-U-N-S 20-922-3593   (HQ)
TURNER FLEISCHER ARCHITECTS INC
67 Lesmill Rd Suite A, North York, ON, M3B 2T8
(416) 425-2222
Emp Here 63   *Sales* 11,437,270
SIC 8712 Architectural services
Peter Turner
Russell Fleischer

John Chow

D-U-N-S 20-518-0727   (SL)
VINCENT ASSOCIATES INC
38 Lesmill Rd, North York, ON, M3B 2T5
(416) 445-5443
Emp Here 45   *Sales* 10,705,545
SIC 8742 Management consulting services
Jamice Vincent

D-U-N-S 20-316-0270   (SL)
VISHAY PRECISION GROUP CANADA ULC
KELK
(*Suby of* VISHAY PRECISION GROUP, INC.)
48 Lesmill Rd, North York, ON, M3B 2T5
(416) 445-5850
Emp Here 98   *Sales* 22,274,322
SIC 3823 Process control instruments
George Oprea
Willam M. Clancy
Steven Klausner
Kathryn Littler

D-U-N-S 20-361-3385   (SL)
VOLANTE SOFTWARE INC
VOLANTE SYSTEMS
49 Coldwater Rd, North York, ON, M3B 1Y8
(416) 988-6333
Emp Here 90   *Sales* 19,246,590
SIC 7372 Prepackaged software
Joseph Lee
Sunil Selby

D-U-N-S 20-901-3895   (HQ)
WESTDALE CONSTRUCTION CO. LIMITED
WESTDALE PROPERTIES
35 Lesmill Rd, North York, ON, M3B 2T3
(416) 703-1877
Sales 44,174,200
SIC 6513 Apartment building operators
Ronald Kimel

D-U-N-S 24-316-7954   (SL)
WYNFORD GROUP INC, THE
WYNFORD TRAVEL SERVICES
101 Duncan Mill Rd Suite 500, North York, ON, M3B 1Z3
(416) 443-9696
Emp Here 70   *Sales* 52,569,860
SIC 4724 Travel agencies
Bernie Koth
Debra Niven
Jeffrey Bowers
Keith Arthur

D-U-N-S 24-365-8999   (SL)
ZEISS, CARL VISION CANADA INC
(*Suby of* CARL-ZEISS-STIFTUNG)
45 Valleybrook Dr, North York, ON, M3B 2S6
(416) 449-4523
Emp Here 90   *Sales* 20,456,010
SIC 3851 Ophthalmic goods
Klaus Leinmueller
John C Dillon

D-U-N-S 24-387-6190   (SL)
ZUCHTER BERK CREATIVE CATERERS INC
1895 Leslie St, North York, ON, M3B 2M3
(416) 386-1086
Emp Here 100   *Sales* 4,551,900
SIC 5812 Eating places
Walter Vaz
Isaac Drookman

North York, ON M3C

D-U-N-S 25-664-9534   (HQ)
1184038 ONTARIO LIMITED
FOOD BASICS
747 Don Mills Rd Suite 60, North York, ON, M3C 1T2
(416) 239-7171
Sales 13,707,600
SIC 5411 Grocery stores

Larry Roth

D-U-N-S 24-387-4307   (HQ)
1667779 ONTARIO LIMITED
52 Prince Andrew Pl, North York, ON, M3C 2H4
(416) 391-5555
Sales 16,354,845
SIC 6712 Bank holding companies
Mark Butler
Geoff Mainprice

D-U-N-S 20-216-6190   (SL)
1971041 ONTARIO LTD
PARKVIEW BMW
1155 Leslie St, North York, ON, M3C 2J6
(416) 444-4269
Emp Here 76   *Sales* 47,825,280
SIC 5511 New and used car dealers
Reg Quinn
Steve Quinn
Karen Willis
Sal Portelli
Katie Quinn

D-U-N-S 24-849-9944   (SL)
2169319 ONTARIO INC
SUNNY FOODMART
747 Don Mills Rd Unit 60, North York, ON, M3C 1T2
(416) 900-1699
Emp Here 80   *Sales* 23,478,160
SIC 5411 Grocery stores
Bill Chen

D-U-N-S 24-245-1131   (SL)
411 LOCAL SEARCH CORP
411.CA
1200 Eglinton Ave E Suite 200, North York, ON, M3C 1H9
(416) 840-2566
Emp Here 150   *Sales* 32,991,450
SIC 8732 Commercial nonphysical research
Neil Romanchych

D-U-N-S 25-846-9790   (SL)
A. JAFFER PHARMACY LTD
SHOPPERS DRUG MART
946 Lawrence Ave E Suite 1330, North York, ON, M3C 1R1
(416) 444-4445
Emp Here 50   *Sales* 12,647,700
SIC 5912 Drug stores and proprietary stores
Akeelo Jaffer

D-U-N-S 24-816-6824   (SL)
ADEASE MEDIA RESEARCH INC
ADEASE MEDIA INTELLIGENCE
150 Ferrand Dr Suite 800, North York, ON, M3C 3E5
(416) 423-2010
Emp Here 50   *Sales* 10,667,900
SIC 8732 Commercial nonphysical research
Herman Campbell

D-U-N-S 24-889-3802   (SL)
ALLIED DON VALLEY HOTEL INC
DON VALLEY HOTEL
(*Suby of* ALLIED HOLDINGS LTD)
175 Wynford Dr, North York, ON, M3C 1J3
(416) 449-4111
Emp Here 206   *Sales* 19,707,608
SIC 7011 Hotels and motels
Kevin Porter

D-U-N-S 20-850-6121   (SL)
ANGUS CONSULTING MANAGEMENT LIMITED
ACML
(*Suby of* ANGUS, H.H. AND ASSOCIATES LIMITED)
1125 Leslie St, North York, ON, M3C 2J6
(416) 443-8300
Emp Here 140   *Sales* 4,475,520
SIC 7349 Building maintenance services, nec
Gary Gale
Don Campbell
Ainsle Yellery

Glen Collins
Robert Bourassa
Paul Lukkaieren
Paul Scriven
Grant Hayward

D-U-N-S 25-732-2255   (SL)
ANGUS SYSTEMS GROUP LIMITED
(*Suby of* ANGUS, H.H. AND ASSOCIATES LIMITED)
1125 Leslie St, North York, ON, M3C 2J6
(416) 385-8550
Emp Here 98   *Sales* 16,351,006
SIC 7372 Prepackaged software
Chris Gale

D-U-N-S 20-412-2428   (HQ)
ANGUS, H.H. AND ASSOCIATES LIMITED
1127 Leslie St, North York, ON, M3C 2J6
(416) 443-8200
Emp Here 165   *Sales* 32,173,020
SIC 8711 Engineering services
Harry Angus
Gary Gale
Glen Collins
Tom Halpenny
Nick Stark
Barbara Bradley
Andrea Wilson
Paul Keenan
Rod Mons
Roger Simpsons

D-U-N-S 24-388-0254   (SL)
ARMSTRONG PARTNERSHIP LP
23 Prince Andrew Pl, North York, ON, M3C 2H2
(416) 444-3050
Emp Here 75   *Sales* 13,987,950
SIC 8743 Public relations services
Mike Armstrong

D-U-N-S 20-159-5873   (SL)
BANNERMAN, BOB MOTORS LIMITED
BANNERMAN, BOB CHRYSLER DODGE & JEEP
888 Don Mills Rd, North York, ON, M3C 1V6
(416) 444-0888
Emp Here 52   *Sales* 32,722,560
SIC 5511 New and used car dealers
Robert Bannerman
Katie Shea

D-U-N-S 25-274-7084   (HQ)
BELL EXPRESSVU INC
(*Suby of* BCE INC)
100 Wynford Dr Suite 300, North York, ON, M3C 4B4
(416) 383-6600
Emp Here 1,170   *Sales* 508,506,880
SIC 4841 Cable and other pay television services
Wade Oosterman
George A. Cope
Alexander J. Du

D-U-N-S 25-977-8694   (HQ)
BELLWOODS CENTRES FOR COMMUNITY LIVING INC
789 Don Mills Rd Suite 701, North York, ON, M3C 1T5
(416) 696-9663
Emp Here 19   *Sales* 12,856,400
SIC 8361 Residential care
Claire Bryden
David Choat
Monica Codjoe
Harold Keller

D-U-N-S 25-168-9626   (HQ)
BGRS LIMITED
(*Suby of* BROOKFIELD ASSET MANAGEMENT INC)
39 Wynford Dr, North York, ON, M3C 3K5
(416) 510-5600
Emp Here 100   *Sales* 133,781,600
SIC 7389 Business services, nec

Traci Morris
Michael Bonin
Richard Ballot
Kent Williams
Thomas Hogan

D-U-N-S 20-109-6166   (HQ)
BRIDGEMARQ REAL ESTATE SERVICES INC
39 Wynford Dr, North York, ON, M3C 3K5
(416) 510-5800
Sales 31,860,753
SIC 6719 Holding companies, nec
Spencer Enright
Philip Soper
Yvonne Ratigan
Sandra Webb
Penny Egan
Paul Zappala
Lorraine Bell
Simon Dean
Colum Bastable
Joe Freedman

D-U-N-S 25-359-4352   (HQ)
C-LIVING INC
71 Barber Greene Rd, North York, ON, M3C 2A2
(416) 391-5777
Sales 11,230,475
SIC 7389 Business services, nec
Reza Banai

D-U-N-S 20-015-5070   (SL)
CANADA PROTECTION PLAN INC
CANADA PROTECTION PLAN
250 Ferrand Dr Suite 1100, North York, ON, M3C 3G8
(416) 447-6060
Emp Here 100   *Sales* 84,806,000
SIC 6411 Insurance agents, brokers, and service
Henry Auyeung
David Slabodkin

D-U-N-S 24-991-1801   (HQ)
CELESTICA INTERNATIONAL INC
(*Suby of* ONEX CORPORATION)
844 Don Mills Rd, North York, ON, M3C 1V7
(416) 448-5800
Sales 848,745,000
SIC 3679 Electronic components, nec
Craig Muhlhauser

D-U-N-S 25-815-7734   (SL)
CENTENNIAL CENTRE OF SCIENCE AND TECHNOLOGY
ONTARIO SCIENCE CENTRE
770 Don Mills Rd, North York, ON, M3C 1T3
(416) 429-4100
Emp Here 300   *Sales* 40,021,800
SIC 8412 Museums and art galleries
Mark Cohon
Robert J. Macdonald
Robert Miller
Sarah Mitchell
Gail Obrien
Sam L. Zuk
Peter Irwin
John R.G Challis
Anthony Cohen
Mary Anne Crummond

D-U-N-S 20-162-2578   (HQ)
COLGATE-PALMOLIVE CANADA INC
(*Suby of* COLGATE-PALMOLIVE COMPANY)
895 Don Mills Rd, North York, ON, M3C 1W3
(416) 421-6000
Emp Here 80   *Sales* 34,082,520
SIC 2844 Toilet preparations
Scott Geffery

D-U-N-S 25-663-2050   (BR)
CORUS MEDIA HOLDINGS INC
GLOBAL TELEVISION
(*Suby of* SHAW COMMUNICATIONS INC)
81 Barber Greene Rd, North York, ON, M3C

2A2
(416) 446-5311
Emp Here 250
SIC 4833 Television broadcasting stations
Patrick O'hara

D-U-N-S 25-462-4687   (SL)
CPAS SYSTEMS INC
(*Suby of* CONDUENT INCORPORATED)
250 Ferrand Dr 7th Floor, North York, ON, M3C 3G8
(416) 422-0563
Emp Here 85   *Sales* 12,255,470
SIC 7371 Custom computer programming services
David Rive
Liam Robertson
Jeanette Willis
James Higginson-Rollins

D-U-N-S 24-390-4245   (BR)
DELOITTE & TOUCHE MANAGEMENT CONSULTANTS
(*Suby of* DELOITTE & TOUCHE MANAGEMENT CONSULTANTS)
1 Concorde Gate Suite 200, North York, ON, M3C 3N6
(416) 601-6150
Emp Here 100
SIC 8111 Legal services
Diane Wilson

D-U-N-S 24-513-3327   (HQ)
ESRI CANADA LIMITED
12 Concorde Pl Suite 900, North York, ON, M3C 3R8
(416) 441-6035
Emp Here 215   *Sales* 67,719,756
SIC 7372 Prepackaged software
Alex Miller
John Kitchen
James Wickson

D-U-N-S 24-192-2681   (SL)
FOREST HILL LEARNING CENTRE LIMITED
CRESTWOOD SCHOOL
411 Lawrence Ave E, North York, ON, M3C 1N9
(416) 444-5858
Emp Here 77   *Sales* 7,742,196
SIC 8211 Elementary and secondary schools
Dalia Eisen
Harold Perry

D-U-N-S 24-333-8477   (HQ)
FOUR SEASONS HOLDINGS INC
(*Suby of* CASCADE INVESTMENT, L.L.C.)
1165 Leslie St, North York, ON, M3C 2K8
(416) 449-1750
Emp Here 100   *Sales* 3,252,712,000
SIC 7011 Hotels and motels
Isadore Sharp
Christian Clerc
John Davison

D-U-N-S 24-666-7935   (HQ)
FOUR SEASONS HOTELS LIMITED
REGENT HOTEL
(*Suby of* CASCADE INVESTMENT, L.L.C.)
1165 Leslie St, North York, ON, M3C 2K8
(416) 449-1750
Emp Here 125   *Sales* 98,059,700
SIC 7011 Hotels and motels
Isadore Sharp
Allan Smith
Bart Carnahan
Peter Nowlan
John Davison

D-U-N-S 24-207-9015   (HQ)
G4S CASH SOLUTIONS (CANADA) LTD
G4S SECURICOR
(*Suby of* G4S PLC)
150 Ferrand Dr Suite 600, North York, ON, M3C 3E5
(416) 645-5555
Emp Here 50   *Sales* 78,750,000

SIC 7381 Detective and armored car services
Edward Jamieson
Han Koren
Alain Roy

D-U-N-S 25-352-9952   (HQ)
GLASSHOUSE SYSTEMS INC
885 Don Mills Road, North York, ON, M3C 1V9
(416) 229-2950
Emp Here 25   *Sales* 21,464,352
SIC 5045 Computers, peripherals, and software
David Antebi

D-U-N-S 24-885-4796   (HQ)
HOME DEPOT OF CANADA INC
(*Suby of* THE HOME DEPOT INC)
1 Concorde Gate Suite 900, North York, ON, M3C 4H9
(416) 609-0852
Emp Here 110   *Sales* 5,058,900,000
SIC 5251 Hardware stores
Michael Rowe

D-U-N-S 20-556-0415   (HQ)
ICICI BANK CANADA
(*Suby of* ICICI BANK LIMITED)
150 Ferrand Dr Suite 1200, North York, ON, M3C 3E5
(416) 847-7881
Sales 53,656,600
SIC 6021 National commercial banks
Sriram Iyer
Anthony Coulthard
Hemang Thanavala

D-U-N-S 20-786-7136   (HQ)
INDEPENDENT ORDER OF FORESTERS, THE
789 Don Mills Rd Suite 1200, North York, ON, M3C 1T9
(416) 429-3000
Emp Here 700   *Sales* 1,353,082,894
SIC 6311 Life insurance
Michael Stramaglia
Sonia Baxendale
Suanne Nielsen
Paul Reaburn
Robert Lamoureux
Christopher Stranahan
Katherine Bardswick
James Bowden
James Boyle
Michael Edge

D-U-N-S 24-350-0332   (HQ)
INFOR (CANADA), LTD
(*Suby of* INFOR, INC.)
250 Ferrand Dr Suite 1200, North York, ON, M3C 3G8
(416) 421-6700
Emp Here 10   *Sales* 18,853,711
SIC 7372 Prepackaged software
Gregory M Giangiordano

D-U-N-S 24-335-7352   (HQ)
INVENTIV CANADA ULC
SIMBROW, JEFFREY ASSOCIATES
895 Don Mills Rd Suite 700, North York, ON, M3C 1W3
(416) 391-5166
Emp Here 55   *Sales* 21,946,560
SIC 8741 Management services
Jeffrey Simbrow
Karen Auslander

D-U-N-S 20-650-7225   (HQ)
ISKIN INC
3 Concorde Gate Unit 311, North York, ON, M3C 3N7
(416) 924-9607
Emp Here 50   *Sales* 13,785,240
SIC 8731 Commercial physical research
Andrew Ackloo

D-U-N-S 24-533-5091   (SL)
IVEDHA INC
18 Wynford Dr Unit 306, North York, ON, M3C

3S2
(416) 424-6614
Emp Here 95   *Sales* 14,230,715
SIC 7373 Computer integrated systems design
Kumar Ratnam

D-U-N-S 24-784-0432   (SL)
JABLONSKY AST AND PARTNERS
1129 Leslie St, North York, ON, M3C 2K5
(416) 447-7405
Emp Here 95   *Sales* 16,716,010
SIC 8711 Engineering services
Paul Ast

D-U-N-S 25-352-1959   (SL)
JANSSEN INC
ORTHO BIOTECH DIV
(*Suby of* JOHNSON & JOHNSON)
19 Green Belt Dr, North York, ON, M3C 1L9
(416) 449-9444
Emp Here 600   *Sales* 198,956,400
SIC 2834 Pharmaceutical preparations
Kelly Martin
Chris Halyk
Louisa Greco
Jennifer Smith

D-U-N-S 20-077-2080   (SL)
JMC MARKETING COMMUNICATIONS CORPORATION
THE Q GROUP
789 Don Mills Rd, North York, ON, M3C 1T5
(416) 424-6644
Emp Here 50   *Sales* 14,164,650
SIC 8741 Management services
Jane-Michele Clark

D-U-N-S 20-333-9643   (HQ)
KIMCOT INC
29 Gervais Dr Unit 203, North York, ON, M3C 1Y9
(416) 854-2772
Emp Here 29   *Sales* 18,479,800
SIC 4899 Communication services, nec
Shamikh Munir

D-U-N-S 24-663-3754   (SL)
KREMBLO INTERNATIONAL TRADE COMPANY INC
49 The Donway W Suite 1401, North York, ON, M3C 3M9
(416) 445-3474
Emp Here 21   *Sales* 17,547,117
SIC 5149 Groceries and related products, nec
Stephen Tripis
Bill Kreatsoulas

D-U-N-S 25-318-1846   (BR)
MCDONALD'S RESTAURANTS OF CANADA LIMITED
MCDONALD'S
(*Suby of* MCDONALD'S CORPORATION)
747 Don Mills Rd Suite 13, North York, ON, M3C 1T2
(416) 429-1266
Emp Here 80
SIC 5812 Eating places
Dyankonyk Cadcallos

D-U-N-S 20-774-2982   (HQ)
MCDONALD'S RESTAURANTS OF CANADA LIMITED
(*Suby of* MCDONALD'S CORPORATION)
1 Mcdonalds Pl, North York, ON, M3C 3L4
(416) 443-1000
Emp Here 300   *Sales* 644,924,092
SIC 5812 Eating places
John Betts
Jeff Mclean
Michael Flores
Dave Simsons

D-U-N-S 20-968-0867   (HQ)
MILLS, BRYAN IRODESSO CORP
(*Suby of* MDC PARTNERS INC.)
1129 Leslie St, North York, ON, M3C 2K5

(416) 447-4740
Emp Here 25   *Sales* 11,714,400
SIC 8748 Business consulting, nec
Nancy Ladenheim
Michael Bertouche
Allan Austin
Shelley Marchant
Glen Nelson
Chris Oberg
Bruce Wigle
Geoffrey Vanderburg
Brenda Hanchar
Jeffrey Martin

D-U-N-S 24-131-9040   (HQ)
MORNEAU SHEPELL INC
895 Don Mills Rd Suite 700, North York, ON,
M3C 1W3
(416) 445-2700
Emp Here 18   *Sales* 547,564,945
SIC 6722 Management investment, open-end
Stephen Liptrap
Rita Fridella
Jamie True
Neil King
Zahid Salman
Gillian Whitebread
Idan Shlesinger
Nigel Branker
Norah Joyce
Julien Ponce

D-U-N-S 24-805-5290   (HQ)
MORNEAU SHEPELL LTD
(*Suby of* MORNEAU SHEPELL INC)
895 Don Mills Rd, North York, ON, M3C 1W3
(416) 445-2700
Emp Here 800   *Sales* 518,712,100
SIC 8999 Services, nec
Stephen Liptrap
Rita Fridella
Norah Joyce
Randal Phillips
Scott Milligan

D-U-N-S 25-213-6494   (HQ)
MR. GREEK RESTAURANTS INC
49 The Donway W Suite 402, North York, ON,
M3C 3M9
(416) 444-3266
Emp Here 5   *Sales* 22,994,730
SIC 6794 Patent owners and lessors
George Raios
Peter Georgopoulos

D-U-N-S 20-195-3028   (SL)
**MULTILINGUAL COMMUNITY INTER-
PRETER SERVICES (ONTARIO)**
MCIS NON-PROFIT LANGUAGE SERVICES
789 Don Mills Rd Suite 1010, North York, ON,
M3C 1T5
(416) 426-7051
Emp Here 25   *Sales* 11,230,475
SIC 7389 Business services, nec
Latha Sukumar

D-U-N-S 25-312-0554   (HQ)
NEWGEN RESTAURANT SERVICES INC
TUCKER'S MARKETPLACE
895 Don Mills Rd Suite 208, North York, ON,
M3C 1W3
(416) 751-8731
Emp Here 5   *Sales* 18,655,600
SIC 5812 Eating places
Nolan Grubert
Oscar Grubert
Wayne A. Sprague
Christine Siwicki

D-U-N-S 25-098-3798   (SL)
ODYSSEY DISTRIBUTION GROUP INC
60 Prince Andrew Pl, North York, ON, M3C
2H4
(647) 288-2222
Emp Here 30   *Sales* 12,580,650
SIC 6712 Bank holding companies
David Cheong

D-U-N-S 25-496-6229   (SL)
ODYSSEY TIME INC
60 Prince Andrew Pl, North York, ON, M3C
2H4
(647) 288-2222
Emp Here 40   *Sales* 20,821,680
SIC 5094 Jewelry and precious stones
David Cheong

D-U-N-S 25-931-4966   (SL)
PANERA BREAD ULC
1066 Don Mills Rd, North York, ON, M3C 0H8
(416) 384-1116
Emp Here 42   *Sales* 11,514,384
SIC 5461 Retail bakeries
Ryan Pimenta

D-U-N-S 20-044-1723   (HQ)
PEARSON CANADA HOLDINGS INC
PEARSON EDUCATION CANADA
(*Suby of* PEARSON PLC)
26 Prince Andrew Pl, North York, ON, M3C
2H4
(416) 447-5101
Emp Here 260
SIC 2731 Book publishing

D-U-N-S 24-919-0125   (HQ)
PEARSON CANADA INC
PEARSON EDUCATION CANADA
(*Suby of* PEARSON PLC)
26 Prince Andrew Pl, North York, ON, M3C
2H4
(416) 447-5101
Sales 96,887,000
SIC 2731 Book publishing
James Reeve

D-U-N-S 24-046-6789   (HQ)
**PRESBYTERIAN CHURCH IN CANADA,
THE**
50 Wynford Dr, North York, ON, M3C 1J7
(416) 441-1111
Sales 17,133,625
SIC 8661 Religious organizations
Richard Fee
Stephen Roche
Stephen Kendall

D-U-N-S 25-704-3562   (BR)
REVERA INC
DONWAY PLACE
(*Suby of* GOVERNMENT OF CANADA)
8 The Donway E Suite 557, North York, ON,
M3C 3R7
(416) 445-7555
Emp Here 120
SIC 8051 Skilled nursing care facilities
Lynn Jennings

D-U-N-S 20-847-3483   (SL)
RIGHT AT HOME REALTY, INC
895 Don Mills Rd Suite 202, North York, ON,
M3C 1W3
(416) 391-3232
Emp Here 1,200   *Sales* 800,270,400
SIC 4731 Freight transportation arrangement
Don Kottick
Howard Drukarsh
Michel Friedman
Eva Liu

D-U-N-S 20-784-0711   (SL)
ROCKPORT HOMES LIMITED
170 The Donway W Suite 307, North York,
ON, M3C 2G3
(416) 444-7391
Emp Here 60   *Sales* 16,256,520
SIC 1522 Residential construction, nec
Burton Winberg
Jack Winberg

D-U-N-S 20-290-3089   (SL)
ROOTS OF EMPATHY
250 Ferrand Dr Suite 1501, North York, ON,
M3C 3G8
(416) 944-3001
Emp Here 25   *Sales* 17,730,300

SIC 8699 Membership organizations, nec
Mary Gordon
Justice Ormston
Lynn Patterson
Tim Sale
Joan Green
Jean-Pierre Boisclair
Christine Hart
Clyde Hertzman
Rod Macgillivary
Patrica Mackenzie

D-U-N-S 24-652-6974   (HQ)
ROYAL LEPAGE LIMITED
(*Suby of* BROOKFIELD ASSET MANAGE-
MENT INC)
39 Wynford Dr, North York, ON, M3C 3K5
(416) 510-5800
Emp Here 2   *Sales* 61,459,200
SIC 6531 Real estate agents and managers
Phillip Soper
Andy Puthon
Gino Romanese
Gurinder Sandhu
Sandra Webb

D-U-N-S 20-846-0584   (SL)
ROYAL LEPAGE SIGNATURE REALTY
49 The Donway W, North York, ON, M3C 3M9
(416) 443-0300
Emp Here 214   *Sales* 72,345,696
SIC 6531 Real estate agents and managers
G E(Ted) Slightham
Chris Slightham

D-U-N-S 24-826-6264   (HQ)
**RR DONELLEY CANADA FINANCIAL COM-
PANY**
BOWNE ENTERPRISE SOLUTIONS, DIV OF
(*Suby of* R. R. DONNELLEY & SONS COM-
PANY)
60 Gervais Dr, North York, ON, M3C 1Z3
(416) 445-8800
Emp Here 300
SIC 2752 Commercial printing, lithographic
Robert Kadis
Robert Hayes
Barry Scruton
Loren Patterson
Bill Penders

D-U-N-S 24-688-0710   (SL)
**SONY MUSIC ENTERTAINMENT CANADA
INC**
RCA RECORDS
(*Suby of* SONY CORPORATION)
150 Ferrand Dr Suite 300, North York, ON,
M3C 3E5
(416) 589-3000
Emp Here 130   *Sales* 90,389,000
SIC 5099 Durable goods, nec
Shane Carter
Stephen Simon
Larry Mcrae
Neil Foster

D-U-N-S 20-733-2110   (BR)
SYMCOR INC
(*Suby of* SYMCOR INC)
8 Prince Andrew Pl, North York, ON, M3C 2H4
(905) 273-1000
Emp Here 800
SIC 8741 Management services
Paul Scherbak

D-U-N-S 25-510-7658   (SL)
THORNBURY FINANCIAL LTD
23 Prince Andrew Pl, North York, ON, M3C
2H2
(416) 444-3050
Emp Here 60   *Sales* 14,057,280
SIC 8743 Public relations services
John Armstrong
Michael Armstrong

D-U-N-S 24-415-0173   (HQ)
TILLEY ENDURABLES, INC

(*Suby of* ALEX TILLEY ENTERPRISES, INC)
60 Gervais Dr, North York, ON, M3C 1Z3
(416) 441-6141
Emp Here 160   *Sales* 35,056,155
SIC 5699 Miscellaneous apparel and acces-
sory stores
Mary-Coleen Shanahan
Alex Tilley
David Kappele
Barbara Rodriguez
Thurstan Berkeley

D-U-N-S 25-509-3718   (BR)
TORONTO DISTRICT SCHOOL BOARD
OVERLAND LEARNING CENTRE
(*Suby of* TORONTO DISTRICT SCHOOL
BOARD)
55 Overland Dr, North York, ON, M3C 2C3
(416) 395-5080
Emp Here 100
SIC 8211 Elementary and secondary schools
Lisa Kattelus

D-U-N-S 20-047-1535   (BR)
TORONTO DISTRICT SCHOOL BOARD
VALLEY PARK MIDDLE SCHOOL
(*Suby of* TORONTO DISTRICT SCHOOL
BOARD)
130 Overlea Blvd, North York, ON, M3C 1B2
(416) 396-2465
Emp Here 95
SIC 8211 Elementary and secondary schools
Nick Stefanoff

D-U-N-S 25-237-8039   (BR)
TORONTO DISTRICT SCHOOL BOARD
GRENOBLE PUBLIC SCHOOL
(*Suby of* TORONTO DISTRICT SCHOOL
BOARD)
9 Grenoble Dr, North York, ON, M3C 1C3
(416) 397-2900
Emp Here 80
SIC 8211 Elementary and secondary schools
Melissa Carson

D-U-N-S 25-509-1001   (HQ)
**TRILLIUM ARCHITECTURAL PRODUCTS
LTD**
(*Suby of* 1667779 ONTARIO LIMITED)
52 Prince Andrew Pl, North York, ON, M3C
2H4
(416) 391-5555
Sales 17,439,786
SIC 5072 Hardware
Mark Butler
Geoff Mainprice

D-U-N-S 24-830-4362   (SL)
**TROJAN CONSOLIDATED INVESTMENTS
LIMITED**
DIAMOND & DIAMOND CERTIFIED MG
18 Wynford Dr Suite 516, North York, ON,
M3C 3S2

Emp Here 160   *Sales* 29,840,960
SIC 8742 Management consulting services
Stephen Robinson
Robert Kleinfeldt
Arthur Paul
Aaron Stein
A Mendelson
Helmut Stern
Arthur Paulson

North York, ON M3H

D-U-N-S 20-310-1134   (HQ)
2360083 ONTARIO LIMITED
COPPA'S FRESH MARKET
4750 Dufferin St, North York, ON, M3H 5S7
(416) 736-6606
Sales 77,880,600
SIC 5411 Grocery stores
Louis Coppa

D-U-N-S 24-411-4138   (SL)
CATERERS (YORK) LIMITED
SWEET YORK DESSERTS
37 Southbourne Ave, North York, ON, M3H
1A4

Emp Here 100   *Sales* 4,287,300
SIC 5812 Eating places
Euclides Batista
Sharon Firestone

D-U-N-S 20-120-6740   (SL)
COMWAVE TELECOM INC
COMWAVE
4884 Dufferin St Unit 1, North York, ON, M3H
5S8
(416) 663-9700
Emp Here 60   *Sales* 12,801,480
SIC 8732 Commercial nonphysical research
Yuval Barzakay

D-U-N-S 20-967-3867   (SL)
CONDOR SECURITY
4610 Dufferin St Unit 1b, North York, ON, M3H
5S4
(416) 410-4035
Emp Here 70   *Sales* 27,697,460
SIC 7381 Detective and armored car services
Shella Zagada

D-U-N-S 20-180-1110   (SL)
CORPORATE TRAVEL MANAGEMENT SO-LUTIONS INC
CTMS
5000 Dufferin St Suite 219b, North York, ON,
M3H 5T5
(416) 665-2867
Emp Here 30   *Sales* 15,599,010
SIC 4724 Travel agencies
Tomer (Tom) Osovitzki
Yair Osovitzki

D-U-N-S 25-512-3531   (HQ)
DEL MANAGEMENT SOLUTIONS INC
DMS GROUP
4810 Dufferin St Suite E, North York, ON, M3H
5S8
(416) 661-3070
Emp Here 45   *Sales* 22,087,100
SIC 6512 Nonresidential building operators
Robert Watt
Paul Smith
Elvio Delzotto

D-U-N-S 20-879-1699   (HQ)
DEL PROPERTY MANAGEMENT INC
109-4800 Dufferin St, North York, ON, M3H
5S9
(416) 661-3151
Emp Here 120   *Sales* 58,644,460
SIC 6531 Real estate agents and managers
Andre Pilish

D-U-N-S 25-858-5736   (HQ)
DMS PROPERTY MANAGEMENT LTD
ASHPRIOR CHARITABLE FOUNDATION
4810 Dufferin St Suite E, North York, ON, M3H
5S8
(416) 661-3070
Emp Here 3   *Sales* 33,919,250
SIC 6513 Apartment building operators
Elvio Delzotto
Rob Watt
Paul Smith

D-U-N-S 20-152-5909   (SL)
DOT BENEFITS CORP
NSP CANADA
555 Wilson Ave, North York, ON, M3H 0C5
(416) 636-4411
Emp Here 20   *Sales* 14,508,780
SIC 6311 Life insurance
Marty Shaw

D-U-N-S 24-353-5759   (SL)
GREAT CONNECTIONS EMPLOYMENT SERVICES INC
5050 Dufferin St Unit 109, North York, ON,

M3H 5T5
(416) 850-5060
Emp Here 50   *Sales* 11,848,500
SIC 7361 Employment agencies
Shaun Levy
Yi He

D-U-N-S 24-394-2302   (SL)
LEVY, JEFF INVESTMENTS LTD
CANADIAN TIRE
4400 Dufferin St Suite 1, North York, ON, M3H
6A8
(416) 667-9777
Emp Here 23   *Sales* 11,455,794
SIC 5531 Auto and home supply stores
Jeff Levy

D-U-N-S 24-366-0156   (HQ)
MANAGEMENT SYSTEMS RESOURCES INC
(*Suby of* DESCARTES SYSTEMS GROUP
INC, THE)
2 Tippett Rd, North York, ON, M3H 2V2
(416) 630-3000
Sales 12,513,525
SIC 7372 Prepackaged software
Raj Manucha
Maria Shepherd
Ann Smokorowski

D-U-N-S 25-509-1159   (SL)
MARY CENTER OF THE ARCHDIOCESE OF TORONTO
MARY CENTER
530 Wilson Ave Suite 210, North York, ON,
M3H 5Y9
(416) 630-5533
Emp Here 80   *Sales* 10,676,720
SIC 8399 Social services, nec
Dominic Conforti

D-U-N-S 25-300-3198   (BR)
METRO ONTARIO INC
METRO
(*Suby of* METRO INC)
600 Sheppard Ave W, North York, ON, M3H
2S1
(416) 636-5136
Emp Here 130
SIC 5411 Grocery stores
Gord Henry

D-U-N-S 24-326-5332   (SL)
MICHAEL S WONG PHARMACY LTD
SHOPPERS DRUG MART
1881 Steeles Ave W Suite 819, North York,
ON, M3H 5Y4
(416) 665-2631
Emp Here 47   *Sales* 11,888,838
SIC 5912 Drug stores and proprietary stores
Michael S Wong

D-U-N-S 20-817-2932   (SL)
NISE N KOSY INCORPORATED
INCREDIBLE CLOTHING COMPANY, THE
120 Overbrook Pl Suite 100, North York, ON,
M3H 4P8
(416) 665-8802
Emp Here 130   *Sales* 17,767,620
SIC 2321 Men's and boy's furnishings
Abe Glowinsky
Mara Dimatteo
Lloyd Stewart
Anh Lam

D-U-N-S 25-221-4937   (SL)
NORTOWN ELECTRICAL CONTRACTORS ASSOCIATES
3845 Bathurst St Suite 102, North York, ON,
M3H 3N2
(416) 638-6700
Emp Here 180   *Sales* 39,209,220
SIC 1731 Electrical work
Harry Marder
Shirley Marder

D-U-N-S 20-171-9622   (SL)
NORTOWN ELECTRICAL CONTRACTORS

LIMITED
3845 Bathurst St Unit 102, North York, ON,
M3H 3N2
(416) 638-6700
Emp Here 185   *Sales* 40,298,365
SIC 1731 Electrical work
Harry Marder
Shirley Marder

D-U-N-S 24-845-1569   (SL)
PROBE INVESTIGATION AND SECURITY SERVICES LTD
PROBE SECURITY
3995 Bathurst St Suite 301, North York, ON,
M3H 5V3
(416) 636-7000
Emp Here 75   *Sales* 29,675,850
SIC 7381 Detective and armored car services
Michael Alter

D-U-N-S 24-206-7549   (SL)
QUALICARE INC
3910 Bathurst St Suite 304, North York, ON,
M3H 5Z3
(416) 630-0202
Emp Here 85   *Sales* 5,487,600
SIC 8059 Nursing and personal care, nec
Brian Church

D-U-N-S 25-418-4435   (SL)
REKAM IMPORT EXPORT INTERNA-TIONAL INC
REKAM
222 Faywood Blvd, North York, ON, M3H 6A9
(416) 630-2892
Emp Here 55   *Sales* 24,594,570
SIC 5043 Photographic equipment and sup-plies
Elena Kaikov

D-U-N-S 20-016-3470   (SL)
RESIDENCES AT ICON INC, THE
4800 Dufferin St, North York, ON, M3H 5S9
(416) 661-9290
Emp Here 200   *Sales* 54,351,200
SIC 6531 Real estate agents and managers
Roman Bukata
Liana Silano

D-U-N-S 25-749-2264   (SL)
SUTTON GROUP ADMIRAL REALTY INC
1881 Steeles Ave W Suite 12, North York, ON,
M3H 5Y4
(416) 739-7200
Emp Here 300   *Sales* 101,419,200
SIC 6531 Real estate agents and managers
Murray Goldkind

D-U-N-S 24-193-1351   (HQ)
TRIDEL CORPORATION
4800 Dufferin St Suite 200, North York, ON,
M3H 5S9
(416) 661-9290
Sales 31,634,400
SIC 6553 Cemetery subdividers and develop-ers
Angelo Del Zotto
Leo Del Zotto
Elvio Del Zotto

D-U-N-S 25-263-3581   (BR)
TYCO INTEGRATED FIRE & SECURITY CANADA, INC
SIMPLEXGRINNELL
(*Suby of* JOHNSON CONTROLS INTERNA-TIONAL PUBLIC LIMITED COMPANY)
5000 Dufferin St, North York, ON, M3H 5T5

Emp Here 100
SIC 7381 Detective and armored car services

D-U-N-S 20-980-7551   (BR)
UNIVERSITY OF TORONTO PRESS
UTP NORTH YORK, DIV OF
(*Suby of* UNIVERSITY OF TORONTO
PRESS)
5201 Dufferin St, North York, ON, M3H 5T8

(416) 667-7791
Emp Here 150
SIC 2731 Book publishing
Kim Stanley

D-U-N-S 20-693-7281   (BR)
UNIVERSITY OF TORONTO PRESS
UTP DISTRIBUTION, DIV OF
(*Suby of* UNIVERSITY OF TORONTO
PRESS)
5201 Dufferin St, North York, ON, M3H 5T8
(416) 667-7791
Emp Here 150
SIC 2731 Book publishing

D-U-N-S 24-171-8134   (HQ)
YUMMY MARKET INC
4400 Dufferin St Unit B-4, North York, ON,
M3H 6A8
(416) 665-0040
Emp Here 150   *Sales* 73,136,320
SIC 5411 Grocery stores
Alexei Tsvetkov
Anna Tsvetkov
Mila Sak

North York, ON M3J

D-U-N-S 25-790-4854   (SL)
1032396 ONTARIO LTD
KJV COURIER SERVICES
3858 Chesswood Dr, North York, ON, M3J
2W6
(416) 398-5155
Emp Here 25   *Sales* 11,087,250
SIC 7389 Business services, nec
Lisa Pileggi

D-U-N-S 24-885-4838   (HQ)
1079746 ONTARIO LIMITED
CRAZY JOE'S DRAPERY STORE
1021 Finch Ave W, North York, ON, M3J 2C7
(416) 650-9996
Emp Here 4   *Sales* 10,006,500
SIC 5131 Piece goods and notions
Chane Czkovits

D-U-N-S 24-596-9993   (HQ)
1669051 NOVA SCOTIA LIMITED
PROVEER
680 Steeprock Dr, North York, ON, M3J 2X1
(416) 635-6500
Emp Here 8   *Sales* 20,426,118
SIC 5085 Industrial supplies
Anthony Hobza
John Douglas Laine

D-U-N-S 24-610-0916   (SL)
1791884 ONTARIO LIMITED
VITO'S NO FRILLS
3685 Keele St Suite 5, North York, ON, M3J
3H6
(866) 987-6453
Emp Here 63   *Sales* 18,489,051
SIC 5411 Grocery stores
Vito Galati

D-U-N-S 24-310-6411   (HQ)
2124688 ONTARIO LIMITED
BROWN'S FUEL
3975 Keele St, North York, ON, M3J 1P1
(416) 665-7594
Emp Here 20   *Sales* 31,430,025
SIC 5172 Petroleum products, nec
Glen Brown

D-U-N-S 24-374-9202   (HQ)
2168587 ONTARIO LTD
UPPER CRUST
55 Canarctic Dr Suite Upper, North York, ON,
M3J 2N7
(416) 661-9455
Sales 34,569,000
SIC 2053 Frozen bakery products, except
bread

David Gelbloom

D-U-N-S 20-369-9140 (SL)
2469447 ONTARIO LIMITED
BUDA JUICE CANADA
14 Ashwarren Rd, North York, ON, M3J 1Z5
(416) 636-7772
Emp Here 50   *Sales* 11,242,750
SIC 2033 Canned fruits and specialties
Sivag Ganesh

D-U-N-S 25-457-8362 (HQ)
806040 ONTARIO LTD
JADACO RECREATION MANAGEMENT
4496 Chesswood Dr, North York, ON, M3J 2B9
(416) 665-6400
Sales 21,946,560
SIC 8741 Management services
Joey Arfin

D-U-N-S 24-057-5584 (SL)
ACCIDENT INJURY MEDICAL ASSESSMENT
1280 Finch Ave W Suite 507, North York, ON, M3J 3K6
(416) 665-4010
Emp Here 20   *Sales* 14,508,780
SIC 6321 Accident and health insurance
Carlo Colacci

D-U-N-S 20-530-7648 (SL)
ALROS PRODUCTS LIMITED
POLYTARP PRODUCTS
350 Wildcat Rd, North York, ON, M3J 2N5
(416) 661-1750
Emp Here 150   *Sales* 23,828,700
SIC 3081 Unsupported plastics film and sheet
Steve Ghantous
Roslyn Lewis
Vinay Kamboj
Janet Spencer

D-U-N-S 20-182-1469 (SL)
ALUMINUM MOLD & PATTERN LTD
15 Vanley Cres, North York, ON, M3J 2B7
(416) 749-3000
Emp Here 75   *Sales* 16,650,075
SIC 3544 Special dies, tools, jigs, and fixtures
Brian Beamish
Susan Beamish

D-U-N-S 20-739-6524 (SL)
AMSCAN DISTRIBUTORS (CANADA) LTD
AMSCAN CANADA
(*Suby of* PARTY CITY HOLDCO INC.)
1225 Finch Ave W, North York, ON, M3J 2E8
(800) 363-6662
Emp Here 20   *Sales* 14,850,400
SIC 5199 Nondurable goods, nec
Gerald Rittenberg
Gabi Tabet
James Harrison

D-U-N-S 25-249-6914 (SL)
ASKAN ARTS LIMITED
PICTURE DEPOT
20 Toro Rd, North York, ON, M3J 2A7
(416) 398-2333
Emp Here 110   *Sales* 21,156,080
SIC 7699 Repair services, nec
Sam Alavy

Askan Alavy

D-U-N-S 20-400-1135 (SL)
AZIZ, J. & A. LIMITED
DOPHES
1635 Flint Rd, North York, ON, M3J 2J6
(416) 787-0365
Emp Here 21   *Sales* 10,464,762
SIC 5131 Piece goods and notions
Joseph Aziz Sr
Joseph D Aziz Jr
Donna Terminesi

D-U-N-S 24-143-7784 (SL)
B K A OFFICE INC
675 Petrolia Rd, North York, ON, M3J 2N6
(416) 665-2466
Emp Here 70   *Sales* 31,302,180
SIC 5065 Electronic parts and equipment, nec
Surendra Patel

D-U-N-S 20-459-5318 (SL)
BEAUTYNEXT GROUP INC
ALUMIER MD
436 Limestone Cres, North York, ON, M3J 2S4
(416) 665-6616
Emp Here 30   *Sales* 33,160,350
SIC 5122 Drugs, proprietaries, and sundries
Daniel Eskin

D-U-N-S 20-249-1098 (SL)
BEST MADE TOYS INTERNATIONAL INC
120 Saint Regis Cres N, North York, ON, M3J 1Z3
(416) 630-6665
Emp Here 50   *Sales* 24,388,384
SIC 5092 Toys and hobby goods and supplies
Sandra Courtman
Heidi Czutrin
Leah Goldband

D-U-N-S 20-260-2975 (SL)
BEST MADE TOYS INTERNATIONAL, ULC
120 Saint Regis Cres N, North York, ON, M3J 1Z3
(416) 630-6665
Emp Here 15   *Sales* 68,162,499
SIC 3942 Dolls and stuffed toys
Carter Pennington
Scott Johnson
Shelly Gobin

D-U-N-S 25-351-6009 (SL)
BETA-CALCO INC
25 Kodiak Cres, North York, ON, M3J 3E5
(416) 531-9942
Emp Here 60   *Sales* 11,426,520
SIC 3645 Residential lighting fixtures
Remy Silver

D-U-N-S 20-002-0861 (SL)
BLUERIVER TRADING LTD
369 Rimrock Road, North York, ON, M3J 3G2
(416) 638-8543
Emp Here 25   *Sales* 20,889,425
SIC 5149 Groceries and related products, nec

D-U-N-S 20-628-2857 (SL)
BRITISH FASTENING SYSTEMS LIMITED
UCAN FASTENING PRODUCTS
155 Champagne Dr Unit 10, North York, ON, M3J 2C6
(416) 631-9400
Emp Here 25   *Sales* 11,875,650
SIC 5085 Industrial supplies
Jeremy Weitz
Harry Weitz

D-U-N-S 20-174-8316 (HQ)
C.G. MAINTENANCE & SANITARY PRODUCTS INC
CG MAINTENANCE
40 Saint Regis Cres, North York, ON, M3J 1Y5

Emp Here 30   *Sales* 19,001,040
SIC 5087 Service establishment equipment
Wilfred Shiff

Richard Senechal

D-U-N-S 20-955-0941 (SL)
CANADA CLEAN FUELS INC
4425 Chesswood Dr, North York, ON, M3J 2C2
(416) 521-9533
Emp Here 10   *Sales* 103,346,185
SIC 4212 Local trucking, without storage
Lucio Angelucci
Arthur Miller
Brian Macdonald

D-U-N-S 24-173-5021 (BR)
CANADA FIBERS LTD
CMC PAPER CONVERERS
(*Suby of* CANADA FIBERS LTD)
35 Vanley Cres Suite 500, North York, ON, M3J 2B7

Emp Here 100
SIC 4953 Refuse systems
Mario Quintieri

D-U-N-S 25-240-8570 (HQ)
CANADA-ISRAEL SECURITIES LIMITED
ISRAEL BONDS
801-1120 Finch Ave W, North York, ON, M3J 3H7
(416) 789-3351
Emp Here 20   *Sales* 16,998,624
SIC 6211 Security brokers and dealers
Israel Maimon
Eric Slavens
Robert Issenman
Michael Florence
George Grossman
George Cohon
Leonard Shapiro

D-U-N-S 25-474-0194 (HQ)
CANADIAN ASSOCIATES OF THE BEN-GURION UNIVERSITY OF NEGEV INC, THE
1000 Finch Ave W Suite 506, North York, ON, M3J 2V5
(416) 665-8054
Emp Here 7   *Sales* 11,341,650
SIC 8399 Social services, nec
Gary Fine
Leon H. Marcus

D-U-N-S 24-390-1949 (SL)
CANADIAN DRAPERY HARDWARE LTD
150 Steeprock Dr, North York, ON, M3J 2T4
(416) 630-6900
Emp Here 35   *Sales* 17,809,960
SIC 5023 Homefurnishings
Michael Ferdman
Morris Ferdman
Susan Ferdman
Jack Ferdman

D-U-N-S 24-856-2352 (SL)
CANCOM SECURITY INC
1183 Finch Ave W Unit 205, North York, ON, M3J 2G2
(416) 763-0000
Emp Here 230   *Sales* 6,037,500
SIC 7381 Detective and armored car services
Ronald Wells
Keith Wells

D-U-N-S 20-161-6703 (HQ)
CAULFEILD APPAREL GROUP LTD
1400 Whitehorse Rd, North York, ON, M3J 3A7
(416) 636-5900
Emp Here 61   *Sales* 54,439,645
SIC 5136 Men's and boy's clothing
Michael Purkis
Craig Wilson
Kelly Pettit
Mario Tomei
Terri Mcmenamin
James Purkis
David I Matheson

D-U-N-S 24-925-2198 (SL)

CENTRE FOR RESEARCH IN EARTH AND SPACE TECHNOLOGY
4850 Keele St, North York, ON, M3J 3K1
(416) 736-5247
Emp Here 67   *Sales* 33,951,312
SIC 8733 Noncommercial research organizations
Ian H Rowe

D-U-N-S 20-290-2578 (SL)
CHEDER CHABAD
900 Alness St Unit 203, North York, ON, M3J 2H6
(416) 663-1972
Emp Here 50   *Sales* 19,870,700
SIC 8699 Membership organizations, nec
Yona Shur

D-U-N-S 24-346-3218 (BR)
CHILDREN'S AID SOCIETY OF TORONTO
(*Suby of* CHILDREN'S AID SOCIETY OF TORONTO)
20 De Boers Dr Suite 250, North York, ON, M3J 0H1
(416) 924-4646
Emp Here 150
SIC 8322 Individual and family services
Corrie Tuyl

D-U-N-S 20-059-4856 (SL)
CITIWELL INTERNATIONAL INC
401 Magnetic Dr Unit 9, North York, ON, M3J 3H9

Emp Here 162   *Sales* 112,638,600
SIC 5092 Toys and hobby goods and supplies
Brenda Ehrentreu
David Rosenberg

D-U-N-S 24-220-1101 (SL)
COLUMBIA BUILDING MAINTENANCE CO LTD
65 Martin Ross Ave Unit 1, North York, ON, M3J 2L6
(416) 663-5020
Emp Here 100   *Sales* 4,020,900
SIC 7349 Building maintenance services, nec
Todd White
Rosemary White
John Fernandes

D-U-N-S 25-239-8888 (BR)
COMMUNITY LIVING TORONTO
NORTH YORK EARLY CHILDHOOD
(*Suby of* COMMUNITY LIVING TORONTO)
1122 Finch Ave W Unit 18, North York, ON, M3J 3J5
(416) 225-7166
Emp Here 100
SIC 8322 Individual and family services
Teresa Strezek

D-U-N-S 24-122-8774 (SL)
COMPUTER METHODS INTERNATIONAL CORP
(*Suby of* COMPUTER FACILITY SERVICES INC)
4850 Keele St, North York, ON, M3J 3K1
(416) 736-0123
Emp Here 90   *Sales* 12,976,380
SIC 7371 Custom computer programming services
Allen Berg
Gordon Rawlins

D-U-N-S 20-293-2182 (SL)
COMWAVE NETWORKS INC
61 Wildcat Rd, North York, ON, M3J 2P5
(866) 288-5779
Emp Here 127   *Sales* 29,015,944
SIC 4899 Communication services, nec
Yuval Barzakay

D-U-N-S 20-290-8021 (HQ)
COVER FX SKIN CARE INC
1681 Flint Rd, North York, ON, M3J 2W8
(866) 424-3332
Sales 55,267,250

SIC 5122 Drugs, proprietaries, and sundries
Lee Graff

D-U-N-S 24-560-2230   (HQ)
CREATIVE BAG CO. LTD, THE
1100 Lodestar Rd Unit 1, North York, ON, M3J 2Z4
(416) 631-6444
Emp Here 15   Sales 10,073,160
SIC 5113 Industrial and personal service paper
Bernie Shapiro

D-U-N-S 24-389-0605   (HQ)
CRIMP CIRCUITS INC
675 Petrolia Rd, North York, ON, M3J 2N6
(416) 665-2466
Emp Here 73   Sales 14,283,150
SIC 3672 Printed circuit boards
Sam Patel

D-U-N-S 20-260-2686   (SL)
CUI-CANADA, INC
(Suby of CUI GLOBAL, INC.)
39 Kodiak Cres, North York, ON, M3J 3E5
(416) 630-8108
Emp Here 130   Sales 31,762,640
SIC 5999 Miscellaneous retail stores, nec
William Clough
Matthew Mckenzie
Daniel Ford

D-U-N-S 20-549-7357   (HQ)
D'AVERSA, NINO BAKERY LIMITED
1 Toro Rd, North York, ON, M3J 2A4
(416) 638-3271
Emp Here 60   Sales 24,945,545
SIC 5461 Retail bakeries
Pasquale D'aversa
Armando D'aversa
Mauro D'aversa

D-U-N-S 24-358-8878   (SL)
DAVID SHAW SILVERWARE NORTH AMERICA LTD
DAVID SHAW TABLEWARE
85 Martin Ross Ave, North York, ON, M3J 2L5
(416) 736-0492
Emp Here 32   Sales 16,657,344
SIC 5094 Jewelry and precious stones
Gerald Greenwood
Robert Dohany

D-U-N-S 20-502-4656   (HQ)
DIAMOND YARNS OF CANADA LTD
155 Martin Ross Ave Suite 3, North York, ON, M3J 2L9
(416) 736-6111
Emp Here 21   Sales 18,563,000
SIC 5199 Nondurable goods, nec
Peter Mulley
Ted Samulak

D-U-N-S 24-919-7252   (HQ)
DIGITCOM   TELECOMMUNICATIONS CANADA INC
DIGITCOM CANADA
250 Rimrock Rd, North York, ON, M3J 3A6
(416) 783-7890
Emp Here 40   Sales 13,349,600
SIC 5999 Miscellaneous retail stores, nec
Jeffrey Wiener
Lynn Conlon

D-U-N-S 24-005-7778   (HQ)
DIRECTIONS EAST TRADING LIMITED
VIVAH FASHION ACCESSORIES & JEWELRY
995 Finch Ave W, North York, ON, M3J 2C7
(416) 661-7188
Emp Here 10   Sales 22,424,500
SIC 5632 Women's accessory and specialty stores
Zellick David Goodbaum

D-U-N-S 20-610-7047   (SL)
DOWNSVIEW   CHRYSLER   PLYMOUTH (1964) LTD

(Suby of WALSH, N.L. HOLDINGS LIMITED)
199 Rimrock Rd, North York, ON, M3J 3C6
(416) 635-1660
Emp Here 105   Sales 50,382,000
SIC 5511 New and used car dealers
Peter Kepecs
Cameron Meehan
Wesley Scott
Neil Walsh

D-U-N-S 20-627-4565   (SL)
DOWNSVIEW LONG TERM CARE CENTRE
3595 Keele St, North York, ON, M3J 1M7
(416) 633-3431
Emp Here 350   Sales 23,914,100
SIC 8051 Skilled nursing care facilities
Christiane Burns

D-U-N-S 24-213-1746   (HQ)
DUROX FLOOR ACCESSORIES LIMITED
255 Steeprock Dr, North York, ON, M3J 2Z5
(416) 630-4883
Emp Here 25   Sales 19,001,040
SIC 5087 Service establishment equipment
Leo Van Vugt

D-U-N-S 25-915-6149   (SL)
DYN EXPORTERS CANADA INC
DYN
387 Limestone Cres, North York, ON, M3J 2R1
(905) 761-9559
Emp Here 200   Sales 48,865,600
SIC 5932 Used merchandise stores
Marc Nanthakumar

D-U-N-S 20-430-0075   (SL)
ENERSHARE TECHNOLOGY CORP
87 Bakersfield St, North York, ON, M3J 1Z4

Emp Here 5   Sales 15,529,285
SIC 4923 Gas transmission and distribution

D-U-N-S 25-726-6387   (SL)
EUROFINS BIOPHARMA PRODUCT TESTING TORONTO, INC
1111 Flint Rd Unit 36, North York, ON, M3J 3C7
(416) 665-2134
Emp Here 100   Sales 22,032,800
SIC 8734 Testing laboratories
Barbara Kovensky
David Gordon
Sohil Mana

D-U-N-S 20-350-7124   (HQ)
EUROFINS   ENVIRONMENT   TESTING CANADA, INC
1111 Flint Rd Unit 36, North York, ON, M3J 3C7
(416) 665-2134
Emp Here 10   Sales 54,351,890
SIC 8734 Testing laboratories
Sylvain Allard
Sohil Mana
Rosalyn Coward

D-U-N-S 24-644-4772   (SL)
FURNCO   FURNITURE   INTERNATIONAL DISTRIBUTORS LTD
DECORIUM
363 Supertest Rd, North York, ON, M3J 2M4
(416) 736-6120
Emp Here 67   Sales 15,571,001
SIC 5712 Furniture stores
Joe Forberg
Gail Forberg
Kathryn Forberg

D-U-N-S 25-147-8046   (HQ)
GLOBAL CONTRACT INC
GLOBAL SEATING, DIV OF
565 Petrolia Rd, North York, ON, M3J 2X8
(416) 739-5000
Emp Here 190   Sales 30,864,400
SIC 2522 Office furniture, except wood
Deanne Masson

D-U-N-S 24-985-1528   (HQ)
GLOBAL UPHOLSTERY CO LIMITED
560 Supertest Rd, North York, ON, M3J 2M6
(416) 661-3660
Sales 438,610,800
SIC 6719 Holding companies, nec
Saul Feldberg
David Feldberg
Ron Flam

D-U-N-S 20-045-1789   (HQ)
GLOBAL UPHOLSTERY CO. INC
GLOBAL TOTAL OFFICE
(Suby of GLOBAL UPHOLSTERY CO LIMITED)
560 Supertest Rd, North York, ON, M3J 2M6
(416) 661-3660
Emp Here 100   Sales 333,997,500
SIC 2522 Office furniture, except wood
Saul Feldberg
Jole Feldberg
David Feldberg

D-U-N-S 24-343-4136   (BR)
GLOBAL UPHOLSTERY CO. INC
THE GLOBAL GROUP
(Suby of GLOBAL UPHOLSTERY CO LIMITED)
1350 Flint Rd, North York, ON, M3J 2J7
(416) 661-3660
Emp Here 80
SIC 6719 Holding companies, nec
Norm Bradford

D-U-N-S 20-913-8218   (BR)
GLOBAL UPHOLSTERY CO. INC
(Suby of GLOBAL UPHOLSTERY CO LIMITED)
565 Petrolia Rd, North York, ON, M3J 2X8
(416) 739-5000
Emp Here 550
SIC 2522 Office furniture, except wood
John Cuda

D-U-N-S 24-611-3476   (HQ)
GLOBAL WOOD CONCEPTS LTD
1300 Flint Rd, North York, ON, M3J 2J7
(416) 663-4191
Emp Here 125   Sales 66,799,500
SIC 2521 Wood office furniture
Israel Vainberg
David Feldberg

D-U-N-S 24-372-9329   (HQ)
GLOBE STAR SYSTEMS INC
GLOBESTAR SYSTEMS
7 Kodiak Cres Suite 100, North York, ON, M3J 3E5
(416) 636-2282
Sales 12,828,100
SIC 3825 Instruments to measure electricity
David Tavares
Mary Digioia

D-U-N-S 24-349-4973   (HQ)
GRIMCO CANADA, INC
GRIMCO SIGN SUPPLY
680 Steeprock Dr, North York, ON, M3J 2X1
(416) 635-6500
Emp Here 25   Sales 23,751,300
SIC 5085 Industrial supplies
Amy Salzman
Robert Hummer

D-U-N-S 25-687-2904   (HQ)
HAGGAR CANADA CO.
CORPORATION HAGGAR CANADA
(Suby of TEXAS CLOTHING HOLDING CORP.)
777 Supertest Rd, North York, ON, M3J 2M9
(416) 652-3777
Emp Here 39   Sales 24,916,100
SIC 5136 Men's and boy's clothing
Michael Stitt
Brian Main
Marc Joseph

D-U-N-S 25-365-8660   (BR)
HOME DEPOT OF CANADA INC
HOME DEPOT
(Suby of THE HOME DEPOT INC)
2375 Steeles Ave W, North York, ON, M3J 3A8
(416) 664-9800
Emp Here 100
SIC 5251 Hardware stores
Jalal Hamad

D-U-N-S 25-403-9340   (SL)
HOUSE INC, THE
620 Supertest Rd Unit 9, North York, ON, M3J 2M5
Emp Here 30   Sales 14,949,660
SIC 5136 Men's and boy's clothing
Steve Kumar
Danielle Rabinowitz
Sandeep (Sonny) Luthra

D-U-N-S 20-429-2367   (SL)
I C G PROPANE
3993 Keele St, North York, ON, M3J 2X6

Emp Here 5   Sales 15,529,285
SIC 4924 Natural gas distribution

D-U-N-S 20-849-5275   (HQ)
IMPERIAL COFFEE AND SERVICES INC
12 Kodiak Cres, North York, ON, M3J 3G5
(416) 638-7404
Sales 80,302,800
SIC 5046 Commercial equipment, nec
Frederick W Steiner
Mark Steiner
Nicholas Kammer
Cindy Meghory
Bernard C Sherman

D-U-N-S 24-044-5184   (HQ)
INTERNATIONAL AQUATIC SERVICES LTD
POOL OF EXPERTS
(Suby of AQUA COASTAL IMPORTS INC)
4496 Chesswood Dr, North York, ON, M3J 2B9
(416) 665-6400
Emp Here 125   Sales 68,642,838
SIC 5999 Miscellaneous retail stores, nec
Greg Cook

D-U-N-S 20-974-0240   (HQ)
JOHNVINCE FOODS
PLANTERS PEANUTS
555 Steeprock Dr, North York, ON, M3J 2Z6
(416) 636-6146
Emp Here 400   Sales 394,193,800
SIC 5145 Confectionery
Vincent Pulla
Joe Pulla
Don Lock
Vincent Cosentino

D-U-N-S 24-830-8496   (HQ)
LIMEN GROUP LTD
46 Lepage Crt Suite B, North York, ON, M3J 1Z9
(416) 638-8880
Emp Here 120   Sales 19,810,482
SIC 1741 Masonry and other stonework
Tony Lima

D-U-N-S 24-117-0419   (BR)
LOBLAWS INC
REAL CANADIAN SUPERSTORE
(Suby of LOBLAW COMPANIES LIMITED)
51 Gerry Fitzgerald Dr Suite 1033, North York, ON, M3J 3N4
(416) 665-7636
Emp Here 280
SIC 5411 Grocery stores
Danny Durance

D-U-N-S 24-760-4718   (BR)
LOVELY IMPORTS & RETAILS LTD
PETRO CANADA
(Suby of LOVELY IMPORTS & RETAILS LTD)
3720 Keele St, North York, ON, M3J 2V9

(416) 636-0568
Emp Here 80
SIC 5541 Gasoline service stations
　Sandeep Varma

　　D-U-N-S 24-185-4124　　(SL)
M & A TILE COMPANY LIMITED
1155 Petrolia Rd, North York, ON, M3J 2X7
(416) 667-8171
Emp Here 50　　*Sales* 11,369,150
SIC 1752 Floor laying and floor work, nec
　Mario Amelio

　　D-U-N-S 24-194-5278　　(SL)
MASTER DESIGN JEWELLERY LIMITED
1001 Petrolia Rd, North York, ON, M3J 2X7

Emp Here 30　　*Sales* 15,616,260
SIC 5094 Jewelry and precious stones
　Vincent Mongia

　　D-U-N-S 25-138-4132　　(SL)
MAXUC TRADING LTD
MTL RECYCLING
79 Martin Ross Ave, North York, ON, M3J 2L5
(416) 667-0888
Emp Here 10　　*Sales* 39,173,850
SIC 5093 Scrap and waste materials
　Chongning Xu
　Liya Zhang

　　D-U-N-S 20-923-7663　　(BR)
MCDONALD'S RESTAURANTS OF CANADA LIMITED
MCDONALD'S RESTAURANT
(*Suby of* MCDONALD'S CORPORATION)
150 Rimrock Rd, North York, ON, M3J 3A6
(416) 630-8381
Emp Here 85
SIC 5812 Eating places
　Katie Grace

　　D-U-N-S 25-354-1668　　(SL)
METARIS INC
(*Suby of* HYDRAULEX INTERNATIONAL HOLDINGS, INC.)
101 Canarctic Dr, North York, ON, M3J 2N7
(416) 638-6000
Emp Here 150　　*Sales* 43,627,500
SIC 3714 Motor vehicle parts and accessories
　Michael Smith
　George Eaton
　Thor Eaton
　Lina Decuzzi

　　D-U-N-S 20-628-7872　　(SL)
METRO HARDWARE & MAINTENANCE INC
72 Martin Ross Ave, North York, ON, M3J 2L4
(416) 633-4293
Emp Here 40　　*Sales* 10,122,360
SIC 5251 Hardware stores
　Abraham Moses

　　D-U-N-S 24-892-9841　　(BR)
METROLINX
(*Suby of* METROLINX)
200 Steeprock Dr, North York, ON, M3J 2T4

Emp Here 700
SIC 4011 Railroads, line-haul operating

　　D-U-N-S 20-058-9369　　(SL)
MIRATEL SOLUTIONS INC
2501 Steeles Ave W Suite 200, North York, ON, M3J 2P1
(416) 650-7850
Emp Here 100　　*Sales* 44,921,900
SIC 7389 Business services, nec
　Tracy Ritson
　Angela Puzzolanti

　　D-U-N-S 20-045-5046　　(SL)
NORTH YORK IRON CORPORATION
1100 Flint Rd, North York, ON, M3J 2J5
(416) 661-2888
Emp Here 15　　*Sales* 15,005,085
SIC 5051 Metals service centers and offices
　Shale Tobe

　Neil Tobe
　Arthur Tobe

　　D-U-N-S 25-148-3293　　(SL)
OLYMPIA JEWELLERY CORP
312 Dolomite Dr Suite 208, North York, ON, M3J 2N2

Emp Here 25　　*Sales* 13,013,550
SIC 5094 Jewelry and precious stones
　Raphael Bazik
　Morris Bazik

　　D-U-N-S 24-704-7017　　(SL)
ONE SOURCE BUSINESS SERVICE
3991 Chesswood Dr, North York, ON, M3J 2R8
(416) 398-0863
Emp Here 49　　*Sales* 11,611,530
SIC 7361 Employment agencies
　Virginia Kaprelian

　　D-U-N-S 25-794-0189　　(SL)
PARAGON HEALTH CARE INC
CASA VERDE HEALTH CENTRE
3595 Keele St, North York, ON, M3J 1M7
(416) 633-3431
Emp Here 250　　*Sales* 16,070,500
SIC 8361 Residential care
　Gerald Harquail

　　D-U-N-S 24-254-5726　　(HQ)
PARTY CITY CANADA INC
(*Suby of* PARTY CITY HOLDCO INC.)
1225 Finch Ave W, North York, ON, M3J 2E8
(416) 631-8455
Sales 183,537,000
SIC 5947 Gift, novelty, and souvenir shop
　William Goodwin
　Reggie Pan

　　D-U-N-S 20-045-6051　　(HQ)
PROGRESS LUV2PAK INTERNATIONAL LTD
LUV 2 PAK
20 Tangiers Rd, North York, ON, M3J 2B2
(416) 638-1221
Sales 19,316,417
SIC 7389 Business services, nec
　David Hertzman

　　D-U-N-S 25-895-9639　　(SL)
PUR COMPANY INC, THE
23 Kodiak Cres, North York, ON, M3J 3E5
(416) 941-7557
Emp Here 35　　*Sales* 29,245,195
SIC 5145 Confectionery
　Jay Klein

　　D-U-N-S 24-335-0758　　(HQ)
R. KIDD FUELS CORP
3993 Keele St, North York, ON, M3J 2X6
(416) 741-2343
Emp Here 35　　*Sales* 52,802,442
SIC 5171 Petroleum bulk stations and terminals
　Manuel Mansueto

　　D-U-N-S 25-274-5393　　(HQ)
R.T. RECYCLING TECHNOLOGY INC
R T PLASTICS
(*Suby of* GLOBAL UPHOLSTERY CO LIMITED)
801 Flint Rd, North York, ON, M3J 2J6
(416) 650-1498
Sales 13,502,930
SIC 3089 Plastics products, nec
　Saul Feldberg

　　D-U-N-S 25-838-4221　　(HQ)
RAM IRON & METAL INC
60 Ashwarren Rd, North York, ON, M3J 1Z5
(416) 630-4545
Sales 12,856,550
SIC 4953 Refuse systems
　Emilio Racco
　Paul Racco
　Peter Racco

　Andrew Racco
　Susana Silva

　　D-U-N-S 20-301-6308　　(SL)
RAPID EQUIPMENT RENTAL LIMITED
5 Saint Regis Cres N Unit 2, North York, ON, M3J 1Y9
(416) 638-7007
Emp Here 110　　*Sales* 36,646,280
SIC 7353 Heavy construction equipment rental
　Frank Heller
　Steven Shinoff
　Trudy Baxter

　　D-U-N-S 20-045-6358　　(HQ)
REGENCY PLASTICS COMPANY LIMITED
50 Brisbane Rd, North York, ON, M3J 2K2
(416) 661-3000
Sales 11,914,350
SIC 3081 Unsupported plastics film and sheet
　David D'ancona
　Abraham D'ancona

　　D-U-N-S 24-400-7345　　(SL)
ROCHON NATIONAL SERVICE
37 Kodiak Cres, North York, ON, M3J 3E5
(416) 398-2888
Emp Here 40　　*Sales* 18,829,240
SIC 1542 Nonresidential construction, nec
　Martin Rochon

　　D-U-N-S 20-182-7180　　(SL)
ROMA LUBE LTD
3975 Keele St, North York, ON, M3J 1P1
(416) 656-4189
Emp Here 18　　*Sales* 18,590,544
SIC 5172 Petroleum products, nec
　Mario Rollo
　Guido Rollo

　　D-U-N-S 24-847-6855　　(SL)
SAFECROSS FIRST AID LTD
21 Kodiak Cres Suite 200, North York, ON, M3J 3E5
(416) 665-0050
Emp Here 30　　*Sales* 22,275,600
SIC 5199 Nondurable goods, nec
　Alan Perry

　　D-U-N-S 24-333-5148　　(HQ)
SANPAUL INVESTMENTS LIMITED
WALKING ON A CLOUD
365 Flint Rd Unit 1, North York, ON, M3J 2J2
(416) 667-8929
Emp Here 3　　*Sales* 17,654,494
SIC 5661 Shoe stores
　David Vella
　Lori-Ann Vella
　Danny Vella

　　D-U-N-S 20-117-6497　　(SL)
SIGA INTERNATIONAL
81 Saint Regis Cres S, North York, ON, M3J 1Y6
(416) 504-7442
Emp Here 45　　*Sales* 22,424,490
SIC 5136 Men's and boy's clothing
　Mark Lucas

　　D-U-N-S 24-355-0386　　(SL)
SKY WINDOW TECHNOLOGIES INC
40 Saint Regis Cres N, North York, ON, M3J 1Z2
(416) 633-1881
Emp Here 50　　*Sales* 10,141,500
SIC 3442 Metal doors, sash, and trim
　Peter Galanis

　　D-U-N-S 25-352-3336　　(SL)
SPONGEZZ INC
79 Saint Regis Cres N, North York, ON, M3J 1Y9
(416) 636-6611
Emp Here 60　　*Sales* 12,113,820
SIC 3089 Plastics products, nec
　Diana Pitsolis

　　D-U-N-S 24-652-8418　　(HQ)

STRAUSSCO HOLDINGS LTD
STARS MENS SHOPS
601 Magnetic Dr Unit 41, North York, ON, M3J 3J2
(416) 650-1404
Emp Here 30　　*Sales* 25,115,440
SIC 5611 Men's and boys' clothing stores
　Harry Strauss

　　D-U-N-S 24-389-6628　　(SL)
SUPERIOR MEDICAL LIMITED
520 Champagne Dr, North York, ON, M3J 2T9
(416) 635-9797
Emp Here 38　　*Sales* 16,992,612
SIC 5047 Medical and hospital equipment

　　D-U-N-S 25-509-3205　　(HQ)
TEKNION CORPORATION
(*Suby of* GLOBAL UPHOLSTERY CO LIMITED)
1150 Flint Rd, North York, ON, M3J 2J5
(416) 661-1577
Emp Here 1,000　　*Sales* 779,327,500
SIC 2522 Office furniture, except wood
　David Feldberg

　　D-U-N-S 20-058-1010　　(HQ)
TEKNION FURNITURE SYSTEMS CO. LIMITED
(*Suby of* GLOBAL UPHOLSTERY CO LIMITED)
1150 Flint Rd, North York, ON, M3J 2J5
(416) 661-3370
Emp Here 90　　*Sales* 86,305,200
SIC 5021 Furniture
　David Feldberg
　Joe Regan
　Scott Deugo

　　D-U-N-S 25-530-8678　　(HQ)
TEKNION HOLDINGS (CANADA) INC
TEKNION FURNITURE SYSTEMS
(*Suby of* GLOBAL UPHOLSTERY CO LIMITED)
1150 Flint Rd, North York, ON, M3J 2J5
(416) 661-1577
Sales 731,018,000
SIC 6712 Bank holding companies
　David Feldberg

　　D-U-N-S 25-148-2188　　(HQ)
TEKNION LIMITED
TEKROLL FORMS, DIV OF
(*Suby of* GLOBAL UPHOLSTERY CO LIMITED)
1150 Flint Rd, North York, ON, M3J 2J5
(416) 661-1577
Emp Here 1,400　　*Sales* 712,528,000
SIC 2522 Office furniture, except wood
　David Feldberg
　Saul Feldberg

　　D-U-N-S 24-463-8532　　(HQ)
TEL-E CONNECT SYSTEMS LTD
CANADA PURE SPRING WATER, DIV OF
7 Kodiak Cres, North York, ON, M3J 3E5
(416) 635-1234
Emp Here 50　　*Sales* 32,674,350
SIC 1731 Electrical work
　David Tavares

　　D-U-N-S 20-628-7419　　(SL)
TETRA PAK CANADA INC
(*Suby of* TETRA LAVAL HOLDINGS B.V.)
20 De Boers Dr Suite 420, North York, ON, M3J 0H1
(647) 775-1837
Emp Here 85　　*Sales* 41,457,050
SIC 5084 Industrial machinery and equipment
　Brian Kennell

　　D-U-N-S 25-793-8597　　(BR)
TORONTO AND REGION CONSERVATION AUTHORITY
BLACK CREEK PIONEER VILLAGE
(*Suby of* TORONTO AND REGION CONSERVATION AUTHORITY)
1000 Murray Ross Pky, North York, ON, M3J

2P3
(416) 736-1740
Emp Here 120
SIC 8412 Museums and art galleries
  Brent Marty

D-U-N-S 20-026-1191   (BR)
TORONTO CATHOLIC DISTRICT SCHOOL BOARD
JAMES CARDINAL MCGUIGAN CATHOLIC SCHOOL
(*Suby of* TORONTO CATHOLIC DISTRICT SCHOOL BOARD)
1440 Finch Ave W, North York, ON, M3J 3G3
(416) 393-5527
Emp Here 100
SIC 8211 Elementary and secondary schools
  Oliver Carroll

D-U-N-S 24-537-5027   (SL)
TORONTO RESEARCH CHEMICALS INC
2 Brisbane Rd, North York, ON, M3J 2J8
(416) 665-9696
Emp Here 75   *Sales* 21,301,575
SIC 2819 Industrial inorganic chemicals, nec
  David Dime
  Charles Dime
  Larry Dime
  Ihor Ruzycky
  Steve Douglas
  Andrew Corbett

D-U-N-S 20-706-2514   (HQ)
TRAFALGAR INDUSTRIES OF CANADA LIMITED
CANADIAN CUSTOM PACKAGING
333 Rimrock Rd, North York, ON, M3J 3J9
(416) 638-1111
Sales 17,757,696
SIC 7389 Business services, nec
  Jeremy Nelson

D-U-N-S 24-736-6151   (SL)
TREND MARKETING WHOLESALE INC
1500 Lodestar Rd, North York, ON, M3J 3C1
(416) 663-3939
Emp Here 45   *Sales* 22,424,490
SIC 5139 Footwear
  Shai Burnstein

D-U-N-S 24-387-4104   (HQ)
TRI-CON CONCRETE FINISHING CO. LTD
835 Supertest Rd Suite 100, North York, ON, M3J 2M9
(416) 736-7700
Sales 24,748,300
SIC 1771 Concrete work
  Frank Guida
  Sandy Guida
  Joe Guida

D-U-N-S 24-503-2946   (SL)
TRILLIUM MARKETING GROUP LTD.
77 Martin Ross Ave, North York, ON, M3J 2L5
(416) 667-3030
Emp Here 35   *Sales* 25,988,200
SIC 5199 Nondurable goods, nec
  Brian Farb

D-U-N-S 20-284-8784   (BR)
UNIVAR CANADA LTD
UNIVAR SOLUTIONS CANADA
(*Suby of* UNIVAR INC.)
777 Supertest Rd, North York, ON, M3J 2M9
(416) 740-5300
Emp Here 130
SIC 4225 General warehousing and storage
  Chis Halberg

D-U-N-S 25-333-1441   (SL)
UNIVERSITY PLUMBING & HEATING LTD
3655 Keele St, North York, ON, M3J 1M8
(416) 630-6010
Emp Here 180   *Sales* 41,951,700
SIC 1711 Plumbing, heating, air-conditioning
  Joe Zentil
  Mario Fattore

D-U-N-S 20-877-8282   (HQ)
VELLA, PAUL SHOES (MISSISSAUGA) LIMITED
WALKING ON A CLOUD
365 Flint Rd Unit 1, North York, ON, M3J 2J2
(416) 667-8929
Emp Here 14   *Sales* 16,325,036
SIC 5661 Shoe stores
  Paul Vella
  Sandra Vella

D-U-N-S 24-069-5945   (SL)
VISUALGATE SYSTEMS INC
64 Bakersfield St, North York, ON, M3J 2W7

Emp Here 27   *Sales* 18,330,921
SIC 6211 Security brokers and dealers
  David Kerzner
  Ron Yekutiel

D-U-N-S 20-936-6574   (HQ)
VPC GROUP INC
ENGINEERED FOAM PRODUCTS CANADA, DIV
150 Toro Rd, North York, ON, M3J 2A9
(416) 630-6633
Emp Here 128   *Sales* 126,279,180
SIC 2824 Organic fibers, noncellulosic
  Peter Farah
  Kevin Day

D-U-N-S 24-133-1995   (SL)
WHOLISTIC CHILD AND FAMILY SERVICES INC
WCFS
601 Magnetic Dr Unit 39, North York, ON, M3J 3J2
(416) 531-5616
Emp Here 49   *Sales* 11,480,112
SIC 8748 Business consulting, nec
  Ramin Mohammadi

D-U-N-S 20-821-7786   (HQ)
YORK UNIVERSITY
4700 Keele St, North York, ON, M3J 1P3
(416) 736-2100
Emp Here 5,000   *Sales* 917,260
SIC 8221 Colleges and universities
  Mamdouh Shoukri
  Gary Brewer
  Marshall Cohen
  Harriet Lewis
  Stan Shapson
  Sheila Embleton

D-U-N-S 20-861-2817   (BR)
YORK UNIVERSITY
COGNITIVE SCIENCE PROGRAM
(*Suby of* YORK UNIVERSITY)
4700 Keele St Rm 428, North York, ON, M3J 1P3
(416) 736-5113
Emp Here 2,000
SIC 8221 Colleges and universities
  Bob Myers

D-U-N-S 20-605-5113   (HQ)
YORKLAND CONTROLS LIMITED
ENVIRONMENTAL CONTROL
2693 Steeles Ave W Suite 661, North York, ON, M3J 2Z8
(416) 661-3306
Emp Here 25   *Sales* 13,862,394
SIC 5074 Plumbing and heating equipment and supplies (hydronics)
  Gavin Barrett
  Gerry Cellucci

North York, ON M3K

D-U-N-S 20-916-4735   (SL)
2031113 ONTARIO LIMITED
YORKDALE VOLKSWAGEN
600 Wilson Ave, North York, ON, M3K 1C9

(416) 741-7480
Emp Here 70   *Sales* 44,049,600
SIC 5511 New and used car dealers
  Tanya Tetreault

D-U-N-S 24-383-4921   (SL)
2069718 ONTARIO LIMITED
BAYWOOD HOMES
1140 Sheppard Ave W Unit 13, North York, ON, M3K 2A2

Emp Here 110   *Sales* 29,803,620
SIC 1521 Single-family housing construction
  Frank Canonaco

D-U-N-S 20-228-5941   (SL)
AGTA HOME HEALTH CARE AND NURSING INC
795 Wilson Ave Suite 102, North York, ON, M3K 1E4
(416) 630-0737
Emp Here 100   *Sales* 27,433,200
SIC 8741 Management services
  Vince Agovino

D-U-N-S 20-850-4829   (SL)
ALTONE INVESTMENTS LIMITED
H & R DEVELOPMENT
3625 Dufferin St Suite 503, North York, ON, M3K 1N4
(416) 638-9002
Emp Here 45   *Sales* 12,982,455
SIC 6512 Nonresidential building operators
  Sandy Hofstedter

D-U-N-S 24-023-3064   (SL)
BATISE INVESTMENTS LIMITED
3625 Dufferin St Unit 503, North York, ON, M3K 1N4
(416) 635-7520
Emp Here 120   *Sales* 18,980,640
SIC 6553 Cemetery subdividers and developers
  Sandor Hofstader
  George Hofstader

D-U-N-S 24-387-0115   (HQ)
BAYWOOD HOMES PARTNERSHIP
1140 Sheppard Ave W Unit 12, North York, ON, M3K 2A2
(416) 633-7333
Emp Here 3   *Sales* 15,817,200
SIC 6552 Subdividers and developers, nec
  Frank Canonaco
  Tony Canonaco
  Ralph Canonaca

D-U-N-S 25-203-5027   (BR)
BOMBARDIER INC
BOMBARDIER AERONAUTIQUE
(*Suby of* BOMBARDIER INC)
123 Garratt Blvd, North York, ON, M3K 1Y5
(416) 633-7310
Emp Here 5,000
SIC 3721 Aircraft
  Mike Arcamore

D-U-N-S 24-624-7928   (HQ)
COCO PAVING INC
COCO ASHPHALT ENGINEERING, DIV OF
949 Wilson Ave, North York, ON, M3K 1G2
(416) 633-9670
Emp Here 50   *Sales* 316,302,860
SIC 1611 Highway and street construction
  Jenny Coco
  Rocky Coco
  Roy Booth

D-U-N-S 24-383-5449   (SL)
ENTERA UTILITY CONTACTORS CO., LIMITED
1011 Wilson Ave, North York, ON, M3K 1G1
(416) 746-9914
Emp Here 100   *Sales* 25,244,200
SIC 1629 Heavy construction, nec
  Stu Warburton

D-U-N-S 24-950-3046   (HQ)
FEDEX FREIGHT CANADA, CORP

(*Suby of* FEDEX CORPORATION)
1011 Wilson Ave, North York, ON, M3K 1G1
(800) 463-3339
Emp Here 80   *Sales* 21,599,130
SIC 4212 Local trucking, without storage
  Doug Duncan
  Pat Reed

D-U-N-S 24-688-6261   (BR)
FLIGHTSAFETY CANADA LTD
FLIGHTSAFETY INTERNATIONAL CANADA
(*Suby of* BERKSHIRE HATHAWAY INC.)
95 Garratt Blvd, North York, ON, M3K 2A5
(416) 638-9313
Emp Here 90
SIC 8299 Schools and educational services, nec
  Patrick Coulter

D-U-N-S 24-858-2434   (SL)
GEP PRODUCTIONS INC
40 Carl Hall Rd Unit 3, North York, ON, M3K 2C1
(416) 398-6869
Emp Here 100   *Sales* 9,403,700
SIC 7812 Motion picture and video production
  Brandie Maher

D-U-N-S 24-560-3493   (SL)
GRIFFEN MANIMPEX LTD
945 Wilson Ave Suite 2, North York, ON, M3K 1E8
(416) 630-7007
Emp Here 120   *Sales* 100,503,960
SIC 5136 Men's and boy's clothing
  Firoz Nasser
  Habib Nasser

D-U-N-S 20-273-8357   (SL)
H & R (U.S.) HOLDINGS INC
3625 Deufferin St Suite 500, North York, ON, M3K 1N4
(416) 635-7520
Emp Here 49   *Sales* 19,183,598
SIC 6798 Real estate investment trusts
  Thomas Hofstedter

D-U-N-S 24-192-4240   (HQ)
H&R DEVELOPMENTS
3625 Dufferin St Suite 503, North York, ON, M3K 1N4
(416) 635-7520
Sales 13,547,100
SIC 1521 Single-family housing construction
  Sandor Hofstedter

D-U-N-S 24-376-2569   (SL)
H&R FINANCE TRUST
3625 Dufferin St Unit 503, North York, ON, M3K 1N4
(416) 635-7520
Emp Here 1   *Sales* 14,920,030
SIC 6726 Investment offices, nec
  Larry Froom
  Thomas J Hofstedter
  Neil Sigler

D-U-N-S 24-709-3685   (HQ)
H&R PROPERTY MANAGEMENT LTD
3625 Dufferin St Suite 409, North York, ON, M3K 1Z2
(416) 635-0163
Emp Here 60   *Sales* 41,888,900
SIC 6531 Real estate agents and managers
  Robert Rubinstein
  Larry Froom

D-U-N-S 25-536-4218   (HQ)
H&R REAL ESTATE INVESTMENT TRUST
3625 Dufferin St Suite 500, North York, ON, M3K 1Z2
(416) 635-7520
Emp Here 7   *Sales* 891,950,973
SIC 6798 Real estate investment trusts
  Thomas J Hofstedter
  Robyn Kestenberg
  Blair Kundell
  Schuyler Levine

Cheryl Fried
Jason Birken
Larry Froom
Nathan Uhr
Robert Dickson
Edward Gilbert

D-U-N-S 25-171-5595   (BR)
HOME DEPOT OF CANADA INC
(*Suby of* THE HOME DEPOT INC)
90 Billy Bishop Way, North York, ON, M3K 2C8
(416) 373-6000
Emp Here 100
SIC 5251 Hardware stores
Nadia Vivan

D-U-N-S 20-122-8272   (SL)
JANICK ELECTRIC LIMITED
1170 Sheppard Ave W Unit 9, North York, ON, M3K 2A3
(416) 635-8989
Emp Here 70   *Sales* 15,248,030
SIC 1731 Electrical work
Janet Wicks

D-U-N-S 24-596-2576   (SL)
KHETIA PHARMACY INC
SHOPPERS DRUG MART 820
1084 Wilson Ave, North York, ON, M3K 1G6
(416) 633-9884
Emp Here 50   *Sales* 12,647,700
SIC 5912 Drug stores and proprietary stores
Jaymesh Khatia

D-U-N-S 20-348-1916   (SL)
NORTH YORK MEDICAL BUILDING INC
1017 Wilson Ave Unit 304, North York, ON, M3K 1Z1
(416) 783-5101
Emp Here 100   *Sales* 18,534,000
SIC 8011 Offices and clinics of medical doctors
Marcel Cohen

D-U-N-S 20-564-5893   (SL)
SEVEN CONTINENTS CORPORATION
945 Wilson Ave Suite 1, North York, ON, M3K 1E8
(416) 784-3717
Emp Here 120   *Sales* 14,859,099
SIC 3999 Manufacturing industries, nec
Kenneth Albright
Steve Singh
Carrie Lane

D-U-N-S 20-257-9272   (SL)
TESKEY CONCRETE COMPANY CORP
(*Suby of* INNOCON INC)
20 Murray Rd, North York, ON, M3K 1T2
(416) 638-0340
Emp Here 65   *Sales* 11,649,235
SIC 3273 Ready-mixed concrete
Roy Teskey
Mark Teskey
Mark Remnant

D-U-N-S 20-045-8032   (SL)
TESKEY CONSTRUCTION COMPANY LTD
20 Murray Rd, North York, ON, M3K 1T2
(416) 638-0340
Emp Here 60   *Sales* 14,771,160
SIC 1794 Excavation work
Mark Teskey
Roy Teskey
Mark Remnant

D-U-N-S 20-035-5167   (BR)
TORONTO DISTRICT SCHOOL BOARD
DOWNSVIEW SECONDARY SCHOOL
(*Suby of* TORONTO DISTRICT SCHOOL BOARD)
7 Hawksdale Rd, North York, ON, M3K 1W3
(416) 395-3200
Emp Here 75
SIC 8211 Elementary and secondary schools
Bruno Berto

D-U-N-S 24-875-6900   (SL)

TRIPLE CANON CORPORATION
1140 Sheppard Ave W Unit 13, North York, ON, M3K 2A2

Emp Here 50   *Sales* 15,943,450
SIC 1521 Single-family housing construction
Frank Canonaco

D-U-N-S 20-057-6630   (SL)
TWO BLOOR RESIDENCES LIMITED
(*Suby of* COMPAGNIE DES CHEMINS DE FER NATIONAUX DU CANADA)
3625 Dufferin St Suite 500, North York, ON, M3K 1Z2
(416) 635-7520
Emp Here 200   *Sales* 92,755,200
SIC 1522 Residential construction, nec
Mark Mandelbaum

D-U-N-S 20-178-0830   (SL)
WAYNE SAFETY INC
1250 Sheppard Ave W, North York, ON, M3K 2A6
(416) 661-1100
Emp Here 25   *Sales* 13,013,550
SIC 5099 Durable goods, nec
Harry Wasserman
Aaron Nisker
Ethel Wasserman

D-U-N-S 20-751-8929   (SL)
ZUREIT HOLDINGS LIMITED
620 Wilson Ave Suite 401, North York, ON, M3K 1Z3
(416) 630-6927
Emp Here 50   *Sales* 20,967,750
SIC 6712 Bank holding companies
Richard Goldberg

North York, ON M3L

D-U-N-S 20-045-0740   (SL)
AMPERE LIMITED
15 Torbarrie Rd, North York, ON, M3L 1G5
(416) 661-3330
Emp Here 100   *Sales* 21,782,900
SIC 1731 Electrical work
Mario Bernardini
Richard Stokes
Kelly Burke

D-U-N-S 24-966-3162   (SL)
COMMERCIAL BAKERIES CORP
45 Torbarrie Rd, North York, ON, M3L 1G5
(416) 247-5478
Emp Here 200   *Sales* 69,138,000
SIC 2052 Cookies and crackers
Anthony Fusco
Phillip Fusco

D-U-N-S 24-925-3196   (SL)
FIRENZA PLUMBING & HEATING LTD
1 Torbarrie Rd, North York, ON, M3L 1G5
(416) 247-7100
Emp Here 70   *Sales* 16,314,550
SIC 1711 Plumbing, heating, air-conditioning
Antonio Baldassarra

D-U-N-S 24-737-2808   (SL)
T.B.T. WINDOWS & DOORS EXTRUSION INC.
27 Torbarrie Rd Unit 25, North York, ON, M3L 1G5
(416) 244-0000
Emp Here 110   *Sales* 62,659,080
SIC 5031 Lumber, plywood, and millwork
Hassan (Sam) Bagherisadr
Rene Khan
Vito Colosonno

North York, ON M3M

D-U-N-S 25-624-2967   (HQ)
BLACK CREEK COMMUNITY HEALTH CENTRE
2202 Jane St Suite 5, North York, ON, M3M 1A4
(416) 249-8000
Sales 12,851,680
SIC 8011 Offices and clinics of medical doctors
Cheryl Presdot

D-U-N-S 24-008-0564   (HQ)
HINCKS-DELLCREST TREATMENT CENTRE, THE
1645 Sheppard Ave W, North York, ON, M3M 2X4
(416) 633-0515
Emp Here 350   *Sales* 28,414,875
SIC 8093 Specialty outpatient clinics, nec
John S Speckkens
Lucy D'souza

D-U-N-S 20-877-1022   (HQ)
LABOURERS INTERNATIONAL UNION OF NORTH AMERICA-LOCAL 183
LIUNA LOCAL 183
1263 Wilson Ave Suite 200, North York, ON, M3M 3G2
(416) 241-1183
Sales 25,509,250
SIC 8631 Labor organizations
Roger Quinn
John Dias

D-U-N-S 24-760-4759   (HQ)
LOVELY IMPORTS & RETAILS LTD
PETRO CANADA
2205 Jane St, North York, ON, M3M 1A5
(416) 248-9814
Emp Here 5   *Sales* 24,903,900
SIC 5541 Gasoline service stations
Malwinder Saini

D-U-N-S 20-593-2739   (BR)
METRO ONTARIO INC
METRO
(*Suby of* METRO INC)
2200 Jane St, North York, ON, M3M 1A4
(416) 241-5732
Emp Here 120
SIC 5411 Grocery stores
Ken Mitchel

D-U-N-S 25-142-5880   (SL)
REX BEAUTY INC.
BEAUTY SUPPLY WAREHOUSE
3304 Keele St, North York, ON, M3M 2H7
(416) 398-9494
Emp Here 30   *Sales* 14,250,780
SIC 5087 Service establishment equipment
Jiyun Choi
Hyck Won Kwon
Hochan Son

North York, ON M3N

D-U-N-S 20-708-6765   (BR)
2063414 ONTARIO LIMITED
LEISUREWORLD CAREGIVING CENTRE NORFINCH
22 Norfinch Dr, North York, ON, M3N 1X1
(416) 623-1120
Emp Here 150
SIC 8051 Skilled nursing care facilities
Anne Deelspra Mcnamara

D-U-N-S 24-918-0563   (SL)
ANTONACCI CLOTHES LIMITED
ANTONACCI FINE CUSTOM TAILORING
99 Norfinch Dr, North York, ON, M3N 1W8
(416) 663-4093
Emp Here 30   *Sales* 14,949,660
SIC 5136 Men's and boy's clothing
Marcello Macaluso

D-U-N-S 20-227-8284   (SL)
B&M EMPLOYMENT INC
168 Oakdale Rd Unit 8, North York, ON, M3N 2S5

Emp Here 50   *Sales* 11,848,500
SIC 7361 Employment agencies
Morzena Jameer

D-U-N-S 20-044-8611   (HQ)
BIC INC
BIC SPORT
(*Suby of* SOCIETE BIC)
155 Oakdale Rd, North York, ON, M3N 1W2
(416) 742-9173
Emp Here 87   *Sales* 99,481,050
SIC 5122 Drugs, proprietaries, and sundries
Kevin Murphy
Angelo Di Placido

D-U-N-S 20-596-9074   (HQ)
CAN-RAD BEAUTY LIMITED
125 Norfinch Dr Suite 100, North York, ON, M3N 1W8
(416) 663-7373
Emp Here 40   *Sales* 42,752,340
SIC 5087 Service establishment equipment
Kenny Wise
Jeff Wise

D-U-N-S 24-850-3430   (BR)
CANADIAN LINEN AND UNIFORM SERVICE CO
(*Suby of* ARAMARK)
75 Norfinch Dr Suite 1, North York, ON, M3N 1W8
(416) 849-5100
Emp Here 140
SIC 7218 Industrial launderers
Lynda Rosmus

D-U-N-S 20-894-6368   (SL)
CANADIAN TENNIS ASSOCIATION
TENNIS CANADA
1 Shoreham Dr Suite 200, North York, ON, M3N 3A7
(416) 665-9777
Emp Here 100   *Sales* 70,921,200
SIC 8699 Membership organizations, nec
Michael Downey
Helene St-Amand

D-U-N-S 25-143-2555   (BR)
CASA BELLA WINDOWS INC
(*Suby of* ALPA LUMBER INC)
124 Norfinch Dr, North York, ON, M3N 1X1
(416) 650-1033
Emp Here 80
SIC 2431 Millwork
Tim Smith

D-U-N-S 20-161-7107   (HQ)
CENTENNIAL OPTICAL LIMITED
(*Suby of* 1455552 ONTARIO LIMITED)
158 Norfinch Dr, North York, ON, M3N 1X6
(416) 739-8539
Emp Here 110   *Sales* 69,595,760
SIC 5049 Professional equipment, nec
Allan Nightingale
Roger De Pinto
Grahame Freeland
Albert Guetta

D-U-N-S 20-513-9806   (BR)
CINTAS CANADA LIMITED
SALLY FOURMY & ASSOCIATES
(*Suby of* CINTAS CORPORATION)
149 Eddystone Ave, North York, ON, M3N 1H5
(416) 743-5070
Emp Here 100
SIC 7218 Industrial launderers
Brandon Rose

D-U-N-S 24-199-1942   (HQ)
CROWN FOOD SERVICE EQUIPMENT LTD
KING METAL SPINNING, A DIV OF
70 Oakdale Rd, North York, ON, M3N 1V9

---

(416) 746-2358
Emp Here 62   *Sales* 22,200,100
SIC 3589 Service industry machinery, nec
 Joe Stritzl
 Edward Mueller
 William Humenick
 Dave Sodi

D-U-N-S 24-827-2239   (SL)
GALATI BROS. SUPERMARKETS (JANE) LIMITED
4734 Jane St, North York, ON, M3N 2L2

Emp Here 60   *Sales* 17,608,620
SIC 5411 Grocery stores
 Antonio Galati
 Frank Galati

D-U-N-S 24-463-5025   (SL)
GARDWELL SECURITY AGENCY INC
168 Oakdale Rd Suite 6b, North York, ON, M3N 2S5
(416) 746-6007
Emp Here 65   *Sales* 25,719,070
SIC 7381 Detective and armored car services
 George Daniel

D-U-N-S 24-926-7451   (HQ)
HTS ENGINEERING LTD
115 Norfinch Dr, North York, ON, M3N 1W8
(416) 661-3400
Emp Here 120   *Sales* 92,008,800
SIC 5075 Warm air heating and air conditioning
 Derek Gordon
 Kevin Little
 Paul Pilutti
 Andy Selin
 Wayne Freethy
 Alan Walcroft

D-U-N-S 20-526-9426   (SL)
KK PRECISION INC
MICRO MACHINE & TOOL, DIV OF
104 Oakdale Rd, North York, ON, M3N 1V9
(416) 742-5911
Emp Here 110   *Sales* 24,420,110
SIC 3599 Industrial machinery, nec
 Vahan Kololian
 Hrair Shahinian
 Lee Chung

D-U-N-S 25-310-8849   (BR)
MCDONALD'S RESTAURANTS OF CANADA LIMITED
MCDONALD'S
(*Suby of* MCDONALD'S CORPORATION)
1831 Finch Ave W Suite 56, North York, ON, M3N 2V2
(416) 636-7601
Emp Here 75
SIC 5812 Eating places
 Melissa Macedo

D-U-N-S 24-924-0094   (HQ)
NELLA CUTLERY (TORONTO) INC
148 Norfinch Dr, North York, ON, M3N 1X8
(416) 740-2424
Emp Here 48   *Sales* 23,751,300
SIC 5087 Service establishment equipment
 Emilio Nella
 Ralph Nella

D-U-N-S 24-195-8230   (HQ)
ONTARIO BAKERY SUPPLIES LIMITED
CAPRI BAGELS & BUNS
84 Oakdale Rd, North York, ON, M3N 1V9
(416) 742-6741
Emp Here 15   *Sales* 14,204,809
SIC 5149 Groceries and related products, nec
 Sam Falcone Sr
 Domenica Falcone

D-U-N-S 25-496-4786   (HQ)
RONKAY MANAGEMENT INC
2000 Sheppard Ave W Suite 304, North York, ON, M3N 1A2
(416) 740-4158
Emp Here 1   *Sales* 11,645,550

SIC 6513 Apartment building operators
 Ronald Kay

D-U-N-S 24-351-0448   (SL)
SUPERIOR EVENTS GROUP INC
LUXE MODERN RENTALS
430 Norfinch Dr, North York, ON, M3N 1Y4
(416) 249-4000
Emp Here 40   *Sales* 11,686,760
SIC 7359 Equipment rental and leasing, nec
 Evan Erinoff
 Peter Jismondi

D-U-N-S 24-555-2302   (SL)
TREND-LINE FURNITURE LTD
166 Norfinch Dr, North York, ON, M3N 1Y4
(416) 650-0504
Emp Here 68   *Sales* 10,493,896
SIC 2512 Upholstered household furniture
 Danny Colalillo
 Giovanna Colalillo

D-U-N-S 24-708-8313   (HQ)
VINYL WINDOW DESIGNS LTD
PERFORMANCE WINDOWS & DOORS, DIVISION OF
550 Oakdale Rd, North York, ON, M3N 1W6
(416) 741-7820
Emp Here 250   *Sales* 142,976,628
SIC 5039 Construction materials, nec
 Philip Spatafora
 Lino D'uva

North York, ON M4A

D-U-N-S 24-047-4239   (HQ)
2585693 ONTARIO INC
PARKWAY HONDA
1681 Eglinton Ave E Suite 1671, North York, ON, M4A 1J6
(416) 752-6666
Sales 76,772,160
SIC 5511 New and used car dealers
 Richard Mcgraw
 Leontina Stefanesecu

D-U-N-S 24-505-7740   (HQ)
A TOWING SERVICE LTD
185 Bartley Dr, North York, ON, M4A 1E6
(416) 656-4000
Emp Here 79   *Sales* 24,080,500
SIC 7549 Automotive services, nec
 Ann Hellebrandt
 Alex Anissimoff

D-U-N-S 20-158-4323   (HQ)
AINSWORTH INC
NATIONAL REFRIGERATION HEATING
(*Suby of* GDI SERVICES AUX IMMEUBLES INC)
131 Bermondsey Rd, North York, ON, M4A 1X4
(416) 751-4420
Emp Here 130   *Sales* 353,263,500
SIC 1731 Electrical work
 Craig Stanford
 Claude Bigras
 John Albers
 Jocelyn Trottier
 Stephane Lavigne

D-U-N-S 20-940-7741   (HQ)
ASTLEY GILBERT LIMITED
42 Carnforth Rd, North York, ON, M4A 2K7
(416) 288-8666
Sales 22,963,780
SIC 2759 Commercial printing, nec

D-U-N-S 24-946-7036   (SL)
CARIBBEAN ICE CREAM COMPANY LTD
TROPICAL TREETS
130 Bermondsey Rd, North York, ON, M4A 1X5
(416) 759-3277
Emp Here 40   *Sales* 33,423,080

SIC 5141 Groceries, general line
 Rumi Keshavjee
 Al Noor Keshavjee

D-U-N-S 20-044-3059   (HQ)
DON VALLEY VOLKSWAGEN LIMITED
1695 Eglinton Ave E, North York, ON, M4A 1J6
(647) 956-0498
Emp Here 41   *Sales* 24,903,900
SIC 5511 New and used car dealers
 Mike Martan
 Joseph Haberbusch
 Anna Haberbusch

D-U-N-S 20-165-4654   (HQ)
FREEMAN FORMALWEAR LIMITED
111 Bermondsey Rd, North York, ON, M4A 2T7
(416) 288-1222
Emp Here 90   *Sales* 13,881,660
SIC 7299 Miscellaneous personal service
 Samuel Freeman
 Leonard Goldstein

D-U-N-S 24-946-4702   (HQ)
INNOVA MEDICAL OPHTHALMICS INC
(*Suby of* LOMBART INSTRUMENTS HOLDINGS, INC.)
48 Carnforth Rd, North York, ON, M4A 2K7
(416) 615-0185
Emp Here 97   *Sales* 63,706,888
SIC 5049 Professional equipment, nec
 Victor Spear
 David Spear

D-U-N-S 20-847-9832   (SL)
LITE-TECH INDUSTRIES LIMITED
161 Bartley Dr, North York, ON, M4A 1E6
(416) 751-5644
Emp Here 50   *Sales* 10,233,650
SIC 3646 Commercial lighting fixtures
 Rosa Samuels

D-U-N-S 24-334-6756   (SL)
MULVEY & BANANI INTERNATIONAL INC
44 Mobile Dr, North York, ON, M4A 2P2
(416) 751-2520
Emp Here 64   *Sales* 11,261,312
SIC 8711 Engineering services
 Myron Washchyshyn
 Diego Battiston

D-U-N-S 20-851-1881   (HQ)
ONTARIO SECONDARY SCHOOL TEACHERS' FEDERATION, THE
OSSTF
60 Mobile Dr Suite 100, North York, ON, M4A 2P3
(416) 751-8300
Emp Here 120   *Sales* 35,116,650
SIC 8621 Professional organizations
 Pierre Cote
 Earl Burt
 James Spray

D-U-N-S 24-131-6848   (SL)
OTG FINANCIAL
ONTARIO TEACHERS GROUP INVESTMENT FUND
57 Mobile Dr, North York, ON, M4A 1H5
(416) 752-9410
Emp Here 25   *Sales* 20,694,425
SIC 6722 Management investment, open-end
 Paulette Wiseman
 Maryanne Taggio

D-U-N-S 25-710-1329   (BR)
PARKWAY AUTOMOTIVE SALES LIMITED
PARKWAY LEASING
(*Suby of* 2585693 ONTARIO INC)
1681 Eglinton Ave E, North York, ON, M4A 1J6

Emp Here 193
SIC 7515 Passenger car leasing
 Jon Damianidis

D-U-N-S 24-318-0309   (BR)
SHOPPERS DRUG MART CORPORATION
SHOPPERS HOME HEALTHCARE
(*Suby of* LOBLAW COMPANIES LIMITED)
104 Bartley Dr, North York, ON, M4A 1C5
(416) 752-8885
Emp Here 90
SIC 5999 Miscellaneous retail stores, nec
 Michael Morse

D-U-N-S 20-717-0499   (HQ)
SHOPPERS HOME HEALTH CARE (ONTARIO) INC
(*Suby of* LOBLAW COMPANIES LIMITED)
104 Bartley Dr, North York, ON, M4A 1C5
(416) 752-8885
Emp Here 63   *Sales* 23,211,160
SIC 5999 Miscellaneous retail stores, nec
 Micheal Mores

D-U-N-S 20-559-3606   (HQ)
T.J. TRADING CO. INC
THREE STAR INDUSTRIES
260 Bartley Dr, North York, ON, M4A 1G5
(416) 661-9506
Sales 11,752,155
SIC 5085 Industrial supplies
 Mukesh Pruthi
 Tajinder Pruthi

D-U-N-S 20-120-0768   (HQ)
TRILLIUM BEVERAGE INC
MILL STREET BREWERY
125 Bermondsey Rd, North York, ON, M4A 1X3
(416) 759-6565
Sales 19,012,950
SIC 2082 Malt beverages
 Stephen Abrams
 Herbert Willer
 Dennis Bennie
 Irvine M. Weitzman
 Mark A Hall
 Alan P Levine

North York, ON M4N

D-U-N-S 20-635-8736   (SL)
2389807 ONTARIO INC
THE MILLER TAVERN
(*Suby of* PEGASUS GROUP INC)
3885 Yonge St, North York, ON, M4N 2P2
(416) 322-5544
Emp Here 75   *Sales* 3,413,925
SIC 5812 Eating places
 Rick Montgomery

D-U-N-S 24-329-6865   (BR)
LOBLAWS INC
LOBLAWS
(*Suby of* LOBLAW COMPANIES LIMITED)
3501 Yonge St, North York, ON, M4N 2N5
(416) 481-8105
Emp Here 200
SIC 5411 Grocery stores
 Aaron French

D-U-N-S 20-698-7732   (BR)
TORONTO DISTRICT SCHOOL BOARD
SUNNY VIEW PUBLIC SCHOOL
(*Suby of* TORONTO DISTRICT SCHOOL BOARD)
450 Blythwood Rd, North York, ON, M4N 1A9
(416) 393-9275
Emp Here 100
SIC 8211 Elementary and secondary schools
 Ted Goldring

D-U-N-S 20-850-8572   (SL)
TORONTO FRENCH SCHOOL
306 Lawrence Ave E, North York, ON, M4N 1T7
(416) 484-6980
Emp Here 235   *Sales* 23,292,965

SIC 8211 Elementary and secondary schools
John Godfrey
Richard Taylor

North York, ON M5M

D-U-N-S 20-772-3060   (SL)
1692038 ONTARIO LTD
DINO'S NOFRILLS
1811 Avenue Rd, North York, ON, M5M 3Z3
(416) 781-3917
Emp Here 50   Sales 13,707,600
SIC 5411 Grocery stores
 Dino Savo

D-U-N-S 25-977-6193   (SL)
BOZIKIS FOOD GROUP
BATON ROUGE RESTAURANT
216 Yonge Blvd, North York, ON, M5M 3H8

Emp Here 80   Sales 20,924,240
SIC 6712 Bank holding companies
 Spiro Bozikis
 George Bozikis

D-U-N-S 25-862-2257   (SL)
CAMP AGUDAH
129 Mcgillivray Ave, North York, ON, M5M 2Y7
(416) 781-7101
Emp Here 200   Sales 18,538,000
SIC 7032 Sporting and recreational camps
 Rabbi Blaustein

D-U-N-S 25-704-0535   (SL)
COMMUNITY FIRST DEVELOPMENTS INC
2171 Avenue Rd Suite 303, North York, ON, M5M 4B4
(416) 932-9249
Emp Here 50   Sales 11,895,050
SIC 8742 Management consulting services
 George Larter
 Eddie Lok
 Christina Wong

D-U-N-S 20-847-0658   (SL)
F D PHARMACY INC
SHOPPERS DRUG MART
1500 Avenue Rd, North York, ON, M5M 3X2
(416) 781-6146
Emp Here 60   Sales 14,659,680
SIC 5912 Drug stores and proprietary stores
 Fabrizio Damiani

D-U-N-S 25-711-4603   (SL)
KALLES, HARVEY REAL ESTATE LTD
2145 Avenue Rd, North York, ON, M5M 4B2
(416) 441-2888
Emp Here 270   Sales 91,277,280
SIC 6531 Real estate agents and managers
 Harvey R. Kalles
 Michael Kalles
 Dena Mintz

D-U-N-S 24-761-9294   (BR)
PUSATERI'S LIMITED
(*Suby of* PUSATERI'S LIMITED)
1539 Avenue Rd, North York, ON, M5M 3X4
(416) 785-9124
Emp Here 300
SIC 5411 Grocery stores
 Frank Luchetta

D-U-N-S 20-657-0132   (HQ)
QUADRA DESIGN STUDIOS INC
Q4 ARCHITECTS
2171 Avenue Rd Suite 302, North York, ON, M5M 4B4
(416) 322-6334
Emp Here 1   Sales 22,460,950
SIC 7389 Business services, nec
 Frances Digiusette

D-U-N-S 20-656-2360   (BR)
TORONTO CATHOLIC DISTRICT SCHOOL BOARD

LORETTO ABBEY HIGHSCHOOL
(*Suby of* TORONTO CATHOLIC DISTRICT SCHOOL BOARD)
101 Mason Blvd, North York, ON, M5M 3E2
(416) 393-5510
Emp Here 75
SIC 8211 Elementary and secondary schools
 Lorie Di Marco

D-U-N-S 20-875-4416   (SL)
TORONTO CRICKET SKATING AND CURL-ING CLUB
141 Wilson Ave, North York, ON, M5M 3A3
(416) 487-4581
Emp Here 125   Sales 9,818,125
SIC 7997 Membership sports and recreation clubs
 Doug Knights

D-U-N-S 20-809-8322   (SL)
TRAVEL DISCOUNTERS
1927 Avenue Rd, North York, ON, M5M 4A2
(416) 481-6701
Emp Here 50   Sales 22,174,500
SIC 7389 Business services, nec
 Lily Singh

North York, ON M5N

D-U-N-S 20-966-0968   (HQ)
HAVERGAL COLLEGE
1451 Avenue Rd, North York, ON, M5N 2H9
(416) 483-3519
Emp Here 150   Sales 29,735,700
SIC 8211 Elementary and secondary schools
 Helen Kay Davy

D-U-N-S 25-476-5415   (SL)
YESHIVA YESODEI HATORAH
77 Glen Rush Blvd, North York, ON, M5N 2T8
(416) 787-1101
Emp Here 90   Sales 8,354,340
SIC 8211 Elementary and secondary schools
 Aher Bornstein

North York, ON M6A

D-U-N-S 24-708-2316   (SL)
1076634 ONTARIO INC
NICHOLLS, DAVE TOYOTA
3080 Dufferin St, North York, ON, M6A 2S6
(416) 243-1550
Emp Here 30   Sales 14,942,340
SIC 5521 Used car dealers
 Ditter Hammer
 David Craig

D-U-N-S 24-888-9925   (SL)
1125278 ONTARIO LTD
DEAN MYERS LEASING (1995)
3180 Dufferin St, North York, ON, M6A 2T1
(416) 256-1405
Emp Here 110   Sales 69,220,800
SIC 5511 New and used car dealers
 Richard Chamberland
 Penny Chamberland

D-U-N-S 20-358-6248   (SL)
1170760 ONTARIO LTD
EUROPEAN BOUTIQUE
1 Yorkdale Rd Unit 402, North York, ON, M6A 3A1
(416) 785-8801
Emp Here 90   Sales 21,989,520
SIC 5944 Jewelry stores
 Eric Sutkiewicz

D-U-N-S 25-855-8394   (SL)
1175469 ONTARIO LTD
REILLY'S SECURITY SERVICES
1120 Caledonia Rd Unit 11, North York, ON, M6A 2W5

(416) 256-3199
Emp Here 200   Sales 5,250,000
SIC 7381 Detective and armored car services
 Carmine Panaro

D-U-N-S 24-938-1278   (SL)
1456882 ONTARIO LTD
MICHEL'S BAGUETTE
3401 Dufferin St, North York, ON, M6A 2T9
(416) 789-3533
Emp Here 50   Sales 13,707,600
SIC 5461 Retail bakeries
 Ali Ghadimi

D-U-N-S 20-911-4045   (SL)
1556890 ONTARIO LTD
MANUALIFE SECURITIES
1 Yorkdale Rd Suite 404, North York, ON, M6A 3A1
(416) 787-1612
Emp Here 26   Sales 17,651,998
SIC 6282 Investment advice
 Josph Dweek

D-U-N-S 20-163-0779   (HQ)
1673612 ONTARIO INC
MIDTOWN HONDA
3400 Dufferin St, North York, ON, M6A 2V1
(416) 789-4101
Emp Here 49   Sales 33,351,840
SIC 5511 New and used car dealers
 Imtihaz Manji
 Brian Tafler

D-U-N-S 24-575-2506   (SL)
593631 ONTARIO LIMITED
DAIRY TREATS
3522 Bathurst St, North York, ON, M6A 2C6

Emp Here 40   Sales 10,966,080
SIC 5461 Retail bakeries
 Shlomo Esses

D-U-N-S 24-963-8669   (HQ)
ALTIMA DENTAL CANADA INC
ALTIMA DENTAL CENTRE
1 Yorkdale Rd Suite 320, North York, ON, M6A 3A1
(416) 785-1828
Emp Here 12   Sales 16,220,880
SIC 8741 Management services
 Sven Grail
 George Christodoulou
 Philip Forster

D-U-N-S 24-594-5626   (SL)
ALWAYS A DOLLAR PLUS
496 Lawrence Ave W, North York, ON, M6A 1A1
(416) 785-8500
Emp Here 49   Sales 13,433,448
SIC 5411 Grocery stores
 Mike Williams

D-U-N-S 24-408-2558   (SL)
BARRYMORE FURNITURE CO. LTD
1168 Caledonia Rd, North York, ON, M6A 2W5
(416) 532-2891
Emp Here 90   Sales 13,888,980
SIC 2512 Upholstered household furniture
 Thomas (Tom) Callahan
 Brian Callahan

D-U-N-S 24-991-6222   (HQ)
BENIX & CO. INC
BARNES & CASTLE
98 Orfus Rd, North York, ON, M6A 1L9
(416) 784-0732
Emp Here 25   Sales 245,900,166
SIC 5719 Miscellaneous homefurnishings
 Fred Benitah

D-U-N-S 20-117-4872   (HQ)
BLEEMAN HOLDINGS LIMITED
BELMONT PROPERTY MANAGEMENT
970 Lawrence Ave W Suite 304, North York, ON, M6A 3B6

(416) 256-3900
Emp Here 10   Sales 33,511,120
SIC 6531 Real estate agents and managers
 Abraham Bleeman
 Nathan S Bleeman
 Aaron Bleeman

D-U-N-S 24-386-8481   (HQ)
BODY SHOP CANADA LIMITED, THE
(*Suby of* NATURA COSMETICOS S/A)
1 Yorkdale Rd Suite 510, North York, ON, M6A 3A1
(416) 782-2948
Emp Here 35   Sales 1,154,546,268
SIC 6794 Patent owners and lessors
 Andrea Goldner
 Jayme Jenkins
 Indra Chanicka

D-U-N-S 24-659-2166   (SL)
BROWN, AL G. & ASSOCIATES
970 Lawrence Ave W Suite 501, North York, ON, M6A 3B6
(416) 787-6176
Emp Here 20   Sales 11,598,480
SIC 6411 Insurance agents, brokers, and ser-vice
 David Brown
 Al G. Brown
 Golda Brown

D-U-N-S 24-765-3686   (HQ)
CALIFORNIA INNOVATIONS INC
36 Dufflaw Rd, North York, ON, M6A 2W1
(416) 590-7700
Sales 55,205,280
SIC 5078 Refrigeration equipment and sup-plies
 Mel Mogil
 Lorne Mogil
 Ron Amber

D-U-N-S 24-525-3617   (HQ)
CANADIAN MENTAL HEALTH ASSOCIA-TION TORONTO BRANCH, THE
CMHA
700 Lawrence Ave W Suite 480, North York, ON, M6A 3B4
(416) 789-7957
Sales 38,041,400
SIC 8011 Offices and clinics of medical doc-tors
 Steve Lurie
 Mary Smith
 Catherine Anastakis

D-U-N-S 20-161-7610   (HQ)
CENTURA (TORONTO) LIMITED
CENTURA FLOOR AND WALL FASHIONS
(*Suby of* CENTURA LIMITED)
950 Lawrence Ave W, North York, ON, M6A 1C4
(416) 785-5165
Emp Here 100   Sales 227,851,200
SIC 5032 Brick, stone, and related material
 Brian Cowie

D-U-N-S 20-113-2870   (HQ)
CENTURA LIMITED
CENTURA TILE
950 Lawrence Ave W, North York, ON, M6A 1C4
(416) 785-5165
Sales 230,147,200
SIC 5023 Homefurnishings
 Brian Cowie

D-U-N-S 25-409-5177   (SL)
CERVELO CYCLES INC
(*Suby of* HOUDSTERMAATSCHAPPIJ WILG B.V.)
15 Leswyn Rd Unit 1, North York, ON, M6A 1J8
(416) 782-6789
Emp Here 50   Sales 11,192,150
SIC 3751 Motorcycles, bicycles and parts
 Robert Reigers

D-U-N-S 24-622-3978   (SL)
COLUMBUS CENTRE OF TORONTO
901 Lawrence Ave W Suite 306, North York,
ON, M6A 1C3
(416) 789-7011
Emp Here 150   *Sales* 11,518,800
SIC 8322 Individual and family services
  Nick Torthetti
  Paul Pellegrini
  Palmacchio Di Iulio
  Ugo Di Federico
  Renzo Pillon

D-U-N-S 25-220-5315   (SL)
DACURY AGENCIES CORPORATION
CLOTHES OUT TRADING
59 Samor Rd, North York, ON, M6A 1J2
(416) 781-2171
Emp Here 22   *Sales* 10,963,084
SIC 5137 Women's and children's clothing

D-U-N-S 20-163-7618   (SL)
**DOMINION SHEET METAL & ROOFING
WORKS**
113 Cartwright Ave Suite 1, North York, ON,
M6A 1V4
(416) 789-0601
Emp Here 70   *Sales* 15,248,030
SIC 1761 Roofing, siding, and sheetMetal
work
  Harry Silverberg
  Sidney Silverberg

D-U-N-S 20-052-2048   (HQ)
FAIRWEATHER LTD
1185 Caledonia Rd, North York, ON, M6A 2X1
(416) 785-1771
Emp Here 50   *Sales* 124,755,000
SIC 5621 Women's clothing stores
  Isaac Benitah

D-U-N-S 20-189-1962   (SL)
**FIRM CAPITAL MORTGAGE INVESTMENT
CORPORATION**
163 Cartwright Ave, North York, ON, M6A 1V5
(416) 635-0221
Emp Here 10   *Sales* 23,294,356
SIC 6726 Investment offices, nec
  Eli Dadouch
  Jonathan Mair
  Victoria Granovski
  Sandy Poklar
  Joseph Fried
  Boris Baril
  Stanley Goldfarb
  Morris Fischtein
  Geoffrey Bledin
  Edward Gilbert

D-U-N-S 25-065-3219   (SL)
FORTINO'S (LAWRENCE & ALLEN) LTD
700 Lawrence Ave W, North York, ON, M6A
3B4
(416) 785-9843
Emp Here 190   *Sales* 55,760,630
SIC 5411 Grocery stores
  Joe Aiello

D-U-N-S 25-172-1767   (SL)
FRAMEWORTH CUSTOM FRAMING INC
1198 Caledonia Rd Unit B, North York, ON,
M6A 2W5
(416) 781-1115
Emp Here 75   *Sales* 20,388,150
SIC 7699 Repair services, nec
  Brian Ehrenworth

D-U-N-S 25-301-1894   (BR)
HUDSON'S BAY COMPANY
BAY, THE
(Suby of HUDSON'S BAY COMPANY)
3401 Dufferin St, North York, ON, M6A 2T9
(416) 789-8011
Emp Here 100
SIC 5311 Department stores
  Stephane Ledoux

D-U-N-S 20-390-2135   (HQ)

INC GROUP INC
INTERNATIONAL CLOTHIERS
1185 Caledonia Rd, North York, ON, M6A 2X1
(416) 785-1771
Emp Here 100   *Sales* 124,755,000
SIC 5611 Men's and boys' clothing stores
  Issac Benitah
  Paul Brener

D-U-N-S 20-980-7700   (SL)
ISA INTERNATIONAL INC
46 Dufflaw Rd, North York, ON, M6A 2W1
(416) 782-9100
Emp Here 35   *Sales* 17,809,960
SIC 5021 Furniture
  Art Sandler
  Kevin Sandler

D-U-N-S 24-775-9277   (SL)
JOSTEN DEVELOPMENTS LIMITED
COUNTRY CLUB TOWERS
1020 Lawrence Ave W Suite 300, North York,
ON, M6A 1C8
(416) 787-1135
Emp Here 30   *Sales* 12,580,650
SIC 6719 Holding companies, nec
  Joseph Tenenbaum

D-U-N-S 25-619-8045   (SL)
KARABUS MANAGEMENT INC
PRICEWATERHOUSECOOPERS, A DIV OF
1 Yorkdale Rd Suite 412, North York, ON, M6A
3A1
Emp Here 43   *Sales* 10,074,384
SIC 8748 Business consulting, nec
  Antony Karabus
  Lawrence Apple
  Stephen Granovsky
  Anthony P. Cancelliere
  Ross Sinclair
  Michael Unger
  Farla Efros
  Isaac Krakovsky

D-U-N-S 20-533-2641   (SL)
KASHRUTH COUNCIL OF CANADA
3200 Dufferin St Suite 308, North York, ON,
M6A 3B2
(416) 635-9550
Emp Here 65   *Sales* 14,321,320
SIC 8734 Testing laboratories
  Mordechai Levin

D-U-N-S 20-921-7173   (BR)
**LONDON   LIFE,   COMPAGNIE
D'ASSURANCE-VIE**
LONDON LIFE INSURANCE COMPANY
(Suby of POWER CORPORATION DU
CANADA)
970 Lawrence Ave W Suite 600, North York,
ON, M6A 3B6

Emp Here 75
SIC 6311 Life insurance
  Edward Seman

D-U-N-S 24-488-8954   (SL)
MAINLINE FASHIONS INC
CLIO/OZ
42 Dufflaw Rd Unit 100, North York, ON, M6A
2W1
(416) 368-1522
Emp Here 58   *Sales* 30,191,436
SIC 5094 Jewelry and precious stones
  Helene Zelovitzky

D-U-N-S 25-819-2533   (HQ)
MANN ENGINEERING LTD
150 Bridgeland Ave Suite 101, North York,
ON, M6A 1Z5
(416) 201-9109
Sales 12,359,987
SIC 1731 Electrical work
  James Mann
  Yawen Wu

D-U-N-S 24-775-9236   (SL)

MARKALTA DEVELOPMENTS LTD
MEDICINE HAT MALL
1020 Lawrence Ave W Suite 300, North York,
ON, M6A 1C8
(416) 787-1135
Emp Here 100   *Sales* 28,443,700
SIC 6512 Nonresidential building operators
  Howard Bisgould

D-U-N-S 24-686-3872   (HQ)
MCI MEDICAL CLINICS INC
DOCTOR'S OFFICE, THE
1 Yorkdale Rd Suite 209, North York, ON, M6A
3A1
(416) 440-4040
Emp Here 15   *Sales* 30,309,200
SIC 8093 Specialty outpatient clinics, nec
  Monte Bail
  Murray Kline
  Paul Davies

D-U-N-S 20-336-8381   (SL)
MEDALLION CORPORATION
MEDALLION DEVELOPMENT
970 Lawrence Ave W Suite 304, North York,
ON, M6A 3B6
(416) 256-3900
Emp Here 100   *Sales* 27,175,600
SIC 6531 Real estate agents and managers
  Abraham Bleeman

D-U-N-S 25-500-8609   (HQ)
MEDALLION PROPERTIES INC
(Suby of BLEEMAN HOLDINGS LIMITED)
970 Lawrence Ave W Suite 304, North York,
ON, M6A 3B6
(416) 256-3900
Emp Here 65   *Sales* 32,254,453
SIC 6531 Real estate agents and managers
  Abraham Bleeman
  Nathan Bleeman
  Aaron Bleeman

D-U-N-S 20-552-8479   (BR)
METRO ONTARIO INC
METRO
(Suby of METRO INC)
3090 Bathurst St, North York, ON, M6A 2A1
(416) 783-1227
Emp Here 300
SIC 5411 Grocery stores
  Paul Bravi

D-U-N-S 24-371-6862   (SL)
MORI LEE ASSOCIATES (CANADA)
1293 Caledonia Rd, North York, ON, M6A 2X7
(416) 789-9911
Emp Here 50   *Sales* 24,916,100
SIC 5131 Piece goods and notions
  Martin Richman

D-U-N-S 24-846-9793   (SL)
MOTEYO INC
ROGERS AUTHORIZED DEALER
3111 Dufferin St, North York, ON, M6A 2S7
(416) 785-3031
Emp Here 33   *Sales* 10,744,800
SIC 5999 Miscellaneous retail stores, nec
  David Tenaglia
  Mark Lewis

D-U-N-S 20-366-7464   (BR)
NORDSTROM CANADA RETAIL, INC
*NORDSTROM YORKDALE SHOPPING CEN-
TRE*
(Suby of NORDSTROM, INC.)
3401 Dufferin St Unit 500, North York, ON,
M6A 2T9
(416) 780-6630
Emp Here 80
SIC 5311 Department stores
  Brynn Herthel

D-U-N-S 24-109-2654   (BR)
OLD NAVY (CANADA) INC
(Suby of THE GAP INC)
1 Yorkdale Rd, North York, ON, M6A 3A1

(416) 787-9384
Emp Here 120
SIC 5651 Family clothing stores
  Angela Rethay

D-U-N-S 25-256-1006   (HQ)
ONTOR LIMITED
*INDUSTRIAL AUTOMATION SYSTEMS, DIV
OF*
12 Leswyn Rd, North York, ON, M6A 1K3
(416) 781-5286
Emp Here 43   *Sales* 42,481,530
SIC 5075 Warm air heating and air condition-
ing
  Robert Elder
  Barry Elder

D-U-N-S 20-802-9764   (HQ)
P.Y.A. IMPORTER LTD
TOSCANO
15 Apex Rd, North York, ON, M6A 2V6
(416) 929-3300
Sales 29,899,320
SIC 5136 Men's and boy's clothing
  Patrick Assaraf
  Elise Latner-Assaraf

D-U-N-S 20-202-0173   (HQ)
PACE INDEPENDENT LIVING
970 Lawrence Ave W Suite 210, North York,
ON, M6A 3B6
(416) 789-7806
Emp Here 50   *Sales* 37,272,240
SIC 8399 Social services, nec
  Joanne Wilson

D-U-N-S 24-221-3106   (HQ)
PAMENSKY, V.J. CANADA INC
64 Samor Rd, North York, ON, M6A 1J6
(416) 781-4617
Emp Here 3   *Sales* 20,122,830
SIC 5063 Electrical apparatus and equipment
  Victor Pamensky
  David Wassyng
  Maurice Pamensky

D-U-N-S 20-172-9696   (HQ)
PETO MACCALLUM LTD
165 Cartwright Ave, North York, ON, M6A 1V5
(416) 785-5110
Emp Here 40   *Sales* 25,023,460
SIC 8711 Engineering services
  Douglas Bonner
  Alnoor Nathoo
  John Dietrich

D-U-N-S 24-752-7591   (HQ)
PICTURE PICTURE COMPANY LTD., THE
PICTURE PICTURE, THE
122 Cartwright Ave, North York, ON, M6A 1V2
(416) 787-9827
Sales 25,442,800
SIC 5023 Homefurnishings
  Ray Hakami
  Alex Gofrani

D-U-N-S 25-497-6434   (HQ)
PINEDALE PROPERTIES LTD
970 Lawrence Ave W Suite 303, North York,
ON, M6A 3B6
(416) 256-2900
Emp Here 58   *Sales* 28,484,452
SIC 6531 Real estate agents and managers
  George Grossman
  Robin Bookbinder
  Yoram Birenzweig
  Alex Grossman

D-U-N-S 20-877-9678   (SL)
PLASTIC PLUS LIMITED
14 Leswyn Rd, North York, ON, M6A 1K2
(416) 789-4307
Emp Here 41   *Sales* 10,519,042
SIC 3851 Ophthalmic goods
  Paul Faibish
  Mark Faibish

D-U-N-S 20-173-1759   (SL)

PLAZA PONTIAC BUICK LIMITED
PLAZA NATIONAL LEASING
3400 Dufferin St, North York, ON, M6A 2V1
(416) 781-5271
Emp Here 75 *Sales* 47,196,000
SIC 5511 New and used car dealers
Herbert Stein

D-U-N-S 25-099-8200 (HQ)
RANDY RIVER INC
111 Orfus Rd, North York, ON, M6A 1M4
(416) 785-1771
Emp Here 20 *Sales* 37,426,500
SIC 5611 Men's and boys' clothing stores
Isaac Benitah
Michael Goldgrub

D-U-N-S 25-711-6921 (BR)
RED LOBSTER HOSPITALITY LLC
RED LOBSTER RESTAURANTS
3200 Dufferin St, North York, ON, M6A 3B2
(416) 785-7930
Emp Here 200
SIC 5812 Eating places
Mark Sozanski

D-U-N-S 25-976-4749 (SL)
REGAL SECURITY INC
1244 Caledonia Rd, North York, ON, M6A 2X5
(416) 633-8558
Emp Here 300 *Sales* 7,875,000
SIC 7381 Detective and armored car services
Nicholas Vetere
Dominic Screnci
Sante Montoni

D-U-N-S 20-012-1825 (HQ)
RIOCAN PROPERTY SERVICES INC
(*Suby of* RIOCAN REAL ESTATE INVEST-MENT TRUST)
700 Lawrence Ave W Suite 315, North York, ON, M6A 3B4
(416) 256-0256
Emp Here 50 *Sales* 169,032,000
SIC 6531 Real estate agents and managers
Edward Sonshine
Frederic Waks
Robert Wolf

D-U-N-S 24-097-8627 (HQ)
SOUTHERN SANITATION INC
WASTECO PEEL DIV
161 Bridgeland Ave, North York, ON, M6A 1Z1
(416) 787-5000
Sales 51,025,600
SIC 4953 Refuse systems
Steve Caudwell

D-U-N-S 25-338-3889 (HQ)
SURECOMP INC
1 Yorkdale Rd Suite 602, North York, ON, M6A 3A1
(416) 781-5545
Sales 41,711,750
SIC 7372 Prepackaged software
Joel Koschitzky
Martin Vaughan

D-U-N-S 25-246-5885 (SL)
T N T GROUP INC
T N T APPLIANCES
65 Dufflaw Rd, North York, ON, M6A 2W2
(416) 781-9156
Emp Here 27 *Sales* 12,073,698
SIC 5064 Electrical appliances, television and radio
David Zolty

D-U-N-S 24-097-3719 (SL)
TAUB, BERNARD & COMPANY
1167 Caledonia Rd, North York, ON, M6A 2X1
(416) 785-5353
Emp Here 75 *Sales* 15,681,375
SIC 8721 Accounting, auditing, and book-keeping
Bernard Taub

D-U-N-S 20-177-0468 (HQ)

TORONTO BARBER & BEAUTY SUPPLY LIMITED
112 Orfus Rd, North York, ON, M6A 1L9
(416) 787-1211
Emp Here 35 *Sales* 99,481,050
SIC 5122 Drugs, proprietaries, and sundries
Nat Kaufman
Cecile Stein
Ethel Ritchie

D-U-N-S 25-107-7541 (BR)
TORONTO DISTRICT SCHOOL BOARD
YORKDALE ADULT LEARNING CENTRE & SECONDARY SCHOOL
(*Suby of* TORONTO DISTRICT SCHOOL BOARD)
38 Orfus Rd, North York, ON, M6A 1L6
(416) 395-3350
Emp Here 75
SIC 8211 Elementary and secondary schools
Eric Dallin

D-U-N-S 20-346-7006 (BR)
TORONTO DISTRICT SCHOOL BOARD
JOHN POLANYI COLLEGIATE INSTITUTE
(*Suby of* TORONTO DISTRICT SCHOOL BOARD)
640 Lawrence Ave W, North York, ON, M6A 1B1
(416) 395-3303
Emp Here 80
SIC 8211 Elementary and secondary schools
Antonio Santos

D-U-N-S 24-424-9983 (SL)
TREND COLOUR LABS INC
TREND COLOUR
1194d Caledonia Rd, North York, ON, M6A 2W5

Emp Here 30 *Sales* 12,525,180
SIC 7384 Photofinish laboratories
Armando Merlo
Rita Merlo

D-U-N-S 24-360-6089 (BR)
TYCO SAFETY PRODUCTS CANADA LTD
DSC
(*Suby of* JOHNSON CONTROLS INTERNA-TIONAL PLC)
95 Bridgeland Ave, North York, ON, M6A 1Y7
(905) 760-3000
Emp Here 600
SIC 3699 Electrical equipment and supplies, nec
Fernando Pimentel

D-U-N-S 20-177-5244 (SL)
UNIVERSAL CHINA LAMP & GLASS COMPANY LIMITED
UNIVERSAL LAMP MFG
121 Cartwright Ave, North York, ON, M6A 1V4
(416) 787-8900
Emp Here 25 *Sales* 11,179,350
SIC 5063 Electrical apparatus and equipment
Charles Feldman
Marla Young

D-U-N-S 20-850-3045 (HQ)
VILLA CHARITIES INC
901 Lawrence Ave W, North York, ON, M6A 1C3
(416) 789-7011
Emp Here 150 *Sales* 345,286,900
SIC 6732 Trusts: educational, religious, etc.
Santo Veltri
Nick Sgro
Pal Di Iulio
Silvi Alzeta-Reali
Sandro D'ercole
Joseph Arcuri
Frank Chiarotto
Joseph J. Fusco
Mario Giampietri
Gina Valee

D-U-N-S 20-182-3130 (HQ)

WILLIAMS-SONOMA CANADA, INC
POTTERY BARN
(*Suby of* WILLIAMS-SONOMA, INC.)
3401 Dufferin St Suite 215, North York, ON, M6A 2T9
(416) 785-1233
Sales 12,782,165
SIC 5712 Furniture stores
Jane Mccrimmon
Seth Jaffe

D-U-N-S 24-779-0538 (BR)
WINNERS MERCHANTS INTERNATIONAL L.P.
WINNERS
(*Suby of* THE TJX COMPANIES INC)
3090 Bathurst St Suite 1, North York, ON, M6A 2A1
(416) 782-4469
Emp Here 110
SIC 5651 Family clothing stores
Antoinette Frazzell

D-U-N-S 25-795-4065 (HQ)
WIRELESS PERSONAL COMMUNICA-TIONS INC
BELL MOBILITY CENTRES
166 Bentworth Ave, North York, ON, M6A 1P7
(416) 667-4189
Emp Here 8 *Sales* 16,280,000
SIC 5999 Miscellaneous retail stores, nec
Steve Winch
Rick Kojfman
David Williamson

D-U-N-S 20-876-6345 (HQ)
YM INC. (SALES)
STITCHES
50 Dufflaw Rd Suite 364, North York, ON, M6A 2W1
(416) 789-1071
Emp Here 400 *Sales* 623,775,000
SIC 5621 Women's clothing stores
Michael Goldgrub
Morley Beallor
Stuart Eustace
Brooke Miller

D-U-N-S 20-175-9768 (SL)
YORKDALE FORD LINCOLN SALES LIM-ITED
3130 Dufferin St, North York, ON, M6A 2S6
(416) 787-4534
Emp Here 62 *Sales* 39,015,360
SIC 5511 New and used car dealers
Simon Yakubowicz

D-U-N-S 25-619-5074 (SL)
YORKDALE SHOPPING CENTRE HOLD-INGS INC
1 Yorkdale Rd Suite 500, North York, ON, M6A 3A1
(416) 256-5066
Emp Here 250 *Sales* 33,919,250
SIC 6512 Nonresidential building operators
Jim Hedrich
John Geddings

D-U-N-S 25-282-6748 (SL)
ZEIFMANS LLP
201 Bridgeland Ave Suite 1, North York, ON, M6A 1Y7
(416) 256-4000
Emp Here 85 *Sales* 17,653,225
SIC 8721 Accounting, auditing, and book-keeping
Laurence Zeifman
Ronald Rutman
Isreal Schon
Edward Kalkstein
Brian Mcgee
Steven Roth
Allan A Rutman
Jason R Price

North York, ON M6B

D-U-N-S 20-200-2338 (SL)
1279317 ONTARIO LTD
STUDIO MUNGE
25 Wingold Ave, North York, ON, M6B 1P8
(416) 588-1668
Emp Here 55 *Sales* 24,707,045
SIC 7389 Business services, nec
Alessandro Munge

D-U-N-S 20-079-6790 (HQ)
ALTERNATIVE PROCESSING SYSTEMS INC
60 Wingold Ave, North York, ON, M6B 1P5
(416) 256-2010
Emp Here 45 *Sales* 11,262,592
SIC 4212 Local trucking, without storage
Ray Leach

D-U-N-S 24-006-0061 (SL)
BIALIK HEBREW DAY SCHOOL
2760 Bathurst St, North York, ON, M6B 3A1
(416) 783-3346
Emp Here 97 *Sales* 9,004,122
SIC 8211 Elementary and secondary schools
Sonia Soron

D-U-N-S 24-683-9166 (SL)
BIOSTEEL SPORTS NUTRITION INC
1-87 Wingold Ave, North York, ON, M6B 1P8
(416) 322-7833
Emp Here 15 *Sales* 16,580,175
SIC 5122 Drugs, proprietaries, and sundries
John Celenza
Matthew Nichol
Stefano Cerone
Michael Cammalleri
Steven Liambas

D-U-N-S 24-265-6488 (SL)
CERAGRES TILE GROUP
170 Tycos Dr, North York, ON, M6B 1W8
(416) 286-3553
Emp Here 49 *Sales* 21,911,526
SIC 5032 Brick, stone, and related material

D-U-N-S 25-921-6703 (SL)
CHD MAINTENANCE LIMITED
274 Viewmount Ave, North York, ON, M6B 1V2
(416) 782-5071
Emp Here 100 *Sales* 4,020,900
SIC 7349 Building maintenance services, nec
M Dacrez

D-U-N-S 25-926-6203 (BR)
DON MICHAEL HOLDINGS INC
ROOTS
(*Suby of* DON MICHAEL HOLDINGS INC)
75 Tycos Dr, North York, ON, M6B 1W3
(416) 781-7540
Emp Here 100
SIC 5651 Family clothing stores
Don Green

D-U-N-S 20-938-6218 (SL)
EITZ CHAIM DAY SCHOOL
1 Viewmount Ave, North York, ON, M6B 1T2
(416) 789-4366
Emp Here 150 *Sales* 14,867,850
SIC 8211 Elementary and secondary schools
Philip Alter
Aaron Grubner

D-U-N-S 25-975-2806 (HQ)
EMPIRE AUCTIONS INC
165 Tycos Dr, North York, ON, M6B 1W6
(416) 784-4261
Emp Here 8 *Sales* 12,128,913
SIC 7389 Business services, nec
Michael Rogozinsky

D-U-N-S 25-066-2723 (SL)
FKK WHOLESALE CASH & CARRY INC
920 Caledonia Rd Suite 2, North York, ON, M6B 3Y1

(416) 783-1197
Emp Here 20   *Sales* 10,702,480
SIC 5145 Confectionery
  Mario Cribari
  Mike Cerra
  Derek Kwok
  Tony Sama

D-U-N-S 24-478-8899   (SL)
GARBO GROUP INC
GARBO CREATIONS
34 Wingold Ave, North York, ON, M6B 1P5
(416) 782-9500
Emp Here 47   *Sales* 24,465,474
SIC 5094 Jewelry and precious stones
  Gary Grundman
  Bonnie Grundman

D-U-N-S 20-004-0686   (BR)
HOME DEPOT OF CANADA INC
HOME DEPOT
(*Suby of* THE HOME DEPOT INC)
825 Caledonia Rd, North York, ON, M6B 3X8
(416) 780-4730
Emp Here 150
SIC 5251 Hardware stores
  George Tserbis

D-U-N-S 20-514-1638   (HQ)
INDEX EXCHANGE INC
74 Wingold Ave, North York, ON, M6B 1P5
(416) 785-5908
Emp Here 275   *Sales* 107,632,035
SIC 7311 Advertising agencies
  John Andrew Casale
  Manny Goncalves
  Gagan Grewal
  Patricia Casele

D-U-N-S 24-185-7804   (HQ)
JAYTEX OF CANADA LIMITED
JAYTEX GROUP
29 Gurney Cres, North York, ON, M6B 1S9
(416) 785-1099
Emp Here 5   *Sales* 49,832,200
SIC 5136 Men's and boy's clothing
  Howie Kasten
  Leo Greenberg
  Eric Grundy
  Roger Flores

D-U-N-S 20-818-8342   (HQ)
JEWISH VOCATIONAL SERVICE OF METROPOLITAN TORONTO
JVS TORONTO
74 Tycos Dr, North York, ON, M6B 1V9
(416) 785-0515
Emp Here 1   *Sales* 23,062,200
SIC 8299 Schools and educational services, nec
  Karen Goldenberg
  Leon Kadish

D-U-N-S 20-045-3421   (SL)
LADY YORK HOLDINGS LTD
LADY YORK FOODS
2939 Dufferin St, North York, ON, M6B 3S7
(416) 781-8585
Emp Here 115   *Sales* 33,749,855
SIC 5411 Grocery stores
  Lucia Torchetti

D-U-N-S 20-172-0794   (HQ)
OCTOPUS PRODUCTS LIMITED
23 Gurney Cres, North York, ON, M6B 1S9
(416) 531-5051
Sales 11,685,520
SIC 5162 Plastics materials and basic shapes
  Thomas Bernard
  Gene Bernard

D-U-N-S 24-764-9015   (SL)
PANAXIS INC
70 Wingold Ave, North York, ON, M6B 1P5
(416) 256-5800
Emp Here 26   *Sales* 12,956,372
SIC 5137 Women's and children's clothing
  Mitchell Linds

  Jennifer Sterling

D-U-N-S 20-172-8896   (SL)
PERL'S MEAT PRODUCTS LIMITED
3015 Bathurst St, North York, ON, M6B 3B5

Emp Here 57   *Sales* 16,728,189
SIC 5421 Meat and fish markets
  Herman Perl
  Brian Perl
  Elliot Perl

D-U-N-S 24-822-2895   (SL)
R.B. INC
79 Wingold Ave Unit 10, North York, ON, M6B 1P8
(416) 787-4998
Emp Here 24   *Sales* 12,493,008
SIC 5091 Sporting and recreation goods
  Richard Browne

D-U-N-S 20-922-6401   (SL)
RE/MAX REALTRON REALTY INC
2815 Bathurst St, North York, ON, M6B 3A4
(416) 782-8882
Emp Here 50   *Sales* 16,356,350
SIC 6531 Real estate agents and managers
  Helen Kamin-Locash

D-U-N-S 20-173-9356   (SL)
RELIABLE CORPORATION
100 Wingold Ave Unit 5, North York, ON, M6B 4K7
(416) 785-0200
Emp Here 29   *Sales* 13,775,754
SIC 5084 Industrial machinery and equipment
  Robert Kahn

D-U-N-S 25-361-3327   (SL)
ROSEDALE SEATING INC
920 Caledonia Rd Unit 3, North York, ON, M6B 3Y1
(647) 348-6666
Emp Here 34   *Sales* 17,301,104
SIC 5021 Furniture
  Anthony Roseman

D-U-N-S 25-253-1041   (HQ)
STONE TILE INTERNATIONAL INC
834 Caledonia Rd Suite 1, North York, ON, M6B 3X9
(416) 515-9000
Emp Here 55   *Sales* 85,444,200
SIC 5032 Brick, stone, and related material
  Sylvia Benchimol

D-U-N-S 24-097-5912   (HQ)
VILLA COLOMBO HOMES FOR THE AGED INC
(*Suby of* VILLA CHARITIES INC)
40 Playfair Ave, North York, ON, M6B 2P9
(416) 789-2113
Sales 35,355,100
SIC 8361 Residential care
  Nick Manocchio
  Fernando Scopa

D-U-N-S 24-452-3700   (SL)
ZANEEN GROUP INC
ZANEEN LIGHTNING
30 Tycos Dr, North York, ON, M6B 1V9
(416) 247-9221
Emp Here 45   *Sales* 20,122,830
SIC 5063 Electrical apparatus and equipment
  Robert Pietrobon
  Florence Pietrobon

North York, ON M6L

D-U-N-S 25-168-4163   (HQ)
CONSEIL SCOLAIRE VIAMONDE
ECOLE ELEMENTAIRE ST-JOSEPH
116 Cornelius Pky, North York, ON, M6L 2K5
(416) 614-0844
Emp Here 50   *Sales* 115,564,581

SIC 8211 Elementary and secondary schools
  Ronald Marion
  Jean-Luc Bernard
  Francoise Fournier

D-U-N-S 24-611-0746   (HQ)
INTERNATIONAL DISTRIBUTION NETWORK CANADA LTD
IDN CANADA
(*Suby of* IDN GLOBAL, INC.)
70 Floral Pky, North York, ON, M6L 2B9
(416) 248-5625
Emp Here 18   *Sales* 21,017,178
SIC 5072 Hardware
  Mark Johnston
  Karen Hoffman Kahl
  Mike Groover

D-U-N-S 24-335-0472   (BR)
METRO ONTARIO INC
METRO
(*Suby of* METRO INC)
1411 Lawrence Ave W, North York, ON, M6L 1A4
(416) 248-5846
Emp Here 150
SIC 5411 Grocery stores
  Benny Marcoecia

D-U-N-S 20-982-2261   (SL)
NORTH PARK NURSING HOME LIMITED
450 Rustic Rd, North York, ON, M6L 1W9
(416) 247-0531
Emp Here 80   *Sales* 5,498,640
SIC 8051 Skilled nursing care facilities
  Nitin Shah
  Chandanbala Shah

D-U-N-S 20-921-7454   (HQ)
ONTARIO FEDERATION FOR CEREBRAL PALSY
OFCP
1630 Lawrence Ave W Unit 104, North York, ON, M6L 1C5
(416) 244-0899
Sales 15,358,400
SIC 8322 Individual and family services
  Victor Gascon
  Clarence Meyers
  Sue Mott
  Ben Toner
  Roly Bergman
  Martti Hyhko

D-U-N-S 20-638-7672   (SL)
SUEDE MASTER (1975) INC
25 Connie St, North York, ON, M6L 2H8
(416) 614-8000
Emp Here 25   *Sales* 11,875,650
SIC 5087 Service establishment equipment
  Brad Maxwell

North York, ON M6M

D-U-N-S 25-274-6706   (HQ)
1120423 ONTARIO LIMITED
COMDA THE CALENDAR PEOPLE
15 Densley Ave, North York, ON, M6M 2P5
(416) 429-2257
Sales 13,055,420
SIC 8743 Public relations services
  Michael Warren
  Susan Kaschuk
  Errol Verasami

D-U-N-S 24-359-7783   (HQ)
1772887 ONTARIO LIMITED
ST. JOSEPH COMMUNICATIONS
(*Suby of* ST. JOSEPH CORPORATION)
15 Benton Rd, North York, ON, M6M 3G2
(416) 364-3333
Emp Here 325   *Sales* 77,509,600
SIC 2721 Periodicals
  Anthony Gagliano

D-U-N-S 20-158-1709   (SL)
ABBOTT OF ENGLAND 1981 LIMITED
ABBOTT
545 Trethewey Dr, North York, ON, M6M 2J4
(416) 789-7663
Emp Here 60   *Sales* 44,551,200
SIC 5199 Nondurable goods, nec
  David Abbott
  Lee Abbott

D-U-N-S 20-165-8481   (SL)
GERTEX HOSIERY INC
MANDERO HOSIERY MILLS, DIV OF
9 Densley Ave, North York, ON, M6M 2P5
(416) 241-2345
Emp Here 86   *Sales* 39,865,760
SIC 5137 Women's and children's clothing
  Aaron Mandelbaum
  Abe Rotenberg
  Herz Mandelbaum

D-U-N-S 20-378-1930   (SL)
LIVE TO SECURE PROTECTIVE SERVICES INC
LTS PROTECTIVE SERVICES
15 Ingram Dr Units 201-702, North York, ON, M6M 2L7
(647) 560-4321
Emp Here 250   *Sales* 6,562,500
SIC 7381 Detective and armored car services
  Cristy Coroa

D-U-N-S 20-786-5056   (HQ)
LOSS PREVENTION SERVICES LIMITED
2221 Keele St Suite 308, North York, ON, M6M 3Z5
(416) 248-1261
Sales 12,344,940
SIC 8744 Management services
  James Burke

D-U-N-S 20-169-8313   (SL)
MAC MOR OF CANADA LTD
21 Benton Rd, North York, ON, M6M 3G2
(416) 596-8237
Emp Here 120   *Sales* 16,400,880
SIC 2329 Men's and boy's clothing, nec
  Max Glicksman
  Morris Glick

D-U-N-S 24-964-4584   (SL)
MELLOW WALK FOOTWEAR INC
17 Milford Ave, North York, ON, M6M 2W1
(416) 241-1312
Emp Here 53   *Sales* 12,372,055
SIC 3143 Men's footwear, except athletic
  Andrew Violi
  Jeffrey Violi
  Robert Violi

D-U-N-S 24-977-9943   (BR)
ST. JOSEPH PRINTING LIMITED
ST JOSEPH PI MEDIA
(*Suby of* ST. JOSEPH CORPORATION)
15 Benton Rd, North York, ON, M6M 3G2
(416) 248-4868
Emp Here 300
SIC 2752 Commercial printing, lithographic
  Doug Templeton

D-U-N-S 20-114-5468   (SL)
STARFIELD LION COMPANY INC
(*Suby of* HAAGEN COOPERATIEF U.A.)
22 Benton Rd, North York, ON, M6M 3G4
(416) 789-4354
Emp Here 63   *Sales* 14,319,207
SIC 3842 Surgical appliances and supplies
  Steve Shorts
  Peggy Curtis
  Loren Lori

D-U-N-S 24-318-1914   (SL)
STINCOR SPECIALTIES LTD
STINCOR PROMOTIONAL SPECIALTIES
15 Densley Ave, North York, ON, M6M 2P5
(416) 243-0293
Emp Here 22   *Sales* 16,335,440
SIC 5199 Nondurable goods, nec

▲ Public Company   ■ Public Company Family Member   **HQ** Headquarters   **BR** Branch   **SL** Single Location

Ian Walker

D-U-N-S 24-408-4992   (SL)
T.G.A. GENERAL CONTRACTING (1980) INC
31 Densley Ave, North York, ON, M6M 2P5
(416) 247-7471
Emp Here 40   *Sales* 12,754,760
SIC 1521 Single-family home construction
Anthony Gagliano

D-U-N-S 25-991-3374   (SL)
YORK MARBLE TILE & TERRAZZO INC
CAPITAL STONEWORKS, DIV OF
2 Sheffield St, North York, ON, M6M 3E6
(416) 235-0161
Emp Here 100   *Sales* 16,238,100
SIC 1743 Terrazzo, tile, marble and mossaic work
Glen Pestrin
Mario Pestrin

North York, ON M9L

D-U-N-S 25-332-9742   (SL)
1100378 ONTARIO LIMITED
WILSON WINDINGS, DIV OF
805 Fenmar Dr, North York, ON, M9L 1C8

Emp Here 50   *Sales* 10,233,650
SIC 3694 Engine electrical equipment
Jan Drzewinski

D-U-N-S 20-700-2937   (SL)
2000007 ONTARIO INC
INKAS ARMORED VEHICLE MANUFACTURING
3605 Weston Rd, North York, ON, M9L 1V7
(416) 744-3322
Emp Here 70   *Sales* 15,669,010
SIC 3711 Motor vehicles and car bodies
David Khazanski

D-U-N-S 24-852-0509   (SL)
2308061 ONTARIO LIMITED
TENDER POULTRY
239 Toryork Dr, North York, ON, M9L 1Y2
(416) 640-1790
Emp Here 85   *Sales* 19,112,675
SIC 2015 Poultry slaughtering and processing
Berardino Furia
Ian Siegal
Danny Rother

D-U-N-S 25-322-6237   (SL)
576195 ONTARIO LIMITED
WISEMAN EXPORT
500 Barmac Dr Suite 2, North York, ON, M9L 2X8
(416) 789-1477
Emp Here 57   *Sales* 28,404,354
SIC 5137 Women's and children's clothing
Neil Rabovsky

D-U-N-S 25-215-0750   (SL)
996660 ONTARIO LIMITED
MOLISANA IMPORTS
63 Signet Dr, North York, ON, M9L 2W5
(416) 747-8707
Emp Here 28   *Sales* 23,396,156
SIC 5141 Groceries, general line
Frank Di Biase
Teresa Di Biase
Anna Di Biase

D-U-N-S 20-112-3507   (HQ)
ABC GROUP LIMITED
(*Suby of* CERBERUS CAPITAL MANAGEMENT, L.P.)
2 Norelco Dr, North York, ON, M9L 2X6
(416) 246-1782
Emp Here 1   *Sales* 365,509,000
SIC 6712 Bank holding companies
Mike Schmidt

Timothy Schmidt

D-U-N-S 24-826-6157   (SL)
ABC PLASTICS LIMITED
SUPREME TOOLING GROUP
(*Suby of* CERBERUS CAPITAL MANAGEMENT, L.P.)
2 Norelco Dr, North York, ON, M9L 2X6
(416) 742-9600
Emp Here 150   *Sales* 28,812,750
SIC 3465 Automotive stampings
David Thompson
Clay Burkett

D-U-N-S 24-421-5893   (HQ)
ABC TECHNOLOGIES INC
ABC GROUP TECH CENTRE
(*Suby of* CERBERUS CAPITAL MANAGEMENT, L.P.)
2 Norelco Dr, North York, ON, M9L 2X6
(416) 246-1782
Emp Here 150   *Sales* 1,528,396,800
SIC 3089 Plastics products, nec
Todd Sheppelman
Derrick Phelps
Mark Poynton
Robert Kunihiro
Timothy Schmidt
Ken Friedman
David Smith
David Ellacott

D-U-N-S 24-817-6067   (HQ)
ALARMFORCE INDUSTRIES INC
(*Suby of* BCE INC)
675 Garyray Dr, North York, ON, M9L 1R2
(416) 445-2001
Sales 43,300,992
SIC 7382 Security systems services
Glen M. Leblanc
Mirko Bibic
Michel Lalande

D-U-N-S 24-845-2369   (SL)
ALPHA OIL INC
490 Garyray Dr, North York, ON, M9L 1P8
(416) 745-6131
Emp Here 35   *Sales* 16,415,175
SIC 5983 Fuel oil dealers
Michael Krula
Teressa Krula
Stefan Krula

D-U-N-S 20-317-3679   (HQ)
APOPHARMA INC
200 Barmac Dr, North York, ON, M9L 2Z7
(416) 749-9300
Sales 13,556,340
SIC 2834 Pharmaceutical preparations
Michael Spino

D-U-N-S 24-310-3699   (BR)
APOTEX INC
APOBIOLOGIX
200 Barmac Dr, North York, ON, M9L 2Z7
(800) 268-4623
Emp Here 4,000
SIC 2834 Pharmaceutical preparations
Bernard Sherman

D-U-N-S 20-320-1673   (BR)
APOTEX INC
285 Garyray Dr, North York, ON, M9L 1P2
(416) 749-9300
Emp Here 500
SIC 2834 Pharmaceutical preparations
Patti Black

D-U-N-S 24-523-9046   (HQ)
APOTEX INTERNATIONAL INC
150 Signet Dr, North York, ON, M9L 1T9
(416) 749-9300
Sales 91,377,250
SIC 6712 Bank holding companies
Jack Kay
Jeremy Disai

D-U-N-S 25-313-9547   (HQ)

APOTEX PHARMACEUTICAL HOLDINGS INC
150 Signet Dr, North York, ON, M9L 1T9
(416) 749-9300
Emp Here 1   *Sales* 689,262,000
SIC 8731 Commercial physical research
Jack Kay
Alex Glasenberg
Jeff Watson

D-U-N-S 24-891-7502   (HQ)
BAD BOY FURNITURE WAREHOUSE LIMITED
BAD BOY FURNITURE & APPLIANCES
500 Fenmar Dr, North York, ON, M9L 2V5
(416) 667-7546
Emp Here 55   *Sales* 80,010,900
SIC 5712 Furniture stores
Blayne Lastman
Tony Balsingham

D-U-N-S 20-159-9313   (SL)
BELMONT MEAT PRODUCTS LIMITED
(*Suby of* PREMIUM BRANDS HOLDINGS CORPORATION)
230 Signet Dr, North York, ON, M9L 1V2
(416) 749-7250
Emp Here 180   *Sales* 62,224,200
SIC 2011 Meat packing plants
W.J. Duffy Smith
David Mclaren

D-U-N-S 20-701-6783   (SL)
BERCO AUTOMOTIVE SUPPLY LIMITED
163 Milvan Dr Suite 1, North York, ON, M9L 1Z8
(416) 749-0231
Emp Here 26   *Sales* 12,950,028
SIC 5511 New and used car dealers
Chester Salvati
Nick Salvati

D-U-N-S 24-075-9340   (HQ)
BERNARDI BUILDING SUPPLY LTD
469 Garyray Dr, North York, ON, M9L 1P9
(416) 741-0941
Sales 17,886,960
SIC 5039 Construction materials, nec
Michael Bernardi
Paul Bernardi
Joseph Bernardi
Michael Burkhart

D-U-N-S 24-707-9267   (HQ)
BURKE'S RESTORATION INC
98 Milvan Dr, North York, ON, M9L 1Z6
(416) 744-2456
Emp Here 5   *Sales* 12,754,760
SIC 1521 Single-family housing construction
Garyk Burke

D-U-N-S 24-138-9832   (SL)
CAMCARB CO2 LTD
155 Signet Dr, North York, ON, M9L 1V1
(416) 745-1304
Emp Here 25   *Sales* 18,258,625
SIC 5169 Chemicals and allied products, nec
Bruce Cameron

D-U-N-S 20-178-0913   (SL)
CANADA SPORTSWEAR CORP
(*Suby of* WEATHERCRAFT HOLDINGS LIMITED)
230 Barmac Dr, North York, ON, M9L 2Z3
(416) 740-8020
Emp Here 55   *Sales* 46,064,315
SIC 5136 Men's and boy's clothing
Ralph Goldfinger
Charles Goldfinger
Regina Goldfinger
Lawrence Goldfinger
Howard Goldfinger

D-U-N-S 25-978-0245   (SL)
CANADIAN GROUP, THE
TCG TOYS
430 Signet Dr Suite A, North York, ON, M9L

2T6
(416) 746-3388
Emp Here 23   *Sales* 11,972,466
SIC 5092 Toys and hobby goods and supplies
Jerry Smith
Michael Albert
Berrie Simpson

D-U-N-S 24-626-0665   (SL)
CANADIAN STARTER DRIVES INC
CSD, A DIV OF
176 Milvan Dr, North York, ON, M9L 1Z9
(416) 748-1458
Emp Here 5   *Sales* 83,286,445
SIC 7538 General automotive repair shops
Frank Colosimo

D-U-N-S 24-737-8714   (HQ)
CLASSIC FIRE PROTECTION INC
645 Garyray Dr, North York, ON, M9L 1P9
(416) 740-3000
Sales 83,613,500
SIC 7389 Business services, nec
Richard Berwick

D-U-N-S 24-181-3179   (SL)
CLEARVIEW INDUSTRIES LTD
CLEARVIEW PATIO DOORS
45 Fenmar Dr, North York, ON, M9L 1M1
(416) 745-6666
Emp Here 200   *Sales* 38,417,000
SIC 3442 Metal doors, sash, and trim
Cathy Gucciardi
Ciro Gucciardi
Tom Marsala

D-U-N-S 24-796-3317   (BR)
COCA-COLA CANADA BOTTLING LIMITED
(*Suby of* COCA-COLA CANADA BOTTLING LIMITED)
24 Fenmar Dr, North York, ON, M9L 1L8
(416) 741-0440
Emp Here 130
SIC 2086 Bottled and canned soft drinks
John Guarino

D-U-N-S 24-963-4528   (HQ)
COMBINED METAL INDUSTRIES INC
(*Suby of* COMBINED METAL HOLDINGS INC)
505 Garyray Dr, North York, ON, M9L 1P9
(416) 743-7730
Emp Here 35   *Sales* 69,530,000
SIC 5093 Scrap and waste materials
Gary Kaplan
Darryl Schull
David Kaplan
Jacques Levinsohn

D-U-N-S 25-474-3727   (SL)
CORE INSURANCE CLAIMS CONTRACTING INC
94 Kenhar Dr Unit 10, North York, ON, M9L 1N2
(416) 740-9400
Emp Here 25   *Sales* 14,498,100
SIC 6411 Insurance agents, brokers, and service
Sam Mazza

D-U-N-S 20-920-6168   (SL)
CUSTOM COLOUR LABS INC
CUSTOM COLOUR IMAGING
5703 Steeles Ave W, North York, ON, M9L 1S7
(416) 630-2020
Emp Here 43   *Sales* 17,014,154
SIC 7384 Photofinish laboratories
Leo Sciarrino

D-U-N-S 20-163-6636   (SL)
DOLENTE CONCRETE & DRAIN CO.
52 High Meadow Pl, North York, ON, M9L 2Z5
(416) 653-6504
Emp Here 50   *Sales* 12,044,200
SIC 1623 Water, sewer, and utility lines
Perry Dolente
Orazio Di Fulviis

D-U-N-S 24-563-4365 (SL)
DORPLEX INDUSTRIES LIMITED
FUSION GLASS WORKS
50 Irondale Dr, North York, ON, M9L 1R8
(416) 739-7794
Emp Here 75 *Sales* 14,406,375
SIC 3442 Metal doors, sash, and trim
 Paul Moseley
 Leon Elmaleh

D-U-N-S 20-405-0124 (SL)
F.& K. MFG., CO., LIMITED
155 Turbine Dr, North York, ON, M9L 2S7
(416) 749-3980
Emp Here 50 *Sales* 11,100,050
SIC 3542 Machine tools, Metal forming type
 Jurgen Walch

D-U-N-S 24-610-4079 (HQ)
FER-PAL CONSTRUCTION LTD
171 Fenmar Dr, North York, ON, M9L 1M7
(416) 742-3713
Sales 45,936,100
SIC 1623 Water, sewer, and utility lines
 Madeleine Paquin
 Shaun Mckaigue
 Kent James
 Ingid Stefancic
 Rejean Loiselle
 Benoit Cote
 Lucio Di Clemente
 Alan Sauriol

D-U-N-S 24-737-1417 (BR)
FGF BRANDS INC
(*Suby of* FGF BRANDS INC)
1295 Ormont Dr, North York, ON, M9L 2W6
(416) 742-7434
Emp Here 80
SIC 5149 Groceries and related products, nec
 Lori Procher

D-U-N-S 24-679-4056 (HQ)
FOOT LOCKER CANADA CO
(*Suby of* FOOT LOCKER, INC.)
230 Barmac Dr, North York, ON, M9L 2Z3
(416) 748-4210
Emp Here 40 *Sales* 374,265,000
SIC 5661 Shoe stores
 Ken C. Hicks
 Giovanna Cipriano
 Paulette Alviti
 Jeffrey L. Berk
 John A. Maurer
 Phillip Reiprich
 Lauren B. Peters
 Robert W. Mchugh
 Jeremy Nowak
 Patricia A. Peck

D-U-N-S 20-817-7543 (SL)
FOUR STAR PLATING INDUSTRIES LIM-ITED
1162 Barmac Dr, North York, ON, M9L 1X5
(416) 745-1742
Emp Here 150 *Sales* 28,812,750
SIC 3471 Plating and polishing
 Frank Lebar

D-U-N-S 20-968-0503 (SL)
GLOBE WHOLESALE MEATS INC
61 Signet Dr, North York, ON, M9L 2W5
(416) 745-7000
Emp Here 28 *Sales* 23,396,156
SIC 5147 Meats and meat products
 Michael Dibiase
 Pat Dibiase

D-U-N-S 20-379-9176 (SL)
GMASJ ONTARIO INC
NU-WAY POTATO PRODUCTS
1290 Ormont Dr, North York, ON, M9L 2V4
(416) 241-9151
Emp Here 35 *Sales* 29,245,195
SIC 5148 Fresh fruits and vegetables
 Michael San Giorgio

D-U-N-S 24-123-3675 (HQ)
HANDI FOODS LTD
MEDITERRANEAN BAKERY
190 Norelco Dr, North York, ON, M9L 1S4
(416) 743-6634
Sales 27,655,200
SIC 2051 Bread, cake, and related products
 George Haddad

D-U-N-S 24-375-3436 (SL)
INKAS CORPORATION
3605 Weston Rd, North York, ON, M9L 1V7
(416) 645-8725
Emp Here 90 *Sales* 26,412,930
SIC 5411 Grocery stores
 David Khazanski

D-U-N-S 20-765-5804 (HQ)
INTERNATIONAL ELECTRONIC COMPO-NENTS INC
IEC
352 Signet Dr, North York, ON, M9L 1V2
(416) 293-2961
Emp Here 8 *Sales* 10,285,002
SIC 5065 Electronic parts and equipment, nec
 Shawn Stone

D-U-N-S 20-182-3937 (HQ)
JACOBS & THOMPSON INC
89 Kenhar Dr, North York, ON, M9L 2R3
(416) 749-0600
Emp Here 109 *Sales* 17,792,096
SIC 3053 Gaskets; packing and sealing de-vices
 Chris Brand

D-U-N-S 20-182-4026 (SL)
JETCO MANUFACTURING LIMITED
36 Milvan Dr, North York, ON, M9L 1Z4
(416) 741-1800
Emp Here 100 *Sales* 19,208,500
SIC 3498 Fabricated pipe and fittings
 Keith Alexander
 Gordon Verk
 Sam Gogas

D-U-N-S 20-187-8407 (SL)
JKL PROPERTIES LTD
32 Penn Dr, North York, ON, M9L 2A9
(416) 740-5671
Emp Here 50 *Sales* 10,619,850
SIC 8748 Business consulting, nec
 Jozef Budziak

D-U-N-S 20-182-4356 (SL)
L & M PRECISION PRODUCTS INC
(*Suby of* L & M SCREW MACHINE HOLD-INGS (1984) LIMITED)
150 Milvan Dr, North York, ON, M9L 1Z9
(416) 741-0700
Emp Here 61 *Sales* 11,717,185
SIC 3451 Screw machine products
 Thomas Liew
 Michael Birch

D-U-N-S 24-652-8558 (HQ)
LG ELECTRONICS CANADA, INC
(*Suby of* LG ELECTRONICS INC.)
20 Norelco Dr Suite, North York, ON, M9L 2X6
(647) 253-6300
Sales 145,061,750
SIC 5064 Electrical appliances, television and radio
 William Cho
 Young Chan Jun

D-U-N-S 24-401-3038 (SL)
LIMA'S GARDENS & CONSTRUCTION INC
116 Toryork Dr, North York, ON, M9L 1X6
(416) 740-9837
Emp Here 70 *Sales* 39,923,660
SIC 1542 Nonresidential construction, nec
 Virgil Lima

D-U-N-S 20-145-5672 (SL)
MACGREGORS MEAT & SEAFOOD LTD
265 Garyray Dr, North York, ON, M9L 1P2

(416) 749-5951
Emp Here 175 *Sales* 60,495,750
SIC 2011 Meat packing plants
 Duncan Macgregor, Sr
 Duncan Macgregor, Jr
 Ed Zervoudakis
 Dean Barger
 John Hercus
 Steve Saunders
 Paul Foster Von Kalben
 John Tarantello
 Jon Palmer
 John Anslow

D-U-N-S 20-565-2584 (SL)
MANUFACT LOGISTICS LTD
MVR CASH AND CARRY
3655 Weston Rd Suite 1, North York, ON, M9L 1V8
(416) 739-8411
Emp Here 90 *Sales* 40,245,660
SIC 5078 Refrigeration equipment and sup-plies
 Michael Commisso
 Robert Commisso
 Vincent Commisso

D-U-N-S 25-167-5088 (HQ)
METRIX READY MIX LTD
777 Fenmar Dr, North York, ON, M9L 1C8
(416) 746-4600
Sales 22,358,700
SIC 5032 Brick, stone, and related material
 Gino Della Fazia

D-U-N-S 20-704-7234 (HQ)
NAILOR INDUSTRIES INC
NAILOR INTERNATIONAL
98 Toryork Dr, North York, ON, M9L 1X6
(416) 744-3300
Sales 67,220,650
SIC 3822 Environmental controls
 Michael Nailor
 Scott Bork

D-U-N-S 20-312-1892 (SL)
NATURE'S VINE PRODUCE INC.
5601 Steeles Ave W Unit 11, North York, ON, M9L 1S7

Emp Here 40 *Sales* 33,423,080
SIC 5148 Fresh fruits and vegetables
 Steve Nalatesta

D-U-N-S 24-383-6033 (SL)
NONUTS BAKING CO INC
(*Suby of* FGF BRANDS INC)
1295 Ormont Dr, North York, ON, M9L 2W6
(905) 532-9517
Emp Here 25 *Sales* 54,106,418
SIC 2051 Bread, cake, and related products
 Sam Ajmera
 Ojus Ajmera
 Tejus Ajmera

D-U-N-S 20-182-5940 (SL)
NORWEST PRECISION LIMITED
460 Signet Dr, North York, ON, M9L 2T6
(416) 742-8082
Emp Here 56 *Sales* 10,756,760
SIC 3499 Fabricated Metal products, nec
 Savino Falcitelli
 Pasquale Falcitelli
 Philip Franco

D-U-N-S 24-555-8234 (SL)
P & P PROJECTS INC
233 Signet Dr Suite 1, North York, ON, M9L 1V3
(416) 398-6197
Emp Here 60 *Sales* 26,953,140
SIC 7389 Business services, nec
 Peter Chamberlain
 Peter Murdoch

D-U-N-S 25-372-2086 (SL)
PERFECT POULTRY INC
239 Toryork Dr, North York, ON, M9L 1Y2

(416) 656-9666
Emp Here 75 *Sales* 25,926,750
SIC 2011 Meat packing plants
 Danny Rother
 Ian Segal

D-U-N-S 25-107-9539 (SL)
PRECISION COMMUNICATION SERVICES CORP
TELMAR NETWORK TECHNOLOGY
99 Signet Dr Unit 200, North York, ON, M9L 1T6
(416) 749-0110
Emp Here 70 *Sales* 16,400,160
SIC 8748 Business consulting, nec
 Hartmut Liebel
 Arthur Smid

D-U-N-S 24-992-6312 (HQ)
PROFILE INDUSTRIES LIMITED
201 Garyray Dr, North York, ON, M9L 2T2
(416) 748-2505
Sales 55,666,250
SIC 2522 Office furniture, except wood
 Saul Feldberg

D-U-N-S 24-428-2930 (SL)
PWS ONTARIO LTD
155 Fenmar Dr, North York, ON, M9L 1M7
(416) 665-8377
Emp Here 40 *Sales* 10,285,240
SIC 4953 Refuse systems
 Carmine Petrilla

D-U-N-S 20-708-4406 (BR)
RCR INTERNATIONAL INC
89 Kenhar Dr, North York, ON, M9L 2R3
(416) 749-0600
Emp Here 100 *Sales* 463,590
SIC 3069 Fabricated rubber products, nec
 Ken Eaton

D-U-N-S 24-752-8565 (SL)
ROADSIDE PAVING LIMITED
125a Toryork Dr Suite A, North York, ON, M9L 1X9
(416) 740-3876
Emp Here 50 *Sales* 14,176,200
SIC 1611 Highway and street construction
 George Gallo

D-U-N-S 24-244-9663 (BR)
SATIN FINISH HARDWOOD FLOORING, LIMITED
15 Fenmar Dr, North York, ON, M9L 1L4
(416) 747-9924
Emp Here 130 *Sales* 273,308
SIC 2426 Hardwood dimension and flooring mills
 Gary Aukstakalnis

D-U-N-S 24-919-9589 (SL)
SENTREX COMMUNICATIONS INC
25 Milvan Dr, North York, ON, M9L 1Y8
(416) 749-7400
Emp Here 100 *Sales* 54,167,070
SIC 1731 Electrical work
 Peter Nicoletti

D-U-N-S 24-581-8823 (HQ)
SENTREX COMMUNICATIONS INC
25 Milvan Dr, North York, ON, M9L 1Y8
(416) 749-7400
Emp Here 95 *Sales* 39,209,220
SIC 1731 Electrical work
 Peter Nicoletti

D-U-N-S 24-853-3072 (HQ)
SHIFT RECYCLING INC
700 Ormont Dr, North York, ON, M9L 2V4
(416) 995-4202
Sales 38,269,200
SIC 4953 Refuse systems
 Gary Diamond
 Craig Miller

D-U-N-S 24-555-1981 (SL)
STATUM DESIGNS INC
180 Norelco Dr, North York, ON, M9L 1S4

(416) 740-4010
Emp Here 80   *Sales* 12,345,760
SIC 2512 Upholstered household furniture
Angelo Gallo
Pasquale Raviele

D-U-N-S 25-212-6883   (HQ)
TAI PAN VACATIONS INC
3668 Weston Rd Unit A, North York, ON, M9L 1W2
(416) 646-8828
Emp Here 20   *Sales* 113,371,640
SIC 4724 Travel agencies
Miranda Cheung

D-U-N-S 20-308-6665   (SL)
TALENT EMPLOYMENT INC
5601 Steeles Ave W Unit 5, North York, ON, M9L 1S7
(416) 748-3982
Emp Here 67   *Sales* 10,409,857
SIC 7361 Employment agencies
Maria Gemma Fuentes

D-U-N-S 20-353-5658   (SL)
TAM ELECTRIC LTD
456 Garyray Dr, North York, ON, M9L 1P7
(416) 743-6214
Emp Here 85   *Sales* 18,515,465
SIC 1731 Electrical work
Frank Talenti

D-U-N-S 24-391-0937   (HQ)
TASCO DISTRIBUTORS INC
TASCO APPLIANCES
84 Kenhar Dr, North York, ON, M9L 1N2
(416) 642-5600
Emp Here 22   *Sales* 16,268,210
SIC 5722 Household appliance stores
James Sayer

D-U-N-S 24-049-5234   (SL)
TRI-KRETE LIMITED
152 Toryork Dr, North York, ON, M9L 1X6
(416) 746-2479
Emp Here 57   *Sales* 13,305,795
SIC 3272 Concrete products, nec
Anthony Bombini
Marc Bombini
Adam Bombini

D-U-N-S 24-391-2842   (BR)
TRIUMPH GEAR SYSTEMS-TORONTO ULC
GENERAL GEAR
(*Suby of* TRIUMPH GROUP, INC.)
11 Fenmar Dr, North York, ON, M9L 1L5
(416) 743-4417
Emp Here 100
SIC 3089 Plastics products, nec
Garen Mikirditsian

D-U-N-S 24-845-3532   (HQ)
TRUE ROCK FINANCIAL INC
TRIMEN PACIFIC
1240 Ormont Dr, North York, ON, M9L 2V4
(905) 669-8333
Emp Here 100   *Sales* 22,200,100
SIC 3589 Service industry machinery, nec
Paul Cesario

D-U-N-S 24-045-4629   (SL)
TUFF CONTROL SYSTEMS LIMITED
5145 Steeles Ave W Suite 201, North York, ON, M9L 1R5

Emp Here 120   *Sales* 3,150,000
SIC 7381 Detective and armored car services
Michael Hearsum
Debi Bellis

D-U-N-S 24-092-0702   (SL)
TYSON TOOL COMPANY LIMITED
75 Ormont Dr, North York, ON, M9L 2S3
(416) 746-3688
Emp Here 23   *Sales* 10,925,598
SIC 5084 Industrial machinery and equipment
Peter Von Richter
Horst Von Richter

D-U-N-S 20-145-8619   (SL)
VAUGHAN METAL POLISHING LIMITED
206 Milvan Dr, North York, ON, M9L 1Z9
(416) 743-7500
Emp Here 60   *Sales* 11,525,100
SIC 3471 Plating and polishing
Tony Parisi

D-U-N-S 25-404-0926   (SL)
VEGFRESH INC
1290 Ormont Dr, North York, ON, M9L 2V4
(416) 667-0518
Emp Here 65   *Sales* 19,076,005
SIC 5461 Retail bakeries
Michael Sangiorgio

D-U-N-S 20-292-3491   (SL)
VIA-CON MASONRY INC
87 Irondale Dr Unit 100, North York, ON, M9L 2S6
(416) 745-0709
Emp Here 80   *Sales* 12,990,480
SIC 1741 Masonry and other stonework
Lino Vitorio

D-U-N-S 25-509-4047   (SL)
VISION COATERS CANADA LTD
73 Penn Dr, North York, ON, M9L 2A6
(416) 746-2988
Emp Here 60   *Sales* 14,771,160
SIC 1799 Special trade contractors, nec
Huucu Nguyen
Kamy Khan

D-U-N-S 20-067-9509   (HQ)
VITA COMMUNITY LIVING SERVICES OF TORONTO
VITA
4301 Weston Rd, North York, ON, M9L 2Y3
(416) 783-6227
Emp Here 2   *Sales* 474,738,330
SIC 8699 Membership organizations, nec
Dunja Monaghan
Brian Naraine

D-U-N-S 20-524-2915   (SL)
WAM INDUSTRIES LTD
(*Suby of* 1836826 ONTARIO INC)
375 Fenmar Dr, North York, ON, M9L 2X4
(416) 741-0660
Emp Here 65   *Sales* 10,030,930
SIC 2541 Wood partitions and fixtures
William Iannaci

D-U-N-S 25-220-0688   (HQ)
WEATHERCRAFT HOLDINGS LIMITED
230 Barmac Dr, North York, ON, M9L 2Z3
(416) 740-8020
Sales 65,791,620
SIC 6712 Bank holding companies
Charles Goldfinger
Ralph Goldfinger
Lorie Goldfinger
Howie Goldfinger
Regina Goldfinger

North York, ON M9M

D-U-N-S 20-327-7959   (BR)
2168587 ONTARIO LTD
UPPER CRUST
(*Suby of* 2168587 ONTARIO LTD)
50 Marmora St, North York, ON, M9M 2X5
(416) 661-7744
Emp Here 900
SIC 2053 Frozen bakery products, except bread
David Gelbloom

D-U-N-S 20-181-8887   (HQ)
ACCURATE MACHINE & TOOL LIMITED
1844 Wilson Ave, North York, ON, M9M 1A1
(416) 742-8301
Emp Here 50   *Sales* 14,403,938
SIC 3469 Metal stampings, nec

Peter Bodi

D-U-N-S 24-680-5972   (SL)
ALCAN PACKAGING CANADA LIMITED
130 Arrow Rd, North York, ON, M9M 2M1

Emp Here 100
SIC 2657 Folding paperboard boxes

D-U-N-S 25-117-5717   (SL)
ALLIED PLASTIC GROUP OF COMPANIES LTD
VICEROY RUBBER AND PLASTICS
707 Arrow Rd, North York, ON, M9M 2L4
(416) 749-7070
Emp Here 80   *Sales* 58,427,600
SIC 5162 Plastics materials and basic shapes
Todd Bruhm

D-U-N-S 20-552-4192   (HQ)
ARROW FURNITURE LTD
35 Arrow Rd, North York, ON, M9M 2L4
(416) 743-1530
Emp Here 37   *Sales* 15,106,195
SIC 5712 Furniture stores
Albert Michaels
Jeff Michaels
Jason Michaels
Debra Watson

D-U-N-S 25-828-4751   (SL)
BAKERY DELUXE COMPANY
50 Marmora St, North York, ON, M9M 2X5
(416) 746-1010
Emp Here 600   *Sales* 292,431,000
SIC 2051 Bread, cake, and related products
Boris Serebryany
Alex Garber

D-U-N-S 20-534-8758   (SL)
BEMIS FLEXIBLE PACKAGING CANADA LIMITED
BEMIS FLEXIBLE PACKAGING MILPRINT, DIV OF
130 Arrow Rd, North York, ON, M9M 2M1
(416) 742-8910
Emp Here 150   *Sales* 29,215,200
SIC 2657 Folding paperboard boxes
Stephane Bois
Chris Huband
Wayne Miller
James Tuck

D-U-N-S 20-967-8515   (SL)
CAMP FORMING LTD
105 Rivalda Rd, North York, ON, M9M 2M6
(416) 745-8680
Emp Here 140   *Sales* 34,647,620
SIC 1771 Concrete work
Jerry Campoli
Frank Campoli
Elmerinda Campoli

D-U-N-S 20-176-7050   (HQ)
CHARLES TENNANT & COMPANY (CANADA) LIMITED
CHARLES TENNANT & COMPANY
(*Suby of* TENNANTS CONSOLIDATED LIMITED)
34 Clayson Rd, North York, ON, M9M 2G8
(416) 741-9264
Emp Here 36   *Sales* 71,831,681
SIC 2869 Industrial organic chemicals, nec
Robert Macphail
Marcelo Ulloa
William Paul Alexander
Andrew Gingell

D-U-N-S 20-185-1214   (SL)
DANIELS, ETLIN
1850 Wilson Ave, North York, ON, M9M 1A1
(416) 741-7336
Emp Here 33   *Sales* 14,756,742
SIC 5063 Electrical apparatus and equipment
David Daniels

D-U-N-S 20-182-1956   (BR)
DOW CHEMICAL CANADA ULC

PACKAGING DIVISION
(*Suby of* DOW INC.)
122 Arrow Rd, North York, ON, M9M 2M1

Emp Here 200
SIC 3081 Unsupported plastics film and sheet

D-U-N-S 20-164-6817   (SL)
ETOBICOKE IRONWORKS LIMITED
141 Rivalda Rd, North York, ON, M9M 2M6
(416) 742-7111
Emp Here 83   *Sales* 15,943,055
SIC 3446 Architectural Metalwork
Ronald Chafee
Michael Whelan

D-U-N-S 24-621-2070   (HQ)
FIERA FOODS COMPANY
50 Marmora St, North York, ON, M9M 2X5
(416) 746-1010
Sales 584,862,000
SIC 2053 Frozen bakery products, except bread
Boris Serebryany
Alex Garber

D-U-N-S 25-180-3706   (SL)
GALATI SUPERMARKETS (FINCH) LIMITED
GALATI BROS SUPERMARKETS
2592 Finch Ave W, North York, ON, M9M 2G3

Emp Here 70   *Sales* 20,543,390
SIC 5411 Grocery stores
Anthony Galati
Frank Galati
Robert Galati
Frank Galati Jr

D-U-N-S 24-181-9473   (SL)
GENERAL SPRINKLERS INC
315 Deerhide Cres Suite 3, North York, ON, M9M 2Z2
(416) 748-1175
Emp Here 80   *Sales* 18,645,200
SIC 1711 Plumbing, heating, air-conditioning
Danny Palumbo
Stefan Starczewski
Emily Palumbo

D-U-N-S 20-411-0498   (SL)
GGP DRUGS LTD
SHOPPERS DRUG MART
2550 Finch Ave W Suite 854, North York, ON, M9M 2G3
(416) 749-5271
Emp Here 50   *Sales* 12,647,700
SIC 5912 Drug stores and proprietary stores
George G Philips

D-U-N-S 20-535-5733   (BR)
GOVERNMENT OF ONTARIO
LAWRENCE SQUARE EMPLOYMENT & SOCIAL SERVICES
(*Suby of* GOVERNMENT OF ONTARIO)
1860 Wilson Ave, North York, ON, M9M 3A7
(416) 392-6500
Emp Here 100
SIC 8399 Social services, nec
Peter Jag

D-U-N-S 20-172-3491   (SL)
GRAND NATIONAL APPAREL INC
GNA
(*Suby of* GNA OTIS HOLDINGS INC)
100 Marmora St Suite 3, North York, ON, M9M 2X5
(416) 746-3511
Emp Here 50   *Sales* 24,916,100
SIC 5136 Men's and boy's clothing
Jeffrey Louis Otis
Marita Anthony
Charles Cheung

D-U-N-S 20-171-2205   (SL)
H. B. MORNINGSTAR INDUSTRIES LIMITED
MORNINGSTAR

335 Clayson Rd, North York, ON, M9M 2H4
(416) 745-3547
Emp Here 30   Sales 14,250,780
SIC 5084 Industrial machinery and equipment
James Ross
Harriet Ross
Ron Cook
Dwight Fowler

D-U-N-S 24-478-2975   (HQ)
HARMAC TRANSPORTATION INC
(Suby of SEABOARD LIQUID CARRIERS LIMITED*)*
55 Arrow Rd, North York, ON, M9M 2L4
(416) 642-0515
Emp Here 100   Sales 45,726,488
SIC 4213 Trucking, except local
Joseph Shannon
Mark Shannon
Todd Stauffer

D-U-N-S 24-858-2087   (BR)
HOME DEPOT OF CANADA INC
IMPORT DISTRIBUTION CENTER
(Suby of THE HOME DEPOT INC*)*
2233 Sheppard Ave W, North York, ON, M9M 2Z7

Emp Here 110
SIC 5251 Hardware stores
Collin Burns

D-U-N-S 24-380-8974   (SL)
J&A CLEANING SOLUTIONS LTD
J + A CLEANING SOLUTIONS
785 Arrow Rd, North York, ON, M9M 2L4
(416) 242-4151
Emp Here 700   Sales 22,377,600
SIC 7349 Building maintenance services, nec
Spyros Kourkoutis
Terry Dellaportas

D-U-N-S 20-168-1699   (SL)
JOYCE FRUIT MARKETS LIMITED
28 Rivalda Rd Suite A, North York, ON, M9M 2M3
(416) 745-4411
Emp Here 21   Sales 17,547,117
SIC 5148 Fresh fruits and vegetables
Dominic Stillo

D-U-N-S 25-406-4116   (BR)
KIRCHHOFF AUTOMOTIVE CANADA INC
(Suby of KIRCHHOFF AUTOMOTIVE HOLD-ING GMBH & CO.KG*)*
114 Clayson Rd, North York, ON, M9M 2H2
(416) 740-2656
Emp Here 250
SIC 3469 Metal stampings, nec
Gaurav Paliwal

D-U-N-S 20-182-7037   (HQ)
KNOLL NORTH AMERICA CORP
(Suby of KNOLL, INC.*)*
1000 Arrow Rd, North York, ON, M9M 2Y7
(416) 741-5453
Emp Here 900   Sales 222,665,000
SIC 2521 Wood office furniture
Gary D Graham

D-U-N-S 24-596-7393   (SL)
MANEL CONTRACTING LTD
41 Rivalda Rd, North York, ON, M9M 2M4
(416) 635-0876
Emp Here 22   Sales 10,356,082
SIC 1542 Nonresidential construction, nec
Michelle Dipietro

D-U-N-S 24-783-5366   (SL)
MANOUCHER FINE FOODS INC
703 Clayson Rd, North York, ON, M9M 2H4
(416) 747-1234
Emp Here 50   Sales 11,242,750
SIC 2051 Bread, cake, and related products
Manoucher Etminan

D-U-N-S 25-188-2502   (SL)
MNM INC

2473 Finch Ave W, North York, ON, M9M 2G1
(416) 744-9675
Emp Here 49   Sales 11,611,530
SIC 7361 Employment agencies
Maher Elladki

D-U-N-S 24-744-8277   (HQ)
NEW HORIZONS CAR & TRUCK RENTALS LTD
DISCOUNT CAR & TRUCK RENTAL
720 Arrow Rd, North York, ON, M9M 2M1
(416) 744-0123
Sales 20,570,600
SIC 4212 Local trucking, without storage
Herb Singer
Rhoda Singer
Barry Singer

D-U-N-S 25-142-1749   (SL)
NORTH AMERICAN CLOTHING INC
22 Lido Rd, North York, ON, M9M 1M6
(416) 741-2626
Emp Here 80   Sales 39,865,760
SIC 5137 Women's and children's clothing
Munier Nasser

D-U-N-S 20-769-7173   (SL)
PRECISION ELECTRONICS CORPORA-TION
PRECISION ELECTRONIC COMPONENTS
70 Bartor Rd, North York, ON, M9M 2G5
(416) 744-8840
Emp Here 60   Sales 11,426,520
SIC 3679 Electronic components, nec
Rudi Both

D-U-N-S 24-314-5377   (SL)
PRIMO FOODS INC
(Suby of SUN-BRITE FOODS INC*)*
56 Huxley Rd, North York, ON, M9M 1H2
(416) 741-9300
Emp Here 115   Sales 39,754,350
SIC 2098 Macaroni and spaghetti
John Iacobelli
John Porco

D-U-N-S 25-320-8920   (BR)
PUROLATOR INC
(Suby of GOVERNMENT OF CANADA*)*
1100 Arrow Rd, North York, ON, M9M 2Z1
(416) 241-4496
Emp Here 250
SIC 4731 Freight transportation arrangement
Jason Key

D-U-N-S 25-405-4380   (SL)
REA INVESTMENTS LIMITED
VON CONSTRUCTION
70 Deerhide Cres, North York, ON, M9M 2Y6
(905) 264-6481
Emp Here 30   Sales 14,121,930
SIC 1542 Nonresidential construction, nec
Angelo Vona
Lucy Vona

D-U-N-S 24-363-5943   (SL)
SALB, H. INTERNATIONAL
49 Rivalda Rd, North York, ON, M9M 2M4
(416) 746-1944
Emp Here 115   Sales 57,307,030
SIC 5136 Men's and boy's clothing
Fatehali Mohammed

D-U-N-S 20-384-6287   (SL)
SALFLEX POLYMERS LTD
(Suby of CERBERUS CAPITAL MANAGE-MENT, L.P.*)*
1925 Wilson Ave, North York, ON, M9M 1A9
(416) 741-0273
Emp Here 45   Sales 12,449,700
SIC 2822 Synthetic rubber
Todd Sheppelman

D-U-N-S 20-175-7127   (HQ)
SOMERVILLE NATIONAL LEASING & RENTALS LTD
(Suby of SOMERVILLE, WILLIAM H. HOLD-INGS INC*)*

75 Arrow Rd, North York, ON, M9M 2L4
(416) 747-7576
Sales 16,998,000
SIC 7515 Passenger car leasing
William Somerville
Shawn Taylor
Brenden Somerville

D-U-N-S 20-299-5994   (SL)
SUPREME INTERNATIONAL CO. CANADA LTD
100 Marmora St Suite 3, North York, ON, M9M 2X5
(416) 746-3511
Emp Here 120   Sales 100,503,960
SIC 5136 Men's and boy's clothing
Jeff Otis

D-U-N-S 25-138-2966   (SL)
TORCAN LIFT EQUIPMENT LTD
115 Rivalda Rd, North York, ON, M9M 2M6
(416) 743-2500
Emp Here 40   Sales 11,686,760
SIC 7353 Heavy construction equipment rental
Joe Picao

D-U-N-S 24-850-5331   (SL)
TRADEX INTERNATIONAL CORP
809 Arrow Rd, North York, ON, M9M 2L4

Emp Here 30   Sales 11,745,060
SIC 6799 Investors, nec
John Georgantopoulos
Anthony Diamond

D-U-N-S 25-361-4549   (BR)
UNIVAR CANADA LTD
UNIVAR SOLUTIONS CANADA
(Suby of UNIVAR INC.*)*
64 Arrow Rd, North York, ON, M9M 2L9
(416) 740-5300
Emp Here 200
SIC 5169 Chemicals and allied products, nec
Dave Hazell

D-U-N-S 20-108-1416   (SL)
VISIONS PERSONNEL SERVICES INC
VPS
2300 Finch Ave W Unit 30, North York, ON, M9M 2Y3
(416) 740-3319
Emp Here 120   Sales 14,973,120
SIC 8741 Management services
Frank Principe

D-U-N-S 20-384-0017   (SL)
WALTER'S SHOE CARE INC
180 Bartor Rd, North York, ON, M9M 2W6
(416) 782-4492
Emp Here 54   Sales 17,611,344
SIC 3999 Manufacturing industries, nec
Timothy D Walter

North York, ON M9N

D-U-N-S 20-178-3602   (SL)
1909203 ONTARIO INC
35 Oak St, North York, ON, M9N 1A1
(416) 245-7991
Emp Here 325   Sales 91,947,375
SIC 3646 Commercial lighting fixtures
William Wiener
Sonia Rowan

D-U-N-S 24-991-9804   (SL)
2931621 CANADA INC
CANADIAN TIRE ASSOCIATE STORE
2625b Weston Rd, North York, ON, M9N 3W1
(416) 247-2196
Emp Here 100   Sales 62,928,000
SIC 5531 Auto and home supply stores
Larry Mcfadden

D-U-N-S 24-995-8794   (BR)

BEST BUY CANADA LTD
(Suby of BEST BUY CO., INC.*)*
2625a Weston Rd, North York, ON, M9N 3V8
(416) 242-6162
Emp Here 80
SIC 5731 Radio, television, and electronic stores
Al Shea

D-U-N-S 25-797-3719   (SL)
CRUICKSHANK FORD
2062 Weston Rd, North York, ON, M9N 1X5
(416) 244-6461
Emp Here 70   Sales 44,049,600
SIC 5511 New and used car dealers
Lou Crovskr

D-U-N-S 20-530-0379   (HQ)
LEON'S FURNITURE LIMITED
LEON'S
45 Gordon Mackay Rd, North York, ON, M9N 3X3
(416) 243-7880
Emp Here 110   Sales 1,699,238
SIC 5712 Furniture stores
Edward Florian Leon
Terrence Leon
Mark Joseph Leon
Dominic Scarangella
Joseph Michael Leon
Peter B Eby
Alan J Lenczner
Mary Ann Leon
Frank Gagliano
Constantine Pefanis

D-U-N-S 25-221-2089   (BR)
LEON'S FURNITURE LIMITED
(Suby of LEON'S FURNITURE LIMITED*)*
10 Suntract Rd, North York, ON, M9N 3N9

Emp Here 160
SIC 5712 Furniture stores
Naeem Zaidi

D-U-N-S 25-310-9169   (BR)
MCDONALD'S RESTAURANTS OF CANADA LIMITED
MCDONALD'S RESTAURANT
(Suby of MCDONALD'S CORPORATION*)*
2625f Weston Rd, North York, ON, M9N 3X2
(416) 241-5505
Emp Here 85
SIC 5812 Eating places
Cathrian Guiar

D-U-N-S 25-318-2174   (BR)
MCDONALD'S RESTAURANTS OF CANADA LIMITED
2080613 ONTARIO INC
(Suby of MCDONALD'S CORPORATION*)*
2020 Jane St, North York, ON, M9N 2V3
(416) 248-6648
Emp Here 110
SIC 5812 Eating places
Julie Thurgood

D-U-N-S 20-644-4296   (SL)
SHEPEHERD GROUP, THE
140 Wendell Ave Suite 9, North York, ON, M9N 3R2
(416) 249-1700
Emp Here 15   Sales 15,523,215
SIC 6331 Fire, marine, and casualty insurance
Neil Shepeherd

D-U-N-S 20-376-9315   (SL)
VISCOR INC
35 Oak St, North York, ON, M9N 1A1
(416) 245-7991
Emp Here 325   Sales 91,947,375
SIC 3646 Commercial lighting fixtures
William Wiener

Northbrook, ON K0H

D-U-N-S 20-699-6568   (BR)
EXTENDICARE (CANADA) INC
PARAMED HOME HEALTH CARE
(*Suby of* EXTENDICARE INC)
124 Lloyd St Rr 1, Northbrook, ON, K0H 2G0
(613) 336-9120
Emp Here 87
SIC 8051 Skilled nursing care facilities
  Bonnie George

Norwich, ON N0J

D-U-N-S 24-302-5368   (SL)
DE JONG, WM ENTERPRISES INC
DE JONG ENTERPRISES
773451 59 Hwy Rr 3, Norwich, ON, N0J 1P0
(519) 424-9007
Emp Here 75   *Sales* 11,114,400
SIC 4213 Trucking, except local
  William (Bill) De Jong
  Scott De Jong
  Marge De Jong

D-U-N-S 20-322-4837   (BR)
SAF-HOLLAND CANADA LIMITED
(*Suby of* SAF-HOLLAND SA)
20 Phoebe St, Norwich, ON, N0J 1P0
(519) 863-3414
Emp Here 92
SIC 3714 Motor vehicle parts and accessories
  Kim Baechler

Norwood, ON K0L

D-U-N-S 20-134-0106   (SL)
STEWART, J. J. MOTORS LIMITED
2239 8 Line, Norwood, ON, K0L 2V0
(705) 639-5383
Emp Here 28   *Sales* 13,946,184
SIC 5521 Used car dealers
  John Stewart

Oakville, ON L6H

D-U-N-S 20-770-0043   (SL)
1057206 ONTARIO LTD
MERRIAM SCHOOL OF MUSIC, THE
2359 Bristol Cir, Oakville, ON, L6H 6P8

Emp Here 100   *Sales* 16,042,600
SIC 8299 Schools and educational services,
nec
  Alan Merriam

D-U-N-S 20-014-4496   (SL)
1161396 ONTARIO INC
S & M ENTERPRISES
2965 Bristol Cir Bldg C, Oakville, ON, L6H 6P9
(905) 829-2229
Emp Here 70   *Sales* 58,490,390
SIC 5145 Confectionery
  Sam Singh

D-U-N-S 24-593-9629   (HQ)
1491222 ONTARIO LTD
PETRO CANADA
450 Dundas St E, Oakville, ON, L6H 7L4
(905) 257-5185
Emp Here 5   *Sales* 24,903,900
SIC 5541 Gasoline service stations
  Emad Mahmoud

D-U-N-S 24-423-4303   (SL)
ALGONQUIN POWER SERVICES CANADA INC
(*Suby of* ALGONQUIN POWER FUND (CANADA) INC)

2845 Bristol Cir, Oakville, ON, L6H 6X5
(905) 465-4500
Emp Here 65   *Sales* 44,191,810
SIC 4911 Electric services
  Ian Robertson

D-U-N-S 24-422-1045   (HQ)
ALIAXIS NORTH AMERICA INC
(*Suby of* ALIAXIS)
1425 North Service Rd E Suite 3, Oakville,
ON, L6H 1A7
(289) 881-0120
Emp Here 100
SIC 6712 Bank holding companies
  Gerard Goyette
  Bernard Lecrocq

D-U-N-S 24-389-5310   (BR)
ALPHORA RESEARCH INC
(*Suby of* ALPHORA RESEARCH INC)
2884 Portland Dr, Oakville, ON, L6H 5W8
(905) 829-9704
Emp Here 80
SIC 8731 Commercial physical research
  Charmaine Fernandes

D-U-N-S 20-065-3459   (HQ)
AMEC FOSTER WHEELER INC
WOOD GROUP
(*Suby of* JOHN WOOD GROUP P.L.C.)
2020 Winston Park Dr Suite 700, Oakville, ON,
L6H 6X7
(905) 829-5400
Emp Here 535   *Sales* 1,937,197,700
SIC 6719 Holding companies, nec
  Grant Ling

D-U-N-S 20-012-0751   (BR)
AMEC FOSTER WHEELER INC
AMEC EC SERVICES
(*Suby of* JOHN WOOD GROUP P.L.C.)
2020 Winston Park Dr Suite 700, Oakville, ON,
L6H 6X7
(905) 829-5400
Emp Here 350
SIC 8711 Engineering services
  Rob Walton

D-U-N-S 20-385-8980   (SL)
ANI PHARMACEUTICALS CANADA INC
(*Suby of* ANI PHARMACEUTICALS, INC.)
400 Iroquois Shore Rd, Oakville, ON, L6H
1M5
(905) 337-4500
Emp Here 100   *Sales* 28,402,100
SIC 2834 Pharmaceutical preparations
  Stephen Carey
  Arthur Przybal
  Robert Schrepfer

D-U-N-S 20-821-8586   (HQ)
ASL DISTRIBUTION SERVICES LIMITED
2160 Buckingham Rd, Oakville, ON, L6H 6M7
(905) 829-5141
Emp Here 140   *Sales* 30,855,900
SIC 4225 General warehousing and storage
  Cole Dolny
  Michael St Louis

D-U-N-S 20-180-4507   (HQ)
ATC-FROST MAGNETICS INC
(*Suby of* STANDEX INTERNATIONAL CORPORATION)
1130 Eighth Line, Oakville, ON, L6H 2R4
(905) 844-6681
Emp Here 34   *Sales* 79,216,200
SIC 3677 Electronic coils and transformers
  Rick Sherrill

D-U-N-S 20-159-4645   (SL)
ATLAS SERVICE COMPANY INC
ATLAS AIR CONDITIONING
2590 Bristol Cir Unit 1, Oakville, ON, L6H 6Z7
(905) 279-3440
Emp Here 60   *Sales* 13,983,900
SIC 1711 Plumbing, heating, air-conditioning
  Roger Grochmal

D-U-N-S 20-410-0028   (SL)
ATLAS VAN LINES (CANADA) LTD
ATLAS CANADA
(*Suby of* ATLAS WORLD GROUP, INC.)
485 North Service Rd E, Oakville, ON, L6H
1A5
(905) 844-0701
Emp Here 97   *Sales* 64,688,524
SIC 4731 Freight transportation arrangement
  Barry Schellenberg
  Shirley C Sveda
  Paul Leader
  Camille Edwards

D-U-N-S 20-159-6111   (SL)
BARD CANADA INC
(*Suby of* BECTON, DICKINSON AND COMPANY)
2715 Bristol Cir Unit 1, Oakville, ON, L6H 6X5
(289) 291-8000
Emp Here 130   *Sales* 29,547,570
SIC 3841 Surgical and medical instruments
  Peter Curry

D-U-N-S 20-041-1924   (SL)
BECTON DICKINSON CANADA INC
B D
2771 Bristol Cir, Oakville, ON, L6H 6R5

Emp Here 200
SIC 5047 Medical and hospital equipment

D-U-N-S 24-823-2696   (HQ)
BIO PED FRANCHISING INC
BIO PED FOOT CARE CENTRE
2150 Winston Park Dr Unit 21, Oakville, ON,
L6H 5V1
(905) 829-0505
Emp Here 12   *Sales* 29,266,020
SIC 6794 Patent owners and lessors
  Robin Scheien

D-U-N-S 20-220-9578   (SL)
BRAR CAPITAL CORP
ENTRIPY CUSTOM CLOTHING
2320 Bristol Cir Unit 3, Oakville, ON, L6H 5S3
(905) 844-1291
Emp Here 150   *Sales* 24,604,050
SIC 2759 Commercial printing, nec
  Jasvinder Brar

D-U-N-S 20-162-1018   (HQ)
C. & J. CLARK CANADA LIMITED
(*Suby of* C&J CLARK LIMITED)
2881 Brighton Rd, Oakville, ON, L6H 6C9
(905) 829-1825
Sales 12,458,050
SIC 5139 Footwear
  George Molyneux

D-U-N-S 25-598-5509   (HQ)
CABLE CONTROL SYSTEMS INC
2800 Coventry Rd, Oakville, ON, L6H 6R1
(905) 829-9910
Sales 24,618,600
SIC 1799 Special trade contractors, nec
  Mike Rauseo

D-U-N-S 24-424-1936   (SL)
CANADA LOYAL FINANCIAL LIMITED
2866 Portland Dr, Oakville, ON, L6H 5W8
(905) 829-5514
Emp Here 60   *Sales* 110,799,540
SIC 6311 Life insurance
  Lawrence Fuller
  Debra Fuller

D-U-N-S 25-264-8258   (HQ)
CANADA LOYAL INSURANCE AGENCY LIMITED
CANADA LOYAL FINANCIAL
2866 Portland Dr, Oakville, ON, L6H 5W8
(905) 829-5514
Emp Here 20   *Sales* 25,441,800
SIC 6411 Insurance agents, brokers, and service
  Lawrence Fuller
  Ken Sterling

  Debra Fuller
  Mona Mann
  Matthew Fuller

D-U-N-S 24-099-2693   (HQ)
CANADIAN HOSPITAL SPECIALTIES LIMITED
2810 Coventry Rd, Oakville, ON, L6H 6R1
(905) 825-9300
Emp Here 25   *Sales* 160,605,600
SIC 5047 Medical and hospital equipment
  Michael Canzoneri
  Gary Enns
  Walter Stothers

D-U-N-S 20-000-3499   (SL)
CHARTWELL CLASSIC OAKVILLE
180 Oak Park Blvd Suite 221, Oakville, ON,
L6H 0A6
(905) 257-0095
Emp Here 49   *Sales* 11,412,639
SIC 6513 Apartment building operators
  Brew Archer

D-U-N-S 20-715-3917   (SL)
CHEUNG, ARTHUR PHARMACY LIMITED
SHOPPERS DRUG MART
240 Leighland Ave, Oakville, ON, L6H 3H6
(905) 842-3730
Emp Here 40   *Sales* 10,118,160
SIC 5912 Drug stores and proprietary stores
  Arthur Cheung

D-U-N-S 20-022-4645   (HQ)
CIPHER PHARMACEUTICALS INC
209 Oak Park Blvd Suite 501, Oakville, ON,
L6H 0M2
(905) 602-5840
Sales 22,749,000
SIC 2834 Pharmaceutical preparations
  Robert D. Tessarolo
  Chris Watters
  Diane Gajewczyk
  Michael Milloy
  Nadine Jutlah
  Mark Beaudet
  Arthur Deboeck
  Christian Godin
  John Mull
  Harold Wolkin

D-U-N-S 24-284-4520   (HQ)
CLARION CANADA INC
(*Suby of* HITACHI, LTD.)
2239 Winston Park Dr, Oakville, ON, L6H 5R1
(905) 829-4600
Emp Here 30   *Sales* 13,415,220
SIC 5064 Electrical appliances, television and
radio
  Philip Albanese
  Hiro Murakami

D-U-N-S 25-819-2814   (HQ)
COLOPLAST CANADA CORPORATION
(*Suby of* COLOPLAST A/S)
2401 Bristol Cir Suite 205a, Oakville, ON, L6H
6P1
(877) 820-7008
Sales 23,700,222
SIC 5047 Medical and hospital equipment
  Michael Alderman

D-U-N-S 20-964-9987   (HQ)
COMMISSIONAIRES (GREAT LAKES)
2947 Portland Dr, Oakville, ON, L6H 5S4
(416) 364-4496
Sales 427,113,400
SIC 7381 Detective and armored car services
  Tom Prins
  Jerry Zhang
  Jan Kwasniewski
  Paul Costello
  Dave Gordon
  Ben Alexander
  Arthur Serales

D-U-N-S 20-053-1564   (SL)
COOPER CONSTRUCTION LIMITED

2381 Bristol Cir Suite C-200, Oakville, ON,
L6H 5S9
(905) 829-0444
Emp Here 30   *Sales* 14,121,930
SIC 1542 Nonresidential construction, nec
William P Cooper
Kenneth A Nevar
Donald Gordon
John Goldspink

D-U-N-S 24-609-6440   (SL)
COORDINATE INDUSTRIES LTD
2251 Winston Park Dr, Oakville, ON, L6H 5R1
(905) 829-0099
Emp Here 105   *Sales* 23,503,515
SIC 3728 Aircraft parts and equipment, nec
Marinko Saric

D-U-N-S 25-512-5379   (HQ)
CORNERSTONE LOGISTICS LP
(*Suby of* TFI INTERNATIONAL INC)
2180 Buckingham Rd Suite 204, Oakville, ON,
L6H 6H1
(905) 339-1456
Emp Here 30   *Sales* 53,351,360
SIC 4731 Freight transportation arrangement
James S. Clark
Gregory W. Rumble
Chantal Martel
Josiane M. Langlois

D-U-N-S 20-535-9359   (HQ)
CTL CORP
(*Suby of* INDUSTRIELLE ALLIANCE, AS-
SURANCE ET SERVICES FINANCIERS INC)
1660 North Service Rd E Suite 102, Oakville,
ON, L6H 7G3
(905) 815-9510
Emp Here 45   *Sales* 13,436,460
SIC 6159 Miscellaneous business credit insti-
tutions
Sean O'brien
Amelie Cantin
Douglas A. Carrothers
Denis Ricard
Normand Pepin
Michel St-Francois
Gerald Bouwers
Edmee Metivier
Jeffrey Newhouse

D-U-N-S 20-408-9742   (HQ)
DAVIS CONTROLS LIMITED
2200 Bristol Cir, Oakville, ON, L6H 5R3
(905) 829-2000
Emp Here 35   *Sales* 19,001,040
SIC 5084 Industrial machinery and equipment
Neil Montgomery

D-U-N-S 25-068-7886   (HQ)
DECOR & MORE INC
1171 Invicta Dr, Oakville, ON, L6H 4M1
(905) 844-1300
Sales 29,199,235
SIC 7389 Business services, nec
Leslee Bell
Kimberley Renkin Mcgibbon

D-U-N-S 20-145-4030   (HQ)
DOALL CANADA INC
DGI SUPPLY
(*Suby of* DOALL COMPANY)
2715 Bristol Cir, Oakville, ON, L6H 6X5
(800) 923-6255
Emp Here 70   *Sales* 65,843,550
SIC 5085 Industrial supplies
Michael Wilkie
Jon Henricks
Jim Hobbs
David Crawford
William Henricks

D-U-N-S 24-265-7008   (SL)
ECO TABS CANADA INC
2429 Lamoka Crt, Oakville, ON, L6H 5Z7
(888) 732-6822
Emp Here 24   *Sales* 11,400,624

SIC 5084 Industrial machinery and equipment
Casparus Groenewald

D-U-N-S 20-164-4416   (SL)
ELLIOTT-MATSUURA CANADA INC
(*Suby of* MATSUURA MACHINERY CORPO-
RATION)
2120 Buckingham Rd, Oakville, ON, L6H 5X2
(905) 829-2211
Emp Here 70   *Sales* 34,141,100
SIC 5084 Industrial machinery and equipment
Frank Haydar

D-U-N-S 20-107-8974   (SL)
EVAULT CANADA INC
(*Suby of* CARBONITE, INC.)
2315 Bristol Cir Unit 200, Oakville, ON, L6H
6P8
(905) 287-2600
Emp Here 100   *Sales* 14,418,200
SIC 7371 Custom computer programming ser-
vices
Terry Cunningham

D-U-N-S 24-525-8280   (SL)
EXCEL-TECH LTD
XLTEK
(*Suby of* NATUS MEDICAL INCORPO-
RATED)
2568 Bristol Cir, Oakville, ON, L6H 5S1
(905) 829-5300
Emp Here 145   *Sales* 39,783,650
SIC 3841 Surgical and medical instruments
Mokbel Sayed
James Hawkins
Steven Murphy
Ron Kurtz

D-U-N-S 20-530-9776   (HQ)
**FAIRVIEW FITTINGS & MANUFACTURING
LIMITED**
1170 Invicta Dr Unit C, Oakville, ON, L6H 6G1
(905) 338-0800
Sales 92,008,800
SIC 5074 Plumbing and heating equipment
and supplies (hydronics)
Leslie Woodward
Keith C Woodward
Jeffrey Woodward
James Forbes

D-U-N-S 20-377-9657   (SL)
FAIRVIEW LTD
1170 Invicta Dr Unit C, Oakville, ON, L6H 6G1
(905) 338-0800
Emp Here 160   *Sales* 37,905,100
SIC 5085 Industrial supplies
Leslie Woodward
Jeffrey Woodward
Robin Pittaway
Kyle Pittaway

D-U-N-S 20-393-1399   (SL)
FAIRVIEW LTD
1170 Invicta Dr Unit C, Oakville, ON, L6H 6G1
(905) 338-0800
Emp Here 140   *Sales* 64,406,160
SIC 5074 Plumbing and heating equipment
and supplies (hydronics)
Leslie Woodward
Kyle Pittaway

D-U-N-S 24-372-8446   (HQ)
FENGATE CORPORATION
2275 Upper Middle Road East Suite 700,
Oakville, ON, L6H 0C3
(289) 288-3822
Emp Here 2   *Sales* 27,335,000
SIC 6712 Bank holding companies
Louis Serafina Jr
Chris Mihailobich

D-U-N-S 25-507-9618   (HQ)
FOURMARK MANUFACTURING INC
2690 Plymouth Dr, Oakville, ON, L6H 6W3
(905) 855-8777
Emp Here 63   *Sales* 12,867,498
SIC 3089 Plastics products, nec

Adam Cruickshank

D-U-N-S 20-966-4858   (HQ)
**GENWORTH FINANCIAL MORTGAGE IN-
SURANCE COMPANY CANADA**
*GENWORTH MORTGAGE INSURANCE
CANADA*
(*Suby of* GENWORTH FINANCIAL, INC.)
2060 Winston Park Dr Suite 300, Oakville, ON,
L6H 5R7
(905) 287-5300
Emp Here 275   *Sales* 587,666,200
SIC 6351 Surety insurance
Brian Hurley
Philip Mayers

D-U-N-S 24-676-3721   (HQ)
GENWORTH MI CANADA INC
(*Suby of* GENWORTH FINANCIAL, INC.)
2060 Winston Park Dr Suite 300, Oakville, ON,
L6H 5R7
(905) 287-5300
Emp Here 203   *Sales* 243,633,607
SIC 6351 Surety insurance
Stuart Levings
Philip Mayers
Debbie Mcpherson
Winsor Macdonell
Craig Sweeney
Mary-Jo Hewat
Michel Cubric
Brian Hurley
Sidney Horn
Andrea Bolger

D-U-N-S 25-145-5945   (HQ)
GEOTAB INC
2440 Winston Park Dr, Oakville, ON, L6H 7V2
(416) 434-4309
Emp Here 19   *Sales* 68,592,500
SIC 3812 Search and navigation equipment
Neil Cawse
Clive Cawse
Dario Murkovic

D-U-N-S 20-719-2092   (SL)
**GLAXOSMITHKLINE CONSUMER HEALTH-
CARE INC**
(*Suby of* GLAXOSMITHKLINE PLC)
2030 Bristol Cir, Oakville, ON, L6H 0H2
(800) 387-7374
Emp Here 150   *Sales* 61,923,150
SIC 5122 Drugs, proprietaries, and sundries
Jennifer Denomme
Diane Williams
Diane Daniel
W. E. Morris
Karen Scollick

D-U-N-S 20-181-9950   (BR)
GLAXOSMITHKLINE INC
(*Suby of* GLAXOSMITHKLINE PLC)
2030 Bristol Cir, Oakville, ON, L6H 0H2

Emp Here 150
SIC 2834 Pharmaceutical preparations
Diane Daniel

D-U-N-S 24-320-3761   (SL)
GOLDEN CROWN FOODS INC
1154 Ballantry Rd, Oakville, ON, L6H 5M9
(905) 334-9178
Emp Here 100   *Sales* 15,536,349
SIC 5146 Fish and seafoods
Bruce Macdonald

D-U-N-S 24-784-3964   (HQ)
GRUNDFOS CANADA INC
(*Suby of* POUL DUE JENSENS FOND)
2941 Brighton Rd, Oakville, ON, L6H 6C9
(905) 829-9533
Sales 42,752,340
SIC 5084 Industrial machinery and equipment
Simon Feddema
Lewis Parps
Rayhan Yoususzai
Grace D'addio

D-U-N-S 25-511-0751   (HQ)
GVA LIGHTING, INC
2771 Bristol Cir, Oakville, ON, L6H 6X5
(905) 569-6044
Sales 19,044,200
SIC 3646 Commercial lighting fixtures
Vladimir Grigorik

D-U-N-S 20-351-6984   (BR)
HALTON DISTRICT SCHOOL BOARD
WHITE OAKS SECONDARY SCHOOL
(*Suby of* HALTON DISTRICT SCHOOL
BOARD)
1330 Montclair Dr, Oakville, ON, L6H 1Z5
(905) 845-5200
Emp Here 200
SIC 8211 Elementary and secondary schools
John Stieva

D-U-N-S 20-289-1128   (BR)
HALTON DISTRICT SCHOOL BOARD
IROQUOIS RIDGE SECONDARY SCHOOL
(*Suby of* HALTON DISTRICT SCHOOL
BOARD)
1123 Glenashton Dr, Oakville, ON, L6H 5M1
(905) 845-0012
Emp Here 100
SIC 8211 Elementary and secondary schools
Darlene White

D-U-N-S 20-336-8949   (BR)
HATCH LTD
(*Suby of* HATCHCOS HOLDINGS LTD)
2265 Upper Middle Rd E Suite 300, Oakville,
ON, L6H 0G5
(905) 855-7600
Emp Here 200
SIC 8711 Engineering services

D-U-N-S 24-596-2261   (SL)
**HAYWARD POOL PRODUCTS CANADA,
INC**
(*Suby of* HAYWARD INDUSTRIES, INC.)
2880 Plymouth Dr, Oakville, ON, L6H 5R4
(905) 829-2880
Emp Here 55   *Sales* 17,937,480
SIC 3949 Sporting and athletic goods, nec
Robert Davis
Francine Neilson
Oscar Davis

D-U-N-S 20-026-3478   (SL)
HIP RESTAURANTS LTD
1011 Upper Middle Rd E Suite C3, Oakville,
ON, L6H 5Z9
(647) 403-2494
Emp Here 100   *Sales* 4,287,300
SIC 5812 Eating places
Brian Meikle
Mike Wilson

D-U-N-S 25-514-2895   (BR)
HOME DEPOT OF CANADA INC
HOME DEPOT
(*Suby of* THE HOME DEPOT INC)
2555 Bristol Cir, Oakville, ON, L6H 5W9
(905) 829-5900
Emp Here 250
SIC 5251 Hardware stores
Ronald Potvin

D-U-N-S 25-504-1766   (HQ)
HUB INTERNATIONAL ONTARIO LIMITED
(*Suby of* HELLMAN & FRIEDMAN LLC)
2265 Upper Middle Rd E Suite 700, Oakville,
ON, L6H 0G5
(905) 847-5500
Emp Here 100   *Sales* 474,610,400
SIC 6411 Insurance agents, brokers, and ser-
vice
Dennis J Pauls
Sharlene Locke
Marianne Paine
Jim Mahood
Kirk James

D-U-N-S 25-301-1852   (BR)

HUDSON'S BAY COMPANY
BAY, THE
(*Suby of* HUDSON'S BAY COMPANY)
240 Leighland Ave, Oakville, ON, L6H 3H6
(905) 842-4811
Emp Here 150
SIC 5311 Department stores
Stacey Sutherland

D-U-N-S 24-626-9385   (SL)
IMPACT XM INC
(*Suby of* IMPACT UNLIMITED, INC.)
1303 North Service Rd E Unit 1, Oakville, ON,
L6H 1A7
(905) 287-4862
Emp Here 80   *Sales* 42,828,160
SIC 5046 Commercial equipment, nec
Jared Pollacco
Charles Pollacco

D-U-N-S 24-194-9890   (HQ)
INDEKA IMPORTS LTD
INDEKA GROUP, THE
2120 Bristol Cir, Oakville, ON, L6H 5R3
(905) 829-3000
Sales 39,865,760
SIC 5139 Footwear
Kamal Sharma
Inder Sharma

D-U-N-S 25-284-9778   (SL)
INTEGRA CANADA ULC
2590 Bristol Cir Unit 1, Oakville, ON, L6H 6Z7
(905) 618-1603
Emp Here 35   *Sales* 15,651,090
SIC 5047 Medical and hospital equipment
Barbara Mansfield

D-U-N-S 24-141-4598   (SL)
KAVCO SALES LTD
CANADIAN TIRE ASSOCIATE STORE
2510 Hyde Park Gate, Oakville, ON, L6H 6M2
(905) 829-5552
Emp Here 90   *Sales* 32,779,350
SIC 5014 Tires and tubes
Mike Kavanagh

D-U-N-S 24-249-3943   (SL)
KEG RESTAURANTS LTD
KEG STEAKHOUSE & BAR, THE
300 Hays Blvd, Oakville, ON, L6H 7P3
(905) 257-2700
Emp Here 90   *Sales* 4,096,710
SIC 5812 Eating places
Al Lynn

D-U-N-S 20-645-8205   (BR)
KINARK CHILD AND FAMILY SERVICES
CHILD AND FAMILY BENEFITS SERVICES
(*Suby of* KINARK CHILD AND FAMILY SER-
VICES)
475 Iroquois Shore Rd, Oakville, ON, L6H
1M3
(905) 844-4110
Emp Here 250
SIC 8322 Individual and family services
Cathy Paul

D-U-N-S 24-862-9339   (HQ)
KOZMA'S MANUFACTURING CO. LTD
K. TOOL & DIE
2751 Plymouth Dr, Oakville, ON, L6H 5R5
(905) 829-3660
Emp Here 60   *Sales* 13,445,950
SIC 3469 Metal stampings, nec
Andrew Kozma Sr
Andrew Kozma Jr

D-U-N-S 20-585-2697   (SL)
**LABOURERS' PENSION FUND OF CEN-
TRAL AND EASTERN CANADA**
1315 North Service Rd E, Oakville, ON, L6H
1A7
(289) 291-3663
Emp Here 35   *Sales* 43,239,630
SIC 6371 Pension, health, and welfare funds
Joseph Mancinelli
Carmen Principato

David D'agostini
Douglas Serroul
Patrick Little
Durval Terceira
Luigi Carrozzi
Manuel Bastos

D-U-N-S 20-169-2381   (HQ)
LEVITT-SAFETY LIMITED
NL TECHNOLOGIES, DIV OF
2872 Bristol Cir, Oakville, ON, L6H 5T5
(905) 829-3668
Emp Here 75   *Sales* 208,590,000
SIC 5099 Durable goods, nec
Bruce Levitt
Tim Dillon
Fraser Gibson
Stephen Haley
Trudy Mcdonald
Heidi Levitt
Giselle Branget
Catherine Macdonald

D-U-N-S 24-383-8823   (BR)
LOBLAWS INC
REAL CANADIAN SUPERSTORE
(*Suby of* LOBLAW COMPANIES LIMITED)
201 Oak Park Blvd Suite 1024, Oakville, ON,
L6H 7T4
(905) 257-9330
Emp Here 100
SIC 5411 Grocery stores
Robert Trotter

D-U-N-S 25-724-5548   (HQ)
LOGIHEDRON INC
2320 Bristol Cir Unit 1, Oakville, ON, L6H 5S3
(905) 823-5767
Emp Here 60   *Sales* 16,459,920
SIC 8741 Management services
Farshogar (Fred) Jasavala

D-U-N-S 24-389-6073   (BR)
LONGO BROTHERS FRUIT MARKETS INC
LONGO'S OAKVILLE FRUIT MARKET
(*Suby of* LONGO BROTHERS FRUIT MAR-
KETS INC)
338 Dundas St E, Oakville, ON, L6H 6Z9
(905) 257-5633
Emp Here 230
SIC 5431 Fruit and vegetable markets
Tony Indovina

D-U-N-S 24-758-0491   (SL)
MAGNUM 2000 INC
1137 North Service Rd E, Oakville, ON, L6H
1A7
(905) 339-1104
Emp Here 65   *Sales* 18,414,500
SIC 7539 Automotive repair shops, nec
Joseph Skupnik
Mary Skupnik
Michael Vella

D-U-N-S 24-319-5927   (HQ)
**MCFADDEN'S HARDWOOD & HARDWARE
INC**
*PANNEAUX ET QUINCAILLERIE MCFAD-
DENS*
(*Suby of* ADOLF WURTH GMBH & CO. KG)
2323 Winston Park Dr Suite 1, Oakville, ON,
L6H 6R7
(416) 674-3333
Emp Here 35   *Sales* 48,764,664
SIC 5072 Hardware
John Stafford
Christoph Lange
Robert Stolz

D-U-N-S 25-204-0480   (HQ)
MDG COMPUTERS CANADA INC
2940 Bristol Cir, Oakville, ON, L6H 6G4
(905) 829-3538
Emp Here 40   *Sales* 267,676,000
SIC 5045 Computers, peripherals, and soft-
ware
Goran Varaklic

Brian Monette

D-U-N-S 25-311-9689   (BR)
METRO ONTARIO INC
METRO
(*Suby of* METRO INC)
1011 Upper Middle Rd E Suite 412, Oakville,
ON, L6H 5Z9
(905) 849-4911
Emp Here 250
SIC 5411 Grocery stores
Suzanne Zybura-Finck

D-U-N-S 24-199-3591   (HQ)
MIELZYNSKI, PETER AGENCIES LIMITED
PMA CANADA
(*Suby of* WILLIAM GRANT & SONS GROUP
LIMITED)
231 Oak Park Blvd Suite 400, Oakville, ON,
L6H 7S8
(905) 257-2116
Emp Here 40   *Sales* 117,254,620
SIC 5182 Wine and distilled beverages
Peter Mielzynski Jr
Ian Bergman
Josh Mitchell
Randy Dionisi
John Torella
Walter Perchal
John Donohue
Ron Wall
Jonathan Yusen
Steven Nathan

D-U-N-S 20-731-2299   (HQ)
MOEN INC
(*Suby of* FORTUNE BRANDS HOME & SE-
CURITY, INC.)
2816 Bristol Cir, Oakville, ON, L6H 5S7
(905) 829-3400
Emp Here 120   *Sales* 64,406,160
SIC 5074 Plumbing and heating equipment
and supplies (hydronics)
Michael J Dennis
John Hammill

D-U-N-S 24-795-1015   (SL)
MUIR TAPES & ADHESIVES LTD
2815 Bristol Cir, Oakville, ON, L6H 6X5
(905) 820-6847
Emp Here 32   *Sales* 15,200,832
SIC 5085 Industrial supplies
Graham Muir Jr

D-U-N-S 24-737-9183   (HQ)
NATIONAL CELLULAR INC
2679 Bristol Cir Suite 8, Oakville, ON, L6H
6Z8
(905) 828-9200
Emp Here 1   *Sales* 22,478,176
SIC 5999 Miscellaneous retail stores, nec
William Folland

D-U-N-S 20-752-3937   (HQ)
NAYLOR GROUP INCORPORATED
455 North Service Rd E, Oakville, ON, L6H
1A5
(905) 338-8000
Emp Here 100   *Sales* 73,128,960
SIC 1711 Plumbing, heating, air-conditioning
Thomas Hitchman
Patricia Lowes
Greg Hitchman
Lauren Hitchman

D-U-N-S 24-684-0438   (HQ)
NEXEO SOLUTIONS CANADA CORP
(*Suby of* UNIVAR INC.)
2450 Bristol Cir, Oakville, ON, L6H 6P6
(800) 387-2376
Sales 100,831,800
SIC 5169 Chemicals and allied products, nec
David Bradley
Stephen Bowater

D-U-N-S 20-558-1544   (SL)
NI-MET METALS INC
2939 Portland Dr Suite 300, Oakville, ON, L6H

5S4
(289) 291-1111
Emp Here 18   *Sales* 91,511,596
SIC 5093 Scrap and waste materials
Anil Shah
Rutvij Shah
Parag Modi

D-U-N-S 20-292-0190   (SL)
NORTHRIDGE LONGTERM CARE CENTER
496 Postridge Dr, Oakville, ON, L6H 7A2
(905) 257-9882
Emp Here 78   *Sales* 5,035,680
SIC 8059 Nursing and personal care, nec
Marilyn Henry

D-U-N-S 20-357-5548   (HQ)
NUCLEUS INDEPENDENT LIVING
3030 Bristol Cir Suite 110, Oakville, ON, L6H
0H2
(905) 829-0555
Emp Here 120   *Sales* 8,199,120
SIC 8051 Skilled nursing care facilities
Beverly Lohn

D-U-N-S 24-352-8465   (BR)
OTTO BOCK HEALTHCARE CANADA LTD
(*Suby of* NADER HOLDING GMBH & CO.
KG)
2897 Brighton Rd, Oakville, ON, L6H 6C9

Emp Here 87
SIC 5047 Medical and hospital equipment
Mark Agro

D-U-N-S 20-322-1544   (HQ)
PCL CONSTRUCTORS CANADA INC
(*Suby of* PCL EMPLOYEES HOLDINGS LTD)
2201 Bristol Cir Suite 500, Oakville, ON, L6H
0J8
(905) 276-7600
Emp Here 500   *Sales* 2,793,568,000
SIC 1542 Nonresidential construction, nec
Chris Gower
Robert Martz
Todd Craigen
Bruce Sonnenberg
Kelly Wallace
Kevi Skinner
Frank Bison

D-U-N-S 24-320-8290   (HQ)
PELMOREX CORP
2655 Bristol Cir, Oakville, ON, L6H 7W1
(905) 829-1159
Emp Here 6   *Sales* 80,909,396
SIC 8999 Services, nec
Sam Sebastian
Pierre L Morrissette
Tawnie Mcnabb
R. Kelly Shaughnessy
Carlos Astorqui

D-U-N-S 24-847-1542   (HQ)
**PELMOREX WEATHER NETWORKS (TELE-
VISION) INC**
WEATHER NETWORK, THE
(*Suby of* PELMOREX CORP)
2655 Bristol Cir, Oakville, ON, L6H 7W1
(905) 829-1159
Emp Here 117   *Sales* 42,952,736
SIC 4833 Television broadcasting stations
Pierre Morrissette
Carlos Astorqui
Bala Gopalakrishnan
Tawnie Mcnabb
Maureen Rogers
Roy Bliss
Geoff Browne
John Dionne
Francis Fox
R. Kelly Shaughnessy

D-U-N-S 20-301-9229   (SL)
PELMOREX WEATHER NETWORKS INC
(*Suby of* PELMOREX CORP)
2655 Bristol Cir, Oakville, ON, L6H 7W1

▲ Public Company   ■ Public Company Family Member   **HQ** Headquarters   **BR** Branch   **SL** Single Location

(905) 829-1159
Emp Here 200   *Sales* 45,694,400
SIC 4833 Television broadcasting stations
Pierre Morrissette
Tawnie Mcnabb

D-U-N-S 25-799-6884   (SL)
PING CANADA CORPORATION
PING CANADA
(*Suby of* KARSTEN MANUFACTURING CORPORATION)
2790 Brighton Rd, Oakville, ON, L6H 5T4
(905) 829-8004
Emp Here 30   *Sales* 15,616,260
SIC 5091 Sporting and recreation goods
Doug Hawken
Dave Wilson

D-U-N-S 24-327-4458   (BR)
PINTY'S DELICIOUS FOODS INC
(*Suby of* OLYMEL S.E.C.)
2714 Bristol Cir, Oakville, ON, L6H 6A1
(905) 829-1130
Emp Here 100
SIC 2015 Poultry slaughtering and processing
Laura Cowan

D-U-N-S 24-664-5899   (SL)
POLYWHEELS MANUFACTURING LTD
1455 North Service Rd E, Oakville, ON, L6H 1A7

Emp Here 300
SIC 3089 Plastics products, nec

D-U-N-S 24-403-0946   (HQ)
PROAX TECHNOLOGIES LTD
2552 Bristol Cir, Oakville, ON, L6H 5S1
(905) 829-2006
Emp Here 25   *Sales* 45,127,470
SIC 5084 Industrial machinery and equipment
Stephen Murray Daub
Theresa Daub

D-U-N-S 24-580-3247   (SL)
PROMATION ENGINEERING LTD
2767 Brighton Rd, Oakville, ON, L6H 6J4
(905) 625-6093
Emp Here 91   *Sales* 20,202,091
SIC 3569 General industrial machinery, nec
Mark Zimny

D-U-N-S 20-705-9049   (HQ)
RALEIGH CANADA LIMITED
(*Suby of* DERBY INTERNATIONAL CORPORATION SA)
2124 London Lane, Oakville, ON, L6H 5V8
(905) 829-5555
Sales 93,072,000
SIC 3751 Motorcycles, bicycles and parts
Farid Vaiya
Edmond Cuthbert
Kenneth Morrison
Adrian Marples
Allan Finden-Croft

D-U-N-S 20-251-2737   (BR)
RICHARDSON INTERNATIONAL LIMITED
RICHARDSON OILSEED EASTERN CANADA
(*Suby of* RICHARDSON, JAMES & SONS, LIMITED)
2835 Bristol Cir, Oakville, ON, L6H 6X5
(905) 829-2942
Emp Here 100
SIC 2079 Edible fats and oils
Eric Murphy

D-U-N-S 24-745-0638   (SL)
ROBERTS, DAVID FOOD CORPORATION
2351 Upper Middle Rd E, Oakville, ON, L6H 6P7
(905) 502-7700
Emp Here 50   *Sales* 41,778,850
SIC 5145 Confectionery
Robert Di Lella
Richard Di Lella
David Abrams

Ronald Merlocco

D-U-N-S 20-342-2134   (SL)
RUTMET INC
2939 Portland Dr Suite 300, Oakville, ON, L6H 5S4
(289) 291-1111
Emp Here 20   *Sales* 93,273,350
SIC 5093 Scrap and waste materials
Anil Shah
Parag Modi
Rudvij Shah

D-U-N-S 24-383-0036   (SL)
SCHWAB TRADING INC
2391 Central Park Dr Unit 608, Oakville, ON, L6H 0E4
(905) 827-6298
Emp Here 3   *Sales* 15,242,740
SIC 6799 Investors, nec
Julio Schwab
Pablo Schwab

D-U-N-S 20-922-3395   (HQ)
SHERIDAN COLLEGE INSTITUTE OF TECHNOLOGY AND ADVANCED LEARNING
1430 Trafalgar Rd, Oakville, ON, L6H 2L1
(905) 845-9430
Emp Here 850   *Sales* 89,207,100
SIC 8222 Junior colleges
Janet Morrison
Wayne Steffler

D-U-N-S 25-192-3587   (HQ)
SHRED-IT INTERNATIONAL ULC
(*Suby of* STERICYCLE, INC.)
1383 North Service Rd E, Oakville, ON, L6H 1A7
(905) 829-2794
Emp Here 700   *Sales* 915,243,000
SIC 7389 Business services, nec
Vincent De Palma
Brenda Frank
Gary Gonsalves
Robert Guice
Colette Raymond
James Rudyk
David Samuel

D-U-N-S 20-234-2051   (HQ)
SIEMENS CANADA LIMITED
SIEMENS NETWORK OF CARING
(*Suby of* SIEMENS AG)
1577 North Service Rd E, Oakville, ON, L6H 0H6
(905) 465-8000
Emp Here 300   *Sales* 1,357,992,000
SIC 3625 Relays and industrial controls
Faisal Kazi
Bo Ouyang

D-U-N-S 20-345-2917   (HQ)
SIEMENS GAMESA RENEWABLE ENERGY LIMITED
(*Suby of* SIEMENS GAMESA RENEWABLE ENERGY SOCIEDAD ANONIMA)
1577 North Service Rd E 4th Fl, Oakville, ON, L6H 0H6
(905) 465-8000
Emp Here 50   *Sales* 191,378,250
SIC 3511 Turbines and turbine generator sets
David Hickey
Muhammad Kamran Aslam

D-U-N-S 24-372-8495   (SL)
SIEMENS HEALTHCARE DIAGNOSTICS LTD
HEALTHCARE DIAGNOSTIC SECTOR
1577 North Service Rd E 2fl, Oakville, ON, L6H 0H6
(905) 564-7333
Emp Here 225   *Sales* 51,140,025
SIC 3841 Surgical and medical instruments
Jim Graziadei
Lisa Pauli

D-U-N-S 24-951-3235   (SL)

D-U-N-S 24-**SIGMA-ALDRICH CANADA CO.**
(*Suby of* MERCK KG AUF AKTIEN)
2149 Winston Park Dr, Oakville, ON, L6H 6J8
(905) 829-9500
Emp Here 70   *Sales* 47,054,840
SIC 5169 Chemicals and allied products, nec
Jean-Christophe Gaumier

D-U-N-S 24-953-5915   (HQ)
SMC PNEUMATICS (CANADA) LTD
(*Suby of* SMC CORPORATION)
2715 Bristol Cir Suite 2, Oakville, ON, L6H 6X5
(905) 812-0400
Emp Here 150   *Sales* 121,932,500
SIC 5084 Industrial machinery and equipment
Dave Armstrong
Yoshiki Takada

D-U-N-S 24-389-5419   (BR)
SNC-LAVALIN INTERNATIONAL INC
SLII
(*Suby of* GROUPE SNC-LAVALIN INC)
2275 Upper Middle Rd E, Oakville, ON, L6H 0C3
(905) 829-8808
Emp Here 250
SIC 8711 Engineering services
Harikrishna Bhavsar

D-U-N-S 20-715-6365   (HQ)
STRONE CORPORATION
2717 Coventry Rd, Oakville, ON, L6H 5V9
(905) 829-2766
Emp Here 5   *Sales* 34,466,040
SIC 1799 Special trade contractors, nec
Roy Blinco
Steve Blinco
Neil Blinco

D-U-N-S 25-243-5193   (HQ)
SYSTEMES WESTCON CANADA (WCSI) INC, LES
(*Suby of* SYNNEX CORPORATION)
1383 Joshuas Creek Dr, Oakville, ON, L6H 7G4
(888) 307-7218
Emp Here 31   *Sales* 31,913,585
SIC 5065 Electronic parts and equipment, nec
Siobhan Byron
Andrew Warren
Kevin Brzezinski
Gino Cotignola
Jay Denton
Mary Ellen O'brien
Matt Karst
Mike Kilduff
Melissa Davis

D-U-N-S 24-384-0670   (SL)
TARRISON PRODUCTS LTD
2780 Coventry Rd, Oakville, ON, L6H 6R1
(905) 825-9665
Emp Here 24   *Sales* 10,732,176
SIC 5046 Commercial equipment, nec
James Witt
Barbara Furlong

D-U-N-S 24-320-1823   (SL)
THEA PHARMA INC
LABTICIAN THEA
(*Suby of* THEA HOLDING)
2150 Winston Park Dr Unit 4, Oakville, ON, L6H 5V1
(905) 829-5283
Emp Here 23   *Sales* 10,285,002
SIC 5048 Ophthalmic goods
Mark Smithyes

D-U-N-S 20-042-1464   (SL)
TORONTO ROCK LACROSSE INC
1132 Invicta Dr, Oakville, ON, L6H 6G1
(416) 596-3075
Emp Here 50   *Sales* 21,186,500
SIC 7941 Sports clubs, managers, and promoters
Brad Waters

D-U-N-S 20-372-7941   (SL)
TRIPAR TRANSPORTATION LP
(*Suby of* TFI INTERNATIONAL INC)
2180 Buckingham Rd, Oakville, ON, L6H 6H1
(905) 829-8500
Emp Here 23   *Sales* 11,959,241
SIC 4731 Freight transportation arrangement

D-U-N-S 25-474-1572   (SL)
ULTIMATE TRAVEL GROUP INC
ULTIMATE GOLF VACATIONS
1660 North Service Rd E Suite 101, Oakville, ON, L6H 7G3
(905) 755-0999
Emp Here 21   *Sales* 10,919,307
SIC 4725 Tour operators
Ron Dawick

D-U-N-S 25-534-3022   (SL)
VIROX TECHNOLOGIES INC
2770 Coventry Rd, Oakville, ON, L6H 6R1
(905) 813-0110
Emp Here 100   *Sales* 27,666,000
SIC 2842 Polishes and sanitation goods
Randall Pilon
Martin Harry

D-U-N-S 25-498-3349   (BR)
WAL-MART CANADA CORP
(*Suby of* WALMART INC.)
234 Hays Blvd, Oakville, ON, L6H 6M4
(905) 257-5740
Emp Here 200
SIC 5311 Department stores
Randy Powers

D-U-N-S 25-108-6799   (SL)
WELLSPRING PHARMACEUTICAL CANADA CORP
(*Suby of* WELLSPRING PHARMACEUTICAL CORPORATION)
400 Iroquois Shore Rd, Oakville, ON, L6H 1M5
(905) 337-4500
Emp Here 120   *Sales* 34,082,520
SIC 2834 Pharmaceutical preparations
Wendy Shusko
Robert Vukovich
Matt Griffitsh

D-U-N-S 24-860-1411   (HQ)
WIELAND ELECTRIC INC
(*Suby of* WIELAND HOLDING GMBH)
2889 Brighton Rd, Oakville, ON, L6H 6C9
(905) 829-8414
Sales 15,651,090
SIC 5063 Electrical apparatus and equipment
Alex Hadjiharalambous
Hana Radomil

D-U-N-S 25-221-2576   (BR)
WINNERS MERCHANTS INTERNATIONAL L.P.
WINNERS
(*Suby of* THE TJX COMPANIES INC)
2460 Winston Churchill Blvd Suite 1, Oakville, ON, L6H 6J5
(905) 829-9086
Emp Here 100
SIC 5651 Family clothing stores
Steve Boyack

D-U-N-S 25-362-6642   (HQ)
WOOD CANADA LIMITED
AMEC EARTH & ENVIRONMENTAL, DIV OF
(*Suby of* JOHN WOOD GROUP P.L.C.)
2020 Winston Park Dr Suite 700, Oakville, ON, L6H 6X7
(905) 829-5400
Emp Here 450   *Sales* 807,861,600
SIC 8741 Management services
Gregory R Gerrish
Steven Toevs
Thomas Grell
Duane E. Gingrich
Brian H. Lamb

D-U-N-S 20-850-7269   (HQ)

WW CANADA LTD
(*Suby of* WEIGHT WATCHERS INTERNA-
TIONAL, INC.)
1415 Joshuas Creek Dr Unit 200, Oakville,
ON, L6H 7G4
(800) 387-8227
Emp Here 120   *Sales* 429,997,248
SIC 8099 Health and allied services, nec
 A Majid Mangalji
 Frereed Mangalji
 Moez Mangalji

   D-U-N-S 25-049-9035   (HQ)
XCG CONSULTING LIMITED
(*Suby of* XCG HOLDINGS INC)
2620 Bristol Cir Suite 300, Oakville, ON, L6H
6Z7
(905) 829-8880
Emp Here 25   *Sales* 17,744,300
SIC 8748 Business consulting, nec
 George Zukovs
 Michael Hulley
 Stephen Nutt

Oakville, ON L6J

   D-U-N-S 20-383-5298   (BR)
673753 ONTARIO LIMITED
TRAFFIX
(*Suby of* 673753 ONTARIO LIMITED)
104-610 Chartwell Rd, Oakville, ON, L6J 4A5
(905) 875-0708
Emp Here 80
SIC 4731 Freight transportation arrangement
 Chuck Snow

   D-U-N-S 20-792-1615   (SL)
81918 ONTARIO LTD
KEVIN'S NO FRILLS
125 Cross Ave Suite 1, Oakville, ON, L6J 2W8
(905) 844-7493
Emp Here 49   *Sales* 13,433,448
SIC 5411 Grocery stores
 Kevin Jesty

   D-U-N-S 24-192-1647   (SL)
A HIGH RISK
349 Davis Rd, Oakville, ON, L6J 2X2
(905) 845-5252
Emp Here 18   *Sales* 10,438,632
SIC 6411 Insurance agents, brokers, and ser-
vice
 Jeffrey Powell

   D-U-N-S 24-368-5679   (SL)
ACI BRANDS INC
(*Suby of* GORAIEB HOLDINGS INC)
2616 Sheridan Garden Dr, Oakville, ON, L6J
7Z2
(905) 829-1566
Emp Here 160   *Sales* 80,262,283
SIC 5137 Women's and children's clothing
 John A Goraieb
 Jeffrey G Goraieb
 Jeffrey Berk
 Paul Eldridge
 John Philp

   D-U-N-S 25-333-5616   (HQ)
ALGONQUIN POWER & UTILITIES CORP
354 Davis Rd, Oakville, ON, L6J 2X1
(905) 465-4500
Sales 1,647,387,000
SIC 6712 Bank holding companies
 Ian E. Robertson
 Kenneth Moore
 Christopher K. Jarratt
 Melissa S. Barnes
 Masheed Saidi
 D. Randy Laney
 George L. Steeves
 Dilek Samil
 Christopher J. Ball
 David Bronicheski

   D-U-N-S 20-528-1400   (HQ)
ALGONQUIN POWER SYSTEMS INC
354 Davis Rd, Oakville, ON, L6J 0C5
(905) 465-4500
Emp Here 50   *Sales* 135,974,800
SIC 4911 Electric services
 Ian Robertson

   D-U-N-S 24-336-1909   (SL)
BTI BLUETOOTH TECHNOLOGIES INC
169 Robinson St, Oakville, ON, L6J 5W7

Emp Here 34   *Sales* 15,203,916
SIC 5065 Electronic parts and equipment, nec
 Anthony Ramsaroop

   D-U-N-S 24-469-2018   (SL)
BURNSTEIN, DR. & ASSOCIATES
CHISHOLM CENTRE
1484 Cornwall Rd, Oakville, ON, L6J 7W5
(905) 844-3240
Emp Here 63   *Sales* 10,106,838
SIC 8299 Schools and educational services,
nec
 Howard A Bernstein
 Jo-Anne Bernstein
 Jarvis Sheraton

   D-U-N-S 25-464-9718   (SL)
CAMBRIAN SOLUTIONS INC
(*Suby of* CAMBRIAN INVESTMENTS INC)
627 Lyons Lane Suite 300, Oakville, ON, L6J
5Z7
(905) 338-3172
Emp Here 42   *Sales* 30,674,490
SIC 5169 Chemicals and allied products, nec
 Peter Jobling

   D-U-N-S 25-833-4747   (SL)
CANFIN CAPITAL GROUP INC
2829 Sherwood Heights Dr Suite 102,
Oakville, ON, L6J 7R7
(905) 829-0020
Emp Here 60   *Sales* 16,459,920
SIC 8741 Management services
 Tony Mahabir

   D-U-N-S 25-302-3501   (HQ)
CARPEDIA GROUP INTERNATIONAL INC
75 Navy St, Oakville, ON, L6J 2Z1
(905) 337-3407
Sales 18,650,600
SIC 8742 Management consulting services
 Peter C Follows
 Gregoire M Trembay
 Mark Follows

   D-U-N-S 24-112-7112   (SL)
**CENTRAL TECHNOLOGY SERVICES COR-
PORATION**
CENTRAL TECHNOLOGY SERVICES
1400 Cornwall Rd Unit 5, Oakville, ON, L6J
7W5
(905) 829-9480
Emp Here 10   *Sales* 54,487,160
SIC 7377 Computer rental and leasing
 Mark Liptok
 Dan O'neil
 Bryce Anger

   D-U-N-S 20-327-3149   (HQ)
**DANA HOSPITALITY LIMITED PARTNER-
SHIP**
(*Suby of* FULCRUM CAPITAL PARTNERS
INC)
2898 South Sheridan Way Suite 200, Oakville,
ON, L6J 7L5
(905) 829-0292
Emp Here 10   *Sales* 77,172,485
SIC 5812 Eating places
 Juri Daniel
 Ralph Mann
 Gary D'andrea
 Ross Munro
 Jim Greenway
 Jackie Taylor

   D-U-N-S 24-538-0555   (SL)

DIRECT EQUIPMENT LTD
1363 Cornwall Rd, Oakville, ON, L6J 7T5
(905) 844-7831
Emp Here 30   *Sales* 14,250,780
SIC 5082 Construction and mining machinery
 Richard Garland

   D-U-N-S 24-523-8337   (SL)
ESCAPE PROOF INC
*ESCAPE PROOF QUALITY INSPECTION
SERVICES*
1496 Durham St, Oakville, ON, L6J 2P3
(289) 837-0813
Emp Here 50   *Sales* 10,131,450
SIC 7549 Automotive services, nec
 Peter Rankin
 Waeil Mohammed

   D-U-N-S 20-699-6295   (BR)
EXTENDICARE INC
*WYNDHAM MANOR LONG-TERM CARE
CENTRE*
(*Suby of* EXTENDICARE INC)
291 Reynolds St Suite 128, Oakville, ON, L6J
3L5
(905) 849-7766
Emp Here 200
SIC 8051 Skilled nursing care facilities
 Stephanie Zajczenko-Opdam

   D-U-N-S 25-687-9347   (SL)
FIELDPOINT SERVICE APPLICATIONS INC
2660 Sherwood Heights Dr Suite 103,
Oakville, ON, L6J 7Y8
(905) 855-2111
Emp Here 30   *Sales* 13,415,220
SIC 5045 Computers, peripherals, and soft-
ware
 Richard Smart
 Philip Smart

   D-U-N-S 25-539-1559   (HQ)
**FIRST CANADIAN TITLE COMPANY LIM-
ITED**
FCT
(*Suby of* FIRST AMERICAN FINANCIAL
CORPORATION)
2235 Sheridan Garden Dr Suite 745, Oakville,
ON, L6J 7Y5
(905) 287-1000
Emp Here 300   *Sales* 1,282,180,800
SIC 6361 Title insurance
 Michael Leblanc
 Gary Finkelstein
 Jennifer Ashton

   D-U-N-S 20-733-0957   (BR)
**FIRST CANADIAN TITLE COMPANY LIM-
ITED**
FIRST CANADIAN TITLE
(*Suby of* FIRST AMERICAN FINANCIAL
CORPORATION)
2235 Sheridan Garden Dr Suite 745, Oakville,
ON, L6J 7Y5
(800) 307-0370
Emp Here 500
SIC 6361 Title insurance
 Tom Gifferdy

   D-U-N-S 20-134-2466   (HQ)
FORD CREDIT CANADA LIMITED
(*Suby of* FORD MOTOR COMPANY)
The Canadian Rd, Oakville, ON, L6J 5C7
(905) 845-2511
Emp Here 27   *Sales* 283,895,790
SIC 6141 Personal credit institutions
 Charles Bilyeu
 John Noone
 Mark Mueller
 Norman Stewart
 Paul Pandos
 Michael Herniak
 Paul Micallef

   D-U-N-S 20-134-2458   (HQ)
**FORD MOTOR COMPANY OF CANADA,
LIMITED**

(*Suby of* FORD MOTOR COMPANY)
1 Canadian Rd, Oakville, ON, L6J 5E4
(905) 845-2511
Emp Here 424   *Sales* 3,839,220,000
SIC 3711 Motor vehicles and car bodies
 Mark Fields
 William Clay Ford
 James Jr Farley
 John Fleming
 Joseph Hinrichs
 Stephen Odell
 Robert Shanks
 Raymond Day
 Felicia Fields
 Raj Nair

   D-U-N-S 24-357-1978   (HQ)
GIYANI METALS CORP
277 Lakeshore Rd E Suite 403, Oakville, ON,
L6J 6J3
(289) 837-0066
Sales 11,671,750
SIC 1061 Ferroalloy ores, except vanadium
 Robin Birchall
 Wajd Boubou
 Aamer Siddiqui
 Jonathan Henry
 Michael Jones
 John Petersen

   D-U-N-S 20-134-2664   (SL)
GLENLEVEN MOTORS LIMITED
GLENLEVEN CHRYSLER
2388 Royal Windsor Dr, Oakville, ON, L6J 7Y2
(905) 845-7575
Emp Here 96   *Sales* 14,942,340
SIC 5511 New and used car dealers
 Eli Faerge
 Gail Guimond

   D-U-N-S 25-154-5133   (SL)
GLOBAL POINT DESIGN INC
2861 Sherwood Heights Dr Unit 27, Oakville,
ON, L6J 7K1
(905) 829-4424
Emp Here 80   *Sales* 29,137,200
SIC 5013 Motor vehicle supplies and new
parts
 John Hoff
 Christopher Mccaig
 Jeff Channell

   D-U-N-S 25-165-3010   (BR)
HALTON DISTRICT SCHOOL BOARD
OAKVILLE TRAFALGAR HIGH SCHOOL
(*Suby of* HALTON DISTRICT SCHOOL
BOARD)
1460 Devon Rd, Oakville, ON, L6J 3L6
(905) 845-2875
Emp Here 91
SIC 8211 Elementary and secondary schools
 Meena Sahi

   D-U-N-S 20-107-1268   (BR)
HOME DEPOT OF CANADA INC
HOME DEPOT
(*Suby of* THE HOME DEPOT INC)
99 Cross Ave, Oakville, ON, L6J 2W7
(905) 815-5000
Emp Here 170
SIC 5251 Hardware stores
 Paul Rex

   D-U-N-S 20-408-1848   (HQ)
IAN MARTIN LIMITED
(*Suby of* MARTIN, IAN TECHNOLOGY
STAFFING LIMITED)
610 Chartwell Rd Suite 101, Oakville, ON, L6J
4A5
(905) 815-1600
Emp Here 60   *Sales* 152,456,000
SIC 7361 Employment agencies
 William Masson
 Robert G. Witterick
 Ratnasingham Singaratnam

   D-U-N-S 24-764-9650   (HQ)

JOANNE FABRICS INC
JF FABRICS
2610 Sheridan Garden Dr, Oakville, ON, L6J 7Z4
(905) 491-3900
Emp Here 10   *Sales* 54,439,645
SIC 5131 Piece goods and notions
Bjarne Hovesen
Donald Cranstoun
Randall Strachan
Shelley Hovesen
Kimberly Krasa

D-U-N-S 24-203-6973   (SL)
KNOWLEDGE MANAGEMENT INNOVATIONS LTD
KNOWLEDGE MANAGEMENT INNOVATIONS
(*Suby of* MSDSONLINE INC.)
586 Argus Rd Suite 201, Oakville, ON, L6J 3J3
(416) 410-4817
Emp Here 39   *Sales* 17,439,786
SIC 5045 Computers, peripherals, and software
Matthew Airhart
Laura Murphy

D-U-N-S 24-251-8053   (SL)
LANDMARK CANADA
2902 South Sheridan Way Suite 10, Oakville, ON, L6J 7L6
(905) 829-5511
Emp Here 25   *Sales* 21,201,500
SIC 6411 Insurance agents, brokers, and service
Gerald Weiner

D-U-N-S 24-525-3120   (SL)
LINKMAX PAPER LTD
2904 South Sheridan Way Suite 303, Oakville, ON, L6J 7L7
(905) 829-0053
Emp Here 12   *Sales* 25,239,007
SIC 5111 Printing and writing paper
Gregory Kuang Lin
Ze Yun Fun
Ao Chen

D-U-N-S 24-407-1564   (SL)
M.E POWELL INSURANCE BROKERS LTD
349 Davis Rd, Oakville, ON, L6J 2X2
(905) 844-3629
Emp Here 40   *Sales* 33,922,400
SIC 6411 Insurance agents, brokers, and service
David Powell

D-U-N-S 25-191-7357   (HQ)
MAGNES GROUP INC, THE
PSA INSURANCE SERVICES, DIV OF
1540 Cornwall Rd Suite 100, Oakville, ON, L6J 7W5
(905) 845-9793
Sales 166,296,780
SIC 6411 Insurance agents, brokers, and service
Donald Vince
Milena Manolas
Belinda Bryce
Paul Hamilton
Jeffrey Bryce
Allison Bryce
Andy Sloan
Roben Stuart

D-U-N-S 24-333-1415   (BR)
MAPLE LEAF FOODS INC
MAPLE LEAF FRESH FOODS
(*Suby of* MAPLE LEAF FOODS INC)
178 South Service Rd E, Oakville, ON, L6J 0A5
(905) 815-6500
Emp Here 200
SIC 5141 Groceries, general line
Andrew Neugebauer

D-U-N-S 25-938-9849   (SL)

MAREK HOSPITALITY INC
(*Suby of* FULCRUM CAPITAL PARTNERS INC)
2898 South Sheridan Way Unit 200, Oakville, ON, L6J 7L5
(905) 829-0292
Emp Here 300   *Sales* 13,991,700
SIC 5812 Eating places
Juri Daniel
John Philp
Lindsay Wilson

D-U-N-S 24-333-8618   (HQ)
MARTIN, IAN TECHNOLOGY STAFFING LIMITED
610 Chartwell Rd Suite 101, Oakville, ON, L6J 4A5
(905) 815-1600
Sales 182,754,500
SIC 6712 Bank holding companies
B William Masson
Ratnasingham Singaratnam

D-U-N-S 24-198-2388   (SL)
MCDONALD, D. SALES & MERCHANDISING LIMITED
MCDONALD SALES MERCHAND
2861 Sherwood Heights Dr Unit 28, Oakville, ON, L6J 7K1
(905) 855-8550
Emp Here 50   *Sales* 22,174,500
SIC 7389 Business services, nec
Jennifer Tulloch

D-U-N-S 20-902-9560   (SL)
MEDIA RESOURCES INC
(*Suby of* MEDIA RESOURCES INTERNATIONAL INC)
1387 Cornwall Rd, Oakville, ON, L6J 7T5
(905) 337-0993
Emp Here 180   *Sales* 58,704,480
SIC 3993 Signs and advertising specialties
Jefferson Rushton

D-U-N-S 24-829-2575   (HQ)
MEDIA RESOURCES INTERNATIONAL INC
MEDIA RESOURCES
1387 Cornwall Rd, Oakville, ON, L6J 7T5
(905) 337-0993
Sales 36,927,900
SIC 1799 Special trade contractors, nec
Keith Edwards
Steve Gallow
Cal Courneya

D-U-N-S 20-629-1155   (SL)
MESSENGER MECHANICAL INCORPORATED
A1 AIR CONDITIONING & HEATING SERVICES
1420 Cornwall Rd Unit 3, Oakville, ON, L6J 7W5
(905) 844-2949
Emp Here 49   *Sales* 10,825,766
SIC 1711 Plumbing, heating, air-conditioning
Paul Messenger
Peter Messenger
Jane Messenger

D-U-N-S 24-966-2255   (SL)
MIG HOLDINGS INC
MONTROSE INTERNATIONAL GROUP
156 Reynolds St, Oakville, ON, L6J 3K9
(905) 339-0229
Emp Here 50   *Sales* 41,778,850
SIC 5149 Groceries and related products, nec
Manik Veerakumar

D-U-N-S 20-442-6720   (HQ)
NEWELL BRANDS CANADA ULC
BERNZOMATIC, DIV OF
586 Argus Rd Suite 400, Oakville, ON, L6J 3J3
(866) 595-0525
Sales 10,410,840
SIC 5099 Durable goods, nec
Paul Harricks

Benjamin Preston
Amit Singh
Robert King

D-U-N-S 20-283-5401   (SL)
NEXUS REAL ESTATE INVESTMENT TRUST
340 Church St, Oakville, ON, L6J 1P1
(416) 613-1262
Emp Here 7   *Sales* 24,342,843
SIC 6798 Real estate investment trusts
Kelly C. Hanczyk
Robert P. Chiasson
Mario Forgione
Bradley Cutsey
Lorne Jacobson
Nicholas Lagopoulos
Ben Rodney

D-U-N-S 20-642-1315   (SL)
OAK-LAND FORD LINCOLN SALES LIMITED
(*Suby of* OAK-LANE PARK INVESTMENTS LIMITED)
570 Trafalgar Rd, Oakville, ON, L6J 3J2
(905) 844-3273
Emp Here 95   *Sales* 59,781,600
SIC 5511 New and used car dealers
David Sanci
Kathy Sanci

D-U-N-S 24-828-3558   (HQ)
OAK-LANE PARK INVESTMENTS LIMITED
570 Trafalgar Rd, Oakville, ON, L6J 3J2
(905) 844-3273
Sales 35,535,500
SIC 6712 Bank holding companies
Leonard Sanci
Peter Lin
Marilyn Sanci

D-U-N-S 24-876-7584   (SL)
OPENAIRE SALES INC
2360 Cornwall Rd Unit B, Oakville, ON, L6J 7T9
(905) 901-8535
Emp Here 50   *Sales* 10,141,500
SIC 3446 Architectural Metalwork
Mark Albertine
Bruce Marsh
David Bolwerk
Deborah Baker

D-U-N-S 25-990-8556   (BR)
ROYAL HOST INC
HOLIDAY INN
(*Suby of* HOLLOWAY LODGING CORPORATION)
590 Argus Rd, Oakville, ON, L6J 3J3
(905) 842-5000
Emp Here 80
SIC 7011 Hotels and motels
Michael Mcfeters

D-U-N-S 25-402-8558   (BR)
ROYAL LEPAGE LIMITED
ROYAL LEPAGE RESIDENTIAL REAL ESTATE SERVICES
(*Suby of* BROOKFIELD ASSET MANAGEMENT INC)
326 Lakeshore Rd E, Oakville, ON, L6J 1J6
(905) 845-4267
Emp Here 95
SIC 6531 Real estate agents and managers
Laurie Panchyshyn

D-U-N-S 25-598-5434   (SL)
SHRED-IT AMERICA INC
(*Suby of* STERICYCLE, INC.)
2794 South Sheridan Way, Oakville, ON, L6J 7T4
(905) 829-2794
Emp Here 27   *Sales* 27,875,988
SIC 6794 Patent owners and lessors
Greg Brophy

D-U-N-S 20-272-3060   (HQ)
SHRED-IT JV LP

(*Suby of* STERICYCLE, INC.)
2794 South Sheridan Way, Oakville, ON, L6J 7T4
(888) 750-6450
Emp Here 1   *Sales* 2,006,724,000
SIC 7389 Business services, nec
David Samuel

D-U-N-S 25-802-9834   (BR)
SOBEYS CAPITAL INCORPORATED
MAPLE GROVE SOBEYS
(*Suby of* EMPIRE COMPANY LIMITED)
511 Maple Grove Dr Suite 4, Oakville, ON, L6J 6X8
(905) 849-0691
Emp Here 180
SIC 5411 Grocery stores
Vivian Barker

D-U-N-S 24-488-9408   (HQ)
SPRIGGS INSURANCE BROKERS LIMITED
159 Church St, Oakville, ON, L6J 1N1
(905) 844-9232
Emp Here 40   *Sales* 125,646,456
SIC 6411 Insurance agents, brokers, and service
Roy Spriggs Sr
Roy J. Spriggs Jr
Mary Spriggs

D-U-N-S 24-976-9837   (SL)
ST. MILDRED'S-LIGHTBOURN SCHOOL
1080 Linbrook Rd, Oakville, ON, L6J 2L1
(905) 845-2386
Emp Here 78   *Sales* 7,240,428
SIC 8211 Elementary and secondary schools
Nancy Richard

D-U-N-S 24-205-2681   (SL)
STERLING IM INC
STERLING HOFFMAN
(*Suby of* MARTIN, IAN TECHNOLOGY STAFFING LIMITED)
610 Chartwell Rd Suite 101, Oakville, ON, L6J 4A5
(416) 979-6701
Emp Here 220   *Sales* 33,540,320
SIC 7361 Employment agencies
Angel Mehta
Steve Brennan

D-U-N-S 20-527-6236   (BR)
SUNRISE NORTH SENIOR LIVING LTD
(*Suby of* WELLTOWER INC.)
456 Trafalgar Rd Suite 312, Oakville, ON, L6J 7X1
(905) 337-1145
Emp Here 100
SIC 8361 Residential care
Stephanie Sanborn

D-U-N-S 20-955-3986   (SL)
TURNKEY MODULAR SYSTEMS INC
TURN-KEY
2590 Sheridan Garden Dr, Oakville, ON, L6J 7R2
(905) 608-8006
Emp Here 70   *Sales* 22,965,390
SIC 3559 Special industry machinery, nec
Paul Hallman
Michael Hallman

D-U-N-S 24-384-0761   (SL)
TVC HOLDINGS LIMITED
2740 Sherwood Heights Dr, Oakville, ON, L6J 7V5
(905) 829-0280
Emp Here 25   *Sales* 11,179,350
SIC 5031 Lumber, plywood, and millwork
Vito Colucci

D-U-N-S 24-080-9376   (SL)
VELUX CANADA INC
(*Suby of* VILLUM FONDEN)
2740 Sherwood Heights Dr, Oakville, ON, L6J 7V5
(905) 829-0280
Emp Here 25   *Sales* 11,179,350

▲ Public Company   ■ Public Company Family Member   / HQ Headquarters   **BR** Branch   **SL** Single Location

SIC 5031 Lumber, plywood, and millwork
Nels Moxness

Oakville, ON L6K

D-U-N-S 25-099-5537   (SL)
ACCESS FLOWER TRADING INC
FLOWERBUYER.COM
(*Suby of* THE WONDERFUL COMPANY LLC)
700 Dorval Dr Suite 405, Oakville, ON, L6K 3V3
(905) 849-1343
Emp Here 30   *Sales* 22,275,600
SIC 5193 Flowers and florists supplies
Blair Campaigne

D-U-N-S 20-936-9396   (SL)
APPLEBY COLLEGE
540 Lakeshore Rd W, Oakville, ON, L6K 3P1
(905) 845-4681
Emp Here 160   *Sales* 15,859,040
SIC 8211 Elementary and secondary schools
Guy Mclean
John See

D-U-N-S 20-607-9675   (SL)
BUDDS CHEVROLET CADILLAC BUICK
GENERAL MOTORS OF CANADA
410 South Service Rd W, Oakville, ON, L6K 2H4
(888) 992-2620
Emp Here 73   *Sales* 45,937,440
SIC 5511 New and used car dealers
Robert Kerr
Sandra Kerr

D-U-N-S 20-964-7528   (HQ)
CENTRAL WEST SPECIALIZED DEVELOP-MENTAL SERVICES
53 Bond St, Oakville, ON, L6K 1L8
(905) 844-7864
Sales 26,877,200
SIC 8322 Individual and family services
James Duncan

D-U-N-S 20-844-0347   (HQ)
COMMUNITY LIVING OAKVILLE
301 Wyecroft Rd, Oakville, ON, L6K 2H2
(905) 844-0146
Emp Here 50   *Sales* 25,883,500
SIC 8399 Social services, nec
Andy Rotsma
Bob Brennan
Jo-Ann Russell-Gyorffy
Scott Williams
Thomas Crawford
John Levasseur
Tom Whelan
John Wilson
Barry Thomson
Eric J. Vanderwall

D-U-N-S 24-335-5898   (BR)
CRH CANADA GROUP INC
DUFFERIN CONSTRUCTION COMPANY, DIV OF
(*Suby of* CRH PUBLIC LIMITED COMPANY)
690 Dorval Dr Suite 200, Oakville, ON, L6K 3W7
(905) 842-2741
Emp Here 150
SIC 8711 Engineering services
Wayne Lazarado

D-U-N-S 20-157-2450   (HQ)
DANA CANADA CORPORATION
SERVICE PARTS DIVISION
(*Suby of* DANA INCORPORATED)
656 Kerr St, Oakville, ON, L6K 3E4
(905) 849-1200
Emp Here 60   *Sales* 581,700,000
SIC 3714 Motor vehicle parts and accessories
Paul Teeple
Rodney R Filcek

William A Jocsak
Paul Fudacz
Rodney W.J. Seyfert
Teresa Mulawa
David J Watson
Gilberto Ceratti

D-U-N-S 24-872-9493   (HQ)
DONATO GROUP INC, THE
700 Kerr St Suite 100, Oakville, ON, L6K 3W5
(905) 337-7777
Emp Here 5   *Sales* 13,991,700
SIC 5812 Eating places
Lou Donato
Nick Veloce

D-U-N-S 25-396-8267   (SL)
EQUIREX LEASING CORP
700 Dorval Dr Unit 302, Oakville, ON, L6K 3V3
(905) 844-4424
Emp Here 70   *Sales* 15,675,870
SIC 6159 Miscellaneous business credit institutions
Lawrence Nadler
Larry Mlynowski
Stuart Forbes
Brian Somer
Leon Solomon
Gabrielle Drazien
Matthew Nadler
Peter Lashchuk

D-U-N-S 25-301-2967   (BR)
EXTENDICARE (CANADA) INC
PARAMED HOME HEALTH CARE
(*Suby of* EXTENDICARE INC)
700 Dorval Dr Suite 111, Oakville, ON, L6K 3V3
(905) 847-1025
Emp Here 500
SIC 8051 Skilled nursing care facilities
Katherine Whelan

D-U-N-S 24-209-4642   (SL)
FORTINOS (OAKVILLE) LTD
FORTINOS 99
173 Lakeshore Rd W, Oakville, ON, L6K 1E7
(905) 845-3654
Emp Here 49   *Sales* 13,433,448
SIC 5411 Grocery stores
Dean Rodo

D-U-N-S 25-958-2088   (SL)
GREEN LIGHT GRAPHICS INC
229 Deane Ave, Oakville, ON, L6K 1N6
(905) 469-8095
Emp Here 75   *Sales* 15,879,300
SIC 7336 Commercial art and graphic design
Janet Stewart

D-U-N-S 20-025-4485   (BR)
HALTON CATHOLIC DISTRICT SCHOOL BOARD
ST THOMAS AQUINAS SECONDARY SCHOOL
(*Suby of* HALTON CATHOLIC DISTRICT SCHOOL BOARD)
124 Dorval Dr, Oakville, ON, L6K 2W1
(905) 842-9494
Emp Here 110
SIC 8211 Elementary and secondary schools
Collin Mcgillicuddy

D-U-N-S 24-849-6783   (SL)
HARVEST PORTFOLIOS GROUP INC
710 Dorval Dr Suite 200, Oakville, ON, L6K 3V7
(416) 649-4541
Emp Here 20   *Sales* 13,933,540
SIC 6722 Management investment, open-end
Michael Kovacs

D-U-N-S 24-489-0133   (SL)
KENNEDY FORD SALES LIMITED
280 South Service Rd W, Oakville, ON, L6K 3X5
(905) 845-1646
Emp Here 55   *Sales* 34,610,400

SIC 5511 New and used car dealers
Robert Nourse
Linda Nourse

D-U-N-S 25-079-0474   (BR)
LOBLAWS SUPERMARKETS LIMITED
LOBLAWS 190
(*Suby of* LOBLAW COMPANIES LIMITED)
173 Lakeshore Rd W, Oakville, ON, L6K 1E7
(905) 845-4946
Emp Here 200
SIC 5411 Grocery stores
Livio Vendramin

D-U-N-S 24-376-5778   (HQ)
LONE STAR GROUP OF COMPANIES LIM-ITED
472 Morden Rd Suite 101, Oakville, ON, L6K 3W4
(905) 845-5852
Sales 32,647,300
SIC 5812 Eating places
Mark Findlay

D-U-N-S 24-350-0522   (HQ)
MADE IN JAPAN JAPANESE RESTAU-RANTS LIMITED
MADE IN JAPAN TERIYAKI EXPERIENCE
700 Kerr St Suite 100, Oakville, ON, L6K 3W5
(905) 337-7777
Emp Here 1   *Sales* 17,420,250
SIC 6794 Patent owners and lessors
Lou Donato

D-U-N-S 24-486-8543   (BR)
METROLAND MEDIA GROUP LTD
OAKVILLE BEAVER
(*Suby of* TORSTAR CORPORATION)
467 Speers Rd Suite 1, Oakville, ON, L6K 3S4
(905) 845-3824
Emp Here 100
SIC 2711 Newspapers
Sandy Pare

D-U-N-S 20-941-8623   (HQ)
MIN-CHEM CANADA LTD
7SEEDS
(*Suby of* 172982 CANADA INC)
460 Wyecroft Rd, Oakville, ON, L6K 2G7
(905) 842-8300
Emp Here 15   *Sales* 14,606,900
SIC 5169 Chemicals and allied products, nec
David Luciani
Bonnie Conner
Jason Slomczewski

D-U-N-S 25-227-0905   (HQ)
OAKVILLE FAMILY YMCA
410 Rebecca St, Oakville, ON, L6K 1K7
(905) 845-3417
Emp Here 25   *Sales* 12,474,800
SIC 8351 Child day care services
Bruce Ireland
Don Jarrett
David Angus
Keith Garton
Bill Rechter
Andrea Stewart
Doug Auld
Tanya Leedale
Don Walker

D-U-N-S 20-514-0655   (BR)
OPEN SOLUTIONS CANADA INC
DATA WEST SOLUTIONS
700 Dorval Dr Suite 202, Oakville, ON, L6K 3V3
(905) 849-1390
Emp Here 85   *Sales* 566,586
SIC 8741 Management services
Colin Brown

D-U-N-S 24-308-8254   (SL)
ORGANIC GARAGE LTD
579 Kerr St, Oakville, ON, L6K 3E1
(905) 849-1648
Emp Here 45   *Sales* 15,456,296
SIC 5411 Grocery stores

Matt Lurie
Olga Balanovskaya
Antonina Szaszkiewicz
Christopher Crupi
Evan Clifford
Ken Villazor
Keith Stein
Kevin Williams

D-U-N-S 25-993-1467   (HQ)
PETHEALTH INC
710 Dorval Dr Suite 400, Oakville, ON, L6K 3V7
(905) 842-2615
Sales 40,222,993
SIC 6411 Insurance agents, brokers, and service
Sean Smith
Alan Maresky
Michelle Cole
Andrei Cornienco
Brad Grucelski
Connie Howard
Kayla Torontow
Steve Zeidman

D-U-N-S 20-528-3489   (SL)
ROBERTSON EADIE & ASSOCIATES
41 Morden Rd Suite 210, Oakville, ON, L6K 3W6
(905) 338-7002
Emp Here 20   *Sales* 11,598,480
SIC 6411 Insurance agents, brokers, and service
Marcus Robertson
Stephen Eadie
John Deinum
John Love

D-U-N-S 24-045-7655   (SL)
ROCCA, LEE FORMING LTD
488 Morden Rd Unit 1, Oakville, ON, L6K 3W4
(905) 842-2543
Emp Here 130   *Sales* 32,004,180
SIC 1794 Excavation work
Lee Rocca

D-U-N-S 24-344-4846   (HQ)
SLEEP MANAGEMENT GROUP LIMITED
466 Speers Rd Unit 4, Oakville, ON, L6K 3W9
(905) 337-0699
Emp Here 20   *Sales* 13,415,220
SIC 5047 Medical and hospital equipment
Kevin Agnew

D-U-N-S 20-534-3452   (SL)
SOUTH OAKVILLE CHRYSLER DODGE JEEP RAM LTD
SOUTH OAKVILLE CHRYSLER FIAT
175 Wyecroft Rd, Oakville, ON, L6K 3S3
(905) 845-6653
Emp Here 40   *Sales* 19,923,120
SIC 5511 New and used car dealers
Reg Nimeck
Gordon Nimeck

D-U-N-S 24-050-1288   (HQ)
WENDY'S RESTAURANTS OF CANADA INC
WENDY'S OLD FASHION HAMBURGERS
(*Suby of* THE WENDY'S COMPANY)
240 Wyecroft Rd, Oakville, ON, L6K 2G7
(905) 337-8041
Emp Here 100   *Sales* 256,514,500
SIC 5812 Eating places
Todd A Penegor
Robert D Wright
Kurt A Kane
Gunther Plosch

Oakville, ON L6L

D-U-N-S 20-111-0760   (SL)
2507246 ONTARIO INC
OAKVILLE INFINITI

2270 South Service Rd W, Oakville, ON, L6L 5M9
(905) 827-7191
Emp Here 35   *Sales* 22,024,800
SIC 5511 New and used car dealers
Jose Martins

D-U-N-S 24-310-4051   (SL)
ACCLAIM HEALTH COMMUNITY CARE SERVICES
ACCLAIM HEALTH
2370 Speers Rd, Oakville, ON, L6L 5M2
(905) 827-8800
Emp Here 350   *Sales* 26,845,350
SIC 8082 Home health care services
Angela Brewer
Gerald Park

D-U-N-S 24-886-8143   (SL)
ALL-CONNECT LOGISTICAL SERVICES INC
ALL CONNECT
2070 Wyecroft Rd, Oakville, ON, L6L 5V6
(905) 847-6555
Emp Here 45   *Sales* 23,398,515
SIC 4731 Freight transportation arrangement
Ian Smith
Georgine Smith

D-U-N-S 20-718-7923   (HQ)
ALLCOLOUR PAINT LIMITED
ALLCOLOUR HOLLOWAY, DIV OF
1257 Speers Rd, Oakville, ON, L6L 2X5
(905) 827-4173
Emp Here 84   *Sales* 35,502,625
SIC 2851 Paints and allied products
Charles Chapman
Robert Chapman

D-U-N-S 20-174-9392   (SL)
ARCH CHEMICALS CANADA, INC
QUATIC CONSUMER PRODUCTS
(*Suby of* LONZA GROUP AG)
160 Warner Dr, Oakville, ON, L6L 6E7
(905) 847-9878
Emp Here 100   *Sales* 73,034,500
SIC 5169 Chemicals and allied products, nec
Larry Mcgregor

D-U-N-S 24-354-2086   (HQ)
BCG LOGISTICS (2000) INC
BCG LOGISTICS GROUP
1300 South Service Rd W, Oakville, ON, L6L 5T7
(905) 238-3444
Sales 15,599,010
SIC 4731 Freight transportation arrangement
Allan Smith
Michael Stephenson

D-U-N-S 20-134-1310   (HQ)
BOT CONSTRUCTION LIMITED
(*Suby of* S. BOT & SONS ENTERPRISES LIMITED)
1224 Speers Rd, Oakville, ON, L6L 5B6
(905) 827-4167
Emp Here 22   *Sales* 13,631,868
SIC 1611 Highway and street construction
Roy Bot
Steve Bot

D-U-N-S 20-881-5449   (HQ)
BUDD, STUART & SONS LIMITED
2454 South Service Rd W, Oakville, ON, L6L 5M9
(905) 845-3577
Emp Here 10   *Sales* 84,952,800
SIC 5511 New and used car dealers
Darryl Budd
Christopher Budd
Terry Budd

D-U-N-S 20-179-5502   (SL)
BUDDS HAMILTON LIMITED
BUDDS BMW OF OAKVILLE
2454 South Service Rd W, Oakville, ON, L6L 5M9

(905) 845-3577
Emp Here 50   *Sales* 24,903,900
SIC 5511 New and used car dealers
Darryl Budd
Stuart Budd
Terrance Budd

D-U-N-S 20-734-8397   (BR)
BUNGE CANADA HOLDINGS 1 ULC
BUNGE CANADA
(*Suby of* BUNGE LIMITED)
2190 South Service Rd W, Oakville, ON, L6L 5N1
(905) 825-7900
Emp Here 75
SIC 2079 Edible fats and oils

D-U-N-S 20-556-0431   (HQ)
BUNGE CANADA HOLDINGS 1 ULC
(*Suby of* BUNGE LIMITED)
2190 South Service Rd W, Oakville, ON, L6L 5N1
(905) 825-7900
Emp Here 1   *Sales* 292,772,709
SIC 6712 Bank holding companies
Larry Clarke

D-U-N-S 24-913-9213   (HQ)
BUNGE OF CANADA LTD
(*Suby of* BUNGE LIMITED)
2190 South Service Rd W, Oakville, ON, L6L 5N1
(905) 825-7900
Sales 365,538,750
SIC 2079 Edible fats and oils
Bruce Croft
Karl Gerrand
Michael C. Lund
Luciano Salvatierra
Todd A. Bastean

D-U-N-S 24-829-1502   (HQ)
CALLISTO INTEGRATION LTD
ASECO INTEGRATED SYSTEMS
635 Fourth Line Unit 16, Oakville, ON, L6L 5W4
(905) 339-0059
Sales 23,705,670
SIC 7373 Computer integrated systems design
Rick Makos
Robert Peters
Brad Walker
Jeffrey Peters

D-U-N-S 24-469-6068   (HQ)
CANTWELL CULLEN & COMPANY INC
(*Suby of* SAFRAN)
1131 South Service Rd W, Oakville, ON, L6L 6K4
(905) 825-3255
Emp Here 128   *Sales* 30,470,720
SIC 3679 Electronic components, nec
Ted Perdue
Stuart Robertson

D-U-N-S 25-535-2965   (HQ)
CARAVAN LOGISTICS INC
2284 Wyecroft Rd, Oakville, ON, L6L 6M1
(905) 338-5885
Emp Here 130   *Sales* 46,095,250
SIC 4213 Trucking, except local
John Iwaniura
Steve Merena
Bohdan Workun

D-U-N-S 20-513-0177   (BR)
CGC INC
(*Suby of* USG NETHERLANDS GLOBAL HOLDINGS B.V.)
735 Fourth Line, Oakville, ON, L6L 5B7
(905) 337-5100
Emp Here 82
SIC 1761 Roofing, siding, and sheetMetal work
John Wesley

D-U-N-S 20-134-1732   (SL)

CLARKSON CONSTRUCTION COMPANY LIMITED
(*Suby of* S. BOT & SONS ENTERPRISES LIMITED)
1224 Speers Rd, Oakville, ON, L6L 5B6
(905) 827-4167
Emp Here 250
SIC 8721 Accounting, auditing, and bookkeeping
Roy Bot
Scott Riddell
John Ross

D-U-N-S 20-254-3299   (SL)
COLDWELL BANKER HOME & FAMILY REALTY LTD
1515 Rebecca St Suite 25, Oakville, ON, L6L 5G8
(905) 825-3305
Emp Here 35   *Sales* 11,449,445
SIC 6531 Real estate agents and managers
Gary Reed

D-U-N-S 20-112-1675   (HQ)
COMPAIR CANADA INC
COMPRESSOR ESSENTIALS DIV.
(*Suby of* GD GLOBAL HOLDINGS UK II LIMITED)
2390 South Service Rd W, Oakville, ON, L6L 5M9
(905) 847-0688
Sales 24,226,326
SIC 5084 Industrial machinery and equipment
Chris Brohman

D-U-N-S 20-566-3235   (SL)
CORBETT'S SKIS & SNOWBOARDS INC
2278 Speers Rd, Oakville, ON, L6L 2X8
(905) 338-7713
Emp Here 50   *Sales* 10,880,650
SIC 5941 Sporting goods and bicycle shops
Chris Tymstra
Kim Tymstra

D-U-N-S 20-353-5844   (BR)
CRH CANADA GROUP INC
DUFFERIN CONSTRUCTION DIV OF
(*Suby of* CRH PUBLIC LIMITED COMPANY)
585 Michigan Dr Suite 1, Oakville, ON, L6L 0G1
(905) 842-2741
Emp Here 100
SIC 1521 Single-family housing construction
Kevin Machej

D-U-N-S 25-404-3110   (BR)
DANA CANADA CORPORATION
THERMAL PRODUCTS - LONG MANUFACTURING
(*Suby of* DANA INCORPORATED)
1400 Advance Rd, Oakville, ON, L6L 6L6
(905) 825-8856
Emp Here 150
SIC 3443 Fabricated plate work (boiler shop)
Jon Head

D-U-N-S 25-104-7072   (HQ)
DE LAGE LANDEN FINANCIAL SERVICES CANADA INC
AGRICREDIT ACCEPTANCE CANADA, A DIV OF
(*Suby of* COOPERATIEVE RABOBANK U.A.)
3450 Superior Crt Unit 1, Oakville, ON, L6L 0C4
(905) 465-3160
Sales 100,975,970
SIC 6159 Miscellaneous business credit institutions
Peter Horan
David Timms
Mark Reichling
Cynthia Losier

D-U-N-S 24-948-9308   (SL)
EL CON
OAKVILLE HYDRO ELECTRICITY, DIV OF
861 Redwood Sq Suite 1900, Oakville, ON,

L6L 6R6
(905) 825-9400
Emp Here 30   *Sales* 15,589,650
SIC 4911 Electric services
Scott Mudie

D-U-N-S 20-690-6997   (SL)
FRUITION MANUFACTURING LIMITED
FRUITION FRUITS & FILLS
(*Suby of* RESTAURANT BRANDS INTERNATIONAL INC)
2379 Speers Rd, Oakville, ON, L6L 2X9
(905) 337-6400
Emp Here 40   *Sales* 33,423,080
SIC 5142 Packaged frozen goods
Marl Pyymaki

D-U-N-S 20-024-7554   (SL)
FUNDS FLOW CANADA INC
INTERNET SECURE
2201 Speers Rd, Oakville, ON, L6L 2X9

Emp Here 30   *Sales* 13,304,700
SIC 7389 Business services, nec
David Pratt

D-U-N-S 25-292-2265   (HQ)
GARDNER DENVER CANADA CORP
(*Suby of* GARDNER DENVER HOLDINGS, INC.)
2390 South Service Rd W, Oakville, ON, L6L 5M9
(905) 847-0688
Sales 27,658,422
SIC 5172 Petroleum products, nec
Darren Sabino

D-U-N-S 24-984-7849   (BR)
GENERAL ELECTRIC CANADA COMPANY
GE LIGHTING CANADA
(*Suby of* GENERAL ELECTRIC COMPANY)
1290 South Service Rd W, Oakville, ON, L6L 5T7
(905) 849-5048
Emp Here 500
SIC 3625 Relays and industrial controls
Elizabeth Sanchez

D-U-N-S 20-707-0830   (HQ)
GOODRICH AEROSPACE CANADA LTD
COLLINS AEROSPACE
(*Suby of* UNITED TECHNOLOGIES CORPORATION)
1400 South Service Rd W, Oakville, ON, L6L 5Y7
(905) 827-7777
Emp Here 580   *Sales* 290,850,000
SIC 3728 Aircraft parts and equipment, nec
Frank Karakas
Tim Whittier
Fabrice Rancoeur
Bob Corbell

D-U-N-S 25-084-4487   (SL)
HALTON ALARM RESPONSE & PROTECTION LTD
HARP SECURITY
760 Pacific Rd Unit 21, Oakville, ON, L6L 6M5
(905) 827-6655
Emp Here 60   *Sales* 23,740,680
SIC 7382 Security systems services
Cam Roberts

D-U-N-S 20-351-6968   (BR)
HALTON DISTRICT SCHOOL BOARD
THOMAS A. BLAKELOCK HIGH SCHOOL
(*Suby of* HALTON DISTRICT SCHOOL BOARD)
1160 Rebecca St, Oakville, ON, L6L 1Y9
(905) 827-1158
Emp Here 123
SIC 8211 Elementary and secondary schools
Brent Coakwell

D-U-N-S 25-278-8138   (SL)
HALTON DISTRICT SCHOOL BOARD
T. A. BLAKELOCK HIGH SCHOOL
1160 Rebecca St, Oakville, ON, L6L 1Y9

(905) 827-1158
Emp Here 125　　*Sales* 12,389,875
SIC 8211 Elementary and secondary schools
Kevin Caughlin
Virginia Hureau
Margaret Kew

D-U-N-S 20-338-5067　　(BR)
HEARN INDUSTRIAL SERVICES INC
(*Suby of* HEARN INDUSTRIAL SERVICES INC)
2189 Speers Rd, Oakville, ON, L6L 2X9
(866) 297-6914
Emp Here 150
SIC 4225 General warehousing and storage
Donald Hearn

D-U-N-S 24-361-7250　　(BR)
HOME DEPOT OF CANADA INC
HOME DEPOT
(*Suby of* THE HOME DEPOT INC)
3300 South Service Rd W, Oakville, ON, L6L 0B1
(905) 469-7110
Emp Here 200
SIC 5251 Hardware stores
Blaine Mcleod

D-U-N-S 20-784-7773　　(HQ)
HOOPER WELDING ENTERPRISES LIMITED
HOOPER WELDING
1390 Advance Rd, Oakville, ON, L6L 6L6
(905) 827-2600
Emp Here 90　　*Sales* 19,208,500
SIC 3443 Fabricated plate work (boiler shop)
Ross Hooper
Chris Hooper

D-U-N-S 20-298-6857　　(BR)
HPG INC
(*Suby of* GENNX360 CAPITAL PARTNERS, L.P.)
2250 Speers Rd, Oakville, ON, L6L 2X8
(905) 825-1218
Emp Here 87
SIC 3728 Aircraft parts and equipment, nec
Dave Wooldriege

D-U-N-S 24-602-4517　　(HQ)
HPG INC
(*Suby of* GENNX360 CAPITAL PARTNERS, L.P.)
2240 Speers Rd, Oakville, ON, L6L 2X8
(905) 825-1218
Sales 13,430,580
SIC 3728 Aircraft parts and equipment, nec
Howard Singleton
Scott Stacey

D-U-N-S 20-052-2097　　(HQ)
INNOMAR STRATEGIES INC
(*Suby of* AMERISOURCEBERGEN CORPORATION)
3470 Superior Crt Suite 2, Oakville, ON, L6L 0C4
(905) 847-4310
Emp Here 10　　*Sales* 479,523,060
SIC 8741 Management services
Guy Payette
Sandra Anderson
Stan Donovan
Jeff Macdonald
Amar Pabla
Kevin West
Jason Zabransky
Jill Lepage

D-U-N-S 24-596-1649　　(BR)
INNVEST HOTELS GP LTD
HOLIDAY INN
(*Suby of* INNVEST HOTELS GP LTD)
2525 Wyecroft Rd, Oakville, ON, L6L 6P8
(905) 847-1000
Emp Here 100
SIC 7011 Hotels and motels
Marcelo Tomazo

D-U-N-S 20-939-3578　　(HQ)
INTERNATIONAL UNION OF OPERATING ENGINEERS LOCAL 793
2245 Speers Rd, Oakville, ON, L6L 6X8
(905) 469-9299
Sales 29,433,750
SIC 8631 Labor organizations
Joe Redshaw
John Anderson
Mike Gallagher

D-U-N-S 20-134-3209　　(HQ)
JELINEK CORK LIMITED
JELINEK CORK GROUP
2260 Speers Rd, Oakville, ON, L6L 2X8
(905) 827-4666
Emp Here 25　　*Sales* 26,027,100
SIC 5099 Durable goods, nec
Jonathan Jelinek
Karina Trummond
Sonny Jelinek

D-U-N-S 20-134-6475　　(BR)
JEMPAK GK INC
1485 Speers Rd, Oakville, ON, L6L 2X5
(905) 827-1123
Emp Here 80　　*Sales* 654,688
SIC 2841 Soap and other detergents
Gary Barone

D-U-N-S 24-850-1728　　(HQ)
JOHN DEERE FINANCIAL INC
(*Suby of* DEERE & COMPANY)
3430 Superior Crt, Oakville, ON, L6L 0C4
(905) 319-9100
Emp Here 130　　*Sales* 203,039,827
SIC 6153 Short-term business credit institutions, except agricultural
David C. Gilmore
Teresa Garside
W. John Grosso
Thomas C. Spitzfaden
Steve A. Watson
Bret C. Thomas

D-U-N-S 24-559-9626　　(SL)
K.L. FINE CARS LTD
HYUNDAI OF OAKVILLE
2500 South Service Rd W, Oakville, ON, L6L 5M9
(905) 845-7791
Emp Here 120　　*Sales* 14,444,262
SIC 5511 New and used car dealers
Ronald Chan
Benjamin Leung

D-U-N-S 24-575-4502　　(BR)
KEG RESTAURANTS LTD
KEG STEAKHOUSE AND BAR, THE
(*Suby of* RECIPE UNLIMITED CORPORATION)
3130 South Service Rd W, Oakville, ON, L6L 6T1
(905) 681-1810
Emp Here 85
SIC 5812 Eating places
Derek Booth

D-U-N-S 24-419-2548　　(HQ)
KPM INDUSTRIES LTD
KING PAVING & MATERIALS COMPANY
555 Michigan Dr Suite 100, Oakville, ON, L6L 0G4
(905) 639-2993
Emp Here 120　　*Sales* 82,028,750
SIC 1611 Highway and street construction
Hugh Macpherson
Henry Hutter
Sheldon Vanderwoude

D-U-N-S 25-333-7000　　(SL)
LAKER ENERGY PRODUCTS LTD
(*Suby of* 981880 ONTARIO INC)
835 Fourth Line, Oakville, ON, L6L 5B8
(905) 332-3231
Emp Here 92　　*Sales* 20,424,092
SIC 3569 General industrial machinery, nec

Christopher Hughes

D-U-N-S 24-737-2402　　(SL)
M & G STEEL LTD
(*Suby of* 2443788 ONTARIO INC)
2285 Speers Rd, Oakville, ON, L6L 2X9
(905) 469-6442
Emp Here 60　　*Sales* 19,950,525
SIC 3441 Fabricated structural Metal
Stephen Dulong
Brian Thompson
Chris Adach

D-U-N-S 20-407-5907　　(HQ)
MANCOR CANADA INC
MANCOR SPEERS RD
2485 Speers Rd, Oakville, ON, L6L 2X9
(905) 827-3737
Emp Here 350　　*Sales* 156,640,764
SIC 3499 Fabricated Metal products, nec
Mike Andrews
Arthur Church

D-U-N-S 20-379-7949　　(BR)
MARK'S WORK WEARHOUSE LTD
MARK'S ACCOUNTS RECEIVABLE
(*Suby of* CANADIAN TIRE CORPORATION, LIMITED)
3449 Superior Crt, Oakville, ON, L6L 0C4
(800) 461-4378
Emp Here 200
SIC 5651 Family clothing stores
James Martino

D-U-N-S 24-010-1915　　(SL)
METRICAN MFG. CO. INC
(*Suby of* METRICAN HOLDINGS LIMITED)
2100 Wyecroft Rd, Oakville, ON, L6L 5V6
(905) 332-3200
Emp Here 70　　*Sales* 15,540,070
SIC 3545 Machine tool accessories
Frank Bosco
Remo Gigliotti

D-U-N-S 20-555-6314　　(BR)
METRO ONTARIO INC
METRO
(*Suby of* METRO INC)
1521 Rebecca St, Oakville, ON, L6L 1Z8
(905) 827-5421
Emp Here 150
SIC 5411 Grocery stores
Pano Tournidis

D-U-N-S 20-718-6164　　(HQ)
MONARCH PLASTICS LIMITED
2335 Speers Rd, Oakville, ON, L6L 2X9
(905) 791-8805
Sales 22,240,120
SIC 3089 Plastics products, nec
Hemang Mehta
Russell Mckay

D-U-N-S 20-515-8798　　(SL)
MOVELINE INC
1317 Speers Rd, Oakville, ON, L6L 2X5
(905) 814-1700
Emp Here 75　　*Sales* 20,320,650
SIC 1522 Residential construction, nec
Daniel Rebernik
Andrew Collins

D-U-N-S 24-319-3117　　(HQ)
NCI CANADA INC
2305 Wyecroft Road, Oakville, ON, L6L 6R2
(905) 727-5545
Emp Here 21　　*Sales* 11,875,650
SIC 5085 Industrial supplies
Clifford Sarjeant
Mike Jackson

D-U-N-S 24-738-2526　　(SL)
OAKVILLE AUTOMOTIVE GROUP INC
OAKVILLE TOYOTA
2375 Wyecroft Rd, Oakville, ON, L6L 6L4
(905) 842-8400
Emp Here 42　　*Sales* 20,919,276

SIC 5511 New and used car dealers
Frank Apa

D-U-N-S 20-181-4931　　(HQ)
OAKVILLE ENTERPRISES CORPORATION
(*Suby of* CORPORATION OF THE TOWN OF OAKVILLE, THE)
861 Redwood Sq Suite 1900, Oakville, ON, L6L 6R6
(905) 825-9400
Sales 101,981,100
SIC 4911 Electric services
Alex Bystrin
Gary Burkett
David Sweezie
Gary Kain

D-U-N-S 24-424-5978　　(HQ)
OAKVILLE HYDRO ELECTRICITY DISTRIBUTION INC
861 Redwood Sq Suite 1900, Oakville, ON, L6L 6R6
(905) 825-9400
Sales 10,025,824
SIC 4911 Electric services
Robert Lister
Gary Burkett
Ray Green
Thomas Hierlihy
Mike Kaptein
Max Khan
Diana Miles
John Mitchell
David Pasieka
Mike Russill

D-U-N-S 24-324-3412　　(HQ)
PROCOR LIMITED
(*Suby of* BERKSHIRE HATHAWAY INC.)
585 Michigan Dr Unit 2, Oakville, ON, L6L 0G1
(905) 827-4111
Sales 20,798,680
SIC 4741 Rental of railroad cars
Ron Waye
Jay Mcgill

D-U-N-S 20-119-9515　　(SL)
ROADWAY OPERATIONS & MAINTENANCE CORPORATION OF ONTARIO INC
ROMCO
1224 Speers Rd, Oakville, ON, L6L 5B6
(905) 827-4167
Emp Here 35　　*Sales* 10,038,271
SIC 1611 Highway and street construction
Roy Bot
Steven Bot

D-U-N-S 20-161-2553　　(SL)
ROCHESTER MIDLAND LIMITED
(*Suby of* ROCHESTER MIDLAND CORPORATION)
851 Progress Crt Suite 1, Oakville, ON, L6L 6K1
(905) 847-3000
Emp Here 65　　*Sales* 18,461,365
SIC 2899 Chemical preparations, nec
Susan Gazley
Harlan D. Calkins

D-U-N-S 24-827-3187　　(BR)
ROPAK CANADA INC
BWAY PACKAGING CANADA
(*Suby of* STONE CANYON INDUSTRIES LLC)
2240 Wyecroft Rd, Oakville, ON, L6L 6M1
(905) 827-9340
Emp Here 135
SIC 3089 Plastics products, nec
Mark Gibson

D-U-N-S 24-842-4991　　(SL)
SAINT-GOBAIN SOLAR GUARD, INC
(*Suby of* COMPAGNIE DE SAINT-GOBAIN)
760 Pacific Rd Unit 1, Oakville, ON, L6L 6M5
(905) 847-2790
Emp Here 50　　*Sales* 14,201,050
SIC 2899 Chemical preparations, nec

▲ Public Company　　■ Public Company Family Member　　**HQ** Headquarters　　**BR** Branch　　**SL** Single Location

Thomas Kinisky
Frank Mackay
Timothy Feagans
Jean-Pierre Floris
Lisa Grossi
M.Shawn Puccio
John Sweeney

D-U-N-S 20-878-1609   (SL)
SHRADER CANADA LIMITED
830 Progress Crt, Oakville, ON, L6L 6K1
(905) 847-0222
Emp Here 75   *Sales* 20,749,500
SIC 2819 Industrial inorganic chemicals, nec
Cliff Addison
Bonnie Malcolm

D-U-N-S 25-053-7404   (BR)
SOBEYS CAPITAL INCORPORATED
(*Suby of* EMPIRE COMPANY LIMITED)
2441 Lakeshore Rd W, Oakville, ON, L6L 5V5
(905) 825-2278
Emp Here 120
SIC 5411 Grocery stores
Marc Poulin

D-U-N-S 25-910-5794   (HQ)
STRATOSPHERE QUALITY, INC
(*Suby of* STRATOSPHERE QUALITY LLC)
1515 Rebecca St, Oakville, ON, L6L 1Z8
(877) 224-8584
Sales 236,079,768
SIC 4785 Inspection and fixed facilities
Tammy Mcewen

D-U-N-S 25-418-6570   (BR)
SUNCOR ENERGY INC
(*Suby of* SUNCOR ENERGY INC)
3275 Rebecca St, Oakville, ON, L6L 6N5
(905) 804-7152
Emp Here 200
SIC 2911 Petroleum refining
Carole Groleau

D-U-N-S 24-847-5915   (HQ)
SUPERIOR SOLUTIONS LTD
GREENLABS CHEMICAL SOLUTIONS
(*Suby of* GDI SERVICES AUX IMMEUBLES INC)
851 Progress Crt, Oakville, ON, L6L 6K1
(800) 921-5527
Emp Here 30   *Sales* 17,100,936
SIC 5087 Service establishment equipment
Craig Rudin
Claude Bigras
Jocelyn Trottier
Stephane Lavigne

D-U-N-S 20-553-8739   (HQ)
TANDET LOGISTICS INC
(*Suby of* TANDET MANAGEMENT INC)
1351 Speers Rd, Oakville, ON, L6L 2X5
(905) 827-4200
Sales 13,370,890
SIC 4213 Trucking, except local
Scott Tilley
Kirk Tilley
Jeff Cockshutt
Corey Cox

D-U-N-S 24-707-8827   (HQ)
TANDET MANAGEMENT INC
1351 Speers Rd, Oakville, ON, L6L 2X5
(905) 827-0501
Emp Here 10   *Sales* 73,025,630
SIC 4213 Trucking, except local
John Tilley
Jeff Cockshutt
Corey Cox

D-U-N-S 24-333-0201   (SL)
TATE ASP ACCESS FLOORS INC
(*Suby of* KINGSPAN GROUP PUBLIC LIMITED COMPANY)
880 Equestrian Crt, Oakville, ON, L6L 6L7
(905) 847-0138
Emp Here 56   *Sales* 10,756,760

SIC 3444 Sheet Metalwork
Russell Shiels
Nelson Martinez
Frank Perri
Ralph Mannion

D-U-N-S 20-845-6624   (HQ)
TISI CANADA INC
TISI INSPECTION SERVICES
(*Suby of* TEAM, INC.)
781 Westgate Rd, Oakville, ON, L6L 6R7
(905) 845-9542
Emp Here 50   *Sales* 203,587,000
SIC 3398 Metal heat treating
Charles Slater
Martin Decamp
John E. G. Gilgan
Authur F Victorson
David C. Palmore
Peter W. Wallace Jr
Ted W. Owen
James Campbell

D-U-N-S 25-796-2795   (HQ)
TOTAL TECH POOLS INC
1380 Speers Rd Suite 1, Oakville, ON, L6L 5V3
(905) 825-1389
Emp Here 23   *Sales* 22,460,950
SIC 7389 Business services, nec
David Warren

D-U-N-S 24-099-9391   (HQ)
VALTROL EQUIPMENT LIMITED
PROCESS AND STEAM SPECIALTIES
2305 Wyecroft Rd, Oakville, ON, L6L 6R2
(905) 828-9900
Sales 16,625,910
SIC 5085 Industrial supplies
David Terry
Stuart Scott

D-U-N-S 20-918-7124   (SL)
VOLVO OF OAKVILLE
770 Pacific Rd, Oakville, ON, L6L 6M5
(905) 825-8088
Emp Here 30   *Sales* 14,942,340
SIC 5511 New and used car dealers
John Martins

D-U-N-S 24-077-1022   (SL)
W.J.B. MOTORS LIMITED
OAKVILLE MAZDA
1291 Speers Rd, Oakville, ON, L6L 2X5
(905) 827-4242
Emp Here 22   *Sales* 10,957,716
SIC 5511 New and used car dealers
Jason Guttman

D-U-N-S 24-708-9097   (HQ)
WIBERG CORPORATION
(*Suby of* INTERNATIONAL FLAVORS & FRAGRANCES INC.)
931 Equestrian Crt, Oakville, ON, L6L 6L7
(905) 825-9900
Emp Here 55   *Sales* 25,926,750
SIC 2099 Food preparations, nec
Richard Welzel
Susanne Jones

D-U-N-S 24-577-5507   (SL)
WOODWARD MEAT PURVEYORS INC
1346 Speers Rd, Oakville, ON, L6L 5V3
(905) 847-7200
Emp Here 24   *Sales* 20,053,848
SIC 5147 Meats and meat products
Brian Woodward
Joanne Woodward

D-U-N-S 20-159-6012   (SL)
YORK BARBELL CO. LTD
1450 South Service Rd W, Oakville, ON, L6L 5T7
(905) 827-6362
Emp Here 50   *Sales* 10,941,200
SIC 3949 Sporting and athletic goods, nec
William Irvine

Oakville, ON L6M

D-U-N-S 20-337-8930   (SL)
1939250 ONTARIO LTD
251 North Service Rd W, Oakville, ON, L6M 3E7
(905) 608-1999
Emp Here 60   *Sales* 15,693,180
SIC 6712 Bank holding companies
Duncan Mccready
Marc Caron
Mike Svetkoff

D-U-N-S 24-359-3626   (SL)
2020455 ONTARIO INC
ACURA OF OAKVILLE
1525 North Service Rd W, Oakville, ON, L6M 2W2
(905) 825-8777
Emp Here 22   *Sales* 10,957,716
SIC 5511 New and used car dealers
Giuseppe Zanchin

D-U-N-S 20-017-0525   (HQ)
ASTOUND GROUP INC, THE
1215 North Service Rd W Unit A, Oakville, ON, L6M 2W2
(905) 465-0474
Emp Here 10   *Sales* 76,270,250
SIC 7389 Business services, nec
Dale Morgan
Darren Hugli
Kevin Morgan

D-U-N-S 25-127-3186   (SL)
BUDD'S MAZDA
1501 North Service Rd W, Oakville, ON, L6M 2W2
(905) 827-4242
Emp Here 30   *Sales* 14,942,340
SIC 5511 New and used car dealers
Terry Budd

D-U-N-S 24-776-6608   (BR)
CHARTWELL MASTER CARE LP
CHARTWELL WATERFORD
(*Suby of* CHARTWELL MASTER CARE LP)
2140 Baronwood Dr, Oakville, ON, L6M 4V6
(905) 827-2405
Emp Here 200
SIC 8052 Intermediate care facilities
Kimberly Widdickombe

D-U-N-S 20-554-7594   (BR)
CHARTWELL RETIREMENT RESIDENCES
WATERFORD LTC RESIDENCE, THE
(*Suby of* CHARTWELL RETIREMENT RESIDENCES)
2140 Baronwood Dr Suite 225, Oakville, ON, L6M 4V6
(905) 827-2405
Emp Here 100
SIC 8059 Nursing and personal care, nec
Jennifer Sarkis

D-U-N-S 20-789-4510   (SL)
COLLIN & DIANA PARKER SALES LTD
CANADIAN TIRE
1100 Kerr St, Oakville, ON, L6M 0L4
(905) 844-0202
Emp Here 100   *Sales* 62,928,000
SIC 5531 Auto and home supply stores
Collin Parker
Diana Parker

D-U-N-S 20-381-4207   (SL)
DIAMOND ESTATES WINES & SPIRITS INC
435 North Service Rd W Unit 100, Oakville, ON, L6M 4X8
(905) 641-1042
Emp Here 8   *Sales* 27,280,167
SIC 5182 Wine and distilled beverages
J. Murray Souter
Thomas Green
Alan Stratton
David Beutel

John L. De Sousa
Keith R. Harris
John Hick
Harold Wolkin

D-U-N-S 24-735-9656   (BR)
DOMINION OF CANADA GENERAL INSURANCE COMPANY, THE
(*Suby of* THE TRAVELERS COMPANIES INC)
1275 North Service Rd W Suite 103, Oakville, ON, L6M 3G4
(905) 825-6400
Emp Here 350
SIC 6411 Insurance agents, brokers, and service
Gerry Jamieson

D-U-N-S 24-684-8373   (SL)
DREW BRADY COMPANY INC
1155 North Service Rd W Unit 6, Oakville, ON, L6M 3E3
(905) 815-1534
Emp Here 12   *Sales* 14,962,833
SIC 5136 Men's and boy's clothing
Ajay Ruia
Rajendra Ruia
Amit Ruia
Sunil Ruia
Vimal Ruia
Alok Ruia

D-U-N-S 24-185-3837   (HQ)
ESSITY CANADA INC
SCA HYGIENE PRODUCTS
1275 North Service Rd W Suite 800, Oakville, ON, L6M 3G4
(905) 339-3539
Emp Here 50   *Sales* 107,070,400
SIC 5047 Medical and hospital equipment
Magnus Groth
Fredrik Rystedt
Anna Savinger Aslund
Mikael Schmidt
Josephine Edwall-Bjorklund
Robert Sjostrom
Kersti Strandqvist
Par Boman
Ewa Bjorling
Annemarie Gardshol

D-U-N-S 20-711-0557   (BR)
HALTON DISTRICT SCHOOL BOARD
WEST OAK PUBLIC SCHOOL
(*Suby of* HALTON DISTRICT SCHOOL BOARD)
2071 Fourth Line, Oakville, ON, L6M 3K1
(905) 469-6119
Emp Here 77
SIC 8211 Elementary and secondary schools
Sean Mccarthy

D-U-N-S 24-008-1802   (BR)
HALTON DISTRICT SCHOOL BOARD
PALERMO PUBLIC SCHOOL
(*Suby of* HALTON DISTRICT SCHOOL BOARD)
2561 Valleyridge Dr, Oakville, ON, L6M 5H4
(905) 469-1138
Emp Here 84
SIC 8211 Elementary and secondary schools
Sheilagh Wright

D-U-N-S 25-192-8250   (BR)
HALTON DISTRICT SCHOOL BOARD
GARTH WEBB SECONDARY SCHOOL
(*Suby of* HALTON DISTRICT SCHOOL BOARD)
2820 Westoak Trails Blvd, Oakville, ON, L6M 4W2
(905) 847-6875
Emp Here 105
SIC 8211 Elementary and secondary schools
Larry O'malley

D-U-N-S 25-138-3717   (BR)
HALTON DISTRICT SCHOOL BOARD

ABBEY PARK HIGH SCHOOL
(Suby of HALTON DISTRICT SCHOOL BOARD)
1455 Glen Abbey Gate, Oakville, ON, L6M 2G5
(905) 827-4101
Emp Here 98
SIC 8211 Elementary and secondary schools
Tara Connor

D-U-N-S 25-511-5289   (HQ)
HALTON HEALTHCARE SERVICES COR-PORATION
MILTON DISTRICT HOSPITAL
3001 Hospital Gate, Oakville, ON, L6M 0L8
(905) 845-2571
Sales 349,000,041
SIC 8062 General medical and surgical hospitals
John Oliver
Mary Wilson Trider
Mags Shorey
Don Newell
Marty Hughes

D-U-N-S 20-558-8820   (SL)
IOVATE HEALTH SCIENCES INTERNA-TIONAL INC
MUSCLETECH
(Suby of KERR INVESTMENT HOLDING CORP)
381 North Service Rd W, Oakville, ON, L6M 0H4
(905) 678-3119
Emp Here 385   Sales 127,663,690
SIC 2833 Medicinals and botanicals
Terry Begley
Paul Gardiner

D-U-N-S 25-361-7989   (HQ)
KERR INVESTMENT HOLDING CORP
381 North Service Rd W, Oakville, ON, L6M 0H4
(905) 678-3119
Sales 109,652,700
SIC 6712 Bank holding companies
Paul Gardiner

D-U-N-S 25-513-1047   (SL)
KIRKWOOD GROUP LTD, THE
1155 North Service Rd W Suite 8, Oakville, ON, L6M 3E3
(905) 849-4346
Emp Here 50   Sales 29,395,800
SIC 5182 Wine and distilled beverages
Peter Kirkwood
Gordon Haist

D-U-N-S 25-535-3203   (SL)
LEXSAN ELECTRICAL INC
3328 Burnhamthorpe Rd W, Oakville, ON, L6M 4H3
(905) 827-1616
Emp Here 3   Sales 18,732,000
SIC 1731 Electrical work
Alexander Moore
Dina Pereira

D-U-N-S 24-859-3274   (SL)
LINCLUDEN INVESTMENT MANAGEMENT LIMITED
1275 North Service Rd W Suite 607, Oakville, ON, L6M 3G4
(905) 825-9000
Emp Here 17   Sales 12,468,684
SIC 6722 Management investment, open-end
Philip Evans
Richard Wong
Lynn Eplett
Peter Chin
James Lampard
Gary Stewart
Brian Brownlee
Wayne Wilson
Todd Parsons

D-U-N-S 24-981-5945   (HQ)
MANULIFE SECURITIES INVESTMENT

SERVICES INC
(Suby of MANULIFE FINANCIAL CORPORA-TION)
1235 North Service Rd W Suite 500, Oakville, ON, L6M 2W2
(905) 469-2100
Sales 1,167,385,000
SIC 6722 Management investment, open-end
Michael Lee-Chinn
Richard Hogeveen
Michael Leman
George Garner
Paul Mckay
Rick K. Annaert

D-U-N-S 24-886-6337   (HQ)
MBEC COMMUNICATIONS INC
THE UPS STORE (FRANCHISOR)
1115 North Service Rd W Unit 1, Oakville, ON, L6M 2V9
(905) 338-9754
Emp Here 20   Sales 17,420,250
SIC 6794 Patent owners and lessors
David Druker
Steven Moorman
Ronald Boratto
Bill Ibberson
Chati Narayan

D-U-N-S 25-136-9955   (BR)
METRO ONTARIO PHARMACIES LIMITED
METRO
(Suby of METRO INC)
280 North Service Rd W, Oakville, ON, L6M 2S2
(905) 337-7694
Emp Here 200
SIC 5411 Grocery stores
Scott Evans

D-U-N-S 20-964-7171   (HQ)
NEW ELECTRIC ENTERPRISES INC
3185 Dundas St W, Oakville, ON, L6M 4J4
(905) 827-2555
Emp Here 75   Sales 32,674,350
SIC 1731 Electrical work
Andy Ketelaars
Roland Vanolst

D-U-N-S 24-771-4579   (SL)
OAKVILLE GYMNASTIC CLUB
1415 Third Line, Oakville, ON, L6M 3G2
(905) 847-7747
Emp Here 80   Sales 11,202,320
SIC 7999 Amusement and recreation, nec
Wayne Hussey

D-U-N-S 20-403-9887   (SL)
OAKVILLE VOLKSWAGEN INC
AUDI CENTRE OAKVILLE
1345 North Service Rd W, Oakville, ON, L6M 2W2
(905) 844-3285
Emp Here 60   Sales 37,756,800
SIC 5511 New and used car dealers
Theodore Seibert

D-U-N-S 20-527-8562   (SL)
PREMIER AUTOMOTIVE GROUP INC
LEXUS OF OAKVILLE
1453 North Service Rd W, Oakville, ON, L6M 2W2
(905) 847-8400
Emp Here 35   Sales 17,432,730
SIC 5511 New and used car dealers
Frank Apa
Joe Zanchin

D-U-N-S 20-978-4367   (BR)
REVERA LONG TERM CARE INC
WEST OAK VILLAGE
(Suby of GOVERNMENT OF CANADA)
2370 Third Line, Oakville, ON, L6M 4E2
(905) 469-3294
Emp Here 250
SIC 8059 Nursing and personal care, nec
Leslie Harris

D-U-N-S 20-879-2457   (HQ)
ROYAL CANADIAN GOLF ASSOCIATION
GOLF CANADA
1333 Dorval Dr Unit 1, Oakville, ON, L6M 4X6
(905) 849-9700
Sales 15,685,437
SIC 8621 Professional organizations
Charlie Beaulieu
Liz Hoffman
Dale Jackson
Laurence Applebaum
Leslie Dunning
David Atkinson
Robert Macdonald
Adam Daifallah
David Mccarthy
Patrick Kelly

D-U-N-S 24-769-7480   (SL)
SCOTIAMCLEOD INC
1235 North Service Rd W Suite 200, Oakville, ON, L6M 2W2
(905) 637-4962
Emp Here 40   Sales 17,739,600
SIC 7389 Business services, nec
Rodney White

D-U-N-S 25-806-4856   (BR)
SOBEYS CAPITAL INCORPORATED
SOBEY'S STORE 777
(Suby of EMPIRE COMPANY LIMITED)
1500 Upper Middle Rd W, Oakville, ON, L6M 0C2
(905) 847-1909
Emp Here 200
SIC 5411 Grocery stores
John Flandja

D-U-N-S 24-352-6253   (HQ)
SUEZ WATER TECHNOLOGIES & SOLU-TIONS CANADA
(Suby of SUEZ)
3239 Dundas St W, Oakville, ON, L6M 4B2
(905) 465-3030
Emp Here 1   Sales 336,106,000
SIC 5169 Chemicals and allied products, nec
Yuvbir Singh
Heiner Markoff
Kevin Cassidy
Deborah Lloyd

D-U-N-S 25-320-1115   (SL)
TAKEDA CANADA INC
(Suby of TAKEDA PHARMACEUTICAL COM-PANY LIMITED)
435 North Service Rd W Suite 101, Oakville, ON, L6M 4X8
(905) 469-9333
Emp Here 220   Sales 90,820,620
SIC 5122 Drugs, proprietaries, and sundries
Michael Egli
Frank Murphy

D-U-N-S 20-294-1365   (SL)
TEMPO CANADA ULC
1175 North Service Rd W Suite 200, Oakville, ON, L6M 2W1
(905) 339-3309
Emp Here 20   Sales 10,006,500
SIC 5169 Chemicals and allied products, nec
Hank Bewolf

D-U-N-S 24-250-2081   (SL)
TOOR & ASSOCIATES INC
BOSTON PIZZA
270 North Service Rd W, Oakville, ON, L6M 2R8
(905) 849-8100
Emp Here 150   Sales 6,827,850
SIC 5812 Eating places
John Wanamaker

Oakville, ON L9T

D-U-N-S 20-161-2116   (HQ)
PSC-POWER SOURCE CANADA LTD
POWER SOURCE CANADA
8400 Parkhill Dr, Oakville, ON, L9T 5V7
(289) 851-6690
Emp Here 27   Sales 15,200,832
SIC 5084 Industrial machinery and equipment
Mark Baillie

Odessa, ON K0H

D-U-N-S 24-864-1461   (SL)
CANADIAN TIRE
1550 Simmons, Odessa, ON, K0H 2H0
(613) 386-3457
Emp Here 30   Sales 14,942,340
SIC 5541 Gasoline service stations
Mike Dugson

D-U-N-S 24-507-6526   (SL)
DOORNEKAMP, H. R. CONSTRUCTION LTD
588 Scotland Rd, Odessa, ON, K0H 2H0
(613) 386-3033
Emp Here 60   Sales 34,220,280
SIC 1542 Nonresidential construction, nec

Ohsweken, ON N0A

D-U-N-S 24-229-3814   (HQ)
GANOHKWA SRA FAMILY ASSAULT SUP-PORT SERVICES
1781 Chiefswood Rd, Ohsweken, ON, N0A 1M0
(519) 445-4324
Emp Here 40   Sales 15,896,560
SIC 8699 Membership organizations, nec
Sandra Montour

D-U-N-S 25-467-1324   (HQ)
GRAND RIVER ENTERPRISES SIX NA-TIONS LIMITED
G R E
2176 Chiefswood Rd, Ohsweken, ON, N0A 1M0
(519) 445-0919
Sales 27,510,450
SIC 2111 Cigarettes
Steve R Williams
Robert Johnson
David R Green

D-U-N-S 20-273-1886   (SL)
SIX NATIONS NATURAL GAS LIMITED PARTNERSHIP
1953 Fourth Line, Ohsweken, ON, N0A 1M0
(519) 445-4213
Emp Here 10   Sales 31,058,570
SIC 4924 Natural gas distribution
Nick Petruzzella

D-U-N-S 24-202-9606   (SL)
SIX NATIONS OF THE GRAND RIVER DE-VELOPMENT CORPORATION
2498 Chiefswood, Ohsweken, ON, N0A 1M0
(519) 753-1950
Emp Here 170   Sales 28,245,901
SIC 8741 Management services
Matt Jamieson
Jean Mckinnon

Oil Springs, ON N0N

D-U-N-S 24-974-5845   (HQ)
CAM-RON INSURANCE BROKERS LIM-ITED
4579 Oil Springs Line, Oil Springs, ON, N0N 1P0
(519) 834-2833
Emp Here 9   Sales 10,176,720

▲ Public Company   ■ Public Company Family Member   **HQ** Headquarters   **BR** Branch   **SL** Single Location

SIC 6411 Insurance agents, brokers, and service
Cheryl Camerond
Gregory Cameron
Agnes Cameron
Karen Hoven
Janet Cameron

Oldcastle, ON N0R

D-U-N-S 24-333-0730   (HQ)
1147048 ONTARIO LIMITED
5000 Regal Dr, Oldcastle, ON, N0R 1L0
(519) 737-7535
Emp Here 1   *Sales* 19,062,960
SIC 3089 Plastics products, nec
Steve Hengsperger

D-U-N-S 24-506-6188   (SL)
A V GAUGE & FIXTURE INC
4000 Delduca Dr, Oldcastle, ON, N0R 1L0
(519) 737-7677
Emp Here 190   *Sales* 42,180,190
SIC 3544 Special dies, tools, jigs, and fixtures
Denis G Levasseur

D-U-N-S 24-364-4432   (SL)
AALBERS TOOL & MOLD INC
5390 Brendan Lane, Oldcastle, ON, N0R 1L0
(519) 737-1369
Emp Here 187   *Sales* 19,441,204
SIC 3544 Special dies, tools, jigs, and fixtures
Gary Aalbers

D-U-N-S 25-459-0136   (HQ)
ADVANTAGE ENGINEERING INC
(*Suby of* 1147048 ONTARIO LIMITED)
5000 Regal Dr, Oldcastle, ON, N0R 1L0
(519) 737-7535
Emp Here 110   *Sales* 19,062,960
SIC 3089 Plastics products, nec
Steve Hengsperger
Lynda Dettinger

D-U-N-S 24-688-9927   (HQ)
AMICO INFRASTRUCTURES INC
AMICO
(*Suby of* AMICONE HOLDINGS LIMITED)
2199 Blackacre Dr Suite 100, Oldcastle, ON, N0R 1L0
(519) 737-1577
Emp Here 35   *Sales* 12,622,100
SIC 1623 Water, sewer, and utility lines
Dominic Amicone
Cindy Prince
Jamie Di Laudo
Dino Fantin
Gary Quenneville
Chris Karpala
Mauro Mastronardi

D-U-N-S 25-401-1604   (SL)
BRIADCO TOOL & MOULD INC
5605 Roscon Industrial Dr, Oldcastle, ON, N0R 1L0
(519) 737-1760
Emp Here 74   *Sales* 30,620,520
SIC 3544 Special dies, tools, jigs, and fixtures
Paul Robinson

D-U-N-S 24-023-4716   (SL)
CIOCIARO CLUB OF WINDSOR INC
3745 North Talbot Rd, Oldcastle, ON, N0R 1L0
(519) 737-6153
Emp Here 85   *Sales* 11,178,775
SIC 8641 Civic and social associations
George Mariani
Carlo Petrilli
Domenic Aversa
Frank Maceroni
Enio Di Donato
Valentino Rossi
Enzo Pappini

Armando Carlini
Nazzareno Conte
Angelo Gesuale

D-U-N-S 25-647-4008   (SL)
CON-TACT MASONRY LTD
2504 Binder Cres Suite 1, Oldcastle, ON, N0R 1L0
(519) 737-1852
Emp Here 85   *Sales* 13,802,385
SIC 1741 Masonry and other stonework
Tony Masciotra

D-U-N-S 24-142-0558   (SL)
CREST MOLD TECHNOLOGY INC
(*Suby of* 971095 ONTARIO INC)
2055 Blackacre Dr Rr 1, Oldcastle, ON, N0R 1L0
(519) 737-1546
Emp Here 66   *Sales* 15,567,760
SIC 3089 Plastics products, nec
William Cipkar
Rose Cipkar

D-U-N-S 20-401-6885   (SL)
ELMARA CONSTRUCTION CO. LIMITED
5365 Walker Rd Rr 1, Oldcastle, ON, N0R 1L0
(519) 737-1253
Emp Here 60   *Sales* 25,364,220
SIC 1541 Industrial buildings and warehouses
Mike Quaggiotto

D-U-N-S 20-316-9313   (HQ)
ESSEX POWER CORPORATION
2199 Blackacre Dr Suite 2, Oldcastle, ON, N0R 1L0
(519) 946-2002
Sales 18,798,420
SIC 4911 Electric services
Raymond Tracey
Gary Mcnamara
Aldo Dicarlo
John Paterson
Ken Antaya
Joe Graziano
Tom Burton
Frank Ricci
William Wark

D-U-N-S 24-193-7499   (HQ)
FLEETWOOD METAL INDUSTRIES INC
FMI
(*Suby of* AK STEEL HOLDING CORPORATION)
1885 Blackacre Dr, Oldcastle, ON, N0R 1L0
(519) 737-1919
Sales 153,235,530
SIC 3469 Metal stampings, nec
Grant Burton
John Clarke
Dave Hillier

D-U-N-S 24-219-0049   (SL)
GLIDER GUARD TOOL & DIE INC
5135 Ure St Suite 1, Oldcastle, ON, N0R 1L0
(519) 737-7313
Emp Here 65   *Sales* 14,430,065
SIC 3544 Special dies, tools, jigs, and fixtures
Roger Cox

D-U-N-S 20-185-3645   (HQ)
GORSKI BULK TRANSPORT INC
5400 Walker Rd, Oldcastle, ON, N0R 1L0
(519) 737-1275
Sales 20,570,600
SIC 4213 Trucking, except local
Ted Gorski Jr
Bernard Gorski

D-U-N-S 20-016-7513   (HQ)
INTEGRITY TOOL & MOLD INC
5015 O'Neil Dr, Oldcastle, ON, N0R 1L0
(519) 737-2650
Emp Here 3   *Sales* 75,225,780
SIC 3089 Plastics products, nec
Paul Digiovanni
Patti Zakoor
Scott Allen

Ed Winter
Dino Desantis
Dave Schraeder
Ryan Hotchkiss
Mike Brouillette
Kevin Booker
Eric Ginter

D-U-N-S 24-823-5608   (SL)
J.F.K. SYSTEMS INC
NARMCO GROUP
3160 Moynahan St, Oldcastle, ON, N0R 1L0
(519) 737-1361
Emp Here 80   *Sales* 17,760,080
SIC 3544 Special dies, tools, jigs, and fixtures
Donald Rodzik

D-U-N-S 24-452-5416   (SL)
KLASSEN, P CUSTOM FAB INC
5140 Ure St, Oldcastle, ON, N0R 1L0
(519) 737-6631
Emp Here 70   *Sales* 13,445,950
SIC 3443 Fabricated plate work (boiler shop)
Peter Klassen

D-U-N-S 24-143-5593   (HQ)
LAKESIDE PLASTICS LIMITED
3786 North Talbot Rd Suite 1, Oldcastle, ON, N0R 1L0
(519) 737-1271
Emp Here 110   *Sales* 78,807,960
SIC 3089 Plastics products, nec
Robert Luckino

D-U-N-S 20-011-1990   (BR)
LAKESIDE PLASTICS LIMITED
(*Suby of* LAKESIDE PLASTICS LIMITED)
5186 O'Neil Dr Rr 1, Oldcastle, ON, N0R 1L0
(519) 737-1271
Emp Here 300
SIC 3089 Plastics products, nec
Owen Hardy

D-U-N-S 24-563-3904   (SL)
M.T.E. CONTROLS CORPORATION
5135 Hennin Dr, Oldcastle, ON, N0R 1L0
(519) 737-7555
Emp Here 50   *Sales* 23,751,300
SIC 5084 Industrial machinery and equipment
Theodore Kuzniak

D-U-N-S 24-363-4375   (HQ)
MANOR TOOL AND DIE LTD
MAX DIE GROUP
5264 Pulleybank St, Oldcastle, ON, N0R 1L0
(519) 737-6537
Sales 22,200,100
SIC 3544 Special dies, tools, jigs, and fixtures
Eleanor Ofner
Anne Marie Ofner

D-U-N-S 20-125-8480   (SL)
MATASSA INCORPORATED
5335 Walker Rd, Oldcastle, ON, N0R 1L0
(519) 737-1506
Emp Here 45   *Sales* 14,999,985
SIC 1541 Industrial buildings and warehouses
Jaqueline Matassa
Frank Matassa

D-U-N-S 24-410-1945   (HQ)
OMEGA TOOL CORP
(*Suby of* 7610955 CANADA INC)
2045 Solar Cres, Oldcastle, ON, N0R 1L0
(519) 737-1201
Sales 44,400,200
SIC 3544 Special dies, tools, jigs, and fixtures
Dave Cecchin
Euclide Cecchin

D-U-N-S 24-381-1101   (SL)
REVSTONE PLASTICS CANADA INC
(*Suby of* REVSTONE INDUSTRIES, LLC)
2045 Solar Cres Rr 1, Oldcastle, ON, N0R 1L0
(519) 737-1201
Emp Here 200   *Sales* 44,400,200
SIC 3544 Special dies, tools, jigs, and fixtures
George S Hofmeister

Richard E Clark

D-U-N-S 24-783-6976   (SL)
SATURN TOOL & DIE (WINDSOR) INC
5175 Hennin Dr, Oldcastle, ON, N0R 1L0

Emp Here 80   *Sales* 17,760,080
SIC 3542 Machine tools, Metal forming type
Frank Ventrella
Mike Ventrella
Rosemary Ventrella
Lisa Ventrella

D-U-N-S 25-396-7483   (SL)
SELECT TOOL INC
3015 North Talbot Rd, Oldcastle, ON, N0R 1L0
(519) 737-6406
Emp Here 145   *Sales* 32,190,145
SIC 3544 Special dies, tools, jigs, and fixtures
Paul Hollister
David Tomassi
John Piruzza

D-U-N-S 24-370-1062   (SL)
TOOLPLAS SYSTEMS INC
1905 Blackacre Dr, Oldcastle, ON, N0R 1L0
(519) 737-9948
Emp Here 165   *Sales* 26,211,570
SIC 3089 Plastics products, nec
John Schultz
Stephane Desbiens

D-U-N-S 24-603-7261   (SL)
WHITFIELD WELDING INC
5425 Roscon Industrial Dr, Oldcastle, ON, N0R 1L0
(519) 737-1814
Emp Here 40   *Sales* 10,873,680
SIC 7692 Welding repair
Ronald Whitfield

D-U-N-S 20-104-2988   (HQ)
WINDSOR METAL TECHNOLOGIES INC
3900 Delduca Dr, Oldcastle, ON, N0R 1L0
(519) 737-7611
Sales 18,672,357
SIC 3544 Special dies, tools, jigs, and fixtures
John Spidalieri
Mike Spidalieri

Orangeville, ON L9W

D-U-N-S 20-114-3794   (SL)
1443237 ONTARIO INC
HALLMARK TOYOTA
713003 1st Line, Orangeville, ON, L9W 2Z2
(519) 941-9291
Emp Here 30   *Sales* 14,942,340
SIC 5511 New and used car dealers
Christopher Pfaff
Brent Scobie

D-U-N-S 20-638-1241   (SL)
4137566 CANADA LTD
CANADIAN TIRE AUTOMOTIVE PARTS
99 First St, Orangeville, ON, L9W 2E8
(519) 941-1090
Emp Here 45   *Sales* 22,413,510
SIC 5531 Auto and home supply stores
Stuart Cameron

D-U-N-S 24-795-9034   (SL)
488491 ONTARIO INC
AVALON RETIREMENT CENTER
355 Broadway Suite 1, Orangeville, ON, L9W 3Y3
(519) 941-5161
Emp Here 250   *Sales* 33,919,250
SIC 6513 Apartment building operators
Alex Jarlette
Erna Baniulis

D-U-N-S 24-209-7673   (SL)
662117 ONTARIO INC

BROWN, JIM & SONS TRUCKING
17 Shannon Crt, Orangeville, ON, L9W 5L8
(519) 941-2950
Emp Here 80   *Sales* 11,855,360
SIC 4212 Local trucking, without storage
James Brown
Brett Brown

        D-U-N-S 20-528-7980   (SL)
891934 ONTARIO LIMITED
ORANGEVILLE HOME HARDWARE BUILD-ING CENTRE
60 Fourth Ave Suite 1, Orangeville, ON, L9W 3Z7
(519) 941-5407
Emp Here 70   *Sales* 18,735,640
SIC 5211 Lumber and other building materials
Royce Hill

        D-U-N-S 20-134-7937   (SL)
941-2401 HEATING LTD
BRYAN'S FUEL
400 Richardson Rd, Orangeville, ON, L9W 4W8
(519) 941-2401
Emp Here 50   *Sales* 23,450,250
SIC 5983 Fuel oil dealers
Roy Bryan

        D-U-N-S 20-158-2699   (HQ)
ACME UNITED LIMITED
ACME
(*Suby of* ACME UNITED CORPORATION)
210 Broadway Suite 204, Orangeville, ON, L9W 5G4
(519) 940-8755
Sales 12,591,450
SIC 5112 Stationery and office supplies
John Ward
Ian Stuart

        D-U-N-S 25-152-9657   (SL)
BLACKSTOCK FORD LINCOLN SALES LTD
207155 9 Hwy, Orangeville, ON, L9W 2Z7
(519) 941-5431
Emp Here 35   *Sales* 17,432,730
SIC 5511 New and used car dealers
Greg Blackstock

        D-U-N-S 24-197-6497   (SL)
CARRUS INVESTMENTS LTD
ORANGEVILLE HONDA
Gd Stn A, Orangeville, ON, L9W 2Z4
(519) 941-6221
Emp Here 35   *Sales* 17,432,730
SIC 5511 New and used car dealers
John Walkinshaw

        D-U-N-S 24-545-5865   (SL)
CCI RESEARCH INC
CCI RESEARCH
71 Broadway, Orangeville, ON, L9W 1K1
(519) 938-9552
Emp Here 50   *Sales* 11,734,800
SIC 8732 Commercial nonphysical research
Ian Macfarlane
Andrew Blunden

        D-U-N-S 24-910-3979   (BR)
CLOROX COMPANY OF CANADA, LTD, THE
(*Suby of* THE CLOROX COMPANY)
101 John St, Orangeville, ON, L9W 2R1
(519) 941-0720
Emp Here 300
SIC 2673 Bags: plastic, laminated, and coated
Cleminson John Hugh

        D-U-N-S 25-876-2970   (SL)
COMPUSTAT CONSULTANTS INC
67 First St, Orangeville, ON, L9W 2E6
(519) 938-9552
Emp Here 200   *Sales* 43,988,600
SIC 8732 Commercial nonphysical research
Ted Hodge
Karen Hodge

        D-U-N-S 20-976-2293   (SL)
DATA CABLE COMPANY INC, THE
31 Robb Blvd, Orangeville, ON, L9W 3L1
(519) 941-7020
Emp Here 65   *Sales* 12,378,730
SIC 3679 Electronic components, nec
Paul Nelson
Richard Fearon
Lita Fearon

        D-U-N-S 24-850-9499   (SL)
DIRECT PLASTICS LTD
NOVOLEX
(*Suby of* OAK HILL CAPITAL PARTNERS, L.P.)
20 Stewart Crt, Orangeville, ON, L9W 3Z9
(519) 942-8511
Emp Here 85   *Sales* 16,555,280
SIC 2673 Bags: plastic, laminated, and coated
Kirk Stover

        D-U-N-S 24-194-3104   (SL)
FITNESS KICKBOXING CANADA INC
10 Second St, Orangeville, ON, L9W 2B5
(519) 942-1625
Emp Here 24   *Sales* 10,169,520
SIC 7941 Sports clubs, managers, and pro-moters
Ross O'donnell

        D-U-N-S 20-730-3892   (HQ)
GORD DAVENPORT AUTOMOTIVE INC
G D AUTO PARTS
74 First St, Orangeville, ON, L9W 2E4
(519) 941-1233
Emp Here 34   *Sales* 16,753,890
SIC 5013 Motor vehicle supplies and new parts
Jim Davenport
John Kallay
Pat Kallay

        D-U-N-S 20-051-0568   (SL)
GREENWOOD CONSTRUCTION COMPANY LIMITED
Hwy 9, Orangeville, ON, L9W 2Y9
(519) 941-0732
Emp Here 80   *Sales* 18,891,090
SIC 3273 Ready-mixed concrete
Sam Greenwood
Joseph Greenwood

        D-U-N-S 20-801-3701   (SL)
GREENWOOD READY MIX LIMITED
Hwy 9, Orangeville, ON, L9W 2Y9
(519) 941-0710
Emp Here 80   *Sales* 45,627,040
SIC 1542 Nonresidential construction, nec
John Samuel Greenwood
Cheryl Irene Greenwood
Joseph Greenwood

        D-U-N-S 24-218-8613   (SL)
HARMONY WHOLE FOODS MARKET (OR-ANGEVILLE) LTD
HARMONY WHOLE FOODS MARKET
163 First St Unit A, Orangeville, ON, L9W 3J8
(519) 941-8961
Emp Here 20   *Sales* 10,702,480
SIC 5149 Groceries and related products, nec
Jennifer Grant

        D-U-N-S 20-921-2752   (SL)
HEADWATERS HEALTH CARE CENTRE
100 Rolling Hills Dr, Orangeville, ON, L9W 4X9
(519) 941-2410
Emp Here 600   *Sales* 50,635,572
SIC 8062 General medical and surgical hospi-tals
Liz Ruegg
Peter Harris
Rob Hamilton
Steve Desrocher

        D-U-N-S 24-387-5569   (SL)

HOFMANN, E. PLASTICS, INC
51 Centennial Rd, Orangeville, ON, L9W 3R1
(519) 943-5050
Emp Here 125   *Sales* 29,145,634
SIC 3089 Plastics products, nec
Paul Kalia

        D-U-N-S 20-192-4045   (BR)
HOME DEPOT OF CANADA INC
HOME DEPOT
(*Suby of* THE HOME DEPOT INC)
49 Fourth Ave, Orangeville, ON, L9W 1G7
(519) 940-9061
Emp Here 150
SIC 5251 Hardware stores
Greg Ruffa

        D-U-N-S 24-059-2105   (HQ)
HONEYCOMB HILL HOLDINGS OF MUL-MUR INC
FOUNDRY, THE
410 Richardson Road, Orangeville, ON, L9W 4W8
(519) 942-9999
Sales 10,746,132
SIC 5074 Plumbing and heating equipment and supplies (hydronics)
Craig Gutowski
Evelyn Fotheringham

        D-U-N-S 24-684-4203   (BR)
JOHNSON CONTROLS NOVA SCOTIA U.L.C.
AUTOMOTIVE SYSTEMS GROUP
(*Suby of* JOHNSON CONTROLS INTERNA-TIONAL PUBLIC LIMITED COMPANY)
120 C Line, Orangeville, ON, L9W 3Z8

Emp Here 350
SIC 2531 Public building and related furniture
Paolucci Domenic

        D-U-N-S 20-024-1565   (SL)
JOPAMAR HOLDINGS INC
HARVEY'S/SWISS CHALET
93 First St, Orangeville, ON, L9W 2E8
(519) 941-4009
Emp Here 78   *Sales* 3,550,482
SIC 5812 Eating places
Mario Medeiros

        D-U-N-S 24-737-8078   (SL)
LJP CORPORATION
ADAMO ESTATE WINERY
(*Suby of* ADAMO HOLDINGS INC)
793522 Mono 3rd Line, Orangeville, ON, L9W 2Y8
(519) 942-0754
Emp Here 50   *Sales* 13,115,450
SIC 0172 Grapes
Nancy Adamo
John Paul Adamo
Julie Adamo
Mario Adamo

        D-U-N-S 25-155-2279   (BR)
MCDONALD'S RESTAURANTS OF CANADA LIMITED
MCDONALD'S
(*Suby of* MCDONALD'S CORPORATION)
95 First St, Orangeville, ON, L9W 2E8
(519) 940-0197
Emp Here 90
SIC 5812 Eating places
Tanvir Khan

        D-U-N-S 25-676-1867   (BR)
METRO ONTARIO INC
METRO
(*Suby of* METRO INC)
150 First St Suite 7, Orangeville, ON, L9W 3T7
(519) 941-6391
Emp Here 140
SIC 5411 Grocery stores
John Sinclair

        D-U-N-S 24-391-2909   (SL)

MOTION MAZDA
753007 2nd Line E, Orangeville, ON, L9W 2Z2
(519) 943-1100
Emp Here 25   *Sales* 12,451,950
SIC 5511 New and used car dealers
Glen Alizadeh

        D-U-N-S 25-221-4549   (SL)
ORANGEVILLE CHRYSLER LIMITED
207 163 Hwy Suite 9, Orangeville, ON, L9W 2Z7
(519) 942-8400
Emp Here 30   *Sales* 14,942,340
SIC 5511 New and used car dealers
Danny Brackett

        D-U-N-S 20-783-1702   (SL)
PINEHURST GROUP, INC
120 C Line, Orangeville, ON, L9W 3Z8
(519) 943-0100
Emp Here 140   *Sales* 21,605,080
SIC 2541 Wood partitions and fixtures
Donald Christie

        D-U-N-S 20-689-1405   (SL)
PINEHURST STORE FIXTURES INC
120 C Line, Orangeville, ON, L9W 3Z8
(519) 943-0100
Emp Here 135   *Sales* 20,833,470
SIC 2542 Partitions and fixtures, except wood
Donald Christie

        D-U-N-S 20-750-2352   (HQ)
R.J. BURNSIDE & ASSOCIATES LIMITED
15 Town Line, Orangeville, ON, L9W 3R4
(519) 941-5331
Emp Here 90   *Sales* 49,282,750
SIC 8711 Engineering services
Robert Burnside
Ian Drever
Bill Yokom
Rui De Carvalho
David Bannister
Mervin Dewasha
Gord Feniak

        D-U-N-S 20-303-3428   (BR)
RECIPE UNLIMITED CORPORATION
KELSEY'S
(*Suby of* RECIPE UNLIMITED CORPORA-TION)
115 Fifth Ave, Orangeville, ON, L9W 5B7
(519) 940-4004
Emp Here 75
SIC 5812 Eating places
Scott Johnston

        D-U-N-S 20-816-7502   (SL)
ROCHLING ENGINEERING PLASTICS LTD
(*Suby of* ROCHLING SE & CO. KG)
21 Tideman Dr, Orangeville, ON, L9W 3K3
(519) 941-5300
Emp Here 110   *Sales* 36,009,845
SIC 3083 Laminated plastics plate and sheet
Tim C Brown
Allison Barrett
Arlene Rentz

        D-U-N-S 20-820-1608   (SL)
ROYAL CHEVROLET-CADILLAC INC
1 Monora Park Dr, Orangeville, ON, L9W 0E1
(519) 941-0420
Emp Here 40   *Sales* 19,923,120
SIC 5511 New and used car dealers
Barry Mckay
Paul Attwell
Todd Mckay

        D-U-N-S 25-499-7588   (SL)
SANOH CANADA, LTD
(*Suby of* SANOH INDUSTRIAL CO.,LTD.)
300 C Line, Orangeville, ON, L9W 3Z8
(519) 941-2229
Emp Here 120   *Sales* 55,338,480
SIC 5013 Motor vehicle supplies and new parts
Connie Fraser

D-U-N-S 20-378-0353 (BR)
SAPUTO INC
WOOLWICH DAIRY
(*Suby of* JOLINA CAPITAL INC)
425 Richardson Rd, Orangeville, ON, L9W 4Z4
(519) 941-9206
Emp Here 97
SIC 2022 Cheese; natural and processed

D-U-N-S 24-326-0291 (BR)
SOBEYS CAPITAL INCORPORATED
(*Suby of* EMPIRE COMPANY LIMITED)
500 Riddell Rd, Orangeville, ON, L9W 5L1
(519) 941-1339
Emp Here 150
SIC 5411 Grocery stores
Derek Leduc

D-U-N-S 24-097-5602 (SL)
TAG INTERNATIONAL INC
TAG PROTECTION SERVICE
75 First St Suite 321, Orangeville, ON, L9W 2E7
(519) 943-0074
Emp Here 49   *Sales* 33,267,227
SIC 6211 Security brokers and dealers
Dean Pavloff

D-U-N-S 25-143-0740 (BR)
UPPER GRAND DISTRICT SCHOOL BOARD, THE
WESTSIDE SECONDARY SCHOOL
(*Suby of* UPPER GRAND DISTRICT SCHOOL BOARD, THE)
300 Alder St, Orangeville, ON, L9W 5A2
(519) 938-9355
Emp Here 75
SIC 8211 Elementary and secondary schools
Deirdre Wilson

Orillia, ON L3V

D-U-N-S 25-497-3134 (SL)
1124178 ONTARIO INC
MORTON METALS
351 West St S, Orillia, ON, L3V 5H1
(705) 327-1300
Emp Here 15   *Sales* 15,005,085
SIC 5051 Metals service centers and offices
Garnet Morton
Gregory Morton

D-U-N-S 25-604-6194 (SL)
1176356 ONTARIO INC
DAVENPORT SUBARU OF ORILLIA
385 West St S, Orillia, ON, L3V 5H2
(705) 329-4277
Emp Here 21   *Sales* 10,459,638
SIC 5511 New and used car dealers
Michael Davenport
Cindy Davenport

D-U-N-S 24-823-4379 (SL)
126074 ONTARIO INC
ORILLIA ASSOCIATION FOR THE HANDI-CAPPED
6 Kitchener St, Orillia, ON, L3V 6Z9
(705) 327-2232
Emp Here 115   *Sales* 7,516,761
SIC 8361 Residential care
Brian Westlake

D-U-N-S 24-768-6087 (SL)
1291292 ONTARIO LIMITED
43 Ontario St, Orillia, ON, L3V 0T7
(705) 326-3586
Emp Here 40   *Sales* 10,966,080
SIC 5411 Grocery stores
Philip Dykes

D-U-N-S 24-703-7997 (SL)
ABERNETHY FOODS (ORILLIA) INC
FOODLAND
80 Fittons Rd W, Orillia, ON, L3V 7A1

(705) 325-9072
Emp Here 55   *Sales* 16,141,235
SIC 5411 Grocery stores
Paul Abernethy

D-U-N-S 24-346-4372 (BR)
CORPORATION OF THE COUNTY OF SIM-COE
TRILLIUM MANOR HOME FOR THE AGED
(*Suby of* CORPORATION OF THE COUNTY OF SIMCOE)
12 Grace Ave, Orillia, ON, L3V 2K2
(705) 325-1504
Emp Here 150
SIC 8361 Residential care
Janice Mccuaig

D-U-N-S 24-059-3137 (SL)
COUNTRY PRODUCE (ORILLIA) LTD
301 Westmount Dr N, Orillia, ON, L3V 6Y4
(705) 325-9902
Emp Here 40   *Sales* 10,966,080
SIC 5431 Fruit and vegetable markets
John Ward

D-U-N-S 24-707-8660 (BR)
FIRSTCANADA ULC
FIRST STUDENT CANADA
(*Suby of* FIRSTGROUP PLC)
445 Laclie St, Orillia, ON, L3V 4P7
(705) 326-7376
Emp Here 85
SIC 4151 School buses
Gerry Richardson

D-U-N-S 25-057-3276 (HQ)
FLSMIDTH LTD
FLS KNELSON
(*Suby of* FLSMIDTH & CO. A/S)
174 West St S, Orillia, ON, L3V 6L4
(705) 325-6181
Emp Here 100   *Sales* 42,131,550
SIC 3532 Mining machinery
Christian Jepsen
George Robles
Brett Knelson
Douglas Corsan
Mike Lloyd
Brad Johnston
Peter Flanagan
Scott Baker
Michael Mcleavy
Stephen Harrington

D-U-N-S 20-849-3825 (SL)
GAMMA SALES INC
100 Hunter Valley Rd, Orillia, ON, L3V 0Y7
(705) 325-3088
Emp Here 30   *Sales* 10,926,450
SIC 5013 Motor vehicle supplies and new parts
Michael Shean

D-U-N-S 25-105-0782 (SL)
HELIX IT INC
9 Ontario St Unit 7, Orillia, ON, L3V 0T7
(705) 327-6564
Emp Here 80   *Sales* 17,426,320
SIC 1731 Electrical work
Robert Loxton

D-U-N-S 25-171-5793 (BR)
HOME DEPOT OF CANADA INC
HOME DEPOT
(*Suby of* THE HOME DEPOT INC)
3225 Monarch Dr, Orillia, ON, L3V 7Z4
(705) 327-6500
Emp Here 150
SIC 5261 Retail nurseries and garden stores
David Craig

D-U-N-S 20-290-6249 (BR)
JARLETTE LTD
LEACOCK CARE CENTRE
25 Museum Dr Suite 204, Orillia, ON, L3V 7T9
(705) 325-9181
Emp Here 160   *Sales* 588,616
SIC 8051 Skilled nursing care facilities

Judy Maltais

D-U-N-S 24-919-5488 (SL)
JIM WILSON CHEVROLET BUICK GMC INC
20 Mulcahy Ct, Orillia, ON, L3V 6H9
(705) 329-2000
Emp Here 65   *Sales* 40,903,200
SIC 5511 New and used car dealers
Jim Wilson

D-U-N-S 25-899-8517 (HQ)
JOHNSTON, RON INSURANCE LTD
448 West St N, Orillia, ON, L3V 5E8
(705) 325-6200
Sales 10,438,632
SIC 6411 Insurance agents, brokers, and service
Douglas Johnston
Dean Johnston
Ronald Johnston
Margaret Beth Johnston

D-U-N-S 24-827-5273 (HQ)
KUBOTA MATERIALS CANADA CORPORA-TION
FAHRAMET, DIV OF
(*Suby of* KUBOTA CORPORATION)
25 Commerce Rd, Orillia, ON, L3V 6L6
(705) 325-2781
Emp Here 325   *Sales* 78,347,700
SIC 3317 Steel pipe and tubes
Yasuhiro Horibe
Daisuke Sugiyama

D-U-N-S 24-216-8284 (SL)
LAUER'S RESTAURANT EQUIPMENT LIM-ITED
3823 Campbell Rd, Orillia, ON, L3V 6H3
(705) 325-9938
Emp Here 35   *Sales* 15,651,090
SIC 5046 Commercial equipment, nec
Ralph Lauer
Therese Lauer

D-U-N-S 20-511-7125 (HQ)
LEADBETTER FOODS INC
(*Suby of* PREMIUM BRANDS HOLDINGS CORPORATION)
255 Hughes Rd, Orillia, ON, L3V 2M2
(705) 325-9922
Emp Here 65   *Sales* 24,198,300
SIC 2011 Meat packing plants
Philip Leadbetter

D-U-N-S 25-536-2584 (SL)
MADISON COUNTY FOOD & BEVERAGE CO. LTD, THE
43 Ontario St, Orillia, ON, L3V 0T7
(705) 326-3586
Emp Here 40   *Sales* 33,423,080
SIC 5149 Groceries and related products, nec
Philip James Dykes
Bonita Anne Dykes

D-U-N-S 24-095-0944 (SL)
MARINE PLAZA TVT
TVT
1753 Division Rd W, Orillia, ON, L3V 6H2
(705) 329-1646
Emp Here 40   *Sales* 19,923,120
SIC 5551 Boat dealers
Henk Ter Veen

D-U-N-S 24-911-0669 (SL)
MARIPOSA MARKET LTD
MARIPOSA MARKET
109 Mississaga St E, Orillia, ON, L3V 1V6
(705) 325-8885
Emp Here 55   *Sales* 13,438,040
SIC 5947 Gift, novelty, and souvenir shop
Robert Willsey

D-U-N-S 24-319-1165 (SL)
MCGILL LOGISTICS INC
Gd Lcd Main, Orillia, ON, L3V 6H8
(705) 329-5891
Emp Here 25   *Sales* 12,999,175
SIC 4731 Freight transportation arrangement

Mac Mcgill

D-U-N-S 24-684-5804 (SL)
MCLEAN & DICKEY LTD
390 Laclie St, Orillia, ON, L3V 4P5
(705) 325-4461
Emp Here 31   *Sales* 17,977,644
SIC 6411 Insurance agents, brokers, and service
Francois Tisi
Bill Hamilton
Danielle Tisi

D-U-N-S 24-318-4573 (SL)
MCLEAN & DICKEY LTD
174 West St S, Orillia, ON, L3V 6L4
(705) 325-4461
Emp Here 21   *Sales* 12,178,404
SIC 6411 Insurance agents, brokers, and service
Danielle Tisi

D-U-N-S 24-333-1696 (BR)
METRO ONTARIO INC
METRO
(*Suby of* METRO INC)
70 Front St N, Orillia, ON, L3V 4R8
(705) 323-9334
Emp Here 60
SIC 5411 Grocery stores
Ngozi Owo

D-U-N-S 20-912-9373 (SL)
ORILLIA BUILDING SUPPLIES (2001) LIM-ITED
HOME HARDWARE BUILDING CENTRE
5 King St, Orillia, ON, L3V 1R2
(705) 326-7371
Emp Here 80   *Sales* 21,412,160
SIC 5251 Hardware stores
John Locke
William (Bill) Ecklund
Michael Tucker

D-U-N-S 25-974-8465 (SL)
ORILLIA DODGE CHRYSLER JEEP INC
(*Suby of* FARQUHAR, THOMAS & SON CO. LIMITED)
450 Memorial Ave, Orillia, ON, L3V 0T7
(705) 325-1331
Emp Here 21   *Sales* 13,214,880
SIC 5511 New and used car dealers
John Farquhar

D-U-N-S 20-059-5630 (HQ)
ORILLIA POWER CORPORATION
(*Suby of* CITY OF ORILLIA, THE)
360 West St S, Orillia, ON, L3V 5G8
(705) 326-7315
Sales 28,197,630
SIC 4911 Electric services
John Mattinson
Patrick Hurley
Larry Brooksbank
Ray Hayhurst
John Cameron
Geoff Hewett
Bruce Jackson

D-U-N-S 20-107-4775 (SL)
ORILLIA POWER DISTRIBUTION CORPO-RATION
ORILLIA POWER
(*Suby of* CITY OF ORILLIA, THE)
360 West St S, Orillia, ON, L3V 5G8
(705) 326-7315
Emp Here 30   *Sales* 18,798,420
SIC 4911 Electric services
John Mattinson
Patrick Hurley

D-U-N-S 20-135-2002 (SL)
PARRY AUTOMOTIVE LIMITED
84 Dunedin St, Orillia, ON, L3V 5T6
(705) 325-1345
Emp Here 28   *Sales* 10,198,020
SIC 5013 Motor vehicle supplies and new

---

parts
Stephen Van Kessel
Susan Peacock
Peter Van Kessel

D-U-N-S 24-364-4481   (SL)
PEARN, ROY E. ENTERPRISES LIMITED
MCDONALD'S RESTAURANT
320 Memorial Ave, Orillia, ON, L3V 5X6
(705) 325-9851
Emp Here 100   *Sales* 4,551,900
SIC 5812 Eating places
Roy Pearn

D-U-N-S 20-515-6727   (BR)
PLASTIQUES BERRY CANADA INC
(Suby of BERRY GLOBAL GROUP, INC.)
301 Forest Ave, Orillia, ON, L3V 3Y7
(705) 326-8921
Emp Here 100
SIC 3081 Unsupported plastics film and sheet
Larry Henshaw

D-U-N-S 20-189-8140   (SL)
QUINAN CONSTRUCTION LIMITED
55 Progress Dr Unit 1, Orillia, ON, L3V 0T7
(705) 325-7704
Emp Here 40   *Sales* 13,333,320
SIC 1541 Industrial buildings and warehouses
Daniel Macnaughton
Ronald Elliott
Richard Leclair
Brian Abbott

D-U-N-S 20-407-1401   (HQ)
R & F CONSTRUCTION INC
R & F CONSTRUCTION
73 Patterson Rd, Orillia, ON, L3V 6H1
(705) 325-5746
Emp Here 54   *Sales* 17,611,230
SIC 1521 Single-family housing construction
Richard Rimkey
David Rimkey

D-U-N-S 24-508-0361   (SL)
RE/MAX ORILLIA REALTY (1996) LTD
97 Neywash St, Orillia, ON, L3V 1X4
(705) 325-1373
Emp Here 50   *Sales* 16,356,350
SIC 6531 Real estate agents and managers

D-U-N-S 25-283-1219   (BR)
REVERA INC
OAK TERRACE
(Suby of GOVERNMENT OF CANADA)
291 Mississaga St W Suite 106, Orillia, ON,
L3V 3B9
(705) 325-2289
Emp Here 95
SIC 8051 Skilled nursing care facilities
Anne Henry

D-U-N-S 20-135-2408   (HQ)
**SANDERSON MONUMENT COMPANY LIM-
ITED**
33 Peter St S, Orillia, ON, L3V 5A8
(705) 326-6131
Emp Here 10   *Sales* 10,504,575
SIC 3281 Cut stone and stone products
Donald Sanderson
Donna Sanderson
Scott Sanderson
Neil Sanderson
William Pashby

D-U-N-S 25-238-2841   (BR)
**SIMCOE COUNTY DISTRICT SCHOOL
BOARD, THE**
*ORILLIA DISTRICT COLLEGIATE & VOCA-
TIONAL INSTITUTE*
(Suby of SIMCOE COUNTY DISTRICT
SCHOOL BOARD, THE)
2 Borland St E, Orillia, ON, L3V 2B4
(705) 728-7570
Emp Here 90
SIC 8211 Elementary and secondary schools
Grant Edwards

D-U-N-S 25-292-4980   (BR)
**SIMCOE COUNTY DISTRICT SCHOOL
BOARD, THE**
TWINS LAKES SECONDARY SCHOOL
(Suby of SIMCOE COUNTY DISTRICT
SCHOOL BOARD, THE)
381 Birch St, Orillia, ON, L3V 2P5
(705) 325-1318
Emp Here 85
SIC 8211 Elementary and secondary schools
Irfan Toor

D-U-N-S 25-238-3070   (BR)
**SIMCOE COUNTY DISTRICT SCHOOL
BOARD, THE**
PARK STREET COLLEGIATE INST
(Suby of SIMCOE COUNTY DISTRICT
SCHOOL BOARD, THE)
233 Park St, Orillia, ON, L3V 5W1

Emp Here 95
SIC 8211 Elementary and secondary schools

D-U-N-S 24-478-0391   (SL)
STORBURN CONSTRUCTION LTD
MCGILL FORMING, DIV OF
Gd, Orillia, ON, L3V 6J3
(705) 326-4140
Emp Here 30   *Sales* 14,121,930
SIC 1542 Nonresidential construction, nec
Frank Burns

D-U-N-S 24-364-4770   (BR)
THERMON HEATING SYSTEMS, INC
(Suby of THERMON GROUP HOLDINGS,
INC.)
1 Hunter Valley Rd, Orillia, ON, L3V 0Y7
(705) 325-3473
Emp Here 190
SIC 3443 Fabricated plate work (boiler shop)
Bruce Thames

D-U-N-S 25-498-2663   (BR)
WAL-MART CANADA CORP
(Suby of WALMART INC.)
175 Murphy Rd, Orillia, ON, L3V 0B5
(705) 325-7403
Emp Here 200
SIC 5311 Department stores
Marty Ovan

D-U-N-S 20-114-7985   (SL)
**WILSON, JIM PONTIAC CHEVROLET
BUICK GMC INC**
Mulcahy Po Box 20 Stn Main, Orillia, ON, L3V
6H9
(705) 325-1322
Emp Here 65   *Sales* 40,903,200
SIC 5511 New and used car dealers
Jim Wilson

Orleans, ON K1C

D-U-N-S 24-268-9321   (SL)
BEAULIEU BAKERY LTD
ORLEANS BAKERY
2122 St. Joseph Blvd, Orleans, ON, K1C 1E6
(613) 837-2525
Emp Here 40   *Sales* 10,966,080
SIC 5461 Retail bakeries
Gabriel Beaulieu

D-U-N-S 25-277-6232   (SL)
**BOURGEOIS-COTE-FORGET & ASSO-
CIATES INSURANCE BROKERS**
2712 St. Joseph Blvd, Orleans, ON, K1C 1G5
(613) 824-0441
Emp Here 18   *Sales* 10,438,632
SIC 6411 Insurance agents, brokers, and ser-
vice
Sylvie Forget

D-U-N-S 20-281-1733   (BR)
CITY OF OTTAWA

*BOB MACQUARRIE RECREATION COM-
PLEX - ORLEANS*
(Suby of CITY OF OTTAWA)
1490 Youville Dr, Orleans, ON, K1C 2X8
(613) 580-9600
Emp Here 75
SIC 7999 Amusement and recreation, nec
France Theriault-Saumur

D-U-N-S 25-246-9648   (SL)
**GUINDON, REJEAN CONSTRUCTION
CORPORATION**
3809 St. Joseph Unit 12, Orleans, ON, K1C
1T1

Emp Here 70   *Sales* 18,965,940
SIC 1521 Single-family housing construction
Rejean Guindon

D-U-N-S 25-301-2637   (BR)
HUDSON'S BAY COMPANY
(Suby of HUDSON'S BAY COMPANY)
110 Place D'Orleans Dr, Orleans, ON, K1C
2L9
(613) 837-8274
Emp Here 200
SIC 5311 Department stores
Giles David

D-U-N-S 24-383-8836   (HQ)
KEAY, JIM FORD LINCOLN SALES LTD
FIX AUTO ORLEANS
1438 Youville Dr, Orleans, ON, K1C 2X8
(613) 841-1010
Emp Here 1   *Sales* 53,488,800
SIC 5511 New and used car dealers
Arthur James Keay
Jason Keay
Lori Keay
Brian Anderson

D-U-N-S 25-769-3655   (BR)
LOBLAWS SUPERMARKETS LIMITED
LOBLAWS
(Suby of LOBLAW COMPANIES LIMITED)
1226 Place D'Orleans Dr Suite 3935, Orleans,
ON, K1C 7K3
(613) 834-4074
Emp Here 100
SIC 5411 Grocery stores
Fern Richer

D-U-N-S 25-479-8226   (SL)
**MOUVEMENT D'IMPLICATION FRANCO-
PHONE D'ORLEANS**
MIFO MOUVEMENT D'IMPLICATION
6600 Carriere St, Orleans, ON, K1C 1J4
(613) 830-6436
Emp Here 45   *Sales* 10,207,485
SIC 8399 Social services, nec
Marie-Claude Doucet

D-U-N-S 20-787-6251   (HQ)
MR. GAS LIMITED
1420 Youville Dr Suite 1, Orleans, ON, K1C
7B3
(613) 824-6777
Emp Here 10   *Sales* 62,928,000
SIC 5541 Gasoline service stations
J H Philippe Gagnon
Donna Gagnon
Gilles Guindon
Andre Gagnon
Mary Ann Gagnon

D-U-N-S 25-395-7237   (SL)
**MYERS ORLEANS CHEVROLET BUICK
GMC INC**
1875 St. Joseph Blvd, Orleans, ON, K1C 7J2
(613) 834-6397
Emp Here 77   *Sales* 48,454,560
SIC 5511 New and used car dealers
Henry Mews
Robert Mews
Harry Mews

D-U-N-S 24-482-1781   (SL)
ORLEANS DODGE CHRYSLER INC

1465 Youville Dr, Orleans, ON, K1C 4R1
(613) 830-1777
Emp Here 60   *Sales* 37,756,800
SIC 5511 New and used car dealers
Maryann Bernard

D-U-N-S 25-926-3457   (BR)
**OTTAWA CATHOLIC DISTRICT SCHOOL
BOARD**
ST MATTHEW HIGH SCHOOL
(Suby of OTTAWA CATHOLIC DISTRICT
SCHOOL BOARD)
6550 Bilberry Dr, Orleans, ON, K1C 2S9
(613) 837-3161
Emp Here 100
SIC 8211 Elementary and secondary schools
Debbie Clark

D-U-N-S 20-705-7972   (SL)
PATHWAY HYUNDAI
1375 Youville Dr, Orleans, ON, K1C 4R1
(613) 837-4222
Emp Here 34   *Sales* 16,934,652
SIC 5521 Used car dealers
Greg Stewart

D-U-N-S 24-885-7039   (SL)
PERFORMANCE MOTORS (OTTAWA) INC
PERFORMANCE MAZDA
(Suby of BERNARD, STAN AUTOMOTIVE
LIMITED)
1469 Youville Dr, Orleans, ON, K1C 4R1
(613) 830-6320
Emp Here 34   *Sales* 21,395,520
SIC 5511 New and used car dealers
Maryann Bernard
Mike Bowland
Doug Sherwood

D-U-N-S 24-684-9587   (BR)
SOEURS DE LA CHARITE D'OTTAWA, LES
RESIDENCE SAINT-LOUIS
(Suby of SOEURS DE LA CHARITE
D'OTTAWA, LES)
879 Hiawatha Park Rd, Orleans, ON, K1C 2Z6
(613) 562-6262
Emp Here 170
SIC 8361 Residential care
Penny Wayne

D-U-N-S 20-519-4413   (HQ)
VEZINA OPTICIANS
5929 Jeanne D'Arc Blvd S Suite Aa, Orleans,
ON, K1C 6V8
(613) 837-1119
Emp Here 10   *Sales* 11,070,400
SIC 5995 Optical goods stores
Robert Vezina

Orleans, ON K1E

D-U-N-S 24-344-5058   (BR)
METRO ONTARIO INC
LOEB FALLINGBROOK
(Suby of METRO INC)
1675e Tenth Line Rd, Orleans, ON, K1E 3P6
(613) 837-2614
Emp Here 120
SIC 5411 Grocery stores
Denyse Charbonneau

D-U-N-S 20-888-9162   (SL)
**PENTAGON-RAYMOND INSURANCE BRO-
KERS INC**
3009 St. Joseph Blvd Unit 101, Orleans, ON,
K1E 1E1
(613) 837-1060
Emp Here 21   *Sales* 12,178,404
SIC 6411 Insurance agents, brokers, and ser-
vice
Joanne Sicotte
Jean Sicotte

D-U-N-S 20-039-5445   (SL)
RAY FRIEL RECREATION COMPLEX

▲ Public Company   ■ Public Company Family Member   **HQ** Headquarters   **BR** Branch   **SL** Single Location

1585 Tenth Line Rd, Orleans, ON, K1E 3E8
(613) 830-2747
Emp Here 225   *Sales* 19,507,500
SIC 7999 Amusement and recreation, nec
Pierre Blais

D-U-N-S 25-769-3085   (BR)
ROYAL LEPAGE LIMITED
ROYAL LEPAGE PERFORMANCE REALTY
(*Suby of* BROOKFIELD ASSET MANAGE-
MENT INC)
250 Centrum Blvd Suite 107, Orleans, ON,
K1E 3J1
(613) 830-3350
Emp Here 80
SIC 6531 Real estate agents and managers
Rick Snell

D-U-N-S 24-686-4458   (SL)
TRIPLE A PHARMACY INC
SHOPPERS DRUG MART
1675e Tenth Line Rd, Orleans, ON, K1E 3P6
(613) 837-6078
Emp Here 59   *Sales* 14,415,352
SIC 5912 Drug stores and proprietary stores
Chesley Woolfrey

Orleans, ON K1W

D-U-N-S 24-350-2627   (SL)
BOSTON PIZZA ORLEANS
3884 Innes Rd, Orleans, ON, K1W 1K9
(613) 590-0881
Emp Here 80   *Sales* 3,641,520
SIC 5812 Eating places
Robert Tuttle

D-U-N-S 24-394-2294   (SL)
CLAUDE L'HEUREUX HOLDINGS INC
CANADIAN TIRE
3910 Innes Rd Suite 422, Orleans, ON, K1W
1K9
(613) 830-7000
Emp Here 173   *Sales* 108,865,440
SIC 5531 Auto and home supply stores
Claude L'heureux

D-U-N-S 25-294-8104   (BR)
WAL-MART CANADA CORP
(*Suby of* WALMART INC.)
3900 Innes Rd, Orleans, ON, K1W 1K9
(613) 837-9399
Emp Here 200
SIC 5311 Department stores
Tim Picotte

Orleans, ON K4A

D-U-N-S 25-496-3887   (HQ)
1213475 ONTARIO INC
PHIL'S CAR WASH & GAS BAR
4358 Innes Rd, Orleans, ON, K4A 3W3
(613) 834-6533
Emp Here 8   *Sales* 50,342,400
SIC 5541 Gasoline service stations
Phillipo Costa

D-U-N-S 20-048-4744   (BR)
AGROPUR COOPERATIVE
NATREL
(*Suby of* AGROPUR COOPERATIVE)
1001 Dairy Dr, Orleans, ON, K4A 3N3
(613) 834-5700
Emp Here 100
SIC 5143 Dairy products, except dried or
canned
Kim Waite

D-U-N-S 24-334-3451   (BR)
**CONSEIL DES ECOLES PUBLIQUES DE
L'EST DE L'ONTARIO**
ECOLE SECONDAIRE PUBLIQUE GISELE-

LALONDE
(*Suby of* CONSEIL DES ECOLES
PUBLIQUES DE L'EST DE L'ONTARIO)
500 Millennium Blvd, Orleans, ON, K4A 4X3
(613) 833-0018
Emp Here 100
SIC 8211 Elementary and secondary schools
Diane Lamoureux

D-U-N-S 25-468-0317   (SL)
**HARTEL FINANCIAL MANAGEMENT COR-
PORATION**
ANDREWS & CO
540 Lacolle Way, Orleans, ON, K4A 0N9
(613) 837-8282
Emp Here 48   *Sales* 10,036,080
SIC 8721 Accounting, auditing, and book-
keeping
David Brighten
Jeff Leblanc

D-U-N-S 20-717-2979   (SL)
HEALTHCARE FOOD SERVICES INC
HEALTHCARE FOOD SERVICES
1010 Dairy Dr, Orleans, ON, K4A 3N3
(613) 841-7786
Emp Here 110   *Sales* 38,025,900
SIC 2099 Food preparations, nec
Brad Mckay
Renso Vettoretti

D-U-N-S 25-095-5648   (BR)
HOME DEPOT OF CANADA INC
HOME DEPOT
(*Suby of* THE HOME DEPOT INC)
2121 Tenth Line Rd Suite 1, Orleans, ON, K4A
4C5
(613) 590-2030
Emp Here 200
SIC 5251 Hardware stores
Kevin Hubich

D-U-N-S 25-311-0175   (BR)
**MCDONALD'S   RESTAURANTS   OF
CANADA LIMITED**
MCDONALD'S #8490
(*Suby of* MCDONALD'S CORPORATION)
4416 Innes Rd, Orleans, ON, K4A 3W3
(613) 841-6633
Emp Here 85
SIC 5812 Eating places
Drew Labelle

D-U-N-S 24-228-3880   (BR)
METRO ONTARIO INC
(*Suby of* METRO INC)
4510 Innes Rd, Orleans, ON, K4A 4C5
(613) 824-8850
Emp Here 109
SIC 5141 Groceries, general line
Andrew Schuweiler

D-U-N-S 25-340-7886   (HQ)
MICON SPORTS LTD
PLAY IT AGAIN SPORTS
2085 Tenth Line Rd, Orleans, ON, K4A 4C5
(613) 731-6006
Emp Here 14   *Sales* 10,880,650
SIC 5941 Sporting goods and bicycle shops
David Jensen
Paul Jensen

D-U-N-S 20-290-6868   (BR)
**OTTAWA CATHOLIC DISTRICT SCHOOL
BOARD**
ST. PETER CATHOLIC HIGH SCHOOL
(*Suby of* OTTAWA CATHOLIC DISTRICT
SCHOOL BOARD)
750 Charlemagne Blvd, Orleans, ON, K4A
3M4
(613) 837-9377
Emp Here 120
SIC 8211 Elementary and secondary schools
Norma Mcdonald

D-U-N-S 25-134-3653   (HQ)
TODAY'S COLONIAL FURNITURE 2000 INC
TODAY'S COLONIAL FURNITURE

1680 Vimont Crt Suite 100, Orleans, ON, K4A
3M3
(613) 837-5900
Emp Here 50   *Sales* 20,916,270
SIC 5712 Furniture stores
Jim Demers
Terry Cole
Vicki Demers
Cyndi Demers

D-U-N-S 25-748-3529   (SL)
TUMBLERS GYMNASTIC CENTRE
330 Vantage Dr, Orleans, ON, K4A 3W1
(613) 834-4334
Emp Here 40   *Sales* 15,896,560
SIC 8699 Membership organizations, nec
Karl Balisch

Oro-Medonte, ON L3V

D-U-N-S 20-705-6599   (HQ)
SPIETH-ANDERSON INTERNATIONAL INC
SPIETH-ANDERSON
135 Forestview Rd, Oro-Medonte, ON, L3V
0R4
(705) 325-2274
Sales 17,937,480
SIC 3949 Sporting and athletic goods, nec
Richard Schell
Brenda Wright

Orono, ON L0B

D-U-N-S 25-340-7456   (SL)
DURHAM CUSTOM MILLWORK INC
19 Tamblyn Rd, Orono, ON, L0B 1M0
(905) 683-8444
Emp Here 70   *Sales* 10,802,540
SIC 2599 Furniture and fixtures, nec
Rod Finney
Gerald Smith

D-U-N-S 24-977-9828   (SL)
ELL-ROD HOLDINGS INC
19 Tamblyn Rd Rr 1, Orono, ON, L0B 1M0
(905) 983-5456
Emp Here 102   *Sales* 19,621,740
SIC 2431 Millwork
Rodney L Finney
Gerald Smith

D-U-N-S 25-119-5830   (SL)
FOUNDATION DISTRIBUTING INC
9 Cobbledick St, Orono, ON, L0B 1M0
(905) 983-1188
Emp Here 35   *Sales* 15,651,090
SIC 5049 Professional equipment, nec
Bob Wood
Colin Prodger
Patrick Chown

D-U-N-S 24-544-1969   (SL)
R.A.C.E. MECHANICAL SYSTEMS INC
9 Cobbledick St, Orono, ON, L0B 1M0
(905) 983-9800
Emp Here 50   *Sales* 11,046,700
SIC 1711 Plumbing, heating, air-conditioning
Terry Timmins
Pat Hegan
Patrick Woodland

Osgoode, ON K0A

D-U-N-S 24-596-1511   (SL)
CARLETON MUSHROOM FARMS LIMITED
6280 Dalmeny Rd, Osgoode, ON, K0A 2W0
(613) 826-2868
Emp Here 34   *Sales* 11,643,878

SIC 0182 Food crops grown under cover
Fernando Medeiros
Fernando Medeiros Jr
Mike Medeiros
Anabela Medeiros

Oshawa, ON L1G

D-U-N-S 24-986-9678   (HQ)
1574942 ONTARIO LIMITED
TIM HORTONS
1802 Simcoe St N, Oshawa, ON, L1G 4X9
(905) 576-2092
Emp Here 1   *Sales* 29,934,654
SIC 5499 Miscellaneous food stores
Robert W Bull
Dorothy Bull

D-U-N-S 25-301-5226   (BR)
**CANADIAN MENTAL HEALTH ASSOCIA-
TION TORONTO BRANCH, THE**
CMHA
(*Suby of* CANADIAN MENTAL HEALTH AS-
SOCIATION TORONTO BRANCH, THE)
60 Bond St W, Oshawa, ON, L1G 1A5
(905) 436-8760
Emp Here 100
SIC 8011 Offices and clinics of medical doc-
tors
Linda Gallacher

D-U-N-S 20-792-1581   (SL)
CHRIS AND BETH NO FRILLS LTD
1050 Simcoe St N Suite 754, Oshawa, ON,
L1G 4W5
(905) 728-3100
Emp Here 60   *Sales* 17,608,620
SIC 5411 Grocery stores
Chris Brown

D-U-N-S 24-805-2453   (BR)
**CORPORATION OF THE REGIONAL MU-
NICIPALITY OF DURHAM, THE**
HILLSDALE TERRACES
(*Suby of* CORPORATION OF THE RE-
GIONAL MUNICIPALITY OF DURHAM, THE)
600 Oshawa Blvd N Suite 208, Oshawa, ON,
L1G 5T9
(905) 579-3313
Emp Here 300
SIC 8741 Management services
John Rankin

D-U-N-S 25-639-4917   (SL)
DHS (OSHAWA) LTD
DHS HEALTH CARE SERVICE
88 Centre St N Suite 1, Oshawa, ON, L1G 4B6
(905) 571-1511
Emp Here 80   *Sales* 18,695,600
SIC 8621 Professional organizations
Jane Jones

D-U-N-S 20-711-3510   (BR)
DURHAM DISTRICT SCHOOL BOARD
*EASTDALE COLLEGIATE & VOCATIONAL
INSTITUTE*
(*Suby of* DURHAM DISTRICT SCHOOL
BOARD)
265 Harmony Rd N, Oshawa, ON, L1G 6L4
(905) 723-8157
Emp Here 100
SIC 8211 Elementary and secondary schools
Bill Levine

D-U-N-S 25-300-8296   (BR)
DURHAM DISTRICT SCHOOL BOARD
O'NEILL COLLEGIATE & VOCATIONAL
(*Suby of* DURHAM DISTRICT SCHOOL
BOARD)
301 Simcoe St N, Oshawa, ON, L1G 4T2
(905) 728-7531
Emp Here 93
SIC 8211 Elementary and secondary schools
Shelley Vanvrile

D-U-N-S 20-769-4639　(SL)
HENRY, KATHERINE PHARMACY LTD
SHOPPERS DRUG MART
300 Taunton Rd E Suite 2, Oshawa, ON, L1G
7T4
(905) 579-1900
Emp Here 40　*Sales* 10,118,160
SIC 5912 Drug stores and proprietary stores
Katherine Henry

D-U-N-S 20-084-5068　(BR)
LAKERIDGE HEALTH
LAKERIDGE HEALTH OSHAWA
(*Suby of* LAKERIDGE HEALTH)
1 Hospital Crt, Oshawa, ON, L1G 2B9
(905) 576-8711
Emp Here 100
SIC 6324 Hospital and medical service plans
Patricia Adolphus

D-U-N-S 20-135-7837　(HQ)
LOVELL DRUGS LIMITED
(*Suby of* LOVELL VENTURES LTD)
52 1/2 Simcoe St N, Oshawa, ON, L1G 4S1
(905) 723-2276
Emp Here 9　*Sales* 27,530,550
SIC 5912 Drug stores and proprietary stores
Arthur Lovell
Edgar Helm
Diana Krik
Roy Wilson
Douglas Sumner
Rita Winn

D-U-N-S 24-140-7712　(SL)
M2 SOLUTIONS INC
M2 FINANCIAL SOLUTIONS
628 Beechwood St, Oshawa, ON, L1G 2R9
(905) 436-1784
Emp Here 100　*Sales* 20,908,500
SIC 8721 Accounting, auditing, and book-
keeping
Timothy James Manery

D-U-N-S 25-300-0707　(BR)
METRO ONTARIO INC
METRO
(*Suby of* METRO INC)
285 Taunton Rd E Suite 4, Oshawa, ON, L1G
3V2
(905) 432-2197
Emp Here 190
SIC 5411 Grocery stores
Michelle Blair

D-U-N-S 20-135-8801　(SL)
MILLS PONTIAC BUICK GMC LTD
240 Bond St E, Oshawa, ON, L1G 1B5
(905) 432-7333
Emp Here 105　*Sales* 66,074,400
SIC 5511 New and used car dealers
Glenn Willson
Lorrie Willson

D-U-N-S 20-180-1136　(SL)
PIC GROUP HOLDINGS LIMITED, THE
111 Simcoe St N, Oshawa, ON, L1G 4S4
(905) 743-4600
Emp Here 1,500　*Sales* 548,263,500
SIC 6712 Bank holding companies
Alan Duffy

D-U-N-S 20-877-5494　(SL)
ROUGHLEY INSURANCE BROKERS LTD
1000 Simcoe St N Suite 205, Oshawa, ON,
L1G 4W4
(905) 576-7770
Emp Here 41　*Sales* 23,776,884
SIC 6411 Insurance agents, brokers, and ser-
vice
James Roughley
Grant Musselman

D-U-N-S 20-553-9419　(SL)
**UNIVERSITY OF ONTARIO INSTITUTE OF
TECHNOLOGY**
2000 Simcoe St N, Oshawa, ON, L1G 0C5

(905) 721-8668
Emp Here 680　*Sales* 139,424,564
SIC 8221 Colleges and universities
Steven Murphy
Craig Elliott
Jennifer Freeman

D-U-N-S 20-414-3069　(HQ)
VALIANT RENTAL PROPERTIES LIMITED
VALIANT PROPERTY MANAGEMENT
177 Nonquon Rd, Oshawa, ON, L1G 3S2
(905) 579-1626
Sales 11,264,421
SIC 6513 Apartment building operators
Elizabeth Kelly

D-U-N-S 20-773-7268　(SL)
**WHITBY HYDRO ENERGY SERVICES COR-
PORATION**
100 Taunton Rd E, Oshawa, ON, L1G 7N1
(905) 668-5878
Emp Here 60　*Sales* 37,596,840
SIC 4911 Electric services
Jim Lavelle

Oshawa, ON L1H

D-U-N-S 25-027-9106　(SL)
473980 ONTARIO LTD
DURHAMWAY BUS LINES, DIV OF
485 Waterloo Crt, Oshawa, ON, L1H 3X2
(905) 433-1392
Emp Here 175　*Sales* 13,172,600
SIC 4151 School buses
Ellen Thomas

D-U-N-S 24-784-5001　(SL)
723926 ONTARIO LIMITED
J.J MCGUIRE GENERAL CONTRACTORS
880 Farewell St Suite 1, Oshawa, ON, L1H
6N6
(905) 436-2554
Emp Here 80　*Sales* 71,602,875
SIC 1541 Industrial buildings and warehouses
Jeff Robinson
Mitch Newbold
Andy Wojtis
Leo Urrasio

D-U-N-S 25-821-2096　(SL)
911 RESTORATION OF DURHAM REGION
500 Raleigh Ave Unit 11, Oshawa, ON, L1H
3T2
(905) 436-9911
Emp Here 14　*Sales* 14,488,334
SIC 6331 Fire, marine, and casualty insurance
Mike Porco

D-U-N-S 24-279-1648　(BR)
A.G. SIMPSON AUTOMOTIVE INC
OSHAWA PLANT
(*Suby of* J2 MANAGEMENT CORP)
901 Simcoe St S, Oshawa, ON, L1H 4L1
(905) 571-2121
Emp Here 510
SIC 3465 Automotive stampings
Andy Matthews

D-U-N-S 20-245-2574　(SL)
AGOSTINO & NANCY'S NO FRILLS
151 Bloor St E, Oshawa, ON, L1H 3M3
(905) 571-6488
Emp Here 100　*Sales* 29,347,700
SIC 5411 Grocery stores
Agostino Battaglia
Nancy Battaglia

D-U-N-S 20-849-9269　(SL)
C H S PHARMACY LIMITED
CLINIC PHARMACY
117 King St E, Oshawa, ON, L1H 1B9
(905) 576-9096
Emp Here 40　*Sales* 10,118,160
SIC 5912 Drug stores and proprietary stores
Erast Huculak

D-U-N-S 24-182-4866　(SL)
**CANNON SECURITY AND PATROL SER-
VICES**
23 Simcoe St S Fl 2, Oshawa, ON, L1H 4G1
(416) 742-9994
Emp Here 150　*Sales* 3,937,500
SIC 7381 Detective and armored car services
Raven Ramnarine

D-U-N-S 20-935-6179　(HQ)
**COMMUNITY　　LIVING　OS-
HAWA/CLARINGTON**
CLOC
39 Wellington Ave E, Oshawa, ON, L1H 3Y1
(905) 576-3011
Emp Here 27　*Sales* 23,141,520
SIC 8361 Residential care
Barbara Feyko
Steven Findlay

D-U-N-S 20-283-4875　(HQ)
**CONCENTRIX TECHNOLOGIES SERVICES
(CANADA) LIMITED**
CONCENTRIX
(*Suby of* SYNNEX CORPORATION)
1189 Colonel Sam Dr, Oshawa, ON, L1H 8W8
(416) 380-3800
Emp Here 4,900　*Sales* 392,681,985
SIC 4899 Communication services, nec
Chris Caldwell
Anil Bhalla
Rosemary Walkem
Jayanta Basu
Aparup Sengupta

D-U-N-S 20-752-3820　(HQ)
**DURHAM COLLEGE OF APPLIED ARTS
AND TECHNOLOGY, THE**
2000 Simcoe St N, Oshawa, ON, L1H 7K4
(905) 721-2000
Emp Here 300　*Sales* 146,629,809
SIC 8222 Junior colleges
Don Lovisa

D-U-N-S 20-025-2406　(BR)
DURHAM DISTRICT SCHOOL BOARD
GROVE SCHOOL
(*Suby of* DURHAM DISTRICT SCHOOL
BOARD)
1356 Simcoe St S, Oshawa, ON, L1H 4M4
(905) 725-7042
Emp Here 80
SIC 8211 Elementary and secondary schools
Marlene Pike

D-U-N-S 24-033-3265　(HQ)
**DURHAM REGION NON PROFIT HOUSING
CORPORATION**
DRYDEN HEIGHTS
28 Albert St, Oshawa, ON, L1H 8S5
(905) 436-6610
Emp Here 20　*Sales* 13,044,288
SIC 6531 Real estate agents and managers
William (Bill) Clapperton
Larry O'connor
April Cullen

D-U-N-S 24-190-1532　(BR)
**ENTERPHASE CHILD AND FAMILY SER-
VICES INC**
(*Suby of* ENTERPHASE CHILD AND FAMILY
SERVICES INC)
250 Harmony Rd S, Oshawa, ON, L1H 6T9

Emp Here 100
SIC 8299 Schools and educational services,
nec
Pam Shaw

D-U-N-S 25-372-2490　(SL)
FREW PETROLEUM CORPORATION
FREW PETROLEUM
190 Wentworth St E, Oshawa, ON, L1H 3V5
(905) 723-3742
Emp Here 10　*Sales* 10,328,080
SIC 5172 Petroleum products, nec
Mark Frew

D-U-N-S 25-666-7270　(BR)
G4S SECURE SOLUTIONS (CANADA) LTD
(*Suby of* G4S PLC)
214 King St E, Oshawa, ON, L1H 1C7
(905) 579-8020
Emp Here 250
SIC 7381 Detective and armored car services
Leschik Don

D-U-N-S 20-403-6677　(SL)
GARRITANO BROS. LTD
881 Nelson St, Oshawa, ON, L1H 5N7
(905) 576-8642
Emp Here 22　*Sales* 10,356,082
SIC 1542 Nonresidential construction, nec
Tony Garritano
Steve Garritano
Alfredo Garritano

D-U-N-S 24-917-4954　(BR)
**GENERAL MOTORS OF CANADA COM-
PANY**
*CANADIAN　REGIONAL　ENGINEERING
CENTRE*
(*Suby of* GENERAL MOTORS COMPANY)
500 Wentworth St E Suite 1, Oshawa, ON,
L1H 3V9
(905) 644-4716
Emp Here 400
SIC 8711 Engineering services
Kenneth Marx

D-U-N-S 20-135-6847　(HQ)
**GENERAL MOTORS OF CANADA COM-
PANY**
(*Suby of* GENERAL MOTORS COMPANY)
1908 Colonel Sam Dr, Oshawa, ON, L1H 8P7
(905) 644-5000
Emp Here 450　*Sales* 2,908,500,000
SIC 3711 Motor vehicles and car bodies
Stephen Carlisle
John Roth
Peter Cho
Ines Craviotto

D-U-N-S 25-204-2064　(BR)
**GENERAL MOTORS OF CANADA COM-
PANY**
SOUTH STAMPING PLANT
(*Suby of* GENERAL MOTORS COMPANY)
1908 Colonel Sam Dr, Oshawa, ON, L1H 8P7
(289) 676-0530
Emp Here 500
SIC 3711 Motor vehicles and car bodies
Don Naughton

D-U-N-S 24-411-9525　(HQ)
HALENDA'S FINE FOODS LTD
HALENDA'S MEATS
915 Nelson St, Oshawa, ON, L1H 5N7
(905) 576-6328
Emp Here 18　*Sales* 17,608,620
SIC 5421 Meat and fish markets
Richard Halenda
Ola Halenda

D-U-N-S 25-354-7764　(HQ)
J & M TIRE INTERNATIONAL INC
717 Drake St, Oshawa, ON, L1H 7R3
(905) 723-3323
Emp Here 116　*Sales* 55,338,480
SIC 5014 Tires and tubes
James Michaud

D-U-N-S 24-470-9077　(HQ)
KERR INDUSTRIES LIMITED
(*Suby of* BAYBRIAR MANAGEMENT SER-
VICES LIMITED)
635 Farewell St, Oshawa, ON, L1H 6N2
(905) 725-6561
Sales 10,482,100
SIC 7549 Automotive services, nec
Bradley Baker

D-U-N-S 24-718-9595　(BR)
LAKERIDGE HEALTH
GLAZIER MEDICAL CENTER
(*Suby of* LAKERIDGE HEALTH)

11 Gibb St, Oshawa, ON, L1H 2J9
(905) 579-1212
Emp Here 100
SIC 8011 Offices and clinics of medical doctors
Fotine Mainville

D-U-N-S 20-980-7296   (HQ)
LAKESHORE MILL SUPPLIES LTD
CCS INDUSTRIALS
150 Wentworth St E, Oshawa, ON, L1H 3V5
(905) 579-5222
Emp Here 16   *Sales* 13,300,728
SIC 5085 Industrial supplies

D-U-N-S 20-135-8496   (SL)
MARACLE PRESS LIMITED
1156 King St E, Oshawa, ON, L1H 1H8
(905) 723-3438
Emp Here 60   *Sales* 14,403,938
SIC 2752 Commercial printing, lithographic
Bruce Fenton
George F. Sittlinger
Bernard Sittlinger

D-U-N-S 20-515-7907   (SL)
MCGUIRE, J.J. GENERAL CONTRACTORS INC
880 Farewell St Suite 1, Oshawa, ON, L1H 6N6
(905) 436-2554
Emp Here 50   *Sales* 23,536,550
SIC 1542 Nonresidential construction, nec
Jeff Robinson
Andy Wojtis
Leo Urrasio
Mitch Newbold

D-U-N-S 24-086-8179   (BR)
METROLAND MEDIA GROUP LTD
OSHAWA THIS WEEK
(*Suby of* TORSTAR CORPORATION)
865 Farewell St, Oshawa, ON, L1H 6N8
(905) 579-4400
Emp Here 200
SIC 2711 Newspapers
Abe Fakhourie

D-U-N-S 20-943-3952   (HQ)
ONTARIO CONFERENCE OF THE SEVENTH-DAY ADVENTISTS CHURCH
1110 King St E, Oshawa, ON, L1H 1H8
(905) 571-1022
Emp Here 5   *Sales* 26,447,242
SIC 8661 Religious organizations
Derrick Nichols

D-U-N-S 24-422-2407   (HQ)
OSCAN ELECTRICAL SUPPLIES LTD
209 Bloor St E, Oshawa, ON, L1H 3M3
(905) 728-3800
Emp Here 20   *Sales* 11,675,820
SIC 5063 Electrical apparatus and equipment
John Osso
Enrico Osso
David Leroy
David Krohn
Jamie Krohn

D-U-N-S 20-823-5036   (HQ)
OSHAWA CLINIC
COURTICE HEALTH CENTRE
117 King St E, Oshawa, ON, L1H 1B9
(905) 723-8551
Emp Here 220   *Sales* 66,572,450
SIC 8011 Offices and clinics of medical doctors
Harry Horricks
Michelle Henry

D-U-N-S 20-013-2202   (SL)
OSHAWA PUC NETWORKS INC
(*Suby of* CORPORATION OF THE CITY OF OSHAWA)
100 Simcoe St S, Oshawa, ON, L1H 7M7
(905) 723-4623
Emp Here 87   *Sales* 59,149,038

SIC 4911 Electric services
Jeff Rosenthal
Irv Harrell
Mark Turney

D-U-N-S 25-663-0633   (SL)
OSHAWA YOUNG WOMEN CHRISTIAN ASSOCIATION, THE
YWCA DURHAM
33 Mcgrigor St, Oshawa, ON, L1H 1X8
(905) 576-6356
Emp Here 45   *Sales* 10,504,575
SIC 3272 Concrete products, nec
Susanne Groen
Wendy Leeder

D-U-N-S 25-455-7036   (SL)
OTHODENT LTD
311 Viola Ave, Oshawa, ON, L1H 3A7
(905) 436-3731
Emp Here 122   *Sales* 27,729,258
SIC 3843 Dental equipment and supplies
William Van Evans

D-U-N-S 20-975-4902   (HQ)
R.M.R REAL ESTATE LIMITED
COLDWELL BANKER
179 King St E, Oshawa, ON, L1H 1C2
(905) 728-9414
Emp Here 15   *Sales* 46,077,790
SIC 6531 Real estate agents and managers
Ralph M Roberto

D-U-N-S 20-606-7662   (SL)
RAGLAN INDUSTRIES INC
5151 Simcoe St N, Oshawa, ON, L1H 0S4
(905) 655-3355
Emp Here 45   *Sales* 10,319,253
SIC 3715 Truck trailers
John Michel
Robert Michel
Harry Michel
Jonathan Michel

D-U-N-S 24-362-2227   (BR)
SECURITAS CANADA LIMITED
(*Suby of* SECURITAS AB)
1908 Colonel Sam Dr, Oshawa, ON, L1H 8P7
(905) 644-6370
Emp Here 90
SIC 6211 Security brokers and dealers
Christine Morton

D-U-N-S 20-644-3272   (BR)
SOBEYS CAPITAL INCORPORATED
FRESHCO
(*Suby of* EMPIRE COMPANY LIMITED)
564 King St E, Oshawa, ON, L1H 1G5
(905) 571-4835
Emp Here 100
SIC 5411 Grocery stores

D-U-N-S 20-086-9373   (BR)
TORSTAR CORPORATION
OSHAWA THIS WEEK NEWSPAPER
(*Suby of* TORSTAR CORPORATION)
865 Farewell St, Oshawa, ON, L1H 6N8
(905) 579-4400
Emp Here 100
SIC 2711 Newspapers
Fred Eismont

D-U-N-S 20-967-5149   (SL)
W. B. WHITE INSURANCE LIMITED
110 King St E, Oshawa, ON, L1H 1B6
(905) 576-6400
Emp Here 36   *Sales* 20,877,264
SIC 6411 Insurance agents, brokers, and service
James Famme

D-U-N-S 25-321-5685   (SL)
WILSON FOODS KINGSWAY LTD
MCDONALD'S 7403
1300 King St E, Oshawa, ON, L1H 8J4
(905) 442-3545
Emp Here 90   *Sales* 3,858,570
SIC 5812 Eating places

Stephen Wilson
Jeannie Wilson

D-U-N-S 25-332-8975   (SL)
WORTH PERSONNEL LTD
219 Wentworth St E, Oshawa, ON, L1H 3V7
(905) 725-5544
Emp Here 130   *Sales* 16,220,880
SIC 8741 Management services
Steven Chandler
Karen Howell

Oshawa, ON L1J

D-U-N-S 25-374-0302   (HQ)
1022481 ONTARIO INC
CONTINENTAL CURRENCY EXCHANGE
419 King St W Suite 2482, Oshawa, ON, L1J 2K5
(905) 576-1600
Emp Here 13   *Sales* 14,805,000
SIC 6099 Functions related to deposit banking
Scott Penfound
James Kerr
John Mace

D-U-N-S 20-524-2725   (SL)
1268558 ONTARIO LIMITED
MACKIE HARLEY-DAVIDSON BUELL
880 Champlain Ave, Oshawa, ON, L1J 7A6
(905) 434-6550
Emp Here 30   *Sales* 18,878,400
SIC 5571 Motorcycle dealers
Ross Mackie
Norman Mackie
Paul Mackie
Dean Mackie
Scott Mackie

D-U-N-S 20-755-3934   (HQ)
AUTO WAREHOUSING COMPANY CANADA LIMITED
(*Suby of* AUTO WAREHOUSING CO.)
1150 Stevenson Rd S Suite 1, Oshawa, ON, L1J 0B3
(905) 725-6549
Emp Here 2   *Sales* 25,478,383
SIC 4789 Transportation services, nec
Stephen Seher
Brian Taylor
Belinda Woodford

D-U-N-S 20-032-8526   (SL)
CANADIAN ASSOCIATION FOR COMMUNITY LIVING
850 King St W Unit 20, Oshawa, ON, L1J 8N5
(905) 436-2500
Emp Here 45   *Sales* 10,207,485
SIC 8399 Social services, nec
Chris Beesley

D-U-N-S 20-794-6190   (BR)
CORPORATION OF THE CITY OF OSHAWA
OSHAWA FIRE SERVICES
(*Suby of* CORPORATION OF THE CITY OF OSHAWA)
199 Adelaide Ave W, Oshawa, ON, L1J 7B1
(905) 433-1239
Emp Here 200
SIC 7389 Business services, nec
Steve Meringer

D-U-N-S 20-209-9839   (HQ)
CROSSBY DEWAR INC
1143 Wentworth St W Suite 201, Oshawa, ON, L1J 8P7
(905) 683-5102
Sales 164,856,300
SIC 1751 Carpentry work
Scott Dewar
John Crossby

D-U-N-S 25-513-0692   (HQ)
DIRECT TIMBER INC
(*Suby of* VELCAN FOREST PRODUCTS

INC)
1181 Thornton Rd S Suite 1, Oshawa, ON, L1J 8P4
(905) 571-4341
Sales 69,506,048
SIC 5031 Lumber, plywood, and millwork
Hovan Tchaglassian
Joseph Carpino

D-U-N-S 24-953-2458   (HQ)
DURHAM CATHOLIC DISTRICT SCHOOL BOARD
650 Rossland Rd W, Oshawa, ON, L1J 7C4
(905) 576-6150
Emp Here 200   *Sales* 207,852,355
SIC 8211 Elementary and secondary schools
Trisha Chapman
Ryan Putnam
Anne O'brien
Kathy Lefort
Tricia Chapman
Theresa Corless
Monique Forster
Jim Mccafferty
Janice Oldman
Paul Paulla

D-U-N-S 24-796-5049   (BR)
DURHAM DISTRICT SCHOOL BOARD
MCLAUGHLIN, R S COLLEGIATE & VOCATIONAL INSTITUTE
(*Suby of* DURHAM DISTRICT SCHOOL BOARD)
570 Stevenson Rd N, Oshawa, ON, L1J 5P1
(905) 728-9407
Emp Here 80
SIC 8211 Elementary and secondary schools
Joyce Thomas

D-U-N-S 25-018-0767   (BR)
DURHAM DISTRICT SCHOOL BOARD
OSHAWA CENTRAL COLLEGIATE
(*Suby of* DURHAM DISTRICT SCHOOL BOARD)
155 Gibb St, Oshawa, ON, L1J 1Y4
Emp Here 75
SIC 8211 Elementary and secondary schools
Lynn Merriman

D-U-N-S 24-027-3102   (HQ)
EHC CANADA, INC
EHC GLOBAL
(*Suby of* EHC GLOBAL INC)
1287 Boundary Rd, Oshawa, ON, L1J 6Z7
(905) 432-3200
Sales 20,868,094
SIC 3534 Elevators and moving stairways
Jeno Eppel
Patrick Robert Bothwell
John Mcintyre

D-U-N-S 24-375-4194   (HQ)
EHC GLOBAL INC
1287 Boundary Rd, Oshawa, ON, L1J 6Z7
(905) 432-3200
Emp Here 1   *Sales* 127,928,150
SIC 6712 Bank holding companies
Jeno Eppel

D-U-N-S 25-398-7788   (SL)
FOREST PARK MOTORS INC
DURHAM DODGE CHRYSLER
799 Bloor St W, Oshawa, ON, L1J 5Y6
(905) 404-0525
Emp Here 44   *Sales* 21,915,432
SIC 5511 New and used car dealers
Bill Hodsoll
Janet Hodsoll

D-U-N-S 25-664-0855   (HQ)
FRASER FORD SALES LIMITED
815 King St W, Oshawa, ON, L1J 2L4
(905) 576-1800
Emp Here 41   *Sales* 36,498,240
SIC 5511 New and used car dealers
Robert Fraser

D-U-N-S 24-101-8394   (BR)
GENERAL MOTORS OF CANADA COM-PANY
(*Suby of* GENERAL MOTORS COMPANY)
461 Park Rd S, Oshawa, ON, L1J 8R3
(905) 845-5456
Emp Here 4,000
SIC 3711 Motor vehicles and car bodies
Jack Willett

D-U-N-S 24-394-9141   (HQ)
H2O POWER LIMITED PARTNERSHIP
560 King St W Unit 2, Oshawa, ON, L1J 7J1
(905) 438-8539
Sales 16,291,964
SIC 4911 Electric services
Jim Gartshore
Marc Mantha
Ron Macleod

D-U-N-S 20-183-6350   (SL)
HAYHURST, GEORGE LIMITED
CANADIAN TIRE #075
441 Gibb St, Oshawa, ON, L1J 1Z4
(905) 728-6272
Emp Here 100   *Sales* 62,928,000
SIC 5531 Auto and home supply stores
George Hayhurst

D-U-N-S 20-176-8996   (BR)
HLS THERAPEUTICS INC
(*Suby of* HLS THERAPEUTICS INC)
940 Thornton Rd S, Oshawa, ON, L1J 7E2
(905) 725-5445
Emp Here 125
SIC 2834 Pharmaceutical preparations
Adam Rowden

D-U-N-S 25-998-3260   (BR)
HUDSON'S BAY COMPANY
BAY, THE
(*Suby of* HUDSON'S BAY COMPANY)
419 King St W, Oshawa, ON, L1J 2K5
(905) 571-1211
Emp Here 100
SIC 5311 Department stores
Sandra Giliso

D-U-N-S 24-028-6559   (HQ)
LAKERIDGE HEALTH
LAKERIDGE HEALTH OSHAWA
850 1/4 Champlain Ave, Oshawa, ON, L1J 8R2
(905) 576-8711
Emp Here 200   *Sales* 333,240,000
SIC 8062 General medical and surgical hospitals
Matthew Anderson
Susan Deryk
Natalie Hovey

D-U-N-S 25-947-7198   (BR)
LOBLAWS SUPERMARKETS LIMITED
REAL CANADIAN SUPERSTORE
(*Suby of* LOBLAW COMPANIES LIMITED)
481 Gibb St, Oshawa, ON, L1J 1Z4
(905) 743-0043
Emp Here 400
SIC 5411 Grocery stores
Ron Mc Mullan

D-U-N-S 20-966-6627   (HQ)
MACKIE MOVING SYSTEMS CORPORA-TION
MACKIE GROUP, THE
(*Suby of* MACKIE TRANSPORTATION HOLDINGS INC)
933 Bloor St W, Oshawa, ON, L1J 5Y7
(905) 728-2400
Emp Here 400   *Sales* 92,190,500
SIC 4231 Trucking terminal facilities
Ross Mackie
Jilles Bernier
Donald Bain
Mike Farger
Dean Mackie
Scott Mackie

Paul Mackie
Norman Mackie

D-U-N-S 24-340-8254   (HQ)
MACKIE TRANSPORTATION HOLDINGS INC
933 Bloor St W, Oshawa, ON, L1J 5Y7
(905) 728-1603
Sales 73,101,800
SIC 6712 Bank holding companies
Ross Mackie
Dean Mackie
Paul Mackie
Norm Mackie
Scott Mackie

D-U-N-S 24-093-5825   (SL)
MCCAM INSURANCE BROKERS LTD
292 King St W, Oshawa, ON, L1J 2J9
(905) 579-0111
Emp Here 25   *Sales* 14,498,100
SIC 6411 Insurance agents, brokers, and service
Colin Mcintosh

D-U-N-S 25-676-2022   (BR)
METRO ONTARIO INC
METRO
(*Suby of* METRO INC)
149 Midtown Dr, Oshawa, ON, L1J 3Z7

Emp Here 100
SIC 5411 Grocery stores
John Mclain

D-U-N-S 24-830-5468   (HQ)
MICROVITE INVESTMENTS LIMITED
DISTICOR MAGAZINE DISTRIBUTION SERVICES
1000 Thornton Rd S Unit B, Oshawa, ON, L1J 7E2
(905) 619-6565
Sales 44,551,200
SIC 5192 Books, periodicals, and newspapers
John Lafranier
Mark Lafranier

D-U-N-S 20-434-0863   (SL)
NORMARK INC
(*Suby of* RAPALA VMC OYJ)
1350 Phillip Murray Ave, Oshawa, ON, L1J 6Z9
(905) 571-3001
Emp Here 20   *Sales* 10,410,840
SIC 5091 Sporting and recreation goods
Gerald Shindler

D-U-N-S 25-981-7369   (SL)
O & O DEVELOPMENTS INC
ICE SPORTS OSHAWA
1401 Phillip Murray Ave, Oshawa, ON, L1J 8C4
(905) 725-6951
Emp Here 75   *Sales* 6,534,600
SIC 7941 Sports clubs, managers, and promoters
Grant Valentine

D-U-N-S 20-770-4388   (SL)
ONTARIO MOTOR SALES LIMITED
140 Bond St W, Oshawa, ON, L1J 8M2
(905) 725-6501
Emp Here 110   *Sales* 69,220,800
SIC 5511 New and used car dealers
Glenn S Willson
Lorrie Willson
Anthony Willson

D-U-N-S 24-719-7155   (HQ)
OSSO HOLDINGS LTD
725 Bloor St W, Oshawa, ON, L1J 5Y6
(905) 576-1700
Emp Here 8   *Sales* 40,245,660
SIC 5063 Electrical apparatus and equipment
James Wamsley

D-U-N-S 24-452-3460   (SL)
PARTICIPATION HOUSE PROJECT

(DURHAM REGION), THE
1255 Terwillegar Ave Unit 9, Oshawa, ON, L1J 7A4
(905) 579-5267
Emp Here 45   *Sales* 10,207,485
SIC 8399 Social services, nec
Marilyn Dow

D-U-N-S 20-534-6067   (SL)
PARTSMAN INC, THE
PARTSMAN, THE
278 Park Rd S, Oshawa, ON, L1J 4H5
(905) 436-3227
Emp Here 26   *Sales* 12,950,028
SIC 5531 Auto and home supply stores
Gary Thibault
Lori May

D-U-N-S 25-088-1174   (SL)
PERRY MECHANICAL INC
DIRECT ENERGY HOME SERVICES
285 Bloor St W, Oshawa, ON, L1J 1R1
(905) 725-3582
Emp Here 30   *Sales* 13,415,220
SIC 5075 Warm air heating and air conditioning
Stephen Perry
Lisa Perry

D-U-N-S 24-726-7420   (BR)
REVERA LONG TERM CARE INC
THORNTONVIEW LONG TERM CARE RESIDENCE
(*Suby of* GOVERNMENT OF CANADA)
186 Thornton Rd S Suite 1103, Oshawa, ON, L1J 5Y2
(905) 576-5181
Emp Here 100
SIC 8051 Skilled nursing care facilities
Heather Power

D-U-N-S 24-622-2681   (SL)
SOUTHERN SUPPLIES LIMITED
(*Suby of* WEGMART LTD)
323 Bloor St W, Oshawa, ON, L1J 6X4
(905) 728-6216
Emp Here 35   *Sales* 15,651,090
SIC 5075 Warm air heating and air conditioning
Walter H Libby
Gordon M Libby
Walter E Libby
Marie Libby
Joanne M Littlejohn
Leanna Meier

D-U-N-S 25-662-2366   (SL)
SUTTON GROUP STATUS REALTY INC
286 King St W, Oshawa, ON, L1J 2J9
(905) 436-0990
Emp Here 49   *Sales* 16,029,223
SIC 6531 Real estate agents and managers
Harry Hayes

D-U-N-S 25-203-0572   (SL)
T.T.O.C.S. LIMITED
EAST SIDE MARIO'S #640
419 King St W Suite Side, Oshawa, ON, L1J 2K5

Emp Here 100   *Sales* 4,551,900
SIC 5812 Eating places
Eric Song

D-U-N-S 24-991-2452   (HQ)
VELCAN FOREST PRODUCTS INC
1240 Skae Dr, Oshawa, ON, L1J 7A1
(905) 571-2477
Emp Here 90   *Sales* 135,835,249
SIC 5031 Lumber, plywood, and millwork
Joseph Carpino
Hovan Tchaglassian
Grace Tchaglassian

D-U-N-S 25-371-1592   (BR)
BEST BUY CANADA LTD
FUTURE SHOP
(*Suby of* BEST BUY CO., INC.)
1471 Harmony Rd N, Oshawa, ON, L1K 0Z6
(905) 433-4455
Emp Here 100
SIC 5731 Radio, television, and electronic stores

D-U-N-S 24-828-1982   (SL)
CANADIAN TIRE ASSOCIATE STORE
1333 Wilson Rd N Suite 336, Oshawa, ON, L1K 2B8
(905) 433-5575
Emp Here 130   *Sales* 81,806,400
SIC 5541 Gasoline service stations
William Beaton
Brad Sayers

D-U-N-S 25-171-5538   (BR)
HOME DEPOT OF CANADA INC
HOME DEPOT
(*Suby of* THE HOME DEPOT INC)
1481 Harmony Rd N, Oshawa, ON, L1K 0Z6
(905) 743-5600
Emp Here 200
SIC 5231 Paint, glass, and wallpaper stores

D-U-N-S 20-528-2098   (SL)
KINGSWAY COLLEGE
1200 Leland Rd, Oshawa, ON, L1K 2H4
(905) 433-1144
Emp Here 150   *Sales* 28,855,500
SIC 2499 Wood products, nec
Lee Richards

D-U-N-S 24-383-8963   (BR)
LOBLAWS INC
REAL CANADIAN SUPERSTORE
(*Suby of* LOBLAW COMPANIES LIMITED)
1385 Harmony Rd N Suite 1043, Oshawa, ON, L1K 0Z6
(905) 433-9569
Emp Here 150
SIC 5411 Grocery stores
Greg Mcneil-Smith

D-U-N-S 25-057-7517   (BR)
METRO ONTARIO INC
A & P FOOD STORES
(*Suby of* METRO INC)
555 Rossland Rd E, Oshawa, ON, L1K 1K8
(905) 579-5862
Emp Here 200
SIC 5411 Grocery stores
Grant Martin

D-U-N-S 20-793-0756   (BR)
SOBEYS CAPITAL INCORPORATED
SOBEYS
(*Suby of* EMPIRE COMPANY LIMITED)
1377 Wilson Rd N, Oshawa, ON, L1K 2Z5
(905) 440-4687
Emp Here 100
SIC 5411 Grocery stores
Sheli Rivers

D-U-N-S 20-789-7518   (BR)
WAL-MART CANADA CORP
(*Suby of* WALMART INC.)
1471 Harmony Rd N Suite 3161, Oshawa, ON, L1K 0Z6
(905) 404-6581
Emp Here 200
SIC 5311 Department stores
Amanda Macisaac

D-U-N-S 25-692-6874   (HQ)
WALTON ENTERPRISES LTD
MIDAS AUTO SERVICE
460 Taunton Rd E, Oshawa, ON, L1K 1A8
(905) 404-1413
Emp Here 5   *Sales* 51,772,655
SIC 7533 Auto exhaust system repair shops
Jack Walton
Irene Walton

Oshawa, ON L1L

D-U-N-S 24-395-9876   (SL)
JAMES CAMPBELL SERVICES LTD
DURHAM KIA
550 Taunton Rd W, Oshawa, ON, L1L 0N8
(905) 571-5420
Emp Here 37   *Sales* 18,428,886
SIC 5511 New and used car dealers
  James Campbell

Otonabee, ON K9J

D-U-N-S 24-284-9842   (SL)
970207 ONTARIO LIMITED
TRENT VALLEY HONDA
851 Highway 7, Otonabee, ON, K9J 6X7
(705) 748-2777
Emp Here 38   *Sales* 18,926,964
SIC 5521 Used car dealers
  Frank Mandeljc
  Monika Carmichael

Ottawa, ON K0A

D-U-N-S 24-629-8699   (HQ)
OZ OPTICS LIMITED
219 Westbrook Rd, Ottawa, ON, K0A 1L0
(613) 831-0981
Sales 65,848,800
SIC 3827 Optical instruments and lenses
  Omur Sezerman
  Garland Best
  Gordon Youle
  Zahide Sezerman
  Shao-Kai Liu

Ottawa, ON K1A

D-U-N-S 20-787-9677   (HQ)
BANK OF CANADA
(*Suby of* GOVERNMENT OF CANADA)
234 Wellington St, Ottawa, ON, K1A 0G9
(613) 782-8111
Emp Here 1,111   *Sales* 1,159,154,222
SIC 6011 Federal reserve banks
  Stephen S. Poloz
  Filipe Dinis
  Carolyn Wilkins
  Carolyn Wilkins
  Norman Betts
  Alan Andrew Borger
  Phyllis Clark
  Colin Dodds
  Monique Jerome-Forget
  Claire Kennedy

D-U-N-S 20-537-1748   (BR)
CANADA POST CORPORATION
BOWDEN PO
(*Suby of* GOVERNMENT OF CANADA)
2701 Riverside Dr, Ottawa, ON, K1A 0B1
(613) 734-8440
Emp Here 3,000
SIC 4311 U.s. postal service
  Deepak Chopra

D-U-N-S 24-269-8181   (HQ)
CANADA POST CORPORATION
INNOVAPOST
(*Suby of* GOVERNMENT OF CANADA)
2701 Riverside Dr, Ottawa, ON, K1A 1L5
(613) 734-8440
Emp Here 2,500   *Sales* 6,444,881,802
SIC 4311 U.s. postal service

Jessica L. Mcdonald
Wayne Cheeseman
Leonard Diplock
John West
Jay Davis
Rod Hart
Manon Fortin
Douglas Greaves
Ann Therese Maceachern
Barbara Mackenzie

D-U-N-S 20-537-5640   (BR)
CANADA POST CORPORATION
CHURCHILL FALLS PO
(*Suby of* GOVERNMENT OF CANADA)
2701 Riverside Dr, Ottawa, ON, K1A 1M2
(613) 734-8440
Emp Here 3,000
SIC 4311 U.s. postal service
  Deppak Chopra

D-U-N-S 20-787-7507   (HQ)
EXPORT DEVELOPMENT CANADA
EDC
(*Suby of* GOVERNMENT OF CANADA)
150 Slater St, Ottawa, ON, K1A 1K3
(613) 598-2500
Emp Here 1,000   *Sales* 1,333,579,935
SIC 6111 Federal and federally sponsored
credit agencies
  Mairead Lavery
  Al Hamdani
  Clive Witter
  Jim Mcardle
  Derek Layne
  Mairead Lavery
  Ken Kember
  Carl Burlock
  Stephanie Butt Thibodeau
  Catherine Decarie

D-U-N-S 20-552-4759   (BR)
NATIONAL RESEARCH COUNCIL CANADA
NRC-FINANCE BRANCH
(*Suby of* GOVERNMENT OF CANADA)
1200 Montreal Rd Building M-58, Ottawa, ON,
K1A 0R6
(613) 993-9200
Emp Here 150
SIC 8741 Management services
  Gisele Goyette

D-U-N-S 20-889-3875   (HQ)
ROYAL CANADIAN MINT
(*Suby of* GOVERNMENT OF CANADA)
320 Sussex Dr, Ottawa, ON, K1A 0G8
(613) 993-8990
Emp Here 400   *Sales* 1,325,093,867
SIC 5094 Jewelry and precious stones
  Sandra Hanington
  J. Marc Brule
  Michel Boucher
  Sean Byrne
  Patrick Hadsipantelis
  Francine Hochereau
  Chris Carkner
  Simon Kamel
  Beverley Lepine
  Jennifer Camelon

D-U-N-S 20-384-2455   (SL)
**STAFF OF THE NON-PUBLIC FUNDS,
CANADIAN FORCES**
101 Colonel By Dr, Ottawa, ON, K1A 0K2
(613) 995-8509
Emp Here 800   *Sales* 165,654,400
SIC 8399 Social services, nec
  Sean Cantelon
  Michael Ward

D-U-N-S 20-788-7316   (HQ)
WELCH LLP
123 Slater St, Ottawa, ON, K1A 1B9
(613) 236-9191
Emp Here 198   *Sales* 44,364,720
SIC 8721 Accounting, auditing, and bookkeeping

Donald (Don) Timmins
John Berry
Michael Burch
Stephen Deblois
Donald (Don) Henderson
George Ireland
William (Bill) Irwin
John Kutschke
Donald (Don) Scott
Garth Steele

Ottawa, ON K1B

D-U-N-S 20-893-2210   (SL)
126677 CANADA LIMITED
LOLACHERS CATERING DIV. OF
1620 Michael St, Ottawa, ON, K1B 3T7
(613) 741-2800
Emp Here 125   *Sales* 5,689,875
SIC 5812 Eating places
  Jonas Moniz
  Eduardo Moniz
  George Moniz
  Manuel Correia

D-U-N-S 20-789-3330   (HQ)
1270477 ONTARIO INC
MAX AUTO SUPPLY
1556 Michael St, Ottawa, ON, K1B 3T7
(613) 741-0337
Emp Here 25   *Sales* 62,928,000
SIC 5511 New and used car dealers
  James Maxwell

D-U-N-S 24-111-3179   (SL)
1496519 ONTARIO INC
BENTO NOUVEAU
2675 Blackwell St Unit 8, Ottawa, ON, K1B
4E4
(613) 747-6660
Emp Here 30   *Sales* 25,067,310
SIC 5141 Groceries, general line
  King Yuen

D-U-N-S 20-646-1423   (SL)
1514498 ONTARIO INC
2445 Sheffield Rd, Ottawa, ON, K1B 3V6
(613) 749-5611
Emp Here 60   *Sales* 13,983,900
SIC 1711 Plumbing, heating, air-conditioning
  Patricia Ethier

D-U-N-S 20-389-8890   (SL)
1551121 ONTARIO INC
ULT POWERTRAIN
1427 Michael St, Ottawa, ON, K1B 3R3
(613) 749-4858
Emp Here 59   *Sales* 11,144,210
SIC 5013 Motor vehicle supplies and new
parts
  Honorio Oliveiro

D-U-N-S 24-685-4632   (SL)
718009 ONTARIO INC
SPRINT COURIER
2617 Edinburgh Pl, Ottawa, ON, K1B 5M1
(613) 742-7171
Emp Here 75   *Sales* 33,691,425
SIC 7389 Business services, nec
  Edward Cook
  Peter Stelcner
  Stewart Stern

D-U-N-S 24-662-1353   (SL)
**AQUATECK WATER SYSTEMS DISTRIBU-
TORS LTD**
2700 Lancaster Rd Suite 116, Ottawa, ON,
K1B 4T7
(613) 526-4613
Emp Here 35   *Sales* 16,625,910
SIC 5084 Industrial machinery and equipment
  Jed Dreifke
  Ronald Dreifke
  Stewart Makinson

D-U-N-S 25-570-3910   (SL)
BLONDEAU TAXI LIMITEE
BLONDEAU TRANSPORTATION
2161 Bantree St, Ottawa, ON, K1B 4X3
Emp Here 170   *Sales* 12,796,240
SIC 4151 School buses
  Hermas Blondeau

D-U-N-S 20-136-5616   (HQ)
BOYD MOVING & STORAGE LTD
1255 Leeds Ave Unit 1, Ottawa, ON, K1B 3W2
(613) 244-4444
Emp Here 99   *Sales* 20,570,600
SIC 4214 Local trucking with storage
  Vera Klein
  Dom Mccormick

D-U-N-S 20-136-5830   (BR)
BRINK'S CANADA LIMITED
BRINK'S CANADA
(*Suby of* THE BRINK'S COMPANY)
2755 Lancaster Rd, Ottawa, ON, K1B 4V8
(613) 521-8650
Emp Here 120
SIC 7381 Detective and armored car services
  James Orendi

D-U-N-S 25-157-4745   (SL)
C-COM SATELLITE SYSTEMS INC
2574 Sheffield Rd, Ottawa, ON, K1B 3V7
(613) 745-4110
Emp Here 23   *Sales* 10,408,985
SIC 3663 Radio and t.v. communications
equipment
  Leslie Klein
  Drew Klein
  Jim Fowles
  Bilal Awada
  Brigitte Legault

D-U-N-S 20-571-4249   (HQ)
CLEAN WATER WORKS INC
1800 Bantree St, Ottawa, ON, K1B 5L6
(613) 745-2444
Emp Here 100   *Sales* 50,488,400
SIC 1623 Water, sewer, and utility lines
  Shane Magee

D-U-N-S 20-893-4786   (SL)
DAVIS, W.R. ENGINEERING LIMITED
1260 Old Innes Rd Suite 606, Ottawa, ON,
K1B 3V3
(613) 748-5500
Emp Here 110   *Sales* 20,948,620
SIC 3674 Semiconductors and related devices
  Willard Roland Davis
  Thomas Davis

D-U-N-S 20-576-6702   (SL)
**DOMUS BUILDING CLEANING COMPANY
LIMITED**
1366 Triole St Suite 200, Ottawa, ON, K1B
3M4
(613) 741-7722
Emp Here 500   *Sales* 15,984,000
SIC 7349 Building maintenance services, nec
  Claude Lecuyer

D-U-N-S 24-844-9746   (HQ)
DRAIN-ALL LTD
ROOTER OTTAWA
1611 Liverpool Crt, Ottawa, ON, K1B 4L1
(613) 739-1070
Emp Here 87   *Sales* 44,647,400
SIC 4953 Refuse systems
  Frank Cardinali
  Clara Cardinali

D-U-N-S 24-268-1302   (SL)
EBAM ENTERPRISES LTD
BAGEL-BAGEL
1616 Michael St, Ottawa, ON, K1B 3T7
(613) 745-8998
Emp Here 20   *Sales* 10,702,480
SIC 5149 Groceries and related products, nec
  Morton White

D-U-N-S 20-011-6239   (SL)
EODC ENGINEERING, DEVELOPING AND LICENSING, INC
EODC
1377 Triole St, Ottawa, ON, K1B 4T4
(613) 748-5549
Emp Here 80   *Sales* 15,366,800
SIC 3462 Iron and steel forgings
Marlies Deisenroth
Philip Lynch

D-U-N-S 24-330-7980   (BR)
FLYNN CANADA LTD
(Suby of FLYNN CANADA LTD)
2780 Sheffield Rd, Ottawa, ON, K1B 3V9
(613) 696-0086
Emp Here 100
SIC 1761 Roofing, siding, and sheetMetal work
Robert Quesnel

D-U-N-S 20-847-3652   (SL)
FRAMOS TECHNOLOGIES INC
(Suby of MOS NORTH AMERICA INC)
2733 Lancaster Dr Suite 210, Ottawa, ON, K1B 0A9
(613) 208-1082
Emp Here 11   *Sales* 13,319,109
SIC 5043 Photographic equipment and supplies
Andreas Franze
Sebastien Dignard
Tenaha Stilzebach

D-U-N-S 25-976-5949   (HQ)
FRED GUY MOVING & STORAGE LTD
1199 Newmarket St, Ottawa, ON, K1B 3V1
(613) 744-8632
Sales 38,055,610
SIC 4214 Local trucking with storage
Wayne Lyttle
Betty Shields

D-U-N-S 20-137-7447   (HQ)
IDEAL ROOFING COMPANY LIMITED
1418 Michael St, Ottawa, ON, K1B 3R2
(613) 746-3206
Emp Here 1   *Sales* 60,807,750
SIC 3444 Sheet Metalwork
Rene Laplante
Claude Laplante

D-U-N-S 24-336-9451   (HQ)
KEYSTONE AUTOMOTIVE INDUSTRIES ON INC
KEYSTONE AUTOMOTIVE
(Suby of LKQ CORPORATION)
1230 Old Innes Rd Suite 401, Ottawa, ON, K1B 3V3
(613) 745-4088
Emp Here 22   *Sales* 21,852,900
SIC 5013 Motor vehicle supplies and new parts
Phil St.Pierre

D-U-N-S 24-103-0824   (BR)
LOBLAWS INC
LOBLAW COMPANIES EAST, DIV OF
(Suby of LOBLAW COMPANIES LIMITED)
2625 Sheffield Rd, Ottawa, ON, K1B 1A8
(613) 741-4756
Emp Here 400
SIC 5141 Groceries, general line
Jim Galloway

D-U-N-S 20-138-1522   (HQ)
MALMBERG TRUCK TRAILER EQUIPMENT LTD
1621 Michael St, Ottawa, ON, K1B 3T3
(613) 741-3360
Emp Here 20   *Sales* 33,251,820
SIC 5082 Construction and mining machinery
Stephen Malmberg

D-U-N-S 25-688-7134   (SL)
MASK MANAGEMENT CONSULTANTS LIMITED
2571 Lancaster Rd, Ottawa, ON, K1B 4L5

(613) 733-7800
Emp Here 60   *Sales* 14,057,280
SIC 8742 Management consulting services
Aurele Simourd
John Cathrae

D-U-N-S 24-522-0301   (SL)
MDS AERO SUPPORT CORPORATION
(Suby of MDS AERO SUPPORT CORPORATION)
1220 Old Innes Rd Suite 200, Ottawa, ON, K1B 3V3
(613) 744-7257
Emp Here 249   *Sales* 49,085,619
SIC 8711 Engineering services
John Jastremski

D-U-N-S 24-600-4931   (HQ)
MDS AERO SUPPORT CORPORATION
1220 Old Innes Rd Suite 200, Ottawa, ON, K1B 3V3
(613) 744-5794
Emp Here 14   *Sales* 24,844,721
SIC 8711 Engineering services
Joe Hajjar
Carole Morris
Wayne Penney
Simon Arbuthnot

D-U-N-S 20-182-3767   (SL)
MDS AEROSPACE CORPORATION
200-1220 Old Innes Rd, Ottawa, ON, K1B 3V3
(613) 744-7257
Emp Here 256   *Sales* 74,457,600
SIC 3724 Aircraft engines and engine parts
John Jastremski

D-U-N-S 25-109-8232   (SL)
METRO WASTE RECYCLING INC
2811 Sheffield Rd, Ottawa, ON, K1B 3V8
(613) 742-1222
Emp Here 75   *Sales* 19,284,825
SIC 4953 Refuse systems
Peter Mcmahon
Al Metauro

D-U-N-S 25-688-3505   (SL)
MICHANIE CONSTRUCTION INC
2825 Sheffield Rd Suite 201, Ottawa, ON, K1B 3V8
(613) 737-7717
Emp Here 30   *Sales* 14,121,930
SIC 1542 Nonresidential construction, nec
Jacques Brunet

D-U-N-S 20-347-1107   (BR)
MILLER PAVING LIMITED
MILLER WASTE SYSTEMS
(Suby of MILLER GROUP INC)
1815 Bantree St, Ottawa, ON, K1B 4L6
(613) 749-2222
Emp Here 100
SIC 4953 Refuse systems
John Larche

D-U-N-S 20-893-3960   (SL)
O A C HOLDINGS LIMITED
OTTAWA ATHLETIC CLUB
2525 Lancaster Rd, Ottawa, ON, K1B 4L5
(613) 523-1540
Emp Here 100   *Sales* 7,639,700
SIC 7991 Physical fitness facilities
Sol Shabinsky

D-U-N-S 20-873-4116   (SL)
OGILVIE SUBARU
SUBARU SALES & SERVICE
1040 Parisien St, Ottawa, ON, K1B 3M8
(613) 745-9191
Emp Here 35   *Sales* 17,432,730
SIC 5511 New and used car dealers
Brendon Brazil

D-U-N-S 25-113-3823   (SL)
OTTAWA EQUIPMENT & HYDRAULIC INC
FORKLIFT DEPOT
2628 Edinburgh Pl, Ottawa, ON, K1B 5M1
(613) 748-9000
Emp Here 22   *Sales* 10,450,572

SIC 5084 Industrial machinery and equipment
Gaston Lachance
Michel Pouliot

D-U-N-S 25-277-5945   (BR)
PINKHAM & SONS BUILDING MAINTENANCE INC
(Suby of PINKHAM & SONS BUILDING MAINTENANCE INC)
1181 Newmarket St Unit M, Ottawa, ON, K1B 3V1
(613) 745-7753
Emp Here 80
SIC 7349 Building maintenance services, nec
Jerry Pinkham

D-U-N-S 24-101-3010   (HQ)
RIVERSIDE OPTICALAB LIMITED
(Suby of ESSILORLUXOTTICA)
2485 Lancaster Rd Unit 10, Ottawa, ON, K1B 5L1
(613) 523-5765
Emp Here 1   *Sales* 14,773,785
SIC 3851 Ophthalmic goods
Charles Plante

D-U-N-S 20-374-6722   (SL)
RJW STONEMASONS LTD
2563 Edinburgh Pl, Ottawa, ON, K1B 5M1
(613) 722-7790
Emp Here 65   *Sales* 10,554,765
SIC 1741 Masonry and other stonework
Robert Watt
Alison Watt
Douglas Watt
Graham Watt

D-U-N-S 20-790-1158   (SL)
ROBADAIR LTD
2400 Lancaster Rd, Ottawa, ON, K1B 3W9
(613) 731-6019
Emp Here 75   *Sales* 14,406,375
SIC 3499 Fabricated Metal products, nec
Jonathan Cross

D-U-N-S 20-639-9818   (SL)
SIMLUC CONTRACTORS LIMITED
2550 Blackwell St, Ottawa, ON, K1B 5R1
(613) 748-0066
Emp Here 60   *Sales* 13,069,740
SIC 1761 Roofing, siding, and sheetMetal work
Martin Languedoc
Fernando Maltez
Stephane Languedoc

D-U-N-S 25-065-1593   (SL)
SIMPLEX INDUSTRIES INC
2762 Sheffield Rd, Ottawa, ON, K1B 3V9
(613) 244-0586
Emp Here 80   *Sales* 11,855,360
SIC 4214 Local trucking with storage
Luc Dompierre
Denis Letourneau

D-U-N-S 20-139-0796   (HQ)
SNELLING PAPER & SANITATION LTD
1410 Triole St, Ottawa, ON, K1B 3M5
(613) 745-7184
Emp Here 59   *Sales* 30,219,480
SIC 5113 Industrial and personal service paper
Randy Graham
Patrick Lahey
Jill Graham

D-U-N-S 24-437-2090   (BR)
SOLUTIONS DE MAINTENANCE APPLIQUEES (AMS) INC
ALLEN MAINTENANCE
(Suby of SOLUTIONS DE MAINTENANCE APPLIQUEES (AMS) INC)
1470 Triole St, Ottawa, ON, K1B 3S6
(613) 241-7794
Emp Here 300
SIC 7349 Building maintenance services, nec
Claude Trudel

D-U-N-S 25-357-3174   (BR)
SURGENOR PONTIAC BUICK LIMITED
SURGENOR TRUCK CENTRE
(Suby of SURGENOR PONTIAC BUICK LIMITED)
1571 Liverpool Crt, Ottawa, ON, K1B 4L1
(613) 745-0024
Emp Here 92
SIC 5511 New and used car dealers
Robert Mitchell

D-U-N-S 24-807-2311   (SL)
UTILITY SERVICES LTD.
1611 Liverpool Crt, Ottawa, ON, K1B 4L1

Emp Here 49   *Sales* 15,624,581
SIC 1521 Single-family housing construction
Frank Cardinali

D-U-N-S 20-051-5570   (SL)
VENTREX VENDING SERVICES INC
1550 Liverpool Crt Unit 6, Ottawa, ON, K1B 4L2
(613) 747-0455
Emp Here 50   *Sales* 22,358,700
SIC 5044 Office equipment
Steven Tremblay
Francois Bastien

Ottawa, ON K1G

D-U-N-S 24-653-1107   (SL)
1084999 ONTARIO INC
TOTAL FIRE PROTECTION
715 Industrial Ave, Ottawa, ON, K1G 0Z1
(613) 228-0073
Emp Here 25   *Sales* 10,437,650
SIC 7382 Security systems services
Christopher Gradwell

D-U-N-S 25-495-4753   (SL)
1222010 ONTARIO INC
AKRAN MARKETING
2000 Thurston Dr Unit 12, Ottawa, ON, K1G 4K7
(613) 739-4000
Emp Here 55   *Sales* 11,644,820
SIC 7311 Advertising agencies

D-U-N-S 24-917-4681   (BR)
3627730 CANADA INC
FREEMAN AUDIO VISUAL
(Suby of TFC NETHERLANDS COOPERATIEF U.A.)
3020 Hawthorne Rd Suite 300, Ottawa, ON, K1G 3J6
(613) 526-3121
Emp Here 80
SIC 7389 Business services, nec
Kevin Wolfe

D-U-N-S 20-393-8548   (SL)
9111735 CANADA INC
ARGON SOLUTION
1730 St. Laurent Blvd Suite 800, Ottawa, ON, K1G 5L1
(343) 996-8101
Emp Here 22   *Sales* 10,450,572
SIC 5084 Industrial machinery and equipment
Steven Bras

D-U-N-S 24-951-6329   (SL)
927912 ONTARIO LIMITED
ORLEANS FRESH FRUIT
(Suby of MELVIN HARTMAN ENTERPRISES LIMITED)
3150 Hawthorne Rd Suite B-1, Ottawa, ON, K1G 5H5
(613) 247-0099
Emp Here 47   *Sales* 39,272,119
SIC 5148 Fresh fruits and vegetables
Melvin Hartman

D-U-N-S 24-827-8475   (HQ)
ABI/ADVANCED BUSINESS INTERIORS

▲ Public Company   ■ Public Company Family Member   **HQ** Headquarters   **BR** Branch   **SL** Single Location

INC
2355 St. Laurent Blvd, Ottawa, ON, K1G 4L2
(613) 738-1003
Emp Here 20   *Sales* 11,517,000
SIC 5712 Furniture stores
William F (Bill) Toutant
David Asselin

D-U-N-S 20-708-9595   (HQ)
ALLEN-VANGUARD CORPORATION
2405 St. Laurent Blvd, Ottawa, ON, K1G 5B4
(613) 739-9646
Sales 22,358,700
SIC 5065 Electronic parts and equipment, nec
Mike Dithurbide

D-U-N-S 24-793-1157   (HQ)
ASBEX LTD
2280 Stevenage Dr Unit 200, Ottawa, ON,
K1G 3W3
(613) 228-1080
Emp Here 5   *Sales* 12,309,300
SIC 1799 Special trade contractors, nec
Normand E Castonguay

D-U-N-S 20-809-4545   (SL)
AVW TELAV AUDIO VISUAL SERVICES
2295 St. Laurent Blvd, Ottawa, ON, K1G 4H6
(613) 526-3121
Emp Here 75   *Sales* 14,351,550
SIC 7359 Equipment rental and leasing, nec
John Murray

D-U-N-S 20-577-3286   (SL)
BEACON LITE LTD
4070 Belgreen Dr, Ottawa, ON, K1G 3N2
(613) 737-7337
Emp Here 150   *Sales* 49,972,200
SIC 7359 Equipment rental and leasing, nec
Gord Thompson
N. Donald Moore
Clark Atchison

D-U-N-S 20-856-6708   (BR)
BREWERS RETAIL INC
BEER STORE, THE
(*Suby of* BREWERS RETAIL INC)
2750 Swansea Cres, Ottawa, ON, K1G 6R8
(613) 738-8615
Emp Here 100
SIC 5921 Liquor stores
Joe Papovich

D-U-N-S 25-543-8699   (SL)
BROFORT INC
2161 Thurston Dr, Ottawa, ON, K1G 6C9
(613) 746-8580
Emp Here 100   *Sales* 19,636,100
SIC 1751 Carpentry work
Renaud Brault

D-U-N-S 24-633-5046   (HQ)
**BUDGET CAR & TRUCK RENTALS OF OT-
TAWA LTD**
851 Industrial Ave, Ottawa, ON, K1G 4L3
(613) 739-4231
Emp Here 10   *Sales* 18,387,680
SIC 7513 Truck rental and leasing, no drivers
Neil Zaret
Avraham Iny
Rick Maguire

D-U-N-S 20-577-2809   (SL)
BYTEK AUTOMOBILES INC
1325 St. Laurent Blvd, Ottawa, ON, K1G 0Z7
(613) 745-6885
Emp Here 35   *Sales* 17,432,730
SIC 5511 New and used car dealers
John Mierins

D-U-N-S 20-788-0766   (HQ)
CAA NORTH & EAST ONTARIO
CAA
2151 Thurston Dr, Ottawa, ON, K1G 6C9
(613) 820-1890
Emp Here 100   *Sales* 23,099,553
SIC 8699 Membership organizations, nec
Christina Hlusko

Robert Keeper
Peter Mcintosh
Vicky Paine-Mantha
Jack Campbell
John Morton
Richard Nowak
Kate Wright
Line Villeneuve
Gerry Brown

D-U-N-S 24-892-8772   (HQ)
**CANADA SCIENCE AND TECHNOLOGY
MUSEUMS CORPORATION**
CANADA AVIATION AND SPACE MUSEUM
(*Suby of* GOVERNMENT OF CANADA)
2421 Lancaster Rd, Ottawa, ON, K1G 5A3
(613) 991-3044
Emp Here 55   *Sales* 24,117,800
SIC 8412 Museums and art galleries
Denise Amyot
Gary Polonsky

D-U-N-S 20-892-9026   (SL)
CANADAWIDE SCIENTIFIC LIMITED
2300 Walkley Rd Suite 4, Ottawa, ON, K1G
6B1
(613) 736-8811
Emp Here 25   *Sales* 11,179,350
SIC 5049 Professional equipment, nec
Antonio Seccareccia
Peter Seccareccia
Carmine Seccareccia

D-U-N-S 25-541-7685   (HQ)
CANADIAN BLOOD SERVICES
1800 Alta Vista Dr, Ottawa, ON, K1G 4J5
(613) 739-2300
Emp Here 400   *Sales* 830,976,351
SIC 8099 Health and allied services, nec

D-U-N-S 20-136-6986   (BR)
**CANADIAN LINEN AND UNIFORM SER-
VICE CO**
(*Suby of* ARAMARK)
1695 Russell Rd, Ottawa, ON, K1G 0N1
(613) 736-9975
Emp Here 160
SIC 7213 Linen supply
Dave Bunton

D-U-N-S 20-787-9057   (HQ)
CANADIAN MEDICAL ASSOCIATION
CANADIAN JOURNAL OF SURGERY
1867 Alta Vista Dr, Ottawa, ON, K1G 5W8
(613) 731-9331
Sales 37,457,760
SIC 8621 Professional organizations
Tim Smith
Laurent Marcoux
Jimmy Mui
Suzanne Strasberg
F. Gigi Osler
Granger Avery
Guruswamy Sridhar
Ann Collins
Rao Tadepalli
Ewan Affleck

D-U-N-S 20-790-1661   (HQ)
**CANADIAN UNION OF PUBLIC EMPLOY-
EES**
CUPE
1375 St. Laurent Blvd, Ottawa, ON, K1G 0Z7
(613) 237-1590
Emp Here 165   *Sales* 158,951,842
SIC 8631 Labor organizations
Mark Hancock
Claude Genereux
Patrick Sid Ryan
Barry O'neill
Donna Ryan
Daniel Legere
Charles Fleury
Candace Rennick
Michael Hurley
Kevin Rebeck

D-U-N-S 24-562-2522   (HQ)
**CAREFOR HEALTH & COMMUNITY SER-
VICES**
760 Belfast Rd, Ottawa, ON, K1G 6M8
(613) 749-7557
Emp Here 95   *Sales* 33,385,601
SIC 8621 Professional organizations
Bob Cerniuk
Bill Chwedchuk
Dorin Lucas
Maria Badek
Steve Perry
Glenna Mackenzie
Norma Strachan
John Kroon
Ruth Pollock
Ian Welton

D-U-N-S 20-013-5775   (BR)
CITY OF OTTAWA
*OTTAWA-CARLETON REGIONAL TRANSIT
COMMISSION*
(*Suby of* CITY OF OTTAWA)
1500 St. Laurent Blvd, Ottawa, ON, K1G 0Z8
(613) 741-6440
Emp Here 4,000
SIC 4111 Local and suburban transit
John Manconi

D-U-N-S 24-891-3600   (BR)
COLABOR LIMITED PARTNERSHIP
SUMMIT FOOD
(*Suby of* GROUPE COLABOR INC)
100 Legacy Rd, Ottawa, ON, K1G 5T8
(613) 737-7000
Emp Here 200
SIC 5141 Groceries, general line
Kim Glover

D-U-N-S 20-058-2406   (HQ)
**COM-NET (COMMUNICATION CABLING
AND NETWORK SOLUTIONS) INC**
2191 Thurston Dr, Ottawa, ON, K1G 6C9
(613) 247-7778
Emp Here 52   *Sales* 19,604,610
SIC 1731 Electrical work
Ross Johnson

D-U-N-S 20-894-2573   (HQ)
COMPUTER MEDIA PRODUCTS LTD
COMPUTER MEDIA GROUP, THE
250 Tremblay Rd Suite 520, Ottawa, ON, K1G
3J8
(613) 226-7071
Emp Here 46   *Sales* 23,253,048
SIC 5045 Computers, peripherals, and soft-
ware
Kevin Rolfe
E Mavis Rolfe

D-U-N-S 25-263-6618   (HQ)
**CONSEIL DES ECOLES PUBLIQUES DE
L'EST DE L'ONTARIO**
CEPEO
2445 St. Laurent Blvd, Ottawa, ON, K1G 6C3
(613) 742-8960
Emp Here 150   *Sales* 182,656,872
SIC 8211 Elementary and secondary schools
Denis Chartrand
Linda Savard
Edith Dumont

D-U-N-S 20-788-6904   (HQ)
COUGHLIN & ASSOCIATES LTD
466 Tremblay Rd, Ottawa, ON, K1G 3R1
(613) 231-2266
Sales 569,532,480
SIC 6411 Insurance agents, brokers, and ser-
vice
Brian Bockstael

D-U-N-S 24-362-8836   (HQ)
**DEW ENGINEERING AND DEVELOPMENT
ULC**
(*Suby of* KEYSTONE HOLDINGS LLC)
3429 Hawthorne Rd, Ottawa, ON, K1G 4G2

(613) 736-5100
Emp Here 200   *Sales* 145,425,000
SIC 3795 Tanks and tank components
Ian Marsh
Neil Hutton

D-U-N-S 24-978-2004   (HQ)
DUSTBANE HOLDINGS INC
25 Pickering Pl, Ottawa, ON, K1G 5P4
(613) 745-6861
Sales 13,077,650
SIC 6712 Bank holding companies
John French
Normand Perron
Pierre Perron

D-U-N-S 24-437-6497   (SL)
DUSTBANE PRODUCTS LIMITED
(*Suby of* DUSTBANE HOLDINGS INC)
25 Pickering Pl, Ottawa, ON, K1G 5P4
(800) 387-8226
Emp Here 50   *Sales* 14,201,050
SIC 2842 Polishes and sanitation goods
Benjamin Merkley
Marc Galarneau
Shannon Hall
Grant Beesley
Dan Cassidy

D-U-N-S 20-714-7096   (BR)
**DYNACARE-GAMMA LABORATORY PART-
NERSHIP**
(*Suby of* LABORATORY CORPORATION OF
AMERICA HOLDINGS)
750 Peter Morand Cres, Ottawa, ON, K1G 6S4
(613) 729-0200
Emp Here 200
SIC 8071 Medical laboratories
Chantel Sinoneau

D-U-N-S 20-528-3158   (SL)
ENCLOSURES DIRECT INC
EDI
2120 Thurston Dr, Ottawa, ON, K1G 6E1
(613) 723-4477
Emp Here 50   *Sales* 10,141,500
SIC 3469 Metal stampings, nec
Steven Christie

D-U-N-S 20-117-9681   (HQ)
EPOCAL INC
(*Suby of* SIEMENS AG)
2060 Walkley Rd, Ottawa, ON, K1G 3P5
(613) 738-6192
Sales 26,881,218
SIC 8731 Commercial physical research
Imants Lauks

D-U-N-S 24-919-5652   (SL)
EURO TILE & STONE INC
3103 Hawthorne Rd, Ottawa, ON, K1G 3V8
(613) 244-4315
Emp Here 50   *Sales* 22,358,700
SIC 5032 Brick, stone, and related material
Benedetto Colasanti

D-U-N-S 24-481-3333   (HQ)
FERANO HOLDINGS LTD
409 Industrial Ave, Ottawa, ON, K1G 0Z1
(613) 523-7731
Emp Here 1   *Sales* 10,462,120
SIC 6712 Bank holding companies
Dominic Ferrarotto

D-U-N-S 25-531-6028   (SL)
FLEMING COMMUNICATIONS INC
FCI
920 Belfast Rd Suite 101, Ottawa, ON, K1G
0Z6
(613) 244-6770
Emp Here 86   *Sales* 38,456,964
SIC 5045 Computers, peripherals, and soft-
ware
Michael Fleming
Geoff Oaks

D-U-N-S 24-269-2507   (HQ)
G.T. WHOLESALE LIMITED

G.T. TABACCO
(Suby of GIANT TIGER STORES LIMITED)
2480 Walkley Rd, Ottawa, ON, K1G 6A9
(613) 521-8222
Emp Here 220   *Sales* 147,289,750
SIC 5194 Tobacco and tobacco products
Gordon Reid
Kevin Little
Greg Farrell

D-U-N-S 25-283-8370   (BR)
GDI SERVICES (CANADA) LP
GDI INTEGRATED FACILITY SERVICES
(Suby of GDI SERVICES AUX IMMEUBLES INC)
800 Industrial Ave Suite 12, Ottawa, ON, K1G 4B8
(613) 247-0065
Emp Here 250
SIC 7349 Building maintenance services, nec
Jim Reklitis

D-U-N-S 20-649-7513   (HQ)
GIANT TIGER STORES LIMITED
MAGASINS TIGRE GEANT, LES
2480 Walkley Rd, Ottawa, ON, K1G 6A9
(613) 521-8222
Emp Here 350   *Sales* 1,216,864,000
SIC 5311 Department stores
Gordon Reid
Scott Reid
Thomas Haig
Paul D. Wood
Greg Farrell
Michael Lewis
Kevin Jackson
Marco Marrone
John Ruddy
Gino Digioacchino

D-U-N-S 20-443-0672   (BR)
GRAND & TOY LIMITED
(Suby of OFFICE DEPOT, INC.)
900 Belfast Rd, Ottawa, ON, K1G 0Z6
(866) 391-8111
Emp Here 140
SIC 5112 Stationery and office supplies
Gary Weatherdon

D-U-N-S 25-529-3581   (SL)
IRIDIAN SPECTRAL TECHNOLOGIES LIMITED
2700 Swansea Cres, Ottawa, ON, K1G 6R8
(613) 741-4513
Emp Here 140   *Sales* 22,240,120
SIC 3081 Unsupported plastics film and sheet
George Laframboise
Brian Sullivan
Douglas Burbidge
Rob Bruce
Monica Coyne

D-U-N-S 20-789-1409   (SL)
KOYMAN GALLERIES LIMITED
KOYMAN GALLERIES
1771 St. Laurent Blvd, Ottawa, ON, K1G 3V4
(613) 526-1562
Emp Here 50   *Sales* 16,280,000
SIC 5999 Miscellaneous retail stores, nec
Marie Koyman
Benjamin Koyman

D-U-N-S 24-574-8637   (SL)
L J C CLEANING SERVICES INC
SERVICEMASTER OF OTTAWA
740 Belfast Rd Unit B, Ottawa, ON, K1G 0Z5
(613) 244-1997
Emp Here 150   *Sales* 85,550,700
SIC 1542 Nonresidential construction, nec
John Cooke

D-U-N-S 20-288-7428   (SL)
LANSDOWNE STADIUM LIMITED PARTNERSHIP
TD PLACE
700 Industrial Ave Unit 220, Ottawa, ON, K1G 0Y9

(613) 232-6767
Emp Here 275   *Sales* 22,692,175
SIC 7941 Sports clubs, managers, and promoters
Bernard Ashe

D-U-N-S 25-130-6726   (SL)
LATCON LTD
3387 Hawthorne Rd, Ottawa, ON, K1G 4G2
(613) 738-9061
Emp Here 65   *Sales* 16,002,090
SIC 1795 Wrecking and demolition work
Leonard Graham
Robert Desormeaux
Vivianne Duval

D-U-N-S 24-104-1938   (SL)
LYCEE CLAUDEL
1635 Riverside Dr, Ottawa, ON, K1G 0E5
(613) 733-8522
Emp Here 80   *Sales* 7,426,080
SIC 8211 Elementary and secondary schools
Yawar Khan
Bruno Bigi
Nicolas Chambrial

D-U-N-S 20-892-7723   (SL)
MARLBORO WINDOW AND DOOR MANUFACTURER LTD
2370 Stevenage Dr, Ottawa, ON, K1G 3W3
(613) 736-1441
Emp Here 40   *Sales* 10,122,360
SIC 5211 Lumber and other building materials
David Dubrofsky
Frank Manitta

D-U-N-S 24-386-9521   (HQ)
MD FINANCIAL MANAGEMENT INC
(Suby of BANK OF NOVA SCOTIA, THE)
1870 Alta Vista Dr Suite 1, Ottawa, ON, K1G 6R7
(613) 731-4552
Emp Here 400   *Sales* 174,686,400
SIC 8741 Management services
Brian F Peters
John Riviere

D-U-N-S 24-267-7490   (HQ)
MD MANAGEMENT LIMITED
MD EQUITY FUND
(Suby of BANK OF NOVA SCOTIA, THE)
1870 Alta Vista Dr, Ottawa, ON, K1G 6R7
(613) 731-4552
Emp Here 20   *Sales* 56,101,500
SIC 8741 Management services
Brian Peters
Lindsay Hugenholtz
Michelle Masson
John Riviere
Daniel Labonte

D-U-N-S 25-995-9260   (HQ)
MD PRIVATE TRUST COMPANY
(Suby of BANK OF NOVA SCOTIA, THE)
1870 Alta Vista Dr, Ottawa, ON, K1G 6R7
(613) 731-8610
Emp Here 8   *Sales* 85,495,538
SIC 6722 Management investment, open-end
Bill Cooke

D-U-N-S 20-299-2178   (HQ)
MED-ENG HOLDINGS ULC
(Suby of MAUI ACQUISITION CORP.)
2400 St. Laurent Blvd, Ottawa, ON, K1G 6C4
(613) 482-8835
Emp Here 5   *Sales* 32,956,905
SIC 3842 Surgical appliances and supplies
Warren Kanders
Scott Timothy O'brien

D-U-N-S 25-058-1600   (SL)
MEDICAL COUNCIL OF CANADA
1021 Thomas Spratt Pl, Ottawa, ON, K1G 5L5

Emp Here 75   *Sales* 21,356,025
SIC 8733 Noncommercial research organizations
Ian Bowmer

Elizabeth Davis

D-U-N-S 24-204-9166   (HQ)
MELVIN HARTMAN ENTERPRISES LIMITED
3150 Hawthorne Rd Suite B-1, Ottawa, ON, K1G 5H5
(613) 247-0099
Sales 39,272,119
SIC 5148 Fresh fruits and vegetables
Melvin Hartman

D-U-N-S 24-344-4887   (BR)
METRO ONTARIO INC
METRO
(Suby of METRO INC)
490 Industrial Ave, Ottawa, ON, K1G 0Y9
(613) 737-1300
Emp Here 100
SIC 5141 Groceries, general line
Mike Meagher

D-U-N-S 24-708-9659   (SL)
MIDEAST FOOD DISTRIBUTORS (1987) LTD
MID EAST FOOD CENTRE
1010 Belfast Rd, Ottawa, ON, K1G 4A2
(613) 244-2525
Emp Here 50   *Sales* 13,707,600
SIC 5499 Miscellaneous food stores
Elias Njaim

D-U-N-S 24-320-4343   (SL)
NIGHT HAWK TECHNOLOGIESTM INC
NIGHT HAWK TECHNOLOGIES
25 Great Oak Pvt, Ottawa, ON, K1G 6P7
(613) 795-8262
Emp Here 5   *Sales* 11,752,155
SIC 8731 Commercial physical research
Guillaume Carle

D-U-N-S 24-686-1736   (HQ)
NORTHERN MICRO INC
(Suby of CONVERGE TECHNOLOGY SOLUTIONS CORP.)
3155 Swansea Cres, Ottawa, ON, K1G 3J3
(613) 226-1117
Emp Here 61   *Sales* 15,762,071
SIC 3571 Electronic computers
Herman Yeh

D-U-N-S 20-615-9295   (SL)
ON CALL CENTRE INC
2405 St. Laurent Blvd Unit B, Ottawa, ON, K1G 5B4
(613) 238-3262
Emp Here 50   *Sales* 22,174,500
SIC 7389 Business services, nec
Stanley Arron
Calvin Smith

D-U-N-S 24-849-0419   (SL)
ONIX LAZER CORPORATION
645 Belfast Rd Unit 1, Ottawa, ON, K1G 4V3

Emp Here 21   *Sales* 10,576,818
SIC 5112 Stationery and office supplies
Roger Brian Kent
Donald W J Finless

D-U-N-S 24-104-1698   (HQ)
OTTAWA CHILDREN'S TREATMENT CENTRE
2211 Thurston Dr, Ottawa, ON, K1G 6C9
(613) 688-2126
Emp Here 50   *Sales* 11,518,800
SIC 8322 Individual and family services
Katheline Stokely
Lori Raycroft

D-U-N-S 25-504-0891   (BR)
OTTAWA-CARLETON DISTRICT SCHOOL BOARD
CANTERBURY HIGH SCHOOL
(Suby of OTTAWA-CARLETON DISTRICT SCHOOL BOARD)
900 Canterbury Ave, Ottawa, ON, K1G 3A7

(613) 731-1191
Emp Here 100
SIC 8211 Elementary and secondary schools
Alan Johnson

D-U-N-S 25-504-0974   (BR)
OTTAWA-CARLETON DISTRICT SCHOOL BOARD
HILLCREST HIGH SCHOOL
(Suby of OTTAWA-CARLETON DISTRICT SCHOOL BOARD)
1900 Dauphin Rd, Ottawa, ON, K1G 2L7
(613) 733-1755
Emp Here 90
SIC 8211 Elementary and secondary schools
Kevin Gilmore

D-U-N-S 20-913-6170   (BR)
PEPSI BOTTLING GROUP (CANADA), ULC, THE
PEPSICO BEVERAGES CANADA
(Suby of PBG INVESTMENT (LUXEMBOURG) SARL)
869 Belfast Rd, Ottawa, ON, K1G 0Z4
(613) 244-9961
Emp Here 200
SIC 5149 Groceries and related products, nec
Daniel Lamirande

D-U-N-S 20-789-6366   (HQ)
PROFESSIONAL INSTITUTE OF THE PUBLIC SERVICE OF CANADA, THE
PIPSC
250 Tremblay Rd, Ottawa, ON, K1G 3J8
(613) 228-6310
Sales 39,872,280
SIC 8631 Labor organizations
Debi Daviau

D-U-N-S 20-891-6098   (SL)
PROLOGIC SYSTEMS LIMITED
2255 St. Laurent Blvd Suite 320, Ottawa, ON, K1G 4K3
(613) 238-1376
Emp Here 60   *Sales* 16,459,920
SIC 8741 Management services
Keith Langley

D-U-N-S 20-893-9819   (HQ)
PROMAXIS SYSTEMS INC
2385 St. Laurent Blvd, Ottawa, ON, K1G 6C3
(613) 737-2112
Sales 21,085,920
SIC 8742 Management consulting services
Sharon Scherlowski
Andrew Knight
Patrick Moore
Thomas Arnold Eyre

D-U-N-S 25-772-8543   (BR)
RED LOBSTER HOSPITALITY LLC
RED LOBSTER RESTAURANTS
1499 St. Laurent Blvd, Ottawa, ON, K1G 0Z9
(613) 744-7560
Emp Here 96
SIC 5812 Eating places
Ian Forrester

D-U-N-S 20-647-2289   (BR)
RESOLVE CORPORATION
2405 St Laurent Blvd, Ottawa, ON, K1G 5B4

Emp Here 250
SIC 7374 Data processing and preparation
Julie Taylor

D-U-N-S 24-437-3510   (HQ)
RICHCRAFT HOMES LTD
2280 St. Laurent Blvd Suite 201, Ottawa, ON, K1G 4K1
(613) 739-7111
Sales 20,562,360
SIC 6553 Cemetery subdividers and developers
Krishan M. Singhal
Manju Singhal

D-U-N-S 24-622-0495   (HQ)

SHALABY ENTERPRISES LIMITED
2310 St. Laurent Blvd, Ottawa, ON, K1G 5H9
(613) 526-5212
Emp Here 40   *Sales* 20,548,395
SIC 6712 Bank holding companies
  Samir Shalaby
  Lynn Shalaby

D-U-N-S 20-787-7903   (HQ)
TANNIS TRADING INC
TANNIS FOOD DISTRIBUTORS
(*Suby of* SYSCO CORPORATION)
2390 Stevenage Dr, Ottawa, ON, K1G 3W3
(613) 736-6000
Emp Here 120   *Sales* 114,674,560
SIC 5149 Groceries and related products, nec
  Theo Tannis
  Michael Tannis
  Eli Tannis
  Kammal Tannis

D-U-N-S 20-798-8697   (BR)
UNITED PARCEL SERVICE CANADA LTD
UPS
(*Suby of* UNITED PARCEL SERVICE, INC.)
2281 Stevenage Dr, Ottawa, ON, K1G 3W1
(613) 670-6061
Emp Here 300
SIC 4215 Courier services, except by air
  Andrew May

D-U-N-S 24-270-6745   (HQ)
URBANDALE CONSTRUCTION LIMITED
2193 Arch St, Ottawa, ON, K1G 2H5
(613) 731-6331
Emp Here 10   *Sales* 15,943,450
SIC 1521 Single-family housing construction
  Richard Sachs
  Lyon Sachs

D-U-N-S 20-139-3303   (HQ)
URBANDALE CORPORATION
2193 Arch St, Ottawa, ON, K1G 2H5
(613) 731-6331
Emp Here 95   *Sales* 22,087,100
SIC 6513 Apartment building operators
  Lyon Sachs
  Richard Sachs
  Ian Lawrence Nadolny

D-U-N-S 20-519-2318   (SL)
VAC SERVICE OF CANADA INC
1001 Thomas Spratt Pl, Ottawa, ON, K1G 5L5

Emp Here 45   *Sales* 83,099,655
SIC 6351 Surety insurance
  Ian Macneil

D-U-N-S 20-894-3472   (HQ)
VICTORIAN ORDER OF NURSES FOR CANADA
VON
2315 St. Laurent Blvd Suite 100, Ottawa, ON, K1G 4J8
(613) 233-5694
Emp Here 60   *Sales* 268,453,500
SIC 8082 Home health care services
  Judith Shamian
  Bob Russell
  Lynn Power
  David McIsaac
  John Gallinger
  Sandy Finnigan
  Hana Gartner
  George Filliter
  Janice Mccallum
  Stan Franklin

D-U-N-S 24-319-5174   (BR)
WAL-MART CANADA CORP
(*Suby of* WALMART INC.)
450 Terminal Ave Suite 1031, Ottawa, ON, K1G 0Z3
(613) 562-0500
Emp Here 120
SIC 5311 Department stores
  Andre Lapensee

D-U-N-S 25-543-8087   (SL)
XSTREAM SOFTWARE INC
2280 St. Laurent Blvd Suite 101, Ottawa, ON, K1G 4K1
(613) 731-9443
Emp Here 100   *Sales* 17,731,100
SIC 7371 Custom computer programming services
  Sunil Sethi
  Lawrence Weinstein

D-U-N-S 20-861-2536   (BR)
YOUTH SERVICES BUREAU OF OTTAWA
WILLIAM E HAY CENTRE
(*Suby of* YOUTH SERVICES BUREAU OF OTTAWA)
3000 Hawthorne Rd, Ottawa, ON, K1G 5Y3
(613) 738-7776
Emp Here 90
SIC 8322 Individual and family services
  Gordon Boyd

Ottawa, ON K1H

D-U-N-S 20-889-4220   (HQ)
AERIC INC
CONFERENCE BOARD OF CANADA, THE
255 Smyth Rd, Ottawa, ON, K1H 8M7
(613) 526-3280
Emp Here 180   *Sales* 43,988,600
SIC 8732 Commercial nonphysical research
  Susan Black
  Glen Hodgson
  Michael Bloom
  David Stewart-Patterson
  Barb Hogberg
  Ian Cullwick
  Jean-Pierre Boisclair
  Bruce Leslie
  Ann Mackenzie
  Ross Roxburgh

D-U-N-S 24-103-4719   (BR)
BLACK & MCDONALD LIMITED
(*Suby of* BLACK & MCDONALD GROUP LIMITED)
2460 Don Reid Dr, Ottawa, ON, K1H 1E1
(613) 526-1226
Emp Here 135
SIC 1731 Electrical work
  Peter Tuck

D-U-N-S 24-139-4852   (SL)
CHEO-AUTISM PROGRAM EASTERN ONTARIO
401 Smyth Rd, Ottawa, ON, K1H 8L1
(613) 745-5963
Emp Here 101   *Sales* 145,298,701
SIC 8699 Membership organizations, nec
  Gabrielle Nadeau
  Lise Bisnare

D-U-N-S 24-100-0066   (HQ)
CHILDRENS HOSPITAL OF EASTERN ONTARIO
CHEO
401 Smyth Rd, Ottawa, ON, K1H 8L1
(613) 737-7600
Sales 277,700,000
SIC 8069 Specialty hospitals, except psychiatric
  Alex Munter
  Darlene Arseneau

D-U-N-S 24-382-7958   (HQ)
DYMON STORAGE CORPORATION
1830 Walkley Rd Unit 1, Ottawa, ON, K1H 8K3
(613) 247-9908
Emp Here 20   *Sales* 46,283,850
SIC 4225 General warehousing and storage
  Brent Wilson
  Glen Luckman

D-U-N-S 24-326-0903   (SL)

DYMON TECHNOLOGIES INC
(*Suby of* DYMON STORAGE CORPORATION)
1830 Walkley Rd Suite 2, Ottawa, ON, K1H 8K3
(613) 247-0888
Emp Here 80   *Sales* 33,511,120
SIC 6531 Real estate agents and managers
  Brent Wilson
  Glen Luckman
  Chris Vigliotti

D-U-N-S 20-894-4397   (HQ)
HANDA TRAVEL SERVICES LTD
TAJ TOURS
2269 Riverside Dr Suite 135, Ottawa, ON, K1H 8K2
(613) 731-1111
Emp Here 24   *Sales* 17,678,878
SIC 4724 Travel agencies
  Inder Handa
  Erna Handa

D-U-N-S 24-104-7356   (HQ)
LARNY HOLDINGS LIMITED
QUICKIE CONVENIENCE STORES
2520 St. Laurent Blvd Suite 201, Ottawa, ON, K1H 1B1
(613) 736-7962
Emp Here 20   *Sales* 42,554,165
SIC 5411 Grocery stores
  Arnold Kimmel
  Lawrence Hartman
  Christopher Wilcox

D-U-N-S 20-714-7161   (BR)
OTTAWA HOSPITAL, THE
RIVERSIDE CAMPUS
(*Suby of* OTTAWA HOSPITAL, THE)
1967 Riverside Dr Suite 323, Ottawa, ON, K1H 7W9
(613) 798-5555
Emp Here 550
SIC 8062 General medical and surgical hospitals

D-U-N-S 20-383-4833   (BR)
OTTAWA HOSPITAL, THE
DEPARTMENT OF OPHTHALMOLOGY
(*Suby of* OTTAWA HOSPITAL, THE)
501 Smyth Rd, Ottawa, ON, K1H 8L6
(613) 737-8899
Emp Here 100
SIC 8011 Offices and clinics of medical doctors
  Steven Gilberg

D-U-N-S 20-507-6649   (SL)
OTTAWA MOULD CRAFT LIMITED
2510 Don Reid Dr, Ottawa, ON, K1H 1E1
(613) 521-6402
Emp Here 120   *Sales* 19,062,960
SIC 3089 Plastics products, nec
  Darcy Cullum
  David Veal
  Kirit Shah
  Shaun Pilkington

D-U-N-S 20-811-2206   (HQ)
PERFORMANCE REALTY LTD
1500 Bank St, Ottawa, ON, K1H 1B8
(613) 733-9100
Sales 13,587,800
SIC 6531 Real estate agents and managers
  Pierre De Varennes

D-U-N-S 20-890-8871   (SL)
RECREATION ASSOCIATION OF THE PUBLIC SERVICE OF CANADA, THE
RA SKI CLUB
2451 Riverside Dr, Ottawa, ON, K1H 7X7
(613) 733-5100
Emp Here 100   *Sales* 7,854,500
SIC 7997 Membership sports and recreation clubs
  Robert Allison
  Irma Bigras
  Ian Bishop

  Gord Cooper
  Fred Costin
  Louise Holmes
  Paul Kelly
  Gregg Kennedy
  Jay Khosla
  M. Mctaggart

D-U-N-S 24-363-0840   (BR)
RGIS CANADA ULC
(*Suby of* THE BLACKSTONE GROUP L P)
2197 Riverside Dr Suite 305, Ottawa, ON, K1H 7X3
(613) 226-4086
Emp Here 100
SIC 7389 Business services, nec

D-U-N-S 25-756-8543   (BR)
ROYAL LEPAGE REAL ESTATE SERVICES LTD
(*Suby of* BRIDGEMARQ REAL ESTATE SERVICES INC)
1500 Bank St Suite 201, Ottawa, ON, K1H 7Z2
(613) 733-9100
Emp Here 90
SIC 6531 Real estate agents and managers
  Thomas Krenn

D-U-N-S 24-424-9020   (BR)
UNIVERSITY OF OTTAWA
FACULTY OF MEDICINE
(*Suby of* UNIVERSITY OF OTTAWA)
451 Smyth Rd Suite Rgn, Ottawa, ON, K1H 8M5
(613) 562-5800
Emp Here 1,000
SIC 8221 Colleges and universities
  Illimar Altosaar

Ottawa, ON K1J

D-U-N-S 25-276-8890   (SL)
CARR & COMPANY INSURANCE BROKERS LTD
1980 Ogilvie Rd, Ottawa, ON, K1J 9L3
(613) 706-1806
Emp Here 30   *Sales* 17,397,720
SIC 6411 Insurance agents, brokers, and service
  Pierre Carr
  Wendy Carr

D-U-N-S 20-247-9713   (SL)
COMBAT
5390 Canotek Rd Unit 20, Ottawa, ON, K1J 1H8

Emp Here 49   *Sales* 10,722,376
SIC 3949 Sporting and athletic goods, nec
  Kurtis Watson

D-U-N-S 20-575-0453   (SL)
DATAVISUAL MARKETING INC
DATAVISUAL
1101 Polytek St Suite 500, Ottawa, ON, K1J 0B3
(613) 741-9898
Emp Here 25   *Sales* 13,013,550
SIC 5099 Durable goods, nec
  Henry Kislich
  Benoit Kislich-Lemyre
  Lisa Kislich-Lemyre
  Vanessa Moriarity

D-U-N-S 20-552-9915   (SL)
FIRST CAPITAL REALTY CORP
SCB PROPERTY MANAGEMENT SERVICES LP
1980 Ogilvie Rd Suite 149, Ottawa, ON, K1J 9L3

Emp Here 200
SIC 8741 Management services

Ottawa, ON K1K

D-U-N-S 24-847-9156   (SL)
1437716 ONTARIO LIMITED
BISSONNETTE YOUR INDEPENDENT GRO-CER
596 Montreal Rd, Ottawa, ON, K1K 0T9
(613) 745-0778
Emp Here 120   *Sales* 35,217,240
SIC 5411 Grocery stores
  Jacques Bissonnette

D-U-N-S 20-268-6564   (HQ)
ASSENT COMPLIANCE INC
525 Coventry Rd, Ottawa, ON, K1K 2C5
(613) 369-8390
Sales 28,836,400
SIC 7371 Custom computer programming services
  Andrew Waitman
  Russell Frederick
  Matthew Whitteker
  Laura Laura

D-U-N-S 20-577-2601   (HQ)
BEL-AIR AUTOMOBILES INC
450 Mcarthur Ave, Ottawa, ON, K1K 1G4
(613) 741-3270
Emp Here 130   *Sales* 91,245,600
SIC 5511 New and used car dealers
  Roland Parent
  Robert Parent
  Michel Parent

D-U-N-S 24-011-8641   (BR)
BEST BUY CANADA LTD
BEST BUY
(*Suby of* BEST BUY CO., INC.)
380 Coventry Rd, Ottawa, ON, K1K 2C6
(613) 212-0333
Emp Here 100
SIC 5731 Radio, television, and electronic stores

D-U-N-S 24-861-5853   (SL)
BIOMEDICAL INDUSTRY GROUP INC
532 Montreal Rd Suite 362, Ottawa, ON, K1K 4R4
(613) 745-4139
Emp Here 49   *Sales* 22,280,051
SIC 5047 Medical and hospital equipment
  Mark Sunderland

D-U-N-S 25-770-7422   (SL)
CANADIAN DINERS (1995) L.P. LTD
PERKINS FAMILY RESTAURANT
1130 St. Laurent Blvd, Ottawa, ON, K1K 3B6
(613) 747-9190
Emp Here 90   *Sales* 4,096,710
SIC 5812 Eating places
  Colin Kinsman
  Terence Whitty

D-U-N-S 20-891-2410   (HQ)
CANADIAN POSTMASTERS AND ASSIS-TANTS ASSOCIATION
281 Queen Mary St, Ottawa, ON, K1K 1X1
(613) 745-2095
Emp Here 9   *Sales* 12,558,780
SIC 8621 Professional organizations
  Leslie Schous
  Shirley Dressler
  Pierrre Charbonneau
  Daniel Maheax

D-U-N-S 20-705-7477   (SL)
CENTRE DE SOINS DE LONGUE DUREE MONTFORT
705 Montreal Rd, Ottawa, ON, K1K 0M9
(613) 746-8602
Emp Here 100   *Sales* 27,433,200
SIC 8741 Management services
  Lisa Grenier

D-U-N-S 25-955-1547   (SL)

CHRISTIE LAKE KIDS
400 Coventry Rd, Ottawa, ON, K1K 2C7
(613) 742-6922
Emp Here 85   *Sales* 1,276,785
SIC 7033 Trailer parks and campsites
  Carole Gagne-Ince

D-U-N-S 24-845-9018   (HQ)
CITE COLLEGIALE, LA
801 Aviation Pky, Ottawa, ON, K1K 4R3
(613) 742-2483
Emp Here 650   *Sales* 20,146,500
SIC 8222 Junior colleges
  Andree Lortie
  Serge Brousseau
  Claude Bergeron
  Marc Tasse

D-U-N-S 20-890-4276   (SL)
CIVIC MOTORS LTD
1171 St. Laurent Blvd, Ottawa, ON, K1K 3B7
(613) 741-6676
Emp Here 50   *Sales* 24,903,900
SIC 5511 New and used car dealers
  Arnie Mierins

D-U-N-S 20-070-2517   (BR)
CONSEIL DES ECOLES CATHOLIQUES DE LANGUE FRANCAISE DU CENTRE-EST
COLLEGE CATHOLIC SAMUEL-GENEST
(*Suby of* CONSEIL DES ECOLES CATHOLIQUES DE LANGUE FRANCAISE DU CENTRE-EST)
704 Carson'S Rd, Ottawa, ON, K1K 2H3
(613) 744-8344
Emp Here 120
SIC 8211 Elementary and secondary schools
  Real Charette

D-U-N-S 20-137-0384   (SL)
CYRVILLE CHRYSLER DODGE JEEP LTD
900 St. Laurent Blvd, Ottawa, ON, K1K 3B3
(613) 745-7051
Emp Here 51   *Sales* 32,093,280
SIC 5511 New and used car dealers
  Adrien Cyr
  Martin Cyr
  Daniele Cyr

D-U-N-S 20-788-7795   (HQ)
HOPITAL MONTFORT
713 Montreal Rd, Ottawa, ON, K1K 0T2
(613) 746-4621
Sales 111,080,000
SIC 8062 General medical and surgical hospitals
  Gerald Savoie
  Pierre Lefebvre
  Marc Joyal
  Danny Purcell

D-U-N-S 25-401-9052   (BR)
HUDSON'S BAY COMPANY
THE BAY
(*Suby of* HUDSON'S BAY COMPANY)
1200 St. Laurent Blvd, Ottawa, ON, K1K 3B8
(613) 748-6105
Emp Here 200
SIC 5311 Department stores
  Annie Katona

D-U-N-S 24-267-6716   (BR)
INTACT INSURANCE COMPANY
ING DIRECT
(*Suby of* INTACT FINANCIAL CORPORA-TION)
1400 St. Laurent Blvd Suite 300, Ottawa, ON, K1K 4H4
(800) 267-1836
Emp Here 100
SIC 6331 Fire, marine, and casualty insurance
  Rick Howe

D-U-N-S 20-174-1662   (SL)
LIXAR I.T. INC
373 Coventry Rd, Ottawa, ON, K1K 2C5
(613) 722-0688
Emp Here 200   *Sales* 33,369,400

SIC 7374 Data processing and preparation
  Bill Syrros
  Emmanuel N. Florakas
  Leroy Wissing
  Michael Sherwin

D-U-N-S 20-442-8833   (HQ)
MARK MOTORS OF OTTAWA (1987) LIM-ITED
MARK MOTORS OF OTTAWA
(*Suby of* MARK HOLDINGS INC)
611 Montreal Rd Suite 1, Ottawa, ON, K1K 0T8
(613) 749-4275
Emp Here 22   *Sales* 32,722,560
SIC 5511 New and used car dealers
  Louis Mrak
  Marguerite Mrak

D-U-N-S 24-103-9700   (BR)
MCDONALD'S   RESTAURANTS   OF CANADA LIMITED
MCDONALD'S 8092
(*Suby of* MCDONALD'S CORPORATION)
594 Montreal Rd, Ottawa, ON, K1K 0T9
(613) 741-0093
Emp Here 85
SIC 5812 Eating places
  Roberto Brenes

D-U-N-S 25-504-0222   (BR)
OTTAWA-CARLETON DISTRICT SCHOOL BOARD
RIDEAU HIGH SCHOOL
(*Suby of* OTTAWA-CARLETON DISTRICT SCHOOL BOARD)
815 St. Laurent Blvd, Ottawa, ON, K1K 3A7

Emp Here 80
SIC 8211 Elementary and secondary schools
  Geordie Walker

D-U-N-S 24-756-7431   (SL)
SHADDY INTERNATIONAL MARKETING LTD
SIM BUSINESS FURNITURE
373 Coventry Rd, Ottawa, ON, K1K 2C5
(613) 749-2053
Emp Here 23   *Sales* 10,285,002
SIC 5044 Office equipment
  Albert Jabara
  Kay Jabara
  Suead Jabara

D-U-N-S 24-100-1114   (HQ)
SKATE CANADA
1200 St. Laurent Blvd Suite 261, Ottawa, ON, K1K 3B8
(613) 747-1007
Sales 117,965,282
SIC 8699 Membership organizations, nec
  Benoit Lavoix
  Dan Thompson
  Bethany Tory
  Marilyn Chidlow
  Bob Dillman
  Jodi Abbott
  Bill Boland
  Leanna Caron
  Helene Gagnon
  Monica Lockie

D-U-N-S 20-615-1813   (HQ)
SURGENOR NATIONAL LEASING LIMITED
HERTZ
881 St. Laurent Blvd, Ottawa, ON, K1K 3B1
(613) 706-4779
Emp Here 11   *Sales* 56,274,625
SIC 7515 Passenger car leasing
  Margaret Mcgurn

D-U-N-S 20-746-6137   (HQ)
SURGENOR PONTIAC BUICK LIMITED
SURGENOR TRUCK CENTRE
939 St. Laurent Blvd, Ottawa, ON, K1K 3B1
(613) 741-0741
Sales 184,720,640

SIC 5511 New and used car dealers
  Patrick Mcgurn
  Michael Mcgurn
  Andrew Mcgurn

D-U-N-S 20-789-6952   (SL)
UNITED WAY/CENTRAIDE OTTAWA
363 Coventry Rd, Ottawa, ON, K1K 2C5
(613) 228-6700
Emp Here 95   *Sales* 126,195,435
SIC 6732 Trusts: educational, religious, etc.
  Michael Allen
  Edward Wolkowycki
  Dennis Jackson
  Eric Girard

Ottawa, ON K1L

D-U-N-S 20-787-8505   (SL)
OXFAM CANADA
39 Mcarthur Ave, Ottawa, ON, K1L 8L7
(613) 237-5236
Emp Here 42   *Sales* 16,095,066
SIC 8399 Social services, nec
  Julie Delahanty
  Tony Cantin
  Leslie Turcotte
  Ricardo Acuna
  Sima Sharifi
  Saad Bashir
  Gerry Barr
  Mary Ellen Maccallum
  Oliver Martin
  Nidhi Tandon

Ottawa, ON K1M

D-U-N-S 24-596-1305   (SL)
ASHBURY COLLEGE INCORPORATED
362 Mariposa Ave, Ottawa, ON, K1M 0T3
(613) 749-5954
Emp Here 120   *Sales* 11,894,280
SIC 8211 Elementary and secondary schools
  Norman Southward
  Gary Godkin
  Alex Milroy
  Bill Palamar
  Richard Dixon
  Lori O'neill

D-U-N-S 20-230-2654   (SL)
GOVERNOR'S WALK LTD
150 Stanley Ave, Ottawa, ON, K1M 2J7
(613) 564-9255
Emp Here 49   *Sales* 11,097,226
SIC 6513 Apartment building operators
  Pat Sosusa

D-U-N-S 20-890-3232   (SL)
SISTERS OF CHARITY OF OTTAWA, THE
COUVENT MONT SAINT JOSEPH
50 Maple Lane, Ottawa, ON, K1M 1G8
(613) 745-1584
Emp Here 75   *Sales* 8,079,525
SIC 8661 Religious organizations
  Susan Corriveau

Ottawa, ON K1N

D-U-N-S 20-735-9790   (BR)
ACCOR CANADA INC
NOVOTEL OTTAWA
(*Suby of* ACCOR)
33 Nicholas St, Ottawa, ON, K1N 9M7
(613) 760-4771
Emp Here 75
SIC 7011 Hotels and motels
  Rafael Ballester

D-U-N-S 24-693-3998 (HQ)
AGA KHAN FOUNDATION CANADA
199 Sussex Dr, Ottawa, ON, K1N 1K6
(613) 237-2532
Emp Here 1 *Sales* 10,452,150
SIC 6732 Trusts: educational, religious, etc.
 Khalil Fhariff

D-U-N-S 25-769-3218 (BR)
BELL MEDIA INC
CTV OTTAWA
(*Suby of* BCE INC)
87 George St, Ottawa, ON, K1N 9H7
(613) 224-1313
Emp Here 100
SIC 4833 Television broadcasting stations
 Richard Gray

D-U-N-S 25-317-4247 (SL)
BOTTEGA NICASTRO INC, LA
64 George St, Ottawa, ON, K1N 5V9
(613) 789-7575
Emp Here 47 *Sales* 12,885,144
SIC 5411 Grocery stores
 Pat Nicastro

D-U-N-S 20-384-4878 (SL)
CANADA GREEN BUILDING COUNCIL
47 Clarence St Suite 202, Ottawa, ON, K1N
9K1
(613) 288-8097
Emp Here 62 *Sales* 16,034,130
SIC 8611 Business associations
 Thomas Mueller
 Stephen Smith
 Ashley Oneill
 Conrad Schartau
 Michele Walkau
 Joanne Perdue
 John Pontarollo
 Andrew Mcallan
 Caroline Bordeaux
 Joanne Mccallum

D-U-N-S 25-458-0764 (SL)
CANADIAN FOUNDATION FOR THE AMER-ICAS
FOCAL
1 Nicholas St Suite 720, Ottawa, ON, K1N 7B7
(613) 562-0005
Emp Here 23 *Sales* 16,311,876
SIC 8699 Membership organizations, nec
 Carlo Dade
 Naume Mutambo
 Kathryn Hewlett-Jobes
 Alain Berranger
 Suzanne Laporte
 Marcelo Grinfeld

D-U-N-S 25-216-3543 (SL)
CFGO
TSN 1200
87 George St, Ottawa, ON, K1N 9H7
(613) 789-2486
Emp Here 49 *Sales* 10,374,476
SIC 7313 Radio, television, publisher repre-sentatives
 Richard Grey

D-U-N-S 24-365-1515 (SL)
CHATEAU LAURIER HOTEL GP INC
1 Rideau St, Ottawa, ON, K1N 8S7
(613) 241-1414
Emp Here 100 *Sales* 9,489,900
SIC 7011 Hotels and motels
 A Majid Mangalji
 Fereed Mangalji

D-U-N-S 25-361-4101 (BR)
FAIRMONT HOTELS & RESORTS INC
FAIRMONT CHATEAU LAURIER
(*Suby of* ACCOR)
1 Rideau St, Ottawa, ON, K1N 8S7
(613) 241-1414
Emp Here 500
SIC 7011 Hotels and motels
 Claude J Sauve

D-U-N-S 24-382-7771 (SL)
FEDERATION OF CANADIAN MUNICIPALI-TIES
FCM
24 Clarence St Suite 2, Ottawa, ON, K1N 5P3
(613) 482-8004
Emp Here 100 *Sales* 25,861,500
SIC 8611 Business associations
 Brock Carlton
 Jean Perrault
 Basil Stewart
 Hans Cunningham
 Berry Vrbanovic

D-U-N-S 20-390-6056 (SL)
FLOW WATER INC
110 Clarence St Suite 202, Ottawa, ON, K1N
5P6
(613) 680-3569
Emp Here 84 *Sales* 23,239,440
SIC 2899 Chemical preparations, nec
 Nicholas Reichenbach

D-U-N-S 24-437-7743 (SL)
GAUTHIER, J C INSURANCE BROKER & ASSOCIATES INC
428 Rideau St Suite 101, Ottawa, ON, K1N
5Z2
(613) 789-4140
Emp Here 26 *Sales* 15,078,024
SIC 6411 Insurance agents, brokers, and ser-vice
 Jean-Claude Gauthier
 Marie-Claude Robert

D-U-N-S 25-449-3075 (BR)
GESCA LTEE
QUOTIDIEN DROIT DIV OF
(*Suby of* GESCA LTEE)
47 Clarence St Suite 222, Ottawa, ON, K1N
9K1
(613) 562-0111
Emp Here 100
SIC 2711 Newspapers
 Jacques Pronovost

D-U-N-S 20-652-1879 (BR)
GOVERNING COUNCIL OF THE SALVA-TION ARMY IN CANADA, THE
(*Suby of* GOVERNING COUNCIL OF THE
SALVATION ARMY IN CANADA, THE)
171 George St, Ottawa, ON, K1N 5W5
(613) 241-1573
Emp Here 150
SIC 8399 Social services, nec
 Sandra Foster

D-U-N-S 24-320-0628 (SL)
GREG KELLY WOOLSTEN CROFT
STRATEGIC COUNSEL, THE
60 George St Suite 205, Ottawa, ON, K1N 1J4
(613) 236-0296
Emp Here 150 *Sales* 32,991,450
SIC 8732 Commercial nonphysical research
 Russell Noseworthy

D-U-N-S 24-421-5492 (BR)
HOCKEY CANADA
(*Suby of* HOCKEY CANADA)
801 King Edward Ave Suite N204, Ottawa,
ON, K1N 6N5
(613) 696-0211
Emp Here 90
SIC 8699 Membership organizations, nec
 Patrick Mceleney

D-U-N-S 20-696-4251 (BR)
HUDSON'S BAY COMPANY
BAY, THE
(*Suby of* HUDSON'S BAY COMPANY)
73 Rideau St, Ottawa, ON, K1N 5W8
(613) 241-7511
Emp Here 100
SIC 5311 Department stores
 Marc Chouinard

D-U-N-S 20-651-0484 (BR)
KEG RESTAURANTS LTD

KEG STEAKHOUSE & BAR, THE
(*Suby of* RECIPE UNLIMITED CORPORA-TION)
75 York St, Ottawa, ON, K1N 5T2
(613) 241-8514
Emp Here 100
SIC 5812 Eating places
 Jay Crossman

D-U-N-S 20-561-4360 (SL)
MAGMIC INC
MAGMIC X
126 York St Suite 400, Ottawa, ON, K1N 5T5
(613) 241-3571
Emp Here 96 *Sales* 17,021,856
SIC 7371 Custom computer programming ser-vices
 John Criswick
 Joshua Ostrowalker
 Phil Giroux

D-U-N-S 25-597-9809 (SL)
MARKET SQUARE LIMITED PARTNERSHIP
COURTYARD BY MARRIOTT OTTAWA
350 Dalhousie St, Ottawa, ON, K1N 7E9
(613) 241-1000
Emp Here 75 *Sales* 6,951,750
SIC 7011 Hotels and motels

D-U-N-S 20-302-2939 (SL)
MAXSYS STAFFING & CONSULTING INC
173 Dalhousie St Suite A, Ottawa, ON, K1N
7C7
(613) 562-9943
Emp Here 1,600 *Sales* 405,584,000
SIC 8748 Business consulting, nec
 Bryan Brulotte
 Mathew Mccaw
 Sylvie Prud'homme

D-U-N-S 25-772-5036 (BR)
MAY COURT CLUB OF OTTAWA, THE
MAY COURT BARGAIN BOX
(*Suby of* MAY COURT CLUB OF OTTAWA,
THE)
228 Laurier Ave E, Ottawa, ON, K1N 6P2
(613) 235-0333
Emp Here 275
SIC 8699 Membership organizations, nec
 Maggie Howsan

D-U-N-S 20-805-0471 (SL)
MONTFORT RENAISSANCE INC
162 Murray St, Ottawa, ON, K1N 5M8
(613) 789-5144
Emp Here 50 *Sales* 16,356,350
SIC 6531 Real estate agents and managers
 Geanne Helene Tardivel
 Michelle Decourville Nicol

D-U-N-S 24-892-8814 (SL)
NATIONAL GALLERY OF CANADA
(*Suby of* GOVERNMENT OF CANADA)
380 Sussex Dr, Ottawa, ON, K1N 9N4
(613) 990-1985
Emp Here 250 *Sales* 14,005
SIC 8412 Museums and art galleries
 David Baxter
 Michael Audain
 Michael Tims
 Alexandra Suda

D-U-N-S 25-775-4366 (BR)
NEWGEN RESTAURANT SERVICES INC
TUCKER'S MARKETPLACE
(*Suby of* NEWGEN RESTAURANT SER-VICES INC)
61 York St, Ottawa, ON, K1N 5T2
(613) 241-6525
Emp Here 80
SIC 5812 Eating places
 Hughes Tom

D-U-N-S 20-270-3591 (BR)
NORDSTROM CANADA RETAIL, INC
NORDSTROM RIDEAU CENTRE
(*Suby of* NORDSTROM, INC.)
50 Rideau St Suite 500, Ottawa, ON, K1N 9J7

(613) 567-7005
Emp Here 80
SIC 5311 Department stores
 Randy Trogler

D-U-N-S 24-366-7532 (SL)
OTTAWA CONVENTION CENTRE CORPO-RATION
SHAW CENTRE
(*Suby of* GOVERNMENT OF ONTARIO)
55 Colonel By Dr, Ottawa, ON, K1N 9J2
(613) 563-1984
Emp Here 393 *Sales* 119,896,833
SIC 7389 Business services, nec
 Patrick Kelly
 Jim Durrell
 Bernie Ashe
 Dick Brown
 Joanne Lefebvre
 Cyril Leeder
 Charles Merovitz
 Bill Milliken
 Patrick W. Murray
 Patricia Parulekar

D-U-N-S 24-965-5374 (SL)
PAUKTUUTIT INUIT WOMEN OF CANADA
1 Nicholas St Suite 520, Ottawa, ON, K1N 7B7
(613) 238-3977
Emp Here 28 *Sales* 11,127,592
SIC 8699 Membership organizations, nec
 Lisapee Sheutiapik
 Tracy O'hearn

D-U-N-S 25-474-4139 (SL)
PERSONAL TOUCH INC
PERSONAL TOUCH COURIER
174 Cobourg St Suite 100, Ottawa, ON, K1N
8H5
(613) 723-5891
Emp Here 40 *Sales* 17,739,600
SIC 7389 Business services, nec
 Stephen Michell

D-U-N-S 24-047-1354 (SL)
PRECISIONERP INCORPORATED
12 York St 4th Fl, Ottawa, ON, K1N 5S6
(613) 226-9900
Emp Here 50 *Sales* 10,619,850
SIC 8748 Business consulting, nec
 Allan O'connor
 Paul Bush

D-U-N-S 25-079-7057 (BR)
RICHTREE MARKET RESTAURANTS INC
MARCHELINO RESTAURANT
(*Suby of* NATURAL MARKETS FOOD
GROUP)
50 Rideau St Suite 115, Ottawa, ON, K1N 9J7

Emp Here 80
SIC 5812 Eating places
 Mark Meagher

D-U-N-S 25-784-3334 (SL)
ROCK THE BYWARD MARKET CORPORA-TION
HARD ROCK CAFE
73 York St, Ottawa, ON, K1N 5T2
(613) 241-2442
Emp Here 100 *Sales* 4,551,900
SIC 5812 Eating places
 Keith Taggart

D-U-N-S 25-658-1252 (SL)
SAGE OTTAWA
700 Sussex Dr Suite 200, Ottawa, ON, K1N
1K4

Emp Here 49 *Sales* 90,486,291
SIC 6331 Fire, marine, and casualty insurance
 Denis Plante

D-U-N-S 25-318-6175 (HQ)
SANDY HILL COMMUNITY HEALTH CEN-TRE INC
221 Nelson St, Ottawa, ON, K1N 1C7
(613) 789-6309
Emp Here 60 *Sales* 10,305,128

▲ Public Company ■ Public Company Family Member **HQ** Headquarters **BR** Branch **SL** Single Location

SIC 8093 Specialty outpatient clinics, nec
Nancy Zahavich
Matthew Garrison
Yvon Lemire

D-U-N-S 24-102-7879   (SL)
SERVICES PHARMACEUTIQUES SOCJETI LTEE
SHOPPERS DRUG MART
50 Rideau St Suite 125, Ottawa, ON, K1N 9J7
(613) 236-2533
Emp Here 65   *Sales* 15,881,320
SIC 5912 Drug stores and proprietary stores
Erik Thibault

D-U-N-S 25-843-3986   (BR)
SHEPHERDS OF GOOD HOPE
(*Suby of* SHEPHERDS OF GOOD HOPE)
256 King Edward Ave, Ottawa, ON, K1N 7M1
(613) 789-8210
Emp Here 100
SIC 8322 Individual and family services
Stephen Bartolo

D-U-N-S 20-747-8033   (HQ)
SOEURS DE LA CHARITE D'OTTAWA, LES
SISTERS OF CHARITY OF OTTAWA
27 Bruyere St, Ottawa, ON, K1N 5C9
(613) 241-2710
Emp Here 5   *Sales* 17,700,910
SIC 8661 Religious organizations
Rachelle Watier
Viviane Bauvais

D-U-N-S 24-965-0029   (BR)
SOEURS DE LA CHARITE D'OTTAWA, LES
ELIZABETH BRUYERE HEALTH CENTRE
(*Suby of* SOEURS DE LA CHARITE D'OTTAWA, LES)
43 Bruyere St, Ottawa, ON, K1N 5C8
(613) 562-0050
Emp Here 950
SIC 8661 Religious organizations
Jean Bartkowiak

D-U-N-S 20-180-4619   (BR)
STARWOOD CANADA ULC
WESTIN OTTAWA, THE
(*Suby of* MARRIOTT INTERNATIONAL, INC.)
11 Colonel By Dr, Ottawa, ON, K1N 9H4
(613) 560-7000
Emp Here 400
SIC 7011 Hotels and motels
John Jarvis

D-U-N-S 24-386-6753   (SL)
STEPHEN MACDONALD PHARMACY INC
SHOPPERS DRUG MART
334 Cumberland St, Ottawa, ON, K1N 7J2
(705) 325-2377
Emp Here 50   *Sales* 12,647,700
SIC 5912 Drug stores and proprietary stores
Stephen Macdonald

D-U-N-S 24-103-3737   (SL)
UNION MISSION FOR MEN, THE
MISSION, THE
35 Waller St, Ottawa, ON, K1N 7G4
(613) 234-1144
Emp Here 104   *Sales* 21,535,072
SIC 8399 Social services, nec
Peter Tilley
Jennifer Parr
Scott Hannant
Garth Steele

D-U-N-S 20-789-0518   (HQ)
UNIVERSITY OF OTTAWA
75 Laurier Ave E, Ottawa, ON, K1N 6N5
(613) 562-5700
Sales 1,045,737,000
SIC 8221 Colleges and universities
Kathryn Butler Malette
Alain Jolicoeur
Kevin Jolicoeur
Paul Beann
Dennis Tyner

Terry Haines
Dennis Tyner
Clark Ribordy
Nancy Wingert
Keith Johnson

D-U-N-S 25-352-6362   (BR)
UNIVERSITY OF OTTAWA
FACULTY OF ENGINEERING DIV SITE
(*Suby of* UNIVERSITY OF OTTAWA)
800 King Edward Ave Suite 2002, Ottawa, ON, K1N 6N5
(613) 562-5800
Emp Here 110
SIC 8221 Colleges and universities
Veronique Jerome

D-U-N-S 24-320-8472   (BR)
UNIVERSITY OF OTTAWA
SCHOOL OF MANAGEMENT
(*Suby of* UNIVERSITY OF OTTAWA)
55 Laurier Ave E Suite 5105, Ottawa, ON, K1N 6N5
(613) 562-5731
Emp Here 150
SIC 8221 Colleges and universities
Marc Albert

D-U-N-S 25-993-3955   (BR)
UNIVERSITY OF OTTAWA
FACULTY OF SOCIAL SCIENCES
(*Suby of* UNIVERSITY OF OTTAWA)
120 Universite Pvt Unit 3010, Ottawa, ON, K1N 6N5
(613) 562-5800
Emp Here 400
SIC 8221 Colleges and universities
Marcel Merette

D-U-N-S 24-309-9657   (HQ)
WIELER HUNT INVESTMENTS INC
EQ3
60 By Ward Market Sq, Ottawa, ON, K1N 7A2
(613) 562-9111
Emp Here 12   *Sales* 11,517,000
SIC 5712 Furniture stores
James Hunt

Ottawa, ON K1P

D-U-N-S 24-426-2676   (SL)
7073674 CANADA LTD
MCDONALD'S
77 Bank St, Ottawa, ON, K1P 5N2
(613) 831-2235
Emp Here 100   *Sales* 4,551,900
SIC 5812 Eating places
Adeel Hashmi

D-U-N-S 20-013-0719   (BR)
ACCENTURE INC
(*Suby of* ACCENTURE INC)
45 O'Connor St Suite 600, Ottawa, ON, K1P 1A4
(613) 750-5000
Emp Here 250
SIC 7379 Computer related services, nec
Karen Pelletier

D-U-N-S 25-407-5013   (HQ)
AIM GROUP INC, THE
130 Albert St Suite 126, Ottawa, ON, K1P 5G4
(613) 230-6991
Sales 14,938,800
SIC 7361 Employment agencies
Meredith Egan

D-U-N-S 20-268-0505   (BR)
BORDEN LADNER GERVAIS LLP
BLG
(*Suby of* BORDEN LADNER GERVAIS LLP)
100 Queen St Suite 1100, Ottawa, ON, K1P 1J9
(613) 237-5160
Emp Here 250

SIC 8111 Legal services
Jeffrey Graham

D-U-N-S 24-948-1128   (SL)
CABLE PUBLIC AFFAIRS CHANNEL INC
CPAC
45 O'Connor St Suite 1750, Ottawa, ON, K1P 1A4

Emp Here 76   *Sales* 17,363,872
SIC 4841 Cable and other pay television services
Ken Stein
Jan Gillies
Edouard Trepanier
Jim Deane
Philip Lind
Yves Mayrand

D-U-N-S 25-027-9395   (SL)
CANADA COUNCIL FOR THE ARTS
(*Suby of* GOVERNMENT OF CANADA)
150 Elgin St, Ottawa, ON, K1P 5V8
(613) 566-4414
Emp Here 275   *Sales* 535,230,025
SIC 6732 Trusts: educational, religious, etc.
Pierre Lassonde
Simon Brault

D-U-N-S 20-789-2407   (HQ)
CANADA DEPOSIT INSURANCE CORPORATION
(*Suby of* GOVERNMENT OF CANADA)
50 O'Connor St 17th Fl, Ottawa, ON, K1P 6L2
(613) 996-2081
Emp Here 70   *Sales* 118,600,128
SIC 6399 Insurance carriers, nec
Peter Routledge
Chantal Richer
M. Claudia Morrow
Dean Cosman
Anthony Carty

D-U-N-S 24-977-7756   (HQ)
CANADA EMPLOYMENT & IMMIGRATION UNION
275 Slater St Unit 1204, Ottawa, ON, K1P 5H9
(613) 236-9634
Emp Here 5   *Sales* 12,908,214
SIC 8631 Labor organizations
Jeanette Meunier-Mckay

D-U-N-S 20-894-7143   (SL)
CANADIAN ASSOCIATION OF PROFESSIONAL EMPLOYEES
CAPE
100 Queen St Suite 400, Ottawa, ON, K1P 1J9
(613) 236-9181
Emp Here 30   *Sales* 11,734,740
SIC 8631 Labor organizations
Claude Torrier

D-U-N-S 24-106-0268   (HQ)
CANADIAN BAR ASSOCIATION, THE
66 Slater St Suite 1200, Ottawa, ON, K1P 5H1
(613) 237-2925
Emp Here 71   *Sales* 28,093,320
SIC 8621 Professional organizations
Cheryl Farrow
Raymond Adlington
Vivene Salmon
Christopher Buchanan
Jason Cooke
Kevin Hache
Jeff Howe
Vincent Larochelle
Thomas Laughlin
Marie Laure Leclercq

D-U-N-S 20-136-6929   (HQ)
CANADIAN BROADCASTING CORPORATION
CBC
(*Suby of* GOVERNMENT OF CANADA)
181 Queen St, Ottawa, ON, K1P 1K9
(613) 288-6000
Emp Here 500   *Sales* 381,671,701

SIC 4833 Television broadcasting stations
Hubert Lacroi
Remi Racine
Judith Purves
Edward Boyd
Rob Jeffrey
Marni Larkin
Terrence Anthony Leier
Norman May
Maureen Mccaw
Marlie Oden

D-U-N-S 24-877-1685   (SL)
CANADIAN CENTRE ON SUBSTANCE ABUSE
75 Albert St Suite 500, Ottawa, ON, K1P 5E7
(613) 235-4048
Emp Here 47   *Sales* 10,027,826
SIC 8732 Commercial nonphysical research
Michel Perron
Anne Richer

D-U-N-S 20-388-8644   (HQ)
CANADIAN CHAMBER OF COMMERCE, THE
275 Slater St Suite 1700, Ottawa, ON, K1P 5H9
(613) 238-4000
Sales 34,751,388
SIC 8699 Membership organizations, nec
Perrin Beatty
Ginny Flood
Phil Noble
Mario Theriault
Christiane Bergevin

D-U-N-S 20-369-1220   (SL)
CANADIAN FOUNDATION FOR HEALTHCARE IMPROVEMENT (CFHI)
150 Kent St Suite 200, Ottawa, ON, K1P 0E4
(613) 728-2238
Emp Here 80   *Sales* 19,321,200
SIC 8621 Professional organizations
Maureen O'neil

D-U-N-S 25-447-4380   (SL)
CANADIAN TOURISM HUMAN RESOURCE COUNCIL
TOURISM HR CANADA
151 Slater St Suite 608, Ottawa, ON, K1P 5H3
(613) 231-6949
Emp Here 30   *Sales* 11,922,420
SIC 8699 Membership organizations, nec
Wendy Swedlove

D-U-N-S 25-771-0889   (SL)
CARON TRANSLATION CENTRE LTD
130 Slater St Suite 700, Ottawa, ON, K1P 6E2
(613) 230-4611
Emp Here 30   *Sales* 13,304,700
SIC 7389 Business services, nec
Michel Caron

D-U-N-S 24-926-3989   (SL)
CBC PENSION BOARD OF TRUSTEES
PENSION FUNDS
99 Bank St Suite 191, Ottawa, ON, K1P 6B9
(613) 688-3900
Emp Here 23   *Sales* 42,473,157
SIC 6371 Pension, health, and welfare funds
Debra Alves
Duncan Durrill

D-U-N-S 25-216-0189   (SL)
CHATEAU OTTAWA HOTEL INC
SHERATON OTTAWA HOTEL
150 Albert St, Ottawa, ON, K1P 5G2
(613) 238-1500
Emp Here 135   *Sales* 12,513,150
SIC 7011 Hotels and motels
Kian Guan Ho

D-U-N-S 24-665-3554   (HQ)
COWATERSOGEMA INTERNATIONAL INC
CONSEILLERS EN GESTION COWATERSOGEMA INTERNATIONAL
275 Slater St Suite 1600, Ottawa, ON, K1P 5H9

(613) 722-6434
Emp Here 50   *Sales* 10,106,856
SIC 8741 Management services
David Baron
Samantha Torrance
Catherine Hebert
Steeve Bergeron
Jeanine Maalouf

D-U-N-S 24-676-5916   (SL)
CRESTVIEW STRATEGY INC
222 Queen St Suite 1201, Ottawa, ON, K1P 5V9
(613) 232-3192
Emp Here 45   *Sales* 10,542,960
SIC 8748 Business consulting, nec
Mark Spiro
Christine Mcmillan
Rob Moore
Chad Rogers
Matthew John

D-U-N-S 20-269-8312   (SL)
DEFENCE UNLIMITED INTERNATIONAL CORP
DEFENCE UNLIMITED
251 Laurier Ave W Suite 900, Ottawa, ON, K1P 5J6
(613) 366-3677
Emp Here 266   *Sales* 177,929,528
SIC 7389 Business services, nec
Stephen Cannon
David Frischman
Jay Gorman
Elizabeth Gaerty
Richard Spencer
Edward Banayoti

D-U-N-S 20-894-5956   (BR)
DELOITTE LLP
(*Suby of* DELOITTE LLP)
100 Queen St Suite 1600, Ottawa, ON, K1P 5T8
(613) 236-2442
Emp Here 300
SIC 8721 Accounting, auditing, and bookkeeping
Nancy Stallone

D-U-N-S 20-789-4296   (BR)
DELOITTE LLP
DELOITTE & TOUCHE MANAGEMENT CONSULTANTS
(*Suby of* DELOITTE LLP)
100 Queen St Suite 800, Ottawa, ON, K1P 5T8
(613) 236-2442
Emp Here 400
SIC 8741 Management services
Michael Runia

D-U-N-S 24-992-0273   (BR)
DENTONS CANADA LLP
(*Suby of* DENTONS CANADA LLP)
99 Bank St Suite 1420, Ottawa, ON, K1P 1H4
(613) 783-9600
Emp Here 75
SIC 8111 Legal services
Thomas Houston

D-U-N-S 24-104-7018   (HQ)
DOHERTY & ASSOCIATES LTD
DOHERTY ET ASSOCIES
(*Suby of* AGF MANAGEMENT LIMITED)
56 Sparks St Suite 700, Ottawa, ON, K1P 5A9
(613) 238-6727
Sales 10,092,933
SIC 6282 Investment advice
Blake C. Goldring
Ian Stuart Sterling
Mark Adams
Judith Gail Goldring
Robert J. Bogart
Kevin Mccredit

D-U-N-S 25-354-6196   (HQ)
EAGLE PROFESSIONAL RESOURCES INC
170 Laurier Ave W Suite 902, Ottawa, ON,

K1P 5V5

Emp Here 15   *Sales* 103,742,730
SIC 7361 Employment agencies
Janis Grantham
Kevin Dee
David O'brien
Frances Mccart
Brendhan Malone
Morley Surcon
Cameron Mccallum
Jonah Laist

D-U-N-S 25-292-1267   (HQ)
EASTERN CANADA RESPONSE CORPORATION LTD
ECRC
275 Slater St Suite 1201, Ottawa, ON, K1P 5H9
(613) 230-7369
Emp Here 7   *Sales* 10,028,109
SIC 4959 Sanitary services, nec
Jim Carson
Paul Pouliotte

D-U-N-S 25-132-3424   (HQ)
ECOLE DE LANGUES DE LA CITE, L'
280 Albert St Suite 500, Ottawa, ON, K1P 5G8
(613) 569-6260
Sales 47,481,000
SIC 8299 Schools and educational services, nec
Michel Plouffe
Denise Veys

D-U-N-S 24-220-8101   (SL)
ELEMENTAL DATA COLLECTION INC
170 Laurier Ave W Suite 400, Ottawa, ON, K1P 5V5
(613) 667-9352
Emp Here 200   *Sales* 43,988,600
SIC 8732 Commercial nonphysical research
Colin Kiviaho
Darcy Zwetko
Rick Lyster

D-U-N-S 20-890-6917   (BR)
ERNST & YOUNG LLP
EY
(*Suby of* ERNST & YOUNG LLP)
99 Bank St Suite 1600, Ottawa, ON, K1P 6B9
(613) 232-1511
Emp Here 184
SIC 8721 Accounting, auditing, and bookkeeping
Gary Zed

D-U-N-S 20-609-7201   (BR)
ESIT CANADA ENTERPRISE SERVICES CO
(*Suby of* DXC TECHNOLOGY COMPANY)
50 O'Connor St Suite 500, Ottawa, ON, K1P 6L2
(613) 266-9442
Emp Here 400
SIC 7376 Computer facilities management

D-U-N-S 20-104-5502   (HQ)
EXIT CERTIFIED CORPORATION
220 Laurier Ave W Suite 1000, Ottawa, ON, K1P 5Z9
(613) 232-3948
Emp Here 25   *Sales* 19,203,240
SIC 8741 Management services
Hees Ham
Timothy Mabey

D-U-N-S 24-633-4528   (SL)
FEDERAL LIBERAL AGENCY OF CANADA, THE
LIBERAL PARTY OF CANADA
350 Albert St Suite 920, Ottawa, ON, K1P 6M8
(613) 237-0740
Emp Here 120   *Sales* 14,973,120
SIC 8741 Management services
John Arnold
John Duffy
Diane Rabbani
John Heralt

Jeremy Broadhurst
Michael Eizenga
Grant Jameson
Elbert Paul
Terrie O'leary
Lloyd Posno

D-U-N-S 20-787-8109   (HQ)
FETHERSTONHAUGH & CO.
FETHERSTONHAUGH
55 Metcalfe St Suite 900, Ottawa, ON, K1P 6L5
(613) 235-4373
Emp Here 300   *Sales* 102,938,000
SIC 8111 Legal services
Ron Fetherstonhaugh

D-U-N-S 20-056-7852   (BR)
FLEETWAY INC
(*Suby of* FLEETWAY INC)
141 Laurier Ave W Suite 800, Ottawa, ON, K1P 5J3
(613) 236-6048
Emp Here 75
SIC 8711 Engineering services
Brent Holden

D-U-N-S 25-769-7524   (BR)
FUJITSU CONSEIL (CANADA) INC
FUJITSU CONSEIL
(*Suby of* FUJITSU CONSULTING (CANADA) HOLDINGS, INC.)
55 Metcalfe St Suite 530, Ottawa, ON, K1P 6L5
(613) 238-2697
Emp Here 100
SIC 8741 Management services
Phillip Stein

D-U-N-S 20-337-6207   (HQ)
GOWLING WLG (CANADA) LLP
160 Elgin St Suite 2600, Ottawa, ON, K1P 1C3
(613) 233-1781
Emp Here 1,200   *Sales* 247,051,200
SIC 8111 Legal services
Peter Lukasiewicz
Karen Byrne
Scott R. Joliffe
T. Gary O'neill
Stephen R. Clarke
R. Ross Wells
Paul R. Basso
Rocco D'angelo
Pasquale C. Palosso
Clara Kisko

D-U-N-S 20-345-4210   (BR)
INNVEST HOTELS LP
OTTAWA MARRIOTT
(*Suby of* INNVEST HOTELS LP)
100 Kent St, Ottawa, ON, K1P 5R7
(613) 238-1122
Emp Here 258
SIC 7011 Hotels and motels
Stephane Pelletier

D-U-N-S 24-849-2626   (SL)
INTENSITY SECURITY INC
45 O'Connor St Suite 1150, Ottawa, ON, K1P 1A4
(613) 755-4094
Emp Here 190   *Sales* 87,408,360
SIC 5072 Hardware
David Hayes

D-U-N-S 20-789-0252   (SL)
INTERNATIONAL DEVELOPMENT RESEARCH CENTRE
I D R C
(*Suby of* GOVERNMENT OF CANADA)
150 Kent St, Ottawa, ON, K1P 0B2
(613) 236-6163
Emp Here 455   *Sales* 92,857,310
SIC 8732 Commercial nonphysical research
Jean Lebel
Sylvain Dofour

D-U-N-S 24-270-2769   (HQ)

JACOBS CONSULTANCY CANADA INC
JACOBS CONSULTANCY
(*Suby of* JACOBS ENGINEERING GROUP INC.)
220 Laurier Ave W Suite 500, Ottawa, ON, K1P 5Z9

Emp Here 191
SIC 8742 Management consulting services
Neil Raynor
Gregory J Landry
Thomas R Hammond
Osama Elshafey
Earl J Mitchell

D-U-N-S 20-805-8755   (SL)
KIDSINKS HOLDINGS INC
LORD ELGIN HOTEL
100 Elgin St, Ottawa, ON, K1P 5K8
(613) 235-3333
Emp Here 75   *Sales* 17,468,325
SIC 6513 Apartment building operators
David Smythe
Jeffery Gillin
Christopher Gillin

D-U-N-S 24-483-6300   (HQ)
LOCKHEED MARTIN CANADA INC
LOCKHEED MARTIN COMMERCIAL ENGINE SOLUTIONS
(*Suby of* LOCKHEED MARTIN CORPORATION)
45 O'Connor St Suite 870, Ottawa, ON, K1P 1A4
(613) 688-0698
Emp Here 600   *Sales* 282,915,000
SIC 3625 Relays and industrial controls
Lorraine Ben
Felix Montanaro
Rosemary Chapdelaine

D-U-N-S 20-801-1044   (SL)
METVIEW REALTY LIMITED
130 Albert St Suite 210, Ottawa, ON, K1P 5G4
(613) 230-5174
Emp Here 50   *Sales* 16,631,444
SIC 6531 Real estate agents and managers
John Mckenna

D-U-N-S 24-101-3986   (SL)
MINING ASSOCIATION OF CANADA, THE
275 Slater St Suite 1100, Ottawa, ON, K1P 5H9
(613) 233-9391
Emp Here 55   *Sales* 14,223,825
SIC 8611 Business associations
Pierre Gratton
Gordon Stothart
Tim Bekhuys
Brent Bergeron
Brendan Cahill
David Clarry
Alan Coutts
Blair Dickerson
Joe Boaro
Peter Sinclair

D-U-N-S 25-357-3547   (HQ)
MINTO HOLDINGS INC
180 Kent St Suite 200, Ottawa, ON, K1P 0B6
(613) 230-7051
Sales 416,680,260
SIC 6712 Bank holding companies
Roger Greenberg

D-U-N-S 25-086-5524   (HQ)
MINTO MANAGEMENT LIMITED
MINTO
(*Suby of* MINTO GROUP INC)
180 Kent St Unit 200, Ottawa, ON, K1P 0B6
(613) 230-7051
Emp Here 10   *Sales* 17,448,809
SIC 6513 Apartment building operators
Roger Greenberg
Eric Mckinney

D-U-N-S 25-772-5622   (HQ)

▲ Public Company   ■ Public Company Family Member   **HQ** Headquarters   **BR** Branch   **SL** Single Location

MINTO PROPERTIES INC
MINTO COMMERCIAL
(*Suby of* MINTO HOLDINGS INC)
180 Kent St Suite 200, Ottawa, ON, K1P 0B6
(613) 786-3000
Emp Here 30   *Sales* 19,878,390
SIC 6512 Nonresidential building operators
  Roger Greenberg

D-U-N-S 20-889-7736   (SL)
NATIONAL ARTS CENTRE CORPORATION
CAFE, LE
(*Suby of* GOVERNMENT OF CANADA)
1 Elgin St, Ottawa, ON, K1P 5W1
(613) 947-7000
Emp Here 600   *Sales* 115,785,600
SIC 8742 Management consulting services
  Daniel Senyk

D-U-N-S 25-400-9566   (HQ)
NAV CANADA
77 Metcalfe St, Ottawa, ON, K1P 5L6
(613) 563-5588
Emp Here 700   *Sales* 1,030,245,111
SIC 4899 Communication services, nec
  Neil R. Wilson
  Rudy Kellar
  Sandy N. Struthers
  Raymond G. Bohn
  Elizabeth Cameron
  Leigh Ann Kirby
  Larry Lachance
  Donna Mathieu
  Claudio Silvestri
  Andrew Norgaard

D-U-N-S 24-924-7180   (BR)
NORTON ROSE FULBRIGHT CANADA S.E.N.C.R.L., S.R.L.
NORTON ROSE FULBRIGHT
(*Suby of* NORTON ROSE FULBRIGHT CANADA S.E.N.C.R.L., S.R.L.)
45 O'Connor St Suite 1600, Ottawa, ON, K1P 1A4
(613) 780-8661
Emp Here 100
SIC 8111 Legal services
  Charles Hurdon

D-U-N-S 24-830-8355   (BR)
ORACLE CANADA ULC
(*Suby of* ORACLE CORPORATION)
45 O'Connor St Suite 400, Ottawa, ON, K1P 1A4
(613) 569-0001
Emp Here 120
SIC 7371 Custom computer programming services
  Hank Dykhuizen

D-U-N-S 20-894-0965   (HQ)
OTTAWA PUBLIC LIBRARY BOARD
120 Metcalfe St, Ottawa, ON, K1P 5M2
(613) 580-2940
Emp Here 120   *Sales* 19,419,435
SIC 8231 Libraries
  Barbara Clubb

D-U-N-S 20-569-3513   (SL)
PARLIAMENTARY CENTRE
255 Albert St Suite 802, Ottawa, ON, K1P 6A9
(613) 237-0143
Emp Here 40   *Sales* 15,896,560
SIC 8699 Membership organizations, nec
  Jean-Paul Ruszkowski
  Peter C Dobell

D-U-N-S 24-437-6067   (BR)
PRICEWATERHOUSECOOPERS LLP
(*Suby of* PRICEWATERHOUSECOOPERS LLP)
99 Bank St Suite 800, Ottawa, ON, K1P 1E4
(613) 237-3702
Emp Here 150
SIC 8721 Accounting, auditing, and book-keeping
  Roxanne Anderson

D-U-N-S 20-291-7469   (SL)
PSHCP ADMINISTRATION AUTHORITY
100 Sparks St Suite 1010, Ottawa, ON, K1P 5B7
(613) 565-1762
Emp Here 12   *Sales* 10,294,586
SIC 6411 Insurance agents, brokers, and service
  Jean-Claude Bouchard
  Chris Aylward
  Edward Gillis
  John Gordon
  Paul Morse
  Pierrette Boyer
  Dominic Laporte
  Tammy Labelle
  Jacques Lambert

D-U-N-S 20-351-5648   (SL)
RAYMOND CHABOT GRANT THORTON CONSULTING INC.
RCGT CONSULTING
116 Albert St, Ottawa, ON, K1P 5G3
(613) 760-3500
Emp Here 75   *Sales* 17,571,600
SIC 8748 Business consulting, nec
  Marco Perron

D-U-N-S 24-103-6862   (SL)
RIDEAU CLUB LIMITED
99 Bank St Suite 1500, Ottawa, ON, K1P 6B9
(613) 233-7787
Emp Here 45   *Sales* 14,158,440
SIC 8699 Membership organizations, nec
  Robert Lams
  Carol Pink

D-U-N-S 25-128-8312   (BR)
SIERRA SYSTEMS GROUP INC
(*Suby of* NIPPON TELEGRAPH AND TELE-PHONE CORPORATION)
220 Laurier Ave W Suite 800, Ottawa, ON, K1P 5Z9
(613) 236-7888
Emp Here 93
SIC 7379 Computer related services, nec
  John Broere

D-U-N-S 24-243-7010   (HQ)
SMART & BIGGAR
55 Metcalfe St Suite 900, Ottawa, ON, K1P 6L5
(613) 232-2486
Emp Here 200   *Sales* 82,350,400
SIC 8111 Legal services
  Keltie Sim Luft

D-U-N-S 20-892-0918   (HQ)
SURANI, B. DRUGS LTD
SHOPPERS DRUG MART
161 Bank St, Ottawa, ON, K1P 5N7
(613) 232-5723
Emp Here 50   *Sales* 19,546,240
SIC 5912 Drug stores and proprietary stores
  Bashir Surani

D-U-N-S 24-858-3242   (HQ)
TREASURY BOARD OF CANADA SECRE-TARIAT
TREASURY BOARD OF CANADA
(*Suby of* GOVERNMENT OF CANADA)
90 Elgin St Fl 8, Ottawa, ON, K1P 0C6
(613) 369-3200
Emp Here 500   *Sales* 365,509,000
SIC 6712 Bank holding companies
  Joyce Murray
  Tony Clement

D-U-N-S 24-357-6167   (HQ)
UR-ENERGY INC
55 Metcalfe St Suite 1300, Ottawa, ON, K1P 6L5
(613) 236-3882
Sales 23,496,000
SIC 1094 Uranium-radium-vanadium ores
  W. William Boberg
  Jeffrey Klenda
  James Franklin

  Paul Macdonnel
  Thomas Parker
  Roger Smith
  Harold A. Backer
  Paul Pitman
  Wayne Heili
  Paul G. Goss

D-U-N-S 20-112-3481   (HQ)
VALCOM CONSULTING GROUP INC
(*Suby of* MACPHERSON, PAUL & ASSO-CIATES LTD)
85 Albert St Suite 300, Ottawa, ON, K1P 6A4
(613) 594-5200
Emp Here 392   *Sales* 71,495,600
SIC 8711 Engineering services
  Paul Macpherson

D-U-N-S 25-300-6621   (BR)
WORKPLACE SAFETY & INSURANCE BOARD, THE
WSIB
(*Suby of* WORKPLACE SAFETY & INSUR-ANCE BOARD, THE)
180 Kent St Suite 400, Ottawa, ON, K1P 0B6
(416) 344-1000
Emp Here 200
SIC 6331 Fire, marine, and casualty insurance
  Pat Lamanna

D-U-N-S 25-360-1488   (BR)
ZAYO CANADA INC
(*Suby of* ZAYO GROUP HOLDINGS, INC.)
45 O'Connor St Suite 1400, Ottawa, ON, K1P 1A4
(613) 688-4688
Emp Here 110
SIC 4899 Communication services, nec
  Ron Mac Donell

Ottawa, ON K1R

D-U-N-S 24-588-8995   (SL)
137077 CANADA INC
HANDYMAN PERSONNEL
203 Rochester St, Ottawa, ON, K1R 7M5
(613) 232-1579
Emp Here 600   *Sales* 44,816,400
SIC 7361 Employment agencies
  Constance Larose

D-U-N-S 24-663-3619   (SL)
ART-IS-IN BAKERY INC
250 City Centre Ave Unit 112, Ottawa, ON, K1R 6K7
(613) 695-1226
Emp Here 50   *Sales* 13,707,600
SIC 5461 Retail bakeries
  Kevin Mathieson

D-U-N-S 20-200-0931   (HQ)
BELLAI BROTHERS CONSTRUCTION LTD
440 Laurier Ave W Suite 200, Ottawa, ON, K1R 7X6
(613) 782-2932
Emp Here 295   *Sales* 153,080,850
SIC 1771 Concrete work
  Pietro Bellai
  Gianni Bellai

D-U-N-S 20-180-0567   (HQ)
BRIDGEHEAD (2000) INC
130 Anderson St, Ottawa, ON, K1R 6T7
(613) 231-5488
Emp Here 40   *Sales* 13,991,700
SIC 5812 Eating places
  Tracey Clark
  Laurie Ouellette

D-U-N-S 24-104-1052   (HQ)
BROWN'S CLEANERS AND TAILORS LIM-ITED
BROWN'S CLEANERS
270 City Centre Ave, Ottawa, ON, K1R 7R7

(613) 235-5181
Emp Here 50   *Sales* 10,891,764
SIC 7216 Drycleaning plants, except rugs
  Malcolm Macgregor

D-U-N-S 24-845-4233   (HQ)
CANADIAN PARKS & WILDERNESS SOCI-ETY
250 City Centre Ave Suite 506, Ottawa, ON, K1R 6K7
(613) 569-7226
Emp Here 11   *Sales* 26,807,330
SIC 8999 Services, nec
  Eric Hebert-Daly
  Oliver Kent

D-U-N-S 24-665-4719   (SL)
CANADIAN PAYMENTS ASSOCIATION
PAYMENTS CANADA
350 Albert St Unit 800, Ottawa, ON, K1R 1A4
(613) 238-4173
Emp Here 75   *Sales* 37,605,771
SIC 8741 Management services
  Gerry Gaetz
  Eileen Mercier
  Anne Butler
  Chuck Hounsell
  Dan Dickinson
  Brenda Clark
  Justin Ferrabee
  Jan Pilbauer
  Sheila Vokey
  Nora Cox

D-U-N-S 24-886-3573   (HQ)
CAPITAL PARKING INC
400 Slater St Suite 2102, Ottawa, ON, K1R 7S7
(613) 593-8820
Emp Here 3   *Sales* 28,330,000
SIC 7521 Automobile parking

D-U-N-S 24-150-7388   (SL)
CIELO PRINT INC
250 City Centre Ave Suite 138, Ottawa, ON, K1R 6K7
(613) 232-1112
Emp Here 27   *Sales* 11,974,230
SIC 7389 Business services, nec
  Mohamed Ali
  John Gagnon

D-U-N-S 24-345-8291   (BR)
CORPORATION MORGUARD
MORGUARD CORPORATION
(*Suby of* CORPORATION MORGUARD)
350 Sparks St Suite 402, Ottawa, ON, K1R 7S8
(613) 237-6373
Emp Here 14
SIC 6519 Real property lessors, nec
  Steve Hebert

D-U-N-S 20-789-6002   (HQ)
DEFENCE CONSTRUCTION (1951) LIM-ITED
DEFENCE CONSTRUCTION CANADA
(*Suby of* GOVERNMENT OF CANADA)
350 Albert St Suite 1900, Ottawa, ON, K1R 1A4
(613) 998-9548
Emp Here 120   *Sales* 112,203,000
SIC 8741 Management services
  James Paul
  Ronald De Vries
  Daniel Benjamin
  Randy Mcgee
  Angelo Ottoni
  Robert Presser

D-U-N-S 20-699-9497   (BR)
DELTA HOTELS LIMITED
DELTA OTTAWA HOTEL AND SUITES
(*Suby of* GOVERNMENT OF THE PROVINCE OF BRITISH COLUMBIA)
361 Queen St, Ottawa, ON, K1R 0C7

Emp Here 200

SIC 8741 Management services
Victor Ferrira

D-U-N-S 20-708-5635 (BR)
DELTA HOTELS NO. 12 LIMITED PARTNER-SHIP
CROWN PLAZA HOTEL
101 Lyon St N, Ottawa, ON, K1R 5T9
(613) 237-1508
Emp Here 180
SIC 7011 Hotels and motels
Zubair Siddiqi

D-U-N-S 24-633-6952 (SL)
EVRIPOS JANITORIAL SERVICES LTD
136 Flora St Suite 1, Ottawa, ON, K1R 5R5
(613) 232-9069
Emp Here 150   *Sales* 4,795,200
SIC 7349 Building maintenance services, nec
John Sigounas

D-U-N-S 24-704-6949 (SL)
IMAGEHOUSE LIMITED
275 Bay St, Ottawa, ON, K1R 5Z5
(613) 238-6232
Emp Here 25   *Sales* 11,230,475
SIC 7389 Business services, nec
Paul Akehurst Sr

D-U-N-S 25-144-4949 (HQ)
INCORPORATION SYNOD DIOCESE OF OT-TAWA
ANGLICAN DIOCESE OF OTTAWA
71 Bronson Ave, Ottawa, ON, K1R 6G6
(613) 232-7124
Emp Here 10   *Sales* 20,824,600
SIC 8661 Religious organizations
Michael Herbert

D-U-N-S 25-411-6999 (HQ)
ITAL-PLUS IMPORTS INC
IMPORTATIONS ITAL-PLUS
925 Gladstone Ave, Ottawa, ON, K1R 6Y3
(613) 230-7166
Emp Here 9   *Sales* 11,698,078
SIC 5141 Groceries, general line
Italo Carnevale
Mario Giannetti

D-U-N-S 20-137-9666 (HQ)
LAPOINTE FISH LIMITED
445 Catherine St, Ottawa, ON, K1R 5T7
(613) 241-1115
Emp Here 4   *Sales* 78,838,760
SIC 5146 Fish and seafoods
Geoffrey Vivian
David Vivian

D-U-N-S 25-302-2271 (SL)
MACY HOLDINGS LIMITED
435 Albert St, Ottawa, ON, K1R 7X4
(613) 238-8858
Emp Here 80   *Sales* 7,591,920
SIC 7011 Hotels and motels
Jacie Levinson
Sandra Levinson

D-U-N-S 24-952-2665 (SL)
METROPOLITAN LIFE INSURANCE COM-PANY
METLIFE
(*Suby of* METLIFE, INC.)
360 Albert St Suite 1750, Ottawa, ON, K1R 7X7

Emp Here 22   *Sales* 50,382,000
SIC 6311 Life insurance
P James Anderson
Karen Sauve

D-U-N-S 24-083-8255 (BR)
MINTO GROUP INC
MINTO FURNISH SUITE
(*Suby of* MINTO GROUP INC)
221 Lyon St N Suite 806, Ottawa, ON, K1R 7X5

Emp Here 120

SIC 6513 Apartment building operators
Emma Osgoode

D-U-N-S 20-118-2891 (HQ)
NASITTUQ CORPORATION
(*Suby of* PAN ARCTIC INUIT LOGISTICS CORP)
360 Albert St Unit 1830, Ottawa, ON, K1R 7X7
(613) 234-9033
Sales 32,441,760
SIC 8741 Management services
Louise Chawner
Ivan Wawryk

D-U-N-S 24-383-2102 (SL)
NATIONAL INDIAN BROTHERHOOD
ASSEMBLY OF FIRST NATIONS
473 Albert St Suite 810, Ottawa, ON, K1R 5B4
(613) 241-6789
Emp Here 105   *Sales* 26,479,950
SIC 8611 Business associations
Bob Watts
Shawn Atleo

D-U-N-S 25-028-6754 (BR)
OSLER, HOSKIN & HARCOURT LLP
CARTHO SERVICES
(*Suby of* OSLER, HOSKIN & HARCOURT LLP)
340 Albert St Suite 1900, Ottawa, ON, K1R 7Y6
(613) 235-7234
Emp Here 94
SIC 8111 Legal services
Julie Somers

D-U-N-S 24-100-2534 (HQ)
OTTAWA-CARLETON ASSOCIATION FOR PERSONS WITH DEVELOPMENTAL DIS-ABILITIES
AHEARN RESIDENCE
250 City Centre Ave Suite 200, Ottawa, ON, K1R 6K7
(613) 569-8993
Emp Here 30   *Sales* 28,105,872
SIC 8322 Individual and family services
David Ferguson
Bill Cowie

D-U-N-S 25-481-2746 (BR)
OTTAWA-CARLETON DISTRICT SCHOOL BOARD
ADULT HIGH SCHOOL
(*Suby of* OTTAWA-CARLETON DISTRICT SCHOOL BOARD)
300 Rochester St Suite 302, Ottawa, ON, K1R 7N4
(613) 239-2416
Emp Here 100
SIC 8211 Elementary and secondary schools
Kevin Bush

D-U-N-S 20-954-7228 (SL)
PERLAW HOLDINGS LIMITED
340 Albert St, Ottawa, ON, K1R 7Y6
(613) 238-2022
Emp Here 100   *Sales* 26,155,300
SIC 6712 Bank holding companies
David H. Hill
Thomas A. Mcdougall

D-U-N-S 24-268-0213 (SL)
PERLEY-ROBERTSON, HILL & MC-DOUGALL LLP/S.R.L.
340 Albert St Suite 1400, Ottawa, ON, K1R 0A5
(613) 238-2022
Emp Here 95   *Sales* 10,533,790
SIC 8111 Legal services
David Hill
Thomas Mcdougall
Trevor Klotz
Paul Kane
David Migicovsky
Paul Bregman
Michael Gerrior
Anthony Mcglynn
Timothy J Thomas

Barbara Nicholls

D-U-N-S 20-138-7149 (SL)
PRESTON HARDWARE (1980) LIMITED
248 Preston St Unit 234, Ottawa, ON, K1R 7R4
(613) 230-7166
Emp Here 120   *Sales* 21,226,856
SIC 5251 Hardware stores
Mario Giannetti
Sandro Giannetti
Mario Frangione

D-U-N-S 24-703-0307 (HQ)
RAYTHEON CANADA LIMITED
ELCAN OPTICAL TECHNOLOGIES, DIV OF
(*Suby of* RAYTHEON COMPANY)
360 Albert St Suite 1640, Ottawa, ON, K1R 7X7
(613) 233-4121
Emp Here 7   *Sales* 383,535,000
SIC 3229 Pressed and blown glass, nec
Thomas Kennedy
Ralph Acaba
Roy Axevedo
Kevin Dasilva
John Harris
Jeanette Hughes
Frank Jimenez
Wesley Kremer
Taylor Lawrence
Randa Newsome

D-U-N-S 24-436-3974 (BR)
SCOTIA CAPITAL INC
SCOTIA MCLEOD
(*Suby of* BANK OF NOVA SCOTIA, THE)
350 Albert St Suite 2100, Ottawa, ON, K1R 1A4
(613) 563-0991
Emp Here 80
SIC 6211 Security brokers and dealers
Tim Wardrop

D-U-N-S 24-101-1139 (HQ)
SOCIAL SCIENCES AND HUMANITIES RE-SEARCH COUNCIL OF CANADA
CONSEIL DE RECHERCHES EN SCIENCES HUMAINES
(*Suby of* GOVERNMENT OF CANADA)
350 Albert St Suite 1610, Ottawa, ON, K1R 1A4
(613) 992-0691
Emp Here 1   *Sales* 21,334,471
SIC 8732 Commercial nonphysical research
Chad Gaffield

D-U-N-S 25-778-8422 (SL)
SOMERSET WEST COMMUNITY HEALTH CENTRE
SOMERSET WEST CHC
55 Eccles St, Ottawa, ON, K1R 6S3
(613) 238-8210
Emp Here 90   *Sales* 6,157,980
SIC 8322 Individual and family services
Jack Mccarthy
Sally Clarke

D-U-N-S 20-787-5857 (SL)
UNIVERSITIES CANADA
350 Albert St Suite 1710, Ottawa, ON, K1R 1B1
(613) 563-1236
Emp Here 80   *Sales* 19,321,200
SIC 8621 Professional organizations
Paul Davidson

D-U-N-S 20-954-6402 (HQ)
WINDMILL DEVELOPMENT GROUP LTD
WINDMILL DEVELOPMENTS
6 Booth St, Ottawa, ON, K1R 6K8
(613) 820-5600
Emp Here 60   *Sales* 17,611,230
SIC 1522 Residential construction, nec
Jonathan Westeinde

Ottawa, ON K1S

D-U-N-S 24-794-1925 (SL)
1039658 ONTARIO INC
WEST COAST VIDEO
1123 Bank St, Ottawa, ON, K1S 3X4

Emp Here 50   *Sales* 11,517,000
SIC 5731 Radio, television, and electronic stores
David Macdonald
Gail Pickwick

D-U-N-S 20-108-8494 (BR)
BMO NESBITT BURNS INC
(*Suby of* BMO NESBITT BURNS INC)
979 Bank St 6th Fl, Ottawa, ON, K1S 5K5
(613) 562-6400
Emp Here 80
SIC 6211 Security brokers and dealers
Rick Hughes

D-U-N-S 25-375-8379 (HQ)
CANADIAN AGENCY FOR DRUGS AND TECHNOLOGIES IN HEALTH (CADTH)
C.C.O.H.T.A.
865 Carling Ave Suite 600, Ottawa, ON, K1S 5S8
(613) 226-2553
Sales 39,058,180
SIC 8731 Commercial physical research
Brian O'rourke
David Agnew

D-U-N-S 24-830-2937 (SL)
CANADIAN MEDICAL PROTECTIVE ASSO-CIATION, THE
875 Carling Ave Suite 928, Ottawa, ON, K1S 5P1
(613) 725-2000
Emp Here 292   *Sales* 68,360,412
SIC 8621 Professional organizations

D-U-N-S 24-751-0808 (HQ)
CARLETON UNIVERSITY
1125 Colonel By Dr, Ottawa, ON, K1S 5B6
(613) 520-2600
Sales 432,593,385
SIC 8221 Colleges and universities
Alastair Summerlee
Rafik Goubran
Pauline Rankin

D-U-N-S 20-577-1868 (SL)
DOW MOTORS (OTTAWA) LIMITED
DOW HONDA
845 Carling Ave, Ottawa, ON, K1S 2E7
(613) 237-2777
Emp Here 62   *Sales* 39,015,360
SIC 5511 New and used car dealers
Jeff Mierins

D-U-N-S 20-891-5608 (BR)
ECONOMICAL MUTUAL INSURANCE COM-PANY
ECONOMICAL INSURANCE GROUP
(*Suby of* ECONOMICAL MUTUAL INSUR-ANCE COMPANY)
343 Preston St Suite 500, Ottawa, ON, K1S 1N4
(613) 567-7060
Emp Here 145
SIC 6331 Fire, marine, and casualty insurance
John Paulon

D-U-N-S 20-889-1291 (SL)
GLEBE CENTRE INCORPORATED, THE
ABBOTTSFORD HOUSE SENIOR CITIZ
950 Bank St, Ottawa, ON, K1S 5G6
(613) 230-5730
Emp Here 220   *Sales* 14,142,040
SIC 8361 Residential care
Susan Le Conte
Carol Burrows

D-U-N-S 20-891-1503 (SL)
INTERNATIONAL ASSOCIATION OF MA-

CHINISTS LABOUR MANAGEMENT PENSION FUND (CANADA)
I.A.M.
200 Isabella St Unit 400, Ottawa, ON, K1S 1V7
(613) 567-8259
Emp Here 6　　　*Sales* 11,079,954
SIC 6371 Pension, health, and welfare funds
Gerald Kirk
Robert Biggar
David Ritchie
Donald Belton
Irene Perry
Jules Molinari

D-U-N-S 20-341-6953　　(SL)
JOULE INC
1031 Bank St, Ottawa, ON, K1S 3W7
(888) 855-2555
Emp Here 75　　　*Sales* 18,113,625
SIC 8621 Professional organizations
Lindee David
Debbie Fischer
Tim Smith
George Davie
Amanda Whitewood
Michael Cloutier
Darren Larsen
Ewan Affleck
Ann Michael
Brian Brodie

D-U-N-S 25-203-2693　　(SL)
LANGUAGES OF LIFE INC
99 Fifth Ave Suite 14, Ottawa, ON, K1S 5K4
(613) 232-9770
Emp Here 600　　*Sales* 401,344,800
SIC 7389 Business services, nec

D-U-N-S 20-788-1736　　(BR)
LOBLAW COMPANIES LIMITED
LOBLAWS
(*Suby of* LOBLAW COMPANIES LIMITED)
64 Isabella St, Ottawa, ON, K1S 1V4
(613) 232-4831
Emp Here 140
SIC 5411 Grocery stores
Michelle Ghent

D-U-N-S 20-889-0616　　(SL)
MCKEEN, D & J HOLDINGS (OTTAWA) INC
MCKEEN GLEBE LOEB
754 Bank St, Ottawa, ON, K1S 3V6
(613) 232-9466
Emp Here 80　　*Sales* 23,478,160
SIC 5411 Grocery stores
James Mckeen

D-U-N-S 25-515-8958　　(BR)
OTTAWA CATHOLIC DISTRICT SCHOOL BOARD
IMMACULATA HIGH SCHOOL
(*Suby of* OTTAWA CATHOLIC DISTRICT SCHOOL BOARD)
140 Main St, Ottawa, ON, K1S 5P4
(613) 237-2001
Emp Here 125
SIC 8211 Elementary and secondary schools
Christopher Mes

D-U-N-S 25-026-7622　　(BR)
OTTAWA-CARLETON DISTRICT SCHOOL BOARD
GLEBE COLLEGIATE INSTITUTE
(*Suby of* OTTAWA-CARLETON DISTRICT SCHOOL BOARD)
212 Glebe Ave, Ottawa, ON, K1S 2C9
(613) 239-2424
Emp Here 110
SIC 8211 Elementary and secondary schools
France Thibault

D-U-N-S 24-796-1329　　(SL)
OWL RAFTING INC
39 First Ave, Ottawa, ON, K1S 2G1
(613) 238-7238
Emp Here 80　　*Sales* 11,202,320

SIC 7999 Amusement and recreation, nec
Dirk Van Wijk

D-U-N-S 20-138-7859　　(HQ)
RANDALL'S PAINTS LIMITED
RANDALL'S DECORATION CENTRES
555 Bank St, Ottawa, ON, K1S 5L7
(613) 233-8441
Emp Here 15　　　*Sales* 21,412,160
SIC 5231 Paint, glass, and wallpaper stores
David Martin
Henk Van Rijswijk
Lee Martin

D-U-N-S 24-891-9474　　(SL)
ROYAL COLLEGE OF PHYSICIANS AND SURGEONS OF CANADA, THE
774 Echo Dr, Ottawa, ON, K1S 5N8
(613) 730-8177
Emp Here 300　　*Sales* 38,044,662
SIC 8621 Professional organizations
Andrew Padmos
Francoise Chagnon

D-U-N-S 25-018-4181　　(BR)
ROYAL LEPAGE REAL ESTATE SERVICES LTD
(*Suby of* BRIDGEMARQ REAL ESTATE SERVICES INC)
165 Pretoria Ave, Ottawa, ON, K1S 1X1
(613) 238-2801
Emp Here 100
SIC 6531 Real estate agents and managers
Russ Perkins

D-U-N-S 20-890-7212　　(SL)
SAINT PAUL UNIVERSITY
CANTERBURY HOUSE BOOKSTORE
223 Main St Suite 267, Ottawa, ON, K1S 1C4
(613) 236-1393
Emp Here 275　　*Sales* 41,082,525
SIC 8221 Colleges and universities
Chantal Beauvais
Luke Roy

D-U-N-S 25-771-1911　　(SL)
SARAZEN REALTY LTD
COLDWELL BANKER SARAZEN REALTY
80 Aberdeen St Suite 300, Ottawa, ON, K1S 5R5
(613) 831-4455
Emp Here 140　　*Sales* 58,644,460
SIC 6531 Real estate agents and managers
Colin Sarazen
Terry Sarazen

D-U-N-S 25-653-5894　　(SL)
SHOEBOX LTD
SHOEBOX AUDIOMETRY
80 Aberdeen St Suite 301, Ottawa, ON, K1S 5R5
(877) 349-9934
Emp Here 55　　　*Sales* 12,500,895
SIC 3841 Surgical and medical instruments
Michael Weider

D-U-N-S 24-326-9458　　(SL)
TEE, FRANK PHARMACIES LTD
SHOPPERS DRUG MART
702 Bank St Suite 700, Ottawa, ON, K1S 3V2
(613) 233-3202
Emp Here 50　　　*Sales* 12,647,700
SIC 5912 Drug stores and proprietary stores
Frank Tee

D-U-N-S 24-313-9990　　(SL)
TITUS INC
343 Preston St Suite 800, Ottawa, ON, K1S 1N4
(613) 820-5111
Emp Here 120　　*Sales* 20,021,640
SIC 7372 Prepackaged software
Jim Barkdoll
Stephane Charbonneau
Mark Cassetta
Anna Lynch
Brad Stilling
Tom Martin

Karyl Parks

D-U-N-S 24-125-9733　　(BR)
XEROX CANADA LTD
(*Suby of* XEROX CORPORATION)
333 Preston St Suite 1000, Ottawa, ON, K1S 5N4
(613) 230-1002
Emp Here 150
SIC 5044 Office equipment
Kevin Murnaghan

D-U-N-S 25-095-1811　　(HQ)
YOUR CREDIT UNION LTD
14 Chamberlain Ave Suite 200, Ottawa, ON, K1S 1V9
(613) 238-8001
Emp Here 30　　　*Sales* 15,351,100
SIC 6062 State credit unions
Kimberley Allo

Ottawa, ON K1V

D-U-N-S 25-769-8027　　(SL)
1179132 ONTARIO LIMITED
WILSON INDEPENDENT
2681 Alta Vista Dr, Ottawa, ON, K1V 7T5
(613) 733-2311
Emp Here 85　　　*Sales* 24,945,545
SIC 5411 Grocery stores
Roger Bureau

D-U-N-S 24-417-1901　　(HQ)
1514660 ONTARIO INC
SHELL
2498 Bank St, Ottawa, ON, K1V 8S2
(613) 523-2027
Emp Here 10　　　*Sales* 14,942,340
SIC 5541 Gasoline service stations
Ali Akil

D-U-N-S 20-349-5754　　(HQ)
1562067 ONTARIO INC
COMMERCIAL TIRE AUTO SERVICE
1720 Bank St, Ottawa, ON, K1V 7Y6

Emp Here 6　　*Sales* 14,942,340
SIC 5531 Auto and home supply stores
Normand Lavoie

D-U-N-S 24-345-7541　　(HQ)
746746 ONTARIO LIMITED
400 Hunt Club Rd, Ottawa, ON, K1V 1C1
(613) 741-0962
Sales 62,007,680
SIC 2752 Commercial printing, lithographic
Ward Griffin
Tracy Griffin

D-U-N-S 25-526-3824　　(SL)
AENOS FOOD SERVICES INC
2455 Kaladar Ave, Ottawa, ON, K1V 8B9
(613) 736-0310
Emp Here 25　　　*Sales* 20,889,425
SIC 5148 Fresh fruits and vegetables
Dimitrios Kampitsis
David Kampitsis

D-U-N-S 20-136-3439　　(SL)
ARTISTIC LANDSCAPE DESIGNS LIMITED
2079 Artistic Pl, Ottawa, ON, K1V 8A8
(613) 733-8220
Emp Here 80　　　*Sales* 8,743,120
SIC 0781 Landscape counseling and planning
Eckhart Schmitz
Eva Schmitz

D-U-N-S 25-777-8100　　(BR)
BAYSHORE HEALTHCARE LTD.
BAYSHORE HEALTHCARE LTD
(*Suby of* BAYSHORE HEALTHCARE LTD.)
310 Hunt Club Rd Suite 202, Ottawa, ON, K1V 1C1
(613) 733-4408
Emp Here 200

SIC 8082 Home health care services
Wendy Alexander

D-U-N-S 25-131-4043　　(BR)
BEST BUY CANADA LTD
FUTURE SHOP
(*Suby of* BEST BUY CO., INC.)
2210 Bank St Unit B1, Ottawa, ON, K1V 1J5
(613) 526-7450
Emp Here 120
SIC 5731 Radio, television, and electronic stores

D-U-N-S 24-986-8829　　(BR)
BRADLEY AIR SERVICES LIMITED
FIRST AIR
(*Suby of* SOCIETE MAKIVIK)
100 Thad Johnson Pvt, Ottawa, ON, K1V 0R1
(613) 254-6200
Emp Here 300
SIC 8322 Individual and family services
Clark Murray

D-U-N-S 25-371-3226　　(SL)
BYEXPRESS CORPORATION
2471 Holly Ln, Ottawa, ON, K1V 7P2
(613) 739-3000
Emp Here 24　　　*Sales* 12,479,208
SIC 4731 Freight transportation arrangement
Tamin Payman

D-U-N-S 20-889-7652　　(HQ)
CANADIAN LABOUR CONGRESS
CLC
2841 Riverside Dr, Ottawa, ON, K1V 8X7
(613) 521-3400
Emp Here 65　　　*Sales* 35,320,500
SIC 8631 Labor organizations
Hassan Yussuff
Marie Clarke-Walker
Donald Lafleur
Barb Byers

D-U-N-S 24-847-2334　　(SL)
DONNELLY PONTIAC BUICK GMC LTD
2496 Bank St, Ottawa, ON, K1V 8S2
(613) 737-5000
Emp Here 68　　　*Sales* 42,791,040
SIC 5511 New and used car dealers
Thomas Donnelly
Dan Mckenna

D-U-N-S 25-105-5422　　(SL)
GLOBAL MART INTERNATIONAL TECHNOLOGY INC
2821 Riverside Dr, Ottawa, ON, K1V 8N4

Emp Here 77　　*Sales* 11,728,363
SIC 7373 Computer integrated systems design
Xi-Nam Dam
Shan Dam

D-U-N-S 24-846-0073　　(SL)
HANNA, NABIL DRUGS LTD
SHOPPERS DRUG MART
2515 Bank St, Ottawa, ON, K1V 0Y4
(613) 523-9999
Emp Here 90　　　*Sales* 21,989,520
SIC 5912 Drug stores and proprietary stores
Nabil Hanna

D-U-N-S 20-176-2114　　(BR)
HOME DEPOT OF CANADA INC
HOME DEPOT
(*Suby of* THE HOME DEPOT INC)
2056 Bank St, Ottawa, ON, K1V 7Z8
(613) 739-5300
Emp Here 125
SIC 5251 Hardware stores
Sarge Compegna

D-U-N-S 20-261-3733　　(SL)
HUNT CLUB AUTOMOTIVE LTD
DONNELLY MITSUBISHI
92 Terry Fox Dr, Ottawa, ON, K1V 0W8
(613) 733-7500
Emp Here 35　　　*Sales* 17,432,730

▲ Public Company　　■ Public Company Family Member　　**HQ** Headquarters　　**BR** Branch　　**SL** Single Location

SIC 5511 New and used car dealers
Maureen Donnelly

D-U-N-S 25-167-1830   (HQ)
HYDRO OTTAWA HOLDING INC
(*Suby of* CITY OF OTTAWA)
3025 Albion Rd N, Ottawa, ON, K1V 9V9
(613) 738-5499
Sales 902,137,726
SIC 4911 Electric services
Bryce Conrad
Geoff Simpson
Lance Jefferies
Julie Lupinacci
Lyne Parent-Garvey
Mark Fernandes
Roger Marsh
Greg Clarke
Jim Durrell
Dale Craig

D-U-N-S 20-697-3633   (BR)
IOGEN BIO-PRODUCTS CORPORATION
(*Suby of* IOGEN CORPORATION)
300 Hunt Club Rd, Ottawa, ON, K1V 1C1
(613) 733-9830
Emp Here 200
SIC 2869 Industrial organic chemicals, nec
Peter Grier

D-U-N-S 20-552-0286   (HQ)
IOGEN BIO-PRODUCTS CORPORATION
(*Suby of* IOGEN CORPORATION)
310 Hunt Club Rd, Ottawa, ON, K1V 1C1
(613) 733-9830
Emp Here 200   *Sales* 61,224,600
SIC 8732 Commercial nonphysical research
Brian E Foody
William Waller
Patrick J Jr Foody

D-U-N-S 24-965-3213   (HQ)
IOGEN CORPORATION
310 Hunt Club Rd, Ottawa, ON, K1V 1C1
(613) 733-9830
Emp Here 48   *Sales* 465,754,250
SIC 2911 Petroleum refining
Brian Foody
Clive Mather
Patrick Foody
Philip Evershed
Ken Wigglesworth
Norman Chirite
Morris Zukerman
John Richardson

D-U-N-S 24-419-3541   (BR)
IOGEN CORPORATION
(*Suby of* IOGEN CORPORATION)
310 Hunt Club Rd, Ottawa, ON, K1V 1C1
(613) 733-9830
Emp Here 100
SIC 2869 Industrial organic chemicals, nec

D-U-N-S 24-389-5971   (SL)
IOGEN ENERGY CORPORATION
310 Hunt Club Rd, Ottawa, ON, K1V 1C1
(613) 733-9830
Emp Here 20   *Sales* 22,106,900
SIC 5122 Drugs, proprietaries, and sundries
William S. Waller
Brian E. Foody
Chris Cooper
Darran Messem
Michael Feldman
John Broadhurst

D-U-N-S 25-091-6884   (SL)
JAZZWORKS
1234 Ridgemont Ave, Ottawa, ON, K1V 6E7
(613) 523-0316
Emp Here 75   *Sales* 7,948,800
SIC 7929 Entertainers and entertainment
groups
Judy Humenick

D-U-N-S 20-892-0785   (SL)

JIM TUBMAN HOLDINGS LTD
JIM TUBMAN CHEVROLET
1770 Bank St, Ottawa, ON, K1V 7Y6
(613) 733-4050
Emp Here 49   *Sales* 24,405,822
SIC 5511 New and used car dealers
Anne Harcourt

D-U-N-S 25-784-6873   (BR)
LOBLAWS INC
LOBLAWS
(*Suby of* LOBLAW COMPANIES LIMITED)
2210c Bank St Suite 1188, Ottawa, ON, K1V
1J5
(613) 733-1377
Emp Here 300
SIC 5411 Grocery stores
Mike Robinson

D-U-N-S 20-789-1433   (HQ)
LOWE-MARTIN COMPANY INC
(*Suby of* 746746 ONTARIO LIMITED)
400 Hunt Club Rd, Ottawa, ON, K1V 1C1
(613) 741-0962
Emp Here 200   *Sales* 72,222,930
SIC 2752 Commercial printing, lithographic
Ward Griffin
Tracy Griffin

D-U-N-S 25-129-4468   (BR)
**MCDONALD'S   RESTAURANTS   OF
CANADA LIMITED**
MCDONALD'S 8571
(*Suby of* MCDONALD'S CORPORATION)
1771 Walkley Rd, Ottawa, ON, K1V 1L2
(613) 733-8354
Emp Here 100
SIC 5812 Eating places
Jerry Formoso

D-U-N-S 25-310-9094   (BR)
**MCDONALD'S   RESTAURANTS   OF
CANADA LIMITED**
MCDONALD'S
(*Suby of* MCDONALD'S CORPORATION)
2380 Bank St, Ottawa, ON, K1V 8S1
(613) 526-1258
Emp Here 130
SIC 5812 Eating places
Ravi Koussa

D-U-N-S 25-676-2063   (BR)
METRO ONTARIO INC
METRO
(*Suby of* METRO INC)
1670 Heron Rd, Ottawa, ON, K1V 0C2
(613) 731-0066
Emp Here 94
SIC 5411 Grocery stores
Glen Wood

D-U-N-S 24-344-4952   (BR)
METRO ONTARIO INC
LOEB
(*Suby of* METRO INC)
2515 Bank St, Ottawa, ON, K1V 0Y4
(613) 731-7410
Emp Here 120
SIC 5411 Grocery stores
Ian Ondrechak

D-U-N-S 25-292-3495   (BR)
METRO ONTARIO INC
METRO
(*Suby of* METRO INC)
3310 Mccarthy Rd, Ottawa, ON, K1V 9S1
(613) 523-2774
Emp Here 85
SIC 5411 Grocery stores
John Paul Guindon

D-U-N-S 20-805-3467   (SL)
OTTAWA FIBRE L.P.
1365 Johnston Rd, Ottawa, ON, K1V 8Z1
(613) 247-7116
Emp Here 84   *Sales* 26,882,850
SIC 3296 Mineral wool
Catherine Skarzenski

D-U-N-S 25-392-9491   (SL)
**OTTAWA   MACDONALD-CARTIER   INTER-
NATIONAL AIRPORT AUTHORITY**
*OTTAWA   INTERNATIONAL   AIRPORT   AU-
THORITY*
1000 Airport Parkway Pvt Suite 2500, Ottawa,
ON, K1V 9B4
(613) 248-2000
Emp Here 125   *Sales* 37,121
SIC 4581 Airports, flying fields, and services
Mark B. Laroche
John Weerdenburg
Ray Butler

D-U-N-S 24-784-1315   (HQ)
OTTAWA MOTOR SALES (1987) LIMITED
DONNELLY FORD LINCOLN
2496 Bank St Suite 40010, Ottawa, ON, K1V
8S2
(613) 733-6931
Sales 88,728,480
SIC 5511 New and used car dealers
Dan Mckenna
Daniel Donnelly
Maureen Donnelly

D-U-N-S 25-504-0263   (BR)
**OTTAWA-CARLETON   DISTRICT   SCHOOL
BOARD**
RIDGEMONT HIGH SCHOOL
(*Suby of*   OTTAWA-CARLETON   DISTRICT
SCHOOL BOARD)
2597 Alta Vista Dr, Ottawa, ON, K1V 7T3
(613) 733-4860
Emp Here 100
SIC 8211 Elementary and secondary schools
Richard King

D-U-N-S 25-504-0859   (BR)
**OTTAWA-CARLETON   DISTRICT   SCHOOL
BOARD**
BROOKFIELD HIGH SCHOOL
(*Suby of*   OTTAWA-CARLETON   DISTRICT
SCHOOL BOARD)
824 Brookfield Rd, Ottawa, ON, K1V 6J3
(613) 733-0610
Emp Here 85
SIC 8211 Elementary and secondary schools
Krista Mcnamara

D-U-N-S 20-138-5572   (SL)
OTTO'S SERVICE CENTRE LIMITED
BMW
660 Hunt Club Rd, Ottawa, ON, K1V 1C1
(613) 725-3048
Emp Here 40   *Sales* 19,923,120
SIC 5511 New and used car dealers
Sonya Koller
Jules Bruehlmann

D-U-N-S 20-833-6433   (SL)
**RAYMOND AND ASSOCIATES ROOFING
INC**
3091 Albion Rd N Suite 5b, Ottawa, ON, K1V
9V9
(613) 274-7508
Emp Here 75   *Sales* 16,337,175
SIC 1761 Roofing, siding, and sheetMetal
work
Alain Raymond

D-U-N-S 20-138-8469   (SL)
RIDEAU BAKERY LIMITED
1666 Bank St, Ottawa, ON, K1V 7Y6
(613) 737-3355
Emp Here 40   *Sales* 10,966,080
SIC 5461 Retail bakeries
Louis Kardish
David Kardish

D-U-N-S 20-442-9435   (HQ)
SANDER GEOPHYSICS LIMITED
S G L
260 Hunt Club Rd, Ottawa, ON, K1V 1C1
(613) 521-9626
Emp Here 157   *Sales* 114,355,430
SIC 1382 Oil and gas exploration services

Stephan Sander
Luise Sander
Reed Archer

D-U-N-S 25-769-7078   (BR)
SIEMENS CANADA LIMITED
BUILDING AUTOMATION
(*Suby of* SIEMENS AG)
2435 Holly Lane, Ottawa, ON, K1V 7P2
(613) 733-9781
Emp Here 110
SIC 1711 Plumbing, heating, air-conditioning
Raymond Rochefort

D-U-N-S 20-787-5816   (SL)
**SOUTHBANK DODGE CHRYSLER (1982)
LTD**
1255 Johnston Rd, Ottawa, ON, K1V 8Z1
(613) 731-1970
Emp Here 85   *Sales* 53,488,800
SIC 5511 New and used car dealers
Al Mcdowell

D-U-N-S 25-354-9182   (SL)
SOUTHBANK FRUIT INC
PRODUCE DEPOT
2446 Bank St Unit 131, Ottawa, ON, K1V 1A4
(613) 521-9653
Emp Here 80   *Sales* 23,478,160
SIC 5431 Fruit and vegetable markets
Daniel Docksteader
Donna-Lee Barstead

D-U-N-S 25-125-6772   (SL)
ST PATRICK'S HOME OF OTTAWA
2865 Riverside Dr, Ottawa, ON, K1V 8N5
(613) 731-4660
Emp Here 255   *Sales* 17,423,130
SIC 8051 Skilled nursing care facilities
Marilyn Willms
Donald Burke
Lyla Graham
Mary Whelan
Alberta Casey
John Duvernet
Linda Chapmin

D-U-N-S 24-595-6867   (BR)
SWISSPORT CANADA INC
SWISSPORT
(*Suby of* SWISSPORT CANADA INC)
130 Thad Johnson Pvt, Ottawa, ON, K1V 0X1
(613) 521-4730
Emp Here 110
SIC 4581 Airports, flying fields, and services
Andrew Fifield

D-U-N-S 20-139-1935   (HQ)
TAGGART CONSTRUCTION LIMITED
3187 Albion Rd S, Ottawa, ON, K1V 8Y3
(613) 521-3000
Emp Here 75   *Sales* 25,244,200
SIC 1623 Water, sewer, and utility lines
James Taggart
Ian Taggart
David Parks
Christopher Taggart

D-U-N-S 24-783-7487   (HQ)
**TAMARACK DEVELOPMENTS CORPORA-
TION**
3187 Albion Rd S, Ottawa, ON, K1V 8Y3
(613) 739-2919
Sales 35,755,650
SIC 1531 Operative builders
Chris Taggart
Scott Parkes
James E Taggart

D-U-N-S 24-382-7631   (SL)
TWIN EQUIPMENT LTD
3091 Albion Rd N, Ottawa, ON, K1V 9V9
(613) 745-7095
Emp Here 45   *Sales* 21,376,170
SIC 5082 Construction and mining machinery
Francois Vachon
Sylvie Larocque-Vachon

D-U-N-S 25-773-7148   (BR)
WAL-MART CANADA CORP
(*Suby of* WALMART INC.)
2210 Bank St, Ottawa, ON, K1V 1J5
(613) 247-1184
Emp Here 311
SIC 5311 Department stores
Rod Fleming

D-U-N-S 20-790-0440   (HQ)
WAR AMPUTATIONS OF CANADA, THE
KEY TAG SERVICE, THE
2827 Riverside Dr Suite 101, Ottawa, ON, K1V 0C4
(613) 731-3821
Emp Here 60   *Sales* 24,330,275
SIC 8641 Civic and social associations
Hugh Clifford Chadderton
David Saunders

Ottawa, ON K1Y

D-U-N-S 24-745-7559   (SL)
ARTECH DIGITAL ENTERTAINMENT INC
ARTECH STUDIOS
6 Hamilton Ave N, Ottawa, ON, K1Y 4R1
(613) 728-4880
Emp Here 70   *Sales* 12,411,770
SIC 7371 Custom computer programming services

D-U-N-S 24-560-8232   (BR)
CANADIAN BANK NOTE COMPANY, LIMITED
(*Suby of* CANADIAN BANK NOTE COMPANY, LIMITED)
975 Gladstone Ave, Ottawa, ON, K1Y 4W5
(613) 722-3421
Emp Here 100
SIC 2759 Commercial printing, nec
Ronald Arends

D-U-N-S 24-946-6582   (HQ)
DISTRICT REALTY CORPORATION
50 Bayswater Ave, Ottawa, ON, K1Y 2E9
(613) 759-8383
Emp Here 20   *Sales* 11,957,264
SIC 6531 Real estate agents and managers
Steven Ramphos

D-U-N-S 20-651-1391   (BR)
GOVERNING COUNCIL OF THE SALVATION ARMY IN CANADA, THE
GOVERNING COUNCIL OF THE SALVATION ARMY IN CANADA,
(*Suby of* GOVERNING COUNCIL OF THE SALVATION ARMY IN CANADA, THE)
1156 Wellington St W Suite 613, Ottawa, ON, K1Y 2Z3
(613) 722-8025
Emp Here 250
SIC 8051 Skilled nursing care facilities
Derrick Gullage

D-U-N-S 20-367-0141   (SL)
LAROCHE PARK COMMUNITY (SPORTS) ASSOCIATION
42 Stonehurst Ave, Ottawa, ON, K1Y 1R4
(613) 722-3944
Emp Here 49   *Sales* 19,473,286
SIC 8699 Membership organizations, nec
Keith Brown

D-U-N-S 20-138-2835   (SL)
MERKLEY SUPPLY LIMITED
100 Bayview Rd, Ottawa, ON, K1Y 4L6
(613) 728-2693
Emp Here 40   *Sales* 18,829,240
SIC 1542 Nonresidential construction, nec
Robert Merkley
Lorne Hartley

D-U-N-S 20-845-5886   (HQ)
MORTGAGE BROKERS CITY INC
MORTGAGE BROKERS OTTAWA

788 Island Park Dr, Ottawa, ON, K1Y 0C2
(613) 274-3490
Emp Here 22   *Sales* 33,591,150
SIC 6163 Loan brokers
Michael Hapke
Frank Napolitano

D-U-N-S 20-894-4942   (HQ)
MRS. TIGGY WINKLE'S LTD
(*Suby of* ANISMAN HOLDINGS INC)
75 Breezehill Ave N, Ottawa, ON, K1Y 2H6
(613) 523-3663
Emp Here 7   *Sales* 10,880,650
SIC 5945 Hobby, toy, and game shops
Maida Anisman
Hymie Anisman

D-U-N-S 24-482-5824   (HQ)
OSGOODE PROPERTIES LTD
1284 Wellington St W, Ottawa, ON, K1Y 3A9
(613) 729-0656
Emp Here 55   *Sales* 24,714,451
SIC 6531 Real estate agents and managers
Stephen Greenberg

D-U-N-S 24-436-4147   (SL)
OTTAWA BAGEL SHOP INC
OTTAWA BAGELSHOP AND DELI
1321 Wellington St W, Ottawa, ON, K1Y 3B6
(613) 722-8753
Emp Here 42   *Sales* 11,514,384
SIC 5461 Retail bakeries
Vincenzo Piazza
Judith Piazza

D-U-N-S 25-774-9309   (HQ)
OTTAWA COMMUNITY IMMIGRANT SERVICES ORGANIZATION
959 Wellington St W, Ottawa, ON, K1Y 2X5
(613) 725-5671
Emp Here 1   *Sales* 49,644,840
SIC 8699 Membership organizations, nec
Hamdi Mohamed
Tyler Meredith
Lise Hebabi
Khatera Akbari

D-U-N-S 25-495-5412   (SL)
OTTAWA HEART INSTITUTE RESEARCH CORPORATION
40 Ruskin St, Ottawa, ON, K1Y 4W7

Emp Here 350   *Sales* 30,666,056
SIC 8733 Noncommercial research organizations
Marion Fraser

D-U-N-S 24-455-3413   (BR)
OTTAWA HOSPITAL, THE
(*Suby of* OTTAWA HOSPITAL, THE)
1053 Carling Ave Suite 119, Ottawa, ON, K1Y 4E9
(613) 722-7000
Emp Here 12,000
SIC 8062 General medical and surgical hospitals

D-U-N-S 25-150-3876   (HQ)
OTTAWA HOSPITAL, THE
RIVERSIDE CAMPUS
1053 Carling Ave, Ottawa, ON, K1Y 4E9
(613) 798-5555
Emp Here 2,000   *Sales* 905,085,755
SIC 8062 General medical and surgical hospitals
Jack Kitts
Nathalie Cadieux
Debra Bournes
Renee Legare
Cameron Love
Shafique Shamji

D-U-N-S 25-359-5532   (BR)
OTTAWA HOSPITAL, THE
OTTAWA REGIONAL CANCER CENTRE
(*Suby of* OTTAWA HOSPITAL, THE)
200 Melrose Ave S, Ottawa, ON, K1Y 4K7

(613) 737-7700
Emp Here 100
SIC 8069 Specialty hospitals, except psychiatric
Greg Doiron

D-U-N-S 20-709-1989   (BR)
OTTAWA HOSPITAL, THE
OTTAWA HEALTH RESEARCH INSTITUTE
(*Suby of* OTTAWA HOSPITAL, THE)
725 Parkdale Ave, Ottawa, ON, K1Y 4E9
(613) 761-4395
Emp Here 1,300
SIC 8733 Noncommercial research organizations
Duncan Stewart

D-U-N-S 24-911-3192   (SL)
SIROIS & SONS GENERAL CONTRACTORS
38 Lynwood Ave, Ottawa, ON, K1Y 2B3

Emp Here 68   *Sales* 28,746,116
SIC 1541 Industrial buildings and warehouses
Louis Sirois
Pierre Sirois

D-U-N-S 25-214-7699   (SL)
UNIVERSITY OF OTTAWA HEART INSTITUTE
40 Ruskin St, Ottawa, ON, K1Y 4W7
(613) 696-7000
Emp Here 750   *Sales* 121,446,906
SIC 8731 Commercial physical research
Thierry Mesana
Jim Orban
Andree Dumulon
Marion Fraser
Hana Pika
Heather Sherrard
Lawrence Soloway
Latifa Belmahdi
Robert Cushman
Graham Fox

D-U-N-S 20-288-9234   (HQ)
WORKSHOPX INC
6 Hamilton Ave N Suite 004, Ottawa, ON, K1Y 4R1
(613) 860-7000
Sales 11,726,975
SIC 8731 Commercial physical research
Noor Marzoky
Nazim Ahmed

Ottawa, ON K1Z

D-U-N-S 20-191-7114   (HQ)
2KEYS CORPORATION
2KEYS SECURITY SOLUTIONS
300-1600 Carling Ave, Ottawa, ON, K1Z 1G3
(613) 860-1620
Emp Here 50   *Sales* 10,845,055
SIC 7379 Computer related services, nec
Robert Pierce
James Anthony Bates
John Scott
Michele Boyle
David Beasant
Allison Dysart
Dimitri Vekris
Ingrid Meier-Villa

D-U-N-S 20-889-5060   (HQ)
ALTERNA SAVINGS AND CREDIT UNION LIMITED
ALTERNA SAVINGS
319 Mcrae Ave, Ottawa, ON, K1Z 0B9
(613) 560-0150
Emp Here 250   *Sales* 68,320,400
SIC 6062 State credit unions
Robert Paterson
Jose Galant

D-U-N-S 25-362-1791   (SL)

BAYCADD SOLUTIONS INC
1296 Carling Ave, Ottawa, ON, K1Z 7K8
(613) 298-4918
Emp Here 70   *Sales* 12,935,860
SIC 4899 Communication services, nec
Bruce Pearson

D-U-N-S 25-086-6209   (SL)
BUSHTUKAH INC
203 Richmond Rd, Ottawa, ON, K1Z 6W4

Emp Here 50   *Sales* 10,880,650
SIC 5941 Sporting goods and bicycle shops
Robert Laughton

D-U-N-S 24-744-2445   (SL)
CAMCO AUTOMOBILES INC
CAMCO ACURA
1475 Carling Ave, Ottawa, ON, K1Z 7L9
(613) 728-8888
Emp Here 50   *Sales* 24,903,900
SIC 5511 New and used car dealers
Arnis Mierins

D-U-N-S 20-136-6770   (SL)
CAMPBELL FORD SALES LTD
1500 Carling Ave, Ottawa, ON, K1Z 0A3
(613) 725-3611
Emp Here 92   *Sales* 57,893,760
SIC 5511 New and used car dealers
Gordon Hoddinott
Robert Turriff

D-U-N-S 20-787-7309   (HQ)
CANADIAN AUTOMOBILE ASSOCIATION
CAA
1545 Carling Ave Suite 500, Ottawa, ON, K1Z 8P9
(613) 247-0117
Emp Here 1   *Sales* 16,691,388
SIC 8699 Membership organizations, nec
Tim Shearman

D-U-N-S 20-746-6038   (HQ)
CANADIAN BANK NOTE COMPANY, LIMITED
CBN COMMERCIAL SOLUTIONS
145 Richmond Rd, Ottawa, ON, K1Z 1A1
(613) 722-3421
Emp Here 500   *Sales* 306,162,920
SIC 2759 Commercial printing, nec
Ronald G Arends
Douglas Arends
Ian Shaw
Gordon C Mckechnie
Craig Bascombe

D-U-N-S 20-889-9443   (SL)
CANADIAN PUBLIC HEALTH ASSOCIATION
1565 Carling Ave Suite 300, Ottawa, ON, K1Z 8R1
(613) 725-3769
Emp Here 65   *Sales* 15,698,475
SIC 8621 Professional organizations
Mark Molnar

D-U-N-S 24-330-0725   (BR)
CARILLION CANADA INC
CARILLION SERVICE ROH
(*Suby of* CARILLION GB LIMITED)
1145 Carling Ave Suite 1317, Ottawa, ON, K1Z 7K4
(613) 722-6521
Emp Here 100
SIC 8741 Management services
Pedro Narbaitz

D-U-N-S 25-769-5205   (SL)
COLDWELL BANKER FIRST OTTAWA REALTY LTD
1419 Carling Ave Suite 219, Ottawa, ON, K1Z 7L6
(613) 728-2664
Emp Here 49   *Sales* 16,029,223
SIC 6531 Real estate agents and managers
Ross Webley

▲ Public Company   ■ Public Company Family Member   **HQ** Headquarters   **BR** Branch   **SL** Single Location

D-U-N-S 24-597-4035   (HQ)
COREL CORPORATION
COREL COMPUTER
(*Suby of* VECTOR CAPITAL MANAGEMENT, L.P.)
1600 Carling Ave Suite 100, Ottawa, ON, K1Z 8R7
(613) 728-8200
Emp Here 450   *Sales* 166,115,700
SIC 7371 Custom computer programming services
  Patrick Nichols
  Jessica Sinden
  Brad Jewett
  Prasannaa Ganesan

D-U-N-S 20-700-7543   (SL)
EMBASSY WEST HOTEL
EMBASSY WEST HOTEL CONFERENCE CENTRE
1400 Carling Ave Suite 517, Ottawa, ON, K1Z 7L8
(613) 729-4321
Emp Here 60   *Sales* 10,135,620
SIC 7011 Hotels and motels
  Sam Greenberg

D-U-N-S 20-937-4979   (SL)
FRATELLI GOUP INC
FRATELLI RESTAURANTS
309 Richmond Rd, Ottawa, ON, K1Z 6X3
(613) 722-6772
Emp Here 80   *Sales* 3,641,520
SIC 5812 Eating places
  Pasquale Valante

D-U-N-S 20-787-8604   (SL)
GINSBERG GLUZMAN FAGE & LEVITZ, LLP
287 Richmond Rd, Ottawa, ON, K1Z 6X4
(613) 728-5831
Emp Here 48   *Sales* 10,036,080
SIC 8721 Accounting, auditing, and bookkeeping
  Leon Gluzman
  Richard W Fage
  Gerald Levitz
  Bruce Johnson
  Jeff Miller
  Deborah Bourchier

D-U-N-S 20-891-5314   (SL)
HALPENNY INSURANCE BROKERS LTD
1550 Laperriere Ave Suite 100, Ottawa, ON, K1Z 7T2
(613) 722-7626
Emp Here 27   *Sales* 15,657,948
SIC 6411 Insurance agents, brokers, and service
  Nick Leadbetter
  Debra Leadbetter

D-U-N-S 24-364-2217   (HQ)
HDR CORPORATION
(*Suby of* HDR, INC.)
300 Richmond Dr Suite 200, Ottawa, ON, K1Z 6X6
(613) 233-6799
Emp Here 53   *Sales* 26,632,111
SIC 8712 Architectural services
  David Lewis

D-U-N-S 20-893-1899   (HQ)
HEART AND STROKE FOUNDATION OF CANADA
1525 Carling Ave Unit 110, Ottawa, ON, K1Z 8R9
(613) 691-4048
Sales 108,689,662
SIC 8399 Social services, nec
  Rebecca Schalm
  Alison Twiner
  John Kelleher
  David Butler-Jones
  Andrew Claerhout
  Marie Elaine Farley
  Nadine Caron

  Andrew Cockwell
  Andrew Pipe
  Zaylin Lalji

D-U-N-S 25-273-4025   (SL)
INCOHO
1960 Scott St Suite 202c, Ottawa, ON, K1Z 8L8
(613) 695-9800
Emp Here 49   *Sales* 12,571,174
SIC 7323 Credit reporting services
  Alex Chapman

D-U-N-S 20-578-4010   (HQ)
J.L. RICHARDS & ASSOCIATES LIMITED
864 Lady Ellen Pl, Ottawa, ON, K1Z 5M2
(613) 728-3571
Sales 40,216,275
SIC 8711 Engineering services
  Guy Cormier
  Stephen Parenteau

D-U-N-S 24-269-2648   (SL)
JALALDIN, NARMIN DRUGS LTD
SHOPPERS DRUG MART
1309 Carling Ave, Ottawa, ON, K1Z 7L3
(613) 722-4277
Emp Here 40   *Sales* 10,118,160
SIC 5912 Drug stores and proprietary stores
  Narmin Jalaldin

D-U-N-S 24-383-9011   (BR)
LOBLAWS INC
REAL CANADIAN SUPERSTORE
(*Suby of* LOBLAW COMPANIES LIMITED)
190 Richmond Rd Suite 1009, Ottawa, ON, K1Z 6W6
(613) 722-5890
Emp Here 200
SIC 5411 Grocery stores
  Chris Wojcik

D-U-N-S 24-374-9541   (SL)
OREZONE GOLD CORPORATION
290 Picton Ave Suite 201, Ottawa, ON, K1Z 8P8
(613) 241-3699
Emp Here 56   *Sales* 14,323,344
SIC 1041 Gold ores
  Patrick G. Downey
  Pascal Marquis
  Peter Tam
  Louis Archambeault
  Ryan Goodman
  Michael H. Halvorson
  Joseph Conway
  Ronald Batt
  Charles Oliver
  Stephen Axcell

D-U-N-S 24-459-6388   (SL)
OTTO'S COLLISION CENTER
OTTO'S SUBARU
1551 Laperriere Ave, Ottawa, ON, K1Z 7T1
(613) 728-7032
Emp Here 40   *Sales* 19,923,120
SIC 5511 New and used car dealers
  Sonia Koller

D-U-N-S 25-094-3586   (HQ)
PYTHIAN GROUP INC, THE
319 Mcrae Ave Unit 700, Ottawa, ON, K1Z 0B9
(613) 565-8696
Sales 73,829,200
SIC 7371 Custom computer programming services
  Paul Vallee
  Keith Millar
  Aaron Lee
  Pavla Selepova
  Ian Cascagnette
  Lori O'neill
  Rob White
  Chris Jones

D-U-N-S 24-975-2551   (HQ)
ROYAL LEPAGE TEAM REALTY

1335 Carling Ave Suite 200, Ottawa, ON, K1Z 8N8
(613) 216-1198
Emp Here 13   *Sales* 12,229,020
SIC 6531 Real estate agents and managers
  Kent Browne

D-U-N-S 20-025-4311   (SL)
T K GROUP INC, THE
T K INSURANCE GROUP
880 Lady Ellen Pl Suite 100, Ottawa, ON, K1Z 5L9
(613) 728-7030
Emp Here 29   *Sales* 24,593,740
SIC 6411 Insurance agents, brokers, and service
  Milan Topolovec

D-U-N-S 24-100-6253   (SL)
WESTBORO AUTO IMPORTS LTD
WESTBORO SUBARU
225 Richmond Rd, Ottawa, ON, K1Z 6W7
(613) 728-5813
Emp Here 50   *Sales* 24,903,900
SIC 5511 New and used car dealers
  Tanya Koller
  Keir Fawcett

Ottawa, ON K2A

D-U-N-S 25-401-8807   (SL)
561028 ONTARIO LIMITED
890 Boyd Ave, Ottawa, ON, K2A 2E3
(613) 798-8020
Emp Here 54   *Sales* 14,123,862
SIC 6712 Bank holding companies
  Paul Ziebarth

D-U-N-S 20-281-0404   (HQ)
8463859 CANADA INC
BABY ENROUTE
416 Richmond Rd, Ottawa, ON, K2A 0G2
(613) 695-3416
Emp Here 10   *Sales* 12,956,372
SIC 5137 Women's and children's clothing
  Qin (Nathan) Xu
  Xi Chen

D-U-N-S 20-136-2332   (HQ)
ADVANCED PREFABS LIMITED
FIREPLACE CENTER & PATIO SHOP, THE
1722 Carling Ave, Ottawa, ON, K2A 1C7
(613) 728-1775
Emp Here 10   *Sales* 10,365,300
SIC 5719 Miscellaneous homefurnishings
  Stephen Cotnam
  Andrew Cotnam

D-U-N-S 20-616-1655   (SL)
AFFILIATED ANIMAL SERVICES
OTTAWA VETERINARY HOSPITAL
900 Boyd Ave, Ottawa, ON, K2A 2E3
(613) 725-1182
Emp Here 60   *Sales* 10,434,300
SIC 0742 Veterinary services, specialties
  Mark Wallar
  Susan Armstrong
  Michael Smith
  John Swatman
  Edward Cottell

D-U-N-S 24-985-1999   (HQ)
CANADIAN INSTITUTE FOR HEALTH INFORMATION
C.I.H.I.
495 Richmond Rd Suite 600, Ottawa, ON, K2A 4B2
(613) 241-7860
Emp Here 150   *Sales* 83,269,347
SIC 8011 Offices and clinics of medical doctors
  David O'toole
  Neala Barton
  Chantal Poirier

  Brent Diverty
  Stephen O'reilly
  Louise Ogilvie
  Caroline Heick
  Kathleen Morris
  Georgina Macdonald
  Cal Marcoux

D-U-N-S 24-918-3781   (SL)
CARLING FRUIT INC
PRODUCE DEPOT
1855 Carling Ave, Ottawa, ON, K2A 1E4
(613) 722-6106
Emp Here 80   *Sales* 23,478,160
SIC 5431 Fruit and vegetable markets
  David Barstead

D-U-N-S 20-136-7786   (SL)
CARLING MOTORS CO LTD
(*Suby of* GORMARK HOLDINGS LIMITED)
1638 Carling Ave, Ottawa, ON, K2A 1C5
(613) 706-8082
Emp Here 64   *Sales* 40,273,920
SIC 5511 New and used car dealers
  John Mierins

D-U-N-S 24-579-1988   (SL)
FIREPLACE CENTRE, THE
811 Boyd Ave, Ottawa, ON, K2A 2C8
(613) 728-1775
Emp Here 49   *Sales* 11,286,660
SIC 5719 Miscellaneous homefurnishings
  Andy Cotnam

D-U-N-S 20-706-1123   (SL)
JEWISH FEDERATION OF OTTAWA
21 Nadolny Sachs Pvt, Ottawa, ON, K2A 1R9
(613) 798-4696
Emp Here 49   *Sales* 22,011,731
SIC 7389 Business services, nec
  Andrea Freedman
  Andrea Freedman

D-U-N-S 25-775-3269   (BR)
MOUNTAIN EQUIPMENT CO-OPERATIVE
MEC
(*Suby of* MOUNTAIN EQUIPMENT CO-OPERATIVE)
366 Richmond Rd, Ottawa, ON, K2A 0E8
(613) 729-2700
Emp Here 120
SIC 5941 Sporting goods and bicycle shops
  Coleen Mooney

D-U-N-S 25-263-6659   (BR)
OTTAWA CATHOLIC DISTRICT SCHOOL BOARD
NOTRE DAME INTERMEDIATE SCHOOL
(*Suby of* OTTAWA CATHOLIC DISTRICT SCHOOL BOARD)
710 Broadview Ave, Ottawa, ON, K2A 2M2
(613) 722-6565
Emp Here 100
SIC 8211 Elementary and secondary schools
  Andre Potvin

D-U-N-S 25-977-1764   (SL)
OTTAWA JEWISH HOME FOR THE AGED
BESS AND MOE GREENBERG FAMILY HILLEL LODGE, THE
10 Nadolny Sachs Pvt, Ottawa, ON, K2A 4G7
(613) 728-3900
Emp Here 140   *Sales* 8,999,480
SIC 8361 Residential care
  Stephen Schneiderman

D-U-N-S 25-501-6255   (BR)
OTTAWA-CARLETON DISTRICT SCHOOL BOARD
BROADVIEW PUBLIC SCHOOL
(*Suby of* OTTAWA-CARLETON DISTRICT SCHOOL BOARD)
590 Broadview Ave, Ottawa, ON, K2A 2L8
(613) 728-1721
Emp Here 80
SIC 8211 Elementary and secondary schools
  Catherine Deschambault

▲ Public Company   ■ Public Company Family Member   **HQ** Headquarters   **BR** Branch   **SL** Single Location

D-U-N-S 25-504-0180   (BR)
OTTAWA-CARLETON DISTRICT SCHOOL BOARD
NEPEAN HIGH SCHOOL
(*Suby of* OTTAWA-CARLETON DISTRICT SCHOOL BOARD)
574 Broadview Ave, Ottawa, ON, K2A 3V8
(613) 722-6551
Emp Here 110
SIC 8211 Elementary and secondary schools
 Patrick Mccarthy

D-U-N-S 25-407-5898   (SL)
OTTAWA-CARLETON MORTGAGE INC
381 Richmond Rd, Ottawa, ON, K2A 0E7
(613) 563-3447
Emp Here 30   *Sales* 20,367,690
SIC 6211 Security brokers and dealers
 Grant King
 Dawn King

D-U-N-S 20-056-8736   (SL)
VALIFF SALES INC
CANADIAN TIRE
1660 Carling Ave Suite 290, Ottawa, ON, K2A 1C5
(613) 725-3111
Emp Here 100   *Sales* 62,928,000
SIC 5531 Auto and home supply stores
 Cliff Hammell
 Valerie Hammell

D-U-N-S 24-100-1759   (SL)
ZIEBARTH ELECTRICAL CONTRACTORS LIMITED
890 Boyd Ave, Ottawa, ON, K2A 2E3
(613) 798-8020
Emp Here 85   *Sales* 18,515,465
SIC 1731 Electrical work
 Johannes Ziebarth
 Paul Ziebarth
 Beatte Ziebarth

Ottawa, ON K2B

D-U-N-S 24-382-5999   (SL)
501548 ONTARIO LTD
OTTAWA HONDA
955 Richmond Rd, Ottawa, ON, K2B 6R1
(613) 726-0333
Emp Here 50   *Sales* 24,903,900
SIC 5511 New and used car dealers
 Kewal Krishan Dilawri

D-U-N-S 24-737-4267   (SL)
715137 ONTARIO LTD
FLAG NATIONAL LEASING
1071 Richmond Rd, Ottawa, ON, K2B 6R2

Emp Here 30   *Sales* 14,942,340
SIC 5521 Used car dealers
 Pawan Dilawri

D-U-N-S 20-216-1597   (SL)
765620 ONTARIO INC
DILAWRI AUTOMOTIVE GROUP
955 Richmond Rd, Ottawa, ON, K2B 6R1
(613) 726-0333
Emp Here 50   *Sales* 25,322,753
SIC 5511 New and used car dealers
 Ram Dilawri
 Swarna Dilawri
 Kapil Dilawri

D-U-N-S 24-383-6434   (SL)
BINKS INSURANCE BROKERS LIMITED
2625 Queensview Dr Suite 100b, Ottawa, ON, K2B 8K2
(613) 226-1350
Emp Here 28   *Sales* 16,237,872
SIC 6411 Insurance agents, brokers, and service
 Harry Binks
 Ward Strickland

 Mark Attley

D-U-N-S 24-829-2161   (HQ)
BOYS & GIRLS CLUB OF OTTAWA
2825 Dumaurier Ave, Ottawa, ON, K2B 7W3
(613) 828-0428
Emp Here 40   *Sales* 10,715,925
SIC 8641 Civic and social associations
 Scott Brantford

D-U-N-S 20-107-7430   (SL)
CUSTOMER EXPRESSIONS CORP
I-SIGHT SOFTWARE
2255 Carling Ave Suite 500, Ottawa, ON, K2B 7Z5
(613) 244-5111
Emp Here 130   *Sales* 29,701,360
SIC 4813 Telephone communication, except radio
 Geoff English
 Ray Gerard

D-U-N-S 24-594-3808   (SL)
FARM BOY SUPERMARKET
1495 Richmond Rd, Ottawa, ON, K2B 6R9
(613) 688-2882
Emp Here 49   *Sales* 13,433,448
SIC 5411 Grocery stores
 Steve Beaulne

D-U-N-S 20-357-8786   (SL)
FERGUSLEA PROPERTIES LIMITED
ACCORA VILLAGE
98 Woodridge Cres, Ottawa, ON, K2B 7S9
(613) 366-5020
Emp Here 100   *Sales* 23,291,100
SIC 6513 Apartment building operators
 Daniel Greenberg

D-U-N-S 24-676-4703   (SL)
FULLER, THOMAS CONSTRUCTION CO. LIMITED
(*Suby of* 1206938 ONTARIO LIMITED)
2700 Queensview Dr, Ottawa, ON, K2B 8H6
(613) 820-6000
Emp Here 35   *Sales* 19,961,830
SIC 1542 Nonresidential construction, nec
 William Fuller

D-U-N-S 25-982-4589   (BR)
GOODLIFE FITNESS CENTRES INC
(*Suby of* GOODLIFE FITNESS CENTRES INC)
2655 Queensview Dr, Ottawa, ON, K2B 8K2

Emp Here 100
SIC 7991 Physical fitness facilities
 David Patchell-Evan

D-U-N-S 24-061-8327   (SL)
HARRIS SECURITY AGENCY
2720 Queensview Dr Suite 1140, Ottawa, ON, K2B 1A5
(613) 726-6713
Emp Here 49   *Sales* 11,480,112
SIC 8748 Business consulting, nec
 Jim Harris

D-U-N-S 25-869-6665   (BR)
LEON'S FURNITURE LIMITED
(*Suby of* LEON'S FURNITURE LIMITED)
2600 Queensview Dr, Ottawa, ON, K2B 8H6
(613) 820-6446
Emp Here 90
SIC 5712 Furniture stores
 Corey Hursp

D-U-N-S 20-138-1209   (SL)
LINCOLN HEIGHTS FORD SALES LIMITED
1377 Richmond Rd, Ottawa, ON, K2B 6R7
(613) 829-2120
Emp Here 50   *Sales* 24,903,900
SIC 5511 New and used car dealers
 Leslie Bell

D-U-N-S 20-614-8553   (HQ)
METCALFE REALTY COMPANY LIMITED
LOCH MARCH GOLF & COUNTRY CLUB,

DIV OF
(*Suby of* FARRELL INVESTMENTS LTD)
2700 Queensview Dr, Ottawa, ON, K2B 8H6
(613) 820-6000
Emp Here 5   *Sales* 31,416,675
SIC 6531 Real estate agents and managers
 Jeanne Fuller
 Antony Fuller
 John Mckenna
 Jan Haubrich
 Nancy Patterson

D-U-N-S 24-344-4945   (BR)
METRO ONTARIO INC
LOEB CANADA
(*Suby of* METRO INC)
1360 Richmond Rd, Ottawa, ON, K2B 8L4
(613) 828-4207
Emp Here 80
SIC 5141 Groceries, general line
 Larry Fulton

D-U-N-S 24-104-1474   (SL)
METRO PLYMOUTH CHRYSLER LTD
METRO CHRYSLER DODGE JEEP
1047 Richmond Rd, Ottawa, ON, K2B 6R1
(613) 596-1006
Emp Here 50   *Sales* 24,903,900
SIC 5511 New and used car dealers
 James Pears Sr

D-U-N-S 25-114-7260   (SL)
NOTRA INC
2725 Queensview Dr Suite 200, Ottawa, ON, K2B 0A1
(613) 738-0887
Emp Here 80   *Sales* 18,743,040
SIC 8748 Business consulting, nec
 Steven Burns

D-U-N-S 25-263-4498   (BR)
OTTAWA-CARLETON DISTRICT SCHOOL BOARD
WOODROFFE SECONDARY HIGH SCHOOL
(*Suby of* OTTAWA-CARLETON DISTRICT SCHOOL BOARD)
2410 Georgina Dr, Ottawa, ON, K2B 7M8
(613) 820-7186
Emp Here 80
SIC 8211 Elementary and secondary schools
 Renald Cousineau

D-U-N-S 24-678-8921   (HQ)
PROSLIDE TECHNOLOGY INC
2650 Queensview Dr Suite 150, Ottawa, ON, K2B 8H6
(613) 526-5522
Emp Here 58   *Sales* 41,718,000
SIC 5091 Sporting and recreation goods
 Richard Hunter
 David Alexander
 Donald Ferrar
 Dave Rozon
 Erin Crowe

D-U-N-S 25-784-5495   (SL)
RAINBOW NATURAL FOODS INC
1487 Richmond Rd, Ottawa, ON, K2B 6R9
(613) 726-9200
Emp Here 50   *Sales* 13,707,600
SIC 5411 Grocery stores
 Michael Kaplan
 Janet Kaplan

D-U-N-S 24-633-3389   (SL)
REMAX GATEWAY REALTY LTD
REMAX METRO CITY REALTY
2255 Carling Ave Suite 101, Ottawa, ON, K2B 7Z5
(613) 288-0090
Emp Here 60   *Sales* 16,305,360
SIC 6531 Real estate agents and managers
 Moses Keoshkerian

D-U-N-S 24-345-7061   (BR)
REVERA LONG TERM CARE INC
CARLINGVIEW MANOR
(*Suby of* GOVERNMENT OF CANADA)

2330 Carling Ave, Ottawa, ON, K2B 7H1
(613) 820-9328
Emp Here 400
SIC 8051 Skilled nursing care facilities
 Kathy Drouin

D-U-N-S 20-892-9620   (HQ)
VERSATERM INC
2300 Carling Ave, Ottawa, ON, K2B 7G1
(613) 820-0311
Sales 14,184,880
SIC 7371 Custom computer programming services
 Warren Loomis
 Ron Meyer

D-U-N-S 24-476-1735   (BR)
WSP CANADA INC
GENIVAR
(*Suby of* AST TRUST COMPANY (CANADA))
2611 Queensview Dr Suite 300, Ottawa, ON, K2B 8K2
(613) 829-2800
Emp Here 175
SIC 8711 Engineering services
 Heather Canon

D-U-N-S 24-366-5866   (HQ)
YOUTH SERVICES BUREAU OF OTTAWA
2675 Queensview Dr, Ottawa, ON, K2B 8K2
(613) 729-1000
Emp Here 30   *Sales* 21,117,800
SIC 8322 Individual and family services
 Wes Richardson
 Mary Conroy
 Jane Fjeld
 Joan Lowe

Ottawa, ON K2C

D-U-N-S 25-214-2369   (SL)
1043133 ONTARIO INC
XTC-COM
1825 Woodward Dr, Ottawa, ON, K2C 0P9
(613) 228-6557
Emp Here 50   *Sales* 14,783,840
SIC 4899 Communication services, nec
 Stewart Duncan
 Douglas Duncan

D-U-N-S 20-610-0583   (SL)
1230172 ONTARIO INC
PARK PLACE RETIREMENT RESIDENCE
110 Central Park Dr Suite 512, Ottawa, ON, K2C 4G3
(613) 727-2773
Emp Here 55   *Sales* 12,810,105
SIC 6513 Apartment building operators
 David Choo

D-U-N-S 25-419-1307   (HQ)
APOLLO MANAGEMENT SERVICES LTD
AMS
1200 Prince Of Wales Dr Suite D, Ottawa, ON, K2C 3Y4
(613) 225-7969
Emp Here 54   *Sales* 23,876,673
SIC 6531 Real estate agents and managers
 Patrick G Charbonneau

D-U-N-S 24-105-2489   (HQ)
ARNON DEVELOPMENT CORPORATION LIMITED
ARNON
1801 Woodward Dr, Ottawa, ON, K2C 0R3
(613) 226-2000
Sales 31,634,400
SIC 6553 Cemetery subdividers and developers
 Gilad Vered
 Ron Vered

D-U-N-S 20-615-3546   (BR)
CARLSON WAGONLIT CANADA
CARLSON WAGONLIT TRAVEL

(Suby of CARLSON WAGONLIT CANADA)
885 Meadowlands Dr Suite 401, Ottawa, ON,
K2C 3N2
(613) 274-6969
Emp Here 80
SIC 4724 Travel agencies
 Pamela Dowsett

D-U-N-S 24-992-8151   (HQ)
COLLIERS PROJECT LEADERS INC
(Suby of COLLIERS INTERNATIONAL
GROUP INC)
2720 Iris St, Ottawa, ON, K2C 1E6
(613) 820-6610
Emp Here 31   *Sales* 35,935,488
SIC 8741 Management services
 Franklin Holtforster
 Oliver Huls

D-U-N-S 20-032-2332   (BR)
**COMPAGNIE D'ASSURANCE BELAIR INC,
LA**
BELAIR DIRECT
(Suby of INTACT FINANCIAL CORPORA-
TION)
1111 Prince Of Wales Dr Suite 200, Ottawa,
ON, K2C 3T2
(613) 744-3279
Emp Here 100
SIC 6411 Insurance agents, brokers, and ser-
vice

D-U-N-S 20-339-9683   (SL)
CONNECT INSURE
1111 Prince Of Wales Dr, Ottawa, ON, K2C
3T2
(613) 723-0670
Emp Here 25   *Sales* 13,280,175
SIC 6289 Security and commodity service
 Michael De Waal

D-U-N-S 24-101-2319   (HQ)
ENERGIE CONVEX ENERGY INC
1771 Woodward Dr, Ottawa, ON, K2C 0P9
(613) 723-3141
Emp Here 19   *Sales* 12,073,698
SIC 5075 Warm air heating and air condition-
ing
 Michel Lalonde
 Francine Lalonde
 Lucie Lalonde

D-U-N-S 24-437-8741   (BR)
EXTENDICARE INC
EXTENDICARE WEST END VILLA
(Suby of EXTENDICARE INC)
2179 Elmira Dr, Ottawa, ON, K2C 3S1
(613) 829-3501
Emp Here 225
SIC 8051 Skilled nursing care facilities
 Lee Kirkwood

D-U-N-S 24-951-8655   (SL)
F. P. RIDEAUVIEW INC
FARMER'S PICK MARKET
1430 Prince Of Wales Dr, Ottawa, ON, K2C
1N6
(613) 225-1240
Emp Here 52   *Sales* 15,260,804
SIC 5411 Grocery stores
 Alfonso Curcio
 Johnny Curcio

D-U-N-S 20-012-4332   (SL)
GLOBAL IQX INC
1111 Prince Of Wales Dr Suite 500, Ottawa,
ON, K2C 3T2
(613) 723-8997
Emp Here 57   *Sales* 10,106,727
SIC 7371 Custom computer programming ser-
vices
 Michael De Waal

D-U-N-S 25-749-4435   (BR)
HOME DEPOT OF CANADA INC
HOME DEPOT
(Suby of THE HOME DEPOT INC)
1900 Baseline Rd, Ottawa, ON, K2C 3Z6

(613) 723-5900
Emp Here 300
SIC 5211 Lumber and other building materials
 Paulo Hribar

D-U-N-S 24-117-0708   (BR)
LOBLAWS SUPERMARKETS LIMITED
LOBLAWS
(Suby of LOBLAW COMPANIES LIMITED)
1980 Baseline Rd, Ottawa, ON, K2C 0C6
(613) 723-3200
Emp Here 100
SIC 5411 Grocery stores
 Trevor Edwards

D-U-N-S 20-951-5530   (SL)
**MYERS CADILLAC CHEVROLET BUICK
GMC INC**
1200 Baseline Rd, Ottawa, ON, K2C 0A6
(613) 225-2277
Emp Here 180   *Sales* 113,270,400
SIC 5511 New and used car dealers
 Henry Mews
 Robert Mews
 Darren Heavens

D-U-N-S 25-398-3373   (HQ)
NOVA NETWORKS INC
1700 Woodward Dr Suite 100, Ottawa, ON,
K2C 3R8
(613) 563-6682
Sales 50,526,400
SIC 7373 Computer integrated systems de-
sign
 Charles Wexler
 Gus Isaac

D-U-N-S 25-265-4348   (BR)
**OTTAWA CATHOLIC DISTRICT SCHOOL
BOARD**
ST. PIUS X HIGH SCHOOL
(Suby of OTTAWA CATHOLIC DISTRICT
SCHOOL BOARD)
1481 Fisher Ave, Ottawa, ON, K2C 1X4
(613) 225-8105
Emp Here 145
SIC 8211 Elementary and secondary schools
 Jennifer Oake

D-U-N-S 24-495-4348   (SL)
PORTIA LEARNING CENTRE INC.
1770 Courtwood Cres Suite 201, Ottawa, ON,
K2C 2B5
(613) 221-9777
Emp Here 20   *Sales* 11,598,480
SIC 6411 Insurance agents, brokers, and ser-
vice
 Karen Mcarthur

D-U-N-S 20-139-0929   (BR)
POSTMEDIA NETWORK INC
OTTAWA CITIZEN, THE
(Suby of POSTMEDIA NETWORK CANADA
CORP)
1101 Baxter Rd, Ottawa, ON, K2C 3M4
(613) 829-9100
Emp Here 300
SIC 2711 Newspapers
 Tammy Walker

D-U-N-S 25-323-1591   (HQ)
**PRECISION TRANSFER TECHNOLOGIES
INC**
1750 Courtwood Cres Suite 104, Ottawa, ON,
K2C 2B5
(613) 729-8987
Emp Here 25   *Sales* 26,027,100
SIC 5099 Durable goods, nec
 Siegried Wolfgang Margies
 Michael Furtner

D-U-N-S 20-303-3378   (BR)
RECIPE UNLIMITED CORPORATION
KELSEY'S
(Suby of RECIPE UNLIMITED CORPORA-
TION)
1100 Baxter Rd, Ottawa, ON, K2C 4B1

Emp Here 80

SIC 5812 Eating places
 Tanya Schwellnus

D-U-N-S 20-787-8364   (HQ)
**REGIONAL GROUP OF COMPANIES INC,
THE**
1737 Woodward Dr Suite 200, Ottawa, ON,
K2C 0P9
(613) 230-2100
Sales 11,413,752
SIC 6531 Real estate agents and managers
 Steven Gordon
 Len Potechin
 David Kardish
 Jeff Gould
 Jim Mccaw

D-U-N-S 24-102-7606   (HQ)
S.L. DEVISON PHARMACIES INC
SHOPPERS DRUG MART
888 Meadowlands Dr, Ottawa, ON, K2C 3R2
(613) 225-6204
Emp Here 70   *Sales* 23,211,160
SIC 5912 Drug stores and proprietary stores
 Shauna Devison

D-U-N-S 20-889-9773   (HQ)
SCOUTS CANADA
1345 Baseline Rd Suite 200, Ottawa, ON, K2C
0A7
(613) 224-0139
Emp Here 40   *Sales* 22,336,608
SIC 8641 Civic and social associations
 Andrew Price
 Ian Mitchell
 Valarie Dillon
 John Petitti
 Gary Trundell
 Peter Valters
 Alan Mimeault
 Kayleigh Kanoza
 Eric Schmitt
 Marc Chamberland

D-U-N-S 25-513-6483   (SL)
T-BASE COMMUNICATIONS INC
885 Meadowlands Dr Suite 401, Ottawa, ON,
K2C 3N2
(613) 236-0866
Emp Here 43   *Sales* 19,316,417
SIC 7389 Business services, nec
 Trevor Lwin
 Bruce Moszcelt
 William Egan
 Kent Weaver
 David Longbottom

D-U-N-S 25-769-6856   (SL)
**VILLA MARCONI LONG TERM CARE CEN-
TRE**
1026 Baseline Rd, Ottawa, ON, K2C 0A6
(613) 727-6201
Emp Here 125   *Sales* 8,540,750
SIC 8051 Skilled nursing care facilities
 Domenico Ricci
 Marco Pagani
 Eolo Bevilacqua
 Madhu Madhavan
 Lina Pavan-Farnworth

Ottawa, ON K2E

D-U-N-S 20-388-4676   (SL)
1150018 ONTARIO INC
GSNETWORKS
15 Capella Crt Unit 115, Ottawa, ON, K2E 7X1
(613) 225-5044
Emp Here 50   *Sales* 10,233,650
SIC 3679 Electronic components, nec
 Ron Nicholas
 Stephen Godding

D-U-N-S 20-350-0202   (SL)
2310884 ONTARIO INC

KIA ON HUNT CLUB
350 West Hunt Club Rd, Ottawa, ON, K2E 1A5
(613) 688-6000
Emp Here 43   *Sales* 21,417,354
SIC 5511 New and used car dealers
 Shiv Dilawri

D-U-N-S 20-136-2456   (SL)
AIRWAY SURGICAL APPLIANCES LTD
(Suby of SURGICAL APPLIANCE INDUS-
TRIES, INC.)
189 Colonnade Rd, Ottawa, ON, K2E 7J4
(613) 723-4790
Emp Here 60   *Sales* 13,637,340
SIC 3842 Surgical appliances and supplies
 Thomas Applegate
 Gary Montgomery

D-U-N-S 24-268-1674   (SL)
**ARMSTRONG MONITORING CORPORA-
TION, THE**
215 Colonnade Rd S, Ottawa, ON, K2E 7K3
(613) 225-9531
Emp Here 53   *Sales* 12,046,317
SIC 3829 Measuring and controlling devices,
nec
 Joanne Johnson

D-U-N-S 24-342-2727   (HQ)
GEODIGITAL INTERNATIONAL INC
1 Antares Dr Unit 140, Ottawa, ON, K2E 8C4
(613) 820-4545
Emp Here 20   *Sales* 43,368,820
SIC 8713 Surveying services
 Alastair Jenkins
 Donald Harkness
 Mark Chamberlain

D-U-N-S 24-858-6476   (HQ)
JAM FILLED ENTERTAINMENT INC
(Suby of BOAT ROCKER MEDIA INC)
65 Auriga Dr Suite 103, Ottawa, ON, K2E 7W6
(613) 366-2550
Emp Here 180   *Sales* 43,054,080
SIC 7812 Motion picture and video production
 Kyle Macdougall

D-U-N-S 24-483-0600   (HQ)
TRI-CO GROUP INC, THE
TRICO EVOLUTION
47-B Antares Dr, Ottawa, ON, K2E 7W6
(613) 736-7777
Sales 12,302,025
SIC 2752 Commercial printing, lithographic
 Usman Shaikh

Ottawa, ON K2G

D-U-N-S 24-437-7214   (SL)
119155 CANADA LIMITED
DAQUIN SALES
159 Cleopatra Dr Suite 100, Ottawa, ON, K2G
5X4
(613) 226-8680
Emp Here 40   *Sales* 19,932,880
SIC 5136 Men's and boy's clothing
 Randy Goyette
 Michael Dupuis

D-U-N-S 20-711-6240   (BR)
**OTTAWA-CARLETON DISTRICT SCHOOL
BOARD**
SIR GUY CARLTON SECONDARY SCHOOL
(Suby of OTTAWA-CARLETON DISTRICT
SCHOOL BOARD)
55 Centrepointe Dr, Ottawa, ON, K2G 5L4
(613) 723-5136
Emp Here 85
SIC 8211 Elementary and secondary schools
 Kevin Bush

D-U-N-S 20-181-7740   (HQ)
**PACIFIC REALM INVESTMENT GROUP
INC.**
20e Castlebrook Lane, Ottawa, ON, K2G 5G3

Sales 18,592,245
SIC 6282 Investment advice
Komei Nakanishi

Ottawa, ON K2H

D-U-N-S 24-396-3472   (HQ)
1460932 ONTARIO LIMITED
PETRO CANADA
2577 Baseline Rd, Ottawa, ON, K2H 7B3
(613) 726-9513
Emp Here 5   *Sales* 19,662,959
SIC 5411 Grocery stores
Radek Szybowski

D-U-N-S 24-804-1464   (SL)
7786395 CANADA INC
GADAR PROMOTIONS
1120 Morrison Dr Unit 1, Ottawa, ON, K2H
8M7
(613) 736-8288
Emp Here 20   *Sales* 10,006,500
SIC 5136 Men's and boy's clothing
Antonio Ricciuti
Garry Graham

D-U-N-S 24-910-4951   (BR)
**CONSEIL DES ECOLES CATHOLIQUES DE
LANGUE FRANCAISE DU CENTRE-EST**
*COLLEGE SCOLAIRE CATHOLIQUE
FRANCO OUEST*
(*Suby of* CONSEIL DES ECOLES
CATHOLIQUES DE LANGUE FRANCAISE
DU CENTRE-EST)
2675 Draper Ave, Ottawa, ON, K2H 7A1

Emp Here 90
SIC 8211 Elementary and secondary schools
Daniel Lepage

D-U-N-S 20-648-7592   (SL)
**EASTERN ONTARIO TACCX SERVICES
LLP**
301 Moody Dr Suite 400, Ottawa, ON, K2H
9C4
(613) 820-8010
Emp Here 49   *Sales* 10,417,476
SIC 8721 Accounting, auditing, and book-
keeping
Ken Tammadge

D-U-N-S 20-357-8018   (SL)
KELLER WILLIAMS INTEGRITY REALTY
245 Menten Pl Unit 100, Ottawa, ON, K2H 9E8
(613) 829-1818
Emp Here 24   *Sales* 16,723,440
SIC 6799 Investors, nec
Gary Keller
John Davis
Bill Soteroff

D-U-N-S 24-815-7927   (HQ)
LEE VALLEY HOLDINGS LIMITED
1090 Morrison Dr, Ottawa, ON, K2H 1C2
(613) 596-0350
Emp Here 4   *Sales* 243,231,000
SIC 3423 Hand and edge tools, nec
Robin Lee
Lillian Lee
Ian Campbell

D-U-N-S 24-101-0958   (HQ)
LEE VALLEY TOOLS LTD
(*Suby of* LEE VALLEY HOLDINGS LIMITED)
1090 Morrison Dr, Ottawa, ON, K2H 1C2
(613) 596-0350
Emp Here 500   *Sales* 250,134,500
SIC 5251 Hardware stores
Leonard Lee
Robin Lee
Lillian Lee

D-U-N-S 20-138-0268   (SL)
LEGERE INDUSTRIAL SUPPLIES LTD

1140 Morrison Dr Unit 110, Ottawa, ON, K2H
8S9
(613) 829-8010
Emp Here 25   *Sales* 11,875,650
SIC 5085 Industrial supplies
Donald Legere
William Legere

D-U-N-S 25-130-3772   (BR)
**OTTAWA CATHOLIC DISTRICT SCHOOL
BOARD**
ST PAUL CATHOLIC HIGH SCHOOL
(*Suby of* OTTAWA CATHOLIC DISTRICT
SCHOOL BOARD)
2675 Draper Ave, Ottawa, ON, K2H 7A1
(613) 820-9705
Emp Here 100
SIC 8211 Elementary and secondary schools
William Barrett

D-U-N-S 20-787-4223   (HQ)
RHODES & WILLIAMS LIMITED
1050 Morrison Dr, Ottawa, ON, K2H 8K7
(613) 226-6590
Sales 120,103,230
SIC 6411 Insurance agents, brokers, and ser-
vice
Trent Young
Cory Young

D-U-N-S 24-886-6105   (HQ)
TECHINSIGHTS INC
(*Suby of* MAPLE BIDCO LIMITED)
1891 Robertson Rd Suite 500, Ottawa, ON,
K2H 5B7
(613) 599-6500
Sales 53,225,370
SIC 8711 Engineering services
Gavin Carter
Michael Mclean
Jason Abt
Andrew Millen

D-U-N-S 24-815-8008   (HQ)
VERITAS TOOLS INC
(*Suby of* LEE VALLEY HOLDINGS LIMITED)
1090 Morrison Dr, Ottawa, ON, K2H 1C2
(613) 596-1922
Emp Here 25   *Sales* 29,187,720
SIC 3423 Hand and edge tools, nec
Leonard Lee
Lillian Lee
Iain Campbell
Robin Lee
Nicole Burns

Ottawa, ON K2J

D-U-N-S 20-137-2067   (SL)
**DUFRESNE PILING COMPANY (1967) LIM-
ITED**
100 Citigate Dr, Ottawa, ON, K2J 6K7
(613) 739-5355
Emp Here 75   *Sales* 18,463,950
SIC 1794 Excavation work
Leonard (Trey) Graham LII
Leonard Graham
Vivianne Gordon
Bill Welch

D-U-N-S 20-442-5144   (HQ)
TOMLINSON, R. W. LIMITED
ONTARIO TRAP ROCK, DIV OF
100 Citigate Dr, Ottawa, ON, K2J 6K7
(613) 822-1867
Emp Here 250   *Sales* 206,554,500
SIC 1411 Dimension stone
Ron Tomlinson
Kevin Cinq-Mars
Christopher Flann
Paul Mccarney
Bert Hendriks
Tim Vizena
Russ Perry

Rob Pierce
Kevin Cinq-Mars
Christopher Flann

Ottawa, ON K2K

D-U-N-S 24-330-3034   (HQ)
ALCATEL-LUCENT CANADA INC
NOKIA NETWORKS
(*Suby of* NOKIA OYJ)
600 March Rd, Ottawa, ON, K2K 2T6
(613) 591-3600
Emp Here 10   *Sales* 28,559,000
SIC 4899 Communication services, nec
Tracy Darling
Richard Harold
James Watt
Kenneth Bellows

D-U-N-S 20-336-8258   (SL)
BETTER SOFTWARE COMPANY INC, THE
303 Terry Fox Dr Suite 101, Ottawa, ON, K2K
3J1
(613) 627-3506
Emp Here 85   *Sales* 18,177,335
SIC 7372 Prepackaged software
Steve Cody
Alex Katz
Bernie Zeisig
Leo Lax
Charles Broderick
Hicham Adra

D-U-N-S 20-379-4185   (BR)
BWXT ITG CANADA, INC
(*Suby of* BWX TECHNOLOGIES, INC.)
447 March Rd, Ottawa, ON, K2K 1X8
(613) 592-3400
Emp Here 150
SIC 2834 Pharmaceutical preparations
Thomas Burnett

D-U-N-S 25-098-3251   (SL)
CIENA CANADA, INC
(*Suby of* CIENA CORPORATION)
385 Terry Fox Dr, Ottawa, ON, K2K 0L1
(613) 670-2000
Emp Here 342   *Sales* 96,059,934
SIC 3571 Electronic computers
Gary Smith
Stephen Alexander
David Rothenstein
James Jr Moylan
James Frodsham
Jane Hobbs
Scott Mcfeely
Jason Phipps
Rick Hamilton
Andrew Petrik

D-U-N-S 20-288-3708   (BR)
CMC ELECTRONIQUE INC
(*Suby of* TRANSDIGM GROUP INCORPO-
RATED)
415 Legget Dr, Ottawa, ON, K2K 2B2
(613) 592-6500
Emp Here 120
SIC 8711 Engineering services
Jean Michel Comtois

D-U-N-S 24-481-1196   (HQ)
**CONVERSANT INTELLECTUAL PROP-
ERTY MANAGEMENT INC**
(*Suby of* STERLING PARTNERS, LLC)
515 Legget Dr Suite 704, Ottawa, ON, K2K
3G4
(613) 576-3000
Emp Here 62   *Sales* 14,091,918
SIC 3825 Instruments to measure electricity
John Lindgren
Carl Schlachte
Normand Yvon Paquette
Barry Joel Reiter
Jerry Woodrow Mills

Ian Giffen
John Peter Veschi

D-U-N-S 20-104-7623   (HQ)
FIDUS SYSTEMS INC
375 Terry Fox Dr, Ottawa, ON, K2K 0J8
(613) 595-0507
Emp Here 50   *Sales* 11,618,035
SIC 8711 Engineering services
Alan Coady
Vicki Coughey
Cameron Redmond
Patrick Gurtler
Scott Turnbull
Mazen Matar
Barbara Szilagyi
Donna Blair
Julian Oscroft
Michael Wakim

D-U-N-S 25-168-0591   (SL)
FLEXTRONICS EMS CANADA INC
(*Suby of* FLEX LTD.)
1280 Teron Rd, Ottawa, ON, K2K 2C1
(613) 895-2056
Emp Here 100   *Sales* 17,873,900
SIC 8711 Engineering services
Yvan Girard
Paul Reid
Carrie Schiff

D-U-N-S 20-552-9410   (HQ)
INNOVAPOST INC
(*Suby of* GOVERNMENT OF CANADA)
365 March Rd, Ottawa, ON, K2K 3N5
(613) 270-6262
Emp Here 290   *Sales* 216,629,280
SIC 7372 Prepackaged software
Bradley Smith
Mary Traversy
Wayne Cheeseman
Barbara Mackenzie
Roslyn Samtleben
Doug Ettinger
John Ferguson

D-U-N-S 24-745-2014   (BR)
METCALFE REALTY COMPANY LIMITED
LOCH MARCH GOLF & COUNTRY CLUB
(*Suby of* FARRELL INVESTMENTS LTD)
1755 Old Carp Rd, Ottawa, ON, K2K 1X7
(613) 839-5401
Emp Here 100
SIC 7992 Public golf courses
Mark Fuller

D-U-N-S 20-378-3287   (SL)
NOKIA CANADA INC
600 March Rd, Ottawa, ON, K2K 2T6
(613) 591-3600
Emp Here 100   *Sales* 18,479,800
SIC 4899 Communication services, nec
Ken Bellows
Richard Herald
Tracy Darling

D-U-N-S 24-359-8815   (HQ)
PRONTOFORMS CORPORATION
2500 Solandt Suite 250, Ottawa, ON, K2K
3G5
(613) 599-8288
Emp Here 5   *Sales* 12,132,506
SIC 7371 Custom computer programming ser-
vices
Alvaro Pombo
Mansell Nelson
Marty Gowling
Glenn Chenier
Mark Scott
Lisa Scian
David Croucher
Terence Matthews
Michael Cristinziano
Jon Shantz

D-U-N-S 20-325-0931   (HQ)
SOLARWINDS MSP CANADA ULC

(Suby of SOLARWINDS CORPORATION)
450 March Rd 2nd Fl, Ottawa, ON, K2K 3K2
(613) 592-6676
Sales 37,909,410
SIC 8731 Commercial physical research
Jp Jauvin
John Blaine
Frank Colletti
Derik Belair

D-U-N-S 25-504-2905   (SL)
TERLIN CONSTRUCTION LTD
(Suby of EMBRYLIN ESTATE LTD)
1240 Teron Road, Ottawa, ON, K2K 2B5
(613) 821-0768
Emp Here 45   Sales 25,665,210
SIC 1542 Nonresidential construction, nec
Terry Mclaughlin

Ottawa, ON K2M

D-U-N-S 25-389-7391   (SL)
IFS AEROSPACE & DEFENSE LTD
(Suby of IGT HOLDING I SARL)
175 Terence Matthews Cres, Ottawa, ON,
K2M 1W8
(613) 576-2480
Emp Here 250   Sales 60,648,160
SIC 7371 Custom computer programming services
Scott Helmer
Jeffrey Cass
Jennifer Ross-Carriere
Derek Menard

Ottawa, ON K2P

D-U-N-S 24-358-3700   (HQ)
1750769 ONTARIO INC
THE WHALESBONE OYSTER HOUSE
504a Kent St, Ottawa, ON, K2P 2B9
(613) 231-3474
Sales 10,702,480
SIC 5146 Fish and seafoods
Joshua Bishop

D-U-N-S 20-782-4066   (SL)
4089171 CANADA INC
BUILDING & MAINTENANCE INDUSTRIES
(BMI)
207 Bank St Suite 405, Ottawa, ON, K2P 2N2
(613) 235-2126
Emp Here 50   Sales 16,666,650
SIC 1541 Industrial buildings and warehouses
Louis Lemieux

D-U-N-S 24-868-4789   (SL)
595799 ONTARIO LTD
BYTOWN INVESTMENTS
180 Maclaren St Suite 1112, Ottawa, ON, K2P
0L3
(613) 232-1121
Emp Here 29   Sales 12,161,295
SIC 6719 Holding companies, nec
Brian Karam

D-U-N-S 20-442-5847   (HQ)
ADGA GROUP CONSULTANTS INC
110 Argyle Ave, Ottawa, ON, K2P 1B4
(613) 237-3022
Emp Here 100   Sales 50,491,350
SIC 8741 Management services
Francoise Gagnon
John Jarvis
Albert Denis Gagnon

D-U-N-S 20-253-3662   (SL)
BRAHAM & ASSOCIATES INC
251 Bank St, Ottawa, ON, K2P 1X3
(613) 294-4589
Emp Here 15   Sales 10,183,845

SIC 6211 Security brokers and dealers
David Braham

D-U-N-S 20-290-4012   (SL)
C.B.U. PUBLICATIONS LTD
420 O'Connor St Suite 1600, Ottawa, ON, K2P
1W4
(613) 230-0721
Emp Here 75   Sales 12,302,025
SIC 2721 Periodicals
Francis Joseph Clarke

D-U-N-S 24-383-4033   (HQ)
CAMBRIAN TRADING HOUSE LTD
CAMBRIAN FLOWER DISTRIBUTION
153 Gilmour St, Ottawa, ON, K2P 0N8
(613) 233-3111
Emp Here 2   Sales 20,048,040
SIC 5193 Flowers and florists supplies
David Hamilton
Pratyaya Hamilton

D-U-N-S 20-789-5715   (HQ)
CANADIAN EGG MARKETING AGENCY
EGG FARMERS OF CANADA
21 Florence St, Ottawa, ON, K2P 0W6
(613) 238-2514
Sales 201,673,765
SIC 5144 Poultry and poultry products
Peter Clarke
Roger Pelissero
John Penner
Tim Lambert
Neil Newlands
Stephanie Polianski
Alison Evans
Bonnie Cohen
Judi Bundrock

D-U-N-S 24-892-6966   (HQ)
CANADIAN MUSEUM OF NATURE
(Suby of GOVERNMENT OF CANADA)
240 Mcleod St, Ottawa, ON, K2P 2R1
(613) 566-4700
Sales 17,301,900
SIC 8412 Museums and art galleries
Florence Minz

D-U-N-S 20-787-8117   (HQ)
CANADIAN NURSES ASSOCIATION
50 Driveway, Ottawa, ON, K2P 1E2
(613) 232-6424
Emp Here 102
SIC 8748 Business consulting, nec

D-U-N-S 20-213-8843   (SL)
CANADIAN PARALYMPIC COMMITTEE
225 Metcalfe St Suite 310, Ottawa, ON, K2P
1P9
(613) 569-4333
Emp Here 37   Sales 26,240,844
SIC 8699 Membership organizations, nec
Henry Storgaard
Gaetan Tardif
Dale Hooper
Hugues Gibeault
Craig Mccord
Rem Langan
Andrea Carey
Jim Westlake
Josh Van Vries
Carla Qualtrough

D-U-N-S 20-966-4275   (HQ)
**CANADIAN REAL ESTATE ASSOCIATION,
THE**
CREA
200 Catherine St 6h Fl, Ottawa, ON, K2P 2K9
(613) 237-7111
Sales 30,111,108
SIC 8611 Business associations
Gary Simonsen
Andrew Peck
Barbara Sukkau
Jason Stephen
Cliff Iverson
Debra Cowan

D-U-N-S 24-974-4285   (HQ)
CANADIAN RED CROSS SOCIETY, THE
400 Cooper St Suite 8000, Ottawa, ON, K2P
2H8
(613) 740-1900
Emp Here 100   Sales 44,601,297
SIC 8322 Individual and family services
Conrad Sauve
Gavin Giles
Alan Dean
Dennis Chow
Peter Collens
Kathleen Mahoney
Alan Pearson
Harvey Wyers
Tami Kjerulf
Michael Beswick

D-U-N-S 24-634-0335   (SL)
**CANADIAN SOCCER ASSOCIATION IN-
CORPORATED, THE**
237 Metcalfe St, Ottawa, ON, K2P 1R2
(613) 237-7678
Emp Here 35   Sales 13,909,490
SIC 8699 Membership organizations, nec
Dominique Maestracci

D-U-N-S 20-891-6858   (HQ)
CANADIAN UNION OF POSTAL WORKERS
CUPW
377 Bank St, Ottawa, ON, K2P 1Y3
(613) 236-7238
Emp Here 75   Sales 43,574,706
SIC 8631 Labor organizations
Mike Palecek
Jan Simpson
Dave Bleakney
George Floresco
Martin Champagne
Beverley Collins

D-U-N-S 25-132-3390   (SL)
**CATHOLIC IMMIGRATION CENTRE OT-
TAWA**
219 Argyle Ave Suite 500, Ottawa, ON, K2P
2H4
(613) 232-9634
Emp Here 80   Sales 3,551,680
SIC 8331 Job training and related services
Carl Nicholson

D-U-N-S 24-104-8206   (HQ)
**CENTRETOWN CITIZENS OTTAWA COR-
PORATION**
415 Gilmour St Unit 200, Ottawa, ON, K2P
2M8
(613) 234-4065
Sales 19,870,700
SIC 8699 Membership organizations, nec
Luke Pelot
Pam Christie
Andrew Mcneil

D-U-N-S 20-892-1775   (SL)
**CENTRETOWN   COMMUNITY   HEALTH
CENTRE**
420 Cooper St, Ottawa, ON, K2P 2N6
(613) 233-4443
Emp Here 80   Sales 6,010,320
SIC 8093 Specialty outpatient clinics, nec
Jeff Morrison
Mike Perry
Donald Shultz
Andrea Madan
Angela Saunders
Marita Killen
Michael Smith
John Julian
Brenda Emerson
Diane Caulfeild

D-U-N-S 20-576-7312   (BR)
CIBC WORLD MARKETS INC
CIBC WOOD GUNDY
(Suby of CANADIAN IMPERIAL BANK OF
COMMERCE)
150 Elgin St, Ottawa, ON, K2P 1L4

(613) 237-5775
Emp Here 100
SIC 6211 Security brokers and dealers
Steve Gallant

D-U-N-S 24-947-4651   (SL)
CLARIDGE HOMES CORPORATION
210 Gladstone Ave Suite 2001, Ottawa, ON,
K2P 0Y6
(613) 233-6030
Emp Here 90   Sales 18,349,470
SIC 6553 Cemetery subdividers and developers
William Malhotra
Josh Frenkel

D-U-N-S 25-973-6239   (HQ)
CLV GROUP INC
485 Bank St Suite 200, Ottawa, ON, K2P 1Z2
(613) 728-2000
Sales 135,225,600
SIC 6531 Real estate agents and managers
Jacie Levinson
Mike Mcgahan

D-U-N-S 24-366-5825   (HQ)
CMI INTERLANGUES INC
INTERLANGUES
412 Maclaren St, Ottawa, ON, K2P 0M8
(613) 236-3763
Emp Here 30   Sales 14,175,222
SIC 8299 Schools and educational services,
nec
Christiane Millet
Claude Tourigny

D-U-N-S 20-014-2631   (SL)
**CO-OPERATIVE DEVELOPMENT FOUNDA-
TION OF CANADA**
275 Bank St Suite 400, Ottawa, ON, K2P 2L6
(613) 238-6711
Emp Here 26   Sales 18,439,512
SIC 8699 Membership organizations, nec
Kelly Mcgiffin
Korinne Collins
Mark Needham
Benoit Andre
Michele Aasgard
Amyn Hyder Ali
Donna Miller
Gioconda Ortega-Alarie
Tracey Kliesch
Erin Hancock

D-U-N-S 25-809-1610   (SL)
**COLDWELL BANKER RHODES & COM-
PANY LTD**
COLDWELL BANKER RHODES & COM-
PANY
100 Argyle Ave, Ottawa, ON, K2P 1B6
(613) 236-9551
Emp Here 60   Sales 16,305,360
SIC 6531 Real estate agents and managers
James Mckeown

D-U-N-S 20-903-6821   (HQ)
DAIRY FARMERS OF CANADA
21 Florence St, Ottawa, ON, K2P 0W6
(613) 236-9997
Sales 81,013,933
SIC 8611 Business associations
Pierre Lampron
Reint-Jan Dykstra
Ralph Dietrich
Burno Letendre
David Wiens
Albert Fledderus
Jeff Peddle
Gerrit Damsteegt
Nick Thurler
David Janssens

D-U-N-S 25-571-6250   (BR)
**DISTRIBUTEL   COMMUNICATIONS   LIM-
ITED**
(Suby of DISTRIBUTEL COMMUNICATIONS
LIMITED)
177 Nepean St Unit 300, Ottawa, ON, K2P

0B4
(613) 237-7055
Emp Here 100
SIC 4899 Communication services, nec
Jacqui Irving

D-U-N-S 25-130-5033   (SL)
EPALS CLASSROOM EXCHANGE INC
EPALS.COM
331 Cooper St Suite 500, Ottawa, ON, K2P
0G5
(613) 562-9847
Emp Here 60   *Sales* 11,087,880
SIC 4813 Telephone communication, except
radio
Jonathan Ewert

D-U-N-S 25-857-2577   (HQ)
ESPIAL GROUP INC
200 Elgin St Suite 1000, Ottawa, ON, K2P 1L5
(613) 230-4770
Emp Here 55   *Sales* 20,218,268
SIC 7371 Custom computer programming ser-
vices
Jaison Dolvane
Yvonne Holland
Michael Mccluskey
Dilshan De Silva
Carl Smith
Kumanan Yogaratnam
Kirk Edwardson

D-U-N-S 20-747-4628   (HQ)
FIDELITAS HOLDING COMPANY LIMITED
*CARTIER PLACE SUITE HOTEL AND RESI-
DENCE*
180 Cooper St, Ottawa, ON, K2P 2L5
(613) 236-5000
Emp Here 80   *Sales* 7,591,920
SIC 7011 Hotels and motels

D-U-N-S 25-157-5841   (HQ)
FOLLETT OF CANADA, INC
(*Suby of* FOLLETT CORPORATION)
381 Kent St Suite 327, Ottawa, ON, K2P 2A8
(613) 230-6148
Emp Here 5   *Sales* 41,047,104
SIC 5942 Book stores
Susan Stephen

D-U-N-S 25-398-7820   (HQ)
G-WLG LP
GOWLINGS
160 Elgin St Suite 2600, Ottawa, ON, K2P 3C3
(613) 233-1781
Sales 67,321,800
SIC 8741 Management services
R. Scott Jolliffe
Karen Byrne

D-U-N-S 20-137-4857   (HQ)
GENERAL BEARING SERVICE INC
PETERBOROUGH BEARINGS
490 Kent St, Ottawa, ON, K2P 2B7
(613) 238-8100
Emp Here 15   *Sales* 44,177,418
SIC 5085 Industrial supplies
Pierre Bouchard

D-U-N-S 24-174-9493   (HQ)
GOWLINGS CANADA INC
160 Elgin St Suite 200, Ottawa, ON, K2P 2C4
(613) 233-1781
Sales 27,720,500
SIC 8111 Legal services
R. Scott Jolliffe
Domenic Crolla
Sharon Mitchell
Stephen Clarke

D-U-N-S 24-482-0940   (SL)
GREENBERG NAIMER GROUP
EMBASSY HOTEL & SUITES
25 Cartier St, Ottawa, ON, K2P 1J2
(613) 237-2111
Emp Here 40   *Sales* 11,377,480
SIC 6512 Nonresidential building operators
Sam Greenberg

Gerald Naimer

D-U-N-S 20-578-3439   (SL)
HOLINSHED RESEARCH GROUP INC
200 Elgin St Suite 1102, Ottawa, ON, K2P 1L5

Emp Here 50   *Sales* 11,932,165
SIC 8732 Commercial nonphysical research
Frank Hall

D-U-N-S 24-288-8287   (SL)
I O T A INFORMATION MANAGEMENT LTD
150 Metcalfe St, Ottawa, ON, K2P 1P1

Emp Here 100   *Sales* 3,783,746
SIC 7379 Computer related services, nec

D-U-N-S 24-334-1406   (SL)
**INTERRENT REAL ESTATE INVESTMENT
TRUST**
485 Bank St Suite 207, Ottawa, ON, K2P 1Z2
(613) 569-5699
Emp Here 273   *Sales* 150,148,089
SIC 6726 Investment offices, nec
Mike Mcgahan
Brad Cutsey
Brian Awrey
Catherine Wood
Dave Nevis
Curt Millar
Will Chan
Victor Stone
Paul Amirault
Paul Bouzanis

D-U-N-S 20-104-7003   (HQ)
IT/NET GROUP INC
150 Elgin St Suite 1800, Ottawa, ON, K2P 2P8
(613) 234-8638
Emp Here 89
SIC 6712 Bank holding companies
Alex Beraskow

D-U-N-S 20-918-8320   (BR)
KPMG LLP
(*Suby of* KPMG LLP)
160 Elgin St Suite 2000, Ottawa, ON, K2P 2P7
(613) 212-5764
Emp Here 200
SIC 8721 Accounting, auditing, and book-
keeping
Robert Wener

D-U-N-S 20-349-2004   (SL)
MASSINE ENTERPRISES INC
*MASSINE'S YOUR INDEPENDENT GRO-
CER*
296 Bank St, Ottawa, ON, K2P 1X8
(613) 234-8692
Emp Here 190   *Sales* 55,760,630
SIC 5411 Grocery stores
David Massine
Kelly Dexter

D-U-N-S 20-718-9437   (SL)
NUTRITION INTERNATIONAL
180 Elgin St 10 Fl, Ottawa, ON, K2P 2K3
(613) 782-6800
Emp Here 70   *Sales* 46,823,560
SIC 7389 Business services, nec
Joel Spicer

D-U-N-S 24-267-9470   (SL)
OTTAWA TOURISM
150 Elgin St Suite 1405, Ottawa, ON, K2P 1L4
(613) 237-5150
Emp Here 31   *Sales* 13,748,190
SIC 7389 Business services, nec
Michael Arokate
Janet Wlodarczyk

D-U-N-S 25-458-9328   (SL)
OTTAWA X PRESS PUBLISHING INC
309 Cooper St Suite 401, Ottawa, ON, K2P
0G5
(613) 237-8226
Emp Here 30   *Sales* 22,275,600
SIC 5192 Books, periodicals, and newspapers

Dara Mottahed

D-U-N-S 24-101-9207   (HQ)
**OTTAWA YOUNG MEN'S AND YOUNG
WOMEN'S CHRISTIAN ASSOCIATION**
YMCA
180 Argyle Ave Suite 1622, Ottawa, ON, K2P
1B7
(613) 237-1320
Emp Here 100   *Sales* 93,644,400
SIC 8621 Professional organizations
Deirdre Speers
Ian Cullwick
Colin Potts

D-U-N-S 25-504-0107   (BR)
**OTTAWA-CARLETON DISTRICT SCHOOL
BOARD**
LISGAR COLLEGIATE INSTITUTE
(*Suby of* OTTAWA-CARLETON DISTRICT
SCHOOL BOARD)
29 Lisgar St, Ottawa, ON, K2P 0B9
(613) 239-2696
Emp Here 85
SIC 8211 Elementary and secondary schools
Patsy Agard

D-U-N-S 25-487-3185   (SL)
PROPERTIES GROUP LTD, THE
236 Metcalfe St, Ottawa, ON, K2P 1R3
(613) 237-2425
Emp Here 25   *Sales* 10,483,875
SIC 6719 Holding companies, nec
Jules Sigler
Brian Lahey

D-U-N-S 25-144-1598   (SL)
PUBLIC HISTORY INC
331 Cooper St Suite 500, Ottawa, ON, K2P
0G5
(613) 236-0713
Emp Here 65   *Sales* 13,868,270
SIC 8732 Commercial nonphysical research
Fred Hosking
Eric Angel
Katherine O'connor

D-U-N-S 20-893-4893   (HQ)
PUBLIC SERVICE ALLIANCE OF CANADA
233 Gilmour St Suite 402, Ottawa, ON, K2P
0P2
(613) 560-2560
Emp Here 200   *Sales* 82,931,019
SIC 8631 Labor organizations
Robyn Benson
Jeannie Baldwin
Magali Picard
Larry Rousseau
Sharon Desousa
Marianne Hladun
Bob Jackson
Julie Docherty
Chris Aylward
Pierre Chartrand

D-U-N-S 24-727-8344   (HQ)
RE/MAX METRO-CITY REALTY LTD
344 Frank St, Ottawa, ON, K2P 0Y1
(613) 288-3300
Emp Here 20   *Sales* 73,697,952
SIC 6531 Real estate agents and managers
Heather F Skuce

D-U-N-S 24-366-6922   (SL)
RENSERVALL LIMITED
BELL BAKER
116 Lisgar St Suite 500, Ottawa, ON, K2P 0C2
(613) 237-3444
Emp Here 27   *Sales* 11,322,585
SIC 6712 Bank holding companies
Joyce Clark
Patricia Ann Webber
Mary Mcininch

D-U-N-S 24-392-7212   (HQ)
SHOPIFY INC
150 Elgin St 8th Floor, Ottawa, ON, K2P 1L4

(613) 241-2828
Emp Here 1,800   *Sales* 1,073,229,000
SIC 7374 Data processing and preparation
Tobi Lutke
Joe Frasca
Brittany Forsyth
Jean-Michel Lemieux
David Lennie
Toby Shannan
Harley Finkelstein
Amy Shapero
Craig Miller
Jeff Weiser

D-U-N-S 24-105-3685   (SL)
**SMITH PETRIE CARR & SCOTT INSUR-
ANCE BROKERS LTD**
359 Kent St Suite 600, Ottawa, ON, K2P 0R6
(613) 237-2871
Emp Here 25   *Sales* 14,498,100
SIC 6411 Insurance agents, brokers, and ser-
vice
Alan Smith
Robert (Bob) Petrie
Brian Scott
Michael Derlis

D-U-N-S 25-103-7222   (SL)
SOCIETE GAMMA INC
240 Bank St Suite 600, Ottawa, ON, K2P 1X4
(613) 233-4407
Emp Here 75   *Sales* 33,691,425
SIC 7389 Business services, nec
Gilles Gamas
Micheline M. Cloutier

D-U-N-S 20-188-3720   (HQ)
TARTAN HOMES CORPORATION
233 Metcalfe St Suite 11, Ottawa, ON, K2P
2C2
(613) 238-2040
Emp Here 30   *Sales* 12,754,760
SIC 1521 Single-family housing construction
Larry Bruce
Ian Nicol
Wesley M Nicol

D-U-N-S 20-507-3406   (HQ)
TELESAT CANADA
(*Suby of* RED ISLE PRIVATE INVESTMENTS
INC)
160 Elgin St Suite 2100, Ottawa, ON, K2P 2P7
(613) 748-0123
Emp Here 87   *Sales* 726,602,054
SIC 4841 Cable and other pay television ser-
vices
Dan Goldberg
Michele Beck
Michel Cayouette
Chris Difrancesco
Patrick Enright
John Flaherty
Michael Bolitho
David Wendling

D-U-N-S 24-952-3416   (HQ)
TRINITY DEVELOPMENT GROUP INC
359 Kent St Suite 400, Ottawa, ON, K2P 0R6

Emp Here 10   *Sales* 14,592,661
SIC 1542 Nonresidential construction, nec
John Ruddy
Dale Proulx

D-U-N-S 20-769-8358   (HQ)
VF SERVICES (CANADA) INC
(*Suby of* VF WORLDWIDE HOLDINGS LTD)
280 Metcalfe St Suite 200, Ottawa, ON, K2P
1R7
(613) 686-9911
Emp Here 3   *Sales* 16,223,360
SIC 8748 Business consulting, nec
Alok Singhal
Olivier De Canson
Radhakrishna Sevgur Bhandary

D-U-N-S 20-890-1249   (SL)
W. H. SCRIVENS & SON LIMITED

▲ Public Company   ■ Public Company Family Member   **HQ** Headquarters   **BR** Branch   **SL** Single Location

SCRIVENS FAMILY OF COMPANIES
270 Maclaren St, Ottawa, ON, K2P 0M3
(613) 236-9101
Emp Here 30   *Sales* 17,397,720
SIC 6411 Insurance agents, brokers, and service
  Peter Scrivens
  Michael Scrivens
  Ole Jensen

Ottawa, ON K2R

D-U-N-S 20-352-3345   (SL)
MOTOR WORKS ONE HOLDINGS INC
BARRHAVEN CHRYSLER DODGE JEEP RAM
510 Motor Works Pvt, Ottawa, ON, K2R 0A5
(613) 656-6526
Emp Here 40   *Sales* 19,923,120
SIC 5511 New and used car dealers
  Shiv Dilawri

D-U-N-S 20-352-3329   (SL)
MOTOR WORKS TWO HOLDINGS INC
BARRHAVEN MAZDA
520 Motor Works Pvt, Ottawa, ON, K2R 0A5
(613) 656-6536
Emp Here 40   *Sales* 19,923,120
SIC 5511 New and used car dealers
  Shiv Dilawri

Ottawa, ON K2V

D-U-N-S 24-436-2893   (HQ)
CALIAN GROUP LTD
770 Palladium Dr, Ottawa, ON, K2V 1C8
(613) 599-8600
Emp Here 500   *Sales* 219,600,542
SIC 8711 Engineering services
  Kevin Ford
  Jacqueline Gauthier
  Sandra Cote
  Scott Murray
  Jerry Johnston
  Lynn Stevens
  Tom Barron
  Kenneth Loeb
  Richard Vickers
  George Weber

D-U-N-S 25-150-7109   (HQ)
CALIAN LTD
(*Suby of* CALIAN GROUP LTD)
4-770 Palladium Dr, Ottawa, ON, K2V 1C8
(613) 599-8600
Emp Here 100   *Sales* 735,996,800
SIC 4899 Communication services, nec
  Kevin Ford

D-U-N-S 20-798-3508   (SL)
DNA GENOTEK INC
(*Suby of* ORASURE TECHNOLOGIES, INC.)
500 Palladium Dr Unit 3000, Ottawa, ON, K2V 1C2
(613) 723-5757
Emp Here 80   *Sales* 18,183,120
SIC 3829 Measuring and controlling devices, nec
  Ian Curry
  Brian Smith
  Rafal Iwasiow
  Scott Rabuka

Otterville, ON N0J

D-U-N-S 24-938-1062   (BR)
FLEETWOOD METAL INDUSTRIES INC
(*Suby of* AK STEEL HOLDING CORPORA-

TION)
71 Dover St, Otterville, ON, N0J 1R0
(519) 879-6577
Emp Here 90
SIC 3469 Metal stampings, nec
  Jeff Blodgett

Owen Sound, ON N4K

D-U-N-S 24-826-5746   (HQ)
BAYSHORE BROADCASTING CORPORATION
CFOS RADIO
270 9 St E, Owen Sound, ON, N4K 5P5
(519) 376-2030
Emp Here 40   *Sales* 13,708,320
SIC 4832 Radio broadcasting stations
  Douglas Caldwell
  Ross Kentner

D-U-N-S 24-269-8236   (BR)
BELLWYCK PACKAGING INC
BELLWYCK PACKAGING SOLUTIONS
(*Suby of* BELLWYCK PACKAGING INC)
Gd, Owen Sound, ON, N4K 5N9
(800) 265-3708
Emp Here 150
SIC 2657 Folding paperboard boxes
  Jeff Sziklai

D-U-N-S 20-648-7626   (BR)
BLUEWATER DISTRICT SCHOOL BOARD
1550 8th St E, Owen Sound, ON, N4K 0A2
(519) 376-2010
Emp Here 100
SIC 8211 Elementary and secondary schools
  Yeo Jim

D-U-N-S 25-145-3767   (HQ)
CARRUTHERS NICOL INSURANCE INC
1230 2nd Ave E, Owen Sound, ON, N4K 2J3
(519) 376-5350
Emp Here 1   *Sales* 25,441,800
SIC 6411 Insurance agents, brokers, and service
  Michael Carruthers

D-U-N-S 24-829-1130   (HQ)
COMMUNITY LIVING OWEN SOUND AND DISTRICT
769 4th Ave E, Owen Sound, ON, N4K 2N5
(519) 371-9251
Emp Here 95   *Sales* 34,580,356
SIC 8399 Social services, nec
  Rick Hill

D-U-N-S 20-560-2790   (BR)
CONTITECH CANADA, INC
(*Suby of* CONTINENTAL AG)
3225 3rd Ave E, Owen Sound, ON, N4K 5N3

Emp Here 120
SIC 3714 Motor vehicle parts and accessories
  James Howell

D-U-N-S 24-991-9945   (SL)
ERSSER, A. J. HOLDINGS LTD
CANADIAN TIRE OWEN SOUND
1605 16th St E, Owen Sound, ON, N4K 5N3
(519) 376-5220
Emp Here 100   *Sales* 62,928,000
SIC 5531 Auto and home supply stores
  Anthony Ersser

D-U-N-S 24-125-8805   (BR)
FIRSTCANADA ULC
FIRST STUDENT CANADA
(*Suby of* FIRSTGROUP PLC)
2180 20th St E, Owen Sound, ON, N4K 5P7
(519) 376-5712
Emp Here 75
SIC 4151 School buses
  Jane Macivor

D-U-N-S 20-901-0081   (HQ)

GAVILLER & COMPANY LLP
GFS PARTNERSHIP
945 3rd Ave E Suite 201, Owen Sound, ON, N4K 2K8
(519) 376-5850
Emp Here 12   *Sales* 10,454,250
SIC 8721 Accounting, auditing, and book-keeping
  K Miller
  Karen Marcell
  John Bujold
  R Caddo
  Joe Heisz
  David Todd
  J H Kearns
  R J Turbitt
  J E Currie
  Sue Martin

D-U-N-S 20-534-5788   (HQ)
GEORGIAN BAY FIRE & SAFETY LTD
1700 20th St E, Owen Sound, ON, N4K 5W9
(519) 376-6120
Emp Here 15   *Sales* 83,436,000
SIC 5099 Durable goods, nec
  Timothy Mckay
  Jeff Taylor

D-U-N-S 24-059-4317   (HQ)
GREY BRUCE HEALTH SERVICES
GBHS LION'S HEAD HOSPITAL
1800 8th St E, Owen Sound, ON, N4K 6M9
(519) 376-2121
Emp Here 850   *Sales* 152,834,880
SIC 8062 General medical and surgical hospitals
  Maureen Solecki
  Brenda Kearney
  Mark Ostland
  Martin Mazza
  Rebecca Cummings
  Judy Shearer
  Tracey Neifer

D-U-N-S 20-772-1494   (HQ)
GREY COUNTY TRANSPORTAION AND PUBLIC SAFETY
595 9th Ave E, Owen Sound, ON, N4K 3E3
(519) 376-2205
Emp Here 1   *Sales* 15,146,520
SIC 1611 Highway and street construction
  Pat Hoy

D-U-N-S 25-741-2551   (SL)
GREY MOTORS AUTOMOTIVE GROUP LTD
717936 Highway 6 N, Owen Sound, ON, N4K 5W9
(519) 376-2240
Emp Here 25   *Sales* 12,451,950
SIC 5511 New and used car dealers
  Jerry Pfeil

D-U-N-S 20-787-6350   (SL)
HIRE RITE PERSONNEL LTD
366 9th St E, Owen Sound, ON, N4K 1P1
(519) 376-6662
Emp Here 95   *Sales* 37,589,410
SIC 7381 Detective and armored car services
  Robin Brent

D-U-N-S 20-107-1185   (BR)
HOME DEPOT OF CANADA INC
HOME DEPOT
(*Suby of* THE HOME DEPOT INC)
1590 20th Ave E, Owen Sound, ON, N4K 5N3
(519) 372-3970
Emp Here 150
SIC 5251 Hardware stores
  Dave Pereira

D-U-N-S 24-412-7445   (BR)
IMPRIMERIES TRANSCONTINENTAL 2005 S.E.N.C.
RBW GRAPHICS
(*Suby of* IMPRIMERIES TRANSCONTINENTAL 2005 S.E.N.C.)
2049 20th St E, Owen Sound, ON, N4K 5R2

---

(519) 376-8330
Emp Here 600
SIC 2732 Book printing
  Derek Smith

D-U-N-S 25-861-9576   (BR)
IMPRIMERIES TRANSCONTINENTAL INC
TRANSCONTINENTAL PRINTING INC
(*Suby of* TRANSCONTINENTAL INC)
1590 20th St E, Owen Sound, ON, N4K 5R2
(519) 371-5171
Emp Here 600
SIC 2752 Commercial printing, lithographic
  Derek Smith

D-U-N-S 25-174-0031   (BR)
ITW CANADA INC
HOBART FOOD EQUIPMENT GROUP (OWEN SOUND) DIV OF
(*Suby of* ITW CANADA INC)
2875 East Bay Shore Road, Owen Sound, ON, N4K 5P5
(519) 376-8886
Emp Here 200
SIC 3639 Household appliances, nec
  Duane Koebel

D-U-N-S 25-256-0461   (HQ)
J.D. MCARTHUR TIRE SERVICES INC
1066 3rd Ave E, Owen Sound, ON, N4K 2L2
(519) 376-3520
Emp Here 39   *Sales* 47,196,000
SIC 5531 Auto and home supply stores
  James Stewart
  Mary Katherine Mcarthur

D-U-N-S 20-266-8989   (SL)
K C AUTOMOTIVE PARTS INC
222 14th St W Suite 130, Owen Sound, ON, N4K 3X8
(519) 376-2501
Emp Here 26   *Sales* 12,950,028
SIC 5531 Auto and home supply stores
  Tim Cox

D-U-N-S 20-982-9910   (SL)
K. C.'S AUTOMOTIVE INC
K. C. AUTO
222r 14th St W, Owen Sound, ON, N4K 3X8
(519) 376-2501
Emp Here 40   *Sales* 14,568,600
SIC 5013 Motor vehicle supplies and new parts
  Kenneth (Ken) Morrison

D-U-N-S 20-879-5088   (SL)
LEE MANOR HOME FOR THE AGED
(*Suby of* CORPORATION OF THE COUNTY OF GREY)
875 6th St E, Owen Sound, ON, N4K 5W5
(519) 376-4420
Emp Here 150
SIC 8051 Skilled nursing care facilities
  Jim Wilson

D-U-N-S 20-607-1482   (SL)
MACDONNELL FUELS LIMITED
317504 Hwy 6 & 10, Owen Sound, ON, N4K 5N6
(519) 376-1916
Emp Here 20   *Sales* 20,656,160
SIC 5172 Petroleum products, nec
  Gary Macdonnell

D-U-N-S 20-901-8464   (HQ)
MACLEAN ENGINEERING & MARKETING CO. LIMITED
1000 6th St E, Owen Sound, ON, N4K 1H1
(705) 445-5707
Emp Here 160   *Sales* 70,219,250
SIC 3532 Mining machinery
  Donald Maclean
  Kevin Maclean
  Casey Verwood
  Bob Wraight
  David Jacques

D-U-N-S 25-300-0731   (BR)
METRO ONTARIO INC

METRO
(*Suby of* METRO INC)
1070 2nd Ave E, Owen Sound, ON, N4K 2H7
(519) 371-0222
Emp Here 85
SIC 5411 Grocery stores
John Garfield

D-U-N-S 20-139-7734   (HQ)
OWEN SOUND LEDGEROCK LIMITED
138436 Ledgerock Rd, Owen Sound, ON, N4K 5P7
(519) 376-0366
Emp Here 70   *Sales* 13,441,425
SIC 3281 Cut stone and stone products
Thomas Stobbe
Lynda Grimoldby
Harold Stobbe

D-U-N-S 20-139-7742   (SL)
OWEN SOUND MOTORS LIMITED
WRIGHT, HAL CHEVROLET CADILLAC
202423 Sunset Strip Hwy 6&21, Owen Sound, ON, N4K 5N7
(519) 376-5580
Emp Here 25   *Sales* 12,451,950
SIC 5511 New and used car dealers
William Wright
Helen Wright
Edward Wright

D-U-N-S 20-139-6926   (SL)
PENINSULA MOTOR SALES LTD
PENINSULA FORD LINCOLN
202392 Sunset Strip, Owen Sound, ON, N4K 5N7
(519) 376-3252
Emp Here 90   *Sales* 56,635,200
SIC 5511 New and used car dealers
Kelly Jennings
Brian Leggat
Craig Beck

D-U-N-S 20-531-1749   (BR)
PPG CANADA INC
(*Suby of* PPG INDUSTRIES, INC.)
1799 20th St E, Owen Sound, ON, N4K 2C3

Emp Here 180
SIC 3211 Flat glass
Tom Closs

D-U-N-S 24-119-3007   (BR)
REVERA LONG TERM CARE INC
SUMMIT PLACE
(*Suby of* GOVERNMENT OF CANADA)
850 4th St E, Owen Sound, ON, N4K 6A3
(519) 376-3213
Emp Here 200
SIC 8051 Skilled nursing care facilities
Diane Kiss

D-U-N-S 20-642-4090   (SL)
SERVICEMASTER OF OWEN SOUND
107 Jason St Unit 1, Owen Sound, ON, N4K 5N7

Emp Here 20   *Sales* 11,598,480
SIC 6411 Insurance agents, brokers, and service
Bud Vallee

D-U-N-S 20-059-6547   (SL)
STEVE'S NO FRILLS LTD
1020 10th St W, Owen Sound, ON, N4K 5S1
(866) 987-6453
Emp Here 49   *Sales* 13,433,448
SIC 5411 Grocery stores
Steve Gillespie

D-U-N-S 24-683-8903   (HQ)
TROY LIFE & FIRE SAFETY LTD
1042 2nd Ave E, Owen Sound, ON, N4K 2H7
(519) 371-4747
Emp Here 40   *Sales* 169,280,000
SIC 1711 Plumbing, heating, air-conditioning
James Mccoubrey
David Heaps

Geoff Bourne
Jeff Vautour
Flaviano Quiquero
Nell Jeffrey
Michael Finlay

D-U-N-S 24-098-7227   (BR)
VICTORIAN ORDER OF NURSES FOR CANADA
VON GREY BRUCE DISTRICT
(*Suby of* VICTORIAN ORDER OF NURSES FOR CANADA)
1280 20th St E, Owen Sound, ON, N4K 6H6
(519) 376-5895
Emp Here 150
SIC 8611 Business associations
Christine Vallis-Tage

D-U-N-S 25-946-1853   (BR)
WAL-MART CANADA CORP
WAL MART
(*Suby of* WALMART INC.)
1555 18th Ave E, Owen Sound, ON, N4K 0E2
(519) 371-6900
Emp Here 250
SIC 5311 Department stores
Jason Marton

Oxford Station, ON K0G

D-U-N-S 24-271-0556   (HQ)
HARVEX AGROMART INC
2109b County Road 20 Rr 2, Oxford Station, ON, K0G 1T0
(613) 258-3445
Emp Here 15   *Sales* 18,563,000
SIC 5191 Farm supplies
Kevin Hill

Pain Court, ON N0P

D-U-N-S 25-061-6935   (SL)
BRAD, D FARM LTD
4939 Bradley Line, Pain Court, ON, N0P 1Z0

Emp Here 38   *Sales* 13,013,746
SIC 0161 Vegetables and melons
D Curtis Bradley
David A Bradley
Barbara Bradley
M Jane Bradley

D-U-N-S 24-099-7429   (SL)
LAPRISE FARMS LTD
7359 Maple Line Suite 1, Pain Court, ON, N0P 1Z0
(519) 352-2968
Emp Here 30   *Sales* 10,274,010
SIC 0191 General farms, primarily crop
Jean Laprise

D-U-N-S 24-424-4963   (SL)
NATURE'S FINEST PRODUCE LTD
6874 Pain Court Line Rr 1, Pain Court, ON, N0P 1Z0
(519) 380-9520
Emp Here 45   *Sales* 12,336,840
SIC 5431 Fruit and vegetable markets
Jason Stallaert
Kevin Stallaert

Palmer Rapids, ON K0J

D-U-N-S 20-045-2733   (SL)
BOUNDLESS ADVENTURES INC
THE BOUNDLESS SCHOOL
7513 River Rd, Palmer Rapids, ON, K0J 2E0
(613) 758-2702
Emp Here 40   *Sales* 12,585,280

SIC 8699 Membership organizations, nec
Steven Gottlieb

D-U-N-S 20-578-3236   (HQ)
GULICK FOREST PRODUCTS LIMITED
6216 Palmer Rd, Palmer Rapids, ON, K0J 2E0
(613) 758-2369
Sales 15,651,090
SIC 5031 Lumber, plywood, and millwork
Glen Gulick
Elizabeth (Betty) Gulick
Grant Gulick
Darlene Coulis

D-U-N-S 20-139-9862   (SL)
NEUMAN, THOMAS J LIMITED
6421 Palmer Rd, Palmer Rapids, ON, K0J 2E0
(613) 758-2555
Emp Here 25   *Sales* 11,179,350
SIC 5031 Lumber, plywood, and millwork
Darwyn Neuman

Palmerston, ON N0G

D-U-N-S 24-993-2435   (SL)
C & M SEEDS MANUFACTURING INC
C & M SEEDS
6180 5th Line Rr 3, Palmerston, ON, N0G 2P0
(519) 343-2126
Emp Here 25   *Sales* 18,563,000
SIC 5191 Farm supplies
John Mclaughlin
Jim Mclaughlin
Anne Schnider

D-U-N-S 25-469-3575   (HQ)
CHALMERS FUELS INC
6630 Hwy 23, Palmerston, ON, N0G 2P0
(519) 343-3023
Sales 22,043,235
SIC 5983 Fuel oil dealers
Nick Brouwer

D-U-N-S 20-844-6252   (SL)
PALEMERSTON AND DISTRICT HOSPITAL
500 Whites Rd Rr 3, Palmerston, ON, N0G 2P0
(519) 343-2030
Emp Here 100   *Sales* 10,213,300
SIC 8062 General medical and surgical hospitals
David Craig

D-U-N-S 20-816-8013   (SL)
SHANTI ENTERPRISES LIMITED
ROYAL TERRACE
600 Whites Rd Rr 3, Palmerston, ON, N0G 2P0
(519) 343-2611
Emp Here 80   *Sales* 5,498,640
SIC 8051 Skilled nursing care facilities
Prakash Ramchandani

D-U-N-S 25-173-7300   (HQ)
TG MINTO CORPORATION
TG MINTO
(*Suby of* TOYODA GOSEI CO., LTD.)
300 Toronto St, Palmerston, ON, N0G 2P0
(519) 343-2800
Emp Here 345   *Sales* 83,584,200
SIC 3089 Plastics products, nec
Kirk Brownell
James Whelan
Kurt Weaver
Katsuya Kato
Kenji Hayashi
Yoshiyuki Fujita

D-U-N-S 20-024-9501   (BR)
UPPER GRAND DISTRICT SCHOOL BOARD, THE
NORWELL DISTRICT SECONDARY SCHOOL
(*Suby of* UPPER GRAND DISTRICT SCHOOL BOARD, THE)

Gd, Palmerston, ON, N0G 2P0
(519) 343-3107
Emp Here 80
SIC 8211 Elementary and secondary schools
Heather Pedjase

Paris, ON N3L

D-U-N-S 20-140-1718   (HQ)
ADVANTAGE MAINTENANCE PRODUCTS LTD
105 Scott Ave, Paris, ON, N3L 3K4
(519) 442-7881
Emp Here 30   *Sales* 21,376,170
SIC 5087 Service establishment equipment
Ron G Underwood
John Underwood
Elbert Hendun

D-U-N-S 20-107-2118   (SL)
BAG TEX PACKAGING INC
10 Spruce St, Paris, ON, N3L 1R6
(519) 442-0499
Emp Here 35   *Sales* 26,289,193
SIC 5199 Nondurable goods, nec
Rick Vanhoucke
Tamie Vanhoucke

D-U-N-S 20-735-0836   (HQ)
BLYLEVEN ENTERPRISES INC
WALTER'S GREENHOUSES & GARDEN CENTRE
363 Governors Rd E, Paris, ON, N3L 3E1
(519) 752-4436
Emp Here 5   *Sales* 10,881,537
SIC 5261 Retail nurseries and garden stores
Walter Blyleven
Diane Hutchinson

D-U-N-S 24-571-4030   (SL)
CALENDAR CLUB OF CANADA LIMITED PARTNERSHIP
CALENDAR CLUB OF CANADA
6 Adams St Suite A, Paris, ON, N3L 3X4
(519) 442-8355
Emp Here 50   *Sales* 12,216,400
SIC 5945 Hobby, toy, and game shops
John Edgar
Ken Edgar

D-U-N-S 24-393-1412   (SL)
CIERE, PIETER ENTERPRISES INC
CANADIAN TIRE
31 Mechanic St, Paris, ON, N3L 1K1
(519) 442-2312
Emp Here 30   *Sales* 14,942,340
SIC 5531 Auto and home supply stores
Pieter Ciere

D-U-N-S 24-682-0034   (SL)
COORSTEK ADVANCED MATERIALS HAMILTON ULC
(*Suby of* KEYSTONE HOLDINGS LLC)
45 Curtis Ave N, Paris, ON, N3L 3W1
(519) 442-6395
Emp Here 60   *Sales* 10,753,140
SIC 3255 Clay refractories
Douglas Gamble
Steven H. Rask
James C. Smulders

D-U-N-S 24-767-9694   (BR)
FIRSTCANADA ULC
FIRST STUDENT CANADA
(*Suby of* FIRSTGROUP PLC)
829 Rest Acres Rd, Paris, ON, N3L 3E3

Emp Here 134
SIC 4142 Bus charter service, except local
Angela Asher

D-U-N-S 20-647-4140   (SL)
KENROD STEEL FABRICATING LIMITED
6 Adams St Suite A, Paris, ON, N3L 3X4

---

(519) 865-7921
Emp Here 50   *Sales* 10,141,500
SIC 3499 Fabricated Metal products, nec
Kevin Rodobolski
Steven Rodobolski
Peter Rodobolski
John Rodobolski

D-U-N-S 20-790-2727   (HQ)
MICHAEL'S EQUIPMENT LTD
105 Scott Ave, Paris, ON, N3L 3K4
(519) 442-0317
Emp Here 8   *Sales* 14,250,780
SIC 5087 Service establishment equipment
Sandra Hardy

D-U-N-S 20-140-1023   (SL)
MISS MARY MAXIM LTD
MARY MAXIM
75 Scott Ave, Paris, ON, N3L 3G5
(519) 442-2266
Emp Here 60   *Sales* 14,659,680
SIC 5961 Catalog and mail-order houses
Rusty Mcphedrain
Rick Ellis
Carol Steed

D-U-N-S 20-530-0155   (SL)
PARASOURCE MARKETING AND DISTRI-BUTION LIMITED
55 Woodslee Ave, Paris, ON, N3L 3E5
(519) 442-7853
Emp Here 35   *Sales* 25,988,200
SIC 5192 Books, periodicals, and newspapers
Gregory Tombs
Hardy Willms

D-U-N-S 24-917-4913   (SL)
PARIS SOUTHERN LIGHTS INC
VMS
6 Adams St Suite A, Paris, ON, N3L 3X4
(519) 442-2988
Emp Here 40   *Sales* 29,700,800
SIC 5199 Nondurable goods, nec
John Edgar
Kenneth Edgar
Mary Ellen Edgar
Harold Edgar

D-U-N-S 20-053-9229   (SL)
PARIS SPRING LTD
LEGGETT & PLATT, DIV OF
(*Suby of* LEGGETT & PLATT, INCORPO-RATED)
41 Woodslee Ave, Paris, ON, N3L 3T5
(519) 442-1502
Emp Here 50   *Sales* 23,751,300
SIC 5085 Industrial supplies
Hal Gimmer

D-U-N-S 24-872-8222   (SL)
PARK LANE TERRACE LIMITED
APANS HEALTH SERVICES
295 Grand River St N, Paris, ON, N3L 2N9
(519) 442-2753
Emp Here 175   *Sales* 11,999,050
SIC 8051 Skilled nursing care facilities
Andrew Schuller

D-U-N-S 20-807-3069   (SL)
PATRIOT FORGE OF PARIS INC
(*Suby of* PATRIOT FORGE CO.)
100 Consolidated Dr, Paris, ON, N3L 3T6
(519) 720-1033
Emp Here 200   *Sales* 38,417,000
SIC 3499 Fabricated Metal products, nec
Frank Carchidi

D-U-N-S 20-733-2532   (BR)
SOBEYS CAPITAL INCORPORATED
(*Suby of* EMPIRE COMPANY LIMITED)
307 Grand River St N, Paris, ON, N3L 2N9
(519) 442-4485
Emp Here 250
SIC 5411 Grocery stores
Keith Carter

D-U-N-S 20-037-4577   (HQ)

TRI-LAD FLANGE AND FITTINGS INC
30 Woodslee Ave, Paris, ON, N3L 3N6
(519) 442-6520
Emp Here 1   *Sales* 10,141,500
SIC 3462 Iron and steel forgings
Donald Musson

D-U-N-S 24-632-6854   (SL)
WHITE STORE EQUIPMENT LTD
21 Woodslee Ave, Paris, ON, N3L 3T6
(519) 442-4461
Emp Here 24   *Sales* 17,820,480
SIC 5199 Nondurable goods, nec
Allan White
Lucy White

Parkhill, ON N0M

D-U-N-S 24-487-0051   (HQ)
ANAGO (NON) RESIDENTIAL RESOURCES INC
ANAGO RESOURCES
252 Delaware St, Parkhill, ON, N0M 2K0
(519) 294-6238
Emp Here 4   *Sales* 10,927,940
SIC 8361 Residential care
Mandy Bennett
Sheryl Blair
Ken Brooks

D-U-N-S 25-759-2048   (HQ)
BEECHWOOD AGRI SERVICES INC
123 King St, Parkhill, ON, N0M 2K0
(519) 294-0474
Emp Here 4   *Sales* 10,273,844
SIC 5153 Grain and field beans
Paul Kramer
John O'neil
Fred O'neil

Parry Sound, ON P2A

D-U-N-S 24-363-1553   (HQ)
COMMUNITY LIVING PARRY SOUND
38 Joseph St, Parry Sound, ON, P2A 2G5
(705) 746-9330
Emp Here 1   *Sales* 10,887,984
SIC 8399 Social services, nec
Jo-Anne Demick

D-U-N-S 24-796-4430   (SL)
CROFTERS FOOD LTD
CROFTERS ORGANIC
7 Great North Rd, Parry Sound, ON, P2A 2X8
(705) 746-6301
Emp Here 55   *Sales* 19,012,950
SIC 2033 Canned fruits and specialties
Gerhard Latka

D-U-N-S 24-685-9508   (SL)
D & F CLOUTIER GROUP ENTERPRISES INC
CANADIAN TIRE ASSOC STORE #78
30 Pine Dr, Parry Sound, ON, P2A 3B8
(705) 746-4033
Emp Here 80   *Sales* 21,412,160
SIC 5251 Hardware stores
Don Cloutier

D-U-N-S 20-941-4325   (SL)
DISTRICT OF PARRY SOUND (WEST) BELVEDERE HEIGHTS HOME FOR THE AGED
BELVEDERE HEIGHTS
21 Belvedere Ave, Parry Sound, ON, P2A 2A2
(705) 746-5871
Emp Here 139   *Sales* 8,935,198
SIC 8361 Residential care
Donna Dellio

D-U-N-S 20-912-9381   (SL)

G & B MCNABB LUMBER COMPANY LIM-ITED
G & B BUILDING CENTRE
22 Seguin St, Parry Sound, ON, P2A 1B1
(705) 746-5825
Emp Here 50   *Sales* 12,652,950
SIC 5211 Lumber and other building materials
Roxann Armstrong
James G. Mcnabb

D-U-N-S 20-528-6631   (SL)
GIBSON'S, TIM HOLDINGS PARRY SOUND LTD
1 Mall Dr, Parry Sound, ON, P2A 3A9
(705) 746-8467
Emp Here 100   *Sales* 4,551,900
SIC 5812 Eating places
Tim Gibson

D-U-N-S 20-004-1887   (BR)
KPMG INC
(*Suby of* KPMG INC)
84 James St, Parry Sound, ON, P2A 1T9
(705) 746-9346
Emp Here 280
SIC 8741 Management services
Dan Ball

D-U-N-S 24-514-9141   (SL)
MORGAN, W. S. CONSTRUCTION LIMITED
19 Bowes St, Parry Sound, ON, P2A 2K7
(705) 746-9686
Emp Here 40   *Sales* 18,829,240
SIC 1542 Nonresidential construction, nec
Wendell Morgan
Kirk Gabel

D-U-N-S 20-650-7837   (HQ)
PARRY SOUND DISTRICT SOCIAL SER-VICES ADMINISTRATION BOARD, THE
ONTARIO WORKS
1 Beechwood Dr, Parry Sound, ON, P2A 1J2
(705) 746-7777
Sales 35,201,560
SIC 8399 Social services, nec
Mark Fisher

D-U-N-S 20-519-4280   (BR)
SHAW-ALMEX INDUSTRIES LIMITED
(*Suby of* SHAW-ALMEX INDUSTRIES LIM-ITED)
17 Shaw Almex Dr, Parry Sound, ON, P2A 2X4
(705) 746-5884
Emp Here 75
SIC 3535 Conveyors and conveying equip-ment
Ken Potter

D-U-N-S 24-317-1852   (BR)
WAL-MART CANADA CORP
WALMART
(*Suby of* WALMART INC.)
1 Pine Dr, Parry Sound, ON, P2A 3C3
(705) 746-1573
Emp Here 130
SIC 5311 Department stores
Scott Jones

D-U-N-S 24-538-8632   (HQ)
WEST PARRY SOUND HEALTH CENTRE
6 Albert St, Parry Sound, ON, P2A 3A4
(705) 746-9321
Emp Here 400   *Sales* 66,648,000
SIC 8062 General medical and surgical hospi-tals
Bill Arvantis
Don Brickett
Cheryl Ward
Donald Sanderson

Pefferlaw, ON L0E

D-U-N-S 20-412-0448   (HQ)

BUCHNER MANUFACTURING INC
30004 Hwy 48, Pefferlaw, ON, L0E 1N0
(705) 437-1734
Emp Here 10   *Sales* 10,141,500
SIC 3444 Sheet Metalwork
Gerry Buchner
John Buchner
Roselind Buchner
Andrew Buchner

D-U-N-S 24-893-6994   (SL)
KENSTRUCT LTD
24533 Park Rd, Pefferlaw, ON, L0E 1N0
(416) 505-9737
Emp Here 50   *Sales* 23,536,550
SIC 1542 Nonresidential construction, nec
Ken Jamieson

D-U-N-S 25-099-6881   (SL)
QUINN'S MARINA LTD
25 Quinn Rd, Pefferlaw, ON, L0E 1N0
(705) 437-1122
Emp Here 25   *Sales* 12,451,950
SIC 5551 Boat dealers
James Murphy Quinn
Timothy Quinn
Edward Michael Quinn

Pembroke, ON K8A

D-U-N-S 25-486-4762   (SL)
1048271 ONTARIO INC
MONCION GROCERS RIVERSIDE MARKET
1200 Pembroke St W, Pembroke, ON, K8A 7T1
(613) 735-5335
Emp Here 65   *Sales* 19,076,005
SIC 5411 Grocery stores

D-U-N-S 20-789-6333   (SL)
113559 ONTARIO LIMITED
MONCION GROCERS PEMBROKE MAR-KET
425 Pembroke St E, Pembroke, ON, K8A 3L1
(613) 735-4136
Emp Here 141   *Sales* 41,380,257
SIC 5411 Grocery stores
Omer Moncion
Gilles Moncion
Jean Moncion

D-U-N-S 24-846-6955   (SL)
760496 ONTARIO LTD
SUPPLES LANDING
201 Joseph St, Pembroke, ON, K8A 8J2
(613) 732-0077
Emp Here 50   *Sales* 13,077,650
SIC 6719 Holding companies, nec
John Habraken

D-U-N-S 24-796-8142   (SL)
868971 ONTARIO INC
PEMBROKE IRVING BIG STOP
1751 Paul Martin Dr, Pembroke, ON, K8A 6W5
(613) 735-7066
Emp Here 73   *Sales* 21,423,821
SIC 5411 Grocery stores
Andre Leclair
Brenda Leclair

D-U-N-S 20-586-4494   (SL)
ALLEN VANGUARD CORP
421 Upper Valley Dr, Pembroke, ON, K8A 6W5
(613) 735-3996
Emp Here 74   *Sales* 16,819,386
SIC 3842 Surgical appliances and supplies
Michele Lair

D-U-N-S 24-269-6201   (HQ)
BUTLER CHEVROLET PONTIAC BUICK CADILLAC LTD
(*Suby of* C B HOLDINGS LTD)
1370 Pembroke St W, Pembroke, ON, K8A 7M3

▲ Public Company   ■ Public Company Family Member   **HQ** Headquarters   **BR** Branch   **SL** Single Location

(613) 735-3147
Emp Here 43   *Sales* 44,049,600
SIC 5511 New and used car dealers
 Charles Butler
 Charlotte Macintosh

D-U-N-S 24-341-0573   (BR)
**CAREFOR HEALTH & COMMUNITY SER-
VICES**
(*Suby* of CAREFOR HEALTH & COMMUNITY
SERVICES)
425 Cecelia St, Pembroke, ON, K8A 1S7
(613) 732-9993
Emp Here 100
SIC 8082 Home health care services
 Stephen Perry

D-U-N-S 20-442-9351   (HQ)
**CASSIDY'S TRANSFER & STORAGE LIM-
ITED**
1001 Mckay St, Pembroke, ON, K8A 6X7
(613) 735-6881
Emp Here 95   *Sales* 23,656,190
SIC 4213 Trucking, except local
 Gordon Robinson
 Dale Robinson
 Danny Robinson
 Mark Robinson

D-U-N-S 20-260-7417   (HQ)
**CHILDREN'S AID SOCIETY OF THE
COUNTY OF RENFREW**
FAMILY & CHILDREN'S SERVICES
77 Mary St Suite 100, Pembroke, ON, K8A
5V4
(613) 735-6866
Sales 11,134,840
SIC 8322 Individual and family services
 Jerry Muldoon

D-U-N-S 20-616-1861   (HQ)
CLOUTHIER, BILL & SONS LTD
VALLEY TRUCK & SPRING SERVICE
17 Brandon Ave, Pembroke, ON, K8A 6W5
(613) 735-4194
Sales 13,946,184
SIC 5511 New and used car dealers
 Todd Clouthier
 Brad Clouthier

D-U-N-S 20-005-6690   (SL)
DENANCO SALES LTD
CANADIAN TIRE
1104 Pembroke St E, Pembroke, ON, K8A
8S2
(613) 735-0000
Emp Here 120   *Sales* 75,513,600
SIC 5531 Auto and home supply stores
 Dennis Beech

D-U-N-S 20-747-1715   (HQ)
**EDMONDS GALLAGHER MCLAUGHLIN IN-
SURANCE BROKERS LIMITED**
EGM
270 Lake St, Pembroke, ON, K8A 7Y9
(613) 735-0621
Emp Here 18   *Sales* 17,809,260
SIC 6411 Insurance agents, brokers, and ser-
vice
 Lisa Edmonds
 Tony Donnelly

D-U-N-S 25-301-3080   (BR)
EXTENDICARE (CANADA) INC
PARAMED HOME HEALTH CARE
(*Suby* of EXTENDICARE INC)
595 Pembroke St E, Pembroke, ON, K8A 3L7

Emp Here 150
SIC 8059 Nursing and personal care, nec
 Marsha Mcgregor

D-U-N-S 24-269-9528   (SL)
GREENWOOD PAVING (PEMBROKE) LTD
1495 Pembroke St W, Pembroke, ON, K8A
7A5
(613) 735-4101
Emp Here 65   *Sales* 16,408,730

SIC 1611 Highway and street construction
 Kent Plummer
 Mark Plummer
 David Plummer

D-U-N-S 24-426-7055   (BR)
HGS CANADA INC
ONLINE SUPPORT
(*Suby* of HINDUJA GLOBAL SOLUTIONS
LIMITED)
100 Crandall St Suite 100, Pembroke, ON,
K8A 6X8
(613) 633-4600
Emp Here 455
SIC 7379 Computer related services, nec
 Eric Olmsted

D-U-N-S 24-361-7268   (BR)
HOME DEPOT OF CANADA INC
HOME DEPOT
(*Suby* of THE HOME DEPOT INC)
27 Robinson Lane, Pembroke, ON, K8A 0A5
(613) 732-6550
Emp Here 100
SIC 5251 Hardware stores
 Bill Lennie

D-U-N-S 25-464-2960   (HQ)
JP2G CONSULTANTS INC
12 International Dr, Pembroke, ON, K8A 6W5
(613) 735-2507
Emp Here 35   *Sales* 17,595,800
SIC 8711 Engineering services
 Joseph Janota

D-U-N-S 20-366-1087   (SL)
KI CANADA CORPORATION
(*Suby* of KRUEGER INTERNATIONAL, INC.)
1000 Olympic Dr, Pembroke, ON, K8A 0E1
(613) 735-5566
Emp Here 200   *Sales* 30,864,400
SIC 2514 Metal household furniture
 Richard Resch
 Michael Pum
 Kelly J. Andersen

D-U-N-S 24-381-6621   (SL)
KRUEGER PEMBROKE LP
1000 Olympic Dr, Pembroke, ON, K8A 0E1

Emp Here 275   *Sales* 61,232,875
SIC 2522 Office furniture, except wood
 Rudy Witlox

D-U-N-S 25-828-2219   (SL)
LAPOINTE BROS PEMBROKE LIMITED
LAPOINTE CHRYSLER
1398 Pembroke St W, Pembroke, ON, K8A
7M3
(613) 735-0634
Emp Here 24   *Sales* 11,953,872
SIC 5511 New and used car dealers
 James Lapointe

D-U-N-S 20-771-0323   (SL)
LAPOINTE CHRYSLER BROS JEEP
1398 Pembroke St W, Pembroke, ON, K8A
7M3
(613) 735-3128
Emp Here 30   *Sales* 14,942,340
SIC 5511 New and used car dealers
 Vic Jones

D-U-N-S 25-292-3370   (BR)
METRO ONTARIO INC
FOOD BASICS
(*Suby* of METRO INC)
1100 Pembroke St E Suite 891, Pembroke,
ON, K8A 6Y7
(613) 735-1846
Emp Here 80
SIC 5411 Grocery stores
 Shane Winniski

D-U-N-S 25-281-1898   (SL)
MIRAMICHI LODGE
725 Pembroke St W Suite 735, Pembroke,
ON, K8A 8S6

(613) 735-0175
Emp Here 200   *Sales* 13,665,200
SIC 8051 Skilled nursing care facilities
 Shelley Sheedy

D-U-N-S 20-140-6055   (HQ)
MULVIHILL DRUG MART LIMITED
1231 Pembroke St W, Pembroke, ON, K8A
5R3
(613) 735-1079
Emp Here 16   *Sales* 10,118,160
SIC 5912 Drug stores and proprietary stores
 Brian Mulvihill
 Joan Weise
 Jane Mulvihill

D-U-N-S 24-383-9198   (SL)
MURPHY FORD SALES LTD
1341 Pembroke St W, Pembroke, ON, K8A
5R3
(613) 735-6861
Emp Here 28   *Sales* 13,946,184
SIC 5511 New and used car dealers
 Michael Murphy
 Reid Murphy
 Mel Abercrombie

D-U-N-S 24-137-9663   (SL)
ONLINE SUPPORT
1200 Pembroke St W Suite 25, Pembroke,
ON, K8A 7T1
(613) 633-4200
Emp Here 100   *Sales* 16,258,400
SIC 7379 Computer related services, nec
 Ross Duff

D-U-N-S 20-081-7067   (SL)
OTTAWA RIVER POWER CORPORATION
283 Pembroke St E, Pembroke, ON, K8A 3K2
(613) 732-3687
Emp Here 26   *Sales* 13,511,030
SIC 4911 Electric services
 Douglas Fee

D-U-N-S 25-534-2610   (SL)
PEMBROKE MDF INC
777 Fibreboard Dr, Pembroke, ON, K8A 6W4
(613) 732-3939
Emp Here 100   *Sales* 19,476,800
SIC 2621 Paper mills
 Felix Bacigalupo
 Juan Andres Camus
 Juan Obach
 Michael Ackman

D-U-N-S 20-892-0538   (HQ)
PEMBROKE REGIONAL HOSPITAL INC
705 Mackay St Suite 732, Pembroke, ON, K8A
1G8
(613) 732-2811
Sales 83,310,000
SIC 8062 General medical and surgical hospitals
 John Wren

D-U-N-S 20-590-8572   (BR)
**RENFREW COUNTY DISTRICT SCHOOL
BOARD**
FELLOWES HIGH SCHOOL
420 Bell St, Pembroke, ON, K8A 2K5
(613) 735-6858
Emp Here 125
SIC 8211 Elementary and secondary schools
 Dean Zadow

D-U-N-S 20-140-6873   (SL)
SHAW, HERB AND SONS LIMITED
31 Sharon St, Pembroke, ON, K8A 7J5
(613) 732-9989
Emp Here 90   *Sales* 40,245,660
SIC 5031 Lumber, plywood, and millwork
 John Shaw
 Dana Shaw
 Herbert Shaw

D-U-N-S 24-847-0379   (SL)
SRB TECHNOLOGIES (CANADA) INC
(*Suby* of SRB TECHNOLOGIES INC.)
320 Boundary Rd E Suite 140, Pembroke, ON,

K8A 6W5
(613) 732-0055
Emp Here 42   *Sales* 13,697,712
SIC 3993 Signs and advertising specialties
 Stephane Levesque
 Michael Dugan

D-U-N-S 20-077-1702   (BR)
WAL-MART CANADA CORP
WAL MART
(*Suby* of WALMART INC.)
1108 Pembroke St E, Pembroke, ON, K8A
8P7
(613) 735-4997
Emp Here 200
SIC 5311 Department stores
 Paul Daniel

Pembroke, ON K8B

D-U-N-S 24-482-1294   (HQ)
1555314 ONTARIO INC
EASTWAY
965 Mackay St, Pembroke, ON, K8B 1A2
(613) 735-4593
Emp Here 22   *Sales* 34,214,972
SIC 7532 Top and body repair and paint shops
 Daniel Bedard

Penetanguishene, ON L9M

D-U-N-S 20-267-9841   (BR)
MAGNA CLOSURES INC
TECHFORM
(*Suby* of MAGNA INTERNATIONAL INC)
11 Centennial Dr Suite 1, Penetanguishene,
ON, L9M 1G8
(705) 549-7406
Emp Here 500
SIC 5013 Motor vehicle supplies and new
parts
 Kevin Sheehan

D-U-N-S 24-048-1481   (SL)
**PENETANGUISHENE GENERAL HOSPITAL
INC, THE**
25 Jeffery St Suite 670, Penetanguishene,
ON, L9M 1K6
(705) 549-7442
Emp Here 175   *Sales* 19,439,000
SIC 8062 General medical and surgical hospi-
tals
 Michael Morris
 Alison Vallance
 Rob Stubbins
 Anne Maher
 Ruth Sullivan
 Rosita Desroches
 James Fahy
 Don Mcdermott
 Robert Keller
 David Webster

D-U-N-S 25-092-3948   (SL)
**WAYPOINT CENTRE FOR MENTAL
HEALTH CARE**
500 Church St, Penetanguishene, ON, L9M
1G3
(705) 549-3181
Emp Here 1,200   *Sales* 95,866,800
SIC 8063 Psychiatric hospitals
 John Barrett-Hamilton
 Susan Plewes
 Catharine Bayles
 Adam Chambers
 Ray Millar
 Eric Preston
 Jennifer Rodgers
 Christa Wessel

Perth, ON K7H

D-U-N-S 24-268-6376   (BR)
3M CANADA COMPANY
(Suby of 3M COMPANY)
2 Craig St, Perth, ON, K7H 3E2
(613) 267-5300
Emp Here 200
SIC 2672 Paper; coated and laminated, nec
  Andy Marg

D-U-N-S 24-437-9707   (SL)
519728 ONTARIO LTD
RIDEAU PIPE & DRILLING SUPPLIES
38 Lanark Rd, Perth, ON, K7H 3C9
(613) 267-5880
Emp Here 35   *Sales* 16,625,910
SIC 5085 Industrial supplies
  Ronald Fournier
  Daryl Ritchie

D-U-N-S 24-911-2400   (SL)
883481 ONTARIO INC
CARSON'S
17100 Highway 7 Rr 6, Perth, ON, K7H 3C8

Emp Here 22   *Sales* 11,142,012
SIC 5571 Motorcycle dealers
  Shawn Carson

D-U-N-S 24-104-5681   (BR)
ALBANY INTERNATIONAL CANADA CORP
(Suby of ALBANY INTERNATIONAL CORP.)
2947 Rideau Ferry Rd, Perth, ON, K7H 3E3
(613) 267-6600
Emp Here 170
SIC 2231 Broadwoven fabric mills, wool
  George Cazalet

D-U-N-S 24-803-0116   (SL)
BROWNLEE, RONALD (1994) LTD
BROWNLEE'S METRO
50 Wilson St W, Perth, ON, K7H 2N4
(613) 267-4921
Emp Here 80   *Sales* 23,478,160
SIC 5411 Grocery stores
  Avis Brownlee
  Brent Brownlee

D-U-N-S 20-140-8499   (HQ)
CALERES CANADA, INC
NATURALIZER
(Suby of CALERES, INC.)
1857 Rogers Rd, Perth, ON, K7H 1P7
(613) 267-0348
Emp Here 35   *Sales* 753,779,700
SIC 5139 Footwear
  Brian Bingley

D-U-N-S 20-140-8580   (HQ)
CENTRAL WIRE INDUSTRIES LTD
TECHALLOY WELDING PRODUCTS
1 North St, Perth, ON, K7H 2S2
(613) 267-3752
Emp Here 100   *Sales* 36,277,600
SIC 3312 Blast furnaces and steel mills
  Larry Smith
  Janice Gilmour

D-U-N-S 20-521-2777   (HQ)
CHILDREN'S AID SOCIETY OF THE COUNTY OF LANARK AND THE TOWN OF SMITHS FALLS, THE
CHILDREN'S AID SOCIETY
8 Herriott St, Perth, ON, K7H 1S9
(613) 264-9991
Emp Here 70   *Sales* 10,676,720
SIC 8399 Social services, nec
  Suzanne Geoffrion
  Allan Hogan

D-U-N-S 25-101-6770   (BR)
CONTRANS GROUP INC
GLEN TAY TRANSPORTATION
42 Lanark Rd, Perth, ON, K7H 3K5

(613) 267-2007
Emp Here 85   *Sales* 426,784
SIC 4482 Ferries
  Dan Robert

D-U-N-S 20-291-4792   (HQ)
ELLARD ENTERPRISES LIMITED
PERTH HOME HARDWARE BUILDING CENTRE
115 Drummond St W, Perth, ON, K7H 2K8
(613) 267-4501
Emp Here 1   *Sales* 20,073,900
SIC 5251 Hardware stores
  Richard Ellard

D-U-N-S 24-269-5963   (SL)
FAMILY WEALTH ADVISORS LTD
22 Foster St, Perth, ON, K7H 1R6
(613) 264-8267
Emp Here 20   *Sales* 14,508,780
SIC 6311 Life insurance
  Brian Noonan
  Patricia Noonan

D-U-N-S 25-482-9179   (SL)
HENDRIKS INDEPENDENT GROCER
80 Dufferin St, Perth, ON, K7H 3A7

Emp Here 100
SIC 5411 Grocery stores

D-U-N-S 20-556-1975   (BR)
HYDRO ONE NETWORKS INC
(Suby of HYDRO ONE LIMITED)
99 Drummond St W, Perth, ON, K7H 3E7
(613) 267-6473
Emp Here 100
SIC 4911 Electric services
  Terry Tysick

D-U-N-S 20-890-5885   (SL)
LANARK LODGE
115 Christie Lake Rd Suite 223, Perth, ON, K7H 3C6
(613) 267-4225
Emp Here 180   *Sales* 11,570,760
SIC 8361 Residential care
  Debroah Pidgeon

D-U-N-S 20-888-9105   (SL)
MCLEAN INSURANCE PROTECTION TEAM INC
58 Foster St, Perth, ON, K7H 1S1
(613) 267-5100
Emp Here 21   *Sales* 12,178,404
SIC 6411 Insurance agents, brokers, and service
  Michael Mclean

D-U-N-S 20-033-2534   (HQ)
OMYA CANADA INC
SNOWHITE
(Suby of OMYA AG)
18595 Hwy 7 W, Perth, ON, K7H 3E4
(613) 267-5367
Emp Here 100   *Sales* 27,025,600
SIC 1499 Miscellaneous nonMetallic minerals, except fuels
  Berndt Kanduth

D-U-N-S 24-205-9074   (SL)
P & R HOFSTATTER SALES LTD
CANADIAN TIRE
45 Dufferin St, Perth, ON, K7H 3A5
(613) 267-3412
Emp Here 100   *Sales* 62,928,000
SIC 5531 Auto and home supply stores
  Pierre Hofstatter
  Robyn Hofstatter

D-U-N-S 24-350-8087   (BR)
PERTH AND SMITHS FALLS DISTRICT HOSPITAL
GREAT WAR MEMORIAL
(Suby of PERTH AND SMITHS FALLS DISTRICT HOSPITAL)
33 Drummond St W, Perth, ON, K7H 2K1
(613) 267-1500
Emp Here 270

SIC 8062 General medical and surgical hospitals
  Linda Bisonette

D-U-N-S 24-381-4188   (SL)
PERTH SOAP MANUFACTURING INC
PERTH SOAP, DIV OF
5 Herriott St, Perth, ON, K7H 3E5
(613) 267-1881
Emp Here 65   *Sales* 18,461,365
SIC 2841 Soap and other detergents
  Grant Lawson
  Rick Duval

D-U-N-S 24-684-6807   (HQ)
SHANDEX PERSONAL CARE MANUFACTURING INC
(Suby of SHANDEX SALES GROUP LIMITED)
5 Herriott St, Perth, ON, K7H 3E5
(613) 267-1881
Sales 18,461,365
SIC 2841 Soap and other detergents
  Rob Staite
  Frank Barrese
  Joyce Shannon
  Christine Shannon
  Jennifer Shannon

Petawawa, ON K8H

D-U-N-S 25-111-2785   (HQ)
WADE GENERAL CONTRACTING LTD
56 Industrial Ave, Petawawa, ON, K8H 2W8
(613) 687-8585
Sales 16,475,585
SIC 1542 Nonresidential construction, nec
  Sharon Godin
  Robert Kumm

Peterborough, ON K9H

D-U-N-S 20-790-2409   (SL)
1441571 ONTARIO INC
TOWERHILL SOBEYS
501 Towerhill Rd, Peterborough, ON, K9H 7S3
(705) 740-9026
Emp Here 160   *Sales* 46,956,320
SIC 5411 Grocery stores
  John Armstrong

D-U-N-S 24-486-8048   (SL)
564205 ONTARIO INC
PETERBOROUGH HYUNDAI SUBARU
1370 Chemong Rd, Peterborough, ON, K9H 0E7
(705) 876-6591
Emp Here 23   *Sales* 11,455,794
SIC 5511 New and used car dealers
  Steve Atkins
  Joseph (Joe) Atkins
  Gordon Atkins

D-U-N-S 20-026-6737   (SL)
ARMSTRONG PLAZA LTD
LIFTLOCK IGA
142 Hunter St E, Peterborough, ON, K9H 1G6
(705) 743-8253
Emp Here 49   *Sales* 13,433,448
SIC 5411 Grocery stores
  Dave Armstrong

D-U-N-S 24-175-6225   (SL)
CAMBIUM INC
52 Hunter St E, Peterborough, ON, K9H 1G5
(705) 742-7900
Emp Here 85   *Sales* 19,914,480
SIC 8748 Business consulting, nec
  John Desbiens
  James Bailey
  David Bucholtz

D-U-N-S 25-941-2539   (HQ)
CAMBIUM INC
52 Hunter St E, Peterborough, ON, K9H 1G5
(705) 742-7900
Emp Here 43   *Sales* 28,137,390
SIC 8748 Business consulting, nec
  John Desbiens
  Jim Bailey
  David Bucholtz
  Stuart Baird
  Steven Williams
  Christopher Fleming

D-U-N-S 24-011-5530   (HQ)
CANADIAN MENTAL HEALTH ASSOCIATION, PETERBOROUGH BRANCH
CMHA
466 George St N, Peterborough, ON, K9H 3R7
(705) 748-6711
Emp Here 40   *Sales* 16,064,600
SIC 8011 Offices and clinics of medical doctors
  Mark Graham
  Joan Peacock

D-U-N-S 25-146-4223   (SL)
CANADIAN TIRE
1050 Chemong Rd, Peterborough, ON, K9H 7S2
(705) 745-1388
Emp Here 30   *Sales* 10,926,450
SIC 5014 Tires and tubes
  Susan O'brien

D-U-N-S 20-845-0965   (SL)
FAIRHAVEN HOME
(Suby of CORPORATION OF THE CITY OF PETERBOROUGH, THE)
881 Dutton Rd, Peterborough, ON, K9H 7S4
(705) 743-4265
Emp Here 280   *Sales* 19,131,280
SIC 8051 Skilled nursing care facilities
  Joy Husack
  Mary-Lynn Koekkoek

D-U-N-S 20-778-9251   (SL)
FAIRHAVEN LONG TERM CARE
881 Dutton Rd, Peterborough, ON, K9H 7S4
(705) 743-0881
Emp Here 300   *Sales* 20,497,800
SIC 8051 Skilled nursing care facilities
  Jo Harris
  Steve Doris

D-U-N-S 20-141-2442   (SL)
FISHERCAST GLOBAL CORPORATION
FISHERCAST
194 Sophia St, Peterborough, ON, K9H 1E5

Emp Here 310
SIC 6712 Bank holding companies

D-U-N-S 20-845-0234   (SL)
ICT GROUP
360 George St N Suite 100, Peterborough, ON, K9H 7E7

Emp Here 49   *Sales* 32,166,736
SIC 5963 Direct selling establishments
  Gary Cave

D-U-N-S 24-084-1846   (BR)
KAWARTHA PARTICIPATION PROJECTS
(Suby of KAWARTHA PARTICIPATION PROJECTS)
440 Water St, Peterborough, ON, K9H 7K6
(705) 745-9434
Emp Here 77
SIC 6531 Real estate agents and managers
  Les Latchford

D-U-N-S 25-082-0594   (SL)
KAWARTHA-HALIBURTON CHILDREN'S AID SOCIETY, THE
1100 Chemong Rd, Peterborough, ON, K9H 7S2

(705) 743-9751
Emp Here 114   *Sales* 8,754,288
SIC 8322 Individual and family services
Hugh Nicholson
Tim Mclaren

D-U-N-S 25-292-3578   (BR)
METRO ONTARIO INC
METRO
(*Suby of* METRO INC)
1154 Chemong Rd Suite 9, Peterborough,
ON, K9H 7J6
(705) 745-3381
Emp Here 100
SIC 5411 Grocery stores
Scott Adair

D-U-N-S 24-677-0353   (BR)
OMNI HEALTH CARE LIMITED PARTNER-SHIP
RIVERVIEW MANOR NURSING HOME
1155 Water St, Peterborough, ON, K9H 3P8
(705) 748-6706
Emp Here 150
SIC 8051 Skilled nursing care facilities
Maryanne Greco

D-U-N-S 24-632-6581   (HQ)
ROMAN CATHOLIC EPISCOPAL CORP OF THE DIOCESE OF PETERBOROUGH
350 Hunter St W, Peterborough, ON, K9H 2M4
(705) 745-5123
Sales 20,824,600
SIC 8661 Religious organizations
Nicolas Deangelis
Joseph Devereaux

D-U-N-S 25-281-2854   (BR)
SECURITAS CANADA LIMITED
(*Suby of* SECURITAS AB)
349a George St N Suite 206, Peterborough,
ON, K9H 3P9
(705) 743-8026
Emp Here 115
SIC 7381 Detective and armored car services
Atik Taraboulsi

D-U-N-S 25-899-5679   (SL)
TRI-COUNTY COMMUNITY SUPPORT SER-VICES
TRI-COUNTY BEHAVIOURAL SERVICES
349a George St N Unit 303, Peterborough,
ON, K9H 3P9
(705) 876-9245
Emp Here 50   *Sales* 11,341,650
SIC 8399 Social services, nec
Gerry Fucile
John Poch

D-U-N-S 25-027-8124   (BR)
VICTORIAN ORDER OF NURSES FOR CANADA
VON   PETERBOROUGH-VICTORIA-HALIBURTON DISTRICT
(*Suby of* VICTORIAN ORDER OF NURSES
FOR CANADA)
360 George St N Suite 25, Peterborough, ON,
K9H 7E7
(705) 745-9155
Emp Here 100
SIC 8082 Home health care services
Cavall Alan

D-U-N-S 25-294-7908   (BR)
WAL-MART CANADA CORP
(*Suby of* WALMART INC.)
1002 Chemong Rd Suite 3071, Peterborough,
ON, K9H 7E2
(705) 742-1685
Emp Here 300
SIC 5311 Department stores
Dean Smith

D-U-N-S 20-964-5449   (HQ)
YOUNG WOMEN'S CHRISTIAN ASSOCIA-TION OF PETERBOROUGH, VICTORIA & HALIBURTON
YWCA OF PETERBOROUGH VICTORIA &

HALIBURTON
216 Simcoe St, Peterborough, ON, K9H 2H7
(705) 743-3526
Emp Here 3   *Sales* 12,011,310
SIC 8399 Social services, nec
Lynn Zimmer
Heather Avery
Theresa Butler-Porter

Peterborough, ON K9J

D-U-N-S 24-240-3967   (SL)
1307299 ONTARIO INC.
SOBEYS
1200 Lansdowne St W, Peterborough, ON,
K9J 2A1
(705) 748-5655
Emp Here 50   *Sales* 13,707,600
SIC 5411 Grocery stores
Allen Armstrong

D-U-N-S 25-365-8199   (SL)
1853865 ONTARIO INC
CHEMONG HOME HARDWARE BUILDING CENTRE
1699 Chemong Rd, Peterborough, ON, K9J
6X2
(705) 748-9111
Emp Here 74   *Sales* 19,806,248
SIC 5211 Lumber and other building materials
Randy Kingdon
Terry Jenkins

D-U-N-S 24-845-7160   (SL)
564242 ONTARIO LIMITED
LIFT LOCK COACH LINES
728 Rye St, Peterborough, ON, K9J 6W9
(705) 745-1666
Emp Here 235   *Sales* 17,688,920
SIC 4141 Local bus charter service
Daryl Bennett
Rob Bennett
Dave Ramey

D-U-N-S 20-141-0230   (SL)
ADAMSON & DOBBIN LIMITED
407 Pido Rd, Peterborough, ON, K9J 6X7
(705) 745-5751
Emp Here 52   *Sales* 12,119,380
SIC 1711 Plumbing, heating, air-conditioning
David Dobbin
William Dobbin
Shane Dobbin

D-U-N-S 20-967-0934   (HQ)
AON INC
(*Suby of* TOBRADSH HOLDINGS INC)
307 Aylmer St N, Peterborough, ON, K9J 7M4
(705) 742-5445
Emp Here 60   *Sales* 144,274,775
SIC 6553 Cemetery subdividers and develop-ers
Ross Smith
Brad Smith
Todd Smith
Domenic Idesanya

D-U-N-S 25-882-6304   (SL)
ARMSTRONG STORE LIMITED
SHERBROOKE IGA
760 Sherbrooke St, Peterborough, ON, K9J
2R1
(705) 742-3321
Emp Here 44   *Sales* 12,062,688
SIC 5411 Grocery stores
Charles Armstrong
David Armstrong

D-U-N-S 24-222-9941   (BR)
BOSTON PIZZA INTERNATIONAL INC
BOSTON PIZZA
(*Suby of* BOSTON PIZZA INTERNATIONAL
INC)
821 Rye St, Peterborough, ON, K9J 6X1

(705) 740-2775
Emp Here 90
SIC 5812 Eating places
Steve Bailey

D-U-N-S 20-524-8750   (HQ)
BRYSTON LTD
677 Neal Dr, Peterborough, ON, K9J 6X7
(705) 742-5325
Emp Here 51   *Sales* 10,093,426
SIC 3651 Household audio and video equip-ment
Christopher Russell
Brian Russell
James Tanner

D-U-N-S 20-354-3855   (HQ)
BWXT NUCLEAR ENERGY CANADA INC
(*Suby of* BWX TECHNOLOGIES, INC.)
1160 Monaghan Rd, Peterborough, ON, K9J
0A8
(855) 696-9588
Sales 13,833,000
SIC 2819 Industrial inorganic chemicals, nec
Mark Ward
Jason Kerr
John Johnson
Theresa Taylor
David Black
Richard Redemacher
N. Kelly Howard
John Macquarrie
Rex Geveden

D-U-N-S 20-084-2289   (BR)
CAMPBELL, JAMES INC
MCDONALD'S
(*Suby of* CAMPBELL, JAMES INC)
978 Lansdowne St W, Peterborough, ON, K9J
1Z9
(705) 743-6731
Emp Here 116
SIC 5812 Eating places
Tara Adamsons

D-U-N-S 20-816-8989   (HQ)
CENTURY 21 UNITED REALTY INC BROK-AGE
387 George St S, Peterborough, ON, K9J 3E1
(705) 743-4444
Emp Here 52   *Sales* 23,038,895
SIC 6531 Real estate agents and managers
Carl Oake

D-U-N-S 24-829-3359   (HQ)
CHARLOTTE PRODUCTS LTD
(*Suby of* SWISH MAINTENANCE LIMITED)
2060 Fisher Dr, Peterborough, ON, K9J 6X6
(705) 740-2880
Sales 12,166,199
SIC 2842 Polishes and sanitation goods
Matthew Strano
Asquith Williams
Mary Batley

D-U-N-S 20-881-5738   (HQ)
COLLINS BARROW KAWARTHAS LLP
272 Charlotte St, Peterborough, ON, K9J 2V4
(705) 742-3418
Emp Here 45   *Sales* 14,537,950
SIC 8721 Accounting, auditing, and book-keeping
Thomas (Tom) Taylor
Robert (Bob) Fisher
Steven (Steve) Porter
Mark Mooney
Herbert (Herb) Gamble
Erik Ellis
Susan Williams
Leah Curtis
Joanna Park
William (Bill) Crowther

D-U-N-S 24-602-4806   (SL)
COMPLETE AVIATION SERVICES LTD
Ss 5 Stn Delivery Centre, Peterborough, ON,
K9J 6X6

(705) 745-8626
Emp Here 30   *Sales* 37,716,030
SIC 5172 Petroleum products, nec
George Johnston

D-U-N-S 25-478-8599   (BR)
CORPORATION OF THE CITY OF PETER-BOROUGH, THE
PETERBOROUGH MEMORIAL CENTRE
(*Suby of* CORPORATION OF THE CITY OF
PETERBOROUGH, THE)
151 Lansdowne St W, Peterborough, ON, K9J
1Y4
(705) 743-3561
Emp Here 75
SIC 8322 Individual and family services
Susan L. Warrington

D-U-N-S 24-369-9183   (BR)
COSTCO WHOLESALE CANADA LTD
COSTCO
(*Suby of* COSTCO WHOLESALE CORPO-RATION)
485 The Parkway, Peterborough, ON, K9J 0B3
(705) 750-2600
Emp Here 250
SIC 5199 Nondurable goods, nec
James Dalton

D-U-N-S 24-364-0674   (SL)
DYNACAST LTD
FISHERCAST
(*Suby of* KDI LUXEMBOURG SARL)
710 Neal Dr, Peterborough, ON, K9J 6X7
(705) 748-9522
Emp Here 200   *Sales* 36,277,600
SIC 3369 Nonferrous foundries, nec
Simon Newman
Adrian Murphy

D-U-N-S 20-551-9981   (BR)
EXTENDICARE (CANADA) INC
EXTENDICARE PETERBOROUGH
(*Suby of* EXTENDICARE INC)
80 Alexander Ave, Peterborough, ON, K9J
6B4
(705) 743-7552
Emp Here 200
SIC 8051 Skilled nursing care facilities
Dawn Baldwin

D-U-N-S 24-925-4426   (SL)
FARMBOY MARKETS LIMITED
754 Lansdowne St W, Peterborough, ON, K9J
1Z3
(705) 745-2811
Emp Here 42   *Sales* 11,514,384
SIC 5411 Grocery stores
John Strano
Bill Strano

D-U-N-S 25-527-3500   (BR)
FLEX-N-GATE CANADA COMPANY
VENTRA PLASTICS PETERBOROUGH
(*Suby of* FLEX-N-GATE LLC)
775 Technology Dr, Peterborough, ON, K9J
6X7
(705) 742-3534
Emp Here 500
SIC 3714 Motor vehicle parts and accessories
Rick Cook

D-U-N-S 25-028-1508   (HQ)
FLYING COLOURS CORP
901 Airport Rd Suite 120, Peterborough, ON,
K9J 0E7
(705) 742-4688
Emp Here 10   *Sales* 13,539,760
SIC 1721 Painting and paper hanging
John Gillespie
Eric Gillespie
Sean Gillespie
Tony Barrett
Debbie Ammann
Alysia Carter
Gabi Hasko
Scott Duncan
Ian Ross

Richard Dabkowski

D-U-N-S 20-141-1063   (BR)
GENERAL ELECTRIC CANADA COMPANY
GE CANADA
(*Suby of* GENERAL ELECTRIC COMPANY)
107 Park St N Suite 2, Peterborough, ON, K9J 7B5
(705) 748-8486
Emp Here 1,300
SIC 3625 Relays and industrial controls
Ross Garland

D-U-N-S 20-968-4799   (SL)
GILL TECHNOLOGIES GLOBAL COMMUNICATIONS INC
150 King St, Peterborough, ON, K9J 2R9
(877) 507-6988
Emp Here 200   *Sales* 45,694,400
SIC 4899 Communication services, nec
George Gill

D-U-N-S 20-813-1677   (SL)
GLOBAL TELESALES OF CANADA INC
(*Suby of* DEUTSCHE LUFTHANSA AG)
1900 Fisher Dr, Peterborough, ON, K9J 6X6
(705) 872-3021
Emp Here 165   *Sales* 110,369,820
SIC 7389 Business services, nec
Andreas Gruenewald

D-U-N-S 24-360-4340   (SL)
HOLIDAY FORD LINCOLN LTD
1555 Lansdowne St W, Peterborough, ON, K9J 7M3
(705) 742-5432
Emp Here 55   *Sales* 34,610,400
SIC 5521 Used car dealers
Ainslie Hogan Jr

D-U-N-S 25-088-1786   (BR)
HOME DEPOT OF CANADA INC
HOME DEPOT
(*Suby of* THE HOME DEPOT INC)
500 Lansdowne St W, Peterborough, ON, K9J 8J7
(705) 876-4560
Emp Here 300
SIC 5211 Lumber and other building materials
Brent Matthews

D-U-N-S 24-792-2318   (SL)
INSTORE FOCUS INC
485 The Parkway, Peterborough, ON, K9J 0B3

Emp Here 35   *Sales* 23,362,673
SIC 5963 Direct selling establishments
Bonnie Vass

D-U-N-S 25-283-6036   (HQ)
KADEX AERO SUPPLY LTD
925 Airport Rd Unit 211a, Peterborough, ON, K9J 0E7
(705) 742-9725
Emp Here 21   *Sales* 13,300,728
SIC 5088 Transportation equipment and supplies
John Lavery
Ken Blow

D-U-N-S 25-213-9258   (SL)
KAWARTHA METALS CORP
1-1961 Fisher Dr, Peterborough, ON, K9J 6X6
(705) 748-6993
Emp Here 26   *Sales* 11,626,524
SIC 5051 Metals service centers and offices
Thomas Elliott

D-U-N-S 20-025-0608   (BR)
KAWARTHA PINE RIDGE DISTRICT SCHOOL BOARD
KENNER COLLEGIATE VOCATIONAL SCHOOL
633 Monaghan Rd, Peterborough, ON, K9J 5J2
(705) 743-2181
Emp Here 150
SIC 8211 Elementary and secondary schools

Craig Allan

D-U-N-S 20-653-6161   (SL)
KIRK CHITICK PETERBOROUGH AUTO
898 Ford St, Peterborough, ON, K9J 5V3
(705) 536-0050
Emp Here 40   *Sales* 19,923,120
SIC 5511 New and used car dealers
Kirk Chitick

D-U-N-S 20-070-9009   (BR)
LABOUR READY TEMPORARY SERVICES LTD
(*Suby of* TRUEBLUE, INC.)
306 George St N Unit 6, Peterborough, ON, K9J 3H2
(705) 760-9111
Emp Here 100
SIC 7361 Employment agencies
Dave Mac Adams

D-U-N-S 24-361-9143   (SL)
LANSDOWNE MALL INC
LANSDOWNE PLACE
645 Lansdowne St W, Peterborough, ON, K9J 7Y5
(705) 748-2961
Emp Here 50   *Sales* 14,424,950
SIC 6512 Nonresidential building operators
Lisa Lafave
Jeffrey Wendling
Stephen Taylor
Barbara Thomson

D-U-N-S 24-737-4564   (SL)
MAXAMA PROTECTION INC
234 Romaine St, Peterborough, ON, K9J 2C5
(705) 745-7500
Emp Here 70   *Sales* 27,697,460
SIC 7381 Detective and armored car services
Aaron Macdonald

D-U-N-S 20-141-4455   (SL)
MCGEE, JACK CHEVROLET CADILLAC LIMITED
1053 Clonsilla Ave, Peterborough, ON, K9J 5Y2
(705) 741-9000
Emp Here 64   *Sales* 40,273,920
SIC 5511 New and used car dealers
David Mcgee
John Robert Mcgee

D-U-N-S 20-773-8402   (HQ)
MCWILLIAMS CARTAGE LIMITED
MCWILLIAMS MOVING & STORAGE
712 The Kingsway, Peterborough, ON, K9J 6W6
(800) 461-6464
Sales 19,542,070
SIC 4213 Trucking, except local
Dan Mcwilliams
Jim Mcwilliams
Mike Mcwilliams
John Mcwilliams

D-U-N-S 24-668-6406   (SL)
MERCEDES BENZ PETERBOROUGH INC
995 Crawford Dr, Peterborough, ON, K9J 3X1
(705) 742-9000
Emp Here 30   *Sales* 14,942,340
SIC 5511 New and used car dealers
Peter Santos

D-U-N-S 24-985-6949   (SL)
MERIT PRECISION MOULDING LIMITED
2035 Fisher Dr, Peterborough, ON, K9J 6X6
(705) 742-4209
Emp Here 50   *Sales* 10,094,850
SIC 3089 Plastics products, nec
Tim Barrie

D-U-N-S 24-964-2661   (BR)
METROLAND MEDIA GROUP LTD
PETERBOROUGH THIS WEEK
(*Suby of* TORSTAR CORPORATION)
884 Ford St, Peterborough, ON, K9J 5V3

(705) 749-3383
Emp Here 120
SIC 2711 Newspapers
Bruce Danford

D-U-N-S 25-282-4842   (BR)
MINUTE MAID COMPANY CANADA INC, THE
MINUTE MAID
(*Suby of* THE COCA-COLA COMPANY)
781 Lansdowne St W, Peterborough, ON, K9J 1Z2
(705) 742-8011
Emp Here 80
SIC 2037 Frozen fruits and vegetables
Daynes Rich

D-U-N-S 20-981-1827   (HQ)
MINUTE MAID COMPANY CANADA INC, THE
(*Suby of* THE COCA-COLA COMPANY)
781 Lansdowne St W, Peterborough, ON, K9J 1Z2
(705) 742-8011
Emp Here 100   *Sales* 197,390,925
SIC 2086 Bottled and canned soft drinks
Vincent R. Timpano
Spencer Enright
Sivarajah Faiyanthan

D-U-N-S 24-627-6823   (SL)
MONKMAN GRACIE & JOHNSTON
261 George St N, Peterborough, ON, K9J 3G9
(705) 742-8863
Emp Here 21   *Sales* 17,809,260
SIC 6411 Insurance agents, brokers, and service
Eric Monkman
David Smith

D-U-N-S 24-585-8659   (HQ)
NEFAB INC
(*Suby of* NEFAB HOLDING AB)
211 Jameson Dr, Peterborough, ON, K9J 6X6
(705) 748-4888
Emp Here 83   *Sales* 19,237,000
SIC 2441 Nailed wood boxes and shook
Rui Garrido
Mark Robinson
Frank Slovacek

D-U-N-S 25-459-5010   (SL)
NIGHTINGALE NURSING REGISTRY LTD
2948 Lakefield Rd, Peterborough, ON, K9J 6X5
(705) 652-6118
Emp Here 100   *Sales* 6,456,000
SIC 8059 Nursing and personal care, nec
Sally Harding

D-U-N-S 24-575-6895   (HQ)
OMNI HEALTH CARE LTD
VILLAGE GREEN
(*Suby of* OMNI HEALTH INVESTMENTS INC)
2020 Fisher Dr Suite 1, Peterborough, ON, K9J 6X6
(705) 748-6631
Emp Here 13   *Sales* 116,154,200
SIC 8051 Skilled nursing care facilities
Patrick Mccarthy
Shawn Riel
Kelly South

D-U-N-S 25-361-4119   (BR)
OMNI HEALTH CARE LTD
SPRINGDALE COUNTRY MANOR
(*Suby of* OMNI HEALTH INVESTMENTS INC)
2020 Fisher Dr, Peterborough, ON, K9J 6X6
(705) 742-8811
Emp Here 75
SIC 8051 Skilled nursing care facilities
Fraser Wilson

D-U-N-S 24-372-2712   (HQ)
OMNI HEALTH INVESTMENTS INC
2020 Fisher Dr, Peterborough, ON, K9J 6X6
(705) 748-6631
Emp Here 1   *Sales* 541,684,338

SIC 6712 Bank holding companies
Patrick Mccarthy

D-U-N-S 20-977-3746   (HQ)
ONTARIO FEDERATION OF ANGLERS AND HUNTERS, THE
OFAH
4601 Guthrie Dr, Peterborough, ON, K9J 0C9
(705) 748-6324
Emp Here 1   *Sales* 17,486,216
SIC 8699 Membership organizations, nec
Mike Reader
Jack Hedman
Frank Wick

D-U-N-S 24-126-2575   (HQ)
PAN-OSTON LTD
660 Neal Dr, Peterborough, ON, K9J 6X7
(705) 748-4811
Sales 14,660,590
SIC 2542 Partitions and fixtures, except wood
Greg Butler

D-U-N-S 20-816-1851   (HQ)
PARIS MARINE LIMITED
2980 Lakefield Rd, Peterborough, ON, K9J 6X5
(705) 652-6444
Sales 10,459,638
SIC 5551 Boat dealers
William J Paris
Deborah Paris

D-U-N-S 20-176-9630   (BR)
PEPSICO CANADA ULC
PEPSI QTG CANADA
(*Suby of* PEPSICO, INC.)
14 Hunter St E, Peterborough, ON, K9J 7B2
(705) 743-6330
Emp Here 700
SIC 2043 Cereal breakfast foods

D-U-N-S 24-645-1892   (HQ)
PETERBOROUGH AUTOMOTIVE & MACHINE LTD
WALKWOOD SUPPLY
898 Ford St, Peterborough, ON, K9J 5V3
(705) 742-2446
Emp Here 40   *Sales* 17,482,320
SIC 5013 Motor vehicle supplies and new parts
Glen Rodney Anderson

D-U-N-S 20-847-2589   (SL)
PETERBOROUGH CLINIC, THE
26 Hospital Dr Suite 204, Peterborough, ON, K9J 7C3
(705) 743-2040
Emp Here 140   *Sales* 26,628,980
SIC 8011 Offices and clinics of medical doctors
Judith A Armstrong
Roy Petticrew

D-U-N-S 25-402-0761   (HQ)
PETERBOROUGH VICTORIA NORTHUMBERLAND AND CLARINGTON CATHOLIC DISTRICT SCHOOL BOARD
PVNC CATHOLIC DISTRICT SCHOOL BOARD
1355 Lansdowne St W, Peterborough, ON, K9J 7M3
(705) 748-4861
Emp Here 70   *Sales* 223,711,583
SIC 8211 Elementary and secondary schools
Michelle Griepsma
David Bernier
Michael Nasello

D-U-N-S 24-370-4470   (BR)
POLYTUBES 2009 INC
POLYTUBES PETERBOROUGH
(*Suby of* POLYTUBES 2009 INC)
416 Pido Rd, Peterborough, ON, K9J 6X7
(705) 740-2872
Emp Here 104
SIC 3084 Plastics pipe
Shawn Watt

D-U-N-S 24-219-9321   (SL)
PROTECTORS GROUP INSURANCE AGEN-CIES (1985) LTD, THE
215 George St N, Peterborough, ON, K9J 3G7
(705) 748-5181
Emp Here 23   *Sales* 13,338,252
SIC 6411 Insurance agents, brokers, and service
Terry Windrum
Patrick Casey
George Mcgillis

D-U-N-S 24-487-1877   (HQ)
RE/MAX EASTERN REALTY INC
64 Hastings St N, Peterborough, ON, K9J 3G3
(705) 743-9111
Emp Here 3   *Sales* 11,350,383
SIC 6531 Real estate agents and managers
John Bowes
John Hope

D-U-N-S 24-284-9743   (SL)
RITZ PLASTICS INC
435 Pido Rd, Peterborough, ON, K9J 6X7
(705) 748-6776
Emp Here 50   *Sales* 10,094,850
SIC 3089 Plastics products, nec
Stephen Akerfeldt

D-U-N-S 24-679-3009   (SL)
ROLLS-ROYCE CIVIL NUCLEAR CANADA LTD
678 Neal Dr, Peterborough, ON, K9J 6X7
(705) 743-2708
Emp Here 85   *Sales* 14,956,430
SIC 8711 Engineering services
Harry Holt
Ian Davis
Geoff Selkirk

D-U-N-S 20-141-6195   (SL)
RUSSELLE ENTERPRISES INC
1400 Lansdowne St W, Peterborough, ON, K9J 2A2
(705) 742-4288
Emp Here 33   *Sales* 16,626,941
SIC 5511 New and used car dealers
Robert M Russelle

D-U-N-S 20-873-4397   (SL)
RUSSELLE TOYOTA INC
1400 Lansdowne St W, Peterborough, ON, K9J 2A2
(705) 742-4288
Emp Here 30   *Sales* 14,942,340
SIC 5511 New and used car dealers
Robert Russelle

D-U-N-S 20-956-3530   (SL)
SAFRAN ELECTRONICS & DEFENSE CANADA INC
(*Suby of* SAFRAN)
2000 Fisher Dr, Peterborough, ON, K9J 6X6
(705) 743-6903
Emp Here 140   *Sales* 15,669,540
SIC 3812 Search and navigation equipment
Serge Aurignac
Ron James
Jeffrey Franks

D-U-N-S 25-787-2671   (SL)
SALKELD, C. & S. ENTERPRISES LTD
CANADIAN TIRE
1200 Lansdowne St W Suite 81, Peterborough, ON, K9J 2A1
(705) 742-0406
Emp Here 105   *Sales* 66,074,400
SIC 5531 Auto and home supply stores
Craig J Salkeld
Sherry G Salkeld

D-U-N-S 24-516-5204   (SL)
SHIMANO CANADA LTD
(*Suby of* SHIMANO INC.)
427 Pido Rd, Peterborough, ON, K9J 6X7
(705) 745-3232
Emp Here 30   *Sales* 15,616,260

SIC 5091 Sporting and recreation goods
Thomas Brooke
Catherine Mitchell
Yoshihiro Hirata
Michael Flavell
Peter Hayden
Jim Lafrance

D-U-N-S 24-805-1034   (BR)
SIEMENS CANADA LIMITED
SIEMENS MILLTRONICS PROCESS INSTRUMENTS
(*Suby of* SIEMENS AG)
1954 Technology Dr, Peterborough, ON, K9J 6X7
(705) 745-2431
Emp Here 350
SIC 3823 Process control instruments
George Ravalico

D-U-N-S 20-786-8647   (HQ)
SIR SANDFORD FLEMING COLLEGE OF APPLIED ARTS AND TECHNOLOGY
FLEMING COLLEGE
599 Brealey Dr, Peterborough, ON, K9J 7B1
(705) 749-5530
Emp Here 650   *Sales* 99,119,000
SIC 8222 Junior colleges
Murray Rodd
Tony Tilly

D-U-N-S 20-141-6682   (HQ)
SWISH MAINTENANCE LIMITED
SWISH
2060 Fisher Dr, Peterborough, ON, K9J 6X6
(705) 745-5763
Emp Here 40   *Sales* 45,884,250
SIC 5999 Miscellaneous retail stores, nec
Shane Mahoney
Anthony Ambler
Michael Ambler
Stephen Ambler
Andre Peters

D-U-N-S 20-552-8263   (BR)
SYSCO CANADA, INC
SYSCO FOOD SERVICES OF ONTARIO
(*Suby of* SYSCO CORPORATION)
65 Elmdale Rd, Peterborough, ON, K9J 6X4
(705) 748-6701
Emp Here 450
SIC 5141 Groceries, general line
Strano Paul

D-U-N-S 20-141-6591   (SL)
SYSCO CENTRAL ONTARIO, INC
(*Suby of* SYSCO CORPORATION)
65 Elmdale Rd, Peterborough, ON, K9J 0G5
(705) 748-6701
Emp Here 550   *Sales* 394,193,800
SIC 5141 Groceries, general line
Paul Strano
Rodney Stroud
Russell Libby

D-U-N-S 20-705-0352   (SL)
TRANS CANADA MOTORS (PETERBOROUGH) LIMITED
A-1 AUTO RENTAL & LEASING
1189 Lansdowne St W, Peterborough, ON, K9J 7M2
(705) 743-4141
Emp Here 38   *Sales* 18,926,964
SIC 5511 New and used car dealers
Paul O'reilly
Dorathy O'reilly

D-U-N-S 20-141-6906   (HQ)
TRENT METALS (2012) LIMITED
TML SUPPLY COMPANY
2040 Fisher Dr, Peterborough, ON, K9J 6X6
(705) 745-4736
Emp Here 50   *Sales* 33,300,150
SIC 3567 Industrial furnaces and ovens
William Edmanson

D-U-N-S 20-141-6948   (HQ)

TRENTWAY-WAGAR INC
COACH CANADA
(*Suby of* COACH USA ADMINISTRATION, INC.)
2015 Fisher Dr Unit 101, Peterborough, ON, K9J 6X6
(705) 748-6411
Emp Here 200   *Sales* 42,160,500
SIC 4131 Intercity and rural bus transportation
James Devlin
Ron English
Ross Kinnear

D-U-N-S 20-181-3545   (SL)
UPPER CANADA FUELS (2001) LIMITED
660 The Queensway, Peterborough, ON, K9J 7H2
(705) 742-8815
Emp Here 12   *Sales* 12,393,696
SIC 5172 Petroleum products, nec
Brent Perrin

D-U-N-S 20-141-7383   (SL)
WINSLOW-GEROLAMY MOTORS LIMITED
1018 Lansdowne St W, Peterborough, ON, K9J 1Z9
(705) 742-3411
Emp Here 65   *Sales* 40,903,200
SIC 5511 New and used car dealers
Michael Winslow
Thomas Gerolamy
Steven Gerolamy

D-U-N-S 20-401-7206   (SL)
YOUNG, ROBERT E CONSTRUCTION LTD
1488 Chemong Rd, Peterborough, ON, K9J 6X2
(705) 745-1488
Emp Here 50   *Sales* 10,206,500
SIC 1442 Construction sand and gravel
Carl Young
Eleanor Young

Peterborough, ON K9L

D-U-N-S 25-186-9079   (SL)
1426159 ONTARIO LIMITED
MORELLO'S INDEPENDANT GROCER
400 Lansdowne St E Suite 1, Peterborough, ON, K9L 0B2
(705) 740-9365
Emp Here 125   *Sales* 36,684,625
SIC 5411 Grocery stores
David Morello
Kimberley Morello

D-U-N-S 20-920-6838   (HQ)
ALF CURTIS HOME IMPROVEMENTS INC
370 Parkhill Rd E, Peterborough, ON, K9L 1C3
(705) 742-4690
Emp Here 45   *Sales* 15,523,816
SIC 5211 Lumber and other building materials
Brent Perry
June Curtis

D-U-N-S 24-418-2833   (BR)
ARAMARK CANADA LTD.
OTONABEE MARKETPLACE
(*Suby of* ARAMARK)
2151 East Bank Dr, Peterborough, ON, K9L 1Z8

Emp Here 90
SIC 5812 Eating places
Pierre Overvelde

D-U-N-S 20-093-9879   (SL)
KAWARTHA CAPITAL CORP
KAWARTHA CAPITAL CONSTRUCTION
580 Ashburnham Dr, Peterborough, ON, K9L 2A2
(705) 750-0440
Emp Here 65   *Sales* 27,477,905
SIC 1541 Industrial buildings and warehouses

Paul Mcleod

D-U-N-S 20-943-7664   (HQ)
PETERBOROUGH UTILITIES SERVICES INC
(*Suby of* CORPORATION OF THE CITY OF PETERBOROUGH, THE)
1867 Ashburnham Dr, Peterborough, ON, K9L 1P8
(705) 748-9300
Emp Here 145   *Sales* 51,899,890
SIC 4941 Water supply
John Stephenson
Byron Thompson
Larry Franks
Jeff Guilbeault
John Wynsma
Wayne Stiver
Carissa Mccaw

Petersburg, ON N0B

D-U-N-S 20-064-9049   (HQ)
DON'S PRODUCE INC
1535 Snyder'S Rd E, Petersburg, ON, N0B 2H0
(519) 634-1077
Sales 25,067,310
SIC 5148 Fresh fruits and vegetables
Gerry Blake
Frank Toscan

Petrolia, ON N0N

D-U-N-S 25-725-6156   (SL)
1401911 ONTARIO LIMITED
REGNIER'S YOUR INDEPENDENT GROCERS
4136 Petrolia Line, Petrolia, ON, N0N 1R0
(519) 882-2211
Emp Here 80   *Sales* 23,478,160
SIC 5411 Grocery stores
Dennis Regnier

D-U-N-S 20-552-7315   (BR)
BLUEWATER HEALTH
(*Suby of* BLUEWATER HEALTH)
450 Blanche St, Petrolia, ON, N0N 1R0
(519) 464-4400
Emp Here 160
SIC 8062 General medical and surgical hospitals
Connie Courtney

D-U-N-S 20-851-0701   (SL)
CHARLOTTE ELEANOR ENGLEHART HOSPITAL
450 Blanche St, Petrolia, ON, N0N 1R0
(519) 882-4325
Emp Here 166   *Sales* 16,341,280
SIC 8062 General medical and surgical hospitals
Marilyne Heath
David Vigar

D-U-N-S 24-420-5667   (BR)
CORPORATION OF THE COUNTY OF LAMBTON
EMERGENCY MEDICAL SERVICES
(*Suby of* CORPORATION OF THE COUNTY OF LAMBTON)
3958 Petrolia Line Rr 4, Petrolia, ON, N0N 1R0
(519) 882-3797
Emp Here 150
SIC 4119 Local passenger transportation, nec
Jeff Brooks

D-U-N-S 24-203-5322   (SL)
ENNISKILLEN PEPPER CO. LTD
4376 Lasalle Line Rr 3, Petrolia, ON, N0N 1R0

(519) 882-3423
Emp Here 40   *Sales* 13,698,680
SIC 0182 Food crops grown under cover
Christine Greydanus
Jack Greydanus
Jocelyn Greydanus-Roelands

D-U-N-S 20-935-7052   (SL)
FIDDICK'S NURSING HOME LIMITED
437 1st Ave, Petrolia, ON, N0N 1R0
(519) 882-0370
Emp Here 130   *Sales* 8,913,580
SIC 8051 Skilled nursing care facilities
Maxine Fiddicks
Michael Fiddicks
Todd Fiddicks

D-U-N-S 25-249-3804   (BR)
LAMBTON KENT DISTRICT SCHOOL BOARD
LAMBTON CENTRAL COLLEGIATE & VOCATIONAL INSTITUTE
(*Suby of* LAMBTON KENT DISTRICT SCHOOL BOARD)
4141 Dufferin Ave, Petrolia, ON, N0N 1R0
(519) 882-1910
Emp Here 115
SIC 8211 Elementary and secondary schools
Bert Phills

D-U-N-S 20-850-4514   (SL)
LAMBTON MEADOWVIEW VILLA
(*Suby of* CORPORATION OF THE COUNTY OF LAMBTON)
3958 Petrolia Line Suite 499, Petrolia, ON, N0N 1R0
(519) 882-1470
Emp Here 150   *Sales* 9,642,300
SIC 8361 Residential care
Ken Herrington

D-U-N-S 20-976-4067   (SL)
MACFARLANE CHEVROLET LIMITED
4219 Oil Heritage Rd Rr 1, Petrolia, ON, N0N 1R0
(519) 882-3804
Emp Here 28   *Sales* 13,946,184
SIC 5511 New and used car dealers
Wayne Macfarlane
Mary Isabelle Macfarlane
Kristin Macfarlane

D-U-N-S 20-346-3963   (SL)
OWS RAILROAD CONSTRUCTION & MAINTENANCE LTD
(*Suby of* UNIVERSAL RAIL SYSTEMS INC)
4320 Discovery Line, Petrolia, ON, N0N 1R0
(519) 882-4996
Emp Here 100   *Sales* 60,648,160
SIC 1629 Heavy construction, nec
Pat Gladwish
Joe Morrison
David Farnsworth
Hermie Ceniza
Patrick O'niel
Ray Sandhu
Tim Mcmillan
Alfred Stanley
Ivor Lee

D-U-N-S 20-376-6683   (SL)
PENTA EQUIPMENT INC
4480 Progress Dr, Petrolia, ON, N0N 1R0
(519) 882-3350
Emp Here 30   *Sales* 14,250,780
SIC 5083 Farm and garden machinery
Glenn Buurma

D-U-N-S 20-032-5793   (SL)
PODOLINSKY EQUIPMENT LTD
6057 Petrolia Line, Petrolia, ON, N0N 1R0
(519) 844-2360
Emp Here 40   *Sales* 13,024,000
SIC 5999 Miscellaneous retail stores, nec
Anne Podolinsky

D-U-N-S 25-687-4421   (BR)
WATERVILLE TG INC

(*Suby of* TOYODA GOSEI CO., LTD.)
4491 Discovery Line, Petrolia, ON, N0N 1R0
(519) 882-4366
Emp Here 205
SIC 3069 Fabricated rubber products, nec
Linda Ryan

Pickering, ON L1V

D-U-N-S 20-708-3051   (SL)
1044912 ONTARIO LIMITED
PINE RIDGE GARDEN GALLERY
2215 Brock Rd N, Pickering, ON, L1V 2R4
(905) 683-5952
Emp Here 40   *Sales* 10,122,360
SIC 5261 Retail nurseries and garden stores
Nicole Rabouin

D-U-N-S 24-992-5132   (SL)
1051107 ONTARIO LTD
MANDARIN RESTAURANT
1725 Kingston Rd Suite 25, Pickering, ON, L1V 4L9
(905) 619-1000
Emp Here 80   *Sales* 3,641,520
SIC 5812 Eating places
Dolores Wai

D-U-N-S 25-712-2325   (BR)
1561716 ONTARIO LTD
LONE STAR TEXAS GRILL
(*Suby of* 1561716 ONTARIO LTD)
705 Kingston Rd, Pickering, ON, L1V 6K3
(905) 420-3334
Emp Here 80
SIC 5812 Eating places
Michael Derkach

D-U-N-S 20-064-9056   (SL)
ANNANDALE LEASING LIMITED
Gd, Pickering, ON, L1V 2R1
(905) 683-5722
Emp Here 35   *Sales* 17,634,634
SIC 5511 New and used car dealers
Don Will

D-U-N-S 24-893-6296   (SL)
BOYER, MICHAEL PONTIAC BUICK GMC (1988) LTD
715 Kingston Rd, Pickering, ON, L1V 1A9
(905) 831-2693
Emp Here 60   *Sales* 37,756,800
SIC 5511 New and used car dealers
Michael Boyer

D-U-N-S 20-411-8566   (HQ)
CENTRE LEASEHOLD IMPROVEMENTS LIMITED
CLI GROUP
1315 Pickering Pky Unit 205, Pickering, ON, L1V 7G5
(905) 492-6131
Emp Here 12   *Sales* 11,768,275
SIC 1542 Nonresidential construction, nec
Raymond Martin
Robert Moore

D-U-N-S 24-923-8718   (HQ)
CHILDREN'S WISH FOUNDATION OF CANADA, THE
1101 Kingston Rd Suite 350, Pickering, ON, L1V 1B5
(905) 839-8882
Emp Here 22   *Sales* 24,806,147
SIC 7389 Business services, nec
Chris Kotsopoulos
Darren Nantes
Jeanette Wakelin
Jim Kapeluck
Rich Gabruch
Tom Novak
Richard Lachance
Nick Leitch
Lloyd Matthews

Sarah Gander

D-U-N-S 25-300-8163   (BR)
DURHAM DISTRICT SCHOOL BOARD
DUNBARTON HIGH SCHOOL
(*Suby of* DURHAM DISTRICT SCHOOL BOARD)
655 Sheppard Ave, Pickering, ON, L1V 1G2
(905) 839-1125
Emp Here 140
SIC 8211 Elementary and secondary schools
Randy Tennant

D-U-N-S 24-505-9530   (SL)
FORMULA FORD SALES LIMITED
940 Kingston Rd, Pickering, ON, L1V 1B3
(905) 420-1449
Emp Here 45   *Sales* 22,413,510
SIC 5511 New and used car dealers
Lou Crkovski

D-U-N-S 24-760-2506   (BR)
HOME DEPOT OF CANADA INC
PICKERING HOME DEPOT
(*Suby of* THE HOME DEPOT INC)
1105a Kingston Rd, Pickering, ON, L1V 1B5
(905) 421-2000
Emp Here 160
SIC 5251 Hardware stores
Matthew Evans

D-U-N-S 20-364-1084   (SL)
LENDCARE CAPITAL INC
1315 Pickering Pkwy Fl 4, Pickering, ON, L1V 7G5
(905) 839-1009
Emp Here 140   *Sales* 31,351,740
SIC 6141 Personal credit institutions
Ali Metel

D-U-N-S 20-708-7912   (BR)
LOBLAWS SUPERMARKETS LIMITED
LOBLAWS
(*Suby of* LOBLAW COMPANIES LIMITED)
1792 Liverpool Rd, Pickering, ON, L1V 4G6
(905) 831-6301
Emp Here 400
SIC 5411 Grocery stores
Terry Bahen

D-U-N-S 24-802-8123   (BR)
LOWE'S COMPANIES CANADA, ULC
(*Suby of* LOWE'S COMPANIES, INC.)
1899 Brock Rd, Pickering, ON, L1V 4H7
(905) 619-7530
Emp Here 100
SIC 5211 Lumber and other building materials
Jeffrey Reed

D-U-N-S 25-310-9219   (BR)
MCDONALD'S RESTAURANTS OF CANADA LIMITED
MCDONALD'S
(*Suby of* MCDONALD'S CORPORATION)
1300 Kingston Rd, Pickering, ON, L1V 3M9
(905) 839-5665
Emp Here 100
SIC 5812 Eating places

D-U-N-S 20-555-6355   (BR)
METRO ONTARIO INC
METRO
(*Suby of* METRO INC)
1822 Whites Rd Suite 11, Pickering, ON, L1V 4M1
(905) 420-8838
Emp Here 208
SIC 5411 Grocery stores
Ted Kucera

D-U-N-S 25-689-4874   (HQ)
MUNICIPAL PROPERTY ASSESSMENT CORPORATION
MPAC
1340 Pickering Pky Suite 101, Pickering, ON, L1V 0C4
(905) 831-4433
Emp Here 200   *Sales* 469,214,578

SIC 7389 Business services, nec
Nicole Mcneill
Carmelo Lipsi
Greg Martino
Sujit Jagdev
Lucy Foster

D-U-N-S 24-122-3387   (BR)
ONTARIO POWER GENERATION INC
O P G
(*Suby of* GOVERNMENT OF ONTARIO)
1675 Montgomery Park Rd, Pickering, ON, L1V 2R5
(905) 839-1151
Emp Here 3,600
SIC 4911 Electric services
Pierre Charlebois

D-U-N-S 25-357-5328   (HQ)
PIC GROUP LTD, THE
TRIGO
(*Suby of* ARDIAN HOLDING)
1305 Pickering Pkwy, Pickering, ON, L1V 3P2
(905) 743-4600
Emp Here 600   *Sales* 18,952,550
SIC 7549 Automotive services, nec
Matthieu Rambaud
Pierre Lewin
Denoit Leblanc
Daniel Jurgens-Mestre
Elaine Retas
Anthony Long
Joe Pellerito

D-U-N-S 24-752-9019   (SL)
PICKERING CAR CORP
PICKERING TOYOTA
557 Kingston Rd, Pickering, ON, L1V 3N7
(416) 798-4800
Emp Here 58   *Sales* 36,498,240
SIC 5511 New and used car dealers
Andrew Chung

D-U-N-S 24-823-4093   (SL)
PROFORMANCE ADJUSTING SOLUTIONS
1101 Kingston Rd Suite 280, Pickering, ON, L1V 1B5

Emp Here 30   *Sales* 31,046,430
SIC 6321 Accident and health insurance
Tammie Norn

D-U-N-S 25-667-3476   (HQ)
RE/MAX FIRST REALTY LTD
1154 Kingston Rd, Pickering, ON, L1V 1B4
(905) 831-3300
Emp Here 1   *Sales* 29,322,230
SIC 6531 Real estate agents and managers
Ronald Gordon

D-U-N-S 20-969-1620   (HQ)
SEARCH ENGINE PEOPLE INC
1305 Pickering Pky Suite 500, Pickering, ON, L1V 3P2
(905) 421-9340
Emp Here 20   *Sales* 16,631,820
SIC 4813 Telephone communication, except radio
Jeffrey Quipp
Jennifer Osborne

D-U-N-S 20-824-2701   (SL)
SHOPPERS DRUG MART
1355 Kingston Rd Suite 618, Pickering, ON, L1V 1B8
(905) 839-4488
Emp Here 47   *Sales* 11,888,838
SIC 5912 Drug stores and proprietary stores
Barry Kawarsky

D-U-N-S 20-611-3412   (SL)
SUTTON GROUP HERITAGE REALTY INC
1755 Pickering Pky Unit 10, Pickering, ON, L1V 6K5
(416) 678-9622
Emp Here 150   *Sales* 62,833,350
SIC 6531 Real estate agents and managers
Rosalind Menary

▲ Public Company   ■ Public Company Family Member   **HQ** Headquarters   **BR** Branch   **SL** Single Location

D-U-N-S 24-851-6440   (SL)
TRANSMONTAIGNE MARKETING CANADA INC
1305 Pickering Pky Suite 101, Pickering, ON, L1V 3P2

Emp Here 50   *Sales* 10,378,161
SIC 2911 Petroleum refining
Charles Dunlap
Richard Pouliot
S. Fabrizio Zichichi

D-U-N-S 20-168-0159   (SL)
VOLVO OF DURHAM
920 Kingston Rd, Pickering, ON, L1V 1B3
(905) 421-9515
Emp Here 25   *Sales* 12,451,950
SIC 5511 New and used car dealers
Lou Crkovski
Steven Baskie

D-U-N-S 24-166-0435   (BR)
WAL-MART CANADA CORP
(*Suby of* WALMART INC.)
1899 Brock Rd Unit B, Pickering, ON, L1V 4H7
(905) 619-9588
Emp Here 200
SIC 5311 Department stores
Drew Cashmore

Pickering, ON L1W

D-U-N-S 20-205-8579   (SL)
1023248 ONTARIO INC
K & K RECYCLING SERVICES
870 Mckay Rd, Pickering, ON, L1W 2Y4
(905) 426-8989
Emp Here 65   *Sales* 29,199,235
SIC 7389 Business services, nec
Kevin Morgan
Ken Sweeney

D-U-N-S 20-638-8134   (SL)
242408 STEEL FABRICATION LIMITED
D & R CUSTOM STEEL FABRICATION
1625 Feldspar Crt, Pickering, ON, L1W 3R7
(905) 831-6172
Emp Here 60   *Sales* 13,320,060
SIC 3589 Service industry machinery, nec
Charlie Reitsma
Dan Engelage
Fred Engelage

D-U-N-S 24-652-7428   (SL)
A.P.S. METAL INDUSTRIES INC
895 Sandy Beach Rd Unit 4, Pickering, ON, L1W 3N7
(905) 831-7698
Emp Here 60   *Sales* 11,525,100
SIC 3444 Sheet Metalwork
Andy Pavletich

D-U-N-S 25-686-3564   (SL)
ABOVE BOARD CONSTRUCTION INC
1731 Orangebrook Crt, Pickering, ON, L1W 3G8
(905) 420-0656
Emp Here 22   *Sales* 10,356,082
SIC 1542 Nonresidential construction, nec
John P Reeves

D-U-N-S 20-605-9263   (SL)
ALLTEMP PRODUCTS COMPANY LIMITED
(*Suby of* 344036 ONTARIO LIMITED)
827 Brock Rd, Pickering, ON, L1W 3J2
(905) 831-3311
Emp Here 37   *Sales* 16,545,438
SIC 5075 Warm air heating and air conditioning
Richard Chalmers
Mary Northam

D-U-N-S 24-809-0354   (SL)
ASPECT RETAIL LOGISTICS INC
1400 Church St, Pickering, ON, L1W 4C1

(905) 428-9947
Emp Here 600   *Sales* 123,423,600
SIC 4225 General warehousing and storage
Roy Drummond

D-U-N-S 20-314-5958   (SL)
AUTOLUX LTD
970 Brock Rd, Pickering, ON, L1W 2A1
(416) 266-1500
Emp Here 120   *Sales* 9,032,640
SIC 4111 Local and suburban transit
Robert Donaldson
Nikolai Choumakevitch

D-U-N-S 24-891-7122   (HQ)
AVERY DENNISON CANADA CORPORATION
FASSOM, DIV OF
(*Suby of* AVERY DENNISON CORPORATION)
1840 Clements Rd, Pickering, ON, L1W 3Y2
(905) 837-4700
Emp Here 100   *Sales* 69,851,030
SIC 2672 Paper; coated and laminated, nec
Kent Kresa
Dean Scarborough
Daniel O'bryant
Lynn Livsey
Sam Baynham

D-U-N-S 24-794-5462   (SL)
B.M.I. CONSTRUCTION CO. LIMITED
1058 Copperstone Dr Suite 1, Pickering, ON, L1W 3V8
(905) 686-4287
Emp Here 50   *Sales* 23,536,550
SIC 1542 Nonresidential construction, nec
Ian Watts
Kevin Coglan
Sherri Daigle

D-U-N-S 20-781-0743   (SL)
BEDWELL VAN LINES LIMITED
1051 Toy Ave, Pickering, ON, L1W 3N9
(905) 686-0002
Emp Here 75   *Sales* 11,243,126
SIC 4214 Local trucking with storage
Jim Bedwell

D-U-N-S 24-876-9424   (SL)
BIG RED OIL PRODUCTS INC
1915 Clements Rd Suite 7, Pickering, ON, L1W 3V1
(905) 420-0001
Emp Here 10   *Sales* 10,328,080
SIC 5172 Petroleum products, nec
Robert Lennox

D-U-N-S 20-150-5260   (HQ)
BURNDY CANADA INC
(*Suby of* HUBBELL INCORPORATED)
870 Brock Rd, Pickering, ON, L1W 1Z8
(905) 752-5400
Emp Here 60   *Sales* 79,216,200
SIC 3643 Current-carrying wiring devices
Albert He
Richard W Davies
Paul J Ashworth

D-U-N-S 20-691-6509   (HQ)
BUSKRO INTERNATIONAL LTD
1738 Orangebrook Crt Unit 1, Pickering, ON, L1W 3G8
(905) 839-6018
Sales 17,760,080
SIC 3577 Computer peripheral equipment, nec
Jeffrey Kropman
Hendrik A. Kropman
Patrick Kropman
Roy P. Kropman
Larry Kropman

D-U-N-S 25-398-7960   (SL)
C F & R SERVICES INC
1920 Clements Rd, Pickering, ON, L1W 3V6
(905) 426-3891
Emp Here 90   *Sales* 21,085,920

SIC 8743 Public relations services
Ronald Peacock

D-U-N-S 24-314-6516   (SL)
C H S PHARMACY LIMITED
MEDICAL PHARMACY
590 Granite Crt Suite 4, Pickering, ON, L1W 3X6
(905) 420-7335
Emp Here 50   *Sales* 12,647,700
SIC 5912 Drug stores and proprietary stores
Syd Shrott

D-U-N-S 20-044-2788   (HQ)
CDA INDUSTRIES INC
CDA NEILSON MARKETING
1055 Squires Beach Rd, Pickering, ON, L1W 4A6
(905) 686-7000
Emp Here 200
SIC 2541 Wood partitions and fixtures
Vincent Devita
Gerry Charbonneau
Ron Terin
Paul Gross
William Malisch
Roland Devita
Terry Holgate
Sherman Hans

D-U-N-S 24-668-9520   (SL)
DOUBLE G GAS SERVICES
962 Alliance Rd, Pickering, ON, L1W 3M9

Emp Here 4   *Sales* 12,423,428
SIC 4925 Gas production and/or distribution
Lew Reilly

D-U-N-S 20-639-3852   (SL)
ECO-TEC INC
(*Suby of* ECO-TEC LIMITED)
1145 Squires Beach Rd, Pickering, ON, L1W 3T9
(905) 427-0077
Emp Here 85   *Sales* 18,870,085
SIC 3559 Special industry machinery, nec
Phillip Simmons
Glenn Towe
Michael Dejak
Jenny Shao
John Reid

D-U-N-S 24-891-8195   (HQ)
ECO-TEC LIMITED
1145 Squires Beach Rd, Pickering, ON, L1W 3T9
(905) 427-0077
Emp Here 6   *Sales* 20,501,250
SIC 6712 Bank holding companies
Phillip Simmons
Robert Strickert
Craig Brown
Jeffrey Potter
Vernon Pace
Mike Dejak

D-U-N-S 24-125-0844   (HQ)
ELLIS PACKAGING LIMITED
1830 Sandstone Manor, Pickering, ON, L1W 3Y1
(905) 831-5777
Sales 23,372,160
SIC 2657 Folding paperboard boxes
Cathie Ellis
Bruce Paterson

D-U-N-S 20-640-6956   (SL)
EMPIRE INVESTIGATIONS AND PROTECTION SERVICES INC
EMPIRE IPS
940 Brock Rd Unit 4, Pickering, ON, L1W 2A1
(905) 426-3909
Emp Here 1,000   *Sales* 26,250,000
SIC 7381 Detective and armored car services

D-U-N-S 24-250-7601   (SL)
ENNIS PAINT CANADA ULC
850 Mckay Rd, Pickering, ON, L1W 2Y4

(905) 686-2770
Emp Here 60   *Sales* 17,041,260
SIC 2851 Paints and allied products
Myriam Burman Plourde
Don Vermeer
Tom Hoolan
Bryce W Anderson
Alex Sekulovski
John Anderson

D-U-N-S 20-287-0650   (SL)
FOURNIER VAN & STORAGE, LIMITED
1051 Toy Ave, Pickering, ON, L1W 3N9
(905) 686-0002
Emp Here 75   *Sales* 11,243,126
SIC 4225 General warehousing and storage
James Bedwell

D-U-N-S 20-267-0654   (HQ)
FRAMATOME CANADA LTD
925 Brock Rd Suite B, Pickering, ON, L1W 2X9
(905) 421-2600
Emp Here 33   *Sales* 16,661,172
SIC 1629 Heavy construction, nec
Nicholas Fehrenvach
William Cooper

D-U-N-S 24-976-8743   (SL)
GFL ENVIRONMENTAL CORP
1070 Toy Ave, Pickering, ON, L1W 3P1
(905) 428-8992
Emp Here 49   *Sales* 14,755,958
SIC 4959 Sanitary services, nec
Patrick Dovigi

D-U-N-S 24-709-3073   (SL)
GUARDIAN VAN LINES LIMITED
1051 Toy Ave, Pickering, ON, L1W 3N9
(905) 686-0002
Emp Here 100   *Sales* 14,819,200
SIC 4212 Local trucking, without storage
James Bedwell

D-U-N-S 20-940-8970   (HQ)
HOLMES & BRAKEL LIMITED
830 Brock Rd, Pickering, ON, L1W 1Z8
(905) 831-6831
Emp Here 40   *Sales* 66,890,800
SIC 7389 Business services, nec
Richard Holmes

D-U-N-S 20-151-6275   (HQ)
HOWARD MARTEN COMPANY LIMITED
902 Dillingham Rd, Pickering, ON, L1W 1Z6
(905) 831-2901
Sales 24,420,110
SIC 3569 General industrial machinery, nec
William Mckay
Brian Whitehead
John Shobridge

D-U-N-S 24-684-8571   (HQ)
HOWARD MARTEN FLUID TECHNOLOGIES INC
902 Dillingham Rd, Pickering, ON, L1W 1Z6
(905) 831-2901
Emp Here 100   *Sales* 43,091,235
SIC 5084 Industrial machinery and equipment
Bill Mckay
Brian Whitehead

D-U-N-S 20-052-2741   (SL)
INTEGRATED DEALER SYSTEMS CANADA LTD
(*Suby of* CONSTELLATION SOFTWARE INC)
1730 Mcpherson Crt Unit 7, Pickering, ON, L1W 3E6
(800) 769-7425
Emp Here 120
SIC 4213 Trucking, except local
Mark Mueller
John Armstrong
Stephen Hawkins

D-U-N-S 24-468-3913   (BR)
JORIKI INC

▲ **Public Company**   ■ **Public Company Family Member**   **HQ** Headquarters   **BR** Branch   **SL** Single Location

JORIKI FOOD AND BEVERAGE
(*Suby of* JORIKI INC)
885 Sandy Beach Rd, Pickering, ON, L1W 3N6
(905) 420-0188
Emp Here 100
SIC 2024 Ice cream and frozen deserts
Yogi Sennick

D-U-N-S 25-667-4631   (SL)
KNIGHTS ON GUARD SECURITY SURVEIL-LANCE SYSTEMS CORPORATION
KNIGHTS ON GUARD PROTECTIVES SER-VICES
1048 Toy Ave Suite 101, Pickering, ON, L1W 3P1
(905) 427-7863
Emp Here 325   *Sales* 8,531,250
SIC 7381 Detective and armored car services
Steve Dimkovski

D-U-N-S 24-756-8132   (HQ)
LENBROOK CORP
LENBROOK GROUP OF COMPANIES, THE
633 Granite Crt, Pickering, ON, L1W 3K1
(905) 831-6333
Emp Here 5   *Sales* 75,432,110
SIC 5065 Electronic parts and equipment, nec
Gordon A Simmonds
Dennis Hill
Terry Mccrae

D-U-N-S 24-122-8147   (HQ)
LENBROOK INDUSTRIES LIMITED
PSB INTERNATIONAL
(*Suby of* LENBROOK CORP)
633 Granite Crt, Pickering, ON, L1W 3K1
(905) 831-6333
Emp Here 82   *Sales* 24,757,460
SIC 3651 Household audio and video equipment
Gordon Simmonds
Dennis Hill
Terry Mccrae

D-U-N-S 20-178-7884   (HQ)
LONG & MCQUADE LIMITED
YORKVILLE SOUND
(*Suby of* LONG HOLDINGS INC)
722 Rosebank Rd, Pickering, ON, L1W 4B2
(905) 837-9785
Emp Here 45   *Sales* 453,395,100
SIC 5736 Musical instrument stores
Steve Long
Jack Long
Frederick Theriault
Michael Klue
Brian Weaver
Jeffrey Long
Jeff Cowling

D-U-N-S 24-314-4479   (HQ)
LONG HOLDINGS INC
722 Rosebank Rd, Pickering, ON, L1W 4B2
(905) 837-9785
Sales 400,054,500
SIC 5736 Musical instrument stores
Steven G Long
Jeffrey Long
John Long
Jack E Long
Carol Long

D-U-N-S 24-937-9900   (HQ)
MAPLERIDGE MECHANICAL CONTACT-ING INC
939 Dillingham Rd, Pickering, ON, L1W 1Z7
(905) 831-0524
Sales 27,967,800
SIC 1711 Plumbing, heating, air-conditioning
Robert Allingham
Michael Gray
Dean Spinello

D-U-N-S 20-031-8988   (HQ)
MASON WINDOWS LIMITED
913 Brock Rd, Pickering, ON, L1W 2X9

(905) 839-1171
Emp Here 100   *Sales* 23,084,400
SIC 2431 Millwork
Robert Mason
Douglas Mason
Linda Mason

D-U-N-S 20-753-1328   (SL)
NELSON INDUSTRIAL INC
1155 Squires Beach Rd, Pickering, ON, L1W 3T9
(905) 428-2240
Emp Here 90   *Sales* 17,287,650
SIC 3499 Fabricated Metal products, nec
Jeff Nelson
Marian Nelson

D-U-N-S 24-352-8457   (BR)
OTTO BOCK HEALTHCARE CANADA LTD
(*Suby of* NADER HOLDING GMBH & CO. KG)
901 Dillingham Rd, Pickering, ON, L1W 2Y5

Emp Here 87
SIC 3842 Surgical appliances and supplies
Mark Agro

D-U-N-S 24-794-9894   (HQ)
PLAYIT INCORPORATED
F.G. BRADLEY'S
831 Brock Rd Unit 1, Pickering, ON, L1W 3L8
(905) 837-7650
Sales 12,216,400
SIC 5945 Hobby, toy, and game shops
Brad Macintosh

D-U-N-S 24-720-3342   (HQ)
PREMIER BRANDS CANADA LTD
680 Granite Crt, Pickering, ON, L1W 4A3
(416) 750-8807
Sales 20,889,425
SIC 5145 Confectionery
Brian Hicks

D-U-N-S 24-026-0141   (HQ)
PROVINCIAL SIGN SERVICE LIMITED
PROVINCIAL SIGN SYSTEMS
1655 Feldspar Crt, Pickering, ON, L1W 3R7
(905) 837-1791
Sales 27,721,560
SIC 3993 Signs and advertising specialties
Paul Cotton

D-U-N-S 25-095-5291   (SL)
PURDUE PHARMA
575 Granite Crt, Pickering, ON, L1W 3W8
(905) 420-6400
Emp Here 300   *Sales* 99,478,200
SIC 2834 Pharmaceutical preparations
David A. Pidduck
Jacqueline Le Saux
Kelly Martin
Kenneth Michalko
Marguerite O'neal
Grant Perry
David Pidduck

D-U-N-S 24-278-6192   (BR)
PUROLATOR INC
(*Suby of* GOVERNMENT OF CANADA)
1075 Squires Beach Rd, Pickering, ON, L1W 3S3
(888) 744-7123
Emp Here 200
SIC 4731 Freight transportation arrangement
Virgin Don

D-U-N-S 20-131-0754   (SL)
QUALITY PACKAGING SOLUTIONS INC
1420 Bayly St Unit 7, Pickering, ON, L1W 3R4

Emp Here 25   *Sales* 11,230,475
SIC 7389 Business services, nec
Joseph Sannella

D-U-N-S 20-119-7550   (HQ)
RCM TECHNOLOGIES CANADA CORP
(*Suby of* R C M TECHNOLOGIES, INC.)

895 Brock Rd, Pickering, ON, L1W 3C1
(905) 837-8333
Emp Here 30   *Sales* 73,110,900
SIC 8999 Services, nec
Rocco Campanelli
Danny White
Robert Black
Craig Sellers
Juan Laverde

D-U-N-S 20-353-5935   (SL)
RENAISSANCE PRINTING INC
1800 Ironstone Manor, Pickering, ON, L1W 3J9
(905) 831-3000
Emp Here 80   *Sales* 13,122,160
SIC 2721 Periodicals
Michael Fredericks
John Bacopulos

D-U-N-S 24-795-7400   (HQ)
SHANDEX SALES GROUP LIMITED
SHANDEX GROUP, THE
1100 Squires Beach Rd, Pickering, ON, L1W 3N8
(905) 420-7407
Sales 19,932,880
SIC 5137 Women's and children's clothing
Gregory Shannon
Robin Staite
Bell Folsom
Frederick J Shannon
Jeffrey Shannon
Jennifer Shannon
Joyce Shannon
Christine Shannon
Shawn Mcnaughton

D-U-N-S 20-315-9926   (SL)
SIGNATURE ALUMINUM CANADA INC
1850 Clements Rd, Pickering, ON, L1W 3R8
(905) 427-6550
Emp Here 148   *Sales* 26,845,424
SIC 3354 Aluminum extruded products
David Pike
Sam Gedy

D-U-N-S 20-771-2092   (SL)
TRIDEN DISTRIBUTORS LIMITED
922 Dillingham Rd, Pickering, ON, L1W 1Z6
(416) 291-2955
Emp Here 30   *Sales* 14,949,660
SIC 5131 Piece goods and notions
Douglas G Ruggles Sr
Kevin Peare

D-U-N-S 24-662-7632   (SL)
UCC INDUSTRIES INTERNATIONAL INC
895 Sandy Beach Rd Unit 12, Pickering, ON, L1W 3N7
(905) 831-7724
Emp Here 14   *Sales* 14,004,746
SIC 5051 Metals service centers and offices
Brent Hughes

D-U-N-S 20-362-6023   (HQ)
WEPAWAUG CANADA CORP
ADAM
(*Suby of* HUBBELL LUXEMBOURG, SARL)
870 Brock Rd, Pickering, ON, L1W 1Z8
(905) 839-1138
Emp Here 3   *Sales* 15,854,300
SIC 6712 Bank holding companies
Maria R. Lee
An-Ping Hsieh
Joseph A. Capozzoli

D-U-N-S 24-659-1564   (HQ)
WESTHALL INVESTMENTS LTD
TRIBUTE COMMUNITIES
1815 Ironstone Manor Unit 1, Pickering, ON, L1W 3W9
(905) 839-3500
Emp Here 1   *Sales* 11,769,885
SIC 6712 Bank holding companies
Alexander Libfeld
Howard Sokolowski

Pickering, ON L1X

D-U-N-S 25-300-8338   (BR)
DURHAM DISTRICT SCHOOL BOARD
PINE RIDGE SECONDARY SCHOOL
(*Suby of* DURHAM DISTRICT SCHOOL BOARD)
2155 Liverpool Rd, Pickering, ON, L1X 1V4
(905) 420-1885
Emp Here 200
SIC 8211 Elementary and secondary schools
Susan Jones

D-U-N-S 25-570-3852   (SL)
RENE GOUPIL JESUITS
2315 Liverpool Rd, Pickering, ON, L1X 1V4
(905) 839-5155
Emp Here 36   *Sales* 14,306,904
SIC 8699 Membership organizations, nec
Alex Kirsten

Picton, ON K0K

D-U-N-S 24-185-3670   (SL)
BAY OF QUINTE MUTUAL INSURANCE CO
13379 Loyalist Pky, Picton, ON, K0K 2T0
(613) 476-2145
Emp Here 25   *Sales* 46,166,475
SIC 6331 Fire, marine, and casualty insurance
Steven Raymond
Donald Martin
Dalton Arthur
Mark Henry
Joseph Mcalpine
George Taylor
Richard Williams
Grant Ketcheson

D-U-N-S 24-354-4041   (HQ)
COMMUNITY LIVING PRINCE EDWARD
67 King St Unit 1, Picton, ON, K0K 2T0
(613) 476-6038
Sales 230,176,160
SIC 8699 Membership organizations, nec
Brian Smith

D-U-N-S 20-711-5135   (BR)
HASTINGS AND PRINCE EDWARD DIS-TRICT SCHOOL BOARD
PRINCE EDWARD AND COLLEGIATE
41 Barker St, Picton, ON, K0K 2T0
(613) 476-2196
Emp Here 100
SIC 8211 Elementary and secondary schools
David Fox

D-U-N-S 25-468-0192   (SL)
PICTON MANOR NURSING HOME LIMITED
9 Hill St, Picton, ON, K0K 2T0

Emp Here 90   *Sales* 6,185,970
SIC 8051 Skilled nursing care facilities
Deborah Skeaff
Margaret Jarvis

D-U-N-S 20-347-5707   (BR)
QUINTE HEALTHCARE CORPORATION
QUINTE HEALTHCARE PRINCE EDWARD COUNTY MEMORIAL
(*Suby of* QUINTE HEALTHCARE CORPORA-TION)
403 Picton Main St, Picton, ON, K0K 2T0
(613) 476-1008
Emp Here 100
SIC 8621 Professional organizations
Lisa Mowbray

D-U-N-S 25-461-8416   (BR)
REVERA LONG TERM CARE INC
VERSA-CARE HALLOWELL HOUSE
(*Suby of* GOVERNMENT OF CANADA)
13628 Loyalist Pky, Picton, ON, K0K 2T0

(613) 476-4444
Emp Here 100
SIC 8051 Skilled nursing care facilities
Janice Wilkes

Pikangikum, ON P0V

D-U-N-S 24-142-3008   (SL)
BRIGHTER FUTURES
Gd, Pikangikum, ON, P0V 2L0
(807) 773-5300
Emp Here 36   *Sales* 30,530,160
SIC 6411 Insurance agents, brokers, and service
Marilyn Ruegsegger

D-U-N-S 24-914-0815   (SL)
PIKANGIKUM EDUCATION AUTHORITY
EENCHOKAY BIRCHSTICK SCHOOL
1 School Rd, Pikangikum, ON, P0V 2L0
(807) 773-1093
Emp Here 95   *Sales* 8,818,470
SIC 8211 Elementary and secondary schools
Kyle Peters

Plainfield, ON K0K

D-U-N-S 25-486-4515   (SL)
MAPLE DALE CHEESE INC
2864 Hwy 37, Plainfield, ON, K0K 2V0
(613) 477-2454
Emp Here 23   *Sales* 19,218,271
SIC 5143 Dairy products, except dried or canned
Paul Henry

Plantagenet, ON K0B

D-U-N-S 20-889-9476   (SL)
656955 ONTARIO LIMITED
PINECREST NURSING HOME
101 Parent St, Plantagenet, ON, K0B 1L0
(613) 673-4835
Emp Here 75   *Sales* 5,154,975
SIC 8051 Skilled nursing care facilities
Marcel Parent

Plattsville, ON N0J

D-U-N-S 24-966-1851   (HQ)
SAINT-GOBAIN CANADA INC
(*Suby of* COMPAGNIE DE SAINT-GOBAIN)
28 Albert St W, Plattsville, ON, N0J 1S0
(519) 684-7441
Emp Here 100   *Sales* 61,365,600
SIC 3291 Abrasive products
Sheri Y Olinyk
John T Crowe
Mark E Mathieson

Point Edward, ON N7T

D-U-N-S 24-028-6377   (SL)
BLUE WATER BRIDGE CANADA
BLUE WATER BRIDGE AUTHORITY
(*Suby of* GOVERNMENT OF CANADA)
1555 Venetian Blvd Suite 436, Point Edward, ON, N7T 0A9
(519) 336-2720
Emp Here 73   *Sales* 48,683,116
SIC 4785 Inspection and fixed facilities
Chuck Chrapko

Cathy Newman
David Joy
Stan Korosec

D-U-N-S 24-305-7106   (SL)
GUILDWOOD INN LIMITED, THE
BEST WESTERN GUILDWOOD INN
1400 Venetian Blvd, Point Edward, ON, N7T 7W6
(519) 337-7577
Emp Here 75   *Sales* 7,117,425
SIC 7011 Hotels and motels
Sheldon Aaron

D-U-N-S 20-414-2798   (SL)
S. M. HEWITT (SARNIA) LIMITED
1555 Venetian Blvd Suite 11 3rd Fl, Point Edward, ON, N7T 0A9
(519) 332-4411
Emp Here 27   *Sales* 14,039,109
SIC 4731 Freight transportation arrangement
Matthew Bogart

Point Edward, ON N7V

D-U-N-S 25-283-5996   (HQ)
CAR-BER TESTING SERVICES INC
CAR-BER TESTING SERVICES
911 Michigan Ave, Point Edward, ON, N7V 1H2
(519) 336-7775
Emp Here 63   *Sales* 20,781,605
SIC 8734 Testing laboratories
Glen Carson
Dianne Carson
Dennis Pearson

D-U-N-S 20-719-1552   (HQ)
EDWARDS DOORS SYSTEMS LIMITED
124 Kendall St, Point Edward, ON, N7V 4G5
(519) 336-4990
Emp Here 20   *Sales* 15,651,090
SIC 5031 Lumber, plywood, and millwork
Gordon Cassidy
William Cassidy
Brian Crombeen

D-U-N-S 24-194-8488   (HQ)
MAGIC REALTY INC
805 Christina St N, Point Edward, ON, N7V 1X6

Emp Here 4   *Sales* 33,511,120
SIC 6531 Real estate agents and managers
Donald Guerette

Pontypool, ON L0A

D-U-N-S 25-203-2891   (SL)
C. D. R. YOUNG'S AGGREGATES INC
31 Hwy 35, Pontypool, ON, L0A 1K0
(705) 277-3972
Emp Here 50   *Sales* 22,358,700
SIC 5032 Brick, stone, and related material
Donald Young

Porcupine, ON P0N

D-U-N-S 20-629-2091   (SL)
GORF CONTRACTING LTD
6855 Hwy 101 E, Porcupine, ON, P0N 1C0
(705) 235-3278
Emp Here 49   *Sales* 14,140,567
SIC 1522 Residential construction, nec
Mark Norkum

D-U-N-S 20-142-2714   (SL)
NORMAC   EQUIPMENT/CONSTRUCTION LIMITED

GORF CONTRACTING
6855 Hwy 101 E, Porcupine, ON, P0N 1C0
(705) 235-3277
Emp Here 49   *Sales* 14,316,281
SIC 7359 Equipment rental and leasing, nec
Mark Norkum
Enrique Gaces

Port Carling, ON P0B

D-U-N-S 24-744-5935   (HQ)
MUSKOKA LUMBER AND BUILDING SUPPLIES CENTRE LIMITED
3687 Hwy 118, Port Carling, ON, P0B 1J0
(705) 765-3105
Emp Here 31   *Sales* 12,652,950
SIC 5211 Lumber and other building materials
Robert Potts
Paul Donaldson

Port Colborne, ON L3K

D-U-N-S 24-610-2495   (SL)
638691 ONTARIO LIMITED
YOUNG AUTOMOTIVE PROFESSIONALS, THE
658 Main St W, Port Colborne, ON, L3K 5V4
(905) 835-8120
Emp Here 30   *Sales* 14,942,340
SIC 5511 New and used car dealers
John Grandilli
Claudio Sceppacerqua

D-U-N-S 24-826-9628   (BR)
ADM AGRI-INDUSTRIES COMPANY
ADM MILLING CO
(*Suby of*   ARCHER-DANIELS-MIDLAND COMPANY)
1 King St Sw, Port Colborne, ON, L3K 5W1
(905) 835-4218
Emp Here 80
SIC 0723 Crop preparation services for market
Quinn Debrouwer

D-U-N-S 24-986-4737   (BR)
ALGOMA CENTRAL CORPORATION
FRASER MARINE & INDUSTRIAL, DIV. OF
(*Suby of* ALGOMA CENTRAL CORPORATION)
1 Chestnut St, Port Colborne, ON, L3K 1R3
(905) 834-4549
Emp Here 100
SIC 3731 Shipbuilding and repairing
Dave Ross

D-U-N-S 24-358-0912   (HQ)
CERES GLOBAL AG CORP
2 Sherwood Forest Ln, Port Colborne, ON, L3K 5V8
(905) 834-5924
Emp Here 10   *Sales* 10,624,140
SIC 6211 Security brokers and dealers
Robert Day
Kyle Egbert
John Carroll
Douglas Speers
Harvey Joel
Gary Mize
James Vanasek

D-U-N-S 25-179-4541   (BR)
DISTRICT SCHOOL BOARD OF NIAGARA
OAKWOOD PUBLIC SCHOOL
255 Omer Ave, Port Colborne, ON, L3K 3Z1
(905) 834-9732
Emp Here 300
SIC 8211 Elementary and secondary schools
Linda Oakes

D-U-N-S 24-206-6566   (SL)

GARON,   LAWRENCE   M   ENTERPRISES LTD
CANADIAN TIRE
287 West Side Rd, Port Colborne, ON, L3K 5L2
(905) 835-1155
Emp Here 40   *Sales* 19,923,120
SIC 5531 Auto and home supply stores
Lawrence Garon

D-U-N-S 24-953-1583   (BR)
IMT PARTNERSHIP
PC FORGE
(*Suby of* IMT PARTNERSHIP)
837 Reuter Rd, Port Colborne, ON, L3K 5V7
(905) 834-7211
Emp Here 115
SIC 3444 Sheet Metalwork
Fred Smiche

D-U-N-S 24-771-1674   (HQ)
INTERNATIONAL MARINE SALVAGE INC
17 Invertose Dr, Port Colborne, ON, L3K 5V5
(905) 835-1203
Emp Here 115   *Sales* 39,863,750
SIC 4953 Refuse systems
Dyllan Elliott
James Ewles
Richard Unyi
Dylan Elliott

D-U-N-S 20-597-7416   (SL)
J. OSKAM STEEL FABRICATORS LIMITED
(*Suby of* HEBELER LLC)
70 Rosedale Ave, Port Colborne, ON, L3K 6G5
(905) 834-7321
Emp Here 70   *Sales* 13,445,950
SIC 3441 Fabricated structural Metal
John Langerak

D-U-N-S 20-143-1624   (SL)
JTL INTEGRATED MACHINE LTD.
857 Reuter Rd, Port Colborne, ON, L3K 5W1
(905) 834-3992
Emp Here 80   *Sales* 17,760,080
SIC 3569 General industrial machinery, nec
Victor Oreskovich

D-U-N-S 25-351-5811   (SL)
MARINE RECYCLING CORPORATION
17 Invertose Dr, Port Colborne, ON, L3K 5V5
(905) 835-1203
Emp Here 40   *Sales* 10,781,960
SIC 4499 Water transportation services,
Jordan Elliott
Morn Wotherspoon

D-U-N-S 25-653-3944   (SL)
MCAVOY BELAN & CAMPBELL INSURANCE AND FINANCIAL SERVICES LTD
MBC FINANCIAL
350 King St, Port Colborne, ON, L3K 4H3
(905) 834-3666
Emp Here 14   *Sales* 11,872,840
SIC 6411 Insurance agents, brokers, and service
Ken Mcavoy
Tim Mcavoy
Millie Belan
Nick Belan
Chuck Campbell
Crystal Campbell
Tammy Mcavoy

D-U-N-S 25-300-0046   (BR)
METRO ONTARIO INC
METRO
(*Suby of* METRO INC)
124 Clarence St, Port Colborne, ON, L3K 3G3
(905) 834-8800
Emp Here 100
SIC 5411 Grocery stores
Paul Cirasolo

D-U-N-S 25-137-3999   (BR)
NIAGARA CATHOLIC DISTRICT SCHOOL BOARD

LAKESHORE CATHOLIC HIGH SCHOOL
(*Suby of* NIAGARA CATHOLIC DISTRICT SCHOOL BOARD)
150 Janet St, Port Colborne, ON, L3K 2E7
(905) 835-2451
Emp Here 150
SIC 8211 Elementary and secondary schools
 Glenn Gifford

D-U-N-S 24-644-2586   (BR)
NIAGARA HEALTH SYSTEM
PORT COLBORNE GENERAL HOSPITAL
(*Suby of* NIAGARA HEALTH SYSTEM)
260 Sugarloaf St, Port Colborne, ON, L3K 2N7
(905) 834-4501
Emp Here 250
SIC 8062 General medical and surgical hospitals
 Caroline Bourque Wiley

D-U-N-S 20-175-8369   (SL)
NOR CLIFF FARMS INC
888 Barrick Rd, Port Colborne, ON, L3K 6H2
(905) 835-0808
Emp Here 48   *Sales* 10,793,040
SIC 2037 Frozen fruits and vegetables
 Nicholas J Secord
 Nina Dilorenzo Secord

D-U-N-S 24-678-4040   (SL)
RAW MATERIALS COMPANY INC
17 Invertose Dr, Port Colborne, ON, L3K 5V5
(905) 835-1203
Emp Here 45   *Sales* 11,570,895
SIC 4953 Refuse systems
 James Ewles
 Michael Macmillan

D-U-N-S 20-610-1495   (SL)
THURSTON MACHINE COMPANY LIMITED
(*Suby of* CANERECTOR INC)
45 Invertose Dr, Port Colborne, ON, L3K 5V8
(905) 834-3606
Emp Here 82   *Sales* 18,204,082
SIC 3547 Rolling mill machinery
 Cecil Hawkins
 Mark Yallin
 Mark Nevar

D-U-N-S 20-143-1616   (BR)
VALE CANADA LIMITED
PORT COLBORNE REFINERY
(*Suby of* VALE S/A)
187 Davis St, Port Colborne, ON, L3K 5W2
(905) 835-6000
Emp Here 200
SIC 7389 Business services, nec
 Del Fraipont

Port Dover, ON N0A

D-U-N-S 20-143-8033   (SL)
ERIE BEACH HOTEL LIMITED
19 Walker St, Port Dover, ON, N0A 1N0
(519) 583-1391
Emp Here 100   *Sales* 9,489,900
SIC 7011 Hotels and motels
 Anderw Schneider

D-U-N-S 20-057-7497   (SL)
LAKESHORE FISH MARKET INC
1 Passmore Ave, Port Dover, ON, N0A 1N0
(519) 428-8949
Emp Here 31   *Sales* 25,902,887
SIC 5146 Fish and seafoods
 James D. Mummery
 Dale W. Mummery
 Rhea Mummery

D-U-N-S 25-203-2370   (SL)
LOWER LAKES TOWING LTD
(*Suby of* AIP, LLC)
517 Main St, Port Dover, ON, N0A 1N0
(519) 583-0982
Emp Here 100   *Sales* 39,372,400

SIC 4449 Water transportation of freight
 Scott F. Bravener
 James Fiddall
 Laurence S. Levy

D-U-N-S 25-944-6003   (BR)
REVERA LONG TERM CARE INC
DOVER CLIFFS
(*Suby of* GOVERNMENT OF CANADA)
501 St George St, Port Dover, ON, N0A 1N0
(519) 583-1422
Emp Here 75
SIC 8051 Skilled nursing care facilities
 Pauline Lyne

Port Elgin, ON N0H

D-U-N-S 25-238-8756   (BR)
BLUEWATER DISTRICT SCHOOL BOARD
SAUGEEN DIST SECONDARY SCHOOL
780 Gustavus St Ss 4, Port Elgin, ON, N0H 2C4
(519) 832-2091
Emp Here 90
SIC 8211 Elementary and secondary schools
 Ron Code

D-U-N-S 24-343-8368   (SL)
CARLSUN ENERGY SOLUTIONS INC
1606 Bruce-Saugeen Tline, Port Elgin, ON, N0H 2C5
(519) 832-4075
Emp Here 40   *Sales* 10,973,280
SIC 8741 Management services
 Jason Van Geel

D-U-N-S 24-336-0125   (SL)
KINGSWAY ARMS MANAGEMENT (AT ELGIN LODGE) INC
551 Mary St, Port Elgin, ON, N0H 2C2
(519) 389-5457
Emp Here 50   *Sales* 11,323,700
SIC 6513 Apartment building operators
 Patrick Byrne
 Graham Parker
 Debbie Wallace

D-U-N-S 24-849-8727   (BR)
UNIFOR
UNIFOR FAMILY EDUCATION CENTER
(*Suby of* UNIFOR)
115 Av Shipley, Port Elgin, ON, N0H 2C5
(519) 389-3200
Emp Here 100
SIC 8631 Labor organizations
 Dean Fowler

Port Hope, ON L1A

D-U-N-S 24-382-3189   (HQ)
2121361 ONTARIO INC
FORM SOLUTIONS
6829 Dale Rd, Port Hope, ON, L1A 3V6
(905) 885-9237
Emp Here 5   *Sales* 10,118,475
SIC 2064 Candy and other confectionery products
 Graham Chapman

D-U-N-S 20-393-9012   (SL)
2508046 ONTARIO LTD
LAURIA VOLKSWAGEN
50 Benson Crt, Port Hope, ON, L1A 3V6
(905) 885-6421
Emp Here 21   *Sales* 10,459,638
SIC 5511 New and used car dealers
 Richard (Bud) Lauria

D-U-N-S 24-388-2065   (SL)
ACCESS COMMUNITY SERVICES INC
160 Walton St, Port Hope, ON, L1A 1N6

(905) 885-6358
Emp Here 85   *Sales* 5,531,375
SIC 8361 Residential care
 Roberta Delatorre
 Helen Sharteet
 Lou Harnesh

D-U-N-S 24-046-2838   (HQ)
AKZO NOBEL WOOD COATINGS LTD
(*Suby of* AKZO NOBEL N.V.)
155 Rose Glen Rd, Port Hope, ON, L1A 3V6
(905) 885-6388
Sales 49,703,675
SIC 2851 Paints and allied products
 Martine Bazinet
 Albert Wemmenhove
 Elliott Vander Meulen

D-U-N-S 24-139-9336   (HQ)
CORPORATION OF TRINITY COLLEGE SCHOOL, THE
55 Deblaquire St N, Port Hope, ON, L1A 4K7
(905) 885-4565
Sales 22,849,470
SIC 8211 Elementary and secondary schools
 Stuart Grainger
 Jeff Prince
 Kathryn Labranche
 Timothy Kennish

D-U-N-S 24-801-7568   (SL)
COURTNEY'S DISTRIBUTING INC
1941 Concession Rd 5, Port Hope, ON, L1A 3V5
(905) 786-1106
Emp Here 30   *Sales* 25,067,310
SIC 5141 Groceries, general line
 Michael Courtney
 Lloyd Courtney
 Robert Brooks

D-U-N-S 24-394-4951   (HQ)
CPK INTERIOR PRODUCTS INC
(*Suby of* FIAT CHRYSLER AUTOMOBILES N.V.)
128 Peter St, Port Hope, ON, L1A 1C4
(905) 885-7231
Sales 116,340,000
SIC 3714 Motor vehicle parts and accessories
 Theodore Renaud
 Paul Gouin

D-U-N-S 24-112-9175   (SL)
DAVIS YOUR INDEPENDENT GROCER
20 Jocelyn St, Port Hope, ON, L1A 3V5
(905) 885-1867
Emp Here 100   *Sales* 29,347,700
SIC 5411 Grocery stores
 Scott Davis

D-U-N-S 20-821-1433   (SL)
DAVIS, GARY FOOD STORES LIMITED
DAVIS VALU-MART
177 Toronto Rd, Port Hope, ON, L1A 3V5

Emp Here 75   *Sales* 22,010,775
SIC 5411 Grocery stores
 Scott Davis

D-U-N-S 24-844-0380   (SL)
EASTON'S 28 RESTAURANTS LTD
HARVEY'S
Hwy 28 & 401, Port Hope, ON, L1A 3V6
(905) 885-1400
Emp Here 160   *Sales* 7,283,040
SIC 5812 Eating places
 Dave Mimnett

D-U-N-S 20-143-9742   (BR)
ESCO LIMITED
(*Suby of* WEIR GROUP PLC(THE))
185 Hope St S, Port Hope, ON, L1A 4C2
(905) 885-6301
Emp Here 150
SIC 3325 Steel foundries, nec
 Bradley Wannamaker

D-U-N-S 20-708-2657   (BR)

EXTENDICARE INC
EXTENDICARE PORT HOPE
(*Suby of* EXTENDICARE INC)
360 Croft St Suite 1124, Port Hope, ON, L1A 4K8
(905) 885-1266
Emp Here 360
SIC 8051 Skilled nursing care facilities
 Jeff Donven

D-U-N-S 20-717-3964   (SL)
GILMER'S BUILDING CENTRE LIMITED
GILMER'S HOME CENTRE
177 Toronto Rd Suite 1, Port Hope, ON, L1A 3V5
(905) 885-4568
Emp Here 50   *Sales* 12,652,950
SIC 5251 Hardware stores
 Jeff Gilmer
 Karen Trizzino
 Lynn Swales

D-U-N-S 25-483-5051   (HQ)
HALIBURTON KAWARTHA PINE RIDGE DISTRICT HEALTH UNIT
200 Roseglen Rd, Port Hope, ON, L1A 3V6
(905) 885-9100
Emp Here 70   *Sales* 35,116,650
SIC 8621 Professional organizations
 Lynn Noseworthy

D-U-N-S 20-384-2422   (SL)
LAKERIDGE CHRYSLER DODGE JEEP LTD
152 Peter St, Port Hope, ON, L1A 1C6
(905) 885-6550
Emp Here 28   *Sales* 13,946,184
SIC 5511 New and used car dealers
 Matthew St. Amand

D-U-N-S 20-606-5948   (SL)
LAURIA HYUNDAI
50 Benson Crt, Port Hope, ON, L1A 3V6
(905) 885-2880
Emp Here 21   *Sales* 10,459,638
SIC 5511 New and used car dealers
 Frank Lauria

D-U-N-S 20-736-5185   (SL)
MCDONALD'S RESTAURANTS
175 Rose Glen Rd, Port Hope, ON, L1A 3V6
(905) 885-2480
Emp Here 80   *Sales* 3,641,520
SIC 5812 Eating places
 Les Andrews

D-U-N-S 25-542-4236   (SL)
NORAG RESOURCES INC
4476 County 10 Rd, Port Hope, ON, L1A 3V5
(905) 753-1180
Emp Here 11   *Sales* 13,314,367
SIC 5153 Grain and field beans
 Benjamin Currelly

D-U-N-S 24-119-4054   (SL)
NORTHUMBERLAND BUILDING MATERIALS LTD
RONA CASHWAY
205 Peter St Suite 368, Port Hope, ON, L1A 3V6
(416) 759-8542
Emp Here 55   *Sales* 14,720,860
SIC 5211 Lumber and other building materials
 Dave Horner

D-U-N-S 24-626-8551   (SL)
QUANTRILL, CHEVROLET BUICK GMC CADILLAC LTD
265 Peter St, Port Hope, ON, L1A 3V6
(905) 885-4573
Emp Here 35   *Sales* 17,432,730
SIC 5511 New and used car dealers
 John Quantrill
 Donna Quantrill

D-U-N-S 24-252-6627   (SL)
SHOPPERS DRUG MART
60 Ontario St, Port Hope, ON, L1A 2T8

▲ Public Company   ■ Public Company Family Member   **HQ** Headquarters   **BR** Branch   **SL** Single Location

(905) 885-1294
Emp Here 40   *Sales* 10,118,160
SIC 5912 Drug stores and proprietary stores
Deo Bahadadur

Port Perry, ON L9L

D-U-N-S 20-702-3818   (HQ)
ADAMSON SYSTEMS ENGINEERING INC
1401 Scugog Line 6, Port Perry, ON, L9L 1B2
(905) 982-0520
Sales 10,233,650
SIC 3651 Household audio and video equipment
Brock Adamson

D-U-N-S 20-118-6298   (SL)
BAAGWATING COMMUNITY ASSOCIATION
GREAT BLUE HERON CHARITY CASINO, DIV OF
(*Suby of* MISSISSAUGAS OF SCUGOG ISLAND FIRST NATION)
22521 Island Rd, Port Perry, ON, L9L 1B6
(905) 985-3337
Emp Here 850   *Sales* 73,695,000
SIC 7999 Amusement and recreation, nec
Joel Gonnella

D-U-N-S 24-816-1424   (SL)
CANPLEX PROFILES INC
1 Easy St, Port Perry, ON, L9L 1B2
(905) 985-2759
Emp Here 40   *Sales* 11,066,400
SIC 2821 Plastics materials and resins
Roman Semeniuk
Nicholas Semeniuk
Michael Semeniuk

D-U-N-S 24-366-3960   (HQ)
COMMUNITY LIVING DURHAM NORTH
60 Vanedward Dr Unit 2, Port Perry, ON, L9L 1G3
(905) 985-8511
Emp Here 20   *Sales* 16,070,500
SIC 8361 Residential care
Glenn Taylor
Teresa Mcguinness

D-U-N-S 25-300-8361   (BR)
DURHAM DISTRICT SCHOOL BOARD
PORT PERRY HIGH SCHOOL
(*Suby of* DURHAM DISTRICT SCHOOL BOARD)
160 Rosa St, Port Perry, ON, L9L 1L7
(905) 985-7337
Emp Here 105
SIC 8211 Elementary and secondary schools
Kandis Thompson

D-U-N-S 25-187-2099   (BR)
LAKERIDGE HEALTH
(*Suby of* LAKERIDGE HEALTH)
451 Paxton St, Port Perry, ON, L9L 1L9
(905) 985-7321
Emp Here 160
SIC 8062 General medical and surgical hospitals
Tina Temmers

D-U-N-S 25-302-1190   (BR)
MAPLE LEAF FOODS INC
SCHNEIDER FOODS
(*Suby of* MAPLE LEAF FOODS INC)
15350 Old Simcoe Rd, Port Perry, ON, L9L 1L8
(905) 985-7373
Emp Here 100
SIC 2038 Frozen specialties, nec
David Jackson

D-U-N-S 24-751-8202   (HQ)
NUTTY CHOCOLATIER CO LTD, THE
NUTTY CHOCOLATIER, THE
182 Queen St, Port Perry, ON, L9L 1B8

(905) 985-2210
Emp Here 23   *Sales* 10,691,928
SIC 5441 Candy, nut, and confectionery stores
Kenneth Koury

D-U-N-S 24-180-6116   (SL)
TECHSTAR PLASTICS INC
15400 Old Simcoe Rd, Port Perry, ON, L9L 1L8
(905) 985-8479
Emp Here 50   *Sales* 10,094,850
SIC 3089 Plastics products, nec
William Barnes
Dave Taylor

D-U-N-S 24-609-8789   (SL)
VO'S YIG #00835
VO'S YIG
1893 Scugog St, Port Perry, ON, L9L 1H9
(905) 985-9772
Emp Here 49   *Sales* 13,433,448
SIC 5411 Grocery stores
Terry Vos
Christine Vos

Port Robinson, ON L0S

D-U-N-S 24-745-5827   (HQ)
ARROW GAMES CORPORATION
(*Suby of* ARROW INTERNATIONAL, INC.)
9515 Montrose Rd Unit 2, Port Robinson, ON, L0S 1K0
(905) 354-7300
Emp Here 60   *Sales* 139,060,000
SIC 5092 Toys and hobby goods and supplies
John E Gallagher Jr
John E Gallagher Sr
Ron Kelly

D-U-N-S 24-802-0138   (SL)
JBI (CANADA) INC
1783 Allanport Rd Rr 1, Port Robinson, ON, L0S 1K0

Emp Here 12   *Sales* 12,393,696
SIC 5172 Petroleum products, nec
Nathan Dobbin

Port Stanley, ON N5L

D-U-N-S 20-965-2288   (SL)
L. R. JACKSON FISHERIES LIMITED
172 Main St, Port Stanley, ON, N5L 1H6
(519) 782-3562
Emp Here 25   *Sales* 20,889,425
SIC 5146 Fish and seafoods
Larry Jackson
Bonnie Jackson

D-U-N-S 24-192-5234   (BR)
ONTARIO MORTGAGE ACTION CENTRE LTD
(*Suby of* ONTARIO MORTGAGE ACTION CENTRE LTD)
288 Bridge St, Port Stanley, ON, N5L 1C3

Emp Here 75
SIC 6162 Mortgage bankers and loan correspondents
Dave Porvidenti

Port Sydney, ON P0B

D-U-N-S 24-801-5539   (SL)
BERT FRENCH & SON LIMITED
FRENCH'S FINE HOMES
126 Greer Rd Suite 1, Port Sydney, ON, P0B 1L0

(705) 385-2311
Emp Here 45   *Sales* 14,349,105
SIC 1521 Single-family housing construction
Lawrence A. French

Powassan, ON P0H

D-U-N-S 24-215-5398   (SL)
EASTHOLME HOME FOR THE AGED
62 Big Bend Ave, Powassan, ON, P0H 1Z0
(705) 724-2005
Emp Here 119   *Sales* 7,649,558
SIC 8361 Residential care
Steve Piekarski

D-U-N-S 24-461-8088   (SL)
QUALITY HARDWOODS LTD
(*Suby of* GOODFELLOW INC)
196 Latour Cres Rr 3, Powassan, ON, P0H 1Z0
(705) 724-2424
Emp Here 50   *Sales* 22,358,700
SIC 5031 Lumber, plywood, and millwork
Peter Van Anelssoorc

Prescott, ON K0E

D-U-N-S 24-366-7953   (SL)
121409 CANADA INC
LOUET NORTH AMERICA
3425 Hands Rd, Prescott, ON, K0E 1T0
(613) 925-4502
Emp Here 24   *Sales* 17,820,480
SIC 5199 Nondurable goods, nec
David Van Stralen
Trudy Van Stralen
Jan Van Stralen

D-U-N-S 24-393-2105   (SL)
BRANCY ONE HOLDINGS LTD
CANADIAN TIRE
140 Prescott Centre Dr, Prescott, ON, K0E 1T0
(613) 925-4217
Emp Here 34   *Sales* 16,934,652
SIC 5531 Auto and home supply stores
Brad O'neill

D-U-N-S 24-737-0344   (BR)
DEEM MANAGEMENT SERVICES LIMITED
WELLINGTON HOUSE
(*Suby of* DEEM MANAGEMENT SERVICES LIMITED)
990 Edward St, Prescott, ON, K0E 1T0
(613) 925-2834
Emp Here 100
SIC 8051 Skilled nursing care facilities
Julie Stresaa

D-U-N-S 24-269-9650   (HQ)
KRISKA HOLDINGS LIMITED
KRISKA TRANSPORTATION
(*Suby of* KRISKA TRANSPORTATION GROUP LIMITED)
850 Sophia St, Prescott, ON, K0E 1T0
(613) 925-5903
Emp Here 265   *Sales* 78,361,925
SIC 4213 Trucking, except local
Mark Seymour
Pierre Carrier

D-U-N-S 20-706-2089   (SL)
O'REILLY'S INDEPENDENT GROCER
150 Prescott Centre Dr, Prescott, ON, K0E 1T0
(613) 925-4625
Emp Here 100   *Sales* 29,347,700
SIC 5411 Grocery stores
Chris O' Reillys

D-U-N-S 20-787-6400   (SL)
PRESCOTT FINISHING INC

823 Walkers St, Prescott, ON, K0E 1T0
(613) 925-2859
Emp Here 65   *Sales* 11,921,195
SIC 2258 Lace and warp knit fabric mills
Jay Derstenfeld
Jeremy Lomas

D-U-N-S 20-289-0344   (HQ)
RIDEAU ST LAWRENCE DISTRIBUTION INC
985 Industrial Rd, Prescott, ON, K0E 1T0
(613) 925-3851
Sales 14,412,122
SIC 4911 Electric services
John Walsh

D-U-N-S 20-747-7704   (SL)
RIVERSIDE PONTIAC BUICK LTD
101 Development Dr, Prescott, ON, K0E 1T0
(613) 925-5941
Emp Here 35   *Sales* 17,432,730
SIC 5511 New and used car dealers
Stephen Birnie
Edwin Macmillan
Stuart Birnie

D-U-N-S 25-932-1693   (SL)
TIM HORTONS
925 Edward St, Prescott, ON, K0E 1T0
(613) 925-1465
Emp Here 40   *Sales* 10,966,080
SIC 5461 Retail bakeries
Ruth Lockett

Princeton, ON N0J

D-U-N-S 20-874-8079   (HQ)
COWAN, FRANK COMPANY LIMITED
75 Main St N, Princeton, ON, N0J 1V0
(519) 458-4331
Sales 166,296,780
SIC 6411 Insurance agents, brokers, and service
Larry Ryan
Barb Szychta

D-U-N-S 24-565-9800   (HQ)
STREEF PRODUCE LIMITED
S P L BRAND
447 Hwy 2, Princeton, ON, N0J 1V0
(519) 458-4311
Emp Here 50   *Sales* 25,389,139
SIC 5148 Fresh fruits and vegetables
Jacob Streef
John Streef
Peter Streef
Christopher Streef
Jaidin Streef
Dylan Streef
Nathan Streef

Puslinch, ON N0B

D-U-N-S 24-467-8343   (HQ)
BARCO MATERIALS HANDLING LIMITED
CHERRY FOREST PRODUCTS
24 Kerr Cres Suite 3, Puslinch, ON, N0B 2J0
(519) 763-1037
Sales 25,008,100
SIC 2426 Hardwood dimension and flooring mills
John Baranski
Bob Baranski
Jacob Baranski

D-U-N-S 20-700-7514   (HQ)
BIOREM INC
7496 Wellington Rd 34, Puslinch, ON, N0B 2J0
(519) 767-9100
Emp Here 6   *Sales* 18,446,765

SIC 3822 Environmental controls
Derek S. Webb
Douglas Newman
Qing Zhao
P. Anthony Ennis
Sandy Ding
Brian Herner

D-U-N-S 20-982-0232   (SL)
BRYAN'S FARM & INDUSTRIAL SUPPLY LTD
4062 Highway 6 Rr 2, Puslinch, ON, N0B 2J0
(519) 837-0710
Emp Here 24   *Sales* 11,400,624
SIC 5083 Farm and garden machinery
Bryan Lillycrop
Ken Lillycrop

D-U-N-S 20-638-2434   (HQ)
CAPITAL PAVING INC
4459 Concession 7, Puslinch, ON, N0B 2J0
(519) 822-4511
Sales 15,146,520
SIC 1611 Highway and street construction
Geoffrey Stephens

D-U-N-S 20-939-6233   (HQ)
CASCADE (CANADA) LTD
(*Suby of* TOYOTA INDUSTRIES CORPORATION)
4 Nicholas Beaver Rd, Puslinch, ON, N0B 2J0
(519) 763-3675
Emp Here 250   *Sales* 91,285,025
SIC 3537 Industrial trucks and tractors
Joseph Pointer
Chandica Harry

D-U-N-S 24-378-2211   (HQ)
CON-CAST PIPE INC
299 Brock Rd S, Puslinch, ON, N0B 2J0
(519) 763-8655
Emp Here 1   *Sales* 17,921,900
SIC 3272 Concrete products, nec
Brian Wood
Romeo Degasperis
Robert Degasperis
James Degasperis
Antonio Degasperis
Mark Wetselaar

D-U-N-S 20-179-4950   (SL)
FARLEY MANUFACTURING INC
6 Kerr Cres, Puslinch, ON, N0B 2J0
(519) 821-5422
Emp Here 50   *Sales* 10,094,850
SIC 3069 Fabricated rubber products, nec
John Simpell
Ralph Farley
Mike Rogen

D-U-N-S 20-645-9724   (HQ)
LAIDLAW CARRIERS VAN LP
BROOKVILLE CARRIERS VAN, DIV OF
21 Kerr Cres, Puslinch, ON, N0B 2J0
(519) 766-0660
Sales 20,570,600
SIC 4213 Trucking, except local
Don Hussey
Tom Etherington

D-U-N-S 24-872-9329   (HQ)
MAMMOET CANADA EASTERN LTD
7504 Mclean Rd E, Puslinch, ON, N0B 2J0
(519) 740-0550
Emp Here 280   *Sales* 67,299,065
SIC 4212 Local trucking, without storage
Keith Guiochet
Jeremy Asher
Travis Anderdson
Kent Lee

D-U-N-S 25-690-4939   (HQ)
MAMMOET CANADA HOLDINGS INC
7504 Mclean Rd E, Puslinch, ON, N0B 2J0
(519) 740-0550
Emp Here 70   *Sales* 255,856,300
SIC 6712 Bank holding companies

Tim Sittler
Roderik Van Seumeren

D-U-N-S 20-179-2681   (BR)
NESTLE CANADA INC
NESTLE WATERS CANADA DIV
(*Suby of* NESTLE S.A.)
101 Brock Rd S, Puslinch, ON, N0B 2J0
(519) 763-9462
Emp Here 200
SIC 5149 Groceries and related products, nec
Daniela Di Loreto Diaz

D-U-N-S 24-423-1940   (SL)
PENTALIFT EQUIPMENT CORPORATION
21 Nicholas Beaver Rd, Puslinch, ON, N0B 2J0
(519) 763-3625
Emp Here 120   *Sales* 26,640,120
SIC 3537 Industrial trucks and tractors
Paul A Pedersen

D-U-N-S 24-414-3129   (HQ)
REN'S FEED AND SUPPLIES LIMITED
REN'S PETS DEPOT
20 Brock Rd N Unit 3, Puslinch, ON, N0B 2J0
(519) 767-5858
Emp Here 25   *Sales* 17,102,960
SIC 5999 Miscellaneous retail stores, nec
Colin Job

D-U-N-S 20-517-8481   (HQ)
ROYAL CANIN CANADA INC
ROYAL CANIN CANADA COMPANY
(*Suby of* MARS, INCORPORATED)
100 Beiber Rd, Puslinch, ON, N0B 2J0
(519) 780-6700
Sales 72,695,199
SIC 5149 Groceries and related products, nec
James Patterson
Brent Matthew

Putnam, ON N0L

D-U-N-S 24-866-4190   (SL)
GOOD FAMILY FOODS
2899 Cromarty Dr, Putnam, ON, N0L 2B0
(519) 269-3700
Emp Here 40   *Sales* 10,492,360
SIC 0182 Food crops grown under cover

Queensville, ON L0G

D-U-N-S 24-963-4544   (SL)
GOODYEAR FARM LTD
139 Ravenshoe Rd, Queensville, ON, L0G 1R0
(905) 478-8388
Emp Here 100   *Sales* 26,230,900
SIC 0191 General farms, primarily crop
Nong Ly

D-U-N-S 20-188-1005   (SL)
LAKEVIEW VEGETABLE PROCESSING INC
21413 Leslie St Rr 1, Queensville, ON, L0G 1R0
(905) 478-2537
Emp Here 30   *Sales* 25,067,310
SIC 5148 Fresh fruits and vegetables
Don Chapman
Jim Chapman

Rama, ON L3V

D-U-N-S 25-320-7567   (SL)
CASINO RAMA INC
5899 Rama Rd, Rama, ON, L3V 6H6

(705) 329-3325
Emp Here 3,400   *Sales* 294,780,000
SIC 7999 Amusement and recreation, nec
Art Frank
Jackie Castel
Sherry Lawson
Brian Ehlers

Red Lake, ON P0V

D-U-N-S 24-161-4531   (SL)
LIVING HOPE NATIVE MINISTRIES
23 Hwy 105 Suite 1, Red Lake, ON, P0V 2M0

Emp Here 30   *Sales* 11,922,420
SIC 8699 Membership organizations, nec
Merle Nisly

D-U-N-S 24-171-1456   (SL)
MACDEN HOLDINGS LTD
RED LAKE IGA
Hwy 105, Red Lake, ON, P0V 2M0
(807) 727-2855
Emp Here 40   *Sales* 10,966,080
SIC 5411 Grocery stores
Warren Lumgair

D-U-N-S 20-832-9813   (SL)
RED LAKE MARGARET COCHENOUR MEMORIAL HOSPITAL CORPORATION, THE
RED LAKE HOSPITAL
51 Hwy 105, Red Lake, ON, P0V 2M0
(807) 727-2231
Emp Here 100   *Sales* 6,534,446
SIC 8062 General medical and surgical hospitals
Paul Chatelain
Eleanor Vachon
Cathy Kaczmarek
Alana Procyk
Anne Billard
Marion Whitton
Leah Gentes
Dave Wilson
Terry Bursey
Arlene Swanwick

Renfrew, ON K7V

D-U-N-S 24-737-6569   (SL)
697739 ONTARIO INC
RENFREW HOME HARDWARE BUILDING CENTRE
555 O'Brien Rd, Renfrew, ON, K7V 3Z3
(613) 432-5138
Emp Here 47   *Sales* 11,893,773
SIC 5251 Hardware stores
Karen Maxwell
Steve Maxwell

D-U-N-S 20-891-4671   (HQ)
COMMUNITY LIVING RENFREW COUNTY SOUTH
326 Raglan St S, Renfrew, ON, K7V 1R5
(613) 432-6763
Sales 22,777,480
SIC 8399 Social services, nec
Jennifer Creeden
Esther Roberts

D-U-N-S 20-787-7804   (BR)
CORPORATION OF THE COUNTY OF RENFREW
BONNECHERE MANOR
(*Suby of* CORPORATION OF THE COUNTY OF RENFREW)
470 Albert St, Renfrew, ON, K7V 4L5
(613) 432-4873
Emp Here 200
SIC 8361 Residential care

Shelley Yantha

D-U-N-S 24-269-0949   (HQ)
DESLAURIER CUSTOM CABINETS INC
550 Hall Ave E, Renfrew, ON, K7V 2S9
(613) 432-5431
Sales 23,148,300
SIC 2541 Wood partitions and fixtures
Ross Staples
Denis Staples
James S Deslaurier

D-U-N-S 20-282-1179   (BR)
GEM HEALTH CARE GROUP LIMITED
GROVES PARK LODGE
(*Suby of* GEM HEALTH CARE GROUP LIMITED)
470 Raglan St N, Renfrew, ON, K7V 1P5
(613) 432-5823
Emp Here 120
SIC 8051 Skilled nursing care facilities
Donna Tinkham

D-U-N-S 20-145-0871   (SL)
MACK MACKENZIE MOTORS LIMITED
547 New St, Renfrew, ON, K7V 1H1
(613) 432-3684
Emp Here 23   *Sales* 11,455,794
SIC 5511 New and used car dealers
Brian Mackenzie

D-U-N-S 24-087-0126   (HQ)
MY BROADCASTING CORPORATION
MY FM 96.1 RENFREW
321b Raglan St S Suite B, Renfrew, ON, K7V 1R6
(613) 432-6936
Emp Here 15   *Sales* 15,707,830
SIC 4832 Radio broadcasting stations
Jon Pole
Andrew Dickson

D-U-N-S 24-823-2498   (SL)
OTTAWA VALLEY GRAIN PRODUCTS INC
OTTAWA VALLEY FUELS
558 Raglan St S, Renfrew, ON, K7V 1R8

Emp Here 2   *Sales* 11,360,888
SIC 5172 Petroleum products, nec
Ronald Wilson

D-U-N-S 20-746-6236   (HQ)
REIS, H.J. INTERNATIONAL LTD
REIS EQUIPMENT CENTER
479 O'Brien Rd, Renfrew, ON, K7V 3Z3
(613) 432-4133
Emp Here 18   *Sales* 23,751,300
SIC 5083 Farm and garden machinery
Joseph Reis

D-U-N-S 24-104-9253   (SL)
RENFREW VICTORIA HOSPITAL
499 Raglan St N, Renfrew, ON, K7V 1P6
(613) 432-4851
Emp Here 450   *Sales* 49,986,000
SIC 8062 General medical and surgical hospitals
Keanan Stone
Randy Penney
Meena Ballantyne
Tom Faloon
Sandi Heins
Shauna Lemenchick
Richard Lester
Philip Marcella
Robert Pelletier
Marg Mcnab-Tubman

D-U-N-S 24-105-3719   (HQ)
SCAPA TAPES NORTH AMERICA LTD
RENFREW TAPE
(*Suby of* SCAPA GROUP PUBLIC LIMITED COMPANY)
609 Barnet Blvd, Renfrew, ON, K7V 0A9
(613) 432-8545
Sales 33,110,560
SIC 2672 Paper; coated and laminated, nec

Steven Eli Head
Eric Springer

D-U-N-S 24-845-2542　　(SL)
TIMES FIBER CANADA LIMITED
(*Suby of* AMPHENOL CORPORATION)
580 O'Brien Rd, Renfrew, ON, K7V 3Z2
(613) 432-8566
Emp Here 100　　*Sales* 19,044,200
SIC 3669 Communications equipment, nec
Zachary Raley
Barry Holt

D-U-N-S 25-294-7783　　(BR)
WAL-MART CANADA CORP
WAL MART
(*Suby of* WALMART INC.)
980 O'Brien Rd Suite 1, Renfrew, ON, K7V
0B4
(613) 432-4676
Emp Here 200
SIC 5311 Department stores

Richards Landing, ON P0R

D-U-N-S 20-145-9153　　(SL)
BERNT GILBERTSON ENTERPRISES LIMITED
GILBERTSON ENTERPRISES
3107 Huron Line Hwy 548, Richards Landing,
ON, P0R 1J0
(705) 246-2076
Emp Here 80　　*Sales* 20,195,360
SIC 1611 Highway and street construction
Donald Gilbertson
Richard Gilbertson
Calvin Gilbertson
Brent Gilbertson
Ruth Gilbertson

Richmond, ON K0A

D-U-N-S 25-360-5240　　(SL)
FIND-A-CAR AUTO SALES & BROKERING INC
6104 Perth St, Richmond, ON, K0A 2Z0

Emp Here 35　　*Sales* 17,432,730
SIC 5521 Used car dealers
Ryan O'connor

D-U-N-S 25-263-5560　　(BR)
OTTAWA-CARLETON DISTRICT SCHOOL BOARD
SOUTH CARLETON HIGH SCHOOL
(*Suby of* OTTAWA-CARLETON DISTRICT
SCHOOL BOARD)
3673 Mcbean St, Richmond, ON, K0A 2Z0
(613) 838-2212
Emp Here 110
SIC 8211 Elementary and secondary schools
Colin Anderson

D-U-N-S 25-913-1910　　(SL)
WALTERS VALU-MART
6179 Perth St, Richmond, ON, K0A 2Z0
(613) 838-8800
Emp Here 45　　*Sales* 12,544,331
SIC 5411 Grocery stores
Christopher King

Richmond, ON L4B

D-U-N-S 24-801-5745　　(HQ)
KIRCHHOFF AUTOMOTIVE CANADA INC
KIRCHHOFF AUTOMOTIVE
(*Suby of* KIRCHHOFF AUTOMOTIVE HOLDING GMBH & CO.KG)

25 Mural St, Richmond, ON, L4B 1J4
(905) 727-8585
Emp Here 149　　*Sales* 145,938,600
SIC 3465 Automotive stampings
Tony Parente
Bo Lindgren
Paul Dilworth
Dinesh Divakaran
Ken Gibbons
Peter Van Schaik

Richmond Hill, ON L4B

D-U-N-S 24-316-2077　　(SL)
10578959 CANADA INC
HOEKERT GROUP
155 East Beaver Creek Rd, Richmond Hill,
ON, L4B 2N1
(905) 904-0596
Emp Here 120　　*Sales* 19,459,700
SIC 6719 Holding companies, nec
Albert Hoekert
Richard Hoekert

D-U-N-S 20-388-1458　　(SL)
11198173 CANADA INC
FLUX LOGISTICS
155 East Beaver Creek Rd Unit 24, Richmond
Hill, ON, L4B 2N1
(905) 904-0612
Emp Here 70　　*Sales* 10,373,440
SIC 4212 Local trucking, without storage
Andrew Hong
Derek Price

D-U-N-S 24-386-1353　　(SL)
1272227 ONTARIO INC
CDC FOODS
21 East Wilmot St Suite 2, Richmond Hill, ON,
L4B 1A3
(905) 763-2929
Emp Here 35　　*Sales* 14,677,425
SIC 6712 Bank holding companies
Vince Dimaria
Pauline Dimaria

D-U-N-S 20-050-0101　　(SL)
1324344 ONTARIO INC
1725 16th Ave Suite 1, Richmond Hill, ON,
L4B 4C6
(905) 882-5563
Emp Here 25　　*Sales* 10,483,875
SIC 6712 Bank holding companies
Sean Morris
Carole Morris
Mohammad Nezarati

D-U-N-S 20-709-0627　　(BR)
2063414 ONTARIO LIMITED
LEISUREWORLD CAREGIVING CENTRE
170 Red Maple Rd, Richmond Hill, ON, L4B
4T8
(905) 731-2273
Emp Here 160
SIC 8051 Skilled nursing care facilities
Sanja Freeborn

D-U-N-S 24-351-5033　　(SL)
2101440 ONTARIO INC
MODERN REQUIREMENTS
30 East Beaver Creek Rd Suite 204, Richmond Hill, ON, L4B 1J2
(416) 469-3131
Emp Here 70　　*Sales* 12,411,770
SIC 7371 Custom computer programming services
Asif Sharif

D-U-N-S 24-927-2717　　(SL)
2714159 CANADA INC
THERMOSHELL
44 East Beaver Creek Rd Unit 16, Richmond
Hill, ON, L4B 1G8
(905) 886-5432
Emp Here 55　　*Sales* 34,610,400

SIC 5541 Gasoline service stations
William Sanford

D-U-N-S 24-196-0954　　(SL)
459324 ONTARIO INC
MASS MANAGEMENT SERVICES
40 East Pearce St, Richmond Hill, ON, L4B
1B7
(905) 764-9533
Emp Here 60　　*Sales* 16,459,920
SIC 8741 Management services
Kathleen Armstrong

D-U-N-S 24-365-6647　　(SL)
ACCOLADE GROUP INC
ACCOLADE GROUP
(*Suby of* ACCOLADE USA INC.)
66 West Beaver Creek Rd, Richmond Hill, ON,
L4B 1G5
(416) 465-7211
Emp Here 100　　*Sales* 13,667,400
SIC 2329 Men's and boy's clothing, nec
Hilton Ngo
Herbert Ngo
Hyman Ngo
Harvey Ngo

D-U-N-S 20-321-2402　　(SL)
ADVANCED MOBILE PAYMENT INC
15 Wertheim Crt Suite 401-403, Richmond
Hill, ON, L4B 3H7
(905) 597-2333
Emp Here 16　　*Sales* 32,533,511
SIC 7371 Custom computer programming services
Parsooa Ahmadieh-Bondar
Homayoon Saghari

D-U-N-S 24-393-5660　　(SL)
ALDACO INDUSTRIES INC
AMVEX
(*Suby of* TENEX CAPITAL MANAGEMENT,
L.P.)
25b East Pearce St Suite 1, Richmond Hill,
ON, L4B 2M9
(905) 764-7736
Emp Here 100　　*Sales* 22,728,900
SIC 3841 Surgical and medical instruments
Albert Sinyor
David Clark Stinson
Mark Hean

D-U-N-S 25-081-8754　　(SL)
ALICE-ALIYA (CANADA) INC
92 Springbrook Dr, Richmond Hill, ON, L4B
3P9
(905) 886-1172
Emp Here 25　　*Sales* 11,875,650
SIC 5085 Industrial supplies
Thomas Kuo

D-U-N-S 20-397-5933　　(HQ)
AMERESCO CANADA INC
(*Suby of* AMERESCO, INC.)
30 Leek Cres Suite 301, Richmond Hill, ON,
L4B 4N4
(888) 483-7627
Emp Here 10　　*Sales* 12,828,100
SIC 3825 Instruments to measure electricity
Robert Mccullough

D-U-N-S 24-382-1688　　(SL)
AMICO CLINICAL SOLUTIONS CORP
85 Fulton Way, Richmond Hill, ON, L4B 2N4
(905) 764-0800
Emp Here 60　　*Sales* 13,637,340
SIC 3841 Surgical and medical instruments
Wayne Benson
Albert Sinyor

D-U-N-S 20-937-5401　　(HQ)
AMICO CORPORATION
85 Fulton Way, Richmond Hill, ON, L4B 2N4
(905) 764-0800
Emp Here 230　　*Sales* 84,263,100
SIC 3569 General industrial machinery, nec
Albert Sinyor
Nicole King

D-U-N-S 25-967-6661　　(SL)
AMICO PATIENT CARE CORPORATION
85 Fulton Way, Richmond Hill, ON, L4B 2N4
(905) 764-0800
Emp Here 62　　*Sales* 27,724,788
SIC 5047 Medical and hospital equipment
Sarah Corey
Erica Berlin

D-U-N-S 24-525-9564　　(SL)
**ANDERSON MERCHANDISERS-CANADA,
INC.**
(*Suby of* ANDERSON MEDIA CORPORATION)
60 Leek Cres Suite B, Richmond Hill, ON, L4B
1H1

Emp Here 375　　*Sales* 260,737,500
SIC 5099 Durable goods, nec
Bill N Lardie
Charles E Taylor

D-U-N-S 25-405-4463　　(HQ)
APPLANIX CORPORATION
(*Suby of* TRIMBLE INC.)
85 Leek Cres, Richmond Hill, ON, L4B 3B3
(289) 695-6000
Sales 22,728,900
SIC 3829 Measuring and controlling devices,
nec
Steve Woolven
Peter Teixeira
Eric Liberty
Michelle Papanikolov
Bruno Scherzinger

D-U-N-S 24-949-9745　　(HQ)
APRI INSURANCE SOLUTIONS INC
165 East Beaver Creek Rd Suite 18, Richmond Hill, ON, L4B 2N2
(866) 877-3600
Emp Here 70　　*Sales* 171,840,006
SIC 6411 Insurance agents, brokers, and service
Darwin Lang
Merv Evdokimenko
Clifford Styles

D-U-N-S 20-251-1986　　(BR)
ARCADIS CANADA INC
(*Suby of* ARCADIS N.V.)
121 Granton Dr Unit 12, Richmond Hill, ON,
L4B 3N4
(905) 764-9380
Emp Here 100
SIC 8748 Business consulting, nec

D-U-N-S 25-507-5475　　(HQ)
ARTAFLEX INC
174 West Beaver Creek Rd, Richmond Hill,
ON, L4B 1B4
(905) 470-0109
Emp Here 220　　*Sales* 70,728,750
SIC 3679 Electronic components, nec
Paul Walker
Trent Carruthers
Shmulik Vlodinger

D-U-N-S 25-221-3889　　(SL)
ASIA LINK COMPUTER INC
ALC MICRO
45a West Wilmot St Unit 5 7, Richmond Hill,
ON, L4B 2P2
(905) 731-1928
Emp Here 55　　*Sales* 24,594,570
SIC 5045 Computers, peripherals, and software
Eric Siu

D-U-N-S 24-795-9521　　(HQ)
**AVENUE INDUSTRIAL SUPPLY COMPANY
LIMITED**
GLOBAL INDUSTRIAL CANADA
(*Suby of* SYSTEMAX INC.)
35 Staples Ave Suite 110, Richmond Hill, ON,
L4B 4W6
(877) 304-1270
Emp Here 35　　*Sales* 23,751,300

SIC 5084 Industrial machinery and equipment
Nelson Rivers
Robert Setnyk

D-U-N-S 20-317-2077   (HQ)
AVI-SPL CANADA LTD
AVI-SPL
(*Suby of* AVI-SPL HOLDINGS, INC.)
35 East Beaver Creek Rd Suite 1, Richmond
Hill, ON, L4B 1B3
(866) 797-5635
Emp Here 75   *Sales* 411,249,600
SIC 4813 Telephone communication, except
radio
John Zettel
Boris Koechlin

D-U-N-S 24-926-3955   (HQ)
AXION INSURANCE SERVICES INC
AXION LEE INSURANCE
(*Suby of* WESTERN FINANCIAL GROUP
INC)
95 Mural St Suite 205, Richmond Hill, ON, L4B
3G2
(905) 731-3118
Emp Here 18   *Sales* 101,625,810
SIC 6411 Insurance agents, brokers, and ser-
vice
Michael Teixeira
Donna Grabowski

D-U-N-S 24-803-0335   (HQ)
BELL AND HOWELL CANADA LTD
30 Mural St Unit 6, Richmond Hill, ON, L4B
1B5
(416) 747-2200
Emp Here 50   *Sales* 21,156,080
SIC 7629 Electrical repair shops
Elisabeth Preston
Paul Halpern
Raymond C French

D-U-N-S 20-292-7166   (SL)
BREVITAS CONSULTING INC
70 East Beaver Creek Rd Suite 24, Richmond
Hill, ON, L4B 3B2
(289) 819-1339
Emp Here 102   *Sales* 19,023,612
SIC 8742 Management consulting services
Anil Peer

D-U-N-S 25-397-2814   (SL)
C.J. MARKETING LTD
50 East Wilmot St, Richmond Hill, ON, L4B
3Z3
(905) 886-8885
Emp Here 48   *Sales* 35,640,960
SIC 5199 Nondurable goods, nec
Brian Chan

D-U-N-S 20-107-6465   (HQ)
**CANADIAN CONTRACT CLEANING SPE-
CIALISTS, INC**
CCCSI
(*Suby of* HARVEST PARTNERS, LP)
10 East Wilmot St Unit 25, Richmond Hill, ON,
L4B 1G9
(905) 707-0410
Emp Here 285   *Sales* 17,742,240
SIC 7349 Building maintenance services, nec
Jeffrey Kaiser
Edward Lam
Ceanne Kaiser

D-U-N-S 24-206-8323   (SL)
CANADIAN TIRE
250 Silver Linden Dr Suite 87, Richmond Hill,
ON, L4B 4W7
(905) 731-3100
Emp Here 50   *Sales* 24,903,900
SIC 5531 Auto and home supply stores
Jeff Levy

D-U-N-S 20-213-6834   (SL)
CANEAST FOODS LIMITED
70 East Beaver Creek Rd Unit 204, Richmond
Hill, ON, L4B 3B2

(905) 771-6051
Emp Here 19   *Sales* 10,167,356
SIC 5141 Groceries, general line
Lisa Mcconnell
Thomas Mcconnell
Graham Mcconnell

D-U-N-S 20-305-5405   (SL)
CANSO CREDIT INCOME FUND
100 York Blvd Suite 501, Richmond Hill, ON,
L4B 1J8
(416) 640-4275
Emp Here 6   *Sales* 35,021,550
SIC 6726 Investment offices, nec
Richard Usher-Jones
Raj Vijh
John Carswell
Timothy Hicks
Raymond Oh
Lee Wong

D-U-N-S 25-405-4927   (SL)
CARLTON ONE ENGAGEMENT ULC
38 Leek Cres 4th Fl, Richmond Hill, ON, L4B
4N8
(905) 477-3971
Emp Here 77   *Sales* 18,040,176
SIC 8742 Management consulting services
Robert Purdy

D-U-N-S 25-369-5720   (HQ)
CATHAY FOREST PRODUCTS CORP
30 Wertheim Crt Suite 14, Richmond Hill, ON,
L4B 1B9

Sales 12,397,020
SIC 0851 Forestry services
Anthony Ng
John Housser
Stephen Miller
Paul Wong
Raymond Lo
John Reynolds

D-U-N-S 24-333-1852   (SL)
CDC FOODS INC
21 East Wilmot St Unit 2, Richmond Hill, ON,
L4B 1A3
(905) 763-2929
Emp Here 40   *Sales* 33,423,080
SIC 5141 Groceries, general line
Vincent Dimaria
Pauline Dimaria

D-U-N-S 24-373-3602   (SL)
**CENTRAL ONTARIO HEALTHCARE PRO-
CUREMENT ALLIANCE**
COHPA
95 Mural St Suite 300, Richmond Hill, ON, L4B
3G2
(905) 886-5319
Emp Here 60   *Sales* 16,401,000
SIC 6712 Bank holding companies
David Yundt

D-U-N-S 20-717-8844   (HQ)
CENTURY 21 ATRIA REALTY INC
1550 16th Ave Unit C Suite 200 South, Rich-
mond Hill, ON, L4B 3K9
(905) 883-1988
Sales 69,641,184
SIC 6531 Real estate agents and managers
Stephen Chow

D-U-N-S 20-278-2231   (HQ)
CHANGEPOINT CANADA ULC
(*Suby of* MARLIN EQUITY PARTNERS, LLC)
30 Leek Cres Suite 300, Richmond Hill, ON,
L4B 4N4
(905) 886-7000
Sales 55,371,900
SIC 7371 Custom computer programming ser-
vices
James Byrnes

D-U-N-S 24-341-0821   (BR)
**COMPAGNIE DE TELEPHONE BELL DU
CANADA OU BELL CANADA, LA**
INFOSTREAM, DIV OF

(*Suby of* BCE INC)
9133 Leslie St, Richmond Hill, ON, L4B 4N1
(905) 762-9137
Emp Here 100
SIC 7379 Computer related services, nec

D-U-N-S 24-793-5679   (HQ)
COMTRONIC COMPUTER INC
30 Kinnear Crt Unit 1, Richmond Hill, ON, L4B
1K8
(905) 881-3606
Emp Here 65   *Sales* 64,242,240
SIC 5045 Computers, peripherals, and soft-
ware
John Tse
Paul Tse

D-U-N-S 20-311-2172   (HQ)
**CONNEX TELECOMMUNICATIONS COR-
PORATION**
44 East Beaver Creek Rd Suite 16, Richmond
Hill, ON, L4B 1G8
(905) 944-6500
Emp Here 2   *Sales* 23,781,450
SIC 6712 Bank holding companies
Sayan Navaratnam
Heung Hung Lee

D-U-N-S 24-991-1103   (HQ)
CONNEX TELECOMMUNICATIONS INC
CONNEX ONTARIO
(*Suby of* CONNEX TELECOMMUNICATIONS
CORPORATION)
44 East Beaver Creek Rd Unit 16, Richmond
Hill, ON, L4B 1G8
(905) 944-6500
Emp Here 300   *Sales* 33,689,511
SIC 4899 Communication services, nec
Sayan Navaratnam
Heung Hung Lee
Peter Manickavasagar

D-U-N-S 24-047-3694   (SL)
**CONTAINER CORPORATION OF CANADA
LTD**
CONTAINER CORPORATION OF CANADA
68 Leek Cres, Richmond Hill, ON, L4B 1H1
(905) 764-3777
Emp Here 135   *Sales* 21,445,830
SIC 3085 Plastics bottles
Norman James Gottlieb

D-U-N-S 25-244-2991   (HQ)
CROCS CANADA INC
(*Suby of* CROCS, INC.)
1455 16th Ave Unit 7, Richmond Hill, ON, L4B
4W5
(905) 747-3366
Emp Here 80   *Sales* 143,287,200
SIC 3021 Rubber and plastics footwear
Douglas Hayes
John P Mccarvel
Stephen Keating

D-U-N-S 20-373-3451   (HQ)
CROWDCARE CORPORATION
WYSDOM.AI
120 East Beaver Creek Rd Suite 202, Rich-
mond Hill, ON, L4B 4V1
(647) 559-9190
Sales 10,092,740
SIC 7371 Custom computer programming ser-
vices
Ian Collins
Jeff Brunet
Artiom Kreimer
Arif Hirani
Karen Chan
Karthik Balakrishnan
Nitin Singhal
Heather Tippin

D-U-N-S 20-260-7230   (SL)
CTL-WDW LTD
9130 Leslie St Unit 204, Richmond Hill, ON,
L4B 0B9
(416) 781-3635
Emp Here 50   *Sales* 12,615,550

SIC 7322 Adjustment and collection services
Francois Sauvageau

D-U-N-S 20-363-9968   (SL)
CWB MAXIUM FINANCIAL INC
(*Suby of* CANADIAN WESTERN BANK)
30 Vogell Rd Suite 1, Richmond Hill, ON, L4B
3K6
(905) 780-6150
Emp Here 55   *Sales* 12,316,755
SIC 6159 Miscellaneous business credit insti-
tutions
Daryl Mccollum

D-U-N-S 20-690-0636   (SL)
DATA ACCESS SOLUTIONS INC
15 Wertheim Crt Unit 107, Richmond Hill, ON,
L4B 3H7
(905) 370-9960
Emp Here 14   *Sales* 21,190,840
SIC 4813 Telephone communication, except
radio
Idin Rangchi
Masoud Gharehgazlou

D-U-N-S 25-275-7240   (HQ)
**DE THOMAS WEALTH MANAGEMENT
CORP**
9033 Leslie St Unit 1, Richmond Hill, ON, L4B
4K3
(905) 731-9800
Emp Here 40   *Sales* 75,134,160
SIC 6282 Investment advice
Tony De Thomasis
Cindy De Thomasis

D-U-N-S 24-610-4640   (HQ)
DECISIONONE CORPORATION
(*Suby of* D1 HOLDINGS, LLC)
44 East Beaver Creek Rd Unit 19, Richmond
Hill, ON, L4B 1G8
(905) 882-1555
Emp Here 50   *Sales* 29,198,225
SIC 7378 Computer maintenance and repair
Paul Lachance
Don Hamilton

D-U-N-S 20-040-4430   (SL)
DELVED LTD
88a E Beaver Creek Rd Unit A, Richmond Hill,
ON, L4B 4A8
(289) 597-5140
Emp Here 29   *Sales* 10,562,235
SIC 5013 Motor vehicle supplies and new
parts

D-U-N-S 20-691-5949   (SL)
DOT-LINE DESIGN LTD
19 East Wilmot St, Richmond Hill, ON, L4B
1A3
(905) 760-1133
Emp Here 20   *Sales* 10,006,500
SIC 5137 Women's and children's clothing
Young Soo Min

D-U-N-S 24-688-9679   (HQ)
**DYNAMIX PROFESSIONAL VIDEO SYS-
TEMS INC**
100 Leek Cres Suite 1, Richmond Hill, ON,
L4B 3E6
(905) 882-4000
Emp Here 25   *Sales* 15,203,916
SIC 5049 Professional equipment, nec
Dave Kinzinger
Maurizio Fraccaro

D-U-N-S 20-164-2097   (HQ)
**EASTERN REFRIGERATION SUPPLY CO.
LIMITED**
CANADIAN REFRIGERATION SUPPLY
30 Vogell Rd Unit 5, Richmond Hill, ON, L4B
3K6
(905) 787-8383
Emp Here 28   *Sales* 18,781,308
SIC 5075 Warm air heating and air condition-
ing
David Merkel
Douglas Merkel

Stacy Albom

D-U-N-S 20-129-6043   (HQ)
EMERSON ELECTRIC CANADA LIMITED
EMERSON POWER TRANSMISSION, DIV OF
(*Suby of* EMERSON ELECTRIC CO.)
66 Leek Cres 2nd Fl, Richmond Hill, ON, L4B 1H1
(905) 762-1010
Emp Here 3,000   *Sales* 1,888,703,985
SIC 5063 Electrical apparatus and equipment
Ryan Garrah
David Distler
John Shivey

D-U-N-S 20-923-8849   (SL)
EMX ENTERPRISES LIMITED
250 Granton Dr, Richmond Hill, ON, L4B 1H7
(905) 764-0040
Emp Here 36   *Sales* 16,098,264
SIC 5065 Electronic parts and equipment, nec
Ernie Legiehn
Marilyn Legiehn

D-U-N-S 25-366-1532   (SL)
ENERGY NETWORK SERVICES INC
ENS
125 West Beaver Creek Rd, Richmond Hill, ON, L4B 1C6
(905) 763-2946
Emp Here 45   *Sales* 15,960,420
SIC 1731 Electrical work
Krishan Bhatia

D-U-N-S 24-830-5484   (HQ)
EUROFASE INC
33 West Beaver Creek Rd, Richmond Hill, ON, L4B 1L8
(905) 695-2055
Sales 69,629,640
SIC 5063 Electrical apparatus and equipment
Joseph Bitton
Jack Bitton
Anthony Zitoli

D-U-N-S 24-985-2559   (BR)
FAIRCHILD TELEVISION LTD
(*Suby of* FAIRCHILD PROPERTY GROUP LTD)
35 East Beaver Creek Rd Unit 8, Richmond Hill, ON, L4B 1B3
(905) 889-8090
Emp Here 200
SIC 4841 Cable and other pay television services
Connie Saphton

D-U-N-S 24-816-3453   (HQ)
FARLEYCO MARKETING INC
FARLEYCO HEALTHCARE
30 East Wilmot St, Richmond Hill, ON, L4B 1A4
(905) 709-2650
Emp Here 15   *Sales* 24,317,590
SIC 5122 Drugs, proprietaries, and sundries
Patsy Farley-Pope
Eric Kalish
Harold Wullfart

D-U-N-S 25-280-5338   (HQ)
FINANCIAL DEBT RECOVERY LIMITED
FDR
40 West Wilmot St Unit 10, Richmond Hill, ON, L4B 1H8
(905) 771-6000
Sales 16,029,680
SIC 7322 Adjustment and collection services
Nicholas Papeo

D-U-N-S 20-746-9420   (HQ)
FLEXMASTER CANADA LIMITED
NOVAFLEX PLASTICS
(*Suby of* DONFLEX HOLDINGS INC)
20 East Pearce St Suite 1, Richmond Hill, ON, L4B 1B7
(905) 731-9411
Emp Here 25   *Sales* 39,960,180

SIC 3599 Industrial machinery, nec
Melinda Donnelly
Kevin Donnelly
John Donnelly

D-U-N-S 25-189-6056   (HQ)
FRESENIUS MEDICAL CARE CANADA INC
(*Suby of* FRESENIUS MEDICAL CARE AG & CO. KGAA)
45 Staples Ave Suite 110, Richmond Hill, ON, L4B 4W6
(905) 770-0855
Emp Here 75   *Sales* 42,828,160
SIC 5047 Medical and hospital equipment
John N. Mcfarlane

D-U-N-S 25-184-0997   (HQ)
FUJI OPTICAL CO LTD
550 Highway 7 E, Richmond Hill, ON, L4B 3Z4
(905) 882-5665
Emp Here 15   *Sales* 13,024,000
SIC 5995 Optical goods stores
David Ng

D-U-N-S 24-993-3334   (HQ)
FUJITEC CANADA, INC
(*Suby of* FUJITEC CO., LTD.)
15 East Wilmot St, Richmond Hill, ON, L4B 1A3
(905) 731-8681
Emp Here 66   *Sales* 80,963,180
SIC 5084 Industrial machinery and equipment
Takakazu Uchiyama
Katsuji Okuda

D-U-N-S 20-818-8920   (SL)
GARDEL METAL PRODUCTS INCORPORATED
140 West Beaver Creek Rd Unit 1, Richmond Hill, ON, L4B 1C2
(905) 881-7992
Emp Here 50   *Sales* 10,141,500
SIC 3499 Fabricated Metal products, nec
James Gardener
Samuel Del Mastro
Tony Gardner

D-U-N-S 20-252-8787   (SL)
GATEWAYS INTERNATIONAL INC
(*Suby of* JOY OF TRAVEL LTD, THE)
30 Wertheim Crt Unit 20, Richmond Hill, ON, L4B 1B9
(905) 889-0483
Emp Here 20   *Sales* 10,399,340
SIC 4725 Tour operators
Eliezer Abitbol

D-U-N-S 24-523-9350   (SL)
GLOBAL COMMERCIAL FINANCIAL INC
45b West Wilmot St Suite 208, Richmond Hill, ON, L4B 2P3
(905) 470-2127
Emp Here 40   *Sales* 15,660,080
SIC 6799 Investors, nec
Joseph Friedman

D-U-N-S 25-404-5156   (SL)
GLOBAL RESP CORPORATION
100 Mural St Suite 201, Richmond Hill, ON, L4B 1J3
(416) 741-7377
Emp Here 38   *Sales* 21,669,360
SIC 6732 Trusts: educational, religious, etc.
Sam Bouji
Frank Gataveckas

D-U-N-S 24-423-0699   (SL)
GLOBAL REWARD SOLUTIONS INC
38 Leek Cres 4th Fl, Richmond Hill, ON, L4B 4N8
(905) 477-3971
Emp Here 77   *Sales* 18,040,176
SIC 8742 Management consulting services
Robert Purdy

D-U-N-S 24-023-6018   (SL)
GRACE FOODS CANADA INC
(*Suby of* GRACEKENNEDY LTD.)

70 West Wilmot St, Richmond Hill, ON, L4B 1H8
(905) 886-1002
Emp Here 52   *Sales* 37,269,232
SIC 5141 Groceries, general line
Sarath (Lucky) Lankage
Julian Weerasinghe

D-U-N-S 24-319-1785   (HQ)
GRIFFIN JEWELLERY DESIGNS INC
50 West Wilmot St Suite 201, Richmond Hill, ON, L4B 1M5
(905) 882-0004
Emp Here 10   *Sales* 24,432,800
SIC 5944 Jewelry stores
Shams Kara
Anise Kara

D-U-N-S 20-936-3092   (SL)
HIBAR SYSTEMS LIMITED
(*Suby of* RABIH HOLDINGS LTD)
35 Pollard St, Richmond Hill, ON, L4B 1A8
(905) 731-2400
Emp Here 150   *Sales* 33,300,150
SIC 3565 Packaging machinery
Iain Mccoll
Stephen Mark

D-U-N-S 25-832-0621   (BR)
HOME DEPOT OF CANADA INC
HOME DEPOT
(*Suby of* THE HOME DEPOT INC)
50 Red Maple Rd, Richmond Hill, ON, L4B 4K1
(905) 763-2311
Emp Here 200
SIC 5251 Hardware stores
Ron Rizzardo

D-U-N-S 25-465-7117   (SL)
INFO FINANCIAL CONSULTING GROUP INC
350 Highway 7 E Suite Ph8, Richmond Hill, ON, L4B 3N2
(905) 886-8811
Emp Here 63   *Sales* 52,149,951
SIC 6722 Management investment, open-end
Gary Yung
Albert Boey
Rocky Chan

D-U-N-S 24-418-6354   (SL)
J.L. INTERNATIONAL
21 East Wilmot St Unit 2, Richmond Hill, ON, L4B 1A3
(905) 763-2929
Emp Here 40   *Sales* 33,423,080
SIC 5141 Groceries, general line
Pauline Di Maria
Vince Di Maria

D-U-N-S 24-937-5064   (HQ)
JAYMOR SECURITIES LTD
JAYMOR GROUP, THE
105 West Beaver Creek Rd Unit 9-10, Richmond Hill, ON, L4B 1C6
(905) 882-1212
Sales 14,936,306
SIC 6211 Security brokers and dealers
Fabrizio Lucchese
William P Myers

D-U-N-S 24-320-3977   (SL)
JINZE (CANADA) CO., LTD
9140 Leslie St Suite 311 & 312, Richmond Hill, ON, L4B 0A9
(905) 762-9300
Emp Here 15   *Sales* 75,080,700
SIC 6799 Investors, nec
William Wu
Kelin Ha
Sherry Ning

D-U-N-S 20-104-3317   (HQ)
JOHNSON CONTROLS CANADA LP
JOHNSON CONTROLS
56 Leek Cres, Richmond Hill, ON, L4B 1H1

(866) 468-1484
Emp Here 200   *Sales* 382,756,500
SIC 8711 Engineering services
Bill Maggins

D-U-N-S 20-168-0766   (HQ)
JOHNSON CONTROLS NOVA SCOTIA U.L.C.
JOHNSON CONTROLS
(*Suby of* JOHNSON CONTROLS INTERNATIONAL PUBLIC LIMITED COMPANY)
56 Leek Cres, Richmond Hill, ON, L4B 1H1
(866) 468-1484
Emp Here 200   *Sales* 667,995,000
SIC 2531 Public building and related furniture
Alex A. Molinaroli
Brian Cadwallader
Susan Davis
Jerome Okarma
Frank Voltolina
Brian Stief
R. Bruce Mcdonald

D-U-N-S 24-330-6219   (BR)
JOHNSON INC
(*Suby of* RSA INSURANCE GROUP PLC)
1595 16th Ave Suite 700, Richmond Hill, ON, L4B 3S5
(905) 764-4900
Emp Here 160
SIC 6411 Insurance agents, brokers, and service
Doug Munn

D-U-N-S 24-694-0274   (HQ)
JOY OF TRAVEL LTD, THE
GATEWAYS INTERNATIONAL
30 Wertheim Crt Unit 20, Richmond Hill, ON, L4B 1B9
(905) 889-1681
Sales 14,559,076
SIC 4725 Tour operators
Loretta Abitbol

D-U-N-S 24-732-8094   (SL)
KEYBASE FINANCIAL GROUP INC
1725 16th Ave Suit1 101, Richmond Hill, ON, L4B 0B3
(905) 709-7911
Emp Here 50   *Sales* 11,895,050
SIC 8742 Management consulting services
Dax Sukhraj

D-U-N-S 25-711-8828   (HQ)
KEYBASE FINANCIAL GROUP INC
1725 16th Ave Suite 101, Richmond Hill, ON, L4B 0B3
(905) 709-7911
Emp Here 32   *Sales* 24,955,200
SIC 8741 Management services
Dax Sukhraj

D-U-N-S 24-925-4475   (SL)
KLEIN INTERNATIONAL LTD
66 West Wilmot St, Richmond Hill, ON, L4B 1H8
(905) 889-4881
Emp Here 18   *Sales* 13,319,109
SIC 5074 Plumbing and heating equipment and supplies (hydronics)
Roy Rezai
Shamsi Mahjour

D-U-N-S 20-647-6004   (HQ)
LEVI STRAUSS & CO. (CANADA) INC
LEVI-STRAUSS
(*Suby of* LEVI STRAUSS & CO.)
1725 16th Ave Suite 200, Richmond Hill, ON, L4B 4C6
(905) 763-4400
Sales 25,574,775
SIC 5632 Women's accessory and specialty stores
Diana Dimitian
Donna Keon

D-U-N-S 24-244-5211   (SL)
LITELINE CORPORATION
90 West Beaver Creek Rd, Richmond Hill, ON,

L4B 1E7
(416) 996-1856
Emp Here 110   *Sales* 17,474,380
SIC 3089 Plastics products, nec
Steven Silverstein
Daniel Silverstein
Mark Silverstein
Helen Silverstein

D-U-N-S 24-808-3946   (SL)
LNB INC
121 Granton Dr Suite 14, Richmond Hill, ON,
L4B 3N4
(905) 882-2500
Emp Here 35   *Sales* 15,522,150
SIC 7389 Business services, nec
Gary Leng

D-U-N-S 24-633-4549   (SL)
MASS ELECTRONICS LTD
MASS ELECTRONICS
(*Suby of* DISTRIBUTION AUTOMOBILITE
INC)
45 West Wilmot St Unit 16-17, Richmond Hill,
ON, L4B 1K1
(905) 764-9533
Emp Here 35   *Sales* 12,747,525
SIC 5013 Motor vehicle supplies and new
parts
Robert Nelson

D-U-N-S 20-193-7476   (SL)
MASSCOMP ELECTRONICS LTD
40 East Pearce St, Richmond Hill, ON, L4B
1B7
(905) 764-9533
Emp Here 25   *Sales* 46,166,475
SIC 6399 Insurance carriers, nec
Kathleen Armstrong

D-U-N-S 20-328-2330   (SL)
MAYHEW INC
28 Sims Cres, Richmond Hill, ON, L4B 2N9
(905) 707-4747
Emp Here 64   *Sales* 32,566,784
SIC 5021 Furniture
Marcia Mayhew
Joan Phillips
Paul Bradshaw
Monica Mayhew

D-U-N-S 20-429-6669   (HQ)
MAZDA CANADA INC
(*Suby of* MAZDA MOTOR CORPORATION)
55 Vogell Rd, Richmond Hill, ON, L4B 3K5
(905) 787-7000
Emp Here 98   *Sales* 57,644,250
SIC 5012 Automobiles and other motor vehi-
cles
Masaharu Kondo
Kory Koreeda
Don Macphee
Stephen Schulze

D-U-N-S 20-026-7495   (SL)
MID-LAND GROUP REALTY INC
330 Highway 7 E Suite 502, Richmond Hill,
ON, L4B 3P8
(905) 709-0828
Emp Here 50   *Sales* 16,356,350
SIC 6531 Real estate agents and managers
Danny Lau
Adrian Lam

D-U-N-S 25-978-8466   (SL)
**MOTORCYCLE INSURANCE BROKERS
INC**
105 West Beaver Creek Rd Suite 1, Richmond
Hill, ON, L4B 1C6
(905) 764-7868
Emp Here 30   *Sales* 25,441,800
SIC 6411 Insurance agents, brokers, and ser-
vice
Jd Smith

D-U-N-S 24-510-5499   (BR)
MULTIMATIC INC
INMET

(*Suby of* MULTIMATIC HOLDINGS INC)
35 West Wilmot St, Richmond Hill, ON, L4B
1L7
(905) 764-5120
Emp Here 256
SIC 3429 Hardware, nec
Michael Welzel

D-U-N-S 24-860-2851   (HQ)
MUNDO MEDIA LTD
120 East Beaver Creek Rd Suite 200, Rich-
mond Hill, ON, L4B 4V1
(416) 342-5646
Sales 22,040,810
SIC 7311 Advertising agencies
Jason Teofilos

D-U-N-S 24-977-4274   (SL)
NEAL BROTHERS INC
50 Vogell Rd Unit 6, Richmond Hill, ON, L4B
3K6
(905) 738-7955
Emp Here 20   *Sales* 10,702,480
SIC 5149 Groceries and related products, nec
Peter Neal
Christopher Neal

D-U-N-S 24-736-7998   (SL)
NOBEL BIOCARE CANADA INC
(*Suby of* DANAHER CORPORATION)
9133 Leslie St Unit 100, Richmond Hill, ON,
L4B 4N1
(905) 762-3500
Emp Here 52   *Sales* 27,838,304
SIC 5047 Medical and hospital equipment
John Cox
Sandy Kokinis

D-U-N-S 24-744-1215   (SL)
**NORTHERN   RESPONSE   (INTERNA-
TIONAL) LTD**
50 Staples Ave, Richmond Hill, ON, L4B 0A7
(866) 584-1694
Emp Here 52   *Sales* 12,705,056
SIC 5963 Direct selling establishments
Richard Stacey

D-U-N-S 25-368-3049   (BR)
NTT DATA CANADA, INC
NTT DATA CANADA, INC.
(*Suby of* NIPPON TELEGRAPH AND TELE-
PHONE CORPORATION)
30 East Beaver Creek Rd Suite 206, Rich-
mond Hill, ON, L4B 1J2

Emp Here 150
SIC 7371 Custom computer programming ser-
vices
Joan Mota

D-U-N-S 25-396-8630   (HQ)
NUTRITION HOUSE CANADA INC
NUTRITION HOUSE
80 West Beaver Creek Rd Unit 12, Richmond
Hill, ON, L4B 1H3
(905) 707-7633
Emp Here 10   *Sales* 61,946,640
SIC 6794 Patent owners and lessors
Wayne Parent
Peter Yim
Kenny Park

D-U-N-S 25-375-8585   (SL)
O'HARA TECHNOLOGIES INC
(*Suby of* DBG HOLDINGS INC)
20 Kinnear Crt, Richmond Hill, ON, L4B 1K8
(905) 707-3286
Emp Here 60   *Sales* 13,320,060
SIC 3559 Special industry machinery, nec
Gilbert O'hara
David O'hara
Brian O'hara
James Laing

D-U-N-S 24-317-7719   (HQ)
OFIELD, CRAIG GROUP LTD
55 Leek Cres, Richmond Hill, ON, L4B 3Y2

(905) 726-5000
Emp Here 1   *Sales* 83,557,700
SIC 5141 Groceries, general line
Craig Ofield

D-U-N-S 20-690-6419   (HQ)
OGO FIBERS INC
9140 Leslie St Suite 312, Richmond Hill, ON,
L4B 0A9
(905) 762-9300
Emp Here 1   *Sales* 23,424,390
SIC 5093 Scrap and waste materials
William Wu
Sherry Ning

D-U-N-S 24-363-3331   (HQ)
OLYMPUS CANADA INC
(*Suby of* OLYMPUS CORPORATION)
25 Leek Cres, Richmond Hill, ON, L4B 4B3
(289) 269-0100
Sales 133,838,000
SIC 5047 Medical and hospital equipment
William (Bill) Collins
Martin Branch

D-U-N-S 24-576-8684   (HQ)
OZAWA CANADA INC
OZAWA AGENCIES
100 East Beaver Creek Rd Unit 2, Richmond
Hill, ON, L4B 1J6
(905) 731-5088
Emp Here 10   *Sales* 13,415,220
SIC 5046 Commercial equipment, nec
T. Andy Ozawa
Sumiko Ozawa

D-U-N-S 25-782-5208   (HQ)
PACIFIC INSURANCE BROKER INC
120 East Beaver Creek Rd Suite 101, Richmond Hill, ON, L4B 4V1
(416) 494-1268
Emp Here 5   *Sales* 11,598,480
SIC 6411 Insurance agents, brokers, and service
Ralph Kar Sun Hui

D-U-N-S 24-764-1863   (HQ)
PACTIV CANADA INC
(*Suby of* PACKAGING HOLDINGS LIMITED)
33 Staples Ave, Richmond Hill, ON, L4B 4W6
(905) 770-8810
Emp Here 25   *Sales* 301,511,880
SIC 5113 Industrial and personal service pa-
per
Ken Bumstead

D-U-N-S 25-398-8141   (SL)
**PARKWAY HOTELS AND CONVENTION
CENTRE INC**
*SHERATON PARKWAY TORONTO NORTH
HOTEL SUITES & CONVENTION CENTRE*
600 Highway 7 E, Richmond Hill, ON, L4B 1B2
(905) 881-2121
Emp Here 300   *Sales* 28,700,400
SIC 7011 Hotels and motels
Simon Kaptyn Sr

D-U-N-S 24-976-3657   (HQ)
PARTYLITE GIFTS, LTD
(*Suby of* THE CARLYLE GROUP L P)
55 East Beaver Creek Rd Unit A, Richmond
Hill, ON, L4B 1E8
(905) 881-6161
Emp Here 65   *Sales* 38,295,335
SIC 5199 Nondurable goods, nec
Gordon Simpson
David Whyte

D-U-N-S 25-374-6333   (SL)
PC OUTLET INC
45a West Wilmot St Suite 17, Richmond Hill,
ON, L4B 2P2

Emp Here 28   *Sales* 12,520,872
SIC 5045 Computers, peripherals, and soft-
ware
Joel Stevens
Paul Busch

Allan Leppick

D-U-N-S 24-116-7738   (SL)
PLATINUM NATURALS LTD
11 Sims Cres Suite 2, Richmond Hill, ON, L4B
1C9
(905) 731-8097
Emp Here 25   *Sales* 27,633,625
SIC 5122 Drugs, proprietaries, and sundries
David Khang

D-U-N-S 20-694-5144   (HQ)
PROTENERGY NATURAL FOODS CORP
125 East Beaver Creek Rd, Richmond Hill,
ON, L4B 4R3
(905) 707-6223
Sales 15,210,360
SIC 2032 Canned specialties
Blaine Hobson
Kevin Tracey
David Marten
Ken Uyede
Joseph Bornbaum

D-U-N-S 24-524-2875   (SL)
PSP USA LLC
35 East Beaver Creek Rd Unit 6, Richmond
Hill, ON, L4B 1B3
(905) 764-1121
Emp Here 30   *Sales* 15,265,680
SIC 5023 Homefurnishings
George Hobson

D-U-N-S 24-938-0106   (SL)
QUADRANT COSMETICS CORP
CALIBRE BEAUTE
20 West Beaver Creek Rd, Richmond Hill, ON,
L4B 3L6
(416) 921-2913
Emp Here 40   *Sales* 13,024,000
SIC 5999 Miscellaneous retail stores, nec
Michael Mclaughlin
Roger Swift

D-U-N-S 20-983-4175   (HQ)
QUALITY UNDERWRITING SERVICES LTD
111 Granton Dr Suite 105, Richmond Hill, ON,
L4B 1L5
(905) 335-8783
Emp Here 45   *Sales* 60,111,300
SIC 7323 Credit reporting services
Alan Shinton
Greg Shinton

D-U-N-S 25-137-1170   (SL)
QVELLA CORPORATION
9133 Leslie St Unit 110, Richmond Hill, ON,
L4B 4N1
(289) 317-0414
Emp Here 70   *Sales* 12,629,050
SIC 8731 Commercial physical research
Tino Alavie
Robert Maaskant
Samad Talebpour

D-U-N-S 25-190-2685   (SL)
RIGHT AT HOME REALTY INC
300 West Beaver Creek Rd Suite 202, Rich-
mond Hill, ON, L4B 3B1
(905) 695-7888
Emp Here 3,600   *Sales* 1,217,030,400
SIC 6531 Real estate agents and managers
Raj Bakshi

D-U-N-S 24-075-7575   (SL)
**ROBERTS,   WALTER   INSURANCE   BRO-
KERS INC**
110 West Beaver Creek Rd Suite 22, Rich-
mond Hill, ON, L4B 1J9
(905) 764-8061
Emp Here 30   *Sales* 17,397,720
SIC 6411 Insurance agents, brokers, and ser-
vice
Rose Roberts
Ronnie Roberts

D-U-N-S 24-389-3240   (HQ)
ROSENEATH CAPITAL CORP

91 Granton Dr, Richmond Hill, ON, L4B 2N5
(905) 882-4740
Sales 11,769,885
SIC 6712 Bank holding companies
Richard Bassett

D-U-N-S 20-808-8331   (SL)
**ROSENEATH DIRECT OPERATING COR-
PORATION**
BASSETT DIRECT
(*Suby of* ROSENEATH CAPITAL CORP)
91 Granton Dr, Richmond Hill, ON, L4B 2N5

Emp Here 45   *Sales* 10,994,760
SIC 5963 Direct selling establishments
Richard Bassett
Donna Van Bilsen
Shelly Wrong

D-U-N-S 20-140-1759   (HQ)
**SANDERSON-HAROLD COMPANY LIM-
ITED, THE**
PARIS KITCHENS
245 West Beaver Creek Rd Unit 2, Richmond
Hill, ON, L4B 1L1
(519) 442-6311
Emp Here 110   *Sales* 26,931,800
SIC 2434 Wood kitchen cabinets
Morris Wolfman

D-U-N-S 20-561-1275   (SL)
SENES HOLDINGS CORP
121 Granton Dr Unit 12, Richmond Hill, ON,
L4B 3N4
(905) 764-9380
Emp Here 75   *Sales* 17,571,600
SIC 8748 Business consulting, nec
Don Gorber

D-U-N-S 24-141-5277   (SL)
SERVCON INC
25 West Beaver Creek Rd Suite 13, Richmond
Hill, ON, L4B 1K2
(905) 881-4300
Emp Here 40   *Sales* 13,333,320
SIC 1541 Industrial buildings and warehouses
Tony Bruccoleri

D-U-N-S 24-374-1407   (SL)
SICK LTD
(*Suby of* SICK HOLDING GMBH)
2 East Beaver Creek Rd Unit 3, Richmond Hill,
ON, L4B 2N3
(905) 771-1444
Emp Here 36   *Sales* 17,100,936
SIC 5084 Industrial machinery and equipment
Craig Smith
Eileen Bogo
Robert Barniskis
Alberto Bertomeu

D-U-N-S 24-693-9722   (HQ)
SOIL ENGINEER LTD
90 West Beaver Creek Rd Suite 100, Rich-
mond Hill, ON, L4B 1E7
(416) 754-8515
Emp Here 80   *Sales* 24,618,600
SIC 1794 Excavation work
Victor Chan

D-U-N-S 25-735-0876   (HQ)
SOLID CADDGROUP INC
SOLID CAD
25b East Pearce St, Richmond Hill, ON, L4B
2M9
(905) 474-1499
Sales 13,415,220
SIC 5045 Computers, peripherals, and soft-
ware
Paul Fordman
Brian Mccorrison
Michael Kugan

D-U-N-S 24-112-4986   (SL)
**STAFF RELIEF HEALTH CARE SERVICES
INC**
350 Highway 7 E Unit Ph4, Richmond Hill, ON,
L4B 3N2

(905) 709-1767
Emp Here 49   *Sales* 11,350,017
SIC 8621 Professional organizations
Susan Dimichele

D-U-N-S 24-889-4412   (HQ)
STAPLES CANADA ULC
BUREAU EN GROS
(*Suby of* SYCAMORE PARTNERS MANAGE-
MENT, L.P.)
6 Staples Ave, Richmond Hill, ON, L4B 4W3
(905) 737-1147
Emp Here 350   *Sales* 2,569,518,000
SIC 5943 Stationery stores
David Boone
Peter Gibel
David Burt

D-U-N-S 24-357-4881   (SL)
STORAGE APPLIANCE CORPORATION
CLICKFREE AUTOMATIC BACK UP
30 West Beaver Creek Rd Unit 115, Richmond
Hill, ON, L4B 3K1
(416) 484-0009
Emp Here 55   *Sales* 24,594,570
SIC 5045 Computers, peripherals, and soft-
ware
Bryan Mcleod
Ian Collins
Gary Connell

D-U-N-S 25-246-8400   (SL)
**SUTTON GROUP-NEW STANDARD RE-
ALTY INC**
360 Highway 7 E Unit L 1, Richmond Hill, ON,
L4B 3Y7
(905) 709-8000
Emp Here 44   *Sales* 14,066,461
SIC 6531 Real estate agents and managers
Louis Chan

D-U-N-S 24-395-3895   (SL)
SUZUKI CANADA INC
100 East Beaver Creek Rd, Richmond Hill,
ON, L4B 1J6
(905) 764-1574
Emp Here 49   *Sales* 24,405,822
SIC 5511 New and used car dealers
Shotaro Sato

D-U-N-S 24-418-1090   (SL)
SWISSMAR LTD
35 East Beaver Creek Rd Unit 6, Richmond
Hill, ON, L4B 1B3
(905) 764-6068
Emp Here 50   *Sales* 25,442,800
SIC 5023 Homefurnishings
George Hobson

D-U-N-S 25-404-1593   (SL)
SYM-TECH INC
SYM-TECH AUTOMOTIVE PROTECTION
(*Suby of* SOHLER-NEUENHAUSER GMBH &
CO. KG)
150 West Beaver Creek Rd Suite 1, Richmond
Hill, ON, L4B 1B4
(905) 889-5390
Emp Here 125   *Sales* 267,121,000
SIC 6399 Insurance carriers, nec
Brad Wells
Chris Cawston
Lindsay Duffield
Derek Sloan
Scott Jaglowitz

D-U-N-S 25-220-1413   (SL)
TAKNOLOGY (CANADA) INC
50 East Pearce St, Richmond Hill, ON, L4B
1B7
(905) 882-2299
Emp Here 40   *Sales* 17,886,960
SIC 5045 Computers, peripherals, and soft-
ware
Raymond Au
George Tunt

D-U-N-S 20-770-0779   (HQ)
TIAN BAO TRAVEL LTD

VACANCES COMPASS HOLIDAYS
60 West Wilmot St Unit 1, Richmond Hill, ON,
L4B 1M6
(905) 695-2229
Emp Here 15   *Sales* 31,198,020
SIC 4724 Travel agencies
Kim Qing Zhang
Pamela Yuton Ye

D-U-N-S 20-847-1847   (SL)
TORONTO MONTESSORI SCHOOLS
8569 Bayview Ave, Richmond Hill, ON, L4B
3M7
(905) 889-6882
Emp Here 100   *Sales* 9,282,600
SIC 8211 Elementary and secondary schools
Michael Durisin
Latif Fazel
Elaine Flett

D-U-N-S 20-177-2423   (HQ)
TRANS-NORTHERN PIPELINES INC
45 Vogell Rd Suite 310, Richmond Hill, ON,
L4B 3P6
(905) 770-3353
Emp Here 38   *Sales* 18,598,881
SIC 4613 Refined petroleum pipelines
W. Alan Sawyer, Jr

D-U-N-S 24-415-1205   (HQ)
TRANSPLACE CANADA LTD
(*Suby of* TRANSPLACE HOLDINGS, INC.)
45a West Wilmot St Unit 213, Richmond Hill,
ON, L4B 2P2
(800) 463-3102
Emp Here 26   *Sales* 15,599,010
SIC 4731 Freight transportation arrangement
Frank Mcguigan
Chris Nester
Leigh Robinson

D-U-N-S 24-093-4778   (HQ)
TUXEDO ROYALE LIMITED
TUXEDO ROYALE FORMAL WEAR
9078 Leslie St Unit 5&6, Richmond Hill, ON,
L4B 3L8
(416) 798-7617
Emp Here 20   *Sales* 14,949,480
SIC 7299 Miscellaneous personal service
Kevin Slaney
Ivan Zichy

D-U-N-S 24-505-5876   (SL)
UNITED WIRE & CABLE (CANADA) INC
1 West Pearce St Unit 303, Richmond Hill, ON,
L4B 3K3
(905) 771-0099
Emp Here 15   *Sales* 15,005,085
SIC 5051 Metals service centers and offices
Marlyn Pawluk

D-U-N-S 25-500-4491   (HQ)
**UPPER CANADA CREATIVE CHILD CARE
CENTRES OF ONTARIO**
30 Fulton Way Unit 4, Richmond Hill, ON, L4B
1E6
(289) 982-1113
Emp Here 18   *Sales* 24,949,600
SIC 8351 Child day care services
John Harlow

D-U-N-S 24-876-5026   (HQ)
UPTOWN COMMUNICATION HOUSE INC
ROGERS AT & T UPTOWN
10 West Pearce St, Richmond Hill, ON, L4B
1B6
(905) 731-7318
Emp Here 7   *Sales* 19,546,240
SIC 5999 Miscellaneous retail stores, nec
Henry Chow

D-U-N-S 20-525-0038   (HQ)
URS CANADA INC
(*Suby of* AECOM)
30 Leek Cres 4th Fl, Richmond Hill, ON, L4B
4N4
(905) 882-9190
Sales 53,621,700

SIC 8711 Engineering services
Paul Hudspith
Murray Thompson

D-U-N-S 20-696-1109   (HQ)
VENTERRA REALTY (CANADA) INC
1725 16th Ave Suite 201, Richmond Hill, ON,
L4B 4C6
(905) 886-1059
Sales 25,133,340
SIC 6531 Real estate agents and managers
John Foresi

D-U-N-S 20-702-4170   (HQ)
VISUAL DEFENCE INC
VDI
9225 Leslie St Suite 7, Richmond Hill, ON,
L4B 3H6
(905) 731-1254
Emp Here 45   *Sales* 20,021,640
SIC 7372 Prepackaged software
Barry Tai

D-U-N-S 20-044-6193   (HQ)
VOLVO CARS OF CANADA CORP
(*Suby of* ZHEJIANG GEELY HOLDING
(GROUP) CO., LTD.)
9130 Leslie St Suite 101, Richmond Hill, ON,
L4B 0B9
(905) 695-9626
Sales 10,926,450
SIC 5012 Automobiles and other motor vehi-
cles
Jeffrey M Pugliese
Alexander Lvivich

D-U-N-S 20-026-7453   (HQ)
W.C.S. FINANCIAL SERVICES INC
20 Wertheim Crt Suite 40, Richmond Hill, ON,
L4B 3A8
(905) 731-1984
Emp Here 13   *Sales* 19,123,452
SIC 6282 Investment advice
Mari-Jayne Woodyatt

D-U-N-S 20-755-4221   (SL)
WATSON GROUP LTD, THE
95 West Beaver Creek Rd Unit 10, Richmond
Hill, ON, L4B 1H2
(905) 889-9119
Emp Here 55   *Sales* 12,818,575
SIC 1711 Plumbing, heating, air-conditioning
John Watson

D-U-N-S 20-360-0288   (HQ)
WELLNESS LIVING SYSTEMS INC
WL MOBILE APPS
30 Fulton Way Bldg 8 Suite 203, Richmond
Hill, ON, L4B 1E6
(888) 668-7728
Emp Here 1   *Sales* 11,547,954
SIC 7372 Prepackaged software
Lin Fridman

D-U-N-S 20-711-4153   (BR)
YORK REGION DISTRICT SCHOOL BOARD
BAYVIEW HILL ELEMENTARY SCHOOL
(*Suby of* YORK REGION DISTRICT SCHOOL
BOARD)
81 Strathearn Ave, Richmond Hill, ON, L4B
2J5
(905) 508-0806
Emp Here 75
SIC 8211 Elementary and secondary schools
Mike Carlin

D-U-N-S 20-847-7448   (HQ)
YORKE TOWNE SUPPLIES LIMITED
1235 Reid St, Richmond Hill, ON, L4B 1G4
(905) 762-1200
Sales 22,275,600
SIC 5198 Paints, varnishes, and supplies
Michael Harrison
Petula Boyce

Richmond Hill, ON L4C

D-U-N-S 20-153-9611 (SL)
1023714 ONTARIO LTD
JIM'S NO FRILLS
10488 Yonge St, Richmond Hill, ON, L4C 3G7
(905) 884-2600
Emp Here 49   *Sales* 13,433,448
SIC 5411 Grocery stores
Jim Marrelli

D-U-N-S 25-726-5785 (HQ)
1118741 ONTARIO LTD
IRPINIA KITCHENS
278 Newkirk Rd, Richmond Hill, ON, L4C 3G7
(905) 780-7722
Sales 13,465,900
SIC 2434 Wood kitchen cabinets
Joseph Marcantonio
Marcello Marcantonio
Nick Rossi

D-U-N-S 20-689-5786 (SL)
2394748 ONTARIO INC
PLAZA KIA
9144 Yonge St, Richmond Hill, ON, L4C 7A1
(905) 763-3688
Emp Here 35   *Sales* 17,432,730
SIC 5511 New and used car dealers
Robert Stein

D-U-N-S 20-375-0877 (SL)
2489736 ONTARIO LIMITED
MAZDA OF RICHMOND HILL
10414 Yonge St, Richmond Hill, ON, L4C 3C3
(905) 780-9999
Emp Here 40   *Sales* 19,923,120
SIC 5511 New and used car dealers
Rick Zanon

D-U-N-S 20-023-3529 (SL)
360 KIDS SUPPORT SERVICES
10415 Yonge St Suite C, Richmond Hill, ON, L4C 0Z3
(905) 475-6694
Emp Here 49   *Sales* 19,473,286
SIC 8699 Membership organizations, nec
Clovis Grant

D-U-N-S 25-708-0648 (SL)
898984 ONTARIO INC
RICHMOND HILL FINE CARS
10427 Yonge St Suite 2, Richmond Hill, ON, L4C 3C2

Emp Here 27   *Sales* 13,448,106
SIC 5511 New and used car dealers
Patrick Ng

D-U-N-S 25-509-2496 (BR)
APOTEX INC
380 Elgin Mills Rd E, Richmond Hill, ON, L4C 5H2
(905) 884-2050
Emp Here 520
SIC 2834 Pharmaceutical preparations
Adnan Abosh

D-U-N-S 25-691-1777 (SL)
ARCON METAL PROCESSING INC
105 Industrial Rd, Richmond Hill, ON, L4C 2Y4

Emp Here 100   *Sales* 19,208,500
SIC 3469 Metal stampings, nec
J. Brian Wisenberg
Alan D Wisenberg

D-U-N-S 24-978-0370 (SL)
BOSS STEEL LIMITED
320 Newkirk Rd, Richmond Hill, ON, L4C 3G7
(888) 301-6403
Emp Here 18   *Sales* 18,006,102
SIC 5051 Metals service centers and offices
Doug Loyst
Steven Walker

D-U-N-S 24-919-0141 (SL)

BRUNO'S FINE FOODS (NORTH) LTD
9665 Bayview Ave Suite 29, Richmond Hill, ON, L4C 9V4
(905) 737-4280
Emp Here 45   *Sales* 12,336,840
SIC 5411 Grocery stores
Bruno Fattore

D-U-N-S 25-144-2364 (SL)
CANADIAN COIN & CURRENCY CORP
10355 Yonge St, Richmond Hill, ON, L4C 3C1
(905) 883-5300
Emp Here 30   *Sales* 15,616,260
SIC 5094 Jewelry and precious stones
Steven Bromberg

D-U-N-S 20-076-8104 (HQ)
CANADIAN VIEWPOINT INC
9350 Yonge St Suite 206, Richmond Hill, ON, L4C 5G2
(905) 770-1770
Emp Here 100   *Sales* 43,988,600
SIC 8732 Commercial nonphysical research
Kim Storer
Carol Udell

D-U-N-S 25-394-3815 (HQ)
CENTURY CELLULAR (RICHMOND HILL) CORPORATION
BELL WORLD
10520 Yonge St Suite 26, Richmond Hill, ON, L4C 3C7
(905) 884-0000
Emp Here 12   *Sales* 26,830,440
SIC 5065 Electronic parts and equipment, nec
Murray Lampert
Norm Snider

D-U-N-S 20-054-1379 (SL)
CESIDIO ALTERNATE ENERGY
298 Demaine Cres, Richmond Hill, ON, L4C 2W5
(416) 822-6750
Emp Here 5   *Sales* 15,529,285
SIC 4924 Natural gas distribution

D-U-N-S 20-875-5249 (HQ)
COMMUNITY LIVING YORK SOUTH
101 Edward Ave, Richmond Hill, ON, L4C 5E5
(905) 884-9110
Emp Here 180   *Sales* 14,784,860
SIC 8361 Residential care
Don Wilkinson
Steve Klein

D-U-N-S 20-407-4777 (SL)
CUSCO FABRICATORS LLC
(*Suby of* HIG CAPITAL MANAGEMENT, INC.)
305 Enford Rd, Richmond Hill, ON, L4C 3E9
(905) 883-1214
Emp Here 75   *Sales* 16,650,075
SIC 3569 General industrial machinery, nec
Stephen Godwin

D-U-N-S 25-829-2903 (SL)
DYNAMIC DIRECT COURIER
57 Newkirk Rd, Richmond Hill, ON, L4C 3G4

Emp Here 25   *Sales* 11,087,250
SIC 7389 Business services, nec
Adrienne Boersma

D-U-N-S 20-164-9167 (HQ)
FAR EAST FOOD PRODUCTS LIMITED
273 Enford Rd, Richmond Hill, ON, L4C 3E9
(905) 883-8717
Sales 10,118,475
SIC 2052 Cookies and crackers
Edmond Lee
Raymond Lee

D-U-N-S 24-058-5646 (SL)
FAR EAST WATCHCASES LTD
TIME CHECK PLUS
120 Newkirk Rd Unit 5&6, Richmond Hill, ON, L4C 9S7
(905) 787-9919
Emp Here 240   *Sales* 21,527,040

SIC 7631 Watch, clock, and jewelry repair
Sudhir Talsania
Nayna Talsania

D-U-N-S 24-965-8089 (SL)
FORREST GREEN CONSULTING CORPORATION
FORREST GREEN GROUP OF COMPANIES
10520 Yonge St Unit 35b, Richmond Hill, ON, L4C 3C7
(905) 884-3103
Emp Here 52   *Sales* 14,265,264
SIC 8741 Management services
Murray Rowe
Murray Sr Rowe

D-U-N-S 24-569-0941 (SL)
GAMMA FOUNDRIES INC
115 Newkirk Rd, Richmond Hill, ON, L4C 3G4
(905) 884-9091
Emp Here 65   *Sales* 14,792,900
SIC 3325 Steel foundries, nec
Adolpho Quiroga

D-U-N-S 25-301-1373 (BR)
HUDSON'S BAY COMPANY
BAY, THE
(*Suby of* HUDSON'S BAY COMPANY)
9350 Yonge St Suite 1999, Richmond Hill, ON, L4C 5G2
(905) 883-1222
Emp Here 250
SIC 5311 Department stores
Gary Hills

D-U-N-S 25-397-2665 (HQ)
INNOCON INC
50 Newkirk Rd, Richmond Hill, ON, L4C 3G3
(905) 508-7676
Emp Here 100   *Sales* 49,285,225
SIC 3273 Ready-mixed concrete
Ken Tanenbaum
Dominique Calabrese
Scott Maynard

D-U-N-S 20-752-3119 (SL)
LEITNER, IRVING DRUGS LTD
SHOPPERS DRUG MART
9350 Yonge St Suite 966, Richmond Hill, ON, L4C 5G2
(905) 884-0555
Emp Here 70   *Sales* 17,102,960
SIC 5912 Drug stores and proprietary stores
Irving Leitner
Gail Leitner

D-U-N-S 20-824-2834 (HQ)
MACKENZIE HEALTH
YORK CENTRAL HOSPITAL
10 Trench St, Richmond Hill, ON, L4C 4Z3
(905) 883-1212
Sales 231,712,880
SIC 8062 General medical and surgical hospitals
Altaf Stationwala
Steven Jackson
Mary-Agnes Wilson
Richard Tam
Terry A. Villella

D-U-N-S 24-795-3177 (SL)
MANSTEEL LTD
105 Industrial Rd Suite 200, Richmond Hill, ON, L4C 2Y4
(905) 780-1488
Emp Here 70   *Sales* 13,445,950
SIC 3441 Fabricated structural Metal
Micheal (Mike) Mansour

D-U-N-S 20-783-3591 (SL)
MARIANN NURSING HOME AND RESIDENCE
MARIANN HOME
9915 Yonge St, Richmond Hill, ON, L4C 1V1
(905) 884-9276
Emp Here 100   *Sales* 6,856,600
SIC 8051 Skilled nursing care facilities
Bernard Boreland

D-U-N-S 20-977-5329 (SL)
NET ELECTRIC LIMITED
120 Newkirk Rd Unit 8, Richmond Hill, ON, L4C 9S7
(905) 737-7760
Emp Here 50   *Sales* 13,968,648
SIC 1731 Electrical work
Ove Bakmand

D-U-N-S 20-517-0300 (SL)
PLAZA AUTO GROUP LTD
9144 Yonge St Suite 200, Richmond Hill, ON, L4C 7A1
(613) 890-4078
Emp Here 500   *Sales* 288,626,000
SIC 5511 New and used car dealers
Morris Stein

D-U-N-S 20-146-1316 (SL)
RATCLIFFS/SEVERN LTD
10537 Yonge St, Richmond Hill, ON, L4C 3C5

Emp Here 160   *Sales* 29,022,080
SIC 3351 Copper rolling and drawing
Robert C Wordham
Jim Dempsey
John Staniforth

D-U-N-S 25-977-2135 (SL)
RESTORERS GROUP INC, THE
344 Newkirk Rd, Richmond Hill, ON, L4C 3G7
(905) 770-1323
Emp Here 31   *Sales* 14,592,661
SIC 1542 Nonresidential construction, nec
Real Parmentier

D-U-N-S 24-660-3708 (SL)
RHCC HOLDINGS LIMITED
RICHMOND HILL COUNTRY CLUB
8905 Bathurst St, Richmond Hill, ON, L4C 0H4
(905) 731-2800
Emp Here 150   *Sales* 11,781,750
SIC 7997 Membership sports and recreation clubs
Morris Macarz
Phillip Macarz

D-U-N-S 20-198-8437 (SL)
ROSEVIEW FLC ELECTRIC INC
51 Roseview Ave, Richmond Hill, ON, L4C 1C6
(647) 667-5618
Emp Here 100   *Sales* 17,731,100
SIC 7371 Custom computer programming services
Tiejun Liu

D-U-N-S 20-364-0230 (SL)
RXSOURCE CORP
556 Edward Ave Unit 74, Richmond Hill, ON, L4C 9Y5
(905) 883-4333
Emp Here 15   *Sales* 16,580,175
SIC 5122 Drugs, proprietaries, and sundries
Alfan Jetha
Yussuf Goolam
Adil Saleh
Alfan Jetha

D-U-N-S 24-664-4587 (HQ)
SEROYAL INTERNATIONAL INC
(*Suby of* NESTLE S.A.)
490 Elgin Mills Rd E, Richmond Hill, ON, L4C 0L8
(905) 508-2050
Sales 49,740,525
SIC 5122 Drugs, proprietaries, and sundries
Rosetta Raso

D-U-N-S 25-459-6687 (SL)
SHOPPERS DRUG MART
10660 Yonge St, Richmond Hill, ON, L4C 3C9
(905) 884-5233
Emp Here 40   *Sales* 10,118,160
SIC 5912 Drug stores and proprietary stores
Nancy Kaiser

D-U-N-S 20-305-0252   (SL)
SIMCOE ESTATES LTD
24 Tannery Crt, Richmond Hill, ON, L4C 7V4
(705) 259-1344
Emp Here 45   *Sales* 14,349,105
SIC 1521 Single-family housing construction
Luigi Orsi

D-U-N-S 20-773-6406   (SL)
SMALL CAR CENTRE LTD
RICHMOND HILL HONDA
77 16th Ave, Richmond Hill, ON, L4C 7A5
(905) 731-8899
Emp Here 60   *Sales* 37,756,800
SIC 5511 New and used car dealers
William Baird
Timothy Baird

D-U-N-S 24-174-5517   (BR)
STOCK TRANSPORTATION LTD
(*Suby of* NATIONAL EXPRESS GROUP PLC)
550 Edward Ave, Richmond Hill, ON, L4C 3K4
(905) 883-6665
Emp Here 250
SIC 4151 School buses

D-U-N-S 24-602-9573   (HQ)
SUE'S PRODUCE WORLD LTD
SUE'S MARKET
205 Don Head Village Blvd Suite 7, Richmond
Hill, ON, L4C 7R4
(905) 737-0520
Sales 13,707,600
SIC 5431 Fruit and vegetable markets
Maylene Shum
Colin Sue
Stanley Sue

D-U-N-S 25-180-5271   (BR)
SUNRISE NORTH ASSISTED LIVING LTD
*SUNRISE ASSISTED LIVING OF RICH-
MOND HILL*
(*Suby of* WELLTOWER INC.)
9800 Yonge St Suite 101, Richmond Hill, ON,
L4C 0P5
(905) 883-6963
Emp Here 75
SIC 8361 Residential care
Mary Wideman

D-U-N-S 25-347-4423   (HQ)
TRILLIUM PRACTICE MANAGEMENT LTD
9625 Yonge St Suite F, Richmond Hill, ON,
L4C 5T2
(905) 918-9573
Emp Here 20   *Sales* 10,973,280
SIC 8741 Management services
Ivo Maider

D-U-N-S 20-817-5422   (SL)
TWIN HILLS FORD LINCOLN LIMITED
10801 Yonge St, Richmond Hill, ON, L4C 3E3
(905) 884-4441
Emp Here 50   *Sales* 24,903,900
SIC 5511 New and used car dealers
Luigi Panetta
Ninetta Panetta

D-U-N-S 20-182-9272   (HQ)
VICTAULIC COMPANY OF CANADA ULC
(*Suby of* VICTAULIC COMPANY)
123 Newkirk Rd, Richmond Hill, ON, L4C 3G5
(905) 884-7444
Emp Here 450   *Sales* 121,615,500
SIC 3494 Valves and pipe fittings, nec
Joseph M Trachtenburg
Gary Moore
Tim Meadows
Mario D'ambrosio
John Malloy

D-U-N-S 20-532-0711   (SL)
WAGONMASTER ENTERPRISES B.C. INC
WAGONMASTER ONTARIO
561 Edward Ave Unit 11, Richmond Hill, ON,
L4C 9W6
(905) 737-4627
Emp Here 16   *Sales* 11,607,024

SIC 6399 Insurance carriers, nec
Tom Carroll

D-U-N-S 20-146-2256   (SL)
WILSON-NIBLETT MOTORS LIMITED
*WILSON-NIBLETT   CHEVROLET
CORVETTE*
10675 Yonge St, Richmond Hill, ON, L4C 3E1
(905) 884-0991
Emp Here 65   *Sales* 40,903,200
SIC 5511 New and used car dealers
Gordon C Wilson Jr
Gordon B Wilson Sr

D-U-N-S 25-221-4606   (BR)
YORK REGION DISTRICT SCHOOL BOARD
LANGSTAFF SECONDARY SCHOOL
(*Suby of* YORK REGION DISTRICT SCHOOL
BOARD)
106 Garden Ave, Richmond Hill, ON, L4C 6M1
(905) 889-6266
Emp Here 100
SIC 8211 Elementary and secondary schools
Richard Cherry

D-U-N-S 25-293-6349   (BR)
YORK REGION DISTRICT SCHOOL BOARD
BAYVIEW SECONDARY SCHOOL
(*Suby of* YORK REGION DISTRICT SCHOOL
BOARD)
10077 Bayview Ave, Richmond Hill, ON, L4C
2L4
(905) 884-4453
Emp Here 135
SIC 8211 Elementary and secondary schools
Brian Schouten

D-U-N-S 25-293-6265   (BR)
YORK REGION DISTRICT SCHOOL BOARD
ALEXANDER MACKENZIE HIGH SCHOOL
(*Suby of* YORK REGION DISTRICT SCHOOL
BOARD)
300 Major Mackenzie Dr W, Richmond Hill,
ON, L4C 3S3
(905) 884-0554
Emp Here 125
SIC 8211 Elementary and secondary schools
Debra Conrad-Knight

D-U-N-S 24-972-9385   (HQ)
YOUR COMMUNITY REALTY INC
*ROYAL LEPAGE YOUR COMMUNITY RE-
ALTY*
9050 Yonge St Suite 100, Richmond Hill, ON,
L4C 9S6
(905) 884-8700
Emp Here 10   *Sales* 10,870,240
SIC 6531 Real estate agents and managers
Vivian Risi

Richmond Hill, ON L4E

D-U-N-S 25-887-3280   (SL)
1207715 ONTARIO INC
ALL-CARE HOME HEALTH & STAFFING
11685 Yonge St Suite 205, Richmond Hill, ON,
L4E 0K7
(905) 770-9450
Emp Here 250   *Sales* 19,175,250
SIC 8082 Home health care services
Maria Dimaio
Ashley Testa

D-U-N-S 20-184-4868   (SL)
**ARTISTIC   DEVELOPMENT   SUPPORT
GROUP**
27 Napanee St, Richmond Hill, ON, L4E 0X3

Emp Here 150   *Sales* 16,662,000
SIC 8062 General medical and surgical hospitals

D-U-N-S 24-348-2853   (SL)
CANADIAN TIRE
11720 Yonge St, Richmond Hill, ON, L4E 0K4

(905) 884-9009
Emp Here 30   *Sales* 14,942,340
SIC 5531 Auto and home supply stores
Michael Medline

D-U-N-S 20-219-5082   (HQ)
VICTOR'S SPECIALTY FOODS LTD
VICKROOS
280 Stouffville Rd, Richmond Hill, ON, L4E
3P4

Emp Here 1   *Sales* 15,735,161
SIC 5159 Farm-product raw materials, nec
Victor Relvas

Richmond Hill, ON L4K

D-U-N-S 25-223-5473   (SL)
XANA INTERNATIONAL INC
55 Administration Rd Units 33 & 34, Richmond
Hill, ON, L4K 4G9
(416) 477-4770
Emp Here 27   *Sales* 12,709,737
SIC 1542 Nonresidential construction, nec
Shane Worthington
Mahmood Kara

Richmond Hill, ON L4S

D-U-N-S 24-329-9661   (SL)
1675001 ONTARIO LIMITED
RICHMOND HILL HYUNDAI
11188 Yonge St, Richmond Hill, ON, L4S 1K9
(905) 884-5100
Emp Here 45   *Sales* 22,413,510
SIC 5511 New and used car dealers
Roger Linton

D-U-N-S 20-387-8483   (SL)
2634912 ONTARIO INC
YONGE NORTH MITSUBISHI
11262 Yonge St, Richmond Hill, ON, L4S 1K9
(905) 770-0005
Emp Here 23   *Sales* 11,455,794
SIC 5511 New and used car dealers
Cheng Liu
Johnny Lam
Man Wai

D-U-N-S 24-485-8536   (SL)
ARCHE DAYBREAK, L'
11339 Yonge St, Richmond Hill, ON, L4S 1L1
(905) 884-3454
Emp Here 100   *Sales* 5,924,700
SIC 8361 Residential care
Carl Macmillan

D-U-N-S 20-561-2856   (HQ)
BMW CANADA INC
BMW GROUP CANADA
(*Suby of* BAYERISCHE MOTOREN WERKE
AG)
50 Ultimate Dr, Richmond Hill, ON, L4S 0C8
(905) 770-1758
Emp Here 203   *Sales* 153,564,282
SIC 5012 Automobiles and other motor vehi-
cles
Hendrik Von Kuenheim
Walter Schauer
Adam Zimmerman
Tom Purves

D-U-N-S 20-304-8095   (SL)
CANROS GRP INC
30 Via Renzo Suite 255, Richmond Hill,
ON, L4S 0B8
(905) 918-0640
Emp Here 6   *Sales* 70,031,228
SIC 3532 Mining machinery
Yuri Tarasov

D-U-N-S 24-253-3789   (SL)

CARA FOODS INTERNATIONAL LTD
KELSEY'S
1620 Elgin Mills Rd E, Richmond Hill, ON, L4S
0B2
(905) 508-4139
Emp Here 100   *Sales* 4,551,900
SIC 5812 Eating places
Jessica Zung

D-U-N-S 25-998-3203   (HQ)
COMPUGEN INC
(*Suby of* COMPUGEN SYSTEMS LTD)
100 Via Renzo Dr, Richmond Hill, ON, L4S
0B8
(905) 707-2000
Emp Here 210   *Sales* 93,885,865
SIC 7373 Computer integrated systems de-
sign
Harry Zarek
David Austin
Michael Charter
Steve Glover
Brian Macintosh
Karen Atkinson

D-U-N-S 24-411-3460   (HQ)
COMPUGEN SYSTEMS LTD
100 Via Renzo Dr, Richmond Hill, ON, L4S
0B8
(905) 707-2000
Sales 146,203,600
SIC 6712 Bank holding companies
Harry Zarek
Frank Fuser
Karen Atkinson
David Austin

D-U-N-S 20-044-9817   (HQ)
COSMO MUSIC COMPANY LTD
COSMO MUSIC
10 Via Renzo Dr, Richmond Hill, ON, L4S 0B6
(905) 770-5222
Sales 46,480,600
SIC 5736 Musical instrument stores
Thomas Hebert
Rudi Brouwers
Mark Hebert
Brenda Hebert

D-U-N-S 24-358-6042   (BR)
COSTCO WHOLESALE CANADA LTD
COSTCO
(*Suby of* COSTCO WHOLESALE CORPO-
RATION)
35 John Birchall Rd Suite 592, Richmond Hill,
ON, L4S 0B2
(905) 780-2100
Emp Here 200
SIC 5099 Durable goods, nec
Frank Chislette

D-U-N-S 24-306-0795   (HQ)
DATA INTEGRITY INC
30 Via Renzo Dr Unit 3, Richmond Hill, ON,
L4S 0B8
(416) 638-0111
Emp Here 5   *Sales* 14,937,660
SIC 5045 Computers, peripherals, and soft-
ware
Norman Filicetti
Robert Seager

D-U-N-S 24-197-8081   (HQ)
**DOUBLE   RAINBOW   CANADA   CHINA
HOLDINGS GROUP INC**
127 Frank Endean Rd, Richmond Hill, ON,
L4S 1V2

Sales 18,592,245
SIC 6211 Security brokers and dealers
Deya Zhao

D-U-N-S 25-129-0755   (SL)
**HOLY   TRINITY   SCHOOL   (CO-
EDUCATIONAL) RICHMOND HILL**
11300 Bayview Ave, Richmond Hill, ON, L4S
1L4

(905) 737-1114
Emp Here 105   *Sales* 10,407,495
SIC 8211 Elementary and secondary schools
George Rotherford

D-U-N-S 24-361-7284   (BR)
HOME DEPOT OF CANADA INC
HOME DEPOT
(*Suby of* THE HOME DEPOT INC)
1706 Elgin Mills Rd E, Richmond Hill, ON, L4S
1M6
(905) 787-7200
Emp Here 100
SIC 5251 Hardware stores
Jessica Bassken

D-U-N-S 24-125-6981   (HQ)
JADE TRAVEL LTD
JADE TOURS
1650 Elgin Mills Rd E Unit 403, Richmond Hill,
ON, L4S 0B2
(905) 787-9288
Emp Here 50   *Sales* 80,027,040
SIC 4725 Tour operators
Doug Vogl
Spencer Ling

D-U-N-S 24-707-4768   (SL)
LA ROCCA CREATIVE CAKES INC
45 Via Renzo Dr, Richmond Hill, ON, L4S 0B4
(905) 884-7275
Emp Here 225   *Sales* 161,261,100
SIC 5149 Groceries and related products, nec
Michael Givens
Harvey Easson
Lina Givens-Easson

D-U-N-S 20-552-8545   (BR)
METRO ONTARIO INC
METRO
(*Suby of* METRO INC)
1070 Major Mackenzie Dr E, Richmond Hill,
ON, L4S 1P3
(905) 770-1400
Emp Here 300
SIC 5411 Grocery stores
Frank Zubiri

D-U-N-S 25-292-1374   (BR)
REVERA INC
BROOKSIDE RETIREMENT RESIDENCE
(*Suby of* GOVERNMENT OF CANADA)
980 Elgin Mills Rd E, Richmond Hill, ON, L4S
1M4
(905) 884-9248
Emp Here 80
SIC 8361 Residential care
Jayson Sukhai

D-U-N-S 20-609-2681   (BR)
REVERA LONG TERM CARE INC
ELGINWOOD LONG TERM CARE
(*Suby of* GOVERNMENT OF CANADA)
182 Yorkland St Suite 1, Richmond Hill, ON,
L4S 2M9
(905) 737-0858
Emp Here 150
SIC 8051 Skilled nursing care facilities
Dian Cairns

D-U-N-S 20-409-0674   (SL)
RICHMOND HILL AUTO PARK LIMITED
RICHMOND HILL TOYOTA
11240 Yonge St, Richmond Hill, ON, L4S 1K9
(905) 889-1189
Emp Here 48   *Sales* 23,907,744
SIC 5511 New and used car dealers
Emaine Kadrie

D-U-N-S 24-320-6187   (SL)
TEK STAFF IT SOLUTIONS INC
30 Via Renzo Dr Suite 200, Richmond Hill,
ON, L4S 0B8
(416) 438-1099
Emp Here 50   *Sales* 11,848,500
SIC 7361 Employment agencies
Jeff Majcenic
Sandra Persaud

D-U-N-S 24-320-1775   (SL)
WIKITOR
129 Rose Branch Dr, Richmond Hill, ON, L4S
1H6
(647) 498-8773
Emp Here 50   *Sales* 10,798,463
SIC 8748 Business consulting, nec
Hamidreza Rahbar

Ridgetown, ON N0P

D-U-N-S 24-320-4210   (SL)
D. PECK PLUMBING
15 Myrtle St, Ridgetown, ON, N0P 2C0
(519) 360-5913
Emp Here 1   *Sales* 43,091,235
SIC 1711 Plumbing, heating, air-conditioning
Dylan Peck

D-U-N-S 20-146-2561   (SL)
DANIELS SERVICE CENTRE LTD
21180 Victoria Rd, Ridgetown, ON, N0P 2C0
(519) 674-5493
Emp Here 50   *Sales* 10,131,450
SIC 7538 General automotive repair shops
Gerard Daniels
Lillian Daniels

D-U-N-S 25-503-1544   (HQ)
KSR INTERNATIONAL INC
DRESDEN INDUSTRIAL
95 Erie St S, Ridgetown, ON, N0P 2C0
(519) 674-5413
Emp Here 450   *Sales* 223,954,500
SIC 3714 Motor vehicle parts and accessories
Rodney Nunn

D-U-N-S 20-652-1101   (BR)
REVERA INC
VILLAGE RETIREMENT, THE
(*Suby of* GOVERNMENT OF CANADA)
9 Myrtle St, Ridgetown, ON, N0P 2C0
(519) 674-5427
Emp Here 100
SIC 8051 Skilled nursing care facilities
Thomas Wellner

D-U-N-S 25-605-5245   (BR)
UNIVERSITY OF GUELPH
RIDGETOWN COLLEGE
(*Suby of* UNIVERSITY OF GUELPH)
120 Main St, Ridgetown, ON, N0P 2C0
(519) 674-1500
Emp Here 100
SIC 8221 Colleges and universities
Ron Pitbaldo

Ridgeway, ON L0S

D-U-N-S 25-509-7263   (SL)
1265767 ONTARIO LIMITED
JOE'S VALU-MART
311 Gorham Rd, Ridgeway, ON, L0S 1N0
(905) 894-5266
Emp Here 37   *Sales* 10,143,624
SIC 5411 Grocery stores
Joe Ambrosio

D-U-N-S 20-848-2083   (SL)
BUFFALO CANOE CLUB
4475 Erie Rd Suite 1, Ridgeway, ON, L0S 1N0
(905) 894-2750
Emp Here 85   *Sales* 6,493,745
SIC 7997 Membership sports and recreation
clubs
Petrea Blais

D-U-N-S 20-852-4066   (SL)
CHERRY HILL CLUB, LIMITED
912 Cherry Hill Blvd, Ridgeway, ON, L0S 1N0
(905) 894-1122
Emp Here 110   *Sales* 8,639,950

SIC 7997 Membership sports and recreation
clubs
Brenda Washburn

Rockcliffe, ON K1M

D-U-N-S 24-103-5179   (SL)
ELMWOOD SCHOOL INCORPORATED
ELMWOOD SCHOOL
261 Buena Vista Rd, Rockcliffe, ON, K1M 0V9
(613) 749-6761
Emp Here 85   *Sales* 7,890,210
SIC 8211 Elementary and secondary schools
Ben Merkley
Tanya Mackin

Rockland, ON K4K

D-U-N-S 24-975-1744   (BR)
**CONSEIL   SCOLAIRE   DE   DISTRICT
CATHOLIQUE DE L'EST ONTARIEN**
*ECOLE   INTERMEDIAIRE   CATHOLIQUE-
PAVILLON ROCKLAND*
(*Suby of* CONSEIL SCOLAIRE DE DISTRICT
CATHOLIQUE DE L'EST ONTARIEN)
1535 Du Parc Ave, Rockland, ON, K4K 1C3
(613) 446-5169
Emp Here 80
SIC 8211 Elementary and secondary schools
Denis Tardif

D-U-N-S 20-774-3530   (SL)
ENTERPRISE PARIS INC
TIM HORTONS
2875 Rue Laporte, Rockland, ON, K4K 1R3
(613) 446-9948
Emp Here 200   *Sales* 9,103,800
SIC 5812 Eating places
Yves Paris

D-U-N-S 24-393-2451   (SL)
JEMARICA INC
CANADIAN TIRE
9040 County Road 17 Suite 623, Rockland,
ON, K4K 1V5
(613) 446-4410
Emp Here 50   *Sales* 12,652,950
SIC 5251 Hardware stores
Richard Marsan

D-U-N-S 20-261-3485   (SL)
LAMARCHE ELECTRIC INC
9374 County Road 17, Rockland, ON, K4K
1K9
(613) 747-8882
Emp Here 65   *Sales* 14,158,885
SIC 1731 Electrical work
Shawn Lamarche

D-U-N-S 24-270-8576   (SL)
POTVIN, A. CONSTRUCTION LTD
8850 County Road 17, Rockland, ON, K4K
1L6
(613) 446-5181
Emp Here 300   *Sales* 139,132,800
SIC 1521 Single-family housing construction
Alain Potvin

D-U-N-S 20-327-9380   (SL)
ROCKLAND HELP CENTRE
2815 Chamberland St, Rockland, ON, K4K
1M7
(613) 446-7594
Emp Here 49   *Sales* 11,114,817
SIC 8399 Social services, nec
Conrad Montcalm

D-U-N-S 24-251-9853   (BR)
WAL-MART CANADA CORP
WALMART
(*Suby of* WALMART INC.)
3001 Richelieu St, Rockland, ON, K4K 0B5

(613) 446-5730
Emp Here 150
SIC 5399 Miscellaneous general merchandise
Dany Plourde

Rockport, ON K0E

D-U-N-S 20-700-4011   (SL)
ROCKPORT BOAT LINE (1994) LIMITED
23 Front St, Rockport, ON, K0E 1V0
(613) 659-3402
Emp Here 75   *Sales* 20,216,175
SIC 4489 Water passenger transportation
Craig Callen-Jones
James Scott
Robert Tennant

Rockton, ON L0R

D-U-N-S 24-707-6698   (HQ)
A.V.K. NURSERY HOLDINGS INC
CONNON NURSERIES
1724 Concession 4, Rockton, ON, L0R 1X0
(905) 659-1518
Sales 74,252,000
SIC 5193 Flowers and florists supplies
Adrian (Art) Vander Kruk

Rockwood, ON N0B

D-U-N-S 20-783-8186   (SL)
DREXLER CONSTRUCTION LIMITED
5274 County Rd 27, Rockwood, ON, N0B 2K0
(519) 856-9526
Emp Here 150   *Sales* 49,217,250
SIC 1623 Water, sewer, and utility lines
Alfred Drexler
Jerome Drexler
Robert Drexler
Kevin Drexler
Martin Drexler
Peter Drexler

Rodney, ON N0L

D-U-N-S 24-990-6280   (BR)
KSR INTERNATIONAL INC
DRESDEN INDUSTRIAL
(*Suby of* KSR INTERNATIONAL INC)
172 Centre St, Rodney, ON, N0L 2C0
(519) 785-0121
Emp Here 320
SIC 3714 Motor vehicle parts and accessories
Darren Negri

Rosslyn, ON P7K

D-U-N-S 20-569-5406   (SL)
HALOW, B. J. & SON CONSTRUCTORS LTD
22 Wing Rd, Rosslyn, ON, P7K 0L2
(807) 939-2533
Emp Here 45   *Sales* 20,122,830
SIC 5032 Brick, stone, and related material
Bruce Halow

D-U-N-S 25-967-1464   (SL)
SUMMIT PIPELINE SERVICES ULC
(*Suby of* API GROUP INC.)
46 Cooper Rd Suite 13, Rosslyn, ON, P7K
0E3
(807) 939-1100
Emp Here 10   *Sales* 19,668,407

▲ Public Company   ■ Public Company Family Member   **HQ** Headquarters   **BR** Branch   **SL** Single Location

SIC 1623 Water, sewer, and utility lines
Michael Throm
Tyler Madgian

Ruscom Station, ON N0R

D-U-N-S 24-856-0406   (SL)
FACCA INCORPORATED
2097 County Rd 31 Suite 1, Ruscom Station, ON, N0R 1R0
(519) 975-0377
Emp Here 120   *Sales* 30,293,040
SIC 1622 Bridge, tunnel, and elevated highway construction
Don Gardionio

D-U-N-S 24-147-6493   (SL)
LHS ENTERPRISES
2916 County Rd 31, Ruscom Station, ON, N0R 1R0

Emp Here 30   *Sales* 20,025,148
SIC 5963 Direct selling establishments
Larry Stieler

Russell, ON K4R

D-U-N-S 24-104-4742   (HQ)
FRECON CONSTRUCTION LIMITED
1235 Russell Rd S, Russell, ON, K4R 1E1
(613) 445-2944
Emp Here 50   *Sales* 21,982,324
SIC 1541 Industrial buildings and warehouses
Dennis Drevniok
Dean Drevniok
Dale Drevniok
Micheline Drevniok

Rutherglen, ON P0H

D-U-N-S 24-822-8124   (SL)
COLUMBIA FOREST PRODUCTS LTD
(*Suby of* COLUMBIA FOREST PRODUCTS, INC.)
Hwy 17 E, Rutherglen, ON, P0H 2E0
(705) 776-7622
Emp Here 145   *Sales* 82,596,060
SIC 5031 Lumber, plywood, and millwork
Harry Demorest
David Drenth

Ruthven, ON N0P

D-U-N-S 24-659-3321   (SL)
617885 ONTARIO LTD
JEM FARMS
1581 County Road 34, Ruthven, ON, N0P 2G0
(519) 326-4907
Emp Here 60   *Sales* 15,738,540
SIC 0182 Food crops grown under cover
Jamie Mastronardi

D-U-N-S 25-221-4689   (SL)
971016 ONTARIO LIMITED
RED ZOO MARKETING
1621 Road 3, Ruthven, ON, N0P 2G0

Emp Here 75   *Sales* 62,668,275
SIC 5148 Fresh fruits and vegetables
Jay Colasanti
Ron Colasanti
William K. Colasanti

D-U-N-S 20-823-8022   (SL)
COLASANTI FARMS LIMITED

1550 Road 3 E, Ruthven, ON, N0P 2G0
(519) 326-3287
Emp Here 190   *Sales* 8,861,410
SIC 5812 Eating places
Joseph Colasanti
Terrance Colasanti

D-U-N-S 20-125-8399   (SL)
M. O. S. ENTERPRISES LIMITED
1475 County Road 34, Ruthven, ON, N0P 2G0
(519) 326-9067
Emp Here 92   *Sales* 7,051,293
SIC 0182 Food crops grown under cover
Annie Mastronardi
Ollie Mastronardi
Jessica Mastronardi
Mark Mastronardi

D-U-N-S 20-769-4290   (HQ)
SUN-BRITE FOODS INC
1532 County Road 34, Ruthven, ON, N0P 2G0
(519) 326-9033
Emp Here 75   *Sales* 46,668,150
SIC 2033 Canned fruits and specialties
Henry Iacobelli
Luigi Saccucci
John Iacobelli

Saint-Pascal-Baylon, ON K0A

D-U-N-S 20-436-6973   (SL)
AUDEAMUS
1546 Rollin Rd, Saint-Pascal-Baylon, ON, K0A 3N0

Emp Here 150   *Sales* 16,662,000
SIC 8062 General medical and surgical hospitals
Katalin Poor

Sarnia, ON N7S

D-U-N-S 25-282-4826   (SL)
1075177 ONTARIO LTD
GENERAL MAINTENANCE SERVICES
1129 Vanier Rd, Sarnia, ON, N7S 3Y6

Emp Here 60   *Sales* 25,364,220
SIC 1541 Industrial buildings and warehouses
Gary Whitson

D-U-N-S 25-463-6525   (SL)
1197283 ONTARIO LIMITED
JONES, DAVY FOODTOWN
1030 Confederation St Unit 2, Sarnia, ON, N7S 6H1
(519) 383-8837
Emp Here 21   *Sales* 17,547,117
SIC 5147 Meats and meat products
David Jones
Gloria Jones

D-U-N-S 20-248-4374   (SL)
629728 ONTARIO LIMITED
ENTROPEX
(*Suby of* UNITEC INC)
1271 Lougar Ave, Sarnia, ON, N7S 5N5
(519) 332-0430
Emp Here 150
SIC 5162 Plastics materials and basic shapes
Keith Bechard

D-U-N-S 20-020-1648   (SL)
ALLIANCE FABRICATING LTD
ALLOY FAB
763 Chester St, Sarnia, ON, N7S 5N2
(519) 336-4328
Emp Here 90   *Sales* 17,287,650
SIC 3499 Fabricated Metal products, nec
Brant Jacklin
John Mcinnis

Charmaine Jacklin
Karen Keenan

D-U-N-S 20-698-7104   (BR)
BEST BUY CANADA LTD
FUTURE SHOP
(*Suby of* BEST BUY CO., INC.)
1380 Exmouth St, Sarnia, ON, N7S 3X9
(519) 542-4388
Emp Here 100
SIC 5731 Radio, television, and electronic stores
Brent Gillen

D-U-N-S 24-355-2218   (SL)
CANADIAN STRUCTURAL & MECHANICAL LTD
1399 Lougar Ave, Sarnia, ON, N7S 5N5
(519) 383-6525
Emp Here 100   *Sales* 23,306,500
SIC 1711 Plumbing, heating, air-conditioning
Paul Douglas
Rick Veenendaal
Douglas Cochrane
Daniel Russell

D-U-N-S 20-973-5869   (SL)
GROOMBRIDGE, W. ENTERPRISES INC
SAMPLER POSTAL OUTLET, THE
1380 London Rd, Sarnia, ON, N7S 1P8

Emp Here 25   *Sales* 11,087,250
SIC 7389 Business services, nec
Chris Groombridge

D-U-N-S 20-108-5557   (BR)
HOME DEPOT OF CANADA INC
HOME DEPOT
(*Suby of* THE HOME DEPOT INC)
1350 Quinn Dr, Sarnia, ON, N7S 6L5
(519) 333-2300
Emp Here 150
SIC 5251 Hardware stores
Terry Lichty

D-U-N-S 20-810-9442   (HQ)
L.A.M.M. INC
LITTLE CAESARS PIZZA
1273 London Rd, Sarnia, ON, N7S 1P3
(519) 383-7727
Emp Here 18   *Sales* 34,840,500
SIC 6794 Patent owners and lessors
Kathleen Mundy

D-U-N-S 20-936-4595   (HQ)
LAMBTON COLLEGE OF APPLIED ARTS & TECHNOLOGY, THE
LAMBTON COLLEGE
1457 London Rd, Sarnia, ON, N7S 6K4
(519) 542-7751
Emp Here 478   *Sales* 89,494,979
SIC 8222 Junior colleges
Judith Morris
Janice Mcmichael-Dennis
Margaret Dragan
Cindy Buchanan
Catherine Large

D-U-N-S 25-249-3705   (BR)
LAMBTON KENT DISTRICT SCHOOL BOARD
ALEXANDER MACKENZIE SECONDARY SCHOOL
(*Suby of* LAMBTON KENT DISTRICT SCHOOL BOARD)
1257 Michigan Ave, Sarnia, ON, N7S 3Y3
(519) 542-5505
Emp Here 80
SIC 8211 Elementary and secondary schools
James Stewart

D-U-N-S 24-420-0031   (BR)
LAMBTON KENT DISTRICT SCHOOL BOARD
ST. CLAIR SECONDARY SCHOOL
(*Suby of* LAMBTON KENT DISTRICT SCHOOL BOARD)

340 Murphy Rd, Sarnia, ON, N7S 2X1
(519) 332-1140
Emp Here 75
SIC 8211 Elementary and secondary schools
Tim Hummel

D-U-N-S 25-297-8697   (BR)
LOBLAWS INC
REAL CANADIAN SUPERSTORE, THE
(*Suby of* LOBLAW COMPANIES LIMITED)
600 Murphy Rd, Sarnia, ON, N7S 5T7
(519) 383-8133
Emp Here 301
SIC 5411 Grocery stores
Al Scott

D-U-N-S 25-360-2981   (BR)
LUXURY HOTELS INTERNATIONAL OF CANADA ULC
LUXURY HOTELS INTERNATIONAL OF CANADA, ULC
(*Suby of* MARRIOTT INTERNATIONAL, INC.)
1337 London Rd, Sarnia, ON, N7S 1P6
(519) 346-4551
Emp Here 350
SIC 7389 Business services, nec
Carol Kameka

D-U-N-S 24-317-9801   (SL)
MAC-WELD MACHINING LTD
MAC-WELD MACHINING AND MANUFACTURING
1324 Lougar Ave, Sarnia, ON, N7S 5N7
(519) 332-1388
Emp Here 75   *Sales* 16,650,075
SIC 3599 Industrial machinery, nec
Alan Merrington
Lynn Merrington

D-U-N-S 20-149-2675   (SL)
PARK LANE CHEVROLET CADILLAC LTD
1290 London Rd, Sarnia, ON, N7S 1P5
(519) 541-8883
Emp Here 50   *Sales* 24,903,900
SIC 5511 New and used car dealers
David Bailey
Brian Bailey
Randy Alexander

D-U-N-S 25-265-3225   (SL)
PATHWAYS HEALTH CENTRE FOR CHILDREN
1240 Murphy Rd, Sarnia, ON, N7S 2Y6
(519) 542-3471
Emp Here 120   *Sales* 9,215,040
SIC 8322 Individual and family services
Jenny Greensmith
Barry Porter
Paul Beaudet
John Mcneil

D-U-N-S 20-148-8806   (SL)
PETER CHARLES ANSLEY HOLDINGS LIMITED
CANADIAN TIRE ASSOCIATE STORE #094
1380 London Rd Unit 300, Sarnia, ON, N7S 1P8
(519) 542-3403
Emp Here 150   *Sales* 94,392,000
SIC 5531 Auto and home supply stores
Peter Ansley

D-U-N-S 25-028-5210   (BR)
REVERA LONG TERM CARE INC
SUMAC LODGE
(*Suby of* GOVERNMENT OF CANADA)
1464 Blackwell Rd, Sarnia, ON, N7S 5M4
(519) 542-3421
Emp Here 103
SIC 8051 Skilled nursing care facilities
Anne Currie

D-U-N-S 20-346-8186   (SL)
REVITAL POLYMERS INC
1271 Lougar Ave, Sarnia, ON, N7S 5N5
(519) 332-0430
Emp Here 90   *Sales* 23,141,790

SIC 4953 Refuse systems
King Hong Leung
Antoine Moucachen

D-U-N-S 20-092-0135   (SL)
SARNIA CARE-A-VAN
1169 Michener Rd, Sarnia, ON, N7S 4W3
(519) 336-3789
Emp Here 45   *Sales* 10,665,068
SIC 8742 Management consulting services
Jim Stevens

D-U-N-S 20-569-6821   (SL)
SARNIA/LAMBTON COMMUNITY CARE ACCESS CENTRE
C C A C
1150 Pontiac Dr, Sarnia, ON, N7S 3A7
(519) 337-1000
Emp Here 70   *Sales* 16,906,050
SIC 8621 Professional organizations
Betty Kuchta

D-U-N-S 25-740-4558   (BR)
STEEVES & ROZEMA ENTERPRISES LIMITED
TWIN LAKES TERRACE
(*Suby of* STEEVES & ROZEMA ENTERPRISES LIMITED)
1310 Murphy Rd Suite 216, Sarnia, ON, N7S 6K5
(519) 542-2939
Emp Here 100
SIC 8059 Nursing and personal care, nec
Cathy Mcintosh

D-U-N-S 25-140-5676   (BR)
STEEVES & ROZEMA ENTERPRISES LIMITED
TRILLIUM VILLA NURSING HOME
(*Suby of* STEEVES & ROZEMA ENTERPRISES LIMITED)
1221 Michigan Ave, Sarnia, ON, N7S 3Y3
(519) 542-5529
Emp Here 180
SIC 8051 Skilled nursing care facilities
Jennifer Allison

D-U-N-S 24-539-7757   (SL)
TEAHEN, R & R BUILDING SUPPLIES LTD
TEAHEN HOME HARDWARE BUILDING CENTRE
1272 London Rd Suite 1707, Sarnia, ON, N7S 1P5
(519) 337-3783
Emp Here 44   *Sales* 11,134,596
SIC 5251 Hardware stores
Robert Teahen

D-U-N-S 20-608-1150   (SL)
TREL OF SARNIA LIMITED
1165 Confederation St, Sarnia, ON, N7S 3Y5
(519) 344-7025
Emp Here 60   *Sales* 13,320,060
SIC 3599 Industrial machinery, nec
Dominic Dicarlo
Ernie Taglione

D-U-N-S 24-486-7222   (HQ)
UNITEC INC
ENTROPEX
1271 Lougar Ave, Sarnia, ON, N7S 5N5
(519) 332-0430
Emp Here 2   *Sales* 15,034,250
SIC 6719 Holding companies, nec
Keith Bechard
Timothy Bechard

D-U-N-S 20-286-9751   (BR)
UNITED ASSOCIATION OF JOURNEYMEN AND APPRENTICES OF THE PLUMBING AND PIPEFITTING INDUSTRY
UA LOCAL 663
(*Suby of* UNITED ASSOCIATION OF JOURNEYMEN AND APPRENTICES OF THE PLUMBING AND PIPEFITTING INDUSTRY)
1151 Confederation St, Sarnia, ON, N7S 3Y5
(519) 337-6261
Emp Here 1,300

SIC 8611 Business associations
Ross Tius

D-U-N-S 24-329-6956   (BR)
WAL-MART CANADA CORP
(*Suby of* WALMART INC.)
1444 Quinn Dr, Sarnia, ON, N7S 6M8
(519) 542-4272
Emp Here 200
SIC 5311 Department stores
Drew Cashmore

D-U-N-S 25-355-4356   (BR)
WORLEYPARSONSCORD LP
(*Suby of* WORLEYPARSONS LIMITED)
1086 Modeland Rd Bldg 1050, Sarnia, ON, N7S 6L2
(519) 332-0160
Emp Here 340
SIC 8742 Management consulting services
Marilyn Gladu

Sarnia, ON N7T

D-U-N-S 24-468-1347   (SL)
2182553 ONTARIO LTD
SENTRY FIRE PROTECTION SERVICES
750 Ontario St Unit 1, Sarnia, ON, N7T 1M6
(519) 383-8880
Emp Here 40   *Sales* 17,968,760
SIC 7389 Business services, nec
Jeffrey Vince

D-U-N-S 20-006-5923   (SL)
612031-376964 ONTARIO LTD
TRIJAN INDUSTRIES
1275 Plank Rd, Sarnia, ON, N7T 7H3
(519) 344-5532
Emp Here 12   *Sales* 12,004,068
SIC 5051 Metals service centers and offices
Lawrence Slipacoff

D-U-N-S 20-273-2103   (SL)
8867038 CANADA INC
ACUTE NETWORK SOLUTIONS
1609 Lena Crt, Sarnia, ON, N7T 7H4
(519) 704-1317
Emp Here 75   *Sales* 13,531,125
SIC 8731 Commercial physical research
Mark Schmidt

D-U-N-S 25-940-8771   (SL)
ARI FLEET SERVICES OF CANADA INC
1000 Degurse Rd, Sarnia, ON, N7T 7H5
(519) 332-3739
Emp Here 32   *Sales* 16,638,944
SIC 4789 Transportation services, nec
James Unger
Mike Williams
Grant Cansfield

D-U-N-S 25-362-8739   (HQ)
ARLANXEO CANADA INC
ENERGIZING CHEMISTRY
(*Suby of* GOVERNMENT OF SAUDI ARABIA)
1265 Vidal St S, Sarnia, ON, N7T 7M2
(519) 337-8251
Emp Here 500   *Sales* 222,322,500
SIC 2822 Synthetic rubber
Dirk Fischer
John Sawyer
Sharon Guo

D-U-N-S 24-976-3384   (BR)
BAYER INC
BAYER HEALTHCARE
(*Suby of* BAYER AG)
1265 Vidal St S, Sarnia, ON, N7T 7M2
(519) 337-8251
Emp Here 900
SIC 2822 Synthetic rubber
Ron Huizingh

D-U-N-S 20-627-4623   (SL)
BAYVIEW CHRYSLER DODGE LTD

255 Indian Rd S, Sarnia, ON, N7T 3W5
(519) 336-2189
Emp Here 50   *Sales* 24,903,900
SIC 5511 New and used car dealers
David Orr
Stephen Orr
Douglas Rothwell
Helen Brown

D-U-N-S 20-188-4264   (HQ)
BLUEWATER HEALTH
89 Norman St, Sarnia, ON, N7T 6S3
(519) 464-4400
Emp Here 600   *Sales* 137,468,576
SIC 8062 General medical and surgical hospitals
Mike Lapaine
Samer Abou-Sweid
Laurie Zimmer
Paula Reaume-Zimmer
Michel Haddad
Shannon Landry
Julia Oosterman
Brian Knott
Paul Wiersma
Fred Vanderheide

D-U-N-S 25-168-4809   (HQ)
BLUEWATER POWER CORPORATION
(*Suby of* CORPORATION OF THE CITY OF SARNIA)
855 Confederation St Suite 716, Sarnia, ON, N7T 2E4
(519) 337-8201
Sales 61,868,534
SIC 4911 Electric services
Janice L. Mcmichael-Dennis
Firman Ventley

D-U-N-S 25-115-3730   (HQ)
BLUEWATER POWER DISTRIBUTION CORPORATION
(*Suby of* CORPORATION OF THE CITY OF SARNIA)
855 Confederation St, Sarnia, ON, N7T 2E4
(519) 337-8201
Sales 45,742,822
SIC 4911 Electric services
Firman Ventley

D-U-N-S 20-596-4778   (SL)
BRAUN ASSOCIATES LIMITED
BRAUN-VALLEY ASSOCIATES
201 Front St N Suite 405, Sarnia, ON, N7T 7T9
(519) 336-4590
Emp Here 130   *Sales* 9,710,220
SIC 7361 Employment agencies
Shelley Weir

D-U-N-S 20-148-8913   (HQ)
CABOT CANADA LTD
(*Suby of* CABOT CORPORATION)
800 Tashamoo Ave, Sarnia, ON, N7T 7N4
(519) 336-2261
Sales 28,402,100
SIC 2895 Carbon black
Dave House
Keith Brown

D-U-N-S 24-339-6236   (BR)
CANADA IMPERIAL OIL LIMITED
(*Suby of* IMPERIAL OIL LIMITED)
602 Christina St S, Sarnia, ON, N7T 7M5
(519) 339-2000
Emp Here 1,000
SIC 5172 Petroleum products, nec
Brian Fairley

D-U-N-S 24-452-2454   (HQ)
CENTRAL MACHINE & MARINE INC
(*Suby of* CANERECTOR INC)
649 Mcgregor Side Rd, Sarnia, ON, N7T 7H5
(519) 337-3722
Sales 13,320,060
SIC 3599 Industrial machinery, nec
Iain Pennington

Bruce Kennedy

D-U-N-S 24-365-7327   (BR)
COMPAGNIE DES CHEMINS DE FER NATIONAUX DU CANADA
C N RAIL
(*Suby of* COMPAGNIE DES CHEMINS DE FER NATIONAUX DU CANADA)
699 Macgregor Rd, Sarnia, ON, N7T 7H8
(519) 339-1253
Emp Here 270
SIC 4011 Railroads, line-haul operating
Russell Hiscock

D-U-N-S 25-457-8511   (BR)
CORPORATION OF THE COUNTY OF LAMBTON
MARSHALL GOWLAND MANOR
(*Suby of* CORPORATION OF THE COUNTY OF LAMBTON)
749 Devine St, Sarnia, ON, N7T 1X3
(519) 336-3720
Emp Here 141
SIC 8361 Residential care
Miller Jackie

D-U-N-S 24-849-5488   (BR)
CORPORATION OF THE COUNTY OF LAMBTON
SARNIA EMS BASE #2
(*Suby of* CORPORATION OF THE COUNTY OF LAMBTON)
6362 Telfer Rd, Sarnia, ON, N7T 7H4
(519) 882-2442
Emp Here 150
SIC 4119 Local passenger transportation, nec
Jeff Brooks

D-U-N-S 20-148-9390   (HQ)
CURRAN & HERRIDGE CONSTRUCTION CO., LIMITED
283 Confederation St, Sarnia, ON, N7T 2A3
(519) 332-3610
Emp Here 2   *Sales* 25,364,220
SIC 1541 Industrial buildings and warehouses
Edward Curran
Raymond Curran

D-U-N-S 24-058-3708   (SL)
CURRAN CONTRACTORS LTD
(*Suby of* CURRAN & HERRIDGE CONSTRUCTION CO., LIMITED)
283 Confederation St, Sarnia, ON, N7T 2A3
(519) 332-3610
Emp Here 60   *Sales* 25,364,220
SIC 1541 Industrial buildings and warehouses
Raymond Curran
Edward Curran
Christopher Curran
Guy Curran

D-U-N-S 25-778-7189   (SL)
DEGROOT'S NURSERIES
1840 London Line, Sarnia, ON, N7T 7H2
(519) 542-3436
Emp Here 49   *Sales* 12,853,141
SIC 0181 Ornamental nursery products

D-U-N-S 20-378-1252   (SL)
DICOCCO CONTRACTORS 2015 INC
550 Mcgregor Side Rd, Sarnia, ON, N7T 7H5
(519) 344-8446
Emp Here 41   *Sales* 13,073,629
SIC 1521 Single-family housing construction
Joseph Digregorio

D-U-N-S 24-588-4655   (SL)
DMW ELECTRICAL INSTRUMENTATION INC
227 Confederation St, Sarnia, ON, N7T 1Z9
(519) 336-3003
Emp Here 160   *Sales* 34,852,640
SIC 1731 Electrical work
Dario Maola

D-U-N-S 25-363-7524   (BR)
DOW CHEMICAL CANADA ULC
(*Suby of* DOW INC.)

▲ Public Company   ■ Public Company Family Member   **HQ** Headquarters   **BR** Branch   **SL** Single Location

Gd Lcd Main, Sarnia, ON, N7T 7H7

Emp Here 300
SIC 2819 Industrial inorganic chemicals, nec
Glen Mutscher

D-U-N-S 20-625-7727 (HQ)
**ELECTROZAD SUPPLY CO. (SARNIA) LIM-
ITED**
625 Scott Rd, Sarnia, ON, N7T 8G3
(519) 336-8550
Sales 11,179,350
SIC 5063 Electrical apparatus and equipment
William Smith
Lewis Mitchell

D-U-N-S 24-987-4918 (HQ)
ELYOD INVESTMENTS LIMITED
TIM HORTONS
775 Exmouth St, Sarnia, ON, N7T 5P7
(519) 332-6741
Emp Here 30 *Sales* 18,195,574
SIC 5461 Retail bakeries
Gordon Best

D-U-N-S 20-148-8517 (HQ)
FENWICK, GLEN MOTORS LIMITED
836 Ontario St, Sarnia, ON, N7T 1N2
(519) 344-7473
Sales 12,451,950
SIC 5511 New and used car dealers
Glen Fenwick
Todd Clark

D-U-N-S 24-315-5215 (HQ)
**GOODWILL INDUSTRIES-ESSEX KENT
LAMBTON INC**
439 Palmerston St S, Sarnia, ON, N7T 3P4
(519) 332-0440
Emp Here 33 *Sales* 17,102,960
SIC 5932 Used merchandise stores
Kevin Smith

D-U-N-S 20-783-6396 (SL)
HENTSCHEL, HART INC
AUTO HOUSE HONDA
755 Confederation St, Sarnia, ON, N7T 1M8
(519) 344-1123
Emp Here 22 *Sales* 10,957,716
SIC 5511 New and used car dealers
Dan Brush

D-U-N-S 24-681-1749 (SL)
IMPERIAL OIL LIMITED
Po Box 3004 Stn Main, Sarnia, ON, N7T 7M5
(519) 339-4015
Emp Here 950 *Sales* 256,743,200
SIC 2911 Petroleum refining
Jon Harding

D-U-N-S 25-203-5506 (BR)
IMPERIAL OIL LIMITED
PRODUCTS & CHEMICALS, DIV OF
(*Suby of* IMPERIAL OIL LIMITED)
453 Christina St N, Sarnia, ON, N7T 5W3
(519) 339-2712
Emp Here 110
SIC 2911 Petroleum refining
Alan Blahey

D-U-N-S 20-771-5475 (SL)
IMPERIAL ROOFING (SARNIA) LTD
313 Gladwish Dr, Sarnia, ON, N7T 7H3
(519) 336-6146
Emp Here 40 *Sales* 10,122,360
SIC 5211 Lumber and other building materials
Wayne Dennis
Vaughn Berry

D-U-N-S 24-361-1501 (SL)
INEOS STYRENICS LTD
872 Tashmoo Ave, Sarnia, ON, N7T 7H5
(519) 339-7339
Emp Here 100 *Sales* 27,666,000
SIC 2865 Cyclic crudes and intermediates
Ian Macdonald

D-U-N-S 24-889-7352 (SL)

INEOS STYROLUTION CANADA LTD
(*Suby of* INEOS AG)
872 Tashmoo Ave, Sarnia, ON, N7T 8A3
(226) 784-2872
Emp Here 85 *Sales* 492,766,300
SIC 2869 Industrial organic chemicals, nec
Brian Lucas

D-U-N-S 24-659-1051 (HQ)
INTERTEC INSTRUMENTATION LTD
(*Suby of* INTERTEC HESS GMBH)
255 Henry Dr, Sarnia, ON, N7T 7H5
(519) 337-2773
Sales 12,186,892
SIC 3299 NonMetallic mineral products,
Martin Hess
Phil Luppke
Steve Scott

D-U-N-S 20-529-3616 (SL)
KEL-GOR LIMITED
1411 Plank Rd, Sarnia, ON, N7T 7H3
(519) 336-9312
Emp Here 125 *Sales* 29,133,125
SIC 1711 Plumbing, heating, air-conditioning
Ronald Gordon
Chris Thomas
Fred Oliver

D-U-N-S 24-390-8170 (HQ)
KIOV INCORPORATED
MCDONALDS RESTAURANT
411 Christina St N, Sarnia, ON, N7T 5V8
(519) 336-1320
Emp Here 200 *Sales* 11,659,750
SIC 5812 Eating places
Colleen Buckley
Peter Buckley

D-U-N-S 20-715-6563 (HQ)
LAMBTON COMMUNICATIONS LIMITED
DAMAR SECURITY SYSTEMS
506 Christina St N, Sarnia, ON, N7T 5W4
(519) 332-1234
Emp Here 50 *Sales* 13,069,740
SIC 1731 Electrical work
Dave Currie
Marie Currie

D-U-N-S 25-249-3523 (BR)
**LAMBTON KENT DISTRICT SCHOOL
BOARD**
*SARNIA COLLEGIATE INSTITUTE & TECH-
NICAL SCHOOL*
(*Suby of* LAMBTON KENT DISTRICT
SCHOOL BOARD)
275 Wellington St, Sarnia, ON, N7T 1H1
(519) 336-6131
Emp Here 100
SIC 8211 Elementary and secondary schools
Linda Jared

D-U-N-S 25-203-2834 (HQ)
**LAMBTON KENT DISTRICT SCHOOL
BOARD**
SARNIA EDUCATION CENTRE
200 Wellington St Suite 2019, Sarnia, ON,
N7T 7L2
(519) 336-1500
Sales 210,664,202
SIC 8211 Elementary and secondary schools

D-U-N-S 20-149-1487 (SL)
LAMBTON MOTORS LIMITED, THE
LAMBTON FORD
(*Suby of* HALL, HAROLD J. INVESTMENTS
INC)
101 Indian Rd S, Sarnia, ON, N7T 3W1
(519) 464-4020
Emp Here 92 *Sales* 57,893,760
SIC 5511 New and used car dealers
Harold Hall
Barbara Stothers

D-U-N-S 20-013-2418 (SL)
LAMSAR INC
608 Mcgregor Rd, Sarnia, ON, N7T 7J2

(519) 332-5010
Emp Here 50 *Sales* 11,046,700
SIC 1711 Plumbing, heating, air-conditioning
Paul Healy
John Healy

D-U-N-S 24-325-9624 (HQ)
LAPORTE, MARCEL PHARMACY INC
SHOPPERS DRUG MART
260 Indian Rd S, Sarnia, ON, N7T 3W4
(519) 337-3727
Emp Here 52 *Sales* 18,080,272
SIC 5912 Drug stores and proprietary stores
Marcel Laport

D-U-N-S 20-411-7642 (SL)
MACKENZIE OIL LIMITED
1486 Plank Rd, Sarnia, ON, N7T 7H3
(519) 336-0521
Emp Here 18 *Sales* 18,590,544
SIC 5172 Petroleum products, nec
Stuart Mackenzie

D-U-N-S 25-695-5279 (BR)
MAGIC REALTY INC
(*Suby of* MAGIC REALTY INC)
380 London Rd, Sarnia, ON, N7T 4W7
(519) 542-4005
Emp Here 90
SIC 6531 Real estate agents and managers
Terry Elliott

D-U-N-S 24-325-9616 (HQ)
MCQUAID, S. PHARMACY LTD
SHOPPERS DRUG MART
510 Exmouth St, Sarnia, ON, N7T 0A5
(519) 344-2409
Emp Here 60 *Sales* 18,324,600
SIC 5912 Drug stores and proprietary stores
Susan Mcquaid

D-U-N-S 24-333-1720 (BR)
METRO ONTARIO INC
FOOD BASIC
(*Suby of* METRO INC)
191 Indian Rd S, Sarnia, ON, N7T 3W3
(519) 344-1500
Emp Here 80
SIC 5411 Grocery stores
Frank Scarpelli

D-U-N-S 24-333-1746 (BR)
METRO ONTARIO INC
METRO
(*Suby of* METRO INC)
560 Exmouth St, Sarnia, ON, N7T 5P5
(519) 337-8308
Emp Here 110
SIC 5411 Grocery stores
Bill Newton

D-U-N-S 20-790-2268 (SL)
MIKE'S NO FRILLS
889 Exmouth St, Sarnia, ON, N7T 5R3
(866) 987-6453
Emp Here 90 *Sales* 26,412,930
SIC 5411 Grocery stores
Mike Mcniel

D-U-N-S 24-176-1761 (SL)
NEL-TEKK INDUSTRIAL SPECIALTIES INC
254 Tecumseh St, Sarnia, ON, N7T 2K9
(519) 332-6813
Emp Here 94 *Sales* 15,263,814
SIC 1742 Plastering, drywall, and insulation
Nelson Guerette

D-U-N-S 25-097-0431 (BR)
NOVA CHEMICALS (CANADA) LTD
(*Suby of* GOVERNMENT OF ABU DHABI)
872 Tashmoo Ave, Sarnia, ON, N7T 7H5
(519) 332-1212
Emp Here 120
SIC 2869 Industrial organic chemicals, nec
Ian Macdonald

D-U-N-S 24-381-1689 (BR)
**ONTARIO ENGLISH CATHOLIC TEACH-
ERS' ASSOCIATION, THE**

**ONTARIO ENGLISH CATHOLIC TEACHERS
ASSOCIATION, THE**
(*Suby of* ONTARIO ENGLISH CATHOLIC
TEACHERS' ASSOCIATION, THE)
281 East St N, Sarnia, ON, N7T 6X8
(519) 332-4550
Emp Here 175
SIC 8641 Civic and social associations
Chad Coene

D-U-N-S 20-525-6022 (BR)
OSPREY MEDIA PUBLISHING INC
OBSERVER, THE
(*Suby of* QUEBECOR MEDIA INC)
140 Front St S Suite Front, Sarnia, ON, N7T
7M8
(519) 344-3641
Emp Here 80
SIC 2711 Newspapers
Daryl Smith

D-U-N-S 20-577-3703 (BR)
OSPREY MEDIA PUBLISHING INC
SARNIA OBSERVER
(*Suby of* QUEBECOR MEDIA INC)
140 Front St S, Sarnia, ON, N7T 7M8
(519) 344-3641
Emp Here 100
SIC 2711 Newspapers
Daryl Smith

D-U-N-S 20-608-1770 (BR)
PLAINS MIDSTREAM CANADA ULC
BP CANADA
(*Suby of* PLAINS GP HOLDINGS, L.P.)
1182 Plank Rd, Sarnia, ON, N7T 7H9
(519) 336-4270
Emp Here 75
SIC 4923 Gas transmission and distribution
Paul Hagger

D-U-N-S 24-946-4389 (HQ)
PLEASE HOLD CANADA INC
STARCHOICEONE SOLUTIONS, A DIV
775 Exmouth St, Sarnia, ON, N7T 5P7
(519) 339-8842
Emp Here 200 *Sales* 67,912,432
SIC 4899 Communication services, nec
Steve Fogel

D-U-N-S 24-182-7146 (HQ)
ROMAX VARIETY LIMITED
MILK MARC VARIETY
900 Wellington St, Sarnia, ON, N7T 1J5
(519) 336-6660
Emp Here 8 *Sales* 12,320,580
SIC 5331 Variety stores
Emile Guibert
Bob Guibert

D-U-N-S 25-733-0365 (BR)
**ROYAL CANADIAN AIR FORCE ASSOCIA-
TION**
A F A C 403 WING
(*Suby of* ROYAL CANADIAN AIR FORCE AS-
SOCIATION)
415 Exmouth St, Sarnia, ON, N7T 8A4
(519) 344-8050
Emp Here 80
SIC 8641 Civic and social associations
John Stewart

D-U-N-S 20-920-1466 (HQ)
**SARNIA AND DISTRICT ASSOCIATION
FOR COMMUNITY LIVING**
WAWANOSH ENTERPRISES
551 Exmouth St Suite 202, Sarnia, ON, N7T
5P6
(519) 332-0560
Emp Here 25 *Sales* 17,662,160
SIC 8322 Individual and family services
Earle Kilner
John Hagens

D-U-N-S 24-397-0832 (SL)
SARNIA FINE CARS 2019 INC
BMW SARNIA
799 Confederation St, Sarnia, ON, N7T 2E4

(519) 332-2886
Emp Here 30   *Sales* 10,926,450
SIC 5012 Automobiles and other motor vehicles
Dan Whitton

D-U-N-S 20-517-7988   (BR)
SNC-LAVALIN INTERNATIONAL INC
SNC LAVALIN ENGINEERS & CONSTRUCTORS
(*Suby of* GROUPE SNC-LAVALIN INC)
265 Front St N Suite 301, Sarnia, ON, N7T 7X1
(519) 336-0201
Emp Here 300
SIC 8711 Engineering services
Rob Stewart

D-U-N-S 24-371-8520   (SL)
ST. JOSEPH'S HOSPICE RESOURCE CENTRE OF SARNIA LAMBTON
475 Christina St N, Sarnia, ON, N7T 5W3
(519) 337-0537
Emp Here 35   *Sales* 13,909,490
SIC 8699 Membership organizations, nec
John Callaghan
Ellen Murphy
Catharine Orr

D-U-N-S 20-149-3848   (HQ)
STEEVES & ROZEMA ENTERPRISES LIMITED
265 Front St N Suite 200, Sarnia, ON, N7T 7X1
(519) 344-8829
Emp Here 35   *Sales* 102,489,000
SIC 8051 Skilled nursing care facilities
Fred Vanderheide
John Scotland
Ralph Rozema

D-U-N-S 20-795-4525   (BR)
SUNCOR ENERGY PRODUCTS INC
(*Suby of* SUNCOR ENERGY INC)
1900 River Rd, Sarnia, ON, N7T 7J3
(519) 337-2301
Emp Here 350
SIC 5172 Petroleum products, nec
Marc Mageau

D-U-N-S 24-058-8269   (SL)
VISION '74 INC
VISION NURSING HOME
229 Wellington St, Sarnia, ON, N7T 1G9
(519) 336-6551
Emp Here 150   *Sales* 10,248,900
SIC 8051 Skilled nursing care facilities
Bernie Bax
Heather Martin

D-U-N-S 25-940-7385   (BR)
WAL-MART CANADA CORP
(*Suby of* WALMART INC.)
Gd Lcd Main, Sarnia, ON, N7T 7H7
(519) 542-1854
Emp Here 150
SIC 5311 Department stores
Eric Paquette

D-U-N-S 24-886-3912   (HQ)
WORLD SOURCE FILTRATION INC
321 Queen St Suite 1, Sarnia, ON, N7T 2S3
(519) 383-7771
Sales 10,450,572
SIC 5085 Industrial supplies
Brad Macswain

Sarnia, ON N7V

D-U-N-S 24-469-3909   (HQ)
509334 ONTARIO INC
SUNRIPE FARMS PRODUCE
1141 Lakeshore Rd, Sarnia, ON, N7V 2V5
(519) 542-1241
Sales 14,967,327

SIC 5431 Fruit and vegetable markets
Wilfred Willemsen

D-U-N-S 25-360-5596   (SL)
CHILDREN'S AID SOCIETY OF THE CITY OF SARNIA AND THE COUNTY OF LAMBTON
SARNIA-LAMBTON CHILDREN'S AID SOCIETY
161 Kendall St, Sarnia, ON, N7V 4G6
(519) 336-0623
Emp Here 131   *Sales* 10,059,752
SIC 8322 Individual and family services
Dawn Flegel

D-U-N-S 20-179-5585   (BR)
WINDSOR-ESSEX CHILDREN'S AID SOCIETY
CHILDREN'S AID SOCIETY
(*Suby of* WINDSOR-ESSEX CHILDREN'S AID SOCIETY)
161 Kendall St, Sarnia, ON, N7V 4G6
(519) 336-0623
Emp Here 83
SIC 8399 Social services, nec
John Beer

Sarnia, ON N7W

D-U-N-S 20-100-5076   (BR)
VICTORIAN ORDER OF NURSES FOR CANADA
VON BATHURST DISTRICT
(*Suby of* VICTORIAN ORDER OF NURSES FOR CANADA)
1705 London Line, Sarnia, ON, N7W 1B2
(519) 542-2310
Emp Here 120
SIC 8082 Home health care services
Vonda Denboer

Sault Ste. Marie, ON P6A

D-U-N-S 25-407-8413   (SL)
510127 ONTARIO LIMITED
BP INVESTMENTS & HOLDINGS
219 Trunk Rd, Sault Ste. Marie, ON, P6A 3S7
(705) 254-7466
Emp Here 100   *Sales* 29,347,700
SIC 5411 Grocery stores
Benjamin Pino

D-U-N-S 20-301-3011   (SL)
ALAGASH INVESTMENTS LIMITED
73 Brock St, Sault Ste. Marie, ON, P6A 3B4
Emp Here 100   *Sales* 5,487,200
SIC 4119 Local passenger transportation, nec
Darryl Buck
Patricia Buck

D-U-N-S 20-823-5416   (HQ)
ALGOMA CENTRAL PROPERTIES INC
(*Suby of* ALGOMA CENTRAL CORPORATION)
293 Bay St, Sault Ste. Marie, ON, P6A 1X3
(705) 946-7220
Emp Here 11   *Sales* 23,876,673
SIC 6531 Real estate agents and managers
Gregory Wight
Robert Leistner
Tim Dool

D-U-N-S 25-502-8235   (HQ)
ALGOMA CENTRAL RAILWAY INC
(*Suby of* COMPAGNIE DES CHEMINS DE FER NATIONAUX DU CANADA)
129 Bay St, Sault Ste. Marie, ON, P6A 1W7
(705) 541-2900
Sales 79,848,400
SIC 4011 Railroads, line-haul operating

Sean Finn
Ghislain Houle
Luc Jobin

D-U-N-S 25-239-0729   (BR)
ALGOMA DISTRICT SCHOOL BOARD
SIR JAMES DUNN COLLEGIATE & VOCATIONAL
(*Suby of* ALGOMA DISTRICT SCHOOL BOARD)
1601 Wellington St E, Sault Ste. Marie, ON, P6A 2R8
(705) 945-7177
Emp Here 100
SIC 8211 Elementary and secondary schools
Joe Maurici

D-U-N-S 24-097-8239   (HQ)
ALGOMA DISTRICT SCHOOL BOARD
644 Albert St E, Sault Ste. Marie, ON, P6A 2K7
(705) 945-7111
Emp Here 60   *Sales* 257,709,400
SIC 8211 Elementary and secondary schools
Mario Turco
Joe Santa Maria
Joe Maurice
Lucia Reece
Kime Collver
Asima Vezina

D-U-N-S 24-507-9889   (SL)
ALGOMA STEEL INC
105 West St, Sault Ste. Marie, ON, P6A 7B4
(705) 945-2351
Emp Here 3,000   *Sales* 1,221,522,000
SIC 3312 Blast furnaces and steel mills
Mike Mcquade
Michael Moraca
Rajat Marwah
Andy Harshaw
Michael Alexander
Michael Bevacqua
Brad Sweeney
Andrew Schultz

D-U-N-S 24-771-6793   (HQ)
ALGOMA UNIVERSITY
ARTHUR A WISHART LIBRARY
1520 Queen St E, Sault Ste. Marie, ON, P6A 2G4
(705) 949-2301
Sales 24,154,036
SIC 8221 Colleges and universities
Asima Vezina
Tim Lavoie
Armando Palstino
Wayne Barnes
Paul Boniferro
Lisa Bell-Murray
James Caicco
Claudette Chevrier-Cachagee
Cathy Denomme
Ray Derosario

D-U-N-S 25-398-9230   (BR)
ARAUCO CANADA LIMITED
(*Suby of* INVERSIONES ANGELINI Y COMPANIA LIMITADA)
657 Base Line, Sault Ste. Marie, ON, P6A 5K6
(705) 253-0770
Emp Here 107
SIC 2493 Reconstituted wood products
Mike Rosso

D-U-N-S 25-134-3711   (BR)
CORPORATION OF THE CITY OF SAULT STE MARIE, THE
SPORTS AND ENTERTAINMENT CENTER
(*Suby of* CORPORATION OF THE CITY OF SAULT STE MARIE, THE)
269 Queen St E, Sault Ste. Marie, ON, P6A 1Y9
(705) 759-5251
Emp Here 150
SIC 7389 Business services, nec
Norm Fera

D-U-N-S 24-006-2513   (HQ)
DAWSON & KEENAN INSURANCE LTD
DAWSON & KEENAN INSURANCE & FINANCIAL SERVICES
121 Brock St, Sault Ste. Marie, ON, P6A 3B6
(705) 949-3740
Emp Here 16   *Sales* 10,438,632
SIC 6411 Insurance agents, brokers, and service
Laurence Day
Graham Lidstone
Elaine Foster

D-U-N-S 20-535-5431   (HQ)
DICK'S GARAGE LIMITED
SOO SUZUKI
967 Trunk Rd, Sault Ste. Marie, ON, P6A 5K9
(705) 759-1133
Emp Here 21   *Sales* 14,942,340
SIC 5511 New and used car dealers
John Dick Sr
Beverley Dick

D-U-N-S 25-718-6783   (HQ)
EAZY EXPRESS INC
Gd Lcd Main, Sault Ste. Marie, ON, P6A 5L1
(705) 253-2222
Sales 100,336,200
SIC 7389 Business services, nec
Joanne Brooks

D-U-N-S 20-588-1654   (BR)
GOVERNMENT OF ONTARIO
ALGOMA UNIVERSITY
(*Suby of* GOVERNMENT OF ONTARIO)
1520 Queen St E, Sault Ste. Marie, ON, P6A 2G4
(705) 949-2301
Emp Here 200
SIC 8221 Colleges and universities
Sean Wyer

D-U-N-S 25-689-4346   (SL)
HURON CENTRAL RAILWAY INC
(*Suby of* GENESEE & WYOMING INC.)
30 Oakland Ave, Sault Ste. Marie, ON, P6A 2T3
(705) 254-4511
Emp Here 50   *Sales* 25,998,350
SIC 4731 Freight transportation arrangement
Louis Gravel
Thomas D Savage
Allison M Fergus
Rene Gilbert Duchesne
Matthew O Walsh

D-U-N-S 24-118-6050   (SL)
INTERNATIONAL BRIDGE ADMINISTRATION
125 Huron St, Sault Ste. Marie, ON, P6A 1R3
(705) 942-4345
Emp Here 35   *Sales* 18,198,845
SIC 4785 Inspection and fixed facilities
Micheline Dube

D-U-N-S 24-097-5284   (SL)
JOHNSON, O M HOLDINGS INC
SUPERIOR DODGE
311 Trunk Rd, Sault Ste. Marie, ON, P6A 3S8
(705) 256-7481
Emp Here 48   *Sales* 23,907,744
SIC 5521 Used car dealers
Greg Nezozv

D-U-N-S 24-466-1968   (SL)
LUCIDIA STUDIOS LTD
123 March St Suite 301, Sault Ste. Marie, ON, P6A 2Z5
(705) 941-9828
Emp Here 29   *Sales* 12,861,210
SIC 7389 Business services, nec
Jeff Elgie
Jr Pierman

D-U-N-S 24-744-5026   (SL)
MAPLE LEAF FOREST PRODUCTS INC
418 Fourth Line W, Sault Ste. Marie, ON, P6A 0B5

▲ Public Company   ■ Public Company Family Member   **HQ** Headquarters   **BR** Branch   **SL** Single Location

(705) 450-2696
Emp Here 24   *Sales* 10,732,176
SIC 5031 Lumber, plywood, and millwork
Peter Tarvudd
Margaret Tarvudd

D-U-N-S 24-333-1647   (BR)
METRO ONTARIO INC
(Suby of METRO INC)
150 Churchill Blvd, Sault Ste. Marie, ON, P6A 3Z9
(705) 254-3923
Emp Here 100
SIC 5411 Grocery stores
Serge Sylvestre

D-U-N-S 20-787-4368   (BR)
METRO ONTARIO INC
FOOD BASICS
(Suby of METRO INC)
625 Trunk Rd, Sault Ste. Marie, ON, P6A 3T1
(705) 949-7260
Emp Here 110
SIC 5411 Grocery stores
Sabrina Maonie

D-U-N-S 24-345-4712   (BR)
NORTH EAST COMMUNITY CARE ACCESS CENTRE
SAULT STE MARIE MAIN OFFICE
(Suby of NORTH EAST COMMUNITY CARE ACCESS CENTRE)
390 Bay St, Sault Ste. Marie, ON, P6A 1X2
(705) 949-1650
Emp Here 85
SIC 8322 Individual and family services
Kerry Munro

D-U-N-S 20-149-5124   (HQ)
OLD STEELCO INC
(Suby of ESSAR STEEL INDIA LIMITED)
105 West St, Sault Ste. Marie, ON, P6A 7B4
(705) 945-2351
Emp Here 2,300   *Sales* 1,180,804,600
SIC 3312 Blast furnaces and steel mills
Kalyan Chosh
David James Rennie
Robert Sandoval
Pramod Shukla
Rajat Marwah

D-U-N-S 25-689-3694   (BR)
OLD STEELCO INC
ESSAR STEEL ALGOMA INC
(Suby of ESSAR STEEL INDIA LIMITED)
Gd, Sault Ste. Marie, ON, P6A 5P2
(705) 945-3172
Emp Here 130
SIC 3312 Blast furnaces and steel mills
Brenda Stenta

D-U-N-S 25-689-3611   (BR)
OLD STEELCO INC
ESSAR STEEL ALGOMA INC
(Suby of ESSAR STEEL INDIA LIMITED)
Gd, Sault Ste. Marie, ON, P6A 5P2
(705) 945-3301
Emp Here 220
SIC 3312 Blast furnaces and steel mills
Jim Rennie

D-U-N-S 20-149-9605   (HQ)
ORANO LIMITED
MERRETT'S PHARMACY
625 Trunk Rd, Sault Ste. Marie, ON, P6A 3T1
(705) 945-8088
Emp Here 12   *Sales* 26,876,080
SIC 5912 Drug stores and proprietary stores
Joseph Disano
Ronald Disano
Sandra Sartor
Ronald Deluco

D-U-N-S 20-149-9696   (SL)
PALMER CONSTRUCTION GROUP INC
845 Old Goulais Bay Rd, Sault Ste. Marie, ON, P6A 0B5

(705) 254-1644
Emp Here 86   *Sales* 21,710,012
SIC 1611 Highway and street construction
Terry Rainone

D-U-N-S 24-966-1513   (SL)
PUC SERVICES INC
765 Queen St E, Sault Ste. Marie, ON, P6A 2A8
(705) 759-6500
Emp Here 150   *Sales* 84,764,250
SIC 4971 Irrigation systems
Robert Brewer
Claudio Stefano
Terry Greco

D-U-N-S 20-726-7928   (SL)
SAULT STAR, LIMITED
SAULT STAR, THE
145 Old Garden River Rd, Sault Ste. Marie, ON, P6A 5M5
(705) 759-3030
Emp Here 98   *Sales* 13,267,828
SIC 2754 Commercial printing, gravure
Jackie Depasquale
Lou Maulucci

D-U-N-S 24-123-4228   (SL)
SAULT STE MARIE HOUSING CORPORATION
180 Brock St, Sault Ste. Marie, ON, P6A 3B7
(705) 946-2077
Emp Here 50   *Sales* 20,944,450
SIC 6531 Real estate agents and managers
Jeff Barban
Pat Mick
David Edgar
Bryan Hanes
Lou Turco

D-U-N-S 20-011-3269   (SL)
SAULT STE. MARIE INNOVATION CENTRE
1520 Queen St E Suite 307, Sault Ste. Marie, ON, P6A 2G4
(705) 942-7927
Emp Here 50   *Sales* 10,667,900
SIC 8732 Commercial nonphysical research
Thomas Vair

D-U-N-S 20-149-8177   (SL)
SUPERIOR DODGE CHRYSLER (1978) LIMITED
311 Trunk Rd, Sault Ste. Marie, ON, P6A 3S8
(705) 256-7481
Emp Here 29   *Sales* 14,444,262
SIC 5511 New and used car dealers
Gregory Johnson
Gerry Beaton

D-U-N-S 20-333-6516   (SL)
UNIVERSAL CONCEPTS
130 Wellington St E, Sault Ste. Marie, ON, P6A 2L5
(705) 575-7521
Emp Here 49   *Sales* 23,065,819
SIC 1542 Nonresidential construction, nec
Blair Mcleod

Sault Ste. Marie, ON P6B

D-U-N-S 24-862-7465   (SL)
170260 CANADA INC
MICROAGE COMPUTER CENTRES
773 Great Northern Rd, Sault Ste. Marie, ON, P6B 0B7
(705) 946-0876
Emp Here 47   *Sales* 10,825,980
SIC 5734 Computer and software stores
Don Bruni
Andy Buffone
Judy Ingram
Jim Bruni

D-U-N-S 25-931-2882   (SL)
985907 ONTARIO LIMITED

WENDY'S RESTAURANT
389 Great Northern Rd, Sault Ste. Marie, ON, P6B 4Z8
(705) 941-9999
Emp Here 90   *Sales* 4,096,710
SIC 5812 Eating places
Patrick Mizzi

D-U-N-S 25-239-0646   (BR)
ALGOMA DISTRICT SCHOOL BOARD
BAWATING COLLEGIATE & VOCATION SCHOOL
(Suby of ALGOMA DISTRICT SCHOOL BOARD)
750 North St, Sault Ste. Marie, ON, P6B 2C5
(705) 945-7177
Emp Here 75
SIC 8211 Elementary and secondary schools
Michael Mccabe

D-U-N-S 24-388-4603   (SL)
ALGOMA POWER INC
(Suby of FORTIS INC)
2 Sackville Rd Suite A, Sault Ste. Marie, ON, P6B 6J6
(705) 256-3850
Emp Here 60   *Sales* 40,792,440
SIC 4911 Electric services
William Daley

D-U-N-S 24-214-0051   (SL)
ARROW PLUMBING INC
GREAT NORTHERN MOTOR & PUMP REPAIR
594 Second Line E, Sault Ste. Marie, ON, P6B 4K1
(705) 759-8316
Emp Here 40   *Sales* 10,122,360
SIC 5251 Hardware stores
Dan Reid
Beverley Reid

D-U-N-S 24-966-1471   (HQ)
BOARD OF HEALTH FOR THE DISTRICT OF ALGOMA HEALTH UNIT
ALGOMA PUBLIC HEALTH
294 Willow Ave, Sault Ste. Marie, ON, P6B 0A9
(705) 942-4646
Emp Here 116   *Sales* 16,707,430
SIC 8011 Offices and clinics of medical doctors
Jeffrey Holmes

D-U-N-S 25-157-2871   (SL)
BOSTON'S CHEV-OLDS-CADILLAC-GEO LTD
415 Pim St, Sault Ste. Marie, ON, P6B 2T9

Emp Here 42   *Sales* 20,919,276
SIC 5511 New and used car dealers
Furgie Boston

D-U-N-S 24-079-8454   (HQ)
CHILDREN'S AID SOCIETY OF ALGOMA
CAS OF ALGOMA
191 Northern Ave E, Sault Ste. Marie, ON, P6B 4H8
(705) 949-0162
Emp Here 59   *Sales* 15,358,400
SIC 8322 Individual and family services
Jim Baraniuk
David Kirk

D-U-N-S 24-848-9296   (HQ)
COMMUNITY LIVING ALGOMA
99 Northern Ave E, Sault Ste. Marie, ON, P6B 4H5
(705) 253-1700
Emp Here 40   *Sales* 31,638,304
SIC 8322 Individual and family services
John Policicchio

D-U-N-S 20-729-8386   (SL)
DEAN'S FOOD BASICS
701 Pine St, Sault Ste. Marie, ON, P6B 3G2
(705) 949-8929
Emp Here 45   *Sales* 12,336,840

SIC 5411 Grocery stores
Dean Wade

D-U-N-S 20-047-4794   (BR)
EXTENDICARE INC
EXTENDICARE VAN DAELE
(Suby of EXTENDICARE INC)
39 Van Daele St, Sault Ste. Marie, ON, P6B 4V3
(705) 949-7934
Emp Here 170
SIC 8051 Skilled nursing care facilities
Janice Dupuis

D-U-N-S 24-452-4427   (SL)
FILEK, STEVE DRUGS LIMITED
SHOPPERS DRUG MART 669
44 Great Northern Rd Suite 669, Sault Ste. Marie, ON, P6B 4Y5
(705) 949-2143
Emp Here 60   *Sales* 14,659,680
SIC 5912 Drug stores and proprietary stores
Steve Filek

D-U-N-S 20-753-7267   (BR)
FIRSTCANADA ULC
LAIDLAW TRANSIT
(Suby of FIRSTGROUP PLC)
70 Industrial Court A, Sault Ste. Marie, ON, P6B 5W6
(705) 759-2192
Emp Here 130
SIC 4151 School buses
Duane Jones

D-U-N-S 20-359-0047   (SL)
FOUNTAIN TIRE (SAULT STE. MARIE) LTD
FOUNTAIN TIRE F406
55 Black Rd, Sault Ste. Marie, ON, P6B 0A3
(705) 254-6664
Emp Here 34   *Sales* 16,934,652
SIC 5531 Auto and home supply stores
Chris Klemm

D-U-N-S 20-389-6985   (SL)
GREAT LAKES POWER LIMITED
243 Industrial Park Cres, Sault Ste. Marie, ON, P6B 5P3
(705) 256-7575
Emp Here 39   *Sales* 20,266,545
SIC 4911 Electric services
Bernard Cardinal

D-U-N-S 20-084-5738   (SL)
GROUP HEALTH CENTRE, THE
240 Mcnabb St, Sault Ste. Marie, ON, P6B 1Y5
(705) 759-5521
Emp Here 75   *Sales* 12,048,450
SIC 8011 Offices and clinics of medical doctors
David Murray
Tom Bonell
Dan Lewis

D-U-N-S 20-406-2384   (SL)
HIGHLAND FORD SALES LIMITED
68 Great Northern Rd, Sault Ste. Marie, ON, P6B 4Y5
(705) 759-5050
Emp Here 50   *Sales* 24,903,900
SIC 5511 New and used car dealers
Darren Smyl

D-U-N-S 25-649-3172   (SL)
HOLLYWOOD BEAUTY SUPPLY
44 Great Northern Rd Suite 51, Sault Ste. Marie, ON, P6B 4Y5
(705) 949-9132
Emp Here 24   *Sales* 11,400,624
SIC 5087 Service establishment equipment
Gerry Giordano

D-U-N-S 20-553-6076   (BR)
HOME DEPOT OF CANADA INC
HOME DEPOT
(Suby of THE HOME DEPOT INC)
530 Great Northern Rd, Sault Ste. Marie, ON,

P6B 4Z9
(705) 254-1150
Emp Here 150
SIC 5251 Hardware stores
Kevin Smith

D-U-N-S 24-419-9865   (HQ)
HURON-SUPERIOR CATHOLIC DISTRICT SCHOOL BOARD
90 Ontario Ave, Sault Ste. Marie, ON, P6B 6G7
(705) 945-5400
Emp Here 38   *Sales* 118,942,800
SIC 8211 Elementary and secondary schools
John Stadnyk
Laurie Aceti
Gerard Rainville
John Caputo
Sandra Turco
Lindsay Liske
Kathleen Rosilius
Elaine Mcdonagh

D-U-N-S 20-349-9301   (SL)
HYDRO ONE SAULT STE. MARIE LP
(Suby of GREAT LAKES POWER TRANSMISSION INC)*
2b Sackville Rd, Sault Ste. Marie, ON, P6B 6J6
(705) 254-7444
Emp Here 55   *Sales* 37,393,070
SIC 4911 Electric services
Duane Fecteau

D-U-N-S 20-020-0421   (BR)
J.J.'S HOSPITALITY LIMITED
PAVILION, THE
(Suby of J.J.'S HOSPITALITY LIMITED)*
360 Great Northern Rd Suite 787, Sault Ste. Marie, ON, P6B 4Z7
(705) 945-7614
Emp Here 150
SIC 7011 Hotels and motels
Donna Hilsinger

D-U-N-S 20-149-8011   (HQ)
J.J.'S HOSPITALITY LIMITED
ALGOMA WATERTOWER INN
360 Great Northern Rd, Sault Ste. Marie, ON, P6B 4Z7
(705) 949-8111
Sales 13,903,500
SIC 7011 Hotels and motels
James Hilsinger
Donna Hilsinger

D-U-N-S 20-786-7672   (SL)
LAWLESS, M.J. HOLDINGS LTD
CANADIAN TIRE
200 Mcnabb St, Sault Ste. Marie, ON, P6B 1Y4
(705) 949-0770
Emp Here 180   *Sales* 81,035,460
SIC 7538 General automotive repair shops
Mat J Lawless

D-U-N-S 20-150-1434   (SL)
LEWIS, MAITLAND ENTERPRISES LTD
MAITLAND FORD LINCOLN MOTORS
1124 Great Northern Rd, Sault Ste. Marie, ON, P6B 0B6
(705) 759-4545
Emp Here 30   *Sales* 14,942,340
SIC 5511 New and used car dealers
Maitland Lewis
Katherine Lewis

D-U-N-S 25-526-5563   (SL)
MAIN FILTER INC
188 Industrial Park Cres, Sault Ste. Marie, ON, P6B 5P2
(705) 256-6622
Emp Here 60   *Sales* 13,320,060
SIC 3569 General industrial machinery, nec
Stephen P. Turmaine
Veniero Peroni

D-U-N-S 24-892-3799   (HQ)

MCDOUGALL ENERGY INC
900 Mcnabb St, Sault Ste. Marie, ON, P6B 6J1
(705) 949-6202
SIC 5983 Fuel oil dealers
Darren Mcdougall

D-U-N-S 24-927-8664   (SL)
MOORE, MIKE & SONS CONSTRUCTION LTD
167 Industrial Court B Unit A, Sault Ste. Marie, ON, P6B 5Z9
(705) 759-3173
Emp Here 35   *Sales* 16,475,585
SIC 1542 Nonresidential construction, nec
Michael Moore

D-U-N-S 24-621-6071   (SL)
NIVTOP HOLDINGS LTD
SERVICE MASTER OF SAULT STE MARIE
105 Black Rd, Sault Ste. Marie, ON, P6B 0A3
(705) 253-3251
Emp Here 50   *Sales* 15,943,450
SIC 1521 Single-family housing construction
Gary Potvin

D-U-N-S 20-903-2044   (HQ)
NORTHERN CREDIT UNION LIMITED
280 Mcnabb St, Sault Ste. Marie, ON, P6B 1Y6
(705) 949-2644
Emp Here 46   *Sales* 46,116,270
SIC 6062 State credit unions
Albert Suraci
Richard Adam

D-U-N-S 20-809-1103   (HQ)
NORTHERN CREDIT UNION LTD
681 Pine St, Sault Ste. Marie, ON, P6B 3G2
(705) 253-9868
Sales 30,900,527
SIC 6062 State credit unions
Wayne Lavallee

D-U-N-S 24-049-0326   (SL)
ONTARIO FINNISH RESTHOME ASSOCIATION, THE
725 North St Suite 209, Sault Ste. Marie, ON, P6B 5Z3
(705) 945-9987
Emp Here 126   *Sales* 9,675,792
SIC 8322 Individual and family services
Lewis Massad
Todd Slotegraaf

D-U-N-S 24-186-1819   (SL)
R F CONTRACTING INC
116 Industrial Park Cres, Sault Ste. Marie, ON, P6B 5P2
(705) 253-1151
Emp Here 50   *Sales* 11,046,700
SIC 1711 Plumbing, heating, air-conditioning
Del Pawliuk
Bernie Farrell

D-U-N-S 20-608-5805   (SL)
RECTOR MACHINE WORKS LTD
190 Sackville Rd, Sault Ste. Marie, ON, P6B 4T6
(705) 256-6221
Emp Here 35   *Sales* 16,625,910
SIC 5084 Industrial machinery and equipment
Harvey Rector
Sandra Rector

D-U-N-S 24-563-8093   (HQ)
S. & T. ELECTRICAL CONTRACTORS LIMITED
S. & T. GROUP
158 Sackville Rd Suite 2, Sault Ste. Marie, ON, P6B 4T6
(705) 942-3043
Sales 58,877,250
SIC 1731 Electrical work
Andrew Sarlo
Dennis Tatasciore

D-U-N-S 24-141-5660   (HQ)
SAULT AREA HOSPITAL
750 Great Northern Rd Suite 1, Sault Ste. Marie, ON, P6B 0A8
(705) 759-3434
Emp Here 1,292   *Sales* 144,404,000
SIC 8062 General medical and surgical hospitals
Ila Watson
Liliana Silvano

D-U-N-S 20-975-4225   (SL)
SAULT COLLEGE OF APPLIED ARTS & TECHNOLOGY, THE
443 Northern Ave E, Sault Ste. Marie, ON, P6B 4J3
(705) 759-2554
Emp Here 526   *Sales* 78,579,666
SIC 8221 Colleges and universities
Ronald Common

D-U-N-S 25-035-1079   (SL)
SAULT STE MARIE & DISTRICT GROUP HEALTH ASSOCIATION
GROUP HEALTH CENTRE
240 Mcnabb St, Sault Ste. Marie, ON, P6B 1Y5
(705) 759-1234
Emp Here 300   *Sales* 57,062,100
SIC 8011 Offices and clinics of medical doctors
Graham Clark

D-U-N-S 20-150-0816   (HQ)
SOO MILL & LUMBER COMPANY LIMITED
(Suby of SOO MILL HOLDINGS LIMITED)*
539 Great Northern Rd, Sault Ste. Marie, ON, P6B 5A1
(705) 759-0533
Emp Here 85   *Sales* 26,765,200
SIC 5211 Lumber and other building materials
D Lynn Hollingsworth
Scott Macpillivray
John Hollingsworth

D-U-N-S 25-142-5625   (HQ)
SYLVAN AUTOMATION LTD
1018 Mcnabb St, Sault Ste. Marie, ON, P6B 6J1
(705) 254-4669
Emp Here 5   *Sales* 13,019,068
SIC 5085 Industrial supplies
Cameron Jefferson
James Kells
Kevin Brazier

Sault Ste. Marie, ON P6C

D-U-N-S 25-220-6230   (SL)
1022013 ONTARIO LIMITED
SUPERIOR INDUSTRIAL SERVICES
1231 Peoples Rd, Sault Ste. Marie, ON, P6C 3W7
(705) 759-5148
Emp Here 100   *Sales* 23,306,500
SIC 1711 Plumbing, heating, air-conditioning
Tony Porco

D-U-N-S 25-239-0687   (BR)
ALGOMA DISTRICT SCHOOL BOARD
KORAH COLLEGIATE AND VOCATIONAL SCHOOL
(Suby of ALGOMA DISTRICT SCHOOL BOARD)*
636 Goulais Ave, Sault Ste. Marie, ON, P6C 5A7
(705) 945-7180
Emp Here 80
SIC 8211 Elementary and secondary schools
Sergio Lacoe

D-U-N-S 25-108-0016   (HQ)
ALGOMA TUBES INC
(Suby of ROCCA & PARTNERS STICHTING ADMINISTRATIEKANTOOR AANDELEN

SAN FAUSTIN)*
547 Wallace Terr, Sault Ste. Marie, ON, P6C 1L9
(705) 946-8130
Sales 223,945,700
SIC 3317 Steel pipe and tubes
Alberto Iperti
Darren Flack

D-U-N-S 24-099-5415   (HQ)
AVERY CONSTRUCTION LIMITED
940 Second Line W Suite B, Sault Ste. Marie, ON, P6C 2L3
(705) 759-4800
Sales 15,146,520
SIC 1611 Highway and street construction
Daniel Avery
Jeff Avery
Mike Artuso

D-U-N-S 20-763-6551   (SL)
BIASUCCI DEVELOPMENTS INC
544 Wellington St W, Sault Ste. Marie, ON, P6C 3T6
(705) 946-8701
Emp Here 26   *Sales* 12,239,006
SIC 1542 Nonresidential construction, nec
Amato Biasucci

D-U-N-S 20-790-2318   (SL)
JOE'S NO FRILLS 796 LIMITED
519 Korah Rd, Sault Ste. Marie, ON, P6C 4J4
(866) 987-6453
Emp Here 45   *Sales* 12,336,840
SIC 5411 Grocery stores
Jiuseppe Policicchio

D-U-N-S 20-149-8706   (SL)
LYONS LTD
LYONS TIM-BR MART
500 Wellington St W, Sault Ste. Marie, ON, P6C 3T5
(705) 759-1555
Emp Here 55   *Sales* 14,720,860
SIC 5211 Lumber and other building materials
David Beaumont
Ruth Beaumont

D-U-N-S 25-300-0699   (BR)
METRO ONTARIO INC
METRO
(Suby of METRO INC)*
275 Second Line W, Sault Ste. Marie, ON, P6C 2J4
(705) 949-0350
Emp Here 75
SIC 5411 Grocery stores
Eric Vachon

D-U-N-S 20-352-0593   (SL)
PALMER PAVING
1121 Peoples Rd, Sault Ste. Marie, ON, P6C 3W4
(705) 254-1644
Emp Here 49   *Sales* 13,892,676
SIC 1611 Highway and street construction
Terri Renoni

Scarborough, ON L9W

D-U-N-S 20-512-2836   (HQ)
AVERTEX UTILITY SOLUTIONS INC
205235 County Rd 109, Scarborough, ON, L9W 0T8
(519) 942-3030
Emp Here 75   *Sales* 37,866,300
SIC 1623 Water, sewer, and utility lines
Jack Kottelenberg
Andrew Blokker
Grant Kottelenberg

D-U-N-S 24-376-6529   (SL)
KREATOR EQUIPMENT & SERVICES INCORPORATED
473036 County Rd 11, Scarborough, ON,

L9W 0R2
(519) 941-7876
Emp Here 50   *Sales* 23,751,300
SIC 5084 Industrial machinery and equipment
Keith Miles
Kathy Miles

D-U-N-S 24-793-2122   (SL)
TIFFANY METAL CASTING LTD
286075 County Rd 10, Scarborough, ON,
L9W 6P5
(519) 941-7026
Emp Here 45   *Sales* 10,504,575
SIC 3321 Gray and ductile iron foundries
John Tiffany
Mark Tiffany
Gord Tiffany

D-U-N-S 24-760-0641   (SL)
TIRE DISCOUNTER GROUP INC
65379 County Rd 3, Scarborough, ON, L9W
7J8
(519) 941-4136
Emp Here 120   *Sales* 55,338,480
SIC 5014 Tires and tubes
Frank Brundle

Scarborough, ON M1B

D-U-N-S 20-297-1649   (SL)
1502026 ONTARIO LTD
AGINCOURT HYUNDAI
80 Auto Mall Dr, Scarborough, ON, M1B 5N5
(416) 291-2929
Emp Here 25   *Sales* 12,451,950
SIC 5511 New and used car dealers
Nicholas Koundouros

D-U-N-S 20-771-2436   (SL)
1571921 ONTARIO LIMITED
GUS' NO FRILLS
51 Tapscott Rd, Scarborough, ON, M1B 4Y7

Emp Here 97   *Sales* 28,467,269
SIC 5411 Grocery stores
Francois Decardalho

D-U-N-S 24-862-2771   (HQ)
A/D FIRE PROTECTION SYSTEMS INC
(*Suby of* RPM INTERNATIONAL INC.)
420 Tapscott Rd Unit 5, Scarborough, ON,
M1B 1Y4
(416) 292-2361
Emp Here 50   *Sales* 11,525,100
SIC 3479 Metal coating and allied services
Bruno Stieg

D-U-N-S 24-185-6343   (SL)
ADLER INTERNATIONAL, LTD
MYRON MANUFACTURING
(*Suby of* MYRON CORP.)
5610 Finch Ave E, Scarborough, ON, M1B
6A6
(416) 291-9000
Emp Here 300   *Sales* 176,747,700
SIC 5199 Nondurable goods, nec
Myron Adler

D-U-N-S 24-792-8641   (HQ)
AMPHENOL CANADA CORP
(*Suby of* AMPHENOL CORPORATION)
605 Milner Ave, Scarborough, ON, M1B 5X6
(416) 291-4401
Emp Here 160   *Sales* 116,049,400
SIC 5065 Electronic parts and equipment, nec
Anthony Davidson
Andrew Toffelmire

D-U-N-S 20-401-4880   (SL)
ASTRA TRADE FINISHING LIMITED
390 Tapscott Rd Suite 1, Scarborough, ON,
M1B 2Y9
(416) 291-2272
Emp Here 60   *Sales* 14,006,100
SIC 2631 Paperboard mills

Jerry Jansen

D-U-N-S 24-708-6499   (SL)
BOARD OF MANAGEMENT OF THE TORONTO ZOO
TORONTO ZOO
361a Old Finch Ave, Scarborough, ON, M1B
5K7
(416) 392-5929
Emp Here 250   *Sales* 34,386,310
SIC 7999 Amusement and recreation, nec
Paul Ainslie
Joshua Vinegar
Cal Bricker
Ming-Tat Cheung
Vanessa Choy
Matthew Cole
Glenn De Baeremaeker
Paul Doyle
Mary Fragedakis
Chin Lee

D-U-N-S 25-405-3796   (SL)
BODY PLUS NUTRITIONAL PRODUCTS INC
130 Mclevin Ave Unit 5, Scarborough, ON,
M1B 3R6
(416) 332-1881
Emp Here 40   *Sales* 33,423,080
SIC 5149 Groceries and related products, nec
Norman Danniels
Elaine Munro

D-U-N-S 20-160-8353   (SL)
BULOVA WATCH COMPANY LIMITED
(*Suby of* CITIZEN WATCH CO., LTD.)
39 Casebridge Crt, Scarborough, ON, M1B
5N4
(416) 751-7151
Emp Here 80   *Sales* 55,624,000
SIC 5094 Jewelry and precious stones
Robert G Humphrey
Sian Williams
Anthony Gaspar
Stephen Nyman
Gerald Hollyer

D-U-N-S 20-104-3374   (SL)
CANADIAN CLOTHING INTERNATIONAL INC
541 Conlins Rd, Scarborough, ON, M1B 5S1
(416) 335-1300
Emp Here 120   *Sales* 100,503,960
SIC 5137 Women's and children's clothing
Raza Nasser

D-U-N-S 25-167-2895   (BR)
CASCADES CANADA ULC
NORAMPAC-LITHOTECH
(*Suby of* CASCADES INC)
5910 Finch Ave E, Scarborough, ON, M1B
5P8
(416) 412-3500
Emp Here 110
SIC 2679 Converted paper products, nec
Patrick Ravary

D-U-N-S 20-850-3490   (HQ)
CHESTER CARTAGE & MOVERS LTD
CHESTER CARTAGE
1995 Markham Rd, Scarborough, ON, M1B
2W3
(416) 754-7716
Sales 26,741,780
SIC 4212 Local trucking, without storage
Harry Cummins
Robert Cummins
Peter Cummins

D-U-N-S 20-324-9925   (HQ)
CINRAM CANADA OPERATIONS ULC
CINRAM GROUP
(*Suby of* NAJAFI COMPANIES, LLC)
2255 Markham Rd, Scarborough, ON, M1B
2W3
(416) 298-8190
Sales 107,070,400
SIC 5045 Computers, peripherals, and soft-

ware
Steve Brown
David Munro
David Ashton
John Bell

D-U-N-S 24-766-2856   (SL)
CINRAM INTERNATIONAL INCOME FUND
2255 Markham Rd, Scarborough, ON, M1B
2W3
(416) 298-8190
Emp Here 8,300   *Sales* 49,261,288,480
SIC 6722 Management investment, open-end
Steven Brown
John Bell
David Ashton

D-U-N-S 24-203-1495   (HQ)
CLT LOGISTICS, INC
CLT INTERNATIONAL
5900 Finch Ave E, Scarborough, ON, M1B
5P8
(416) 686-4199
Emp Here 35   *Sales* 60,793,975
SIC 5122 Drugs, proprietaries, and sundries
Beryl Wilkinson

D-U-N-S 25-202-5762   (HQ)
COMMON COLLECTION AGENCY INC
CCA
5900 Finch Ave E Suite 200a, Scarborough,
ON, M1B 5P8
(416) 297-7077
Sales 19,902,056
SIC 7322 Adjustment and collection services
Dennis Hickey
Jeff Kerslake
Todd Koyama-Asada
Rob Yarmo

D-U-N-S 25-147-0498   (SL)
CTI INDUSTRIES INC
5621 Finch Ave E Unit 3, Scarborough, ON,
M1B 2T9
(416) 297-8738
Emp Here 150   *Sales* 28,566,300
SIC 3679 Electronic components, nec
Joe Bornbaum
Roman Brenner
Peter Caulfield
George Mcpherson
Dino Berardi
Jeffery Me

D-U-N-S 20-151-5509   (HQ)
DART CANADA INC
2121 Markham Rd, Scarborough, ON, M1B
2W3
(416) 293-2877
Emp Here 410   *Sales* 165,436,650
SIC 2656 Sanitary food containers
Steven Schildt
Bruno Pazienza

D-U-N-S 24-645-4961   (SL)
DIETRON TOOL & DIE INC
64 Melford Dr, Scarborough, ON, M1B 6B7
(416) 297-5858
Emp Here 70   *Sales* 15,540,070
SIC 3544 Special dies, tools, jigs, and fixtures
John Scrymgeour
Cheryl Scrymgeour

D-U-N-S 24-183-7996   (HQ)
DONALCO INC
(*Suby of* DONALCO WESTERN INC)
20 Melford Dr Unit 10, Scarborough, ON, M1B
2X6
(416) 292-7118
Emp Here 30   *Sales* 17,233,020
SIC 1799 Special trade contractors, nec
Bradley Hart
Ronald Murphy
Edward Brennan

D-U-N-S 24-138-4627   (SL)
EN-PLAS INC
1395 Morningside Ave, Scarborough, ON,

M1B 3J1
(416) 286-3030
Emp Here 30   *Sales* 14,250,780
SIC 5084 Industrial machinery and equipment
Allan Lemieux

D-U-N-S 20-288-9242   (HQ)
EOS CANADA INC
EOS NCN
(*Suby of* KG ATLAS VERMOGENSVERWAL-
TUNGSGESELLSCHAFT & CO.)
325 Milner Ave Suite 1111, Scarborough, ON,
M1B 5N1
(647) 436-2605
Emp Here 96   *Sales* 29,053,795
SIC 7322 Adjustment and collection services
Paul Leary Jr
Jim Shaw
Paul Leary Sr.
Abdul Wahid

D-U-N-S 25-057-7202   (SL)
EXECWAY CONSTRUCTION LTD
10157 Sheppard Ave E, Scarborough, ON,
M1B 1G1
(416) 286-2019
Emp Here 45   *Sales* 14,999,985
SIC 1541 Industrial buildings and warehouses
Robert Wayment
Dan Campbell

D-U-N-S 25-536-8458   (SL)
FOOD DIRECTIONS INC
120 Melford Dr Unit 8, Scarborough, ON, M1B
2X5
(416) 609-0016
Emp Here 50   *Sales* 11,242,750
SIC 2098 Macaroni and spaghetti
Allen Lau

D-U-N-S 25-404-0116   (HQ)
FORTRESS TECHNOLOGY INC
51 Grand Marshall Dr, Scarborough, ON, M1B
5N6
(416) 754-2898
Sales 19,319,565
SIC 3812 Search and navigation equipment
Stephen Gidman
Dino Rosati

D-U-N-S 24-686-4557   (HQ)
FREEWAY FORD SALES LIMITED
EAST METRO AUTO LEASING, DIV OF
958 Milner Ave, Scarborough, ON, M1B 5V7
(416) 293-3077
Emp Here 1   *Sales* 40,903,200
SIC 5511 New and used car dealers
Linda Marshall

D-U-N-S 24-652-9499   (BR)
GROUPE PAGES JAUNES CORP
(*Suby of* PAGES JAUNES LIMITEE)
325 Milner Ave Suite 4, Scarborough, ON,
M1B 5N1
(416) 412-5000
Emp Here 100
SIC 2741 Miscellaneous publishing
Dave Stanyon

D-U-N-S 25-289-2419   (SL)
HAMILTON, T & SON ROOFING INC
20 Thornmount Dr, Scarborough, ON, M1B
3J4
(416) 755-5522
Emp Here 53   *Sales* 11,544,937
SIC 1761 Roofing, siding, and sheetMetal
work
Tom Hamilton

D-U-N-S 25-514-3091   (BR)
HOME DEPOT OF CANADA INC
HOME DEPOT
(*Suby of* THE HOME DEPOT INC)
60 Grand Marshall Dr, Scarborough, ON, M1B
5N6
(416) 283-3166
Emp Here 100
SIC 5251 Hardware stores

Michelle Garcia

D-U-N-S 20-383-9738   (SL)
INGENIOUS PACKAGING, INC
(*Suby of* RESOURCE LABEL GROUP, LLC)
999 Progress Ave, Scarborough, ON, M1B
6J1
(416) 292-6600
Emp Here 150   *Sales* 29,215,200
SIC 2672 Paper; coated and laminated, nec
Michael Apperson

D-U-N-S 25-227-3966   (SL)
INSURANCE PORTFOLIO INC
10 Milner Business Crt Suite 800, Scarborough, ON, M1B 3C6
(416) 754-3910
Emp Here 25   *Sales* 14,498,100
SIC 6411 Insurance agents, brokers, and service
Phillip Tyrwhitt

D-U-N-S 20-648-6354   (BR)
INVESTORS GROUP INC
INVESTORS GROUP FINANCIAL SERVICES
(*Suby of* POWER CORPORATION DU
CANADA)
305 Milner Ave Suite 701, Scarborough, ON,
M1B 3V4
(416) 292-7229
Emp Here 100
SIC 6162 Mortgage bankers and loan correspondents
Gabe Chiodo

D-U-N-S 24-320-2156   (SL)
IWN CONSULTING INC
10 Milner Business Crt Suite 300, Scarborough, ON, M1B 3C6
(416) 827-2727
Emp Here 104   *Sales* 15,247,125
SIC 7371 Custom computer programming services
Najeeb Ahmad

D-U-N-S 24-822-8827   (HQ)
KNP HEADWEAR INC
50 Melham Crt, Scarborough, ON, M1B 2E5
(416) 298-8516
Emp Here 45   *Sales* 27,906,032
SIC 5136 Men's and boy's clothing
Philip Chong

D-U-N-S 24-567-7377   (SL)
LILY CUPS INC
2121 Markham Rd, Scarborough, ON, M1B
2W3
(416) 293-2877
Emp Here 45   *Sales* 22,664,610
SIC 5113 Industrial and personal service paper
David Mcintyre

D-U-N-S 24-771-7390   (HQ)
MASTERMIND LP
MASTERMIND EDUCATIONAL
415 Milner Ave Suite 4, Scarborough, ON,
M1B 2L1
(416) 321-8984
Sales 73,414,800
SIC 5945 Hobby, toy, and game shops
John T Loh

D-U-N-S 20-845-5191   (SL)
MYRON MANUFACTURING CORP (USA)
(*Suby of* MYRON CORP.)
5610 Finch Ave E, Scarborough, ON, M1B
6A6
(647) 288-5300
Emp Here 350   *Sales* 206,205,650
SIC 5199 Nondurable goods, nec
Allan Courneya

D-U-N-S 25-095-8597   (SL)
NATIONAL PHARMACY
70 Melford Dr Suite 7, Scarborough, ON, M1B
1Y9

(416) 265-9000
Emp Here 40   *Sales* 10,118,160
SIC 5912 Drug stores and proprietary stores
Paul Baui

D-U-N-S 20-702-4188   (HQ)
**O.T.T. LEGAL SERVICES PROFESSIONAL
CORPORATION**
1504 Markham Rd, Scarborough, ON, M1B
2V9
(416) 292-2022
Emp Here 8   *Sales* 11,679,694
SIC 7389 Business services, nec
Christopher Conway

D-U-N-S 24-704-9026   (SL)
PAULDONLAM INVESTMENTS INC
FORMULA HONDA
2240 Markham Rd, Scarborough, ON, M1B
2W4
(416) 754-4555
Emp Here 95   *Sales* 59,781,600
SIC 5511 New and used car dealers
Basil Cultrera

D-U-N-S 20-911-3864   (BR)
PEPSICO CANADA ULC
FRITO LAY CANADA
(*Suby of* PEPSICO, INC.)
1 Water Tower Gate, Scarborough, ON, M1B
6C5
(416) 284-3200
Emp Here 210
SIC 5145 Confectionery
Scott Dickson

D-U-N-S 24-911-8142   (HQ)
RE/MAX ROUGE RIVER REALTY LTD
6758 Kingston Rd Unit 1, Scarborough, ON,
M1B 1G8
(416) 286-3993
Emp Here 1   *Sales* 54,036,681
SIC 6531 Real estate agents and managers
David Pearce
Dolores Pearce

D-U-N-S 20-874-6537   (SL)
REX PAK LIMITED
85 Thornmount Dr, Scarborough, ON, M1B
5V3
(416) 755-3324
Emp Here 155   *Sales* 103,680,740
SIC 7389 Business services, nec
Louis Sabatini
Devin Sabatani

D-U-N-S 24-010-6351   (SL)
SCARBOROUGH TRUCK CENTRE INC
1810 Markham Rd, Scarborough, ON, M1B
2W2

Emp Here 25   *Sales* 12,451,950
SIC 5511 New and used car dealers
John Marotta
Andrew Kovacic

D-U-N-S 24-415-1817   (SL)
SCARSVIEW MOTORS LTD
SCARSVIEW CHRYSLER DODGE JEEP
951 Milner Ave, Scarborough, ON, M1B 5X4
(416) 281-6200
Emp Here 40   *Sales* 19,923,120
SIC 5511 New and used car dealers
Sudhir Chopra
Neelam Chopra

D-U-N-S 24-316-3920   (SL)
SIGMA MOULDERS
150 Mclevin Ave, Scarborough, ON, M1B 4Z7
(416) 297-0088
Emp Here 105   *Sales* 16,680,090
SIC 3089 Plastics products, nec
Sam Grundland
Herbert Magister

D-U-N-S 24-252-6684   (SL)
SIGMAPAC ENGINEERED SERVICES INC
71 Melford Dr Unit 1, Scarborough, ON, M1B
2G6

(866) 805-4256
Emp Here 80   *Sales* 35,937,520
SIC 7389 Business services, nec
Walter Rosati

D-U-N-S 25-710-4281   (SL)
SOMERVILLE MERCHANDISING INC
5760 Finch Ave E, Scarborough, ON, M1B 5J9
(416) 754-7228
Emp Here 70   *Sales* 22,829,520
SIC 3993 Signs and advertising specialties
Bob Muzyka
Shashi Budakoti

D-U-N-S 24-523-6158   (SL)
STEELCORE CONSTRUCTION LTD
1295 Morningside Ave Unit 27, Scarborough,
ON, M1B 4Z4
(416) 282-4888
Emp Here 26   *Sales* 27,421,695
SIC 1542 Nonresidential construction, nec
Themis Tzovolos
Rob Difrancesco

D-U-N-S 20-176-5658   (SL)
TALBOT SALES LIMITED
CARDINAL FASTENERS
120 Venture Dr, Scarborough, ON, M1B 3L6
(416) 286-3666
Emp Here 30   *Sales* 14,250,780
SIC 5085 Industrial supplies
Gordon Turner

D-U-N-S 20-151-8008   (HQ)
TEVA CANADA LIMITED
TEVA NOVOPHARM
(*Suby of* TEVA PHARMACEUTICAL INDUSTRIES LIMITED)
30 Novopharm Crt, Scarborough, ON, M1B
2K9
(416) 291-8876
Emp Here 300   *Sales* 464,231,600
SIC 2834 Pharmaceutical preparations
Leslie Dan
Doug Sommerville
Suzanne Brand

D-U-N-S 20-025-0723   (BR)
TORONTO DISTRICT SCHOOL BOARD
LESTER B PEARSON COLLEGIATE INSTITUTE
(*Suby of* TORONTO DISTRICT SCHOOL
BOARD)
150 Tapscott Rd, Scarborough, ON, M1B 2L2
(416) 396-5892
Emp Here 114
SIC 8211 Elementary and secondary schools
Denise De Paola

D-U-N-S 25-679-0643   (HQ)
TURF OPERATIONS SCARBOROUGH INC
WEED MAN
80 Auto Mall Dr, Scarborough, ON, M1B 5N5
(416) 269-8333
Emp Here 100   *Sales* 43,476,250
SIC 0782 Lawn and garden services
Roger Mongeon

D-U-N-S 25-294-8179   (BR)
WAL-MART CANADA CORP
(*Suby of* WALMART INC.)
785 Milner Ave, Scarborough, ON, M1B 3C3
(416) 281-2929
Emp Here 250
SIC 5311 Department stores
Maria Della Grotta

D-U-N-S 24-418-2494   (SL)
ZEDD CUSTOMER SOLUTIONS LP
325 Milner Ave, Scarborough, ON, M1B 5N1
(416) 745-1333
Emp Here 100   *Sales* 44,921,900
SIC 7389 Business services, nec
Mark Gross

Scarborough, ON M1C

D-U-N-S 20-549-0035   (SL)
989116 ONTARIO LIMITED
SENCORE COMPANY
503 Centennial Rd N, Scarborough, ON, M1C
2A5
(416) 208-5441
Emp Here 1,200
SIC 5112 Stationery and office supplies

D-U-N-S 24-046-5161   (SL)
C A S COMMUNICATIONS SERVICES LIMITED
COMMUNICATION SERVICES
503 Centennial Rd N, Scarborough, ON, M1C
2A5
(416) 724-8333
Emp Here 25   *Sales* 11,087,250
SIC 7389 Business services, nec
Norman Rhora
Maxine Rhora

D-U-N-S 24-936-5610   (BR)
GOVERNING COUNCIL OF THE UNIVERSITY OF TORONTO, THE
UNIVERSITY OF TORONTO - SCARBOROUGH CAMPUS (UTSC)
(*Suby of* GOVERNING COUNCIL OF THE
UNIVERSITY OF TORONTO, THE)
1265 Military Trail Suite 303, Scarborough,
ON, M1C 1A4
(416) 287-7033
Emp Here 500
SIC 8221 Colleges and universities
Kim Mclean

D-U-N-S 24-057-9136   (SL)
JAMAL, OME PHARMACY LTD
SHOPPERS DRUG MART
265 Port Union Rd, Scarborough, ON, M1C
2L3
(416) 284-9229
Emp Here 45   *Sales* 11,382,930
SIC 5912 Drug stores and proprietary stores
Ome Jamal

D-U-N-S 25-300-0418   (BR)
METRO ONTARIO INC
METRO
(*Suby of* METRO INC)
261 Port Union Rd, Scarborough, ON, M1C
2L3
(416) 284-7792
Emp Here 130
SIC 5411 Grocery stores
Gary Fitzgerald

D-U-N-S 24-375-8450   (SL)
MIHIR INTERNATIONAL
531 Meadowvale Rd, Scarborough, ON, M1C
1S7
(416) 989-2445
Emp Here 48   *Sales* 22,595,088
SIC 1542 Nonresidential construction, nec
Mihir Kapadia

D-U-N-S 25-898-4467   (SL)
NEBRASKA COLLISION CENTRE INC
6511 Kingston Rd, Scarborough, ON, M1C
1L5
(416) 282-5794
Emp Here 50   *Sales* 10,131,450
SIC 7532 Top and body repair and paint shops
Bradley Dumoulin

D-U-N-S 24-337-0673   (BR)
**ROYAL CANADIAN LEGION ONTARIO
COMMAND,THE**
ROYAL CANADIAN LEGION ONTARIO COMMAND
(*Suby of* ROYAL CANADIAN LEGION ONTARIO COMMAND,THE)
45 Lawson Rd, Scarborough, ON, M1C 2J1
(416) 281-2992
Emp Here 120
SIC 8641 Civic and social associations

D-U-N-S 20-025-3776 (BR)
TORONTO DISTRICT SCHOOL BOARD
SIR OLIVER MOWAT C I
(*Suby of* TORONTO DISTRICT SCHOOL BOARD)
5400 Lawrence Ave E, Scarborough, ON, M1C 2C6
(416) 396-6802
Emp Here 100
SIC 8211 Elementary and secondary schools
Anthony Hack

D-U-N-S 20-301-0673 (SL)
WIND POWER MEDIA INC
49 Feagan Dr, Scarborough, ON, M1C 3B6
(416) 471-4420
Emp Here 105   *Sales* 26,616,450
SIC 8748 Business consulting, nec
Peter Wolstencroft
Louis Wisferford
Robert Baniles

Scarborough, ON M1E

D-U-N-S 20-790-2219 (SL)
1594414 ONTARIO LIMITED
FRANK'S NO FRILLS
4473 Kingston Rd, Scarborough, ON, M1E 2N7
(416) 281-9140
Emp Here 45   *Sales* 12,336,840
SIC 5411 Grocery stores
Frank Palmieri

D-U-N-S 24-707-9494 (SL)
BEECHGROVE COUNTRY FOODS INC
20 Minuk Acres, Scarborough, ON, M1E 4Y6
(416) 283-8777
Emp Here 55   *Sales* 19,012,950
SIC 2011 Meat packing plants
Mary Donnolly

D-U-N-S 25-403-5132 (HQ)
BERRY PLASTICS CANADA INC
(*Suby of* BERRY GLOBAL GROUP, INC.)
595 Coronation Dr, Scarborough, ON, M1E 2K4
(416) 281-6000
Emp Here 86   *Sales* 14,138,362
SIC 3081 Unsupported plastics film and sheet
David Lai Thom
Nat Mcgrath
Dave Oxley
Brendan Barba
Paul Feeney
Larry Noll

D-U-N-S 25-226-0971 (SL)
BLACK PALM AVIARIES OF CANADA INC
LOAN ARRANGER, THE
4251 Kingston Rd, Scarborough, ON, M1E 2M5
(416) 283-4262
Emp Here 27   *Sales* 13,448,106
SIC 5511 New and used car dealers
Frank Bozz

D-U-N-S 25-035-1368 (SL)
CHEVALIER AUTOMOBILES INC
ACTION HONDA
(*Suby of* CHEVALIER INTERNATIONAL HOLDINGS LIMITED)
4334 Kingston Rd, Scarborough, ON, M1E 2M8
(416) 281-1234
Emp Here 48   *Sales* 30,205,440
SIC 5511 New and used car dealers
Philipe So

D-U-N-S 24-737-7419 (HQ)
DIGITAL SPECIALTY CHEMICALS LIMITED
470 Coronation Dr, Scarborough, ON, M1E 4Y4
(416) 231-2991
Sales 13,279,680

SIC 2819 Industrial inorganic chemicals, nec
Ravi Gukathasan
James Guy

D-U-N-S 20-937-7928 (SL)
ESTONIAN RELIEF COMMITTEE IN CANADA
EHATARE RETIREMENT AND NURSING HOME
40 Old Kingston Rd, Scarborough, ON, M1E 3J5
(416) 724-6144
Emp Here 60   *Sales* 42,552,720
SIC 8699 Membership organizations, nec
Ruth Mcfarlane

D-U-N-S 20-923-9573 (BR)
EXTENDICARE INC
EXTENDICARE GUILDWOOD
(*Suby of* EXTENDICARE INC)
60 Guildwood Pky Suite 327, Scarborough, ON, M1E 1N9
(416) 266-7711
Emp Here 182
SIC 8051 Skilled nursing care facilities
Andy Barros

D-U-N-S 20-356-8738 (HQ)
HALLTECH INC
POLYCOL, UNE DIVISION DE HALLTECH
(*Suby of* HALLTECH HOLDING CORP)
465 Coronation Dr, Scarborough, ON, M1E 2K2
(416) 284-6111
Sales 13,833,000
SIC 2891 Adhesives and sealants
Vince Contento
Al Deli

D-U-N-S 25-365-5450 (HQ)
HENRY COMPANY CANADA INC
(*Suby of* HNC PARENT, INC.)
15 Wallsend Dr, Scarborough, ON, M1E 3X6
(416) 724-2000
Sales 19,881,470
SIC 2851 Paints and allied products
Frank Ready
John Dobson
Vic Patel
Christian Nolte

D-U-N-S 24-953-0320 (BR)
METRO ONTARIO INC
FOOD BASICS
(*Suby of* METRO INC)
2900 Ellesmere Rd Suite 587, Scarborough, ON, M1E 4B8
(416) 284-5320
Emp Here 122
SIC 5411 Grocery stores
God Win

D-U-N-S 24-313-8620 (SL)
ROHM AND HAAS CANADA LP
DOW ADVANCED MATERIALS
(*Suby of* DOW INC.)
2 Manse Rd, Scarborough, ON, M1E 3T9
(416) 284-4711
Emp Here 125   *Sales* 55,580,625
SIC 2899 Chemical preparations, nec
Gregory Johnston

D-U-N-S 20-025-1630 (BR)
SEVEN OAKS HOMES INC
SEVEN OAKS HOMES FOR THE AGED
(*Suby of* SEVEN OAKS HOMES INC)
9 Neilson Rd, Scarborough, ON, M1E 5E1
(416) 392-3500
Emp Here 150
SIC 8051 Skilled nursing care facilities
Gayle Campbell

D-U-N-S 20-700-2358 (BR)
TORONTO CATHOLIC DISTRICT SCHOOL BOARD
ST. JOHN PAUL LL CATHOLIC SECONDARY SCHOOL
(*Suby of* TORONTO CATHOLIC DISTRICT

SCHOOL BOARD)
685 Military Trail, Scarborough, ON, M1E 4P6
(416) 393-5531
Emp Here 130
SIC 8211 Elementary and secondary schools
Paul Mcalpine

D-U-N-S 20-025-1085 (BR)
TORONTO DISTRICT SCHOOL BOARD
WEST HILL COLLEGIATE INSTITUTE
(*Suby of* TORONTO DISTRICT SCHOOL BOARD)
350 Morningside Ave, Scarborough, ON, M1E 3G3
(416) 396-6864
Emp Here 100
SIC 8211 Elementary and secondary schools
Gillian Gibbons

D-U-N-S 25-153-1372 (BR)
TORONTO DISTRICT SCHOOL BOARD
MAPLEWOOD HIGH SCHOOL
(*Suby of* TORONTO DISTRICT SCHOOL BOARD)
120 Galloway Rd, Scarborough, ON, M1E 1W7
(416) 396-6765
Emp Here 100
SIC 8211 Elementary and secondary schools
Duncan Le Blanc

D-U-N-S 20-025-2489 (BR)
TORONTO DISTRICT SCHOOL BOARD
SIR WILFRID LAURIER COLLEGIATE INSTITUTE
(*Suby of* TORONTO DISTRICT SCHOOL BOARD)
145 Guildwood Pky, Scarborough, ON, M1E 1P5
(416) 396-6820
Emp Here 100
SIC 8211 Elementary and secondary schools
Marios Tenentes

Scarborough, ON M1G

D-U-N-S 20-881-3501 (HQ)
CENTENNIAL COLLEGE OF APPLIED ARTS & TECHNOLOGY, THE
BIBLIOCENTRE, DIV OF
941 Progress Ave, Scarborough, ON, M1G 3T8
(416) 289-5000
Emp Here 150   *Sales* 211,433,040
SIC 8222 Junior colleges
Ann Buller
Brad Chapman
Rosanna Cavallaro
Yves Deschenes
Marilyn Herie
Craig Stephenson
Taylan Tatli
Jin Li
Tracey Lloyd

D-U-N-S 25-222-1890 (BR)
EXTENDICARE (CANADA) INC
EXTENDICARE SCARBOROUGH
(*Suby of* EXTENDICARE INC)
3830 Lawrence Ave E Suite 103, Scarborough, ON, M1G 1R6
(416) 439-1243
Emp Here 160
SIC 8051 Skilled nursing care facilities
Vania Sakelaris

D-U-N-S 24-875-5290 (BR)
TORONTO DISTRICT SCHOOL BOARD
WOBURN COLLEGIATE INSTITUTE
(*Suby of* TORONTO DISTRICT SCHOOL BOARD)
2222 Ellesmere Rd, Scarborough, ON, M1G 3M3
(416) 396-4575
Emp Here 100

SIC 8211 Elementary and secondary schools
Karen Hume

Scarborough, ON M1H

D-U-N-S 24-784-6447 (SL)
1210670 ONTARIO INC
SCARBOROUGH CITY CAB
1940 Ellesmere Rd Unit 18, Scarborough, ON, M1H 2V7
(416) 438-5151
Emp Here 200   *Sales* 15,054,400
SIC 4121 Taxicabs
Rachhpal Dhillon

D-U-N-S 24-389-4537 (SL)
6875866 CANADA INC
40 Production Dr, Scarborough, ON, M1H 2X8
(905) 513-1097
Emp Here 70   *Sales* 31,445,330
SIC 7389 Business services, nec
Daniel Popent

D-U-N-S 20-717-7197 (HQ)
A. T. DESIGNS INSIGNIA LTD
70 Production Dr, Scarborough, ON, M1H 2X8
(800) 288-0111
Sales 21,198,840
SIC 3961 Costume jewelry
Trevor Temple

D-U-N-S 20-082-3651 (SL)
BEEFEATERS INC
SHOPCO FOOD PROVISIONERS
885 Progress Ave Suite 318, Scarborough, ON, M1H 3G3
(416) 289-1554
Emp Here 40   *Sales* 33,423,080
SIC 5147 Meats and meat products
Norman Gaal

D-U-N-S 20-012-7368 (SL)
BESTILE APPAREL INC
841 Progress Ave, Scarborough, ON, M1H 2X4

Emp Here 25   *Sales* 12,458,050
SIC 5136 Men's and boy's clothing
Simon Chang

D-U-N-S 25-691-0704 (HQ)
CAREMED SERVICES INC
WE CARE HOME HEALTH SERVICES
1200 Markham Rd Suite 220, Scarborough, ON, M1H 3C3
(416) 438-4577
Emp Here 110   *Sales* 9,272,770
SIC 8082 Home health care services
Richard Pillsworth
Judith Pillsworth

D-U-N-S 24-242-3395 (HQ)
CHASE PAYMENTECH SOLUTIONS
100 Consilium Pl Suite 1400, Scarborough, ON, M1H 3E3
(416) 940-6300
Sales 133,781,600
SIC 7389 Business services, nec
Sam Jawad

D-U-N-S 24-285-9387 (HQ)
CIGNA LIFE INSURANCE COMPANY OF CANADA
(*Suby of* CIGNA CORPORATION)
100 Consilium Pl Suite 301, Scarborough, ON, M1H 3E3
(416) 290-6666
Sales 12,418,572
SIC 6321 Accident and health insurance
Eman Hassan

D-U-N-S 24-376-5513 (SL)
DECOR STRUCTURES CORP
SUMMERWOOD PRODUCTS
735 Progress Ave, Scarborough, ON, M1H

2W7
(416) 498-9379
Emp Here 25   *Sales* 18,563,000
SIC 5191 Farm supplies
Peter Harvey

D-U-N-S 25-500-6116   (HQ)
FIRST FINANCIAL UNDERWRITING SERVICES INC
111 Grangeway Ave Suite 300, Scarborough, ON, M1H 3E9
(416) 750-7388
Emp Here 25   *Sales* 21,248,280
SIC 6211 Security brokers and dealers
Ali Jalali

D-U-N-S 25-704-4305   (SL)
FOX, JOHN A LTD
CANADIAN TIRE
3553 Lawrence Ave E, Scarborough, ON, M1H 1B2
(416) 431-3888
Emp Here 40   *Sales* 19,923,120
SIC 5531 Auto and home supply stores
John A Fox

D-U-N-S 25-624-2926   (SL)
GREEN LIGHT COURIER INC
705 Progress Ave Suite 26, Scarborough, ON, M1H 2X1

Emp Here 30   *Sales* 13,304,700
SIC 7389 Business services, nec
Scott Cluett

D-U-N-S 25-227-0236   (SL)
GROWING TYKES CHILD CARE
GROWING TYKES LEARNING CENTRE
910 Markham Rd, Scarborough, ON, M1H 2Y2
(416) 438-4088
Emp Here 85   *Sales* 5,190,865
SIC 8351 Child day care services
Cecelia Cianflocca

D-U-N-S 20-552-0588   (HQ)
HAKIM OPTICAL LABORATORY LIMITED
HAKIM OPTICAL FACTORY OUTLET
3430 Lawrence Ave E, Scarborough, ON, M1H 1A9
(416) 439-3416
Emp Here 60   *Sales* 119,299,050
SIC 5995 Optical goods stores
Karim Hakim
Ricu Haras

D-U-N-S 20-008-7703   (SL)
INNOVATIVE DETAILING SERVICES INC
695 Markham Rd Suite 29, Scarborough, ON, M1H 2A5
(416) 438-6004
Emp Here 28   *Sales* 12,417,720
SIC 7389 Business services, nec
Jay Finna

D-U-N-S 24-326-9581   (SL)
IP, JERRY PHARMACY INC
SHOPPERS DRUG MART
1235 Mccowan Rd, Scarborough, ON, M1H 3K3
(416) 412-1353
Emp Here 45   *Sales* 11,382,930
SIC 5912 Drug stores and proprietary stores
Jerry Ip

D-U-N-S 25-272-8589   (BR)
KEG RESTAURANTS LTD
KEG STEAKHOUSE & BAR, THE
(*Suby of* RECIPE UNLIMITED CORPORATION)
60 Estate Dr, Scarborough, ON, M1H 2Z1
(416) 438-1452
Emp Here 100
SIC 5812 Eating places
Lynn Forbes

D-U-N-S 25-944-3349   (BR)
LOBLAWS SUPERMARKETS LIMITED
LOBLAWS NO 105

(*Suby of* LOBLAW COMPANIES LIMITED)
3401 Lawrence Ave E, Scarborough, ON, M1H 1B2
(416) 438-4392
Emp Here 450
SIC 5411 Grocery stores
Dave Ali

D-U-N-S 20-878-5956   (SL)
MARCHANT'S SCHOOL SPORT LIMITED
849 Progress Ave, Scarborough, ON, M1H 2X4
(416) 439-9400
Emp Here 30   *Sales* 15,616,260
SIC 5091 Sporting and recreation goods
Bruce Marchant
Mary Marchant
Darryl Marchant

D-U-N-S 24-242-3317   (HQ)
OMRON CANADA INC
(*Suby of* OMRON CORPORATION)
100 Consilium Pl Suite 802, Scarborough, ON, M1H 3E3
(416) 986-6766
Emp Here 70   *Sales* 78,333,345
SIC 5065 Electronic parts and equipment, nec
Ted Butson
Arthur Kitamura
John A Abraham
J Mark Stinson
Deepak Sharma

D-U-N-S 24-383-1315   (SL)
OMRON ELECTRONIC COMPONENTS CANADA, INC
(*Suby of* OMRON CORPORATION)
100 Consilium Pl Suite 802, Scarborough, ON, M1H 3E3
(416) 286-6465
Emp Here 50   *Sales* 22,358,700
SIC 5065 Electronic parts and equipment, nec
Michael Snow
Ron Gee

D-U-N-S 25-978-9378   (SL)
RIO TEXTILES EXPORTERS LTD
1840 Ellesmere Rd, Scarborough, ON, M1H 2V5

Emp Here 60   *Sales* 14,659,680
SIC 5932 Used merchandise stores
Noordin Nanji
Karim Nanji
Zulficar Nanji
Khatoon Nanji

D-U-N-S 20-323-1212   (HQ)
SCARBOROUGH CENTRE FOR HEALTHY COMMUNITIES
629 Markham Rd Unit 2, Scarborough, ON, M1H 2A4
(416) 642-9445
Emp Here 1   *Sales* 10,835,822
SIC 8011 Offices and clinics of medical doctors
Jeanie Joaquin
Vincent Correia
Melisse Willems
Rachna Chaudhary
Hugh Hasan

D-U-N-S 24-351-0844   (SL)
SIMPRO SOLUTIONS INC
100 Consilium Pl Unit 601, Scarborough, ON, M1H 3E3
(416) 915-9571
Emp Here 300   *Sales* 200,672,400
SIC 7389 Business services, nec
Andy Jasuja
Tony Nadra

D-U-N-S 20-007-9601   (HQ)
TELE-MOBILE COMPANY
TELUS MOBILITY
200 Consilium Pl Suite 1600, Scarborough, ON, M1H 3J3

(800) 308-5992
Emp Here 500   *Sales* 1,672,720,000
SIC 4899 Communication services, nec
Darren Entwistle

D-U-N-S 20-025-2893   (BR)
TORONTO DISTRICT SCHOOL BOARD
CEDARBRAE COLLEGIATE INSTITUTE
(*Suby of* TORONTO DISTRICT SCHOOL BOARD)
550 Markham Rd, Scarborough, ON, M1H 2A2
(416) 396-4400
Emp Here 120
SIC 8211 Elementary and secondary schools
Jinah Park

D-U-N-S 20-704-6228   (HQ)
TOYOTA CANADA INC
(*Suby of* TOYOTA MOTOR CORPORATION)
1 Toyota Pl, Scarborough, ON, M1H 1H9
(416) 438-6320
Emp Here 425   *Sales* 345,865,500
SIC 5012 Automobiles and other motor vehicles
Larry Hutchinson
Donald Campbell
Larry Baldesarra
Tetsuo Komuro
Real Tanguay

D-U-N-S 24-126-6845   (HQ)
VIMY RIDGE GROUP LTD, THE
NUCRO-TECHNICS
2000 Ellesmere Rd Unit 16, Scarborough, ON, M1H 2W4
(416) 438-6727
Emp Here 140   *Sales* 34,463,100
SIC 8731 Commercial physical research
John Fanaras
Constantine Fanaras

Scarborough, ON M1J

D-U-N-S 24-011-4160   (BR)
CANADA TORONTO EAST MISSION
(*Suby of* CORPORATION OF THE PRESIDENT OF THE CHURCH OF JESUS CHRIST OF LATTER-DAY SAINTS)
30 Seminole Ave, Scarborough, ON, M1J 1N1

Emp Here 200
SIC 8661 Religious organizations
Tad R Callister

D-U-N-S 20-730-5475   (SL)
EASTWAY CHRYSLER DODGE JEEP LTD
2851 Eglinton Ave E, Scarborough, ON, M1J 2E2
(416) 264-2501
Emp Here 40   *Sales* 19,923,120
SIC 5511 New and used car dealers

D-U-N-S 25-171-5488   (BR)
HOME DEPOT OF CANADA INC
HOME DEPOT
(*Suby of* THE HOME DEPOT INC)
2911 Eglinton Ave E, Scarborough, ON, M1J 2E5
(416) 289-2500
Emp Here 150
SIC 5231 Paint, glass, and wallpaper stores
Emmanuel Espenida

D-U-N-S 24-572-9293   (SL)
KODICOM CANADA
2811 Eglinton Ave E, Scarborough, ON, M1J 2E1
(416) 261-2266
Emp Here 40   *Sales* 17,886,960
SIC 5063 Electrical apparatus and equipment
Karen Ryu

D-U-N-S 24-756-8017   (SL)
LAU, REGINALD DRUGS LTD

SHOPPERS DRUG MART #501
685 Mccowan Rd, Scarborough, ON, M1J 1K2
(416) 431-4822
Emp Here 40   *Sales* 10,118,160
SIC 5912 Drug stores and proprietary stores
Reginald Lau

D-U-N-S 24-380-0930   (BR)
LOBLAWS INC
REAL CANADIAN SUPERSTORE
(*Suby of* LOBLAW COMPANIES LIMITED)
755 Brimley Rd, Scarborough, ON, M1J 1C5
(416) 279-0802
Emp Here 75
SIC 5411 Grocery stores
Julka Copovic

D-U-N-S 25-300-2737   (BR)
METRO ONTARIO INC
METRO
(*Suby of* METRO INC)
3221 Eglinton Ave E, Scarborough, ON, M1J 2H7
(416) 261-4204
Emp Here 300
SIC 5411 Grocery stores
Kurt Spears

D-U-N-S 20-410-5191   (SL)
STARR, MARVIN PONTIAC BUICK CADILLAC INC
(*Suby of* MSPB INVESTMENTS LIMITED)
3132 Eglinton Ave E, Scarborough, ON, M1J 2H1

Emp Here 100
SIC 5511 New and used car dealers
Marvin Starr
Nick Basaliga

D-U-N-S 20-025-0285   (BR)
TORONTO DISTRICT SCHOOL BOARD
CEDAR DRIVE JUNIOR PUBLIC SCHOOL
(*Suby of* TORONTO DISTRICT SCHOOL BOARD)
21 Gatesview Ave, Scarborough, ON, M1J 3G4
(416) 396-6120
Emp Here 80
SIC 8211 Elementary and secondary schools
Lana Cumberbatch

Scarborough, ON M1K

D-U-N-S 25-695-5717   (SL)
1137283 ONTARIO LTD
SCARBOROUGH KIA
2594 Eglinton Ave E Suite 2592, Scarborough, ON, M1K 2R5
(416) 266-4594
Emp Here 25   *Sales* 12,451,950
SIC 5511 New and used car dealers
Carmen Vigliatore
Frank Vigliatore
Peter Romer

D-U-N-S 24-183-5453   (SL)
CARMEN & FRANKS GARAGE LTD
SCARBOROUGH SUBARU AND SUZUKI
2584 Eglinton Ave E, Scarborough, ON, M1K 2R5
(416) 261-7219
Emp Here 30   *Sales* 14,942,340
SIC 5511 New and used car dealers
Carmen Vigliatore
Frank Vigliatore

D-U-N-S 25-209-0675   (SL)
ELITE CONCEPTS INC
1079 Midland Ave, Scarborough, ON, M1K 4G7
(416) 827-3007
Emp Here 41   *Sales* 18,334,134
SIC 5046 Commercial equipment, nec
Phil Chu

▲ Public Company   ■ Public Company Family Member   **HQ** Headquarters   **BR** Branch   **SL** Single Location

D-U-N-S 25-513-8190   (SL)
ELIZABETH GRANT INTERNATIONAL INC
381 Kennedy Rd, Scarborough, ON, M1K 2A1
(877) 751-1999
Emp Here 30   *Sales* 33,160,350
SIC 5122 Drugs, proprietaries, and sundries
Marion Witz

D-U-N-S 20-983-8879   (SL)
HOME LUMBER INC
(*Suby of* ALPA LUMBER INC)
714 Birchmount Rd, Scarborough, ON, M1K 1R4
(416) 759-4441
Emp Here 60   *Sales* 16,059,120
SIC 5251 Hardware stores
John Di Poce
Donald A Maciver
George Frankfort
Giovanni Guglietti
Carmen Guglietti

D-U-N-S 20-178-0009   (SL)
I3 INTERNATIONAL INC
I3DVR INTERNATIONAL
(*Suby of* 3826058 CANADA INC)
780 Birchmount Rd Unit 16, Scarborough, ON, M1K 5H4
(416) 261-2266
Emp Here 61   *Sales* 11,616,962
SIC 3699 Electrical equipment and supplies, nec
Jack Hoang
Bob Hoang
Grace Baba
Vy Hoang

D-U-N-S 20-655-8996   (SL)
MID-SCARBOROUGH   COMMUNITY RECREATION CENTER
2467 Eglinton Ave E, Scarborough, ON, M1K 2R1
(416) 267-0714
Emp Here 150   *Sales* 14,242,950
SIC 7999 Amusement and recreation, nec
Mark Latremouille

D-U-N-S 20-524-3582   (SL)
PAYMENTECH CANADA DEBIT, INC
(*Suby of* JPMORGAN CHASE & CO.)
888 Birchmount Rd Suite 7, Scarborough, ON, M1K 5L1
(416) 288-3027
Emp Here 200   *Sales* 284,627,600
SIC 6211 Security brokers and dealers
Drew Brown

D-U-N-S 20-166-8605   (SL)
PRINTLINX CORPORATION
POSTLINX
(*Suby of* PITNEY BOWES INC.)
1170 Birchmount Rd Suite 1, Scarborough, ON, M1K 5M1
(416) 752-8100
Emp Here 120   *Sales* 24,044,520
SIC 7331 Direct mail advertising services
Greg Mackenzie
Michael Price
Jeff Mackinnon

D-U-N-S 20-940-0571   (SL)
SPARK AUTO ELECTRIC CO LTD
401 Birchmount Rd, Scarborough, ON, M1K 1N3
(416) 690-3133
Emp Here 40   *Sales* 14,568,600
SIC 5013 Motor vehicle supplies and new parts
Stavros Bintas
Peter Bintas

D-U-N-S 24-663-1477   (SL)
SUN VALLEY SUPERMARKET INCORPORATED
468 Danforth Rd, Scarborough, ON, M1K 1C6
(416) 264-2323
Emp Here 48   *Sales* 13,159,296
SIC 5411 Grocery stores

Gerry Aravantinos
Steve Aravantinos

D-U-N-S 25-332-6656   (SL)
TUBULAR STEEL INC
285 Raleigh Ave, Scarborough, ON, M1K 1A5
(416) 261-2089
Emp Here 150   *Sales* 89,618,100
SIC 5051 Metals service centers and offices
Robert D Mckinnon

Scarborough, ON M1L

D-U-N-S 25-695-6293   (SL)
1216809 ONTARIO LIMITED
SCARBOROUGH TOYOTA NATCO LEASING
1897 Eglinton Ave E, Scarborough, ON, M1L 2L6
(416) 751-4892
Emp Here 150   *Sales* 94,392,000
SIC 5511 New and used car dealers
Gerry Macdonald

D-U-N-S 20-708-7920   (SL)
1992013 ONTARIO LTD
ALI'S NO FRILLS
1880 Eglinton Ave E, Scarborough, ON, M1L 2L1
(416) 750-4400
Emp Here 50   *Sales* 13,707,600
SIC 5411 Grocery stores
Ron Dickie
Denise Dickie

D-U-N-S 20-275-3513   (HQ)
8956642 CANADA CORP
FV FOODS
757 Warden Ave Unit 4, Scarborough, ON, M1L 4B5
(416) 759-2000
Emp Here 40   *Sales* 11,242,750
SIC 2051 Bread, cake, and related products
Allan Ocampo

D-U-N-S 20-771-1508   (HQ)
AVIVA   INSURANCE   COMPANY   OF CANADA
(*Suby of* GENERAL ACCIDENT PLC)
2206 Eglinton Ave E Suite 160, Scarborough, ON, M1L 4S8
(416) 288-1800
Emp Here 20   *Sales* 123,541,800
SIC 6331 Fire, marine, and casualty insurance
Igal Mayer
A Warren Moysey
Brian W Barr
J Charles Caty
James D. Hewitt
Ross Betteridge
Robert M Fitzgerald
Gregory Somerville
Robin Spencer
Gillian Platt

D-U-N-S 20-846-3935   (SL)
BROADVIEW FOUNDATION
CHESTER VILLAGE
3555 Danforth Ave, Scarborough, ON, M1L 1E3
(416) 466-2173
Emp Here 218   *Sales* 14,013,476
SIC 8361 Residential care
Warren Brown
Alan Dorman

D-U-N-S 24-988-0621   (SL)
CALADO AND LIMA HOME IMPROVEMENT INC
15 Mansion Ave, Scarborough, ON, M1L 1A5
(416) 782-0110
Emp Here 34   *Sales* 10,841,546
SIC 1521 Single-family housing construction
Sonia Lima

D-U-N-S 24-049-9426   (SL)

CANADIAN KAWASAKI MOTORS INC
(*Suby of* KAWASAKI HEAVY INDUSTRIES, LTD.)
101 Thermos Rd, Scarborough, ON, M1L 4W8
(416) 445-7775
Emp Here 50   *Sales* 18,210,750
SIC 5012 Automobiles and other motor vehicles
Goro Takahashi
Pat Chambers
Stephen Pike
Shinichi Juri

D-U-N-S 24-610-7882   (SL)
CHANDLER, DEAN ROOFING LIMITED
275 Comstock Rd, Scarborough, ON, M1L 2H2
(416) 751-7840
Emp Here 60   *Sales* 13,069,740
SIC 1761 Roofing, siding, and sheetMetal work
Kenneth Goodale

D-U-N-S 25-508-0491   (SL)
COSMETICA LABORATORIES INC
1960 Eglinton Ave E, Scarborough, ON, M1L 2M5
(416) 615-2400
Emp Here 500   *Sales* 222,322,500
SIC 2844 Toilet preparations
Michael Kehoe
Marlene Oilgisser
Rob Murray
Douglas Bradley
Howard Rimerman
Robyn Sacks

D-U-N-S 24-124-6875   (SL)
DONWAY FORD SALES LIMITED
DONWAY LEASING
(*Suby of* METROPOLITAN MOTORS LIMITED)
1975 Eglinton Ave E, Scarborough, ON, M1L 2N1
(416) 751-2200
Emp Here 90   *Sales* 56,635,200
SIC 5511 New and used car dealers

D-U-N-S 25-139-0613   (SL)
ELLAS BANQUET HALL AND CONFERENCE CENTRE LTD
35 Danforth Rd, Scarborough, ON, M1L 3W5

Emp Here 300   *Sales* 26,908,800
SIC 7299 Miscellaneous personal service
Anastasios Dimacopoulos
Elizabeth Diamcopolous

D-U-N-S 24-952-4166   (SL)
FPC FLEXIBLE PACKAGING CORPORATION
(*Suby of* JACOBSON PARTNERS, L.P.)
1891 Eglinton Ave E, Scarborough, ON, M1L 2L7
(416) 288-3060
Emp Here 125   *Sales* 24,346,000
SIC 2671 Paper; coated and laminated packaging
Donald Iwacha
Bernard Matte
John Avery
Raj Thangavelu

D-U-N-S 24-892-6172   (BR)
G&K SERVICES CANADA INC
(*Suby of* CINTAS CORPORATION)
940 Warden Ave Suite 1, Scarborough, ON, M1L 4C9
(647) 933-2627
Emp Here 150
SIC 2326 Men's and boy's work clothing
Christopher Macdonald

D-U-N-S 20-151-1789   (HQ)
GRIFFITH FOODS LIMITED
(*Suby of* GRIFFITH FOODS GROUP INC.)
757 Pharmacy Ave, Scarborough, ON, M1L 3J8

(416) 288-3050
Emp Here 300   *Sales* 170,584,750
SIC 2099 Food preparations, nec
Brian Griffith
Tc Chatterjee
Matt West
Jennifer Convery
Stelios Paschalidis
Oscar Lizarazu
Eugenio Torres
Dhiren Kanwar

D-U-N-S 20-172-7252   (HQ)
HILLMAN GROUP CANADA ULC, THE
HILLMAN CANADA
55 Milne Ave, Scarborough, ON, M1L 4N3
(416) 694-3351
Emp Here 200   *Sales* 145,938,600
SIC 3452 Bolts, nuts, rivets, and washers
Scott Ride
Douglas D. Roberts
Michael Costello

D-U-N-S 25-301-1613   (BR)
HUDSON'S BAY COMPANY
BAY, THE
(*Suby of* HUDSON'S BAY COMPANY)
1 Eglinton Sq, Scarborough, ON, M1L 2K1
(416) 759-4771
Emp Here 300
SIC 5311 Department stores
Mike Hickling

D-U-N-S 20-923-3766   (SL)
INA GRAFTON GAGE HOME OF TORONTO
IGGH
40 Bell Estate Rd Suite 402, Scarborough, ON, M1L 0E2
(416) 422-4890
Emp Here 105   *Sales* 13,101,480
SIC 8741 Management services
Charles Hain
Denise Bedard-Eldridge
Bharat Kalra

D-U-N-S 20-554-8084   (BR)
IPEX INC
IPEX MANAGEMENT
(*Suby of* ALIAXIS)
807 Pharmacy Ave, Scarborough, ON, M1L 3K2
(416) 445-3400
Emp Here 77
SIC 3088 Plastics plumbing fixtures
Kyle Beazley

D-U-N-S 20-903-4339   (SL)
JOHN BEAD CORPORATION LIMITED
20 Bertrand Ave, Scarborough, ON, M1L 2P4
(416) 757-3287
Emp Here 48   *Sales* 24,986,016
SIC 5092 Toys and hobby goods and supplies
Michael John
Joe Maio
Betty John

D-U-N-S 24-710-8264   (SL)
KINGSCROSS HYUNDAI MOTOR SPORTS INC
23 Civic Rd, Scarborough, ON, M1L 2K6
(416) 757-7700
Emp Here 40   *Sales* 19,923,120
SIC 5511 New and used car dealers
Maria Ho

D-U-N-S 24-923-8445   (SL)
KINGSCROSS MOTOR SPORTS INC
1957 Eglinton Ave E, Scarborough, ON, M1L 2M3
(416) 755-6283
Emp Here 40   *Sales* 19,923,120
SIC 5511 New and used car dealers
Thomas Cho

D-U-N-S 20-935-1386   (SL)
KRONOS FOODS LTD
371 Danforth Rd, Scarborough, ON, M1L 3X8

▲ Public Company   ■ Public Company Family Member   **HQ** Headquarters   **BR** Branch   **SL** Single Location

(416) 690-1990
Emp Here 38   *Sales* 31,751,926
SIC 5141 Groceries, general line
Jim Panagiotopoulos
Andy Panagiotopoulos
Chris Panagiotopoulos

D-U-N-S 24-522-5250   (SL)
LAMBDA THERAPEUTIC RESEARCH INC
LAMBDA CANADA
(*Suby of* LAMBDA THERAPEUTIC RE-SEARCH LIMITED)
460 Comstock Rd, Scarborough, ON, M1L 4S4
(416) 752-3636
Emp Here 105   *Sales* 23,094,015
SIC 8732 Commercial nonphysical research
Saleh Hussain
Mohammed Hussain
Imran Ahmad

D-U-N-S 24-391-7973   (SL)
LEROUX, K. D. SALES LTD
CANADIAN TIRE
1901 Eglinton Ave E, Scarborough, ON, M1L 2L8
(416) 615-2666
Emp Here 70   *Sales* 44,049,600
SIC 5531 Auto and home supply stores
Pamela Leroux

D-U-N-S 20-700-9267   (HQ)
MARSAN FOODS LIMITED
160 Thermos Rd, Scarborough, ON, M1L 4W2
(416) 755-9262
Sales 34,569,000
SIC 2038 Frozen specialties, nec
Graeme Jewett
James Jewett
Kenneth Jewett

D-U-N-S 25-310-8971   (BR)
MCDONALD'S RESTAURANTS OF CANADA LIMITED
MCDONALDS
(*Suby of* MCDONALD'S CORPORATION)
3150 St Clair Ave E, Scarborough, ON, M1L 1V6
(416) 751-9014
Emp Here 94
SIC 5812 Eating places
Rob Marshella

D-U-N-S 25-212-7279   (SL)
METRO PAPER INDUSTRIES INC
MPI PAPER MILLS
111 Manville Rd, Scarborough, ON, M1L 4J2
(416) 757-2737
Emp Here 106   *Sales* 20,645,408
SIC 2676 Sanitary paper products
Karim Jadavji
Amin Jadavji

D-U-N-S 20-227-3462   (HQ)
MIBRO PARTNERS
MIBRO GROUP, THE
111 Sinnott Rd, Scarborough, ON, M1L 4S6
(416) 285-9000
Emp Here 75   *Sales* 69,006,600
SIC 5072 Hardware
Bill Condie
Leon Lapidus

D-U-N-S 25-531-7067   (HQ)
OAK LEAF CONFECTIONS CO.
(*Suby of* MIGROS-GENOSSENSCHAFTS-BUND)
440 Comstock Rd, Scarborough, ON, M1L 2H6
(416) 751-0740
Sales 112,098,550
SIC 2064 Candy and other confectionery products
Philip Terranova

D-U-N-S 20-151-8420   (HQ)
PAISLEY PRODUCTS OF CANADA INCORPORATED

40 Upton Rd, Scarborough, ON, M1L 2B9
(416) 751-3700
Emp Here 31   *Sales* 17,886,960
SIC 5063 Electrical apparatus and equipment
Randolph Paisley
Andre Schonfeld
Ruth Paisley
Marlon Paisley

D-U-N-S 25-810-0452   (SL)
PLUMBERS AND STEAMFITTERS UNION LOCAL 46
UNITED ASSOCIATION LOCAL 46
936 Warden Ave Suite 46, Scarborough, ON, M1L 4C9
(416) 759-6791
Emp Here 30   *Sales* 11,734,740
SIC 8631 Labor organizations
Joesepth Dimaso

D-U-N-S 25-084-5534   (BR)
PRIME RESTAURANTS INC
EAST SIDE MARIO'S
(*Suby of* RECIPE UNLIMITED CORPORA-TION)
12 Lebovic Ave Suite 9, Scarborough, ON, M1L 4V9
(416) 285-6631
Emp Here 75
SIC 5812 Eating places
John Deluca

D-U-N-S 20-114-2838   (HQ)
PROLOGIX DISTRIBUTION SERVICES
120 Sinnott Rd, Scarborough, ON, M1L 4N1
(416) 615-3064
Emp Here 250   *Sales* 212,097,240
SIC 5192 Books, periodicals, and newspapers
Mitch Massicotte

D-U-N-S 20-817-1827   (SL)
PROVIDENCE HEALTHCARE
3276 St Clair Ave E, Scarborough, ON, M1L 1W1
(416) 285-3666
Emp Here 1,150   *Sales* 683,100,922
SIC 8069 Specialty hospitals, except psychiatric
Josie Walsh
Gretchen Van Riesen
Virginia West
Jim Elliott
James Fox
Peter Nord
Sal Bevan
Maggie Bruneau
Joe Calderone
Alan Cheatley

D-U-N-S 20-159-0528   (HQ)
S. A. ARMSTRONG LIMITED
ARMSTRONG FLUID TECHNOLOGY
23 Bertrand Ave, Scarborough, ON, M1L 2P3
(416) 755-2291
Emp Here 100   *Sales* 561,754,000
SIC 3561 Pumps and pumping equipment
Charles Armstrong
James Armstrong
Lex Van Der Weerd

D-U-N-S 20-610-8599   (HQ)
SCARBOROUGH NISSAN (1989) LIMITED
1941 Eglinton Ave E, Scarborough, ON, M1L 2M4
(416) 751-3511
Sales 37,756,800
SIC 5511 New and used car dealers
Kenneth Yoo

D-U-N-S 24-285-4669   (SL)
SOLARFECTIVE PRODUCTS LIMITED
55 Hymus Rd, Scarborough, ON, M1L 2C6
(416) 421-3800
Emp Here 65   *Sales* 14,773,785
SIC 3861 Photographic equipment and supplies
Anise Odeh

D-U-N-S 20-165-2542   (SL)
SPECIALTIES GRAPHIC FINISHERS LTD
946 Warden Ave, Scarborough, ON, M1L 4C9
(416) 701-0111
Emp Here 126   *Sales* 20,667,402
SIC 2789 Bookbinding and related work
Norman Beange
Pauline Beange

D-U-N-S 25-475-9335   (HQ)
STARBOARD SEAFOOD (ONTARIO) INC
(*Suby of* FRUITS DE MER STARBOARD INC)
33 Upton Rd, Scarborough, ON, M1L 2C1
(416) 752-2828
Sales 16,711,540
SIC 5146 Fish and seafoods
Alfred Yan
Norman Yan
Peter Yan
Raymond Chan
Emil Yan

D-U-N-S 24-986-2293   (BR)
STOCK TRANSPORTATION LTD
(*Suby of* NATIONAL EXPRESS GROUP PLC)
17 Upton Rd, Scarborough, ON, M1L 2C1
(416) 754-4949
Emp Here 253
SIC 4151 School buses
Debbie Black

D-U-N-S 20-391-9290   (SL)
TIGER AUTO PARTS INC
117 Sinnott Rd, Scarborough, ON, M1L 4S6
(888) 664-6618
Emp Here 35   *Sales* 17,432,730
SIC 5531 Auto and home supply stores
Abdul Sakhi

D-U-N-S 24-462-7600   (SL)
TRADITION FINE FOODS LTD
663 Warden Ave, Scarborough, ON, M1L 3Z5
(416) 444-4777
Emp Here 150   *Sales* 73,107,750
SIC 2053 Frozen bakery products, except bread
Thomas Glowcewski
Peter Glowczewski
Danuta Glowczewski
Catherine Glowczewski

D-U-N-S 24-764-1004   (SL)
TRANS-CONTINENTAL TEXTILE EX-PORTERS INC
16 Upton Rd, Scarborough, ON, M1L 2B8
(416) 285-8951
Emp Here 65   *Sales* 32,390,930
SIC 5137 Women's and children's clothing
Shamshudin Rajani
Amin Rajani
Karima Rajani

D-U-N-S 24-434-0126   (HQ)
V.H. FUELS INC
PETRO CANADA
1896 Eglinton Ave E, Scarborough, ON, M1L 2L9
(416) 751-8896
Emp Here 1   *Sales* 14,942,340
SIC 5541 Gasoline service stations
Vikram Heer

D-U-N-S 25-498-2705   (BR)
WAL-MART CANADA CORP
(*Suby of* WALMART INC.)
800 Warden Ave, Scarborough, ON, M1L 4T7
(416) 615-2697
Emp Here 170
SIC 5311 Department stores
Mace Pickket

D-U-N-S 24-744-9218   (SL)
WESTBURY NATIONAL SHOW SYSTEMS LTD
772 Warden Ave, Scarborough, ON, M1L 4T7
(416) 752-1371
Emp Here 140   *Sales* 46,640,720

SIC 7359 Equipment rental and leasing, nec
David Bennett
Robert Sandolowich
Frank Gerstein

Scarborough, ON M1M

D-U-N-S 20-973-7642   (SL)
CHARLIE'S MEAT & SEAFOOD SUPPLY LTD
61 Skagway Ave, Scarborough, ON, M1M 3T9
(416) 261-1312
Emp Here 65   *Sales* 54,312,505
SIC 5147 Meats and meat products
Jim Cheung

D-U-N-S 20-151-2456   (SL)
HERITAGE FORD SALES LIMITED
HERITAGE AUTO LEASING, DIV OF
2660 Kingston Rd, Scarborough, ON, M1M 1L6
(416) 261-3311
Emp Here 70   *Sales* 44,049,600
SIC 5511 New and used car dealers
Earl Bleeks
Greg Bleeks

D-U-N-S 24-720-9281   (SL)
INTELLIGARDE INTERNATIONAL INC
3090 Kingston Rd Suite 400, Scarborough, ON, M1M 1P2
(416) 760-0000
Emp Here 130   *Sales* 3,412,500
SIC 7381 Detective and armored car services
Ross Mcleod

D-U-N-S 25-365-0931   (SL)
JCS NURSING & HOME CARE SERVICES INC
3464 Kingston Rd Suite 207a, Scarborough, ON, M1M 1R5
(416) 265-1687
Emp Here 50   *Sales* 14,164,650
SIC 8741 Management services
Lyra Joy Tupas

D-U-N-S 20-106-4826   (BR)
NIKE CANADA CORP
(*Suby of* NIKE, INC.)
260 Brimley Rd, Scarborough, ON, M1M 3H8
(416) 264-8505
Emp Here 250
SIC 5091 Sporting and recreation goods
Bill Strong

D-U-N-S 20-079-2583   (BR)
TORONTO CATHOLIC DISTRICT SCHOOL BOARD
BLESSED CARDINAL NEWMAN SEC-ONDARY SCHOOL
(*Suby of* TORONTO CATHOLIC DISTRICT SCHOOL BOARD)
100 Brimley Rd S, Scarborough, ON, M1M 3X4
(416) 393-5519
Emp Here 100
SIC 8211 Elementary and secondary schools
Joan Tschernow

D-U-N-S 20-025-2943   (BR)
TORONTO DISTRICT SCHOOL BOARD
R. H. KING ACADEMY
(*Suby of* TORONTO DISTRICT SCHOOL BOARD)
3800 St Clair Ave E, Scarborough, ON, M1M 1V3
(416) 396-5550
Emp Here 100
SIC 8211 Elementary and secondary schools
David Rowan

D-U-N-S 24-684-7966   (SL)
VERSATECH MECHANICAL LTD
50 Skagway Ave Suite A, Scarborough, ON, M1M 3V1

(416) 292-9220
Emp Here 50   *Sales* 11,046,700
SIC 1711 Plumbing, heating, air-conditioning
Peter Soknacki

Scarborough, ON M1N

D-U-N-S 25-722-6993   (SL)
1576610 ONTARIO LTD
ROD & JOE'S NO FRILLS
2471 Kingston Rd, Scarborough, ON, M1N
1V4
(416) 261-4569
Emp Here 49   *Sales* 13,433,448
SIC 5411 Grocery stores
Rod Muller

D-U-N-S 20-151-5491   (HQ)
ELI LILLY CANADA INC
(*Suby of* ELI LILLY AND COMPANY)
3650 Danforth Ave, Scarborough, ON, M1N
2E8
(416) 694-3221
Emp Here 400   *Sales* 132,637,600
SIC 2834 Pharmaceutical preparations
Lisa Elias Matar
Nicholas B. Lemen
Lauren Fischer
Karen Mckay
Doron Sagman

D-U-N-S 24-379-3143   (SL)
HEALTH TRANS SERVICES INC
HEALTH TRANS
104 Blantyre Ave, Scarborough, ON, M1N
2R5

Emp Here 80   *Sales* 11,855,360
SIC 4213 Trucking, except local
Michael Quinn

D-U-N-S 20-800-6085   (SL)
MIDLAND GARDENS INC
130 Midland Ave Suite 1006, Scarborough,
ON, M1N 4E6
(416) 264-2301
Emp Here 49   *Sales* 13,881,357
SIC 8741 Management services
Shawn Steele

Scarborough, ON M1P

D-U-N-S 25-274-8934   (SL)
1216037 ONTARIO INC
(*Suby of* SCEPTER HOLDINGS INC)
170 Midwest Rd, Scarborough, ON, M1P 3A9
(416) 751-9445
Emp Here 200   *Sales* 31,771,600
SIC 3089 Plastics products, nec
Perry Elliot

D-U-N-S 20-275-0311   (SL)
1905405 ONTARIO LIMITED
AT EAZE
300 Borough Dr Unit 267, Scarborough, ON,
M1P 4P5
(416) 290-6863
Emp Here 92   *Sales* 16,504,432
SIC 5651 Family clothing stores
Asad Halai
Feroz Halai
Shahnaz Halai
Asim Halai

D-U-N-S 20-974-3587   (BR)
2063414 ONTARIO LIMITED
LEISUREWORLD CAREGIVING CENTRE
1000 Ellesmere Rd Suite 333, Scarborough,
ON, M1P 5G2
(416) 291-0222
Emp Here 75
SIC 8051 Skilled nursing care facilities

Denise Brown

D-U-N-S 20-252-0003   (SL)
2281445 ONTARIO INC
NEW ORLEANS PIZZA
77 Progress Ave, Scarborough, ON, M1P 2Y7
(416) 288-8515
Emp Here 40   *Sales* 15,660,080
SIC 6794 Patent owners and lessors
Tom Michalopoulos

D-U-N-S 25-499-8073   (HQ)
2549204 ONTARIO INC
TIM HORTONS
1 William Kitchen Rd Suite 1, Scarborough,
ON, M1P 5B7
(416) 293-1010
Emp Here 35   *Sales* 17,608,620
SIC 5461 Retail bakeries
Mark Wafer

D-U-N-S 24-848-5633   (HQ)
ABCO MOVING SERVICES INC
ABCO OFFICE INSTALLATION
2480 Lawrence Ave E Suite 1, Scarborough,
ON, M1P 2R7
(416) 750-0118
Emp Here 42   *Sales* 11,078,370
SIC 1799 Special trade contractors, nec
Michael (Mike) Menzies

D-U-N-S 20-168-4537   (SL)
ABCORP CA LTD
AB NOTE NORTH AMERICA
(*Suby of* AMERICAN BANKNOTE CORPO-
RATION)
15 Golden Gate Crt, Scarborough, ON, M1P
3A4
(416) 293-3842
Emp Here 80   *Sales* 10,513,404
SIC 3089 Plastics products, nec
Wulfred Kronenberg
Eva Chan
James Simpson
David Koberd

D-U-N-S 24-507-3437   (HQ)
ACTIVE EXHAUST CORP
1865 Birchmount Rd, Scarborough, ON, M1P
2J5
(416) 445-9610
Sales 268,251,500
SIC 5084 Industrial machinery and equipment
Peter Hampton

D-U-N-S 24-726-9715   (SL)
ALLEN, CENTURY 21 WENDA REALTY LTD
2025 Midland Ave, Scarborough, ON, M1P
3E2
(416) 293-3900
Emp Here 35   *Sales* 11,449,445
SIC 6531 Real estate agents and managers
Wenda Allen

D-U-N-S 24-095-0824   (SL)
ALLIED-HALO INDUSTRIES INC
345 Nantucket Blvd, Scarborough, ON, M1P
2P2
(416) 751-2042
Emp Here 65   *Sales* 15,173,275
SIC 2673 Bags: plastic, laminated, and
coated
Hershey Friedman
June Deleon

D-U-N-S 20-818-5850   (HQ)
AMHERST CONCRETE PUMPING LIMITED
105 Nantucket Blvd, Scarborough, ON, M1P
2N5
(416) 752-2431
Emp Here 10   *Sales* 12,374,150
SIC 1771 Concrete work
David Welstead
Valerie Brennan
Terence Welstead
Jonathan Welstead

D-U-N-S 20-150-2978   (HQ)

AMHERST CRANE RENTALS LIMITED
105 Nantucket Blvd, Scarborough, ON, M1P
2N5
(416) 752-2602
Sales 19,135,400
SIC 7359 Equipment rental and leasing, nec
Jonathan Welstead

D-U-N-S 24-388-4483   (HQ)
ARRAY CANADA INC
ARRAY MARKETING
45 Progress Ave, Scarborough, ON, M1P 2Y6
(416) 299-4865
Emp Here 100   *Sales* 211,654,400
SIC 3993 Signs and advertising specialties
Thomas Hendren
Kevin Pattrick

D-U-N-S 20-544-0808   (BR)
ATLANTIC PACKAGING PRODUCTS LTD
(*Suby of* ATLANTIC PACKAGING PROD-
UCTS LTD)
111 Progress Ave, Scarborough, ON, M1P
2Y9
(416) 298-5456
Emp Here 200
SIC 2679 Converted paper products, nec

D-U-N-S 24-309-4229   (HQ)
ATLANTIC PACKAGING PRODUCTS LTD
FLEXIBLE PACKAGING, DIV OF
111 Progress Ave, Scarborough, ON, M1P
2Y9
(416) 298-8101
Emp Here 200   *Sales* 882,328,800
SIC 2679 Converted paper products, nec
Irving Granovsky
John Cherry
Dave Boles
Bob Hagan
Paul Doyle

D-U-N-S 20-214-6879   (SL)
AUTOMOTIVE WHOLESALE INC
TORONTO AUTO GROUP, DIV OF
2380 Lawrence Ave E, Scarborough, ON, M1P
2R5
(416) 285-6363
Emp Here 40   *Sales* 19,923,120
SIC 5511 New and used car dealers
Anil Puri

D-U-N-S 24-060-5642   (HQ)
BEDESSEE IMPORTS LTD
2 Golden Gate Crt, Scarborough, ON, M1P
3A5
(416) 292-2400
Sales 25,067,310
SIC 5142 Packaged frozen goods
Lionel Bedessee
Rayman Bedessee

D-U-N-S 24-213-3445   (SL)
BEL VOLT SALES LIMITED
1350 Birchmount Rd, Scarborough, ON, M1P
2E4
(416) 757-2277
Emp Here 25   *Sales* 11,179,350
SIC 5063 Electrical apparatus and equipment
Tony Cocco

D-U-N-S 20-815-9392   (SL)
BERG CHILLING SYSTEMS INC
51 Nantucket Blvd, Scarborough, ON, M1P
2N5
(416) 755-2221
Emp Here 100   *Sales* 22,200,100
SIC 3585 Refrigeration and heating equipment
Donald Berggren

D-U-N-S 25-371-1717   (BR)
BEST BUY CANADA LTD
BEST BUY
(*Suby of* BEST BUY CO., INC.)
480 Progress Ave, Scarborough, ON, M1P
5J1
(416) 296-7020
Emp Here 170

SIC 5731 Radio, television, and electronic
stores
Nick Hill

D-U-N-S 20-409-4643   (BR)
BRICK WAREHOUSE LP, THE
(*Suby of* BRICK WAREHOUSE LP, THE)
19 William Kitchen Rd, Scarborough, ON,
M1P 5B7
(416) 751-3383
Emp Here 80
SIC 5712 Furniture stores
John Macdonald

D-U-N-S 24-248-1500   (SL)
CABLESHOPPE INC, THE
CSI
1410 Birchmount Rd, Scarborough, ON, M1P
2E3
(416) 293-3634
Emp Here 125   *Sales* 27,228,625
SIC 1731 Electrical work
Monte Muphulingam

D-U-N-S 20-161-0524   (SL)
**CAMERON ADVERTISING DISPLAYS LIM-
ITED**
CAMAD
12 Nantucket Blvd, Scarborough, ON, M1P
2N4
(416) 752-7220
Emp Here 60   *Sales* 12,703,440
SIC 7319 Advertising, nec
Robert Deveau
Daniel Deveau

D-U-N-S 25-120-6512   (BR)
CANADA POST CORPORATION
SCARBOROUGH STATION D
(*Suby of* GOVERNMENT OF CANADA)
280 Progress Ave, Scarborough, ON, M1P
5H8
(416) 299-4577
Emp Here 500
SIC 4311 U.s. postal service
George Duguay

D-U-N-S 24-830-5950   (SL)
CANADA TAXES
TORONTO EAST TAX SERVICES OFFICE
200 Town Centre Crt Suite 475, Scarborough,
ON, M1P 4Y3
(800) 267-6999
Emp Here 49   *Sales* 22,011,731
SIC 7389 Business services, nec
Don Alton

D-U-N-S 25-531-1516   (HQ)
CHAIRMAN'S BRAND CORPORATION
COFFEE TIME
77 Progress Ave, Scarborough, ON, M1P 2Y7
(416) 288-8515
Emp Here 50   *Sales* 154,866,600
SIC 6794 Patent owners and lessors
Anastasios Michalopoulos
Steven Michalopoulos

D-U-N-S 25-403-2717   (SL)
CIRCUIT CENTER INC
175 Midwest Rd, Scarborough, ON, M1P 3A6
(416) 285-5550
Emp Here 70   *Sales* 13,330,940
SIC 3672 Printed circuit boards
Reza Javdan

D-U-N-S 24-860-0397   (SL)
CITIGUARD SECURITY SERVICES INC
1560 Brimley Rd Suite 201, Scarborough, ON,
M1P 3G9
(416) 431-6888
Emp Here 150   *Sales* 3,937,500
SIC 7381 Detective and armored car services
Steve Bosovski

D-U-N-S 24-844-2360   (HQ)
CLIFFORD MASONRY (ONTARIO) LIMITED
1190 Birchmount Rd, Scarborough, ON, M1P
2B8

---

(416) 691-2341
Sales 57,033,800
SIC 1542 Nonresidential construction, nec
Sam Trigila
Tony Serafico
Phil Puype

D-U-N-S 24-992-2279   (SL)
CLIFFORD RESTORATION LIMITED
(*Suby of* CLIFFORD MASONRY (ONTARIO) LIMITED)
1190 Birchmount Rd, Scarborough, ON, M1P 2B8
(416) 691-2341
Emp Here 40   *Sales* 22,813,520
SIC 1542 Nonresidential construction, nec
Sam Trigila
Tony Serafico
Phil Puype

D-U-N-S 24-911-6633   (HQ)
COFFEE TIME DONUTS INCORPORATED
COFFEE TIME
(*Suby of* CHAIRMAN'S BRAND CORPORATION)
77 Progress Ave, Scarborough, ON, M1P 2Y7
(416) 288-8515
Sales 20,904,300
SIC 6794 Patent owners and lessors
Anastasios (Tom) Michalopoulos

D-U-N-S 25-312-6072   (SL)
CONCORD COORDINATES INC
2220 Midland Ave Unit 21 23, Scarborough, ON, M1P 3E6

Emp Here 50   *Sales* 24,916,100
SIC 5136 Men's and boy's clothing
Peter Kwan
Anna Kwan

D-U-N-S 20-771-4569   (HQ)
COVER-ALL COMPUTER SERVICES CORP
1170 Birchmount Rd, Scarborough, ON, M1P 5E3
(416) 752-8100
Emp Here 60   *Sales* 21,690,110
SIC 7372 Prepackaged software
Mike Coverdale
James Coverdale
Jim Meighan

D-U-N-S 24-860-4530   (SL)
DOM INTERNATIONAL LIMITED
10 Golden Gate Crt, Scarborough, ON, M1P 3A5
(416) 265-3993
Emp Here 50   *Sales* 41,778,850
SIC 5146 Fish and seafoods
Domenic Porporo
Mario Porporo

D-U-N-S 20-641-6562   (SL)
ECON-O-PAC LIMITED
490 Midwest Rd, Scarborough, ON, M1P 3A9
(416) 750-7200
Emp Here 175   *Sales* 117,058,900
SIC 7389 Business services, nec
Howard Nisenbaum
Elliott Warsh
Irving Walsh
Nathan Hartley
Norman Scolnick

D-U-N-S 20-938-3827   (SL)
FALCON FASTENERS LIMITED
251 Nantucket Blvd, Scarborough, ON, M1P 2P2
(416) 751-8284
Emp Here 185   *Sales* 50,569,750
SIC 6719 Holding companies, nec
Martin Leistner

D-U-N-S 24-208-8086   (HQ)
FORTRAN TRAFFIC SYSTEMS LIMITED
(*Suby of* GUILD ELECTRIC HOLDINGS LIMITED)
470 Midwest Rd, Scarborough, ON, M1P 4Y5

(416) 288-1320
Emp Here 50   *Sales* 10,233,650
SIC 3669 Communications equipment, nec
Peter Lengyel
Andrew Lengyel

D-U-N-S 25-509-6588   (SL)
FRIPES EXPORT LTD
310 Midwest Rd, Scarborough, ON, M1P 3A9
(416) 752-5046
Emp Here 120   *Sales* 29,319,360
SIC 5932 Used merchandise stores
R Dharsi

D-U-N-S 24-965-4542   (SL)
GOLDEN GATE HIDE & LEATHER LTD
21a Cosentino Dr, Scarborough, ON, M1P 3A3
(416) 299-7195
Emp Here 15   *Sales* 11,137,800
SIC 5199 Nondurable goods, nec
Ming Tser Pai
Chih Pin Pai
Yu Feng Pai
Chih Hsang Pai

D-U-N-S 25-717-8707   (BR)
GOODLIFE FITNESS CENTRES INC
(*Suby of* GOODLIFE FITNESS CENTRES INC)
1911 Kennedy Rd, Scarborough, ON, M1P 2L9
(416) 297-7279
Emp Here 165
SIC 7991 Physical fitness facilities
Robyn Gebien

D-U-N-S 25-990-9596   (HQ)
GUILD ELECTRIC HOLDINGS LIMITED
470 Midwest Rd, Scarborough, ON, M1P 4Y5
(416) 288-8222
Emp Here 5   *Sales* 153,080,850
SIC 1731 Electrical work
Andrew Lengyel
Peter Lengyel
Gary Lengyel
Audrey Lengyel
Amy Lengyel

D-U-N-S 20-166-4661   (HQ)
GUILD ELECTRIC LIMITED
(*Suby of* GUILD ELECTRIC HOLDINGS LIMITED)
470 Midwest Rd, Scarborough, ON, M1P 4Y5
(416) 288-8222
Sales 117,754,500
SIC 1731 Electrical work
Gary Lengyel
Andrew Lengyel
Peter Lengyel

D-U-N-S 24-910-5602   (BR)
HEROUX-DEVTEK INC
MAGTRON
(*Suby of* HEROUX-DEVTEK INC)
1480 Birchmount Rd, Scarborough, ON, M1P 2E3
(416) 757-2366
Emp Here 75
SIC 3443 Fabricated plate work (boiler shop)
Hans Kleiner

D-U-N-S 24-892-6677   (BR)
HIGHLAND FARMS INC
HIGHLAND FARMS SUPERMARKETS
(*Suby of* HIGHLAND FARMS INC)
850 Ellesmere Rd, Scarborough, ON, M1P 2W5
(416) 298-1999
Emp Here 125
SIC 5411 Grocery stores
Steve Cooper

D-U-N-S 25-278-8989   (SL)
HIND, CRAIG DODGE CHRYSLER LIMITED
2180 Lawrence Ave E, Scarborough, ON, M1P 2P8

Emp Here 55   *Sales* 34,610,400

SIC 5511 New and used car dealers
Craig Hind

D-U-N-S 24-120-1180   (BR)
HUDSON'S BAY COMPANY
(*Suby of* HUDSON'S BAY COMPANY)
300 Borough Dr Suite 2, Scarborough, ON, M1P 4P5
(416) 296-0555
Emp Here 300
SIC 5311 Department stores
Melanie Logan

D-U-N-S 20-151-3504   (SL)
J & K DIE CASTING LIMITED
18 Golden Gate Crt, Scarborough, ON, M1P 3A5
(416) 293-8229
Emp Here 45   *Sales* 10,504,575
SIC 3369 Nonferrous foundries, nec
Warren Kawaguchi

D-U-N-S 25-170-4946   (SL)
JITE TECHNOLOGIES INC
11 Progress Ave Unit 25, Scarborough, ON, M1P 4S7
(416) 298-6447
Emp Here 500   *Sales* 141,457,500
SIC 3678 Electronic connectors
Gang Chai
D. James Misener
Colin Digout

D-U-N-S 24-660-2460   (BR)
KRAFT HEINZ CANADA ULC
DAD'S COOKIES
(*Suby of* THE KRAFT HEINZ COMPANY)
370 Progress Ave, Scarborough, ON, M1P 2Z4
(416) 291-3713
Emp Here 161
SIC 2051 Bread, cake, and related products
Robert Tyrrell

D-U-N-S 25-304-1156   (BR)
KRAFT HEINZ CANADA ULC
(*Suby of* THE KRAFT HEINZ COMPANY)
1440 Birchmount Rd, Scarborough, ON, M1P 2E3

Emp Here 100
SIC 2099 Food preparations, nec
Heidi Strassguertl

D-U-N-S 24-331-0377   (HQ)
LIFELABS LP
LIFELABS MEDICAL LABORATORY SERVICES
1290 Ellesmere Rd, Scarborough, ON, M1P 2X9
(416) 291-1464
Emp Here 600   *Sales* 977,913,000
SIC 8071 Medical laboratories
Jos Wintermans

D-U-N-S 24-838-9202   (SL)
MCCOWAN DESIGN & MANUFACTURING LTD
1760 Birchmount Rd, Scarborough, ON, M1P 2H7
(416) 291-7111
Emp Here 60   *Sales* 14,659,680
SIC 5999 Miscellaneous retail stores, nec
Frank Ruffolo
Anthony Ruffolo

D-U-N-S 20-038-9349   (BR)
MCGREGOR INDUSTRIES INC
JET KNITTING
(*Suby of* MCGREGOR INDUSTRIES INC)
1360 Birchmount Rd, Scarborough, ON, M1P 2E3

Emp Here 200
SIC 2252 Hosiery, nec
Ines Carrita

D-U-N-S 20-078-7625   (BR)
METRO ONTARIO INC

METRO
(*Suby of* METRO INC)
16 William Kitchen Rd Suite 535, Scarborough, ON, M1P 5B7
(416) 321-0500
Emp Here 240
SIC 5411 Grocery stores
John Paton

D-U-N-S 24-194-2481   (HQ)
MISTER COFFEE & SERVICES INC
2045 Midland Ave Suite 1, Scarborough, ON, M1P 3E2
(416) 293-3333
Emp Here 68   *Sales* 34,140,644
SIC 7389 Business services, nec
Robert Hale
Marilyn Hale
Paul Cherry

D-U-N-S 20-080-3836   (SL)
NEW STAR REAL ESTATE LTD
1450 Midland Ave Unit 206, Scarborough, ON, M1P 4Z8
(416) 288-0800
Emp Here 100   *Sales* 27,175,600
SIC 6531 Real estate agents and managers
Anita Saini

D-U-N-S 20-360-0437   (SL)
ORIGINAL CHIMNEYS INC
EVA'S ORIGINAL CHIMNEY
300 Borough Dr, Scarborough, ON, M1P 4P5
(416) 697-8884
Emp Here 45   *Sales* 10,118,475
SIC 2051 Bread, cake, and related products
Kristin Butler

D-U-N-S 20-151-9311   (HQ)
PIZZA NOVA RESTAURANTS LIMITED
PIZZA NOVA TAKE-OUT
2247 Midland Ave Suite 12, Scarborough, ON, M1P 4R1
(416) 439-0051
Emp Here 150   *Sales* 9,327,800
SIC 5812 Eating places
Samuel Primucci

D-U-N-S 24-363-4339   (SL)
PLEXPACK CORP
1160 Birchmount Rd Unit 2, Scarborough, ON, M1P 2B8
(416) 291-8085
Emp Here 30   *Sales* 14,250,780
SIC 5084 Industrial machinery and equipment
Paul Irvine
Lisa Hunt

D-U-N-S 24-771-7002   (SL)
PLEXTRON HOLDINGS INC
2045 Midland Ave, Scarborough, ON, M1P 3E2
(416) 293-1156
Emp Here 120   *Sales* 19,062,960
SIC 3089 Plastics products, nec
Paul Irvine
Wilfred G Lewitt

D-U-N-S 24-827-8053   (HQ)
POWERTRADE ELECTRIC LTD
255 Midwest Rd, Scarborough, ON, M1P 3A6
(416) 757-3008
Sales 10,285,002
SIC 5063 Electrical apparatus and equipment
Tak Wai Yam

D-U-N-S 20-151-9907   (SL)
RAPID REFRIGERATION MANUFACTURING COMPANY LIMITED
1550 Birchmount Rd, Scarborough, ON, M1P 2H1
(416) 285-8282
Emp Here 75   *Sales* 16,650,075
SIC 3585 Refrigeration and heating equipment
Albert Sausik
Albert Sausik Jr
Hilda Sausik

D-U-N-S 20-047-8084   (BR)
REVERA LONG TERM CARE INC
KENNEDY LODGE NURSING HOME
(*Suby of* GOVERNMENT OF CANADA)
1400 Kennedy Rd, Scarborough, ON, M1P
4V6
(416) 752-8282
Emp Here 200
SIC 8051 Skilled nursing care facilities
 Joseph Peterson

D-U-N-S 20-152-0384   (SL)
ROADSPORT LIMITED
ROADSPORT HONDA
940 Ellesmere Rd, Scarborough, ON, M1P
2W8
(416) 291-9501
Emp Here 75   *Sales* 47,196,000
SIC 5511 New and used car dealers
 Christopher Gauthier

D-U-N-S 25-227-0871   (SL)
ROSALIE HALL
3020 Lawrence Ave E, Scarborough, ON, M1P
2T7
(416) 438-6880
Emp Here 49   *Sales* 11,114,817
SIC 8399 Social services, nec
 Alan Nickell

D-U-N-S 24-870-0838   (SL)
S.R.V. INDUSTRIAL SUPPLY INC
2500 Lawrence Ave E Suite 12, Scarborough,
ON, M1P 2R7
(416) 757-1020
Emp Here 40   *Sales* 20,821,680
SIC 5093 Scrap and waste materials
 Sam Ragah

D-U-N-S 24-793-0852   (SL)
SAE POWER COMPANY
(*Suby of* COLM CAMPBELL CO INC)
1810 Birchmount Rd, Scarborough, ON, M1P
2H7
(416) 298-0560
Emp Here 60   *Sales* 11,426,520
SIC 3679 Electronic components, nec
 Colm Noel Campbell
 David Allan Brown

D-U-N-S 24-320-1590   (HQ)
SCARBOROUGH AND ROUGE HOSPITAL
SRH
3050 Lawrence Ave E, Scarborough, ON, M1P
2V5
(416) 438-2911
Sales 150,166,000
SIC 8062 General medical and surgical hospitals
 Elizabeth Buller
 Cara Flemming
 Rhonda Lewis
 Linda Calhoun
 Rick Gowrie
 Michele James
 Nurallah Rahim
 Mark Vimr
 Naresh Mohan
 David Belous

D-U-N-S 20-273-6724   (HQ)
SCEPTER CANADA INC
(*Suby of* MYERS INDUSTRIES, INC.)
170 Midwest Rd, Scarborough, ON, M1P 3A9
(416) 751-9445
Sales 66,867,360
SIC 3089 Plastics products, nec
 Robert Torokvei
 Terry Elliot

D-U-N-S 20-610-7880   (HQ)
**SHOREWOOD PACKAGING CORP. OF
CANADA LIMITED**
AGI SHOREWOOD
(*Suby of* WESTROCK COMPANY)
2220 Midland Ave Unit 50, Scarborough, ON,
M1P 3E6

(416) 940-2400
Emp Here 300   *Sales* 147,422,437
SIC 2657 Folding paperboard boxes
 Fernando Pimentel

D-U-N-S 25-812-1490   (BR)
SILGAN PLASTICS CANADA INC
(*Suby of* SILGAN HOLDINGS INC.)
1200 Ellesmere Rd, Scarborough, ON, M1P
2X4
(416) 293-8233
Emp Here 120
SIC 3089 Plastics products, nec
 Mike Lane

D-U-N-S 20-388-2829   (SL)
TDI-DYNAMIC CANADA ULC
DYNAMIC TEAM SPORTS
1870 Birchmount Rd, Scarborough, ON, M1P
2J7
(877) 722-2003
Emp Here 100   *Sales* 13,667,400
SIC 2321 Men's and boy's furnishings
 Jim Walker

D-U-N-S 25-366-2357   (HQ)
TEKRAN INSTRUMENTS CORPORATION
(*Suby of* THE CHURCHILL COMPANIES)
330 Nantucket Blvd, Scarborough, ON, M1P
2P4
(416) 449-3084
Sales 11,364,450
SIC 3821 Laboratory apparatus and furniture
 Karl Wilber

D-U-N-S 20-058-9641   (SL)
TIGER NORTH AMERICA INC
1170 Birchmount Rd, Scarborough, ON, M1P
5E3
(416) 752-8100
Emp Here 120   *Sales* 24,044,520
SIC 7331 Direct mail advertising services
 Anthony Keenan
 Frank Mangialardi
 Heather Waldman

D-U-N-S 20-026-8501   (BR)
TORONTO DISTRICT SCHOOL BOARD
BENDALE BUSINESS & TECHNICAL INSTITUTE
(*Suby of* TORONTO DISTRICT SCHOOL
BOARD)
1555 Midland Ave, Scarborough, ON, M1P
3C1
(416) 396-6695
Emp Here 100
SIC 8211 Elementary and secondary schools
 Colin Dye

D-U-N-S 20-025-0855   (BR)
TORONTO DISTRICT SCHOOL BOARD
DAVID & MARY THOMSON COLLEGIATE INSTITUTE
(*Suby of* TORONTO DISTRICT SCHOOL
BOARD)
2740 Lawrence Ave E, Scarborough, ON, M1P
2S7
(416) 396-5525
Emp Here 100
SIC 8221 Colleges and universities
 William Papconstantino

D-U-N-S 25-458-0988   (SL)
TORONTO PROFESSIONAL FIREFIGHTERS ASSOCIATION LOCAL 3888
14 Cosentino Dr, Scarborough, ON, M1P 3A2
(416) 466-1167
Emp Here 30   *Sales* 11,734,740
SIC 8631 Labor organizations
 Frank Ramaganano

D-U-N-S 24-424-2624   (BR)
TRENCH LIMITED
(*Suby of* SIEMENS AG)
390 Midwest Rd, Scarborough, ON, M1P 3B5
(416) 751-8570
Emp Here 175
SIC 3612 Transformers, except electric

D-U-N-S 24-330-0469   (BR)
WAL-MART CANADA CORP
(*Suby of* WALMART INC.)
300 Borough Dr Suite 2, Scarborough, ON,
M1P 4P5
(416) 290-1916
Emp Here 200
SIC 5311 Department stores

D-U-N-S 20-178-8106   (SL)
YOUNG & YOUNG TRADING CO. LIMITED
328 Nantucket Blvd Unit 8, Scarborough, ON,
M1P 2P4
(416) 288-9298
Emp Here 30   *Sales* 25,067,310
SIC 5141 Groceries, general line
 Marie Young

Scarborough, ON M1R

D-U-N-S 25-657-8154   (SL)
1123932 ONTARIO INC
SCARBORO MAZDA
2124 Lawrence Ave E, Scarborough, ON,
M1R 3A3
(416) 752-0970
Emp Here 26   *Sales* 12,950,028
SIC 5511 New and used car dealers
 Ken Gyles

D-U-N-S 25-924-5249   (SL)
1249592 ONTARIO LTD
QUALITY AUTO WHOLESALERS
2110 Lawrence Ave E, Scarborough, ON,
M1R 3A3
(416) 750-8885
Emp Here 26   *Sales* 12,950,028
SIC 5511 New and used car dealers
 Saan Mestah

D-U-N-S 20-195-3549   (HQ)
1451805 ONTARIO LTD
PRO LINE MANAGEMENT
2 Principal Rd Unit 10, Scarborough, ON, M1R
4Z3
(416) 497-4363
Sales 14,164,650
SIC 8741 Management services
 Raymond Hooker
 Don Hall

D-U-N-S 24-692-6489   (SL)
APPAREL RESOURCE GROUP INC
A R G
80 Rolark Dr, Scarborough, ON, M1R 4G2

Emp Here 75   *Sales* 37,374,150
SIC 5137 Women's and children's clothing
 Michael Friedmann
 George Friedmann

D-U-N-S 20-717-6538   (SL)
BOBRICK WASHROOM EQUIPMENT COMPANY
(*Suby of* THE BOBRICK CORPORATION)
45 Rolark Dr, Scarborough, ON, M1R 3B1
(416) 298-1611
Emp Here 70   *Sales* 13,445,950
SIC 3431 Metal sanitary ware
 William Louchheim
 Jerald Otchis
 Marlon Inniss

D-U-N-S 25-793-9801   (SL)
CANADIAN FINE MOTORS INC
1882 Lawrence Ave E, Scarborough, ON,
M1R 2Y5
(416) 588-8899
Emp Here 30   *Sales* 14,942,340
SIC 5521 Used car dealers
 Sam Atout

D-U-N-S 24-950-3319   (SL)
CANTEX CANADA LIMITED
2 Rolark Dr, Scarborough, ON, M1R 4G2

(416) 751-4567
Emp Here 50   *Sales* 24,916,100
SIC 5131 Piece goods and notions
 Fatehaly Gulamhusein
 Mehmood Gulamhusein

D-U-N-S 25-756-3999   (BR)
COSTCO WHOLESALE CANADA LTD
PRICE CLUB SCARBOROUGH
(*Suby of* COSTCO WHOLESALE CORPORATION)
1411 Warden Ave Suite 537, Scarborough,
ON, M1R 2S3
(416) 288-0033
Emp Here 75
SIC 5099 Durable goods, nec

D-U-N-S 20-553-2708   (HQ)
DURABOND PRODUCTS LIMITED
55 Underwriters Rd, Scarborough, ON, M1R
3B4
(416) 759-4133
Sales 10,236,420
SIC 2891 Adhesives and sealants
 Guido Rapone
 Nick Petrakis
 Grace Liu

D-U-N-S 20-404-5538   (SL)
INGADALE INDUSTRIES INC
48 Crockford Blvd, Scarborough, ON, M1R
3C3
(416) 752-6266
Emp Here 65   *Sales* 14,430,065
SIC 3599 Industrial machinery, nec
 Gregory Holdsworth

D-U-N-S 25-530-8140   (SL)
K-WOOD KITCHENS INC
32 Continental Pl, Scarborough, ON, M1R 2T4
(416) 335-4027
Emp Here 30   *Sales* 15,265,680
SIC 5021 Furniture
 Simon Chan
 Philip Lee
 Jane Wong

D-U-N-S 20-647-2292   (SL)
MAGIC WHITE INC
80 Crockford Blvd, Scarborough, ON, M1R
3C3
(416) 751-2802
Emp Here 25   *Sales* 18,258,625
SIC 5169 Chemicals and allied products, nec
 Jim Anastasiadis

D-U-N-S 20-151-6663   (SL)
MCMULLEN & WARNOCK INC
70 Crockford Blvd, Scarborough, ON, M1R
3C3

Emp Here 22   *Sales* 10,356,082
SIC 1542 Nonresidential construction, nec
 Stuart Mcmullen
 Andrew Mcmullen
 Beryl Mcmullen

D-U-N-S 25-300-3388   (BR)
METRO ONTARIO INC
METRO
(*Suby of* METRO INC)
15 Ellesmere Rd, Scarborough, ON, M1R 4B7
(416) 391-0626
Emp Here 200
SIC 5411 Grocery stores
 Jack Chow

D-U-N-S 24-079-9825   (BR)
PATTISON, JIM INDUSTRIES LTD
PATTISON SIGN GROUP, DIV OF
(*Suby of* PATTISON, JIM GROUP INC)
555 Ellesmere Rd, Scarborough, ON, M1R
4E8
(416) 759-1111
Emp Here 130
SIC 3993 Signs and advertising specialties
 Rick Macina

D-U-N-S 25-187-1935   (SL)

PETER'S FOOD & DRUG BASICS
2131 Lawrence Ave E, Scarborough, ON,
M1R 5G4
(416) 759-7625
Emp Here 90   *Sales* 26,412,930
SIC 5411 Grocery stores
Leon Peter

D-U-N-S 25-997-4251   (SL)
PFC FLEXIBLE CIRCUITS LIMITED
11 Canadian Rd Suite 7, Scarborough, ON,
M1R 5G1
(416) 750-8433
Emp Here 100   *Sales* 19,044,200
SIC 3679 Electronic components, nec
Steve Kelly
Anish Somaiya

D-U-N-S 24-828-0497   (SL)
PROGRESSIVE ANODIZERS INC
41 Crockford Blvd, Scarborough, ON, M1R
3B7
(416) 751-5487
Emp Here 60   *Sales* 11,525,100
SIC 3471 Plating and polishing
Arthur Leal

D-U-N-S 20-404-6429   (SL)
**SHOREWOOD CARTON CORPORATION
LIMITED**
44 Rolark Dr, Scarborough, ON, M1R 4G2
(416) 940-2436
Emp Here 140   *Sales* 27,267,520
SIC 2657 Folding paperboard boxes
Fernando Pimentel

D-U-N-S 25-400-3031   (HQ)
TRACTEL LTD
SWINGSTAGE, DIV OF
(Suby of TRACTEL GMBH)
1615 Warden Ave, Scarborough, ON, M1R
2T3
(416) 298-8822
Sales 18,248,075
SIC 3446 Architectural Metalwork
Thierry Bertrand
Matthieu Terray

D-U-N-S 24-862-3894   (HQ)
TRACTEL NORTH AMERICA INC
(Suby of TRACTEL GMBH)
1615 Warden Ave, Scarborough, ON, M1R
2T3
(416) 298-8822
Emp Here 85   *Sales* 31,309,855
SIC 3446 Architectural Metalwork
Denis Pradon
Thierry Bertrand

D-U-N-S 24-124-5174   (SL)
WEXFORD RESIDENCE INC, THE
WEXFORD, THE
1860 Lawrence Ave E, Scarborough, ON,
M1R 5B1
(416) 752-8877
Emp Here 200   *Sales* 12,856,400
SIC 8361 Residential care
Sandra Bassett

D-U-N-S 25-270-3350   (BR)
WOOD CANADA LIMITED
AMEC EARTH & ENVIRONMENTAL, DIV OF
(Suby of JOHN WOOD GROUP P.L.C.)
104 Crockford Blvd, Scarborough, ON, M1R
3C3
(416) 751-6565
Emp Here 100
SIC 8711 Engineering services
George Chow

Scarborough, ON M1S

D-U-N-S 24-936-9075   (SL)
1155760 ONTARIO LIMITED
AGINCOURT MAZDA

5500 Finch Ave E, Scarborough, ON, M1S
0C7
(416) 283-7100
Emp Here 55   *Sales* 34,610,400
SIC 5511 New and used car dealers
Kap Dilawri

D-U-N-S 25-974-6881   (SL)
1387208 ONTARIO LTD
APACO IMAGING LAB
190 Milner Ave, Scarborough, ON, M1S 5B6
(416) 293-9943
Emp Here 38   *Sales* 15,865,228
SIC 7384 Photofinish laboratories
Domenic Rubino
David B Wood
Timothy K Wood
Richard Sojecki

D-U-N-S 24-135-8519   (SL)
1615517 ONTARIO INC
5215 Finch Ave E Unit 203, Scarborough, ON,
M1S 0C2
(416) 321-6969
Emp Here 160   *Sales* 43,736,000
SIC 6719 Holding companies, nec
Raja Mahendran
Vanessa Vanessa

D-U-N-S 24-079-8350   (SL)
2138894 ONTARIO INC
METRO PROTECTIVE SERVICES
140 Shorting Rd, Scarborough, ON, M1S 3S6
(416) 240-0911
Emp Here 151   *Sales* 3,963,750
SIC 7381 Detective and armored car services
Frank Decurtis

D-U-N-S 24-632-0469   (SL)
602390 ONTARIO LIMITED
OCEAN SEAFOOD COMPANY
81 Scottfield Dr, Scarborough, ON, M1S 5R4
(416) 740-9000
Emp Here 35   *Sales* 29,245,195
SIC 5146 Fish and seafoods
Patrick Lay
Amy Lay

D-U-N-S 24-388-4350   (SL)
AGINCOURT NISSAN LIMITED
AGINCOURT NISSAN
1871 Mccowan Rd, Scarborough, ON, M1S
4L4
(416) 291-1188
Emp Here 80   *Sales* 50,342,400
SIC 5511 New and used car dealers
Robert Stephen

D-U-N-S 24-046-7761   (SL)
**AJAX MAINTENANCE & SHIPPING SUP-
PLIES CO LTD**
100 Commander Blvd, Scarborough, ON,
M1S 3H7
(416) 291-7601
Emp Here 38   *Sales* 18,050,988
SIC 5087 Service establishment equipment
Nicholas Shaw

D-U-N-S 25-974-1585   (HQ)
ALFA LAVAL INC
(Suby of ALFA LAVAL AB)
101 Milner Ave, Scarborough, ON, M1S 4S6
(416) 299-6101
Emp Here 50   *Sales* 47,502,600
SIC 5085 Industrial supplies
Ashley Davis

D-U-N-S 25-402-4318   (SL)
APPAREL TRIMMINGS INC
APP-TRIM
20 Commander Blvd, Scarborough, ON, M1S
3L9
(416) 298-8836
Emp Here 160   *Sales* 21,867,840
SIC 2387 Apparel belts
Francis Liu

D-U-N-S 24-156-2859   (HQ)

ARMOUR VALVE LTD
(Suby of EDCAIR HOLDINGS INC)
126 Milner Ave, Scarborough, ON, M1S 3R2
(416) 299-0780
Emp Here 19   *Sales* 12,350,676
SIC 5085 Industrial supplies
Ian Braff

D-U-N-S 20-150-3562   (SL)
AUTOMATIC COATING LIMITED
211 Nugget Ave, Scarborough, ON, M1S 3B1
(416) 335-7500
Emp Here 80   *Sales* 8,992,956
SIC 3479 Metal coating and allied services
Bradley Bamford
Harold Bamford
Jocelyn Bamford

D-U-N-S 25-369-4764   (BR)
BELL MEDIA INC
(Suby of BCE INC)
9 Channel Nine Crt, Scarborough, ON, M1S
4B5
(416) 332-5000
Emp Here 2,000
SIC 4833 Television broadcasting stations
Sam Dynes

D-U-N-S 20-075-1290   (SL)
**BRIMELL AUTOMOTIVE SERVICES LIM-
ITED**
BRIMELL GROUP, THE
5060 Sheppard Ave E, Scarborough, ON,
M1S 4N3
(416) 292-2241
Emp Here 75   *Sales* 21,247,500
SIC 7532 Top and body repair and paint shops
Mark Dozian
Michael Dozian

D-U-N-S 20-550-0945   (SL)
BRIMELL MOTORS LIMITED
BRIMELL TOYOTA
5060 Sheppard Ave E, Scarborough, ON,
M1S 4N3
(416) 292-2241
Emp Here 55   *Sales* 34,610,400
SIC 5511 New and used car dealers
Mark Bozian

D-U-N-S 20-150-5419   (HQ)
C & S AUTO PARTS LIMITED
COLLINS AUTO PARTS
151 Nugget Ave, Scarborough, ON, M1S 3B1
(416) 754-8500
Emp Here 1   *Sales* 24,402,405
SIC 5013 Motor vehicle supplies and new
parts
A William Collins

D-U-N-S 20-379-0696   (SL)
CANADIAN TAMIL ACADEMY
8 Milner Ave, Scarborough, ON, M1S 3P8
(416) 757-2006
Emp Here 123   *Sales* 12,332,839
SIC 8211 Elementary and secondary schools
Vinasithamby Thurairajah

D-U-N-S 20-965-4123   (SL)
CATELECTRIC INC
125 Commander Blvd, Scarborough, ON,
M1S 3M7
(416) 299-4864
Emp Here 50   *Sales* 10,141,500
SIC 3479 Metal coating and allied services
David Lund
Shaun Reid

D-U-N-S 24-138-4981   (SL)
CENTURY 21 CAMDEC REAL ESTATE LTD
4544 Sheppard Ave E Suite 100, Scarbor-
ough, ON, M1S 1V2
(416) 298-2800
Emp Here 32   *Sales* 10,468,064
SIC 6531 Real estate agents and managers
Camille De Castro
Rupert De Castro

D-U-N-S 20-134-3014   (SL)
CENTURY 21 REGAL REALTY INC
4030 Sheppard Ave E Suite 2, Scarborough,
ON, M1S 1S6
(416) 291-0929
Emp Here 140   *Sales* 58,644,460
SIC 6531 Real estate agents and managers
John D'andrade
Jennifer D'andrade

D-U-N-S 24-000-2951   (BR)
CINRAM CANADA OPERATIONS ULC
(Suby of NAJAFI COMPANIES, LLC)
400 Nugget Ave, Scarborough, ON, M1S 4A4
(416) 332-9000
Emp Here 500
SIC 3652 Prerecorded records and tapes
John Bell

D-U-N-S 24-522-0046   (SL)
CISCO SYSTEMS CO.
SCIENTIFIC-ATLANTA CANADA
100 Middlefield Rd Unit 1, Scarborough, ON,
M1S 4M6
(416) 299-6888
Emp Here 150   *Sales* 87,037,050
SIC 5065 Electronic parts and equipment, nec
Evan B Sloves
Mark T Gorman
Nitin S Kawale

D-U-N-S 20-050-4699   (HQ)
**COAST TO COAST NEWSSTAND SER-
VICES LTD**
5230 Finch Ave E Suite 1, Scarborough, ON,
M1S 4Z9
(416) 754-3900
Emp Here 1   *Sales* 18,563,000
SIC 5192 Books, periodicals, and newspapers
Glenn Morgan

D-U-N-S 20-549-3484   (SL)
CRYSTAL CLAIRE COSMETICS INC
(Suby of CRYSTAL GROUP HOLDINGS INC.)
165 Milner Ave, Scarborough, ON, M1S 4G7
(416) 421-1882
Emp Here 827   *Sales* 367,721,415
SIC 2844 Toilet preparations
Roger Hwang

D-U-N-S 20-288-6230   (HQ)
CRYSTAL GROUP HOLDINGS INC.
165 Milner Ave, Scarborough, ON, M1S 4G7
(416) 421-9299
Emp Here 55   *Sales* 137,065,875
SIC 6712 Bank holding companies
Roger Hwang

D-U-N-S 25-127-9782   (SL)
CRYSTAL INTERNATIONAL (GROUP) INC.
CRYSTAL INTERNATIONAL
(Suby of CRYSTAL GROUP HOLDINGS INC.)
165 Milner Ave, Scarborough, ON, M1S 4G7
(416) 421-9299
Emp Here 55   *Sales* 15,621,155
SIC 2844 Toilet preparations
Roger Hwang

D-U-N-S 20-163-0092   (SL)
D & L SALES LIMITED
ROYAL SPECIALTY SALES
150 Middlefield Rd, Scarborough, ON, M1S
4L6
(416) 423-1133
Emp Here 25   *Sales* 18,563,000
SIC 5199 Nondurable goods, nec
Kenneth Feldbloom

D-U-N-S 25-279-8194   (SL)
DATCOM
1361 Huntingwood Dr Unit 13, Scarborough,
ON, M1S 3J1
(416) 293-2866
Emp Here 16   *Sales* 16,005,424
SIC 5051 Metals service centers and offices
Jeff Quinn
Bilal Sibai

▲ Public Company   ■ Public Company Family Member   **HQ** Headquarters   **BR** Branch   **SL** Single Location

D-U-N-S 20-056-4891 (SL)
DERMA SCIENCES CANADA INC
(*Suby of* INTEGRA LIFESCIENCES HOLD-
INGS CORPORATION)
104 Shorting Rd, Scarborough, ON, M1S 3S4
(416) 299-4003
Emp Here 115   *Sales* 32,662,415
SIC 2834 Pharmaceutical preparations
Frederic Eigner
Stephen T. Wills
Geoffrey Reid

D-U-N-S 20-192-7642 (HQ)
DOMINET CORPORATION
10 Compass Crt, Scarborough, ON, M1S 5R3
(416) 646-5232
Emp Here 1   *Sales* 43,049,952
SIC 3944 Games, toys, and children's vehicles
John Dominelli

D-U-N-S 24-597-3003 (SL)
DUVET COMFORT INC
130 Commander Blvd, Scarborough, ON, M1S 3H7
(416) 754-1455
Emp Here 75   *Sales* 10,250,550
SIC 2329 Men's and boy's clothing, nec
Johnny Yiu
Frankie Chu
Yuk Chung Lee

D-U-N-S 20-822-8049 (SL)
**EAST-COURT FORD LINCOLN SALES LIM-
ITED**
QUICKLANE
4700 Sheppard Ave E, Scarborough, ON, M1S 3V6
(416) 292-1171
Emp Here 62   *Sales* 39,015,360
SIC 5511 New and used car dealers
Ray Sahi

D-U-N-S 25-507-7802 (SL)
ELECTRONIC IMAGING SYSTEMS CORP
1361 Huntingwood Dr Unit 8, Scarborough, ON, M1S 3J1
(416) 292-0900
Emp Here 150   *Sales* 25,027,050
SIC 7374 Data processing and preparation
Joe Wells
Rose Kramer

D-U-N-S 20-844-8068 (SL)
EM DYNAMICS INC
160 Commander Blvd, Scarborough, ON, M1S 3C8
(416) 293-8385
Emp Here 146   *Sales* 26,891,900
SIC 3499 Fabricated Metal products, nec
Baldev Sidhu
Nirbhai Sidhu

D-U-N-S 25-092-6276 (BR)
ESTEE LAUDER COSMETICS LTD
(*Suby of* THE ESTEE LAUDER COMPANIES
INC)
161 Commander Blvd, Scarborough, ON, M1S 3K9
(416) 292-1111
Emp Here 200
SIC 5122 Drugs, proprietaries, and sundries
Sue Connely-King

D-U-N-S 20-295-2982 (HQ)
ESTEE LAUDER COSMETICS LTD
MAC COSMETICS
(*Suby of* THE ESTEE LAUDER COMPANIES
INC)
161 Commander Blvd, Scarborough, ON, M1S 3K9
(416) 292-1111
Sales 49,703,675
SIC 2844 Toilet preparations
Fabrizio Freda
Carl Haney
Sara Moss
Michael O'hare
Tracey T Travis

D-U-N-S 25-406-3217 (SL)
FORWARD SIGNS INC
60 Emblem Crt, Scarborough, ON, M1S 1B1
(416) 291-4477
Emp Here 80   *Sales* 26,090,880
SIC 3993 Signs and advertising specialties
Simon Ho
Philip Ho

D-U-N-S 20-770-2341 (HQ)
GRAIN PROCESS ENTERPRISES LIMITED
105 Commander Blvd, Scarborough, ON, M1S 3M7
(416) 291-3226
Emp Here 30   *Sales* 11,242,750
SIC 2041 Flour and other grain mill products
George Birinyi Sr
George Birinyi Jr
Irene Evans
Irene Birinyi

D-U-N-S 24-359-5803 (SL)
GRANDVIEW SALES & DISTRIBUTION LTD
CANADIAN TIRE
4630 Sheppard Ave E Suite 264, Scarbor-
ough, ON, M1S 3V5
(416) 291-7791
Emp Here 200   *Sales* 125,856,000
SIC 5531 Auto and home supply stores
Stephen Grand

D-U-N-S 20-183-0903 (SL)
**HIGHLAND FEATHER MANUFACTURING
INC**
171 Nugget Ave, Scarborough, ON, M1S 3B1
(416) 754-7443
Emp Here 40   *Sales* 20,354,240
SIC 5023 Homefurnishings
Nai Jian Chen
Cheney Q Chen
Jian Guang Duan
John Fischook
Ping Yu Leung

D-U-N-S 20-400-2208 (SL)
HOGAN CHEVROLET BUICK GMC LIMITED
(*Suby of* ROY FOSS MOTORS LTD)
5000 Sheppard Ave E, Scarborough, ON, M1S 4L9
(416) 291-5054
Emp Here 110   *Sales* 69,220,800
SIC 5511 New and used car dealers
Drew Foss
Roy Foss

D-U-N-S 24-666-4635 (SL)
HOMELIFE/ACES REALTY & INS. LTD
4002 Sheppard Ave E Unit 216, Scarborough, ON, M1S 4R5
(416) 298-8880
Emp Here 35   *Sales* 11,449,445
SIC 6531 Real estate agents and managers
Linda Dato
Waldo Buzon

D-U-N-S 20-167-5139 (SL)
INDEPENDENT ELECTRIC SUPPLY INC
48 Milner Ave, Scarborough, ON, M1S 3P8
(416) 291-0048
Emp Here 50   *Sales* 22,358,700
SIC 5063 Electrical apparatus and equipment
Robert Branscombe

D-U-N-S 24-346-3283 (BR)
**INFORMATION COMMUNICATION SER-
VICES (ICS) INC**
ICS COURIER SERVICES
(*Suby of* TFI INTERNATIONAL INC)
80 Cowdray Crt, Scarborough, ON, M1S 4N1
(416) 642-2477
Emp Here 100
SIC 7389 Business services, nec
Lynn Margison

D-U-N-S 24-212-3008 (HQ)
INTERNATIONAL GROUP, INC, THE
INTERNATIONAL WAXES

(*Suby of* IGI HOLDINGS, INC)
50 Salome Dr, Scarborough, ON, M1S 2A8
(416) 293-4151
Sales 27,025,600
SIC 2911 Petroleum refining
Ross Reucassel
John Reucassel
David Imrie

D-U-N-S 25-246-5398 (SL)
INVESTIGATORS GROUP INC, THE
2061 Mccowan Rd Suite 2, Scarborough, ON, M1S 3Y6
(416) 955-9450
Emp Here 100   *Sales* 39,567,800
SIC 7381 Detective and armored car services
William Joynt
Sean Gladney
Bill Thompson

D-U-N-S 24-802-9530 (SL)
ITN FOOD CORPORATION
40 Commander Blvd, Scarborough, ON, M1S 3S2
(416) 321-2052
Emp Here 28   *Sales* 23,396,156
SIC 5149 Groceries and related products, nec
Mohammed Ansari
Lateef Ansari

D-U-N-S 25-511-1098 (SL)
JAMEI COMPANY LTD
180 Commander Blvd, Scarborough, ON, M1S 3C8
(416) 293-8385
Emp Here 130   *Sales* 17,767,620
SIC 2335 Women's, junior's, and misses'
dresses
John Chau

D-U-N-S 20-291-7873 (SL)
JERICO SPORTSWEAR LTD
120 Commander Blvd, Scarborough, ON, M1S 3H7
(416) 288-0822
Emp Here 75   *Sales* 10,250,550
SIC 2339 Women's and misses' outerwear,
nec
Aziz Andani
Arzina Maherali

D-U-N-S 25-317-2985 (SL)
KING'S EMBROIDERY LTD
225 Nugget Ave Suite 6, Scarborough, ON, M1S 3L2
(416) 292-7471
Emp Here 30   *Sales* 13,304,700
SIC 7389 Business services, nec
Sam Yu
Paul Cheng

D-U-N-S 24-452-8626 (HQ)
LELAND INDUSTRIES INC
95 Commander Blvd, Scarborough, ON, M1S 3S9
(416) 291-5308
Emp Here 123   *Sales* 54,726,975
SIC 3429 Hardware, nec
Byron Nelson
Jason Nelson
Dwayne Nelson
Denis Ebata

D-U-N-S 20-552-2964 (HQ)
LONGFORD INTERNATIONAL LTD
41 Lamont Ave, Scarborough, ON, M1S 1A8
(416) 298-6622
Sales 22,200,100
SIC 3565 Packaging machinery
Edward Paterson
Ralph Viegas
Edward Cook

D-U-N-S 20-168-6664 (SL)
LOUISE KOOL & GALT LIMITED
EDUCATIONAL, DIV
2123 Mccowan Rd, Scarborough, ON, M1S 3Y6

(416) 293-0312
Emp Here 21   *Sales* 10,931,382
SIC 5092 Toys and hobby goods and supplies
James Robb

D-U-N-S 20-902-3084 (SL)
**MIDAS REALTY CORPORATION OF
CANADA INC**
(*Suby of* TBC CORPORATION)
105 Commander Blvd, Scarborough, ON, M1S 3M7
(416) 291-4261
Emp Here 125
SIC 6531 Real estate agents and managers
John R Moore
Roger E Appleton

D-U-N-S 24-985-4373 (HQ)
NRT TECHNOLOGY CORP
(*Suby of* DOMINET CORPORATION)
10 Compass Crt, Scarborough, ON, M1S 5R3
(416) 646-5232
Emp Here 130   *Sales* 44,976,560
SIC 3944 Games, toys, and children's vehicles
John Dominelli
Rosa Laricchia
Gary Lindsay
Michael Dominelli
Josh Sidsworth
Jackie Dominelli

D-U-N-S 24-393-5694 (BR)
PHARMA MEDICA RESEARCH INC
(*Suby of* 2065424 ONTARIO LIMITED)
4770 Sheppard Ave E Suite 2, Scarborough, ON, M1S 3V6
(416) 759-5554
Emp Here 263
SIC 8731 Commercial physical research
Zenith Xu

D-U-N-S 25-323-2862 (HQ)
QUALITY NATURAL FOODS CANADA INC
420 Nugget Ave Suite 1, Scarborough, ON, M1S 4A4
(416) 261-8700
Emp Here 32   *Sales* 33,423,080
SIC 5149 Groceries and related products, nec
Jarnail Singh
Robert Balcom
Rajdai Singh
Vicente Trius
J. Bradley Holland
David Gore
Sarah Davis
Peter Mcmahon

D-U-N-S 20-560-4341 (SL)
**QUEST AUTOMOTIVE LEASING SERVICES
LTD**
QUEST AUTOMOTIVE LEASING SERVICES
(*Suby of* HIND, CRAIG HOLDINGS LTD)
4960 Sheppard Ave E, Scarborough, ON, M1S 4A7
(416) 298-7600
Emp Here 110   *Sales* 69,220,800
SIC 5511 New and used car dealers
Craig Hind
Lance Hanson

D-U-N-S 20-106-8033 (SL)
ROGERS SPORTSNET INC
(*Suby of* ROGERS COMMUNICATIONS INC)
9 Channel Nine Crt, Scarborough, ON, M1S 4B5
(416) 764-6000
Emp Here 250   *Sales* 83,636,000
SIC 4833 Television broadcasting stations
Anthony Viner

D-U-N-S 24-555-9893 (SL)
SATISFASHION INC
33 Commander Blvd Suite 1, Scarborough, ON, M1S 3E7

Emp Here 80   *Sales* 15,936,320
SIC 2337 Women's and misses' suits and
coats

Kelly Wong
Wayne Wong

D-U-N-S 24-337-0277   (HQ)
SEALY CANADA LTD
(*Suby of* TEMPUR SEALY INTERNATIONAL, INC.)
145 Milner Ave, Scarborough, ON, M1S 3R1
(416) 699-7170
Emp Here 145   *Sales* 93,519,300
SIC 2515 Mattresses and bedsprings
Larry Rogers

D-U-N-S 20-355-5490   (SL)
SIB ENTERPRISES INC
393 Nugget Ave, Scarborough, ON, M1S 4G3
(416) 292-7792
Emp Here 65   *Sales* 15,881,320
SIC 5932 Used merchandise stores
Ali Bawa

D-U-N-S 20-610-8797   (HQ)
SKF CANADA LIMITED
(*Suby of* AB SKF)
40 Executive Crt, Scarborough, ON, M1S 4N4
(416) 299-1220
Emp Here 90   *Sales* 79,987,720
SIC 5085 Industrial supplies
Joao Ricciarelli
Paul Winter
Tom Karch
Frank Bijnens

D-U-N-S 20-260-5739   (BR)
SOFINA FOODS INC
VIENNA MEAT PRODUCTS
(*Suby of* SOFINA FOODS INC)
170 Nugget Ave, Scarborough, ON, M1S 3A7
(416) 297-1062
Emp Here 100
SIC 2013 Sausages and other prepared meats

D-U-N-S 24-632-1814   (SL)
SOLIDWEAR ENTERPRISES LIMITED
59 Milner Ave, Scarborough, ON, M1S 3P6
(416) 298-2667
Emp Here 166   *Sales* 30,444,898
SIC 2253 Knit outerwear mills
Arthur Lee

D-U-N-S 24-099-3600   (HQ)
SOUTHWEST BINDING SYSTEMS LTD
SOUTHWEST PLASTIC BINDINGS
20 Dovedale Crt, Scarborough, ON, M1S 5A7
(416) 285-7044
Emp Here 76   *Sales* 43,702,392
SIC 5084 Industrial machinery and equipment
Louis Cordeiro

D-U-N-S 24-386-4923   (HQ)
SURATI SWEET MART LIMITED
300 Middlefield Rd, Scarborough, ON, M1S 5B1
(416) 752-3366
Sales 11,242,750
SIC 2051 Bread, cake, and related products
Mansukh Sheth
Haren Sheth

D-U-N-S 24-006-5920   (HQ)
TFI FOODS LTD
(*Suby of* TAI FOONG INVESTMENTS LTD)
44 Milner Ave, Scarborough, ON, M1S 3P8
(416) 299-7575
Emp Here 55   *Sales* 79,379,815
SIC 5146 Fish and seafoods
David Lam
Sherman Lam

D-U-N-S 25-790-9770   (SL)
TIAN BAO TRAVEL CO INC
4002 Sheppard Ave E Unit 106a, Scarborough, ON, M1S 4R5
(416) 292-9990
Emp Here 30   *Sales* 11,560,800
SIC 4724 Travel agencies
Kim Zhang

D-U-N-S 20-711-3148   (BR)
TORONTO DISTRICT SCHOOL BOARD
AGINCOURT COLLEGIATE INSTITUTE
(*Suby of* TORONTO DISTRICT SCHOOL BOARD)
2621 Midland Ave, Scarborough, ON, M1S 1R6
(416) 396-6675
Emp Here 120
SIC 8211 Elementary and secondary schools
Roy Hu

D-U-N-S 20-119-8251   (BR)
TORONTO DISTRICT SCHOOL BOARD
(*Suby of* TORONTO DISTRICT SCHOOL BOARD)
52 Mcgriskin Rd, Scarborough, ON, M1S 5C5
(416) 396-7610
Emp Here 100
SIC 8211 Elementary and secondary schools
Ali Abdi

D-U-N-S 20-077-8160   (BR)
TORONTO DISTRICT SCHOOL BOARD
SIR WILLIAM OSLER HIGH SCHOOL
(*Suby of* TORONTO DISTRICT SCHOOL BOARD)
1050 Huntingwood Dr, Scarborough, ON, M1S 3H5
(416) 396-6830
Emp Here 102
SIC 8211 Elementary and secondary schools
Kathleen Pelaia

D-U-N-S 25-355-0347   (SL)
TRIMONT MFG. INC
TS TECH CO
(*Suby of* TS TECH CO., LTD.)
115 Milner Ave Suite 2, Scarborough, ON, M1S 4L7
(416) 640-2045
Emp Here 260   *Sales* 61,490,780
SIC 2211 Broadwoven fabric mills, cotton
Steven Li

D-U-N-S 24-244-5328   (HQ)
UMBRA LTD
40 Emblem Crt, Scarborough, ON, M1S 1B1
(416) 299-0088
Sales 115,073,600
SIC 5023 Homefurnishings

D-U-N-S 24-010-3697   (HQ)
YAMAHA CANADA MUSIC LTD
(*Suby of* YAMAHA CORPORATION)
135 Milner Ave, Scarborough, ON, M1S 3R1
(416) 298-1311
Emp Here 80   *Sales* 73,701,800
SIC 5099 Durable goods, nec
Yosuke Mikami
John R Finley
Yoshihiro Doi

D-U-N-S 25-360-1850   (BR)
YEE HONG CENTRE FOR GERIATRIC CARE
YEE HONG CENTRE SCARBOROUGH FINCH
(*Suby of* YEE HONG CENTRE FOR GERIATRIC CARE)
60 Scottfield Dr Suite 428, Scarborough, ON, M1S 5T7
(416) 321-3000
Emp Here 200
SIC 8059 Nursing and personal care, nec
Tilda Hui

Scarborough, ON M1T

D-U-N-S 20-940-4990   (SL)
2051183 ONTARIO INC
HONG TAI SUPERMARKET
2555 Victoria Park Ave Suite 19, Scarborough, ON, M1T 1A3

(416) 773-1166
Emp Here 40   *Sales* 10,966,080
SIC 5411 Grocery stores
Wei Cheng Yei

D-U-N-S 20-185-1458   (HQ)
EASTERN CONSTRUCTION COMPANY LIMITED
2075 Kennedy Rd Suite 1200, Scarborough, ON, M1T 3V3
(416) 497-7110
Emp Here 37   *Sales* 114,067,600
SIC 1542 Nonresidential construction, nec
Frank Decaria
Ronald Littlejohns
Renato Tacconelli
Bryan Arnold

D-U-N-S 20-031-8566   (SL)
FOSTER PONTIAC BUICK INC
FOSTER KIA
3445 Sheppard Ave E, Scarborough, ON, M1T 3K5
(416) 291-9745
Emp Here 65   *Sales* 40,903,200
SIC 5511 New and used car dealers
Mark Murphy
Stewart Esplin

D-U-N-S 20-074-0301   (BR)
HOLLISWEALTH INC
DUNDEE SECURITY
(*Suby of* BANK OF NOVA SCOTIA, THE)
2075 Kennedy Rd Suite 500, Scarborough, ON, M1T 3V3
(416) 292-0869
Emp Here 75
SIC 8742 Management consulting services
Allan Proos

D-U-N-S 24-215-7279   (HQ)
INTERNATIONAL LUMBER INC
3410 Sheppard Ave E Suite 400, Scarborough, ON, M1T 3K4
(416) 754-1020
Emp Here 25   *Sales* 20,122,830
SIC 5031 Lumber, plywood, and millwork
Bernard Noik

D-U-N-S 24-228-4326   (BR)
LONDON LIFE, COMPAGNIE D'ASSURANCE-VIE
LONDON LIFE INSURANCE COMPANY
(*Suby of* POWER CORPORATION DU CANADA)
2075 Kennedy Rd Suite 300, Scarborough, ON, M1T 3V3

Emp Here 100
SIC 6411 Insurance agents, brokers, and service
Rick Smith

D-U-N-S 20-837-4707   (SL)
MILLER MAINTENANCE LIMITED
2064 Kennedy Rd, Scarborough, ON, M1T 3V1
(416) 332-1360
Emp Here 3,500   *Sales* 1,148,402,500
SIC 1611 Highway and street construction
Monique Mcnabb

D-U-N-S 25-137-5366   (SL)
NURSING & HOMEMAKERS INC
NHI
2347 Kennedy Rd Suite 204, Scarborough, ON, M1T 3T8
(416) 754-0700
Emp Here 350   *Sales* 72,473,800
SIC 8399 Social services, nec
Delores Lawrence

D-U-N-S 24-173-4883   (BR)
RECIPE UNLIMITED CORPORATION
SWISS CHALET ROTISSERIE GRILL
(*Suby of* RECIPE UNLIMITED CORPORATION)
2555 Victoria Park Ave Suite 19, Scarborough,

ON, M1T 1A3
(416) 494-9693
Emp Here 80
SIC 5812 Eating places
Alan Sinn

D-U-N-S 25-172-5487   (BR)
RED LOBSTER HOSPITALITY LLC
RED LOBSTER RESTAURANTS
3252 Sheppard Ave E, Scarborough, ON, M1T 3K3
(416) 491-2507
Emp Here 90
SIC 5812 Eating places

D-U-N-S 20-784-4010   (HQ)
SHEPHERD VILLAGE INC
SHEPHERD LODGE
3760 Sheppard Ave E, Scarborough, ON, M1T 3K9
(416) 609-5700
Sales 18,641,780
SIC 8361 Residential care
Wendy Beckles

D-U-N-S 20-025-5862   (BR)
TORONTO DISTRICT SCHOOL BOARD
STEPHEN LEACOCK COLLEGIATE INSTITUTE
(*Suby of* TORONTO DISTRICT SCHOOL BOARD)
2450 Birchmount Rd, Scarborough, ON, M1T 2M5
(416) 396-8000
Emp Here 100
SIC 8211 Elementary and secondary schools
Mike Poirier

D-U-N-S 25-297-7772   (BR)
WAL-MART CANADA CORP
WALMART
(*Suby of* WALMART INC.)
3850 Sheppard Ave E Suite 3000, Scarborough, ON, M1T 3L4
(416) 291-4100
Emp Here 420
SIC 5311 Department stores

Scarborough, ON M1V

D-U-N-S 20-690-7326   (SL)
1519694 ONTARIO INC
NORTH KEE TRADING COMPANY
135 Select Ave Unit 8-9, Scarborough, ON, M1V 4A5
(416) 754-0483
Emp Here 55   *Sales* 19,012,950
SIC 2015 Poultry slaughtering and processing
Simon Wu

D-U-N-S 24-771-5774   (HQ)
683949 ONTARIO LIMITED
NESA
155 Dynamic Dr, Scarborough, ON, M1V 5L8
(416) 366-6372
Emp Here 1   *Sales* 23,079,360
SIC 7629 Electrical repair shops
Dominic Renda

D-U-N-S 20-731-4782   (HQ)
ALL-WELD COMPANY LIMITED
AURORA FILTERS
49 Passmore Ave, Scarborough, ON, M1V 4T1
(416) 299-3311
Emp Here 40   *Sales* 10,141,500
SIC 3499 Fabricated Metal products, nec
William A Dunsmoor
Scott Dunsmoor
Susan Dunsmoor
James Dunsmoor

D-U-N-S 25-825-3301   (BR)
ALL-WELD COMPANY LIMITED
(*Suby of* ALL-WELD COMPANY LIMITED)

14 Passmore Ave, Scarborough, ON, M1V 2R6
(416) 293-3638
Emp Here 80
SIC 7539 Automotive repair shops, nec
James Dunsmoor

D-U-N-S 20-210-2021   (SL)
ALLIANCE ENVIRONMENTAL & ABATEMENT CONTRACTORS INC
589 Middlefield Rd Unit 14, Scarborough, ON, M1V 4Y6
(416) 298-4500
Emp Here 36   *Sales* 10,841,112
SIC 4953 Refuse systems
Dean Power
Robert Lewis

D-U-N-S 25-117-9024   (SL)
ARSENAL CLEANING SERVICES LTD
80 Nashdene Rd Unit 7, Scarborough, ON, M1V 5E4
(416) 321-8777
Emp Here 110   *Sales* 3,516,480
SIC 7349 Building maintenance services, nec
Aris Paparafiou
George Kandelas

D-U-N-S 24-848-7555   (SL)
ARTEX SPORTSWEAR INC
40 Tiffield Ave Unit 9, Scarborough, ON, M1V 5B6
(416) 755-3382
Emp Here 80   *Sales* 14,672,240
SIC 2253 Knit outerwear mills
Archie So
Edward Leung

D-U-N-S 24-639-7215   (BR)
ATLANTIC PACKAGING PRODUCTS LTD
ADD INK
(*Suby of* ATLANTIC PACKAGING PRODUCTS LTD)
118 Tiffield Rd, Scarborough, ON, M1V 5N2
(800) 268-5620
Emp Here 75
SIC 2653 Corrugated and solid fiber boxes
William White

D-U-N-S 24-207-1004   (BR)
ATLANTIC PACKAGING PRODUCTS LTD
(*Suby of* ATLANTIC PACKAGING PRODUCTS LTD)
55 Milliken Blvd, Scarborough, ON, M1V 1V3
(416) 298-5508
Emp Here 100
SIC 2653 Corrugated and solid fiber boxes
Robin Washer

D-U-N-S 24-098-2822   (BR)
ATLANTIC PACKAGING PRODUCTS LTD
(*Suby of* ATLANTIC PACKAGING PRODUCTS LTD)
45 Milliken Blvd, Scarborough, ON, M1V 1V3
(416) 298-5566
Emp Here 150
SIC 2676 Sanitary paper products
Tony Taccogna

D-U-N-S 20-555-3753   (SL)
ATLAS PAPER BAG COMPANY LIMITED
90 Dynamic Dr, Scarborough, ON, M1V 2V1
(416) 293-2125
Emp Here 100   *Sales* 23,343,500
SIC 2674 Bags: uncoated paper and multiwall
Charles Provvidenza
John Calvo
Mike Rochon

D-U-N-S 20-279-9862   (SL)
AVG (OEAM) INC
605 Middlefield Rd Unit 1, Scarborough, ON, M1V 5B9
(416) 321-2978
Emp Here 35   *Sales* 17,432,730
SIC 5531 Auto and home supply stores
Ayaz Somani

D-U-N-S 25-366-7836   (SL)
AVG (OEM) INC
50 Tiffield Rd Unit 1, Scarborough, ON, M1V 5B7
(416) 321-2978
Emp Here 100   *Sales* 36,421,500
SIC 5013 Motor vehicle supplies and new parts
Ayaz Somani
Karim Suleman

D-U-N-S 20-401-6844   (SL)
CALSCO SOLVENTS LIMITED
CANADIAN ALCOHOL CO
4120 Midland Ave, Scarborough, ON, M1V 4S8
(416) 293-0123
Emp Here 20   *Sales* 10,006,500
SIC 5169 Chemicals and allied products, nec
Norman Craig

D-U-N-S 20-937-5393   (SL)
CARDINAL CARETAKERS CO LIMITED
80 Dynamic Dr, Scarborough, ON, M1V 2V1

Emp Here 80   *Sales* 3,216,720
SIC 7349 Building maintenance services, nec
Michael Donovan
Linda Chaloner

D-U-N-S 25-825-1073   (HQ)
CAREFIRST SENIORS AND COMMUNITY SERVICES ASSOCIATION
300 Silver Star Blvd, Scarborough, ON, M1V 0G2
(416) 502-2323
Emp Here 20   *Sales* 21,787,200
SIC 8322 Individual and family services
Paul Tam
Sheila Neysmith
Michael Wong
Janet Lee
Olivia Mui
Helen Leung

D-U-N-S 24-209-5859   (HQ)
CENTURY 21 PERCY FULTON LTD
2911 Kennedy Rd, Scarborough, ON, M1V 1S8
(416) 298-0465
Emp Here 185   *Sales* 83,777,800
SIC 6531 Real estate agents and managers
Clare Fulton

D-U-N-S 20-650-5021   (HQ)
D. CRUPI & SONS LIMITED
CRUPI GROUP, THE
(*Suby of* CRUPI HOLDINGS LIMITED)
85 Passmore Ave, Scarborough, ON, M1V 4S9
(416) 291-1986
Emp Here 120   *Sales* 98,434,500
SIC 1611 Highway and street construction
Cosimo Crupi

D-U-N-S 25-346-1532   (HQ)
ECI TECHNOLOGY GROUP INC
815 Middlefield Rd Unit 1-2, Scarborough, ON, M1V 2P9
(416) 291-2220
Emp Here 77   *Sales* 18,663,316
SIC 3679 Electronic components, nec
Ramesh Patel
Jashvant Patel
Ashok Patel
Kanaiyalel Patel
Shailesh Patel

D-U-N-S 25-353-7401   (SL)
ECO II MANUFACTURING INC
3391 Mcnicoll Ave Unit 6, Scarborough, ON, M1V 2V4
(416) 292-0220
Emp Here 75   *Sales* 17,507,625
SIC 2673 Bags: plastic, laminated, and coated
Stephen Klunowski
Scott Andrews

D-U-N-S 25-330-5775   (HQ)
GROUPE SEB CANADA INC
(*Suby of* SEB SA)
36 Newmill Gate, Scarborough, ON, M1V 0E2
(416) 297-4131
Emp Here 75   *Sales* 22,358,700
SIC 5064 Electrical appliances, television and radio
Fabrice Dupont
Luc Gaudemard
Philippe Sumeire
Pierre Guibert
Patrizia Banducci

D-U-N-S 24-577-0730   (SL)
HARDING DISPLAY CORP
150 Dynamic Dr, Scarborough, ON, M1V 5A5
(416) 754-3215
Emp Here 100   *Sales* 32,613,600
SIC 3993 Signs and advertising specialties
William Harding
Glen Harding

D-U-N-S 20-372-0177   (SL)
HARDING GROUP LIMITED, THE
150 Dynamic Dr, Scarborough, ON, M1V 5A5
(416) 754-3215
Emp Here 110   *Sales* 18,995,525
SIC 8743 Public relations services
Robert Harding
John Harding
Kevin Mason
Russel Harding
Glen Harding
William Harding

D-U-N-S 25-404-1304   (SL)
HIGH LIFE HEATING, AIR CONDITIONING & SECURITY INC
102 Passmore Ave, Scarborough, ON, M1V 4S9
(416) 298-2987
Emp Here 50   *Sales* 11,046,700
SIC 1711 Plumbing, heating, air-conditioning
Stephen Yeung
Rosanna Yeung

D-U-N-S 20-181-5201   (HQ)
JACCO TOURS (ONTARIO) INC
633 Silver Star Blvd Unit 122, Scarborough, ON, M1V 5N1
(416) 332-0808
Emp Here 1   *Sales* 18,718,812
SIC 4724 Travel agencies
Danny Li

D-U-N-S 24-847-5428   (HQ)
JORIKI INC
3431 Mcnicoll Ave, Scarborough, ON, M1V 2V3
(416) 754-2747
Sales 27,655,200
SIC 2033 Canned fruits and specialties
Yogi Sennik

D-U-N-S 24-408-2285   (SL)
K-LINE INSULATORS LIMITED
50 Passmore Ave, Scarborough, ON, M1V 4T1
(416) 292-2008
Emp Here 75   *Sales* 14,283,150
SIC 3644 Noncurrent-carrying wiring devices
Mark K Kellett
Anthony Carreira
Allan Kellett

D-U-N-S 24-391-6884   (SL)
KOBAY ENSTEL LIMITED
125 Nashdene Rd Unit 5, Scarborough, ON, M1V 2W3
(416) 292-7088
Emp Here 300   *Sales* 72,969,300
SIC 3469 Metal stampings, nec
Gavin Galansky

D-U-N-S 25-708-0879   (HQ)
L. HANSEN'S FORWARDING LTD
HANSEN'S RELEASING COMPANY

105 Nashdene Rd, Scarborough, ON, M1V 2W3
(416) 293-9135
Sales 30,855,900
SIC 4213 Trucking, except local
Michael Hansen
Karin Stewart

D-U-N-S 24-858-2210   (BR)
LOWE'S COMPANIES CANADA, ULC
(*Suby of* LOWE'S COMPANIES, INC.)
6005 Steeles Ave E, Scarborough, ON, M1V 5P7
(416) 940-4827
Emp Here 150
SIC 5211 Lumber and other building materials
Atif Usmani

D-U-N-S 24-576-8908   (SL)
MILPLEX CIRCUIT (CANADA) INC
70 Maybrook Dr, Scarborough, ON, M1V 4B6
(416) 292-8645
Emp Here 60   *Sales* 11,426,520
SIC 3672 Printed circuit boards
Natu Patel
Pravin Patel
Kanchan Patel

D-U-N-S 20-990-6846   (BR)
MON SHEONG FOUNDATION
(*Suby of* MON SHEONG FOUNDATION)
2030 Mcnicoll Ave, Scarborough, ON, M1V 5P4
(416) 291-3898
Emp Here 160
SIC 8051 Skilled nursing care facilities
Stella Leung

D-U-N-S 20-920-9493   (SL)
NATIONAL SHOE SPECIALTIES LIMITED
3015 Kennedy Rd Unit 8-18, Scarborough, ON, M1V 1E7
(416) 292-7181
Emp Here 37   *Sales* 16,545,438
SIC 5047 Medical and hospital equipment
Ernie Hinrichs
Joan Hinrichs
Wayne Hinrichs

D-U-N-S 24-576-0087   (HQ)
NMC DYNAPLAS LTD
H2O PERFORMANCE PADDLES
(*Suby of* NATIONAL MOLDING, LLC)
380 Passmore Ave, Scarborough, ON, M1V 4B4
(416) 293-3855
Sales 31,771,600
SIC 3089 Plastics products, nec
Gregory J. Walton
Jason Foulds

D-U-N-S 24-365-4626   (HQ)
OC CANADA HOLDINGS COMPANY
OWENS CORNING
(*Suby of* OWENS CORNING)
3450 Mcnicoll Ave, Scarborough, ON, M1V 1Z5
(416) 292-4000
Emp Here 1   *Sales* 155,203,830
SIC 3296 Mineral wool
Robert Kwong
Mark Giveins
Rodney Nowland
Steve Krull

D-U-N-S 24-478-9855   (BR)
PUROLATOR INC
(*Suby of* GOVERNMENT OF CANADA)
90 Silver Star Blvd, Scarborough, ON, M1V 4V8
(888) 744-7123
Emp Here 300
SIC 4731 Freight transportation arrangement
Virgin Don

D-U-N-S 20-624-5243   (HQ)
RACING FORENSICS INC
3015 Kennedy Rd Unit 2, Scarborough, ON,

M1V 1E7
(416) 479-4489
Sales 50,092,750
SIC 7319 Advertising, nec
Richard Tso

D-U-N-S 24-877-1610   (SL)
RE/MAX GOLDENWAY REALTY INC
RE/MAX
3390 Midland Ave Unit 7, Scarborough, ON,
M1V 5K3
(416) 299-8199
Emp Here 45   *Sales* 14,720,715
SIC 6531 Real estate agents and managers
Shusing Ng

D-U-N-S 24-659-7181   (SL)
SHEUNG KEE TRADING COMPANY INC
3411 Mcnicoll Ave Unit 11, Scarborough, ON,
M1V 2V6
(905) 471-4481
Emp Here 14   *Sales* 11,698,078
SIC 5141 Groceries, general line
Andrew Ouyang
Pui Lam Auyeung
Peter Auyeung
Philip Auyeung

D-U-N-S 25-092-1194   (HQ)
**THYSSENKRUPP ELEVATOR (CANADA)
LIMITED**
THYSSENKRUPP ELEVATOR
(*Suby of* THYSSENKRUPP AG)
410 Passmore Ave Unit 1, Scarborough, ON,
M1V 5C3
(416) 291-2000
Emp Here 150   *Sales* 254,851,200
SIC 1796 Installing building equipment
Ryan Wilson
Richard T. Hussey

D-U-N-S 20-705-5039   (HQ)
**THYSSENKRUPP NORTHERN ELEVATOR
CORPORATION**
(*Suby of* THYSSENKRUPP AG)
410 Passmore Ave Unit 1, Scarborough, ON,
M1V 5C3
(416) 291-2000
Emp Here 225   *Sales* 467,098,451
SIC 3534 Elevators and moving stairways
Kevin Lavallee

D-U-N-S 24-688-6899   (SL)
TIP TOP BINDERY LTD
335 Passmore Ave, Scarborough, ON, M1V
4B5
(416) 609-3281
Emp Here 500   *Sales* 82,013,500
SIC 2789 Bookbinding and related work
Cal Johnson
Dean Johnson

D-U-N-S 24-243-6496   (BR)
**TORONTO CATHOLIC DISTRICT SCHOOL
BOARD**
MARY WARD CATHOLIC HIGH SCHOOL
(*Suby of* TORONTO CATHOLIC DISTRICT
SCHOOL BOARD)
3200 Kennedy Rd, Scarborough, ON, M1V
3S8
(416) 393-5544
Emp Here 100
SIC 8211 Elementary and secondary schools
Carmela Giardini

D-U-N-S 20-100-1166   (BR)
TORONTO DISTRICT SCHOOL BOARD
ALBERT CAMPBELL C.I.
(*Suby of* TORONTO DISTRICT SCHOOL
BOARD)
1550 Sandhurst Cir, Scarborough, ON, M1V
1S6
(416) 396-6684
Emp Here 120
SIC 8211 Elementary and secondary schools
Carol Richards-Sauer

D-U-N-S 20-822-0640   (SL)

TOY-SPORT AGENCIES LIMITED
120 Dynamic Dr Suite 22, Scarborough, ON,
M1V 5C8
(905) 640-6598
Emp Here 5   *Sales* 11,793,600
SIC 7389 Business services, nec
Brigitte Ward
Jack Ward

D-U-N-S 20-524-5087   (HQ)
TRENCH LIMITED
TRENCH CANADA COIL PRODUCTS
(*Suby of* SIEMENS AG)
71 Maybrook Dr, Scarborough, ON, M1V 4B6
(416) 298-8108
Emp Here 300   *Sales* 148,530,375
SIC 3699 Electrical equipment and supplies,
nec
Marco Michel
Norman Hyde-Whipp

D-U-N-S 20-769-3656   (HQ)
TRICIFIC ENTERPRISES INC
155 Dynamic Dr, Scarborough, ON, M1V 5L8
(905) 470-8811
Emp Here 29   *Sales* 17,809,960
SIC 5023 Homefurnishings
Lawrence Chen
Sidney Chen

D-U-N-S 24-765-3061   (BR)
WAL-MART CANADA CORP
(*Suby of* WALMART INC.)
5995 Steeles Ave E Suite Side, Scarborough,
ON, M1V 5P7
(416) 298-1210
Emp Here 200
SIC 5311 Department stores
Erin Mackey

D-U-N-S 24-964-4253   (SL)
**WRIGHT, GEORGE A. & SON (TORONTO)
LIMITED**
21 State Crown Blvd, Scarborough, ON, M1V
4B1
(416) 261-6499
Emp Here 55   *Sales* 12,210,055
SIC 3599 Industrial machinery, nec
Jamie Meikle

D-U-N-S 25-512-7367   (HQ)
**YEE HONG CENTRE FOR GERIATRIC
CARE**
YEE HONG
2311 Mcnicoll Ave, Scarborough, ON, M1V
5L3

Emp Here 200   *Sales* 64,776,600
SIC 8051 Skilled nursing care facilities
Joseph Wong
Helen Hayward
Ron Knowles
Susan Roher
Lynn Bennett
Albert Tseng
Andrew Wang
Susan Eng
Peter Chung
Florence Wong

Scarborough, ON M1W

D-U-N-S 24-325-1027   (HQ)
1072667 ONTARIO LIMITED
3370 Pharmacy Ave, Scarborough, ON, M1W
3K4
(416) 494-1444
Emp Here 1   *Sales* 95,032,340
SIC 6712 Bank holding companies
Roman Arbesman

D-U-N-S 25-406-9115   (BR)
BANK OF MONTREAL
BANK OF MONTREAL INSTITUTE FOR

LEARNING
(*Suby of* BANK OF MONTREAL)
3550 Pharmacy Ave, Scarborough, ON, M1W
3Z3
(416) 490-4300
Emp Here 100
SIC 6021 National commercial banks
Richard Rudderham

D-U-N-S 25-703-7721   (BR)
EXTENDICARE INC
TENDERCARE NURSING HOME
(*Suby of* EXTENDICARE INC)
1020 Mcnicoll Ave Suite 547, Scarborough,
ON, M1W 2J6
(416) 499-2020
Emp Here 300
SIC 8051 Skilled nursing care facilities
Frances Marpis

D-U-N-S 25-691-0639   (HQ)
GREAT GULF GROUP OF COMPANIES INC
3751 Victoria Park Ave, Scarborough, ON,
M1W 3Z4
(416) 449-1340
Sales 20,320,650
SIC 1521 Single-family housing construction
Jerry Patava

D-U-N-S 24-412-2735   (HQ)
GREAT GULF HOMES LIMITED
GREAT GULF HOMES
3751 Victoria Park Ave, Scarborough, ON,
M1W 3Z4
(416) 449-1340
Sales 14,349,105
SIC 1521 Single-family housing construction
Elly Reisman
Norman Reisman
Harry Rosenbaum

D-U-N-S 24-987-4827   (SL)
GULFVIEW CONTRACTING LTD
3751 Victoria Park Ave, Scarborough, ON,
M1W 3Z4
(416) 449-1340
Emp Here 45   *Sales* 14,349,105
SIC 1521 Single-family housing construction
Seymour Joffe

D-U-N-S 24-876-9580   (SL)
HOMELIFE GOLD PACIFIC REALTY INC
3601 Victoria Park Ave Suite 401, Scarbor-
ough, ON, M1W 3Y3
(416) 490-1068
Emp Here 140   *Sales* 58,644,460
SIC 6531 Real estate agents and managers
Bernard Wong

D-U-N-S 25-310-7957   (BR)
HOOPER-HOLMES CANADA LIMITED
PORTAMEDIC
(*Suby of* HOOPER-HOLMES CANADA LIM-
ITED)
1059 Mcnicoll Ave, Scarborough, ON, M1W
3W6
(416) 493-2800
Emp Here 100
SIC 6411 Insurance agents, brokers, and ser-
vice

D-U-N-S 24-121-4410   (HQ)
HOOPER-HOLMES CANADA LIMITED
1059 Mcnicoll Ave, Scarborough, ON, M1W
3W6
(416) 493-2800
Emp Here 100   *Sales* 1,186,526,000
SIC 6411 Insurance agents, brokers, and ser-
vice
Daniel Gauvin
Ira Greenspoon

D-U-N-S 20-139-4517   (HQ)
LEICA GEOSYSTEMS LTD
3761 Victoria Park Ave Unit 1, Scarborough,
ON, M1W 3S2
(416) 497-2460
Emp Here 15   *Sales* 20,122,830

SIC 5049 Professional equipment, nec
Sudha Sachdeva

D-U-N-S 25-300-2810   (BR)
METRO ONTARIO INC
METRO
(*Suby of* METRO INC)
2900 Warden Ave, Scarborough, ON, M1W
2S8
(416) 497-6734
Emp Here 120
SIC 5411 Grocery stores
Grant Martin

D-U-N-S 24-805-5209   (BR)
NUCAP INDUSTRIES INC
GRIP METAL
(*Suby of* 1072667 ONTARIO LIMITED)
3370 Pharmacy Ave, Scarborough, ON, M1W
3K4
(416) 494-1444
Emp Here 100
SIC 3714 Motor vehicle parts and accessories
Neisha Bacchus

D-U-N-S 25-246-8343   (HQ)
NUCAP INDUSTRIES INC
GRIP METAL
(*Suby of* 1072667 ONTARIO LIMITED)
3370 Pharmacy Ave, Scarborough, ON, M1W
3K4
(416) 494-1444
Emp Here 160   *Sales* 75,621,000
SIC 3714 Motor vehicle parts and accessories
Roman Arbesman
David Weichenberg

D-U-N-S 24-387-6695   (HQ)
OVERSEAS MISSIONARY FELLOWSHIP
OMF INTERNATIONAL
10 Huntingdale Blvd, Scarborough, ON, M1W
2S5
(905) 568-9971
Sales 10,772,700
SIC 8661 Religious organizations
Jon Fuller

D-U-N-S 20-924-2437   (SL)
PHOENIX GEOPHYSICS LIMITED
(*Suby of* ELLIOTT, G GEOPHYSICS INC)
3781 Victoria Park Ave Unit 3, Scarborough,
ON, M1W 3K5
(416) 491-7340
Emp Here 50   *Sales* 11,364,450
SIC 3829 Measuring and controlling devices,
nec
Leo Fox
Yann Avram
Davra Young

D-U-N-S 24-417-9339   (SL)
RE/MAX CROSSROADS REALTY INC
1055 Mcnicoll Ave, Scarborough, ON, M1W
3W6
(416) 491-4002
Emp Here 130   *Sales* 54,455,570
SIC 6531 Real estate agents and managers
Barney Johnson

D-U-N-S 24-197-7255   (HQ)
SAYAL PURCHASING SERVICES INC
SAYAL ELECTRONICS
3791 Victoria Park Ave Unit 1, Scarborough,
ON, M1W 3K6
(416) 494-8999
Emp Here 24   *Sales* 13,415,220
SIC 5065 Electronic parts and equipment, nec
Paul Sayal
Kevin Sayal

D-U-N-S 20-176-8926   (HQ)
SHEFFIELD MOVING AND STORAGE INC
4069 Gordon Baker Rd, Scarborough, ON,
M1W 2P3
(416) 291-1200
Emp Here 20   *Sales* 82,282,400
SIC 4214 Local trucking with storage
John Novak

D-U-N-S 25-475-7933   (SL)
SINCERE REALTY INC
1033 Mcnicoll Ave, Scarborough, ON, M1W
3W6
(416) 497-8900
Emp Here 67   *Sales* 18,207,652
SIC 6531 Real estate agents and managers
Victor Ng

D-U-N-S 24-198-2214   (SL)
ST. PAUL'S L'AMOREAUX CENTRE
3333 Finch Ave E, Scarborough, ON, M1W
2R9
(416) 493-3333
Emp Here 130   *Sales* 17,638,010
SIC 6513 Apartment building operators
James Koffman
Larry Burke

D-U-N-S 24-216-0711   (SL)
**T & L FOOD MERCHANDISING SERVICES
LTD**
PROMOTIONS
78 Pinemeadow Blvd, Scarborough, ON,
M1W 1P2
(416) 497-6573
Emp Here 250   *Sales* 46,626,500
SIC 8743 Public relations services
Lucille Cantafio

D-U-N-S 20-699-6485   (BR)
TENDERCARE NURSING HOMES LIMITED
MOLL BERCZY HAUS
1020 Mcnicoll Ave Suite 436, Scarborough,
ON, M1W 2J6
(416) 497-3639
Emp Here 275
SIC 8051 Skilled nursing care facilities
Francis Martis

D-U-N-S 20-079-2898   (BR)
TORONTO DISTRICT SCHOOL BOARD
L'AMOREAUX COLLEGIATE INSTITUTE
(*Suby of* TORONTO DISTRICT SCHOOL
BOARD)
2501 Bridletowne Cir, Scarborough, ON, M1W
2K1
(416) 396-6745
Emp Here 100
SIC 8211 Elementary and secondary schools
Huw Chinnery

D-U-N-S 24-985-9547   (SL)
TRIPLEWELL ENTERPRISES LTD
3440 Pharmacy Ave Unit 9, Scarborough, ON,
M1W 2P8
(416) 498-5637
Emp Here 450   *Sales* 119,400,750
SIC 2399 Fabricated textile products, nec
Lincoln Wong

D-U-N-S 20-692-3109   (SL)
TUCKER HI-RISE CONSTRUCTION INC
3755 Victoria Park Ave, Scarborough, ON,
M1W 3Z4
(416) 441-2730
Emp Here 50   *Sales* 16,666,650
SIC 1541 Industrial buildings and warehouses
Micheal Mcgrath

D-U-N-S 20-550-8054   (SL)
WASIP LTD
3771 Victoria Park Ave, Scarborough, ON,
M1W 3Z5
(416) 297-5020
Emp Here 39   *Sales* 20,301,138
SIC 5099 Durable goods, nec
John Brindley
Paul Brindley
Helen Brindley
Mala Brindley

D-U-N-S 20-942-2104   (HQ)
WEBCOM INC
(*Suby of* MARQUIS IMPRIMEUR INC)
3480 Pharmacy Ave, Scarborough, ON, M1W
2S7
(416) 496-1000
Sales 31,165,130

SIC 2732 Book printing
Michael Collinge

Scarborough, ON M1X

D-U-N-S 24-849-7638   (SL)
A.K.D. TRADING INC
10 Newgale Gate Suite 5, Scarborough, ON,
M1X 1C5
(416) 299-7384
Emp Here 50   *Sales* 41,778,850
SIC 5141 Groceries, general line
Wendell Ng-See-Quan

D-U-N-S 20-706-5889   (SL)
ABBEYWOOD MOVING & STORAGE INC
WILSON RELOCATION
480 Finchdene Sq, Scarborough, ON, M1X
1C2
(416) 292-1107
Emp Here 85   *Sales* 12,596,320
SIC 4213 Trucking, except local
Randy Wilson
Bruce Edwards

D-U-N-S 25-411-8904   (SL)
ANTEK MADISON PLASTICS CORP
100 Finchdene Sq, Scarborough, ON, M1X
1C1
(416) 321-1170
Emp Here 24   *Sales* 17,528,280
SIC 5162 Plastics materials and basic shapes
James Angelopoulos
Victor Tay

D-U-N-S 24-964-3396   (HQ)
BERENDSEN FLUID POWER LTD
(*Suby of* MIDCON INVESTORS INC)
35 Ironside Cres Unit A, Scarborough, ON,
M1X 1G5
(416) 335-5557
Emp Here 30   *Sales* 47,502,600
SIC 5084 Industrial machinery and equipment
Ian Hill
Valerie Lister

D-U-N-S 25-370-8085   (BR)
BLACK & MCDONALD LIMITED
*BLACK & MCDONALD SHEET METAL AND
CUSTOM FABRICATION*
(*Suby of* BLACK & MCDONALD GROUP LIM-
ITED)
35 Pullman Crt, Scarborough, ON, M1X 1E4
(416) 298-9977
Emp Here 200
SIC 1711 Plumbing, heating, air-conditioning
Macdonald Larry

D-U-N-S 24-383-8732   (BR)
BLACK & MCDONALD LIMITED
(*Suby of* BLACK & MCDONALD GROUP LIM-
ITED)
31 Pullman Crt, Scarborough, ON, M1X 1E4
(416) 298-9977
Emp Here 500
SIC 1711 Plumbing, heating, air-conditioning
Judy Stratton

D-U-N-S 25-239-3764   (SL)
**BREMNER, GORDON C. INTERNATIONAL
INC**
BREMNER INTERNATIONAL
420 Finchdene Sq, Scarborough, ON, M1X
1C2
(416) 321-6943
Emp Here 25   *Sales* 12,999,175
SIC 4731 Freight transportation arrangement
Gordon C Bremner
Virginia Bremner

D-U-N-S 20-077-3013   (SL)
**C.M.S. COMMERCIAL MECHANICAL SER-
VICES LTD**
COMMERCIAL MECHANICAL SERVICES
2721 Markham Rd Unit 10, Scarborough, ON,

M1X 1L5
(416) 609-9992
Emp Here 100   *Sales* 23,306,500
SIC 1711 Plumbing, heating, air-conditioning
Clive Lacey

D-U-N-S 20-648-6529   (SL)
**CANADIAN FITNESS PROFESSIONALS
INC**
CAN-FIT-PRO, DIV OF
225 Select Ave Suite 110, Scarborough, ON,
M1X 0B5
(416) 493-3515
Emp Here 100   *Sales* 14,002,900
SIC 7999 Amusement and recreation, nec
Nathalie Lacombe
Maureen Hagan

D-U-N-S 24-727-1554   (SL)
DURAPAINT INDUSTRIES LIMITED
247 Finchdene Sq Suite 1, Scarborough, ON,
M1X 1B9
(416) 754-3664
Emp Here 65   *Sales* 12,485,525
SIC 3471 Plating and polishing
Elio Zarlenga

D-U-N-S 24-772-2317   (SL)
EUCLID'S HOLDINGS LTD
JIM'S BROTHER TRADING CO
275 Finchdene Sq Unit 1, Scarborough, ON,
M1X 1B9
(416) 321-8002
Emp Here 35   *Sales* 29,245,195
SIC 5141 Groceries, general line
Che Keung Jim

D-U-N-S 24-324-0876   (HQ)
**FIRAN TECHNOLOGY GROUP CORPORA-
TION**
FTG AEROSPACE - TORONTO
250 Finchdene Sq, Scarborough, ON, M1X
1A5
(416) 299-4000
Emp Here 200   *Sales* 84,196,064
SIC 3672 Printed circuit boards
Bradley C. Bourne
Melinda Diebel
Hardeep Heer
Michael Labrador
Hitesh Talati
Chris Woodland
Peter Dimopoulos
Randy Drake
Bryan Clark

D-U-N-S 24-948-0708   (SL)
G & P MILLWORK LTD
191 Finchdene Sq, Scarborough, ON, M1X
1E3
(416) 298-4204
Emp Here 50   *Sales* 13,514,526
SIC 2431 Millwork
Peter Diamond
Gerald Diamond

D-U-N-S 20-408-8702   (SL)
GOLDY METALS INC
STANDARD AUTO WRECKERS
1216 Sewells Rd, Scarborough, ON, M1X 1S1
(416) 286-8686
Emp Here 110   *Sales* 76,483,000
SIC 5093 Scrap and waste materials
Kenneth Gold

D-U-N-S 25-504-5353   (SL)
GRUVEN INC
19 Newgale Gate, Scarborough, ON, M1X
1B6
(416) 292-7331
Emp Here 150   *Sales* 20,501,100
SIC 2389 Apparel and accessories, nec
Jimmy Yiu
Susan Lau
David Rushton

D-U-N-S 24-978-2178   (SL)
KOPPERT CANADA LIMITED

(*Suby of* STICHTING ADMINISTRATIEKAN-
TOOR LIVEHOLDING)
40 Ironside Cres Unit 3, Scarborough, ON,
M1X 1G4
(416) 291-0040
Emp Here 18   *Sales* 19,896,210
SIC 5122 Drugs, proprietaries, and sundries
Paul Goodspeed

D-U-N-S 24-876-2734   (SL)
KROEGER INC
455 Finchdene Sq, Scarborough, ON, M1X
1B7
(416) 752-4382
Emp Here 24   *Sales* 12,493,008
SIC 5092 Toys and hobby goods and supplies
Grant Chatman
David Charbonneau

D-U-N-S 24-046-7019   (SL)
MANNARICH FOOD INC
131 Finchdene Sq Unit 10, Scarborough, ON,
M1X 1A6
(905) 471-9656
Emp Here 60   *Sales* 50,134,620
SIC 5142 Packaged frozen goods
Matthew Lo
Raphael Lo

D-U-N-S 20-151-6671   (SL)
MCNICOL STEVENSON LIMITED
EXPOSYSTEMS CANADA
3640 Mcnicoll Ave Suite B, Scarborough, ON,
M1X 1G5
(416) 291-2933
Emp Here 30   *Sales* 13,304,700
SIC 7389 Business services, nec
Nigel Vance-Lousada
Dale Hartney

D-U-N-S 24-917-4269   (BR)
MORRISON LAMOTHE INC
141 Finchdene Sq, Scarborough, ON, M1X
1A7
(416) 291-9121
Emp Here 200
SIC 2038 Frozen specialties, nec
Judy Martin

D-U-N-S 20-267-9130   (SL)
NASHA METAL EXPORT INC
88 Misty Hills Trail, Scarborough, ON, M1X
1T3
(647) 765-8952
Emp Here 30   *Sales* 15,616,260
SIC 5093 Scrap and waste materials
Iyyappan Kamalam
Jothy Iyyappan

D-U-N-S 25-989-8385   (SL)
NOWPAC INC
780 Tapscott Rd Unit 5, Scarborough, ON,
M1X 1A3
(416) 321-5799
Emp Here 100   *Sales* 23,428,800
SIC 8743 Public relations services
Anna Calder

D-U-N-S 24-361-6328   (HQ)
NUTRALAB CANADA CORP
(*Suby of* HONSON PHARMATECH GROUP,
LTD)
980 Tapscott Rd, Scarborough, ON, M1X 1C3
(905) 752-1823
Emp Here 50   *Sales* 17,041,260
SIC 2834 Pharmaceutical preparations
Peter Ou

D-U-N-S 25-283-7273   (SL)
PROTAGON DISPLAY INC
719 Tapscott Rd, Scarborough, ON, M1X 1A2
(416) 293-9500
Emp Here 90   *Sales* 17,529,120
SIC 2653 Corrugated and solid fiber boxes
Larry Titchner
Jeffrey Lynch
Peter Nodwell
Scott Chapman

▲ Public Company   ■ Public Company Family Member   **HQ** Headquarters   **BR** Branch   **SL** Single Location

D-U-N-S 20-114-1689   (SL)
PROTECTIVE TROOPS RESPONSE FORCE
15 Weaver Dr, Scarborough, ON, M1X 1V2
(905) 233-4873
Emp Here 30   *Sales* 11,870,340
SIC 7381 Detective and armored car services
  Wasim Ali

D-U-N-S 20-596-3945   (HQ)
SCHINDLER ELEVATOR CORPORATION
(*Suby of* SCHINDLER HOLDING AG)
3640 Mcnicoll Ave Unit A, Scarborough, ON, M1X 1G5
(416) 332-8280
Emp Here 100   *Sales* 93,445,440
SIC 1796 Installing building equipment
  Jeff Coles
  Thomas Koch

D-U-N-S 25-366-8446   (SL)
STRIKE FIRST CORPORATION
777 Tapscott Rd, Scarborough, ON, M1X 1A2
(416) 299-7767
Emp Here 40   *Sales* 17,739,600
SIC 7389 Business services, nec
  Patricia William

D-U-N-S 24-910-4928   (HQ)
TAI FOONG INVESTMENTS LTD
TFI FOODS
2900 Markham Rd, Scarborough, ON, M1X 1E6
(416) 299-7575
Emp Here 3   *Sales* 81,050,969
SIC 5146 Fish and seafoods
  David Lam
  Sherman Lam

D-U-N-S 24-887-1704   (SL)
VIVA   HEALTHCARE   PACKAGING (CANADA) LTD
1663 Neilson Rd Suite 13, Scarborough, ON, M1X 1T1
(416) 321-0622
Emp Here 200   *Sales* 31,771,600
SIC 3083 Laminated plastics plate and sheet
  May Chan

D-U-N-S 25-386-6149   (SL)
VIVA MEDIA PACKAGING (CANADA) LTD
1663 Neilson Rd Suite 13, Scarborough, ON, M1X 1T1
(416) 321-0622
Emp Here 1,500   *Sales* 358,218,000
SIC 3089 Plastics products, nec
  May Chan
  Ky Choi

D-U-N-S 20-152-4956   (SL)
WILLIAMS BROTHERS CORPORATION, THE
777 Tapscott Rd, Scarborough, ON, M1X 1A2
(416) 299-7767
Emp Here 54   *Sales* 10,372,590
SIC 3442 Metal doors, sash, and trim
  William G Williams

Schomberg, ON L0G

D-U-N-S 20-761-3741   (SL)
614128 ONTARIO LTD
TRISAN CONSTRUCTION
5878 Highway 9, Schomberg, ON, L0G 1T0
(416) 410-3839
Emp Here 60   *Sales* 15,146,520
SIC 1611 Highway and street construction
  Angelo Santorelli

D-U-N-S 24-891-4590   (SL)
ALLSTONE QUARRY PRODUCTS INC
16105 Highway 27 Rr 1, Schomberg, ON, L0G 1T0
(905) 939-8491
Emp Here 40   *Sales* 17,886,960
SIC 5032 Brick, stone, and related material

Jose Melo

D-U-N-S 20-767-6656   (HQ)
B.C. PRECISION INC
B.C. INSTRUMENTS
41 Proctor Rd, Schomberg, ON, L0G 1T0
(905) 939-7323
Emp Here 132   *Sales* 35,076,158
SIC 3545 Machine tool accessories
  Roger Conzelman
  Robert Wheeler
  Bruce Conzelman

D-U-N-S 24-451-4618   (HQ)
BROOKDALE   TREELAND   NURSERIES LIMITED
BTN
6050 17th Sideroad, Schomberg, ON, L0G 1T0
(905) 859-4571
Emp Here 75   *Sales* 25,353,750
SIC 0181 Ornamental nursery products
  Jeff Olsen

D-U-N-S 20-374-6784   (HQ)
CANADIAN KROWN DEALERS INC
KROWN RUST CONTROL SYSTEMS
35 Magnum Dr, Schomberg, ON, L0G 1T0
(905) 939-8750
Emp Here 1   *Sales* 16,797,935
SIC 5169 Chemicals and allied products, nec
  Freeman Young
  Dan Cotton
  George Jackson
  Gilles Letourneau
  Paul Shaheen
  Christopher Mercer
  Pierre Leger

D-U-N-S 25-529-1593   (SL)
SHOWA CANADA INC
(*Suby of* SHOWA CORPORATION)
1 Showa Crt, Schomberg, ON, L0G 1T0
(905) 939-0575
Emp Here 325   *Sales* 94,526,250
SIC 3714 Motor vehicle parts and accessories
  Akira Kuriyama
  Rick Wolak

D-U-N-S 24-418-5620   (BR)
SILANI SWEET CHEESE LIMITED
(*Suby of* SILANI SWEET CHEESE LIMITED)
4205 2nd Line, Schomberg, ON, L0G 1T0
(416) 324-3290
Emp Here 185
SIC 2022 Cheese; natural and processed
  Isawar Saxena

Schumacher, ON P0N

D-U-N-S 24-183-3912   (HQ)
DISTRICT SCHOOL BOARD ONTARIO NORTH EAST
153 Croatia Ave, Schumacher, ON, P0N 1G0
(705) 360-1151
Emp Here 30   *Sales* 39,647,600
SIC 8211 Elementary and secondary schools
  Saunders Porter
  Linda Knight
  Jergun Leukert

D-U-N-S 20-037-8698   (BR)
EXTENDICARE (CANADA) INC
EXTENDICARE TIMMINS
(*Suby of* EXTENDICARE INC)
15 Hollinger Lane, Schumacher, ON, P0N 1G0

Emp Here 147
SIC 8059 Nursing and personal care, nec
  Kelly Tremblay

D-U-N-S 24-348-9940   (HQ)
TORBA RESTAURANTS INC

WENDY'S RESTAURANTS
6 Father Costello Dr, Schumacher, ON, P0N 1G0
(705) 267-4150
Sales 37,311,200
SIC 5812 Eating places
  Kirsten Summers

Scotland, ON N0E

D-U-N-S 20-878-3266   (SL)
KOMIENSKI LIMITED
4665 Highway 24 Rr 3, Scotland, ON, N0E 1R0
(519) 446-2315
Emp Here 40   *Sales* 13,698,680
SIC 0161 Vegetables and melons
  Tom Komienski

Seaforth, ON N0K

D-U-N-S 25-362-5826   (HQ)
1090349 ONTARIO INC
S & B MANAGEMENT
95 Main St S, Seaforth, ON, N0K 1W0
(519) 527-1631
Emp Here 2   *Sales* 20,967,750
SIC 6712 Bank holding companies

D-U-N-S 20-518-1287   (SL)
450252 ONTARIO LTD
SEAFORTH FOOD MARKET
(*Suby of* 1090349 ONTARIO INC)
95 Main St S, Seaforth, ON, N0K 1W0
(519) 527-1631
Emp Here 50   *Sales* 13,707,600
SIC 5411 Grocery stores

D-U-N-S 24-333-2256   (SL)
E.D. SMITH & SONS, LP
151 Main St S, Seaforth, ON, N0K 1W0
(800) 263-9246
Emp Here 185   *Sales* 63,952,650
SIC 2035 Pickles, sauces, and salad dressings
  Mike Barr

D-U-N-S 25-460-7948   (SL)
PROVINCIAL NURSING HOME LIMITED PARTNERSHIP
SEAFORTH MANOR RETIREMENT LIVING AND LONG TERM CARE
100 James St, Seaforth, ON, N0K 1W0
(519) 527-0030
Emp Here 75   *Sales* 5,142,450
SIC 8051 Skilled nursing care facilities
  Cathy Stewart

D-U-N-S 20-755-1300   (SL)
SMITH, WAYNE & HAROLD CONSTRUCTION LIMITED
55 Birch St, Seaforth, ON, N0K 1W0
(519) 527-1079
Emp Here 25   *Sales* 11,768,275
SIC 1542 Nonresidential construction, nec
  Harold Smith

D-U-N-S 24-947-4321   (SL)
VINCENT FARM EQUIPMENT (SEAFORTH) INC
42787 Hydroline Rd, Seaforth, ON, N0K 1W0
(519) 527-0120
Emp Here 20   *Sales* 10,000,000
SIC 5083 Farm and garden machinery
  Marlen Vincent
  Bryan Vincent
  Barry Vincent

Searchmont, ON P0S

D-U-N-S 24-356-2860   (HQ)
SEARCHMONT SKI ASSOCIATION INC
SEARCHMONT RESORT
103 Searchmont Resort Rd, Searchmont, ON, P0S 1J0
(705) 781-2340
Emp Here 158   *Sales* 1,159,541
SIC 7011 Hotels and motels
  Kristy Rachkowski
  Travis Mccormack
  Brian Macdonald
  Janet Gawne
  Tyler Epp
  Joe Derosario
  Andrea Reibmayr

Sebringville, ON N0K

D-U-N-S 20-921-0210   (SL)
410648 ONTARIO LIMITED
WOODCOCK BROTHERS
(*Suby of* WOODCOCK HOLDINGS INC)
225 Huron Rd, Sebringville, ON, N0K 1X0
(519) 393-6194
Emp Here 140   *Sales* 28,798,840
SIC 4213 Trucking, except local
  Brad Woodcock
  Susan Woodcock

D-U-N-S 20-607-5616   (HQ)
LUCKHART TRANSPORT LTD
4049 Perth County Rd 135, Sebringville, ON, N0K 1X0
(519) 393-6128
Emp Here 79   *Sales* 16,456,480
SIC 4212 Local trucking, without storage
  Douglas Luckhart
  Thomas Luckhart
  Howard Luckhart
  Marjorie Luckhart

D-U-N-S 24-101-3734   (SL)
WOODCOCK   TRANSPORTATION   SERVICES INC
225 Heron Rd, Sebringville, ON, N0K 1X0
(519) 393-5353
Emp Here 30   *Sales* 11,560,800
SIC 4731 Freight transportation arrangement
  Brad Woodcock

Seguin, ON P2A

D-U-N-S 24-198-2297   (SL)
KROPF INDUSTRIAL INC
CONOLIFT
1 Quebec Dr, Seguin, ON, P2A 0B2
(705) 378-2453
Emp Here 69   *Sales* 10,378,296
SIC 3448 Prefabricated Metal buildings and components
  Darin Kropf
  Kara Kropf
  Jordan Kropf
  Derrick Gingrich
  Timothy Gingrich

Shallow Lake, ON N0H

D-U-N-S 20-152-8643   (SL)
SHOULDICE DESIGNER STONE LTD
281227 Shouldice Block Rd Suite 281, Shallow Lake, ON, N0H 2K0
(800) 265-3174
Emp Here 100   *Sales* 23,343,500
SIC 3271 Concrete block and brick
  Steve Shouldice

Brad Shouldice
June Shouldice

Shannonville, ON K0K

D-U-N-S 25-220-4144   (SL)
ASPEN-DUNHILL HOLDINGS LTD
FREE FLOW PETROLIUM
Highway 2 W Suite 6, Shannonville, ON, K0K
3A0
(613) 966-6895
Emp Here 30   *Sales* 14,942,340
SIC 5541 Gasoline service stations
Steven Morris

Shanty Bay, ON L0L

D-U-N-S 24-120-4986   (SL)
CARRIAGE HILLS VACATION OWNERS AS-SOCIATION
90 Highland Dr, Shanty Bay, ON, L0L 2L0
(705) 835-5858
Emp Here 137   *Sales* 12,698,530
SIC 7011 Hotels and motels
Emily Burns

D-U-N-S 24-204-0801   (SL)
HITCH HOUSE INC, THE
1490 11 Hwy S, Shanty Bay, ON, L0L 2L0
(705) 722-0008
Emp Here 50   *Sales* 24,903,900
SIC 5571 Motorcycle dealers
David Mckee
Pamela Mckee
Thomas Stoate

Sharon, ON L0G

D-U-N-S 24-616-8947   (SL)
1748271 ONTARIO INC
36 Maplehyrn Ave, Sharon, ON, L0G 1V0
(519) 457-2863
Emp Here 45   *Sales* 29,540,880
SIC 5963 Direct selling establishments
Randy Robertson

D-U-N-S 24-727-1257   (HQ)
677957 ONTARIO INC
VINCE'S COUNTRY MARKET
19101 Leslie St, Sharon, ON, L0G 1V0
(905) 478-8241
Sales 23,478,160
SIC 5411 Grocery stores
Carmen Trimarchi
Mario Testa
Brian Johns

D-U-N-S 24-419-4296   (HQ)
AMG METALS INC
21 Bales Dr W, Sharon, ON, L0G 1V0
(905) 953-4111
Emp Here 50   *Sales* 11,675,820
SIC 3365 Aluminum foundries
Mileo Monte
John Pierson
Matthew Powell
William Powell

D-U-N-S 20-157-0850   (HQ)
GEO. A. KELSON COMPANY LIMITED
2 Bales Dr W, Sharon, ON, L0G 1V0
(905) 898-3400
Emp Here 150   *Sales* 34,959,750
SIC 1711 Plumbing, heating, air-conditioning
Rod Kelson
Larry Kelson

D-U-N-S 24-505-8466   (SL)

KING CAPON LIMITED
18347 Warden Ave, Sharon, ON, L0G 1V0
(905) 478-2382
Emp Here 19   *Sales* 10,167,356
SIC 5144 Poultry and poultry products
Thomas Appleton
Diane Appleton

D-U-N-S 20-577-7431   (BR)
TANDET MANAGEMENT INC
(*Suby of* TANDET MANAGEMENT INC)
2510 Davis Dr, Sharon, ON, L0G 1V0
(905) 953-5457
Emp Here 300
SIC 4212 Local trucking, without storage
Jeff Cockshutt

D-U-N-S 20-557-5306   (SL)
TECHNICORE UNDERGROUND INC
102 Bales Drive E, Sharon, ON, L0G 1V0
(905) 898-4889
Emp Here 200   *Sales* 50,488,400
SIC 1622 Bridge, tunnel, and elevated high-way construction
Lynn Jackson
Patrick Michaud

Shelburne, ON L0N

D-U-N-S 24-858-4539   (SL)
BLUE MOUNTAIN PLASTICS INC
400 Second Line, Shelburne, ON, L0N 1S5
(519) 925-3550
Emp Here 35   *Sales* 10,539,970
SIC 4953 Refuse systems
Ryan L'abbe

Shelburne, ON L9V

D-U-N-S 20-349-8456   (BR)
CORPORATION OF THE COUNTY OF DUF-FERIN, THE
DUFFERIN OAKS HOME FOR SENIOR CITI-ZENS
(*Suby of* CORPORATION OF THE COUNTY OF DUFFERIN, THE)
151 Centre St, Shelburne, ON, L9V 3R7
(519) 925-2140
Emp Here 164
SIC 8322 Individual and family services

D-U-N-S 20-304-3922   (SL)
GILLAM FAMILY HOLDINGS LIMITED
SHELBURNE HOME HARDWARE
725 Steeles St, Shelburne, ON, L9V 3M7
(519) 925-3991
Emp Here 60   *Sales* 16,059,120
SIC 5251 Hardware stores
Bill Gillam

D-U-N-S 25-502-3103   (HQ)
ICE RIVER SPRINGS WATER CO. INC
485387 County Rd 11, Shelburne, ON, L9V 3N5
(519) 925-2929
Emp Here 150   *Sales* 143,343,200
SIC 5149 Groceries and related products, nec
Jamie Gott
Sandy Gott
James Dickson
Paul Dawdall

D-U-N-S 25-510-1982   (SL)
KTH SHELBURNE MFG. INC
(*Suby of* KTH PARTS INDUSTRIES, INC.)
300 2nd Line, Shelburne, ON, L9V 3N4
(519) 925-3030
Emp Here 430   *Sales* 125,065,500
SIC 3714 Motor vehicle parts and accessories
Yosuke Sewa
Ted Scott

Tim Inoue

D-U-N-S 24-974-5993   (BR)
UPPER GRAND DISTRICT SCHOOL BOARD, THE
CENTRE DUFFERIN DISTRICT HIGH SCHOOL
(*Suby of* UPPER GRAND DISTRICT SCHOOL BOARD, THE)
150 Fourth Ave, Shelburne, ON, L9V 3R5
(519) 925-3834
Emp Here 100
SIC 8211 Elementary and secondary schools
Pat Hamilton

Simcoe, ON N3Y

D-U-N-S 20-639-6889   (SL)
AITKEN MOTORS LTD
AITKEN CHEVROLET
51 Queensway E, Simcoe, ON, N3Y 4M5
(519) 426-1793
Emp Here 24   *Sales* 11,953,872
SIC 5511 New and used car dealers
Paul Cripps

D-U-N-S 25-593-1958   (HQ)
ANNEX PUBLISHING & PRINTING INC
ANNEX BUSINESS MEDIA
105 Donly Dr S, Simcoe, ON, N3Y 4N5
(519) 428-3471
Emp Here 77   *Sales* 13,450,214
SIC 2721 Periodicals
Micheal Fredericks
Susan Fredericks

D-U-N-S 20-003-4648   (SL)
ANNISONS LTD
CANADIAN TIRE
140 Queensway E, Simcoe, ON, N3Y 4Y7
(519) 426-1513
Emp Here 95   *Sales* 34,600,425
SIC 5014 Tires and tubes
Douglas W Annis
T. Annis

D-U-N-S 24-720-5636   (SL)
BLUE STAR FORD LINCOLN SALES LTD
121 Queensway E, Simcoe, ON, N3Y 4M5
(519) 426-3673
Emp Here 37   *Sales* 18,428,886
SIC 5511 New and used car dealers
Robert Kowtaluk

D-U-N-S 20-293-1056   (BR)
BRANT HALDIMAND NORFOLK CATHOLIC DISTRICT SCHOOL BOARD
HOLY TRINITY CATHOLIC HIGH SCHOOL
(*Suby of* BRANT HALDIMAND NORFOLK CATHOLIC DISTRICT SCHOOL BOARD)
128 Evergreen Hill Rd, Simcoe, ON, N3Y 4K1
(519) 429-3600
Emp Here 125
SIC 8211 Elementary and secondary schools
Floyd Kennedy

D-U-N-S 20-153-2652   (HQ)
BRUCE R. SMITH LIMITED
51 Park Rd, Simcoe, ON, N3Y 4J9
(519) 426-0904
Emp Here 7   *Sales* 21,845,992
SIC 4212 Local trucking, without storage
Beth Knoll

D-U-N-S 24-619-7375   (SL)
CHATHAM, W. T ASSOCIATES LTD
83 Maple St, Simcoe, ON, N3Y 2G1
(519) 426-0379
Emp Here 6   *Sales* 18,948,562
SIC 4925 Gas production and/or distribution

D-U-N-S 24-827-6941   (HQ)
CLARK, H. PHARMACY INC
PHARMASAVE
454 Norfolk St S, Simcoe, ON, N3Y 2X3

---

(519) 426-6580
Emp Here 1   *Sales* 16,369,976
SIC 5912 Drug stores and proprietary stores

D-U-N-S 24-011-7213   (BR)
COMCARE (CANADA) LIMITED
COMCARE HEALTH SERVICES
(*Suby of* COMCARE (CANADA) LIMITED)
8 Queensway E Suite 4, Simcoe, ON, N3Y 4M3
(519) 426-5122
Emp Here 80
SIC 8059 Nursing and personal care, nec
Kelly Speeding

D-U-N-S 25-034-6541   (SL)
COMMUNITY LIVING ACCESS SUPPORT SERVICES
COMMUNITY LIVING ACCESS
89 Culver St, Simcoe, ON, N3Y 2V5
(519) 426-0007
Emp Here 100   *Sales* 13,345,900
SIC 8399 Social services, nec
Patricia Morris
Vivian Fuller

D-U-N-S 20-845-3241   (BR)
CORPORATION OF NORFOLK COUNTY
NORVIEW LODGE
(*Suby of* CORPORATION OF NORFOLK COUNTY)
44 Rob Blake Way, Simcoe, ON, N3Y 0E3
(519) 426-0902
Emp Here 110
SIC 8051 Skilled nursing care facilities
Bill Nolan

D-U-N-S 20-153-0425   (SL)
DEMEYERE CHRYSLER LIMITED
144 Queensway E, Simcoe, ON, N3Y 4K8
(519) 426-3010
Emp Here 30   *Sales* 14,942,340
SIC 5511 New and used car dealers
Douglas Derek Demeyere

D-U-N-S 24-347-6327   (SL)
ESSEX GROUP CANADA INC
SUPERIOR ESSEX
(*Suby of* LS CORP.)
20 Gilbertson Dr Suite 20, Simcoe, ON, N3Y 4L5
(519) 428-3900
Emp Here 147   *Sales* 26,664,036
SIC 3351 Copper rolling and drawing
David Reed

D-U-N-S 20-024-9766   (BR)
GRAND ERIE DISTRICT SCHOOL BOARD
SIMCOE COMPOSITE SCHOOL
(*Suby of* GRAND ERIE DISTRICT SCHOOL BOARD)
40 Wilson Ave, Simcoe, ON, N3Y 2E5
(519) 426-4664
Emp Here 100
SIC 8211 Elementary and secondary schools
Alison High

D-U-N-S 20-015-7515   (SL)
HALDIMAND HEALTH AND SEPTIC INSP
HALDIMAND NORFOLK HEALTH UNIT
12 Gilbertson Dr, Simcoe, ON, N3Y 4L1
(519) 426-6170
Emp Here 49   *Sales* 11,114,817
SIC 8399 Social services, nec
Marlene Miranda

D-U-N-S 20-026-1092   (SL)
HALDIMAND-NORFOLK COMMUNITY CARE ACCESS CENTRE
HAMILTON NIAGARA HALDIMAND-BRANT CCAC
76 Victoria St, Simcoe, ON, N3Y 1L5
(519) 426-7400
Emp Here 60   *Sales* 16,459,920
SIC 8741 Management services
John Elgersma
Megan Allen
Larry Horwood

D-U-N-S 25-498-6169   (HQ)
HALDIMAND-NORFOLK COMMUNITY SE-NIOR SUPPORT SERVICES INC
SENIOR SUPPORT SERVICES
230 Victoria St, Simcoe, ON, N3Y 4K2
(519) 426-6060
Emp Here 10   *Sales* 10,743,750
SIC 8611 Business associations
Guy Bryan
Patricia Verdone

D-U-N-S 20-640-6605   (SL)
HENDERSON RECREATION EQUIPMENT LIMITED
11 Gilbertson Dr, Simcoe, ON, N3Y 4K8
(519) 426-9380
Emp Here 54   *Sales* 17,611,344
SIC 3949 Sporting and athletic goods, nec
Gordon Henderson

D-U-N-S 24-335-9796   (SL)
JARJA FLORAL INTERNATIONAL CORP
JARJA FLORAL
577 Charlotteville Road 8, Simcoe, ON, N3Y 4K5
(519) 582-3930
Emp Here 56   *Sales* 14,689,304
SIC 0181 Ornamental nursery products
Jan Gerrit Oosterveld
Raymond Oosterveld
Wybe Kornelis Vanderveen

D-U-N-S 20-822-1390   (SL)
MANN, R. E. BROKERS LTD
TRI-COUNTY INSURACE GROUP
28 Colborne St N, Simcoe, ON, N3Y 3T9
(519) 426-2551
Emp Here 26   *Sales* 15,078,024
SIC 6411 Insurance agents, brokers, and service
Fred Morison

D-U-N-S 20-772-6191   (HQ)
MAPLEWOOD NURSING HOME LIMITED
CEDARWOOD VILLAGE
500 Queensway W Suite 210, Simcoe, ON, N3Y 4R4
(519) 426-8305
Emp Here 100   *Sales* 27,608,875
SIC 6513 Apartment building operators
George Kaniuk
Evelyn Kaniuk
Christine Kaniuk

D-U-N-S 25-300-2703   (BR)
METRO ONTARIO INC
FOOD BASICS
(*Suby of* METRO INC)
150 West St, Simcoe, ON, N3Y 5C1
(519) 426-2010
Emp Here 75
SIC 5411 Grocery stores
Doug Davis

D-U-N-S 24-977-1338   (SL)
NELSON, NELSON FOODS INC
TIM HORTONS
15 Queensway E, Simcoe, ON, N3Y 4Y2
(519) 428-0101
Emp Here 50   *Sales* 13,707,600
SIC 5461 Retail bakeries
Pauline Nelson
Grant Nelson

D-U-N-S 20-153-1969   (SL)
NORFOLK FRUIT GROWERS' ASSOCIATION, THE
99 Queensway E, Simcoe, ON, N3Y 4M5
(519) 426-6931
Emp Here 30   *Sales* 11,247,798
SIC 5148 Fresh fruits and vegetables
Marshall Schuyler
Harold Schooley
Richard Pearson
Les Vajda
Tom Haskett
Tom O'neill

D-U-N-S 24-488-0316   (SL)
NORFOLK GENERAL HOSPITAL
365 West St, Simcoe, ON, N3Y 1T7
(519) 426-0130
Emp Here 500   *Sales* 38,313,173
SIC 8062 General medical and surgical hospitals
Kelly Isfan
Tom Thomson
John Thorpe
Nancy Gabel
Susan Graham
Brian Miller
Beth Snowden
Thomas White
Veronica Pepper
Ellen Coffey

D-U-N-S 24-388-9508   (SL)
NORFOLK POWER DISTRIBUTION INC
(*Suby of* CORPORATION OF NORFOLK COUNTY)
70 Victoria St, Simcoe, ON, N3Y 1L5
(519) 426-4440
Emp Here 50   *Sales* 31,330,700
SIC 4911 Electric services
Fred Druyf

D-U-N-S 24-206-9594   (SL)
RASSAUN SERVICES INC
22 Boswell Dr, Simcoe, ON, N3Y 4N5
(519) 426-0150
Emp Here 100   *Sales* 19,208,500
SIC 3441 Fabricated structural Metal
Kevin Saunders

D-U-N-S 20-153-2397   (HQ)
ROULSTON'S DISCOUNT DRUGS LIMITED
ROULSTON'S PHARMACY
17 Norfolk St S, Simcoe, ON, N3Y 2V8
(519) 426-1731
Emp Here 43   *Sales* 24,677,128
SIC 5912 Drug stores and proprietary stores
Mark Stephens
Blair Snow
Steve Flexman

D-U-N-S 25-309-1870   (BR)
SOBEYS CAPITAL INCORPORATED
SOBEYS
(*Suby of* EMPIRE COMPANY LIMITED)
438 Norfolk St S, Simcoe, ON, N3Y 2X3
(519) 426-4799
Emp Here 125
SIC 5411 Grocery stores
Mike Feff

D-U-N-S 24-408-1451   (SL)
STRAWBERRY TYME INC
1250 St John'S Rd W, Simcoe, ON, N3Y 4K1
(519) 426-3099
Emp Here 50   *Sales* 13,707,600
SIC 5431 Fruit and vegetable markets
Gary Cooper
Sandra Cooper

D-U-N-S 25-353-1610   (SL)
TOWNSEND BUTCHERS INC
419 Concession 14 Townsend, Simcoe, ON, N3Y 4K3
(519) 426-6750
Emp Here 23   *Sales* 19,218,271
SIC 5147 Meats and meat products
Steve Miedema
Jeff Miedema

D-U-N-S 24-346-7078   (SL)
TOYOTETSU CANADA, INC
(*Suby of* TOYODA IRON WORKS CO.,LTD.)
88 Park Rd, Simcoe, ON, N3Y 4J9
(519) 428-6500
Emp Here 302   *Sales* 73,455,762
SIC 3465 Automotive stampings
Norifumi Taniguchi

D-U-N-S 20-980-7015   (BR)
UNILEVER CANADA INC
GOOD HUMOR BREYERS

(*Suby of* UNILEVER PLC)
175 Union St, Simcoe, ON, N3Y 2B1
(519) 426-1673
Emp Here 350
SIC 2024 Ice cream and frozen deserts
Brad Allender

D-U-N-S 20-004-0660   (BR)
ZEHRMART INC
REAL CANADIAN SUPERSTORE
(*Suby of* LOBLAW COMPANIES LIMITED)
125 Queensway E, Simcoe, ON, N3Y 5M7
(519) 426-7743
Emp Here 220
SIC 5411 Grocery stores
Guane Flood

Sioux Lookout, ON P8T

D-U-N-S 25-542-1950   (HQ)
13089980 ONTARIO LTD
MORGAN ESSO
1 Black Bear Rd, Sioux Lookout, ON, P8T 1B3
(807) 737-2250
Emp Here 1   *Sales* 11,360,888
SIC 5171 Petroleum bulk stations and terminals
Darrell Morgan

D-U-N-S 24-966-8930   (BR)
BEARSKIN LAKE AIR SERVICE LP
BEARSKIN AIRLINES
(*Suby of* EXCHANGE INCOME CORPORATION)
7 Airport Rd, Sioux Lookout, ON, P8T 1J6
(807) 737-3473
Emp Here 110
SIC 4522 Air transportation, nonscheduled
Terri Busch

D-U-N-S 20-153-3536   (SL)
MICHIELI'S SUPERMARKET LIMITED
JOHNNY'S FRESH MARKET
79 Queen St, Sioux Lookout, ON, P8T 1A3
(807) 737-1630
Emp Here 100   *Sales* 29,347,700
SIC 5411 Grocery stores

D-U-N-S 25-499-5624   (HQ)
NORTHERN NISHNAWBE EDUCATION COUNCIL
21 King St, Sioux Lookout, ON, P8T 1B9
(807) 737-2002
Emp Here 25   *Sales* 27,132,000
SIC 8299 Schools and educational services, nec
Randy Feurst

D-U-N-S 20-180-8040   (HQ)
SIOUX LOOKOUT MENO-YA-WIN HEALTH CENTRE PLANNING CORPORATION
WILLIAM A.(BILL) GEORGE EXTENDED CARE FACILITY
1 Meno Ya Win Way, Sioux Lookout, ON, P8T 1B4
(807) 737-3030
Emp Here 100   *Sales* 30,547,000
SIC 8062 General medical and surgical hospitals
Roger Walker
Gordon Hill
Knowles Mcgill

D-U-N-S 24-579-3562   (SL)
SKYCARE AIR AMBULANCE
17 Airport Rd, Sioux Lookout, ON, P8T 1A3
(807) 737-0038
Emp Here 49   *Sales* 15,912,946
SIC 4522 Air transportation, nonscheduled
Frank Behrendt

D-U-N-S 20-002-6487   (HQ)
TIKINAGAN CHILD & FAMILY SERVICES
63 King St, Sioux Lookout, ON, P8T 1B1

(807) 737-3466
Sales 23,037,600
SIC 8322 Individual and family services
Michael Hardy

Smiths Falls, ON K7A

D-U-N-S 20-708-7037   (BR)
BAYSHORE HEALTHCARE LTD.
BAYSHORE HEALTHCARE LTD
(*Suby of* BAYSHORE HEALTHCARE LTD.)
94 Beckwith St N, Smiths Falls, ON, K7A 2C1
(613) 283-1400
Emp Here 200
SIC 8082 Home health care services
Anita Fitches

D-U-N-S 25-510-2030   (SL)
BRANCH FINANCE CORPORATION LIMITED
BRANCH VENTURE CAPITAL SERVICE
5 Chambers St, Smiths Falls, ON, K7A 2Y2
(613) 283-5555
Emp Here 46   *Sales* 32,053,260
SIC 6799 Investors, nec
S. G. Robertson
A. M. Kelly
Brett Robertson

D-U-N-S 25-572-5277   (SL)
BROADVIEW NURSING CENTRE LIMITED
210 Brockville St, Smiths Falls, ON, K7A 3Z4
(613) 283-1845
Emp Here 85   *Sales* 5,842,305
SIC 8051 Skilled nursing care facilities
Leonard Parsons

D-U-N-S 20-251-3016   (HQ)
CANOPY GROWTH CORPORATION
1 Hershey Dr, Smiths Falls, ON, K7A 0A8
(855) 558-9333
Sales 30,368,433
SIC 6712 Bank holding companies
Bruce Linton
Mark Zekulin
Tim Saunders
John Bell
Peter Stringham
Murray Goldman
Chris Schnarr

D-U-N-S 20-008-6135   (BR)
COMCARE (CANADA) LIMITED
COMCARE HEALTH SERVICES
(*Suby of* COMCARE (CANADA) LIMITED)
52 Abbott St N Unit 3, Smiths Falls, ON, K7A 1W3
Emp Here 80
SIC 7363 Help supply services
Dawn Risebrough

D-U-N-S 24-704-8663   (SL)
FAIR, MIKE CHEVROLET BUICK GMC CADILLAC LTD
199 Lombard St, Smiths Falls, ON, K7A 5B8
(613) 283-3882
Emp Here 33   *Sales* 16,436,574
SIC 5511 New and used car dealers
Mike Fair
Doris Ferguson
Wayne Lanning

D-U-N-S 20-153-4666   (SL)
GUILDLINE INSTRUMENTS LIMITED
21 Gilroy St, Smiths Falls, ON, K7A 5B7
(613) 283-3000
Emp Here 40   *Sales* 10,262,480
SIC 3825 Instruments to measure electricity
Richard Timmins
Peter Doit

D-U-N-S 24-826-7551   (BR)
HERSHEY CANADA INC
(*Suby of* HERSHEY COMPANY)

▲ Public Company   ■ Public Company Family Member   **HQ** Headquarters   **BR** Branch   **SL** Single Location

1 Hershey Dr, Smiths Falls, ON, K7A 4T8

Emp Here 500
SIC 2066 Chocolate and cocoa products
Rene Albert

D-U-N-S 20-334-6866   (BR)
METROLAND MEDIA GROUP LTD
PERFORMANCE PRINTING
(*Suby of* TORSTAR CORPORATION)
65 Lorne St, Smiths Falls, ON, K7A 3K8
(800) 267-7936
Emp Here 150
SIC 2711 Newspapers
Michael Mount

D-U-N-S 24-393-0489   (SL)
PARISIEN, J.W. ENTERPRISES LTD
CANADIAN TIRE
10 Ferrara Dr Suite 98, Smiths Falls, ON, K7A 5K4
(613) 283-3906
Emp Here 49   *Sales* 24,405,822
SIC 5531 Auto and home supply stores
Jean Parisien

D-U-N-S 20-894-3068   (HQ)
PERFORMANCE PRINTING LIMITED
PERFORMANCE   PRINTING   SPECIALTY PUBLICATIONS
(*Suby of* TORSTAR CORPORATION)
65 Lorne St, Smiths Falls, ON, K7A 3K8
(613) 283-5650
Sales 19,459,700
SIC 2711 Newspapers
Ian Oliver
Peter Bishop

D-U-N-S 24-103-5401   (HQ)
PERTH AND SMITHS FALLS DISTRICT HOSPITAL
60 Cornelia St W, Smiths Falls, ON, K7A 2H9
(613) 283-2330
Emp Here 270   *Sales* 42,072,625
SIC 8062 General medical and surgical hospitals
Beverley Mcfarlane
Wayne Johnson
Cheryl Becket
Michele Bellows
Jay Brennan
Leslie Drynan
John Fenik
Warren Hollis
Anil Kuchinad
Bruce Laing

D-U-N-S 20-153-5291   (SL)
QUATTROCCHI, JOSEPH & COMPANY LIMITED
63 Church St W, Smiths Falls, ON, K7A 1R2
(613) 283-4980
Emp Here 40   *Sales* 33,423,080
SIC 5148 Fresh fruits and vegetables
Joseph Quattrocchi Jr
Vince Quattrocchi
Frances Quattrocchi
James Quattrocchi
Joseph Quattrocchi

D-U-N-S 20-153-5416   (SL)
RIDEAU LUMBER (SMITH'S FALLS) LIMITED
RIDEAU   HOME   HARDWARE   BUILDING CENTRE
58 Abbott St N, Smiths Falls, ON, K7A 1W5
(613) 283-2211
Emp Here 50   *Sales* 12,652,950
SIC 5211 Lumber and other building materials
Scott Fleming
Jim Ireton
Trevor Lloyd
Clayton Fleming

D-U-N-S 25-628-8424   (HQ)
STREET MOTOR SALES LTD
STREET KIA

171 Lombard St, Smiths Falls, ON, K7A 5B8
(613) 284-0023
Emp Here 20   *Sales* 16,934,652
SIC 5521 Used car dealers
Bev Street
Robert Street

D-U-N-S 20-577-3088   (SL)
TOWN & COUNTRY CHRYSLER LIMITED
245 Lombard St, Smiths Falls, ON, K7A 5B8
(613) 283-7555
Emp Here 36   *Sales* 17,930,808
SIC 5511 New and used car dealers
Bradley J Kyle

D-U-N-S 24-318-0812   (BR)
WAL-MART CANADA CORP
WALMART
(*Suby of* WALMART INC.)
114 Lombard St, Smiths Falls, ON, K7A 5B8
(613) 284-0838
Emp Here 120
SIC 5311 Department stores
Jason Salmon

D-U-N-S 20-153-5895   (HQ)
WILLS TRANSFER LIMITED
146 Hwy 15, Smiths Falls, ON, K7A 4S7
(613) 283-0225
Emp Here 62   *Sales* 31,061,606
SIC 4225 General warehousing and storage

Smithville, ON L0R

D-U-N-S 25-967-9830   (SL)
2408234 ONTARIO INC
SMITHVILLE FOODLAND
239 St Catharines St, Smithville, ON, L0R 2A0
(905) 957-3374
Emp Here 70   *Sales* 20,543,390
SIC 5411 Grocery stores
Mike Macqueen
Erin Macqueen

D-U-N-S 24-380-7257   (SL)
EHS CANADA INC
2964 South Grimsby Rd 18 Rr 1, Smithville, ON, L0R 2A0
(905) 643-3343
Emp Here 43   *Sales* 10,074,384
SIC 8748 Business consulting, nec
William Abbott

D-U-N-S 24-363-3760   (HQ)
HARBISONWALKER   INTERNATIONAL CORP
(*Suby of* HARBISONWALKER INTERNATIONAL HOLDINGS, INC.)
2689 Industrial Park Rd, Smithville, ON, L0R 2A0
(905) 957-3311
Emp Here 30   *Sales* 11,671,750
SIC 3297 Nonclay refractories
Carol Jackson
Brad Cramer
Judy Weisseg
Don Abrino
Ross Wilkin

D-U-N-S 24-964-3701   (SL)
MCFEETERS G., ENTERPRISES INC
2825 South Grimsby Rd 21, Smithville, ON, L0R 2A0
(905) 643-6167
Emp Here 50   *Sales* 26,027,100
SIC 5099 Durable goods, nec
Greg Mcfeeters

D-U-N-S 25-470-0321   (SL)
PEACOCK VANDERHOUT & VANDYK INSURANCE BROKERS LTD
MEESTER INSURANCE BROKERS, DIV OF
Hwy 20 Village Square Mall, Smithville, ON, L0R 2A0

(905) 957-2333
Emp Here 18   *Sales* 10,438,632
SIC 6411 Insurance agents, brokers, and service
Brian Vanderhout

D-U-N-S 24-488-1926   (SL)
SHELDRICK, J. W. SANITATION LTD
(*Suby of* MODERN LANDFILL, INC.)
4278 London Rd, Smithville, ON, L0R 2A0
(905) 957-3165
Emp Here 60   *Sales* 19,134,600
SIC 4953 Refuse systems
Richard Washuta

D-U-N-S 20-533-9054   (SL)
SICARD HOLIDAY CAMPERS LIMITED
SICARD RV
7526 Regional Road 20, Smithville, ON, L0R 2A0
(905) 957-3344
Emp Here 75   *Sales* 47,196,000
SIC 5561 Recreational vehicle dealers
Gary Sicard
Blair Sicard

D-U-N-S 20-716-5085   (HQ)
STANPAC INC
2790 Thompson Rd, Smithville, ON, L0R 2A0
(905) 957-3326
Sales 268,375,010
SIC 2675 Die-cut paper and board
Andrew Witt
Matthew Witt
Ian Killins
Murray Bain
Dave Kuzmich
Brent Roszell

Smooth Rock Falls, ON P0L

D-U-N-S 24-164-2656   (SL)
COMMUNITY CLUB
219 5th St, Smooth Rock Falls, ON, P0L 2B0
(705) 338-2336
Emp Here 100   *Sales* 14,528,205
SIC 8641 Civic and social associations
Emilliene Blanchette

D-U-N-S 24-364-7831   (SL)
SMOOTH ROCK FALLS HOSPITAL CORPORATION
107 Kelly Rd, Smooth Rock Falls, ON, P0L 2B0
(705) 338-2781
Emp Here 90   *Sales* 9,191,970
SIC 8062 General medical and surgical hospitals
Fabien Hebert

South Lancaster, ON K0C

D-U-N-S 24-718-9723   (HQ)
ROB MCINTOSH CHINA INC
ROB MCINTOSH CHINA STORES
20369 South Service Rd, South Lancaster, ON, K0C 2C0
(613) 347-2461
Emp Here 35   *Sales* 46,480,600
SIC 5719 Miscellaneous homefurnishings
Robin Mcintosh
Barbara Mcintosh
Peter Mcintosh

South Porcupine, ON P0N

D-U-N-S 20-007-9072   (BR)
KINROSS GOLD CORPORATION
PROCUPINE JOINT VENTURES

(*Suby of* KINROSS GOLD CORPORATION)
4315 Goldmine Rd, South Porcupine, ON, P0N 1H0

Emp Here 285
SIC 1041 Gold ores
Chris Cormier

South River, ON P0A

D-U-N-S 25-975-7180   (BR)
PHOENIX BUILDING COMPONENTS INC
(*Suby of* PHOENIX BUILDING COMPONENTS INC)
93 Ottawa Ave, South River, ON, P0A 1X0
(705) 386-0007
Emp Here 100
SIC 2439 Structural wood members, nec

South Woodslee, ON N0R

D-U-N-S 25-650-0273   (SL)
COUNTRY VILLAGE HEALTH CARE CENTRE
440 County Rd 8 Suite 8, South Woodslee, ON, N0R 1V0
(519) 839-4812
Emp Here 130   *Sales* 8,882,380
SIC 8051 Skilled nursing care facilities
Jane Brooks-Keller

Southampton, ON N0H

D-U-N-S 24-120-7984   (SL)
SOUTHAMPTON CARE CENTRE INC
140 Grey St S, Southampton, ON, N0H 2L0
(519) 797-3220
Emp Here 80   *Sales* 5,498,640
SIC 8051 Skilled nursing care facilities
David Jarlette

Sparta, ON N0L

D-U-N-S 20-153-9160   (SL)
VANDENBRINK FARM EQUIPMENT INC
7565 Quaker Rd, Sparta, ON, N0L 2H0
(519) 775-2601
Emp Here 20   *Sales* 10,000,000
SIC 5083 Farm and garden machinery
Henry Vandenbrink
Anne Vandenbrink

Spencerville, ON K0E

D-U-N-S 20-788-4123   (SL)
GRENVILLE MUTUAL INSURANCE COMPANY
GRENVILLE MUTUAL
3005 County Rd 21, Spencerville, ON, K0E 1X0
(613) 258-9988
Emp Here 18   *Sales* 18,627,858
SIC 6331 Fire, marine, and casualty insurance
Ross Lincoln
James (Jim) Locke
Ivan Petersen
Hebert Ferguson
Ron Greaves
Gordon Smith

▲ Public Company   ■ Public Company Family Member   **HQ** Headquarters   **BR** Branch   **SL** Single Location

Springbrook, ON K0K

D-U-N-S 20-153-9509   (SL)
MCKEOWN, WILLIAM MOTOR SALES LIMITED
MCKEOWN MOTOR SALES
2589 Springbrook Rd, Springbrook, ON, K0K 3C0
(613) 395-3883
Emp Here 25   *Sales* 12,451,950
SIC 5541 Gasoline service stations
William Mckeown
Allan Mckeown
Grace Mckeown

Springwater, ON L9X

D-U-N-S 20-036-2978   (HQ)
BRADFORD GREENHOUSES LIMITED
BRADFORD GREENHOUSES GARDEN GALLERY
4346 Hwy 90, Springwater, ON, L9X 1T7
(705) 725-9913
Emp Here 150   *Sales* 70,262,500
SIC 5261 Retail nurseries and garden stores
Anthony Ferragine
Domenic Ferragine
Len Ferragine
Sam Gallo
Eileen Graham

St Agatha, ON N0B

D-U-N-S 20-975-5222   (BR)
ANGIE'S KITCHEN LIMITED
(*Suby of* ANGIE'S KITCHEN LIMITED)
1761 Erb'S Rd, St Agatha, ON, N0B 2L0
(519) 747-1700
Emp Here 90
SIC 5812 Eating places
Teresa Huegle

D-U-N-S 25-877-9818   (SL)
BRI-AL FISHER SERVICES INC
FISHER'S ESSO SERVICE
1678 Erb'S Rd, St Agatha, ON, N0B 2L0
(519) 747-1606
Emp Here 28   *Sales* 13,946,184
SIC 5541 Gasoline service stations
Brian Fisher

D-U-N-S 25-080-3160   (SL)
HERRLE FARMS LTD
1253 Erb'S Rd, St Agatha, ON, N0B 2L0
(519) 886-7576
Emp Here 50   *Sales* 17,123,350
SIC 0181 Ornamental nursery products
Howard Herrle

D-U-N-S 20-268-2654   (SL)
HERRLE'S COUNTRY FARM MARKET LTD
1253 Erb'S Rd, St Agatha, ON, N0B 2L0
(519) 886-7576
Emp Here 45   *Sales* 15,411,015
SIC 0191 General farms, primarily crop
James Herrle
Joanne Herrle-Braun

D-U-N-S 25-487-1916   (HQ)
KIDS LINK/ NDSA
1855 Notre Dame Dr, St Agatha, ON, N0B 2L0
(519) 746-5437
Emp Here 1   *Sales* 63,829,080
SIC 8699 Membership organizations, nec
Sonia Pouyat

D-U-N-S 24-688-9083   (SL)
T R SAND & GRAVEL INC
REGIONAL FLEET SERVICE
1417 Notre Dame Dr Rr 1, St Agatha, ON,

N0B 2L0
(519) 747-4173
Emp Here 22   *Sales* 10,957,716
SIC 5521 Used car dealers
Anthony Hartleib
Ronald Strauss

St Albert, ON K0A

D-U-N-S 20-146-7669   (SL)
ST-ALBERT CHEESE CO-OPERATIVE INC
150 St Paul St, St Albert, ON, K0A 3C0
(613) 987-2872
Emp Here 70   *Sales* 24,198,300
SIC 2022 Cheese; natural and processed
Denis Latour

St Anns, ON L0R

D-U-N-S 20-224-7875   (BR)
FIRSTCANADA ULC
(*Suby of* FIRSTGROUP PLC)
4598 Sixteen Rd, St Anns, ON, L0R 1Y0

Emp Here 200
SIC 4151 School buses
Pat Ruber

St Catharines, ON L2M

D-U-N-S 20-641-2587   (SL)
1434378 ONTARIO INC
COMMERICAL CLEANING SERVICE
151 Cushman Rd, St Catharines, ON, L2M 6T4
(905) 688-9220
Emp Here 249   *Sales* 7,960,032
SIC 7349 Building maintenance services, nec
Chris Draayer
Jason Rawsthorne
Gloria Gonzales

D-U-N-S 20-390-0485   (SL)
AMAX HEALTH INC
27 Seapark Dr Unit 1, St Catharines, ON, L2M 6S5
(905) 682-8070
Emp Here 7   *Sales* 15,651,090
SIC 5047 Medical and hospital equipment

D-U-N-S 20-388-4309   (SL)
AMAX HEALTH INC
27 Seapark Dr Unit 1, St Catharines, ON, L2M 6S5
(905) 682-8070
Emp Here 50   *Sales* 22,358,700
SIC 5047 Medical and hospital equipment
Peter Jugoon
Leslie Jaggan

D-U-N-S 20-537-0604   (HQ)
ARLIE'S SPORT SHOP (DOWNTOWN) LTD
BOATHOUSE
17 Keefer Rd, St Catharines, ON, L2M 6K4
(905) 684-8134
Sales 17,939,600
SIC 5621 Women's clothing stores
Jamie Katzman

D-U-N-S 24-124-2189   (SL)
BICKNELL, PETER AUTOMOTIVE INC
PETE'S AUTOMOTIVE
117 Cushman Rd, St Catharines, ON, L2M 6S9
(905) 685-3184
Emp Here 44   *Sales* 21,417,354
SIC 5511 New and used car dealers
Peter Bicknell
Nancy Bicknell

D-U-N-S 24-860-4555   (SL)
CANAFRIC INC
MORTIMER'S FINE FOODS
15 Seapark Dr, St Catharines, ON, L2M 6S5
(905) 688-9588
Emp Here 35   *Sales* 29,245,195
SIC 5142 Packaged frozen goods
Nurudden Somji
Husein Merali
Suvrut Pandya

D-U-N-S 24-098-3288   (SL)
DAN NEL COACH LINES COMPANY LIMITED
(*Suby of* DAN NEL COACH LINES COMPANY (1985) INC)
12 Keefer Rd Suite 10, St Catharines, ON, L2M 7N9
(905) 934-1124
Emp Here 100   *Sales* 7,527,200
SIC 4151 School buses
June Jobson

D-U-N-S 25-468-6843   (HQ)
DEFLECTO CANADA LTD
(*Suby of* JORDAN INDUSTRIES, INC.)
221 Bunting Rd, St Catharines, ON, L2M 3Y2
(905) 641-8872
Sales 21,705,605
SIC 3444 Sheet Metalwork
John Williams

D-U-N-S 24-625-8917   (SL)
EASTWOOD WOOD SPECIALTIES LTD
6 Peacock Bay, St Catharines, ON, L2M 7N8
(905) 937-3030
Emp Here 75   *Sales* 14,427,750
SIC 2426 Hardwood dimension and flooring mills
Ferdinand Neufeld
Rudi Neufeld
Diane Neufeld
Edith Neufeld

D-U-N-S 20-754-3596   (HQ)
ELMWOOD GROUP LIMITED, THE
CABICO
570 Welland Ave, St Catharines, ON, L2M 5V6
(905) 688-5205
Sales 14,427,750
SIC 2434 Wood kitchen cabinets
Rudy Sawatzky
Robert Wiens

D-U-N-S 25-350-7651   (BR)
ELMWOOD GROUP LIMITED, THE
ELMWOOD KITCHEN
(*Suby of* ELMWOOD GROUP LIMITED, THE)
570 Welland Ave, St Catharines, ON, L2M 5V6
(905) 688-5205
Emp Here 75
SIC 3429 Hardware, nec
Rudy Sawatzky

D-U-N-S 24-388-0973   (HQ)
FILTERFAB COMPANY
COMPAGNIE FILTERFAB
(*Suby of* ALSCO INC.)
16 Seapark Dr, St Catharines, ON, L2M 6S6
(905) 684-8363
Sales 16,650,075
SIC 3569 General industrial machinery, nec
John Eugster
James R. Smith
Lisa Lindberg

D-U-N-S 24-372-1110   (HQ)
FREW ENERGY LIMITED
180 Cushman Rd, St Catharines, ON, L2M 6T6
(905) 685-7334
Emp Here 16   *Sales* 125,720,100
SIC 5172 Petroleum products, nec
Mark Frew

D-U-N-S 25-025-2376   (HQ)
HOPE & HARDER INSURANCE BROKERS INC

512 Welland Ave, St Catharines, ON, L2M 5V5
(905) 935-4667
Emp Here 19   *Sales* 21,201,500
SIC 6411 Insurance agents, brokers, and service
William Hope
David Harder

D-U-N-S 24-985-9299   (SL)
LIGHTNING CIRCUITS INC
12 Seapark Dr, St Catharines, ON, L2M 6S6
(905) 984-4006
Emp Here 25   *Sales* 11,179,350
SIC 5065 Electronic parts and equipment, nec
Robert Jeysman

D-U-N-S 20-282-8687   (SL)
NEPTUNUS YACHTS INTERNATIONAL INC
8 Keefer Rd, St Catharines, ON, L2M 7N9
(905) 937-3737
Emp Here 57   *Sales* 11,019,012
SIC 3731 Shipbuilding and repairing
Elaine Hristovski
Milenko Soso

D-U-N-S 25-866-6379   (BR)
NIAGARA CATHOLIC DISTRICT SCHOOL BOARD
HOLY CROSS SECONDARY SCHOOL
(*Suby of* NIAGARA CATHOLIC DISTRICT SCHOOL BOARD)
460 Linwell Rd, St Catharines, ON, L2M 2P9
(905) 937-6446
Emp Here 100
SIC 8211 Elementary and secondary schools
Tony Bozza

D-U-N-S 24-058-0530   (SL)
NIAGARA INA GRAFTON GAGE HOME OF THE UNITED CHURCH
NIAGARA INA GRAFTON GAGE VILLAGE
413 Linwell Rd Suite 4212, St Catharines, ON, L2M 7Y2
(905) 935-6822
Emp Here 100   *Sales* 5,924,700
SIC 8361 Residential care
Patrick O'neill

D-U-N-S 25-465-7679   (SL)
PVS CONTRACTORS INC
113 Cushman Rd Unit 5, St Catharines, ON, L2M 6S9
(905) 984-5414
Emp Here 112   *Sales* 28,273,504
SIC 1623 Water, sewer, and utility lines
Richard Dekker

D-U-N-S 24-526-2589   (HQ)
QUICKSERVICE TECHNOLOGIES INC
QUICKSERVICE TECHNOLOGY SYSTEMS
610 Welland Ave, St Catharines, ON, L2M 5V6
(905) 687-8440
Emp Here 44   *Sales* 29,066,310
SIC 5044 Office equipment
Philip Turner
Garry Messenger
Tim Nugent

D-U-N-S 20-790-2300   (SL)
RON'S NO FRILLS
525 Welland Ave Suite 1316, St Catharines, ON, L2M 6P3
(905) 685-4096
Emp Here 49   *Sales* 13,433,448
SIC 5411 Grocery stores
Ron Anderson

D-U-N-S 20-146-8030   (SL)
SAM ADELSTEIN & CO. LIMITED
PUBLIC METAL SUPPLY DIV OF
492 Welland Ave, St Catharines, ON, L2M 5V5
(905) 988-9336
Emp Here 35   *Sales* 18,218,970
SIC 5093 Scrap and waste materials
Albert Adelstein
Brian Adelstein
Mark Adelstein

D-U-N-S 20-769-8205   (BR)
SOBEYS CAPITAL INCORPORATED
(*Suby of* EMPIRE COMPANY LIMITED)
400 Scott St, St Catharines, ON, L2M 3W4
(905) 935-9974
Emp Here 150
SIC 5411 Grocery stores
Nikki Unrau

D-U-N-S 20-821-2738   (SL)
ST JOSEPHS BAKERY (NIAGARA) INC
53 Facer St, St Catharines, ON, L2M 5H7
(905) 937-4411
Emp Here 24   *Sales* 20,053,848
SIC 5149 Groceries and related products, nec
Joseph Kedzierski
Babara Kedzierski

D-U-N-S 25-535-9267   (SL)
STAR SUPPLY INC
530 Eastchester Ave E, St Catharines, ON,
L2M 7P3
(905) 641-1240
Emp Here 50   *Sales* 23,751,300
SIC 5084 Industrial machinery and equipment
Al Edwards

D-U-N-S 25-213-0406   (HQ)
TORA INVESTMENTS INC
TORA
15 Cushman Rd, St Catharines, ON, L2M 6S7
(905) 227-5088
Emp Here 3   *Sales* 67,529,550
SIC 7549 Automotive services, nec
Ray Ling
Mike Paladichuk

D-U-N-S 25-369-0994   (BR)
TORA INVESTMENTS INC
(*Suby of* TORA INVESTMENTS INC)
453 Eastchester Ave E, St Catharines, ON,
L2M 6S2
(905) 685-5409
Emp Here 80
SIC 7549 Automotive services, nec
Scott Demont

D-U-N-S 24-391-0341   (SL)
TRANSCOM WORLDWIDE (NORTH AMER-ICA) INC
300 Bunting Rd 4, St Catharines, ON, L2M 3Y3
(905) 323-3939
Emp Here 1,100   *Sales* 251,319,200
SIC 4899 Communication services, nec
Kaarle Soinienn
Neil Rae
Christopher Kendall

D-U-N-S 25-498-3224   (BR)
WAL-MART CANADA CORP
(*Suby of* WALMART INC.)
525 Welland Ave, St Catharines, ON, L2M 6P3
(905) 685-4100
Emp Here 200
SIC 5311 Department stores
John Lake

D-U-N-S 25-652-3671   (BR)
WASTE MANAGEMENT OF CANADA COR-PORATION
(*Suby of* WASTE MANAGEMENT, INC.)
124 Cushman Rd, St Catharines, ON, L2M 6T6
(905) 687-9605
Emp Here 85
SIC 4953 Refuse systems
Dale Sett

St Catharines, ON L2N

D-U-N-S 24-796-7060   (SL)
1264316 ONTARIO INC
DAYS INN
89 Meadowvale Dr, St Catharines, ON, L2N
3Z8
(905) 934-5400
Emp Here 200   *Sales* 18,538,000
SIC 7011 Hotels and motels
Chris Nitsopolous

D-U-N-S 20-380-4401   (SL)
1991943 ONTARIO INC
ST. CATHARINES NISSAN
155 Scott St, St Catharines, ON, L2N 1H3
(888) 511-2862
Emp Here 25   *Sales* 12,451,950
SIC 5511 New and used car dealers
David Scherle

D-U-N-S 20-769-1838   (SL)
859689 ONTARIO INC
SATURN OF ST CATHARINES
158 Scott St, St Catharines, ON, L2N 1H1

Emp Here 30   *Sales* 14,942,340
SIC 5511 New and used car dealers
Bill Magee

D-U-N-S 25-147-7014   (BR)
BAYSHORE HEALTHCARE LTD.
BAYSHORE HEALTHCARE LTD
(*Suby of* BAYSHORE HEALTHCARE LTD.)
282 Linwell Rd Suite 205, St Catharines, ON,
L2N 6N5
(905) 688-5214
Emp Here 125
SIC 8322 Individual and family services
Stuart Cottrelle

D-U-N-S 20-937-8611   (SL)
BOLDT POOL CONSTRUCTION LTD
BOLDT POOLS & SPAS
20 Nihan Dr, St Catharines, ON, L2N 1L1
(905) 934-0937
Emp Here 34   *Sales* 11,070,400
SIC 5999 Miscellaneous retail stores, nec
Ted Boldt
Kristine Boldt
Peter Boldt
Fern Boldt

D-U-N-S 24-964-0413   (SL)
BRAIN MATTERS
314 Lake St Suite 2, St Catharines, ON, L2N
4H4

Emp Here 27   *Sales* 11,464,389
SIC 8999 Services, nec
Lee Gerdes

D-U-N-S 24-121-3425   (BR)
CANADA POST CORPORATION
(*Suby of* GOVERNMENT OF CANADA)
163 Scott St, St Catharines, ON, L2N 1H3
(905) 934-9792
Emp Here 90
SIC 4311 U.s. postal service
Cathy Goertz

D-U-N-S 25-529-3144   (BR)
COSTCO WHOLESALE CANADA LTD
COSTCO
(*Suby of* COSTCO WHOLESALE CORPO-RATION)
3 North Service Rd, St Catharines, ON, L2N
7R1
(905) 646-2008
Emp Here 225
SIC 5141 Groceries, general line
Ann Sinclair

D-U-N-S 20-410-9540   (SL)
COSTINIUK, D PHARMACY LTD
SHOPPERS DRUG MART
600 Ontario St, St Catharines, ON, L2N 7H8
(905) 937-3532
Emp Here 43   *Sales* 10,877,022
SIC 5912 Drug stores and proprietary stores
David Costiniuk

D-U-N-S 25-065-3631   (SL)
FIVE BROTHERS HOSPITALITY PARTNER-

SHIP
HOLIDAY INN
2 North Service Rd, St Catharines, ON, L2N
4G9
(905) 934-8000
Emp Here 90   *Sales* 8,342,100
SIC 7011 Hotels and motels
John Nitsopoulos
Chris Nitsopoulos
Peter Nitsopoulos
James Nitsopoulos
Angelo Nitsopoulos

D-U-N-S 20-639-6181   (SL)
HENLEY HOUSE LTD, THE
20 Ernest St Suite 2045, St Catharines, ON,
L2N 7T2
(905) 937-9703
Emp Here 160   *Sales* 10,970,560
SIC 8051 Skilled nursing care facilities
John Bergin

D-U-N-S 20-147-2859   (HQ)
HENLEY MOTORS LIMITED
HENLEY HONDA
308 Lake St, St Catharines, ON, L2N 4H3
(905) 934-3379
Emp Here 1   *Sales* 19,425,042
SIC 5511 New and used car dealers
Alex Di Genis

D-U-N-S 25-354-9703   (BR)
HOME DEPOT OF CANADA INC
HOME DEPOT
(*Suby of* THE HOME DEPOT INC)
20 Ymca Dr, St Catharines, ON, L2N 7R6
(905) 937-5900
Emp Here 250
SIC 5251 Hardware stores
Keith Dobson

D-U-N-S 25-651-7442   (SL)
JOHN BEAR BUICK GMC LTD
(*Suby of* BEAR, JOHN C. HOLDINGS LTD)
333 Lake St, St Catharines, ON, L2N 7T3
(905) 934-2571
Emp Here 70   *Sales* 44,049,600
SIC 5511 New and used car dealers
John Bear
Jamie Lalande

D-U-N-S 25-500-9409   (SL)
LINCOLN FABRICS HOLDINGS LIMITED
63 Lakeport Rd, St Catharines, ON, L2N 4P6

Emp Here 56   *Sales* 10,270,568
SIC 2299 Textile goods, nec
David Howes

D-U-N-S 25-641-1299   (HQ)
LING & LING ENTERPRISES LTD
PETRO CANADA
533 Lake St, St Catharines, ON, L2N 4H6
(905) 937-7719
Emp Here 5   *Sales* 13,707,600
SIC 5411 Grocery stores
Chong Ling

D-U-N-S 25-292-3735   (BR)
METRO ONTARIO INC
METRO
(*Suby of* METRO INC)
101 Lakeshore Rd, St Catharines, ON, L2N
2T6
(905) 934-0131
Emp Here 130
SIC 5411 Grocery stores
Larry Smatana

D-U-N-S 25-483-8303   (HQ)
MOMENTUM REALTY INC
COLDWELL BANKER MOMENTUM REALTY
353 Lake St, St Catharines, ON, L2N 7G4
(905) 935-8001
Emp Here 30   *Sales* 25,133,340
SIC 6531 Real estate agents and managers
Peggy Rose

D-U-N-S 25-129-5796   (HQ)
MORZOC INVESTMENT INC
TIM HORTONS
275 Geneva St, St Catharines, ON, L2N 2E9
(905) 935-0071
Emp Here 25   *Sales* 13,707,600
SIC 5461 Retail bakeries
Joe Zoccoli

D-U-N-S 24-875-0093   (SL)
PERFORMANCE GROUP 262 LAKE INC
PERFORMANCE LEXUS TOYOTA
(*Suby of* AUTOTREND HOLDINGS INC)
262 Lake St, St Catharines, ON, L2N 4H1
(905) 934-7246
Emp Here 25   *Sales* 34,610,400
SIC 5511 New and used car dealers
Glen Alizadeh
M. Steven Alizadeh
May Allison

D-U-N-S 24-407-0731   (SL)
PERFORMANCE HYUNDAI
268 Lake St, St Catharines, ON, L2N 4H1
(905) 937-7000
Emp Here 25   *Sales* 12,451,950
SIC 5511 New and used car dealers
Rein Knol

D-U-N-S 24-795-0710   (SL)
PINDER'S LOCK & SECURITY INC
PINDER'S SECURITY PRODUCTS
25 Nihan Dr, St Catharines, ON, L2N 1L2
(905) 934-6333
Emp Here 37   *Sales* 16,545,438
SIC 5065 Electronic parts and equipment, nec
Gregory (Greg) Pinder
Norman Schwenker

D-U-N-S 25-028-5202   (BR)
REVERA LONG TERM CARE INC
VERSA CARE CENTER
(*Suby of* GOVERNMENT OF CANADA)
168 Scott St, St Catharines, ON, L2N 1H2
(905) 934-3321
Emp Here 240
SIC 8051 Skilled nursing care facilities
Thomas Wellner

D-U-N-S 20-770-6222   (SL)
TABOR MANOR LONG TERM CARE FACIL-ITY
1 Tabor Dr, St Catharines, ON, L2N 1V9
(905) 934-2548
Emp Here 49   *Sales* 90,486,291
SIC 6351 Surety insurance
Tim Siemens

D-U-N-S 24-060-4868   (HQ)
YMCA OF NIAGARA
25 Ymca Dr, St Catharines, ON, L2N 7P9
(905) 646-9622
Emp Here 250   *Sales* 1,179,652,820
SIC 8699 Membership organizations, nec
Steve Butz
Tom Kretz

St Catharines, ON L2P

D-U-N-S 24-596-8276   (SL)
ABSOLUTE PALLET & CRATE INC
NCAC REGIONAL TRAINING CENTRE, DIV OF
104 Dunkirk Rd, St Catharines, ON, L2P 3H5

Emp Here 35   *Sales* 10,539,970
SIC 4953 Refuse systems
Ronald Dubchiak
Jake Sinke
Brian Mcgillion

D-U-N-S 25-637-5627   (HQ)
COMMUNITY CARE ACCESS CENTRE NIA-GARA
PLACEMENT CO-ORDINATION SVC

149 Hartzel Rd, St Catharines, ON, L2P 1N6
(905) 684-9441
Emp Here 50   *Sales* 14,573,190
SIC 8082 Home health care services
Catherine Chisholm

D-U-N-S 20-289-8834   (BR)
DISTRICT SCHOOL BOARD OF NIAGARA
KERNAHAN PARK SECONDARY SCHOOL
91 Bunting Rd, St Catharines, ON, L2P 3G8
(905) 684-9461
Emp Here 75
SIC 8211 Elementary and secondary schools
Barb Edde

D-U-N-S 20-893-7388   (SL)
HELPING LIMITED
SERVICEMASTER CLEAN OF NIAGARA
114 Dunkirk Rd Unit 1, St Catharines, ON,
L2P 3H5
(905) 646-9890
Emp Here 88   *Sales* 3,538,392
SIC 7349 Building maintenance services, nec
Michael Helpard

D-U-N-S 20-800-5715   (SL)
LATHAM DISTRIBUTORS
475 Glendale Ave, St Catharines, ON, L2P
3Y2
(905) 682-3344
Emp Here 30   *Sales* 25,357,637
SIC 5149 Groceries and related products, nec
Patrick Latham

D-U-N-S 24-387-3226   (HQ)
NIAGARA BATTERY & TIRE LTD
79 Hartzel Rd, St Catharines, ON, L2P 1M9
(905) 682-1844
Sales 50,342,400
SIC 5531 Auto and home supply stores
Gordon Singleton
Chris Singleton

D-U-N-S 25-639-5542   (SL)
SHANNON'S, GREG FOOD BASICS
149 Hartzel Rd, St Catharines, ON, L2P 1N6
(905) 684-7439
Emp Here 45   *Sales* 12,336,840
SIC 5411 Grocery stores
Greg Shannon

D-U-N-S 24-387-8415   (HQ)
TIW STEEL PLATEWORK INC
(*Suby of* CANERECTOR INC)
23 Smith St, St Catharines, ON, L2P 3J7
(905) 684-9421
Emp Here 30   *Sales* 45,486,120
SIC 3441 Fabricated structural Metal
Jacques Dion

D-U-N-S 20-147-9367   (SL)
TRADEWOOD INDUSTRIES LIMITED
TRADEWOOD WINDOWS & DOORS
7 Wright St, St Catharines, ON, L2P 3J2
(905) 641-4949
Emp Here 70   *Sales* 10,910,410
SIC 2431 Millwork
David Tausendfreundt
Richard Krysiak
Nanni Tausenfreund

D-U-N-S 25-502-2501   (SL)
TRENERGY INC
87 Grantham Ave, St Catharines, ON, L2P
2Y8
(905) 687-8736
Emp Here 125   *Sales* 24,010,625
SIC 3443 Fabricated plate work (boiler shop)
Victor Oreskovich
Spencer Fox

D-U-N-S 25-169-7454   (SL)
TUFFORD NURSING HOME LTD
312 Queenston St, St Catharines, ON, L2P
2X4
(905) 682-0411
Emp Here 85   *Sales* 5,842,305
SIC 8051 Skilled nursing care facilities

Mike Walter

D-U-N-S 25-934-0453   (BR)
UNGER NURSING HOMES LIMITED
TUFFORD NURSING HOME
(*Suby of* UNGER NURSING HOMES LIMITED)
312 Queenston St, St Catharines, ON, L2P
2X4
(905) 682-0503
Emp Here 90
SIC 8051 Skilled nursing care facilities
Greg Latanik

St Catharines, ON L2R

D-U-N-S 20-878-1898   (SL)
295823 ONTARIO INC
TROJAN SECURITY AND INVESTIGATION SERVICES
31 Raymond St, St Catharines, ON, L2R 2T3
(905) 685-4279
Emp Here 75   *Sales* 29,675,850
SIC 7381 Detective and armored car services
Henry Becker

D-U-N-S 24-644-8179   (SL)
301061 ONTARIO LIMITED
DELTA BINGO
227 Church St, St Catharines, ON, L2R 3E8

Emp Here 165   *Sales* 15,667,245
SIC 7999 Amusement and recreation, nec
John Johnstone
John Cameron

D-U-N-S 24-388-2974   (SL)
407994 ONTARIO LIMITED
SPECIALTY PRINT
417 Lakeshore Rd, St Catharines, ON, L2R
7K6
(905) 646-6247
Emp Here 103   *Sales* 16,894,781
SIC 2754 Commercial printing, gravure
James Johnson

D-U-N-S 20-149-5058   (HQ)
ALGOMA CENTRAL CORPORATION
63 Church St Suite 600, St Catharines, ON,
L2R 3C4
(905) 687-7888
Emp Here 30   *Sales* 385,268,195
SIC 4432 Freight transportation on the great
lakes
Gregg Ruhl
J. Wesley Newton
Brad Tiffin
Mario Battista
Fredrik Hanson
Christopher A.L. Lazarz
Steve Wright
Bruce Partridge
Jeffrey M. Derosario
Cathy Smith

D-U-N-S 25-330-5742   (BR)
ALGOMA CENTRAL CORPORATION
ALGOMA CENTRAL MARINE
(*Suby of* ALGOMA CENTRAL CORPORATION)
63 Church St Suite 600, St Catharines, ON,
L2R 3C4

Emp Here 100
SIC 4432 Freight transportation on the great
lakes
Al Vanagas

D-U-N-S 20-280-3573   (SL)
APEX-NIAGARA TOOL LTD
(*Suby of* BAIN CAPITAL, LP)
54 Catherine St, St Catharines, ON, L2R 7R5
(905) 704-1797
Emp Here 43   *Sales* 11,509,036
SIC 5251 Hardware stores

Bill Mcmaster

D-U-N-S 20-820-1822   (HQ)
ARCHER TRUCK SERVICES LIMITED
260 Dunkirk Rd, St Catharines, ON, L2R 7K6
(905) 685-6532
Emp Here 26   *Sales* 22,911,588
SIC 5511 New and used car dealers
G. Robert Butter
Scott Mcghie
Herman Heikoop

D-U-N-S 20-146-8618   (SL)
BAKKER, J. C. & SONS LIMITED
1360 Third St Suite 3, St Catharines, ON, L2R
6P9
(905) 935-4533
Emp Here 45   *Sales* 33,413,400
SIC 5193 Flowers and florists supplies
John C Bakker Iii
Kenneth Bakker
Gerald Dehaan

D-U-N-S 24-537-5951   (SL)
BROUWER CONSTRUCTION (1981) LTD
1880 King St, St Catharines, ON, L2R 6P7
(905) 984-3060
Emp Here 18   *Sales* 23,360,948
SIC 1542 Nonresidential construction, nec
Albert Brouwer

D-U-N-S 25-320-1458   (HQ)
CANADIAN CANNABIS CLINICS
80 King Street, St Catharines, ON, L2R 7G1
(289) 273-3851
Sales 28,531,050
SIC 8011 Offices and clinics of medical doctors

D-U-N-S 24-193-1844   (HQ)
CANADIAN MENTAL HEALTH ASSOCIATION, NIAGARA BRANCH
CMHA
15 Wellington St, St Catharines, ON, L2R 5P7
(905) 641-5222
Emp Here 20   *Sales* 11,245,220
SIC 8011 Offices and clinics of medical doctors
George Kurzawa
Michael Lethby

D-U-N-S 24-392-8392   (BR)
CANERECTOR INC
NIAGARA STRUCTURAL STEEL, DIV OF
(*Suby of* CANERECTOR INC)
23 Smith St, St Catharines, ON, L2R 6Y6
(905) 684-2022
Emp Here 100
SIC 3441 Fabricated structural Metal
Iain Fox

D-U-N-S 25-178-9160   (SL)
CANTEC SECURITY SERVICES INC
140 Welland Ave Unit 5, St Catharines, ON,
L2R 2N6
(905) 687-9500
Emp Here 318   *Sales* 8,347,500
SIC 7381 Detective and armored car services
Gregory Hoadley

D-U-N-S 20-147-9375   (SL)
CHECKPOINT CHRYSLER LTD
PERFORMANCE CHRYSLER DODGE JEEP
357 Ontario St, St Catharines, ON, L2R 5L3
(905) 688-2802
Emp Here 85   *Sales* 53,488,800
SIC 5511 New and used car dealers
John Mann
Cam Champion

D-U-N-S 20-606-8421   (SL)
CULLEN, BRIAN MOTORS LIMITED
386 Ontario St, St Catharines, ON, L2R 5L8
(905) 684-8745
Emp Here 75   *Sales* 47,196,000
SIC 5511 New and used car dealers
Brian Cullen
Tim O'brien

Bob Cullen
Debbie Faris
Peter Kotsilidis

D-U-N-S 25-755-1986   (BR)
DISTRICT SCHOOL BOARD OF NIAGARA
ST CATHARINES COLLEGIATE
34 Catherine St, St Catharines, ON, L2R 5E7
(905) 687-7301
Emp Here 90
SIC 8211 Elementary and secondary schools
Tammy Zonneveld

D-U-N-S 20-824-1992   (HQ)
DIXON COMMERCIAL INVESTIGATORS (1982) INC
91 Geneva St, St Catharines, ON, L2R 4M9
(905) 688-0447
Emp Here 49   *Sales* 10,586,200
SIC 7322 Adjustment and collection services
John M Dixon

D-U-N-S 20-755-0211   (SL)
ED LEARN FORD LINCOLN LTD
375 Ontario St, St Catharines, ON, L2R 5L3
(905) 684-8791
Emp Here 83   *Sales* 23,513,900
SIC 7515 Passenger car leasing
Andrew O'jamie
Mark Jeweiss
Frank Trivieri

D-U-N-S 20-147-1331   (SL)
FBT INC
413 Lakeshore Rd, St Catharines, ON, L2R
7K6
(905) 937-3333
Emp Here 80   *Sales* 17,760,080
SIC 3541 Machine tools, Metal cutting type
Kenneth Forstinger
Robert Forstinger
Koleen Forstinger
Celine Forstinger

D-U-N-S 25-638-4876   (BR)
FIRSTONTARIO CREDIT UNION LIMITED
(*Suby of* FIRSTONTARIO CREDIT UNION
LIMITED)
3969 Montrose, St Catharines, ON, L2R 6Z4
(905) 685-5555
Emp Here 300
SIC 6062 State credit unions
Janice Cheel

D-U-N-S 24-317-5291   (BR)
GENERAL MOTORS OF CANADA COMPANY
ST CATHARINES ENGINE PLANT
(*Suby of* GENERAL MOTORS COMPANY)
570 Glendale Ave, St Catharines, ON, L2R
7B3
(905) 641-6424
Emp Here 2,000
SIC 3465 Automotive stampings
Caroline Watts

D-U-N-S 20-878-9524   (HQ)
GOODWILL INDUSTRIES NIAGARA
111 Church St, St Catharines, ON, L2R 3C9
(905) 641-5285
Emp Here 10   *Sales* 14,659,680
SIC 5932 Used merchandise stores
Saulis Zemaitis
Eleanor Lancaster
Karen Drobnich
Laura Hills
Catharine Streeter

D-U-N-S 25-075-2516   (SL)
HAMDANI TEXTILES LTD
55 Catherine St, St Catharines, ON, L2R 5E9
(905) 682-6666
Emp Here 40   *Sales* 19,932,880
SIC 5131 Piece goods and notions
Hassan Hamdani

D-U-N-S 24-719-7429   (SL)
HINAN, T.R. CONSTRUCTION LIMITED

31 Church St, St Catharines, ON, L2R 3B7

Emp Here 52   *Sales* 29,657,576
SIC 1542 Nonresidential construction, nec
 Terry Hinan
 Patti Hinan

      D-U-N-S 20-690-4190   (SL)
IFC NORTH AMERICA INC
(*Suby of* INTERNATIONAL FURAN CHEMI-
CALS B.V.)
63 Church St Suite 301, St Catharines, ON,
L2R 3C4
(905) 685-8560
Emp Here 4   *Sales* 15,764,494
SIC 5169 Chemicals and allied products, nec
 Alexander Vanzijl

      D-U-N-S 20-607-4270   (HQ)
JACK VAN KLAVEREN LIMITED
J V K
(*Suby of* GRAYVIN HOLDINGS LIMITED)
1894 Seventh St, St Catharines, ON, L2R 6P9
(905) 641-5599
Emp Here 50   *Sales* 51,976,400
SIC 5191 Farm supplies
 Robert Murch
 Glenn Fozard

      D-U-N-S 20-532-4346   (HQ)
JEFFERY'S GREENHOUSES INC
1036 Lakeshore Rd W, St Catharines, ON,
L2R 6P9
(905) 934-0514
Sales 17,050,085
SIC 0181 Ornamental nursery products
 James Jeffery
 Sandy Jeffery

      D-U-N-S 25-478-1636   (SL)
**KANNEGIETER-ZIMMERMAN INSURANCE
BROKERS LIMITED**
K & Z INSURANCE
131 Ontario St, St Catharines, ON, L2R 5J9
(905) 688-9170
Emp Here 70   *Sales* 59,364,200
SIC 6411 Insurance agents, brokers, and ser-
vice
 Mark Sherk
 Rick Sherk

      D-U-N-S 24-161-5645   (SL)
KENMORE MANAGEMENT INC
KENMORE HOMES
151 James St, St Catharines, ON, L2R 5C4

Emp Here 42   *Sales* 19,770,702
SIC 1542 Nonresidential construction, nec
 Dorris Sherman

      D-U-N-S 20-800-5723   (SL)
MCDONALD'S RESTAURANTS
385 Ontario St, St Catharines, ON, L2R 5L3
(905) 688-0244
Emp Here 80   *Sales* 3,641,520
SIC 5812 Eating places
 Peter Macisaac

      D-U-N-S 24-092-8937   (SL)
NEWMAN BROS. LIMITED
72 Welland Ave, St Catharines, ON, L2R 2M9
(905) 641-8111
Emp Here 80   *Sales* 33,818,960
SIC 1541 Industrial buildings and warehouses
 Douglas H Newman
 Phillip Martens
 Jason Walsh
 Philip C. Martens
 Jason D. Walsh
 Dian Holmes
 Diane Holmes

      D-U-N-S 24-355-3166   (BR)
NIAGARA HEALTH SYSTEM
ST. CATHARINES GENERAL SITE
(*Suby of* NIAGARA HEALTH SYSTEM)
142 Queenston St, St Catharines, ON, L2R
2Z7

(905) 684-7271
Emp Here 800
SIC 8062 General medical and surgical hospi-
tals
 Suzanne Johnston

      D-U-N-S 24-247-0495   (SL)
NIAGARA ICEDOGS HOCKEY CLUB INC
35 Queen St, St Catharines, ON, L2R 5G4
(905) 687-3641
Emp Here 25   *Sales* 10,593,250
SIC 7941 Sports clubs, managers, and pro-
moters
 Denise Burke
 Bill Burke

      D-U-N-S 25-361-3939   (HQ)
NORTHLAND FLORAL INC
1703 South Service Rd, St Catharines, ON,
L2R 6P9
(905) 646-2828
Sales 18,563,000
SIC 5193 Flowers and florists supplies
 Mark Buys
 John Buys
 Garett Vanderwal

      D-U-N-S 20-769-1556   (SL)
OJEKA GALLERY INC
TIM HORTONS
212 Welland Ave, St Catharines, ON, L2R 2P3
(905) 682-4129
Emp Here 42   *Sales* 11,514,384
SIC 5461 Retail bakeries
 Dal Bains

      D-U-N-S 25-717-8996   (BR)
OSPREY MEDIA PUBLISHING INC
ST CATHARINES STANDARD, THE
(*Suby of* QUEBECOR MEDIA INC)
17 Queen St, St Catharines, ON, L2R 5G4
(905) 684-7251
Emp Here 160
SIC 2711 Newspapers
 Judy Bullis

      D-U-N-S 24-098-2553   (SL)
PENGLAD FARMS INC
3930 Ninth St, St Catharines, ON, L2R 6P9
(905) 684-7861
Emp Here 40   *Sales* 13,024,000
SIC 5992 Florists
 Wayne Houtby
 Catharina Houtby

      D-U-N-S 20-147-7130   (HQ)
**PERFORMANCE CARS (ST CATHARINES)
LIMITED**
PERFORMANCE MERCEDES-BENZ
371 Ontario St, St Catharines, ON, L2R 5L3
(905) 685-3838
Sales 12,451,950
SIC 5511 New and used car dealers
 Campbell Champion
 John Mann
 William Anderson

      D-U-N-S 24-783-5200   (HQ)
**RE/MAX GARDEN CITY REALTY INC BRO-
KERAGE**
161 Carlton St Suite 123, St Catharines, ON,
L2R 1R5
(905) 641-1110
Emp Here 75   *Sales* 78,430,848
SIC 6531 Real estate agents and managers
 Wayne Quirk

      D-U-N-S 24-408-3408   (SL)
**REGIONAL DOORS & HARDWARE (NIA-
GARA) LIMITED**
44 Scott St W, St Catharines, ON, L2R 1C9
(905) 684-8161
Emp Here 45   *Sales* 20,122,830
SIC 5031 Lumber, plywood, and millwork
 Jim Dove
 Rick Jenkins
 Gerry Decharme

      D-U-N-S 20-783-3575   (SL)

RIDLEY COLLEGE
2 Ridley Rd, St Catharines, ON, L2R 7C3
(905) 684-1889
Emp Here 200   *Sales* 29,878,200
SIC 8221 Colleges and universities
 Georgina Black
 Jim Parke

      D-U-N-S 25-638-8562   (HQ)
**ROYAL LEPAGE NIAGARA REAL ESTATE
CENTRE**
33 Maywood Ave, St Catharines, ON, L2R
1C5
(905) 688-4561
Emp Here 50   *Sales* 135,225,600
SIC 6531 Real estate agents and managers
 Margie Spence

      D-U-N-S 20-147-8377   (SL)
**SCHENCK FARMS & GREENHOUSES CO.
LIMITED**
1396 South Service Rd, St Catharines, ON,
L2R 6P9
(905) 684-5478
Emp Here 50   *Sales* 73,384,600
SIC 5159 Farm-product raw materials, nec
 Louis M. Schenck
 Robert C. Schenck

      D-U-N-S 20-648-2494   (HQ)
SEAWAY MARINE TRANSPORT
63 Church St Suite 600, St Catharines, ON,
L2R 3C4
(905) 988-2600
Emp Here 59   *Sales* 40,013,520
SIC 4731 Freight transportation arrangement
 Ken Bloch Soerensen

      D-U-N-S 25-203-5647   (SL)
SEAWAY SELF UNLOADERS
63 Church St Suite 503, St Catharines, ON,
L2R 3C4
(905) 988-2600
Emp Here 100   *Sales* 26,954,900
SIC 4424 Deep sea domestic transportation of
freight
 Ken Bloch Soerensen
 Tim Dool

      D-U-N-S 20-854-9779   (SL)
SPORT BY ABILITY NIAGARA
8 Napier St, St Catharines, ON, L2R 6B4

Emp Here 31   *Sales* 12,319,834
SIC 8699 Membership organizations, nec
 Paul Rylett

      D-U-N-S 24-098-0334   (SL)
**SPRING VALLEY GARDENS (NIAGARA)
INC**
1330 Fifth St Louth, St Catharines, ON, L2R
6P9
(905) 935-9002
Emp Here 40   *Sales* 29,700,800
SIC 5193 Flowers and florists supplies
 John Van Koeveringe
 Jake Van Koeveringe
 Ron Van Koeveringe

      D-U-N-S 24-915-1965   (SL)
SPRING VALLEY GARDENS INC
1846 Seventh St, St Catharines, ON, L2R 6P9
(905) 682-9002
Emp Here 49   *Sales* 16,780,883
SIC 0181 Ornamental nursery products
 John Vankauvering

      D-U-N-S 24-885-4663   (SL)
ST. CATHARINES STANDARD GROUP INC
1 St. Paul St Suite 10, St Catharines, ON, L2R
7L4
(905) 684-7251
Emp Here 150   *Sales* 24,604,050
SIC 2711 Newspapers
 Paul Mccuaig
 Brad O'neill

      D-U-N-S 25-684-0224   (BR)

**ST. LAWRENCE SEAWAY MANAGEMENT
CORPORATION, THE**
(*Suby of* ST. LAWRENCE SEAWAY MAN-
AGEMENT CORPORATION, THE)
508 Glendale Ave, St Catharines, ON, L2R
6V8
(905) 641-1932
Emp Here 200
SIC 4432 Freight transportation on the great
lakes
 Alvina Ghirardi

      D-U-N-S 20-831-8605   (HQ)
VERGE INSURANCE BROKERS LIMITED
131 Ontario St, St Catharines, ON, L2R 5J9
(905) 688-9170
Sales 120,103,230
SIC 6411 Insurance agents, brokers, and ser-
vice
 Mark Sherk

      D-U-N-S 24-859-8559   (HQ)
W. S. TYLER CANADA LTD
HAVER & BOECKER CANADA
(*Suby of* HAVER & BOECKER OHG)
225 Ontario St, St Catharines, ON, L2R 7J2
(905) 688-2644
Emp Here 75   *Sales* 31,339,080
SIC 3496 Miscellaneous fabricated wire prod-
ucts
 Karen Thompson
 Caroline Mann

St Catharines, ON L2S

      D-U-N-S 20-146-8782   (HQ)
BEATTIE STATIONERY LIMITED
BEATTIE'S BASICS
399 Vansickle Rd Suite 3056, St Catharines,
ON, L2S 3T4
(905) 688-4040
Emp Here 60   *Sales* 23,859,810
SIC 5943 Stationery stores

      D-U-N-S 20-773-5416   (HQ)
BROCK UNIVERSITY
*BROCK UNIVERSITY WELLNESS INSTI-
TUTE, DIV OF*
1812 Sir Isaac Brock Way, St Catharines, ON,
L2S 3A1
(905) 688-5550
Emp Here 800   *Sales* 194,208,300
SIC 8221 Colleges and universities
 David Howes
 Jack N. Lightstone
 Steven Pillar
 Joanne Mckee

      D-U-N-S 24-991-9416   (SL)
DRAVES, BRIAN H MERCHANDISING LTD
CANADIAN TIRE
431 Louth St Suite 90, St Catharines, ON, L2S
4A2
(905) 682-9275
Emp Here 100   *Sales* 26,765,200
SIC 5251 Hardware stores
 Brian Draves
 Lynda Draves

      D-U-N-S 24-470-8533   (HQ)
**DURWARD JONES BARKWELL & COM-
PANY LLP**
DJB
20 Corporate Park Dr Suite 300, St
Catharines, ON, L2S 3W2
(905) 684-9221
Emp Here 30   *Sales* 23,291,478
SIC 8721 Accounting, auditing, and book-
keeping

      D-U-N-S 24-677-0833   (HQ)
EXOCOR LTD
(*Suby of* SAUGATUCK CAPITAL CO LIMITED
PARTNERSHIP)

----

271 Ridley Rd W Suite 2, St Catharines, ON,
L2S 0B3
(905) 704-0603
Sales 16,625,910
SIC 5085 Industrial supplies
Leo Walsh

D-U-N-S 25-280-0990   (BR)
EXTENDICARE INC
EXTENDICARE ST. CATHERINES
(*Suby of* EXTENDICARE INC)
283 Pelham Rd, St Catharines, ON, L2S 1X7
(905) 688-3311
Emp Here 265
SIC 8051 Skilled nursing care facilities
Mike Boyle

D-U-N-S 20-147-3873   (SL)
KALA'S HARDWARE LIMITED
KALA'S HOME HARDWARE
1380 Fourth Ave Suite 3, St Catharines, ON,
L2S 0B8
(905) 688-5520
Emp Here 28   *Sales* 12,520,872
SIC 5072 Hardware
Yvonne Kala
Victor Kala
Christine Macintosh

D-U-N-S 20-404-9506   (HQ)
LIFCO HYDRAULICS LTD
HYDRAULICS INTEGRATED SYSTEMS
250 Martindale Rd, St Catharines, ON, L2S
0B2
(905) 641-0033
Emp Here 20   *Sales* 11,875,650
SIC 5084 Industrial machinery and equipment
Edward Berkhout

D-U-N-S 20-699-7848   (HQ)
MERIDIAN CREDIT UNION LIMITED
75 Corporate Park Dr Suite 1, St Catharines,
ON, L2S 3W3
(905) 937-4222
Emp Here 100   *Sales* 270,451,988
SIC 6062 State credit unions
Bill Maurin
John Murphy
Tamara Paton
Gary Genik
Leo Gautreau
Anne Berend
David Baldarelli
Tim Smart
Don Ariss
Richard Owen

D-U-N-S 20-975-2211   (HQ)
NIAGARA HEALTH SYSTEM
WELLAND HOSPITAL SITE
1200 Fourth Ave, St Catharines, ON, L2S 0A9
(905) 378-4647
Emp Here 900   *Sales* 533,184,000
SIC 8062 General medical and surgical hospitals
Thomas E. Stewart
Suzanne Johnston
Angela Zangari

D-U-N-S 24-733-2443   (BR)
PRIMERICA FINANCIAL SERVICES LTD
(*Suby of* PRIMERICA, INC.)
251 St. Paul St W Suite 1, St Catharines, ON,
L2S 2E4
(905) 687-9374
Emp Here 120
SIC 6411 Insurance agents, brokers, and service
John Carlo Gigone

D-U-N-S 24-218-7979   (HQ)
RANKIN CONSTRUCTION INC
(*Suby of* RANKIN ENGINEERING INC)
222 Martindale Rd, St Catharines, ON, L2S
0B2
(905) 684-1111
Emp Here 60   *Sales* 14,771,160
SIC 1794 Excavation work

Thomas A Rankin
Brian Rankin
Wendy Wing
Stojan Tritchew
Dave Pagnan

D-U-N-S 20-699-1510   (SL)
RCI VENTURES INC.
222 Martindale Rd, St Catharines, ON, L2S
0B2
(905) 684-1111
Emp Here 60   *Sales* 14,771,160
SIC 1796 Installing building equipment
Thomas A. Rankin

D-U-N-S 20-878-3225   (SL)
SHEEHAN & ROSIE LTD
70 St. Paul St W, St Catharines, ON, L2S 2C5
(905) 688-3713
Emp Here 25   *Sales* 14,498,100
SIC 6411 Insurance agents, brokers, and service
Gordon Sheehan
David Sheehan

D-U-N-S 25-638-5642   (SL)
ST CATHARINES MAINSTREAM NON PROFIT HOUSING PROJECT
263 Pelham Rd, St Catharines, ON, L2S 1X7
(905) 934-3924
Emp Here 49   *Sales* 19,473,286
SIC 8699 Membership organizations, nec
Kevin Berswick

D-U-N-S 24-312-4059   (HQ)
TRI-MEDIA INTEGRATED MARKETING TECHNOLOGIES INC
20 Corporate Park Dr Suite 103, St
Catharines, ON, L2S 3W2

Emp Here 5   *Sales* 13,745,695
SIC 7311 Advertising agencies
Albert Lannantuono
Alf Stutzmann
Rick Dillon
Dennis Sherbakov
Keith Cummings
Wilmer Otto
Gary Jordan

D-U-N-S 24-329-6840   (BR)
WAL-MART CANADA CORP
(*Suby of* WALMART INC.)
420 Vansickle Rd Suite 2, St Catharines, ON,
L2S 0C7
(905) 687-9212
Emp Here 200
SIC 5311 Department stores
Fred Stone

St Catharines, ON L2T

D-U-N-S 25-301-2058   (BR)
HUDSON'S BAY COMPANY
BAY, THE
(*Suby of* HUDSON'S BAY COMPANY)
221 Glendale Ave, St Catharines, ON, L2T
2K9
(905) 688-4441
Emp Here 200
SIC 5311 Department stores
Andrew Fraser

D-U-N-S 25-403-2576   (SL)
INTERLAKE ACQUISITION CORPORATION LIMITED
INTERLAKE PAPER
(*Suby of* DUNN PAPER HOLDINGS, INC.)
45 Merritt St, St Catharines, ON, L2T 1J4
(905) 680-3000
Emp Here 160   *Sales* 31,162,880
SIC 2621 Paper mills
Russell Taylor
David Morris

D-U-N-S 24-157-7431   (BR)
KEG RESTAURANTS LTD
(*Suby of* RECIPE UNLIMITED CORPORATION)
344 Glendale Ave, St Catharines, ON, L2T
4E3
(905) 680-4585
Emp Here 100
SIC 5812 Eating places
Micheal Callihoo

D-U-N-S 24-771-7739   (SL)
MARTIN HOME & AUTO LTD
CANADIAN TIRE ASSOCIATE STORE
300 Glendale Ave, St Catharines, ON, L2T
2L5
(905) 227-7481
Emp Here 50   *Sales* 24,903,900
SIC 5531 Auto and home supply stores
Joseph Martin

D-U-N-S 25-162-9788   (BR)
NIAGARA CATHOLIC DISTRICT SCHOOL BOARD
DENIS MORRIS CATHOLIC HIGH SCHOOL
(*Suby of* NIAGARA CATHOLIC DISTRICT SCHOOL BOARD)
40 Glen Morris Dr, St Catharines, ON, L2T
2M9
(905) 684-8731
Emp Here 90
SIC 8211 Elementary and secondary schools
Danny Dilorenzo

D-U-N-S 24-007-2009   (SL)
NIAGARA PENINSULA CHILDREN'S CENTRE
567 Glenridge Ave, St Catharines, ON, L2T
4C2
(905) 688-3553
Emp Here 100   *Sales* 8,183,300
SIC 8069 Specialty hospitals, except psychiatric
Timothy Wright

D-U-N-S 24-321-4645   (BR)
PF RESOLU CANADA INC
ABITIBI BOWATER
(*Suby of* RESOLUTE FOREST PRODUCTS INC)
2 Allanburg Rd S, St Catharines, ON, L2T
3W9
(905) 227-5000
Emp Here 125
SIC 2621 Paper mills
Gordon Cole

D-U-N-S 20-205-7977   (BR)
UNIFOR
CAW LOCAL 4401
(*Suby of* UNIFOR)
20 Walnut St, St Catharines, ON, L2T 1H5
(905) 227-7717
Emp Here 600
SIC 8631 Labor organizations
Jim Macdougall

St Catharines, ON L2W

D-U-N-S 20-153-9249   (SL)
1271591 ONTARIO INC
BAZAAR MARKETING
261 Martindale Rd Unit 14, St Catharines, ON,
L2W 1A2
(905) 688-7755
Emp Here 44   *Sales* 22,903,848
SIC 5092 Toys and hobby goods and supplies
Timothy Stuart
Len Stuart

D-U-N-S 24-140-6347   (HQ)
CHILDREN'S AID SOCIETY OF THE NIAGARA REGION, THE
FAMILY & CHILDREN'S SERVICES NIAGARA

82 Hannover Dr, St Catharines, ON, L2W 1A4
(905) 937-7731
Emp Here 100   *Sales* 34,556,400
SIC 8322 Individual and family services
Willian J Charron

D-U-N-S 24-827-2775   (HQ)
FIRE MONITORING OF CANADA INC
235 Martindale Rd Unit 19, St Catharines, ON,
L2W 1A5
(905) 688-0600
Emp Here 16   *Sales* 11,679,694
SIC 7389 Business services, nec
James Asselstine
Roy Karens
Al Isaac
Harold Smith
Don Ward

D-U-N-S 24-388-9938   (HQ)
LADSON PROPERTIES LIMITED
CHARTER BUILDING CO DIV OF
235 Martindale Rd Unit 14, St Catharines, ON,
L2W 1A5
(905) 684-6542
Emp Here 21   *Sales* 14,121,930
SIC 1542 Nonresidential construction, nec
Donald Ward
Jeff Gradner

D-U-N-S 20-414-4422   (SL)
MENTHOLATUM COMPANY OF CANADA LIMITED, THE
(*Suby of* ROHTO PHARMACEUTICAL CO.,
LTD.)
45 Hannover Dr Unit 2, St Catharines, ON,
L2W 1A3
(905) 688-1665
Emp Here 12   *Sales* 13,264,140
SIC 5122 Drugs, proprietary, and sundries
Greg Lewis
Francis Chan
Jim Ingham

D-U-N-S 24-483-7415   (SL)
MERIT CONTRACTORS NIAGARA
235 Martindale Rd Suite 3, St Catharines, ON,
L2W 1A5
(905) 641-2374
Emp Here 38   *Sales* 21,672,844
SIC 1542 Nonresidential construction, nec
Dennis R Kowalchuk

D-U-N-S 25-597-7936   (SL)
PRO WELLNESS HEALTH SERVICES INC
110 Hannover Dr Suite B107, St Catharines,
ON, L2W 1A4
(905) 682-1059
Emp Here 90   *Sales* 7,494,480
SIC 8082 Home health care services
Jerry Bilton

D-U-N-S 25-249-5452   (SL)
ROMAN DELI LTD
ANTIPASTOS DI ROMA
87 Hannover Dr Suite 3, St Catharines, ON,
L2W 1A3
(905) 641-5211
Emp Here 80   *Sales* 66,846,160
SIC 5147 Meats and meat products
Sergio Sforza
Dominic Disersino
Natalino Garosolo

D-U-N-S 25-017-4083   (SL)
YOUNGS INSURANCE BROKERS INC
110b Hannover Dr Suite 106, St Catharines,
ON, L2W 1A4
(905) 688-1100
Emp Here 14   *Sales* 10,156,146
SIC 6351 Surety insurance
S Valleriani

St Clements, ON N0B

▲ Public Company   ■ Public Company Family Member   **HQ** Headquarters   **BR** Branch   **SL** Single Location

D-U-N-S 20-129-5029   (HQ)
STEED & EVANS LIMITED
3000 Ament Line, St Clements, ON, N0B 2M0
(519) 744-7315
Emp Here 20   *Sales* 50,488,400
SIC 1611 Highway and street construction
Malcolm Matheson

St Davids, ON L0S

D-U-N-S 24-057-7197   (HQ)
CHATEAU DES CHARMES WINES LTD
1025 York Rd, St Davids, ON, L0S 1P0
(905) 262-4219
Emp Here 40   *Sales* 14,659,680
SIC 5921 Liquor stores
Roger A Gordon
Paul M Bosc
Paul A. Bosc

St Eugene, ON K0B

D-U-N-S 24-885-7443   (SL)
1048547 ONTARIO INC
SKOTIDAKIS GOAT FARM
185 County Rd 10, St Eugene, ON, K0B 1P0
(613) 674-3183
Emp Here 180   *Sales* 62,224,200
SIC 2022 Cheese; natural and processed
John Skotidakis
Antigoni Skotidakis

St George Brant, ON N0E

D-U-N-S 24-744-5885   (HQ)
S.N.S. INDUSTRIAL PRODUCTS LIMITED
S.N.S. AUTOMATION PRODUCTS
142 Sugar Maple Rd, St George Brant, ON, N0E 1N0
(519) 448-3055
Emp Here 8   *Sales* 16,625,910
SIC 5084 Industrial machinery and equipment
Don Sanfilippo

D-U-N-S 24-804-5510   (HQ)
TIM HORTON CHILDREN'S FOUNDATION, INC
264 Glen Morris Rd Suite 2, St George Brant, ON, N0E 1N0
(519) 448-1248
Emp Here 25   *Sales* 27,969,096
SIC 7032 Sporting and recreational camps
William Moir
Donald Schroeder

D-U-N-S 20-316-0044   (BR)
TIM HORTON CHILDREN'S FOUNDATION, INC
TIM HORTON ONONDAGA FARMS
(*Suby of* TIM HORTON CHILDREN'S FOUN-DATION, INC)
264 Glen Morris Rd, St George Brant, ON, N0E 1N0
(519) 448-1264
Emp Here 95
SIC 7032 Sporting and recreational camps
Barb Weeden

St Isidore, ON K0C

D-U-N-S 20-523-0035   (HQ)
1649313 ONTARIO INC
LEVAC PROPANE
5552 Rue St Catharine, St Isidore, ON, K0C 2B0

(613) 524-2079
Sales 13,438,040
SIC 5984 Liquefied petroleum gas dealers
Jean-Marc Levac

D-U-N-S 25-925-2567   (SL)
MAISONNEUVE LALONDE SOULIGNY COURTIERS D'ASSURANCE LTEE
Gd, St Isidore, ON, K0C 2B0
(613) 524-2174
Emp Here 36   *Sales* 20,877,264
SIC 6411 Insurance agents, brokers, and service
Paul Maisonneuve

D-U-N-S 20-148-1678   (SL)
MENARD, J. R. LIMITED
5 Ranger St, St Isidore, ON, K0C 2B0
(613) 524-2885
Emp Here 30   *Sales* 13,415,220
SIC 5039 Construction materials, nec
Luc Rouleau
Francois Rouleau
Jean-Guy Quesnel

D-U-N-S 24-482-3506   (HQ)
MLS INSURANCE BROKERS INC
4741 St Catherine St, St Isidore, ON, K0C 2B0
(613) 524-2174
Emp Here 9   *Sales* 29,682,100
SIC 6411 Insurance agents, brokers, and service
Paul Maisonneuve
Daniel Maisonneuve
Josee Souligny

D-U-N-S 24-891-6205   (HQ)
PRODUITS DALMEN PRODUCTS LTD
5630 St Catherine St, St Isidore, ON, K0C 2B0
(613) 524-2268
Emp Here 1   *Sales* 10,564,675
SIC 3442 Metal doors, sash, and trim
Dominic Alary
Jasmine Menard

St Jacobs, ON N0B

D-U-N-S 20-148-1793   (HQ)
HOME HARDWARE STORES LIMITED
34 Henry St, St Jacobs, ON, N0B 2N0
(519) 664-2252
Emp Here 1,420   *Sales* 2,424,608,819
SIC 5211 Lumber and other building materials
Kevin Macnab
Dianne Mctavish
Scott Bryant
Grant Knowlton
Gino Gualtieri
John Dyksterhuis
Darrin Noble
Joel Marks
Marianne Thompson
Rob Wallace

D-U-N-S 24-007-1530   (SL)
MERCEDES CORP
1386 King St N, St Jacobs, ON, N0B 2N0
(519) 664-2293
Emp Here 350   *Sales* 93,346,050
SIC 5712 Furniture stores
Marcus Shantz
Ross Shantz
David Howey

D-U-N-S 24-047-8826   (HQ)
QUARRY INTEGRATED COMMUNICATIONS INC
1440 King St N Unit 1, St Jacobs, ON, N0B 2N0
(877) 723-2999
Sales 20,037,100
SIC 7311 Advertising agencies
Alan Quarry
Ken Whyte
Maurice Allin

Sarah Hardwood
Jay Fournier
Glen Drummond

D-U-N-S 24-617-8383   (BR)
QUARRY INTEGRATED COMMUNICA-TIONS INC
(*Suby of* QUARRY INTEGRATED COMMUNI-CATIONS INC)
1440 King St N Suite 1, St Jacobs, ON, N0B 2N0
(877) 723-2999
Emp Here 80
SIC 7311 Advertising agencies
Ken Whyte

St Marys, ON N4X

D-U-N-S 25-294-0739   (SL)
2008788 ONTARIO LIMITED
CALEDON TUBING, DIV OF
(*Suby of* MARTINREA INTERNATIONAL INC)
580 James St S, St Marys, ON, N4X 1B3
(519) 349-2850
Emp Here 72   *Sales* 13,059,936
SIC 3317 Steel pipe and tubes
Pat D'eramo
Brenda Chambers

D-U-N-S 24-335-0357   (BR)
CASCADES CANADA ULC
NORAMPAC ST. MARYS
(*Suby of* CASCADES INC)
304 James St S, St Marys, ON, N4X 1B7
(519) 284-1840
Emp Here 151
SIC 2653 Corrugated and solid fiber boxes
Steve Cousins

D-U-N-S 24-861-8696   (BR)
DANA CANADA CORPORATION
(*Suby of* DANA INCORPORATED)
500 James St S, St Marys, ON, N4X 1B4

Emp Here 500
SIC 3714 Motor vehicle parts and accessories
Chris Speece

D-U-N-S 24-463-3046   (HQ)
FARM-FLEET INC
ONTARIO AG EQUIPMENT SALES AGENCY, A DIVISION OF
23703 Wellburn Rd Rr 3, St Marys, ON, N4X 1C6
(519) 461-1499
Emp Here 10   *Sales* 11,400,624
SIC 5083 Farm and garden machinery
Paul Stubbens
Carolyn Noble

D-U-N-S 24-193-6434   (HQ)
FAWCETT TRACTOR SUPPLY LTD
2126 Road 120, St Marys, ON, N4X 1C5
(519) 284-2379
Sales 11,875,650
SIC 5083 Farm and garden machinery
Jeffrey Fawcett

D-U-N-S 25-673-6489   (SL)
FINNIE DISTRIBUTING (1997) INC
4188 Perth Line Suite 9, St Marys, ON, N4X 1C5
(519) 284-2080
Emp Here 49   *Sales* 36,383,480
SIC 5191 Farm supplies
Gary Richardson
Linda Richardson

D-U-N-S 24-248-5824   (HQ)
GRA HAM ENERGY LIMITED
88 Queen St W, St Marys, ON, N4X 1A9
(519) 284-3420
Sales 25,171,200
SIC 5541 Gasoline service stations
Bruce Graham

Charles Hammond
Richard Hammond

D-U-N-S 20-249-4506   (HQ)
INOAC CANADA LIMITED
(*Suby of* INOUE RUBBER CO.,LTD.)
575 James St S, St Marys, ON, N4X 1C6
(519) 349-2170
Sales 52,538,640
SIC 3089 Plastics products, nec
Andrew Dargavell

D-U-N-S 20-279-2107   (SL)
INOAC INTERIOR SYSTEMS LP
(*Suby of* INOUE RUBBER CO.,LTD.)
575 James St S, St Marys, ON, N4X 1C6
(519) 349-2170
Emp Here 250   *Sales* 59,703,000
SIC 3089 Plastics products, nec
Tatsuo Yamamoto
Andrew Dargavell

D-U-N-S 20-818-9308   (SL)
KINGSWAY LODGE ST. MARYS LTD
310 Queen St E, St Marys, ON, N4X 1C8
(519) 284-2921
Emp Here 78   *Sales* 5,361,174
SIC 8051 Skilled nursing care facilities
Scott Mackay

D-U-N-S 20-178-3722   (BR)
MAPLE LEAF FOODS INC
SCHNEIDER FOODS
(*Suby of* MAPLE LEAF FOODS INC)
1865 Perth Road Suite 139, St Marys, ON, N4X 1C8
(519) 229-8900
Emp Here 400
SIC 2015 Poultry slaughtering and processing
Shawn Wedow

D-U-N-S 20-148-2809   (SL)
MCLEAN TAYLOR CONSTRUCTION LIM-ITED
(*Suby of* MCLEAN TAYLOR HOLDINGS LIM-ITED)
25 Water St N, St Marys, ON, N4X 1B1
(519) 284-2580
Emp Here 120   *Sales* 39,373,800
SIC 1622 Bridge, tunnel, and elevated high-way construction
Scott Taylor
Ken Mclean
Michael Doupe
Scott Schiedel
Paul Taylor

D-U-N-S 24-184-2061   (SL)
PATTERSON GRAIN LIMITED
23364 Wellburn Rd Suite 3, St Marys, ON, N4X 1C6
(519) 461-1829
Emp Here 10   *Sales* 12,103,970
SIC 5153 Grain and field beans
Allan Patterson
Steve Bradley
Dorothy Patterson

D-U-N-S 24-859-0478   (SL)
PERTH COUNTRY INGREDIENTS INC
20 Thames Rd, St Marys, ON, N4X 1C4
(519) 284-3449
Emp Here 30   *Sales* 11,565,570
SIC 0254 Poultry hatcheries
Mary Walz
Auftin Currah

D-U-N-S 24-422-2154   (SL)
RONALD D. BAILEY GROCERY LIMITED
STONETOWN FOODLAND MARKET
Gd, St Marys, ON, N4X 1A6
(519) 284-2631
Emp Here 50   *Sales* 13,707,600
SIC 5411 Grocery stores
Craig Macdonald

D-U-N-S 20-875-3293   (SL)
ST MARYS MEMORIAL HOSPITAL

HURON PERTH HEALTHCARE ALLIANCE-ST MARYS MEMORIAL HOSPITAL
(*Suby of* HURON PERTH HEALTHCARE ALLIANCE)
267 Queen St W, St Marys, ON, N4X 1B6
(519) 284-1330
Emp Here 100   *Sales* 11,108,000
SIC 8062 General medical and surgical hospitals
Andrew Williams

D-U-N-S 25-332-5682   (BR)
ST. MARYS CEMENT INC. (CANADA)
CBM CANADA BUILDING MATERIALS
(*Suby of* HEJOASSU ADMINISTRACAO S/A)
585 Water St S, St Marys, ON, N4X 1B6
(519) 284-1020
Emp Here 75
SIC 3241 Cement, hydraulic
Jim Storey

D-U-N-S 20-148-3187   (SL)
STM BG AUTO INC
449 Queen St W, St Marys, ON, N4X 1B7
(519) 284-3310
Emp Here 26   *Sales* 12,950,028
SIC 5511 New and used car dealers
Chris West
Tom Welker

D-U-N-S 24-028-1006   (SL)
STONE TOWN CONSTRUCTION LIMITED
(*Suby of* MCLEAN TAYLOR HOLDINGS LIMITED)
25 Water St N, St Marys, ON, N4X 1B1
(519) 284-2580
Emp Here 100   *Sales* 25,244,200
SIC 1629 Heavy construction, nec
Robert Taylor
Scott Taylor
Murray Mclean

D-U-N-S 20-124-1569   (SL)
ULCH TRANSPORT LIMITED
100 South Service Rd, St Marys, ON, N4X 1A9
(519) 349-2340
Emp Here 70   *Sales* 10,373,440
SIC 4212 Local trucking, without storage
Robert Wilhelm
Joe Wilhelm

D-U-N-S 20-819-9133   (SL)
VETERINARY PURCHASING COMPANY LIMITED
485 Queen St W, St Marys, ON, N4X 1B7
(519) 284-1211
Emp Here 200   *Sales* 237,486,306
SIC 5047 Medical and hospital equipment
Rick Culbert
Pat Hinnegan
Gregory Burke
Janet Walsh
George Wood
Jeff Buckland
Tim Zaharchuk

St Thomas, ON N5P

D-U-N-S 24-359-5662   (SL)
1787930 ONTARIO INC
MESSENGER FREIGHT SYSTEMS
150 Dennis Rd, St Thomas, ON, N5P 0B6
(519) 631-9604
Emp Here 75   *Sales* 38,997,525
SIC 4731 Freight transportation arrangement
Louise Vonk

D-U-N-S 24-991-0670   (SL)
969774 ONTARIO LIMITED
ELGIN CONSTRUCTION
140 Burwell Rd, St Thomas, ON, N5P 3R8
(519) 631-5041
Emp Here 53   *Sales* 13,379,426

SIC 1611 Highway and street construction
James Nicli
Bob Nicli

D-U-N-S 25-215-2103   (SL)
ARVA INDUSTRIES INC
43 Gaylord Rd, St Thomas, ON, N5P 3R9
(519) 637-1855
Emp Here 43   *Sales* 12,763,719
SIC 3599 Industrial machinery, nec
Paul Smith
Shawn Smith
John Smith
Todd Smith
Kevin Spicer

D-U-N-S 20-848-8189   (HQ)
BUCKLAND CUSTOMS BROKERS LIMITED
BUCKLAND FREIGHT SERVICES
73 Gaylord Rd, St Thomas, ON, N5P 3R9
(519) 631-4944
Emp Here 90   *Sales* 78,693,256
SIC 4731 Freight transportation arrangement
Craig Smith
Shirley Smith
John Merrylees

D-U-N-S 20-692-7712   (HQ)
CANADIAN IPG CORPORATION
CANADIAN IPG
130 Woodworth Ave, St Thomas, ON, N5P 3K1
(519) 637-1945
Emp Here 38   *Sales* 21,851,196
SIC 5084 Industrial machinery and equipment
Rodney Malloy
Dale Stewart
William Buckborough

D-U-N-S 20-903-7407   (HQ)
COMMUNITY LIVING ELGIN
ELGIN A.C.L.
400 Talbot St, St Thomas, ON, N5P 1B8
(519) 631-9222
Emp Here 20   *Sales* 16,713,320
SIC 8361 Residential care
Tom Mccallum
David Round
Mary Cosyns

D-U-N-S 25-517-8436   (BR)
CORPORATION OF THE COUNTY OF ELGIN
ELGIN MANOR HOME FOR SENIORS
(*Suby of* CORPORATION OF THE COUNTY OF ELGIN)
39232 Fingal Line, St Thomas, ON, N5P 3S5
(519) 631-0620
Emp Here 110
SIC 8361 Residential care
Pat Vandevenne

D-U-N-S 24-951-9679   (SL)
DISBROWE PONTIAC BUICK CADILLAC LTD
116 Edward St, St Thomas, ON, N5P 4E6
(519) 631-2224
Emp Here 55   *Sales* 34,610,400
SIC 5511 New and used car dealers
Carl Ansingh

D-U-N-S 20-409-1391   (HQ)
DOWLER-KARN LIMITED
43841 Talbot Line, St Thomas, ON, N5P 3S7
(519) 631-3810
Emp Here 48   *Sales* 212,809,140
SIC 5172 Petroleum products, nec
Dave Karn
John Karn
Barb Molinaro
Dan Kelly
Neil Flegel

D-U-N-S 24-026-9050   (SL)
ELGIN MANOR HOME FOR SR CITIZENS
A COUNTY OF ELGIN
39262 Fingal Line, St Thomas, ON, N5P 3S5

(519) 631-0620
Emp Here 100   *Sales* 5,924,700
SIC 8361 Residential care
Pat Vandevenne

D-U-N-S 25-488-4083   (SL)
ELGIN ST. THOMAS HEALTH UNIT
ELGIN ST. THOMAS PUBLIC HEALTH
1230 Talbot St, St Thomas, ON, N5P 1G9
(519) 631-9900
Emp Here 65   *Sales* 15,698,475
SIC 8621 Professional organizations
Cynthia St John

D-U-N-S 20-148-4953   (SL)
FERGUSON BROS. OF ST. THOMAS LIMITED
43850 Ferguson Line Suite 6, St Thomas, ON, N5P 3T1
(519) 631-3463
Emp Here 11   *Sales* 13,314,367
SIC 5153 Grain and field beans
Colin Ferguson
Joyce Ferguson

D-U-N-S 20-553-1630   (SL)
FOREST CITY CASTINGS INC
10 Highbury Ave, St Thomas, ON, N5P 4C7
(519) 633-2999
Emp Here 80   *Sales* 18,674,800
SIC 3365 Aluminum foundries
Michael Vandenboom
Scott Mcrae

D-U-N-S 24-463-7500   (SL)
GKN SINTER METALS - ST THOMAS LTD
(*Suby of* MELROSE INDUSTRIES PLC)
7 Michigan Blvd, St Thomas, ON, N5P 1H1
(519) 631-4880
Emp Here 160   *Sales* 29,022,080
SIC 3399 Primary Metal products
Kristina Schmitt

D-U-N-S 20-148-5331   (HQ)
HARTZ CANADA INC
(*Suby of* UNICHARM CORPORATION)
1125 Talbot St, St Thomas, ON, N5P 3W7
(519) 631-7660
Emp Here 14   *Sales* 14,850,400
SIC 5199 Nondurable goods, nec
William Ecker

D-U-N-S 24-326-2719   (BR)
LOBLAWS INC
REAL CANADIAN SUPERSTORE
(*Suby of* LOBLAW COMPANIES LIMITED)
1063 Talbot St Unit 50, St Thomas, ON, N5P 1G4
(519) 637-6358
Emp Here 200
SIC 5411 Grocery stores
Nick Merucci

D-U-N-S 25-399-0576   (BR)
MAGNA INTERNATIONAL INC
FORMET INDUSTRIES
(*Suby of* MAGNA INTERNATIONAL INC)
1 Cosma Crt, St Thomas, ON, N5P 4J5
(519) 633-8400
Emp Here 1,200
SIC 3714 Motor vehicle parts and accessories
Mark Johnson

D-U-N-S 24-346-4554   (BR)
MASCO CANADA LIMITED
(*Suby of* MASCO CORPORATION)
35 Currah Rd, St Thomas, ON, N5P 3R2

Emp Here 100
SIC 3432 Plumbing fixture fittings and trim
Terry Gillard

D-U-N-S 24-953-7002   (HQ)
MASCO CANADA LIMITED
DELTA FAUCET CANADA
(*Suby of* MASCO CORPORATION)
350 South Edgeware Rd, St Thomas, ON, N5P 4L1

(519) 633-5050
Emp Here 410   *Sales* 109,453,950
SIC 3432 Plumbing fixture fittings and trim
Kenneth Roberts
William Simpson

D-U-N-S 20-558-2104   (SL)
MUSTANG DRINKWARE INC
MUSTANG PRODUCTS
35 Currah Rd, St Thomas, ON, N5P 3R2
(519) 631-3030
Emp Here 54   *Sales* 17,611,344
SIC 3949 Sporting and athletic goods, nec
Bradley Sparling
Angela Sparling

D-U-N-S 24-414-3178   (SL)
N WELCH PHARMACY SERVICES INC
SHOPPERS DRUG MART
107 Edward St Suite 101, St Thomas, ON, N5P 1Y8
(519) 633-4402
Emp Here 50   *Sales* 12,647,700
SIC 5912 Drug stores and proprietary stores
Norma Welch

D-U-N-S 24-576-5896   (SL)
NORTH STAR MANUFACTURING (LONDON) LTD
NORTH STAR VINYL WINDOWS AND DOORS
(*Suby of* CORNERSTONE BUILDING BRANDS, INC.)
40684 Talbot Line, St Thomas, ON, N5P 3T2
(519) 637-7899
Emp Here 210   *Sales* 50,150,520
SIC 3089 Plastics products, nec
Ron Cauchi
Pat Rooke

D-U-N-S 24-991-9432   (SL)
SCHMIDT, JACK SUPPLIES LIMITED
CANADIAN TIRE
1063 Talbot St Unit 25, St Thomas, ON, N5P 1G4
(519) 631-4910
Emp Here 60   *Sales* 37,756,800
SIC 5531 Auto and home supply stores
Jack Schmidt

D-U-N-S 24-336-3293   (BR)
SMP MOTOR PRODUCTS LTD
UNIMOTOR, DIVISION OF
(*Suby of* STANDARD MOTOR PRODUCTS, INC.)
33 Gaylord Rd, St Thomas, ON, N5P 3R9
(519) 633-8422
Emp Here 170
SIC 3621 Motors and generators
Denis Kerrigan

D-U-N-S 20-050-3451   (SL)
ST THOMAS ENERGY INC
135 Edward St, St Thomas, ON, N5P 4A8
(519) 631-5550
Emp Here 20   *Sales* 10,393,100
SIC 4911 Electric services
Brian Hollywood
Dana Witt

D-U-N-S 20-010-0241   (BR)
ST. JOSEPH'S HEALTH CARE, LONDON
REGIONAL MENTAL HEALTH CARE, ST THOMAS
(*Suby of* ST. JOSEPH'S HEALTH CARE, LONDON)
Gd, St Thomas, ON, N5P 3T4
(519) 631-8510
Emp Here 667
SIC 8093 Specialty outpatient clinics, nec
Michelle Campbell

D-U-N-S 24-347-1591   (HQ)
ST. THOMAS FORD LINCOLN SALES LIMITED
ST. THOMAS FORD LINCOLN
1012 Talbot St, St Thomas, ON, N5P 1G3
(519) 631-5080
Emp Here 3   *Sales* 24,903,900

SIC 5511 New and used car dealers
Bruce Dumouchelle
John Stollery

D-U-N-S 24-361-7474   (SL)
TAKUMI STAMPING CANADA INC
(Suby of TAKAGI HOLDINGS CO.,LTD.)
100 Dennis Rd, St Thomas, ON, N5P 0B6
(519) 633-6070
Emp Here 120   *Sales* 23,050,200
SIC 3465 Automotive stampings
Osanu Iwata
Naoyuki Ito
Christine Cote

D-U-N-S 25-033-7631   (BR)
THAMES VALLEY DISTRICT SCHOOL BOARD
ARTHUR VOADEN SECONDARY SCHOOL
(Suby of THAMES VALLEY DISTRICT SCHOOL BOARD)
41 Flora St, St Thomas, ON, N5P 2X5
(519) 631-3770
Emp Here 80
SIC 8211 Elementary and secondary schools
Dan Clarke

D-U-N-S 20-786-8563   (SL)
TRU-DIE LIMITED
236 Edward St, St Thomas, ON, N5P 1Z5
(519) 633-1040
Emp Here 55   *Sales* 12,210,055
SIC 3545 Machine tool accessories
Donald C Tregenza
Hazel Tregenza

D-U-N-S 24-773-1784   (SL)
VANGUARD NETWORKING INC
1217 Talbot St, St Thomas, ON, N5P 1G8

Emp Here 49   *Sales* 54,161,905
SIC 5122 Drugs, proprietaries, and sundries
Kevin Danylchuk

D-U-N-S 24-329-0256   (BR)
WAL-MART CANADA CORP
(Suby of WALMART INC.)
1063 Talbot St Unit 60, St Thomas, ON, N5P 1G4
(519) 631-1253
Emp Here 200
SIC 5311 Department stores
Dave Commission

D-U-N-S 20-148-7758   (SL)
YARMOUTH GROUP INC, THE
YARMOUTH CRANE SERVICE
9462 Tower Rd, St Thomas, ON, N5P 3S7
(519) 631-2663
Emp Here 56   *Sales* 10,756,760
SIC 3499 Fabricated Metal products, nec
Bob Bishop
Richard Bishop

St Thomas, ON N5R

D-U-N-S 24-771-9651   (SL)
808269 ONTARIO INC
ST THOMAS FOOD MARKET
(Suby of EMPIRE COMPANY LIMITED)
20 William St, St Thomas, ON, N5R 3G9
(519) 633-9370
Emp Here 43   *Sales* 11,788,536
SIC 5411 Grocery stores
John Braund
Sharon Braund

D-U-N-S 25-347-6287   (BR)
CARESSANT-CARE NURSING AND RETIREMENT HOMES LIMITED
(Suby of CARESSANT-CARE NURSING AND RETIREMENT HOMES LIMITED)
15 Bonnie Pl, St Thomas, ON, N5R 5T8
(519) 633-6493
Emp Here 100

SIC 8051 Skilled nursing care facilities
Vicki Martinez

D-U-N-S 25-354-9190   (SL)
ELGIN CHRYSLER LTD
275 Wellington St, St Thomas, ON, N5R 2S6
(519) 633-2200
Emp Here 25   *Sales* 12,451,950
SIC 5511 New and used car dealers
Doris Demuymck
Micheal Stollery

D-U-N-S 25-521-7903   (SL)
ELGIN MALL
417 Wellington St Suite 53, St Thomas, ON, N5R 5J5
(519) 633-4060
Emp Here 100   *Sales* 22,087,100
SIC 6512 Nonresidential building operators
Lucas Blois

D-U-N-S 24-000-5392   (SL)
GEERLINKS BUILDING CENTRE AND FURNITURE LIMITED
GEERLINKS HOME HARDWARE BUILDING CENTRE AND FURNIT
295 Wellington St, St Thomas, ON, N5R 2S6
(519) 631-2910
Emp Here 50   *Sales* 12,652,950
SIC 5251 Hardware stores
Harry Geerlinks
Frank Geerlinks

D-U-N-S 25-300-0590   (BR)
METRO ONTARIO INC
METRO
(Suby of METRO INC)
417 Wellington St Suite 1, St Thomas, ON, N5R 5J5
(519) 633-8780
Emp Here 80
SIC 5411 Grocery stores
Brian Pugh

D-U-N-S 20-940-5109   (SL)
ST. THOMAS-ELGIN GENERAL HOSPITAL, THE
189 Elm St, St Thomas, ON, N5R 5C4
(519) 631-2030
Emp Here 950   *Sales* 65,219,627
SIC 8062 General medical and surgical hospitals
Paul Collins
Malcolm Hopkins
Nancy Whitmore
Brenda Lambert

D-U-N-S 20-361-9085   (SL)
STATION PARK LOGISTICS
28 Majestic Crt, St Thomas, ON, N5R 0B9
(519) 207-3399
Emp Here 1   *Sales* 14,024,887
SIC 4731 Freight transportation arrangement
Jeff Coffey

D-U-N-S 20-068-0747   (BR)
THAMES VALLEY DISTRICT SCHOOL BOARD
PARKSIDE COLLEGIATE INSTITUTE
(Suby of THAMES VALLEY DISTRICT SCHOOL BOARD)
241 Sunset Dr, St Thomas, ON, N5R 3C2
(519) 633-0090
Emp Here 80
SIC 8211 Elementary and secondary schools
Andrew Smith

D-U-N-S 24-621-2117   (SL)
TISDELLE ENTERPRISES (EXPRESS) LIMITED
TIM HORTONS
6 Princess Ave Suite 5, St Thomas, ON, N5R 3V2
(519) 631-0116
Emp Here 300   *Sales* 13,991,700
SIC 5812 Eating places
Brian Tisdelle

St Williams, ON N0E

D-U-N-S 20-181-5045   (SL)
ST. WILLIAMS NURSERY AND ECOLOGY CENTRE INC
885 24 Hwy E, St Williams, ON, N0E 1P0
(519) 586-9116
Emp Here 150   *Sales* 30,992,550
SIC 0851 Forestry services
Allan Arthur

Staples, ON N0P

D-U-N-S 25-047-7762   (SL)
POMAS FARMS INC
1057 Hwy 77, Staples, ON, N0P 2J0
(519) 326-4410
Emp Here 130   *Sales* 21,973,250
SIC 0161 Vegetables and melons
Juan Braun
Daniel Braun
David Braun
Maria Klassen

Stayner, ON L0M

D-U-N-S 20-921-0442   (BR)
REINHART FOODS LIMITED
(Suby of REINHART FOODS LIMITED)
7449 Hwy 26, Stayner, ON, L0M 1S0
(705) 428-2422
Emp Here 110
SIC 2099 Food preparations, nec
Louise Watt

D-U-N-S 20-312-8129   (SL)
TUNDRA INTERNATIONAL INC
TUNDRA RESCUE
1393 Centre Line Rd, Stayner, ON, L0M 1S0
(705) 428-0544
Emp Here 50   *Sales* 12,887,734
SIC 8742 Management consulting services
Brent Stockford

D-U-N-S 24-378-3615   (SL)
TUNDRA STRATEGIES, INC
TUNDRA
1393 Centre Line Rd, Stayner, ON, L0M 1S0.
(705) 734-7700
Emp Here 55   *Sales* 12,885,840
SIC 8742 Management consulting services
Rob Macintyre

Stevensville, ON L0S

D-U-N-S 24-101-4849   (SL)
DMI CANADA INC
(Suby of OTTER TAIL CORPORATION)
2677 Winger Rd, Stevensville, ON, L0S 1S0
(905) 382-5793
Emp Here 142   *Sales* 31,524,142
SIC 3523 Farm machinery and equipment
Paul Smith

D-U-N-S 24-952-3226   (SL)
GIBBONS, V. CONTRACTING LTD
1755 Stevensville Rd, Stevensville, ON, L0S 1S0
(905) 382-2393
Emp Here 42   *Sales* 10,117,128
SIC 1623 Water, sewer, and utility lines
Vaughn Gibbons

D-U-N-S 24-011-1690   (SL)
STEVENSVILLE LAWN SERVICE INC
2821 Stevensville Rd Rr 2, Stevensville, ON,

L0S 1S0
(905) 382-2124
Emp Here 50   *Sales* 14,176,200
SIC 1611 Highway and street construction
Terry Tykolis
Tim Tykolis
Marianne Tykolis

D-U-N-S 20-270-3534   (BR)
ZAVCOR TRUCKING LIMITED
ZAVCOR LOGISTICS
(Suby of ZAVCOR TRUCKING LIMITED)
3650 Eagle St, Stevensville, ON, L0S 1S0
(905) 382-3444
Emp Here 120
SIC 4213 Trucking, except local
Gregory Davis

D-U-N-S 24-850-4862   (HQ)
ZAVCOR TRUCKING LIMITED
TRUK-KING, DIV OF
3650 Eagle St, Stevensville, ON, L0S 1S0
(905) 382-3444
Sales 17,485,010
SIC 4213 Trucking, except local
Kirk Zavitz
Gregory Zavitz
Robert Kranyak

Stirling, ON K0K

D-U-N-S 25-119-5400   (SL)
MANORCARE PARTNERS
STIRLING MANOR NURSING HOME
218 Edward St, Stirling, ON, K0K 3E0
(613) 395-2596
Emp Here 85   *Sales* 5,828,110
SIC 8051 Skilled nursing care facilities
Charmaine Jordan

D-U-N-S 20-154-1422   (SL)
WELLS FORD SALES LTD
48 Belleville Rd, Stirling, ON, K0K 3E0
(613) 395-3375
Emp Here 30   *Sales* 14,942,340
SIC 5511 New and used car dealers
Allan Wells
Steven Wells
Michael Wells

Stittsville, ON K2S

D-U-N-S 24-103-5153   (SL)
BRADLEY'S COMMERCIAL INSURANCE LIMITED
1469 Stittsville Main St, Stittsville, ON, K2S 0C8
(613) 836-2473
Emp Here 60   *Sales* 50,883,600
SIC 6411 Insurance agents, brokers, and service
Ross W. Bradley
Chantal Pelletier

D-U-N-S 20-704-7080   (SL)
FIRST OTTAWA REALTY INC
COLDWELL BANKER FIRST OTTAWA REALTY
2 Hobin St, Stittsville, ON, K2S 1C3
(613) 831-9628
Emp Here 121   *Sales* 50,685,569
SIC 6531 Real estate agents and managers
Ross Webley

D-U-N-S 24-422-1086   (BR)
GROUPE EMBALLAGE SPECIALISE S.E.C.
SMITH INDUSPAC OTTAWA
(Suby of GROUPE EMBALLAGE SPECIALISE S.E.C.)
140 Iber Rd, Stittsville, ON, K2S 1E9

---

(613) 742-6766
Emp Here 90
SIC 3086 Plastics foam products
Paul Gaulin

D-U-N-S 20-747-5369   (SL)
LAURYSEN KITCHENS LTD
2415 Carp Rd, Stittsville, ON, K2S 1B3
(613) 836-5353
Emp Here 100   *Sales* 15,586,300
SIC 2434 Wood kitchen cabinets
William (Bill) Laurysen
Caroline Castrucci
Audrey Laurysen

D-U-N-S 20-404-0174   (SL)
LEGRAND AV CANADA ULC
113 Iber Rd, Stittsville, ON, K2S 1E7
(613) 836-2501
Emp Here 29   *Sales* 12,968,046
SIC 5046 Commercial equipment, nec
Scott Gill
Neil Andison
Steve Schneider
James Laperriere
John Selldorff
Franck Lemery
David Beugin

D-U-N-S 24-523-2033   (SL)
LLOYD DOUGLAS SOLUTIONS INC
130 Iber Rd, Stittsville, ON, K2S 1E9
(613) 369-5189
Emp Here 80   *Sales* 17,760,080
SIC 3578 Calculating and accounting equipment
Jim Burke
Don Burke
Tony Morgan
Andrew Dale

D-U-N-S 24-875-9847   (SL)
MADIX ENGINEERING INC
L-D TOOL & DIE
139 Iber Rd, Stittsville, ON, K2S 1E7
(613) 591-1474
Emp Here 75   *Sales* 15,142,275
SIC 3089 Plastics products, nec
David Tait
Lawrence Dickson

D-U-N-S 20-804-4342   (SL)
MAHOGANY SALON & SPA LTD
1261 Stittsville Main St Unit 1, Stittsville, ON, K2S 2E4
(613) 836-3334
Emp Here 90   *Sales* 6,875,730
SIC 7991 Physical fitness facilities
Catherine Wood

D-U-N-S 25-673-8808   (SL)
MIDDLE ATLANTIC PRODUCTS-CANADA, INC
(*Suby of* LEGRAND)
113 Iber Rd, Stittsville, ON, K2S 1E7
(613) 836-2501
Emp Here 23   *Sales* 10,285,002
SIC 5046 Commercial equipment, nec
Neil Andison
Robert J. (Bob) Schluter

D-U-N-S 24-847-0825   (SL)
MOR-WEN RESTAURANTS LTD
GLEN SCOTTISH PUB & RESTAURANT
1010 Stittsville Main St, Stittsville, ON, K2S 1B9
(613) 831-2738
Emp Here 80   *Sales* 3,641,520
SIC 5812 Eating places
Kathleen Mcconville
John Mcconville
Luchana Mcconville

D-U-N-S 25-131-3003   (BR)
OTTAWA CATHOLIC DISTRICT SCHOOL BOARD
SACRED HEART CATHOLIC HIGH SCHOOL
(*Suby of* OTTAWA CATHOLIC DISTRICT

SCHOOL BOARD)
Sacred Heart Catholic High School, Stittsville, ON, K2S 1X4
(613) 831-6643
Emp Here 130
SIC 8211 Elementary and secondary schools
Valerie Mcgillis

D-U-N-S 25-411-7203   (HQ)
SANI-SOL INC
REPAREX
149 Iber Rd, Stittsville, ON, K2S 1E7
(613) 831-3698
Emp Here 19   *Sales* 32,865,525
SIC 5169 Chemicals and allied products, nec
David Duncan

D-U-N-S 20-288-9197   (BR)
SPECIALTY CARE INC
SPECIALTY CARE FAMILY
(*Suby of* SPECIALTY CARE INC)
5501 Abbott St E, Stittsville, ON, K2S 2C5
(613) 836-0331
Emp Here 100
SIC 8051 Skilled nursing care facilities
Janice Martin

D-U-N-S 20-763-5681   (HQ)
T.A. MORRISON & CO. INC
TAMCO
(*Suby of* CHAPPELL BOYS HOLDINGS INC)
27 Iber Rd, Stittsville, ON, K2S 1E6
(613) 831-7000
Sales 10,262,480
SIC 3822 Environmental controls

D-U-N-S 24-437-9004   (SL)
TRIPLE K TRANSPORT LTD
(*Suby of* POOLE CREEK MANAGEMENT COMPANY LTD)
6640 Hazeldean Rd, Stittsville, ON, K2S 1B9
(613) 836-7333
Emp Here 65   *Sales* 13,370,890
SIC 4213 Trucking, except local
Keith D. Sabiston

Stoney Creek, ON L8E

D-U-N-S 20-698-2022   (BR)
1589711 ONTARIO INC
WENTWORTH MOLD, DIV OF
(*Suby of* 1589711 ONTARIO INC)
566 Arvin Ave Unit 3, Stoney Creek, ON, L8E 5P1

Emp Here 130
SIC 3544 Special dies, tools, jigs, and fixtures
Walter Kuskowski

D-U-N-S 24-419-1248   (BR)
ACIER NOVA INC
NOVA STEEL PROCESSING
(*Suby of* 3195538 CANADA INC)
830 South Service Rd, Stoney Creek, ON, L8E 5M7
(905) 643-3300
Emp Here 75
SIC 3312 Blast furnaces and steel mills
Vince Gallo

D-U-N-S 20-836-0540   (SL)
AESTHETICS LANDSCAPE CONTRACTORS
1092 Highway 8, Stoney Creek, ON, L8E 5H8
(905) 643-9933
Emp Here 30   *Sales* 14,250,780
SIC 5083 Farm and garden machinery
Greg Davis

D-U-N-S 20-177-5827   (SL)
ALDON INVESTMENTS LTD
46 Community Ave, Stoney Creek, ON, L8E 2Y3
(905) 664-2126
Emp Here 100   *Sales* 26,155,300

SIC 6712 Bank holding companies
Lou Albanese

D-U-N-S 20-052-5004   (SL)
ARMOUR STEEL SUPPLY LIMITED
540 Seaman St, Stoney Creek, ON, L8E 3X7
(905) 388-7751
Emp Here 24   *Sales* 10,732,176
SIC 5051 Metals service centers and offices
John Bruzzese
Marilyn Bruzzese

D-U-N-S 24-626-3214   (HQ)
ASI GROUP LTD
566 Arvin Ave, Stoney Creek, ON, L8E 5P1
(905) 643-3283
Emp Here 105   *Sales* 30,293,040
SIC 1629 Heavy construction, nec
Carmen Sferrazza
Barry Grant

D-U-N-S 24-311-7509   (HQ)
ASSOCIATED BRANDS INC
(*Suby of* TREEHOUSE FOODS, INC.)
944 Highway 8, Stoney Creek, ON, L8E 5S3
(905) 643-1211
Emp Here 200   *Sales* 243,692,500
SIC 2099 Food preparations, nec
Scott Greenwood
Brent Belzberg
Eric Berke

D-U-N-S 24-421-5026   (SL)
BALL HARRISON HANSELL EMPLOYEE BENEFITS INSURANCE AGENCY LTD
1040 South Service Rd, Stoney Creek, ON, L8E 6G3
(905) 643-1017
Emp Here 15   *Sales* 10,881,585
SIC 6321 Accident and health insurance
Ronald Hansell

D-U-N-S 24-720-6204   (HQ)
BARTEK INGREDIENTS INC
(*Suby of* TORQUEST PARTNERS INC)
421 Seaman St, Stoney Creek, ON, L8E 3J4
(905) 662-1127
Sales 28,402,100
SIC 2869 Industrial organic chemicals, nec
Raffaele Brancato
David Tapajna

D-U-N-S 20-373-0887   (SL)
BARTERPAY INC
102-1040 South Service Rd, Stoney Creek, ON, L8E 6G3
(905) 777-0660
Emp Here 60   *Sales* 26,953,140
SIC 7389 Business services, nec
John Porter
Gavin Duncan

D-U-N-S 25-294-9185   (BR)
BREWERS RETAIL INC
BEER STORE, THE
(*Suby of* BREWERS RETAIL INC)
414 Dewitt Rd, Stoney Creek, ON, L8E 4B7
(905) 664-7921
Emp Here 100
SIC 5921 Liquor stores
Michael Nickell

D-U-N-S 25-987-8630   (HQ)
C J I PROPERTIES INC
237 Arvin Ave, Stoney Creek, ON, L8E 5S6
(905) 664-8448
Sales 31,435,250
SIC 6712 Bank holding companies
William Baird Jones
Syd Wilkinson

D-U-N-S 20-154-2164   (HQ)
CANADIAN CURTIS REFRIGERATION INC
881 Arvin Ave, Stoney Creek, ON, L8E 5N8
(905) 643-1977
Emp Here 62   *Sales* 16,650,075
SIC 3585 Refrigeration and heating equipment

Michael Gilhespy

D-U-N-S 24-947-5609   (HQ)
CORESLAB INTERNATIONAL INC
332 Jones Rd Suite 8, Stoney Creek, ON, L8E 5N2
(905) 643-0220
Emp Here 4   *Sales* 27,335,000
SIC 6712 Bank holding companies
Lou Franciosa
Mario Franciosa
Dominic Franciosa
Sidney Spiegel

D-U-N-S 24-044-6117   (SL)
CRANE SERVICE SYSTEMS INC
419 Millen Rd, Stoney Creek, ON, L8E 2P6
(905) 664-9900
Emp Here 29   *Sales* 13,027,351
SIC 7389 Business services, nec
Kenneth Vandenberg

D-U-N-S 20-053-1812   (HQ)
CRANE, JOHN CANADA INC
(*Suby of* SMITHS GROUP PLC)
423 Green Rd, Stoney Creek, ON, L8E 3A1
(905) 662-6191
Emp Here 120   *Sales* 50,105,586
SIC 3499 Fabricated Metal products, nec
Chris Steele
Fern Lebeille

D-U-N-S 24-601-8964   (BR)
CRANE, JOHN CANADA INC
(*Suby of* SMITHS GROUP PLC)
423 Green Rd, Stoney Creek, ON, L8E 3A1
(905) 662-6191
Emp Here 90
SIC 3061 Mechanical rubber goods
Chrish Steele

D-U-N-S 24-179-3996   (SL)
DEFAVERI GROUP CONTRACTING INC
1259 Arvin Ave, Stoney Creek, ON, L8E 0H7
(905) 560-2555
Emp Here 40   *Sales* 13,333,320
SIC 1541 Industrial buildings and warehouses
Giovanni Defaveri

D-U-N-S 24-119-9228   (SL)
DEL WINDOWS & DOORS INC
241 Arvin Ave, Stoney Creek, ON, L8E 2L9
(905) 561-4335
Emp Here 100   *Sales* 20,189,700
SIC 3089 Plastics products, nec
Edward Bremer

D-U-N-S 20-053-3040   (SL)
DIANA DOLLS FASHIONS INC
KUSHIES BABY
555 Barton St, Stoney Creek, ON, L8E 5S1
(905) 643-9118
Emp Here 160   *Sales* 134,005,280
SIC 5137 Women's and children's clothing
Sam Perez
Susan Malinowski

D-U-N-S 20-393-7164   (SL)
DINAMIX ALLIANCE INC
35 Sunnyhurst Ave Suite 2, Stoney Creek, ON, L8E 5M9
(905) 643-9979
Emp Here 50   *Sales* 41,778,850
SIC 5142 Packaged frozen goods
Zanna Cicnska

D-U-N-S 24-223-1850   (SL)
DYNAMIC & PROTO CIRCUITS INC
DAPC
869 Barton St, Stoney Creek, ON, L8E 5G6

Emp Here 100   *Sales* 19,044,200
SIC 3672 Printed circuit boards
Mark Stevens
Carl Hewitt

D-U-N-S 24-364-3376   (SL)
E. M. PRECISE TOOL LTD

216 Arvin Ave Unit A, Stoney Creek, ON, L8E
2L8
(905) 664-2644
Emp Here 22   *Sales* 10,450,572
SIC 5084 Industrial machinery and equipment
  David Macniven
  Yvonne Macniven
  Peter Lemmen

D-U-N-S 20-186-9591   (HQ)
E.D. SMITH FOODS, LTD
(*Suby of* TREEHOUSE FOODS, INC.)
944 Highway 8, Stoney Creek, ON, L8E 5S3
(905) 643-1211
Emp Here 10   *Sales* 175,458,600
SIC 2033 Canned fruits and specialties
  Ian Maton
  Llewellyn S Smith
  John Cooper
  Keiran Kelly

D-U-N-S 25-829-3000   (SL)
EARL PADDOCK TRANSPORTATION INC
199 Arvin Ave, Stoney Creek, ON, L8E 2L9
(905) 667-8755
Emp Here 115   *Sales* 23,656,190
SIC 4213 Trucking, except local
  Scott Paddock
  Cameron Paddock
  Phyllis Paddock

D-U-N-S 24-488-0076   (SL)
EQUIPMENT CORPS INC
1256 Arvin Ave, Stoney Creek, ON, L8E 0H7
(905) 545-1234
Emp Here 25   *Sales* 11,875,650
SIC 5082 Construction and mining machinery
  James T Bedard

D-U-N-S 25-911-6028   (BR)
EXTENDICARE INC
STONEY CREEK LIFECARE CENTRE
(*Suby of* EXTENDICARE INC)
199 Glover Rd, Stoney Creek, ON, L8E 5J2
(905) 643-1795
Emp Here 80
SIC 8051 Skilled nursing care facilities
  Stephanie Opdam

D-U-N-S 20-560-5363   (SL)
FABRIS INC.
1216 South Service Rd, Stoney Creek, ON,
L8E 5C4
(905) 643-4111
Emp Here 114   *Sales* 25,308,114
SIC 3599 Industrial machinery, nec
  Carole Fabris

D-U-N-S 25-977-7811   (HQ)
FIRSTONTARIO CREDIT UNION LIMITED
970 South Service Rd Suite 301, Stoney
Creek, ON, L8E 6A2
(905) 387-0770
Emp Here 156   *Sales* 85,400,500
SIC 6062 State credit unions
  Kelly Mcgiffin
  Barry Doan
  Carey Smith
  Otto Penner

D-U-N-S 24-390-6539   (HQ)
FLOCOR INC
(*Suby of* ENTREPRISES MIRCA INC, LES)
470 Seaman St, Stoney Creek, ON, L8E 2V9
(905) 664-9230
Emp Here 40   *Sales* 82,807,920
SIC 5074 Plumbing and heating equipment
and supplies (hydronics)
  Martin Deschenes
  Francois Deschenes
  Marc Lapierre
  Jacques Deschenes
  Tom Murray

D-U-N-S 20-708-1832   (BR)
FLYNN CANADA LTD
(*Suby of* FLYNN CANADA LTD)

890 Arvin Ave, Stoney Creek, ON, L8E 5Y8
(905) 643-9515
Emp Here 90
SIC 1761 Roofing, siding, and sheetMetal
work
  Blair Holmes

D-U-N-S 25-103-9913   (SL)
FURNITURE INVESTMENT GROUP INC
ASHLEY FURNITURE HOME STORE
563 Barton St, Stoney Creek, ON, L8E 5S1

Emp Here 62   *Sales* 14,408,986
SIC 5712 Furniture stores
  Bob Binkley
  Dennis Novosel
  Mark Macdiarmid

D-U-N-S 25-214-4969   (SL)
GARRTECH INC
910 Arvin Ave, Stoney Creek, ON, L8E 5Y8
(905) 643-6414
Emp Here 60   *Sales* 13,320,060
SIC 3544 Special dies, tools, jigs, and fixtures
  Anthony Paget
  John Parente
  Robert Fazackerley
  Graeme Lambert
  Russell Norman

D-U-N-S 20-038-9682   (HQ)
GLASROCK PRODUCTS INC
GLASROCK OMI
274 South Service Rd Suite 268, Stoney
Creek, ON, L8E 2N9
(905) 664-5300
Emp Here 25   *Sales* 21,376,170
SIC 5085 Industrial supplies
  Jeff Dibenedetto

D-U-N-S 24-923-5987   (SL)
GRECO MANAGEMENT INC
21 Teal Ave, Stoney Creek, ON, L8E 2P1
(905) 560-0661
Emp Here 65   *Sales* 13,590,525
SIC 8721 Accounting, auditing, and book-
keeping
  Marsha Rice
  Elsa Greco
  Mary Greco
  Filimena Greco
  Emilia Greco

D-U-N-S 20-136-4598   (BR)
**HAMILTON-WENTWORTH   DISTRICT
SCHOOL BOARD, THE**
ORCHARD PARK SECONDARY SCHOOL
(*Suby of* HAMILTON-WENTWORTH DIS-
TRICT SCHOOL BOARD, THE)
200 Dewitt Rd, Stoney Creek, ON, L8E 4M5
(905) 573-3550
Emp Here 90
SIC 8211 Elementary and secondary schools
  Marco Barzetti

D-U-N-S 20-127-3778   (HQ)
HARRIS STEEL GROUP INC
(*Suby of* NUCOR CORPORATION)
318 Arvin Ave, Stoney Creek, ON, L8E 2M2
(905) 662-0611
Emp Here 110   *Sales* 486,462,000
SIC 3499 Fabricated Metal products, nec
  Gary Richmond
  Douglas Deighton
  Eugene Mcmanus

D-U-N-S 24-719-1430   (HQ)
HARRIS STEEL ULC
FISHER & LUDLOW, DIV OF
(*Suby of* NUCOR CORPORATION)
318 Arvin Ave, Stoney Creek, ON, L8E 2M2
(905) 662-0611
Emp Here 150   *Sales* 340,523,400
SIC 3449 Miscellaneous Metalwork
  John Harris
  Douglas Deighton
  Robert Roe

D-U-N-S 24-668-6062   (SL)
I-CUBED INDUSTRY INNOVATORS INC
999 Barton St, Stoney Creek, ON, L8E 5H4
(905) 643-8685
Emp Here 60   *Sales* 13,320,060
SIC 3569 General industrial machinery, nec
  David Bunker

D-U-N-S 20-732-2632   (HQ)
INTEGRATED MARKET SOLUTIONS INC
266 South Service Rd, Stoney Creek, ON,
L8E 2N9
(905) 662-9194
Emp Here 29   *Sales* 11,803,316
SIC 1623 Water, sewer, and utility lines
  George Vehi

D-U-N-S 24-827-0142   (SL)
JANCO STEEL LTD
925 Arvin Ave, Stoney Creek, ON, L8E 5N9
(905) 643-3535
Emp Here 140   *Sales* 83,643,560
SIC 5051 Metals service centers and offices
  Allan Schutten

D-U-N-S 24-751-5521   (SL)
JAYNE INDUSTRIES INC
550 Seaman St, Stoney Creek, ON, L8E 3X7
(905) 643-9200
Emp Here 64   *Sales* 14,939,840
SIC 3297 Nonclay refractories
  Duncan Robson
  Chris Cashin

D-U-N-S 20-054-2074   (HQ)
JONES, CHARLES INDUSTRIAL LIMITED
(*Suby of* C J I PROPERTIES INC)
237 Arvin Ave, Stoney Creek, ON, L8E 5S6
(905) 664-8448
Emp Here 34   *Sales* 56,088,950
SIC 5085 Industrial supplies
  William Baird Jones
  Syd Wilkinson

D-U-N-S 25-398-6921   (SL)
KENWAL CANADA INC
1100 South Service Rd Suite 317, Stoney
Creek, ON, L8E 0C5
(905) 643-8930
Emp Here 11   *Sales* 11,003,729
SIC 5051 Metals service centers and offices
  Norman Katzman
  Frank Jerneycic
  Kenneth Eisenberg

D-U-N-S 24-751-8913   (SL)
KLINGSPOR INC
KLINGSPOR ENGINEERED ABBRASIVES
(*Suby of* KLINGSPOR AG)
1175 Barton St Unit 1, Stoney Creek, ON, L8E
5H1
(905) 643-0770
Emp Here 36   *Sales* 17,100,936
SIC 5085 Industrial supplies
  Bruce Jonson
  Jim Gallino

D-U-N-S 20-934-9257   (HQ)
KUBES STEEL INC
930 Arvin Ave, Stoney Creek, ON, L8E 5Y8
(905) 643-1229
Emp Here 40   *Sales* 15,366,800
SIC 3499 Fabricated Metal products, nec
  Joe Kubes
  John Freond
  Ted Slade

D-U-N-S 25-332-3406   (SL)
L.P. CUSTOM MACHINING LTD
211 Barton St, Stoney Creek, ON, L8E 2K3

Emp Here 80   *Sales* 17,760,080
SIC 3599 Industrial machinery, nec
  David Singh

D-U-N-S 24-363-8947   (HQ)
LOSANI HOMES (1998) LTD
LOSANI HOMES

430 Mcneilly Rd, Stoney Creek, ON, L8E 5E3
(905) 643-7386
Sales 37,700,010
SIC 6531 Real estate agents and managers
  Fred Losani
  Lino Losani

D-U-N-S 25-140-6252   (SL)
**MACK SALES & SERVICE OF STONEY
CREEK LTD**
STONEY CREEK MACK
330 South Service Rd, Stoney Creek, ON,
L8E 2R4
(905) 662-4240
Emp Here 30   *Sales* 14,942,340
SIC 5511 New and used car dealers
  John Jr Slotegraaf
  Boyd Brenton

D-U-N-S 24-355-1798   (SL)
MCGOWAN INSULATIONS LTD
345 Barton St, Stoney Creek, ON, L8E 2L2
(905) 549-1844
Emp Here 70   *Sales* 17,233,020
SIC 1799 Special trade contractors, nec
  Robert Mcgowan Sr.

D-U-N-S 24-199-7493   (SL)
MEAT FACTORY LIMITED, THE
TMF FOODS
46 Community Ave, Stoney Creek, ON, L8E
2Y3
(905) 664-2126
Emp Here 100   *Sales* 34,569,000
SIC 2013 Sausages and other prepared
meats
  Lou Albanese

D-U-N-S 20-920-9704   (HQ)
METRO FREIGHTLINER HAMILTON INC
METRO TRUCK
475 Seaman St, Stoney Creek, ON, L8E 2R2
(905) 561-6110
Emp Here 50   *Sales* 44,049,600
SIC 5511 New and used car dealers
  John Cappellazzo

D-U-N-S 25-089-2155   (SL)
MID WEST COAST CANADA INC
PACKERS LOGISTICS SOLUTIONS, DIV OF
400 Jones Rd Suite 106, Stoney Creek, ON,
L8E 5P4
(905) 578-9993
Emp Here 70   *Sales* 10,373,440
SIC 4213 Trucking, except local
  Martin S Paddock

D-U-N-S 24-964-7009   (BR)
**MOHAWK COLLEGE OF APPLIED ARTS
AND TECHNOLOGY, THE**
MOHAWK COLLEGE STARRT INSTITUTE
(*Suby of* MOHAWK COLLEGE OF APPLIED
ARTS AND TECHNOLOGY, THE)
481 Barton St, Stoney Creek, ON, L8E 2L7
(905) 662-9796
Emp Here 80
SIC 8222 Junior colleges
  Cheryl Fowler

D-U-N-S 20-248-0427   (SL)
NARROFLEX INC
(*Suby of* WENTWORTH TEXTILES INC)
590 South Service Rd, Stoney Creek, ON,
L8E 2W1
(905) 643-6066
Emp Here 170   *Sales* 31,178,510
SIC 2241 Narrow fabric mills
  Xavier Joseph

D-U-N-S 25-482-3800   (SL)
NORSTAR WINDOWS & DOORS LTD
944 South Service Rd, Stoney Creek, ON,
L8E 6A2
(905) 643-9333
Emp Here 70   *Sales* 13,445,950
SIC 3442 Metal doors, sash, and trim
  John Vacca

D-U-N-S 24-339-8760   (BR)
OLDCASTLE BUILDING PRODUCTS CANADA, INC
MATERIAUX DE CONSTRUCTION OLDCAS-TLE CANADA INC, LES
(*Suby of* CRH PUBLIC LIMITED COMPANY)
682 Arvin Ave, Stoney Creek, ON, L8E 5R4

Emp Here 80
SIC 3272 Concrete products, nec
 Brad Thomson

D-U-N-S 25-306-2715   (BR)
ORLICK INDUSTRIES LIMITED
(*Suby of* ORLICK INDUSTRIES LIMITED)
500 Seaman St, Stoney Creek, ON, L8E 2V9
(905) 662-5954
Emp Here 200
SIC 3365 Aluminum foundries
 David Knowles

D-U-N-S 20-012-9927   (HQ)
PARKER HANNIFIN CANADA
PARKER FILTRATION CANADA
(*Suby of* PARKER-HANNIFIN CORPORA-TION)
1100 South Service Rd Unit 318, Stoney Creek, ON, L8E 0C5
(905) 309-8230
Emp Here 20   *Sales* 182,570,050
SIC 3593 Fluid power cylinders and actuators
 Lynn Moline

D-U-N-S 24-369-8854   (HQ)
PEARSON DUNN INSURANCE INC
(*Suby of* ARTHUR J. GALLAGHER & CO.)
435 Mcneilly Rd Suite 103, Stoney Creek, ON, L8E 5E3
(905) 575-1122
Emp Here 5   *Sales* 42,403,000
SIC 6411 Insurance agents, brokers, and ser-vice
 Trevor Waldron

D-U-N-S 20-923-8443   (SL)
PNEU-HYD INDUSTRIES LIMITED
375 Green Rd Unit 1, Stoney Creek, ON, L8E 4A5
(905) 664-5540
Emp Here 66   *Sales* 41,532,480
SIC 5531 Auto and home supply stores
 Douglas Rogers

D-U-N-S 24-142-0728   (HQ)
PRO INSUL LIMITED
468 Arvin Ave, Stoney Creek, ON, L8E 2M9
(905) 662-6161
Emp Here 50   *Sales* 27,819,018
SIC 1799 Special trade contractors, nec
 James Flower
 Paul Mitchell

D-U-N-S 24-952-1634   (SL)
RESIDENTIAL ENERGY SAVING PROD-UCTS INC
201 Barton St Unit 3, Stoney Creek, ON, L8E 2K3
(905) 578-2292
Emp Here 45   *Sales* 12,986,235
SIC 1522 Residential construction, nec
 Richard Hames
 Joe Zaborski

D-U-N-S 25-362-9505   (BR)
SAMUEL, SON & CO., LIMITED
NELSON STEEL
(*Suby of* SAMUEL, SON & CO., LIMITED)
400 Glover Rd, Stoney Creek, ON, L8E 5X1
(905) 662-1404
Emp Here 100
SIC 3479 Metal coating and allied services
 Graham Oakley

D-U-N-S 20-794-3007   (BR)
SAMUEL, SON & CO., LIMITED
SAMUEL PLATE SALES
(*Suby of* SAMUEL, SON & CO., LIMITED)
12 Teal Ave, Stoney Creek, ON, L8E 3Y5

(800) 263-1316
Emp Here 160
SIC 5051 Metals service centers and offices
 Mark Samuel

D-U-N-S 25-673-5572   (HQ)
SELKIRK CANADA CORPORATION
(*Suby of* SELKIRK AMERICAS, L.P.)
375 Green Rd Suite 1, Stoney Creek, ON, L8E 4A5
(905) 662-6600
Emp Here 50   *Sales* 19,714,090
SIC 3259 Structural clay products, nec
 Tim Valters

D-U-N-S 20-140-3581   (HQ)
SHAW-ALMEX INDUSTRIES LIMITED
SHAW ALMEX FUSION CANADA, DIV OF
323 Glover Rd, Stoney Creek, ON, L8E 5M2
(905) 643-7750
Emp Here 25   *Sales* 112,350,800
SIC 3535 Conveyors and conveying equip-ment
 Timothy Shaw

D-U-N-S 20-876-3961   (SL)
SOLAR ERECTORS LTD
(*Suby of* CORESLAB INTERNATIONAL INC)
332 Jones Rd Unit 1, Stoney Creek, ON, L8E 5N2
(905) 643-1829
Emp Here 80   *Sales* 19,798,640
SIC 1771 Concrete work
 Lou Franciosa
 Domenic Franciosa

D-U-N-S 20-154-3907   (SL)
STAALDUINEN FLORAL LIMITED
1255 Arvin Ave, Stoney Creek, ON, L8E 0H7
(905) 643-2703
Emp Here 40   *Sales* 13,024,000
SIC 5992 Florists
 Brian Van Staalduinen
 Gerta Van Staalduinen
 Duane Van Staalduinen
 Wendy Van Staalduinen
 Brian Van Staalduinen Jr

D-U-N-S 20-505-4745   (HQ)
STONEY CREEK FURNITURE LIMITED
(*Suby of* 1077337 ONTARIO LIMITED)
395 Lewis Rd, Stoney Creek, ON, L8E 5N5
(905) 643-4121
Sales 29,050,375
SIC 5712 Furniture stores
 Dennis Novosel
 Jim Fee
 Jim Carruthers

D-U-N-S 24-140-4417   (HQ)
TAYLOR STEEL INC
477 Arvin Ave, Stoney Creek, ON, L8E 2N1
(905) 662-4925
Sales 298,727,000
SIC 5051 Metals service centers and offices
 Michael Taylor
 William Bourque

D-U-N-S 20-336-9590   (BR)
TAYLOR STEEL INC
(*Suby of* TAYLOR STEEL INC)
395 Green Rd, Stoney Creek, ON, L8E 5V4
(905) 662-5555
Emp Here 80
SIC 4225 General warehousing and storage
 Brian Deams

D-U-N-S 20-699-4258   (HQ)
TIERCON CORP
(*Suby of* J2 MANAGEMENT CORP)
591 Arvin Ave, Stoney Creek, ON, L8E 5N7
(905) 643-4176
Sales 145,425,000
SIC 3714 Motor vehicle parts and accessories
 Joseph Loparco
 Joseph Leon

D-U-N-S 20-320-1736   (BR)

TIERCON CORP
(*Suby of* J2 MANAGEMENT CORP)
352 Arvin Ave, Stoney Creek, ON, L8E 2M4
(905) 662-1097
Emp Here 100
SIC 3714 Motor vehicle parts and accessories
 Michelle Sund

D-U-N-S 25-181-1238   (HQ)
TOP LIFT ENTERPRISES INC
42 Pinelands Ave, Stoney Creek, ON, L8E 5X9
(905) 662-4137
Emp Here 25   *Sales* 83,889,560
SIC 5084 Industrial machinery and equipment
 Emidio Greco
 David Shea
 Ronaldo Greco
 Falco Greco

D-U-N-S 24-007-7388   (BR)
TOROMONT INDUSTRIES LTD
(*Suby of* TOROMONT INDUSTRIES LTD)
460 South Service Rd, Stoney Creek, ON, L8E 2P8
(905) 561-5901
Emp Here 80
SIC 7699 Repair services, nec
 Tim Hurt

D-U-N-S 20-921-0454   (BR)
TOROMONT INDUSTRIES LTD
BATTLEFIELD EQUIPMENT RENTALS
(*Suby of* TOROMONT INDUSTRIES LTD)
880 South Service Rd, Stoney Creek, ON, L8E 5M7
(905) 643-9410
Emp Here 80
SIC 7359 Equipment rental and leasing, nec
 Ryan Jeffcoate

D-U-N-S 24-736-2585   (SL)
TRANSAXLE PARTS HAMILTON INC
730 South Service Rd Unit 1, Stoney Creek, ON, L8E 5S7
(905) 643-0700
Emp Here 30   *Sales* 10,926,450
SIC 5013 Motor vehicle supplies and new parts
 Tom Neelin

D-U-N-S 24-023-6232   (HQ)
TUBE-MAC PIPING TECHNOLOGIES LTD
853 Arvin Ave Suite 1, Stoney Creek, ON, L8E 5N8
(905) 643-8823
Sales 24,618,600
SIC 1799 Special trade contractors, nec
 Gary Mackay
 Neil Smith
 Sandra Mackay
 Geoffrey Mackay
 Chris Peitchinis

D-U-N-S 24-198-9615   (HQ)
VENETOR CRANE LTD
(*Suby of* 1090319 ONTARIO INC)
45 Oriole Ave, Stoney Creek, ON, L8E 5C4
(905) 643-7943
Emp Here 170   *Sales* 66,629,600
SIC 7353 Heavy construction equipment rental
 Louis Beraldo
 Miranda Beraldo

D-U-N-S 25-148-2691   (HQ)
VERMEER CANADA INC
VERMEER SALES & SERVICES
1100 South Service Rd Suite 423, Stoney Creek, ON, L8E 0C5
(289) 765-5260
Emp Here 20   *Sales* 19,001,040
SIC 5084 Industrial machinery and equipment
 Chris Burelle
 Peter Trombetta

D-U-N-S 24-847-2326   (HQ)
WABTEC CANADA INC

UNIFIN INTERNATIONAL, DIV OF
(*Suby of* WESTINGHOUSE AIR BRAKE TECHNOLOGIES CORPORATION)
475 Seaman St, Stoney Creek, ON, L8E 2R2
(905) 561-8700
Emp Here 300   *Sales* 196,323,750
SIC 3743 Railroad equipment
 William E Cassling
 Alvaro Garcia-Tunon
 George A Socher
 James Norval Watson

D-U-N-S 24-704-1395   (HQ)
WENTWORTH TEXTILES INC
NARROFLEX
590 South Service Rd, Stoney Creek, ON, L8E 2W1
(905) 643-6066
Emp Here 250   *Sales* 111,156,410
SIC 2241 Narrow fabric mills
 Xavier Joseph
 Andrew Ma
 Keyvan Ghahary

D-U-N-S 24-626-0715   (SL)
WHEEL'S AUTOMOTIVE DEALER SUP-PLIES INC
WHEELS ADS
600 Arvin Ave, Stoney Creek, ON, L8E 5P1
(800) 465-8831
Emp Here 30   *Sales* 14,942,340
SIC 5511 New and used car dealers
 Richard Ashworth

D-U-N-S 20-134-6418   (SL)
WHITE OAK TRANSPORT LIMITED
365 Lewis Rd, Stoney Creek, ON, L8E 5N4
(905) 643-9500
Emp Here 75   *Sales* 11,703,210
SIC 4213 Trucking, except local
 Stephen Sharples

D-U-N-S 20-116-6621   (SL)
ZELUS MATERIAL HANDLING INC
730 South Service Rd, Stoney Creek, ON, L8E 5S7
(905) 643-4928
Emp Here 50   *Sales* 10,185,800
SIC 7699 Repair services, nec
 Jason White
 Bryan White
 Patricia White

Stoney Creek, ON L8G

D-U-N-S 25-633-5340   (SL)
CLARION NURSING HOMES LIMITED
337 Highway 8, Stoney Creek, ON, L8G 1E7
(905) 664-2281
Emp Here 120   *Sales* 8,227,920
SIC 8051 Skilled nursing care facilities
 Michael Janjic

D-U-N-S 25-598-0120   (HQ)
COMPLETE COMMUNICATION SYSTEMS INC
ROGERS WIRELESS
905 Queenston Rd, Stoney Creek, ON, L8G 1B6
(905) 664-1158
Emp Here 20   *Sales* 16,280,000
SIC 5999 Miscellaneous retail stores, nec
 Rene Monaro

D-U-N-S 25-059-0429   (BR)
CREDIT VALLEY ANIMAL CENTRE LIM-ITED
EASTSIDE PET VET HOSPITAL
(*Suby of* CREDIT VALLEY ANIMAL CENTRE LIMITED)
111 Highway 8, Stoney Creek, ON, L8G 1C1
(905) 662-6719
Emp Here 100
SIC 0742 Veterinary services, specialties

Bonnie Machin

D-U-N-S 20-652-0988   (SL)
FORTINOS FIESTA MALL LTD
102 Highway 8, Stoney Creek, ON, L8G 4H3
(905) 662-3772
Emp Here 49   *Sales* 13,433,448
SIC 5411 Grocery stores
Dwayne Peterson

D-U-N-S 20-940-4974   (BR)
FORTINOS SUPERMARKET LTD
(*Suby of* LOBLAW COMPANIES LIMITED)
102 Highway 8, Stoney Creek, ON, L8G 4H3
(905) 664-2886
Emp Here 250
SIC 5141 Groceries, general line
Joe Caruso

D-U-N-S 25-292-6829   (BR)
**HAMILTON-WENTWORTH   CATHOLIC
SCHOOL BOARD**
*CARDINAL   NEWMAN   SECONDARY
SCHOOL*
(*Suby of* HAMILTON-WENTWORTH
CATHOLIC SCHOOL BOARD)
127 Gray Rd, Stoney Creek, ON, L8G 3V3
(905) 523-2314
Emp Here 120
SIC 8211 Elementary and secondary schools
Dean Di Francesco

D-U-N-S 20-798-7814   (SL)
RIBAK PHARMA LTD
SHOPPERS DRUG MART
377 Highway 8 Suite 369, Stoney Creek, ON,
L8G 1E7
(905) 662-9996
Emp Here 50   *Sales* 12,647,700
SIC 5912 Drug stores and proprietary stores
Faisal Kabir

D-U-N-S 24-891-7445   (HQ)
STATE REALTY LIMITED
ROYAL LEPAGE
115 Highway 8, Stoney Creek, ON, L8G 1C1
(905) 662-6666
Emp Here 76   *Sales* 80,426,688
SIC 6531 Real estate agents and managers
Tony Chiarella

D-U-N-S 24-324-7249   (SL)
STONEY CREEK DISTRIBUTION LTD
135 King St E, Stoney Creek, ON, L8G 0B2

Emp Here 55   *Sales* 19,012,950
SIC 2024 Ice cream and frozen deserts
Alec Kepecs

D-U-N-S 25-246-3856   (SL)
**THOMAS HEALTH CARE CORPORATION,
THE**
NEW VILLAGE RETIREMENT HOME
490 Highway 8, Stoney Creek, ON, L8G 1G6
(905) 573-4900
Emp Here 63   *Sales* 13,914,873
SIC 6513 Apartment building operators
Augustus C Thomas
Conrad Thomas
Rita Thomas
Shirley Thomas

D-U-N-S 24-783-4161   (HQ)
**TRIPEMCO   BURLINGTON   INSURANCE
GROUP LIMITED**
99 Highway 8, Stoney Creek, ON, L8G 1C1
(905) 664-2266
Emp Here 16   *Sales* 17,809,260
SIC 6411 Insurance agents, brokers, and ser-
vice
Paul Vaccarrello

Stoney Creek, ON L8J

D-U-N-S 24-911-4539   (HQ)

ACUMEN INSURANCE GROUP INC
835 Paramount Dr Suite 301, Stoney Creek,
ON, L8J 0B4
(905) 574-7000
Emp Here 21   *Sales* 20,353,440
SIC 6411 Insurance agents, brokers, and ser-
vice
Salvatore Bagazzoli

D-U-N-S 20-710-8288   (BR)
**HAMILTON-WENTWORTH   DISTRICT
SCHOOL BOARD, THE**
SALTFLEET DISTRICT HIGH SCHOOL
(*Suby of* HAMILTON-WENTWORTH DIS-
TRICT SCHOOL BOARD, THE)
108 Highland Rd W, Stoney Creek, ON, L8J
2T2
(905) 573-3000
Emp Here 100
SIC 8211 Elementary and secondary schools
Kevin Graham

D-U-N-S 20-154-2743   (SL)
HIGHLAND PACKERS LTD
432 Highland Rd E, Stoney Creek, ON, L8J
3G4
(905) 662-8396
Emp Here 125   *Sales* 43,211,250
SIC 2011 Meat packing plants
Janneka Dejonge

D-U-N-S 20-100-5050   (BR)
MAPLE LEAF FOODS INC
(*Suby of* MAPLE LEAF FOODS INC)
92 Highland Rd E, Stoney Creek, ON, L8J
2W6
(905) 662-8883
Emp Here 100
SIC 2015 Poultry slaughtering and processing
Terry Mcgowan

D-U-N-S 20-644-7463   (BR)
REVERA LONG TERM CARE INC
RIDGEVIEW LONG TERM CARE CENTER
(*Suby of* GOVERNMENT OF CANADA)
385 Highland Rd W, Stoney Creek, ON, L8J
3X9
(905) 561-3332
Emp Here 100
SIC 8051 Skilled nursing care facilities
Nanne D"ambrosio

D-U-N-S 24-329-2229   (SL)
WINNERS HOME CENTRAL INC
DUCK SUCKERS
2105 Rymal Rd E, Stoney Creek, ON, L8J 2R8
(905) 560-0800
Emp Here 33   *Sales* 22,994,730
SIC 6794 Patent owners and lessors
David Vanderploeg
John Lewis
Anthony B Nunoo

Stouffville, ON L4A

D-U-N-S 24-522-7843   (SL)
2194747 ONTARIO INC
STOUFFVILLE TOYOTA
1288 Millard St, Stouffville, ON, L4A 0W7
(416) 921-1288
Emp Here 50   *Sales* 24,903,900
SIC 5511 New and used car dealers
Paul Baxter
Kevin Baxter
Lambertus Dekkema
Richard Muir
Thomas N Wright

D-U-N-S 20-374-6677   (SL)
2449616 ONTARIO INC
STOUFFVILLE HONDA
35 Automall Blvd, Stouffville, ON, L4A 0W7
(289) 451-0087
Emp Here 35   *Sales* 17,432,730
SIC 5511 New and used car dealers

Kevin Pearson

D-U-N-S 20-792-1524   (SL)
994731 ONTARIO LTD
STEVE & LIZ'S NO FRILLS 265
5710 Main St, Stouffville, ON, L4A 8B1
(866) 987-6453
Emp Here 50   *Sales* 13,707,600
SIC 5411 Grocery stores
Steve Balsdon

D-U-N-S 25-370-7251   (BR)
ALPA ROOF TRUSSES INC
ALPA ROOF TRUSSES
(*Suby of* ALPA LUMBER INC)
5532 Slaters Rd, Stouffville, ON, L4A 2G7
(905) 713-6616
Emp Here 130
SIC 2439 Structural wood members, nec
Nelson Santos

D-U-N-S 24-596-4663   (HQ)
**CHRISTIAN   BLIND   MISSION   INTERNA-
TIONAL**
CDM CANADA
Gd, Stouffville, ON, L4A 7Z9
(905) 640-6464
Emp Here 39   *Sales* 171,528,374
SIC 8661 Religious organizations
Ed Epp
Jill Bartley
Jonathan Liteplo
Ruby Klassen
Brenda Ben
Wayne Feasby
Don Gerke
Ruth Kuelker
Andrew Mills
Randal Phillips

D-U-N-S 20-812-1470   (BR)
CLUBLINK CORPORATION ULC
EMERALD HILLS GOLF & COUNTRY CLUB
(*Suby of* TWC ENTERPRISES LIMITED)
14001 Warden Ave, Stouffville, ON, L4A 3T4
(905) 888-1100
Emp Here 100
SIC 7992 Public golf courses
Jamie Al-Jbouri

D-U-N-S 24-075-2782   (SL)
COOK (CANADA) INC
(*Suby of* COOK GROUP INCORPORATED)
165 Mostar St, Stouffville, ON, L4A 0Y2
(905) 640-7110
Emp Here 69   *Sales* 36,939,288
SIC 5047 Medical and hospital equipment
William Bobbie
Carl Cook

D-U-N-S 20-979-8834   (HQ)
DRUXY'S INC
DRUXY'S FAMOUS DELI SANDWICHES
52 Abbotsford Rd, Stouffville, ON, L4A 2C1
(416) 385-9500
Emp Here 4   *Sales* 18,655,600
SIC 5812 Eating places
Bruce Druxerman
Harold Druxerman
Peter Druxerman

D-U-N-S 24-597-4175   (HQ)
FRANCIS POWELL & CO. LIMITED
180 Ram Forest Rd, Stouffville, ON, L4A 2G8
(905) 727-2518
Sales 14,176,200
SIC 1611 Highway and street construction
Dwight Powell
William Powell
Nancy Wallingford

D-U-N-S 24-075-6184   (SL)
JMX CONTRACTING INC
(*Suby of* JMX LEASING INC)
130 Ram Forest Rd, Stouffville, ON, L4A 2G8
(905) 241-2224
Emp Here 150   *Sales* 25,472,480
SIC 1795 Wrecking and demolition work

Jeffrey Norton
Charlie Dahl

D-U-N-S 20-404-5694   (HQ)
**K-LINE MAINTENANCE & CONSTRUCTION
LIMITED**
12731 Highway 48, Stouffville, ON, L4A 4A7
(905) 640-2002
Emp Here 75   *Sales* 35,326,350
SIC 1731 Electrical work
Mark Kellett
Mark Kellett
Allan G. Kellett
Rupen Shah
Ken Ramnarine
Neil Johnston

D-U-N-S 24-817-9327   (HQ)
KAITLIN GROUP LTD, THE
28 Sandiford Dr Suite 201, Stouffville, ON,
L4A 1L8
(905) 642-7050
Sales 22,217,244
SIC 1521 Single-family housing construction
William J Daniel
Gary A Daniel

D-U-N-S 20-033-3813   (HQ)
KING COLE DUCKS LIMITED
(*Suby of* KING COLE HOLDINGS LIMITED)
15351 Warden Ave, Stouffville, ON, L4A 2V5
(905) 836-9461
Emp Here 142   *Sales* 30,992,550
SIC 0259 Poultry and eggs, nec
Robert Murby
Joanne Grant

D-U-N-S 25-106-7609   (SL)
KOTT LUMBER
14 Anderson Blvd, Stouffville, ON, L4A 7X4
(905) 642-4400
Emp Here 60   *Sales* 26,830,440
SIC 5031 Lumber, plywood, and millwork
Paul Kruyne
Bernie Ashe
Owen Griffiths

D-U-N-S 20-818-1529   (SL)
LEBOVIC ENTERPRISES LIMITED
12045 Mccowan Rd, Stouffville, ON, L4A 4C3
(905) 640-7361
Emp Here 25   *Sales* 10,483,875
SIC 6712 Bank holding companies
Joseph Lebovic
Wolf Lebovic

D-U-N-S 20-552-8586   (BR)
METRO ONTARIO INC
METRO
(*Suby of* METRO INC)
5612 Main St, Stouffville, ON, L4A 8B7
(905) 642-8600
Emp Here 300
SIC 5411 Grocery stores
John Mcerlain

D-U-N-S 20-708-8159   (SL)
MYRSA MANAGEMENT SERVICES LTD
LOAD LISTER
3 Anderson Blvd Suite 1, Stouffville, ON, L4A
7X4
(416) 291-9756
Emp Here 41   *Sales* 17,193,555
SIC 6712 Bank holding companies
Headley Thomas

D-U-N-S 24-389-4987   (SL)
**POWELL (RICHMOND HILL) CONTRACT-
ING LIMITED**
(*Suby of* FRANCIS POWELL & CO. LIMITED)
180 Ram Forest Rd, Stouffville, ON, L4A 2G8
(905) 727-2518
Emp Here 50   *Sales* 12,622,100
SIC 1611 Highway and street construction
Dwight Powell
William Powell
Nancy Wallingford

D-U-N-S 24-326-5746 (HQ)
PVK DRUGS LIMITED
SHOPPERS DRUG MART
5710 Main St Unit 3, Stouffville, ON, L4A 8A9
(905) 640-2700
Sales 12,647,700
SIC 5912 Drug stores and proprietary stores
 Paul Kuras
 Rasa Kuras

D-U-N-S 24-467-8418 (HQ)
RICHVALE YORK BLOCK INC
5 Cardico Dr, Stouffville, ON, L4A 2G5
(416) 213-7444
Emp Here 40 *Sales* 10,753,140
SIC 3271 Concrete block and brick
 Luciano Teseo
 Stanley Stank

D-U-N-S 24-251-6582 (HQ)
SANDFORD - BLACKSTOCK INVESTMENTS LIMITED
37 Sandiford Dr Unit 300, Stouffville, ON, L4A 3Z2

Sales 18,592,245
SIC 6282 Investment advice

D-U-N-S 20-154-5449 (SL)
SCHELL LUMBER LIMITED
SCHELL COUNTRY DEPOT
33 Edward St, Stouffville, ON, L4A 1A4
(905) 640-3440
Emp Here 45 *Sales* 11,387,655
SIC 5211 Lumber and other building materials
 Harry Schell
 Percy Schell
 Ron Schell
 Steve Schell

D-U-N-S 20-031-9655 (SL)
STANMORE EQUIPMENT LIMITED
3 Anderson Blvd, Stouffville, ON, L4A 7X4
(416) 291-1928
Emp Here 32 *Sales* 15,200,832
SIC 5082 Construction and mining machinery
 Hedley R Thomas

D-U-N-S 25-964-7220 (BR)
STOCK TRANSPORTATION LTD
(*Suby of* NATIONAL EXPRESS GROUP PLC)
24 Cardico Dr, Stouffville, ON, L4A 2G5

Emp Here 275
SIC 4111 Local and suburban transit
 Robbin Forbes

D-U-N-S 24-198-8422 (SL)
SUTTON GROUP - TOWN AND COUNTRY REALTY LTD
6209 Main St, Stouffville, ON, L4A 4H8
(905) 640-0888
Emp Here 33 *Sales* 10,795,191
SIC 6531 Real estate agents and managers
 John Walley

D-U-N-S 25-321-9422 (BR)
TEVA CANADA LIMITED
(*Suby of* TEVA PHARMACEUTICAL INDUSTRIES LIMITED)
5691 Main St, Stouffville, ON, L4A 1H5
(416) 291-8888
Emp Here 110
SIC 2834 Pharmaceutical preparations
 Simon Graham

D-U-N-S 24-329-8705 (BR)
WAL-MART CANADA CORP
(*Suby of* WALMART INC.)
1050 Hoover Park Dr, Stouffville, ON, L4A 0K2
(905) 640-8848
Emp Here 200
SIC 5311 Department stores
 Mario Pilozzi

D-U-N-S 25-297-9687 (BR)
YORK REGION DISTRICT SCHOOL BOARD
STOUFFVILLE DISTRICT SECONDARY SCHOOL
(*Suby of* YORK REGION DISTRICT SCHOOL BOARD)
801 Hoover Park Dr, Stouffville, ON, L4A 0A4
(905) 640-1433
Emp Here 80
SIC 8211 Elementary and secondary schools
 Corey Chesham

Stratford, ON N4Z

D-U-N-S 20-178-5305 (SL)
AISIN CANADA INC
AISIN
(*Suby of* AISIN SEIKI CO., LTD.)
180 Wright Blvd, Stratford, ON, N4Z 1H3
(519) 271-1575
Emp Here 350 *Sales* 85,130,850
SIC 3465 Automotive stampings
 Katsunori Nakanishi

D-U-N-S 20-104-9207 (SL)
C. R. PLASTIC PRODUCTS INC
CRP PRODUCTS
1172 Erie St, Stratford, ON, N4Z 0A1
(519) 271-1283
Emp Here 200 *Sales* 30,864,400
SIC 2519 Household furniture, nec
 Jamie Bailey
 Bruce Ballantyne

D-U-N-S 25-812-8529 (SL)
COFFEE COOP, THE
TIM HORTONS
693 Erie St, Stratford, ON, N4Z 1A1
(519) 271-6127
Emp Here 40 *Sales* 10,966,080
SIC 5461 Retail bakeries
 Robbin Cooper

D-U-N-S 20-178-6774 (SL)
FIO AUTOMOTIVE CANADA CORPORATION
(*Suby of* FUTABA INDUSTRIAL CO., LTD.)
220 Dunn Rd, Stratford, ON, N4Z 0A7
(519) 275-6070
Emp Here 350 *Sales* 85,130,850
SIC 3465 Automotive stampings
 Dave Martin
 Yoshikazu Kuwahara
 Takayuki Yoshida
 Shingo Tsuchiya

D-U-N-S 24-225-2356 (SL)
HAYASHI CANADA INC
(*Suby of* HAYASHI TELEMPU CORPORATION)
300 Dunn Rd, Stratford, ON, N4Z 0A7
(519) 271-5600
Emp Here 150 *Sales* 36,484,650
SIC 3465 Automotive stampings
 Robert Macdonald
 Takashi Kobayashi
 Yoshiki Asada
 Norio Takami

D-U-N-S 25-528-6882 (SL)
MAGEST INC
(*Suby of* MAGEST GROUP LIMITED, THE)
25 Wright Blvd, Stratford, ON, N4Z 1H3
(519) 272-1001
Emp Here 57 *Sales* 10,188,123
SIC 8711 Engineering services
 Gary Martin

D-U-N-S 20-535-1158 (SL)
NOVATRONICS INC
CURTISS-WRIGHT CONTROLS EM TECHNOLOGIES
(*Suby of* CURTISS-WRIGHT CORPORATION)
789 Erie St, Stratford, ON, N4Z 1A2
(519) 271-3880
Emp Here 140 *Sales* 38,411,800

SIC 3812 Search and navigation equipment
 Martin R Benante
 Doug Wright
 Peter Van Drunen
 Glen E Tynan
 Michael J Denton
 Paul J Ferdenzi
 Robert Shaw
 Harry Jakubowitz
 Marc S O'casal

D-U-N-S 25-194-2595 (BR)
SCHAEFFLER AEROSPACE CANADA INC
FAG AEROSPACE INC
(*Suby of* INA-HOLDING SCHAEFFLER GMBH & CO. KG)
151 Wright Blvd, Stratford, ON, N4Z 1H3
(519) 271-3230
Emp Here 250
SIC 3369 Nonferrous foundries, nec
 Patrick Poulin

D-U-N-S 24-846-0701 (BR)
SOBEYS CAPITAL INCORPORATED
SOBEYS
(*Suby of* EMPIRE COMPANY LIMITED)
30 Queensland Rd, Stratford, ON, N4Z 1H4
(519) 273-2631
Emp Here 140
SIC 5411 Grocery stores
 Karl Grobbecker

D-U-N-S 20-156-5397 (SL)
SOMMERS MOTOR-GENERATOR SALES LIMITED
70 Packham Ave, Stratford, ON, N4Z 0A6
(519) 655-2396
Emp Here 32 *Sales* 14,309,568
SIC 5063 Electrical apparatus and equipment
 Chris Mcgregor

Stratford, ON N5A

D-U-N-S 20-213-9437 (BR)
1032451 B.C. LTD
BEACON HERALD, THE
(*Suby of* QUEBECOR MEDIA INC)
16 Packham Rd, Stratford, ON, N5A 6T6
(519) 271-2220
Emp Here 100
SIC 2711 Newspapers
 David Carter

D-U-N-S 20-918-6027 (SL)
1441246 ONTARIO INC
STRATFORD HOME HARDWARE BUILDING CENTRE
3010 Line 34, Stratford, ON, N5A 6S5
(519) 271-4370
Emp Here 40 *Sales* 10,122,360
SIC 5251 Hardware stores
 Steve Straus

D-U-N-S 20-849-9145 (HQ)
402424 ONTARIO LIMITED
CARMAN'S FOTO SOURCE
257 Monteith Ave, Stratford, ON, N5A 2P6
(519) 271-4552
Emp Here 15 *Sales* 20,501,250
SIC 6712 Bank holding companies
 Rick Carman

D-U-N-S 20-547-3049 (HQ)
ADVANCED DESIGN SOLUTIONS INC
533 Romeo St S Suite 1, Stratford, ON, N5A 4V3
(519) 271-7810
Sales 19,208,500
SIC 3499 Fabricated Metal products, nec
 Mark Booker

D-U-N-S 20-913-6857 (BR)
AVON MAITLAND DISTRICT SCHOOL BOARD
STRATFORD NORTHWESTERN SECONDARY SCHOOL
428 Forman Ave, Stratford, ON, N5A 6R7
(519) 271-9740
Emp Here 100
SIC 8211 Elementary and secondary schools
 Deborah Mc Nair

D-U-N-S 24-473-8998 (SL)
BUY SELL TRADE
STRICTLAND BUDGET LOT
945 Erie St, Stratford, ON, N5A 6S4
(519) 271-6824
Emp Here 49 *Sales* 18,146,692
SIC 5013 Motor vehicle supplies and new parts
 Richard Edmunds

D-U-N-S 20-152-8437 (SL)
CHRIMA IRON WORK LIMITED
CHRIMA METAL FABRICATION
559 Douro St, Stratford, ON, N5A 0E3
(519) 271-5399
Emp Here 70 *Sales* 13,445,950
SIC 3499 Fabricated Metal products, nec
 William Christian
 Dan Christian

D-U-N-S 20-154-6678 (HQ)
CLEAVER-BROOKS OF CANADA LIMITED
CHEMINEE LINING E.
(*Suby of* HARBOUR GROUP LTD.)
161 Lorne Ave W, Stratford, ON, N5A 6S4
(519) 271-9220
Emp Here 117 *Sales* 24,010,625
SIC 3443 Fabricated plate work (boiler shop)
 Robert St Denis

D-U-N-S 20-154-9102 (HQ)
COOPER-STANDARD AUTOMOTIVE CANADA LIMITED
(*Suby of* COOPER-STANDARD HOLDINGS INC.)
703 Douro St, Stratford, ON, N5A 3T1
(519) 271-3360
Sales 119,406,000
SIC 3069 Fabricated rubber products, nec
 Bryan Magoffin
 Keith Stephenson
 Howard Hallam

D-U-N-S 24-664-9263 (BR)
COOPER-STANDARD AUTOMOTIVE CANADA LIMITED
SEALING SYSTEMS GROUP
(*Suby of* COOPER-STANDARD HOLDINGS INC.)
703 Douro St, Stratford, ON, N5A 3T1
(519) 271-3360
Emp Here 369
SIC 2891 Adhesives and sealants

D-U-N-S 20-955-9108 (HQ)
CRANE PLUMBING CANADA CORP
FIAT PRODUCTS, A DIV OF
15 Crane Ave, Stratford, ON, N5A 6S4

Emp Here 130
SIC 3431 Metal sanitary ware
 Kevin Oak
 Larry Coburn

D-U-N-S 25-822-5580 (SL)
CREDIT BUREAU OF STRATFORD (1970) LTD
CREDIT RISK MANAGEMENT CANADA
61 Lorne Ave E Suite 96, Stratford, ON, N5A 6S4
(519) 271-6211
Emp Here 50 *Sales* 12,615,550
SIC 7323 Credit reporting services
 Doug Forster
 Tracy Ivanyshyn

D-U-N-S 20-154-8120 (SL)
CULLITON INC
473 Douro St, Stratford, ON, N5A 3S9
(519) 271-1981
Emp Here 150 *Sales* 40,627,200

SIC 1711 Plumbing, heating, air-conditioning
 Timothy Culliton

D-U-N-S 25-487-0736   (SL)
DILL, W.C. & COMPANY INC
STRATFORD AUCTION
Perth Line Suite 26, Stratford, ON, N5A 6S3

Emp Here 24   *Sales* 10,643,760
SIC 7389 Business services, nec
 William Dill

D-U-N-S 24-676-4539   (SL)
EG INDUSTRIES CANADA, ULC
EG TRANSPIRE
(*Suby of* ERNIE GREEN INDUSTRIES, INC.)
291 Griffith Rd Unit 2, Stratford, ON, N5A 6S4
(519) 273-3733
Emp Here 95   *Sales* 15,091,510
SIC 3089 Plastics products, nec
 Derrick Redding
 Vince Ellerbrock
 Mark Sockness
 Darrel Hollanbacher

D-U-N-S 24-677-3753   (BR)
F&P MFG INC
F&P MFG., INC
(*Suby of* F-TECH INC.)
275 Wright Blvd, Stratford, ON, N5A 7Y1

Emp Here 500
SIC 3714 Motor vehicle parts and accessories
 Kiyoshi Horiuchi

D-U-N-S 25-035-2515   (HQ)
FAMME & CO. PROFESSIONAL CORPORATION
125 Ontario St, Stratford, ON, N5A 3H1
(519) 271-7581
Emp Here 40   *Sales* 12,461,100
SIC 8721 Accounting, auditing, and book-keeping
 Franklin Famme

D-U-N-S 20-879-9262   (SL)
FINCH, BARRY ENTERPRISES LTD
CANADIAN TIRE ASSOCIATE STORE
1093 Ontario St, Stratford, ON, N5A 6W6
(519) 273-2080
Emp Here 110   *Sales* 69,220,800
SIC 5531 Auto and home supply stores
 Barry Finch

D-U-N-S 24-564-7060   (BR)
FIRSTCANADA ULC
FIRST STUDENT CANADA
(*Suby of* FIRSTGROUP PLC)
4321 Line 34, Stratford, ON, N5A 6S7
(519) 393-6727
Emp Here 80
SIC 4151 School buses
 Brian Pawley

D-U-N-S 24-947-3851   (HQ)
GODERICH-EXETER RAILWAY COMPANY LIMITED
(*Suby of* GENESEE & WYOMING INC.)
101 Shakespeare St Suite 2, Stratford, ON, N5A 3W5
(519) 271-4441
Emp Here 42   *Sales* 12,668,803
SIC 4011 Railroads, line-haul operating
 Doug Mackenzie
 Sherri Haggith

D-U-N-S 24-354-3985   (HQ)
GOWANSTOWN POULTRY LIMITED
17 Pine St, Stratford, ON, N5A 1W2
(519) 275-2240
Sales 17,348,355
SIC 0254 Poultry hatcheries
 Mark Finnimore

D-U-N-S 20-154-7510   (HQ)
HENDRICKSON CANADA ULC
HENDRICKSON SPRING
(*Suby of* THE BOLER COMPANY)

532 Romeo St S, Stratford, ON, N5A 4V4
(519) 271-4840
Emp Here 250   *Sales* 12,456,367
SIC 3493 Steel springs, except wire
 Matthew Boler
 Matthew Joy
 Paul Schouwstra

D-U-N-S 24-009-2049   (HQ)
HUNTER STEEL SALES LTD
500 Lorne Ave E, Stratford, ON, N5A 6S4
(519) 273-3151
Emp Here 14   *Sales* 24,147,396
SIC 5051 Metals service centers and offices
 Douglas Hunter
 Mark Hunter
 Steven Hunter
 Lynda Mckenzie

D-U-N-S 20-177-1693   (HQ)
HURON PERTH HEALTHCARE ALLIANCE
CLINTON PUBLIC HOSPITAL, THE
46 General Hospital Dr, Stratford, ON, N5A 2Y6
(519) 271-2120
Emp Here 300   *Sales* 192,976,000
SIC 8742 Management consulting services
 Anne Campbell

D-U-N-S 20-047-7565   (SL)
HURON-PERTH CHILDREN'S AID SOCIETY
CHILD WELFARE
639 Lorne Ave E, Stratford, ON, N5A 6S4
(519) 271-5290
Emp Here 110   *Sales* 8,447,120
SIC 8322 Individual and family services
 John Brightwell
 Thomas F. Knight

D-U-N-S 20-051-3161   (BR)
INDUSTRIES SPECTRA PREMIUM INC, LES
SPI
(*Suby of* INDUSTRIES SPECTRA PREMIUM INC, LES)
533 Romeo St S, Stratford, ON, N5A 4V3
(519) 275-3802
Emp Here 250
SIC 3714 Motor vehicle parts and accessories
 Owen Cathi

D-U-N-S 20-154-7700   (HQ)
INTERNATIONAL GRAPHICS ULC
VALUE GRAPHICS
(*Suby of* TAYLOR CORPORATION)
505 Douro St, Stratford, ON, N5A 3S9
(519) 271-3010
Sales 24,346,000
SIC 2678 Stationery products
 Warren Dinsmore

D-U-N-S 20-702-8606   (SL)
JUTZI, D.H. LIMITED
(*Suby of* JUTZI HOLDINGS INC)
279 Lorne Ave E, Stratford, ON, N5A 6S4
(519) 271-9831
Emp Here 32   *Sales* 20,136,960
SIC 5541 Gasoline service stations
 David E Jutzi
 Dean Jutzi
 Brian Jutzi

D-U-N-S 24-426-0258   (SL)
MVA STRATFORD INC
753 Ontario St, Stratford, ON, N5A 7Y2
(519) 275-2203
Emp Here 140   *Sales* 11,094,675
SIC 3089 Plastics products, nec
 Alex Muradov
 Viktoriya Muradova

D-U-N-S 24-370-9438   (SL)
OMEX MANUFACTURING ULC
AC OMEX
(*Suby of* ANDERSON-COOK, INC.)
251 Lorne Ave W, Stratford, ON, N5A 6S4
(519) 273-5760
Emp Here 100   *Sales* 24,432,800

SIC 5962 Merchandising machine operators
 Kim C Anderson
 Douglas W Spittal
 Rick Slawek

D-U-N-S 24-590-8921   (HQ)
ONTARIO HOME OXYGEN AND RESPIRATORY SERVICES INC
ONTARIO HOME HEALTH
29 Monteith Ave, Stratford, ON, N5A 7J9
(519) 273-1744
Emp Here 12   *Sales* 14,309,568
SIC 5047 Medical and hospital equipment
 Richard Gautreau
 Doug Pinder
 Williams M. Schlotzhauer

D-U-N-S 24-545-2149   (SL)
ORR INSURANCE BROKERS INC
50 Cobourg St, Stratford, ON, N5A 3E5
(519) 271-4340
Emp Here 27   *Sales* 15,657,948
SIC 6411 Insurance agents, brokers, and service
 Richard Orr
 Jeff Orr

D-U-N-S 24-924-3379   (HQ)
RE/MAX A-B REALTY LTD
88 Wellington St, Stratford, ON, N5A 2L2
(519) 273-2821
Emp Here 42   *Sales* 13,587,800
SIC 6531 Real estate agents and managers
 John Wolfe

D-U-N-S 24-387-3119   (BR)
REVERA LONG TERM CARE INC
HILLSIDE MANOR
(*Suby of* GOVERNMENT OF CANADA)
5066 Line 34 Suite 8, Stratford, ON, N5A 6S6
(519) 393-5132
Emp Here 86
SIC 8051 Skilled nursing care facilities
 Wendy Gilmour

D-U-N-S 24-044-8089   (BR)
RIDEAU COUNCIL 2444
RIDEAU COUNCIL
93 Morgan St, Stratford, ON, N5A 7V2
(519) 272-9700
Emp Here 250
SIC 8641 Civic and social associations

D-U-N-S 24-308-9468   (SL)
ROULSTON PHARMACY LTD
SHOPPERS DRUG MART
211 Ontario St Unit 1, Stratford, ON, N5A 3H3
(519) 271-8600
Emp Here 50   *Sales* 12,647,700
SIC 5912 Drug stores and proprietary stores
 Paul Roulston

D-U-N-S 24-829-2823   (HQ)
SAMSONITE CANADA INC
(*Suby of* SAMSONITE INTERNATIONAL SA)
305 C H Meier Blvd, Stratford, ON, N5A 0H4
(519) 271-5040
Emp Here 40   *Sales* 33,835,230
SIC 5099 Durable goods, nec
 Keith Pehlke
 Paul Hanley
 Paul Decorso

D-U-N-S 20-018-2951   (SL)
SAUNDERS AUTOMOTIVE LIMITED
STRATFORD HYUNDAI
640 Lorne Ave E, Stratford, ON, N5A 6S4
(519) 271-9227
Emp Here 25   *Sales* 12,451,950
SIC 5511 New and used car dealers
 Todd Saunders

D-U-N-S 20-848-0723   (HQ)
SCHAEFFLER AEROSPACE CANADA INC
(*Suby of* INA-HOLDING SCHAEFFLER GMBH & CO. KG)
801 Ontario St, Stratford, ON, N5A 6T2

(519) 271-3230
Emp Here 1   *Sales* 112,631,677
SIC 3568 Power transmission equipment, nec
 Robert Hillstrom

D-U-N-S 20-154-7189   (HQ)
SCHAEFFLER CANADA INC
(*Suby of* INA-HOLDING SCHAEFFLER GMBH & CO. KG)
801 Ontario St, Stratford, ON, N5A 7Y2
(519) 271-3231
Emp Here 375   *Sales* 105,328,875
SIC 3562 Ball and roller bearings
 Juergen Geissinger
 Ralph Moore
 Bob Hillstrom
 Frank Lange
 Ella Bernhard
 Bruce Warmbold
 Kelly Walsh

D-U-N-S 25-081-6832   (SL)
SELECTRA INC
SELECTRA CONTROLS
750 Douro St, Stratford, ON, N5A 0E3
(519) 271-0322
Emp Here 80   *Sales* 17,426,320
SIC 1731 Electrical work
 Paul Siegner
 Derek Luckhardt

D-U-N-S 20-154-9011   (HQ)
SINCLAIR PHARMACY (1980) LTD
GUARDIAN DRUGS
12 Wellington St, Stratford, ON, N5A 2L2
(519) 271-8940
Emp Here 30   *Sales* 10,118,160
SIC 5912 Drug stores and proprietary stores
 Cathy Hawkins
 Jan Elligsen
 Marc Michaud
 Theresa Ryan

D-U-N-S 20-936-7135   (SL)
SPRUCE LODGE HOME FOR THE AGED
643 West Gore St, Stratford, ON, N5A 1L4
(519) 271-4090
Emp Here 158   *Sales* 10,156,556
SIC 8361 Residential care
 Peter Bolland

D-U-N-S 24-885-9050   (BR)
STACKPOLE INTERNATIONAL POWDER METAL, LTD.
STACKPOLE INTERNATIONAL POWDER METAL, LTD
(*Suby of* JOHNSON ELECTRIC HOLDINGS LIMITED)
128 Monteith Ave, Stratford, ON, N5A 2P5
(519) 271-6060
Emp Here 300
SIC 3714 Motor vehicle parts and accessories
 Jim Mcmaster

D-U-N-S 20-561-3487   (BR)
STEELCRAFT INC
(*Suby of* HANSON CAPITAL CORPORATION)
904 Downie Rd, Stratford, ON, N5A 6T3
(519) 271-4750
Emp Here 85
SIC 3443 Fabricated plate work (boiler shop)
 Chris Dowson

D-U-N-S 24-073-6087   (SL)
STRATFORD CHILDREN'S SERVICES INC
508 Erie St, Stratford, ON, N5A 2N6
(519) 273-3623
Emp Here 75   *Sales* 9,903,000
SIC 8093 Specialty outpatient clinics, nec
 Brenda Mason
 David Macdonald

D-U-N-S 20-154-9243   (SL)
STRATFORD MOTOR PRODUCTS (1984) LTD
824 Ontario St, Stratford, ON, N5A 3K1

(519) 271-5900
Emp Here 40   *Sales* 19,923,120
SIC 5511 New and used car dealers
Steve Jarrett
Murray Matthison

D-U-N-S 20-552-9444   (HQ)
STRATFORD SHAKESPEAREAN FESTI-VAL OF CANADA, THE
STRATFORD FESTIVAL THEATRE OF CANADA
55 Queen St, Stratford, ON, N5A 4M9
(519) 271-4040
Emp Here 650   *Sales* 97,378,450
SIC 7922 Theatrical producers and services
Joy Wishart
Antoni Cimolino

D-U-N-S 25-819-9884   (SL)
STRATFORD-PERTH FAMILY YMCA
204 Downie St, Stratford, ON, N5A 1X4
(519) 271-0480
Emp Here 100   *Sales* 7,639,700
SIC 7997 Membership sports and recreation clubs
Mimi Price
Corrine Hyde

D-U-N-S 24-011-2631   (SL)
TAYLOR FLUID SYSTEMS INC
81 Griffith Rd, Stratford, ON, N5A 6S4
(519) 273-2811
Emp Here 25   *Sales* 11,875,650
SIC 5085 Industrial supplies
David Campbell
Peter Willmore
Chris Taylor

D-U-N-S 24-151-5852   (SL)
TIM HORTONS
166 Ontario St, Stratford, ON, N5A 3H4
(519) 273-2421
Emp Here 125   *Sales* 36,684,625
SIC 5461 Retail bakeries
Mark Moore

D-U-N-S 25-347-6550   (SL)
TORA STRATFORD LIMITED
GIANT TIGER
477 Huron St, Stratford, ON, N5A 5T8
(519) 272-2029
Emp Here 60   *Sales* 12,320,580
SIC 5399 Miscellaneous general merchandise
Stephen Vandeerkuyl

D-U-N-S 20-025-6258   (BR)
TRI-COUNTY MENNONITE HOMES ASSO-CIATION
GREENWOOD COURT, DIV OF
(*Suby of* TRI-COUNTY MENNONITE HOMES ASSOCIATION)
90 Greenwood Dr Suite 117, Stratford, ON, N5A 7W5
(519) 273-4662
Emp Here 85
SIC 8059 Nursing and personal care, nec
Robert Veitch

D-U-N-S 20-303-3972   (BR)
VICWEST INC
(*Suby of* VICWEST INC)
362 Lorne Ave E, Stratford, ON, N5A 6S4
(519) 271-5553
Emp Here 75
SIC 3444 Sheet Metalwork
Tom Nugent

Strathroy, ON N7G

D-U-N-S 20-900-8747   (HQ)
AUTOTUBE LIMITED
300 High St E, Strathroy, ON, N7G 4C5
(519) 245-1742
Sales 14,511,040
SIC 3312 Blast furnaces and steel mills

Peter Hall

D-U-N-S 25-147-4573   (BR)
CORPORATION OF THE COUNTY OF MID-DLESEX
STRATHMERE LODGE
(*Suby of* CORPORATION OF THE COUNTY OF MIDDLESEX)
599 Albert St, Strathroy, ON, N7G 1X1
(519) 245-2520
Emp Here 160
SIC 8361 Residential care
Larry Hills

D-U-N-S 25-759-2055   (SL)
CROPLEY, PAUL J & D SALES LTD
CANADIAN TIRE
24614 Adelaide Rd, Strathroy, ON, N7G 2P8
(519) 245-2704
Emp Here 49   *Sales* 24,405,822
SIC 5531 Auto and home supply stores
Paul Cropley

D-U-N-S 24-387-5262   (SL)
CUDDY FARMS LIMITED 2008
28429 Centre Rd, Strathroy, ON, N7G 3H6
(519) 245-1592
Emp Here 300   *Sales* 56,360,700
SIC 0253 Turkeys and turkey eggs
John Flaherty
Doug Hill
Peggy Foster
John Cameron
John Scott Chambers

D-U-N-S 25-672-5987   (HQ)
CUDDY GROUP LIMITED
CUDDY FARMS
28429 Centre Rd, Strathroy, ON, N7G 3H6
(519) 245-1592
Sales 71,489,482
SIC 0253 Turkeys and turkey eggs
John Flaherty
Doug Hill

D-U-N-S 24-412-1802   (SL)
DORTMANS BROS. BARN EQUIP. INC
2234 Egremont Dr Suite 5, Strathroy, ON, N7G 3H6
(519) 247-3435
Emp Here 20   *Sales* 10,000,000
SIC 5083 Farm and garden machinery
John Dortmans
Rita Dortmans

D-U-N-S 25-239-1552   (SL)
DOWNHAM NURSERIES (1993) INC
390 York St, Strathroy, ON, N7G 2E5

Emp Here 30   *Sales* 22,650,249
SIC 5193 Flowers and florists supplies

D-U-N-S 20-146-2678   (HQ)
GRAY, L. H. & SON LIMITED
GRAY RIDGE EGGS
(*Suby of* GRAY RIDGE INVESTMENTS LIM-ITED)
644 Wright St, Strathroy, ON, N7G 3H8
(519) 245-0480
Emp Here 100   *Sales* 172,011,840
SIC 5144 Poultry and poultry products
William Gray
Mike Walsh
Scott Brookshaw

D-U-N-S 24-335-9858   (SL)
KML WINDOWS INC
(*Suby of* ANDERSEN CORPORATION)
71 Second St, Strathroy, ON, N7G 3H8
(519) 245-2270
Emp Here 350   *Sales* 85,130,850
SIC 3442 Metal doors, sash, and trim
Chris Parker

D-U-N-S 20-610-6403   (HQ)
LANGS BUS LINES LIMITED
66 Zimmerman Ave, Strathroy, ON, N7G 2G7

(519) 245-2350
Emp Here 118   *Sales* 22,581,600
SIC 4151 School buses
Douglas Langs

D-U-N-S 20-874-8058   (HQ)
LONDON TIRE SALES LIMITED
290 Ellor St, Strathroy, ON, N7G 2L4
(519) 245-1133
Emp Here 26   *Sales* 11,654,880
SIC 5014 Tires and tubes
Evan Campbell
Scott Campbell
James Campbell

D-U-N-S 20-155-0878   (SL)
MACDONALD, LARRY CHEVROLET LTD
28380 Centre Rd, Strathroy, ON, N7G 3C4
(519) 245-0410
Emp Here 28   *Sales* 13,946,184
SIC 5521 Used car dealers
Randy Cullen

D-U-N-S 20-050-5626   (SL)
MCDONNELL MOTORS LTD
359 Caradoc St S, Strathroy, ON, N7G 2P5
(519) 245-0840
Emp Here 22   *Sales* 10,957,716
SIC 5511 New and used car dealers
Barry Mcdonnell
Kevin Mcdonnell

D-U-N-S 25-035-3299   (HQ)
MCROBERT FUELS LIMITED
4755 Egremont Dr Suite 1, Strathroy, ON, N7G 3H3
(519) 246-1019
Sales 10,328,080
SIC 5171 Petroleum bulk stations and termi-nals
Raymond Mcrobert
Pennie Mcrobert

D-U-N-S 24-369-4036   (HQ)
MERIDIAN LIGHTWEIGHT TECHNOLO-GIES HOLDINGS INC
(*Suby of* WANFENG AUTO HOLDING GROUP CO., LTD.)
25 Mcnab St, Strathroy, ON, N7G 4H6
(519) 246-9600
Emp Here 30   *Sales* 154,726,120
SIC 3364 Nonferrous die-castings except alu-minum
Terry Luo

D-U-N-S 24-359-8765   (HQ)
MERIDIAN LIGHTWEIGHT TECHNOLO-GIES INC
MAGNESIUM PRODUCTS
(*Suby of* WANFENG AUTO HOLDING GROUP CO., LTD.)
25 Mcnab St, Strathroy, ON, N7G 4H6
(519) 246-9600
Emp Here 35   *Sales* 134,367,420
SIC 3364 Nonferrous die-castings except alu-minum
Terry Luo
Frank Chen

D-U-N-S 24-443-0062   (SL)
MERIDIAN LIGHTWEIGHT TECHNOLO-GIES INC
800 Wright St, Strathroy, ON, N7G 4H7
(519) 246-9620
Emp Here 49   *Sales* 11,438,315
SIC 3369 Nonferrous foundries, nec
Terry Luo
Kevin O'brian

D-U-N-S 24-826-4509   (BR)
MERIDIAN LIGHTWEIGHT TECHNOLO-GIES INC
MAGNESIUM PRODUCTS DIVISION
(*Suby of* WANFENG AUTO HOLDING GROUP CO., LTD.)
155 High St E, Strathroy, ON, N7G 1H4
(519) 245-4040
Emp Here 400

SIC 3364 Nonferrous die-castings except alu-minum
Matt Macdonald

D-U-N-S 24-463-0174   (HQ)
MIDDLESEX COMMUNITY LIVING
82 Front St W, Strathroy, ON, N7G 1X7
(519) 245-1301
Sales 11,341,650
SIC 8399 Social services, nec
Sherri Kroll

D-U-N-S 24-369-4044   (HQ)
MLTH HOLDINGS INC
25 Mcnab St, Strathroy, ON, N7G 4H6
(519) 246-9600
Emp Here 1   *Sales* 138,893,420
SIC 6712 Bank holding companies
Terry Lou

D-U-N-S 20-376-4451   (SL)
NATIONAL EGG INC
644 Wright St, Strathroy, ON, N7G 3H8
(519) 245-0480
Emp Here 50   *Sales* 42,262,729
SIC 5144 Poultry and poultry products
William Gray
Michael Walsh
Scott Brookshaw
John Leitch

D-U-N-S 20-934-8382   (SL)
SPRUCEDALE CARE CENTRE INC
96 Kittridge Ave E Suite 115, Strathroy, ON, N7G 2A8
(519) 245-2808
Emp Here 114   *Sales* 7,816,524
SIC 8051 Skilled nursing care facilities
Gordon Giffen
Charles Micalles

D-U-N-S 24-721-3825   (SL)
STRATHROY MIDDLESEX GENERAL HOS-PITAL
395 Carrie St Suite 360, Strathroy, ON, N7G 3C9
(519) 245-5295
Emp Here 400   *Sales* 44,432,000
SIC 8062 General medical and surgical hospi-tals
Todd Stepanuik

D-U-N-S 25-629-1287   (SL)
TOWN & COUNTRY MUTUAL INSURANCE COMPANY
79 Caradoc St N, Strathroy, ON, N7G 2M5
(519) 246-1132
Emp Here 20   *Sales* 14,508,780
SIC 6331 Fire, marine, and casualty insurance
Robert Pearson

D-U-N-S 20-394-1273   (SL)
VARI-FORM MANUFACTURING INC
(*Suby of* FIAT CHRYSLER AUTOMOBILES N.V.)
233 Lothian Ave, Strathroy, ON, N7G 4J1
(519) 245-5200
Emp Here 250   *Sales* 60,807,750
SIC 3469 Metal stampings, nec
Michael Resha
Al Whitted
Eric Cronander
Mike Tonietto

D-U-N-S 24-319-5190   (BR)
WAL-MART CANADA CORP
WALMART
(*Suby of* WALMART INC.)
150 Carroll St E, Strathroy, ON, N7G 4G2
(519) 245-7200
Emp Here 125
SIC 5311 Department stores
Mike Intzandt

Sturgeon Falls, ON P2B

D-U-N-S 20-155-3575   (SL)
ALOUETTE BUS LINES LTD
194 Front St Suite Front, Sturgeon Falls, ON,
P2B 2J3
(705) 753-3911
Emp Here 100   *Sales* 5,487,200
SIC 4151 School buses
Mike Brideau

D-U-N-S 24-178-8145   (BR)
COMMUNITY LIVING WEST NIPISSING
120 Nipissing St, Sturgeon Falls, ON, P2B 1J6
(705) 753-3143
Emp Here 100
SIC 8059 Nursing and personal care, nec
Chantal Savage

D-U-N-S 20-264-7137   (BR)
DSI UNDERGROUND CANADA LTD
(*Suby of* TENSION II LUXCO SARL)
15 Toulouse Cres, Sturgeon Falls, ON, P2B
0A5
(705) 753-4872
Emp Here 150
SIC 3532 Mining machinery

D-U-N-S 24-765-4262   (SL)
MARCHAND, PIERRE STORE INC
CANADIAN TIRE
12011 Highway 17 E, Sturgeon Falls, ON, P2B
2S7
(705) 753-2630
Emp Here 48   *Sales* 23,907,744
SIC 5531 Auto and home supply stores
Pierre Marchand

D-U-N-S 25-894-3349   (HQ)
RIVET, J. G. BROKERS LIMITED
RIVET INSURANCE
229 Main St Suite 1, Sturgeon Falls, ON, P2B
1P5
(705) 753-0130
Emp Here 6   *Sales* 20,353,440
SIC 6411 Insurance agents, brokers, and ser-
vice
Jean-Luc Rivet
Francois Rivet
Martin Rivet
Rita Rivet
Serge Rivet

D-U-N-S 24-796-0016   (BR)
SYSCO CANADA, INC
SYSCO FOOD SERVICES
(*Suby of* SYSCO CORPORATION)
106 Bay St, Sturgeon Falls, ON, P2B 3G6
(705) 753-4444
Emp Here 95
SIC 5141 Groceries, general line
Cliff Sinclair

D-U-N-S 25-162-5760   (SL)
**WEST NIPISSING GENERAL HOSPITAL,
THE**
725 Coursol Rd Suite 427, Sturgeon Falls,
ON, P2B 2Y6
(705) 753-3110
Emp Here 250   *Sales* 20,033,622
SIC 8062 General medical and surgical hospi-
tals
Cynthia Desormiers
Collin Bourgeois
Sylvie Belanger
Janet Parsons
Vince Susini
Ben Lalonde
Klere Bourgault
Julie Duhaime
Charles Goulard
Howard Longfellow

Sudbury, ON P3A

D-U-N-S 24-288-6802   (SL)
1124980 ONTARIO INC
HEALTH CARE PHARMACY
1276 Lasalle Blvd Suite 683, Sudbury, ON,
P3A 1Y8
(705) 566-5551
Emp Here 50   *Sales* 12,647,700
SIC 5912 Drug stores and proprietary stores
Arnold Lapienis
Yves Fortin
Jean R Paquette

D-U-N-S 25-673-5796   (SL)
343315 ONTARIO LTD
LARO CONSTRUCTION
916 Lapointe St, Sudbury, ON, P3A 5N8
(705) 521-1575
Emp Here 34   *Sales* 11,333,322
SIC 1541 Industrial buildings and warehouses
Larry Therrien
Marc Therrien
Claudette Therrien

D-U-N-S 24-205-6609   (HQ)
510172 ONTARIO LTD
DIESEL ELECTRIC SERVICE
(*Suby of* AMEN HOLDINGS INC)
100 Foundry St, Sudbury, ON, P3A 4R7
(705) 674-5626
Emp Here 37   *Sales* 14,997,481
SIC 3743 Railroad equipment
Milad Gebrael Mansour

D-U-N-S 24-891-1794   (SL)
862390 ONTARIO INC
TRU-NOR TRUCK CENTRES
1035 Falconbridge Rd, Sudbury, ON, P3A
4M9
(705) 560-6625
Emp Here 65   *Sales* 40,903,200
SIC 5511 New and used car dealers
Donald Leuschen

D-U-N-S 24-418-9171   (SL)
AIRCO LTD
1510 Old Falconbridge Rd, Sudbury, ON, P3A
4N8
(705) 673-2210
Emp Here 48   *Sales* 12,037,155
SIC 7623 Refrigeration service and repair
Peter Richter Jr
Kelly Richter

D-U-N-S 20-391-6205   (SL)
BEYOND WIRELESS INC
444 Barrydowne Rd Unit 3, Sudbury, ON, P3A
3T3
(705) 525-7091
Emp Here 260   *Sales* 59,402,720
SIC 4812 Radiotelephone communication
Derek Bain
Jamie Mcnain

D-U-N-S 20-845-0049   (HQ)
**CAMBRIAN COLLEGE OF APPLIED ARTS
& TECHNOLOGY, THE**
1400 Barrydowne Rd, Sudbury, ON, P3A 3V8
(705) 566-8101
Emp Here 830   *Sales* 84,251,150
SIC 8222 Junior colleges
Bill Best
Kristine Morrissey

D-U-N-S 20-939-0152   (SL)
CAMBRIAN FORD SALES INC
1615 Kingsway St, Sudbury, ON, P3A 4S9
(705) 560-3673
Emp Here 60   *Sales* 44,049,600
SIC 5511 New and used car dealers
Stephen Mcculloch
Scott Mcculloch
D. Bruce Mcculloch

D-U-N-S 20-732-7466   (SL)
CAR LOT ETC INC, THE
2231 Lasalle Blvd, Sudbury, ON, P3A 2A9
(705) 560-3999
Emp Here 25   *Sales* 12,451,950

SIC 5521 Used car dealers
Carl Prescott

D-U-N-S 24-365-1981   (HQ)
**CHILDREN'S AID SOCIETY OF THE DIS-
TRICTS OF SUDBURY AND MANITOULIN,
THE**
319 Lasalle Blvd Unit 3, Sudbury, ON, P3A
1W7
(705) 566-3113
Emp Here 190   *Sales* 18,430,080
SIC 8322 Individual and family services
Colette Prevoft

D-U-N-S 24-977-7178   (BR)
CITY OF GREATER SUDBURY, THE
PIONEER MANOR DIVISION
(*Suby of* CITY OF GREATER SUDBURY,
THE)
960 Notre Dame Ave Suite D, Sudbury, ON,
P3A 2T4
(705) 566-4270
Emp Here 400
SIC 8059 Nursing and personal care, nec
Randy Hotta

D-U-N-S 24-182-9175   (HQ)
**COLLINS BARROW, SUDBURY - NIPISSING
LLP**
1174 St. Jerome St, Sudbury, ON, P3A 2V9
(705) 560-5592
Emp Here 60   *Sales* 14,537,950
SIC 8721 Accounting, auditing, and book-
keeping
Sherry Hakansson

D-U-N-S 20-715-6068   (SL)
**CROSSTOWN OLDSMOBILE CHEVROLET
LTD**
280 Falconbridge Rd, Sudbury, ON, P3A 5K3
(705) 566-4804
Emp Here 60   *Sales* 37,756,800
SIC 5511 New and used car dealers
Merle Gray
Vince Pollesel

D-U-N-S 20-020-6253   (BR)
EXTENDICARE INC
EXTENDICARE FALCONBRIDGE
(*Suby of* EXTENDICARE INC)
281 Falconbridge Rd, Sudbury, ON, P3A 5K4
(705) 566-7980
Emp Here 200
SIC 8051 Skilled nursing care facilities
James Foreman

D-U-N-S 24-846-1261   (HQ)
**GRANT AGGREGATE & INDUSTRIAL SUP-
PLY INC**
2578 Lasalle Blvd, Sudbury, ON, P3A 4R7
(705) 524-2711
Emp Here 31   *Sales* 20,426,118
SIC 5084 Industrial machinery and equipment
David Morris
Shaun Morris
Gilles Chenard

D-U-N-S 25-495-3250   (HQ)
HITE SERVICES LIMITED
790 Lapointe St, Sudbury, ON, P3A 5N8
(705) 524-5333
Sales 15,722,665
SIC 7389 Business services, nec
Ritchie Castonguay
Luc Bidal

D-U-N-S 20-190-4245   (BR)
HYDRO ONE NETWORKS INC
(*Suby of* HYDRO ONE LIMITED)
957 Falconbridge Rd, Sudbury, ON, P3A 5K8
(705) 566-8955
Emp Here 100
SIC 4911 Electric services
Greg Towns

D-U-N-S 25-309-7372   (BR)
**INDUSTRIELLE ALLIANCE, ASSURANCE
ET SERVICES FINANCIERS INC**

(*Suby of* INDUSTRIELLE ALLIANCE, AS-
SURANCE ET SERVICES FINANCIERS INC)
1210 Lasalle Blvd, Sudbury, ON, P3A 1Y5
(705) 524-5755
Emp Here 100
SIC 6411 Insurance agents, brokers, and ser-
vice
Al Stonier

D-U-N-S 20-155-7899   (SL)
**LACROIX CONSTRUCTION CO. (SUD-
BURY) LTD**
861 Lapointe St, Sudbury, ON, P3A 5N8
(705) 566-1294
Emp Here 40   *Sales* 13,333,320
SIC 1541 Industrial buildings and warehouses
Murray Lacroix

D-U-N-S 24-377-0042   (BR)
LOBLAWS INC
REAL CANADIAN SUPERSTORE
(*Suby of* LOBLAW COMPANIES LIMITED)
1485 Lasalle Blvd, Sudbury, ON, P3A 5H7
(705) 521-1031
Emp Here 200
SIC 5411 Grocery stores
Mike Porter

D-U-N-S 24-476-5236   (SL)
LYNSOS INC
PAT & MARIO'S RESTAURANT
1463 Lasalle Blvd, Sudbury, ON, P3A 1Z8
(705) 560-2500
Emp Here 90   *Sales* 4,096,710
SIC 5812 Eating places
George Moutsatsos

D-U-N-S 24-024-6272   (SL)
MANITOU MECHANICAL LTD
874 Lapointe St, Sudbury, ON, P3A 5N8
(705) 566-5702
Emp Here 50   *Sales* 16,666,650
SIC 1541 Industrial buildings and warehouses
Thomas Lachance
Julie Zulich

D-U-N-S 20-402-1398   (HQ)
MASLACK SUPPLY LIMITED
488 Falconbridge Rd, Sudbury, ON, P3A 4S4
(705) 566-1270
Emp Here 51   *Sales* 45,602,496
SIC 5082 Construction and mining machinery
John Maslack

D-U-N-S 20-754-4651   (SL)
MCNAMARA, MERVIN J. INC
CANADIAN TIRE ASSOCIATE STORE
1066 Barrydowne Rd Suite 278, Sudbury, ON,
P3A 3V3
(705) 566-9735
Emp Here 200   *Sales* 125,856,000
SIC 5531 Auto and home supply stores
Mervin Mcnamara

D-U-N-S 20-595-0355   (SL)
NIM DISPOSAL LTD
2755 Lasalle Blvd, Sudbury, ON, P3A 4R7
(705) 566-9363
Emp Here 30   *Sales* 15,616,260
SIC 5093 Scrap and waste materials
Joan Greenspoon

D-U-N-S 25-819-8571   (HQ)
NORTH HERITAGE REALTY INC
*ROYAL LEPAGE NORTH HERITAGE RE-
ALTY*
860 Lasalle Blvd, Sudbury, ON, P3A 1X5
(705) 688-0007
Sales 25,971,118
SIC 6531 Real estate agents and managers
Alex Dumas

D-U-N-S 24-419-6325   (BR)
**PEPSI BOTTLING GROUP (CANADA), ULC,
THE**
PEPSICO BEVERAGES CANADA
(*Suby of* PBG INVESTMENT (LUXEM-
BOURG) SARL)

801 Lapointe St, Sudbury, ON, P3A 5N8
(705) 525-4000
Emp Here 110
SIC 2086 Bottled and canned soft drinks
Trevor Grant

D-U-N-S 20-059-9491   (BR)
PERSONA COMMUNICATIONS INC
AMAZING PERSONA, THE
(*Suby of* TIDNISH HOLDINGS LIMITED)
500 Barrydowne Rd Unit 15, Sudbury, ON,
P3A 3T3
(705) 560-1560
Emp Here 100
SIC 4841 Cable and other pay television services
Collette Rivet

D-U-N-S 25-464-4529   (SL)
**PIQUETTE, ROGER L. INSURANCE
AGENCY INC**
1210 Lasalle Blvd, Sudbury, ON, P3A 1Y5
(705) 524-5755
Emp Here 83   *Sales* 70,388,980
SIC 6411 Insurance agents, brokers, and service
Al Stonier
Margaret Stonier

D-U-N-S 20-156-0463   (HQ)
RAINBOW CONCRETE INDUSTRIES LIMITED
2477 Maley Dr, Sudbury, ON, P3A 4R7
(705) 566-1740
Emp Here 90   *Sales* 21,506,280
SIC 3271 Concrete block and brick
Boris Naneff
Rade Brujic

D-U-N-S 25-239-9969   (BR)
RAINBOW DISTRICT SCHOOL BOARD
LASALLE SECONDARY SCHOOL
(*Suby of* RAINBOW DISTRICT SCHOOL
BOARD)
1545 Kennedy St, Sudbury, ON, P3A 2G1
(705) 566-2280
Emp Here 100
SIC 8211 Elementary and secondary schools
Jeff Mckibbon

D-U-N-S 25-281-2896   (BR)
SECURITAS CANADA LIMITED
(*Suby of* SECURITAS AB)
767 Barrydowne Rd Suite 301, Sudbury, ON,
P3A 3T6
(705) 675-3654
Emp Here 130
SIC 7381 Detective and armored car services
Robert Pilon

D-U-N-S 25-419-2958   (SL)
SMITH'S MARKETS INC
971 Lasalle Blvd, Sudbury, ON, P3A 1X7
(705) 560-3663
Emp Here 50   *Sales* 13,707,600
SIC 5431 Fruit and vegetable markets
Marshall Smith
Greg Smith

D-U-N-S 20-015-9523   (SL)
STUART OLSON INDUSTRIAL CONSTRUCTORS INC
(*Suby of* STUART OLSON INC)
670 Falconbridge Rd Unit 1, Sudbury, ON,
P3A 4S4
(705) 222-4848
Emp Here 197   *Sales* 53,357,056
SIC 1711 Plumbing, heating, air-conditioning
Tyler Roberge
Yvon Kermen
Gary Schnase

D-U-N-S 20-851-6831   (SL)
SUDBURY MANAGEMENT SERVICES LIMITED
MANPOWER
1901 Lasalle Blvd, Sudbury, ON, P3A 2A3

Emp Here 50   *Sales* 11,848,500
SIC 7363 Help supply services
Gerald Cronin
Keane Cronin

D-U-N-S 24-418-2523   (HQ)
**SUDBURY WINDOW MANUFACTURING
LTD**
902 Newgate Ave, Sudbury, ON, P3A 5J9
(705) 560-5700
Sales 10,094,850
SIC 3089 Plastics products, nec
Jack St Amand
Mariette St Amand

D-U-N-S 20-394-0499   (SL)
SWSE ATHLETIC TEAMS LTD
874 Lapointe St, Sudbury, ON, P3A 5N8
(705) 675-7973
Emp Here 50   *Sales* 21,186,500
SIC 7941 Sports clubs, managers, and promoters
Dario Zulich

D-U-N-S 24-218-4406   (HQ)
TESC CONTRACTING COMPANY LTD
874 Lapointe St, Sudbury, ON, P3A 5N8
(705) 566-5702
Sales 16,666,650
SIC 1541 Industrial buildings and warehouses
Don Bennett
Julie Zulich
Frank Leduc

D-U-N-S 24-302-6648   (HQ)
TRACKS & WHEELS EQUIPMENT BROKERS INC
GENERAL BREAKERS CANADA
400 Hwy 69 N, Sudbury, ON, P3A 4S9
(705) 566-5438
Emp Here 80   *Sales* 47,502,600
SIC 5082 Construction and mining machinery
Mike Gougan

D-U-N-S 24-770-8878   (SL)
TRIBURY CONSTRUCTION (1995) INC
1549 Fairburn St, Sudbury, ON, P3A 1N6
(705) 560-8743
Emp Here 25   *Sales* 11,768,275
SIC 1542 Nonresidential construction, nec
Robert Cecchetto
John Nipius

D-U-N-S 25-294-8625   (BR)
WAL-MART CANADA CORP
(*Suby of* WALMART INC.)
1349 Lasalle Blvd Suite 3097, Sudbury, ON,
P3A 1Z2
(705) 566-3700
Emp Here 250
SIC 5311 Department stores
Bell Newlove

Sudbury, ON P3B

D-U-N-S 24-180-9656   (HQ)
B. MCDOWELL EQUIPMENT LIMITED
2018 Kingsway, Sudbury, ON, P3B 4J8
(705) 566-8190
Emp Here 20   *Sales* 23,751,300
SIC 5084 Industrial machinery and equipment
Kevin Mcdowell

D-U-N-S 25-977-1798   (HQ)
**CONSEIL SCOLAIRE DE DISTRICT DU
GRAND NORD DE L'ONTARIO**
CSPGNO
296 Van Horne St, Sudbury, ON, P3B 1H9
(705) 671-1533
Emp Here 60   *Sales* 39,647,600
SIC 8211 Elementary and secondary schools
Jean Marc Aubin
Louise D'amour
Marc Guthier

D-U-N-S 25-097-2320   (BR)
COSTCO WHOLESALE CANADA LTD
COSTCO
(*Suby of* COSTCO WHOLESALE CORPORATION)
1465 Kingsway, Sudbury, ON, P3B 0A5
(705) 524-8255
Emp Here 200
SIC 5141 Groceries, general line
Jamie Robero

D-U-N-S 25-171-5678   (BR)
HOME DEPOT OF CANADA INC
HOME DEPOT
(*Suby of* THE HOME DEPOT INC)
1500 Marcus Dr, Sudbury, ON, P3B 4K5
(705) 525-2960
Emp Here 100
SIC 5251 Hardware stores
Kyle Meeks

D-U-N-S 20-155-7568   (SL)
JUTRAS, PHIL & SON LIMITED
JUTRAS AUTO SALES
(*Suby of* TRANSPORATION JUTRAS
TRANSPORATION INC)
2042 Kingsway, Sudbury, ON, P3B 4J8
(705) 525-5560
Emp Here 57   *Sales* 11,725,242
SIC 4212 Local trucking, without storage
Denise Jutras

D-U-N-S 20-922-2942   (SL)
LAKING MOTORS INC
LAKING TOYOTA
695 Kingsway, Sudbury, ON, P3B 2E4
(705) 674-7534
Emp Here 45   *Sales* 22,413,510
SIC 5511 New and used car dealers
Christopher Laking

D-U-N-S 24-858-2194   (BR)
LOWE'S COMPANIES CANADA, ULC
(*Suby of* LOWE'S COMPANIES, INC.)
1199 Marcus Dr, Sudbury, ON, P3B 4K6
(705) 521-7200
Emp Here 150
SIC 5211 Lumber and other building materials
Larry Gauci

D-U-N-S 24-199-1462   (HQ)
NORTHERN YOUTH SERVICES INC
3200 Bancroft Dr, Sudbury, ON, P3B 1V3
(705) 524-3354
Emp Here 75   *Sales* 25,883,500
SIC 8399 Social services, nec
Beverley Crockford

D-U-N-S 25-001-6045   (HQ)
SUDBURY DEVELOPMENTAL SERVICES
CGSDS/SHDVGS
245 Mountain St, Sudbury, ON, P3B 2T8
(705) 674-1451
Emp Here 20   *Sales* 12,856,400
SIC 8361 Residential care
Mila Wong

Sudbury, ON P3C

D-U-N-S 25-099-5024   (HQ)
BOUDREAU-ESPLEY-PITRE CORPORATION
BESTECH
1040 Lorne St Unit 3, Sudbury, ON, P3C 4R9
(705) 675-7720
Emp Here 100   *Sales* 21,448,680
SIC 8711 Engineering services
Marc Boudreau
Denis Pitre

D-U-N-S 24-393-5934   (HQ)
**CAISSE POPULAIRE DES VOYAGEURS
INC**
CAISSE POPULAIRE

531 Notre Dame Ave, Sudbury, ON, P3C 5L1
(705) 674-4234
Sales 10,745,770
SIC 6062 State credit unions
Jean-Marc Spencer

D-U-N-S 20-155-5125   (SL)
CARRINGTONS BUILDING CENTRE LTD
BEAVER LUMBER
82 Lorne St, Sudbury, ON, P3C 4N8
(705) 673-9511
Emp Here 40   *Sales* 10,122,360
SIC 5211 Lumber and other building materials
Robert Tate
Russell Tate

D-U-N-S 25-488-4653   (BR)
CLAIMSECURE INC
(*Suby of* CLAIMSECURE INC)
40 Elm St Suite 225, Sudbury, ON, P3C 0A2
(705) 673-2541
Emp Here 100
SIC 6324 Hospital and medical service plans
Bonnie Jussila

D-U-N-S 20-710-4097   (BR)
**CONSEIL SCOLAIRE DE DISTRICT
CATHOLIQUE DU NOUVEL-ONTARIO,
LE**
(*Suby of* CONSEIL SCOLAIRE DE DISTRICT
CATHOLIQUE DU NOUVEL-ONTARIO, LE)
201 Jogues St, Sudbury, ON, P3C 5L7
(705) 673-5626
Emp Here 100
SIC 8211 Elementary and secondary schools
Monique Smith

D-U-N-S 25-482-9799   (BR)
**CONSEIL SCOLAIRE DE DISTRICT
CATHOLIQUE DU NOUVEL-ONTARIO,
LE**
COLLEGE NOTRE-DAME
(*Suby of* CONSEIL SCOLAIRE DE DISTRICT
CATHOLIQUE DU NOUVEL-ONTARIO, LE)
100 Levis St, Sudbury, ON, P3C 2H1
(705) 674-7484
Emp Here 80
SIC 8211 Elementary and secondary schools
Johanne Chretien

D-U-N-S 25-095-3551   (HQ)
**CONSEIL SCOLAIRE DE DISTRICT
CATHOLIQUE DU NOUVEL-ONTARIO,
LE**
201 Jogues St, Sudbury, ON, P3C 5L7
(705) 673-5626
Emp Here 50   *Sales* 144,019,907
SIC 8211 Elementary and secondary schools
Andre Bidal
Anne Dechaine
Paul Gervais
Loise Dube
Garry Bruneau
Paul Demers
Normand Courtemanche
Marc Larochelle
Louise Essiembre
Suzanne Salituri

D-U-N-S 20-007-9205   (BR)
CTV SPECIALTY TELEVISION INC
(*Suby of* BCE INC)
699 Frood Rd, Sudbury, ON, P3C 5A3
(705) 674-8301
Emp Here 75
SIC 4833 Television broadcasting stations
Lund Scott

D-U-N-S 20-530-1922   (HQ)
DALRON CONSTRUCTION LIMITED
130 Elm St, Sudbury, ON, P3C 1T6
(705) 560-9770
Sales 27,094,200
SIC 1521 Single-family housing construction
Ronald Arnold
David Arnold
Frank Arnold

Philip Arnold

D-U-N-S 20-155-5799   (HQ)
DIBRINA SURE BENEFITS CONSULTING INC
DIBRINA SURE GROUP
(Suby of ARTHUR J. GALLAGHER & CO.)
62 Frood Rd Suite 302, Sudbury, ON, P3C 4Z3
(705) 688-9393
Emp Here 20   *Sales* 147,819,360
SIC 6411 Insurance agents, brokers, and service
 Michael Dibrina
 Tim Lychy
 Diego Favero
 Ehren Baldauf
 Jeff St. Cyr
 Frank Cinotti

D-U-N-S 25-752-9826   (SL)
DIBRINA SURE FINANCIAL GROUP INC
(Suby of ARTHUR J. GALLAGHER & CO.)
62 Frood Rd Suite 302, Sudbury, ON, P3C 4Z3
(705) 688-9011
Emp Here 35   *Sales* 32,871,195
SIC 6282 Investment advice
 Michael Dibrina
 Tim Lychy
 Aurel Malo
 Diego Favero
 Ehren Baldauf
 Jeff St.Cyr
 Frank Cinotti

D-U-N-S 24-153-9290   (SL)
DUMAS YOUR INDEPENDENT GROCERS
82 Lorne St, Sudbury, ON, P3C 4N8
(705) 671-3051
Emp Here 130   *Sales* 38,152,010
SIC 5411 Grocery stores
 Alexander Dumas

D-U-N-S 20-155-6453   (SL)
EVANS LUMBER AND BUILDERS SUPPLY LIMITED
EVANS HOME BUILDING CENTRE
172 Pine St, Sudbury, ON, P3C 1X3
(705) 674-1921
Emp Here 58   *Sales* 15,523,816
SIC 5211 Lumber and other building materials
 Judi Fex
 John Carrey

D-U-N-S 25-321-8770   (BR)
GOLDER ASSOCIATES LTD
(Suby of GOLDER ASSOCIATES CORPORATION)
33 Mackenzie St Suite 100, Sudbury, ON, P3C 4Y1
(705) 524-6861
Emp Here 100
SIC 8711 Engineering services
 Kevin Beauchamp

D-U-N-S 24-951-7319   (SL)
ICAN INDEPENDENCE CENTRE AND NETWORK
765 Brennan Rd, Sudbury, ON, P3C 1C4
(705) 673-0655
Emp Here 77   *Sales* 5,279,582
SIC 8051 Skilled nursing care facilities
 Valerie Scarfone

D-U-N-S 24-896-4272   (BR)
METRO ONTARIO INC
FOOD BASICS
(Suby of METRO INC)
400 Notre Dame Ave, Sudbury, ON, P3C 5K5
(705) 675-5845
Emp Here 120
SIC 5411 Grocery stores
 Daniel Bremner

D-U-N-S 20-251-5560   (HQ)
NORTH EAST COMMUNITY CARE ACCESS CENTRE
CCAC

40 Elm St Suite 41-C, Sudbury, ON, P3C 1S8
(705) 522-3461
Emp Here 1   *Sales* 10,248,900
SIC 8059 Nursing and personal care, nec
 Richard Joly
 Tom Trainor

D-U-N-S 20-943-4414   (HQ)
NORTHERN COMMUNICATION SERVICES INC
TRUE STEEL SECURITY
230 Alder St, Sudbury, ON, P3C 4J2
(705) 677-6744
Emp Here 60   *Sales* 56,857,180
SIC 7389 Business services, nec
 Norman Bradley
 Mike Bradley
 Andre Lacroix
 John Whitehead
 Michael Chance

D-U-N-S 20-849-8766   (HQ)
O.C.P. CONSTRUCTION SUPPLIES INC
1072 Webbwood Dr, Sudbury, ON, P3C 3B7
(705) 674-7073
Emp Here 10   *Sales* 15,651,090
SIC 5032 Brick, stone, and related material
 Dick Cousineau
 Rick Cousineau
 Pauline Adams

D-U-N-S 20-981-0998   (SL)
ORACLEPOLL RESEARCH LTD
130 Elm St Suite 102, Sudbury, ON, P3C 1T6
(705) 674-9591
Emp Here 60   *Sales* 12,801,480
SIC 8732 Commercial nonphysical research
 Paul Seccastina

D-U-N-S 20-751-7988   (SL)
RASTALL MINE SUPPLY LIMITED
RASTALL NUT & BOLT CO
268 Hemlock St, Sudbury, ON, P3C 1H9
(705) 675-2431
Emp Here 29   *Sales* 13,775,754
SIC 5085 Industrial supplies
 Donald Rastall
 Thomas Primeau
 Mary-Helen Primeau
 Jacqueline Rastall

D-U-N-S 20-156-0620   (HQ)
RELIABLE WINDOW CLEANERS (SUDBURY) LIMITED
RELIABLE MAINTENANCE PRODUCT
345 Regent St, Sudbury, ON, P3C 4E1
(705) 675-5281
Emp Here 130   *Sales* 83,889,560
SIC 5087 Service establishment equipment
 Albert Bertuzzi
 Robert Bertuzzi
 Noah Jr Bertuzzi

D-U-N-S 24-632-0840   (HQ)
ROMAN CATHOLIC EPISCOPAL CORP OF THE DIOCESE OF SAULT STE MARIE, IN ONTARIO CANADA
30 Ste. Anne Rd, Sudbury, ON, P3C 5E1
(705) 674-2727
Emp Here 129   *Sales* 13,535,990
SIC 8661 Religious organizations
 Jean-Louis Plouffe

D-U-N-S 24-498-8429   (SL)
SCOUTS FRANCOPHONES DIST. DE
30 Ste. Anne Rd, Sudbury, ON, P3C 5E1
(705) 560-4499
Emp Here 49   *Sales* 11,114,817
SIC 8399 Social services, nec
 Marc Forget

D-U-N-S 24-093-1493   (SL)
SOCIETY CARUSO CLUB OF SUDBURY
CARUSO CLUB
385 Haig St, Sudbury, ON, P3C 1C5
(705) 675-1357
Emp Here 80   *Sales* 15,051,680

SIC 8641 Civic and social associations
 Jiavanni Cimino

D-U-N-S 20-156-1172   (HQ)
SOUCIE-SALO SAFETY INC
1300 Lorne St, Sudbury, ON, P3C 5N1
(705) 674-8092
Sales 13,953,016
SIC 5136 Men's and boy's clothing
 Paul Villgren

D-U-N-S 25-239-9530   (HQ)
SUDBURY CATHOLIC DISTRICT SCHOOL BOARD
165a D'Youville St, Sudbury, ON, P3C 5E7
(705) 674-4231
Emp Here 25   *Sales* 79,159,110
SIC 8211 Elementary and secondary schools
 Catherine Mccullough
 Jody Cameron
 Barry Macdonald

Sudbury, ON P3E

D-U-N-S 20-967-9968   (SL)
375414 ONTARIO LIMITED
SHOP, THE
2240 Long Lake Rd, Sudbury, ON, P3E 5H4
(705) 682-4463
Emp Here 30   *Sales* 14,942,340
SIC 5599 Automotive dealers, nec
 Ronald Kanerva
 Eric Kanerva

D-U-N-S 24-720-7087   (SL)
4 CORNERS PHARMACYSTEMS INC
PLAZA 69 PHARMACY
1935 Paris St Suite 69, Sudbury, ON, P3E 3C6
(705) 523-3730
Emp Here 40   *Sales* 10,118,160
SIC 5912 Drug stores and proprietary stores
 Walter Mozek

D-U-N-S 24-838-1860   (SL)
AGILIS NETWORKS
500 Regent St Suite 250, Sudbury, ON, P3E 3Y2
(705) 675-0516
Emp Here 50   *Sales* 10,590,200
SIC 7373 Computer integrated systems design
 Josey Frescura

D-U-N-S 24-243-6863   (BR)
ALEXANDER CENTRE INDUSTRIES LIMITED
FISHER WAVY
(Suby of ALEXANDER CENTRE INDUSTRIES LIMITED)
1297 Kelly Lake Rd, Sudbury, ON, P3E 5P5
(705) 674-4291
Emp Here 150
SIC 3273 Ready-mixed concrete
 Bryan Dixon

D-U-N-S 24-344-5165   (BR)
BAYSHORE HEALTHCARE LTD.
BAYSHORE HEALTHCARE LTD
(Suby of BAYSHORE HEALTHCARE LTD.)
2120 Regent St Suite 8, Sudbury, ON, P3E 3Z9
(705) 523-6668
Emp Here 300
SIC 8082 Home health care services
 Lucie Parenteau

D-U-N-S 20-155-4730   (HQ)
BRISTOL MACHINE WORKS LIMITED
2100 Algonquin Rd, Sudbury, ON, P3E 4Z6
(705) 522-1550
Emp Here 61   *Sales* 22,200,100
SIC 3599 Industrial machinery, nec
 Ray Morin
 Alain Theriault

D-U-N-S 24-802-2618   (SL)
BRISTOW, TERRY DRUGS LTD
SHOPPERS DRUG MART
2015 Long Lake Rd, Sudbury, ON, P3E 4M8
(705) 522-3030
Emp Here 55   *Sales* 13,438,040
SIC 5912 Drug stores and proprietary stores
 Terry Bristow

D-U-N-S 20-847-2720   (HQ)
CAMBRIAN INSURANCE BROKERS LIMITED
130 Paris St Suite 1, Sudbury, ON, P3E 3E1
(705) 673-5000
Emp Here 27   *Sales* 36,466,580
SIC 6411 Insurance agents, brokers, and service
 James F Smith
 Lisa Hansen-Smith
 Shelly Bradley

D-U-N-S 20-586-8156   (BR)
CITY OF GREATER SUDBURY, THE
GREATER SUDBURY TRANSIT
(Suby of CITY OF GREATER SUDBURY, THE)
1700 Kingsway Rd, Sudbury, ON, P3E 3L7
(705) 675-3333
Emp Here 150
SIC 4111 Local and suburban transit
 Glenn Evans

D-U-N-S 20-595-0629   (SL)
COURVILLE, DAN CHEVROLET LTD
2601 Regent St, Sudbury, ON, P3E 6K6
(705) 523-2438
Emp Here 30   *Sales* 14,942,340
SIC 5511 New and used car dealers
 Dan Courville
 Denis Lauzon

D-U-N-S 20-527-6264   (SL)
DELLELCE CONSTRUCTION & EQUIPMENT LTD
CITY RENTALS
1375 Regent St Suite 2, Sudbury, ON, P3E 6K4
Emp Here 125   *Sales* 25,713,250
SIC 4212 Local trucking, without storage
 Nicholas Dellelce

D-U-N-S 24-991-9713   (SL)
DEMERS, MICHEL STORE INC
CANADIAN TIRE
2259 Regent St, Sudbury, ON, P3E 5M9
(705) 523-5800
Emp Here 100   *Sales* 62,928,000
SIC 5531 Auto and home supply stores
 Michel Demers

D-U-N-S 20-657-0301   (SL)
DIBRINA & ASSOCIATES
7 Cedar St Suite 202, Sudbury, ON, P3E 1A2
(705) 688-9011
Emp Here 49   *Sales* 41,554,940
SIC 6411 Insurance agents, brokers, and service
 Michael Dibrina

D-U-N-S 24-626-4936   (BR)
E.S. FOX LIMITED
(Suby of E.S. FOX LIMITED)
1349 Kelly Lake Rd Suite 1, Sudbury, ON, P3E 5P5
(705) 522-3357
Emp Here 100
SIC 1541 Industrial buildings and warehouses
 John Bee

D-U-N-S 25-868-6955   (BR)
EXTENDICARE INC
EXTENDICARE YORK
(Suby of EXTENDICARE INC)
333 York St, Sudbury, ON, P3E 5J3
(705) 674-4221
Emp Here 300

SIC 8051 Skilled nursing care facilities
Sandra Moroso

D-U-N-S 24-345-9687   (BR)
G4S SECURE SOLUTIONS (CANADA) LTD
(*Suby of* G4S PLC)
1351 D Kelly Lake Rd Unit 9, Sudbury, ON,
P3E 5P5
(705) 524-1519
Emp Here 350
SIC 7381 Detective and armored car services
Kim Giroux

D-U-N-S 20-047-5395   (SL)
GREATER SUDBURY HYDRO INC
(*Suby of* GREATER SUDBURY UTILITIES
INC)
500 Regent St, Sudbury, ON, P3E 3Y2
(705) 675-7536
Emp Here 93   *Sales* 63,228,282
SIC 4911 Electric services
Doug Reeves
Stan Pawlowicz

D-U-N-S 24-796-3846   (HQ)
GREATER SUDBURY UTILITIES INC
500 Regent St Suite 250, Sudbury, ON, P3E
3Y2
(705) 675-7536
Sales 73,426,392
SIC 4911 Electric services
Frank Kallonen
Nancy Whissell
Brian Mcmillan

D-U-N-S 25-419-1851   (HQ)
HEALTH SCIENCES NORTH
41 Ramsey Lake Rd, Sudbury, ON, P3E 5J1
(705) 523-7100
Emp Here 3,800   *Sales* 351,944,981
SIC 8062 General medical and surgical hospi-
tals
Dominic Giroux
Joe Pilon
Chris Bourdon
David Mcneil
Viviane Lapointe
Paul St. George
Mark Hartman
Rhonda Watson
Gaston Roy
Janet Mcelhaney

D-U-N-S 24-966-4009   (SL)
**HEALTH SCIENCES NORTH RESEARCH
INSTITUTE**
41 Ramsey Lake Rd, Sudbury, ON, P3E 5J1
(705) 523-7300
Emp Here 90   *Sales* 45,606,240
SIC 8733 Noncommercial research organiza-
tions
Nicole Everest
Floyd Laughren
Janet Mcelhaney
Chris Redmond
Dominic Giroux
Mark Hartman
Paul St George
Michelle Joly
Sheila Cote-Meek
Geoffrey Lougheed

D-U-N-S 24-049-7297   (HQ)
LAURENTIAN PUBLISHING LIMITED
NORTHERN LIFE NEWSPAPER
158 Elgin St, Sudbury, ON, P3E 3N5
(705) 673-5120
Emp Here 15   *Sales* 19,683,240
SIC 2711 Newspapers
Michael Atkins

D-U-N-S 20-294-8188   (HQ)
MANSOUR MINING TECHNOLOGIES INC
MMTI
2502 Elm, Sudbury, ON, P3E 4R8
(705) 682-0671
Sales 58,527,600

SIC 5082 Construction and mining machinery
Stephan Bay
Francis J Cooke
Nathan Gibb
Steve Groot

D-U-N-S 24-333-1662   (BR)
METRO ONTARIO INC
(*Suby of* METRO INC)
1933 Regent St, Sudbury, ON, P3E 5R2

Emp Here 85
SIC 5411 Grocery stores
Jan Browning

D-U-N-S 20-049-3166   (SL)
MIKE DOYLE DODGE CHRYSLER INC
2555 Regent St, Sudbury, ON, P3E 6K6
(705) 523-1101
Emp Here 47   *Sales* 23,409,666
SIC 5511 New and used car dealers
Mike Doyle

D-U-N-S 24-893-3165   (SL)
MILMAN INDUSTRIES INC
2502 Elm St, Sudbury, ON, P3E 4R6
(705) 682-9277
Emp Here 200   *Sales* 44,174,200
SIC 6512 Nonresidential building operators
Gilles Lebeau

D-U-N-S 24-175-3388   (BR)
**NORTHERN ONTARIO SCHOOL OF
MEDICINE**
(*Suby of* NORTHERN ONTARIO SCHOOL
OF MEDICINE)
935 Ramsey Lake Rd, Sudbury, ON, P3E 2C6
(705) 675-4883
Emp Here 110
SIC 8221 Colleges and universities
Kim Daynard

D-U-N-S 20-104-5569   (SL)
NORTHERN VOICE & DATA INC
174 Douglas St, Sudbury, ON, P3E 1G1
(705) 674-2729
Emp Here 30   *Sales* 13,415,220
SIC 5065 Electronic parts and equipment, nec
Gates Poulin
Monique Forsyth

D-U-N-S 25-405-7565   (HQ)
NRCS INC
31 Larch St Suite 200, Sudbury, ON, P3E 1B7
(705) 688-1288
Emp Here 35   *Sales* 15,836,557
SIC 8093 Specialty outpatient clinics, nec
Michael Sheridan

D-U-N-S 20-156-0232   (HQ)
PIONEER CONSTRUCTION INC
1 Ceasar Rd, Sudbury, ON, P3E 5P3
(705) 560-7200
Sales 25,244,200
SIC 1611 Highway and street construction
James Wallace
Martin Gran
Phill Annett

D-U-N-S 25-542-6736   (HQ)
RAINBOW DISTRICT SCHOOL BOARD
69 Young St, Sudbury, ON, P3E 3G5
(705) 377-4615
Emp Here 50   *Sales* 138,766,600
SIC 8211 Elementary and secondary schools
Doreen Dewar
Norm Blaseg

D-U-N-S 24-350-7303   (SL)
REASBECK CONSTRUCTION INC
1085 Kelly Lake Rd, Sudbury, ON, P3E 5P5
(705) 222-1800
Emp Here 70   *Sales* 29,591,590
SIC 1541 Industrial buildings and warehouses
Micheal Reasbeck

D-U-N-S 24-443-8342   (SL)
REGENCY MALL

469 Bouchard St Suite 203, Sudbury, ON, P3E
2K8
(705) 522-4722
Emp Here 48   *Sales* 13,652,976
SIC 6512 Nonresidential building operators
Bruno Michel

D-U-N-S 24-802-2068   (SL)
**ST. JOSEPH'S CONTINUING CARE CEN-
TRE OF SUDBURY**
*ST. JOSEPH'S CONTINUING CARE CEN-
TRE*
1140 South Bay Rd, Sudbury, ON, P3E 0B6
(705) 674-2846
Emp Here 100   *Sales* 10,213,300
SIC 8062 General medical and surgical hospi-
tals
Jo-Anne Palkovits
Joseph Pintur
Barb Desjardins

D-U-N-S 20-547-4716   (SL)
ST. JOSEPH'S VILLA OF SUDBURY, INC
1250 Southbay Rd, Sudbury, ON, P3E 6L9

Emp Here 150   *Sales* 10,248,900
SIC 8059 Nursing and personal care, nec
Jo-Anne Palkovits
Joseph Pintur
Rey Ingriselli
Ehren Baldauf
Kari Gervais
Lianne Valiquette
Barb Desjardins
Kim Long
Karen Caverson
Bev Lafoley

D-U-N-S 24-048-1523   (SL)
SUDBURY HOSPITAL SERVICES
(*Suby of* HEALTH SCIENCES NORTH)
363 York St, Sudbury, ON, P3E 2A8
(705) 674-2158
Emp Here 90   *Sales* 9,610,380
SIC 7219 Laundry and garment services, nec
Terry Watters
Vicki Kaminski

D-U-N-S 24-380-7356   (SL)
SUDBURY REGENT STREET INC
HOMEWOOD SUITES BY HILTON
(*Suby of* VRANCOR PROPERTY MANAGE-
MENT INC)
2270 Regent St, Sudbury, ON, P3E 0B4
(705) 523-8100
Emp Here 100   *Sales* 9,269,000
SIC 7011 Hotels and motels
Darko Vranich

D-U-N-S 20-116-0988   (SL)
VISTA SUDBURY HOTEL INC
RADISSON HOTEL SUDBURY
85 Ste Anne Rd, Sudbury, ON, P3E 4S4
(705) 675-1123
Emp Here 75   *Sales* 7,117,425
SIC 7011 Hotels and motels
Paul Pedro

D-U-N-S 24-859-7312   (BR)
WESTON BAKERIES LIMITED
695 Martindale Rd, Sudbury, ON, P3E 4H6
(705) 673-4185
Emp Here 100
SIC 2051 Bread, cake, and related products

D-U-N-S 25-300-6787   (BR)
**WORKPLACE SAFETY & INSURANCE
BOARD, THE**
(*Suby of* WORKPLACE SAFETY & INSUR-
ANCE BOARD, THE)
30 Cedar St, Sudbury, ON, P3E 1A4
(705) 677-4260
Emp Here 130
SIC 6331 Fire, marine, and casualty insurance

D-U-N-S 24-044-9793   (HQ)
YOUNG MENS CHRISTIAN ASSOCIATION

YMCA SUDBURY
140 Durham St, Sudbury, ON, P3E 3M7
(705) 673-9136
Emp Here 90   *Sales* 32,747,235
SIC 8641 Civic and social associations
Tom Coon

Sudbury, ON P3G

D-U-N-S 25-204-0233   (SL)
**TERANORTH CONSTRUCTION & ENGI-
NEERING LIMITED**
799 Luoma Rd, Sudbury, ON, P3G 1J4
(705) 523-1540
Emp Here 50   *Sales* 14,176,200
SIC 1611 Highway and street construction
Carlo Bot
Jim Bot

Sudbury, ON P3L

D-U-N-S 24-977-5396   (SL)
1558775 ONTARIO LIMITED
*WAT SUPPLY SANITATION & PAPER PROD-
UCTS*
80 National St, Sudbury, ON, P3L 1M5
(705) 673-8218
Emp Here 23   *Sales* 10,925,598
SIC 5087 Service establishment equipment
Wallace Gillard
Janice Gillard

Summerstown, ON K0C

D-U-N-S 20-890-8889   (BR)
NESEL FAST FREIGHT INCORPORATED
(*Suby of* NESEL FAST FREIGHT INCORPO-
RATED)
19216 Hay Rd, Summerstown, ON, K0C 2E0

Emp Here 100
SIC 4213 Trucking, except local
Carolyn Carriere

D-U-N-S 24-862-8299   (BR)
PACTIV CANADA INC
RENO FOOD PACKAGING
6870 Richmond Rd, Summerstown, ON, K0C
2E0
(613) 931-1439
Emp Here 100
SIC 3089 Plastics products, nec
Jack Lindsay

Sunderland, ON L0C

D-U-N-S 25-352-0506   (BR)
STOCK TRANSPORTATION LTD
(*Suby of* NATIONAL EXPRESS GROUP PLC)
36 12 Hwy, Sunderland, ON, L0C 1H0
(705) 357-3187
Emp Here 250
SIC 4151 School buses
Anne Cameron

D-U-N-S 20-156-3236   (HQ)
SUNDERLAND CO-OPERATIVE INC
1 River St, Sunderland, ON, L0C 1H0
(705) 357-3491
Emp Here 30   *Sales* 10,744,800
SIC 5999 Miscellaneous retail stores, nec
Urs Kressibucher
Gary Jebson
Jim Lockie

▲ Public Company   ■ Public Company Family Member   **HQ** Headquarters   **BR** Branch   **SL** Single Location

Sundridge, ON P0A

D-U-N-S 24-409-2755   (HQ)
KENT TRUSSES LIMITED
204 Forest Lake Rd, Sundridge, ON, P0A 1Z0
(705) 384-5326
Emp Here 70   *Sales* 10,214,498
SIC 2439 Structural wood members, nec
  Julio Cacoilo

D-U-N-S 25-846-9543   (SL)
SUNDRIDGE HAPPY GANG, THE
110 Main St E, Sundridge, ON, P0A 1Z0
(705) 384-7351
Emp Here 140   *Sales* 10,931,697
SIC 8322 Individual and family services
  Robert Walker
  Carmen Stenhouse

Sutton West, ON L0E

D-U-N-S 20-156-4119   (SL)
1323339 ONTARIO LIMITED
SOBEYS
20954 Dalton Rd, Sutton West, ON, L0E 1R0
(905) 722-5671
Emp Here 70   *Sales* 20,543,390
SIC 5411 Grocery stores
  Gerry Derouin

D-U-N-S 24-345-9604   (BR)
CORPORATION OF THE TOWN OF GEORGINA, THE
COMMUNITY LIVING GEORGINA
(*Suby of* CORPORATION OF THE TOWN OF GEORGINA, THE)
26943 48 Hwy Rr 2, Sutton West, ON, L0E 1R0
(905) 722-8947
Emp Here 100
SIC 8361 Residential care
  Susan Rome

D-U-N-S 20-156-3848   (HQ)
INLAND AND MARINE SALVAGE LIMITED
INLAND IRON & METALS
4408 York Rd Suite 32, Sutton West, ON, L0E 1R0
(905) 473-2600
Emp Here 40   *Sales* 11,313,764
SIC 4953 Refuse systems
  Howard Scott
  William G Scott
  Stuart Scott
  Edward Windsor

D-U-N-S 20-877-1386   (SL)
KANNAMPUZHA HOLDINGS LTD
RIVER GLEN HAVEN NURSING HOME
160 High St, Sutton West, ON, L0E 1R0
(905) 722-3631
Emp Here 200   *Sales* 13,713,200
SIC 8051 Skilled nursing care facilities
  Tom Kannampuzha

D-U-N-S 25-293-5853   (BR)
YORK REGION DISTRICT SCHOOL BOARD
SUTTON DISTRICT HIGH SCHOOL
(*Suby of* YORK REGION DISTRICT SCHOOL BOARD)
20798 Dalton Rd, Sutton West, ON, L0E 1R0
(905) 722-3281
Emp Here 150
SIC 8211 Elementary and secondary schools
  Dawn Laliberte

Sydenham, ON K0H

D-U-N-S 25-305-4993   (BR)

LIMESTONE DISTRICT SCHOOL BOARD
SYDENHAM HIGH SCHOOL
2860 Rutledge Rd, Sydenham, ON, K0H 2T0
(613) 376-3612
Emp Here 80
SIC 8211 Elementary and secondary schools
  Brent Pickering

D-U-N-S 25-062-2644   (SL)
TROUSDALE'S I G A
5 George St, Sydenham, ON, K0H 2T0
(613) 376-6609
Emp Here 40   *Sales* 10,966,080
SIC 5411 Grocery stores
  David Stacey

Tara, ON N0H

D-U-N-S 20-306-3664   (SL)
PARTNER AG SERVICES LTD
3694 Bruce Rd 10, Tara, ON, N0H 2N0
(519) 934-2343
Emp Here 30   *Sales* 14,250,780
SIC 5083 Farm and garden machinery
  Ben Rier
  Frank Hogervorst
  Darrel Penner
  Sheri Rier
  Russ Cavanagh

D-U-N-S 24-125-2923   (HQ)
SPRUCEDALE AGROMART LIMITED
291 Young St, Tara, ON, N0H 2N0
(519) 934-2340
Emp Here 12   *Sales* 15,592,920
SIC 5191 Farm supplies
  Frank Coulter
  Jim Reid
  Rob Helm

Tavistock, ON N0B

D-U-N-S 24-627-4104   (BR)
ALIMENTS SAPUTO LIMITEE
SAPUTO
(*Suby of* JOLINA CAPITAL INC)
284 Hope St W, Tavistock, ON, N0B 2R0
(519) 655-2337
Emp Here 240
SIC 2022 Cheese; natural and processed
  Grant Hutchinson

D-U-N-S 25-469-0035   (BR)
CARESSANT-CARE NURSING AND RE-TIREMENT HOMES LIMITED
MAPLES HOME FOR SENIORS, THE
(*Suby of* CARESSANT-CARE NURSING AND RETIREMENT HOMES LIMITED)
94 William St S Suite 202, Tavistock, ON, N0B 2R0
(519) 655-2344
Emp Here 75
SIC 8051 Skilled nursing care facilities
  Lois Riehl

D-U-N-S 24-095-3760   (SL)
PEOPLE CARE CENTRES INC
PEOPLE CARE TAVISTOCK
28 William St N, Tavistock, ON, N0B 2R0
(519) 655-2031
Emp Here 100   *Sales* 6,873,300
SIC 8051 Skilled nursing care facilities
  Brent Gingerich
  Mary Gingerich

D-U-N-S 24-414-0612   (HQ)
SOUTH EASTHOPE MUTUAL INSURANCE COMPANY
62 Woodstock St N, Tavistock, ON, N0B 2R0
(519) 655-2011
Sales 21,201,500

SIC 6411 Insurance agents, brokers, and service
  Frank Rider
  Glen Blair
  Ronald Mckay

D-U-N-S 20-148-2031   (HQ)
W-S FEED & SUPPLIES LIMITED
W-S FEEDS
45 Maria St, Tavistock, ON, N0B 2R0
(519) 664-2237
Emp Here 15   *Sales* 20,741,400
SIC 2048 Prepared feeds, nec
  Paul Wideman
  Darren Wideman

Tecumseh, ON N8N

D-U-N-S 25-108-6484   (SL)
1266192 ONTARIO LTD
ONFREIGHT LOGISTICS
302 Patillo Rd Suite 1, Tecumseh, ON, N8N 2L9
(519) 727-4578
Emp Here 70   *Sales* 10,373,440
SIC 4212 Local trucking, without storage
  Steve Ondejko

D-U-N-S 24-538-1660   (SL)
DUNN PAVING LIMITED
485 Little Baseline Rd, Tecumseh, ON, N8N 2L9
(519) 727-3838
Emp Here 70   *Sales* 17,670,940
SIC 1611 Highway and street construction
  Michael Dunn

D-U-N-S 20-699-6246   (BR)
EXTENDICARE INC
EXTENDICARE TECUMSEH
(*Suby of* EXTENDICARE INC)
2475 St. Alphonse St Suite 1238, Tecumseh, ON, N8N 2X2
(519) 739-2998
Emp Here 100
SIC 8051 Skilled nursing care facilities
  James Egan

D-U-N-S 24-987-6368   (HQ)
FLEX-N-GATE CANADA COMPANY
(*Suby of* FLEX-N-GATE LLC)
538 Blanchard Pk, Tecumseh, ON, N8N 2L9
(519) 727-3931
Sales 72,969,300
SIC 3465 Automotive stampings
  James Zsebok
  Shahid Khan
  Timothy Graham
  Kevin Hamilton

D-U-N-S 20-530-2136   (HQ)
G.W. ANGLIN MANUFACTURING INC
220 Patillo Rd Suite 1, Tecumseh, ON, N8N 2L9
(519) 727-4398
Emp Here 70   *Sales* 23,050,200
SIC 3499 Fabricated Metal products, nec
  Loris Boschin

D-U-N-S 20-186-1838   (HQ)
MCBRIDE METAL FABRICATING CORPO-RATION
AMERIMARK, DIV OF
305 Patillo Rd, Tecumseh, ON, N8N 2L9
(519) 727-6640
Emp Here 60   *Sales* 19,208,500
SIC 3465 Automotive stampings
  Mark Jutras
  Gerard Jutras
  Marie Jutras

D-U-N-S 20-792-5285   (BR)
MCDONALD'S RESTAURANTS OF CANADA LIMITED
MCDONALD'S

(*Suby of* MCDONALD'S CORPORATION)
1631 Manning Rd, Tecumseh, ON, N8N 2L9
(519) 735-8122
Emp Here 80
SIC 5812 Eating places
  Lisa Mulligan

D-U-N-S 20-350-9187   (SL)
PARAMITA ENTERPRISES LIMITED
FOUR SEASONS HOTEL TORONTO
538 Blanchard Pk, Tecumseh, ON, N8N 2L9
(519) 727-2323
Emp Here 475   *Sales* 45,442,300
SIC 7011 Hotels and motels
  Shadid Khan
  Tim Graham
  Dave Ekblad

D-U-N-S 20-035-0413   (HQ)
ST-CLAIR INSURANCE BROKERS INC
13340 Lanoue St, Tecumseh, ON, N8N 5E1
(519) 259-1955
Sales 10,176,720
SIC 6411 Insurance agents, brokers, and service

D-U-N-S 20-192-7543   (HQ)
TRQSS, INC
QUALITY SAFETY SYSTEMS COMPANY
(*Suby of* TOKAI RIKA CO., LTD.)
255 Patillo Rd, Tecumseh, ON, N8N 2L9
(519) 973-7400
Emp Here 700   *Sales* 238,801,500
SIC 2399 Fabricated textile products, nec
  Mark Dolsen
  John Dinardo
  Yasutaka Watanabe
  Kouji Buma
  Mikio Kato

D-U-N-S 20-409-4809   (HQ)
VENTRA GROUP CO
VENTRA PLASTICS MISSISSAUGA SPD
(*Suby of* FLEX-N-GATE LLC)
538 Blanchard Pk, Tecumseh, ON, N8N 2L9
(519) 727-3931
Emp Here 900   *Sales* 1,721,832,000
SIC 3714 Motor vehicle parts and accessories
  James Zsebok
  David Ekblad
  Shahid Rafiq Khan

Teeswater, ON N0G

D-U-N-S 20-156-6759   (HQ)
HURON BAY CO-OPERATIVE INC
15 Hilcrest St, Teeswater, ON, N0G 2S0
(519) 392-6862
Emp Here 19   *Sales* 31,892,840
SIC 5999 Miscellaneous retail stores, nec
  Jeffrey Hurst

Terrace Bay, ON P0T

D-U-N-S 25-092-2411   (SL)
AV TERRACE BAY INC
21 Mill Rd, Terrace Bay, ON, P0T 2W0
(807) 825-1075
Emp Here 350   *Sales* 68,168,800
SIC 2611 Pulp mills
  Vinod Tiwari

D-U-N-S 24-967-5240   (HQ)
SPADONI MOTORS LIMITED
NATIONAL CAR RENTAL
(*Suby of* SPADONI BROS. LIMITED)
Hwy 17, Terrace Bay, ON, P0T 2W0
(807) 825-4561
Emp Here 15   *Sales* 12,451,950
SIC 5521 Used car dealers
  Patrick Spadoni

Micheal Spadoni

D-U-N-S 24-607-9974   (SL)
TERRACE BAY ENTERPRISES LIMITED
EMPERIAL MOTEL
Hwy 17 3 Simcoe Plaza, Terrace Bay, ON, P0T 2W0
(807) 825-3226
Emp Here 30   *Sales* 14,942,340
SIC 5541 Gasoline service stations
Frank Trichilo

D-U-N-S 24-323-6366   (SL)
TERRACE BAY PULP INC
21 Mill Rd, Terrace Bay, ON, P0T 2W0

Emp Here 50   *Sales* 11,671,750
SIC 2611 Pulp mills
Wolfgang Gericke
Taras Sawula
Robert Baxter

Thamesville, ON N0P

D-U-N-S 25-173-5809   (SL)
768308 ONTARIO INC
SUNSHINE ASPARAGUS FARMS
30043 Jane Rd, Thamesville, ON, N0P 2K0
(519) 692-4416
Emp Here 50   *Sales* 11,242,750
SIC 2035 Pickles, sauces, and salad dressings
John Jaques
Claudia Jaques

D-U-N-S 24-862-1658   (SL)
KEARNEY, B. R. ENTERPRISES LTD
KEARNEY PLANTERS
14232 Turin Line, Thamesville, ON, N0P 2K0
(519) 678-3206
Emp Here 20   *Sales* 10,000,000
SIC 5083 Farm and garden machinery
Barry Kearney

Thessalon, ON P0R

D-U-N-S 25-481-2514   (SL)
ALGOMA MANOR NURSING HOME
ALGOMA MANOR
145 Dawson St, Thessalon, ON, P0R 1L0
(705) 842-2840
Emp Here 110   *Sales* 7,071,020
SIC 8361 Residential care
Barbara Harten
Tammy Campbell
Frances Leveques
Darlene Inch

D-U-N-S 24-124-8491   (SL)
ALGOMA MUTUAL INSURANCE COMPANY
131 Main St, Thessalon, ON, P0R 1L0
(705) 842-3345
Emp Here 14   *Sales* 10,156,146
SIC 6331 Fire, marine, and casualty insurance
Cameron Ross
Vernon Bailey

D-U-N-S 24-369-1313   (HQ)
BIRCHLAND PLYWOOD - VENEER LIMITED
50 Genelle St, Thessalon, ON, P0R 1L0
(705) 842-2430
Emp Here 1   *Sales* 11,542,200
SIC 2435 Hardwood veneer and plywood
Mike Morgan
Bruce Morgan

D-U-N-S 20-156-8649   (SL)
MIDWAY LUMBER MILLS LIMITED
41 Sherwood Rd, Thessalon, ON, P0R 1L0
(705) 842-3246
Emp Here 75   *Sales* 20,073,900
SIC 5211 Lumber and other building materials

Michael Morgan

D-U-N-S 20-551-0907   (SL)
MISSISSAGI POWER TRUST
4917 129 Hwy, Thessalon, ON, P0R 1L0
(705) 842-3377
Emp Here 23   *Sales* 14,412,122
SIC 4911 Electric services
Ian Kerr
Donald Tremblay
Colin Clark
Richard Legault

D-U-N-S 25-892-5275   (SL)
RENEWABLE ENERGY SOLUTIONS THESSALON
48 Feltham Rd, Thessalon, ON, P0R 1L0
(705) 842-6911
Emp Here 5   *Sales* 15,529,285
SIC 4924 Natural gas distribution

Thornbury, ON N0H

D-U-N-S 25-684-0992   (HQ)
BREAKER TECHNOLOGY LTD
BTI
(*Suby of* ASTEC INDUSTRIES, INC.)
35 Elgin St, Thornbury, ON, N0H 2P0
(519) 599-2015
Sales 26,640,120
SIC 3532 Mining machinery
Donald Sissons

Thorndale, ON N0M

D-U-N-S 25-684-6080   (HQ)
AGRONOMY COMPANY OF CANADA LTD
AGROMART GROUP
17554 Plover Mills Rd, Thorndale, ON, N0M 2P0
(519) 461-9057
Sales 15,592,920
SIC 5191 Farm supplies
Gaetan Desroches
Andre Mercure
Jean-Francois Harel
Jean-Yves Caron
Kenneth O'hagan

D-U-N-S 24-287-8668   (HQ)
IDEAL DRAIN TILE LIMITED
1100 Ideal Dr, Thorndale, ON, N0M 2P0
(519) 473-2669
Emp Here 20   *Sales* 35,535,500
SIC 6712 Bank holding companies
Scott Barbour

D-U-N-S 20-557-5645   (HQ)
IDEAL PIPE
1100 Ideal Dr, Thorndale, ON, N0M 2P0
(519) 473-2669
Emp Here 46   *Sales* 19,208,500
SIC 3498 Fabricated pipe and fittings
Gerald Randall Clarke

Thornhill, ON L3T

D-U-N-S 25-508-3404   (SL)
1200839 ONTARIO LIMITED
M.C. JANITORIAL SYSTEMS
2900 Steeles Ave E Suite 210, Thornhill, ON, L3T 4X1
(905) 889-4224
Emp Here 100   *Sales* 4,020,900
SIC 7349 Building maintenance services, nec
Tina Ferlaino

D-U-N-S 24-469-5565   (SL)
1263815 ONTARIO INC

NORTH TORONTO MAZDA
7079 Yonge St, Thornhill, ON, L3T 2A7
(905) 763-3688
Emp Here 28   *Sales* 13,946,184
SIC 5511 New and used car dealers
Carlo Sistilli
Jerry Jarosz
Carl Ritter

D-U-N-S 20-010-0753   (SL)
1456661 ONTARIO INCORPORATED
TEXPRESS
300 John St Suite 87552, Thornhill, ON, L3T 5W4
(905) 669-1103
Emp Here 74   *Sales* 15,222,244
SIC 4212 Local trucking, without storage
Laya Jalaie
Mehdi Takyan
Hossein F.Fard
Hans Gustavson

D-U-N-S 20-354-6650   (SL)
2521153 ONTARIO INC
WPSL SECURITY SOLUTIONS
300 John St Suite 310, Thornhill, ON, L3T 5W4
(416) 222-7144
Emp Here 130   *Sales* 3,412,500
SIC 7381 Detective and armored car services
Slava Levin
Darren Strom

D-U-N-S 20-512-6027   (BR)
ACCENTURE BUSINESS SERVICES FOR UTILITIES INC
(*Suby of* ACCENTURE INC)
123 Commerce Valley Dr E Suite 500, Thornhill, ON, L3T 7W8

Emp Here 350
SIC 8741 Management services

D-U-N-S 20-982-8826   (BR)
ACKLANDS - GRAINGER INC
AGI
(*Suby of* W.W. GRAINGER, INC.)
50 Minthorn Blvd, Thornhill, ON, L3T 7X8
(905) 763-3474
Emp Here 500
SIC 5084 Industrial machinery and equipment
Dean Johnson

D-U-N-S 25-389-2251   (HQ)
ACKLANDS - GRAINGER INC
AGI
(*Suby of* W.W. GRAINGER, INC.)
123 Commerce Valley Dr E Suite 700, Thornhill, ON, L3T 7W8
(905) 731-5516
Emp Here 350   *Sales* 1,077,883,300
SIC 5085 Industrial supplies
John Kaul
George Mcclean
Jason Moore

D-U-N-S 20-228-2948   (HQ)
ADASTRA CORPORATION
8500 Leslie St Suite 600, Thornhill, ON, L3T 7M8
(905) 881-7946
Emp Here 280   *Sales* 147,658,400
SIC 7371 Custom computer programming services
Darren Edery
Oliver Fuchs
Nelio Lucas
Ilia Bolotine
Shameer Kanji
Rob Turner
Krasen Paskalev
Shannon Corless
Zeeshan Saeed
Shauna Walker

D-U-N-S 24-235-5514   (SL)
ADVENTURE VALLEY INC

ADVENTURE VALLEY
7015 Leslie St, Thornhill, ON, L3T 6L6
(905) 731-2267
Emp Here 100   *Sales* 14,002,900
SIC 7999 Amusement and recreation, nec
Kevin Gandy

D-U-N-S 24-462-7634   (HQ)
AT&T ENTERPRISES CANADA CO
(*Suby of* AT&T INC.)
55 Commerce Valley Dr W Suite 700, Thornhill, ON, L3T 7V9
(905) 762-7390
Emp Here 130   *Sales* 50,181,600
SIC 4899 Communication services, nec
David Denault
Mary Livingston
Maria Sbrocchi
Thomas Brown
Matthew Mototsune

D-U-N-S 20-117-0920   (HQ)
AT&T GLOBAL SERVICES CANADA CO
(*Suby of* AT&T INC.)
55 Commerce Valley Dr W Suite 700, Thornhill, ON, L3T 7V9
(905) 762-7390
Emp Here 100   *Sales* 22,847,200
SIC 4899 Communication services, nec
David Dorman
David Stroud
Justin Simms
Mary Livingston
David Aspinall

D-U-N-S 24-951-3763   (HQ)
BANK OF CHINA (CANADA) LTD
(*Suby of* CHINA INVESTMENT CORPORATION)
50 Minthorn Blvd Suite 600, Thornhill, ON, L3T 7X8
(905) 771-6886
Emp Here 32   *Sales* 53,656,600
SIC 6021 National commercial banks
Aihua Li

D-U-N-S 25-890-8409   (HQ)
BMC SOFTWARE CANADA INC
(*Suby of* BOXER PARENT COMPANY INC.)
50 Minthorn Blvd Suite 200, Thornhill, ON, L3T 7X8
(905) 707-4600
Emp Here 45   *Sales* 10,692,550
SIC 7372 Prepackaged software
Paul Capombassis

D-U-N-S 25-059-4041   (HQ)
CAA CLUB GROUP
CAA SOUTH CENTRAL ONTARIO
60 Commerce Valley Dr E, Thornhill, ON, L3T 7P9
(905) 771-3000
Emp Here 250   *Sales* 147,921,000
SIC 8699 Membership organizations, nec
Bill Graham
Hank Keyzers
Rhonda English
Teddy Chien
Cindy Hillaby
Larry Sheffit
Sue Selby
Linda Matthews
Bill Wright
Robert Wong

D-U-N-S 20-351-9525   (SL)
CAA INSURANCE COMPANY
60 Commerce Valley Dr E, Thornhill, ON, L3T 7P9
(905) 771-3000
Emp Here 300   *Sales* 641,090,400
SIC 6331 Fire, marine, and casualty insurance
Earlene Huntley

D-U-N-S 24-384-0720   (HQ)
CAA TRAVEL (SOUTH CENTRAL ONTARIO) INC.
60 Commerce Valley Dr E, Thornhill, ON, L3T

7P9
(905) 771-3000
Emp Here 250   Sales 316,350,400
SIC 4724 Travel agencies
Dina Palozzi
Ajay Tellis
Michael Elliott
Art Leitch
Amy Bryson
Susan Waywell
William Carter
Mervin A C Daub
William Graham
Janet Lafortune

D-U-N-S 20-528-8769   (SL)
CAMILION SOLUTIONS, INC
123 Commerce Valley Dr E Suite 800, Thornhill, ON, L3T 7W8

Emp Here 100   Sales 14,418,200
SIC 7371 Custom computer programming services
Ross Orette
Dave Conte
Neil Ohm
Rober Logan
Brian Antonen
Raymond Chang
David Adderley
Andrew Pinkerton

D-U-N-S 20-609-2314   (HQ)
CHEMLINE PLASTICS LIMITED
55 Guardsman Rd, Thornhill, ON, L3T 6L2
(905) 889-7890
Sales 12,825,702
SIC 5085 Industrial supplies
William Ruddock
Richard Ruddock
David Burke
Valerie Burke

D-U-N-S 20-573-4416   (BR)
CIBC WORLD MARKETS INC
CIBC WOOD GUNDY
(*Suby of* CANADIAN IMPERIAL BANK OF COMMERCE)
123 Commerce Valley Dr E Suite 100, Thornhill, ON, L3T 7W8
(905) 762-2300
Emp Here 90
SIC 6211 Security brokers and dealers
Ross Serrier

D-U-N-S 25-319-8774   (SL)
CIS INSURANCE BROKERS (CANADA) LTD
505 Highway 7 E Suite 328, Thornhill, ON, L3T 7T1
(905) 889-2268
Emp Here 33   Sales 19,137,492
SIC 6411 Insurance agents, brokers, and service
Louis Luk

D-U-N-S 25-403-2451   (SL)
CLUB AUTO ROADSIDE SERVICES LTD
(*Suby of* CANADIAN AUTOMOBILE ASSOCIATION)
60 Commerce Valley Dr E, Thornhill, ON, L3T 7P9
(905) 771-4001
Emp Here 75   Sales 33,764,775
SIC 7549 Automotive services, nec
Sean Grasby

D-U-N-S 20-552-8081   (SL)
CMN GLOBAL INC
GENERALI GLOBAL HEALTH SERVICES
(*Suby of* ASSICURAZIONI GENERALI SPA)
150 Commerce Valley Dr W Suite 900, Thornhill, ON, L3T 7Z3
(905) 669-4333
Emp Here 150   Sales 28,531,050
SIC 8011 Offices and clinics of medical doctors
Marco Gizacomelli

Paul Tidy
Denis Lou

D-U-N-S 24-745-1818   (HQ)
COMPUTER TALK TECHNOLOGY INC
150 Commerce Valley Dr W Unit 800, Thornhill, ON, L3T 7Z3
(905) 882-5000
Emp Here 70   Sales 10,813,650
SIC 7371 Custom computer programming services
Mandle Cheung

D-U-N-S 20-011-7658   (SL)
CONTENT MANAGEMENT CORPORATION
MULTIVIEW CANADA
(*Suby of* MULTI-VIEW, INC.)
50 Minthorn Blvd Suite 800, Thornhill, ON, L3T 7X8
(905) 889-6555
Emp Here 100   Sales 16,684,700
SIC 7376 Computer facilities management
Scott Bedford
Dan Maitland

D-U-N-S 20-716-9843   (SL)
D & D ASSOCIATES LTD
D & D ASSOCIATES LEASING
8199 Yonge St Suite 401, Thornhill, ON, L3T 2C6
(905) 881-5575
Emp Here 25   Sales 12,636,475
SIC 6733 Trusts, nec
David Ciobotaru

D-U-N-S 24-918-5174   (HQ)
DUPLIUM CORP
35 Minthorn Blvd, Thornhill, ON, L3T 7N5
(905) 709-9930
Sales 20,037,100
SIC 7334 Photocopying and duplicating services
Bernie Anderson
Robert Hashimoto
Kalman Weber
Michael Jackson
Brian Harley

D-U-N-S 24-707-5039   (BR)
ERNST & YOUNG LLP
(*Suby of* ERNST & YOUNG LLP)
175 Commerce Valley Dr W Suite 600, Thornhill, ON, L3T 7P6

Emp Here 125
SIC 8721 Accounting, auditing, and bookkeeping
Pam Tzogas

D-U-N-S 24-313-8026   (HQ)
EVERLINK PAYMENT SERVICES INC
125 Commerce Valley Dr W Unit 100, Thornhill, ON, L3T 7W4
(905) 946-5898
Sales 11,844,000
SIC 6099 Functions related to deposit banking
Mark Ripplinger
Duane Gomes
Bryan Beattie
Todd Clark
Jim Hanisch
David Becker
Bob Reczka
Keith Nixon

D-U-N-S 20-070-8167   (HQ)
EXTREME FITNESS GROUP INC
8281 Yonge St, Thornhill, ON, L3T 2C7
(905) 709-1248
Emp Here 140   Sales 18,811,250
SIC 7991 Physical fitness facilities

D-U-N-S 20-206-7950   (SL)
FAGA GROUP INC
137 Langstaff Rd E, Thornhill, ON, L3T 3M6
(905) 881-2552
Emp Here 50   Sales 11,135,898
SIC 1794 Excavation work

Carmen Tullio

D-U-N-S 25-318-9708   (BR)
FIRSTCANADA ULC
1ST STUDENT CANADA
(*Suby of* FIRSTGROUP PLC)
120 Doncaster Ave, Thornhill, ON, L3T 1L3
(905) 764-6662
Emp Here 200
SIC 4151 School buses
Laura Clarke

D-U-N-S 20-300-7372   (SL)
FOSS NATIONAL LEASING LTD.
FOSS FLEET MANAGEMENT
125 Commerce Valley Dr W Suite 801, Thornhill, ON, L3T 7W4
(905) 886-2522
Emp Here 60   Sales 16,998,000
SIC 7515 Passenger car leasing
Jeffery Hartley
Karen Foss
Roy Foss
John Thomas

D-U-N-S 24-872-4908   (SL)
GALDERMA CANADA INC
(*Suby of* NESTLE S.A.)
55 Commerce Valley Dr W Suite 400, Thornhill, ON, L3T 7V9
(905) 762-2500
Emp Here 62   Sales 25,594,902
SIC 5122 Drugs, proprietaries, and sundries
Wendy Adams

D-U-N-S 24-751-0571   (SL)
HOMELIFE BAYVIEW REALTY INC
505 Highway 7 E Suite 201, Thornhill, ON, L3T 7T1
(416) 845-0000
Emp Here 320   Sales 108,180,480
SIC 6531 Real estate agents and managers
Tom Tauro
Steven Schmeiser

D-U-N-S 20-578-4486   (SL)
HOMELIFE PROSPERITY LAND REALTY INC
2900 Steeles Ave E Suite 211, Thornhill, ON, L3T 4X1
(905) 707-8020
Emp Here 25   Sales 14,666,015
SIC 6411 Insurance agents, brokers, and service
Bruce Sin

D-U-N-S 20-288-1616   (HQ)
ILLUMITI INC
(*Suby of* ILLUMITI CORP.)
123 Commerce Valley Dr E Suite 500, Thornhill, ON, L3T 7W8
(905) 737-1066
Emp Here 20   Sales 21,085,920
SIC 8748 Business consulting, nec
Nir Orbach
Dror Orbach

D-U-N-S 25-375-0236   (BR)
INTEC BILLING CANADA LTD
(*Suby of* INTEC BILLING CANADA LTD)
123 Commerce Valley Dr E, Thornhill, ON, L3T 7W8

Emp Here 250
SIC 5045 Computers, peripherals, and software
Catherine Gill

D-U-N-S 24-452-9095   (SL)
LEO PHARMA INC
(*Suby of* LEO FONDET)
123 Commerce Valley Dr E Suite 400, Thornhill, ON, L3T 7W8
(905) 886-9822
Emp Here 50   Sales 55,267,250
SIC 5122 Drugs, proprietaries, and sundries
Christian Scheuer
Sharmayne Mistry

W. Brian Rose

D-U-N-S 24-876-8095   (HQ)
LEXMARK CANADA INC
(*Suby of* NINESTAR GROUP COMPANY LIMITED)
125 Commerce Valley Dr W Unit 600, Thornhill, ON, L3T 7W4
(905) 763-0560
Emp Here 135   Sales 122,060,256
SIC 5045 Computers, peripherals, and software
Todd Hamblin
Todd Greenwood
Matthew Barnicoat

D-U-N-S 25-459-3387   (SL)
MATRIX RESEARCH LIMITED
55 Doncaster Ave Suite 280, Thornhill, ON, L3T 1L7
(905) 707-1300
Emp Here 50   Sales 11,734,800
SIC 8732 Commercial nonphysical research
Alec Svoboda
Tanya Svoboda
Karel Ferus

D-U-N-S 25-672-3362   (BR)
METRO ONTARIO INC
FOOD BASICS
(*Suby of* METRO INC)
8190 Bayview Ave, Thornhill, ON, L3T 2S2
(905) 731-2300
Emp Here 80
SIC 5411 Grocery stores
George Thistel

D-U-N-S 20-385-4492   (SL)
MNZ GLOBAL INC
300 John St Suite 503, Thornhill, ON, L3T 5W4
(905) 597-0207
Emp Here 10   Sales 10,185,201
SIC 5051 Metals service centers and offices
Mehdi Bukhari

D-U-N-S 20-771-1904   (HQ)
MORRISON HERSHFIELD GROUP INC
125 Commerce Valley Dr W Suite 300, Thornhill, ON, L3T 7W4
(416) 499-3110
Emp Here 96   Sales 228,443,125
SIC 6712 Bank holding companies
Anthony Karakatsanis
Catherine Karakatsanis
Kevin Chouinard
Jon Mccarthy
Rob Selby
Jim Weir
David Pavey
Pelly Shafto
Scott Steiding
Raymond Mantha

D-U-N-S 25-214-6766   (HQ)
MORRISON HERSHFIELD LIMITED
(*Suby of* MORRISON HERSHFIELD GROUP INC)
125 Commerce Valley Dr W Unit 300, Thornhill, ON, L3T 7W4
(416) 499-3110
Emp Here 305   Sales 133,654,818
SIC 8711 Engineering services
Anthony Karakatsanis
Catherine Karakatsanis
David Pavey
James Lew
James Weir
Pierre Gallant

D-U-N-S 24-767-1154   (SL)
MULTI-SECTOR NON PROFIT
105 Commerce Valley Dr W Unit 310, Thornhill, ON, L3T 7W3
(905) 889-6200
Emp Here 20   Sales 11,598,480
SIC 6411 Insurance agents, brokers, and ser-

vice
Martin Kogan

D-U-N-S 20-410-4152   (HQ)
NORMAC KITCHENS LIMITED
59 Glen Cameron Rd, Thornhill, ON, L3T 5W2
(905) 889-1342
Emp Here 105   *Sales* 29,624,980
SIC 2434 Wood kitchen cabinets
Hans Marcus
Bianca Marcus
Andrew Marcus

D-U-N-S 20-251-0223   (SL)
ON TRACK SAFETY LTD
29 Ruggles Ave, Thornhill, ON, L3T 3S4
(905) 660-5969
Emp Here 70   *Sales* 31,445,330
SIC 7389 Business services, nec
Paul Furlano

D-U-N-S 24-310-6924   (HQ)
ONX ENTERPRISE SOLUTIONS LTD
(*Suby of* CINCINNATI BELL INC.)
165 Commerce Valley Dr W Suite 300, Thornhill, ON, L3T 7V8
(905) 881-4414
Emp Here 125   *Sales* 266,605,296
SIC 5045 Computers, peripherals, and software
Paul Khawaja
Eric Miller
David M.Greulich

D-U-N-S 20-369-7610   (SL)
ORION TRAVEL INSURANCE COMPANY
COMPAGNIE D'ASSURANCE VOYAGE
ORION
(*Suby of* CAA CLUB GROUP)
60 Commerce Valley Dr E, Thornhill, ON, L3T 7P9
(905) 771-3000
Emp Here 200
SIC 6321 Accident and health insurance
Earlene Huntley

D-U-N-S 20-903-9064   (HQ)
PARTNERS IN CREDIT INC
50 Minthorn Blvd Suite 700, Thornhill, ON, L3T 7X8
(905) 886-0555
Emp Here 20   *Sales* 19,266,884
SIC 7322 Adjustment and collection services
Vincent Fiore
Gary Abel
Anthony Fiore
Mike Spence

D-U-N-S 24-326-3154   (SL)
PATEL, SAMIR PHARMACY LTD
SHOPPERS DRUG MART
298 John St, Thornhill, ON, L3T 6M8
(905) 886-3711
Emp Here 50   *Sales* 12,647,700
SIC 5912 Drug stores and proprietary stores
Samir Patel

D-U-N-S 20-703-5333   (HQ)
RAYWAL LIMITED PARTNERSHIP, THE
RAYWAL CABINETS
68 Green Lane, Thornhill, ON, L3T 6K8
(905) 889-6243
Sales 28,855,500
SIC 2434 Wood kitchen cabinets
Brian Mcgee

D-U-N-S 24-522-0152   (HQ)
REAL MATTERS INC
50 Minthorn Blvd Suite 401, Thornhill, ON, L3T 7X8
(905) 739-1212
Emp Here 50   *Sales* 302,976,000
SIC 7371 Custom computer programming services
Jason Smith
Bill Herman
Nathan Chandler
Loren Cooke

Kim Montgomery
Craig Rowsell
Ryan Smith
Kevin Walton
Blaine Hobson
Robert Courteau

D-U-N-S 24-342-2149   (BR)
RECIPE UNLIMITED CORPORATION
MONTANA'S COOKHOUSE
(*Suby of* RECIPE UNLIMITED CORPORATION)
2910 Steeles Ave E, Thornhill, ON, L3T 7X1
(905) 709-0550
Emp Here 75
SIC 5812 Eating places
Christopher Mitchell

D-U-N-S 25-735-5560   (BR)
RED LOBSTER HOSPITALITY LLC
RED LOBSTER RESTAURANTS
7291 Yonge St, Thornhill, ON, L3T 2A9
(905) 731-3550
Emp Here 80
SIC 5812 Eating places
Susan Rocha

D-U-N-S 25-794-9735   (BR)
REVERA INC
GLYNNWOOD
(*Suby of* GOVERNMENT OF CANADA)
7700 Bayview Ave Suite 518, Thornhill, ON, L3T 5W1
(905) 881-9475
Emp Here 110
SIC 8051 Skilled nursing care facilities
Meirav Schwartzman

D-U-N-S 20-336-5630   (SL)
ROCKMAN PSYCHOLOGY PROFES-
SIONAL CORPORATION
YORK REGION PSYCHOLOGICAL SERVICES
7191 Yonge St Suite 801, Thornhill, ON, L3T 0C4
(416) 602-3230
Emp Here 40   *Sales* 14,449,480
SIC 8049 Offices of health practitioner
Hannah Rockman

D-U-N-S 20-234-1400   (HQ)
SHERWIN-WILLIAMS CANADA INC
DIVERSIFIED BRANDS DIV OF
(*Suby of* THE SHERWIN-WILLIAMS COMPANY)
8500 Leslie St Suite 220, Thornhill, ON, L3T 7M8

Sales 73,644,875
SIC 5198 Paints, varnishes, and supplies
Judy Belaske
Robert Liebel

D-U-N-S 20-848-6985   (SL)
SHOULDICE HOSPITAL LIMITED
SHOULDICE SURGERY
7750 Bayview Ave Suite 370, Thornhill, ON, L3T 4A3
(905) 889-1125
Emp Here 180   *Sales* 14,729,940
SIC 8069 Specialty hospitals, except psychiatric
E Byrnes Shouldice
Catherine Shouldice

D-U-N-S 25-362-0900   (BR)
SIEMENS CANADA LIMITED
SIEMENS TANGO SOFTWARE
(*Suby of* SIEMENS AG)
55 Commerce Valley Dr W Suite 400, Thornhill, ON, L3T 7V9

Emp Here 170
SIC 7371 Custom computer programming services
Bozzo Grace

D-U-N-S 25-150-6622   (HQ)

SOFINA FOODS INC
EAST HURON POULTRY, DIV OF
100 Commerce Valley Dr W Suite 900, Thornhill, ON, L3T 0A1
(905) 747-3333
Emp Here 400   *Sales* 292,431,000
SIC 2013 Sausages and other prepared meats
Micheal Latifi

D-U-N-S 20-289-8263   (SL)
SPORTBALL LTD
SPORTBALL
39 Glen Cameron Rd Unit 8, Thornhill, ON, L3T 1P1
(905) 882-4473
Emp Here 120   *Sales* 11,394,360
SIC 7999 Amusement and recreation, nec
Carmella Gelgor
Mark Gelgor
John Mallinick

D-U-N-S 20-700-5773   (HQ)
TERAGO INC
55 Commerce Valley Dr W Suite 800, Thornhill, ON, L3T 7V9
(866) 837-2465
Emp Here 100   *Sales* 41,161,148
SIC 4813 Telephone communication, except radio
Antonio Ciciretto
Mark Lau
Duncan Mcgregor
Ron Perrotta
Christopher Taylor
Geoff Kereluik
Candice Levy
David Charron
Matthew Gerber
Michael Martin

D-U-N-S 25-101-1771   (HQ)
TERAGO NETWORKS INC
TERAGO
(*Suby of* TERAGO INC)
55 Commerce Valley Dr W Suite 800, Thornhill, ON, L3T 7V9
(866) 837-2461
Emp Here 55   *Sales* 31,986,080
SIC 4813 Telephone communication, except radio
Stewart Lyons
Joe Frodan
Ryan Lausman
Jeffrey Yim

D-U-N-S 20-293-1031   (SL)
TRAVEL HEALTHCARE INSURANCE SO-
LUTIONS INC
STUDENTGUARD HEALTH INSURANCE
300 John St Suite 405, Thornhill, ON, L3T 5W4
(905) 731-8140
Emp Here 50   *Sales* 92,332,950
SIC 6321 Accident and health insurance
Keith A Segal
Maryann A Brown
Clark Hortsing

D-U-N-S 24-342-1356   (SL)
TRIANGLE LOGISTICS SOLUTIONS INC
8500 Leslie St Suite 320, Thornhill, ON, L3T 7M8
(416) 747-6474
Emp Here 15   *Sales* 11,524,275
SIC 4213 Trucking, except local
Alfred Emdon

D-U-N-S 20-848-9583   (HQ)
UNIVERSAL LOGISTICS INC
125 Commerce Valley Dr W Suite 750, Thornhill, ON, L3T 7W4
(905) 882-4880
Emp Here 50   *Sales* 46,682,440
SIC 4731 Freight transportation arrangement
Michael Glionna
David Glionna

Mark Glionna
Paul Glionna
Judith Glionna

D-U-N-S 24-093-8985   (HQ)
VERI-CHEQUE LTD
VERI-CREDIT
(*Suby of* LOURON LEASING LTD)
8500 Leslie St Suite 500, Thornhill, ON, L3T 7M8
(905) 709-0928
Emp Here 15   *Sales* 80,302,170
SIC 6351 Surety insurance
Ronald Renwick

D-U-N-S 20-903-6839   (SL)
WALLMARC WOOD INDUSTRIES LIMITED
59 Glen Cameron Rd, Thornhill, ON, L3T 5W2
(905) 889-1342
Emp Here 150   *Sales* 73,159,500
SIC 5084 Industrial machinery and equipment
Hans Marcus

D-U-N-S 24-078-1732   (HQ)
WINSHAM FABRIK CANADA LTD
25 Minthorn Blvd, Thornhill, ON, L3T 7N5
(905) 882-1827
Emp Here 55   *Sales* 33,075,640
SIC 5023 Homefurnishings
Muhammad Husein Sr
Sultana Husein

D-U-N-S 20-358-3166   (HQ)
WSP CANADA GROUP LIMITED
(*Suby of* AST TRUST COMPANY (CANADA))
100 Commerce Valley Dr W, Thornhill, ON, L3T 0A1
(905) 882-1100
Sales 1,715,039,700
SIC 8711 Engineering services
Hugo Blasutta
Barbara Oberleitner
Andre Desautels
Josee Gagnon
Victoria Trim

D-U-N-S 25-151-0376   (BR)
YORK CATHOLIC DISTRICT SCHOOL
BOARD
ST ROBERT CATHOLIC HIGH SCHOOL
(*Suby of* YORK CATHOLIC DISTRICT SCHOOL BOARD)
8101 Leslie St, Thornhill, ON, L3T 7P4
(905) 889-4982
Emp Here 140
SIC 8211 Elementary and secondary schools
Jennifer Sarna

D-U-N-S 25-297-9471   (BR)
YORK REGION DISTRICT SCHOOL BOARD
THORNLEA SECONDARY SCHOOL
(*Suby of* YORK REGION DISTRICT SCHOOL BOARD)
8075 Bayview Ave, Thornhill, ON, L3T 4N4
(905) 889-9696
Emp Here 120
SIC 8211 Elementary and secondary schools
Joseph Foti

Thornhill, ON L4J

D-U-N-S 20-705-2189   (SL)
1290357 ONTARIO LIMITED
JUSTIN'S NO FRILLS
1054 Centre St, Thornhill, ON, L4J 3M8
(905) 882-2240
Emp Here 160   *Sales* 46,956,320
SIC 5411 Grocery stores
Justin Lesnick

D-U-N-S 24-166-9360   (SL)
1543738 ONTARIO LIMITED
WILLOWDALE SUBARU
222 Steeles Ave W, Thornhill, ON, L4J 1A1

(416) 221-8876
Emp Here 30 *Sales* 14,942,340
SIC 5511 New and used car dealers
Paul Staples

D-U-N-S 24-144-1851 (SL)
1633578 ONTARIO LIMITED
LANDROVER JAGUAR THORNHILL
434 Steeles Ave W, Thornhill, ON, L4J 6X6
(905) 889-0080
Emp Here 30 *Sales* 14,942,340
SIC 5511 New and used car dealers
Sylvester Chuang
Pauline Chuang

D-U-N-S 25-984-6830 (HQ)
1850178 ONTARIO LIMITED
ACURA OF NORTH TORONTO
7064 Yonge St, Thornhill, ON, L4J 1V7
(905) 882-9660
Sales 54,118,080
SIC 5511 New and used car dealers
Kapil Dilawri

D-U-N-S 20-550-9552 (HQ)
2024232 ONTARIO INC
GALLERIA SUPERMARKET
7040 Yonge St Unit B1, Thornhill, ON, L4J 1V7
(905) 882-0040
Emp Here 1 *Sales* 17,608,620
SIC 5411 Grocery stores
Jeffery Min

D-U-N-S 20-251-6279 (SL)
CALCULATED INCENTIVES INC
109 Rosedale Heights Dr, Thornhill, ON, L4J 4V9

Emp Here 15 *Sales* 11,137,800
SIC 5199 Nondurable goods, nec

D-U-N-S 24-513-8433 (HQ)
COLOR STEELS INC
(*Suby of* RUSSEL METALS INC)
251 Racco Pky, Thornhill, ON, L4J 8X9
(905) 879-0300
Emp Here 60 *Sales* 31,302,180
SIC 5051 Metals service centers and offices
David Sanderson

D-U-N-S 20-391-4549 (SL)
COMMERCIAL SWITCHGEAR LIMITED
CSL COMMERCIAL SWITCHGEAR LIMITED
175 Racco Pkwy, Thornhill, ON, L4J 8X9
(905) 669-9270
Emp Here 55 *Sales* 10,474,310
SIC 3613 Switchgear and switchboard apparatus
Gifford Scott

D-U-N-S 24-950-6957 (HQ)
CONCORD FOOD CENTRE INC
1438 Centre St, Thornhill, ON, L4J 3N1
(905) 886-2180
Emp Here 10 *Sales* 29,347,700
SIC 5411 Grocery stores
Joe Greco
Rina Virgilio

D-U-N-S 20-526-2264 (SL)
CRODA CANADA LIMITED
(*Suby of* CRODA INTERNATIONAL PUBLIC LIMITED COMPANY)
221 Racco Pky Unit A, Thornhill, ON, L4J 8X9
(905) 886-1383
Emp Here 14 *Sales* 10,224,830
SIC 5169 Chemicals and allied products, nec
Fredoon Khory
Esther Cheng

D-U-N-S 24-150-4062 (SL)
FRUIT OF THE LAND INC
1 Promenade Cir, Thornhill, ON, L4J 4P8
(905) 761-9611
Emp Here 20 *Sales* 10,702,480
SIC 5141 Groceries, general line
Michael Kurtz
Stacey Kurtz

D-U-N-S 20-911-3625 (SL)
GOODLAD, JOHN P. SALES INC
CANADIAN TIRE STORE 321
8081 Dufferin St, Thornhill, ON, L4J 8R9
(905) 889-7455
Emp Here 96 *Sales* 25,694,592
SIC 5251 Hardware stores
John P. Goodlad
Bonnie Goodlad

D-U-N-S 24-169-7106 (SL)
HOMELIFE FRONTIER REALTY INC
7620 Yonge St Suite 400, Thornhill, ON, L4J 1V9
(416) 218-8800
Emp Here 50 *Sales* 16,356,350
SIC 6531 Real estate agents and managers
Frank Yu

D-U-N-S 20-081-9634 (BR)
J.F. & L. RESTAURANTS LIMITED
PICKLE BARREL RESTAURANT
(*Suby of* J.F. & L. RESTAURANTS LIMITED)
1 Promenade Cir, Thornhill, ON, L4J 4P8

Emp Here 100
SIC 5812 Eating places
Dina Naghaway

D-U-N-S 20-395-1356 (SL)
LYY LIFE INC
147 Ner Israel Dr, Thornhill, ON, L4J 8Z7
(647) 673-8888
Emp Here 102 *Sales* 6,979,044
SIC 8322 Individual and family services
Ming Liu

D-U-N-S 25-251-6588 (SL)
NEWTON, ALAN REAL ESTATE LTD
370 Steeles Ave W Suite 102, Thornhill, ON, L4J 6X1
(905) 764-7200
Emp Here 60 *Sales* 16,305,360
SIC 6531 Real estate agents and managers
Alan Newton

D-U-N-S 20-524-8875 (SL)
NORTH YORK CHEVROLET OLDSMOBILE LTD
7200 Yonge St, Thornhill, ON, L4J 1V8
(905) 881-5000
Emp Here 150 *Sales* 94,392,000
SIC 5511 New and used car dealers
Michael Croxon
Derrick Gilpin
Jackey Robb

D-U-N-S 25-117-2342 (BR)
RE/MAX REALTRON REALTY INC
(*Suby of* RE/MAX REALTRON REALTY INC)
7646 Yonge St, Thornhill, ON, L4J 1V9
(416) 802-0707
Emp Here 85
SIC 6531 Real estate agents and managers
Susan Kruger

D-U-N-S 20-183-8141 (HQ)
ROY FOSS MOTORS LTD
CANSTEM LEASING SERVICES
7200 Yonge St Unit 1, Thornhill, ON, L4J 1V8
(905) 886-2000
Emp Here 117 *Sales* 126,995,440
SIC 5511 New and used car dealers
Roy Foss
John Thomas

D-U-N-S 24-319-5856 (HQ)
SISLEY MOTORS LIMITED
SISLEY FOR HONDA
88 Steeles Ave W, Thornhill, ON, L4J 1A1
(416) 223-3111
Sales 66,074,400
SIC 5511 New and used car dealers
Hugh Sisley

D-U-N-S 20-806-2609 (BR)
SOBEYS CAPITAL INCORPORATED
SOBEYS STORE 794

(*Suby of* EMPIRE COMPANY LIMITED)
9200 Bathurst St, Thornhill, ON, L4J 8W1
(905) 731-7600
Emp Here 100
SIC 5411 Grocery stores
Pina Sanone

D-U-N-S 20-549-4615 (HQ)
SUNRISE NORTH SENIOR LIVING LTD
(*Suby of* WELLTOWER INC.)
484 Steeles Ave W, Thornhill, ON, L4J 0C7
(905) 731-4300
Emp Here 6 *Sales* 17,468,640
SIC 8741 Management services
Rob Forrester
Mark Decosta

D-U-N-S 20-185-0810 (BR)
T & T SUPERMARKET INC
(*Suby of* LOBLAW COMPANIES LIMITED)
1 Promenade Cir, Thornhill, ON, L4J 4P8
(905) 763-8113
Emp Here 200
SIC 5411 Grocery stores
Gerald Way

D-U-N-S 20-850-7426 (SL)
THORNHILL GOLF & COUNTRY CLUB
7994 Yonge St, Thornhill, ON, L4J 1W3
(905) 881-3000
Emp Here 120 *Sales* 9,425,400
SIC 7997 Membership sports and recreation clubs
Matthew Budco

D-U-N-S 24-218-9140 (SL)
TORONTO SMART CARS LTD
NORTH YORK CHRYSLER JEEP DODGE
7200 Yonge St Suite 1, Thornhill, ON, L4J 1V8
(905) 762-1020
Emp Here 60 *Sales* 37,756,800
SIC 5511 New and used car dealers
Massoud (Tom) Jamali

D-U-N-S 25-664-4840 (SL)
TRANSGLOBAL FINE CARS LTD
BMW AUTOHAUS
480 Steeles Ave W, Thornhill, ON, L4J 1A2
(905) 886-3380
Emp Here 30 *Sales* 14,942,340
SIC 5511 New and used car dealers
Pauline Chuang

D-U-N-S 24-779-5636 (SL)
TRANSOCEANIC FINE CARS LTD
VOLVO VILLA
220 Steeles Ave W, Thornhill, ON, L4J 1A1
(905) 886-8800
Emp Here 50 *Sales* 24,903,900
SIC 5511 New and used car dealers
Sylvester Chuang

D-U-N-S 20-184-2205 (SL)
TRANSWORLD FINE CARS LTD
VOLKSWAGEN VILLA
222 Steeles Ave W, Thornhill, ON, L4J 1A1
(905) 886-6880
Emp Here 35 *Sales* 17,432,730
SIC 5511 New and used car dealers
Sylvester Chuang
Pauline Chuang

D-U-N-S 24-412-6389 (HQ)
TRUE NORTH IMAGING INC
REPRODUCTIVE IMAGING
7330 Yonge St Suite 120, Thornhill, ON, L4J 7Y7
(905) 889-5926
Emp Here 8 *Sales* 11,707,200
SIC 8071 Medical laboratories
Gerald Hartman
Alex Hartman

D-U-N-S 20-389-9847 (HQ)
VAUNTEK HOLDINGS INC.
8707 Dufferin St Suite 10, Thornhill, ON, L4J 0A6

Sales 10,462,120
SIC 6712 Bank holding companies
Ron Kleiner

D-U-N-S 24-728-9101 (SL)
WILLOWDALE NISSAN LTD
7200 Yonge St Suite 881, Thornhill, ON, L4J 1V8
(905) 881-3900
Emp Here 60 *Sales* 37,756,800
SIC 5511 New and used car dealers
Hans Falkenberg

D-U-N-S 25-297-9430 (BR)
YORK REGION DISTRICT SCHOOL BOARD
VAUGHAN SECONDARY SCHOOL
(*Suby of* YORK REGION DISTRICT SCHOOL BOARD)
1401 Clark Ave W, Thornhill, ON, L4J 7R4
(905) 660-1397
Emp Here 120
SIC 8211 Elementary and secondary schools
Maria Maiato

D-U-N-S 25-197-7450 (SL)
YYZ TRAVEL SERVICES (INT'L) INC
CANADIAN GATEWAY
7851 Dufferin St Suite 100, Thornhill, ON, L4J 3M4
(905) 660-7000
Emp Here 40 *Sales* 20,798,680
SIC 4725 Tour operators
Vicky Zaltsman

Thorold, ON L2V

D-U-N-S 24-341-3858 (SL)
1729787 ONTARIO LIMITED
BIG RED MARKETS
133 Front St N Suite 1, Thorold, ON, L2V 0A3
(905) 227-2015
Emp Here 70 *Sales* 58,490,390
SIC 5144 Poultry and poultry products
John William Hessels

D-U-N-S 20-871-7343 (SL)
2023649 ONTARIO LIMITED
KE MARR SUPERMARKET
9 Pine St N, Thorold, ON, L2V 3Z9
(905) 227-0533
Emp Here 75 *Sales* 22,010,775
SIC 5411 Grocery stores
Todd Marr

D-U-N-S 24-764-2994 (SL)
581917 ONTARIO LIMITED
THOROLD AUTO PARTS & RECYCLERS
1108 Beaver Dam Rd, Thorold, ON, L2V 3Y7
(905) 227-4118
Emp Here 40 *Sales* 19,923,120
SIC 5531 Auto and home supply stores
Leonard Serravalle

D-U-N-S 24-736-5133 (SL)
633569 ONTARIO LIMITED
BIG RED MARKET
206 Richmond St, Thorold, ON, L2V 4L8
(905) 227-1575
Emp Here 60 *Sales* 50,134,620
SIC 5141 Groceries, general line
John Hessels
Daniel Timmins

D-U-N-S 24-989-0349 (SL)
BETHESDA COMMUNITY SERVICES INC
3280 Schmon Pky, Thorold, ON, L2V 4Y6
(905) 684-6918
Emp Here 49 *Sales* 11,114,817
SIC 8399 Social services, nec
Brian Davies

D-U-N-S 25-255-2989 (HQ)
BETHESDA HOME FOR THE MENTALLY HANDICAPPED INC
BETHESDA PROGRAMS

3280 Schmon Pky, Thorold, ON, L2V 4Y6
(905) 684-6918
Sales 103,534,000
SIC 8399 Social services, nec
Brian Davies

D-U-N-S 25-203-4244   (HQ)
BOOK DEPOT INC
67 Front St N, Thorold, ON, L2V 1X3
(905) 680-7230
Emp Here 50   *Sales* 117,831,800
SIC 5192 Books, periodicals, and newspapers
Valerie Tun
Bill Van Vliet

D-U-N-S 25-282-7993   (HQ)
BRAIN INJURY COMMUNITY RE-ENTRY (NIAGARA) INC
3340 Schmon Pkwy Unit 2, Thorold, ON, L2V 4Y6
(905) 687-6788
Emp Here 30   *Sales* 28,368,316
SIC 8399 Social services, nec
Nick Ostryhon
Sandra Harding
Frank Greco

D-U-N-S 24-920-3209   (HQ)
CAA NIAGARA
3271 Schmon Pky, Thorold, ON, L2V 4Y6
(905) 984-8585
Emp Here 30   *Sales* 215,790,150
SIC 8699 Membership organizations, nec
Pat Neilson
Doug Stones

D-U-N-S 24-386-1838   (BR)
EXTENDICARE (CANADA) INC
PARAMED HOME HEALTH CARE
(*Suby of* EXTENDICARE INC)
3550 Schmon Pky Suite 4, Thorold, ON, L2V 4Y6
(905) 685-6501
Emp Here 175
SIC 8049 Offices of health practitioner
Ken Cook

D-U-N-S 24-760-2571   (HQ)
GEORGIA-PACIFIC CANADA LP
(*Suby of* KOCH INDUSTRIES, INC.)
319 Allanburg Rd, Thorold, ON, L2V 5C3
(905) 451-0620
Emp Here 100   *Sales* 220,582,200
SIC 2679 Converted paper products, nec
Gerald Finlayson

D-U-N-S 20-157-2468   (SL)
HENDERSON'S PHARMACY LIMITED
HENDERSON'S PHARMASAVE
15 Front St S, Thorold, ON, L2V 1W8
(905) 227-2511
Emp Here 50   *Sales* 12,647,700
SIC 5912 Drug stores and proprietary stores

D-U-N-S 20-967-6535   (SL)
IAFRATE MACHINE WORKS LIMITED
(*Suby of* 707300 ONTARIO LIMITED)
1150 Beaverdams Rd, Thorold, ON, L2V 4T3
(905) 227-6141
Emp Here 74   *Sales* 14,214,290
SIC 3499 Fabricated Metal products, nec
Al Iafrate
Costantino Iafrate
Bruno Iafrate

D-U-N-S 24-773-2063   (SL)
LANDMARK HOME SOLUTIONS INC
3430 Schmon Pky, Thorold, ON, L2V 4Y6
(905) 646-8995
Emp Here 90   *Sales* 14,027,670
SIC 2431 Millwork
Steve Mason

D-U-N-S 24-420-2219   (SL)
RUSKCAST INC
110 Ormond St S, Thorold, ON, L2V 4J6
(905) 227-4011
Emp Here 18   *Sales* 18,006,102

SIC 5051 Metals service centers and offices
Jeffery Rusk
Robyn Rusk

D-U-N-S 20-147-9193   (HQ)
STOKES SEEDS LIMITED
296 Collier Rd S, Thorold, ON, L2V 5B6
(905) 688-4300
Emp Here 75   *Sales* 26,230,900
SIC 0181 Ornamental nursery products
John Gale

Thunder Bay, ON P7A

D-U-N-S 24-427-5590   (SL)
1548732 ONTARIO LIMITED
SHOPPERS DRUG MART
640 River St, Thunder Bay, ON, P7A 3S4
(807) 345-8012
Emp Here 50   *Sales* 12,647,700
SIC 5912 Drug stores and proprietary stores
Hannu Uurainen

D-U-N-S 25-304-5108   (SL)
CANADIAN MENTAL HEALTH ASSOCIA-TION, THUNDER BAY BRANCH
CMHA
200 Van Norman St, Thunder Bay, ON, P7A 4B8
(807) 345-5564
Emp Here 60   *Sales* 14,490,900
SIC 8621 Professional organizations
Maurice Fortin

D-U-N-S 24-775-4666   (BR)
CORPORATION OF THE CITY OF THUN-DER BAY, THE
DAWSON COURT HOME FOR THE AGED
(*Suby of* CORPORATION OF THE CITY OF THUNDER BAY, THE)
523 Algoma St N, Thunder Bay, ON, P7A 5C2

Emp Here 225
SIC 8361 Residential care
Don Holmstrom

D-U-N-S 24-333-1589   (BR)
METRO ONTARIO INC
METRO
(*Suby of* METRO INC)
640 River St, Thunder Bay, ON, P7A 3S4
(807) 345-8342
Emp Here 300
SIC 5411 Grocery stores
Brian Mcnamara

D-U-N-S 25-500-8237   (HQ)
OPTIONS NORTHWEST PERSONAL SUP-PORT SERVICES
95 Cumberland St N, Thunder Bay, ON, P7A 4M1
(807) 344-4994
Sales 54,873,020
SIC 8399 Social services, nec
Bernard Travis

D-U-N-S 20-948-1241   (SL)
PORT ARTHUR HEALTH CENTRE INC, THE
194 Court St N, Thunder Bay, ON, P7A 4V7
(807) 345-2332
Emp Here 75   *Sales* 12,048,450
SIC 8011 Offices and clinics of medical doc-tors
Allan Kirk

D-U-N-S 24-917-3022   (SL)
ROACH'S TAXI (1988) LTD
CALL ROACH'S YELLOW TAXI
216 Camelot St, Thunder Bay, ON, P7A 4B1
(807) 344-8481
Emp Here 100   *Sales* 5,487,200
SIC 4121 Taxicabs
Tim Cordone

D-U-N-S 24-039-7414   (BR)

SISTERS OF ST. JOSEPH OF SAULT STE. MARIE, THE
LAKEHEAD PSYCHIATRIC HOSPITAL
(*Suby of* SISTERS OF ST. JOSEPH OF SAULT STE. MARIE, THE)
580 Algoma St N, Thunder Bay, ON, P7A 8C5
(807) 343-4300
Emp Here 488
SIC 8063 Psychiatric hospitals
Kathy Sanderson

D-U-N-S 25-264-9983   (BR)
THUNDER BAY CATHOLIC DISTRICT SCHOOL BOARD
ST IGNATIUS HIGH SCHOOL
(*Suby of* THUNDER BAY CATHOLIC DIS-TRICT SCHOOL BOARD)
285 Gibson St, Thunder Bay, ON, P7A 2J6
(807) 344-8433
Emp Here 105
SIC 8211 Elementary and secondary schools
Pino Tassone

D-U-N-S 20-142-9263   (SL)
THUNDER BAY ELECTRONICS LIMITED
CHFD CHANNEL 4
87 Hill St N, Thunder Bay, ON, P7A 5V6
(807) 346-2600
Emp Here 150   *Sales* 34,270,800
SIC 4833 Television broadcasting stations
H Fraser Dougall
Elizabeth Dougall

D-U-N-S 20-116-1200   (SL)
THUNDER BAY HYDRO ELECTRICITY DIS-TRIBUTION INC
34 Cumberland St N Suite 101, Thunder Bay, ON, P7A 4L4
(807) 343-1111
Emp Here 150   *Sales* 101,981,100
SIC 4911 Electric services
Robert Mace
Cynthia (Cindy) Speziale
Manuel Derosa
Tim Wilson

Thunder Bay, ON P7B

D-U-N-S 25-502-6825   (SL)
1191460 ONTARIO INC
PERFORMANCE MOTORS
545 Thirteenth Ave, Thunder Bay, ON, P7B 7B4
(807) 345-2552
Emp Here 26   *Sales* 12,950,028
SIC 5511 New and used car dealers
Bruno Niederer

D-U-N-S 25-116-5049   (SL)
1204626 ONTARIO INC
MAKKINGA CONTRACTING & EQUIPMENT RENTAL
570 Squier Pl, Thunder Bay, ON, P7B 6M2
(807) 935-2792
Emp Here 50   *Sales* 11,008,400
SIC 1794 Excavation work
John Makkinga

D-U-N-S 24-172-8955   (SL)
1670747 ONTARIO INC
PETRO CANADA
720 Hewitson St, Thunder Bay, ON, P7B 5Z1
(807) 623-3996
Emp Here 12   *Sales* 12,393,696
SIC 5172 Petroleum products, nec
Joe Mastrangelo
Darlene Mastrangelo

D-U-N-S 20-044-6862   (SL)
539290 ONTARIO LTD
SMITH'S R V CENTRE
940 Cobalt Cres, Thunder Bay, ON, P7B 5W3
(807) 346-9399
Emp Here 30   *Sales* 14,942,340

SIC 5561 Recreational vehicle dealers
Scott Smith
Mary Smith

D-U-N-S 20-554-6414   (SL)
967003 ONTARIO LIMITED
581 Red River Rd, Thunder Bay, ON, P7B 1H4
(807) 344-6666
Emp Here 65   *Sales* 17,000,945
SIC 6712 Bank holding companies
Andrew Christie

D-U-N-S 20-944-9933   (SL)
APEX INVESTIGATION & SECURITY INC
391 Oliver Rd, Thunder Bay, ON, P7B 2G2
(807) 344-8491
Emp Here 200   *Sales* 5,250,000
SIC 7381 Detective and armored car services
Gary S. Boyer

D-U-N-S 24-032-1583   (BR)
ARAMARK CANADA LTD.
ARAMARK MANAGED SERVICES
(*Suby of* ARAMARK)
955 Oliver Rd, Thunder Bay, ON, P7B 5E1
(807) 343-8142
Emp Here 100
SIC 5812 Eating places
Liz Mckinnon

D-U-N-S 20-142-3225   (HQ)
ARNONE TRANSPORT LIMITED
300 Water St S, Thunder Bay, ON, P7B 6P6
(807) 345-1478
Emp Here 47   *Sales* 11,930,948
SIC 4213 Trucking, except local
Leonard Arnone

D-U-N-S 20-169-6072   (SL)
BADANAI MOTORS LTD
BADANAI CHEVROLET OLDSMOBILE CADILLAC
399 Memorial Ave, Thunder Bay, ON, P7B 3Y4
(807) 683-4900
Emp Here 60   *Sales* 37,756,800
SIC 5511 New and used car dealers
George Badanai

D-U-N-S 25-543-3740   (HQ)
BARRA HOLDINGS INC
SHOPPERS HOME HEALTH CARE
285 Memorial Ave, Thunder Bay, ON, P7B 6H4
(807) 345-6564
Emp Here 50   *Sales* 19,134,500
SIC 6712 Bank holding companies
James Crooks
Suzanne Crooks

D-U-N-S 20-142-3506   (HQ)
BENNETT'S BAKERY LIMITED
PERSIAN MAN
899 Tungsten St, Thunder Bay, ON, P7B 6H2
(807) 344-2931
Emp Here 12   *Sales* 30,080,772
SIC 5149 Groceries and related products, nec
Santino Nucci
Joseph Nucci
Danny Nucci

D-U-N-S 25-411-7856   (SL)
BOYER HOLDINGS INC
391 Oliver Rd, Thunder Bay, ON, P7B 2G2
(807) 344-8491
Emp Here 200   *Sales* 54,670,000
SIC 6712 Bank holding companies
Gary S Boyer

D-U-N-S 20-710-3219   (SL)
BRUNO'S CONTRACTING (THUNDER BAY) LIMITED
665 Hewitson St, Thunder Bay, ON, P7B 5V5
(807) 623-1855
Emp Here 200   *Sales* 50,488,400
SIC 1611 Highway and street construction
Bruno Digregorio
Silvio Digregorio
John Simperl

▲ Public Company   ■ Public Company Family Member   **HQ** Headquarters   **BR** Branch   **SL** Single Location

D-U-N-S 24-916-2405   (SL)
BUCHANAN SALES INC
BUCHANAN LUMBER SALES
1120 Premier Way, Thunder Bay, ON, P7B 0A3

Emp Here 40   *Sales* 20,821,680
SIC 5099 Durable goods, nec
Hal Brindley
Russell York

D-U-N-S 24-671-2975   (SL)
CANADIAN TIRE GAS BAR
943 Fort William Rd, Thunder Bay, ON, P7B 3A6
(807) 346-8070
Emp Here 25   *Sales* 12,451,950
SIC 5541 Gasoline service stations
Michael Medline

D-U-N-S 24-915-7942   (BR)
CANCER CARE ONTARIO
NORTHWESTERN ONTARIO REGIONAL CANCER CENTRE
(*Suby of* CANCER CARE ONTARIO)
980 Oliver Rd, Thunder Bay, ON, P7B 6V4
(807) 343-1610
Emp Here 150
SIC 8731 Commercial physical research
Andrea Docherty

D-U-N-S 25-357-7126   (HQ)
CHRISTIE, B. L. INVESTMENTS INC
LOWERYS BASICS
581 Red River Rd, Thunder Bay, ON, P7B 1H4
(807) 344-6666
Emp Here 1   *Sales* 15,881,320
SIC 5943 Stationery stores
Brian Christie
Scott Christie
Kim Christie
Shawn Christie
Andrew Christie

D-U-N-S 20-374-9304   (SL)
CHRONICLE JOURNAL, THE
75 Cumberland St S, Thunder Bay, ON, P7B 1A3
(807) 343-6200
Emp Here 70   *Sales* 11,481,890
SIC 2711 Newspapers
Clinton Harris

D-U-N-S 25-611-9074   (HQ)
CONTACT NORTH/CONTACT NORD
1139 Alloy Dr Suite 104, Thunder Bay, ON, P7B 6M8
(807) 344-1616
Emp Here 40   *Sales* 48,244,000
SIC 8742 Management consulting services
Maxim Jean-Louis
Debby Sefton
Alan Spacek

D-U-N-S 25-612-7184   (BR)
CORPORATION OF THE CITY OF THUNDER BAY, THE
TBAY TEL MOBILITY
(*Suby of* CORPORATION OF THE CITY OF THUNDER BAY, THE)
1046 Lithium Dr, Thunder Bay, ON, P7B 6G3
(807) 623-4400
Emp Here 400
SIC 4899 Communication services, nec
Kevin Burns

D-U-N-S 24-818-9698   (HQ)
CROOKS, J R HEALTH CARE SERVICES INC
SHOPPERS HOME HEALTH CARE
(*Suby of* BARRA HOLDINGS INC)
285 Memorial Ave, Thunder Bay, ON, P7B 6H4
(807) 345-6564
Emp Here 48   *Sales* 16,614,304
SIC 5999 Miscellaneous retail stores, nec
Jim Crooks
Suzanne Crooks

D-U-N-S 20-142-4611   (SL)
DINGWELL'S MACHINERY AND SUPPLY LIMITED
963 Alloy Dr, Thunder Bay, ON, P7B 5Z8
(807) 623-4477
Emp Here 65   *Sales* 12,485,525
SIC 3499 Fabricated Metal products, nec
Rob Bell
Frank Marini

D-U-N-S 20-048-9607   (SL)
DOMINION MOTORS (THUNDER BAY-1984) LTD
882 Copper Cres, Thunder Bay, ON, P7B 6C9
(807) 343-2277
Emp Here 55   *Sales* 34,610,400
SIC 5511 New and used car dealers
John Dolcetti

D-U-N-S 25-358-2886   (HQ)
DST CONSULTING ENGINEERS INC
605 Hewitson St, Thunder Bay, ON, P7B 5V5
(807) 623-2929
Emp Here 120   *Sales* 30,564,369
SIC 8711 Engineering services
Mike Fabius

D-U-N-S 20-758-3725   (HQ)
EQUIPMENT WORLD INC
988 Alloy Dr, Thunder Bay, ON, P7B 6A5
(807) 623-9561
Emp Here 37   *Sales* 29,926,638
SIC 5084 Industrial machinery and equipment
Peter Knudsen
Lyle Knudsen

D-U-N-S 20-245-7318   (BR)
GATEWAY CASINOS & ENTERTAINMENT LIMITED
GATEWAY CASINO THUNDER BAY
(*Suby of* GATEWAY CASINOS & ENTERTAINMENT LIMITED)
50 Cumberland St S, Thunder Bay, ON, P7B 5L4
(877) 656-4263
Emp Here 300
SIC 7999 Amusement and recreation, nec
Jordi Psikla

D-U-N-S 24-512-8520   (SL)
GRANT THORTON
979 Alloy Dr Suite 300, Thunder Bay, ON, P7B 5Z8
(807) 346-7302
Emp Here 49   *Sales* 10,245,165
SIC 8721 Accounting, auditing, and bookkeeping
Tom Boyle

D-U-N-S 20-556-0688   (BR)
HOME DEPOT OF CANADA INC
HOME DEPOT
(*Suby of* THE HOME DEPOT INC)
359 Main St, Thunder Bay, ON, P7B 5L6
(807) 624-1100
Emp Here 175
SIC 5251 Hardware stores
Win Budden

D-U-N-S 24-631-0221   (HQ)
HOOD LOGGING EQUIPMENT CANADA INCORPORATED
Gd Stn Csc, Thunder Bay, ON, P7B 5E6
(807) 939-2641
Emp Here 35   *Sales* 18,050,988
SIC 5082 Construction and mining machinery
Bruce Hynnes
Beverley Hynnes

D-U-N-S 20-142-5865   (SL)
INTERCITY INDUSTRIAL SUPPLY LIMITED
(*Suby of* DESCOURS ET CABAUD SA)
669 Squier St, Thunder Bay, ON, P7B 4A7
(807) 345-2324
Emp Here 26   *Sales* 12,350,676
SIC 5085 Industrial supplies
Craig Urquhart

Neil Gillingham

D-U-N-S 24-851-3293   (HQ)
IRON RANGE BUS LINES INC
1141 Golf Links Rd, Thunder Bay, ON, P7B 7A3
(807) 345-7387
Sales 18,818,000
SIC 4142 Bus charter service, except local
Jason Logozzo

D-U-N-S 20-104-8753   (SL)
JONES, TOM CORPORATION
560 Squier St, Thunder Bay, ON, P7B 4A8
(807) 345-0511
Emp Here 50   *Sales* 23,536,550
SIC 1542 Nonresidential construction, nec
Tom Jones Sr

D-U-N-S 24-427-0658   (BR)
KEG RESTAURANTS LTD
KEG STEAKHOUSE & BAR, THE
(*Suby of* RECIPE UNLIMITED CORPORATION)
735 Hewitson St, Thunder Bay, ON, P7B 6B5
(807) 623-1960
Emp Here 100
SIC 5812 Eating places
Bob Stewart

D-U-N-S 25-238-1231   (BR)
LAKEHEAD DISTRICT SCHOOL BOARD
HAMMARSKJOLD HIGH SCHOOL
80 Clarkson St S, Thunder Bay, ON, P7B 4W8
(807) 767-1631
Emp Here 155
SIC 8211 Elementary and secondary schools
Charles Bishop

D-U-N-S 20-591-7383   (BR)
LAKEHEAD DISTRICT SCHOOL BOARD
ECOLE GRON MORGAN PUBLIC SCHOOL
174 Marlborough St, Thunder Bay, ON, P7B 4G4
(807) 345-1468
Emp Here 85
SIC 8211 Elementary and secondary schools
Carolyn Carlson

D-U-N-S 20-167-5787   (HQ)
LAKEHEAD MOTORS LIMITED, THE
951 Memorial Ave, Thunder Bay, ON, P7B 4A1
(807) 344-0584
Emp Here 75   *Sales* 47,196,000
SIC 5521 Used car dealers
Michael Comuzzi

D-U-N-S 20-073-7927   (BR)
LAKEHEAD UNIVERSITY
(*Suby of* LAKEHEAD UNIVERSITY)
955 Oliver Rd Suite 2008, Thunder Bay, ON, P7B 5E1
(807) 343-8500
Emp Here 2,000
SIC 8221 Colleges and universities
Frederick Gilbert

D-U-N-S 20-948-3064   (HQ)
LAKEHEAD UNIVERSITY
955 Oliver Rd, Thunder Bay, ON, P7B 5E1
(807) 343-8110
Emp Here 1,000   *Sales* 133,703,717
SIC 8221 Colleges and universities
Michael Pawlowski
Rita Blais
Kevin Cleghorn
Colin Bruce
Brian Stevenson

D-U-N-S 25-834-9547   (SL)
LAKEHEAD UNIVERSITY STUDENT UNION
OUTPOST, THE
955 Oliver Rd, Thunder Bay, ON, P7B 5E1
(807) 343-8500
Emp Here 80   *Sales* 3,641,520
SIC 5812 Eating places
Kerri Law

D-U-N-S 25-270-1503   (BR)
LOBLAWS INC
REAL CANADIAN SUPERSTORE 1504
(*Suby of* LOBLAW COMPANIES LIMITED)
600 Harbour Expy, Thunder Bay, ON, P7B 6P4
(807) 343-4500
Emp Here 300
SIC 5411 Grocery stores
Kyle Lavalee

D-U-N-S 20-142-6772   (HQ)
LOWERYS, LIMITED
LOWERYS BASICS
(*Suby of* CHRISTIE, B. L. INVESTMENTS INC)
540 Central Ave, Thunder Bay, ON, P7B 6B4
(807) 344-6666
Emp Here 38   *Sales* 15,881,320
SIC 5943 Stationery stores
Brian L Christie
Kim Christie
Andrew Christie
Shawn Christie

D-U-N-S 24-039-1821   (SL)
MAROSTICA MOTORS LIMITED
1142 Alloy Dr, Thunder Bay, ON, P7B 6M9
(807) 346-5809
Emp Here 50   *Sales* 24,903,900
SIC 5511 New and used car dealers
Ronald Marostica

D-U-N-S 20-142-7218   (HQ)
MCKEVITT TRUCKING LIMITED
(*Suby of* MO-ANN HOLDINGS LTD)
1200 Carrick St, Thunder Bay, ON, P7B 5P9
(807) 623-0054
Emp Here 140   *Sales* 32,912,960
SIC 4213 Trucking, except local
John Mckevitt Sr
Shirley Mckevitt

D-U-N-S 24-203-1149   (SL)
METALS CREEK RESOURCES CORP
945 Cobalt Cres, Thunder Bay, ON, P7B 5Z4
(807) 345-4990
Emp Here 50   *Sales* 12,309,300
SIC 1799 Special trade contractors, nec
Alexander Stares
Michael Macisaac
Wayne Reid
Nikolaos S. Tsimidis
Michael Stares
Malvin Spooner
Pat Mohan
Lorne Woods

D-U-N-S 24-617-0950   (HQ)
MGM ELECTRIC LIMITED
724 Macdonell St, Thunder Bay, ON, P7B 4A6
(807) 345-7767
Emp Here 24   *Sales* 11,626,524
SIC 5063 Electrical apparatus and equipment
Terence Mcdonald
Douglas Chadwick
Edward Fukishima

D-U-N-S 20-126-8260   (SL)
NEARING, ROBERT C. HOLDINGS INC
CANADIAN TIRE INTER CITY
939 Fort William Rd Suite 83, Thunder Bay, ON, P7B 3A6
(807) 623-1999
Emp Here 50   *Sales* 18,210,750
SIC 5015 Motor vehicle parts, used
Robert C Nearing

D-U-N-S 20-289-7174   (HQ)
NORTHERN DIABETES HEALTH NETWORK INC
1204 Roland St Unit A, Thunder Bay, ON, P7B 5M4
(807) 624-1720
Emp Here 1   *Sales* 10,730,178
SIC 8699 Membership organizations, nec
Susan Griffis

▲ Public Company   ■ Public Company Family Member   **HQ** Headquarters   **BR** Branch   **SL** Single Location

D-U-N-S 20-635-7761   (HQ)
NORTHERN ONTARIO SCHOOL OF MEDICINE
955 Oliver Rd Suite 2005, Thunder Bay, ON, P7B 5E1
(807) 766-7300
Emp Here 90   *Sales* 19,994,400
SIC 8062 General medical and surgical hospitals
  Roger Strasser
  Dorothy Wright

D-U-N-S 24-376-3224   (SL)
NORTHERN SAWMILLS INC
NORTHERN WOOD
490 Maureen St, Thunder Bay, ON, P7B 6T2

Emp Here 300   *Sales* 83,517,000
SIC 2491 Wood preserving
  Wolf Gericke
  Harry Mercer
  John Twigg

D-U-N-S 24-266-8630   (SL)
ORCHARD, VALI PHARMACY INC
SHOPPERS DRUG MART
1186 Memorial Ave Unit 1, Thunder Bay, ON, P7B 5K5
(807) 623-3601
Emp Here 60   *Sales* 14,659,680
SIC 5912 Drug stores and proprietary stores
  Vali Orchard
  Larry Gislason

D-U-N-S 24-915-7066   (SL)
P & A MANAGEMENT LTD
MANPOWER
1205 Amber Dr Unit 106, Thunder Bay, ON, P7B 6M4
(807) 346-8367
Emp Here 100   *Sales* 15,537,100
SIC 7363 Help supply services
  Florentine Bahlieda

D-U-N-S 20-436-0440   (SL)
PINEWOOD FORD LIMITED
(*Suby of* 169749 CANADA LTD)
640 Memorial Ave, Thunder Bay, ON, P7B 3Z5
(807) 344-9611
Emp Here 75   *Sales* 47,196,000
SIC 5511 New and used car dealers
  Darryl Burton

D-U-N-S 25-353-2535   (SL)
PIONEER RIDGE HOME FOR THE AGED
750 Tungsten St, Thunder Bay, ON, P7B 6R1
(807) 684-3910
Emp Here 80   *Sales* 4,739,760
SIC 8361 Residential care
  Greg Alexander

D-U-N-S 24-327-6008   (HQ)
PREMIER GOLD MINES LIMITED
1100 Russell St Suite 200, Thunder Bay, ON, P7B 5N2
(807) 346-1390
Emp Here 50   *Sales* 204,294,896
SIC 1481 NonMetallic mineral services
  Ewan Downie
  John Begeman
  Stephen Mcgibbon
  Charlie Ronkos
  Brent Kristof
  Kerri Chaboyer-Jean
  Matthew Gollat
  Steve Filipovic
  Tony Makuch
  Ron Little

D-U-N-S 20-433-8115   (HQ)
R.C. MOFFATT SUPPLY LIMITED
MOFFATT SUPPLY & SPECIALTIES
1135 Russell St, Thunder Bay, ON, P7B 5M6
(807) 626-0040
Emp Here 8   *Sales* 28,501,560
SIC 5082 Construction and mining machinery
  David Perry

D-U-N-S 20-048-2656   (SL)
RE/MAX FIRST CHOICE REALTY LTD
846 Macdonell St, Thunder Bay, ON, P7B 5J1
(807) 344-5700
Emp Here 32   *Sales* 10,468,064
SIC 6531 Real estate agents and managers
  Mario Tegola

D-U-N-S 24-718-1308   (SL)
RENCO FOODS LTD
161 Court St S, Thunder Bay, ON, P7B 2X7
(807) 345-3947
Emp Here 41   *Sales* 11,240,232
SIC 5411 Grocery stores
  Rocco Larizza
  Naz Larizza

D-U-N-S 24-231-9622   (SL)
SPORTOP MARKETING INC
(*Suby of* OASIS ORIGINALS INC)
875 Tungsten St Unit C, Thunder Bay, ON, P7B 6H2
(807) 346-5400
Emp Here 25   *Sales* 18,563,000
SIC 5199 Nondurable goods, nec
  Gary Littlefield
  Derek Geddes

D-U-N-S 20-832-8997   (HQ)
SUPERIOR SAFETY INC
782 Macdonell St, Thunder Bay, ON, P7B 4A6
(807) 344-3473
Emp Here 36   *Sales* 44,246,070
SIC 5099 Durable goods, nec
  Douglas Coppin
  Susan Coppin

D-U-N-S 24-757-0013   (BR)
TETRA TECH CANADA INC
(*Suby of* TETRA TECH, INC.)
725 Hewitson St, Thunder Bay, ON, P7B 6B5
(807) 345-5453
Emp Here 78
SIC 8711 Engineering services
  Shayne Smith

D-U-N-S 24-775-4740   (HQ)
THUNDER BAY DISTRICT HEALTH UNIT
999 Balmoral St, Thunder Bay, ON, P7B 6E7
(807) 625-5900
Emp Here 175   *Sales* 46,822,200
SIC 8621 Professional organizations
  Maria Harding
  David Williams

D-U-N-S 25-674-5712   (SL)
THUNDER BAY MARINE SERVICES (1998) LTD
100 Main St Suite 600, Thunder Bay, ON, P7B 6R9
(807) 344-9221
Emp Here 30   *Sales* 12,580,650
SIC 6712 Bank holding companies
  Sharon Dawson

D-U-N-S 25-054-5480   (HQ)
THUNDER BAY REGIONAL HEALTH SCIENCES CENTRE
NORTHERN SUPPLY CHAIN
980 Oliver Rd Rm 1480, Thunder Bay, ON, P7B 6V4
(807) 684-6500
Sales 298,188,262
SIC 8062 General medical and surgical hospitals
  Jean Bartkowiak
  Rhonda Ellacott
  Mark Henderson
  Steven Kennedy
  Rod Morrison
  Roxanne Deslauriers
  Cathy Covino
  Tracie Smith
  Janet Northan
  Peter Myllymaa

D-U-N-S 24-502-5015   (SL)
TIM HORTONS

1127 Oliver Rd, Thunder Bay, ON, P7B 7A4
(807) 344-0880
Emp Here 40   *Sales* 10,966,080
SIC 5461 Retail bakeries
  Kevin Matson

D-U-N-S 20-142-9479   (SL)
TWIN CITY REFRESHMENTS LIMITED
637 Squier St, Thunder Bay, ON, P7B 4A7
(807) 344-8651
Emp Here 25   *Sales* 16,411,600
SIC 5963 Direct selling establishments
  Allan Miahalcin

D-U-N-S 20-921-0629   (BR)
VON CANADA FOUNDATION
VICTORIAN ORDER OF NURSES
214 Red River Rd Suite 200, Thunder Bay, ON, P7B 1A6
(807) 344-0012
Emp Here 100
SIC 8082 Home health care services
  Jone Wekner

D-U-N-S 25-294-8617   (BR)
WAL-MART CANADA CORP
(*Suby of* WALMART INC.)
777 Memorial Ave, Thunder Bay, ON, P7B 6S2
(807) 346-9441
Emp Here 400
SIC 5311 Department stores
  Ryan Colanago

D-U-N-S 24-851-3371   (BR)
WSP CANADA INC
GENIVAR
(*Suby of* AST TRUST COMPANY (CANADA))
1269 Premier Way, Thunder Bay, ON, P7B 0A3
(807) 625-6700
Emp Here 140
SIC 8711 Engineering services
  Johnn Bradika

Thunder Bay, ON P7C

D-U-N-S 24-913-6797   (BR)
BOMBARDIER TRANSPORTATION CANADA INC
BOMBARIDER TRANSPORT
(*Suby of* BOMBARDIER INC)
1001 Montreal St, Thunder Bay, ON, P7C 4V6
(807) 475-2810
Emp Here 650
SIC 3743 Railroad equipment
  Andre Navarri

D-U-N-S 20-836-0099   (HQ)
CONFEDERATION COLLEGE OF APPLIED ARTS AND TECHNOLOGY, THE
CONFEDERATION COLLEGE
1450 Nakina Dr, Thunder Bay, ON, P7C 4W1
(807) 475-6110
Emp Here 700   *Sales* 54,263,958
SIC 8222 Junior colleges
  Jim Madder
  Bob Backstrom
  Gwen Dubois
  Don Campbelli
  Marilyn Gouthro
  Dick O'donnell

D-U-N-S 24-819-9580   (HQ)
COURTESY FREIGHT SYSTEMS LTD
(*Suby of* MULLEN GROUP LTD)
340 Simpson St, Thunder Bay, ON, P7C 3H7
(807) 623-3278
Sales 13,337,280
SIC 4231 Trucking terminal facilities
  Aody Dorby

D-U-N-S 24-967-8780   (SL)
GRANDVIEW LODGE HOME FOR THE AGED

200 Lillie St N, Thunder Bay, ON, P7C 5Y2

Emp Here 250   *Sales* 16,070,500
SIC 8361 Residential care
  Don Holmstrom

D-U-N-S 25-026-6293   (BR)
LAKEHEAD DISTRICT SCHOOL BOARD
SIR WINSTON CHURCHILL C. & V.I.
130 Churchill Dr W, Thunder Bay, ON, P7C 1V5

Emp Here 100
SIC 8211 Elementary and secondary schools
  Art Warwick

D-U-N-S 20-050-4694   (HQ)
LOUDON BROS. LIMITED
830a Athabasca St, Thunder Bay, ON, P7C 3E6
(807) 623-5458
Sales 30,443,320
SIC 5194 Tobacco and tobacco products
  Patrick Gleeson
  Peter Gleeson

D-U-N-S 24-915-3508   (SL)
PEROGY - POLISH HALL
818 Spring St, Thunder Bay, ON, P7C 3L6

Emp Here 49   *Sales* 19,473,286
SIC 8699 Membership organizations, nec
  Jan Slis

D-U-N-S 24-037-1211   (SL)
PHILPOT & DELGATY LTD
800 Victoria Ave E, Thunder Bay, ON, P7C 0A2
(807) 623-9022
Emp Here 22   *Sales* 12,758,328
SIC 6411 Insurance agents, brokers, and service
  William Covello
  Pauline Mascarin

D-U-N-S 24-242-1761   (BR)
SAFETY NET SECURITY LTD
(*Suby of* SAFETY NET SECURITY LTD)
857 May St N, Thunder Bay, ON, P7C 3S2
(807) 623-1844
Emp Here 100
SIC 5065 Electronic parts and equipment, nec
  Peter Corrado

D-U-N-S 24-819-0217   (HQ)
THUNDER BAY CATHOLIC DISTRICT SCHOOL BOARD
459 Victoria Ave W, Thunder Bay, ON, P7C 0A4
(807) 625-1555
Emp Here 67   *Sales* 97,241,305
SIC 8211 Elementary and secondary schools
  John De Faveri
  Tom Mustapic
  David Fulton
  Bob Hupka
  Tony Romeo
  Eleanor Ashe
  Doug Demeo
  Phil Colosimo
  Kathy O'brien
  Philip Pelletier

D-U-N-S 24-655-9850   (SL)
VENSHORE MECHANICAL LTD
1019 Northern Ave, Thunder Bay, ON, P7C 5L6
(807) 623-6414
Emp Here 50   *Sales* 11,653,250
SIC 1711 Plumbing, heating, air-conditioning
  John Jurcik
  James Moshonsky
  Michael Fodchuck
  Timothy Stevens
  Richard Jedruch
  Wayne Fossum

D-U-N-S 24-375-5451   (HQ)

WESTERN STAR SALES THUNDER BAY LTD
BOYER TRUCK SALES
3150 Arthur St W, Thunder Bay, ON, P7C 4V1
(807) 939-2537
Emp Here 30   *Sales* 16,934,652
SIC 5511 New and used car dealers
 Lionel Boyer
 Darryl Boyer

Thunder Bay, ON P7E

D-U-N-S 24-423-1143   (SL)
1796640 ONTARIO LIMITED
CAN-OP
(*Suby of* BCP IV UK FUEL HOLDINGS II LIMITED)
920 Commerce St, Thunder Bay, ON, P7E 6E9
(807) 475-9555
Emp Here 15   *Sales* 18,858,015
SIC 5172 Petroleum products, nec
 David Clara
 Terry Redden
 Robert Macminn

D-U-N-S 24-426-7944   (BR)
BEARSKIN LAKE AIR SERVICE LP
BEARSKIN AIRLINES
(*Suby of* EXCHANGE INCOME CORPORATION)
216 Round Blvd Suite 2, Thunder Bay, ON, P7E 3N9
(807) 475-0006
Emp Here 160
SIC 4512 Air transportation, scheduled
 Cliff Friesen

D-U-N-S 24-826-3381   (HQ)
BEARSKIN LAKE AIR SERVICE LP
BEARSKIN AIRLINES
(*Suby of* EXCHANGE INCOME CORPORATION)
1475 Walsh St W, Thunder Bay, ON, P7E 4X6
(807) 577-1141
Emp Here 100   *Sales* 53,395,600
SIC 4512 Air transportation, scheduled
 Brad Martin

D-U-N-S 25-542-4673   (SL)
CENTRAL CANADA FUELS & LUBRICANTS INC
910 Commerce St, Thunder Bay, ON, P7E 6E9
(807) 475-4259
Emp Here 20   *Sales* 20,656,160
SIC 5172 Petroleum products, nec
 Bob Gill
 Bob Macminn

D-U-N-S 24-172-1810   (HQ)
CLARA INDUSTRIAL SERVICES LIMITED
1130 Commerce St, Thunder Bay, ON, P7E 6E9
(807) 475-4608
Emp Here 30   *Sales* 11,847,290
SIC 1721 Painting and paper hanging
 David Clara
 Daniele Clara
 Mark Clara
 Terry Redden

D-U-N-S 24-852-4399   (SL)
EXCALIBUR MOTORCYCLE WORKS LIMITED
1425 Walsh St W, Thunder Bay, ON, P7E 4X6
(807) 622-0007
Emp Here 25   *Sales* 12,451,950
SIC 5571 Motorcycle dealers

D-U-N-S 24-916-4104   (SL)
FINN WAY GENERAL CONTRACTOR INC
1301 Walsh St W, Thunder Bay, ON, P7E 4X6
(807) 767-2426
Emp Here 35   *Sales* 16,475,585

SIC 1542 Nonresidential construction, nec
 David K Karimi
 Nancy N Karimi

D-U-N-S 20-694-9526   (SL)
GRID LINK CORP
1499 Rosslyn Rd, Thunder Bay, ON, P7E 6W1
(807) 683-0350
Emp Here 70   *Sales* 15,248,030
SIC 1731 Electrical work
 Jody Bernst
 Neal Stubbs

D-U-N-S 24-851-8060   (SL)
GRK CANADA LIMITED
GRK FASTENERS
(*Suby of* ITW CANADA INC)
1499 Rosslyn Rd, Thunder Bay, ON, P7E 6W1
(807) 474-4300
Emp Here 36   *Sales* 17,100,936
SIC 5085 Industrial supplies
 Mark Ristow
 Mary Ann Spiegel

D-U-N-S 24-427-9097   (SL)
KAPOOR, VINAY DRUGS LTD
SHOPPERS DRUG MART
900 Arthur St E, Thunder Bay, ON, P7E 5M8
(807) 623-2390
Emp Here 40   *Sales* 10,118,160
SIC 5912 Drug stores and proprietary stores
 Vinay Kapoor

D-U-N-S 24-915-0046   (SL)
MAINTAIR AVIATION SERVICES LTD
316 Hector Dougall Way, Thunder Bay, ON, P7E 6M6
(807) 475-5915
Emp Here 50   *Sales* 62,860,050
SIC 5172 Petroleum products, nec
 Brock Marshall
 Gail Marshall

D-U-N-S 24-333-1597   (BR)
METRO ONTARIO INC
(*Suby of* METRO INC)
505 Arthur St W, Thunder Bay, ON, P7E 5R5
(807) 475-0276
Emp Here 250
SIC 5411 Grocery stores
 Serge Sylestre

D-U-N-S 24-333-1605   (BR)
METRO ONTARIO INC
METRO (SUPERMARKETS)
(*Suby of* METRO INC)
1101 Arthur St W, Thunder Bay, ON, P7E 5S2
(807) 577-3910
Emp Here 100
SIC 5411 Grocery stores
 Chris Sorel

D-U-N-S 20-281-5460   (SL)
MOVATI ATHLETIC (THUNDER BAY) INC.
1185 Arthur St W, Thunder Bay, ON, P7E 6E2
(807) 623-6223
Emp Here 75   *Sales* 5,729,775
SIC 7991 Physical fitness facilities
 Chuck Kelly
 Dan Pompilii

D-U-N-S 24-774-8536   (SL)
NORTH AMERICAN KILN SERVICES INC
960 Walsh St W, Thunder Bay, ON, P7E 4X4
(807) 622-7728
Emp Here 50   *Sales* 12,044,200
SIC 1629 Heavy construction, nec
 Richard Posehn
 Susan Posehn

D-U-N-S 20-967-4246   (SL)
NORTHERN OASIS MARKETING & DIRECT SALES
701 Montreal St, Thunder Bay, ON, P7E 3P2
(807) 623-5249
Emp Here 30   *Sales* 14,250,780
SIC 5085 Industrial supplies
 Paul Currie

D-U-N-S 24-585-2855   (SL)
PERHOL CONSTRUCTION LTD
1450 Rosslyn Rd, Thunder Bay, ON, P7E 6W1
(807) 474-0930
Emp Here 30   *Sales* 14,121,930
SIC 1542 Nonresidential construction, nec
 Jim Hollinsworth

D-U-N-S 24-348-7118   (BR)
PF RESOLU CANADA INC
(*Suby of* RESOLUTE FOREST PRODUCTS INC)
2001 Neebing Ave, Thunder Bay, ON, P7E 6S3
(807) 475-2110
Emp Here 216
SIC 2421 Sawmills and planing mills, general
 Maxime Langlais

D-U-N-S 24-208-9899   (BR)
PF RESOLU CANADA INC
RESOLUTE FORCE PRODUCT
(*Suby of* RESOLUTE FOREST PRODUCTS INC)
2001 Neebing Ave, Thunder Bay, ON, P7E 6S3
(807) 475-2400
Emp Here 1,000
SIC 2621 Paper mills
 Remi Lalonee

D-U-N-S 24-749-3414   (SL)
QUALITY MARKET (THUNDER BAY) INC
146 Centennial Sq, Thunder Bay, ON, P7E 1H3

Emp Here 46   *Sales* 12,610,992
SIC 5411 Grocery stores
 David Stezenko
 Danny Stezenko

D-U-N-S 24-851-1966   (HQ)
R B D MARKETING INC
BUDGET RENT A CAR
230 Waterloo St S, Thunder Bay, ON, P7E 2C3
(807) 622-3366
Sales 11,332,000
SIC 7514 Passenger car rental
 Gerald Kirk
 David Currie

D-U-N-S 24-352-1429   (BR)
REVERA LONG TERM CARE INC
PINEWOOD COURT
(*Suby of* GOVERNMENT OF CANADA)
2625 Walsh St E Suite 1127, Thunder Bay, ON, P7E 2E5
(807) 577-1127
Emp Here 95
SIC 8361 Residential care
 Cheryl Grant

D-U-N-S 24-778-2803   (SL)
TARANIS CONTRACTING GROUP LTD
1473 Rosslyn Rd, Thunder Bay, ON, P7E 6W1
(807) 475-5443
Emp Here 100   *Sales* 25,244,200
SIC 1611 Highway and street construction
 Ryan Jones

D-U-N-S 25-219-9559   (HQ)
THUNDER AIRLINES LIMITED
310 Hector Dougall Way, Thunder Bay, ON, P7E 6M6
(807) 475-4211
Emp Here 65   *Sales* 24,028,020
SIC 4522 Air transportation, nonscheduled
 Kenneth (Ken) Bittle

D-U-N-S 25-224-9230   (BR)
THUNDER BAY CATHOLIC DISTRICT SCHOOL BOARD
ST PATRICK HIGH SCHOOL
(*Suby of* THUNDER BAY CATHOLIC DISTRICT SCHOOL BOARD)
621 Selkirk St S, Thunder Bay, ON, P7E 1T9

(807) 623-5218
Emp Here 150
SIC 8211 Elementary and secondary schools
 Francis Veneruz

D-U-N-S 24-607-7457   (SL)
THUNDER BAY FLIGHT REFUELING LIMITED
304 Hector Dougall Way, Thunder Bay, ON, P7E 6M6
(807) 577-1178
Emp Here 10   *Sales* 10,328,080
SIC 5172 Petroleum products, nec
 Gary Linger

D-U-N-S 24-547-0844   (SL)
THUNDER BAY HYDRAULICS LTD
TITAN WORLDWIDE MATERIALS HANDLING SOLUTIONS, DIV OF
701 Montreal St, Thunder Bay, ON, P7E 3P2
(807) 623-3151
Emp Here 30   *Sales* 14,250,780
SIC 5084 Industrial machinery and equipment
 Jay Currie
 Karl Currie
 Diane Currie

D-U-N-S 20-944-6202   (HQ)
THUNDER BAY TRUCK CENTRE INC
PETERBILT
(*Suby of* THUNDER BAY TRUCK CENTRE HOLDINGS INC)
1145 Commerce St, Thunder Bay, ON, P7E 6E8
(807) 577-5793
Emp Here 28   *Sales* 13,111,740
SIC 5012 Automobiles and other motor vehicles
 Carolyn Igo
 Theodore Kaemingh

D-U-N-S 25-099-0363   (SL)
WESTFORT FOODS INC
111 Frederica St E, Thunder Bay, ON, P7E 3V4
(807) 623-4220
Emp Here 40   *Sales* 10,966,080
SIC 5411 Grocery stores
 Bob Van Dyk
 Larry Rowthorn
 Robert Van Dyk

Thunder Bay, ON P7G

D-U-N-S 24-081-2834   (SL)
FISHER WAVY INC
1344 Oliver Rd, Thunder Bay, ON, P7G 1K4
(807) 345-5925
Emp Here 49   *Sales* 11,438,315
SIC 3273 Ready-mixed concrete

D-U-N-S 20-646-4294   (BR)
PIONEER CONSTRUCTION INC
(*Suby of* PIONEER CONSTRUCTION INC)
1344 Oliver Rd, Thunder Bay, ON, P7G 1K4
(807) 345-2338
Emp Here 100
SIC 1611 Highway and street construction
 Fred Hakala

Thunder Bay, ON P7J

D-U-N-S 20-049-1389   (SL)
LOCH LOMOND SKI AREA LIMITED
(*Suby of* 368770 ONTARIO LIMITED)
1800 Loch Lomond Rd, Thunder Bay, ON, P7J 1E9
(807) 475-7787
Emp Here 70   *Sales* 19,134,500
SIC 6712 Bank holding companies
 Ward Bond

▲ Public Company   ■ Public Company Family Member   **HQ** Headquarters   **BR** Branch   **SL** Single Location

Thunder Bay, ON P7K

D-U-N-S 24-426-6763   (BR)
COMPAGNIE DES CHEMINS DE FER NA-TIONAUX DU CANADA
C N
(Suby of COMPAGNIE DES CHEMINS DE FER NATIONAUX DU CANADA)
1825 Broadway Ave, Thunder Bay, ON, P7K 1M8

Emp Here 85
SIC 4011 Railroads, line-haul operating
Earl Taylor

D-U-N-S 25-673-7917   (SL)
LEVAERO AVIATION INC
2039 Derek Burney Dr, Thunder Bay, ON, P7K 0A1
(807) 475-5353
Emp Here 56   Sales 35,239,680
SIC 5599 Automotive dealers, nec
Robert Arnone
Steven Davey

D-U-N-S 20-210-2609   (SL)
STONE, BRUCE ENTERPRISES LTD
CANADIAN TIRE
1221 Arthur St W, Thunder Bay, ON, P7K 1A7
(807) 475-4235
Emp Here 115   Sales 23,614,445
SIC 5311 Department stores
Donald Bruce Stone
Linda Stone

Tilbury, ON N0P

D-U-N-S 24-624-8645   (HQ)
908593 ONTARIO LIMITED
EAGLE TRAVEL PLAZA
3613 Queen'S Line, Tilbury, ON, N0P 2L0
(519) 682-3235
Emp Here 23   Sales 24,405,822
SIC 5541 Gasoline service stations
Sarbjit Dhillon
Mandhir Dhillon

D-U-N-S 24-120-1230   (BR)
A.P. PLASMAN INC
A.P. PLASMAN INC.
(Suby of APP HOLDINGS LP)
24 Industrial Park Rd, Tilbury, ON, N0P 2L0
(519) 682-1155
Emp Here 120
SIC 7532 Top and body repair and paint shops
Mark Mateman

D-U-N-S 25-534-3741   (HQ)
AUTOLIV CANADA INC
(Suby of AUTOLIV, INC.)
20 Autoliv Dr, Tilbury, ON, N0P 2L0
(519) 682-1083
Emp Here 491   Sales 159,201,000
SIC 2394 Canvas and related products
Jan Carlson
Lars Westerberg

D-U-N-S 24-032-8216   (BR)
DIVERSICARE CANADA MANAGEMENT SERVICES CO., INC
TILBURY MANOR NURSING HOME
(Suby of DCMS HOLDINGS INC)
16 Fort St, Tilbury, ON, N0P 2L0
(519) 682-0243
Emp Here 84
SIC 8059 Nursing and personal care, nec
Jennifer Middleeton

D-U-N-S 20-007-1392   (SL)
DPM INSURANCE GROUP
31 Queen St N, Tilbury, ON, N0P 2L0

(519) 682-0202
Emp Here 42   Sales 35,618,520
SIC 6411 Insurance agents, brokers, and service
Robert Dillon

D-U-N-S 24-779-3201   (HQ)
IFS INTERNATIONAL FREIGHT SYSTEMS INC
18900 County Road 42 Rr 5, Tilbury, ON, N0P 2L0
(519) 682-3544
Emp Here 10   Sales 11,108,124
SIC 4213 Trucking, except local
Michael Donahue
Stephen Mcginty

D-U-N-S 24-564-6088   (SL)
K-TILBURY FOOD MARKET LTD
TILBURY FOOD MARKET
15 Queen St S, Tilbury, ON, N0P 2L0
(519) 682-3245
Emp Here 48   Sales 13,159,296
SIC 5411 Grocery stores
Merrick Mccall
Denise Mccall

D-U-N-S 24-339-2284   (SL)
KNECHTEL'S FOOD MARKET
TILBURY FOODLAND
15 Queen S, Tilbury, ON, N0P 2L0
(519) 682-3245
Emp Here 40   Sales 10,966,080
SIC 5411 Grocery stores
Merrick Mccall

D-U-N-S 24-385-2472   (SL)
LANOUE, ANDRE ORGANIZATION INC
85 Mill St W, Tilbury, ON, N0P 2L0
(519) 682-2424
Emp Here 40   Sales 19,923,120
SIC 5511 New and used car dealers
Craig Lanoue
Duane Lanoue

D-U-N-S 24-335-3070   (HQ)
MAHLE FILTER SYSTEMS CANADA, ULC
(Suby of M A H L E - S T I F T U N G GESELLSCHAFT MIT BESCHRANKTER HAFTUNG)
16 Industrial Park Rd, Tilbury, ON, N0P 2L0
(519) 682-0444
Emp Here 100   Sales 65,673,300
SIC 3089 Plastics products, nec
Jorg Stratmann
Michael Glowatzki

D-U-N-S 25-487-1767   (SL)
RALY AUTOMOTIVE GROUP LTD
TILBURY CHRYSLER
76 Mill St W, Tilbury, ON, N0P 2L0
(519) 682-3131
Emp Here 35   Sales 17,432,730
SIC 5511 New and used car dealers
Thomas Charles Mayhew

D-U-N-S 20-359-8552   (BR)
RS TECHNOLOGIES INC
RS COMPOSITE UTILITY POLES
(Suby of RS TECHNOLOGIES INC)
22 Industrial Park Rd, Tilbury, ON, N0P 2L0
(519) 682-1110
Emp Here 100
SIC 2499 Wood products, nec
Domenic Varacalli

D-U-N-S 24-365-7277   (HQ)
SMITH, JACK FUELS LTD
351 Queen St N, Tilbury, ON, N0P 2L0
(519) 682-0111
Emp Here 8   Sales 13,426,504
SIC 5172 Petroleum products, nec
Jack Smith
Lynne Smith
Mark Smith

D-U-N-S 25-972-5633   (SL)
TILBURY AUTO SALES AND RV INC.

20600 County Road 42, Tilbury, ON, N0P 2L0
(866) 980-2512
Emp Here 25   Sales 12,451,950
SIC 5511 New and used car dealers
Lindsay Belanger

Tillsonburg, ON N4G

D-U-N-S 24-120-8292   (BR)
1032451 B.C. LTD
TILLSONBURG NEWS
(Suby of QUEBECOR MEDIA INC)
25 Townline Rd Suite 190, Tillsonburg, ON, N4G 2R5
(519) 688-6397
Emp Here 100
SIC 2711 Newspapers
Mike Walsh

D-U-N-S 24-339-2284   (HQ)
1596101 ONTARIO INC
35 Townline Rd, Tillsonburg, ON, N4G 2R5
(519) 688-5803
Emp Here 3   Sales 109,652,700
SIC 6712 Bank holding companies
Christopher Wood
Henry Spanjers
Erwin Hawel

D-U-N-S 20-532-1953   (HQ)
AUTONEUM CANADA LTD
1451 Bell Mill Sideroad, Tillsonburg, ON, N4G 4H8
(519) 842-6411
Emp Here 40   Sales 80,411,020
SIC 2299 Textile goods, nec
Richard Derr
John Lenga
Scott Cole
Jeffrey S Miller

D-U-N-S 25-673-1183   (HQ)
BREEZE DRIED INC
BREEZE WOOD FOREST PRODUCTS
1300 Jackson Suite 2, Tillsonburg, ON, N4G 4G7
(519) 688-0224
Emp Here 1   Sales 13,081,160
SIC 2426 Hardwood dimension and flooring mills
David Townsend
Laura Townsend

D-U-N-S 25-170-8699   (SL)
COTNAM, DAN DRUGS LTD
SHOPPERS DRUG MART
200 Broadway St, Tillsonburg, ON, N4G 5A7
(519) 842-3521
Emp Here 50   Sales 12,647,700
SIC 5912 Drug stores and proprietary stores
Dan Cotnam

D-U-N-S 20-133-9363   (SL)
DEGROOT-HILL CHEVROLET BUICK GMC LTD
Hwy 3, Tillsonburg, ON, N4G 4H3
(519) 842-9026
Emp Here 26   Sales 12,950,028
SIC 5511 New and used car dealers
Reme Degroote
Gordon Hill

D-U-N-S 20-971-2426   (HQ)
EAST ELGIN CONCRETE FORMING LIMITED
FOREST CITY CONCRETE FINISHING, DIV OF
10 Elm St, Tillsonburg, ON, N4G 0A7
(519) 842-6667
Emp Here 65   Sales 19,798,640
SIC 1771 Concrete work
Tyson Van Leeuwen
Robyn Hanson

D-U-N-S 20-627-4227   (SL)

EICHENBERG MOTORS (1971) LIMITED
39 Broadway St, Tillsonburg, ON, N4G 3P2
(519) 842-5953
Emp Here 22   Sales 10,957,716
SIC 5511 New and used car dealers
David Moore

D-U-N-S 24-309-1449   (SL)
ELECTRICAL COMPONENTS CANADA, INC
(Suby of ELECTRICAL COMPONENTS INTERNATIONAL, INC.)
91 Lincoln St, Tillsonburg, ON, N4G 2P9
(519) 842-9063
Emp Here 105   Sales 19,996,410
SIC 3679 Electronic components, nec
Paul Chaney
Paul Csanyi

D-U-N-S 24-380-3751   (SL)
ERIE GREENHOUSE STRUCTURES INC
ERIE STRUCTURES
500 Hwy 3 Unit 2, Tillsonburg, ON, N4G 4G8
(519) 688-6809
Emp Here 25   Sales 11,768,275
SIC 1542 Nonresidential construction, nec
William Dendekker
Ben Fehr
Leona Dendekker

D-U-N-S 20-812-0498   (BR)
FLEETWOOD METAL INDUSTRIES INC
(Suby of AK STEEL HOLDING CORPORATION)
21 Clearview Dr, Tillsonburg, ON, N4G 4G8
(519) 737-1919
Emp Here 280
SIC 3469 Metal stampings, nec
John Hantz

D-U-N-S 20-984-0594   (SL)
FREUDENBERG-NOK, INC
FREUDENBERG-NOK SEALING TECHNOLOGIES
(Suby of FREUDENBERG & CO. KG)
65 Spruce St, Tillsonburg, ON, N4G 5C4
(519) 842-6451
Emp Here 140   Sales 19,053,425
SIC 3053 Gaskets; packing and sealing devices
Matthew Portu
John Vettor
Falko Bauaen

D-U-N-S 20-628-8599   (HQ)
GUARDIAN INDUSTRIES CANADA CORP
(Suby of KOCH INDUSTRIES, INC.)
10 Rouse St, Tillsonburg, ON, N4G 5W8
(416) 674-6945
Emp Here 175   Sales 80,542,350
SIC 3211 Flat glass
James Boudreault
Dave Zanin

D-U-N-S 24-676-9900   (HQ)
HOOVER ENTERPRISES INC
81 Lincoln St, Tillsonburg, ON, N4G 5Y4
(519) 842-2890
Emp Here 47   Sales 21,766,560
SIC 3312 Blast furnaces and steel mills
Tobias Hoover
Steven Martin
Jacob Wall
Solomon Hoover

D-U-N-S 20-267-7910   (BR)
INOVATA FOODS CORP
(Suby of PASTA MILL LTD, THE)
98 Spruce St, Tillsonburg, ON, N4G 5V3

Emp Here 180
SIC 2099 Food preparations, nec
Bob Mccoll

D-U-N-S 24-451-5680   (SL)
J/E BEARING & MACHINE LTD
68 Spruce St, Tillsonburg, ON, N4G 5V3

▲ Public Company   ■ Public Company Family Member   **HQ** Headquarters   **BR** Branch   **SL** Single Location

(519) 842-8476
Emp Here 60   *Sales* 29,263,800
SIC 5085 Industrial supplies
Joe L Volkaert Jr
Patricia Hendricks

D-U-N-S 20-536-5505   (BR)
JOHNSON CONTROLS NOVA SCOTIA U.L.C.
(*Suby of* JOHNSON CONTROLS INTERNATIONAL PUBLIC LIMITED COMPANY)
100 Townline Rd, Tillsonburg, ON, N4G 2R7
(519) 842-5971
Emp Here 350
SIC 2531 Public building and related furniture
Ken Mackenzie

D-U-N-S 24-876-0019   (HQ)
KITCHENER FOREST PRODUCTS INC
(*Suby of* TOWNSEND LUMBER INC)
1300 Jackson, Tillsonburg, ON, N4G 4G7
(519) 842-7381
Emp Here 1   *Sales* 11,626,524
SIC 5031 Lumber, plywood, and millwork
Michael Penner
Laura Townsend

D-U-N-S 20-313-6957   (SL)
KOTELES FARMS LIMITED
164700 New Rd Suite 2, Tillsonburg, ON, N4G 4G7
(519) 842-5425
Emp Here 35   *Sales* 11,986,345
SIC 0161 Vegetables and melons
Joseph Koteles
Irene Koteles

D-U-N-S 24-350-9994   (BR)
MAPLEWOOD NURSING HOME LIMITED
(*Suby of* MAPLEWOOD NURSING HOME LIMITED)
73 Bidwell St, Tillsonburg, ON, N4G 3T8
(519) 842-3563
Emp Here 120
SIC 8051 Skilled nursing care facilities
George Kaniuk

D-U-N-S 24-845-8648   (HQ)
MARWOOD INTERNATIONAL INC
(*Suby of* 1058347 ONTARIO LIMITED)
35 Townline Rd, Tillsonburg, ON, N4G 2R5
(519) 688-1144
Emp Here 127   *Sales* 122,157,000
SIC 3714 Motor vehicle parts and accessories
Christopher Arthur Wood
Leon Thoonen
Henry William Spanjers
Erwin Johann Hawel

D-U-N-S 25-300-0350   (BR)
METRO ONTARIO INC
(*Suby of* METRO INC)
225 Broadway St, Tillsonburg, ON, N4G 3R2
(519) 842-3625
Emp Here 150
SIC 5411 Grocery stores
Gerry Finley

D-U-N-S 20-793-0715   (BR)
SOBEYS CAPITAL INCORPORATED
(*Suby of* EMPIRE COMPANY LIMITED)
678 Broadway St, Tillsonburg, ON, N4G 3S9
(519) 688-1734
Emp Here 100
SIC 5411 Grocery stores
Jeffrey Shultz

D-U-N-S 20-157-6121   (SL)
STAUFFER MOTORS LIMITED
685 Broadway St, Tillsonburg, ON, N4G 4H1
(519) 842-3646
Emp Here 29   *Sales* 14,444,262
SIC 5511 New and used car dealers
John Hartmell
Bonnie Harris

D-U-N-S 20-512-2075   (HQ)
TFT GLOBAL INC

(*Suby of* 1596101 ONTARIO INC)
25 Townline Rd Suite 200, Tillsonburg, ON, N4G 2R5
(519) 842-4540
Emp Here 30   *Sales* 55,314,300
SIC 4225 General warehousing and storage
Joanne Vandergunst
Ronda Polk
Kim Parker

D-U-N-S 25-249-1469   (BR)
THAMES VALLEY DISTRICT SCHOOL BOARD
GLENDALE HIGH SCHOOL
(*Suby of* THAMES VALLEY DISTRICT SCHOOL BOARD)
37 Glendale Dr Suite 16, Tillsonburg, ON, N4G 1J6
(519) 842-4207
Emp Here 80
SIC 8211 Elementary and secondary schools
Jenny Vanbommel

D-U-N-S 20-358-2838   (BR)
THK RHYTHM AUTOMOTIVE CANADA LIMITED
(*Suby of* THK CO., LTD.)
1417 Bell Mill Sideroad, Tillsonburg, ON, N4G 4G9
(519) 688-4200
Emp Here 200
SIC 3089 Plastics products, nec

D-U-N-S 25-481-2779   (SL)
TILLSONBURG & DISTRICT MULTI-SERVICE CENTRE INC
96 Tillson Ave, Tillsonburg, ON, N4G 3A1
(519) 842-9000
Emp Here 49   *Sales* 11,114,817
SIC 8399 Social services, nec
Marlene Pink

D-U-N-S 25-338-3095   (SL)
TILLSONBURG DISTRICT MEMORIAL HOSPITAL TRUST
167 Rolph St Suite 3100, Tillsonburg, ON, N4G 3Y9
(519) 842-3611
Emp Here 320   *Sales* 19,242,915
SIC 8062 General medical and surgical hospitals
Crystal Houze
Larry Phillips
Larry Phillips
Scot Bolton
Frank Deutsch
Brian Holowachuk
Dan Dockx
Dan Rasokas
Jane Esseltine
Josie Edwards

D-U-N-S 24-850-7209   (SL)
TOTAL SWINE GENETICS INC
223277 Ostrander Rd Suite 7, Tillsonburg, ON, N4G 4H1
(519) 877-4350
Emp Here 20   *Sales* 24,207,940
SIC 5159 Farm-product raw materials, nec
Arnold Ypma

D-U-N-S 20-180-1487   (HQ)
TOWNSEND LUMBER INC
1300 Jackson Suite 2, Tillsonburg, ON, N4G 4G7
(519) 842-7381
Emp Here 10   *Sales* 22,358,700
SIC 5031 Lumber, plywood, and millwork
Michael Penner
Laura Townsend

D-U-N-S 25-294-8864   (BR)
WAL-MART CANADA CORP
(*Suby of* WALMART INC.)
400 Simcoe St, Tillsonburg, ON, N4G 4X1
(519) 842-7770
Emp Here 100
SIC 5311 Department stores

Ray Corriveau

D-U-N-S 20-522-2326   (SL)
WELLMASTER PIPE AND SUPPLY INC
WELLMASTER CARTS
1494 Bell Mill Sideroad, Tillsonburg, ON, N4G 5Y1
(519) 688-0500
Emp Here 55   *Sales* 20,605,882
SIC 3533 Oil and gas field machinery
Douglas White

D-U-N-S 24-054-4833   (SL)
XCEL FABRICATION & DESIGN LTD
24 Clearview Dr, Tillsonburg, ON, N4G 4G8
(519) 688-3193
Emp Here 65   *Sales* 10,003,188
SIC 3441 Fabricated structural Metal
Diedrich Braun
Agatha Braun

D-U-N-S 24-221-2512   (BR)
ZF AUTOMOTIVE CANADA LIMITED
BRAKING & SUSPENSION PRODUCT CENTER
(*Suby of* ZEPPELIN-STIFTUNG)
101 Spruce St, Tillsonburg, ON, N4G 5C4
(519) 688-4200
Emp Here 270
SIC 3714 Motor vehicle parts and accessories
Robert Davies

Timmins, ON P4N

D-U-N-S 25-369-0812   (HQ)
1562246 ONTARIO INC
THE BRICK
108 Third Ave, Timmins, ON, P4N 1C3
(705) 264-2274
Emp Here 28 .   *Sales* 11,056,320
SIC 5712 Furniture stores
Brian Vacchino
Cheryl Vacchino

D-U-N-S 25-962-8712   (SL)
2355291 ONTARIO IN
NPLH DRILLING
92 Balsam St S Suite 1, Timmins, ON, P4N 2C8
(705) 268-7956
Emp Here 60   *Sales* 14,006,100
SIC 1081 Metal mining services
Daniel Blaquiere

D-U-N-S 25-373-4701   (BR)
AIR CREEBEC INC
Gd Lcd Main, Timmins, ON, P4N 7C4
(705) 264-9521
Emp Here 140
SIC 4512 Air transportation, scheduled
Anne-Marie Farrington

D-U-N-S 25-320-5181   (HQ)
AUBE, J.-P. RESTAURANT SERVICES LTD
MCDONALDS
522 Algonquin Blvd E Unit 520, Timmins, ON, P4N 1B7
(705) 264-7323
Emp Here 80   *Sales* 4,551,900
SIC 5812 Eating places
Jean-Paul Aube

D-U-N-S 24-122-7271   (HQ)
BMT INSURANCE BROKERS LIMITED
BMT INSURANCE & FINANCIAL SERVICES
65 Maple St S, Timmins, ON, P4N 1Y6
(705) 268-9988
Emp Here 22   *Sales* 21,201,500
SIC 6411 Insurance agents, brokers, and service
Joel Bergeron

D-U-N-S 24-225-7876   (HQ)
CANADIAN MENTAL HEALTH ASSOCIATION-COCHRANE-TIMISKAMING

BRANCH
CMHA
330 Second Ave Suite 201, Timmins, ON, P4N 8A4
(705) 267-8100
Emp Here 50   *Sales* 22,824,840
SIC 8011 Offices and clinics of medical doctors
Clark Mcfarland

D-U-N-S 25-196-1504   (HQ)
COCHRANE DISTRICT SOCIAL SERVICES ADMINISTRATION BOARD
COCHRANE DSSAB
500 Algonquin Blvd E, Timmins, ON, P4N 1B7
(705) 268-7722
Emp Here 80   *Sales* 41,413,600
SIC 8399 Social services, nec
Brian Marks

D-U-N-S 20-965-2668   (HQ)
COCHRANE TEMISKAMING RESOURCE CENTRE
INFANCY AND EARLY CHILDHOOD SERVICES
600 Toke St, Timmins, ON, P4N 6W1
(705) 267-8181
Emp Here 50   *Sales* 11,052,825
SIC 8052 Intermediate care facilities
Gary Dowe

D-U-N-S 24-125-3566   (SL)
COMMUNITY LIVING TIMMINS INTERGRATION COMMUNAUTAIRE
166 Brousseau Ave, Timmins, ON, P4N 5Y4
(705) 268-8811
Emp Here 100   *Sales* 6,842,200
SIC 8322 Individual and family services
Johanne Rondeau
Robert Tremblay
Therese Bergerson-Hopson
Odile Robichaud
Veronica Farrell

D-U-N-S 24-183-3854   (HQ)
CONSEIL SCOLAIRE CATHOLIQUE DE DISTRICT DES GRANDES RIVIERES, LE
896 Riverside Dr, Timmins, ON, P4N 3W2
(705) 267-1421
Emp Here 70   *Sales* 88,839,278
SIC 8211 Elementary and secondary schools
Denis Belanger
Marc Bedard
Alphonse Aisnworth
Charlotte Laforest
Michel St-Louis
Marcel Joliat
Denise Labelle

D-U-N-S 24-411-4880   (SL)
CY RHEAULT CONSTRUCTION LTD
273 Third Ave Suite 404, Timmins, ON, P4N 1E2
(705) 268-3445
Emp Here 70   *Sales* 39,923,660
SIC 1542 Nonresidential construction, nec
Roger Rheault
Carole Rheault-Gibouleau

D-U-N-S 24-184-2004   (SL)
DAVIDSON DELAPLANTE INSURANCE BROKERS LTD
100 Third Ave, Timmins, ON, P4N 1C3
(705) 268-1011
Emp Here 30   *Sales* 17,397,720
SIC 6411 Insurance agents, brokers, and service
Pierre Delaplante
William M. Davidson

D-U-N-S 25-401-1117   (SL)
EPITRON INC
841 Pine St S, Timmins, ON, P4N 8S3
(705) 267-7382
Emp Here 20   *Sales* 12,454,208
SIC 5063 Electrical apparatus and equipment
Thomas Skwarok

Jethro Skwarok
Jane Skwarok

D-U-N-S 24-228-1553 (BR)
G4S SECURE SOLUTIONS (CANADA) LTD
(Suby of G4S PLC)
211 Craig St, Timmins, ON, P4N 4A2
(705) 268-7040
Emp Here 80
SIC 7381 Detective and armored car services
Jim Moores

D-U-N-S 20-404-8300 (SL)
GAETAN VERREAULT FUELS LIMITED
Highway 101 W, Timmins, ON, P4N 7H9
(705) 268-4199
Emp Here 15   Sales 15,671,548
SIC 5172 Petroleum products, nec
Gaetan Verreault

D-U-N-S 24-915-3060 (SL)
GREENER STEEL INC
352 Railway St, Timmins, ON, P4N 2P6
(705) 268-7197
Emp Here 49   Sales 21,911,526
SIC 5051 Metals service centers and offices
George Scott

D-U-N-S 24-821-0320 (HQ)
IMERYS TALC CANADA INC
(Suby of GROUPE BRUXELLES LAMBERT)
100 Water Tower Rd, Timmins, ON, P4N 7J5
(705) 268-2208
Sales 18,647,664
SIC 1499 Miscellaneous nonMetallic minerals, except fuels
Brian Hanrahan

D-U-N-S 20-817-4482 (SL)
J & B CYCLE & MARINE CO. LTD
950 Riverside Dr, Timmins, ON, P4N 3W2
(705) 267-1417
Emp Here 30   Sales 14,942,340
SIC 5599 Automotive dealers, nec
Robert Racine
Dennis Langevin
Richard Lacroix

D-U-N-S 25-687-0239 (HQ)
NORTHEASTERN CATHOLIC DISTRICT SCHOOL BOARD
383 Birch St N, Timmins, ON, P4N 6E8
(705) 268-7443
Emp Here 25   Sales 29,548,692
SIC 8211 Elementary and secondary schools
Glenn Sheculski
Mary-Lou Pollon
Richard Brassard
Martin Drainville
Peter Delguidice
Fred Salvador, Jr
Elizabeth King
Denis Lincez
Colleen Landers
Steve Malciw

D-U-N-S 25-772-6187 (SL)
NORTHEC CONSTRUCTION INC
2401 Airport Rd, Timmins, ON, P4N 7C3
(705) 531-3370
Emp Here 100   Sales 25,244,200
SIC 1629 Heavy construction, nec
Marie-Claude Houle

D-U-N-S 20-157-9364 (SL)
NORTHERN ALLIED SUPPLY COMPANY LIMITED
NORTHERN ALLIED STEEL SERVICE CENTRE
352 Railway St, Timmins, ON, P4N 2P6
(705) 264-5291
Emp Here 30   Sales 13,415,220
SIC 5051 Metals service centers and offices
George Scott
Bruce Scott

D-U-N-S 20-341-5104 (SL)
NORTHERN TRANSPORT SERVICES INC

NORTHERN TAXI
36 Pine St S Suite 200, Timmins, ON, P4N 2J8
(705) 268-6868
Emp Here 49   Sales 21,731,010
SIC 7389 Business services, nec
Dauda Raji

D-U-N-S 24-022-1148 (SL)
O S S T F DISTRICT 1
111 Wilson Ave Suite E, Timmins, ON, P4N 2S8
Emp Here 28   Sales 10,952,424
SIC 8631 Labor organizations
William Mcgillis

D-U-N-S 20-207-6258 (SL)
R HOME SECURITY LTD
ADVANCED SECURITY AND INVESTIGATION SERVICES
28 Columbus Ave, Timmins, ON, P4N 3H3
(705) 267-5547
Emp Here 125   Sales 83,613,500
SIC 7389 Business services, nec
Ron Short

D-U-N-S 20-081-4791 (BR)
RELIABLE WINDOW CLEANERS (SUDBURY) LIMITED
RELIABLE CLEANING SERVICES
167 Wilson Ave, Timmins, ON, P4N 2T2
(705) 360-1194
Emp Here 100
SIC 1799 Special trade contractors, nec
Gary Griffith

D-U-N-S 20-753-8513 (HQ)
RLP MACHINE & STEEL FABRICATION INC
RLP MACHINE
259 Reliable Lane, Timmins, ON, P4N 7W7
(705) 267-1445
Emp Here 50   Sales 38,417,000
SIC 3441 Fabricated structural Metal
Stephen Symes
Robert Parcey
Monica Parcey

D-U-N-S 20-246-0627 (SL)
ROY, G.R. CONSTRUCTION LTD
Gd Lcd Main, Timmins, ON, P4N 7C4
(705) 266-3585
Emp Here 50   Sales 16,666,650
SIC 1541 Industrial buildings and warehouses
Rene Roy

D-U-N-S 20-157-9885 (HQ)
SENATOR HOTELS LIMITED
DAYS INN
14 Mountjoy St S, Timmins, ON, P4N 1S4
(705) 267-6211
Emp Here 80   Sales 10,195,900
SIC 7011 Hotels and motels
Charmaine Aube

D-U-N-S 24-663-5734 (SL)
T.T.S. HOLDINGS INC
85 Pine St S, Timmins, ON, P4N 2K1
(705) 264-7200
Emp Here 45   Sales 18,870,975
SIC 6712 Bank holding companies
James Martin

D-U-N-S 20-273-2330 (BR)
TEMBEC INC
(Suby of RAYONIER A.M. GLOBAL HOLDINGS LUXEMBOURG SCS)
5310 Hwy 101 W, Timmins, ON, P4N 7J3
(705) 268-1462
Emp Here 200
SIC 2611 Pulp mills
Alan Thorne

D-U-N-S 24-348-5559 (SL)
TIMBERLAND FORD INC
445 Algonquin Blvd W, Timmins, ON, P4N 2S4
(705) 268-3673
Emp Here 27   Sales 13,448,106

SIC 5511 New and used car dealers
Michael Gougeon

D-U-N-S 25-671-5418 (SL)
TIMMINS AND DISTRICT HOSPITAL
700 Ross Ave E Suite 1559, Timmins, ON, P4N 8P2
(705) 267-2131
Emp Here 700   Sales 68,422,959
SIC 8062 General medical and surgical hospitals
Blaisse Macneil
Maggie Matear
David Thomas
Gaeetan Malette
Harry Voogjarv
Iain Martin
Leon Laforest
Doug Arnold
Jacklyn Bernardi
Joan Ludiwg

Timmins, ON P4P

D-U-N-S 24-709-2091 (SL)
900261 ONTARIO LTD
LEVIS FOODLAND
670 Airport Rd Suite 200, Timmins, ON, P4P 1J2
(705) 268-5020
Emp Here 50   Sales 13,707,600
SIC 5411 Grocery stores
Daniel Levis

D-U-N-S 24-991-7402 (SL)
MIKEY'S GENERAL SALES & REPAIR LTD
1301 Airport Rd, Timmins, ON, P4P 0A8
(705) 268-6050
Emp Here 25   Sales 12,451,950
SIC 5571 Motorcycle dealers
Michael Mason

Timmins, ON P4R

D-U-N-S 24-816-5391 (HQ)
BUCKET SHOP INC, THE
STEELTEC, DIV OF
(Suby of PEPCO CORP)
24 Government Rd S, Timmins, ON, P4R 1N4
(705) 531-2658
Emp Here 45   Sales 47,502,600
SIC 5085 Industrial supplies
Ross Woodward
Paul Woodward

D-U-N-S 20-157-7376 (SL)
BUPONT MOTORS INC
TIMMINS NISSAN
1180 Riverside Dr, Timmins, ON, P4R 1A2
(705) 268-2226
Emp Here 35   Sales 17,432,730
SIC 5511 New and used car dealers
Urgel R Gravel

D-U-N-S 20-629-5409 (SL)
CHENIER MOTORS LTD
1276 Riverside Dr, Timmins, ON, P4R 1A4
(705) 264-9528
Emp Here 25   Sales 12,451,950
SIC 5541 Gasoline service stations
Richard Chenier

D-U-N-S 24-361-7300 (BR)
HOME DEPOT OF CANADA INC
HOME DEPOT
(Suby of THE HOME DEPOT INC)
2143 Riverside Dr, Timmins, ON, P4R 0A1
(705) 360-8750
Emp Here 100
SIC 5251 Hardware stores
Bill Lennie

D-U-N-S 20-216-5143 (SL)
KIA OF TIMMINS
STEWART VEHICLE LEASING
1285 Riverside Dr, Timmins, ON, P4R 1A6
(705) 267-8291
Emp Here 22   Sales 10,957,716
SIC 5511 New and used car dealers
Bruce Stewart

D-U-N-S 20-158-0206 (SL)
TIMMINS GARAGE INCORPORATED
1395 Riverside Dr, Timmins, ON, P4R 1A6
(705) 268-4122
Emp Here 55   Sales 34,610,400
SIC 5511 New and used car dealers
James Mascioli
Elena Mascioli
Norman Mascioli

D-U-N-S 24-765-5558 (HQ)
TIMMINS KENWORTH LTD
NEW LISKEARD KENWORTH
4041 Hwy 101 W, Timmins, ON, P4R 0E8
(705) 268-7800
Emp Here 20   Sales 14,942,340
SIC 5511 New and used car dealers
Dwight Michaud
Nicole Michaud

Tiverton, ON N0G

D-U-N-S 24-346-4596 (BR)
ATOMIC ENERGY OF CANADA LIMITED
AECL
(Suby of GOVERNMENT OF CANADA)
Gd, Tiverton, ON, N0G 2T0

Emp Here 190
SIC 2819 Industrial inorganic chemicals, nec
Rick Janzen

D-U-N-S 25-145-7404 (HQ)
BRUCE POWER L.P.
177 Tie Rd Municipal Kincardine Rr 2, Tiverton, ON, N0G 2T0
(519) 361-2673
Sales 3,425,999,200
SIC 4911 Electric services
Mike Rencheck
Kevin Kelly
Cathy Sprague
Len Clewett

D-U-N-S 20-943-4042 (BR)
MUNICIPALITY OF KINCARDINE, THE
BRUCE TELECOM
(Suby of MUNICIPALITY OF KINCARDINE, THE)
3145 Hwy 21 N, Tiverton, ON, N0G 2T0
(519) 368-2000
Emp Here 80
SIC 4813 Telephone communication, except radio
Michael Andrews

Toronto, ON M1B

D-U-N-S 24-152-0712 (SL)
ALLIED TECHNICAL SALES INC
885 Milner Ave, Toronto, ON, M1B 5V8
(416) 282-1010
Emp Here 125   Sales 14,703,720
SIC 8712 Architectural services
William Petro
Rob Fenwick

D-U-N-S 24-610-7783 (SL)
APO PRODUCTS LTD
5590 Finch Ave E Unit 1, Toronto, ON, M1B 1T1
(416) 321-5412
Emp Here 25   Sales 20,889,425

▲ Public Company   ■ Public Company Family Member   **HQ** Headquarters   **BR** Branch   **SL** Single Location

SIC 5141 Groceries, general line
Rodolfo Ong

D-U-N-S 25-517-4641   (SL)
INTERPHARM LTD
VITAL HEALTH PRODUCTS
30 Novopharm Crt, Toronto, ON, M1B 2K9
(800) 663-5903
Emp Here 75
SIC 5122 Drugs, proprietaries, and sundries

D-U-N-S 20-128-4213   (HQ)
MAC'S CONVENIENCE STORES INC
DEPANNEURS MAC'S, LES
(*Suby of* ALIMENTATION COUCHE-TARD INC)
305 Milner Ave Suite 400, Toronto, ON, M1B 0A5
(416) 291-4441
Emp Here 110   *Sales* 1,337,031,922
SIC 6712 Bank holding companies
Jean Bernier
Sylvain Aubry
Karinne Bouchard
Claude Tessier

D-U-N-S 20-133-8698   (SL)
TTM TECHNOLOGIES INC
8150 Sheppard Ave E Suite 1, Toronto, ON, M1B 5K2
(416) 208-2159
Emp Here 50   *Sales* 18,210,750
SIC 5013 Motor vehicle supplies and new parts
Thomas T. Edman

D-U-N-S 24-393-6924   (SL)
VIASYSTEMS TORONTO INC
MEMBER OF TTM TECHNOLOGIES
(*Suby of* TTM TECHNOLOGIES, INC.)
8150 Sheppard Ave E, Toronto, ON, M1B 5K2
(416) 208-2100
Emp Here 485   *Sales* 137,213,775
SIC 3672 Printed circuit boards
Thomas Edman
Brian Barber
Canice Chung
Kent Hardwick
Dale Knecht
Shawn Powers
Todd Schull

D-U-N-S 24-093-4336   (SL)
VOYSUS GROUP INC
5900 Finch Ave East Unit 200b, Toronto, ON, M1B 5P8
(416) 291-0224
Emp Here 30   *Sales* 13,304,700
SIC 7389 Business services, nec
Imran Butt
Mahdi Raza

Toronto, ON M1K

D-U-N-S 20-393-0854   (SL)
NELSON EDUCATION LTD
1120 Birchmount Rd, Toronto, ON, M1K 5G4
(416) 752-9100
Emp Here 331   *Sales* 64,139,194
SIC 2731 Book publishing
Steven Brown
Atish Banerjea
John Brecker
David Kirsch
John Bell
Jessica Mosher
David Ashton

Toronto, ON M1L

D-U-N-S 20-404-5892   (SL)

METAPLAST CIRCUITS LIMITED
(*Suby of* ANOTEX INC)
180 Hymus Rd, Toronto, ON, M1L 2E1
(416) 285-5000
Emp Here 62   *Sales* 11,807,404
SIC 3672 Printed circuit boards
John Angaritis
John Mikelson

D-U-N-S 20-120-7920   (SL)
ROSSCLAIR CONTRACTORS INC
(*Suby of* R.O.M CONTRACTORS LIMITED)
59 Comstock Rd Suite 1, Toronto, ON, M1L 2G6
(416) 285-0190
Emp Here 52   *Sales* 29,657,576
SIC 1542 Nonresidential construction, nec
John Richardson
Anne Richardson
Kathy Hogeveen

Toronto, ON M1P

D-U-N-S 24-301-9320   (SL)
KEILHAUER LTD
1450 Birchmount Rd, Toronto, ON, M1P 2E3
(416) 759-5665
Emp Here 260   *Sales* 57,892,900
SIC 2521 Wood office furniture
Mike Keilhauer
Barry Moore
Steve Keilhauer
Meghan Sherwin

D-U-N-S 20-982-6890   (HQ)
MARKDOM PLASTIC PRODUCTS LIMITED
MARKDOM
1220 Birchmount Rd, Toronto, ON, M1P 2C3
(416) 752-4290
Emp Here 185   *Sales* 34,614,158
SIC 3089 Plastics products, nec
Joerg Dietterle

D-U-N-S 20-173-5438   (HQ)
QUALITY KNITTING LIMITED
1210 Birchmount Rd, Toronto, ON, M1P 2C3
(416) 598-2422
Sales 18,340,300
SIC 2253 Knit outerwear mills
Nathan Kleinman
Sidney Kleinman
Howard Kleinman

D-U-N-S 25-513-9370   (HQ)
TELLZA INC
PHONETIME
190 Borough Dr Suite 3302, Toronto, ON, M1P 0B6

Emp Here 24   *Sales* 549,020,408
SIC 4899 Communication services, nec
Mike Vazquez
Anuj Sethi
Luciano Garavaglia

Toronto, ON M1R

D-U-N-S 25-194-1951   (SL)
INVODANE ENGINEERING LTD
44 Metropolitan Rd, Toronto, ON, M1R 2T6
(416) 443-8049
Emp Here 75   *Sales* 13,196,850
SIC 8711 Engineering services
Paul Laursen

Toronto, ON M1T

D-U-N-S 20-369-7552   (SL)

DASONG ZAO CAMPAIGN, THE
3469 Sheppard Ave E, Toronto, ON, M1T 3K5
(647) 641-7292
Emp Here 50   *Sales* 13,916,639
SIC 8651 Political organizations
Dasong Zao

D-U-N-S 24-991-2734   (HQ)
SKYLINK AVIATION INC
100 Sheppard Ave E Suite 760, Toronto, ON, M1T 3L3
(416) 924-9000
Emp Here 34   *Sales* 32,037,360
SIC 4512 Air transportation, scheduled
David Dacquino
Mark Massad

D-U-N-S 20-027-6411   (SL)
VOLKSWAGEN MIDTOWN
3450 Sheppard Ave E, Toronto, ON, M1T 3K4
(416) 291-6456
Emp Here 33   *Sales* 16,436,574
SIC 5511 New and used car dealers
Ken Laird

Toronto, ON M1V

D-U-N-S 24-826-2789   (SL)
BPONOVO INC
CALLNOVO
3660 Midland Ave Unit V3022, Toronto, ON, M1V 0B8
(416) 479-0416
Emp Here 120   *Sales* 27,416,640
SIC 4899 Communication services, nec

D-U-N-S 20-138-3742   (HQ)
MORRISON LAMOTHE INC
825 Middlefield Rd Unit 1, Toronto, ON, M1V 4Z7
(416) 291-6762
Emp Here 50   *Sales* 170,584,750
SIC 2038 Frozen specialties, nec
John M Pigott
David Williams
Allan Halter
David C Pigott
Kelly Kubrick

D-U-N-S 20-844-6625   (SL)
SAMCO MACHINERY LIMITED
351 Passmore Ave, Toronto, ON, M1V 3N8
(416) 285-0619
Emp Here 132   *Sales* 29,304,132
SIC 3542 Machine tools, Metal forming type
Robert Repovs
Rahu Gana
Jaswinder Bhatti
Gerry Birmingham
Rachel Martinez
Mona Seusan

D-U-N-S 24-097-5367   (BR)
WAR AMPUTATIONS OF CANADA, THE
KEY TAG SERVICE
(*Suby of* WAR AMPUTATIONS OF CANADA, THE)
1 Maybrook Dr, Toronto, ON, M1V 5K9
(416) 412-0600
Emp Here 100
SIC 8699 Membership organizations, nec
David Saunders

Toronto, ON M1X

D-U-N-S 24-333-8600   (HQ)
BELLWYCK PACKAGING INC
BELLWYCK PACKAGING SOLUTIONS
21 Finchdene Sq, Toronto, ON, M1X 1A7
(416) 752-1210
Emp Here 135   *Sales* 154,407,540

SIC 2657 Folding paperboard boxes
John Vella
Jeffrey Sziklai
Greg Keizer
John Mcveigh
Bruce Wells

D-U-N-S 20-903-3935   (SL)
FELLOWES CANADA LTD
(*Suby of* FELLOWES, INC.)
1261 Tapscott Rd, Toronto, ON, M1X 1S9
(905) 475-6320
Emp Here 45   *Sales* 22,664,610
SIC 5113 Industrial and personal service paper
James Edmonds
James E Fellowes

D-U-N-S 24-926-8293   (SL)
NIENKAMPER FURNITURE & ACCESSORIES INC
(*Suby of* INTERNATIONAL CONTRACT FURNISHINGS, INC.)
257 Finchdene Square, Toronto, ON, M1X 1B9
(416) 298-5700
Emp Here 115   *Sales* 25,606,475
SIC 2522 Office furniture, except wood
Klaus Nienkamper
Romesh Jayarajah
James Kasschau
Ann-Marie Snook

D-U-N-S 20-259-5872   (SL)
NUGALE PHARMACEUTICAL INC
41 Pullman Crt, Toronto, ON, M1X 1E4
(416) 298-7275
Emp Here 50   *Sales* 16,556,763
SIC 2834 Pharmaceutical preparations
Wynn Xie

Toronto, ON M2H

D-U-N-S 20-551-0605   (HQ)
CCL INDUSTRIES INC
ETIQUETTES CCL MONTREAL
111 Gordon Baker Rd Suite 801, Toronto, ON, M2H 3R1
(416) 756-8500
Emp Here 1,200   *Sales* 3,912,943,473
SIC 2672 Paper; coated and laminated, nec
Geoffrey T. Martin
Lalitha Vaidyanathan
Jim Sellors
Mark Mcclendon
Sean P. Washchuk
Peter Fleissner
Donald G. Lang
Vincent J. Galifi
Edward E. Guillet
Kathleen L. Keller-Hobson

D-U-N-S 25-685-3912   (HQ)
DAPASOFT INC
111 Gordon Baker Suite 600, Toronto, ON, M2H 3R1
(416) 847-4080
Sales 17,731,100
SIC 7371 Custom computer programming services
Stephen Chan
Elaine Chan

D-U-N-S 25-306-1758   (HQ)
ICOM INFORMATION & COMMUNICATIONS L.P.
EPSILON TARGETING, DIV OF
(*Suby of* ALLIANCE DATA SYSTEMS CORPORATION)
111 Gordon Baker Rd Suite 300, Toronto, ON, M2H 3R1
(647) 795-9600
Emp Here 250   *Sales* 55,205,693
SIC 8732 Commercial nonphysical research

Catherine Mcintyre
John Wen

D-U-N-S 25-509-3528   (SL)
MINI-MICRO SUPPLY INC. CANADA
524 Gordon Baker Rd, Toronto, ON, M2H 3B4
(905) 305-7671
Emp Here 25   *Sales* 11,179,350
SIC 5045 Computers, peripherals, and software
Henry Han

D-U-N-S 20-923-0101   (SL)
THE HIDI GROUP INC
THE HIDI GROUP
155 Gordon Baker Rd Suite 200, Toronto, ON, M2H 3N5
(416) 364-2100
Emp Here 150   *Sales* 26,810,850
SIC 8711 Engineering services
Jamie Hidi
Jessica Merenda

Toronto, ON M2J

D-U-N-S 25-300-3628   (HQ)
A.G. SIMPSON AUTOMOTIVE INC
AGS AUTOMOTIVE SYSTEMS
(*Suby of* J2 MANAGEMENT CORP)
200 Yorkland Blvd Suite 800, Toronto, ON, M2J 5C1
(416) 438-6650
Emp Here 120   *Sales* 222,209,400
SIC 3714 Motor vehicle parts and accessories
Joseph Peter Loparco
Joseph Leon

D-U-N-S 20-391-8388   (SL)
CROFAM MANAGEMENT INC
501 Consumers Rd, Toronto, ON, M2J 5E2
(416) 391-0400
Emp Here 85   *Sales* 16,265,090
SIC 7359 Equipment rental and leasing, nec
George Crothers
Mary Crothers
Kelly Crothers
Julie Crothers

D-U-N-S 20-809-9130   (SL)
INNOVATIVE VISION MARKETING INC
515 Consumers Rd 6th Floor, Toronto, ON, M2J 4Z2
(416) 321-8189
Emp Here 100   *Sales* 18,479,800
SIC 4899 Communication services, nec
Puneet Sharma
Sajan Choksi

D-U-N-S 20-181-3404   (HQ)
J2 MANAGEMENT CORP
200 Yorkland Blvd Suite 800, Toronto, ON, M2J 5C1
(416) 438-6650
Emp Here 1   *Sales* 365,509,000
SIC 6712 Bank holding companies
Joe Loparco

D-U-N-S 20-005-5581   (SL)
JRP GROUP INSURANCE SOLUTIONS INC
2 Lansing Sq Unit 207, Toronto, ON, M2J 4P8
(647) 776-0906
Emp Here 49   *Sales* 41,554,940
SIC 6411 Insurance agents, brokers, and service
Richard Parridge
Michael Bonneville

D-U-N-S 24-387-2769   (HQ)
JUVENILE DIABETES RESEARCH FOUNDATION CANADA
235 Yorkland Blvd Suite 600, Toronto, ON, M2J 4Y8
(647) 789-2000
Emp Here 45   *Sales* 13,345,900
SIC 8399 Social services, nec

D-U-N-S 20-398-0698   (SL)
NORTH YORK REHABILITATION CENTRE CORP
2255 Sheppard Ave E Suite 300, Toronto, ON, M2J 4Y1
(416) 497-4477
Emp Here 27   *Sales* 27,941,787
SIC 6321 Accident and health insurance
Elizabeth De Sousa
Daniella Guerriero
Rocco Guerriero

D-U-N-S 20-644-0526   (HQ)
NOVITEX ENTERPRISE SOLUTIONS CANADA, INC
(*Suby of* EXELA TECHNOLOGIES, INC.)
2225 Sheppard Ave E Suite 1008, Toronto, ON, M2J 5C2
(416) 886-2540
Sales 64,259,640
SIC 8741 Management services
Simon Fisher
Shane Jordan

D-U-N-S 20-724-5007   (HQ)
PARADISE HOMES CORP
1 Herons Hill Way, Toronto, ON, M2J 0G2
(416) 756-1972
Emp Here 1   *Sales* 20,320,650
SIC 1521 Single-family housing construction
Eddy Weisz

D-U-N-S 24-926-9457   (HQ)
TOYS, TOYS, TOYS INC
1800 Sheppard Ave E, Toronto, ON, M2J 5A7
(416) 773-1950
Sales 12,216,400
SIC 5945 Hobby, toy, and game shops
Steven Reiken

D-U-N-S 24-409-8570   (HQ)
VISION TRAVEL DT ONTARIO-WEST INC
SM+I
251 Consumers Rd Suite 700, Toronto, ON, M2J 4R3
(416) 487-5385
Emp Here 50   *Sales* 83,361,500
SIC 4724 Travel agencies
Arend Roos
Robert Filkin
Michael Yirilli
Brian Robertson
Edward Adams
Joe Ostrov
Bob Potter
Stephanie Anevich
Ian Race
Jonathan Rubin

D-U-N-S 24-205-5973   (SL)
YESUP ECOMMERCE SOLUTIONS INC
YES ADVERTISING
200 Consumers Rd Suite 308, Toronto, ON, M2J 4R4
(416) 499-8009
Emp Here 50   *Sales* 11,734,800
SIC 8731 Commercial physical research
Patrick Zeng
Jeff Zeng

Toronto, ON M2K

D-U-N-S 24-167-2745   (SL)
BAGHAI DEVELOPMENT LIMITED
PARADISE FARMS
678 Sheppard Ave E Unit H, Toronto, ON, M2K 1B7
(416) 449-5994
Emp Here 40   *Sales* 15,420,760
SIC 0212 Beef cattle, except feedlots
Shane Baghai

Toronto, ON M2L

D-U-N-S 20-784-0422   (SL)
GRANITE CLUB
2350 Bayview Ave, Toronto, ON, M2L 1E4
(416) 449-8713
Emp Here 440   *Sales* 57,866,600
SIC 8641 Civic and social associations
Susanne Willans
Lori Tymchyk
Suzanne Villeneuve

Toronto, ON M2M

D-U-N-S 20-848-4949   (SL)
TYNDALE UNIVERSITY COLLEGE & SEMINARY
3377 Bayview Ave, Toronto, ON, M2M 3S4
(416) 226-6380
Emp Here 110   *Sales* 16,433,010
SIC 8221 Colleges and universities
Gary Nelson
Winston Ling
Randy Henderson

Toronto, ON M2N

D-U-N-S 20-652-1119   (BR)
ACCOR CANADA INC
NOVOTEL TORONTO NORTH YORK
(*Suby of* ACCOR)
3 Park Home Ave, Toronto, ON, M2N 6L3
(416) 733-2929
Emp Here 75
SIC 7011 Hotels and motels
Melih Yanik

D-U-N-S 24-325-5908   (SL)
B3INTELLIGENCE LTD
100 Sheppard Ave E Suite 503, Toronto, ON, M2N 6N5
(416) 549-8000
Emp Here 90   *Sales* 19,202,220
SIC 8732 Commercial nonphysical research
Walter Ramdeholl

D-U-N-S 20-418-7744   (HQ)
COLAS CANADA INC
(*Suby of* BOUYGUES)
4950 Yonge St Suite 2400, Toronto, ON, M2N 6K1
(416) 293-5443
Emp Here 25   *Sales* 889,519,765
SIC 1611 Highway and street construction
Louis R. Gabanna
Frederic Roussel
Jean Yves Llenas
Francois Vachon
Terrence (Terry) Gale
Herve Le Bouc
Eric Haentjens

D-U-N-S 24-463-7161   (HQ)
ECKLER LTD
5140 Yonge St Suite 1700, Toronto, ON, M2N 6L7
(416) 429-3330
Emp Here 120   *Sales* 90,170,110
SIC 8999 Services, nec
Bill Weiland

D-U-N-S 20-107-4817   (SL)
LEARNING PARTNERSHIP CANADA, THE
45 Sheppard Ave E Suite 400, Toronto, ON, M2N 5W9
(416) 440-5100
Emp Here 40   *Sales* 15,896,560
SIC 8699 Membership organizations, nec
Ron Canuel

Toronto, ON M2P

D-U-N-S 24-389-2978   (HQ)
DORCHESTER CORPORATION, THE
4120 Yonge St Suite 215, Toronto, ON, M2P 2C6
(416) 628-6238
Emp Here 13   *Sales* 24,388,350
SIC 6799 Investors, nec
Morris Shohet

D-U-N-S 24-596-9506   (SL)
SEGAL LLP
502-4101 Yonge St, Toronto, ON, M2P 1N6
(416) 391-4499
Emp Here 60   *Sales* 12,461,100
SIC 8721 Accounting, auditing, and bookkeeping
Stanley Segal
Gerald Sanders
Michael Dennis
Leslie Nevsky
Michael Daren
Robbie Rotin
Dan Natali
John Cleveland-Iliffe
Andrew Shalit
Larry Citrullo

Toronto, ON M2R

D-U-N-S 20-071-3255   (SL)
O.L.E.G. ENERGY CORPORATION
1319 Steeles Avenue W, Toronto, ON, M2R 3N2
(416) 886-4798
Emp Here 5   *Sales* 15,709,144
SIC 4924 Natural gas distribution

Toronto, ON M3A

D-U-N-S 24-802-4309   (SL)
682770 ONTARIO INC
ITC SYSTEMS
49 Railside Rd, Toronto, ON, M3A 1B3
(416) 289-2244
Emp Here 51   *Sales* 10,296,747
SIC 3089 Plastics products, nec
Campbell Richardson
Dan Bodolai

Toronto, ON M3B

D-U-N-S 25-338-6312   (HQ)
RE/MAX HALLMARK REALTY LTD
1 Duncan Mill Rd Unit 101, Toronto, ON, M3B

D-U-N-S 24-978-3973   (SL)
PERICHEM TRADING INC
4711 Yonge St 10f, Toronto, ON, M2N 6K8
(416) 479-5498
Emp Here 4   *Sales* 97,729,194
SIC 6799 Investors, nec
Mehmet Alp Erkaya

D-U-N-S 20-300-0880   (SL)
TEMPLETON INTERNATIONAL STOCK FUND
FRANKLIN TEMPLETON INVESTMENTS
5000 Yonge St Suite 900, Toronto, ON, M2N 0A7
(416) 364-4672
Emp Here 49   *Sales* 40,561,073
SIC 6722 Management investment, open-end
Martin Cobb

3J5
(416) 424-3170
Emp Here 25   *Sales* 13,587,800
SIC 6531 Real estate agents and managers
Ted Lorimer

D-U-N-S 20-273-2699   (SL)
RED ROSE REALTY INC
101 Duncan Mill Rd Unit G5, Toronto, ON,
M3B 1Z3
(416) 640-0512
Emp Here 45   *Sales* 14,720,715
SIC 6531 Real estate agents and managers
Bob Refani

D-U-N-S 20-413-7145   (HQ)
SCICAN LTD
1440 Don Mills Rd, Toronto, ON, M3B 3P9
(416) 445-1600
Emp Here 171   *Sales* 63,928,210
SIC 3843 Dental equipment and supplies
John Westermeier
Arthur Zwingenberger
Aaron Holtzman

D-U-N-S 20-393-3481   (SL)
VAULT CREDIT CORPORATION
41 Scarsdale Rd Suite 5, Toronto, ON, M3B
2R2
(416) 499-8466
Emp Here 40   *Sales* 11,331,720
SIC 8741 Management services
Daniel Wittlin
Harman Aujla
Amy Ma

Toronto, ON M3C

D-U-N-S 25-404-7434   (HQ)
CELESTICA INC
(*Suby of* ONEX CORPORATION)
844 Don Mills Rd, Toronto, ON, M3C 1V7
(416) 448-5800
Emp Here 100   *Sales* 6,633,200,000
SIC 3589 Service industry machinery, nec
Rob Mionis
Jack Lawless
Jason Phillips
Mandeep Chawla
Betty Delbianco
Todd Cooper
Nicolas Pujet
William Etherington
Dan Dimaggio
Laurette Koellner

D-U-N-S 20-369-7644   (HQ)
CELESTICA INTERNATIONAL LP
(*Suby of* ONEX CORPORATION)
844 Don Mills Rd, Toronto, ON, M3C 1V7
(416) 448-2559
Emp Here 700   *Sales* 567,244,575
SIC 3672 Printed circuit boards
Rob Mionis
Mandeep Chawla
Paul Blom

D-U-N-S 20-051-5604   (SL)
METEX INC
789 Don Mills Road, Suite 218, Toronto, ON,
M3C 1T5
(416) 203-8388
Emp Here 100   *Sales* 21,385,100
SIC 7372 Prepackaged software
David Dai

D-U-N-S 24-462-1645   (HQ)
ONTARIO LUNG ASSOCIATION
18 Wynford Dr Suite 401, Toronto, ON, M3C
0K8
(416) 864-9911
Emp Here 40   *Sales* 25,883,500
SIC 8399 Social services, nec
Ross Reid
Cathy Newton

Lynn Blanchard
Warren Chant
Robert Kelly

D-U-N-S 24-524-8331   (HQ)
ROYAL LEPAGE REAL ESTATE SERVICES
LTD
ROYAL LEPAGE
(*Suby of* BRIDGEMARQ REAL ESTATE SER-
VICES INC)
39 Wynford Dr 3 Fl, Toronto, ON, M3C 3K5
(416) 510-5810
Sales 41,888,900
SIC 6531 Real estate agents and managers

Toronto, ON M3J

D-U-N-S 20-433-7176   (HQ)
1512081 ONTARIO LTD
ABRAMS
93 Toro Rd, Toronto, ON, M3J 2A4
(416) 398-2500
Sales 19,831,000
SIC 7549 Automotive services, nec
Joseph Gagne

D-U-N-S 20-350-6589   (HQ)
ACASTA ENTERPRISES INC
ACASTA
1 Apollo Pl, Toronto, ON, M3J 0H2

Emp Here 10   *Sales* 287,160,774
SIC 8732 Commercial nonphysical research
Ian Kidson
Edward Vesel
Geoff Beattie
Robert Schwartz
Jay Schwartz

D-U-N-S 24-771-8919   (SL)
ASIGRA INC
79 Brisbane Road, Toronto, ON, M3J 2K3
(416) 736-8111
Emp Here 100   *Sales* 17,731,100
SIC 7371 Custom computer programming ser-
vices
David Farajun
Eran Farajun
Sara Farajun

D-U-N-S 20-398-4521   (SL)
BLUEBIX SOLUTIONS INCORPORATED
1110 Finch Ave W Suite 612, Toronto, ON,
M3J 2T2
(416) 319-5486
Emp Here 100   *Sales* 15,537,100
SIC 7361 Employment agencies
Sanjay Bonthapally
Suresh Mani

D-U-N-S 24-951-3438   (SL)
CMIC SUCCESS LTD
4850 Keele St, Toronto, ON, M3J 3K1
(416) 736-0123
Emp Here 49   *Sales* 10,663,037
SIC 5942 Book stores
Allen Berg

D-U-N-S 24-831-0666   (SL)
DALTON CHEMICAL LABORATORIES INC
DALTON PHARMA SERVICES
349 Wildcat Rd, Toronto, ON, M3J 2S3
(416) 661-2102
Emp Here 80   *Sales* 22,132,800
SIC 2834 Pharmaceutical preparations
Peter Pekos
Natalie Lazarowych

D-U-N-S 24-122-1647   (HQ)
GRIFFIN CENTRE MENTAL HEALTH SER-
VICES
1126 Finch Ave W Unit 16, Toronto, ON, M3J
3J6
(416) 222-1153
Emp Here 20   *Sales* 16,915,813

SIC 8361 Residential care
Barbara Macdonalds
Deanna Dannell
Kenneth Edwards
Debbie Carwana
Cathi Duncan
Barbara Hanssmann
Nadine Rubie
Rudolph Stewart
Gabriella Cappelletti
Catia Valenti

D-U-N-S 20-045-3744   (SL)
LONG ISLAND DISTRIBUTING CO. LIM-
ITED
425 Alness St, Toronto, ON, M3J 2H4

Emp Here 40   *Sales* 20,042,100
SIC 5099 Durable goods, nec

D-U-N-S 20-388-5181   (SL)
STALCO INC
64 Bakersfield St, Toronto, ON, M3J 2W7
(647) 367-2459
Emp Here 50   *Sales* 19,268,000
SIC 4783 Packing and crating
Steven Page
Lorne Taylor

D-U-N-S 24-992-6507   (SL)
TEXTBOOKRENTAL CA, INC
34 Ashwarrren Rd, Toronto, ON, M3J 1Z7

Emp Here 30   *Sales* 19,693,920
SIC 5961 Catalog and mail-order houses
Brandon Luft

Toronto, ON M3K

D-U-N-S 20-397-2216   (SL)
DE HAVILLAND AIRCRAFT OF CANADA
LIMITED
(*Suby of* LONGVIEW AVIATION CAPITAL
CORP)
123 Garratt Blvd, Toronto, ON, M3K 1Y5
(416) 633-7310
Emp Here 1,200   *Sales* 349,020,000
SIC 3721 Aircraft
David Curtis
Sean Marshman
Laurelle Funk

Toronto, ON M3M

D-U-N-S 25-529-2435   (HQ)
HUMBER RIVER HOSPITAL
HRH
1235 Wilson Ave, Toronto, ON, M3M 0B2
(416) 242-1000
Emp Here 1,400   *Sales* 333,240,000
SIC 8062 General medical and surgical hospi-
tals
Barbara Collins
Scott Jarrett
Ray Martin
Karen Adams
Narendra Singh
Marg Czaus
Paul Allison
Craig Baxter
Deborah Pankhurst
John Rossetti

Toronto, ON M3N

D-U-N-S 20-690-1659   (BR)
HUMBER RIVER HOSPITAL
(*Suby of* HUMBER RIVER HOSPITAL)

2111 Finch Ave W, Toronto, ON, M3N 1N1
(416) 744-2500
Emp Here 800
SIC 8062 General medical and surgical hospi-
tals
Darlene Barnes

Toronto, ON M4A

D-U-N-S 24-593-5924   (SL)
SELECT FOOD PRODUCTS LIMITED
120 Sunrise Ave, Toronto, ON, M4A 1B4
(416) 759-9316
Emp Here 150   *Sales* 51,853,500
SIC 2099 Food preparations, nec
Andrew Mitchell

D-U-N-S 20-044-5872   (HQ)
THISTLE PRINTING LIMITED
35 Mobile Dr, Toronto, ON, M4A 2P6
(416) 288-1288
Sales 14,598,403
SIC 2752 Commercial printing, lithographic
Erik Robinson
Bryan Hockaday
John Diclemente

Toronto, ON M4B

D-U-N-S 24-875-7528   (HQ)
AIRBORN FLEXIBLE CIRCUITS INC
(*Suby of* AIRBORN INTERCONNECT, INC.)
11 Dohme Ave, Toronto, ON, M4B 1Y7
(416) 752-2224
Sales 30,470,720
SIC 3672 Printed circuit boards
Michael Fielding
Dean F. Mastantuono

D-U-N-S 20-159-2516   (HQ)
ATLAS POLAR COMPANY LIMITED
HIAB QUEBEC
60 Northline Rd, Toronto, ON, M4B 3E5
(416) 751-7740
Emp Here 70   *Sales* 35,626,950
SIC 5084 Industrial machinery and equipment
Robert Parr
Laura Parr
Cecilia Lee

D-U-N-S 20-328-7177   (SL)
B & R HOLDINGS INC
32 Cranfield Rd, Toronto, ON, M4B 3H3
(416) 701-9800
Emp Here 100   *Sales* 23,343,500
SIC 2672 Paper; coated and laminated, nec
Rhys Seymour

D-U-N-S 24-708-2303   (SL)
DAVID YOUNGSON & ASSOCIATES LIM-
ITED
12 Cranfield Rd Unit 200, Toronto, ON, M4B
3G8
(416) 441-9696
Emp Here 28   *Sales* 20,790,560
SIC 5199 Nondurable goods, nec
David Youngson
Karin Schuster
Ray Shikatani
Helen Voronka

D-U-N-S 20-691-4058   (SL)
EVAGELOU ENTERPRISES INC
CRANFIELD GENERAL CONTRACTING
39 Cranfield Rd, Toronto, ON, M4B 3H6
(416) 285-4774
Emp Here 150   *Sales* 16,017,300
SIC 7299 Miscellaneous personal service
Frank Evagelou

D-U-N-S 24-075-5892   (SL)
GILLAM GROUP INC

36 Northline Rd, Toronto, ON, M4B 3E2
(416) 486-6776
Emp Here 60   *Sales* 119,703,150
SIC 8742 Management consulting services
Marcus Gillam
Joel Parke
Temple Harris

D-U-N-S 24-279-1028   (BR)
IPEX INC
IPEX MANAGEMENT
(*Suby of* ALIAXIS)
11 Bermondsey Rd, Toronto, ON, M4B 1Z3
(416) 751-3820
Emp Here 100
SIC 3089 Plastics products, nec
Kyle Beazley

D-U-N-S 24-418-0501   (SL)
KIANGTEX COMPANY LIMITED
46 Hollinger Rd, Toronto, ON, M4B 3G5
(416) 750-3771
Emp Here 120   *Sales* 100,503,960
SIC 5137 Women's and children's clothing

D-U-N-S 20-168-4628   (HQ)
KIDD, H.A. AND COMPANY LIMITED
5 Northline Rd, Toronto, ON, M4B 3P2
(416) 364-6451
Emp Here 85   *Sales* 15,576,120
SIC 3965 Fasteners, buttons, needles, and pins
Barton Earle
Darlene Devine
Douglas Earle

D-U-N-S 24-326-9300   (SL)
MONTY PHARMACY LTD
SHOPPERS DRUG MART
812 O'Connor Dr, Toronto, ON, M4B 2S9
(416) 285-5822
Emp Here 50   *Sales* 12,647,700
SIC 5912 Drug stores and proprietary stores
Lucija Djurovic-Djukic

D-U-N-S 24-096-4130   (HQ)
R.O.M CONTRACTORS LIMITED
25 Curity Ave Unit 4, Toronto, ON, M4B 3M2
(416) 285-0190
Sales 10,462,120
SIC 6712 Bank holding companies
John Richardson

D-U-N-S 24-469-7124   (SL)
ST. CLAIR O'CONNOR COMMUNITY INC
2701 St Clair Ave E Suite 211, Toronto, ON, M4B 1M5
(416) 757-8757
Emp Here 80   *Sales* 4,739,760
SIC 8361 Residential care
Walter Friesen

D-U-N-S 25-406-4918   (SL)
STAR OFFICE INSTALLIONS LTD
85 Northline Rd, Toronto, ON, M4B 3E9
(416) 750-1104
Emp Here 25   *Sales* 10,483,875
SIC 6712 Bank holding companies
Luciano Puopolo
Peter Tosh

D-U-N-S 24-287-0962   (SL)
TANG APPAREL CO. LIMITED
50 Northline Rd, Toronto, ON, M4B 3E2
(416) 603-0021
Emp Here 80   *Sales* 10,933,920
SIC 2337 Women's and misses' suits and coats
James Tang

D-U-N-S 20-200-9481   (SL)
TOP RANK BUSINESS ASSOCIATES GROUP OF COMPANY INC
2863 St Clair Ave E, Toronto, ON, M4B 1N4

Emp Here 150
SIC 8741 Management services

Toronto, ON M4C

D-U-N-S 20-977-2784   (SL)
1719094 ONTARIO INC
HOME INSTEAD SENIOR CARE
953 Woodbine Ave, Toronto, ON, M4C 4B6
(416) 698-1384
Emp Here 65   *Sales* 17,831,580
SIC 8741 Management services
John Colin Macdonald

D-U-N-S 25-275-7000   (SL)
A WAY EXPRESS COURIER SERVICE
2168 Danforth Ave, Toronto, ON, M4C 1K3
(416) 424-4471
Emp Here 60   *Sales* 26,953,140
SIC 7389 Business services, nec
Laurie Hall

D-U-N-S 24-196-4675   (HQ)
BIRTHRIGHT
BIRTHRIGHT INTERNATIONAL
777 Coxwell Ave, Toronto, ON, M4C 3C6
(416) 469-1111
Emp Here 5   *Sales* 45,554,960
SIC 8399 Social services, nec
Louise R Summerhill
Mary Berney
Stephanie Fox

D-U-N-S 24-642-1379   (SL)
CANADIAN TIRE
2681 Danforth Ave Suite 273, Toronto, ON, M4C 1L4
(416) 690-6069
Emp Here 30   *Sales* 14,942,340
SIC 5531 Auto and home supply stores
Ray Macdonald

D-U-N-S 24-199-4235   (SL)
ISON T.H. AUTO SALES INC
TORONTO HONDA
2300 Danforth Ave, Toronto, ON, M4C 1K6
(416) 423-2300
Emp Here 63   *Sales* 39,644,640
SIC 5511 New and used car dealers
Jordan Ison

D-U-N-S 24-024-0973   (BR)
METRO ONTARIO INC
DOMINION
(*Suby of* METRO INC)
1500 Woodbine Ave, Toronto, ON, M4C 4G9
(416) 422-0076
Emp Here 100
SIC 5411 Grocery stores
Jim Pupo

D-U-N-S 25-692-9332   (BR)
NEIGHBOURHOOD GROUP COMMUNITY SERVICES, THE
STEPHENSON SENIOR LINK HOME
(*Suby of* NEIGHBOURHOOD GROUP COMMUNITY SERVICES, THE)
11 Coatsworth Cres, Toronto, ON, M4C 5P8
(416) 691-7407
Emp Here 105
SIC 8322 Individual and family services
Jenny Destesano

D-U-N-S 25-529-8457   (HQ)
NEIGHBOURHOOD GROUP COMMUNITY SERVICES, THE
3036 Danforth Ave, Toronto, ON, M4C 1N2
(416) 691-7407
Sales 14,998,425
SIC 8322 Individual and family services
Mary Christie
Philip Fernandez
Marguerite Rea
Jennifer Rae
Robert Gore

D-U-N-S 20-898-8167   (SL)
OP PROMOTIONS INC
1017 Woodbine Ave Unit 408, Toronto, ON,

M4C 4C3
(416) 425-0363
Emp Here 100   *Sales* 23,428,800
SIC 8743 Public relations services
Michael Melton

D-U-N-S 25-090-2947   (BR)
SOBEYS CAPITAL INCORPORATED
(*Suby of* EMPIRE COMPANY LIMITED)
2451 Danforth Ave Suite 938, Toronto, ON, M4C 1L1
(416) 698-6868
Emp Here 120
SIC 5411 Grocery stores
Nick Lucarelli

D-U-N-S 24-170-9588   (SL)
ST. PIERRE, BARRY PHARMACY LTD
SHOPPERS DRUG MART
1500 Woodbine Ave, Toronto, ON, M4C 4G9
(416) 429-2529
Emp Here 70   *Sales* 17,102,960
SIC 5912 Drug stores and proprietary stores
Barry St. Pierre

D-U-N-S 25-139-0597   (BR)
TORONTO DISTRICT SCHOOL BOARD
EAST YORK COLLEGIATE INSTITUTE
(*Suby of* TORONTO DISTRICT SCHOOL BOARD)
650 Cosburn Ave, Toronto, ON, M4C 2V2
(416) 396-2355
Emp Here 200
SIC 8211 Elementary and secondary schools
John Bratina

D-U-N-S 20-819-7541   (SL)
TORONTO EAST GENERAL GIFT SHOP
825 Coxwell Ave, Toronto, ON, M4C 3E7
(416) 469-6050
Emp Here 61   *Sales* 14,904,008
SIC 5947 Gift, novelty, and souvenir shop
Gail Brodeur

D-U-N-S 24-008-9243   (HQ)
TORONTO EAST HEALTH NETWORK
MICHAEL GARRON HOSPITAL
825 Coxwell Ave, Toronto, ON, M4C 3E7
(416) 461-8272
Emp Here 2,000   *Sales* 333,240,000
SIC 8062 General medical and surgical hospitals
Sarah Downey
Wolf Klassen
Carmine Stumpo
Irene Andress
Robert Orr
Sarah Chow
Mitze Mourinho
Ian Fraser
Susan Armstrong
Imogen Coe

D-U-N-S 25-900-9137   (SL)
TORONTO KIA
2222 Danforth Ave, Toronto, ON, M4C 1K3
(416) 421-9000
Emp Here 25   *Sales* 12,451,950
SIC 5511 New and used car dealers
Gregory Kensit

D-U-N-S 20-413-3904   (SL)
VANDENBURG, ROMEO DRUG COMPANY LTD
SHOPPERS DRUG MART
3003 Danforth Ave, Toronto, ON, M4C 1M9
(416) 694-2131
Emp Here 50   *Sales* 12,647,700
SIC 5912 Drug stores and proprietary stores
Romeo Vandenburg

Toronto, ON M4E

D-U-N-S 20-376-9161   (SL)
BUILT TO SELL INC

VALUE BUILDER SYSTEM
2175 Queen St E Unit 302, Toronto, ON, M4E 1E5
(416) 628-9754
Emp Here 15   *Sales* 96,407,296
SIC 5734 Computer and software stores
John Warrillow

D-U-N-S 24-964-4204   (SL)
DAVIS & WILLMOT INC
2060 Queen St E Suite 51504, Toronto, ON, M4E 1C9

Emp Here 75   *Sales* 39,040,650
SIC 5094 Jewelry and precious stones

D-U-N-S 20-329-7536   (SL)
ESTATE REALTY LTD
ROYAL LEPAGE ESTATE REALTY
1052 Kingston Rd, Toronto, ON, M4E 1T4
(416) 690-5100
Emp Here 145   *Sales* 61,442,377
SIC 6531 Real estate agents and managers

D-U-N-S 24-695-3330   (SL)
INKAS FINANCE CORP
2192 Gerrard St E, Toronto, ON, M4E 2C7
(416) 686-4587
Emp Here 100   *Sales* 23,428,800
SIC 8742 Management consulting services
David Khazanski
Margarita Simkin
David Tsyrlin
Paul Khakhan
Llia Klytchkov

D-U-N-S 20-260-9157   (SL)
PEGASUS COMMUNITY PROJECT
931 Kingston Rd, Toronto, ON, M4E 1S6
(416) 691-5651
Emp Here 35   *Sales* 13,909,490
SIC 8699 Membership organizations, nec
Sheryl Gailbraigh

D-U-N-S 25-531-6911   (BR)
RE/MAX HALLMARK REALTY LTD
(*Suby of* RE/MAX HALLMARK REALTY LTD)
2237 Queen St E, Toronto, ON, M4E 1G1
(416) 357-1059
Emp Here 130
SIC 6531 Real estate agents and managers
Joy Robertson

D-U-N-S 24-306-4797   (BR)
REVERA LONG TERM CARE INC
VERSA CARE
(*Suby of* GOVERNMENT OF CANADA)
77 Main St, Toronto, ON, M4E 2V6
(416) 690-3001
Emp Here 120
SIC 8051 Skilled nursing care facilities
Elizabeth Bradshaw

Toronto, ON M4G

D-U-N-S 25-188-9564   (SL)
1437384 ONTARIO LIMITED
TREMBLETTS VALU-MART
1500 Bayview Ave, Toronto, ON, M4G 3B4
(416) 486-8294
Emp Here 40   *Sales* 10,966,080
SIC 5411 Grocery stores
Warn Schindel

D-U-N-S 20-808-9255   (SL)
ACCORD SPECIALIZED INVESTIGATIONS & SECURITY
1560 Bayview Ave Suite 300, Toronto, ON, M4G 3B8
(416) 322-2013
Emp Here 75   *Sales* 29,675,850
SIC 7382 Security systems services
Kim Kane

D-U-N-S 20-160-5227   (SL)

AMSTERDAM BREWING CO. LIMITED
45 Esandar Dr Unit 2, Toronto, ON, M4G 4C5
(416) 504-1040
Emp Here 50   *Sales* 11,242,750
SIC 2082 Malt beverages
  Jefferson Carefoote

        D-U-N-S 20-325-8678   (SL)
ASTOR & YORK RETAIL BC LTD
1721 Bayview Ave Unit 202, Toronto, ON,
M4G 3C1
(416) 434-2900
Emp Here 120   *Sales* 50,266,680
SIC 6531 Real estate agents and managers
  Corey Samuel

        D-U-N-S 20-527-8737   (SL)
B.L.T. CONSTRUCTION SERVICES INC
953a Eglinton Ave E, Toronto, ON, M4G 4B5
(416) 755-2505
Emp Here 55   *Sales* 23,250,535
SIC 1541 Industrial buildings and warehouses
  Mark Watts
  John Watts
  Paul Watts
  Jack Watts

        D-U-N-S 25-214-6428   (SL)
BRENNAN PONTIAC BUICK GMC LTD
1860 Bayview Ave, Toronto, ON, M4G 0C3
(416) 485-0350
Emp Here 60   *Sales* 37,756,800
SIC 5511 New and used car dealers
  Mark Brennan

        D-U-N-S 20-163-6842   (SL)
BRIAN DOMELLE ENTERPRISES LIMITED
CANADIAN TIRE ASSOCIATE STORE
459-825 Eglinton Ave E, Toronto, ON, M4G
4G9
(416) 422-0303
Emp Here 150   *Sales* 40,147,800
SIC 5251 Hardware stores
  Brian Domelle
  Devon Parsons
  Regan Franklin
  Tristan Styner
  Jordan Domelle

        D-U-N-S 20-552-9126   (HQ)
**CANADIAN NATIONAL INSTITUTE FOR
THE BLIND, THE**
CNIB
1929 Bayview Ave, Toronto, ON, M4G 3E8
(416) 486-2500
Emp Here 250   *Sales* 61,178,367
SIC 8331 Job training and related services
  John M. Rafferty
  Pamela Gow-Boyd
  Diane Bergeron
  John Mulka
  Rob Hindley
  Keith Gordon
  Garry Nenson
  Maria Ash
  Angela Bonfanti
  Craig Lillico

        D-U-N-S 20-073-3843   (BR)
**CENTRE FOR ADDICTION AND MENTAL
HEALTH**
QUEEN STREET MENTAL HEALTH
(*Suby of* CENTRE FOR ADDICTION AND
MENTAL HEALTH)
175 Brentcliffe Rd, Toronto, ON, M4G 0C5
(416) 425-3930
Emp Here 1,000
SIC 8093 Specialty outpatient clinics, nec
  Jackie Jagoda

        D-U-N-S 25-462-8928   (SL)
**COLDWELL BANKER PROPERTIES UN-
LIMITED REALTY LTD**
874 Eglinton Ave E, Toronto, ON, M4G 2L1
(416) 424-1300
Emp Here 45   *Sales* 14,720,715
SIC 6531 Real estate agents and managers

  Wendy Leblanc

        D-U-N-S 20-848-9633   (SL)
DONWOOD INSTITUTE, THE
*CENTRE FOR ADDICTION MENTAL
HEALTH*
175 Brentcliffe Rd, Toronto, ON, M4G 0C5
(416) 425-3930
Emp Here 100   *Sales* 8,183,300
SIC 8069 Specialty hospitals, except psychi-
atric
  Steven Sharp
  Peter Moore
  Pamela Jeffery
  David Korn
  Mike Prociw
  Melinie Wozick

        D-U-N-S 20-328-1456   (SL)
EVENT RENTAL GROUP GP INC
210 Wicksteed Ave, Toronto, ON, M4G 2C3
(416) 759-2611
Emp Here 30   *Sales* 13,476,570
SIC 7389 Business services, nec
  Gregory A. Halton
  Blake Lyon
  Ronald Halton
  Simon Martin
  Sam Reisman

        D-U-N-S 20-786-0958   (HQ)
**HOLLAND BLOORVIEW KIDS REHABILI-
TATION HOSPITAL**
150 Kilgour Rd, Toronto, ON, M4G 1R8
(416) 425-6220
Emp Here 500   *Sales* 94,418,000
SIC 8069 Specialty hospitals, except psychi-
atric
  Julia Hanigsberg
  Tom Chau
  Diana Savage

        D-U-N-S 20-647-4475   (HQ)
**HOLLAND BLOORVIEW KIDS REHABILI-
TATION HOSPITAL FOUNDATION**
150 Kilgour Rd, Toronto, ON, M4G 1R8
(416) 424-3809
Sales 17,021,088
SIC 8699 Membership organizations, nec
  Sandra Hawken
  Julie Forrest
  Sarah Barker
  Dayna Bleeman
  Donna Inch

        D-U-N-S 20-108-5318   (BR)
HOME DEPOT OF CANADA INC
HOME DEPOT
(*Suby of* THE HOME DEPOT INC)
101 Wicksteed Ave, Toronto, ON, M4G 4H9
(416) 467-2300
Emp Here 200
SIC 5251 Hardware stores
  Sandra Carlucci

        D-U-N-S 20-167-2748   (HQ)
HOUSE OF METALS COMPANY LIMITED
(*Suby of* 556212 ONTARIO LIMITED)
45 Commercial Rd, Toronto, ON, M4G 1Z3
(416) 421-1572
Sales 11,179,350
SIC 5051 Metals service centers and offices
  Tom Lobel
  Daniel Bitton

        D-U-N-S 25-318-2000   (BR)
HU-A-KAM ENTERPRISES INC
MCDONALD'S
(*Suby of* HU-A-KAM ENTERPRISES INC)
1787 Bayview Ave, Toronto, ON, M4G 3C5
(416) 292-0459
Emp Here 76
SIC 5812 Eating places
  Hilda Cavaro

        D-U-N-S 24-859-1810   (BR)
LEVITT-SAFETY LIMITED

NL TECHNOLOGIES
(*Suby of* LEVITT-SAFETY LIMITED)
33 Laird Dr, Toronto, ON, M4G 3S8
(416) 425-6659
Emp Here 300
SIC 5999 Miscellaneous retail stores, nec
  Robert Fiset

        D-U-N-S 20-169-3330   (HQ)
**LINCOLN ELECTRIC COMPANY OF
CANADA LP**
INDALCO ALLOYS, A DIV OF
(*Suby of* LINCOLN ELECTRIC HOLDINGS,
INC.)
179 Wicksteed Ave, Toronto, ON, M4G 2B9
(416) 421-2600
Emp Here 245   *Sales* 70,219,250
SIC 3548 Welding apparatus
  Joseph Doria

        D-U-N-S 25-504-5338   (BR)
LOBLAWS SUPERMARKETS LIMITED
LOBLAWS
(*Suby of* LOBLAW COMPANIES LIMITED)
301 Moore Ave, Toronto, ON, M4G 1E1
(416) 425-0604
Emp Here 100
SIC 5411 Grocery stores
  Ross Bonomo

        D-U-N-S 20-081-6242   (SL)
MARANT CONSTRUCTION LIMITED
(*Suby of* MARANT HOLDINGS LIMITED)
200 Wicksteed Ave, Toronto, ON, M4G 2B6
(416) 425-6650
Emp Here 66   *Sales* 37,642,308
SIC 1542 Nonresidential construction, nec
  Gino Vettoretto

        D-U-N-S 20-170-6223   (HQ)
MERCEDES-BENZ CANADA INC
(*Suby of* DAIMLER AG)
98 Vanderhoof Ave, Toronto, ON, M4G 4C9
(416) 425-3550
Emp Here 289   *Sales* 783,961,800
SIC 5012 Automobiles and other motor vehi-
cles
  Brian D. Fulton
  Robert Muller
  Joachim Schmidt
  Hannu Ylanko
  Christian Spelter
  Tim A Reuss
  James C M Rossitier

        D-U-N-S 24-355-7308   (BR)
RESOLVE CORPORATION
210 Wicksteed Ave, Toronto, ON, M4G 2C3

Emp Here 130
SIC 8743 Public relations services

        D-U-N-S 24-124-0274   (SL)
**ROY FOSS SATURN SAAB OF LEASIDE
LTD**
MIDTOWN SATURN SAAB ISUZU
957 Eglinton Ave E, Toronto, ON, M4G 4B5

Emp Here 60   *Sales* 37,756,800
SIC 5511 New and used car dealers
  Roy Foss
  Karen Foss-Ricci
  Paul Hartley

        D-U-N-S 25-791-4960   (SL)
SELECT BAIT & FISHING SUPPLIES INC
45 Research Rd, Toronto, ON, M4G 2G8
(416) 429-5656
Emp Here 45   *Sales* 33,413,400
SIC 5199 Nondurable goods, nec
  Ioannis Karadimas

        D-U-N-S 24-309-1514   (SL)
SHASHI FOODS INC
(*Suby of* CLARIUS INC)
55 Esandar Dr, Toronto, ON, M4G 4H2
(416) 645-0611
Emp Here 30   *Sales* 10,370,700

SIC 2044 Rice milling
  Sujay Shah
  Ajay Shah

        D-U-N-S 25-844-2854   (BR)
ST. MARYS CEMENT INC. (CANADA)
CBM-CANADA BUILDING MAT CO
(*Suby of* HEJOASSU ADMINISTRACAO S/A)
55 Industrial St, Toronto, ON, M4G 3W9
(416) 423-1300
Emp Here 200
SIC 3273 Ready-mixed concrete

        D-U-N-S 20-174-7268   (HQ)
ST. MARYS CEMENT INC. (CANADA)
ST. MARYS CEMENT CO
(*Suby of* HEJOASSU ADMINISTRACAO S/A)
55 Industrial St, Toronto, ON, M4G 3W9
(416) 423-1300
Emp Here 75   *Sales* 357,966,000
SIC 3241 Cement, hydraulic
  Martin (Matty) Fallon
  Celso Martini
  Bram Vermeulen
  Gerry Hahn
  Michael Pengelly

        D-U-N-S 20-048-5238   (BR)
TORONTO DISTRICT SCHOOL BOARD
*NORTHLEA ELEMENTARY & MIDDLE
SCHOOL*
(*Suby of* TORONTO DISTRICT SCHOOL
BOARD)
305 Rumsey Rd, Toronto, ON, M4G 1R4
(416) 396-2395
Emp Here 75
SIC 8211 Elementary and secondary schools
  David Ehrlich

        D-U-N-S 24-347-9982   (BR)
TORONTO REHABILITATION INSTITUTE
(*Suby of* UNIVERSITY HEALTH NETWORK)
520 Sutherland Dr, Toronto, ON, M4G 3V9
(416) 597-3422
Emp Here 500
SIC 8093 Specialty outpatient clinics, nec
  Milos Popovic

        D-U-N-S 24-625-2399   (SL)
UNICELL LIMITED
50 Industrial St, Toronto, ON, M4G 1Y9
(416) 421-6845
Emp Here 75   *Sales* 16,788,225
SIC 3713 Truck and bus bodies
  Roger Martin
  Scott Vader
  David Martin

        D-U-N-S 24-575-7786   (SL)
WRAP-IT-UP INC
660 Eglinton Ave E, Toronto, ON, M4G 2K2

Emp Here 78   *Sales* 21,008,412
SIC 5947 Gift, novelty, and souvenir shop

Toronto, ON M4H

        D-U-N-S 20-610-0062   (HQ)
1461148 ONTARIO CORP
PETRO CANADA
8 Thorncliffe Park Dr, Toronto, ON, M4H 1H4
(416) 421-3723
Emp Here 5   *Sales* 24,903,900
SIC 5541 Gasoline service stations
  Samir Lamy

        D-U-N-S 24-206-7242   (SL)
BEE-CLEAN (TORONTO) LTD
BEE-CLEAN BUILDING MAINTENANCE
2 Thorncliffe Park Dr Unit 22, Toronto, ON,
M4H 1H2
(416) 410-6181
Emp Here 249   *Sales* 7,960,032
SIC 7349 Building maintenance services, nec
  Jose Correia

▲ Public Company   ■ Public Company Family Member   **HQ** Headquarters   **BR** Branch   **SL** Single Location

Peter Dobrowolfki

D-U-N-S 24-685-3993 (SL)
CANADA NATIONAL OWN COMPANY (CNOC)
71 Thorncliffe Park Dr Suite 403, Toronto, ON, M4H 1L3
(647) 520-9004
Emp Here 100 *Sales* 103,244,400
SIC 6799 Investors, nec
Malik Shiza

D-U-N-S 24-289-1075 (HQ)
CANAM BUILDING ENVELOPE SPECIALISTS INC
(*Suby of* RPM INTERNATIONAL INC.)
50 Beth Nealson Dr, Toronto, ON, M4H 1M6
(416) 467-3485
Emp Here 19 *Sales* 10,732,176
SIC 5033 Roofing, siding, and insulation
Anthony Woods
William Boyd

D-U-N-S 24-723-3542 (SL)
DEBEERS CANADA EXPLORATION
65 Overlea Blvd Suite 300, Toronto, ON, M4H 1P1
(416) 645-1710
Emp Here 49 *Sales* 15,665,545
SIC 1382 Oil and gas exploration services
Martin Doyle

D-U-N-S 20-163-7550 (HQ)
DOMINION REGALIA LIMITED
4 Overlea Blvd, Toronto, ON, M4H 1A4
(416) 752-9987
Emp Here 16 *Sales* 13,120,704
SIC 2353 Hats, caps, and millinery
Alan Boothe
Geoffrey Boothe

D-U-N-S 20-163-8640 (HQ)
DOROTHEA KNITTING MILLS LIMITED
PARKHURST KNITWEAR
51 Beth Nealson Dr, Toronto, ON, M4H 0A4
(416) 421-3773
Emp Here 175 *Sales* 70,950,900
SIC 2253 Knit outerwear mills
Steven Borsook
Lisa Borsook
Cathi Borsook-Freedman

D-U-N-S 24-627-2595 (HQ)
GOVERNING COUNCIL OF THE SALVATION ARMY IN CANADA, THE
BOOTH INDUSTRIES, A DIV OF
2 Overlea Blvd, Toronto, ON, M4H 1P4
(416) 425-2111
Emp Here 250 *Sales* 142,699,284
SIC 8399 Social services, nec
Brian Peddle
Paul R Goodyear
Sandra Rice
Lee Graves
Mark Tillsley

D-U-N-S 25-105-8327 (SL)
IQBAL FOODS CORPORATION
2 Thorncliffe Park Dr Unit 10, Toronto, ON, M4H 1H2
(416) 467-0177
Emp Here 55 *Sales* 45,956,735
SIC 5141 Groceries, general line
Iqbal Malek
Nazim Tajuddin
Anwar Tejani

D-U-N-S 20-844-8209 (HQ)
MARCH OF DIMES CANADA
10 Overlea Blvd, Toronto, ON, M4H 1A4
(416) 425-3463
Emp Here 80 *Sales* 81,478,388
SIC 8331 Job training and related services
Andria Spindel
Jerry Lucas
Michael Cole
Peter Rumyee
Zullfikar Chaggan

Jenelle Ross
Cameron Whale

D-U-N-S 25-300-3461 (BR)
METRO ONTARIO INC
FOOD BASICS
(*Suby of* METRO INC)
45 Overlea Blvd Suite 2, Toronto, ON, M4H 1C3
(416) 421-1732
Emp Here 180
SIC 5411 Grocery stores
Jean Miljevic

D-U-N-S 20-923-3741 (HQ)
MOUNT PLEASANT GROUP OF CEMETERIES
65 Overlea Blvd Suite 500, Toronto, ON, M4H 1P1
(416) 696-7866
Emp Here 15 *Sales* 37,232,200
SIC 6553 Cemetery subdividers and developers
Glenn Mcclary
Lucy Lombardi
Louise Maclean

D-U-N-S 20-166-9249 (SL)
R.G. HENDERSON & SON LIMITED
FOOD EQUIPMENT PARTS & SERVICE
100 Thorncliffe Park Dr Suite 416, Toronto, ON, M4H 1L9
(416) 422-5580
Emp Here 64 *Sales* 17,397,888
SIC 7699 Repair services, nec
William Blum
Rick Blum
Ronald Boyce

D-U-N-S 25-193-0806 (HQ)
RPM CANADA
TREMCO CANADA
(*Suby of* RPM INTERNATIONAL INC.)
220 Wicksteed Ave, Toronto, ON, M4H 1G7
(416) 421-3300
Emp Here 450 *Sales* 333,483,750
SIC 2851 Paints and allied products
Kathie Rogers

D-U-N-S 25-058-0479 (HQ)
SILTECH CORPORATION
225 Wicksteed Ave, Toronto, ON, M4H 1G5
(416) 424-4567
Emp Here 130 *Sales* 36,922,730
SIC 2869 Industrial organic chemicals, nec
Richard Vrckovnik
Dag Enhorning
Milan Vrckovnik

D-U-N-S 24-213-7685 (SL)
SPECIAL OLYMPICS ONTARIO INC
65 Overlea Blvd Suite 200, Toronto, ON, M4H 1P1
(416) 447-8326
Emp Here 27 *Sales* 10,730,178
SIC 8699 Membership organizations, nec
Glen Macdonell
Armand La Barge
Robert Wilkes

D-U-N-S 20-299-8050 (SL)
TI GROUP INC
115 Thorncliffe Park Dr, Toronto, ON, M4H 1M1
(416) 696-2853
Emp Here 200 *Sales* 32,805,400
SIC 2752 Commercial printing, lithographic
Peter Spring
Alice Chan
David Smith

D-U-N-S 20-104-1683 (SL)
TI HOLDINGS INC
115 Thorncliffe Park Dr, Toronto, ON, M4H 1M1
(416) 696-2853
Emp Here 51 *Sales* 13,339,203
SIC 6712 Bank holding companies

David Smith
Timothy K Wood

D-U-N-S 25-265-0791 (BR)
TORONTO DISTRICT SCHOOL BOARD
THORNCLIFFE PARK PUBLIC SCHOOL
(*Suby of* TORONTO DISTRICT SCHOOL BOARD)
80 Thorncliffe Park Dr, Toronto, ON, M4H 1K3
(416) 396-2460
Emp Here 110
SIC 8211 Elementary and secondary schools
Jeffrey Crane

Toronto, ON M4J

D-U-N-S 25-721-3348 (HQ)
1185985 ONTARIO INC
EAST YORK HEARING CENTER
1573 Danforth Ave, Toronto, ON, M4J 1N8
(905) 607-1322
Emp Here 8 *Sales* 17,198,060
SIC 8099 Health and allied services, nec
Rhonda Martin
Lisa Martin

D-U-N-S 25-882-4341 (SL)
AMPHORA MAINTENANCE SERVICES INC
707a Danforth Ave, Toronto, ON, M4J 1L2
(416) 461-0401
Emp Here 95 *Sales* 3,819,855
SIC 7349 Building maintenance services, nec
Savvas Krotiris
Tony Krotiris
George Krotiris

D-U-N-S 20-041-1606 (SL)
COLDWELL CASE REALTY
836 Danforth Ave, Toronto, ON, M4J 1L6
(416) 690-7771
Emp Here 49 *Sales* 16,029,223
SIC 6531 Real estate agents and managers
Doug Fraser

D-U-N-S 25-512-3135 (SL)
DAILY SEAFOOD INC
135 Blake St, Toronto, ON, M4J 3E2
(416) 461-9449
Emp Here 35 *Sales* 29,245,195
SIC 5146 Fish and seafoods
Timen Ho
Jessie Ho

D-U-N-S 24-218-1899 (SL)
KNORR BRAKE LIMITED
(*Suby of* STELLA VERMOGENSVERWALTUNGS GMBH)
101 Condor Ave, Toronto, ON, M4J 3N2
(416) 461-4343
Emp Here 75 *Sales* 16,788,225
SIC 3743 Railroad equipment
Paul Morgan

D-U-N-S 20-010-2306 (SL)
L'ARCHE TORONTO HOMES INC
186 Floyd Ave, Toronto, ON, M4J 2J1
(416) 406-2869
Emp Here 35 *Sales* 11,012,120
SIC 8699 Membership organizations, nec
Jean Vanier
Raphael Arens

D-U-N-S 24-334-3035 (SL)
MAPLE LEAF TAXI-CAB LIMITED
1245 Danforth Ave Suite 203, Toronto, ON, M4J 5B5
(416) 465-2445
Emp Here 250 *Sales* 18,818,000
SIC 4121 Taxicabs
Andres Leonidis

D-U-N-S 24-863-5380 (SL)
ST LEONARDS SOCIETY OF TORONTO
779 Danforth Ave, Toronto, ON, M4J 1L2

(416) 462-1596
Emp Here 30 *Sales* 11,922,420
SIC 8699 Membership organizations, nec
Sonya Spencer

D-U-N-S 20-697-6230 (BR)
TORONTO CATHOLIC DISTRICT SCHOOL BOARD
ST. PATRICK CATHOLIC SECONDARY SCHOOL
(*Suby of* TORONTO CATHOLIC DISTRICT SCHOOL BOARD)
49 Felstead Ave, Toronto, ON, M4J 1G3
(416) 393-5546
Emp Here 75
SIC 8211 Elementary and secondary schools
Sandra Mudryj

D-U-N-S 25-531-1607 (BR)
TORONTO DISTRICT SCHOOL BOARD
MONARCH PARK COLLEGIATE
(*Suby of* TORONTO DISTRICT SCHOOL BOARD)
1 Hanson St, Toronto, ON, M4J 1G6
(416) 393-0190
Emp Here 90
SIC 8211 Elementary and secondary schools
Cynthia Abernathy

D-U-N-S 25-319-8733 (BR)
TORONTO TRANSIT COMMISSION
(*Suby of* TORONTO TRANSIT COMMISSION)
400 Greenwood Ave, Toronto, ON, M4J 4Y5
(416) 393-3176
Emp Here 200
SIC 4111 Local and suburban transit
Malcolm Mackay

D-U-N-S 24-608-9858 (HQ)
WOODGREEN COMMUNITY SERVICES
815 Danforth Ave Suite 100, Toronto, ON, M4J 1L2
(416) 645-6000
Emp Here 50 *Sales* 41,413,600
SIC 8399 Social services, nec
Anne Babcock
Thomas Hofmann
Larry Whatmore

Toronto, ON M4K

D-U-N-S 24-545-3667 (SL)
546073 ONTARIO LIMITED
BIG CARROT NATURAL FOOD MARKET
348 Danforth Ave Suite 8, Toronto, ON, M4K 1N8
(416) 466-2129
Emp Here 100 *Sales* 29,347,700
SIC 5499 Miscellaneous food stores
Daiva Koyzanauskaf
Tony Lichtenberg

D-U-N-S 25-341-3587 (SL)
602726 ONTARIO LTD
PAPE I G A
623 Danforth Ave, Toronto, ON, M4K 1R2
(416) 466-5371
Emp Here 45 *Sales* 12,336,840
SIC 5411 Grocery stores
Ken Kyriacou

D-U-N-S 24-195-4825 (HQ)
CONREZ GROUP LTD, THE
LEGS BEAUTIFUL
366 Danforth Ave Suite A, Toronto, ON, M4K 1N8
(416) 449-7444
Emp Here 1 *Sales* 72,271,080
SIC 6794 Patent owners and lessors
Ian Collins
Andrew Kerekes

D-U-N-S 25-520-4380 (BR)
GOVERNING COUNCIL OF THE SALVA-

TION ARMY IN CANADA, THE
GOVERNING COUNCIL OF THE SALVATION ARMY IN CANADA,
(Suby of GOVERNING COUNCIL OF THE SALVATION ARMY IN CANADA, THE)
1132 Broadview Ave, Toronto, ON, M4K 2S5
(416) 425-1052
Emp Here 120
SIC 8399 Social services, nec
Jeff Robertson

D-U-N-S 20-487-8610   (SL)
IMMEDIATE RESPONSE FORCE INC
IMMEDIATE RESPONSE SERVICE
1127 Broadview Ave Unit B, Toronto, ON, M4K 2S6
(647) 987-0002
Emp Here 178   *Sales* 591,320
SIC 8748 Business consulting, nec
Muhammad Ashar

D-U-N-S 24-382-3288   (BR)
LOBLAWS INC
LOBLAWS
(Suby of LOBLAW COMPANIES LIMITED)
720 Broadview Ave, Toronto, ON, M4K 2P1
(416) 778-8762
Emp Here 100
SIC 5411 Grocery stores
Ross Bonomo

D-U-N-S 20-784-3632   (SL)
NISBET LODGE
740 Pape Ave, Toronto, ON, M4K 3S7
(416) 469-1105
Emp Here 100   *Sales* 5,924,700
SIC 8361 Residential care
William Louth
Craig S Lougheed
Glen Moorehouse
John Cambridge
Lorna Gard
Kenneth Morlock
Carol Morris
David Wilson
John Wray

D-U-N-S 24-279-2125   (SL)
SIGNATURES CRAFT SHOWS LTD
SIGNATURES CRAFT SHOWS
37 Langley Ave, Toronto, ON, M4K 1B4
(416) 465-8055
Emp Here 30   *Sales* 13,304,700
SIC 7389 Business services, nec
John Ladoucer

D-U-N-S 25-988-4245   (BR)
SOBEYS CAPITAL INCORPORATED
SOBEYS 611
(Suby of EMPIRE COMPANY LIMITED)
1015 Broadview Ave Suite 718, Toronto, ON, M4K 2S1
(416) 421-5906
Emp Here 130
SIC 5141 Groceries, general line
Bill Mcewan

D-U-N-S 24-462-8780   (SL)
SUN VALLEY FRUIT MARKET & GRO-CERIES (DANFORTH) LTD
SUN VALLEY FINE FOODS
583 Danforth Ave, Toronto, ON, M4K 1P9
(416) 264-2323
Emp Here 45   *Sales* 12,336,840
SIC 5431 Fruit and vegetable markets
Gerry Aravantinos
Steve Aravantinos

D-U-N-S 25-237-9391   (BR)
TORONTO DISTRICT SCHOOL BOARD
CITY ADULT LEARNING CENTRE
(Suby of TORONTO DISTRICT SCHOOL BOARD)
1 Danforth Ave, Toronto, ON, M4K 1M8
(416) 393-9740
Emp Here 100
SIC 8211 Elementary and secondary schools

Richard Bilkszto

D-U-N-S 24-418-0092   (SL)
URBAN REALTY INC
ROYAL LEPAGE URBAN REALTY
840 Pape Ave, Toronto, ON, M4K 3T6
(416) 461-9900
Emp Here 75   *Sales* 20,381,700
SIC 6531 Real estate agents and managers
Diane Speer

Toronto, ON M4L

D-U-N-S 20-159-7887   (SL)
BEACH SUPERMARKETS LIMITED
BEACH I G A
2040 Queen St E, Toronto, ON, M4L 1J4
(416) 694-3011
Emp Here 50   *Sales* 13,707,600
SIC 5411 Grocery stores
Nick Kyriacous

D-U-N-S 24-779-6972   (SL)
HALO SECURITY INC
SECURITY MANAGEMENT SERVICES
1574 Queen St E Suite 1, Toronto, ON, M4L 1G1
(416) 360-1902
Emp Here 150   *Sales* 3,937,500
SIC 7381 Detective and armored car services
Sean O'brien

D-U-N-S 24-348-5844   (SL)
PILOT COFFEE CORP
50 Wagstaff Dr, Toronto, ON, M4L 3W9
(416) 546-4006
Emp Here 25   *Sales* 20,889,425
SIC 5149 Groceries and related products, nec
Jessie Wilkin
Robert Wilkin
Andrew Wilkin
Michelle Wilkin

Toronto, ON M4M

D-U-N-S 20-582-7657   (HQ)
2176542 ONTARIO LTD
BMW TORONTO
11 Sunlight Park Rd, Toronto, ON, M4M 1B5
(416) 623-4269
Sales 75,513,600
SIC 5521 Used car dealers
Thomas R Quinn

D-U-N-S 20-375-1669   (SL)
2232556 ONTARIO INC
MINI DOWNTOWN
11 Sunlight Park Rd, Toronto, ON, M4M 1B5
(416) 623-6464
Emp Here 50   *Sales* 24,903,900
SIC 5511 New and used car dealers
Patrick Quinn
Scott Quinn

D-U-N-S 24-413-7139   (SL)
498326 ONTARIO LIMITED
DOWNTOWN TOYOTA
677 Queen St E, Toronto, ON, M4M 1G6
(416) 465-5471
Emp Here 48   *Sales* 23,907,744
SIC 5511 New and used car dealers
Gary Grimme
Arthur Keller

D-U-N-S 24-097-3883   (HQ)
BAIRD MACGREGOR INSURANCE BRO-KERS INC
825 Queen St E, Toronto, ON, M4M 1H8
(416) 778-8000
Emp Here 67   *Sales* 129,341,940
SIC 6411 Insurance agents, brokers, and ser-vice

Philomena Comerford
Corrie Da Prato
Harry Mcgregor
Jack Baird

D-U-N-S 24-452-4377   (HQ)
CANROOF CORPORATION INC
(Suby of GOLDIS ENTERPRISES, INC.)
560 Commissioners St, Toronto, ON, M4M 1A7
(416) 461-8122
Emp Here 95   *Sales* 29,441,720
SIC 5211 Lumber and other building materials
Saul Koschitzky
Martin Vaughn
Henry Koschitzky

D-U-N-S 24-793-4813   (BR)
CASCADES CANADA ULC
CASCADES   BOXBOARD   GROUP TORONTO
(Suby of CASCADES INC)
495 Commissioners St, Toronto, ON, M4M 1A5
(416) 461-8261
Emp Here 150
SIC 2631 Paperboard mills
Tony Wong

D-U-N-S 24-795-1460   (SL)
CHAI POULTRY INC
HIGH KOSHER POULTRY
115 Saulter St S, Toronto, ON, M4M 3K8

Emp Here 100   *Sales* 83,557,700
SIC 5144 Poultry and poultry products

D-U-N-S 24-602-5233   (SL)
CHEUNG, HARRY PHARMACIES LTD
SHOPPERS DRUG MART
970 Queen St E Suite 823, Toronto, ON, M4M 1J8
(416) 462-0062
Emp Here 60   *Sales* 14,659,680
SIC 5912 Drug stores and proprietary stores
Harry Cheung

D-U-N-S 20-163-4268   (HQ)
DEMPSEY CORPORATION
47 Davies Ave, Toronto, ON, M4M 2A9
(416) 461-0844
Emp Here 35   *Sales* 51,124,150
SIC 5169 Chemicals and allied products, nec
Benjamin Dempsey

D-U-N-S 20-174-6653   (SL)
DIVERSIFIED TECHNOLOGY SYSTEMS INC
1043 Gerrard St E, Toronto, ON, M4M 1Z7
(416) 486-6587
Emp Here 51   *Sales* 11,948,688
SIC 8748 Business consulting, nec
Gavin Bridge
Paul Armstrong

D-U-N-S 20-902-1992   (SL)
HARIRI PONTARINI ARCHITECTS LLP
235 Carlaw Ave Suite 301, Toronto, ON, M4M 2S1
(416) 929-4901
Emp Here 60   *Sales* 10,557,480
SIC 8712 Architectural services
Siamak Hariri
David Pontarini

D-U-N-S 24-918-5786   (HQ)
HAVANA HOUSE CIGAR AND TOBACCO MERCHANTS LTD
9 Davies Ave Suite 112, Toronto, ON, M4M 2A6
(416) 406-6644
Emp Here 20   *Sales* 10,017,448
SIC 5993 Tobacco stores and stands
Jose Leugo

D-U-N-S 20-850-9141   (SL)
HERITAGE NURSING HOMES INC

1195 Queen St E Suite 229, Toronto, ON, M4M 1L6

Emp Here 160   *Sales* 10,970,560
SIC 8051 Skilled nursing care facilities
Daniel Glick
Marilyn Glick

D-U-N-S 24-045-3084   (SL)
HING LEE MOTORS LIMITED
SUBARU
601 Eastern Ave, Toronto, ON, M4M 1E3
(416) 461-2323
Emp Here 30   *Sales* 14,942,340
SIC 5511 New and used car dealers
Tom Leung
Paul Leung

D-U-N-S 20-039-7029   (BR)
LOBLAWS INC
LOBLAWS
(Suby of LOBLAW COMPANIES LIMITED)
17 Leslie St, Toronto, ON, M4M 3H9
(416) 469-2897
Emp Here 300
SIC 5411 Grocery stores
Pat Kelly

D-U-N-S 25-139-8095   (BR)
MAYFAIR TENNIS COURTS LIMITED
MAYFAIR RAQUET & FITNESS CLUBS
801 Lake Shore Blvd E, Toronto, ON, M4M 1A9
(416) 466-3770
Emp Here 80
SIC 7997 Membership sports and recreation clubs
Barbara Cougar

D-U-N-S 24-344-5140   (BR)
METROLINX
GO TRANSIT
(Suby of METROLINX)
580 Commissioners St, Toronto, ON, M4M 1A7
(416) 393-4111
Emp Here 350
SIC 4131 Intercity and rural bus transportation
Janet O'sullivan

D-U-N-S 20-378-3340   (SL)
NO FIXED ADDRESS INC
50 Carroll St, Toronto, ON, M4M 3G3
(416) 947-8584
Emp Here 60   *Sales* 12,022,260
SIC 7311 Advertising agencies
David Lafond
Serge Rancourt
Mark Carpenter
Olav Peter
Jennifer Siripong
Dave Federico
David Jowett
Serge Rancourt

D-U-N-S 25-669-0165   (SL)
NOUVEAU TASTE INC
38 Mcgee St, Toronto, ON, M4M 2K9
(416) 778-6300
Emp Here 20   *Sales* 10,702,480
SIC 5142 Packaged frozen goods
Fred Cheung

D-U-N-S 20-822-6548   (HQ)
O'SHANTER DEVELOPMENT COMPANY LTD
245 Carlaw Ave Suite 107, Toronto, ON, M4M 2S1
(416) 466-2642
Emp Here 25   *Sales* 15,460,970
SIC 6513 Apartment building operators
William Krehm
Johnathan Khrem
Adam Khrem

D-U-N-S 24-393-1388   (SL)
OLIVER, PETER M SALES LTD
CANADIAN TIRE EXPRESS

1015 Lake Shore Blvd E Suite 654, Toronto, ON, M4M 1B4
(416) 778-0102
Emp Here 150   *Sales* 94,392,000
SIC 5531 Auto and home supply stores
Peter Oliver

D-U-N-S 20-184-9127   (SL)
P. G. DISPOSAL SERVICE LTD
1-800-GOT-JUNK?
9 Dibble St Suite 1, Toronto, ON, M4M 2E7
(416) 467-8717
Emp Here 50   *Sales* 15,057,100
SIC 4953 Refuse systems
Paul Guy
Derick Ladurantaye

D-U-N-S 24-390-1852   (SL)
PTC AUTOMOTIVE LTD
GRAND TOURING AUTOMOBILES
777 Dundas St E, Toronto, ON, M4M 0E2
(416) 530-1366
Emp Here 40   *Sales* 19,923,120
SIC 5511 New and used car dealers
Paul Cummings
Donal Robidas
John Morabito

D-U-N-S 20-209-3410   (BR)
PUROLATOR INC
(*Suby of* GOVERNMENT OF CANADA)
20 Morse St, Toronto, ON, M4M 2P6
(416) 461-9031
Emp Here 350
SIC 4731 Freight transportation arrangement
Jamie Wright

D-U-N-S 24-079-2259   (HQ)
SO, JAMES REALTY LTD
259 Broadview Ave, Toronto, ON, M4M 2G6
(416) 465-2412
Emp Here 70   *Sales* 46,077,790
SIC 6531 Real estate agents and managers
James So

D-U-N-S 24-720-4415   (SL)
SOUTH RIVERDALE COMMUNITY HEALTH CENTRE
955 Queen St E, Toronto, ON, M4M 3P3
(416) 461-1925
Emp Here 80   *Sales* 12,851,680
SIC 8011 Offices and clinics of medical doctors
Lynne Raskin

D-U-N-S 25-341-0708   (HQ)
TD FINANCING SERVICES HOME INC
(*Suby of* TORONTO-DOMINION BANK, THE)
25 Booth Ave Suite 101, Toronto, ON, M4M 2M3
(416) 463-4422
Emp Here 200   *Sales* 158,601,000
SIC 6141 Personal credit institutions
Erik De Witte
Shailesh Kotwal
Christine Morris
Manjit Singh
Raymond Chun
Mark Clearihue
Sandra Mundy
Catherine Sampson

D-U-N-S 24-524-4491   (SL)
TOONBOX ENTERTAINMENT LTD
100 Broadview Ave Unit 400, Toronto, ON, M4M 3H3
(416) 362-8783
Emp Here 160   *Sales* 14,266,080
SIC 7812 Motion picture and video production
Hong Kim
Soo (Sue) Jung

D-U-N-S 25-237-9425   (BR)
TORONTO DISTRICT SCHOOL BOARD
RIVERDALE COLLEGIATE INSTITUTE
(*Suby of* TORONTO DISTRICT SCHOOL BOARD)
1094 Gerrard St E, Toronto, ON, M4M 2A1

(416) 393-9820
Emp Here 101
SIC 8211 Elementary and secondary schools
Kenneth Harvey

D-U-N-S 25-513-8026   (SL)
URBACON BUILDINGS GROUP CORP
URBACON
750 Lake Shore Blvd E, Toronto, ON, M4M 3M3
(416) 865-9405
Emp Here 80   *Sales* 9,982,080
SIC 8741 Management services
Marco Mancini
Ron Carinci

D-U-N-S 20-804-5331   (BR)
URBACON LIMITED
URBACON LIMITED/URBACON LIMITEE
(*Suby of* URBACON LIMITED)
750 Lake Shore Blvd E, Toronto, ON, M4M 3M3
(416) 865-9405
Emp Here 80
SIC 1541 Industrial buildings and warehouses
Nicole Fairman

D-U-N-S 24-524-9552   (HQ)
URBACON LIMITED
750 Lake Shore Blvd E, Toronto, ON, M4M 3M3
(416) 865-9405
Sales 79,897,293
SIC 1541 Industrial buildings and warehouses
Marco Mancini
Antonio Mancini

D-U-N-S 25-808-3211   (SL)
WILLYS URBANE CULTURE
276 Carlaw Ave Suite 218b, Toronto, ON, M4M 3L1
(416) 462-2038
Emp Here 20   *Sales* 10,006,500
SIC 5136 Men's and boy's clothing
David Setka

D-U-N-S 24-074-8749   (SL)
WINGBACK ENTERPRISES LIMITED
ADELAIDE CLUB, THE
(*Suby of* CAMBRIDGE GROUP INC)
1 First Ave, Toronto, ON, M4M 1W7
(416) 367-9957
Emp Here 80   *Sales* 6,283,600
SIC 7991 Physical fitness facilities
Clive Caldwell

Toronto, ON M4N

D-U-N-S 20-556-0035   (SL)
1095086 ONTARIO INC
GEMINI SOLUTIONS
3080 Yonge St Suite 4054, Toronto, ON, M4N 3N1
Emp Here 42   *Sales* 11,484,242
SIC 5072 Hardware

D-U-N-S 25-940-6817   (SL)
CSH FOUR TEDDINGTON PARK INC
CHARTWELL SENIOR HOUSING
(*Suby of* CHARTWELL MASTER CARE LP)
4 Teddington Park Ave, Toronto, ON, M4N 2C3
(416) 481-2986
Emp Here 47   *Sales* 10,946,817
SIC 6513 Apartment building operators
Brent Binions
Vlad Volodarski

D-U-N-S 24-218-8790   (SL)
D DENISON CONSULTANTS
1535 Mount Pleasant Rd, Toronto, ON, M4N 2V1
(416) 484-1893
Emp Here 46   *Sales* 10,777,248
SIC 8748 Business consulting, nec
Dan Denison

D-U-N-S 25-096-8898   (SL)
FUJIFILM VISUALSONICS INC
(*Suby of* FUJIFILM HOLDINGS CORPORATION)
3080 Yonge St Suite 6100, Toronto, ON, M4N 3N1
(416) 484-5000
Emp Here 60   *Sales* 13,637,340
SIC 3829 Measuring and controlling devices, nec
Anil Amlani
Randy Aucoin
Sam Ifergan
Doug Armstrong
William Clarke
Jeff Courtney
Harold Wodlinger
Steven Chackowicz
Larry Mcdowell
Lori Loparco

D-U-N-S 20-640-9740   (HQ)
GOWAY TRAVEL LIMITED
PACESETTER TRAVEL
3284 Yonge St Suite 500, Toronto, ON, M4N 3M7
(416) 322-1034
Emp Here 140   *Sales* 152,241,800
SIC 4725 Tour operators
Bruce Hodge
Claire Hodge
Peter Lacy

D-U-N-S 25-674-1356   (HQ)
GRID METALS CORP
3335 Yonge St Suite 304, Toronto, ON, M4N 2M1
(416) 955-4773
Emp Here 7   *Sales* 238,754,900
SIC 1021 Copper ores
Robin E. Dunbar
David Black
Rodger Roden
Thomas W. Meredith
Ted Munden

D-U-N-S 25-443-7924   (SL)
INSTITUTE FOR CLINICAL EVALUATIVE SCIENCES
ICES CENTRAL
2075 Bayview Ave Suite G106, Toronto, ON, M4N 3M5
(416) 480-4055
Emp Here 90   *Sales* 17,393,827
SIC 8733 Noncommercial research organizations
Michael Schull
Harry Deeg
Matthew Anderson
Anne Corbett
Colleen Flood
Laura Formusa
Murray Glendining
Harriet Macmillan
Geoffrey Rowan
Kathy Watts

D-U-N-S 20-079-1643   (HQ)
PACESETTER TRAVEL LIMITED
3284 Yonge St Suite 300, Toronto, ON, M4N 3M7
(416) 322-1031
Emp Here 115   *Sales* 90,030,420
SIC 4724 Travel agencies
Bruce Hodge
Claire Hodge

D-U-N-S 24-382-2223   (SL)
RESEARCH NOW INC
E-REWARDS
(*Suby of* CITIGROUP INC.)
3080 Yonge St Suite 2000, Toronto, ON, M4N 3N1
(800) 599-7938
Emp Here 152   *Sales* 34,922,608
SIC 8731 Commercial physical research
Kurt Knapton

D-U-N-S 20-770-7373   (SL)
ROSEDALE GOLF ASSOCIATION LIMITED, THE
ROSEDALE GOLF CLUB
1901 Mount Pleasant Rd, Toronto, ON, M4N 2W3
(416) 485-9321
Emp Here 110   *Sales* 8,639,950
SIC 7997 Membership sports and recreation clubs
William Vining

D-U-N-S 25-512-2400   (BR)
ROYAL LEPAGE LIMITED
LEPAGE ON YONGE
(*Suby of* BROOKFIELD ASSET MANAGEMENT INC)
3080 Yonge St Suite 2060, Toronto, ON, M4N 3N1
(416) 487-4311
Emp Here 96
SIC 6531 Real estate agents and managers
Trish Manning

D-U-N-S 20-046-6345   (HQ)
SUNNYBROOK HEALTH SCIENCES CENTRE
SUNNYBROOK HOSPITAL
2075 Bayview Ave, Toronto, ON, M4N 3M5
(416) 480-6100
Emp Here 7,000   *Sales* 882,520,338
SIC 8062 General medical and surgical hospitals
Andy Smith
Jocelyn Charles
Janet Bodley
Craig Duhamel
Kristen Winter
Michael Julius
Ari Zaretsky
Kunal Patel
Dan Cass
Ru Taggar

D-U-N-S 24-684-0065   (SL)
SUNNYBROOK RESEARCH INSTITUTE
2075 Bayview Ave, Toronto, ON, M4N 3M5
(416) 480-6100
Emp Here 480   *Sales* 105,572,640
SIC 8732 Commercial nonphysical research
Michael Julius
Grace Cheng

D-U-N-S 25-976-3902   (SL)
VOX INTEGRATED SOLUTIONS MODEL INC
36 Glengowan Rd, Toronto, ON, M4N 1E8
(905) 840-7477
Emp Here 61   *Sales* 10,815,971
SIC 7371 Custom computer programming services
James (Jim) Heaton

D-U-N-S 24-222-4954   (SL)
ZUCKER, SIMON & ASSOCIATES
3080 Yonge St Suite 5010, Toronto, ON, M4N 3N1
(416) 489-8277
Emp Here 40   *Sales* 33,423,080
SIC 5141 Groceries, general line
Simon Zucker

Toronto, ON M4P

D-U-N-S 24-219-1679   (SL)
1619214 ONTARIO LIMITED
SABON
2552 Yonge St, Toronto, ON, M4P 2J2
(416) 485-0303
Emp Here 45   *Sales* 10,365,300
SIC 5719 Miscellaneous homefurnishings
Orit Natan

D-U-N-S 20-286-6067   (SL)

2188262 ONTARIO LTD
AVANT SLEEP
586 Eglinton Ave E Unit 208, Toronto, ON,
M4P 1P2
(416) 802-2382
Emp Here 50   *Sales* 22,358,700
SIC 5047 Medical and hospital equipment
Kostas Tsambourlianos

D-U-N-S 24-061-0618   (HQ)
ACCORD FINANCIAL LTD
(*Suby of* ACCORD FINANCIAL CORP)
40 Eglinton Ave E Suite 602, Toronto, ON,
M4P 3A2
(416) 961-0007
Sales 28,688,633
SIC 8741 Management services
Simon Hitzig
Jean Rene Bates
Carmen Perrelli
Ken Hitzig
Thomas Henderson

D-U-N-S 24-381-2281   (SL)
**ALITHYA DIGITAL TECHNOLOGY CORPO-
RATION**
SYSTEMWARE INNOVATIONS
2300 Yonge St Suite 1800, Toronto, ON, M4P
1E4
(416) 932-4700
Emp Here 110   *Sales* 15,860,020
SIC 7371 Custom computer programming ser-
vices
Nigel Fonseca
David Tremaine
Jim Picha
Ed Mischkot
Iain Mckone
Jeff Mcdougall

D-U-N-S 20-113-5667   (BR)
BELL MEDIA INC
ASTRAL TELEVISION NETWORK, DIV OF
(*Suby of* BCE INC)
50 Eglinton Ave E Suite 1, Toronto, ON, M4P
1A6
(416) 924-6664
Emp Here 175
SIC 4833 Television broadcasting stations
Sabina Blaskovic

D-U-N-S 20-153-5304   (SL)
CAMP WINSTON FOUNDATION
55 Eglinton Ave E Suite 312, Toronto, ON,
M4P 1G8
(416) 487-6229
Emp Here 45   *Sales* 17,883,630
SIC 8699 Membership organizations, nec
Gerald Enchin

D-U-N-S 24-987-3407   (SL)
**CANADIAN   BENEFITS   CONSULTING
GROUP INC**
2300 Yonge St Suite 3000, Toronto, ON, M4P
1E4
(416) 483-5896
Emp Here 12   *Sales* 12,418,572
SIC 6321 Accident and health insurance
Roy Rastrick

D-U-N-S 24-985-2039   (BR)
**CANADIAN INSTITUTE FOR HEALTH IN-
FORMATION**
CIHI
(*Suby of* CANADIAN INSTITUTE FOR
HEALTH INFORMATION)
90 Eglinton Ave E Suite 300, Toronto, ON,
M4P 2Y3
(416) 481-2002
Emp Here 300
SIC 8361 Residential care
Graham Scott

D-U-N-S 25-322-5809   (SL)
CANADIAN INSURANCE BROKERS INC
1 Eglinton Ave E Suite 415, Toronto, ON, M4P
3A1

(416) 486-0951
Emp Here 35   *Sales* 20,297,340
SIC 6411 Insurance agents, brokers, and ser-
vice
Jason Jenkins

D-U-N-S 20-296-6552   (SL)
CT REAL ESTATE INVESTMENT TRUST
CT REIT
2180 Yonge St, Toronto, ON, M4P 2V8
(416) 480-2029
Emp Here 10   *Sales* 358,190,307
SIC 6798 Real estate investment trusts
Ken Silver
Kimberley Graham
Kevin Salsberg
Clint Elenko
Lesley Gibson
David Laidley
Heather Briant
Greg Hicks
Anna Martini
Dean Mccann

D-U-N-S 25-510-7716   (BR)
DECIMA INC
OPINION SEARCH (OSI)
2345 Yonge St Suite 704, Toronto, ON, M4P
2E5
(416) 962-9109
Emp Here 90
SIC 8732 Commercial nonphysical research
Ruby Huxter

D-U-N-S 24-391-9383   (SL)
EYERETURN MARKETING INC
(*Suby of* TORSTAR CORPORATION)
110 Eglinton Ave E Suite 701, Toronto, ON,
M4P 2Y1
(416) 929-4834
Emp Here 52   *Sales* 10,419,292
SIC 7319 Advertising, nec
Renee Hill
Ian Hewetson

D-U-N-S 24-858-5940   (SL)
HARRIS/DECIMA
(*Suby of* NIELSEN HOLDINGS PLC)
2345 Yonge St Suite 405, Toronto, ON, M4P
2E5
(416) 716-4903
Emp Here 100
SIC 8732 Commercial nonphysical research
Richard Cooper

D-U-N-S 20-923-7379   (HQ)
**HEART AND STROKE FOUNDATION OF
ONTARIO**
HSFO
2300 Yonge St Suite 1300, Toronto, ON, M4P
1E4
(416) 489-7111
Emp Here 200   *Sales* 136,384
SIC 8399 Social services, nec
Rocco Rossi
Mike Leclair
David Sculthorpe
Bill Thomas
Shannon Von Kaldenberg
Laura Syron
Vicky Alexiou
Lisa Chicules
Bruce Terry
Tom Mcallister

D-U-N-S 20-175-3287   (SL)
HOTSPEX INC
40 Eglinton Ave E Suite 801, Toronto, ON,
M4P 3A2
(416) 487-5439
Emp Here 63   *Sales* 13,441,554
SIC 8732 Commercial nonphysical research
Shane Skillen

D-U-N-S 25-341-7471   (SL)
IN-SYNC CONSUMER INSIGHT CORP
IN-SYNC
90 Eglinton Ave E Suite 403, Toronto, ON,

M4P 2Y3
(416) 932-0921
Emp Here 65   *Sales* 13,868,270
SIC 8732 Commercial nonphysical research
Janet Winkler

D-U-N-S 25-404-3052   (SL)
INTELYSIS CORP
2619 Yonge St Suite 200, Toronto, ON, M4P
2J1
(416) 216-6962
Emp Here 40   *Sales* 10,092,440
SIC 7323 Credit reporting services
Bashir Rahemtulla
Sandy Boucher

D-U-N-S 20-527-5126   (SL)
JOHN WILEY & SONS CANADA LIMITED
(*Suby of* JOHN WILEY & SONS, INC.)
90 Eglinton Ave E Suite 300, Toronto, ON,
M4P 2Y3
(416) 236-4433
Emp Here 125   *Sales* 20,503,375
SIC 2731 Book publishing
Brian Napack
Matthew Kissner

D-U-N-S 20-812-0324   (HQ)
K & G APARTMENT HOLDINGS INC
KG GROUP RENTAL OFFICE
305 Roehampton Ave, Toronto, ON, M4P 0B2
(416) 487-3050
Emp Here 1   *Sales* 13,587,800
SIC 6531 Real estate agents and managers
Sam Goldband

D-U-N-S 24-452-2280   (HQ)
KERNELS POPCORN LIMITED
KERNELS
40 Eglinton Ave E Suite 250, Toronto, ON,
M4P 3A2
(416) 487-4194
Emp Here 10   *Sales* 20,543,390
SIC 5441 Candy, nut, and confectionery
stores
Scott Staiman

D-U-N-S 24-850-7936   (SL)
KNOWROAMING LTD.
90 Eglinton Ave E Suite 701, Toronto, ON,
M4P 2Y3
(416) 482-8193
Emp Here 250   *Sales* 57,118,000
SIC 4899 Communication services, nec
Matthew Stein

D-U-N-S 24-253-3912   (SL)
KOGNITIVE MARKETING INC
150 Eglinton Ave E Suite 801, Toronto, ON,
M4P 1E8
(416) 534-5651
Emp Here 80   *Sales* 16,937,920
SIC 7311 Advertising agencies
Josh Singer

D-U-N-S 25-951-3778   (SL)
LABRASH SECURITY SERVICES LTD
55 Eglinton Ave E Suite 403, Toronto, ON,
M4P 1G8
(416) 487-4864
Emp Here 120   *Sales* 3,150,000
SIC 7381 Detective and armored car services
Mark Labrash

D-U-N-S 24-335-0530   (BR)
METRO ONTARIO INC
METRO
(*Suby of* METRO INC)
40 Eglinton Ave E, Toronto, ON, M4P 3A2
(416) 759-1952
Emp Here 150
SIC 5411 Grocery stores
Lith Martell

D-U-N-S 20-552-8552   (BR)
METRO ONTARIO INC
DOMINION
(*Suby of* METRO INC)
2300 Yonge St Suite 752, Toronto, ON, M4P

1E4
(416) 483-7340
Emp Here 250
SIC 5411 Grocery stores
Mike Orford

D-U-N-S 20-552-8784   (BR)
METRO ONTARIO INC
METRO
(*Suby of* METRO INC)
656 Eglinton Ave E, Toronto, ON, M4P 1P1
(416) 482-7422
Emp Here 300
SIC 5411 Grocery stores
Tom Sanders

D-U-N-S 24-525-3013   (HQ)
MMCC SOLUTIONS CANADA COMPANY
TELEPERFORMANCE CANADA
(*Suby of* TELEPERFORMANCE SE)
75 Eglinton Ave E, Toronto, ON, M4P 3A4
(416) 922-3519
Emp Here 500   *Sales* 1,003,362,000
SIC 7389 Business services, nec
Dean Duncan
Jeffrey K. Balagna

D-U-N-S 24-526-0872   (HQ)
**NATURE CONSERVANCY OF CANADA,
THE**
245 Eglinton Ave E Suite 410, Toronto, ON,
M4P 3J1
(416) 932-3202
Emp Here 65   *Sales* 71,421,091
SIC 8999 Services, nec
John Lounds
Bruce Maclellan
Michael Bradstreet
Jane Gilbert
Stewart Hardacre
Lisa Mclaughlin
Mark Rittinger
Linda Stephenson
Bob Alexander
Kamal Rajani

D-U-N-S 20-979-7633   (SL)
**NORTH TORONTO BASEBALL ASSOCIA-
TION**
2708 Yonge St, Toronto, ON, M4P 3J4
(519) 740-3900
Emp Here 26   *Sales* 10,332,764
SIC 8699 Membership organizations, nec
Jim Lisser

D-U-N-S 20-374-7295   (SL)
OLIVER & BONACINI HOSPITALITY INC
2323 Yonge St Suite 303, Toronto, ON, M4P
2C9
(416) 485-8047
Emp Here 1,500   *Sales* 69,958,500
SIC 5812 Eating places
Andrew Oliver
Phil Wylie
Lee Chung
Cliff Snell
Theresa Suraci
Gloria Gomes-Cabral

D-U-N-S 25-678-5135   (SL)
**PARACHUTE LEADERS IN INJURY PRE-
VENTION**
PARACHUTE
150 Eglinton Ave E Suite 300, Toronto, ON,
M4P 1E8
(647) 776-5100
Emp Here 30   *Sales* 11,922,420
SIC 8699 Membership organizations, nec
Louise Logan

D-U-N-S 20-344-9244   (HQ)
POWER WORKERS UNION
244 Eglinton Ave E, Toronto, ON, M4P 1K2
(416) 481-4491
Emp Here 40   *Sales* 4,556,832,000
SIC 8631 Labor organizations
Donald Mackinnon

Robert Walker
Jeff Parnell
Mel Hyatt

D-U-N-S 24-352-2963   (HQ)
PROFESSIONAL COMPUTER CONSUL-TANTS GROUP LTD
PROCOM
2323 Yonge St Suite 400, Toronto, ON, M4P 2C9
(416) 483-0766
Emp Here 100   *Sales* 25,027,050
SIC 7379 Computer related services, nec
Frank Mccrea

D-U-N-S 20-261-5035   (HQ)
RIOCAN MANAGEMENT INC
2300 Yonge St Suite 500, Toronto, ON, M4P 1E4
(800) 465-2733
Sales 893,684,792
SIC 6531 Real estate agents and managers
Raghunath Davloor
Jonathan Gitlin
Edward Sonshine
Cynthia Devine
Danny Kissoon

D-U-N-S 25-862-7140   (HQ)
RIOCAN REAL ESTATE INVESTMENT TRUST
2300 Yonge St Suite 500, Toronto, ON, M4P 1E4
(416) 866-3033
Emp Here 100   *Sales* 870,181,316
SIC 6798 Real estate investment trusts
Edward Sonshine
Jonathan Gitlin
Qi Tang
John Ballantyne
Jeff Ross
Andrew Duncan
Jennifer Suess
Anushka Grant
Frank Keller
Kevin Miller

D-U-N-S 20-514-7932   (HQ)
RIOCAN RETAIL VALUE L.P.
2300 Yonge St Suite 500, Toronto, ON, M4P 1E4
(416) 866-3033
Emp Here 1   *Sales* 10,452,150
SIC 6799 Investors, nec
Edward Sonshine

D-U-N-S 24-599-3303   (SL)
RIZWAN CHAMPSI PHARMACY INC
SHOPPERS DRUG MART
2345 Yonge St, Toronto, ON, M4P 2E5
(416) 487-5411
Emp Here 49   *Sales* 32,166,736
SIC 5961 Catalog and mail-order houses
Art Mandel

D-U-N-S 25-691-2775   (BR)
SCHWARTZ LEVITSKY FELDMAN LLP
SCHWARTZ   LEVITSKY   FELDMAN S.E.N.C.R.L.
(*Suby of* SCHWARTZ LEVITSKY FELDMAN LLP)
2300 Yonge St Suite 1500, Toronto, ON, M4P 1E4
(416) 785-5353
Emp Here 80
SIC 8721 Accounting, auditing, and book-keeping
Morty Lober

D-U-N-S 24-425-8963   (HQ)
SP DATA CAPITAL ULC
1 Eglinton Ave E 8th Fl, Toronto, ON, M4P 3A1
(416) 915-3300
Emp Here 150   *Sales* 367,899,400
SIC 7389 Business services, nec
Dan Plashkes

D-U-N-S 25-685-6261   (SL)

TERRALINK TECHNOLOGIES CANADA INC
(*Suby of* TERRALINK TECHNOLOGIES MANAGEMENT LTD)
181 Eglinton Ave E Suite 206, Toronto, ON, M4P 1J4
(416) 593-0700
Emp Here 85   *Sales* 12,255,470
SIC 7371 Custom computer programming services
Ron Lewin

D-U-N-S 20-698-8003   (BR)
TORONTO DISTRICT SCHOOL BOARD
NORTH TORONTO COLLEGIATE INSTI-TUTE
(*Suby of* TORONTO DISTRICT SCHOOL BOARD)
17 Broadway Ave, Toronto, ON, M4P 1T7
(416) 393-9180
Emp Here 100
SIC 8211 Elementary and secondary schools
William Mack

D-U-N-S 25-019-5062   (BR)
TORONTO DISTRICT SCHOOL BOARD
NORTHERN SECONDARY SCHOOL
(*Suby of* TORONTO DISTRICT SCHOOL BOARD)
851 Mount Pleasant Rd, Toronto, ON, M4P 2L5
(416) 393-0270
Emp Here 200
SIC 8211 Elementary and secondary schools
Roni Felsen

D-U-N-S 25-092-7100   (BR)
TOYS 'R' US (CANADA) LTD
TOYS 'R' US
(*Suby of* FAIRFAX FINANCIAL HOLDINGS LIMITED)
2300 Yonge St, Toronto, ON, M4P 1E4
(416) 322-1599
Emp Here 75
SIC 5945 Hobby, toy, and game shops
Tom Via

D-U-N-S 20-818-6106   (HQ)
UNITED STEELWORKERS OF AMERICA
(*Suby of* UNITED STEELWORKERS)
234 Eglinton Ave E Suite 800, Toronto, ON, M4P 1K7
(416) 487-1571
Emp Here 50   *Sales* 71,200,500
SIC 8631 Labor organizations
Ken Newmann

D-U-N-S 25-343-4559   (HQ)
YORKDALE CAFE LTD
TIM HORTONS
2377 Yonge St Suite 823, Toronto, ON, M4P 2C8
(416) 484-4231
Emp Here 25   *Sales* 42,554,165
SIC 5461 Retail bakeries
George Brown
Steve Brown
Danial Brown

Toronto, ON M4R

D-U-N-S 24-720-2948   (HQ)
ALZHEIMER SOCIETY OF CANADA
20 Eglinton Ave W Suite 1200, Toronto, ON, M4R 1K8
(416) 488-8772
Sales 12,771,231
SIC 8399 Social services, nec

D-U-N-S 20-845-2755   (HQ)
CAMP WAHANOWIN LIMITED
227 Eglinton Ave W, Toronto, ON, M4R 1A9
(416) 482-2600
Emp Here 10   *Sales* 28,700,400
SIC 7032 Sporting and recreational camps

Harold Nashman

D-U-N-S 20-120-5080   (HQ)
CENTRIC HEALTH CORPORATION
20 Eglinton Ave W Suite 2100, Toronto, ON, M4R 1K8
(416) 927-8400
Sales 93,809,058
SIC 8742 Management consulting services
David Murphy
Paul Rakowski
Ryan Stempfle
Andrew Mok
Nina Freier
Yazdi Bharucha
Ingrid Davis
John Ewing
Rik Ganderton

D-U-N-S 24-665-9106   (SL)
CORNERSTONE GROUP OF COMPANIES LIMITED
SEARCH & WEB SERVICES
20 Eglinton Ave W 4th Floor, Toronto, ON, M4R 1K8
(416) 932-9555
Emp Here 200   *Sales* 37,301,200
SIC 8742 Management consulting services
Ossie Hinds
Robert Coles
Donald Lange
Justin Webb
Stuart Young
Jim Grant
Dan Vickruck
Julio Tavares
George Tsiribis

D-U-N-S 25-530-4933   (SL)
CREATIVE TRAVEL SOLUTIONS INC
AIRLINERS, DIV OF
118 Eglinton Ave W Suite 500, Toronto, ON, M4R 2G4
(416) 485-6387
Emp Here 30   *Sales* 15,599,010
SIC 4724 Travel agencies
J R Arora

D-U-N-S 20-288-9119   (SL)
IMKT DIRECT SOLUTIONS CORPORATION
IMARKETING SOLUTIONS GROUP
90 Eglinton Ave W Suite 300, Toronto, ON, M4R 2E4
(416) 633-4646
Emp Here 450   *Sales* 301,008,600
SIC 7389 Business services, nec
Andrew Langhorne

D-U-N-S 25-467-0276   (HQ)
LIFEMARK HEALTH CORP
MARKHAM PHYSIOTHERAPY CLINIC
(*Suby of* AUDAX GROUP, L.P.)
20 Eglinton Ave W Suite 600, Toronto, ON, M4R 1K8
(416) 485-1344
Emp Here 100   *Sales* 227,319,000
SIC 8093 Specialty outpatient clinics, nec
Peter Stymiest
Liez Ballantyne
Ajay Chadha

D-U-N-S 25-220-7139   (SL)
OCASI - ONTARIO COUNCIL OF AGENCIES SERVING IMMIGRANTS
OCASI
110 Eglinton Ave W Suite 200, Toronto, ON, M4R 1A3
(416) 322-4950
Emp Here 35   *Sales* 13,909,490
SIC 8699 Membership organizations, nec
Debbie Douglas

D-U-N-S 24-421-0170   (SL)
RUBY CORP
20 Eglinton Ave W Suite 1200, Toronto, ON, M4R 1K8

(416) 480-2334
Emp Here 140   *Sales* 14,949,480
SIC 7299 Miscellaneous personal service
Rob Segal
James Millership
Rizwan Jiwan
Trevor Sykes

D-U-N-S 20-973-8947   (HQ)
SENIOR DISCOVERY TOURS INC
225 Eglinton Ave W, Toronto, ON, M4R 1A9
(416) 322-1500
Emp Here 19   *Sales* 21,838,614
SIC 4725 Tour operators
Danny Shay
Oedile Daniels

D-U-N-S 20-845-3969   (SL)
ST. CLEMENT'S SCHOOL
21 St Clements Ave, Toronto, ON, M4R 1G8
(416) 483-4835
Emp Here 90   *Sales* 8,354,340
SIC 8211 Elementary and secondary schools
Brian Denega
Carol Ann Millington
Martha Perry

D-U-N-S 20-784-7484   (SL)
YONGE EGLINTON CENTRE MANAGE-MENT SERVICES IN TRUST
20 Eglinton Ave W Suite 401, Toronto, ON, M4R 1K8
(416) 489-2300
Emp Here 75   *Sales* 21,637,425
SIC 6512 Nonresidential building operators
Minaz Ebrahim

Toronto, ON M4S

D-U-N-S 20-005-3788   (SL)
1365992 ONTARIO LTD
MOUNT PLEASANT IGA #7607
710 Mount Pleasant Rd, Toronto, ON, M4S 2N6
(416) 483-1290
Emp Here 49   *Sales* 13,433,448
SIC 5411 Grocery stores
Renato Razzolini

D-U-N-S 20-159-0965   (SL)
ART SHOPPE LIMITED
2131 Yonge St, Toronto, ON, M4S 2A7
(416) 487-3211
Emp Here 75   *Sales* 17,430,225
SIC 5712 Furniture stores
Martin Offman
Allan Offman

D-U-N-S 25-532-0012   (HQ)
AU LIT FINE LINENS INC
AU LIT
2049 Yonge St, Toronto, ON, M4S 2A2
(416) 489-7992
Emp Here 1   *Sales* 11,620,150
SIC 5719 Miscellaneous homefurnishings
Margueret Byron
Jack Nordin
Joanna Goodman
Miguel Cardinal

D-U-N-S 25-118-7415   (BR)
BOSLEY REAL ESTATE LTD
(*Suby of* BOSLEY REAL ESTATE LTD)
290 Merton St, Toronto, ON, M4S 1A9
(416) 322-8000
Emp Here 75
SIC 6531 Real estate agents and managers
Brian Torry

D-U-N-S 25-119-2530   (HQ)
CANADIAN COUNCIL ON REHABILITA-TION AND WORK, THE
CCRW
477 Mount Pleasant Rd Suite 105, Toronto, ON, M4S 2L9

(416) 260-3060
Emp Here 1   *Sales* 10,542,960
SIC 8748 Business consulting, nec
Ashley Caldwell
Jennifer Dinn
Tony Dolan
Corrine Gannon
Naqsh (Nick) Kochar
Kathy Malley
Carol Thiessen
Jon Wollaston

D-U-N-S 20-161-3668   (HQ)
CANADIAN TIRE CORPORATION, LIMITED
PARTSOURCE
2180 Yonge St, Toronto, ON, M4S 2B9
(416) 480-3000
Emp Here 50   *Sales* 10,657,928,587
SIC 5531 Auto and home supply stores
Stephen G. Wetmore
Allan Macdonald
Dean Mccann
Mahes Wickramasinghe
Iain Kennedy
Jim Christie
John Koryl
Robyn Collver
Susan O'brien
Lisa Greatrix

D-U-N-S 25-405-0263   (HQ)
CANADIAN TIRE REAL ESTATE LIMITED
(*Suby of* CANADIAN TIRE CORPORATION,
LIMITED)
2180 Yonge St, Toronto, ON, M4S 2B9
(416) 480-3000
Emp Here 70   *Sales* 33,511,120
SIC 6531 Real estate agents and managers
Ken Silver

D-U-N-S 20-849-0573   (HQ)
CANADIAN UNICEF COMMITTEE
UNICEF CANADA
2200 Yonge St Suite 1100, Toronto, ON, M4S
2C6
(416) 482-4444
Emp Here 80   *Sales* 29,675,077
SIC 8399 Social services, nec
David Morley
Mabel Wong
Donald Fox
Christopher Simard

D-U-N-S 25-998-1579   (SL)
DESTINY SOLUTIONS INC
40 Holly St Suite 800, Toronto, ON, M4S 3C3
(416) 480-0500
Emp Here 69   *Sales* 12,234,459
SIC 7371 Custom computer programming services
Shaul Kuper
Peter De Vries

D-U-N-S 20-849-1837   (HQ)
FIRSTBROOK CASSIE & ANDERSON LIMITED
1867 Yonge St Suite 300, Toronto, ON, M4S
1Y5
(416) 486-1421
Emp Here 64   *Sales* 138,580,650
SIC 6411 Insurance agents, brokers, and service
Donald Anderson
Brenda Rose
Andrew Osbourne
John Vanbilsen
Jeffrey Smith
David Hore
Martin R Hefferon
J T Cassie
Ronald Firstbrook

D-U-N-S 24-343-2288   (SL)
FLEXTRACK INC
2200 Yonge St Suite 801, Toronto, ON, M4S
2C6
(416) 545-5288
Emp Here 45   *Sales* 12,344,940

SIC 8741 Management services
Frank Mccrea
Allison Mccrea

D-U-N-S 20-303-9490   (HQ)
GIRL GUIDES OF CANADA
50 Merton St, Toronto, ON, M4S 1A3
(416) 487-5281
Sales 10,831,170
SIC 8641 Civic and social associations
Deborah Del Duca
Jill Zelmanovits
Robyn Mcdonald

D-U-N-S 20-180-6135   (SL)
GREENWOOD COLLEGE SCHOOL
443 Mount Pleasant Rd, Toronto, ON, M4S
2L8
(416) 482-9811
Emp Here 91   *Sales* 8,447,166
SIC 8211 Elementary and secondary schools
Donald Lewtas
Sarah Bruce
Glen Stewart
Kelly Giannoccaro
Richard Wernham
Julia West
Vivian Abdelmessih
Jennifer Bermingham
Stephen Bowman
Ferg Devins

D-U-N-S 20-773-0441   (HQ)
HANSCOMB LIMITED
40 Holly St Suite 900, Toronto, ON, M4S 3C3
(416) 487-3811
Emp Here 22   *Sales* 13,716,600
SIC 8741 Management services
Arthur Ma
Ted Flaxman
Paul Westbrook
Susan Neil
Paul Westrook

D-U-N-S 20-879-6839   (SL)
KOLTER PROPERTY MANAGEMENT LIMITED
KOLTER PROPERTY COMPANY
2200 Yonge St Suite 1600, Toronto, ON, M4S
2C6

Emp Here 119
SIC 6512 Nonresidential building operators

D-U-N-S 25-318-4048   (HQ)
MERRITHEW CORPORATION
STOTT PILATES
2200 Yonge St Suite 500, Toronto, ON, M4S
2C6
(416) 482-4050
Sales 104,295,000
SIC 5091 Sporting and recreation goods
Lindsay Merrithew
Moira Merrithew

D-U-N-S 25-460-1727   (SL)
MERRITHEW INTERNATIONAL INC
(*Suby of* MERRITHEW CORPORATION)
2200 Yonge St Suite 500, Toronto, ON, M4S
2C6
(416) 482-4050
Emp Here 75   *Sales* 9,009,675
SIC 8299 Schools and educational services,
nec
Lindsay Merrithew
Moira Merrithew

D-U-N-S 24-757-8008   (SL)
ONTARIO CINEMAS INC
LANSDOWNE CINEMA
745 Mount Pleasant Rd Suite 300, Toronto,
ON, M4S 2N4
(416) 481-1186
Emp Here 100   *Sales* 9,403,700
SIC 7832 Motion picture theaters, except
drive-in
Norman Stern

D-U-N-S 20-939-3974   (HQ)
**ONTARIO EDUCATIONAL COMMUNICA-
TIONS AUTHORITY, THE**
TVONTARIO
(*Suby of* GOVERNMENT OF ONTARIO)
2180 Yonge St, Toronto, ON, M4S 2B9
(416) 484-2600
Sales 81,632,800
SIC 8733 Noncommercial research organizations
Lisa Dewilde
Peter O'brian

D-U-N-S 24-465-9996   (SL)
PINO ALEJANDRO
*SOTHEBY'S INTERNATIONAL REALTY
CANADA, BROKERAGE*
1867 Yonge St Suite 100, Toronto, ON, M4S
1Y5
(416) 960-9995
Emp Here 49   *Sales* 13,316,044
SIC 6531 Real estate agents and managers
John Poole

D-U-N-S 20-895-5307   (HQ)
PROCOM CONSULTANTS GROUP LTD
PROCOM
2200 Yonge St Suite 700, Toronto, ON, M4S
2C6
(416) 483-0766
Emp Here 5   *Sales* 25,349,000
SIC 8748 Business consulting, nec
Frank T Mccrea
Kent Mccrea
Mark Galloway

D-U-N-S 24-222-6611   (SL)
REUVEN INTERNATIONAL LIMITED
ROXBOROUGH POULTRY
(*Suby of* S&Z INTERNATIONAL INC)
1881 Yonge St Suite 201, Toronto, ON, M4S
3C4
(416) 929-1496
Emp Here 32   *Sales* 26,738,464
SIC 5142 Packaged frozen goods
Paul Stott
John Barker

D-U-N-S 24-652-0928   (SL)
**ROYAL INTERNATIONAL COLLECTABLES
INC**
2161 Yonge St Suite 608, Toronto, ON, M4S
3A6

Emp Here 35   *Sales* 18,218,970
SIC 5094 Jewelry and precious stones

D-U-N-S 20-709-2532   (BR)
ROYAL LEPAGE LIMITED
(*Suby of* BROOKFIELD ASSET MANAGE-
MENT INC)
477 Mount Pleasant Rd Unit 210, Toronto, ON,
M4S 2L9
(416) 489-2121
Emp Here 250
SIC 7389 Business services, nec
Phillip Soper

D-U-N-S 20-004-5941   (BR)
ROYAL LEPAGE LIMITED
JOHNSTON & DANIEL
(*Suby of* BROOKFIELD ASSET MANAGE-
MENT INC)
477 Mount Pleasant Rd, Toronto, ON, M4S
2L9
(416) 489-2121
Emp Here 160
SIC 6531 Real estate agents and managers
Don Kottick

D-U-N-S 20-645-5987   (SL)
RUTLEDGE FLOWERS AT YORKDALE INC
635 Mount Pleasant Rd Suite A, Toronto, ON,
M4S 2M9
(416) 783-6355
Emp Here 85   *Sales* 20,767,880
SIC 5992 Florists
John Benson

D-U-N-S 20-305-3160   (SL)
S&P DATA CORP
1920 Yonge St, Toronto, ON, M4S 3E2
(844) 877-3282
Emp Here 100   *Sales* 66,890,800
SIC 7389 Business services, nec
Dan Plashkes
Ken Crema
Brian Cato
Kevin Lacomb
David Borts
Steve Murphy

D-U-N-S 20-227-7542   (HQ)
**SENIOR PEOPLES' RESOURCES IN
NORTH TORONTO INCORPORATED**
SPRINT
140 Merton St, Toronto, ON, M4S 1A1
(416) 481-6411
Sales 10,075,554
SIC 8322 Individual and family services
Stacy Landau

D-U-N-S 20-817-1793   (HQ)
SKICAN LIMITED
745 Mount Pleasant Rd Suite 300, Toronto,
ON, M4S 2N4
(416) 488-1169
Emp Here 20   *Sales* 13,519,142
SIC 4725 Tour operators
Robin Nasmith
Sheila Nasmith
Julia Atkinson

D-U-N-S 24-181-4516   (HQ)
SPORTING LIFE INC
(*Suby of* FAIRFAX FINANCIAL HOLDINGS
LIMITED)
130 Merton St 6th Fl, Toronto, ON, M4S 1A4
(416) 485-1685
Emp Here 240   *Sales* 119,299,050
SIC 5941 Sporting goods and bicycle shops
Brian Mcgrath
David Russell
Patty Russell
Sharon Mcgrath
Julie Loi

D-U-N-S 20-901-9397   (SL)
**STATTEN, TAYLOR CAMP COMPANY, LIM-
ITED**
STATTEN, TAYLOR CAMPS
59 Hoyle Ave, Toronto, ON, M4S 2X5
(416) 486-6959
Emp Here 260   *Sales* 24,873,680
SIC 7032 Sporting and recreational camps

D-U-N-S 20-001-0036   (SL)
SUTTON GRANITE HILL REALTY INC
2010 Yonge St Suite 200, Toronto, ON, M4S
1Z9

Emp Here 45   *Sales* 12,229,020
SIC 6531 Real estate agents and managers
Elmar Moser

D-U-N-S 20-408-4271   (HQ)
TORONTO TRANSIT COMMISSION
TTC
1900 Yonge St Suite 400, Toronto, ON, M4S
1Z2
(416) 393-4000
Emp Here 450   *Sales* 631,564,290
SIC 4111 Local and suburban transit
Karen Stintz
Peter Milczyn
Michael Roche
Maria Augimeri
Vincent Crisanti
Frank Di Giorgio
Norm Kelly
Denzil Minnan-Wong
Cesar Palacio
John Parker

D-U-N-S 24-097-5722   (HQ)
VHA HOME HEALTHCARE

▲ Public Company   ■ Public Company Family Member   **HQ** Headquarters   **BR** Branch   **SL** Single Location

30 Soudan Ave Suite 500, Toronto, ON, M4S
1V6
(416) 489-2500
Emp Here 100   *Sales* 80,273,000
SIC 8059 Nursing and personal care, nec
Carol Annett
Alan Ely
Susan Houston
Catherine Seguin
Diane Pirner
Joel Kohm
Denis Long
Donna-Dale Smith
Vikas Sharma
Jeff Litwin

D-U-N-S 20-874-9788   (SL)
WELLS GORDON LIMITED
THE BRITON HOUSE
720 Mount Pleasant Rd, Toronto, ON, M4S
2N6
(416) 487-3392
Emp Here 150   *Sales* 8,887,050
SIC 8361 Residential care
Russel B Wells
John Wells
Gary Patriquin
Mark Wells

D-U-N-S 20-880-5788   (HQ)
YMCA OF GREATER TORONTO
YMCA
2200 Yonge St Suite 300, Toronto, ON, M4S
2C6
(416) 928-9622
Emp Here 165   *Sales* 197,035,205
SIC 8699 Membership organizations, nec
Medhat Mahdy
Diane Sinuber
Lesley Davidson
Gayle Gioiosa
Laura Graham-Prentice
Michael Hall
Melanie Laflamme
Linda Cottes
Nora Gorman
Sandra Kalpouzos

Toronto, ON M4T

D-U-N-S 20-290-4954   (HQ)
1404136 ONTARIO LIMITED
NEW BALANCE TORONTO
1510 Yonge St, Toronto, ON, M4T 1Z6
(416) 962-8662
Emp Here 35   *Sales* 12,557,720
SIC 5651 Family clothing stores
Sean Mcgrath
David Russell

D-U-N-S 20-762-3380   (HQ)
CANADIAN OLYMPIC COMMITTEE
21 St Clair Ave E Suite 900, Toronto, ON, M4T
1L9
(416) 962-0262
Emp Here 40   *Sales* 49,644,840
SIC 8699 Membership organizations, nec
Tricia Smith

D-U-N-S 20-921-8130   (HQ)
CANADIAN SPECIAL OLYMPICS INC
SPECIAL OLYMPICS CANADA
60 St Clair Ave E Suite 700, Toronto, ON, M4T
1N5
(416) 927-9050
Emp Here 12   *Sales* 70,921,200
SIC 8699 Membership organizations, nec
Deborah Bright

D-U-N-S 20-552-1201   (HQ)
**CINEPLEX ENTERTAINMENT LIMITED
PARTNERSHIP**
CINEPLEX ENTERTAINMENT
(*Suby* of CINEPLEX INC)

1303 Yonge St, Toronto, ON, M4T 2Y9
(416) 323-6600
Emp Here 200   *Sales* 322,905,600
SIC 7832 Motion picture theaters, except
drive-in
Ellis Jacob

D-U-N-S 20-552-1169   (HQ)
CINEPLEX INC
CINEPLEX ENTERTAINMENT
1303 Yonge St Suite 300, Toronto, ON, M4T
2Y9
(416) 323-6600
Emp Here 300   *Sales* 1,224,200,546
SIC 7822 Motion picture and tape distribution
Ellis Jacob
Michael Kennedy
Anne Fitzgerald
Gord Nelson
Dan Mcgrath
Cindy Bush
Ian Greenberg
Joan Dea
Sarabjit Marwah
Edward Sonshine

D-U-N-S 24-096-6622   (HQ)
CINEPLEX ODEON CORPORATION
GALAXY CINEMAS
(*Suby* of CINEPLEX INC)
1303 Yonge St, Toronto, ON, M4T 2Y9
(416) 323-6600
Emp Here 100   *Sales* 179,392,000
SIC 7832 Motion picture theaters, except
drive-in
Ellis Jacob
Gord Nelson

D-U-N-S 24-329-3334   (SL)
CITADEL INCOME FUND
1300 Yonge St Suite 300, Toronto, ON, M4T
1X3
(416) 361-9673
Emp Here 2   *Sales* 11,809,055
SIC 6726 Investment offices, nec
Wayne Pushka
Robert Parent
Michael Burns
Gary Nest

D-U-N-S 24-843-6800   (HQ)
CLAIRVEST GROUP INC
22 St Clair Ave E Suite 1700, Toronto, ON,
M4T 2S3
(416) 925-9270
Sales 100,076,147
SIC 6726 Investment offices, nec
Kenneth Rotman
Jeff Parr
Michael Wagman
Michael Castellarin
Mitchell Green
Robbie Isenberg
Douglas Horn
Mohit Kansal
Andrew Whiting
Kingsley Gifford

D-U-N-S 24-211-2035   (HQ)
CROHN'S AND COLITIS CANADA
CCFC
60 St Clair Ave E Suite 600, Toronto, ON, M4T
1N5
(416) 920-5035
Emp Here 18   *Sales* 11,603,278
SIC 8399 Social services, nec
Andrew Dalglish

D-U-N-S 20-819-6469   (SL)
CROWE SOBERMAN LLP
2 St Clair Ave E Suite 1100, Toronto, ON, M4T
2T5
(416) 964-7633
Emp Here 180   *Sales* 37,383,300
SIC 8721 Accounting, auditing, and bookkeeping
Jerry Cukier

Eric Bornstein
Ravinder Sanghera

D-U-N-S 20-704-5928   (SL)
DELISLE CLUB
EXTREME FITNESS
1521 Yonge St Suite 303, Toronto, ON, M4T
1Z2

Emp Here 75   *Sales* 5,729,775
SIC 7991 Physical fitness facilities
David Luck

D-U-N-S 24-977-4084   (HQ)
FRASTELL PROPERTY MANAGEMENT INC
22 St Clair Ave E Suite 1500, Toronto, ON,
M4T 2S3
(416) 499-3333
Sales 14,221,850
SIC 6512 Nonresidential building operators
Victor Lopez

D-U-N-S 25-137-9269   (HQ)
GALAXY ENTERTAINMENT INC
GALAXY CINEMAS
1303 Yonge St Suite 100, Toronto, ON, M4T
2Y9
(416) 323-6600
Emp Here 20   *Sales* 17,939,200
SIC 7832 Motion picture theaters, except
drive-in
Ellis Jacob
Dan Mcgrath
Anne Fitzgerald
Gordon Nelson
Howard Beck
Timothy Duncanson

D-U-N-S 20-521-5408   (HQ)
GENERATION ADVISORS INC
(*Suby* of 1346049 ONTARIO LIMITED)
22 St Clair Ave E, Toronto, ON, M4T 2S3
(416) 361-1498
Emp Here 17   *Sales* 10,092,933
SIC 6282 Investment advice
Herbert Abramson
Randall Abramson
Adam Abramson
Bryan Rakusin
Jeremy Rakusin

D-U-N-S 24-359-7205   (HQ)
**GENERATION PORTFOLIO MANAGEMENT
CORP**
22 St Clair Ave E, Toronto, ON, M4T 2S3
(416) 361-1498
Emp Here 1   *Sales* 13,578,460
SIC 6282 Investment advice
Randall Abramson

D-U-N-S 20-178-2513   (HQ)
GEORGE WESTON LIMITED
22 St Clair Ave E Suite 1901, Toronto, ON,
M4T 2S7
(416) 922-2500
Emp Here 120   *Sales* 36,819,497,936
SIC 5141 Groceries, general line
Galen G. Weston
Richard Dufresne
Gordon A.M. Curie
Rashid Wasti
Allan Bifield
Khush Dadyburjor
Andrew Bunston
Nadeem Mansour
John Williams
Alannah Weston

D-U-N-S 20-598-5620   (SL)
HEATH ST HOUSING CO-OP INC
232 Heath St E, Toronto, ON, M4T 1S9
(416) 486-8169
Emp Here 49   *Sales* 11,412,639
SIC 6513 Apartment building operators
Angelina Mcmayo

D-U-N-S 24-757-8347   (SL)
HOMESERVICE CLUB OF CANADA LTD

1255 Yonge St, Toronto, ON, M4T 1W6
(416) 925-1111
Emp Here 35   *Sales* 10,100,405
SIC 1522 Residential construction, nec
Richard David Felton

D-U-N-S 25-052-1101   (SL)
IQPC WORLDWIDE COMPANY
*INTERNATIONAL QUALITY AND PRODUC-
TIVITY CENTRE*
(*Suby* of PENTON LEARNING SYSTEMS
L.L.C.)
60 St Clair Ave E Suite 304, Toronto, ON, M4T
1N5
(416) 597-4700
Emp Here 75   *Sales* 50,168,100
SIC 7389 Business services, nec
Robert Shannon
Richard Worden

D-U-N-S 25-306-1741   (BR)
LOBLAWS SUPERMARKETS LIMITED
ST CLAIR MARKET
(*Suby* of LOBLAW COMPANIES LIMITED)
12 St Clair Ave E, Toronto, ON, M4T 1L7
(416) 960-8108
Emp Here 100
SIC 5411 Grocery stores
Erin French

D-U-N-S 25-059-0866   (SL)
**MAPLE LEAF INTERNATIONAL CONSULT-
ING INC**
27 St Clair Ave E Suite 1145, Toronto, ON,
M4T 1L8
(416) 724-6475
Emp Here 47   *Sales* 12,893,604
SIC 8741 Management services
Sonny Pitchumani
Lisa Ryder
Randal Nelson

D-U-N-S 24-216-7088   (SL)
MIMERI INVESTMENTS LTD
*CAREER PARTNERS INTERNATIONAL/
HAZELL & ASSOCIATES*
1220 Yonge St, Toronto, ON, M4T 1W1
(416) 961-3700
Emp Here 39   *Sales* 11,048,427
SIC 8741 Management services
Michael Hazell
Melanie Hazell

D-U-N-S 24-320-2120   (SL)
**MULRONEY, CAROLINE LEADERSHIP
CAMPAIGN**
1491 Yonge St Suite 201, Toronto, ON, M4T
1Z4
(416) 922-0573
Emp Here 50   *Sales* 13,916,639
SIC 8651 Political organizations
Andrew Boddington

D-U-N-S 25-369-3162   (HQ)
NEXONIA TECHNOLOGIES INC
(*Suby* of K1 INVESTMENT MANAGEMENT,
LLC)
2 St Clair Ave E Suite 750, Toronto, ON, M4T
2T5
(416) 480-0688
Emp Here 69   *Sales* 14,015,148
SIC 7374 Data processing and preparation
Hassan Askari
Eric White
Steven Horniak
Pascal Paradis-Theberge

D-U-N-S 20-551-0063   (SL)
**NUCLEAR WASTE MANAGEMENT ORGA-
NIZATION (NWMO)**
NWMO
22 St Clair Ave E 6th Fl, Toronto, ON, M4T 2S3
(416) 934-9814
Emp Here 130   *Sales* 51,731,804
SIC 8999 Services, nec
Laurie Swami
Mahrez Ben Belfadhel

Jennifer Spragge
Doug Taylor
Lisa Frizzell
Georgina Kossivas

D-U-N-S 20-880-5440 (HQ)
ONTARIO ENGLISH CATHOLIC TEACH-ERS' ASSOCIATION, THE
OECTA
65 St Clair Ave E Suite 400, Toronto, ON, M4T 2Y8
(416) 925-2493
Sales 14,490,900
SIC 8621 Professional organizations
Liz Stuart

D-U-N-S 20-511-9394 (SL)
ONTARIO HIV TREATMENT NETWORK, THE
1300 Yonge St Suite 600, Toronto, ON, M4T 1X3
(416) 642-6486
Emp Here 50   *Sales* 11,684,750
SIC 8621 Professional organizations
Evans Collins
Lynne Leonard
Ken Logue
Neil Mcgregor

D-U-N-S 24-597-5565 (SL)
PRIME QUADRANT CORP
2 St Clair Ave E Suite 800, Toronto, ON, M4T 2T5
(647) 749-4118
Emp Here 32   *Sales* 21,725,536
SIC 6282 Investment advice
Mo Lidsky

D-U-N-S 20-391-6445 (SL)
PRIME QUADRANT FOUNDATION
2 St Clair Ave E Suite 800, Toronto, ON, M4T 2T5
(647) 749-4118
Emp Here 35   *Sales* 13,909,490
SIC 8699 Membership organizations, nec
Mo Lidsky

D-U-N-S 20-020-5203 (SL)
PROSPER CANADA
60 St Clair Avenue E Suite 700, Toronto, ON, M4T 1N5
(416) 665-2828
Emp Here 25   *Sales* 17,420,250
SIC 6733 Trusts, nec
Koker Christensen

D-U-N-S 20-001-4012 (SL)
RE/MAX UNIQUE INC
1251 Yonge St, Toronto, ON, M4T 1W6
(416) 928-6833
Emp Here 60   *Sales* 16,305,360
SIC 6531 Real estate agents and managers
John Meehan

D-U-N-S 20-650-9734 (SL)
REINGOLD, M. DRUGS LIMITED
SHOPPERS DRUG MART
1507 Yonge St, Toronto, ON, M4T 1Z2
(416) 923-7700
Emp Here 40   *Sales* 10,118,160
SIC 5912 Drug stores and proprietary stores
Mel Reingold

D-U-N-S 20-258-2917 (HQ)
ROMAN CATHOLIC EPISCOPAL CORPO-RATION FOR THE DIOCESE OF TORONTO, IN CANADA
CATHOLIC PASTORAL CENTRE
1155 Yonge St, Toronto, ON, M4T 1W2
(416) 934-3400
Sales 20,824,600
SIC 8661 Religious organizations
William Dunlop

D-U-N-S 24-061-0196 (HQ)
ROMAN CATHOLIC EPISCOPAL CORPO-RATION FOR THE DIOCESE OF TORONTO, IN CANADA

SACRED HEART CHURCH
1155 Yonge St Suite 603, Toronto, ON, M4T 1W2
(416) 934-0606
Emp Here 120   *Sales* 93,710,700
SIC 8661 Religious organizations
Thomas Collins

D-U-N-S 24-367-0895 (SL)
TERRA FIRMA CAPITAL CORPORATION
22 St Clair Ave E Suite 200, Toronto, ON, M4T 2S3
(416) 792-4700
Emp Here 20   *Sales* 13,236,711
SIC 6159 Miscellaneous business credit institutions
Glenn Watchorn
Dov Meyer
Mano Thiyagarajah
Seth Greenspan
Scott Sadleir
Carolyn Montgomery
John Kaplan
Seymour Temkin
Chris Bart
Philip Reichmann

D-U-N-S 20-784-3905 (HQ)
WITTINGTON INVESTMENTS, LIMITED
22 St Clair Ave E Suite 2001, Toronto, ON, M4T 2S3
(416) 967-7990
Emp Here 20   *Sales* 314,770,640
SIC 6512 Nonresidential building operators
W Galen Weston
Robert J Dart
Anthony R. Graham
Garry Weston
John D Stevenson

D-U-N-S 24-910-9521 (SL)
YORK SCHOOL, THE
1320 Yonge St, Toronto, ON, M4T 1X2
(416) 926-1325
Emp Here 90   *Sales* 16,191,228
SIC 8211 Elementary and secondary schools
Stephen Karam
Sara Bellamy
Warren Bongard
John Brown
Lynn Clarfield
Joel Feldberg
Andrew Kay
Gene Mcburney
Allison Menkes
Lloyd A. Perlmutter

D-U-N-S 20-822-8791 (HQ)
YOUNG WOMEN'S CHRISTIAN ASSOCIA-TION OF GREATER TORONTO
YWCA TORONTO
80 Woodlawn Ave E, Toronto, ON, M4T 1C1
(416) 923-8454
Emp Here 180   *Sales* 37,272,240
SIC 8399 Social services, nec
Heather Mcgregor

Toronto, ON M4V

D-U-N-S 25-254-5835 (SL)
154644 CANADA INC
SENIORS FOR SENIORS
40 St Clair Ave W Unit 102, Toronto, ON, M4V 1M2
(416) 481-2733
Emp Here 200   *Sales* 13,713,200
SIC 8059 Nursing and personal care, nec
Peter Cook

D-U-N-S 24-390-9046 (BR)
ASTRAL MEDIA RADIO INC
(*Suby of* ASTRAL MEDIA RADIO INC)
2 St Clair Ave W Suite 200, Toronto, ON, M4V 1L6

(416) 323-5200
Emp Here 150
SIC 4832 Radio broadcasting stations
Sherry O'neil

D-U-N-S 20-646-9413 (SL)
BADMINTON AND RACQUET CLUB OF TORONTO, THE
25 St Clair Ave W, Toronto, ON, M4V 1K6
(416) 921-2159
Emp Here 100   *Sales* 7,639,700
SIC 7997 Membership sports and recreation clubs
John Sauquier
Catharine Bolla

D-U-N-S 25-251-0995 (SL)
BASKIN FINANCIAL SERVICES INC
BASKIN WEALTH SERVICES
95 St Clair Ave W Suite 900, Toronto, ON, M4V 1N6
(416) 969-9540
Emp Here 25   *Sales* 16,973,075
SIC 6282 Investment advice
David P. Baskin
Barry Schwartz

D-U-N-S 24-213-3783 (SL)
BISHOP STRACHAN SCHOOL, THE
298 Lonsdale Rd, Toronto, ON, M4V 1X2
(416) 483-4325
Emp Here 150   *Sales* 14,867,850
SIC 8211 Elementary and secondary schools
Nathalie Little

D-U-N-S 20-012-1858 (BR)
CANADIAN CANCER SOCIETY
ONTARIO DIVISION
(*Suby of* CANADIAN CANCER SOCIETY)
55 St Clair Ave W Suite 500, Toronto, ON, M4V 2Y7
(416) 961-7223
Emp Here 200
SIC 8399 Social services, nec
Michael Loo

D-U-N-S 20-786-0990 (HQ)
CANADIAN CANCER SOCIETY
55 St Clair Ave W Suite 300, Toronto, ON, M4V 2Y7
(416) 961-7223
Emp Here 240   *Sales* 114,285,492
SIC 8399 Social services, nec
Lynne Hudson
Robert Lawrie
Paula Roberts
Sara Oates
Alison Staples
Suzanne Dubois
Sylvie Poissant
Andre Beaulieu
Denis Lalonde
Andre Leger

D-U-N-S 20-202-0256 (SL)
CCI ENTERTAINMENT LTD
210 St Clair Ave W 4 Fl, Toronto, ON, M4V 1R2
(416) 964-8750
Emp Here 60   *Sales* 16,401,000
SIC 6712 Bank holding companies
Arnie Zipursky
Charles Salzon
Gordon Mcilquham
Murray Palay

D-U-N-S 24-625-3009 (SL)
CORPORATION OF COUNCIL OF MINIS-TERS OF EDUCATION CANADA, THE
COUNCIL OF MINISTERS OF EDUCATION CANADA
95 St Clair Ave W Suite 1106, Toronto, ON, M4V 1N6
(416) 962-8100
Emp Here 44   *Sales* 10,282,580
SIC 8621 Professional organizations
Kelly Lamrock
John Kershaw

D-U-N-S 20-285-1465 (BR)
DESJARDINS SECURITE FINANCIERE, COMPAGNIE D'ASSURANCE VIE
DESJARDINS FINANCIAL SECURITY
(*Suby of* FEDERATION DES CAISSES DES-JARDINS DU QUEBEC)
95 St Clair Ave W Suite 100, Toronto, ON, M4V 1N7
(416) 926-2700
Emp Here 460
SIC 6311 Life insurance
Bill Packham

D-U-N-S 24-486-5879 (HQ)
EQUITABLE BANK
(*Suby of* EQUITABLE GROUP INC)
30 St Clair Ave W Suite 700, Toronto, ON, M4V 3A1
(416) 515-7000
Sales 80,484,900
SIC 6021 National commercial banks
Andrew Moor
Austin Beutel
Eric Beutel
Joseph Dickstein
Eric Kirzner
David Legresley
Lynn Mcdonald
Katherine Rethy
Morris Shohet
Vincenza Sera

D-U-N-S 24-327-6214 (HQ)
EQUITABLE GROUP INC
30 St Clair Ave W Suite 700, Toronto, ON, M4V 3A1
(416) 515-7000
Emp Here 91   *Sales* 285,076,676
SIC 6163 Loan brokers
Andrew Moor
Kim Kukulowicz
Darren Lorimer
Ron Tratch
Dan Dickinson
Brian Leland
Jody Sperling
Tim Wilson
Mahima Poddar
David Legresley

D-U-N-S 24-309-6109 (HQ)
FUSION BRANDS INC
FUSION BEAUTY
40 St Clair Ave W Suite 200, Toronto, ON, M4V 1M2
(800) 261-9110
Emp Here 20   *Sales* 27,633,625
SIC 5122 Drugs, proprietaries, and sundries
Caroline Pieper-Vogt
Neil Shinder
Lenora Zelikovitz
Eugene Melnyk

D-U-N-S 25-674-0564 (SL)
HANFENG EVERGREEN INC
2 St Clair Ave W Suite 610, Toronto, ON, M4V 1L5

Emp Here 600   *Sales* 353,495,400
SIC 5191 Farm supplies
Xinduo Yu
Loudon Frank Mclean Owen
David J. Thomson
Joanne Yan
Edwin Nordholm

D-U-N-S 20-356-3002 (HQ)
HEARINGLIFE CANADA LTD
HEARINGLIFE
(*Suby of* WILLIAM DEMANT FONDEN)
1 St Clair Ave W Suite 800, Toronto, ON, M4V 1K7
(416) 925-9223
Emp Here 1   *Sales* 26,520,550
SIC 8093 Specialty outpatient clinics, nec
Gino Chouinard

D-U-N-S 24-309-8584   (SL)
HIGHVAIL SYSTEMS INC
1 St Clair Ave W Suite 1201, Toronto, ON, M4V
1K6
(416) 867-3000
Emp Here 23   *Sales* 10,285,002
SIC 5045 Computers, peripherals, and software
Bradley Brodkin
Krys Armatys
Dino Chronopoulos

D-U-N-S 24-046-6227   (HQ)
IBI GROUP
55 St Clair Ave W Suite 700, Toronto, ON, M4V
2Y7
(416) 596-1930
Emp Here 250   *Sales* 241,220,000
SIC 8742 Management consulting services
Bruce Han
Dusica Pavlovic

D-U-N-S 24-127-1902   (HQ)
IBI GROUP INC
55 St Clair Ave W Suite 700, Toronto, ON, M4V
2Y7
(416) 596-1930
Sales 279,208,967
SIC 8711 Engineering services
Scott Stewart
David M Thom
Lorraine Bell
Jane Sillberg
Stephen Taylor
Dale Richmond
Juri Pill
Angela Holtham
Claudia Krywiak
John Reid

D-U-N-S 20-303-4640   (BR)
IBI GROUP INC
(*Suby of* IBI GROUP INC)
95 St Clair Ave W Suite 200, Toronto, ON, M4V
1N6
(416) 596-1930
Emp Here 125
SIC 8712 Architectural services
Tim Gorley

D-U-N-S 20-185-5517   (HQ)
JAMIESON LABORATORIES LTD
JAMIESON
(*Suby of* JAMIESON WELLNESS INC)
2 St Clair Ave W, Toronto, ON, M4V 1L5
(416) 960-0052
Emp Here 100   *Sales* 252,011,440
SIC 2833 Medicinals and botanicals
Mark Hornick
Chris Snowden

D-U-N-S 20-847-1896   (HQ)
KENAIR APARTMENTS LIMITED
500 Avenue Rd, Toronto, ON, M4V 2J6
(416) 923-7557
Sales 11,645,550
SIC 6513 Apartment building operators
Keneth Rotenberg
Ronald Schmidt
David Kapelus
Robert Mckenzie

D-U-N-S 24-845-9562   (HQ)
KINGSWAY FINANCIAL SERVICES INC
KFSI
45 St Clair Ave W Ste 400, Toronto, ON, M4V
1K9
(416) 848-1171
Sales 216,595,002
SIC 6331 Fire, marine, and casualty insurance
John T Fitzgerald
William A. Hickey Jr.
Paul Hogan
Terence Kavanagh
Joseph Stilwell
Gregory Hannon
Doug Levine

D-U-N-S 20-786-7599   (HQ)
MANDRAKE MANAGEMENT CONSULTANTS CORPORATION
55 St Clair Ave W Suite 401, Toronto, ON, M4V
2Y7
(416) 922-5400
Emp Here 46   *Sales* 13,983,390
SIC 7361 Employment agencies
Harold Perry
Stefan Danis

D-U-N-S 20-553-1333   (HQ)
MEDICAL FACILITIES CORPORATION
45 St Clair Ave W Suite 200, Toronto, ON, M4V
1K9
(416) 848-7380
Emp Here 889   *Sales* 431,602,000
SIC 8062 General medical and surgical hospitals
Robert O. Horrar
Jimmy Porter
James D. Rolfe
David Watson
Jeffrey C. Lozon
David R. Bellaire
Stephen Dineley
Dale Lawr
Reza Shahim
Erin S. Enright

D-U-N-S 25-832-6065   (SL)
MILBORNE REAL ESTATE INC
385 Madison Ave, Toronto, ON, M4V 2W7
(416) 928-9998
Emp Here 60   *Sales* 16,305,360
SIC 6531 Real estate agents and managers
Hunter Milborne

D-U-N-S 25-098-7419   (HQ)
MONTECO LTD
55 St Clair Ave W Suite 408, Toronto, ON, M4V
2Y7
(416) 960-9968
Emp Here 2   *Sales* 16,129,710
SIC 3299 NonMetallic mineral products,
Scott Monteith
Joseph Monteith
Michael Brandt

D-U-N-S 20-566-9901   (SL)
NATIONAL CANCER INSTITUTE OF CANADA
NCIC
10 Alcorn Ave Suite 200, Toronto, ON, M4V
3B1
(416) 961-7223
Emp Here 37   *Sales* 10,535,639
SIC 8733 Noncommercial research organizations
Michael Wosnick
Elizabeth Eisenhauer

D-U-N-S 24-736-3989   (HQ)
NORTHLAND POWER INC
30 St Clair Ave W 12 Fl, Toronto, ON, M4V
3A1
(416) 962-6262
Emp Here 300   *Sales* 1,179,293,616
SIC 4911 Electric services
Mike Crawley
James C. Temerty
Michael Shadbolt
Morten Melin
Troy Patton
Paul Bradley
Russell Goodman
John Brace
Linda L. Bertoldi
Marie Bountrogianni

D-U-N-S 24-333-0508   (HQ)
PARK LAWN CORPORATION
2 St Clair Ave W Suite 1300, Toronto, ON, M4V
1L5
(416) 231-1462
Sales 112,307,505
SIC 7261 Funeral service and crematories

Andrew Clark
Brad Green
Lorie Johnson
Linda Gilbert
Suzanne Cowan
Nicolas Mulroney
Joseph Leeder
Jay Dodds
Winz Martina Casagrande
John Ward

D-U-N-S 20-408-5419   (SL)
ROLEX CANADA LTD
50 St Clair Ave W, Toronto, ON, M4V 3B7
(416) 968-1100
Emp Here 50   *Sales* 26,027,100
SIC 5094 Jewelry and precious stones
Luca Bermasconi

D-U-N-S 25-703-6467   (BR)
ROYAL LEPAGE REAL ESTATE SERVICES LTD
(*Suby of* BRIDGEMARQ REAL ESTATE SERVICES INC)
55 St Clair Ave W, Toronto, ON, M4V 2Y7
(416) 921-1112
Emp Here 115
SIC 6531 Real estate agents and managers
Ryan Duffy

D-U-N-S 24-338-9561   (SL)
SWIFT TRADE SECURITIES LTD
55 St Clair Ave W Suite 900, Toronto, ON, M4V
2Y7
(416) 351-0000
Emp Here 50   *Sales* 33,946,150
SIC 6211 Security brokers and dealers
Peter Beck

D-U-N-S 20-511-8560   (SL)
TRUESTAR HEALTH INC
TRUE STAR CONSULTING
55 St Clair Ave W Suite 600, Toronto, ON, M4V
2Y7

Emp Here 60   *Sales* 14,184,098
SIC 8621 Professional organizations
Tim Mulcahy
David Schleich

D-U-N-S 24-422-5616   (HQ)
TURNER & TOWNSEND CM2R INC
2 St Clair Ave W 12th Fl, Toronto, ON, M4V
1L5
(416) 925-1424
Emp Here 55   *Sales* 10,188,123
SIC 8713 Surveying services
Gregory Curran
Gerard Mccabe
Manoj Ravindran
Mark Jones
Jeremy Lathom-Sharp

D-U-N-S 25-220-0183   (HQ)
UNIFOR LEGAL SERVICES PLAN
1 St Clair Ave W Suite 600, Toronto, ON, M4V
3C3
(416) 960-2410
Emp Here 10   *Sales* 11,088,200
SIC 8111 Legal services
Stephen Ginsberg

D-U-N-S 20-923-7411   (HQ)
UPPER CANADA COLLEGE
200 Lonsdale Rd, Toronto, ON, M4V 1W6
(416) 488-1125
Sales 19,823,800
SIC 8211 Elementary and secondary schools
Jim Power
Michael Macmillan

D-U-N-S 25-477-7758   (HQ)
WELLESLEY INSTITUTE
10 Alcorn Ave Suite 300, Toronto, ON, M4V
3A9
(416) 972-1010
Sales 21,276,360
SIC 8699 Membership organizations, nec

Rick Blickstead
Peter Warrian
Susan Williams
Minda Davis

D-U-N-S 20-407-4991   (HQ)
WZMH ARCHITECTS
95 St Clair Ave W Suite 1500, Toronto, ON,
M4V 1N6
(416) 961-4111
Emp Here 70   *Sales* 14,299,120
SIC 8712 Architectural services
Carl Blanchaer

Toronto, ON M4W

D-U-N-S 20-159-1518   (HQ)
333308 ONTARIO LTD
(*Suby of* FAIRFAX FINANCIAL HOLDINGS
LIMITED)
55 Bloor St W Suite 506, Toronto, ON, M4W
1A5
(416) 964-2900
Emp Here 90   *Sales* 27,888,360
SIC 5719 Miscellaneous homefurnishings
Alan J Stark

D-U-N-S 24-032-2003   (SL)
6142974 CANADA INC
LUSIGHT RESEARCH
175 Bloor St E Suite 606, Toronto, ON, M4W
3R8
(416) 934-1436
Emp Here 40   *Sales* 21,248,280
SIC 6282 Investment advice
Paul Warme
Philip Harrison
Paul Sparrow

D-U-N-S 24-849-0104   (SL)
ACCUMARK PARTNERS INC
BOOMU MARKETING DIV OF
(*Suby of* MDC PARTNERS INC.)
2 Bloor St E Suite 2600, Toronto, ON, M4W
1A8
(416) 446-7758
Emp Here 55   *Sales* 10,257,830
SIC 8743 Public relations services
Thomas Green
David Sharpe
David Peres
Troy Yung
Nicole Gallucci

D-U-N-S 20-291-4099   (SL)
AGELLAN COMMERCIAL REIT HOLDINGS INC
(*Suby of* ELAD CANADA INC)
890 Yonge St Ste 505, Toronto, ON, M4W 3P4
(416) 593-6800
Emp Here 15   *Sales* 10,452,150
SIC 6798 Real estate investment trusts
Frank Camenzuli
Terra Attard
Daniel Millett
Christopher Caswell

D-U-N-S 24-952-8688   (SL)
ALL HEALTH SERVICES INC
PARMED ACADEMY
66 Collier St Unit 9d, Toronto, ON, M4W 1L9
(416) 515-1151
Emp Here 50   *Sales* 11,848,500
SIC 7361 Employment agencies
Marilyn Anden
Lita Azarcon

D-U-N-S 20-769-5461   (SL)
ALL LANGUAGES LTD
421 Bloor St E Suite 306, Toronto, ON, M4W
3T1
(647) 427-8308
Emp Here 38   *Sales* 16,852,620
SIC 7389 Business services, nec
Adele Salvagne

Paul Penzo

D-U-N-S 20-260-4112   (HQ)
ALL SENIORS CARE HOLDINGS INC
175 Bloor St E Suite 601, Toronto, ON, M4W 3R8
(416) 323-3773
Sales 271,354,000
SIC 6513 Apartment building operators
George Kuhl

D-U-N-S 24-204-9232   (HQ)
ALL SENIORS CARE LIVING CENTRES LTD
(*Suby of* ALL SENIORS CARE HOLDINGS INC)
175 Bloor St E Suite 601, Toronto, ON, M4W 3R8
(416) 323-3773
Emp Here 40   *Sales* 144,883,701
SIC 6513 Apartment building operators
George Kuhl
Micheal Kuhl
Joshua Kuhl
Michael Fraser
Lily Goodman

D-U-N-S 24-858-4117   (SL)
ALLIANCE ATLANTIS COMMUNICATIONS INC
121 Bloor St E Suite 1500, Toronto, ON, M4W 3M5
(416) 967-1174
Emp Here 871   *Sales* 202,346,035
SIC 4899 Communication services, nec

D-U-N-S 24-822-7118   (SL)
BAIN & COMPANY CANADA, INC
(*Suby of* BAIN & COMPANY, INC.)
2 Bloor St E, Toronto, ON, M4W 1A8
(416) 929-1888
Emp Here 80   *Sales* 14,920,480
SIC 8742 Management consulting services
Pierre Lavallee
Michael Collins
Orit Gadish

D-U-N-S 24-337-4964   (SL)
BAY-BLOOR RADIO INC
55 Bloor St W, Toronto, ON, M4W 1A5
(416) 967-1122
Emp Here 50   *Sales* 11,517,000
SIC 5731 Radio, television, and electronic stores
Mark Mandlsohn

D-U-N-S 25-359-7934   (BR)
BBDO CANADA CORP
PROXIMITY CANADA, DIV OF
(*Suby of* OMNICOM GROUP INC.)
2 Bloor St W Suite 3200, Toronto, ON, M4W 3E2
(416) 972-1505
Emp Here 200
SIC 7311 Advertising agencies
Marcus Evans

D-U-N-S 24-423-5904   (HQ)
BBDO CANADA CORP
BBDO
(*Suby of* OMNICOM GROUP INC.)
2 Bloor St W Suite Suite 3200, Toronto, ON, M4W 3R6
(416) 972-1505
Emp Here 195   *Sales* 71,754,690
SIC 7311 Advertising agencies
Philip Filippopoulos

D-U-N-S 24-184-1626   (HQ)
BLACK & MCDONALD GROUP LIMITED
2 Bloor St E Suite 2100, Toronto, ON, M4W 1A8
(416) 920-5100
Sales 1,354,240,000
SIC 1711 Plumbing, heating, air-conditioning
John Bruce Mcdonald
William Ian Mcdonald

D-U-N-S 20-160-2216   (HQ)

BLACK & MCDONALD LIMITED
(*Suby of* BLACK & MCDONALD GROUP LIMITED)
2 Bloor St E Suite 2100, Toronto, ON, M4W 1A8
(416) 920-5100
Emp Here 12   *Sales* 1,489,664,000
SIC 1711 Plumbing, heating, air-conditioning
W. Ian Mcdonald
John Bruce Mcdonald
William Mcdonald
Seaz Rahim

D-U-N-S 20-846-2812   (SL)
BRANKSOME HALL
10 Elm Ave, Toronto, ON, M4W 1N4
(416) 920-9741
Emp Here 150   *Sales* 14,867,850
SIC 8211 Elementary and secondary schools
Karen Murton
Judy Gordon

D-U-N-S 20-160-8759   (SL)
BURNETT, LEO COMPANY LTD
175 Bloor St E North Tower Suite 1200, Toronto, ON, M4W 3R9
(416) 925-5997
Emp Here 300   *Sales* 60,111,300
SIC 7311 Advertising agencies
Judy John
David Kennedy
Thomas Beckett

D-U-N-S 25-487-8101   (SL)
BUSINESS TRAVEL NETWORK INC
1027 Yonge St Suite 103, Toronto, ON, M4W 2K9
(416) 924-6000
Emp Here 80   *Sales* 41,597,360
SIC 4724 Travel agencies
Milka Cook

D-U-N-S 24-388-4988   (HQ)
CANADA COLORS AND CHEMICALS (EASTERN) LIMITED
(*Suby of* CANADA COLORS AND CHEMICALS LIMITED)
175 Bloor St E Suite 1300, Toronto, ON, M4W 3R8
(416) 443-5500
Emp Here 24   *Sales* 218,468,900
SIC 5169 Chemicals and allied products, nec
Brian Job
Carol Maclean

D-U-N-S 20-161-1001   (HQ)
CANADA COLORS AND CHEMICALS LIMITED
CCC PLASTICS
175 Bloor St E Suite 1300, Toronto, ON, M4W 3R8
(416) 443-5500
Emp Here 21   *Sales* 73,034,500
SIC 5162 Plastics materials and basic shapes
Guy Carr-Harris
Deborah Hewison
Brian Job

D-U-N-S 20-388-2089   (BR)
CANADIAN BLOOD SERVICES
(*Suby of* CANADIAN BLOOD SERVICES)
2 Bloor St W, Toronto, ON, M4W 3E2
(613) 739-2300
Emp Here 100
SIC 8099 Health and allied services, nec
Jennifer Biemans

D-U-N-S 24-077-3267   (HQ)
CANADIAN PAYROLL ASSOCIATION, THE
250 Bloor St E Suite 1600, Toronto, ON, M4W 1E6
(416) 487-3380
Sales 12,930,750
SIC 8611 Business associations
Patrick Culhane

D-U-N-S 25-473-3280   (BR)
CANON CANADA INC

BUSINESS SOLUTIONS DIVISION
(*Suby of* CANON INC.)
175 Bloor St E Suite 1200, Toronto, ON, M4W 3R8
(416) 491-9330
Emp Here 225
SIC 5999 Miscellaneous retail stores, nec
Eric Turcot

D-U-N-S 24-079-8421   (SL)
CHARTERED PROFESSIONAL ACCOUNTANTS OF ONTARIO
CPA ONTARIO
69 Bloor St E, Toronto, ON, M4W 1B3
(416) 962-1841
Emp Here 120   *Sales* 28,093,320
SIC 8621 Professional organizations
Rod Barr
Nora Murrant
Brian Leader

D-U-N-S 20-606-1855   (HQ)
CHISHOLM, RONALD A. LIMITED
2 Bloor St W Suite 3300, Toronto, ON, M4W 3K3
(416) 967-6000
Emp Here 115   *Sales* 107,507,400
SIC 5141 Groceries, general line
Timothy Frith
Paul Buzbuzian
Zoran Perusina
Gregg Badger
Yuval Hason
Jeffrey S. Ryley

D-U-N-S 25-400-1241   (HQ)
CHOICE PROPERTIES REAL ESTATE INVESTMENT TRUST
C R E I T
175 Bloor St E Suite 1400n, Toronto, ON, M4W 3R8
(416) 324-7840
Emp Here 1   *Sales* 870,508,058
SIC 6798 Real estate investment trusts
Stephen E Johnson
Rael Diamond
Mario Barrafato
Kerry D. Adams
Christie J.B. Clark
Graeme Eadie
Anthony R. Graham
Karen A. Kinsley
R. Michael Latimer
John Morrison

D-U-N-S 25-399-2184   (HQ)
CITCO (CANADA) INC
2 Bloor St E Suite 2700, Toronto, ON, M4W 1A8
(416) 966-9200
Sales 207,394,672
SIC 8742 Management consulting services
Kieran Conway

D-U-N-S 25-264-1840   (HQ)
CONTAX INC
893 Yonge St, Toronto, ON, M4W 2H2
(416) 927-1913
Emp Here 30   *Sales* 13,716,600
SIC 8741 Management services
Michael Pearson
Glen Wallace

D-U-N-S 24-652-4805   (HQ)
CORITY SOFTWARE INC
CORITY
250 Bloor St E 1st Fl, Toronto, ON, M4W 1E6
(416) 863-6800
Sales 46,143,250
SIC 7371 Custom computer programming services
Mark Wallace
Shanti Atkins
Greg Durand
John Easton
Michael Couture
Ryan Magee

D-U-N-S 20-592-6236   (HQ)
CREIT MANAGEMENT L.P.
175 Bloor St E Suite 500n, Toronto, ON, M4W 3R8
(416) 628-7771
Sales 318,818,925
SIC 6531 Real estate agents and managers
Stephen Johnson
Rael Diamond
Mario Barrafata
Deborah Barrett
John Brough
Anthony Fell
Andrew Hoffman
Michael Latimer
Reay Mackay
Dale Ponder

D-U-N-S 20-810-0540   (BR)
DIALOG
DIALOG DESIGN
(*Suby of* DIALOG)
2 Bloor St E Suite 1000, Toronto, ON, M4W 1A8
(416) 966-0220
Emp Here 100
SIC 7361 Employment agencies
Nicole Mackereth

D-U-N-S 24-245-8763   (SL)
ENVIRONICS ANALYTICS GROUP LTD
ENVIRONICS ANALYTICS
33 Bloor St E Suite 400, Toronto, ON, M4W 3H1
(416) 969-2733
Emp Here 100   *Sales* 21,335,800
SIC 8732 Commercial nonphysical research
Jan Kestle

D-U-N-S 25-486-6148   (HQ)
EVERGREEN ENVIROMENTAL FOUNDATION
EVERGREEN
550 Bayview Ave Suite 300, Toronto, ON, M4W 3X8
(416) 596-1495
Sales 12,964,773
SIC 8748 Business consulting, nec

D-U-N-S 24-587-8293   (BR)
FOUR SEASONS HOTELS LIMITED
(*Suby of* CASCADE INVESTMENT, L.L.C.)
60 Yorkville Ave, Toronto, ON, M4W 0A4
(416) 964-0411
Emp Here 450
SIC 7011 Hotels and motels
Dimitrios Zarikos

D-U-N-S 24-551-9371   (SL)
FRESHII INC
1055 Yonge St, Toronto, ON, M4W 2L2
(647) 350-2001
Emp Here 178   *Sales* 21,650,000
SIC 5812 Eating places
Matthew Corrin
Craig De Pratto
Adam Corrin
Ashley Dalziel
Paul Huges
Neil Pasricha
Jeffrey Burchell
Marc Kielburger
Michele Romanow
Heather Briant

D-U-N-S 24-844-9845   (HQ)
GAP (CANADA) INC
(*Suby of* THE GAP INC)
60 Bloor St W Suite 1501, Toronto, ON, M4W 3B8
(416) 921-2225
Emp Here 65   *Sales* 748,530,000
SIC 5651 Family clothing stores
Pierre Pronovost

D-U-N-S 25-344-8997   (HQ)
GLOBAL KNOWLEDGE NETWORK (CANADA) INC

(*Suby of* GK HOLDINGS, INC.)
2 Bloor St E Unit 3100, Toronto, ON, M4W 1A8
(613) 254-6530
Emp Here 5   *Sales* 20,338,488
SIC 8741 Management services
Sean Dolan
Paul Renucci
Lawrence Franco
Brian Holland
Robert Kalainikas
Satish Shetty
Robert Kalainikas
Michael Fox
Kevin Pawsey
Robb Kaufmann

D-U-N-S 25-984-8641   (SL)
GROUPEX INC
GROUPEX-SOLUTIONS
3 Rowanwood Ave, Toronto, ON, M4W 1Y5
(416) 968-0000
Emp Here 94   *Sales* 22,023,072
SIC 8748 Business consulting, nec
Laurie Dudo
Theodore Smith
Farham Khan
Aman Dassi

D-U-N-S 20-384-2885   (SL)
GROUPEX LIMITED
3 Rowanwood Ave, Toronto, ON, M4W 1Y5
(416) 968-0000
Emp Here 57   *Sales* 13,354,416
SIC 8748 Business consulting, nec
Theodore Smith
Farhan Khan
Patricia Wallenius

D-U-N-S 25-092-4052   (SL)
H K STRATEGIES CANADA
160 Bloor St E Suite 700, Toronto, ON, M4W 0A2
(416) 413-1218
Emp Here 49   *Sales* 11,480,112
SIC 8743 Public relations services
Michael Coates

D-U-N-S 25-498-1004   (SL)
HASTON, NANCY & ASSOCIATES INC
175 Bloor St E Suite 807, Toronto, ON, M4W 3R8

Emp Here 80   *Sales* 10,563,200
SIC 8093 Specialty outpatient clinics, nec
Nancy Haston

D-U-N-S 20-221-3484   (HQ)
HOLT, RENFREW & CIE, LIMITEE
CAFE HOLT TMA482, 017
60 Bloor St W Suite 1100, Toronto, ON, M4W 3B8
(416) 922-2333
Emp Here 200   *Sales* 286,936,500
SIC 5621 Women's clothing stores
Mark Derbyshire
Lorraine E Kuska
Hilary Weston
Isabelle Hudon
Alannah Weston
Paul Kelly
Anthony R Graham
Robert John Dart
Galen W.G Weston

D-U-N-S 25-104-4806   (BR)
HOLT, RENFREW & CIE, LIMITEE
HOLT RENFREW
50 Bloor St W Suite 200, Toronto, ON, M4W 1A1
(416) 922-2333
Emp Here 100
SIC 5621 Women's clothing stores
Scott Harris

D-U-N-S 25-721-1524   (BR)
HUDSON'S BAY COMPANY
THE BAY
(*Suby of* HUDSON'S BAY COMPANY)

2 Bloor St E Suite 52, Toronto, ON, M4W 3H7
(416) 972-3313
Emp Here 600
SIC 5311 Department stores
Roger Humphries

D-U-N-S 20-702-8288   (BR)
HUDSON'S BAY COMPANY
(*Suby of* HUDSON'S BAY COMPANY)
2 Bloor St E Suite 52, Toronto, ON, M4W 3H7
(416) 972-3333
Emp Here 300
SIC 5311 Department stores
Poole June

D-U-N-S 24-024-4400   (SL)
HUTCHINSON SMILEY LIMITED
HSL
890 Yonge St Suite 1002, Toronto, ON, M4W 3P4

Emp Here 50   *Sales* 11,895,050
SIC 8742 Management consulting services
Robert W. Sydia
Robert A. Sydia

D-U-N-S 20-005-4034   (BR)
INDIGO BOOKS & MUSIC INC
(*Suby of* INDIGO BOOKS & MUSIC INC)
55 Bloor St W, Toronto, ON, M4W 1A5
(416) 925-3536
Emp Here 100
SIC 5942 Book stores
Colleen Logan

D-U-N-S 20-651-1516   (BR)
IPSOS LIMITED PARTNERSHIP
IPSOS REID
(*Suby of* IPSOS)
160 Bloor St E Suite 300, Toronto, ON, M4W 1B9
(416) 925-4444
Emp Here 300
SIC 8732 Commercial nonphysical research
Andrew Cochrane

D-U-N-S 25-531-3140   (BR)
IPSOS-ASI, LTD
IPSOS REID
(*Suby of* IPSOS)
160 Bloor St E Suite 300, Toronto, ON, M4W 1B9
(416) 925-4444
Emp Here 90
SIC 8732 Commercial nonphysical research
Angela Sweeney

D-U-N-S 25-096-1844   (HQ)
IPSOS-ASI, LTD
(*Suby of* IPSOS)
160 Bloor St E Suite 300, Toronto, ON, M4W 1B9
(416) 324-2900
Emp Here 33   *Sales* 127,551,250
SIC 8732 Commercial nonphysical research
Jacquie Matthews
James T. Smith
Sheryl Goodman
James Thompson
Debra Mason
Didier Truchot

D-U-N-S 25-130-6866   (SL)
J.W.T ENTERPRISES INC
160 Bloor St E Suite 8th, Toronto, ON, M4W 3P7
(416) 926-7300
Emp Here 200   *Sales* 40,074,200
SIC 7311 Advertising agencies
Antonio Piget
Rob Elliot

D-U-N-S 20-343-7012   (SL)
JOLERA INC
365 Bloor St E 2 Fl, Toronto, ON, M4W 3L4
(416) 410-1011
Emp Here 85   *Sales* 19,754,255
SIC 5734 Computer and software stores

Alex Shan
Joseph Khunaysir

D-U-N-S 20-281-1717   (SL)
JUNIPER PARK TBWA COMMUNICATIONS ULC
33 Bloor St E, Toronto, ON, M4W 3H1
(416) 413-7301
Emp Here 128   *Sales* 25,647,488
SIC 7311 Advertising agencies
Jill Nykoliation
Kathleen Brown
Laura White
Jackie Wiseman
Shanta Maula

D-U-N-S 20-176-2846   (SL)
JUNVIR INVESTMENTS LIMITED
SUMMERHILL MARKET
446 Summerhill Ave, Toronto, ON, M4W 2E4
(416) 921-2714
Emp Here 225   *Sales* 43,304,400
SIC 5411 Grocery stores
Robert Mcmullen
Christina Mcmullen
Bradley Mcmullen

D-U-N-S 20-079-2146   (SL)
K2 & ASSOCIATES INVESTMENT MANAGEMENT INC
2 Bloor St W Suite 801, Toronto, ON, M4W 3E2
(416) 365-2155
Emp Here 15   *Sales* 10,450,155
SIC 6726 Investment offices, nec
Shawn Kimel

D-U-N-S 24-986-8621   (HQ)
KANTAR CANADA INC
KANTAR MILLWARD BROWN
(*Suby of* WPP PLC)
2 Bloor St E Suite 900, Toronto, ON, M4W 3H8
(416) 924-5751
Emp Here 1   *Sales* 18,695,155
SIC 8732 Commercial nonphysical research
Scott Negginson
Michael Hecimovic
Phil Cadieux
Carole Ross
Morgan Mulvihill
Mary Graham
Margot Acton
Rhonda Grunier
Janet Cloud
Derick Barrett

D-U-N-S 24-926-7311   (HQ)
KBS+P CANADA INC
2 Bloor St E Suite 137, Toronto, ON, M4W 3J4
(416) 260-7000
Emp Here 30   *Sales* 21,038,955
SIC 7311 Advertising agencies
Terry Johnson
Tony Battaglia
Richard Brott

D-U-N-S 25-529-4175   (SL)
KLICK INC
KLICK HEALTH
175 Bloor St E Suite 301, Toronto, ON, M4W 3R8
(416) 214-4977
Emp Here 450   *Sales* 75,081,150
SIC 7379 Computer related services, nec
Leerom Segal
Peter Cordy
Glen Webster

D-U-N-S 20-526-8733   (HQ)
MANUFACTURERS LIFE INSURANCE COMPANY, THE
(*Suby of* MANULIFE FINANCIAL CORPORATION)
200 Bloor St E Suite 1, Toronto, ON, M4W 1E5
(416) 926-3000
Emp Here 1,500   *Sales* 38,465,424,000
SIC 6311 Life insurance

Roy Gori
Jim Gallagher
Philip Witherington

D-U-N-S 25-530-9791   (SL)
MANULIFE ASSET MANAGEMENT LIMITED
MANULIFE MUTUAL FUNDS
(*Suby of* MANULIFE FINANCIAL CORPORATION)
200 Bloor St E Suite 1, Toronto, ON, M4W 1E5
(416) 581-8300
Emp Here 345   *Sales* 189,747,585
SIC 6722 Management investment, open-end
Kai Sotorp
Kevin Adolphe
Brian Carmichael
Beth Mcgoldrick
Warren Thompson
J. Roy Firth
Bruce Gordon
Roger Renaud
Bernard Letendre
Richard Coles

D-U-N-S 20-337-9651   (SL)
MANULIFE CANADIAN REAL ESTATE INVESTMENT FUND
250 Bloor St Fl 15, Toronto, ON, M4W 1E5
(416) 926-5500
Emp Here 49   *Sales* 13,316,044
SIC 6531 Real estate agents and managers
Kevin Adolphe

D-U-N-S 25-101-7042   (HQ)
MANULIFE FINANCIAL CORPORATION
MANULIFE MFC INVESTMENT MANAGEMENT
200 Bloor St E, Toronto, ON, M4W 1E5
(416) 926-3000
Emp Here 1,000   *Sales* 29,544,751,144
SIC 6411 Insurance agents, brokers, and service
Michael J. Doughty
John M. Cassaday
Roy Gori
Ronalee H. Ambrose
Joseph P. Caron
Susan F. Dabarno
Sheila S. Fraser
Tsun-Yan Hsieh
P. Thomas Jenkins
Donald R. Lindsay

D-U-N-S 24-761-0145   (SL)
MANULIFE FINANCIAL SERVICES INC
(*Suby of* MANULIFE FINANCIAL CORPORATION)
200 Bloor St E Suite 1, Toronto, ON, M4W 1E5
(416) 926-3000
Emp Here 500   *Sales* 96,488,000
SIC 8742 Management consulting services
Gordon M Hill
John Mceachen

D-U-N-S 20-380-9355   (SL)
MANULIFE US REGIONAL BANK TRUST
200 Bloor St E North Tower, Toronto, ON, M4W 1E5
(416) 926-3000
Emp Here 13   *Sales* 75,880,025
SIC 6726 Investment offices, nec
Roy Gori
Michael Doughty
Paul Lorentz
James (Jim) Gallagher
Scott Hartz
Shamus Weiland
Rahim Hirji
Philip Witherington
Rahul Joshi
Linda Mantia

D-U-N-S 20-338-4045   (HQ)
MARU GROUP CANADA INC
MARU VCR & C
(*Suby of* MARU GROUP HOLDINGS LIM-

ITED)
2 Bloor St E Suite 1600, Toronto, ON, M4W 1A8
(647) 258-1416
Sales 17,595,440
SIC 8732 Commercial nonphysical research
  Edward Morawski
  Amanda Ram

D-U-N-S 20-003-8086   (SL)
MASTERCARD CANADA, INC
(*Suby of* MASTERCARD INCORPORATED)
121 Bloor St E Suite 600, Toronto, ON, M4W 3M5
(416) 365-6655
Emp Here 63   *Sales* 14,108,283
SIC 6153 Short-term business credit institutions, except agricultural
  Kevin Stanton
  Craig Penney

D-U-N-S 25-109-2409   (SL)
MILLENNIUM RESEARCH GROUP INC
DECISION RESOURCES GROUP (DRG)
(*Suby of* PIRAMAL ENTERPRISES LIMITED)
175 Bloor St E Suite 400, Toronto, ON, M4W 3R8
(416) 364-7776
Emp Here 180   *Sales* 45,628,200
SIC 8748 Business consulting, nec
  Jon Sandler
  Chris Obrien
  Carolyn Mcmeekin
  Tim Lyden
  Carol Barry
  Ken Lambe
  Michael Weiss
  Thomas Halliday
  Meredith Ressi
  Ken Mclaren

D-U-N-S 25-100-9858   (HQ)
MINDSHARE CANADA
EXCELERATOR MEDIA, DIV OF
(*Suby of* WPP PLC)
160 Bloor St E Suite 700, Toronto, ON, M4W 0A2
(416) 987-5100
Sales 32,059,360
SIC 7311 Advertising agencies
  Karen Nayler

D-U-N-S 25-102-7918   (HQ)
NORR LIMITED
(*Suby of* INGENIUM GROUP INC)
175 Bloor St E, Toronto, ON, M4W 3R8
(416) 929-0200
Emp Here 192   *Sales* 43,368,820
SIC 8712 Architectural services
  Brian Gerstmar

D-U-N-S 20-180-3652   (HQ)
OLD NAVY (CANADA) INC
(*Suby of* THE GAP INC)
60 Bloor St W Suite 1501, Toronto, ON, M4W 3B8
(416) 921-2711
Emp Here 10   *Sales* 62,377,500
SIC 5651 Family clothing stores
  Lauri Shanahan
  Santiago Marin

D-U-N-S 24-992-4325   (HQ)
OMNICOM CANADA CORP
MARKETSTAR
(*Suby of* OMNICOM GROUP INC.)
2 Bloor St W Suite 2900, Toronto, ON, M4W 3E2
(416) 972-7571
Emp Here 9   *Sales* 180,494,600
SIC 8743 Public relations services
  Frank Palmer
  Kathleen Brown
  Keith Bremer
  Jackie Wiseman

D-U-N-S 25-000-4207   (BR)
OMNICOM CANADA CORP

ANDERSON DDB HEALTH & LIFESTYLE
(*Suby of* OMNICOM GROUP INC.)
33 Bloor St E Suite 1300, Toronto, ON, M4W 3H1
(416) 960-3830
Emp Here 80
SIC 7311 Advertising agencies
  Kevin Brady

D-U-N-S 25-530-5443   (SL)
PLAZA II CORPORATION, THE
TORONTO MARRIOTT BLOOR YORKVILLE
(*Suby of* LARCO INVESTMENTS LTD)
90 Bloor St E, Toronto, ON, M4W 1A7
(416) 922-9155
Emp Here 100   *Sales* 9,269,000
SIC 7011 Hotels and motels
  Aminmohammed J Lalji

D-U-N-S 20-337-0882   (HQ)
POLARIS INFRASTRUCTURE INC
2 Bloor St W Suite 2700it, Toronto, ON, M4W 3E2
(416) 849-2587
Emp Here 20   *Sales* 60,106,603
SIC 1731 Electrical work
  Marc Murnaghan
  Shane Downey
  Jorge Bernhard
  James Lawless
  Jaime Guillen
  C. Thomas Ogryzlo

D-U-N-S 24-683-8457   (HQ)
POSTMEDIA NETWORK CANADA CORP
365 Bloor St E, Toronto, ON, M4W 3L4
(416) 383-2300
Emp Here 100   *Sales* 601,918,512
SIC 2711 Newspapers
  Paul Godfrey
  Peter Sharpe
  Janet Ecker
  Wendy Henkelman
  Mary Junck
  David Pecker
  Daniel Rotstein
  Graham Savage

D-U-N-S 24-424-3254   (HQ)
POSTMEDIA NETWORK INC
POSTMEDIA INTEGRATED ADVERTISING
(*Suby of* POSTMEDIA NETWORK CANADA CORP)
365 Bloor St E Suite 1601, Toronto, ON, M4W 3L4
(416) 383-2300
Emp Here 200   *Sales* 968,870,000
SIC 2711 Newspapers
  Paul Godfrey
  Andrew Macleod
  Brian Bidulka
  Gillian Akai
  Michelle Hall
  Rod Phillips
  Peter Sharpe
  Graham Savage
  Janet Ecker
  Wendy Henkelman

D-U-N-S 20-554-4617   (SL)
PROOF INC
33 Bloor St E Suite 900, Toronto, ON, M4W 3H1
(416) 920-9000
Emp Here 50   *Sales* 10,383,700
SIC 8743 Public relations services
  Bruce Maclellan

D-U-N-S 20-107-5673   (HQ)
PUBLICIS MEDIA CANADA INC
ZENITH MEDIA
(*Suby of* PUBLICIS GROUPE HOLDINGS B.V.)
175 Bloor St E 9th Floor, Toronto, ON, M4W 3R8
(437) 222-5200
Emp Here 80   *Sales* 20,037,100

SIC 7311 Advertising agencies
  Kristine Lyrette

D-U-N-S 25-075-1729   (SL)
ROGERS COMMUNICATIONS CANADA INC
CHATR MOBILE
(*Suby of* ROGERS COMMUNICATIONS INC)
333 Bloor St E Fl 8, Toronto, ON, M4W 1G9
(800) 485-9745
Emp Here 1,000   *Sales* 334,544,000
SIC 4813 Telephone communication, except radio
  Joe Natale

D-U-N-S 24-331-0260   (HQ)
ROGERS COMMUNICATIONS CANADA INC
(*Suby of* ROGERS COMMUNICATIONS INC)
333 Bloor St E 9th Fl, Toronto, ON, M4W 1G9
(416) 935-7777
Emp Here 5   *Sales* 799,652,000
SIC 4841 Cable and other pay television services
  Edward Rogers

D-U-N-S 20-164-9068   (HQ)
ROGERS COMMUNICATIONS INC
ROGERS COMMUNICATIONS PARTNERS
333 Bloor St E, Toronto, ON, M4W 1G9
(416) 935-7777
Emp Here 5,000   *Sales* 11,444,307,792
SIC 4899 Communication services, nec
  Joseph M. Natale
  Rick Brace
  Phil Hartling
  Dean Prevost
  Tony Staffieri
  Graeme Mcphail
  Jorge Fernandes
  Jim Reid
  Lisa Durocher
  Edward S. Rogers

D-U-N-S 25-274-9072   (HQ)
ROGERS MEDIA INC
(*Suby of* ROGERS COMMUNICATIONS INC)
333 Bloor St E, Toronto, ON, M4W 1G9
(416) 935-8200
Emp Here 30   *Sales* 620,076,800
SIC 2721 Periodicals
  Anthony Viner
  John Hinnen

D-U-N-S 20-111-2229   (SL)
ROGERS SPORTS GROUP INC
(*Suby of* ROGERS COMMUNICATIONS INC)
333 Bloor St E, Toronto, ON, M4W 1G9
(416) 935-8200
Emp Here 250
SIC 4832 Radio broadcasting stations
  David P. Miller

D-U-N-S 24-215-1157   (SL)
ROYAL COLLEGE OF DENTAL SURGEONS OF ONTARIO
6 Crescent Rd, Toronto, ON, M4W 1T1
(416) 961-6555
Emp Here 45   *Sales* 10,516,275
SIC 8621 Professional organizations
  Irwin Fefergrad
  Greg Moors

D-U-N-S 24-419-1706   (SL)
SAATCHI & SAATCHI ADVERTISING INC
SAATCHI & SAATCHI
(*Suby of* PUBLICIS GROUPE S.A.)
2 Bloor St E Suite 600, Toronto, ON, M4W 1A8
(416) 359-9595
Emp Here 50   *Sales* 10,586,200
SIC 7311 Advertising agencies
  Stuart Payne
  Brett Channer

D-U-N-S 20-554-9137   (SL)
SKYLINK SECURITY INC
1027 Yonge St, Toronto, ON, M4W 2K9
(416) 922-5017
Emp Here 200   *Sales* 187,835,400

SIC 6211 Security brokers and dealers
  Meir Livneh

D-U-N-S 25-283-4403   (HQ)
SPAFAX CANADA INC
(*Suby of* WPP PLC)
2 Bloor St E Suite 1020, Toronto, ON, M4W 1A8
(416) 350-2425
Emp Here 20   *Sales* 51,976,400
SIC 5199 Nondurable goods, nec
  Richard Staunton
  Simon Ogden

D-U-N-S 24-057-6850   (HQ)
SPECTRUM HEALTH CARE LTD
2 Bloor St E Suite 1200, Toronto, ON, M4W 1A8
(416) 964-0322
Sales 92,041,200
SIC 8082 Home health care services
  Mitchell Gallinger

D-U-N-S 25-092-4334   (SL)
STARCOM MEDIAVEST GROUP SMG
STARCOM WORLDWIDE
175 Bloor St E Suite 1200n, Toronto, ON, M4W 3R9
(416) 927-3300
Emp Here 200   *Sales* 40,074,200
SIC 7311 Advertising agencies
  Bruce Neve

D-U-N-S 20-414-1360   (SL)
STOLLERY, FRANK LIMITED
STOLLERY'S
1 Bloor St W, Toronto, ON, M4W 1A3

Emp Here 56   *Sales* 10,046,176
SIC 5611 Men's and boys' clothing stores
  Ed Whaley
  Patricia Whaley

D-U-N-S 25-949-7725   (SL)
TEMPLE AND TEMPLE TOURS INC
TNT TOURS
819 Yonge St 2nd Fl, Toronto, ON, M4W 2G9
(416) 928-3227
Emp Here 35   *Sales* 13,487,600
SIC 4725 Tour operators
  David Temple
  John Temple

D-U-N-S 20-176-7894   (HQ)
THOMPSON, J. WALTER COMPANY LIMITED
JWT
(*Suby of* WPP PLC)
160 Bloor St E Suite 1100, Toronto, ON, M4W 3P7
(416) 926-7300
Emp Here 150   *Sales* 40,074,200
SIC 7311 Advertising agencies
  Susan Kim-Kirkland
  Brent Choi

D-U-N-S 20-703-1670   (HQ)
TIMBERCREEK ASSET MANAGEMENT INC
25 Price St, Toronto, ON, M4W 1Z1
(416) 306-9967
Emp Here 10   *Sales* 185,007,940
SIC 6282 Investment advice
  R. Blair Tamblyn
  Elina Nam
  Ugo Bizzarri
  Jeff Hutchison
  Gigi Wong

D-U-N-S 20-337-9664   (SL)
TIMBERCREEK FINANCIAL CORP
25 Price St, Toronto, ON, M4W 1Z1
(416) 923-9967
Emp Here 600   *Sales* 239,306,400
SIC 6162 Mortgage bankers and loan correspondents
  Cam Goodnough
  Carrie Morris
  Peter Hawkings

Gigi Wong
Ugo Bizzarri
Blair Tamblyn
W. Glenn Shyba
Steven R. Scott
Zelick I. Altman
Derek J. Watchorn

D-U-N-S 20-273-9736   (SL)
**TIMBERCREEK INVESTMENT MANAGE-
MENT INC**
25 Price St, Toronto, ON, M4W 1Z1
(416) 306-9967
Emp Here 100   *Sales* 53,120,700
SIC 6282 Investment advice
R. Blair Tamblyn

D-U-N-S 20-917-8206   (SL)
TIMBERCREEK INVESTMENTS INC
25 Price St, Toronto, ON, M4W 1Z1
(416) 923-9967
Emp Here 58   *Sales* 11,825,214
SIC 6553 Cemetery subdividers and developers
Blair Tamblyn
Aimee Gaudet

D-U-N-S 20-115-2282   (HQ)
**TORONTO COMMUNITY HOUSING COR-
PORATION**
(*Suby of* CORPORATION OF THE CITY OF
TORONTO)
931 Yonge St Suite 400, Toronto, ON, M4W
2H2
(416) 981-5500
Emp Here 50   *Sales* 473,289,600
SIC 6531 Real estate agents and managers
Len Koroneos
Bronwyn Krog
Howie Wong
Deborah Simon
Mitzie Hunter

D-U-N-S 20-292-0711   (BR)
TORONTO DISTRICT SCHOOL BOARD
*ROSEDALE HEIGHTS SCHOOL OF THE
ARTS*
(*Suby of* TORONTO DISTRICT SCHOOL
BOARD)
711 Bloor St E, Toronto, ON, M4W 1J4
(416) 393-1580
Emp Here 85
SIC 8211 Elementary and secondary schools
Barrie Sketchley

D-U-N-S 24-047-0633   (HQ)
TORONTO PUBLIC LIBRARY BOARD
789 Yonge St, Toronto, ON, M4W 2G8
(416) 397-5946
Emp Here 380   *Sales* 112,949,775
SIC 8231 Libraries
Larry Hughson

D-U-N-S 20-921-8387   (HQ)
TOWERS WATSON CANADA INC
(*Suby of* WILLIS TOWERS WATSON PUBLIC
LIMITED COMPANY)
175 Bloor St E Suite 1701, Toronto, ON, M4W
3T6
(416) 960-2700
Emp Here 50   *Sales* 42,460,700
SIC 8999 Services, nec
Kevin Aselstine
William Gulliver

D-U-N-S 20-009-1999   (HQ)
TOWLE, RUSSELL L ENTERPRISES LTD
MARVEL BEAUTY SCHOOL
25 Yorkville Ave, Toronto, ON, M4W 1L1
(416) 923-0993
Emp Here 140   *Sales* 13,454,400
SIC 7231 Beauty shops
James Muir
William Crump
Garth Evans
Margaret Muir
Donald Evans

D-U-N-S 24-418-2861   (HQ)
UNILEVER CANADA INC
UNILEVER BEST FOODS
(*Suby of* UNILEVER PLC)
160 Bloor St E Suite 1400, Toronto, ON, M4W
3R2
(416) 415-3000
Emp Here 200   *Sales* 1,657,109,000
SIC 2099 Food preparations, nec
Gary Wade
John Leboutillier
John Coyne
Paulo Decastro
Julie Teh-Ching
Gabor Szekendi

D-U-N-S 24-171-0420   (BR)
VALUMART LTD
VALUMART
55 Bloor St W, Toronto, ON, M4W 1A5
(416) 923-8831
Emp Here 100
SIC 5411 Grocery stores
Tim Arnold

D-U-N-S 25-318-5490   (SL)
VETERINARY REFERRAL CLINIC
920 Yonge St Suite 117, Toronto, ON, M4W
3C7
(416) 920-2002
Emp Here 50   *Sales* 11,016,400
SIC 8734 Testing laboratories
Douglas Mason
Allan Norris
Susan Cochrane
Sharon French
Craig Miller
Jocelyn Wellington
Kevin Isakow

D-U-N-S 20-292-5442   (SL)
VR TRAVEL LTD
2 Bloor St W Suite 2120, Toronto, ON, M4W
3E2

Emp Here 49   *Sales* 18,882,640
SIC 4724 Travel agencies
Ole Svendsen
Jan Stojberg

D-U-N-S 24-991-0548   (SL)
WANG, MAURICE DRUGS LTD
SHOPPERS DRUG MART
20 Bloor St E, Toronto, ON, M4W 3G7
(416) 967-7787
Emp Here 40   *Sales* 10,118,160
SIC 5912 Drug stores and proprietary stores
Maurice Wang

D-U-N-S 24-858-0313   (SL)
WAVEMAKER CANADA ULC
(*Suby of* WPP PLC)
160 Bloor St E 5th Fl, Toronto, ON, M4W 3S7
(416) 987-9100
Emp Here 95   *Sales* 19,035,245
SIC 7311 Advertising agencies
Ann Stewart
Kelly Clark
Barren Hardenan

D-U-N-S 24-350-9564   (SL)
WEST FACE CAPITAL INC
2 Bloor St E Suite 3000, Toronto, ON, M4W
1A8
(647) 724-8900
Emp Here 30   *Sales* 22,003,560
SIC 6722 Management investment, open-end
Gregory A Boland

D-U-N-S 24-304-7610   (HQ)
**WPP GROUP CANADA COMMUNICATIONS
LIMITED**
HILL AND KNOWLTON CANADA, DIV OF
(*Suby of* WPP PLC)
160 Bloor St E Suite 800, Toronto, ON, M4W
1B9
(416) 987-5121
Emp Here 95   *Sales* 26,110,840

SIC 8743 Public relations services
Jack Chairman
Lars Erik Grnntun

D-U-N-S 25-203-5738   (BR)
XEROX CANADA LTD
(*Suby of* XEROX CORPORATION)
33 Bloor St E, Toronto, ON, M4W 3H1
(416) 921-0210
Emp Here 500
SIC 5044 Office equipment
Jim Doherty

D-U-N-S 24-386-6472   (SL)
**YONGE-ROSEDALE CHARITABLE FOUN-
DATION**
DAVENHILL SENIOR LIVING
877 Yonge St Suite 1603, Toronto, ON, M4W
3M2
(416) 923-8887
Emp Here 95   *Sales* 20,982,745
SIC 6513 Apartment building operators
Glen Roadknight

D-U-N-S 25-469-8061   (BR)
**YOUNG & RUBICAM GROUP OF COMPA-
NIES ULC, THE**
BLUE HIVE
(*Suby of* WPP PLC)
60 Bloor St W Suite 8, Toronto, ON, M4W 3B8

Emp Here 102
SIC 7311 Advertising agencies

D-U-N-S 20-300-9261   (SL)
**YOUNG & RUBICAM GROUP OF COMPA-
NIES ULC, THE**
MEC CANADA
(*Suby of* WPP PLC)
160 Bloor St E Suite 500, Toronto, ON, M4W
1B9
(416) 987-9100
Emp Here 80   *Sales* 16,029,680
SIC 7311 Advertising agencies
Michele Pauchuck
Nick Williams

Toronto, ON M4X

D-U-N-S 25-914-5506   (SL)
AGE D'OR SACRE-COEUR TORONTO, L'
474 Ontario St, Toronto, ON, M4X 1M7
(416) 923-3724
Emp Here 49   *Sales* 11,114,817
SIC 8399 Social services, nec
Lisa Vineyard

Toronto, ON M4Y

D-U-N-S 25-990-0439   (HQ)
1094285 ONTARIO LIMITED
IL FORNELLO RESTAURANT
112 Isabella St, Toronto, ON, M4Y 1P1
(416) 920-9410
Sales 11,659,750
SIC 5812 Eating places
Ian Sorbie

D-U-N-S 20-845-1401   (HQ)
**ALLIANCE OF CANADIAN CINEMA, TELE-
VISION & RADIO ARTISTS**
A C T R A NATIONAL
625 Church St, Toronto, ON, M4Y 2G1
(416) 489-1311
Emp Here 70   *Sales* 34,176,240
SIC 8631 Labor organizations
David Sparrow

D-U-N-S 20-812-9044   (HQ)
ANGLICAN CHURCH OF CANADA
ANGLICAN APPEAL
80 Hayden St Suite 400, Toronto, ON, M4Y

3G2
(416) 924-9192
Sales 14,577,220
SIC 8661 Religious organizations
Frederick Hiltz

D-U-N-S 24-120-3368   (SL)
BRYDSON GROUP LTD
ELMWOOD SPA, THE
557 Church St, Toronto, ON, M4Y 2E2
(416) 964-4525
Emp Here 200   *Sales* 15,709,000
SIC 7991 Physical fitness facilities
Cherry Brydson
Marie Pickton
Stephen J. Griggs

D-U-N-S 20-850-6238   (SL)
CANADA'S NATIONAL BALLET SCHOOL
400 Jarvis St, Toronto, ON, M4Y 2G6
(416) 964-3780
Emp Here 150   *Sales* 12,377,550
SIC 7911 Dance studios, schools, and halls
Jeffrey Melanson
Mavis Stains
Charles Richards
Judith Gelber
Troy Maxwell

D-U-N-S 20-551-6701   (HQ)
**CAR PARK MANAGEMENT SERVICES LIM-
ITED**
40 Isabella St, Toronto, ON, M4Y 1N1
(416) 920-3382
Emp Here 12   *Sales* 67,529,550
SIC 7521 Automobile parking
Gerard Mclean
Catherine Zwarych
Paul Mclean
Carol Mclean

D-U-N-S 24-704-4985   (SL)
CASEY HOUSE HOSPICE INC
119 Isabella St, Toronto, ON, M4Y 1P2
(416) 962-7600
Emp Here 80   *Sales* 5,485,280
SIC 8051 Skilled nursing care facilities
Stephanie Karapita
Gayle Janes
Guy Bethell
Josee Bertrand
Mike R. Mckeon

D-U-N-S 20-902-5741   (HQ)
**CATHOLIC CHILDREN'S AID SOCIETY OF
TORONTO, THE**
26 Maitland St, Toronto, ON, M4Y 1C6
(416) 395-1500
Emp Here 100   *Sales* 38,396,000
SIC 8322 Individual and family services
Janice Robinson
Richard Piatti

D-U-N-S 20-851-1741   (HQ)
CHILDREN'S AID SOCIETY OF TORONTO
30 Isabella St, Toronto, ON, M4Y 1N1
(416) 924-4646
Emp Here 450   *Sales* 174,831,138
SIC 8322 Individual and family services
David Rivard
Janet Morrison
Sangeeta Subramanian
Wayne Zronik
Tony Quan
Nancy Dale
Lisa Lifshitz
Liz Rykert

D-U-N-S 25-059-3480   (HQ)
**ELEMENTARY TEACHERS FEDERATION
OF ONTARIO**
ETFO
136 Isabella St, Toronto, ON, M4Y 0B5
(416) 962-3836
Emp Here 92   *Sales* 34,176,240
SIC 8631 Labor organizations
Sam Hammond

Susan Swackhammer
James Mccormack
Maureen Weinberger
Gene Lewis

D-U-N-S 25-956-0675   (BR)
ELEMENTARY TEACHERS FEDERATION OF ONTARIO
(*Suby of* ELEMENTARY TEACHERS FEDER-ATION OF ONTARIO)
136 Isabella St, Toronto, ON, M4Y 0B5
(416) 962-3836
Emp Here 120
SIC 8631 Labor organizations

D-U-N-S 24-242-5069   (BR)
GOVERNING COUNCIL OF THE UNIVER-SITY OF TORONTO, THE
GOVERNING COUNCIL OF THE UNIVER-SITY OF TORONTO
(*Suby of* GOVERNING COUNCIL OF THE UNIVERSITY OF TORONTO, THE)
10 St Mary St Suite 700, Toronto, ON, M4Y 2W8
(416) 978-1000
Emp Here 200
SIC 8221 Colleges and universities
Bruce Kidd

D-U-N-S 25-272-8621   (BR)
KEG RESTAURANTS LTD
KEG STEAKHOUSE & BAR, THE
(*Suby of* RECIPE UNLIMITED CORPORA-TION)
515 Jarvis St, Toronto, ON, M4Y 2H7
(416) 964-6609
Emp Here 100
SIC 5812 Eating places
Tap Alakorpi

D-U-N-S 24-410-0889   (SL)
OOLAGEN COMMUNITY SERVICES
YOUTH MENTAL HEALTH
65 Wellesley St E Suite 500, Toronto, ON, M4Y 1G7
(416) 395-0660
Emp Here 50   *Sales* 19,870,700
SIC 8699 Membership organizations, nec
Robert Engel

D-U-N-S 20-076-2040   (SL)
OSI-WORLDWIDE INC
10 St Mary St Suite 602, Toronto, ON, M4Y 1P9
(416) 960-9752
Emp Here 13   *Sales* 13,453,453
SIC 6311 Life insurance
Ray Husain

D-U-N-S 20-943-1998   (SL)
PAR-S DRUGS LTD
SHOPPERS DRUG MART
465 Yonge St, Toronto, ON, M4Y 1X4
(416) 408-4000
Emp Here 53   *Sales* 12,949,384
SIC 5912 Drug stores and proprietary stores
Par Singh

D-U-N-S 20-327-7389   (HQ)
RAPPORT CREDIT UNION LIMITED
18 Grenville St Suite 1, Toronto, ON, M4Y 3B3
(416) 314-6772
Emp Here 30   *Sales* 14,890,567
SIC 6062 State credit unions
Kim Leak

D-U-N-S 20-112-1618   (BR)
ROGERS COMMUNICATIONS CANADA INC
(*Suby of* ROGERS COMMUNICATIONS INC)
1 Mount Pleasant Rd Suite 115, Toronto, ON, M4Y 2Y5
(416) 764-2000
Emp Here 3,000
SIC 6712 Bank holding companies

D-U-N-S 24-772-3935   (SL)
SALVATION ARMY TORONTO GRACE HEALTH CENTER, THE

(*Suby of* GOVERNING COUNCIL OF THE SALVATION ARMY IN CANADA, THE)
650 Church St, Toronto, ON, M4Y 2G5
(416) 925-2251
Emp Here 275   *Sales* 17,195,686
SIC 8051 Skilled nursing care facilities
Jake Tran

D-U-N-S 25-531-1904   (BR)
SUNNYBROOK HEALTH SCIENCES CEN-TRE
ORTHOPAEDIC & ATHRITIC CAMPUS
(*Suby of* SUNNYBROOK HEALTH SCI-ENCES CENTRE)
43 Wellesley St E Suite 327, Toronto, ON, M4Y 1H1
(416) 967-8500
Emp Here 350
SIC 8069 Specialty hospitals, except psychi-atric
Terry Houghton

D-U-N-S 24-487-1588   (SL)
SUPER FRESHMART LTD
524 Church St, Toronto, ON, M4Y 2E1

Emp Here 103   *Sales* 21,150,329
SIC 5331 Variety stores
Daniel Choi

D-U-N-S 25-103-7933   (HQ)
TC BIZZ.COM CORP
STAG SHOP
449 Church St, Toronto, ON, M4Y 2C5
(416) 323-0772
Emp Here 5   *Sales* 15,881,320
SIC 5947 Gift, novelty, and souvenir shop
Peter Horea

D-U-N-S 20-711-2603   (BR)
TORONTO DISTRICT SCHOOL BOARD
JARVIS COLLEGIATE INSTITUTE
(*Suby of* TORONTO DISTRICT SCHOOL BOARD)
495 Jarvis St, Toronto, ON, M4Y 2G8
(416) 393-0140
Emp Here 100
SIC 8211 Elementary and secondary schools
Michael Harvey

D-U-N-S 24-337-8643   (HQ)
TURNING POINT YOUTH SERVICES
95 Wellesley St E, Toronto, ON, M4Y 2X9
(416) 925-9250
Emp Here 60   *Sales* 19,965,920
SIC 8322 Individual and family services
Jeanetta Hoffman
Colin Dart

D-U-N-S 25-131-4902   (HQ)
UNIVERSITY OF TORONTO PRESS
10 St Mary St Suite 700, Toronto, ON, M4Y 2W8
(416) 978-2239
Emp Here 200   *Sales* 48,443,500
SIC 2731 Book publishing
John Yates
Roger Parkinson
Frank Anderson
Carol Moore
Catherine Riggall

D-U-N-S 20-799-8548   (SL)
WELLESLEY CENTRAL PLACE
160 Wellesley St E Suite 2044, Toronto, ON, M4Y 1J2
(416) 929-9385
Emp Here 150   *Sales* 10,284,900
SIC 8051 Skilled nursing care facilities
Heather Colyer

D-U-N-S 20-006-7168   (SL)
YONGE STREET HOTEL LTD
COURTYARD BY MARRIOTT, THE
475 Yonge St, Toronto, ON, M4Y 1X7
(416) 924-0611
Emp Here 250   *Sales* 23,917,000
SIC 7011 Hotels and motels

Lori Levine
Ronit Keith

Toronto, ON M5A

D-U-N-S 20-640-5318   (HQ)
1032451 B.C. LTD
THE TORONTO SUN
(*Suby of* QUEBECOR MEDIA INC)
333 King St E Unit 1, Toronto, ON, M5A 0E1
(416) 947-2222
Emp Here 30   *Sales* 1,162,644,000
SIC 2711 Newspapers
Julia Kamula

D-U-N-S 25-167-2580   (SL)
1263528 ONTARIO LIMITED
GUVERNMENT NIGHT CLUB, THE
132 Queens Quay E, Toronto, ON, M5A 0S1

Emp Here 200   *Sales* 9,103,800
SIC 5813 Drinking places
Charles Khabouth

D-U-N-S 25-193-4456   (SL)
1784007 ONTARIO LTD
LUCIANO'S NO FRILLS
200 Front St E Suite 3458, Toronto, ON, M5A 4T9
(416) 368-8484
Emp Here 49   *Sales* 13,433,448
SIC 5411 Grocery stores
Luciano Graziano

D-U-N-S 20-915-1211   (HQ)
2041098 ONTARIO LIMITED
METCAP LIVING
260 Richmond St E Unit 300, Toronto, ON, M5A 1P4
(416) 340-1600
Emp Here 1   *Sales* 12,229,020
SIC 6531 Real estate agents and managers
Lucy Tao

D-U-N-S 20-341-1012   (SL)
2456317 ONTARIO LTD
CANADIAN STANDARD HOME SERVICES
431 Richmond St E, Toronto, ON, M5A 1R1
(647) 490-4839
Emp Here 100   *Sales* 19,135,400
SIC 7359 Equipment rental and leasing, nec
Raymond Kalonga

D-U-N-S 20-548-7486   (SL)
4 ON THE FLOOR SEATING COMPANY LIM-ITED
13 Polson St, Toronto, ON, M5A 1A4
(416) 466-3376
Emp Here 110   *Sales* 63,290,480
SIC 5021 Furniture
Derek Hellyer
Greg Henderson

D-U-N-S 25-367-8213   (SL)
709528 ONTARIO LTD
OPP FOODS
246 Parliament St, Toronto, ON, M5A 3A4

Emp Here 40   *Sales* 15,660,080
SIC 6794 Patent owners and lessors
Joe Schiavone
Vito Schiavone

D-U-N-S 24-693-9623   (HQ)
718878 ONTARIO LIMITED
MESSENGERS INTERNATIONAL,THE
529 Richmond St E Unit 104, Toronto, ON, M5A 1R4
(416) 365-0155
Emp Here 75   *Sales* 73,579,880
SIC 7389 Business services, nec
Frank D'angelo

D-U-N-S 20-212-2877   (SL)
7226438 CANADA INC

VOILA LEARNING
80 Sackville St Rm 315, Toronto, ON, M5A 3E5
(416) 834-5951
Emp Here 70   *Sales* 11,229,820
SIC 8299 Schools and educational services, nec
Hosni Zaouali

D-U-N-S 25-344-0556   (SL)
ALUMNAE THEATRE COMPANY
70 Berkeley St, Toronto, ON, M5A 2W6
(416) 364-4170
Emp Here 100   *Sales* 15,136,900
SIC 7922 Theatrical producers and services
Sheila Macdonald-Tait

D-U-N-S 24-525-8561   (HQ)
ARTSMARKETING SERVICES INC
260 King St E Suite 500, Toronto, ON, M5A 4L5
(416) 941-9000
Emp Here 20   *Sales* 668,908,000
SIC 7389 Business services, nec
Ava Paulin
Robert Brown

D-U-N-S 24-128-3543   (BR)
AUTODESK CANADA CIE
(*Suby of* AUTODESK, INC.)
210 King St E, Toronto, ON, M5A 1J7
(416) 362-9181
Emp Here 275
SIC 7371 Custom computer programming ser-vices
David Wharry

D-U-N-S 20-557-7930   (SL)
BASSETT & WALKER INTERNATIONAL INC
BWI
2 Berkeley St Suite 502, Toronto, ON, M5A 4J5
(416) 363-7070
Emp Here 28   *Sales* 23,396,156
SIC 5142 Packaged frozen goods
Nicholas Walker
Nicholas M Walker
Allan Bean

D-U-N-S 20-388-1433   (SL)
BOAT ROCKER RIGHTS INC
595 Adelaide St E, Toronto, ON, M5A 1N8
(416) 591-0065
Emp Here 602   *Sales* 86,797,564
SIC 7371 Custom computer programming ser-vices
Jon Rutherford
John Young
Shannon Valliant
Sam Traub

D-U-N-S 20-785-2591   (HQ)
CANADIAN OPERA COMPANY
227 Front St E, Toronto, ON, M5A 1E8
(416) 363-6671
Emp Here 1   *Sales* 10,786,536
SIC 7922 Theatrical producers and services
Justin Linden
Paul A Bernards
John H. Macfarlane
Alexander Neef
Rob Lamb

D-U-N-S 20-108-7512   (SL)
CANDEAL.CA INC
152 King St E Suite 400, Toronto, ON, M5A 1J3
(416) 814-7800
Emp Here 20   *Sales* 13,578,460
SIC 6231 Security and commodity exchanges
Jayson Horner

D-U-N-S 24-207-5104   (HQ)
CANOE INC
RESEAU CANOE
(*Suby of* QUEBECOR MEDIA INC)
333 King St E Suite 1, Toronto, ON, M5A 0E1

(416) 947-2154
Emp Here 440   *Sales* 147,199,360
SIC 4813 Telephone communication, except radio
Pierre K Peladeau
Claudine Tremblay
Serge Gouin
Jean-Francois Pruneau

D-U-N-S 20-161-7719   (SL)
CENTRE AUTO COLLISION LIMITED
CENTRE HONDA
354 Richmond St E, Toronto, ON, M5A 1P7
(416) 364-1116
Emp Here 75   *Sales* 21,247,500
SIC 7532 Top and body repair and paint shops
Paul Schmelzer
Lillian Schmelzer

D-U-N-S 20-088-4927   (BR)
CLARENDON FOUNDATION (CHESHIRE HOMES) INC
25 Henry Lane Terr Suite 442, Toronto, ON, M5A 4B6

Emp Here 80
SIC 8699 Membership organizations, nec
Claire Bryden

D-U-N-S 20-390-9171   (HQ)
COCA-COLA CANADA BOTTLING LIMITED
335 King St E, Toronto, ON, M5A 1L1
(416) 424-6000
Sales 2,826,833,000
SIC 2086 Bottled and canned soft drinks
Todd Parsons

D-U-N-S 20-179-4039   (HQ)
COCA-COLA REFRESHMENTS CANADA COMPANY
COCA-COLA BOTTLING
(*Suby of* THE COCA-COLA COMPANY)
335 King St E, Toronto, ON, M5A 1L1
(416) 424-6000
Emp Here 383   *Sales* 2,729,356,000
SIC 2086 Bottled and canned soft drinks
Kevin Warren
Jeffrey Kirsh
Kathy Loveless
Christopher Nolan

D-U-N-S 20-162-5753   (SL)
COOPER'S IRON & METAL INC
130 Commissioners St, Toronto, ON, M5A 1A8
(416) 461-0733
Emp Here 45   *Sales* 23,424,390
SIC 5093 Scrap and waste materials
Alan Schwartz
Irving Cooper
Martin Schwartz

D-U-N-S 25-862-8478   (SL)
CORE ARCHITECTS INC
130 Queens Quay E Suite 700, Toronto, ON, M5A 0P6
(416) 343-0400
Emp Here 115   *Sales* 20,554,985
SIC 8712 Architectural services
Babak Eslahjou
Charles Gane
Deni Poletti

D-U-N-S 25-976-5196   (HQ)
CORUS ENTERTAINMENT INC
25 Dockside Dr, Toronto, ON, M5A 0B5
(416) 479-7000
Emp Here 200   *Sales* 1,339,883,643
SIC 4832 Radio broadcasting stations
Doug Murphy
Barbara Williams
Judy Adams
John Gossling
Dale Hancocks
Shawn Kelly
Cheryl Fullerton
Greg Mclelland
Colin Bohm
Gary Maavara

D-U-N-S 24-676-8381   (HQ)
CORUS MEDIA HOLDINGS INC
GLOBAL TELEVISION
(*Suby of* SHAW COMMUNICATIONS INC)
25 Dockside Dr, Toronto, ON, M5A 0B5
(416) 479-7000
Emp Here 250   *Sales* 498,754,376
SIC 4833 Television broadcasting stations
Paul Robertson
Michael French

D-U-N-S 24-737-5843   (HQ)
COTA HEALTH
550 Queen St E Suite 201, Toronto, ON, M5A 1V2
(888) 785-2779
Emp Here 1   *Sales* 11,604,060
SIC 8049 Offices of health practitioner
Sandra Hanmer

D-U-N-S 20-383-2998   (SL)
CRYSTAL INFOSOFT
186 Frederick St, Toronto, ON, M5A 4L4

Emp Here 849   *Sales* 122,410,518
SIC 7371 Custom computer programming services
Ricky Khanna
Rahul Vaghela

D-U-N-S 24-844-1222   (SL)
D.C. DRUGS LIMITED
SHOPPERS DRUG MART
467 Parliament St, Toronto, ON, M5A 3A3
(416) 925-4121
Emp Here 45   *Sales* 11,382,930
SIC 5912 Drug stores and proprietary stores
Douglas Chow

D-U-N-S 24-409-0114   (SL)
DANIEL ET DANIEL CATERING INC
248 Carlton St, Toronto, ON, M5A 2L1
(416) 968-9275
Emp Here 90   *Sales* 3,858,570
SIC 5812 Eating places
Daniel Clairet
Daniel Megly

D-U-N-S 24-313-9974   (HQ)
DANIELS CORPORATION, THE
130 Queens Quay E 8 Fl, Toronto, ON, M5A 0P6
(416) 598-2129
Emp Here 1   *Sales* 72,271,080
SIC 6799 Investors, nec
John Daniels
Mitchell Cohen
Tommas Dutton

D-U-N-S 20-341-6169   (SL)
DANIELS GROUP INC, THE
130 Queens Quay E 8 Fl, Toronto, ON, M5A 0P6
(416) 598-2129
Emp Here 110   *Sales* 46,077,790
SIC 6531 Real estate agents and managers
John Daniels

D-U-N-S 24-384-9267   (SL)
DANIELS HR CORPORATION
(*Suby of* DANIELS CORPORATION, THE)
130 Queens Quay E 8 Fl, Toronto, ON, M5A 0P6
(416) 598-2129
Emp Here 110   *Sales* 139,132,800
SIC 1522 Residential construction, nec
Mitchell Cohen

D-U-N-S 24-368-4177   (SL)
DANIELS LR CORPORATION
(*Suby of* DANIELS CORPORATION, THE)
130 Queens Quay E 8 Fl, Toronto, ON, M5A 0P6
(416) 598-2129
Emp Here 200   *Sales* 35,747,800
SIC 8712 Architectural services
John Daniels

D-U-N-S 24-361-5585   (SL)
DANIELS MIDTOWN CORPORATION
(*Suby of* DANIELS CORPORATION, THE)
130 Queens Quay E 8 Fl, Toronto, ON, M5A 0P6
(416) 598-2129
Emp Here 150   *Sales* 69,566,400
SIC 1522 Residential construction, nec
John H Daniels
Mitchell S Cohen
Gary Polenz
Tom Dutton
Niall Haggart

D-U-N-S 20-378-0361   (SL)
DECIEM DISTRIBUTION INC
517 Richmond St E, Toronto, ON, M5A 1R4
(416) 203-3992
Emp Here 40   *Sales* 13,024,000
SIC 5999 Miscellaneous retail stores, nec
Brandon Truaxe
Pasquale Cusano
Niall Henry
Michael Basler

D-U-N-S 20-313-3665   (SL)
DECIEM INC
517 Richmond St E, Toronto, ON, M5A 1R4
(416) 203-3992
Emp Here 40   *Sales* 13,024,000
SIC 5999 Miscellaneous retail stores, nec
Brandon Truaxe
Pasquale Cusano
Niall Henry
Michael Basler

D-U-N-S 20-941-9605   (HQ)
DIXON HALL
58 Sumach St, Toronto, ON, M5A 3J7
(416) 863-0499
Sales 16,894,240
SIC 8322 Individual and family services
Mercedes Watson

D-U-N-S 24-008-9532   (SL)
DOWNTOWN AUTOMOTIVE INC
DOWNTOWN MAZDA
259 Lake Shore Blvd E, Toronto, ON, M5A 3T7

Emp Here 40   *Sales* 19,923,120
SIC 5511 New and used car dealers
Dieter Hammer

D-U-N-S 24-045-4330   (SL)
DOWNTOWN FINE CARS INC
DOWNTOWN PORCHE
68 Parliament St, Toronto, ON, M5A 0B2
(416) 603-9988
Emp Here 80   *Sales* 50,342,400
SIC 5511 New and used car dealers
Peter A Kircher
Helen Ching

D-U-N-S 20-316-2651   (SL)
EGALE CANADA HUMAN RIGHTS TRUST
185 Carlton St, Toronto, ON, M5A 2K7
(888) 204-7777
Emp Here 30   *Sales* 11,922,420
SIC 8699 Membership organizations, nec
Kendall Forde

D-U-N-S 24-756-7209   (SL)
EMPIRE SANDY INC
151 Queens Quay E, Toronto, ON, M5A 1B6
(416) 364-3244
Emp Here 60   *Sales* 31,198,020
SIC 4725 Tour operators
Norman Rogers

D-U-N-S 24-893-6239   (HQ)
FERCAN DEVELOPMENTS INC
193 King St E Suite 200, Toronto, ON, M5A 1J5
(416) 867-9899
Emp Here 1   *Sales* 10,194,150
SIC 6553 Cemetery subdividers and developers
Vince De Rosa

D-U-N-S 25-509-3809   (HQ)
FIRST GULF DEVELOPMENT CORPORATION
351 King St E 13th Fl, Toronto, ON, M5A 0L6
(416) 773-7070
Sales 12,653,760
SIC 6552 Subdividers and developers, nec
David Gerofsky
John Macneil
David Carreiro
Brian Harrison
Victor Settino
Jonathan Weinberg
Andre Mhelic
Derek Goring
Thom Jackman
Solito Mallari

D-U-N-S 20-700-2416   (HQ)
FIRST NICKEL INC
120 Front St E Suite 206, Toronto, ON, M5A 4L9
(416) 362-7050
Emp Here 43   *Sales* 396,333,134
SIC 1061 Ferroalloy ores, except vanadium
Thomas M. Boehlert
Paul Davis
Vernon C. Baker
Alfred Colas
C. David A. Comba
William J. Anderson
Joao Paulo Simoes Carrelo
Russell Cranswick

D-U-N-S 24-664-3936   (SL)
FORT YORK C MOTORS LP
TORONTO CHRYSLER DODGE JEEP RAM
(*Suby of* AUTOCANADA INC)
321 Front St E, Toronto, ON, M5A 1G3
(416) 368-7000
Emp Here 49   *Sales* 24,405,822
SIC 5511 New and used car dealers
Paul Stern
Lilian Poon

D-U-N-S 24-760-8263   (SL)
GLOBE AND MAIL INC, THE
(*Suby of* THOMSON COMPANY INC, THE)
351 King St E Suite 1600, Toronto, ON, M5A 0N1
(416) 585-5000
Emp Here 850   *Sales* 500,785,150
SIC 5192 Books, periodicals, and newspapers
Phillip Crawley
Sue Gaudi
David W Binet
W Geoffrey Beattie
Ronald Close
Kevin Crull
David Thomson
Sandra Mason

D-U-N-S 24-822-6227   (SL)
HARRIS INSTITUTE FOR THE ARTS INCORPORATED, THE
118 Sherbourne St, Toronto, ON, M5A 2R2
(416) 367-0162
Emp Here 75   *Sales* 13,245,075
SIC 8249 Vocational schools, nec
John Harris

D-U-N-S 20-558-4514   (HQ)
HEALTHCARE PROPERTIES HOLDINGS LTD
284 King St E Suite 100, Toronto, ON, M5A 1K4
(416) 366-2000
Emp Here 50   *Sales* 27,335,000
SIC 6719 Holding companies, nec
Paul Dalla Lana
Peter Riggin
Mike Brady
Lauchie Macleod
Carlo Dalla Lana
Austin Phillips
Michael Diminno
Sean Nakamoto

Solito Mallari
Sabrena Man

D-U-N-S 20-528-8652   (SL)
INFINIUM CAPITAL CORPORATION
GALIAM SECURITY CANADA
106 Front St E Suite 200, Toronto, ON, M5A 1E1

Emp Here 35   *Sales* 24,161,958
SIC 6211 Security brokers and dealers
Sergei Tchetvertnykh
Alan Grujic

D-U-N-S 20-283-4339   (SL)
KBS+P CANADA LP KBS+P CANADA SEC
340 King St E 4th Fl Suite 500, Toronto, ON, M5A 1K8
(416) 260-7000
Emp Here 120   *Sales* 24,044,520
SIC 7311 Advertising agencies
Matt Hassel
Annie Aubert
Sacha Ouimet
Richard Brott
Matt Hassell
Cameron Wykes
Maria Spensieri

D-U-N-S 20-170-4327   (HQ)
MCGREGOR INDUSTRIES INC
MCGREGOR HOSIERY MILLS
63 Polson St, Toronto, ON, M5A 1A4
(416) 591-9191
Emp Here 40   *Sales* 125,629,950
SIC 5136 Men's and boy's clothing
Earl Lipson
Carl Grilo
Jordan Lipson
Abbey Lipson
Anthony Segal
Gary Smith
Frank Burke

D-U-N-S 20-967-3409   (HQ)
MCLEAN HALLMARK INSURANCE GROUP LTD
(*Suby of* NFP INTERMEDIATE HOLDINGS B CORP.)
184 Front St E Suite 601, Toronto, ON, M5A 4N3
(416) 364-4000
Sales 96,082,584
SIC 6411 Insurance agents, brokers, and service
Darren Mclean

D-U-N-S 20-375-0443   (SL)
ME TO WE SHOP INC
145 Berkeley St, Toronto, ON, M5A 2X1
(416) 964-8942
Emp Here 76   *Sales* 18,568,928
SIC 5999 Miscellaneous retail stores, nec
Roxane Joyal
Beatriz Gancedo

D-U-N-S 24-323-4213   (SL)
ME TO WE STYLE INC
ME TO WE RESPONSIBLE STYLE
145 Berkeley St, Toronto, ON, M5A 2X1
(416) 964-8942
Emp Here 100   *Sales* 17,939,600
SIC 5651 Family clothing stores
Oliver Madison
Marc Kielburger
Jim Berk
Victor Li
Craig Kielburger

D-U-N-S 20-375-0583   (SL)
ME TO WE TRIPS INC
145 Berkeley St, Toronto, ON, M5A 2X1
(416) 964-8942
Emp Here 156   *Sales* 104,035,152
SIC 4724 Travel agencies
Russ Mcleod
Roxanne Joyal

D-U-N-S 20-011-4010   (HQ)
METCAP LIVING INC
260 Richmond St E Suite 300, Toronto, ON, M5A 1P4
(416) 340-1600
Sales 50,709,600
SIC 6531 Real estate agents and managers
Brent D Merrill
Guy Alberga
Alanne O'gallagher
Robert Burke

D-U-N-S 20-011-3970   (HQ)
METCAP LIVING MANAGEMENT INC
260 Richmond St E Suite 300, Toronto, ON, M5A 1P4
(416) 340-1600
Emp Here 40   *Sales* 13,587,800
SIC 6531 Real estate agents and managers
Brent Merrill
Lucy Tao
Gregory Sullivan
Bruce Stewart
Jack Rabinovitch
Kenneth Rotenberg

D-U-N-S 25-496-6997   (HQ)
METIS NATION OF ONTARIO
75 Sherbourne St Suite 311, Toronto, ON, M5A 2P9
(416) 977-9881
Emp Here 20   *Sales* 31,060,200
SIC 8399 Social services, nec
Margaret Froh
France Picotte
Sharon Cadeau
Tim Pile
Joseph Poitras

D-U-N-S 20-596-7847   (HQ)
MORIYAMA & TESHIMA ARCHITECTS
117 George St, Toronto, ON, M5A 2N4
(416) 925-4484
Emp Here 6   *Sales* 10,724,340
SIC 8712 Architectural services
Ajon Moriyama
Jason Moriyama
Diarmuid Nash
Daniel Teramura

D-U-N-S 20-846-9841   (HQ)
NELVANA LIMITED
(*Suby of* CORUS ENTERTAINMENT INC)
25 Dockside Dr, Toronto, ON, M5A 0B5
(416) 479-7000
Sales 31,393,600
SIC 7812 Motion picture and video production
Doug Murphy
Tom Peddie

D-U-N-S 24-320-4776   (HQ)
ONLIA HOLDINGS INC
351 King St E Suite 801, Toronto, ON, M5A 1L1
(416) 479-2260
Sales 29,682,100
SIC 6411 Insurance agents, brokers, and service
Pieter Louter

D-U-N-S 25-351-7502   (HQ)
PIRATE GROUP INC
260 King St E Suite 507, Toronto, ON, M5A 4L5
(416) 594-3784
Sales 11,039,782
SIC 8999 Services, nec
Terry O'reilly
Tom Eydmundson
Tom Goudie
Chris Tait
Bill Kostenko
Terry Miele

D-U-N-S 24-763-1851   (BR)
QUEBECOR MEDIA INC
QUEBECOR MEDIA INC
(*Suby of* QUEBECOR MEDIA INC)

333 King St E Suite 1, Toronto, ON, M5A 3X5
(416) 222-2222
Emp Here 300
SIC 7319 Advertising, nec
Jason Woldinger

D-U-N-S 25-108-0487   (HQ)
QUEST SOFTWARE CANADA INC
FASTLANE TECHNOLOGIES
(*Suby of* FRANCISCO PARTNERS MANAGEMENT, L.P.)
260 King St E, Toronto, ON, M5A 4L5
(416) 933-5000
Emp Here 150   *Sales* 65,338,842
SIC 7371 Custom computer programming services
Douglas F. Garn
J Michael Vaughn
Enrico D'amico
Vincent Smith

D-U-N-S 20-808-9461   (SL)
QUINTINMANUS MARKETING GROUP INC
258 Adelaide St E Suite 400, Toronto, ON, M5A 1N1

Emp Here 100   *Sales* 23,428,800
SIC 8743 Public relations services
Garry Johnson

D-U-N-S 24-946-7825   (SL)
RED BRANCH EXECUTIVE SEARCH & RECRUITMENT
232-366 Adelaide St E, Toronto, ON, M5A 3X9
(416) 862-2525
Emp Here 45   *Sales* 10,663,650
SIC 7361 Employment agencies
Michael Hill

D-U-N-S 24-828-2907   (HQ)
SAS INSTITUTE (CANADA) INC
(*Suby of* SAS INSTITUTE INC.)
280 King St E Unit 500, Toronto, ON, M5A 1K7
(416) 363-4424
Emp Here 200   *Sales* 85,104,360
SIC 7372 Prepackaged software

D-U-N-S 24-927-2303   (HQ)
SIMEX INC
SIMEX-IWERKS ENTERTAINMENT
600-210 King St E, Toronto, ON, M5A 1J7
(416) 597-1585
Emp Here 30   *Sales* 17,760,080
SIC 3571 Electronic computers
Michael Needham
Shiori Sudo
Moses Znaimer
Donald Gordon

D-U-N-S 20-802-4278   (SL)
SOMERSET CHEVROLET CORVETTE LTD
SOMERSET CHEV
291 Lake Shore Blvd E, Toronto, ON, M5A 1B9
(416) 368-8878
Emp Here 25   *Sales* 12,451,950
SIC 5511 New and used car dealers
Sadelone Nymptha

D-U-N-S 24-963-5046   (HQ)
T4G LIMITED
340 King St E Suite 300, Toronto, ON, M5A 1K8
(416) 462-4200
Emp Here 135   *Sales* 35,872,105
SIC 7379 Computer related services, nec
Geoff Flood
Micheal Cottenden

D-U-N-S 24-805-0242   (SL)
THINK RESEARCH CORPORATION
351 King St E Suite 500, Toronto, ON, M5A 0L6
(416) 977-1955
Emp Here 140   *Sales* 20,185,480
SIC 7371 Custom computer programming services
Sachin Aggarwal
Christopher O'connor

Mark Sakamoto
Kirsten Lewis
Roger Beharry Lall
Joanna Carroll
Saurabh Mukhi

D-U-N-S 24-977-6626   (BR)
TOROMONT INDUSTRIES LTD
CIMCO REFRIGERATION
(*Suby of* TOROMONT INDUSTRIES LTD)
65 Villiers St, Toronto, ON, M5A 3S1
(416) 465-7581
Emp Here 850
SIC 3585 Refrigeration and heating equipment
Dave Malinauskas

D-U-N-S 20-902-0999   (SL)
TORONTO HUMANE SOCIETY, THE
11 River St, Toronto, ON, M5A 4C2
(416) 392-2273
Emp Here 100   *Sales* 9,636,342
SIC 8699 Membership organizations, nec
Jacques Messier
Andy Robling
Dominique Rousselle
Kathy Mcdonald
Stephen Steele
Gillian Armstrong
Marcie Laking
Cathy Kinloch
Shelley Austin
Martin Buckle

D-U-N-S 25-696-2119   (HQ)
TORONTO TOURS LTD
259 Lake Shore Blvd E, Toronto, ON, M5A 3T7
(416) 868-0400
Emp Here 25   *Sales* 15,599,010
SIC 4725 Tour operators
John Ryan

D-U-N-S 25-720-3047   (SL)
TRANSASIAN FINE CARS LTD
DOWNTOWN ACURA
183 Front St E, Toronto, ON, M5A 1E7
(416) 867-1577
Emp Here 35   *Sales* 17,432,730
SIC 5511 New and used car dealers
Sylvester Chuang

D-U-N-S 24-365-3891   (SL)
TRANSCONTINENTAL FINE CARS LTD
AUDI DOWNTOWN TORONTO
328 Bayview Ave, Toronto, ON, M5A 3R7
(416) 961-2834
Emp Here 70   *Sales* 44,049,600
SIC 5511 New and used car dealers
Chuang Sylvester
Paul Roach

D-U-N-S 20-984-1332   (SL)
UNIVERIS CORPORATION
111 George St 3rd Fl, Toronto, ON, M5A 2N4
(416) 979-3700
Emp Here 80   *Sales* 14,184,880
SIC 7371 Custom computer programming services
Carmine Tullio
Richard Binnendyk

D-U-N-S 24-075-1727   (HQ)
VISTEK LTD
496 Queen St E, Toronto, ON, M5A 4G8
(416) 365-1777
Emp Here 120   *Sales* 48,865,600
SIC 5946 Camera and photographic supply stores
Ronald Silverstein

D-U-N-S 20-551-3596   (SL)
VOL-HAM AUTOMOTIVE INC
VOLVO OF TORONTO
43 Eastern Ave, Toronto, ON, M5A 1H1
(416) 868-1880
Emp Here 50   *Sales* 24,903,900
SIC 5511 New and used car dealers

Dieter Hammer

D-U-N-S 20-530-0403   (SL)
WADDINGTON MCLEAN & COMPANY LIMITED
WADDINGTON AUTIONEER
275 King St E, Toronto, ON, M5A 1K2
(416) 504-9100
Emp Here 24   *Sales* 10,643,760
SIC 7389 Business services, nec
Donald Mclean
Ronald Mclean
Allister Mclean

D-U-N-S 20-336-6823   (SL)
WALRUS FOUNDATION, THE
411 Richmond St E Suite B15, Toronto, ON,
M5A 3S5
(416) 971-5004
Emp Here 31   *Sales* 12,319,834
SIC 8699 Membership organizations, nec
Robin Mclay
Bruce Bennett
Jodi Butts

D-U-N-S 24-015-0966   (HQ)
WE CHARITY
339 Queen St E, Toronto, ON, M5A 1S9
(416) 925-5894
Emp Here 10   *Sales* 31,874,373
SIC 8699 Membership organizations, nec
Michelle Douglas
Victor Li

D-U-N-S 20-290-7353   (HQ)
**WEBER SHANDWICK WORLDWIDE
(CANADA) INC**
GOLLIN HARRIS
(*Suby of* THE INTERPUBLIC GROUP OF
COMPANIES INC)
351 King St E Suite 800, Toronto, ON, M5A
0L6
(416) 964-6444
Emp Here 48   *Sales* 13,055,420
SIC 8743 Public relations services
Greg Power

D-U-N-S 24-976-8268   (SL)
WESTMINSTER SELECT TRADING CORPORATION
397 Dundas St E, Toronto, ON, M5A 2A7
(416) 363-2727
Emp Here 25   *Sales* 13,013,550
SIC 5094 Jewelry and precious stones

D-U-N-S 24-758-1200   (SL)
YTV CANADA, INC
(*Suby of* CORUS ENTERTAINMENT INC)
25 Dockside Dr, Toronto, ON, M5A 0B5
(416) 479-7000
Emp Here 150   *Sales* 34,270,800
SIC 4833 Television broadcasting stations
Paul W Robertson
Chris Nalborczyk

D-U-N-S 24-361-6369   (SL)
ZULU ALPHA KILO INC
260 King St E Suite B 101, Toronto, ON, M5A
4L5
(416) 777-9858
Emp Here 55   *Sales* 11,644,820
SIC 7311 Advertising agencies
Zak Mroueh

Toronto, ON M5B

D-U-N-S 24-424-1720   (HQ)
541907 ONTARIO LIMITED
HOLIDAY INN
30 Carlton St Suite 1, Toronto, ON, M5B 2E9
(416) 977-6655
Sales 18,538,000
SIC 7011 Hotels and motels
Gian Noldin
Renate Weidner

D-U-N-S 20-819-2575   (SL)
ARSANDCO INVESTMENTS LIMITED
BEST WESTERN PRIMROSE HOTEL, THE
111 Carlton St, Toronto, ON, M5B 2G3
(416) 977-8000
Emp Here 150   *Sales* 13,903,500
SIC 7011 Hotels and motels
Joseph Rubin
Al Rappaport

D-U-N-S 24-138-9316   (SL)
ASSURIS
250 Yonge St Suite 3110, Toronto, ON, M5B
2L7
(416) 359-2001
Emp Here 20   *Sales* 11,598,480
SIC 6411 Insurance agents, brokers, and service
Gordon Dunning

D-U-N-S 20-981-9465   (SL)
BOND PLACE HOTEL LTD
65 Dundas St E, Toronto, ON, M5B 2G8
(416) 362-6061
Emp Here 80   *Sales* 7,591,920
SIC 7011 Hotels and motels
Jules Kofman
Stephen Pustil
Harry Rubin

D-U-N-S 25-520-3192   (BR)
CADILLAC FAIRVIEW CORPORATION LIMITED, THE
TORONTO EATON CENTRE
(*Suby of* ONTARIO TEACHERS' PENSION
PLAN BOARD)
220 Yonge St Suite 110, Toronto, ON, M5B
2H1
(416) 598-8700
Emp Here 140
SIC 6512 Nonresidential building operators
Graham Crowder

D-U-N-S 25-354-5131   (SL)
COLLEGES OF APPLIED ARTS & TECHNOLOGY PENSION PLAN
CAAT PENSION PLAN
250 Yonge St Unit 2900, Toronto, ON, M5B
2L7
(416) 673-9000
Emp Here 35   *Sales* 64,633,065
SIC 6371 Pension, health, and welfare funds
Paul Owens
Sharon Chandler
Martin Kogan
Julie Cays

D-U-N-S 25-972-4706   (BR)
CONSEILLERS EN GESTION ET INFORMATIQUE CGI INC
CGI
(*Suby of* CGI INC)
250 Yonge St Suite 2000, Toronto, ON, M5B
2L7
(416) 363-7827
Emp Here 400
SIC 8741 Management services

D-U-N-S 24-387-1076   (SL)
COVENANT HOUSE TORONTO
20 Gerrard St E, Toronto, ON, M5B 2P3
(416) 598-4898
Emp Here 150   *Sales* 11,518,800
SIC 8322 Individual and family services
Ruth Dacosta
Cindy Metzler

D-U-N-S 20-276-5889   (SL)
DEMAC MEDIA INC
211 Yonge St Suite 600, Toronto, ON, M5B
1M4
(416) 670-1322
Emp Here 90   *Sales* 8,618,247
SIC 7372 Prepackaged software
Matthew Joseph Bertulli
Christopher Bertulli
Dmitri Colomvakos

D-U-N-S 25-518-5456   (HQ)
DION, DURRELL & ASSOCIATES INC
250 Yonge St Suite 2, Toronto, ON, M5B 2L7
(416) 408-2626
Emp Here 70   *Sales* 48,740,600
SIC 8999 Services, nec
Ian Durrell
Silvain Dion
Cheri Niven
Patrick Mahoney

D-U-N-S 24-308-9922   (BR)
FIDELITY INVESTMENTS CANADA ULC
(*Suby of* FMR LLC)
250 Yonge St Suite 700, Toronto, ON, M5B
2L7

Emp Here 250
SIC 6722 Management investment, open-end
Dan Dupont

D-U-N-S 25-304-6833   (BR)
GAP (CANADA) INC
GAP
(*Suby of* THE GAP INC)
260 Yonge St, Toronto, ON, M5B 2L9
(416) 599-8802
Emp Here 160
SIC 5651 Family clothing stores
Renita Hansrag

D-U-N-S 25-721-2035   (BR)
GAP (CANADA) INC
BANANA REPUBLIC
(*Suby of* THE GAP INC)
220 Yonge St, Toronto, ON, M5B 2H1
(416) 595-6336
Emp Here 75
SIC 5651 Family clothing stores
Karen Doobay

D-U-N-S 25-371-3184   (SL)
GOODLAW SERVICES INC
250 Yonge St Suite 2400, Toronto, ON, M5B
2L7
(416) 979-2211
Emp Here 600   *Sales* 66,529,200
SIC 8111 Legal services
Byron Sonberg

D-U-N-S 20-770-0675   (HQ)
HERZING INSTITUTES OF CANADA INC
HERZING COLLEGE
(*Suby of* HERZING UNIVERSITY, LTD.)
220 Yonge St Suite 202, Toronto, ON, M5B
2H1
(416) 599-6996
Emp Here 25   *Sales* 15,521,200
SIC 8244 Business and secretarial schools
Henry Herzing
George Hood

D-U-N-S 24-827-8004   (HQ)
HOMES FIRST SOCIETY
90 Shuter St, Toronto, ON, M5B 2K6
(416) 214-1870
Emp Here 1   *Sales* 56,736,960
SIC 8699 Membership organizations, nec
Kate Stark

D-U-N-S 24-140-3013   (HQ)
HRC CANADA INC
HARD ROCK CAFE CANADA
(*Suby of* THE SEMINOLE TRIBE OF
FLORIDA INC)
279 Yonge St, Toronto, ON, M5B 1N8
(416) 362-3636
Emp Here 80   *Sales* 10,260,580
SIC 5813 Drinking places
Hamish Dodds

D-U-N-S 25-082-6435   (BR)
INDIGO BOOKS & MUSIC INC
INDIGO
(*Suby of* INDIGO BOOKS & MUSIC INC)
220 Yonge St Suite 103, Toronto, ON, M5B
2H1

(416) 591-3622
Emp Here 100
SIC 5942 Book stores
Rachel Dionne

D-U-N-S 24-679-6796   (SL)
ISG SEARCH INC
229 Yonge St Suite 408, Toronto, ON, M5B
1N9
(416) 775-4800
Emp Here 45   *Sales* 32,603,268
SIC 7361 Employment agencies
Taki Giourgas
Vince Roti
Virginia Forno

D-U-N-S 24-977-1056   (SL)
**LAWYERS PROFESSIONAL INDEMNITY
COMPANY**
LAWPRO
(*Suby of* LAW SOCIETY OF UPPER
CANADA, THE)
250 Yonge St Suite 3101, Toronto, ON, M5B
2L7
(416) 598-5800
Emp Here 110   *Sales* 522,071,440
SIC 6411 Insurance agents, brokers, and service
Daniel Pinnington
Duncan Gosnell
Steve Jorgensen

D-U-N-S 24-423-4381   (HQ)
LEE HECHT HARRISON-CANADA CORP
(*Suby of* ADECCO GROUP AG)
250 Yonge St Suite 2800, Toronto, ON, M5B
2L7
(416) 922-7561
Emp Here 5   *Sales* 18,743,040
SIC 8742 Management consulting services
Russell Sheppard
Todd J. King

D-U-N-S 20-651-0120   (SL)
M I C A
229 Yonge St Suite 400, Toronto, ON, M5B
1N9

Emp Here 50   *Sales* 10,798,463
SIC 8748 Business consulting, nec
Alexandria Sugarman

D-U-N-S 24-751-5182   (HQ)
MEGA URANIUM LTD
211 Yonge St Suite 502, Toronto, ON, M5B
1M4
(416) 643-7630
Emp Here 10   *Sales* 25,577,400
SIC 1094 Uranium-radium-vanadium ores
Richard Patricio
Carmelo Marrelli
Albert Contardi
Larry Goldberg
Arni Johannson
Douglas Reeson
Stewart Taylor

D-U-N-S 24-335-0571   (BR)
METRO ONTARIO INC
METRO
(*Suby of* METRO INC)
89 Gould St, Toronto, ON, M5B 2R1
(416) 862-7171
Emp Here 160
SIC 5411 Grocery stores

D-U-N-S 24-687-5256   (HQ)
NORTHAM REALTY ADVISORS LIMITED
(*Suby of* NORTHAM REALTY HOLDINGS
LIMITED)
2 Carlton St Suite 909, Toronto, ON, M5B 1J3
(416) 977-7151
Sales 29,322,230
SIC 6531 Real estate agents and managers
Patrick Handreke
Craig Walters
Rod Finlayson

D-U-N-S 24-335-4495   (SL)

▲ Public Company   ■ Public Company Family Member   **HQ** Headquarters   **BR** Branch   **SL** Single Location

NOW COMMUNICATIONS INC
NOW MAGAZINE
189 Church St, Toronto, ON, M5B 1Y7
(416) 364-1300
Emp Here 110   *Sales* 18,042,970
SIC 2721 Periodicals
Michael Hollett

D-U-N-S 20-545-2506   (SL)
ONTARIO HEALTHY COMMUNITY COALI-TION
2 Carlton St Suite 1810, Toronto, ON, M5B 1J3

Emp Here 26   *Sales* 10,332,764
SIC 8699 Membership organizations, nec
Lorna Heidenheim

D-U-N-S 24-704-3896   (HQ)
OPERATION SPRINGBOARD
SPRINGBOARD
2 Carlton St Suite 800, Toronto, ON, M5B 1J3
(416) 977-0089
Emp Here 20   *Sales* 15,358,400
SIC 8322 Individual and family services
Brad Lambert
Margaret Stanowski

D-U-N-S 24-062-5301   (SL)
PALIN FOUNDATION, THE
OAKHAM HOUSE
63 Gould St, Toronto, ON, M5B 1E9
(416) 979-5250
Emp Here 130   *Sales* 13,881,660
SIC 7299 Miscellaneous personal service
Eric Newstadt

D-U-N-S 25-810-8331   (SL)
PAUL GOLDMAN DRUGS LTD
SHOPPERS DRUG MART
220 Yonge St Suite 824, Toronto, ON, M5B 2H1
(416) 979-9373
Emp Here 126   *Sales* 30,785,328
SIC 5912 Drug stores and proprietary stores
Paul Goldman

D-U-N-S 25-733-2536   (HQ)
PROCEPT ASSOCIATES LTD
250 Yonge St Suite 2201-49, Toronto, ON, M5B 2L7
(416) 693-5559
Emp Here 10   *Sales* 13,716,600
SIC 8741 Management services
Carlo Barrettara
Keith Farndale

D-U-N-S 20-772-3123   (HQ)
RYERSON UNIVERSITY
350 Victoria St, Toronto, ON, M5B 2K3
(416) 979-5000
Sales 594,301,809
SIC 8221 Colleges and universities
Mohamed Lachemi

D-U-N-S 20-175-4751   (HQ)
SEARS CANADA INC
SEARS CATALOGUE, DIV OF
290 Yonge St Suite 700, Toronto, ON, M5B 2C3

Emp Here 2,900   *Sales* 1,991,921,263
SIC 5311 Department stores
Steven Bissell

D-U-N-S 24-682-1115   (HQ)
SIGNAL HILL EQUITY PARTNERS INC
2 Carlton St Suite 1700, Toronto, ON, M5B 1J3
(416) 847-1502
Sales 83,517,000
SIC 2434 Wood kitchen cabinets
Patrick Handreke
James C. Johnson
Imran Siddiqui
Carl Elia
Stephen Orr

D-U-N-S 25-446-3052   (SL)
ST MICHAEL'S HOSPITAL FOUNDATION

30 Bond St, Toronto, ON, M5B 1W8
(416) 864-5000
Emp Here 37   *Sales* 49,149,801
SIC 6732 Trusts: educational, religious, etc.
Frank Techar
Gregory Belton
David Cooper
Julie Di Lorenzo
William Downe
Nicole C. Eaton
Timothy K. Griffin
Gwen Harvey
Ken Hugessen
John Hunkin

D-U-N-S 24-319-2820   (HQ)
ST VINCENT DE PAUL SOCIETY
TORONTO CENTRAL COUNCIL
240 Church St, Toronto, ON, M5B 1Z2
(416) 364-5577
Emp Here 7   *Sales* 25,262,296
SIC 8399 Social services, nec
Frank Boscariol
John Gant
Nick Volk
Anna Meyer
Alan King

D-U-N-S 20-177-0948   (HQ)
TORONTO HYDRO CORPORATION
(*Suby of* CORPORATION OF THE CITY OF TORONTO)
14 Carlton St Suite 6, Toronto, ON, M5B 1K5
(416) 542-8000
Emp Here 370   *Sales* 2,632,660,815
SIC 4911 Electric services
Anthony Haines
Aida Cipolla
Amanda Klein
Ben Lapianta
Ave Lethbridge
Dino Priore
Chris Tyrrell
Robert Wong
Laura Foster
David Mcfadden

D-U-N-S 20-521-7552   (HQ)
TORONTO HYDRO-ELECTRIC SYSTEM LIMITED
(*Suby of* CORPORATION OF THE CITY OF TORONTO)
14 Carlton St, Toronto, ON, M5B 1K5
(416) 542-3100
Emp Here 170   *Sales* 1,053,804,700
SIC 4911 Electric services
Anthony Haines
Jean-Sebastien Couillard

D-U-N-S 20-106-3562   (BR)
WINNERS MERCHANTS INTERNATIONAL L.P.
WINNERS
(*Suby of* THE TJX COMPANIES INC)
444 Yonge St Unit G3, Toronto, ON, M5B 2H4
(416) 598-8800
Emp Here 175
SIC 5651 Family clothing stores
Antoinette Ferrezo

D-U-N-S 20-550-3324   (SL)
WORLD TRADE GROUP (NORTH AMER-ICA) INC
WORLD TRADE GROUP
211 Yonge St, Toronto, ON, M5B 1M4
(416) 214-3400
Emp Here 75   *Sales* 34,081,636
SIC 7389 Business services, nec
Victor Lewis

D-U-N-S 20-780-4241   (SL)
ZARA
ZARA CANADA
220 Yonge St Suite C-4a, Toronto, ON, M5B 2H1
(647) 288-0333
Emp Here 55   *Sales* 46,489,001

SIC 5141 Groceries, general line
Vela Campbell

Toronto, ON M5C

D-U-N-S 25-598-0096   (SL)
1174976 ONTARIO INC
ROSE WATER SUPER CLUB
19 Toronto St, Toronto, ON, M5C 2R1
(416) 214-5888
Emp Here 250   *Sales* 11,659,750
SIC 5812 Eating places
Nick Didonato

D-U-N-S 24-787-9443   (SL)
24/7 CUSTOMER CANADA, INC
INTELLIRESPONSE
(*Suby of* 24 7.AI, INC.)
20 Toronto St Suite 530, Toronto, ON, M5C 2B8
(416) 214-9337
Emp Here 125   *Sales* 18,022,750
SIC 7371 Custom computer programming services
Pv Kannan
Shanmugam Nagarajan
Brent Bowman
Rohan Ganeson
Michael Moritz
Ram Shriram
George Shaheen

D-U-N-S 20-813-2923   (SL)
AFRICAN GOLD GROUP, INC
151 Yonge St 11th Fl, Toronto, ON, M5C 2W7
(647) 775-8538
Emp Here 15   *Sales* 35,813,235
SIC 1041 Gold ores
Stephan Theron
Stan Bharti
Bruce Humphrey
John Begeman
Marco J. Durante
Sam Jonah
Pierre Pettigrew
Ryan Ptolemy

D-U-N-S 20-706-5152   (HQ)
AGNICO EAGLE MINES LIMITED
145 King St E Suite 400, Toronto, ON, M5C 2Y7
(416) 947-1212
Emp Here 100   *Sales* 2,191,221,000
SIC 1041 Gold ores
Sean Boyd
Ammar Al-Joundi
Donald Allan
Alain Blackburn
Louise Grondin
David Smith
Jean Robitaille
R. Gregory Laing
Yvon Sylvestre
Chris Vollmershausen

D-U-N-S 20-699-0405   (HQ)
ALDRIDGE MINERALS INC
10 King St E Suite 300, Toronto, ON, M5C 1C3

Sales 57,301,176
SIC 1041 Gold ores
Han Ilhan
Ahmet Sentrk
Serdar Akca
Oya Misirdali
Jim O'neill
Baran Umut Baycan
Ahmet Tacyildiz
Mike Widmer
Gage Jull
Talha Ozkul

D-U-N-S 24-338-1303   (SL)
ARROW CAPITAL MANAGEMENT INC

36 Toronto St Suite 750, Toronto, ON, M5C 2C5
(416) 323-0477
Emp Here 30   *Sales* 20,367,690
SIC 6211 Security brokers and dealers
James Mcgovern

D-U-N-S 20-300-2969   (SL)
ARROW DIVERSIFIED FUND
36 Toronto St Suite 750, Toronto, ON, M5C 2C5
(416) 323-0477
Emp Here 30   *Sales* 25,120,927
SIC 6722 Management investment, open-end
Tim Mc Govern

D-U-N-S 25-171-1081   (HQ)
ASSANTE CAPITAL MANAGEMENT LTD
ASSANTE WEALTH MANAGEMENT
(*Suby of* ASSANTE WEALTH MANAGEMENT (CANADA) LTD)
2 Queen St E Suite 1900, Toronto, ON, M5C 3G7
(416) 348-9994
Emp Here 2   *Sales* 1,147,049,228
SIC 6211 Security brokers and dealers
Joseph C Canavan
Steven J Donald

D-U-N-S 20-369-8522   (HQ)
AST TRUST COMPANY (CANADA)
1 Toronto St Suite 1200, Toronto, ON, M5C 2V6
(416) 682-3800
Emp Here 50   *Sales* 20,088,936
SIC 8741 Management services
Margot Jordan
Mark Mulima
Frank Turzanski
Mary-Lou Duffy
Mark Cohen
Charito De Vera
Candace Covent
Nelia Andrade
Margaret Dupuis

D-U-N-S 24-849-2840   (SL)
ATACAMA PACIFIC GOLD CORPORATION
25 Adelaide St E Suite 1900, Toronto, ON, M5C 3A1
(416) 861-8267
Emp Here 5   *Sales* 11,937,745
SIC 1041 Gold ores
Carl Hansen
Albert Schneider
Thomas Pladsen
Marcio Fonseca
Robert Suttie

D-U-N-S 25-704-0464   (SL)
ATRIUM MORTGAGE INVESTMENT COR-PORATION
20 Adelaide St E Suite 900, Toronto, ON, M5C 2T6
(416) 867-1053
Emp Here 14   *Sales* 44,209,476
SIC 6163 Loan brokers
Robert Goodall
Jennifer Scoffield
Mark Silver
Peter P. Cohos
Robert H. Degasperis
Andrew Grant
Nancy Lockhart
Maurice Kagan

D-U-N-S 24-212-2672   (SL)
AUTOMOTIVE PROPERTIES REAL ESTATE INVESTMENT TRUST
133 King St E Suite 300, Toronto, ON, M5C 1G6
(647) 789-2440
Emp Here 5   *Sales* 36,581,454
SIC 6719 Holding companies, nec
Milton Lamb
Andrew Kalra
Kapil Dilawri

Stuart Lazier
James Matthews
John Morrison
Louis Forbes

D-U-N-S 25-253-7428   (HQ)
BANK OF NOVA SCOTIA TRUST COM-PANY, THE
SCOTIA WEALTH MANAGEMENT
(*Suby of* BANK OF NOVA SCOTIA, THE)
1 Queen St E Suite 1200, Toronto, ON, M5C 2W5
(416) 866-7829
Sales 402,424,500
SIC 6021 National commercial banks
Steven George Cannon
Roxana Tavana
Emily Tan
Rajagopal Viswanathan
Gerald Girard
Roula Kataras
Abdurrehman Muhammadi
Glen Gowland
James Ian Mcphedran

D-U-N-S 24-337-0801   (SL)
BDO CANADA & ASSOCIATES LTD
36 Toronto St Suite 600, Toronto, ON, M5C 2C5
(416) 369-3100
Emp Here 2,400   *Sales* 498,444,000
SIC 8721 Accounting, auditing, and book-keeping
Randy J Berry
Gilles Chaput
Keith Farlinger
Russelle Weir

D-U-N-S 25-532-4097   (SL)
BESRA GOLD INC
10 King St E Suite 500, Toronto, ON, M5C 1C3
(416) 572-2525
Emp Here 1,681   *Sales* 429,956,094
SIC 1081 Metal mining services
David A. Seton
Kevin Michael Tomlinson
Jeffrey D. Klam
Darin Lee
Jane Bell
Paul Seton
John A.G. Seton
Nathaniel Jon Morda
Leslie Robinson

D-U-N-S 20-175-9581   (HQ)
BLACKWOOD PARTNERS CORPORATION
110 Yonge St Suite 1500, Toronto, ON, M5C 1T4
(416) 603-3900
Emp Here 20   *Sales* 53,533,089
SIC 6282 Investment advice
Carmen Bruccoleri
Jonathan Button
John Hayes
Michael Cairns

D-U-N-S 20-847-5301   (SL)
BLANEY MCMURTRY LLP
2 Queen St E Suite 1500, Toronto, ON, M5C 3G5
(416) 593-1221
Emp Here 200   *Sales* 22,176,400
SIC 8111 Legal services
Barry Grant

D-U-N-S 24-379-0206   (HQ)
BRADKEN CANADA MANUFACTURED PRODUCTS LTD
CAST METAL SERVICES
(*Suby of* HITACHI, LTD.)
90 Richmond St E Suite 4000, Toronto, ON, M5C 1P1
(416) 975-8251
Emp Here 5   *Sales* 203,587,000
SIC 3325 Steel foundries, nec
Kevin Mcdermed
Steven Perry

D-U-N-S 20-639-6736   (HQ)
BROADGRAIN COMMODITIES INC
(*Suby of* BROADGRAIN HOLDINGS INC)
18 King St E Suite 900, Toronto, ON, M5C 1C4
(416) 504-0070
Emp Here 55   *Sales* 494,437,800
SIC 5153 Grain and field beans
Zaid Qadoumi
Ghazi Qadoumi
David Hanna
Brian Hazzard
Brian Cooper

D-U-N-S 24-342-9912   (SL)
CANADA GUARANTY MORTGAGE INSUR-ANCE COMPANY
1 Toronto St Suite 400, Toronto, ON, M5C 2V6
(416) 640-8924
Emp Here 50   *Sales* 51,744,050
SIC 6351 Surety insurance
Andrew Charles

D-U-N-S 20-574-9794   (HQ)
CANADA PENSION PLAN INVESTMENT BOARD
CPP INVESTMENT BOARD
(*Suby of* GOVERNMENT OF CANADA)
1 Queen St E, Toronto, ON, M5C 2W5
(416) 868-4075
Sales 31,785,674,965
SIC 6719 Holding companies, nec
Mark Machin
Neil Beaumont
Alain Carrier
Edwin Cass
Shane Feeney
Michel Leduc
Geoffrey Rubin
Mary Sullivan
Patrice Walch-Watson
John Graham

D-U-N-S 20-610-2642   (SL)
CANADIAN GENERAL INVESTMENTS LIM-ITED
CGI
10 Toronto St, Toronto, ON, M5C 2B7
(416) 366-2931
Emp Here 7   *Sales* 11,794,551
SIC 6726 Investment offices, nec
Vanessa L Morgan
Michael A Smedley
Jonathan A Morgan
D. Greg Eckel
Clive W. Robinson
D. Christopher King
Alex Sulzer
Niall C.T. Brown
James F. Billett
Frank Fuernkranz

D-U-N-S 24-169-8633   (SL)
CANADIAN LIFE AND HEALTH INSUR-ANCE OMBUDSERVICE
CLHIO
20 Toronto St Suite 710, Toronto, ON, M5C 2B8
(416) 777-9002
Emp Here 12   *Sales* 12,418,572
SIC 6311 Life insurance
Marjolaine Cantin

D-U-N-S 20-410-4756   (HQ)
CANADIAN PRESS, THE
BROADCAST NEWS
36 King St E Suite 301, Toronto, ON, M5C 2L9
(416) 364-0321
Emp Here 150   *Sales* 106,778,350
SIC 7383 News syndicates
Charles Messina

D-U-N-S 20-696-7239   (HQ)
CATLIN CANADA INC
(*Suby of* AXA)
100 Yonge St Suite 1200, Toronto, ON, M5C 2W1

(416) 928-5586
Emp Here 10   *Sales* 10,183,845
SIC 6211 Security brokers and dealers
Mike Hansen

D-U-N-S 25-323-4132   (HQ)
CB RICHARD ELLIS GLOBAL CORPORATE SERVICES LTD
(*Suby of* CBRE GROUP, INC.)
18 King St E Unit 1100, Toronto, ON, M5C 1C4
(416) 775-3975
Emp Here 10   *Sales* 27,135,400
SIC 6512 Nonresidential building operators
Blake Hutcheson
Jeff Cook

D-U-N-S 24-828-6296   (HQ)
CHAMPION IRON MINES LIMITED
(*Suby of* CHAMPION IRON LIMITED)
20 Adelaide St E Suite 200, Toronto, ON, M5C 2T6
(416) 866-2200
Emp Here 5   *Sales* 23,875,490
SIC 1081 Metal mining services
Michael O'keeffe
Estepa Jorge
Paul Ankcorn
Andrew Love
Gary Lawler
Miles Nagamatsu
David Cataford

D-U-N-S 20-551-9791   (HQ)
CI FINANCIAL CORP
2 Queen St E, Toronto, ON, M5C 3G7
(416) 364-1145
Emp Here 500   *Sales* 1,695,392,779
SIC 6282 Investment advice

D-U-N-S 20-849-7131   (HQ)
CI INVESTMENTS INC
(*Suby of* CI FINANCIAL CORP)
1 Queen St E Suite 2000, Toronto, ON, M5C 3W5
(416) 364-1145
Sales 996,196,600
SIC 6282 Investment advice
Derek J Green
David Pauli
Douglas Jamieson
Chris Von Boetticher
Imran Malik
James Lawrence

D-U-N-S 24-861-8043   (BR)
CITIBANK CANADA
CITIBANK VISA
(*Suby of* CITIGROUP INC.)
1 Toronto St Suite 1200, Toronto, ON, M5C 2V6
(416) 369-6399
Emp Here 400
SIC 6153 Short-term business credit institu-tions, except agricultural
Janicky Carlota

D-U-N-S 25-397-0487   (HQ)
CONSTELLATION SOFTWARE INC
20 Adelaide St E Suite 1200, Toronto, ON, M5C 2T6
(416) 861-2279
Emp Here 10   *Sales* 3,060,100,000
SIC 7371 Custom computer programming ser-vices
Mark Leonard
Jamal Baksh
Mark Miller
Bernard Anzarouth
Lawrence Cunningham
Meredith (Sam) Hayes
Robert Kittel
Paul Mcfeeters
Jeff Bender
Lori O'neill

D-U-N-S 24-376-2965   (HQ)
CORSA COAL CORP
110 Yonge St Suite 601, Toronto, ON, M5C

1T4
Emp Here 4   *Sales* 96,986,000
SIC 1081 Metal mining services
George Dethlefsen
Kevin Harrigan
Larry Evans
Robert Sturdivant
John Craig
Alan De'ath
Arthur Einav
Robert Scott
Ronald Stovash
Kai Xia

D-U-N-S 20-176-9556   (SL)
CPP INVESTMENT BOARD REAL ESTATE HOLDINGS INC
(*Suby of* GOVERNMENT OF CANADA)
1 Queen St E Suite 2500, Toronto, ON, M5C 2W5
(416) 868-4075
Emp Here 200   *Sales* 73,101,800
SIC 6719 Holding companies, nec
Mark Wiseman
Robert Brooks
Tahira Hassan
Douglas Mahaffy

D-U-N-S 24-618-6832   (HQ)
CPPIB EQUITY INVESTMENTS INC
CPP INVESTMENT BOARD
1 Queen St E Suite 2500, Toronto, ON, M5C 2W5
(416) 868-4075
Sales 1,992,393,200
SIC 6211 Security brokers and dealers
Mark Nachian

D-U-N-S 24-407-1999   (HQ)
CRANBROOK GLEN ENTERPRISES LIM-ITED
HENRY'S CAMERA
(*Suby of* GILAMY HOLDINGS INC)
119 Church St, Toronto, ON, M5C 2G5
(416) 868-0872
Emp Here 75   *Sales* 73,414,800
SIC 5946 Camera and photographic supply stores
Andrew Stein
Gillian Stein
Julie Welsh
Gaye Stein

D-U-N-S 24-045-9362   (HQ)
CREDIT UNION CENTRAL OF CANADA
CANADIAN CENTRAL
151 Yonge St Suite 1000, Toronto, ON, M5C 2W7
(416) 232-1262
Emp Here 56   *Sales* 15,675,870
SIC 6111 Federal and federally sponsored credit agencies
David Phillips
Scott Kennedy
Sean Jackson
Stephen Fitzpatrick
Garth Manness
Daniel Burns
Dave Mcclane
Paul Mcneil
Donald Rolfe
Graham Wetter

D-U-N-S 25-318-8452   (HQ)
CUSHMAN & WAKEFIELD ASSET SER-VICES ULC
SOCIETE DE GESTION 20 VIC
(*Suby of* CUSHMAN & WAKEFIELD PLC)
1 Queen St E Suite 300, Toronto, ON, M5C 2W5
(416) 955-0595
Emp Here 60   *Sales* 253,548,000
SIC 6531 Real estate agents and managers
Randy Scharfe
Michael Cogliano
Mark Banting

Marv Holmen
George Buckles
Marv Holmen

D-U-N-S 20-705-8004   (SL)
DIVERSIFIED GLOBAL ASSET MANAGEMENT CORP
DGAM
77 King St E Suite 4310, Toronto, ON, M5C
1G3
(416) 644-7587
Emp Here 22   *Sales* 11,686,554
SIC 6211 Security brokers and dealers
George Main
F. Graham Thouret
Mike Moscaritolo
Jeff Lucassen
Ray Carroll
Simon Griffiths
Warren Wright
David Hay
Lindsay Holtz
Ryan Barry

D-U-N-S 24-327-9085   (HQ)
DRA AMERICAS INC
(*Suby of* DRA INTERNATIONAL LIMITED)
44 Victoria St Suite 300, Toronto, ON, M5C
1Y2
(416) 800-8797
Emp Here 11   *Sales* 10,308,672
SIC 8742 Management consulting services
Wray Anthony Carvelas
Andre Van Wyk
Andrew Naude
Kenneth Lund

D-U-N-S 25-274-9460   (HQ)
DREAM ASSET MANAGEMENT CORPORATION
DREAM ALTERNATIVES
30 Adelaide St E Suite 301, Toronto, ON, M5C
3H1
(416) 365-3535
Emp Here 50   *Sales* 125,083,680
SIC 6531 Real estate agents and managers
Ned Goodman
P. Jane Gavan
Michael J. Cooper
Robert Hughes
Joanne Ferstman
Richard N. Gateman
Jennifer Lee Koss
Vicky Schiff
Vincenza Sera

D-U-N-S 20-273-9355   (SL)
DREAM GLOBAL REAL ESTATE INVESTMENT TRUST
DREAM GLOBAL REIT
30 Adelaide St E Suite 301, Toronto, ON, M5C
3H1
(416) 365-3535
Emp Here 140   *Sales* 76,999,020
SIC 6722 Management investment, open-end
P. Jane Gavan
Bruce Traversy
Michael Schwobel
Rajeev Viswanathan
Alexander Sannikov
Detlef Bierbaum
R. Sacha
Michael J. Cooper
P. Jane Gavan
Christian Schede

D-U-N-S 20-259-6821   (SL)
DREAM HARD ASSET ALTERNATIVES TRUST
30 Adelaide St E Suite 301, Toronto, ON, M5C
3H1
(416) 365-3535
Emp Here 10   *Sales* 43,324,771
SIC 6722 Management investment, open-end
Adam Reeds
Mikhail Arkaev
Kim Lefever

Pauline Alimchandani
Lindsay Brand
Amar Bhalla
James Eaton
Joanne Ferstman
David Kaufman
Karine Macindoe

D-U-N-S 20-255-7849   (SL)
DREAM INDUSTRIAL LP
30 Adelaide St E Suite 301, Toronto, ON, M5C
3H1
(416) 365-3535
Emp Here 300   *Sales* 101,419,200
SIC 6531 Real estate agents and managers
Jane Gavin

D-U-N-S 20-381-4215   (SL)
DREAM INDUSTRIAL REAL ESTATE INVESTMENT TRUST
DREAM INDUSTRIAL REIT
30 Adelaide Street E Suite 301, Toronto, ON,
M5C 3H1
(416) 365-3535
Emp Here 6   *Sales* 20,865,294
SIC 6798 Real estate investment trusts
Brain Pauls
Joe Ladeluca
Nick Stryland
Andrew Reial
Ayesha Shafiq
Lenis Quan

D-U-N-S 20-360-0320   (SL)
DREAM OFFICE LP
30 Adelaide St E Suite 301, Toronto, ON, M5C
3H1
(416) 365-3535
Emp Here 200   *Sales* 67,612,800
SIC 6531 Real estate agents and managers
Jane Gavan

D-U-N-S 24-684-9665   (HQ)
DREAM OFFICE MANAGEMENT CORP
(*Suby of* DUNDEE REAL ESTATE INVESTMENT TRUST)
30 Adelaide St E Suite 301, Toronto, ON, M5C
3H1
(416) 365-3535
Emp Here 50   *Sales* 41,888,900
SIC 6531 Real estate agents and managers
Michael J. Cooper
Michael Knowlton
Jean Gavan
Jo Ladeluca
John Page
Chris Holtved
Randy Cameron

D-U-N-S 20-380-9632   (SL)
DREAM OFFICE REAL ESTATE INVESTMENT TRUST
DREAM OFFICE REIT
30 Adelaide St E Suite 301, Toronto, ON, M5C
3H1
(416) 365-3535
Emp Here 5   *Sales* 17,387,745
SIC 6798 Real estate investment trusts
Michael J. Cooper
Andrew Reial
Ayesha Shafiq
Gordon Wadley
Jay Jiang

D-U-N-S 20-293-6126   (HQ)
DREAM UNLIMITED CORP
DREAM REIT INDUSTRIAL
30 Adelaide St E Suite 301, Toronto, ON, M5C
3H1
(416) 365-3535
Emp Here 20   *Sales* 257,658,401
SIC 6553 Cemetery subdividers and developers
Michael J. Cooper
Pauline Alimchandani
Daniel Marinovic
Lindsay Brand

Jason Lester
Joanne Ferstman
James Eaton
Richard Gateman
P. Jane Gavan
Duncan Jackman

D-U-N-S 24-947-2978   (HQ)
DUNDEE CORPORATION
1 Adelaide St E Suite 2000, Toronto, ON, M5C
2V9
(416) 350-3388
Emp Here 12   *Sales* 117,268,524
SIC 6211 Security brokers and dealers
Jonathan Goodman
Bob Sellars
Richard McIntrye
Geoffrey Morphy
Sivan Fox
Perina Montesano
Mark Pereira
Allen Palmiere
A. Murray Sinclair
Andrew Molson

D-U-N-S 24-844-1230   (HQ)
DUNDEE PRECIOUS METALS INC
1 Adelaide St E Suite 500, Toronto, ON, M5C
2V9
(416) 365-5191
Sales 377,111,000
SIC 1041 Gold ores
Rick Howes
Kelly Stark-Anderson
Hume Kyle
David Rae
Michael Dorfman
Richard Gosse
Nikolay Hristov
John Lindsay
Paul Proulx
Alex Wilson

D-U-N-S 25-996-3130   (HQ)
ENERGY FUELS INC
82 Richmond St E Suite 308, Toronto, ON,
M5C 1P1
(416) 214-2810
Sales 39,864,000
SIC 1031 Lead and zinc ores
Stephen Antony
Daniel Zang
W. Paul Goranson
Mark Chalmers
David Frydenlund
Curtis Moore
J. Birks Bovaird
Paul Carroll
Bruce Hansen
Dennis Higgs

D-U-N-S 20-697-0233   (HQ)
ESKA INC
ESKA WATER
(*Suby of* MORGAN STANLEY)
25 Adelaide St E Suite 1000, Toronto, ON,
M5C 3A1
(416) 504-2222
Emp Here 20   *Sales* 21,506,280
SIC 3221 Glass containers
James Delsnyder
Michael Mcgrath

D-U-N-S 25-096-2347   (SL)
EXCHANGE SOLUTIONS INC
36 Toronto St Suite 1200, Toronto, ON, M5C
2C5
(416) 646-7000
Emp Here 100   *Sales* 12,477,600
SIC 8741 Management services
Mike Hughes
Robert Jewell
Steven Hoffman
Alan Grant
Geoffrey S. Oblak
Brett J. Rome
Harry D'andrea

Maureen Drew
Shane O'neil

D-U-N-S 20-372-7818   (SL)
FIRST ASSET INVESTMENT GRADE BOND ETF
2 Queen St E Suite 1200, Toronto, ON, M5C
3G7
(416) 642-1289
Emp Here 20   *Sales* 14,167,885
SIC 6722 Management investment, open-end
Manash Goswami
Lijon Geeverghese

D-U-N-S 20-307-0701   (HQ)
FIRST COBALT CORP
140 Yonge St Suite 201, Toronto, ON, M5C
1X6
(416) 900-3891
Sales 23,875,490
SIC 1081 Metal mining services
Trent Mell
Ryan Snyder
Frank Santaguida
Peter Campbell
Paul Matysek
Robert Cross
Garett Macdonald
Ross Phillips
John Pollesel
Jeff Swinoga

D-U-N-S 20-550-6475   (HQ)
FIRST INSURANCE FUNDING OF CANADA INC
20 Toronto St Suite 700, Toronto, ON, M5C
2B8
(888) 232-2238
Emp Here 55   *Sales* 601,504,000
SIC 6159 Miscellaneous business credit institutions
Stuart Bruce
John Martin
Brian Day
David Caringi
Marcus Albertson
Crystal Macklin

D-U-N-S 20-300-5103   (SL)
FIRSTASSET CANADIAN COVERTIBLE DEBENTURE FUND
FIRST ASSET
2 Queen St E Suite 1200, Toronto, ON, M5C
3G7
(416) 642-1289
Emp Here 35   *Sales* 28,972,195
SIC 6722 Management investment, open-end
Rohit D. Mehta

D-U-N-S 24-365-8973   (SL)
FORESTERS ASSET MANAGEMENT INC
20 Adelaide St E Suite 1500, Toronto, ON,
M5C 2T6
(800) 828-1540
Emp Here 15   *Sales* 10,881,585
SIC 6371 Pension, health, and welfare funds
Gregory Ross
Andrew Berwick
Suzann Pennington

D-U-N-S 24-318-5147   (SL)
FOYSTON, GORDON & PAYNE INC
(*Suby of* AFFILIATED MANAGERS GROUP,
INC.)
1 Adelaide St E Suite 2600, Toronto, ON, M5C
2V9
(416) 362-4725
Emp Here 53   *Sales* 78,125,233
SIC 6722 Management investment, open-end
Bryan Pilsworth
Donald Foyston
Stephen Copeland

D-U-N-S 24-793-7634   (HQ)
FRED VICTOR CENTRE
59 Adelaide St E Suite 600, Toronto, ON, M5C
1K6

(416) 364-8228
Emp Here 10   *Sales* 11,600,096
SIC 6513 Apartment building operators
Pamela Bryant
Mark Aston
David Hrynyk

D-U-N-S 24-857-2765   (SL)
GCIC LTD
1 Adelaide St E Suite 2800, Toronto, ON, M5C
2V9
(416) 350-3250
Emp Here 800   *Sales* 430,049,270
SIC 6159 Miscellaneous business credit insti-
tutions
Jordy Warren Chilcott
Simon Mielniczuk
Jim Morris
Robin Lacey

D-U-N-S 20-269-7546   (SL)
GEOLOGICAL INDUSTRY RESEARCH INC
140 Yonge St, Toronto, ON, M5C 1X6
(416) 477-1164
Emp Here 49   *Sales* 15,220,272
SIC 8999 Services, nec
Stefan Quinn

D-U-N-S 24-341-8287   (HQ)
GLOBAL MAXFIN CAPITAL INC
(*Suby of* GLOBAL RESP CORPORATION)
15 Toronto St Suite 202, Toronto, ON, M5C
2E3
(416) 741-1445
Emp Here 4   *Sales* 12,220,614
SIC 6211 Security brokers and dealers
Sam Bouji

D-U-N-S 24-575-2290   (HQ)
**GOODMAN & COMPANY, INVESTMENT
COUNSEL LTD**
*CONSEILLERS EN PLACEMENTS GOOD-
MAN & COMPANY*
1 Adelaide St E Suite 2100, Toronto, ON, M5C
2V9
(416) 363-9097
Emp Here 330   *Sales* 601,987,374
SIC 6282 Investment advice
David Goodman
David Jason Goodman

D-U-N-S 20-293-2240   (SL)
GPVTL CANADA INC
PIVOTAL SOFTWARE
(*Suby of* DELL TECHNOLOGIES INC.)
1 Toronto St Suite 1100, Toronto, ON, M5C
2V6
(416) 907-9470
Emp Here 270   *Sales* 49,834,710
SIC 7371 Custom computer programming ser-
vices
Paul T. Dacier
Mark H. Glenn
Andrew Cohen
Orrin Bean
Robert Kozlov
Scott Erkilla

D-U-N-S 20-215-1627   (HQ)
GREENFIELD GLOBAL, INC
COMMERCIAL ALCOHOL DIV OF
20 Toronto St Suite 1400, Toronto, ON, M5C
2B8
(416) 304-1700
Emp Here 25   *Sales* 319,475,400
SIC 2869 Industrial organic chemicals, nec
Robert Gallant
Kenneth E Field
Gary Mcinerney
Stewart Davidson

D-U-N-S 25-529-7004   (SL)
HELIX APPLICATIONS INC
82 Richmond St Suite 203 The Canadian Venture Building, Toronto, ON, M5C 1P1
(416) 848-6865
Emp Here 50   *Sales* 119,377,450
SIC 1041 Gold ores

Brian Hinchcliffe
Steven Cuthill
Brad Dunne
Mike Sutton
Trevor Maurice Gabriel
Rufus Round

D-U-N-S 20-180-4155   (SL)
HMZ METALS INC
2 Toronto St Suite 500, Toronto, ON, M5C 2B6

Emp Here 400   *Sales* 162,869,600
SIC 3339 Primary nonferrous Metals, nec

D-U-N-S 20-117-8733   (SL)
HUBIO SOLUTIONS INC
20 Victoria St, Toronto, ON, M5C 2N8
(416) 364-6306
Emp Here 52   *Sales* 23,253,048
SIC 5045 Computers, peripherals, and soft-
ware
Mark Williams
Lisa Reed
Glen Piller
Paul Reed

D-U-N-S 25-354-9034   (BR)
HUDSON'S BAY COMPANY
ROOM, THE
(*Suby of* HUDSON'S BAY COMPANY)
176 Yonge St, Toronto, ON, M5C 2L7
(416) 861-6251
Emp Here 1,200
SIC 5311 Department stores
Rich Montgomery

D-U-N-S 20-935-2467   (HQ)
**INCORPORATED SYNOD OF THE DIO-
CESE OF TORONTO, THE**
ANGLICAN DIOCESE OF TORONTO
135 Adelaide St E, Toronto, ON, M5C 1L8
(416) 363-6021
Emp Here 35   *Sales* 62,473,800
SIC 8661 Religious organizations
Colin R Johnson
Stuart Mann
P.E. Finlay

D-U-N-S 25-305-2963   (BR)
INNVEST PROPERTIES CORP
QUALITY HOTEL
(*Suby of* INNVEST PROPERTIES CORP)
111 Lombard St, Toronto, ON, M5C 2T9
(416) 367-5555
Emp Here 80
SIC 7011 Hotels and motels
Stock Nancy

D-U-N-S 20-822-7918   (HQ)
INSURANCE INSTITUTE OF CANADA, THE
18 King St E Suite 600, Toronto, ON, M5C 1C4
(416) 362-8586
Sales 10,282,580
SIC 8621 Professional organizations
Peter G Hohman
Jean-Francois Blais
Mary Dimitriou

D-U-N-S 24-138-6457   (HQ)
INTER-ROCK MINERALS INC
2 Toronto St 5th Fl, Toronto, ON, M5C 2B6
(416) 367-3003
Emp Here 2   *Sales* 51,890,000
SIC 1481 NonMetallic mineral services
Michael B. Crombie
David Briggs
Keith Belingheri
Robert Crombie
David R. Crombie
Scott Kelly
Frank Van De Water

D-U-N-S 25-255-0371   (SL)
**INTERNATIONAL CHAMPIONSHIP MAN-
AGEMENT LIMITED**
MARCUS EVANS
(*Suby of* MARCUS EVANS WORLDWIDE

HOLDINGS (IOM) LTD)
20 Toronto St, Toronto, ON, M5C 2B8
(416) 955-0375
Emp Here 120
SIC 7941 Sports clubs, managers, and promoters
Marcus Evan

D-U-N-S 20-059-1142   (SL)
**INTERNATIONAL FINANCIAL DATA SER-
VICES (CANADA) LIMITED**
IFDS
30 Adelaide St E Suite 1, Toronto, ON, M5C
3G9
(416) 506-8000
Emp Here 600   *Sales* 853,882,800
SIC 6289 Security and commodity service
Katherine Macmillan
Dennis Gregoris
Giuseppe Desario
Terrence Metzger
Simon Hudson-Lund
Susan Dargan

D-U-N-S 20-364-0420   (HQ)
JAMIESON WELLNESS INC
1 Adelaide St E Suite 2200, Toronto, ON, M5C
2V9
(833) 223-2666
Emp Here 14   *Sales* 242,422,825
SIC 2833 Medicinals and botanicals
Mark Hornick
Robert Chan
Joel Scales
Paul Galbraith
Don Bird
Christopher Snowden
Regan Stewart
John Doherty
David Williams
Heather Allen

D-U-N-S 20-384-3735   (SL)
KINETIC HEALTH INC
140 Yonge St, Toronto, ON, M5C 1X6
(416) 302-4724
Emp Here 39   *Sales* 10,005,918
SIC 3842 Surgical appliances and supplies
Jean-Francois Gauthier
Jelena Neylan

D-U-N-S 24-422-1060   (SL)
KING EDWARD REALTY INC
OMNI KING EDWARD
37 King St E, Toronto, ON, M5C 1E9
(416) 863-9700
Emp Here 225   *Sales* 21,525,300
SIC 7011 Hotels and motels
Alex Shnaider
Gil Blutrich
Simon Serruya
Jason Lester

D-U-N-S 25-192-6390   (HQ)
LEADFX INC
ENIRGI GROUP
1 Adelaide St E, Toronto, ON, M5C 2V9
(416) 867-9298
Emp Here 6   *Sales* 33,425,686
SIC 1081 Metal mining services
Andrew Worland
Stephen Dennis
David Dreisinger
David Warner
Michel Marier
George Molyviatis

D-U-N-S 20-334-4338   (HQ)
LEEDE JONES GABLE INC
110 Yonge St Suite 600, Toronto, ON, M5C
1T4
(416) 365-8000
Sales 10,624,140
SIC 6211 Security brokers and dealers
Alvin Ritchie
Bradley Hemingson
Catherine Vinterlik

Charles Laddish
Donald Ross
Glenn Beitz
Gordon Medland
J. Victor Taboika
James Clark Macdonald
James W Dale

D-U-N-S 25-251-5788   (HQ)
LOFT COMMUNITY SERVICES
15 Toronto St Suite 9, Toronto, ON, M5C 2E3

Emp Here 14   *Sales* 19,198,000
SIC 8322 Individual and family services
Terry Mccullum

D-U-N-S 20-322-1429   (HQ)
LOGIQ3 CORP
(*Suby of* LOGIQ3 INC)
60 Adelaide St E Unit 1300, Toronto, ON, M5C
3E4
(416) 340-7435
Sales 62,823,228
SIC 6411 Insurance agents, brokers, and ser-
vice
Chris Murumets
Ray Didonna
Simon Bell
Brian Wilkinson
Carmela Tedesco
Natalie Ho
Dylan Friedmann
Mitch Ocampo
Sanjay Thakrar

D-U-N-S 20-112-2160   (HQ)
MANDALAY RESOURCES CORPORATION
76 Richmond St E Suite 330, Toronto, ON,
M5C 1P1
(647) 260-1566
Sales 112,168,000
SIC 1041 Gold ores
Dominic Duffy
Chris Gregory
Toni Streczynski
Belinda Labatte
Nick Dwyer
Bradford A. Mills
Peter Rhys Jones
Amy Freedman
Braam Jonker
Rob Doyle

D-U-N-S 24-130-8191   (SL)
MAVRIX AMERICAN GROWTH FUND
MATRIX ASSET MANAGEMENT
36 Lombard St Suite 2200, Toronto, ON, M5C
2X3
(416) 362-3077
Emp Here 26   *Sales* 21,522,202
SIC 6722 Management investment, open-end
Dvid Levi

D-U-N-S 25-202-6893   (SL)
MERCANTILE EXCHANGE CORPORATION
8 King St E 14th Fl, Toronto, ON, M5C 1B5
(416) 368-3680
Emp Here 55   *Sales* 10,257,500
SIC 6099 Functions related to deposit banking
Stephen Lau

D-U-N-S 24-339-8679   (HQ)
MERRILL CORPORATION CANADA
(*Suby of* MERRILL CORPORATION)
3000-1 Adelaide St E, Toronto, ON, M5C 2V9
(416) 214-2448
Sales 13,778,268
SIC 2752 Commercial printing, lithographic
Aivars Beikmanis

D-U-N-S 25-864-9938   (SL)
**MORGAN MEIGHEN & ASSOCIATES LIM-
ITED**
10 Toronto St, Toronto, ON, M5C 2B7
(416) 366-2931
Emp Here 18   *Sales* 12,540,186
SIC 6726 Investment offices, nec

Michael Smedley
Vanessa Morgan
Jonathan Morgan

D-U-N-S 20-108-8221   (HQ)
NAVIGANT CONSULTING LTD
NAVIGANT
(*Suby of* NAVIGANT CONSULTING, INC.)
1 Adelaide St E Suite 1250, Toronto, ON, M5C
2V9
(416) 777-2440
Emp Here 35   *Sales* 16,785,540
SIC 8742 Management consulting services
William Goodyear
Richard Fischer
Ben Perks
Wayne Koprowski
Robert Macdonald

D-U-N-S 24-525-6412   (SL)
NEXGEN FINANCIAL LIMITED PARTNER-SHIP
(*Suby of* NATIXIS INVESTMENT MAN-AGERS CANADA CORP)
36 Toronto St Suite 1070, Toronto, ON, M5C
2C5
(416) 775-3700
Emp Here 30   *Sales* 15,936,210
SIC 6282 Investment advice
Patrick Lincoln

D-U-N-S 20-171-9598   (HQ)
NORBORD INC
1 Toronto St Suite 600, Toronto, ON, M5C
2W4
(416) 365-0705
Emp Here 100   *Sales* 2,424,000,000
SIC 2435 Hardwood veneer and plywood
Peter C. Wijnbergen
Robin E. Lampard
Nigel Banks
Alan Mcmeekin
Mark R. Dubois-Phillips
Kevin Burke
Jack Cockwell
Pierre Dupuis
Paul Gagne
Peter Gordon

D-U-N-S 24-784-7148   (HQ)
NORBORD INDUSTRIES INC
(*Suby of* NORBORD INC)
1 Toronto St Unit 600, Toronto, ON, M5C 2W4
(416) 365-0705
Emp Here 100   *Sales* 723,814,000
SIC 2431 Millwork
Peter Wijnbergen
Robin Lampard
Nigel Banks
Michael Dawson

D-U-N-S 25-683-7501   (SL)
NORTHSTAR RESEARCH PARTNERS INC
18 King St E Suite 1500, Toronto, ON, M5C
1C4
(416) 907-7100
Emp Here 50   *Sales* 11,734,800
SIC 8732 Commercial nonphysical research
Stephen Tile
Joanne Orr

D-U-N-S 25-253-1207   (HQ)
ONTARIO PUBLIC SERVICE EMPLOYEES UNION PENSION PLAN TRUST FUND
OPSEU PENSION TRUST
1 Adelaide St E Suite 1200, Toronto, ON, M5C
3A7
(416) 681-6161
Emp Here 140   *Sales* 427,393,600
SIC 6371 Pension, health, and welfare funds
Charles Eigl

D-U-N-S 24-683-4027   (SL)
OPTIMUS SBR INC
30 Adelaide St E Suite 600, Toronto, ON, M5C
3G8
(416) 962-7500
Emp Here 40   *Sales* 11,331,720

SIC 8741 Management services
Kevin Gauci
Guiseppe Oppedisano
John Whincup

D-U-N-S 20-968-3135   (HQ)
PARTNERS INDEMNITY INSURANCE BRO-KERS LTD
10 Adelaide St E Suite 400, Toronto, ON, M5C
1J3
(416) 366-5243
Emp Here 15   *Sales* 36,466,580
SIC 6411 Insurance agents, brokers, and service
Barry Downs

D-U-N-S 24-369-3665   (SL)
PELANGIO EXPLORATION INC
82 Richmond St E, Toronto, ON, M5C 1P1
(905) 336-3828
Emp Here 50   *Sales* 10,443,600
SIC 1041 Gold ores
Ingrid Hibbard
Paul Rokeby
Warren Bates
Sam Torkornoo
Kevin Filo
David Mosher
Carl Nurmi
David K. Paxton
Kevin P. Thomson
J.C. St-Amour

D-U-N-S 20-288-9507   (SL)
PLATFORM INSURANCE MANAGEMENT INC
20 Toronto St Suite 440, Toronto, ON, M5C
2B8
(416) 434-4322
Emp Here 23   *Sales* 13,338,252
SIC 6411 Insurance agents, brokers, and service
Shaun Mcpherson
Matthew Francis
Charles Quenneville
Scott Beitel

D-U-N-S 24-893-8776   (HQ)
PRIMARIS MANAGEMENT INC
(*Suby of* H&R REAL ESTATE INVESTMENT TRUST)
1 Adelaide St E Suite 900, Toronto, ON, M5C
2V9
(416) 642-7800
Emp Here 75   *Sales* 39,271,050
SIC 8741 Management services
Tom Hofstedter
Lesley Gibson
Toran Eggert
Brenda Huggins
Larry Froom
Patrick Sullivan
Mordecai Bobrowsky
Robyn Kestenberg

D-U-N-S 20-552-3009   (HQ)
PRIMARIS RETAIL REAL ESTATE INVEST-MENT TRUST
(*Suby of* H&R REAL ESTATE INVESTMENT TRUST)
1 Adelaide St E Suite 900, Toronto, ON, M5C
2V9
(416) 642-7800
Emp Here 7   *Sales* 44,221,830
SIC 6726 Investment offices, nec
John Morrison
Roland Cardy
Louis Forbes
Kerry D. Adams
William Biggar
Ian Collier
Kenneth Field
Brent Hollister

D-U-N-S 20-709-3191   (BR)
PUBLICIS CANADA INC
(*Suby of* PUBLICIS GROUPE HOLDINGS

B.V.)
111 Queen St E Suite 200, Toronto, ON, M5C
1S2
(416) 925-7733
Emp Here 260
SIC 7311 Advertising agencies
Julie Myers

D-U-N-S 20-012-0934   (HQ)
PYXIS REAL ESTATE EQUITIES INC
95 King St E Suite 201, Toronto, ON, M5C 1G4
(416) 815-0201
Sales 20,534,300
SIC 5311 Department stores
David Jubb
Susan Mcgowan

D-U-N-S 24-026-2555   (SL)
RED SEAL NOTARY INC
25 Adelaide St E Unit 100, Toronto, ON, M5C
3A1
(416) 922-7325
Emp Here 25   *Sales* 11,087,250
SIC 7389 Business services, nec
Javad Heydary
Marjan Heydary
Paul Hakimi

D-U-N-S 25-530-0519   (SL)
REGAL CONSOLIDATED VENTURES LIM-ITED
20 Adelaide St E Suite 1100, Toronto, ON,
M5C 2T6
(416) 642-0602
Emp Here 50   *Sales* 11,671,750
SIC 1081 Metal mining services
Robert Brissenden

D-U-N-S 25-977-8090   (HQ)
ROUTE1 INC
8 King St E Suite 600, Toronto, ON, M5C 1B5
(416) 848-8391
Emp Here 15   *Sales* 19,885,581
SIC 7371 Custom computer programming services
Brian Brunetti
Yamian Quintero
Peter Chodos

D-U-N-S 25-372-0155   (HQ)
SCALAR DECISIONS INC
1 Toronto St 3rd Fl, Toronto, ON, M5C 2V6
(416) 202-0020
Emp Here 100   *Sales* 69,318,400
SIC 7379 Computer related services, nec
Paul Kerr
Michael Maillet
Karolina Tallar
Glenn Kaul
Ella Trubacheva
Eric Ng

D-U-N-S 25-248-5966   (SL)
SCOTIALIFE FINANCIAL SERVICES INC
(*Suby of* BANK OF NOVA SCOTIA, THE)
100 Yonge St Suite 400, Toronto, ON, M5C
2W1
(416) 866-7075
Emp Here 50   *Sales* 92,332,950
SIC 6321 Accident and health insurance
Robert James Grant
Jennifer Gilbert
Antonio Pergola

D-U-N-S 25-106-1156   (HQ)
SENTRY INVESTMENTS
NCE RESOURCES
2 Queen St E Fl 12, Toronto, ON, M5C 3G7
(416) 861-8729
Sales 89,221,815
SIC 6282 Investment advice
John F Driscoll
Gordon Thompson
Brian Mcostrich

D-U-N-S 25-512-7995   (HQ)
SKYLINE INVESTMENTS INC
(*Suby of* THE ILDC GROUP LTD)

36 King St E Suite 700, Toronto, ON, M5C 2L9
(416) 368-2565
Sales 176,073,738
SIC 6512 Nonresidential building operators
Blake Lyon
Robert Waxman
Bruce Riggins
Paul Mondell
Shimshon Marfogel
Gil Blutrich
Ruhama Avraham
Lana Sherman
Mordechai Keret
Rami Shriki

D-U-N-S 20-251-7363   (SL)
SLALOM CONSULTING ULC
(*Suby of* SLALOM, LLC)
8 King St E Unit 2000, Toronto, ON, M5C 1B5
(416) 366-5390
Emp Here 50   *Sales* 11,714,400
SIC 8748 Business consulting, nec
Wayne Ingram

D-U-N-S 24-409-4967   (HQ)
ST ANDREW GOLDFIELDS LTD
SAS GOLDMINES
(*Suby of* KIRKLAND LAKE GOLD LTD)
20 Adelaide St E Suite 1500, Toronto, ON,
M5C 2T6
(416) 815-9855
Sales 127,887,000
SIC 1041 Gold ores
Duncan Middlemiss
Ben Au
Doug Cater
Linda Weinzettl
Herbert Abramson
Michael Churchill
John Hick
Duncan Middlemiss
Donald Njegovan
Eric Robin

D-U-N-S 20-819-8416   (HQ)
ST. JOHN COUNCIL FOR ONTARIO
ST. JOHN AMBULANCE
15 Toronto St Suite 800, Toronto, ON, M5C
2E3
(416) 923-8411
Emp Here 15   *Sales* 27,740,900
SIC 8611 Business associations
Allan Smith
Robert White
Paul Philip Clarke
Richard Neville
Geoffrey Lougheed

D-U-N-S 20-310-2132   (SL)
STRATEGIC UNDERWRITING MANAGERS INC
SUM INSURANCE
18 King St E Suite 903, Toronto, ON, M5C 1C4
(416) 603-7864
Emp Here 19   *Sales* 11,018,556
SIC 6411 Insurance agents, brokers, and service
Jeff Somerville
Travis Budd
Stan Lam
Serge Nelanson
Andy Henke
William Andrus
Rick Degrace
Brian Reeve

D-U-N-S 24-425-1125   (HQ)
SYMPHONY SENIOR LIVING INC
20 Toronto St Suite 440, Toronto, ON, M5C
2B8
(416) 366-3888
Emp Here 489   *Sales* 67,838,500
SIC 6513 Apartment building operators
Lisa Brush
Lisa Wernham
Jessica Kim

▲ Public Company   ■ Public Company Family Member   **HQ** Headquarters   **BR** Branch   **SL** Single Location

D-U-N-S 25-215-4661 (SL)
TANZANIAN ROYALTY EXPLORATION CORPORATION
82 Richmond St W Suite 208, Toronto, ON, M5C 1P1
(844) 364-1830
Emp Here 15 *Sales* 35,813,235
SIC 1081 Metal mining services
Jeffrey Duval
Jim Sinclair
Norman Betts
William M. Harvey
Ulrich Rath
Rosalind Morrow
Marco Guidi

D-U-N-S 20-193-7948 (BR)
TERANET INC
(*Suby of* TERANET INC)
1 Adelaide St E Suite 600, Toronto, ON, M5C 2V9
(416) 360-5263
Emp Here 300
SIC 7371 Custom computer programming services
Aris Kaplanis

D-U-N-S 24-222-0002 (SL)
TORKIN MANES LLP
151 Yonge St Suite 1500, Toronto, ON, M5C 2W7
(416) 863-1188
Emp Here 150 *Sales* 16,632,300
SIC 8111 Legal services
Ronald Manes
Barry Arbus
Barry Cohen
Jeffrey Cohen

D-U-N-S 20-555-7689 (SL)
TORONTO PARKING AUTHORITY, THE
GREENP
(*Suby of* CORPORATION OF THE CITY OF TORONTO)
33 Queen St E, Toronto, ON, M5C 1R5
(416) 393-7275
Emp Here 341 *Sales* 30,586,336
SIC 7521 Automobile parking
Gwyn Thomas
Michael Tziretas
Gerard Daigle
Barry Martin
Sam Roussos
Geraldine Kozorys

D-U-N-S 20-919-2959 (SL)
TRAVEL EDGE (CANADA) INC
VOYAGE WORLDVIEW (CANADA)
2 Queen St E Suite 200, Toronto, ON, M5C 3G7
(416) 649-9093
Emp Here 85 *Sales* 9,601,571
SIC 4724 Travel agencies
Jeffrey Willner
Romeo Cuter
Michelle Drover
John Hiscock
Saeideh Fard

D-U-N-S 20-105-8190 (HQ)
TRAVELEX CANADA LIMITED
TRAVELEX GLOBAL BUSINESS PAYMENTS
(*Suby of* TP FINANCING 3 LIMITED)
100 Yonge St, Toronto, ON, M5C 2W1
(416) 359-3700
Emp Here 500 *Sales* 117,703,152
SIC 6099 Functions related to deposit banking
Judy Adams

D-U-N-S 24-514-5321 (SL)
TULLETT PREBON CANADA LIMITED
(*Suby of* TP ICAP PLC)
1 Toronto St Suite 803, Toronto, ON, M5C 2V6
(416) 941-0606
Emp Here 70 *Sales* 13,818,000
SIC 6099 Functions related to deposit banking
Christopher Woolcock

D-U-N-S 24-378-8903 (HQ)
U3O8 CORP
36 Toronto St Suite 1050, Toronto, ON, M5C 2C5
(416) 868-1491
Sales 310,381,370
SIC 1081 Metal mining services
Richard Spencer
David Constable
Hugo Bastias
Gabriel Bastias
Elpidio Reis
John Ross
Keith Barron
David Franklin
Pablo Marcet
David Marsh

D-U-N-S 20-532-0315 (SL)
UNIGOLD INC
44 Victoria St Suite 504, Toronto, ON, M5C 1Y2
(416) 866-8157
Emp Here 5 *Sales* 11,937,745
SIC 1081 Metal mining services
Joseph Del Campo
John Green
Wesley Hanson
Joseph Hamilton
Charles Page
Daniel Danis
Jose Acero
Ruben Padilla

D-U-N-S 24-366-0466 (SL)
VELOCITY TRADE CANADA LTD.
VELOCITYTRADE
(*Suby of* VELOCITY TRADE HOLDINGS LTD)
100 Yonge St Unit 1800, Toronto, ON, M5C 2W1
(416) 855-2800
Emp Here 70 *Sales* 65,742,390
SIC 6211 Security brokers and dealers
Simon Grayson
Gregory Morgan
Simon Law
Jim Kennwy

D-U-N-S 24-366-0441 (HQ)
VELOCITY TRADE HOLDINGS LTD
VELOCITY FOREIGN EXCHANGE SERVICES
100 Yonge St Suite 1800, Toronto, ON, M5C 2W1
(416) 855-2800
Emp Here 15 *Sales* 10,067,400
SIC 6099 Functions related to deposit banking
Greg Morgan
Simon Law
Simon Grayson

D-U-N-S 24-992-9126 (HQ)
VERIZON CANADA LTD
VERIZON BUSINESS
(*Suby of* VERIZON COMMUNICATIONS INC.)
1 Adelaide St E Suite 2400, Toronto, ON, M5C 2V9
(416) 933-6500
Sales 39,525,656
SIC 4899 Communication services, nec
Margaret Jodha

D-U-N-S 24-215-0276 (HQ)
VRETTA INC
120 Adelaide St E, Toronto, ON, M5C 1K9
(866) 522-9228
Sales 15,722,665
SIC 7389 Business services, nec
Anand Karat

D-U-N-S 25-101-7166 (SL)
WARD EMPIRE GROUP INC, THE
2 Lombard St Suite 203, Toronto, ON, M5C 1M1
(416) 366-7227
Emp Here 200 *Sales* 38,417,000

SIC 3441 Fabricated structural Metal
Guy Nelson
Steve Lockwood

D-U-N-S 25-509-3031 (SL)
WATT CARMICHAEL INC
1 Queen St E Suite 1900, Toronto, ON, M5C 2W6
(416) 864-1500
Emp Here 16 *Sales* 10,862,768
SIC 6211 Security brokers and dealers
Harry J Carmichael
Roger Rowan
Martin Sims
Stafford W Higgins
Craig Schleyer

D-U-N-S 20-035-9169 (SL)
WHITE GOLD CORP
82 Richmond St E, Toronto, ON, M5C 1P1
(416) 643-3880
Emp Here 5 *Sales* 11,937,745
SIC 1041 Gold ores
David D'onofrio
Jodie Gibson
Robert Carpenter
Maruf Raza
Sean Bromley

D-U-N-S 20-344-4307 (SL)
WILSON CONTINGENT TALENT SOLUTIONS, INC
WILSONCTS
44 Victoria St Suite 2000, Toronto, ON, M5C 1Y2
(416) 440-0097
Emp Here 200 *Sales* 50,698,000
SIC 8748 Business consulting, nec
Paul Dodd
Stan Hamersak

Toronto, ON M5E

D-U-N-S 24-523-3569 (HQ)
ALLOYCORP MINING INC
67 Yonge St Suite 501, Toronto, ON, M5E 1J8
(416) 847-0376
Emp Here 5 *Sales* 23,875,490
SIC 1061 Ferroalloy ores, except vanadium
Mario B. Caron
Shane Uren
Graham Du Preez
Daniella Dimitrov
Robert Francis
John Stubbs

D-U-N-S 24-857-2633 (SL)
ALPHAPRO MANAGEMENT INC
26 Wellington St E Suite 700, Toronto, ON, M5E 1S2
(416) 933-5745
Emp Here 45 *Sales* 33,005,340
SIC 6722 Management investment, open-end
Mark Arthur

D-U-N-S 24-805-6934 (BR)
ALTUS GEOMATICS LIMITED PARTNERSHIP
ALTUS GROUP
(*Suby of* ALTUS GROUP LIMITED)
33 Yonge St Suite 500, Toronto, ON, M5E 1G4
(416) 641-9500
Emp Here 250
SIC 8713 Surveying services

D-U-N-S 25-373-4941 (HQ)
ALTUS GROUP LIMITED
33 Yonge St Suite 500, Toronto, ON, M5E 1G4
(416) 641-9500
Emp Here 274 *Sales* 386,957,246
SIC 6722 Management investment, open-end
Robert Courteau
Carl Farrell
Michael Commons

Liana Turrin
Angelo Bartolini
Raymond Mikulich
Eric W. Slavens
Diane Macdiarmid
Tony Gaffney
Janet Woodruff

D-U-N-S 24-721-0099 (SL)
BARNES COMMUNICATIONS INC
ROADSHOW ACADEMY, DIV OF
1 Yonge St Suite 1504, Toronto, ON, M5E 1E5
(416) 367-5000
Emp Here 1 *Sales* 14,936,306
SIC 6282 Investment advice
Kenneth Barnes
Gary Kapsa
Marianna Barnes

D-U-N-S 20-818-1941 (HQ)
BDO CANADA LLP
20 Wellington St E Suite 500, Toronto, ON, M5E 1C5
(416) 865-0111
Emp Here 150 *Sales* 406,676,600
SIC 8721 Accounting, auditing, and bookkeeping
Pat Kramer
Dave Simkins
Mary Parkes
Travis Leppky
Armand Capisciolto
John Wonfor

D-U-N-S 25-821-4550 (HQ)
BMO LIFE ASSURANCE COMPANY
60 Yonge St, Toronto, ON, M5E 1H5
(416) 596-3900
Emp Here 230 *Sales* 1,186,526,000
SIC 6411 Insurance agents, brokers, and service
Peter C. Mccarthy
Myra Cridland
Paul Dubal
David Mackie
Crawford William Spratt
J. Peter Eccleton
Maurice Hudon
Thomas Brian
Charyl Gaplin
Rebecca Tascona

D-U-N-S 20-699-8440 (SL)
BMO LIFE INSURANCE COMPANY
(*Suby of* BANK OF MONTREAL)
60 Yonge St 11th Floor, Toronto, ON, M5E 1H5
(416) 596-3900
Emp Here 200 *Sales* 427,393,600
SIC 6311 Life insurance
Gordon Henderson

D-U-N-S 25-510-8250 (HQ)
CADILLAC VENTURES INC
65 Front St E Suite 200, Toronto, ON, M5E 1B5
(416) 203-7722
Emp Here 11 *Sales* 28,650,588
SIC 1041 Gold ores
Norman Brewster
Leo O'shaughnessy
Youliang Wang
Neil Novak
Maurice Stekel
James Burke
Jesus Fernandez Lopez
Jianxiong Liu
Raja Singh
Sam Wang

D-U-N-S 25-602-4910 (HQ)
CANADIAN APARTMENT PROPERTIES REAL ESTATE INVESTMENT TRUST
CAPREIT
11 Church St Suite 401, Toronto, ON, M5E 1W1
(416) 861-9404
Emp Here 125 *Sales* 493,343,721

SIC 6722 Management investment, open-end
Mark Kenney
Trish Macpherson
Jonathan Fleischer
Scott Bunker
Priyanka Taneja
Chin Dhushenthen
Ivano De Luca
Stephen Co
Corinne Pruzanski
Scott Cryer

D-U-N-S 25-283-5418 (SL)
CANADIAN COPYRIGHT LICENSING AGENCY
ACCESS COPYRIGHT
1 Yonge St Suite 800, Toronto, ON, M5E 1E5
(416) 868-1620
Emp Here 40 *Sales* 27,872,400
SIC 6794 Patent owners and lessors
Maureen Cavan
Surendra Bungaroo
Bill Zerter
Michael O'reilly

D-U-N-S 20-785-4068 (SL)
CANADIAN FOOTBALL LEAGUE
C F L
50 Wellington St E 3rd Fl, Toronto, ON, M5E 1C8
(416) 322-9650
Emp Here 32 *Sales* 22,694,784
SIC 8699 Membership organizations, nec
Randy Ambrosie
Douglas Allison
Michael Copeland
Rob Assimakopoulos

D-U-N-S 20-291-6909 (SL)
CANADIAN MEDIA FUND
50 Wellington St E, Toronto, ON, M5E 1C8
(416) 214-4400
Emp Here 50 *Sales* 281,085,558
SIC 8399 Social services, nec
Valerie Creighton
Stephane Cardin
Sandra Collins
Alain Cousineau
Cheryl Barker
Glenn Wong
Alison Clayton
Guy Fournier
David Mclennan
Rob Scarth

D-U-N-S 24-801-4680 (SL)
CANADIAN TURNER CONSTRUCTION COMPANY LTD
(Suby of ACS, ACTIVIDADES DE CONSTRUCCION Y SERVICIOS, SA)
48 Yonge St, Toronto, ON, M5E 1G6
(416) 607-8300
Emp Here 28 *Sales* 15,969,464
SIC 1542 Nonresidential construction, nec
William Moser
Stephen M Christo
John A Diciurcio
Lars Leitner

D-U-N-S 20-986-1900 (HQ)
CHAPAIS ENERGIE, SOCIETE EN COMMANDITE
67 Yonge St Suite 810, Toronto, ON, M5E 1J8

Emp Here 2 *Sales* 16,918,578
SIC 4911 Electric services
Daryle Moffatt

D-U-N-S 24-119-5809 (HQ)
CIBC MORTGAGES INC
FIRSTLINE MORTGAGES
(Suby of CANADIAN IMPERIAL BANK OF COMMERCE)
33 Yonge St Suite 700, Toronto, ON, M5E 1G4
(416) 865-1999
Emp Here 5 *Sales* 11,237,200
SIC 6163 Loan brokers

Tim Mezik

D-U-N-S 25-520-6682 (SL)
COVINGTON CAPITAL CORPORATION
87 Front St E Suite 400, Toronto, ON, M5E 1B8
(416) 504-5419
Emp Here 15 *Sales* 11,001,780
SIC 6722 Management investment, open-end
Grant Brown
Kenneth (Chip) Vallis
Scott Clark
Jeff Park
Phil Reddon
Jim Laird
Lisa Low

D-U-N-S 20-979-7369 (SL)
CROSSWINDS INTERNET COMMUNICATIONS INC
1 Yonge St, Toronto, ON, M5E 1E5
(416) 364-2202
Emp Here 100 *Sales* 18,479,800
SIC 4813 Telephone communication, except radio
Tony Holmes

D-U-N-S 20-287-5956 (SL)
DIGITAL CONCEPT INC
1 Yonge St Suite 1801, Toronto, ON, M5E 1W7

Emp Here 37 *Sales* 16,545,438
SIC 5065 Electronic parts and equipment, nec
Fidel Douglas

D-U-N-S 24-222-7437 (SL)
DUFFERIN TRAVEL INC
TRAVEL TRUST INTERNATIONAL
35 The Esplanade Suite 200, Toronto, ON, M5E 1Z4
(416) 369-1750
Emp Here 22 *Sales* 11,439,274
SIC 4725 Tour operators
Rocky Racco
Elena Racco

D-U-N-S 24-140-9650 (BR)
EAGLE PROFESSIONAL RESOURCES INC
(Suby of EAGLE PROFESSIONAL RESOURCES INC)
67 Yonge St Suite 200, Toronto, ON, M5E 1J8
(416) 861-1492
Emp Here 100
SIC 7361 Employment agencies
Olga Grishin

D-U-N-S 24-644-3998 (SL)
ESPLANADE (TORONTO) SPAGHETTI CORP
OLD SPAGHETTI FACTORY, THE
(Suby of ESPLANADE RESTAURANTS LTD)
54 The Esplanade, Toronto, ON, M5E 1A6
(416) 864-9761
Emp Here 150 *Sales* 6,995,850
SIC 5812 Eating places
Peter Hnatiuw

D-U-N-S 20-117-2090 (SL)
FRONT STREET CAPITAL 2004
33 Yonge St Suite 600, Toronto, ON, M5E 1G4
(416) 597-9595
Emp Here 28 *Sales* 23,177,756
SIC 6722 Management investment, open-end
Gary Selke
David Conway

D-U-N-S 24-131-1765 (SL)
FRONT STREET DIVERSIFIED INCOME FUND
FRONT STREET CAPITAL
33 Yonge St Suite 600, Toronto, ON, M5E 1G4
(416) 597-9595
Emp Here 33 *Sales* 24,203,916
SIC 6722 Management investment, open-end
Gary Selke

D-U-N-S 20-300-4510 (SL)
FRONT STREET SPECIAL OPPORTUNI-

TIES CANADIAN FUND
33 Yonge St Suite 600, Toronto, ON, M5E 1G4
(416) 597-9595
Emp Here 30 *Sales* 25,250,976
SIC 6722 Management investment, open-end
John Serpa

D-U-N-S 20-648-3765 (HQ)
GLOBALIVE COMMUNICATIONS CORP
48 Yonge St Suite 1200, Toronto, ON, M5E 1G6
(416) 640-1088
Emp Here 1,200 *Sales* 274,166,400
SIC 4899 Communication services, nec
Anthony Lacavera
Simon Lockie
Brice Scheschuk

D-U-N-S 20-810-5903 (BR)
GWL REALTY ADVISORS INC
(Suby of POWER CORPORATION DU CANADA)
33 Yonge St Suite 1000, Toronto, ON, M5E 1S9
(416) 507-2929
Emp Here 100
SIC 6531 Real estate agents and managers
Heidi Labrash

D-U-N-S 24-993-4365 (SL)
HOCKEY HALL OF FAME AND MUSEUM
HHOF
30 Yonge St, Toronto, ON, M5E 1X8
(416) 360-7735
Emp Here 100 *Sales* 9,136,900
SIC 8412 Museums and art galleries
William C. Hay
Jeffery Denomme

D-U-N-S 25-998-4078 (HQ)
HOLLISWEALTH INC
(Suby of BANK OF NOVA SCOTIA, THE)
26 Wellington St E Suite 700, Toronto, ON, M5E 1S2
(416) 350-3250
Emp Here 3 *Sales* 429,838,584
SIC 6719 Holding companies, nec
Glen Gowland

D-U-N-S 20-300-4742 (SL)
HORIZONS ACTIVE CORPORATE BOND ETF
26 Wellington St E Suite 700, Toronto, ON, M5E 1S2
(416) 933-5754
Emp Here 1 *Sales* 452,430,569
SIC 6722 Management investment, open-end
Howard Atkinson
Steven Hawkins

D-U-N-S 20-300-6036 (SL)
HORIZONS ACTIVE DIVERSIFIED INCOME ETF INC
26 Wellington St E Suite 700, Toronto, ON, M5E 1S2
(416) 933-5745
Emp Here 45 *Sales* 10,542,960
SIC 8742 Management consulting services

D-U-N-S 20-300-4734 (SL)
HORIZONS ACTIVE HIGH YIELD BOND ETF
26 Wellington St E Suite 700, Toronto, ON, M5E 1S2
(416) 933-5745
Emp Here 1 *Sales* 108,856,718
SIC 6722 Management investment, open-end
Steven J. Hawkins

D-U-N-S 24-513-2006 (SL)
HOT HOUSE RESTAURANT AND BAR
35 Church St, Toronto, ON, M5E 1T3
(416) 366-7800
Emp Here 95 *Sales* 4,324,305
SIC 5812 Eating places
Andrew Laffey
Elinor Laffey

D-U-N-S 25-691-2007 (SL)

INDIA BREWERIES INC
1 Yonge St Suite 1801, Toronto, ON, M5E 1W7
(416) 214-1855
Emp Here 20 *Sales* 10,006,500
SIC 5181 Beer and ale
Peter Harvey
Steven Judge

D-U-N-S 24-664-0742 (SL)
INTERNATIONAL DATA CORPORATION (CANADA) LTD
IDC CANADA
(Suby of INTERNATIONAL DATA GROUP, INC.)
33 Yonge St Suite 420, Toronto, ON, M5E 1G4
(416) 369-0033
Emp Here 50 *Sales* 10,667,900
SIC 8732 Commercial nonphysical research
Chris Sullivan
Lorne Drennan
Vito Mabrucco

D-U-N-S 24-588-5041 (BR)
KEG RESTAURANTS LTD
KEG STEAKHOUSE & BAR, THE
(Suby of RECIPE UNLIMITED CORPORATION)
56 The Esplanade, Toronto, ON, M5E 1A7
(416) 367-0685
Emp Here 95
SIC 5812 Eating places
Angie Shelley

D-U-N-S 20-818-5843 (HQ)
LIQUOR CONTROL BOARD OF ONTARIO, THE
LCBO
(Suby of GOVERNMENT OF ONTARIO)
55 Lake Shore Blvd E Suite 876, Toronto, ON, M5E 1A4
(416) 365-5900
Emp Here 100 *Sales* 4,970,710,095
SIC 5921 Liquor stores
Bonnie Brooks
George Soleas
Rob Dutton
Nancy Cardinal
Bob Clevely
Bob Downey
Penny Wyger
Pat Ford
Michael Eubanks

D-U-N-S 24-121-0942 (BR)
LIQUOR CONTROL BOARD OF ONTARIO, THE
LCBO FINANCIAL OFFICE
(Suby of GOVERNMENT OF ONTARIO)
1 Yonge St 13th Floor, Toronto, ON, M5E 1E5
(416) 365-5778
Emp Here 85
SIC 5921 Liquor stores
Carol Lyons

D-U-N-S 24-216-5074 (SL)
MARTIN MERRY & REID LIMITED
3 Church St Suite 404, Toronto, ON, M5E 1M2
(416) 366-3333
Emp Here 25 *Sales* 14,498,100
SIC 6411 Insurance agents, brokers, and service
David Browne

D-U-N-S 24-333-1563 (BR)
METRO ONTARIO INC
METRO
(Suby of METRO INC)
80 Front St E Suite 804, Toronto, ON, M5E 1T4
(416) 703-9393
Emp Here 220
SIC 5411 Grocery stores
Frank Raso

D-U-N-S 20-181-7231 (HQ)
MGI SECURITIES INC
26 Wellington St E Suite 900, Toronto, ON,

M5E 1S2
(416) 864-6477
Emp Here 60   *Sales* 112,701,240
SIC 6211 Security brokers and dealers
 Andrea Jones
 Donald Mcfarlane
 Gordon Crawford

D-U-N-S 20-073-4502   (SL)
NEXUS PROTECTIVE SERVICES LIMITED
56 The Esplanade Suite 510, Toronto, ON,
M5E 1A7
(416) 815-7575
Emp Here 75   *Sales* 29,675,850
SIC 7381 Detective and armored car services
 John Lamb
 Fred Cozol

D-U-N-S 24-537-5720   (SL)
OGILVYONE WORLDWIDE LTD
(*Suby of* WPP PLC)
33 Yonge St Suite 1100, Toronto, ON, M5E
1X6
(416) 363-9514
Emp Here 75   *Sales* 13,987,950
SIC 8743 Public relations services
 Guy Stevenson

D-U-N-S 24-830-9551   (BR)
OLDE YORKE ESPLANADE HOTELS LTD
NOVOTEL TORONTO CENTRE HOTEL
(*Suby of* OLDE YORKE ESPLANADE HO-
TELS LTD)
45 The Esplanade, Toronto, ON, M5E 1W2
(416) 367-8900
Emp Here 80
SIC 7011 Hotels and motels
 Michael Singer

D-U-N-S 24-059-8169   (SL)
**ONTARIO ASSOCIATION OF CHILDREN'S
AID SOCIETIES**
OACAS
75 Front St E Suite 308, Toronto, ON, M5E
1V9
(416) 987-7725
Emp Here 45   *Sales* 11,265,356
SIC 8611 Business associations
 Margaret Bowman
 Rachel Daigneault
 Lisa Sarsfield
 David Rivard
 Maria Odumodu
 Dawn Flegel
 Anne-Marie Burrus
 Rachel Daigneault
 Don Mckay
 Nancy Macgillivray

D-U-N-S 25-322-9785   (HQ)
ONTARIO CLEAN WATER AGENCY
OCWA
(*Suby of* GOVERNMENT OF ONTARIO)
1 Yonge St Suite 1700, Toronto, ON, M5E 1E5
(416) 314-5600
Emp Here 100   *Sales* 131,200,052
SIC 4941 Water supply
 Elizabeth Mclaren
 Michael R. Garrett
 Art Leitch
 Juli Abouchar
 John Bergsma
 Susan Fletcher
 Allan Gunn
 Doug Lawson
 Gino Nicolini

D-U-N-S 20-293-0975   (SL)
ONTARIO RIBS INC
TONY ROMA'S
56 The Esplanade Suite 201, Toronto, ON,
M5E 1A7
(416) 864-9775
Emp Here 1   *Sales* 23,589,585
SIC 5812 Eating places
 Peter Hnatiw

D-U-N-S 20-629-5581   (SL)

OPENLANE CANADA INC
11 Church St Suite 200, Toronto, ON, M5E
1W1
(416) 861-1366
Emp Here 90   *Sales* 32,779,350
SIC 5012 Automobiles and other motor vehi-
cles
 Gary Edelstein
 Clive Kinross
 Michael Stein

D-U-N-S 24-556-3812   (HQ)
PENEQUITY REALTY CORPORATION
33 Yonge St Suite 901, Toronto, ON, M5E 1G4
(416) 408-3080
Sales 29,799,972
SIC 6722 Management investment, open-end
 David V. Johnston
 Glenn A. Miller
 Leger Xavier
 Neil Miller
 Lawrence Burke
 Stacey Lenathen

D-U-N-S 20-299-9959   (SL)
**PICTON MAHONEY LONG SHORT EQUITY
FUND**
33 Yonge St Suite 830, Toronto, ON, M5E 1G4
(416) 955-4108
Emp Here 49   *Sales* 40,561,073
SIC 6722 Management investment, open-end
 Dave Picton

D-U-N-S 20-213-3658   (HQ)
REDPATH SUGAR LTD
(*Suby of* FANJUL CORP.)
95 Queens Quay E, Toronto, ON, M5E 1A3
(416) 366-3561
Emp Here 350   *Sales* 219,323,250
SIC 2061 Raw cane sugar

D-U-N-S 20-300-1391   (SL)
RETURN ON INNOVATION ADVISORS LTD
43 Front St E Suite 301, Toronto, ON, M5E
1B3
(416) 361-6162
Emp Here 33   *Sales* 24,484,244
SIC 6722 Management investment, open-end
 Joe Dasilca

D-U-N-S 20-352-3659   (SL)
ROYAL LEGAL SOLUTIONS P.C. INC
1 Yonge St Suite 1801, Toronto, ON, M5E 1W7

Emp Here 490   *Sales* 55,245,982
SIC 8111 Legal services
 Ahmed Ali

D-U-N-S 25-174-0080   (HQ)
SHOPSY'S HOSPITALITY INC
SHOPSY'S DELI
33 Yonge St, Toronto, ON, M5E 1G4
(905) 474-3333
Emp Here 4   *Sales* 11,659,750
SIC 5812 Eating places
 Mark Weber

D-U-N-S 24-767-2160   (SL)
**SOUTH AMERICAN GOLD AND COPPER
COMPANY LIMITED**
67 Yonge St Suite 1201, Toronto, ON, M5E
1J8
(416) 369-9115
Emp Here 49   *Sales* 10,002,370
SIC 1081 Metal mining services
 Stephen Houghton

D-U-N-S 20-772-3008   (SL)
ST LAWRENCE CENTRE FOR THE ARTS
27 Front St E, Toronto, ON, M5E 1B4
(416) 366-7723
Emp Here 249   *Sales* 33,783,573
SIC 6512 Nonresidential building operators
 Clyde Wagner
 Mary Ellen Heiman
 Richard Carter
 Raymond Hallett
 Nathan Gilbert

D-U-N-S 24-209-6782   (HQ)
STREET CAPITAL GROUP INC
STREET CAPITAL BANK OF CANADA
1 Yonge St Suite 2401, Toronto, ON, M5E 1E5
(647) 259-7873
Emp Here 115   *Sales* 98,140,094
SIC 6719 Holding companies, nec
 Duncan Hannay
 Lea Ray
 Marissa Lauder
 Gary Taylor
 Greg Parker
 R. Adam Levy
 Alfonso Casciato
 Ronald Appleby
 Tom Bermingham
 W. Ed Gettings

D-U-N-S 24-082-8012   (HQ)
T.E. FINANCIAL CONSULTANTS LTD
T.E. WEALTH
26 Wellington St E Suite 800, Toronto, ON,
M5E 1S2
(416) 366-1451
Emp Here 46   *Sales* 149,429,490
SIC 6282 Investment advice
 Timothy Egan
 Mark Arthur
 Gerry Deboer
 Steven Belchetz

D-U-N-S 20-305-2006   (SL)
**THEREDPIN.COM REALTY INC., BROKER-
AGE**
RED PIN, THE
5 Church St, Toronto, ON, M5E 1M2
(416) 800-0812
Emp Here 40   *Sales* 13,085,080
SIC 6531 Real estate agents and managers
 Matthew Eric Lem

D-U-N-S 24-097-4634   (HQ)
TORONTO STAR NEWSPAPERS LIMITED
TORONTO STAR
(*Suby of* TORSTAR CORPORATION)
1 Yonge St Suite 400, Toronto, ON, M5E 1E6
(416) 869-4000
Emp Here 1,122   *Sales* 304,225,180
SIC 2711 Newspapers
 Jagoda Pike
 Frederic Karen
 Peter Bishop

D-U-N-S 20-177-1417   (HQ)
TORSTAR CORPORATION
1 Yonge St, Toronto, ON, M5E 1E5
(416) 869-4010
Emp Here 20   *Sales* 594,886,180
SIC 2752 Commercial printing, lithographic
 John Boynton
 Lorenzo Demarchi
 Marie E. Beyette
 Jennifer Barber
 Ian Oliver
 Neil Oliver
 John A. Honderich
 Daryl Aitken
 Elaine B. Berger
 Campbell R. Harvey

D-U-N-S 20-346-5976   (SL)
**TRANSCRIPT HEROES TRANSCRIPTION
SERVICES INC**
1 Yonge St Suite 1801, Toronto, ON, M5E 1W7
(647) 478-5188
Emp Here 30   *Sales* 13,458,794
SIC 7389 Business services, nec
 Andrew Dodson

D-U-N-S 20-114-1244   (BR)
TRAVELBRANDS INC
HOLIDAY NETWORK, THE
(*Suby of* RED LABEL HOLDINGS INC)
26 Wellington St E, Toronto, ON, M5E 1S2
(416) 364-5100
Emp Here 500
SIC 4725 Tour operators

Reza Aumeeruddy

D-U-N-S 24-522-5185   (HQ)
UNIT PARK MANAGEMENT INC
1 Yonge St Suite 1510, Toronto, ON, M5E 1E5
(416) 366-7275
Emp Here 1   *Sales* 67,529,550
SIC 7521 Automobile parking
 Peter Meramveliotakis

D-U-N-S 25-306-7888   (SL)
UNITED WAY OF GREATER TORONTO
*UNITED WAY TORONTO AND YORK RE-
GION*
26 Wellington St E Fl 12, Toronto, ON, M5E
1S2
(416) 777-2001
Emp Here 200   *Sales* 287,720,200
SIC 8699 Membership organizations, nec
 Daniele Zanotti
 Louise Bellingham
 Julia Gorman
 Michael Herrera
 Rahima Mamdani
 Amy Tong

D-U-N-S 24-369-5363   (HQ)
**VERTICA AU SERVICE DES RESIDENTS
INC**
(*Suby of* POWER CORPORATION DU
CANADA)
33 Yonge St Suite 1000, Toronto, ON, M5E
1S9
(416) 507-2929
Emp Here 1   *Sales* 67,612,800
SIC 6531 Real estate agents and managers
 W. Paul Finkbeiner
 Anne S. Morash
 Tanyss M.I. Price
 Robert Siddal
 Ralf B. Dost
 Todd Spencer

D-U-N-S 20-271-8409   (SL)
VIP SITTERS INC
PETRELOCATE
22 Leader Lane Suite 540, Toronto, ON, M5E
0B2
(416) 999-6666
Emp Here 92   *Sales* 13,791,568
SIC 4212 Local trucking, without storage
 Kyle Freeman
 Vincent Freeman

D-U-N-S 20-652-1838   (SL)
WESTERN ASSURANCE COMPANY
10 Wellington St E, Toronto, ON, M5E 1C5
(416) 366-7511
Emp Here 50   *Sales* 28,996,200
SIC 6411 Insurance agents, brokers, and ser-
vice
 Shawn Desantis

D-U-N-S 25-998-0894   (HQ)
WORKOPOLIS INC
WORKOPOLIS.COM
1 Yonge St Suite 402, Toronto, ON, M5E 1E6
(416) 957-8300
Emp Here 200   *Sales* 16,432,680
SIC 7361 Employment agencies
 Chris Goodridge
 Lorenzo Demarchi
 Patrick Buchholz
 Patrick Clouatre

D-U-N-S 20-285-6753   (BR)
**WPP GROUP CANADA COMMUNICATIONS
LIMITED**
OGILVY CANADA
(*Suby of* WPP PLC)
33 Yonge St, Toronto, ON, M5E 1X6
(416) 367-3573
Emp Here 80
SIC 7311 Advertising agencies
 Laurie Young

D-U-N-S 25-191-0360   (BR)
WPP GROUP CANADA COMMUNICATIONS

LIMITED
OGILVY & ACTION DIV
(*Suby of* WPP PLC)
33 Yonge St Suite 1100, Toronto, ON, M5E
1X6
(416) 367-3573
Emp Here 236
SIC 7311 Advertising agencies

D-U-N-S 25-193-0491   (SL)
YAK COMMUNICATIONS INC
(*Suby of* GLOBALIVE COMMUNICATIONS
CORP)
48 Yonge St Suite 1202, Toronto, ON, M5E
1G6
(800) 490-7235
Emp Here 151   *Sales* 34,499,272
SIC 4899 Communication services, nec
Anthony Lacavera

Toronto, ON M5G

D-U-N-S 24-167-3347   (SL)
678925 ONTARIO INC
S B R GLOBAL
14 College St, Toronto, ON, M5G 1K2
(416) 962-7500
Emp Here 50   *Sales* 14,164,650
SIC 8741 Management services
Stevan Ralth

D-U-N-S 24-204-7152   (HQ)
AMEC FOSTER WHEELER NCL LIMITED
AMEC
(*Suby of* JOHN WOOD GROUP P.L.C.)
700 University Ave Suite 200, Toronto, ON,
M5G 1X6
(416) 592-2102
Emp Here 308   *Sales* 155,969,920
SIC 8999 Services, nec
James P Rippon
Charles Caza
Charles Mountain

D-U-N-S 20-787-0064   (HQ)
ARTHRITIS SOCIETY, THE
393 University Ave Suite 1700, Toronto, ON,
M5G 1E6
(416) 979-7228
Emp Here 55   *Sales* 73,219,440
SIC 7389 Business services, nec
Janet Yale
Ronald Smith

D-U-N-S 25-101-6812   (HQ)
B2B BANK
B2B
(*Suby of* BANQUE LAURENTIENNE DU
CANADA)
199 Bay St Suite 600, Toronto, ON, M5G 1M5
(647) 826-7979
Emp Here 100   *Sales* 27,364,866
SIC 6021 National commercial banks
Francois Desjardin
Deborah Rose
Michel C. Trudeau
Stephane Therrien
Francois Laurin
Eva Stamadianos

D-U-N-S 24-422-7450   (SL)
B2B BANK FINANCIAL SERVICES INC
B2B BANK DEALER SERVICES
(*Suby of* BANQUE LAURENTIENNE DU
CANADA)
199 Bay St Suite 610, Toronto, ON, M5G 1M5
(416) 926-0221
Emp Here 335   *Sales* 476,751,230
SIC 6282 Investment advice
Deborah Rose
Francois Desjardins
Diane Lafresnaye
Theodore Ikonomou

D-U-N-S 20-292-7810   (SL)
BAYVIEW HOSPITALITY INC
*DOUBLETREE BY HILTON TORONTO
DOWNTOWN*
108 Chestnut St, Toronto, ON, M5G 1R3
(416) 977-5000
Emp Here 250   *Sales* 23,917,000
SIC 7011 Hotels and motels
Alnoor Gulamani

D-U-N-S 20-943-0321   (SL)
BELL, TEMPLE
393 University Ave Suite 1300, Toronto, ON,
M5G 1E6
(416) 581-8200
Emp Here 98   *Sales* 10,866,436
SIC 8111 Legal services
Cameron C.R. Godden
Donald G. Cormack
David A. Tompkins
Brian E. Lucas
Hugh G. Brown
Lisa E. Hamilton
Frank J. Kosturik
Andrew K. Lee
Joseph A Baldanza
Katherine E Kolnhofer

D-U-N-S 20-291-8962   (BR)
BRUCE POWER L.P.
(*Suby of* BRUCE POWER L.P.)
700 University Ave Suite 200, Toronto, ON,
M5G 1X6
(519) 361-2673
Emp Here 3,700
SIC 4911 Electric services
Cheryl Cottrill

D-U-N-S 20-812-1017   (SL)
BT LAW LIMITED PARTNERSHIP
393 University Ave Suite 1300, Toronto, ON,
M5G 1E6
(416) 581-8200
Emp Here 50   *Sales* 13,716,600
SIC 8741 Management services
Rose Devoe

D-U-N-S 20-524-5210   (HQ)
**CANADA LIFE ASSURANCE COMPANY,
THE**
(*Suby of* POWER CORPORATION DU
CANADA)
330 University Ave Suite 2, Toronto, ON, M5G
1R8
(416) 597-1440
Emp Here 50   *Sales* 10,575,372,546
SIC 6311 Life insurance
R. Jeffrey Orr
Paul A. Mahon
Laurie A. Speers
Paul (Jr.) Desmarais
Andre Desmarais
Marcel R. Coutu
Chaviva M. Hosek
Henri-Paul Rousseau
Brian E. Walsh
Gregory D. Tretiak

D-U-N-S 25-996-5226   (HQ)
CANADA LIFE FINANCIAL CORPORATION
(*Suby of* POWER CORPORATION DU
CANADA)
330 University Ave, Toronto, ON, M5G 1R7
(416) 597-1440
Emp Here 20   *Sales* 2,697,051,000
SIC 6351 Surety insurance
D. Allen Loney
William W. Lovatt
Laurie A. Speers
Raymond Mcfeetors
Marcel Coutu
Andre Desmarais
Paul Desmarais, Jr
H. David Graves
Michael L. Hepher
Chaviva M. Hosek

D-U-N-S 20-984-0891   (SL)
CANADA LIFE MORTGAGE SERVICES LTD
(*Suby of* POWER CORPORATION DU
CANADA)
330 University Ave, Toronto, ON, M5G 1R8
(416) 597-6981
Emp Here 50   *Sales* 11,237,200
SIC 6163 Loan brokers
Peter G. Munro
Harvey A. Andres
Anthony G. Reznik

D-U-N-S 24-336-5988   (HQ)
**CANADIAN EXECUTIVE SERVICE ORGA-
NIZATION**
CESO
700 Bay St Suite 800, Toronto, ON, M5G 1Z6
(416) 961-2376
Emp Here 21   *Sales* 35,460,600
SIC 8699 Membership organizations, nec
Wendy Harris
Scott Wetmore
Lou Naumovski
David Ross
Hope Sanderson
Skirrow Christopher
Whyte Laureen
Martine Normand
Glen Nolan
Robert Noble

D-U-N-S 20-291-0928   (SL)
CANADIAN NUCLEAR SOCIETY
655 Bay St, Toronto, ON, M5G 2K4
(416) 977-7620
Emp Here 26   *Sales* 11,039,782
SIC 8999 Services, nec
Adriaan Buijs
David Novog
Dorin Nichita
Jadranka Popovic
Duane Pendergast
Ed Hinchley
Eric Williams
Frank Doyle
Jeremy Whitlock
Jim Harvie

D-U-N-S 24-365-7665   (HQ)
CANCER CARE ONTARIO
620 University Ave Suite 1500, Toronto, ON,
M5G 2L7
(416) 971-9800
Sales 1,398,278,757
SIC 8733 Noncommercial research organiza-
tions
Michael Sherar
Elizabeth Carson
Jason Garey
Rebecca Harvey
Paula Knight
Garth Mattheson
Robin Mcleod
Linda Rabeneck
Etham Roushani
Ratan Ralliaram

D-U-N-S 24-425-4178   (SL)
CLEARESULT CANADA INC
(*Suby of* CLEARESULT CONSULTING INC.)
393 University Ave Suite 1622, Toronto, ON,
M5G 1E6
(416) 504-3400
Emp Here 115   *Sales* 20,554,985
SIC 8711 Engineering services
Ryan Shaw

D-U-N-S 20-943-2376   (SL)
**COLLEGE OF PHYSICIANS AND SUR-
GEONS OF ONTARIO**
80 College St, Toronto, ON, M5G 2E2
(416) 967-2600
Emp Here 250   *Sales* 58,527,750
SIC 8621 Professional organizations
James Wright
Rayudu Koka

Clark Mcintosh
Douglas Anderson

D-U-N-S 25-311-9812   (BR)
**COMPAGNIE D'ASSURANCE BELAIR INC,
LA**
BELAIR DIRECT
(*Suby of* INTACT FINANCIAL CORPORA-
TION)
700 University Ave Suite 1100, Toronto, ON,
M5G 0A2
(416) 250-6363
Emp Here 300
SIC 6331 Fire, marine, and casualty insurance
Melanie Muise

D-U-N-S 25-069-5855   (HQ)
COU HOLDING ASSOCIATION INC
THE COUNCIL OF ONTARIO UNIVERSITIES
180 Dundas St W Suite 1100, Toronto, ON,
M5G 1Z8
(416) 979-2165
Emp Here 35   *Sales* 16,906,050
SIC 8621 Professional organizations
Ian Clark
Silvia Reesor

D-U-N-S 24-322-0428   (HQ)
CROWN PROPERTY MANAGEMENT INC
(*Suby of* CROWN REALTY PARTNERS)
400 University Ave Suite 1900, Toronto, ON,
M5G 1S5
(416) 927-1851
Emp Here 8   *Sales* 25,133,340
SIC 6531 Real estate agents and managers
Stephan Von Buttlar
Gary Samuel
Alan Rowe
Les Miller
Harvey Barth
Brian Johnson
Michael Pittana

D-U-N-S 20-880-8105   (HQ)
DIABETES CANADA
522 University Ave Suite 1400, Toronto, ON,
M5G 2R5
(416) 363-3373
Emp Here 150   *Sales* 37,028,696
SIC 8699 Membership organizations, nec
Jan Hux
Anna Kennedy
John Reidy

D-U-N-S 20-967-6597   (HQ)
ECHO POWER GENERATION INC
777 Bay St Suite 1910, Toronto, ON, M5G 2C8
(416) 364-6513
Emp Here 1   *Sales* 14,412,122
SIC 4911 Electric services
Joseph Fuda

D-U-N-S 25-338-2840   (SL)
EPSTEIN COLE LLP
393 University Ave Suite 2200, Toronto, ON,
M5G 1E6
(416) 862-9888
Emp Here 68   *Sales* 10,472,748
SIC 8111 Legal services
Richard Greene
Philip Epstein
Kenneth Cole

D-U-N-S 24-976-6429   (SL)
**EXPORT-IMPORT TRADE CENTRE OF
CANADA AND U.S.A. LIMITED**
EXIMCAN CANADA
481 University Ave Unit 301, Toronto, ON,
M5G 2E9
(416) 979-7967
Emp Here 20   *Sales* 10,702,480
SIC 5141 Groceries, general line
Haresh Mehta
Mike Mehta

D-U-N-S 20-858-5901   (SL)
FACILITY ASSOCIATION
777 Bay St Suite 2400, Toronto, ON, M5G 2C8

---

(416) 863-1750
Emp Here 36   *Sales* 66,479,724
SIC 6331 Fire, marine, and casualty insurance
David Simpson
Robert Tistale

D-U-N-S 20-652-4691   (BR)
FETHERSTONHAUGH & CO.
BIGGAR
(*Suby of* FETHERSTONHAUGH & CO.)
438 University Ave Suite 1500, Toronto, ON,
M5G 2K8
(416) 598-4209
Emp Here 85
SIC 8111 Legal services
Mark Evans

D-U-N-S 20-259-5054   (SL)
FIDELITY CLEARING CANADA ULC
483 Bay St Suite 300, Toronto, ON, M5G 2N7
(416) 307-5200
Emp Here 49   *Sales* 35,939,148
SIC 6722 Management investment, open-end
Edward Johnson

D-U-N-S 20-284-7679   (SL)
FIDELITY CLEARING CANADA ULC
483 Bay St, Toronto, ON, M5G 2N7
(416) 216-6357
Emp Here 140   *Sales* 199,239,320
SIC 6211 Security brokers and dealers
Tisha Lawton
Lawrence Mccann
Stephen Cosburn
Ronald White
Bryan Moffitt
Scott Mackenzie

D-U-N-S 24-721-2046   (HQ)
FIDELITY INVESTMENTS CANADA ULC
(*Suby of* FMR LLC)
483 Bay St Suite 200, Toronto, ON, M5G 2N7
(416) 307-5200
Emp Here 600   *Sales* 4,541,127,650
SIC 6722 Management investment, open-end
Robert Strickland

D-U-N-S 20-300-5475   (SL)
**FIDELITY RSP GLOBAL OPPORTUNITES
FUND**
FIDELITY INVESTMENTS CANADA ULC
483 Bay St Suite 300, Toronto, ON, M5G 2N7
(416) 307-5200
Emp Here 49   *Sales* 41,030,848
SIC 6722 Management investment, open-end
Rob Strickland

D-U-N-S 20-369-4372   (BR)
**GOVERNING COUNCIL OF THE UNIVER-
SITY OF TORONTO, THE**
DEPARTMENT OF PAEDIATRICS
(*Suby of* GOVERNING COUNCIL OF THE
UNIVERSITY OF TORONTO, THE)
555 University Ave Rm 1436d, Toronto, ON,
M5G 1X8
(416) 813-6122
Emp Here 263
SIC 8221 Colleges and universities
Ronald D. Cohn

D-U-N-S 25-362-0363   (BR)
**GOVERNING COUNCIL OF THE UNIVER-
SITY OF TORONTO, THE**
REHABILITATION SCIENCES INSTITUTE
(*Suby of* GOVERNING COUNCIL OF THE
UNIVERSITY OF TORONTO, THE)
500 University Ave Suite 160, Toronto, ON,
M5G 1V7
(416) 946-8554
Emp Here 120
SIC 8221 Colleges and universities
Angela Colantonio

D-U-N-S 25-079-2140   (BR)
**GOVERNING COUNCIL OF THE UNIVER-
SITY OF TORONTO, THE**
FACULTY OF DENTISTRY
(*Suby of* GOVERNING COUNCIL OF THE

UNIVERSITY OF TORONTO, THE)
124 Edward St, Toronto, ON, M5G 1G6
(416) 979-4927
Emp Here 304
SIC 8221 Colleges and universities
David Mock

D-U-N-S 20-911-3005   (BR)
**GOVERNING COUNCIL OF THE UNIVER-
SITY OF TORONTO, THE**
DEPARTMENT OF MEDICINE
(*Suby of* GOVERNING COUNCIL OF THE
UNIVERSITY OF TORONTO, THE)
190 Elizabeth St, Toronto, ON, M5G 2C4
(416) 978-8383
Emp Here 500
SIC 8221 Colleges and universities
Gillian Hawker

D-U-N-S 20-297-1045   (BR)
**GOVERNING COUNCIL OF THE UNIVER-
SITY OF TORONTO, THE**
*DEPARTMENT OF LABORATORY MEDICINE
& PATHOBIOLOGY*
(*Suby of* GOVERNING COUNCIL OF THE
UNIVERSITY OF TORONTO, THE)
100 College St Rm 110, Toronto, ON, M5G
1L5
(416) 978-4059
Emp Here 393
SIC 8221 Colleges and universities
Rita Kandel

D-U-N-S 24-120-2220   (BR)
**GOVERNING COUNCIL OF THE UNIVER-
SITY OF TORONTO, THE**
*DEPARTMENT OF OBSTETRICS AND GY-
NAECOLOGY*
(*Suby of* GOVERNING COUNCIL OF THE
UNIVERSITY OF TORONTO, THE)
123 Edward St Suite 1200, Toronto, ON, M5G
1E2
(416) 978-2668
Emp Here 285
SIC 8221 Colleges and universities
John Kingdom

D-U-N-S 24-174-9501   (BR)
**GOVERNING COUNCIL OF THE UNIVER-
SITY OF TORONTO, THE**
*GOVERNING COUNCIL OF THE UNIVER-
SITY OF TORONTO*
(*Suby of* GOVERNING COUNCIL OF THE
UNIVERSITY OF TORONTO, THE)
101 College St Rm 15-701, Toronto, ON, M5G
1L7
(416) 634-8755
Emp Here 119
SIC 8221 Colleges and universities
Thomas Kislinger

D-U-N-S 25-530-8835   (SL)
GRAYMATTER DIRECT (CANADA) INC
BOXPILOT
600 Bay St Suite 400, Toronto, ON, M5G 1M6
(416) 341-0623
Emp Here 30   *Sales* 13,304,700
SIC 7389 Business services, nec
Mika Kaitila
Koray Parmaks

D-U-N-S 20-918-8676   (BR)
**GREAT-WEST LIFE ASSURANCE COM-
PANY, THE**
(*Suby of* POWER CORPORATION DU
CANADA)
330 University Ave Suite 400, Toronto, ON,
M5G 1R7
(416) 552-5050
Emp Here 100
SIC 6311 Life insurance
Allen Loney

D-U-N-S 25-099-9166   (HQ)
GUYANA GOLDFIELDS INC
375 University Av Suite 802, Toronto, ON,
M5G 2J5

(416) 628-5936
Emp Here 13   *Sales* 187,890,000
SIC 1041 Gold ores
Scott Caldwell
Suresh Kalathil
Ron Stewart
Perry Holloway
Jacqueline Wagenaar
Forbes Gemmell
Christopher Stackhouse
Lisa Zangari
Rohit Tellis
Rene Marion

D-U-N-S 24-979-7655   (HQ)
GWL REALTY ADVISORS INC
*RICH IN TRADITION, FOCUSED ON THE
FUTURE*
(*Suby of* POWER CORPORATION DU
CANADA)
330 University Ave Suite 300, Toronto, ON,
M5G 1R7
(416) 552-5959
Emp Here 250   *Sales* 618,388,000
SIC 6282 Investment advice
Brian R. Allison
W. Paul Finkbeiner
Robert G. Siddall
Robert J. Ritchie
Ruth Ann Mcconkey
Helen Kasdorf

D-U-N-S 20-547-8766   (HQ)
H&M HENNES & MAURITZ INC
(*Suby of* RAMSBURY INVEST AB)
1 Dundas St W Suite 1808, Toronto, ON, M5G
1Z3
(416) 623-4300
Emp Here 30   *Sales* 249,510,000
SIC 5651 Family clothing stores
Karl-Johan Persson
Stefan Persson
Chelsia Wharton
Jyrki Peter Tervonen
Helena Helmersson
Toni Galli

D-U-N-S 24-124-9213   (SL)
**HOSPITAL FOR SICK CHILDREN FOUNDA-
TION INC, THE**
SICK KIDS FOUNDATION
525 University Ave 14th Fl, Toronto, ON, M5G
2L3
(416) 813-5320
Emp Here 150   *Sales* 215,790,150
SIC 8699 Membership organizations, nec
Ted Garrard
David Estok
Heather Broll
Adrian Horwood
Rosalie Mcgovern
Grant Stirling
Robin Cardozo
John Francis
Christian Lassonde
Kathleen Taylor

D-U-N-S 20-851-1808   (HQ)
HOSPITAL FOR SICK CHILDREN, THE
SICK KIDS HOSPITAL
555 University Ave, Toronto, ON, M5G 1X8
(416) 813-1500
Emp Here 6,700   *Sales* 725,662,823
SIC 8069 Specialty hospitals, except psychi-
atric
Ronald Cohn
Megan Evans
Karen Kinnear
Laurie Harrison
Jeff Mainland
Susan O'dowd

D-U-N-S 20-565-6999   (HQ)
HOSPITAL LOGISTICS INC
PLEXXUS LOGISTICS
1 Dundas St W Suite 1700, Toronto, ON, M5G
1Z3

(416) 673-5600
Emp Here 50   *Sales* 22,358,700
SIC 5047 Medical and hospital equipment
David Yundt
Mary Byczok
Andrea Englert-Rygus
Pedro Gomes
Paul Holland
Connie Curtis
Lorena Ferino
Bruce Bond
Mike Nader
Brian Gabel

D-U-N-S 20-832-1104   (SL)
HUB INTERNATIONAL HKMB LIMITED
(*Suby of* HELLMAN & FRIEDMAN LLC)
595 Bay St Suite 900, Toronto, ON, M5G 2E3
(416) 597-0008
Emp Here 235   *Sales* 1,115,334,440
SIC 6411 Insurance agents, brokers, and ser-
vice
Robert Keilty

D-U-N-S 25-528-9282   (HQ)
HYDRO ONE INC
(*Suby of* HYDRO ONE LIMITED)
483 Bay St Suite 1000, Toronto, ON, M5G 2P5
(416) 345-5000
Emp Here 3,000   *Sales* 4,659,337,719
SIC 4911 Electric services
Mayo Schmidt
David Denison
Gregory Kiraly
Judy Mckellar
Paul Dobson
Patrick Meneley
Ferio Pugliese
James Scarlett
Chris Lopez
Gale Rubenstein

D-U-N-S 20-343-6142   (HQ)
HYDRO ONE LIMITED
483 Bay St 8th Fl South Tower, Toronto, ON,
M5G 2P5
(416) 345-5000
Emp Here 20   *Sales* 4,662,327,300
SIC 4911 Electric services
Mark Poweska
Saylor Millitz-Lee
Brad Bowness
Chris Lopez
Darlene Bradley
Jason Fitzsimmons
Tom Woods
Cherie Brant
Blair Cowper-Smith
Anne Giardini

D-U-N-S 25-094-5458   (HQ)
HYDRO ONE NETWORKS INC
(*Suby of* HYDRO ONE LIMITED)
483 Bay St Suite 1000, Toronto, ON, M5G 2P5
(416) 345-5000
Emp Here 500   *Sales* 2,697,060,158
SIC 4911 Electric services
Paul Dobson

D-U-N-S 20-179-6500   (HQ)
HYDRO ONE REMOTE COMMUNITIES INC
(*Suby of* HYDRO ONE LIMITED)
483 Bay St Suite 1000, Toronto, ON, M5G 2P5

Emp Here 3   *Sales* 28,197,630
SIC 4911 Electric services
Myles Darcey
Laura Formusa
Peter Gregg
Maureen Wareham

D-U-N-S 20-264-3110   (SL)
**IA CLARINGTON GLOBAL TACTICAL IN-
COME FUND INC**
522 University Ave Suite 700, Toronto, ON,
M5G 1Y7
(416) 860-9880
Emp Here 49   *Sales* 41,030,848

SIC 6722 Management investment, open-end
Carl Mustos

D-U-N-S 24-130-1725   (SL)
IA CLARINGTON INVESTMENTS INC
522 University Ave Unit 700, Toronto, ON,
M5G 1W7
(416) 860-9880
Emp Here 119   *Sales* 175,413,259
SIC 6722 Management investment, open-end
Yvon Charest

D-U-N-S 24-131-3811   (HQ)
IA CLARINGTON INVESTMENTS INC
JOVFINANCIAL
(*Suby of* INDUSTRIELLE ALLIANCE, AS-
SURANCE ET SERVICES FINANCIERS INC)
522 University Ave Suite 700, Toronto, ON,
M5G 1W7
(416) 860-9880
Emp Here 80   *Sales* 75,134,160
SIC 6282 Investment advice
Normand Pepin
Carl Mustos
Yvon Charest
Amelie Cantin
Theresa Currie
Andre Dubuc
Lisa Pankratz
Gerald Bouwers

D-U-N-S 24-131-0775   (SL)
IA CLERINGTON INVESTMENTS INC
522 University Ave Suite 700, Toronto, ON,
M5G 1W7
(416) 860-9880
Emp Here 200   *Sales* 294,812,200
SIC 6722 Management investment, open-end
Carl Muspos

D-U-N-S 20-290-8591   (SL)
INNOVATION INSTITUTE OF ONTARIO
IIO
101 College St Suite HI20, Toronto, ON, M5G
1L7

Emp Here 80   *Sales* 14,920,480
SIC 8742 Management consulting services
Kenneth Knox
Janet Faas
Nicole Westwood
Nancy Hanley

D-U-N-S 25-804-4940   (SL)
INSTITUTE FOR WORK & HEALTH
481 University Ave Suite 800, Toronto, ON,
M5G 2E9
(416) 927-2027
Emp Here 88   *Sales* 11,744,392
SIC 8399 Social services, nec
Cameron Mustard
Mary Cicinelli

D-U-N-S 20-820-6482   (HQ)
INSURANCE BUREAU OF CANADA
INSURANCE INFORMATION DIVISION
777 Bay St Suite 2400, Toronto, ON, M5G 2C8
(416) 362-2031
Emp Here 35   *Sales* 186,491,100
SIC 6411 Insurance agents, brokers, and ser-
vice
Don Forgeron
David Mcgown
Sally Turney
Kim Donaldson
Craig Stewart
Bill Adams
Amanda Dean
Johanne Lamanque
Aaron Sutherland
Kenn Lalonde

D-U-N-S 24-902-5461   (HQ)
INTACT FINANCIAL CORPORATION
700 University Ave Suite 1500, Toronto, ON,
M5G 0A1
(416) 341-1464
Emp Here 3,000   *Sales* 8,025,267,772

SIC 6331 Fire, marine, and casualty insurance
Charles Brindamour
Jean-Francois Blais
Louis Gagnon
Mark Tullis
Don Fox
Patrick Barbeau
Martin Beaulieu
Alan Blair
Sonya Cote
Frederick Cotnoir

D-U-N-S 20-771-6473   (HQ)
INTACT INSURANCE COMPANY
(*Suby of* INTACT FINANCIAL CORPORA-
TION)
700 University Ave Suite 1500, Toronto, ON,
M5G 0A1
(416) 341-1464
Emp Here 200   *Sales* 7,693,084,800
SIC 6331 Fire, marine, and casualty insurance
Charles Brindamour
Louis Gagnon
Francoise Guenette
Yves Brouillette
Stephen G Snyder
Marcel Cote
Eileen Mercier
Timothy H Penner
Louise Roy
Claude Dussault

D-U-N-S 20-124-7579   (SL)
INTACT INVESTMENT MANAGEMENT, INC
(*Suby of* INTACT FINANCIAL CORPORA-
TION)
700 University Ave Suite 1500, Toronto, ON,
M5G 0A1
(416) 341-1464
Emp Here 17   *Sales* 11,541,691
SIC 6282 Investment advice
Marc Provost
Charles Brindamour
Mark Tullis

D-U-N-S 24-931-2661   (HQ)
ITAFOS
1 Dundas St W Suite 2500, Toronto, ON, M5G
1Z3
(416) 367-2200
Emp Here 8   *Sales* 109,886,994
SIC 1475 Phosphate rock
Brian Zatarain
Brent De Jong
Evgenij Iorich
Mhamed Ibnabdeljalil
G. David Delaney
Ron Wilkinson
Anthony Cina
George Burdette

D-U-N-S 24-625-1896   (HQ)
KIDS HELP PHONE
439 University Ave Suite 300, Toronto, ON,
M5G 1Y8
(416) 586-5437
Emp Here 150   *Sales* 15,358,400
SIC 8322 Individual and family services
Katherine Hay
Susan Morris
Hatty Reisman

D-U-N-S 20-120-9546   (SL)
KINECTRICS NSS INC
KINECTRICS
393 University Ave 4th Flr, Toronto, ON, M5G
1E6
(416) 592-7000
Emp Here 500   *Sales* 112,763,500
SIC 8999 Services, nec
David Harris

D-U-N-S 25-197-3228   (HQ)
LEGAL AID ONTARIO
Legal Aid Ontario, Toronto, ON, M5G 2H1
(416) 979-1446
Emp Here 750   *Sales* 154,407,000

SIC 8111 Legal services
Bob Ward
John Mccamus

D-U-N-S 24-477-0590   (HQ)
LMS PROLINK LTD
480 University Ave Suite 800, Toronto, ON,
M5G 1V2
(416) 595-7484
Emp Here 30   *Sales* 31,378,220
SIC 6411 Insurance agents, brokers, and ser-
vice
Joseph Mccabe
Wolf K Leue
Walter Skomra
Virginia Mavroudi

D-U-N-S 25-537-1916   (SL)
**LUMINEX MOLECULAR DIAGNOSTICS,
INC**
(*Suby of* LUMINEX CORPORATION)
439 University Ave Suite 900, Toronto, ON,
M5G 1Y8
(416) 593-4323
Emp Here 90   *Sales* 48,181,680
SIC 5047 Medical and hospital equipment
Patrick J. Balthrop Sr
Jeremy Bridge-Cook

D-U-N-S 24-334-1547   (SL)
LUNENFELD RESEARCH INSTITUTE
600 University Ave Rm 850, Toronto, ON, M5G
1X5
(416) 586-8811
Emp Here 49   *Sales* 13,952,603
SIC 8733 Noncommercial research organizations
James Woodgett

D-U-N-S 24-926-4813   (BR)
**LUXURY HOTELS INTERNATIONAL OF
CANADA ULC**
*LUXURY HOTELS INTERNATIONAL OF
CANADA, ULC*
(*Suby of* MARRIOTT INTERNATIONAL, INC.)
525 Bay St, Toronto, ON, M5G 2L2
(416) 597-9200
Emp Here 350
SIC 7011 Hotels and motels
George Camalier

D-U-N-S 20-647-1901   (SL)
MD FINANCIAL MANAGEMENT LIMITED
MD FUNDS MANAGEMENT LIMITED
522 University Ave Suite 1100, Toronto, ON,
M5G 1W7
(416) 598-1442
Emp Here 49   *Sales* 11,792,161
SIC 8742 Management consulting services
Gordon Krupa

D-U-N-S 20-771-9378   (HQ)
MEDIA BUYING SERVICES ULC
1 Dundas St W Suite 2800, Toronto, ON, M5G
1Z3
(416) 961-1255
Emp Here 50   *Sales* 21,172,400
SIC 7319 Advertising, nec
David Campbell
Marilyn Dixon

D-U-N-S 24-385-9605   (HQ)
MEDIACOM CANADA
(*Suby of* WPP PLC)
1 Dundas St W Suite 2800, Toronto, ON, M5G
1Z3
(416) 342-6500
Sales 30,055,650
SIC 7319 Advertising, nec
Stephen Allan
Christine Fang

D-U-N-S 24-860-9299   (SL)
MITCHELL SANDHAM INC
MITCHELL SANDHAM PASTOR DIV
438 University Ave Suite 2000, Toronto, ON,
M5G 2K8
(416) 862-1750
Emp Here 1   *Sales* 21,457,188

SIC 6411 Insurance agents, brokers, and ser-
vice
Peter Mitchell
Norman Sandham

D-U-N-S 20-628-8057   (SL)
**NATIVE CHILD AND FAMILY SERVICES OF
TORONTO**
30 College St, Toronto, ON, M5G 1K2
(416) 969-8510
Emp Here 80   *Sales* 10,676,720
SIC 8399 Social services, nec
Mae Maracle
Ruth Koleszar-Green
Stephen Lindley
Dawn Maracle
Erica Riley
Kenneth Richard
Heather Levecque
Barbara Fallon
Joanne Meyer
Krystal Abotossaway

D-U-N-S 20-708-6393   (BR)
NEW HORIZON SYSTEM SOLUTIONS INC
CAP GEMINI
(*Suby of* CAPGEMINI)
700 University Ave Suite 200, Toronto, ON,
M5G 1X6

Emp Here 500
SIC 7374 Data processing and preparation
Stephen Power

D-U-N-S 20-771-7059   (HQ)
**NORDIC INSURANCE COMPANY OF
CANADA, THE**
(*Suby of* INTACT FINANCIAL CORPORA-
TION)
700 University Ave Suite 1500, Toronto, ON,
M5G 0A1
(416) 932-0044
Sales 160,604,340
SIC 6331 Fire, marine, and casualty insurance
Claude Dussault
Mark Tullis

D-U-N-S 24-683-7145   (HQ)
**NORTHWEST HEALTHCARE PROPERTIES
REAL ESTATE INVESTMENT TRUST**
*NORTHWEST HEALTHCARE PROPERTIES
REIT*
180 Dundas St W Suite 1100, Toronto, ON,
M5G 1Z8
(416) 366-2000
Emp Here 5   *Sales* 265,026,394
SIC 6798 Real estate investment trusts
Paul Dalla Lana
Bernard Crotty
Brian Petersen
Bernard Crotty
Colin Loudon
C. David Naylor
Robert Baron
Karen Weaver
Shailen Chande
Peter Riggin

D-U-N-S 24-354-8315   (SL)
**OFFICE DES TELECOMMUNICATIONS ED-
UCATIVES DE LANGUE FRANCAISE DE
L'ONTARIO**
OTEFLO
21 College St Suite 600, Toronto, ON, M5G
2B3
(416) 968-3536
Emp Here 140   *Sales* 12,557,440
SIC 7812 Motion picture and video production
Leonie Tchatat
Gisele Chretien
Alain-Michel Sekula
Pierre C Belanger
Diane Desaulniers
L. Anne Gagne
Janine Griffore
Paul Lalonde

D-U-N-S 20-315-9165   (SL)
ONTARIO INFRASTRUCTURE AND LANDS CORPORATION
INFRASTRUCTURE ONTARIO
(Suby of GOVERNMENT OF ONTARIO)
1 Dundas St W Suite 2000, Toronto, ON, M5G 2L5
(416) 327-3937
Emp Here 22   *Sales* 219,243,842
SIC 8748 Business consulting, nec
  Ehren Cory
  Kathy Milsom
  Deb Barrett
  Linda Robinson
  Bruce Bodden
  Johanne Brossard
  Colleen Campbell
  Patrick Dillon
  Lawrence Kelly
  Gadi Mayman

D-U-N-S 20-554-0219   (SL)
ONTARIO INSTITUTE FOR CANCER RESEARCH
661 University Ave Suite 510, Toronto, ON, M5G 0A3
(416) 977-7599
Emp Here 200   *Sales* 70,936,466
SIC 8733 Noncommercial research organizations
  Jeff Courtney
  Janet Manzo
  Calvin Stiller
  Elizabeth Eisenhauer
  Mark Lievonen
  Michael Power
  Graham Scott
  David Parkinson
  John Morrison
  Michael Sherar

D-U-N-S 25-528-9241   (HQ)
ONTARIO POWER GENERATION INC
O P G
(Suby of GOVERNMENT OF ONTARIO)
700 University Ave, Toronto, ON, M5G 1X6
(416) 592-2555
Emp Here 800   *Sales* 4,041,174,366
SIC 4911 Electric services
  Jeffrey Lyash
  Carlo Crozzoli
  Christopher Ginther
  Ken Hartwick
  Barb Keenan
  Dietmar Reiner
  Catriona King
  Jennifer Rowe
  Bernard Lord
  William Coley

D-U-N-S 25-317-3900   (HQ)
ONTARIO REALTY CORPORATION
1 Dundas St W Suite 2000, Toronto, ON, M5G 1Z3
(416) 327-3937
Emp Here 165   *Sales* 104,799,840
SIC 6531 Real estate agents and managers
  Gail Kigour
  Mitch Kowalski
  Karen Weaver
  Mitchell Abrahams

D-U-N-S 24-341-4229   (SL)
ONTARIO TELEMEDICINE NETWORK
OTN
438 University Ave Suite 200, Toronto, ON, M5G 2K8
(416) 446-4110
Emp Here 260   *Sales* 29,840,315
SIC 7363 Help supply services
  Edward Brown
  Gilad Epstein
  Palvinder Gill
  Sue Good
  Payam Pakravan
  Laurie Poole

  Marcia Visser
  Stephen Sorocky
  Anne Brace
  Matthew Anderson

D-U-N-S 20-299-3015   (SL)
PARA-MED HEALTH SERVICES INC
480 University Ave Suite 708, Toronto, ON, M5G 1V2
(416) 977-5008
Emp Here 49   *Sales* 10,360,168
SIC 8611 Business associations
  Jim Topping

D-U-N-S 24-989-9050   (HQ)
PATHWAYS TO EDUCATION CANADA
439 University Ave Suite 1600, Toronto, ON, M5G 1Y8
(416) 646-0123
Emp Here 20   *Sales* 22,573,005
SIC 8211 Elementary and secondary schools
  David Hughes
  Dianne Bascombe
  Cathy Yanosik
  David Garland
  Elizabeth Sharp
  Christy Moorhead

D-U-N-S 24-911-4182   (SL)
PRINCESS MARGARET CANCER FOUNDATION, THE
THE RIDE TO CONQUER CANCER
700 University Ave 10th Floor, Toronto, ON, M5G 1Z5
(416) 946-6560
Emp Here 100   *Sales* 72,468,619
SIC 8399 Social services, nec
  Michael Burns
  Glenn Ives
  Asha Raheja
  Sherri Freedman
  Christine Lasky
  Greg Lichti
  Steve Merker
  Laura Syron
  Clayton Atto
  Ivy Cuervo

D-U-N-S 20-309-2200   (SL)
PRINCESS MARGARET CANCER FOUNDATION, THE
THE RIDE TO CONQUER CANCER
610 University Ave, Toronto, ON, M5G 2M9
(416) 946-6560
Emp Here 100   *Sales* 8,183,300
SIC 8069 Specialty hospitals, except psychiatric
  Laura Syron
  Greg Lichti
  Christy Atto
  Jill Nelson
  St Rose Genance
  Malka Greene
  Richard Cadieux

D-U-N-S 24-850-9874   (SL)
PROLINK BROKER NETWORK INC
480 University Ave Suite 800, Toronto, ON, M5G 1V2
(416) 595-7484
Emp Here 40   *Sales* 23,587,105
SIC 6411 Insurance agents, brokers, and service
  Derick Leu

D-U-N-S 25-810-2227   (HQ)
RANDSTAD INTERIM INC
GROUPE RANDSTAD
(Suby of RANDSTAD N.V.)
777 Bay St Suite 2000, Toronto, ON, M5G 2C8
(800) 540-3594
Emp Here 32   *Sales* 69,824,848
SIC 7361 Employment agencies
  Linda Smith
  Marc-Etienne Julien
  Arturo Ayala Salazar
  Lyne Bertoldi

D-U-N-S 25-528-6452   (SL)
RUDD SERVICES LTD
123 Edward St Suite 825, Toronto, ON, M5G 1E2
(416) 597-6995
Emp Here 50   *Sales* 11,872,250
SIC 8099 Health and allied services, nec
  Warren Rudd

D-U-N-S 20-105-9214   (SL)
SELECTCARE WORLDWIDE CORP
(Suby of CO-OPERATORS GROUP LIMITED, THE)
438 University Ave Suite 1201, Toronto, ON, M5G 2K8
(416) 340-7265
Emp Here 25   *Sales* 46,166,475
SIC 6321 Accident and health insurance
  Mark Sylvia

D-U-N-S 24-946-4777   (SL)
SIMBAS LIMITED
330 University Ave Suite 504, Toronto, ON, M5G 1R7
(416) 595-1155
Emp Here 100   *Sales* 15,401,100
SIC 8111 Legal services
  Michael Stuart

D-U-N-S 20-880-8949   (HQ)
SINAI HEALTH SYSTEM
MOUNT SINAI HOSPITAL
600 University Ave, Toronto, ON, M5G 1X5
(416) 596-4200
Emp Here 3,000   *Sales* 457,417,339
SIC 8062 General medical and surgical hospitals
  Gary Newton
  Jane Merkley
  Maureen Shandling
  John Aldis
  Susan Brown
  Melanie De Wit
  Sandra Dietrich
  Gerry Dimnik
  Stephen Goldsmith
  Jacqueline James

D-U-N-S 24-387-7078   (SL)
TATA CONSULTANCY SERVICES CANADA INC
TCCI
(Suby of TATA CONSULTANCY SERVICES LIMITED)
400 University Ave 25th Fl, Toronto, ON, M5G 1S5
(647) 790-7200
Emp Here 3,000   *Sales* 649,860,000
SIC 7379 Computer related services, nec
  Roy Soumen
  Surya Kant
  Dharmesh Gandhi
  Alfred Page

D-U-N-S 20-515-1975   (SL)
THORNHILL RESEARCH INC
(Suby of THORNHILL SCIENTIFIC INC)
210 Dundas St W Suite 200, Toronto, ON, M5G 2E8
(416) 597-1325
Emp Here 25   *Sales* 12,668,400
SIC 8733 Noncommercial research organizations
  Kipton Lade
  Veso Tijanic
  Joseph Fisher
  Ludwik Fedorko
  Steve Iscoe

D-U-N-S 24-875-1968   (HQ)
TORONTO GENERAL & WESTERN HOSPITAL FOUNDATION
190 Elizabeth St, Toronto, ON, M5G 2C4
(416) 340-3935
Sales 43,479,020
SIC 7389 Business services, nec
  Tennys J.M. Hanson

  David W. Smith

D-U-N-S 25-511-5040   (HQ)
TORONTO REHABILITATION INSTITUTE
TORONTO REHAB
(Suby of UNIVERSITY HEALTH NETWORK)
550 University Ave, Toronto, ON, M5G 2A2
(416) 597-3422
Emp Here 1,000   *Sales* 136,391,400
SIC 8093 Specialty outpatient clinics, nec
  Mark Rochon
  Jim Elliott
  Georgia Gerring
  Gaetan Tardif
  Carol Boettcher
  Karima Velji
  Geoff Fernie
  Winston Ling

D-U-N-S 24-386-8556   (HQ)
TOTTEN INSURANCE GROUP INC
(Suby of HELLMAN & FRIEDMAN LLC)
20 Dundas St W Suite 910, Toronto, ON, M5G 2C2
(416) 342-1159
Emp Here 20   *Sales* 474,610,400
SIC 6411 Insurance agents, brokers, and service
  Heather Masterson
  Theresa Teixeira
  Gerry Kennedy
  Barb Dinan
  Richard Belanger
  John Rhuland
  Terry Gudmundson
  Marco Andolfatto

D-U-N-S 20-649-8995   (HQ)
TRILLIUM GIFT OF LIFE NETWORK
483 Bay St South Tower 4th Floor, Toronto, ON, M5G 2C9
(416) 363-4001
Sales 57,957,120
SIC 8099 Health and allied services, nec
  Ronnie Gavsie
  Debbie Lanktree

D-U-N-S 20-846-9486   (HQ)
UNIVERSITY HEALTH NETWORK
200 Elizabeth St, Toronto, ON, M5G 2C4
(416) 340-3111
Emp Here 3,500   *Sales* 1,650,250,111
SIC 8062 General medical and surgical hospitals
  Peter Pisters
  John Mulvihill

D-U-N-S 25-361-7237   (BR)
UNIVERSITY HEALTH NETWORK
ADVANCED MEDICAL DISCOVERIES INSTITUTE
(Suby of UNIVERSITY HEALTH NETWORK)
620 University Ave Suite 706, Toronto, ON, M5G 2C1
(416) 946-2294
Emp Here 90
SIC 8733 Noncommercial research organizations
  Denis Bouchard

D-U-N-S 25-426-3726   (BR)
UNIVERSITY HEALTH NETWORK
TORONTO GENERAL HOSPITAL
(Suby of UNIVERSITY HEALTH NETWORK)
200 Elizabeth St Suite 224, Toronto, ON, M5G 2C4
(416) 340-3111
Emp Here 200
SIC 8011 Offices and clinics of medical doctors

D-U-N-S 20-389-2401   (HQ)
UPFIELD CANADA INC
480 University Ave Suite 803, Toronto, ON, M5G 1V2
(416) 595-5300
Sales 10,189,571
SIC 2079 Edible fats and oils

Dan Bajor
Michael Faherty

D-U-N-S 24-363-7522   (SL)
WITRON CANADA CORPORATION
WITRON LOGISTIK+INFORMATIK
(Suby of WITRON VERMOGENSVERWAL-TUNGS GMBH)
480 University Ave Suite 1500, Toronto, ON, M5G 1V2
(416) 598-7096
Emp Here 50   *Sales* 11,714,400
SIC 8742 Management consulting services
Helmut Prieschenk
Harald Schroeps

Toronto, ON M5H

D-U-N-S 20-292-1883   (SL)
1 KING WEST INC
STINSON CREATIVE
1 King St W, Toronto, ON, M5H 1A1
(416) 548-8100
Emp Here 200   *Sales* 31,634,400
SIC 6553 Cemetery subdividers and developers
Harry Stinson

D-U-N-S 25-372-8927   (SL)
1576640 ONTARIO LTD
CERTEX SOLUTIONS
157 Adelaide St W Suite 207, Toronto, ON, M5H 4E7

Emp Here 438   *Sales* 23,441,400
SIC 8741 Management services

D-U-N-S 20-323-0537   (SL)
180 UNIVERSITY HOTEL LIMITED PARTNERSHIP
SHANGRI-LA HOTEL TORONTO
188 University Ave, Toronto, ON, M5H 0A3
(647) 788-8888
Emp Here 150   *Sales* 13,903,500
SIC 7011 Hotels and motels
Richard Cooke

D-U-N-S 20-328-4989   (SL)
500PX, INC
(Suby of VISUAL CHINA GROUP CO., LTD.)
20 Duncan St Unit 100, Toronto, ON, M5H 3G8
(647) 465-1033
Emp Here 71   *Sales* 16,221,512
SIC 4813 Telephone communication, except radio
Andy Yang

D-U-N-S 24-632-9502   (HQ)
582219 ONTARIO INC
KETCHUM CANADA
214 King St W Suite 508, Toronto, ON, M5H 3S6
(416) 340-9710
Emp Here 1   *Sales* 22,220,892
SIC 8741 Management services
Marnie A Spears
Ross Mcgregor
Mike Logue

D-U-N-S 25-529-1916   (SL)
A.U.G. SIGNALS LTD
73 Richmond St W Suite 103, Toronto, ON, M5H 4E8
(416) 923-4425
Emp Here 147   *Sales* 33,773,838
SIC 8731 Commercial physical research
George Lampropoulos

D-U-N-S 20-007-9049   (BR)
ACCENTURE INC
(Suby of ACCENTURE INC)
40 King St W Suite 4800, Toronto, ON, M5H 3Y2

(416) 641-5220
Emp Here 100
SIC 8741 Management services
Deborah Giesen

D-U-N-S 24-130-9280   (SL)
ACKER FINLEY CANADA FOCUS FUND
181 University Ave Suite 1400, Toronto, ON, M5H 3M7
(416) 777-9005
Emp Here 20   *Sales* 14,669,040
SIC 6722 Management investment, open-end
Brian Acker

D-U-N-S 25-151-9476   (SL)
ALLANA POTASH CORP
65 Queen St W Suite 805, Toronto, ON, M5H 2M5
(416) 861-5800
Emp Here 100   *Sales* 41,310,900
SIC 1474 Potash, soda, and borate minerals

D-U-N-S 20-354-7377   (SL)
ALLIED WORLD SPECIALTY INSURANCE COMPANY
200 King St W Suite 1600, Toronto, ON, M5H 3T4
(647) 558-1120
Emp Here 12   *Sales* 18,491,125
SIC 6331 Fire, marine, and casualty insurance
Gordon Kerr

D-U-N-S 20-191-3576   (HQ)
AMERICAS SILVER CORPORATION
145 King St W Suite 2870, Toronto, ON, M5H 1J8
(416) 848-9503
Emp Here 13   *Sales* 68,354,000
SIC 1081 Metal mining services
Darren Blasutti
Peter Mcrae
Shawn Wilson
Daren Dell
Warren Varga
Alex Davidson
Alan Edwards
Bradley Kipp
Gordon Pridham
Manuel Rivera

D-U-N-S 20-007-9965   (HQ)
AMICA MATURE LIFESTYLES INC
(Suby of AMICA SENIOR LIFESTYLES INC)
20 Queen St W Suite 2700, Toronto, ON, M5H 3R3
(416) 487-2020
Emp Here 50   *Sales* 107,608,068
SIC 8361 Residential care
Douglas Maclatchy
Bob Kallone
Art Ayres

D-U-N-S 25-092-8046   (HQ)
AMICA SENIOR LIFESTYLES INC
BAYBRIDGE SENIOR LIVING
20 Queen St W Suite 3200, Toronto, ON, M5H 3R3
(416) 487-2020
Emp Here 25   *Sales* 507,096,000
SIC 6531 Real estate agents and managers
Douglas J. Maclatchy
Bob Kallonen
Robert I. Ezer
Robert Wickham
Sandy Ardern
Amy R. Holland
Joan Wilson
Andrea Prashad

D-U-N-S 25-511-5792   (HQ)
ANACONDA MINING INC
150 York St Suite 410, Toronto, ON, M5H 3S5
(416) 304-6622
Emp Here 12   *Sales* 24,055,438
SIC 1041 Gold ores
Dustin Angelo
Kevin Bullock
Lynn Hammond

Allan Cramm
Paul Mcneill
Robert Dufour
Gordana Slepcev
Jonathan Fitzgerald
Lewis Mawrick
Maruf Raza

D-U-N-S 24-313-3134   (SL)
ASIAN MINERAL RESOURCES LIMITED
120 Adelaide St W Suite 2500, Toronto, ON, M5H 1T1
(416) 360-3412
Emp Here 552   *Sales* 1,317,927,048
SIC 1061 Ferroalloy ores, except vanadium
Duncan Blount
Paula Kember
Christopher Castle
Norm Yurik

D-U-N-S 24-966-3840   (SL)
ASSOCIATION OF MUNICIPALITIES OF ONTARIO
AMO
200 University Ave Suite 801, Toronto, ON, M5H 3C6
(416) 971-9856
Emp Here 28   *Sales* 26,296,956
SIC 6282 Investment advice
Russ Powers
Patricia Vanini
Nancy Plumridge

D-U-N-S 20-650-4537   (SL)
AUDICO SERVICES LIMITED PARTNERSHIP
SMITH NIXON
390 Bay St Suite 1900, Toronto, ON, M5H 2Y2
(416) 361-1622
Emp Here 75   *Sales* 15,681,375
SIC 8721 Accounting, auditing, and bookkeeping
Bob Reid

D-U-N-S 24-348-7043   (HQ)
AURA MINERALS INC
155 University Ave Suite 1240, Toronto, ON, M5H 3B7
(416) 649-1033
Emp Here 15   *Sales* 157,711,000
SIC 1041 Gold ores
Rodrigo Barbosa
Ryan Goodman
Fernando A. Cornejo
Sergio Castanho
Paulo Carlos De Brito
Stephen Keith
Philip Reade

D-U-N-S 25-405-9785   (SL)
AVALON ADVANCED MATERIALS INC
130 Adelaide St W Suite 1901, Toronto, ON, M5H 3P5
(416) 364-4938
Emp Here 15   *Sales* 35,813,235
SIC 1021 Copper ores
Donald Bubar
R. James Andersen
David Marsh
William Mercer
Pierre Neatby
Mark Wiseman
Brian Maceachen
Alan Ferry
Kenneth Thomas
Jane Pagel

D-U-N-S 24-313-3043   (HQ)
AVION GOLD CORPORATION
65 Queen St W Suite 820, Toronto, ON, M5H 2M5
(416) 861-9500
Emp Here 5   *Sales* 255,774,000
SIC 1081 Metal mining services
John Begeman
James C. Coleman
Michael E. Beckett

Neil Woodyer
Jorge L. Gamarci
Wayne Mcmanus
Mark Connelly
Dr. Antony Harwood

D-U-N-S 20-850-2534   (HQ)
AVISON YOUNG ADVISORS AND MANAGERS INC
(Suby of GREINER-PACAUD MANAGEMENT ASSOCIATES)
257 Adelaide St W Suite 400, Toronto, ON, M5H 1X9
(416) 343-0078
Emp Here 35   *Sales* 67,612,800
SIC 6531 Real estate agents and managers
Gary Hudson
Susan Russell
Siobhan Kenny
Richard Kwon

D-U-N-S 25-214-5289   (BR)
AVIVA INSURANCE COMPANY OF CANADA
(Suby of GENERAL ACCIDENT PLC)
121 King St W Suite 1400, Toronto, ON, M5H 3T9

Emp Here 130
SIC 6411 Insurance agents, brokers, and service
Glenn Cooper

D-U-N-S 20-700-5930   (HQ)
AY HOLDINGS ONTARIO INC
150 York St Suite 900, Toronto, ON, M5H 3S5
(416) 955-0000
Sales 20,501,250
SIC 6712 Bank holding companies
Mark Fieder
Rob Ishoj

D-U-N-S 20-770-5989   (HQ)
BANK OF NOVA SCOTIA, THE
BANQUE SCOTIA
44 King St W Scotia Plaza, Toronto, ON, M5H 1H1
(416) 866-6161
Emp Here 1,100   *Sales* 22,224,313,700
SIC 6733 Trusts, nec
Brian J. Porter
Ian Arellano
Terry Fryett
Glen Gowland
Mike Henry
Rania Llewellyn
James Mcphedran
James Neate
Gillian Riley
Shawn Rose

D-U-N-S 24-238-2120   (HQ)
BARKERVILLE GOLD MINES LTD
155 University Ave Suite 1410, Toronto, ON, M5H 3B7
(416) 775-3671
Emp Here 15   *Sales* 71,626,470
SIC 1041 Gold ores
Chris Lodder
Chris Pharness
Maggie Layman
Sean Masse
Jason Kosec
Andres Tinajero
Sean Roosen
Thomas J. Obradovich
Anthony Makuch
Morris Prychidny

D-U-N-S 24-707-6466   (SL)
BEARD WINTER LLP
130 Adelaide St W Suite 701, Toronto, ON, M5H 2K4
(416) 593-5555
Emp Here 110   *Sales* 12,197,020
SIC 8111 Legal services
David Beard

Richard Winter

D-U-N-S 25-674-3311   (SL)
BELO SUN MINING CORP
65 Queen St W Suite 800, Toronto, ON, M5H
2M5
(416) 309-2137
Emp Here 70   *Sales* 17,904,180
SIC 1041 Gold ores
  Peter Tagliamonte
  Mark Eaton
  Joe Milbourne
  Stephane Amireault
  Neil Said
  Stan Bharti
  Carol Fries
  William Clarke
  Bruce Humphrey
  Denis Arsenault

D-U-N-S 24-181-3492   (HQ)
BERESKIN & PARR LLP
BERESKIN & PARR MANAGEMENT
40 King St W 4th Fl, Toronto, ON, M5H 3Y2
(416) 364-7311
Emp Here 180   *Sales* 46,939,728
SIC 8111 Legal services
  Daniel Bereskin

D-U-N-S 24-377-5470   (HQ)
BERKLEY CANADA INC
(*Suby of* W. R. BERKLEY CORPORATION)
145 King St W Suite 1000, Toronto, ON, M5H
1J8
(416) 304-1178
Emp Here 1   *Sales* 14,773,272
SIC 6351 Surety insurance
  Andrew Steen
  Sayf Ali
  Graham Toon
  Carl Spensieri
  Liam Brown
  Craig Spencer
  Brian Yoshikuni
  Ashley Beales
  Jeanette Lawrence
  Kate Tang

D-U-N-S 25-420-0074   (SL)
**BFL CANADA RISK AND INSURANCE SER-
VICES INC**
181 University Ave Suite 1700, Toronto, ON,
M5H 3M7
(416) 599-5530
Emp Here 40   *Sales* 33,922,400
SIC 6411 Insurance agents, brokers, and ser-
vice
  Barry Lorenzetti
  Robert Nicholls
  Adelino Buna
  Joseph Pare
  Edward Gathercole
  Frank Howden

D-U-N-S 24-836-9741   (HQ)
BLUE GOOSE CAPITAL CORP
80 Richmond St W Suite 1502, Toronto, ON,
M5H 2A4
(416) 363-5151
Emp Here 1   *Sales* 13,675,900
SIC 0259 Poultry and eggs, nec
  Ben Nikolaevsky

D-U-N-S 24-340-2893   (HQ)
BOARDSUITE CORP
GOVERNANCEGLOBAL
372 Bay St Suite 1800, Toronto, ON, M5H
2W9

Emp Here 25   *Sales* 10,692,550
SIC 7372 Prepackaged software
  Oscar A Jofre Jr
  Marshall Rosichuk
  Sean Griffin
  Sean Harrison
  Adrian Banica
  Dean Peloso

Randy Thompson
Charles Walker

D-U-N-S 20-771-1813   (HQ)
**BOILER INSPECTION AND INSURANCE
COMPANY OF CANADA, THE**
HSB BI&I
(*Suby*   *of*   MUNCHENER
RUCKVERSICHERUNGS-GESELLSCHAFT
AG IN MUNCHEN)
390 Bay St Suite 2000, Toronto, ON, M5H 2Y2
(416) 363-5491
Emp Here 100   *Sales* 84,813
SIC 6331 Fire, marine, and casualty insurance
  John Mulvihill
  Dave Picot
  Derrick Hughes
  Jean Dubois
  Brian Storey
  David Pivato
  Barbara Hanley
  Mark Moore

D-U-N-S 25-102-8973   (HQ)
BORDEN LADNER GERVAIS LLP
BLG
22 Adelaide St W Suite 3400, Toronto, ON,
M5H 4E3
(416) 367-6000
Emp Here 600   *Sales* 370,576,800
SIC 8111 Legal services

D-U-N-S 25-365-5203   (SL)
BOREALIS INVESTMENTS INC
(*Suby of* OMERS ADMINISTRATION COR-
PORATION)
100 Adelaide St W Suite 900, Toronto, ON,
M5H 0E2
(416) 361-1011
Emp Here 500
SIC 6719 Holding companies, nec
  Paul Haggins

D-U-N-S 20-327-7715   (SL)
BRIO GOLD INC
(*Suby of* YAMANA GOLD INC)
22 Adelaide St W Unit 2020, Toronto, ON,
M5H 4E3
(416) 860-6310
Emp Here 10   *Sales* 217,891,000
SIC 1081 Metal mining services
  Gil Clausen
  Joseph M. Longpre
  Vitor Belo
  Lance Newman
  Mark Stevens
  Letitia Wong
  Sarah A. Strunk
  John Gravelle
  Daniel Racine
  William Washington

D-U-N-S 24-684-9087   (HQ)
BRISBIN BROOK BEYNON, ARCHITECTS
BRISBIN BROOK BEYNON, INTERIORS
14 Duncan St Suite 400, Toronto, ON, M5H
3G8
(416) 591-8999
Emp Here 50   *Sales* 11,618,035
SIC 8712 Architectural services
  Brian Brisbin
  Murray Beynon
  Ritchard Brisbin
  Greg Alexander

D-U-N-S 24-357-3495   (HQ)
**BROADRIDGE FINANCIAL SOLUTIONS
(CANADA) INC**
(*Suby of* BROADRIDGE FINANCIAL SOLU-
TIONS, INC.)
4 King St W Suite 500, Toronto, ON, M5H 1B6
(416) 350-0999
Sales 20,021,640
SIC 7374 Data processing and preparation
  Michael Dignam

D-U-N-S 25-536-1263   (BR)

BROADRIDGE SOFTWARE LIMITED
A D P DATAPHIE
(*Suby of* BROADRIDGE FINANCIAL SOLU-
TIONS, INC.)
4 King St W Suite 500, Toronto, ON, M5H 1B6
(416) 350-0999
Emp Here 100
SIC 7371 Custom computer programming ser-
vices
  Michael Dignam

D-U-N-S 24-334-0952   (SL)
BUFFALO COAL CORP
65 Queen St W, Toronto, ON, M5H 2M5
(416) 309-2957
Emp Here 573   *Sales* 58,686,230
SIC 1221 Bituminous coal and lignite-surface
mining
  Rowan Karstel
  Graham Du Preez
  Craig Wiaggill
  Robert Francis
  Eddie Scholtz

D-U-N-S 20-160-9823   (HQ)
**CADILLAC FAIRVIEW CORPORATION LIM-
ITED, THE**
(*Suby of* ONTARIO TEACHERS' PENSION
PLAN BOARD)
20 Queen St W Suite 500, Toronto, ON, M5H
3R4
(416) 598-8200
Emp Here 200   *Sales* 225,862,560
SIC 6512 Nonresidential building operators
  John Sullivan
  Cathal O'connor
  Robert Michaels
  Robert G Bertram
  Barbara Zvan
  Chuck Crovitz
  Craig Macnab
  Jane Rowe
  John Curtin Jr.
  Nora Aufreiter

D-U-N-S 24-286-4320   (HQ)
CALDWELL SECURITIES LTD
150 King St W Suite 1710, Toronto, ON, M5H
1J9
(416) 862-7755
Emp Here 36   *Sales* 20,717,073
SIC 6211 Security brokers and dealers
  Brendan Thomas North Caldwell
  Dennis Freeman
  Angela Stirpe
  Charles B Hughson
  Thomas S Caldwell
  Robert M Callander
  Sally Haldenby-Haba

D-U-N-S 20-848-4758   (HQ)
CAMBRIDGE GROUP OF CLUB
CAMBRIDGE CLUB
100 Richmond St W Suite 444, Toronto, ON,
M5H 3K6
(416) 862-1077
Sales 33,860,250
SIC 7991 Physical fitness facilities
  Clive Caldwell

D-U-N-S 25-284-0046   (HQ)
CAMBRIDGE MERCANTILE CORP
CAMBRIDGE GLOBAL PAYMENTS
(*Suby of* FLEETCOR TECHNOLOGIES, INC.)
212 King St W Suite 400, Toronto, ON, M5H
1K5
(416) 646-6401
Emp Here 175   *Sales* 75,899,850
SIC 6099 Functions related to deposit banking
  Gary Mcdonald
  Mark Frey
  Gary Krikler
  Carole Palmer

D-U-N-S 24-227-4111   (SL)
CANADA HEALTH INFOWAY
150 King St W Suite 1300, Toronto, ON, M5H

1J9
(416) 979-4606
Emp Here 50   *Sales* 10,619,850
SIC 8748 Business consulting, nec
  Richard Alvarez

D-U-N-S 20-966-4408   (HQ)
**CANADIAN DEPOSITORY FOR SECURI-
TIES LIMITED, THE**
CDS
85 Richmond St W, Toronto, ON, M5H 2C9
(416) 365-8400
Emp Here 385   *Sales* 690,221,930
SIC 6289 Security and commodity service
  Jay Rajarathinam
  John Mckenzie

D-U-N-S 20-350-2588   (SL)
**CANADIAN INTERNATIONAL MILITARY
GAMES CORPORATION**
INVICTUS GAMES TORONTO 2017
357 Bay St Suite 300, Toronto, ON, M5H 2T7
(416) 364-0001
Emp Here 74   *Sales* 52,481,688
SIC 8699 Membership organizations, nec
  James Eaton
  Michael Burns
  Matthew Kelleher

D-U-N-S 24-349-4858   (SL)
**CANADIAN PARTNERSHIP AGAINST CAN-
CER CORPORATION**
145 King St W Ste 900, Toronto, ON, M5H 1J8
(416) 915-9222
Emp Here 150   *Sales* 39,081,955
SIC 8733 Noncommercial research organiza-
tions
  Shelly Jamieson

D-U-N-S 20-813-2592   (SL)
**CANADIAN PUBLIC ACCOUNTABILITY
BOARD**
CPAB
150 York St Suite 900, Toronto, ON, M5H 3S5
(416) 913-8260
Emp Here 25   *Sales* 14,139,865
SIC 8721 Accounting, auditing, and book-
keeping
  Brian A Hunt
  Keneth J.A. Vallilee
  Glen Fagan
  Kam Grewal

D-U-N-S 25-302-3246   (SL)
**CANADIAN SHAREOWNERS ASSOCIA-
TION**
CANADIAN SHAREOWNER INVESTMENT
170 University Ave Suite 704, Toronto, ON,
M5H 3B3
(416) 595-9600
Emp Here 20   *Sales* 13,578,460
SIC 6282 Investment advice
  John Bart

D-U-N-S 20-896-5397   (SL)
**CANADIAN SOCIETY OF IMMIGRATION
CONSULTANTS**
390 Bay St Suite 1600, Toronto, ON, M5H 2Y2
(416) 572-2800
Emp Here 25   *Sales* 11,087,250
SIC 7389 Business services, nec
  Ross Eastley
  John Ryan
  Holly Gracey

D-U-N-S 25-146-8724   (HQ)
CAPGEMINI CANADA INC
CONSULTANTS CAPGEMINI
(*Suby of* CAPGEMINI)
200 University Ave Suite 1100, Toronto, ON,
M5H 3C6
(416) 365-4400
Emp Here 100   *Sales* 173,678,400
SIC 8742 Management consulting services
  Sanjay Tugnait
  Vanda Vicars
  Michael Chayet

Thierry Delaporte

D-U-N-S 20-818-5488 (HQ)
CASSELS BROCK & BLACKWELL LLP
40 King St W Suite 2100, Toronto, ON, M5H 3C2
(416) 869-5300
Emp Here 450   *Sales* 113,231,800
SIC 8111 Legal services
Marshall A Cohen
Walter Bowen
David R Peterson
Bruce A Thomas
Crawford R Spencer
Philip Spencer
Peter Steinmetz
Ralph Lean
Ian Blue

D-U-N-S 20-269-9088 (SL)
CBRE CALEDON CAPITAL MANAGEMENT INC
(*Suby of* CBRE GROUP, INC.)
141 Adelaide St W Suite 1500, Toronto, ON, M5H 3L5
(416) 861-0700
Emp Here 30   *Sales* 44,221,830
SIC 6722 Management investment, open-end
Dennis Pellarin
Robert Chen
Noi Spyratos
Aaron Vale
Lee Anderson
Adam Wylychenko
Toms Lokmanis
David Rogers
Martin Day
Stephen Dowd

D-U-N-S 24-421-0472 (HQ)
CBRE LIMITEE
(*Suby of* CBRE LIMITED PARTNERSHIP)
145 King St W Suite 1100, Toronto, ON, M5H 1J8
(416) 362-2244
Emp Here 1,800   *Sales* 7,858,190,000
SIC 8748 Business consulting, nec
Mark Renzoni
Nicolette Desouza
Peter D. Senst
Laurence H. Midler

D-U-N-S 24-206-9446 (BR)
CBRE LIMITEE
CBRE LIMITED
(*Suby of* CBRE LIMITED PARTNERSHIP)
40 King St W Suite 4100, Toronto, ON, M5H 3Y2
(416) 947-7661
Emp Here 80
SIC 6531 Real estate agents and managers
Ralph Barton

D-U-N-S 24-364-2803 (HQ)
CDS CLEARING AND DEPOSITORY SERVICES INC
(*Suby of* CANADIAN DEPOSITORY FOR SECURITIES LIMITED, THE)
85 Richmond St W, Toronto, ON, M5H 2C9
(416) 365-8400
Sales 569,255,200
SIC 6211 Security brokers and dealers
Ian Gilhooley
Tom Marley
Mark Weseluck
Keith Evans
Steve Blake

D-U-N-S 25-681-0813 (HQ)
CGX ENERGY INC
333 Bay St Suite 1100, Toronto, ON, M5H 2R2
(416) 364-5569
Sales 42,378,777
SIC 1389 Oil and gas field services, nec
Suresh Narine
Tralisa Maraj
Dennis Mills

Erik Lyngberg

D-U-N-S 24-828-7575 (SL)
CIBC SECURITIES INC
(*Suby of* CANADIAN IMPERIAL BANK OF COMMERCE)
200 King St W Suite 700, Toronto, ON, M5H 4A8
(416) 980-2211
Emp Here 750   *Sales* 412,494,750
SIC 6722 Management investment, open-end
Stephen Geist
Jennifer Hubbard
Norah Mccarthy
Thomas Mccready
Daniel Donnelly
Victor Dodig

D-U-N-S 20-329-7072 (SL)
CLEANMARK GROUP INC
141 Adelaide St W Suite 1000, Toronto, ON, M5H 3L5
(416) 364-0677
Emp Here 425   *Sales* 13,586,400
SIC 7349 Building maintenance services, nec
John Vavitsas

D-U-N-S 24-423-7447 (SL)
COBALT 27 CAPITAL CORP
4 King St W Suite 401, Toronto, ON, M5H 1B6
(647) 846-7765
Emp Here 5   *Sales* 11,937,745
SIC 1061 Ferroalloy ores, except vanadium
Anthony Milewski
Justin Cochrane
Kathryn Witter
Cindy Davis
Frank Estergaard
Nicholas French
John Kanellitsas
Candace Macgibbon
Philip Williams

D-U-N-S 24-892-9382 (SL)
COLLINS BARROW TORONTO LLP
11 King St W Suite 700, Toronto, ON, M5H 4C7
(416) 480-0160
Emp Here 130   *Sales* 26,999,050
SIC 8721 Accounting, auditing, and bookkeeping
Marvin Martenfeld
Ken Maiden
Maruf Raza
John Sinclair
Rhonda Klosler
Chris Nitsopoulos
Susan Maynard
Mary Louise Hall
Stephen Mccourt
Sheldon Carr

D-U-N-S 20-937-4156 (SL)
CONSULATE GENERAL OF THE REPUBLIC OF KOREA COMMERCIAL SECTION
KOREA BUSINESS CENTRE
65 Queen St W Suite 600, Toronto, ON, M5H 2M5
(416) 368-3399
Emp Here 43   *Sales* 29,962,830
SIC 6799 Investors, nec
Kwang Hee Kim

D-U-N-S 20-347-6838 (SL)
COUGAR GLOBAL INVESTMENTS LIMITED PARTNERSHIP
357 Bay St Suite 1001, Toronto, ON, M5H 2T7
(416) 368-5255
Emp Here 15   *Sales* 10,183,845
SIC 6211 Security brokers and dealers
James Breech

D-U-N-S 24-682-1313 (SL)
CST INVESTOR SERVICES INC
320 Bay St Suite 1000, Toronto, ON, M5H 4A6
(888) 402-1644
Emp Here 20   *Sales* 13,578,460

SIC 6231 Security and commodity exchanges
Mark C Healy
Marty Flanigan
Robert M Carney Sr.
Vincient J. Ioria
Bill Spiers

D-U-N-S 20-322-4006 (SL)
CUCO RESOURCES LTD
155 University Ave Suite 1230, Toronto, ON, M5H 3B7
(647) 247-1381
Emp Here 50   *Sales* 11,671,750
SIC 1021 Copper ores
Chetan Chug
Imran Patel
John Brough
Kenneth Thomas
George Ireland
Malik Talib
Bob Buchan
Peter Gundy

D-U-N-S 20-554-2087 (SL)
D&D SECURITIES INC
150 York St Suite 1714, Toronto, ON, M5H 3S5
(416) 363-0201
Emp Here 38   *Sales* 20,185,866
SIC 6211 Security brokers and dealers
Paul Morgante
Egon Lechner
Richard Papazian

D-U-N-S 24-760-3983 (HQ)
DAS LEGAL PROTECTION INSURANCE COMPANY LIMITED
(*Suby of* MUNCHENER RUCKVERSICHERUNGS-GESELLSCHAFT AG IN MUNCHEN)
390 Bay St Suite 1610, Toronto, ON, M5H 2Y2
(416) 342-5400
Sales 53,553,111
SIC 6331 Fire, marine, and casualty insurance
Barbara Haynes

D-U-N-S 20-966-0711 (HQ)
DBRS LIMITED
DOMINION BOND RATING SERVICES
181 University Ave Suite 700, Toronto, ON, M5H 3M7
(416) 593-5577
Emp Here 135   *Sales* 249,049,150
SIC 6289 Security and commodity service
Walter Schroeder
Daniel Curry
Connie Silva

D-U-N-S 24-939-8439 (HQ)
DEALNET CAPITAL CORP
4 King St W Suite 1700, Toronto, ON, M5H 1B6
(905) 695-8557
Emp Here 4   *Sales* 14,815,587
SIC 6159 Miscellaneous business credit institutions
Brent Houlden
Harold Bridge
Sanjeev Motwani
Siddharth Kakkar
Barclay Morton
Peter Soon
Kathryn Houlden
Richard Carl
Joanne De Laurentiis
Matthew Lewis

D-U-N-S 24-333-6567 (HQ)
DELOITTE LLP
8 Adelaide St W Suite 200, Toronto, ON, M5H 0A9
(416) 601-6150
Emp Here 90   *Sales* 1,578,406,000
SIC 8721 Accounting, auditing, and bookkeeping
Anthony Viel
Glenn Ives

Kenneth J Fredeen

D-U-N-S 24-000-3025 (BR)
DELOITTE LLP
DELOITTE MANAGEMENT SERVICES
(*Suby of* DELOITTE LLP)
22 Adelaide St W Suite 200, Toronto, ON, M5H 0A9
(416) 601-6150
Emp Here 350
SIC 8721 Accounting, auditing, and bookkeeping
Alan Mcardle

D-U-N-S 24-677-0437 (SL)
DELOITTE MANAGEMENT SERVICES LP
DELOITTE
121 King St W Suite 300, Toronto, ON, M5H 3T9
(416) 775-2364
Emp Here 7,000   *Sales* 1,293,971,000
SIC 8721 Accounting, auditing, and bookkeeping
Frank Vettese

D-U-N-S 24-324-7728 (BR)
DOMINION OF CANADA GENERAL INSURANCE COMPANY, THE
(*Suby of* THE TRAVELERS COMPANIES INC)
165 University Ave., Toronto, ON, M5H 3B9
(416) 362-7231
Emp Here 200
SIC 6411 Insurance agents, brokers, and service
Ina Blanchard

D-U-N-S 24-024-6504 (HQ)
DOMINION OF CANADA GENERAL INSURANCE COMPANY, THE
(*Suby of* THE TRAVELERS COMPANIES INC)
165 University Ave Suite 101, Toronto, ON, M5H 3B9
(416) 362-7231
Emp Here 200   *Sales* 2,136,968,000
SIC 6331 Fire, marine, and casualty insurance
Brigid Murphy
Duncan Nr Jackman
Mark J Fuller
Deanna Rosenswig
Mark M Taylor
Clive Rowe
Douglas Townsend

D-U-N-S 20-302-2728 (HQ)
DRAGADOS CANADA INC
150 King St W Suite 2103, Toronto, ON, M5H 1J9
(647) 260-5001
Emp Here 1   *Sales* 317,615,320
SIC 1629 Heavy construction, nec
Diego Zumaquero
Ignacio Segura Surinach

D-U-N-S 20-822-1549 (HQ)
DRAKE INTERNATIONAL INC
DRAKE PERSONNEL
320 Bay St Suite 1400, Toronto, ON, M5H 4A6
(416) 216-1000
Emp Here 60   *Sales* 194,204,400
SIC 7361 Employment agencies
Karen Meredith
Robert W Pollock

D-U-N-S 24-195-0146 (SL)
DUCARTOR HOLDINGS LTD
130 Adelaide St W Suite 701, Toronto, ON, M5H 2K4
(416) 593-5555
Emp Here 80   *Sales* 21,946,560
SIC 8741 Management services
Julie Holmes

D-U-N-S 20-874-8954 (HQ)
E-L FINANCIAL CORPORATION LIMITED
165 University Ave 10th Fl, Toronto, ON, M5H 3B8

(416) 947-2578
Emp Here 8   *Sales* 816,242,359
SIC 6282 Investment advice
Duncan N.R. Jackman
Richard B. Carty
Scott F. Ewert
Fahad Khan
Susan C. Clifford
James F Billett
Michael J. Cooper
William J. Corcoran
Henry N.R. Jackman
Victoria D. Jackman

D-U-N-S 24-687-9043   (HQ)
EMC CORPORATION OF CANADA
(*Suby of* DELL TECHNOLOGIES INC.)
120 Adelaide St W Suite 1400, Toronto, ON,
M5H 1T1
(416) 628-5973
Emp Here 100   *Sales* 49,715,229
SIC 3577 Computer peripheral equipment,
nec
Michael Ruettgers
Larry Murray
Roger Stone
Richard J Egan

D-U-N-S 25-807-4025   (HQ)
ENTUITIVE CORPORATION
200 University Ave 7th Fl, Toronto, ON, M5H
3C6
(416) 477-5832
Sales 27,704,545
SIC 8711 Engineering services
David Stevenson

D-U-N-S 24-477-0707   (HQ)
ENWAVE ENERGY CORPORATION
(*Suby of* BROOKFIELD ASSET MANAGE-
MENT INC)
333 Bay St Suite 710, Toronto, ON, M5H 2R2
(416) 392-6838
Emp Here 30   *Sales* 39,556,650
SIC 4961 Steam and air-conditioning supply
Carlyle Coutinho
Alex Sotirov
Joyce Lee
Geoff Olsen

D-U-N-S 20-392-5557   (SL)
**EPIC INVESTMENT SERVICES LIMITED
PARTNERSHIP**
141 Adelaide St W Suite 1201, Toronto, ON,
M5H 3L5
(416) 497-9332
Emp Here 113   *Sales* 38,201,232
SIC 6531 Real estate agents and managers
Gordon Thompson

D-U-N-S 25-462-8712   (SL)
EQUITY FINANCIAL TRUST COMPANY
HAVENTREE BANK
200 University Ave Suite 400, Toronto, ON,
M5H 3C6
(416) 504-5050
Emp Here 125   *Sales* 177,892,250
SIC 6289 Security and commodity service
Terrance Martinuk
Nick Kyprianou

D-U-N-S 20-818-2006   (HQ)
ERNST & YOUNG LLP
EY
(*Suby of* ERNST & YOUNG LLP)
100 Adelaide St W Suite 3100, Toronto, ON,
M5H 0B3
(416) 864-1234
Emp Here 3,000   *Sales* 610,014,900
SIC 8721 Accounting, auditing, and book-
keeping
Alycia Calvert
Jay Hutchison
Massimo Marinelli
Murray Mcdonald
Stephen Shea
Linda Williams
Doris Stamml

D-U-N-S 20-513-3965   (HQ)
EURO SUN MINING INC
65 Queen St W Suite 800, Toronto, ON, M5H
2M5
(416) 368-7744
Sales 1,007,545,678
SIC 1041 Gold ores
G. Scott Moore
Randall Ruff
Brad Humphrey
Peter Tagliamonte
Stan Moore
David Danziger
Michael Barton
Matthew Simpson
Eva Bellissimo
Paul Bozoki

D-U-N-S 20-067-8436   (HQ)
FASKEN MARTINEAU DUMOULIN LLP
FASKEN MARTINEAU
333 Bay St Suite 2400, Toronto, ON, M5H 2T6
(416) 366-8381
Emp Here 530   *Sales* 348,548,068
SIC 8111 Legal services
Martin Denyes
William Westerlingh
Eric Beddard
Peter Feldberg
Clarke Barnes
Robert Maxwell
Al Gourley
Nancy Rendle
Robert Garmaise

D-U-N-S 20-770-5484   (SL)
FEDERATION OF ONTARIO NATURALISTS
ONTARIO NATURE
214 King St W Suite 612, Toronto, ON, M5H
3S6
(416) 444-8419
Emp Here 30   *Sales* 11,922,420
SIC 8699 Membership organizations, nec
Caroline Schultz
Joe Mccalmont

D-U-N-S 24-362-9826   (HQ)
FELIX GLOBAL CORP
80 Richmond St W Suite 1000, Toronto, ON,
M5H 2A4
(416) 512-7244
Sales 11,714,400
SIC 8742 Management consulting services
Jim Graham

D-U-N-S 25-343-9749   (SL)
FIGURE 3
200 University Ave Suite 200, Toronto, ON,
M5H 3C6
(416) 363-6993
Emp Here 26   *Sales* 11,679,694
SIC 7389 Business services, nec
Christopher Wright
Allan Guinan
Caroline Hughes

D-U-N-S 20-383-8123   (SL)
FIORE GOLD LTD
120 Adelaide St W Suite 1410, Toronto, ON,
M5H 1T1
(416) 639-1426
Emp Here 10   *Sales* 10,696,000
SIC 1041 Gold ores
Tim Warman
James C. Wilbourn
Barry O'shea
Ross Maclean
Mark H. Bailey
Anne Labelle
Peter Tallman
Matt Manson
Kenneth A. Brunk
Peter T. Hemstead

D-U-N-S 24-253-1858   (SL)
FLIGHT NETWORK LTD
FLIGHTNETWORK.COM

145 King St W Suite 1401, Toronto, ON, M5H
1J8
(905) 829-8699
Emp Here 94   *Sales* 48,876,898
SIC 4724 Travel agencies
Kiran Budhdev
Pravina Budhdev
Naman Budhdev
Tejal Budhdev

D-U-N-S 25-203-5266   (SL)
FRANMED CONSULTANTS (1993) INC
150 York St Suite 1500, Toronto, ON, M5H
3S5
(416) 350-7706
Emp Here 50   *Sales* 14,164,650
SIC 8741 Management services
Robert W Francis
Shaun Francis

D-U-N-S 24-886-2419   (SL)
**FREEDOM INTERNATIONAL BROKERAGE
COMPANY**
181 University Ave Suite 1500, Toronto, ON,
M5H 3M7
(416) 367-2588
Emp Here 55   *Sales* 51,654,735
SIC 6211 Security brokers and dealers
Peter Mcrae
Michael Woolnough

D-U-N-S 25-682-0986   (HQ)
FRONTERA ENERGY CORPORATION
333 Bay St Suite 1100, Toronto, ON, M5H 2R2
(416) 362-7735
Emp Here 30   *Sales* 1,371,706,000
SIC 1381 Drilling oil and gas wells
Richard Herbert
Gabriel De Alba
Renata Campagnaro
Erik Lyngberg
Duncan Nightingale
Grayson Andersen
Alejandra Honours
Alejandro Pineros
Luis F. Alarcon
W. Ellis Armstrong

D-U-N-S 20-365-0650   (SL)
FUEL TRADE INTERNATIONAL INC
FUEL TRADE
(*Suby of* DARO INDUSTRIES INC)
180 University Ave Unit 5204, Toronto, ON,
M5H 0A2
(416) 313-2912
Emp Here 30   *Sales* 37,716,030
SIC 5172 Petroleum products, nec
Robert Daninnger
Konstantinos Kazinakis
Ralf Gerhard Otto

D-U-N-S 24-562-8433   (HQ)
FUJITSU CANADA, INC
(*Suby of* FUJITSU LIMITED)
155 University Ave Suite 1600, Toronto, ON,
M5H 3B7
(905) 286-9666
Emp Here 50   *Sales* 42,481,530
SIC 5045 Computers, peripherals, and soft-
ware
David Shearer
Craig Smith
Danielle Parent

D-U-N-S 20-638-9967   (HQ)
FUJITSU FRONTECH CANADA INC
(*Suby of* FUJITSU LIMITED)
155 University Ave Suite 1600, Toronto, ON,
M5H 3B7
(800) 668-8325
Sales 12,776,574
SIC 7699 Repair services, nec
Michitaka Sugawara
Carlos A. Cerqueira
Maura Corrigan

D-U-N-S 20-259-1798   (SL)
FURA GEMS INC

FURA
65 Queen St W Suite 800, Toronto, ON, M5H
2M5
(416) 861-2269
Emp Here 282   *Sales* 116,496,738
SIC 1499 Miscellaneous nonMetallic minerals,
except fuels
Dev Shetty
Ashim Roy
Rupak Sen
Ryan Ptolemy
Scott Moore
Gaurav Gupta

D-U-N-S 20-259-9734   (HQ)
**GALLAGHER, ARTHUR J. CANADA LIM-
ITED**
(*Suby of* ARTHUR J. GALLAGHER & CO.)
181 University Ave Unit 1200, Toronto, ON,
M5H 3M7
(416) 260-5333
Emp Here 20   *Sales* 92,387,100
SIC 6411 Insurance agents, brokers, and ser-
vice
Ken Keenan
Vyvienne Wade
William Mark Shedden
Thomas J Gallagher
Kevin Neiles
Philip Gaunce
Greg Metcalfe

D-U-N-S 20-977-3431   (SL)
GARDINER ROBERTS LLP
22 Adelaide St W Unit 3600, Toronto, ON,
M5H 4E3
(416) 865-6600
Emp Here 140   *Sales* 15,523,480
SIC 8111 Legal services
David E Fine
Robert Rossow
Evert Van Noudenberg
Robert J Picard
Lori D Mark

D-U-N-S 25-183-0738   (SL)
**GENSLER ARCHITECTURE & DESIGN
CANDA, INC**
GENSLER
(*Suby of* M. ARTHUR GENSLER JR. & AS-
SOCIATES, INC.)
150 King St W Suite 1400, Toronto, ON, M5H
1J9
(416) 601-3890
Emp Here 70   *Sales* 12,511,730
SIC 8712 Architectural services
Eric Ginsburg
Joseph Brancato
Jordan Goldstein
Judy Pesek
Andy Cohen
Ray Shick
Julia Simet
Dan Winey
Jun Xia
Diane Hoskins

D-U-N-S 24-037-6348   (SL)
GHR SYSTEMS INC
11 King St W Suite 600, Toronto, ON, M5H
4C7
(416) 360-5775
Emp Here 49   *Sales* 11,012,456
SIC 6159 Miscellaneous business credit institutions
Rick Arends

D-U-N-S 24-383-7031   (SL)
GLENSTONE CAPITAL CORPORATION
(*Suby of* RSA INSURANCE GROUP PLC)
181 University Ave Suite 1000, Toronto, ON,
M5H 3M7
(416) 682-5300
Emp Here 105
SIC 6331 Fire, marine, and casualty insurance
Steve Faraone

D-U-N-S 20-077-4052   (SL)
GLOBAL SKILLS INC
366 Bay St 10th Fl, Toronto, ON, M5H 4B2
(416) 907-8400
Emp Here 50   *Sales* 11,848,500
SIC 7361 Employment agencies
 Michael Mancuso
 Michelle Lynn Harrison

D-U-N-S 24-803-0058   (SL)
GLUSKIN SHEFF + ASSOCIATES INC
GS
(*Suby of* ONEX CORPORATION)
333 Bay St Suite 5100, Toronto, ON, M5H 2R2
(416) 681-6000
Emp Here 40   *Sales* 37,567,080
SIC 6282 Investment advice
 Jeff Moody
 Nancy Lockhart
 Peter Mann
 Peter Zaltz
 Jim Bantis
 Lindsay Quinn
 David Morris
 Paul Beeston
 Ann Davis
 Wilfred Gobert

D-U-N-S 24-347-7580   (HQ)
GMP CAPITAL INC
GMP SECURITIES
145 King St W Suite 300, Toronto, ON, M5H
1J8
(416) 367-8600
Sales 134,793,568
SIC 6211 Security brokers and dealers
 Harris Fricker
 Kevin M. Sullivan
 Stephen Harris
 Deborah Starkman
 Donald A. Wright
 David G. Brown
 David C. Ferguson
 Kishore Kapoor
 Fiona L. Macdonald
 Eugene C. Mcburney

D-U-N-S 25-273-8190   (HQ)
GMP SECURITIES L.P.
(*Suby of* GMP CORP)
145 King St W Suite 300, Toronto, ON, M5H
1J8
(416) 367-8600
Emp Here 100   *Sales* 314,513,498
SIC 6211 Security brokers and dealers
 Kevin M Sullivan
 J. Robert Fraser
 Eugene C Mcburney
 Mark Wellings
 Lorne M. Sugarman
 Jason J. Robertson
 Bob Bastianon
 Ed Charron
 Leo Ciccone

D-U-N-S 24-313-0221   (SL)
GOBIMIN INC
120 Adelaide St W Suite 2110, Toronto, ON,
M5H 1T1
(416) 915-0133
Emp Here 250   *Sales* 103,277,250
SIC 1481 NonMetallic mineral services
 Felipe Tan
 Joyce Ko
 Hubert Marleau
 Dominic Cheng
 Maxime Lemieux
 Ma Jianqing

D-U-N-S 20-301-8262   (HQ)
GOLDEN STAR RESOURCES LTD
150 King St W Suite 1200, Toronto, ON, M5H
1J9
(416) 583-3800
Emp Here 100   *Sales* 273,017,000
SIC 1041 Gold ores
 Andrew Wray

 Tim Baker
 Martin Raffield
 Andre Van Niekerk
 Daniel Owiredu
 Robert Vallis
 Tania Shaw
 Karen Walsh
 Mitch Wasel
 Philipa Varris

D-U-N-S 20-771-6838   (HQ)
GOODMANS LLP
333 Bay St Suite 3400, Toronto, ON, M5H 2S7
(416) 979-2211
Emp Here 600   *Sales* 129,701,880
SIC 8111 Legal services
 Dale Lastman
 Allan Leibel
 Byron Sonberg

D-U-N-S 20-111-1866   (HQ)
GRAN COLOMBIA GOLD CORP
401 Bay St Suite 2400, Toronto, ON, M5H 2Y4
(416) 360-4653
Emp Here 2,098   *Sales* 268,525,000
SIC 1081 Metal mining services
 Lombardo Paredes Arenas
 Serafino Iacono
 Miguel De La Campa
 Jose Ignacio Noguera
 Alessandro Cecchi
 De Lyle Bloomquist
 Hernan Martinez
 Jaime Peres Branger
 Robert Metcalfe
 Monica De Greiff

D-U-N-S 20-503-8201   (HQ)
GRAVITAS FINANCIAL INC
333 Bay St Suite 1700, Toronto, ON, M5H 2R2
(647) 252-1674
Sales 10,230,122
SIC 6282 Investment advice
 Ernie Eves
 Peter Liabotis
 Vikas Ranjan
 Vishy Karamadam
 Gerry Goldberg
 Yongbiao Ding

D-U-N-S 25-283-5566   (SL)
GREAT LAKES COMMODITIES INC
320 Bay St, Toronto, ON, M5H 4A6
(416) 864-0856
Emp Here 31   *Sales* 21,400,592
SIC 6221 Commodity contracts brokers, dealers
 John Mcbride

D-U-N-S 24-215-9135   (SL)
GREEN AND SPIEGEL, LLP
150 York St 5th Fl, Toronto, ON, M5H 3S5
(416) 862-7880
Emp Here 75   *Sales* 8,316,150
SIC 8111 Legal services
 Mendel Green
 Stephen W Green
 Evan Green

D-U-N-S 20-287-4186   (SL)
GREEN EARTH NANO SCIENCE INC
181 University Ave Suite 2200, Toronto, ON,
M5H 3M7
(416) 800-0969
Emp Here 44   *Sales* 13,250,248
SIC 4959 Sanitary services, nec
 Piotr Chrzaniecki

D-U-N-S 20-341-1095   (SL)
GREEN ESSENTIAL SERVICES INC
250 University Ave Suite 200, Toronto, ON,
M5H 3E5
(866) 820-2284
Emp Here 50   *Sales* 16,280,000
SIC 5999 Miscellaneous retail stores, nec
 Dennis Kiriopoulos

D-U-N-S 20-552-1565   (HQ)

GRIFFITHS MCBURNEY CANADA CORP
ACQUISITION GMP
(*Suby of* GMP CORP)
145 King St W Suite 1100, Toronto, ON, M5H
1J8
(416) 367-8600
Emp Here 10   *Sales* 256,164,840
SIC 6211 Security brokers and dealers
 Harris A. Fricker
 Deborah J. Starkman

D-U-N-S 20-369-0362   (SL)
HAMPTON FINANCIAL CORPORATION
141 Adelaide St W Suite 1800, Toronto, ON,
M5H 3L5
(416) 862-7800
Emp Here 107   *Sales* 13,351,032
SIC 8741 Management services
 Peter M. Debb
 Joe Pavao
 Robert Sherman
 Steven Small
 Richard Carl
 John H. Sununu
 Jason Mackey

D-U-N-S 25-512-5775   (SL)
HAMPTON SECURITIES LIMITED
141 Adelaide St W Suite 1800, Toronto, ON,
M5H 3L5
(416) 862-7800
Emp Here 100   *Sales* 93,917,700
SIC 6211 Security brokers and dealers
 Peter Deeb
 Cheryl De Montigny
 Joe Pavao
 Jason Mackey

D-U-N-S 20-527-5134   (HQ)
HARLEQUIN ENTERPRISES LIMITED
HARLEQUIN BOOKS
(*Suby of* NEWS CORPORATION)
22 Adelaide Street W 41st Fl, Toronto, ON,
M5H 4E3
(416) 445-5860
Sales 193,774,000
SIC 2731 Book publishing
 Craig Swinwood
 Leo Macdonald
 Christina Clifford
 John Reindl
 Christine Greco
 Kirk Marshall

D-U-N-S 20-044-2671   (HQ)
HARPERCOLLINS CANADA LIMITED
(*Suby of* NEWS CORP UK & IRELAND LIMITED)
22 Adelaide St W, Toronto, ON, M5H 4E3
(416) 975-9334
Emp Here 100   *Sales* 91,908,804
SIC 5192 Books, periodicals, and newspapers
 David Kent
 Wayne Playter

D-U-N-S 20-874-8715   (HQ)
HAY GROUP LIMITED
HAY GROUP, THE
(*Suby of* KORN FERRY)
121 King St W Suite 700, Toronto, ON, M5H
3T9
(416) 868-1371
Emp Here 80   *Sales* 16,220,880
SIC 8741 Management services
 Christopher Matthews
 Teresa Ahuja

D-U-N-S 24-418-5737   (SL)
HDR ARCHITECTURE ASSOCIATES, INC
HDR/G&G
255 Adelaide St W, Toronto, ON, M5H 1X9
(647) 777-4900
Emp Here 77   *Sales* 13,548,766
SIC 8712 Architectural services
 John Greenan

D-U-N-S 20-221-2700   (HQ)
HILTON CANADA CO.

HILTON TORONTO
(*Suby of* HILTON WORLDWIDE HOLDING LLP)
145 Richmond St W, Toronto, ON, M5H 2L2
(416) 869-3456
Emp Here 7   *Sales* 153,068,800
SIC 7011 Hotels and motels
 Ted R Ratcliff
 Kevin J Jacobs
 Joseph Berger
 W Steven Standefer
 Denis Mccarthy
 Robert Harper
 David Marote

D-U-N-S 24-810-6742   (HQ)
HITACHI DATA SYSTEMS INC
(*Suby of* HITACHI, LTD.)
11 King St W Suite 1400, Toronto, ON, M5H
4C7
(416) 494-4114
Emp Here 95   *Sales* 20,315,845
SIC 7372 Prepackaged software
 Minoru Kosuge
 Barry Morrison

D-U-N-S 24-632-7720   (HQ)
HOME CAPITAL GROUP INC
145 King St W Suite 2300, Toronto, ON, M5H
1J8
(416) 360-4663
Sales 279,454,196
SIC 7389 Business services, nec
 Yousry Bissada
 Mike Forshee
 Ed Karthaus
 Dinah J. Henderson
 Benjy Katchen
 David Cluff
 Brad Kotush
 Anthony Stilo
 Amy Bruyea
 John Hong

D-U-N-S 20-077-3401   (HQ)
HOME TRUST COMPANY
(*Suby of* HOME CAPITAL GROUP INC)
145 King St W Suite 2300, Toronto, ON, M5H
1J8
(416) 775-5000
Emp Here 300   *Sales* 101,947,540
SIC 6021 National commercial banks
 Bonita Then
 Yousry Bissada
 Chris Ahlvik
 Cathy Sutherland
 John Harry
 Brian Mosko
 Brad Kotush
 Chris Whyte
 David Cluff
 Pino Decina

D-U-N-S 20-772-5123   (BR)
HUDSON'S BAY COMPANY
HBC
(*Suby of* HUDSON'S BAY COMPANY)
401 Bay St Suite 601, Toronto, ON, M5H 2Y4
(866) 225-8251
Emp Here 80
SIC 5311 Department stores

D-U-N-S 20-770-1616   (BR)
HY'S OF CANADA LTD
HY'S STEAKHOUSE
(*Suby of* HY'S OF CANADA LTD)
120 Adelaide St W Suite 101, Toronto, ON,
M5H 1T1
(416) 364-6600
Emp Here 100
SIC 5812 Eating places
 Chris Meybr

D-U-N-S 25-203-8633   (HQ)
IAMGOLD CORPORATION
MINE WESTWOOD
401 Bay St Suite 3200, Toronto, ON, M5H 2Y4

▲ Public Company   ■ Public Company Family Member   **HQ** Headquarters   **BR** Branch   **SL** Single Location

(416) 360-4710
Emp Here 55   *Sales* 1,111,000,000
SIC 1041 Gold ores
Stephen J. J. Letwin
Carol Banducci
Gordon Stothart
Benjamin Little
Craig Macdougall
Jeffery Snow
Donald Charter
John Caldwell
Richard Hall
Mahendra Naik

D-U-N-S 24-910-2864   (HQ)
IMPERIAL CAPITAL CORPORATION
200 King St W Suite 1701, Toronto, ON, M5H
3T4
(416) 362-3658
Sales 10,862,768
SIC 6211 Security brokers and dealers
Stephen D. Lister
Jeffrey L. Rosenthal
Edward Truant

D-U-N-S 25-529-0041   (HQ)
**INDEPENDENT ELECTRICITY SYSTEM OP-
ERATOR**
IESO
120 Adelaide St W Suite 1600, Toronto, ON,
M5H 1P9
(905) 855-6100
Emp Here 20   *Sales* 509,905,500
SIC 4911 Electric services
Peter Gregg
Kimberly Marshall
Leonard Kula
Timothy O'neill
Cynthia Chaplin
Murray Elston
Susanna Han
Christopher Henderson
Ersilia Serafini
Deborah Whale

D-U-N-S 20-637-9914   (HQ)
INDEPENDENT TRADING GROUP (ITG) INC
4 King St W Suite 402, Toronto, ON, M5H 1B6
(416) 941-0046
Emp Here 8   *Sales* 12,899,537
SIC 6211 Security brokers and dealers
Dave Houlding
Doug Christie
Robin Russell
Brian Jones

D-U-N-S 25-278-1042   (HQ)
**INDUSTRIAL AND COMMERCIAL BANK OF
CHINA (CANADA)**
(*Suby of* INDUSTRIAL AND COMMERCIAL
BANK OF CHINA LIMITED)
333 Bay St Suite 3710, Toronto, ON, M5H 2R2
(416) 366-5588
Emp Here 40   *Sales* 20,144,700
SIC 6021 National commercial banks
Cedric Ng
David K.P. Li

D-U-N-S 24-453-5407   (HQ)
INFORMATION BUILDERS (CANADA) INC
(*Suby of* INFORMATION BUILDERS, INC.)
150 York St Suite 1000, Toronto, ON, M5H
3S5
(416) 364-0349
Sales 44,717,400
SIC 5045 Computers, peripherals, and soft-
ware
Gerald Cohen

D-U-N-S 20-706-0158   (BR)
INFOROUTE SANTE DU CANADA INC
CANADA HEALTH INFOWAY
(*Suby of* INFOROUTE SANTE DU CANADA
INC)
150 King St Suite 1308, Toronto, ON, M5H
1J9
(416) 979-4606
Emp Here 75

SIC 7338 Secretarial and court reporting
Jean Gangdein

D-U-N-S 25-195-1166   (HQ)
INFOTEK CONSULTING SERVICES INC
80 Richmond St W Suite 400, Toronto, ON,
M5H 2A4
(416) 365-0337
Emp Here 1   *Sales* 25,027,050
SIC 7379 Computer related services, nec
Kelly Amaral

D-U-N-S 20-315-8878   (SL)
INMET ANATOLIA LIMITED
330 Bay St Suite 1000, Toronto, ON, M5H 2S8
(416) 361-6400
Emp Here 220   *Sales* 525,260,780
SIC 1081 Metal mining services
Jochen Tilk
Steven Astritis

D-U-N-S 25-691-0928   (SL)
INQUENT TECHNOLOGIES INC
150 York St, Toronto, ON, M5H 3S5
(416) 645-4600
Emp Here 150   *Sales* 34,270,800
SIC 4813 Telephone communication, except
radio
Kelly Hagen
Jesse Rasch
Wayne Bigby

D-U-N-S 20-983-8130   (HQ)
INSIGHT SPORTS LTD
INSIGHT SPORTS NETWORKS
184 Pearl St Suite 302, Toronto, ON, M5H 1L5
(416) 593-0915
Sales 15,993,040
SIC 4833 Television broadcasting stations
Michael Rubinstein
Sean Luxton
Corey Russell
John Brunton
Lawrence Tanenbaum
Geoff Browne
Michael Griffiths

D-U-N-S 20-731-5800   (SL)
INTEGRAL WEALTH SECURITIES LIMITED
(*Suby of* INTEGRAL WEALTH MANAGE-
MENT INC)
56 Temperance St Suite 900, Toronto, ON,
M5H 3V5
(416) 203-2000
Emp Here 15   *Sales* 10,183,845
SIC 6211 Security brokers and dealers
Darryl Sherriff
John Gibson

D-U-N-S 25-512-1717   (SL)
**INTERCONTINENTAL GOLD AND METALS
LTD**
365 Bay St Suite 400, Toronto, ON, M5H 2V1
(647) 985-2785
Emp Here 10   *Sales* 22,604,888
SIC 1081 Metal mining services
Gorden Glenn
John Anderson
Chris Irwin
Ali Zamani

D-U-N-S 25-353-1727   (SL)
INTERHEALTH CANADA LIMITED
357 Bay St Suite 600, Toronto, ON, M5H 2T7
(416) 362-4681
Emp Here 8   *Sales* 65,982,900
SIC 8732 Commercial nonphysical research
Stephen Parsons
Shashikant Nayak
Christopher Barldrop

D-U-N-S 24-359-2602   (HQ)
INVESQUE INC
333 Bay St Suite 3400, Toronto, ON, M5H 2S7

Emp Here 7   *Sales* 109,388,000
SIC 8361 Residential care
Scott White

Adam Zeiger
Vineet Bedi
Bryan Hickman
Dennis Dechow
Azin Lotfi
Scott Higgs
Donna Brandin

D-U-N-S 24-375-3428   (HQ)
**INVESTMENT INDUSTRY REGULATORY
ORGANIZATION OF CANADA**
IIROC
121 King St W Suite 1600, Toronto, ON, M5H
3T9
(416) 364-0604
Emp Here 160   *Sales* 53,896
SIC 8611 Business associations
Susan Wolburgh Jenah
Daniel Leclair
Daniel Muzuka
Gerry Rocchi
Grant Vingoe
Kerry Adams
Michelle Khalili
Robert Lesourd
Roger Casgrain
Ronald S Lloyd

D-U-N-S 20-383-5210   (SL)
IQ OFFICE SUITES HOLDINGS INC
IQ OFFICE SUITES
150 King St W Suite 200, Toronto, ON, M5H
1J9
(888) 744-2292
Emp Here 25   *Sales* 11,087,250
SIC 7389 Business services, nec
Kane Willmott

D-U-N-S 25-975-9603   (HQ)
**JONES LANG LASALLE REAL ESTATE
SERVICES, INC**
(*Suby of* JONES LANG LASALLE INCORPO-
RATED)
22 Adelaide St W 26th Fl East Tower, Toronto,
ON, M5H 4E3
(416) 304-6000
Emp Here 50   *Sales* 41,888,900
SIC 6531 Real estate agents and managers
Rick Urbanczyk

D-U-N-S 25-291-2472   (SL)
**KING'S HEALTH CENTRE CORPORATION
THE**
250 University Ave, Toronto, ON, M5H 3E5

Emp Here 220
SIC 8093 Specialty outpatient clinics, nec

D-U-N-S 20-187-0990   (HQ)
KINGSETT CAPITAL INC
40 King St W Suite 3700, Toronto, ON, M5H
3Y2
(416) 687-6700
Emp Here 22   *Sales* 34,840,500
SIC 6798 Real estate investment trusts
Jon E Love
Anna Kennedy
Kamran Abbasi
Charles Blue
Kandiah Aravinthan
David Vernon
Andy Baines
Ingrid Beausoleil

D-U-N-S 24-625-0542   (SL)
KOSKIE MINSKY LLP
20 Queen St W Unit 900, Toronto, ON, M5H
3R3
(416) 977-8353
Emp Here 125   *Sales* 13,860,250
SIC 8111 Legal services
Lawrence Banack
Stephen Wahl
Mark Zigler
Kirk Baert
Andrew Hatnay
Arleen Huggins

Ari Kaplan
Jeffrey Long
Michael Mazzuca
Alistair Esterbauer

D-U-N-S 24-874-5754   (HQ)
KPMG INC
333 Bay St Suite 4600, Toronto, ON, M5H 2S5
(416) 777-8500
Emp Here 60   *Sales* 34,937,280
SIC 8741 Management services
Joseph A Tucker
Robert Sanderson

D-U-N-S 20-770-4156   (HQ)
KPMG LLP
333 Bay St Suite 4600, Toronto, ON, M5H 2S5
(416) 777-8500
Emp Here 150   *Sales* 924,265,000
SIC 8721 Accounting, auditing, and book-
keeping
Bill Thomas
Mary Lou Maher
Mario Paron
Peter Doyle
Axel Thesburg
John Herhalt
Greg Wiebe
Jean-Pierre Desrosiers
Beth Wilson

D-U-N-S 24-890-9376   (HQ)
LAC DES ILES MINES LTD
(*Suby of* NORTH AMERICAN PALLADIUM
LTD)
130 Adelaide St W Suite 2116, Toronto, ON,
M5H 3P5
(807) 448-2000
Sales 72,895,590
SIC 1099 Metal ores, nec
G Fraser B Sinclair
Trent C A Mell
David J Passfield
James D Excell

D-U-N-S 25-509-3007   (HQ)
LAKE SHORE GOLD CORP
(*Suby of* PAN AMERICAN SILVER CORP)
181 University Ave, Toronto, ON, M5H 3M7
(416) 703-6298
Emp Here 15   *Sales* 120,113,620
SIC 1382 Oil and gas exploration services
Anthony P. Makuch
Phil Yee
Eric Kallio
Alasdair Federico
Christina Ouellette
Mark Utting
Peter Van Alphen
Natasha Vaz
Merushe Verli
Alan Moon

D-U-N-S 24-060-9834   (HQ)
LAW SOCIETY OF UPPER CANADA, THE
130 Queen St W Suite 100, Toronto, ON, M5H
2N6
(416) 644-4886
Sales 163,833,900
SIC 8111 Legal services
Robert Lapper
Janet Minor

D-U-N-S 24-120-3525   (BR)
LAW SOCIETY OF UPPER CANADA, THE
BARREAU DU HAUT CANADA
(*Suby of* LAW SOCIETY OF UPPER
CANADA, THE)
130 Queen St W Suite 100, Toronto, ON, M5H
2N6
(416) 947-3315
Emp Here 525
SIC 8111 Legal services
John Peddie

D-U-N-S 25-185-0301   (SL)
LEGAL LINK CORPORATION, THE

333 Bay St Suite 400, Toronto, ON, M5H 2R2
(416) 348-0432
Emp Here 20   *Sales* 11,734,690
SIC 8732 Commercial nonphysical research
Vince Saroli

D-U-N-S 25-520-3879   (BR)
LERNERS LLP
(*Suby of* LERNERS LLP)
130 Adelaide St W Suite 2400, Toronto, ON, M5H 3P5
(416) 867-3076
Emp Here 150
SIC 8111 Legal services
Michelle Medel

D-U-N-S 25-221-3509   (HQ)
LINDT & SPRUNGLI (CANADA), INC
(*Suby of* CHOCOLADEFABRIKEN LINDT & SPRUNGLI AG)
181 University Ave Suite 900, Toronto, ON, M5H 3M7
(416) 351-8566
Emp Here 73   *Sales* 75,201,930
SIC 5145 Confectionery
Rudi Blatter

D-U-N-S 24-829-7681   (HQ)
LRI ENGINEERING INC
LRI
170 University Ave 3rd Fl, Toronto, ON, M5H 3B3
(416) 515-9331
Sales 17,968,760
SIC 7389 Business services, nec
Eric Esselink
Jon Winton
Michael Devine

D-U-N-S 25-235-4170   (HQ)
LUNDIN MINING CORPORATION
150 King St W Suite 1500, Toronto, ON, M5H 1J9
(416) 342-5560
Sales 1,725,589,000
SIC 1021 Copper ores
Marie Inkster
Jinhee Magie
Peter Richardson
Andrew Hastings
Jean-Claude Lalumiere
Peter Rockandel
Mikael Schauman
Steve Gatley
Derek Riehm
Ciara Talbot

D-U-N-S 20-291-2994   (HQ)
MAGRIS RESOURCES INC
333 Bay St Suite 1101, Toronto, ON, M5H 2R2
(416) 901-9877
Sales 1,391,019,600
SIC 6799 Investors, nec
Anne-Marie Vcelik

D-U-N-S 20-582-0975   (SL)
MARKET REGULATION SERVICES INC
145 King St W Unit 900, Toronto, ON, M5H 1J8
(416) 646-7204
Emp Here 75   *Sales* 17,571,600
SIC 8742 Management consulting services
Martina Wood

D-U-N-S 24-127-4054   (SL)
MAVRIX FUND MANAGEMENT INC
212 King St W Suite 501, Toronto, ON, M5H 1K5
(416) 362-3077
Emp Here 43   *Sales* 22,841,901
SIC 6282 Investment advice
Malvin C Spooner
Raymond M Steele
William Shaw
A. Kirk Purdy
Kenneth R Yurichuk
Pierre Saint-Laurent
Martine Guimond

D-U-N-S 25-403-3319   (SL)
MCAN MORTGAGE CORPORATION
200 King St W Suite 600, Toronto, ON, M5H 3T4
(416) 572-4880
Emp Here 61   *Sales* 57,843,183
SIC 6798 Real estate investment trusts
Karen H. Weaver
Dipti Patel
Joseph Shaw
Martin Beaudry
Carl Brown
Emily Randle
Mike Jensen
Sylvia Pinto
Ian Sutherland
Susan Dore

D-U-N-S 24-325-1043   (HQ)
MCAP COMMERCIAL LP
200 King St W Suite 400, Toronto, ON, M5H 3T4
(416) 598-2665
Sales 105,734,000
SIC 6162 Mortgage bankers and loan correspondents
Derek Norton
Mark Aldridge

D-U-N-S 20-114-4891   (HQ)
MCAP SERVICE CORPORATION
200 King St W Suite 400, Toronto, ON, M5H 3T4
(416) 598-2665
Emp Here 211   *Sales* 396,502,500
SIC 6162 Mortgage bankers and loan correspondents
Derek Norton
Steve Holman
Susan Dore
Steven Maker
Gordon Herridge
Jack Shapiro
Patricia Somers
Cheryl Preston
Robert May

D-U-N-S 24-857-9513   (HQ)
MCEWEN MINING INC
150 King St W Suite 2800, Toronto, ON, M5H 1J9
(647) 258-0395
Sales 128,822,000
SIC 1041 Gold ores
Robert Mcewen
Chris Stewart
Andrew Iaboni
Simon Quick
Sylvian Guerard
Donald Brown
Luke Willis
Michele Ashby
Michael Stein
Allen Ambrose

D-U-N-S 20-151-6572   (HQ)
MCGRAW-HILL RYERSON LIMITED
HIGHER EDUCATION, DIV OF
(*Suby of* S&P GLOBAL INC.)
145 King St W West Suite 1501, Toronto, ON, M5H 1J8
(800) 245-2914
Sales 45,924,438
SIC 2731 Book publishing
David L. Swail
Hendrik J. Kranenburg
Manon R. Vennat
Gordon Dyer
Clive Powell
Marshall Morris
Ian Macdonald
Susan M. Armstrong
Robert J. Bahash
J. Mark Deslauriers

D-U-N-S 24-678-5021   (SL)
MCLEAN WATSON INVESTMENTS INC

(*Suby of* MCLEAN WATSON CAPITAL INC)
141 Adelaide St W Suite 1200, Toronto, ON, M5H 3L5
(416) 363-2000
Emp Here 120   *Sales* 170,776,560
SIC 6211 Security brokers and dealers
Loudon F. Owen
John F Eckert

D-U-N-S 24-130-1279   (SL)
MCLEAN, BUDDEN CANADIAN EQUITY GROWTH FUND
145 King St W Suite 2525, Toronto, ON, M5H 1J8
(416) 862-9800
Emp Here 25   *Sales* 20,694,425
SIC 6722 Management investment, open-end

D-U-N-S 24-131-4413   (SL)
MCLEAN, BUDDEN LIMITED
MCLEAN BUDDEN HIGH INCOME EQUITY FUND
145 King St W Suite 2525, Toronto, ON, M5H 1J8
(416) 862-9800
Emp Here 45   *Sales* 37,249,965
SIC 6722 Management investment, open-end
Roger Beauchemin

D-U-N-S 20-967-9927   (HQ)
MEDCAN HEALTH MANAGEMENT INC
MEDCAN
150 York St Suite 1500, Toronto, ON, M5H 3S5
(416) 350-5900
Sales 28,531,050
SIC 8011 Offices and clinics of medical doctors
Shaun Francis
Ashim Khemani
Andrew Rinzema
Neal Shah

D-U-N-S 20-181-3891   (SL)
MIGAO CORPORATION
200 University Ave Suite300, Toronto, ON, M5H 4H1
(416) 869-1108
Emp Here 1,196   *Sales* 377,255,345
SIC 1474 Potash, soda, and borate minerals

D-U-N-S 24-564-4489   (HQ)
MILLER THOMSON LLP
40 King St W Unit 5800, Toronto, ON, M5H 3S1
(416) 595-8500
Sales 82,350,400
SIC 8111 Legal services
Chris Issar
Orest Szot
John N Turner
Judd D Whiteside
Larry Bertuzzi

D-U-N-S 20-153-0305   (HQ)
MILTOM MANAGEMENT LP
40 King St W Suite 5800, Toronto, ON, M5H 3S1
(416) 595-8500
Emp Here 300   *Sales* 182,754,500
SIC 6712 Bank holding companies
Gerald Courage

D-U-N-S 20-278-8055   (SL)
MINCORE INC
80 Richmond St W Suite 1502, Toronto, ON, M5H 2A4
(416) 214-1766
Emp Here 50   *Sales* 11,671,750
SIC 1081 Metal mining services
David Jones
Francisco Zepeda
Dino Titaro
Terry Bell

D-U-N-S 24-563-8440   (SL)
MINDEN GROSS LLP
145 King St W Suite 2200, Toronto, ON, M5H

4G2
(416) 362-3711
Emp Here 150   *Sales* 16,632,300
SIC 8111 Legal services
Reuben M Rosenblatt
Jules Berman

D-U-N-S 20-379-0347   (SL)
MLG BLOCKCHAIN CONSULTING LTD
214 King St W Suite 210, Toronto, ON, M5H 3S6
(647) 377-3489
Emp Here 40   *Sales* 11,331,720
SIC 8741 Management services
Michael Gord
Kyle Fry
Brian Leiberman

D-U-N-S 24-366-0532   (BR)
MNP LLP
(*Suby of* MNP LLP)
111 Richmond St W Suite 300, Toronto, ON, M5H 2G4
(416) 596-1711
Emp Here 100
SIC 8721 Accounting, auditing, and bookkeeping
Blain Mathieson

D-U-N-S 24-829-4381   (SL)
MONITOR COMPANY CANADA
(*Suby of* DELOITTE LLP)
8 Adelaide St W Ste 20, Toronto, ON, M5H 0A9
(416) 408-4800
Emp Here 5,000
SIC 8741 Management services
Ken Fredeen

D-U-N-S 20-322-0017   (SL)
MORTGAGE CENTRE (CANADA) INC, THE
MCC
(*Suby of* DOMINION LENDING CENTRES INC)
123 Queen St W Suite 403, Toronto, ON, M5H 3M9
(416) 865-9750
Emp Here 50   *Sales* 34,840,500
SIC 6798 Real estate investment trusts
Gary Mauris
Edward Cocciolli
Chris Kayat

D-U-N-S 24-772-0998   (SL)
MUNICH LIFE MANAGEMENT CORPORATION LTD
(*Suby of* MUNCHENER RUCKVERSICHERUNGS-GESELLSCHAFT AG IN MUNCHEN)
390 Bay St Suite 2600, Toronto, ON, M5H 2Y2
(416) 359-2200
Emp Here 160   *Sales* 341,914,880
SIC 6311 Life insurance
Mary Forest
Douglas Tozer
Lloyd Milani
Bernard Naumann
Jackie Puchalski
Saskia Goedhart
Richard Letarte

D-U-N-S 20-771-6879   (HQ)
MUNICH REINSURANCE COMPANY OF CANADA
(*Suby of* MUNCHENER RUCKVERSICHERUNGS-GESELLSCHAFT AG IN MUNCHEN)
390 Bay St Suite 2300, Toronto, ON, M5H 2Y2
(416) 366-9206
Emp Here 110   *Sales* 277,805,840
SIC 6331 Fire, marine, and casualty insurance
Kenneth Irvin
D. Murray Paton
John Lower
Gary Gray
Peter Mccutcheon
Robert Jemmett

James Brierley
Anthony Fall
John Phelan

D-U-N-S 20-192-5281 (HQ)
MUTUAL FUND DEALERS ASSOCIATION OF CANADA
121 King St W Suite 1000, Toronto, ON, M5H 3T9
(416) 361-6332
Emp Here 80 *Sales* 23,411,100
SIC 8621 Professional organizations
Mark Gordon
Lea Hansen
Dawn Russell
Doug Thomson
Janet Woodruff
Robert Sellars
Bill Charles
Steven Donald
Stephen Geist
Sonny Goldstein

D-U-N-S 24-366-8985 (SL)
NATIONAL CLUB, THE
303 Bay St, Toronto, ON, M5H 2R1
(416) 364-3247
Emp Here 80 *Sales* 19,321,200
SIC 8621 Professional organizations
William Morari

D-U-N-S 20-296-4532 (SL)
NDX GROWTH & INCOME FUND
121 King St W Suite 2600, Toronto, ON, M5H 3T9
(416) 681-3966
Emp Here 21 *Sales* 17,383,317
SIC 6726 Investment offices, nec
Allan Leung

D-U-N-S 20-372-7391 (SL)
NEO PERFORMANCE MATERIALS INC
121 King St W Suite 1740, Toronto, ON, M5H 3T9
(416) 367-8588
Emp Here 10 *Sales* 454,195,000
SIC 3499 Fabricated Metal products, nec
Geoffrey R Bedford
Rahim Suleman
Kevin D Morris
Jeffrey R Hogan
Greg Kroll
Frank Timmerman

D-U-N-S 24-951-2443 (HQ)
NEO PERFORMANCE MATERIALS ULC
(*Suby of* MOLYCORP, INC.)
121 King St W Suite 1740, Toronto, ON, M5H 3T9
(416) 367-8588
Emp Here 15 *Sales* 586,486,755
SIC 2819 Industrial inorganic chemicals, nec
Geoffrey Bedford
Rahim Suleman
Kevin Morris
Jeffrey Hogan
Shannon Song
Frank Timmerman

D-U-N-S 24-388-9495 (SL)
NESSCAP ENERGY INC
40 King St W Suite 5800, Toronto, ON, M5H 3S1
(416) 596-2127
Emp Here 8 *Sales* 17,193,109
SIC 3675 Electronic capacitors

D-U-N-S 20-357-9354 (SL)
NEWGIOCO GROUP INC
130 Adelaide St W Suite 701, Toronto, ON, M5H 2K4
(647) 229-0136
Emp Here 15 *Sales* 17,914,316
SIC 7999 Amusement and recreation, nec
Michele Ciavarella
Alessandro Marcelli
Luca Pasquini
Mark J. Korb

Federico Reisenauer
Gabriele Peroni
Franco Salvagni
Julia Lesnykh
Quirinio Mancini
Robert Stabile

D-U-N-S 24-319-3989 (HQ)
NIGHTHAWK GOLD CORP
141 Adelaide St W Suite 301, Toronto, ON, M5H 3L5
(647) 794-4313
Sales 19,100,392
SIC 1041 Gold ores
Michael Byron
Suzette N. Ramcharan
Michael Leskovec
Morris Prychidny
Ernie Eves
Brian Howlett
Luc Lessard
Brent Peters

D-U-N-S 24-848-5224 (HQ)
NIOBEC INC
(*Suby of* MAGRIS RESOURCES INC)
333 Bay St Suite 1101, Toronto, ON, M5H 2R2
(416) 901-9877
Emp Here 1 *Sales* 127,887,000
SIC 1081 Metal mining services
Aaron Regent
Matthew Fenton
Steve Astritis
Anne Marie Vcelik
Warren Gilman
Ranjit Dandekar

D-U-N-S 24-828-8177 (SL)
NORONT RESOURCES LTD
212 King St W Suite 501, Toronto, ON, M5H 1K5
(416) 367-1444
Emp Here 33 *Sales* 78,789,117
SIC 1041 Gold ores
Alan Coutts
Ryan Weston
Glenn Nolan
Mark Baker
Gregory Rieveley
Paul Parisotto
Jean Paul Gladu
John Pollesel
Bo Liu
Sybil Veenman

D-U-N-S 20-193-9886 (HQ)
NORTHBRIDGE FINANCIAL CORPORATION
(*Suby of* FAIRFAX FINANCIAL HOLDINGS LIMITED)
105 Adelaide St W Suite 700, Toronto, ON, M5H 1P9
(416) 350-4400
Sales 7,593,766,400
SIC 6411 Insurance agents, brokers, and service
Silvy Wright
Lambert Morvan
Craig Pinnock

D-U-N-S 25-312-7369 (HQ)
NORTHBRIDGE GENERAL INSURANCE CORPORATION
(*Suby of* FAIRFAX FINANCIAL HOLDINGS LIMITED)
105 Adelaide St W 4th Fl, Toronto, ON, M5H 1P9
(416) 350-4400
Sales 3,205,452,000
SIC 6331 Fire, marine, and casualty insurance
Silvy Wright

D-U-N-S 25-405-6195 (BR)
NORTHBRIDGE GENERAL INSURANCE CORPORATION
(*Suby of* FAIRFAX FINANCIAL HOLDINGS LIMITED)

105 Adelaide St W Unit 700, Toronto, ON, M5H 1P9
(416) 350-4300
Emp Here 600
SIC 6331 Fire, marine, and casualty insurance
Silvy Wright

D-U-N-S 20-628-7190 (BR)
NORTHBRIDGE INDEMNITY INSURANCE CORPORATION
(*Suby of* FAIRFAX FINANCIAL HOLDINGS LIMITED)
105 Adelaide St W Unit 700, Toronto, ON, M5H 1P9
(855) 620-6262
Emp Here 800
SIC 6411 Insurance agents, brokers, and service
Silvy Wright

D-U-N-S 20-511-7476 (HQ)
NORTHBRIDGE PERSONAL INSURANCE CORPORATION
(*Suby of* FAIRFAX FINANCIAL HOLDINGS LIMITED)
105 Adelaide St W, Toronto, ON, M5H 1P9
(416) 350-4400
Emp Here 10 *Sales* 98,833,440
SIC 6331 Fire, marine, and casualty insurance
Silvy Wright
Jane Gardner-Robinson
Fabian Richenberger

D-U-N-S 24-946-8216 (SL)
NORTHERN TRUST COMPANY, CANADA
NORTHERN TRUST GLOBAL ADVISORS
(*Suby of* NORTHERN TRUST CORPORATION)
145 King St W Suite 1910, Toronto, ON, M5H 1J8
(416) 365-7161
Emp Here 55 *Sales* 81,073,355
SIC 6722 Management investment, open-end
Robert Baillie

D-U-N-S 24-376-3708 (BR)
NORTHSTAR HOSPITALITY LIMITED PARTNERSHIP
HILTON TORONTO, THE
(*Suby of* NORTHSTAR HOSPITALITY LIMITED PARTNERSHIP)
145 Richmond St W Suite 212, Toronto, ON, M5H 2L2
(416) 869-3456
Emp Here 100
SIC 7011 Hotels and motels

D-U-N-S 25-509-3569 (HQ)
NORTHWEST MUTUAL FUNDS INC/NORDOUEST FONDS MUTUELS INC
155 University Ave Suite 400, Toronto, ON, M5H 3B7
(416) 594-6633
Emp Here 28 *Sales* 35,594,411
SIC 6722 Management investment, open-end
Michael Butler
Leslie Wood

D-U-N-S 24-576-2984 (SL)
NT GLOBAL ADVISORS INC
(*Suby of* NORTHERN TRUST CORPORATION)
145 King St W Suite 1910, Toronto, ON, M5H 1J8
(416) 366-2020
Emp Here 24 *Sales* 10,624,140
SIC 6282 Investment advice
Robert J Baillie

D-U-N-S 25-373-7233 (SL)
OMBUDSMAN FOR BANKING SERVICES AND INVESTMENTS
OBSI
401 Bay St Suite 1505, Toronto, ON, M5H 2Y4
(416) 287-2877
Emp Here 20 *Sales* 13,578,460
SIC 6282 Investment advice
Sarah Bradley

Joelle Harfouche

D-U-N-S 25-530-9940 (HQ)
OMD CANADA
(*Suby of* OMNICOM GROUP INC.)
67 Richmond St W Suite 2, Toronto, ON, M5H 1Z5
(416) 681-5600
Emp Here 175 *Sales* 78,588,470
SIC 7319 Advertising, nec
Cathy Collier
Michael Pitre
Lorraine Hughes

D-U-N-S 24-411-6752 (HQ)
OMERS ADMINISTRATION CORPORATION
OMERS
100 Adelaide St W Suite 900, Toronto, ON, M5H 0E2
(416) 369-2400
Emp Here 500 *Sales* 1,482,895,769
SIC 6371 Pension, health, and welfare funds
Michael Latimer
Annesley Wallace
Jenny Tsouvalis
Upton Jeans
Michael Kelly
Rodney Hill
Jonathan Simmons

D-U-N-S 20-695-9871 (HQ)
OMERS PRIVATE EQUITY INC
(*Suby of* OMERS ADMINISTRATION CORPORATION)
100 Adelaide St W Suite 900, Toronto, ON, M5H 0E2
(416) 864-3200
Sales 5,692,552,000
SIC 6282 Investment advice
Michael Rolland
Robert C Hedges

D-U-N-S 24-893-9720 (HQ)
OMERS REALTY CORPORATION
PROMENADES DE LA CATHEDRALE, LES
(*Suby of* OMERS ADMINISTRATION CORPORATION)
130 Adelaide St W Suite 1100, Toronto, ON, M5H 3P5
(416) 369-2400
Emp Here 15 *Sales* 91,377,250
SIC 6719 Holding companies, nec
E.M. Blake Hutcheson
Michael Kitt
Robert M. Aziz
Judith E. George

D-U-N-S 24-382-0847 (HQ)
ONTARIO PENSION BOARD
200 King St W Suite 2200, Toronto, ON, M5H 3X6
(416) 364-8558
Sales 203,843,970
SIC 6371 Pension, health, and welfare funds
Mark Fuller
M Vinzenza Sera
M David Brown

D-U-N-S 25-070-7163 (SL)
ONTARIO PHARMACISTS' ASSOCIATION
155 University Ave Suite 600, Toronto, ON, M5H 3B7
(416) 441-0788
Emp Here 85 *Sales* 20,528,775
SIC 8621 Professional organizations
Amedeoo Zottola
Tina Perlman
Akeel Jaffer
Bruce Faulkner
Donnie Edwards
Ken Burns
Bill Wilson
Renee St-Jean
Jack Pinkus
Robert Modestino

D-U-N-S 25-535-7451 (SL)
ONTARIO SECURITIES COMMISSION

20 Queen St W 22 Flr, Toronto, ON, M5H 3R3
(416) 593-8314
Emp Here 400   *Sales* 44,352,800
SIC 8111 Legal services
  Tim Moseley

D-U-N-S 25-405-0883   (SL)
OPEN ACCESS LIMITED
1 Richmond St W Suite 800, Toronto, ON, M5H 3W4
(416) 364-4444
Emp Here 40   *Sales* 23,196,960
SIC 6411 Insurance agents, brokers, and service
  John Warren Laing
  Catherine Marsh
  Ron Feddersen

D-U-N-S 24-866-9913   (HQ)
ORVANA MINERALS CORP
170 University Ave Suite 900, Toronto, ON, M5H 3B3
(416) 369-1629
Sales 137,999,000
SIC 1081 Metal mining services
  Juan Gavidia
  Nuria Menendez
  Gordon Pridham
  Ed Guimaraes
  Sara Magner
  Alan Edwards
  George Darling
  Alfredo Garcia

D-U-N-S 25-251-3809   (HQ)
OSISKO MINING INC
155 University Ave Suite 1440, Toronto, ON, M5H 3B7
(416) 848-9504
Sales 15,346,440
SIC 1081 Metal mining services
  John F. Burzynski
  Sean Roosen
  Robert Wares
  Jose Vizquerra-Benavides
  Don Njegovan
  Alix Drapack
  Alexandria Marcotte
  Lili Mance
  Patrick Patrick
  Keith Mckay

D-U-N-S 20-639-6756   (HQ)
OXFORD PROPERTIES GROUP INC
(*Suby of* OMERS ADMINISTRATION CORPORATION)
100 Adelaide St W Suite 900, Toronto, ON, M5H 0E2
(416) 865-8300
Emp Here 100   *Sales* 176,380,100
SIC 6512 Nonresidential building operators
  Blake Hutcheson
  Ann Clavelle
  Robert Aziz
  Michael Kitt
  Colin Loudon

D-U-N-S 20-954-6675   (SL)
PARADIGM QUEST INC
390 Bay St Suite 1800, Toronto, ON, M5H 2Y2
(416) 366-8606
Emp Here 190   *Sales* 100,447,300
SIC 6162 Mortgage bankers and loan correspondents
  Kathy Gregory
  Donald Zuill
  John Bordignon
  Sally Aitken
  Sharon Fitzpatrick
  Rich Hewitt
  Chris Mariani
  Sam Stravato

D-U-N-S 20-351-4948   (SL)
PAYPROP CANADA LIMITED
357 Bay St Unit 500, Toronto, ON, M5H 2T7

(416) 735-7600
Emp Here 80   *Sales* 14,184,880
SIC 7371 Custom computer programming services
  Mislav Majic

D-U-N-S 20-361-0456   (SL)
PAYTM LABS INC
PAYTM
(*Suby of* ONE 97 COMMUNICATIONS LIMITED)
220 Adelaide St W, Toronto, ON, M5H 1W7
(647) 360-8331
Emp Here 50   *Sales* 10,692,550
SIC 7372 Prepackaged software
  Harinder Pal Singh Takhar
  Vijay Shekhar Sharma

D-U-N-S 20-340-8364   (SL)
PEAK POWER INC
214 King St W Suite 414, Toronto, ON, M5H 3S6
(647) 226-1834
Emp Here 25   *Sales* 15,665,350
SIC 4911 Electric services
  Derek Lim Soo
  Matthew Sachs

D-U-N-S 20-526-8852   (SL)
PLUSONE INC
347 Bay St Suite 506, Toronto, ON, M5H 2R7
(416) 861-1662
Emp Here 68   *Sales* 18,654,576
SIC 8741 Management services
  Don Mccaw
  Joseph Brandt

D-U-N-S 25-998-3666   (HQ)
POINTS INTERNATIONAL LTD
111 Richmond St W Suite 700, Toronto, ON, M5H 2G4
(416) 595-0000
Sales 376,245,000
SIC 8742 Management consulting services
  T. Robert Maclean
  Christopher Barnard
  Peter Lockhard
  Erick Georgiou
  Jay Malowney
  Owen Tran
  Inez Murdoch
  David Adams
  Leontine Atkins
  Christopher J.D. Barnard

D-U-N-S 25-214-8945   (HQ)
POLAR CAPITAL CORPORATION
372 Bay St, Toronto, ON, M5H 2W9
(416) 367-4364
Emp Here 23   *Sales* 14,873,796
SIC 6211 Security brokers and dealers
  Paul Sabourin
  Reid Drury
  Stephen Mulherin
  Tom Sabourin
  T. Gerald Jackson

D-U-N-S 25-520-5759   (HQ)
POLLITT & CO. INC
(*Suby of* 2186217 ONTARIO INC)
330 Bay St Suite 405, Toronto, ON, M5H 2S8
(416) 365-3313
Emp Here 13   *Sales* 10,183,845
SIC 6211 Security brokers and dealers
  Murray H. Pollitt
  John Christie
  Charles Bourke
  Graeme Lang

D-U-N-S 24-356-3884   (HQ)
PURE INDUSTRIAL REAL ESTATE TRUST
PIRET
(*Suby of* BLACKSTONE PROPERTY PARTNERS L.P.)
121 King St W Suite 2100, Toronto, ON, M5H 3T9
(416) 479-8590
Emp Here 16   *Sales* 176,662,311

SIC 6722 Management investment, open-end
  Teresa Neto
  Kantaro Goto
  Allan T. Sato
  Charlie Deeks

D-U-N-S 25-676-6395   (HQ)
QMX GOLD CORPORATION
65 Queen St W Suite 800, Toronto, ON, M5H 2M5
(416) 861-5899
Emp Here 30   *Sales* 33,506,394
SIC 1081 Metal mining services
  Brad Humphrey
  Michael Timmins
  David Rigg
  Andreas Rompel
  Stephane Amireault
  Ralph Lean
  Bruce Humphrey
  Deborah Battiston

D-U-N-S 24-028-5726   (SL)
REGISTERED NURSES ASSOCIATION OF ONTARIO
RNAO
158 Pearl St, Toronto, ON, M5H 1L3
(416) 599-1925
Emp Here 55   *Sales* 13,283,325
SIC 8621 Professional organizations
  Doris Grinspun
  Nancy Campbell

D-U-N-S 25-487-8283   (SL)
REINSURANCE MANAGEMENT ASSOCIATES INC
RMA
170 University Ave Suite 500, Toronto, ON, M5H 3B3
(416) 408-2602
Emp Here 27   *Sales* 49,859,793
SIC 6311 Life insurance
  John Chamberlain
  Claire Myles
  Jason Arnell

D-U-N-S 24-991-1918   (SL)
RETAIL READY FOODS INC
130 Adelaide St W Suite 810, Toronto, ON, M5H 3P5
(905) 812-8555
Emp Here 39   *Sales* 32,587,503
SIC 5147 Meats and meat products
  John Ferraro

D-U-N-S 20-699-9166   (HQ)
RICHTREE MARKET RESTAURANTS INC
(*Suby of* NATURAL MARKETS FOOD GROUP)
14 Queen St W, Toronto, ON, M5H 3X4
(416) 366-8986
Emp Here 12   *Sales* 28,926,500
SIC 5812 Eating places
  Gabriel De Alba
  Matt Williams
  William Jean
  Newton Glassman
  Jane Chan

D-U-N-S 20-942-8655   (HQ)
RIDOUT & MAYBEE LLP
250 University Ave 5th Fl, Toronto, ON, M5H 3E5
(416) 868-1482
Emp Here 50   *Sales* 14,414,660
SIC 8111 Legal services
  David Greer

D-U-N-S 24-354-9206   (HQ)
ROBINSON SOLUTIONS INC
(*Suby of* 2082486 ONTARIO INC)
390 Bay St Suite 1520, Toronto, ON, M5H 2Y2
(416) 479-7440
Emp Here 10   *Sales* 35,213,598
SIC 8741 Management services
  Bernie Robinson
  Michael Robinson

D-U-N-S 25-528-9092   (SL)
ROXGOLD INC
360 Bay St Suite 500, Toronto, ON, M5H 2V6
(416) 203-6401
Emp Here 171   *Sales* 168,859,000
SIC 1041 Gold ores
  John Dorward
  Eric Pick
  Vince Sapuppo
  Iain Cox
  Paul Criddle
  Oliver Lennox-King
  Richard Colterjohn
  John Knowles
  Kate Harcourt
  Norm Pitcher

D-U-N-S 24-555-8825   (HQ)
ROYAL NICKEL CORPORATION
141 Adelaide St W Suite 1608, Toronto, ON, M5H 3L5
(416) 363-0649
Emp Here 20   *Sales* 89,613,721
SIC 1061 Ferroalloy ores, except vanadium
  Mark Selby
  Peter Goudie
  John Leddy
  Johnna Muinonen
  Alger St-Jean
  Scott Hand
  Wendy Kei
  Peter Goudie
  Warwick Morley-Jepson
  Frank Marzoli

D-U-N-S 20-188-4876   (HQ)
ROYNAT CAPITAL INC
ROYNAT EQUITY PARTNERS
(*Suby of* BANK OF NOVA SCOTIA, THE)
40 King St W, Toronto, ON, M5H 3Y2
(416) 933-2730
Emp Here 25   *Sales* 79,300,500
SIC 6159 Miscellaneous business credit institutions
  Renie Llewellyn
  Jeff Chernin
  Wray Stannard

D-U-N-S 20-410-0317   (HQ)
SCOTIA CAPITAL INC
PATRIMOINE HOLLIS
(*Suby of* BANK OF NOVA SCOTIA, THE)
40 King St W, Toronto, ON, M5H 3Y2
(416) 863-7411
Emp Here 500   *Sales* 2,703,962,200
SIC 6211 Security brokers and dealers
  Glenda Caratao
  Massimo Ceschia

D-U-N-S 24-891-6769   (HQ)
SCOTIA WEALTH INSURANCE SERVICES INC
SCOTIACAPITAL
(*Suby of* BANK OF NOVA SCOTIA, THE)
40 King St W, Toronto, ON, M5H 1H1
(416) 863-7272
Emp Here 7   *Sales* 42,403,000
SIC 6411 Insurance agents, brokers, and service
  Robert Mcgavin
  Chris Whittaker
  Glenda Caratao
  Michel Martil
  Alex Cruickshank
  Alex R. Besharat
  Edward Keohane

D-U-N-S 24-685-2920   (SL)
SECURITY COMPASS INC
257 Adelaide St W Suite 500, Toronto, ON, M5H 1X9
(888) 777-2211
Emp Here 100   *Sales* 17,731,100
SIC 7371 Custom computer programming services
  Nishchal Bhalla

David Rea

D-U-N-S 20-304-0332   (HQ)
SERCO CANADA INC
(*Suby of* SERCO GROUP PLC)
330 Bay St Suite 400, Toronto, ON, M5H 2S8
(416) 225-3788
Sales 134,643,600
SIC 8741 Management services
Paul Dalglish
Alan Casey
Anthony Vantellingen
Gary Shankman
David Goldberg
Keith Hoffman
Dirk Smith
Terry Caldarone
Cynthia Elderkin
Michaal Plymack

D-U-N-S 24-349-6937   (SL)
SGGG FUND SERVICES INC.
121 King St W Unit 300, Toronto, ON, M5H 3T9
(416) 967-0038
Emp Here 120   *Sales* 24,922,200
SIC 8721 Accounting, auditing, and book-keeping
Sharon Grosman

D-U-N-S 24-985-2443   (HQ)
SHERRITT INTERNATIONAL CORPORA-TION
22 Adelaide St W Suite 4220, Toronto, ON, M5H 4E3
(416) 924-4551
Emp Here 700   *Sales* 115,913,796
SIC 1081 Metal mining services
David Pathe
Steve Wood
Elvin Saruk
Tim Dobson
Ward Sellers
Andrew Snowden
Karen Trenton
Timothy Baker
Peter Gillin
Adrian Loader

D-U-N-S 20-772-7801   (HQ)
SHIBLEY RIGHTON LLP
250 University Ave Suite 700, Toronto, ON, M5H 3E5
(416) 214-5200
Emp Here 68   *Sales* 11,396,814
SIC 8111 Legal services
Richard Shibley
Sandra E Dawe

D-U-N-S 24-942-9521   (SL)
SHIMMERMAN PENN LLP
111 Richmond St W Suite 300, Toronto, ON, M5H 2G4
(416) 964-7200
Emp Here 48   *Sales* 10,036,080
SIC 8721 Accounting, auditing, and book-keeping
Irwin Choleva
Doug Hartkorn

D-U-N-S 24-377-3848   (BR)
SIERRA SYSTEMS GROUP INC
SIERRA SYSTEMS
(*Suby of* NIPPON TELEGRAPH AND TELE-PHONE CORPORATION)
150 York St Suite 1910, Toronto, ON, M5H 3S5
(416) 777-1212
Emp Here 105
SIC 7379 Computer related services, nec
Greg Pelling

D-U-N-S 20-357-7846   (SL)
SLATE OFFICE II L.P.
SLATE OFFICE MANAGEMENT
(*Suby of* SLATE ASSET MANAGEMENT L.P.)
121 King St W Suite 200, Toronto, ON, M5H 3T9

(416) 644-4264
Emp Here 60   *Sales* 61,946,640
SIC 6798 Real estate investment trusts
Brady Welch
Blair Welch

D-U-N-S 20-123-6842   (SL)
SLATE OFFICE REIT
121 King St W Suite 200, Toronto, ON, M5H 3T9
(416) 644-4264   *Sales* 159,124,852
Emp Here 9
SIC 6798 Real estate investment trusts
Scott Antoniak
Lisa Rowe
Robert Armstrong
Steve Hodgson
Lindsay Stiles
Brandon Donnelly
Andrew Broad
Katie Fasken
Jeremy Kaupp
Michael Sheehan

D-U-N-S 20-344-9202   (SL)
SLATE RETAIL REAL ESTATE INVEST-MENT TRUST
SKATE ASSET MANAGEMENT
121 King St W Suite 200, Toronto, ON, M5H 3T9
(416) 644-4264
Emp Here 16   *Sales* 144,213,000
SIC 6798 Real estate investment trusts
Greg Stevenson
Lisa Rowe
Brandon Donnelly
Will Miller
David Dunn
Tyler Pridham
Robert Armstrong
Ryan Robert
Andrew Agatep
Ramsey Ali

D-U-N-S 20-374-6180   (SL)
SPERIDIAN TECHNOLOGIES CANADA INC
357 Bay St Suite 402, Toronto, ON, M5H 2T7
(416) 613-1621
Emp Here 1,500   *Sales* 219,910,449
SIC 7371 Custom computer programming services
Girish Panicker

D-U-N-S 25-212-9374   (SL)
SPRUCEGROVE INVESTMENT MANAGE-MENT LTD
181 University Ave Suite 1300, Toronto, ON, M5H 3M7
(416) 363-5854
Emp Here 25   *Sales* 13,280,175
SIC 6282 Investment advice
Peter Clark
Ian Fyfe
John Watson

D-U-N-S 25-511-6345   (SL)
STADIUM CONSULTANTS INTERNA-TIONAL INC
S C I
14 Duncan St, Toronto, ON, M5H 3G8
(416) 591-6777
Emp Here 50   *Sales* 11,714,400
SIC 8742 Management consulting services
Brian Brisbin
Murray Beynon
Richard Brisbin

D-U-N-S 25-669-1692   (HQ)
STARWOOD CANADA ULC
SHERATON HOTEL
(*Suby of* MARRIOTT INTERNATIONAL, INC.)
123 Queen St W Suite 100, Toronto, ON, M5H 2M9
(416) 947-4955
Sales 38,267,200
SIC 7011 Hotels and motels
Jason Cohen
Todd Noonan

Jennifer Bishop

D-U-N-S 24-550-5979   (SL)
STRATHBRIDGE ASSET MANAGEMENT INC
121 King St W Suite 2600, Toronto, ON, M5H 3T9
(416) 681-3900
Emp Here 20   *Sales* 14,508,780
SIC 6371 Pension, health, and welfare funds
John Mulvihill

D-U-N-S 20-119-2817   (SL)
SUTHERLAND UNION INC
335 Bay St Suite 1000, Toronto, ON, M5H 2R3

Emp Here 5   *Sales* 28,197,474
SIC 5112 Stationery and office supplies

D-U-N-S 24-363-6636   (SL)
SWISS RE LIFE & HEALTH CANADA
(*Suby of* SWISS RE AG)
150 King St W Suite 1000, Toronto, ON, M5H 1J9
(416) 947-3800
Emp Here 72   *Sales* 88,950,096
SIC 6321 Accident and health insurance
Brenda Buckingham

D-U-N-S 20-773-1845   (HQ)
SWISS REINSURANCE COMPANY CANADA
(*Suby of* SWISS RE AG)
150 King St W Suite 2200, Toronto, ON, M5H 1J9
(416) 408-0272
Emp Here 71   *Sales* 96,362,604
SIC 6331 Fire, marine, and casualty insurance
Peter Forstmoser
Benedict Hentsch
Bob Scott
John Jr Smith
Kasper Villiger
Thomas Hodler
Walter Kielholz
Jakob Baer
Thomas Bechtler
Raymund Breu

D-U-N-S 24-514-5750   (SL)
TALISKER CORPORATION
145 Adelaide St W Suite 500, Toronto, ON, M5H 4E5
(416) 864-0213
Emp Here 29   *Sales* 11,353,558
SIC 6799 Investors, nec
Jack Bistricer
Jeff Levine

D-U-N-S 24-393-6528   (HQ)
TAO GROUP HOLDINGS CORP
11 King St W Suite 1600, Toronto, ON, M5H 4C7
(416) 309-7557
Emp Here 3   *Sales* 16,401,000
SIC 6712 Bank holding companies
Ken Toten
Albert Ottoni
John Abraham

D-U-N-S 24-393-6510   (HQ)
TAO SOLUTIONS INC
(*Suby of* TAO GROUP HOLDINGS CORP)
11 King St W Suite 1600, Toronto, ON, M5H 4C7
(416) 309-7557
Sales 11,179,350
SIC 5045 Computers, peripherals, and soft-ware
Aaron Seaton
Ryan Pereira

D-U-N-S 20-735-0674   (HQ)
TECK METALS LTD
(*Suby of* TECK RESOURCES LIMITED)
11 King St W Suite 1700, Toronto, ON, M5H 4C7
(647) 788-3000
Sales 477,509,800

SIC 1081 Metal mining services
Donald Lindsay
Ronald Millos
Peter Rozee

D-U-N-S 24-998-3818   (SL)
TEMPERENCECO INC
CHASE AND CHASE FISH & OYSTER, THE
10 Temperance St Suite 202, Toronto, ON, M5H 1Y4
(647) 348-7000
Emp Here 150   *Sales* 6,827,850
SIC 5812 Eating places
Michael Jason Kimel
Steven Eric Salm
Jeffrey Kimel

D-U-N-S 24-368-1512   (BR)
TETRA TECH CANADA INC
(*Suby of* TETRA TECH, INC.)
330 Bay St Suite 900, Toronto, ON, M5H 2S8
(416) 368-9080
Emp Here 90
SIC 8711 Engineering services
Tim Maunula

D-U-N-S 20-114-3836   (SL)
THIINC LOGISTICS INC
120 Adelaide St W Suite 2150, Toronto, ON, M5H 1T1
(416) 862-5552
Emp Here 75   *Sales* 17,571,600
SIC 8742 Management consulting services
John Gilmore
Don Marshall

D-U-N-S 25-110-0749   (HQ)
THOMSON COMPANY INC, THE
65 Queen St W Suite 2400, Toronto, ON, M5H 2M8
(416) 364-8700
Emp Here 4   *Sales* 10,657,570,000
SIC 2731 Book publishing
Geoffrey W. Beattie
Peter Thomson
David Binet
Greg Dart
Winston Boy
Patrick Phillips
Debra Barrett

D-U-N-S 24-666-8032   (HQ)
THOMSON REUTERS CANADA LIMITED
THOMSON REUTERS (FINANCIAL & RISK) CANADA, A DIV OF
(*Suby of* THOMSON COMPANY INC, THE)
333 Bay St Suite 400, Toronto, ON, M5H 2R2
(416) 687-7500
Emp Here 300   *Sales* 180,421,600
SIC 8999 Services, nec
Paula Monaghan
Terra Rebick
Heather O'hagan

D-U-N-S 24-217-5776   (HQ)
THOMSON REUTERS CORPORATION
(*Suby of* THOMSON COMPANY INC, THE)
333 Bay St, Toronto, ON, M5H 2R2
(416) 687-7500
Emp Here 3,400   *Sales* 5,501,000,000
SIC 7299 Miscellaneous personal service
James C. Smith
David W. Craig
Brian Peccarelli
Susan Taylor Martin
Gonzalo Lissarrague
Stephane Bello
Gus Carlson
Richard H. King
Neil Masterson
Brian Scanlon

D-U-N-S 20-784-5835   (SL)
THOMSON ROGERS
390 Bay St Suite 3100, Toronto, ON, M5H 1W2
(416) 868-3100
Emp Here 100   *Sales* 11,088,200

SIC 8111 Legal services
Alan Farrer
Roger T Beaman
Desmond H Dixon
David R Neill
Patrick D Schmidt
Leslie C Brown
Richard C Halpern
Stephen J D D'agostino
David R Tenszen
Leonard H Kunka

D-U-N-S 20-876-7736   (SL)
THOMSON, WILLIAM E ASSOCIATES INC
THOMSON ASSOCIATES
390 Bay St Suite 1102, Toronto, ON, M5H 2Y2
(416) 947-1300
Emp Here 35   *Sales* 18,807,579
SIC 6211 Security brokers and dealers
William Thomson

D-U-N-S 20-609-2975   (HQ)
TIMMINCO LIMITED
TIMMINCO METALS, DIV OF
150 King St W Suite 2401, Toronto, ON, M5H 1J9
(416) 364-5171
Emp Here 10   *Sales* 199,515,260
SIC 3339 Primary nonferrous Metals, nec
Heinz Schimmelbusch
Arthur R Spector
Robert J Dietrich
Peter D Rayner
Jack L Messman
Mickey M. Yaksich
Michael Winfield
John W W Hick
John C Fox

D-U-N-S 20-181-9757   (HQ)
TMX GROUP LIMITED
TSX
100 Adelaide St W Suite 300, Toronto, ON, M5H 1S3
(416) 947-4670
Emp Here 500   *Sales* 619,445,144
SIC 6231 Security and commodity exchanges
Luc Fortin
Lou Eccleston
Cheryl Graden
Mary Lou Hukezalie
John Mckenzie
Jay Rajarathinam
Charles Winograd
Luc Bertrand
Christian Exshaw
Marie Giguere

D-U-N-S 24-047-7141   (HQ)
TOWERS WATSON ULC
(*Suby of* WILLIS TOWERS WATSON PUBLIC LIMITED COMPANY)
20 Queen St W Suite 2800, Toronto, ON, M5H 3R3
(416) 960-2700
Sales 33,660,900
SIC 8741 Management services
John Haley
Mark Mactas
David B. Friend
Michael J. Hayes

D-U-N-S 20-280-7707   (BR)
TRAVELERS INSURANCE COMPANY OF CANADA
(*Suby of* THE TRAVELERS COMPANIES INC)
165 University Ave Suite 101, Toronto, ON, M5H 3B9
(416) 362-7231
Emp Here 500
SIC 6351 Surety insurance

D-U-N-S 25-254-0109   (HQ)
TRAVELERS INSURANCE COMPANY OF CANADA
THE DOMINION OF CANADA GENERAL IN-

SURANCE COMPANY
(*Suby of* THE TRAVELERS COMPANIES INC)
20 Queen St W Suite 300, Toronto, ON, M5H 3R3
(416) 360-8183
Emp Here 130   *Sales* 480,817,800
SIC 6351 Surety insurance
George Petropoulos
Robert Burns
Phil Baker
Desmond Su-Chan

D-U-N-S 24-848-6677   (HQ)
TREDD INSURANCE BROKERS LTD
141 Adelaide St W Suite 1410, Toronto, ON, M5H 3L5
(416) 306-6000
Emp Here 9   *Sales* 18,557,568
SIC 6411 Insurance agents, brokers, and service
Ian Eddy
Ronald Trecroce

D-U-N-S 24-242-2546   (SL)
TRICOM SECURITY SERVICES INC
20 Queen St W, Toronto, ON, M5H 3R3
(416) 651-7890
Emp Here 49   *Sales* 15,954,400
SIC 5999 Miscellaneous retail stores, nec
Dio De Brito

D-U-N-S 20-819-2021   (HQ)
TSX INC
TORONTO STOCK EXCHANGE
(*Suby of* TMX GROUP LIMITED)
100 Adelaide St W Suite 300, Toronto, ON, M5H 4H1
(888) 873-8392
Emp Here 300   *Sales* 425,141,750
SIC 6231 Security and commodity exchanges
Lou Eccleston
Jean Desgagne
Luc Fortin
Cheryl Graden
Mary Lou Hukezalie
John Mckenzie
James Oosterbaan
Eric Sinclair
Nicholas Thadaney
Luc Bertrand

D-U-N-S 24-334-3027   (HQ)
UBS BANK (CANADA)
154 University Ave Suite 700, Toronto, ON, M5H 3Y9
(416) 343-1800
Emp Here 82   *Sales* 28,437,998
SIC 6021 National commercial banks
Sarah Bevin
Martin Liechti
John F. Angus
Geoffrey R. Walker

D-U-N-S 20-300-5715   (HQ)
UGE INTERNATIONAL LTD
56 Temperance St 7 Fl, Toronto, ON, M5H 3V5
(416) 789-4655
Sales 20,934,836
SIC 1711 Plumbing, heating, air-conditioning
Nick Blitterswyk
Xiangrong Xie
Scott Matthews
Robert Van Duynhoven
Mateo Chaskel
Christina Boyd
Michael Doolan
Baoxin Yang
Joyce Ferris
Chris Varrone

D-U-N-S 20-344-1274   (SL)
UNITED BUNKERS INVESTORS CORPORATION
180 University Ave Suite 04, Toronto, ON, M5H 0A2
(416) 567-0089
Emp Here 17   *Sales* 46,616,560

SIC 6111 Federal and federally sponsored credit agencies
Osama Eissa
Konstantino Kazinakis

D-U-N-S 24-312-8993   (HQ)
URANIUM ONE INC
(*Suby of* ROSATOM, GK)
333 Bay St Suite 1200, Toronto, ON, M5H 2R2
(647) 788-8500
Emp Here 22   *Sales* 301,300,000
SIC 1094 Uranium-radium-vanadium ores
Eduards Smirnovs
Jane Luck
Vasily Konstantinov
Guerman Kornilov
Vladimir Hlavinka

D-U-N-S 24-850-1355   (SL)
URBANA CORPORATION
150 King St W Suite 1702, Toronto, ON, M5H 1J9
(416) 595-9106
Emp Here 5   *Sales* 29,184,625
SIC 6726 Investment offices, nec
Thomas S Caldwell
Sylvia Stinson
Harry Liu
Bethann Colle
Michael Gundy
George Elliott
Charles Pennock

D-U-N-S 20-896-7617   (SL)
VENGROWTH ASSET MANAGEMENT INC
105 Adelaide St W Suite 1000, Toronto, ON, M5H 1P9
(416) 971-6656
Emp Here 72   *Sales* 19,751,904
SIC 8741 Management services
Michael Cohen
David Ferguson
Allen Lupyrypa
Earl Storie
Pat Dipietro
Luc Marengere
Graham Mcbride

D-U-N-S 20-966-1722   (HQ)
VERAX SOLUTIONS CORPORATION
120 Adelaide St W Suite 1501, Toronto, ON, M5H 1T1
(416) 363-3030
Emp Here 1   *Sales* 45,628,200
SIC 8748 Business consulting, nec
Sid Thomas

D-U-N-S 20-187-4539   (HQ)
VESTAS-CANADIAN WIND TECHNOLOGY, INC
VESTAS.COM
(*Suby of* VESTAS WIND SYSTEMS A/S)
65 Queen St W Suite 2000, Toronto, ON, M5H 2M5
(647) 837-6101
Emp Here 5   *Sales* 20,168,925
SIC 3443 Fabricated plate work (boiler shop)
Cynthia Wong

D-U-N-S 20-140-2000   (SL)
VIKING LIMITED PARTNERSHIP
FILION WAKELY THORUP ANGELETTI
333 Bay St Suite 2500, Toronto, ON, M5H 2R2
(416) 408-3221
Emp Here 44   *Sales* 12,070,608
SIC 8741 Management services
Lia Lomtadze-Dedina

D-U-N-S 24-827-7592   (SL)
VISA CANADA INC
40 King St W Suite 3710, Toronto, ON, M5H 3Y2
(416) 367-8472
Emp Here 115
SIC 8741 Management services

D-U-N-S 20-177-2324   (HQ)
WELLS FARGO FINANCIAL CORPORA-

TION CANADA
WELLS FARGO CAPITAL FINANCE
(*Suby of* WELLS FARGO & COMPANY)
40 King St W Suite 3200, Toronto, ON, M5H 3Y2
(800) 626-2805
Emp Here 20   *Sales* 52,867,000
SIC 6159 Miscellaneous business credit institutions
Carmella Massari
Richard Valade
Jeahnette Cavaliere
Bruce A Miller
Eric Torkelson
Wyetta Hammer
Art Bailey

D-U-N-S 20-944-3514   (HQ)
WOODBRIDGE COMPANY LIMITED, THE
(*Suby of* THOMSON COMPANY INC, THE)
65 Queen St W Suite 2400, Toronto, ON, M5H 2M8
(416) 364-8700
Emp Here 70   *Sales* 20,102,995,000
SIC 6712 Bank holding companies
David Binet
Geoffrey Beattie

Toronto, ON M5J

D-U-N-S 24-219-6702   (SL)
1548383 ONTARIO INC
RADISSONADMIRAL HOTEL
249 Queens Quay W Suite 109, Toronto, ON, M5J 2N5
(416) 203-3333
Emp Here 110   *Sales* 10,195,900
SIC 7011 Hotels and motels
Deepak Ruparell
Narenda Patel
Nan Patel
Vinod Patel

D-U-N-S 24-987-3282   (HQ)
3 FOR 1 PIZZA & WINGS INC
10 Bay St Suite 802, Toronto, ON, M5J 2R8
(416) 360-0888
Emp Here 2   *Sales* 556,407,840
SIC 6794 Patent owners and lessors

D-U-N-S 20-250-9456   (SL)
30 FORENSIC ENGINEERING INC
40 University Ave Suite 800, Toronto, ON, M5J 1T1
(416) 368-1700
Emp Here 91   *Sales* 16,012,178
SIC 8711 Engineering services
Christopher Giffin
Jamie Catania

D-U-N-S 24-805-6413   (HQ)
8961182 CANADA INC
BROOKFIELD PROPERTIES
(*Suby of* BROOKFIELD ASSET MANAGEMENT INC)
181 Bay St Suite 330, Toronto, ON, M5J 2T3
(416) 363-9491
Emp Here 90   *Sales* 202,838,400
SIC 6531 Real estate agents and managers
Jan Sucharda
Keith Hyde
Michelle Campbell
Bryan Davis
Brett Fox

D-U-N-S 24-951-9604   (SL)
979786 ONTARIO LIMITED
LOOSE MOOSE TAP & GRILL, THE
146 Front St W, Toronto, ON, M5J 1G2
(416) 977-8840
Emp Here 110   *Sales* 5,007,090
SIC 5812 Eating places
Robert Smith

D-U-N-S 20-294-4369 (SL)
ABERDEEN ASIA-PACIFIC INCOME IN-VESTMENT COMPANY LIMITED
161 Bay St, Toronto, ON, M5J 2S1

Emp Here 20 *Sales* 21,973,706
SIC 6726 Investment offices, nec
Megan Kennedy
Matthew Keener
Kenneth Akintewe
Nicholas Bishop
Siddharth Dahiya
Thomas Drissner
Martin J. Gilbert
Alan Goodson
Bev Hendry
Lin-Jing Leong

D-U-N-S 20-934-1825 (HQ)
ACE INA INSURANCE
25 York St Suite 1400, Toronto, ON, M5J 2V5
(416) 368-2911
Emp Here 187 *Sales* 408,160,888
SIC 6331 Fire, marine, and casualty insurance
David Brosnam
Karen Barkley
Shawn Doherty
Timothy O'donnell
Jess Bush
James W Blaney
Richard M Freborough

D-U-N-S 20-377-1071 (SL)
ACUITYADS HOLDINGS INC
181 Bay St Suite 320, Toronto, ON, M5J 2T3
(416) 218-9888
Emp Here 83 *Sales* 45,801,659
SIC 7371 Custom computer programming services
Tal Hayek
Sheldon Pollack
Sarel Meirovich
Joe Ontman
Nathan Mekuz
Rachel Kapcan
Igal Mayer
Roger Dent
Yishay Waxman
Jonathan Pollack

D-U-N-S 20-911-7308 (HQ)
ADECCO EMPLOYMENT SERVICES LIMITED
ROEVIN TECHNICAL PEOPLE
(*Suby of* ADECCO GROUP AG)
20 Bay St Suite 800, Toronto, ON, M5J 2N8
(416) 646-3322
Emp Here 40 *Sales* 63,879,064
SIC 7361 Employment agencies
Gilbert Boileau
Douglas Hamlyn
Sohail Dossani
Nicolette Mueller
Marylynn Dalgety

D-U-N-S 20-381-0846 (SL)
AGELLAN COMMERCIAL REAL ESTATE INVESTMENT TRUST
156 Front St W Suite 303, Toronto, ON, M5J 2L6
(416) 593-6800
Emp Here 11 *Sales* 79,600,480
SIC 6722 Management investment, open-end
Frank Camenzuli
Rosalia Lau
Christopher Caswell
Daniel Millett
Terra Attard
Glen Ladouceur
Renzo Barazzuol
Dayna Gibbs
Rafael Lazer
Dov Meyer

D-U-N-S 20-844-8563 (HQ)
AIG INSURANCE COMPANY OF CANADA

AIG INSURANCE CANADA
(*Suby of* AMERICAN INTERNATIONAL GROUP, INC.)
145 Wellington St W Suite 1400, Toronto, ON, M5J 1H8
(416) 596-3000
Sales 747,938,800
SIC 6331 Fire, marine, and casualty insurance
Gary A Mcmillan
Lynn Oldfield
Raymond Lui
Serge R Leger
Kevin Kelley
Maurice R Greenberg
Crawford Spratt
Marc Lipman

D-U-N-S 20-850-7947 (SL)
AIRD & BERLIS LLP
181 Bay St Suite 1800, Toronto, ON, M5J 2T9
(416) 863-1500
Emp Here 450 *Sales* 92,644,200
SIC 8111 Legal services
Steve Zakem

D-U-N-S 25-538-2723 (HQ)
ALAMOS GOLD INC
181 Bay St Suite 3910, Toronto, ON, M5J 2T3
(416) 368-9932
Sales 651,800,000
SIC 1041 Gold ores
John Mccluskey
Paul J. Murphy
Christine Barwell
Chris Bostwick
Luis Chavez
Andrew Cormier
Nils Engelstad
Greg Fisher
Scott Parsons
Colin Webster

D-U-N-S 24-386-8762 (SL)
ALPHA TRADING SYSTEMS INC
70 York St Suite 1501, Toronto, ON, M5J 1S9
(416) 563-5896
Emp Here 50 *Sales* 11,714,400
SIC 8742 Management consulting services
Pruyn Haskins
Dilprit Grewal
Ed Cass
Jean-Guy Brunelle
Ray Tucker
John Reilly
James Ehrensperger

D-U-N-S 20-770-4214 (HQ)
AON CANADA INC
AON RISK SOLUTION
(*Suby of* AON PLC)
20 Bay St Suite 2400, Toronto, ON, M5J 2N8
(416) 868-5500
Emp Here 396 *Sales* 6,169,935,200
SIC 6411 Insurance agents, brokers, and service
Christine Lithgow
Lily Choo
Fayeanne Beattie

D-U-N-S 20-786-9884 (HQ)
AON REED STENHOUSE INC
(*Suby of* AON PLC)
20 Bay St Suite 2400, Toronto, ON, M5J 2N8
(416) 868-5500
Emp Here 314 *Sales* 932,455,500
SIC 6411 Insurance agents, brokers, and service
Christine Lithgow
Gilles Corriveau
James Millard
Grant Assman
Lily Choo
James A. Hubbard
Jonh W. King

D-U-N-S 24-218-3440 (HQ)
APPLE CANADA INC

APPLE STORE
(*Suby of* APPLE INC.)
120 Bremner Blvd Suite 1600, Toronto, ON, M5J 0A8
(647) 943-4400
Emp Here 100 *Sales* 80,302,800
SIC 5045 Computers, peripherals, and software
John Hagias
Derek Smith

D-U-N-S 24-368-1801 (HQ)
AVISON YOUNG (CANADA) INC
(*Suby of* AY HOLDINGS ONTARIO INC)
18 York St Suite 400, Toronto, ON, M5J 2T8
(416) 955-0000
Emp Here 60 *Sales* 92,628,480
SIC 8742 Management consulting services
Mark E. Rose
Todd Throndson
Cory Wosnack
Michael Brown

D-U-N-S 24-848-9957 (HQ)
AVISON YOUNG COMMERCIAL REAL ESTATE (ONTARIO) INC
(*Suby of* AY HOLDINGS ONTARIO INC)
18 York St Suite 400, Toronto, ON, M5J 2T8
(416) 955-0000
Emp Here 60 *Sales* 31,416,675
SIC 6531 Real estate agents and managers
Mark Fieder
Robert Ishoj
Robin White
David Warren

D-U-N-S 25-790-5232 (SL)
BADALI'S, JOE PIAZZA ON FRONT INC
BADALI'S, JOE ITALIAN RESTAURANT & BAR
156 Front St W, Toronto, ON, M5J 2L6
(416) 977-3064
Emp Here 85 *Sales* 3,869,115
SIC 5812 Eating places
Micheal O'connor

D-U-N-S 24-227-5340 (HQ)
BAROMETER CAPITAL MANAGEMENT INC
1 University Ave Suite 1800, Toronto, ON, M5J 2P1
(416) 775-3080
Sales 21,248,280
SIC 6211 Security brokers and dealers
Roy Scaini
Gregory M Guichon
David Burrows

D-U-N-S 24-387-0490 (HQ)
BARRICK GOLD CORPORATION
HOLT-MCDERMOTT MINES
161 Bay St Suite 3700, Toronto, ON, M5J 2S1
(416) 861-9911
Emp Here 1,000 *Sales* 7,243,000,000
SIC 1041 Gold ores
Mark Bristow
Rob Krcmarov
Graham Shuttleworth
Kevin Thomson
Mark Hill
Willem Jacobs
Catherine Raw
John L. Thornton
Gustavo Cisneros
Christopher Coleman

D-U-N-S 20-819-1700 (HQ)
BDO CANADA LIMITED
BDO DUNWOODY
123 Front St W Suite 1200, Toronto, ON, M5J 2M2
(416) 865-0210
Emp Here 50 *Sales* 33,264,600
SIC 8111 Legal services
Pat Kramer

D-U-N-S 24-778-7419 (HQ)
BEACH & ASSOCIATES LIMITED

95 Wellington St W Suite 1120, Toronto, ON, M5J 2N7
(416) 368-9680
Sales 550,548,064
SIC 6411 Insurance agents, brokers, and service
Jonathan Beach
John Cartwright

D-U-N-S 24-169-8914 (BR)
BEASLEY, WILLIAM ENTERPRISES LIMITED
CENTREVILLE AMUSEMENT PARK
(*Suby of* BEASLEY, WILLIAM ENTERPRISES LIMITED)
9 Queens Quay W, Toronto, ON, M5J 2H3
(416) 203-0405
Emp Here 500
SIC 7996 Amusement parks
William Beasley

D-U-N-S 25-915-7519 (SL)
BEAZLEY CANADA LIMITED
(*Suby of* BEAZLEY PLC)
55 University Ave Suite 550, Toronto, ON, M5J 2H7
(416) 601-2155
Emp Here 37 *Sales* 68,366,454
SIC 6411 Insurance agents, brokers, and service
Adrian Cox
Clive Washbourn
Martin Bride
Neil Maidment

D-U-N-S 20-177-8334 (HQ)
BENTALL KENNEDY LP
(*Suby of* BENTALLGREENOAK (CANADA) LIMITED PARTNERSHIP)
1 York St Suite 1100, Toronto, ON, M5J 0B6
(416) 681-3400
Sales 187,835,400
SIC 6282 Investment advice
Gary Whitelaw

D-U-N-S 24-344-7559 (BR)
BENTALLGREENOAK (CANADA) LIMITED PARTNERSHIP
(*Suby of* BENTALLGREENOAK (CANADA) LIMITED PARTNERSHIP)
1 York St Suite 1100, Toronto, ON, M5J 0B6
(416) 681-3400
Emp Here 150
SIC 6531 Real estate agents and managers
Katherine Weiss

D-U-N-S 20-371-5540 (SL)
BERKSHIRE HATHAWAY SPECIALTY INSURANCE
(*Suby of* BERKSHIRE HATHAWAY INC.)
200 Bay St, Toronto, ON, M5J 2J2
(647) 846-7803
Emp Here 10 *Sales* 10,348,810
SIC 6311 Life insurance
Dale Geistkemper

D-U-N-S 25-098-2493 (SL)
BLUE RIBBON INCOME FUND
181 Bay St Suite 2930, Toronto, ON, M5J 2T3
(416) 642-6000
Emp Here 3 *Sales* 17,510,775
SIC 6722 Management investment, open-end
M. Paul Bloom
Mark A. Caranci
Adina Bloom Somer
Patricia Meredith
Arthur R.A. Scace
Ken S. Woolner
Craig T. Kikuchi

D-U-N-S 25-991-6484 (BR)
BLUE TREE HOTELS INVESTMENT (CANADA), LTD
WESTIN HARBOUR CASTLE
(*Suby of* BLUE TREE HOTELS INVESTMENT (CANADA), LTD)
Westin Harbour Castle, Toronto, ON, M5J 1A6

(416) 869-1600
Emp Here 750
SIC 7011 Hotels and motels
 Rekha Khote

D-U-N-S 20-105-2870   (SL)
BONASOURCE INC
144 Front St W Suite 725, Toronto, ON, M5J
2L7
(416) 410-4059
Emp Here 125   *Sales* 21,097,426
SIC 7374 Data processing and preparation
 Dmitri Buterin

D-U-N-S 20-514-3576   (HQ)
BOREALIS CAPITAL CORPORATION
(*Suby of* OMERS ADMINISTRATION COR-
PORATION)
200 Bay St Suite 200, Toronto, ON, M5J 2J2
(416) 361-1011
Emp Here 100   *Sales* 213,470,700
SIC 6282 Investment advice
 Michael Nobrega

D-U-N-S 20-551-9775   (HQ)
**BOREALIS HOLDINGS TRUST MANAGE-
MENT INC**
(*Suby of* OMERS ADMINISTRATIQN COR-
PORATION)
200 Bay St S Suite 2100, Toronto, ON, M5J
2J2
(416) 361-1011
Emp Here 5   *Sales* 153,080,850
SIC 1731 Electrical work
 Gerard Mcgrath

D-U-N-S 24-318-1901   (HQ)
**BOREALIS INFRASTRUCTURE MANAGE-
MENT INC**
(*Suby of* OMERS ADMINISTRATION COR-
PORATION)
200 Bay St Suite 2100, Toronto, ON, M5J 2J2
(416) 361-1011
Sales 11,197,050
SIC 6162 Mortgage bankers and loan corre-
spondents
 Michael Rolland
 Rick Byers
 Michael Kelly
 John Knowlton
 Ryan Doersam
 Sebastien Sherman
 Paul Gill
 Michael Holland
 Reena Sagoo

D-U-N-S 20-818-5942   (HQ)
**BOSTON CONSULTING GROUP OF
CANADA LIMITED, THE**
(*Suby of* THE BOSTON CONSULTING
GROUP INC)
181 Bay St Suite 2400, Toronto, ON, M5J 2T3
(416) 955-4200
Sales 15,597,000
SIC 8741 Management services
 Cliff Grevler
 George Stalk
 David Pecaut
 Joe Manget
 Hans-Paul Buerknar

D-U-N-S 24-184-1352   (HQ)
BPO PROPERTIES LTD
(*Suby of* BROOKFIELD OFFICE PROPER-
TIES INC)
181 Bay St Suite 330, Toronto, ON, M5J 2T3
(416) 363-9491
Emp Here 1   *Sales* 453,127,712
SIC 6719 Holding companies, nec

D-U-N-S 20-291-3237   (SL)
BRANDES INVESTMENT PARTNERS & CO.
BRANDES INVESTMENT PARTNERS
(*Suby of* BRANDES INVESTMENT PART-
NERS, INC.)
20 Bay St Suite 400, Toronto, ON, M5J 2N8
(416) 306-5700
Emp Here 50   *Sales* 46,958,850

SIC 6282 Investment advice
 Oliver Murray

D-U-N-S 25-793-8951   (SL)
BRANT SECURITIES LIMITED
220 Bay St Suite 300, Toronto, ON, M5J 2W4
(416) 596-4599
Emp Here 23   *Sales* 12,217,761
SIC 6211 Security brokers and dealers
 Keith Mcmeekin
 Hugh Jackson
 Alex Squires
 John Davies
 John Housser

D-U-N-S 20-296-6669   (SL)
BROMPTON FUNDS LIMITED
181 Bay St Suite 2930, Toronto, ON, M5J 2T3
(416) 642-9061
Emp Here 20   *Sales* 13,933,540
SIC 6722 Management investment, open-end
 Mark Caranci

D-U-N-S 20-522-5126   (SL)
BROMPTON GROUP LIMITED
BROMPTON FUNDS
181 Bay St Suite 2930, Toronto, ON, M5J 2T3
(416) 642-6000
Emp Here 20   *Sales* 13,933,540
SIC 6722 Management investment, open-end
 Mark Caranci

D-U-N-S 24-313-1526   (SL)
BROMPTON SPLIT BANC CORP
181 Bay St Suite 2930, Toronto, ON, M5J 2T3
(416) 642-9061
Emp Here 10   *Sales* 58,369,250
SIC 6726 Investment offices, nec
 Mark A. Caranci
 Christopher Cullen
 Michael D. Clare
 Kathryn A.H. Banner
 Laura Lau
 Ann P. Wong
 Michelle L. Tiraborelli
 Craig T. Kikuchi
 Christopher S.L. Hoffmann
 Raymond Pether

D-U-N-S 20-527-1935   (HQ)
BROOKFIELD ASSET MANAGEMENT INC
181 Bay St Suite 300, Toronto, ON, M5J 2T3
(416) 363-9491
Emp Here 200   *Sales* 43,038,208,642
SIC 6512 Nonresidential building operators
 Bruce Flatt
 Barry Blattman
 Jeff Blidner
 Leonardo Anguiano
 Larry Antonatos
 Jason Baine
 Luis Barreto
 Mark Bishop
 Michael Botha
 Carlos Castro

D-U-N-S 24-805-6405   (SL)
BROOKFIELD CAPITAL PARTNERS II L.P.
181 Bay St Suite 300, Toronto, ON, M5J 2T3
(416) 363-9491
Emp Here 1,002   *Sales* 159,175,716
SIC 3088 Plastics plumbing fixtures
 Robert Harding

D-U-N-S 24-367-4327   (HQ)
BROOKFIELD CAPITAL PARTNERS LTD
(*Suby of* BROOKFIELD ASSET MANAGE-
MENT INC)
181 Bay St Suite 300, Toronto, ON, M5J 2T3
(416) 363-9491
Emp Here 5   *Sales* 41,515,110
SIC 8741 Management services
 Gary Franko

D-U-N-S 20-321-3889   (HQ)
**BROOKFIELD INFRASTRUCTURE PART-
NERS L.P.**

181 Bay St Suite 300, Toronto, ON, M5J 2T3
(416) 363-9491
Sales 2,115,000,000
SIC 8711 Engineering services
 Sam Pollock
 Justin Beber
 Marcos Almeida
 Michael Ryan
 Bahir Manios

D-U-N-S 20-264-3508   (SL)
BROOKFIELD PRIVATE EQUITY INC
181 Bay St Suite 300, Toronto, ON, M5J 2T3
(416) 363-9491
Emp Here 49   *Sales* 35,939,148
SIC 6722 Management investment, open-end
 Bruce Flatt

D-U-N-S 25-364-8422   (SL)
**BROOKFIELD PROPERTIES MANAGE-
MENT CORPORATION**
(*Suby of* BROOKFIELD ASSET MANAGE-
MENT INC)
181 Bay St Suite 300, Toronto, ON, M5J 2T3
(416) 369-2300
Emp Here 100   *Sales* 41,888,900
SIC 6531 Real estate agents and managers
 Jan Sucharda

D-U-N-S 20-348-4860   (SL)
BROOKFIELD PROPERTY PARTNERS L.P.
181 Bay St Suite 300, Toronto, ON, M5J 2T3
(416) 363-9491
Emp Here 300   *Sales* 1,043,264,700
SIC 6798 Real estate investment trusts
 Jan Suchsarda

D-U-N-S 20-380-9462   (SL)
**BROOKFIELD RENEWABLE PARTNERS
L.P.**
181 Bay St Suite 300, Toronto, ON, M5J 2T3
(416) 363-9491
Emp Here 12   *Sales* 2,056,627,125
SIC 4911 Electric services
 Sachin Shah
 Richard Legault
 Harry Goldgut
 Jeffrey Blidner
 Eleazar De Carvalho Filho
 John Van Egmond
 David Mann
 Lou Maroun
 Patricia Zuccotti
 Lars Josefsson

D-U-N-S 25-302-2206   (HQ)
BURGUNDY ASSET MANAGEMENT LTD
181 Bay St Suite 4510, Toronto, ON, M5J 2T3
(416) 869-3222
Sales 61,046,505
SIC 6211 Security brokers and dealers
 H. Anthony Arrell
 Richard E. Rooney
 Stephen G. Mitchell
 Allan Macdonald
 David P. Vanderwood
 Craig Pho
 Kelly Battle

D-U-N-S 24-327-8954   (HQ)
CALLIDUS CAPITAL CORPORATION
181 Bay St Unit 4620, Toronto, ON, M5J 2T3
(416) 945-3016
Emp Here 5   *Sales* 263,819,496
SIC 8741 Management services
 Newton Glassman
 David M. Reese
 James Riley
 Dan Nohdomi
 James (Jay) Roger
 Bradley W. Ashley
 Tibor Donath
 David Sutin

D-U-N-S 25-793-9629   (SL)
**CAMERON & ASSOCIATES INSURANCE
CONSULTANTS LTD**

55 York St Suite 400, Toronto, ON, M5J 1R7
(416) 350-5822
Emp Here 25   *Sales* 14,498,100
SIC 6411 Insurance agents, brokers, and ser-
vice
 Jim Cameron

D-U-N-S 20-305-5249   (SL)
CAN-60 INCOME ETF
95 Wellington St W Suite 1400, Toronto, ON,
M5J 2N7
(416) 642-1289
Emp Here 45   *Sales* 37,681,391
SIC 6722 Management investment, open-end
 Rudy Luukko

D-U-N-S 25-320-7849   (HQ)
CANADA LANDS COMPANY CLC LIMITED
CN TOWER
(*Suby of* GOVERNMENT OF CANADA)
1 University Ave Suite 1700, Toronto, ON, M5J
2P1
(416) 214-1250
Emp Here 40   *Sales* 153,819,120
SIC 6531 Real estate agents and managers
 John Mcbain
 Robert Howald
 Matthew Topscott
 Neil Jones
 Teresa Law
 Rodger Martin
 Basil Cavis
 Greg Barker
 Grant Walsh
 Clint Hames

D-U-N-S 20-765-5861   (SL)
**CANADIAN AVIATION INSURANCE MAN-
AGERS LTD**
CAIG
(*Suby of* BERKSHIRE HATHAWAY INC.)
200 Bay St Suite 2310, Toronto, ON, M5J 2J1
(416) 865-0252
Emp Here 15   *Sales* 12,720,900
SIC 6411 Insurance agents, brokers, and ser-
vice
 Kyle Anderson

D-U-N-S 20-753-6590   (HQ)
**CANADIAN FUR SHOP OF SAITOH LIM-
ITED**
65 Harbour Sq Suite 1204, Toronto, ON, M5J
2L4
(416) 364-5885
Emp Here 1   *Sales* 12,216,400
SIC 5948 Luggage and leather goods stores
 Asae Saitoh

D-U-N-S 20-878-0452   (SL)
CANADIAN MARKETING ASSOCIATION
CMA
55 University Ave Suite 603, Toronto, ON, M5J
2H7
(416) 391-2362
Emp Here 40   *Sales* 10,344,600
SIC 8611 Business associations
 John Wiltshire
 Peter Furnish
 Janine Keogh
 Uwe Stueckmann
 Heather Tulk
 Aldo Cundari
 John Boynton
 Jan Kestle
 Steve Mast
 Brent Cuthbertson

D-U-N-S 20-296-2304   (SL)
**CAPITAL INTERNATIONAL ASSET MAN-
AGEMENT (CANADA), INC.**
CAPITAL GROUP
181 Bay St Suite 3730, Toronto, ON, M5J 2T3
(416) 815-2134
Emp Here 15   *Sales* 11,001,780
SIC 6722 Management investment, open-end
 Tim Armour

D-U-N-S 20-297-2704   (HQ)

CAPSERVCO LIMITED PARTNERSHIP
50 Bay St Suite 1200, Toronto, ON, M5J 3A5
(416) 366-4240
Sales 15,576,375
SIC 8721 Accounting, auditing, and book-keeping
Phillip Noble
David Peneycad

D-U-N-S 20-290-0697 (HQ)
CATALYST CAPITAL GROUP INC, THE
181 Bay St Suite 4700, Toronto, ON, M5J 2T3
(416) 945-3003
Emp Here 6 *Sales* 41,388,850
SIC 6726 Investment offices, nec
Newton Glassman

D-U-N-S 25-852-7688 (HQ)
CENTERRA GOLD INC
1 University Ave Suite 1500, Toronto, ON, M5J 2P1
(416) 204-1953
Emp Here 50 *Sales* 1,129,336,000
SIC 1081 Metal mining services
Scott G. Perry
Gordon Reid
Darren Millman
Dennis C. Kwong
Stephen Lang
Bruce Walter
Sheryl Pressler
Richard Connor
Eduard Kubatov
Michael Parrett

D-U-N-S 20-405-7246 (SL)
CHANGFENG ENERGY INC.
55 University Ave, Toronto, ON, M5J 2H7

Emp Here 5 *Sales* 15,529,285
SIC 4923 Gas transmission and distribution
H. Lin

D-U-N-S 20-262-2122 (HQ)
CIBC ASSET MANAGEMENT INC
18 York St Suite 140, Toronto, ON, M5J 2T8
(416) 364-5620
Sales 26,560,350
SIC 6282 Investment advice
Heather Kaine
John Braive
Stephen Geist
Frank Vivacqua
Peter Lee
Patrick Mckenna

D-U-N-S 25-675-0027 (HQ)
CIBC MELLON GLOBAL SECURITIES SERVICES COMPANY
1 York St Suite 500, Toronto, ON, M5J 0B6
(416) 643-5000
Emp Here 734 *Sales* 203,878,674
SIC 6091 Nondeposit trust facilities
Steven R. Wolff
Richard Anton
Karen Rowe
Rob Ferguson
Claire Johnson
Kelly Hastings
Daniel (Dan) Smith
Shane Kuros
Tedford Mason
Maple Tam

D-U-N-S 24-919-4879 (HQ)
CIBC MELLON TRUST COMPANY
1 York St Suite 900, Toronto, ON, M5J 0B6
(416) 643-5000
Emp Here 400 *Sales* 685,952,516
SIC 6211 Security brokers and dealers
Tom Monahan
Rob Ferguson
Richard Anton
Claire Johnson
Sue Simone
Duncan Webb
Kelly Hastings

Benjamin Kenton
Daniel (Dan) Smith
Elizabeth Earle

D-U-N-S 20-410-2917 (HQ)
CIBC WORLD MARKETS INC
(*Suby of* CANADIAN IMPERIAL BANK OF COMMERCE)
161 Bay St, Toronto, ON, M5J 2S1
(416) 594-7000
Emp Here 50 *Sales* 3,557,845,000
SIC 6211 Security brokers and dealers
Victor G. Dodig
Michael G. Capatides
Harry Culham

D-U-N-S 20-152-9737 (BR)
CIBC WORLD MARKETS INC
CIBC WOOD GUNDY
(*Suby of* CANADIAN IMPERIAL BANK OF COMMERCE)
181 Bay St Suite 600, Toronto, ON, M5J 2T3

Emp Here 100
SIC 6211 Security brokers and dealers
Amanda Bush

D-U-N-S 24-877-1776 (HQ)
CISCO SYSTEMS CANADA CO
(*Suby of* CISCO SYSTEMS, INC.)
88 Queens Quay W Suite 2700, Toronto, ON, M5J 0B8
(416) 306-7000
Emp Here 200 *Sales* 174,074,100
SIC 5065 Electronic parts and equipment, nec
Bernadette Wightman
Mark Gorman
Douglas Scott
Evan Sloves

D-U-N-S 24-209-4258 (HQ)
CITIBANK CANADA
DINERS CLUB-EN ROUTE
(*Suby of* CITIGROUP INC.)
123 Front St W Suite 1900, Toronto, ON, M5J 2M3
(416) 947-5500
Emp Here 600 *Sales* 427,072,500
SIC 6021 National commercial banks
Kenneth Quinn
Charles G Alexander
Stanley H Hart
Kevin J Murray
Lucy Ciuriak
Howard L Beck
Marc Lalonde
Radcliff R Latimer
George A Boa
Andrew L Kreeger

D-U-N-S 24-985-0454 (SL)
CITICORP VENDOR FINANCE, LTD
CITICAPITAL
(*Suby of* CITIGROUP INC.)
123 Front St W Suite 1500, Toronto, ON, M5J 2M3
(800) 991-4046
Emp Here 92 *Sales* 20,602,572
SIC 6159 Miscellaneous business credit institutions
Steve Klein
Michael Lin

D-U-N-S 24-952-7375 (HQ)
CITIGROUP GLOBAL MARKETS CANADA INC
(*Suby of* CITIGROUP INC.)
161 Bay St Suite 4600, Toronto, ON, M5J 2S1
(416) 866-2300
Emp Here 39 *Sales* 21,248,280
SIC 6211 Security brokers and dealers
Robert J Gemmell
Stanley Hartt

D-U-N-S 20-765-4260 (HQ)
CNW GROUP LTD
CANADA NEWSWIRE

(*Suby of* UBM PLC)
88 Queens Quay W Suite 3000, Toronto, ON, M5J 0B8
(416) 863-9350
Emp Here 215 *Sales* 83,636,000
SIC 4899 Communication services, nec
Nichol Guillot

D-U-N-S 20-335-0624 (BR)
COLLIERS INTERNATIONAL GROUP INC
(*Suby of* COLLIERS INTERNATIONAL GROUP INC)
181 Bay St Suite 1400, Toronto, ON, M5J 2V1
(416) 777-2200
Emp Here 80
SIC 6531 Real estate agents and managers
Daniel Holmes

D-U-N-S 20-716-2723 (HQ)
COLLIERS MACAULAY NICOLLS INC
COLLIERS INTERNATIONAL
181 Bay St Unit 1400, Toronto, ON, M5J 2V1
(416) 777-2200
Sales 42,872,300
SIC 8611 Business associations
John Arnoldi
Scott Addison
Ken Norris

D-U-N-S 20-180-5640 (HQ)
COMMONWEALTH LEGAL INC
RICOH CANADA, DIV OF
(*Suby of* WEST CANADIAN INDUSTRIES GROUP LTD)
145 Wellington St W Suite 901, Toronto, ON, M5J 1H8
(416) 703-3755
Emp Here 40 *Sales* 10,780,770
SIC 8111 Legal services
Karen Brookman
Martin Felsky

D-U-N-S 20-263-9972 (HQ)
COMPLETE INNOVATIONS HOLDINGS INC
FLEET COMPLETE
88 Queens Quay W Suite 200, Toronto, ON, M5J 0B8
(905) 944-0863
Sales 10,092,740
SIC 7371 Custom computer programming services
Tony Lourakis
Jamal Raza
Dror Nir
George Kypreos
Dave Prusinski
Jerry Leong
Larry Indovina

D-U-N-S 20-698-5298 (SL)
COMPUTERSHARE CANADA INC
(*Suby of* COMPUTERSHARE LIMITED)
100 University Ave Suite 800, Toronto, ON, M5J 2Y1
(416) 263-9200
Emp Here 500 *Sales* 182,754,500
SIC 6712 Bank holding companies
Stuart Swartz
David Nugent
Toni De Luca
Mark Jacobs

D-U-N-S 25-115-7004 (HQ)
COMPUTERSHARE TRUST COMPANY OF CANADA
(*Suby of* COMPUTERSHARE LIMITED)
100 University Ave Suite 800, Toronto, ON, M5J 2Y1
(416) 263-9200
Emp Here 400 *Sales* 5,198,604,400
SIC 6733 Trusts, nec
Wayne Newling
Sharon Tulloch
Lindsay Horwood
Paul H Farrar
William Braithwaite
Robert Fairweather

Brian Puckier
Hector Mcfadyen
Steve Rothbloom

D-U-N-S 20-351-3379 (HQ)
CONVERGE TECHNOLOGY PARTNERS INC
(*Suby of* CONVERGE TECHNOLOGY SOLUTIONS CORP.)
161 Bay St Suite 4420, Toronto, ON, M5J 2S1

Sales 10,692,550
SIC 7372 Prepackaged software
Shaun Maine
Shane Maine
Nathan Chan

D-U-N-S 20-381-9789 (HQ)
CONVERGE TECHNOLOGY SOLUTIONS CORP.
161 Bay St Suite 2325, Toronto, ON, M5J 2S1
(416) 360-3995
Sales 348,115,132
SIC 7371 Custom computer programming services
Shaun Maine
Brian Phillips
Ralph Garcea

D-U-N-S 20-121-1781 (SL)
CORMARK SECURITIES (USA) LIMITED
(*Suby of* CORMARK SECURITIES INC)
220 Bay St Suite 2800, Toronto, ON, M5J 2W4
(416) 362-7485
Emp Here 100
SIC 6211 Security brokers and dealers
Scott Lamacraft

D-U-N-S 24-384-4735 (HQ)
CORMARK SECURITIES INC
200 Bay St S Suite 2800, Toronto, ON, M5J 2J2
(416) 362-7485
Emp Here 75 *Sales* 149,429,490
SIC 6211 Security brokers and dealers
Scott Lamacraft
Jim Kofman
Peter Charton
Jeff Kennedy
Tim Foote
Susan Streeter

D-U-N-S 20-733-5522 (SL)
CORPORATION OF MASSEY HALL AND ROY THOMSON HALL, THE
MASSEY HALL
60 Simcoe St, Toronto, ON, M5J 2H5
(416) 593-4822
Emp Here 315 *Sales* 19,258,215
SIC 6512 Nonresidential building operators
Deane Cameron
Richard Hamm
Eileen Costello
Susan Aglukark
John Kim Bell
Gary Berman
Michael Burns
Linda Campbell
Colin Chapin
Dan Coholan

D-U-N-S 25-104-0077 (SL)
COVENTREE INC
161 Bay St 27th Fl, Toronto, ON, M5J 2S1
(416) 815-0700
Emp Here 27 *Sales* 14,342,589
SIC 6211 Security brokers and dealers
Geoffrey Cornish
G. Wesley Voorheis
Peter Dey

D-U-N-S 25-340-6912 (HQ)
CUSHMAN & WAKEFIELD ULC
(*Suby of* CUSHMAN & WAKEFIELD PLC)
161 Bay St Suite 1500, Toronto, ON, M5J 2S1
(416) 862-0611
Emp Here 200 *Sales* 212,980,320

SIC 6531 Real estate agents and managers
Glenn Rufrano

D-U-N-S 20-547-4120   (HQ)
D+H LIMITED PARTNERSHIP
DAVIS HENDERSON INTERCHEQUES
(*Suby of* VISTA EQUITY PARTNERS MANAGEMENT, LLC)
120 Bremner Blvd 30th Fl, Toronto, ON, M5J 0A8
(416) 696-7700
Emp Here 500   *Sales* 2,087,059,500
SIC 6211 Security brokers and dealers
Gerrard Schmid
Paul Damp
Young Park
Brian Kyle
Yves Denomme
Bob Noftall
David Caldwell

D-U-N-S 24-376-4029   (SL)
DATA & AUDIO-VISUAL ENTERPRISES HOLDINGS INC
MOBILICITY
161 Bay St Suite 2300, Toronto, ON, M5J 2S1
(416) 361-1959
Emp Here 200   *Sales* 54,670,000
SIC 6712 Bank holding companies
John Bitove
Frank Penny
Stewart Lyons

D-U-N-S 20-790-6736   (HQ)
DELOITTE & TOUCHE MANAGEMENT CONSULTANTS
181 Bay St Suite 1400, Toronto, ON, M5J 2V1
(416) 601-6150
Emp Here 120   *Sales* 37,924,614
SIC 8741 Management services
Kate Peacock

D-U-N-S 25-536-4812   (HQ)
DENISON MINES CORP
1100 40 University Ave, Toronto, ON, M5J 1T1
(416) 979-1991
Emp Here 10   *Sales* 11,788,486
SIC 1094 Uranium-radium-vanadium ores
David D. Cates
Mac Mcdonald
Dale Verran
Tim Gabruch
Michael J. Schoonderwoerd
Amanda Willett
Catherine J.G. Stefan
W. Robert Dengler
Brian D. Edgar
Ron F. Hochstein

D-U-N-S 25-092-9416   (HQ)
DENTALCORP HEALTH SERVICES ULC
181 Bay St Ste 2600, Toronto, ON, M5J 2T3
(416) 558-8338
Sales 24,151,500
SIC 8621 Professional organizations
Graham Rosenberg
Tom Weber
Richard Maisel
Julia Croll
Leona Lau
Stuart Omsen
Michelle Mcara
Andrew Weir
Matt Shulist
Joe Farra

D-U-N-S 20-393-9822   (SL)
DENTSU AEGIS NETWORK ENTERPRISE SOLUTIONS INC
DENTSU AGENT NETWORK
1 University Ave 10fl, Toronto, ON, M5J 2P1
(416) 473-6287
Emp Here 1,500   *Sales* 300,556,500
SIC 7311 Advertising agencies
Annette Warring
Jeff Greenspoon

D-U-N-S 20-122-9205   (HQ)
DH CORPORATION
FINASTRA
(*Suby of* VISTA EQUITY PARTNERS MANAGEMENT, LLC)
120 Bremner Blvd 30 Floor, Toronto, ON, M5J 0A8
(416) 696-7700
Sales 1,242,497,831
SIC 7371 Custom computer programming services
Simon Paris
Tom Kilroy
John Shatka
Karen Weaver
William Neville

D-U-N-S 24-375-4111   (SL)
DHX MEDIA (TORONTO PROD) LTD
207 Queens Quay W Suite 550, Toronto, ON, M5J 1A7
(416) 363-8034
Emp Here 100   *Sales* 9,403,700
SIC 7812 Motion picture and video production
Steven Denure
Anne Loi

D-U-N-S 24-564-5437   (HQ)
DUMAS CONTRACTING LTD
DUMAS MINING
(*Suby of* PALA HOLDCO (LUXEMBOURG) II SARL)
200 Bay St Suite 2301, Toronto, ON, M5J 2J1
(416) 594-2525
Emp Here 20   *Sales* 281,351,400
SIC 1081 Metal mining services
Richard Labelle
Daniel Dumas
Wayne Mohns
Michael Psihogios
Larry Zuccherato
Wayne Mohns
8teven Chambers
Michael Psihogios

D-U-N-S 24-330-1350   (HQ)
EASTWEST GOLD CORPORATION
(*Suby of* KINROSS GOLD CORPORATION)
25 York St 17 Fl, Toronto, ON, M5J 2V5
(416) 365-5123
Emp Here 15   *Sales* 179,041,800
SIC 1041 Gold ores
Brant E. Hinze
Shelley Riley
Frank De Costanzo
Ram Gill

D-U-N-S 20-348-4365   (HQ)
ECN CAPITAL CORP
200 Bay St North Tower Suite 1625, Toronto, ON, M5J 2J1
(416) 646-4710
Emp Here 10   *Sales* 176,490,000
SIC 6159 Miscellaneous business credit institutions
Steven Hudson
Jim Nikopoulos
Loreto Grimaldi
Michael Lepore
Algis Vaitonis
William Lovatt
Pierre Lortie
David Morris
Paul Stoyan
Donna Toth

D-U-N-S 24-373-8403   (SL)
ECOBEE INC
207 Queens Quay W Suite 600, Toronto, ON, M5J 1A7
(877) 932-6233
Emp Here 110   *Sales* 50,604,840
SIC 5075 Warm air heating and air conditioning
Stuart Lombard
Derrick Boyce
Chris Carradine

Mark Malchiondo
Jon Prosser
Hesham Fahmy
Rahul Raj

D-U-N-S 24-849-0740   (HQ)
ECUHOME CORPORATION
73 Simcoe St Suite 308, Toronto, ON, M5J 1W9
(416) 593-9313
Emp Here 6   *Sales* 15,896,560
SIC 8699 Membership organizations, nec
Kate Bird

D-U-N-S 24-563-5441   (HQ)
ELEMENT FLEET MANAGEMENT CORP
161 Bay St Suite 3600, Toronto, ON, M5J 2S1
(416) 386-1067
Emp Here 100   *Sales* 662,216,501
SIC 8742 Management consulting services
Jay Forbes
Karen L. Martin
Mary Barcellos
Vito Culmone
John Wall
Kathryn Parkinson
Brian V. Tobin
Keith Graham
Paul D. Damp
Joan Lamm-Tennant

D-U-N-S 25-351-4905   (SL)
ENTRO COMMUNICATIONS INC
33 Harbour Sq Suite 202, Toronto, ON, M5J 2G2
(416) 368-1095
Emp Here 50   *Sales* 10,941,200
SIC 3993 Signs and advertising specialties
Wayne Mccutcheon
Andrew Kuzyk

D-U-N-S 24-858-3960   (SL)
FA CAPITAL MANAGEMENT INC
95 Wellington St W Suite 1400, Toronto, ON, M5J 2N7
(416) 642-1289
Emp Here 30   *Sales* 24,833,310
SIC 6722 Management investment, open-end
Barry H. Gordon

D-U-N-S 20-785-4969   (HQ)
FAIRFAX FINANCIAL HOLDINGS LIMITED
95 Wellington St W Suite 800, Toronto, ON, M5J 2N7
(416) 367-4941
Emp Here 44   *Sales* 17,757,700,000
SIC 6282 Investment advice
V. Prem Watsa
Paul Rivett
Jean Cloutier
Peter Clarke
Jennifer Allen
John Varnell
Bradley Martin
Eric Salsberg
Ronald Schokking
Vinodh Loganadhan

D-U-N-S 20-257-9173   (HQ)
FAIRFAX INDIA HOLDINGS CORPORATION
(*Suby of* FAIRFAX FINANCIAL HOLDINGS LIMITED)
95 Wellington St W Suite 800, Toronto, ON, M5J 2N7
(416) 367-4755
Emp Here 5   *Sales* 166,518,000
SIC 6719 Holding companies, nec
Chandran Ratnaswami
V. Prem Watsa
John Varnell
Keir Hunt
Jennifer Allen
Anthony F. Griffiths
Christopher Hodgson
Alan Horn
Deepak Parekh
Sumit Maheshwari

D-U-N-S 24-425-3766   (HQ)
FERONIA INC
181 Bay St Suite 1800, Toronto, ON, M5J 2T9
(647) 987-7663
Emp Here 100   *Sales* 29,121,951
SIC 2076 Vegetable oil mills, nec
Frank Braeken
Yanick Vernet
Gilles Marit
Sherree Schaefer
David White
Nicholas Thompson
Monique Gieskes
David Osborne
Kalaa Mpinga
Larry Seruma

D-U-N-S 20-300-5491   (SL)
FIRST ASSET CAN FINANCIALS COVERED CALL ETF
95 Wellington St W Suite 1400, Toronto, ON, M5J 2N7
(416) 642-1289
Emp Here 40   *Sales* 33,111,080
SIC 6722 Management investment, open-end
Barry Gordon

D-U-N-S 24-676-3689   (SL)
FIRST ASSET OPPORTUNITY FUND
95 Wellington St W Suite 1400, Toronto, ON, M5J 2N7
(416) 642-1289
Emp Here 40   *Sales* 27,156,920
SIC 6211 Security brokers and dealers
Edward Akkawi

D-U-N-S 24-862-1740   (HQ)
FIRST NATIONAL FINANCIAL CORPORATION
100 University Ave Suite 700, Toronto, ON, M5J 1V6
(416) 593-1100
Emp Here 230   *Sales* 405,918,893
SIC 6798 Real estate investment trusts
Stephen Smith
Moray Tawse
Lisa White
Jeremy Wedgbury
Jeremy Wedgbury
Hilda Wong
Scott Mckenzie
Robert Inglis
John Brough
Duncan Jackman

D-U-N-S 20-210-9984   (SL)
FIRST NATIONAL FINANCIAL LP
100 University Ave Suite 1200, Toronto, ON, M5J 1V6
(416) 593-1100
Emp Here 665   *Sales* 466,783,645
SIC 6162 Mortgage bankers and loan correspondents
Stephen Smith
Robert Inglis
Stanley Beck
John Brough
Robert Courteau
Duncan Jackman
Robert Mitchell

D-U-N-S 24-924-5945   (SL)
FRIEDBERG MERCANTILE GROUP LTD
FRIEDBERG DIRECT
(*Suby of* FCMI FINANCIAL CORPORATION)
181 Bay St Suite 250, Toronto, ON, M5J 2T3
(416) 364-1171
Emp Here 40   *Sales* 37,567,080
SIC 6221 Commodity contracts brokers, dealers
Albert D Friedberg
Henry Fenig
Daniel Gordon
Enrique Zauderer

D-U-N-S 24-860-0293   (SL)
GALANE GOLD LTD

181 Bay St Suite 1800, Toronto, ON, M5J 2T9
(647) 987-7663
Emp Here 178   *Sales* 44,650,021
SIC 1041 Gold ores
Nick Brodie
Gavin Vandervegt
Ravi Sood
Ian Egan
Amar Bhalla
Wayne Hatton-Jones

D-U-N-S 20-818-5009   (HQ)
GRANT THORNTON LLP
12th-50 Bay St, Toronto, ON, M5J 2Z8
(416) 366-4240
Emp Here 35   *Sales* 212,580,950
SIC 8721 Accounting, auditing, and book-keeping
Kevin Ladner
Phil Noble
Alexander Athol Macbeath
John Garritsen
Jim Copeland

D-U-N-S 25-839-3313   (SL)
GREAT LAKES SCHOONER COMPANY LIMITED
249 Queens Quay W Suite 111, Toronto, ON, M5J 2N5
(416) 260-6355
Emp Here 55   *Sales* 14,825,195
SIC 4489 Water passenger transportation
Damian Ivers
Shey Clark
Trina Ivers

D-U-N-S 24-367-0080   (HQ)
GREINER-PACAUD MANAGEMENT ASSOCIATES
70 University Ave Suite 1200, Toronto, ON, M5J 2M4
(416) 864-0040
Sales 10,881,585
SIC 6371 Pension, health, and welfare funds
Tony Pacaud
Robert Burns

D-U-N-S 24-575-7963   (BR)
HALF, ROBERT CANADA INC
(*Suby of* ROBERT HALF INTERNATIONAL INC.)
181 Bay St Suite 820, Toronto, ON, M5J 2T3
(416) 350-2010
Emp Here 85
SIC 7361 Employment agencies
Gena Griffin

D-U-N-S 20-849-7818   (HQ)
HALF, ROBERT CANADA INC
ACCOUNTEMPS, DIV OF
(*Suby of* ROBERT HALF INTERNATIONAL INC.)
181 Bay St Suite 820, Toronto, ON, M5J 2T3
(416) 203-7656
Emp Here 375   *Sales* 37,347,000
SIC 7361 Employment agencies
Greg Scileppi
David King

D-U-N-S 24-789-7320   (SL)
HALF, ROBERT INTERNATIONAL
ROBERT HALF LEGAL
181 Bay St Suite 820, Toronto, ON, M5J 2T3
(416) 365-3153
Emp Here 49   *Sales* 11,611,530
SIC 7361 Employment agencies
Harold Messmer
Paul Gentzkow
Robert Glass
Keith Waddell

D-U-N-S 24-815-8305   (SL)
HAMBLIN, WATSA INVESTMENT COUNSEL LTD
(*Suby of* FAIRFAX FINANCIAL HOLDINGS LIMITED)
95 Wellington St W Suite 802, Toronto, ON,

M5J 2N7
(416) 366-9544
Emp Here 20   *Sales* 10,624,140
SIC 6282 Investment advice
Prem Watsa

D-U-N-S 20-981-7139   (HQ)
HARBOURFRONT CORPORATION (1990)
HARBOURFRONT CENTRE
235 Queens Quay W, Toronto, ON, M5J 2G8
(416) 973-4000
Emp Here 200   *Sales* 28,826,463
SIC 7922 Theatrical producers and services
Marah Braye
Neil Kerr

D-U-N-S 25-255-0298   (BR)
HEENAN BLAIKIE S.E.N.C.R.L.
200 Bay St, Toronto, ON, M5J 2J4
(514) 898-5398
Emp Here 300
SIC 8111 Legal services
Susan Wilson

D-U-N-S 25-531-4189   (SL)
HIRERIGHT CANADA CORPORATION
(*Suby of* DUFF & PHELPS, LLC)
70 University Ave Suite 200, Toronto, ON, M5J 2M4
(416) 956-5000
Emp Here 75   *Sales* 5,602,050
SIC 7361 Employment agencies
Jenifer Deloach
Sabrina H Perel
Lowell Pancer

D-U-N-S 25-679-9859   (SL)
HONEY BADGER EXPLORATION INC
145 Wellington St W Suite 101, Toronto, ON, M5J 1H8
(416) 364-7029
Emp Here 100   *Sales* 23,343,500
SIC 1081 Metal mining services
Quentin Yarie
Tara Gilfillan
Craig Scherba
Kevin Tanas
Chad Gilfillan
Quentin Yarie
Petra Decher

D-U-N-S 25-230-6238   (SL)
HOOPP INVESTMENT MANAGEMENT LIMITED
HEALTH CARE OF ONTARIO PENSION PLAN
1 York St Suite 1900, Toronto, ON, M5J 0B6
(416) 369-9212
Emp Here 150   *Sales* 55,124,658,243
SIC 6371 Pension, health, and welfare funds
Jim Keohane
John Riviere
David L. Miller
Marcelle Goldenberg
Ronald Meredith-Jones
David Alexander
Dan Anderson
Lesley Bell
Warren Chant
Helen Fetterly

D-U-N-S 24-910-6832   (BR)
HSBC BANK CANADA
(*Suby of* HSBC HOLDINGS PLC)
70 York St Suite 800, Toronto, ON, M5J 1S9
(416) 868-8000
Emp Here 300
SIC 6021 National commercial banks
Ramez Chwaf

D-U-N-S 25-116-1204   (BR)
HSBC SECURITIES (CANADA) INC
HSBC
(*Suby of* HSBC HOLDINGS PLC)
70 York St Suite 800, Toronto, ON, M5J 1S9
(416) 868-8000
Emp Here 110

SIC 6211 Security brokers and dealers
Michael Miller

D-U-N-S 25-511-1007   (HQ)
HUDBAY MINERALS INC
25 York St Suite 800, Toronto, ON, M5J 2V5
(416) 362-8181
Emp Here 1,455   *Sales* 1,472,366,000
SIC 1081 Metal mining services
Alan Hair
Eugene Lei
David S Bryson
Cashel Meagher
Jon Douglas
David Clarry
Patrick Donnelly
Robert Assabgui
Adrienne Balzo
Javier Del Rio

D-U-N-S 25-790-1223   (HQ)
HULL GROUP INC, THE
181 Bay St Suite 4200, Toronto, ON, M5J 2T3
(416) 865-0131
Sales 10,200,567
SIC 6712 Bank holding companies
Thomas Hull

D-U-N-S 20-378-1740   (SL)
HYUNDAI CAPITAL LEASE INC
SERVICE DES FINANCES DE HYUNDAI MOTORS / HYUNDAI MOTORS FINANCE DEPARTMENT
(*Suby of* HYUNDAI CAPITAL CANADA INC)
123 Front St W Suite 1000, Toronto, ON, M5J 2M3
(647) 943-1887
Emp Here 100   *Sales* 45,019,700
SIC 7515 Passenger car leasing
George Steinsky

D-U-N-S 24-326-7361   (HQ)
INNVEST HOTELS LP
200 Bay St Suite 2200, Toronto, ON, M5J 2W4
(416) 607-7100
Emp Here 150   *Sales* 287,004,000
SIC 7011 Hotels and motels
Majid Mangalji
Fereed Mangalji
Moez Mangalji
Sadru Mangalji

D-U-N-S 24-771-4298   (HQ)
INNVEST PROPERTIES CORP
200 Bay St Suite 2200, Toronto, ON, M5J 2J2
(416) 607-7100
Emp Here 100   *Sales* 430,506,000
SIC 7011 Hotels and motels
Anthony Messiana
George Kosziwka

D-U-N-S 20-557-6551   (HQ)
INNVEST REAL ESTATE INVESTMENT TRUST
200 Bay St Suite 3205, Toronto, ON, M5J 2J1
(416) 607-7100
Emp Here 1,500   *Sales* 774,910,800
SIC 7011 Hotels and motels
Lydia Chen
Jeff Hyslop
Lisa Conway
George Kosziwka

D-U-N-S 25-997-5100   (HQ)
INTEGRATED ASSET MANAGEMENT CORP
IAM
70 University Ave Suite 1200, Toronto, ON, M5J 2M4
(416) 360-7667
Emp Here 9   *Sales* 10,888,737
SIC 8741 Management services
John F K Robertson
David Mather
Thomas Felkai
Victor Koloshuk
Jean-Christophe Greck

David H Atkins
Robert L Brooks
John Crocker
Bruce D. Day
Veronika Hirsch

D-U-N-S 25-975-9611   (HQ)
INTELEX CORPORATION
70 University Ave Suite 800, Toronto, ON, M5J 2M4
(416) 599-6009
Sales 75,674,930
SIC 7371 Custom computer programming services
Mark Jaine

D-U-N-S 25-332-3430   (SL)
INTELEX TECHNOLOGIES INC
(*Suby of* INTELEX CORPORATION)
70 University Ave Suite 800, Toronto, ON, M5J 2M4
(416) 599-6009
Emp Here 500   *Sales* 92,286,500
SIC 7371 Custom computer programming services
Craig Halliday
Mark Jaine
James Rumble

D-U-N-S 24-937-6468   (SL)
INTERAC CORP
200 Bay St Suite 2400, Toronto, ON, M5J 2J1
(416) 362-8550
Emp Here 280   *Sales* 52,221,680
SIC 8742 Management consulting services
Mark O'connell
Berry Campbell
Jerry Mcdonald

D-U-N-S 20-269-0038   (BR)
INTERPUBLIC GROUP OF COMPANIES CANADA, INC, THE
UM CANADA
(*Suby of* THE INTERPUBLIC GROUP OF COMPANIES INC)
207 Queens Quay W Suite 2, Toronto, ON, M5J 1A7
(647) 260-2116
Emp Here 105
SIC 7336 Commercial art and graphic design
Mike Segreto

D-U-N-S 20-356-9285   (SL)
IQ PARTNERS INC
144 Front St W Suite 600, Toronto, ON, M5J 2L7
(416) 599-4700
Emp Here 44   *Sales* 10,308,672
SIC 8748 Business consulting, nec
Randy Quarin
Jamie Danziger
Bruce Powell
Mark Rouse
Ross Campbell

D-U-N-S 20-291-4354   (SL)
ISHARES U.S. HIGH YIELD BOND INDEX ETF (CAD-HEDGED)
BLACK ROCK
161 Bay St Suite 2500, Toronto, ON, M5J 2S1
(416) 643-4000
Emp Here 49   *Sales* 40,561,073
SIC 6722 Management investment, open-end
David Stephenson

D-U-N-S 20-059-0375   (SL)
ISOBAR CANADA INC
(*Suby of* DENTSU INC.)
1 University Ave Fl 6, Toronto, ON, M5J 2P1
(416) 646-2340
Emp Here 70   *Sales* 14,025,970
SIC 7311 Advertising agencies
Louise Gauthier
Scott Hughes

D-U-N-S 25-406-2185   (HQ)
JONES BROWN INC
SIMMLANDS INSURANCE BROKERS DIV

OF
(*Suby of* ARTHUR J. GALLAGHER & CO.)
145 Wellington St W Suite 1200, Toronto, ON,
M5J 1H8
(416) 408-1920
Emp Here 60   *Sales* 474,610,400
SIC 6411 Insurance agents, brokers, and service
Rod Campbell
John Lindsay
Lola Thake
Grant Robinson
Peter Bryant
Wendy Sinclair
Jeffrey Charles
Trevor Waldron
Krista Franklin

D-U-N-S 24-977-8390   (HQ)
KINROSS GOLD CORPORATION
KGC
25 York St 17th Fl, Toronto, ON, M5J 2V5
(416) 365-5123
Emp Here 3,927   *Sales* 3,212,600,000
SIC 1081 Metal mining services
J. Paul Rollinson
Paul Tomory
Geoffrey Gold
Andrea S. Freeborough
Catherine Mcleod-Seltzer
Ian Atkinson
John A. Brough
Kerry D. Dyte
Ave G. Lethbridge
Kelly J. Osborne

D-U-N-S 20-333-6987   (HQ)
KIRKLAND LAKE GOLD LTD
200 Bay St Suite 3120, Toronto, ON, M5J 2J1
(416) 840-7884
Emp Here 18   *Sales* 747,495,000
SIC 104 ¡ Gold ores
Anthony Makuch
Brian Hagan
Mark Utting
Raymond Yip
Ian Holland
John Landmark
Doug Cater
Pierre Rocque
Alasdair Federico
Philip Yee

D-U-N-S 20-703-0073   (HQ)
KITCHEN TABLE INCORPORATED, THE
KITCHEN TABLE GROCERY STORES
12 Queens Quay W Suite 416, Toronto, ON,
M5J 2V7
(416) 778-4800
Emp Here 17   *Sales* 44,266,720
SIC 5411 Grocery stores
John Rumig
Gehl Martin
Ian Shiach

D-U-N-S 25-520-4992   (HQ)
KNEBEL WATTERS & ASSOCIATES INC
KWA PARTNERS
10 Bay St Suite 605, Toronto, ON, M5J 2R8
(416) 362-4300
Emp Here 30   *Sales* 10,195,056
SIC 8748 Business consulting, nec
Ronald Dahms
Robert Potvin

D-U-N-S 24-766-3698   (HQ)
LABATT BREWING COMPANY LIMITED
(*Suby of* ANHEUSER-BUSCH INBEV)
207 Queens Quay W Suite 299, Toronto, ON,
M5J 1A7
(416) 361-5050
Emp Here 20   *Sales* 1,462,155,000
SIC 2082 Malt beverages
Marcelo Abud
Daniel Preston
Pamela Sidey
Charlie Angelakos

D-U-N-S 24-888-1450   (HQ)
LARGO RESOURCES LTD
55 University Ave Suite 1105, Toronto, ON,
M5J 2H7
(416) 861-9797
Emp Here 10   *Sales* 395,285,754
SIC 1094 Uranium-radium-vanadium ores
Mark A. Smith
Paulo Misk
Ernest Cleave
Luciano Chaves
Alberto Arias
Daniel Tellechea
David Brace
Koko Yamamoto
Jonathan Lee

D-U-N-S 24-904-1179   (HQ)
LEGG MASON CANADA INC
*LEGG MASON GLOBAL ASSET MANAGE-
MENT*
(*Suby of* LEGG MASON INC)
220 Bay St Suite 1400, Toronto, ON, M5J 2W4
(416) 860-0616
Emp Here 18   *Sales* 20,661,894
SIC 6282 Investment advice
Richard Vandermey
Richard Bernard
Elizabeth Davis
Joseph Larocque
Terence Johnson
David Gregoire
Lori Mackay
Janet Case

D-U-N-S 24-329-2419   (SL)
LIFE & BANC SPLIT CORP
181 Bay St Suite 2930, Toronto, ON, M5J 2T3
(416) 642-6000
Emp Here 10   *Sales* 58,369,250
SIC 6722 Management investment, open-end
Peter A. Braaten
Mark A. Caranci
Raymond R. Pether
David E. Roode
Lorne Zeiler
Moyra E. Mackay
Arthur R.A. Scace
Ken S. Woolner
James W. Davie
Craig T. Kikuchi

D-U-N-S 20-290-7908   (SL)
LM SERVICES LIMITED PARTNERSHIP
181 Bay St Suite 2500, Toronto, ON, M5J 2T3

Emp Here 153   *Sales* 19,090,728
SIC 8741 Management services
Mary Martin

D-U-N-S 20-921-3370   (HQ)
**MACQUARIE CAPITAL MARKETS CANADA
LTD**
(*Suby of* MACQUARIE GROUP LIMITED)
181 Bay St Suite 3100, Toronto, ON, M5J 2T3
(416) 848-3500
Emp Here 100   *Sales* 177,892,250
SIC 6211 Security brokers and dealers
John Budreski
Chris Salapoutis
Kasia Pawlowski

D-U-N-S 24-171-9686   (BR)
**MACQUARIE CAPITAL MARKETS CANADA
LTD**
(*Suby of* MACQUARIE GROUP LIMITED)
181 Bay St Suite 900, Toronto, ON, M5J 2T3
(416) 848-3500
Emp Here 125
SIC 6211 Security brokers and dealers
Kevin Dalton

D-U-N-S 20-026-0409   (HQ)
MACQUARIE NORTH AMERICA LTD
MACQUARIE CAPITAL MARKETS CANADA
(*Suby of* MACQUARIE GROUP LIMITED)
181 Bay St Suite 3100, Toronto, ON, M5J 2T3

(416) 607-5000
Emp Here 59   *Sales* 15,293,492
SIC 8742 Management consulting services
Gregory Smith
Michael Bernstein
David Fleck
Nicholas Hann
Matthew Rady

D-U-N-S 20-170-0218   (HQ)
**MAPLE LEAF SPORTS & ENTERTAINMENT
LTD**
AIR CANADA CENTRE
50 Bay St Suite 500, Toronto, ON, M5J 2L2
(416) 815-5400
Emp Here 500   *Sales* 45,384,350
SIC 7941 Sports clubs, managers, and pro-
moters
Michael Friisdahl
Cynthia Devine
Dale Lastman
Lawrence Tanenbaum
George Cope
Edward Rogers
Anthony Staffieri
Siim Vanaselja
Bernard Le Duc
Greg Kinch

D-U-N-S 20-296-2098   (SL)
**MARQUEST 2013-1 MINING SUPER FLOW-
THROUGH LIMITED PARTNERSHIP**
161 Bay St Suite 4420, Toronto, ON, M5J 2S1
(416) 777-7350
Emp Here 25   *Sales* 20,694,425
SIC 6722 Management investment, open-end
Gerry Brockelspy

D-U-N-S 20-300-1458   (SL)
MARQUEST INVESTMENT COUNSEL INC
161 Bay St Suite 4420, Toronto, ON, M5J 2S1
(416) 777-7350
Emp Here 20   *Sales* 13,933,540
SIC 6722 Management investment, open-end
Gerry Brocksby

D-U-N-S 20-769-5347   (HQ)
MARSH CANADA LIMITED
(*Suby of* MARSH & MCLENNAN COMPA-
NIES, INC.)
120 Bremner Blvd Suite 800, Toronto, ON,
M5J 0A8
(416) 868-2600
Emp Here 500   *Sales* 4,746,104,000
SIC 6411 Insurance agents, brokers, and ser-
vice
Alan Garner
Peter Cleyn
James Abernethy

D-U-N-S 25-687-1799   (BR)
MARSH CANADA LIMITED
(*Suby of* MARSH & MCLENNAN COMPA-
NIES, INC.)
120 Bremner Blvd Suite 800, Toronto, ON,
M5J 0A8
(416) 868-2600
Emp Here 250
SIC 6411 Insurance agents, brokers, and ser-
vice
William Mc Aller

D-U-N-S 20-412-5777   (HQ)
MCKAY, W. G. LIMITED
40 University Ave Suite 602, Toronto, ON, M5J
1J9
(416) 593-1380
Emp Here 35   *Sales* 43,347,980
SIC 4731 Freight transportation arrangement
Winfield C Mckay
Winfield L Mckay
Ken Tracy
Cheryl D Dottin
Noreen Mckay

D-U-N-S 20-783-9853   (HQ)
MCMILLAN LLP
181 Bay St Suite 4400, Toronto, ON, M5J 2T3

(416) 865-7000
Emp Here 350   *Sales* 164,700,800
SIC 8111 Legal services
Teresa Dufort
David Dunlop
Steven Wortley
Tim Murphy

D-U-N-S 24-314-7899   (HQ)
MCW CONSULTANTS LTD
207 Queens Quay W Suite 615, Toronto, ON,
M5J 1A7
(416) 598-2920
Emp Here 120   *Sales* 83,780,675
SIC 8711 Engineering services
David Bellamy
George Bellamy
John Sloan
Collin Rabnett

D-U-N-S 24-322-3240   (SL)
MCW CUSTOM ENERGY SOLUTIONS LTD
MCW CES
207 Queens Quay W Suite 615, Toronto, ON,
M5J 1A7
(416) 598-2920
Emp Here 50   *Sales* 23,078,839
SIC 8711 Engineering services
David Bellamy
Colin Rabnett
John Sloan
George Bellamy

D-U-N-S 20-334-7872   (HQ)
MELTWATER NEWS CANADA INC
(*Suby of* MELTWATER HOLDING B.V.)
25 York St Suite 1200, Toronto, ON, M5J 2V5
(416) 641-4902
Emp Here 80   *Sales* 16,684,700
SIC 7372 Prepackaged software
Jessica Roman
Nicole Clark

D-U-N-S 20-769-9752   (HQ)
MERCER (CANADA) LIMITED
MERCER
(*Suby of* MARSH & MCLENNAN COMPA-
NIES, INC.)
120 Bremner Blvd Suite 800, Toronto, ON,
M5J 0A8
(416) 868-2000
Emp Here 600   *Sales* 994,619,200
SIC 6411 Insurance agents, brokers, and ser-
vice
Ted Singeris
Audrey Mckinney
Denise Mitchell
Donald Shaw Webster
Marvin Ens
James A Giesinger
Kenneth Hugessen
Bernard Morency
Richard Brennan
Robert Dumas

D-U-N-S 24-126-9401   (BR)
MERCER (CANADA) LIMITED
(*Suby of* MARSH & MCLENNAN COMPA-
NIES, INC.)
70 University Ave Suite 900, Toronto, ON, M5J
2M4
(416) 868-2000
Emp Here 100
SIC 8742 Management consulting services
Jack Pheroet

D-U-N-S 20-731-4618   (SL)
MERRILL LYNCH & CO., CANADA LTD
(*Suby of* BANK OF AMERICA CORPORA-
TION)
181 Bay St Suite 400, Toronto, ON, M5J 2V8
(416) 369-7400
Emp Here 345   *Sales* 490,982,610
SIC 6211 Security brokers and dealers
Mark Dickerson
Lynn Paterson

D-U-N-S 20-731-5169   (HQ)

MERRILL LYNCH CANADA INC
MERRILL LYNCH FUTURES
(*Suby of* BANK OF AMERICA CORPORATION)
181 Bay St Suite 400, Toronto, ON, M5J 2V8
(416) 369-7400
Emp Here 200   *Sales* 426,941,400
SIC 6211 Security brokers and dealers
Lynn Paterson
Mark Dickerson

D-U-N-S 20-306-4563   (SL)
MESSAGEPOINT INC
207 Queens Quay W Suite 802, Toronto, ON, M5J 1A7
(416) 410-8956
Emp Here 65   *Sales* 15,228,720
SIC 8748 Business consulting, nec
Nick Romano
Steve Biancaniello
Olga Borovicka
Bruce Macinnis

D-U-N-S 24-367-4376   (BR)
METROLINX
GO TRANSIT
(*Suby of* METROLINX)
20 Bay St Suite 600, Toronto, ON, M5J 2W3
(416) 869-3200
Emp Here 500
SIC 4011 Railroads, line-haul operating
Mark Childs

D-U-N-S 24-677-0734   (HQ)
METROLINX
GO TRANSIT, DIV OF
97 Front St W Suite 200, Toronto, ON, M5J 1E6
(416) 874-5900
Emp Here 1,500   *Sales* 1,580,105,600
SIC 4011 Railroads, line-haul operating
J Robert S Prichard
Robert Siddall

D-U-N-S 25-352-3948   (HQ)
MODIS CANADA INC
(*Suby of* ADECCO GROUP AG)
10 Bay St Suite 700, Toronto, ON, M5J 2R8
(416) 367-2020
Emp Here 80   *Sales* 9,710,220
SIC 7361 Employment agencies
Lynn Bouchard
Nicolette Mueller
Rakesh Das

D-U-N-S 20-764-8593   (HQ)
MORGAN STANLEY CANADA LIMITED
(*Suby of* MORGAN STANLEY)
181 Bay St Suite 3700, Toronto, ON, M5J 2T3
(416) 943-8400
Sales 69,499,098
SIC 6211 Security brokers and dealers
James P.Gorman
Colm Kelleher
Jonathan Pruzan

D-U-N-S 24-957-1225   (HQ)
MOUNTAIN PROVINCE DIAMONDS INC
161 Bay St Suite 1410, Toronto, ON, M5J 2S1
(416) 361-3562
Sales 235,746,221
SIC 1499 Miscellaneous nonMetallic minerals, except fuels
Stuart Brown
Reid Mackie
Tom E. Mccandless
Perry Ing
Jonathan Christopher James Comerford
David E. Whittle
Karen Goracke
Tom Peregoodoff
William Lamb
Brett Desmond

D-U-N-S 24-335-3039   (HQ)
MS MEDIA GP HOLDING LIMITED
(*Suby of* OMERS ADMINISTRATION COR-

PORATION)
25 York St Suite 900, Toronto, ON, M5J 2V5
(416) 362-0885
Sales 57,689,400
SIC 7383 News syndicates
Michael Graham
Michael Nowlan
Vipon Ghai
Teresa Lee
Michael Lank

D-U-N-S 24-360-1593   (HQ)
MUFG BANK, LTD., CANADA BRANCH
(*Suby of* MITSUBISHI UFJ FINANCIAL GROUP, INC.)
200 Bay St Suite 1700, Toronto, ON, M5J 2J1
(416) 865-0220
Emp Here 72   *Sales* 122,389,868
SIC 6211 Security brokers and dealers
Takashi Ando
Angelo Bisutti
Normand Bernier
William Saywell
John A Paterson
M Joseph Regan
James Kennedy
Donald Brown

D-U-N-S 24-729-0117   (SL)
NATIONAL HOCKEY LEAGUE PLAYERS ASSOCIATION, THE
NHLPA
20 Bay St Suite 1700, Toronto, ON, M5J 2N8
(416) 313-2300
Emp Here 45   *Sales* 10,516,275
SIC 8621 Professional organizations
Michelle Allen

D-U-N-S 24-376-3955   (SL)
NERIUM BIOTECHNOLOGY, INC
220 Bay St Unit 500, Toronto, ON, M5J 2W4
(416) 862-7330
Emp Here 100   *Sales* 311,498
SIC 8731 Commercial physical research
Dennis K. Knocke
Joseph B. Nester
J. Peter Nettlefield
John F. O'donnell
Maxwell A. Polinsky
Gustavo A. Ulloa Jr

D-U-N-S 20-970-8309   (HQ)
NEW GOLD INC
181 Bay St Suite 3320, Toronto, ON, M5J 2T3
(416) 324-6000
Emp Here 33   *Sales* 604,500,000
SIC 1481 NonMetallic mineral services
Renaud Adams
Lisa Damiani
Martin Wallace
Robert J. Chausse
Anne Day
Ian Pearce
Gillian Davidson
James Gowans
Margaret Mulligan
Marilyn Schonberner

D-U-N-S 20-369-3015   (SL)
NINEPOINT PARTNERS LP
200 Bay St Suite 2700, Toronto, ON, M5J 2J1
(416) 362-7172
Emp Here 100   *Sales* 93,917,700
SIC 6282 Investment advice
John Wilson

D-U-N-S 24-540-1997   (HQ)
NORTH AMERICAN PALLADIUM LTD
One University Ave Suite 1601, Toronto, ON, M5J 2P1
(416) 360-7590
Emp Here 250   *Sales* 300,814,874
SIC 1099 Metal ores, nec
Jim Gallagher
Timothy Hill
David Peck
Wayne Scott

Erin Satterthwaite
J. Peter Gordon
David Nowak
John W. Jentz
Dean Chambers
Gregory P. Fauquier

D-U-N-S 24-342-4822   (HQ)
NORTHWATER CAPITAL INC
181 Bay St Suite 4700, Toronto, ON, M5J 2T3
(416) 360-5435
Sales 27,335,000
SIC 6712 Bank holding companies
David Patterson
Daniel Mills

D-U-N-S 24-326-4020   (BR)
NORTON ROSE FULBRIGHT CANADA S.E.N.C.R.L., S.R.L.
(*Suby of* NORTON ROSE FULBRIGHT CANADA S.E.N.C.R.L., S.R.L.)
200 Bay St Suite 3800, Toronto, ON, M5J 2Z4
(416) 216-4000
Emp Here 300
SIC 8111 Legal services
Andrew Flemming

D-U-N-S 20-345-5449   (SL)
OLE MEDIA MANAGEMENT (GP) L.P.
120 Bremner Blvd Suite 2900, Toronto, ON, M5J 0A8
(416) 850-1163
Emp Here 80   *Sales* 13,122,160
SIC 2741 Miscellaneous publishing
Denis Dinsmore

D-U-N-S 25-513-4645   (HQ)
OLIVER, WYMAN LIMITED
(*Suby of* MARSH & MCLENNAN COMPANIES, INC.)
120 Bremner Blvd Suite 800, Toronto, ON, M5J 0A8
(416) 868-2200
Emp Here 99   *Sales* 14,224,464
SIC 8741 Management services
John Romeo

D-U-N-S 24-310-7997   (HQ)
ONCAP II L.P.
161 Bay St, Toronto, ON, M5J 2S1
(416) 214-4300
Emp Here 1   *Sales* 337,541,118
SIC 6719 Holding companies, nec
Michael Lay
Wole James
Aly Hadibhai
Adam Shantz
Stephen Marshall
Stefan Bars

D-U-N-S 24-488-2650   (HQ)
ONEX CORPORATION
161 Bay St, Toronto, ON, M5J 2S1
(416) 362-7711
Sales 23,785,000,000
SIC 6282 Investment advice
Gerry Schwartz
Ewout Heersink
Robert Le Blanc
Seth Mersky
Anthony Munk
Chris Govan
David Copeland
Andrea Daly
Donald Lewtas
Emma Thompson

D-U-N-S 24-852-5292   (SL)
ONEX PARTNERS ADVISOR GP INC
161 Bay St Suite 4900, Toronto, ON, M5J 2S1
(416) 362-7711
Emp Here 30   *Sales* 15,936,210
SIC 6282 Investment advice
Gerald W. Schwartz
Ewout R Heersink
Donald W Lewtas
Seth M Mersky

Andrew J Sheiner

D-U-N-S 24-924-5630   (SL)
OPTIMA COMMUNICATIONS INTERNATIONAL INC
144 Front St W Suite 200, Toronto, ON, M5J 2L7
(416) 581-1236
Emp Here 500   *Sales* 114,236,000
SIC 4899 Communication services, nec
Don Macleod

D-U-N-S 24-385-0588   (SL)
OWN INC
(*Suby of* CORUS ENTERTAINMENT INC)
181 Bay St Suite 1630, Toronto, ON, M5J 2T3
(416) 642-3770
Emp Here 100
SIC 4833 Television broadcasting stations
Heather Shaw

D-U-N-S 25-940-9696   (HQ)
PARADIGM CAPITAL INC
95 Wellington St W Suite 2101, Toronto, ON, M5J 2N7
(416) 361-9892
Emp Here 2   *Sales* 37,567,080
SIC 6211 Security brokers and dealers
David Roland
Peter Dey
Ian Joseph
John Bellamy
Daniel Kim
Jonathan Hill
Michael Ward
Michael Roland

D-U-N-S 20-381-0957   (SL)
PARTNERS VALUE INVESTMENTS LP
181 Bay St Suite 210, Toronto, ON, M5J 2T3
(647) 503-6513
Emp Here 7   *Sales* 12,792,815
SIC 6719 Holding companies, nec
Brian D. Lawson
Frank N.C. Lochan
Loretta M. Corso
John P. Barratt
Edward C. Kress
Ralph Zarboni
Adil Mawani

D-U-N-S 20-706-6098   (SL)
PEOPLES FINANCIAL CORPORATION
(*Suby of* MACQUARIE GROUP LIMITED)
95 Wellington St W Suite 915, Toronto, ON, M5J 2N7
(416) 861-1315
Emp Here 120   *Sales* 63,440,400
SIC 6162 Mortgage bankers and loan correspondents
Grant Mackenzie
Frank Ganis
Mike Barrett

D-U-N-S 24-350-4037   (SL)
PINNACLE CATERERS LTD
40 Bay St Suite 300, Toronto, ON, M5J 2X2
(416) 815-6036
Emp Here 500   *Sales* 4,551,900
SIC 5812 Eating places
John Corkill

D-U-N-S 25-191-1509   (HQ)
POLYCORP LTD
B F GOODRICH
123 Front St W Suite 905, Toronto, ON, M5J 2M2
(416) 364-2241
Emp Here 100   *Sales* 83,584,200
SIC 3069 Fabricated rubber products, nec
Peter Snucins
Andrew Haber

D-U-N-S 20-104-3507   (HQ)
PRESIDENT'S CHOICE BANK
PRESIDENTS CHOICE FINANCIAL
(*Suby of* LOBLAW COMPANIES LIMITED)
25 York St Suite 7fl, Toronto, ON, M5J 2V5

(416) 204-2600
Emp Here 62   *Sales* 37,301,200
SIC 8742 Management consulting services
Donald Reid
Anthony Graham
David Boone
Kevin Lengyell
Lisa Swartzman

D-U-N-S 20-793-1312   (HQ)
PRICEWATERHOUSECOOPERS LLP
PWC
18 York St Suite 2600, Toronto, ON, M5J 0B2
(416) 863-1133
Emp Here 2,200   *Sales* 1,201,544,500
SIC 8721 Accounting, auditing, and book-keeping
Bill Mcfarland
Tahir Ayub
Serge Gattesco
Christopher Kong
Brian Mclean
Tracey Riley
Nicolas Marcoux

D-U-N-S 24-417-2222   (HQ)
PRODIGY VENTURES INC
161 Bay St Suite 4420, Toronto, ON, M5J 2S1
(416) 488-7700
Sales 12,844,556
SIC 6799 Investors, nec
Tom Beckerman
Jeff Watts
Doug Woolridge
Pierre Roberge
Andrew Hilton
Robert Maclean
Stephen Moore
Gayemarie Brown

D-U-N-S 20-268-5426   (SL)
PROLIFIO INVESTMENT & ASSET MANAGEMENT CORP
161 Bay St, Toronto, ON, M5J 2S1
(416) 948-5505
Emp Here 22   *Sales* 14,936,306
SIC 6282 Investment advice
Mathew Lowenbraun

D-U-N-S 24-005-7810   (HQ)
PURVES REDMOND LIMITED
70 University Ave Suite 400, Toronto, ON, M5J 2M4
(416) 362-4246
Emp Here 20   *Sales* 21,201,500
SIC 6411 Insurance agents, brokers, and service
Peter Redmond
Robert Purves

D-U-N-S 20-363-9534   (SL)
QUISITIVE TECHNOLOGY SOLUTIONS, INC
161 Bay St Suite 2325, Toronto, ON, M5J 2S1
(519) 574-5520
Emp Here 10   *Sales* 12,606,724
SIC 7372 Prepackaged software
Mike Reinhart
Will Clevenger
Scotty Perkins
Steven Balusek
Kevin Castillo
Tami Anders
Stephanie Ratza
Dave Guebert
Gord Mcmillan
Phil Sorgen

D-U-N-S 25-311-9614   (SL)
QUORUM FUNDING CORPORATION
70 York St Suite 1720, Toronto, ON, M5J 1S9

Emp Here 16   *Sales* 11,334,308
SIC 6726 Investment offices, nec
Wanda Dorosz
Gary Mah

D-U-N-S 20-550-9081   (HQ)

RBC ASSET MANAGEMENT INC
(*Suby of* ROYAL BANK OF CANADA)
200 Bay St, Toronto, ON, M5J 2J5
(416) 974-9419
Sales 284,627,600
SIC 6282 Investment advice
Dan Chornous

D-U-N-S 20-561-2849   (HQ)
RBC DOMINION SECURITIES INC
RBC CAPITAL MARKETS
(*Suby of* ROYAL BANK OF CANADA)
200 Bay St, Toronto, ON, M5J 2W7
(416) 842-2000
Emp Here 1,000   *Sales* 7,542,631,400
SIC 6282 Investment advice
Anthony Fell
David John Agnew

D-U-N-S 24-826-0267   (HQ)
RBC DOMINION SECURITIES LIMITED
(*Suby of* ROYAL BANK OF CANADA)
200 Bay St 9th Floor, Toronto, ON, M5J 2J5
(416) 842-4088
Sales 1,423,138,000
SIC 6211 Security brokers and dealers
Terri-Lee Weeks
Troy Maxwell
Douglas Mcgregor

D-U-N-S 24-365-4741   (BR)
RBC INVESTOR SERVICES TRUST
(*Suby of* ROYAL BANK OF CANADA)
200 Bay St, Toronto, ON, M5J 2J5

Emp Here 100
SIC 6282 Investment advice
Douglas Mcgregor

D-U-N-S 20-378-1328   (SL)
RBC VENTURES INC
(*Suby of* ROYAL BANK OF CANADA)
20 Bay St 17th Fl, Toronto, ON, M5J 2N8
(416) 846-3465
Emp Here 170   *Sales* 24,510,940
SIC 7371 Custom computer programming services
Richard Thomas

D-U-N-S 20-036-6461   (HQ)
RE/MAX CONDOS PLUS CORPORATION
45 Harbour Sq, Toronto, ON, M5J 2G4
(416) 203-6636
Sales 12,772,532
SIC 6531 Real estate agents and managers
Jamie Johnston
Greta Greenhow

D-U-N-S 25-107-9877   (HQ)
REGUS BUSINESS CENTRE LTD
161 Bay St, Toronto, ON, M5J 2S1
(416) 572-2200
Emp Here 8   *Sales* 13,476,570
SIC 7389 Business services, nec
Mark Dixon
Johnnie Mike Irving
Katherine Latimer
Rudolf Lobo
Leslie Wittlin

D-U-N-S 25-513-1104   (HQ)
RGA INTERNATIONAL CORPORATION
(*Suby of* REINSURANCE GROUP OF AMERICA, INCORPORATED)
161 Bay St Suite 4600, Toronto, ON, M5J 2S1
(416) 943-6770
Sales 13,077,650
SIC 6712 Bank holding companies
Graham Watson
Paul Nitsou

D-U-N-S 25-221-3186   (HQ)
ROINS FINANCIAL SERVICES LIMITED
(*Suby of* RSA INSURANCE GROUP PLC)
18 York St Suite 410, Toronto, ON, M5J 2T8
(416) 366-7511
Emp Here 9   *Sales* 1,666,115,400

SIC 6331 Fire, marine, and casualty insurance
Marcel J Bundock
George Anderson
Simon Lee
Shelley Miller
Rowan Saunders
Robert Mcfarlane
Guy Dufresne
Charles White
Bo Rickard Gustafson

D-U-N-S 20-292-0773   (HQ)
ROSCOE POSTLE ASSOCIATES INC
RPA
55 University Ave Suite 501, Toronto, ON, M5J 2H7
(416) 947-0907
Emp Here 35   *Sales* 14,861,245
SIC 8999 Services, nec
Deborah Mccombe
Graham Clow
Richard Lambert
William Roscoe
Wayne Valliant

D-U-N-S 24-845-4696   (HQ)
ROTHSCHILD (CANADA) INC
(*Suby of* ROTHSCHILD & CO)
161 Bay St Suite 4230, Toronto, ON, M5J 2S1
(416) 369-9600
Sales 10,624,140
SIC 6211 Security brokers and dealers
N. Hogo H. Dryland
Stephen Ledoux
John M. Carroll
Shawn D. Mcreynolds
James Arthur Lawrence

D-U-N-S 20-879-3612   (HQ)
ROYAL & SUN ALLIANCE INSURANCE COMPANY OF CANADA
RSA
(*Suby of* RSA INSURANCE GROUP PLC)
18 York St Suite 800, Toronto, ON, M5J 2T8
(416) 366-7511
Emp Here 400   *Sales* 3,269,561,040
SIC 6331 Fire, marine, and casualty insurance
Martin Thompson
Marcel Bundock

D-U-N-S 25-287-1900   (HQ)
ROYAL BANK HOLDING INC
(*Suby of* ROYAL BANK OF CANADA)
200 Bay St 9th Floor, Toronto, ON, M5J 2J5
(416) 974-7493
Sales 3,864,925,000
SIC 6211 Security brokers and dealers
David R. Allgood
Antonella Deo
Peter Armenio
W. James Westlake
Janice R. Fukakusa
Barbara Stymiest

D-U-N-S 20-333-2952   (BR)
ROYAL BANK OF CANADA
RBC AUTOMOTIVE FINANCE
(*Suby of* ROYAL BANK OF CANADA)
88 Queens Quay W Suite 300, Toronto, ON, M5J 0B8
(416) 955-2777
Emp Here 150
SIC 6021 National commercial banks
Grant Simons

D-U-N-S 20-524-7372   (HQ)
ROYAL BANK OF CANADA
200 Bay St, Toronto, ON, M5J 2J5
(416) 974-3940
Emp Here 500   *Sales* 21,462,640,000
SIC 6021 National commercial banks
David Mckay
Rod Bolger
Helena Gottschling
Mark Hughes
Doug Guzman
A. Douglas Mcgregor

Jennifer Tory
Mike Dobbins
Kathleen P. Taylor
David Denison

D-U-N-S 20-397-7657   (SL)
ROYAL YORK OPERATIONS LP
FAIRMONT ROYAL YORK
(*Suby of* KINGSETT CAPITAL INC)
100 Front St W, Toronto, ON, M5J 1E3
(416) 368-2511
Emp Here 1,300   *Sales* 115,989,606
SIC 7011 Hotels and motels
Edwin Frizzell
Jawad Qamar

D-U-N-S 24-963-4023   (HQ)
RPM TECHNOLOGIES CORPORATION
(*Suby of* BROADRIDGE FINANCIAL SOLUTIONS, INC.)
120 Bremner Blvd Suite 2300, Toronto, ON, M5J 0A8
(416) 214-6232
Sales 33,369,400
SIC 7372 Prepackaged software
David Poppleton

D-U-N-S 20-693-9030   (HQ)
SALESFORCE.COM CANADA CORPORATION
(*Suby of* SALESFORCE.COM, INC.)
20 Bay St Suite 800, Toronto, ON, M5J 2N8
(647) 258-3800
Sales 13,716,600
SIC 8741 Management services
Marc Benioff
Stephen Edward Houck

D-U-N-S 24-952-3077   (SL)
SCARBOROUGH TOWN CENTRE HOLDINGS INC
(*Suby of* OMERS ADMINISTRATION CORPORATION)
200 Bay St Suite 900, Toronto, ON, M5J 2J2
(416) 865-8300
Emp Here 90   *Sales* 19,878,390
SIC 6512 Nonresidential building operators
Gawain Smart

D-U-N-S 20-298-5636   (HQ)
SIERRA METALS INC
161 Bay St Suite 4260, Toronto, ON, M5J 2S1
(416) 366-7777
Emp Here 100   *Sales* 232,371,000
SIC 1021 Copper ores
Igor Gonzales
Alonso Lujan
Mike Mcallister
Ed Guimaraes
Gordon Babcock
Alberto Arias
Doug Cater
Steven Dean
Dionisio Romero Paoletti
Jose Alberto Vizquerra-Benavides

D-U-N-S 25-160-0730   (SL)
SIGMA BUSINESS SOLUTIONS INC
55 York St Suite 900, Toronto, ON, M5J 1R7
(416) 368-2000
Emp Here 115   *Sales* 16,580,930
SIC 7371 Custom computer programming services
Ameer Ramsundar
Dave Chanchalani

D-U-N-S 20-514-6710   (SL)
SIGMA SOFTWARE SOLUTIONS INC
55 York St Suite 1100, Toronto, ON, M5J 1R7
(416) 368-2000
Emp Here 100   *Sales* 17,731,100
SIC 7371 Custom computer programming services
Craig Denson
Andy Jasuja

D-U-N-S 24-125-2266   (SL)

▲ Public Company   ■ Public Company Family Member   **HQ** Headquarters   **BR** Branch   **SL** Single Location

SIGMA SYSTEMS GROUP INC
(*Suby of* HANSEN TECHNOLOGIES LIMITED)
55 York St Suite 1100, Toronto, ON, M5J 1R7
(416) 943-9696
Emp Here 150   *Sales* 21,627,300
SIC 7371 Custom computer programming services
Tim Spencer
Robert Levine

    D-U-N-S 20-938-0133   (BR)
SIR CORP
JACK ASTOR'S BAR AND GRILL
(*Suby of* SIR CORP)
144 Front St W, Toronto, ON, M5J 2L7
(416) 585-2121
Emp Here 195
SIC 5812 Eating places
Trevor Brodi

    D-U-N-S 25-536-7617   (HQ)
SOFTCOM INC
MYHOSTING.COM
(*Suby of* HNA TECHNOLOGY CO., LTD.)
88 Queens Quay W Suite 2610, Toronto, ON, M5J 0B8
(416) 957-7400
Sales 13,708,320
SIC 4813 Telephone communication, except radio
Turker Sokullu
Firat Eren
Michael Carr

    D-U-N-S 24-141-3699   (HQ)
SPENCER STUART & ASSOCIATES (CANADA) LTD
1 University Ave Unit 1900, Toronto, ON, M5J 2P1
(416) 361-0311
Emp Here 30   *Sales* 10,973,280
SIC 8741 Management services
John Koopmana
David Rasmussen

    D-U-N-S 24-352-9786   (HQ)
SPROTT ASSET MANAGEMENT INC
(*Suby of* SPROTT INC)
200 Bay St Suite 2700, Toronto, ON, M5J 2J1
(416) 955-5885
Sales 93,917,700
SIC 6282 Investment advice
Eric Sprott
Anne Spork
Iryna Gordiyenko

    D-U-N-S 24-130-3747   (SL)
SPROTT BULL/BEAR RSP
200 Bay St Suite 2700, Toronto, ON, M5J 2J1
(416) 943-6707
Emp Here 49   *Sales* 40,561,073
SIC 6722 Management investment, open-end
Eric Sprott

    D-U-N-S 24-127-4393   (SL)
SPROTT CANADIAN EQUITY FUND
NINEPOINT PARTNERS
200 Bay St Suite 2700, Toronto, ON, M5J 2J1
(416) 362-7172
Emp Here 49   *Sales* 40,561,073
SIC 6722 Management investment, open-end
John Wilson
James Fox

    .D-U-N-S 20-303-3873   (HQ)
SPROTT INC
200 Bay St Suite 2600, Toronto, ON, M5J 2J1
(416) 943-8099
Sales 82,837,047
SIC 6282 Investment advice
Peter Grosskopf
Whitney George
Rick Rule
Arthur Einav
John Ciampaglia
Edward C. Coyne

Dan Elder
Tim Sorensen
Greg Caione
Tom Ulrich

    D-U-N-S 24-683-7160   (HQ)
SPROTT PHYSICAL GOLD & SILVER TRUST
(*Suby of* SPROTT INC)
200 Bay St Suite 2600, Toronto, ON, M5J 2J1
(877) 403-2310
Sales 54,999,300
SIC 6726 Investment offices, nec
Peter Grosskopf
Kevin Hibbert
Whitney George
John Ciampaglia
Rick Rule
Arthur Einav
Steve Yuzpe

    D-U-N-S 24-014-6535   (HQ)
SPROTT RESOURCE HOLDINGS INC
200 Bay St Suite 2600, Toronto, ON, M5J 2J1
(855) 943-8099
Sales 24,789,935
SIC 1011 Iron ores
Michael Harrison
Michael Staresinic
Arthur Einav
Andrew Stronach
Terrence Lyons
Rick Rule
Donald K. Charter
Xinting Wang
Lenard Boggio
Ron Hochstein

    D-U-N-S 20-716-2806   (SL)
STARCAN CORPORATION
211 Queens Quay W Suite 908, Toronto, ON, M5J 2M6
(416) 361-0255
Emp Here 600   *Sales* 219,305,400
SIC 6712 Bank holding companies
Grant Burton

    D-U-N-S 24-352-7848   (HQ)
STARS GROUP INC, THE
AMAYA
200 Bay St Suite 3205, Toronto, ON, M5J 2J3
(437) 371-5742
Emp Here 351   *Sales* 2,029,238,000
SIC 3944 Games, toys, and children's vehicles
Brian Kyle
Rafael (Rafi) Ashkenazi
Marlon D. Goldstein
Jerry Bowskill
Robin Chhabra
Guy Nigel Templer
Divyesh (Dave) Gadhia
David Lazzarato
Alfred F Hurley Jr.
Harlan W. Goodson

    D-U-N-S 24-346-7086   (HQ)
STONE INVESTMENT GROUP LIMITED
40 University Ave Suite 901, Toronto, ON, M5J 1T1
(416) 364-9188
Emp Here 5   *Sales* 12,363,542
SIC 6719 Holding companies, nec
Richard Stone
James A. Elliott
Hari Panday
Mark Lerohl

    D-U-N-S 20-726-3773   (HQ)
SUN LIFE ASSURANCE COMPANY OF CANADA
(*Suby of* SUN LIFE FINANCIAL INC)
1 York St, Toronto, ON, M5J 0B6
(416) 979-9966
Emp Here 970   *Sales* 22,240,880,324
SIC 6311 Life insurance
Dean Connor
James Sutcliffe

John Clappison
Krystyna Hoeg
David Kerr
Mitchell Merin
Hugh Segal
William Anderson
Richard Booth
David Ganong

    D-U-N-S 25-998-4052   (HQ)
SUN LIFE FINANCIAL INC
1 York St, Toronto, ON, M5J 0B6
(416) 979-9966
Emp Here 1,000   *Sales* 20,466,479,694
SIC 6411 Insurance agents, brokers, and service
Dean A. Connor
Kevin P. Dougherty
Colm J. Freyne
Melissa J. Kennedy
Mark Saunders
Linda Dougherty
Helena Pagano
Kevin D. Strain
William D. Anderson
Stephanie L. Coyles

    D-U-N-S 20-348-0884   (HQ)
SUPERIOR GOLD INC
70 University Ave Suite 1410, Toronto, ON, M5J 2M4
(647) 925-1291
Sales 107,514,000
SIC 1041 Gold ores
Chris Bradbrook
Brian Szeto
Paul Olmsted
Keith Boyle
Fredrick (Lappies) Labuschagne
Mark Welling
Tamara Brown
Rene Marion
Michael Mulroney

    D-U-N-S 25-528-9944   (HQ)
TD ASSET MANAGEMENT INC
(*Suby of* TORONTO-DOMINION BANK, THE)
161 Bay St Suite 3200, Toronto, ON, M5J 2T2
(416) 361-5400
Sales 147,406,100
SIC 6722 Management investment, open-end
Tim Wiggan
Jennifer Soward
David Kelly
Margo Paul
Sandra Cimoroni
R. Michael Thorfinnson
Timothy Thompson
Atanaska Novakova

    D-U-N-S 24-378-4217   (SL)
TDAM USA INC
(*Suby of* TORONTO-DOMINION BANK, THE)
161 Bay St Suite 3200, Toronto, ON, M5J 2T2
(416) 982-6681
Emp Here 20   *Sales* 14,669,040
SIC 6722 Management investment, open-end
Barbara Palk

    D-U-N-S 20-019-9458   (HQ)
TERANET ENTERPRISES INC
(*Suby of* TERANET INC)
123 Front St W Suite 700, Toronto, ON, M5J 2M2
(416) 360-5263
Sales 73,829,200
SIC 7371 Custom computer programming services
Elgin Farewell

    D-U-N-S 24-911-2640   (HQ)
TERANET INC
123 Front St W Suite 700, Toronto, ON, M5J 2M2
(416) 360-5263
Emp Here 250   *Sales* 147,658,400
SIC 7371 Custom computer programming ser-

vices
Elgin Farewell
Peter Vukanovich
Eduardo Alzamora
Kerri Brass
Greg Kowal
Agostino Russo
Julia Reed
Dennis Barnhart
Ryan Doersam

    D-U-N-S 20-773-0946   (SL)
THOMAS I. HULL INSURANCE LIMITED
THE HULL GROUP
(*Suby of* HULL GROUP INC, THE)
220 Bay St Suite 600, Toronto, ON, M5J 2W4
(416) 865-0131
Emp Here 30   *Sales* 25,441,800
SIC 6411 Insurance agents, brokers, and service
Thomas Hull
Lindsay Panning
Myrian G Attard

    D-U-N-S 20-304-6701   (SL)
TMAC RESOURCES INC
95 Wellington St W Suite 1010, Toronto, ON, M5J 2N7
(416) 628-0216
Emp Here 454   *Sales* 134,942,156
SIC 1041 Gold ores
Jason Neal
Ronald P. Gagel
Julia Micks
Oliver Curran
Dave King
Alex Buchan
Gil Lawson
Maarten Theunissen
Terry Mcgibbon
John Lydall

    D-U-N-S 20-556-8009   (HQ)
TORONTO CONVENTION & VISITORS ASSOCIATION
TOURISM TORONTO
207 Queens Quay W Suite 405, Toronto, ON, M5J 1A7
(416) 203-2600
Sales 20,931,770
SIC 8611 Business associations
Johanne Belanger
Peter Doyle
Robert Housez
Nick Eaves
Maurice Bitran
Michael Copeland
Peter Kingsbury
Andy Loges

    D-U-N-S 20-647-0536   (HQ)
TORONTO PORT AUTHORITY
PORTS TORONTO
(*Suby of* CORPORATION OF THE CITY OF TORONTO)
60 Harbour St, Toronto, ON, M5J 1B7
(416) 863-2000
Emp Here 80   *Sales* 44,153,848
SIC 4581 Airports, flying fields, and services
Geoffrey A. Wilson
Alan J. Paul
Gene Cabral
Craig Manuel
Robert Poirier
G. Mark Curry
Jan Innes
Amanda Walton
Darin Deschamps
Hellen Siwanowicz

    D-U-N-S 24-666-2357   (SL)
TORONTO TERMINALS RAILWAY COMPANY LIMITED, THE
TTR
50 Bay St Suite 1400, Toronto, ON, M5J 3A5
(416) 864-3440
Emp Here 225   *Sales* 73,825,875

SIC 1629 Heavy construction, nec
George Huggins
James Robbins
Tony Marquis
Michael Farkouh

D-U-N-S 20-119-1108   (SL)
TORONTO WATERFRONT REVITALIZA-TION CORPORATION
WATERFRONT TORONTO
20 Bay St Suite 1310, Toronto, ON, M5J 2N8
(416) 214-1344
Emp Here 85   *Sales* 37,967,102
SIC 8748 Business consulting, nec
Helen Burstyn
Michael Nobrege

D-U-N-S 20-290-8526   (HQ)
TORQUEST PARTNERS INC
161 Bay St Suite 4240, Toronto, ON, M5J 2S1
(416) 956-7022
Sales 27,335,000
SIC 6712 Bank holding companies
Brent Belzberg
Eric Berke
Daniel Sonshine
Matthew Chapman
Michael Hollend

D-U-N-S 20-327-2104   (SL)
TRADE ALLIANCE & INVESTMENT CORP
161 Bay St, Toronto, ON, M5J 2S1

Emp Here 23   *Sales* 15,615,229
SIC 6282 Investment advice
Joshua Reisman
Carl Krasik
Colleen Davies

D-U-N-S 25-674-2784   (SL)
TRIAX DIVERSIFIED HIGH-YIELD TRUST
95 Wellington St W Suite 1400, Toronto, ON, M5J 2N7
(416) 362-2929
Emp Here 25   *Sales* 20,694,425
SIC 6726 Investment offices, nec
Barry H. Gordon
Edward Akkawi
Karen Wagman
Paul Dinelle
Charlene A. Schikowsky
Paul Dinelle
Edward Akkawi
Karen Wagman
Rohit Mehta
John Stephenson

D-U-N-S 25-172-3680   (SL)
TRILOGY RETAIL ENTERPRISES L.P
161 Bay St Suite 4900, Toronto, ON, M5J 2S1
(416) 943-4110
Emp Here 6,000   *Sales* 2,193,054,000
SIC 6712 Bank holding companies

D-U-N-S 25-167-2838   (HQ)
TRIOVEST REALTY ADVISORS INC
(*Suby of* CORIL HOLDINGS LTD)
40 University Ave Suite 1200, Toronto, ON, M5J 1T1
(416) 362-0045
Emp Here 50   *Sales* 211,290,000
SIC 6531 Real estate agents and managers
Vince Brown
David Robins
Yves-Andre Godon
Scott Ball

D-U-N-S 24-873-8031   (HQ)
UBS GLOBAL ASSET MANAGEMENT (CANADA) INC
161 Bay St Suite 4000, Toronto, ON, M5J 2S1
(416) 681-5200
Emp Here 20   *Sales* 13,578,460
SIC 6282 Investment advice
Thomas D. Johnston

D-U-N-S 24-327-6073   (HQ)

VALE CANADA LIMITED
(*Suby of* VALE S/A)
200 Bay St Suite 1500 Royal Bank Plz, Toronto, ON, M5J 2K2
(416) 361-7511
Emp Here 200   *Sales* 3,456,363,410
SIC 1629 Heavy construction, nec
Eduardo Bartolomeo
Gilberto Antonio Vieira
Fernando Jorge Buso Gomes
Alexandre Pereira
Luciano Siani Pires

D-U-N-S 24-142-0371   (BR)
VIA RAIL CANADA INC
(*Suby of* GOVERNMENT OF CANADA)
65 Front St W Suite 222, Toronto, ON, M5J 1E6
(888) 842-7245
Emp Here 600
SIC 4111 Local and suburban transit

D-U-N-S 20-988-6840   (SL)
WATTS' GROUP LIMITED
156 Front St W Suite 610, Toronto, ON, M5J 2L6
(416) 755-1374
Emp Here 120   *Sales* 5,462,280
SIC 5812 Eating places
Lisa Jodhan

D-U-N-S 25-361-2493   (HQ)
WESDOME GOLD MINES LTD
MINES D'OR WESDOME
220 Bay St Suite 1200, Toronto, ON, M5J 2W4
(416) 360-3743
Emp Here 10   *Sales* 87,971,672
SIC 1041 Gold ores
Duncan Middlemiss
Ben Au
Marc-Andre Pelletier
Lindsay Dunlop
Michael Michaud
Stacy Kimmett
Heather Laxton
Vincent K. Ramcharan
Charles Page
Nadine Miller

D-U-N-S 25-384-3130   (HQ)
WESTAIM CORPORATION, THE
70 York St Suite 1700, Toronto, ON, M5J 1S9
(416) 969-3333
Emp Here 8   *Sales* 40,195,220
SIC 6211 Security brokers and dealers
J. Cameron Macdonald
Joseph Schenk
Glenn Macneil
Robert T. Kittel
Ian W. Delaney
Bruce V. Walter
John W. Gildner
Stephen Cole

D-U-N-S 20-915-5063   (SL)
XPV WATER PARTNERS INC
VRG CAPITAL
40 University Ave Suite 801, Toronto, ON, M5J 1T1
(416) 581-8850
Emp Here 16   *Sales* 11,607,024
SIC 6351 Surety insurance
Kingsley Ward

D-U-N-S 25-538-5866   (HQ)
YAMANA GOLD INC
200 Bay St Royal Bank Plaza North Tower Ste 2200, Toronto, ON, M5J 2J3
(416) 815-0220
Emp Here 40   *Sales* 1,798,500,000
SIC 1041 Gold ores
Daniel Racine
Peter Marrone
Richard Campbell
Ross Gallinger
Jason Leblanc
Gerardo Fernandez

Yohann Bouchard
Henry Marsden
Sofia Tsakos
Nigel Lees

D-U-N-S 24-289-0226   (SL)
YORK CONDOMINIUM CORPORATION NO. 510
HARBOURSIDE
55 Harbour Sq Suite 3212, Toronto, ON, M5J 2L1
(416) 362-1174
Emp Here 62   *Sales* 25,971,118
SIC 6531 Real estate agents and managers
Ruth Wormitt

Toronto, ON M5K

D-U-N-S 24-135-8568   (SL)
1367313 ONTARIO INC
THORNTON GROUT FINNIGAN LLP
100 Wellington St Suite 3200, Toronto, ON, M5K 1K7
(416) 304-1616
Emp Here 40   *Sales* 16,774,200
SIC 6712 Bank holding companies
Robert Thornton

D-U-N-S 24-423-8648   (SL)
373813 ONTARIO LIMITED
TORYCO SERVICES
Gd, Toronto, ON, M5K 1N2
(416) 865-0040
Emp Here 250   *Sales* 31,194,000
SIC 8741 Management services
Les Viner

D-U-N-S 20-374-4862   (SL)
AGF EMERGING MARKETS BOND FUND
66 Wellington St W Suite 3100, Toronto, ON, M5K 1E9
(905) 214-8204
Emp Here 49   *Sales* 36,355,392
SIC 6722 Management investment, open-end
Blake Goldring
Judy Goldring

D-U-N-S 20-300-2589   (SL)
AGF GLOBAL MANAGEMENT LIMITED
66 Wellington St W 31st Fl Toronto Dominion Bank Tower, Toronto, ON, M5K 1E6
(416) 367-1900
Emp Here 45   *Sales* 37,249,965
SIC 6722 Management investment, open-end
Blake C. Goldring

D-U-N-S 20-264-2112   (SL)
AGF GLOBAL RESOURCES CLASS
66 Wellington St W, Toronto, ON, M5K 1E9
(905) 214-8203
Emp Here 49   *Sales* 36,355,392
SIC 6722 Management investment, open-end
Blake Goldring
Judy Goldring

D-U-N-S 25-274-9866   (HQ)
AGF INVESTMENTS INC
(*Suby of* AGF MANAGEMENT LIMITED)
66 Wellington St W Suite 3100, Toronto, ON, M5K 1E9
(416) 367-1900
Sales 1,867,816,000
SIC 6722 Management investment, open-end
Blake Goldring
Kevin Mccreadie
Robert J. Bogart
Judith Gail Goldring
Mark Adams

D-U-N-S 20-656-1594   (BR)
AGF MANAGEMENT LIMITED
(*Suby of* AGF MANAGEMENT LIMITED)
66 Wellington St W Fl 31, Toronto, ON, M5K 1E9

(800) 268-8583
Emp Here 700
SIC 6282 Investment advice

D-U-N-S 20-752-3390   (HQ)
AGF MANAGEMENT LIMITED
FONDS AGF, LES
66 Wellington St W Suite 3300, Toronto, ON, M5K 1E9
(416) 367-1900
Emp Here 400   *Sales* 323,721,631
SIC 6211 Security brokers and dealers
Blake Goldring
W. Robert Farquharson
Kevin Mccreadie
Judy Goldring
Adrian Basaraba
Chris Jackson
Kathleen Camilli
Douglas Derry
G. Wayne Squibb
Sarah Davis

D-U-N-S 20-259-9247   (SL)
AGF U.S SMALL-MID CAP FUND
66 Wellington St W, Toronto, ON, M5K 1E9
(905) 214-8203
Emp Here 49   *Sales* 36,355,392
SIC 6722 Management investment, open-end
Blake Goldring
Judy Goldring

D-U-N-S 20-372-8290   (SL)
AGFIQ ENHANCED CORE CANADIAN EQUITY ETF
66 Wellington St W Suite 3100, Toronto, ON, M5K 1E9
(905) 214-8204
Emp Here 49   *Sales* 35,939,148
SIC 6722 Management investment, open-end
Blake Goldring
Judy Goldring

D-U-N-S 25-119-1008   (HQ)
AP FOUNDERS LP
ALTAS PARTNERS
79 Wellington St W Suite 3500, Toronto, ON, M5K 1K7
(416) 306-9800
Sales 12,899,537
SIC 6282 Investment advice
Andrew Sheiner
Christopher Mcelhone
Paul Nicoletti

D-U-N-S 25-093-0356   (SL)
ASCENDANT RESOURCES INC
79 Wellington St W Suite 2100, Toronto, ON, M5K 1H1
(647) 796-0066
Emp Here 659   *Sales* 85,618,000
SIC 1081 Metal mining services
Chris Buncic
Cliff Hale-Sanders
Rohan Hazelton
Neil Ringdahl
Robert Campbell
Maria Virginia Anzola
Mark Brennan
Robert Campbell
Guillermo Kaelin
Kurt Menchen

D-U-N-S 20-284-7711   (SL)
ASTON HILL VIP INCOME FUND
77 King St W Suite 2110, Toronto, ON, M5K 2A1
(416) 583-2300
Emp Here 5   *Sales* 23,630,020
SIC 6733 Trusts, nec
Mark Caranci
Christopher Cullen
Moyra Mackay
Michelle Tiraborelli
Craig Kikuchi

D-U-N-S 25-219-3805   (SL)
ATS AUTOMATION

---

100 Wellington St W, Toronto, ON, M5K 1J3
(416) 601-1555
Emp Here 20   *Sales* 13,129,280
SIC 5962 Merchandising machine operators
Andrew Hider

D-U-N-S 20-275-3232   (BR)
BDO CANADA LLP
(*Suby of* BDO CANADA LLP)
66 Wellington St W Suite 3600, Toronto, ON,
M5K 1H1
(416) 865-0200
Emp Here 180
SIC 8748 Business consulting, nec

D-U-N-S 20-552-1177   (SL)
BIRCH HILL EQUITY PARTNERS II LTD
(*Suby of* TORONTO-DOMINION BANK, THE)
100 Wellington St W Suite 2300, Toronto, ON,
M5K 1B7
(416) 775-3800
Emp Here 50   *Sales* 46,958,850
SIC 6211 Security brokers and dealers
Joseph P Wiley
Stephen J Dent
John B Macintyre
Peter Zissis
Pierre J Schuurmans
Michael R Mazan
Michael J Salamon
Paul R Henry
David G Samuel
William A Lambert

D-U-N-S 20-695-0615   (HQ)
BIRCH HILL EQUITY PARTNERS MANAGEMENT INC
100 Wellington St W Suite 2300, Toronto, ON,
M5K 1A1
(416) 775-3800
Sales 51,592,135
SIC 6726 Investment offices, nec
Geoff Reed
Steve Gunn
Vince De Palma
Martin Connell
Bill Sanford
Anna Wu
Peter Zissis

D-U-N-S 20-881-0598   (HQ)
CANADIAN LIFE AND HEALTH INSURANCE ASSOCIATION INC
CLHIA
79 Wellington St W Suite 2300, Toronto, ON,
M5K 1G8
(416) 777-2221
Emp Here 1   *Sales* 14,999,670
SIC 8611 Business associations
Stephen Frank
Angela Albini
Wendy Hope

D-U-N-S 24-319-1447   (SL)
CASTLE RESOURCES INC
79 Wellington St W Suite 2100, Toronto, ON,
M5K 1H1
(416) 593-8300
Emp Here 5   *Sales* 11,937,745
SIC 1081 Metal mining services
Tim Mann
Jennifer Ta
Tony Croll
Lester Fernandez
Tyler Mitchelson

D-U-N-S 20-267-1249   (HQ)
CNA CANADA, INC
(*Suby of* LOEWS CORPORATION)
66 Wellington St W Suite 3700, Toronto, ON,
M5K 1J5
(416) 542-7300
Emp Here 90   *Sales* 541,055,856
SIC 6411 Insurance agents, brokers, and service
Gary Owcar
Denis Dei Cont

Gale Lockbaum

D-U-N-S 24-387-6336   (BR)
COMPAGNIE DE TELEPHONE BELL DU CANADA OU BELL CANADA, LA
Q9 NETWORKS
(*Suby of* BCE INC)
100 Wellington St W, Toronto, ON, M5K 1J3
(416) 365-7200
Emp Here 99
SIC 4813 Telephone communication, except radio
Osama Arafat

D-U-N-S 25-528-5892   (HQ)
CONTINENTAL CASUALTY COMPANY
CNA CANADA
(*Suby of* LOEWS CORPORATION)
66 Wellington St W Suite 3700, Toronto, ON,
M5K 1E9
(416) 542-7300
Emp Here 135   *Sales* 384,654,240
SIC 6331 Fire, marine, and casualty insurance
Gary Owcar

D-U-N-S 20-587-5149   (HQ)
DELTA HOTELS LIMITED
(*Suby of* GOVERNMENT OF THE PROVINCE OF BRITISH COLUMBIA)
77 King St W Suite 2300, Toronto, ON, M5K 2A1
Emp Here 750   *Sales* 311,940,000
SIC 8741 Management services
Hank Stackhouse
Ken Lambert

D-U-N-S 20-784-7062   (HQ)
DENTONS CANADA LLP
F M C
77 King St W Suite 400, Toronto, ON, M5K 2A1
(416) 863-4511
Emp Here 504   *Sales* 283,903,004
SIC 8111 Legal services
Beth Wilson
Chris Pinnington

D-U-N-S 25-253-3690   (SL)
DICKINSON WRIGHT LLP
DW MANAGEMENT COMPANY
(*Suby of* DICKINSON WRIGHT PLLC)
222 Bay St 18th Fl, Toronto, ON, M5K 1H1
(416) 777-0101
Emp Here 75   *Sales* 8,316,150
SIC 8111 Legal services
Eric Kay
Michael Miller

D-U-N-S 20-772-7074   (HQ)
ERNST & YOUNG INC
222 Bay St, Toronto, ON, M5K 1J7
(416) 864-1234
Sales 265,674,600
SIC 6733 Trusts, nec
Murray A Mcdonald

D-U-N-S 24-331-0229   (BR)
ERNST & YOUNG LLP
ORENDA CORPORATE FINANCE
(*Suby of* ERNST & YOUNG LLP)
222 Bay St 16th Flr, Toronto, ON, M5K 1J7
(416) 943-2040
Emp Here 200
SIC 8721 Accounting, auditing, and bookkeeping
Tony Ianni

D-U-N-S 24-965-8233   (HQ)
FENGATE CAPITAL MANAGEMENT LTD
77 King St W Unit 4230, Toronto, ON, M5K 2A1
(416) 488-4184
Emp Here 50   *Sales* 93,917,700
SIC 6211 Security brokers and dealers
Lou Serafini Jr
Pranav Pandya

D-U-N-S 24-335-5521   (SL)
FIRST URANIUM CORPORATION
(*Suby of* SIMMER AND JACK MINES LTD)
77 King St W Suite 400, Toronto, ON, M5K 0A1
(416) 306-3072
Emp Here 500
SIC 1094 Uranium-radium-vanadium ores
Mary Batoff
Emma Oosthuizen

D-U-N-S 24-564-6914   (BR)
FITNESS INSTITUTE LIMITED, THE
THE TORONTO ATHLETIC CLUB
(*Suby of* CAMBRIDGE GROUP OF CLUB)
79 Wellington St. W 36th Fl, Toronto, ON, M5K 1J5
(416) 865-0900
Emp Here 75
SIC 7991 Physical fitness facilities
Steve Roest

D-U-N-S 20-786-7532   (HQ)
FOGLER, RUBINOFF LLP
MELLOY MANAGEMENT
77 King St W Suite 3000, Toronto, ON, M5K 2A1
(416) 864-9700
Emp Here 195   *Sales* 22,176,400
SIC 8111 Legal services
Lloyd Fogler
Mel Rubinoff
Sydney Conn
Norman May
Michael Appleton

D-U-N-S 24-374-2389   (HQ)
FTI CONSULTING CANADA ULC
(*Suby of* FTI CONSULTING, INC.)
79 Wellington St W Suite 2010, Toronto, ON, M5K 1B1
(416) 649-8100
Emp Here 5   *Sales* 11,714,400
SIC 8748 Business consulting, nec
Dave Bannister
Eric B Miller
Ronald Reno
Gregg Watson

D-U-N-S 24-803-3086   (HQ)
GOLDMAN SACHS CANADA INC
(*Suby of* THE GOLDMAN SACHS GROUP INC)
77 King St W Suite 3400, Toronto, ON, M5K 2A1
(416) 343-8900
Sales 51,654,735
SIC 6211 Security brokers and dealers
James T. Kiernan
Stefano Zuliani
George Estey

D-U-N-S 20-551-8702   (HQ)
GRANITE REIT INC
77 King St W, Toronto, ON, M5K 2A1
(647) 925-7500
Sales 174,431,752
SIC 6798 Real estate investment trusts
Kevan Gorrie
Ilias Konstantopoulos
Lorne Kumer

D-U-N-S 20-259-3547   (SL)
HARMONY CANADIAN EQUITY POOL
66 Wellington St W, Toronto, ON, M5K 1E9
(905) 214-8203
Emp Here 49   *Sales* 36,355,392
SIC 6722 Management investment, open-end
Blake Goldring
Judy Goldring

D-U-N-S 20-259-3745   (SL)
HARMONY FUNDS
AGF HARMONY FUNDS
66 Wellington St W Suite 3100, Toronto, ON, M5K 1E9
(905) 214-8204
Emp Here 49   *Sales* 36,355,392

SIC 6722 Management investment, open-end
Blake Goldring
Judy Goldring

D-U-N-S 20-259-3380   (SL)
HARMONY GROWTH PLUS PORTFOLIO
AGF
66 Wellington St W Suite 3100, Toronto, ON, M5K 1E9
(905) 214-8204
Emp Here 49   *Sales* 36,355,392
SIC 6722 Management investment, open-end
Blake Goldring
Judy Goldring

D-U-N-S 20-259-3794   (SL)
HARMONY MONEY MARKET POOL
66 Wellington St W Suite 3100, Toronto, ON, M5K 1E9
(905) 214-8204
Emp Here 49   *Sales* 36,355,392
SIC 6722 Management investment, open-end
Blake Goldring
Judy Goldring

D-U-N-S 24-046-6649   (HQ)
HICKS MORLEY HAMILTON STEWART STORIE LLP
77 King St W 39th Fl Td Centre, Toronto, ON, M5K 2A1
(416) 362-1011
Emp Here 197   *Sales* 53,527,760
SIC 8111 Legal services
Stephen J Shamie
D Brent Labord
Vincent Panetta

D-U-N-S 24-130-1733   (SL)
HILLSDALE CANADIAN PERFORMANCE EQUITY
100 Wellington St W Suite 2100, Toronto, ON, M5K 1J3
(416) 913-3900
Emp Here 30   *Sales* 24,833,310
SIC 6722 Management investment, open-end
Christoper Guthrie

D-U-N-S 20-179-5304   (SL)
HILLSDALE INVESTMENT MANAGEMENT INC
100 Wellington St W Suite 2100, Toronto, ON, M5K 1J3
(416) 913-3900
Emp Here 25   *Sales* 13,280,175
SIC 6282 Investment advice
Christopher Guthrie

D-U-N-S 24-645-0969   (HQ)
LANNICK GROUP INC
LANNICK ASSOCIATES
77 King St W Suite 4110, Toronto, ON, M5K 2A1
(416) 340-1500
Emp Here 45   *Sales* 10,099,115
SIC 7361 Employment agencies
Peter Jeewan

D-U-N-S 24-215-6842   (HQ)
MATTAMY HOMES LIMITED
66 Wellington St W, Toronto, ON, M5K 1G8
(905) 829-2424
Emp Here 150   *Sales* 55,848,300
SIC 6552 Subdividers and developers, nec
Peter Gilgan
Brad Carr
Mary Federau
Bill Tofflemire

D-U-N-S 20-823-0441   (HQ)
MCCARTHY TETRAULT LLP
66 Wellington St W Suite 5300, Toronto, ON, M5K 1E6
(416) 362-1812
Emp Here 800   *Sales* 308,814,000
SIC 8111 Legal services
David Leonard
Tracie Crooks
Carol Kemp

Sarit E. Batner
Suzanne V. Murphy
Linda Brown
John S.Osler

D-U-N-S 24-425-6269   (SL)
MELLOY MANAGEMENT LIMITED
77 King St W Suite 3000, Toronto, ON, M5K
1G8
(416) 864-9700
Emp Here 150   *Sales* 18,716,400
SIC 8741 Management services
Karen Schremps

D-U-N-S 24-417-2404   (HQ)
MERUS LABS INTERNATIONAL INC
100 Wellington St W Suite 2110, Toronto, ON,
M5K 1H1
(905) 726-0995
Emp Here 11   *Sales* 70,678,401
SIC 2834 Pharmaceutical preparations
Barry Fishman
Frank Fokkinga
Frank Rotmann
Geoff Morrow
Michael Bumby
Michael Cloutier
David Guebert
Robert Pollock
Tim Sorensen
Theresa Firestone

D-U-N-S 20-764-3024   (HQ)
**MFS INVESTMENT MANAGEMENT
CANADA LIMITED**
(*Suby of* SUN LIFE FINANCIAL INC)
77 King St W Suite 3500, Toronto, ON, M5K
2A1
(416) 862-9800
Emp Here 70   *Sales* 75,134,160
SIC 6282 Investment advice
Peter Kotsopoulos

D-U-N-S 20-171-0142   (HQ)
MITSUI & CO. (CANADA) LTD
(*Suby of* MITSUI & CO., LTD.)
66 Wellington St W Suite 3510, Toronto, ON,
M5K 1K2
(416) 365-3800
Emp Here 41   *Sales* 36,444,694
SIC 5051 Metals service centers and offices
Fumiaki Miyamoto
Koki Oba
Terence A. Mcnally

D-U-N-S 24-826-7788   (SL)
MT SERVICES LIMITED PARTNERSHIP
66 Wellington St W Rd Suite 5300, Toronto,
ON, M5K 1E6
(416) 601-8200
Emp Here 1,000   *Sales* 110,882,000
SIC 8111 Legal services
Thomas Oakes
David Leonard

D-U-N-S 24-760-6986   (SL)
NIAGARA ACQUISITION GP INC
66 Wellington St W Suite 4400, Toronto, ON,
M5K 1H6
(416) 687-6700
Emp Here 100   *Sales* 27,175,600
SIC 6531 Real estate agents and managers
Jon Love

D-U-N-S 24-391-2735   (HQ)
**NORTHLEAF CAPITAL PARTNERS
(CANADA) LTD**
NORTHLEAF CAPITAL ADVISERS
79 Wellington St W, Toronto, ON, M5K 1N9
(866) 964-4141
Emp Here 37   *Sales* 50,715,558
SIC 6282 Investment advice
Rob Maclellan
Daniel Dupont
Michael Flood
Gavin Foo
Stephen Foote

D-U-N-S 20-357-9602   (SL)
**NORTHLEAF INFRASTRUCTURE CAPITAL
PARTNERS II LP**
79 Wellington St W Fl 6, Toronto, ON, M5K
1N9
(866) 964-4141
Emp Here 86   *Sales* 80,769,222
SIC 6282 Investment advice
Stewart Waugh

D-U-N-S 24-379-5635   (HQ)
PRIMERO MINING CORP
(*Suby of* FIRST MAJESTIC SILVER CORP)
79 Wellington St W Td South Tower Suite
2100, Toronto, ON, M5K 1H1
(416) 814-3160
Sales 153,975,948
SIC 1041 Gold ores
Joseph Conway
Damien Marantelli
Kevin Jennings
Tamara Brown
H. Maura Lendon
James Mallory
Louis Toner
Wade Nesmith
David Demers
Grant Edey

D-U-N-S 20-394-1047   (SL)
PRO COUNT STAFFING INC
(*Suby of* LANNICK GROUP INC)
77 King St W Suite 4110, Toronto, ON, M5K
2A1
(416) 340-1500
Emp Here 100
SIC 7361 Employment agencies
Peter Jeewan

D-U-N-S 20-294-1514   (SL)
**QUANTUM INTERNATIONAL INCOME
CORP**
79 Wellington St W Suite 1630, Toronto, ON,
M5K 1H1
(416) 477-3400
Emp Here 10   *Sales* 25,744,248
SIC 0971 Hunting, trapping, game propaga-
tion
Manu K. Sekhri
Chad Williams
Peter Shippen
Mark Lerohl
Sheila Ogilvie-Harris
Ryan Bouskill

D-U-N-S 24-127-2017   (SL)
RBC O'SHAUGHNESSY U.S. VALUE FUND
GLOBAL ASSET MANAGEMENT
77 King St W, Toronto, ON, M5K 2A1
(800) 463-3863
Emp Here 49   *Sales* 40,561,073
SIC 6722 Management investment, open-end
Jim O Shaughnessy
Patrick O'shaughnessy

D-U-N-S 24-923-0632   (HQ)
**RGA LIFE REINSURANCE COMPANY OF
CANADA**
(*Suby of* REINSURANCE GROUP OF AMER-
ICA, INCORPORATED)
77 King St W Suite 2300, Toronto, ON, M5K
2A1
(416) 682-0000
Emp Here 14   *Sales* 121,070,964
SIC 6311 Life insurance
David A Pelletier
Alain Neemeh
Robert Mallette
Jackie Deforest
Josee Malboeuf
Brian Louth
Gary Walters
Patricia O'keeffe
Dominique Faribault
Micheline Dionne

D-U-N-S 24-014-8148   (HQ)

**ROYAL TRUST CORPORATION OF
CANADA**
(*Suby of* ROYAL BANK OF CANADA)
77 King St W Suite 3800, Toronto, ON, M5K
2A1
(416) 974-1400
Sales 268,283,000
SIC 6021 National commercial banks
Gordon Nixon

D-U-N-S 24-631-8653   (SL)
SCOTIA MORTGAGE AUTHORITY
(*Suby of* BANK OF NOVA SCOTIA, THE)
79 Wellingston St W Suite 3400, Toronto, ON,
M5K 1K7
(416) 350-7400
Emp Here 700   *Sales* 370,069,000
SIC 6162 Mortgage bankers and loan corre-
spondents
John Webster

D-U-N-S 20-562-2629   (SL)
TD ASSET FINANCE CORP
(*Suby of* TORONTO-DOMINION BANK, THE)
55 King St W, Toronto, ON, M5K 1A2
(416) 982-2322
Emp Here 100
SIC 6159 Miscellaneous business credit insti-
tutions
Edward P. Hawara
Numaan Butt
Lian Yuen

D-U-N-S 24-860-8549   (SL)
TD CAPITAL GROUP LIMITED
(*Suby of* TORONTO-DOMINION BANK, THE)
100 Wellington St W, Toronto, ON, M5K 1A2
(800) 430-6095
Emp Here 25   *Sales* 23,479,425
SIC 6211 Security brokers and dealers
Jane Stubbington
Sandra Mundy
Richard G. Greene
Robert Linklater
Adam Newman

D-U-N-S 20-552-1334   (SL)
TD INVESTMENT SERVICES INC
(*Suby of* TORONTO-DOMINION BANK, THE)
55 King St W, Toronto, ON, M5K 1A2
(416) 944-5728
Emp Here 50   *Sales* 26,560,350
SIC 6282 Investment advice
William Hatanaka

D-U-N-S 25-193-8544   (SL)
TD LIFE INSURANCE COMPANY
TD INSURANCE
(*Suby of* TORONTO-DOMINION BANK, THE)
55 King St W, Toronto, ON, M5K 1A2

Emp Here 200   *Sales* 427,393,600
SIC 6311 Life insurance
Sean E. Kilburn
Bernard T. Dorval
Jim Senn
David G. Duncan

D-U-N-S 24-889-5799   (HQ)
TD SECURITIES INC
(*Suby of* TORONTO-DOMINION BANK, THE)
66 Wellington St W, Toronto, ON, M5K 1A2
(416) 307-8500
Emp Here 1,600   *Sales* 3,557,845,000
SIC 6211 Security brokers and dealers
Bob Dorrance
John F. Coombs
William J. (Bill) Furlong

D-U-N-S 20-865-2727   (BR)
TD WATERHOUSE CANADA INC
TD WEALTH
(*Suby of* TORONTO-DOMINION BANK, THE)
79 Wellington St W 10th Fl, Toronto, ON, M5K
1A1
(416) 307-6672
Emp Here 97

SIC 6211 Security brokers and dealers
Kirste Spencer

D-U-N-S 20-707-6915   (HQ)
**TD WATERHOUSE PRIVATE INVESTMENT
COUNSEL INC**
(*Suby of* TORONTO-DOMINION BANK, THE)
66 Wellington St W, Toronto, ON, M5K 1A2
(416) 308-1933
Sales 235,849,760
SIC 6722 Management investment, open-end
John Miller
David Kelli

D-U-N-S 24-524-6942   (HQ)
TERANGA GOLD CORPORATION
77 King St W Suite 2110, Toronto, ON, M5K
2A1
(416) 594-0000
Emp Here 50   *Sales* 312,628,000
SIC 1041 Gold ores
Richard S. Young
David Mallo
David Savarie
Navin Dyal
Paul Chawrun
Alan R. Hill
Jendayi E. Frazer
William J. Biggar
Edward S. Goldenberg
Christopher R. Lattanzi

D-U-N-S 20-268-6150   (HQ)
TORONTO-DOMINION BANK, THE
TD CANADA TRUST
55 King St W, Toronto, ON, M5K 1A2
(416) 982-5722
Emp Here 5,000   *Sales* 22,804,055,000
SIC 6021 National commercial banks
Gregory B. Braca
Philip Aquilino
Ernie Diaz
Chris Giamo
Patrick Mclean
Adam Newman
Anita O'dell
Jim Peterson
Manjit Singh
Gregory Smith

D-U-N-S 24-118-0475   (BR)
TORONTO-DOMINION BANK, THE
TD BANK
(*Suby of* TORONTO-DOMINION BANK, THE)
66 Wellington St W, Toronto, ON, M5K 1A2
(416) 982-7650
Emp Here 100
SIC 6021 National commercial banks
Rabha Arjune

D-U-N-S 20-980-5589   (HQ)
TORYS LLP
79 Wellington St W Suite 3000, Toronto, ON,
M5K 1N2
(416) 865-0040
Sales 164,700,800
SIC 8111 Legal services
Les Viner
Adam S. Armstrong
Dany H. Assaf

D-U-N-S 20-968-5114   (SL)
WEIRFOULDS LLP
66 Wellington St W Suite 4100, Toronto, ON,
M5K 1B7
(416) 365-1110
Emp Here 170   *Sales* 18,849,940
SIC 8111 Legal services
Bill Ross
Jeff Cowan
Alec Clute
Ken Prehogan
Glenn W Ackerley
Lisa Borsook
John Buhlman
Raj Anand
Dee Nevett

Toronto, ON M5L

D-U-N-S 20-393-3416   (HQ)
ALTIUM PACKAGING CANADA INC
(*Suby of* LOEWS CORPORATION)
199 Bay St Suite 4000, Toronto, ON, M5L 1A9

Sales 14,850,400
SIC 5199 Nondurable goods, nec
Sean Fallmann
Jeff Brubaker
Brian Hankin
Dan Ferus
Mark Shafer
Patrick Keese
Louis Lettes
Julie Davis
Richard Sehring
Beth Duncan

D-U-N-S 24-309-5101   (HQ)
ASSANTE   WEALTH   MANAGEMENT
(CANADA) LTD
199 Bay St Suite 2700, Toronto, ON, M5L 1E2
(416) 348-9994
Emp Here 3   Sales 432,031,638
SIC 6712 Bank holding companies
Joseph Canavan
Steven J Donald
Douglas Jamieson

D-U-N-S 20-293-7579   (HQ)
AVESORO RESOURCES INC
199 Bay St Suite 5300, Toronto, ON, M5L 1B9

Emp Here 10   Sales 282,798,000
SIC 1041 Gold ores
Serhan Umurhan
Geoff Eyre
Mehmet Nazif Gunal
David Netherway
Jean-Guy Martin
Loudon Owen

D-U-N-S 24-058-3732   (HQ)
BLAKE, CASSELS & GRAYDON LLP
199 Bay St Suite 4000, Toronto, ON, M5L 1A9
(416) 863-2400
Emp Here 700   Sales 205,876,000
SIC 8111 Legal services
Robert Granatstein
Richard Prupas
Brock Gibson

D-U-N-S 24-738-3524   (SL)
BLAKES SERVICES INC
199 Bay St, Toronto, ON, M5L 1A9
(416) 863-2603
Emp Here 117   Sales 14,598,792
SIC 8741 Management services
Jim Christie
Joel Shafer

D-U-N-S 20-936-0056   (HQ)
CANADIAN BANKERS ASSOCIATION, THE
199 Bay St 30th Fl, Toronto, ON, M5L 1G2
(416) 362-6092
Emp Here 50   Sales 15,516,900
SIC 8611 Business associations
Neil Parmenter
Terry Campbell
Anne Wetlaufer

D-U-N-S 20-268-6119   (HQ)
CANADIAN IMPERIAL BANK OF COM-
MERCE
199 Bay St Commerce Crt W, Toronto, ON,
M5L 1A2
(416) 980-3096
Emp Here 3,000   Sales 13,774,054,232
SIC 6021 National commercial banks
Victor G. Dodig
Michael G. Capatides
Harry Culham
Laura Dottori-Attanasio

Kevin Glass
Jon Hountalas
Deepak Khandelwal
Christina Kramer
Kevin Patterson
Larry D. Richman

D-U-N-S 20-944-1211   (HQ)
CHUBB   INSURANCE   COMPANY   OF
CANADA
(*Suby of* CHUBB LIMITED)
199 Bay St Suite 2500, Toronto, ON, M5L 1E2
(416) 863-0550
Emp Here 250   Sales 897,526,560
SIC 6331 Fire, marine, and casualty insurance
Ellen Moore
Andy Hollenberg
Grant Mcewen

D-U-N-S 24-310-8078   (HQ)
CIBC ASSET MANAGEMENT HOLDINGS
INC
(*Suby of* CANADIAN IMPERIAL BANK OF
COMMERCE)
Commerce Crt W, Toronto, ON, M5L 1A2
(416) 980-2211
Emp Here 1   Sales 93,917,700
SIC 6282 Investment advice
Victor Dodig

D-U-N-S 25-531-9170   (HQ)
CIBC INVESTOR SERVICES INC
CIBC INVESTORS EDGE
(*Suby of* CANADIAN IMPERIAL BANK OF
COMMERCE)
199 Bay St, Toronto, ON, M5L 1A2
(416) 980-3343
Sales 26,560,350
SIC 6282 Investment advice
Marybeth Jordan
Thomas Mccready
Daniel Donnelly
Norah Mccarthy
Michael Martin
Monique Gravel
Victor Dodig

D-U-N-S 24-324-6522   (HQ)
DETOUR GOLD CORPORATION
199 Bay St Suite 4100, Toronto, ON, M5L 1E2
(416) 304-0800
Emp Here 425   Sales 77,600,000
SIC 1041 Gold ores
Mick Mcmullen
Ruben Wallin
Dan Schmelzer
Laurie Gaborit
Kelly Barrowcliffe
Carl Deluca
Frazer W. Bourchier
Patrice Merrin
Andre Falzon
Steven Feldman

D-U-N-S 20-185-1354   (SL)
DEUTSCHE BANK AG- CANADA BRANCH
(*Suby of* DEUTSCHE BANK AG)
199 Bay St Suite 4700, Toronto, ON, M5L 1E9
(416) 682-8000
Emp Here 90   Sales 24,145,470
SIC 6021 National commercial banks
Daniel Sooley

D-U-N-S 24-355-1830   (HQ)
FRANCO-NEVADA CORPORATION
199 Bay St Suite 2000, Toronto, ON, M5L 1G9
(416) 306-6300
Sales 653,200,000
SIC 1041 Gold ores
David Harquail
Paul Brink
Sandip Rana
Lloyd Hong
Pierre Lassonde
Tom Albanese
Derek Evans

Catharine Farrow
Louis Gignac
Jennifer Maki

D-U-N-S 20-769-5263   (HQ)
GUARDIAN CAPITAL GROUP LIMITED
199 Bay St Suite 3100, Toronto, ON, M5L 1E8
(416) 364-8341
Emp Here 70   Sales 130,024,348
SIC 6282 Investment advice
George Mavroudis
Leslie Lee
A. Michael Christodoulou
Matthew Turner
Vern Christensen
Donald Yi
James Anas
Petros Christodoulou
George Mavroudis
Barry Myers

D-U-N-S 20-821-2027   (HQ)
GUARDIAN CAPITAL LP
199 Bay St Suite 3100, Toronto, ON, M5L 1E8
(416) 364-8341
Sales 75,134,160
SIC 6282 Investment advice
J.J. Woolverton

D-U-N-S 20-702-3730   (HQ)
MACKIE RESEACH CAPITAL CORPORA-
TION
MRCC
199 Bay St Suite 4500, Toronto, ON, M5L 1G2
(416) 860-7600
Emp Here 150   Sales 498,098,300
SIC 6211 Security brokers and dealers
Patrick Walsh
Geoffrey Whitlam
Andrew Selbie

D-U-N-S 20-386-1179   (SL)
PAYLESS SHOESOURCE GP INC
4000-199 St Bay, Commerce Court W,
Toronto, ON, M5L 1A9

Emp Here 100   Sales 17,939,600
SIC 5661 Shoe stores
Lorelei Lane

D-U-N-S 20-386-1174   (SL)
PAYLESS SHOESOURCE LP
4000-199 St Bay, Toronto, ON, M5L 1A9

Emp Here 100   Sales 17,939,600
SIC 5661 Shoe stores
Jessica Gale

D-U-N-S 24-350-0993   (SL)
PORTEX MINERALS INC
SRA
199 Bay St W Suite 2901, Toronto, ON, M5L
1G1
(416) 786-3876
Emp Here 260   Sales 620,762,740
SIC 1041 Gold ores
Peter Chodos
Victor P. Wyprysky
Terence Chandler
Richard Bishop
Patrick Raleigh
Geoffrey Douglas Stanley

D-U-N-S 24-099-9102   (HQ)
SCOR CANADA REINSURANCE COMPANY
(*Suby of* SCOR SE)
199 Bay St Suite 2800, Toronto, ON, M5L 1G1
(416) 869-3670
Sales 68,326,383
SIC 6331 Fire, marine, and casualty insurance
Henry Klecan
Stanley Fung

D-U-N-S 20-259-3489   (SL)
SENTRY ENHANCED CORPORATE BOND
FUND
199 Bay St Suite 2700, Toronto, ON, M5L 1E2

(416) 861-8729
Emp Here 49   Sales 41,030,848
SIC 6722 Management investment, open-end
Sean Bristoll

D-U-N-S 24-045-6111   (HQ)
STIKEMAN ELLIOTT LLP
5300 Commerce Crt W Suite 199, Toronto,
ON, M5L 1B9
(416) 869-5500
Emp Here 40   . Sales 82,350,400
SIC 8111 Legal services
Marc Barbeau
Patrick L. Benaroche
Louis P. Belanger
Jean Fontaine
Jean-Marc Huot
John W. Leopold
Andre Roy
Elizabeth Breen
Laurent G. Fortier
Peter J. Cullen

D-U-N-S 24-320-4337   (HQ)
TMS INTERNATIONAL CANADA LIMITED
(*Suby of* TMS INTERNATIONAL CORP.)
199 Bay St Suite 5300, Toronto, ON, M5L 1B9

Emp Here 2   Sales 31,232,520
SIC 5093 Scrap and waste materials
Jonathan Fingeret
Robert Garbaty
William Miller

D-U-N-S 20-393-5957   (SL)
VENTUREKIDS TECH ORGANIZATION
30 Wellington St W 5th Fl, Toronto, ON, M5L
1E2
(416) 985-6839
Emp Here 45   Sales 10,207,485
SIC 8399 Social services, nec
Takara Small

D-U-N-S 20-300-1664   (SL)
WPT INDUSTRIAL REAL ESTATE INVEST-
MENT TRUST
199 Bay St Suite 4000, Toronto, ON, M5L 1A9
(800) 230-9505
Emp Here 9   Sales 95,244,000
SIC 6021 National commercial banks
Scott Frederiksen
Milo D. Arkema
Sarah B. Kavanagh
Louie Dinunzio
Stuart H.B. Smith
Robert T. Wolf
Pamela J. Spackman
Judd K. Gilats
Matthew J. Cimino

Toronto, ON M5M

D-U-N-S 25-202-4658   (BR)
RICHTREE MARKET RESTAURANTS INC
MARCHE MOVENPICK
(*Suby of* NATURAL MARKETS FOOD
GROUP)
40 Yonge Blvd, Toronto, ON, M5M 3G5
(416) 366-8986
Emp Here 200
SIC 5812 Eating places
Williams Matt

Toronto, ON M5N

D-U-N-S 24-783-8840   (SL)
A.D.H. DRUGS LIMITED
SHOPPERS DRUG MART
550 Eglinton Ave W Suite 506, Toronto, ON,
M5N 1B6
(416) 485-3093
Emp Here 75   Sales 18,324,600

SIC 5912 Drug stores and proprietary stores
Howard Trifler

D-U-N-S 20-369-7859   (SL)
CG CANADIAN GLOVE CORP
67 Kimbark Blvd, Toronto, ON, M5N 2X9
(416) 939-5066
Emp Here 305   *Sales* 49,266,589
SIC 3069 Fabricated rubber products, nec
Amirhossein Farajzdeh-Ahari

D-U-N-S 20-823-8964   (SL)
LEVIN, FISCHER LIMITED
525 Eglinton Ave W, Toronto, ON, M5N 1B1
(416) 487-5277
Emp Here 31   *Sales* 10,140,937
SIC 6531 Real estate agents and managers
Dov J Levin

D-U-N-S 25-254-5983   (BR)
REVERA INC
FOREST HILL PLACE
(*Suby of* GOVERNMENT OF CANADA)
645 Castlefield Ave Suite 716, Toronto, ON,
M5N 3A5
(416) 785-1511
Emp Here 120
SIC 8051 Skilled nursing care facilities
Hartini Kumar

D-U-N-S 25-344-3733   (SL)
SLAVENS ASSOCIATES
SLAVENS, PAUL AND ASSOCIATES
435 Eglinton Ave W, Toronto, ON, M5N 1A4
(416) 483-4337
Emp Here 40   *Sales* 13,085,080
SIC 6531 Real estate agents and managers
Paul Slavens

Toronto, ON M5P

D-U-N-S 24-141-3384   (SL)
BETH TZEDEC CONGREGATION INC
BETH TZEDEC MEMORIAL PARK
1700 Bathurst St, Toronto, ON, M5P 3K3
(416) 781-3511
Emp Here 100   *Sales* 10,772,700
SIC 8661 Religious organizations
Randy Spiegel

D-U-N-S 24-413-9978   (HQ)
CAMP WINNEBAGOE INC
4 Silverwood Ave, Toronto, ON, M5P 1W4
(416) 486-1110
Emp Here 1   *Sales* 12,513,150
SIC 7032 Sporting and recreational camps
Bernard Lustig
Jill Lustig

D-U-N-S 24-545-6132   (HQ)
FOREST HILL REAL ESTATE INC
441 Spadina Rd, Toronto, ON, M5P 2W3
(416) 488-2875
Emp Here 105   *Sales* 84,516,000
SIC 6531 Real estate agents and managers
David Fingold
Jeffrey Wagman

D-U-N-S 25-710-1188   (SL)
ST. MICHAEL'S COLLEGE SCHOOL
ST. MICHAEL'S ARENA
1515 Bathurst St, Toronto, ON, M5P 3H4
(416) 653-4483
Emp Here 110   *Sales* 10,210,860
SIC 8211 Elementary and secondary schools
Joseph Redican
Gino Saccone

Toronto, ON M5R

D-U-N-S 20-176-9119   (SL)
1561109 ONTARIO INC

PRODUCT EXCELLENCE
40 Bernard Ave, Toronto, ON, M5R 1R2
(416) 460-0980
Emp Here 30   *Sales* 33,160,350
SIC 5122 Drugs, proprietaries, and sundries
Norman Paul
Ralph Phillips
Annette Ryan
Shiam Pasupathay

D-U-N-S 25-321-7525   (BR)
2063414 ONTARIO LIMITED
LEISUREWORLD CAREGIVING CENTRE
225 St. George St, Toronto, ON, M5R 2M2
(416) 967-3985
Emp Here 200
SIC 8051 Skilled nursing care facilities
Elizabeth Bryce

D-U-N-S 25-486-5355   (SL)
601092 ONTARIO LIMITED
VERMONT SQUARE
914 Bathurst St, Toronto, ON, M5R 3G5
(416) 533-9473
Emp Here 200   *Sales* 13,713,200
SIC 8051 Skilled nursing care facilities
George Kuhl

D-U-N-S 25-404-7129   (SL)
924169 ONTARIO LIMITED
SPAMEDICA CANADA
66 Avenue Rd Unit 4, Toronto, ON, M5R 3N8
(416) 922-2868
Emp Here 60   *Sales* 11,120,400
SIC 8011 Offices and clinics of medical doctors
Stephen Mulholland

D-U-N-S 20-363-2646   (HQ)
9580166 CANADA INC
MOBILE KLINIK
(*Suby of* MOBILE SERVICE CENTER CANADA LIMITED)
15 Prince Arthur Ave, Toronto, ON, M5R 1B2
(647) 282-2802
Emp Here 25   *Sales* 10,185,800
SIC 7629 Electrical repair shops
Alain Adam
Robert Bruce
Kenneth Campbell

D-U-N-S 20-323-3940   (SL)
B&N MANAGEMENT
51 Tranby Ave, Toronto, ON, M5R 1N4
(613) 321-7401
Emp Here 100   *Sales* 15,537,100
SIC 7361 Employment agencies
Maurice Naufal
Mountaha Saikaly

D-U-N-S 24-095-3638   (SL)
BLYTH & COMPANY TRAVEL LIMITED
13 Hazelton Ave, Toronto, ON, M5R 2E1
(416) 964-2569
Emp Here 35   *Sales* 13,487,600
SIC 4724 Travel agencies
Sam G Blyth

D-U-N-S 20-344-0420   (HQ)
BLYTH EDUCATIONAL GROUP INC
BLYTH EDUCATION
160 Avenue Rd, Toronto, ON, M5R 2H8
(416) 960-3552
Emp Here 10   *Sales* 15,969,870
SIC 8748 Business consulting, nec
Monique Grignard

D-U-N-S 20-423-6426   (HQ)
BONNETERIE BELLA INC.
1191 Bathurst St, Toronto, ON, M5R 3H4
(416) 537-2137
Sales 31,178,510
SIC 2251 Women's hosiery, except socks
Albert Werner

D-U-N-S 24-964-5201   (HQ)
C5 GROUP INC
1329 Bay St Suite 300, Toronto, ON, M5R 2C4

(416) 926-8200
Emp Here 4   *Sales* 91,377,250
SIC 6719 Holding companies, nec
Toby Belman
David Gray

D-U-N-S 20-784-9191   (HQ)
CALDWELL PARTNERS INTERNATIONAL INC, THE
165 Avenue Rd Suite 600, Toronto, ON, M5R 3S4
(416) 920-7702
Emp Here 50   *Sales* 46,129,604
SIC 7311 Advertising agencies
John Wallace
Chris Beck
Pamela Cioffi
Michael Falagario
Caroline Lomot
G. Edmund King
Paul Daoust
Kathryn Welsh

D-U-N-S 20-190-6216   (HQ)
CAMTX CORPORATION
106 Avenue Rd, Toronto, ON, M5R 2H3
(416) 920-0500
Emp Here 10   *Sales* 11,004,180
SIC 2211 Broadwoven fabric mills, cotton
Fred Litwin
Mark Litwin
Stanley Abramowitz
Mark Dawber
Sol Nayman
Alan Kornblum

D-U-N-S 24-817-9574   (HQ)
CANADA DEVELOPMENT INVESTMENT CORPORATION
CDIC
(*Suby of* GOVERNMENT OF CANADA)
1240 Bay St Suite 302, Toronto, ON, M5R 2A7
(416) 966-2221
Sales 233,720,572
SIC 6719 Holding companies, nec
William C. Ross
Michael Carter
Andrew Stafl
Patrice Walch-Watson
Benita M Warmbold
Mary Ritchie
John James Hillyard
Ted Howell
Mary Beth Montcalm

D-U-N-S 20-821-2118   (HQ)
CANADIAN HEARING SOCIETY
271 Spadina Rd, Toronto, ON, M5R 2V3
(416) 928-2502
Emp Here 100   *Sales* 26,446,457
SIC 5999 Miscellaneous retail stores, nec
Julia Dumanian
Stephanus Greeff
Chantal Graveline
Gary Malkowski
Shane Silver

D-U-N-S 20-529-2592   (HQ)
CARA HOLDINGS LIMITED
21 Bedford Rd Suite 200, Toronto, ON, M5R 2J9
(905) 760-2244
Emp Here 4   *Sales* 654,718,282
SIC 5812 Eating places
H Gail Regan
Sanish Samuel
Peter L. Gaunt
Colin Stewart Robertson
Paul James Phelan
Vali Jean-Marie Bennet
Stephen John David Christie
Larry Hynes
Helen Doris Phelan
Sharon G. Phelan

D-U-N-S 20-351-2876   (SL)
CHG BLOOR HOLDINGS INC

PLANTA YORKVILLE
1221 Bay St, Toronto, ON, M5R 3P5
(647) 348-7000
Emp Here 109   *Sales* 5,045,018
SIC 5812 Eating places
Steven Eric Salm
Michael Jason Kimel

D-U-N-S 20-379-7258   (SL)
COLD PRESS CORP, THE
CEDAR JUICE
(*Suby of* GREENSPACE BRANDS INC)
176 St George St, Toronto, ON, M5R 2M7
(416) 934-5034
Emp Here 80   *Sales* 3,980,075
SIC 5149 Groceries and related products, nec
Matthew Von Teichman
Cindy Leung
Greg Guyatt
Aaron Skelton

D-U-N-S 24-096-7075   (SL)
COLLEGE OF NURSES OF ONTARIO
101 Davenport Rd, Toronto, ON, M5R 3P1
(416) 928-0900
Emp Here 135   *Sales* 31,604,985
SIC 8621 Professional organizations
Sandra Ireland
Gail Siskind
Paul Reinhard
Anne Coghlan
Ravi Prathivathi
Cathy Stanford
Heather Campbell

D-U-N-S 20-772-7629   (HQ)
COMMUNITY LIVING TORONTO
20 Spadina Rd, Toronto, ON, M5R 2S7
(416) 968-0650
Emp Here 100   *Sales* 99,829,600
SIC 8322 Individual and family services
Angela Bradley
Bruce Rivers
Flavian Pinto

D-U-N-S 20-803-8476   (BR)
COMMUNITY LIVING TORONTO
(*Suby of* COMMUNITY LIVING TORONTO)
20 Spadina Rd Suite 257, Toronto, ON, M5R 2S7
(416) 968-0650
Emp Here 100
SIC 8742 Management consulting services
Gary Pruden

D-U-N-S 20-771-1599   (HQ)
GEORGE BROWN COLLEGE OF APPLIED ARTS AND TECHNOLOGY, THE
GEORGE BROWN COLLEGE
500 Macpherson Ave, Toronto, ON, M5R 1M3
(416) 415-2000
Emp Here 60   *Sales* 99,119,000
SIC 8222 Junior colleges
Michael Eubanks
Anne Sado
Eugene Harrigan
Ric Ho

D-U-N-S 24-714-7882   (BR)
GOVERNING COUNCIL OF THE UNIVERSITY OF TORONTO, THE
DEPARTMENT OF ENGLISH
(*Suby of* GOVERNING COUNCIL OF THE UNIVERSITY OF TORONTO, THE)
170 St. George St, Toronto, ON, M5R 2M8
(416) 978-3190
Emp Here 137
SIC 8221 Colleges and universities
Paul Stevens

D-U-N-S 20-369-4344   (BR)
GOVERNING COUNCIL OF THE UNIVERSITY OF TORONTO, THE
DEPARTMENT OF PHILOSOPHY
(*Suby of* GOVERNING COUNCIL OF THE UNIVERSITY OF TORONTO, THE)
170 St. George St 4 Fl, Toronto, ON, M5R

2M8
(416) 978-3311
Emp Here 158
SIC 8221 Colleges and universities
Martin Pickave

D-U-N-S 20-264-9455   (HQ)
GREENSPACE BRANDS INC
176 St George St, Toronto, ON, M5R 2M7
(416) 934-5034
Sales 44,819,625
SIC 5149 Groceries and related products, nec
Matthew Von Teichman
James Haggarty
Roger Daher
Blair Tamblyn
Maria Pacella
Micheal Lovsin
Cindy Leung
Aaron Skelton

D-U-N-S 24-804-3007   (SL)
GTA GOLF & COUNTRY CLUB
800 Bathurst St Unit 1, Toronto, ON, M5R 3M8
(416) 762-2530
Emp Here 120   *Sales* 2,052,664
SIC 7997 Membership sports and recreation
clubs

D-U-N-S 24-804-3015   (SL)
GTA GOLF & COUNTRY CLUB
800 Bathurst St Unit 1, Toronto, ON, M5R 3M8
(416) 762-2530
Emp Here 120   *Sales* 2,052,664
SIC 7997 Membership sports and recreation
clubs

D-U-N-S 24-804-3023   (SL)
GTA GOLF & COUNTRY CLUB
800 Bathurst St Unit 1, Toronto, ON, M5R 3M8
(416) 762-2530
Emp Here 120   *Sales* 2,052,664
SIC 7997 Membership sports and recreation
clubs

D-U-N-S 24-804-3031   (SL)
GTA GOLF & COUNTRY CLUB
800 Bathurst St Unit 1, Toronto, ON, M5R 3M8
(416) 762-2531
Emp Here 120   *Sales* 26,979,563
SIC 7997 Membership sports and recreation
clubs

D-U-N-S 24-804-3049   (SL)
GTA GOLF & COUNTRY CLUB
800 Bathurst St Unit 1, Toronto, ON, M5R 3M8
(416) 762-2530
Emp Here 120   *Sales* 2,052,664
SIC 7997 Membership sports and recreation
clubs

D-U-N-S 24-804-3056   (SL)
GTA GOLF & COUNTRY CLUB
800 Bathurst St Unit 1, Toronto, ON, M5R 3M8
(416) 762-2530
Emp Here 120   *Sales* 2,052,664
SIC 7997 Membership sports and recreation
clubs

D-U-N-S 24-804-3106   (SL)
GTA GOLF & COUNTRY CLUB
800 Bathurst St Unit 1, Toronto, ON, M5R 3M8
(416) 762-2530
Emp Here 120   *Sales* 2,052,664
SIC 7997 Membership sports and recreation
clubs

D-U-N-S 24-804-3114   (SL)
GTA GOLF & COUNTRY CLUB
800 Bathurst St Unit 1, Toronto, ON, M5R 3M8
(416) 762-2530
Emp Here 120   *Sales* 2,052,664
SIC 7997 Membership sports and recreation
clubs

D-U-N-S 24-804-3122   (SL)
GTA GOLF & COUNTRY CLUB
800 Bathurst St Unit 1, Toronto, ON, M5R 3M8

(416) 762-2530
Emp Here 120   *Sales* 2,052,664
SIC 7997 Membership sports and recreation
clubs

D-U-N-S 24-804-3130   (SL)
GTA GOLF & COUNTRY CLUB
800 Bathurst St Unit 1, Toronto, ON, M5R 3M8
(416) 762-2530
Emp Here 120   *Sales* 2,052,664
SIC 7997 Membership sports and recreation
clubs

D-U-N-S 24-804-3148   (SL)
GTA GOLF & COUNTRY CLUB
800 Bathurst St Unit 1, Toronto, ON, M5R 3M8
(416) 762-2530
Emp Here 120   *Sales* 2,052,664
SIC 7997 Membership sports and recreation
clubs

D-U-N-S 24-804-3155   (SL)
GTA GOLF & COUNTRY CLUB
800 Bathurst St Unit 1, Toronto, ON, M5R 3M8
(416) 762-2530
Emp Here 120   *Sales* 2,052,664
SIC 7997 Membership sports and recreation
clubs

D-U-N-S 24-804-3163   (SL)
GTA GOLF & COUNTRY CLUB
800 Bathurst St Unit 1, Toronto, ON, M5R 3M8
(416) 762-2530
Emp Here 120   *Sales* 2,052,664
SIC 7997 Membership sports and recreation
clubs

D-U-N-S 24-804-3171   (SL)
GTA GOLF & COUNTRY CLUB
800 Bathurst St Unit 1, Toronto, ON, M5R 3M8
(416) 762-2530
Emp Here 120   *Sales* 2,052,664
SIC 7997 Membership sports and recreation
clubs

D-U-N-S 24-804-3189   (SL)
GTA GOLF & COUNTRY CLUB
800 Bathurst St Unit 1, Toronto, ON, M5R 3M8
(416) 762-2530
Emp Here 120   *Sales* 2,052,664
SIC 7997 Membership sports and recreation
clubs

D-U-N-S 24-804-3197   (SL)
GTA GOLF & COUNTRY CLUB
800 Bathurst St Unit 1, Toronto, ON, M5R 3M8
(416) 762-2530
Emp Here 120   *Sales* 2,052,664
SIC 7997 Membership sports and recreation
clubs

D-U-N-S 24-804-3064   (SL)
GTA GOLF & COUNTRY CLUB
800 Bathurst St Unit 1, Toronto, ON, M5R 3M8
(416) 762-2530
Emp Here 120   *Sales* 2,052,664
SIC 7997 Membership sports and recreation
clubs

D-U-N-S 24-804-3072   (SL)
GTA GOLF & COUNTRY CLUB
800 Bathurst St Unit 1, Toronto, ON, M5R 3M8
(416) 762-2530
Emp Here 120   *Sales* 2,052,664
SIC 7997 Membership sports and recreation
clubs

D-U-N-S 24-804-3080   (SL)
GTA GOLF & COUNTRY CLUB
800 Bathurst St Unit 1, Toronto, ON, M5R 3M8
(416) 762-2530
Emp Here 120   *Sales* 2,052,664
SIC 7997 Membership sports and recreation
clubs

D-U-N-S 20-551-3419   (SL)
**LOEWEN, ONDAATJE, MCCUTCHEON LIM-
ITED**
(*Suby of* LOM BANCORP LIMITED)

148 Yorkville Ave Suite 3, Toronto, ON, M5R
1C2
(416) 964-4400
Emp Here 35   *Sales* 18,592,245
SIC 6211 Security brokers and dealers
Garrett Herman
Paul Deslauriers

D-U-N-S 24-124-8467   (HQ)
MARKIO DESIGNS INC
CAPEZIO
1200 Bay St Suite 600, Toronto, ON, M5R 2A5
(416) 929-9629
Emp Here 8   *Sales* 14,351,680
SIC 5661 Shoe stores
David Markowitz
Faye Markowitz
May Yang
Ilana Markowitz

D-U-N-S 24-805-9201   (SL)
MARWA HOLDINGS INC
61 Yorkville Ave Ph 914, Toronto, ON, M5R
1B7

Emp Here 30   *Sales* 20,367,690
SIC 6211 Security brokers and dealers
Allan Rosenberg
Mihaela Zavoanu

D-U-N-S 25-530-8306   (SL)
MINTO FURNISHED SUITES
61 Yorkville Ave Suite 200, Toronto, ON, M5R
1B7
(416) 923-1000
Emp Here 35   *Sales* 15,522,150
SIC 7389 Business services, nec
Randall Proffit

D-U-N-S 24-171-3721   (SL)
NART DRUGS INC
SHOPPERS DRUG MART
292 Dupont St, Toronto, ON, M5R 1V9
(416) 972-0232
Emp Here 50   *Sales* 12,647,700
SIC 5912 Drug stores and proprietary stores
Tim Tran

D-U-N-S 20-384-7350   (SL)
NOTHING BUT NATURE INC
176 St. George St, Toronto, ON, M5R 2M7
(416) 934-5034
Emp Here 50   *Sales* 41,778,850
SIC 5149 Groceries and related products, nec
Matthew Von-Teichman

D-U-N-S 24-213-7792   (SL)
**ONTARIO COLLEGE OF PHARMA-
CISTS ORDRE DES PHARMACIENS DE
L'ONTARIO**
483 Huron St, Toronto, ON, M5R 2R4
(416) 962-4861
Emp Here 50   *Sales* 13,526,898
SIC 8621 Professional organizations
Deanna Williams
Stephen Clement
Bonnie Hauser

D-U-N-S 20-819-8473   (HQ)
ONTARIO DENTAL ASSOCIATION, THE
O D A
4 New St, Toronto, ON, M5R 1P6
(416) 922-3900
Sales 11,684,750
SIC 8621 Professional organizations
Frank Bevilacqua

D-U-N-S 25-052-1358   (SL)
PRINCETON REVIEW CANADA INC, THE
PRINCETON REVIEW, THE
(*Suby of* EDUCATION HOLDINGS 1, INC.)
1255 Bay St Suite 550, Toronto, ON, M5R 2A9
(416) 944-8001
Emp Here 200   *Sales* 50,698,000
SIC 8748 Business consulting, nec
Blaise Moritz

D-U-N-S 20-172-0604   (HQ)

PRINTING HOUSE LIMITED, THE
TPH
1403 Bathurst St, Toronto, ON, M5R 3H8
(416) 536-6113
Emp Here 50   *Sales* 106,575,700
SIC 2752 Commercial printing, lithographic
Earle O'born
Jamie O'born
Yvonne Bland
Scott O'born

D-U-N-S 24-793-0043   (SL)
RAINBOW NURSING REGISTRY LTD
344 Dupont St Suite 402c, Toronto, ON, M5R
1V9
(416) 922-7616
Emp Here 100   *Sales* 17,020,500
SIC 8049 Offices of health practitioner
Elca Crooks

D-U-N-S 24-864-0695   (SL)
RE:SOUND
RESOUND MUSIC LICENSING COMPANY
1235 Bay St Suite 900, Toronto, ON, M5R 3K4
(416) 968-8870
Emp Here 49   *Sales* 34,143,690
SIC 6794 Patent owners and lessors
Ian Mackay
Peter Steinmetz
Stephen Waddell
Annie Morin
Lyette Bouchard
Stuart Johnston
David Jandrisch
Graham Henderson

D-U-N-S 24-610-3188   (HQ)
ROBINSON GROUP LIMITED
263 Davenport Rd, Toronto, ON, M5R 1J9
(416) 960-2444
Emp Here 1   *Sales* 10,837,680
SIC 1521 Single-family housing construction
Christopher Robinson

D-U-N-S 20-821-6457   (SL)
ROYAL CANADIAN YACHT CLUB, THE
141 St. George St Suite 218, Toronto, ON,
M5R 2L8
(416) 967-7245
Emp Here 120   *Sales* 9,425,400
SIC 7997 Membership sports and recreation
clubs
David Brightling

D-U-N-S 20-042-1316   (SL)
ROYAL ST GEORGE'S COLLEGE
120 Howland Ave, Toronto, ON, M5R 3B5
(416) 533-9481
Emp Here 75   *Sales* 135,075,720
SIC 8211 Elementary and secondary schools
Paul Clark

D-U-N-S 20-327-8846   (SL)
RP DEBT OPPORTUNITIES FUND
RP INVESTMENT AND ADVISOR LP
39 Hazelton Ave, Toronto, ON, M5R 2E3
(647) 776-1777
Emp Here 40   *Sales* 33,111,080
SIC 6722 Management investment, open-end
Richard Pilosos

D-U-N-S 20-327-2133   (SL)
SCIERADE INVESTMENT CORPORATION
1235 Bay St, Toronto, ON, M5R 3K4
(647) 244-6707
Emp Here 26   *Sales* 17,651,998
SIC 6282 Investment advice
Sophie Cooper
Dieter Prinz

D-U-N-S 25-721-0583   (SL)
SOTTO SOTTO RISTORANTE LIMITED
116 Avenue Rd Unit A, Toronto, ON, M5R 2H4
(416) 962-0011
Emp Here 80   *Sales* 3,641,520
SIC 5812 Eating places
Marisa Rocca

D-U-N-S 20-408-4735   (SL)
STANDARD SECURITIES CAPITAL COR-PORATION
24 Hazelton Ave, Toronto, ON, M5R 2E2

Emp Here 35   *Sales* 23,762,305
SIC 6211 Security brokers and dealers
Mark A. Marcello

D-U-N-S 20-626-9151   (SL)
STARKMAN SURGICAL SUPPLY INC
STARKMAN HOME HEALTH CARE DEPOT
1243 Bathurst St, Toronto, ON, M5R 3H3
(416) 534-8411
Emp Here 30   *Sales* 11,179,350
SIC 5047 Medical and hospital equipment
Andrew Starkman

D-U-N-S 20-336-6609   (SL)
STUDENT ASSOCIATION OF GEORGE BROWN COLLEGE
142 Kendal Ave Rm E100, Toronto, ON, M5R 1M3
(416) 415-5000
Emp Here 30   *Sales* 11,922,420
SIC 8699 Membership organizations, nec
Naqeeb Omar
Ron Greenberg
Brittney Steeves

D-U-N-S 25-683-0787   (HQ)
SUPER-FIT KNITTING MILLS INC
1191 Bathurst St, Toronto, ON, M5R 3H4
(416) 537-2137
Emp Here 15   *Sales* 14,949,660
SIC 5137 Women's and children's clothing
Albert Werner

D-U-N-S 25-121-3120   (SL)
SUTTON GROUP-ASSOCIATES REALTY INC
358 Davenport Rd, Toronto, ON, M5R 1K6
(416) 966-0300
Emp Here 120   *Sales* 50,266,680
SIC 6531 Real estate agents and managers
Henry Balaban

D-U-N-S 20-845-9792   (SL)
TORONTO AGED MEN'S AND WOMEN'S HOMES, THE
BELMONT HOUSE
55 Belmont St Suite 403, Toronto, ON, M5R 1R1
(416) 964-9231
Emp Here 190   *Sales* 12,213,580
SIC 8361 Residential care
Maria Elias
Michelle Noble
Dennis Donavan

D-U-N-S 20-172-6473   (SL)
VILLAGE MANOR (TO) LTD
MADISON AVENUE PUB
(*Suby of* VILLAGE MANOR LTD)
14 Madison Ave, Toronto, ON, M5R 2S1
(416) 927-1722
Emp Here 100   *Sales* 4,551,900
SIC 5813 Drinking places
Isabel Manore

D-U-N-S 24-874-7990   (HQ)
VILLAGE MANOR LTD
14 Madison Ave, Toronto, ON, M5R 2S1
(416) 927-1722
Emp Here 1   *Sales* 27,335,000
SIC 6712 Bank holding companies
Isabel Manore

D-U-N-S 20-269-9237   (SL)
VOGOGO INC
5 Hazelton Ave Suite 300, Toronto, ON, M5R 2E1
(647) 715-3707
Emp Here 6   *Sales* 13,705,730
SIC 6099 Functions related to deposit banking
John Kennedy Fitzgerald
Jordan Greenberg
Paul Leggett

Dale Johnson
Gino L. Demichele
Thomas Burton English

D-U-N-S 24-421-5398   (SL)
WERTEX HOSIERY INCORPORATED
1191 Bathurst St, Toronto, ON, M5R 3H4
(416) 537-2137
Emp Here 135   *Sales* 113,066,955
SIC 5137 Women's and children's clothing
Ernest Werner

D-U-N-S 24-052-8745   (SL)
WOOD, BRENDAN INTERNATIONAL LTD
17 Prince Arthur Ave, Toronto, ON, M5R 1B2
(416) 924-8110
Emp Here 45   *Sales* 12,748,185
SIC 8741 Management services
Brendan Wood

Toronto, ON M5S

D-U-N-S 25-359-7090   (BR)
955 BAY STREET HOSPITALITY INC
SUTTON PLACE GRANDE LIMITED
(*Suby of* NORTHLAND PROPERTIES COR-PORATION)
955 Bay St, Toronto, ON, M5S 2A2

Emp Here 250
SIC 7011 Hotels and motels
Nick Vesely

D-U-N-S 24-214-6574   (SL)
ACCESS RESEARCH INC
FORUM RESEARCH
180 Bloor St W Suite 1402, Toronto, ON, M5S 2V6
(416) 960-9603
Emp Here 49   *Sales* 11,500,104
SIC 8732 Commercial nonphysical research
Lorne Bozinoff

D-U-N-S 24-613-1957   (HQ)
ACCORD FINANCIAL CORP
77 Bloor St W 18 Fl, Toronto, ON, M5S 1M2
(416) 961-0007
Emp Here 10   *Sales* 35,575,719
SIC 6159 Miscellaneous business credit institutions
Thomas (Tom) Henderson
Ken Hitzig
Robert S. Sandler
Stephen D. Warden
John J. Swidler
David Beutel
Gary J. Prager
Simon Hitzig

D-U-N-S 24-794-5418   (BR)
ARAMARK CANADA LTD.
(*Suby of* ARAMARK)
21 Classic Ave Suite 1008, Toronto, ON, M5S 2Z3
(416) 598-2424
Emp Here 85
SIC 5812 Eating places
Larysa Ihnatowycz

D-U-N-S 20-984-0990   (HQ)
BOOKMASTERS LTD
BOOK CITY
501 Bloor St W Suite 30, Toronto, ON, M5S 1Y2
(416) 961-4496
Emp Here 20   *Sales* 17,102,960
SIC 5942 Book stores
J Frans Donker
Gini Donker
John Snyder

D-U-N-S 24-986-7953   (SL)
CANADIAN ASSOCIATION FOR CO-OPERATIVE EDUCATION
720 Spadina Ave Suite 202, Toronto, ON, M5S

2T9
(416) 483-3311
Emp Here 50   *Sales* 11,684,750
SIC 8621 Professional organizations
Julie Walchi
Christina Campo

D-U-N-S 20-936-5337   (SL)
CANADIAN MUSICAL REPRODUCTION RIGHTS AGENCY LIMITED, THE
CMRRA
56 Wellesley St W Suite 320, Toronto, ON, M5S 2S3
(416) 926-1966
Emp Here 50   *Sales* 19,575,100
SIC 6794 Patent owners and lessors
David Basskin
Fred Merrit
Michael Mccarty

D-U-N-S 20-515-1934   (BR)
CENTRE FOR ADDICTION AND MENTAL HEALTH
(*Suby of* CENTRE FOR ADDICTION AND MENTAL HEALTH)
33 Russell St, Toronto, ON, M5S 2S1
(416) 535-8501
Emp Here 250
SIC 8093 Specialty outpatient clinics, nec
Paul Garfinkel

D-U-N-S 24-737-7310   (HQ)
CLUB MONACO CORP
CABAN
(*Suby of* RALPH LAUREN CORPORATION)
157 Bloor St W, Toronto, ON, M5S 1P7
(416) 591-8837
Emp Here 150   *Sales* 162,181,500
SIC 5621 Women's clothing stores
John Mehas
Gary Miller

D-U-N-S 20-259-6169   (HQ)
COLLIERS INTERNATIONAL GROUP INC
1140 Bay St Suite 4000, Toronto, ON, M5S 2B4
(416) 960-9500
Emp Here 5,860   *Sales* 2,825,427,000
SIC 6531 Real estate agents and managers
David Bowden
Jay Hennick
Scott Addison
James Macqueen
Synthia Kloot
John Duda
Keri Fraser
Lex Perry
Mihai Strusievici
Peter Cohen

D-U-N-S 24-377-3905   (SL)
CYMBRIA CORPORATION
(*Suby of* EDGEPOINT INVESTMENT GROUP INC)
150 Bloor St W Suite 500, Toronto, ON, M5S 2X9
(416) 963-9353
Emp Here 11   *Sales* 26,286,429
SIC 6726 Investment offices, nec
Tye Bousada
Goeff Macdonald
Diane Rossi
Norman Tang
Patrick Farmer
Ugo Bizzarri
James Macdonald
Reena Carter
Richard Whiting

D-U-N-S 20-647-2243   (HQ)
EDELMAN PUBLIC RELATIONS WORLD-WIDE CANADA INC
150 Bloor St W Suite 300, Toronto, ON, M5S 2X9
(416) 979-1120
Emp Here 65   *Sales* 14,920,480
SIC 8743 Public relations services

John Clinton
Danny London
Jay Lefton
Inna Prissiajniouk

D-U-N-S 20-305-5645   (SL)
EDGEPOINT CANADIAN PORTFOLIO
150 Bloor St W Suite 200, Toronto, ON, M5S 2X9
(416) 963-9353
Emp Here 39   *Sales* 32,657,205
SIC 6722 Management investment, open-end
Patrick Farmer

D-U-N-S 20-305-3434   (SL)
EDGEPOINT WEALTH MANAGEMENT INC
EDGEPOINT
150 Bloor St W Suite 500, Toronto, ON, M5S 2X9
(416) 963-9353
Emp Here 36   *Sales* 26,404,272
SIC 6722 Management investment, open-end
Patrick Farmer

D-U-N-S 24-815-8024   (HQ)
FIRSTSERVICE CORPORATION
1140 Bay St Suite 4000, Toronto, ON, M5S 2B4
(416) 960-9500
Emp Here 500   *Sales* 1,931,473,000
SIC 6519 Real property lessors, nec
D. Scott Patterson
Douglas G. Cooke
Alex Nguyen
Roger M. Thompson
Jeremy Rakusin
Chuck M. Fallon
Charlie E. Chase
Jay Hennick
Bernard I. Ghert
Brendan Calder

D-U-N-S 20-848-5052   (SL)
FULLER LANDAU LLP
151 Bloor St W, Toronto, ON, M5S 1S4
(416) 645-6500
Emp Here 50   *Sales* 10,454,250
SIC 8721 Accounting, auditing, and book-keeping
H. Zerker
B. D. Hoffe
R. H. Berkovitz
S. Hameer
B.C. Roher
G. F. Abrahamson
S. J. Pasquale
M. B. Epstein
L. S. Cappell
J. R. Dessau

D-U-N-S 20-295-7981   (SL)
GEDCO
1033 Bay St Suite 212, Toronto, ON, M5S 3A5
(416) 961-1777
Emp Here 8   *Sales* 11,741,536
SIC 5153 Grain and field beans
Haifa Reda
Mohamed Reda
Saleh Reda
Iman Reda

D-U-N-S 24-119-9756   (BR)
GOVERNING COUNCIL OF THE UNIVER-SITY OF TORONTO, THE
DEPARTMENT OF ELECTRICAL ENGI-NEERS
(*Suby of* GOVERNING COUNCIL OF THE UNIVERSITY OF TORONTO, THE)
40 St. George St Rm 4113, Toronto, ON, M5S 2E4
(416) 978-1655
Emp Here 100
SIC 8221 Colleges and universities
Brian Beuerlein

D-U-N-S 24-205-8787   (BR)
GOVERNING COUNCIL OF THE UNIVER-SITY OF TORONTO, THE

GOVERNING COUNCIL OF THE UNIVER-
SITY OF TORONTO
(Suby of GOVERNING COUNCIL OF THE
UNIVERSITY OF TORONTO, THE)
35 St. George St Suite 173, Toronto, ON, M5S
1A4
(416) 978-3099
Emp Here 78
SIC 8221 Colleges and universities
 Brent Sleep

D-U-N-S 24-312-5403   (BR)
GOVERNING COUNCIL OF THE UNIVER-
SITY OF TORONTO, THE
GOVERNING COUNCIL OF THE UNIVER-
SITY OF TORONTO
(Suby of GOVERNING COUNCIL OF THE
UNIVERSITY OF TORONTO, THE)
10 King'S College Rd Suite 3302, Toronto,
ON, M5S 3G4
(416) 978-6025
Emp Here 104
SIC 8221 Colleges and universities
 Ravin Balakrishnan

D-U-N-S 24-207-3836   (BR)
GOVERNING COUNCIL OF THE UNIVER-
SITY OF TORONTO, THE
DEPARTMENT OF PHYSIOLOGY
(Suby of GOVERNING COUNCIL OF THE
UNIVERSITY OF TORONTO, THE)
1 King'S College Circle 3rd Fl, Toronto, ON,
M5S 1A8

Emp Here 121
SIC 8221 Colleges and universities
 Graham L. Collingridge

D-U-N-S 20-293-8184   (BR)
GOVERNING COUNCIL OF THE UNIVER-
SITY OF TORONTO, THE
JOHN H. DANIELS FACULTY OF ARCHITEC-
TURE, LANDSCAPE AND DESIGN
(Suby of GOVERNING COUNCIL OF THE
UNIVERSITY OF TORONTO, THE)
1 Spadina Cres, Toronto, ON, M5S 2J5
(416) 978-5038
Emp Here 118
SIC 8221 Colleges and universities
 Richard M. Sommer

D-U-N-S 20-641-9871   (HQ)
GOVERNING COUNCIL OF THE UNIVER-
SITY OF TORONTO, THE
UNIVERSITY OF TORONTO
27 King'S College Cir, Toronto, ON, M5S 1A1
(416) 978-2196
Emp Here 9,000   Sales 2,414,595,312
SIC 8221 Colleges and universities
 David Naylor
 Bryn Macpherson
 Catherine Rigall
 Judith Wolfson
 Angela Hildyard
 Rivi Frankle

D-U-N-S 24-000-6044   (BR)
GOVERNING COUNCIL OF THE UNIVER-
SITY OF TORONTO, THE
DEPARTMENT OF IMMUNOLOGY
(Suby of GOVERNING COUNCIL OF THE
UNIVERSITY OF TORONTO, THE)
1 King'S College Circle Rm 7207, Toronto,
ON, M5S 1A8

Emp Here 80
SIC 8221 Colleges and universities
 Juan Carlos Zuniga-Pflucker

D-U-N-S 20-124-7827   (BR)
GOVERNING COUNCIL OF THE UNIVER-
SITY OF TORONTO, THE
DEPARTMENT OF CHEMICAL ENGINEER-
ING & APPLIED CHEMISTRY
(Suby of GOVERNING COUNCIL OF THE
UNIVERSITY OF TORONTO, THE)
200 College St Unit 217, Toronto, ON, M5S

3E5
(416) 978-6204
Emp Here 120
SIC 8221 Colleges and universities
 Grant Allen

D-U-N-S 20-301-3680   (BR)
GOVERNING COUNCIL OF THE UNIVER-
SITY OF TORONTO, THE
DEPARTMENT OF CHEMISTRY
(Suby of GOVERNING COUNCIL OF THE
UNIVERSITY OF TORONTO, THE)
80 St. George St, Toronto, ON, M5S 3H6
(416) 978-3564
Emp Here 119
SIC 8221 Colleges and universities
 Robert A. Batey

D-U-N-S 20-344-6430   (BR)
GOVERNING COUNCIL OF THE UNIVER-
SITY OF TORONTO, THE
DEPARTMENT OF SOCIOLOGY
(Suby of GOVERNING COUNCIL OF THE
UNIVERSITY OF TORONTO, THE)
725 Spadina Ave, Toronto, ON, M5S 2J4
(416) 946-4058
Emp Here 79
SIC 8221 Colleges and universities
 Scott Schieman

D-U-N-S 20-369-4356   (BR)
GOVERNING COUNCIL OF THE UNIVER-
SITY OF TORONTO, THE
DEPARTMENT OF MOLECULAR GENETICS
(Suby of GOVERNING COUNCIL OF THE
UNIVERSITY OF TORONTO, THE)
1 King'S College Cir Rm 4396, Toronto, ON,
M5S 1A8
(416) 978-3730
Emp Here 115
SIC 8221 Colleges and universities
 Leah Cowen

D-U-N-S 20-369-4328   (BR)
GOVERNING COUNCIL OF THE UNIVER-
SITY OF TORONTO, THE
DEPARTMENT OF MATHEMATICS
(Suby of GOVERNING COUNCIL OF THE
UNIVERSITY OF TORONTO, THE)
40 St. George St Rm 6290, Toronto, ON, M5S
2E4
(416) 978-3323
Emp Here 154
SIC 8221 Colleges and universities
 Jeremy Quastel

D-U-N-S 20-153-1212   (BR)
GOVERNING COUNCIL OF THE UNIVER-
SITY OF TORONTO, THE
DEPARTMENT OF ELECTRICAL COM-
PUTER & ENGINEERING
(Suby of GOVERNING COUNCIL OF THE
UNIVERSITY OF TORONTO, THE)
10 King'S College Rd Rm 1024, Toronto, ON,
M5S 3H5
(416) 978-3112
Emp Here 84
SIC 8221 Colleges and universities
 Farid N. Najm

D-U-N-S 20-153-1139   (BR)
GOVERNING COUNCIL OF THE UNIVER-
SITY OF TORONTO, THE
DEPARTMENT OF COMPUTER SYSTEMS &
NETWORKS RESEARCH GROUP
(Suby of GOVERNING COUNCIL OF\THE
UNIVERSITY OF TORONTO, THE)
40 St. George St Rm Ba 5165, Toronto, ON,
M5S 2E4

Emp Here 80
SIC 8221 Colleges and universities
 Sharon Dickinson

D-U-N-S 20-716-4364   (BR)
GOVERNING COUNCIL OF THE UNIVER-
SITY OF TORONTO, THE
DEPARTMENT OF GEOGRAPHY & PLAN-

NING
(Suby of GOVERNING COUNCIL OF THE
UNIVERSITY OF TORONTO, THE)
100 St. George St Rm 5047, Toronto, ON,
M5S 3G3
(416) 978-3375
Emp Here 76
SIC 8221 Colleges and universities
 Virginia Maclaren

D-U-N-S 20-107-8812   (BR)
GOVERNING COUNCIL OF THE UNIVER-
SITY OF TORONTO, THE
DEPARTMENT OF ECOLOGY AND EVOLU-
TIONARY
(Suby of GOVERNING COUNCIL OF THE
UNIVERSITY OF TORONTO, THE)
25 Willcocks Street, Toronto, ON, M5S 3B2

Emp Here 86
SIC 8221 Colleges and universities
 Donald Jackson

D-U-N-S 20-512-6076   (BR)
GOVERNING COUNCIL OF THE UNIVER-
SITY OF TORONTO, THE
GOVERNING COUNCIL OF THE UNIVER-
SITY OF TORONTO
(Suby of GOVERNING COUNCIL OF THE
UNIVERSITY OF TORONTO, THE)
105 St. George St Suite 275, Toronto, ON,
M5S 3E6
(416) 978-4574
Emp Here 300
SIC 8221 Colleges and universities
 Roger Martin

D-U-N-S 20-555-0812   (BR)
GOVERNING COUNCIL OF THE UNIVER-
SITY OF TORONTO, THE
GOVERNING COUNCIL OF THE UNIVER-
SITY OF TORONTO
(Suby of GOVERNING COUNCIL OF THE
UNIVERSITY OF TORONTO, THE)
150 St. George St, Toronto, ON, M5S 3G7
(416) 978-4622
Emp Here 100
SIC 8221 Colleges and universities
 Ettore Damiano

D-U-N-S 20-912-3749   (BR)
GOVERNING COUNCIL OF THE UNIVER-
SITY OF TORONTO, THE
DEPARTMENT OF PHARMACOLOGY AND
TOXICOLOGY
(Suby of GOVERNING COUNCIL OF THE
UNIVERSITY OF TORONTO, THE)
1 King'S College Cir Rm 4207, Toronto, ON,
M5S 1A8
(416) 978-2728
Emp Here 97
SIC 8221 Colleges and universities
 Ruth Alexander-Ross

D-U-N-S 25-987-9799   (BR)
GOVERNING COUNCIL OF THE UNIVER-
SITY OF TORONTO, THE
FACULTY OF KINESIOLOGY AND PHYSI-
CAL EDUCATION
(Suby of GOVERNING COUNCIL OF THE
UNIVERSITY OF TORONTO, THE)
55 Harbord St Suite 1048, Toronto, ON, M5S
2W6
(416) 978-7375
Emp Here 218
SIC 8221 Colleges and universities
 Ira Jacobs

D-U-N-S 20-192-5513   (BR)
GOVERNING COUNCIL OF THE UNIVER-
SITY OF TORONTO, THE
FACULTY OF MEDICINE
(Suby of GOVERNING COUNCIL OF THE
UNIVERSITY OF TORONTO, THE)
1 King'S College Cir Suite 2109, Toronto, ON,
M5S 1A8
(416) 978-6585
Emp Here 200

SIC 8221 Colleges and universities
 Pat Arnold

D-U-N-S 20-190-8402   (BR)
GOVERNING COUNCIL OF THE UNIVER-
SITY OF TORONTO, THE
MUNK SCHOOL OF GLOBAL AFFAIRS
(Suby of GOVERNING COUNCIL OF THE
UNIVERSITY OF TORONTO, THE)
1 Devonshire Pl, Toronto, ON, M5S 3K7
(416) 946-8900
Emp Here 100
SIC 8221 Colleges and universities
 Randall Hansen

D-U-N-S 24-766-9331   (BR)
GOVERNING COUNCIL OF THE UNIVER-
SITY OF TORONTO, THE
FACULTY OF ARTS AND SCIENCE
(Suby of GOVERNING COUNCIL OF THE
UNIVERSITY OF TORONTO, THE)
100 St. George St, Toronto, ON, M5S 3G3
(416) 978-3383
Emp Here 1,806
SIC 8221 Colleges and universities

D-U-N-S 24-227-7643   (BR)
GOVERNING COUNCIL OF THE UNIVER-
SITY OF TORONTO, THE
GOVERNING COUNCIL OF THE UNIVER-
SITY OF TORONTO
(Suby of GOVERNING COUNCIL OF THE
UNIVERSITY OF TORONTO, THE)
144 College St, Toronto, ON, M5S 3M2
(416) 978-2889
Emp Here 150
SIC 8221 Colleges and universities
 Heather Boon

D-U-N-S 24-926-3005   (BR)
GOVERNING COUNCIL OF THE UNIVER-
SITY OF TORONTO, THE
JOSEPH L. ROTMAN SCHOOL OF MAN-
AGEMENT
(Suby of GOVERNING COUNCIL OF THE
UNIVERSITY OF TORONTO, THE)
105 St. George St, Toronto, ON, M5S 3E6
(416) 978-5703
Emp Here 137
SIC 8221 Colleges and universities
 Tiff Macklem

D-U-N-S 20-411-5919   (HQ)
HARRY ROSEN INC
77 Bloor St W Suite 5, Toronto, ON, M5S 1M2
(416) 935-9200
Emp Here 100   Sales 112,279,500
SIC 5611 Men's and boys' clothing stores
 Larry Rosen
 Jeff Farbstein
 Conrad Frejlich
 Manuel Maciel

D-U-N-S 25-293-7289   (BR)
HARRY ROSEN INC
HARRY ROSEN MENS WEAR
(Suby of HARRY ROSEN INC)
82 Bloor St W, Toronto, ON, M5S 1L9
(416) 972-0556
Emp Here 100
SIC 5611 Men's and boys' clothing stores
 Alan Whitfield

D-U-N-S 24-119-9327   (BR)
IMARKETING SOLUTIONS GROUP INC
(Suby of IMARKETING SOLUTIONS GROUP
INC)
80 Bloor St W Suite 601, Toronto, ON, M5S
2V1
(416) 646-3128
Emp Here 250
SIC 8399 Social services, nec
 Orazio Puglia

D-U-N-S 25-052-3487   (SL)
INSTITUTE OF PUBLIC ADMINISTRATION
OF CANADA, THE

▲ Public Company   ■ Public Company Family Member   HQ Headquarters   BR Branch   SL Single Location

IPAC
1075 Bay St Suite 401, Toronto, ON, M5S 2B1
(416) 924-8787
Emp Here 46   *Sales* 13,098,362
SIC 8733 Noncommercial research organizations
Robert Taylor

D-U-N-S 24-388-7817   (SL)
MASTER AND FELLOWS OF MASSEY COLLEGE, THE
MASSEY COLLEGE
4 Devonshire Pl, Toronto, ON, M5S 2E1
(416) 978-2892
Emp Here 50   *Sales* 11,931,050
SIC 6514 Dwelling operators, except apartments
John Fraser

D-U-N-S 25-791-2162   (SL)
MAYTREE FOUNDATION, THE
170 Bloor St W Suite 804, Toronto, ON, M5S 1T9
(416) 944-1101
Emp Here 27   *Sales* 19,148,724
SIC 8699 Membership organizations, nec
Alan Broadbend
Judy Broadbent
Ratna Omidvar
Jane Millan
Daniel Burns

D-U-N-S 20-552-8701   (BR)
METRO ONTARIO INC
METRO
(*Suby of* METRO INC)
425 Bloor St W, Toronto, ON, M5S 1X6
(416) 923-9099
Emp Here 300
SIC 5411 Grocery stores
Paul Bravi

D-U-N-S 20-913-4357   (SL)
MILES NADAL JEWISH COMMUNITY CENTRE
750 Spadina Ave, Toronto, ON, M5S 2J2
(416) 944-8002
Emp Here 100   *Sales* 9,266,500
SIC 8322 Individual and family services
Ellen Cole

D-U-N-S 24-627-2660   (HQ)
MUGGS, J J INC
J J MUGGS GOURMET GRILL
500 Bloor St W, Toronto, ON, M5S 1Y3
(416) 531-7638
Emp Here 10   *Sales* 16,323,650
SIC 5812 Eating places
Ted Nikolao

D-U-N-S 20-881-4392   (HQ)
ONTARIO INSTITUTE FOR STUDIES IN EDUCATION OF THE UNIVERSITY OF TORONTO
O I S E
252 Bloor St W Suite 100, Toronto, ON, M5S 1V6
(416) 978-0005
Emp Here 485   *Sales* 102,041,000
SIC 8733 Noncommercial research organizations
Glen A. Jones

D-U-N-S 20-845-9677   (HQ)
ONTARIO MEDICAL ASSOCIATION
150 Bloor St W Suite 900, Toronto, ON, M5S 3C1
(416) 599-2580
Emp Here 200   *Sales* 70,233,300
SIC 8621 Professional organizations
Allan O'dette
Sandy Zidaric

D-U-N-S 20-938-6150   (HQ)
ONTARIO NURSES' ASSOCIATION
85 Grenville St Suite 400, Toronto, ON, M5S 3A2

(416) 964-8833
Emp Here 109   *Sales* 46,992,330
SIC 8631 Labor organizations
Lesley Bell
Linda Haslam-Stroud
Dan Anderson
Noelle Andrews
Gloria Lynn

D-U-N-S 24-418-1590   (HQ)
ONTARIO TRILLIUM FOUNDATION
800 Bay St Suite 2, Toronto, ON, M5S 3A9
(416) 963-4927
Sales 22,394,100
SIC 6111 Federal and federally sponsored credit agencies
Robin Cardozo
Anne Pashley

D-U-N-S 24-610-7973   (HQ)
PUSATERI'S LIMITED
PUSATERI'S FINE FOODS
77 Bloor St W Suite 1803, Toronto, ON, M5S 1M2
(416) 785-9100
Emp Here 300   *Sales* 86,608,800
SIC 5411 Grocery stores
Frank Luchetta
Ida Pusateri

D-U-N-S 25-514-2598   (HQ)
REALSTAR MANAGEMENT PARTNERSHIP
77 Bloor St W Suite 2000, Toronto, ON, M5S 1M2
(416) 923-2950
Emp Here 100   *Sales* 15,721,776
SIC 8741 Management services
Wayne Squibb
Judy Meisels

D-U-N-S 24-563-5826   (HQ)
REALSTAR PROPERTY MANAGEMENT LIMITED
77 Bloor St W Suite 2000, Toronto, ON, M5S 1M2
(416) 923-2950
Emp Here 100   *Sales* 108,541,600
SIC 6514 Dwelling operators, except apartments
Wayne Squibb
Jonas Prince

D-U-N-S 20-703-2785   (SL)
ROYAL ONTARIO MUSEUM FOUNDATION, THE
ROM GOVERNORS
100 Queen'S Pk, Toronto, ON, M5S 2C6
(416) 586-5660
Emp Here 26   *Sales* 10,332,764
SIC 8699 Membership organizations, nec
Janet Carding
Robert Pierce
Linda Hasenfratz

D-U-N-S 20-641-9780   (SL)
ROYAL ONTARIO MUSEUM, THE
(*Suby of* GOVERNMENT OF ONTARIO)
100 Queen'S Pk, Toronto, ON, M5S 2C6
(416) 586-8000
Emp Here 430   *Sales* 45,089,800
SIC 8412 Museums and art galleries
Mark Engstrom
William Graesser
Glenn Dobbin
Chris Koester

D-U-N-S 24-911-8878   (SL)
SEE REALTY INC
991 Bay St, Toronto, ON, M5S 3C4

Emp Here 100   *Sales* 27,175,600
SIC 6531 Real estate agents and managers
Danny See

D-U-N-S 20-200-2544   (BR)
SODEXO CANADA LTD
SODEXHO
(*Suby of* SODEXO)

21 Sussex Ave Unit 3, Toronto, ON, M5S 1J6

Emp Here 180
SIC 5812 Eating places
Francine Brown

D-U-N-S 20-977-0820   (BR)
SODEXO CANADA LTD
(*Suby of* SODEXO)
41 Classic Ave, Toronto, ON, M5S 2Z3

Emp Here 80
SIC 5812 Eating places
Chris Fry

D-U-N-S 25-278-0838   (SL)
SURREY PLACE CENTRE
2 Surrey Pl, Toronto, ON, M5S 2C2
(416) 925-5141
Emp Here 292   *Sales* 60,463,856
SIC 8399 Social services, nec
Steven Finlay
Alain Mootoo
Bruce Wilson
Elizabeth Scott

D-U-N-S 24-793-8350   (SL)
TAN, KENNY PHARMACY INC
SHOPPERS DRUG MART
360 Bloor St W Suite 806, Toronto, ON, M5S 1X1
(416) 961-2121
Emp Here 80   *Sales* 19,546,240
SIC 5912 Drug stores and proprietary stores
Kenny Tan

D-U-N-S 24-506-3607   (HQ)
TD WATERHOUSE CANADA INC
(*Suby of* TORONTO-DOMINION BANK, THE)
77 Bloor St W Suite 3, Toronto, ON, M5S 1M2
(416) 982-7686
Emp Here 1,200   *Sales* 2,846,276,000
SIC 6211 Security brokers and dealers
John See
Gerry O'mahoney
Bruce Shewfelt
Kathleen Devenny

D-U-N-S 24-886-1320   (HQ)
TIFFANY & CO. CANADA
(*Suby of* TIFFANY & CO.)
150 Bloor St W Suite M108, Toronto, ON, M5S 2X9
(416) 921-3900
Emp Here 65   *Sales* 28,097,720
SIC 5944 Jewelry stores
Andrea Hopson

D-U-N-S 25-092-8124   (BR)
TORONTO DISTRICT SCHOOL BOARD
CENTRAL TECHNICAL SCHOOL
(*Suby of* TORONTO DISTRICT SCHOOL BOARD)
725 Bathurst St, Toronto, ON, M5S 2R5
(416) 393-0060
Emp Here 220
SIC 8211 Elementary and secondary schools
Rick Tarasuk

D-U-N-S 24-680-8310   (HQ)
TRICON CAPITAL GROUP INC
7 St Thomas St Suite 801, Toronto, ON, M5S 2B7
(416) 925-7228
Emp Here 50   *Sales* 276,134,000
SIC 6719 Holding companies, nec
Gary Berman
Wissam Francis
David Veneziano
Sandra Pereira
David Mark
Wojtek Nowak
Rick Rick
Alan Leela
Gina Mcmullan
Jonathan Ellenzweig

D-U-N-S 25-065-3235   (SL)

U OF T INNIS RESIDENCE
111 St. George St, Toronto, ON, M5S 2E8
(416) 978-2512
Emp Here 38   *Sales* 10,326,728
SIC 6531 Real estate agents and managers
Tim Morgan

D-U-N-S 20-784-9415   (HQ)
UNIVERSITY OF ST MICHAEL'S COLLEGE, THE
ST. MICHAEL COLLEGE
81 St Mary St, Toronto, ON, M5S 1J4
(416) 926-1300
Sales 11,263,600
SIC 8221 Colleges and universities
David Sylzester
Randy Boyagoda

D-U-N-S 24-738-3540   (SL)
UNIVERSITY OF TORONTO ENGINEERING SOCIETY, THE
10 King'S College Rd Suite B740, Toronto, ON, M5S 3G4
(416) 978-2917
Emp Here 76   *Sales* 10,858,804
SIC 8641 Civic and social associations
David Chung

D-U-N-S 20-247-9952   (HQ)
URBAN DINING GROUP INC
GABBY'S RESTAURANT GROUP
192 Bloor St W Suite 201, Toronto, ON, M5S 1T8
(416) 967-9671
Emp Here 25   *Sales* 13,991,700
SIC 5812 Eating places
Todd Sherman
Andrew Last
Grant Warfield

D-U-N-S 20-105-2904   (BR)
VICTORIA UNIVERSITY
NORTHROP FRYE HALL
(*Suby of* VICTORIA UNIVERSITY)
75 Queen'S Park Cres E, Toronto, ON, M5S 1K7
(416) 585-4467
Emp Here 150
SIC 8742 Management consulting services
David Keeling

D-U-N-S 24-659-4444   (HQ)
VICTORIA UNIVERSITY
VICTORIA COLLEGE
140 Charles St W, Toronto, ON, M5S 1K9
(416) 585-4524
Emp Here 1   *Sales* 44,817,300
SIC 8221 Colleges and universities
William Robins

D-U-N-S 24-410-5185   (HQ)
VISION NEW WAVE TRAVEL INC
1075 Bay St, Toronto, ON, M5S 2B1
(416) 928-3113
Emp Here 1   *Sales* 36,679,060
SIC 4724 Travel agencies
Brian Robertson
Gloria Pelchovitz

D-U-N-S 25-332-4446   (SL)
WINDSOR ARMS DEVELOPMENT CORPORATION
THE WINDSOR ARMS HOTEL
18 Saint Thomas St, Toronto, ON, M5S 3E7
(416) 971-9666
Emp Here 100   *Sales* 9,489,900
SIC 7011 Hotels and motels
George Friedmann
Stan Grossman

D-U-N-S 24-388-9099   (HQ)
WOMEN'S COLLEGE HOSPITAL
WOMEN'S COLLEGE RESEARCH INSTITUTE
76 Grenville St, Toronto, ON, M5S 1B2
(416) 323-6400
Sales 118,368,088
SIC 8062 General medical and surgical hospi-

tals
Marilyn Emery
Heather Mcpherson
Cynthia Whitehead
Danielle Martin
Mary Lou Toop
Paula Rochon
Wendy Cukier
Benita Warmbold
Hania Amad
Viola Antao

Toronto, ON M5T

D-U-N-S 20-786-8639 (SL)
ART GALLERY OF ONTARIO
317 Dundas St W Suite 535, Toronto, ON, M5T 1G4
(416) 977-0414
Emp Here 475 *Sales* 49,808,500
SIC 8412 Museums and art galleries
Stephan Jost
Julian Cox
Mike Mahoney
Rocco Saverino

D-U-N-S 25-722-7488 (SL)
BURDIFILEK INC
183 Bathurst St Suite 300, Toronto, ON, M5T 2R7
(416) 703-4334
Emp Here 25 *Sales* 11,087,250
SIC 7389 Business services, nec
Paul Filek
Diego Burdi

D-U-N-S 24-385-5090 (SL)
CENTRE FOR PHENOGENOMICS INC, THE
TCP
25 Orde St, Toronto, ON, M5T 3H7
(647) 837-5811
Emp Here 60 *Sales* 17,084,820
SIC 8733 Noncommercial research organizations
Lise Phaneuf
Colin Mckerlie

D-U-N-S 20-353-6706 (SL)
CHSM & C MANAGEMENT
474 Bathurst St Suite 300, Toronto, ON, M5T 2S6
(416) 964-1115
Emp Here 80 *Sales* 12,320,880
SIC 8111 Legal services
Jayne Ivall

D-U-N-S 20-379-6235 (BR)
COGNIZANT TECHNOLOGY SOLUTIONS CANADA, INC
IDEA COUTURE
(*Suby of* COGNIZANT TECHNOLOGY SOLUTIONS CORPORATION)
241 Spadina Ave Suite 500, Toronto, ON, M5T 2E2
(647) 827-0412
Emp Here 175
SIC 7379 Computer related services, nec
Idris Mootee

D-U-N-S 20-692-1780 (HQ)
DOMINION VOTING SYSTEMS CORPORATION
215 Spadina Ave Suite 200, Toronto, ON, M5T 2C7
(416) 762-8683
Sales 47,502,600
SIC 5087 Service establishment equipment
John Poulos
Ivan Lobo

D-U-N-S 24-660-6370 (SL)
DRAGON CITY DEVELOPMENTS INC
131 Baldwin St, Toronto, ON, M5T 1L7
(416) 596-8885
Emp Here 40 *Sales* 11,539,960

SIC 6512 Nonresidential building operators
Henry Hung
Daniel Hung

D-U-N-S 20-392-8606 (SL)
GEORGE BROWN COLLEGE OF APPLIED ARTS AND TECHNOLOGY, THE
160 Kendal Ave Suite 126a, Toronto, ON, M5T 2T9
(416) 415-5000
Emp Here 1,200 *Sales* 222,884,200
SIC 8221 Colleges and universities
Anne Sado
Chris Mcgrath
Cory Ross
Karen Thompson
Leslie Quinlan
Rick Huijbregts
Paul Ruppert
Adel Esayed
Colin Simpson
Ian Austin

D-U-N-S 24-345-0355 (BR)
GOVERNING COUNCIL OF THE UNIVERSITY OF TORONTO, THE
GOVERNING COUNCIL OF THE UNIVERSITY OF TORONTO
(*Suby of* GOVERNING COUNCIL OF THE UNIVERSITY OF TORONTO, THE)
340 College St Suite 400, Toronto, ON, M5T 3A9
(416) 978-4321
Emp Here 175
SIC 8221 Colleges and universities
Sherif El-Defrawy

D-U-N-S 25-137-9467 (BR)
GOVERNING COUNCIL OF THE UNIVERSITY OF TORONTO, THE
DEPARTMENT OF FAMILY AND COMMUNITY MEDICINE
(*Suby of* GOVERNING COUNCIL OF THE UNIVERSITY OF TORONTO, THE)
263 Mccaul St 3 Fl, Toronto, ON, M5T 1W7
(416) 978-5938
Emp Here 120
SIC 8221 Colleges and universities
Michael Kidd

D-U-N-S 24-802-4718 (BR)
GOVERNING COUNCIL OF THE UNIVERSITY OF TORONTO, THE
DEPARTMENT OF MEDICAL IMAGING
(*Suby of* GOVERNING COUNCIL OF THE UNIVERSITY OF TORONTO, THE)
263 Mccaul St, Toronto, ON, M5T 1W7
(416) 978-6801
Emp Here 270
SIC 8221 Colleges and universities
Alan Moody

D-U-N-S 24-720-2752 (BR)
GOVERNING COUNCIL OF THE UNIVERSITY OF TORONTO, THE
DEPARTMENT OF PSYCHIATRY
(*Suby of* GOVERNING COUNCIL OF THE UNIVERSITY OF TORONTO, THE)
250 College St 8 Fl, Toronto, ON, M5T 1R8
(416) 979-6948
Emp Here 109
SIC 8221 Colleges and universities
Benoit H. Mulsant

D-U-N-S 20-291-8855 (BR)
GOVERNING COUNCIL OF THE UNIVERSITY OF TORONTO, THE
LAWRENCE S. BLOOMBERG FACULTY OF NURSING
(*Suby of* GOVERNING COUNCIL OF THE UNIVERSITY OF TORONTO, THE)
155 College St Suite 130, Toronto, ON, M5T 1P8
(416) 978-2392
Emp Here 80
SIC 8221 Colleges and universities
Linda Johnston

D-U-N-S 25-360-9424 (BR)
GREAT-WEST LIFE ASSURANCE COMPANY, THE
CANADA LIFE
(*Suby of* POWER CORPORATION DU CANADA)
190 Simcoe St, Toronto, ON, M5T 3M3
(416) 597-1440
Emp Here 2,000
SIC 6311 Life insurance
Raymond Mcfeetors

D-U-N-S 20-959-4217 (HQ)
GREENPEACE CANADA
33 Cecil St, Toronto, ON, M5T 1N1
(416) 597-8408
Emp Here 42 *Sales* 13,045,284
SIC 8399 Social services, nec
Bruce Cox
Larry Brown
Peter Blyer
John Doherty
Ann Rowan
Brigid Rowan
Hugo Sequin
Bev Thorpe

D-U-N-S 20-107-6150 (SL)
GRIP LIMITED
(*Suby of* DENTSU INC.)
179 John St, Toronto, ON, M5T 1X4
(416) 340-7111
Emp Here 95 *Sales* 19,035,245
SIC 7311 Advertising agencies
Scott Dube
Randy Stein
Rich Pryce-Jones
David Chiavegato
Bob Shanks
David Crichton

D-U-N-S 25-412-1866 (SL)
HCH LAZERMAN INC
278 Bathurst St, Toronto, ON, M5T 2S3
(416) 504-2154
Emp Here 70 *Sales* 15,540,070
SIC 3555 Printing trades machinery
Hugo Hynn

D-U-N-S 24-826-4645 (SL)
JUMP PLUS STORES ULC
275 College St, Toronto, ON, M5T 1S2
(416) 927-8000
Emp Here 100 *Sales* 23,240,300
SIC 5734 Computer and software stores
Daniel Schneeweiss
Joseph Schneeweiss

D-U-N-S 24-028-8969 (SL)
K.M. BAKERY
KIM MOON BAKERY
438 Dundas St W, Toronto, ON, M5T 1G7

Emp Here 50 *Sales* 13,707,600
SIC 5461 Retail bakeries
Lien Ly

D-U-N-S 20-784-5934 (SL)
MICHENER INSTITUTE OF EDUCATION AT UHN, THE
MINISTRY OF HEALTH AND LONG TERM CARE
(*Suby of* UNIVERSITY HEALTH NETWORK)
222 Saint Patrick St Suite 414, Toronto, ON, M5T 1V4
(416) 596-3101
Emp Here 150 *Sales* 10,931,374
SIC 8221 Colleges and universities
Peter Pisters
Brian Hodges
Emma Pavlov
Justine Jackson
Bella Martin

D-U-N-S 20-785-4274 (HQ)
ONTARIO COLLEGE OF ART & DESIGN UNIVERSITY

OCAD UNIVERSITY
100 Mccaul St Suite 500, Toronto, ON, M5T 1W1
(416) 977-6000
Emp Here 400 *Sales* 55,730,839
SIC 8221 Colleges and universities
Sarah Diamond
Peter Fraser

D-U-N-S 20-300-9113 (SL)
PATHFACTORY INC
174 Spadina Ave Suite 600, Toronto, ON, M5T 2C2
(416) 304-9400
Emp Here 100 *Sales* 16,684,700
SIC 7372 Prepackaged software
Mark Opauszky
Nick Edouard
Scott Mcnabb
Dwayne Walker
Elle Woulfe
Heather Foeh
Stephen Streich
Scott Mcnabb
Gregg Michaelson
Paul Teshima

D-U-N-S 20-535-1849 (HQ)
PIGEON BRANDS INC
PIGEON BRANDING + DESIGN
179 John St 2nd Fl, Toronto, ON, M5T 1X4
(416) 532-9950
Emp Here 60 *Sales* 16,029,680
SIC 7336 Commercial art and graphic design
Thomas Pigeon

D-U-N-S 25-106-2758 (SL)
POINTS.COM INC
(*Suby of* POINTS INTERNATIONAL LTD)
171 John St Suite 500, Toronto, ON, M5T 1X3
(416) 595-0000
Emp Here 125 *Sales* 18,022,750
SIC 7371 Custom computer programming services
Robert Maclean
Christopher Barnard
Anthony Lam

D-U-N-S 20-175-4207 (SL)
SILVERSTEIN'S BAKERY LIMITED
(*Suby of* SILVERSTEIN'S HOLDINGS INC)
195 Mccaul St, Toronto, ON, M5T 1W6
(416) 598-3478
Emp Here 130
SIC 2051 Bread, cake, and related products
Harvey Silverstein
Murray Appleby

D-U-N-S 25-172-8721 (HQ)
SILVERSTEIN'S HOLDINGS INC
195 Mccaul St, Toronto, ON, M5T 1W6
(416) 598-3478
Sales 34,569,000
SIC 2051 Bread, cake, and related products
Harvey Silverstein
Murray Appleby

D-U-N-S 25-862-5656 (SL)
SPEAKERS' SPOTLIGHT INC
SPEAKERS' SPOTLIGHT
179 John St Suite 302, Toronto, ON, M5T 1X4
(416) 345-1559
Emp Here 34 *Sales* 15,273,446
SIC 7389 Business services, nec
Martin Perelmuter
Farah Perelmuter
Cindy Sheridan
Sundance Filardi
Kelly Macdonald
Jennifer Bovaconti
Marnie Ballane
Donna Carreiro

D-U-N-S 25-226-6804 (HQ)
ST STEPHENS COMMUNITY HOUSE
ST STEPHENS COMMUNITY HOUSE DAYCARE

91 Bellevue Ave, Toronto, ON, M5T 2N8
(416) 925-2103
Emp Here 1   *Sales* 24,848,160
SIC 8399 Social services, nec
Leanne Regendanz

D-U-N-S 25-669-2385   (HQ)
TAOIST TAI CHI SOCIETY OF CANADA
134 D'Arcy St, Toronto, ON, M5T 1K3
(416) 656-2110
Emp Here 4   *Sales* 10,332,764
SIC 8699 Membership organizations, nec
Joseph Karner
David Frame

D-U-N-S 25-535-2387   (SL)
TORONTO CENTRAL COMMUNITY CARE ACCESS CENTRE
TORONTO CENTRAL CCAC
250 Dundas St W Suite 305, Toronto, ON, M5T 2Z5
(416) 506-9888
Emp Here 250   *Sales* 359,650,250
SIC 8699 Membership organizations, nec
Flavian Pinto

D-U-N-S 24-766-3086   (SL)
URBAN STRATEGIES INC
197 Spadina Ave Suite 600, Toronto, ON, M5T 2C8
(416) 340-9004
Emp Here 50   *Sales* 11,714,400
SIC 8748 Business consulting, nec
Cindy Rottenberg-Walker
Melanie Hare
Connie Pasqualitto

D-U-N-S 25-846-9394   (BR)
YONGE STREET MISSION, THE
EVERGREEN CENTRE FOR STREET YOUTH
(*Suby of* YONGE STREET MISSION, THE)
365 Spadina Ave, Toronto, ON, M5T 2G3
(416) 929-9614
Emp Here 130
SIC 8322 Individual and family services
Angie Draskovic

Toronto, ON M5V

D-U-N-S 20-122-8249   (SL)
1390835 ONTARIO LIMITED
TOYOTA ON FRONT
528 Front St W Suite 325, Toronto, ON, M5V 1B8
(416) 703-7700
Emp Here 45   *Sales* 22,413,510
SIC 5511 New and used car dealers
Shahin Alizadeh
Thomas Powers
Michael Stein

D-U-N-S 20-551-4412   (HQ)
1607138 ONTARIO LIMITED
(*Suby of* DHX MEDIA LTD)
266 King St W Suite 200, Toronto, ON, M5V 1H8
(416) 977-3238
Sales 29,662,974
SIC 7922 Theatrical producers and services
Michael Hirsh
Toper Taylor
Kevin O'grady
Aaron Ames
John Loh

D-U-N-S 24-208-5608   (BR)
2945-8171 QUEBEC INC
STINGRAY COURRIER SERVICE
296 Richmond St W Suite 401, Toronto, ON, M5V 1X2
(416) 979-0000
Emp Here 100
SIC 7389 Business services, nec
Douglas Castor

D-U-N-S 20-343-9898   (SL)
3119696 CANADA INC
QMS COURIER
269 Richmond St W Suite 201, Toronto, ON, M5V 1X1
(416) 368-1623
Emp Here 50   *Sales* 22,174,500
SIC 7389 Business services, nec
Paul Etheridge
Michael George

D-U-N-S 20-345-2755   (SL)
3798143 CANADA INC
PRICEMETRIX
155 Wellington St W Suite 2901, Toronto, ON, M5V 3H6
(416) 955-0514
Emp Here 60   *Sales* 16,459,920
SIC 8741 Management services
Doug Trott
Jeff Marsden
Patrick Kennedy
Christopher Payne

D-U-N-S 24-360-7889   (SL)
4116372 CANADA INC
266 King St W Suite 200, Toronto, ON, M5V 1H8
(416) 977-3238
Emp Here 70   *Sales* 19,134,500
SIC 6712 Bank holding companies
Lisa Melchior
Michael Hirsh
John Loh
Joseph Wiley

D-U-N-S 24-388-4025   (SL)
576794 ONTARIO LTD
FRESH AND WILD FOOD MARKET
69 Spadina Ave, Toronto, ON, M5V 3P8
(416) 979-8155
Emp Here 45   *Sales* 12,336,840
SIC 5411 Grocery stores
Peter Papadopoulos

D-U-N-S 20-770-4797   (HQ)
601712 ONTARIO INC
JAMES MOTO ENTERPRISES
315 Adelaide St W, Toronto, ON, M5V 1P8
(416) 977-2603
Emp Here 70   *Sales* 21,868,000
SIC 6712 Bank holding companies
James Matsumoto

D-U-N-S 24-357-8254   (SL)
ACCEL HIGH RISE CONSTRUCTION LTD
66 Portland St Suite 801, Toronto, ON, M5V 2M6

Emp Here 30   *Sales* 14,121,930
SIC 1542 Nonresidential construction, nec
Peter Freed
Anthony Corsetti

D-U-N-S 24-255-4710   (SL)
ACCELERATED CONNECTIONS INC
(*Suby of* GTT COMMUNICATIONS, INC.)
155 Wellington St W Suite 3740, Toronto, ON, M5V 3H1
(416) 637-3432
Emp Here 92   *Sales* 75,099,800
SIC 4899 Communication services, nec
Michael Garbe

D-U-N-S 20-896-9431   (HQ)
ACCLAIM ABILITY MANAGEMENT INC
82 Peter St, Toronto, ON, M5V 2G5
(416) 486-9706
Emp Here 1   *Sales* 13,716,600
SIC 8741 Management services
Tony Fasulo

D-U-N-S 25-989-6181   (HQ)
ACCOR MANAGEMENT CANADA INC
155 Wellington St W Suite 3300, Toronto, ON, M5V 0C3
(416) 874-2600
Emp Here 200   *Sales* 8,891,083,200

SIC 6531 Real estate agents and managers
Heather Mccroy
Barbara Kilner
Sara Glenn

D-U-N-S 20-193-7955   (HQ)
ACCOR SERVICES CANADA INC
(*Suby of* ACCOR)
155 Wellington St W Suite 3300, Toronto, ON, M5V 0C3
(416) 874-2600
Sales 91,377,250
SIC 6712 Bank holding companies
Kevin Frid

D-U-N-S 24-783-2900   (SL)
ACI WORLDWIDE (CANADA) INC
(*Suby of* ACI WORLDWIDE, INC.)
200 Wellington St W Suite 700, Toronto, ON, M5V 3C7
(416) 813-3000
Emp Here 100   *Sales* 53,535,200
SIC 5045 Computers, peripherals, and software
Rob Cameron
Scott Behrens
Dennis P. Byrnes
Ross England
Geoffrey T. Parker

D-U-N-S 20-410-3337   (HQ)
ADAMSON ASSOCIATES
401 Wellington St W 3rd Flr, Toronto, ON, M5V 1E7
(416) 967-1500
Sales 35,747,800
SIC 8712 Architectural services
David Jansen
Greg Dunn
William Bradley
Richard Edwards

D-U-N-S 20-183-6496   (HQ)
ALLIED PROPERTIES REAL ESTATE INVESTMENT TRUST
134 Peter St Suite 1700, Toronto, ON, M5V 2H2
(416) 977-9002
Emp Here 19   *Sales* 66,073,431
SIC 6798 Real estate investment trusts
Michael R. Emory
Thomas Burns
Cecilia Williams
Doug Riches
David Pitfield
Tim Low
Hugh Clark
Luqman Ahmad
Tyrone Bowers
Andrew Groenewegen

D-U-N-S 25-504-7441   (HQ)
AMERICA ONLINE CANADA INC
AOL CANADA
(*Suby of* VERIZON COMMUNICATIONS INC.)
99 Spadina Ave Suite 200, Toronto, ON, M5V 3P8
(416) 263-8100
Emp Here 100   *Sales* 80,148,400
SIC 7319 Advertising, nec
Jonathan Lister
John Hamovitch
George Haman

D-U-N-S 24-099-4868   (SL)
ANT & BEE CORPORATION
123 John St, Toronto, ON, M5V 2E2
(416) 646-2811
Emp Here 120   *Sales* 8,963,280
SIC 7361 Employment agencies
Stafford Burrowes
Alex Borba

D-U-N-S 24-377-3244   (HQ)
AON BENFIELD CANADA ULC
(*Suby of* AON PLC)
225 King St W Suite 1000, Toronto, ON, M5V

3M2
(416) 979-3300
Sales 38,023,500
SIC 8748 Business consulting, nec
Robert Mclean
David Sloan
Joseph I O'connell
Maureen Mackay
William D Farmer
Peter Bennett
Desmond Dosramos

D-U-N-S 20-771-6994   (HQ)
AON HEWITT INC
(*Suby of* AON PLC)
225 King St W Suite 1600, Toronto, ON, M5V 3M2
(416) 542-5500
Emp Here 180   *Sales* 180,421,600
SIC 8999 Services, nec
Jeff Jackson
Vanessa Bonomo
Allan Shapira
David Seabrook
Rejean Tremblay
Shaun Miller

D-U-N-S 20-778-5960   (SL)
ARTON BEADS CRAFT INC
523 Queen St W, Toronto, ON, M5V 2B4
(416) 504-1168
Emp Here 25   *Sales* 11,875,650
SIC 5088 Transportation equipment and supplies
River Chiang

D-U-N-S 20-657-5250   (SL)
AUDIENCEVIEW
2nd Floor, Toronto, ON, M5V 3C7
(416) 687-2100
Emp Here 49   *Sales* 11,480,112
SIC 8748 Business consulting, nec
Michael Bryce

D-U-N-S 20-652-4386   (BR)
BELL MEDIA INC
GLOBE AND MAIL
(*Suby of* BCE INC)
444 Front St W, Toronto, ON, M5V 2S9
(416) 585-5000
Emp Here 800
SIC 5192 Books, periodicals, and newspapers
Phillip Crawley

D-U-N-S 20-114-1483   (BR)
BELL MEDIA INC
REPORT ON BUSINESS TELEVISION
(*Suby of* BCE INC)
720 King St W Suite 1000, Toronto, ON, M5V 2T3

Emp Here 95
SIC 7922 Theatrical producers and services
Jack Fleischmann

D-U-N-S 20-719-1495   (HQ)
BELL MEDIA INC
ASTRAL MEDIA OUTDOOR
(*Suby of* BCE INC)
299 Queen St W, Toronto, ON, M5V 2Z5
(416) 591-5757
Emp Here 1,200   *Sales* 1,003,632,000
SIC 4833 Television broadcasting stations
Randy Lennox
Jon Arklay
Erasmo Tiseo

D-U-N-S 24-326-8948   (SL)
BENSIMON BYRNE INC
225 Wellington St W, Toronto, ON, M5V 3G7
(416) 922-2211
Emp Here 110   *Sales* 22,040,810
SIC 7311 Advertising agencies
Jack Bensimon
Colleen Peddie

D-U-N-S 25-983-0193   (SL)
BIBLIOCOMMONS INC

---

119 Spadina Ave Suite 1000, Toronto, ON, M5V 2L1
(647) 436-6381
Emp Here 75   *Sales* 13,298,325
SIC 7374 Data processing and preparation
Patrick Kennedy

D-U-N-S 20-514-7338   (BR)
BLAST RADIUS INC
(*Suby of* WPP PLC)
99 Spadina Ave Suite 200, Toronto, ON, M5V 3P8
(416) 214-4220
Emp Here 160
SIC 7374 Data processing and preparation
David Feldt

D-U-N-S 24-286-2313   (SL)
BLUE ELEPHANT REALTY INC
548 King St W Suite 202, Toronto, ON, M5V 1M3
(416) 504-6133
Emp Here 50   *Sales* 16,356,350
SIC 6531 Real estate agents and managers
Blair Johnson
Mark Wadden

D-U-N-S 25-100-0170   (SL)
BRONSKILL & CO. INC
(*Suby of* FREEMAN DECORATING CO.)
662 King St W Suite 101, Toronto, ON, M5V 1M7
(416) 703-8689
Emp Here 29   *Sales* 13,027,351
SIC 7389 Business services, nec
Reginald Bronskill

D-U-N-S 24-418-0597   (SL)
BRUNICO COMMUNICATIONS LTD
366 Adelaide St W Suite 100, Toronto, ON, M5V 1R9
(416) 408-2300
Emp Here 90   *Sales* 14,762,430
SIC 2721 Periodicals
Russell Goldstein
Mary Maddever
Jocelyn Christie
Claire Macdonald
Linda Lovegrove

D-U-N-S 20-769-4055   (HQ)
BUCK CONSULTANTS LIMITED
(*Suby of* BUCK GLOBAL, LLC)
155 Wellington St W Suite 3000, Toronto, ON, M5V 3L3
(416) 865-0060
Sales 50,698,000
SIC 8748 Business consulting, nec
Gregory Fayarchuk

D-U-N-S 20-696-9821   (HQ)
BULLFROG POWER INC
366 Adelaide St W Suite 701, Toronto, ON, M5V 1R9
(416) 360-3464
Sales 28,197,630
SIC 4911 Electric services
Anthony Santilli
Ron Seftel

D-U-N-S 20-919-4369   (BR)
CABINET DE RELATIONS PUBLIQUES NATIONAL INC, LE
NATIONAL PUBLIC RELATIONS INC
(*Suby of* GROUPE CONSEIL RES PUBLICA INC)
320 Front St W Suite 1600, Toronto, ON, M5V 3B5
(416) 586-0180
Emp Here 100
SIC 8743 Public relations services
Rick Murray

D-U-N-S 20-073-3801   (BR)
CANADA LANDS COMPANY CLC LIMITED
CN TOWER
(*Suby of* GOVERNMENT OF CANADA)
301 Front St W, Toronto, ON, M5V 2T6

(416) 868-6937
Emp Here 250
SIC 6531 Real estate agents and managers
Sarfaraz Haq

D-U-N-S 24-376-2817   (SL)
CANADIAN BANC CORP
200 Front St W Suite 2510, Toronto, ON, M5V 3K2
(416) 304-4440
Emp Here 5   *Sales* 29,184,625
SIC 6722 Management investment, open-end
S. Wayne Finch
Laura L. Johnson
Silvia Gomes
Peter F. Cruickshank
Michael W. Sharp
John D. Steep
William C. Thornhill

D-U-N-S 25-992-4124   (BR)
CANADIAN BROADCASTING CORPORATION
CBC
(*Suby of* GOVERNMENT OF CANADA)
205 Wellington St W Unit 9a211, Toronto, ON, M5V 3G7
(416) 205-3072
Emp Here 400
SIC 4833 Television broadcasting stations
Magda Cristestu

D-U-N-S 20-879-4651   (BR)
CANADIAN BROADCASTING CORPORATION
CBC
(*Suby of* GOVERNMENT OF CANADA)
250 Front St W, Toronto, ON, M5V 3G5
(416) 205-3311
Emp Here 3,000
SIC 4832 Radio broadcasting stations
Natasha Ramsahai

D-U-N-S 20-004-2963   (BR)
CANADIAN BROADCASTING CORPORATION
TV NEWS
(*Suby of* GOVERNMENT OF CANADA)
205 Wellington St W Rm 4e301 B, Toronto, ON, M5V 3G7
(416) 205-5807
Emp Here 3,000
SIC 4833 Television broadcasting stations
Tony Burman

D-U-N-S 25-093-1979   (HQ)
CAPSTONE INFRASTRUCTURE CORPORATION
155 Wellington St W Suite 2930, Toronto, ON, M5V 3H1
(416) 649-1300
Emp Here 200   *Sales* 139,209,512
SIC 4911 Electric services
David Eva
Aileen Gien
Andrew Kennedy
Paul Smith
Paul Malan
Adele Malo
Gary Eade
Janet Woodruff
Richard Knowles
Michael Smerdon

D-U-N-S 25-256-0446   (HQ)
CARAT CANADA INC
AEGIS TRADE
(*Suby of* DENTSU INC.)
276 King St W Suite 400, Toronto, ON, M5V 1J2
(416) 504-3965
Emp Here 115   *Sales* 32,460,102
SIC 7311 Advertising agencies
Scott Hughes
Dave Wein
Filippopoulos Philip

D-U-N-S 24-025-6813   (SL)

CARL SQUARED PRODUCTIONS INC
PORTFOLIO ENTERTAINMENT
901 King St W Suite 301, Toronto, ON, M5V 3H5
(416) 483-9773
Emp Here 75   *Sales* 11,352,675
SIC 7922 Theatrical producers and services
Joy Rosen
Lisa Olsman

D-U-N-S 20-592-3340   (SL)
CENTRAL TORONTO COMMUNITY HEALTH CENTRES
QUEEN WEST COMMUNITY HEALTH CENTRE
168 Bathurst St Suite 3199, Toronto, ON, M5V 2R4
(416) 703-8480
Emp Here 49   *Sales* 11,583,680
SIC 8621 Professional organizations

D-U-N-S 25-872-2326   (SL)
CHARTERED PROFESSIONAL ACCOUNTANTS OF CANADA
CPA CANADA
277 Wellington St W Suite 600, Toronto, ON, M5V 3H2
(416) 977-3222
Emp Here 200   *Sales* 33,214
SIC 8621 Professional organizations
Kevin Dancey
Lou Ragagnin
Heather Whyte
Stephen A.Anisman

D-U-N-S 20-259-4453   (BR)
CINEFLIX MEDIA INC
(*Suby of* CINEFLIX MEDIA INC)
110 Spadina Ave Suite 400, Toronto, ON, M5V 2K4
(416) 531-2500
Emp Here 200
SIC 7929 Entertainers and entertainment groups

D-U-N-S 20-085-6198   (BR)
CINEPLEX ODEON CORPORATION
SCOTIABANK THEATER TORONTO
(*Suby of* CINEPLEX INC)
259 Richmond St W, Toronto, ON, M5V 3M6
(416) 368-5600
Emp ·Here 200
SIC ·7832 Motion picture theaters, except drive-in
Rafiq Khimani

D-U-N-S 25-362-8390   (BR)
COMPAGNIE DE TELEPHONE BELL DU CANADA OU BELL CANADA, LA
(*Suby of* BCE INC)
21 Canniff St, Toronto, ON, M5V 3G1
(647) 393-3039
Emp Here 200
SIC 4813 Telephone communication, except radio

D-U-N-S 24-172-9961   (BR)
COMPAGNIE DES CHEMINS DE FER NATIONAUX DU CANADA
CN RAILS
(*Suby of* COMPAGNIE DES CHEMINS DE FER NATIONAUX DU CANADA)
277 Front St W, Toronto, ON, M5V 2X4
(888) 888-5909
Emp Here 21,967
SIC 4111 Local and suburban transit
Mark Hallman

D-U-N-S 20-020-8403   (HQ)
CONCORD ADEX INC
23 Spadina Ave, Toronto, ON, M5V 3M5
(416) 813-0333
Sales 23,536,550
SIC 1542 Nonresidential construction, nec
Terrence Hiu

D-U-N-S 20-341-8611   (SL)
CONTINENTAL GOLD INC

155 Wellington St W Suite 2920, Toronto, ON, M5V 3H1
(416) 583-5610
Emp Here 372   *Sales* 95,147,928
SIC 1041 Gold ores
Ari Sussman
Leon Teicher
Ana Milena Vasquez
Jairo Ivan Ariza
Carlos Franco Echavarria
Omar Ossma
Guillermo Salgado
Amanda Duran Casas
Christopher Sattler
Paul J. Murphy

D-U-N-S 20-215-4407   (HQ)
CORBY SPIRIT AND WINE LIMITED
(*Suby of* PERNOD RICARD)
225 King St W Suite 1100, Toronto, ON, M5V 3M2
(416) 479-2400
Emp Here 50   *Sales* 107,029,472
SIC 2085 Distilled and blended liquors
R. Patrick O'driscoll
Stephane Cote
Melissa Hanesworth
Anne Martin
Marc A. Valencia
Antonio Sanchez Villarreal
Angel Li
George Mccarthy
Claude Boulay
Robert Llewellyn

D-U-N-S 24-322-0519   (BR)
CRITICAL MASS INC
425 Adelaide St W, Toronto, ON, M5V 3C1
(416) 673-5275
Emp Here 80
SIC 7374 Data processing and preparation
Jaime Escobar

D-U-N-S 24-052-8125   (HQ)
CSI GLOBAL EDUCATION INC
CSI
(*Suby of* MOODY'S CORPORATION)
200 Wellington St W Suite 1200, Toronto, ON, M5V 3G2
(416) 364-9130
Emp Here 110   *Sales* 20,349,000
SIC 8299 Schools and educational services, nec
Roberta Wilton
Jerry Fahrer
Steve Rosen

D-U-N-S 24-555-4449   (HQ)
CUNDARI GROUP LTD
CUNDARI
26 Duncan St, Toronto, ON, M5V 2B9
(416) 510-1771
Emp Here 100   *Sales* 22,040,810
SIC 7311 Advertising agencies
Aldo Cundari
Maria Orsini
Jennifer Steinmann

D-U-N-S 20-286-9129   (HQ)
DAN AGENCY INC
360I CANADA
(*Suby of* DENTSU INC.)
276 King St W Suite 100, Toronto, ON, M5V 1J2
(416) 929-9700
Emp Here 100   *Sales* 20,037,100
SIC 7311 Advertising agencies
Michel Ostiguy
Claude Carrier
Annie Rizen
Nicholas Rey
Bryan Wiener
Timothy Andree
Yushin Soga
James Cran

D-U-N-S 20-784-5090   (HQ)

DAVIES WARD PHILLIPS & VINEBERG LLP
155 Wellington St W, Toronto, ON, M5V 3J7
(416) 863-0900
Sales 82,350,400
SIC 8111 Legal services
William O'reilly

D-U-N-S 20-354-4960   (SL)
DBRAND INC
500 King St W 3rd Fl, Toronto, ON, M5V 1L9
(647) 282-3711
Emp Here 65   *Sales* 11,371,530
SIC 5999 Miscellaneous retail stores, nec
Adam Ijaz
Musawar Ijaz

D-U-N-S 24-926-4441   (HQ)
DELUXE TORONTO LTD
DELUXE LABORATORIES
(*Suby of* MACANDREWS & FORBES INCOR-
PORATED)
901 King St W Suite 700, Toronto, ON, M5V
3H5
(416) 364-4321
Emp Here 370   *Sales* 40,363,200
SIC 7819 Services allied to motion pictures
Cyril Drabinsky
Nick Iannelli
Diane Cuthbert

D-U-N-S 20-934-6787   (HQ)
DERMALOGICA (CANADA) LTD
(*Suby of* UNILEVER PLC)
720 King St W Suite 300, Toronto, ON, M5V
2T3
(416) 368-2286
Sales 38,687,075
SIC 5122 Drugs, proprietaries, and sundries
Raymond Wurwand

D-U-N-S 20-976-2608   (SL)
**DIAMOND AND SCHMITT ARCHITECTS IN-
CORPORATED**
384 Adelaide St W Suite 300, Toronto, ON,
M5V 1R7
(416) 862-8800
Emp Here 135   *Sales* 24,129,765
SIC 8712 Architectural services
A.J. Diamond
Donald Schmitt
Gary Mccluskie
Martin Davidson
David Dow

D-U-N-S 20-358-1905   (SL)
DIF INFRA IV CANADA LTD
100 Wellington St W, Toronto, ON, M5V 1E3
(647) 748-2088
Emp Here 46   *Sales* 33,738,792
SIC 6722 Management investment, open-end
Paul Huebener

D-U-N-S 24-358-0268   (SL)
DIVIDEND 15 SPLIT CORP
200 Front St W Suite 2510, Toronto, ON, M5V
3K2
(416) 304-4443
Emp Here 6   *Sales* 35,021,550
SIC 6722 Management investment, open-end
S Wayne Finch
Peter Cruickshank
Laura Johnson
Michael Sharp
John Steep
William Thornhill

D-U-N-S 24-680-6512   (SL)
DIVIDEND SELECT 15 CORP
200 Front St W Suite 2510, Toronto, ON, M5V
3K2
(416) 304-4443
Emp Here 6   *Sales* 35,021,550
SIC 6722 Management investment, open-end
Wayne Finch
Laura L. Johnson
Silvia Gomes

D-U-N-S 24-309-8154   (HQ)

DOME PRODUCTIONS INC
1 Blue Jays Way Suite 3400, Toronto, ON,
M5V 1J3
(416) 341-2001
Emp Here 45   *Sales* 17,831,580
SIC 8741 Management services
Mary Ellen Carlyle
Joseph Latka

D-U-N-S 20-177-1292   (HQ)
DOUBLETEX
352 Adelaide St W, Toronto, ON, M5V 1R8
(416) 593-0320
Emp Here 5   *Sales* 18,340,300
SIC 2211 Broadwoven fabric mills, cotton
Richard Zuckerman
Alan Zuckerman
Stuart Zuckerman

D-U-N-S 20-153-0180   (SL)
DOWNTOWN EATERY (1993) LTD
FOR YOUR EYES ONLY
563 King St W, Toronto, ON, M5V 1M1
(416) 585-9200
Emp Here 45   *Sales* 14,652,000
SIC 5995 Optical goods stores
Sam Dahab

D-U-N-S 20-954-8622   (SL)
DYSON CANADA LIMITED
(*Suby of* DYSON JAMES GROUP LIMITED)
312 Adelaide St W, Toronto, ON, M5V 1R2
(416) 849-5821
Emp Here 35   *Sales* 16,625,910
SIC 5087 Service establishment equipment
Andrew Peter Robinson
Peter Richardson
Max Conze
Benjamin Temple
Glenn Andrew
Martin Mccourt

D-U-N-S 24-858-3044   (SL)
**EF   INTERNATIONAL   LANGUAGE
SCHOOLS (CANADA) LIMITED**
SALES OFFICE
127 Portland St, Toronto, ON, M5V 2N4
(800) 387-1463
Emp Here 125   *Sales* 13,347,750
SIC 7299 Miscellaneous personal service
Goran Rannefors

D-U-N-S 25-115-6279   (SL)
ELOQUA CORPORATION
(*Suby of* ORACLE CORPORATION)
553 Richmond St W Suite 214, Toronto, ON,
M5V 1Y6
(416) 864-0440
Emp Here 200   *Sales* 33,369,400
SIC 7372 Prepackaged software
Joseph Payne
Steve Woods
Ralph Riekers
Paul Teshima
Abe Wagner
Alex Shootman

D-U-N-S 24-826-6723   (HQ)
ENTERTAINMENT ONE LTD
134 Peter St Suite 700, Toronto, ON, M5V 2H2
(416) 646-2400
Sales 44,848,000
SIC 7812 Motion picture and video production
Darren Dennis Throop
Allan Leighton
Joseph Sparacio
Linda Robinson
Mark Opzoomer
Michael Friisdahl
Mitzi Reaugh
Robert Mcfarlane
Scott Lawrence

D-U-N-S 24-827-1129   (HQ)
ESC CORPORATE SERVICES LTD
(*Suby of* INFORMATION SERVICES COR-
PORATION)

445 King St W Suite 400, Toronto, ON, M5V
1K4
(416) 595-7177
Sales 12,152,450
SIC 6541 Title abstract offices
Christopher Valentine

D-U-N-S 20-300-1875   (SL)
EURO RSCG HEALTHCARE (CANADA) INC
EURO RSCG LIFE INTERACTION, DIV OF
(*Suby of* VIVENDI)
473 Adelaide St W Suite 300, Toronto, ON,
M5V 1T1
(416) 925-9005
Emp Here 50   *Sales* 10,586,200
SIC 7311 Advertising agencies
Pamela Stewart
Lisa Williams

D-U-N-S 24-163-4091   (HQ)
**EXPERIENTIAL   MARKETING   LIMITED
PARTNERSHIP**
XMC
49 Bathurst St Suite 101, Toronto, ON, M5V
2P2
(416) 703-3589
Sales 10,598,400
SIC 7922 Theatrical producers and services
Steven Lewis
Peri Luel

D-U-N-S 20-213-5869   (HQ)
FAIRMONT HOTELS & RESORTS INC
(*Suby of* ACCOR)
155 Wellington St W Suite 3300, Toronto, ON,
M5V 0C3
(416) 874-2600
Emp Here 200   *Sales* 2,870,040,000
SIC 7011 Hotels and motels
Chris Cahilo
Terence Badour
Mark Rozells
Paula Mcmullan
Allison Keppy
Thomas Storey
Kevin Jacobs
Iain Morton
Brian Mcdonald
Thomas Griffiths

D-U-N-S 24-355-7852   (SL)
FINANCIAL 15 SPLIT CORP
200 Front St W Suite 2510, Toronto, ON, M5V
3K2
(416) 304-4443
Emp Here 5   *Sales* 29,184,625
SIC 6722 Management investment, open-end
Laura L. Johnson
Peter Cruickshank
Michael W. Sharp
John D. Steep
Wayne Finch
William Thornhill

D-U-N-S 20-818-4689   (HQ)
**FINANCIAL ADVISORS ASSOCIATION OF
CANADA, THE**
ADVOCIS
10 Lower Spadina Ave Suite 600, Toronto, ON,
M5V 2Z2
(416) 444-5251
Sales 14,223,825
SIC 8611 Business associations
Gregory Pollock

D-U-N-S 20-180-8461   (HQ)
**FRENCH CONNECTION (CANADA) LIM-
ITED**
(*Suby of* FRENCH CONNECTION GROUP
PLC)
111 Peter St Suite 406, Toronto, ON, M5V 2H1
(416) 640-6160
Emp Here 15   *Sales* 31,394,300
SIC 5651 Family clothing stores
Stephen Marks
Elizabeth Hardy
Neil Williams

D-U-N-S 24-143-2632   (BR)
FUJITSU CONSEIL (CANADA) INC
FUJITSU CONSULTING
(*Suby of* FUJITSU CONSULTING (CANADA)
HOLDINGS, INC.)
200 Front St W Suite 2300, Toronto, ON, M5V
3K2
(416) 363-8661
Emp Here 150
SIC 7379 Computer related services, nec
Linda Aquino

D-U-N-S 20-338-2320   (SL)
FUTUREVAULT INC
441 King St W Unit 200, Toronto, ON, M5V
1K4
(416) 560-7808
Emp Here 25   *Sales* 11,087,250
SIC 7389 Business services, nec
Bradley Rosenberg

D-U-N-S 24-951-3177   (HQ)
G ADVENTURES INC
19 Charlotte St Suite 200, Toronto, ON, M5V
2H5
(416) 260-0999
Emp Here 375   *Sales* 158,175,200
SIC 4725 Tour operators
Bruce Poon Tip
Saul Mendel

D-U-N-S 20-050-2131   (HQ)
GIVEX CANADA CORP
134 Peter St Suite 1400, Toronto, ON, M5V
2H2
(416) 350-9660
Emp Here 117   *Sales* 21,356,416
SIC 7374 Data processing and preparation
Don Gray

D-U-N-S 20-344-1001   (SL)
GOLDMONEY INC
334 Adelaide St W Unit 307, Toronto, ON,
M5V 0M1
(647) 499-6748
Emp Here 40   *Sales* 455,643,734
SIC 7372 Prepackaged software
Roy Sebag
James Turk
John Butler
Josh Crumb
Mahendra Naik
Stefan Wieler
Alessandro Premoli
Steve Fray
Paul Mennega
Mike Bushy

D-U-N-S 25-208-0254   (SL)
GREEN CIRCLE SALONS INC
401 Richmond St W Suite 371, Toronto, ON,
M5V 3A8
(647) 341-6812
Emp Here 35   *Sales* 10,539,970
SIC 4953 Refuse systems
Shane Price

D-U-N-S 20-220-6298   (HQ)
GREY ADVERTISING ULC
GREY CANADA
(*Suby of* WPP PLC)
46 Spadina Ave Suite 500, Toronto, ON, M5V
2H8
(416) 486-0700
Emp Here 75   *Sales* 114,465,815
SIC 7311 Advertising agencies
Stephanie Nerlich
Leah Power

D-U-N-S 24-247-3622   (HQ)
GUESTLOGIX INC
111 Peter St Suite 407, Toronto, ON, M5V 2H1
(647) 317-1517
Emp Here 120   *Sales* 48,591,721
SIC 3577 Computer peripheral equipment,
nec
Brett Proud
Chris Gardner

Thomas Drohan
Andy Archer
Patrick Leung
Louis Belanger-Martin
Stephen Clampett
Kim Eaton

D-U-N-S 24-429-4146   (HQ)
HACHETTE DISTRIBUTION SERVICES (CANADA) INC
LS TRAVEL RETAIL NORTH AMERICA
(*Suby of* LAGARDERE SCA)
370 King St W Suite 600, Toronto, ON, M5V 1J9
(416) 863-6400
Emp Here 100   *Sales* 275,305,500
SIC 5947 Gift, novelty, and souvenir shop
Gerald Savaria

D-U-N-S 25-503-6733   (SL)
HANSON PUBLICATIONS INC.
111 Peter St,Ste 406, Toronto, ON, M5V 2H1

Emp Here 250   *Sales* 15,325,200
SIC 2741 Miscellaneous publishing

D-U-N-S 20-358-7316   (HQ)
HAVAS CANADA HOLDINGS, INC
HAVAS MEDIA
473 Adelaide St W Suite 300, Toronto, ON, M5V 1T1
(416) 920-6864
Emp Here 100   *Sales* 28,051,940
SIC 7311 Advertising agencies
Thomas Olesinski

D-U-N-S 20-170-8716   (HQ)
HERMAN MILLER CANADA, INC
WORKPLACE RESOURCE
(*Suby of* HERMAN MILLER, INC.)
462 Wellington St W Suite 200, Toronto, ON, M5V 1E3
(416) 366-3300
Emp Here 60   *Sales* 80,551,520
SIC 5021 Furniture
Paulo Carmini
Hezron Timothy Lopez
W. Bruce Clark
Brian Walker

D-U-N-S 25-221-9662   (SL)
HIVE STRATEGIC MARKETING INC, THE
544 King St W, Toronto, ON, M5V 1M3
(416) 923-3800
Emp Here 125   *Sales* 23,313,250
SIC 8743 Public relations services
Andy Krupski

D-U-N-S 24-385-4460   (HQ)
HOGG ROBINSON CANADA INC
HRG NORTH AMERICA
(*Suby of* HOGG ROBINSON GROUP LIMITED)
370 King St W Suite 700, Toronto, ON, M5V 1J9
(416) 593-8866
Emp Here 70   *Sales* 135,083,200
SIC 8742 Management consulting services
Greg Treasure
Randy Nanek
Michal Grey

D-U-N-S 24-421-4446   (SL)
HOTEL 550 WELLINGTON GP LTD
THOMPSON TORONTO
550 Wellington St W, Toronto, ON, M5V 2V4
(416) 640-7778
Emp Here 99   *Sales* 9,395,001
SIC 7011 Hotels and motels
Peter Freed
Anthony Cohen

D-U-N-S 20-372-8050   (SL)
ICON INFRASTRUCTURE LLP
155 Wellington St W Suite 2930, Toronto, ON, M5V 3H1
(416) 649-1331
Emp Here 29   *Sales* 15,405,003

SIC 6211 Security brokers and dealers

D-U-N-S 24-421-0584   (SL)
IMAGINE FINANCIAL LTD
IMAGINE INSURANCE
460 Richmond St W Suite 100, Toronto, ON, M5V 1Y1
(416) 730-8488
Emp Here 45   *Sales* 26,096,580
SIC 6411 Insurance agents, brokers, and service
Robin Ingle

D-U-N-S 25-091-0049   (SL)
INC RESEARCH TORONTO, INC
INC RESEARCH
(*Suby of* SYNEOS HEALTH, INC.)
720 King St W 7th Fl, Toronto, ON, M5V 2T3
(416) 963-9338
Emp Here 200   *Sales* 101,347,200
SIC 8733 Noncommercial research organizations
Pierre Geoffroy

D-U-N-S 20-131-8040   (BR)
INDIGO BOOKS & MUSIC INC
INDIGO.CHAPTERS.CA
(*Suby of* INDIGO BOOKS & MUSIC INC)
82 Peter St Suite 300, Toronto, ON, M5V 2G5
(416) 598-8000
Emp Here 100
SIC 5942 Book stores
Jessica Kiel

D-U-N-S 20-162-2495   (HQ)
INDIGO BOOKS & MUSIC INC
CHAPTERS
620 King St W, Toronto, ON, M5V 1M6
(416) 364-4499
Emp Here 200   *Sales* 824,980,780
SIC 5942 Book stores
Heather Reisman
Kirsten Chapman
Gil Dennis
Hugues Simard
Kathleen Flynn
Tod Morehead
Bo Parizadeh
Frank Clegg
Jonathan Deitcher
Mitchell Goldhar

D-U-N-S 20-012-6493   (SL)
INFUSION DEVELOPMENT INC
INFUSION DEVELOPMENT CANADA
(*Suby of* ACCENTURE PUBLIC LIMITED COMPANY)
200 Wellington St W, Toronto, ON, M5V 3C7
(416) 593-6595
Emp Here 115   *Sales* 19,187,405
SIC 7379 Computer related services, nec
Greg Brill
Sheldon Fernandez
Alim Somani
William(Bill) Baldasti

D-U-N-S 20-984-0672   (SL)
INGLE INTERNATIONAL INC.
460 Richmond St W Suite 100, Toronto, ON, M5V 1Y1
(416) 730-8488
Emp Here 51   *Sales* 11,461,944
SIC 6141 Personal credit institutions
Robin Ingle

D-U-N-S 24-761-1242   (HQ)
INTERAXON INC
555 Richmond St W, Suite 900, Toronto, ON, M5V 3B1
(416) 598-8989
Sales 13,476,570
SIC 7389 Business services, nec
Ariel Garten

D-U-N-S 20-144-0448   (SL)
INTERCONTINENTAL TORONTO CENTRE, THE
225 Front St W, Toronto, ON, M5V 2X3

(416) 597-1400
Emp Here 300   *Sales* 28,700,400
SIC 7011 Hotels and motels
Alexi Hakim
Paul Mitchell

D-U-N-S 20-364-2694   (SL)
INTERTAIN GROUP LIMITED, THE
(*Suby of* JPJ GROUP PLC)
24 Duncan St 2 Fl, Toronto, ON, M5V 2B8
(647) 641-8404
Emp Here 7   *Sales* 356,429,748
SIC 5734 Computer and software stores
Andrew Ross Mciver
Neil Geoffrey Goulden
Robert Bressler
Nigel Brewster
David Danziger
Paul Pathak
Keith Laslop

D-U-N-S 20-360-0283   (BR)
JAM FILLED ENTERTAINMENT INC
(*Suby of* BOAT ROCKER MEDIA INC)
364 Richmond St W Suite 100, Toronto, ON, M5V 1X6
(613) 366-2550
Emp Here 250
SIC 7812 Motion picture and video production
Kyle Macdougall

D-U-N-S 20-967-6902   (SL)
JOURNALISTS FOR HUMAN RIGHTS (JHR)
147 Spadina Ave Suite 206, Toronto, ON, M5V 2L7
(416) 413-0240
Emp Here 26   *Sales* 10,332,764
SIC 8699 Membership organizations, nec
Ben Peterson

D-U-N-S 24-804-9343   (HQ)
KANETIX LTD
INSURANCEHOTLINE COM
360 Adelaide St W Suite 100, Toronto, ON, M5V 1R7
(416) 599-9779
Sales 42,403,000
SIC 6411 Insurance agents, brokers, and service
Igal Mayer
Matt Lutzko
Leonie Tait
Umair Suria

D-U-N-S 25-819-7495   (BR)
KEG RESTAURANTS LTD
KEG STEAKHOUSE & BAR, THE
(*Suby of* RECIPE UNLIMITED CORPORATION)
560 King St W, Toronto, ON, M5V 0L5
(416) 364-7227
Emp Here 85
SIC 5812 Eating places
Angie Shally

D-U-N-S 25-214-5024   (SL)
KPMB ARCHITECTS
322 King St W, Toronto, ON, M5V 1J2
(416) 977-5104
Emp Here 101   *Sales* 18,052,639
SIC 8712 Architectural services
Bruce Kuwabara
Marianne Mckenna
Shirley Blumberg

D-U-N-S 25-087-7354   (BR)
LARCO INVESTMENTS LTD
RENAISSANCE HOTEL
(*Suby of* LARCO INVESTMENTS LTD)
1 Blue Jays Way Suite 1, Toronto, ON, M5V 1J4
(416) 341-7100
Emp Here 200
SIC 7011 Hotels and motels
Mark Ive

D-U-N-S 25-050-1905   (SL)
LAST BEST PLACE CORP, THE

MONTANA
145 John St, Toronto, ON, M5V 2E4

Emp Here 90   *Sales* 3,858,570
SIC 5812 Eating places
Larry Sdao
Evengelos Pitsadiotis

D-U-N-S 20-578-0377   (SL)
LEONARDO WORLDWIDE CORPORATION
111 Peter St Suite 530, Toronto, ON, M5V 2H1
(416) 593-6634
Emp Here 78   *Sales* 13,830,258
SIC 7374 Data processing and preparation
Paolo Boni
Victor Robison
Mark Charlinski
Stephen Mcdonald

D-U-N-S 20-379-1921   (SL)
LIFT CO. LTD
77 Peter St Suite 200, Toronto, ON, M5V 2G4
(647) 239-6804
Emp Here 45   *Sales* 10,365,300
SIC 5734 Computer and software stores
Matei Olaru

D-U-N-S 20-281-1840   (SL)
LS TRAVEL RETAIL NORTH AMERICA INC
370 King St W Suite 703, Toronto, ON, M5V 1J9
(416) 863-6400
Emp Here 100   *Sales* 24,432,800
SIC 5947 Gift, novelty, and souvenir shop
Gregg Paradies
Gerald Savaria
Wei Huang
Vadim Motlik
Ivana Krpan
Dag Inge Rasmussen

D-U-N-S 20-819-6220   (HQ)
MACKENZIE FINANCIAL CORPORATION
MACKENZIE MAXXUM DIVIDEND GROWTH FUND
(*Suby of* POWER CORPORATION DU CANADA)
180 Queen St W Suite 1600, Toronto, ON, M5V 3K1
(800) 387-0614
Emp Here 1,100   *Sales* 7,588,002,500
SIC 6722 Management investment, open-end
Barry Mcinerney
Tony Elavia

D-U-N-S 20-299-9801   (SL)
MACKENZIE INVESTMENTS
MACKENZIE FINANCIAL
180 Queen St W, Toronto, ON, M5V 3K1
(416) 922-5322
Emp Here 25   *Sales* 20,694,425
SIC 6722 Management investment, open-end
Barry Mcinerney

D-U-N-S 25-997-1638   (HQ)
MAPLECORE LTD
MAPLE MUSIC
230 Richmond St W Suite 11, Toronto, ON, M5V 3E5
(416) 961-1040
Sales 13,304,700
SIC 7389 Business services, nec
Grant Dexter
Mike Alkier

D-U-N-S 20-928-1435   (HQ)
MARKEL CANADA LIMITED
(*Suby of* MARKEL CORPORATION)
200 Wellington St W Unit 400, Toronto, ON, M5V 3C7
(416) 601-1133
Emp Here 2   *Sales* 12,816,097
SIC 6712 Bank holding companies
Karen Barkley

D-U-N-S 20-019-5923   (HQ)
MCCAIN FOODS LIMITED
MCCAIN GLOBAL SOURCING

(*Suby of* MCCAIN FOODS GROUP INC)
439 King St W Suite 500, Toronto, ON, M5V
1K4
(416) 955-1700
Emp Here 1,100   *Sales* 9,747,700,000
SIC 2037 Frozen fruits and vegetables
Dirk Van De Van De Put
Max Koeune
Allison D Mccain
Andrew Mccain
Scott Mccain
J-P Bisnaire
Jacques Bougie
Janet Plaut Giesselam
Victor Young
Jose Boisjoli

D-U-N-S 20-170-3741   (HQ)
MCCANN WORLDGROUP CANADA INC
MACLAREN MCCANN INTERACTIVE
(*Suby of* THE INTERPUBLIC GROUP OF
COMPANIES INC)
200 Wellington St W Suite 1300, Toronto, ON,
M5V 0N6
(416) 594-6000
Emp Here 650   *Sales* 239,182,300
SIC 7311 Advertising agencies
Simon Sikorski
Erwin Buck
Diane Ridgway-Cross
Jennifer Powell
Patrick O'donovan
Nadia D'alessandro
Mark Dicks
John Alabaszowski
Lindsey Feasby
Caroline Murphy

D-U-N-S 25-170-6503   (SL)
MEDIA PROFILE INC
579 Richmond St W Suite 500, Toronto, ON,
M5V 1Y6
(416) 504-8464
Emp Here 50   *Sales* 13,716,600
SIC 8741 Management services
Alison King
David Wills
John Thibodeau
Adrienne Simic
Patrick Erlich
Susan Reisler
Jennifer Alsop-Lee
Stephanie Bell
Nelli Sofiyenko

D-U-N-S 24-680-2511   (SL)
MERCATUS TECHNOLOGIES INC
545 King St W Suite 500, Toronto, ON, M5V
1M1
(416) 603-3406
Emp Here 70   *Sales* 10,092,740
SIC 7371 Custom computer programming ser-
vices
Sylvain Perrier
Bernie Nisker
Tony Shuparsky
Dave Conte
Bohdan Zabawskyj
Kevin Kidd
Brandon Eady
Djen Choo
Tim Zimmerman
Andrew Chang

D-U-N-S 20-938-0898   (HQ)
MERIT TRAVEL GROUP INC
MERIT VACATIONS
(*Suby of* MERIT HOLDINGS INC)
111 Peter St Suite 200, Toronto, ON, M5V 2H1
(416) 364-3775
Emp Here 84   *Sales* 197,719,000
SIC 4724 Travel agencies
Michael Merrithew
Louise De Granpre

D-U-N-S 20-121-2540   (SL)
METFIN PROPERTIES LIMITED PARTNER-

SHIP
ALL-CANADIAN SELF STORAGE
266 King St W Suite 405, Toronto, ON, M5V
1H8
(416) 360-0122
Emp Here 50   *Sales* 34,840,500
SIC 6799 Investors, nec
John Donald

D-U-N-S 24-936-5370   (HQ)
**METROPOLITAN TORONTO CONVENTION
CENTRE CORPORATION**
METRO TORONTO CONVENTION CENTRE
(*Suby of* GOVERNMENT OF ONTARIO)
255 Front St, Toronto, ON, M5V 2W6
(416) 585-8000
Sales 305,081,000
SIC 7389 Business services, nec
Barry Smith
John Houghton
Esther Lee
Walter G. Oster
David Chisholm
Vince Quattrociocchi
Richard Willett
Imtiaz Dhanjee
Judi L. Cohen
Brian Smith

D-U-N-S 24-771-2177   (HQ)
**METROPOLITAN   TORONTO   WATER-
WORKS SYSTEM**
(*Suby of* CORPORATION OF THE CITY OF
TORONTO)
55 John St, Toronto, ON, M5V 3C6
(416) 392-8211
Sales 198,348,345
SIC 4971 Irrigation systems
Barry Gutteridge

D-U-N-S 25-281-9883   (HQ)
**MING PAO NEWSPAPERS (CANADA) LIM-
ITED**
MING PAO DAILY NEWS
(*Suby of* MEDIA CHINESE INTERNATIONAL
LIMITED)
23 Spadina Ave, Toronto, ON, M5V 3M5
(416) 321-0088
Emp Here 230   *Sales* 68,789,770
SIC 2711 Newspapers
Ka Ming Lui
Kiew Chiong Tiong
Mary Chan
Dewitt Liew
Ngiik Siong Tiong Liew

D-U-N-S 20-108-7744   (HQ)
MIRVISH PRODUCTIONS LTD
284 King St W Suite 400, Toronto, ON, M5V
1J2
(416) 593-0351
Sales 21,196,800
SIC 7922 Theatrical producers and services
David Mirvish

D-U-N-S 20-170-9649   (HQ)
MIRVISH, ED ENTERPRISES LIMITED
ROYAL ALEXANDRA THEATRE
284 King St W Suite 400, Toronto, ON, M5V
1J2
(416) 593-0351
Emp Here 100   *Sales* 15,897,600
SIC 7922 Theatrical producers and services
David Mirvish

D-U-N-S 24-976-5236   (SL)
**MOODY'S ANALYTICS GLOBAL EDUCA-
TION (CANADA), INC**
(*Suby of* MOODY'S CORPORATION)
200 Wellington St W, Toronto, ON, M5V 3C7
(416) 364-9130
Emp Here 100   *Sales* 12,012,900
SIC 8299 Schools and educational services,
nec
Mark Almeida
Simon Parmar

D-U-N-S 20-704-0908   (HQ)
NATIONAL BALLET OF CANADA, THE
470 Queens Quay W, Toronto, ON, M5V 3K4
(416) 345-9686
Sales 25,869,810
SIC 7922 Theatrical producers and services
James Kudelka
Kevin Garland

D-U-N-S 24-131-4702   (HQ)
NEWPORT PARTNERS HOLDINGS LP
469 King St W, Toronto, ON, M5V 3M4
(416) 867-7555
Emp Here 1   *Sales* 36,714,258,250
SIC 6722 Management investment, open-end
John Bell

D-U-N-S 20-153-0719   (HQ)
NEWPORT PRIVATE WEALTH INC
469 King St W Suite C, Toronto, ON, M5V 1K4
(416) 867-7555
Sales 13,578,460
SIC 6282 Investment advice
David Lloyd
Mark A. Kenney
Douglas Brown

D-U-N-S 20-425-5707   (HQ)
NIKE CANADA CORP
(*Suby of* NIKE, INC.)
200 Wellington St W, Toronto, ON, M5V 3C7
(416) 581-1585
Emp Here 150   *Sales* 417,180,000
SIC 5091 Sporting and recreation goods
Mark Parker
Maria Montano
John Coburn
Robert Woodruff
Bernard Pliska
Andy Campion
Monique Matheson
Eric Sprunk

D-U-N-S 20-351-4476   (SL)
NOBUL CORPORATION
200 Wellington St W, Toronto, ON, M5V 3C7
(416) 543-3710
Emp Here 60   *Sales* 10,638,660
SIC 7371 Custom computer programming ser-
vices
Regan Mcgee

D-U-N-S 20-337-9474   (SL)
**NORTH AMERICAN FINANCIAL 15 SPLIT
CORP**
200 Front St West Suite 2510, Toronto, ON,
M5V 3K2
(416) 304-4440
Emp Here 5   *Sales* 29,184,625
SIC 6722 Management investment, open-end
S. Wayne Finch
Laura L. Johnson
Peter F. Cruickshank
Silvia Gomes
Michael W Sharp
John D Steep
William C. Thornhill

D-U-N-S 20-378-6673   (SL)
NUCO NETWORKS INC
AION FOUNDATION
129 Spadina Ave Suite 200, Toronto, ON, M5V
2L3
(647) 290-3419
Emp Here 100   *Sales* 17,731,100
SIC 7371 Custom computer programming ser-
vices
Matthew Spoke
Kesem Frank

D-U-N-S 20-391-5827   (SL)
OATH (CANADA) CORP
99 Spadina Ave Suite 200, Toronto, ON, M5V
3P8
(416) 263-8100
Emp Here 120   *Sales* 27,416,640
SIC 4899 Communication services, nec

D-U-N-S 25-398-3845   (BR)
OMNICOM CANADA CORP
PHD CANADA, DIV OF
(*Suby of* OMNICOM GROUP INC.)
96 Spadina Ave 7th Floor, Toronto, ON, M5V
2J6
(416) 922-0217
Emp Here 135
SIC 7319 Advertising, nec
Cam Reston

D-U-N-S 20-515-1967   (SL)
ONEMETHOD INC
225 Wellington St W, Toronto, ON, M5V 3G7
(416) 649-0180
Emp Here 50   *Sales* 11,734,800
SIC 8732 Commercial nonphysical research
Amin Todai

D-U-N-S 20-559-3259   (HQ)
ONTARIO CENTRES OF EXCELLENCE INC
*CENTRE FOR COMMUNICATIONS AND IN-
FORMATION TECHNOLOGY, DIV OF*
325 Front St Suite 300, Toronto, ON, M5V 2Y1
(416) 861-1092
Emp Here 41   *Sales* 81,063,167
SIC 8732 Commercial nonphysical research
Thomas Corr
David Chabot
William Ballios
David Mcfadden
Peter Annan

D-U-N-S 24-816-1614   (HQ)
ONTARIO HOSPITAL ASSOCIATION
OHA
200 Front St W Suite 2800, Toronto, ON, M5V
3L1
(416) 205-1300
Sales 27,828,052
SIC 8742 Management consulting services
Anthony Dale

D-U-N-S 24-350-4128   (SL)
OPENLANE CANADA INC
OPENLANE / ADESA CANADA
(*Suby of* KAR AUCTION SERVICES, INC.)
370 King St W Suite 500, Toronto, ON, M5V
1J9
(416) 861-5777
Emp Here 150   *Sales* 86,587,800
SIC 5521 Used car dealers
Peter Kelly
Rebecca Polak
James P. Hallet
Gary Edelstein
Sheryl Watson

D-U-N-S 20-172-3673   (SL)
OUTDOOR OUTFITS LIMITED
372 Richmond St W Suite 400, Toronto, ON,
M5V 1X6
(416) 598-4111
Emp Here 40   *Sales* 19,932,880
SIC 5136 Men's and boy's clothing

D-U-N-S 24-406-9977   (HQ)
P P I FINANCIAL GROUP (EASTERN) LTD
200 Front St W Suite 2400, Toronto, ON, M5V
3K5
(416) 494-7707
Sales 28,834,040
SIC 6411 Insurance agents, brokers, and ser-
vice
James Burton
Joseph Dickstein
Gary Mcleod

D-U-N-S 20-329-3394   (HQ)
**PENGUIN RANDOM HOUSE CANADA LIM-
ITED**
(*Suby of* BERTELSMANN STIFTUNG)
320 Front St W Suite 1400, Toronto, ON, M5V
3B6
(416) 364-4449
Emp Here 100   *Sales* 25,424,185
SIC 2731 Book publishing
Bradley Martin

Douglas Foot

D-U-N-S 20-078-9316   (SL)
PLANNING ALLIANCE INC
REGIONALARCHITECTS
317 Adelaide St W Suite 205, Toronto, ON,
M5V 1P9
(416) 593-6499
Emp Here 60   *Sales* 10,724,340
SIC 8712 Architectural services
John Van Nostrand
Adrian Dicastri
Peter Clewes
Ralph Bergman
Rudy Wallman
Patricia Hanson

D-U-N-S 24-101-2827   (HQ)
PORTER AIRLINES INC
(*Suby of* PORTER AVIATION HOLDINGS
INC)
4 Toronto Island Airport, Toronto, ON, M5V
1A1
(416) 203-8100
Sales 26,697,800
SIC 4581 Airports, flying fields, and services
Robert Deluce
Michael Deluce
Jeffrey Brown
Kevin Jackson
Paul Moreira

D-U-N-S 24-678-4453   (HQ)
POTENTIA RENEWABLES INC
200 Wellington St W Suite 1102, Toronto, ON,
M5V 3G2
(416) 703-1911
Sales 14,057,280
SIC 8748 Business consulting, nec
Jeff Jenner
Ben Greenhouse
Kirk Lloyd

D-U-N-S 20-228-1783   (SL)
**PREMIERE CONFERENCING (CANADA)
LIMITED**
(*Suby of* SIRIS CAPITAL GROUP, LLC)
225 King St W Suite 900, Toronto, ON, M5V
3M2
(416) 516-5170
Emp Here 75   *Sales* 17,135,400
SIC 4899 Communication services, nec
Frank Cianciulli
Tony Lacavera

D-U-N-S 24-227-0234   (HQ)
PVH CANADA, INC
CALVIN KLEIN
(*Suby of* PVH CORP.)
555 Richmond St W Suite 1106, Toronto, ON,
M5V 3B1
(416) 309-7200
Emp Here 100   *Sales* 418,766,500
SIC 5136 Men's and boy's clothing
Emanuel Chirico
Michael A. Shaffer
Mark D. Fischer
Richard Deck

D-U-N-S 20-355-1957   (HQ)
Q4 INC
A-469 King St W, Toronto, ON, M5V 1K4
(416) 626-7829
Sales 20,855,875
SIC 7374 Data processing and preparation
Darrell Heaps
Adam Frederick
Matt Twydell
Mark Wicks
Ryan Levenberg
Corey Bonkowski
Taryn Shulman
Alex Corotphi

D-U-N-S 20-325-5245   (HQ)
QOC HEALTH INC
436 Wellington St W Unit 601, Toronto, ON,
M5V 1E3

(647) 725-9660
Sales 38,779,839
SIC 6321 Accident and health insurance
Chancellor Crawford
Raymond Shih
John Semple
Sarah Sharpe

D-U-N-S 25-367-3438   (HQ)
QUICKPLAY MEDIA CO
(*Suby of* AT&T INC.)
901 King St W Unit 200, Toronto, ON, M5V
3H5
(416) 586-6200
Sales 18,277,760
SIC 4813 Telephone communication, except
radio
Wayne Purboo
Bruce Bishop
Scott Hamilton
Sanjay Sondhi
Mark Hayland
Samir Ahuja

D-U-N-S 25-719-4316   (HQ)
**QUIZNO'S CANADA RESTAURANT COR-
PORATION**
355 King St W Suite 300, Toronto, ON, M5V
1J6
(647) 259-0333
Sales 34,840,500
SIC 6794 Patent owners and lessors
James Boyd
Steve Sheffer
Patrick Meyers

D-U-N-S 24-121-0462   (HQ)
RBC INVESTOR SERVICES TRUST
(*Suby of* ROYAL BANK OF CANADA)
155 Wellington St W 7 Fl, Toronto, ON, M5V
3H1
(416) 955-6251
Emp Here 100   *Sales* 284,627,600
SIC 6282 Investment advice
Shawn L Murphy
Robert B Bennett
James M Daigle

D-U-N-S 24-027-8275   (HQ)
**RBC PHILLIPS, HAGER & NORTH INVEST-
MENT COUNSEL INC**
(*Suby of* ROYAL BANK OF CANADA)
155 Wellington St W Fl 17, Toronto, ON, M5V
3H1
(416) 956-9618
Emp Here 8   *Sales* 93,917,700
SIC 6211 Security brokers and dealers
Vijay Parmar
Randy Mitchell
Nathalie Gagnon

D-U-N-S 20-361-4966   (BR)
RECIPE UNLIMITED CORPORATION
MILESTONE'S GRILL AND BAR
(*Suby of* RECIPE UNLIMITED CORPORA-
TION)
132 John St, Toronto, ON, M5V 2E3

Emp Here 100
SIC 5812 Eating places
Ian Elgar

D-U-N-S 24-255-6319   (HQ)
RED BULL CANADA LTD
(*Suby of* RED BULL GMBH)
381 Queen St W Suite 200, Toronto, ON, M5V
2A5
(416) 593-1629
Emp Here 1   *Sales* 22,469,850
SIC 2086 Bottled and canned soft drinks
John Hankin
Tim O'hara
Rudolf Theierl

D-U-N-S 20-044-4321   (HQ)
REED ELSEVIER CANADA LTD
(*Suby of* RELX PLC)
555 Richmond St W Suite 1100, Toronto, ON,

M5V 3B1
(416) 253-3640
Sales 14,762,430
SIC 2731 Book publishing
Cathy Thrist

D-U-N-S 20-260-6653   (HQ)
RESOLVER INC
(*Suby of* KLASS CAPITAL CORPORATION)
111 Peter St Suite 804, Toronto, ON, M5V 2H1
(416) 622-2299
Emp Here 105   *Sales* 15,860,020
SIC 7371 Custom computer programming ser-
vices
Will Anderson

D-U-N-S 24-171-6476   (SL)
**RITZ-CARLTON HOTEL COMPANY OF
CANADA LIMITED, THE**
(*Suby of* MARRIOTT INTERNATIONAL, INC.)
181 Wellington St W, Toronto, ON, M5V 3G7
(416) 585-2500
Emp Here 400   *Sales* 38,267,200
SIC 7011 Hotels and motels
Jake Eujack
Tim P Terceira

D-U-N-S 24-392-8368   (SL)
**ROGERS BLUE JAYS BASEBALL PART-
NERSHIP**
TORONTO BLUE JAYS BASEBALL CLUB
1 Blue Jays Way Suite 3200, Toronto, ON,
M5V 1J1
(416) 341-1000
Emp Here 250   *Sales* 20,629,250
SIC 7941 Sports clubs, managers, and pro-
moters
Paul Beeston
Lynda Kolody

D-U-N-S 20-109-0524   (SL)
SAPIENT CANADA INC
(*Suby of* PUBLICIS GROUPE S.A.)
134 Peter St Suite 1200, Toronto, ON, M5V
2H2
(416) 645-1500
Emp Here 130   *Sales* 21,690,110
SIC 7379 Computer related services, nec
Trevor Vandorsser

D-U-N-S 20-278-1787   (SL)
SCORE MEDIA VENTURES INC
SCR
500 King St W, Toronto, ON, M5V 1L9
(416) 479-8812
Emp Here 220   *Sales* 31,720,040
SIC 7371 Custom computer programming ser-
vices
Benjie Levy
John Levy

D-U-N-S 24-356-1979   (SL)
SCORE TELEVISION NETWORK LTD, THE
HEADLINE SPORTS
(*Suby of* SCORE MEDIA INC)
370 King St W Suite 435, Toronto, ON, M5V
1J9
(416) 977-6787
Emp Here 110   *Sales* 25,131,920
SIC 4841 Cable and other pay television ser-
vices
John Levy

D-U-N-S 24-967-4933   (HQ)
SCRIBBLE TECHNOLOGIES INC
SCRIBBLELIVE
49 Spadina Ave Unit 303, Toronto, ON, M5V
2J1
(416) 364-8118
Emp Here 55   *Sales* 13,681,454
SIC 7372 Prepackaged software
Efrem Ainsley

D-U-N-S 20-388-6069   (SL)
SECURITY COMPASS LTD
390 Queens Quay W Suite 209, Toronto, ON,
M5V 3A6

(888) 777-2211
Emp Here 173   *Sales* 24,943,486
SIC 7371 Custom computer programming ser-
vices
Nishchal Bhalla
John Phyper
Brian Horn
Ehsan Foroughi
Krishna Raja
David Rea
Rohit Sethi
Michelle Dizon
Michelle Brooks
Altaz Valani

D-U-N-S 20-804-3112   (SL)
SOLUTIA SDO LTD
30 Duncan St Unit 202, Toronto, ON, M5V 2C3
(416) 204-9797
Emp Here 85   *Sales* 7,697,584
SIC 8742 Management consulting services
Sam D'aurizio
Jackie Clark
Troy Loder
Robert Emer
Frank D'addio

D-U-N-S 20-553-9682   (HQ)
SPIN MASTER CORP
225 King St W Suite 200, Toronto, ON, M5V
3M2
(416) 364-6002
Sales 1,631,537,000
SIC 6712 Bank holding companies
Anton Rabie
Ronnen Harary
Ben Varadi
Ben Gadbois
Mark Segal
Bill Hess
Chris Beardall
Christopher Harrs
Krista Diberardino
Laura Henderson

D-U-N-S 24-985-0363   (HQ)
SPIN MASTER LTD
SPIN MASTER FILM PRODUCTION
(*Suby of* SPIN MASTER CORP)
225 King St W Suite 200, Toronto, ON, M5V
1B6
(416) 364-6002
Emp Here 300   *Sales* 105,827,200
SIC 3944 Games, toys, and children's vehicles
Ronnen Harary
Anton Rabie
Ben Varadi
Chris Beardall

D-U-N-S 25-690-9763   (HQ)
STEAM WHISTLE BREWING INC
255 Bremner Blvd, Toronto, ON, M5V 3M9
(416) 362-2337
Sales 24,198,300
SIC 2082 Malt beverages
Cameron Heaps
Frank Heaps
Greg Taylor
Richard Armstrong
John Craig
Donald Woodley
Adrian Joseph

D-U-N-S 25-862-7942   (SL)
STRATEGY INSTITUTE INC
401 Richmond St W Suite 401, Toronto, ON,
M5V 3A8
(416) 944-9200
Emp Here 25   *Sales* 11,087,250
SIC 7389 Business services, nec
David Laird

D-U-N-S 24-745-6593   (SL)
STRATICOM PLANNING ASSOCIATES INC
(*Suby of* BROOKFIELD ASSET MANAGE-
MENT INC)
366 Adelaide St W, Toronto, ON, M5V 1R9

(416) 362-7407
Emp Here 40   *Sales* 17,968,760
SIC 7389 Business services, nec
  John Khajadourian

    D-U-N-S 25-327-7073   (HQ)
SUPERIOR PLUS CORP
SUPERIOR GAS LIQUIDS
200 Wellington St W Suite 401, Toronto, ON,
M5V 3C7
(416) 345-8050
Sales 2,067,116,723
SIC 2819 Industrial inorganic chemicals, nec
  Luc Desjardins
  Beth Summers
  Darren Hribar
  Shawn Vammen
  John Engelen
  Julien Houle
  Rob Dorran
  Inder Minhas
  Harry Kanwar
  Erin Seaman

    D-U-N-S 24-340-6555   (HQ)
SUPERIOR PLUS LP
SUPERIOR PROPANE
(*Suby of* SUPERIOR PLUS CORP)
200 Wellington St W Suite 401, Toronto, ON,
M5V 3C7
(416) 345-8050
Emp Here 15   *Sales* 174,360,150
SIC 5984 Liquefied petroleum gas dealers
  Grant Billing
  Luc Desjardins
  Darren Hribar
  John Engelen

    D-U-N-S 24-946-8273   (HQ)
SWATCH GROUP (CANADA) LTD, THE
(*Suby of* THE SWATCH GROUP AG)
555 Richmond St W Suite 1105, Toronto, ON,
M5V 3B1
(416) 703-1667
Emp Here 34   *Sales* 31,232,520
SIC 5094 Jewelry and precious stones
  John Maraston

    D-U-N-S 20-121-2094   (HQ)
SYMBILITY SOLUTIONS INC
(*Suby of* CORELOGIC, INC.)
111 Peter St Suite 900, Toronto, ON, M5V 2H1
(647) 775-8601
Emp Here 45   *Sales* 75,484,632
SIC 5045 Computers, peripherals, and software
  James R. Swayze
  Wes Jones
  John Burega
  Blair Baxter
  Marc-Oliver Huyn
  Joel Moreno

    D-U-N-S 24-707-6425   (SL)
T B W A CHIAT/DAY
(*Suby of* OMNICOM GROUP INC.)
10 Lower Spadina Ave, Toronto, ON, M5V 2Z2
(416) 642-1380
Emp Here 93   *Sales* 18,634,503
SIC 7311 Advertising agencies
  Steve Hancock
  David Fong

    D-U-N-S 20-325-6602   (SL)
TARGET PARK GROUP INC
525 King St W Suite 300, Toronto, ON, M5V
1K4
(416) 425-7275
Emp Here 60   *Sales* 16,998,000
SIC 7521 Automobile parking
  Hercules Modopoulos
  Chris Mckay

    D-U-N-S 24-760-3298   (HQ)
TAXI CANADA LTD
(*Suby of* WPP PLC)
495 Wellington St W Suite 102, Toronto, ON,
M5V 1E9

(416) 342-8294
Emp Here 140   *Sales* 76,880,025
SIC 7311 Advertising agencies
  Robert Guenette
  Paul Lavoie
  Nancy Beattie
  Ronald Wilson
  Andrew Packwood

    D-U-N-S 20-256-7426   (SL)
THE&PARTNERSHIP INC
(*Suby of* WPP PLC)
99 Spadina Ave Unit 100, Toronto, ON, M5V
3P8
(647) 252-6801
Emp Here 50   *Sales* 13,716,600
SIC 8741 Management services
  Andrew Bailey
  Christopher Andrews
  Victoria Davies

    D-U-N-S 20-305-2840   (SL)
THESCORE INC
500 King St W 4th Fl, Toronto, ON, M5V 1L9
(416) 479-8812
Emp Here 9   *Sales* 21,026,257
SIC 7372 Prepackaged software
  John Levy
  Benjie Levy
  Ethan Ross
  Sally Farrell
  Joe Ross
  Tom Hearne
  John Albright
  Ralph Lean
  Lorry Schneider

    D-U-N-S 25-507-6176   (HQ)
TICKETMASTER CANADA HOLDINGS ULC
(*Suby of* LIVE NATION ENTERTAINMENT,
INC.)
1 Blue Jays Way Suite 3900, Toronto, ON,
M5V 1J3
(416) 345-9200
Emp Here 1   *Sales* 270,476,660
SIC 6712 Bank holding companies

    D-U-N-S 24-523-3874   (HQ)
TICKETMASTER CANADA LP
TICKETMASTER
(*Suby of* LIVE NATION ENTERTAINMENT,
INC.)
1 Blue Jays Way Suite 3900, Toronto, ON,
M5V 1J3
(416) 345-9200
Emp Here 100   *Sales* 64,158,000
SIC 7999 Amusement and recreation, nec
  Thomas Worrall

    D-U-N-S 24-793-3146   (SL)
TORONTO IMAGE WORKS LIMITED
80 Spadina Ave Suite 207, Toronto, ON, M5V
2J4
(416) 703-1999
Emp Here 35   *Sales* 14,612,710
SIC 7384 Photofinish laboratories
  Ed Burtynsky
  Jeannie Baxter

    D-U-N-S 20-983-8648   (SL)
**TORONTO INTERNATIONAL FILM FESTI-
VAL INC**
FILM CIRCUIT, DIV OF
350 King St W Suite 477, Toronto, ON, M5V
3X5
(416) 967-7371
Emp Here 60   *Sales* 42,552,720
SIC 8699 Membership organizations, nec
  Michele Maheux
  Allen Karp

    D-U-N-S 24-385-2378   (BR)
TORSTAR CORPORATION
TORSTAR
(*Suby of* TORSTAR CORPORATION)
590 King St W Suite 400, Toronto, ON, M5V
1M3

Emp Here 200

SIC 2752 Commercial printing, lithographic
  Eduardo Mandri

    D-U-N-S 20-351-4013   (SL)
TRADEGECKO SOFTWARE CANADA LTD
409 King St W Suite 201, Toronto, ON, M5V
1K1
(647) 621-5456
Emp Here 90   *Sales* 21,085,920
SIC 8742 Management consulting services
  Cameron Priest
  Nathalie Benzing
  Bradley Priest

    D-U-N-S 24-952-6141   (SL)
UKEN STUDIOS INC
UKEN GAME
266 King St W 2nd Fl, Toronto, ON, M5V 1H8
(416) 616-8901
Emp Here 80   *Sales* 17,108,080
SIC 7372 Prepackaged software
  Chris Ye
  Mark Lampert

    D-U-N-S 20-295-5324   (SL)
UNATA INC
504 Wellington St W Suite 200, Toronto, ON,
M5V 1E3
(416) 305-9977
Emp Here 90   *Sales* 26,412,930
SIC 5411 Grocery stores
  Christopher Bryson

    D-U-N-S 20-527-9537   (SL)
UNION ADVERTISING CANADA LP
UNION CREATIVE
(*Suby of* MDC PARTNERS INC.)
479 Wellington St W, Toronto, ON, M5V 1E7
(416) 598-4944
Emp Here 100   *Sales* 20,037,100
SIC 7311 Advertising agencies
  Subtej Nijjar
  Lance Martin
  Martin Belanger
  Boni Griffith

    D-U-N-S 24-120-6544   (BR)
UNITED PARCEL SERVICE CANADA LTD
UPS
(*Suby of* UNITED PARCEL SERVICE, INC.)
12 Mercer St, Toronto, ON, M5V 1H3

Emp Here 80
SIC 4513 Air courier services
  Larry Sutton

    D-U-N-S 24-812-0565   (SL)
UTOURS INC
345 Adelaide St W Suite 400, Toronto, ON,
M5V 1R5
(416) 479-3972
Emp Here 65   *Sales* 15,228,720
SIC 8742 Management consulting services
  David Diamond

    D-U-N-S 25-726-6536   (HQ)
VALTECH DIGITAL CANADA INC
(*Suby of* VALTECH SOLUTIONS, INC.)
49 Spadina Ave Suite 205, Toronto, ON, M5V
2J1
(416) 203-2997
Emp Here 75   *Sales* 13,347,760
SIC 7374 Data processing and preparation
  Shannon Ryan
  Randolph Woods
  Daniel Roberge

    D-U-N-S 20-300-1763   (SL)
VANGUARD FTSE CANADA INDEX ETF
155 Wellington St W Suite 3720, Toronto, ON,
M5V 3H1
(888) 293-6728
Emp Here 10   *Sales* 58,369,250
SIC 6722 Management investment, open-end
  Atul Tiwari

    D-U-N-S 20-305-2832   (SL)
VANGUARD FTSE DEVELOPED EX NORTH

AMERICA INDEX ETF
155 Wellington St W Suite 3720, Toronto, ON,
M5V 3H1
(888) 293-6728
Emp Here 17   *Sales* 99,227,725
SIC 6726 Investment offices, nec
  Atul Tiwari

    D-U-N-S 20-310-8592   (SL)
VANGUARD INVESTMENTS CANADA INC.
155 Wellington St W Suite 3720, Toronto, ON,
M5V 3H1
(416) 263-7100
Emp Here 49   *Sales* 33,267,227
SIC 6282 Investment advice
  Atul Tiwari

    D-U-N-S 20-696-9706   (SL)
VEREQUEST INCORPORATED
370 Queens Quay W Suite 301, Toronto, ON,
M5V 3J3
(416) 362-6777
Emp Here 50   *Sales* 11,714,400
SIC 8742 Management consulting services
  Sharon Oatway

    D-U-N-S 25-282-1525   (SL)
VERITAS COMMUNICATIONS INC
(*Suby of* MDC PARTNERS INC.)
370 King St W Suite 800, Toronto, ON, M5V
1J9
(416) 482-2248
Emp Here 60   *Sales* 15,209,400
SIC 8748 Business consulting, nec
  Krista Webster

    D-U-N-S 25-978-1151   (SL)
VISION GROUP OF COMPANIES LTD, THE
HOCKEY HOUSE 2010
99 Blue Jays Way Suite 300, Toronto, ON,
M5V 9G9
(416) 341-2474
Emp Here 30   *Sales* 15,599,010
SIC 4725 Tour operators
  Jordan Bitove

    D-U-N-S 20-163-6099   (HQ)
**WALT DISNEY COMPANY (CANADA) LTD,
THE**
BUENA VISTA TELEVISION DISTRIBUTION
(*Suby of* THE WALT DISNEY COMPANY)
200 Front St W Suite 2900, Toronto, ON, M5V
3L4
(416) 596-7000
Emp Here 20   *Sales* 82,595,520
SIC 6794 Patent owners and lessors
  Susan Patterson
  Peter Noonan

    D-U-N-S 20-113-5337   (HQ)
WATT INTERNATIONAL INC
590 King St W Suite 300, Toronto, ON, M5V
1M3
(416) 364-9384
Emp Here 1   *Sales* 22,460,950
SIC 7389 Business services, nec
  Vince Guzzi
  Mike Grace
  Genovese Geoffrey

    D-U-N-S 24-330-8983   (SL)
WELLINGTON WINDSOR HOLDINGS LTD
*RESIDENCE INN TORONTO DOWN-
TOWN/ENTERTAINMENT DISTRICT*
255 Wellington St W, Toronto, ON, M5V 3P9
(416) 581-1800
Emp Here 75   *Sales* 7,117,425
SIC 7011 Hotels and motels
  Steve Gupta

    D-U-N-S 24-171-9058   (SL)
WEYLAND, LAURA PHARMACY LTD
SHOPPERS DRUG MART
388 King St W Suite 1320, Toronto, ON, M5V
1K2
(416) 597-6550
Emp Here 50   *Sales* 12,647,700
SIC 5912 Drug stores and proprietary stores

Laura Weyland

D-U-N-S 20-184-8111   (SL)
WHITE CLARKE NORTH AMERICA INC
(*Suby of* WHITE CLARKE & PARTNERS LIMITED)
901 King St W Suite 202, Toronto, ON, M5V 3H5
(416) 467-1900
Emp Here 60   *Sales* 15,209,400
SIC 8748 Business consulting, nec
Debbie Carroll
Dara Clarke
Edward White

D-U-N-S 20-851-1659   (HQ)
WORKPLACE SAFETY & INSURANCE BOARD, THE
WSIB
200 Front St W Suite 101, Toronto, ON, M5V 3J1
(416) 344-1000
Emp Here 2,500   *Sales* 9,381,289,520
SIC 6331 Fire, marine, and casualty insurance
Thomas Teahen
Pamela Steer

D-U-N-S 25-166-6319   (SL)
WORLD TRAVEL PROTECTION CANADA INC
WORLD TRAVEL PROTECTION
(*Suby of* ZURICH INSURANCE GROUP AG)
901 King St W Suite 300, Toronto, ON, M5V 3H5
(416) 205-4618
Emp Here 70   *Sales* 129,341,940
SIC 6411 Insurance agents, brokers, and service
Will Mcaleer
Grace Patenall
Mark Panturescu

D-U-N-S 20-587-0061   (HQ)
WORLD WILDLIFE FUND CANADA
WWF - CANADA
410 Adelaide St W Suite 400, Toronto, ON, M5V 1S8
(416) 489-8800
Emp Here 83   *Sales* 18,852,932
SIC 8699 Membership organizations, nec
Megan Leslie
David Martin
Anne Giardini
Anne-Marie Boucher
Bruce Poon Tip
Eriel Deranger
James Biggar
John Fitzpatrick
Lloyd Bryant
Marilyn De Mara

D-U-N-S 24-752-9456   (HQ)
YOUNG & RUBICAM GROUP OF COMPANIES ULC, THE
(*Suby of* WPP PLC)
495 Wellington St W Suite 102, Toronto, ON, M5V 1E9

Emp Here 145   *Sales* 30,055,650
SIC 7311 Advertising agencies
Chris Jordan

D-U-N-S 20-650-5435   (HQ)
ZAYO CANADA INC
ALLSTREAM
(*Suby of* ZAYO GROUP HOLDINGS, INC.)
200 Wellington St W Suite 800, Toronto, ON, M5V 3C7
(416) 363-4444
Emp Here 120   *Sales* 811,603,744
SIC 4899 Communication services, nec
Dan Caruso
Jack Waters
Brad Korch
John Sandoval
Matt Steinfort

D-U-N-S 20-771-1607   (HQ)

ZEIDLER PARTNERSHIP ARCHITECTS
315 Queen St W Unit 200, Toronto, ON, M5V 2X2
(416) 596-8300
Emp Here 95   *Sales* 35,483,580
SIC 8712 Architectural services
Vaidila Banelis
Andrea Richardson
Stephen Carruthers
Eberhard H Zeidler
Alan Munn
Tarek Elkhatib
Francise Kwok
Gerald Stein
Jurgen Henze
Donald (Don) Vetere

Toronto, ON M5W

D-U-N-S 25-528-9548   (SL)
LABRADOR IRON ORE ROYALTY CORPORATION
40 King St W, Toronto, ON, M5W 2X6
(416) 863-7133
Emp Here 2,620   *Sales* 99,216,599
SIC 6211 Security brokers and dealers
John F. Tuer
William H. Mcneil
Robert O. Hansen
James C. Mccartney
Sandra L. Rosch
Alan R. Thomas
Wiiliam J. Corcoran
Mark J. Fuller
Patricia M. Volker

D-U-N-S 24-326-3808   (SL)
SCITI TRUST
40 King St W, Toronto, ON, M5W 2X6
(416) 863-7411
Emp Here 6   *Sales* 35,021,550
SIC 6722 Management investment, open-end
Brian Mcchesney
Stephen D. Pearce
Robert Hall
Robert Williams
John Newman
Stephens Lowden
J. Nicholas Ross

Toronto, ON M5X

D-U-N-S 24-336-8375   (HQ)
4384768 CANADA INC
100 King St W Suite 6600, Toronto, ON, M5X 2A1
(905) 624-7337
Emp Here 2   *Sales* 110,383,718
SIC 6712 Bank holding companies
Darren Throop
Peter Pigott
Patrice Theroux
Giles Willits

D-U-N-S 20-321-5918   (BR)
AIMIA INC
(*Suby of* AIMIA INC)
130 King St W Suite 1600, Toronto, ON, M5X 2A2
(905) 214-8699
Emp Here 200
SIC 8743 Public relations services
Dorin Brebeanu

D-U-N-S 24-685-8042   (SL)
AIMIA PROPRIETARY LOYALTY CANADA INC
(*Suby of* AIMIA INC)
130 King St W Suite 1600, Toronto, ON, M5X 2A2

(905) 214-8699
Emp Here 200   *Sales* 37,301,200
SIC 8743 Public relations services
Georgia Couvavas
Edouard Vo-Quang
Steven Leonard
Mark Grafton

D-U-N-S 24-761-6159   (HQ)
ALMONTY INDUSTRIES INC
100 King St W Suite 5700, Toronto, ON, M5X 1C7.
(647) 438-9766
Emp Here 20   *Sales* 49,889,248
SIC 1061 Ferroalloy ores, except vanadium
Lewis Black
Marion Mcgrath
Mark Gelmon
Daniel D'amato
Mark Trachuk
Thomas Gutschlag
Michael Costa

D-U-N-S 25-977-5252   (HQ)
ARGONAUT GOLD INC
1 First Canadian Place Suite 3400, Toronto, ON, M5X 1A4

Sales 144,780,000
SIC 1081 Metal mining services
Peter Dougherty
David Ponczoch
William Zisch
W. Robert Rose
Daniel Symons
James Kofman
Ian Atkinson
Christopher Lattanzi
Peter Mordaunt
Dale Peniuk

D-U-N-S 25-416-1573   (HQ)
ATLANTA GOLD INC
100 King St W Suite 5600, Toronto, ON, M5X 1C9
(416) 777-0013
Sales 11,937,745
SIC 1041 Gold ores
Allan J. Folk
Manabu Kameda
Marz Kord

D-U-N-S 25-996-5796   (HQ)
BANK OF MONTREAL HOLDING INC
(*Suby of* BANK OF MONTREAL)
100 King St W 21st Floor, Toronto, ON, M5X 1A1
(416) 359-5003
Sales 1,423,138,000
SIC 6211 Security brokers and dealers
Chris Hughes
Olaf Sheikh
Bernadette Murphy

D-U-N-S 20-708-7342   (BR)
BANQUE NATIONALE DU CANADA
(*Suby of* BANQUE NATIONALE DU CANADA)
130 King St W Suite 3200, Toronto, ON, M5X 2A2
(647) 252-5380
Emp Here 100
SIC 6021 National commercial banks

D-U-N-S 25-254-7559   (HQ)
BANRO CORPORATION
100 King St W Suite 7070, Toronto, ON, M5X 2A1
(416) 366-2221
Sales 228,346,000
SIC 1041 Gold ores
John Clarke
Donat Madilo
Arnold T Kondrat
Desire Sangara
David C Langille
Geoffrey G Farr
Daniel K Madilo

Richard Brissenden
Peter Cowley
Derrick Weyrauch

D-U-N-S 20-329-7478   (SL)
BANRO INVESTMENT SOLUTIONS CORP
100 King St W Unit 5602, Toronto, ON, M5X 2A2
(416) 948-5271
Emp Here 29   *Sales* 20,019,908
SIC 6282 Investment advice
Steve White

D-U-N-S 24-511-5436   (BR)
BENNETT JONES LLP
(*Suby of* BENNETT JONES LLP)
3400 One First Canadian Pl, Toronto, ON, M5X 1A4
(416) 863-1200
Emp Here 176
SIC 8111 Legal services
Stephen Bowman

D-U-N-S 24-366-8936   (SL)
BMO ASSET MANAGEMENT INC
(*Suby of* BMO NESBITT BURNS INC)
100 King St W 43rd Floor, Toronto, ON, M5X 1A1
(416) 359-5000
Emp Here 35   *Sales* 32,871,195
SIC 6282 Investment advice
Kevin Gopaul
Barry Merritt Cooper
Stella Vranes
Ben Iraya
Nelson Avila
Thomas Burian
Richard Wilson
Joan Z. Mohammed

D-U-N-S 25-537-2534   (HQ)
BMO INVESTMENTS INC
BMO FONDS D'INVESTISSEMENT
(*Suby of* BANK OF MONTREAL)
100 King St W 43rd Floor, Toronto, ON, M5X 1A1
(416) 359-5003
Sales 723,778,700
SIC 6722 Management investment, open-end
Kevin Gopaul
Barry M. Cooper
Ross F. Kappele
Penelope Muradya
Joan Z. Mohammed
Viki Lazaris
Thomas Burian
Robert Schaufer

D-U-N-S 24-828-1800   (HQ)
BMO INVESTORLINE INC
(*Suby of* BANK OF MONTREAL)
100 King St W 21st Floor, Toronto, ON, M5X 2A1
(416) 867-6300
Emp Here 150   *Sales* 426,941,400
SIC 6211 Security brokers and dealers
Susan M. Payne
Viki Lazaris
Robertson Lucas Seabrook
Silvio Stroescu

D-U-N-S 24-018-9076   (HQ)
BMO NESBITT BURNS INC
BMO CAPITAL MARKETS
100 King St W Unit 1, Toronto, ON, M5X 2A1
(416) 643-1778
Emp Here 800   *Sales* 5,938,754,874
SIC 6211 Security brokers and dealers
Tim Churchill-Smith
Patrick C. Forrest
Dave L. Foraie
Gregory M. Sternig
Jeff A. Katzin
Michael Dorfman

D-U-N-S 20-002-6545   (BR)
BMO NESBITT BURNS INC
(*Suby of* BMO NESBITT BURNS INC)

---

100 King St W Fl 38, Toronto, ON, M5X 1H3
(416) 365-6029
Emp Here 80
SIC 6211 Security brokers and dealers
 Jason Kahng

D-U-N-S 24-311-4126   (BR)
BMO NESBITT BURNS INC
BANK OF MONTREAL SECURITIES CANADA
(*Suby of* BMO NESBITT BURNS INC)
1 First Canadian Pl 21st Fl, Toronto, ON, M5X 1H3
(416) 359-4000
Emp Here 3,000
SIC 6211 Security brokers and dealers
 Thomas Milroy

D-U-N-S 25-096-4855   (HQ)
BMO PRIVATE INVESTMENT COUNSEL INC
(*Suby of* BMO NESBITT BURNS INC)
100 King St W, Toronto, ON, M5X 1H3
(416) 359-5001
Emp Here 150   *Sales* 284,627,600
SIC 6211 Security brokers and dealers
 Barry Cooper

D-U-N-S 24-131-0445   (SL)
CANADIAN SCIENCE AND TECHNOLOGY GROWTH FUND INC
130 King St W Suite 2200, Toronto, ON, M5X 2A2
Emp Here 29   *Sales* 21,270,108
SIC 6722 Management investment, open-end
 Joanne Breseiani

D-U-N-S 20-368-8721   (SL)
CAPCO
100 King St W Suite 5010, Toronto, ON, M5X 1C7
(416) 923-4570
Emp Here 45   *Sales* 10,542,960
SIC 8742 Management consulting services
 Lance Levy

D-U-N-S 25-114-7377   (HQ)
CARTHOS SERVICES LP
1 1st Canadian Pl, Toronto, ON, M5X 1B8
(416) 362-2111
Emp Here 400   *Sales* 67,321,800
SIC 8741 Management services
 Kenneth Whiteside

D-U-N-S 24-250-2396   (SL)
CHES SPECIAL RISK INC
130 King St W 19th Fl, Toronto, ON, M5X 1C9
(647) 480-1515
Emp Here 30   *Sales* 17,397,720
SIC 6411 Insurance agents, brokers, and service
 Doug Everett

D-U-N-S 24-385-2568   (HQ)
CLAIRE'S STORES CANADA CORP
(*Suby of* CLAIRE'S INC.)
100 King St W Suite 6600, Toronto, ON, M5X 2A1
(800) 252-4737
Emp Here 1   *Sales* 87,328,500
SIC 5632 Women's accessory and specialty stores
 Eugene S Khan
 Karen Newberry
 Per Brodin

D-U-N-S 25-370-0215   (HQ)
CNSX MARKETS INC
CANADIAN SECURITIES EXCHANGE
100 King St W Suite 7210, Toronto, ON, M5X 1E1
(416) 572-2000
Emp Here 25   *Sales* 15,936,210
SIC 6231 Security and commodity exchanges
 Richard Carleton
 Robert Cook
 Pina De Santis

 Mark Faulkner
 David Timpany
 James Black
 Jamie Anderson
 Adam Conyers

D-U-N-S 24-364-9014   (SL)
COLOSSUS MINERALS INC
100 King St W Suite 5600, Toronto, ON, M5X 1C9

Emp Here 43   *Sales* 10,037,705
SIC 1041 Gold ores
 Claudio Mancuso
 John Frostiak
 David Anthony
 Tom Bruington
 Lesley Duncan
 Jason Brooks
 Luis Albano Tondo
 Graham Long
 Ann Wilkinson
 Alden Greenhouse

D-U-N-S 20-358-3612   (HQ)
CONNOR CLARK & LUNN PRIVATE CAPITAL LTD
130 King St W Unit 1400, Toronto, ON, M5X 2A2
(416) 214-6325
Emp Here 50   *Sales* 875,538,750
SIC 6722 Management investment, open-end
 Michael Freund
 Tim Griffith
 Patrick Robitaillie
 Steve Affleck
 Lindsay Holtz
 Michael Walsh

D-U-N-S 20-374-0811   (SL)
CONNOR, CLARK & LUNN WHOLESALE FINANCE INC
130 King Street W Suite 1400, Toronto, ON, M5X 1C8
(416) 862-2020
Emp Here 130   *Sales* 187,150,685
SIC 6211 Security brokers and dealers

D-U-N-S 20-360-2946   (SL)
CPT GLOBAL CONSULTING CORPORATION
100 King St W Suite 5600, Toronto, ON, M5X 1C9
(416) 642-2886
Emp Here 49   *Sales* 11,792,161
SIC 8742 Management consulting services
 Gerard Francis Tuddenham

D-U-N-S 20-195-2632   (HQ)
CREDIT SUISSE SECURITIES (CANADA) INC
(*Suby of* CREDIT SUISSE GROUP AG)
1 First Canadian Pl Suite 2900, Toronto, ON, M5X 1C9
(416) 352-4500
Emp Here 150   *Sales* 213,470,700
SIC 6211 Security brokers and dealers
 Ronald Lloyd
 Andrew Stewart

D-U-N-S 20-300-3603   (HQ)
CRIUS ENERGY TRUST
100 King St W Suite 3400, Toronto, ON, M5X 1A4
(416) 644-1753
Emp Here 8   *Sales* 1,235,112,000
SIC 4924 Natural gas distribution
 Michael Fallquist
 Marcie C. Zlotnik
 Daniel Sullivan
 Robert Huggard
 Ali Hedayat
 Robert Gries
 Brian Burden
 James A. Ajello
 Barbara Clay
 Roop S. Bhullar

D-U-N-S 24-119-6356   (BR)
DAVIS MANAGEMENT LTD
(*Suby of* DAVIS MANAGEMENT LTD)
100 King St W Unit 60, Toronto, ON, M5X 2A1
(416) 365-3500
Emp Here 130
SIC 8111 Legal services
 Elizabeth Armstrong

D-U-N-S 24-971-8839   (SL)
DEEPAK INTERNATIONAL LTD
1 First Canadian Pl Unit 6000, Toronto, ON, M5X 1B5

Emp Here 37   *Sales* 101,862,619
SIC 3915 Jewelers' materials and lapidary work
 Deepak Kumar

D-U-N-S 24-985-9109   (SL)
DOLCE INTERNATIONAL (ONTARIO) CO.
IVEY TANGERINE LEADERSHIP CENTRE
(*Suby of* WYNDHAM HOTELS & RESORTS, INC.)
130 King St W, Toronto, ON, M5X 2A2
(416) 861-9600
Emp Here 120   *Sales* 16,279,200
SIC 8299 Schools and educational services, nec
 Lu Lu Pucl

D-U-N-S 20-052-5694   (SL)
EDGESTONE CAPITAL EQUITY PARTNERS INC
(*Suby of* EDGESTONE CAPITAL GP HOLDCO INC)
130 King St W Suite 600, Toronto, ON, M5X 2A2
(416) 860-3740
Emp Here 33   *Sales* 48,644,013
SIC 6722 Management investment, open-end
 Samuel L. Duboc
 Gilbert S. Palter
 Bryan Kerdman

D-U-N-S 20-200-9093   (SL)
EVEREST INSURANCE COMPANY OF CANADA
PREMIERE INSURANCE
(*Suby of* EVEREST RE GROUP, LTD.)
130 King St W Suite 2520, Toronto, ON, M5X 2A2
(416) 487-3900
Emp Here 25   *Sales* 46,193,550
SIC 6411 Insurance agents, brokers, and service
 Mark Teitelbaum

D-U-N-S 20-385-5262   (SL)
FIRST GENERAL ENTERPRISES (ONTARIO) LTD
130 King St Suite 1800, Toronto, ON, M5X 1E3
(416) 665-6680
Emp Here 100   *Sales* 25,032,655
SIC 1799 Special trade contractors, nec
 Frank Mirabelli
 Randy Millar
 Charles Sabourin

D-U-N-S 20-300-7646   (SL)
FLEXITI FINANCIAL INC
FLEXITI FINANCIAL
130 King St W Suite 1740, Toronto, ON, M5X 1E1
(416) 583-1860
Emp Here 150   *Sales* 79,300,500
SIC 6163 Loan brokers
 Peter Kalen
 Joe Prodan
 Jerome Peeters
 Geoffrey Browne
 Barry Pickford
 Paul Smith
 Martin Parizeau

D-U-N-S 20-171-8269   (HQ)
GLENCORE CANADA CORPORATION

MINE RAGLAN
(*Suby of* GLENCORE PLC)
100 King St W Suite 6900, Toronto, ON, M5X 2A1
(416) 775-1200
Emp Here 350   *Sales* 3,452,949,000
SIC 1021 Copper ores
 William M Aniley
 Benny S Levene
 Stephen K Young
 Douglas W Knight
 James D Wallace

D-U-N-S 20-015-6003   (BR)
GOWLING WLG (CANADA) LLP
(*Suby of* GOWLING WLG (CANADA) LLP)
1 First Canadian Pl 100 King St W Suite 1600, Toronto, ON, M5X 1G5
(416) 862-7525
Emp Here 524
SIC 8111 Legal services
 Karyn Bradley

D-U-N-S 20-896-7484   (SL)
GROWTHWORKS CAPITAL LTD
130 King St W Suite 2200, Toronto, ON, M5X 2A2

Emp Here 100   *Sales* 27,433,200
SIC 8741 Management services
 Timothy Lee

D-U-N-S 20-255-8201   (SL)
HEALTHCARE SPECIAL OPPURTUNITIES FUND
130 King St W Suite 2130, Toronto, ON, M5X 2A2
(416) 362-4141
Emp Here 10   *Sales* 14,740,610
SIC 6722 Management investment, open-end
 Michael B. Decter
 Beryl Mccallum
 Andrew Pink
 Marc Robinson
 Ron E Bailey
 Graham Scott

D-U-N-S 20-378-0937   (SL)
IFG - INTERNATIONAL FINANCIAL GROUP (US) LTD
100 King St W Suite 910, Toronto, ON, M5X 1B1
(416) 645-2434
Emp Here 1,200   *Sales* 91,140,315
SIC 7361 Employment agencies
 Joseph Taylor
 Greg Currie
 Scott Hargreaves

D-U-N-S 24-523-0672   (SL)
IFG - INTERNATIONAL FINANCIAL GROUP LTD
100 King St W Suite 910, Toronto, ON, M5X 1B1
(416) 645-2434
Emp Here 110   *Sales* 22,845,350
SIC 8721 Accounting, auditing, and bookkeeping
 Joe Taylor
 Raffi Toughlouian
 Tracy Macintyre
 Ken Sugar
 Greg Currie
 Gary Fogelman
 Jason Plosz
 Scott Allen
 Kelly Mcfeeters
 Bruce Jardine

D-U-N-S 24-391-9300   (HQ)
INTERPUBLIC GROUP OF COMPANIES CANADA, INC, THE
FCB CANADA
(*Suby of* THE INTERPUBLIC GROUP OF COMPANIES INC)
100 King St W Suite 6200, Toronto, ON, M5X 1B8

(416) 545-5563
Emp Here 5   Sales 67,869,300
SIC 7336 Commercial art and graphic design
Tyler Turnbull
Monica Hofmann
Andrew Bonzoni
Francisco Quiroga
Asad Husain

D-U-N-S 20-304-5869   (HQ)
JAGUAR MINING INC
100 King St W 56th Fl, Toronto, ON, M5X 1C9
(416) 847-1854
Sales 94,918,000
SIC 1041 Gold ores
Benjamin Guenther
Thomas S. Weng
Kevin Weston
Richard Falconer
Edward Reeser
Luis Ricardo Miraglia
Robert Getz
Jonathan (Jon) Victor Hill
Jean-Marc Lopez
Hashim Ahmed

D-U-N-S 25-536-4044   (SL)
KARMIN EXPLORATION INC
100 King St W Suite 5700, Toronto, ON, M5X 1C7
(416) 367-0369
Emp Here 100   Sales 238,754,900
SIC 1081 Metal mining services
David Brace
John A Iannozzi
Larry Ciccarelli
Richard Faucher
Terence Ortslan
Luis Rodrguez Maritegui Canny

D-U-N-S 20-460-4248   (SL)
KS CIRCUITS INC
100 King St W Suite 5600, Toronto, ON, M5X 1C9
(416) 913-5438
Emp Here 150   Sales 34,463,100
SIC 8731 Commercial physical research
Kajenbran Selvachandiran

D-U-N-S 25-100-2093   (SL)
LARAMIDE RESOURCES LTD
130 King St W Suite 3680, Toronto, ON, M5X 2A2
(416) 599-7363
Emp Here 10   Sales 23,875,490
SIC 1081 Metal mining services
Marc Henderson
John Booth
Greg Ferron
Chris Irwin
Raffi Babikian
Scott Patterson
Paul Wilkens
Dennis Gibson
Bryn Jones

D-U-N-S 24-372-0567   (SL)
LONCOR RESOURCES INC
100 King St W Suite 7070, Toronto, ON, M5X 2A1
(416) 361-2510
Emp Here 79   Sales 188,616,371
SIC 1041 Gold ores
Arnold T. Kondrat
Donat Madilo
William R. Wilson
Richard J. Lachcik

D-U-N-S 24-131-9685   (SL)
MAVRIX GLOBAL FUND INC
MATRIX
130 King St W Suite 2200, Toronto, ON, M5X 2A2
(416) 362-3077
Emp Here 24   Sales 17,602,848
SIC 6722 Management investment, open-end
David Levi

D-U-N-S 25-194-9723   (SL)
MCCAGUE BORLACK LLP
130 King St W Suite 2700, Toronto, ON, M5X 2A2
(416) 860-0001
Emp Here 180   Sales 19,958,760
SIC 8111 Legal services
Paul Mccague
Howard Borlack
Doug Mcinnis

D-U-N-S 25-213-9787   (HQ)
MFL MANAGEMENT LIMITED
100 King St W, Toronto, ON, M5X 2A1
(416) 362-0714
Sales 12,316,755
SIC 6159 Miscellaneous business credit institutions
Murray Brasseur
Garth Jestley
Sylvia Stinnson
Dennis Dunlop
Shelagh White

D-U-N-S 24-537-3345   (HQ)
MIDDLEFIELD GROUP LIMITED
100 King St W Suite 5855, Toronto, ON, M5X 2A1
(416) 362-0714
Sales 24,601,500
SIC 6719 Holding companies, nec
Garth Jestley
Anthony Traub
James Parsons
Sylvia Stinson

D-U-N-S 20-388-2881   (SL)
MULTIPLEX CANADA HSP HOLDINGS LIMITED
130 King St W Suite 2350, Toronto, ON, M5X 2A2
(416) 359-8559
Emp Here 50   Sales 14,164,650
SIC 8741 Management services
John Flecker
Steve Crosby
Ashley Muldoon
Ralph Tulipano

D-U-N-S 20-281-5361   (SL)
MULTIPLEX CONSTRUCTION CANADA LIMITED
(Suby of MULTIPLEX CANADA HOLDINGS LIMITED)
130 King St W Suite 2350, Toronto, ON, M5X 2A2
(416) 359-8559
Emp Here 90   Sales 11,229,840
SIC 8741 Management services
John Flecker
Ashley Muldoon
Hamish Pryor
Steven Crosby
Derek Gorgi
Pankaj Sayal

D-U-N-S 20-379-5724   (SL)
NBF INC
NATIONAL BANK INDEPENDENT NETWORK
(Suby of FINANCIERE BANQUE NATIONALE INC)
130 King St W Suite 3000, Toronto, ON, M5X 1J9
(416) 869-3707
Emp Here 225   Sales 1,313,308,125
SIC 6722 Management investment, open-end
Patrick Primerano
Martin Gagnon

D-U-N-S 20-309-7647   (SL)
NEWS MARKETING CANADA CORP
(Suby of NEWS CORPORATION)
100 King St W Suite 7000, Toronto, ON, M5X 1A4
(416) 775-3000
Emp Here 50   Sales 11,714,400

SIC 8743 Public relations services
Omar El Kady
William Vanderburg
Chris Mixson
Adam North

D-U-N-S 20-122-7332   (HQ)
NORANDA INCOME FUND
100 King St W Suite 6900, Toronto, ON, M5X 2A1
(416) 775-1500
Sales 931,298,000
SIC 6722 Management investment, open-end
Eva Carissimi
Paul Einarson
Jean Pierre Ouellet
Chris Eskdale
Yihua Xiao
Francois Roy
Anthony Lloyd
Barry Tissenbaum
Dirk Vollrath
Ken Klassen

D-U-N-S 20-365-3753   (HQ)
ONE10 CANADA HOLDINGS ULC
(Suby of ONE10 LLC)
130 King St W Suite 1600, Toronto, ON, M5X 2A2
(905) 214-8699
Sales 13,716,600
SIC 8741 Management services
Robert Miller

D-U-N-S 20-876-1908   (HQ)
OSLER, HOSKIN & HARCOURT LLP
100 King St W Suite 4600 First Canadian Place, Toronto, ON, M5X 1B8
(416) 362-2111
Emp Here 700   Sales 226,463,600
SIC 8111 Legal services
Brian Levitt
Kimberly Wharram
Craig Fields

D-U-N-S 20-271-8508   (HQ)
RESTAURANT BRANDS INTERNATIONAL INC
POPEYES
130 King St W Suite 300, Toronto, ON, M5X 1E1
(905) 339-5724
Emp Here 100   Sales 5,357,000,000
SIC 5812 Eating places
Alex Macedo
Jill Granat
Matthew Dunnigan
Joshua Kobza
Jose E. Cil
Daniel Schwartz
Alexandre Behring
Marcello Caira
Joao Mauricio Giffoni De Castro Neves
Martin E. Franklin

D-U-N-S 24-688-6089   (SL)
RUSSELL INVESTMENTS CANADA LIMITED
(Suby of THE NORTHWESTERN MUTUAL LIFE INSURANCE COMPANY)
100 King St W Suite 5900, Toronto, ON, M5X 2A1
(416) 362-8411
Emp Here 70   Sales 129,341,940
SIC 6411 Insurance agents, brokers, and service
David Feather
David Steele

D-U-N-S 20-321-6502   (SL)
STANDARD & POORS'S RATING SERVICES
(Suby of S&P GLOBAL INC.)
130 King St W Suite 1100, Toronto, ON, M5X 2A2
(416) 507-2500
Emp Here 110   Sales 156,545,180

SIC 6289 Security and commodity service
Robert Palombi

D-U-N-S 20-251-9914   (SL)
STRATAPRIME SOLUTIONS, INC
STRATAPRIME
1 First Canadian Place Suite 350, Toronto, ON, M5X 1C1
(647) 693-7656
Emp Here 25   Sales 11,087,250
SIC 7389 Business services, nec
Paul Melnyk
Andrew Livingstone
Andrew Livingstone
Penny Woolley

D-U-N-S 25-528-9530   (SL)
TALISKER RESOURCES LTD
100 King Street W 70 Floor, Toronto, ON, M5X 1A9
(416) 361-2808
Emp Here 53   Sales 49,776,381
SIC 6282 Investment advice
Terry Harbort
Ruben Padilla
Andres Tinajero
Tom Obradovich
Brent Gilchrist
Paul Wood
Blair Zaritsky

D-U-N-S 24-852-8734   (SL)
TANGO GOLD MINES INCORPORATED
130 King St W, Toronto, ON, M5X 2A2
(416) 479-4433
Emp Here 7   Sales 10,575,109
SIC 1081 Metal mining services
Samer Khalaf
Terry L. Tucker
Donna Moroney
Kevin Gallagher
Simon Van Der Loo

D-U-N-S 20-640-6548   (HQ)
TDL GROUP CORP, THE
TIM HORTONS
(Suby of RESTAURANT BRANDS INTERNATIONAL INC)
130 King St Suite 300, Toronto, ON, M5X 1E1
(905) 845-6511
Emp Here 450   Sales 1,334,078,400
SIC 6794 Patent owners and lessors
Marc Caira
Paul House
Garry Fraser
Glen Mortimer
James Nesbitt
David Mcmullen
Michelle Wettlaufer
Peter Fragnelli
David Blackmore
Michael Myskiw

D-U-N-S 24-861-3952   (HQ)
TOREX GOLD RESOURCES INC
130 King St W Suite 740, Toronto, ON, M5X 2A2
(647) 260-1500
Sales 442,900,000
SIC 1081 Metal mining services
Fred Stanford
Mark Thorpe
Anne Stephen
Gabriela Sanchez
Dawson Proudfoot
Mary Batoff
Jason Simpson
Steven Thomas
A. Terrance Macgibbon
Andrew Adams

D-U-N-S 20-259-2127   (HQ)
TRILOGY INTERNATIONAL PARTNERS INC
100 King St W Suite 7050, Toronto, ON, M5X 1C7
(416) 360-6390
Sales 20,694,425

SIC 6722 Management investment, open-end
Sanjil Shah

D-U-N-S 20-140-2257   (SL)
VIRTU ITG CANADA CORP
(Suby of VIRTU FINANCIAL, INC.)
130 King St W Suite 1040, Toronto, ON, M5X
2A2
(416) 874-0900
Emp Here 80   *Sales* 113,851,040
SIC 6211 Security brokers and dealers
Joseph Etienne Phaneuf
David Gregory Harris
Daljit Bhartt
Douglas Clark
Gregory Leonard Davies

D-U-N-S 25-681-4096   (HQ)
WILLIS CANADA INC
WILLIS TOWERS WATSON
(Suby of WILLIS TOWERS WATSON PUBLIC
LIMITED COMPANY)
100 King St W Suite 4700, Toronto, ON, M5X
1K7
(416) 368-9641
Emp Here 100   *Sales* 569,532,480
SIC 6411 Insurance agents, brokers, and ser-
vice
Richard T Hynes
Sarah Flint
Daniel Beaudry
Eric Brooks
Derek Smyth

D-U-N-S 20-967-9869   (HQ)
ZURICH CANADIAN HOLDINGS LIMITED
(Suby of ZURICH INSURANCE GROUP AG)
100 King St W Suite 5500, Toronto, ON, M5X
1C9
(416) 586-3000
Sales 128,050,500
SIC 6712 Bank holding companies
David Levinson
Paolo D'ambrosio
Jill Lankin
Scott Thomas
Lori Cassidy
Ilona Niemi
Kevin Doyle
Greg Irvine
Maria Jones
Jennifer Arezes

D-U-N-S 20-771-4551   (HQ)
ZURICH INSURANCE COMPANY LTD
(Suby of ZURICH INSURANCE GROUP AG)
100 King St W Suite 5500, Toronto, ON, M5X
2A1
(416) 586-3000
Emp Here 50   *Sales* 949,220,800
SIC 6411 Insurance agents, brokers, and ser-
vice
Alister Campbell
Gordon E Thompson
Nigel Ayers

Toronto, ON M6A

D-U-N-S 24-925-7411   (SL)
970910 ONTARIO INC
PRESTIGE MOTORS
147 Bentworth Ave, Toronto, ON, M6A 1P6

Emp Here 24   *Sales* 11,953,872
SIC 5521 Used car dealers
Gino Arconti
Flavio Arconti

D-U-N-S 20-596-5189   (HQ)
**BAYCREST CENTRE FOR GERIATRIC
CARE**
BAYCREST HOSPITAL
3560 Bathurst St, Toronto, ON, M6A 2E1
(416) 785-2500
Sales 164,398,400

SIC 8069 Specialty hospitals, except psychi-
atric
William E. Reichman
Brian Mackie

D-U-N-S 20-351-3184   (HQ)
CENTURA (OTTAWA) LIMITED
CENTURA OTTAWA
950 Lawrence Ave W, Toronto, ON, M6A 1C4
(416) 785-5151
Emp Here 10   *Sales* 287,684,000
SIC 5023 Homefurnishings
Brian Cowie

D-U-N-S 20-380-9728   (SL)
FIRM CAPITAL PROPERTY TRUST
FIRM CAPITAL
163 Cartwright Ave, Toronto, ON, M6A 1V5
(416) 635-0221
Emp Here 1   *Sales* 15,135,686
SIC 6021 National commercial banks
Robert Mckee
Sergio Elport
Joseph Fried
Sandy Poklar
Eli Dadouch

D-U-N-S 25-173-5791   (SL)
GRANDMOTHER'S PIE SHOPPE INC
65 Samor Rd, Toronto, ON, M6A 1J2
(416) 782-9000
Emp Here 40   *Sales* 10,966,080
SIC 5461 Retail bakeries
Joe Lasac

D-U-N-S 25-475-9210   (SL)
**GRILLO BARRISTERS PROFESSIONAL
CORPORATION**
GRILLO BARRISTERS
38 Apex Rd Unit A, Toronto, ON, M6A 2V2
(416) 614-6000
Emp Here 73   *Sales* 11,242,803
SIC 8111 Legal services
Sal Grillo

D-U-N-S 20-022-5495   (SL)
MCCARTHY ELLIS MERCANTILE LTD
CANADIAN TIRE
700 Lawrence Ave W, Toronto, ON, M6A 3B4
(289) 442-2851
Emp Here 40   *Sales* 25,171,200
SIC 5531 Auto and home supply stores

D-U-N-S 24-989-5848   (HQ)
MEVOTECH LP
240 Bridgeland Ave, Toronto, ON, M6A 1Z4
(416) 783-7800
Sales 41,503,860
SIC 5013 Motor vehicle supplies and new
parts
Ezer Mevorach
Taly Mevorach
Katya Forsyth
Harry Van Drunen
Scott Stone
Brian Rossi
Mike Duggan
Allan Bartolini
Ed Simone
Assaf Bar-Menachem

D-U-N-S 24-869-1420   (HQ)
OLYMPIA TILE INTERNATIONAL INC
OLYMPIA TILE + STONE
1000 Lawrence Ave W, Toronto, ON, M6A 1C6
(416) 785-6666
Emp Here 300   *Sales* 512,665,200
SIC 5032 Brick, stone, and related material
Ralph Reichmann
Paul Reichmann

D-U-N-S 24-666-2980   (SL)
WEG ELECTRIC MOTORS
64 Samor Rd, Toronto, ON, M6A 1J6
(416) 781-4617
Emp Here 49   *Sales* 21,911,526
SIC 5063 Electrical apparatus and equipment

Victor Pamansky

Toronto, ON M6B

D-U-N-S 24-573-4913   (SL)
1557483 ONTARIO INC
CANADIAN TIRE
2471 Dufferin St, Toronto, ON, M6B 3P6

Emp Here 30   *Sales* 14,942,340
SIC 5531 Auto and home supply stores
Mamdouh Sivin

D-U-N-S 25-989-7577   (SL)
**COMPASS CONSTRUCTION RESOURCES
LTD**
2700 Dufferin St Unit 77, Toronto, ON, M6B
4J3
(416) 789-9819
Emp Here 35   *Sales* 16,475,585
SIC 1542 Nonresidential construction, nec
Christopher Dossett

D-U-N-S 20-163-0746   (SL)
DALTON COMPANY LTD, THE
1140 Castlefield Ave, Toronto, ON, M6B 1E9
(416) 789-4195
Emp Here 40   *Sales* 13,333,320
SIC 1541 Industrial buildings and warehouses
Andrew Dalton
Peter John Dalton
Randy Dalton

D-U-N-S 20-784-4606   (HQ)
DON MICHAEL HOLDINGS INC
ROOTS CANADA
1400 Castlefield Ave Suite 2, Toronto, ON,
M6B 4N4
(416) 781-3574
Emp Here 350   *Sales* 959,286,000
SIC 3143 Men's footwear, except athletic
Jim A. Gabel
Michael Budman
Don Green

D-U-N-S 20-164-3897   (SL)
ELECTRO CANADA LIMITED
30 Tycos Dr, Toronto, ON, M6B 1V9

Emp Here 450
SIC 3714 Motor vehicle parts and accessories

D-U-N-S 20-839-2725   (SL)
HOME IMPROVEMENT PEOPLE INC, THE
1120 Castlefield Ave, Toronto, ON, M6B 1E9
(905) 760-7607
Emp Here 55   *Sales* 14,901,810
SIC 1521 Single-family housing construction
Bentzion Berkovits
Daniel Berkovits

D-U-N-S 24-826-4293   (SL)
JACOBS CATERING LTD
2828 Bathurst St Suite 502, Toronto, ON, M6B
3A7
(905) 886-3832
Emp Here 106   *Sales* 4,825,014
SIC 5812 Eating places
Kalman Lowenthal

D-U-N-S 24-918-7394   (HQ)
KITCHEN STUFF PLUS INC
(Suby of HALPERN, MARK HOLDINGS INC)
125 Tycos Dr, Toronto, ON, M6B 1W6
(416) 944-2847
Emp Here 25   *Sales* 80,010,900
SIC 5719 Miscellaneous homefurnishings
Mark Halpern

D-U-N-S 24-676-6807   (HQ)
L'OCCITANE CANADA CORP
2700 Dufferin St Unit 89, Toronto, ON, M6B
4J3
(416) 782-0005
Emp Here 5   *Sales* 12,216,400

SIC 5999 Miscellaneous retail stores, nec
David Boynton
Cory Sherman
Marcin Jasiak
Reinold Sherman
David Mcconnachie

D-U-N-S 20-333-9148   (SL)
ROOTS CORPORATION
1400 Castlefield Ave Suite 2, Toronto, ON,
M6B 4N4
(416) 781-3574
Emp Here 2,450   *Sales* 261,653,243
SIC 3143 Men's footwear, except athletic
James A. Gabel
James Connell
Almira Cuizon
Priscilla Shum
Jim Rudyk
Erol Uzumeri
Gregory David
Dale H. Lastman
Richard P. Mavrinac
Eric Zinterhofer

D-U-N-S 24-371-9866   (SL)
ROYAL SUPPLY CHAIN INC
65a Wingold Ave, Toronto, ON, M6B 1P8
(647) 344-8142
Emp Here 15   *Sales* 15,179,960
SIC 4731 Freight transportation arrangement
Richard Cohen
Jonathan Cohen

D-U-N-S 20-692-5781   (HQ)
WEAVERS ART INC
1400 Castlefield Ave, Toronto, ON, M6B 4N4
(416) 923-7929
Emp Here 18   *Sales* 22,011,731
SIC 7389 Business services, nec
Michael Pourvakil

Toronto, ON M6C

D-U-N-S 20-004-7004   (SL)
DINOFF, S. DRUGS LIMITED
SHOPPERS DRUG MART STORE
523 St Clair Ave W, Toronto, ON, M6C 1A1
(416) 538-1155
Emp Here 50   *Sales* 12,647,700
SIC 5912 Drug stores and proprietary stores
Stan Dinoff

D-U-N-S 20-178-2179   (SL)
**LEESE ENTERPRISES INTERNATIONAL
INC**
1210 Eglinton Ave W, Toronto, ON, M6C 2E3
(416) 781-8404
Emp Here 25   *Sales* 20,889,425
SIC 5145 Confectionery
Michael Leese

D-U-N-S 20-171-9648   (HQ)
NORTOWN FOODS LIMITED
892 Eglinton Ave W, Toronto, ON, M6C 2B6
(416) 789-2921
Emp Here 18   *Sales* 12,336,840
SIC 5411 Grocery stores
Michael Klein
Brian Klein

D-U-N-S 20-753-2037   (SL)
PHC PROPERTY MANAGEMENT CORP
UNITY APARTMENTS, DIV OF
875 Eglinton Ave W Suite 300, Toronto, ON,
M6C 3Z9
(416) 789-2664
Emp Here 62   *Sales* 13,694,002
SIC 6513 Apartment building operators
Leon Platt
Jack Jacobson
Albert Goldman
Elliot Rosenberg
John Rothman

D-U-N-S 24-683-9059   (SL)
PROSCAFF NORTH AMERICA INC
148 Dewbourne Ave, Toronto, ON, M6C 1Z2
(416) 783-7500
Emp Here 30   *Sales* 13,415,220
SIC 5049 Professional equipment, nec
Colin Spurrell
Cristian Stefan

D-U-N-S 24-978-3247   (SL)
RUBY SEAS INTERNATIONAL INC
1061 Eglinton Ave W Suite 202, Toronto, ON,
M6C 2C9
(416) 787-3474
Emp Here 12   *Sales* 52,109,328
SIC 5146 Fish and seafoods
David Rubenstein
Veronika Margulis

D-U-N-S 25-343-9962   (HQ)
**SKILLS FOR CHANGE OF METRO
TORONTO**
SKILLS FOR CHANGE
791 St Clair Ave W, Toronto, ON, M6C 1B7
(416) 658-3101
Emp Here 77   *Sales* 5,095,307
SIC 8331 Job training and related services
Althea Gordon
Michelle Surace
Diana Welgus
Eiraj Sohail
Jason Lee
Jasmine Jackson
Nadeem Ladha
Kleva Gruda

Toronto, ON M6E

D-U-N-S 20-356-1779   (SL)
41068 TORONTO HYUNDAI
2460 Dufferin St, Toronto, ON, M6E 3T3
(416) 787-9789
Emp Here 30   *Sales* 14,942,340
SIC 5511 New and used car dealers
Benny Leung

D-U-N-S 24-098-4260   (SL)
415841 ONTARIO LIMITED
SCARBOROUGH LEXUS TOYOTA
2000 Eglinton Ave W, Toronto, ON, M6E 2J9
(416) 751-1530
Emp Here 121   *Sales* 76,142,880
SIC 5511 New and used car dealers
Betty Rowntree

D-U-N-S 20-170-7171   (HQ)
**BLACK FEATHER HOLDINGS INCORPO-
RATED**
CANADA GOOSE
(*Suby of* BAIN CAPITAL, LP)
250 Bowie Ave, Toronto, ON, M6E 4Y2
(416) 780-9850
Emp Here 20   *Sales* 13,667,400
SIC 2339 Women's and misses' outerwear,
nec
Daniel Reiss
David Reiss
Malca Reiss

D-U-N-S 20-329-3519   (HQ)
CANADA GOOSE HOLDINGS INC
(*Suby of* BAIN CAPITAL, LP)
250 Bowie Ave, Toronto, ON, M6E 4Y2
(416) 780-9850
Sales 307,358,686
SIC 2331 Women's and misses' blouses and
shirts
Dani Reiss
Scott Cameron
David Forrest
Pat Sherlock
Carrie Baker
Ana Mihaljevic
John Moran

Spencer Orr
Kara Mackillop
Jacob Pat

D-U-N-S 24-989-8078   (HQ)
CANADA GOOSE INC
250 Bowie Ave, Toronto, ON, M6E 4Y2
(416) 780-9850
Emp Here 5   *Sales* 18,713,250
SIC 5611 Men's and boys' clothing stores
Daniel Reiss
John Black
Ryan Cotton
Joshua Bekenstein
Kevin Spreekmeester

D-U-N-S 20-880-8824   (HQ)
COSTI IMMIGRANT SERVICES
1710 Dufferin St, Toronto, ON, M6E 3P2
(416) 658-1600
Emp Here 20   *Sales* 30,716,800
SIC 8322 Individual and family services
Mario Calla
Frank Mendicino
Bruno Suppa
Mike Yealland

D-U-N-S 25-805-7116   (SL)
COURIER COMPANY LTD, THE
1219 St Clair Ave W, Toronto, ON, M6E 1B5
(416) 504-7373
Emp Here 30   *Sales* 13,304,700
SIC 7389 Business services, nec
Al Weiss

D-U-N-S 20-164-5074   (HQ)
ELTE CARPETS LIMITED
80 Ronald Ave, Toronto, ON, M6E 5A2
(416) 785-7885
Sales 34,860,450
SIC 5713 Floor covering stores
Kenneth Metrick
Laurence Metrick
Mary Ann Metrick
Frederick Metrick

D-U-N-S 24-685-9946   (SL)
FABRICMASTER INC
76 Miranda Ave Suite 2, Toronto, ON, M6E
5A1
(416) 658-2205
Emp Here 25   *Sales* 12,458,050
SIC 5131 Piece goods and notions
Howard Yesovitch
Steve Pippert

D-U-N-S 24-693-8997   (HQ)
MENDOCINO CLOTHING COMPANY LTD
M BOUTIQUE
496 Gilbert Ave, Toronto, ON, M6E 4X5
(416) 847-0590
Emp Here 25   *Sales* 56,139,750
SIC 5621 Women's clothing stores
Norma Kaplan
Jan Kaplan

D-U-N-S 25-194-9756   (SL)
**NORTHWEST PROTECTION SERVICES
LTD**
1951 Eglinton Ave W Unit 201, Toronto, ON,
M6E 2J7
(416) 787-1448
Emp Here 1,200   *Sales* 31,500,000
SIC 7381 Detective and armored car services
Bruce Mcbean

D-U-N-S 25-460-8326   (SL)
**RECONNECT COMMUNITY HEALTH SER-
VICES**
1281 St. Clair Ave W, Toronto, ON, M6E 1B8
(416) 248-2050
Emp Here 300   *Sales* 22,731,900
SIC 8093 Specialty outpatient clinics, nec
Mohamed Badsha

D-U-N-S 24-023-3379   (SL)
ST. HILDA'S TOWERS, INC
2339 Dufferin St, Toronto, ON, M6E 4Z5

(416) 781-6621
Emp Here 100   *Sales* 5,924,700
SIC 8361 Residential care
Derwyn Shea
Rodney Seyffert
Joyce Myers
Gary Posner

D-U-N-S 20-955-3648   (SL)
SUSANNE LANG FRAGRANCE INC
(*Suby of* LVMH MOET HENNESSY LOUIS
VUITTON)
670 Caledonia Rd Unit 100, Toronto, ON, M6E
4V9
(416) 961-1234
Emp Here 125   *Sales* 35,502,625
SIC 2844 Toilet preparations
Susanne Langmuir
Kimberley Thomas
Cindy Park

D-U-N-S 20-923-5134   (SL)
**SUTTON GROUP-SECURITY REAL ESTATE
INC**
1239 St Clair Ave W, Toronto, ON, M6E 1B5
(416) 654-1010
Emp Here 50   *Sales* 16,356,350
SIC 6531 Real estate agents and managers
Jo Volpentesta

D-U-N-S 20-290-9326   (BR)
TORONTO DISTRICT SCHOOL BOARD
OAKWOOD COLLEGIATE INSTITUTE
(*Suby of* TORONTO DISTRICT SCHOOL
BOARD)
991 St Clair Ave W, Toronto, ON, M6E 1A3
(416) 393-1780
Emp Here 75
SIC 8211 Elementary and secondary schools
Steve Yee

Toronto, ON M6G

D-U-N-S 25-995-4790   (HQ)
1100833 ONTARIO LIMITED
FAEMA
672 Dupont St Suite 201, Toronto, ON, M6G
1Z6
(416) 535-1555
Emp Here 43   *Sales* 11,620,150
SIC 5722 Household appliance stores
Mike Didondato
Pat Didondato
Lorenzo Didondato
Rocco Didonadato
Joe Didondato

D-U-N-S 24-011-4343   (BR)
CANADA TORONTO EAST MISSION
*CHURCH OF JESUS CHRIST OF LATTER
DAY SAINTS, THE*
(*Suby of* CORPORATION OF THE PRESI-
DENT OF THE CHURCH OF JESUS CHRIST
OF LATTER-DAY SAINTS)
851 Ossington Ave, Toronto, ON, M6G 3V2
(416) 531-0535
Emp Here 100
SIC 8661 Religious organizations
Lind Strom

D-U-N-S 25-319-9699   (SL)
**CHRISTIE GARDENS APARTMENTS AND
CARE INC**
600 Melita Cres, Toronto, ON, M6G 3Z4
(416) 530-1330
Emp Here 100   *Sales* 6,856,600
SIC 8051 Skilled nursing care facilities
Heather James

D-U-N-S 24-987-6426   (SL)
FIESTA FARMS INC
200 Christie St, Toronto, ON, M6G 3B6
(416) 537-1235
Emp Here 63   *Sales* 18,489,051
SIC 5411 Grocery stores

Joseph Virgona

D-U-N-S 24-685-2990   (HQ)
GENEEN AUTOMOBILES LIMITED
740 Dupont St, Toronto, ON, M6G 1Z6
(416) 530-1880
Sales 24,903,900
SIC 5511 New and used car dealers
David Geneen
Nizar Moredina

D-U-N-S 25-220-4565   (SL)
GENUINE HEALTH INC
200-491 College St, Toronto, ON, M6G 1A5
(877) 500-7888
Emp Here 43   *Sales* 47,529,835
SIC 5122 Drugs, proprietaries, and sundries
Stewart Brown

D-U-N-S 24-991-5554   (SL)
HELLENIC HOME FOR THE AGE INC
33 Winona Dr, Toronto, ON, M6G 3Z7
(416) 654-7700
Emp Here 90   *Sales* 5,332,230
SIC 8361 Residential care
Peter Xenias
Irene Keroglidis
John Fanaras
Mike Neroulas
Nicholas Nitsias

D-U-N-S 20-845-1294   (SL)
HENGAB INVESTMENTS LIMITED
*NEW CANADIANS LUMBER & BUILDING
SUPPLIES*
804 Dupont St, Toronto, ON, M6G 1Z6
(416) 531-2401
Emp Here 65   *Sales* 17,397,380
SIC 5211 Lumber and other building materials
Roger Henriques
Joe Gabriel

D-U-N-S 20-167-1955   (SL)
HONEST ED'S LIMITED
(*Suby of* MIRVISH, ED ENTERPRISES LIM-
ITED)
581 Bloor St W Suite 1, Toronto, ON, M6G 1K3
(416) 537-1574
Emp Here 210   *Sales* 31,942,680
SIC 5311 Department stores
David Mirvish

D-U-N-S 24-197-6662   (HQ)
KEW MEDIA GROUP INC
672 Dupont St, Toronto, ON, M6G 1Z6
(647) 956-1965
Emp Here 8   *Sales* 152,908,072
SIC 7812 Motion picture and video production
Steven Silver
Peter Sussman
Geoff Webb
Rick Kwak
Madeleine Cohen
Julie Bristow
David Fleck
Maish Kagan
Patrice Merrin
Stephen Pincus

D-U-N-S 25-374-9220   (BR)
LOBLAWS SUPERMARKETS LIMITED
LOBLAWS
(*Suby of* LOBLAW COMPANIES LIMITED)
650 Dupont St Suite 1029, Toronto, ON, M6G
4B1
(416) 588-3756
Emp Here 400
SIC 5141 Groceries, general line
Terry Bahen

D-U-N-S 25-300-3248   (BR)
METRO ONTARIO INC
DOMINION SAVER CENTER
(*Suby of* METRO INC)
735 College St, Toronto, ON, M6G 1C5
(416) 533-2515
Emp Here 200

SIC 5411 Grocery stores
Michael Breen

D-U-N-S 24-744-1686   (HQ)
RADIO 1540 LIMITED
CHIN RADIO/TV INTERNATIONAL
622 College St Suite 2, Toronto, ON, M6G 1B6
(416) 531-9991
Emp Here 70   *Sales* 13,859,850
SIC 4832 Radio broadcasting stations
Lenny Lombardi
Teresa Lombardi
Donina Lombardi

D-U-N-S 25-360-6578   (BR)
SOBEYS CAPITAL INCORPORATED
SOBEYS ONTARIO
(*Suby of* EMPIRE COMPANY LIMITED)
840 Dupont St, Toronto, ON, M6G 1Z8
(416) 534-3588
Emp Here 90
SIC 5411 Grocery stores
Alev Cosgun

D-U-N-S 20-653-4898   (BR)
TORONTO CATHOLIC DISTRICT SCHOOL BOARD
ST. RAYMOND SEPARATE SCHOOL
(*Suby of* TORONTO CATHOLIC DISTRICT SCHOOL BOARD)
270 Barton Ave, Toronto, ON, M6G 1R4
(416) 393-5293
Emp Here 250
SIC 8211 Elementary and secondary schools
Ann Marie Verre

D-U-N-S 25-214-3870   (BR)
TORONTO DISTRICT SCHOOL BOARD
CENTRAL TORONTO ACADEMY
(*Suby of* TORONTO DISTRICT SCHOOL BOARD)
570 Shaw St, Toronto, ON, M6G 3L6
(416) 393-0030
Emp Here 86
SIC 8211 Elementary and secondary schools
Iwona Kurman

D-U-N-S 20-025-2604   (BR)
TORONTO DISTRICT SCHOOL BOARD
HARBORD COLLEGIATE INSTITUTE
(*Suby of* TORONTO DISTRICT SCHOOL BOARD)
286 Harbord St, Toronto, ON, M6G 1G5
(416) 393-1650
Emp Here 90
SIC 8211 Elementary and secondary schools
Vince Meade

Toronto, ON M6H

D-U-N-S 25-343-4484   (SL)
1080414 ONTARIO LIMITED
(*Suby of* G.H. JOHNSON'S TRADING COMPANY LIMITED)
950 Dupont St, Toronto, ON, M6H 1Z2
(416) 532-6700
Emp Here 80
SIC 6719 Holding companies, nec
Patrick Johnson

D-U-N-S 20-295-0606   (SL)
887252 ONTARIO LIMITED
NOSSO TALHO PARTNERSHIP
1042 Bloor St W, Toronto, ON, M6H 1M3
(416) 531-7462
Emp Here 65   *Sales* 19,076,005
SIC 5421 Meat and fish markets
Julio Lima

D-U-N-S 20-168-1145   (SL)
960667 ONTARIO LIMITED
JOMAR ELECTRIC
777 Saint Clarens Ave, Toronto, ON, M6H 3X3
(416) 536-2194
Emp Here 90   *Sales* 23,539,770

SIC 6712 Bank holding companies
Joseph Edell

D-U-N-S 20-385-3585   (SL)
AURACLEAN BUILDING MAINTENANCE INC
AURACLEAN
104 Greenlaw Ave, Toronto, ON, M6H 3V5
(416) 561-6137
Emp Here 120   *Sales* 3,203,503
SIC 7349 Building maintenance services, nec
Mario Camilleri
Victor Camilleri

D-U-N-S 24-886-6089   (HQ)
CANADIAN CAPITAL CORPORATION
1022 Bloor St W Suite 300, Toronto, ON, M6H 1M2
(416) 495-0909
Emp Here 3   *Sales* 20,501,250
SIC 6712 Bank holding companies
Gus Baril

D-U-N-S 25-342-8601   (BR)
CATHOLIC CHILDREN'S AID SOCIETY OF TORONTO, THE
(*Suby of* CATHOLIC CHILDREN'S AID SOCIETY OF TORONTO, THE)
900 Dufferin St Suite 219, Toronto, ON, M6H 4A9
(416) 395-1500
Emp Here 180
SIC 8322 Individual and family services
Anabela Cardoso

D-U-N-S 24-005-8131   (SL)
DOVERCOURT BAPTIST FOUNDATION
NEW HORIZONS TOWER
1140 Bloor St W, Toronto, ON, M6H 4E6
(416) 536-6111
Emp Here 90   *Sales* 5,332,230
SIC 8361 Residential care
Ken Sweatman

D-U-N-S 24-383-8005   (SL)
G.H. JOHNSONS FURNITURE INC
JOHNSONS BUSINESS INTERIORS
950 Dupont St, Toronto, ON, M6H 1Z2
(613) 736-7000
Emp Here 25   *Sales* 12,721,400
SIC 5021 Furniture
Elyse Summers

D-U-N-S 20-702-0652   (SL)
H.A.S. NOVELTIES LIMITED
H A S MARKETING
300 Geary Ave, Toronto, ON, M6H 2C5
(416) 593-1101
Emp Here 50   *Sales* 10,941,200
SIC 3993 Signs and advertising specialties
Randy Sterling

D-U-N-S 25-321-7442   (BR)
LONG & MCQUADE LIMITED
LONG & MCQUADE MUSICAL INSTRUMENTS
(*Suby of* LONG HOLDINGS INC)
925 Bloor St W, Toronto, ON, M6H 1L5
(416) 588-7886
Emp Here 75
SIC 7359 Equipment rental and leasing, nec
Jordan Small

D-U-N-S 24-386-0939   (SL)
MAGNUM PROTECTIVE SERVICES LIMITED
1043 Bloor St W, Toronto, ON, M6H 1M4
(416) 591-1566
Emp Here 100   *Sales* 39,567,800
SIC 7381 Detective and armored car services
Hyo Lee

D-U-N-S 25-310-8880   (BR)
MCDONALD'S RESTAURANTS OF CANADA LIMITED
MCDONALD'S
(*Suby of* MCDONALD'S CORPORATION)
1185 Dupont St, Toronto, ON, M6H 2A5

(416) 536-4188
Emp Here 90
SIC 5812 Eating places
Chuck Coolen

D-U-N-S 24-849-6325   (SL)
NITTA GELATIN CANADA, INC
(*Suby of* NITTA GELATIN INC.)
60 Paton Rd, Toronto, ON, M6H 1R8
(416) 532-5111
Emp Here 42   *Sales* 11,928,882
SIC 2899 Chemical preparations, nec
Raymond Merz
Noryuki Tsuji
Noromichi Soga
Jurgen Gallert
Juergen Gallert

D-U-N-S 20-967-6431   (SL)
PRODUCTIVE SECURITY INC
940 Lansdowne Ave, Toronto, ON, M6H 3Z4
(416) 535-9341
Emp Here 60   *Sales* 23,740,680
SIC 7381 Detective and armored car services
Sanjay Rupani

D-U-N-S 20-265-5861   (SL)
ROYAL LE PAGE SUPREME
1245 Dupont St, Toronto, ON, M6H 2A6
(416) 543-0979
Emp Here 40   *Sales* 10,870,240
SIC 6531 Real estate agents and managers
Lucy Ramos

D-U-N-S 20-704-0502   (HQ)
SPAR ROOFING & METAL SUPPLIES LIMITED
SPAR-MARATHON ROOFING SUPPLIES
1360 Bloor St W, Toronto, ON, M6H 1P2
(416) 534-8421
Emp Here 15   *Sales* 10,122,360
SIC 5211 Lumber and other building materials
Craig Glynn

D-U-N-S 25-795-7415   (SL)
ST. HELEN SEAFOODS INC
138 Saint Helens Ave, Toronto, ON, M6H 0B8
(416) 536-5111
Emp Here 40   *Sales* 33,985,216
SIC 5146 Fish and seafoods
Steven Chow

D-U-N-S 25-294-8989   (BR)
WAL-MART CANADA CORP
(*Suby of* WALMART INC.)
900 Dufferin St Suite 3106, Toronto, ON, M6H 4B1
(416) 537-2561
Emp Here 100
SIC 5311 Department stores
Wendt Dave

Toronto, ON M6J

D-U-N-S 20-985-4517   (SL)
1476182 ONTARIO LIMITED
PARKDALE PRICE CHOPPER
22 Northcote Ave, Toronto, ON, M6J 3K3
(416) 537-4124
Emp Here 60   *Sales* 17,608,620
SIC 5411 Grocery stores
Marco Amati

D-U-N-S 20-275-1616   (SL)
2161457 ONTARIO INC
DESIGNAGENCY
845 Adelaide St W, Toronto, ON, M6J 3X1
(416) 703-2022
Emp Here 30   *Sales* 13,304,700
SIC 7389 Business services, nec
Allen Chan

D-U-N-S 20-772-3792   (SL)
341822 ONTARIO INC
MAYNARD NURSING HOME

28 Halton St, Toronto, ON, M6J 1R3
(416) 533-5198
Emp Here 84   *Sales* 5,773,572
SIC 8051 Skilled nursing care facilities
Julie Music

D-U-N-S 20-314-5461   (SL)
BEWORKS INC
(*Suby of* KYU INVESTMENT INCORPORATED)
946 Queen St W, Toronto, ON, M6J 1G8
(416) 920-1921
Emp Here 50   *Sales* 11,714,400
SIC 8742 Management consulting services
Kelly Peters
Dhushanthan Thevarajah
Wardah Malik

D-U-N-S 24-564-0909   (SL)
CECCONI SIMONE INC
1335 Dundas St W, Toronto, ON, M6J 1Y3
(416) 588-5900
Emp Here 30   *Sales* 13,304,700
SIC 7389 Business services, nec
Elaine Cecconi
Anna Simone

D-U-N-S 20-785-5271   (HQ)
CENTRE FOR ADDICTION AND MENTAL HEALTH
CAMH
1001 Queen St W Suite 301, Toronto, ON, M6J 1H4
(416) 535-8501
Emp Here 1,500   *Sales* 285,778,061
SIC 8093 Specialty outpatient clinics, nec
Catherine Zahn
Darrell Gregersen
Tracey Macarthur
Kim Bellissimo
David Cunic
Damian Jankowicz
Bruce Pollock
Hilary Rodrigues
Ivan Silver
Stephen Sokolov

D-U-N-S 24-422-7661   (SL)
CENTRE FOR ADDICTION AND MENTAL HEALTH FOUNDATION
100 Stokes St Fl 5, Toronto, ON, M6J 1H4
(416) 979-6909
Emp Here 50   *Sales* 19,870,700
SIC 8699 Membership organizations, nec
Deborah Gillis
Jamie Anderson
Peter Doyle

D-U-N-S 20-651-9600   (SL)
DRAKE HOTEL PROPERTIES (DHP) INC
THE DRAKE HOTEL
1150 Queen St W, Toronto, ON, M6J 1J3
(416) 531-5042
Emp Here 195   *Sales* 18,074,550
SIC 7011 Hotels and motels
Jeffrey Stober
William Simpson

D-U-N-S 24-779-8150   (HQ)
GATHER INVESTMENTS LIMITED
DOWNTOWN LUMBER & BUILDING SUPPLIES CO
172 Ossington Ave, Toronto, ON, M6J 2Z7
(416) 532-2813
Sales 12,044,340
SIC 5211 Lumber and other building materials
Helder Estevez
Gil Henriques
Julio Henriques
Tony Tavares

D-U-N-S 24-320-3003   (HQ)
GREENHOUSE JUICE COMPANY ULC
9 Ossington Ave, Toronto, ON, M6J 2Y8
(647) 351-0188
Emp Here 10   *Sales* 13,707,600
SIC 5499 Miscellaneous food stores

Anthony Green

D-U-N-S 24-006-6548   (SL)
HOUSE OF HORVATH INC
77 Ossington Ave, Toronto, ON, M6J 2Z2
(416) 534-4254
Emp Here 50   *Sales* 37,126,000
SIC 5194 Tobacco and tobacco products
Joseph Horvath

D-U-N-S 20-388-5736   (SL)
INFINITY & ASSOCIATES LLP / INC
36 Lisgar St Suite 623w, Toronto, ON, M6J
0C7
(888) 508-6277
Emp Here 75   *Sales* 33,691,425
SIC 7389 Business services, nec
Nakone Vongkham

D-U-N-S 20-400-8635   (SL)
KNIX WEAR INC
KNIX TEEN
70 Claremont St 2nd Fl, Toronto, ON, M6J
2M5
(647) 715-9446
Emp Here 40   *Sales* 21,441,429
SIC 5632 Women's accessory and specialty
stores
Joanna Griffith

D-U-N-S 25-370-8390   (BR)
KRAFT HEINZ CANADA ULC
CADBURY
(*Suby of* THE KRAFT HEINZ COMPANY)
277 Gladstone Ave, Toronto, ON, M6J 3L9
(416) 667-6224
Emp Here 250
SIC 2064 Candy and other confectionery
products
Ed Pizale

D-U-N-S 24-848-9101   (SL)
PEACOCK PARADE INC, THE
828 Richmond St W, Toronto, ON, M6J 1C9

Emp Here 18   *Sales* 11,816,352
SIC 5961 Catalog and mail-order houses
Jan Gandhi
Gurpreet (Nancy) Sahota
Lorne Gertner

D-U-N-S 20-311-1612   (SL)
PROVINCIAL PROTECTION INC
J.B. GEARS CANADA
36 Lisgar St Suite 623w, Toronto, ON, M6J
0C7
(888) 508-6277
Emp Here 75   *Sales* 33,691,425
SIC 7389 Business services, nec
Nakone Vongkham

D-U-N-S 20-635-8702   (SL)
PULP & FIBER INC
COMMUNITY, THE
822 Richmond St W Suite 400, Toronto, ON,
M6J 1C9
(416) 361-0030
Emp Here 64   *Sales* 11,339,785
SIC 8743 Public relations services
Art Mandalas
David Smulowitz

D-U-N-S 24-237-5368   (HQ)
RESTAURANTS CANADA
CRFA
1155 Queen St W, Toronto, ON, M6J 1J4
(416) 923-8416
Emp Here 35   *Sales* 12,930,750
SIC 8611 Business associations
Shanna Munro
Carmine Aquino
Shery Ross
Joyce Reynolds
Brad Kramble

D-U-N-S 24-141-5892   (SL)
WOOLFITT'S ART ENTERPRISES INC
1153 Queen St W, Toronto, ON, M6J 1J4

(416) 536-7878
Emp Here 20   *Sales* 10,410,840
SIC 5092 Toys and hobby goods and supplies
Benjamin Woolfitt

Toronto, ON M6K

D-U-N-S 24-877-2774   (SL)
3161234 MANITOBA LIMITED
RISE HEALTHWARE
64 Jefferson Ave Unit 3, Toronto, ON, M6K
1Y4
(416) 589-6563
Emp Here 46   *Sales* 13,439,774
SIC 7359 Equipment rental and leasing, nec
Byron Darlison
Vic Toews

D-U-N-S 25-418-8907   (HQ)
500 STAFFING INC, THE
67 Mowat Ave Suite 411, Toronto, ON, M6K
3E3

Emp Here 145   *Sales* 14,938,800
SIC 7361 Employment agencies
William (Bill) Masson

D-U-N-S 20-560-2266   (SL)
ACHIEVERS SOLUTIONS INC
(*Suby of* BHN HOLDINGS, INC.)
190 Liberty St Suite 100, Toronto, ON, M6K
3L5
(888) 622-3343
Emp Here 240   *Sales* 36,589,440
SIC 7361 Employment agencies
Shrey Bhatia
Kaizer Suleman
Alfred Lin
John Albright
Aris Zakinphinos
David Brennan

D-U-N-S 20-287-2735   (HQ)
ANTHEM MEDIA GROUP INC
*ANTHEM MEDIA SPORTS & ENTERTAIN-
MENT*
171 East Liberty St Suite 230, Toronto, ON,
M6K 3P6
(416) 987-7841
Sales 11,087,880
SIC 4833 Television broadcasting stations
Leonard Asper

D-U-N-S 24-489-0984   (SL)
**BOARD OF GOVERNORS OF EXHIBITION
PLACE, THE**
(*Suby of* CORPORATION OF THE CITY OF
TORONTO)
100 Princes Blvd Suite 1, Toronto, ON, M6K
3C3
(416) 263-3600
Emp Here 120   *Sales* 10,404,000
SIC 7999 Amusement and recreation, nec
Mark Grimes
Dianne Young
Fatima Scagnol
Hardat Persaud

D-U-N-S 20-818-4556   (SL)
BOULEVARD CLUB LIMITED, THE
1491 Lake Shore Blvd W, Toronto, ON, M6K
3C2
(416) 532-3341
Emp Here 100   *Sales* 7,639,700
SIC 7997 Membership sports and recreation
clubs
Anne Geddes

D-U-N-S 20-823-5010   (SL)
**CANADIAN NATIONAL EXHIBITION ASSO-
CIATION**
CNEA
210 Princes Blvd, Toronto, ON, M6K 3C3
(416) 263-3600
Emp Here 1,500   *Sales* 112,867,500

SIC 7996 Amusement parks
Jim Mcmillen

D-U-N-S 24-999-9322   (SL)
**COMPREHENSIVE CARE INTERNATIONAL
INC**
173 Dufferin St Suite 200, Toronto, ON, M6K
3H7
(416) 531-5950
Emp Here 49   *Sales* 11,480,112
SIC 8742 Management consulting services
Debra Delaney

D-U-N-S 20-288-6123   (BR)
COSSETTE COMMUNICATION INC
(*Suby of* COSSETTE COMMUNICATION
INC)
32 Atlantic Ave, Toronto, ON, M6K 1X8
(416) 922-2727
Emp Here 300
SIC 4899 Communication services, nec

D-U-N-S 20-161-7214   (SL)
DESIGNER FABRIC OUTLET LTD
DESIGNER FABRICS
1360 Queen St W, Toronto, ON, M6K 1L7
(416) 531-2810
Emp Here 30   *Sales* 14,949,660
SIC 5131 Piece goods and notions
Sheldon Fainer
Beverley Fainer
Paula Fainer

D-U-N-S 25-791-4333   (SL)
ELM GROVE LIVING CENTRE INC
35 Elm Grove Ave Suite 209, Toronto, ON,
M6K 2J2
(416) 537-2465
Emp Here 115   *Sales* 7,885,090
SIC 8051 Skilled nursing care facilities
Edward Brown

D-U-N-S 24-802-7190   (SL)
FIRST CAPITAL ASSET MANAGEMENT LP
(*Suby of* FIRST CAPITAL REALTY INC)
85 Hanna Ave Suite 400, Toronto, ON, M6K
3S3
(416) 504-4114
Emp Here 300   *Sales* 101,419,200
SIC 6531 Real estate agents and managers
Adam Paul

D-U-N-S 25-397-9827   (HQ)
FIRST CAPITAL REALTY INC
85 Hanna Ave Suite 400, Toronto, ON, M6K
3S3
(416) 504-4114
Emp Here 17   *Sales* 553,107,429
SIC 6512 Nonresidential building operators
Adam Paul
Kay Brekken
Jordan Robins
Jodi Shpigel
Carmine Francella
Maryanne Mcdougald
Alison Harnick
Dori Segal
Jon N Hagan
Allan Kimberley

D-U-N-S 24-991-6370   (SL)
FORREC LTD
FORREC DESIGN
219 Dufferin St Suite 100c, Toronto, ON, M6K
3J1
(416) 696-8686
Emp Here 70   *Sales* 39,923,660
SIC 1542 Nonresidential construction, nec
D.Cale Heit
Steven Rhys
Anthony Van Dam
Gordon Dorrett

D-U-N-S 20-364-1188   (SL)
FORTY CREEK DISTILLERY LTD
GRUPPO CAMPARI
(*Suby of* LAGFIN)
1 Pardee Ave Suite 102, Toronto, ON, M6K

3H1
(905) 945-9225
Emp Here 100   *Sales* 34,569,000
SIC 2085 Distilled and blended liquors

D-U-N-S 24-377-4325   (HQ)
LIVE NATION CANADA, INC
MOLSOM AMPHITHEATRE
(*Suby of* LIVE NATION ENTERTAINMENT,
INC.)
909 Lake Shore Blvd W Suite 300, Toronto,
ON, M6K 3L3
(416) 260-5600
Sales 21,090,816
SIC 7922 Theatrical producers and services
Michael Rapino
Kert Eric
Kathy Willard

D-U-N-S 20-052-0307   (HQ)
MARCATUS QED INC
43 Hanna Ave Unit C-424, Toronto, ON, M6K
1X1
(416) 255-0099
Sales 46,792,312
SIC 5149 Groceries and related products, nec
Murali Sundaralingam
Alec Wong

D-U-N-S 25-173-6948   (SL)
**MARKETING   STORE   WORLDWIDE
(CANADA) L.P., THE**
MARKETING STORE, THE
(*Suby of* THE HAVI GROUP LIMITED PART-
NERSHIP)
1209 King St W, Toronto, ON, M6K 1G2
(416) 583-3931
Emp Here 80   *Sales* 14,920,480
SIC 8743 Public relations services
John Hilbrich
Mark Eden
Paul Hains

D-U-N-S 25-220-6685   (SL)
**MEDIEVAL TIMES DINNER & TOURNA-
MENT (TORONTO) INC**
(*Suby of* MEDIEVAL TIMES ENTERTAIN-
MENT, INC.)
10 Dufferin St, Toronto, ON, M6K 3C3
(416) 260-1170
Emp Here 165   *Sales* 7,695,435
SIC 5812 Eating places
Mory Di Maurizio
Kenneth Kim

D-U-N-S 20-410-2466   (SL)
MEJURI INC
18 Mowat Ave Unit C, Toronto, ON, M6K 3E8
(416) 731-2600
Emp Here 42   *Sales* 11,752,155
SIC 5944 Jewelry stores
Noura Sakkijha
Majed Masad

D-U-N-S 24-320-4239   (HQ)
MEJURI INC
18 Mowat Ave, Toronto, ON, M6K 3E8
(416) 731-2600
Emp Here 76   *Sales* 19,710,652
SIC 5632 Women's accessory and specialty
stores
Noura Sakkijha
Majed Masad

D-U-N-S 20-552-8743   (BR)
METRO ONTARIO INC
METRO
(*Suby of* METRO INC)
100 Lynn Williams St Suite 572, Toronto, ON,
M6K 3N6
(416) 588-1300
Emp Here 250
SIC 5411 Grocery stores

D-U-N-S 20-550-0650   (HQ)
**PEOPLESOURCE STAFFING SOLUTIONS
INC**
67 Mowat Ave Suite 411, Toronto, ON, M6K

3E3
(905) 277-4455
Emp Here 20   *Sales* 10,189,710
SIC 7361 Employment agencies
John Nalli
Frank Cianciulli

D-U-N-S 24-387-1402   (HQ)
RAKUTEN KOBO INC
(*Suby of* RAKUTEN,INC.)
135 Liberty St Suite 101, Toronto, ON, M6K
1A7
(416) 977-8737
Sales 55,061,100
SIC 5942 Book stores
Michael Tamblyn
Takahito Aiki
Spencer Low
Alan Macnevin
Dan Budlovsky
Scott Cleaver
Pieter Swinkels
Dave Anderson
Trevor Hunter
Kyosuke Murota

D-U-N-S 24-425-3378   (SL)
RIVET CANADA
219 Dufferin St Suite 200a, Toronto, ON, M6K
3J1
(416) 483-3624
Emp Here 49   *Sales* 10,374,476
SIC 7311 Advertising agencies
Angele Elvesque

D-U-N-S 20-351-4971   (SL)
ROAM MOBILITY HOLDINGS, INC
(*Suby of* TUCOWS INC)
96 Mowat Ave, Toronto, ON, M6K 3M1
(416) 535-0123
Emp Here 450   *Sales* 150,544,800
SIC 4899 Communication services, nec
Elliot Noss
Dave Singh
Justen Burdette

D-U-N-S 24-581-6751   (SL)
ROYAL LE PAGE REAL ESTATE
905 King St W, Toronto, ON, M6K 3G9
(416) 271-1569
Emp Here 40   *Sales* 10,870,240
SIC 6531 Real estate agents and managers
Patricia Manning

D-U-N-S 20-251-5482   (HQ)
SIM VIDEO INTERNATIONAL INC
SIM DIGITAL
1 Atlantic Ave Suite 110, Toronto, ON, M6K
3E7
(416) 979-9958
Sales 19,988,880
SIC 7359 Equipment rental and leasing, nec
James Haggarty
Robert Sim
Stephen R. Brooks
Alex Sandahl

D-U-N-S 24-219-2099   (SL)
SINKING SHIP ENTERTAINMENT INC
1179 King St W Suite 302, Toronto, ON, M6K
3C5
(416) 533-8172
Emp Here 123   *Sales* 10,394,181
SIC 7812 Motion picture and video production
James Anthony Johnson
Blair Arthur Powers
Matthew James Rupert Bishop

D-U-N-S 24-313-1617   (SL)
SIRIUS XM CANADA HOLDINGS INC
135 Liberty St 4th Floor, Toronto, ON, M6K
1A7
(416) 408-6000
Emp Here 80   *Sales* 260,594,631
SIC 4832 Radio broadcasting stations
Mark Redmond
Jason Redman
Paul Cunningham

Mark Knapton
John Lewis
Oliver Jaakkola
Ian Gordon

D-U-N-S 24-204-3250   (SL)
SIRIUS XM CANADA INC
(*Suby of* LIBERTY MEDIA CORPORATION)
135 Liberty St Suite 400, Toronto, ON, M6K
1A7
(416) 513-7470
Emp Here 140   *Sales* 31,986,080
SIC 4832 Radio broadcasting stations
Mark Redmond
Mark Redmond
Paul Cunningham
John Lewis
Oliver Jaakkola

D-U-N-S 24-886-4415   (HQ)
SOFTCHOICE CORPORATION
(*Suby of* BIRCH HILL EQUITY PARTNERS
MANAGEMENT INC)
173 Dufferin St Suite 200, Toronto, ON, M6K
3H7
(416) 588-9002
Emp Here 600   *Sales* 249,173,550
SIC 7371 Custom computer programming services
David Macdonald
Simon Parmar
Kevin Wright
Anna Filipopoulos
Linda Millage

D-U-N-S 20-296-0514   (SL)
SOFTCHOICE LP
(*Suby of* BIRCH HILL EQUITY PARTNERS
MANAGEMENT INC)
173 Dufferin St Suite 200, Toronto, ON, M6K
3H7
(416) 588-9000
Emp Here 600
SIC 7371 Custom computer programming services
David Macdonald

D-U-N-S 25-213-2113   (SL)
STRATEGIC COACH INC, THE
33 Fraser Ave Suite 201, Toronto, ON, M6K
3J9
(416) 531-7399
Emp Here 80   *Sales* 21,946,560
SIC 8741 Management services
Dan Sullivan
Barbara Sue Smith

D-U-N-S 25-312-3665   (HQ)
STRATEGIC COMMUNICATIONS INC
1179 King St W Suite 202, Toronto, ON, M6K
3C5
(416) 537-6100
Emp Here 1   *Sales* 23,428,800
SIC 8748 Business consulting, nec
Robert Penner

D-U-N-S 25-340-3182   (SL)
TORONTO ARTSCAPE INC
TORONTO ARTSCAPE FOUNDATION
171 East Liberty St Suite 224, Toronto, ON,
M6K 3P6
(416) 392-1038
Emp Here 100   *Sales* 13,345,900
SIC 8399 Social services, nec
Tim Jones
Loriann Girvan
Pru Robie

D-U-N-S 20-698-7492   (BR)
TORONTO DISTRICT SCHOOL BOARD
QUEEN VICTORIA PUBLIC SCHOOL
(*Suby of* TORONTO DISTRICT SCHOOL
BOARD)
100 Close Ave, Toronto, ON, M6K 2V3
(416) 530-0683
Emp Here 100
SIC 8211 Elementary and secondary schools
Madelaine Allan

D-U-N-S 25-238-1009   (BR)
TORONTO DISTRICT SCHOOL BOARD
PARKDALE COLLEGIATE INSTITUTE
(*Suby of* TORONTO DISTRICT SCHOOL
BOARD)
209 Jameson Ave, Toronto, ON, M6K 2Y3
(416) 393-9000
Emp Here 75
SIC 8211 Elementary and secondary schools
Alisa Cashore

D-U-N-S 20-192-8186   (HQ)
TUCOWS INC
96 Mowat Ave, Toronto, ON, M6K 3M1
(416) 535-0123
Emp Here 195   *Sales* 346,013,000
SIC 4813 Telephone communication, except
radio
Elliot Noss
David Woroch
Michael Goldstein
Jason Silverstein
Jody Stocks
Ross Rader
Jessica Johannson
Dave Singh
Allen Karp
Rawleigh Ralls

D-U-N-S 25-691-1363   (HQ)
TUCOWS.COM CO
(*Suby of* TUCOWS INC)
96 Mowat Ave, Toronto, ON, M6K 3M1
(416) 535-0123
Sales 34,270,800
SIC 4813 Telephone communication, except
radio
Elliot Noss
Michael Cooperman

D-U-N-S 20-555-1067   (BR)
VISION 7 COMMUNICATIONS INC
COSSETTE
(*Suby of* VISION 7 INTERNATIONAL INC)
32 Atlantic Ave, Toronto, ON, M6K 1X8
(647) 253-0570
Emp Here 350
SIC 4899 Communication services, nec
Lisa Mae

D-U-N-S 25-340-5708   (SL)
WELCOME PHARMACY (QUEEN) LTD
PARKDALE GUARDIAN DRUGS
1488 Queen St W, Toronto, ON, M6K 1M4
(416) 533-2391
Emp Here 28   *Sales* 30,949,660
SIC 5122 Drugs, proprietaries, and sundries
Andrew Ng

D-U-N-S 20-300-4924   (SL)
ZOOMER MEDIA LIMITED
70 Jefferson Ave, Toronto, ON, M6K 1Y4
(416) 367-5353
Emp Here 100   *Sales* 21,335,800
SIC 8732 Commercial nonphysical research
Moses Znaimer

D-U-N-S 24-372-6242   (HQ)
ZOOMERMEDIA LIMITED
70 Jefferson Ave, Toronto, ON, M6K 1Y4
(416) 607-7735
Emp Here 5   *Sales* 40,394,435
SIC 7313 Radio, television, publisher representatives
Moses Znaimer
Lynn Kozak
Leanne Wright
Julia Johnston
Laas Turnbull
Omri Tintpulver
David Vickers
David Morgenthau
Peter Palframan
Chandran Ratnaswami

Toronto, ON M6L

D-U-N-S 25-294-8948   (BR)
WAL-MART CANADA CORP
(*Suby of* WALMART INC.)
1305 Lawrence Ave W, Toronto, ON, M6L 1A5
(416) 244-1171
Emp Here 260
SIC 5311 Department stores
Scott Thomas

Toronto, ON M6M

D-U-N-S 20-059-9418   (SL)
1508235 ONTARIO INC
MICRO FORUM SERVICES GROUP
1 Woodborough Ave, Toronto, ON, M6M 5A1
(416) 654-8008
Emp Here 55   *Sales* 10,474,310
SIC 3651 Household audio and video equipment
Frank Stipo
Noble Musa
Barbara Baiocchi

D-U-N-S 24-952-9074   (HQ)
**COMMISSO BROS. & RACCO ITALIAN
BAKERY INC**
8 Kincort St, Toronto, ON, M6M 3E1
(416) 651-7671
Sales 20,741,400
SIC 2051 Bread, cake, and related products
Tony Commisso
Giuseppe Racco
Frank Pizzimenti

D-U-N-S 24-078-3852   (SL)
DEE, ROSE E. (INTERNATIONAL) LIMITED
1450 Castlefield Ave, Toronto, ON, M6M 1Y6
(416) 658-2222
Emp Here 140   *Sales* 117,254,620
SIC 5131 Piece goods and notions
Steve Pippert
Warren Kimel

D-U-N-S 20-555-5345   (HQ)
**FABRICLAND DISTRIBUTORS (WESTERN)
CORP**
FABRICLAND
1450 Castlefield Ave, Toronto, ON, M6M 1Y6
(416) 658-2200
Emp Here 4   *Sales* 24,432,800
SIC 5949 Sewing, needlework, and piece
goods
Manuel Kimel
Marcel Fuhrer

D-U-N-S 20-551-8673   (HQ)
FABRICLAND DISTRIBUTORS INC
1450 Castlefield Ave, Toronto, ON, M6M 1Y6
(416) 658-2200
Emp Here 50   *Sales* 137,652,750
SIC 5949 Sewing, needlework, and piece
goods
Warren Kimel

D-U-N-S 25-202-6703   (SL)
GOLDRICH PRINTPAK INC
100 Industry St, Toronto, ON, M6M 4L8
(416) 769-9000
Emp Here 65   *Sales* 15,173,275
SIC 2657 Folding paperboard boxes
Leslie Goldberg

D-U-N-S 25-215-1923   (HQ)
HODDOR LIGHTING INC
SESCOLITE LIGHTING
1461 Castlefield Ave, Toronto, ON, M6M 1Y4
(416) 651-6570
Emp Here 25   *Sales* 10,458,135
SIC 5719 Miscellaneous homefurnishings
Doug Grand

▲ Public Company   ■ Public Company Family Member   **HQ** Headquarters   **BR** Branch   **SL** Single Location

D-U-N-S 25-936-9635   (BR)
IRVING CONSUMER PRODUCTS LIMITED
IRVING, J D
(*Suby of* IRVING, J. D. LIMITED)
1551 Weston Rd, Toronto, ON, M6M 4Y4
(416) 246-6666
Emp Here 400
SIC 2676 Sanitary paper products
Tim Latanville

D-U-N-S 20-311-9284   (BR)
IRVING CONSUMER PRODUCTS LIMITED
JD IRVING
(*Suby of* IRVING, J. D. LIMITED)
1551 Weston Rd, Toronto, ON, M6M 4Y4
(416) 246-6666
Emp Here 400
SIC 2676 Sanitary paper products
Bill Viger

D-U-N-S 25-511-5834   (SL)
ITIF INC
25 Bertal Rd Unit 9, Toronto, ON, M6M 4M7

Emp Here 25   *Sales* 11,179,350
SIC 5046 Commercial equipment, nec
Tony Bennett

D-U-N-S 20-402-5886   (SL)
KINCORT BAKERY LIMITED
8 Kincort St, Toronto, ON, M6M 3E1
(416) 651-7671
Emp Here 60   *Sales* 15,693,180
SIC 6719 Holding companies, nec
Frank Commisso
Joe Commisso
Michael Commisso

D-U-N-S 24-033-9775   (BR)
LOBLAW PROPERTIES LIMITED
REAL CANADIAN WHOLESALE CLUB, THE
(*Suby of* LOBLAW COMPANIES LIMITED)
605 Rogers Rd Suite 208, Toronto, ON, M6M
1B9
(416) 653-1951
Emp Here 80
SIC 5411 Grocery stores
Davis Joseph

D-U-N-S 20-050-6942   (SL)
**MILLWORKS CUSTOM MANUFACTURING
(2001) INC**
MCM 2001
25 Bertal Rd Unit 9, Toronto, ON, M6M 4M7
(416) 760-0222
Emp Here 85   *Sales* 13,248,355
SIC 2431 Millwork
Gregory Rybak
Sean Baldwin

D-U-N-S 20-171-2858   (HQ)
MOTORCADE INDUSTRIES INC
MOTORCADE AUTO PARTS
(*Suby of* GROUPE MONACO AUTOMOTIVE
INC)
90 Kincort St, Toronto, ON, M6M 5G1
(416) 614-6118
Emp Here 70   *Sales* 69,173,100
SIC 5013 Motor vehicle supplies and new
parts
Jerold Winter

D-U-N-S 20-079-0249   (BR)
NUCLEUS INDEPENDENT LIVING
(*Suby of* NUCLEUS INDEPENDENT LIVING)
30 Denarda St Suite 309, Toronto, ON, M6M
5C3
(416) 244-1234
Emp Here 150
SIC 8361 Residential care
Anne Newman

D-U-N-S 20-761-5506   (SL)
OFFICE COFFEE SOLUTIONS LTD
82 Industry St, Toronto, ON, M6M 4L7
(416) 516-9333
Emp Here 25   *Sales* 11,179,350
SIC 5046 Commercial equipment, nec

Claudio David

D-U-N-S 24-631-5766   (BR)
REVERA INC
HAROLD & GRACE BAKER CENTRE
(*Suby of* GOVERNMENT OF CANADA)
1 Northwestern Ave, Toronto, ON, M6M 2J7
(416) 654-2889
Emp Here 200
SIC 8051 Skilled nursing care facilities
Milena Sujer

D-U-N-S 24-925-2529   (HQ)
ROCHON BUILDING CORPORATION
*ROCHON NATIONAL SMALL PROJECT DIV
OF*
74 Industry St, Toronto, ON, M6M 4L7
(416) 638-6666
Sales 34,220,280
SIC 1542 Nonresidential construction, nec
Martin Rochon

D-U-N-S 24-721-4125   (SL)
ST CLAIR WEST SERVICES FOR SENIORS
2562 Eglinton Ave W Suite 202, Toronto, ON,
M6M 1T4
(416) 787-2114
Emp Here 90   *Sales* 12,011,310
SIC 8399 Social services, nec
Susan Rego
Sujata Ganglu

D-U-N-S 24-937-1980   (BR)
TORONTO DISTRICT SCHOOL BOARD
YORK MEMORIAL COLLEGIATE INSTITUTE
(*Suby of* TORONTO DISTRICT SCHOOL
BOARD)
2690 Eglinton Ave W, Toronto, ON, M6M 1T9
(416) 394-3000
Emp Here 150
SIC 8211 Elementary and secondary schools
Suzana Greenaway

D-U-N-S 25-300-9153   (BR)
TORONTO DISTRICT SCHOOL BOARD
YORK HUMBER HIGH SCHOOL
(*Suby of* TORONTO DISTRICT SCHOOL
BOARD)
100 Emmett Ave, Toronto, ON, M6M 2E6
(416) 394-3280
Emp Here 75
SIC 8211 Elementary and secondary schools
Rhonda Davy

D-U-N-S 24-966-1828   (SL)
UNION ELECTRIC LIGHTING CO. LTD
UNION LIGHTING & FURNISHINGS
1491 Castlefield Ave, Toronto, ON, M6M 1Y3
(416) 652-2200
Emp Here 82   *Sales* 19,057,046
SIC 5719 Miscellaneous homefurnishings
Mark Naimer

D-U-N-S 20-845-3654   (SL)
WEST PARK HEALTHCARE CENTRE
82 Buttonwood Ave Suite 1121, Toronto, ON,
M6M 2J5
(416) 243-3600
Emp Here 900   *Sales* 99,972,000
SIC 8069 Specialty hospitals, except psychi-
atric
Anne-Marie Malek
Jay Cooper
Donna Ronzetti
Christianne Abou-Saab
Michael Bonnah

Toronto, ON M6N

D-U-N-S 24-133-6622   (SL)
1222433 ONTARIO INC
STARK IRON & METAL
144 Union St, Toronto, ON, M6N 3M9
(416) 654-3464
Emp Here 30   *Sales* 15,616,260

SIC 5093 Scrap and waste materials
Steven Stark

D-U-N-S 24-896-5303   (SL)
1416018 ONTARIO LIMITED
DENI'S FOOD BASICS
853 Jane St, Toronto, ON, M6N 4C4
(416) 762-7975
Emp Here 72   *Sales* 21,130,344
SIC 5411 Grocery stores
Denis Veillette

D-U-N-S 24-333-8845   (SL)
A.C.D. WHOLESALE MEATS LTD
140 Ryding Ave, Toronto, ON, M6N 1H2
(416) 766-2200
Emp Here 30   *Sales* 25,067,310
SIC 5147 Meats and meat products
Albert Domingues

D-U-N-S 24-844-0661   (SL)
BENNY STARK LIMITED
200 Union St, Toronto, ON, M6N 3M9
(416) 654-3464
Emp Here 55   *Sales* 28,629,810
SIC 5093 Scrap and waste materials
Stephen Stark
Martin Gollan

D-U-N-S 20-528-0522   (SL)
**BERNARD ATHLETIC KNIT & ENTER-
PRISES LIMITED**
ATHLETIC KNIT
2 Scarlett Rd, Toronto, ON, M6N 4J6
(416) 766-6151
Emp Here 250   *Sales* 209,383,250
SIC 5137 Women's and children's clothing
Bernard Sliwin

D-U-N-S 20-042-1308   (BR)
CANADA BREAD COMPANY, LIMITED
CENTRAL BAKERY DEMPSTER
(*Suby of* GRUPO BIMBO, S.A.B. DE C.V.)
130 Cawthra Ave, Toronto, ON, M6N 3C2
(416) 626-4382
Emp Here 100
SIC 2051 Bread, cake, and related products
Luciano Masella

D-U-N-S 20-162-4673   (HQ)
CONSOLIDATED BOTTLE CORPORATION
HUMPHREY COSBURN PLASTICS
(*Suby of* BAKBOOK FINANCIAL INC)
77 Union St, Toronto, ON, M6N 3N2
(800) 561-1354
Emp Here 82   *Sales* 70,699,080
SIC 5199 Nondurable goods, nec
Sam Susswein
Hengen Chow
Stephen Bubnich
Jonathan Rutman

D-U-N-S 24-008-0887   (SL)
CONSULTEC LTD
139 Mulock Ave, Toronto, ON, M6N 1G9
(416) 236-2426
Emp Here 70   *Sales* 12,511,730
SIC 8711 Engineering services
George Ochrym
Alexander Ochrym

D-U-N-S 20-164-7476   (SL)
**EVERLITE LUGGAGE MANUFACTURING
LIMITED**
BUSHMASTER HUNTING & FISHING
451 Alliance Ave, Toronto, ON, M6N 2J1
(416) 763-4040
Emp Here 50   *Sales* 26,027,100
SIC 5099 Durable goods, nec
Philip La Rosa
Rita La Rosa
Cosimo La Rosa
Joseph La Rosa
Nina La Rosa

D-U-N-S 25-791-2618   (SL)
GENESIS MEAT PACKERS INC
70 Glen Scarlett Rd, Toronto, ON, M6N 1P4

Emp Here 50   *Sales* 11,242,750
SIC 2011 Meat packing plants
Joe Petronaci

D-U-N-S 25-754-2944   (BR)
HOME DEPOT OF CANADA INC
HOME DEPOT
(*Suby of* THE HOME DEPOT INC)
2121 St Clair Ave W, Toronto, ON, M6N 5A8
(416) 766-2800
Emp Here 300
SIC 5251 Hardware stores

D-U-N-S 20-341-3372   (SL)
ICON INSULATION INC
935 Weston Rd, Toronto, ON, M6N 3R4
(647) 945-9648
Emp Here 135   *Sales* 21,921,435
SIC 1742 Plastering, drywall, and insulation
Ken Demelo
Stephen Hubbert
Dave Caley
Debbie Plener

D-U-N-S 20-175-2037   (SL)
KEN SHAW MOTORS LIMITED
SHAW, KEN LEXUS TOYOTA
2336 St Clair Ave W, Toronto, ON, M6N 1K8
(416) 766-0055
Emp Here 75   *Sales* 47,196,000
SIC 5511 New and used car dealers
Kennedy Shaw, Sr
Ken Shaw, Jr
Paul Shaw

D-U-N-S 24-344-5108   (BR)
MAPLE LEAF FOODS INC
(*Suby of* MAPLE LEAF FOODS INC)
100 Ethel Ave, Toronto, ON, M6N 4Z7
(416) 767-5151
Emp Here 700
SIC 2015 Poultry slaughtering and processing
Michael Foster

D-U-N-S 24-173-8231   (BR)
**MCDONALD'S RESTAURANTS OF
CANADA LIMITED**
MCDONALD'S
(*Suby of* MCDONALD'S CORPORATION)
630 Keele St, Toronto, ON, M6N 3E2
(416) 604-1496
Emp Here 100
SIC 5812 Eating places
John Porfilio

D-U-N-S 24-364-1417   (SL)
MORGAN SOLAR INC
100 Symes Rd Unit 100a, Toronto, ON, M6N
0A8
(416) 203-1655
Emp Here 51   *Sales* 11,717,454
SIC 8731 Commercial physical research
Asif Ansari
Hugo Navarro
Thomas Rand
Angeles Santamaria Martin
Nicholas Morgan
Sean Carton
Philip Chang
Stefan Myrskog
John Paul Morgan
Eric Nicolas Morgan

D-U-N-S 24-322-6987   (HQ)
**NATIONAL RUBBER TECHNOLOGIES
CORP**
(*Suby of* KINDERHOOK INDUSTRIES, LLC)
35 Cawthra Ave, Toronto, ON, M6N 5B3
(416) 657-1111
Sales 117,830,925
SIC 2822 Synthetic rubber
Terry Tomlinson
Manuel Estragadimho
Corwynne Carruthers

D-U-N-S 24-324-0020   (BR)
NATIONAL RUBBER TECHNOLOGIES

CORP
(*Suby of* KINDERHOOK INDUSTRIES, LLC)
394 Symington Ave, Toronto, ON, M6N 2W3
(416) 657-1111
Emp Here 130
SIC 2822 Synthetic rubber
Greg Bavington

D-U-N-S 20-172-1115   (HQ)
OLD MILL PONTIAC BUICK CADILLAC LIMITED
EZEE LEASING
2595 St Clair Ave W, Toronto, ON, M6N 4Z5
(416) 766-2443
Sales 50,342,400
SIC 5511 New and used car dealers
Lou Vavaroutsos
Stu Esplen
Joseph Pede

D-U-N-S 20-176-4479   (HQ)
PHANTOM INDUSTRIES INC
207 Weston Rd, Toronto, ON, M6N 4Z3
(416) 762-7177
Emp Here 475   *Sales* 125,346,590
SIC 2251 Women's hosiery, except socks
Alex Strasser
Ronnie Strasser
Franca Rossini
Frank Marascio

D-U-N-S 25-088-6645   (BR)
RECIPE UNLIMITED CORPORATION
CARA OPERATIONS LIMITED
(*Suby of* RECIPE UNLIMITED CORPORATION)
590 Keele St, Toronto, ON, M6N 3E2
(416) 760-7893
Emp Here 100
SIC 5812 Eating places
Lisa Amorim

D-U-N-S 24-829-8119   (SL)
RYDING-REGENCY MEAT PACKERS LTD
70 Glen Scarlett Rd, Toronto, ON, M6N 1P4
(416) 763-1611
Emp Here 100   *Sales* 83,557,700
SIC 5147 Meats and meat products
Guiseppe Petronaci
Greg Bennett

D-U-N-S 20-175-3910   (SL)
SILVANO COLOR LABORATORIES LIMITED
355 Weston Rd, Toronto, ON, M6N 4Y7

Emp Here 38   *Sales* 15,865,228
SIC 7384 Photofinish laboratories
Silvano Venuto Jr.
John Sacilotto

D-U-N-S 24-062-9469   (HQ)
ST. HELEN'S MEAT PACKERS LIMITED
55 Glen Scarlett Rd, Toronto, ON, M6N 1P5
(416) 769-1788
Sales 107,507,400
SIC 5147 Meats and meat products
Marsha Bielak
Robert Bielak
Marilyn Gold
Sylvia Bielak

D-U-N-S 24-991-9887   (SL)
TALLON, TIMOTHY J SALES INC
CANADIAN TIRE 182
2129 St Clair Ave W Suite 182, Toronto, ON, M6N 5B4
(416) 766-8141
Emp Here 200   *Sales* 125,856,000
SIC 5531 Auto and home supply stores
Timothy Tallon

D-U-N-S 20-176-7209   (SL)
TERRAZZO MOSAIC & TILE COMPANY LIMITED
TMT
900 Keele St, Toronto, ON, M6N 3E7

(416) 653-6111
Emp Here 75   *Sales* 12,178,575
SIC 1743 Terrazzo, tile, marble and mossaic work
Carlo Onorati
Enzo Costantino

D-U-N-S 20-700-2275   (BR)
TORONTO CATHOLIC DISTRICT SCHOOL BOARD
OUR LADY OF VICTORY CATHOLIC SCHOOL
(*Suby of* TORONTO CATHOLIC DISTRICT SCHOOL BOARD)
70 Guestville Ave, Toronto, ON, M6N 4N3
(416) 393-5247
Emp Here 100
SIC 8211 Elementary and secondary schools
Laura Warburton

D-U-N-S 20-067-9228   (BR)
TORONTO CATHOLIC DISTRICT SCHOOL BOARD
ARCHBISHOP ROMERO CATHOLIC SECONDARY SCHOOL
(*Suby of* TORONTO CATHOLIC DISTRICT SCHOOL BOARD)
99 Humber Blvd, Toronto, ON, M6N 2H4
(416) 393-5555
Emp Here 100
SIC 8211 Elementary and secondary schools
Nancy Mancini

D-U-N-S 25-294-5191   (BR)
TORONTO DISTRICT SCHOOL BOARD
GEORGE SYME COMMUNITY SCHOOL
(*Suby of* TORONTO DISTRICT SCHOOL BOARD)
69 Pritchard Ave, Toronto, ON, M6N 1T6
(416) 394-2340
Emp Here 90
SIC 8211 Elementary and secondary schools
Ali Jahangir

D-U-N-S 20-171-7154   (HQ)
UNICER FOODS LTD
370 Alliance Ave, Toronto, ON, M6N 2H8
(416) 766-9535
Sales 20,053,848
SIC 5141 Groceries, general line
Jose Cerqueira
Dulce Cerqueira
Frank Cerqueira
Andrew Cerqueira

D-U-N-S 24-319-1090   (BR)
WAL-MART CANADA CORP
WAL-MART
(*Suby of* WALMART INC.)
2525 St Clair Ave W, Toronto, ON, M6N 4Z5
(416) 763-7325
Emp Here 120
SIC 5311 Department stores
Carlos Goncalves

D-U-N-S 24-869-1974   (SL)
WEST YORK CHEVROLET INC
1785 St Clair Ave W, Toronto, ON, M6N 1J6
(416) 656-1200
Emp Here 60   *Sales* 37,756,800
SIC 5511 New and used car dealers
William Seedhouse
Deeter Rieckermann

D-U-N-S 20-178-5763   (HQ)
WOLF, PAUL LIGHTING & ELECTRIC SUPPLY LIMITED
425 Alliance Ave, Toronto, ON, M6N 2J1
(416) 504-8195
Emp Here 45   *Sales* 22,358,700
SIC 5063 Electrical apparatus and equipment
Dean Hamill
Bruce Milligan
Domenic Calabria
Scott Schooley
Cosmo Amato

Toronto, ON M6P

D-U-N-S 20-278-0946   (SL)
1882540 ONTARIO INC
WHAT A BLOOM CANADA
1444 Dupont St Unit 11, Toronto, ON, M6P 4H3
(416) 516-1569
Emp Here 47   *Sales* 34,898,440
SIC 5193 Flowers and florists supplies
Cesario Ginjo

D-U-N-S 20-262-0142   (SL)
1924345 ONTARIO INC
FRESHBOOKS
1655 Dupont St Suite 250, Toronto, ON, M6P 3T1
(416) 481-6946
Emp Here 184   *Sales* 38,214,040
SIC 8721 Accounting, auditing, and book-keeping
Michael Mcderment
Joseph Sawada
Levi Cooperman
Shawn Cadeau
Mark Girvan
Rich Laferty
Steve Bujouves
Richard Kwok
Jeremy Bailey
Avru Laurie

D-U-N-S 20-175-7101   (SL)
570026 ONTARIO LIMITED
SOLWAY METAL SALES
26 Ernest Ave, Toronto, ON, M6P 3M7
(416) 531-1131
Emp Here 15   *Sales* 15,005,085
SIC 5051 Metals service centers and offices
Jack Bettel
Howard Bettel

D-U-N-S 25-171-2782   (HQ)
GOVAN BROWN & ASSOCIATES LIMITED
GOVAN BROWN CONSTRUCTION MANAGERS
108 Vine Ave, Toronto, ON, M6P 1V7
(416) 703-5100
Emp Here 85   *Sales* 15,597,000
SIC 8741 Management services
John Brown
Ralph Govan
Jonathan Taylor

D-U-N-S 24-347-6616   (SL)
HORTICULTURAL SOCIETIES OF PARKDALE & TORONTO
1938 Bloor St W, Toronto, ON, M6P 3K8
(416) 486-0898
Emp Here 200   *Sales* 51,550,679
SIC 8748 Business consulting, nec
Judy Whalen

D-U-N-S 20-190-0789   (HQ)
MIMRAN, JOSEPH & ASSOCIATES INC
PINK TARTAN
1485 Dupont St, Toronto, ON, M6P 3S2
(416) 516-0641
Emp Here 10   *Sales* 17,939,600
SIC 5699 Miscellaneous apparel and accessory stores
Kimberley Newport-Mimran
Joseph Mimran

D-U-N-S 25-940-4192   (SL)
NAVANTIS INC
21 Randolph Ave Suite 200, Toronto, ON, M6P 4G4
(416) 532-5554
Emp Here 161   *Sales* 26,862,367
SIC 7379 Computer related services, nec
Frank Clegg
Jason Martin
Rick Gaisser

D-U-N-S 20-385-7672   (SL)
OUAT MEDIA INC
CHANNEL ZERO
(*Suby of* CHANNEL ZERO INC)
2844 Dundas St W, Toronto, ON, M6P 1Y7
(416) 492-1595
Emp Here 100
SIC 4833 Television broadcasting stations
Romen Podzyhun
C.J. Millar
Chris Fuoco

D-U-N-S 20-628-8966   (SL)
RE MAX WEST REALTY BROKERAGE INC
REMAX QUEST REALITY
1678 Bloor St W, Toronto, ON, M6P 1A9
(416) 769-1616
Emp Here 100   *Sales* 27,175,600
SIC 6531 Real estate agents and managers
Frank Costaltial

D-U-N-S 24-685-2300   (SL)
SCOUT LOGISTICS CORPORATION
3351 Dundas St W, Toronto, ON, M6P 2A6
(416) 630-7268
Emp Here 25   *Sales* 12,999,175
SIC 4731 Freight transportation arrangement
Lorne Swartz
Hannah Abrams

D-U-N-S 24-616-8574   (SL)
SWEET POTATO INC, THE
108 Vine Ave, Toronto, ON, M6P 1V7
(416) 762-4848
Emp Here 50   *Sales* 41,778,850
SIC 5149 Groceries and related products, nec
Digs Dorfman
Cj Chiddy

D-U-N-S 24-765-1383   (SL)
TREBAS INSTITUTE ONTARIO INC
2340 Dundas St W Suite 2, Toronto, ON, M6P 4A9
(416) 966-3066
Emp Here 75   *Sales* 8,766,525
SIC 8221 Colleges and universities
David Leonard

Toronto, ON M6R

D-U-N-S 20-983-8726   (SL)
AUTHENTIC CONCIERGE AND SECURITY SERVICES INC
PILLAR SECURITY
2333 Dundas St W Suite 206, Toronto, ON, M6R 3A6
(416) 777-1812
Emp Here 55   *Sales* 21,762,290
SIC 7381 Detective and armored car services
Fapsah Bennai

D-U-N-S 20-190-1317   (SL)
CANADIAN DENTAL RELIEF INTERNATIONAL
203 Parkside Dr, Toronto, ON, M6R 2Z2

Emp Here 150   *Sales* 16,662,000
SIC 8062 General medical and surgical hospitals
Brian Eckert

D-U-N-S 25-791-5116   (SL)
CONSUMER/SURVIVOR BUSINESS COUNCIL OF ONTARIO
ONTARIO COUNCIL OF ALTERNATIVE BUSINESSES
1499 Queen St W Suite 203, Toronto, ON, M6R 1A3
(416) 504-1693
Emp Here 160   *Sales* 33,130,880
SIC 8399 Social services, nec
Pat Fowler

D-U-N-S 20-847-1185   (HQ)
FAMILY SERVICE TORONTO

202-128a Sterling Rd, Toronto, ON, M6R 2B7
(416) 595-9230
Emp Here 120   *Sales* 11,518,800
SIC 8322 Individual and family services
Margaret Hancock
Harlan Schonfeld
Fran Odette
Miriam Digiuseppe
Tanbir Grover
Derek Ballantyne

D-U-N-S 24-915-1866   (SL)
HUGH'S ROOM
2261 Dundas St W, Toronto, ON, M6R 1X6
(416) 533-5483
Emp Here 49   *Sales* 14,136,451
SIC 6512 Nonresidential building operators
Richard Parson

D-U-N-S 24-802-7869   (SL)
MAINTENANCE ASSISTANT INC
FIIX SOFTWARE
35 Golden Ave Suite A-201, Toronto, ON, M6R
2J5
(647) 317-9055
Emp Here 50   *Sales* 10,692,550
SIC 7372 Prepackaged software
Marc Castel
Daryl Sedgman
James Novak

D-U-N-S 24-803-1122   (BR)
NESTLE CANADA INC
(*Suby of* NESTLE S.A.)
72 Sterling Rd, Toronto, ON, M6R 2B6
(416) 535-2181
Emp Here 505
SIC 2064 Candy and other confectionery
products
Eda Siliplic

D-U-N-S 20-714-7658   (SL)
ONTARIO FAMILY GROUP HOMES INC
146 Westminster Ave, Toronto, ON, M6R 1N7
(416) 532-6234
Emp Here 75   *Sales* 4,880,625
SIC 8361 Residential care
Lynda Parsons
Cindy Alexander

D-U-N-S 24-419-7042   (HQ)
ROWE FARM MEATS LIMITED
ROWE FARM
105 Roncesvalles Ave, Toronto, ON, M6R 2K9
(416) 532-3738
Emp Here 10   *Sales* 41,778,850
SIC 5147 Meats and meat products
Jamie Cooney

D-U-N-S 20-817-2064   (HQ)
**ST STANISLAUS-ST CASIMIR'S POLISH
PARISHES CREDIT UNION LIMITED**
220 Roncesvalles Ave, Toronto, ON, M6R 2L7
(416) 537-2181
Emp Here 50   *Sales* 10,713,806
SIC 6062 State credit unions
Andrzej Pitek
Robert Jagielski
Elibieta Morgan
Lucyna Jankowicz
Mark Taborowski
Kazimierz Babiarz
Peter Mazurkiewicz
Miros'aw Ruta
Alfred Zawadzki
Bill Botha

D-U-N-S 20-608-2448   (HQ)
ST. JOSEPH'S HEALTH CENTRE
30 The Queensway, Toronto, ON, M6R 1B5
(416) 530-6000
Sales 222,160,000
SIC 8062 General medical and surgical hospitals
Elizabeth Buller
Daniel Cass
Maria Dyck

David Graham
Mike Heenan
Mary Macleod
Jenni Glad-Timmons

D-U-N-S 20-809-4271   (SL)
ST. JOSEPH'S PROVINCE HOUSE INC
419 Parkside Dr, Toronto, ON, M6R 2Z7
(416) 604-7992
Emp Here 48   *Sales* 19,075,872
SIC 8699 Membership organizations, nec
Hugh O Neil

Toronto, ON M6S

D-U-N-S 20-817-9200   (HQ)
ARBOR MEMORIAL SERVICES INC
ARBOR MEMORIAL
2 Jane St Suite 101, Toronto, ON, M6S 4W8
(416) 763-3230
Emp Here 135   *Sales* 754,882,855
SIC 6553 Cemetery subdividers and developers
Brian Snowdon
David Scanlan
Michael J Scanlan
Laura Ancheta
Gary D Rogerson

D-U-N-S 24-092-6386   (SL)
CHUNG, A. T. PHARMACY LIMITED
SHOPPERS DRUG MART
2290 Bloor St W Suite 989, Toronto, ON, M6S
1N9
(416) 769-1105
Emp Here 40   *Sales* 10,118,160
SIC 5912 Drug stores and proprietary stores
Tony Chung

D-U-N-S 20-164-7500   (SL)
CORONA JEWELLERY COMPANY LTD
CORONA COMPANY
16 Ripley Ave, Toronto, ON, M6S 3P1
(416) 762-2222
Emp Here 60   *Sales* 19,568,160
SIC 3911 Jewelry, precious Metal

D-U-N-S 24-173-5930   (SL)
HUMBERVIEW GROUP LTD
2500 Bloor St W, Toronto, ON, M6S 1R7

Emp Here 700   *Sales* 404,076,400
SIC 5511 New and used car dealers
John C Esplen

D-U-N-S 24-344-4333   (SL)
INTRACHEM INDUSTRIES INC
476 Armadale Ave, Toronto, ON, M6S 3X9
(416) 760-0929
Emp Here 41   *Sales* 29,944,145
SIC 5169 Chemicals and allied products, nec
Fawzi Kfoury

D-U-N-S 25-538-6070   (HQ)
NAUTILUS MINERALS INC
2100 Bloor St W Suite 6125, Toronto, ON,
M6S 5A5
(416) 551-1100
Emp Here 8   *Sales* 19,950,372
SIC 1081 Metal mining services
Michael Johnston
Tariq Al Barwani
Stuart Mackenzie
Mohammed Ali Al Barwani
Jay Layman
Jonathan Whitworth
Glenn Withers

D-U-N-S 20-077-2767   (SL)
NETWORK MESSENGER INC
34 Magwood Crt, Toronto, ON, M6S 2M5
(416) 777-2278
Emp Here 25   *Sales* 11,087,250
SIC 7389 Business services, nec
Jonathan Davies

D-U-N-S 25-193-2513   (BR)
NORTHERN REFLECTIONS LTD
(*Suby of* NORTHERN ACQUISITION HOLDINGS CORP)
2198 Bloor St W, Toronto, ON, M6S 1N4
(416) 769-8378
Emp Here 108
SIC 5621 Women's clothing stores
Lalonnie Biggar

D-U-N-S 24-462-8319   (SL)
RUNNYMEDE HEALTHCARE CENTRE
625 Runnymede Rd, Toronto, ON, M6S 3A3
(416) 762-7316
Emp Here 200   *Sales* 13,665,200
SIC 8051 Skilled nursing care facilities
Connie Dejak

D-U-N-S 20-177-3926   (HQ)
TURNER & PORTER FUNERAL DIRECTORS LIMITED
TURNER & PORTER
380 Windermere Ave, Toronto, ON, M6S 3L4
(416) 767-7452
Emp Here 12   *Sales* 11,425,674
SIC 7261 Funeral service and crematories
Doug Porter

Toronto, ON M7A

D-U-N-S 25-430-6140   (SL)
CALL2RECYCLE CANADA, INC
5140 Yonge St Unit 1570, Toronto, ON, M7A
2K2
(888) 224-9764
Emp Here 100   *Sales* 18,138,800
SIC 3356 Nonferrous rolling and drawing, nec
Jeff Haltrecht
Carl Smith
Maury Mccausland
Saquib Vali
Gordon Gow
Harriet Velazquez
Jules Lapointe
Katherine Larocque

D-U-N-S 20-868-3461   (BR)
GOVERNMENT OF ONTARIO
OFFICE OF THE CHIEF INFORMATION OFFICER
(*Suby of* GOVERNMENT OF ONTARIO)
900 Bay St Suite 200, Toronto, ON, M7A 1L2
(866) 797-0000
Emp Here 250
SIC 7299 Miscellaneous personal service
Soussan Tabari

D-U-N-S 24-336-1040   (BR)
GOVERNMENT OF ONTARIO
ONTARIO MINISTRY OF LABOUR
(*Suby of* GOVERNMENT OF ONTARIO)
400 University Ave 14th Flr, Toronto, ON, M7A
1T7
(416) 326-7600
Emp Here 500
SIC 8111 Legal services
Kevin Flynn

D-U-N-S 24-375-4129   (HQ)
HALLCON CORPORATION
(*Suby of* SOUTHFIELD CAPITAL ADVISORS,
LLC)
5775 Yonge St Suite 1010, Toronto, ON, M7A
2E5
(416) 964-9191
Emp Here 250   *Sales* 217,490,900
SIC 4741 Rental of railroad cars
Anton G Plut
Kevin A Ramsay
Brian Kirk
Kevin Blair Melnyk
Bradley Wayne Ashley

D-U-N-S 20-980-4681   (HQ)

**MULTIPLE SCLEROSIS SOCIETY OF
CANADA**
MS
250 Dundas St W Unit 500, Toronto, ON, M7A
1G1
(416) 922-6065
Emp Here 100   *Sales* 39,197,487
SIC 8399 Social services, nec
Sylvia Leonard
Gayelene Bonenfant
John Folka
Valerie Hussey
Francois Coupal
John Clifford
Marie Josee Comtois
Rahil Dattu
Tom Feasby
Bonnie Gleim

Toronto, ON M8V

D-U-N-S 25-419-3196   (SL)
BONDI PRODUCE CO. LTD
188 New Toronto St, Toronto, ON, M8V 2E8
(416) 252-7799
Emp Here 50   *Sales* 41,778,850
SIC 5148 Fresh fruits and vegetables
Gaspare Bondi

Toronto, ON M8W

D-U-N-S 24-688-1601   (BR)
FCA CANADA INC
ETOBICOKE CASTING PLANT
(*Suby of* FIAT CHRYSLER AUTOMOBILES
N.V.)
15 Browns Line, Toronto, ON, M8W 3S3
(416) 253-2300
Emp Here 450
SIC 3365 Aluminum foundries
Mike Butz

D-U-N-S 20-173-8242   (SL)
FOAMEX CANADA INC
415 Evans Ave, Toronto, ON, M8W 2T2

Emp Here 208   *Sales* 66,501,985
SIC 2821 Plastics materials and resins

D-U-N-S 25-294-5456   (HQ)
FREEMAN EXPOSITIONS, LTD
FREEMAN
(*Suby of* FREEMAN DECORATING CO.)
61 Browns Line, Toronto, ON, M8W 3S2
(416) 252-3361
Emp Here 38   *Sales* 30,177,882
SIC 7389 Business services, nec
Martin Cymbal
Joe Popolo

Toronto, ON M8X

D-U-N-S 24-875-3303   (HQ)
DISTRIBUTEL COMMUNICATIONS LIMITED
3300 Bloor St W Suite 800, Toronto, ON, M8X
2X2
(416) 324-2861
Emp Here 31   *Sales* 25,360,392
SIC 4899 Communication services, nec
Matt Stein
Gerry Vanderpost

D-U-N-S 24-383-7015   (HQ)
EDUCATOURS LTD
BRIGHTSPARK
(*Suby of* TUI AG)
3280 Bloor St W Suite 901, Toronto, ON, M8X

▲ Public Company   ■ Public Company Family Member   **HQ** Headquarters   **BR** Branch   **SL** Single Location

2X3
(416) 251-3390
Sales 23,918,482
SIC 4725 Tour operators
Linda Philp

D-U-N-S 20-924-3658   (SL)
LONTOURS CANADA LIMITED
GLOBUS FAMILY OF BRANDS
3280 Bloor St W 4 Fl Suite 400, Toronto, ON, M8X 2X3
(800) 268-3636
Emp Here 35   *Sales* 13,487,600
SIC 4724 Travel agencies
Steve Mccullough
Antonella Santia

D-U-N-S 20-383-2514   (SL)
MOTUS BANK
(*Suby of* MERIDIAN CREDIT UNION LIMITED)
3280 Bloor St W Centre Tower Suite 700, Toronto, ON, M8X 2X3
(905) 988-1000
Emp Here 100
SIC 6021 National commercial banks
David Baldarelli

D-U-N-S 25-711-0049   (SL)
ONTARIO PC PARTY
56 Aberfoyle Cres Unit 400, Toronto, ON, M8X 2W4
(416) 861-0020
Emp Here 50   *Sales* 13,669,750
SIC 8651 Political organizations
Jag Badwal
Marc Marzotto
Siri Vallipuranathar
Kaydee Richmond
Luca Bucci
Elanor Brodie
Zack Goldford
Andrew Brande
Gaggan Gill
Alanna Newman

D-U-N-S 25-972-3781   (SL)
STARLIGHT U.S. MULTI-FAMILY (NO.5) CORE FUND
STARLIGHT INVESTMENTS
3280 Bloor St W Suite 1400, Toronto, ON, M8X 2X3
(416) 234-8444
Emp Here 4   *Sales* 99,327,000
SIC 6722 Management investment, open-end
Daniel Drimmer
Evan Kirsh
Martin Liddell
David Hanick

D-U-N-S 20-300-0435   (SL)
TRUE NORTH COMMERCIAL REIT
3280 Bloor St W Suite 1400, Toronto, ON, M8X 2X3
(416) 234-8444
Emp Here 7   *Sales* 66,006,425
SIC 6722 Management investment, open-end
Daniel Drimmer
Alon Ossip
Jeff Baryshnik
William Biggar
Roland Cardy
Sandy Poklar
Tracy Sherren

Toronto, ON M8Y

D-U-N-S 20-163-7105   (HQ)
DOMINION CITRUS LIMITED
DOMINION FARM PRODUCE, DIV OF
165 The Queensway Suite 302, Toronto, ON, M8Y 1H8
(416) 242-8341
Emp Here 10   *Sales* 12,533,655

SIC 5148 Fresh fruits and vegetables
Paul Scarafile
Jean Corriveau
Ted Cira
Tony Tomizza
Les Watson
Joe Nobrega

D-U-N-S 24-677-0387   (HQ)
TOMATO KING 2010 INC
165 The Queensway Suite 232, Toronto, ON, M8Y 1H8
(416) 259-5410
Emp Here 10   *Sales* 110,422,020
SIC 5148 Fresh fruits and vegetables
Vincent Carpino
Giuseppe Mazarese
Lorenzo Scala

Toronto, ON M8Z

D-U-N-S 24-018-2969   (SL)
1541094 ONTARIO INC
427 QEW KIA
1581 The Queensway Suite 2, Toronto, ON, M8Z 1T8
(416) 253-5001
Emp Here 22   *Sales* 10,957,716
SIC 5561 Recreational vehicle dealers
Amit Sachdeva

D-U-N-S 20-369-2884   (SL)
AUTOLOAN SOLUTIONS LTD
AUTOLOANS.CA
80 Jutland Rd, Toronto, ON, M8Z 2G6
(888) 300-9769
Emp Here 70   *Sales* 15,732,080
SIC 6141 Personal credit institutions
Roger Ryall

D-U-N-S 24-875-2644   (SL)
CORPORATE ASSETS INC
373 Munster Ave, Toronto, ON, M8Z 3C8
(416) 962-9600
Emp Here 30   *Sales* 13,304,700
SIC 7389 Business services, nec
Ryan Haas

D-U-N-S 24-320-3229   (SL)
KINECTRICS NCL INC
800 Kipling Ave Unit 2, Toronto, ON, M8Z 5G5
(416) 592-2102
Emp Here 65   *Sales* 16,408,730
SIC 1623 Water, sewer, and utility lines
David Harris
Lawrence Gibbons
Nancy Macdonald Exel

D-U-N-S 20-734-2023   (BR)
MORRISON LAMOTHE INC
399 Evans Ave, Toronto, ON, M8Z 1K9
(416) 255-7731
Emp Here 80
SIC 2038 Frozen specialties, nec
Jintao Metz

D-U-N-S 24-632-7209   (SL)
NATIONAL TIME EQUIPMENT CO LTD
31 Coronet Rd, Toronto, ON, M8Z 2L8
(416) 252-2293
Emp Here 25   *Sales* 13,013,550
SIC 5094 Jewelry and precious stones
John Stockwell

D-U-N-S 20-347-9647   (SL)
QUEENSWAY REAL ESTATE BROKERAGE INC
8 Hornell St, Toronto, ON, M8Z 1X2
(416) 259-4000
Emp Here 32   *Sales* 10,468,064
SIC 6531 Real estate agents and managers
Bill Dincod

D-U-N-S 20-387-9861   (SL)
STRUCTO NORTH AMERICA INC

200 Evans Ave Unit 11, Toronto, ON, M8Z 1J7
(877) 787-8286
Emp Here 70   *Sales* 11,481,890
SIC 2752 Commercial printing, lithographic
Huub Van Esbroeck

D-U-N-S 20-178-5185   (HQ)
WING HING LUNG LIMITED
WINGS FOOD PRODUCTS
(*Suby of* VENTURA FOODS, LLC)
550 Kipling Ave, Toronto, ON, M8Z 5E9
(416) 531-5768
Emp Here 50   *Sales* 20,741,400
SIC 2098 Macaroni and spaghetti
Kenneth Lee

Toronto, ON M9B

D-U-N-S 20-551-6164   (HQ)
EASTERN MEAT SOLUTIONS INC
302 The East Mall Suite 500, Toronto, ON, M9B 6C7
(416) 252-2791
Emp Here 26   *Sales* 25,067,310
SIC 5147 Meats and meat products
Robert Vanden Broek
Mark Ishoy
James Krall
Rick Laferriere
Brian White

D-U-N-S 25-921-0904   (SL)
LOGIT GROUP INC, THE
302 The East Mall Suite 400, Toronto, ON, M9B 6C7
(416) 236-4770
Emp Here 200   *Sales* 43,988,600
SIC 8732 Commercial nonphysical research
Anthony Molinaro
Paul Molinaro
Salvatore Pisani

D-U-N-S 25-399-1434   (HQ)
NEWCOM MEDIA INC
TODAY'S TRUCKING MAGAZINE
5353 Dundas St W Suite 400, Toronto, ON, M9B 6H8
(416) 614-2200
Emp Here 25   *Sales* 13,614,241
SIC 2721 Periodicals
Jim Glionna
Peter Fryters

Toronto, ON M9C

D-U-N-S 24-159-7475   (SL)
BRACKNELL CORPORATION
195 The West Mall Ste 302, Toronto, ON, M9C 5K1

Emp Here 7,000   *Sales* 843,661,000
SIC 1711 Plumbing, heating, air-conditioning

D-U-N-S 24-026-9415   (HQ)
CANWORLD FOODS LTD
320 North Queen St Suite 100, Toronto, ON, M9C 5K4
(416) 233-1900
Emp Here 20   *Sales* 20,889,425
SIC 5147 Meats and meat products
Michael Costa
John C. Mezenberg

D-U-N-S 20-512-7959   (HQ)
CDW CANADA CORP
(*Suby of* CDW CORPORATION)
185 The West Mall Suite 1700, Toronto, ON, M9C 1B8
(647) 288-5700
Sales 45,504,920
SIC 5045 Computers, peripherals, and software

Ginette Adragna
Mary Ann Yule
Josh Roberts
Daniel Reio
Ginette Adragna

D-U-N-S 20-411-9036   (HQ)
DIAGEO CANADA INC
(*Suby of* DIAGEO PLC)
401 The West Mall Suite 800, Toronto, ON, M9C 5P8
(416) 626-2000
Emp Here 70   *Sales* 682,339,000
SIC 2085 Distilled and blended liquors
Paul Walsh
Franz Humer
Deirdre Mahlan
Peggy Bruzelius
Laurence Danon
Betsy Holden
Philip Scott
Todd Stitzer
Paul Tunnacliffe

D-U-N-S 20-699-1684   (SL)
INNOVATIVE TRAILER DESIGN INDUSTRIES INC
161 The West Mall, Toronto, ON, M9C 4V8
(416) 620-7755
Emp Here 85   *Sales* 19,026,655
SIC 3715 Truck trailers
Benito Difranco
Domenic Alvaro
Dionisio Difranco
Tracey Slater

D-U-N-S 20-168-9924   (SL)
PARMALAT FOOD INC
405 The West Mall 10th Floor, Toronto, ON, M9C 5J1

Emp Here 180
SIC 2023 Dry, condensed and evaporated dairy products

D-U-N-S 24-032-6686   (SL)
TELEPARTNERS
5407 Eglinton Ave W Suite 103, Toronto, ON, M9C 5K6
(416) 621-7600
Emp Here 25   *Sales* 11,230,475
SIC 7389 Business services, nec
Gary Pudles

D-U-N-S 25-535-8103   (BR)
TRILLIUM HEALTH PARTNERS
QUEENSWAY HEALTH CENTRE
(*Suby of* TRILLIUM HEALTH PARTNERS)
150 Sherway Dr, Toronto, ON, M9C 1A5
(416) 259-6671
Emp Here 400
SIC 8062 General medical and surgical hospitals
Michelle Diemanuele

D-U-N-S 24-026-8862   (SL)
WD-40 COMPANY (CANADA) LTD
(*Suby of* WD-40 COMPANY)
5399 Eglinton Ave W Suite 214, Toronto, ON, M9C 5K6
(416) 622-9881
Emp Here 11   *Sales* 13,829,211
SIC 5172 Petroleum products, nec
Daniel Derdes
Diane L Gazzola

Toronto, ON M9L

D-U-N-S 20-942-9182   (HQ)
APOTEX INC
150 Signet Dr, Toronto, ON, M9L 1T9
(416) 401-7328
Emp Here 1,000   *Sales* 2,652,752,000
SIC 2834 Pharmaceutical preparations

Jeff Watson
Pere Paton
Klaus Martin
Michael Spino
Gordon Fahner
Pradeep Bhadauria
Jordan Berman
Jean-Luc Giraud
Peter Kalins
Steven Liberty

D-U-N-S 20-547-8717   (HQ)
CROWN METAL PACKAGING CANADA LP
(*Suby of* CROWN HOLDINGS INC.)
21 Fenmar Dr, Toronto, ON, M9L 2Y9
(416) 741-6002
Emp Here 25   *Sales* 19,208,500
SIC 3411 Metal cans
Barry Curran

D-U-N-S 20-116-0277   (HQ)
FACES COSMETICS INC
FACES
520 Garyray Dr, Toronto, ON, M9L 1R1
(416) 746-7575
Emp Here 20   *Sales* 29,319,360
SIC 5999 Miscellaneous retail stores, nec
Ramesh Jolly

D-U-N-S 20-183-2743   (HQ)
FGF BRANDS INC
1295 Ormont Dr, Toronto, ON, M9L 2W6
(905) 761-3333
Emp Here 125   *Sales* 1,218,462,500
SIC 2051 Bread, cake, and related products
Ojus Ajmera
Sam Ajmera
Jeremy Knoll
Sundaram Sambamoorthy

D-U-N-S 20-343-4600   (SL)
MULTISEAL INC
4255 Weston Rd, Toronto, ON, M9L 1W8
(416) 743-6017
Emp Here 80   *Sales* 19,694,880
SIC 1799 Special trade contractors, nec
Robert Barbieri
Jack Vitali

D-U-N-S 20-388-1438   (SL)
NWI PRECISION TUBE ULC
9 Fenmar Dr, Toronto, ON, M9L 1L5
(416) 743-4417
Emp Here 220   *Sales* 63,987,000
SIC 3728 Aircraft parts and equipment, nec
Bruce Van Nus

D-U-N-S 24-344-5538   (HQ)
PROGISTIX-SOLUTIONS INC
(*Suby of* GOVERNMENT OF CANADA)
99 Signet Dr Suite 300, Toronto, ON, M9L 0A2
(416) 401-7000
Emp Here 388   *Sales* 74,602,400
SIC 8742 Management consulting services
James H Eckler
Cal Hart

D-U-N-S 20-294-6141   (HQ)
TRIUMPH GEAR SYSTEMS-TORONTO ULC
TGST
(*Suby of* TRIUMPH GROUP, INC.)
9 Fenmar Dr, Toronto, ON, M9L 1L5
(416) 743-4417
Emp Here 120   *Sales* 44,768,600
SIC 3728 Aircraft parts and equipment, nec
Bruce Van Nus

Toronto, ON M9M

D-U-N-S 20-734-7956   (HQ)
CANADA FIBERS LTD
CMC PAPER CONVERTERS
130 Arrow Rd, Toronto, ON, M9M 2M1
(416) 253-0400
Emp Here 74   *Sales* 39,040,650

SIC 5093 Scrap and waste materials
Joe Miranda
Anne Carter

D-U-N-S 25-969-6701   (SL)
DECK STORE INC, THE
789 Arrow Rd Suite 10, Toronto, ON, M9M 2L4
(416) 749-3963
Emp Here 49   *Sales* 12,399,891
SIC 5211 Lumber and other building materials
Alain Villenvue

D-U-N-S 25-311-9036   (SL)
NUTRIAG LTD
62 Arrow Rd, Toronto, ON, M9M 2L8
(416) 636-1555
Emp Here 60   *Sales* 16,599,600
SIC 2874 Phosphatic fertilizers
Martin Bloomberg

D-U-N-S 20-609-4153   (SL)
PRECISION ELECTRONIC CORPORATION
70 Bartor Rd, Toronto, ON, M9M 2G5
(416) 744-8840
Emp Here 65   *Sales* 12,378,730
SIC 3679 Electronic components, nec

D-U-N-S 20-513-6869   (SL)
SUCCESSION CAPITAL CORPORATION
88 Arrow Rd, Toronto, ON, M9M 2L8
(416) 223-1700
Emp Here 5   *Sales* 284,627,600
SIC 6211 Security brokers and dealers
Bradley Nathan
Allan Kates
Marvin Poudwinski
Kathryn Wortsman

Toronto, ON M9N

D-U-N-S 20-716-3952   (BR)
2063414 ONTARIO LIMITED
WESTON TERRACE CARE COMMUNITY
2005 Lawrence Ave W Suite 323, Toronto, ON, M9N 3V4
(416) 243-8879
Emp Here 220
SIC 8051 Skilled nursing care facilities
Michael Bastian

D-U-N-S 24-335-2481   (SL)
ANNETTE'S DONUTS LIMITED
1965 Lawrence Ave W, Toronto, ON, M9N 1H5
(416) 656-3444
Emp Here 84   *Sales* 29,037,960
SIC 2051 Bread, cake, and related products
Nicolas Yannopoulos
Ariadni Yannopoulos

D-U-N-S 25-794-2565   (SL)
DRISCOLL, J. F. INVESTMENT CORP
130 King St, Toronto, ON, M9N 1L5
(416) 365-7532
Emp Here 35   *Sales* 18,592,245
SIC 6282 Investment advice
John Driscoll

D-U-N-S 25-213-4101   (SL)
FUNDSERV INC
130 King St Unit 1700, Toronto, ON, M9N 1L5
(416) 362-2400
Emp Here 100   *Sales* 22,427,339
SIC 8741 Management services
Katherine Macmillan
Mark Hubbard
Cameron Murray
Brad Badeau
Jim Russell
Bruno Carchidi
David Mccullum
Ghion Shewangzaw
Doug Bennet
Robert J. Bogard

D-U-N-S 20-087-8838   (BR)

GDI SERVICES (CANADA) LP
(*Suby of* GDI SERVICES AUX IMMEUBLES INC)
130 King St, Toronto, ON, M9N 1L5
(416) 364-0643
Emp Here 200
SIC 1799 Special trade contractors, nec
Tony Meneses

D-U-N-S 20-378-2800   (SL)
INFINITE OUTSOURCING SOLUTIONS INC
2100 Lawrence Ave W Unit 202a, Toronto, ON, M9N 3W3
(647) 247-5490
Emp Here 300   *Sales* 43,254,600
SIC 7371 Custom computer programming services
Ragavan Baladurai

D-U-N-S 25-322-8365   (SL)
INTEGRATED BUSINESS ANALYSIS, INC
IBA
(*Suby of* IBA HOLDINGS INC.)
130 King St, Toronto, ON, M9N 1L5
(800) 531-7100
Emp Here 85
SIC 8742 Management consulting services
Greg Steinberg
Scott Wood

D-U-N-S 24-359-1604   (BR)
LOBLAWS INC
REAL CANADIAN SUPERSTORE WESTON
(*Suby of* LOBLAW COMPANIES LIMITED)
2549 Weston Rd, Toronto, ON, M9N 2A7
(416) 246-1906
Emp Here 100
SIC 5411 Grocery stores
Peter Christopolous

D-U-N-S 25-098-6296   (HQ)
NORSTONE FINANCIAL CORPORATION
130 King St, Toronto, ON, M9N 1L5
(416) 860-6245
Emp Here 2   *Sales* 284,627,600
SIC 6211 Security brokers and dealers
Steven Chepa

D-U-N-S 24-989-2543   (SL)
PETRO ASSETS INC
SENTRY SELECT
130 King St Suite 2850, Toronto, ON, M9N 1L5
(416) 364-8788
Emp Here 150   *Sales* 41,002,500
SIC 6712 Bank holding companies
John Driscoll

D-U-N-S 20-008-7687   (BR)
TORONTO DISTRICT SCHOOL BOARD
WESTON COLLEGIATE INSTITUTE
(*Suby of* TORONTO DISTRICT SCHOOL BOARD)
100 Pine St, Toronto, ON, M9N 2Y9
(416) 394-3250
Emp Here 130
SIC 8211 Elementary and secondary schools
Ian Botnick

D-U-N-S 20-813-3350   (SL)
Y FIRM MANAGEMENT INC
2700-130 King St, Toronto, ON, M9N 1L5
(416) 860-8370
Emp Here 50   *Sales* 14,164,650
SIC 8741 Management services
Cindy Davies

Toronto, ON M9P

D-U-N-S 20-129-0054   (SL)
JENSEN HUGHES CONSULTING CANADA LTD
2150 Islington Ave Suite 100, Toronto, ON, M9P 3V4
(647) 559-1251
Emp Here 49   *Sales* 11,480,112

SIC 8748 Business consulting, nec
Peter Senez

Toronto, ON M9V

D-U-N-S 20-809-6961   (SL)
CENTURY 21 PEOPLE'S CHOICE REALTY INC
1780 Albion Rd Suite 2, Toronto, ON, M9V 1C1
(416) 742-8000
Emp Here 60   *Sales* 16,305,360
SIC 6531 Real estate agents and managers
Virendra Srivastava

Toronto, ON M9W

D-U-N-S 20-772-8221   (HQ)
AECON CONSTRUCTION GROUP INC
AECON UTILITIES
(*Suby of* AECON GROUP INC)
20 Carlson Crt Suite 800, Toronto, ON, M9W 7K6
(416) 293-7004
Emp Here 250   *Sales* 2,984,229,016
SIC 1541 Industrial buildings and warehouses

D-U-N-S 24-157-0527   (SL)
AXIOM REAL-TIME METRICS INC
1 City View Dr, Toronto, ON, M9W 5A5
(905) 845-9779
Emp Here 70   *Sales* 12,411,770
SIC 7371 Custom computer programming services
Andrew Schachter

D-U-N-S 24-804-1639   (SL)
DELVIRO INC
DELVIRO ENERGY
94 Brockport Dr, Toronto, ON, M9W 7J8
(416) 502-3434
Emp Here 125   *Sales* 23,805,250
SIC 3646 Commercial lighting fixtures
Joseph Delonghi
Kevin Moorhead
Kimberley Delonghi

D-U-N-S 25-511-5107   (SL)
FRESENIUS KABI CANADA LTD
(*Suby of* FRESENIUS SE & CO. KGAA)
165 Galaxy Blvd Suite 100, Toronto, ON, M9W 0C8
(905) 770-3711
Emp Here 95   *Sales* 39,217,995
SIC 5122 Drugs, proprietaries, and sundries
John Ducker
Matthew Rotenburg

D-U-N-S 20-011-4481   (HQ)
HAMILTON KENT INC
(*Suby of* ALIAXIS)
77 Carlingview Dr, Toronto, ON, M9W 5E6
(416) 675-9873
Sales 30,183,020
SIC 3053 Gaskets; packing and sealing devices
Bernard Gregoire

D-U-N-S 24-505-3665   (BR)
HOLT, RENFREW & CIE, LIMITEE
HOLT RENFREW
396 Humberline Dr, Toronto, ON, M9W 6J7
(416) 675-9200
Emp Here 100
SIC 5632 Women's accessory and specialty stores

D-U-N-S 20-182-3812   (HQ)
INTERFAST INC
(*Suby of* WESCO AIRCRAFT HOLDINGS, INC.)
22 Worcester Rd, Toronto, ON, M9W 5X2

▲ Public Company   ■ Public Company Family Member   **HQ** Headquarters   **BR** Branch   **SL** Single Location

(416) 674-0770
Emp Here 100   *Sales* 66,706,380
SIC 5072 Hardware
 S Douglas Woollings
 Conrad Lennert
 Pauline Mainville

D-U-N-S 24-007-7834   (SL)
LENWORTH METAL PRODUCTS LIMITED
275 Carrier Dr, Toronto, ON, M9W 5Y8

Emp Here 120   *Sales* 7,621,600
SIC 3499 Fabricated Metal products, nec

D-U-N-S 20-271-5025   (SL)
LOVSUNS TUNNELING CANADA LIMITED
(*Suby of* LIAONING CENSCIENCE INDUS-
TRY CO., LTD.)
441 Carlingview Dr, Toronto, ON, M9W 5G7
(647) 255-0018
Emp Here 75   *Sales* 16,650,075
SIC 3531 Construction machinery
 Shuangzhong Liu
 Harry Tian
 Hongyu Xue

D-U-N-S 20-306-3581   (SL)
M. BLOCK CANADA, ULC
M. BLOCK & SONS
(*Suby of* M. BLOCK & SONS, INC.)
134 Bethridge Rd, Toronto, ON, M9W 1N3
(705) 252-6471
Emp Here 20   *Sales* 10,177,120
SIC 5023 Homefurnishings
 Bruce Levy
 Peter Levy
 Edward Roels
 William Moore

D-U-N-S 25-791-3475   (SL)
NIKO COSMETICS INC
STUDIO NIKO
397 Humberline Dr Unit 7, Toronto, ON, M9W
5T5

Emp Here 100   *Sales* 8,962,900
SIC 7231 Beauty shops
 Niko Papadatos

D-U-N-S 24-339-2565   (HQ)
PUMA CANADA INC
(*Suby of* PUMA SE)
175 Boul Galaxy Suite 201, Toronto, ON, M9W
0C9
(416) 481-7862
Emp Here 50   *Sales* 173,825,000
SIC 5091 Sporting and recreation goods
 Jay Piccola
 Michael Laemmermann
 Peter Mastrostefano
 Cyril Hottot
 Luc Cousineau
 Edward M. Pletcher

D-U-N-S 20-145-7645   (HQ)
S & C ELECTRIC CANADA LTD
(*Suby of* S & C ELECTRIC COMPANY)
90 Belfield Rd, Toronto, ON, M9W 1G4
(416) 249-9171
Emp Here 295   *Sales* 99,020,250
SIC 3613 Switchgear and switchboard appa-
ratus

D-U-N-S 24-525-0308   (HQ)
**SEMPLE GOODER ROOFING CORPORA-
TION**
SLOPED CONCRETE SOLUTIONS
1365 Martin Grove Rd, Toronto, ON, M9W 4X7
(416) 743-5370
Emp Here 190   *Sales* 41,692,536
SIC 1761 Roofing, siding, and sheetMetal
work
 Mark Baxter
 Peter Mcgoey
 Bill Gray
 Marla Hammond

D-U-N-S 20-373-4363   (SL)

STANDARD FIRE PROTECTION INC
254 Attwell Dr, Toronto, ON, M9W 5B2
(416) 240-7980
Emp Here 30   *Sales* 13,304,700
SIC 7389 Business services, nec
 Paul Di Lucia

D-U-N-S 20-785-7827   (SL)
UHAUL COMPANY OF EASTERN ONTARIO
240 Rexdale Blvd, Toronto, ON, M9W 1R2
(416) 335-1250
Emp Here 60   *Sales* 11,614,214
SIC 7359 Equipment rental and leasing, nec
 Anthony Grocott

D-U-N-S 20-818-6445   (HQ)
WOODBINE ENTERTAINMENT GROUP
WOODBINE RACETRACK
555 Rexdale Blvd, Toronto, ON, M9W 5L2
(416) 675-7223
Emp Here 1,000   *Sales* 222,795,900
SIC 7948 Racing, including track operation
 Joe Aschaiek
 Bill Ford
 Jorge Soares
 Michelle Soans
 David Vivenes
 Tom Via

Toronto, ON N5K

D-U-N-S 24-325-3833   (HQ)
GREENFIELD ENERGY CENTRE LP
66 Wellington St W Suite 3515, Toronto, ON,
N5K 1H1
(416) 362-0978
Sales 47,591,180
SIC 4911 Electric services
 Rick Dejongad

Toronto, ON T5K

D-U-N-S 20-388-6234   (SL)
JTL GROUP CORP
37 Advance Rd, Toronto, ON, T5K 1P2

Emp Here 300   *Sales* 11,371,530
SIC 4213 Trucking, except local
 Timothy Troy
 Robert Yeates
 John Ferguson

Torrance, ON P0C

D-U-N-S 20-780-9497   (BR)
YMCA OF GREATER TORONTO
YMCA CAMP PINE CREST
(*Suby of* YMCA OF GREATER TORONTO)
1090 Gullwing Lake Rd Rr 1, Torrance, ON,
P0C 1M0
(705) 762-3377
Emp Here 174
SIC 7032 Sporting and recreational camps
 Andrea Balmer

Tottenham, ON L0G

D-U-N-S 20-703-8360   (SL)
1339022 ONTARIO LTD
COUNTRY SIGNS
75 Industrial Rd, Tottenham, ON, L0G 1W0
(800) 748-0277
Emp Here 25   *Sales* 11,230,475
SIC 7389 Business services, nec
 Bradley Butterfield

D-U-N-S 20-246-0247   (HQ)
BIG SHO FOODS LTD
TIM HORTONS
130 Queen St N, Tottenham, ON, L0G 1W0
(905) 936-6157
Emp Here 3   *Sales* 13,991,700
SIC 5812 Eating places
 Gerry Lawlor

D-U-N-S 24-663-2277   (HQ)
F&P MFG INC
(*Suby of* F-TECH INC.)
1 Nolan Rd, Tottenham, ON, L0G 1W0
(905) 936-3435
Emp Here 630   *Sales* 557,897,648
SIC 3714 Motor vehicle parts and accessories
 Andrew Kochanek
 Kiyoshi Horiuchi
 Stuart Fraser
 Yasuyuki Ikezawa
 Geoff Smith
 Kuniwiko Ito
 Kevin Menaab
 Snella Clayton
 Kenji Yamamoto

D-U-N-S 25-338-4119   (HQ)
FIBER CONNECTIONS INC
80 Queen St S, Tottenham, ON, L0G 1W0
(800) 353-1127
Emp Here 25   *Sales* 13,330,940
SIC 3679 Electronic components, nec
 Larry Fingler
 Paul Fujiwara
 Geoff Laycock
 Scott Fingler

D-U-N-S 25-224-8729   (BR)
**SIMCOE MUSKOKA CATHOLIC DISTRICT
SCHOOL BOARD**
ST. THOMAS AQUINAS HIGH SCHOOL
(*Suby of* SIMCOE MUSKOKA CATHOLIC
DISTRICT SCHOOL BOARD)
2 Nolan Rd, Tottenham, ON, L0G 1W0
(905) 936-4743
Emp Here 80
SIC 8211 Elementary and secondary schools
 Frank Kewin

D-U-N-S 24-189-3937   (BR)
SOBEYS CAPITAL INCORPORATED
TOTTENHAM FOODLAND STORE
(*Suby of* EMPIRE COMPANY LIMITED)
260 Queen St N, Tottenham, ON, L0G 1W0
(905) 936-1077
Emp Here 120
SIC 5411 Grocery stores
 Joann Leduc

D-U-N-S 25-976-9065   (SL)
TITAN METALS LTD
5982 6th Line, Tottenham, ON, L0G 1W0
(905) 729-4347
Emp Here 60   *Sales* 13,069,740
SIC 1761 Roofing, siding, and sheetMetal
work
 Andrew Minialoff

D-U-N-S 24-280-0241   (BR)
VENTRA GROUP CO
VMA TOTTENHAM
(*Suby of* FLEX-N-GATE LLC)
65 Industrial Rd, Tottenham, ON, L0G 1W0
(905) 936-4245
Emp Here 250
SIC 3465 Automotive stampings
 Elgin Dewar

Townsend, ON N0A

D-U-N-S 24-220-5169   (SL)
**CHILDREN'S AID SOCIETY OF
HALDIMAND AND NORFOLK, THE**
CASHN

70 Town Centre Dr, Townsend, ON, N0A 1S0
(519) 587-5437
Emp Here 140   *Sales* 10,750,880
SIC 8322 Individual and family services
 Bernadette Gallegher
 Chad Deblock

Trenton, ON K8V

D-U-N-S 24-139-6894   (SL)
A L NEILSON FAMILY PHARMACY LTD
SHOPPERS DRUG MART
90 Dundas St W, Trenton, ON, K8V 3P3
(613) 392-1212
Emp Here 50   *Sales* 12,647,700
SIC 5912 Drug stores and proprietary stores
 Andrea Neilson

D-U-N-S 25-503-9133   (BR)
CASCADES CANADA ULC
*CASCADES CONTAINER BOARD PACKAG-
ING*
(*Suby of* CASCADES INC)
300 Marmora St, Trenton, ON, K8V 5R8

Emp Here 140
SIC 2679 Converted paper products, nec
 Beniot Dionne

D-U-N-S 24-924-3304   (HQ)
**CROWN RIDGE HEALTH CARE SERVICES
INC**
CROWN RIDGE PLACE
106 Crown St, Trenton, ON, K8V 6R3
(613) 392-1289
Emp Here 150   *Sales* 13,699,629
SIC 8051 Skilled nursing care facilities
 Gregory Freeman
 Fred Freeman

D-U-N-S 24-666-5343   (SL)
DECA CABLES INC
150 North Murray St, Trenton, ON, K8V 6R8
(613) 392-3585
Emp Here 90   *Sales* 17,287,650
SIC 3496 Miscellaneous fabricated wire prod-
ucts
 Domenic Di Pietrantonio
 Darryl Edgett

D-U-N-S 20-787-3159   (SL)
DOMTECH INC
40 Davis St E, Trenton, ON, K8V 6S4
(613) 394-4884
Emp Here 100   *Sales* 23,343,500
SIC 3357 Nonferrous wiredrawing and insulat-
ing
 Timothy Bannon
 Jagdeep Singh

D-U-N-S 24-524-9305   (HQ)
ELECTRO CABLES INC
(*Suby of* TRIPEX MANUFACTURING LIM-
ITED)
9 Riverside Dr, Trenton, ON, K8V 5P8
(613) 394-4896
Sales 18,682,964
SIC 3357 Nonferrous wiredrawing and insulat-
ing
 Peter Davis
 Beatrix Davis

D-U-N-S 25-321-8614   (BR)
ERB TRANSPORT LIMITED
(*Suby of* ERB ENTERPRISES INC)
4 Riverside Dr, Trenton, ON, K8V 5P8
(613) 965-6633
Emp Here 170
SIC 4212 Local trucking, without storage
 Al Mcinroy

D-U-N-S 24-700-7664   (SL)
EYES N. OPTICS
73 Dundas St W Suite A, Trenton, ON, K8V

▲ Public Company   ■ Public Company Family Member   **HQ** Headquarters   **BR** Branch   **SL** Single Location

3P4
(613) 392-3040
Emp Here 21   *Sales* 10,931,382
SIC 5093 Scrap and waste materials
Jim Ham

D-U-N-S 25-180-1999   (SL)
FRAZIER INDUSTRIAL CO., LTD
FRACAN STRUCTURAL STEEL
(*Suby of* FRAZIER INDUSTRIAL COMPANY)
163 North Murray St, Trenton, ON, K8V 6R7
(613) 394-6621
Emp Here 100   *Sales* 19,208,500
SIC 3441 Fabricated structural Metal
Jerry Jansen

D-U-N-S 25-690-4442   (SL)
GLOBALMED INC
(*Suby of* SCHAUENBURG INTERNATIONAL GMBH)
155 Murray St N, Trenton, ON, K8V 5R5
(613) 394-9844
Emp Here 180   *Sales* 40,912,020
SIC 3841 Surgical and medical instruments
Allan Flieler
Deborah Harris
John Seniuk

D-U-N-S 25-831-1158   (BR)
HASTINGS AND PRINCE EDWARD DISTRICT SCHOOL BOARD
TRENTON HIGH SCHOOL
15 Fourth Ave, Trenton, ON, K8V 5N4
(613) 392-1227
Emp Here 75
SIC 8211 Elementary and secondary schools
Ken Manderville

D-U-N-S 25-585-9944   (SL)
KOTSOVOS RESTAURANTS LIMITED
TOMASSO'S ITALIAN GRILLE
35 Front St, Trenton, ON, K8V 4N3
(613) 392-4333
Emp Here 80   *Sales* 3,641,520
SIC 5812 Eating places
Athanasios Kotsovos
Andrew Kotsovos
Michael Kotsovos
Cynthia Kotsovos

D-U-N-S 20-179-0367   (SL)
LANGE & FETTER MOTORS LIMITED
52 Dundas St E, Trenton, ON, K8V 1K7
(613) 392-6561
Emp Here 25   *Sales* 12,451,950
SIC 5511 New and used car dealers
Richard Lange

D-U-N-S 20-154-1356   (HQ)
MCCURDY CHEVROLET OLSMOBILE PONTIAC BUICK GMC LTD
174 Trenton-Frankford Rd, Trenton, ON, K8V 5R6
(613) 392-1245
Sales 34,610,400
SIC 5511 New and used car dealers
Don Mccurdy

D-U-N-S 25-300-0517   (BR)
METRO ONTARIO INC
(*Suby of* METRO INC)
53 Quinte St, Trenton, ON, K8V 3S8
(613) 394-2525
Emp Here 110
SIC 5411 Grocery stores
Brian Mccartney

D-U-N-S 20-179-0573   (HQ)
MIRTREN CONTRACTORS LIMITED
18 Stockdale Rd, Trenton, ON, K8V 5P6
(613) 392-6511
Sales 54,752,448
SIC 1542 Nonresidential construction, nec
Daniel Miron

D-U-N-S 20-536-7907   (BR)
MOORE CANADA CORPORATION
R.R. DONNELLEY

(*Suby of* R. R. DONNELLEY & SONS COMPANY)
8 Douglas Rd, Trenton, ON, K8V 5R4
(613) 392-1205
Emp Here 135
SIC 2761 Manifold business forms
Mark Hockley

D-U-N-S 24-337-3016   (SL)
MURRAY TOWNSHIP FARMS LTD
Gd Lcd Main, Trenton, ON, K8V 5P9
(613) 392-8068
Emp Here 45   *Sales* 15,411,015
SIC 0191 General farms, primarily crop
Colin Crews

D-U-N-S 25-616-3601   (HQ)
MYSTICAL DISTRIBUTING COMPANY LTD
6 Foster Stearns Rd, Trenton, ON, K8V 5R5
(613) 394-7056
Emp Here 17   *Sales* 20,821,680
SIC 5092 Toys and hobby goods and supplies
Mark Phillips
Rod Cameron
Wendy Cameron

D-U-N-S 20-879-9429   (BR)
NESTLE CANADA INC
(*Suby of* NESTLE S.A.)
1 Douglas Rd, Trenton, ON, K8V 5S7
(613) 394-4712
Emp Here 200
SIC 2037 Frozen fruits and vegetables
Michael Strong

D-U-N-S 20-057-5103   (HQ)
NVENT THERMAL CANADA LTD
PYROTENAX
250 West St, Trenton, ON, K8V 5S2
(613) 392-6571
Sales 23,036,276
SIC 3315 Steel wire and related products
Nick Rogerson

D-U-N-S 25-628-8762   (BR)
QUINTE HEALTHCARE CORPORATION
TRENTON MEMORIAL HOSPITAL
(*Suby of* QUINTE HEALTHCARE CORPORATION)
242 King St, Trenton, ON, K8V 5S6
(613) 392-2540
Emp Here 375
SIC 8062 General medical and surgical hospitals
Mary Claire Egberts

D-U-N-S 25-621-6250   (SL)
RE/MAX TRENT VALLEY REALTY LTD
447 Dundas St W, Trenton, ON, K8V 3S4
(613) 243-2209
Emp Here 34   *Sales* 11,122,318
SIC 6531 Real estate agents and managers
Craig Kerr

D-U-N-S 25-690-5076   (BR)
SAPUTO INC
SAPUTO DAIRY PRODUCTS CANADA G.P.
(*Suby of* JOLINA CAPITAL INC)
7 Riverside Drive, Trenton, ON, K8V 5R7
(613) 392-6762
Emp Here 150
SIC 2022 Cheese; natural and processed
Trevor Braun

D-U-N-S 24-142-0053   (SL)
SENIOR CAPITAL CORP LTD
21 Albert St, Trenton, ON, K8V 4S4
(613) 394-3317
Emp Here 25   *Sales* 10,483,875
SIC 6719 Holding companies, nec
Even James

D-U-N-S 20-986-9135   (SL)
SMYLIE'S YOUR INDEPENDENT GROCER
293 Dundas St E, Trenton, ON, K8V 1M1
(613) 392-0297
Emp Here 160   *Sales* 46,956,320
SIC 5411 Grocery stores

John Smylie

D-U-N-S 20-733-9503   (BR)
SOBEYS CAPITAL INCORPORATED
PRICE CHOPPER
(*Suby of* EMPIRE COMPANY LIMITED)
30 Ontario St, Trenton, ON, K8V 5S9
(613) 394-2791
Emp Here 85
SIC 5411 Grocery stores
Clarence Blakely

D-U-N-S 24-506-4019   (BR)
SONOCO CANADA CORPORATION
(*Suby of* SONOCO PRODUCTS COMPANY)
5 Bernard Long Rd, Trenton, ON, K8V 5P6
(613) 394-6903
Emp Here 130
SIC 2631 Paperboard mills
Chris Freeman

D-U-N-S 20-873-1799   (SL)
SPELMER CHRYSLER JEEP DODGE SALES LTD
51 Highway 33, Trenton, ON, K8V 5R1
(613) 394-3945
Emp Here 21   *Sales* 10,459,638
SIC 5511 New and used car dealers
Jason Spelmer

D-U-N-S 24-192-4385   (SL)
TIM HORTONS
221 R.C.A.F. Rd, Trenton, ON, K8V 5P8
(613) 965-0555
Emp Here 26   *Sales* 11,530,740
SIC 7389 Business services, nec
Josephine Robertson

D-U-N-S 20-179-1324   (HQ)
TRENTON COLD STORAGE INC
TCS GROUP
21 Albert St, Trenton, ON, K8V 4S4
(613) 394-3317
Emp Here 50   *Sales* 61,711,800
SIC 4222 Refrigerated warehousing and storage
Eben James Jr
Stanley Bigford

D-U-N-S 20-259-6649   (BR)
TRENTON COLD STORAGE INC
FRASER GLENBURNIE
(*Suby of* TRENTON COLD STORAGE INC)
17489 Telephone Rd, Trenton, ON, K8V 5P4
(613) 394-3317
Emp Here 100
SIC 4225 General warehousing and storage
Carl Derusha

D-U-N-S 24-302-6432   (HQ)
TRENTON DISTRIBUTORS LIMITED
TDL CANADA
75 Huff Ave, Trenton, ON, K8V 0H3
(613) 392-3875
Emp Here 27   *Sales* 9,597,883,322
SIC 5063 Electrical apparatus and equipment
Shawn Tennier
Susan Tennier

D-U-N-S 24-184-2426   (HQ)
TRENTON MEMORIAL HOSPITAL
242 King St, Trenton, ON, K8V 3X1
(613) 392-2541
Sales 41,655,000
SIC 8062 General medical and surgical hospitals
Mike Murphy
Susan White
Marie Claire Egberts

D-U-N-S 20-178-9518   (SL)
TRULIFE LIMITED
(*Suby of* TRULIFE GROUP LIMITED)
39 Davis St E, Trenton, ON, K8V 4K8
(613) 392-6528
Emp Here 110   *Sales* 25,001,790
SIC 3842 Surgical appliances and supplies
Noel Murphy

John Benson

D-U-N-S 20-651-2035   (BR)
VICTORIAN ORDER OF NURSES FOR CANADA
VON HASTINGS-NORTHUMBERLAND-PE DISTRICT
(*Suby of* VICTORIAN ORDER OF NURSES FOR CANADA)
80 Division St Suite 14, Trenton, ON, K8V 5S5
(613) 392-4181
Emp Here 350
SIC 8082 Home health care services
Lori Cooper

D-U-N-S 24-318-0820   (BR)
WAL-MART CANADA CORP
WALMART
(*Suby of* WALMART INC.)
Hwy 2 At 2nd Dughill Rd, Trenton, ON, K8V 5P7
(613) 394-2191
Emp Here 150
SIC 5311 Department stores
Bob Garrah

D-U-N-S 24-121-1309   (HQ)
WILKINSON & COMPANY LLP
71 Dundas St W, Trenton, ON, K8V 3P4
(888) 713-7283
Emp Here 25   *Sales* 11,422,675
SIC 8721 Accounting, auditing, and bookkeeping
James Coward
Robert Deacon
Jeffrey Snider
Jeffrey Lay
Kurt Gregoire
Wayne Phillips
Robert Robertson
Robert Yager
Jennifer Fischer
Brian Kehoe

Trout Creek, ON P0H

D-U-N-S 24-026-4077   (SL)
LADY ISABELLE NURSING HOME LTD
102 Corkery St, Trout Creek, ON, P0H 2L0
(705) 723-5232
Emp Here 75   *Sales* 5,154,975
SIC 8051 Skilled nursing care facilities
Sadie Newman

Troy, ON L0R

D-U-N-S 20-054-6596   (SL)
ARCHIE MCCOY (HAMILTON) LIMITED
MCCOY FOUNDRY
1890 Highway 5 W, Troy, ON, L0R 2B0
(519) 647-3411
Emp Here 65   *Sales* 15,173,275
SIC 3321 Gray and ductile iron foundries
Harry Mccoy
Paul Mccoy
Jean Mccoy

Tweed, ON K0K

D-U-N-S 20-031-1533   (SL)
M & M MARKETS LTD
TWEED VALUE MART
58a Victoria St N, Tweed, ON, K0K 3J0
(613) 478-2014
Emp Here 39   *Sales* 10,691,928
SIC 5411 Grocery stores
Brian Gall

▲ Public Company   ■ Public Company Family Member   **HQ** Headquarters   **BR** Branch   **SL** Single Location

D-U-N-S 20-705-3844 (HQ)
WOODS, DON FUELS LIMITED
20 River St, Tweed, ON, K0K 3J0
(613) 478-3039
Emp Here 9 *Sales* 37,716,030
SIC 5172 Petroleum products, nec
Donald Woods
Brian Woods

Unionville, ON L3P

D-U-N-S 25-056-2865 (SL)
MARKHAM CENTENNIAL CENTRE
8600 Mccowan Rd, Unionville, ON, L3P 3M2
(905) 294-6111
Emp Here 115 *Sales* 7,868,530
SIC 8322 Individual and family services
Barbara Roth

D-U-N-S 20-711-4187 (BR)
YORK REGION DISTRICT SCHOOL BOARD
MARKVILLE SECONDARY SCHOOL
(*Suby of* YORK REGION DISTRICT SCHOOL BOARD)
1000 Carlton Rd, Unionville, ON, L3P 7P5
(905) 940-8840
Emp Here 110
SIC 8211 Elementary and secondary schools
Patricia Obadia

Unionville, ON L3R

D-U-N-S 24-736-6318 (HQ)
1008803 ONTARIO LTD
PETRO CANADA
4780 Highway 7 E, Unionville, ON, L3R 1M8
(905) 477-2003
Emp Here 1 *Sales* 24,903,900
SIC 5541 Gasoline service stations
Ali-Reza Lour-Razavi-Nabi
Akram Khajouei Nejad
Hamid-Reza Lour-Razavi-Nabi

D-U-N-S 24-995-8752 (BR)
BEST BUY CANADA LTD
FUTURE SHOP
(*Suby of* BEST BUY CO., INC.)
8601 Warden Ave Suite 1, Unionville, ON, L3R 0B5

Emp Here 105
SIC 5731 Radio, television, and electronic stores

D-U-N-S 24-727-5027 (SL)
BRUHAM AUTOMOTIVE INC
MARKHAM ACURA
5201 Highway 7 E, Unionville, ON, L3R 1N3
(905) 948-8222
Emp Here 50 *Sales* 24,903,900
SIC 5511 New and used car dealers
Michael Brugel
Dick Hammer

D-U-N-S 20-981-4714 (SL)
COLLEY, BORLAND & VALE INSURANCE BROKERS LIMITED
4591 Highway 7 E Suite 200, Unionville, ON, L3R 1M6
(905) 477-2720
Emp Here 26 *Sales* 15,078,024
SIC 6411 Insurance agents, brokers, and service
Philip Colley
Donald Vale
Sheena Colley

D-U-N-S 20-811-1463 (SL)
DEREK K. HO PHARMACY LTD
SHOPPERS DRUG MART
8601 Warden Ave, Unionville, ON, L3R 0B5

(905) 479-0772
Emp Here 50 *Sales* 12,647,700
SIC 5912 Drug stores and proprietary stores
Derek Ho

D-U-N-S 24-423-6352 (HQ)
INTERNATIONAL CIGAR STORES LIMITED
ICS GROUP
170 Main St, Unionville, ON, L3R 2G9
(905) 940-1515
Emp Here 12 *Sales* 17,102,960
SIC 5947 Gift, novelty, and souvenir shop
Robert Kadlovski

D-U-N-S 24-254-8464 (SL)
MARKHAM INFINITI LIMITED
4340 Highway 7 E, Unionville, ON, L3R 1L9
(905) 752-0881
Emp Here 30 *Sales* 14,942,340
SIC 5511 New and used car dealers
Robert Stephen

D-U-N-S 24-758-3040 (SL)
MARKVILLE FORD LINCOLN LIMITED
8210 Kennedy Rd, Unionville, ON, L3R 5X3
(905) 474-1350
Emp Here 55 *Sales* 34,610,400
SIC 5511 New and used car dealers
Craig Riley

D-U-N-S 20-641-9108 (BR)
MCDONALD'S RESTAURANTS OF CANADA LIMITED
MCDONALD'S RESTAURANTS
(*Suby of* MCDONALD'S CORPORATION)
5225 Highway 7 E, Unionville, ON, L3R 1N3
(905) 477-2891
Emp Here 90
SIC 5812 Eating places
Stacey Salvalaggio

D-U-N-S 20-535-2255 (SL)
NORTH MARKHAM MOTORS LTD
MARKHAM HONDA
8220 Kennedy Rd, Unionville, ON, L3R 5X3
(905) 477-2451
Emp Here 67 *Sales* 42,161,760
SIC 5511 New and used car dealers
Kap Dilawri

D-U-N-S 25-990-9257 (HQ)
RE/MAX ALL-STARS REALTY INC.
RE/MAX
5071 Highway 7 E, Unionville, ON, L3R 1N3
(905) 477-0011
Emp Here 43 *Sales* 23,038,895
SIC 6531 Real estate agents and managers
Marlene Wrong
June Williamson
Leslie Benczik
Daniel Sarafian
Leo Barraso

D-U-N-S 24-345-9414 (BR)
RECIPE UNLIMITED CORPORATION
MILESTONES GRILL & BAR
(*Suby of* RECIPE UNLIMITED CORPORATION)
3760 Highway 7 E, Unionville, ON, L3R 0N2
(905) 760-2244
Emp Here 150
SIC 5812 Eating places
Peter Kraft

D-U-N-S 24-855-5109 (SL)
RFI CANADA PARTNERSHIP
178 Main St, Unionville, ON, L3R 2G9
(905) 534-1044
Emp Here 100 *Sales* 83,557,700
SIC 5149 Groceries and related products, nec
Grant Smith

D-U-N-S 24-058-5935 (BR)
SHERIDAN NURSERIES LIMITED
(*Suby of* SHERIDAN NURSERIES LIMITED)
4077 Highway 7 E, Unionville, ON, L3R 1L5
(905) 477-2253
Emp Here 90

SIC 0181 Ornamental nursery products
Joe Ohearn

D-U-N-S 25-406-9982 (HQ)
STUART, W H MUTUALS LTD
W. H. STUART & ASSOCIATES
16 Main St, Unionville, ON, L3R 2E4
(905) 305-0880
Emp Here 10 *Sales* 41,388,850
SIC 6722 Management investment, open-end
Howard Stuart
Diane Stuart

D-U-N-S 20-209-9052 (SL)
SUNRISE OF MARKHAM LIMITED
SUNRISE ASSISTED LIVING UNIONVILLE
38 Swansea Rd, Unionville, ON, L3R 5K2
(905) 947-4566
Emp Here 84 *Sales* 5,759,544
SIC 8051 Skilled nursing care facilities
Paul Klaasen
David W Feader
Thomas Newell
Therese Klasssen
Brian Swinton
Tiffany Tomasso

D-U-N-S 24-407-5909 (SL)
TOWN & COUNTRY MOTORS (1989) LIMITED
TOWN & COUNTRY BMW
8111 Kennedy Rd, Unionville, ON, L3R 5M2
(905) 948-2948
Emp Here 126 *Sales* 79,289,280
SIC 5511 New and used car dealers
Jim Cochrane

D-U-N-S 20-106-8587 (SL)
TRANSASIAN FINE CARS LTD
ACURA IN MARKHAM
5201 Highway 7 E, Unionville, ON, L3R 1N3
(905) 948-8866
Emp Here 60 *Sales* 37,756,800
SIC 5511 New and used car dealers
Sylvester Chuang
Paul Roach
Pauline Chuang

D-U-N-S 20-754-5708 (SL)
UNIONVILLE MOTORS (1973) LIMITED
4630 Highway 7 E, Unionville, ON, L3R 1M5

Emp Here 60 *Sales* 37,756,800
SIC 5511 New and used car dealers
Kelly Jamieson
Dennis Hext
John Jamieson

D-U-N-S 24-454-0571 (SL)
VILLAGE NISSAN LIMITED
VILLAGE NISSAN
25 South Unionville Ave, Unionville, ON, L3R 6B8
(905) 604-0147
Emp Here 30 *Sales* 14,942,340
SIC 5511 New and used car dealers
Scott Campbell
Christopher Campbell

Unionville, ON L6G

D-U-N-S 24-026-1180 (SL)
BRECKLES INSURANCE BROKERS LIMITED
85 Enterprise Blvd Suite 401, Unionville, ON, L6G 0B5
(905) 752-4747
Emp Here 51 *Sales* 94,234,842
SIC 6411 Insurance agents, brokers, and service
Ben Malik
Chris Conitlio
Elena D'agostini
Emilia Voicu

D-U-N-S 24-910-3086 (HQ)
GARY JONAS COMPUTING LTD
JONAS SOFTWARE
(*Suby of* CONSTELLATION SOFTWARE INC)
8133 Warden Ave Suite 400, Unionville, ON, L6G 1B3
(905) 470-4600
Sales 46,143,250
SIC 7371 Custom computer programming services
Barry Symmons
Jeff Mckee

D-U-N-S 24-817-6174 (BR)
WORLEYPARSONSCORD LP
(*Suby of* WORLEYPARSONS LIMITED)
8133 Warden Ave, Unionville, ON, L6G 1B3
(905) 940-4774
Emp Here 75
SIC 8711 Engineering services

Utopia, ON L0M

D-U-N-S 20-133-7185 (SL)
DECAST LTD
8807 County Road 56, Utopia, ON, L0M 1T0
(800) 461-5632
Emp Here 180 *Sales* 32,259,420
SIC 3272 Concrete products, nec
Silvio De Gasperis

D-U-N-S 20-693-5020 (HQ)
PHOENIX BUILDING COMPONENTS INC
5650 Sideroad 30, Utopia, ON, L0M 1T0
(705) 733-3843
Emp Here 130 *Sales* 21,153,879
SIC 2439 Structural wood members, nec
Grant Gibbons
Tom Partridge
Jim Francis

D-U-N-S 24-235-7742 (SL)
REED ATWOOD BUILDERS (ONTARIO) INC
8693 6th Line, Utopia, ON, L0M 1T0
(705) 797-0553
Emp Here 49 *Sales* 23,065,819
SIC 1542 Nonresidential construction, nec
Brad Harrington

Utterson, ON P0B

D-U-N-S 25-456-2127 (SL)
EMMONS GREENHOUSES INC
WINDERMERE GARDEN CENTRE
1453 Deebank Rd, Utterson, ON, P0B 1M0
(705) 769-3238
Emp Here 35 *Sales* 11,986,345
SIC 0181 Ornamental nursery products
Richard Emmons

D-U-N-S 24-891-2750 (SL)
PEERLESS SECURITY LTD
PEERLESS GROUP
544 Greer Rd, Utterson, ON, P0B 1M0
(705) 645-4108
Emp Here 60 *Sales* 13,069,740
SIC 1731 Electrical work
Douglas Spiller

Uxbridge, ON L4A

D-U-N-S 24-365-9328 (BR)
FORTERRA PRESSURE PIPE, ULC
102 Prouse Rd, Uxbridge, ON, L4A 7X4
(905) 642-4383
Emp Here 75
SIC 3272 Concrete products, nec

Steve Gates

Uxbridge, ON L9P

D-U-N-S 24-764-7357   (SL)
643487 ONTARIO LIMITED
PINE VALLEY PACKAGING
1 Parratt Rd, Uxbridge, ON, L9P 1R1
(905) 862-0830
Emp Here 60   *Sales* 16,431,426
SIC 3086 Plastics foam products
Steve Richards
Michael Clee

D-U-N-S 25-895-7679   (SL)
994794 ONTARIO INC
PET VALU
4 Banff Rd Suite 3, Uxbridge, ON, L9P 1S9
(905) 852-6977
Emp Here 40   *Sales* 13,024,000
SIC 5999 Miscellaneous retail stores, nec
Art Mathews

D-U-N-S 20-179-4153   (HQ)
ALEX WILLIAMSON MOTOR SALES LIMITED
WILLIAMSON LEASING
259 Toronto St S, Uxbridge, ON, L9P 1R1
(905) 852-3332
Emp Here 85   *Sales* 72,367,200
SIC 5511 New and used car dealers
Peter Williamson
Alexander Williamson Jr
Alexander (Todd) Williamson Jr
James Williamson

D-U-N-S 20-728-3834   (SL)
BENNETT DESIGN ASSOCIATES INC
(*Suby of* BIG BLUE OPPORTUNITIES INC)
10 Douglas Rd Unit 2, Uxbridge, ON, L9P 1S9
(905) 852-4617
Emp Here 40   *Sales* 17,968,760
SIC 7389 Business services, nec
Sue Bennett

D-U-N-S 24-525-3018   (HQ)
CHOKO MOTORSPORTS INC
CHOKO AUTHENTIC APPAREL
19 Anderson Blvd, Uxbridge, ON, L9P 0C7
(905) 642-1010
Sales 20,929,524
SIC 5136 Men's and boy's clothing
Edward Hakonson
Hilda Hakonson

D-U-N-S 24-318-8369   (BR)
EXCO TECHNOLOGIES LIMITED
CASTOOL TOOLING SYSTEMS
(*Suby of* EXCO TECHNOLOGIES LIMITED)
2 Parratt Rd, Uxbridge, ON, L9P 1R1
(905) 852-0121
Emp Here 101
SIC 3545 Machine tool accessories
Paul Robbins

D-U-N-S 24-319-0378   (SL)
HELA SPICE CANADA INC
HELA CANADA
(*Suby of* HELA GEWURZWERK HERMANN LAUE GMBH)
119 Franklin St, Uxbridge, ON, L9P 1J5
(905) 852-5100
Emp Here 40   *Sales* 33,423,080
SIC 5149 Groceries and related products, nec
Walter Knecht
Anita Kokot-Larsen

D-U-N-S 24-991-9408   (SL)
HIGGINS, PATRICK J ENTERPRISES LTD
CANADIAN TIRE STORE #127
327 Toronto St S, Uxbridge, ON, L9P 1Z7
(905) 852-3315
Emp Here 100   *Sales* 62,928,000
SIC 5531 Auto and home supply stores

Patrick Higgins

D-U-N-S 24-000-4148   (HQ)
KOCH-GLITSCH CANADA LP
18 Dallas St, Uxbridge, ON, L9P 1C6
(905) 852-3381
Sales 24,420,110
SIC 3559 Special industry machinery, nec
Michael Mcguire
Tom Pattinson

D-U-N-S 24-802-6937   (BR)
MARKHAM STOUFFVILLE HOSPITAL
UXBRIDGE COTTAGE HOSPITAL
(*Suby of* MARKHAM STOUFFVILLE HOSPITAL)
4 Campbell Dr, Uxbridge, ON, L9P 1S4
(905) 852-9771
Emp Here 100
SIC 8062 General medical and surgical hospitals
Ranjeet Wallia

D-U-N-S 20-187-3879   (SL)
PINE VALLEY PACKAGING GROUP INC
1 Parratt Rd, Uxbridge, ON, L9P 1R1
(905) 862-0830
Emp Here 8   *Sales* 16,860,674
SIC 5199 Nondurable goods, nec
Elizabeth Richards
Donna Clee

D-U-N-S 25-028-5350   (BR)
REVERA LONG TERM CARE INC
REACHVIEW VILLAGE
(*Suby of* GOVERNMENT OF CANADA)
130 Reach St Suite 25, Uxbridge, ON, L9P 1L3
(905) 852-5191
Emp Here 85
SIC 8051 Skilled nursing care facilities
Barbara Andrews

D-U-N-S 20-207-2208   (SL)
SCARSIN CORPORATION
2 Brock St W Suite 201, Uxbridge, ON, L9P 1P2
(905) 852-0086
Emp Here 66   *Sales* 11,702,526
SIC 7371 Custom computer programming services
Paul Minshull
Jill Minshull

D-U-N-S 24-918-5380   (HQ)
UTECH ELECTRONICS
25 Anderson Blvd, Uxbridge, ON, L9P 0C7
(416) 609-2900
Emp Here 20   *Sales* 13,415,220
SIC 5065 Electronic parts and equipment, nec
Keith Mccrone
Christopher Riley

D-U-N-S 24-317-2025   (BR)
WAL-MART CANADA CORP
WALMART
(*Suby of* WALMART INC.)
6 Welwood Dr, Uxbridge, ON, L9P 1Z7
(905) 862-0721
Emp Here 150
SIC 5311 Department stores
Vincent Caruana

Val Caron, ON P3N

D-U-N-S 20-058-0459   (SL)
1011191 ONTARIO INC
METRO VAL-EAST
3140 Old Hwy 69 N Suite 28, Val Caron, ON, P3N 1G3
(705) 897-4958
Emp Here 100   *Sales* 29,347,700
SIC 5411 Grocery stores
Lionel Dutrisac
Gilles Dutrisac

D-U-N-S 24-627-3122   (HQ)
CONSBEC INC
2736 Belisle Dr, Val Caron, ON, P3N 1B3
(705) 897-4971
Emp Here 75   *Sales* 20,925,810
SIC 1799 Special trade contractors, nec
Reginald Walker

D-U-N-S 20-179-1345   (BR)
JARLETTE LTD
VALLEY EAST LONG TERM CARE
2100 Main St, Val Caron, ON, P3N 1S7
(705) 897-7695
Emp Here 150
SIC 8059 Nursing and personal care, nec

D-U-N-S 24-192-8290   (SL)
MOBILE PARTS INC
(*Suby of* FULCRUM CAPITAL PARTNERS INC)
2472 Evans Rd, Val Caron, ON, P3N 1P5
(705) 897-4955
Emp Here 52   *Sales* 13,337,398
SIC 5082 Construction and mining machinery
Greg Collings
Roger Morin
Richard Telenko

D-U-N-S 25-197-7302   (HQ)
NICKEL CENTRE PHARMACY INC
VAL EST PHARMACY
3140 Old Hwy 69 N Suite 17, Val Caron, ON, P3N 1G3
(705) 897-1867
Emp Here 20   *Sales* 10,880,650
SIC 5947 Gift, novelty, and souvenir shop
Carlo Berardi
Enrico Berardi

D-U-N-S 25-497-4645   (SL)
SCR MINING & TUNNELLING INC
2797 White St, Val Caron, ON, P3N 1B2
(705) 897-1932
Emp Here 150   *Sales* 37,866,300
SIC 1629 Heavy construction, nec
Richard Seguin
Claude Seguin

D-U-N-S 25-526-1281   (SL)
WHITSON MANUFACTURING INC
2725 Belisle Dr, Val Caron, ON, P3N 1B3
(705) 897-4971
Emp Here 40   *Sales* 13,093,760
SIC 2892 Explosives
Reginald F Walker

Val Rita, ON P0L

D-U-N-S 20-846-3711   (SL)
VAL RITA TIRE SALES LTD
MURRAY OK TIRE & TOWING
96 Government Rd, Val Rita, ON, P0L 2G0
(705) 335-8496
Emp Here 32   *Sales* 15,938,496
SIC 5541 Gasoline service stations
Rejean Murray
Justin Murray
Martin Murray

Vanier, ON K1L

D-U-N-S 25-250-3149   (SL)
176026 CANADA INC
AMOR CONSTRUCTION
134 Saint Paul St Unit 2a, Vanier, ON, K1L 6A3
(613) 742-7550
Emp Here 80   *Sales* 7,834,770
SIC 1542 Nonresidential construction, nec
Jude Gauvreau
Rock Gauvreau

D-U-N-S 24-229-3079   (SL)
1799795 ONTARIO LIMITED
LABOUR GROUP
171 Montreal Rd, Vanier, ON, K1L 6E4
(613) 745-5720
Emp Here 50   *Sales* 11,848,500
SIC 7361 Employment agencies
Nicholas Caravatta

D-U-N-S 25-773-7619   (BR)
LOBLAWS INC
LOBLAWS
(*Suby of* LOBLAW COMPANIES LIMITED)
100 Mcarthur Ave, Vanier, ON, K1L 8H5
(613) 744-0705
Emp Here 260
SIC 5411 Grocery stores
Roslyn Gascon

D-U-N-S 20-889-5151   (HQ)
MANTHA INSURANCE BROKERS LTD
295 Montreal Rd, Vanier, ON, K1L 6B8
(613) 746-1450
Emp Here 40   *Sales* 33,922,400
SIC 6411 Insurance agents, brokers, and service
Paul Mantha
Sylvie Mantha
Fernand Mantha

D-U-N-S 25-772-4740   (SL)
MANTHA REAL ESTATE & INSURANCE INC
295 Montreal Rd, Vanier, ON, K1L 6B8
(613) 830-3000
Emp Here 40   *Sales* 23,196,960
SIC 6411 Insurance agents, brokers, and service
Fernand Mantha

D-U-N-S 24-344-5074   (BR)
METRO ONTARIO INC
METRO
(*Suby of* METRO INC)
50 Beechwood Ave, Vanier, ON, K1L 8B3
(613) 744-6676
Emp Here 100
SIC 5411 Grocery stores
Karen Sauvel

D-U-N-S 25-747-1755   (SL)
PARTAGE VANIER FOOD BANK
161 Marier Ave, Vanier, ON, K1L 5R8
(613) 747-2839
Emp Here 46   *Sales* 10,434,318
SIC 8399 Social services, nec
Dianne Nadeau

D-U-N-S 24-435-9774   (HQ)
UNIGLOBE PREMIERE TRAVEL PLANNERS INC
24 Selkirk St Suite 100, Vanier, ON, K1L 0A4
(613) 230-7411
Sales 15,079,043
SIC 4724 Travel agencies

Vankleek Hill, ON K0B

D-U-N-S 20-128-9063   (HQ)
H & I ENTERPRISES (VANKLEEK) LTD
HERB'S TRAVEL PLAZA
21160 Service Rd, Vankleek Hill, ON, K0B 1R0
(613) 525-2120
Sales 19,923,120
SIC 5541 Gasoline service stations
Hubert Denis Vink
Joanne Vink
Nathalie Vink

D-U-N-S 20-507-8595   (SL)
VANKLEEK HILL LIVESTOCK EXCHANGE LIMITED
1239 Ridge Rd, Vankleek Hill, ON, K0B 1R0
(613) 678-3008
Emp Here 11   *Sales* 13,314,367

▲ Public Company   ■ Public Company Family Member   HQ Headquarters   BR Branch   SL Single Location

SIC 5154 Livestock
Francois Tremblay

Vars, ON K0A

D-U-N-S 25-372-2185   (HQ)
2967-3183 QUEBEC INC
300 Rue Universelle Ss 4, Vars, ON, K0A 3H0
(613) 443-0044
Sales 13,654,423
SIC 3713 Truck and bus bodies
Jean-Marie Bibeau
Jean Huard
Marcel Bibeau

D-U-N-S 20-294-2975   (BR)
**ADESA AUCTIONS CANADA CORPORA-
TION**
ADESA OTTAWA
(*Suby of* KAR AUCTION SERVICES, INC.)
1717 Burton Rd, Vars, ON, K0A 3H0
(613) 443-4400
Emp Here 150
SIC 5012 Automobiles and other motor vehi-
cles
Jason Mcclenaham

D-U-N-S 24-541-1780   (SL)
ATELIERS BEAU-ROC INC, LES
(*Suby of* 2967-3183 QUEBEC INC)
300 Rue Universelle, Vars, ON, K0A 3H0
(613) 443-0044
Emp Here 50   *Sales* 11,192,150
SIC 3713 Truck and bus bodies
Jean-Marie Bibeau
Daniel Tremblay
Joel Bibeau

D-U-N-S 20-040-0463   (HQ)
J. R. BRISSON EQUIPMENT LTD
121 St Pierre Rd, Vars, ON, K0A 3H0
(613) 443-3300
Emp Here 24   *Sales* 17,100,936
SIC 5082 Construction and mining machinery
Daniel Riendeau

D-U-N-S 20-556-6250   (SL)
LDC PRECISION CONCRETE INC
112 Clement St, Vars, ON, K0A 3H0
(613) 822-2872
Emp Here 60   *Sales* 14,848,980
SIC 1771 Concrete work
Rocco Crea

D-U-N-S 25-477-5836   (SL)
LOUIS W. BRAY CONSTRUCTION LIMITED
308 Corduroy Rd, Vars, ON, K0A 3H0
(613) 938-6711
Emp Here 100   *Sales* 25,244,200
SIC 1611 Highway and street construction
Michael Bray
Doug Dillion
Jim Flegg

D-U-N-S 25-673-0508   (HQ)
PNE CORPORATION
279 Entreprise Rd, Vars, ON, K0A 3H0
(613) 443-2181
Emp Here 25   *Sales* 29,213,800
SIC 5169 Chemicals and allied products, nec
Andre Alie
Yann Baillargeon

D-U-N-S 20-542-6950   (BR)
TOMLINSON, R. W. LIMITED
ONTARIO TRAP ROCK, DIV OF
(*Suby of* TOMLINSON, R. W. LIMITED)
8125 Russell Rd, Vars, ON, K0A 3H0
(613) 835-3395
Emp Here 75
SIC 5211 Lumber and other building materials

Vaughan, ON L4H

D-U-N-S 20-286-3064   (SL)
BRANDALLIANCE, INC
BRANDALLIANCE ONTARIO
10 Roybridge Gate Suite 202, Vaughan, ON,
L4H 3M8
(905) 819-0155
Emp Here 260   *Sales* 153,181,340
SIC 5199 Nondurable goods, nec
Mark Roy
Ian Mclearon
Nicholas Thompson
Jr Pete Kmech
Francois Mizoduchi
Alan Chippindale

D-U-N-S 25-684-6650   (HQ)
MODERN/NIAGARA GROUP INC
MNGI
8125 Hwy 50, Vaughan, ON, L4H 4S6
(613) 591-1338
Emp Here 275   *Sales* 81,254,400
SIC 1711 Plumbing, heating, air-conditioning
John Mcaninch
Terry Dunlop
Tony Sottile

D-U-N-S 24-719-9524   (SL)
ROYPLAST LIMITED
ROYALGUARD VINYL CO DIV
91 Royal Group Crt, Vaughan, ON, L4H 1X9

Emp Here 400
SIC 3089 Plastics products, nec

D-U-N-S 24-357-8445   (SL)
STATE WINDOW CORPORATION
STATE
220 Hunter'S Valley Rd, Vaughan, ON, L4H
3V9
(416) 646-1421
Emp Here 200   *Sales* 38,417,000
SIC 3442 Metal doors, sash, and trim
Christopher Liberta

D-U-N-S 24-367-9425   (HQ)
WORLD WIDE LOGISTICS INC
330 New Huntington Rd Suite 101, Vaughan,
ON, L4H 4C9
(416) 213-9522
Emp Here 35   *Sales* 19,102,068
SIC 4731 Freight transportation arrangement
Shipon Howlader
Sukhdev Dhaliwal
Parvin Howlader
Dwijo Banerjie
Patricia Ccorimanya

Vaughan, ON L4K

D-U-N-S 24-143-5945   (SL)
2022839 ONTARIO INC
8500 Keele St, Vaughan, ON, L4K 2A6
(905) 532-1455
Emp Here 400   *Sales* 286,686,400
SIC 5141 Groceries, general line
Jeffrey Min

D-U-N-S 25-220-4953   (HQ)
ADVANTAGE CAR & TRUCK RENTALS LTD
ADVANTAGE CAR & TRUCK RENTALS
110 Jardin Dr Suite 13, Vaughan, ON, L4K
2T7
(416) 493-5250
Emp Here 9   *Sales* 28,330,000
SIC 7514 Passenger car rental
Bruce Taylor
Craig Hind

D-U-N-S 20-050-1483   (SL)
**CANADIAN RENEWABLE ENERGY
ACADEMY**
445 Edgeley Boulevard, Vaughan, ON, L4K

4G1
(647) 832-0553
Emp Here 5   *Sales* 15,529,285
SIC 4924 Natural gas distribution

D-U-N-S 20-304-6073   (SL)
CHOICE CANNING COMPANY INC
(*Suby of* CHOICE TRADING CORPORATION
PRIVATE LIMITED)
3100 Steeles Ave W Suite 603, Vaughan, ON,
L4K 3R1
(905) 918-3866
Emp Here 3   *Sales* 11,752,155
SIC 5146 Fish and seafoods
Jose Thomas
Anna Jose

D-U-N-S 25-347-7038   (BR)
**COMPAGNIE DES CHEMINS DE FER NA-
TIONAUX DU CANADA**
MACMILLAN YARD
(*Suby of* COMPAGNIE DES CHEMINS DE
FER NATIONAUX DU CANADA)
1 Administration Rd, Vaughan, ON, L4K 1B9
(905) 669-3128
Emp Here 1,000
SIC 4011 Railroads, line-haul operating
Ian Thomson

D-U-N-S 24-387-4286   (HQ)
**CONSTRUCTION DISTRIBUTION & SUP-
PLY COMPANY INC**
DISCOUNTERS WAREHOUSE DIV.
300 Confederation Pkwy Unit 3, Vaughan, ON,
L4K 4T8
(416) 665-8006
Emp Here 40   *Sales* 26,765,200
SIC 5211 Lumber and other building materials
Stan Lazar
Gary Muzin
David Lazar

D-U-N-S 24-412-2818   (SL)
DOUGH DELIGHT LTD
CANADA BREAD DOUGH DELIGHT
144 Viceroy Rd, Vaughan, ON, L4K 2L8

Emp Here 200
SIC 2051 Bread, cake, and related products

D-U-N-S 20-321-7070   (BR)
FRESHPOINT VANCOUVER LTD
FRESHPOINT VANCOUVER, LTD
(*Suby of* SYSCO CORPORATION)
1400 Creditstone Rd Unit A, Vaughan, ON,
L4K 0E2

Emp Here 100
SIC 5148 Fresh fruits and vegetables
Dave Alho

D-U-N-S 20-278-7222   (HQ)
GFL ENVIRONMENTAL INC
BLANCHARD
100 New Park Pl Suite 500, Vaughan, ON,
L4K 0H9
(905) 326-0101
Emp Here 50   *Sales* 1,140,027,000
SIC 4953 Refuse systems
Patrick Dovigi
Mindy Gilbert
Dino Chiesa
Adam Gross
Shahir Guindi
Arun Nayar
Paolo Notarnicola
Michael Pan
Blake Sumler
Raymond Svider

D-U-N-S 20-398-3494   (SL)
GREAT CLIPS, INC
3100 N Rutherford Rd Suite 201, Vaughan,
ON, L4K 0G6

Emp Here 270   *Sales* 24,217,920
SIC 7231 Beauty shops
Steve Hockett

Rob Doggins
Rachelle Johnson

D-U-N-S 24-692-3395   (SL)
ITS ELECTRONICS INC
*MICROWAVE COMPONENETS AND SUB-
SYSTEMS*
3280 Langstaff Rd Unit B, Vaughan, ON, L4K
5B6
(905) 660-0405
Emp Here 67   *Sales* 12,759,614
SIC 3663 Radio and t.v. communications
equipment
Ilya Tchaplia
Martin Exon
Shan Liang

D-U-N-S 24-171-1428   (SL)
KOREA FOOD TRADING LTD
8500 Keele St, Vaughan, ON, L4K 2A6
(905) 532-0325
Emp Here 23   *Sales* 19,218,271
SIC 5149 Groceries and related products, nec
Jeffrey Min

D-U-N-S 24-358-4740   (HQ)
LEGRAND CANADA INC
(*Suby of* LEGRAND)
9024 Keele St, Vaughan, ON, L4K 2N2
(905) 738-9195
Emp Here 55   *Sales* 11,426,520
SIC 3643 Current-carrying wiring devices
John Selldorff
Antoine Burel
Thomas Macerollo
James Laperrierre

D-U-N-S 20-112-2319   (HQ)
MARTINREA AUTOMOTIVE INC
ATLAS FLUID SYSTEM, DIV OF
(*Suby of* MARTINREA INTERNATIONAL INC)
3210 Langstaff Rd, Vaughan, ON, L4K 5B2
(289) 982-3000
Emp Here 400   *Sales* 729,693,000
SIC 3499 Fabricated Metal products, nec
Nick Orlando
Robert Wildeboer

D-U-N-S 25-202-7883   (HQ)
MARTINREA INTERNATIONAL INC
HYDROFORM SOLUTIONS, DIV OF
3210 Langstaff Rd, Vaughan, ON, L4K 5B2
(416) 749-0314
Emp Here 100   *Sales* 2,776,851,816
SIC 3499 Fabricated Metal products, nec

D-U-N-S 24-978-0669   (HQ)
MARTINREA METALLIC CANADA INC
(*Suby of* MARTINREA INTERNATIONAL INC)
3210 Langstaff Rd, Vaughan, ON, L4K 5B2
(416) 749-0314
Emp Here 250   *Sales* 72,969,300
SIC 3465 Automotive stampings

D-U-N-S 20-384-2828   (SL)
**PENGUIN PICK-UP LIMITED PARTNER-
SHIP**
PENGUINPICKUP
700 Applewood Cres Unit 1, Vaughan, ON,
L4K 5X3
(905) 760-6200
Emp Here 85   *Sales* 17,485,010
SIC 4215 Courier services, except by air
Egil Nielsen

D-U-N-S 20-292-3194   (SL)
SAFETY FIRST ONTARIO INC
SAFETY FIRST FIRE PREVENTION
41 Courtland Ave Unit 1, Vaughan, ON, L4K
3T3
(905) 738-4999
Emp Here 23   *Sales* 10,200,270
SIC 7389 Business services, nec
David King

D-U-N-S 25-289-8663   (SL)
**SMARTCENTRES REAL ESTATE INVEST-
MENT TRUST**

SMARTCENTRES
3200 Highway 7, Vaughan, ON, L4K 5Z5
(905) 326-6400
Emp Here 337   *Sales* 51,779,376
SIC 6512 Nonresidential building operators
Peter Forde
Rudy Gobin
Stephen Champion
Fernando Vescio
Peter E. Sweeney
Mauro Pambianchi
Mitchell Goldhar
Jamie Mcvicar
Kevin Pshebniski
Michael Young

D-U-N-S 20-784-8839   (SL)
VAN HORNE CONSTRUCTION LIMITED
51a Caldari Rd Unit 1m, Vaughan, ON, L4K
4G3
(905) 677-5150
Emp Here 13   *Sales* 37,344,150
SIC 1542 Nonresidential construction, nec
Fesih Mert

D-U-N-S 24-382-2496   (SL)
VESTACON LIMITED
3 Bradwick Dr, Vaughan, ON, L4K 2T4
(416) 440-7970
Emp Here 22   *Sales* 10,356,082
SIC 1542 Nonresidential construction, nec
Daniel Passera
Sam Falzone

D-U-N-S 20-045-1520   (SL)
WAI CANADA INC
535 Millway Ave Suite 1, Vaughan, ON, L4K
3V4
(905) 660-7274
Emp Here 49   *Sales* 24,405,822
SIC 5531 Auto and home supply stores
Bernie Ceresne

D-U-N-S 20-119-1645   (HQ)
WASTE CONNECTIONS, INC
610 Applewood Cres, Vaughan, ON, L4K 0C3
(905) 532-7510
Emp Here 80   *Sales* 4,630,488,000
SIC 4953 Refuse systems
Ronald J. Mittelstaedt
Worthing F. Jackman
Keith P. Gordon
Gregory Thibodeaux
Scott I. Schreiber
Susan R. Netherton
Shawn W. Mandel
Eric O. Hansen
Robert M. Cloninger
Michelle L. Little

Vaughan, ON L4L

D-U-N-S 24-684-6302   (SL)
FORMGLAS PRODUCTS LTD
(*Suby of* FORMGLAS HOLDINGS INC)
181 Regina Rd, Vaughan, ON, L4L 8M3
(416) 635-8030
Emp Here 395   *Sales* 13,168,916
SIC 3299 NonMetallic mineral products,
John Chettleburgh

D-U-N-S 20-718-1350   (SL)
**KENTUCKY FRIED CHICKEN CANADA
COMPANY**
(*Suby of* YUM BRANDS, INC.)
191 Creditview Rd Unit 100, Vaughan, ON,
L4L 9T1
(416) 664-5200
Emp Here 100   *Sales* 103,244,400
SIC 6794 Patent owners and lessors
Nicolas Burquier
Nivera Wallani

D-U-N-S 24-141-2154   (HQ)

MAGNOTTA WINERY CORPORATION
271 Chrislea Rd, Vaughan, ON, L4L 8N6
(905) 738-9463
Emp Here 75   *Sales* 36,988,830
SIC 2084 Wines, brandy, and brandy spirits
Bert Felice
Fulvio Deangelis

D-U-N-S 24-045-3217   (SL)
ORGANIZED INTERIORS INC
ORGANIZED INTERIORS
201 Chrislea Rd, Vaughan, ON, L4L 8N6
(905) 264-5678
Emp Here 90   *Sales* 40,245,660
SIC 5072 Hardware
Mike Albo
Vince Petrozza

D-U-N-S 24-391-1455   (HQ)
SUSTAINCO INC
1 Royal Gate Blvd, Vaughan, ON, L4L 8Z7
(905) 850-8686
Sales 11,032,014
SIC 6799 Investors, nec
Emlyn J. David
Nicholas Price
Chris Hazelton
Michael Galloro
Adam Szweras

Vaughan, ON L6A

D-U-N-S 24-329-1924   (SL)
CANADA'S WONDERLAND COMPANY
(*Suby of* CEDAR FAIR, L.P.)
9580 Jane St, Vaughan, ON, L6A 1S6
(905) 832-7000
Emp Here 100   *Sales* 7,854,500
SIC 7996 Amusement parks
Richard Kinzel
Raffi Kaprelyan

D-U-N-S 20-646-7706   (HQ)
**FABCO PLASTICS WHOLESALE (ON-
TARIO) LIMITED**
FABCO PLASTICS WHOLESALE
2175 Teston Rd, Vaughan, ON, L6A 1T3
(905) 832-0600
Sales 36,517,250
SIC 5162 Plastics materials and basic shapes
William Kehren

D-U-N-S 20-190-1001   (SL)
MARYNA (PRIVATE) LIMITED
9926 Keele St Unit 5444, Vaughan, ON, L6A
3Y4

Emp Here 2,000   *Sales* 1,083,470,000
SIC 6726 Investment offices, nec

D-U-N-S 20-373-3931   (SL)
MCF HIGHRISE FORMING INC
2900 Highway 7 W, Vaughan, ON, L6A 0K9
(416) 988-9235
Emp Here 60   *Sales* 25,364,220
SIC 1541 Industrial buildings and warehouses
Gabriel Coreelleccu

Verner, ON P0H

D-U-N-S 20-179-5598   (HQ)
**CO-OPERATIVE REGIONALE DE
NIPISSING-SUDBURY LIMITED**
4 Rue Principale, Verner, ON, P0H 2M0
(705) 594-2354
Sales 100,240,200
SIC 5191 Farm supplies
John Wilkins
Conrad Bedard
Denis Katonguay

Verona, ON K0H

D-U-N-S 20-577-8368   (SL)
REID'S FOODLAND
BROOKS IGA
6145 Highway 38, Verona, ON, K0H 2W0
(613) 374-2112
Emp Here 50   *Sales* 13,707,600
SIC 5411 Grocery stores
Cleint Reid

D-U-N-S 20-224-7685   (SL)
REVELL FORD LINCOLN
6715 Main St, Verona, ON, K0H 2W0
(613) 374-2612
Emp Here 35   *Sales* 17,432,730
SIC 5521 Used car dealers
Harry Revell

D-U-N-S 20-179-6026   (SL)
REVELL MOTORS SALES LIMITED
REVELL FORD LINCOLN MERCURY
6628 38 Hwy, Verona, ON, K0H 2W0
(613) 374-2133
Emp Here 38   *Sales* 18,926,964
SIC 5511 New and used car dealers
Harry Revell
Allan Revell
Larry Revell

Vienna, ON N0J

D-U-N-S 20-556-3224   (HQ)
**MAX UNDERHILL'S FARM SUPPLY LIM-
ITED**
56532 Calton Line Suite 1, Vienna, ON, N0J
1Z0
(519) 866-3632
Sales 14,107,880
SIC 5191 Farm supplies
Jonathan R. Sebok
Andrew J. Sebok
John Sebok
Marnie Sebok
Diane Deline
Scott Howle
Ken O'hagan
Andre Mcclure

D-U-N-S 20-316-0932   (SL)
PIHOKKER FARMS INC
58126 Calton Line Rr 1, Vienna, ON, N0J 1Z0
(519) 866-5030
Emp Here 40   *Sales* 13,698,680
SIC 0161 Vegetables and melons
Frank Pihokker
Maggie Pihokker

Vineland, ON L0R

D-U-N-S 24-488-9507   (SL)
984379 ONTARIO INC
VINELAND ESTATES WINERY
3620 Moyer Rd, Vineland, ON, L0R 2C0
(905) 562-7088
Emp Here 50   *Sales* 11,242,750
SIC 2084 Wines, brandy, and brandy spirits
Allan Schmidt

D-U-N-S 25-350-3296   (BR)
**BETHESDA HOME FOR THE MENTALLY
HANDICAPPED INC**
BETHESDA PROGRAMS
(*Suby of* BETHESDA HOME FOR THE MEN-
TALLY HANDICAPPED INC)
3950 Fly Rd Rr 1, Vineland, ON, L0R 2C0
(905) 562-4184
Emp Here 100
SIC 8399 Social services, nec

Marlene Goerz

D-U-N-S 24-184-4252   (SL)
JORDAN LION PARK
2769 4 Ave, Vineland, ON, L0R 2C0

Emp Here 31   *Sales* 12,319,834
SIC 8699 Membership organizations, nec
Glen Corfield

D-U-N-S 25-973-3152   (HQ)
PLASTRUCT CANADA INC
IPOLY
4305 Spring Creek Rd, Vineland, ON, L0R
2C0
(905) 563-4000
Emp Here 1   *Sales* 16,797,935
SIC 5162 Plastics materials and basic shapes
Nick Koppelaar

D-U-N-S 20-977-5634   (SL)
**UNITED MENNONITE HOME FOR THE
AGED**
4024 23rd St, Vineland, ON, L0R 2C0
(905) 562-7385
Emp Here 200   *Sales* 12,856,400
SIC 8361 Residential care
Ronald Wiens

Vineland Station, ON L0R

D-U-N-S 20-309-9056   (SL)
GGS STRUCTURES INC
3559 North Service Rd, Vineland Station, ON,
L0R 2E0
(905) 562-7341
Emp Here 50   *Sales* 23,536,550
SIC 1542 Nonresidential construction, nec
Leigh Coulter
Gerry Harrison

D-U-N-S 24-288-7230   (SL)
GROWERS GREENHOUSE SUPPLIES INC
3559 North Service Rd, Vineland Station, ON,
L0R 2E0
(905) 562-7341
Emp Here 60   *Sales* 44,551,200
SIC 5191 Farm supplies
Gerald Harrison
Leigh Coulter

D-U-N-S 24-455-5728   (HQ)
PRIVA NORTH AMERICA INC
PRIVA BUILDING INTELLIGENCE
(*Suby of* STICHTING BEHEER PRIVA
GROUP)
3468 South Service Rd Ss 1, Vineland Station,
ON, L0R 2E0
(905) 562-7351
Sales 10,262,480
SIC 3823 Process control instruments
Mike Marino

D-U-N-S 24-665-7241   (SL)
VINELAND MANUFACTURING LTD
4937 Victoria Ave Suite 1, Vineland Station,
ON, L0R 2E0
(905) 562-7308
Emp Here 55   *Sales* 12,311,365
SIC 3714 Motor vehicle parts and accessories
Suzanne Court
Douglas Major
Michael Court
Philip Court

Virgil, ON L0S

D-U-N-S 24-004-4656   (SL)
2079421 ONTARIO LIMITED
PHIL'S VALU-MART
1551 Niagara Stone Rd, Virgil, ON, L0S 1T0

(905) 468-3286
Emp Here 50   *Sales* 13,707,600
SIC 5411 Grocery stores
Phil Leboudec

D-U-N-S 20-133-5085   (SL)
HERITAGE PLACE CARE FACILITY
Gd, Virgil, ON, L0S 1T0
(905) 468-1111
Emp Here 80   *Sales* 5,548,810
SIC 8059 Nursing and personal care, nec
Kim Siemens

D-U-N-S 20-179-7099   (SL)
NIAGARA MOTORS LIMITED
1537 Niagara Stone Rd, Virgil, ON, L0S 1T0
(905) 468-2145
Emp Here 50   *Sales* 24,903,900
SIC 5511 New and used car dealers
David W Dick

D-U-N-S 20-051-3042   (HQ)
NIAGARA ORCHARD & VINEYARD CORP
LOUCH NIAGARA
1550 Hwy 55, Virgil, ON, L0S 1T0
(905) 468-3297
Emp Here 4   *Sales* 12,533,655
SIC 5148 Fresh fruits and vegetables
Arnold Lepp

D-U-N-S 25-366-1862   (SL)
NIAGARA-ON-THE-LAKE HYDRO INC
(*Suby of* NIAGARA-ON-THE-LAKE, TOWN
OF)
8 Henegan Rd, Virgil, ON, L0S 1T0
(905) 468-4235
Emp Here 20   *Sales* 12,532,280
SIC 4911 Electric services
Jim Huntingdon

D-U-N-S 24-286-3975   (SL)
**PENNER BUILDING CENTRE AND
BUILDERS SUPPLIES LIMITED**
HOME HARDWARE
700 Penner St, Virgil, ON, L0S 1T0
(905) 468-3242
Emp Here 60   *Sales* 16,059,120
SIC 5251 Hardware stores
Harry Penner
Kevin Penner

D-U-N-S 20-179-7149   (SL)
**PENNER LUMBER & BUILDERS' SUP-
PLIES LIMITED**
PENNER BUILDING CENTRE
700 Penner St, Virgil, ON, L0S 1T0
(905) 468-3242
Emp Here 70   *Sales* 18,735,640
SIC 5211 Lumber and other building materials
Kevin Penner

Vittoria, ON N0E

D-U-N-S 24-848-6086   (SL)
SCOTLYNN INVESTMENTS INC
1150 Vittoria Rd, Vittoria, ON, N0E 1W0
(519) 426-2700
Emp Here 200   *Sales* 54,670,000
SIC 6712 Bank holding companies
Scott Biddle

D-U-N-S 20-327-4725   (SL)
SCOTLYNN SWEETPAC GROWERS INC
1150 Vittoria Rd, Vittoria, ON, N0E 1W0
(519) 426-2700
Emp Here 200   *Sales* 33,805,000
SIC 0161 Vegetables and melons
Scott Biddle

Walkerton, ON N0G

D-U-N-S 25-849-7239   (SL)

1087299 ONTARIO LTD
TIM HORTONS
10 Mcnab St, Walkerton, ON, N0G 2V0
(519) 881-2794
Emp Here 38   *Sales* 10,417,776
SIC 5461 Retail bakeries
Cathy Patterson

D-U-N-S 24-354-3118   (HQ)
1340560 ONTARIO INC
LITTLE ROCK FARM TRUCKING
7 Industrial Rd, Walkerton, ON, N0G 2V0
(519) 881-4055
Emp Here 2   *Sales* 11,769,885
SIC 6712 Bank holding companies
Mark Reuber
Daniel Reuber

D-U-N-S 24-522-0061   (SL)
1788317 ONTARIO INC
18 Industrial Rd, Walkerton, ON, N0G 2V0
(519) 881-0187
Emp Here 40   *Sales* 10,638,080
SIC 6712 Bank holding companies
Allan Beitz
Joseph Bester
Patrick Fischer
Jeffray Harper
Thomas Inglis
Trevor Reading

D-U-N-S 25-238-9689   (BR)
**BRUCE-GREY CATHOLIC DISTRICT
SCHOOL BOARD**
SACRED HEART HIGH SCHOOL
(*Suby of* BRUCE-GREY CATHOLIC DIS-
TRICT SCHOOL BOARD)
450 Robinson St, Walkerton, ON, N0G 2V0
(519) 881-1900
Emp Here 80
SIC 8211 Elementary and secondary schools
Glen Miller

D-U-N-S 20-717-8083   (BR)
CANPAR TRANSPORT L.P.
(*Suby of* CANPAR TRANSPORT L.P.)
18 Industrial Rd, Walkerton, ON, N0G 2V0
(519) 881-2770
Emp Here 120
SIC 4731 Freight transportation arrangement

D-U-N-S 20-047-4356   (HQ)
**COMMUNITY LIVING WALKERTON AND
DISTRICT**
19 Durham St E, Walkerton, ON, N0G 2V0
(519) 881-0233
Emp Here 25   *Sales* 14,938,800
SIC 7361 Employment agencies
Brodie Hart

D-U-N-S 24-726-5507   (HQ)
**CRAIG, MCDONALD, REDDON INSUR-
ANCE BROKERS LTD**
12 Colborne St S, Walkerton, ON, N0G 2V0
(519) 881-2701
Emp Here 9   *Sales* 27,137,920
SIC 6411 Insurance agents, brokers, and ser-
vice
Daniel Craig
Bill Reddon
Bruce Mcdonald
Jim Diemert

D-U-N-S 20-179-8360   (SL)
ERNEWEIN, JOHN LIMITED
RURAL AGRI LEASING, DIV OF
18 Industrial Rd, Walkerton, ON, N0G 2V0
(519) 881-0187
Emp Here 45   *Sales* 20,122,830
SIC 5039 Construction materials, nec
John Ernewein
Jeff Harper
Allan Beitz
Trevor Reading
Mary Ernewein
Randy Willick
Jack Lacey

Ian Inglis
Joe Bester
Patrick Fischer

D-U-N-S 24-793-6839   (SL)
FIRE EMERGENCY SERVICE
510 Napier St E, Walkerton, ON, N0G 2V0
(519) 881-0642
Emp Here 25   *Sales* 11,230,475
SIC 7389 Business services, nec
Mike Murphy

D-U-N-S 20-084-7650   (BR)
HAMMOND MUSEUM OF RADIO
(*Suby of* HAMMOND MUSEUM OF RADIO)
15 Industrial Rd, Walkerton, ON, N0G 2V0
(519) 881-3552
Emp Here 75
SIC 3612 Transformers, except electric
Tom Holman

D-U-N-S 20-179-8717   (SL)
LARSEN & SHAW LIMITED
575 Durham St W, Walkerton, ON, N0G 2V0
(519) 881-1320
Emp Here 100   *Sales* 19,208,500
SIC 3429 Hardware, nec
Mary Jane Bushell
Steven Caslick
John Larsen

D-U-N-S 25-017-4497   (HQ)
MCINTEE , WILFRED & CO. LIMITED
11 Durham St, Walkerton, ON, N0G 2V0
(519) 881-2270
Emp Here 8   *Sales* 39,794,455
SIC 6531 Real estate agents and managers
Wilfred Mcintee

D-U-N-S 25-778-6400   (SL)
MURPHY'S VALU-MART
1200 Younge St S, Walkerton, ON, N0G 2V0
(519) 881-2280
Emp Here 49   *Sales* 13,433,448
SIC 5411 Grocery stores
Mike Murphy

D-U-N-S 24-892-4425   (HQ)
SOUTH BRUCE GREY HEALTH CENTRE
21 Mcgivern St, Walkerton, ON, N0G 2V0
(519) 881-1220
Emp Here 80   *Sales* 44,876,320
SIC 8062 General medical and surgical hospi-
tals
Paul Rosebush

D-U-N-S 20-112-7821   (SL)
WESTARIO POWER INC
24 Eastridge Rd, Walkerton, ON, N0G 2V0
(519) 507-6937
Emp Here 46   *Sales* 23,904,130
SIC 4911 Electric services
George Bridge

Wallaceburg, ON N8A

D-U-N-S 20-547-7222   (HQ)
1528593 ONTARIO INC
SELECT FINISHING
6941 Base Line, Wallaceburg, ON, N8A 4L3
(519) 627-7885
Emp Here 60   *Sales* 30,733,600
SIC 3479 Metal coating and allied services
George Bogaert
Peter Bogaert
Jordan Bogaert
Gregory Bogaert

D-U-N-S 24-426-3666   (BR)
AARKEL TOOL AND DIE INC
(*Suby of* 8913897 CANADA INC)
760 Lowe Ave, Wallaceburg, ON, N8A 5H5
(519) 627-9601
Emp Here 150
SIC 3544 Special dies, tools, jigs, and fixtures

Joe Bianco

D-U-N-S 25-897-8550   (BR)
AARKEL TOOL AND DIE INC
(*Suby of* 8913897 CANADA INC)
740 Lowe Ave, Wallaceburg, ON, N8A 5H5
(519) 627-9601
Emp Here 80
SIC 3544 Special dies, tools, jigs, and fixtures
Richard Dunn

D-U-N-S 24-889-0543   (HQ)
AARKEL TOOL AND DIE INC
(*Suby of* 8913897 CANADA INC)
17 Elm Dr S, Wallaceburg, ON, N8A 5E8
(519) 627-6078
Sales 33,608,383
SIC 3544 Special dies, tools, jigs, and fixtures
Larry Delaey
Mary Van Santvoort

D-U-N-S 20-178-1890   (HQ)
ACCURCAST CORPORATION
333 Arnold St, Wallaceburg, ON, N8A 3P3
(519) 627-2227
Emp Here 55   *Sales* 29,521,800
SIC 6712 Bank holding companies
Mitchell Goldman

D-U-N-S 20-178-1858   (SL)
ACCURCAST INC
(*Suby of* ACCURCAST CORPORATION)
333 Arnold St, Wallaceburg, ON, N8A 3P3
(519) 627-2227
Emp Here 104   *Sales* 18,864,352
SIC 3365 Aluminum foundries
Mitchell Goldman
Jeffrey Mclaughlin
Stanley Marchalewicz

D-U-N-S 24-360-7244   (SL)
ARRK CANADA HOLDINGS, INC
17 Elm Dr S, Wallaceburg, ON, N8A 5E8
(519) 627-6078
Emp Here 160   *Sales* 43,544,573
SIC 5261 Retail nurseries and garden stores

D-U-N-S 20-738-6900   (SL)
CANADIAN TIRE
74 Mcnaughton Ave Suite 135, Wallaceburg,
ON, N8A 1R9
(519) 627-4251
Emp Here 25   *Sales* 12,451,950
SIC 5531 Auto and home supply stores
Peter Marshall

D-U-N-S 20-787-3758   (SL)
COMMUNITY LIVING WALLACEBURG
1100 Dufferin Ave, Wallaceburg, ON, N8A
2W1
(519) 627-0776
Emp Here 140   *Sales* 99,289,680
SIC 8699 Membership organizations, nec
David Katzman
Kristen Williams
Caroline Mortier

D-U-N-S 20-051-8137   (SL)
ECR INTERNATIONAL LTD
(*Suby of* ECR INTERNATIONAL, INC.)
6800 Base Line, Wallaceburg, ON, N8A 2K6
(519) 627-0791
Emp Here 70   *Sales* 15,540,070
SIC 3585 Refrigeration and heating equip-
ment
Michael Paparone
Brian Brown

D-U-N-S 24-209-3250   (HQ)
LAMBTON CONVEYOR LIMITED
102 Arnold St, Wallaceburg, ON, N8A 3P4
(519) 627-8228
Sales 31,080,140
SIC 3535 Conveyors and conveying equip-
ment
Christopher Moorhouse
Patricia Moorhouse
Dorothea Moorhouse

D-U-N-S 20-025-2646   (BR)
LAMBTON KENT DISTRICT SCHOOL BOARD
WALLACEBURG DISTRICT SECONDARY SCHOOL
(*Suby of* LAMBTON KENT DISTRICT SCHOOL BOARD)
920 Elgin St, Wallaceburg, ON, N8A 3E1
(519) 627-3368
Emp Here 90
SIC 8211 Elementary and secondary schools
Reberta Buchanan

D-U-N-S 20-968-5403   (HQ)
LAPOINTE-FISHER NURSING HOME, LIMITED
FAIRFIELD PARK
1934 Dufferin Ave, Wallaceburg, ON, N8A 4M2
(519) 627-1663
Emp Here 120   *Sales* 17,764,760
SIC 8051 Skilled nursing care facilities
Dan Bailey
Joanne Vink

D-U-N-S 20-408-1160   (SL)
OAKS RETIREMENT VILLAGE INC
80 Mcnaughton Ave Suite 114, Wallaceburg, ON, N8A 1R9
(519) 627-9292
Emp Here 70   *Sales* 16,303,770
SIC 6513 Apartment building operators
Ben Carter

D-U-N-S 20-180-0687   (SL)
RIVERVIEW AUTOMOBILE LIMITED
854 Murray St, Wallaceburg, ON, N8A 1W4
(519) 627-6014
Emp Here 25   *Sales* 12,451,950
SIC 5511 New and used car dealers
John Fleischmann Jr
Julie Fleischmann

D-U-N-S 20-895-9106   (HQ)
RULMECA CANADA LIMITED
(*Suby of* RULMECA HOLDING SPA)
75 Mason St, Wallaceburg, ON, N8A 4L7
(519) 627-2277
Sales 13,320,060
SIC 3535 Conveyors and conveying equipment
Joseph Hartney
Marco Ghisalberti
Fabio Ghisalberti

D-U-N-S 25-168-3298   (HQ)
ST. CLAIR CATHOLIC DISTRICT SCHOOL BOARD
420 Creek St, Wallaceburg, ON, N8A 4C4
(519) 627-6762
Sales 109,030,900
SIC 8211 Elementary and secondary schools
Paul Wubben

D-U-N-S 20-180-0711   (HQ)
ST. CLAIR TECHNOLOGIES INC
827 Dufferin Ave, Wallaceburg, ON, N8A 2V5
(519) 627-1673
Emp Here 60   *Sales* 159,967,500
SIC 3714 Motor vehicle parts and accessories
David Thomas
Ronald Bishop
Charles Hess
David Hess
Paul Hess
Randal Hess
Jodi Pilon
Daniel Reid

D-U-N-S 24-412-8369   (BR)
TRAVELERS TRANSPORTATION SERVICES INC
(*Suby of* TRAVELERS TRANSPORTATION SERVICES INC)
735 Gillard St, Wallaceburg, ON, N8A 5G7
(519) 627-5848
Emp Here 85

SIC 4213 Trucking, except local
Roger Macclatchey

D-U-N-S 20-700-1319   (BR)
WABTEC CANADA INC
WABTEC FOUNDRY
(*Suby of* WESTINGHOUSE AIR BRAKE TECHNOLOGIES CORPORATION)
40 Mason St, Wallaceburg, ON, N8A 4M1
(519) 627-1244
Emp Here 180
SIC 3321 Gray and ductile iron foundries
Paul Teron

D-U-N-S 24-609-0661   (BR)
WAL-MART CANADA CORP
WALMART
(*Suby of* WALMART INC.)
60 Mcnaughton Ave Unit 16, Wallaceburg, ON, N8A 1R9
(519) 627-8840
Emp Here 176
SIC 5311 Department stores
Martin Genier

D-U-N-S 20-180-0984   (HQ)
WALLACEBURG AUTOMOTIVE INC
NAPA AUTO PARTS
330 Selkirk St, Wallaceburg, ON, N8A 3X7
(519) 627-2288
Emp Here 6   *Sales* 15,938,496
SIC 5511 New and used car dealers
David Elliott
Jean Elliott

Wallenstein, ON N0B

D-U-N-S 25-600-5075   (SL)
COUNTRY POULTRY
7705 4th Line Suite 2, Wallenstein, ON, N0B 2S0
(519) 698-9930
Emp Here 30   *Sales* 11,760,089
SIC 0212 Beef cattle, except feedlots
Paul Martin

D-U-N-S 24-818-3928   (SL)
TRIMAR STEEL
3595 Ament Line Rr 3, Wallenstein, ON, N0B 2S0
(519) 699-5444
Emp Here 11   *Sales* 11,003,729
SIC 5051 Metals service centers and offices
Enoch Martin

D-U-N-S 24-425-8518   (HQ)
WALLENSTEIN FEED & SUPPLY LTD
7307 Wellington Road 86, Wallenstein, ON, N0B 2S0
(519) 669-5143
Sales 29,700,800
SIC 5191 Farm supplies
Lloyd Martin
Rick Martin

Walton, ON N0K

D-U-N-S 20-180-1644   (SL)
MCGAVIN FARM EQUIPMENT LTD
MCGAVIN FARM SUPPLIES
83145 Brussels Line, Walton, ON, N0K 1Z0
(519) 887-6365
Emp Here 20   *Sales* 10,000,000
SIC 5083 Farm and garden machinery
Neil Mcgavin
Jeff Mcgavin
Marie Mcgavin

Warkworth, ON K0K

D-U-N-S 24-987-3712   (HQ)
ALLEN, G & B INSURANCE BROKERS LIMITED
ALLEN INSURANCE
45 Dominion St, Warkworth, ON, K0K 3K0
(705) 924-2632
Emp Here 17   *Sales* 28,834,040
SIC 6411 Insurance agents, brokers, and service
Bryce D Allen

Warwick Township, ON N0N

D-U-N-S 20-823-7321   (SL)
BIRNAM EXCAVATING LTD
7046 Nauvoo Rd, Warwick Township, ON, N0N 1J4
(519) 828-3449
Emp Here 60   *Sales* 15,146,520
SIC 1623 Water, sewer, and utility lines
Mark Van Bree
Teresa Van Bree

Wasaga Beach, ON L9Z

D-U-N-S 20-994-8343   (BR)
LOBLAWS INC
REAL CANADIAN SUPERSTORE
(*Suby of* LOBLAW COMPANIES LIMITED)
25 45th St S, Wasaga Beach, ON, L9Z 1A7
(705) 429-4315
Emp Here 200
SIC 5411 Grocery stores
Randy Rutledge

D-U-N-S 25-943-4579   (SL)
WASAGA 500 GO-KARTS LTD
152 River Rd W, Wasaga Beach, ON, L9Z 2X2
(705) 322-2594
Emp Here 30   *Sales* 14,942,340
SIC 5599 Automotive dealers, nec
Robert Croll

Waterdown, ON L0R

D-U-N-S 20-574-0389   (BR)
ATTRIDGE TRANSPORTATION INCORPORATED
(*Suby of* ATTRIDGE TRANSPORTATION INCORPORATED)
27 Mill St S, Waterdown, ON, L0R 2H0
(905) 690-2632
Emp Here 650
SIC 4141 Local bus charter service
Jim Attridge

D-U-N-S 20-179-5627   (BR)
JARLETTE LTD
ALEXANDER PLACE LONG TERM CARE
329 Parkside Dr E, Waterdown, ON, L0R 2H0
(905) 689-2662
Emp Here 120   *Sales* 588,616
SIC 8051 Skilled nursing care facilities
Cathie Robitille

D-U-N-S 20-647-5621   (HQ)
OPTA MINERALS INC
ROSSBORQUGH CANADA
(*Suby of* SUNOPTA INC)
407 Parkside Dr, Waterdown, ON, L0R 2H0
(905) 689-7361
Emp Here 45   *Sales* 69,036,300
SIC 3291 Abrasive products
David Kruse
Jeremy Kendall
Sylvain Levert
Steven Bromley

Waterdown, ON L8B

D-U-N-S 24-612-2209   (SL)
2156110 ONTARIO LIMITED
FORTINO'S #00081
(*Suby of* LOBLAW COMPANIES LIMITED)
115 Hamilton St N Suite 81, Waterdown, ON, L8B 1A8
(905) 690-6446
Emp Here 110   *Sales* 32,282,470
SIC 5411 Grocery stores
John Macdonald

D-U-N-S 20-468-7966   (SL)
EVERWORKS INC
64 Spring Creek Dr, Waterdown, ON, L8B 0X4
(905) 208-1668
Emp Here 50   *Sales* 11,895,050
SIC 8742 Management consulting services
John Alesi

D-U-N-S 24-393-9423   (SL)
FILES, JIM & DEANNA SALES & SERVICES LIMITED
CANADIAN TIRE
11 Clappison Ave Suite 220, Waterdown, ON, L8B 0Y2
(905) 690-3486
Emp Here 70   *Sales* 44,049,600
SIC 5531 Auto and home supply stores
Jim Files
Deanna Files

D-U-N-S 20-590-5461   (BR)
HAMILTON-WENTWORTH DISTRICT SCHOOL BOARD, THE
WATERDOWN DISTRICT HIGH SCHOOL
(*Suby of* HAMILTON-WENTWORTH DISTRICT SCHOOL BOARD, THE)
215 Parkside Dr, Waterdown, ON, L8B 1B9
(905) 689-6692
Emp Here 100
SIC 8211 Elementary and secondary schools
Michelle Visca

D-U-N-S 20-770-9841   (SL)
HORTICO INC
723 Robson Rd, Waterdown, ON, L8B 1H2
(905) 689-6984
Emp Here 40   *Sales* 13,698,680
SIC 0181 Ornamental nursery products
John Vanderkruk
Philip Vanderkruk

D-U-N-S 20-437-1155   (SL)
HOUSE OF HOPE SOCIETY INCORPORATED
87 Bousfield Rise, Waterdown, ON, L8B 0T4

Emp Here 150   *Sales* 16,662,000
SIC 8062 General medical and surgical hospitals
Melvin Schrader

D-U-N-S 24-735-9219   (SL)
STRYKER CANADA LP
(*Suby of* STRYKER CORPORATION)
2 Medicorum Place, Waterdown, ON, L8B 1W2
(905) 690-5700
Emp Here 195   *Sales* 104,393,640
SIC 5047 Medical and hospital equipment
John Brown
Si Johnson
Cecelia Moffat
Bill Vanderburg
Dave Simpson

D-U-N-S 20-109-0193   (BR)
YMCA OF HAMILTON/BURLINGTON/BRANTFORD
YMCA
(*Suby of* YMCA OF HAMILTON/BURLINGTON/BRANTFORD)
207 Parkside Dr, Waterdown, ON, L8B 1B9

(905) 690-3555
Emp Here 75
SIC 7997 Membership sports and recreation clubs
Michael Braithwaite

Waterford, ON N0E

D-U-N-S 24-302-6457   (HQ)
BRADSHAW BROS. PETROLEUM LTD.
B B FAMILY CONVENIENCE
308 Main St S, Waterford, ON, N0E 1Y0
(519) 443-8611
Emp Here 15   *Sales* 14,070,150
SIC 5983 Fuel oil dealers
Brenda Bradshaw

D-U-N-S 20-277-9922   (SL)
MILES PRODUCE LTD
1701 Old Highway 24, Waterford, ON, N0E 1Y0
(519) 443-7227
Emp Here 49   *Sales* 16,780,883
SIC 0161 Vegetables and melons
Kevin Miles

Waterloo, ON N2J

D-U-N-S 20-688-9870   (HQ)
1449132 ONTARIO LIMITED
BEAT GOES ON, THE
343 Weber St N, Waterloo, ON, N2J 3H8
(519) 579-8243
Emp Here 5   *Sales* 11,517,000
SIC 5736 Musical instrument stores
John Rocchetta

D-U-N-S 24-593-9637   (HQ)
1579149 ONTARIO LTD
PETRO CANADA
106 Bridgeport Rd E, Waterloo, ON, N2J 2J9
(519) 746-0139
Emp Here 5   *Sales* 24,903,900
SIC 5541 Gasoline service stations
Susan Kaake

D-U-N-S 20-351-7925   (SL)
1928321 ONTARIO INC
SETTLEMENT CO
23 King St N, Waterloo, ON, N2J 2W6
(519) 954-6622
Emp Here 20   *Sales* 10,702,480
SIC 5149 Groceries and related products, nec
Rob Theodosiou
Ian Pattenden
Brian Prudham

D-U-N-S 24-822-3257   (SL)
793337 ONTARIO INC
FLYING DOG, THE
341 Marsland Dr, Waterloo, ON, N2J 3Z2
(519) 886-7730
Emp Here 200   *Sales* 9,103,800
SIC 5813 Drinking places
Barry Humphrey
Gary Stewart
Susan Stewart

D-U-N-S 25-471-8356   (SL)
828590 ONTARIO INC
TIM HORTONS
94 Bridgeport Rd E, Waterloo, ON, N2J 2J9
(519) 746-6804
Emp Here 39   *Sales* 10,691,928
SIC 5461 Retail bakeries
Patricia Mcgrinder

D-U-N-S 20-390-3393   (HQ)
ACTIVA CONSTRUCTION INC
55 Columbia St E Suite 1, Waterloo, ON, N2J 4N7

(519) 886-9400
Sales 27,094,200
SIC 1521 Single-family housing construction
Domenico-Antonio Giovinazzo
Laurie Klassen

D-U-N-S 20-850-2229   (SL)
ADLYS HOTELS INC
HUETHER HOTEL
59 King St N, Waterloo, ON, N2J 2X2
(519) 886-3350
Emp Here 100   *Sales* 4,551,900
SIC 5812 Eating places
Sonia Adlys

D-U-N-S 20-940-8368   (SL)
BAST TIRECRAFT
1 Bast Pl, Waterloo, ON, N2J 4G8
(519) 664-2282
Emp Here 25   *Sales* 15,732,000
SIC 5531 Auto and home supply stores
Wayne Moser

D-U-N-S 24-778-7088   (SL)
BOUCHER & JONES INC
BOUCHER & JONES FUELS
155 Roger St Suite 1, Waterloo, ON, N2J 1B1
(519) 653-3501
Emp Here 30   *Sales* 37,716,030
SIC 5171 Petroleum bulk stations and terminals

D-U-N-S 24-212-0629   (BR)
CRAWFORD & COMPANY (CANADA) INC
CRAWFORD CLASS ACTION SERVICES
(*Suby of* CRAWFORD & COMPANY)
180 King St S Unit 610, Waterloo, ON, N2J 1P8
(519) 578-9800
Emp Here 120
SIC 6411 Insurance agents, brokers, and service

D-U-N-S 24-664-4066   (SL)
DONOVAN INSURANCE BROKERS INC
72 Regina St N, Waterloo, ON, N2J 3A5
(519) 886-3150
Emp Here 21   *Sales* 12,178,404
SIC 6411 Insurance agents, brokers, and service
Kevin Donovan

D-U-N-S 20-017-3487   (HQ)
DSI RECYCLING SYSTEMS INC
(*Suby of* 1054579 ONTARIO INC)
1595 Lobsinger Line Suite 1, Waterloo, ON, N2J 4G8
(519) 664-3586
Sales 11,626,524
SIC 5074 Plumbing and heating equipment and supplies (hydronics)
Ron Lugowski
Dean Burbacher

D-U-N-S 25-971-3303   (SL)
EAST SIDE MARIO'S
450 King St N Suite Side, Waterloo, ON, N2J 2Z6
(226) 647-2587
Emp Here 90   *Sales* 4,096,710
SIC 5812 Eating places
Robert Cuttie

D-U-N-S 20-843-9778   (HQ)
EQUITABLE LIFE INSURANCE COMPANY OF CANADA, THE
1 Westmount Rd N, Waterloo, ON, N2J 4C7
(519) 886-5210
Emp Here 425   *Sales* 1,068,484,000
SIC 6311 Life insurance
Ronald E. Beettham
Douglas W. Dodds
Rita Burak
Douglas L. Derry
Maureen A. Farrow
Paul D. Mitchell
Marc J. Somerville
Donald N. Stevens

C. Lee F. Watchorn
David S. Weinberg

D-U-N-S 20-873-2060   (SL)
FORD LINCOLN
455 King St N, Waterloo, ON, N2J 2Z5
(877) 339-6067
Emp Here 80   *Sales* 50,342,400
SIC 5511 New and used car dealers
Dan Devoer

D-U-N-S 20-578-4304   (SL)
GLENBRIAR HOME HARDWARE
PLUMBING SHOWPLACE
262 Weber St N, Waterloo, ON, N2J 3H6
(519) 886-2950
Emp Here 49   *Sales* 12,399,891
SIC 5251 Hardware stores
Jeff Sauder

D-U-N-S 20-302-3432   (BR)
HAUSER INDUSTRIES INC
HAUSER COMPANY STORE
(*Suby of* JOHN HAUSER IRONWORKS HOLDINGS INC)
330 Weber St N, Waterloo, ON, N2J 3H6
(800) 268-7328
Emp Here 235
SIC 5712 Furniture stores
Lisa Schnarr

D-U-N-S 24-543-4626   (HQ)
HAUSER INDUSTRIES INC
HAUSER CONTRACT
(*Suby of* JOHN HAUSER IRONWORKS HOLDINGS INC)
330 Weber St N, Waterloo, ON, N2J 3H6
(519) 747-1138
Emp Here 75   *Sales* 13,117,370
SIC 2514 Metal household furniture
Ernie Hauser
Eric Hauser
Christopher Hauser
Jason Hauser
Stephanie Hauser
Holly Hauser
Donald Pickett

D-U-N-S 24-373-0590   (SL)
HEALTH INTEGRATION NETWORK OF WATERLOO WELLINGTON
WATERLOO WELLINGTON LHIN
141 Weber St S, Waterloo, ON, N2J 2A9
(519) 748-2222
Emp Here 560   *Sales* 131,102,160
SIC 8621 Professional organizations
Bruce Lauckner

D-U-N-S 20-342-3025   (HQ)
HEARTLAND FARM MUTUAL INC
100 Erb St E, Waterloo, ON, N2J 1L9
(519) 886-4530
Sales 111,187,620
SIC 6331 Fire, marine, and casualty insurance
Carlos Rodrigues
Les Card
David Balodis
Jim Zyta
Josie Gaffney
Larry Nickel
Helen Johns
Andrew Dyment
Betty Semeniuk
Bruce Pearson

D-U-N-S 24-129-7261   (SL)
INSCRIBER TECHNOLOGY CORPORATION
26 Peppler St, Waterloo, ON, N2J 3C4
(519) 570-9111
Emp Here 90   *Sales* 16,226,384
SIC 7371 Custom computer programming services
Dan Mance
Mike Bernhardt

D-U-N-S 20-241-1075   (SL)

INTELLIGENT MECHATRONICS SYSTEMS INC.
IMS
(*Suby of* TRAK GLOBAL GROUP LIMITED)
435 King St N, Waterloo, ON, N2J 2Z5
(519) 745-8887
Emp Here 108   *Sales* 24,674,976
SIC 4899 Communication services, nec
Tracey Weaver

D-U-N-S 20-358-2291   (HQ)
KOGNITIV CORPORATION
187 King St S, Waterloo, ON, N2J 1R1
(226) 476-1124
Sales 16,684,700
SIC 7372 Prepackaged software
Peter Schwartz
Kamal Pastakia
Don Tapscott
John Bowey
Mark Rider
Ken Teslia
Rick Nathan
Mark Lerohi

D-U-N-S 24-829-9950   (BR)
KPMG LLP
(*Suby of* KPMG LLP)
115 King St S Suite 201, Waterloo, ON, N2J 5A3
(519) 747-8800
Emp Here 170
SIC 8721 Accounting, auditing, and bookkeeping
Frank Boutzis

D-U-N-S 20-786-6930   (SL)
MAR-JOHN'S NURSERY LTD
JOHN'S NURSERY
1060 Lobsinger Line, Waterloo, ON, N2J 4G8
(519) 664-2482
Emp Here 30   *Sales* 22,275,600
SIC 5191 Farm supplies
John Albrecht
Mary Albrecht
John D Albrecht

D-U-N-S 24-525-5575   (HQ)
MARTIN'S FAMILY FRUIT FARM LTD
1420 Lobsinger Line Unit 1, Waterloo, ON, N2J 4G8
(519) 664-2750
Sales 16,902,500
SIC 0175 Deciduous tree fruits
Leighton Martin
Florence Martin
Steve Martin
Ken Martin
Kevin Martin

D-U-N-S 24-868-3633   (SL)
MCDONALD, PHIL ENTERPRISES LTD
CANADIAN TIRE ASSOCIATE STORE
400 Weber St N, Waterloo, ON, N2J 3J3
(519) 885-1050
Emp Here 110   *Sales* 29,441,720
SIC 5251 Hardware stores
Phil Mcdonald

D-U-N-S 24-108-0592   (SL)
MIDWESTERN ONTARIO SERVICE EXPERT
BOEHMERS CRONIN EMERY ACCENT HEATING & COOLING
826 King St N Unit 14, Waterloo, ON, N2J 4G8
(519) 664-2974
Emp Here 49   *Sales* 11,286,660
SIC 5722 Household appliance stores
Ralph Simmone

D-U-N-S 25-974-7157   (SL)
NANCY LOPEZ GOLF
185 Weber St S, Waterloo, ON, N2J 2B1
(866) 649-1759
Emp Here 47   *Sales* 10,457,704
SIC 3949 Sporting and athletic goods, nec
Susan Summers

D-U-N-S 20-180-6759   (SL)
ONTARIO DIE COMPANY LIMITED
ODC TOOLING & MOLDS
119 Roger St, Waterloo, ON, N2J 1A4
(519) 576-8950
Emp Here 110   *Sales* 21,129,350
SIC 3423 Hand and edge tools, nec
Ronald Levene

D-U-N-S 20-787-3985   (SL)
PARKWAY FORD SALES (1996) LTD
PARKWAY VEHICLE LEASING
455 King St N, Waterloo, ON, N2J 2Z5
(519) 884-5110
Emp Here 65   *Sales* 40,903,200
SIC 5511 New and used car dealers
Michael Stollery
Ken Bast
Carolyn Zenger

D-U-N-S 25-408-4783   (SL)
RAF ENTERPRISES INC
FORBES WATERLOO TOYOTA
300 Weber St N, Waterloo, ON, N2J 3H6
(519) 885-2000
Emp Here 35   *Sales* 17,432,730
SIC 5511 New and used car dealers
Lynn Forbes

D-U-N-S 20-201-1750   (HQ)
REMAX SOLID GOLD REALTY (II) LTD
180 Weber St S, Waterloo, ON, N2J 2B2
(519) 888-7110
Emp Here 1   *Sales* 10,326,728
SIC 6531 Real estate agents and managers
Ken Cameron

D-U-N-S 24-025-6896   (SL)
RIDETONES INC
161 Roger St, Waterloo, ON, N2J 1B1
(519) 745-8887
Emp Here 50   *Sales* 24,903,900
SIC 5531 Auto and home supply stores
Otman Basir

D-U-N-S 20-875-7914   (SL)
ROSENDALE FARMS LIMITED
544 Sawmill Rd, Waterloo, ON, N2J 4G8
(519) 744-4941
Emp Here 11   *Sales* 16,144,612
SIC 5153 Grain and field beans
Larry Shantz
Murray Shantz
Diane Shantz
Carol Shantz
Brad Shantz
Brian Shantz

D-U-N-S 25-608-0789   (BR)
SOBEYS CAPITAL INCORPORATED
SOBEY'S 649
(*Suby of* EMPIRE COMPANY LIMITED)
94 Bridgeport Rd E, Waterloo, ON, N2J 2J9
(519) 885-4170
Emp Here 100
SIC 5411 Grocery stores
John Smith

D-U-N-S 20-692-8702   (SL)
SUDS EXPRESS INC
SUDS
130 Dearborn Pl, Waterloo, ON, N2J 4N5
(519) 886-0561
Emp Here 50   *Sales* 10,131,450
SIC 7542 Carwashes
George Walsh
Peter Walsh

D-U-N-S 24-850-0464   (HQ)
**SUN LIFE FINANCIAL INVESTMENT SER-
VICES (CANADA) INC**
(*Suby of* SUN LIFE FINANCIAL INC)
227 King St S, Waterloo, ON, N2J 1R2
(519) 888-2290
Sales 32,283,303
SIC 6722 Management investment, open-end
John Garramone

D-U-N-S 20-180-7526   (SL)
SWAN DUST CONTROL LIMITED
35 University Ave E, Waterloo, ON, N2J 2V9
(519) 885-4450
Emp Here 45   *Sales* 13,147,605
SIC 7359 Equipment rental and leasing, nec
Christopher Tank
Brian Tank

D-U-N-S 24-985-7012   (SL)
TAYLOR & GRANT SPECIALTIES LIMITED
151 Weber St S Suite 2, Waterloo, ON, N2J 2A9

Emp Here 90   *Sales* 75,201,930
SIC 5145 Confectionery
T Dundee Staunton
Jim Schulz

D-U-N-S 20-404-0018   (HQ)
TOURNAMENT SPORTS MARKETING INC
185 Weber St S, Waterloo, ON, N2J 2B1
(519) 888-6500
Emp Here 64   *Sales* 33,835,230
SIC 5091 Sporting and recreation goods
Kim D Bauer

D-U-N-S 20-120-0446   (HQ)
TWINCORP INC
KFC
316 Marsland Dr, Waterloo, ON, N2J 3Z1
(519) 885-4600
Emp Here 10   *Sales* 93,278,000
SIC 5812 Eating places
Barney Strassburger

D-U-N-S 24-326-6009   (SL)
V.A. HEALTH CARE INC
SHOPPERS DRUG MART
50 Weber St N, Waterloo, ON, N2J 3G7
(519) 880-8083
Emp Here 45   *Sales* 11,382,930
SIC 5912 Drug stores and proprietary stores
Veneta Anand

D-U-N-S 24-381-1804   (SL)
VALIDUS RESEARCH INC
(*Suby of* AMERICAN INTERNATIONAL
GROUP, INC.)
187 King St S Suite 201, Waterloo, ON, N2J 1R1
(519) 783-9100
Emp Here 17   *Sales* 14,417,020
SIC 6411 Insurance agents, brokers, and ser-
vice
Jason Miller

D-U-N-S 24-564-8167   (SL)
WATERLOO DODGE CHRYSLER LTD
DEAN MYERS CHRYSLER DODGE
150 Weber St S, Waterloo, ON, N2J 2A8
(519) 743-0300
Emp Here 30   *Sales* 14,942,340
SIC 5511 New and used car dealers
Dean Myers

D-U-N-S 20-786-5585   (SL)
WATERLOO MOTOR INN LIMITED
WATERLOO INN CONFERRANCE HOTEL
475 King St N, Waterloo, ON, N2J 2Z5
(519) 885-0721
Emp Here 125   *Sales* 11,586,250
SIC 7011 Hotels and motels
Mary D'alton
Charles (Chuck) Groocock
Lawrence Bingeman

D-U-N-S 24-419-8557   (HQ)
**WATERLOO NORTH HYDRO HOLDING
CORPORATION**
526 Country Squire Rd, Waterloo, ON, N2J 4G8
(519) 886-5090
Sales 42,033,535
SIC 6712 Bank holding companies
Rene Gatien
Virgina Dybenko
Bill Strauss

Glen Wright
Brenda Holloran
Tim Jackson
Ross Kelterborn
Chuck Martin
Ian Mclean
Henrik Noesgaard

D-U-N-S 24-218-6583   (SL)
WATERLOO NORTH HYDRO INC
(*Suby of* WATERLOO NORTH HYDRO
HOLDING CORPORATION)
526 Country Squire Rd, Waterloo, ON, N2J 4G8
(519) 886-5090
Emp Here 128   *Sales* 87,023,872
SIC 4911 Electric services
Rene Gatien
Albert Singh

D-U-N-S 25-771-8684   (SL)
WATERLOO POTTERS' WORKSHOP
75 King St S, Waterloo, ON, N2J 1P2
(519) 885-5570
Emp Here 49   *Sales* 19,473,286
SIC 8699 Membership organizations, nec
Ester Debries

D-U-N-S 25-228-1464   (BR)
**WATERLOO REGION DISTRICT SCHOOL
BOARD**
BLUEVALE COLLEGIATE INSTITUTE
(*Suby of* WATERLOO REGION DISTRICT
SCHOOL BOARD)
80 Bluevale St N, Waterloo, ON, N2J 3R5
(519) 885-4620
Emp Here 130
SIC 8211 Elementary and secondary schools
Mark Hunniford

D-U-N-S 25-969-9452   (HQ)
**WATERLOO   WELLINGTON   LOCAL
HEALTH INTEGRATION NETWORK**
141 Weber St S, Waterloo, ON, N2J 2A9
(519) 748-2222
Emp Here 200   *Sales* 82,827,200
SIC 8399 Social services, nec
Bruce Lauckner
Zeynep Danis
Andrew Davidson
Steven Harrison
Karyn Lumsden
Kunuk Rhee

D-U-N-S 20-873-8596   (SL)
WRIGHT AUTO SALES INC
35 Weber St N, Waterloo, ON, N2J 3G5
(519) 742-5622
Emp Here 35   *Sales* 17,432,730
SIC 5521 Used car dealers
Larry Wright

D-U-N-S 25-297-8721   (BR)
ZEHRMART INC
ZEHRS MARKETS
(*Suby of* LOBLAW COMPANIES LIMITED)
315 Lincoln Rd Suite 1, Waterloo, ON, N2J 4H7
(519) 885-1360
Emp Here 165
SIC 5411 Grocery stores
Travis Gowland

Waterloo, ON N2K

D-U-N-S 25-625-6413   (SL)
ARCA FINANCIAL GROUP INC
237 Labrador Dr, Waterloo, ON, N2K 4M8
(519) 745-8500
Emp Here 31   *Sales* 21,046,613
SIC 6282 Investment advice
Christine Black
Mark Leech
John Lunz

Bill Vollmer

D-U-N-S 24-288-7784   (SL)
**BARBER-COLLINS SECURITY SERVICES
LTD**
245 Labrador Dr Unit 1, Waterloo, ON, N2K 4M8
(519) 745-1111
Emp Here 400   *Sales* 10,500,000
SIC 7381 Detective and armored car services
Paul Collins

D-U-N-S 24-564-5353   (HQ)
BLACKBERRY LIMITED
2200 University Ave E, Waterloo, ON, N2K 0A7
(519) 888-7465
Emp Here 500   *Sales* 904,000,000
SIC 7371 Custom computer programming ser-
vices
John Chen
Billy Ho
Nita White-Ivy
Vito Giallorenzo
Steve Rai
Alex Thurber
Neelam Sandhu
Mark Wilson
Steve Capelli
Steven E. Zipperstein

D-U-N-S 24-684-6773   (HQ)
BRANDALLIANCE ONTARIO INC
640 Bridge St W, Waterloo, ON, N2K 4M9
(519) 746-2055
Emp Here 1   *Sales* 40,096,080
SIC 5199 Nondurable goods, nec
Louis Smerechanski
Bjorn Bevenborn

D-U-N-S 20-068-0382   (BR)
**CORPORATION OF THE CITY OF WATER-
LOO, THE**
CITY OF WATERLOO SERVICE CENTER
(*Suby of* CORPORATION OF THE CITY OF
WATERLOO, THE)
265 Lexington Crt, Waterloo, ON, N2K 1W9
(519) 886-2310
Emp Here 100
SIC 7389 Business services, nec
Tim Anderson

D-U-N-S 20-981-0944   (HQ)
DEEM MANAGEMENT SERVICES LIMITED
229 Lexington Rd, Waterloo, ON, N2K 2E1
(519) 772-1026
Emp Here 3   *Sales* 14,211,808
SIC 8051 Skilled nursing care facilities
Donald Dal Bianco

D-U-N-S 20-507-0126   (SL)
PARKWOOD MENNONITE HOME INC
PARKWOOD MENNONITE HOME
726 New Hampshire St, Waterloo, ON, N2K 4M1
(519) 885-4810
Emp Here 150   *Sales* 10,248,900
SIC 8051 Skilled nursing care facilities
Duane Eby
Tim Kennel

D-U-N-S 20-102-6304   (BR)
QUALIDEC CORPORATION
MCDONALD'S
55 Northfield Dr E, Waterloo, ON, N2K 3T6

Emp Here 75
SIC 5812 Eating places
Joel Sider

D-U-N-S 25-616-4724   (SL)
**TREATMENT CENTRE OF WATERLOO RE-
GION, THE**
ROTARY CHILDREN'S CENTRE
500 Hallmark Rd, Waterloo, ON, N2K 3P5
(519) 886-8886
Emp Here 150   *Sales* 8,887,050
SIC 8361 Residential care

▲ Public Company   ■ Public Company Family Member   **HQ** Headquarters   **BR** Branch   **SL** Single Location

Stephen Swatridge

D-U-N-S 25-362-8010 (HQ)
**WASTE MANAGEMENT OF CANADA COR-
PORATION**
(Suby of WASTE MANAGEMENT, INC.)
219 Labrador Dr Suite 100, Waterloo, ON,
N2K 4M8
(519) 886-3974
Emp Here 30 *Sales* 1,074,882,600
SIC 4953 Refuse systems
Donald P Wright
Cal Bricker
Jeff Harris
Linda J Smith
Edward R Schauble
Cherie Rice
Greg A Robertson

D-U-N-S 20-653-3023 (BR)
**WATERLOO REGION DISTRICT SCHOOL
BOARD**
LESTER B PEARSON PUBLIC SCHOOL
*(Suby of WATERLOO REGION DISTRICT
SCHOOL BOARD)*
520 Chesapeake Dr, Waterloo, ON, N2K 4G5
(519) 880-0300
Emp Here 75
SIC 8211 Elementary and secondary schools
Greg Jespersen

D-U-N-S 20-180-6916 (HQ)
WISMER DEVELOPMENTS INC
PILLER SAUSAGES
443 Wismer St, Waterloo, ON, N2K 2K6
(519) 743-1412
Sales 131,593,950
SIC 2013 Sausages and other prepared
meats
Wilhelm Huber Sr
Wilhelm Huber Jr
John Nunn
Henry Huber

Waterloo, ON N2L

D-U-N-S 20-552-0336 (BR)
AGFA HEALTHCARE INC
(Suby of AGFA-GEVAERT)
375 Hagey Blvd, Waterloo, ON, N2L 6R5
(519) 746-2900
Emp Here 250
SIC 7371 Custom computer programming ser-
vices
Johan Demeester

D-U-N-S 24-918-0852 (BR)
ATC-FROST MAGNETICS INC
*(Suby of STANDEX INTERNATIONAL COR-
PORATION)*
550 Parkside Dr Unit D6, Waterloo, ON, N2L
5V4
(905) 844-6681
Emp Here 130
SIC 3677 Electronic coils and transformers
Steve Nolan

D-U-N-S 20-117-7990 (HQ)
ATHLETICA SPORT SYSTEMS INC
ATHLETICA
*(Suby of FULCRUM CAPITAL PARTNERS
INC)*
554 Parkside Dr, Waterloo, ON, N2L 5Z4
(519) 747-1856
Sales 19,568,160
SIC 3949 Sporting and athletic goods, nec
Andrew Mcrae
Patrick (Pat) Westfall
Paul Eldridge
Klemens Wilhelm

D-U-N-S 20-129-8502 (SL)
BUSTARD BROTHERS LIMITED
BUSTARD CHRYSLER

575 Davenport Rd, Waterloo, ON, N2L 5Z3
(519) 884-5888
Emp Here 38 *Sales* 18,926,964
SIC 5511 New and used car dealers
Bill Bustard
Brent Ravelle

D-U-N-S 25-034-7267 (SL)
**CALEY ORTHODONTIC LABORATORY
LIMITED**
151 Park St, Waterloo, ON, N2L 1Y5
(519) 742-1467
Emp Here 40 *Sales* 10,262,480
SIC 3843 Dental equipment and supplies
Paul Caley

D-U-N-S 25-560-0371 (SL)
CKMS-FM 100.3
SOUND FM
200 University Ave W, Waterloo, ON, N2L 3G1

Emp Here 120 *Sales* 27,416,640
SIC 4832 Radio broadcasting stations
Steve Krysak

D-U-N-S 24-390-5069 (HQ)
**COMMUNITY SUPPORT CONNECTIONS-
MEALS ON WHEELS AND MORE**
MEALS ON WHEELS
420 Weber St N Unit L, Waterloo, ON, N2L
4E7
(519) 772-8787
Emp Here 12 *Sales* 10,503,424
SIC 5963 Direct selling establishments
Dale Howatt

D-U-N-S 25-775-7781 (BR)
**CORPORATION OF THE CITY OF WATER-
LOO, THE**
*WATERLOO MEMORIAL RECREATION
COMPLEX*
*(Suby of CORPORATION OF THE CITY OF
WATERLOO, THE)*
101 Father David Bauer Dr, Waterloo, ON,
N2L 0B4
(519) 886-1177
Emp Here 80
SIC 7299 Miscellaneous personal service
Lois Amos-Herter

D-U-N-S 24-400-1090 (SL)
DELN CONSTRUCTION INC
550 Conestogo Rd, Waterloo, ON, N2L 4E3
(519) 880-9863
Emp Here 37 *Sales* 11,798,153
SIC 1521 Single-family housing construction
Herman Derksen

D-U-N-S 20-180-5074 (SL)
DEMUTH STEEL PRODUCTS INC
419 Albert St, Waterloo, ON, N2L 3V2
(519) 884-2980
Emp Here 27 *Sales* 12,825,702
SIC 5083 Farm and garden machinery
Joe Stanic
Eric Vallieres

D-U-N-S 20-771-1706 (HQ)
**ECONOMICAL MUTUAL INSURANCE COM-
PANY**
111 Westmount Rd S, Waterloo, ON, N2L 2L6
(519) 570-8200
Emp Here 500 *Sales* 4,273,936,000
SIC 6331 Fire, marine, and casualty insurance
Karen Gavan
John H Bowey
Phil Mather
Ed Berko
Linda Goss
Michael Gagnier
Innes Dey
Jorge Arruda
Tom Reikman
Pamela Derksen

D-U-N-S 20-875-5264 (HQ)
FAITHLIFE FINANCIAL
470 Weber St N, Waterloo, ON, N2L 6J2

(519) 886-4610
Emp Here 75 *Sales* 21,379,007
SIC 6311 Life insurance
Karen Bjerland
Sheryl Teed Callum
Geoff Bellew
Julie Halgren
R. Paul Hogan
Bruce Ratzlaff
Walter Rugland
Stephen Taylor
Ronald Walter
Dale Wilcox

D-U-N-S 25-319-8956 (HQ)
GHD CONTRACTORS LIMITED
455 Phillip St, Waterloo, ON, N2L 3X2
(519) 884-0510
Emp Here 14 *Sales* 17,902,924
SIC 1629 Heavy construction, nec
Stephen Quigley
Edward Roberts
Michael Moran

D-U-N-S 20-248-4499 (HQ)
GHD LIMITED
(Suby of GHD GROUP LIMITED)
455 Phillip St, Waterloo, ON, N2L 3X2
(519) 884-0510
Emp Here 1 *Sales* 130,188,975
SIC 8711 Engineering services
Ashley Wright
Stephen M. Quigley
Mark Jolly

D-U-N-S 24-098-0573 (SL)
JAPAN AUTO LEASING INC
WATERLOO HONDA
545 King St N, Waterloo, ON, N2L 5Z6
(519) 746-4120
Emp Here 59 *Sales* 37,127,520
SIC 5511 New and used car dealers
Robin Lowe
Phyllis Lowe
Karen Carter

D-U-N-S 20-738-7239 (SL)
KEG STEAKHOUSE & BAR, THE
42 Northfield Dr E, Waterloo, ON, N2L 6A1
(519) 725-4444
Emp Here 85 *Sales* 3,869,115
SIC 5812 Eating places
James Mozes
Mychael Button
Eric Deboer

D-U-N-S 20-270-1249 (HQ)
KIK INTERACTIVE INC.
KIK
420 Weber St N Suite I, Waterloo, ON, N2L
4E7
(226) 868-0056
Emp Here 96 *Sales* 18,022,750
SIC 7371 Custom computer programming services

D-U-N-S 25-092-2486 (SL)
KRAUS CARPET LP
KRAUS FLOORS WITHMORE
65 Northfield Dr W, Waterloo, ON, N2L 0A8
(519) 884-2310
Emp Here 350 *Sales* 82,776,050
SIC 2273 Carpets and rugs
Shawn Davies

D-U-N-S 25-526-2057 (HQ)
LUBRICOR INC
*(Suby of QUAKER CHEMICAL CORPORA-
TION)*
475 Conestogo Rd, Waterloo, ON, N2L 4C9
(519) 884-8455
Emp Here 22 *Sales* 37,716,030
SIC 5172 Petroleum products, nec
Jorma Braks
Jeff Murray

D-U-N-S 25-965-6536 (HQ)
LUTHERWOOD

139 Father David Bauer Dr Suite 1, Waterloo,
ON, N2L 6L1
(519) 783-3710
Emp Here 67 *Sales* 72,473,800
SIC 8399 Social services, nec
John Colangeli

D-U-N-S 20-279-4673 (BR)
**MANUFACTURERS LIFE INSURANCE
COMPANY, THE**
MANULIFE FINANCIAL
*(Suby of MANULIFE FINANCIAL CORPORA-
TION)*
500 King St N, Waterloo, ON, N2L 5W6
(519) 747-7000
Emp Here 300
SIC 6311 Life insurance

D-U-N-S 24-911-2228 (SL)
MEGTEC TURBOSONIC INC
(Suby of DURR AG)
550 Parkside Dr Unit A14, Waterloo, ON, N2L
5V4
(519) 885-5513
Emp Here 33 *Sales* 15,675,858
SIC 5084 Industrial machinery and equipment
Egbert Van Everdingen
Edward Spink
David Hobson
Robert Allan
Mohit Uberoi
Greg Linn

D-U-N-S 24-000-5632 (HQ)
**MEGTEC TURBOSONIC TECHNOLOGIES
INC**
(Suby of DURR AG)
550 Parkside Dr Unit A14, Waterloo, ON, N2L
5V4
(519) 885-5513
Emp Here 30 *Sales* 21,376,170
SIC 5084 Industrial machinery and equipment
Egbert Van Everdingen
Edward Spink

D-U-N-S 20-278-9181 (BR)
MILLER THOMSON LLP
(Suby of MILLER THOMSON LLP)
295 Hagey Blvd Suite 300, Waterloo, ON, N2L
6R5
(519) 579-3660
Emp Here 100
SIC 8111 Legal services
Eve Munro

D-U-N-S 24-785-1561 (HQ)
NAVBLUE INC
(Suby of AIRBUS SE)
295 Hagey Blvd Suite 200, Waterloo, ON, N2L
6R5
(519) 747-1170
Sales 47,066,115
SIC 7371 Custom computer programming ser-
vices
Michael Hulley

D-U-N-S 24-340-9427 (SL)
NAVTECH INC
*(Suby of CAMBRIDGE INFORMATION
GROUP, INC.)*
295 Hagey Blvd Suite 200, Waterloo, ON, N2L
6R5
(519) 747-1170
Emp Here 240 *Sales* 47,311,440
SIC 8711 Engineering services
Mike Hulley
Sean Doherty

D-U-N-S 20-138-3952 (SL)
ONE-EIGHTY CORP
20 Erb St W Suite 803, Waterloo, ON, N2L 1T2
(519) 884-2003
Emp Here 30 *Sales* 14,942,340
SIC 5521 Used car dealers
Achim H.J. Mueller
Kerry Mueller

D-U-N-S 25-280-6849 (HQ)

ONTARIO TEACHERS' INSURANCE PLAN INC
OTIP/RAEO
125 Northfield Dr W Suite 100, Waterloo, ON, N2L 6K4
(519) 888-9683
Emp Here 150   *Sales* 427,393,600
SIC 6371 Pension, health, and welfare funds
Randy Mcglynn
Bernard Ethier
Wayne Cushman

D-U-N-S 24-850-3187   (HQ)
OPEN TEXT CORPORATION
275 Frank Tompa Dr, Waterloo, ON, N2L 0A1
(519) 888-7111
Emp Here 500   *Sales* 2,815,241,000
SIC 7372 Prepackaged software
Mark J. Barrenechea
P. Thomas Jenkins
Madhu Ranganathan
Muhi Majzoub
Gordon A. Davies
James Mcgourlay
Prentiss Donohue
Simon Harrison
David Jamieson
Patricia E. Nagle

D-U-N-S 20-808-5048   (BR)
PEAK REALTY LTD
(*Suby of* PEAK REALTY LTD)
410 Conestogo Rd Suite 210, Waterloo, ON, N2L 4E2
(519) 747-0231
Emp Here 75
SIC 6411 Insurance agents, brokers, and service

D-U-N-S 24-771-3167   (HQ)
PEAK REALTY LTD
PEAK
139 Northfield Dr W Suite 104, Waterloo, ON, N2L 5A6
(519) 662-4900
Emp Here 50   *Sales* 35,605,565
SIC 6531 Real estate agents and managers
Paul Ruby

D-U-N-S 20-139-9347   (SL)
PERIMETER INSTITUTE
PERIMETER INSTITUTE FOR THEORETICAL PHYSICS
31 Caroline St N, Waterloo, ON, N2L 2Y5
(519) 569-7600
Emp Here 85   *Sales* 43,072,560
SIC 8733 Noncommercial research organizations
Neil Turok
John Reid
Lynn Watt
Douglas T. Wright
Sue Scanlan
Donald Campbell
Ken Cork
Cosimo Fiorenza
Peter Godsoe
Mike Lazaridis

D-U-N-S 20-180-7047   (BR)
RAYTHEON CANADA LIMITED
(*Suby of* RAYTHEON COMPANY)
400 Phillip St, Waterloo, ON, N2L 6R7
(519) 885-0110
Emp Here 400
SIC 3669 Communications equipment, nec
Anne Bulikl

D-U-N-S 25-609-7130   (BR)
RE/MAX TWIN CITY REALTY INC
(*Suby of* RE/MAX TWIN CITY REALTY INC)
83 Erb St W, Waterloo, ON, N2L 6C2
(519) 885-0200
Emp Here 120
SIC 6531 Real estate agents and managers
Adrian Baas

D-U-N-S 20-912-5025   (SL)
RENISON UNIVERSITY COLLEGE
265 Westmount Rd N, Waterloo, ON, N2L 3G7
(519) 884-4404
Emp Here 85   *Sales* 9,574,060
SIC 8221 Colleges and universities
Barbara Checketts
Glenn Carpwright

D-U-N-S 24-024-8885   (SL)
RIVERSIDE DOOR & TRIM INC
520 Conestogo Rd, Waterloo, ON, N2L 4E2
(519) 578-3265
Emp Here 50   *Sales* 11,369,150
SIC 1751 Carpentry work
Stelios Gianniots
George Gianniots
Mario Gianniots

D-U-N-S 20-056-6904   (HQ)
SANDVINE INCORPORATED ULC
(*Suby of* SANDVINE LTD)
408 Albert St, Waterloo, ON, N2L 3V3
(519) 880-2600
Sales 142,946,770
SIC 3825 Instruments to measure electricity
David Caputo
Tom Donnelly
Brad Siim
Angelo Compagnoni

D-U-N-S 24-342-9789   (HQ)
SANDVINE LTD
408 Albert St, Waterloo, ON, N2L 3V3
(519) 880-2600
Sales 142,946,770
SIC 3825 Instruments to measure electricity
Lyndon Cantor
Tom Carter
Alan Petry
Brian Decker
Andrew Kowal
Mark Driedger
Richard Deggs
Samir Marwaha

D-U-N-S 25-495-4993   (BR)
SAP CANADA INC
SAP SYBASE OFFICES
(*Suby of* SAP SE)
445 Wes Graham Way, Waterloo, ON, N2L 6R2
(519) 886-3700
Emp Here 250
SIC 7371 Custom computer programming services
Terry Stepien

D-U-N-S 20-068-0390   (SL)
SCHARF REALTY LTD
ROYAL LEPAGE SCHARF REALTY
50 Westmount Rd N, Waterloo, ON, N2L 2R5
(519) 747-2040
Emp Here 60   *Sales* 16,305,360
SIC 6531 Real estate agents and managers
Ted Scharf

D-U-N-S 20-565-3277   (HQ)
SOLOWAVE DESIGN INC
(*Suby of* SOLOWAVE INVESTMENTS LIMITED)
103 Bauer Pl Suite 5, Waterloo, ON, N2L 6B5
(519) 323-3833
Sales 32,613,600
SIC 3949 Sporting and athletic goods, nec
Richard Boyer

D-U-N-S 24-325-2579   (HQ)
SOLOWAVE INVESTMENTS LIMITED
103 Bauer Pl Suite 5, Waterloo, ON, N2L 6B5
(519) 725-5379
Emp Here 4   *Sales* 32,613,600
SIC 3949 Sporting and athletic goods, nec
Richard Boyer

D-U-N-S 25-399-1459   (BR)
STANTEC CONSULTING LTD
(*Suby of* STANTEC INC)

300 Hagey Blvd Suite 100, Waterloo, ON, N2L 0A4
(519) 579-4410
Emp Here 325
SIC 8711 Engineering services
Paul Allen

D-U-N-S 20-300-7232   (BR)
STANTEC GEOMATICS LTD
(*Suby of* STANTEC INC)
300 Hagey Blvd Suite 100, Waterloo, ON, N2L 0A4
(519) 579-4410
Emp Here 340
SIC 8713 Surveying services
Brian Campbell

D-U-N-S 20-180-4911   (HQ)
STEELCRAFT INC
(*Suby of* HANSON CAPITAL CORPORATION)
446 Albert St, Waterloo, ON, N2L 3V3
(519) 884-4320
Emp Here 80   *Sales* 85,130,850
SIC 3443 Fabricated plate work (boiler shop)
Paul Summers
Keith Zehr
Graham Barraclough
Richard Findlay
Tom Davidson Jr.
Brian Jones
Gary Pooley
David Sutherland
Mark Drolet

D-U-N-S 20-848-8833   (HQ)
UNIVERSITY OF WATERLOO
200 University Ave W, Waterloo, ON, N2L 3G1
(519) 888-4567
Sales 312,824,754
SIC 8221 Colleges and universities

D-U-N-S 20-144-7596   (HQ)
VALLEY BLADES LIMITED
435 Phillip St, Waterloo, ON, N2L 3X2
(519) 885-5500
Emp Here 75   *Sales* 18,870,085
SIC 3531 Construction machinery
Dale Baier

D-U-N-S 24-992-2188   (SL)
VIA PERSONNEL SERVICES LTD
105 Bauer Pl, Waterloo, ON, N2L 6B5

Emp Here 50   *Sales* 11,848,500
SIC 7361 Employment agencies
Richard Bennett

D-U-N-S 20-292-6507   (SL)
WATERLOO CONSERVATIVE EDA
420 Erb St W Unit 5 Ste 424, Waterloo, ON, N2L 6K6
(519) 888-8300
Emp Here 30   *Sales* 11,922,420
SIC 8699 Membership organizations, nec
Samuel Marshall

D-U-N-S 24-659-2737   (HQ)
WATERLOO MANUFACTURING COMPANY LIMITED
505 Dotzert Crt Unit 1, Waterloo, ON, N2L 6A7
(519) 884-0600
Sales 10,285,002
SIC 5074 Plumbing and heating equipment and supplies (hydronics)
John J Kraemer Jr
Brian Taylor

D-U-N-S 24-320-2380   (SL)
WATERLOO NISSAN INC
141 Northfield Dr W, Waterloo, ON, N2L 5A6
(866) 99-9411
Emp Here 50   *Sales* 24,903,900
SIC 5511 New and used car dealers
Terry Yates
Glen Yates
Kathryn Elizabeth Yates
Paolo Grisafi

Heather Louise Albini
Roy Yates

D-U-N-S 25-174-0692   (BR)
WATERLOO REGION DISTRICT SCHOOL BOARD
WATERLOO COLLEGIATE INSTITUTE
(*Suby of* WATERLOO REGION DISTRICT SCHOOL BOARD)
300 Hazel St, Waterloo, ON, N2L 3P2
(519) 884-9590
Emp Here 250
SIC 8211 Elementary and secondary schools
Nelson Custhbert

D-U-N-S 20-881-5506   (HQ)
WILFRID LAURIER UNIVERSITY
75 University Ave W, Waterloo, ON, N2L 3C5
(519) 884-1970
Emp Here 800   *Sales* 257,957,995
SIC 8221 Colleges and universities
Max Blouw
Jim Butler

Waterloo, ON N2T

D-U-N-S 25-996-5759   (SL)
CANADA INTERNATIONAL TRAVEL SERVICE INC
794 Paris Blvd, Waterloo, ON, N2T 2Z2
(519) 746-0579
Emp Here 34   *Sales* 13,102,240
SIC 4724 Travel agencies
Fulu Mao

D-U-N-S 24-389-6164   (SL)
DN PHARMACY INC
SHOPPERS DRUG MART
658 Erb St W, Waterloo, ON, N2T 2Z7
(519) 886-3530
Emp Here 45   *Sales* 11,382,930
SIC 5912 Drug stores and proprietary stores
Dragana Nedeljkovic

D-U-N-S 20-566-5958   (SL)
GPS PRODUCTS INC
622 Frieburg Dr, Waterloo, ON, N2T 2Y4
(519) 885-7235
Emp Here 100   *Sales* 36,421,500
SIC 5015 Motor vehicle parts, used
David Godwin

D-U-N-S 20-300-5124   (BR)
SOBEYS CAPITAL INCORPORATED
SOBEYS
(*Suby of* EMPIRE COMPANY LIMITED)
450 Columbia St W, Waterloo, ON, N2T 2W1
(519) 880-9143
Emp Here 100
SIC 5411 Grocery stores
Kevin Clouston

D-U-N-S 24-337-0751   (SL)
YOUNG, J. & S. MERCHANTS LTD
CANADIAN TIRE
656 Erb St W, Waterloo, ON, N2T 2Z7
(519) 884-1255
Emp Here 60   *Sales* 37,756,800
SIC 5531 Auto and home supply stores
Justin Young

D-U-N-S 25-297-8689   (BR)
ZEHRMART INC
ZEHRS MARKET
(*Suby of* LOBLAW COMPANIES LIMITED)
450 Erb St W, Waterloo, ON, N2T 1H4
(519) 886-4900
Emp Here 350
SIC 5411 Grocery stores
Jared Dickie

Waterloo, ON N2V

D-U-N-S 20-388-1961   (SL)
2615267 ONTARIO INC
DAVENPORT REALTY BROKERAGE
620 Davenport Rd Unit 33, Waterloo, ON, N2V 2C2
(226) 777-5833
Emp Here 34   *Sales* 11,122,318
SIC 6531 Real estate agents and managers
Steven Smith
Wes Watson
Cathy Zalman

D-U-N-S 24-393-8946   (SL)
AERYON LABS INC
(*Suby of* FLIR SYSTEMS, INC.)
575 Kumpf Dr, Waterloo, ON, N2V 1K3
(519) 489-6726
Emp Here 150   *Sales* 41,155,500
SIC 3861 Photographic equipment and supplies
William Mchale
John Vukovic
John Bagocius
Pete Keller
Chuck Lownie
David Proulx
April Clarke
Brad Young
Eric Ritter

D-U-N-S 25-824-6016   (BR)
AIRWAYS TRANSIT SERVICE LIMITED
(*Suby of* AIRWAYS TRANSIT SERVICE LIMITED)
99 Northland Rd Unit A, Waterloo, ON, N2V 1Y8
(519) 658-5521
Emp Here 160
SIC 4131 Intercity and rural bus transportation
Ross Fergeson

D-U-N-S 20-329-2503   (SL)
ARCTIC PACKAGING INDUSTRIES INC
(*Suby of* CRAWFORD PACKAGING INC)
295 Frobisher Dr, Waterloo, ON, N2V 2G4
(519) 885-2161
Emp Here 15   *Sales* 11,137,800
SIC 5199 Nondurable goods, nec
Clarence Covey
John Ashby

D-U-N-S 20-115-9055   (HQ)
ASSANTE FINANCIAL MANAGEMENT LTD
(*Suby of* ASSANTE WEALTH MANAGEMENT (CANADA) LTD)
855 Birchmount Dr, Waterloo, ON, N2V 2R7
(519) 886-3257
Emp Here 6   *Sales* 42,637,140
SIC 8741 Management services
Stephen Ellis
Rodney Ancrum
Hal Button
Shaun Devlin
John Howard
Timothy Pryor
Nick Mancini
Donald Yi
Michael Nairne

D-U-N-S 25-009-0342   (SL)
BGL CONTRACTORS CORP
608 Colby Dr, Waterloo, ON, N2V 1A2
(519) 725-5000
Emp Here 25   *Sales* 11,768,275
SIC 1542 Nonresidential construction, nec
Gordon Robb
Jason Robb
John Moylan

D-U-N-S 25-353-2493   (SL)
BRENNER & ASSOCIATES INC
630 Superior Dr, Waterloo, ON, N2V 2C6
(519) 746-0439
Emp Here 57   *Sales* 15,580,950
SIC 6712 Bank holding companies
Michael Brenner

Barbara Martin

D-U-N-S 25-350-9566   (SL)
BRENNER MECHANICAL INC
630 Superior Dr, Waterloo, ON, N2V 2C6
(519) 746-0439
Emp Here 47   *Sales* 10,383,898
SIC 1711 Plumbing, heating, air-conditioning
Michael Brenner

D-U-N-S 24-850-4078   (HQ)
CAMPANA SYSTEMS INC
103 Randall Dr Unit 2, Waterloo, ON, N2V 1C5
(226) 336-8085
Sales 13,408,926
SIC 7371 Custom computer programming services

D-U-N-S 20-769-4220   (SL)
CANTON POULTRY MEATS INC
670 Superior Dr, Waterloo, ON, N2V 2C6
(519) 746-1390
Emp Here 40   *Sales* 33,423,080
SIC 5144 Poultry and poultry products
Shu Man

D-U-N-S 24-024-7627   (HQ)
CARLSTAR GROUP ULC, THE
(*Suby of* THE CARLSTAR GROUP LLC)
645 Mcmurray Rd, Waterloo, ON, N2V 2B7
(519) 885-0630
Sales 28,501,560
SIC 5085 Industrial supplies
Jacob Thomas
Max Narancich
Laren Harmon
Jonathan Mathews

D-U-N-S 25-592-3880   (HQ)
CHERVIN INC
20 Benjamin Rd, Waterloo, ON, N2V 2J9
(519) 885-3542
Sales 20,833,470
SIC 2511 Wood household furniture
Kevin Bauman
Darren Huber
Marvin Bauman
Michael Good

D-U-N-S 25-156-6816   (SL)
DAKON CONSTRUCTION LTD
275 Frobisher Dr Unit 1, Waterloo, ON, N2V 2G4
(519) 746-0920
Emp Here 30   *Sales* 14,121,930
SIC 1542 Nonresidential construction, nec
Dennis Kuepfer
James Kuepfer
Ryan Turk
Susann Kuepfer

D-U-N-S 24-304-8550   (HQ)
DESCARTES SYSTEMS GROUP INC, THE
120 Randall Dr, Waterloo, ON, N2V 1C6
(519) 746-8110
Emp Here 240   *Sales* 237,439,000
SIC 7371 Custom computer programming services
Edward Ryan
J.Scott Pagan
Raimond Diederik
Chris Jones
Ken Wood
Bob Parker
Allan Brett
Michael Verhoeve
Eric Demirian
Chris Hewat

D-U-N-S 20-607-9790   (HQ)
DONALD CHOI CANADA LIMITED
147 Bathurst Dr, Waterloo, ON, N2V 1Z4
(519) 886-5010
Sales 10,529,782
SIC 5072 Hardware
Donald Choi
Bo Choi

D-U-N-S 24-744-2775   (SL)
FISCHER CANADA STAINLESS STEEL TUBING INC
(*Suby of* FISCHER GROUP SE & CO. KG)
190 Frobisher Dr Suite 2, Waterloo, ON, N2V 2A2
(519) 746-0088
Emp Here 100   *Sales* 19,208,500
SIC 3498 Fabricated pipe and fittings
Thomas Prell
Uta Prell
Karl Corning
Hans Fischer

D-U-N-S 24-469-4055   (HQ)
FORTRESS GROUP INC
85 Baffin Pl, Waterloo, ON, N2V 2C1
(519) 747-4604
Emp Here 10   *Sales* 11,179,350
SIC 5075 Warm air heating and air conditioning
David Kaytor

D-U-N-S 25-033-7235   (BR)
GROTE INDUSTRIES CO.
GROTE ELECTRONICS, DIV. OF
(*Suby of* GROTE INDUSTRIES, INC.)
95 Bathurst Dr, Waterloo, ON, N2V 1N2
(519) 884-4991
Emp Here 100
SIC 2821 Plastics materials and resins
Luigi Tavernese

D-U-N-S 20-124-5768   (SL)
H & O CENTERLESS GRINDING COMPANY LTD
45 Bathurst Dr, Waterloo, ON, N2V 1N2
(519) 884-0322
Emp Here 102   *Sales* 22,644,102
SIC 3599 Industrial machinery, nec
Thomas Johansson

D-U-N-S 24-927-2402   (SL)
HANDTMANN CANADA LIMITED
(*Suby of* ARTHUR HANDTMANN FAMILIEN-STIFTUNG)
654 Colby Dr, Waterloo, ON, N2V 1A2
(519) 725-3666
Emp Here 30   *Sales* 14,250,780
SIC 5084 Industrial machinery and equipment
Tom Kittle
Nancy Reynold

D-U-N-S 25-671-4353   (BR)
HOME DEPOT OF CANADA INC
HOME DEPOT
(*Suby of* THE HOME DEPOT INC)
600 King St N, Waterloo, ON, N2V 2J5
(519) 883-0580
Emp Here 250
SIC 5211 Lumber and other building materials
Marlyn Price

D-U-N-S 24-357-5409   (HQ)
LEGGETT & PLATT CANADA CO
NORTHFIELD METAL PRODUCTS
(*Suby of* LEGGETT & PLATT, INCORPORATED)
195 Bathurst Dr, Waterloo, ON, N2V 2B2
(519) 884-1860
Sales 18,138,800
SIC 3312 Blast furnaces and steel mills
Robert Stuart
Brian Anauo
Shonna Koch
Kristen Beerly
Jason Higdon
Sheri Mossbeck

D-U-N-S 24-965-9954   (SL)
LIBRARY BOUND INC
100 Bathurst Dr Unit 2, Waterloo, ON, N2V 1V6
(519) 885-3233
Emp Here 30   *Sales* 22,275,600
SIC 5192 Books, periodicals, and newspapers
Heather Bindseil

Paul Clarke

D-U-N-S 25-278-5936   (HQ)
M&T PRINTING GROUP LIMITED
M & T INSTAPRINT
675 Davenport Rd, Waterloo, ON, N2V 2E2
(519) 804-0017
Emp Here 45   *Sales* 25,046,375
SIC 7336 Commercial art and graphic design
Don Froome

D-U-N-S 24-986-4026   (SL)
MCM GROUP LTD
WORLD WONDERS
730 Bridge St W Suite 1, Waterloo, ON, N2V 2J4
(519) 725-3800
Emp Here 29   *Sales* 21,533,080
SIC 5199 Nondurable goods, nec
Trevor Misch
Kevin Misch

D-U-N-S 24-385-9618   (HQ)
MELLOUL-BLAMEY CONSTRUCTION INC
(*Suby of* MELLOUL-BLAMEY ENTERPRISES INC)
700 Rupert St, Waterloo, ON, N2V 2B5
(519) 886-8850
Sales 18,250,816
SIC 1542 Nonresidential construction, nec
Joel M. Melloul
Bernard Melloul
Jeff Heimpel
Jeffrey Shantz
Steve Hanley
David Blamey

D-U-N-S 24-325-8501   (HQ)
MELLOUL-BLAMEY ENTERPRISES INC
700 Rupert St Unit A, Waterloo, ON, N2V 2B5
(519) 886-8850
Emp Here 2   *Sales* 23,234,750
SIC 6712 Bank holding companies
Bernard Melloul
David Blamey

D-U-N-S 25-995-8585   (HQ)
MENNONITE ECONOMIC DEVELOPMENT ASSOCIATES OF CANADA
MEDA
155 Frobisher Dr Suite I-106, Waterloo, ON, N2V 2E1
(519) 725-1633
Emp Here 45   *Sales* 21,848,883
SIC 8699 Membership organizations, nec
Allan Sauder
Albert Friesen
Gary Leis
Zachary Bishop

D-U-N-S 20-181-6506   (SL)
MULTI-TECH SYSTEMS INTERNATIONAL INC
592 Colby Drive, Waterloo, ON, N2V 1A2
(905) 825-3825
Emp Here 40   *Sales* 19,001,040
SIC 5084 Industrial machinery and equipment
Eamonn Godsell
Tim Childs
Dan Michaelis

D-U-N-S 20-171-4730   (HQ)
NCR CANADA CORP
FINANCIAL SOLUTION, DIV OF
(*Suby of* NCR CORPORATION)
50 Northland Rd, Waterloo, ON, N2V 1N3
(519) 880-7700
Emp Here 200   *Sales* 642,422,400
SIC 5044 Office equipment
William Nuti
Nicholas Hames
Luc Villeneuve

D-U-N-S 24-198-7692   (HQ)
NORTHERN DIGITAL INC
NDI
(*Suby of* ROPER TECHNOLOGIES, INC.)
103 Randall Dr, Waterloo, ON, N2V 1C5

▲ Public Company   ■ Public Company Family Member   **HQ** Headquarters   **BR** Branch   **SL** Single Location

(519) 884-5142
Emp Here 125   *Sales* 61,733,250
SIC 3841 Surgical and medical instruments
David Rath
Gary Barfoot

D-U-N-S 20-349-2293   (SL)
ODCO, INC
H&O CYLINDRICAL PRECISION
45 Bathurst Dr, Waterloo, ON, N2V 1N2
(519) 884-0322
Emp Here 70   *Sales* 12,560,030
SIC 3599 Industrial machinery, nec
Thomas Johansson
Kara Johansson

D-U-N-S 20-184-1108   (HQ)
**ONWARD MANUFACTURING COMPANY
LIMITED**
(*Suby of* ONWARD MULTI-CORP INC)
585 Kumpf Dr, Waterloo, ON, N2V 1K3
(519) 885-4540
Sales 113,166,000
SIC 3631 Household cooking equipment
Ted Witzel
Terry Witzel
Tim Witzel

D-U-N-S 24-719-3865   (HQ)
ONWARD MULTI-CORP INC
585 Kumpf Dr, Waterloo, ON, N2V 1K3
(519) 885-4540
Emp Here 250   *Sales* 84,874,500
SIC 3631 Household cooking equipment
Ted Witzel Jr
Tim Witzel
Terrance Witzel

D-U-N-S 24-360-8697   (SL)
QUADRO ENGINEERING CORP
(*Suby of* IDEX CORPORATION)
613 Colby Dr, Waterloo, ON, N2V 1A1
(226) 270-6017
Emp Here 95   *Sales* 21,090,095
SIC 3541 Machine tools, Metal cutting type
Keith Mcintosh

D-U-N-S 24-745-7187   (SL)
SCHAAF FOODS INC
130 Frobisher Dr Suite 6, Waterloo, ON, N2V
1Z9
(519) 747-1655
Emp Here 28   *Sales* 23,396,156
SIC 5149 Groceries and related products, nec
John Schaaf
Lavina Schaff

D-U-N-S 25-222-0595   (SL)
SEPTIMATECH GROUP INC
106 Randall Dr, Waterloo, ON, N2V 1K5
(519) 746-7463
Emp Here 59   *Sales* 13,098,059
SIC 3565 Packaging machinery
Sharron L Gilbert
Gord Beaton
Glen Bell
Quinn Martin
Amanda Collins

D-U-N-S 20-112-8175   (SL)
SUNWEST FOODS PROCESSORS LTD
DC FOODS & SUNRISE FARMS
35 Northland Rd, Waterloo, ON, N2V 1Y8
(519) 747-5546
Emp Here 90   *Sales* 38,046,330
SIC 1541 Industrial buildings and warehouses
Donald Kilimnik
Robert Curik

D-U-N-S 24-677-0569   (HQ)
TELEDYNE DALSA, INC
(*Suby of* TELEDYNE TECHNOLOGIES INC)
605 Mcmurray Rd, Waterloo, ON, N2V 2E9
(519) 886-6000
Emp Here 350
SIC 3827 Optical instruments and lenses

D-U-N-S 24-684-9996   (HQ)

U.B.P. SERVICES LIMITED
151 Frobisher Dr Suite E220, Waterloo, ON,
N2V 2C9
(519) 725-8818
Emp Here 20   *Sales* 40,626,498
SIC 6371 Pension, health, and welfare funds
Mark Hall
Paul Gillis

D-U-N-S 24-244-7001   (HQ)
UNITECH LUBRICANTS AMERICA
155 Frobisher Dr Unit 218, Waterloo, ON, N2V
2E1
(519) 208-2900
Sales 27,658,422
SIC 5172 Petroleum products, nec

D-U-N-S 24-198-3964   (HQ)
**VIESSMANN MANUFACTURING COMPANY
INC**
(*Suby of* VIESSMANN WERKE GMBH & CO
KG)
750 Mcmurray Rd, Waterloo, ON, N2V 2G5
(519) 885-6300
Sales 13,445,950
SIC 3433 Heating equipment, except electric
Michael Luz

D-U-N-S 24-947-4834   (HQ)
VIRTEK VISION INTERNATIONAL INC
785 Bridge St W Suite 8, Waterloo, ON, N2V
2K1
(519) 746-7190
Sales 10,093,426
SIC 3699 Electrical equipment and supplies,
nec
Hal Osthus
Katherine Campbell
Michael Elia
Michael Lyon

D-U-N-S 24-726-6463   (SL)
W.H. LUBRICANTS LTD
185 Frobisher Dr, Waterloo, ON, N2V 2E6
(519) 513-9805
Emp Here 11   *Sales* 11,360,888
SIC 5172 Petroleum products, nec
Richard Habsch
Walter Habsch
Gabriele Habsch

D-U-N-S 24-587-3377   (BR)
**WASTE MANAGEMENT OF CANADA COR-
PORATION**
WASTE MANAGEMENT
(*Suby of* WASTE MANAGEMENT, INC.)
645 Conrad Pl, Waterloo, ON, N2V 1C4
(519) 886-6932
Emp Here 100
SIC 4953 Refuse systems
David Lee

D-U-N-S 24-877-0927   (HQ)
WATERLOO MAPLE INC
MAPLESOFT
(*Suby of* FUJI SOFT INCORPORATED)
615 Kumpf Dr, Waterloo, ON, N2V 1K8
(519) 747-2373
Sales 20,855,875
SIC 7372 Prepackaged software
James Cooper
Tom Lee
Rick Brock
Richard Hodgson
Chris Howlett
Keith Geddes
John Whitney
Stephen Watt

Watford, ON N0M

D-U-N-S 20-180-8300   (SL)
GROGAN FORD LINCOLN INC
5271 Nauvoo Rd, Watford, ON, N0M 2S0

(519) 876-2730
Emp Here 22   *Sales* 10,957,716
SIC 5511 New and used car dealers
Larry Grogan
Bonnie-Jeanne Grogan

D-U-N-S 24-406-6767   (HQ)
WATFORD ROOF TRUSS LIMITED
(*Suby of* MOFFATT & POWELL LIMITED)
330 Front St, Watford, ON, N0M 2S0
(519) 876-2612
Sales 28,855,500
SIC 2439 Structural wood members, nec
Keith Moffatt
David Powell
John Duffield

Wawa, ON P0S

D-U-N-S 24-386-9492   (SL)
DONALD L. DAVIDSON FUELS LTD
ESSO AGENT
54 Pinewood Dr, Wawa, ON, P0S 1K0
(705) 856-2166
Emp Here 12   *Sales* 12,393,696
SIC 5171 Petroleum bulk stations and termi-
nals
Scott Davidson

D-U-N-S 20-180-9050   (SL)
HAMAN, B. & A. LIMITED
WAWA VALU-MART
36 Mission Rd, Wawa, ON, P0S 1K0
(705) 856-2555
Emp Here 40   *Sales* 10,966,080
SIC 5411 Grocery stores
Gilles Begin
Line Begin

D-U-N-S 24-575-4544   (HQ)
LADY DUNN HEALTH CENTRE
17 Government Rd, Wawa, ON, P0S 1K0
(705) 856-2335
Sales 10,213,300
SIC 8062 General medical and surgical hospi-
tals
Kadean Ogilvie-Pinter

Webbwood, ON P0P

D-U-N-S 25-822-6158   (SL)
**BRIGGS, GEORGE L. AERIE 4269 FRATER-
NAL ORDER OF EAGLES**
3 Centre St, Webbwood, ON, P0P 2G0
(705) 869-4269
Emp Here 40   *Sales* 16,163,921
SIC 8699 Membership organizations, nec
Ronald Harris

Welland, ON L3B

D-U-N-S 25-640-4658   (HQ)
**A CHILD'S WORLD FAMILY CHILD CARE
SERVICES OF NIAGARA**
344 Avon St, Welland, ON, L3B 6E5
(905) 735-1162
Emp Here 1   *Sales* 11,289,694
SIC 8351 Child day care services
Kim Cole

D-U-N-S 20-699-3961   (SL)
ATLAS TUBE CANADA ULC
ENERGEX TUBE
160 Dain Ave, Welland, ON, L3B 5Y6
(905) 735-7473
Emp Here 480   *Sales* 195,443,520
SIC 3317 Steel pipe and tubes
Ron Bedard
Ken Hunter

Vic Alboini
William S Grant
Thomas G Milne
Wesley Roitman

D-U-N-S 20-180-9951   (HQ)
BOSCH REXROTH CANADA CORP
(*Suby of* R O B E R T B O S C H S T I F T U
N G GESELLSCHAFT MIT BESCHRANKTER
HAFTUNG)
490 Prince Charles Dr S, Welland, ON, L3B
5X7
(905) 735-0510
Emp Here 200   *Sales* 126,877,244
SIC 5084 Industrial machinery and equipment
John Mataya
Paul Cooke

D-U-N-S 24-587-5026   (HQ)
CANADA FORGINGS INC
CANFORGE
130 Hagar Welland, Welland, ON, L3B 5P8
(905) 735-1220
Sales 15,162,040
SIC 3462 Iron and steel forgings
Scott Naar

D-U-N-S 24-314-1207   (SL)
CANADIAN TIRE
158 Primeway Drive, Welland, ON, L3B 0A1
(905) 732-1371
Emp Here 30   *Sales* 10,926,450
SIC 5014 Tires and tubes
Stephen Wetmore

D-U-N-S 20-648-6198   (BR)
CANADIAN TIRE SERVICES LIMITED
CTFS
(*Suby of* CANADIAN TIRE CORPORATION,
LIMITED)
1000 East Main St, Welland, ON, L3B 3Z3
(905) 735-3131
Emp Here 1,000
SIC 6153 Short-term business credit institu-
tions, except agricultural
Cindy Avey

D-U-N-S 24-489-0166   (SL)
E.D. PRODUCTS LTD
90 Atlas Ave, Welland, ON, L3B 6H5
(905) 732-9473
Emp Here 110   *Sales* 20,948,620
SIC 3679 Electronic components, nec
Joe Deman

D-U-N-S 25-624-2801   (SL)
FOYER RICHELIEU WELLAND
655 Tanguay Ave, Welland, ON, L3B 6A1
(905) 734-1400
Emp Here 96   *Sales* 5,687,712
SIC 8361 Residential care
Andre Trembley
Normand Lecompte
Camille Bernard
Clarisse Maurice

D-U-N-S 25-352-3120   (SL)
HYDAC CORPORATION
(*Suby of* H Y D A C TECHNOLOGY GMBH)
14 Federal Rd, Welland, ON, L3B 3P2
(905) 714-9322
Emp Here 34   *Sales* 16,150,884
SIC 5084 Industrial machinery and equipment
Alexander Dieter

D-U-N-S 20-044-9098   (HQ)
**INDEXABLE CUTTING TOOLS OF CANADA
LIMITED**
66 Clark St, Welland, ON, L3B 5W6
(905) 735-8665
Emp Here 30   *Sales* 11,387,655
SIC 5251 Hardware stores
John Precious
Bill Palangio

D-U-N-S 24-385-2444   (SL)
**INFINITY RUBBER TECHNOLOGY GROUP
INC**

100 Kennedy St, Welland, ON, L3B 0B4
(905) 735-6366
Emp Here 62   *Sales* 12,517,614
SIC 3069 Fabricated rubber products, nec
 James Chung
 Kent Barber

D-U-N-S 24-223-3914   (SL)
LIFT LINE MACHINERY LTD
495 Prince Charles Dr S, Welland, ON, L3B
5X1
(905) 788-0971
Emp Here 35   *Sales* 16,625,910
SIC 5084 Industrial machinery and equipment
 Tim Morgan

D-U-N-S 24-384-2547   (SL)
PANELS.CA ONTARIO INC
123 Centre St, Welland, ON, L3B 0E1
(905) 734-6060
Emp Here 70   *Sales* 10,910,410
SIC 2426 Hardwood dimension and flooring
mills
 Martin Pena

D-U-N-S 20-825-6276   (HQ)
PENFINANCIAL CREDIT UNION LIMITED
247 East Main St, Welland, ON, L3B 3X1
(905) 735-4801
Emp Here 15   *Sales* 12,439,094
SIC 6062 State credit unions
 Ken Janzen
 Reg Sonnenberg
 Frank Perugino

D-U-N-S 25-178-7446   (SL)
PENINSULA SECURITY SERVICES LTD
50 Division St, Welland, ON, L3B 3Z6
(905) 732-2337
Emp Here 125   *Sales* 3,281,250
SIC 7381 Detective and armored car services
 Philip Lance

D-U-N-S 25-306-1154   (SL)
PROCON CONSTRUCTORS INC
401 Enterprise Dr, Welland, ON, L3B 6H8
(905) 732-0322
Emp Here 80   *Sales* 17,426,320
SIC 1731 Electrical work
 Rico Leone
 Michael Leone

D-U-N-S 20-641-4364   (BR)
**REGIONAL MUNICIPALITY OF NIAGARA,
THE**
D.H. RAPELJE LODGE
(*Suby of* REGIONAL MUNICIPALITY OF NIA-
GARA, THE)
277 Plymouth Rd, Welland, ON, L3B 6E3
(905) 714-7428
Emp Here 200
SIC 8361 Residential care
 Kim Eros

D-U-N-S 24-334-9458   (HQ)
SL MARKETING INC
SL MARKETING
555 Brown Rd, Welland, ON, L3B 5N4
(905) 714-4000
Emp Here 30   *Sales* 20,821,680
SIC 5093 Scrap and waste materials
 Stewart Lehmann
 Stephen Lehmann

D-U-N-S 20-181-4399   (SL)
**TIMMS, R CONSTRUCTION AND ENGI-
NEERING LIMITED, THE**
TIMBRO
34 East Main St Suite B, Welland, ON, L3B
3W3
(905) 734-4513
Emp Here 22   *Sales* 10,356,082
SIC 1542 Nonresidential construction, nec
 Roy Timms
 Marion Timms

D-U-N-S 24-327-4508   (BR)
WAL-MART CANADA CORP

(*Suby of* WALMART INC.)
102 Primeway Dr, Welland, ON, L3B 0A1
(905) 735-3500
Emp Here 250
SIC 5311 Department stores
 Dave Commission

D-U-N-S 25-051-9584   (SL)
**WELLAND & DISTRICT SOCIETY FOR THE
PREVENTION OF CRUELTY TO ANIMALS**
SPCA
60 Provincial St, Welland, ON, L3B 5W7
(905) 735-1552
Emp Here 23   *Sales* 16,311,876
SIC 8699 Membership organizations, nec
 Arnold Paulson
 Sheryl Nemeth
 Sherly Cohen
 Mike Duerden
 Glen Bowes
 John Harrington
 Lynn Whiteley

D-U-N-S 24-140-9101   (HQ)
**WELLAND ASSOCIATION FOR COMMU-
NITY LIVING**
535 Sutherland Ave, Welland, ON, L3B 5A4
(905) 735-0081
Emp Here 230   *Sales* 50,731,660
SIC 8399 Social services, nec
 Shelia Kiess
 Barbara Vyrostko

D-U-N-S 25-107-3060   (SL)
**WELLAND HYDRO-ELECTRIC SYSTEMS
CORP**
950 East Main St, Welland, ON, L3B 3Y9

Emp Here 38   *Sales* 19,746,890
SIC 4911 Electric services
 Rimas Slavickas

D-U-N-S 20-181-5008   (HQ)
WHITING EQUIPMENT CANADA INC
(*Suby of* G. K. ENTERPRISES, INC.)
350 Alexander St, Welland, ON, L3B 2R3
(905) 732-7585
Emp Here 65   *Sales* 148,864,810
SIC 3559 Special industry machinery, nec
 Rudi Kroeker
 Nick Sestili
 Martin Sear
 Jeff Kahn

D-U-N-S 24-794-7369   (HQ)
WINOA CANADA INC
(*Suby of* ELASTIKOS HOLDINGS III SARL)
650 Rusholme Rd, Welland, ON, L3B 5N7
(905) 735-4691
Emp Here 56   *Sales* 10,573,921
SIC 3291 Abrasive products
 Jean-Charles Peluchon
 William Koshub
 Jeff Glaser

D-U-N-S 24-795-5396   (HQ)
YOUNGS INSURANCE BROKERS INC
55 East Main St, Welland, ON, L3B 3W4
(905) 735-7212
Emp Here 10   *Sales* 33,922,400
SIC 6411 Insurance agents, brokers, and ser-
vice
 Sandy Valleriani
 George Fairgrieve
 Patty Valleriani

Welland, ON L3C

D-U-N-S 25-967-9822   (SL)
1847674 ONTARIO INC
SOBEYS
609 South Pelham Rd, Welland, ON, L3C 3C7
(905) 735-7467
Emp Here 105   *Sales* 12,745,952

SIC 5411 Grocery stores
 Mike Zolli
 Joanne Zolli

D-U-N-S 24-422-2196   (SL)
**BERTIE AND CLINTON MUTUAL INSUR-
ANCE COMPANY**
BCM INSURANCE COMPANY
1003 Niagara St, Welland, ON, L3C 1M5
(905) 735-1234
Emp Here 35   *Sales* 36,220,835
SIC 6331 Fire, marine, and casualty insurance
 Paul Demare
 Howard Augustine

D-U-N-S 20-784-7401   (SL)
DORAL HOLDINGS LIMITED
SEAWAY MALL
800 Niagara St, Welland, ON, L3C 5Z4
(905) 734-9900
Emp Here 45   *Sales* 12,982,455
SIC 6512 Nonresidential building operators
 S Michael Belcastro
 Michael Allen

D-U-N-S 20-844-4042   (BR)
FIRSTCANADA ULC
LAIDLAW EDUCATIONAL SERVICES
(*Suby of* FIRSTGROUP PLC)
1049 Niagara St, Welland, ON, L3C 1M5
(905) 735-5944
Emp Here 130
SIC 4151 School buses
 Gerry Mcilhone

D-U-N-S 20-718-8053   (HQ)
**GILLESPIE PONTIAC BUICK CADILLAC
LIMITED**
GILLESPIE AUTO CENTRE
16 Lincoln St, Welland, ON, L3C 5J1
(905) 735-7151
Emp Here 3   *Sales* 32,722,560
SIC 5511 New and used car dealers
 Bernie Law
 James Richardson
 Heather Richardson

D-U-N-S 24-037-5043   (BR)
LOBLAWS SUPERMARKETS LIMITED
ZEHRS FOOD PLUS
(*Suby of* LOBLAW COMPANIES LIMITED)
821 Niagara St, Welland, ON, L3C 1M4
(905) 732-9010
Emp Here 150
SIC 5411 Grocery stores
 Derek Mckenna

D-U-N-S 24-395-3879   (SL)
MIKE KNAPP FORD SALES LIMITED
607 Niagara St, Welland, ON, L3C 1L9
(905) 732-3673
Emp Here 35   *Sales* 17,432,730
SIC 5511 New and used car dealers
 Mike Knapp

D-U-N-S 20-591-6179   (BR)
**NIAGARA CATHOLIC DISTRICT SCHOOL
BOARD**
NOTRE DAME HIGH SCHOOL
(*Suby of* NIAGARA CATHOLIC DISTRICT
SCHOOL BOARD)
64 Smith St, Welland, ON, L3C 4H4
(905) 788-3060
Emp Here 120
SIC 8211 Elementary and secondary schools
 John Crocco

D-U-N-S 24-972-7066   (HQ)
**NIAGARA CATHOLIC DISTRICT SCHOOL
BOARD**
427 Rice Rd, Welland, ON, L3C 7C1
(905) 562-1321
Emp Here 80   *Sales* 297,357,000
SIC 8211 Elementary and secondary schools
 Dan Wipple
 John Dekker
 William Tumalt

D-U-N-S 20-980-8328   (HQ)
**NIAGARA COLLEGE OF APPLIED ARTS &
TECHNOLOGY**
NIAGARA COLLEGE CANADA
100 Niagara College Blvd, Welland, ON, L3C
7L3
(905) 735-2211
Emp Here 500   *Sales* 99,119,000
SIC 8222 Junior colleges
 John Scott
 Daniel J Patterson
 Mary Turner

D-U-N-S 20-181-3508   (SL)
PUPO'S SUPERMARKET LIMITED
195 Maple Ave, Welland, ON, L3C 5G6
(905) 735-5615
Emp Here 80   *Sales* 23,478,160
SIC 5411 Grocery stores
 Paul Pupo Jr.
 Leonard Pupo
 James Pupo
 Gerald Pupo
 Richard Pupo

D-U-N-S 20-181-4274   (SL)
TALLMAN TRANSPORTS LIMITED
1003 Niagara St, Welland, ON, L3C 1M5
(416) 735-1410
Emp Here 75   *Sales* 11,114,400
SIC 4213 Trucking, except local
 Pattie Lenson
 Douglas Tallman

D-U-N-S 20-937-3075   (SL)
**VERMEER GREENHOUSES (WELLAND)
INC**
*VERMEER'S GARDEN CENTRE & FLOWER
SHOP*
684 South Pelham Rd, Welland, ON, L3C 3C8
(905) 735-5744
Emp Here 50   *Sales* 16,280,000
SIC 5992 Florists
 Karin Vermeer
 Gerry Vermeer

D-U-N-S 24-926-0985   (HQ)
VESUVIUS CANADA INC
(*Suby of* VESUVIUS PLC)
333 Prince Charles Dr, Welland, ON, L3C 5A6
(905) 732-4441
Emp Here 110   *Sales* 31,363,325
SIC 3297 Nonclay refractories
 Jeffrey D. Kelly
 William Kelly
 Thomas J. Serravalle

D-U-N-S 25-644-3599   (BR)
**WATCH TOWER BIBLE AND TRACT SOCI-
ETY OF CANADA**
KINGDOM HALL JEHOVAH'S WITNESS
(*Suby of* WATCH TOWER BIBLE AND TRACT
SOCIETY OF CANADA)
390 Clare Ave, Welland, ON, L3C 5R2

Emp Here 92
SIC 8661 Religious organizations
 Don Gordon

D-U-N-S 20-117-9053   (BR)
YMCA OF NIAGARA
YMCA
(*Suby of* YMCA OF NIAGARA)
310 Woodland Rd, Welland, ON, L3C 7N3
(905) 735-9622
Emp Here 250
SIC 8641 Civic and social associations
 Jody Kyle

D-U-N-S 20-789-4689   (BR)
ZEHRMART INC
ZEHRS MARKETS
(*Suby of* LOBLAW COMPANIES LIMITED)
821 Niagara St, Welland, ON, L3C 1M4
(905) 732-9380
Emp Here 130
SIC 5411 Grocery stores

▲ Public Company   ■ Public Company Family Member   **HQ** Headquarters   **BR** Branch   **SL** Single Location

Valerie Clark

Wellesley, ON N0B

D-U-N-S 20-181-5495 (HQ)
LEIS FEED AND SUPPLY LIMITED
1214 Queens Bush Rd, Wellesley, ON, N0B 2T0
(519) 656-2810
Emp Here 10 *Sales* 17,077,960
SIC 5191 Farm supplies
Gary Leis
William Cook
Brian Sauder
John Lichti

D-U-N-S 25-407-6862 (HQ)
LEIS PET DISTRIBUTING INC
ATLANTIC PET DISTRIBUTING, DIV OF
(*Suby of* 1096294 ONTARIO INC)
1315 Hutchison Rd, Wellesley, ON, N0B 2T0
(519) 656-3559
Emp Here 64 *Sales* 28,882,014
SIC 5149 Groceries and related products, nec
Gary Leis

West Lorne, ON N0L

D-U-N-S 20-605-7986 (SL)
ERIE FLOORING & WOOD PRODUCTS LIMITED
1191 Jane St, West Lorne, ON, N0L 2P0
(519) 768-1200
Emp Here 150 *Sales* 28,855,500
SIC 2426 Hardwood dimension and flooring mills
Andy Pastor
David Zimmerman
Chris Austin

D-U-N-S 20-181-8481 (SL)
MILNER-RIGSBY CO. LIMITED, THE
ROCKLAND FLOORING
(*Suby of* ROCKLAND INDUSTRIAL PRODUCTS, LLC)
139 Elm St, West Lorne, ON, N0L 2P0
(519) 768-1250
Emp Here 100 *Sales* 22,384,300
SIC 3713 Truck and bus bodies
Mark Chorney
Henry Bens

D-U-N-S 20-697-7782 (SL)
WEST LORNE BIOOIL CO-GENERATION LIMITED PARTNERSHIP
191 Jane St, West Lorne, ON, N0L 2P0

Emp Here 100 *Sales* 27,480,138
SIC 2911 Petroleum refining
Nathan Numer

West Montrose, ON N0B

D-U-N-S 25-554-7606 (SL)
WINTERMAR FARMS (1989) LTD
CRIBIT SEEDS
265 Katherine St S Suite 1, West Montrose, ON, N0B 2V0
(519) 664-3701
Emp Here 20 *Sales* 14,850,400
SIC 5191 Farm supplies
Quentin Martin
Keith Martin
Craig Martin
Jason Martin
Andrew Bauman

Wheatley, ON N0P

D-U-N-S 24-522-1481 (SL)
BOLTHOUSE FARMS CANADA INC
303 Milo Rd, Wheatley, ON, N0P 2P0
(519) 825-3412
Emp Here 100 *Sales* 29,347,700
SIC 5431 Fruit and vegetable markets
Phil Kooy
Scott Laporta
Lyndon Richardson
Tracy Marchant Saiki

D-U-N-S 24-560-6991 (SL)
DEGOEYS NURSERY AND FLOWERS
1501 Rd 6, Wheatley, ON, N0P 2P0
(519) 326-8813
Emp Here 22 *Sales* 16,335,440
SIC 5191 Farm supplies
John G Degoey
Jane Degoeys

D-U-N-S 20-342-0187 (SL)
HACIENDA NORTH FARMS INC
2961 Talbot Trail, Wheatley, ON, N0P 2P0
(519) 800-5062
Emp Here 32 *Sales* 10,958,944
SIC 0161 Vegetables and melons
Abram Braun
Elisabet Braun
Carlos Braun
Johnny Braun

D-U-N-S 24-985-5172 (SL)
JOHN O'S FOODS INC
827 Drovers Rd, Wheatley, ON, N0P 2P0
(519) 825-4673
Emp Here 50 *Sales* 41,778,850
SIC 5142 Packaged frozen goods
John Omstead

D-U-N-S 20-183-0932 (HQ)
OMSTEAD FOODS LIMITED
SNOWCREST PACKERS
303 Milo Rd, Wheatley, ON, N0P 2P0
(519) 825-4611
Sales 12,342,360
SIC 4222 Refrigerated warehousing and storage
Bill Stafford
Rick Bremner
Norm Vanderee
Blair Hyslop

D-U-N-S 24-302-7877 (HQ)
PRESTEVE FOODS LIMITED
20954 Erie St S, Wheatley, ON, N0P 2P0
(519) 825-4677
Sales 89,589,500
SIC 5146 Fish and seafoods
Ulysses Pratas
Jose Pratas
Clara Pratas

D-U-N-S 24-043-6704 (BR)
PRESTEVE FOODS LIMITED
(*Suby of* PRESTEVE FOODS LIMITED)
20954 Erie St S, Wheatley, ON, N0P 2P0
(519) 825-4677
Emp Here 200
SIC 5146 Fish and seafoods
Ulysses Prasam

Whitby, ON L1N

D-U-N-S 20-303-0353 (SL)
1257391 ONTARIO LIMITED
PROMOTIONAL PRODUCTS FULFILLMENT & DISTRIBUTION
80 William Smith Dr, Whitby, ON, L1N 9W1
(905) 668-5060
Emp Here 45 *Sales* 18,870,975

SIC 6712 Bank holding companies
Kathy Perna

D-U-N-S 25-143-9766 (HQ)
1378045 ONTARIO INC
THE MANUFACTURING & TECHNOLOGY CENTRE
220 Water St, Whitby, ON, L1N 0G9
(905) 666-7669
Emp Here 160 *Sales* 34,619,040
SIC 7629 Electrical repair shops
Howard Humphrey

D-U-N-S 20-597-6082 (SL)
1413249 ONTARIO INC
DENNY'S RESTAURANT
75 Consumers Dr Suite 17, Whitby, ON, L1N 9S2
(905) 665-6575
Emp Here 95 *Sales* 4,324,305
SIC 5812 Eating places
Kumar Arul

D-U-N-S 24-423-2844 (SL)
1527619 ONTARIO LIMITED
WHITBY MAZDA
5 Sunray St, Whitby, ON, L1N 8Y3
(905) 668-6881
Emp Here 38 *Sales* 18,926,964
SIC 5511 New and used car dealers
Dominic Mesiano

D-U-N-S 20-748-2014 (BR)
476982 BRITISH COLUMBIA LTD
BOSTON PIZZA
75 Consumers Dr, Whitby, ON, L1N 9S2

Emp Here 75
SIC 5812 Eating places

D-U-N-S 24-708-2712 (SL)
715837 ONTARIO INC
MOTORCITY MITSUBISHI
1520 Dundas St E, Whitby, ON, L1N 2K7
(905) 430-2351
Emp Here 35 *Sales* 17,432,730
SIC 5511 New and used car dealers
Anne Nurse
Ernie Bugelli

D-U-N-S 24-947-9080 (HQ)
921983 ONTARIO INC
CANADA WINDOWS & DOORS
119 Consumers Dr, Whitby, ON, L1N 1C4
(905) 665-9565
Emp Here 39 *Sales* 10,706,080
SIC 5211 Lumber and other building materials
Andy Van Hoof

D-U-N-S 24-387-8142 (BR)
AECOM CANADA LTD
(*Suby of* AECOM)
300 Water St Suite 1, Whitby, ON, L1N 9J2
(905) 668-9363
Emp Here 300
SIC 8711 Engineering services
Doug Allingham

D-U-N-S 24-772-3604 (SL)
AJAX JEEP EAGLE LTD
MENZIES CHRYSLER
1602 Champlain Ave, Whitby, ON, L1N 6A7
(905) 683-4100
Emp Here 45 *Sales* 22,413,510
SIC 5511 New and used car dealers
Todd Menzies

D-U-N-S 24-394-4035 (SL)
ASCS CANADIAN SIGNAL CORPORATION
(*Suby of* VERITAS CAPITAL MANAGEMENT LLC)
606 Beech St W, Whitby, ON, L1N 7T8
(905) 665-4300
Emp Here 80 *Sales* 15,235,360
SIC 3679 Electronic components, nec
Keith Buckley
Paul Weldon
Troy Depuma

Alex Condie

D-U-N-S 20-102-8177 (HQ)
ATLANTIC COATED PAPERS LTD
1605 Mcewen Dr, Whitby, ON, L1N 7L4
(416) 299-1675
Emp Here 60 *Sales* 16,555,280
SIC 2672 Paper; coated and laminated, nec
David Granovsky
Jim Dubay
Sylvain Jutras

D-U-N-S 24-312-0974 (BR)
ATLANTIC PACKAGING PRODUCTS LTD
ATLANTIC NEWSPRINT COMPANY, DIV
(*Suby of* ATLANTIC PACKAGING PRODUCTS LTD)
1900 Thickson Rd S, Whitby, ON, L1N 9E1
(905) 686-5944
Emp Here 100
SIC 2621 Paper mills
Nina Baba

D-U-N-S 24-372-2795 (SL)
BALL PACKAGING PRODUCTS CANADA CORP
METAL BEVERAGE PACKAGING, DIV OF
(*Suby of* BALL CORPORATION)
1506 Wentworth St, Whitby, ON, L1N 7C1
(905) 666-3600
Emp Here 190 *Sales* 46,213,890
SIC 3411 Metal cans
R David Hoover
John A Hayes
Raymond J Seabrook
Charles E Baker
Scott C Morrison
Maurice P Chiasson
Douglas K Bradford

D-U-N-S 24-830-5153 (SL)
CAM-SCOTT TRANSPORT LTD
1900 Boundary Rd, Whitby, ON, L1N 8P8
(905) 438-9555
Emp Here 115 *Sales* 23,656,190
SIC 4212 Local trucking, without storage
Glenn Weddel
Pat Weddel

D-U-N-S 24-002-1985 (BR)
CAREMED SERVICES INC
WE CARE HOME HEALTH SERVICES
(*Suby of* CAREMED SERVICES INC)
1450 Hopkins St Suite 205, Whitby, ON, L1N 2C3
(905) 666-6656
Emp Here 80
SIC 8059 Nursing and personal care, nec
Richard Pillsworth

D-U-N-S 24-183-2844 (SL)
CDN TECHNOLOGY
901 Burns St E, Whitby, ON, L1N 0E6
(905) 430-7295
Emp Here 49 *Sales* 10,028,977
SIC 3699 Electrical equipment and supplies, nec

D-U-N-S 24-095-1306 (SL)
CORBETT CREEK WATER POLLUTION CONTROL PLANT
CORBETT CREEK W C P C P
2400 Forbes St, Whitby, ON, L1N 8M3
(905) 576-9844
Emp Here 25 *Sales* 11,875,650
SIC 5084 Industrial machinery and equipment
Tom Sloley

D-U-N-S 24-976-8896 (BR)
CORPORATION OF THE REGIONAL MUNICIPALITY OF DURHAM, THE
REGION OF DURHAM WORKS DEPARTMENT
(*Suby of* CORPORATION OF THE REGIONAL MUNICIPALITY OF DURHAM, THE)
105 Consumers Dr, Whitby, ON, L1N 6A3
(905) 668-7721
Emp Here 200

SIC 4941 Water supply
Cliff Curtis

D-U-N-S 25-721-3843 (BR)
CORPORATION OF THE REGIONAL MU-NICIPALITY OF DURHAM, THE
FAIRVIEW LODGE HOME FOR AGED
(*Suby of* CORPORATION OF THE RE-GIONAL MUNICIPALITY OF DURHAM, THE)
632 Dundas St W, Whitby, ON, L1N 5S3
(905) 668-5851
Emp Here 200
SIC 8361 Residential care
Laura Macdermaid

D-U-N-S 25-658-0507 (BR)
CORPORATION OF THE TOWN OF WHITBY, THE
IROQUOIS PARK SPORTS CENTRE, THE
500 Victoria St W, Whitby, ON, L1N 9G4
(905) 668-7765
Emp Here 100
SIC 7999 Amusement and recreation, nec
Greg Scott

D-U-N-S 25-370-3235 (HQ)
CULINARY PAPERS INC
MCNAIRN PACKAGING
(*Suby of* MCNAIRN PACKAGING, INC.)
125 Consumers Dr, Whitby, ON, L1N 1C4
(905) 668-7533
Sales 27,462,288
SIC 2671 Paper; coated and laminated pack-aging
Scott Miller

D-U-N-S 25-300-8288 (BR)
DURHAM DISTRICT SCHOOL BOARD
HENRY STREET HIGH SCHOOL
(*Suby of* DURHAM DISTRICT SCHOOL BOARD)
600 Henry St, Whitby, ON, L1N 5C7
(905) 666-5500
Emp Here 120
SIC 8211 Elementary and secondary schools
Chrystal Bryan

D-U-N-S 20-087-0207 (BR)
DURHAM DISTRICT SCHOOL BOARD
ANDERSON COLLEGIATE VOCATIONAL IN-STITUTE
(*Suby of* DURHAM DISTRICT SCHOOL BOARD)
400 Anderson St, Whitby, ON, L1N 3V6
(905) 668-5809
Emp Here 93
SIC 8211 Elementary and secondary schools
Sarah Macdonald

D-U-N-S 25-350-7222 (HQ)
DURHAM MENTAL HEALTH SERVICES
519 Brock St S, Whitby, ON, L1N 4K8
(905) 666-0831
Emp Here 50   *Sales* 10,009,425
SIC 8399 Social services, nec
Robert Adams

D-U-N-S 20-085-7170 (SL)
DURHAM REGION PLANNING
1615 Dundas St E Suite 4, Whitby, ON, L1N 2L1
(905) 723-1365
Emp Here 45   *Sales* 10,542,960
SIC 8742 Management consulting services
Alex Georgieff

D-U-N-S 20-554-6737 (SL)
EWING INTERNATIONAL INC
1445 Hopkins St, Whitby, ON, L1N 2C2
(416) 291-1675
Emp Here 50   *Sales* 10,141,500
SIC 3463 Nonferrous forgings
David Myles
Norm Myles

D-U-N-S 24-736-0837 (BR)
FISHER SCIENTIFIC COMPANY
(*Suby of* THERMO FISHER SCIENTIFIC

INC.)
111 Scotia Crt, Whitby, ON, L1N 6J6
(905) 725-7341
Emp Here 90
SIC 5049 Professional equipment, nec
Ernie Jones

D-U-N-S 20-852-4892 (HQ)
GERDAU AMERISTEEL CORPORATION
GERDAU AMERISTEEL METALS RECY-CLING
(*Suby of* METALURGICA GERDAU S/A.)
1 Gerdau Crt, Whitby, ON, L1N 7G8
(905) 668-8811
Emp Here 500   *Sales* 1,954,435,200
SIC 3312 Blast furnaces and steel mills
Mario Longhi
Phillip E Casey
Andre Gerdau Johannpeter
Joseph J Heffernan
Jorge Gerdau Johannpeter
J Spencer Lanthier
Arthur Scace
Frederico C Gerdau Johannpeter
Richard Mccoy
Claudio Gerdau Johannpeter

D-U-N-S 20-005-4941 (SL)
GLOBAL RESEARCH EPICENTER AGAINST HUMAN TRAFFICKIN
301 Saint John St W, Whitby, ON, L1N 1N6

Emp Here 150   *Sales* 16,662,000
SIC 8062 General medical and surgical hospi-tals
Kim Derry

D-U-N-S 20-383-2717 (BR)
GOVERNMENT OF ONTARIO
CENTRAL EAST LOCAL HEALTH INTEGRA-TION NETWORK
(*Suby of* GOVERNMENT OF ONTARIO)
920 Champlain Crt, Whitby, ON, L1N 6K9
(905) 430-3308
Emp Here 350
SIC 8059 Nursing and personal care, nec
Stewart Sutley

D-U-N-S 25-624-3296 (SL)
HARDIMAN, MOUNT &ASSOCIATES IN-SURANCE BROKERS LIMITED
1032 Brock St S Suite 5, Whitby, ON, L1N 4L8
(905) 668-1477
Emp Here 23   *Sales* 13,338,252
SIC 6411 Insurance agents, brokers, and ser-vice
Jim Hardiman
Barry Mount

D-U-N-S 25-664-2109 (BR)
HOME DEPOT OF CANADA INC
HOME DEPOT
(*Suby of* THE HOME DEPOT INC)
1700 Victoria St E, Whitby, ON, L1N 9K6
(905) 571-5900
Emp Here 225
SIC 5251 Hardware stores
Tom Scholtz

D-U-N-S 20-358-0790 (SL)
HYDRX FARMS LTD
209 Dundas St E, Whitby, ON, L1N 5R7
(844) 493-7922
Emp Here 33   *Sales* 10,802,352
SIC 2834 Pharmaceutical preparations
Har Grover
Alex Massis
Thil Hemans

D-U-N-S 24-421-4982 (HQ)
INTEVA PRODUCTS CANADA, ULC
INTEVA OSHAWA PLANT
(*Suby of* THE RENCO GROUP INC)
1555 Wentworth St, Whitby, ON, L1N 9T6
(905) 666-4600
Sales 54,023,640
SIC 7532 Top and body repair and paint shops

Robert Cooper

D-U-N-S 25-315-8877 (BR)
INVESTORS GROUP FINANCIAL SER-VICES INC
(*Suby of* POWER CORPORATION DU CANADA)
1614 Dundas St E Unit 111, Whitby, ON, L1N 8Y8
(905) 434-8400
Emp Here 129
SIC 8741 Management services
David Roth

D-U-N-S 20-170-5100 (SL)
J. H. MCNAIRN LIMITED
MCNAIRN PACKAGING
(*Suby of* MCNAIRN PACKAGING, INC.)
125 Consumers Dr, Whitby, ON, L1N 1C4
(905) 668-7533
Emp Here 180   *Sales* 35,058,240
SIC 2671 Paper; coated and laminated pack-aging
Brent Quinn
Scott Lafonde

D-U-N-S 25-709-7915 (SL)
LAARK ENTERPRISES LIMITED
TIM HORTONS
516 Brock St N, Whitby, ON, L1N 4J2
(905) 430-3703
Emp Here 50   *Sales* 13,707,600
SIC 5461 Retail bakeries
Andre Lauzon

D-U-N-S 20-920-8263 (BR)
LAKERIDGE HEALTH
LAKERIDGE HEALTH WHITBY
(*Suby of* LAKERIDGE HEALTH)
300 Gordon St Suite 779, Whitby, ON, L1N 5T2
(905) 668-6831
Emp Here 250
SIC 8069 Specialty hospitals, except psychi-atric
Catharine Tunney

D-U-N-S 25-317-6150 (BR)
LIQUOR CONTROL BOARD OF ONTARIO, THE
LCBO
(*Suby of* GOVERNMENT OF ONTARIO)
2000 Boundary Rd, Whitby, ON, L1N 7G4
(905) 723-3417
Emp Here 300
SIC 4225 General warehousing and storage
Bruce Pizzoleto

D-U-N-S 20-273-4117 (SL)
MACKIE TRANSPORTATION INC
1900 Boundary Rd Unit 2, Whitby, ON, L1N 8P8
(905) 728-1000
Emp Here 100   *Sales* 13,533,840
SIC 4213 Trucking, except local
Dean Mackie
Sarah Mackie
Shawn Mackie

D-U-N-S 20-848-6084 (HQ)
MAKITA CANADA INC
(*Suby of* MAKITA CORPORATION)
1950 Forbes St, Whitby, ON, L1N 7B7
(905) 571-2200
Emp Here 98   *Sales* 90,628,668
SIC 5072 Hardware
Hideyuki Terajima
Shiro Hori

D-U-N-S 20-183-2730 (SL)
MARIGOLD FORD LINCOLN SALES LIM-ITED
1120 Dundas St E, Whitby, ON, L1N 2K2
(905) 668-5893
Emp Here 47   *Sales* 23,409,666
SIC 5511 New and used car dealers
Terry Souch

D-U-N-S 25-637-9421 (SL)
MASON, GREG SERVICES INC
ONTARIO HYUNDAI
1505 Dundas St E, Whitby, ON, L1N 2K6
(905) 668-5100
Emp Here 30   *Sales* 14,942,340
SIC 5511 New and used car dealers
Greg Mason

D-U-N-S 25-512-0255 (SL)
MEADWELL MOWAT FENNELL
413 Dundas St E, Whitby, ON, L1N 2J2
(905) 668-3579
Emp Here 22   *Sales* 18,657,320
SIC 6411 Insurance agents, brokers, and ser-vice
David Meadwell
Noel Mowat
Ron Fennell

D-U-N-S 25-214-9182 (SL)
METALS PLUS LTD
1610 Mcewen Dr Unit 1-3, Whitby, ON, L1N 8V7
(905) 721-0050
Emp Here 12   *Sales* 12,004,068
SIC 5051 Metals service centers and offices
Occo Van Tijn
Susan Van Tijn
Gareth Raggett

D-U-N-S 24-333-1670 (BR)
METRO ONTARIO INC
METRO
(*Suby of* METRO INC)
70 Thickson Rd S, Whitby, ON, L1N 7T2
(905) 668-5334
Emp Here 100
SIC 5411 Grocery stores
Garth Cameron

D-U-N-S 25-214-7996 (SL)
MULTI-PLASTICS CANADA CO
55 Moore Crt, Whitby, ON, L1N 9Z8
(905) 430-7511
Emp Here 39   *Sales* 28,483,455
SIC 5162 Plastics materials and basic shapes
John Parsio
Doug Caillier
Lynn Begley

D-U-N-S 24-640-6982 (SL)
NATURAL GAS CUSTOM PIPING
244 Brock St S, Whitby, ON, L1N 4K1

Emp Here 5   *Sales* 15,790,468
SIC 4925 Gas production and/or distribution
Timor Shukur

D-U-N-S 24-378-9588 (SL)
NEMATO CORP
1605 Mcewen Dr, Whitby, ON, L1N 7L4

Emp Here 75   *Sales* 17,507,625
SIC 3299 NonMetallic mineral products,
Steven Andrews
Franca Dekever
Jerry Lozinski

D-U-N-S 20-359-1904 (HQ)
NORTH AMERICAN STEEL EQUIPMENT INC
300 Hopkins St, Whitby, ON, L1N 2B9
(905) 668-3300
Sales 29,629,824
SIC 2542 Partitions and fixtures, except wood
Rolf Fabricius
Tania Fabricius

D-U-N-S 20-183-2433 (SL)
NURSE CHEVROLET CADILLAC LTD
(*Suby of* 360435 ONTARIO LIMITED)
1530 Dundas St E, Whitby, ON, L1N 2K7
(905) 668-4044
Emp Here 140   *Sales* 88,099,200
SIC 5511 New and used car dealers
Mary Nurse

D-U-N-S 24-535-0926   (SL)
ONTARIO SHORES CENTRE FOR MENTAL HEALTH SCIENCES
700 Gordon St, Whitby, ON, L1N 5S9
(905) 668-5881
Emp Here 1,300   *Sales* 103,855,700
SIC 8063 Psychiatric hospitals
Karim Mamdani

D-U-N-S 25-965-7455   (SL)
OPTIMA COMMUNICATIONS INC
1615 Dundas St E Suite 300, Whitby, ON, L1N 2L1
(905) 448-2300
Emp Here 49   *Sales* 15,954,400
SIC 5999 Miscellaneous retail stores, nec
Don Macleod

D-U-N-S 20-216-8162   (SL)
OWASCO CANADIAN CAR & CAMPER RENTAL LTD
2030 Champlain Ave, Whitby, ON, L1N 6A7
(905) 579-7573
Emp Here 30   *Sales* 15,193,652
SIC 5561 Recreational vehicle dealers
Bob Verwey

D-U-N-S 20-899-0999   (SL)
PARTNERS IN COMMUNITY NURSING
1001 Burns St E Unit 2, Whitby, ON, L1N 6A6
(905) 665-1711
Emp Here 120   *Sales* 14,973,120
SIC 8741 Management services
Theresa Henderson

D-U-N-S 20-547-5333   (BR)
PATHEON INC
(*Suby of* THERMO FISHER SCIENTIFIC INC.)
111 Consumers Dr, Whitby, ON, L1N 5Z5
(905) 668-3368
Emp Here 500
SIC 2834 Pharmaceutical preparations
Paul Fitzgerald

D-U-N-S 24-365-8924   (SL)
PHOENIX RESTORATION INC
1100 Burns St E, Whitby, ON, L1N 6M6
(905) 665-7600
Emp Here 40   *Sales* 13,333,320
SIC 1541 Industrial buildings and warehouses
Vincent Brannigan
Michael Brannigan

D-U-N-S 24-805-5589   (BR)
PIC GROUP LTD, THE
(*Suby of* ARDIAN HOLDING)
202 South Blair St Unit 12, Whitby, ON, L1N 8X9
(416) 676-5659
Emp Here 140
SIC 4225 General warehousing and storage
Shelly Robinson

D-U-N-S 25-711-9750   (SL)
PIONEER FOOD COURTS INC
1 Paisley Crt, Whitby, ON, L1N 9L2
(905) 665-1217
Emp Here 80   *Sales* 17,669,680
SIC 6512 Nonresidential building operators

D-U-N-S 20-300-3830   (SL)
PRIMERICA FINANCIAL SERVICES LTD
(*Suby of* PRIMERICA, INC.)
1615 Dundas St E Suite 200, Whitby, ON, L1N 2L1
(905) 436-8499
Emp Here 100
SIC 6411 Insurance agents, brokers, and service
Raymond Young

D-U-N-S 25-478-2873   (SL)
PRINGLE CREEK I G A
SOBEY'S
728 Anderson St Unit 4, Whitby, ON, L1N 3V6
(905) 668-5538
Emp Here 60   *Sales* 17,608,620

SIC 5411 Grocery stores
Peter Plastina

D-U-N-S 24-611-3765   (SL)
PROMOTIONAL   PRODUCTS   FULFILL-MENT & DISTRIBUTION LT
PPFD
80 William Smith Dr, Whitby, ON, L1N 9W1
(905) 668-5060
Emp Here 60   *Sales* 26,953,140
SIC 7389 Business services, nec
Gilbert Kee
Kathy Perna

D-U-N-S 24-197-6281   (SL)
R. P. OIL LIMITED
1111 Burns St E Unit 3, Whitby, ON, L1N 6A6
(905) 666-2313
Emp Here 14   *Sales* 14,459,312
SIC 5172 Petroleum products, nec
Larry Harris

D-U-N-S 24-342-7957   (BR)
RECIPE UNLIMITED CORPORATION
SWISS CHALET ROTISSERIE & GRILL
(*Suby of* RECIPE UNLIMITED CORPORATION)
175 Consumers Dr, Whitby, ON, L1N 1C4
(905) 666-1411
Emp Here 75
SIC 5812 Eating places
Craig Frampton

D-U-N-S 24-048-0210   (HQ)
RIVETT   ARCHITECTURAL   HARDWARE LTD
111 Industrial Dr Unit 1, Whitby, ON, L1N 5Z9
(905) 668-4455
Emp Here 25   *Sales* 14,756,742
SIC 5072 Hardware
Ray Pickell
Joan Pickell

D-U-N-S 25-202-5861   (HQ)
RLM MANUFACTURING INC
701 Rossland Rd E Unit 370, Whitby, ON, L1N 8Y9
(905) 434-4567
Emp Here 3   *Sales* 12,210,055
SIC 3569 General industrial machinery, nec
Richard Mckinley

D-U-N-S 25-527-7410   (SL)
ROGERS, JOHN C. SHEET METAL LTD
2300 Forbes St, Whitby, ON, L1N 8M3
(905) 571-2422
Emp Here 50   *Sales* 11,046,700
SIC 1711 Plumbing, heating, air-conditioning
George Brown

D-U-N-S 24-314-0386   (SL)
ROSS DREY LIMITED
CANADIAN TIRE
155 Consumers Dr, Whitby, ON, L1N 1C4
(905) 668-5828
Emp Here 100   *Sales* 62,928,000
SIC 5531 Auto and home supply stores
Ross Leckie

D-U-N-S 24-873-8957   (SL)
RPG SUPPLY INC
40 Sunray St, Whitby, ON, L1N 8Y3
(905) 430-8170
Emp Here 30   *Sales* 10,926,450
SIC 5013 Motor vehicle supplies and new parts
Robert Addie
Paul Cumming

D-U-N-S 24-387-2087   (HQ)
RPM CANADA COMPANY FINANCE ULC
RPM CANADA
(*Suby of* RPM INTERNATIONAL INC.)
95 Sunray St, Whitby, ON, L1N 9C9
(905) 430-3333
Emp Here 450   *Sales* 355,716,000
SIC 2851 Paints and allied products
Frank C. Sullivan

Keith R. Smiley
P. Kelly Tomkins

D-U-N-S 25-634-3963   (BR)
SAINT ELIZABETH HEALTH CARE
(*Suby of* SAINT ELIZABETH HEALTH CARE)
420 Green St Suite 202, Whitby, ON, L1N 8R1
(905) 430-6997
Emp Here 150
SIC 8361 Residential care
Lynn Park

D-U-N-S 24-976-8979   (SL)
SB PHARMACY SERVICES LTD
SHOPPERS DRUG MART
1801 Dundas St E, Whitby, ON, L1N 7C5
(905) 436-1050
Emp Here 65   *Sales* 15,881,320
SIC 5912 Drug stores and proprietary stores
Susan Bowser
Eric Ellis

D-U-N-S 25-195-3030   (HQ)
SERNAS GROUP INC, THE
SRM ASSOCIATES
110 Scotia Crt Unit 41, Whitby, ON, L1N 8Y7
(905) 432-7878
Sales 37,535,190
SIC 8711 Engineering services
Rej Webster

D-U-N-S 24-844-9506   (HQ)
SOFT-MOC INC
1400 Hopkins St Unit 3-4, Whitby, ON, L1N 2C3
(905) 665-8119
Emp Here 30   *Sales* 49,902,000
SIC 5661 Shoe stores
Bryan Bardocz

D-U-N-S 24-395-3846   (SL)
STAR ONE MOTOR CO
MERCEDES BENZ
250 Thickson Rd S, Whitby, ON, L1N 9Z1
(905) 666-8805
Emp Here 30   *Sales* 14,942,340
SIC 5511 New and used car dealers
Dick Hammer

D-U-N-S 20-971-2624   (HQ)
STONHARD LTD
RPM CANANDA, DIVISION OF
95 Sunray St, Whitby, ON, L1N 9C9
(705) 749-1460
Sales 39,272,200
SIC 1752 Floor laying and floor work, nec
Alan Brooks

D-U-N-S 24-412-5100   (SL)
SUNNYCREST NURSING HOMES LIMITED
SUNNY CREST RETIREMENT VILLA
1635 Dundas St E, Whitby, ON, L1N 2K9
(905) 576-0111
Emp Here 140   *Sales* 9,599,240
SIC 8051 Skilled nursing care facilities
Candace Lewis

D-U-N-S 25-221-0190   (HQ)
SURNET INSURANCE GROUP INC
1621 Mcewen Dr Suite 50, Whitby, ON, L1N 9A5
(905) 433-2378
Emp Here 6   *Sales* 25,441,800
SIC 6411 Insurance agents, brokers, and service
Brian R Thompson
Kelly Thompson

D-U-N-S 24-353-2350   (SL)
TRANSCONTINENTAL   PACKAGING WHITBY ULC
(*Suby of* TRANSCONTINENTAL INC)
201 South Blair St, Whitby, ON, L1N 5S6
(905) 668-5811
Emp Here 150   *Sales* 29,215,200
SIC 2671 Paper; coated and laminated packaging
Ron Tutak

D-U-N-S 25-528-8771   (BR)
TST SOLUTIONS L.P.
TST AUTOMOTIVE SERVICES
(*Suby of* TST SOLUTIONS L.P.)
1601 Tricont Ave, Whitby, ON, L1N 7N5

Emp Here 150
SIC 4225 General warehousing and storage
Wayne Goodwin

D-U-N-S 24-826-9602   (BR)
VENTRA GROUP CO
VENTRA OSHAWA SPD, DIV OF
(*Suby of* FLEX-N-GATE LLC)
200 Montecorte St, Whitby, ON, L1N 9V8

Emp Here 80
SIC 3714 Motor vehicle parts and accessories
David Ekblad

D-U-N-S 24-367-8062   (SL)
WEGU MANUFACTURING INC
1707 Harbour St, Whitby, ON, L1N 9G6
(905) 668-2359
Emp Here 105   *Sales* 29,822,205
SIC 2821 Plastics materials and resins
Angela Lowe
Anastasios Votis

D-U-N-S 24-485-2786   (HQ)
WENZEL INTERNATIONAL INC
CROVEN CRYSTALS
(*Suby of* WENZEL ASSOCIATES, INC.)
500 Beech St W, Whitby, ON, L1N 7T8
(905) 668-3324
Sales 16,187,570
SIC 3679 Electronic components, nec
Luke Mueller

D-U-N-S 25-159-6128   (SL)
WHITBY-OSHAWA IMPORTS LTD
WHITBY-OSHAWA HONDA
300 Thickson Rd S, Whitby, ON, L1N 9Z1
(905) 666-1772
Emp Here 58   *Sales* 16,431,400
SIC 7515 Passenger car leasing
Bentley Hammer

Whitby, ON L1P

D-U-N-S 20-753-5469   (SL)
C & C MOTOR SALES LTD
SUBARU AUTHORISED DEALERS
1705 Dundas St W, Whitby, ON, L1P 1Y9
(905) 430-6666
Emp Here 22   *Sales* 10,957,716
SIC 5511 New and used car dealers
Idalo Cappuccitti

D-U-N-S 20-711-3817   (BR)
DURHAM CATHOLIC DISTRICT SCHOOL BOARD
ALL   SAINT   CATHOLIC   SECONDARY SCHOOL
(*Suby of* DURHAM CATHOLIC DISTRICT SCHOOL BOARD)
3001 Country Lane, Whitby, ON, L1P 1M1
(905) 666-7753
Emp Here 135
SIC 8211 Elementary and secondary schools
Mark Lacey

D-U-N-S 20-646-5804   (BR)
DURHAM DISTRICT SCHOOL BOARD
DONALD A WILSON SECONDARY SCHOOL
(*Suby of* DURHAM DISTRICT SCHOOL BOARD)
681 Rossland Rd W, Whitby, ON, L1P 1Y1
(905) 665-5057
Emp Here 120
SIC 8211 Elementary and secondary schools
Stephen Nevills

D-U-N-S 24-373-1234   (HQ)

VIRGIN & ALL SAINTS CO. LTD, THE
PETRO CANADA
1755 Dundas St W, Whitby, ON, L1P 1Y9
(905) 665-9270
Emp Here 5   *Sales* 24,903,900
SIC 5541 Gasoline service stations
Mona Aziz

D-U-N-S 25-638-3951   (SL)
WHITBY TOYOTA COMPANY
1025 Dundas St W, Whitby, ON, L1P 1Z1
(905) 668-4792
Emp Here 45   *Sales* 22,413,510
SIC 5511 New and used car dealers
Ian Kingsley

Whitby, ON L1R

D-U-N-S 20-010-7717   (SL)
AINSWORTH MANAGEMENT SERVICES INC
SERVICEMASTER OF DURHAM CONTRACT SERVICES
56 Carlinds Dr, Whitby, ON, L1R 3B9
(905) 666-9156
Emp Here 100   *Sales* 4,020,900
SIC 7349 Building maintenance services, nec
Richard Ainsworth

D-U-N-S 20-086-9399   (BR)
CORPORATION OF THE REGIONAL MUNICIPALITY OF DURHAM, THE
MAINTENANCE DEPOT
(*Suby of* CORPORATION OF THE REGIONAL MUNICIPALITY OF DURHAM, THE)
825 Conlin Rd, Whitby, ON, L1R 3K3
(905) 655-3344
Emp Here 100
SIC 1611 Highway and street construction
John Tryon

D-U-N-S 20-015-4982   (BR)
DURHAM CATHOLIC DISTRICT SCHOOL BOARD
FATHER LEO J AUSTIN
(*Suby of* DURHAM CATHOLIC DISTRICT SCHOOL BOARD)
1020 Dryden Blvd, Whitby, ON, L1R 2A2
(905) 666-2010
Emp Here 200
SIC 8211 Elementary and secondary schools
Paul Perron

D-U-N-S 20-773-5960   (HQ)
DURHAM DISTRICT SCHOOL BOARD
400 Taunton Rd E, Whitby, ON, L1R 2K6
(905) 686-2711
Emp Here 250   *Sales* 650,878,987
SIC 8211 Elementary and secondary schools
Lou Vavougios
Edward Hodgins
Terry Henderson
Martin Beckett

D-U-N-S 24-719-9938   (HQ)
HARD-CO CONSTRUCTION LTD
HARD-CO SAND & GRAVEL, DIV OF
625 Conlin Rd, Whitby, ON, L1R 2W8
(905) 655-2001
Emp Here 30   *Sales* 27,768,620
SIC 1611 Highway and street construction
Barry Harding
Larry Harding

D-U-N-S 24-383-8807   (BR)
LOBLAWS INC
REAL CANADIAN SUPERSTORE
(*Suby of* LOBLAW COMPANIES LIMITED)
200 Taunton Rd W Suite 1058, Whitby, ON, L1R 3H8
(905) 665-1164
Emp Here 150
SIC 5411 Grocery stores
Sarah Power

D-U-N-S 25-709-4417   (BR)
LOBLAWS SUPERMARKETS LIMITED
LA ROSA'S NOFRILLS
(*Suby of* LOBLAW COMPANIES LIMITED)
3100 Garden St Unit 2, Whitby, ON, L1R 2G8
(866) 987-6453
Emp Here 220
SIC 5411 Grocery stores
Steve Canini

D-U-N-S 24-858-2780   (BR)
LOWE'S COMPANIES CANADA, ULC
LOWES HOME IMPROVEMENT WAREHOUSE
(*Suby of* LOWE'S COMPANIES, INC.)
4005 Garrard Rd, Whitby, ON, L1R 0J1
(905) 433-2870
Emp Here 150
SIC 5211 Lumber and other building materials
Paul Santos

D-U-N-S 24-848-5278   (HQ)
MARVIN ENTERPRISES INC
MARVIN CANDY & DISPLAYS
3627 Cochrane St, Whitby, ON, L1R 2T2
(905) 665-5686
Emp Here 10   *Sales* 12,533,655
SIC 5145 Confectionery
Vince Cotroneo
Marna Cotroneo

D-U-N-S 24-335-0464   (BR)
METRO ONTARIO INC
METRO
(*Suby of* METRO INC)
4111 Thickson Rd N, Whitby, ON, L1R 2X3
(905) 655-1553
Emp Here 200
SIC 5411 Grocery stores
John Sparacino

D-U-N-S 25-108-8852   (SL)
PERFORMA LUBRICANTS INTERNATIONAL INC
42 Montrose Cres, Whitby, ON, L1R 1C5
(905) 668-1440
Emp Here 11   *Sales* 11,360,888
SIC 5172 Petroleum products, nec
Guy R Smith

D-U-N-S 25-561-9814   (SL)
SWAN SOURCE
47 Butterfield Cres, Whitby, ON, L1R 1K5
(647) 967-6723
Emp Here 5   *Sales* 15,529,285
SIC 4924 Natural gas distribution

D-U-N-S 24-329-6980   (BR)
WAL-MART CANADA CORP
(*Suby of* WALMART INC.)
4100 Baldwin St S, Whitby, ON, L1R 3H8
(905) 655-0206
Emp Here 200
SIC 5311 Department stores
Rob Walton

White River, ON P0M

D-U-N-S 20-257-1733   (SL)
WHITE RIVER FOREST PRODUCTS GP INC
315 Hwy 17, White River, ON, P0M 3G0
(807) 822-1818
Emp Here 167   *Sales* 46,763,036
SIC 2421 Sawmills and planing mills, general
Frank Dottori
Thomas Kennedy
Norm Jaehrling
Jason Linkewich
Angelo Eazzoni

D-U-N-S 20-305-4143   (SL)
WHITE RIVER FOREST PRODUCTS LTD
315 Hwy 17, White River, ON, P0M 3G0

(807) 822-1818
Emp Here 65   *Sales* 12,504,050
SIC 2426 Hardwood dimension and flooring mills
Frank Dottori
Tom Bagdon
Norm Jaehrling
Jason Linkewich
Marlene Sabourin
Dino Tarini

Whitevale, ON L0H

D-U-N-S 24-578-6400   (SL)
TBG ENVIRONMENTAL INC
425 Whitevale Rd Unit 5, Whitevale, ON. L0H 1M0
(905) 620-1222
Emp Here 180   *Sales* 19,672,020
SIC 0782 Lawn and garden services
Mark Bradley
Janna Bradley

Whitney, ON K0J

D-U-N-S 20-719-1529   (SL)
COUPLES RESORT INC
BEAR TRAIL
139 Galeairy Lake Rd, Whitney, ON, K0J 2M0
(613) 637-1179
Emp Here 75   *Sales* 6,951,750
SIC 7011 Hotels and motels
Gertrude Sorensen
John Sorensen
Evelyne Lasage
Mark Sorensen
Paul Sorensen

D-U-N-S 20-183-3746   (SL)
MCRAE LUMBER COMPANY LIMITED
MCRAE MILLS
384 Hay Creek Rd, Whitney, ON, K0J 2M0
(613) 637-2190
Emp Here 70   *Sales* 10,910,410
SIC 2411 Logging
John Mcrae
Robert Mcrae

D-U-N-S 24-470-3583   (SL)
MCRAE MILLS LIMITED
160 Hay Creek Rd, Whitney, ON, K0J 2M0
(613) 637-2977
Emp Here 60   *Sales* 16,059,120
SIC 5211 Lumber and other building materials
Robert Mcrae
John Mcrae

Wiarton, ON N0H

D-U-N-S 25-350-0672   (BR)
CORPORATION OF THE COUNTY OF BRUCE, THE
GATEWAY HAVEN
(*Suby of* CORPORATION OF THE COUNTY OF BRUCE, THE)
671 Frank St, Wiarton, ON, N0H 2T0
(519) 534-1113
Emp Here 95
SIC 8051 Skilled nursing care facilities
Charles Young

Wikwemikong, ON P0P

D-U-N-S 20-560-2220   (SL)
MANITOWABI, ANDREW GROUP

2174 Wikwemikong Way, Wikwemikong, ON, P0P 2J0
(705) 859-3788
Emp Here 35   *Sales* 22,024,800
SIC 5541 Gasoline service stations
Lester Manitowabi
James Manitowabi
Farrell Manitowabi
Jennifer Manitowabi
Walter Manitowabi
Judy Manitowabi
Sharon Manitowabi

D-U-N-S 25-322-9710   (SL)
WIKWEMIKONG TRIBAL POLICE
2074 Wikwemikong Way, Wikwemikong, ON, P0P 2J0
(705) 859-3141
Emp Here 30   *Sales* 11,870,340
SIC 7381 Detective and armored car services
Gary Reid
Myles Webkamigad

Wilsonville, ON N0E

D-U-N-S 25-203-5654   (SL)
PROCYK FARMS (1994) LIMITED
Gd, Wilsonville, ON, N0E 1Z0
(519) 443-4516
Emp Here 104   *Sales* 33,805,000
SIC 0161 Vegetables and melons
Paul Procyk
Rod Wheeler
Mike Procyk
Dan Procyk

Winchester, ON K0C

D-U-N-S 24-104-1540   (SL)
DUNDAS MANOR LTD
533 Clarence St Suite 970, Winchester, ON. K0C 2K0
(613) 774-2293
Emp Here 104   *Sales* 7,130,864
SIC 8051 Skilled nursing care facilities
Jill Alguire
Ross Alquire

D-U-N-S 20-649-4403   (BR)
PARMALAT CANADA INC
(*Suby of* PARMALAT SPA)
490 Gordon St, Winchester, ON, K0C 2K0
(613) 774-2310
Emp Here 215
SIC 2022 Cheese; natural and processed
Elaine Derooy

D-U-N-S 24-382-8589   (SL)
RIDEAU AUCTIONS INC
Gd, Winchester, ON, K0C 2K0
(613) 774-2735
Emp Here 30   *Sales* 13,304,700
SIC 7389 Business services, nec
Hunter Mccaig

D-U-N-S 20-153-7925   (HQ)
WEAGANT FARM SUPPLIES LIMITED
TOPLINE TRAILER & EQUIPMENT SALES, DIV OF
11250 County Rd 43, Winchester, ON, K0C 2K0
(613) 774-2887
Emp Here 37   *Sales* 12,949,384
SIC 5999 Miscellaneous retail stores, nec
Robert Weagant
Laird Allan Weagant
David Black
Sandra Weagant
Elise Weagant
Barbara Black

D-U-N-S 24-966-1539   (SL)

WINCHESTER DISTRICT MEMORIAL HOSPITAL
566 Louise St Rr 4, Winchester, ON, K0C 2K0
(613) 774-2420
Emp Here 280   *Sales* 31,102,400
SIC 8062 General medical and surgical hospitals
Trudy Reid
Michelle Blouin
Lynn Hall
Peter Sorby

Windermere, ON P0B

D-U-N-S 24-035-8585   (SL)
1090769 ONTARIO INC
2508 Windermere Rd, Windermere, ON, P0B 1P0
(705) 769-3611
Emp Here 107   *Sales* 9,917,830
SIC 7011 Hotels and motels
Jim Twiss
Stanly Goodman
Bill Wakefield

Windham Centre, ON N0E

D-U-N-S 20-202-5533   (SL)
MK SAFETY NET CANADA
1038 Windham Centre Rd, Windham Centre, ON, N0E 2A0

Emp Here 150   *Sales* 16,662,000
SIC 8062 General medical and surgical hospitals

Windsor, ON N0R

D-U-N-S 20-186-7769   (SL)
WINDSOR PALLET LIMITED
2890 N Talbot, Windsor, ON, N0R 1K0
(519) 737-1406
Emp Here 38   *Sales* 18,050,988
SIC 5085 Industrial supplies
Louis Calsavara Jr

Windsor, ON N8N

D-U-N-S 24-764-4255   (SL)
734046 ONTARIO LIMITED
TECUMSEH HOME HARDWARE
1613 Lesperance Rd, Windsor, ON, N8N 1Y2
(519) 735-3400
Emp Here 40   *Sales* 10,122,360
SIC 5251 Hardware stores
Larry Seguin

D-U-N-S 20-549-8442   (BR)
A.P. PLASMAN INC
A.P. PLASMAN INC.
(*Suby of* APP HOLDINGS LP)
418 Silver Creek Industrial Dr, Windsor, ON, N8N 4Y3
(519) 727-4545
Emp Here 520
SIC 3089 Plastics products, nec
Randy Marenette

D-U-N-S 24-751-4776   (SL)
ACM PANELWORX INC
357 Croft Dr, Windsor, ON, N8N 2L9
(519) 739-2380
Emp Here 47   *Sales* 21,017,178
SIC 5051 Metals service centers and offices
Timothy Mrkajl

Mark Mrkalj

D-U-N-S 20-515-9614   (HQ)
APPLESHORE RESTAURANTS INC
APPLEBEE'S
11865 County Rd 42, Windsor, ON, N8N 2M1
(519) 979-7800
Sales 62,388,000
SIC 8741 Management services
Robert Troup
Ken Troup
Paul Moore
Brian Moore

D-U-N-S 25-169-6860   (SL)
BABINEAU, D. DRUGS INC
SHOPPERS DRUG MART
11500 Tecumseh Rd E Suite 1118, Windsor, ON, N8N 1L7
(519) 735-2121
Emp Here 65   *Sales* 15,881,320
SIC 5912 Drug stores and proprietary stores
David Babineau

D-U-N-S 20-290-7155   (SL)
BANWELL GARDENS
3000 Banwell Rd, Windsor, ON, N8N 0B3
(519) 735-3204
Emp Here 150   *Sales* 10,284,900
SIC 8051 Skilled nursing care facilities
Gwen Waddick

D-U-N-S 24-034-6085   (BR)
COMMUNITY LIVING ESSEX COUNTY
ESSEX COUNTY ASSOCIATION FOR COMMUNITY LIVING
(*Suby of* COMMUNITY LIVING ESSEX COUNTY)
13158 Tecumseh Rd E, Windsor, ON, N8N 3T6
(519) 979-0057
Emp Here 600
SIC 8322 Individual and family services
Nancy Wallace - Dero

D-U-N-S 24-745-4952   (HQ)
CONCORDE PRECISION MACHINING INC
CONCORD MACHINE TOOL, DIV OF
(*Suby of* REKO INTERNATIONAL GROUP INC)
469 Silver Creek Industrial Dr, Windsor, ON, N8N 4W2
(519) 727-3287
Emp Here 50   *Sales* 36,630,165
SIC 3544 Special dies, tools, jigs, and fixtures
Diane Reko

D-U-N-S 25-214-3904   (HQ)
CONCOURS MOLD INC
(*Suby of* CRESTVIEW PARTNERS, L.P.)
465 Jutras Dr S, Windsor, ON, N8N 5C4
(519) 727-9949
Sales 44,400,200
SIC 3544 Special dies, tools, jigs, and fixtures
Andy Aiton
Lou Meneses
Don Turner

D-U-N-S 20-397-8424   (SL)
CRAWFORD GENERAL CONTRACTING INC
507 Birkdale Crt, Windsor, ON, N8N 4B3
(519) 567-8411
Emp Here 29   *Sales* 18,681,312
SIC 1542 Nonresidential construction, nec
Stephen Crawford
Jomil Crawford

D-U-N-S 24-737-9030   (SL)
CS WIND CANADA INC
(*Suby of* CS WIND CORPORATION)
9355 Anchor Dr, Windsor, ON, N8N 5A8
(519) 735-0973
Emp Here 100   *Sales* 22,200,100
SIC 3523 Farm machinery and equipment
Jinhee Won
Jennifer Shilson
Bang Cham Kim

D-U-N-S 24-486-4542   (SL)
DIEFFENBACHER NORTH AMERICA INC
(*Suby of* DIEFFENBACHER VERMO-GENSVERWALTUNGS GMBH + CO. KG)
9495 Twin Oaks Dr, Windsor, ON, N8N 5B8
(519) 979-6937
Emp Here 60   *Sales* 13,320,060
SIC 3542 Machine tools, Metal forming type
Colin Folco
Heiko Heitlinger
Wolf-Gerd Dieffenbacher
Peter Lynch

D-U-N-S 24-341-5499   (SL)
ECOTEMP MANUFACTURING INC
(*Suby of* ECOTEMP INTERNATIONAL INC)
8400 Twin Oaks Dr, Windsor, ON, N8N 5C2

Emp Here 60   *Sales* 11,426,520
SIC 3679 Electronic components, nec
Lynn Johner

D-U-N-S 24-778-7047   (HQ)
ERIE ARCHITECTURAL PRODUCTS INC
477 Jutras Dr S, Windsor, ON, N8N 5C4
(519) 727-0372
Sales 12,677,610
SIC 3442 Metal doors, sash, and trim
Ron Stronks

D-U-N-S 20-822-9559   (BR)
G&K SERVICES CANADA INC
G&K SERVICES - WINDSOR
(*Suby of* CINTAS CORPORATION)
9085 Twin Oaks Dr, Windsor, ON, N8N 5B8
(519) 979-5913
Emp Here 115
SIC 7213 Linen supply
Chris Moore

D-U-N-S 20-880-4203   (HQ)
GREEN SHIELD CANADA
8677 Anchor Dr, Windsor, ON, N8N 5G1
(519) 739-1133
Emp Here 344   *Sales* 505,666,980
SIC 6324 Hospital and medical service plans
Zahid Salman
Scot Hopkins
Mila Lucio
Brent Allen
Carmen Hogen

D-U-N-S 20-113-4918   (BR)
LINAMAR CORPORATION
EXKOR MANUFACTURING
(*Suby of* LINAMAR CORPORATION)
3590 Valtec Crt, Windsor, ON, N8N 5E6
(519) 739-3465
Emp Here 200
SIC 3714 Motor vehicle parts and accessories
Kevin Applegate

D-U-N-S 24-333-1639   (BR)
METRO ONTARIO INC
METRO
(*Suby of* METRO INC)
11729 Tecumseh Rd E, Windsor, ON, N8N 1L8
(519) 979-9366
Emp Here 100
SIC 5411 Grocery stores
Rick Lucier

D-U-N-S 20-059-3551   (SL)
POLYTECH CANADA INC
5505 Rhodes Dr, Windsor, ON, N8N 2M1

Emp Here 40   *Sales* 29,213,800
SIC 5169 Chemicals and allied products, nec

D-U-N-S 25-651-7632   (HQ)
QUALITY MODELS LIMITED
Q M PLASTICS, DIV OF
478 Silver Creek Industrial Dr Suite 1, Windsor, ON, N8N 4Y3
(519) 727-4255
Emp Here 117   *Sales* 19,857,250
SIC 3089 Plastics products, nec

William Szekesy

D-U-N-S 24-123-7387   (HQ)
REKO INTERNATIONAL GROUP INC
469 Silver Creek Industrial Dr, Windsor, ON, N8N 4W2
(519) 727-3287
Emp Here 200   *Sales* 32,361,971
SIC 3544 Special dies, tools, jigs, and fixtures
Diane Reko
Maria Ann Thompson
Marilyn Crowley
Andrew J. Szonyi
John Sartz

D-U-N-S 24-849-9530   (SL)
REKO MANUFACTURING GROUP INC
(*Suby of* REKO INTERNATIONAL GROUP INC)
469 Silver Creek Industrial Dr, Windsor, ON, N8N 4W2
(519) 727-3287
Emp Here 215   *Sales* 60,388,555
SIC 3544 Special dies, tools, jigs, and fixtures
Diane Reko

D-U-N-S 24-744-9788   (HQ)
RIVERVIEW STEEL CO. LTD
(*Suby of* ANOBILE ENTERPRISES CORP)
8165 Anchor Dr, Windsor, ON, N8N 5B7
(519) 979-5576
Emp Here 60   *Sales* 18,781,308
SIC 5051 Metals service centers and offices
Michael Anobile
Cheryl Anobile

D-U-N-S 20-793-2927   (BR)
UNITED PARCEL SERVICE CANADA LTD
UPS
(*Suby of* UNITED PARCEL SERVICE, INC.)
5325 Rhodes Dr, Windsor, ON, N8N 2M1
(519) 251-7050
Emp Here 100
SIC 7389 Business services, nec
Patryk Konopacki

D-U-N-S 25-095-8154   (BR)
VALIANT MACHINE & TOOL INC
VALIANT TOOL & GAGE
9355 Anchor Dr, Windsor, ON, N8N 5A8
(519) 974-5200
Emp Here 75
SIC 3541 Machine tools, Metal cutting type
Nick Sauro

D-U-N-S 24-314-9635   (HQ)
ZF AUTOMOTIVE CANADA LIMITED
TRW AUTOMOTIVE
(*Suby of* ZEPPELIN-STIFTUNG)
3355 Munich Crt, Windsor, ON, N8N 5G2
(519) 739-9861
Emp Here 50   *Sales* 36,421,500
SIC 5013 Motor vehicle supplies and new parts
Luke Razny
John C. Plant

Windsor, ON N8P

D-U-N-S 20-642-2987   (SL)
SNR NURSING HOMES LTD
HERON TERRACE
11550 Mcnorton St, Windsor, ON, N8P 1T9
(519) 979-6730
Emp Here 180   *Sales* 10,664,460
SIC 8361 Residential care
John Scotland

Windsor, ON N8R

D-U-N-S 20-216-7578   (SL)
1461616 ONTARIO INC

▲ Public Company   ■ Public Company Family Member   **HQ** Headquarters   **BR** Branch   **SL** Single Location

VOLKSWAGEN OF WINDSOR
10280 Tecumseh Rd E, Windsor, ON, N8R 1A2
(519) 735-7706
Emp Here 26   *Sales* 12,950,028
SIC 5511 New and used car dealers
Gus Revenberg

D-U-N-S 20-384-4071   (SL)
1681230 ONTARIO INC
WINDSOR CHRYSLER
10380 Tecumseh Rd E, Windsor, ON, N8R 1A7
(519) 979-9900
Emp Here 110   *Sales* 69,220,800
SIC 5511 New and used car dealers
Philip Diemer

D-U-N-S 20-357-6376   (SL)
2494719 ONTARIO INC
AUDI WINDSOR
10980 Tecumseh Rd E, Windsor, ON, N8R 1A8
(519) 956-7700
Emp Here 26   *Sales* 12,950,028
SIC 5511 New and used car dealers
Chris Leavens

D-U-N-S 25-669-4050   (SL)
EASTWAY SALES & LEASING INC
EASTWAY TOYOTA & LEXUS OF WINDSOR
9375 Tecumseh Rd E, Windsor, ON, N8R 1A1
(519) 979-1900
Emp Here 40   *Sales* 19,923,120
SIC 5511 New and used car dealers
Talal (Terry) Rafih

D-U-N-S 25-175-2820   (SL)
OVERSEAS MOTORS (WINDSOR) INC
MERCEDES-BENZ WINDSOR
9225 Tecumseh Rd E, Windsor, ON, N8R 1A1
(519) 254-0358
Emp Here 30   *Sales* 14,942,340
SIC 5511 New and used car dealers
Terry Rafih

D-U-N-S 24-708-6069   (HQ)
REVENBERG, GUS PONTIAC BUICK HUMMER GMC LTD
10150 Tecumseh Rd E, Windsor, ON, N8R 1A2
(519) 979-2800
Sales 62,928,000
SIC 5511 New and used car dealers
Gus Revenberg
Mel Duncan
Jerry Revenberg

D-U-N-S 24-816-1127   (BR)
SECURITAS CANADA LIMITED
PINKERTON'S OF CANADA
(*Suby of* SECURITAS AB)
11210 Tecumseh Rd E, Windsor, ON, N8R 1A8
(519) 979-1317
Emp Here 160
SIC 7381 Detective and armored car services
Roderick Beattie

Windsor, ON N8S

D-U-N-S 24-892-4508   (HQ)
ACROLAB TECHNOLOGIES INC
7475 Tranby Ave, Windsor, ON, N8S 2B7
(519) 944-5900
Emp Here 14   *Sales* 11,508,332
SIC 6712 Bank holding companies
Joseph Ouellette
John Hodgins

D-U-N-S 24-180-3121   (SL)
EVERYDAY STYLE LTD
7675 Tranby Ave, Windsor, ON, N8S 2B7
(519) 258-7905
Emp Here 50   *Sales* 32,823,200

SIC 5963 Direct selling establishments
Marjorie Rau
Carl Rau

D-U-N-S 25-249-1014   (BR)
GREATER ESSEX COUNTY DISTRICT SCHOOL BOARD
RIVERSIDE SECONDARY SCHOOL
(*Suby of* GREATER ESSEX COUNTY DISTRICT SCHOOL BOARD)
8465 Jerome St, Windsor, ON, N8S 1W8
(519) 948-4116
Emp Here 80
SIC 8211 Elementary and secondary schools
Ted Laurendeau

D-U-N-S 24-543-4253   (HQ)
MEDA LIMITED
1575 Lauzon Rd, Windsor, ON, N8S 3N4
(519) 944-7221
Emp Here 196   *Sales* 35,747,800
SIC 8711 Engineering services
Carole Lawn
David Lawn

D-U-N-S 25-300-0004   (BR)
METRO ONTARIO INC
A & P STORES
(*Suby of* METRO INC)
6740 Wyandotte St E, Windsor, ON, N8S 1P6
(519) 948-5676
Emp Here 100
SIC 5411 Grocery stores
Troy Steward

D-U-N-S 25-410-8590   (SL)
WINDSOR SPITFIRES INC
8787 Mchugh St, Windsor, ON, N8S 0A1
(519) 254-9256
Emp Here 35   *Sales* 14,830,550
SIC 7941 Sports clubs, managers, and promoters
Steve Riolo

Windsor, ON N8T

D-U-N-S 25-686-9363   (SL)
1363199 ONTARIO LIMITED
MOTION SPECIALTIES WINDSOR
5923 Tecumseh Rd E Suite 1, Windsor, ON, N8T 1E4
(519) 252-2011
Emp Here 26   *Sales* 11,626,524
SIC 5047 Medical and hospital equipment
John Fase

D-U-N-S 20-185-2043   (SL)
147766 CANADA INC
WINDSOR HONDA
7180 Tecumseh Rd E, Windsor, ON, N8T 1E6
(519) 945-8100
Emp Here 25   *Sales* 12,451,950
SIC 5511 New and used car dealers
Robert Kerr
Mike Wheatley
Fred Mclennan

D-U-N-S 24-197-6534   (HQ)
1498403 ONTARIO INC
PETRO CANADA
7400 Tecumseh Rd E, Windsor, ON, N8T 1E9
(519) 974-7116
Emp Here 5   *Sales* 24,903,900
SIC 5541 Gasoline service stations
Shiraz Ajmeri
Femida Ajmeri

D-U-N-S 20-568-6491   (HQ)
782659 ONTARIO LTD
PARKER CONSTRUCTION
2910 Jefferson Blvd, Windsor, ON, N8T 3J2
(519) 944-1212
Sales 12,754,760
SIC 1521 Single-family housing construction
James Parker

D-U-N-S 20-804-2031   (HQ)
ASSEMBLE-RITE, LTD
SPENCERARL DIV OF
(*Suby of* SPENCERARL NEW YORK, INC.)
2755 Lauzon Pky, Windsor, ON, N8T 3H5
(519) 945-8464
Emp Here 12   *Sales* 14,349,240
SIC 8741 Management services
Joanne Surace

D-U-N-S 20-184-7688   (HQ)
BUTCHER ENGINEERING ENTERPRISES LIMITED, THE
BUTCHER ENTERPRISES
2755 Lauzon Pky, Windsor, ON, N8T 3H5
(519) 944-9200
Emp Here 150   *Sales* 158,175,200
SIC 4783 Packing and crating
William Spencer
L Christopher Butcher
David Butcher
Linda Spencer
Denis Blondin

D-U-N-S 25-156-1593   (SL)
CENTRE COMMUNAUTAIRE FRANCO-PHONE WINDSOR-ESSEX-KENT INC
PLACE CONCORDE
7515 Forest Glade Dr, Windsor, ON, N8T 3P5
(519) 948-5545
Emp Here 100   *Sales* 8,962,900
SIC 7299 Miscellaneous personal service
Didier Marotte

D-U-N-S 25-114-8698   (HQ)
CONSEIL SCOLAIRE CATHOLIQUE PROVIDENCE
7515 Forest Glade Dr, Windsor, ON, N8T 3P5
(519) 948-9227
Sales 71,960,394
SIC 8211 Elementary and secondary schools
Janine Griffore
Celine Verville

D-U-N-S 20-185-1631   (HQ)
ELECTROZAD SUPPLY COMPANY LIMITED
2900 Jefferson Blvd, Windsor, ON, N8T 3J2
(519) 944-2900
Emp Here 48   *Sales* 65,567,911
SIC 5063 Electrical apparatus and equipment
William Smith
John Jenner

D-U-N-S 25-368-5960   (BR)
FORD MOTOR COMPANY OF CANADA, LIMITED
(*Suby of* FORD MOTOR COMPANY)
7654 Tecumseh Rd E, Windsor, ON, N8T 1E9
(519) 944-8564
Emp Here 1,000
SIC 3714 Motor vehicle parts and accessories

D-U-N-S 24-909-6611   (BR)
FORD MOTOR COMPANY OF CANADA, LIMITED
ESSEX ALUMINUM PLANT
(*Suby of* FORD MOTOR COMPANY)
6500 Cantelon Dr, Windsor, ON, N8T 0A6
(519) 251-4401
Emp Here 700
SIC 3711 Motor vehicles and car bodies
Lloyd Maisonville

D-U-N-S 20-361-4078   (SL)
FORTIS CONSTRUCTION GROUP INC
(*Suby of* FORTIS GROUP INC)
3070 Jefferson Blvd, Windsor, ON, N8T 3G9
(519) 419-7828
Emp Here 96   *Sales* 40,582,752
SIC 1541 Industrial buildings and warehouses
Scott Woodall
Maximillian De Angelis
Tyler Beckett

D-U-N-S 20-346-1975   (HQ)
FORTIS GROUP INC

3070 Jefferson Blvd, Windsor, ON, N8T 3G9
(519) 419-7828
Sales 26,241,600
SIC 6712 Bank holding companies
Scott Woodall
Tyler Beckett
Maximilian De Angelis
Denise Hillman

D-U-N-S 25-635-9423   (HQ)
GUARDIAN ALARM COMPANY OF CANADA LTD
2885 Lauzon Pky Suite 105, Windsor, ON, N8T 3H5
(519) 258-4646
Emp Here 1   *Sales* 18,370,264
SIC 7382 Security systems services
Matt Fraibert
Milton Pierce

D-U-N-S 20-014-7663   (SL)
HEARN AUTOMOTIVE INC
(*Suby of* DBS-HEARN INC)
6630 Tecumseh Rd E, Windsor, ON, N8T 1E6

Emp Here 70   *Sales* 15,669,010
SIC 3714 Motor vehicle parts and accessories
Donald M (Jr.) Hearn

D-U-N-S 24-024-1179   (BR)
HOME DEPOT OF CANADA INC
HOME DEPOT
(*Suby of* THE HOME DEPOT INC)
6570 Tecumseh Rd E, Windsor, ON, N8T 1E6
(519) 974-5420
Emp Here 150
SIC 5251 Hardware stores
Frank Blake

D-U-N-S 24-512-9374   (SL)
HOSPICE OF WINDSOR AND ESSEX COUNTY INC, THE
6038 Empress St, Windsor, ON, N8T 1B5
(519) 974-7100
Emp Here 80   *Sales* 10,676,720
SIC 8399 Social services, nec
Colleen Reaume

D-U-N-S 20-205-1525   (SL)
J B FOOD SERVICES INC
7605 Tecumseh Rd E, Windsor, ON, N8T 3H1
(519) 251-1125
Emp Here 40   *Sales* 33,423,080
SIC 5141 Groceries, general line
Bill Lattimer

D-U-N-S 25-310-9573   (BR)
MCDONALD'S RESTAURANTS OF CANADA LIMITED
MCDONALD'S
(*Suby of* MCDONALD'S CORPORATION)
7777 Tecumseh Rd E, Windsor, ON, N8T 1G3
(519) 945-4751
Emp Here 100
SIC 5812 Eating places

D-U-N-S 24-369-2386   (BR)
METRO ONTARIO INC
FOOD BASICS
(*Suby of* METRO INC)
2090 Lauzon Rd, Windsor, ON, N8T 2Z3
(519) 944-7335
Emp Here 120
SIC 5411 Grocery stores
Elaine Chatwood

D-U-N-S 24-851-2092   (SL)
PRISTINE LED INC
3215 Jefferson Blvd Suite 100, Windsor, ON, N8T 2W7

Emp Here 25   *Sales* 11,179,350
SIC 5063 Electrical apparatus and equipment
Bruce Melmer

D-U-N-S 20-201-1891   (HQ)
RE/MAX PREFERRED REALTY LTD
6505 Tecumseh Rd E Suite 1, Windsor, ON,

N8T 1E7
(519) 944-5955
Emp Here 75   *Sales* 64,927,795
SIC 6531 Real estate agents and managers
Glen Muir

D-U-N-S 25-925-5404   (BR)
RED LOBSTER HOSPITALITY LLC
RED LOBSTER RESTAURANTS
6575 Tecumseh Rd E, Windsor, ON, N8T 1E7
(519) 948-7677
Emp Here 90
SIC 5812 Eating places
Taltas Mike

D-U-N-S 24-302-2167   (SL)
ROSE CITY FORD SALES LIMITED
6333 Tecumseh Rd E, Windsor, ON, N8T 1E7
(519) 948-7800
Emp Here 73   *Sales* 45,937,440
SIC 5511 New and used car dealers
John Chisholm
William Chisholm
Sophia Chisholm

D-U-N-S 20-186-3677   (SL)
SKELLY, ROBERT E. LIMITED
CANADIAN TIRE
5415 Tecumseh Rd E, Windsor, ON, N8T 1C5
(519) 948-8111
Emp Here 100   *Sales* 62,928,000
SIC 5531 Auto and home supply stores
Robert E. Skelly
Bernice Skelly

D-U-N-S 20-702-8767   (SL)
SOLCZ GROUP INC
6555 Hawthorne Dr, Windsor, ON, N8T 3G6
(519) 974-5200
Emp Here 5   *Sales* 360,498,734
SIC 6712 Bank holding companies
Michael J Solcz
Martin Solcz
Leonard Solcz
Michael Solcz

D-U-N-S 20-051-3898   (HQ)
VALIANT CORPORATION
6555 Hawthorne Dr, Windsor, ON, N8T 3G6
(519) 974-5200
Sales 219,305,400
SIC 6712 Bank holding companies
Degui Mao
Tony Elias
Nick Sauro
Tao Liu
Yongliang Zhang

D-U-N-S 20-186-5920   (HQ)
VALIANT MACHINE & TOOL INC
VALIANT AUTOMATION & ASSEMBLY, DIV OF
6555 Hawthorne Dr, Windsor, ON, N8T 3G6
(519) 974-5200
Emp Here 300   *Sales* 184,978,920
SIC 3548 Welding apparatus
Martin Solcz
Anthony Elias
Tony Sauro
Leonard Solcz
Michael J. Solcz

D-U-N-S 24-876-6305   (SL)
VALIANT TOOL & MOLD INC
6775 Hawthorne Dr, Windsor, ON, N8T 3B8
(519) 251-4800
Emp Here 50   *Sales* 10,094,850
SIC 3089 Plastics products, nec
Tony Elias
Nick Sauro
Ze Chen
Tao Liu

D-U-N-S 25-504-1683   (BR)
VENTRA GROUP CO
VENTRA PLASTICS DIVISIONS
(*Suby of* FLEX-N-GATE LLC)
2800 Kew Dr, Windsor, ON, N8T 3C6

(519) 944-1102
Emp Here 250
SIC 3089 Plastics products, nec
Dave Richards

D-U-N-S 24-512-0472   (BR)
WAL-MART CANADA CORP
(*Suby of* WALMART INC.)
7100 Tecumseh Rd E Suite 3115, Windsor, ON, N8T 1E6
(519) 945-3065
Emp Here 150
SIC 5311 Department stores
Darel Porter

D-U-N-S 24-407-9265   (HQ)
WORLDWIDE SLEEP CENTRE LIMITED
WORLDWIDE MATTRESS OUTLET
2525 Jefferson Blvd, Windsor, ON, N8T 2W5
(519) 944-3552
Emp Here 12   *Sales* 11,517,000
SIC 5712 Furniture stores
David Turner

Windsor, ON N8W

D-U-N-S 24-560-5985   (HQ)
591182 ONTARIO LIMITED
WOLVERINE FREIGHT SYSTEM
2500 Airport Rd, Windsor, ON, N8W 5E7
(519) 966-8970
Sales 38,720,010
SIC 4212 Local trucking, without storage
Christopher John
Michael John

D-U-N-S 24-305-9052   (HQ)
ADVANCE BEAUTY SUPPLY LIMITED
ADVANCE BEAUTY & ESTHETICS SUPPLY
2979 Tecumseh Rd E, Windsor, ON, N8W 1G6
(519) 944-0904
Emp Here 14   *Sales* 11,875,650
SIC 5087 Service establishment equipment
Philip Rice

D-U-N-S 25-321-4324   (BR)
ALLIED SYSTEMS (CANADA) COMPANY
(*Suby of* ALLIED SYSTEMS HOLDINGS, INC.)
1790 Provincial Rd, Windsor, ON, N8W 5W3

Emp Here 100
SIC 4213 Trucking, except local
Ernie Godden

D-U-N-S 20-528-4024   (SL)
ANM INDUSTRIES (2005) INC
2500 Central Ave, Windsor, ON, N8W 4J5
(519) 258-2550
Emp Here 65   *Sales* 12,485,525
SIC 3471 Plating and polishing
Jerry Lev

D-U-N-S 24-195-5920   (SL)
BELYER INSURANCE LTD
EASYINSURE
(*Suby of* HELLMAN & FRIEDMAN LLC)
3390 Walker Rd Suite 300, Windsor, ON, N8W 3S1
(519) 915-4667
Emp Here 23   *Sales* 19,505,380
SIC 6411 Insurance agents, brokers, and service
Leendert Meyer
Grant Belanger

D-U-N-S 20-851-8803   (SL)
BUCKINGHAM REALTY (WINDSOR) LTD
4573 Tecumseh Rd E, Windsor, ON, N8W 1K6
(519) 948-8171
Emp Here 45   *Sales* 14,720,715
SIC 6531 Real estate agents and managers
Jason Paine
Stan Dunn

D-U-N-S 20-941-0786   (SL)
CAVALIER TOOL & MANUFACTURING LTD
3450 Wheelton Dr, Windsor, ON, N8W 5A7
(519) 944-2144
Emp Here 140   *Sales* 31,080,140
SIC 3544 Special dies, tools, jigs, and fixtures
Brian Bendig

D-U-N-S 20-812-0845   (SL)
CAW COMMUNITY CHILD CARE AND DE-VELOPMENTAL SERVICES INC
3450 Ypres Ave Suite 100, Windsor, ON, N8W 5K9

Emp Here 70   *Sales* 16,712,500
SIC 8611 Business associations
Anna Angelidis

D-U-N-S 24-966-4707   (HQ)
CENTOCO PLASTICS LIMITED
2450 Central Ave, Windsor, ON, N8W 4J3
(519) 948-2300
Sales 14,427,750
SIC 2499 Wood products, nec
Anthony Toldo

D-U-N-S 20-583-3874   (HQ)
CENTRAL STAMPINGS LIMITED
NARMCO GROUP
2525 Central Ave, Windsor, ON, N8W 4J6
(519) 945-1111
Emp Here 230   *Sales* 58,375,440
SIC 3469 Metal stampings, nec
John Rodzik
Donald Rodzik
Annette Trepanier

D-U-N-S 20-919-4278   (SL)
CLARICA LIFE INSURANCE COMPANY
3200 Deziel Dr Suite 508, Windsor, ON, N8W 5K8
(519) 974-3200
Emp Here 35   *Sales* 64,633,065
SIC 6311 Life insurance
Ralph Hanoski

D-U-N-S 24-964-5516   (SL)
COLONIAL TOOL GROUP INC
COLONIAL
(*Suby of* COLONIAL TOOL GROUP HOLD-INGS LIMITED)
1691 Walker Rd, Windsor, ON, N8W 3P1
(519) 253-2461
Emp Here 55   *Sales* 12,210,055
SIC 3541 Machine tools, Metal cutting type
Paul Thrasher
Brett Froats
Thomas Alterman

D-U-N-S 24-449-5094   (BR)
COMMUNITY LIVING WINDSOR
2840 Temple Dr, Windsor, ON, N8W 5J5
(519) 944-2464
Emp Here 80
SIC 8322 Individual and family services
Steve Shearer

D-U-N-S 24-320-6229   (SL)
CONTI ELECTRIC COMPANY OF CANADA
(*Suby of* CONTI CORPORATION)
2861 Temple Dr, Windsor, ON, N8W 5E5
(519) 250-8212
Emp Here 100
SIC 1731 Electrical work
John Conti

D-U-N-S 20-523-5968   (BR)
CORPORATION OF THE CITY OF WIND-SOR
ENVIRONMENTAL SERVICES DIVISION OF PUBLIC WORKS DEPARTMENT
(*Suby of* CORPORATION OF THE CITY OF WINDSOR)
3540 North Service Rd E, Windsor, ON, N8W 5X2
(519) 974-2277
Emp Here 120
SIC 4959 Sanitary services, nec

Ron Mcconnell

D-U-N-S 25-529-3060   (BR)
COSTCO WHOLESALE CANADA LTD
COSTCO
(*Suby of* COSTCO WHOLESALE CORPO-RATION)
4411 Walker Rd Suite 534, Windsor, ON, N8W 3T6
(519) 972-1899
Emp Here 200
SIC 5399 Miscellaneous general merchandise
Lee Baker

D-U-N-S 24-420-5662   (HQ)
CYPHER SYSTEMS GROUP INC
(*Suby of* HELLMAN & FRIEDMAN LLC)
3600 Rhodes Dr, Windsor, ON, N8W 5A4
(519) 945-4943
Sales 25,952,760
SIC 7371 Custom computer programming services
Brian Schwab
John Savage
Stephen Savage

D-U-N-S 24-024-8950   (HQ)
ELLWOOD SPECIALTY METALS COMPANY
ESM
(*Suby of* ELLWOOD GROUP, INC.)
3282 St Etienne Blvd, Windsor, ON, N8W 5E1
(519) 944-4411
Sales 24,259,264
SIC 5051 Metals service centers and offices
Robert Rizk
David Heath

D-U-N-S 24-121-1999   (BR)
FCA CANADA INC
CHRYSLER CANADA
(*Suby of* FIAT CHRYSLER AUTOMOBILES N.V.)
2410 Walker Rd, Windsor, ON, N8W 3P6
(519) 973-2000
Emp Here 330
SIC 4212 Local trucking, without storage
Fred Pernal

D-U-N-S 20-786-3895   (SL)
FOGOLAR FURLAN WINDSOR
FOGOLAR FURLAN CLUB
1800 North Service Rd E, Windsor, ON, N8W 1Y3
(519) 966-2230
Emp Here 80   *Sales* 11,430,320
SIC 8641 Civic and social associations
Ceasar Pecile
Lou Villalta

D-U-N-S 25-281-4926   (BR)
G4S SECURE SOLUTIONS (CANADA) LTD
(*Suby of* G4S PLC)
3372 Mannheim Way, Windsor, ON, N8W 5J9
(519) 255-1441
Emp Here 300
SIC 7381 Detective and armored car services
Robert Mailloux

D-U-N-S 24-361-5127   (BR)
GATES CANADA INC
GATES-WINDSOR OPERATIONS, DIV OF
(*Suby of* GATES INDUSTRIAL CORPORA-TION PLC)
3303 St Etienne Blvd, Windsor, ON, N8W 5B1
(519) 945-4200
Emp Here 150
SIC 3568 Power transmission equipment, nec
Bob Mcclellan

D-U-N-S 24-919-6825   (BR)
GENERAL MOTORS OF CANADA COM-PANY
WINDSOR TRANSMISSION PLANT
(*Suby of* GENERAL MOTORS COMPANY)
1550 Kildare Rd, Windsor, ON, N8W 2W4
(519) 255-4161
Emp Here 1,290
SIC 3714 Motor vehicle parts and accessories

▲ Public Company   ■ Public Company Family Member   **HQ** Headquarters   **BR** Branch   **SL** Single Location

Lewis Campbell

D-U-N-S 24-779-1601   (HQ)
GENTHERM CANADA ULC
(Suby of GENTHERM INCORPORATED)
3445 Wheelton Dr, Windsor, ON, N8W 5A6
(519) 948-4808
Sales 22,384,300
SIC 3714 Motor vehicle parts and accessories
Thomas Liedl
Vincent Sebastiano

D-U-N-S 25-249-0933   (BR)
**GREATER ESSEX COUNTY DISTRICT
SCHOOL BOARD**
WF HERMAN SCHOOL
*(Suby of GREATER ESSEX COUNTY DIS-
TRICT SCHOOL BOARD)*
1930 Rossini Blvd, Windsor, ON, N8W 4P5
(519) 944-4700
Emp Here 80
SIC 8211 Elementary and secondary schools
Thomas Halliwill

D-U-N-S 24-654-5297   (HQ)
GROUND EFFECTS LTD
INTERNATIONAL SEATING & DECOR
(Suby of OLYMPUS PARTNERS, L.P.)
4505 Rhodes Dr, Windsor, ON, N8W 5R8
(519) 944-3800
Emp Here 130   *Sales* 196,323,750
SIC 3714 Motor vehicle parts and accessories
James Scott
Mark Kupko

D-U-N-S 20-307-3416   (BR)
GROUND EFFECTS LTD
INTERNATIONAL SEATING & DECOR
(Suby of OLYMPUS PARTNERS, L.P.)
2775 St Etienne Blvd, Windsor, ON, N8W 5B1
(519) 944-3800
Emp Here 100
SIC 3714 Motor vehicle parts and accessories
Scott Hebert

D-U-N-S 24-335-5984   (SL)
HBPO CANADA INC
(Suby of HELLA GMBH & CO. KGAA)
2570 Central Ave, Windsor, ON, N8W 4J5
(519) 251-4300
Emp Here 115   *Sales* 33,447,750
SIC 3711 Motor vehicles and car bodies
Emmanuel Boudon
Richard Ling
John Bulger
Jen Keller
Martin Schueler

D-U-N-S 24-407-2732   (HQ)
HOLLAND CLEANING SOLUTIONS LTD
4590 Rhodes Dr, Windsor, ON, N8W 5C2
(519) 948-4373
Emp Here 20   *Sales* 18,988,970
SIC 5169 Chemicals and allied products, nec
Michael Shalhoub

D-U-N-S 24-361-7326   (BR)
HOME DEPOT OF CANADA INC
HOME DEPOT
(Suby of THE HOME DEPOT INC)
1925 Division Rd, Windsor, ON, N8W 1Z7
(519) 967-3700
Emp Here 100
SIC 5251 Hardware stores
Bill Lennie

D-U-N-S 20-750-5587   (SL)
INSPECTIONAIR GAUGE LIMITED
3298 Riberdy Rd, Windsor, ON, N8W 3T9
(519) 966-1232
Emp Here 50   *Sales* 12,828,100
SIC 3825 Instruments to measure electricity
Donald C Tregenza
Hazel Tregenza

D-U-N-S 24-624-3323   (SL)
KAUTEX CORPORATION
KAUTEX TEXTRON

(Suby of TEXTRON INC.)
2701 Kautex Dr, Windsor, ON, N8W 5B1
(519) 974-6656
Emp Here 500   *Sales* 145,425,000
SIC 3714 Motor vehicle parts and accessories
Klaus Konig
Larry Reid

D-U-N-S 20-387-8269   (SL)
KB COMPONENTS CANADA INC
(Suby of VARI-FORM GROUP, LLC)
2900 St Etienne Blvd, Windsor, ON, N8W 5E6
(519) 974-6596
Emp Here 65   *Sales* 11,618,035
SIC 8711 Engineering services
David Ulrich

D-U-N-S 25-973-6304   (SL)
KOOLINI ITALIAN CUISINI LIMITED
KOOLINI EATERY
1520 Tecumseh Rd E, Windsor, ON, N8W 1C4
(519) 254-5665
Emp Here 150   *Sales* 6,827,850
SIC 5812 Eating places
Leo Deluca

D-U-N-S 25-482-1465   (HQ)
KS CENTOCO WHEEL CORPORATION
2450 Central Ave, Windsor, ON, N8W 4J3
(519) 974-2727
Sales 53,510,820
SIC 3429 Hardware, nec
Anthony P Toldo

D-U-N-S 24-556-6187   (HQ)
LASER TRANSPORT INC
3380 Wheelton Dr, Windsor, ON, N8W 5A7
(519) 974-3435
Sales 26,741,780
SIC 4213 Trucking, except local
Angelo Pernasilici

D-U-N-S 20-997-8233   (BR)
LOBLAWS INC
REAL CANADIAN SUPERSTORE
(Suby of LOBLAW COMPANIES LIMITED)
4371 Walker Rd Suite 567, Windsor, ON, N8W
3T6
(519) 972-8335
Emp Here 330
SIC 5411 Grocery stores
Paul Boileau

D-U-N-S 20-185-7828   (HQ)
MANZ CONTRACTING SERVICES INC
MANZ DECOR CENTRE
2680 Temple Dr, Windsor, ON, N8W 5J5
(519) 974-2899
Sales 12,693,525
SIC 1721 Painting and paper hanging
Patricia Batten
Dave Batten

D-U-N-S 25-318-1739   (BR)
**MCDONALD'S   RESTAURANTS   OF
CANADA LIMITED**
MCDONALD'S 8046
(Suby of MCDONALD'S CORPORATION)
2780 Tecumseh Rd E, Windsor, ON, N8W 1G3
(519) 945-3634
Emp Here 85
SIC 5812 Eating places
George A. Cohon

D-U-N-S 20-192-1157   (HQ)
PANGEO CORPORATION
(Suby of PANGEO HOLDINGS LTD)
3000 Temple Dr, Windsor, ON, N8W 5J6
(519) 737-1678
Sales 12,747,525
SIC 5013 Motor vehicle supplies and new
parts
Brian Pan

D-U-N-S 24-372-9667   (HQ)
PANGEO HOLDINGS LTD
3000 Temple Dr, Windsor, ON, N8W 5J6

(519) 737-1678
Emp Here 1   *Sales* 365,509,000
SIC 6712 Bank holding companies
Brian Pan

D-U-N-S 24-307-4960   (HQ)
PERFORMANCE FORD SALES INC
(Suby of 1495754 ONTARIO LTD)
1150 Provincial Rd, Windsor, ON, N8W 5W2
(519) 972-6500
Sales 41,532,480
SIC 5511 New and used car dealers
Talal Rafih

D-U-N-S 25-690-1133   (SL)
PINNACLE CHRYSLER JEEP DODGE INC
2300 Tecumseh Rd E, Windsor, ON, N8W 1E5
(519) 254-1196
Emp Here 75   *Sales* 47,196,000
SIC 5511 New and used car dealers
Terry Rafih
Munawwar Ali

D-U-N-S 20-916-1848   (SL)
PROVINCIAL CHRYSLER LTD
1001 Provincial Rd, Windsor, ON, N8W 5V9
(519) 250-5500
Emp Here 80   *Sales* 24,903,900
SIC 5511 New and used car dealers
Sherry Levasseur

D-U-N-S 20-641-1709   (BR)
PUROLATOR INC
(Suby of GOVERNMENT OF CANADA)
4520 North Service Rd E, Windsor, ON, N8W
5X2
(519) 945-1363
Emp Here 75
SIC 7389 Business services, nec
Barbara Dinning

D-U-N-S 24-390-8980   (SL)
RODFAM HOLDINGS LIMITED
2575 Airport Rd, Windsor, ON, N8W 1Z4
(519) 969-3350
Emp Here 1,500   *Sales* 548,263,500
SIC 6712 Bank holding companies
Donald Rodzik
John Rodzik

D-U-N-S 24-727-5787   (HQ)
SERVICE MOLD + AEROSPACE INC
2711 St Etienne Blvd, Windsor, ON, N8W 5B1
(519) 945-3344
Sales 12,432,056
SIC 3544 Special dies, tools, jigs, and fixtures
Martin Schuurman
Vicki Schuurman

D-U-N-S 20-522-9508   (SL)
**SMARTCOVERAGE INSURANCE AGENCY
INC**
3600 Rhodes Dr, Windsor, ON, N8W 5A4
(519) 974-7067
Emp Here 80   *Sales* 147,732,720
SIC 6331 Fire, marine, and casualty insurance
John Savage

D-U-N-S 20-411-6255   (SL)
SPIROL INDUSTRIES LIMITED
*(Suby of SPIROL INTERNATIONAL HOLD-
ING CORPORATION)*
3103 St Etienne Blvd, Windsor, ON, N8W 5B1
(519) 974-3334
Emp Here 71   *Sales* 18,338,383
SIC 3429 Hardware, nec
Thomas Buchta
Hans Koehl
Jeffrey Koehl

D-U-N-S 20-186-4782   (SL)
TAMAR BUILDING PRODUCTS (1981) LTD
3957 Walker Rd, Windsor, ON, N8W 3T4
(519) 969-7060
Emp Here 43   *Sales* 18,123,000
SIC 5039 Construction materials, nec
Gary Gascoigne
Dorene M. Brown

D-U-N-S 24-181-8975   (SL)
TAMWIN HOLDINGS LIMITED
3957 Walker Rd, Windsor, ON, N8W 3T4
(519) 969-7060
Emp Here 40   *Sales* 10,462,120
SIC 6712 Bank holding companies
William Gascoigne

D-U-N-S 24-252-9621   (BR)
VALUE VILLAGE STORES, INC
VALUE VILLAGE
(Suby of SAVERS, INC.)
4322 Walker Rd, Windsor, ON, N8W 3T5
(519) 250-0199
Emp Here 100
SIC 5399 Miscellaneous general merchandise
Ken Alterman

D-U-N-S 25-637-1725   (HQ)
WATSON, T.J. ENTERPRISES INC
TIM HORTONS
4255 Tecumseh Rd E, Windsor, ON, N8W 1K2
(519) 250-0955
Emp Here 5   *Sales* 18,655,600
SIC 5812 Eating places
Tim Watson
Pat Hayes

D-U-N-S 24-470-8723   (SL)
**WINDSOR ESSEX COUNTY HUMANE SO-
CIETY**
1375 Provincial Rd, Windsor, ON, N8W 5V8
(519) 966-5751
Emp Here 27   *Sales* 10,730,178
SIC 8699 Membership organizations, nec
Melanie Coulter
Kelvin Leddy

D-U-N-S 25-361-8979   (BR)
WINDSOR MOLD INC
(Suby of 873740 ONTARIO INC)
1628 Durham Pl, Windsor, ON, N8W 2Z8
(519) 258-7300
Emp Here 250
SIC 3544 Special dies, tools, jigs, and fixtures

D-U-N-S 25-161-9052   (SL)
WINDSOR PENNYSAVER
WEBCO PRINTING
4525 Rhodes Dr Unit 400, Windsor, ON, N8W
5R8

Emp Here 80   *Sales* 13,342,859
SIC 2741 Miscellaneous publishing
Dave Calibaba

D-U-N-S 20-771-5319   (HQ)
WINDSOR REGIONAL HOSPITAL
1995 Lens Ave, Windsor, ON, N8W 1L9
(519) 254-5577
Emp Here 1,300   *Sales* 244,376,000
SIC 8062 General medical and surgical hospi-
tals
David Musyj
Gay Wrye
Daniel Germain

D-U-N-S 20-769-7066   (SL)
WINDSOR STAR PRINT PLANT
3000 Starway Ave, Windsor, ON, N8W 5P1
(519) 255-5730
Emp Here 200   *Sales* 32,805,400
SIC 2759 Commercial printing, nec
Doug Shillington

Windsor, ON N8X

D-U-N-S 25-221-4655   (SL)
658771 ONTARIO LTD
REMARK FARMS
2727 Howard Ave, Windsor, ON, N8X 3X4
(519) 972-1440
Emp Here 90   *Sales* 26,412,930
SIC 5431 Fruit and vegetable markets
Cliff Remark

Paul Remark

D-U-N-S 24-874-8485   (SL)
882819 ONTARIO LTD
MORRICE TRANSPORTATION
3049 Devon Dr, Windsor, ON, N8X 4L3
(519) 250-8008
Emp Here 210   *Sales* 43,198,260
SIC 4213 Trucking, except local
Richard C Morrice

D-U-N-S 24-214-9672   (HQ)
944746 ONTARIO INC
WHEEL COVERS UNLIMITED
2594 Howard Ave, Windsor, ON, N8X 3W5
(519) 966-2006
Sales 13,214,880
SIC 5531 Auto and home supply stores
Paul Soulliere
Rose Soulliere
Marie Soulliere

D-U-N-S 24-974-2495   (HQ)
ALL-RISKS INSURANCE BROKERS LIMITED
1591 Ouellette Ave, Windsor, ON, N8X 1K5
(519) 253-6376
Emp Here 15   *Sales* 27,137,920
SIC 6411 Insurance agents, brokers, and service
Brian Lazarus
Paul Lemmon

D-U-N-S 20-976-4984   (HQ)
ANCHOR DANLY INC
(*Suby of* HIDDEN HARBOR CAPITAL PARTNERS, LLC)
2590 Ouellette Ave, Windsor, ON, N8X 1L7
(519) 966-4431
Emp Here 160   *Sales* 235,936,680
SIC 3544 Special dies, tools, jigs, and fixtures
Paul Brisebois

D-U-N-S 25-639-2515   (SL)
ASSEMBLY INTERNATIONAL INC
3233 Devon Dr, Windsor, ON, N8X 4L5

Emp Here 75   *Sales* 27,316,125
SIC 5013 Motor vehicle supplies and new parts
Chain Sandhu

D-U-N-S 20-184-7126   (SL)
BORDER STEEL LIMITED
3209 Devon Dr, Windsor, ON, N8X 4L5
(519) 966-0760
Emp Here 20   *Sales* 20,006,780
SIC 5051 Metals service centers and offices
Terry Tingle
Matthew Tingle
Gary Tingle

D-U-N-S 24-311-8341   (SL)
BRENTWOOD FOUNDATION
2335 Dougall Ave Suite 42, Windsor, ON, N8X 1S9
(519) 946-3115
Emp Here 45   *Sales* 17,883,630
SIC 8699 Membership organizations, nec
Don Russell

D-U-N-S 24-365-9203   (SL)
C.J.C. COULTER INVESTMENTS 2006 INC
COULTER'S FURNITURE
1324 Windsor Ave, Windsor, ON, N8X 3L9
(519) 253-7422
Emp Here 50   *Sales* 11,517,000
SIC 5712 Furniture stores
Craig Coulter
Charles J Coulter
June Coulter

D-U-N-S 20-293-0731   (SL)
CANADA AGRIGROW
1243 Elm Ave, Windsor, ON, N8X 2B6
(519) 915-8882
Emp Here 15   *Sales* 11,137,800
SIC 5191 Farm supplies

Mohamed Mahmoud
Ehab Elsayed
Hanan Elsayed
Hagar Elsayed

D-U-N-S 24-764-6482   (SL)
CANADIAN CAPSULE EQUIPMENT LIMITED
2510 Ouellette Ave Suite 102, Windsor, ON, N8X 1L4
(519) 966-1122
Emp Here 60   *Sales* 13,320,060
SIC 3559 Special industry machinery, nec
William Hreceniuk
Striana Victorov
Herman Victorov

D-U-N-S 24-479-1901   (HQ)
CANADIAN MENTAL HEALTH ASSOCIATION, WINDSOR-ESSEX COUNTY BRANCH
CMHA
1400 Windsor Ave, Windsor, ON, N8X 3L9
(519) 255-7440
Sales 16,064,600
SIC 8011 Offices and clinics of medical doctors
Pamela Hines

D-U-N-S 20-290-1133   (SL)
CANARX SERVICES INC
235 Eugenie St W Suite 105d, Windsor, ON, N8X 2X7
(519) 973-1735
Emp Here 60   *Sales* 66,320,700
SIC 5122 Drugs, proprietaries, and sundries

D-U-N-S 24-891-2990   (HQ)
DEERBROOK REALTY INC
59 Eugenie St E, Windsor, ON, N8X 2X9
(519) 972-1000
Emp Here 71   *Sales* 31,416,675
SIC 6531 Real estate agents and managers
Kelly Zlotnik

D-U-N-S 25-711-7325   (BR)
EXTENDICARE (CANADA) INC
PARAMED HOME HEALTH CARE
(*Suby of* EXTENDICARE INC)
880 North Service Rd E Suite 301, Windsor, ON, N8X 3J5
(519) 966-5200
Emp Here 300
SIC 8059 Nursing and personal care, nec
Paula Thomas

D-U-N-S 24-337-3102   (BR)
FGL SPORTS LTD
SPORT CHEK
(*Suby of* CANADIAN TIRE CORPORATION, LIMITED)
3100 Howard Ave, Windsor, ON, N8X 3Y8
(519) 972-8379
Emp Here 85
SIC 5941 Sporting goods and bicycle shops
Karl Bierworth

D-U-N-S 20-185-2738   (SL)
FREED STORAGE LIMITED
FREED'S OF WINDSOR
1526 Ottawa St, Windsor, ON, N8X 2G5
(519) 258-6532
Emp Here 65   *Sales* 11,660,740
SIC 5611 Men's and boys' clothing stores
Gerald Freed
Alan Orman
Keith White

D-U-N-S 24-325-9467   (SL)
GAUTHIER, VINCE R. DRUGS LTD
SHOPPERS DRUG MART
500 Tecumseh Rd E, Windsor, ON, N8X 2S2
(519) 253-1115
Emp Here 79   *Sales* 19,301,912
SIC 5912 Drug stores and proprietary stores
Vince Gauthier

D-U-N-S 25-056-5090   (SL)

GRAY, TOM BUILDING CENTRES INC
GRAY HOME HARDWARE BUILDING CENTRES
700 Tecumseh Rd W, Windsor, ON, N8X 1H2
(519) 254-1143
Emp Here 54   *Sales* 14,453,208
SIC 5211 Lumber and other building materials
Thomas Gray
Carol Gray

D-U-N-S 20-590-6048   (BR)
GREATER ESSEX COUNTY DISTRICT SCHOOL BOARD
W C KENNEDY COLLEGIATE INSTITUTE
(*Suby of* GREATER ESSEX COUNTY DISTRICT SCHOOL BOARD)
245 Tecumseh Rd E, Windsor, ON, N8X 2R2
(519) 254-6475
Emp Here 80
SIC 8211 Elementary and secondary schools
A Safranyos

D-U-N-S 25-106-1057   (HQ)
HALLER GROUP INC
1537 Mcdougall St, Windsor, ON, N8X 3M9
(519) 254-4635
Sales 10,483,875
SIC 6712 Bank holding companies
Mark Haller
Vergil Costa

D-U-N-S 25-636-1254   (BR)
HOWELL DATA SYSTEMS INC
(*Suby of* HOWELL DATA SYSTEMS INC)
250 Tecumseh Rd E, Windsor, ON, N8X 2R3

Emp Here 200
SIC 5999 Miscellaneous retail stores, nec
Chuck Chrapko

D-U-N-S 20-184-7209   (BR)
HUDSON'S BAY COMPANY
THE BAY
(*Suby of* HUDSON'S BAY COMPANY)
3030 Howard Ave, Windsor, ON, N8X 4T3
(519) 966-4666
Emp Here 300
SIC 5311 Department stores
Jay Williams

D-U-N-S 25-976-2201   (SL)
IGB AUTOMOTIVE LTD
3090 Marentette Ave, Windsor, ON, N8X 4G2
(519) 250-5777
Emp Here 352   *Sales* 102,379,200
SIC 3714 Motor vehicle parts and accessories
Josef Hilmer
Tom Fortushniok

D-U-N-S 20-329-5746   (SL)
INTEGRITY HD INC
3126 Devon Dr, Windsor, ON, N8X 4L2
(519) 946-1400
Emp Here 52   *Sales* 11,544,052
SIC 3545 Machine tool accessories
Zeno Hadadean
David Schild
Paul Digiovanni

D-U-N-S 20-185-6051   (SL)
KAPCO TOOL & DIE LIMITED
3200 Devon Dr, Windsor, ON, N8X 4L4
(519) 966-0320
Emp Here 68   *Sales* 15,096,068
SIC 3544 Special dies, tools, jigs, and fixtures
Mat Rodvik

D-U-N-S 24-977-1908   (SL)
MID SOUTH CONTRACTORS ULC
(*Suby of* MOTOR CITY ELECTRIC CO.)
3110 Devon Dr, Windsor, ON, N8X 4L2
(519) 966-6163
Emp Here 120   *Sales* 28,261,080
SIC 1731 Electrical work
Dale Wieczorek
Denise Hodgins

D-U-N-S 20-527-6079   (SL)

MOXIE'S CLASSIC GRILL
3100 Howard Ave Unit 20, Windsor, ON, N8X 3Y8
(519) 250-3390
Emp Here 150   *Sales* 6,995,850
SIC 5812 Eating places
Jason Dolsen

D-U-N-S 24-384-0746   (HQ)
PBL INSURANCE LIMITED
PBL
(*Suby of* NFP INTERMEDIATE HOLDINGS B CORP.)
150 Ouellette Pl Suite 100, Windsor, ON, N8X 1L9
(519) 254-1633
Emp Here 30   *Sales* 972,951,320
SIC 6411 Insurance agents, brokers, and service
Michael P Robinson
Albert Weerts
Timothy A Fuerth
Mandeep Singh
John Boynton
Chipman A Purdom

D-U-N-S 20-786-1774   (SL)
PEDLER, BOB REAL ESTATE LIMITED
280 Edinborough St, Windsor, ON, N8X 3C4
(519) 966-3750
Emp Here 46   *Sales* 15,047,842
SIC 6531 Real estate agents and managers
Bob Pedler
Greig Pedler

D-U-N-S 24-802-8862   (HQ)
PETER ANTHONY DESIGNS INC
2700 Ouellette Ave, Windsor, ON, N8X 1L7
(519) 969-7332
Sales 15,432,200
SIC 2599 Furniture and fixtures, nec
Anthony G Toldo

D-U-N-S 20-995-1305   (BR)
PIC GROUP LTD, THE
(*Suby of* ARDIAN HOLDING)
1303 Mcdougall St, Windsor, ON, N8X 3M6
(519) 252-1611
Emp Here 75
SIC 7549 Automotive services, nec
Neil Taylor

D-U-N-S 20-186-4907   (HQ)
TEPPERMAN, N. LIMITED
TEPPERMAN'S
2595 Ouellette Ave, Windsor, ON, N8X 4V8
(519) 969-9700
Emp Here 1   *Sales* 80,010,900
SIC 5712 Furniture stores
William Tepperman
Andrew Tepperman
Noah Tepperman
Nelly Tedesco
Michael Horrobin
Rochelle Tepperman

D-U-N-S 25-367-8056   (HQ)
THYSSENKRUPP SUPPLY CHAIN SERVICES CA, INC
THYSSENKRUPP INDUSTRIAL SERVICES CANADA
(*Suby of* THYSSENKRUPP AG)
2491 Ouellette Ave, Windsor, ON, N8X 1L5
(519) 977-8420
Emp Here 50   *Sales* 14,399,420
SIC 4225 General warehousing and storage
Brian Diephuis

D-U-N-S 20-186-5151   (SL)
TITAN TOOL & DIE LIMITED
2801 Howard Ave, Windsor, ON, N8X 3Y1
(519) 966-1234
Emp Here 103   *Sales* 10,150,380
SIC 3469 Metal stampings, nec
Jozsef Szecsei
Darlene Szecsei-Albano

D-U-N-S 24-259-1622   (SL)

UNIVERSAL HEALTH PRODUCTS
635 Tecumseh Rd W, Windsor, ON, N8X 1H4
(519) 258-6717
Emp Here 32   *Sales* 14,309,568
SIC 5047 Medical and hospital equipment
So Abiad

D-U-N-S 20-564-4524   (BR)
VENTRA GROUP CO
VELTRI HOWARD DIV
(*Suby of* FLEX-N-GATE LLC)
1425 Howard Ave, Windsor, ON, N8X 5C9
(519) 258-3509
Emp Here 189
SIC 3465 Automotive stampings
Perry Silvaggi

D-U-N-S 24-326-3949   (HQ)
WFS ENTERPRISES INC
(*Suby of* W.W. GRAINGER, INC.)
730 North Service Rd E, Windsor, ON, N8X 3J3
(519) 966-2202
Emp Here 1   *Sales* 91,693,240
SIC 5085 Industrial supplies
Richard C Thurston
Frank Brull
Fernand Mireault
David Marcon
James R Cornies
Leo Viselli
Thomas Hyatt
David Manders
Mark Rennison

D-U-N-S 20-186-7520   (HQ)
WFS LTD
(*Suby of* W.W. GRAINGER, INC.)
730 North Service Rd E, Windsor, ON, N8X 3J3
(519) 966-2202
Emp Here 60   *Sales* 121,932,500
SIC 5085 Industrial supplies
Richard Thurston

D-U-N-S 25-929-8933   (SL)
WINDSOR ESSEX COMMUNITY HEALTH CENTRE
WE CHC
1361 Ouellette Ave Unit 101, Windsor, ON, N8X 1J6
(519) 253-8481
Emp Here 125   *Sales* 9,599,000
SIC 8322 Individual and family services
Kathryn Hengl
William Mcclounie
Toni Scislowski
Elaine Clark
Tina Heinrichs
Bob Fetherston
Helen Bolton
John Mowat

D-U-N-S 24-874-7511   (HQ)
WINDSOR FAMILY CREDIT UNION LIMITED
WFCU
3000 Marentette Ave, Windsor, ON, N8X 4G2
(519) 974-1181
Emp Here 20   *Sales* 15,156,100
SIC 6062 State credit unions
Martin Komsa
Martin D Gillis
Eddie Francis

D-U-N-S 20-731-9245   (BR)
WINDSOR MOLD INC
EMRICK PLASTICS, DIV OF
(*Suby of* 873740 ONTARIO INC)
310 Ellis St E, Windsor, ON, N8X 2H2
(519) 258-3211
Emp Here 100
SIC 3089 Plastics products, nec
Tom Herm

D-U-N-S 20-654-4095   (BR)
WINDSOR-ESSEX CATHOLIC DISTRICT SCHOOL BOARD, THE

CATHOLIC CENTRAL SECONDARY SCHOOL
(*Suby of* WINDSOR-ESSEX CATHOLIC DISTRICT SCHOOL BOARD, THE)
441 Tecumseh Rd E, Windsor, ON, N8X 2R7
(519) 256-3171
Emp Here 100
SIC 8211 Elementary and secondary schools
Sherrilynn Colley-Vegh

D-U-N-S 24-665-3232   (SL)
WOODALL CONSTRUCTION CO. LIMITED
620 North Service Rd E, Windsor, ON, N8X 3J3
(519) 966-3381
Emp Here 25   *Sales* 10,568,425
SIC 1541 Industrial buildings and warehouses
Frederick David Woodall
John Woodall
Robert Alan Woodall

D-U-N-S 25-300-6829   (BR)
WORKPLACE SAFETY & INSURANCE BOARD, THE
WSIB
(*Suby of* WORKPLACE SAFETY & INSURANCE BOARD, THE)
2485 Ouellette Ave, Windsor, ON, N8X 1L5
(800) 387-0750
Emp Here 150
SIC 6331 Fire, marine, and casualty insurance
Dane Clark

D-U-N-S 20-186-9286   (HQ)
ZALEV BROTHERS CO
FERROUS PROCESSING & TRADING
200 Grand Marais Rd E, Windsor, ON, N8X 3H2
(519) 966-0620
Sales 52,054,200
SIC 5093 Scrap and waste materials
Howard Sherman
Joanie Streicher

Windsor, ON N8Y

D-U-N-S 25-638-9693   (SL)
AMBASSADOR BUILDING MAINTENANCE LIMITED
628 Monmouth Rd, Windsor, ON, N8Y 3L1
(519) 255-1107
Emp Here 170   *Sales* 5,434,560
SIC 7349 Building maintenance services, nec
Karin Krouger

D-U-N-S 24-765-3236   (SL)
AMICA AT WINDSOR
4909 Riverside Dr E Suite 207, Windsor, ON, N8Y 0A4
(519) 948-5500
Emp Here 80   *Sales* 17,669,680
SIC 6513 Apartment building operators
Lisa Rufo

D-U-N-S 20-071-8307   (BR)
BAYSHORE HEALTHCARE LTD.
BAYSHORE HEALTHCARE LTD
(*Suby of* BAYSHORE HEALTHCARE LTD.)
1275 Walker Rd Suite 10, Windsor, ON, N8Y 4X9
(519) 973-5411
Emp Here 225
SIC 8082 Home health care services
Mike Thoms

D-U-N-S 24-946-5428   (HQ)
CHAMPION PRODUCTS CORP
2601 Wyandotte St E, Windsor, ON, N8Y 0A5
(519) 252-5414
Emp Here 50   *Sales* 32,737,770
SIC 5113 Industrial and personal service paper
Ashok Sood
Amit Sood

D-U-N-S 20-184-8769   (HQ)
CHECKER INDUSTRIAL LTD
3345 Wyandotte St E, Windsor, ON, N8Y 1E9
(519) 258-2022
Emp Here 60   *Sales* 33,251,820
SIC 5085 Industrial supplies
William Mechanic
Kenn Morris

D-U-N-S 20-185-1987   (SL)
ESSEX TERMINAL RAILWAY COMPANY, THE
1601 Lincoln Rd, Windsor, ON, N8Y 2J3
(519) 973-8222
Emp Here 81   *Sales* 32,338,602
SIC 4013 Switching and terminal services

D-U-N-S 20-710-5771   (BR)
GREATER ESSEX COUNTY DISTRICT SCHOOL BOARD
WALKER VILLE SECONDARY SCHOOL
(*Suby of* GREATER ESSEX COUNTY DISTRICT SCHOOL BOARD)
2100 Richmond St, Windsor, ON, N8Y 1L4
(519) 252-6514
Emp Here 80
SIC 8211 Elementary and secondary schools
J. Proctor

D-U-N-S 25-340-8926   (HQ)
GRECO ALUMINUM RAILINGS LTD
ALUMA-FENCE
3255 Wyandotte St E, Windsor, ON, N8Y 1E9
(519) 966-4210
Emp Here 1   *Sales* 15,366,800
SIC 3446 Architectural Metalwork
Dino Aleo
Larry Greco

D-U-N-S 20-338-3849   (HQ)
HEARN INDUSTRIAL SERVICES INC
2480 Seminole St, Windsor, ON, N8Y 1X3
(226) 674-3200
Emp Here 40   *Sales* 23,656,190
SIC 4225 General warehousing and storage
Bradley Hearn
Donald Hearn
Steven Hearn

D-U-N-S 20-186-6373   (HQ)
HIRAM WALKER & SONS LIMITED
(*Suby of* PERNOD RICARD)
2072 Riverside Dr E, Windsor, ON, N8Y 4S5
(519) 254-5171
Emp Here 350   *Sales* 243,692,500
SIC 2085 Distilled and blended liquors
Roland P Driscoll
Thierry R J Pourchette
Marc Valencia
Sharon Mayers
Garry Quick
Frederick Villain
Katherine Anne Mcleod
Claude Boulay
Philippe A X Dreano
Paul G Holub

D-U-N-S 20-185-6523   (SL)
L-K METAL PRODUCTS CO. LIMITED
1595 Lincoln Rd, Windsor, ON, N8Y 2J3
(519) 256-1861
Emp Here 31   *Sales* 13,862,394
SIC 5075 Warm air heating and air conditioning
Silver Leach
Margaret Leach

D-U-N-S 20-349-9561   (SL)
LEGACY PERSONNEL SOLUTIONS INC
2480 Seminole St, Windsor, ON, N8Y 1X3
(519) 419-5073
Emp Here 49   *Sales* 11,611,530
SIC 7361 Employment agencies
Lisa Hearn

D-U-N-S 24-425-2987   (HQ)
MORTERM LIMITED

1601 Lincoln Rd, Windsor, ON, N8Y 2J3
(519) 973-8200
Sales 27,560,680
SIC 4491 Marine cargo handling

D-U-N-S 20-814-7723   (BR)
SUNRISE NORTH SENIOR LIVING LTD
(*Suby of* WELLTOWER INC.)
5065 Riverside Dr E Suite 203, Windsor, ON, N8Y 5B3
(519) 974-5858
Emp Here 85
SIC 8059 Nursing and personal care, nec
Robin Naimane

D-U-N-S 24-380-3686   (SL)
VALCO MANUFACTURING INC
1235 St Luke Rd, Windsor, ON, N8Y 4W7
(519) 971-9666
Emp Here 78   *Sales* 17,316,078
SIC 3541 Machine tools, Metal cutting type
Ze Chen
Tao Liu
Tony Elias
Nick Sauro

D-U-N-S 25-635-8011   (HQ)
WINDSOR-ESSEX CHILDREN'S AID SOCIETY
WE-CAS
1671 Riverside Dr E, Windsor, ON, N8Y 5B5
(519) 252-1171
Sales 44,927,138
SIC 8322 Individual and family services
William Bevan
Michael Lockbaum
Kelly Gherasim

Windsor, ON N9A

D-U-N-S 20-524-2527   (SL)
1118528 ONTARIO INC
KELCOM TELEMESSAGING
1172 Goyeau St, Windsor, ON, N9A 1J1
(519) 977-5757
Emp Here 27   *Sales* 11,974,230
SIC 7389 Business services, nec
Paul Kerry

D-U-N-S 20-552-7539   (BR)
A.P. PLASMAN INC
A.P. PLASMAN INC.
(*Suby of* APP HOLDINGS LP)
5265 Outer Dr, Windsor, ON, N9A 6J3
(519) 737-9602
Emp Here 400
SIC 3089 Plastics products, nec
David Wiskell

D-U-N-S 25-362-8226   (BR)
A.P. PLASMAN INC
A.P. PLASMAN INC.
(*Suby of* APP HOLDINGS LP)
5265 Outer Dr Suite 2, Windsor, ON, N9A 6J3
(519) 737-9602
Emp Here 250
SIC 3089 Plastics products, nec
David Wiskel

D-U-N-S 20-190-1324   (HQ)
A.P. PLASMAN INC
BUILD-A-MOLD, DIV OF
(*Suby of* APP HOLDINGS LP)
5245 Burke St, Windsor, ON, N9A 6J3
(519) 737-6984
Emp Here 100   *Sales* 262,693,200
SIC 3089 Plastics products, nec
David Wiskel
Tony Romanello
Jeff Rose
Mila Lucio
Jason Keys
Tim Berezowski

D-U-N-S 24-150-5911   (SL)

ABSOLUTE TOOL TECHNOLOGIES INC
5455 Outer Dr, Windsor, ON, N9A 6J3
(519) 737-9428
Emp Here 53   *Sales* 11,766,053
SIC 3544 Special dies, tools, jigs, and fixtures
Denis Comartin
Jeffrey Pillon
Anthony Piazza
Gietano Scalia

D-U-N-S 20-117-7578   (BR)
ACTIVE INDUSTRIAL SOLUTIONS INC
(*Suby of* ACTIVE INDUSTRIAL SOLUTIONS
INC)
5250 Pulleyblank St, Windsor, ON, N9A 6J3

Emp Here 175
SIC 3544 Special dies, tools, jigs, and fixtures
Mike Bragagnolo

D-U-N-S 25-393-9334   (HQ)
ACTIVE INDUSTRIAL SOLUTIONS INC
ACTIVE BURGESS MOULD & DESIGN
2155 North Talbot Rd Suite 3, Windsor, ON,
N9A 6J3
(519) 737-1341
Emp Here 250   *Sales* 98,306,950
SIC 3544 Special dies, tools, jigs, and fixtures
Michael Bragagnolo
Donald Jackson
Randy Levine
Catherine Herring

D-U-N-S 20-373-2235   (BR)
ADVANTAGE ENGINEERING INC
(*Suby of* 1147048 ONTARIO LIMITED)
2030 North Talbot Rd, Windsor, ON, N9A 6J3
(519) 737-7535
Emp Here 200
SIC 3089 Plastics products, nec
Mark Rauth

D-U-N-S 24-215-9499   (BR)
BASF CANADA INC
(*Suby of* BASF SE)
845 Wyandotte St W, Windsor, ON, N9A 5Y1
(519) 256-3155
Emp Here 100
SIC 2851 Paints and allied products
Dennis Watt

D-U-N-S 24-136-8088   (SL)
BREAKAWAY GAMING CENTRE
655 Crawford Ave, Windsor, ON, N9A 5C7
(519) 256-0001
Emp Here 75   *Sales* 10,502,175
SIC 7999 Amusement and recreation, nec
Annette Hunter

D-U-N-S 25-097-7238   (HQ)
**CHRYSLER FINANCIAL SERVICES
CANADA INC**
(*Suby of* CERBERUS CAPITAL MANAGE-
MENT, L.P.)
1 Riverside Dr W, Windsor, ON, N9A 5K3
(519) 973-2000
Emp Here 30   *Sales* 140,626,220
SIC 6153 Short-term business credit institu-
tions, except agricultural
Brian Chillman
Michael J Dodge
Gilman Thomas F

D-U-N-S 24-337-1650   (BR)
**CORPORATION OF THE CITY OF WIND-
SOR**
WINDSOR FIRE & RESCUE SERVICES
(*Suby of* CORPORATION OF THE CITY OF
WINDSOR)
815 Goyeau St, Windsor, ON, N9A 1H7
(519) 253-6573
Emp Here 270
SIC 7389 Business services, nec
David T Fields

D-U-N-S 20-575-1329   (SL)
CSH DEVONSHIRE SENIORS INC

(*Suby of* CHARTWELL RETIREMENT RESI-
DENCES)
901 Riverside Dr W, Windsor, ON, N9A 7J6
(519) 252-2273
Emp Here 110
SIC 6513 Apartment building operators

D-U-N-S 25-051-8693   (SL)
DETROIT & CANADA TUNNEL
555 Goyeau St, Windsor, ON, N9A 1H1
(519) 258-7424
Emp Here 100   *Sales* 5,487,200
SIC 4111 Local and suburban transit
Neil Belitsky

D-U-N-S 20-407-6079   (SL)
EL-BRIS LIMITED
ELLIS GENERAL CONTRACTOR
933 Goyeau St, Windsor, ON, N9A 1H7

Emp Here 50   *Sales* 15,943,450
SIC 1521 Single-family housing construction
James W Ellis

D-U-N-S 20-285-3198   (SL)
EMPIRE ROOFING CORPORATION
4810 Walker Rd, Windsor, ON, N9A 6J3
(519) 969-7101
Emp Here 150   *Sales* 32,674,350
SIC 1761 Roofing, siding, and sheetMetal
work
Kenneth Gascoigne

D-U-N-S 25-978-8099   (HQ)
ENWIN UTILITIES LTD
(*Suby of* WINDSOR CANADA UTILITIES
LTD)
787 Ouellette Ave Suite 517, Windsor, ON,
N9A 4J4
(519) 255-2727
Emp Here 339   *Sales* 294,257,600
SIC 4911 Electric services
Helga Reidel
Jim Brown
Garry Rossi
Byron Thompson

D-U-N-S 20-184-8868   (HQ)
FCA CANADA INC
CHRYSLER CANADA
(*Suby of* FIAT CHRYSLER AUTOMOBILES
N.V.)
1 Riverside Dr W, Windsor, ON, N9A 5K3
(519) 973-2000
Emp Here 500   *Sales* 3,492,526,800
SIC 3711 Motor vehicles and car bodies
Reid Bigland
Lorraine Shalhoub

D-U-N-S 24-376-4409   (BR)
FCA CANADA INC
CHRYSLER WINDSOR
(*Suby of* FIAT CHRYSLER AUTOMOBILES
N.V.)
2199 Chrysler Ctr, Windsor, ON, N9A 4H6
(519) 973-2000
Emp Here 5,000
SIC 3711 Motor vehicles and car bodies
Marcel Breau

D-U-N-S 25-195-3261   (BR)
**FORD MOTOR COMPANY OF CANADA,
LIMITED**
(*Suby of* FORD MOTOR COMPANY)
2900 Trenton St, Windsor, ON, N9A 7B2
(519) 257-2000
Emp Here 1,000
SIC 3322 Malleable iron foundries
Robert Mrdjenovich

D-U-N-S 24-120-8029   (BR)
**FORD MOTOR COMPANY OF CANADA,
LIMITED**
(*Suby of* FORD MOTOR COMPANY)
3223 Lauzon Pky, Windsor, ON, N9A 6X3
(519) 944-8784
Emp Here 1,000

SIC 5521 Used car dealers
Tony Sazoni

D-U-N-S 20-646-4666   (BR)
**FORD MOTOR COMPANY OF CANADA,
LIMITED**
FORD WINDSOR ENGINE PLANT
(*Suby of* FORD MOTOR COMPANY)
1000 Henry Ford Centre Dr, Windsor, ON,
N9A 7E8
(519) 257-2020
Emp Here 500
SIC 3519 Internal combustion engines, nec
Shaun Whitaed

D-U-N-S 25-674-3501   (HQ)
**GREATER ESSEX COUNTY DISTRICT
SCHOOL BOARD**
451 Park St W, Windsor, ON, N9A 5V4
(519) 255-3200
Emp Here 100   *Sales* 430,353,560
SIC 8211 Elementary and secondary schools
Penny Allen
Warren Kennedy
Gale Simko-Hatfield

D-U-N-S 24-388-0148   (SL)
HAWK PLASTICS LTD
5295 Burke St, Windsor, ON, N9A 6J3
(519) 737-1452
Emp Here 60   *Sales* 12,113,820
SIC 3089 Plastics products, nec
Matt Urquhart
Sherry Urquhart
Len Scurto

D-U-N-S 20-874-9023   (SL)
HOLWIN TOOLING SYSTEMS INC
5270 Burke St, Windsor, ON, N9A 6J3
(519) 737-7550
Emp Here 25   *Sales* 11,875,650
SIC 5084 Industrial machinery and equipment
Loi Nguyen
Frank Piccolo

D-U-N-S 24-910-5438   (BR)
INNVEST PROPERTIES CORP
*WATERFRONT HOTEL - DOWNTOWN
WINDSOR*
(*Suby of* INNVEST PROPERTIES CORP)
277 Riverside Dr W, Windsor, ON, N9A 5K4
(519) 973-5555
Emp Here 150
SIC 7011 Hotels and motels
Bernard Baggoo

D-U-N-S 25-098-9589   (SL)
KODIAK CALL CENTRE LTD
525 Windsor Ave, Windsor, ON, N9A 1J4

Emp Here 115   *Sales* 76,924,420
SIC 7389 Business services, nec
Wendy Luxford

D-U-N-S 20-007-8496   (SL)
LIBERTY REALTY (1998) LTD
1125 Mercer St, Windsor, ON, N9A 1N8

Emp Here 45   *Sales* 14,720,715
SIC 6531 Real estate agents and managers
Joe Montaleone

D-U-N-S 20-185-8560   (SL)
**MERCHANTS PAPER COMPANY WINDSOR
LIMITED**
975 Crawford Ave, Windsor, ON, N9A 5C8
(519) 977-9977
Emp Here 50   *Sales* 25,182,900
SIC 5113 Industrial and personal service pa-
per
Carl Cohen

D-U-N-S 25-477-8541   (HQ)
MERITAS CARE CORPORATION
REGENCY PARK LTC HOME
567 Victoria Ave, Windsor, ON, N9A 4N1
(519) 254-1141
Emp Here 91   *Sales* 31,194,000

SIC 8741 Management services
Frederick Babbie

D-U-N-S 25-300-0632   (BR)
METRO ONTARIO INC
FOOD BASICS
(*Suby of* METRO INC)
880 Goyeau St, Windsor, ON, N9A 1H8
(519) 258-3064
Emp Here 110
SIC 5411 Grocery stores
Lou Raffoul

D-U-N-S 20-185-9220   (SL)
MORTON WHOLESALE LTD
5188 Walker Rd, Windsor, ON, N9A 6J3
(519) 737-6961
Emp Here 90   *Sales* 26,412,930
SIC 5411 Grocery stores
Robert Calcott
Phil Quenneville
Mary Lynn Calcott
Rick Grenon

D-U-N-S 20-700-2127   (BR)
POSTMEDIA NETWORK INC
WINDSOR STAR, THE
(*Suby of* POSTMEDIA NETWORK CANADA
CORP)
167 Ferry St, Windsor, ON, N9A 0C5
(519) 255-5720
Emp Here 300
SIC 2711 Newspapers
James Venney

D-U-N-S 20-750-5579   (SL)
**PREMIER CHEVROLET CADILLAC BUICK
GMC INC**
KANE, DAN CHEVROLET BUICK GM
500 Division Rd, Windsor, ON, N9A 6M9
(519) 969-6000
Emp Here 80   *Sales* 50,342,400
SIC 5511 New and used car dealers
Craig Lanoue
Thomas Mayhew

D-U-N-S 20-357-9391   (BR)
**PRESTRESSED SYSTEMS INCORPO-
RATED**
*INTERNATIONAL PRECAST SOLUTIONS,
DIVISION OF*
(*Suby of* PRESTRESSED SYSTEMS INCOR-
PORATED)
4955 Walker Rd, Windsor, ON, N9A 6J3
(519) 737-1216
Emp Here 100
SIC 3272 Concrete products, nec
Loris Collavino

D-U-N-S 20-876-3029   (HQ)
**PRESTRESSED SYSTEMS INCORPO-
RATED**
4955 Walker Rd, Windsor, ON, N9A 6J3
(519) 737-1216
Sales 57,530,250
SIC 3272 Concrete products, nec
Donald Little
Kenneth Borman
Valentino Collavino
Paul Phillips
Sonia Walton
Loris Collavino

D-U-N-S 20-569-6813   (SL)
RIDGE NATIONAL INC
100 Ouellette Ave Suite 1004, Windsor, ON,
N9A 6T3
(519) 256-2112
Emp Here 50   *Sales* 14,176,200
SIC 1611 Highway and street construction
Joe Lepera

D-U-N-S 24-379-9843   (SL)
SPM AUTOMATION (CANADA) INC
5445 Outer Dr, Windsor, ON, N9A 6J3
(519) 737-0320
Emp Here 45   *Sales* 13,517,964
SIC 3569 General industrial machinery, nec

Christian Peter Holtkamp
Lisa Lapico

D-U-N-S 25-524-4394   (SL)
STANDARD TOOL & MOLD INC
(*Suby of* JIN HU HOLDINGS INC)
5110 Halford Dr, Windsor, ON, N9A 6J3
(519) 737-1778
Emp Here 60   *Sales* 13,320,060
SIC 3544 Special dies, tools, jigs, and fixtures
Jin Hu

D-U-N-S 25-483-8659   (HQ)
STERLING MUTUALS INC
880 Ouellette Ave, Windsor, ON, N9A 1C7
(519) 256-8999
Emp Here 20   *Sales* 12,748,968
SIC 6211 Security brokers and dealers
Nelson Cheng
Rocky Ieraci

D-U-N-S 24-154-5578   (HQ)
SUTHERLAND GLOBAL SERVICES CANADA ULC
(*Suby of* SUTHERLAND GLOBAL SERVICES INC.)
500 Ouellette Ave, Windsor, ON, N9A 1B3
(800) 591-9395
Emp Here 20   *Sales* 79,773,192
SIC 7361 Employment agencies
Dilip Vellodi
Satish Raman

D-U-N-S 24-700-4166   (SL)
TIMBERWOLF FOREST PRODUCTS INC
2015 North Talbot Rd, Windsor, ON, N9A 6J3

Emp Here 27   *Sales* 12,825,702
SIC 5085 Industrial supplies
Thomas Manherz

D-U-N-S 24-393-0653   (SL)
TRANSIT LOGISTICS SOLUTIONS INC
TLS
4455 County Rd 42, Windsor, ON, N9A 6J3
(519) 967-0911
Emp Here 150   *Sales* 9,667,169
SIC 4213 Trucking, except local
Davor Novakovic

D-U-N-S 24-308-2997   (SL)
UNIQUE TOOL & GAUGE INC
1505 Moro Dr, Windsor, ON, N9A 6J3
(519) 737-1159
Emp Here 70   *Sales* 19,586,925
SIC 3544 Special dies, tools, jigs, and fixtures
Robert King
Darcy King

D-U-N-S 20-186-6175   (HQ)
VIKING PUMP OF CANADA INC
(*Suby of* IDEX CORPORATION)
661 Grove Ave, Windsor, ON, N9A 6G7
(519) 256-5438
Emp Here 31   *Sales* 32,301,768
SIC 5084 Industrial machinery and equipment
Jeff Mcmillin

D-U-N-S 20-329-6819   (SL)
WECAN- WINDSOR ETHICS CAPITAL ANGEL NETWORK
720 Ouellette Ave, Windsor, ON, N9A 1C2
(519) 259-9836
Emp Here 30   *Sales* 15,936,210
SIC 6282 Investment advice
Colin Mckillop

D-U-N-S 25-192-3447   (HQ)
WINDSOR CANADA UTILITIES LTD
ENWIN
787 Ouellette Ave, Windsor, ON, N9A 4J4
(519) 255-2727
Emp Here 288   *Sales* 538,911,776
SIC 4911 Electric services
Victor J Neufeld
Martin J Komsa
Tom Kosnik
Phil Partington

Joe Levack
M Jacqueline Merlo
Edgar Francis
Joyce Zuk
Fulvio Valentinis
Victoria Zuber

D-U-N-S 24-991-7295   (SL)
WINDSOR CASINO LIMITED
CAESARS WINDSOR
(*Suby of* HAMLET HOLDING, LLC)
377 Riverside Dr E, Windsor, ON, N9A 7H7
(519) 258-7878
Emp Here 3,000   *Sales* 287,004,000
SIC 7011 Hotels and motels
Kevin Laforet
Terry Black
Wallace Barr

D-U-N-S 20-397-1049   (SL)
WINDSOR INTERNATIONAL FILM FESTIVAL
WIFF
101 University Ave W, Windsor, ON, N9A 5P4
(226) 826-9433
Emp Here 250   *Sales* 268,223
SIC 7999 Amusement and recreation, nec
Vincent Georgie
Hayden Freker
Lynne Watts

D-U-N-S 24-467-5752   (SL)
WINDSOR UTILITIES COMMISSION
787 Ouellette Ave, Windsor, ON, N9A 4J4
(519) 255-2727
Emp Here 49   *Sales* 10,360,168
SIC 8611 Business associations
Bill Marra

D-U-N-S 25-403-7625   (BR)
WINDSOR-ESSEX CATHOLIC DISTRICT SCHOOL BOARD, THE
ST. THOMAS OF VILLANOVA SECONDARY SCHOOL
(*Suby of* WINDSOR-ESSEX CATHOLIC DISTRICT SCHOOL BOARD, THE)
2800 North Town Line Rd, Windsor, ON, N9A 6Z6
(519) 734-6444
Emp Here 150
SIC 8211 Elementary and secondary schools
Patrick Hickson

D-U-N-S 20-581-3012   (HQ)
WINDSOR-ESSEX COUNTY HOUSING CORPORATION
(*Suby of* CORPORATION OF THE CITY OF WINDSOR)
945 Mcdougall St, Windsor, ON, N9A 1L9
(519) 254-1681
Emp Here 20   *Sales* 13,587,800
SIC 6531 Real estate agents and managers
Jim Steele
Glenda Ward
Sheila Smallwood
George Robson
Janice Campbell

D-U-N-S 20-899-7671   (HQ)
YOUNG MEN'S CHRISTIAN ASSOCIATION OF WINDSOR AND ESSEX COUNTY
YMCA OF WINDSOR-ESSEX COUNTY
500 Victoria Ave, Windsor, ON, N9A 4M8
(519) 258-3881
Emp Here 75   *Sales* 172,632,120
SIC 8699 Membership organizations, nec
Shaun Elliot
Denise Simpson

Windsor, ON N9B

D-U-N-S 20-184-8041   (SL)
CANADIAN ENGINEERING AND TOOL COMPANY LIMITED, THE

2265 South Cameron Blvd, Windsor, ON, N9B 3P6
(519) 969-1618
Emp Here 110   *Sales* 24,420,110
SIC 3544 Special dies, tools, jigs, and fixtures
Donald Tregenza
Hazel Tregenza

D-U-N-S 25-249-0891   (BR)
GREATER ESSEX COUNTY DISTRICT SCHOOL BOARD
CENTURY SECONDARY SCHOOL
(*Suby of* GREATER ESSEX COUNTY DISTRICT SCHOOL BOARD)
1375 California Ave, Windsor, ON, N9B 2Z8
(519) 253-2481
Emp Here 75
SIC 8211 Elementary and secondary schools
Joan Rankin

D-U-N-S 25-652-6245   (BR)
METRO ONTARIO INC
METRO
(*Suby of* METRO INC)
2750 Tecumseh Rd W, Windsor, ON, N9B 3P9
(519) 256-1891
Emp Here 125
SIC 5411 Grocery stores
Bob Comber

D-U-N-S 20-057-6044   (HQ)
MOE'S TRANSPORT TRUCKING INC
1333 College Ave, Windsor, ON, N9B 1M8
(519) 253-8442
Emp Here 1   *Sales* 35,998,550
SIC 4213 Trucking, except local
Moe Faddoul
Kay Marie Abi-Samra

D-U-N-S 25-282-3414   (SL)
MORRISON, DAVID W. ENTERPRISES LTD
CANADIAN TIRE
2650 Tecumseh Rd W, Windsor, ON, N9B 3R1
(519) 252-7743
Emp Here 60   *Sales* 37,756,800
SIC 5531 Auto and home supply stores
David Morrison

D-U-N-S 20-786-3549   (HQ)
UNIVERSITY OF WINDSOR
401 Sunset Ave Suite G07, Windsor, ON, N9B 3P4
(519) 253-3000
Sales 224,086,500
SIC 8221 Colleges and universities
Alan Wildeman
John Bergholtz
Eric Harbottle

D-U-N-S 25-542-8070   (HQ)
WINDSOR-ESSEX CATHOLIC DISTRICT SCHOOL BOARD, THE
1325 California Ave, Windsor, ON, N9B 3Y6
(519) 253-2481
Emp Here 100   *Sales* 201,415,454
SIC 8211 Elementary and secondary schools
Paul Picard
Barbara Holland
Mary Dimenna
Fred Alexander
Fabio Costante
Frank Ditomasso
Bernie Mastromattei
Lisa Soulliere
Susan Tope
Fulvio Valentinis

Windsor, ON N9C

D-U-N-S 24-976-6551   (SL)
792716 ONTARIO LTD
SHUR LOK PRODUCTS
735 Prince Rd, Windsor, ON, N9C 2Z2
(519) 256-6700
Emp Here 75   *Sales* 16,788,225

SIC 3714 Motor vehicle parts and accessories
Peter Kelly
Grant Bourdeau

D-U-N-S 20-281-5619   (BR)
A.P. PLASMAN INC
A.P. PLASMAN INC.
(*Suby of* APP HOLDINGS LP)
635 Sprucewood Ave, Windsor, ON, N9C 0B3
(519) 791-9119
Emp Here 200
SIC 3089 Plastics products, nec

D-U-N-S 24-372-1201   (HQ)
ADM AGRI-INDUSTRIES COMPANY
ADM COCOA, DIV OF
(*Suby of* ARCHER-DANIELS-MIDLAND COMPANY)
5550 Maplewood Dr, Windsor, ON, N9C 0B9
(519) 972-8100
Emp Here 125   *Sales* 487,385,000
SIC 2079 Edible fats and oils
David J. Smith
Steven Mills
Mark Kolkhorst
Ronald Bandler

D-U-N-S 20-329-6256   (SL)
AVANCEZ ASSEMBLY CANADA, ULC
(*Suby of* AVANCEZ, LLC)
599 Sprucewood Ave, Windsor, ON, N9C 0B3
(226) 221-8800
Emp Here 50   *Sales* 10,094,850
SIC 3011 Tires and inner tubes
Kathryn Nichols

D-U-N-S 24-688-4225   (SL)
CANADIAN ELECTROCOATING LTD
NARMCO GROUP
945 Prince Rd, Windsor, ON, N9C 2Z4
(519) 977-7523
Emp Here 140   *Sales* 26,891,900
SIC 3479 Metal coating and allied services
Donald Rodzik
Gail Rodzik

D-U-N-S 24-844-1727   (HQ)
CATALENT ONTARIO LIMITED
CATALENT WINDSOR OPERATIONS
(*Suby of* CATALENT, INC.)
2125 Ambassador Dr, Windsor, ON, N9C 3R5
(519) 969-5404
Emp Here 350   *Sales* 222,322,500
SIC 2899 Chemical preparations, nec
Aris Gennadios
Eric Andrus
Marie Campagna

D-U-N-S 20-689-3500   (SL)
DJ GALVANIZING CORPORATION
(*Suby of* ARCELORMITTAL)
300 Sprucewood Ave, Windsor, ON, N9C 0B7
(519) 250-2120
Emp Here 104   *Sales* 19,976,840
SIC 3479 Metal coating and allied services
Paul Dunmore

D-U-N-S 24-699-9937   (BR)
ELECTROMAC GROUP INC, THE
CANNON AUTOMOTIVE SOLUTIONS
(*Suby of* AK STEEL HOLDING CORPORATION)
600 Sprucewood Ave, Windsor, ON, N9C 0B2
(519) 969-4632
Emp Here 100
SIC 3544 Special dies, tools, jigs, and fixtures
James Richards

D-U-N-S 25-413-0263   (HQ)
ELECTROMAC GROUP INC, THE
(*Suby of* AK STEEL HOLDING CORPORATION)
1965 Ambassador Dr, Windsor, ON, N9C 3R5
(519) 969-4632
Emp Here 110   *Sales* 64,456,215
SIC 3469 Metal stampings, nec
O'neil (Desmond) Griffiths

D-U-N-S 20-358-5864   (SL)
ENNOVA FACADES INC
620 Sprucewood Ave, Windsor, ON, N9C 0B2
(519) 969-1740
Emp Here 125   *Sales* 24,010,625
SIC 3449 Miscellaneous Metalwork
Michal Chlumecky

D-U-N-S 20-939-5839   (SL)
FAHRHALL MECHANICAL CONTRACTORS LIMITED
FAHRHALL MECHANICAL HOME COMFORT
3822 Sandwich St, Windsor, ON, N9C 1C1
(519) 969-7822
Emp Here 70   *Sales* 16,314,550
SIC 1711 Plumbing, heating, air-conditioning
Brad Vollmer
Peter Hill

D-U-N-S 24-324-3933   (HQ)
FARROW GROUP INC
2001 Huron Church Rd, Windsor, ON, N9C 2L6
(519) 252-4415
Sales 168,134,140
SIC 6712 Bank holding companies
Richard Farrow
John Farrow
Randy Motley
Romeo Girardi
Brian Wikston

D-U-N-S 20-528-4235   (HQ)
FARROW, RUSSELL A. LIMITED
FARROW INTERNATIONAL
(*Suby of* FARROW GROUP INC)
2001 Huron Church Rd, Windsor, ON, N9C 2L6
(519) 966-3003
Emp Here 75   *Sales* 237,262,800
SIC 4731 Freight transportation arrangement
Richard Farrow
John Farrow
Randy Motley
Romeo Girardi
Brian Wikston

D-U-N-S 25-180-9281   (BR)
K+S SEL WINDSOR LTEE
(*Suby of* K+S AG)
30 Prospect Ave, Windsor, ON, N9C 3G3
(519) 255-5400
Emp Here 110
SIC 2899 Chemical preparations, nec
Gilles Carrier

D-U-N-S 20-185-6457   (HQ)
K-SCRAP RESOURCES LTD
110 Hill Ave, Windsor, ON, N9C 3B8
(519) 254-5188
Sales 15,616,260
SIC 5093 Scrap and waste materials
John Rodzik
William Carter
Donald Rodzik

D-U-N-S 25-260-0213   (SL)
LOU ROMANO WATER RECLAMATION PLANT
4155 Ojibway Pky, Windsor, ON, N9C 4A5
(519) 253-7217
Emp Here 35   *Sales* 10,403,470
SIC 4941 Water supply
Tony Bietola

D-U-N-S 24-470-3294   (SL)
MARYVALE ADOLESCENT FAMILY SERVICE
3640 Wells St, Windsor, ON, N9C 1T9
(519) 258-0484
Emp Here 200   *Sales* 12,856,400
SIC 8361 Residential care
Connie Martin

D-U-N-S 24-347-9511   (BR)
MCDONALD'S RESTAURANTS OF CANADA LIMITED

MCDONALD'S RESTAURANT
(*Suby of* MCDONALD'S CORPORATION)
5631 Ojibway Pky, Windsor, ON, N9C 4J5
(519) 250-5311
Emp Here 102
SIC 5812 Eating places
June Reybrok

D-U-N-S 25-318-1564   (BR)
MCDONALD'S RESTAURANTS OF CANADA LIMITED
MCDONALD'S 8065
(*Suby of* MCDONALD'S CORPORATION)
883 Huron Church Rd, Windsor, ON, N9C 2K3
(519) 258-3531
Emp Here 101
SIC 5812 Eating places
Rita Webb

D-U-N-S 20-010-3765   (HQ)
NEMAK OF CANADA CORPORATION
ESSEX ALUMINUM PLANT
(*Suby of* ALFA, S.A.B. DE C.V.)
4600 G N Booth Dr, Windsor, ON, N9C 4G8
(519) 250-2500
Sales 30,835,960
SIC 3334 Primary aluminum
Lloyd Maisonville
Manuel Rivera
Salvador Ramos

D-U-N-S 20-337-5196   (HQ)
PPHC NORTH LTD
(*Suby of* AK STEEL HOLDING CORPORATION)
1965 Ambassador Dr, Windsor, ON, N9C 3R5
(519) 969-4632
Sales 365,509,000
SIC 6712 Bank holding companies
Desmond Griffiths

D-U-N-S 24-765-0542   (SL)
PRINCE METAL PRODUCTS LTD
945 Prince Rd, Windsor, ON, N9C 2Z4
(519) 977-5333
Emp Here 140   *Sales* 31,338,020
SIC 3714 Motor vehicle parts and accessories
Donald Rodzik

D-U-N-S 24-690-0856   (SL)
RADIOCO LTD
KELCOM MOBILITY SOLUTIONS WINDSOR
1983 Ambassador Dr, Windsor, ON, N9C 3R5
(519) 250-9100
Emp Here 30   *Sales* 13,415,220
SIC 5065 Electronic parts and equipment, nec
Wayne Eric Wood
Thomas St. Denis
Timothy Schweyer
Dale E Carr
Paul Morgan

D-U-N-S 25-213-8664   (SL)
SOUTHWESTERN MANUFACTURING INC
3710 Peter St, Windsor, ON, N9C 1J9
(519) 985-6161
Emp Here 200   *Sales* 38,417,000
SIC 3499 Fabricated Metal products, nec
Vincent Schiller

D-U-N-S 24-250-6363   (SL)
STERLING MARINE FUELS
3565 Russell St, Windsor, ON, N9C 1E8
(519) 253-4694
Emp Here 30   *Sales* 14,942,340
SIC 5551 Boat dealers
Peter Kelly

D-U-N-S 20-731-7801   (SL)
TEE-BEE-QUE LIMITED
TBQ'S OTHER PASTRY PLACE & CAFE
1855 Huron Church Rd, Windsor, ON, N9C 2L6

Emp Here 150   *Sales* 6,827,850
SIC 5812 Eating places
Thomas K Racovitis
Marilynn Racovitis

Christos Stoiantsis
Valerie Stoiantsis

D-U-N-S 24-026-8656   (HQ)
VOLLMER INC
3822 Sandwich St, Windsor, ON, N9C 1C1
(519) 966-6100
Sales 108,339,200
SIC 1711 Plumbing, heating, air-conditioning
Bradley Gerald Vollmer

D-U-N-S 20-701-1701   (HQ)
WINDSOR MOLD INC
WINDSOR MOLD TOOLING, DIV OF
(*Suby of* 873740 ONTARIO INC)
4035 Malden Rd, Windsor, ON, N9C 2G4
(519) 972-9032
Emp Here 4   *Sales* 22,200,100
SIC 3544 Special dies, tools, jigs, and fixtures
Keith Henry
Colin Dodd
Gregory Mahoney

D-U-N-S 25-407-3497   (BR)
WINDSOR MOLD INC
(*Suby of* 873740 ONTARIO INC)
4035 Malden Rd, Windsor, ON, N9C 2G4
(519) 972-9032
Emp Here 180
SIC 3544 Special dies, tools, jigs, and fixtures
Schooly Jem

D-U-N-S 25-636-4035   (BR)
WINDSOR REGIONAL HOSPITAL
WINDSOR REGIONAL CHILDREN CENTRE
(*Suby of* WINDSOR REGIONAL HOSPITAL)
3901 Connaught Ave, Windsor, ON, N9C 4H4
(519) 257-5215
Emp Here 75
SIC 8093 Specialty outpatient clinics, nec
Mary Broga

D-U-N-S 25-249-4026   (BR)
WINDSOR-ESSEX CATHOLIC DISTRICT SCHOOL BOARD, THE
ASSUMPTION COLLEGE CATHOLIC HIGH SCHOOL
(*Suby of* WINDSOR-ESSEX CATHOLIC DISTRICT SCHOOL BOARD, THE)
1100 Huron Church Rd, Windsor, ON, N9C 2K7
(519) 256-7801
Emp Here 90
SIC 8211 Elementary and secondary schools
Joseph Ibrahim

Windsor, ON N9E

D-U-N-S 20-889-2393   (SL)
CHILDREN'S HOUSE MONTESSORI, THE
2611 Labelle St, Windsor, ON, N9E 4G4
(519) 969-5278
Emp Here 100   *Sales* 6,106,900
SIC 8351 Child day care services
Julie Di Ponio Roy
Liz Price

D-U-N-S 20-026-0540   (BR)
GREATER ESSEX COUNTY DISTRICT SCHOOL BOARD
VINCENT MASSEY SECONDARY SCHOOL
(*Suby of* GREATER ESSEX COUNTY DISTRICT SCHOOL BOARD)
1800 Liberty St, Windsor, ON, N9E 1J2
(519) 969-2530
Emp Here 100
SIC 8211 Elementary and secondary schools
Larry Ash

D-U-N-S 24-308-0715   (BR)
LOBLAWS INC
REAL CANADIAN SUPERSTORE
(*Suby of* LOBLAW COMPANIES LIMITED)
2950 Dougall Ave Suite 18, Windsor, ON, N9E 1S2

---

(519) 969-3087
Emp Here 100
SIC 2051 Bread, cake, and related products
John Findlater

D-U-N-S 24-688-8630   (BR)
MCDONALD'S RESTAURANTS OF CANADA LIMITED
MANNAH FOODS
(*Suby of* MCDONALD'S CORPORATION)
3354 Dougall Ave, Windsor, ON, N9E 1S6
(519) 966-0454
Emp Here 115
SIC 5812 Eating places
Lina Jido

D-U-N-S 24-004-4706   (SL)
RIGHT TO LIFE ASSOCIATION OF WINDSOR AND AREA
WINDSOR ESSEX COUNTY RIGHT TO LIFE
3021 Dougall Ave, Windsor, ON, N9E 1S3
(519) 969-7555
Emp Here 45   *Sales* 17,883,630
SIC 8699 Membership organizations, nec
Beryl Caves

D-U-N-S 20-965-6149   (SL)
VALENTE, REMO REAL ESTATE (1990) LIMITED
2985 Dougall Ave, Windsor, ON, N9E 1S1
(519) 966-7777
Emp Here 70   *Sales* 19,022,920
SIC 6531 Real estate agents and managers
Remo Valente

D-U-N-S 25-652-6435   (BR)
WAL-MART CANADA CORP
(*Suby of* WALMART INC.)
3120 Dougall Ave, Windsor, ON, N9E 1S7
(519) 969-8121
Emp Here 280
SIC 5311 Department stores
Williamson Jay

D-U-N-S 20-555-8591   (SL)
WINDSOR WHOLESALE BAIT LTD
500 Northwood St, Windsor, ON, N9E 4Z2
(519) 966-8540
Emp Here 35   *Sales* 25,988,200
SIC 5199 Nondurable goods, nec
Tuan Huynh

D-U-N-S 25-225-1624   (BR)
WINDSOR-ESSEX CATHOLIC DISTRICT SCHOOL BOARD, THE
HOLY NAMES HIGH SCHOOL
(*Suby of* WINDSOR-ESSEX CATHOLIC DISTRICT SCHOOL BOARD, THE)
1400 Northwood St, Windsor, ON, N9E 1A4
(519) 966-2504
Emp Here 120
SIC 8211 Elementary and secondary schools
Brendan Roberts

Windsor, ON N9G

D-U-N-S 25-570-6988   (BR)
CORPORATION OF THE CITY OF WINDSOR
HURON LODGE HOME FOR THE AGED
(*Suby of* CORPORATION OF THE CITY OF WINDSOR)
1881 Cabana Rd W, Windsor, ON, N9G 1C7
(519) 253-6060
Emp Here 250
SIC 8361 Residential care
Mary Bateman

D-U-N-S 20-213-2028   (BR)
EXTENDICARE INC
EXTENDICARE SOUTHWOOD LAKES
(*Suby of* EXTENDICARE INC)
1255 North Talbot Rd, Windsor, ON, N9G 3A4
(519) 945-7249
Emp Here 160

▲ Public Company   ■ Public Company Family Member   **HQ** Headquarters   **BR** Branch   **SL** Single Location

SIC 8051 Skilled nursing care facilities
Susan Petahtegoose

D-U-N-S 24-991-9200   (SL)
WRANK ENTERPRISES LTD
CANADIAN TIRE
3920 Dougall Ave, Windsor, ON, N9G 1X2
(519) 966-3650
Emp Here 100   *Sales* 62,928,000
SIC 5531 Auto and home supply stores
William P Vander Linden

Windsor, ON N9H

D-U-N-S 24-325-9418   (SL)
CRAIG, JAN DRUG STORE LTD
SHOPPERS DRUG MART
6020 Malden Rd, Windsor, ON, N9H 1S8
(519) 969-9971
Emp Here 56   *Sales* 13,682,368
SIC 5912 Drug stores and proprietary stores
Jan Craig

D-U-N-S 25-410-7113   (SL)
ROSATI CONSTRUCTION INC
6555 Malden Rd, Windsor, ON, N9H 1T5
(519) 734-6511
Emp Here 45   *Sales* 14,999,985
SIC 1541 Industrial buildings and warehouses
Anthony Rosati
Nicholas Rosati

D-U-N-S 20-377-4091   (HQ)
WINDSOR MACHINE & STAMPING (2009) LTD
WINDSOR MACHINE GROUP
1555 Talbot Rd Suite 401, Windsor, ON, N9H 2N2
(519) 737-7155
Sales 18,226,653
SIC 3312 Blast furnaces and steel mills
Gregory Peltier
Christopher Peltier
David Zultek

Windsor, ON N9J

D-U-N-S 20-184-8579   (HQ)
CENTERLINE (WINDSOR) LIMITED
415 Morton Dr, Windsor, ON, N9J 3T8
(519) 734-8464
Emp Here 200   *Sales* 98,306,950
SIC 3599 Industrial machinery, nec
Michael Beneteau
Donald Beneteau
David Beneteau
Christopher Beneteau

D-U-N-S 20-034-7524   (SL)
DEAN CONSTRUCTION COMPANY LIMITED
2720 Front Rd, Windsor, ON, N9J 2N5
(519) 734-8999
Emp Here 55   *Sales* 13,884,310
SIC 1629 Heavy construction, nec
Brooks Dean
Americo Dean Jr
Barbara Dean
Americo Dean Iii

D-U-N-S 25-115-9059   (SL)
FRONT CONSTRUCTION INDUSTRIES INC
FRONT CONSTRUCTION
740 Morton Dr Unit 1, Windsor, ON, N9J 3V2
(519) 250-8229
Emp Here 23   *Sales* 10,826,813
SIC 1542 Nonresidential construction, nec
Mario Baggio
Paul Merritt

D-U-N-S 24-595-4149   (BR)
K+S SEL WINDSOR LTEE

(Suby of K+S AG)
200 Morton Dr, Windsor, ON, N9J 3W9
(519) 972-2201
Emp Here 300
SIC 1479 Chemical and fertilizer mining
David Church

D-U-N-S 24-008-8963   (HQ)
PAPP PLASTICS AND DISTRIBUTING LIMITED
6110 Morton Industrial Pky, Windsor, ON, N9J 3W3
(519) 734-1112
Emp Here 1   *Sales* 17,272,683
SIC 3089 Plastics products, nec
Michael Papp
Marco Castilla
Kim Segarac

D-U-N-S 24-185-7218   (HQ)
RE-DOE MOLD COMPANY LIMITED
665 Morton Dr, Windsor, ON, N9J 3T9
(519) 734-6161
Emp Here 90   *Sales* 22,200,100
SIC 3544 Special dies, tools, jigs, and fixtures
Patrick Endo
Edward Regan
Shirley Regan
Paul Taylor
Ken Leblanc

D-U-N-S 20-125-6757   (SL)
REAUME CHEVROLET LTD
REAUME CHEVROLET BUICK GMC
500 Front Rd, Windsor, ON, N9J 1Z9
(519) 734-7844
Emp Here 60   *Sales* 37,756,800
SIC 5511 New and used car dealers
Richard Reaume
Jeffrey Reaume
Craig Reaume
Jennifer Natyshak-Reaume

D-U-N-S 20-278-2272   (SL)
REJUDICARE SYNERGY LTD
WAREHOUSE
6220 Westar Dr, Windsor, ON, N9J 0B5
(519) 734-6600
Emp Here 22   *Sales* 24,317,590
SIC 5122 Drugs, proprietaries, and sundries
Roger Odette

Windsor, ON N9K

D-U-N-S 20-245-9124   (BR)
SOBEYS CAPITAL INCORPORATED
(Suby of EMPIRE COMPANY LIMITED)
19 Amy Croft Dr, Windsor, ON, N9K 1C7
(519) 735-4110
Emp Here 193
SIC 5411 Grocery stores
Rob Hayes

Wingham, ON N0G

D-U-N-S 25-804-4817   (BR)
AVON MAITLAND DISTRICT SCHOOL BOARD
MADILL, F E SECONDARY SCHOOL
231 Madill Dr E, Wingham, ON, N0G 2W0
(519) 357-1800
Emp Here 100
SIC 8211 Elementary and secondary schools
Daby Green

D-U-N-S 25-868-9736   (HQ)
FOXTON FUELS LIMITED
50 North St W, Wingham, ON, N0G 2W0
(519) 357-2664
Emp Here 9   *Sales* 16,524,928
SIC 5171 Petroleum bulk stations and termi-

nals
Mark Foxton

D-U-N-S 20-369-1928   (SL)
PENGUIN POWER SOLAR
2118 Huron Bruce Rd, Wingham, ON, N0G 2W0
(519) 274-2179
Emp Here 250   *Sales* 67,712,000
SIC 1711 Plumbing, heating, air-conditioning
Jaret Henhoeffer

D-U-N-S 24-023-4385   (HQ)
ROYAL HOMES LIMITED
213 Arthur St, Wingham, ON, N0G 2W0
(519) 357-2606
Sales 22,314,804
SIC 2452 Prefabricated wood buildings
Pieter Venema
Douglas Kuyvenhoven
Klaas Jorritsma

D-U-N-S 20-302-0011   (BR)
WESCAST INDUSTRIES INC
WESCAST INDUSTRIES MACHINING WINGHAM
(Suby of MIANYANG SCIENCE TECHNOLOGY CITY DEVELOPMENT INVESTMENT (GROUP) CO., LTD.)
100 Water St, Wingham, ON, N0G 2W0
(519) 357-3450
Emp Here 75
SIC 3714 Motor vehicle parts and accessories
Raymond Finnie

D-U-N-S 25-371-6419   (BR)
WESCAST INDUSTRIES INC
WINGHAM CASTINGS
(Suby of MIANYANG SCIENCE TECHNOLOGY CITY DEVELOPMENT INVESTMENT (GROUP) CO., LTD.)
200 Water St, Wingham, ON, N0G 2W0
(519) 357-3450
Emp Here 400
SIC 3714 Motor vehicle parts and accessories
Trevor Grubb

D-U-N-S 24-478-1001   (SL)
WINGHAM AND DISTRICT HOSPITAL
LISTOWEL & WINGHAM HOSPITALS ALLIANCE
270 Carling Terr, Wingham, ON, N0G 2W0
(519) 357-3210
Emp Here 200   *Sales* 13,238,298
SIC 8062 General medical and surgical hospitals
Karl Ellis
Amy Miller
Andy Mcbride
Angela Stanley
Trevor Seip
Tim Lewis

Wolfe Island, ON K0H

D-U-N-S 20-114-3687   (SL)
CANADIAN RENEWABLE ENERGY CORPORATION
(Suby of TRANSALTA CORPORATION)
4 Line Rd Suite 209, Wolfe Island, ON, K0H 2Y0
(613) 385-2045
Emp Here 20   *Sales* 12,532,280
SIC 4911 Electric services
Trudy De Ruiter

Woodbridge, ON L4H

D-U-N-S 24-123-8229   (HQ)
329985 ONTARIO LIMITED
KISKO PRODUCTS

50 Royal Group Cres Unit 1, Woodbridge, ON, L4H 1X9
(905) 652-2363
Sales 32,840,550
SIC 2024 Ice cream and frozen deserts
Mark Joseps
Glenor Josephs
Randolph Joseph
Mike Mcalary

D-U-N-S 25-985-0899   (SL)
407 ETR CONCESSION COMPANY LIMITED
(Suby of FERROVIAL SA)
6300 Steeles Ave W, Woodbridge, ON, L4H 1J1
(905) 265-4070
Emp Here 450   *Sales* 177,947,100
SIC 4785 Inspection and fixed facilities
Jose Tamarez
Louis Tamariz

D-U-N-S 25-953-7181   (HQ)
407 INTERNATIONAL INC
(Suby of FERROVIAL SA)
6300 Steeles Ave W, Woodbridge, ON, L4H 1J1
(905) 265-4070
Emp Here 600
SIC 4785 Inspection and fixed facilities
Andres Sacristan
David Mcfadden
Geoffrey Liang
Andrew Alley
Michael Bernasiewicz
Francisco Clemente Sanchez
George Davie
Enrique Diaz-Rato Revuelta
Laura Formusa
Denis Jasmin

D-U-N-S 24-801-9028   (HQ)
864884 ONTARIO INC
AXXESS LOGISTICS, DIV OF
180 New Huntington Rd Unit 1, Woodbridge, ON, L4H 0P5
(905) 264-6670
Emp Here 64   *Sales* 35,256,060
SIC 5112 Stationery and office supplies
Gianna Ponzi
Gianfranco (John) Ponzi
Daniele Ponzi

D-U-N-S 20-809-7506   (HQ)
ACCURISTIX
ACCURISTIX ADVANCING HEALTHCARE LOGISTIC
122 Stone Ridge Rd, Woodbridge, ON, L4H 0A5
(905) 829-9927
Sales 29,827,370
SIC 4225 General warehousing and storage
Marlyn Forbes
Cameron Joyce

D-U-N-S 24-330-0303   (BR)
ADIDAS CANADA LIMITED
ADIDAS GROUP
(Suby of ADIDAS AG)
8100 27 Hwy Suite 1, Woodbridge, ON, L4H 3N2
(905) 266-4200
Emp Here 280
SIC 5139 Footwear
Katie Beattie

D-U-N-S 20-158-3531   (HQ)
ADIDAS CANADA LIMITED
ROCKPORT CANADA
(Suby of ADIDAS AG)
8100 27 Hwy Suite 1, Woodbridge, ON, L4H 3N2
(905) 266-4200
Emp Here 150   *Sales* 486,710,000
SIC 5091 Sporting and recreation goods
Steven Ralph
Natalie Knight
Robert Adam

▲ Public Company   ■ Public Company Family Member   **HQ** Headquarters   **BR** Branch   **SL** Single Location

Daniel Gervais

D-U-N-S 20-052-7500 (SL)
ALLIANCE STORE FIXTURES INC
370 New Huntington Rd, Woodbridge, ON,
L4H 0R4
(905) 660-5944
Emp Here 74   *Sales* 11,419,828
SIC 2542 Partitions and fixtures, except wood
Fernando (Freddy) Policano
Giuseppe (Joe) Policano
Vincenzo (Vince) Nasso

D-U-N-S 24-008-4095 (SL)
BEN MACHINE PRODUCTS COMPANY IN-CORPORATED
BMP
(*Suby of* EXCHANGE INCOME CORPORA-TION)
8065 Huntington Rd Suite 1, Woodbridge, ON,
L4H 3T9
(905) 856-7707
Emp Here 120   *Sales* 24,259,264
SIC 3499 Fabricated Metal products, nec
Michael Iacovelli
Adrian Iacovelli
Ivan Del Giudice
Dianne Spencer

D-U-N-S 20-183-8877 (HQ)
BRADSHAW CANADA HOLDINGS, INC
(*Suby of* ONCAP II L.P.)
200 Zenway Blvd Suite 3, Woodbridge, ON,
L4H 0L6
(905) 264-2246
Sales 10,862,768
SIC 6211 Security brokers and dealers
David Brown

D-U-N-S 20-955-5387 (SL)
BURNAC PRODUCE LIMITED
PRO PAK PACKAGING
(*Suby of* BURNAC CORPORATION)
80 Zenway Blvd, Woodbridge, ON, L4H 3H1
(905) 856-9064
Emp Here 191   *Sales* 136,892,756
SIC 5148 Fresh fruits and vegetables
Frank Defrancesco
Jacques Lavergne
Anas Helwani
Joe Losurdo

D-U-N-S 25-367-5763 (SL)
CANADIAN TOLLING COMPANY INTERNA-TIONAL INC
407 ETR
(*Suby of* FERROVIAL SA)
6300 Steeles Ave W, Woodbridge, ON, L4H
1J1
(905) 265-4070
Emp Here 500   *Sales* 197,719,000
SIC 4785 Inspection and fixed facilities
Jose Tamaliz
Enrique Diaz-Rato Revuelta
Louis St-Maurice
Robert Ives

D-U-N-S 20-357-9370 (HQ)
CANNTRUST HOLDINGS INC
9200 Weston Rd, Woodbridge, ON, L4H 2P8
(647) 872-2300
Sales 34,603,674
SIC 5993 Tobacco stores and stands
Peter Aceto
Eric Paul
Mark Litwin
Ian Abramowitz
Bernard Yeung
Andrea Kirk
Adam Jerusalim
Brady Green
Chris Lucky
Ilana Platt

D-U-N-S 24-368-3997 (HQ)
CAPITAL SEWER SERVICES INC
401 Vaughan Valley Blvd, Woodbridge, ON,

L4H 3B5
(905) 522-0522
Emp Here 10   *Sales* 14,771,160
SIC 1799 Special trade contractors, nec
Gary Bates
Maryline Fatia
Jeff Hoover

D-U-N-S 20-296-0779 (HQ)
CERTAINTEED CANADA, INC
DECOUSTICS
(*Suby of* COMPAGNIE DE SAINT-GOBAIN)
61 Royal Group Cres, Woodbridge, ON, L4H
1X9
(905) 652-5200
Emp Here 50   *Sales* 17,921,900
SIC 3296 Mineral wool
Richard Juggery
Adriano Mazzaferro
Christian Kellett
Matthew Madeksza

D-U-N-S 20-172-7047 (HQ)
COATS CANADA INC
COATS BELL
(*Suby of* COATS GROUP PLC)
10 Roybridge Gate Suite 200, Woodbridge,
ON, L4H 3M8
(905) 850-9200
Emp Here 20   *Sales* 11,451,924
SIC 5092 Toys and hobby goods and supplies
John Arbour

D-U-N-S 24-694-1421 (SL)
CONAIR CONSUMER PRODUCTS ULC
DANNY PROFESSIONAL SERVICES
100 Conair Pky, Woodbridge, ON, L4H 0L2
(905) 851-5162
Emp Here 85   *Sales* 38,009,790
SIC 5064 Electrical appliances, television and
radio
Leonardo P Rizzuto
Paul Sullivan

D-U-N-S 20-164-9662 (HQ)
CONSOLIDATED FASTFRATE INC
FASTFRATE
9701 Highway 50, Woodbridge, ON, L4H 2G4
(905) 893-2600
Emp Here 250   *Sales* 165,942,900
SIC 4213 Trucking, except local
Ronald Tepper
Manny Calandrino
George Bichara
Patricia Scott
Ahmet A. Taran
Alfonso Triolo
Sebastian Carta
Kim Wonfor
Richard Rose
Tony Kelly

D-U-N-S 20-215-6857 (HQ)
CRANE CANADA CO.
VALVE MANUFACTURING, DIV OF
(*Suby of* CRANE CO.)
141 Royal Group Cres, Woodbridge, ON, L4H
1X9
(416) 244-5351
Emp Here 85   *Sales* 374,088,910
SIC 5085 Industrial supplies
Eric Fast
Tom Frazer

D-U-N-S 20-016-6713 (SL)
CUTLER FOREST PRODUCTS INC
CUTLER GROUP
81 Royal Group Cres Unit A, Woodbridge, ON,
L4H 1X9
(905) 212-1414
Emp Here 120   *Sales* 68,355,360
SIC 5031 Lumber, plywood, and millwork
Jonathan Glick
Mike Creador

D-U-N-S 25-500-8328 (SL)
D & V ELECTRONICS LTD

(*Suby of* MOTORCAR PARTS OF AMERICA
INC)
130 Zenway Blvd, Woodbridge, ON, L4H 2Y7
(905) 264-7646
Emp Here 106   *Sales* 11,675,820
SIC 3694 Engine electrical equipment
William Hardy
Kalina Loukanov

D-U-N-S 20-400-3938 (HQ)
DIVERSIFIED ULBRICH OF CANADA
(*Suby of* ULBRICH STAINLESS STEELS
INC)
150 New Huntington Rd Unit 1, Woodbridge,
ON, L4H 4N4
(416) 663-7130
Emp Here 6   *Sales* 11,003,729
SIC 5051 Metals service centers and offices
F. Christopher Ulbrich
John Cei
Barry Arbus

D-U-N-S 24-320-3040 (HQ)
DYNAMIC TIRE INC
(*Suby of* SAILUN GROUP CO., LTD.)
211 Hunter'S Valley Rd, Woodbridge, ON,
L4H 3V9
(905) 595-5558
Emp Here 30   *Sales* 14,568,600
SIC 5014 Tires and tubes
Robert Sherkin
Changkun Ji
Yanhua Liu
Shengyun Zhou
Zhaoling Yu

D-U-N-S 25-977-6792 (HQ)
ENERGI FENESTRATION SOLUTIONS, LTD
(*Suby of* PROFILE HOLDINGS SARL)
30 Royal Group Cres, Woodbridge, ON, L4H
1X9
(905) 851-6637
Emp Here 100   *Sales* 121,615,500
SIC 3442 Metal doors, sash, and trim
Jesse Hawthorne

D-U-N-S 24-346-2561 (HQ)
ETHAN ALLEN (CANADA) INC
ETHAN ALLEN HOME INTERIORS
(*Suby of* ETHAN ALLEN INTERIORS INC.)
205 Trade Valley Dr Suite B, Woodbridge, ON,
L4H 3N6
(905) 264-7686
Emp Here 18   *Sales* 25,099,524
SIC 5712 Furniture stores
Edward Teplitz

D-U-N-S 25-366-1698 (BR)
FLYNN CANADA LTD
(*Suby of* FLYNN CANADA LTD)
141 Royal Group Cres, Woodbridge, ON, L4H
1X9
(905) 671-3971
Emp Here 250
SIC 1761 Roofing, siding, and sheetMetal
work

D-U-N-S 24-874-2215 (SL)
FOTIOU FRAMES LIMITED
135 Rainbow Creek Dr, Woodbridge, ON, L4H
0A4
(800) 668-8420
Emp Here 45   *Sales* 22,898,520
SIC 5023 Homefurnishings
Louis Rodriguez
Carlos Rodriguez
Manuel Anton

D-U-N-S 24-644-2979 (SL)
GLOBAL NET TRADE
50 Parisienne Rd, Woodbridge, ON, L4H 0V4
(905) 417-9470
Emp Here 30   *Sales* 13,476,570
SIC 7389 Business services, nec
Allan Pollett

D-U-N-S 20-294-3932 (BR)
HOME DEPOT OF CANADA INC

HOME DEPOT RDC 7275
(*Suby of* THE HOME DEPOT INC)
8966 Huntington Rd, Woodbridge, ON, L4H
3V1
(905) 265-4400
Emp Here 400
SIC 4225 General warehousing and storage
Shawn Gregory

D-U-N-S 20-733-9854 (HQ)
HUSKY FOOD IMPORTERS & DISTRIBU-TORS LIMITED
155 Rainbow Creek Dr, Woodbridge, ON, L4H
0A4
(905) 850-8288
Sales 41,778,850
SIC 5145 Confectionery
Gordon Hufsky
John Hufsky

D-U-N-S 20-017-3131 (BR)
IMPRIMERIES TRANSCONTINENTAL INC
TRANSCONTINENTAL PRINTING INC
(*Suby of* TRANSCONTINENTAL INC)
100 Royal Group Cres Unit B, Woodbridge,
ON, L4H 1X9
(905) 663-1216
Emp Here 110
SIC 2711 Newspapers
Gary Huges

D-U-N-S 24-330-5948 (SL)
J.D. COLLINS FIRE PROTECTION COM-PANY INC
101 Innovation Dr Unit 1, Woodbridge, ON,
L4H 0S3
(905) 660-4535
Emp Here 32   *Sales* 14,191,680
SIC 7389 Business services, nec
John Collins

D-U-N-S 20-258-6756 (SL)
JR CERTUS CONSTRUCTION CO. LTD
81 Zenway Blvd Unit 3, Woodbridge, ON, L4H
0S5
(647) 494-0150
Emp Here 25   *Sales* 34,114,590
SIC 1542 Nonresidential construction, nec
Joseph Aquino
David Aquino
Matthew Aquino

D-U-N-S 24-738-1700 (SL)
KORSON FURNITURE IMPORTS LTD
7933 Huntington Rd Unit 1, Woodbridge, ON,
L4H 0S9
(905) 850-1530
Emp Here 24   *Sales* 12,212,544
SIC 5021 Furniture
Vince Napolitano

D-U-N-S 25-104-5431 (HQ)
KUMON CANADA INC
KUMON CENTRE OF BEACON HILL
(*Suby of* KUMON INSTITUTE OF EDUCA-TION CO., LTD.)
6240 Highway 7 Suite 300, Woodbridge, ON,
L4H 4G3
(416) 490-1434
Emp Here 95   *Sales* 20,349,000
SIC 8299 Schools and educational services,
nec
Lisa Kaul
Kazuomi Shibata

D-U-N-S 20-129-2919 (HQ)
LONGO BROTHERS FRUIT MARKETS INC
LONGO'S FRUIT MARKET
8800 Huntington Rd, Woodbridge, ON, L4H
3M6
(905) 264-4100
Emp Here 125   *Sales* 1,154,784,000
SIC 5411 Grocery stores
Anthony J Longo
Thomas Longo
Gus Longo

D-U-N-S 24-375-3477 (HQ)

MACTRANS LOGISTICS INC
MACTRANS
(*Suby of* CARRIER ALLIANCE INC)
81 Zenway Blvd Unit 16, Woodbridge, ON, L4H 0S5
(905) 856-6800
Emp Here 19   *Sales* 12,999,175
SIC 4731 Freight transportation arrangement
Joel Mackay
Rico Covello

D-U-N-S 20-737-7859   (SL)
MCDONALDS RESTAURANT OF CANADA INC
9200 Weston Rd Unit E, Woodbridge, ON, L4H 2P8
(905) 832-0424
Emp Here 120   *Sales* 5,596,680
SIC 5812 Eating places
Christie Schlicter

D-U-N-S 20-625-2470   (SL)
METRO BEAUTY SUPPLY LIMITED
315 New Huntington Rd, Woodbridge, ON, L4H 0R5
(800) 263-2365
Emp Here 50   *Sales* 23,751,300
SIC 5087 Service establishment equipment
Luigi Miraglia

D-U-N-S 24-335-0514   (BR)
METRO ONTARIO INC
(*Suby of* METRO INC)
9600 Islington Ave, Woodbridge, ON, L4H 2T1
(905) 893-1618
Emp Here 300
SIC 5411 Grocery stores

D-U-N-S 20-555-7853   (HQ)
MODERN NIAGARA TORONTO INC
MODERN NIAGARA HVAC SERVICES
(*Suby of* MODERN/NIAGARA GROUP INC)
8125 Highway 50, Woodbridge, ON, L4H 4S6
(416) 749-6031
Emp Here 25   *Sales* 34,959,750
SIC 1711 Plumbing, heating, air-conditioning
Craig Pickering
Robert Silberstein
Douglas Rankin

D-U-N-S 24-389-7233   (SL)
NIIGON MACHINES LTD
372 New Enterprise Way, Woodbridge, ON, L4H 0S8
(905) 265-0277
Emp Here 80   *Sales* 17,760,080
SIC 3569 General industrial machinery, nec
Robert Schad

D-U-N-S 25-353-2105   (SL)
NOVEL MECHANICAL INC
111 Zenway Blvd Unit 23, Woodbridge, ON, L4H 3H9

Emp Here 45   *Sales* 10,057,178
SIC 1711 Plumbing, heating, air-conditioning
Pat Corapi

D-U-N-S 24-857-2419   (SL)
OMTRANS LOGISTICS INC
111 Zenway Blvd Unit 5, Woodbridge, ON, L4H 3H9
(416) 921-2255
Emp Here 105   *Sales* 70,023,660
SIC 4731 Freight transportation arrangement
Ritesh Malik

D-U-N-S 20-341-3067   (SL)
ORANGE PASTRIES INC
39 Turning Leaf Dr, Woodbridge, ON, L4H 2J5
(289) 236-0270
Emp Here 49   *Sales* 11,017,895
SIC 2051 Bread, cake, and related products
Samira Sebou
Severio Hennessy
Walid Sebou
Matthew Toledano
Derek Lewis

D-U-N-S 25-253-1934   (HQ)
OWEN & COMPANY LIMITED
KINGSDOWN CANADA
51 Stone Ridge Rd Suite Lbby, Woodbridge, ON, L4H 0A5
(905) 265-9203
Emp Here 180   *Sales* 46,759,650
SIC 2515 Mattresses and bedsprings
Hugh Owen
Cindy Anisman
Michael James

D-U-N-S 25-089-5729   (HQ)
PRECISION TRUCK LINES INC
8111 Huntington Rd, Woodbridge, ON, L4H 0S6
(905) 851-1996
Emp Here 30   *Sales* 13,782,302
SIC 4213 Trucking, except local
Vishnu Ramdeen
Simon Arjoon

D-U-N-S 25-214-3615   (SL)
PRO-LINE AUTOMATION SYSTEMS LTD
303 Vaughan Valley Blvd, Woodbridge, ON, L4H 3B5
(905) 264-6230
Emp Here 45   *Sales* 21,376,170
SIC 5084 Industrial machinery and equipment
Leon Gimelshtein
Vinod Ramnauth

D-U-N-S 24-816-2919   (HQ)
QUANTUM PLUS LTD
500 New Enterprise Way, Woodbridge, ON, L4H 0R3
(905) 264-3700
Sales 90,389,000
SIC 5099 Durable goods, nec
Gary Preszcator
Kent Graham
Raj Saini
Martin Hughes

D-U-N-S 24-079-1392   (SL)
RAVINE MUSHROOM (1983) LIMITED
4101 King-Vaughan Rd, Woodbridge, ON, L4H 1E4
(905) 833-5498
Emp Here 60   *Sales* 15,738,540
SIC 0182 Food crops grown under cover
Luciano Quattrociocchi
Frank Quattrociocchi
Frank Oddi

D-U-N-S 24-380-7729   (HQ)
ROBERTSON ELECTRIC WHOLESALE 2008 LIMITED
REW
180 New Huntington Rd Unit 2, Woodbridge, ON, L4H 0P5
(905) 856-9311
Emp Here 100   *Sales* 145,061,750
SIC 5063 Electrical apparatus and equipment
Rick Campbell
Chris Campbell
Michael Kergon

D-U-N-S 24-477-2224   (HQ)
ROLARK STAINLESS STEEL INC
(*Suby of* JACQUET METAL SERVICE)
71 Conair Pkwy, Woodbridge, ON, L4H 0S4
(416) 798-7770
Emp Here 52   *Sales* 33,538,050
SIC 5051 Metals service centers and offices
Radoslav Matijevic

D-U-N-S 20-304-7188   (HQ)
ROYAL GROUP, INC
ROYAL BUILDING PRODUCTS
30 Royal Group Cres, Woodbridge, ON, L4H 1X9
(905) 264-0701
Sales 333,997,500
SIC 2519 Household furniture, nec
Mark Orcutt
Mark Badger
Guy Prentice

Corbet Elder

D-U-N-S 20-512-9906   (BR)
ROYAL GROUP, INC
ROYAL OUTDOOR PRODUCTS, DIV OF
(*Suby of* WESTLAKE CHEMICAL CORPORATION)
100 Royal Group Cres Unit B, Woodbridge, ON, L4H 1X9
(905) 264-2989
Emp Here 400
SIC 3448 Prefabricated Metal buildings and components
Pat Welford

D-U-N-S 20-557-3363   (HQ)
ROYAL GROUP, INC
STEELWOOD DOORS
(*Suby of* WESTLAKE CHEMICAL CORPORATION)
10 Roybridge Gate Suite 201, Woodbridge, ON, L4H 3M8
(905) 264-1660
Emp Here 3,500   *Sales* 2,149,308,000
SIC 3089 Plastics products, nec
Simon Bates
Scott D. Bates
Paul Czachor
Guy Prentice
Michael Boulanger

D-U-N-S 20-647-6454   (BR)
ROYAL GROUP, INC
CROWN PLASTICS EXTUSSION CO
(*Suby of* WESTLAKE CHEMICAL CORPORATION)
111 Royal Group Cres, Woodbridge, ON, L4H 1X9

Emp Here 150
SIC 3089 Plastics products, nec

D-U-N-S 24-340-7439   (BR)
ROYAL GROUP, INC
ROYAL WINDOW & DOOR PROFILES PLANT 2
(*Suby of* WESTLAKE CHEMICAL CORPORATION)
71 Royal Group Cres Suite 2, Woodbridge, ON, L4H 1X9
(905) 264-5500
Emp Here 178
SIC 5039 Construction materials, nec
Pino Consolmagno

D-U-N-S 24-963-9584   (HQ)
RYCOM INC
6201 7 Hwy Unit 8, Woodbridge, ON, L4H 0K7
(905) 264-4800
Emp Here 45   *Sales* 26,830,440
SIC 5065 Electronic parts and equipment, nec
Casey Witkowicz
Pat Mancuso

D-U-N-S 24-872-3421   (HQ)
SONAVOX CANADA INC
(*Suby of* KOALA FINANCIAL GROUP LTD)
100-261 Milani Blvd, Woodbridge, ON, L4H 4E3
(905) 265-2060
Sales 13,645,836
SIC 8731 Commercial physical research
Joe Riggi
Yang Ching Yau
Soh Yong Seng

D-U-N-S 20-705-1855   (SL)
STERLING TILE & CARPET
505 Cityview Blvd Unit 1, Woodbridge, ON, L4H 0L8
(905) 585-4800
Emp Here 100   *Sales* 16,238,100
SIC 1743 Terrazzo, tile, marble and mossaic work
Al Silver
Mark Silver

D-U-N-S 24-138-3215   (SL)

SUNVIEW PATIO DOORS LTD
500 Zenway Blvd, Woodbridge, ON, L4H 0S7
(905) 851-1006
Emp Here 75   *Sales* 33,538,050
SIC 5039 Construction materials, nec
Alex Diiorio
Jerry Diiorio
Lino Diiorio
Sandro Diiorio

D-U-N-S 24-320-1874   (SL)
TAYLOR MADE GOLF CANADA LTD
6240 Highway 7 Suite 100, Woodbridge, ON, L4H 4G3
(800) 668-9883
Emp Here 50   *Sales* 26,027,100
SIC 5091 Sporting and recreation goods
David Abeles
Bill Reimus
Laura Garrett
Chuck Presto
David Brownie
Todd Beach
Brian Bazzel
Brian Coffman
David Bradley
David Silvers

D-U-N-S 25-065-1627   (SL)
TOOLWAY INDUSTRIES LTD
31 Conair Pky, Woodbridge, ON, L4H 0S4
(905) 326-5450
Emp Here 76   *Sales* 36,101,976
SIC 5084 Industrial machinery and equipment
Asher Peres

D-U-N-S 24-857-5966   (HQ)
TRI-COR CONSTRUCTION INC
310 Vaughan Valley Blvd Unit 1, Woodbridge, ON, L4H 3C3

Emp Here 3   *Sales* 11,768,275
SIC 1542 Nonresidential construction, nec
Deborah Lucchette

D-U-N-S 24-503-4280   (HQ)
TRU TECH CORPORATION
TRU TECH DOORS
20 Vaughan Valley Blvd, Woodbridge, ON, L4H 0B1
(905) 856-0096
Sales 24,010,625
SIC 3442 Metal doors, sash, and trim
John Careri
James Wilson

D-U-N-S 24-685-7614   (HQ)
TRULITE GLASS & ALUMINUM SOLUTIONS CANADA, ULC
(*Suby of* TRULITE GLASS & ALUMINUM SOLUTIONS, LLC)
20 Royal Group Cres, Woodbridge, ON, L4H 1X9
(905) 605-7040
Emp Here 155   *Sales* 57,530,250
SIC 3211 Flat glass
Paul Schmitz
David Mccallen
Ron Miller

D-U-N-S 20-624-9013   (HQ)
ULBRICH OF CANADA INC
DIVERSIFIED ULBRICH - TORONTO
(*Suby of* ULBRICH STAINLESS STEELS & SPECIAL METALS, INC.)
150 New Huntington Rd Unit 1, Woodbridge, ON, L4H 4N4
(416) 663-7130
Emp Here 23   *Sales* 20,122,830
SIC 5051 Metals service centers and offices
S Fay Sulley
Barry S Arbus
Frederick C Ulbrich Lll
Frederick C Ulbrich Jr
John J Cei Jr

D-U-N-S 24-335-5450   (SL)

V.I.C. SAFETY INCORPORATED
377 Vaughan Valley Blvd, Woodbridge, ON, L4H 3B5
(905) 850-0838
Emp Here 21   *Sales* 10,464,762
SIC 5136 Men's and boy's clothing
Vince Vinelli
Maurice Cugliari

D-U-N-S 25-977-4206   (HQ)
VISION EXTRUSIONS GROUP LIMITED
201 Zenway Blvd, Woodbridge, ON, L4H 3H9
(905) 265-9970
Sales 63,543,200
SIC 3089 Plastics products, nec
Vic De Zen
Francesco Bisogno
James Digiorgio

D-U-N-S 20-849-1233   (HQ)
WATSON BUILDING SUPPLIES INC
50 Royal Group Cres Unit 2, Woodbridge, ON, L4H 1X9
(905) 669-1898
Emp Here 81   *Sales* 111,077,460
SIC 5039 Construction materials, nec
Douglas Skrepnek
Robert Bucci
Carmine Bucci
Adolf Gust
Tony Rinomato
Leo Rinomato

D-U-N-S 20-295-7452   (SL)
WEBER-STEPHEN (CANADA) COMPANY
(*Suby of* WEBER-STEPHEN PRODUCTS LLC)
1 Roybridge Gate, Woodbridge, ON, L4H 4E6
(905) 850-8999
Emp Here 25   *Sales* 12,721,400
SIC 5023 Homefurnishings
Tony Ferraro
Dale Wytiaz
Philip John Zadeik

D-U-N-S 24-378-9554   (HQ)
WSB TITAN INC
(*Suby of* GMS INC.)
50 Royal Group Cres Unit 2, Woodbridge, ON, L4H 1X9
(905) 669-1898
Sales 12,477,600
SIC 8741 Management services
Douglas Skrepnek

D-U-N-S 20-711-4682   (BR)
YORK CATHOLIC DISTRICT SCHOOL BOARD
ST AGNES OF ASSISI ELEMENTARY SCHOOL
(*Suby of* YORK CATHOLIC DISTRICT SCHOOL BOARD)
120 La Rocca Ave, Woodbridge, ON, L4H 2A9
(905) 303-4646
Emp Here 80
SIC 8211 Elementary and secondary schools
Amalia Scott

D-U-N-S 20-711-4393   (BR)
YORK REGION DISTRICT SCHOOL BOARD
EMILY CARR SECONDARY SCHOOL
(*Suby of* YORK REGION DISTRICT SCHOOL BOARD)
4901 Rutherford Rd, Woodbridge, ON, L4H 3C2
(905) 850-5012
Emp Here 100
SIC 8211 Elementary and secondary schools
Paolo Burzese

D-U-N-S 20-117-1712   (SL)
ZZEN DESIGN BUILD LIMITED
(*Suby of* ZZEN GROUP OF COMPANIES LIMITED)
100 Zenway Blvd, Woodbridge, ON, L4H 2Y7
(905) 264-5962
Emp Here 30   *Sales* 43,441,809

SIC 7372 Prepackaged software
Vic De Zen
Joseph Sgro
Lu Galasso
Sergio De Zen

Woodbridge, ON L4L

D-U-N-S 20-375-0646   (SL)
10365289 CANADA INC
MARCOMM INTEGRATED BUSINESS SOLUTIONS
7777 Weston Rd 8th Fl, Woodbridge, ON, L4L 0G9
(905) 695-1700
Emp Here 100   *Sales* 21,782,900
SIC 1731 Electrical work
Rick Boyd

D-U-N-S 25-302-8112   (HQ)
1146898 ONTARIO INC
MASTER BUILDING MATERIALS
101 Westcreek Dr, Woodbridge, ON, L4L 9N6
(905) 850-2212
Emp Here 17   *Sales* 10,732,176
SIC 5039 Construction materials, nec
Antonio Iacobelli
Luigi Iacobelli

D-U-N-S 20-324-8075   (SL)
1359238 ONTARIO INC.
CELLULAR POINT
643 Chrislea Rd Unit 3, Woodbridge, ON, L4L 8A3
(905) 669-3882
Emp Here 130   *Sales* 29,701,360
SIC 4813 Telephone communication, except radio
Brinder Singh Maker

D-U-N-S 20-515-3047   (SL)
1428309 ONTARIO LTD
ALTA INFINITI
5585 Highway 7, Woodbridge, ON, L4L 1T5
(877) 694-8654
Emp Here 25   *Sales* 12,451,950
SIC 5511 New and used car dealers
Joe Zanchin

D-U-N-S 20-999-7480   (SL)
2012865 ONTARIO INC
HIGGINS COHN BRAND MANAGEMENT
71 Silton Rd Unit 8, Woodbridge, ON, L4L 7Z8
(905) 856-8252
Emp Here 22   *Sales* 18,382,694
SIC 5141 Groceries, general line
Patrick Higgins
Jonathan Cohn

D-U-N-S 20-972-9784   (BR)
2063414 ONTARIO LIMITED
WOODBRIDGE VISTA CARE COMMUNITY
5400 Steeles Ave W, Woodbridge, ON, L4L 9S1
(905) 856-7200
Emp Here 200
SIC 8051 Skilled nursing care facilities
Lucie Fontaine

D-U-N-S 24-679-2118   (HQ)
2261079 ONTARIO LTD
METAL SUPERMARKETS
100 Haist Ave Unit B, Woodbridge, ON, L4L 5V4
(905) 851-0173
Emp Here 5   *Sales* 13,415,220
SIC 5051 Metals service centers and offices
Christopher Hare
Scott Turner

D-U-N-S 20-272-8309   (SL)
2443499 ONTARIO INC
PATISSERIE MONACO
48 Caster Ave, Woodbridge, ON, L4L 5Z1

(905) 771-0637
Emp Here 25   *Sales* 20,889,425
SIC 5149 Groceries and related products, nec
Mohamed Alibhai

D-U-N-S 24-966-4046   (SL)
4 STAR DRYWALL (99) LTD
115 Sharer Rd Unit 1, Woodbridge, ON, L4L 8Z3
(905) 660-9676
Emp Here 200   *Sales* 32,476,200
SIC 1742 Plastering, drywall, and insulation
Robert Pirocchi
Tony Alves
Emidio Tramontozzi
Frank Pirocchi

D-U-N-S 25-458-7124   (SL)
706017 ONTARIO CORP
NU TREND CONSTRUCTION CO
101 Caster Ave, Woodbridge, ON, L4L 5Z2
(905) 851-3189
Emp Here 120   *Sales* 32,513,040
SIC 1521 Single-family housing construction
John Gabriele
Frank Gabriele

D-U-N-S 24-991-4409   (HQ)
770976 ONTARIO LIMITED
TIM HORTONS
100 Whitmore Rd, Woodbridge, ON, L4L 7K4
(905) 850-1477
Sales 57,739,200
SIC 5461 Retail bakeries
Ralph Sheperd

D-U-N-S 24-952-6401   (HQ)
972683 ONTARIO INC
O'NEIL ELECTRIC SUPPLY
150 Creditview Rd, Woodbridge, ON, L4L 9N4
(416) 798-7722
Emp Here 1   *Sales* 13,077,650
SIC 6712 Bank holding companies
Michael O'neil

D-U-N-S 20-322-4654   (SL)
ABC GROUP
ABC GROUP TRANSPORTATION
100 Hanlan Rd Suite 3, Woodbridge, ON, L4L 4V8
(905) 392-0485
Emp Here 450   *Sales* 6,058,200
SIC 6712 Bank holding companies
William Baker
Jensen Linonale
Mark Baker

D-U-N-S 20-112-3739   (HQ)
ACOSTA CANADA CORPORATION
ACOSTA CANADA
(*Suby of* ACOSTA INC.)
250 Rowntree Dairy Rd, Woodbridge, ON, L4L 9J7
(905) 264-0466
Emp Here 150   *Sales* 329,689,360
SIC 5141 Groceries, general line
Shaun Mckenna

D-U-N-S 25-221-2386   (SL)
ACROSS CANADA CONSTRUCTION LTD
220 Regina Rd, Woodbridge, ON, L4L 8L6
(905) 264-9500
Emp Here 22   *Sales* 10,356,082
SIC 1542 Nonresidential construction, nec
Peter Trezzi

D-U-N-S 24-526-6739   (SL)
ADRIATIC INSURANCE BROKERS LTD
10 Director Crt Suite 100, Woodbridge, ON, L4L 7E8
(905) 851-8555
Emp Here 37   *Sales* 21,457,188
SIC 6411 Insurance agents, brokers, and service
Don Bowden
Joseph Sorbara

D-U-N-S 20-936-7366   (SL)
ALL TEAM GLASS & MIRROR LTD

281 Hanlan Rd, Woodbridge, ON, L4L 3R7
(905) 851-7711
Emp Here 45   *Sales* 10,504,575
SIC 3231 Products of purchased glass
Leander Timoll
Mark Timoll
Aldo Piazza

D-U-N-S 25-509-2132   (HQ)
ANATOLIA GROUP INC
8300 Huntington Rd, Woodbridge, ON, L4L 1A5
(905) 771-3800
Emp Here 40   *Sales* 20,122,830
SIC 5032 Brick, stone, and related material
Galip Elmaagacli
Cengiz Elmaagacli
Berrin Elmaagacli
Saadet Elmaagacli
Bekir Elmaagacli

D-U-N-S 20-999-6722   (SL)
ANCO CONTRACTING INC
140 Regina Rd Unit 15, Woodbridge, ON, L4L 8N1
(905) 652-2353
Emp Here 40   *Sales* 17,886,960
SIC 5032 Brick, stone, and related material
Tony Catanzariti

D-U-N-S 24-562-8730   (HQ)
AQUARIUM SERVICES WAREHOUSE OUTLETS INC
BIG AL'S AQUARIUM SERVICES
441 Chrislea Rd, Woodbridge, ON, L4L 8N4
(905) 851-1858
Emp Here 50   *Sales* 77,433,300
SIC 6794 Patent owners and lessors
Allan Saul
Tally Saul

D-U-N-S 20-400-1325   (SL)
ASL PRINT FX LTD
1 Royal Gate Blvd Unit A, Woodbridge, ON, L4L 8Z7
(416) 798-7310
Emp Here 81   *Sales* 13,286,187
SIC 2759 Commercial printing, nec
Charles W Maclean
Yvonne Baker
Stay Daly

D-U-N-S 24-523-9749   (HQ)
ASSA ABLOY DOOR GROUP INC
(*Suby of* ASSA ABLOY AB)
101 Ashbridge Cir, Woodbridge, ON, L4L 3R5
(416) 749-2111
Sales 30,733,600
SIC 3442 Metal doors, sash, and trim
Thanasis Molokotos
Jeffrey Mereschuk
Shane Magee

D-U-N-S 25-504-3077   (SL)
ATS TEST INC
(*Suby of* ATS AUTOMATION TOOLING SYSTEMS INC)
600 Chrislea Rd, Woodbridge, ON, L4L 8K9
(905) 850-8600
Emp Here 50   *Sales* 11,364,450
SIC 3823 Process control instruments
Maria Perrella

D-U-N-S 25-991-2491   (HQ)
AUDIO VISUAL SERVICES (CANADA) CORPORATION
PRESENTATION SERVICES AUDIO VISUAL
(*Suby of* PSAV HOLDINGS LLC)
180 Trowers Rd Unit 28, Woodbridge, ON, L4L 8A6
(647) 724-0880
Emp Here 10   *Sales* 78,327,600
SIC 7359 Equipment rental and leasing, nec
Digby J Davies
Robert K Ellis
Patricia Chiuppi-Silverio

D-U-N-S 24-985-3029   (HQ)

AVENUE MOTOR WORKS INC
681 Rowntree Dairy Rd, Woodbridge, ON, L4L 5T9
(905) 850-2268
Emp Here 40   *Sales* 29,137,200
SIC 5013 Motor vehicle supplies and new parts
John Bosschaert

D-U-N-S 20-097-3191   (SL)
BASECRETE INC
396 Chrislea Rd, Woodbridge, ON, L4L 8A8
(905) 265-9983
Emp Here 31   *Sales* 14,592,661
SIC 1542 Nonresidential construction, nec
Tony Smeriglio

D-U-N-S 25-090-1956   (SL)
BAUMAN, T & W ENTERPRISES INC
INTERSTATE BATTERY SYSTEMS OF BRAMPTON
7835 Highway 50 Unit 14 & 15, Woodbridge, ON, L4L 1A5
(905) 264-0080
Emp Here 28   *Sales* 10,198,020
SIC 5013 Motor vehicle supplies and new parts
Vernon Timothy Bauman
Wendy Michelle Bauman

D-U-N-S 20-743-4767   (BR)
BEST BUY CANADA LTD
BEST BUY
(*Suby of* BEST BUY CO., INC.)
7850 Weston Rd Suite 1, Woodbridge, ON, L4L 9N8
(905) 264-3191
Emp Here 145
SIC 5731 Radio, television, and electronic stores
Carol Graziani

D-U-N-S 20-145-9708   (SL)
BEST WAY STONE LIMITED
8821 Weston Rd, Woodbridge, ON, L4L 1A6
(416) 747-0988
Emp Here 50   *Sales* 11,671,750
SIC 3272 Concrete products, nec
Frank Pacitto
Paul Pignatelli

D-U-N-S 20-016-2837   (BR)
BRICK WAREHOUSE LP, THE
(*Suby of* BRICK WAREHOUSE LP, THE)
137 Chrislea Rd, Woodbridge, ON, L4L 8N6
(905) 850-5300
Emp Here 130
SIC 5712 Furniture stores
Armando Lopez

D-U-N-S 25-279-6180   (SL)
BROOKLIN ESTATES GENERAL PARTNER INC.
3700 Steeles Ave W Suite 800, Woodbridge, ON, L4L 8M9
(905) 850-8508
Emp Here 92   *Sales* 18,757,236
SIC 6553 Cemetery subdividers and developers
Joseph Sorbara
Edward Sorbara

D-U-N-S 24-488-2080   (SL)
CAMPIO FURNITURE LIMITED
CAMPIO GROUP
5770 Highway 7 Unit 1, Woodbridge, ON, L4L 1T8
(905) 850-6636
Emp Here 90   *Sales* 13,888,980
SIC 2512 Upholstered household furniture
Vito Servello

D-U-N-S 20-526-2975   (HQ)
CANADA COMPOUND CORPORATION
391 Rowntree Dairy Rd, Woodbridge, ON, L4L 8H1
(905) 856-5005
Sales 20,053,848

SIC 5149 Groceries and related products, nec
Mike Wallace

D-U-N-S 20-582-5644   (BR)
CANADA POST CORPORATION
(*Suby of* GOVERNMENT OF CANADA)
21 Haist Ave Suite 1, Woodbridge, ON, L4L 5V5
(905) 851-1237
Emp Here 80
SIC 4311 U.s. postal service
Steven Hewitt

D-U-N-S 24-097-1945   (SL)
CANADIAN THERMO WINDOWS INC
MAGIC WINDOW
75 Rowntree Dairy Rd, Woodbridge, ON, L4L 6C8
(905) 856-8805
Emp Here 65   *Sales* 12,485,525
SIC 3442 Metal doors, sash, and trim
Sol Goldenberg
Yael Goldenberg

D-U-N-S 20-638-9876   (HQ)
CARPENTER CANADA CO
(*Suby of* CARPENTER CO.)
500 Hanlan Rd, Woodbridge, ON, L4L 3P6
(416) 743-5689
Emp Here 105   *Sales* 26,508,735
SIC 1751 Carpentry work
Dave Lemire
Stanley Pauley
Mark Willard

D-U-N-S 25-074-9517   (SL)
CARPENTERS DISTRICT COUNCIL OF ONTARIO TRAINING TRUST FUND, THE
CDC
222 Rowntree Dairy Rd, Woodbridge, ON, L4L 9T2

Emp Here 100   *Sales* 70,921,200
SIC 8699 Membership organizations, nec
Tony Iannuzzi
Mike Yorke
Tom Cardinal

D-U-N-S 20-913-3086   (SL)
CARPENTERS LOCAL UNION 27 JOINT APPRENTICESHIP AND TRAINING TRUST FUND INC
222 Rowntree Dairy Rd, Woodbridge, ON, L4L 9T2
(905) 652-5507
Emp Here 75   *Sales* 3,538,575
SIC 8331 Job training and related services
Eddie Thornton

D-U-N-S 20-177-7922   (HQ)
CATERPILLAR OF CANADA CORPORATION
(*Suby of* CATERPILLAR INC.)
3700 Steeles Ave W Suite 902, Woodbridge, ON, L4L 8K8
(905) 265-5802
Sales 87,791,400
SIC 5082 Construction and mining machinery
Tim Salmon
Ty Rakestraw
Brian Westlake

D-U-N-S 20-177-4742   (SL)
CHICAGO 58 FOOD PRODUCTS LIMITED
CHICAGO 58
135 Haist Ave, Woodbridge, ON, L4L 5V6
(905) 265-1044
Emp Here 12   *Sales* 10,026,924
SIC 5147 Meats and meat products
Sidney Starkman
Ted Bernholtz
Moshe Ami

D-U-N-S 25-512-6070   (SL)
CITYWIDE DOOR & HARDWARE INC
(*Suby of* AVANTE LOGIXX INC)
80 Vinyl Crt, Woodbridge, ON, L4L 4A3

(905) 265-2444
Emp Here 45   *Sales* 15,037,600
SIC 5072 Hardware
Michael Shearer
Tony Bancheri
Domenic Greco
Joseph Shearer
Daniel Shearer

D-U-N-S 24-827-3443   (SL)
CLOVER INSURANCE GROUP
3800 Steeles Ave W Suite 201, Woodbridge, ON, L4L 4G9
(905) 851-7774
Emp Here 36   *Sales* 20,877,264
SIC 6411 Insurance agents, brokers, and service
Joseph Coccia

D-U-N-S 25-075-3212   (SL)
COG-VEYOR SYSTEMS INC
371 Hanlan Rd, Woodbridge, ON, L4L 3T1
(416) 798-7333
Emp Here 30   *Sales* 14,250,780
SIC 5084 Industrial machinery and equipment
David Osmond

D-U-N-S 24-831-2613   (SL)
COMMDOOR ALUMINUM
471 Chrislea Rd Suite 1, Woodbridge, ON, L4L 8N6
(416) 743-3667
Emp Here 45   *Sales* 10,504,575
SIC 3365 Aluminum foundries
Gianfranco Dimarco

D-U-N-S 24-408-1832   (HQ)
COMPACT MOULD LIMITED
120 Haist Ave, Woodbridge, ON, L4L 5V4
(905) 851-7724
Sales 13,320,060
SIC 3544 Special dies, tools, jigs, and fixtures
Miguel Petrucci
Gaston Petrucci
Aldino Petrucci

D-U-N-S 24-665-7522   (SL)
CONCORD STEEL CENTRE LIMITED
147 Ashbridge Cir, Woodbridge, ON, L4L 3R5
(905) 856-1717
Emp Here 80   *Sales* 35,773,920
SIC 5051 Metals service centers and offices
Bruno Bellisario
Marco Bellisario
Sachin Shah

D-U-N-S 24-844-9571   (HQ)
CONSOLIDATED DEALERS CO-OPERATIVE INC
441 Hanlan Rd, Woodbridge, ON, L4L 3T1
(905) 264-7022
Emp Here 46   *Sales* 21,852,900
SIC 5013 Motor vehicle supplies and new parts
Thomas Langton
Janette Andrade
Trevor Dawson

D-U-N-S 24-319-4099   (HQ)
COREIO INC
55 Director Crt, Woodbridge, ON, L4L 4S5
(905) 264-8520
Sales 187,373,200
SIC 5045 Computers, peripherals, and software
David Naiman
Scott Glen

D-U-N-S 24-876-9804   (HQ)
CORNERSTONE INSURANCE BROKERS LTD
(*Suby of* INTACT FINANCIAL CORPORATION)
8001 Weston Rd Suite 300, Woodbridge, ON, L4L 9C8
(905) 856-1981
Emp Here 25   *Sales* 157,058,070
SIC 6411 Insurance agents, brokers, and ser-

vice
Daniella Bonia

D-U-N-S 20-113-2342   (BR)
CORPORATION OF THE CITY OF VAUGHAN, THE
AL PALLADINI COMMUNITY CENTRE
(*Suby of* CORPORATION OF THE CITY OF VAUGHAN, THE)
9201 Islington Ave, Woodbridge, ON, L4L 1A6
(905) 832-8564
Emp Here 100
SIC 8322 Individual and family services
Janis Lee

D-U-N-S 24-666-8982   (SL)
CORTINA KITCHENS INC
70 Regina Rd, Woodbridge, ON, L4L 8L6
(905) 264-6464
Emp Here 100   *Sales* 19,237,000
SIC 2434 Wood kitchen cabinets
Peter Tommasino
Paul Tommasino
Tony Tommasino
Gino Tersigni

D-U-N-S 25-529-3227   (BR)
COSTCO WHOLESALE CANADA LTD
COSTCO
(*Suby of* COSTCO WHOLESALE CORPORATION)
71 Colossus Dr Suite 547, Woodbridge, ON, L4L 9J8
(905) 264-8337
Emp Here 200
SIC 5199 Nondurable goods, nec

D-U-N-S 20-545-5178   (SL)
COVENTRY NORTH JAGUAR LAND ROVER
123 Auto Park Cir, Woodbridge, ON, L4L 9S5
(647) 990-3433
Emp Here 25   *Sales* 12,451,950
SIC 5511 New and used car dealers
Lou Crkovski

D-U-N-S 20-774-4699   (SL)
DECOR-REST FURNITURE LTD
511 Chrislea Rd Suite 8, Woodbridge, ON, L4L 8N6
(905) 856-5956
Emp Here 220   *Sales* 48,986,300
SIC 2512 Upholstered household furniture
Angelo Marzilli Sr
Christina Marzilli

D-U-N-S 24-951-6543   (SL)
DELTA BEVERAGES INC
21 Marycroft Ave, Woodbridge, ON, L4L 5Y6
(905) 850-8077
Emp Here 50   *Sales* 11,242,750
SIC 2086 Bottled and canned soft drinks
Sam Koundouros

D-U-N-S 24-075-2840   (SL)
DENTSPLY CANADA LTD
(*Suby of* DENTSPLY SIRONA INC.)
161 Vinyl Crt, Woodbridge, ON, L4L 4A3
(905) 851-6060
Emp Here 80   *Sales* 42,828,160
SIC 5047 Medical and hospital equipment
Bret W Wise
Debora M Rasin
Judy Dautovich

D-U-N-S 20-387-9676   (SL)
DMC MINING SERVICES LTD
(*Suby of* KGHM POLSKA MIEDZ S A)
191 Creditview Rd Suite 400, Woodbridge, ON, L4L 9T1
(905) 780-1980
Emp Here 520
SIC 1081 Metal mining services
Michal Jezioro
Joan Beck
Rebecca Ng

D-U-N-S 24-183-9455   (HQ)
DOBBIN SALES LIMITED

51 Terecar Dr Unit 2, Woodbridge, ON, L4L 0B5
(905) 264-5465
Sales 11,179,350
SIC 5074 Plumbing and heating equipment and supplies (hydronics)
Bruce Laing
Jason Boyd

D-U-N-S 20-045-0633 (HQ)
DUNNE, WILLIAM M & ASSOCIATES LIMITED
10 Director Crt Suite 300, Woodbridge, ON, L4L 7E8
(905) 856-5240
Sales 37,600,965
SIC 5141 Groceries, general line
Robert Brema
Michael Crosby

D-U-N-S 24-867-1075 (HQ)
EDDIE BAUER OF CANADA INC
EDDIE BAUER SPORTSWEAR
201 Aviva Park Dr, Woodbridge, ON, L4L 9C1
(800) 426-8020
Emp Here 50 *Sales* 87,328,500
SIC 5699 Miscellaneous apparel and accessory stores
Fabian Mansson
Ron Gaston

D-U-N-S 25-076-5468 (SL)
EGAN TEAMBOARD INC
(*Suby of* EGAN VISUAL INC)
300 Hanlan Rd, Woodbridge, ON, L4L 3P6
(905) 851-2826
Emp Here 200 *Sales* 30,864,400
SIC 2521 Wood office furniture
James Egan

D-U-N-S 20-554-3267 (HQ)
EGAN VISUAL INC
300 Hanlan Rd, Woodbridge, ON, L4L 3P6
(905) 851-2826
Emp Here 100 *Sales* 20,061,860
SIC 2599 Furniture and fixtures, nec
Sean Brown

D-U-N-S 20-973-6453 (SL)
ELECTRICITY DISTRIBUTORS ASSOCIATION
EDA
3700 Steeles Ave W Suite 1100, Woodbridge, ON, L4L 8K8
(905) 265-5300
Emp Here 40 *Sales* 10,344,600
SIC 8611 Business associations
Charlie Macaluso
Max Cananzi
Jac Vanderbaan
Rene Gatien
Brian Bentz
Jim Hogan
Ed Houghton
Robert Mace
Blair Peberdy
Vinay Sharma

D-U-N-S 24-770-8357 (SL)
ELITREX PLUMBING LTD
120 Sharer Rd, Woodbridge, ON, L4L 8P4
(905) 264-7418
Emp Here 48 *Sales* 10,604,832
SIC 1711 Plumbing, heating, air-conditioning
Massimo Arduini
Claudio Zarpellon

D-U-N-S 25-215-2194 (SL)
EXCENTROTECH PRECISION INC
55 Westcreek Dr, Woodbridge, ON, L4L 9N6
(905) 856-1801
Emp Here 55 *Sales* 12,311,365
SIC 3728 Aircraft parts and equipment, nec
Tony Petricca
Nick Ciccone

D-U-N-S 24-310-6684 (HQ)

EXTREME RETAIL CANADA INC
BUCK OR TWO
11 Director Crt Suite 554, Woodbridge, ON, L4L 4S5
(905) 265-3160
Emp Here 30 *Sales* 24,388,350
SIC 6794 Patent owners and lessors
Frank Spain
Tom Norwell
Ken Opper
Dusan Miklas
Greg Miklas
Ted Agnew

D-U-N-S 20-052-1560 (SL)
EXTRUDEX ALUMINUM LIMITED
411 Chrislea Rd, Woodbridge, ON, L4L 8N4
(416) 745-4444
Emp Here 150 *Sales* 27,208,200
SIC 3354 Aluminum extruded products
Andrew Gucciardi

D-U-N-S 24-720-8077 (SL)
FESTA JUICE COMPANY LTD
(*Suby of* MAGNOTTA WINERY CORPORATION)
271 Chrislea Rd, Woodbridge, ON, L4L 8N6
(905) 850-5557
Emp Here 15 *Sales* 12,533,655
SIC 5149 Groceries and related products, nec
Rossana Magnotta
Gabe Magnotta

D-U-N-S 24-654-8486 (SL)
FLEMING DOOR PRODUCTS LTD.
(*Suby of* ASSA ABLOY AB)
101 Ashbridge Cir, Woodbridge, ON, L4L 3R5
(800) 263-7515
Emp Here 45 *Sales* 12,044,340
SIC 5211 Lumber and other building materials
William Strong

D-U-N-S 25-274-1889 (HQ)
FORMGLAS HOLDINGS INC
181 Regina Rd, Woodbridge, ON, L4L 8M3
(416) 635-8030
Sales 13,777,883
SIC 6712 Bank holding companies
John Chettleburgh

D-U-N-S 25-080-5371 (SL)
FORTINO'S (HIGHWAY 7 & ANSLEY) LTD
3940 Highway 7, Woodbridge, ON, L4L 9C3
(905) 851-5642
Emp Here 275 *Sales* 52,927,600
SIC 5411 Grocery stores
Joey Cosentino

D-U-N-S 25-369-5258 (BR)
G-TEL ENGINEERING INC
(*Suby of* OAKVILLE HYDRO ELECTRICITY DISTRIBUTION INC)
200 Hanlan Rd, Woodbridge, ON, L4L 3P6
(905) 856-1162
Emp Here 200
SIC 8748 Business consulting, nec
Trac Ngo

D-U-N-S 20-165-6543 (HQ)
GANZ
GANZ CANADA
1 Pearce Rd, Woodbridge, ON, L4L 3T2
(905) 851-6661
Emp Here 550 *Sales* 441,869,250
SIC 5199 Nondurable goods, nec
Howard Ganz
Owen Rogers

D-U-N-S 20-346-9221 (SL)
GEMSTAR SECURITY SERVICE LTD
4000 Steeles Ave W Unit 29, Woodbridge, ON, L4L 4V9
(905) 850-8517
Emp Here 100 *Sales* 39,567,800
SIC 7381 Detective and armored car services
Dave Catalano

D-U-N-S 25-033-3739 (SL)

GLOBAL PLUMBING & HEATING INC
601 Rowntree Dairy Rd Suite 1, Woodbridge, ON, L4L 5T8
(905) 851-4212
Emp Here 80 *Sales* 18,645,200
SIC 1711 Plumbing, heating, air-conditioning
Victor Dicarlo
Lucy Dicarlo

D-U-N-S 24-817-0664 (SL)
GRACIOUS LIVING CORPORATION
7200 Martin Grove Rd, Woodbridge, ON, L4L 9J3
(905) 264-5660
Emp Here 415 *Sales* 65,926,070
SIC 3089 Plastics products, nec
Enzo Macri
Vito Galloro
Lou Farrace

D-U-N-S 20-413-9083 (HQ)
GRAND & TOY LIMITED
OFFICEMAXMD GRAND&TOY
(*Suby of* OFFICE DEPOT, INC.)
200 Aviva Park Dr, Woodbridge, ON, L4L 9C7
(416) 401-6300
Emp Here 210 *Sales* 266,862,798
SIC 5943 Stationery stores
John Baigrie
Marla Allan
Stan Dabic
Darlene Quashie Henry

D-U-N-S 25-115-1759 (BR)
GRAND & TOY LIMITED
(*Suby of* OFFICE DEPOT, INC.)
200 Aviva Park Dr, Woodbridge, ON, L4L 9C7
(866) 391-8111
Emp Here 500
SIC 5112 Stationery and office supplies
Josie O"brian

D-U-N-S 20-182-3051 (HQ)
GRANDE CHEESE COMPANY LIMITED
468 Jevlan Dr, Woodbridge, ON, L4L 8L4
(905) 856-6880
Emp Here 50 *Sales* 64,644,030
SIC 2022 Cheese; natural and processed
Albert Contardi
Gino Contardi
Rocco Rossi

D-U-N-S 20-166-4026 (SL)
GRIFFITHS, H. COMPANY LIMITED
140 Regina Rd Suite 15, Woodbridge, ON, L4L 8N1
(905) 850-7070
Emp Here 50 *Sales* 11,046,700
SIC 1711 Plumbing, heating, air-conditioning
Mel Prowse

D-U-N-S 20-328-0958 (HQ)
HDS CANADA, INC
HD SUPPLY CONSTRUCTION & INDUSTRIAL - BRAFASCO
(*Suby of* HD SUPPLY HOLDINGS, INC.)
100 Galcat Dr, Woodbridge, ON, L4L 0B9
(905) 850-8085
Emp Here 120 *Sales* 215,300,592
SIC 5072 Hardware
Vasken Altounian
Joseph Deangelo
Dan Mcdevitt
Evan Levitt
Jeffrey R. Monday
William P. Stengel
Marc A. Gonzalez
James F. Brumsey
Malinda A. Miller

D-U-N-S 25-368-3346 (SL)
HEARTLAND SERVICES GROUP LIMITED
40 Trowers Rd Unit 1, Woodbridge, ON, L4L 7K6
(905) 265-9667
Emp Here 200 *Sales* 6,393,600
SIC 7349 Building maintenance services, nec

Jonathan Heart

D-U-N-S 24-886-0637 (HQ)
HIGHFIELD HOLDINGS INC
TRADE SECRETS
101 Jevlan Dr Suite 1, Woodbridge, ON, L4L 8C2
(905) 264-2799
Sales 17,420,250
SIC 6794 Patent owners and lessors
Joseph Bellotti

D-U-N-S 25-250-4931 (BR)
HOME DEPOT OF CANADA INC
HOME DEPOT
(*Suby of* THE HOME DEPOT INC)
140 Northview Blvd, Woodbridge, ON, L4L 8T2
(905) 851-1800
Emp Here 200
SIC 5251 Hardware stores
Emmanuele Barbaro

D-U-N-S 25-459-1829 (SL)
HOMELIFE/ROYALCORP REAL ESTATE INC
HOMELIFE
4040 Steeles Ave W Unit 12, Woodbridge, ON, L4L 4Y5
(905) 856-6611
Emp Here 42 *Sales* 13,739,334
SIC 6531 Real estate agents and managers
Frank Andriano

D-U-N-S 20-290-8419 (HQ)
HUB FINANCIAL INC
(*Suby of* HELLMAN & FRIEDMAN LLC)
3700 Steeles Ave W Unit 1001, Woodbridge, ON, L4L 8K8
(905) 264-1634
Emp Here 56 *Sales* 536,309,752
SIC 6411 Insurance agents, brokers, and service
Terri Diflorio

D-U-N-S 20-388-8321 (SL)
INTEGRICON PROPERTY RESTORATION AND CONSTRUCTION GROUP INC
219 Westcreek Dr, Woodbridge, ON, L4L 9T7
(416) 736-0395
Emp Here 80 *Sales* 19,798,640
SIC 1771 Concrete work
Neal Weir
Darryl D'silva

D-U-N-S 24-320-1970 (SL)
INTERNATIONAL CUSTOMER CARE SERVICES INC
3800 Steeles Ave W Unit 100e, Woodbridge, ON, L4L 4G9
(905) 850-4760
Emp Here 80 *Sales* 15,032,486
SIC 4899 Communication services, nec
Jorge Aguirre-Barrios

D-U-N-S 24-545-2453 (SL)
INVESTMENTS HARDWARE LIMITED
IHL
250 Rowntree Dairy Rd, Woodbridge, ON, L4L 9J7
(905) 851-8974
Emp Here 70 *Sales* 31,302,180
SIC 5072 Hardware
Domenic Digiorgio
Rose Martino
Vincenzina De Francesco

D-U-N-S 20-845-3712 (SL)
ISLINGTON MOTOR SALES LIMITED
ALTA NISSAN
7625 Martin Grove Rd Suite B, Woodbridge, ON, L4L 2C5
(905) 851-1279
Emp Here 45 *Sales* 22,413,510
SIC 5511 New and used car dealers
Giuseppe (Joe) Zanchin
Edward Wong

D-U-N-S 20-172-3772   (HQ)
JAN K. OVERWEEL LIMITED
(*Suby of* JKO HOLDINGS INC)
3700 Steeles Ave W Suite 702, Woodbridge, ON, L4L 8K8
(905) 850-9010
Emp Here 45   *Sales* 45,956,735
SIC 5141 Groceries, general line
Arthur Pelliccione
Patrick Pelliccione
Art Pelliccione
Teresa Pelliccione

D-U-N-S 25-136-0962   (SL)
JARDIN BANQUET & CONFERENCE CEN-TRE INC, LE
8440 27 Hwy, Woodbridge, ON, L4L 1A5
(905) 851-2200
Emp Here 150   *Sales* 16,017,300
SIC 7299 Miscellaneous personal service
Carlo Parentela
Mara Vanan

D-U-N-S 20-548-1687   (HQ)
KGHM INTERNATIONAL LTD
(*Suby of* KGHM POLSKA MIEDZ S A)
191 Creditview Rd Suite 400, Woodbridge, ON, L4L 9T1
(647) 265-9191
Emp Here 15   *Sales* 204,619,200
SIC 1081 Metal mining services
Wojciech Kedzia
Marin Chludzinski
Robert Nowak
Robert Macdonald

D-U-N-S 24-015-1782   (SL)
KHALSA UNION TRADING COMPANY
418 Hanlan Rd Suite 17, Woodbridge, ON, L4L 4Z1
(905) 851-7999
Emp Here 30   *Sales* 25,067,310
SIC 5149 Groceries and related products, nec
Jagpal Manota

D-U-N-S 25-360-1041   (BR)
KNOLL NORTH AMERICA CORP
(*Suby of* KNOLL, INC.)
600 Rowntree Dairy Rd, Woodbridge, ON, L4L 5T8
(416) 741-5453
Emp Here 200
SIC 2514 Metal household furniture
Jane Eccleston

D-U-N-S 25-282-4354   (SL)
KRISTUS DARZS LATVIAN HOME
11290 Pine Valley Dr, Woodbridge, ON, L4L 1A6
(905) 832-3300
Emp Here 115   *Sales* 7,857,490
SIC 8051 Skilled nursing care facilities
Lauma Stikuts

D-U-N-S 24-122-9251   (SL)
L.H.M. TECHNOLOGIES INC
446 Rowntree Dairy Rd, Woodbridge, ON, L4L 8H2
(905) 856-2466
Emp Here 88   *Sales* 19,536,088
SIC 3541 Machine tools, Metal cutting type
Lovro Gotovac
Marko Gotovac
Katarina Gotovac

D-U-N-S 24-953-4546   (SL)
LEADER PLUMBING & HEATING INC
91 Haist Ave Unit 3, Woodbridge, ON, L4L 5V5
(905) 264-1162
Emp Here 90   *Sales* 20,975,850
SIC 1711 Plumbing, heating, air-conditioning
Glenn Bortolus
David Breda

D-U-N-S 20-346-0670   (SL)
LIFTKING MANUFACTURING CORP
LIFTKING
(*Suby of* LANCO INTERNATIONAL INC.)

7135 Islington Ave, Woodbridge, ON, L4L 1V9
(905) 851-3988
Emp Here 80   *Sales* 17,760,080
SIC 3537 Industrial trucks and tractors
Michael Lanigan
Mark Aldrovandi
Stephen Bayers
Frank Calomino

D-U-N-S 24-094-7622   (HQ)
LITENS AUTOMOTIVE PARTNERSHIP
LITENS AUTOMOTIVE GROUP
730 Rowntree Dairy Rd, Woodbridge, ON, L4L 5T7
(905) 856-0200
Emp Here 700   *Sales* 364,846,500
SIC 3429 Hardware, nec
Paul Robinson
David Glover

D-U-N-S 20-699-9596   (BR)
LONGO BROTHERS FRUIT MARKETS INC
LONGO'S FRUIT MARKET
(*Suby of* LONGO BROTHERS FRUIT MAR-KETS INC)
8401 Weston Rd, Woodbridge, ON, L4L 1A6
(905) 850-6161
Emp Here 120
SIC 5411 Grocery stores
Joe Vruzzese

D-U-N-S 20-132-6576   (SL)
LUBRIZOL CANADA LIMITED
LUBRIZOL CANADA
(*Suby of* BERKSHIRE HATHAWAY INC.)
3700 Steeles Ave W Suite 201, Woodbridge, ON, L4L 8K8
(905) 264-4646
Emp Here 130   *Sales* 35,133,280
SIC 2992 Lubricating oils and greases
Tom Curtis
Paul Sampson

D-U-N-S 24-006-8668   (SL)
MACRI CATERING LIMITED
71 Winges Rd, Woodbridge, ON, L4L 6B5
(905) 851-8030
Emp Here 260   *Sales* 12,126,140
SIC 5812 Eating places
Vincenzo Macri
Marisa Filippelli

D-U-N-S 20-042-6716   (BR)
MAGNA POWERTRAIN INC
M S M
(*Suby of* MAGNA INTERNATIONAL INC)
390 Hanlan Rd, Woodbridge, ON, L4L 3P6
(905) 851-6791
Emp Here 380
SIC 3714 Motor vehicle parts and accessories
Jose Melo

D-U-N-S 24-822-2952   (SL)
MALFAR MECHANICAL INC
144 Woodstream Blvd Suite 7, Woodbridge, ON, L4L 7Y3
(905) 850-1242
Emp Here 55   *Sales* 12,818,575
SIC 1711 Plumbing, heating, air-conditioning
Frank Micoli

D-U-N-S 24-024-2966   (HQ)
MARANELLO MOTORS LIMITED
MARANELLO BMW
55 Auto Park Cir, Woodbridge, ON, L4L 8R1
(416) 213-5699
Sales 125,856,000
SIC 5511 New and used car dealers
Remo Ferri

D-U-N-S 25-283-6051   (HQ)
MARANELLO SPORTS INC
FERRARI OF ONTARIO
200 Auto Park Cir, Woodbridge, ON, L4L 8R1
(416) 749-5325
Emp Here 24   *Sales* 31,464,000
SIC 5511 New and used car dealers

Remo Ferri

D-U-N-S 24-426-4086   (BR)
MARTINREA INTERNATIONAL INC
ALFIELD INDUSTRIES
(*Suby of* MARTINREA INTERNATIONAL INC)
30 Aviva Park Dr, Woodbridge, ON, L4L 9C7
(905) 264-0149
Emp Here 500
SIC 3499 Fabricated Metal products, nec
Rob Wildeboer

D-U-N-S 24-378-5420   (SL)
MARZILLI INTERNATIONAL INC
511 Chrislea Rd, Woodbridge, ON, L4L 8N6
(289) 268-2040
Emp Here 250   *Sales* 38,580,500
SIC 2512 Upholstered household furniture
Angelo Marzilli Sr

D-U-N-S 25-253-0183   (SL)
MAXIMUM REALTY CORPORATION
ROYAL LEPAGE
7694 Islington Ave, Woodbridge, ON, L4L 1W3
(905) 856-7653
Emp Here 70   *Sales* 19,022,920
SIC 6531 Real estate agents and managers
Marchello Miceli
Mirella Miceli

D-U-N-S 20-113-9594   (HQ)
MEDEX. FISH IMPORTING & EXPORTING CO. LTD
OCEAN MIRACLE SEAFOOD
(*Suby of* PREMIUM BRANDS HOLDINGS CORPORATION)
189 Westcreek Dr, Woodbridge, ON, L4L 9N6
(905) 856-8188
Emp Here 110   *Sales* 143,343,200
SIC 5146 Fish and seafoods
Massimo D'elia
Will Kalutycz
David Carriere
George Paleologou

D-U-N-S 24-334-4889   (SL)
MIKE AND MIKE'S INC
1 Royal Gate Blvd Unit F, Woodbridge, ON, L4L 8Z7
(416) 987-2772
Emp Here 50   *Sales* 41,778,850
SIC 5149 Groceries and related products, nec
Mike Fronte
Mike Dattoli

D-U-N-S 25-106-4676   (HQ)
NEXT PLUMBING & HYDRONICS SUPPLY INC
FULFORD SUPPLY
300 Galcat Dr, Woodbridge, ON, L4L 0B9
(289) 304-2000
Emp Here 55   *Sales* 35,773,920
SIC 5074 Plumbing and heating equipment and supplies (hydronics)
Michael Storfer
Brahm Swirsky
Robert Farrugia

D-U-N-S 20-923-1760   (HQ)
NORANCO INC
PCC AEROSTRUCTURES GTA WOOD-BRIDGE
(*Suby of* BERKSHIRE HATHAWAY INC.)
710 Rowntree Dairy Rd, Woodbridge, ON, L4L 5T7
(905) 264-2050
Emp Here 200   *Sales* 121,615,500
SIC 3499 Fabricated Metal products, nec
David Camilleri
Terence Fernandes

D-U-N-S 24-364-0906   (SL)
NUFORM BUILDING TECHNOLOGIES INC.
100 Galcat Dr Unit 2, Woodbridge, ON, L4L 0B9
(905) 652-0001
Emp Here 85   *Sales* 17,161,245

SIC 3089 Plastics products, nec
Daniel Tiberini
Galliano Tiberini

D-U-N-S 20-935-4323   (SL)
NUMBER 7 HONDA SALES LIMITED
NUMBER 7 HONDA
5555 Highway 7, Woodbridge, ON, L4L 1T5
(905) 851-2258
Emp Here 60   *Sales* 16,998,000
SIC 7538 General automotive repair shops
Giuseppe Zanchin

D-U-N-S 20-145-6563   (HQ)
O'NEIL, EARL ELECTRIC SUPPLY LIMITED
O'NEIL ELECTRIC SUPPLY
(*Suby of* 972683 ONTARIO INC)
150 Creditview Rd, Woodbridge, ON, L4L 9N4
(416) 798-7722
Emp Here 30   *Sales* 22,358,700
SIC 5063 Electrical apparatus and equipment
Earl O'neil
Michael O'neil

D-U-N-S 20-045-5210   (HQ)
ONTARIO BELTING & POWER TRANSMIS-SION CO. LTD
371 Hanlan Rd, Woodbridge, ON, L4L 3T1
(416) 798-7333
Emp Here 25   *Sales* 14,250,780
SIC 5085 Industrial supplies
David Osmond
Tim Osmond

D-U-N-S 24-413-4078   (HQ)
ONTARIO SOCCER ASSOCIATION INCOR-PORATED, THE
ONTARIO SOCCER
7601 Martin Grove Rd, Woodbridge, ON, L4L 9E4
(905) 264-9390
Sales 13,909,490
SIC 8699 Membership organizations, nec
Peter Augruso
Johnny Misley

D-U-N-S 20-169-1800   (HQ)
ORIANA FINANCIAL GROUP OF CANADA LTD
4300 Steeles Ave W Unit 34, Woodbridge, ON, L4L 4C2
(905) 265-8315
Emp Here 1   *Sales* 10,113,480
SIC 6163 Loan brokers
Michael Hall

D-U-N-S 25-710-7300   (SL)
OZERY'S PITA BREAK PARTNERSHIP
OZERY'S PITA BREAK
11 Director Crt, Woodbridge, ON, L4L 4S5
(905) 265-1143
Emp Here 140   *Sales* 100,340,240
SIC 5149 Groceries and related products, nec
Guy Ozery

D-U-N-S 25-462-2269   (SL)
PAGGOS, MARIO DRUGS LTD
SHOPPERS DRUG MART # 930
4000 Highway 7, Woodbridge, ON, L4L 8Z2
(905) 851-2199
Emp Here 65   *Sales* 15,881,320
SIC 5912 Drug stores and proprietary stores
Mario Paggos

D-U-N-S 20-513-4468   (HQ)
PERKINELMER   HEALTH   SCIENCES CANADA, INC
PERKINELMER
(*Suby of* PERKINELMER, INC.)
501 Rowntree Dairy Rd Unit 6, Woodbridge, ON, L4L 8H1
(905) 851-4585
Emp Here 10   *Sales* 29,066,310
SIC 5049 Professional equipment, nec
Ian Brown
Gary F Budzey
Robert E Milnes

John L Healy

D-U-N-S 20-597-7291   (SL)
PINE VIEW AUTO SALES INC
PINE VIEW HYUNDAI
3790 Highway 7, Woodbridge, ON, L4L 9C3
(905) 851-2851
Emp Here 40   *Sales* 16,774,200
SIC 6712 Bank holding companies
Frank Romeo
Anna De Santis
Domenic Romeo

D-U-N-S 25-107-4431   (SL)
PINNACLE PHARMACEUTICS LTD
7611 Pine Valley Dr Suite 31, Woodbridge, ON, L4L 0A2
(905) 430-7541
Emp Here 45   *Sales* 49,740,525
SIC 5122 Drugs, proprietaries, and sundries
Tom Measor

D-U-N-S 24-666-7810   (SL)
PIPE-ALL PLUMBING & HEATING LTD
141 Strada Dr, Woodbridge, ON, L4L 5V9
(905) 851-1927
Emp Here 95   *Sales* 22,141,175
SIC 1711 Plumbing, heating, air-conditioning
Frank Caschera

D-U-N-S 20-045-5798   (HQ)
PIZZAVILLE INC
741 Rowntree Dairy Rd Unit 1, Woodbridge, ON, L4L 5T9
(905) 850-0070
Emp Here 50   *Sales* 61,946,640
SIC 6794 Patent owners and lessors
Angelo Contardi

D-U-N-S 20-278-2173   (SL)
PONG GAME STUDIOS LIMITED
201 Creditview Rd, Woodbridge, ON, L4L 9T1
(905) 264-3555
Emp Here 70   *Sales* 12,411,770
SIC 7371 Custom computer programming services
Fernando Di Carlo

D-U-N-S 20-852-6913   (SL)
POTTRUFF & SMITH INVESTMENTS INC
8001 Weston Rd Suite 300, Woodbridge, ON, L4L 9C8
(905) 265-7470
Emp Here 125   *Sales* 34,168,750
SIC 6719 Holding companies, nec
Gary Pottruff

D-U-N-S 24-313-5568   (SL)
PRIMA AUTO SALES LIMITED
PRIMA MAZDA
7635 Martin Grove Rd, Woodbridge, ON, L4L 2C5
(905) 850-8111
Emp Here 35   *Sales* 17,432,730
SIC 5511 New and used car dealers
Giuseppe (Joe) Zanchin

D-U-N-S 24-910-4761   (SL)
PRIMO MECHANICAL INC
253 Jevlan Dr Unit 15, Woodbridge, ON, L4L 7Z6
(905) 851-6718
Emp Here 80   *Sales* 18,645,200
SIC 1711 Plumbing, heating, air-conditioning
Leo Agozzino
Charlie Agozzino

D-U-N-S 25-685-8507   (SL)
PROCASE CONSULTING INC
180 Caster Ave Suite 55, Woodbridge, ON, L4L 5Y7
(905) 856-7479
Emp Here 45   *Sales* 12,344,940
SIC 8741 Management services
Lev Moltyaner

D-U-N-S 20-857-5324   (HQ)
PROVO LTD
620 Rowntree Dairy Rd, Woodbridge, ON, L4L

5T8
(905) 851-8520
Emp Here 15   *Sales* 12,073,698
SIC 5051 Metals service centers and offices
Haskell Greenberg
Leonard Greenberg
Elliot Greenberg

D-U-N-S 24-388-4595   (SL)
PS TRAVEL INSURANCE BROKERS INC
(*Suby of* MANULIFE FINANCIAL CORPORATION)
8001 Weston Rd Suite 300, Woodbridge, ON, L4L 9C8
(416) 798-8001
Emp Here 50   *Sales* 42,403,000
SIC 6411 Insurance agents, brokers, and service
Gary Pottruff

D-U-N-S 20-347-8743   (HQ)
RAVINE MUSHROOM FARMS INC
131 Marycroft Ave Unit 3, Woodbridge, ON, L4L 5Y6
(905) 264-6173
Sales 13,304,700
SIC 7389 Business services, nec
Simone Quattrociocchi
Luciano Quattrociocchi

D-U-N-S 25-791-9043   (SL)
RDA INC
290 Rowntree Dairy Rd, Woodbridge, ON, L4L 9J7
(905) 652-8680
Emp Here 90   *Sales* 76,325,400
SIC 6411 Insurance agents, brokers, and service
Peter Rocca

D-U-N-S 20-292-0992   (SL)
REMAX EXCELLENCE REALTY INC
3700 Steeles Ave W, Woodbridge, ON, L4L 8K8
(905) 856-1111
Emp Here 100   *Sales* 27,175,600
SIC 6531 Real estate agents and managers
Patricia Tostanzo

D-U-N-S 20-172-2170   (HQ)
REVERSOMATIC MANUFACTURING LTD
790 Rowntree Dairy Rd, Woodbridge, ON, L4L 5V3
(905) 851-6701
Sales 16,650,075
SIC 3564 Blowers and fans
Joseph Salerno
Peter Salerno

D-U-N-S 24-885-5363   (SL)
RICH PRODUCTS OF CANADA LIMITED
(*Suby of* RICH PRODUCTS CORPORATION)
149 Rowntree Dairy Rd Suite 1, Woodbridge, ON, L4L 6E1
(905) 850-3836
Emp Here 50   *Sales* 17,284,500
SIC 2024 Ice cream and frozen deserts
Frank Cannataro
Nick Lucchese

D-U-N-S 20-530-6467   (HQ)
ROMA MOULDING INC
360 Hanlan Rd, Woodbridge, ON, L4L 3P6
(905) 850-1500
Emp Here 85   *Sales* 28,855,500
SIC 2499 Wood products, nec
John Gareri
Tony Gareri
Michael Pallotta

D-U-N-S 25-508-0608   (HQ)
ROYAL AUTOMOTIVE GROUP LTD
STAMP-A-TRON MANUFACTURING, DIV OF
(*Suby of* MARTINREA INTERNATIONAL INC)
30 Aviva Park Dr, Woodbridge, ON, L4L 9C7
(416) 749-0314
Sales 26,861,160
SIC 3714 Motor vehicle parts and accessories

Vince Passarelli

D-U-N-S 24-946-8562   (BR)
ROYAL GROUP, INC
NAPCO
(*Suby of* WESTLAKE CHEMICAL CORPORATION)
131 Regalcrest Crt, Woodbridge, ON, L4L 8P3
(905) 652-0461
Emp Here 150
SIC 3084 Plastics pipe

D-U-N-S 20-091-0235   (SL)
ROYAL LE PAGE MAXIMUM REALTY
7694 Islington Ave, Woodbridge, ON, L4L 1W3
(416) 324-2626
Emp Here 70   *Sales* 29,322,230
SIC 6531 Real estate agents and managers
Mar Cello

D-U-N-S 24-365-8507   (SL)
S.L.K. MARKETING LIMITED
126 Trowers Rd, Woodbridge, ON, L4L 5Z4
(905) 856-4343
Emp Here 30   *Sales* 22,275,600
SIC 5199 Nondurable goods, nec
Sharon Kohut

D-U-N-S 20-564-7621   (SL)
SANYO CANADA INC
(*Suby of* PANASONIC CORPORATION)
201 Creditview Rd, Woodbridge, ON, L4L 9T1
(905) 760-9944
Emp Here 50   *Sales* 22,358,700
SIC 5064 Electrical appliances, television and radio
Walter Buzzelli
Koshi Terakawa

D-U-N-S 20-901-6864   (SL)
SCHON, GEORGE MOTORS LIMITED
WOODBRIDGE TOYOTA
7685 Martin Grove Rd, Woodbridge, ON, L4L 1B5
(905) 851-3993
Emp Here 55   *Sales* 34,610,400
SIC 5511 New and used car dealers
Giuseppe Zanchin

D-U-N-S 24-737-1297   (SL)
SEACORE SEAFOOD INC
81 Aviva Park Dr, Woodbridge, ON, L4L 9C1
(905) 856-6222
Emp Here 50   *Sales* 58,490,390
SIC 5146 Fish and seafoods
Joseph Nestico
Antonio Cristoforo
Gerry Battaglia

D-U-N-S 25-508-6597   (SL)
SELECT DRYWALL & ACOUSTICS INC
75 Sharer Rd Suite 2, Woodbridge, ON, L4L 8Z3
(905) 856-8249
Emp Here 180   *Sales* 29,228,580
SIC 1742 Plastering, drywall, and insulation
Ed Tatone

D-U-N-S 20-152-5755   (HQ)
SILANI SWEET CHEESE LIMITED
661 Chrislea Rd Unit 14, Woodbridge, ON, L4L 0C4
(905) 792-3811
Sales 69,138,000
SIC 2022 Cheese; natural and processed
Joe Lanzino
Michael Talarico
Vince Lanzino

D-U-N-S 24-322-1251   (BR)
SILGAN PLASTICS CANADA INC
COUSINS CURRIE DIVISION OF SILGAN PLASTICS CANADA
(*Suby of* SILGAN HOLDINGS INC.)
400 Rowntree Dairy Rd, Woodbridge, ON, L4L 8H2
(416) 746-8300
Emp Here 155

SIC 3089 Plastics products, nec
Peter Fillmor

D-U-N-S 20-118-7775   (HQ)
SORBARA SERVICES LIMITED
3700 Steeles Ave W Suite 800, Woodbridge, ON, L4L 8M9
(905) 850-6154
Sales 21,946,560
SIC 8741 Management services
Edward Sorbara
Joseph Sorbara

D-U-N-S 24-318-2227   (HQ)
SOROC TECHNOLOGY INC
607 Chrislea Rd, Woodbridge, ON, L4L 8A3
(905) 265-8000
Emp Here 210   *Sales* 240,908,400
SIC 5045 Computers, peripherals, and software
Rudy Cheddie
Barbara Hopper

D-U-N-S 24-140-9945   (SL)
SPECTRA ANODIZING LTD
201 Hanlan Rd, Woodbridge, ON, L4L 3R7
(905) 851-1141
Emp Here 60   *Sales* 11,525,100
SIC 3471 Plating and polishing
David Hudson
Alexandria Hudson

D-U-N-S 20-977-2656   (SL)
SPEEDY ELECTRICAL CONTRACTORS LIMITED
114 Caster Ave Suite A, Woodbridge, ON, L4L 5Y9
(905) 264-2344
Emp Here 230   *Sales* 54,167,070
SIC 1731 Electrical work
Albert Passero

D-U-N-S 24-652-2585   (BR)
SPICERS CANADA ULC
SPICERS
(*Suby of* CNG CANADA HOLDING INC.)
200 Galcat Dr, Woodbridge, ON, L4L 0B9
(905) 265-5000
Emp Here 200
SIC 5111 Printing and writing paper
James Tovell

D-U-N-S 20-268-1847   (HQ)
SPICERS CANADA ULC
(*Suby of* CNG CANADA HOLDING INC.)
200 Galcat Dr, Woodbridge, ON, L4L 0B9
(905) 265-5000
Emp Here 200   *Sales* 477,393,810
SIC 5111 Printing and writing paper
Cory James Turner
Meherab Chothia
Howard Herman

D-U-N-S 20-999-7001   (SL)
SRIULLI LONG TERM CARE
VILLA LEONARDO GAMBIN
40 Friuli Crt, Woodbridge, ON, L4L 9T3
(905) 856-3939
Emp Here 200   *Sales* 12,250,800
SIC 8052 Intermediate care facilities
Annette Zuccaro Vanin

D-U-N-S 20-992-9376   (SL)
STANDARD PAINT SYSTEMS LTD
80 Ashbridge Cir Unit 1-4, Woodbridge, ON, L4L 3R5

Emp Here 100   *Sales* 17,120,720
SIC 1721 Painting and paper hanging
Tony Petratos

D-U-N-S 24-182-1693   (SL)
STAR QUALITY OFFICE FURNITURE MFG LTD
10 Westcreek Dr Suite 16, Woodbridge, ON, L4L 9R5
(416) 741-8000
Emp Here 70   *Sales* 16,268,210

SIC 5712 Furniture stores
Fred Monsoor
Ken Aviss
Jonathan Mansoor
Joe Lampert

D-U-N-S 20-279-1331   (SL)
STATEVIEW HOMES LTD
410 Chrislea Rd Unit 1, Woodbridge, ON, L4L 8B5
(905) 851-1849
Emp Here 50   *Sales* 15,943,450
SIC 1521 Single-family housing construction
Dino Taurasi
Carlo Taurasi
Daniel Ciccone

D-U-N-S 25-992-2268   (SL)
STAXI CORPORATION LIMITED
120 Jevlan Dr Unit 4b, Woodbridge, ON, L4L 8G3
(877) 677-8294
Emp Here 25   *Sales* 11,875,650
SIC 5087 Service establishment equipment
Andrew J Hart
Graham Card

D-U-N-S 20-114-7399   (SL)
STELLAR METAL PRODUCTS INC
STELLAR METAL
609 Hanlan Rd, Woodbridge, ON, L4L 4R8
(289) 371-0218
Emp Here 25   *Sales* 11,179,350
SIC 5046 Commercial equipment, nec
Branko Lebar
Peter Stellnberger

D-U-N-S 20-176-4131   (SL)
SUPERSTYLE FURNITURE LTD
123 Ashbridge Cir, Woodbridge, ON, L4L 3R5
(905) 850-6060
Emp Here 90   *Sales* 13,888,980
SIC 2512 Upholstered household furniture
Giovanni Colalillo
Dominic Colalillo

D-U-N-S 24-026-3376   (HQ)
TACC CONSTRUCTION CO. LTD
270 Chrislea Rd, Woodbridge, ON, L4L 8A8
(905) 856-8500
Sales 164,057,500
SIC 1623 Water, sewer, and utility lines
Silvio De Gasperis
Carlos De Gasperis
Carlo Vitali

D-U-N-S 25-899-5299   (SL)
TACC CONSTRUCTION LTD
270 Chrislea Rd, Woodbridge, ON, L4L 8A8
(905) 856-8500
Emp Here 80   *Sales* 20,195,360
SIC 1623 Water, sewer, and utility lines
Silvio Degasperis
Carlo Degasperis
Michael Degasperis
Jenny Commisso
Carlo Vitali

D-U-N-S 25-397-9561   (SL)
TEL-STAR MARKETING GROUP (1993) LTD
64 Trowers Rd Unit 2, Woodbridge, ON, L4L 7K5

Emp Here 22   *Sales* 16,335,440
SIC 5194 Tobacco and tobacco products
Wayne Cogswell
Rosanne Cogswell

D-U-N-S 24-025-5463   (SL)
TOPPITS FOODS LTD
TOPPITS
301 Chrislea Rd, Woodbridge, ON, L4L 8N4
(905) 850-8900
Emp Here 62   *Sales* 44,436,392
SIC 5146 Fish and seafoods
Brian Xiao
Chris Glowienka

D-U-N-S 20-190-5689   (BR)
TORONTO STAR NEWSPAPERS LIMITED
VAUGHAN PRESS CENTRE
(*Suby of* TORSTAR CORPORATION)
1 Century Pl, Woodbridge, ON, L4L 8R2
(416) 502-8273
Emp Here 500
SIC 2711 Newspapers
Dean Zavarise

D-U-N-S 24-216-7369   (SL)
TORY TAPE LTD
230 Trowers Rd Unit 9-11, Woodbridge, ON, L4L 7J1
(416) 410-1404
Emp Here 28   *Sales* 13,300,728
SIC 5085 Industrial supplies
Gerald Meagher

D-U-N-S 20-997-5593   (SL)
TRIAD INTERNATIONAL CORP
690 Rowntree Dairy Rd Suite 201, Woodbridge, ON, L4L 5T7
(905) 264-9031
Emp Here 15   *Sales* 10,183,845
SIC 6289 Security and commodity service
Anthony Addesi

D-U-N-S 25-198-9323   (BR)
UNITED BROTHERHOOD OF CARPEN-TERS JOINERS AMERICA LOCAL 83
DRYWALL ACOUSTIC LATHING & INSULA-TION
(*Suby of* UNITED BROTHERHOOD OF CAR-PENTERS JOINERS AMERICA LOCAL 83)
222 Rowntree Dairy Rd Suite 598, Woodbridge, ON, L4L 9T2
(416) 749-0675
Emp Here 4,000
SIC 8631 Labor organizations
Tony Innuzzi

D-U-N-S 25-087-8543   (SL)
UNITED THERMO GROUP LTD
DIRECT ENERGY
261 Trowers Rd, Woodbridge, ON, L4L 5Z8
(905) 851-0500
Emp Here 50   *Sales* 11,046,700
SIC 1711 Plumbing, heating, air-conditioning
Ron Caicco

D-U-N-S 25-150-3447   (HQ)
UPSTREAM WORKS SOFTWARE LTD
777 Weston Rd Suite 1000, Woodbridge, ON, L4L 0G9
(905) 660-0969
Sales 14,894,124
SIC 7371 Custom computer programming services
Robert Mcdougall
Douglas Hay

D-U-N-S 24-523-1738   (SL)
VISUAL ELEMENTS MANUFACTURING INC
VISUAL ELEMENTS
21 Regina Rd, Woodbridge, ON, L4L 8L9
(905) 761-5222
Emp Here 90   *Sales* 13,888,980
SIC 2541 Wood partitions and fixtures
Robert Turk

D-U-N-S 20-512-6134   (SL)
WINDOW CITY INDUSTRIES INC
5690 Steeles Ave W, Woodbridge, ON, L4L 9T4
(905) 265-9975
Emp Here 50   *Sales* 11,671,750
SIC 3231 Products of purchased glass
Jafar Bagheri-Sadr
Yousef Bagheri-Sadr
Mohammad Bagheri-Sadr
Hossein Bagheri-Sadr

D-U-N-S 25-282-1566   (SL)
WINDOWCITY MFRS. INC
5690 Steeles Ave W, Woodbridge, ON, L4L 9T4

(905) 265-9975
Emp Here 175   *Sales* 31,363,325
SIC 3231 Products of purchased glass
Jeff Sadr
Joseph Sadr
Matthew Sadr
Hossein Sadr

D-U-N-S 24-784-8476   (SL)
WOODBRIDGE LUMBER INC
(*Suby of* ALPA LUMBER INC)
8100 Kipling Ave, Woodbridge, ON, L4L 2A1
(905) 581-2804
Emp Here 26   *Sales* 11,626,524
SIC 5031 Lumber, plywood, and millwork
John Di Poce
George Frankfort
Carmen Guglietti
Donald Maciver

D-U-N-S 24-873-3651   (SL)
WOODBRIDGE PALLET LTD
7200 Martin Grove Rd, Woodbridge, ON, L4L 9J3
(905) 856-3332
Emp Here 85   *Sales* 23,106,570
SIC 7699 Repair services, nec
Lino Di Poce
Ryan Scobie

D-U-N-S 24-096-4841   (HQ)
YALE INDUSTRIAL TRUCKS INC
(*Suby of* YIT HOLDINGS INC)
340 Hanlan Rd, Woodbridge, ON, L4L 3P6
(905) 851-6620
Emp Here 58   *Sales* 74,134,960
SIC 5084 Industrial machinery and equipment
Alan Mcfadyen

D-U-N-S 25-151-0384   (BR)
YORK CATHOLIC DISTRICT SCHOOL BOARD
HOLY CROSS CATHOLIC ACADEMY
(*Suby of* YORK CATHOLIC DISTRICT SCHOOL BOARD)
7501 Martin Grove Rd, Woodbridge, ON, L4L 1A5
(905) 851-6699
Emp Here 200
SIC 8211 Elementary and secondary schools
Iolanda Faraone

D-U-N-S 25-100-4537   (BR)
YORK CATHOLIC DISTRICT SCHOOL BOARD
FATHER BRESSANI CATHOLIC HIGH SCHOOL
(*Suby of* YORK CATHOLIC DISTRICT SCHOOL BOARD)
250 Ansley Grove Rd, Woodbridge, ON, L4L 3W4
(905) 851-6643
Emp Here 110
SIC 8211 Elementary and secondary schools
Eugene Pivato

D-U-N-S 20-183-0122   (SL)
YORK SHEET METAL LIMITED
227 Westcreek Dr, Woodbridge, ON, L4L 9T7
(416) 742-8242
Emp Here 98   *Sales* 18,824,330
SIC 3444 Sheet Metalwork
Jimmy Scaturchio

D-U-N-S 24-827-5505   (HQ)
YORKWEST PLUMBING SUPPLY INC
201 Aviva Park Dr, Woodbridge, ON, L4L 9C1
(905) 856-9466
Emp Here 51   *Sales* 26,383,266
SIC 5074 Plumbing and heating equipment and supplies (hydronics)
Carlo Perfetto
Gabe Pizzardi
Tullio Capone

D-U-N-S 24-602-4376   (SL)
Z.M.C. METAL COATING INC
Z.M.C. WINDOW COVERINGS SUPPLIES

40 Gaudaur Rd Suite 3, Woodbridge, ON, L4L 4S6
(905) 856-3838
Emp Here 50   *Sales* 10,141,500
SIC 3479 Metal coating and allied services
Philip Ng
Alfred Poon

Woodstock, ON N0J

D-U-N-S 25-186-5614   (SL)
GUNTER TRANSPORTATION LTD
445 Springbank Ave S, Woodstock, ON, N0J 1E4
(519) 539-9222
Emp Here 90   *Sales* 13,337,280
SIC 4212 Local trucking, without storage
John Gunter

Woodstock, ON N4S

D-U-N-S 24-145-8384   (SL)
2079608 ONTARIO INC
WOODSTOCK FORD
1455 Dundas St, Woodstock, ON, N4S 7V9
(519) 537-5614
Emp Here 26   *Sales* 12,950,028
SIC 5511 New and used car dealers
Darrin Lester

D-U-N-S 25-619-5967   (SL)
990731 ONTARIO INC
INDUSTRIAL PARTS SERVICE
1401 Dundas St, Woodstock, ON, N4S 7V9
(519) 537-8095
Emp Here 23   *Sales* 10,925,598
SIC 5084 Industrial machinery and equipment
Judy Stewart
Jeff Runnells

D-U-N-S 20-081-7455   (SL)
A & A ENTERPRISES INC
LADY GODIVA'S
354 Dundas St, Woodstock, ON, N4S 1B4

Emp Here 26   *Sales* 19,305,520
SIC 5199 Nondurable goods, nec
James Bender

D-U-N-S 20-279-5068   (BR)
ACIER NOVA INC
NOVA STEEL INC
(*Suby of* 3195538 CANADA INC)
807 Pattullo Ave, Woodstock, ON, N4S 7W3
(519) 537-6639
Emp Here 100
SIC 3312 Blast furnaces and steel mills
Rick Roese

D-U-N-S 24-254-8712   (SL)
ANDERSON, GORD AUTOMOTIVE GROUP INC
1267 Dundas St, Woodstock, ON, N4S 7V9
(519) 537-2326
Emp Here 75   *Sales* 47,196,000
SIC 5511 New and used car dealers
Dale Anderson
Keith Chapman

D-U-N-S 24-321-4306   (HQ)
ARCELORMITTAL TUBULAR PRODUCTS CANADA G.P.
(*Suby of* ARCELORMITTAL)
193 Givins St, Woodstock, ON, N4S 5Y8
(519) 537-6671
Emp Here 450   *Sales* 218,137,500
SIC 3714 Motor vehicle parts and accessories
Lakshmi N Mittal
Aditya Mittal
Brian Aranha

D-U-N-S 20-561-3821   (BR)

ARCELORMITTAL TUBULAR PRODUCTS CANADA G.P.
(*Suby of* ARCELORMITTAL)
193 Givins St, Woodstock, ON, N4S 5Y8
(519) 537-6671
Emp Here 485
SIC 3714 Motor vehicle parts and accessories
Ian Mclean

D-U-N-S 24-735-3258   (SL)
AZ GROUP
847 Berkshire Dr, Woodstock, ON, N4S 8R6
(519) 421-2423
Emp Here 49   *Sales* 11,895,509
SIC 8611 Business associations
Jerry Traweek

D-U-N-S 20-187-2223   (BR)
BRIDGESTONE CANADA INC
FIRESTONE TEXTILES
(*Suby of* BRIDGESTONE CORPORATION)
1200 Dundas St, Woodstock, ON, N4S 7V9
(519) 537-6231
Emp Here 250
SIC 2296 Tire cord and fabrics
Robert Galway

D-U-N-S 20-179-7540   (BR)
CARESSANT-CARE NURSING AND RE-TIREMENT HOMES LIMITED
(*Suby of* CARESSANT-CARE NURSING AND RETIREMENT HOMES LIMITED)
81 Fyfe Ave, Woodstock, ON, N4S 8Y2
(519) 539-6461
Emp Here 200
SIC 8051 Skilled nursing care facilities
Bonnie Hudge

D-U-N-S 24-125-6023   (HQ)
CARESSANT-CARE NURSING AND RE-TIREMENT HOMES LIMITED
264 Norwich Ave, Woodstock, ON, N4S 3V9
(519) 539-0408
Emp Here 16   *Sales* 85,680,804
SIC 8051 Skilled nursing care facilities
James Lavelle
Arlene Christianson

D-U-N-S 20-327-4899   (BR)
CARGILL LIMITED
AGRIBRANDS PURINA CANADA
(*Suby of* CARGILL, INCORPORATED)
404 Main St, Woodstock, ON, N4S 7X5
(519) 539-8561
Emp Here 75
SIC 2048 Prepared feeds, nec

D-U-N-S 24-751-5096   (HQ)
CARRIER CENTERS INC
645 Athlone Ave, Woodstock, ON, N4S 7V8
(519) 539-0971
Sales 24,405,822
SIC 5511 New and used car dealers
Robert Long

D-U-N-S 20-407-0221   (HQ)
CARRIER TRUCK CENTER INC
CARRIER EMERGENCY
(*Suby of* ROYALEX INCORPORATED)
645 Athlone Ave, Woodstock, ON, N4S 7V8
(519) 539-9837
Emp Here 45   *Sales* 173,175,600
SIC 5531 Auto and home supply stores
Robert R. Long
Betty Long
Marvin Long
Michael Paquette

D-U-N-S 20-088-7755   (HQ)
CENTURY 21 HERITAGE HOUSE LTD
871 Dundas St, Woodstock, ON, N4S 1G8
(519) 539-5646
Sales 40,632,233
SIC 6531 Real estate agents and managers
Michael Slager

D-U-N-S 25-483-3403   (HQ)
CHILDREN'S AID SOCIETY OF OXFORD

COUNTY
712 Peel St, Woodstock, ON, N4S 0B4
(519) 539-6176
Emp Here 85   *Sales* 6,157,980
SIC 8322 Individual and family services
Bruce Burbank

D-U-N-S 25-312-2451   (SL)
COMMUNITY CARE ACCESS CENTRE - OXFORD
CCAC OXFORD
1147 Dundas St, Woodstock, ON, N4S 8W3
(519) 539-1284
Emp Here 75   *Sales* 5,349,675
SIC 8082 Home health care services
John Oosterink

D-U-N-S 24-196-0038   (SL)
FAIRCREST FARMS LIMITED
455017 45th Line, Woodstock, ON, N4S 7V7
(519) 537-8713
Emp Here 13   *Sales* 15,735,161
SIC 5153 Grain and field beans
Roger Minler

D-U-N-S 24-463-0141   (BR)
GENERAL MOTORS OF CANADA COM-PANY
GM CANADA WOODSTOCK PDC 36
(*Suby of* GENERAL MOTORS COMPANY)
1401 Parkinson Rd, Woodstock, ON, N4S 7W3
(519) 539-6136
Emp Here 250
SIC 4226 Special warehousing and storage, nec
Scott Williamson

D-U-N-S 24-184-2764   (BR)
GUARANTEE COMPANY OF NORTH AMERICA, THE
THE GUARANTEE
954 Dundas St, Woodstock, ON, N4S 7Z9
(519) 539-9868
Emp Here 100
SIC 6411 Insurance agents, brokers, and service
Ron Burns

D-U-N-S 25-842-0439   (SL)
HOAM LTD
KELSEY'S RESTAURANT
525 Norwich Ave, Woodstock, ON, N4S 9A2
(519) 421-7300
Emp Here 78   *Sales* 3,550,482
SIC 5812 Eating places
Simon Amicucci

D-U-N-S 24-664-3977   (SL)
HYD-MECH GROUP LIMITED
(*Suby of* AKSIA GROUP SOCIETA' DI GESTIONE DEL RISPARMIO SPA)
1079 Parkinson Rd, Woodstock, ON, N4S 7W3
(519) 539-6341
Emp Here 126   *Sales* 30,824,165
SIC 3569 General industrial machinery, nec
William Giacometti
Michael Miller

D-U-N-S 24-338-1469   (SL)
LAIDLAW CARRIERS BULK GP INC
MARCO TRANSPORT
(*Suby of* CONTRANS CORP)
240 Universal Rd, Woodstock, ON, N4S 7W3
(519) 539-0471
Emp Here 32   *Sales* 16,638,944
SIC 4731 Freight transportation arrangement
Gregory W. Rumble
Chantal Martel
Josiane M. Langlois

D-U-N-S 20-691-5519   (HQ)
LAIDLAW CARRIERS BULK LP
240 Universal Rd, Woodstock, ON, N4S 7W3
(519) 539-0471
Emp Here 10   *Sales* 20,570,600
SIC 4213 Trucking, except local

Stanley Dunford
Scott Talbot

D-U-N-S 24-576-6332   (SL)
LAMPREA BUILDING MATERIALS LTD
HOME HARDWARE BUILDING CENTRE - WOODSTOCK
1147 Dundas St Suite 1, Woodstock, ON, N4S 8W3
(519) 421-0484
Emp Here 50   *Sales* 12,652,950
SIC 5211 Lumber and other building materials
John Lamprea

D-U-N-S 24-150-1076   (SL)
LEVEL 1 ACS INC
225 Main St, Woodstock, ON, N4S 1T1
(519) 539-8619
Emp Here 24   *Sales* 10,781,256
SIC 7389 Business services, nec
Genny Mcgurvin

D-U-N-S 20-783-6250   (BR)
METRO ONTARIO INC
FOOD BASICS
(*Suby of* METRO INC)
868 Dundas St, Woodstock, ON, N4S 1G7
(519) 537-7021
Emp Here 125
SIC 5411 Grocery stores
Suzanne Schiemann

D-U-N-S 25-672-1879   (SL)
MTO METAL PRODUCTS LTD
1205 Welford Pl Suite 54, Woodstock, ON, N4S 7W3
(519) 537-8257
Emp Here 60   *Sales* 11,525,100
SIC 3429 Hardware, nec
Bryan Remington

D-U-N-S 24-565-5709   (HQ)
NASG CANADA INC
NORTH AMERICA STAMPING GROUP
975 Pattulo Ave E, Woodstock, ON, N4S 7W3
(519) 539-7491
Emp Here 50   *Sales* 58,375,440
SIC 3469 Metal stampings, nec
Gordon Hurd
Fred Gehring
Michael Haughey

D-U-N-S 20-301-8478   (SL)
OTTAWAY MOTOR EXPRESS (2010) INC
(*Suby of* MCCAIN FOODS GROUP INC)
520 Beards Lane Unit B, Woodstock, ON, N4S 7W3
(519) 602-3026
Emp Here 60   *Sales* 12,342,360
SIC 4212 Local trucking, without storage
John Doucet
Peter Ottaway

D-U-N-S 20-642-1729   (HQ)
OWL DISTRIBUTION INC
(*Suby of* GILLFOR DISTRIBUTION INC)
220 Universal Rd, Woodstock, ON, N4S 7W3
(519) 539-8115
Sales 22,358,700
SIC 5031 Lumber, plywood, and millwork
Harvey Hunt

D-U-N-S 24-311-0249   (SL)
PROMAT INC
594711 County Rd 59 S, Woodstock, ON, N4S 7V8
(519) 456-2284
Emp Here 19   *Sales* 37,905,100
SIC 3496 Miscellaneous fabricated wire products
Larry Wood
Jack Bosman
Hilco Stevens
Jodi Ritter
Andrew Jenkins

D-U-N-S 20-923-1687   (SL)
ROBERTS WELDING & FABRICATING LTD

BRON
873 Devonshire Ave, Woodstock, ON, N4S 8Z4
(519) 421-0036
Emp Here 75   *Sales* 16,650,075
SIC 3531 Construction machinery
Ronald Hall
Robert Hall
Barbara Hall
Ernest Collinson

D-U-N-S 20-447-5610   (BR)
ROBINSON SOLUTIONS INC
(*Suby of* 2082486 ONTARIO INC)
715106 Oxford Rd Suite 4, Woodstock, ON, N4S 7V9
(519) 653-1111
Emp Here 125
SIC 8741 Management services
Ninos Ismail

D-U-N-S 20-187-2694   (HQ)
SAF-HOLLAND CANADA LIMITED
(*Suby of* SAF-HOLLAND SA)
595 Athlone Ave, Woodstock, ON, N4S 7V8
(519) 537-2366
Emp Here 185   *Sales* 74,166,750
SIC 3714 Motor vehicle parts and accessories
Kim Baechler
Joseph Fransen

D-U-N-S 20-819-8452   (SL)
SIERRA CONSTRUCTION (WOODSTOCK) LIMITED
1401 Dundas St, Woodstock, ON, N4S 7V9
(519) 421-9689
Emp Here 90   *Sales* 51,330,420
SIC 1542 Nonresidential construction, nec
Clifford Zaluski

D-U-N-S 25-147-0928   (SL)
SILVERTHORNE PHARMACY LTD
SHOPPERS DRUG MART
959 Dundas St Suite 1, Woodstock, ON, N4S 1H2
(519) 537-2042
Emp Here 44   *Sales* 11,129,976
SIC 5912 Drug stores and proprietary stores
Lisa Silverthorne

D-U-N-S 25-349-8653   (HQ)
SUTTON GROUP-RIGHT WAY REAL ES-TATE INC
28 Perry St, Woodstock, ON, N4S 3C2
(519) 539-6194
Emp Here 1   *Sales* 10,326,728
SIC 6531 Real estate agents and managers
Dave Redford

D-U-N-S 20-938-3202   (BR)
THAMES VALLEY DISTRICT SCHOOL BOARD
COLLEGE AVENUE SECONDARY SCHOOL
(*Suby of* THAMES VALLEY DISTRICT SCHOOL BOARD)
700 College Ave, Woodstock, ON, N4S 2C8
(519) 539-0020
Emp Here 80
SIC 8211 Elementary and secondary schools
Tiffany Birtch

D-U-N-S 20-938-3210   (BR)
THAMES VALLEY DISTRICT SCHOOL BOARD
HURON PARK SECONDARY SCHOOL
(*Suby of* THAMES VALLEY DISTRICT SCHOOL BOARD)
900 Cromwell St, Woodstock, ON, N4S 5B5
(519) 537-2347
Emp Here 80
SIC 8211 Elementary and secondary schools
Tim Doherty

D-U-N-S 20-373-4723   (BR)
TIGERCAT INDUSTRIES INC
(*Suby of* TIGERCAT INTERNATIONAL INC)
1403 Dundas St, Woodstock, ON, N4S 7V9

(519) 537-3000
Emp Here 300
SIC 3531 Construction machinery
Michael Fischer

D-U-N-S 20-187-4815   (HQ)
TIMBERLAND EQUIPMENT LIMITED
459 Industrial Ave, Woodstock, ON, N4S 7L1
(519) 537-6262
Emp Here 130   *Sales* 28,860,130
SIC 3531 Construction machinery
Mark Gabourie
Bradley Vollmershausen
Lisa Disalle

D-U-N-S 24-317-1472   (HQ)
TOYOTA BOSHOKU CANADA, INC
(*Suby of* TOYOTA BOSHOKU CORPORA-
TION)
230 Universal Rd, Woodstock, ON, N4S 7W3
(519) 421-7556
Sales 31,771,600
SIC 3089 Plastics products, nec
Shuhei Toyoda
Shuichi Koyama

D-U-N-S 24-362-1492   (BR)
**TOYOTA   MOTOR   MANUFACTURING
CANADA INC**
(*Suby of* TOYOTA MOTOR CORPORATION)
715106 Oxford Rd Suite 4, Woodstock, ON,
N4S 7V9

Emp Here 260
SIC 3711 Motor vehicles and car bodies

D-U-N-S 24-370-4876   (BR)
**TOYOTA   MOTOR   MANUFACTURING
CANADA INC**
TOYOTA MOTOR MANUFACTURING
(*Suby of* TOYOTA MOTOR CORPORATION)
1717 Dundas St, Woodstock, ON, N4S 0A4
(519) 653-1111
Emp Here 250
SIC 3711 Motor vehicles and car bodies

D-U-N-S 24-364-4304   (BR)
TOYOTA TSUSHO CANADA INC
WOODSTOCK SERVICE CENTRE
(*Suby of* TOYOTA TSUSHO CORPORATION)
270 Beards Lane, Woodstock, ON, N4S 7W3
(519) 533-5577
Emp Here 100
SIC 5013 Motor vehicle supplies and new
parts
Ramone Luzcano

D-U-N-S 20-175-6496   (SL)
TRAVEL CENTRE CANADA INC, THE
WOODSTOCK 230 TRAVEL CENTRE
(*Suby of* TRAVELCENTERS OF AMERICA
LLC)
535 Mill St, Woodstock, ON, N4S 7V6
(519) 421-3144
Emp Here 120   *Sales* 141,872,760
SIC 5172 Petroleum products, nec
Michelle Argoso

D-U-N-S 24-335-5641   (HQ)
UVALUX INTERNATIONAL INC
*ADVANCED UVALUX SUN TANNING EQUIP-
MENT*
(*Suby of* RANHEAVEN HOLDINGS INC)
470 Industrial Ave, Woodstock, ON, N4S 7L1
(519) 421-1212
Emp Here 50   *Sales* 31,302,180
SIC 5064 Electrical appliances, television and
radio
William Van Haeren
Antonia Van Haeren

D-U-N-S 25-294-8492   (BR)
WAL-MART CANADA CORP
(*Suby of* WALMART INC.)
499 Norwich Ave, Woodstock, ON, N4S 9A2
(519) 539-5120
Emp Here 250
SIC 5311 Department stores

David D'agostino

D-U-N-S 20-788-3799   (SL)
WOODSTOCK FLYING CLUB
Gd Lcd Main, Woodstock, ON, N4S 7W4
(519) 539-3303
Emp Here 30   *Sales* 12,122,941
SIC 8699 Membership organizations, nec
Luc Tuolin

D-U-N-S 20-014-6426   (SL)
WOODSTOCK HYDRO SERVICES INC
16 Graham St Suite 1598, Woodstock, ON,
N4S 6J6
(519) 537-7172
Emp Here 37   *Sales* 19,227,235
SIC 4911 Electric services
Ross Mcmillan
Elizabeth Carswell
John Krill

D-U-N-S 24-667-1080   (SL)
**WOODSTOCK   INDEPENDENT   GROCER
ASSOCIATE, INC.**
FOODLAND STORE 6301
645 Dundas St Suite 1, Woodstock, ON, N4S
1E4
(519) 421-3420
Emp Here 85   *Sales* 24,945,545
SIC 5411 Grocery stores
Christopher Chapman

D-U-N-S 24-366-8709   (BR)
ZF AUTOMOTIVE CANADA LIMITED
TRW AUTOMOTIVE
(*Suby of* ZEPPELIN-STIFTUNG)
155 Beards Lane, Woodstock, ON, N4S 7W3
(519) 537-2331
Emp Here 150
SIC 3714 Motor vehicle parts and accessories
David Hammond

Woodstock, ON N4T

D-U-N-S 20-903-5351   (HQ)
JEAMAR WINCHES CORPORATION
125 Bysham Park Dr, Woodstock, ON, N4T
1R2
(519) 537-8855
Sales 11,675,820
SIC 3531 Construction machinery
Gregory Leslie
James M Leslie

D-U-N-S 25-032-1601   (BR)
SOBEYS CAPITAL INCORPORATED
SOBEY'S READY TO SERVE 640
(*Suby of* EMPIRE COMPANY LIMITED)
379 Springbank Ave N, Woodstock, ON, N4T
1R3
(519) 421-3340
Emp Here 150
SIC 5411 Grocery stores
Sheila Wammes

Woodstock, ON N4V

D-U-N-S 24-544-0979   (SL)
552653 ONTARIO INC
ALTADORE QUALITY HOTEL & SUITES
580 Bruin Blvd, Woodstock, ON, N4V 1E5
(519) 537-5586
Emp Here 100   *Sales* 9,489,900
SIC 7011 Hotels and motels
Joe Odumodo
Willard Mckay
John Findlay

D-U-N-S 20-187-1605   (SL)
CANADA STAMPINGS LTD
(*Suby of* VAST INDUSTRIAL CORP)
1299 Commerce Way, Woodstock, ON, N4V

0A2
(519) 537-6245
Emp Here 36   *Sales* 18,074,450
SIC 3469 Metal stampings, nec
Douglas Hamilton

D-U-N-S 24-540-4991   (HQ)
CONTRANS CORP
1179 Ridgeway Rd, Woodstock, ON, N4V 1E3
(519) 421-4600
Sales 493,437,150
SIC 6712 Bank holding companies
Stanley G. Dunford
Gregory W. Rumble
James S Clark
D. Jamieson Miller
Robert Burgess
Archie Leach

D-U-N-S 24-338-1451   (SL)
CONTRANS HOLDING II LP
1179 Ridgeway Rd, Woodstock, ON, N4V 1E3
(519) 421-4600
Emp Here 400   *Sales* 146,203,600
SIC 6712 Bank holding companies
Stanley George Dunford

D-U-N-S 24-925-0002   (BR)
DBG CANADA LIMITED
(*Suby of* DBG GROUP LTD)
980 Juliana Dr, Woodstock, ON, N4V 1B9

Emp Here 90
SIC 3469 Metal stampings, nec
Philipe Mantia

D-U-N-S 20-156-8078   (HQ)
EXECULINK TELECOM INC
1127 Ridgeway Rd, Woodstock, ON, N4V 1E3
(877) 393-2854
Emp Here 10   *Sales* 23,989,560
SIC 4813 Telephone communication, except
radio
Ian Stevens
Keith Stevens
John Downs

D-U-N-S 24-469-1812   (SL)
HARVAN MANUFACTURING LTD
(*Suby of* VLEUTEN HOLDINGS INC)
612 Jack Ross Ave, Woodstock, ON, N4V 1B6
(519) 537-8311
Emp Here 50   *Sales* 23,751,300
SIC 5085 Industrial supplies
Harry Vleuten
Joanne Vleuten
Paul Vleuten
Lisa Ross

D-U-N-S 25-365-8587   (BR)
HOME DEPOT OF CANADA INC
HOME DEPOT
(*Suby of* THE HOME DEPOT INC)
901 Juliana Dr, Woodstock, ON, N4V 1B9
(519) 421-5500
Emp Here 126
SIC 5251 Hardware stores
Jim Talbot

D-U-N-S 24-966-3261   (HQ)
KERRY (CANADA) INC
AGRINOVE
(*Suby of* KERRY GROUP PUBLIC LIMITED
COMPANY)
615 Jack Ross Ave, Woodstock, ON, N4V 1B7
(519) 537-3461
Emp Here 65   *Sales* 243,692,500
SIC 2099 Food preparations, nec
Gerard Behan
Lanny Schimmel
Gary S. Fogler

D-U-N-S 20-180-5368   (SL)
LELY CANADA INC
1015 Ridgeway Rd, Woodstock, ON, N4V 1E2
(519) 602-6737
Emp Here 20   *Sales* 10,000,000

SIC 5083 Farm and garden machinery
Peter Langebeeke

D-U-N-S 20-941-8409   (SL)
**OXFORD   MILKWAY   TRANSPORT   CO-
OPERATIVE**
103 Longworth Lane, Woodstock, ON, N4V
1G6
(519) 539-2302
Emp Here 48   *Sales* 16,465,920
SIC 5963 Direct selling establishments
James Knudsen
Cindy Crawford

D-U-N-S 24-232-3447   (SL)
TRIGON CONSTRUCTION INC
35 Ridgeway Cir, Woodstock, ON, N4V 1C9
(519) 602-2222
Emp Here 75   *Sales* 42,775,350
SIC 1542 Nonresidential construction, nec
Bill Van Haeren

D-U-N-S 24-764-1970   (HQ)
VUTEQ CANADA INC
(*Suby of* VUTEQ CORPORATION)
920 Keyes Dr, Woodstock, ON, N4V 1C2
(519) 421-0011
Emp Here 750   *Sales* 218,045,200
SIC 3089 Plastics products, nec
Ezio Andreola
Zaitsu Tatsuo
Christopher Spence
Nancy Olenio

D-U-N-S 20-315-3762   (BR)
VUTEQ CANADA INC
(*Suby of* VUTEQ CORPORATION)
885 Keyes Dr, Woodstock, ON, N4V 1C3
(519) 421-0011
Emp Here 350
SIC 3465 Automotive stampings

D-U-N-S 24-602-8203   (HQ)
**WOODSTOCK   GENERAL   HOSPITAL
TRUST**
310 Juliana Dr, Woodstock, ON, N4V 0A4
(519) 421-4211
Sales 111,080,000
SIC 8062 General medical and surgical hospi-
tals
Natasa Veljovic
Wilma Boughtflower

Woodville, ON K0M

D-U-N-S 20-999-5849   (SL)
**KAWARTHA LAKES COOPERATIVE AUC-
TION MARKET INC**
580 Woodville Rd, Woodville, ON, K0M 2T0
(705) 439-4444
Emp Here 40   *Sales* 48,415,880
SIC 5154 Livestock
Ivan Bell

Wroxeter, ON N0G

D-U-N-S 20-783-7527   (HQ)
HYNDMAN TRANSPORT (1972) LIMITED
HYNDMAN TRANSPORT
(*Suby of* CELADON)
1001 Belmore Line, Wroxeter, ON, N0G 2X0
(519) 335-3575
Emp Here 174   *Sales* 42,038,868
SIC 4213 Trucking, except local
Mike Campbell
George Kerr
Norm Maclennan
Clare Newell
Jeff Sippel
Lisa Kawalez

▲ Public Company   ■ Public Company Family Member   **HQ** Headquarters   **BR** Branch   **SL** Single Location

D-U-N-S 25-410-5893   (HQ)
HYNDMAN TRANSPORT LIMITED
1001 Belmore Line, Wroxeter, ON, N0G 2X0
(519) 335-3575
Emp Here 1   *Sales* 43,070,000
SIC 4731 Freight transportation arrangement
Michael Campbell

Wyoming, ON N0N

D-U-N-S 24-744-6198   (SL)
1197243 ONTARIO LTD
RON CLARK MOTORS
425 Broadway St, Wyoming, ON, N0N 1T0
(519) 845-3352
Emp Here 25   *Sales* 12,451,950
SIC 5511 New and used car dealers
Todd Clark
Randy Clark

D-U-N-S 25-195-5696   (HQ)
ADVANTAGE FARM EQUIPMENT LTD
392 Broadway St, Wyoming, ON, N0N 1T0
(519) 845-3346
Emp Here 23   *Sales* 24,861,625
SIC 5999 Miscellaneous retail stores, nec
Donald Hendrick
Donald Mcnally
Daniel Janicek
Paul Hendrick

D-U-N-S 24-023-4161   (HQ)
**CORPORATION OF THE COUNTY OF
LAMBTON**
789 Broadway St, Wyoming, ON, N0N 1T0
(519) 845-0801
Emp Here 60   *Sales* 129,058,840
SIC 8741 Management services
Jim Burns
Ron Van Horne
John Innes

D-U-N-S 24-991-2213   (SL)
HURONWEB OFFSET PRINTING INC
HURONWEB PRINTING
395 Broadway St, Wyoming, ON, N0N 1T0
(519) 845-0821
Emp Here 63   *Sales* 10,333,701
SIC 2752 Commercial printing, lithographic
Chris Cooke

D-U-N-S 24-877-1263   (SL)
SIPKENS NURSERIES LTD
3261 London Line, Wyoming, ON, N0N 1T0
(519) 542-8353
Emp Here 30   *Sales* 22,275,600
SIC 5193 Flowers and florists supplies
Kenneth Sipken
Jennifer Sipken

D-U-N-S 20-180-1735   (HQ)
**WANSTEAD FARMERS CO-OPERATIVE
CO., LIMITED**
5495 Elevator St, Wyoming, ON, N0N 1T0
(519) 845-3301
Emp Here 13   *Sales* 10,586,750
SIC 5191 Farm supplies
John Turvey
Dave Minielly

York., ON N0A

D-U-N-S 24-355-4354   (SL)
BARTSIDE FARMS
3302 Haldimand Road 9, York., ON, N0A 1R0
(905) 692-2766
Emp Here 10   *Sales* 12,103,970
SIC 5154 Livestock
Wayne Bartels

▲ Public Company   ■ Public Company Family Member   **HQ** Headquarters   **BR** Branch   **SL** Single Location

Albany, PE C0B

D-U-N-S 20-549-9218   (SL)
ATLANTIC BEEF PRODUCTS INC
(*Suby of* ATLANTIC BEEF PRODUCERS CO-
OPERATIVE LTD)
95 Train Station Rd, Albany, PE, C0B 1A0
(902) 437-2727
Emp Here 100   *Sales* 34,569,000
SIC 2011 Meat packing plants
  James Casey
  Mike Nabuurs
  Suzanne Iwankow
  John Colwill
  Tony Overmars
  Karl Larsen
  Mitch Maclean

D-U-N-S 20-631-6077   (SL)
ROBINSON, ERIC C. INC
INGLESIDE FARM
1804 Rte 115, Albany, PE, C0B 1A0
(902) 437-6666
Emp Here 30   *Sales* 25,067,310
SIC 5148 Fresh fruits and vegetables
  John Robinson
  Andrew Robinson
  Lori Robinson
  Deborah Robinson
  Mary Robinson
  Susan Robinson
  Alan J. Robinson
  Julia Robinson
  Hazel Robinson

Alberton, PE C0B

D-U-N-S 20-084-6355   (HQ)
WESTERN HOSPITAL
*WESTERN HOSPITAL & MAPPLEWOOD
MANOR*
148 Popular St, Alberton, PE, C0B 1B0
(902) 853-8650
Emp Here 150   *Sales* 16,662,000
SIC 8062 General medical and surgical hospi-
tals
  Paul Young

Bedeque, PE C0B

D-U-N-S 20-188-5394   (SL)
FUTURE SEAFOODS INC
FUTURE AUTO & MARINE
358 New Rd, Bedeque, PE, C0B 1C0
(902) 887-3012
Emp Here 30   *Sales* 25,067,310
SIC 5146 Fish and seafoods
  Brian Lewis
  Ted Boutilier
  Erskine Lewis

Belfast, PE C0A

D-U-N-S 24-511-3969   (SL)
BELFAST MINI MILLS LTD
1820 Garfield Rd, Belfast, PE, C0A 1A0
(902) 659-2430
Emp Here 18   *Sales* 18,952,550
SIC 3552 Textile machinery
  Douglas Nobles
  Linda Nobles
  Richard Hannams

D-U-N-S 24-534-2527   (SL)
GILLIS, JOHN M MEMORIAL LODGE

3134 Garfield Rd, Belfast, PE, C0A 1A0
(902) 659-2337
Emp Here 49   *Sales* 13,442,268
SIC 8741 Management services
  Douglas Mackenzie

Belle River, PE C0A

D-U-N-S 24-605-8101   (SL)
BELLE RIVER ENTERPRISES LTD
Gd, Belle River, PE, C0A 1B0
(902) 962-2248
Emp Here 60   *Sales* 20,741,400
SIC 2092 Fresh or frozen packaged fish

Bloomfield Station, PE C0B

D-U-N-S 20-172-5830   (SL)
SOUTH SHORE SEAFOODS LTD
6 Foy Rd, Bloomfield Station, PE, C0B 1E0
(902) 853-4052
Emp Here 100   *Sales* 83,557,700
SIC 5146 Fish and seafoods
  David Dalton

Borden-Carleton, PE C0B

D-U-N-S 20-293-8333   (SL)
J.D. FOX ENTERPRISES INC
GATEWAY PETROLEUM
141 Abegweit Blvd, Borden-Carleton, PE, C0B
1X0
(902) 437-2600
Emp Here 30   *Sales* 14,942,340
SIC 5541 Gasoline service stations
  Jamie Fox
  Debra Fox

D-U-N-S 25-148-6494   (HQ)
MACDOUGALL STEEL ERECTORS INC
168 Industrial Dr, Borden-Carleton, PE, C0B
1X0
(902) 855-2100
Emp Here 30   *Sales* 11,525,100
SIC 3441 Fabricated structural Metal
  Dave Clark
  Kirk Mackinnon

D-U-N-S 25-060-9914   (BR)
MASTER PACKAGING INC
(*Suby of* MASTER PACKAGING INC)
23784 Trans Canada Highway, Borden-
Carleton, PE, C0B 1X0
(902) 437-3737
Emp Here 100
SIC 3554 Paper industries machinery
  Jean Pierre Delage

D-U-N-S 25-125-3746   (HQ)
STRAIT CROSSING BRIDGE LIMITED
CONFEDERATION BRIDGE
(*Suby of* STRAIT CROSSING DEVELOP-
MENT INC)
104 Abegweit Blvd Suite 2032, Borden-
Carleton, PE, C0B 1X0
(902) 437-7300
Sales 20,798,680
SIC 4785 Inspection and fixed facilities
  J David Pirie
  Jean Yves Tassini
  Michel Le Chasseur

D-U-N-S 24-993-6378   (HQ)
STRAIT CROSSING DEVELOPMENT INC
104 Abegweit Blvd, Borden-Carleton, PE, C0B
1X0
(902) 437-7300
Sales 38,679,736

SIC 4785 Inspection and fixed facilities
  David Pirie
  Jean-Yves Tassini

Brackley, PE C1E

D-U-N-S 20-560-4312   (HQ)
3237681 CANADA INC
PADERNO
(*Suby of* 4145151 CANADA INC)
489 Brackley Point Rd -Rte 15, Brackley, PE,
C1E 1Z3
(902) 629-1500
Sales 20,683,867
SIC 5719 Miscellaneous homefurnishings
  A. James Casey
  Timothy Casey
  Ernest Brennan
  Curtis Macmillan
  Frederick Hyndman
  Doug Wright

D-U-N-S 24-849-1727   (HQ)
4145151 CANADA INC
489 Brackley Point Rd - Rte 15, Brackley, PE,
C1E 1Z3
(902) 629-1500
Sales 54,826,350
SIC 6712 Bank holding companies
  Timothy J. Casey

D-U-N-S 24-130-9475   (HQ)
PADINOX INC
PADERNO COOKWEAR
(*Suby of* 4145151 CANADA INC)
489 Brackley Point Rd Rte 15, Brackley, PE,
C1E 1Z3
(902) 629-1500
Emp Here 85   *Sales* 59,129,235
SIC 3631 Household cooking equipment
  James Casey
  Tim Casey
  Curtis Macmillan
  Ernest Brennan
  Fred Hyndman
  Joan Casey
  Doug Wright

Cardigan, PE C0A

D-U-N-S 24-127-6807   (SL)
MACDONALD, J A COMPANY
*CARDIGAN LOBSTER SUPPERS & JOCKS
LOUNGE*
4557 Wharf Rd, Cardigan, PE, C0A 1G0
(902) 583-2020
Emp Here 20   *Sales* 10,702,480
SIC 5146 Fish and seafoods
  John Macdonald

D-U-N-S 20-017-7475   (SL)
MCKENNA BROS (1989) LIMITED
4109 48 Rd, Cardigan, PE, C0A 1G0
(902) 583-2951
Emp Here 8   *Sales* 15,063,640
SIC 5148 Fresh fruits and vegetables
  Kevin Mckenna
  Shawn Mckenna

D-U-N-S 25-895-4072   (BR)
RODD MANAGEMENT LIMITED
RODD-BRUDENELL RIVER RESORT
(*Suby of* RODD MANAGEMENT LIMITED)
86 Dewars Ln, Cardigan, PE, C0A 1G0
(902) 652-2332
Emp Here 100
SIC 7011 Hotels and motels
  Blair Smith

Charlottetown, PE C1A

D-U-N-S 24-312-6369   (SL)
ADVANTAGE DELIVERY SERVICE
47 Kensington Rd, Charlottetown, PE, C1A
5H6
(902) 940-3971
Emp Here 30   *Sales* 13,304,700
SIC 7389 Business services, nec
  Robbie Keen

D-U-N-S 25-631-1341   (BR)
ATLANTIC WHOLESALERS LTD
CHARLOTTETOWN SUPER STORE
(*Suby of* LOBLAW COMPANIES LIMITED)
465 University Ave, Charlottetown, PE, C1A
4N9
(902) 569-2850
Emp Here 270
SIC 5411 Grocery stores
  Macdonald Phil

D-U-N-S 20-100-1539   (SL)
B J'S TRUCK PARTS INC
B J'S TRUCK CENTRE
502 Brackley Pt Rd, Charlottetown, PE, C1A
8C2
(902) 566-4205
Emp Here 24   *Sales* 11,953,872
SIC 5531 Auto and home supply stores
  William Macdonald

D-U-N-S 25-410-6867   (HQ)
BAY FERRIES LIMITED
94 Water St, Charlottetown, PE, C1A 1A6
(902) 566-3838
Emp Here 30   *Sales* 49,215,500
SIC 4449 Water transportation of freight
  Mark Macdonald
  Gordon Macrae
  Donald Cormier
  Danny Bartlett
  Gerard Stevenson

D-U-N-S 25-839-5412   (BR)
**CANADIAN CORPS OF COMMISSION-
AIRES NATIONAL OFFICE, THE**
(*Suby of* CANADIAN CORPS OF COMMIS-
SIONAIRES NATIONAL OFFICE, THE)
15 St. Peters Rd, Charlottetown, PE, C1A 5N1
(902) 894-7026
Emp Here 180
SIC 8621 Professional organizations
  Allan Mackinnon

D-U-N-S 24-341-6765   (HQ)
CENTURY 21 COLONIAL REALTY INC
111 St. Peters Rd, Charlottetown, PE, C1A
5P1
(902) 566-2121
Emp Here 35   *Sales* 10,326,728
SIC 6531 Real estate agents and managers
  John Ives
  Joel Ives

D-U-N-S 24-128-8950   (SL)
CITY CAB INC
168 Prince St, Charlottetown, PE, C1A 4R6
(902) 892-6567
Emp Here 80   *Sales* 4,389,760
SIC 4121 Taxicabs
  Joe Corrigian

D-U-N-S 20-105-5071   (SL)
COASTAL CULTURE INC
COASTAL CULTURE
156 Queen St, Charlottetown, PE, C1A 4B5
(902) 894-3146
Emp Here 48   *Sales* 10,445,424
SIC 5947 Gift, novelty, and souvenir shop
  Beryl Cudmore
  Christopher Cudmore

D-U-N-S 24-352-8481   (HQ)
COMMANDER HOLDINGS INC
3 Mount Edward Rd, Charlottetown, PE, C1A
5R7

(902) 566-2295
Sales 11,725,125
SIC 5983 Fuel oil dealers
Daniel Macisaac

D-U-N-S 24-626-9075   (SL)
CONFEDERATION CENTRE BOX OFFICE
145 Richmond St, Charlottetown, PE, C1A
1J1
(902) 628-1864
Emp Here 49   *Sales* 13,937,413
SIC 6512 Nonresidential building operators
Jessie Inman

D-U-N-S 20-728-7087   (HQ)
**COOKE, CHARLIE INSURANCE AGENCY
LTD**
125 Pownal St Suite 1, Charlottetown, PE,
C1A 3W4
(902) 566-5666
Emp Here 19   *Sales* 23,745,680
SIC 6411 Insurance agents, brokers, and ser-
vice
Jeffrey Cooke
Harold Saint
Charles Cooke

D-U-N-S 24-754-5627   (BR)
DELTA HOTELS LIMITED
DELTA PRINCE EDWARD HOTEL
(*Suby of* GOVERNMENT OF THE
PROVINCE OF BRITISH COLUMBIA)
18 Queen St, Charlottetown, PE, C1A 4A1
(902) 566-2222
Emp Here 140
SIC 8741 Management services
Michael Bird

D-U-N-S 25-323-9362   (SL)
DELTAWARE SYSTEMS INC
(*Suby of* MAXIMUS, INC.)
176 Great George St Suite 300, Charlotte-
town, PE, C1A 4K9
(902) 368-8122
Emp Here 75   *Sales* 10,813,650
SIC 7371 Custom computer programming ser-
vices
Robert Lawlor

D-U-N-S 20-728-1890   (HQ)
FAIR ISLE FORD SALES LTD
Gd Stn Central, Charlottetown, PE, C1A 7K1
(902) 368-3673
Emp Here 46   *Sales* 37,127,520
SIC 5511 New and used car dealers
Peter Macdonald
Dianne Mackay

D-U-N-S 20-908-5364   (SL)
**FATHERS OF CONFEDERATION BUILD-
INGS TRUST**
CONFEDERATION CENTRE OF THE ARTS
145 Richmond St, Charlottetown, PE, C1A
1J1
(902) 629-1166
Emp Here 80   *Sales* 10,854,160
SIC 6512 Nonresidential building operators
H. Wayne Hambly
Jessie Inman
Kim Macleod
Colin J. Mcmillan
Michael Schurman

D-U-N-S 20-780-0897   (SL)
GARDEN HOME (1986) INCORPORATED
310 North River Rd, Charlottetown, PE, C1A
3M4
(902) 892-4131
Emp Here 90   *Sales* 6,185,970
SIC 8051 Skilled nursing care facilities
Robert Nutbrown

D-U-N-S 20-017-4613   (HQ)
HILLSIDE MOTORS (1973) LTD
113 St. Peters Rd, Charlottetown, PE, C1A
5P3
(902) 368-2438
Emp Here 1   *Sales* 19,923,120
SIC 5511 New and used car dealers

Robert Delong
Alan Delong

D-U-N-S 20-273-2892   (BR)
HOLLAND COLLEGE
ADMISSION OFFICE
(*Suby of* HOLLAND COLLEGE)
4 Sydney St, Charlottetown, PE, C1A 1E9
(902) 894-6805
Emp Here 80
SIC 8221 Colleges and universities
Albert Roach

D-U-N-S 24-129-6672   (HQ)
HOLLAND COLLEGE
140 Weymouth St, Charlottetown, PE, C1A
4Z1
(902) 629-4217
Emp Here 150   *Sales* 42,303,900
SIC 8221 Colleges and universities
Alex Macaulay
Keith Dewar
Jake Baird
Ken Heckbert

D-U-N-S 20-781-6364   (HQ)
HYNDMAN & COMPANY LTD
57 Queen St, Charlottetown, PE, C1A 4A5
(902) 566-4244
Emp Here 37   *Sales* 35,618,520
SIC 6411 Insurance agents, brokers, and ser-
vice
Fred Hyndman

D-U-N-S 25-651-8952   (SL)
**INSURANCE COMPANY OF PRINCE ED-
WARD ISLAND, THE**
ICPEI
(*Suby of* SGI CANADA INSURANCE SER-
VICES LTD)
14 Great George St Suite 3, Charlottetown,
PE, C1A 4J6
(902) 368-3675
Emp Here 12   *Sales* 24,836,550
SIC 6331 Fire, marine, and casualty insurance
Charlie Cooke
Don Thompson

D-U-N-S 20-589-2672   (HQ)
ISLAND COASTAL SERVICES LTD
GREEN GABLES GOLF COURSE, DIV OF
155 Belvedere Ave, Charlottetown, PE, C1A
2Y9
(902) 892-1062
Emp Here 10   *Sales* 18,933,150
SIC 1629 Heavy construction, nec
David Blair Maclauchlan

D-U-N-S 24-362-5337   (HQ)
ISLANDSAND HOLDINGS INC
SUBWAY
150 Queen St, Charlottetown, PE, C1A 4B5
(902) 368-1728
Emp Here 100   *Sales* 4,551,900
SIC 5812 Eating places
Irwin Dawson

D-U-N-S 20-198-3843   (SL)
K CRAWFORD PHARMACY INC
SHOPPERS DRUG MART
403 University Ave, Charlottetown, PE, C1A
4N7
(902) 892-3433
Emp Here 50   *Sales* 12,647,700
SIC 5912 Drug stores and proprietary stores
Kenneth Crawford

D-U-N-S 24-628-8773   (HQ)
KENMAC ENERGY INC
(*Suby of* COMMANDER HOLDINGS INC)
3 Mount Edward Rd, Charlottetown, PE, C1A
5R7
(902) 566-2295
Sales 11,725,125
SIC 5983 Fuel oil dealers
Daniel Macisaac
Gordon Matthews

D-U-N-S 20-226-3083   (HQ)
MARITIME ELECTRIC COMPANY, LIMITED
(*Suby of* FORTIS INC)
180 Kent St, Charlottetown, PE, C1A 1N9
(800) 670-1012
Emp Here 85   *Sales* 118,977,950
SIC 4911 Electric services
John Gaudet
Keith O'neill
Karen Creighton
Steven D. Loggie
James D. Bradley
Earl Ludlow
D Blair Maclauchlan
Brian Thompson
Jacqueline Macintyre
Robert Sear

D-U-N-S 25-502-1990   (HQ)
MASTER PACKAGING INC
60 Belvedere Ave, Charlottetown, PE, C1A
6B1
(902) 368-3737
Emp Here 15   *Sales* 110,291,100
SIC 2653 Corrugated and solid fiber boxes
Mary Jean Irving

D-U-N-S 25-146-8302   (BR)
MEDIAS TRANSCONTINENTAL INC
GUARDIAN, THE
(*Suby of* TRANSCONTINENTAL INC)
165 Prince St, Charlottetown, PE, C1A 4R7
(902) 629-6000
Emp Here 75
SIC 2711 Newspapers
Don Brander

D-U-N-S 20-443-4609   (SL)
MITTON, V CO LTD
DAIRY QUEEN BRAZIER STORE
365 University Ave, Charlottetown, PE, C1A
4N2
(902) 892-1892
Emp Here 80   *Sales* 3,641,520
SIC 5812 Eating places
Orris Mitton
David Mitton
Brian Mitton
Debbie Bowman

D-U-N-S 20-017-5859   (HQ)
MURPHY'S PHARMACIES INC
MURPHY'S KENSINGTON PHARM DIV
41 St. Peters Rd, Charlottetown, PE, C1A 5N1
(902) 894-4447
Emp Here 10   *Sales* 62,833,350
SIC 6531 Real estate agents and managers
Raymond (Ray) Murphy
Carolyn Murphy
Paul Evoy

D-U-N-S 24-342-0593   (HQ)
MURPHY, D.P. INC
OAK ACRES CHILDREN'S CAMP
250 Brackley Point Rd, Charlottetown, PE,
C1A 6Y9
(902) 368-3727
Emp Here 15   *Sales* 230,956,800
SIC 5461 Retail bakeries
Daniel P. Murphy
Laurie Dove

D-U-N-S 24-114-1543   (SL)
**NATIONAL PORT SECURITY SERVICES
INC**
379 Queen St, Charlottetown, PE, C1A 4C9
(902) 892-9977
Emp Here 65   *Sales* 15,228,720
SIC 8748 Business consulting, nec
J Dave Power
David A Power

D-U-N-S 20-443-3759   (HQ)
NORTHUMBERLAND FERRIES LIMITED
94 Water St, Charlottetown, PE, C1A 1A6
(902) 566-3838
Sales 86,619,280

SIC 4449 Water transportation of freight
Mitchell Maclean
Gordon Macrae

D-U-N-S 20-630-6334   (HQ)
PEI BUSINESS DEVELOPMENT INC
(*Suby of* PROVINCE OF PEI)
94 Euston St, Charlottetown, PE, C1A 1W4
(902) 368-5800
Sales 21,826,630
SIC 8731 Commercial physical research
Michael Mayne

D-U-N-S 24-574-1145   (SL)
POLYCLINIC PROFESSIONAL CENTRE INC
POLYCLINIC, THE
199 Grafton St Suite 307, Charlottetown, PE,
C1A 1L2
(902) 629-8810
Emp Here 100   *Sales* 18,534,000
SIC 8011 Offices and clinics of medical doc-
tors
Allen Profitt
Matthew Crockett
Raymond Cooke

D-U-N-S 20-300-8636   (SL)
PORTSMOUTH ATLANTIC LIMITED
(*Suby of* PORTSMOUTH AVIATION HOLD-
INGS LIMITED)
20 Great George St Suite 103, Charlottetown,
PE, C1A 4J6
(902) 978-1400
Emp Here 130
SIC 8748 Business consulting, nec
Simon Escott
Allen Dillon

D-U-N-S 20-905-0939   (HQ)
**PRINCE EDWARD ISLAND LIQUOR CON-
TROL COMMISSION**
P.E.I. LIQUOR CONTROL COMMISSION
(*Suby of* PROVINCE OF PEI)
3 Garfield St, Charlottetown, PE, C1A 6A4
(902) 368-5710
Emp Here 19   *Sales* 20,556,144
SIC 5921 Liquor stores
Andrew Macmillan
Quentin Bevan
Pauline Wood
Carl Adams
James C. Macleod
Andrew Macmillan
David Stewart

D-U-N-S 20-009-0160   (BR)
PROVINCE OF PEI
INNOVATION PEI
(*Suby of* PROVINCE OF PEI)
94 Euston St, Charlottetown, PE, C1A 1W4
(902) 368-6300
Emp Here 75
SIC 6111 Federal and federally sponsored
credit agencies
David Keedwell

D-U-N-S 20-191-9755   (BR)
PROVINCE OF PEI
HILLSBOROUGH HOSPITAL
(*Suby of* PROVINCE OF PEI)
115 Dacon Grove Lane, Charlottetown, PE,
C1A 7N5
(902) 368-5400
Emp Here 350
SIC 8063 Psychiatric hospitals
Tina Lowther

D-U-N-S 20-706-2626   (BR)
PROVINCE OF PEI
QUEEN ELIZABETH HOSPITAL
(*Suby of* PROVINCE OF PEI)
60 Riverside Dr, Charlottetown, PE, C1A 8T5
(902) 894-2111
Emp Here 2,000
SIC 8062 General medical and surgical hospi-
tals
Tracey Bomeau

D-U-N-S 24-263-1471   (HQ)
RAYLINK LTD
TRAVEL STORE, THE
134 Kent St, Charlottetown, PE, C1A 8R8
(902) 629-8400
Emp Here 10   *Sales* 23,398,515
SIC 4724 Travel agencies
Gary Rayner

D-U-N-S 24-993-6030   (SL)
SHERWOOD HARDWARE LTD
HOME HARDWARE CHARLOTTETOWN
115 St. Peters Rd, Charlottetown, PE, C1A
5P3
(902) 892-8509
Emp Here 50   *Sales* 12,652,950
SIC 5251 Hardware stores
Paul Johnston
Leslie Wong

D-U-N-S 20-905-2448   (HQ)
UNIVERSITY OF PRINCE EDWARD ISLAND
UPEI
550 University Ave, Charlottetown, PE, C1A
4P3
(902) 628-4353
Emp Here 700   *Sales* 102,357,449
SIC 8221 Colleges and universities
Tom Cullen
Alaa Abd-El-Aziz
Christian Lacroix
Jackie Podger
Robert Gilmour
M. Lynn Murray
Don Mcdougall
Duncan Shaw
Pat Sinnott
Shawn Murphy

D-U-N-S 24-804-3150   (HQ)
VOGUE OPTICAL GROUP INC
VOGUE OPTICAL
(*Suby of* CANADIAN DEPOSITORY FOR SE-
CURITIES LIMITED, THE)
5 Brackley Point Rd, Charlottetown, PE, C1A
6X8
(902) 566-3326
Emp Here 30   *Sales* 47,169,009
SIC 5995 Optical goods stores
John Macleod
W. John Bennett
Antoine Amiel
Martial Gagne
C. Emmett Pearson
Richard Cherney

D-U-N-S 24-629-5471   (SL)
WILBUR, DAVID PRODUCTS LTD
RALSTON FUELS
(*Suby of* PARKLAND FUEL CORPORATION)
155 Belvedere Ave, Charlottetown, PE, C1A
2Y9

Emp Here 90   *Sales* 113,148,090
SIC 5172 Petroleum products, nec
Blair Maclauchlan
Wade Maclauchlan
Donna Maclauchlan
Roger Maclauchlan

D-U-N-S 24-878-3342   (HQ)
**WORKERS COMPENSATION BOARD OF
PRINCE EDWARD ISLAND**
(*Suby of* PROVINCE OF PEI)
14 Weymouth St, Charlottetown, PE, C1A 4Y1
(902) 368-5680
Sales 45,693,372,872
SIC 6331 Fire, marine, and casualty insurance
Stuart Affleck
Luanne Gallant
Annette Johnson
Margaret Stewart
Mike Annear
Angus Houston
Charlene Mcinnis
Sandy Mackay
Harvey Larkin

Charlottetown, PE C1E

D-U-N-S 24-956-3677   (SL)
120601 CANADA INC
MERMAID MARINE PRODUCTS
26 Fourth St, Charlottetown, PE, C1E 2B3
(902) 566-1220
Emp Here 30   *Sales* 14,250,780
SIC 5084 Industrial machinery and equipment
Patrick Villeneuve

D-U-N-S 20-559-6419   (HQ)
3 POINTS AVIATION CORP
91 Watts Ave, Charlottetown, PE, C1E 2B7
(902) 628-8846
Emp Here 63   *Sales* 38,477,106
SIC 5088 Transportation equipment and supplies
John Druken

D-U-N-S 24-932-5473   (HQ)
A.P.M. LANDMARK INC
A P M PROPERTIES
16 Mccarville St, Charlottetown, PE, C1E 2A6
(902) 569-8400
Sales 114,067,600
SIC 1542 Nonresidential construction, nec
Timothy Banks

D-U-N-S 25-643-4069   (SL)
ADVANTAGE COMMUNICATIONS INC
265 Brackley Point Rd, Charlottetown, PE,
C1E 2A3
(902) 892-1585
Emp Here 230   *Sales* 52,548,560
SIC 4899 Communication services, nec
Kent Macphee
Jeff Willis

D-U-N-S 24-330-1590   (HQ)
APM CONSTRUCTION SERVICES INC
16 Mccarville St, Charlottetown, PE, C1E 2A6
(902) 569-8400
Emp Here 40   *Sales* 146,662,320
SIC 1542 Nonresidential construction, nec
Tim Banks
Duane Lamont
Terry Palmer

D-U-N-S 24-391-5043   (BR)
BIOVECTRA INC
(*Suby of* BIOVECTRA INC)
29 Mccarville St, Charlottetown, PE, C1E 2A7
(902) 566-9116
Emp Here 200
SIC 2834 Pharmaceutical preparations
Mark Walman

D-U-N-S 20-630-2093   (HQ)
BIOVECTRA INC
11 Aviation Ave, Charlottetown, PE, C1E 0A1
(902) 566-9116
Emp Here 220   *Sales* 60,648,160
SIC 2834 Pharmaceutical preparations
Oliver Technow
Heather Delage
Mark Wellman
Scott Doncaster
Marc Sauer
George Rowat
Lester Wood
Darren Macgregor

D-U-N-S 20-908-5869   (SL)
CAMPBELL'S CONCRETE LTD
CAMPBELL'S CONCRETE
420 Mount Edward Rd, Charlottetown, PE,
C1E 2A1
(902) 368-3442
Emp Here 27   *Sales* 12,073,698
SIC 5032 Brick, stone, and related material
Allan Martin
Ross White
Melanie Martin
Shirley Martin

D-U-N-S 25-643-4168   (SL)
COGSDALE CORPORATION
(*Suby of* CONSTELLATION SOFTWARE
INC)
3 Lower Malpeque Rd, Charlottetown, PE,
C1E 1R4
(902) 892-3101
Emp Here 103   *Sales* 14,850,746
SIC 7371 Custom computer programming ser-
vices
Terry Ridyard
Dana Lendorf-Mccarthy
Benjamin Moradian
Todd Ramsey
Linda Perna
Casey Dowd
Judy Wells

D-U-N-S 25-355-3028   (HQ)
COWS PRINCE EDWARD ISLAND INC
COWS
397 Capital Dr, Charlottetown, PE, C1E 2E2
(902) 566-5558
Sales 19,134,500
SIC 6712 Bank holding companies
Scott Linkletter

D-U-N-S 20-252-0800   (HQ)
GREENISLE ENVIRONMENTAL INC
SUPERIOR TRUCK AND TRAILER
7 Superior Cres, Charlottetown, PE, C1E 2A1
(902) 892-1333
Sales 12,856,550
SIC 4953 Refuse systems
John Edward Clark

D-U-N-S 25-672-7801   (HQ)
HGS CANADA INC
(*Suby of* HINDUJA GLOBAL SOLUTIONS
LIMITED)
82 Hillstrom Ave, Charlottetown, PE, C1E 2C6
(902) 370-3200
Emp Here 25   *Sales* 367,063,400
SIC 7379 Computer related services, nec
Ross Beattie
John Hooper
Tracy Laughlin

D-U-N-S 24-386-9661   (SL)
ISLAND ABBEY FOODS LTD
ISLAND ABBEY FOOD SCIENCE
20 Innovation Way, Charlottetown, PE, C1E
0K4
(902) 367-9722
Emp Here 25   *Sales* 20,889,425
SIC 5149 Groceries and related products, nec
John L Rowe

D-U-N-S 24-207-0162   (SL)
ISLAND EMS INC
229 Sherwood Rd, Charlottetown, PE, C1E
0E5
(902) 892-9995
Emp Here 160   *Sales* 12,043,520
SIC 4119 Local passenger transportation, nec
Eric Sande

D-U-N-S 20-813-4999   (SL)
JOLOWAY LTD
CAPITAL HONDA
40 Lower Malpeque Rd, Charlottetown, PE,
C1E 1R3
(902) 566-1101
Emp Here 22   *Sales* 10,957,716
SIC 5511 New and used car dealers
Paul Mckenna
Pam Mckenna

D-U-N-S 24-393-0182   (SL)
MACEACHERN, K & A HOLDINGS LTD
CANADIAN TIRE
202 Buchanan Dr, Charlottetown, PE, C1E
2H8
(902) 892-8586
Emp Here 100   *Sales* 20,534,300
SIC 5311 Department stores
Kenneth Maceachern
Geoff Hyson

D-U-N-S 20-017-8176   (SL)
MACSWEEN ENTERPRISES LTD
MAGIC WOK
161 Maypoint Rd Suite 14, Charlottetown, PE,
C1E 1X6
(902) 892-8002
Emp Here 55   *Sales* 16,141,235
SIC 5411 Grocery stores
Lorne Macsween

D-U-N-S 25-720-3802   (SL)
MCINNIS EXPRESS LTD
2 Macaleer Dr, Charlottetown, PE, C1E 2A1
(902) 892-9333
Emp Here 35   *Sales* 15,522,150
SIC 7389 Business services, nec
Thane Nunn
Clayton Nunn

D-U-N-S 20-523-7787   (SL)
**P.E.I.   VEGETABLE   GROWERS   CO-
OPERATIVE ASSOCIATION, LIMITED**
PEI VEGETABLE GROWERS
280 Sherwood Rd, Charlottetown, PE, C1E
0E4
(902) 892-5361
Emp Here 20   *Sales* 10,702,480
SIC 5148 Fresh fruits and vegetables
Donald Read
Edward Dykerman

D-U-N-S 25-631-2406   (HQ)
PARKER REALTY LTD
COLDWELL BANKER
535 North River Rd Suite 1, Charlottetown,
PE, C1E 1J6
(902) 566-4663
Emp Here 50   *Sales* 13,587,800
SIC 6531 Real estate agents and managers
Della Parker

D-U-N-S 20-780-4485   (SL)
PREBILT STRUCTURES LTD
PREBILT STEEL
423 Mount Edward Rd, Charlottetown, PE,
C1E 2A1
(902) 892-8577
Emp Here 55   *Sales* 10,564,675
SIC 3441 Fabricated structural Metal
Duncan Shaw
Gary Macleod
Norman Macleod

D-U-N-S 24-955-6598   (SL)
**PRINCE EDWARD ISLAND UNION OF PUB-
LIC SECTOR EMPLOYEES**
4 Enman Cres, Charlottetown, PE, C1E 1E6
(902) 892-5335
Emp Here 45   *Sales* 17,602,110
SIC 8631 Labor organizations
Karen Jackson

D-U-N-S 24-966-7945   (BR)
PROVINCE OF PEI
BEACH GROVE NURSING HOME
(*Suby of* PROVINCE OF PEI)
200 Beach Grove Rd, Charlottetown, PE, C1E
1L3
(902) 368-6750
Emp Here 200
SIC 8051 Skilled nursing care facilities
Andrew Mcdougal

D-U-N-S 20-037-4978   (BR)
PROVINCE OF PEI
QUEEN REGION HOME CARE
(*Suby of* PROVINCE OF PEI)
165 John Yeo Dr, Charlottetown, PE, C1E 3J3
(902) 368-4790
Emp Here 100
SIC 8059 Nursing and personal care, nec
Eva Mol

D-U-N-S 24-878-1262   (SL)
PT ENTERPRISES INC
DIVERSIFIED METAL ENGINEERING
54 Hillstrom Ave, Charlottetown, PE, C1E 2C6

▲ Public Company   ■ Public Company Family Member   **HQ** Headquarters   **BR** Branch   **SL** Single Location

(902) 628-6900
Emp Here 60   *Sales* 13,320,060
SIC 3556 Food products machinery
 Peter Toombs

D-U-N-S 24-188-5912   (SL)
RELIABLE MOTORS LTD
14 John Yeo Dr, Charlottetown, PE, C1E 3H6
(902) 566-4409
Emp Here 30   *Sales* 14,942,340
SIC 5511 New and used car dealers
 Brent Maclennan
 Phyllis Maclennan

D-U-N-S 25-357-5971   (BR)
RESOLVE CORPORATION
50 Watts Ave, Charlottetown, PE, C1E 2B8
(902) 629-3000
Emp Here 400
SIC 7389 Business services, nec
 John Brennan

D-U-N-S 24-357-6530   (SL)
SEKISUI DIAGNOSTICS P.E.I. INC
(*Suby of* SEKISUI CHEMICAL CO., LTD.)
70 Watts Ave Suite 24, Charlottetown, PE,
C1E 2B9
(902) 566-1396
Emp Here 100   *Sales* 28,402,100
SIC 2819 Industrial inorganic chemicals, nec
 Jerome Harold Casey
 Paul John O'connor
 Misuhisa Manabe
 Christopher Wayne Brandy

D-U-N-S 20-798-8739   (SL)
SHERWOOD TIMBER MART INC
SHERWOOD BMR
423 Mount Edward Rd, Charlottetown, PE,
C1E 2A1
(902) 368-3648
Emp Here 49   *Sales* 12,399,891
SIC 5211 Lumber and other building materials
 Gary Macleod

D-U-N-S 24-943-6460   (BR)
SOBEYS CAPITAL INCORPORATED
SOBEYS
(*Suby of* EMPIRE COMPANY LIMITED)
679 University Ave, Charlottetown, PE, C1E
1E5
(902) 566-3218
Emp Here 135
SIC 5411 Grocery stores
 Tim Arnett

D-U-N-S 20-444-2263   (HQ)
SUPERIOR SANITATION SERVICES LTD
7 Superior Cres, Charlottetown, PE, C1E 2A1
(902) 892-1333
Sales 17,999,170
SIC 4953 Refuse systems
 Edward Clark

D-U-N-S 20-085-0472   (BR)
**UNITED BROTHERHOOD OF CARPEN-
TERS JOINERS AMERICA LOCAL 83**
*UNITED BROTHERHOOD OF CARPEN-
TERS LOCAL 1338*
(*Suby of* UNITED BROTHERHOOD OF CAR-
PENTERS JOINERS AMERICA LOCAL 83)
22 Enman Cres, Charlottetown, PE, C1E 1E6
(902) 566-1414
Emp Here 268
SIC 8631 Labor organizations
 Paul Chiasson

D-U-N-S 20-646-1340   (SL)
VISION RESEARCH INC
94 Watts Ave, Charlottetown, PE, C1E 2C1
(902) 569-7300
Emp Here 60   *Sales* 17,084,820
SIC 8733 Noncommercial research organiza-
tions
 Douglas Mcmonagle

D-U-N-S 24-329-8721   (BR)
WAL-MART CANADA CORP
(*Suby of* WALMART INC.)

80 Buchanan Dr, Charlottetown, PE, C1E 2E5
(902) 628-4600
Emp Here 200
SIC 5311 Department stores
 Carl Givens

Cornwall, PE C0A

D-U-N-S 20-728-4670   (HQ)
BULK CARRIERS (P.E.I) LIMITED
779 Bannockburn Rd, Cornwall, PE, C0A 1H0
(902) 675-2600
Sales 20,570,600
SIC 4213 Trucking, except local
 John Kelly
 Carlotta Kelly

Elmira, PE C0A

D-U-N-S 20-205-0717   (SL)
**ST COLUMBIA CATHOLIC WOMEN
LEAGUE FAIRFIELD**
3849 East Point Rd -Rte 16, Elmira, PE, C0A
1K0
(902) 357-2695
Emp Here 49   *Sales* 19,698,824
SIC 8699 Membership organizations, nec
 Margaret Stewart

Georgetown, PE C0A

D-U-N-S 20-272-1957   (SL)
EASTERN FABRICATORS INC
341 Georgetown Rd, Georgetown, PE, C0A
1L0
(902) 283-3229
Emp Here 53   *Sales* 10,180,505
SIC 3441 Fabricated structural Metal
 Todd Cormier
 Paul Livingston
 Chris Chaisson
 Reagh Ellis
 Rob Mayhew

D-U-N-S 25-895-4593   (BR)
IRVING SHIPBUILDING INC
EAST ISLE SHIPYARD
(*Suby of* IRVING SHIPBUILDING INC)
115 Water St, Georgetown, PE, C0A 1L0

Emp Here 100
SIC 3731 Shipbuilding and repairing
 Stephen O'brien

Hunter River, PE C0A

D-U-N-S 20-780-6340   (SL)
**NEW GLASGOW RECREATION CENTRE
(1980) INC**
NEW GLASGOW LOBSTER SUPPERS
604 Rte 258 Rr 3, Hunter River, PE, C0A 1N0
(902) 964-2810
Emp Here 110   *Sales* 5,130,290
SIC 5812 Eating places
 William Nicholson
 Jean Macrae
 Sterling Macrae
 Thelma Nicholson
 Carl Nicholson

Kensington, PE C0B

D-U-N-S 24-340-0330   (SL)
**KENSINGTON AGRICULTURAL SERVICES
LTD**
15 Park Rd, Kensington, PE, C0B 1M0
(902) 836-3212
Emp Here 27   *Sales* 12,825,702
SIC 5083 Farm and garden machinery
 Earle Clarke
 George Stewart
 James Mciver
 James Hickey

D-U-N-S 20-267-1140   (SL)
PINE ACRES (HAMPTON) LIMITED
PINE ACRES RV
24965 Route 2, Kensington, PE, C0B 1M0
(902) 836-5040
Emp Here 41   *Sales* 20,421,198
SIC 5561 Recreational vehicle dealers
 Edwin Brown

D-U-N-S 24-804-7201   (SL)
PRINCE EDWARD AQUA FARMS INC
ISLAND GOLD
Gd, Kensington, PE, C0B 1M0
(902) 886-2220
Emp Here 50   *Sales* 11,242,750
SIC 2092 Fresh or frozen packaged fish
 Debbie Ramsey
 Jerry Adams
 David Cole

D-U-N-S 24-128-4926   (SL)
**PRINCE EDWARD ISLAND GRAIN ELEVA-
TORS CORPORATION**
(*Suby of* PROVINCE OF PEI)
62 Victoria St, Kensington, PE, C0B 1M0
(902) 836-8935
Emp Here 14   *Sales* 20,547,688
SIC 5153 Grain and field beans
 Alvin Keenan
 Earle Smith
 Rollin Andrew
 James Mciver
 Nelson Mackinnon
 Denton Ellis
 Robert Mulligan

Lennox Island, PE C0B

D-U-N-S 20-366-0469   (SL)
MINIGOO FISHERIES INC
195 Eagle Feather Trail, Lennox Island, PE,
C0B 1P0

Emp Here 20   *Sales* 16,711,540
SIC 5146 Fish and seafoods
 Heather Pothier
 Chief Matilda Ramjattan
 Mary Moore-Phillips
 Janet Banks
 Corrine Dyment
 Gerry Thomas

Moncton, PE C1E

D-U-N-S 20-753-9417   (SL)
VANCO FARMS LTD
280 Crooked Creek Rd -Rte 251, Moncton,
PE, C1E 0M1
(902) 651-2970
Emp Here 100   *Sales* 26,230,900
SIC 0191 General farms, primarily crop
 Phil Vannieuwenhuyzen

Montague, PE C0A

D-U-N-S 25-152-5812   (HQ)

**ASPIN KEMP & ASSOCIATES HOLDING
CORP**
AKA GROUP OF COMPANIES
23 Brook St, Montague, PE, C0A 1R0
(902) 361-3135
Sales 27,335,000
SIC 6712 Bank holding companies
 Jason Aspin
 Neale Kemp

D-U-N-S 20-334-0369   (HQ)
ASPIN KEMP & ASSOCIATES INC
(*Suby of* ASPIN KEMP & ASSOCIATES
HOLDING CORP)
23 Brook St, Montague, PE, C0A 1R0
(902) 361-3135
Emp Here 5   *Sales* 24,381,996
SIC 8711 Engineering services
 Jason Conrad Aspin
 Ravi Naidu

D-U-N-S 20-004-0637   (BR)
ATLANTIC WHOLESALERS LTD
REAL ATLANTIC SUPERSTORE, THE
(*Suby of* LOBLAW COMPANIES LIMITED)
509 Main St, Montague, PE, C0A 1R0
(902) 838-5421
Emp Here 105
SIC 5411 Grocery stores
 Brian Barry

D-U-N-S 20-029-1537   (BR)
EASTERN SCHOOL DISTRICT
MONTAGUE REGIONAL HIGH SCHOOL
(*Suby of* EASTERN SCHOOL DISTRICT)
274 Valleyfield Rd, Montague, PE, C0A 1R0
(902) 838-0835
Emp Here 80
SIC 8211 Elementary and secondary schools
 Seana Evans-Renaud

D-U-N-S 20-017-8838   (SL)
KINGS COUNTY CONSTRUCTION LIMITED
5284a A Macdonald Hwy, Montague, PE, C0A
1R0
(902) 838-2191
Emp Here 67   *Sales* 16,913,614
SIC 1611 Highway and street construction
 Harry Annear
 Sandra Annear

D-U-N-S 20-930-2819   (SL)
KINGS COUNTY MEMORIAL HOSPITAL
409 Mcintyre Ave, Montague, PE, C0A 1R0
(902) 838-0777
Emp Here 76   *Sales* 7,762,108
SIC 8062 General medical and surgical hospi-
tals
 Terry Campbell
 Marie Wood

D-U-N-S 20-377-0029   (SL)
RED ROCK SEAFOODS LTD
546 Main St, Montague, PE, C0A 1R0
(902) 549-5087
Emp Here 20   *Sales* 11,693,572
SIC 5146 Fish and seafoods
 Glen Fewer
 Ryan Hynes

D-U-N-S 24-943-6346   (BR)
SOBEYS CAPITAL INCORPORATED
(*Suby of* EMPIRE COMPANY LIMITED)
Gd, Montague, PE, C0A 1R0
(902) 838-3388
Emp Here 80
SIC 5411 Grocery stores
 Brad Butler

Morell, PE C0A

D-U-N-S 20-114-4180   (SL)
P.E.I. MUSSEL KING (1994) INC
318 Red Head Rd, Morell, PE, C0A 1S0

---

(902) 961-3300
Emp Here 70   *Sales* 14,463,190
SIC 0913 Shellfish
 Russell Dockendorff, Sr
 Linda Smith
 Esther Dockendorff
 Scott Dockendorff
 Donna Macdonald
 Russell Dockendorff, Jr
 Dorothy Dockendorff
 Stewart Dockendorff

D-U-N-S 25-380-9388   (SL)
WYMAN, JASPER & SON CANADA INC
(*Suby of* JASPER WYMAN & SON)
41 Mcquin Rd, Morell, PE, C0A 1S0
(902) 961-3330
Emp Here 50   *Sales* 41,778,850
SIC 5142 Packaged frozen goods
 Edward Flanagan
 John D Duncan
 Elizabeth Doudoumopoulos

Mount Albion, PE C1B

D-U-N-S 20-554-9574   (SL)
VANCO FARMS LTD
9311 Trans Canada Hwy - Rte 1, Mount Albion, PE, C1B 0R4
(902) 651-2005
Emp Here 60   *Sales* 50,134,620
SIC 5148 Fresh fruits and vegetables
 Phillip Vannieuwenhuyzen
 Rit Vannieuwenhuyzen
 Willem Vannieuwenhuyzen

Murray Harbour, PE C0A

D-U-N-S 24-420-9842   (SL)
BEACH POINT PROCESSING COMPANY
75 Wharf Lane, Murray Harbour, PE, C0A 1V0
(902) 962-4340
Emp Here 100   *Sales* 34,569,000
SIC 2091 Canned and cured fish and seafoods
 Jordan Mazetta
 Thomas Mazetta
 Paul Mazetta
 Richard Wilkins
 Zachary Mazetta

North Rustico, PE C0A

D-U-N-S 20-780-8648   (SL)
AVONLEA VILLAGE
Gd, North Rustico, PE, C0A 1X0
(902) 963-3050
Emp Here 45   *Sales* 23,398,515
SIC 4725 Tour operators
 Scott Linkletter

O'Leary, PE C0B

D-U-N-S 25-999-4259   (SL)
O'LEARY POTATO PACKERS LTD
85 Ellis Ave, O'Leary, PE, C0B 1V0

Emp Here 30   *Sales* 25,067,310
SIC 5148 Fresh fruits and vegetables
 Warren Ellis
 Orville Willis

Slemon Park, PE C0B

D-U-N-S 20-566-2500   (HQ)
MDS COATING TECHNOLOGIES CORPORATION
(*Suby of* MDS AEROSPACE CORPORATION)
60 Aerospace Blvd, Slemon Park, PE, C0B 2A0
(902) 888-3900
Emp Here 68   *Sales* 14,406,375
SIC 3479 Metal coating and allied services
 Hans Odoerfer
 Phil Rodger
 Kerry Butler

D-U-N-S 24-878-1569   (HQ)
SLEMON PARK CORPORATION
30 Aerospace Blvd Unit A, Slemon Park, PE, C0B 2A0
(902) 432-1700
Sales 35,605,565
SIC 6531 Real estate agents and managers
 Shawn Mccarvill

Souris, PE C0A

D-U-N-S 25-313-0603   (SL)
AGRAWEST INVESTMENTS LIMITED
AGRAWEST FOODS
30 Hope St, Souris, PE, C0A 2B0
(902) 687-1400
Emp Here 90   *Sales* 31,112,100
SIC 2034 Dried and dehydrated fruits, vegetables and soup mixes
 Wally Browning

D-U-N-S 20-753-9599   (BR)
OCI HOLDINGS INC
(*Suby of* OCI HOLDINGS INC)
20 Hope St, Souris, PE, C0A 2B0
(902) 687-1245
Emp Here 800
SIC 5146 Fish and seafoods
 Pam Perrot

D-U-N-S 20-084-6264   (BR)
PROVINCE OF PEI
COLVILLE MANOR
(*Suby of* PROVINCE OF PEI)
20 Macphee Ave, Souris, PE, C0A 2B0
(902) 687-7090
Emp Here 75
SIC 8051 Skilled nursing care facilities
 Shelley Connick

D-U-N-S 24-343-4800   (SL)
ROLLO BAY HOLDINGS LTD
677 2 Rte Rr 4, Souris, PE, C0A 2B0
(902) 687-3333
Emp Here 45   *Sales* 15,411,015
SIC 0134 Irish potatoes
 Raymond Keenan
 Alvin Keenan Jr

St-Peters Bay, PE C0A

D-U-N-S 24-187-8750   (HQ)
MILLIGANS FISHERIES LTD
1968 Cardigan Road, St-Peters Bay, PE, C0A 2A0
(902) 961-2651
Emp Here 1   *Sales* 16,171,884
SIC 7389 Business services, nec
 Philip Milligan

Stratford, PE C1B

D-U-N-S 20-929-2937   (HQ)
EASTERN SCHOOL DISTRICT
234 Shakespeare Dr, Stratford, PE, C1B 2V8
(902) 368-6990
Sales 247,797,500
SIC 8211 Elementary and secondary schools
 Marjorie Steeves

D-U-N-S 25-665-7412   (SL)
GREAT HOBBIES INC
17 Glen Stewart Dr Suite 1, Stratford, PE, C1B 2A8
(902) 569-3289
Emp Here 50   *Sales* 10,880,650
SIC 5945 Hobby, toy, and game shops
 James Ewing
 Mark Bowlan
 Gary Stephen

D-U-N-S 24-347-3191   (BR)
HOME HARDWARE STORES LIMITED
(*Suby of* HOME HARDWARE STORES LIMITED)
14 Kinlock Rd, Stratford, PE, C1B 1R1

Emp Here 75
SIC 5211 Lumber and other building materials
 George Birt

D-U-N-S 24-214-9811   (SL)
NUTRACELLE
9 Carriage Lane, Stratford, PE, C1B 2G9
(877) 229-1207
Emp Here 12   *Sales* 10,026,924
SIC 5149 Groceries and related products, nec

D-U-N-S 20-904-3488   (SL)
REDDIN FARM EQUIPMENT LTD
JOHN DEERE
(*Suby of* NORJOHN HOLDINGS LTD)
237 Mason Rd, Stratford, PE, C1B 2G1
(902) 569-2500
Emp Here 35   *Sales* 16,625,910
SIC 5083 Farm and garden machinery
 John Reddin
 Norma Reddin

D-U-N-S 25-364-3944   (BR)
SOBEYS CAPITAL INCORPORATED
(*Suby of* EMPIRE COMPANY LIMITED)
9 Kinlock Rd Suite 621, Stratford, PE, C1B 1P8
(902) 894-3800
Emp Here 100
SIC 5411 Grocery stores
 Kevin Jones

Summerside, PE C1N

D-U-N-S 20-018-1055   (HQ)
AMALGAMATED DAIRIES LIMITED
ADL QUALITY PRODUCTS
79 Water St Suite 1, Summerside, PE, C1N 1A6
(902) 888-5088
Emp Here 100   *Sales* 109,661,625
SIC 2026 Fluid milk
 James Bradley
 Thane Macewen
 Gail Ellis
 Jamie Macphail
 Lee Turner
 Chad Mann

D-U-N-S 24-349-1482   (SL)
ARSENAULT BROS. CONSTRUCTION LTD
5 Hillside Ave, Summerside, PE, C1N 4H3
(902) 888-2689
Emp Here 45   *Sales* 12,192,390
SIC 1522 Residential construction, nec
 Carl Arsenault
 Anne Marie Arsenault
 William Albert Arsenault
 Joel Arsenault

Clarence Arsenault

D-U-N-S 25-656-5698   (BR)
ATLANTIC WHOLESALERS LTD
REAL ATLANTIC SUPERSTORE, THE
(*Suby of* LOBLAW COMPANIES LIMITED)
535 Granville St, Summerside, PE, C1N 6N4
(902) 888-1581
Emp Here 250
SIC 5411 Grocery stores
 Michael French

D-U-N-S 20-017-3227   (SL)
CALLBECKS LTD
CALLBECKS HOME HARDWARE
613 Water St E, Summerside, PE, C1N 4H8
(902) 436-1100
Emp Here 55   *Sales* 14,720,860
SIC 5211 Lumber and other building materials
 Ronald Macdonald
 Donna Macdonald

D-U-N-S 20-523-8827   (SL)
CLARK'S AUTO CENTRE LTD
CLARK'S TOYOTA
110 Walker Ave, Summerside, PE, C1N 6V9
(902) 436-5800
Emp Here 25   *Sales* 12,451,950
SIC 5511 New and used car dealers
 David Clark
 Scott Clark

D-U-N-S 20-145-3719   (HQ)
CURRAN & BRIGGS LIMITED
ADVANCE RENTALS DIV OF
40 All Weather Hwy, Summerside, PE, C1N 4J8
(902) 436-2163
Emp Here 50   *Sales* 19,185,592
SIC 1611 Highway and street construction
 Rick Kennedy
 David Riehl
 Marion Riehl

D-U-N-S 24-419-3590   (SL)
FITZGERALD & SNOW (2010) LTD
190 Greenwood Dr, Summerside, PE, C1N 4K2
(902) 436-9256
Emp Here 60   *Sales* 34,220,280
SIC 1542 Nonresidential construction, nec
 Vernon Mcquillan

D-U-N-S 20-018-1246   (SL)
HEMPHILL PONTIAC BUICK CHEVROLET GMC LIMITED
HEMPHILL GM
34 Water St, Summerside, PE, C1N 4T8
(877) 759-1458
Emp Here 35   *Sales* 17,432,730
SIC 5511 New and used car dealers
 Brian Hemphill

D-U-N-S 20-781-5226   (SL)
LINKLETTER'S WELDING LTD
26 Av Linkletter Suite 3, Summerside, PE, C1N 4J9
(902) 887-2652
Emp Here 48   *Sales* 10,656,048
SIC 3523 Farm machinery and equipment
 Wayne Linkletter

D-U-N-S 20-018-1899   (SL)
MACDONALD, D. ALEX LIMITED
MACDONALD, D. ALEX FORD LINCOLN
25 Water St, Summerside, PE, C1N 1A3
(902) 436-6653
Emp Here 35   *Sales* 17,432,730
SIC 5511 New and used car dealers
 Peter Macdonald

D-U-N-S 20-801-1879   (BR)
MCKENNCO INC
MCDONALD'S
(*Suby of* MCKENNCO INC)
481 Granville St, Summerside, PE, C1N 4P7
(902) 436-5462
Emp Here 100

SIC 5812 Eating places
Martha Macleod

D-U-N-S 24-606-6567   (SL)
NOYE ENTERPRISES INC
87 Ottawa St, Summerside, PE, C1N 1W2

Emp Here 29   *Sales* 13,651,199
SIC 1542 Nonresidential construction, nec
Randy William Noye

D-U-N-S 25-380-7259   (BR)
OLD DUTCH FOODS LTD
HUMPTY DUMPTY OLD DUTCH FOODS
(*Suby of* OLD DUTCH FOODS LTD)
4 Slemon Park Dr, Summerside, PE, C1N 4K4
(902) 888-5160
Emp Here 100
SIC 2096 Potato chips and similar snacks
Glen Mackinnon

D-U-N-S 25-542-9961   (SL)
PRINCE COUNTY HORSEMAN'S CLUB INC
SUMMERSIDE RACEWAY
477 Notre Dame St, Summerside, PE, C1N 1T2

Emp Here 30   *Sales* 12,711,900
SIC 7948 Racing, including track operation
Eric Johnson

D-U-N-S 20-904-4718   (SL)
PRINCE COUNTY HOSPITAL
65 Roy Boates Ave, Summerside, PE, C1N 6M8
(902) 438-4200
Emp Here 425   *Sales* 47,209,000
SIC 8062 General medical and surgical hospitals
Arlene Gallant

D-U-N-S 24-126-8366   (SL)
PRINCE EDWARD ISLAND MUTUAL INSURANCE COMPANY
116 Walker Ave, Summerside, PE, C1N 6V9
(902) 436-2185
Emp Here 35   *Sales* 64,633,065
SIC 6331 Fire, marine, and casualty insurance
Blair Campbell
Rudy Smith
Terrance Shea
Stewart Macrae
Claude Dorgan
Gordon Vessey
Percy Affleck
James Doyle
Brian Mackinley
Brian Annear

D-U-N-S 25-656-5201   (BR)
PROVINCE OF PEI
SUMMERSET MANOR
(*Suby of* PROVINCE OF PEI)
15 Frank Mellish St, Summerside, PE, C1N 0H3
(902) 888-8310
Emp Here 100
SIC 8052 Intermediate care facilities
Gayle Lamont

D-U-N-S 20-554-7719   (BR)
RESOLVE CORPORATION
150 Industrial Cres, Summerside, PE, C1N 5N6
(902) 432-7500
Emp Here 350
SIC 7389 Business services, nec
Bonnie Gallant

D-U-N-S 24-943-6064   (BR)
SOBEYS CAPITAL INCORPORATED
SOBEYS #425
(*Suby of* EMPIRE COMPANY LIMITED)
868-475 Granville St, Summerside, PE, C1N 3N9
(902) 436-5795
Emp Here 100
SIC 5411 Grocery stores

Corey Rochford

D-U-N-S 20-018-2426   (SL)
SUMMERSIDE CHRYSLER DODGE (1984) LTD
3 Water St, Summerside, PE, C1N 1A2
(902) 436-9141
Emp Here 23   *Sales* 11,455,794
SIC 5511 New and used car dealers
Richard Ripley
Patricia Ripley

D-U-N-S 24-955-7992   (HQ)
VECTOR AEROSPACE ENGINE SERVICES-ATLANTIC INC
(*Suby of* STANDARDAERO AVIATION HOLDINGS, INC.)
800 Aerospace Blvd, Summerside, PE, C1N 4P6
(902) 436-1333
Emp Here 400   *Sales* 142,808,400
SIC 4581 Airports, flying fields, and services
Jeff Poirier
Mark O'keefe
Tracy Connelly Mcgilley
Claire Silvester
Darren Smith

D-U-N-S 24-120-9464   (BR)
WAL-MART CANADA CORP
(*Suby of* WALMART INC.)
511 Granville St, Summerside, PE, C1N 5J4
(902) 432-3570
Emp Here 200
SIC 5311 Department stores
Jeff Sheculski

Tignish, PE C0B

D-U-N-S 20-179-6849   (SL)
L. & S. MARKETING LTD
142 Dalton Ave, Tignish, PE, C0B 2B0
(902) 882-3105
Emp Here 20   *Sales* 10,702,480
SIC 5146 Fish and seafoods
Shawn Hogan

D-U-N-S 25-706-1556   (SL)
PERRY'S CONSTRUCTION & READY MIX LTD
190 Centennial Dr, Tignish, PE, C0B 2B0
(902) 882-3166
Emp Here 35   *Sales* 10,100,405
SIC 1522 Residential construction, nec
Harley Perry

Vernon Bridge, PE C0A

D-U-N-S 24-754-8597   (SL)
VISSER, GERRIT & SONS (1991) INC
GWR VISSER FARMS
6346 Trans Canada Hwy - Rte 1, Vernon Bridge, PE, C0A 2E0
(902) 651-2371
Emp Here 25   *Sales* 20,889,425
SIC 5148 Fresh fruits and vegetables
Randy Visser
William Visser

Wellington Station, PE C0B

D-U-N-S 20-337-3910   (SL)
ACADIAN SUPREME INC
8323 11 Rte, Wellington Station, PE, C0B 2E0
(902) 854-2675
Emp Here 50   *Sales* 41,778,850
SIC 5146 Fish and seafoods
Jeffrey Malloy

Marcel Duguay
Janell Macdonald
Darrell Roche
Peter Buhl
Paul Grant

D-U-N-S 20-063-8307   (HQ)
COMISSION SCOLAIRE DE LANGUE FRANCAISE, LA
FRENCH LANGUAGE SCHOOL BOARD
1596 124 Rte, Wellington Station, PE, C0B 2E0
(902) 854-2975
Emp Here 36   *Sales* 13,480,184
SIC 8211 Elementary and secondary schools
Gilles Benoit

D-U-N-S 20-781-2371   (SL)
WELLINGTON CONSTRUCTION CO LTD
1742 124 Rte, Wellington Station, PE, C0B 2E0
(902) 854-2650
Emp Here 30   *Sales* 14,121,930
SIC 1542 Nonresidential construction, nec
David Arsenault
Roger Arsenault

York, PE C0A

D-U-N-S 20-018-2921   (HQ)
VESEY'S HOLDINGS LTD
VESEYS
(*Suby of* B & S HOLDINGS LTD)
411 York Rd Hwy Suite 25, York, PE, C0A 1P0
(902) 368-7333
Sales 17,767,750
SIC 6712 Bank holding companies
Beverly E Simpson
Shirley Simpson
Gerry Simpson

D-U-N-S 24-537-4587   (SL)
VESEY'S SEEDS LTD
(*Suby of* B & S HOLDINGS LTD)
411 York Rd, York, PE, C0A 1P0
(902) 368-7333
Emp Here 65   *Sales* 18,174,347
SIC 5261 Retail nurseries and garden stores
Gerry Simpson

Acton Vale, QC J0H

D-U-N-S 20-290-6079   (SL)
9303-6952 QUEBEC INC
355 Rue Bonin, Acton Vale, QC, J0H 1A0
(450) 546-3279
Emp Here 73   *Sales* 19,093,369
SIC 6712 Bank holding companies
Yves St-Germain
Yves Perazzelli
Guy Laurendeau

D-U-N-S 24-650-6067   (SL)
AIRBOSS ENGINEERED PRODUCTS INC
AIRBOSS & DESING (TMA494,030)
(Suby of AIRBOSS OF AMERICA CORP)
970 Rue Landry, Acton Vale, QC, J0H 1A0
(450) 546-2776
Emp Here 240   *Sales* 57,314,880
SIC 3069 Fabricated rubber products, nec
P. Grenville Schoch
Lisa Swartzman
Daniel Gagnon
Chris Figel
Yvan Ambeault

D-U-N-S 20-187-7487   (SL)
CARRIERE D'ACTON VALE LTEE
525 116 Rte, Acton Vale, QC, J0H 1A0
(450) 546-3201
Emp Here 45   *Sales* 10,350,855
SIC 3273 Ready-mixed concrete
Maurice Halde
Julien Halde

D-U-N-S 24-082-9069   (SL)
CLUB DE GOLF ACTON VALE INC
1000 Rte 116, Acton Vale, QC, J0H 1A0
(450) 549-5885
Emp Here 64   *Sales* 5,729,775
SIC 7992 Public golf courses
Jocelyne Coderre
Daniel Coderre

D-U-N-S 24-086-1885   (BR)
COMMISSION SCOLAIRE DE SAINT-HYACINTHE, LA
POLYVALENTE ROBERT OUIMET
(Suby of COMMISSION SCOLAIRE DE SAINT-HYACINTHE, LA)
1450 3e Av, Acton Vale, QC, J0H 1A0
(450) 546-5575
Emp Here 100
SIC 8211 Elementary and secondary schools
Andree Leduc

D-U-N-S 20-419-0193   (HQ)
COMPAGNIE BEAULIEU CANADA
BEAULIEU CANADA
(Suby of BEAULIEU HOLDINGS OF CANADA, INC.)
335 Rue De Roxton, Acton Vale, QC, J0H 1A0
(450) 546-5000
Emp Here 75   *Sales* 139,536,770
SIC 2273 Carpets and rugs
Mieke D. Hanssens
Benoit Leclair

D-U-N-S 25-391-9310   (SL)
EQUIPEMENTS PIERRE CHAMPIGNY LTEE
PRODUIT MOBICAB CANADA
280 Rue Bonin Rr 4, Acton Vale, QC, J0H 1A0
(450) 546-0999
Emp Here 25   *Sales* 12,451,950
SIC 5599 Automotive dealers, nec
Pierre Champigny

D-U-N-S 20-187-7834   (SL)
JOLY, ERNEST & FILS INC
PROVIGO
1530 Rue D'Acton, Acton Vale, QC, J0H 1A0
(450) 546-7733
Emp Here 60   *Sales* 17,608,620
SIC 5411 Grocery stores
Denis Joly

Marcel Joly

D-U-N-S 24-893-5335   (SL)
LIFE SCIENCE NUTRITIONALS INC
SUPPLMENTS ALIMENTAIRES LSN, LES
1190 Rue Lemay, Acton Vale, QC, J0H 1A0
(450) 546-0101
Emp Here 82   *Sales* 22,686,120
SIC 2833 Medicinals and botanicals
Carlyn Solomon
Michael White

D-U-N-S 24-388-0338   (HQ)
LIFE SCIENCE NUTRITIONALS INCORPORATED
SUPPLEMENTS ALIMENTAIRES LSN, LES
575 Rue De Roxton, Acton Vale, QC, J0H 1A0
(866) 942-2429
Sales 19,988,598
SIC 8731 Commercial physical research
Carlyn Solomon
David J. Koo
Andrew B. Hochman
Joseph F. Damico
Lester B. Knight
James Utts
John Dahldorf

D-U-N-S 20-187-7347   (SL)
PATISSERIE GAUDET INC
BOULANGERIE BEAUSEJOUR
1048 Rue Macdonald, Acton Vale, QC, J0H 1A0
(450) 546-3221
Emp Here 50   *Sales* 11,242,750
SIC 2051 Bread, cake, and related products
Lyne Lamothe
Maher Mahjoub
Peter S. Martin

D-U-N-S 20-317-5807   (HQ)
PRODUITS MOBILICAB CANADA INC
280 Rue Bonin, Acton Vale, QC, J0H 1A0
(450) 546-0999
Emp Here 25   *Sales* 11,432,055
SIC 5088 Transportation equipment and supplies
Robert Charest

Adstock, QC G0N

D-U-N-S 24-909-3881   (SL)
BERCOMAC LIMITEE
92 Rue Fortin N, Adstock, QC, G0N 1S0
(418) 422-2252
Emp Here 50   *Sales* 11,100,050
SIC 3523 Farm machinery and equipment
Alain Acteau
Sylvie Vachon
Sebastien Acteau

D-U-N-S 20-255-5496   (HQ)
BOULANGERIE ST-METHODE INC
(Suby of GROUPE BSM INC)
14 Rue Principale E, Adstock, QC, G0N 1S0
(418) 422-2246
Emp Here 180   *Sales* 50,040,640
SIC 5461 Retail bakeries
Benoit Faucher
Carl Pouliot

D-U-N-S 25-258-7092   (SL)
CONFECTION ST METHODE INC
228 Rue Notre-Dame N, Adstock, QC, G0N 1S0
(418) 422-2206
Emp Here 90   *Sales* 17,928,360
SIC 2325 Men's and boys' trousers and slacks
Sylvain Lachance
Nancy Jacques
Vickey Jacques

Albanel, QC G8M

D-U-N-S 20-187-8592   (SL)
COOPERATIVE D'ALBANEL
287 Rue De L'Eglise, Albanel, QC, G8M 3J9
(418) 279-3183
Emp Here 35   *Sales* 11,434,836
SIC 5411 Grocery stores
Andre St-Pierre
Adele Gaudreault

Alma, QC G8B

D-U-N-S 24-499-1683   (SL)
130395 CANADA INC
NORDEX ENR
200 Rue Des Pins O Bureau 201, Alma, QC, G8B 6P9
(418) 668-0420
Emp Here 40   *Sales* 18,675,367
SIC 1794 Excavation work
Yvon Potvin
Alain Potvin
Jean-Marc Potvin
Richard Gaudreault

D-U-N-S 20-214-4080   (SL)
2742-7608 QUEBEC INC
PIECES D'AUTOS JMR ALMA
225 Av Du Pont S, Alma, QC, G8B 2T7
(418) 668-3061
Emp Here 25   *Sales* 12,451,950
SIC 5531 Auto and home supply stores
Jean-Francois Claveau

D-U-N-S 25-973-5173   (SL)
9075-5125 QUEBEC INC
ALMA HONDA
2625 Av Du Pont S Bureau 1, Alma, QC, G8B 5V2
(418) 480-4776
Emp Here 30   *Sales* 14,942,340
SIC 5511 New and used car dealers
Martin Ouellet
Gilles Bernard

D-U-N-S 24-890-8113   (SL)
9124-4269 QUEBEC INC
TIM HORTONS
1049 Av Du Pont S, Alma, QC, G8B 0E8
(418) 662-1178
Emp Here 100   *Sales* 4,287,300
SIC 5812 Eating places
Claude Gauthier
Marlene Gagnon

D-U-N-S 24-353-9249   (SL)
9165-2214 QUEBEC INC
LAVAL FORTIN ADAMS
130 Rue Notre-Dame O, Alma, QC, G8B 2K1
(819) 964-0057
Emp Here 75   *Sales* 31,705,275
SIC 1541 Industrial buildings and warehouses
Johnny Adams
Charles Deslauriers

D-U-N-S 24-746-3359   (HQ)
ALCO-TMI INC
995 Rue Bombardier, Alma, QC, G8B 6H2
(418) 669-1911
Sales 11,653,250
SIC 1711 Plumbing, heating, air-conditioning
Marc Lepage
Normand Bouchard
Lucie Lavoie
Francois Potvin
Martin Cossette

D-U-N-S 24-908-1621   (SL)
ALMA FORD INC
1570 Av Du Pont S, Alma, QC, G8B 6N1
(418) 662-6695
Emp Here 26   *Sales* 12,950,028
SIC 5511 New and used car dealers

Jocelyn Gaudreault
Daniel Simard

D-U-N-S 20-192-4243   (HQ)
B.P.D.L. INC
890 Rue Des Pins O, Alma, QC, G8B 7R3
(418) 668-6161
Sales 11,190,360
SIC 8742 Management consulting services
Robert Bouchard
Guy Bouchard
Christine Bouchard
Joane Bergeron

D-U-N-S 20-253-3881   (SL)
BETON PREFABRIQUE DU RICHELIEU INC
BPDR
890 Rue Des Pins O, Alma, QC, G8B 7R3
(418) 668-6161
Emp Here 50   *Sales* 11,671,750
SIC 3273 Ready-mixed concrete
Robert Bouchard
Camil Sauve
Eric Caron

D-U-N-S 24-464-2096   (HQ)
BETONS PREFABRIQUES DU LAC INC
BPDL
890 Rue Des Pins O, Alma, QC, G8B 7R3
(418) 668-6161
Emp Here 100   *Sales* 83,099,250
SIC 3272 Concrete products, nec
Robert Bouchard
Christine Bouchard
Guy Bouchard
Joane Bergeron

D-U-N-S 25-899-1959   (HQ)
BETONS PREFABRIQUES TRANS-CANADA INC
890 Rue Des Pins O, Alma, QC, G8B 7R3
(418) 668-6161
Emp Here 5   *Sales* 13,611,565
SIC 1771 Concrete work
Robert Bouchard
Guy Bouchard
Lino Pansieri
Gaetan Bouchard
Robert Bouchard

D-U-N-S 20-767-7647   (SL)
BOUILLOIRE FALMEC INC
BSI EQUIPEMENTIER
200 Rue Des Pins O Bureau 109, Alma, QC, G8B 6P9
(418) 668-0788
Emp Here 50   *Sales* 10,141,500
SIC 3443 Fabricated plate work (boiler shop)
Luc Martel
Claude Asselin

D-U-N-S 24-841-9095   (SL)
CAFE MARC ROBITAILLE INC
850 Av Tanguay, Alma, QC, G8B 5Y3
(418) 668-8022
Emp Here 19   *Sales* 10,167,356
SIC 5149 Groceries and related products, nec
Marc Robitaille
Gisele Fortin

D-U-N-S 20-547-6562   (HQ)
CAISSE POPULAIRE DESJARDINS D'ALMA
CENTRE DE SERVICES LABRECQUE
600 Rue Collard, Alma, QC, G8B 1N4
(418) 669-1414
Emp Here 70   *Sales* 23,386,096
SIC 6062 State credit unions
Michel Caron
Regis Tremblay
Gladys Harvey
Caroline Laberge
Audrey Cote
Michel Desgagne
Carl Fleury
Jany Fortin
Michel Lefebvre

Annie Gilbert

D-U-N-S 24-908-4146   (SL)
**CENTRE LOCAL DES SERVICES COMMU-
NAUTAIRES LE NOROIS**
C L S C LE NOROIS
100 Rue Saint-Joseph, Alma, QC, G8B 7A6
(418) 668-4563
Emp Here 200   *Sales* 41,413,600
SIC 8399 Social services, nec
Jacques Levesque

D-U-N-S 24-011-6447   (BR)
**COMMISSION SCOLAIRE DU LAC-ST-
JEAN**
*CENTRE DE FORMATION PROFESSION-
NELLE PAVILLON BEGIN*
850 Av B?Gin, Alma, QC, G8B 2X6
(418) 669-6063
Emp Here 150
SIC 8211 Elementary and secondary schools
Sandra Larouche

D-U-N-S 20-188-0564   (SL)
**COOPERATIVE DES CONSOMMATEURS
D'ALMA**
COOP IGA CARREFOUR
705 Av Du Pont N, Alma, QC, G8B 6T5
(418) 662-7405
Emp Here 100   *Sales* 27,415,200
SIC 5411 Grocery stores
Andre Simard
Serge Tremblay

D-U-N-S 25-463-1179   (SL)
**CORPORATION REGIONALE DE DEVEL-
OPPEMENT DE LA RECUPERATION ET DU
RECYCLAGE REGION 02**
GROUPE-CODERR
1000 Boul Saint-Jude, Alma, QC, G8B 3L1
(418) 668-8502
Emp Here 50   *Sales* 12,216,400
SIC 5932 Used merchandise stores
Gerald Tremblay
Jacques Belanger
Patrice Gobeil
Ghislain Fournier
Marcel Duguay
Claude Coude
Diane Martel
Dany D Guerin
Ludger Cote
Robin Labonte

D-U-N-S 20-187-9574   (SL)
DUBE, R. LTEE
METRO DUBE
370 Av Begin, Alma, QC, G8B 2W8
(418) 662-3611
Emp Here 200   *Sales* 58,695,400
SIC 5411 Grocery stores
Andre Dube
Richard Dube
Louis Dube

D-U-N-S 20-187-9558   (HQ)
DUCHESNE AUTO LTEE
DUCHESNE CHEVROLET OLDSMOBILE
450 Boul De Quen, Alma, QC, G8B 5P5
(418) 662-3431
Emp Here 30   *Sales* 24,903,900
SIC 5511 New and used car dealers
Daniel Duchesne
Jean-Michel Duchesne

D-U-N-S 25-298-6278   (SL)
GESTION ALAIN LAFOREST INC
MARCHAND CANADIAN TIRE DE STE-FOY
50 Boul Saint-Luc, Alma, QC, G8B 6K1
(418) 662-6618
Emp Here 66   *Sales* 13,552,638
SIC 5311 Department stores
Alain Laforest

D-U-N-S 20-716-9561   (BR)
HYDRO-QUEBEC
(*Suby of* GOUVERNEMENT DE LA

PROVINCE DE QUEBEC)
Gd, Alma, QC, G8B 5V5
(418) 668-1400
Emp Here 800
SIC 4911 Electric services
Paul Desroches

D-U-N-S 20-290-0841   (SL)
LA GALERIE DU JOUET JFA INC
GALERIE DU JOUET
1435 Av Du Pont S, Alma, QC, G8B 2V9
(418) 662-6221
Emp Here 26   *Sales* 13,534,092
SIC 5092 Toys and hobby goods and supplies
Michel Tremblay
Audrey Tremblay

D-U-N-S 20-187-9681   (SL)
LAVAL FORTIN LTEE
GROUPE LFL
(*Suby of* 9102-4976 QUEBEC INC)
130 Rue Notre-Dame O, Alma, QC, G8B 2K1
(418) 668-3321
Emp Here 50   *Sales* 21,136,850
SIC 1541 Industrial buildings and warehouses
Charles Deslauriers
Lynda Noel
Robin Larouche
Gaston Munger

D-U-N-S 20-102-2295   (BR)
MEGABURO INC
(*Suby of* SOCIETE FINANCIERE GRENCO
INC)
440 Rue Collard, Alma, QC, G8B 1N2
(418) 668-4591
Emp Here 250
SIC 5712 Furniture stores
Pierre Girard

D-U-N-S 24-790-6282   (HQ)
MODE CHOC (ALMA) LTEE
MODE CHOC
1055 Av Du Pont S Bureau 50, Alma, QC, G8B
2V7
(418) 668-2346
Emp Here 100   *Sales* 62,377,500
SIC 5651 Family clothing stores
Marlene Hudon
Jessika Roussy
Raymond Roussy

D-U-N-S 20-640-4928   (HQ)
PAPIERS SOLIDERR INC, LES
PAPIERS CODERR
525 Av Du Pont S, Alma, QC, G8B 2T9
(418) 668-5377
Emp Here 1   *Sales* 14,607,600
SIC 2679 Converted paper products, nec
Simon Coutu
Ludger Cote
Patrice Gobeil

D-U-N-S 24-339-8125   (BR)
PAPIERS SOLIDERR INC, LES
COLLECTES CODERR
(*Suby of* PAPIERS SOLIDERR INC, LES)
1025 Rue Des Pins O, Alma, QC, G8B 7V7
(418) 668-1234
Emp Here 130
SIC 4212 Local trucking, without storage
Gerald Tremblay

D-U-N-S 20-188-0978   (BR)
PF RESOLU CANADA INC
*PRODUITS FORESTIERS RESOLU USINE
ALMA*
(*Suby of* RESOLUTE FOREST PRODUCTS
INC)
1100 Rue Melancon O, Alma, QC, G8B 7G2
(418) 668-9400
Emp Here 338
SIC 2621 Paper mills
Michel Leroux

D-U-N-S 24-701-8794   (SL)
PORTE EVOLUTION INC
1500 Boul Saint-Jude, Alma, QC, G8B 3L4

(418) 668-6688
Emp Here 49   *Sales* 11,286,660
SIC 5712 Furniture stores
Sandra Duschesne

D-U-N-S 25-850-0545   (BR)
PROMUTEL DU LAC AU FJORD
(*Suby of* PROMUTUEL DU LAC AU FJORD)
790 Av Du Pont S, Alma, QC, G8B 2V4
(418) 662-6595
Emp Here 80
SIC 6411 Insurance agents, brokers, and ser-
vice
Gaetane Boivin

D-U-N-S 20-016-2431   (BR)
RIO TINTO ALCAN INC
(*Suby of* RIO TINTO PLC)
3000 Rue Des Pins O, Alma, QC, G8B 5W2
(418) 480-6000
Emp Here 1,000
SIC 3399 Primary Metal products
Guy Gaudrault

D-U-N-S 20-277-9658   (SL)
SOUDURES EXPRESS INC
995 Av Bombardier, Alma, QC, G8B 6H2
(418) 669-1911
Emp Here 60   *Sales* 16,310,520
SIC 7692 Welding repair
Marc Lepage
Martin Cossette
Normand Bouchard
Lucie Lavoie

D-U-N-S 20-119-4235   (HQ)
TREMBLAY ASSURANCE LTEE
ASSURANCE 5000
575 Boul De Quen, Alma, QC, G8B 5Z1
(418) 662-6413
Sales 46,166,475
SIC 6331 Fire, marine, and casualty insurance
Rachel Maltais
Alain Fortin
Isabelle Tremblay
Yannick Tremblay

D-U-N-S 24-207-4255   (BR)
WAL-MART CANADA CORP
WALMART
(*Suby of* WALMART INC.)
1755 Av Du Pont S Bureau 5795, Alma, QC,
G8B 7W7
(418) 480-3887
Emp Here 100
SIC 5311 Department stores
Melanie Cote

Alma, QC G8C

D-U-N-S 20-290-3712   (SL)
9283-9034 QUEBEC INC
PEXAL-TECALUM CANADA
2185 Boul Eugene-Robitaille, Alma, QC, G8C
0H5
(418) 769-3113
Emp Here 17   *Sales* 16,143,360
SIC 3354 Aluminum extruded products
Jean-Francois Harvey
Jean-Francois Harvey
Dany Tremblay
Marc Sansalvador Asina
Pierre Pelletier

Alma, QC G8E

D-U-N-S 20-195-5796   (SL)
CHARCUTERIE L. FORTIN LIMITEE
ALIMENTS PHILIPS
(*Suby of* NUTRINOR COOPERATIVE)
5371 Av Du Pont N, Alma, QC, G8E 1T9

(418) 347-3365
Emp Here 85   *Sales* 29,383,650
SIC 2013 Sausages and other prepared
meats
Yves Girard
Paul Pomerleau
Daniel Asselin

D-U-N-S 24-054-6072   (SL)
CUMAF DU LAC
5791 Av Du Pont N, Alma, QC, G8E 1X1

Emp Here 25   *Sales* 11,419,358
SIC 7389 Business services, nec
Ande Menard

D-U-N-S 20-195-5739   (HQ)
ELECTRO SAGUENAY LTEE
245 Rue Des Huarts, Alma, QC, G8E 2G1
(418) 347-3371
Emp Here 15   *Sales* 26,506,410
SIC 1623 Water, sewer, and utility lines
Jean-Pierre Fleury
Andrea Tremblay

D-U-N-S 24-758-6019   (SL)
LOCATION A.L.R. INC
211 Rue Du Mistral, Alma, QC, G8E 2E2
(418) 347-4665
Emp Here 70   *Sales* 17,670,940
SIC 1611 Highway and street construction
Miguel Savard
Maxime Lavoie
Jerome Maltais

Amos, QC J9T

D-U-N-S 24-710-3344   (SL)
9056-4725 QUEBEC INC
AMOS TOYOTA
(*Suby of* GESTION 3 T INC)
1151 111 Rte E, Amos, QC, J9T 1N2
(819) 732-7000
Emp Here 28   *Sales* 13,946,184
SIC 5511 New and used car dealers
Remi Drolet
Claude Tardif

D-U-N-S 24-842-8914   (HQ)
AGRITIBI R.H. INC
2711 Rte 111 E Bureau 2, Amos, QC, J9T 3A1
(819) 732-6296
Sales 10,450,572
SIC 5083 Farm and garden machinery
Daniel Rivard
Vanessa Grenier

D-U-N-S 24-051-5957   (SL)
AMOPHARM INC
BRUNET
82 1re Av E, Amos, QC, J9T 4B2
(819) 727-1234
Emp Here 52   *Sales* 12,705,056
SIC 5912 Drug stores and proprietary stores
Christian Viens
Michael Ahern

D-U-N-S 20-962-3032   (SL)
**ASSURANCES COTE, GUIMOND, LAFOND
& ASSOCIES INC**
221 1re Av E, Amos, QC, J9T 1H5
(819) 732-5371
Emp Here 35   *Sales* 20,297,340
SIC 6411 Insurance agents, brokers, and ser-
vice
Florian Lafond
Andre Lesage

D-U-N-S 20-188-2198   (HQ)
BEN DESHAIES INC
BDI DISTRIBUTION
431 6e Rue O, Amos, QC, J9T 2V5
(819) 732-6466
Emp Here 200   *Sales* 207,847,640
SIC 5141 Groceries, general line

Francis Deshaies
Patrick Deshaies
Philippe Deshaies
Richard Deshaies
Renee Deshaies
Rejean Deshaies

D-U-N-S 25-337-1017   (HQ)
CAISSE DESJARDINS D'AMOS
CENTRE DE SERVICE CHRIST-ROI
2 Rue Principale N, Amos, QC, J9T 2K6

Emp Here 60   *Sales* 16,886,210
SIC 6062 State credit unions
Andre Talbot
Jean-Robert Gagnon
Benoit Godbout
Simon Letendre
Roch Ouellet
Maryse Thibault
Valerie Dugas
Luc Cloutier
Gysele B Lebreux
Robert Dufresne

D-U-N-S 24-346-7375   (BR)
**CENTRE DE SANTE ET DE SERVICE SOCI-
AUX LES ESKERS DE L'ABITIBI**
CLSC LES ESKERS
632 1re Rue O, Amos, QC, J9T 2N2
(819) 732-3271
Emp Here 800
SIC 8062 General medical and surgical hospi-
tals
Lise Dicaire

D-U-N-S 24-022-1564   (HQ)
CENTRE DU CAMION D'AMOS INC
145 Rte 111 E, Amos, QC, J9T 3A2
(819) 732-6471
Sales 21,395,520
SIC 5531 Auto and home supply stores
Alain Sayeur
Claude Ouellet
Pascal Sayeur
Stephane Carignan

D-U-N-S 20-885-8381   (HQ)
CLAIR FOYER INC
841 3e Rue O, Amos, QC, J9T 2T4
(819) 732-6511
Emp Here 20   *Sales* 11,849,400
SIC 8361 Residential care
Real Bordeleau
Denis Plourde

D-U-N-S 20-855-8445   (SL)
**CLUB COOPERATIF DE CONSOMMATION
D'AMOS**
CLUB COOP D'AMOS
421 12e Av E, Amos, QC, J9T 3H1
(819) 732-5281
Emp Here 100   *Sales* 29,347,700
SIC 5411 Grocery stores
Paul Bourget
Laurent Corriveau
Jean-Pierre Marcotte
Jean-Charles Breton
Eudes Martin

D-U-N-S 25-337-1009   (BR)
COMMISSION SCOLAIRE HARRICANA
POLYVALENTE DE LA FORET
850 1re Rue E, Amos, QC, J9T 2H8
(819) 732-3221
Emp Here 106
SIC 8211 Elementary and secondary schools
Marie-Helene Grondin

D-U-N-S 25-233-5690   (BR)
COMMISSION SCOLAIRE HARRICANA
ECOLE SECONDAIRE LA CALYPSO
800 1re Rue E, Amos, QC, J9T 2H8
(819) 732-3221
Emp Here 75
SIC 8211 Elementary and secondary schools
Yannick Roy

D-U-N-S 24-055-0053   (HQ)
COMMUNICATIONS POMERLEAU INC
VITRERIE POMERLEAU
111 Boul Mercier, Amos, QC, J9T 2P2
(819) 732-5377
Emp Here 22   *Sales* 12,794,432
SIC 4899 Communication services, nec
Dominic Maheux
Guillaume Dallaire
Marc Trudel
Gino Trudel

D-U-N-S 24-650-9780   (SL)
DISTRIBUTIONS NORYVE INC
JEAN COUTU 108
76 1re Av O Bureau 108, Amos, QC, J9T 1T8
(819) 732-3306
Emp Here 54   *Sales* 13,193,712
SIC 5912 Drug stores and proprietary stores

D-U-N-S 24-108-9846   (SL)
ENTREPRENEURS BLANCHET INC, LES
722 Av De L'Industrie, Amos, QC, J9T 4L9
(819) 732-5520
Emp Here 40   *Sales* 11,340,960
SIC 1611 Highway and street construction
Rejean Blanchet
Jean-Guy Blanchet
Gilles Blanchet

D-U-N-S 20-188-2420   (SL)
GARAGE TARDIF LTEE
(*Suby of* GESTION 3 T INC)
1222 111 Rte E, Amos, QC, J9T 1N1
(819) 732-5314
Emp Here 32   *Sales* 20,136,960
SIC 5521 Used car dealers
Yvan Gagnon

D-U-N-S 25-285-9699   (HQ)
GROUPE ROUILLIER INC
824 Av Des Forestiers Bureau 57, Amos, QC,
J9T 4L4
(819) 727-9269
Sales 26,241,600
SIC 6712 Bank holding companies
Mario Rouillier

D-U-N-S 20-860-6074   (BR)
IAMGOLD CORPORATION
IAMGOLD CORPORATION
(*Suby of* IAMGOLD CORPORATION)
118 Rte 109 N, Amos, QC, J9T 3A3
(819) 732-8268
Emp Here 190
SIC 1041 Gold ores
Eric Tremblay

D-U-N-S 24-614-6419   (BR)
MATERIAUX BLANCHET INC
(*Suby of* MATERIAUX BLANCHET INC)
2771 Rte De L'Aeroport, Amos, QC, J9T 3A8
(819) 732-6581
Emp Here 165
SIC 2421 Sawmills and planing mills, general
Rosaire Dube

D-U-N-S 24-941-8294   (HQ)
PETROLES ALCASYNA (1993) INC, LES
(*Suby of* GESTIGROUP LAPOINTE INC)
511 Rue Principale S, Amos, QC, J9T 2J8
(819) 732-5334
Emp Here 1   *Sales* 50,288,040
SIC 5172 Petroleum products, nec
Alain Lapointe
Danielle Grenier
Stephane Gobeil

D-U-N-S 25-097-1108   (BR)
PF RESOLU CANADA INC
(*Suby of* RESOLUTE FOREST PRODUCTS
INC)
801 Rue Des Papetiers, Amos, QC, J9T 3X5
(819) 727-1515
Emp Here 140
SIC 2621 Paper mills
Michel Roy

D-U-N-S 24-863-3687   (HQ)
**PRO MUTUEL L'ABITIBIENNE, SOCIETE
MUTUELLE D'ASSURANCE GENERALE**
GROUPE PROMUTUEL
282 1re Av E, Amos, QC, J9T 1H3
(819) 732-1531
Emp Here 30   *Sales* 120,103,230
SIC 6411 Insurance agents, brokers, and ser-
vice
Yvan Levesque
Yvan Rose

D-U-N-S 20-188-3394   (SL)
SOMA AUTO INC
FORD
42 10e Av O, Amos, QC, J9T 1W8
(819) 732-3205
Emp Here 25   *Sales* 12,451,950
SIC 5511 New and used car dealers
Yves Roy
Rene Trudel

D-U-N-S 25-336-9789   (SL)
SUPERMARCHE GUY CORRIVEAU INC
PROVIGO CORRIVEAU
511 7e Rue O, Amos, QC, J9T 2Y3

Emp Here 50   *Sales* 13,707,600
SIC 5411 Grocery stores
Guy Corriveau
Yves Drouin

D-U-N-S 20-281-5213   (BR)
TRANSPORT TFI 23 S.E.C.
BERGERON MAYBOIS, DIV OF
200 Rue Des Routiers, Amos, QC, J9T 3A6
(819) 727-1304
Emp Here 100
SIC 4212 Local trucking, without storage
Dany Rouillard

D-U-N-S 24-084-1684   (HQ)
TRIONEX INC
HYDRAULIQUE NES
121 Rue Des Metiers, Amos, QC, J9T 4M4
(819) 732-5327
Sales 18,526,014
SIC 5084 Industrial machinery and equipment
Michel G. Drapeau
Antony Drapeau
Pierre Dulac
Samuel Dennis-Larocque

Amqui, QC G5J

D-U-N-S 24-843-2429   (BR)
AGROPUR COOPERATIVE
AGROPUR DIV. NATREL
(*Suby of* AGROPUR COOPERATIVE)
466 132 Rte O Bureau 1320, Amqui, QC, G5J
2G7
(418) 629-3133
Emp Here 80
SIC 2026 Fluid milk

D-U-N-S 20-087-0033   (HQ)
AIDE-MAISON VALLEE DE LA MATAPEDIA
VILLA GEORGES FOURNIER
20a Rue Desbiens Bureau 100, Amqui, QC,
G5J 3P1
(418) 629-5812
Emp Here 111   *Sales* 9,445,416
SIC 8322 Individual and family services
Nadia St-Pierre
Monique Tanguay

D-U-N-S 20-954-7298   (HQ)
**COMMISSION SCOLAIRE DES MONTS-ET-
MAREES**
93 Av Du Parc Bureau 3, Amqui, QC, G5J 2L8
(418) 629-6200
Emp Here 300   *Sales* 99,119,000
SIC 8211 Elementary and secondary schools
Leopold Marquis

Berthe Simard

D-U-N-S 25-232-0924   (HQ)
**COMMISSION SCOLAIRE DES MONTS-ET-
MAREES**
93 Av Du Parc Bureau 3, Amqui, QC, G5J 2L8
(418) 629-6200
Emp Here 25   *Sales* 118,942,800
SIC 8211 Elementary and secondary schools
Marquis Leopold
Simard Berthe

D-U-N-S 20-086-4093   (BR)
**COMMISSION SCOLAIRE DES MONTS-ET-
MAREES**
*COMMISSION SCOLAIRE DES MONTS-ET-
MAREES*
(*Suby of* COMMISSION SCOLAIRE DES
MONTS-ET-MAREES)
95 Av Du Parc, Amqui, QC, G5J 2L8
(418) 629-6200
Emp Here 90
SIC 8211 Elementary and secondary schools
Stephane Bedard

D-U-N-S 24-729-3723   (SL)
FENE-TECH INC
(*Suby of* HERIGE)
264 Boul Saint-Benoit E, Amqui, QC, G5J 2C5
(418) 629-4675
Emp Here 95   *Sales* 15,091,510
SIC 3089 Plastics products, nec
Denis Dufour
Bruno Cadudal
William D. Hart
Bruno Cadudal

D-U-N-S 25-484-0226   (SL)
IMPRESSION ALLIANCE 9000 INC
ALLIANCE 9000
142 Rue Du Pont, Amqui, QC, G5J 2R3
(418) 629-5256
Emp Here 100   *Sales* 16,402,700
SIC 2732 Book printing
Christian Viens
Andre Bellavance
Thania Paquet
Guylaine Lavoie
Raymonde Viens-Bellavance
Pascale Rioux
Celine Raymond
Antonin Michaud

D-U-N-S 24-336-9803   (HQ)
**MATAPEDIENNE COOPERATIVE AGRI-
COLE, LA**
COOP MATAPEDIENNE, LA
90 Rue Proulx Bureau 550, Amqui, QC, G5J
3G3
(418) 629-4401
Emp Here 15   *Sales* 13,024,000
SIC 5999 Miscellaneous retail stores, nec
Renald Dumais
Bruno Robichaud

D-U-N-S 20-317-5880   (SL)
RENO-VALLEE INC
RONA
358 Boul Saint-Benoit O, Amqui, QC, G5J 2G3
(418) 629-3800
Emp Here 49   *Sales* 12,399,891
SIC 5251 Hardware stores
Vincent Vadnais

Ange-Gardien, QC J0E

D-U-N-S 24-934-9010   (SL)
2956-2584 QUEBEC INC
ENTREPRISES A & W ROY, LES
98 235 Rte, Ange-Gardien, QC, J0E 1E0
(450) 293-6115
Emp Here 65   *Sales* 19,076,005
SIC 5411 Grocery stores
Andre Roy

Karl Roy

D-U-N-S 24-677-8849   (HQ)
AGROMEX INC
FERME BETHANIE
(*Suby of* F. MENARD INC)
251 235 Rte, Ange-Gardien, QC, J0E 1E0
(450) 293-3694
Emp Here 150   *Sales* 228,641,100
SIC 2011 Meat packing plants
Luc Menard
Yvon Paquette
Francois Menard
Pierre Menard

D-U-N-S 24-858-2975   (HQ)
ALIMPLUS INC
(*Suby of* ATTILA INC)
340 235 Rte, Ange-Gardien, QC, J0E 1E0
(450) 293-3626
Sales 71,671,600
SIC 5141 Groceries, general line
Daniel Le Rossignol
Rene Fournier
Jeff York
Eric Phaneuf
Anna Martini

D-U-N-S 24-523-1647   (SL)
CHOCOLATS COLOMBE
128 235 Rte, Ange-Gardien, QC, J0E 1E0
(450) 293-0129
Emp Here 20   *Sales* 10,702,480
SIC 5149 Groceries and related products, nec
Colombe Menard

D-U-N-S 20-188-6090   (HQ)
F. MENARD INC
FERME BETHANIE
251 Rte 235, Ange-Gardien, QC, J0E 1E0
(450) 293-3694
Emp Here 30   *Sales* 165,293,600
SIC 0213 Hogs
Luc Menard
Francois Menard
Fulgence Menard
Pierre Menard

D-U-N-S 24-901-6189   (HQ)
LAREAU, FRANK INC
TOP BEDDING
150 Rue Lague, Ange-Gardien, QC, J0E 1E0
(450) 293-2602
Emp Here 30   *Sales* 14,427,750
SIC 2421 Sawmills and planing mills, general
Louis-Philippe Cordeau

Anjou, QC H1A

D-U-N-S 24-249-5666   (SL)
SOFA TO GO
12900 Boul Industrille, Anjou, QC, H1A 4Z6
(514) 387-7632
Emp Here 49   *Sales* 11,286,660
SIC 5712 Furniture stores
Stephane Morin

Anjou, QC H1E

D-U-N-S 20-873-2821   (SL)
3725766 CANADA INC
MAZDA PRESIDENT
7050 Boul Henri-Bourassa E, Anjou, QC, H1E 7K7
(514) 354-7901
Emp Here 35   *Sales* 17,432,730
SIC 5511 New and used car dealers
Carole Azouz
Gabriel Azouz

D-U-N-S 25-899-9671   (SL)

COMMERCE AUTOMOBILE S.G.C. CORPO-RATION
NISSAN GABRIEL
7010 Boul Henri-Bourassa E, Anjou, QC, H1E 7K7
(514) 324-7777
Emp Here 37   *Sales* 18,428,886
SIC 5511 New and used car dealers
Gabriel Azouz

Anjou, QC H1J

D-U-N-S 24-904-2367   (HQ)
159519 CANADA INC
9031 Boul Parkway, Anjou, QC, H1J 1N4
(514) 325-8700
Sales 23,234,750
SIC 6712 Bank holding companies
Michael Marfoglia

D-U-N-S 20-703-2157   (HQ)
2163-2088 QUEBEC INC
J.E. MONDOU
10400 Rue Renaude-Lapointe, Anjou, QC, H1J 2V7
(514) 322-5300
Sales 75,660,363
SIC 6712 Bank holding companies
Jules Legault
Philippe Legault

D-U-N-S 25-502-3749   (SL)
2790173 CANADA INC
7900 Rue Jarry, Anjou, QC, H1J 1H1
(514) 353-1710
Emp Here 40   *Sales* 17,739,600
SIC 7389 Business services, nec
Pietro Iannicca

D-U-N-S 20-051-8525   (SL)
2945-2901 QUEBEC INC
10251 Boul Ray-Lawson, Anjou, QC, H1J 1L6
(514) 493-6113
Emp Here 33   *Sales* 13,998,994
SIC 6719 Holding companies, nec
Dominique Jean-Denis
Luis Ravello

D-U-N-S 20-212-2896   (SL)
3213463 CANADA INC
ALIMENTS MEJIVANO +, LES
7545 Av M.-B.-Jodoin, Anjou, QC, H1J 2H9
(514) 528-1150
Emp Here 24   *Sales* 20,053,848
SIC 5149 Groceries and related products, nec
Guy Meloche
Philippe Gadoua
Pascal Gadoua

D-U-N-S 20-031-1889   (HQ)
9019-4002 QUEBEC INC
INFOLASER
9601 Boul Parkway, Anjou, QC, H1J 1P3
(514) 352-0858
Sales 22,664,610
SIC 5112 Stationery and office supplies
Maxime L'heureux
Nicolas Malric

D-U-N-S 20-302-8014   (SL)
9272-8781 QUEBEC INC
REFRIGERATION METROPOLITAINE COM-MERCIALE
11020 Boul Parkway, Anjou, QC, H1J 1R6
(514) 270-7181
Emp Here 26   *Sales* 11,626,524
SIC 5078 Refrigeration equipment and supplies
Rolland De Castris

D-U-N-S 20-230-6528   (SL)
9330-4855 QUEBEC INC
7900 Rue Jarry, Anjou, QC, H1J 1H1
(514) 353-1710
Emp Here 120   *Sales* 23,372,160

SIC 2673 Bags: plastic, laminated, and coated
Pietro Iannicca
Alphonse D'amore

D-U-N-S 20-400-5557   (SL)
9395-8098 QUEBEC INC
DISTRIBUTION VIANDES DECARIE
9595 Boul Metropolitain E, Anjou, QC, H1J 3C1
(514) 744-6641
Emp Here 50   *Sales* 41,778,850
SIC 5147 Meats and meat products
Eric Riendeau

D-U-N-S 24-330-0634   (SL)
A.Y.K. INTERNATIONAL INC
8250 Rue Edison, Anjou, QC, H1J 1S8
(514) 279-4648
Emp Here 25   *Sales* 12,458,050
SIC 5136 Men's and boy's clothing
Asher Krausz

D-U-N-S 24-987-7333   (SL)
ADHESIFS PROMA INC
CERA-PRO ECOLOGICAL
9801 Boul Parkway, Anjou, QC, H1J 1P3
(514) 852-8585
Emp Here 20   *Sales* 10,006,500
SIC 5169 Chemicals and allied products, nec
Eric James Broggi
Fulvia Rodighiero-Broggi

D-U-N-S 24-814-2655   (SL)
ALIMENTS MULTIBAR INC, LES
NELLSON
(*Suby of* NELLSON NUTRACEUTICAL, LLC)
9000 Boul Des Sciences, Anjou, QC, H1J 3A9
(514) 355-1151
Emp Here 765   *Sales* 548,287,740
SIC 5142 Packaged frozen goods
James Better
Nadia Decobellis
Manuel Martinez
Jean Filion

D-U-N-S 20-213-0605   (SL)
ALIMENTS OUIMET-CORDON BLEU INC
CLARK
(*Suby of* HOLDING O.C.B. INC)
8383 Rue J.-Rene-Ouimet, Anjou, QC, H1J 2P8
(514) 352-3000
Emp Here 150   *Sales* 73,107,750
SIC 2032 Canned specialties
J.-Robert Ouimet
Robert Mckenzie
John Leboutillier
Louis Roquet
Luc Villeneuve

D-U-N-S 20-010-7691   (SL)
ALIMENTS RUSTICA INC, LES
ALIMENTS MIA, LES
10301 Rue Colbert, Anjou, QC, H1J 2G5
(514) 325-9009
Emp Here 170   *Sales* 121,841,720
SIC 5149 Groceries and related products, nec
Joseph Richard Morgante
Vincent Giove
Assunta Morgante

D-U-N-S 25-977-2648   (SL)
ALIMENTS SUNCHEF INC
SUNCHEF FARMS
9750 Boul Des Sciences, Anjou, QC, H1J 0A1
(514) 272-3238
Emp Here 400   *Sales* 194,954,000
SIC 2015 Poultry slaughtering and processing
Theodore Eliopoulos

D-U-N-S 20-183-3949   (BR)
ALIMPLUS INC
(*Suby of* ATTILA INC)
9777 Rue Colbert, Anjou, QC, H1J 1Z9
(514) 274-5662
Emp Here 100

SIC 5141 Groceries, general line
Pierre Tanguay

D-U-N-S 24-226-9165   (SL)
ALTA PRECISION INC
11120 Rue Colbert, Anjou, QC, H1J 2X4
(514) 353-0919
Emp Here 100   *Sales* 22,200,100
SIC 3599 Industrial machinery, nec
Guillermo Jr. Alonso
Sonia Alonso
Jose Mathieu
Jacques St-Laurent
Jean-Pierre Dube
Jacques Blais

D-U-N-S 24-903-0875   (HQ)
AMERICAN & EFIRD CANADA INCOR-POREE
AMERCIAN & EFIRD
(*Suby of* AMERICAN & EFIRD LLC)
8301 Boul Ray-Lawson, Anjou, QC, H1J 1X9
(514) 352-4800
Sales 15,589,255
SIC 2284 Thread mills
Craig G Stover
John L. Miller
Mario Di Stefano

D-U-N-S 24-920-5212   (SL)
AMEUBLEMENTS ARTELITE INC
ARTELITE
(*Suby of* 155124 CANADA INC)
10251 Boul Ray-Lawson, Anjou, QC, H1J 1L6
(514) 493-6113
Emp Here 45   *Sales* 10,458,135
SIC 5712 Furniture stores
Georges Sayegh
Adi (Adolf) Koschier
Caroline Sayegh

D-U-N-S 24-600-7314   (SL)
ATELIER ABACO INC
ABACO PHARMA
9100 Rue Claveau, Anjou, QC, H1J 1Z4
(514) 355-6182
Emp Here 91   *Sales* 40,878,929
SIC 7389 Business services, nec
Daniel Perreault
Roger Pedneault

D-U-N-S 20-735-8342   (HQ)
BOUTIQUE MARIE CLAIRE INC
GROUPE MARIE CLAIRE
8501 Boul Ray-Lawson, Anjou, QC, H1J 1K6
(514) 354-0650
Emp Here 250   *Sales* 149,706,000
SIC 5621 Women's clothing stores
Real Lafrance
Sylvain Lafrance
Marie-Claude Lafrance
Martin Lafrance
Stephanie Lafrance

D-U-N-S 24-379-0800   (SL)
C.T.M. ADHESIVES INC
C.T.M. ADHESIF
8320 Rue Grenache, Anjou, QC, H1J 1C5
(514) 321-5540
Emp Here 14   *Sales* 10,224,830
SIC 5169 Chemicals and allied products, nec
Michelangelo Delle Donne
Vasilios Voulelikas
Michael Spineti
Giuseppe Matteo
Maddalena Rao
Giovanni Delle Donne
Lucio Verrillo
Aurora Escobedo Spineti
Giuseppe Spineti

D-U-N-S 24-612-8953   (SL)
CAMIONS INTER-ANJOU INC
8300 Rue Edison, Anjou, QC, H1J 1S8
(514) 353-9720
Emp Here 75   *Sales* 27,316,125
SIC 5012 Automobiles and other motor vehi-

cles
Nathalie Halle
Steve Halle

D-U-N-S 20-227-3512   (HQ)
CENTRE DE TELEPHONE MOBILE LTEE
C.T.M. GATINEAU
9680 Boul Du Golf Bureau 1, Anjou, QC, H1J
2Y7
(514) 645-9271
Emp Here 60   *Sales* 23,211,160
SIC 5999 Miscellaneous retail stores, nec
Richard Tremblay
Lyne Tremblay

D-U-N-S 20-764-7140   (SL)
CHAINES DE TRACTION QUEBEC LTEE
(*Suby of* 119278 CANADA INC)
9401 Boul Parkway, Anjou, QC, H1J 1N4
(514) 353-9210
Emp Here 25   *Sales* 11,179,350
SIC 5072 Hardware
Raymond Perrault
Diane Perrault

D-U-N-S 24-870-6756   (SL)
CHAUSSURES RALLYE INC
10001 Boul Ray-Lawson, Anjou, QC, H1J 1L6
(514) 353-5888
Emp Here 90   *Sales* 18,170,730
SIC 3021 Rubber and plastics footwear
Pardo Vitulli
Pasquale Vitulli

D-U-N-S 20-027-7891   (SL)
CHAUSSURES S T C INC, LES
10100 Rue Colbert, Anjou, QC, H1J 2J8
(514) 351-0675
Emp Here 49   *Sales* 24,417,778
SIC 5139 Footwear
Rene Mellerin

D-U-N-S 20-601-5596   (HQ)
COBRA FIXATIONS CIE LTEE
(*Suby of* COBRA INTERNATIONAL SYS-
TEMES DE FIXATIONS CIE LTEE)
8051 Boul Metropolitain E, Anjou, QC, H1J
1J8
(514) 354-2240
Sales 32,613,600
SIC 3965 Fasteners, buttons, needles, and
pins
Pierre Mcduff
Richard Labelle

D-U-N-S 25-974-6113   (HQ)
**COBRA INTERNATIONAL SYSTEMES DE
FIXATIONS CIE LTEE**
8051 Boul Metropolitain E, Anjou, QC, H1J
1J8
(514) 354-2240
Emp Here 65   *Sales* 100,514,975
SIC 6712 Bank holding companies
Pierre Mcduff
Richard Labelle
Jocelyne Mousseau Mcduff

D-U-N-S 24-228-3901   (HQ)
COFORCE INC
INFO-FLEX
11301 Rue Mirabeau, Anjou, QC, H1J 2S2
(514) 354-3430
Emp Here 330   *Sales* 25,854,144
SIC 8361 Residential care
Bani Juarez
Diane Lebel
Lise Boies
Martine Barry
Francine Laperriere
Caroline Martineau
Sebastien Richer

D-U-N-S 24-295-7785   (SL)
CONCORDIA FURNITURE LTD
MPF MEUBLES PACIFIQUE
11001 Rue Secant, Anjou, QC, H1J 1S6
(514) 355-5100
Emp Here 50   *Sales* 11,517,000

SIC 5712 Furniture stores
Joseph Florio Trust
James Florio

D-U-N-S 25-222-9851   (SL)
CONFORT EXPERT INC
9771 Boul Metropolitain E, Anjou, QC, H1J
0A4
(514) 640-7711
Emp Here 60   *Sales* 13,983,900
SIC 1711 Plumbing, heating, air-conditioning
Pierre Boule
Alain Pouliot
Pierre Dupuis
Gilbert Boule
Enrique Paz
Gilbert Boule
Pierre-Marc Lamoureux
Pierre Dupuis

D-U-N-S 24-904-2375   (HQ)
CONSULTANTS DE L'ARCTIQUE INC, LES
10200 Rue Mirabeau, Anjou, QC, H1J 1T6
(514) 353-3552
Sales 21,226,856
SIC 7389 Business services, nec
Robert Pelletier
Melanie Normandin

D-U-N-S 20-192-1538   (BR)
COSTCO WHOLESALE CANADA LTD
(*Suby of* COSTCO WHOLESALE CORPO-
RATION)
7373 Rue Bombardier, Anjou, QC, H1J 2V2
(514) 493-4814
Emp Here 200
SIC 5099 Durable goods, nec
Yves Paradis

D-U-N-S 20-215-6287   (HQ)
COURCHESNE, LAROSE, LIMITEE
(*Suby of* MICHAL INC)
9761 Boul Des Sciences, Anjou, QC, H1J 0A6
(514) 525-6381
Sales 114,674,560
SIC 5148 Fresh fruits and vegetables
Alain Routhier
Michel Routhier

D-U-N-S 20-965-2952   (SL)
DECO SIGNALISATION INC
9225 Rue Du Parcours, Anjou, QC, H1J 3A8
(514) 494-1004
Emp Here 60   *Sales* 19,568,160
SIC 3993 Signs and advertising specialties
Philippe Desautels

D-U-N-S 24-354-4285   (HQ)
DISPRO INC
ISOLATION DISPRO
10280 Boul Ray-Lawson, Anjou, QC, H1J 1L8
(514) 354-5251
Emp Here 42   *Sales* 22,358,700
SIC 5033 Roofing, siding, and insulation
Robert Ouellette
Ginette Ouellette
Luc Barriault

D-U-N-S 20-552-0427   (HQ)
**DISTRIBUTION HARTCO SOCIETE EN
COMMANDITE**
DISTRIBUTION HARTCO
9393 Boul Louis-H.-Lafontaine, Anjou, QC,
H1J 1Z1
(514) 354-3810
Sales 133,838,000
SIC 5045 Computers, peripherals, and soft-
ware
Harry Hart

D-U-N-S 24-241-3271   (SL)
**DISTRIBUTION HARTCO SOCIETE EN
COMMANDITE**
HARTCO DISTRIBUTION LP
9393 Boul Metropolitain E, Anjou, QC, H1J
3C7
(514) 354-0580
Emp Here 45   *Sales* 10,365,300

SIC 5734 Computer and software stores
Harry Hart

D-U-N-S 24-677-7098   (SL)
DISTRIBUTIONS GYPCO (1988) INC
GYPCO DISTRIBUTION
9550 Boul Ray-Lawson, Anjou, QC, H1J 1L3
(514) 352-0150
Emp Here 75   *Sales* 33,538,050
SIC 5072 Hardware
Normand Proulx
Gratien Proulx

D-U-N-S 20-216-9207   (HQ)
DOMINION & GRIMM INC
8250 Rue Marconi, Anjou, QC, H1J 1B2
(514) 351-3000
Emp Here 1   *Sales* 52,054,200
SIC 5099 Durable goods, nec
Vincent Pepin
Stephane Pepin

D-U-N-S 20-216-9355   (SL)
DOMINION NEON INC
DOMINION SIGNS
9225 Rue Du Parcours, Anjou, QC, H1J 3A8
(514) 354-6366
Emp Here 55   *Sales* 24,594,570
SIC 5046 Commercial equipment, nec
Rhea Fontaine

D-U-N-S 25-116-2301   (HQ)
DORSON LTEE
*ATELIER D'OUTILS ELECTRIQUES SHER-
BROOKE*
8551 Boul Parkway, Anjou, QC, H1J 1N1
(514) 351-0160
Sales 12,350,676
SIC 5082 Construction and mining machinery
Claude D'orsonnens
Lise D'orsonnens
Michel D'orsonnens
Martin D'orsonnens

D-U-N-S 20-421-1163   (HQ)
E-Z-EM CANADA INC
BRACCO IMAGING CANADA
(*Suby of* BRACCO SPA)
11065 Boul Louis-H.-Lafontaine, Anjou, QC,
H1J 2Z4
(514) 353-5820
Sales 35,843,800
SIC 3295 Minerals, ground or treated
Luc Raymond
Fulvio Uggeri
Eric M. Levy
Roberto Desimini

D-U-N-S 24-510-4088   (SL)
**EDIFICE DES ROUTIERS LOCAL 1999
CANADA INC.**
9393 Rue Edison Bureau 100, Anjou, QC, H1J
1T4
(514) 355-1110
Emp Here 30   *Sales* 11,734,740
SIC 8631 Labor organizations
Herve Trudel
Herve Trudel

D-U-N-S 24-818-6921   (SL)
EMBALLAGES DELTAPAC INC
7575 Boul Metropolitain E, Anjou, QC, H1J
1J8
(514) 352-5546
Emp Here 26   *Sales* 13,095,108
SIC 5113 Industrial and personal service paper
Anne Perreault

D-U-N-S 20-715-4407   (BR)
ENERGIR INC
BUREAU D'AFFAIRE D'ANJOU
(*Suby of* NOVERCO INC)
11441 Av L.-J.-Forget, Anjou, QC, H1J 2Z8
(514) 356-8777
Emp Here 85
SIC 4924 Natural gas distribution
Lucie Picard

D-U-N-S 20-423-3829   (HQ)
ENSEIGNES INNOVA INC, LES
GROUPE BO CONCEPT
9900 Boul Du Golf, Anjou, QC, H1J 2Y7
(514) 323-6767
Sales 11,087,250
SIC 7389 Business services, nec
Marc Noel
Roger Perron

D-U-N-S 20-183-8534   (SL)
ENSEIGNES TRANSWORLD CIE
ENSEIGNES TRANS-CANADA
9310 Boul Parkway, Anjou, QC, H1J 1N7
(514) 352-8030
Emp Here 100   *Sales* 32,613,600
SIC 3993 Signs and advertising specialties
Pat Lopez
Christophe Chambonnet

D-U-N-S 25-248-6019   (SL)
ENSEIGNES VISION DEK-OR INC
9225 Rue Du Parcours, Anjou, QC, H1J 3A8
(514) 354-8383
Emp Here 49   *Sales* 10,722,376
SIC 3993 Signs and advertising specialties
Philippe Desautels

D-U-N-S 24-319-7295   (BR)
ENTREPRISES MICROTEC INC, LES
ALARM CAP
(*Suby of* STANLEY BLACK & DECKER, INC.)
8125 Boul Du Golf, Anjou, QC, H1J 0B2
(514) 388-8177
Emp Here 92
SIC 5063 Electrical apparatus and equipment
Claude Boisclair

D-U-N-S 20-654-8484   (SL)
ENTREPRISES S.J.M. INC, LES
8501 Rue Jarry, Anjou, QC, H1J 1H7
(514) 321-2160
Emp Here 500   *Sales* 182,754,500
SIC 6712 Bank holding companies
Jacques Majeau
Majeau Dominique
Majeau Edith

D-U-N-S 24-900-9291   (SL)
ENVIROPLAST INC
11060 Boul Parkway, Anjou, QC, H1J 1R6
(514) 352-6060
Emp Here 40   *Sales* 10,285,240
SIC 4953 Refuse systems
Stephane Begin
Yvan Charlebois

D-U-N-S 20-500-1464   (HQ)
EQUIPEMENTS TWIN INC
(*Suby of* 3979385 CANADA INC)
10401 Boul Parkway, Anjou, QC, H1J 1R4
(514) 353-1190
Emp Here 1   *Sales* 14,568,600
SIC 5013 Motor vehicle supplies and new
parts
Louis Beaulieu
Francois Beaulieu

D-U-N-S 20-416-5641   (SL)
ETALEX INC
(*Suby of* 101056 CANADA LTEE)
8501 Rue Jarry, Anjou, QC, H1J 1H7
(514) 351-2000
Emp Here 100   *Sales* 15,432,200
SIC 2542 Partitions and fixtures, except wood
Dominique Majeau
Jacinthe Majeau
Edith Majeau

D-U-N-S 20-229-5754   (SL)
EXCAVATIONS PAYETTE LTEE, LES
CIMAX LA BELLECHASSOISE
(*Suby of* FAYOLLE CANADA INC)
7900 Rue Bombardier, Anjou, QC, H1J 1A4
(514) 322-4800
Emp Here 50   *Sales* 12,309,300
SIC 1794 Excavation work

Eric Rioux
Luc Guttin
Hugues Fastrel
Bruno Fayolle
Nancy Isabelle

D-U-N-S 20-117-3377   (SL)
FROMAGES CDA INC
8895 3e Croissant, Anjou, QC, H1J 1B6
(514) 648-7997
Emp Here 25   *Sales* 20,889,425
SIC 5143 Dairy products, except dried or canned
Daniel Allard

D-U-N-S 20-895-7584   (HQ)
G.C.M. CONSULTANTS INC
9496 Boul Du Golf, Anjou, QC, H1J 3A1
(514) 351-8350
Emp Here 124   *Sales* 27,220,716
SIC 8711 Engineering services
Normand Thouin
Yves Malouin
Alex Leduc
Daniel Mayrand
Nathaniel Tiffany
Marc-Andre Richer

D-U-N-S 24-336-7955   (HQ)
GASTIER M.P. INC
CHARLES BELANGER & FILS
(*Suby of* BOUYGUES)
10400 Boul Du Golf, Anjou, QC, H1J 2Y7
(514) 325-4220
Sales 117,754,500
SIC 1731 Electrical work
Sylvain Gadoury
Paul Gerard Sheridan
Edward Michael Peeke
Claude Ganache

D-U-N-S 20-727-0455   (SL)
GENEQ INC
10700 Rue Secant, Anjou, QC, H1J 1S5
(514) 354-2511
Emp Here 35   *Sales* 15,651,090
SIC 5049 Professional equipment, nec
Rene Parise
Nathalie Parise

D-U-N-S 20-220-8518   (SL)
GEO A. HALL INC
8800 6e Croissant, Anjou, QC, H1J 1A1
(514) 352-5550
Emp Here 75   *Sales* 11,114,400
SIC 4212 Local trucking, without storage
Robert Hall
Beverley Hall

D-U-N-S 24-355-6623   (SL)
GESTION JUSTERO INC
ALUMINART ARCHITECTURAL
11001 Rue Colbert, Anjou, QC, H1J 2S1
(514) 355-7484
Emp Here 50   *Sales* 10,141,500
SIC 3442 Metal doors, sash, and trim
Jean Lefebvre

D-U-N-S 24-703-6937   (SL)
GESTION TECHNIQUE D'IMMEUBLES
9000 Rue De L'Innovation, Anjou, QC, H1J 2X9
(514) 354-6666
Emp Here 26   *Sales* 12,239,006
SIC 1542 Nonresidential construction, nec
Jean-Yves Roy

D-U-N-S 20-883-5520   (HQ)
GROUPE A&A SPECIALISTE DU DOCUMENT (MONTREAL) INC, LE
GROUPE A&A, LE
10985 Boul Louis-H.-Lafontaine Bureau 101, Anjou, QC, H1J 2E8
(514) 325-7700
Sales 22,358,700
SIC 5044 Office equipment
Andre Lamarche

Roch Contant
Hugo Contant

D-U-N-S 24-422-8636   (HQ)
GROUPE ENERGIE BDL INC
JOSEPH ELIE
10390 Boul Louis-H.-Lafontaine, Anjou, QC, H1J 2T3
(514) 493-3576
Sales 32,687,226
SIC 5172 Petroleum products, nec
Patrick Boule
Pierre Boule
Gilbert Boule
Pierre Boule
Pierre-Marc Lamoureux

D-U-N-S 20-698-5249   (HQ)
GROUPE LOU-TEC INC
CHEF DE FILE EN LOCATION DESSIN
8500 Rue Jules-Leger, Anjou, QC, H1J 1A7
(514) 356-0047
Emp Here 5   *Sales* 10,723,673
SIC 6712 Bank holding companies
Jasmin Asselin
Carold Breton
Christian Hetu
Mathieu Pelletier
Jean-Marc Dallaire
Gilles C. Lachance

D-U-N-S 20-220-7007   (SL)
GUARD-X INC
10600 Boul Parkway, Anjou, QC, H1J 1R6
(514) 277-2127
Emp Here 50   *Sales* 23,751,300
SIC 5087 Service establishment equipment
Denis Verville
Guy Verville

D-U-N-S 24-050-7541   (BR)
GUAY INC
10801 Rue Colbert, Anjou, QC, H1J 2G5
(514) 354-4420
Emp Here 100
SIC 7353 Heavy construction equipment rental
Louis-Pierre Fortune

D-U-N-S 25-849-2552   (SL)
HACHETTE DISTRIBUTION SERVICES (CANADA) INC
EXPRESS MAGAZINE
8155 Rue Larrey, Anjou, QC, H1J 2L5
(514) 355-3334
Emp Here 100   *Sales* 16,402,700
SIC 2721 Periodicals
Francois Lesle

D-U-N-S 20-107-1227   (BR)
HOME DEPOT OF CANADA INC
HOME DEPOT
(*Suby of* THE HOME DEPOT INC)
11300 Rue Renaude-Lapointe, Anjou, QC, H1J 2V7
(514) 356-3650
Emp Here 130
SIC 5251 Hardware stores
Michel Cote

D-U-N-S 25-683-0654   (SL)
HORIZON CONNEXTIONS INC
9660 Boul Du Golf, Anjou, QC, H1J 2Y7

Emp Here 85   *Sales* 18,515,465
SIC 1731 Electrical work
Pierre Lescarbeau

D-U-N-S 25-072-7864   (BR)
IMPRIMERIES TRANSCONTINENTAL INC
TRANSCONTINENTAL PRINTING INC
(*Suby of* TRANSCONTINENTAL INC)
10807 Rue Mirabeau, Anjou, QC, H1J 1T7
(514) 355-4134
Emp Here 180
SIC 2711 Newspapers
Daniel Brooke

D-U-N-S 20-271-0174   (SL)
INDUSTRIES COVER INC
VITRERIE BAIE ST-PAUL
(*Suby of* KOCH INDUSTRIES, INC.)
9300 Boul Ray-Lawson, Anjou, QC, H1J 1Y6
(514) 353-3880
Emp Here 250   *Sales* 59,125,750
SIC 2241 Narrow fabric mills
James Boudreault
Jeffrey A Knight
Richard Zoulek

D-U-N-S 20-763-5764   (HQ)
INDUSTRIES JOHN LEWIS LTEE
(*Suby of* GESTION REMABEC INC)
8545 Rue Jules-Leger, Anjou, QC, H1J 1A8
(514) 352-2950
Emp Here 3   *Sales* 19,237,000
SIC 2499 Wood products, nec
Rejean Pare
Roger Tremblay
Eric Bouchard

D-U-N-S 20-632-7702   (SL)
INDUSTRIES UNICOR INC
9151 Rue Claveau, Anjou, QC, H1J 2C8
(514) 353-0857
Emp Here 60   *Sales* 12,113,820
SIC 3089 Plastics products, nec
Jaynul Sheriff
Sarakhanu Alibhai Sheriff

D-U-N-S 24-869-9100   (SL)
INTERNATIONAL MINICUT INC
(*Suby of* 8061076 CANADA INC)
8400 Boul Du Golf, Anjou, QC, H1J 3A1
(514) 352-6464
Emp Here 50   *Sales* 13,382,600
SIC 5251 Hardware stores
Yunkyun Yu
Heather Hyunhae Lee
Tae Seob Yoon
Seok Young Hong

D-U-N-S 20-227-5129   (HQ)
J. E. MONDOU LTEE
VET DIET
(*Suby of* 2163-2088 QUEBEC INC)
10400 Rue Renaude-Lapointe, Anjou, QC, H1J 2V7
(514) 322-5300
Emp Here 50   *Sales* 37,625,085
SIC 5999 Miscellaneous retail stores, nec
Jules Legault
Philippe Legault

D-U-N-S 24-500-2910   (HQ)
KARLO CORPORATION SUPPLY & SERVICES
DISTRIBUTION DU PHARE
10801 Boul Ray-Lawson Bureau 100, Anjou, QC, H1J 1M5
(514) 255-5017
Emp Here 27   *Sales* 17,100,936
SIC 5088 Transportation equipment and supplies
Michael J. Liantonio
Sanda Hiliuta
Robert Steen Kledal
Soren Jorgensen

D-U-N-S 24-788-0834   (SL)
LABORATOIRE ATLAS INC
9600 Boul Des Sciences, Anjou, QC, H1J 3B6
(514) 254-7188
Emp Here 50   *Sales* 14,201,050
SIC 2834 Pharmaceutical preparations
Mario Ostiguy
Mario Picard
Raynald Ostiguy
Andre Pinsonneault
Camil Poulin
Pierre Lizotte
Andre Boudreau

D-U-N-S 24-668-1670   (HQ)
LAFCO OUTILLAGE INC

7700 Rue Bombardier, Anjou, QC, H1J 0A2
(514) 327-7556
Emp Here 21   *Sales* 12,825,702
SIC 5085 Industrial supplies
Rene Lafreniere
Serge Lafreniere

D-U-N-S 25-196-0852   (SL)
LAVERGNE GROUPE INC
LAVERGNE
(*Suby of* 6187820 CANADA INC)
8800 1er Croissant, Anjou, QC, H1J 1C8
(514) 354-5757
Emp Here 100   *Sales* 15,885,800
SIC 3087 Custom compound purchased resins
Jean-Luc Lavergne

D-U-N-S 25-784-4282   (BR)
LOGIC-CONTROLE INC
8002 Rue Jarry, Anjou, QC, H1J 1H5
(514) 493-1162
Emp Here 150
SIC 7521 Automobile parking
Philippe Warren

D-U-N-S 20-210-2513   (SL)
LUSTRE ARTCRAFT DE MONTREAL LTEE
ARTCRAFT
8525 Rue Jules-Leger, Anjou, QC, H1J 1A8
(514) 353-7200
Emp Here 85   *Sales* 16,187,570
SIC 3645 Residential lighting fixtures
Stephen Cohen

D-U-N-S 25-105-6545   (SL)
MARCHE D'ALIMENTATION MARCANIO (ANJOU) INC
MARCHE METRO MARCANIO
7172 Rue Bombardier, Anjou, QC, H1J 2Z9
(514) 352-5447
Emp Here 100   *Sales* 29,347,700
SIC 5411 Grocery stores
Frank Marcanio
Sabatino Marcanio

D-U-N-S 24-933-7783   (SL)
MARFOGLIA CONSTRUCTION INC
(*Suby of* 159519 CANADA INC)
9031 Boul Parkway, Anjou, QC, H1J 1N4
(514) 325-8700
Emp Here 55   *Sales* 31,368,590
SIC 1542 Nonresidential construction, nec
Michael Marfoglia
Mathew Marfoglia
Gabrielle Marfoglia

D-U-N-S 20-226-6433   (SL)
MAYRAND LIMITEE
ENTREPRISES SMART&FINAL, LES
(*Suby of* ATTILA INC)
9701 Boul Louis-H.-Lafontaine, Anjou, QC, H1J 2A3
(514) 255-9330
Emp Here 145   *Sales* 103,923,820
SIC 5141 Groceries, general line
Daniel Le Rossignol
Rene Fournier
Jeff York
Eric Phaneuf
Anna Martini

D-U-N-S 24-169-4033   (HQ)
MIP INC
LE FOND DU PRESIDENT DE MIP
9100 Boul Ray-Lawson, Anjou, QC, H1J 1K8
(514) 356-1224
Sales 86,233,875
SIC 2392 Household furnishings, nec
David Arditi
Tor Lund
Aviyam Friedman
Michael Freund
Adam Jezewski
Jeff Wigle

D-U-N-S 25-356-8851   (HQ)

MODE LE GRENIER INC
LE GRENIER
8501 Boul Ray-Lawson, Anjou, QC, H1J 1K6
(514) 354-0650
Emp Here 83   *Sales* 40,171,110
SIC 5621 Women's clothing stores
Real Lafrance
Sylvain Lafrance
Claude Lanquette
Marie-Claude Lafrance
Martin Lafrance
Stephanie Lafrance

D-U-N-S 24-508-8208   (HQ)
MONIDEX DISTRIBUTION INTERNATIONAL INC
10700 Rue Colbert, Anjou, QC, H1J 2H8
(514) 323-9932
Sales 28,408,770
SIC 5013 Motor vehicle supplies and new parts
Salvatore Polletta
Richard Sforzin

D-U-N-S 20-563-3410   (BR)
MOORE CANADA CORPORATION
TOPS PRODUCTS CANADA
(*Suby of* R. R. DONNELLEY & SONS COMPANY)
11150 Av L.-J.-Forget, Anjou, QC, H1J 2K9
(514) 353-9090
Emp Here 120
SIC 2782 Blankbooks and looseleaf binders

D-U-N-S 25-073-4027   (SL)
NATIONAL HERRING IMPORTING COMPANY LTD
NATIONAL HERRING H.J.S.
9820 Boul Ray-Lawson, Anjou, QC, H1J 1L1
(514) 274-4774
Emp Here 25   *Sales* 20,889,425
SIC 5146 Fish and seafoods
Samuel (Sam) Friedman
David Friedman

D-U-N-S 24-768-1133   (SL)
NEXTRUSION INC
10500 Rue Colbert, Anjou, QC, H1J 2H8
(514) 355-6868
Emp Here 50   *Sales* 10,094,850
SIC 3089 Plastics products, nec
Vic De Zen
Gerald Gravel
Jean-Michel Lerdu
Sergio De Zen
James De Zen

D-U-N-S 25-729-5121   (BR)
OLYMEL S.E.C.
FLAMINGO
(*Suby of* OLYMEL S.E.C.)
7770 Rue Grenache, Anjou, QC, H1J 1C3
(514) 353-2830
Emp Here 240
SIC 2011 Meat packing plants
Stephane Lacasse

D-U-N-S 20-229-4047   (SL)
PASTENE ENTERPRISES ULC
LES ENTREPRISES PASTENE
(*Suby of* THE PASTENE COMPANIES LTD)
9101 Rue De L'Innovation, Anjou, QC, H1J 2X9
(514) 353-7997
Emp Here 23   *Sales* 19,218,271
SIC 5141 Groceries, general line
John Franciosa
Vincent Tangredi

D-U-N-S 20-972-7197   (SL)
PAVAGE C.S.F. INC
11101 Rue Mirabeau, Anjou, QC, H1J 2S2
(514) 352-7430
Emp Here 40   *Sales* 11,340,960
SIC 1611 Highway and street construction
Dominic Cammalleri
Calogero Fucale

D-U-N-S 24-115-0945   (SL)
PEPCO ENERGY CORP
PEPCO
10220 Boul Louis-H.-Lafontaine, Anjou, QC, H1J 2T3
(514) 493-7000
Emp Here 11   *Sales* 11,360,888
SIC 5172 Petroleum products, nec
Jean-Guy Pepin

D-U-N-S 24-527-5557   (HQ)
PNEUS SP INC
9135 Rue Edison, Anjou, QC, H1J 1T4
(514) 354-7444
Emp Here 43   *Sales* 42,791,040
SIC 5531 Auto and home supply stores
Pierre Marois
Sylvain Marois
Colette Marois
Richard Marois

D-U-N-S 20-230-7518   (HQ)
POWRMATIC DU CANADA LTEE
(*Suby of* STAMM INTERNATIONAL CORPORATION)
9530 Boul Ray-Lawson, Anjou, QC, H1J 1L1
(514) 493-6400
Emp Here 10   *Sales* 33,538,050
SIC 5075 Warm air heating and air conditioning
Claude Lapierre
Stamm Marilyn Skony
Emilio A Dominianni

D-U-N-S 24-226-4690   (BR)
PRAXAIR CANADA INC
(*Suby of* LINDE PUBLIC LIMITED COMPANY)
8151 Boul Metropolitain E, Anjou, QC, H1J 1X6
(514) 353-3340
Emp Here 101
SIC 5169 Chemicals and allied products, nec
Lynda Bellefleur

D-U-N-S 20-972-4038   (SL)
PRODUITS & SERVICES DE LA CONSTRUCTION (MONTREAL) INC
POLY-TECH M.P
9711 Rue Colbert, Anjou, QC, H1J 1Z9
(514) 355-9650
Emp Here 50   *Sales* 22,358,700
SIC 5039 Construction materials, nec
Stephane Begin
Colin Benoit-Dunnigan

D-U-N-S 20-229-5978   (SL)
PRODUITS D'ENTREPOSAGE PEDLEX LTEE, LES
10000 Boul Du Golf, Anjou, QC, H1J 2Y7
(514) 324-5310
Emp Here 40   *Sales* 17,886,960
SIC 5046 Commercial equipment, nec
Pierre Poirier
Francis Poirier
Yves Poirier

D-U-N-S 20-223-7509   (SL)
PRODUITS DE FIL DE FER LAURENTIEN LTEE
10500 Rue Secant, Anjou, QC, H1J 1S3
(514) 351-8814
Emp Here 50   *Sales* 10,141,500
SIC 3499 Fabricated Metal products, nec
Gino Del Prete
Antonio Arcaro
Nicolina Del Prete
Carmela Del Preta

D-U-N-S 20-210-1697   (HQ)
PRODUITS DE SECURITE NORTH LTEE
HONEYWELL LIFE SAFETY
10550 Boul Parkway, Anjou, QC, H1J 2K4
(514) 351-7233
Emp Here 220   *Sales* 109,748,000
SIC 3842 Surgical appliances and supplies
John Montigny

Joshua P. Foster
John J. Tus
Kenneth Friesen

D-U-N-S 24-330-3117   (HQ)
PRODUITS LABELINK INC, LES
ETIQUETTES FLEXO
9201 Rue Claveau, Anjou, QC, H1J 2C8
(514) 328-1887
Emp Here 50   *Sales* 11,481,890
SIC 2759 Commercial printing, nec
Stephen Bouchard
William Mcdougall
Donald K Jackson

D-U-N-S 20-362-8102   (HQ)
PROMAG DISPLAYCORR CANADA INC
DISPLAY-CORR
11150 Av L.-J.-Forget, Anjou, QC, H1J 2K9
(514) 352-9511
Emp Here 30   *Sales* 22,200,100
SIC 3577 Computer peripheral equipment, nec
Raffaele Pagnotta
Francois Cadieux
Francesco Perrone

D-U-N-S 24-346-6195   (SL)
PROSYS TECH CORPORATION
7751 Rue Jarry, Anjou, QC, H1J 1H3
(450) 681-7744
Emp Here 100   *Sales* 22,200,100
SIC 3571 Electronic computers
Georges Hebert
Piero D'amore
Daniel Hebert
Kerrigan Turner
Maurizio Iulianella

D-U-N-S 20-183-6975   (SL)
RBC BEARINGS CANADA, INC
AEROSPATIALE SARGENT CANADA
(*Suby of* RBC BEARINGS INCORPORATED)
8121 Rue Jarry, Anjou, QC, H1J 1H6
(514) 352-9425
Emp Here 100   *Sales* 22,384,300
SIC 3724 Aircraft engines and engine parts
Chantale Tremblay
Daniel A. Bergeron
Thomas J. Williams
Maria Riccio

D-U-N-S 24-110-0676   (BR)
REYNOLDS AND REYNOLDS (CANADA) LIMITED
(*Suby of* UNIVERSAL COMPUTER SYSTEMS, INC.)
11075 Boul Louis-H.-Lafontaine, Anjou, QC, H1J 3A3
(514) 355-7550
Emp Here 80
SIC 5045 Computers, peripherals, and software
Chantal Lachapelle

D-U-N-S 20-331-8894   (SL)
RITE CORPORATION
ENTREPRISES RITE, LES
10250 Boul Parkway, Anjou, QC, H1J 2K4
(514) 324-8900
Emp Here 30   *Sales* 14,250,780
SIC 5085 Industrial supplies
Craig C. Brown

D-U-N-S 20-422-3762   (SL)
ROLAND GRENIER CONSTRUCTION LTEE
9150 Rue Claveau, Anjou, QC, H1J 1Z4
(514) 252-1818
Emp Here 85   *Sales* 48,478,730
SIC 1542 Nonresidential construction, nec
Real Grenier
Stephane Grenier
Sandro Arancio
Patrick Gernier
Mathieu Archambault

D-U-N-S 24-365-9898   (BR)

ROTISSERIES ST-HUBERT LTEE, LES
MEILLEURES MARQUES
(*Suby of* RECIPE UNLIMITED CORPORATION)
9050 Imp De L'Invention, Anjou, QC, H1J 3A7
(514) 324-5400
Emp Here 154
SIC 5145 Confectionery

D-U-N-S 24-768-6322   (SL)
SALAISON ALPHA LTEE
10800 Boul Du Golf, Anjou, QC, H1J 2Y7
(514) 593-8430
Emp Here 60   *Sales* 50,134,620
SIC 5147 Meats and meat products
Nick Tountas
Panagiota Tountas
Terry Tountas

D-U-N-S 24-175-8770   (HQ)
SERTI INFORMATIQUE INC
SERTI INFORMATION SOLUTIONS
7555 Rue Beclard, Anjou, QC, H1J 2S5
(514) 493-1909
Emp Here 100   *Sales* 107,070,400
SIC 5045 Computers, peripherals, and software
Louis Laporte
Michel Beauchemin
Francis Gingras

D-U-N-S 20-331-5221   (BR)
SERTI INFORMATIQUE INC
(*Suby of* SERTI INFORMATIQUE INC)
10975 Boul Louis-H.-Lafontaine Unite 201, Anjou, QC, H1J 2E8
(514) 493-1909
Emp Here 200
SIC 5045 Computers, peripherals, and software

D-U-N-S 20-852-6751   (BR)
SOCIETE DE TRANSPORT DE MONTREAL
(*Suby of* SOCIETE DE TRANSPORT DE MONTREAL)
8150 Rue Larrey, Anjou, QC, H1J 2J5
(514) 280-5913
Emp Here 560
SIC 4111 Local and suburban transit
Pierre Gagnon

D-U-N-S 24-347-3076   (SL)
SOLUTION MORNEAU INC
(*Suby of* GESTION DENIS MORNEAU (1993) INC)
9601 Boul Des Sciences, Anjou, QC, H1J 0A6
(514) 325-2727
Emp Here 30   *Sales* 21,360,993
SIC 4212 Local trucking, without storage
Andre Morneau
Micheline Morneau

D-U-N-S 25-542-5498   (SL)
SOLUTIONS D'AIR NORTEK QUEBEC, INC
VAPAC
(*Suby of* MELROSE INDUSTRIES PLC)
9100 Rue Du Parcours, Anjou, QC, H1J 2Z1
(514) 354-7776
Emp Here 400   *Sales* 112,350,800
SIC 3585 Refrigeration and heating equipment
Joe Naccarello
Mario Tougas
Raymond Daigle
John Albert
Kevin Donnelly

D-U-N-S 24-922-6457   (SL)
SOLUTIONS D'EMBALLAGES PENTAFLEX INC
7905 Rue Jarry, Anjou, QC, H1J 2C3
(514) 353-4330
Emp Here 35   *Sales* 15,522,150
SIC 7389 Business services, nec
Hershey Friedman
Shuly Vorhand
Serge Capozzo

D-U-N-S 24-580-7631   (HQ)
STEAMATIC METROPOLITAIN INC
S.M.I. QUEBEC CONSTRUCTION
8351 Boul Louis-H.-Lafontaine, Anjou, QC,
H1J 3B4
(514) 351-7500
Emp Here 30   *Sales* 14,771,160
SIC 1799 Special trade contractors, nec
Serge Lavoie
Alexandre Ashby
Claire Castonguay
Claude Bigras
Andrew Fortier
Catherine Chevalier

D-U-N-S 24-254-3007   (SL)
**STUDIO DE PHOTOS DES ECOLES QUE-
BECOISES INC**
SPEQ PHOTO
8300 Rue De L'Industrie, Anjou, QC, H1J 1S7
(514) 351-8275
Emp Here 95   *Sales* 8,514,755
SIC 7221 Photographic studios, portrait

D-U-N-S 24-349-8458   (SL)
SUPERMARCHE LAFRANCE INC
7172 Rue Bombardier, Anjou, QC, H1J 2Z9
(514) 352-1386
Emp Here 45   *Sales* 12,336,840
SIC 5411 Grocery stores
Guy Lafrance

D-U-N-S 20-180-8479   (SL)
SYMBOTIC CANADA ULC
AXIUM AUTOMATION
(*Suby of* SYMBOL TECHNOLOGIES
CANADA, ULC)
10925 Boul Louis-H.-Lafontaine, Anjou, QC,
H1J 2E8
(514) 352-0500
Emp Here 100   *Sales* 17,873,900
SIC 8711 Engineering services
Richard B Cohen
Corey Dufresne
Jacob M Gearwar

D-U-N-S 25-683-8830   (HQ)
TECHNO SPORT INTERNATIONAL LTEE
TECHNO MOTOSPORT
7850 Rue Bombardier Bureau 263, Anjou, QC,
H1J 2G3
(514) 356-2151
Sales 100,503,960
SIC 5136 Men's and boy's clothing
Luc Beauchamp
Sylvain Beauchamp
Stephan Boutin
Daniel Beauchamp

D-U-N-S 24-394-6303   (HQ)
TECHNOLOGIES METAFORE INC
METAFORE
9393 Boul Louis-H.-Lafontaine, Anjou, QC,
H1J 1Z1
(514) 354-3810
Emp Here 1,000   *Sales* 184,573,000
SIC 7371 Custom computer programming ser-
vices
Hary Hart
Michael Lemieux
Jeffrey Hart
Frank Fuser

D-U-N-S 24-679-6619   (HQ)
TEXTILES ELITE INC
TEXTILES ELITE FABRICS
9200 Rue Claveau, Anjou, QC, H1J 1Z4
(514) 352-2291
Emp Here 15   *Sales* 10,464,762
SIC 5131 Piece goods and notions
Frank Iemma

D-U-N-S 24-404-2057   (SL)
TEXTILES ROBLIN INC
9151 Boul Louis-H.-Lafontaine, Anjou, QC,
H1J 1Z1
(514) 353-8100
Emp Here 20   *Sales* 10,006,500

SIC 5131 Piece goods and notions
Robert Guigui

D-U-N-S 20-707-1416   (HQ)
TISSUS MASTER LTEE, LES
AVANT-GARDE FABRICS
(*Suby of* LASAGER LTEE)
7963 Rue Alfred, Anjou, QC, H1J 1J3
(514) 351-9715
Sales 13,188,268
SIC 5131 Piece goods and notions
Erich Imbach
Bobby Imbach

D-U-N-S 25-407-4818   (SL)
TRANSPORT LOGI-PRO INC.
9001 Rue Du Parcours, Anjou, QC, H1J 2Y1
(514) 493-1717
Emp Here 200   *Sales* 143,343,200
SIC 5147 Meats and meat products
Conrad Boivin

D-U-N-S 20-267-4511   (BR)
TRANSPORT MORNEAU INC
(*Suby of* GESTION DENIS MORNEAU (1993)
INC)
9601 Boul Des Sciences, Anjou, QC, H1J 0A6
(514) 325-2727
Emp Here 120
SIC 4213 Trucking, except local

D-U-N-S 20-216-9496   (HQ)
VENTES ALLAJOY LTEE
8301 Rue J.-Rene-Ouimet, Anjou, QC, H1J
2H7
(514) 374-9010
Sales 24,604,050
SIC 2782 Blankbooks and looseleaf binders
David Chaitman

D-U-N-S 20-333-2010   (SL)
VERRERIE WALKER LTEE, LA
(*Suby of* PLACEMENTS HARRICO LTEE,
LES)
9551 Boul Ray-Lawson, Anjou, QC, H1J 1L5
(514) 352-3030
Emp Here 100   *Sales* 17,921,900
SIC 3231 Products of purchased glass
Lee Harrison
Ross Christie
Thomas Kennedy

D-U-N-S 20-220-3303   (SL)
**VETEMENTS GOLDEN BRAND (CANADA)
LTEE**
BRITTANY INTERNATIONAL
(*Suby of* TAILORED BRANDS, INC.)
9393 Boul Metropolitain E, Anjou, QC, H1J
3C7
(514) 272-8841
Emp Here 35   *Sales* 17,441,270
SIC 5136 Men's and boy's clothing
Jamie Bragg
Laura Ann Smith
Bruce Thorn

D-U-N-S 24-324-2559   (SL)
VIANDES MONTCALM INC, LES
LES VIANDES INTERCITE
(*Suby of* GORDON FOOD SERVICE, INC.)
7755 Rue Grenache, Anjou, QC, H1J 1C4
(514) 327-1310
Emp Here 25   *Sales* 20,889,425
SIC 5147 Meats and meat products
Dean Noble
Frank Geier
David L Gray
Daniel A Gordon

D-U-N-S 20-237-3015   (HQ)
WEST PENETONE INC
(*Suby of* PENETONE CORPORATION)
10900 Rue Secant, Anjou, QC, H1J 1S5
(514) 355-4660
Emp Here 40   *Sales* 11,062,646
SIC 2842 Polishes and sanitation goods
Jean Richard

Bruce Muretta
Volkert Lindloge
Jesus Alberto Medina

D-U-N-S 24-290-8940   (SL)
WM QUEBEC INC
RCI ENVIRONMENT
9501 Boul Ray-Lawson Bureau 114, Anjou,
QC, H1J 1L4
(514) 352-1596
Emp Here 49   *Sales* 14,755,958
SIC 4953 Refuse systems
Brad Muter

Anjou, QC H1K

D-U-N-S 25-222-7350   (SL)
ASSURANCES JOE ANGELONE INC
7811 Boul Louis-H.-Lafontaine Bureau 201,
Anjou, QC, H1K 4E4
(514) 353-1331
Emp Here 18   *Sales* 10,438,632
SIC 6411 Insurance agents, brokers, and ser-
vice
Joseph Angelone

D-U-N-S 25-246-2577   (SL)
**COMENCO SERVICES AUX IMMEUBLES
INC**
COMENCO
8150 Boul Metropolitain E Bureau 310, Anjou,
QC, H1K 1A1
(514) 389-7233
Emp Here 45   *Sales* 14,720,715
SIC 6531 Real estate agents and managers
Francois Lafleur
Benoit De Grosbois

D-U-N-S 24-680-4942   (SL)
CONSTRUCTION PASCAL
8020 Boul Metropolitain E, Anjou, QC, H1K
1A1
(514) 493-1054
Emp Here 30   *Sales* 14,121,930
SIC 1542 Nonresidential construction, nec
Pascal Lanoue

D-U-N-S 24-125-4841   (BR)
**FEDERATION DES CAISSES DESJARDINS
DU QUEBEC**
DOMAINE L'HYPOTHEQUE
(*Suby of* FEDERATION DES CAISSES DES-
JARDINS DU QUEBEC)
7755 Boul Louis-H.-Lafontaine Bureau 30711,
Anjou, QC, H1K 4M6
(514) 376-4420
Emp Here 200
SIC 6162 Mortgage bankers and loan corre-
spondents
Pierre Lemay

D-U-N-S 25-393-1018   (HQ)
**FRATERNITE   NATIONALE   DES
CHARPENTIERS-MENUISIERS (SECTION
LOCALE 9)**
9100 Boul Metropolitain E, Anjou, QC, H1K
4L2
(514) 374-5871
Sales 10,952,424
SIC 8631 Labor organizations
Erick Angers

D-U-N-S 20-910-8930   (BR)
GROUPE ROY SANTE INC
CENTRE LE ROYER
(*Suby of* GESTION ROYAL-MIG INC)
7351 Av Jean-Desprez Bureau 103, Anjou,
QC, H1K 5A6
(514) 493-9397
Emp Here 120
SIC 8051 Skilled nursing care facilities
Diane Gauthier

D-U-N-S 24-590-4438   (SL)
HARDY,   NORMAND   &   ASSOCIES

S.E.N.C.R.L.
7875 Boul Louis-H.-Lafontaine Bureau 200,
Anjou, QC, H1K 4E4
(514) 355-1550
Emp Here 49   *Sales* 10,245,165
SIC 8721 Accounting, auditing, and book-
keeping
Mario Hardy
Gilbert Normand
Gilles Brouillard
Marcel Lemay

D-U-N-S 25-747-6762   (BR)
METRO INC
METRO
(*Suby of* METRO INC)
6500 Boul Joseph-Renaud, Anjou, QC, H1K
3V4
(514) 354-0282
Emp Here 75
SIC 5411 Grocery stores
Giovanni Russo

D-U-N-S 25-390-4155   (SL)
**SERVICES PROFESSIONNELS DES AS-
SUREURS PLUS INC**
S P A PLUS
8290 Boul Metropolitain E, Anjou, QC, H1K
1A2
Emp Here 50   *Sales* 22,174,500
SIC 7389 Business services, nec
Maurice Poirier

D-U-N-S 20-797-7187   (BR)
**SYNDICAT CANADIEN DES COMMUNICA-
TIONS DE L'ENERGIE ET DU PAPIER**
LOCAL 98
8290 Boul Metropolitain E, Anjou, QC, H1K
1A2
(514) 259-7237
Emp Here 650
SIC 8631 Labor organizations
Patrice Lepine

Anjou, QC H1M

D-U-N-S 20-793-6287   (HQ)
**ASSOCIATION PROVINCIALE DES CON-
STRUCTEURS D'HABITATIONS DU QUE-
BEC INC**
A. P. C. H. Q.
5930 Boul Louis-H.-Lafontaine, Anjou, QC,
H1M 1S7
(514) 353-9960
Emp Here 215   *Sales* 60,525,600
SIC 8611 Business associations
Jean Pierre Sirard
Monique Campeau

D-U-N-S 24-222-9933   (BR)
BOSTON PIZZA INTERNATIONAL INC
BOSTON PIZZA
(*Suby of* BOSTON PIZZA INTERNATIONAL
INC)
7300 Boul Des Roseraies, Anjou, QC, H1M
2T5
(514) 788-4848
Emp Here 90
SIC 5812 Eating places
Martin Lalancette

D-U-N-S 24-815-2332   (HQ)
**COMITE PARITAIRE DES AGENTS DE SE-
CURITE**
7450 Boul Des Galeries D'Anjou Unite 490,
Anjou, QC, H1M 3M3
(514) 493-9105
Emp Here 29   *Sales* 12,517,056
SIC 8631 Labor organizations
Sylvain Laplante
Bernard Desjardins

D-U-N-S 20-764-9336   (HQ)
COMPAGNIE D'ASSURANCE BELAIR INC,

LA
BELAIR DIRECT
(*Suby of* INTACT FINANCIAL CORPORATION)
7101 Rue Jean-Talon E Bureau 300, Anjou, QC, H1M 3T6
(514) 270-1700
Emp Here 450   *Sales* 1,987,380,240
SIC 6331 Fire, marine, and casualty insurance
Louis Gagnon
Yves Poulin
Francoise Guenette
Eileen Mercier
Carol Stephenson
Charles Brindamour
Claude Dussault
Stephen G. Snyder
Timothy H. Penner
Janet De Silva

D-U-N-S 24-870-1708   (SL)
ELIE, JOSEPH LTEE
(*Suby of* SUNCOR ENERGY INC)
7400 Boul Des Galeries D'Anjou Unite 300, Anjou, QC, H1M 3M2
(514) 493-2930
Emp Here 55   *Sales* 13,438,040
SIC 5983 Fuel oil dealers
Pat Lizotte
Boris J. Jackman

D-U-N-S 20-219-0161   (SL)
FORTIER AUTO (MONTREAL) LTEE
LOCATION FORTIER DIV
7000 Boul Louis-H.-Lafontaine, Anjou, QC, H1M 2X3
(514) 353-9821
Emp Here 100   *Sales* 62,928,000
SIC 5511 New and used car dealers
Michel Salotti

D-U-N-S 20-271-4739   (SL)
GARANTIE DE CONSTRUCTION RESIDENTIELLE (GCR), LA
GARANTIE CONSTRUCTION RESIDENTIELLE
7171 Rue Jean-Talon E Bureau 200, Anjou, QC, H1M 3N2
(514) 657-2333
Emp Here 35   *Sales* 36,220,835
SIC 6351 Surety insurance
Jacques Leroux

D-U-N-S 24-762-7730   (HQ)
GROUPE ULTIMA INC
7100 Rue Jean-Talon E Bureau 210, Anjou, QC, H1M 3S3
(514) 722-0024
Sales 110,864,520
SIC 6411 Insurance agents, brokers, and service
Rene Vocelle
Andre Roy
Dany Murray
Andre Deschambault
Michel Chapdelaine
Yves Brassard
Anne-Stephanie Mamane
Francois Dufault
Rachelle Maltais
Yvon Lareau

D-U-N-S 24-813-9719   (BR)
INTACT INSURANCE COMPANY
INTACT ASSURANCE
(*Suby of* INTACT FINANCIAL CORPORATION)
7101 Rue Jean-Talon E Bureau 1000, Anjou, QC, H1M 0A5
(514) 388-5466
Emp Here 350
SIC 6331 Fire, marine, and casualty insurance
Carol Stephenson

D-U-N-S 24-522-9161   (BR)
METRO INC
ALEXANDRE GAUDET

(*Suby of* METRO INC)
7151 Rue Jean-Talon E, Anjou, QC, H1M 3N8
(514) 356-5800
Emp Here 200
SIC 5141 Groceries, general line
Claude Dussault

D-U-N-S 20-294-2889   (SL)
PAFCO INSURANCE
7100 Rue Jean-Talon E Bureau 300, Anjou, QC, H1M 3S3
(514) 351-8711
Emp Here 30   *Sales* 17,397,720
SIC 6411 Insurance agents, brokers, and service
Jacinthe Giroux

D-U-N-S 24-548-1759   (SL)
RE/MAX EXCELLENCE INC
7130 Rue Beaubien E, Anjou, QC, H1M 1B2
(514) 354-6240
Emp Here 43   *Sales* 14,066,461
SIC 6531 Real estate agents and managers
Josee Pellegrino
Michael La Polla

D-U-N-S 20-763-9188   (SL)
SAJY COMMUNICATIONS INC
TONIK-GROUPIMAGE
7070 Rue Beaubien E, Anjou, QC, H1M 1B2
(514) 521-4301
Emp Here 100   *Sales* 16,402,700
SIC 2791 Typesetting
Marc Roberge

Asbestos, QC J1T

D-U-N-S 25-233-2820   (BR)
COMMISSION SCOLAIRE DES SOMMETS
ECOLE SECONDAIRE DE L'ESCALE
(*Suby of* COMMISSION SCOLAIRE DES SOMMETS)
430 5e Av, Asbestos, QC, J1T 1X2
(819) 879-5413
Emp Here 80
SIC 8211 Elementary and secondary schools
Jocelyne Baugeois

D-U-N-S 20-188-9003   (SL)
COOP ALIMENTAIRE DE LA REGION D'ASBESTOS
CENTRE COMMERCIAL D'ASBESTOS
511 1re Av, Asbestos, QC, J1T 3P6
(819) 879-5427
Emp Here 100   *Sales* 27,415,200
SIC 5411 Grocery stores
Andre Rosa

D-U-N-S 24-760-0919   (SL)
FRECHETTE, JOSEE PHARMACIE
JEAN-COUTU
525 1re Av, Asbestos, QC, J1T 4R1
(819) 879-6969
Emp Here 65   *Sales* 71,847,425
SIC 5122 Drugs, proprietaries, and sundries
Josee Frechette

Ascot Corner, QC J0B

D-U-N-S 24-792-6827   (SL)
135456 CANADA INC
CREATIONS JADE
5547 Rte 112, Ascot Corner, QC, J0B 1A0
(819) 822-1833
Emp Here 22   *Sales* 16,335,440
SIC 5199 Nondurable goods, nec
Bruno Maher
Serge Maher

Auclair, QC G0L

D-U-N-S 24-381-3904   (SL)
GROUPEMENT FORESTIER DE L'EST DU LAC TEMISCOUATA INC
710 Rue Du Clocher, Auclair, QC, G0L 1A0
(418) 899-6673
Emp Here 150   *Sales* 28,855,500
SIC 2411 Logging
Gerald Lavoie
Reginald Tremblay

Ayer'S Cliff, QC J0B

D-U-N-S 24-225-2344   (SL)
EVEREST EQUIPMENT CO
EVEREST
1077 Rue Westmount, Ayer'S Cliff, QC, J0B 1C0
(819) 838-4257
Emp Here 95   *Sales* 21,265,085
SIC 3713 Truck and bus bodies
Lyle Roarke
Richard J. Wehrle
Robert H. George
Jeffery A. Leonard

D-U-N-S 24-820-9991   (SL)
WULFTEC INTERNATIONAL INC
MSS CANADA
(*Suby of* ODYSSEY CAPITAL PARTNERS V, LLC)
209 Rue Wulftec, Ayer'S Cliff, QC, J0B 1C0
(819) 838-4232
Emp Here 180   *Sales* 87,791,400
SIC 5084 Industrial machinery and equipment
Stephane Jonca

Baie D Urfe, QC H9X

D-U-N-S 25-093-0802   (SL)
ALTIUS EPICES ET ASSAISONNEMENTS INC
ALIMENT ENCORE GOURMET
19000 Aut Transcanadienne, Baie D Urfe, QC, H9X 3S4
(514) 457-2200
Emp Here 55   *Sales* 19,012,950
SIC 2099 Food preparations, nec
Laurence Bloom
Arash Ilkhani
Costa Arkalis

D-U-N-S 24-251-0808   (HQ)
SEIGNIORY CHEMICAL PRODUCTS LTD
SCP SCIENCE
21800 Av Clark-Graham, Baie D Urfe, QC, H9X 4B6
(514) 457-0701
Sales 31,302,180
SIC 5049 Professional equipment, nec
George Feilders

Baie-Comeau, QC G4Z

D-U-N-S 24-759-1423   (SL)
2630-6241 QUEBEC INC
HAMILTON & BOURASSA (1988) ENR
305 Boul La Salle, Baie-Comeau, QC, G4Z 2L5
(418) 296-9191
Emp Here 40   *Sales* 19,923,120
SIC 5571 Motorcycle dealers
Germain Deschenes

D-U-N-S 20-702-8965   (BR)
ALCOA CANADA CIE

ALUMINERIE DE BAIE COMEAU
(*Suby of* ALUMINERIE LAURALCO SARL)
100 Rte Maritime, Baie-Comeau, QC, G4Z 2L6
(418) 296-3311
Emp Here 700
SIC 3354 Aluminum extruded products
Pierre Morin

D-U-N-S 20-695-6653   (SL)
CONSTRUCTIONS BOB-SON INC
2264 Av Du Labrador, Baie-Comeau, QC, G4Z 3C4
(418) 296-0064
Emp Here 50   *Sales* 14,340,388
SIC 1611 Highway and street construction
Boby Miller

D-U-N-S 24-803-4030   (SL)
DISTRIBUTION COTE-NORD INC
12 Av Romeo-Vezina, Baie-Comeau, QC, G4Z 2W2
(418) 296-3300
Emp Here 26   *Sales* 21,725,002
SIC 5142 Packaged frozen goods
Dominic Savard
Raphael Girard
Carl Rodrigue

D-U-N-S 20-858-1330   (SL)
ENTREPRISES R & G ST-LAURENT INC
2081 Av Du Labrador, Baie-Comeau, QC, G4Z 3B9
(418) 589-5453
Emp Here 20   *Sales* 15,669,540
SIC 1794 Excavation work
Yann St-Laurent
Real St-Laurent

D-U-N-S 24-820-3952   (SL)
FABRICATION FRANSI INC
32 Av Babin, Baie-Comeau, QC, G4Z 3A6
(418) 296-6021
Emp Here 110   *Sales* 21,156,080
SIC 7692 Welding repair
Richard Imbeault

D-U-N-S 20-643-4631   (HQ)
GROUPE CONSEIL TDA INC
(*Suby of* GESTION TDA INC)
26 Boul Comeau, Baie-Comeau, QC, G4Z 3A8
(418) 296-6711
Emp Here 88   *Sales* 16,086,510
SIC 8711 Engineering services
Jacques Parent
Etienne Chapados
Gilles Cote
Myriam Hotte
Lavoie Steve

D-U-N-S 25-389-8159   (BR)
PF RESOLU CANADA INC
ABITIBI-CONSOLIDATED, DIVISION BAIE-COMEAU
(*Suby of* RESOLUTE FOREST PRODUCTS INC)
20 Av Marquette, Baie-Comeau, QC, G4Z 1K6
(418) 296-3371
Emp Here 290
SIC 2679 Converted paper products, nec
Gaston Joncas

D-U-N-S 24-354-6400   (SL)
RENALD COTE 2007 INC
R.C.I.
48 Av William-Dobell, Baie-Comeau, QC, G4Z 1T7
(418) 296-2854
Emp Here 70   *Sales* 17,233,020
SIC 1794 Excavation work
Marc Riverin
Mario Laberge

D-U-N-S 24-884-3948   (SL)
TRANSPORT BAIE-COMEAU INC
(*Suby of* GESTION JEAN FOURNIER INC)
62 Av William-Dobell, Baie-Comeau, QC, G4Z

1T7
(418) 296-5229
Emp Here 60   *Sales* 12,342,360
SIC 4213 Trucking, except local
Jean-Pierre Fournier
Jean Fournier
Lucille Larouche Fournier

Baie-Comeau, QC G5C

D-U-N-S 20-949-7494   (SL)
CEGEP DE BAIE-COMEAU
537 Boul Blanche, Baie-Comeau, QC, G5C 2B2
(418) 589-5707
Emp Here 186   *Sales* 27,786,726
SIC 8221 Colleges and universities
Roger Lapointe

D-U-N-S 20-176-7238   (BR)
CENTRE DE PROTECTION ET DE READAPTATION DE LA COTE-NORD
CENTRE JEUNESSE COTE NORD
835 Boul Jolliet, Baie-Comeau, QC, G5C 1P5
(418) 589-9927
Emp Here 650
SIC 8361 Residential care
Alcide Huard

D-U-N-S 25-358-4460   (HQ)
COMMISSION SCOLAIRE DE L'ESTUAIRE
620 Rue Jalbert, Baie-Comeau, QC, G5C 0B8
(418) 589-0806
Emp Here 3   *Sales* 99,119,000
SIC 8211 Elementary and secondary schools
Alain Ouellet
Nadine Desrosiers

D-U-N-S 24-758-6431   (SL)
FLECHE AUTO (1987) LTEE, LA
707 Boul Lafleche, Baie-Comeau, QC, G5C 1C6
(418) 589-3714
Emp Here 25   *Sales* 12,451,950
SIC 5511 New and used car dealers
Jean-Marc Hins

D-U-N-S 24-349-6390   (SL)
FONDATION DU CENTRE DE SANTE ET DE SERVICES SOCIAUX DE MANICOUAGAN
(*Suby of* GOUVERNEMENT DE LA PROVINCE DE QUEBEC)
635 Boul Jolliet, Baie-Comeau, QC, G5C 1P1
(418) 589-3701
Emp Here 900
SIC 8062 General medical and surgical hospitals

D-U-N-S 25-298-5833   (SL)
GESTION BENOIT GUILLEMETTE INC
CANADIAN TIRE BAIE COMEAU
650 Rue De Parfondeval Bureau 265, Baie-Comeau, QC, G5C 3R3
(418) 589-9924
Emp Here 70   *Sales* 44,049,600
SIC 5531 Auto and home supply stores
Benoit Guillemette

D-U-N-S 24-466-0221   (SL)
GROUPE DE LA COTE INC
VETEMENTS NORFIL, LES
332 Rue De Puyjalon, Baie-Comeau, QC, G5C 1M5
(418) 589-8397
Emp Here 75   *Sales* 10,250,550
SIC 2326 Men's and boy's work clothing
Claude Belzile

D-U-N-S 25-365-7167   (BR)
HYDRO-QUEBEC
TRANSENERGIE ET PRODUCTION, DIVISIONS DE
(*Suby of* GOUVERNEMENT DE LA PROVINCE DE QUEBEC)
1161 Rue Mccormick, Baie-Comeau, QC,

G5C 2S7
(418) 295-1507
Emp Here 100
SIC 4911 Electric services
Gilles Poirier

D-U-N-S 24-941-9995   (SL)
MARTIN & BELZILE INC
PHARMACIE JEAN COUTU #89
691 Boul Lafleche Bureau 89, Baie-Comeau, QC, G5C 1C4
(418) 589-4969
Emp Here 60   *Sales* 14,659,680
SIC 5912 Drug stores and proprietary stores
Dany Belzile

D-U-N-S 20-003-4911   (BR)
PF RESOLU CANADA INC
PRODUITS FORESTIERS RESOLUT SCIERIE OUTARDES
(*Suby of* RESOLUTE FOREST PRODUCTS INC)
1 Ch De La Scierie, Baie-Comeau, QC, G5C 2S9
(418) 589-9229
Emp Here 136
SIC 5099 Durable goods, nec
Gervais Goulet

D-U-N-S 20-030-4439   (BR)
PROVIGO DISTRIBUTION INC
MAXI BAIE-COMEAU
(*Suby of* LOBLAW COMPANIES LIMITED)
570 Boul Lafleche, Baie-Comeau, QC, G5C 1C3
(418) 589-9020
Emp Here 84
SIC 5411 Grocery stores
Luc D'anjou

D-U-N-S 25-991-6005   (BR)
WAL-MART CANADA CORP
WALMART BAIE COMEAU
(*Suby of* WALMART INC.)
630 Boul Lafleche Bureau 3002, Baie-Comeau, QC, G5C 2Y3
(418) 589-9971
Emp Here 120
SIC 5311 Department stores
Mario Tardis

Baie-D'Urfe, QC H9X

D-U-N-S 20-317-7548   (SL)
BOULANGERIES RENE ULC, LES
375 Av Lee, Baie-D'Urfe, QC, H9X 3S3
(514) 457-4500
Emp Here 50   *Sales* 11,242,750
SIC 2051 Bread, cake, and related products
Dale W. Tremblay
Thomas A. Mcrae
Janelle M. Sykes
Justin W. Grubbs

D-U-N-S 20-213-4052   (HQ)
CIE CANADA TIRE INC, LA
DISTRIBUTION ST-DAVID
21500 Aut Transcanadienne, Baie-D'Urfe, QC, H9X 4B7
(514) 457-0155
Emp Here 26   *Sales* 36,421,500
SIC 5014 Tires and tubes
William Granatstein
Gabriel Granatstein

D-U-N-S 24-252-1904   (SL)
DAVID BROWN SYSTEM (CANADA) INC
ENTREPRISE UNIGEAR
20375 Av Clark-Graham, Baie-D'Urfe, QC, H9X 3T5
(514) 457-7700
Emp Here 55   *Sales* 12,210,055
SIC 3566 Speed changers, drives, and gears
Thomas Burley
Karen Ann Tulley

David Armitt
Roshan Mehra

D-U-N-S 24-730-1849   (SL)
DISTRIBUTIONS D'ACIER ANICA INC, LES
ACIER ANICA
540 Av Firing, Baie-D'Urfe, QC, H9X 3T2
(514) 457-3071
Emp Here 11   *Sales* 11,003,729
SIC 5051 Metals service centers and offices
Andre Dagenais

D-U-N-S 20-410-7767   (SL)
FCNQ CONSTRUCTION INC
19400 Av Clark-Graham, Baie-D'Urfe, QC, H9X 3R8
(514) 457-9375
Emp Here 100   *Sales* 57,033,800
SIC 1542 Nonresidential construction, nec
Francois Day
Ali Tuktu Tulugak
Morin Janique
Luc Bourassa
Sarollie Weetaluktuk
Maggie Saviadjuk

D-U-N-S 20-205-8152   (HQ)
FEDERATION DES COOPERATIVES DU NOUVEAU-QUEBEC
FCNQ
19950 Av Clark-Graham, Baie-D'Urfe, QC, H9X 3R8
(514) 457-9371
Sales 153,695,490
SIC 5172 Petroleum products, nec
Ali Tuktu Tulugak
Sarollie Weetaluktuk
Mary Johannes
Charlie Tukkiapik
Janique Morin
Maggie Saviadjuk
Francois Day

D-U-N-S 25-167-6961   (SL)
G PRODUCTION INC
G.P.C.I.
(*Suby of* NESTLE S.A.)
19400 Aut Transcanadienne, Baie-D'Urfe, QC, H9X 3S4
(514) 457-3366
Emp Here 250   *Sales* 82,898,500
SIC 2834 Pharmaceutical preparations
Cecile Dussart
Stuart Raetzman
Stevens Murray
Pierre Streit

D-U-N-S 24-821-3407   (HQ)
GUITABEC INC
GUITARES GODIN
19420 Av Clark-Graham, Baie-D'Urfe, QC, H9X 3R8
(514) 457-7977
Emp Here 25   *Sales* 121,701,280
SIC 3931 Musical instruments
Patrick Godin
Robert Godin
Daniel Roy

D-U-N-S 24-175-2245   (SL)
HOLDING SECURITE C M LTEE, LE
19400 Av Cruickshank, Baie-D'Urfe, QC, H9X 3P1
(514) 457-6650
Emp Here 52   *Sales* 13,600,756
SIC 6712 Bank holding companies
Cedomir Draca
Gerald Spenard

D-U-N-S 20-760-9504   (HQ)
INDUSTRIES JAM LTEE, LES
B&J MUSIC
(*Suby of* DCC PUBLIC LIMITED COMPANY)
21000 Aut Transcanadienne, Baie-D'Urfe, QC, H9X 4B7
(514) 457-2555
Sales 278,120,000
SIC 5099 Durable goods, nec

Martin Szpiro
Stuart Frenkel
Stephen Casey
Timothy Griffin

D-U-N-S 20-231-7103   (HQ)
INDUSTRIES REHAU INC
FIRST PIPE
(*Suby of* REHAU INCORPORATED)
625 Av Lee, Baie-D'Urfe, QC, H9X 3S3
(514) 905-0345
Emp Here 100   *Sales* 132,540,660
SIC 3089 Plastics products, nec

D-U-N-S 25-200-9105   (SL)
INTERNATIONAL SUPPLIERS AND CONTRACTORS INC
INTERSAC
19400 Av Cruickshank, Baie-D'Urfe, QC, H9X 3P1
(514) 457-5362
Emp Here 100   *Sales* 30,620,520
SIC 5169 Chemicals and allied products, nec
Jean Banna
Arel Banna
Antonio Banna

D-U-N-S 20-375-3124   (HQ)
INVESTISSEMENTS SKYFOLD LTEE
(*Suby of* DORMAKABA HOLDING AG)
325 Av Lee, Baie-D'Urfe, QC, H9X 3S3
(514) 735-5410
Sales 25,968,250
SIC 6712 Bank holding companies
Stefano Aurelio Zocca
Sandra Heller
Bernd Brinker

D-U-N-S 24-835-0670   (HQ)
LABORATOIRES ITR CANADA INC, LES
19601 Av Clark-Graham, Baie-D'Urfe, QC, H9X 3T1
(514) 457-7400
Sales 45,950,800
SIC 8731 Commercial physical research
Kumi Yamanouchi
Tetsutaka Hirakawa
Naoki Yamanouchi
Hiroshi Yamanouchi

D-U-N-S 24-698-3571   (BR)
MARTIN-BROWER OF CANADA CO
(*Suby of* REYES HOLDINGS, L.L.C.)
475 Av Lee, Baie-D'Urfe, QC, H9X 3S3
(514) 457-4411
Emp Here 120
SIC 5141 Groceries, general line
Warren Dafoe

D-U-N-S 24-516-2888   (SL)
MATRICES CARRITEC INC, LES
575 Boul Morgan, Baie-D'Urfe, QC, H9X 3T6
(514) 457-7779
Emp Here 75   *Sales* 11,574,150
SIC 2542 Partitions and fixtures, except wood
Tamer Shaaban

D-U-N-S 24-689-6807   (HQ)
MERIAL CANADA INC
(*Suby of* C.H. BOEHRINGER SOHN AG & CO. KG)
20000 Av Clark-Graham, Baie-D'Urfe, QC, H9X 4B6
(514) 457-1555
Emp Here 30   *Sales* 19,029,407
SIC 2834 Pharmaceutical preparations
Richard Mole
Susan Blair
Guido Hoeller
Ywe Looper

D-U-N-S 24-406-4200   (SL)
MONTREAL TRACTEUR INC
21601 Av Clark-Graham, Baie-D'Urfe, QC, H9X 3T5
(514) 457-8100
Emp Here 26   *Sales* 12,350,676
SIC 5084 Industrial machinery and equipment

▲ Public Company   ■ Public Company Family Member   **HQ** Headquarters   **BR** Branch   **SL** Single Location

Concezio Masciotra
Angelo Masciotra

D-U-N-S 24-321-0218　　(SL)
NDT TECHNOLOGIES INC
EDDYTRON
20275 Av Clark-Graham, Baie-D'Urfe, QC,
H9X 3T5
(514) 457-7650
Emp Here 50　　*Sales* 12,828,100
SIC 3825 Instruments to measure electricity
Jaroslav J. Slaba

D-U-N-S 20-194-6035　　(SL)
PEINTURE UCP INC
ASCOT
19500 Aut Transcanadienne, Baie-D'Urfe, QC,
H9X 3S4
(514) 457-1512
Emp Here 50　　*Sales* 13,833,000
SIC 2851 Paints and allied products
Erno Jakabovits
Zoltan Jakabovits

D-U-N-S 25-393-7502　　(SL)
RECYCAN INC
20500 Av Clark-Graham, Baie-D'Urfe, QC,
H9X 4B6
(514) 457-0322
Emp Here 50　　*Sales* 15,057,100
SIC 4953 Refuse systems
Gilles Malouin
Maxime Couture
Philippe Cote

D-U-N-S 20-220-8328　　(HQ)
ROLF C. HAGEN INC
AVANT
20500 Aut Transcanadienne, Baie-D'Urfe, QC,
H9X 0A2
(514) 457-0914
Emp Here 125　　*Sales* 589,159,000
SIC 5199 Nondurable goods, nec
Jr. Rolf Hagen
Tom Hagen
Dieter Hagen
J.W. Joergensen
Bradley C. Rogers
Mark Hagen
Thomas Marshall

D-U-N-S 20-112-9488　　(SL)
ROS-MAR INC
19500 Av Clark-Graham, Baie-D'Urfe, QC,
H9X 3R8
(514) 694-2178
Emp Here 160　　*Sales* 26,548,279
SIC 2752 Commercial printing, lithographic
Frank Carbone

D-U-N-S 24-179-0435　　(HQ)
ROS-MAR LITHO INC
PAPERWORKS INDUSTRIES
(*Suby of* SUN CAPITAL PARTNERS, INC.)
19500 Av Clark-Graham, Baie-D'Urfe, QC,
H9X 3R8
(514) 694-2178
Sales 26,244,320
SIC 2752 Commercial printing, lithographic
Kevin Kwilinski
Michael P. Whitcombe

D-U-N-S 20-013-1642　　(BR)
SAMUEL, SON & CO., LIMITED
METAUX AERONAUTIQUE SAMUEL
(*Suby of* SAMUEL, SON & CO., LIMITED)
21525 Av Clark-Graham, Baie-D'Urfe, QC,
H9X 3T5
(800) 361-3483
Emp Here 198
SIC 5051 Metals service centers and offices
Emile Beaulieu

D-U-N-S 24-990-3931　　(HQ)
SCHOLLE IPN CANADA LTD
AUTOFILL PRODUCTS
(*Suby of* SCHOLLE IPN CORPORATION)
22000 Av Clark-Graham, Baie-D'Urfe, QC,

H9X 4B6
(514) 457-1569
Sales 19,476,800
SIC 2673 Bags: plastic, laminated, and
coated
Eli Carmeli
Jerry Trousdale
Tom Bickford
Alec Marketos
Jerry Trousdale
Jay Goffin

D-U-N-S 20-856-5572　　(SL)
SKYFOLD INC
SKYFOLD CLASSIC
(*Suby of* DORMAKABA HOLDING AG)
325 Av Lee, Baie-D'Urfe, QC, H9X 3S3
(514) 457-4767
Emp Here 95　　*Sales* 18,248,075
SIC 3449 Miscellaneous Metalwork
Christoph Jacob
Sandra Heller
Bernd Brinker

D-U-N-S 24-787-5289　　(HQ)
STYROCHEM CANADA LTEE
19250 Av Clark-Graham, Baie-D'Urfe, QC,
H9X 3R8
(514) 457-3226
Sales 21,301,575
SIC 2821 Plastics materials and resins
Aubry Pat
Glenn Wredenhagen
Gaetan D'agostino

D-U-N-S 24-848-5562　　(SL)
TOMRA CANADA INC
LES SYSTEMES TOMRA
(*Suby of* TOMRA SYSTEMS ASA)
20500 Av Clark-Graham, Baie-D'Urfe, QC,
H9X 4B6
(514) 457-4177
Emp Here 55　　*Sales* 26,825,150
SIC 5084 Industrial machinery and equipment
Alain Nault
Walter F Garigliano
Stefan Ranstand
Espen Gundersen

D-U-N-S 24-680-1369　　(HQ)
TRICOTS MAXIME INC, LES
19500 Av Clark-Graham, Baie-D'Urfe, QC,
H9X 3R8
(514) 336-0445
Emp Here 10　　*Sales* 34,708,224
SIC 2258 Lace and warp knit fabric mills
Denis Theriault
Maxime Theriault
Helene Massicotte

Baie-Du-Febvre, QC J0G

D-U-N-S 25-666-1372　　(HQ)
COVILAC COOPERATIVE AGRICOLE
40 Rue De L'Eglise, Baie-Du-Febvre, QC, J0G
1A0
(450) 783-6491
Emp Here 35　　*Sales* 22,174,500
SIC 7389 Business services, nec
Jeannine Chartrand
Muriel Dubois
Jean Roy
Richard Laroche
Jessy Pelletier
Martin Paquette
Jean Landry

D-U-N-S 24-405-0357　　(SL)
SOGETEL
37 Rue Verville, Baie-Du-Febvre, QC, J0G
1A0
(450) 783-1005
Emp Here 165　　*Sales* 37,697,880
SIC 4813 Telephone communication, except

radio
Jean-Philippe Saia
Maurice Proulx
Yvon Brunelle

Baie-Saint-Paul, QC G3Z

D-U-N-S 20-872-5150　　(SL)
BFCO INC
5 Rue Paul-Rene-Tremblay, Baie-Saint-Paul,
QC, G3Z 3E4
(418) 435-3682
Emp Here 110　　*Sales* 21,160,700
SIC 2499 Wood products, nec
Marie-Josee Bouchard
Joel Ostrov

D-U-N-S 25-232-3597　　(BR)
**COMMISSION SCOLAIRE DE
CHARLEVOIX, LA**
*ECOLES ET CENTRES EDUCATIF SAINT
AUBIN*
(*Suby of* COMMISSION SCOLAIRE DE
CHARLEVOIX, LA)
200 Rue Saint-Aubin Unite 102, Baie-Saint-
Paul, QC, G3Z 2R2
(418) 435-2824
Emp Here 80
SIC 8211 Elementary and secondary schools
Robert Labb

D-U-N-S 25-232-7879　　(HQ)
**COMMISSION SCOLAIRE DE
CHARLEVOIX, LA**
CENTRE ADMINISTRATIF
200 Rue Saint-Aubin, Baie-Saint-Paul, QC,
G3Z 2R2
(418) 435-2824
Sales 59,471,400
SIC 8211 Elementary and secondary schools
Martine Vallee
Pierre Girard

D-U-N-S 20-189-4763　　(HQ)
**ENTREPRISES JACQUES DUFOUR & FILS
INC, LES**
106 Rue Sainte-Anne, Baie-Saint-Paul, QC,
G3Z 1P5
(418) 435-2445
Emp Here 30　　*Sales* 37,866,300
SIC 1611 Highway and street construction
Gilles Dufour
Yvon Dufour

D-U-N-S 20-582-5110　　(SL)
GARAGE JEAN-ROCH THIBEAULT INC
HYUNDAI JEAN-ROCH THIBEAULT
909 Boul Monseigneur-De Laval, Baie-Saint-
Paul, QC, G3Z 2V9
(418) 435-2379
Emp Here 25　　*Sales* 12,451,950
SIC 5511 New and used car dealers
Nicolas Thibeault
Sebastien Thibeault

D-U-N-S 25-198-1643　　(HQ)
**PROMUTUEL CHARLEVOIX-
MONTMORENCY**
951 Boul Monseigneur-De Laval, Baie-Saint-
Paul, QC, G3Z 2W3
(418) 435-2793
Emp Here 15　　*Sales* 46,166,475
SIC 6331 Fire, marine, and casualty insurance
Jean-Baptiste Pedneault
Thomas-Louis Gaudreault

D-U-N-S 24-115-1638　　(SL)
**PROMUTUEL DU LAC AU FLEUVE, SO-
CIETE MUTUELLE D'ASSURANCE GEN-
ERALE**
*PROMUTUEL ASSURANCE DU LAC AU
FLEUVE*
951 Boul Monseigneur-De Laval, Baie-Saint-
Paul, QC, G3Z 2W3

(418) 435-2793
Emp Here 49　　*Sales* 41,554,940
SIC 6411 Insurance agents, brokers, and ser-
vice
Omer Bouchard

D-U-N-S 24-885-0547　　(SL)
SUPERMARCHE G.C. INC
MARCHE I G A
1020 Boul Monseigneur-De Laval Bureau 1,
Baie-Saint-Paul, QC, G3Z 2W6
(418) 435-5210
Emp Here 80　　*Sales* 23,478,160
SIC 5411 Grocery stores
Cyrille Tremblay
Claude Menard
Pierre Menard
Gerard Raymond Tremblay

Beaconsfield, QC H9W

D-U-N-S 25-209-8322　　(SL)
9007-8361 QUEBEC INC
PHARMAPRIX
50 Boul Saint-Charles, Beaconsfield, QC,
H9W 2X3
(514) 697-4550
Emp Here 40　　*Sales* 10,118,160
SIC 5912 Drug stores and proprietary stores
Nada Nasreddine

D-U-N-S 25-846-0278　　(SL)
9038-5477 QUEBEC INC
HEALTH ACCESS
482 Boul Beaconsfield Bureau 204, Beaconsfield, QC, H9W 4C4
(514) 695-3131
Emp Here 100　　*Sales* 6,456,000
SIC 8059 Nursing and personal care, nec
Donna Byrne

D-U-N-S 24-828-9931　　(SL)
CWT CONCIERGE
53 Maple Cres, Beaconsfield, QC, H9W 4T3
(514) 695-7215
Emp Here 26　　*Sales* 13,519,142
SIC 4724 Travel agencies
Christopher Woodcock

D-U-N-S 20-531-3625　　(BR)
LESTER B. PEARSON SCHOOL BOARD
BEACONSFIELD HIGH SCHOOL
250 Beaurepaire Dr, Beaconsfield, QC, H9W
5G7
(514) 697-7220
Emp Here 100
SIC 8211 Elementary and secondary schools
Michelle Harper

D-U-N-S 25-794-3423　　(BR)
METRO RICHELIEU INC
METRO PLUS BEACONSFIELD
(*Suby of* METRO INC)
50 Boul Saint-Charles Bureau 17, Beacons-
field, QC, H9W 2X3
(514) 695-5811
Emp Here 85
SIC 5411 Grocery stores
Philippe Birdjandi

Bearn, QC J0Z

D-U-N-S 24-706-2235　　(BR)
RAYONIER A.M. CANADA G.P.
TEMBEC
(*Suby of* RAYONIER A.M. CANADA G.P.)
67 Rue Principale S, Bearn, QC, J0Z 1G0
(819) 726-3551
Emp Here 150
SIC 2421 Sawmills and planing mills, general
Rejean Parent

Beauceville, QC G5X

D-U-N-S 20-213-9429   (BR)
AGROPUR COOPERATIVE
*AGROPUR DIVISION FROMAGE ET PRO-
DUITS FONCTIONNELS*
(*Suby of* AGROPUR COOPERATIVE)
75 Av Lambert, Beauceville, QC, G5X 3N5
(418) 774-9848
Emp Here 125
SIC 2022 Cheese; natural and processed
Nathalie Doyer

D-U-N-S 24-706-3605   (SL)
ARBORICULTURE DE BEAUCE INC
364e Rte Du President-Kennedy, Beauceville,
QC, G5X 1N9
(418) 774-6217
Emp Here 200   *Sales* 34,781,000
SIC 0721 Crop planting and protection
Denis Rancourt
Jean-Guy Rancourt
Charles-Yvan Guenette

D-U-N-S 24-890-8105   (SL)
**AUXILIAIRES BENEVOLES DU CENTRE
D'HEBERGEMENT DE BEAUCEVILLE
(CBH)**
253 108 Rte, Beauceville, QC, G5X 2Z3
(418) 774-3304
Emp Here 500   *Sales* 37,886,500
SIC 8093 Specialty outpatient clinics, nec
Michel Beaulieu
Lise Poulin
Julie Cloutier
Eva-Reine Morin
Helene Pare
Mariette Plante
Pierrette Mathieu
Berthe Roy

D-U-N-S 25-794-9933   (SL)
BEAUCE AUTO (2000) INC
405 Boul Renault, Beauceville, QC, G5X 1N7
(418) 774-9801
Emp Here 29   *Sales* 14,444,262
SIC 5511 New and used car dealers
Pierre Couture
Roger Hebert

D-U-N-S 24-513-3900   (SL)
BETON CHEVALIER INC
152 39e Av, Beauceville, QC, G5X 3S4
(418) 774-4747
Emp Here 49   *Sales* 12,399,891
SIC 5211 Lumber and other building materials
Bernard Chevallier

D-U-N-S 24-907-9963   (SL)
BOIS OUVRE DE BEAUCEVILLE (1992) INC
(*Suby of* SECHOIRS DE BEAUCE INC)
201 134e Rue, Beauceville, QC, G5X 3H9
(418) 774-3606
Emp Here 60   *Sales* 11,542,200
SIC 2431 Millwork
Jean-Francois Drouin
Nicholas Drouin
Steeve Drouin

D-U-N-S 25-077-5678   (BR)
IMPRIMERIES TRANSCONTINENTAL INC
TRANSCONTINENTAL PRINTING INC
(*Suby of* TRANSCONTINENTAL INC)
150 181e Rue, Beauceville, QC, G5X 3P3
(418) 774-3367
Emp Here 500
SIC 2752 Commercial printing, lithographic
Jacquies Gregoire

D-U-N-S 24-146-5541   (HQ)
MENUISEROX INC
SECHOIRS DE LERY
159 181e Rue, Beauceville, QC, G5X 2S9
(418) 774-9019
Sales 10,580,350

SIC 2431 Millwork
Simon Boucher
Jacquot Veilleux
Guillaume Boucher
Bruno Tardif

D-U-N-S 24-207-3021   (SL)
PNEUS BEAUCERONS INC, LES
DISTRIBUTION LPB 2012
538 Boul Renault, Beauceville, QC, G5X 1N2
(418) 774-3404
Emp Here 26   *Sales* 12,950,028
SIC 5531 Auto and home supply stores
Yvan Poulin

D-U-N-S 24-907-1226   (SL)
PORTES PATIO NOVATECH INC
PORTES PATIO RESIVER
(*Suby of* 7347456 CANADA INC)
100 181e Rue, Beauceville, QC, G5X 2T1
(418) 774-2949
Emp Here 250   *Sales* 63,922,500
SIC 3231 Products of purchased glass
Jean Champagne
Harold Savard
Raymond Ouellette

D-U-N-S 20-000-5739   (HQ)
**PROMUTUEL BEAUCE SOCIETE
MUTUELLE D'ASSURANCE GENERALE**
650 Boul Renault, Beauceville, QC, G5X 3P2
(418) 774-3621
Emp Here 32   *Sales* 65,300,620
SIC 6411 Insurance agents, brokers, and ser-
vice
Jean Roy
Jean-Denis Morin

D-U-N-S 24-438-6491   (SL)
**PROMUTUEL BEAUCE-ETCHEMINS, SO-
CIETE MUTUELLE D'ASSURANCE GEN-
ERALE**
PROMUTUEL ASSURANCE
650 Boul Renault, Beauceville, QC, G5X 3P2

Emp Here 50   *Sales* 28,996,200
SIC 6411 Insurance agents, brokers, and ser-
vice
Anne Vaillancourt

D-U-N-S 20-189-7444   (HQ)
RENE BERNARD INC
88 Av Lambert, Beauceville, QC, G5X 3N4
(418) 774-3382
Sales 11,179,350
SIC 5031 Lumber, plywood, and millwork
Michel Bernard
Daniel Bernard
Eric Bernard

D-U-N-S 24-760-0075   (SL)
ROYAL MAT INC
132 181e Rue, Beauceville, QC, G5X 2S8
(418) 774-3694
Emp Here 150   *Sales* 23,828,700
SIC 3069 Fabricated rubber products, nec
Francois Hardy
Jacques Foisy

D-U-N-S 25-977-8538   (SL)
SECHOIRS DE BEAUCE INC
201 134e Rue, Beauceville, QC, G5X 3H9
(418) 774-3606
Emp Here 69   *Sales* 10,754,547
SIC 2431 Millwork
Jean-Francois Drouin
Nicholas Drouin
Steeve Grondin

Beauharnois, QC J6N

D-U-N-S 20-712-3360   (BR)
**COMMISSION SCOLAIRE DE LA VALLEE-
DES-TISSERANDS, LA**
ECOLES SECONDAIRES PATRIOTES DE

BEAUHARNOIS
250 Rue Gagnon, Beauharnois, QC, J6N 2W8
(450) 225-2260
Emp Here 75
SIC 8211 Elementary and secondary schools
Robert Byette

D-U-N-S 25-231-3031   (SL)
**FAVREAU, GENDRON ASSURANCE ET
SERVICES FINANCIERS INC**
*MAILLOUX, ROCHON ASSURANCE ET
SERVICES FINANCIERS*
505 Rue Des E?Rables, Beauharnois, QC,
J6N 1T3
(450) 429-3755
Emp Here 26   *Sales* 48,013,134
SIC 6311 Life insurance

Beaupre, QC G0A

D-U-N-S 20-554-6703   (SL)
161251 CANADA INC
355 Rue Dupont, Beaupre, QC, G0A 1E0
(418) 827-8347
Emp Here 50   *Sales* 20,967,750
SIC 6712 Bank holding companies
Jean-Guy Larouche

D-U-N-S 25-198-0629   (HQ)
CARON & GUAY INC
CARON ET GUAY, PORTES & FENETRES
95 Rue Industrielle, Beaupre, QC, G0A 1E0
(418) 827-2459
Emp Here 80   *Sales* 23,828,700
SIC 3089 Plastics products, nec
Alain Guay
Jean-Francois Duclos

D-U-N-S 24-148-3577   (SL)
**CENTRE DE RENOVATION RAYMOND
BOIES INC**
215 Rue Lachance, Beaupre, QC, G0A 1E0
(418) 827-4531
Emp Here 50   *Sales* 13,382,600
SIC 5211 Lumber and other building materials
Emma Boies
Lucie Boies
Christine Boies
Jacques Boies
Emma Boies

D-U-N-S 24-345-5602   (BR)
**CENTRE DE SANTE ET DE SERVICES SO-
CIAUX DE QUEBEC-NORD**
CLSC ORLEANS
(*Suby of* GOUVERNEMENT DE LA
PROVINCE DE QUEBEC)
11000 Rue Des Montagnards, Beaupre, QC,
G0A 1E0
(418) 827-3726
Emp Here 350
SIC 8062 General medical and surgical hospi-
tals
Martin Bedard

D-U-N-S 25-232-7002   (BR)
**COMMISSION SCOLAIRE DES
PREMIERES-SEIGNEURIES**
*COMMISSION SCOLAIRE DES
PREMIERES-SEIGNEURIES*
(*Suby of* COMMISSION SCOLAIRE DES
PREMIERES-SEIGNEURIES)
10975 Boul Sainte-Anne, Beaupre, QC, G0A
1E0
(418) 821-8053
Emp Here 100
SIC 8211 Elementary and secondary schools
Michel Legare

D-U-N-S 24-941-1752   (HQ)
**CORPORATION FINANCIERE QUEBE-
COISE INC**
500 Boul Du Beau-Pre, Beaupre, QC, G0A
1E0

(418) 827-5211
Emp Here 1   *Sales* 88,453,178
SIC 6712 Bank holding companies
Charles Sirois
Maurice Roussin
Charles Sirois
Eric Tordjman
Francois-Charles Sirois
Sebastien Roy

D-U-N-S 24-781-8482   (SL)
**FONDATION DE L'HOPITAL SAINTE-ANNE-
DE-BEAUPRE INC**
11000 Rue Des Montagnards, Beaupre, QC,
G0A 1E0
(418) 827-3726
Emp Here 44   *Sales* 19,765,636
SIC 7389 Business services, nec
Martin Roy
Blais-Giroux Blais
Claude Maltais
Pierre Boutet
Pierre Tremblay
Johanne Paradis
Lucie Boies
Germain Tremblay
Steeve Vigneault

D-U-N-S 24-890-7974   (BR)
**GOUVERNEMENT DE LA PROVINCE DE
QUEBEC**
*CENTRE DE SANTE ET DE SERVICES SO-
CIAUX QUEBECNORD*
(*Suby of* GOUVERNEMENT DE LA
PROVINCE DE QUEBEC)
11000 Rue Des Montagnards Rr 1, Beaupre,
QC, G0A 1E0
(418) 661-5666
Emp Here 500
SIC 8361 Residential care
Lucie Lacroix

D-U-N-S 25-785-2798   (SL)
STATION MONT-SAINTE-ANNE INC
ANECDOTE, L'
(*Suby of* RESORTS OF THE CANADIAN
ROCKIES INC)
2000 Boul Du Beau-Pre Bureau 400, Beaupre,
QC, G0A 1E0
(418) 827-4561
Emp Here 150   *Sales* 13,903,500
SIC 7011 Hotels and motels
Larry Moeller
Daniel Rochon

Becancour, QC G9H

D-U-N-S 24-678-2952   (SL)
ALUMINERIE DE BECANCOUR INC
5555 Rue Pierre-Thibault Bureau 217, Becan-
cour, QC, G9H 2T7
(819) 294-6101
Emp Here 1,000   *Sales* 243,231,000
SIC 3463 Nonferrous forgings
Nicole Coutu
Christian Fortin

D-U-N-S 24-424-9462   (HQ)
ARKEMA CANADA INC
(*Suby of* ARKEMA)
655 Boul Alphonse-Deshaies, Becancour, QC,
G9H 2Y8
(819) 294-9965
Sales 34,082,520
SIC 2819 Industrial inorganic chemicals, nec
Richard Rowe
Dori L Mansur Ratka
Pierre Papin
Patricia Maccarthy
Philippe Philippe
Dean Adams

D-U-N-S 20-314-0553   (SL)
AUTOCAR HELIE INC.

GROUPE HELIE
3505 Boul De Port-Royal, Becancour, QC, G9H 1Y2
(819) 371-1177
Emp Here 100   *Sales* 5,487,200
SIC 4151 School buses
Pierre Helie
Normand Helie

D-U-N-S 20-251-2810   (SL)
BLANCHARD, A. INC
4350 Av Arseneault, Becancour, QC, G9H 1V8
(819) 233-2349
Emp Here 30   *Sales* 14,942,340
SIC 5511 New and used car dealers
Huguette Richard
Albert Blanchard
Normand Richard

D-U-N-S 20-502-8988   (SL)
BOUVET, ANDRE LTEE
1840 Boul De Port-Royal, Becancour, QC, G9H 0K7
(819) 233-2357
Emp Here 50   *Sales* 11,008,400
SIC 1794 Excavation work
Claude Bouvet
Clemence Bergeron Bouvet

D-U-N-S 25-363-0727   (HQ)
CAISSE DESJARDINS GODEFROY
CENTRE DE SERVICES BECANCOUR
4265 Boul De Port-Royal, Becancour, QC, G9H 1Z3
(819) 233-2333
Emp Here 25   *Sales* 14,326,924
SIC 6062 State credit unions
Dominique Raiche
Christian Savard
Leo Courchesne
Katia St-Onge
Jean Pinard
Raymond Arseneault
Claude Comeau
Josiane Grenier
Francine Pare Lampron
Nancy Trottier

D-U-N-S 24-404-6900   (HQ)
CANADOIL FORGE LTEE
805 Boul Alphonse-Deshaies, Becancour, QC, G9H 2Y8
(819) 294-6600
Emp Here 90   *Sales* 19,208,500
SIC 3462 Iron and steel forgings
Giacomo Sozzi
Gianluca Forcella
Martin Toutant

D-U-N-S 24-987-9438   (SL)
CEPSA CHIMIE BECANCOUR INC
(*Suby of* COMPAIIA ESPAIOLA DE PETROLEOS SAU)
5250 Boul Becancour, Becancour, QC, G9H 3X3
(819) 294-1414
Emp Here 64   *Sales* 18,177,344
SIC 2819 Industrial inorganic chemicals, nec
Jose Manuel Martinez Sanchez
Jose Aurelio Tellez Menchen
Agustin Bonilla
Victor Bermejo
Pierre Lahaie
Luc Van Hoecke
Jose Maria Cuadro
Loreano Alban

D-U-N-S 20-542-1712   (SL)
DESHAIES, JEAN-PAUL INC
14875 Boul Becancour, Becancour, QC, G9H 2L7
(819) 222-5623
Emp Here 15   *Sales* 15,492,120
SIC 5172 Petroleum products, nec
Jean-Paul Deshaies
Lucie Deshaies

(819) 294-2900
Emp Here 60   *Sales* 10,883,280
SIC 3353 Aluminum sheet, plate, and foil
Aldredo Riviere
Alfredo Luis Riviere
Stephane Amyot

D-U-N-S 25-370-3425   (BR)
TELEBEC, SOCIETE EN COMMANDITE
TELEBEC
(*Suby of* TELEBEC, SOCIETE EN COMMAN-DITE)
625 Av Godefroy, Becancour, QC, G9H 1S3

Emp Here 250
SIC 4813 Telephone communication, except radio
Danielle Godin

D-U-N-S 24-341-9657   (SL)
TRANSCANADA QUEBEC INC
(*Suby of* TC ENERGY CORPORATION)
7005 Boul Raoul-Duchesne, Becancour, QC, G9H 4X6
(819) 294-1282
Emp Here 30   *Sales* 18,798,420
SIC 4911 Electric services
Wendy L. Hanrahan
Donald J Degrandis

D-U-N-S 24-351-8099   (SL)
VIANDES SEFICLO INC
1660 Av Le Neuf, Becancour, QC, G9H 2E4
(819) 233-2653
Emp Here 100   *Sales* 34,569,000
SIC 2015 Poultry slaughtering and processing
Benoit Hogue
Philippe L. Labelle
Alain Michel
Robert Janody

Bedford, QC J0J

D-U-N-S 24-346-5577   (BR)
CENTRE DE SANTE ET DE SERVICES SO-CIAUX LA POMMERAIE
CSSS DE BEDFORD
34 Rue Saint-Joseph, Bedford, QC, J0J 1A0
(450) 248-4304
Emp Here 400
SIC 8621 Professional organizations
Diane Daigle

D-U-N-S 24-890-8022   (SL)
CENTRE HOSPITALIER DE BEDFORD
34 Rue Saint-Joseph, Bedford, QC, J0J 1A0
(450) 248-4304
Emp Here 100   *Sales* 12,287,700
SIC 8069 Specialty hospitals, except psychiatric
Claude Codere
Pierre Cabot

D-U-N-S 24-228-2887   (HQ)
EXELTOR INC
(*Suby of* GROZ-BECKERT KG)
110 Rue De La Riviere, Bedford, QC, J0J 1A0
(450) 248-4343
Sales 39,685,200
SIC 3965 Fasteners, buttons, needles, and pins
Philip S Champagne
Hans-Jurgen Haug
Karl-Heinz Mattes
Arvid K Rafaelsen
Thomas Lindner

D-U-N-S 24-389-5005   (SL)
KOYO BEARINGS CANADA INC
ROULEMENTS KOYO CANADA
(*Suby of* JTEKT CORPORATION)
4 Rue Victoria S, Bedford, QC, J0J 1A0
(450) 248-3316
Emp Here 225   *Sales* 109,739,250
SIC 5085 Industrial supplies

D-U-N-S 25-526-0762   (HQ)
FROMAGERIE L'ANCETRE INC
1615 Boul De Port-Royal, Becancour, QC, G9H 1X7
(819) 233-9157
Sales 11,242,750
SIC 2022 Cheese; natural and processed
Pascal Desilets
Joseph Boily
Dominic Hamel
Madeleine Desilets Lacourse

D-U-N-S 20-251-2950   (SL)
GUILLEMETTE, MAURICE INC
3635 Boul De Port-Royal, Becancour, QC, G9H 1Y2
(819) 233-2354
Emp Here 28   *Sales* 20,790,560
SIC 5191 Farm supplies
Georgette Guillemette

D-U-N-S 24-296-1431   (SL)
HYDREXCEL INC
665 Av Dutord Bureau 294, Becancour, QC, G9H 2Z6
(819) 294-2728
Emp Here 50   *Sales* 23,751,300
SIC 5084 Industrial machinery and equipment
Mario Blanchette

D-U-N-S 24-370-5782   (BR)
OLIN CANADA ULC
OLIN PRODUITS CHLORALCALIS
(*Suby of* OLIN CANADA ULC)
675 Boul Alphonse-Deshaies, Becancour, QC, G9H 2Y8
(819) 294-6633
Emp Here 175
SIC 2819 Industrial inorganic chemicals, nec
Pierre Ducharme

D-U-N-S 20-928-4298   (HQ)
SILICIUM BECANCOUR INC
TIMMINCO SOLAR
(*Suby of* TIMMINCO LIMITED)
6500 Rue Yvon-Trudeau, Becancour, QC, G9H 2V8
(819) 294-6000
Sales 34,660,444
SIC 3674 Semiconductors and related devices
Rene Boisvert
Robert Dietrich
Peter A M Kalins
John Fenger

D-U-N-S 24-522-6555   (SL)
SILICIUM QUEBEC SOCIETE EN COMMAN-DITE
SILICIUM BECANCOUR
6500 Rue Yvon-Trudeau, Becancour, QC, G9H 2V8
(819) 294-6000
Emp Here 50   *Sales* 10,233,650
SIC 3674 Semiconductors and related devices
Brian D'amico

D-U-N-S 24-863-7506   (SL)
SOCIETE EN COMMANDITE AUBERGE GODEFROY
17575 Boul Becancour, Becancour, QC, G9H 1A5
(819) 233-2200
Emp Here 80   *Sales* 7,415,200
SIC 7011 Hotels and motels
Guy Boisclair
Andre Parent
Claude Heon
Luc Bouvet
Jocelyn Hebert
Solange Rouleau Boisclair
Leon Bouvet

D-U-N-S 20-277-6001   (SL)
SURAL LAMINATED PRODUCTS OF CANADA INC
6900 Boul Raoul-Duchesne, Becancour, QC, G9H 2V2

Carol Belanger
James Gregory
David Basinski
Kenneth Hopkins
Noboyoshi Hisda
Tomokazu Takahashi
Yoshio Tsuji

D-U-N-S 20-415-1294   (SL)
SUPER MARCHE PLOUFFE INC
METRO
5 Av Des Pins, Bedford, QC, J0J 1A0
(450) 248-2968
Emp Here 65   *Sales* 19,076,005
SIC 5411 Grocery stores
Jean-Claude Plouffe

Beloeil, QC J3G

D-U-N-S 20-185-0091   (SL)
AUVENTS MULTIPLES INC
MULTIPLE AWNINGS
1505a Rue De L'Industrie, Beloeil, QC, J3G 0S5
(450) 446-4182
Emp Here 75   *Sales* 14,406,375
SIC 3444 Sheet Metalwork
Pierre Galarineau
Luc Leboeuf
Simon Dufresne
Jean-Francois Tremblay

D-U-N-S 24-849-6130   (SL)
BOISE ST-FRANCIS INC, LE
1981 Rue Bernard-Pilon, Beloeil, QC, J3G 4S5
(450) 446-8221
Emp Here 50   *Sales* 16,356,350
SIC 6531 Real estate agents and managers
Patrice St-Pierre

D-U-N-S 20-580-4201   (BR)
CANADA POST CORPORATION
BUREAU DE POSTES DE BELOEIL
(*Suby of* GOVERNMENT OF CANADA)
595 Boul Sir-Wilfrid-Laurier, Beloeil, QC, J3G 4J1

Emp Here 75
SIC 4311 U.s. postal service

D-U-N-S 24-085-5171   (HQ)
CHAPDELAINE ASSURANCE ET SER-VICES FINANCIERS INC
ULTIMA
220 Rue Brebeuf, Beloeil, QC, J3G 5P3
(450) 464-2112
Emp Here 28   *Sales* 38,162,700
SIC 6411 Insurance agents, brokers, and service
Michel Chapdelaine
Andre Coriveau

D-U-N-S 25-240-5154   (BR)
COMMISSION SCOLAIRE DES PATRIOTES
ECOLE SAINT MATHIEU
(*Suby of* COMMISSION SCOLAIRE DES PA-TRIOTES)
225 Rue Hubert, Beloeil, QC, J3G 2S8
(450) 467-9309
Emp Here 80
SIC 8211 Elementary and secondary schools
Johanne Massie

D-U-N-S 25-240-5477   (BR)
COMMISSION SCOLAIRE DES PATRIOTES
ECOLE SECONDAIRE POLYBEL
(*Suby of* COMMISSION SCOLAIRE DES PA-TRIOTES)
725 Rue De Levis, Beloeil, QC, J3G 2M1
(450) 467-0262
Emp Here 200
SIC 8211 Elementary and secondary schools
Michel Langis

D-U-N-S 20-207-0469   (SL)
CONSTRUCTION PAROX INC
1655 Rue De L'Industrie, Beloeil, QC, J3G 0S5
(450) 813-9655
Emp Here 35   *Sales* 10,100,405
SIC 1522 Residential construction, nec
Martin Letendre
Richard Verreault
Robert Deslandes

D-U-N-S 20-381-4020   (HQ)
DEMERS   BRAUN   MANUFACTURIER D'AMBULANCES INC
28 Rue Richelieu, Beloeil, QC, J3G 4N5
(450) 467-4683
Sales 33,576,450
SIC 3713 Truck and bus bodies
Alain Brunelle
Marie-Claude Boisvert
John Veitch
Andre Lavoie
Lawrence N. Stevenson
Kimberly L. Braun

D-U-N-S 24-683-3227   (HQ)
DEMERS,   AMBULANCE   MANUFACTURER INC
(*Suby of* DEMERS BRAUN MANUFAC-TURIER D'AMBULANCES INC)
28 Rue Richelieu, Beloeil, QC, J3G 4N5
(450) 467-4683
Sales 43,627,500
SIC 3713 Truck and bus bodies
Alain Brunelle
Marie-Claude Boisvert
Lawrence N. Stevenson
John Veitch
Andre Lavoie
Kimberly L. Braun

D-U-N-S 25-323-7697   (SL)
FIBROCAP INC
FIBROBEC, DIV OF
201 Rue Saint-Georges, Beloeil, QC, J3G 4N4
(450) 467-8611
Emp Here 100   *Sales* 22,384,300
SIC 3713 Truck and bus bodies
Frederic Albert
Frederic Chabanne
Philippe Steiger

D-U-N-S 20-190-3671   (SL)
GRENIER ELPHEGE INC
(*Suby of* PLACEMENTS CHABOT ET CORMIER INC, LES)
40 Boul Sir-Wilfrid-Laurier, Beloeil, QC, J3G 4E8
(450) 467-4279
Emp Here 12   *Sales* 10,026,924
SIC 5149 Groceries and related products, nec
Francois Cormier
Leon Chabot

D-U-N-S 20-997-5010   (HQ)
INDUSTRIES BONNEVILLE LTEE, LES
ECONO-FAB
(*Suby of* GROUPE BONNEVILLE INC, LE)
601 Rue De L'Industrie, Beloeil, QC, J3G 0S5
(450) 464-1001
Emp Here 200   *Sales* 69,597,500
SIC 2452 Prefabricated wood buildings
Andre Bonneville
Normand Bonneville
Dany Bonneville
Eric Bonneville

D-U-N-S 20-221-5559   (SL)
JIMEXS INC
1360 Rue Louis-Marchand, Beloeil, QC, J3G 6S3

Emp Here 30   *Sales* 13,415,220
SIC 5072 Hardware
Jean-Pierre Desmarais
Pascal Godbout

D-U-N-S 24-249-4636   (SL)

MARCHE RIENDEAU BELOEIL INC
METRO PLUS RIENDEAU BELOEIL
(*Suby of* ENTREPRISES GAETAN RIEN-DEAU INC, LES)
1030 Rue Saint-Jean-Baptiste, Beloeil, QC, J3G 0J1
(450) 536-1113
Emp Here 50   *Sales* 14,673,850
SIC 5411 Grocery stores
Gaetan Riendeau

D-U-N-S 20-190-4133   (SL)
MARCHES PEPIN INC, LES
IGA PEPIN
865 Boul Yvon-L'Heureux N, Beloeil, QC, J3G 6P5
(450) 467-3512
Emp Here 450   *Sales* 86,608,800
SIC 5411 Grocery stores
Bernard Pepin

D-U-N-S 20-501-5159   (SL)
OUTILLAGE PLACIDE MATHIEU INC
(*Suby of* 1864-8808 QUEBEC INC)
670 Rue Picard, Beloeil, QC, J3G 5X9
(450) 467-3565
Emp Here 30   *Sales* 14,250,780
SIC 5084 Industrial machinery and equipment
Christian Mathieu
Sylvie Mathieu
Solange Mathieu

D-U-N-S 25-198-2195   (SL)
RE/MAX EXTRA INC
365 Boul Sir-Wilfrid-Laurier Bureau 202, Be-loeil, QC, J3G 4T2
(450) 464-1000
Emp Here 49   *Sales* 16,029,223
SIC 6531 Real estate agents and managers
Joyce Paduano

D-U-N-S 20-738-2854   (SL)
SOCIETE PRIBEX LTEE, LA
JEAN COUTU #087
350 Boul Sir-Wilfrid-Laurier, Beloeil, QC, J3G 4G7
(450) 467-0296
Emp Here 53   *Sales* 12,949,384
SIC 5912 Drug stores and proprietary stores
Claude Lemonde
Nathalie Lemonde

D-U-N-S 25-663-0385   (BR)
TRANSDEV QUEBEC INC
LIMOCAR DE LA VALLEE
(*Suby of* TRANSDEV CANADA INC)
1500 Rue Louis-Marchand, Beloeil, QC, J3G 6S3
(450) 446-8899
Emp Here 80
SIC 4131 Intercity and rural bus transportation
Julie Monette

D-U-N-S 20-887-2903   (SL)
TREMBLAY, ANDREE P. PHARMACIEN ENR
PHARMACIE JEAN-COUTU
350 Boul Sir-Wilfrid-Laurier, Beloeil, QC, J3G 4G7
(450) 467-0296
Emp Here 50   *Sales* 12,647,700
SIC 5912 Drug stores and proprietary stores
Andre Patrick Tremblay
Therese Meunier

Berthierville, QC J0K

D-U-N-S 24-581-6699   (HQ)
AUTOMOBILE PAILLE INC
700 Av Gilles-Villeneuve, Berthierville, QC, J0K 1A0
(450) 836-6291
Sales 10,957,716
SIC 5511 New and used car dealers
Claude Paille

D-U-N-S 20-022-8593   (BR)
COMMISSION SCOLAIRE DES SAMARES
ECOLE PIERRE-DE-LESTAGE
(*Suby of* COMMISSION SCOLAIRE DES SAMARES)
881 Rue Pierre-De-Lestage, Berthierville, QC, J0K 1A0
(450) 758-3599
Emp Here 81
SIC 8211 Elementary and secondary schools
Judith Biron

D-U-N-S 20-190-5189   (HQ)
EBI ENERGIE INC
FBI ENERGY
670 Rue De Montcalm, Berthierville, QC, J0K 1A0
(450) 836-8111
Emp Here 10   *Sales* 12,309,300
SIC 1794 Excavation work
Pierre Sylvestre
Rene Sylvestre

D-U-N-S 24-542-6200   (HQ)
EBI ENVIRONNEMENT INC
EBI ENVIRONNEMENT/CDT
670 Rue De Montcalm, Berthierville, QC, J0K 1A0
(450) 836-8111
Emp Here 10   *Sales* 12,856,550
SIC 4953 Refuse systems
Pierre Sylvestre
Rene Sylvestre

D-U-N-S 20-357-0551   (HQ)
FLEET INFORMATIQUE INC
FLEET HEBERGEMENT
750 Rue Notre-Dame Bureau D, Berthierville, QC, J0K 1A0
(450) 836-4877
Emp Here 13   *Sales* 10,285,002
SIC 5045 Computers, peripherals, and soft-ware
Mathieu Fleet

D-U-N-S 24-662-4147   (HQ)
GESTION CEJEMAR INC
MCDONALD'S
1040 Av Gilles-Villeneuve, Berthierville, QC, J0K 1A0
(450) 836-1238
Emp Here 5   *Sales* 11,659,750
SIC 5812 Eating places
Martin Harvey

D-U-N-S 24-252-3363   (BR)
GROUPE CHAMPLAIN INC
CHSLD LE CHATEAU
1231 Rue Dr Olivier-M.-Gendron Pr, Berthierville, QC, J0K 1A0
(450) 836-6241
Emp Here 100
SIC 8361 Residential care
Claude Campeau

D-U-N-S 20-568-8653   (SL)
JEAN COUTU GERMAIN CHARTIER & LIVIO PAROLIN (AFFILIATED PHARMA-CIES)
790 Av Gilles-Villeneuve, Berthierville, QC, J0K 1A0
(450) 836-3733
Emp Here 49   *Sales* 12,394,746
SIC 5912 Drug stores and proprietary stores
Germain Chartier
Livio Parolin

D-U-N-S 24-993-8713   (SL)
MARCHE CROISETIERE BERTHIER INC
EPICERIE I G A
1071 Av Gilles-Villeneuve, Berthierville, QC, J0K 1A0
(450) 836-3775
Emp Here 130   *Sales* 38,152,010
SIC 5411 Grocery stores
Bruno Lambert
Johanne Martel
Sylvie Lambert

Robert Croisetiere

D-U-N-S 24-742-6430   (HQ)
MATRA PLAST INDUSTRIES INC
HI-CORE, DIV OF
(*Suby of* INTEPLAST GROUP CORPORA-TION)
420 Rue Notre-Dame, Berthierville, QC, J0K 1A0
(450) 836-7071
Sales 10,325,770
SIC 3089 Plastics products, nec
Herman Sterling
Robert H Wang
Benjamin Tsao
Joseph Wang

D-U-N-S 24-763-5915   (SL)
MEUBLES D'AUTRAY INC
1180 Rue Gregoire, Berthierville, QC, J0K 1A0
(450) 836-3187
Emp Here 45   *Sales* 10,232,235
SIC 1751 Carpentry work
Richard C.A Darveau

D-U-N-S 20-120-7276   (BR)
OLYMEL S.E.C.
OLYMEL/FLAMINGO
(*Suby of* OLYMEL S.E.C.)
580 Rue Laferriere, Berthierville, QC, J0K 1A0
(450) 836-1651
Emp Here 490
SIC 2011 Meat packing plants
Patrick Bonin

D-U-N-S 24-354-8430   (SL)
OUTILS A. RICHARD CO
120 Rue Jacques-Cartier, Berthierville, QC, J0K 1A0
(450) 836-3766
Emp Here 150   *Sales* 42,157,500
SIC 5251 Hardware stores
Francois Panfili
Richard M Clemence
Richard R. Clemence

D-U-N-S 25-639-5138   (HQ)
PAPIERS C.C.T. INC
830 Rue Saint-Viateur, Berthierville, QC, J0K 1A0
(450) 836-3846
Sales 11,066,400
SIC 2821 Plastics materials and resins
Jacques Chevrette
Yves Therrien

D-U-N-S 24-501-2307   (SL)
PARENT, ALAIN INC
DISTRIBUTION PARAL
640 Rue Notre-Dame, Berthierville, QC, J0K 1A0
(450) 836-4480
Emp Here 75   *Sales* 62,668,275
SIC 5143 Dairy products, except dried or canned
Alain Parent
Denis Parent

D-U-N-S 20-622-4610   (SL)
PIECES D'AUTOS M.R. INC., LES
NAPA PIECES D AUTO
125 Rue D'Iberville, Berthierville, QC, J0K 1A0
(450) 836-7001
Emp Here 25   *Sales* 12,661,377
SIC 5531 Auto and home supply stores
Jean-Francois Racine

Bishopton, QC J0B

D-U-N-S 20-026-1274   (BR)
SHERMAG IMPORT INC
(*Suby of* GROUPE BERMEX INC)
10 Rue Bishop, Bishopton, QC, J0B 1G0

(819) 884-1145
Emp Here 125
SIC 2511 Wood household furniture
Claude Oreilly

Blainville, QC J7B

D-U-N-S 20-249-3318   (SL)
AUTOMOBILES ST-EUSTACHE INC
16 Rue De Braine, Blainville, QC, J7B 1Z1
(514) 927-8977
Emp Here 45   *Sales* 22,413,510
SIC 5511 New and used car dealers
Gilles Pilon

D-U-N-S 20-706-6973   (BR)
CLUBLINK CORPORATION ULC
CLUB DE GOLF FONTAINEBLEAU
(*Suby of* TWC ENTERPRISES LIMITED)
1 Boul De Fontainebleau, Blainville, QC, J7B
1L4
(450) 434-7569
Emp Here 80
SIC 7992 Public golf courses
Frederick St-Germain

D-U-N-S 24-349-5939   (BR)
SUNRISE NORTH SENIOR LIVING LTD
*MAISON DE VIE SUNRISE DE
FONTAINEBLEAU*
(*Suby of* WELLTOWER INC.)
50 Boul Des Chateaux, Blainville, QC, J7B
0A3
(450) 420-2727
Emp Here 80
SIC 8361 Residential care
Christine Lachaine

Blainville, QC J7C

D-U-N-S 24-902-8812   (SL)
2782677 CANADA INC
HYUNDAI BLAINVILLE
1053 Boul Du Cure-Labelle, Blainville, QC,
J7C 2M2
(450) 434-5484
Emp Here 22   *Sales* 10,957,716
SIC 5511 New and used car dealers
Antonio Gennarelli

D-U-N-S 24-934-1355   (SL)
2848-7403 QUEBEC INC
HONDA DE BLAINVILLE
700 Boul Du Cure-Labelle, Blainville, QC, J7C
2J6
(450) 435-1122
Emp Here 61   *Sales* 38,386,080
SIC 5511 New and used car dealers
Claude Leclair

D-U-N-S 20-511-7992   (SL)
9088-3570 QUEBEC INC
ENERTEC RAIL EQUIPEMENT
40 Rue Emilien-Marcoux Bureau 109,
Blainville, QC, J7C 0B5
(450) 420-9814
Emp Here 30   *Sales* 15,599,010
SIC 4789 Transportation services, nec
Jean Desrosiers
Julie Desrosiers
Suzanne Prevost

D-U-N-S 25-989-1195   (SL)
9106-5235 QUEBEC INC
BEADERS CHOICE
1044 Boul Du Cure-Labelle, Blainville, QC,
J7C 2M5
(450) 939-4799
Emp Here 26   *Sales* 13,761,719
SIC 5094 Jewelry and precious stones
Simon Labrecque

D-U-N-S 20-856-7719   (SL)

D-U-N-S 9183-7252 QUEBEC INC

9183-7252 QUEBEC INC
XEBEC
730 Boul Industriel, Blainville, QC, J7C 3V4
(450) 979-8700
Emp Here 60   *Sales* 13,320,060
SIC 3567 Industrial furnaces and ovens
Kurt Sorschak
David B. Ostro
Lynn Moline

D-U-N-S 20-370-3400   (SL)
9306-8906 QUEBEC INC
1083 Boul Du Cure-Labelle Bureau 110,
Blainville, QC, J7C 3M9
(450) 435-1981
Emp Here 50   *Sales* 12,860,419
SIC 5912 Drug stores and proprietary stores
Marie-Claude Favreau
Simon Favreau-Pelchat

D-U-N-S 25-291-4486   (SL)
9323-7055 QUEBEC INC
KOMET INTERNATIONAL
(*Suby of* GROUPE AQUADIS INC, LE)
1190 Boul Michele-Bohec, Blainville, QC, J7C
5S4
(450) 433-2210
Emp Here 45   *Sales* 20,122,830
SIC 5074 Plumbing and heating equipment
and supplies (hydronics)
Francois Nadeau
Guy Nadeau
Gilles Nadeau
Marc Nadeau

D-U-N-S 20-859-0158   (SL)
ACIER PROFILE S.B.B. INC
USINAGE SBB
10 Rue Emilien-Marcoux, Blainville, QC, J7C
0B5
(450) 970-3055
Emp Here 50   *Sales* 22,358,700
SIC 5063 Electrical apparatus and equipment
Patrick Gharzani

D-U-N-S 24-321-3480   (HQ)
APGN INC
GAP NEUROS
(*Suby of* GROUPE AVIATION ET PUIS-
SANCE INC)
1270 Boul Michele-Bohec, Blainville, QC, J7C
5S4
(450) 939-0799
Sales 31,492,835
SIC 3564 Blowers and fans
Omar Hammoud

D-U-N-S 24-871-7860   (SL)
AUTO PLUS J.F. HAMEL INC
ACURA PLUS
255 Boul De La Seigneurie O, Blainville, QC,
J7C 4N3
(450) 435-4455
Emp Here 43   *Sales* 21,417,354
SIC 5511 New and used car dealers
Jean-Francois Hamel

D-U-N-S 24-769-8426   (SL)
**AUTOLOG, GESTION DE LA PRODUCTION
INC**
AUTOLOG
1240 Boul Michele-Bohec, Blainville, QC, J7C
5S4
(450) 434-8389
Emp Here 100   *Sales* 14,703,720
SIC 7379 Computer related services, nec
Sylvain Magnan

D-U-N-S 24-685-2052   (HQ)
BAIN DEPOT INC
BAIN DEPOT
1200 Boul Michele-Bohec, Blainville, QC, J7C
5S4
(450) 433-6930
Emp Here 25   *Sales* 34,860,450
SIC 5719 Miscellaneous homefurnishings
Marc Nadeau
Guy Nadeau

Gilles Nadeau
Francois Nadeau

D-U-N-S 24-016-9750   (SL)
BERLINES TRANSIT INC
ENTRETIEN MECANIQUE BT
719 Boul Industriel Bureau 102b, Blainville,
QC, J7C 3V3
(450) 437-3589
Emp Here 100   *Sales* 5,487,200
SIC 4151 School buses
Christian Cyr
Philippe Cyr

D-U-N-S 20-436-3659   (SL)
BLAINVILLE CHRYSLER DODGE INC
249 Boul De La Seigneurie O, Blainville, QC,
J7C 4N3
(450) 419-5337
Emp Here 49   *Sales* 24,405,822
SIC 5511 New and used car dealers
Eric Corso

D-U-N-S 24-402-8911   (SL)
BLAINVILLE FORD INC
600 Boul Du Cure-Labelle, Blainville, QC, J7C
2H9
(450) 430-9181
Emp Here 40   *Sales* 19,923,120
SIC 5511 New and used car dealers
Rene Arsenault

D-U-N-S 24-474-2268   (SL)
BOISVERT PONTIAC BUICK LTD
470 Boul Du Cure-Labelle, Blainville, QC, J7C
2H2
(450) 430-9400
Emp Here 70   *Sales* 44,049,600
SIC 5511 New and used car dealers
Guy Boisvert

D-U-N-S 24-769-7683   (HQ)
BRASSEURS DU NORD INC, LES
BOREALE
875 Boul Michele-Bohec Bureau 221,
Blainville, QC, J7C 5J6
(450) 979-8400
Sales 51,853,500
SIC 2082 Malt beverages
Daniel Tremblay
Yvan Nantel
Martin Ostiguy
Laura Urtnowski
Alain Denis

D-U-N-S 24-634-8973   (HQ)
CADROPORTE MANUFACTURIER INC
700 Boul Industriel, Blainville, QC, J7C 3V4
(450) 434-9000
Emp Here 30   *Sales* 11,387,655
SIC 5211 Lumber and other building materials
Andre Plante

D-U-N-S 24-126-2364   (BR)
**CAISSE POPULAIRE DESJARDINS DE
L'ENVOLEE**
(*Suby of* CAISSE POPULAIRE DESJARDINS
DE L'ENVOLEE)
1070 Boul Du Cure-Labelle, Blainville, QC,
J7C 2M7
(450) 430-4603
Emp Here 75
SIC 6062 State credit unions
Alain Martineau

D-U-N-S 24-341-6661   (HQ)
CENTRAIDE LAURENTIDES
COMPTOIR D'ENTRAIDE DE LACHUTE
880 Boul Michele-Bohec Bureau 107,
Blainville, QC, J7C 5E2
(450) 436-1584
Sales 11,679,694
SIC 7389 Business services, nec
Serge Paquette
Charles Michaud
Suzanne M Piche

D-U-N-S 20-721-5211   (HQ)

CHARCUTERIE LA TOUR EIFFEL INC
CHARCUTERIE DE BRETAGE
(*Suby of* MCCAIN FOODS GROUP INC)
1020 Boul Michele-Bohec, Blainville, QC, J7C
5E2
(450) 979-0001
Emp Here 100   *Sales* 69,138,000
SIC 2011 Meat packing plants
Ken Carrier
Darryl Rowe
Jillian Moffat
Michael J Campbell

D-U-N-S 24-890-1696   (SL)
CLUB DE GOLF LE BLAINVILLIER INC
200 Rue Du Blainvillier, Blainville, QC, J7C
4X6
(450) 433-1444
Emp Here 110   *Sales* 8,639,950
SIC 7997 Membership sports and recreation
clubs
Olivier Dolbec
Marcel-Paul Raymond
Pierre Laplante
Michel Drouin
Serge Boucher
Bernard Gauthier
Pierre Lamothe
Louise Lessard
Martine Morissette

D-U-N-S 20-290-9156   (SL)
COFFRAGES ATLANTIQUE INC
(*Suby of* INVESTISSEMENTS ATLANTIQUE
INC)
41 Rue Gaston-Dumoulin, Blainville, QC, J7C
6B4
(450) 437-5353
Emp Here 150   *Sales* 31,856,400
SIC 1799 Special trade contractors, nec
Sebastien Boyer

D-U-N-S 20-418-3198   (SL)
CONSTRUCTION BAU-VAL INC
PAVAGES DORVAL, LES
(*Suby of* GESTION PAVAGES DORVAL 2000
INC)
87 Rue Emilien-Marcoux Bureau 101,
Blainville, QC, J7C 0B4
(514) 788-4660
Emp Here 40   *Sales* 10,097,680
SIC 1611 Highway and street construction
Adrien Vigneault
Luc Lachapelle
Jean-Pierre Malo

D-U-N-S 24-163-4836   (HQ)
CORTEX DISTRIBUTION LTD
40 Rue Emilien-Marcoux Bureau 10, Blainville,
QC, J7C 0B5
(450) 686-9999
Emp Here 14   *Sales* 11,875,650
SIC 5087 Service establishment equipment
Patrick English
Ginette Lalonde

D-U-N-S 25-356-6590   (SL)
D.L.G.L. IMMOBILIERE LTEE
850 Boul Michele-Bohec, Blainville, QC, J7C
5E2
(450) 979-4646
Emp Here 95   *Sales* 16,844,545
SIC 7371 Custom computer programming services
Jacques Guenette

D-U-N-S 25-337-8996   (SL)
D.L.G.L. LTEE
850 Boul Michele-Bohec, Blainville, QC, J7C
5E2
(450) 979-4646
Emp Here 90   *Sales* 15,957,990
SIC 7371 Custom computer programming services
Jacques Guenette

D-U-N-S 24-637-0282   (HQ)
DISTRIBUTIONS CHRISTIAN PELLERIN

INC
719 Boul Industriel Bureau 101, Blainville, QC, J7C 3V3
(450) 434-4641
Sales 18,382,694
SIC 5149 Groceries and related products, nec
Christian Pellerin
Santo A. Sata

D-U-N-S 24-053-8306   (HQ)
DUCHESNAY INC
BACINIL
(*Suby of* 3104-0330 QUEBEC INC)
950 Boul Michele-Bohec, Blainville, QC, J7C 5E2
(450) 433-7734
Sales 28,402,100
SIC 2834 Pharmaceutical preparations
Pierre Boivin
Eric Gervais

D-U-N-S 24-800-7510   (SL)
EUROFRET CANADA INC
1140 Boul Michele-Bohec, Blainville, QC, J7C 5N5
(450) 430-1313
Emp Here 40   *Sales* 20,798,680
SIC 4731 Freight transportation arrangement
Robert Morin

D-U-N-S 25-392-5150   (SL)
FENETRES MAGISTRAL WINDOWS INC
705 Boul Industriel, Blainville, QC, J7C 3V3
(450) 433-8733
Emp Here 200   *Sales* 31,771,600
SIC 3089 Plastics products, nec
Martin Charron
Claude Charron
Michel Theoret
Stephane Charron

D-U-N-S 20-332-5402   (HQ)
FIX AUTO CANADA INC
99 Rue Emilien-Marcoux Bureau 101, Blainville, QC, J7C 0B4
(450) 433-1414
Sales 26,533,570
SIC 7532 Top and body repair and paint shops
Steve Leal
Gabrielle Comtois
Jorge Arruda
Isaac David Marshall
Robert Hattem
Daniel Hogg

D-U-N-S 20-381-5526   (SL)
GAZ METROPOLITAIN
1230 Boul Michele-Bohec, Blainville, QC, J7C 5S4
(450) 419-5000
Emp Here 5   *Sales* 15,529,285
SIC 4924 Natural gas distribution

D-U-N-S 24-900-6396   (HQ)
GESTION J.C. FAVREAU LTEE
1083 Boul Du Cure-Labelle Bureau 110, Blainville, QC, J7C 3M9
(450) 435-1981
Emp Here 1   *Sales* 13,077,650
SIC 6712 Bank holding companies
Jean-Claude Favreau

D-U-N-S 20-052-3111   (SL)
GESTION M.L.B. CARDINAL LTEE
CANADIAN TIRE BLAINVILLE
500 Boul De La Seigneurie O Bureau 649, Blainville, QC, J7C 5T7
(450) 419-4700
Emp Here 70   *Sales* 14,374,010
SIC 5311 Department stores
Michel Cardinal
Louise Boudreau

D-U-N-S 20-296-8108   (SL)
GIRAFE SANTE INC
617 Boul Du Cure-Labelle Bureau 100, Blainville, QC, J7C 2J1

Emp Here 100   *Sales* 15,537,100
SIC 7361 Employment agencies
Dany Savard
France Gamache

D-U-N-S 20-266-5139   (HQ)
GROUPE AVIATION ET PUISSANCE INC
1270 Boul Michele-Bohec, Blainville, QC, J7C 5S4
(450) 939-0799
Emp Here 1   *Sales* 15,540,070
SIC 3564 Blowers and fans
Omar Hammoud

D-U-N-S 20-314-2336   (HQ)
GROUPE DCM INC
ENTREPRISE DE SOUDURE AEROSPA-TIALE, DIV DE
890 Boul Michele-Bohec, Blainville, QC, J7C 5E2
(450) 435-9210
Emp Here 100   *Sales* 18,743,660
SIC 7371 Custom computer programming services
Eric-Hertel Ledoux
Yves Martel
Ghislain Lefebvre
Pierre Brouillard
Rejean Bourque
Guillaume Gasparri

D-U-N-S 24-354-6371   (SL)
GROUPE J.C.F. LTEE
PHARMACIE JEAN COUTU
(*Suby of* GESTION J.C. FAVREAU LTEE)
1083 Boul Du Cure-Labelle Bureau 110, Blainville, QC, J7C 3M9
(450) 435-1981
Emp Here 50   *Sales* 12,216,400
SIC 5912 Drug stores and proprietary stores
Jean-Claude Favreau

D-U-N-S 24-293-8470   (HQ)
GROUPE PANDA DETAIL INC
CHAUSSURES PANDA
1060 Boul Michele-Bohec Bureau 108, Blainville, QC, J7C 5E2
(579) 637-9741
Emp Here 1   *Sales* 17,939,600
SIC 5661 Shoe stores
Linda Goulet
Claude Goulet

D-U-N-S 24-821-2685   (SL)
HAMEL AUTOS DE BLAINVILLE INC
HAMEL BMW
620 Boul De La Seigneurie O Bureau 517, Blainville, QC, J7C 5T7
(450) 437-5050
Emp Here 49   *Sales* 24,405,822
SIC 5521 Used car dealers
Jean-Francois Hamel

D-U-N-S 20-008-7000   (HQ)
HITACHI SYSTEMS SECURITY INC
SYSTEMES DE SECURITE HITACHI
(*Suby of* HITACHI, LTD.)
955 Boul Michele-Bohec Bureau 244, Blainville, QC, J7C 5J6
(450) 430-8166
Sales 16,684,700
SIC 7376 Computer facilities management
Fadi Albatal
Daniel Gaudreau
Kenji Kuroki
Kansuke Kuroyanagi
Akira Kusakabe
Robert Lawrie
Masahiro Takano

D-U-N-S 24-052-6764   (SL)
INDUSTRIES TROVAC LIMITEE, LES
CYCLO VAC
3 Rue Marcel-Ayotte, Blainville, QC, J7C 5L7
(450) 434-2233
Emp Here 50   *Sales* 10,233,650
SIC 3635 Household vacuum cleaners

Marc Bruneau

D-U-N-S 20-972-3329   (SL)
LABORATOIRE RIVA INC
660 Boul Industriel, Blainville, QC, J7C 3V4
(450) 434-7482
Emp Here 100   *Sales* 28,402,100
SIC 2834 Pharmaceutical preparations
Andre St-Denis
Olivier St-Denis

D-U-N-S 24-761-7678   (SL)
LABORATOIRES NICAR INC, LES
ALIMENTS NUTRIK
10 Rue Gaston-Dumoulin Bureau 500, Blainville, QC, J7C 0A3
(450) 979-0400
Emp Here 17   *Sales* 37,582,141
SIC 5122 Drugs, proprietaries, and sundries
Regent Racine
Andree Allard

D-U-N-S 20-205-1058   (HQ)
LUSSIER, SIMON LTEE
16 Boul De La Seigneurie E, Blainville, QC, J7C 3V5
(450) 435-6591
Emp Here 10   *Sales* 13,415,220
SIC 5031 Lumber, plywood, and millwork
Jean-Pierre Lussier
Mario Lussier
Mathieu Lussier

D-U-N-S 20-979-5400   (HQ)
MANUFACTURE EXM LTEE
870 Boul Michele-Bohec, Blainville, QC, J7C 5E2
(450) 979-4373
Sales 10,233,650
SIC 3613 Switchgear and switchboard apparatus
Maurizio Ciocca
Steven M Shein
Paola Ciocca

D-U-N-S 25-311-1116   (BR)
MCDONALD'S RESTAURANTS OF CANADA LIMITED
RESTAURANTS MCDONALD'S
(*Suby of* MCDONALD'S CORPORATION)
797 Boul Du Cure-Labelle, Blainville, QC, J7C 3P5
(450) 979-7131
Emp Here 75
SIC 5812 Eating places
Valerie Potvin

D-U-N-S 20-012-7715   (HQ)
MONDOFIX INC
ENTREPRISE MONDOFIX
99 Rue Emilien-Marcoux Bureau 101, Blainville, QC, J7C 0B4
(450) 433-1414
Sales 13,936,200
SIC 6794 Patent owners and lessors
Steve Leal
Daniel Hogg
Jorge Arruda
David Marshall
Robert Hattem

D-U-N-S 20-738-4785   (SL)
MONTOUR LTEE
LEBON
1080 Boul Michele-Bohec, Blainville, QC, J7C 5N5
(450) 433-1312
Emp Here 45   *Sales* 10,118,475
SIC 2099 Food preparations, nec
Marc Montour

D-U-N-S 24-175-7228   (SL)
MOULURES M. WARNET INC
MOULURES WARNET
110 Rue Marius-Warnet, Blainville, QC, J7C 5P9
(450) 437-1209
Emp Here 50   *Sales* 12,652,950

SIC 5211 Lumber and other building materials
Gilles Warnet

D-U-N-S 24-337-9372   (HQ)
NEOPHARM LABS INC
BIOPHARM
865 Boul Michele-Bohec, Blainville, QC, J7C 5J6
(450) 435-8864
Sales 11,016,400
SIC 8734 Testing laboratories
Morris Adler

D-U-N-S 20-381-6611   (BR)
OLYMEL S.E.C.
TRIUMPH FOODS
(*Suby of* OLYMEL S.E.C.)
1020 Boul Michele-Bohec, Blainville, QC, J7C 5E2
(450) 979-0001
Emp Here 200
SIC 2013 Sausages and other prepared meats

D-U-N-S 24-388-0544   (SL)
PETITE BRETONNE (DISTRIBUTION) INC, LA
1210 Boul Michele-Bohec, Blainville, QC, J7C 5S4
(450) 420-9159
Emp Here 19   *Sales* 10,167,356
SIC 5149 Groceries and related products, nec
Serge Bohec

D-U-N-S 24-352-8929   (SL)
PETITE BRETONNE INC, LA
CROISSANTERIE BLANVILLE
1210 Boul Michele-Bohec, Blainville, QC, J7C 5S4
(450) 435-3381
Emp Here 50   *Sales* 11,242,750
SIC 2051 Bread, cake, and related products
Serge Bohec
Audrey Laurin
Dominique Bohec
Charles Bergeron-Vachon
Marcel Ostiguy
Pierre Lafrance
Ghislain Perron

D-U-N-S 24-526-9543   (SL)
PRODUITS M.G.D. INC, LES
LAURENTIDES J'EN MANGES
680 Boul Industriel, Blainville, QC, J7C 3V4
(450) 437-1414
Emp Here 26   *Sales* 13,095,108
SIC 5113 Industrial and personal service paper
Michel Jolicoeur Jr
Johanne Poulin

D-U-N-S 25-647-8272   (SL)
PROSERVIN INC
1250 Boul Michele-Bohec Unite 400, Blainville, QC, J7C 5S4
(450) 433-1002
Emp Here 25   *Sales* 11,768,275
SIC 1542 Nonresidential construction, nec
Eric Boulay

D-U-N-S 24-993-8465   (SL)
PUBCO PRODUITS INTERNATIONALS INC
32 Boul De La Seigneurie E, Blainville, QC, J7C 3V5
(450) 433-4272
Emp Here 80   *Sales* 3,496,504
SIC 3083 Laminated plastics plate and sheet
Wayne Zacard
Nicole Heroux
Tammy Zacard
Patrick Zacard

D-U-N-S 20-962-7355   (SL)
RDC CONTROLE LTEE
1100 Boul Michele-Bohec, Blainville, QC, J7C 5N5
(450) 434-0216
Emp Here 100   *Sales* 22,728,900

SIC 3823 Process control instruments
Donald Codey

D-U-N-S 24-889-8728   (SL)
RECYCLAGE AUTOMOBILES GRAVEL INC
677 Boul Du Cure-Labelle, Blainville, QC, J7C
2J5
(450) 435-8335
Emp Here 40   *Sales* 14,568,600
SIC 5013 Motor vehicle supplies and new
parts
Jean Guy Gravel
Stephane Gravel

D-U-N-S 25-369-4608   (SL)
RPM ENVIRONNEMENT LTEE
RPM ECO
100 Rue Marius-Warnet, Blainville, QC, J7C
5P9
(450) 435-0777
Emp Here 100   *Sales* 25,713,100
SIC 4953 Refuse systems
Dominic Payette

D-U-N-S 25-024-2088   (SL)
SEIGNEURIE BLAINVILLE INC, LA
9 Boul De La Seigneurie E, Blainville, QC, J7C
4G6
(450) 434-3313
Emp Here 200   *Sales* 58,695,400
SIC 5411 Grocery stores
Serge Girard
Julie Girard
Isabelle Girard

D-U-N-S 25-484-9321   (SL)
SERVICE CUISINE G.P. INC
82 Rue Real-Benoit, Blainville, QC, J7C 5J1
(450) 979-9921
Emp Here 130   *Sales* 5,917,470
SIC 5812 Eating places
Gaetan Pilon

D-U-N-S 20-323-8287   (HQ)
SPI SANTE SECURITE INC
60 Rue Gaston-Dumoulin, Blainville, QC, J7C
0A3
(450) 420-2012
Emp Here 40   *Sales* 27,530,550
SIC 5999 Miscellaneous retail stores, nec
Martin Tremblay
Marc Duchesne

D-U-N-S 25-139-0030   (SL)
SPI SECURITE INC
60 Rue Gaston-Dumoulin, Blainville, QC, J7C
0A3
(450) 967-0911
Emp Here 49   *Sales* 12,571,538
SIC 3842 Surgical appliances and supplies
Robert Courteau

D-U-N-S 24-322-3047   (HQ)
STABLEX CANADA INC
760 Boul Industriel, Blainville, QC, J7C 3V4
(450) 430-9230
Sales 31,891,000
SIC 4953 Refuse systems
Jeffrey R. Feeler
Simon G. Bell
Steven D. Welling
Wayne R. Ipsen
Eric Lance Gerratt
Jeffrey R. Fuller
Guy Thibault

D-U-N-S 24-976-4460   (HQ)
SYNERGIE CANADA INC
GROUPE SYNERGIE XPRESS, LE
(*Suby of* GESTION NGMA INC)
60 Rue Emilien-Marcoux, Blainville, QC, J7C
0B5
(450) 939-5757
Emp Here 52   *Sales* 25,998,077
SIC 4731 Freight transportation arrangement
Marc-Andre Guindon
Carl Lariviere
Sebastien Suicco

D-U-N-S 24-788-5429   (SL)
SYSCOMAX INC
(*Suby of* GROUPE SYSCOMAX INC, LE)
1060 Boul Michele-Bohec Bureau 106,
Blainville, QC, J7C 5E2
(450) 434-0008
Emp Here 40   *Sales* 16,909,480
SIC 1541 Industrial buildings and warehouses
Sylvain Robitaille
Melissa Robitaille
Jean-Philip Robitaille

D-U-N-S 24-367-7973   (SL)
SYSTEME INTERIEUR EXCEL + INC
735 Boul Industriel Bureau 107, Blainville, QC,
J7C 3V3
(450) 477-4585
Emp Here 70   *Sales* 11,366,670
SIC 1742 Plastering, drywall, and insulation
Robert Tavano

D-U-N-S 25-381-0634   (SL)
TOITURES HOGUE INC, LES
745 Boul Industriel, Blainville, QC, J7C 3V3
(450) 435-6336
Emp Here 150   *Sales* 18,473,400
SIC 1761 Roofing, siding, and sheetMetal
work
Jocelyn Hogue
Lynda Hogue

D-U-N-S 25-139-3385   (BR)
UNITED PARCEL SERVICE CANADA LTD
UPS
(*Suby of* UNITED PARCEL SERVICE, INC.)
71 Rue Omer-Deserres, Blainville, QC, J7C
5N3
(450) 979-9390
Emp Here 100
SIC 4212 Local trucking, without storage
Claude Trotier

D-U-N-S 20-313-9514   (HQ)
XEBEC ADSORPTION INC
730 Boul Industriel, Blainville, QC, J7C 3V4
(450) 979-8700
Sales 11,553,098
SIC 3567 Industrial furnaces and ovens
Kurt Sorschak
Louis Dufour
Prabhu Rao
Joseph H. Petrowski
Guy Saint-Jacques
William Beckett

Bois-Des-Filion, QC J6Z

D-U-N-S 25-243-2620   (HQ)
AIREAU QUALITE CONTROLE INC
AQC
660 Rue De La Sabliere, Bois-Des-Filion, QC,
J6Z 4T7
(450) 621-6661
Emp Here 27   *Sales* 13,415,220
SIC 5075 Warm air heating and air condition-
ing
Martin Brisebois
Francois Charest

D-U-N-S 24-864-9394   (SL)
**CLUB PISCINE PLUS QUEBEC C.P.P.Q.
INC, LE**
888 Boul Industriel, Bois-Des-Filion, QC, J6Z
4V1
(450) 965-9249
Emp Here 25   *Sales* 17,420,250
SIC 6794 Patent owners and lessors
Martin Rathe
Robert Aumont
Norbert Levasseur
Gerald Naud
Jean-Francois Mauger
Terry Martyniuk
Andre Duguay

Annick Aumont

D-U-N-S 24-138-7534   (SL)
COMPAGNIE TOP TUBES
*REPUBLIC TECHNOLOGIES CANADA, DIV
DE*
870 Boul Industriel, Bois-Des-Filion, QC, J6Z
4V7
(450) 621-9600
Emp Here 80   *Sales* 26,090,880
SIC 3999 Manufacturing industries, nec
Donald R Levin
Seth I. Gold
Stephane David

D-U-N-S 24-819-1517   (SL)
**DAIGNEAULT FERLAND ASSURANCES
INC**
DFA
181 Rue Henry-Bessemer Bureau 103, Bois-
Des-Filion, QC, J6Z 4S9
(450) 621-3666
Emp Here 14   *Sales* 10,156,146
SIC 6311 Life insurance
Yves Daigneault

D-U-N-S 24-954-8132   (SL)
EMSPEC INC
(*Suby of* GROUPE RI2 INC, LE)
904 Rue Jacques Paschini, Bois-Des-Filion,
QC, J6Z 4W4
(450) 430-5522
Emp Here 35   *Sales* 15,651,090
SIC 5063 Electrical apparatus and equipment
Daniel Mongrain
Gabriel Di Tomaso

D-U-N-S 24-001-0467   (SL)
**F.I.D. FUTUR INTERNATIONAL DIVERSIFIE
INC**
926 Rue Jacques Paschini, Bois-Des-Filion,
QC, J6Z 4W4
(450) 621-4230
Emp Here 25   *Sales* 25,811,100
SIC 6799 Investors, nec
Zack Monahoyios

D-U-N-S 24-649-6384   (SL)
MARCHE MONTEE GAGNON INC
I G A
50 Montee Gagnon, Bois-Des-Filion, QC, J6Z
2L1
(450) 621-2266
Emp Here 135   *Sales* 39,619,395
SIC 5411 Grocery stores
Francois Girard
Serge Girard
Jean-Francois Rioux

D-U-N-S 20-230-4226   (HQ)
PLAD EQUIPEMENT LTEE
680 Rue De La Sabliere, Bois-Des-Filion, QC,
J6Z 4T7
(450) 965-0224
Emp Here 40   *Sales* 14,430,065
SIC 3561 Pumps and pumping equipment
Regeant Miron

D-U-N-S 20-416-7860   (SL)
TRANSPORT LAURENTIEN LTEE
926 Rue Jacques Paschini Bureau 300, Bois-
Des-Filion, QC, J6Z 4W4
(450) 628-2372
Emp Here 180   *Sales* 37,027,080
SIC 4212 Local trucking, without storage
Claire Bouchard

D-U-N-S 25-364-7622   (SL)
TRANSPORT TFI 16, S.E.C.
GOLDEN INTERNATIONAL TRANSPORT
801 Boul Industriel Bureau 228, Bois-Des-
Filion, QC, J6Z 4T3
(450) 628-8000
Emp Here 175   *Sales* 35,998,550
SIC 4214 Local trucking with storage
Theresa D'urso
Martin Godbout

Bois-Franc, QC J9E

D-U-N-S 25-365-3265   (BR)
LOUISIANA-PACIFIC CANADA LTD
(*Suby of* LOUISIANA-PACIFIC CORPORA-
TION)
1012 Ch Du Parc-Industriel, Bois-Franc, QC,
J9E 3A9
(819) 449-7030
Emp Here 180
SIC 2431 Millwork

Boisbriand, QC J7E

D-U-N-S 25-503-1270   (HQ)
**GROUPE CONSEIL PARISELLA VINCELLI,
ASSOCIES INC**
PVA CONSULTING GROUP
(*Suby of* GESTION PARISELLA VINCELLI
INC)
20865 Ch De La Cote N Unite 200, Bois-
briand, QC, J7E 4H5
(450) 970-1970
Sales 17,831,580
SIC 8741 Management services

D-U-N-S 20-277-0160   (SL)
PAVAGE DION INC
ENTREPRISE DE PAVAGE DION
20855 Ch De La Cote N, Boisbriand, QC, J7E
4H5
(450) 435-0333
Emp Here 50   *Sales* 11,008,400
SIC 1794 Excavation work
Robert Dion
Alain Dion
Louis-Philippe Dion
Caroline Dion

Boisbriand, QC J7G

D-U-N-S 24-394-5131   (SL)
4525663 CANADA INC
SALAISONS DESCO, LES
87 Rue Prevost, Boisbriand, QC, J7G 3A1
(450) 437-7182
Emp Here 120   *Sales* 41,482,800
SIC 2013 Sausages and other prepared
meats
Guy Chevalier

D-U-N-S 25-395-7021   (HQ)
BOUTIQUE OPTION INC
120 Ch De La Grande-Cote, Boisbriand, QC,
J7G 1B9
(450) 433-2999
Emp Here 5   *Sales* 17,939,600
SIC 5621 Women's clothing stores
Madeleine Mayer Legault
Germain A Legault

D-U-N-S 20-289-0240   (HQ)
COH PROJETS ET SERVICES INC
(*Suby of* GROUPE REEL)
801 Boul Du Cure-Boivin, Boisbriand, QC.
J7G 2J2
(450) 430-6500
Emp Here 1   *Sales* 22,200,100
SIC 3531 Construction machinery
Jacques Rigollot
Sebastien Darveau
Jean-Luc Duconseil

D-U-N-S 24-489-5140   (HQ)
DEMILEC INC
PREMILEC
(*Suby of* HUNTSMAN CORPORATION)
870 Boul Du Cure-Boivin, Boisbriand, QC.
J7G 2A7

---

(866) 345-3916
Sales 11,066,400
SIC 2899 Chemical preparations, nec
Peter Riley Huntsman
Kevin Clyde Hardman
Sean Douglas
David M Stryker

D-U-N-S 20-302-1522   (HQ)
DESTINATIONS ESCAPA INC
CLUB VOYAGE DUMOULIN
362 Ch De La Grande-Cote, Boisbriand, QC,
J7G 1B1
(514) 338-1160
Emp Here 6   *Sales* 15,599,010
SIC 4724 Travel agencies
Stephane Corbeil
Genevieve Dupuy Duplessis

D-U-N-S 20-221-1454   (HQ)
DOUGLAS BARWICK INC
(*Suby of* MARSHALL-BARWICK HOLDINGS
INC)
599 Boul Du Cure-Boivin, Boisbriand, QC,
J7G 2A8
(450) 435-3643
Emp Here 3   *Sales* 14,022,205
SIC 3498 Fabricated pipe and fittings
Alain Laberge
Tim Buckland
Amanda Hawkins
William Nickel
Pierre Desormeaux

D-U-N-S 20-240-1498   (SL)
**GROUPE PICHE CONSTRUCTION (2005)
INC**
755 Boul Du Cure-Boivin Bureau 100, Bois-
briand, QC, J7G 2J2
(450) 433-0783
Emp Here 75   *Sales* 17,571,600
SIC 8742 Management consulting services
Yourik Piche

D-U-N-S 20-220-7049   (HQ)
GUAY BEAUTE INC
585 Boul Du Cure-Boivin, Boisbriand, QC,
J7G 2A8
(514) 273-9991
Sales 21,376,170
SIC 5087 Service establishment equipment
Jean-Paul Hetu
Jean Hetu
Pierre Hetu

D-U-N-S 24-319-8538   (SL)
JENO NEUMAN ET FILS INC
COLLECTION IME
95 Boul Des Entreprises, Boisbriand, QC, J7G
2T1
(450) 430-5901
Emp Here 61   *Sales* 30,397,642
SIC 5137 Women's and children's clothing
Philip Quadros
Shilom Neuman
David H Neuman

D-U-N-S 24-709-6290   (SL)
PERFIX INC
FABRICATION PERFIX
645 Boul Du Cure-Boivin, Boisbriand, QC,
J7G 2J2
(450) 435-0540
Emp Here 100   *Sales* 15,432,200
SIC 2522 Office furniture, except wood
Marc Tardif

D-U-N-S 20-562-1097   (HQ)
REEL COH INC
COH
(*Suby of* GROUPE REEL)
801 Boul Du Cure-Boivin, Boisbriand, QC,
J7G 2J2
(450) 430-6500
Emp Here 150   *Sales* 67,691,357
SIC 3531 Construction machinery
Jacques Rigollot
Sebastien Darveau

Marie-Andree Gravel
Jean-Luc Duconseil
Marie-France Pommaret

D-U-N-S 25-673-7677   (SL)
SERVICE ALIMENTAIRE DESCO INC
97 Rue Prevost, Boisbriand, QC, J7G 3A1
(450) 437-7182
Emp Here 160   *Sales* 55,310,400
SIC 2015 Poultry slaughtering and processing
Guy Chevalier

D-U-N-S 24-680-0143   (BR)
SIGNIFY CANADA LTD
LUMEC
(*Suby of* KONINKLIJKE PHILIPS N.V.)
640 Boul Du Cure-Boivin, Boisbriand, QC,
J7G 2A7
(450) 430-7040
Emp Here 300
SIC 3646 Commercial lighting fixtures
Jean Bernard Goguen

D-U-N-S 24-824-7343   (SL)
SIMO MANAGEMENT
150 Rue Chauvin, Boisbriand, QC, J7G 2N5

Emp Here 49   *Sales* 21,911,526
SIC 5074 Plumbing and heating equipment
and supplies (hydronics)
Marc Verreault

D-U-N-S 25-458-9872   (SL)
SUPERMARCHES DAIGLE, JACQUES INC
IGA
25 Boul Des Entreprises, Boisbriand, QC, J7G
3K6
(450) 430-1396
Emp Here 500   *Sales* 96,232,000
SIC 5411 Grocery stores
Luc Daigle
Robert Daigle

Boisbriand, QC J7H

D-U-N-S 24-458-5329   (SL)
113712 CANADA INC
DISTRIBUTION FARINEX
3780 Rue La Verendrye, Boisbriand, QC, J7H
1R5
(450) 437-7077
Emp Here 85   *Sales* 60,920,860
SIC 5149 Groceries and related products, nec
Cedric O'hayon
Gerard O'hayon
Lisette Ouaknine

D-U-N-S 25-024-0074   (BR)
2755-4609 QUEBEC INC
LIMOCAR BASSES LAURENTIDES ENR
(*Suby of* TRANSDEV CANADA INC)
4243 Rue Marcel-Lacasse, Boisbriand, QC,
J7H 1N4
(450) 435-8899
Emp Here 200
SIC 4131 Intercity and rural bus transportation

D-U-N-S 24-573-3865   (SL)
9109-9861 QUEBEC INC
PETRO CANADA
2525 Boul De La Grande-Allee, Boisbriand,
QC, J7H 1E3
(450) 430-4475
Emp Here 49   *Sales* 24,405,822
SIC 5541 Gasoline service stations
Pierre Turgeon

D-U-N-S 24-245-0158   (SL)
9135-3904 QUEBEC INC
IMPORTS DRAGON
2515 Av De La Renaissance, Boisbriand, QC,
J7H 1T9
(514) 667-0623
Emp Here 30   *Sales* 15,616,260
SIC 5092 Toys and hobby goods and supplies

Stephane Tetrault

D-U-N-S 25-775-4747   (SL)
ABIPA CANADA INC
(*Suby of* FONDS DE SOLIDARITE DES TRA-
VAILLEURS DU QUEBEC (F.T.Q.))
3700 Av Des Grandes Tourelles, Boisbriand,
QC, J7H 0A1
(450) 963-6888
Emp Here 100   *Sales* 22,384,300
SIC 3721 Aircraft
Pierre Racine
Marcel Tetreault
Jean Blondin
Sonia Leveque
Guy Bibeau
Claude Lauzon
Martin Ostiguy
Jean Wilhelmy
Jean Blondin
Nick Malorni

D-U-N-S 24-993-9729   (SL)
ALIMENTS O SOLE MIO INC, LES
ALIMENTS NONNA ROSA, LES
4600 Rue Ambroise-Lafortune, Boisbriand,
QC, J7H 0G1
(450) 435-4111
Emp Here 100   *Sales* 34,569,000
SIC 2098 Macaroni and spaghetti
Alfredo Napolitano
Gennaro Napolitano
Luigi Napolitano
Fiore Napolitano

D-U-N-S 20-292-5574   (SL)
**AP&C REVETEMENTS & POUDRES
AVANCEES INC**
AP&C UNE SOCIETE DE GE ADDITIVE
(*Suby of* GENERAL ELECTRIC COMPANY)
3765 Rue La Verendrye Bureau 110, Bois-
briand, QC, J7H 1R8
(450) 434-1004
Emp Here 100   *Sales* 19,208,500
SIC 3479 Metal coating and allied services
Alain Dupont
Helena Miller
Jocelyne Lagueux

D-U-N-S 20-927-2863   (HQ)
BMI CANADA INC
3437 Boul De La Grande-Allee, Boisbriand,
QC, J7H 1H5
(450) 434-1313
Sales 13,415,220
SIC 5074 Plumbing and heating equipment
and supplies (hydronics)
Marc Bouthillette

D-U-N-S 20-584-8281   (BR)
CANADA POST CORPORATION
POSTE CANADA
(*Suby of* GOVERNMENT OF CANADA)
4570 Rue Ambroise-Lafortune, Boisbriand,
QC, J7H 0E5
(450) 435-4527
Emp Here 100
SIC 4311 U.s. postal service
Yannick Lemaire

D-U-N-S 20-712-1570   (BR)
**COMMISSION SCOLAIRE DE LA
SEIGNEURIE-DES-MILLE-ILES**
*COMMISSION SCOLAIRE DE LA
SEIGNEURIE-DES-MILLE-ILE*
(*Suby of* COMMISSION SCOLAIRE DE LA
SEIGNEURIE-DES-MILLE-ILES)
2700 Rue Jean-Charles-Bonenfant, Bois-
briand, QC, J7H 1P1
(450) 433-5455
Emp Here 149
SIC 8211 Elementary and secondary schools
Lise Lambert

D-U-N-S 24-354-4421   (BR)
COSTCO WHOLESALE CANADA LTD
COSTCO

(*Suby of* COSTCO WHOLESALE CORPO-
RATION)
3600 Av Des Grandes Tourelles, Boisbriand,
QC, J7H 0A1
(450) 420-4500
Emp Here 200
SIC 5099 Durable goods, nec
Daniel Paradis

D-U-N-S 24-769-1736   (SL)
DIMENSIONS PORTES ET FENETRES INC
DIMENSION DOORS
4065 Rue Alfred-Laliberte, Boisbriand, QC,
J7H 1P7
(450) 430-4486
Emp Here 130   *Sales* 74,051,640
SIC 5031 Lumber, plywood, and millwork
Francois Audette
Remy Audette
Mathieu Audette
Micheline Pesant

D-U-N-S 24-837-3813   (HQ)
ELASTO PROXY INC
(*Suby of* GESTIONS CLYVIN INC)
4035 Rue Lavoisier, Boisbriand, QC, J7H 1N1
(450) 434-2744
Emp Here 20   *Sales* 22,275,600
SIC 5199 Nondurable goods, nec
Doug Sharpe
Donna Sharpe

D-U-N-S 25-977-3174   (SL)
ELOPAK CANADA INC
(*Suby of* FERD JHA AS)
3720 Av Des Grandes Tourelles, Boisbriand,
QC, J7H 0A1
(450) 970-2846
Emp Here 318   *Sales* 61,620,132
SIC 2754 Commercial printing, gravure
Regis Rehel
Martin Deslauriers
Marie Colalillo

D-U-N-S 24-727-3852   (SL)
ENTREPRISES Z-TECH INC., LES
4230 Rue Marcel-Lacasse, Boisbriand, QC,
J7H 1N3

Emp Here 26   *Sales* 11,626,524
SIC 5072 Hardware
Raoul Moulinie

D-U-N-S 24-295-5474   (SL)
EQUIPEMENTS QUE-MONT INC, LES
3685 Av Des Grandes Tourelles, Boisbriand,
QC, J7H 0E2
(514) 331-0302
Emp Here 24   *Sales* 10,533,642
SIC 5014 Tires and tubes
Dominic Labelle
Francine Page Warren

D-U-N-S 24-822-6578   (HQ)
EVALUATIONS BIGRAS INC, LES
1919 Boul Lionel-Bertrand Bureau 103, Bois-
briand, QC, J7H 1N8
(450) 420-6555
Emp Here 10   *Sales* 15,523,215
SIC 6311 Life insurance
Sylvain Bigras

D-U-N-S 25-167-9015   (HQ)
GROUPE BEAUDET INC, LE
6455 Rue Doris-Lussier Bureau 110, Bois-
briand, QC, J7H 0E8
(514) 990-5833
Emp Here 1   *Sales* 10,996,300
SIC 7992 Public golf courses
Sylvain Beaudet
Regent L. Beaudet

D-U-N-S 20-543-2065   (SL)
GROUPE BUGATTI INC, LE
BUGATTI INTERNATIONAL
1963 Boul Lionel-Bertrand, Boisbriand, QC,
J7H 1N8

(514) 832-1010
Emp Here 50   *Sales* 26,027,100
SIC 5099 Durable goods, nec
Andrew Hattem
Jason Bishara
Benoit Larose
Freddie Afshar

D-U-N-S 20-300-7281   (SL)
GROUPE COMMENSAL INC
3737 Boul De La Grande-Allee, Boisbriand,
QC, J7H 1M6
(450) 979-5772
Emp Here 50   *Sales* 11,242,750
SIC 2032 Canned specialties
George Kyres

D-U-N-S 24-346-4521   (BR)
HOME DEPOT OF CANADA INC
(*Suby of* THE HOME DEPOT INC)
2400 Boul Du Faubourg, Boisbriand, QC, J7H
1S3
(450) 971-6061
Emp Here 140
SIC 5251 Hardware stores
Carlos Munoz

D-U-N-S 24-799-0831   (SL)
JOCELYN CROTEAU INC
AUBAINERIE, L'
2300 Boul Du Faubourg, Boisbriand, QC, J7H
1S3
(450) 435-0216
Emp Here 150   *Sales* 30,801,450
SIC 5311 Department stores
Jocelyn Croteau

D-U-N-S 25-025-2475   (HQ)
KAESER COMPRESSEURS CANADA INC
(*Suby of* KELLIGER & RUTSCHLE GMBH
MALERGESCHAFT)
3760 Rue La Verendrye, Boisbriand, QC, J7H
1R5
(450) 971-1414
Sales 12,350,676
SIC 5084 Industrial machinery and equipment
Harald Helgo Wagenknecht
Pierre D. Grenier
Thomas Kaeser
Tina-Maria Vlantoussi-Kaeser

D-U-N-S 25-674-3386   (SL)
KIEWIT ENGINEERING CANADA CO.
(*Suby of* PETER KIEWIT SONS', INC.)
4333 Boul De La Grande-Allee, Boisbriand,
QC, J7H 1M7
(450) 435-5756
Emp Here 50   *Sales* 12,622,100
SIC 1629 Heavy construction, nec
Ernie M. Elko
Bruce W. Ballai
Gregory D. Brokke
Anne E. Begley
Richard W. Colf

D-U-N-S 24-000-5657   (SL)
**KIEWIT-NUVUMIUT, SOCIETE EN COPAR-
TICIPATION**
4333 Boul De La Grande-Allee, Boisbriand,
QC, J7H 1M7
(450) 435-5756
Emp Here 50   *Sales* 11,671,750
SIC 1081 Metal mining services
Jean Garon

D-U-N-S 24-357-9625   (SL)
KIEWIT-PARSONS, UN PARTENARIAT
4333 Boul De La Grande-Allee, Boisbriand,
QC, J7H 1M7
(450) 435-5756
Emp Here 200   *Sales* 65,623,000
SIC 1622 Bridge, tunnel, and elevated high-
way construction
Louis Chapdelaine

D-U-N-S 24-422-3306   (SL)
KINOVA INC
KINOVA ROBOTICS

4333 Boul De La Grande-Allee, Boisbriand,
QC, J7H 1M7
(514) 277-3777
Emp Here 135   *Sales* 8,091,273
SIC 3549 Metalworking machinery, nec
Charles Deguire
Louis-Joseph Caron L'ecuyer
Eric Labbe
Marc Dufresne
Hochan Lee

D-U-N-S 20-058-3594   (HQ)
KONTRON CANADA INC
TECHNOLOGIES INOCYBE
(*Suby of* S&T AG)
4555 Rue Ambroise-Lafortune, Boisbriand,
QC, J7H 0A4
(450) 437-5682
Sales 36,760,640
SIC 8731 Commercial physical research
Robert Courteau
Veronique Benard
Hannes Niederhauser
Leo Chan

D-U-N-S 20-253-5274   (SL)
KPH TURCOT, UN PARTENARIAT S.E.N.C
4333 Boul De La Grande-Allee, Boisbriand,
QC, J7H 1M7
(450) 435-5756
Emp Here 750   *Sales* 139,879,500
SIC 8742 Management consulting services
Huguette Emond

D-U-N-S 20-034-2870   (SL)
**L.C. ENTREPRENEURS GENERAUX (2000)
LTEE**
L.C. 2000
4045 Rue Lavoisier, Boisbriand, QC, J7H 1N1
(450) 682-1951
Emp Here 50   *Sales* 23,536,550
SIC 1542 Nonresidential construction, nec
Guy Brodeur
Felix Lachapelle
Jacques Wazen
Anthony Lamarre

D-U-N-S 20-738-6459   (SL)
**L.C. ENTREPRENEURS GENERAUX (2000)
LTEE**
4045 Rue Lavoisier, Boisbriand, QC, J7H 1N1
(450) 682-1951
Emp Here 30   *Sales* 14,121,930
SIC 1542 Nonresidential construction, nec
Guy Brodeur
Felix Lachapelle
Jacques Wazen
Anthony Lamarre

D-U-N-S 24-860-4451   (SL)
LOGISTIQUE CANAMEX INC
1933 Boul Lionel-Bertrand, Boisbriand, QC,
J7H 1N8
(450) 434-1939
Emp Here 20   *Sales* 10,399,340
SIC 4731 Freight transportation arrangement
Sylvain Jarry
Sylvain Grou

D-U-N-S 24-353-4336   (SL)
MAITRE SALADIER INC
(*Suby of* RECIPE UNLIMITED CORPORA-
TION)
1755 Boul Lionel-Bertrand, Boisbriand, QC,
J7H 1N8
(450) 435-0674
Emp Here 200   *Sales* 97,477,000
SIC 2099 Food preparations, nec
Kenneth J. Grondin
Gilles Corriveau
Dave Lantz
Diane Bouchard
Sophie Gagne

D-U-N-S 24-288-3127   (SL)
MEILLEURES MARQUES LTEE
(*Suby of* RECIPE UNLIMITED CORPORA-

TION)
1755 Boul Lionel-Bertrand, Boisbriand, QC,
J7H 1N8
(450) 435-0674
Emp Here 100   *Sales* 71,671,600
SIC 5142 Packaged frozen goods
Kenneth J. Grondin
Pierre Rivard
Dave Lantz

D-U-N-S 25-323-6186   (HQ)
PLAISIRS GASTRONOMIQUES INC
CROQUE-MOI
3740 Rue La Verendrye, Boisbriand, QC, J7H
1R5
(450) 433-1970
Emp Here 300   *Sales* 160,837,050
SIC 2099 Food preparations, nec
Christophe Beauvais
Olivier Beauvais
Jean-Philippe Beauvais

D-U-N-S 20-308-9578   (SL)
PMR INC
(*Suby of* INVESTISSEMENTS PMR INC)
4640 Boul De La Grande-Allee, Boisbriand,
QC, J7H 1S7
(450) 420-7361
Emp Here 50   *Sales* 25,821,414
SIC 3339 Primary nonferrous Metals, nec
Patrick Dupere
Christian Thibault

D-U-N-S 24-018-3699   (SL)
PROLOGUE INC
1650 Boul Lionel-Bertrand, Boisbriand, QC,
J7H 1N7
(450) 434-0306
Emp Here 105   *Sales* 61,861,695
SIC 5192 Books, periodicals, and newspapers
Blaise Renaud

D-U-N-S 25-246-3294   (SL)
PROTECTION INCENDIE POLYGON INC
(*Suby of* SECURITE POLYGON INC)
1935 Boul Lionel-Bertrand, Boisbriand, QC,
J7H 1N8
(450) 430-7516
Emp Here 200   *Sales* 97,546,000
SIC 5087 Service establishment equipment
Jean-Pierre Asselin
Kenneth W Graham
Aleksandar Hoffman
Marc Gagnon
Robert Lapierre
Alain Rousseau
Maurice Lareau
Peter Domenjoz
Jean-Pierre Asselin
Rene Belanger

D-U-N-S 25-359-3081   (HQ)
PROTECTION INCENDIE VIKING INC
PYROSPEC
(*Suby of* SECURITE POLYGON INC)
1935 Boul Lionel-Bertrand, Boisbriand, QC,
J7H 1N8
(450) 430-7516
Emp Here 60   *Sales* 261,111,150
SIC 5063 Electrical apparatus and equipment
Jean-Pierre Asselin
Line Menard
Maurice Lareau
Aleksandar Hoffman
Marc Gagnon
Marc Girouard
Jonathan Roger
Peter Robert Domenjoz

D-U-N-S 20-010-8889   (SL)
**RAUFOSS AUTOMOTIVE COMPONENTS
CANADA INC**
RAUFOSS TECHNOLOGY
(*Suby of* CAG HANDELS-GMBH & CO.KG)
4050 Rue Lavoisier, Boisbriand, QC, J7H 1R4
(450) 419-4911
Emp Here 100   *Sales* 22,384,300

SIC 3714 Motor vehicle parts and accessories
Jean Meredith
Volkmar Dittrich
Guylaine Belanger
Gerhard Anger

D-U-N-S 20-565-7588   (HQ)
SECURITE POLYGON INC
SCS CANADA
1935 Boul Lionel-Bertrand, Boisbriand, QC,
J7H 1N8
(450) 430-7516
Sales 317,024,500
SIC 5087 Service establishment equipment
Jean-Pierre Asselin
Line Menard
Domenjoz Peter
Jonathan Roger
Maurice Lareau

D-U-N-S 24-649-9537   (HQ)
SOTECH-NITRAM INC
3975 Boul De La Grande-Allee, Boisbriand,
QC, J7H 1M6
(450) 975-2100
Emp Here 19   *Sales* 13,519,142
SIC 4731 Freight transportation arrangement
Jacinthe Martin

D-U-N-S 24-354-7267   (BR)
SPECIALITES LASSONDE INC
MONDIV, DIV DE SPECIALITES LASSONDE
(*Suby of* 3346625 CANADA INC)
3810 Rue Alfred-Laliberte, Boisbriand, QC,
J7H 1P8
(450) 979-0717
Emp Here 75
SIC 2033 Canned fruits and specialties
Vito Monopoli

D-U-N-S 24-316-7363   (BR)
**TRANSPORT JAGUAR INTERNATIONAL
INC**
3777 Rue La Fayette O, Boisbriand, QC, J7H
1N5
(450) 433-8000
Emp Here 45   *Sales* 10,119,096
SIC 4213 Trucking, except local
Gerry Lemay
Sebastien Lacasse

D-U-N-S 20-857-1471   (BR)
VETEMENTS S & F (CANADA) LTEE
VETEMENTS S F CANADA, LES
(*Suby of* VETEMENTS S & F (CANADA)
LTEE)
3720 Rue La Verendrye, Boisbriand, QC, J7H
1R5

Emp Here 300
SIC 2311 Men's and boy's suits and coats
Sereo Dilucas

D-U-N-S 25-868-5858   (SL)
VITRERIE VERTECH (2000) INC
VERTECH FENEXPERT
4275 Boul De La Grande-Allee, Boisbriand,
QC, J7H 1M7
(450) 430-6161
Emp Here 50   *Sales* 11,369,150
SIC 1751 Carpentry work
Martin Bergeron

D-U-N-S 20-569-5534   (BR)
WASTE CONNECTIONS OF CANADA INC
ENVIRO CONNEXIONS
(*Suby of* WASTE CONNECTIONS, INC)
4141 Boul De La Grande-Allee, Boisbriand,
QC, J7H 1M7
(450) 435-2627
Emp Here 200
SIC 4953 Refuse systems
Richard Poirier

Boischatel, QC G0A

D-U-N-S 24-942-8103   (SL)
9274-8706 QUEBEC INC
J. D. DODGE CHRYSLER JEEP
5740 Boul Sainte-Anne, Boischatel, QC, G0A 1H0
(418) 822-2424
Emp Here 45   *Sales* 22,413,510
SIC 5511 New and used car dealers
Pierre Tremblay
Richard Laplante

D-U-N-S 20-242-2440   (SL)
AUTO FRANK & MICHEL INC
5790 Boul Sainte-Anne Rr 1, Boischatel, QC, G0A 1H0
(418) 822-2252
Emp Here 45   *Sales* 22,413,510
SIC 5511 New and used car dealers
Frank Theetge

D-U-N-S 20-174-0177   (SL)
AUTO FRANK ET MICHEL INC
5790 Boul Sainte-Anne, Boischatel, QC, G0A 1H0
(418) 822-6686
Emp Here 60   *Sales* 37,756,800
SIC 5511 New and used car dealers
Donald Theetge
Benoit Theetge

D-U-N-S 20-873-2461   (HQ)
CONGEBEC CAPITAL LTEE
5780 Boul Sainte-Anne, Boischatel, QC, G0A 1H0
(418) 822-4077
Emp Here 1   *Sales* 82,239,525
SIC 6719 Holding companies, nec
Laurier Pedneault

D-U-N-S 24-822-0600   (SL)
PRO-PERFORMANCE G. P. L. INC
5750 Boul Sainte-Anne, Boischatel, QC, G0A 1H0
(418) 822-3838
Emp Here 25   *Sales* 12,451,950
SIC 5599 Automotive dealers, nec
Michel Gosselin
Martin Ratte
Marie Laberge

Bon-Conseil, QC J0C

D-U-N-S 20-714-5819   (BR)
AGROPUR COOPERATIVE
NARTEL
(*Suby of* AGROPUR COOPERATIVE)
81 Rue Saint-Felix, Bon-Conseil, QC, J0C 1A0
(819) 336-2727
Emp Here 180
SIC 5143 Dairy products, except dried or canned
Francois Despeau

D-U-N-S 24-933-7411   (SL)
LAMBERT & GRENIER INC
1244 Ch Quatre-Saisons, Bon-Conseil, QC, J0C 1A0
(819) 336-2613
Emp Here 26   *Sales* 10,903,230
SIC 6719 Holding companies, nec
Denis Lambert

D-U-N-S 20-419-8113   (SL)
PIERCON LTEE
387 Rue Notre-Dame, Bon-Conseil, QC, J0C 1A0
(819) 336-3777
Emp Here 50   *Sales* 11,500,950
SIC 3281 Cut stone and stone products
Philippe St-Pierre
Charles St-Pierre

D-U-N-S 24-395-3259   (SL)
SIXPRO INC

1576 10e Rang De Simpson, Bon-Conseil, QC, J0C 1A0
(819) 336-2117
Emp Here 180   *Sales* 9,145,644
SIC 3479 Metal coating and allied services
Richard Bourbeau
Claude Fournier
Sylvain Parenteau
Nathalie Joyal
Denis Valois
Marc Paquin

Bonaventure, QC G0C

D-U-N-S 20-190-9256   (SL)
MAGASIN CO-OP DE BONAVENTURE
IGA
168 Av De Grand-Pre, Bonaventure, QC, G0C 1E0
(418) 534-2020
Emp Here 69   *Sales* 18,916,488
SIC 5411 Grocery stores
Stephen Merry

Boucherville, QC J4B

D-U-N-S 24-612-0422   (SL)
147755 CANADA INC
1501 Rue Ampere Bureau 200, Boucherville, QC, J4B 5Z5
(450) 655-2441
Emp Here 250   *Sales* 91,377,250
SIC 6712 Bank holding companies
Yves Gagnon
Gilles Jean
Peter Keays
Lucie Boies
Jocelyn Letourneau
David Stroddard
Bernard Miron

D-U-N-S 25-165-8936   (HQ)
162069 CANADA INC
EXTRA MULTI-RESSOURCES
1263 Rue Volta, Boucherville, QC, J4B 7M7
(450) 670-1110
Emp Here 425   *Sales* 17,817,800
SIC 7361 Employment agencies
Gilles Fournier

D-U-N-S 24-902-8341   (SL)
2945-9344 QUEBEC INC
MAZDA DUVAL
1540 Rue Ampere, Boucherville, QC, J4B 7L4
(450) 449-7929
Emp Here 40   *Sales* 19,923,120
SIC 5511 New and used car dealers
Luc Duval
Hugues Loranger

D-U-N-S 25-099-2179   (HQ)
2945-9708 QUEBEC INC
TOYOTA DUVAL
1175 Rue Ampere, Boucherville, QC, J4B 7M6
(450) 655-2350
Sales 13,077,650
SIC 6712 Bank holding companies
Luc Duval

D-U-N-S 25-202-4211   (SL)
2953-6778 QUEBEC INC
S.R.M. PLOMBERIE & CHAUFFAGE
549 Rue De Verrazano Bureau 3000, Boucherville, QC, J4B 7W2
(450) 449-1516
Emp Here 525   *Sales* 142,195,200
SIC 1711 Plumbing, heating, air-conditioning
Eddy Junior Savoie
Carmelle Savoie Ouellette
Nathalie Savoie

D-U-N-S 20-760-8662   (HQ)
4270797 CANADA INC
(*Suby of* CHEMARKETING INDUSTRIES INC)
1270 Rue Nobel, Boucherville, QC, J4B 5H1
(450) 645-0296
Emp Here 38   *Sales* 11,066,400
SIC 2899 Chemical preparations, nec
James Robert Fell

D-U-N-S 20-290-6095   (HQ)
7577010 CANADA INC
BMR MATCO
(*Suby of* GESTION BMR INC)
1501 Rue Ampere Bureau 200, Boucherville, QC, J4B 5Z5
(450) 655-2441
Emp Here 1   *Sales* 281,050,000
SIC 5211 Lumber and other building materials
Ghislain Gervais
Luc Forget
Muriel Dubois
Jean-Francois Harel
Martin Juneau

D-U-N-S 20-547-4856   (HQ)
9138-4438 QUEBEC INC
CENTRE DES CONGRES DE BOUCHEV-ERVILLE
1228 Rue Nobel, Boucherville, QC, J4B 5H1
(450) 655-9966
Emp Here 2   *Sales* 24,601,500
SIC 6712 Bank holding companies
Danielle Beaulieu

D-U-N-S 24-368-2486   (SL)
9164-2033 QUEBEC INC
HOTEL MORTAGNE
(*Suby of* 9138-4438 QUEBEC INC)
1228 Rue Nobel, Boucherville, QC, J4B 5H1
(450) 655-9966
Emp Here 90   *Sales* 8,342,100
SIC 7011 Hotels and motels
Danielle Beaulieu

D-U-N-S 20-270-5836   (SL)
9314-8591 QUEBEC INC
EMMI CANADA
(*Suby of* GENOSSENSCHAFT ZEN-TRALSCHWEIZER MILCHPRODUZENTEN ZMP)
1250 Rue Nobel Bureau 200, Boucherville, QC, J4B 5H1
(450) 645-2211
Emp Here 20   *Sales* 16,711,540
SIC 5143 Dairy products, except dried or canned
Linda Methot
Matthias Kunz
Francois Huguenin
Jorg Riboni

D-U-N-S 25-242-8453   (SL)
ACIER INOXYDABLE FAFARD INC
S.T.A.F. INOXYDABLE
21 Rue De Montgolfier, Boucherville, QC, J4B 8C4
(450) 641-4349
Emp Here 60   *Sales* 14,006,100
SIC 3312 Blast furnaces and steel mills
Jean-Francois Fafard
France Letendre

D-U-N-S 24-858-9269   (BR)
ADP CANADA CO
DEALER SERVICES GROUP
(*Suby of* AUTOMATIC DATA PROCESSING, INC.)
204 Boul De Montarville, Boucherville, QC, J4B 6S2

Emp Here 110
SIC 7374 Data processing and preparation
Louis-Yves Cloutier

D-U-N-S 24-395-1675   (HQ)
ATELIER LA FLECHE DE FER INC, L'

AFFI
1730 Rue Eiffel, Boucherville, QC, J4B 7W1
(450) 552-9150
Emp Here 350   *Sales* 25,563,648
SIC 8322 Individual and family services
Daniel Perreault
Roger Pedneault
Jean-Charles Dagenais
Pierre Bariteau
Fernand R. Plante
Pierre Hebert
Denis Roy
Mireille Berichon
Sylvie L'ecuyer

D-U-N-S 20-277-1403   (HQ)
AURREA SIGNATURE INC
AURREA SIGNATURE MD
1205 Rue Ampere Bureau 201, Boucherville, QC, J4B 7M6
(450) 650-2151
Emp Here 10   *Sales* 25,441,800
SIC 6411 Insurance agents, brokers, and service
Marc Peliel
Christian Laroche

D-U-N-S 24-364-8073   (HQ)
AZELIS CANADA INC
ADDITIFS DE PERFORMANCE ELITE
(*Suby of* AZELIS US HOLDING, INC.)
1570 Rue Ampere Bureau 106, Boucherville, QC, J4B 7L4
(450) 449-6363
Emp Here 50   *Sales* 60,499,080
SIC 5169 Chemicals and allied products, nec
Frank Bergonzi
Jean-Pierre Pelchat
Bernard Vinet
Terence Moriarty
Joseph Balducci

D-U-N-S 24-376-6248   (HQ)
BAU-VAL INC
3RETC
210 Boul De Montarville Bureau 2006, Boucherville, QC, J4B 6T3
(514) 875-4270
Emp Here 11   *Sales* 40,538,400
SIC 1429 Crushed and broken stone, nec
Luc Lachapelle
Jean-Pierre Malo

D-U-N-S 25-152-2074   (HQ)
BEAUDEV GESTIONS INC
HALLMARK
102 Ch Du Tremblay, Boucherville, QC, J4B 6Z6

Emp Here 2   *Sales* 14,659,680
SIC 5947 Gift, novelty, and souvenir shop
Jacques Beaulieu
Huguette Beaulieu
Eric Beaulieu
Alain Beaulieu

D-U-N-S 20-211-3908   (SL)
BELANGER LAMINES INC
BELANGER-VT INDUSTRIES
(*Suby of* V-T INDUSTRIES INC.)
1435 Rue Joliot-Curie, Boucherville, QC, J4B 7M4
(450) 449-3447
Emp Here 150   *Sales* 23,148,300
SIC 2541 Wood partitions and fixtures
Jean-Yves Brochu
Nancy Bedard
Douglas E. Clausen

D-U-N-S 25-344-4970   (HQ)
BELL TECHNICAL SOLUTIONS INC
(*Suby of* BCE INC)
75 Rue J.-A.-Bombardier Suite 200, Boucherville, QC, J4B 8P1
(450) 449-1120
Emp Here 90   *Sales* 588,772,500
SIC 1731 Electrical work

Declan Brady
Michel Lalande

D-U-N-S 20-860-3092   (SL)
BELLEMONT POWELL LTEE
(*Suby of* C.B. POWELL LIMITED)
1570 Rue Ampere Unite 508, Boucherville,
QC, J4B 7L4
(450) 641-2661
Emp Here 22   *Sales* 18,382,694
SIC 5141 Groceries, general line
Dino Fareese
Emile Bonneville

D-U-N-S 24-311-1544   (BR)
BEST BUY CANADA LTD
FUTURE SHOP
(*Suby of* BEST BUY CO., INC.)
584 Ch De Touraine Bureau 101, Boucherville,
QC, J4B 8S5

Emp Here 80
SIC 5999 Miscellaneous retail stores, nec

D-U-N-S 24-811-5714   (SL)
BILODEAU, L. & FILS LTEE
1405 Rue Graham-Bell Bureau 101,
Boucherville, QC, J4B 6A1
(450) 449-6542
Emp Here 49   *Sales* 25,478,383
SIC 4724 Travel agencies
Isabelle Bilodeau

D-U-N-S 20-191-0015   (SL)
BOISVERT, P.E. AUTO LTEE
BOISVERT AUTO
2 Boul Marie-Victorin, Boucherville, QC, J4B
1V5
(514) 527-8215
Emp Here 140   *Sales* 88,099,200
SIC 5511 New and used car dealers
Pierre Boisvert
Lisette Boisvert
Francois Boisverrt

D-U-N-S 24-527-5169   (HQ)
BRIDOR INC
BOULANGERIE AU PAIN DORE
1370 Rue Graham-Bell, Boucherville, QC, J4B
6H5
(450) 641-1265
Emp Here 100   *Sales* 194,954,000
SIC 2053 Frozen bakery products, except
bread
Louis Le Duff
Pascale Closson-Duquette
Guillaume Avenet
Maryvonne Guillou

D-U-N-S 24-329-8069   (HQ)
CAISSE DESJARDINS DE BOUCHERVILLE
CENTRE DE SERVICES FORT ST-LOUIS
1071 Boul De Montarville, Boucherville, QC,
J4B 6R2
(450) 655-9041
Emp Here 30   *Sales* 14,781,805
SIC 6062 State credit unions
Paul Dulude
Claude Dupras
Guy Chauvin
Mireille Noiseux
Philippe Archambault
Simon Robert
Lydia Halley-Soucy
Linda Labbe

D-U-N-S 24-110-4967   (HQ)
CAMIONS LAGUE INC
205 Ch Du Tremblay, Boucherville, QC, J4B
6L6
(450) 655-6940
Sales 14,165,000
SIC 7538 General automotive repair shops
Genevieve Lague
Maryline Lague
Jean-Philippe Lague

D-U-N-S 24-741-6738   (BR)

CARQUEST CANADA LTD
CARQUEST DISTRIBUTION CENTER
(*Suby of* ADVANCE AUTO PARTS, INC.)
1670 Rue Eiffel Bureau 100, Boucherville, QC,
J4B 7W1
(450) 641-5757
Emp Here 150
SIC 4225 General warehousing and storage
Guy Lagace

D-U-N-S 20-214-5090   (SL)
CELANESE CANADA ULC
50 Boul Marie-Victorin Bureau 100,
Boucherville, QC, J4B 1V5
(450) 655-0396
Emp Here 50   *Sales* 13,833,000
SIC 2819 Industrial inorganic chemicals, nec
Pierre Morin
Christopher W. Jensen
Scott Richardson
Peacock Iii James R.

D-U-N-S 24-890-8139   (SL)
CENTRE D'ACCEUIL JEANNE CREVIER
151 Rue De Muy, Boucherville, QC, J4B 4W7

Emp Here 80   *Sales* 4,739,760
SIC 8361 Residential care
Gisele Lacoste

D-U-N-S 25-359-5581   (BR)
CINTAS CANADA LIMITED
SALLY FOURMY & ASSOCIATES
(*Suby of* CINTAS CORPORATION)
1470 Rue Nobel, Boucherville, QC, J4B 5H3
(450) 449-4747
Emp Here 85
SIC 7218 Industrial launderers
James Dawe

D-U-N-S 20-502-4870   (SL)
CLARK, DROUIN, LEFEBVRE INC
1301 Rue Gay-Lussac, Boucherville, QC, J4B
7K1
(450) 449-4171
Emp Here 200   *Sales* 143,343,200
SIC 5141 Groceries, general line
Yvan Normandeau
Pierre Taillebois

D-U-N-S 24-865-8494   (SL)
CLOTURE SPEC-II INC
65 Rue De Montgolfier, Boucherville, QC, J4B
8C4
(450) 449-7732
Emp Here 30   *Sales* 13,415,220
SIC 5039 Construction materials, nec
Gaston Miousse
Daniel Miousse

D-U-N-S 20-929-0972   (HQ)
COMPROD INC
COMMUNICATIONS COMPROD
88 Boul Industriel, Boucherville, QC, J4B 2X2
(450) 641-1454
Emp Here 67   *Sales* 15,307,624
SIC 4899 Communication services, nec
Gilles Racine
Claudette Racine
Fernando Apolinario

D-U-N-S 24-835-5018   (HQ)
CONSTRUCTION DJL INC
*CARRIERE MONT-BRUNO DIVISION DE
CONSTRUCTION DJL*
(*Suby of* VINCI)
1550 Rue Ampere Bureau 200, Boucherville,
QC, J4B 7L4
(450) 641-8000
Emp Here 40   *Sales* 98,434,500
SIC 1611 Highway and street construction
Patrick Sulliot
Xavier Lansade
Philippe Princet

D-U-N-S 20-338-9924   (SL)
CONSULTANTS LUPIEN ROULEAU INC
FILATURE EXPERT

1550 Rue Ampere Bureau 301, Boucherville,
QC, J4B 5Z5
(450) 449-7333
Emp Here 25   *Sales* 11,087,250
SIC 7389 Business services, nec
Roch Rouleau

D-U-N-S 20-109-6406   (BR)
COOP FEDEREE, LA
OLYMEL
(*Suby of* COOP FEDEREE, LA)
1580 Rue Eiffel, Boucherville, QC, J4B 5Y1
(450) 449-6344
Emp Here 200
SIC 5191 Farm supplies
Richard Davies

D-U-N-S 24-340-5474   (BR)
COSTCO WHOLESALE CANADA LTD
COSTCO WHOLESALE
(*Suby of* COSTCO WHOLESALE CORPO-
RATION)
635 Ch De Touraine, Boucherville, QC, J4B
5E4
(450) 645-2631
Emp Here 200
SIC 5099 Durable goods, nec
Francois Gauthier

D-U-N-S 20-277-2133   (BR)
CRT - EBC, S.E.N.C.
(*Suby of* CRT - EBC, S.E.N.C.)
95 Rue J.-A.-Bombardier Bureau 4,
Boucherville, QC, J4B 8P1

Emp Here 100
SIC 7363 Help supply services

D-U-N-S 20-237-6513   (HQ)
DANONE INC
DANONE CANADA
(*Suby of* DANONE)
100 Rue De Lauzon, Boucherville, QC, J4B
1E6
(450) 655-7331
Emp Here 400   *Sales* 219,323,250
SIC 2026 Fluid milk
Pedro Silveira
Isabelle Rayle-Doiron
Clemence Delcourt

D-U-N-S 24-935-4382   (HQ)
DANS UN JARDIN CANADA INC
PARFUMERIES DANS UN JARDIN CANADA
(*Suby of* 3903842 CANADA INC)
240 Boul Industriel, Boucherville, QC, J4B
2X4
(450) 449-2121
Emp Here 40   *Sales* 45,884,250
SIC 5999 Miscellaneous retail stores, nec
Real Lafrance
Eric Arminjon

D-U-N-S 24-942-0027   (HQ)
DANS UN JARDIN INC
(*Suby of* 3903842 CANADA INC)
240 Boul Industriel, Boucherville, QC, J4B
2X4
(450) 449-2121
Sales 91,377,250
SIC 6712 Bank holding companies
Gilles Sansregret
Real Lafrance
Sylvain Lafrance
Martin Lafrance

D-U-N-S 20-919-4294   (HQ)
DESLAURIERS & ASSOCIES INC
210 Boul De Montarville Bureau 3015,
Boucherville, QC, J4B 6T3
(450) 641-1911
Emp Here 14   *Sales* 20,353,440
SIC 6411 Insurance agents, brokers, and ser-
vice
Stephan Bernatchez

D-U-N-S 20-332-3332   (SL)
DISTRIBUTION STOX INC

DISTRIBU-PNEUS
235 Rue J.-A.-Bombardier, Boucherville, QC,
J4B 8P1
(450) 449-0362
Emp Here 250   *Sales* 115,288,500
SIC 5014 Tires and tubes
Jocelyn Bernard
Denis Desharnais
Bruno Leclair
Martin Labrecque
Stephane Ratte
Normand Lavoie
Gilles C. Lachance

D-U-N-S 24-696-2307   (SL)
**DISTRIBUTIONS ALIMENTAIRES LE MAR-
QUIS INC**
MARQUIS
1630 Rue Eiffel Bureau 1, Boucherville, QC,
J4B 7W1
(450) 645-1999
Emp Here 100
SIC 7389 Business services, nec
Jopseph Pulla
Moody Talaat

D-U-N-S 24-590-9726   (SL)
**DISTRIBUTIONS ALIMENTAIRES LE MAR-
QUIS INC**
PLANTERS
1250 Rue Nobel Bureau 190, Boucherville,
QC, J4B 5H1
(450) 655-4764
Emp Here 80   *Sales* 66,846,160
SIC 5141 Groceries, general line
Carl Leblanc
Joe Pulla

D-U-N-S 24-323-7203   (SL)
DUBREUIL, GILLES LTEE
CANADIAN TIRE
1055 Boul De Montarville Bureau 332,
Boucherville, QC, J4B 6P5
(450) 655-6950
Emp Here 100   *Sales* 36,421,500
SIC 5014 Tires and tubes
Gilles Dubreuil

D-U-N-S 25-200-7232   (SL)
DUVAL VOLKSWAGEN INC
VOLKSWAGEN
(*Suby of* 2945-9708 QUEBEC INC)
1301 Rue Ampere, Boucherville, QC, J4B 5Z5
(450) 679-0890
Emp Here 35   *Sales* 17,432,730
SIC 5511 New and used car dealers
Luc Duval
Marc-Andre Ladouceur

D-U-N-S 20-736-2138   (SL)
EBENISTERIE NORCLAIR INC
NORCLAIR
155 Rue Jules-Leger, Boucherville, QC, J4B
7K8
(450) 641-1737
Emp Here 100   *Sales* 23,240,300
SIC 5712 Furniture stores
Steve Pilon
Andre Lachance
Mario Leduc
Alain Valiquette

D-U-N-S 24-864-9527   (HQ)
EMBALLAGES CARROUSEL INC, LES
CAVALIER ET DESSIN
1401 Rue Ampere, Boucherville, QC, J4B 6C5
(450) 655-2025
Emp Here 100   *Sales* 209,383,250
SIC 5113 Industrial and personal service pa-
per
Brigitte Jalbert
Martin Boily

D-U-N-S 24-024-9933   (BR)
EMPIRE SPORTS INC
(*Suby of* EMPIRE SPORTS INC)
1155c Place Nobel, Boucherville, QC, J4B

7L3
(450) 645-9998
Emp Here 80
SIC 5941 Sporting goods and bicycle shops
Phil Grise

D-U-N-S 20-265-6013   (HQ)
EUROVIA QUEBEC CONSTRUCTION INC
EUROVIA QC CONSTRUCTION
(*Suby of* VINCI)
1550 Rue Ampere Bureau 200, Boucherville,
QC, J4B 7L4
(450) 641-8000
Emp Here 150   *Sales* 656,230,000
SIC 1611 Highway and street construction
Christophe Verweirde
Patrick Sulliot
Xavier Lansade
Xavier Neuschwander
Gabriel Duchesne

D-U-N-S 20-277-5813   (SL)
**EUROVIA QUEBEC GRANDS PROJETS
INC**
EUROVIA QC GP
(*Suby of* VINCI)
1550 Rue Ampere Bureau 200, Boucherville,
QC, J4B 7L4
(450) 641-8000
Emp Here 100   *Sales* 25,244,200
SIC 1611 Highway and street construction
Christophe Verweirde
Xavier Lansade
Patrick Sulliot
Gabriel Duchesne

D-U-N-S 24-005-1529   (SL)
FONDATION SOURCE BLEU
*MAISON DE SOINS PALLIATIFS SOURCE
BLEUE*
1130 Rue De Montbrun, Boucherville, QC,
J4B 8W6
(450) 641-3165
Emp Here 49   *Sales* 19,473,286
SIC 8699 Membership organizations, nec
Claude Beauchamp

D-U-N-S 20-039-1918   (SL)
**FOURNITURE DE PLANCHERS INNOVAT-
IFS INC**
1280   Rue   Graham-Bell   Bureau   1,
Boucherville, QC, J4B 6H5
(450) 641-4566
Emp Here 10   *Sales* 18,626,625
SIC 1752 Floor laying and floor work, nec
Joseph Lui
William Friend

D-U-N-S 24-205-4000   (SL)
GAZ METRO PLUS INC
GMP
(*Suby of* NOVERCO INC)
1350 Rue Nobel Bureau 100, Boucherville,
QC, J4B 5H3
(450) 641-6300
Emp Here 57   *Sales* 10,962,696
SIC 7699 Repair services, nec
Stephanie Trudeau
Nathalie Longval
Carole Carle
Andre G. Nadeau
Mario Gagne

D-U-N-S 24-871-4552   (HQ)
GESTION J. M. BRASSEUR INC
1361 Rue Graham-Bell, Boucherville, QC, J4B
6A1
(450) 655-3155
Sales 34,569,000
SIC 2047 Dog and cat food
Jacinthe Brasseur
Jocelyn Brasseur
Jean Brasseur

D-U-N-S 20-013-0974   (SL)
GESTION MICHEL JULIEN INC
115 Rue De Lauzon, Boucherville, QC, J4B

1E7
(450) 641-3150
Emp Here 110   *Sales* 30,068,500
SIC 6712 Bank holding companies
Julien Michel

D-U-N-S 24-814-1079   (HQ)
GRAYMONT (QC) INC
BULL DOG
(*Suby of* GRAYMONT LIMITED)
25 Rue De Lauzon Bureau 206, Boucherville,
QC, J4B 1E7
(450) 449-2262
Emp Here 100   *Sales* 144,588,150
SIC 1422 Crushed and broken limestone
Weir J. Graham
Stephane Godin
Chris Davies
Celia Helen Johnson
Steve Boulay

D-U-N-S 20-194-6050   (HQ)
GROUPE BMR INC
BMR AGRIZONE
(*Suby of* GESTION BMR INC)
1501 Rue Ampere Bureau 200, Boucherville,
QC, J4B 5Z5
(450) 655-2441
Emp Here 70   *Sales* 730,487,040
SIC 5039 Construction materials, nec
Ghislain Gervais
Murial Dubois
Jean-Francois Harel
Mathieu Couture
Martin Juneau

D-U-N-S 24-353-5528   (BR)
GROUPE BMR INC
BMR
(*Suby of* GESTION BMR INC)
1660 Rue Eiffel, Boucherville, QC, J4B 7W1
(450) 655-2441
Emp Here 130
SIC 5072 Hardware

D-U-N-S 25-088-5787   (BR)
GROUPE BOUTIN INC
128 Ch Du Tremblay, Boucherville, QC, J4B
6Z6
(450) 449-7373
Emp Here 500
SIC 4213 Trucking, except local
Jacques Ladouceur

D-U-N-S 24-942-4482   (BR)
GROUPE CANAM INC
INDUSTRIES TANGUAY
(*Suby of* CANAM LUX PARENT COMPANY
SARL)
270 Ch Du Tremblay, Boucherville, QC, J4B
5X9
(418) 251-3152
Emp Here 140
SIC 3531 Construction machinery
Rene Guizzetti

D-U-N-S 20-139-2375   (BR)
GROUPE CANAM INC
MUROX
(*Suby of* CANAM LUX PARENT COMPANY
SARL)
270 Ch Du Tremblay, Boucherville, QC, J4B
5X9
(866) 506-4000
Emp Here 150
SIC 3441 Fabricated structural Metal
Anne Quirion

D-U-N-S 25-883-1684   (BR)
GROUPE CANAM INC
(*Suby of* CANAM LUX PARENT COMPANY
SARL)
200 Boul Industriel, Boucherville, QC, J4B
2X4
(450) 641-8770
Emp Here 80
SIC 3441 Fabricated structural Metal
Alain Leduc

D-U-N-S 24-388-9396   (HQ)
GROUPE COLABOR INC
*BERTRAND DISTRIBUTEUR EN ALIMENTA-
TION*
1620 Boul De Montarville, Boucherville, QC,
J4B 8P4
(450) 449-4911
Emp Here 10   *Sales* 911,933,025
SIC 5141 Groceries, general line
Lionel Ettedgui
Michel Delisle
Daniel Valiquette
Elisabeth Tremblay
Mathieu Dumulong
John Hemeon
Robert Cloutier
Robert J. Briscoe
Robert B. Johnston
Marc Baillargeon

D-U-N-S 25-496-1485   (SL)
GROUPE INTERSAND CANADA INC, LE
INTERSAND CANADA
125 Rue De La Barre, Boucherville, QC, J4B
2X6
(450) 449-7070
Emp Here 50   *Sales* 11,671,750
SIC 3295 Minerals, ground or treated
Stephane Chevigny

D-U-N-S 20-980-1315   (HQ)
GROUPE MASTER INC, LE
(*Suby of* GESTION GROUPE MASTER INC)
1675 Boul De Montarville, Boucherville, QC,
J4B 7W4
(514) 527-2301
Emp Here 190   *Sales* 322,030,800
SIC 5075 Warm air heating and air condition-
ing
Michel Ringuet
Jacques Foisy
Louis St-Laurent
Alain Fournier
Jean-Francois Routhier
Marc Paiement

D-U-N-S 24-870-0155   (BR)
GROUPE ROBERT INC
TRANSPORT ROBERT
(*Suby of* GROUPE ROBERT INC)
20 Boul Marie-Victorin, Boucherville, QC, J4B
1V5
(514) 521-1011
Emp Here 500
SIC 4212 Local trucking, without storage
Claude Robert

D-U-N-S 20-514-4723   (BR)
GROUPE ROBERT INC
CENTRE DE DISTRIBUTION ROBERT
(*Suby of* GROUPE ROBERT INC)
65 Rue De Vaudreuil, Boucherville, QC, J4B
1K7
(514) 521-1416
Emp Here 200
SIC 4225 General warehousing and storage
Rejean Lacharite

D-U-N-S 25-865-1660   (BR)
GROUPE ROBERT INC
ROBERT TRANSPORT
(*Suby of* GROUPE ROBERT INC)
20 Boul Marie-Victorin, Boucherville, QC, J4B
1V5
(514) 521-1011
Emp Here 100
SIC 4213 Trucking, except local
Jean-Yves Letarte

D-U-N-S 20-015-8256   (HQ)
GROUPE SIMONEAU INC, LE
1541 Rue De Coulomb, Boucherville, QC, J4B
8C5
(450) 641-9140
Sales 12,828,100
SIC 3823 Process control instruments
Nancy Simoneau

D-U-N-S 24-053-1038   (HQ)
GROUPE SPORTSCENE INC
CAGE AUX SPORTS, LA
1180 Place Nobel Bureau 102, Boucherville,
QC, J4B 5L2
(450) 641-3011
Emp Here 52   *Sales* 75,879,827
SIC 5812 Eating places
Jean Bedard
Charles St-Germain
Louis-Francois Marcotte
Jeanne Lebrun
Jean-Francois Dube
Josee Pepin
Francois-Xavier Pilon
Annick Mongeau
Rene Vachon
Nelson Gentiletti

D-U-N-S 24-789-2193   (SL)
GROUPE ULTRAGEN LTEE, LE
50 Rue De Lauzon, Boucherville, QC, J4B 1E6
(450) 650-0770
Emp Here 75   *Sales* 13,196,850
SIC 8711 Engineering services
Khac Trong Truong
Steve Surveyer

D-U-N-S 24-388-4777   (SL)
HNA ACQUISITION ULC
(*Suby of* CELANESE CORPORATION)
50 Boul Marie-Victorin, Boucherville, QC, J4B
1V5
(450) 655-0396
Emp Here 250   *Sales* 111,161,250
SIC 2821 Plastics materials and resins
Pierre Morin

D-U-N-S 20-726-4722   (BR)
HONDA CANADA INC
ACURA
(*Suby of* HONDA MOTOR CO., LTD.)
1750 Rue Eiffel, Boucherville, QC, J4B 7W1
(450) 641-9062
Emp Here 115
SIC 5012 Automobiles and other motor vehi-
cles
Pierre Langevin

D-U-N-S 20-646-9392   (BR)
IKEA CANADA LIMITED PARTNERSHIP
IKEA
(*Suby of* QINGDAO HONGYISEN CON-
STRUCTION ENGINEERING SERVICE CO.,
LTD.)
586 Ch De Touraine, Boucherville, QC, J4B
5E4

Emp Here 300
SIC 5712 Furniture stores
Nancy Leblanc

D-U-N-S 20-016-8271   (HQ)
IMAGIX IMAGERIE MEDICALE INC
SOUTH SHORE RADIOLOGISTS
600 Boul Du Fort-Saint-Louis Unite 202,
Boucherville, QC, J4B 1S7
(450) 655-2430
Emp Here 50   *Sales* 12,048,450
SIC 8011 Offices and clinics of medical doc-
tors
Maurice Dufresne

D-U-N-S 24-340-7298   (BR)
IMPRIMERIES TRANSCONTINENTAL INC
TRANSCONTINENTAL PRINTING INC
(*Suby of* TRANSCONTINENTAL INC)
1603 Boul De Montarville, Boucherville, QC,
J4B 5Y2
(450) 655-2801
Emp Here 500
SIC 2752 Commercial printing, lithographic

D-U-N-S 24-812-8613   (SL)
INDUSTRIE LEMIEUX INC
MECFAB
(*Suby of* CANERECTOR INC)

1401 Rue Graham-Bell, Boucherville, QC, J4B
6A1
(450) 655-7910
Emp Here 95   *Sales* 18,248,075
SIC 3444 Sheet Metalwork
Eric Smits
Tim Buckland
Amanda Hawkins
William Nickel
Pierre Desormeaux

D-U-N-S 20-221-8814   (SL)
INDUSTRIES D'ACIER INOXYDABLE LIMI-TEE
1440 Rue Graham-Bell, Boucherville, QC, J4B
6H5
(450) 449-4000
Emp Here 110   *Sales* 19,952,680
SIC 3312 Blast furnaces and steel mills
Real Bourret
Alain Bourret
Guy Bourret

D-U-N-S 24-812-9017   (HQ)
INDUSTRIES SPECTRA PREMIUM INC, LES
1421 Rue Ampere, Boucherville, QC, J4B 5Z5
(450) 641-3090
Emp Here 900   *Sales* 462,138,900
SIC 3433 Heating equipment, except electric
Jacques Mombleau
Henri-Paul Boyer
Michel Baril
Michel Maheux
Marc Guay
Yvan Landry
Rene Vachon
Claire Barra

D-U-N-S 25-626-7345   (SL)
INOX DISTRIBUTION INC
INOX
1440   Rue   Graham-Bell   Bureau   A,
Boucherville, QC, J4B 6H5
(450) 449-9200
Emp Here 10   *Sales* 10,003,390
SIC 5051 Metals service centers and offices
Alain Bourret
Real Bourret
Guy Bourret

D-U-N-S 25-968-9701   (SL)
INTER-BOUCHERVILLE INC
50 Ch Du Tremblay, Boucherville, QC, J4B
6Z5
(450) 655-5050
Emp Here 30   *Sales* 14,942,340
SIC 5511 New and used car dealers
Nathalie Halle
Albert Pepin

D-U-N-S 24-351-5892   (SL)
INVESTISSEMENT CRB INC
585 Ch De Touraine, Boucherville, QC, J4B
5E4
(450) 655-1340
Emp Here 125   *Sales* 33,456,500
SIC 5251 Hardware stores
Louis Turcotte
Daniel Gervais

D-U-N-S 24-613-0637   (HQ)
ISN CANADA GROUP HOLDINGS INC
DISTRIBUTION P.D.G.
88 Ch Du Tremblay, Boucherville, QC, J4B
6Z6
(514) 327-0222
Emp Here 20   *Sales* 16,025,460
SIC 5013 Motor vehicle supplies and new
parts
Bruce D. Weber
Martin Cote

D-U-N-S 20-563-2198   (SL)
J.L. FREEMAN, S.E.C.
1250 Rue Nobel Bureau 200, Boucherville,
QC, J4B 5H1

(450) 641-4520
Emp Here 50   *Sales* 41,778,850
SIC 5141 Groceries, general line
Carole St-Charles

D-U-N-S 24-164-4835   (BR)
JOHNVINCE FOODS
ALIM JONHVINCE
(*Suby of* JOHNVINCE FOODS)
1630 Rue Eiffel Bureau 1, Boucherville, QC,
J4B 7W1
(450) 645-1999
Emp Here 100
SIC 4783 Packing and crating
Carl Leblanc

D-U-N-S 24-921-7076   (SL)
JOURNAL LA RELEVE INC
528 Rue Saint-Charles, Boucherville, QC, J4B
3M5
(450) 641-4844
Emp Here 21   *Sales* 15,592,920
SIC 5192 Books, periodicals, and newspapers
Charles Desmarteau Jr
Jean-Claude Messier

D-U-N-S 20-215-5545   (HQ)
LA COMPAGNIE D'IMPORTATION DE COS-METIQUES LIMITEE
C.I.C IMPORTATIONS NATURELLES
1380 Rue Newton Bureau 203, Boucherville,
QC, J4B 5H2
(450) 449-1236
Sales 14,369,485
SIC 5122 Drugs, proprietaries, and sundries
Louis Pilon

D-U-N-S 24-676-8782   (SL)
LABORATOIRE DU-VAR INC
1460 Rue Graham-Bell, Boucherville, QC, J4B
6H5
(450) 641-4740
Emp Here 60   *Sales* 16,599,600
SIC 2844 Toilet preparations
Paul Salloum

D-U-N-S 24-769-6131   (SL)
LABORATOIRES SUISSE INC, LES
BAKTERA
1310 Rue Nobel, Boucherville, QC, J4B 5H3
(450) 444-9808
Emp Here 18   *Sales* 19,896,210
SIC 5122 Drugs, proprietaries, and sundries
Louis Pilon

D-U-N-S 25-323-7747   (BR)
LOBLAWS INC
PROVIGO BOUCHERVILLE
(*Suby of* LOBLAW COMPANIES LIMITED)
1001 Boul De Montarville Bureau 1,
Boucherville, QC, J4B 6P5
(450) 449-0081
Emp Here 75
SIC 5411 Grocery stores
Sylvain Daginas

D-U-N-S 25-209-8231   (HQ)
MAGCHEM INC
AERODET
(*Suby of* GROUPE SOCOMORE)
1271 Rue Ampere Bureau 101, Boucherville,
QC, J4B 5Z5
(450) 641-8500
Sales 14,606,900
SIC 5169 Chemicals and allied products, nec
Andrew Leech
Frederic Lescure

D-U-N-S 20-225-4140   (HQ)
MAGNETO, HYDRAULIQUE & PNEUMA-TIQUE INC
1375 Rue Gay-Lussac, Boucherville, QC, J4B
7K1
(450) 655-2551
Emp Here 41   *Sales* 12,504,732
SIC 7699 Repair services, nec
Daniel Garceau
Benoit Garceau

Alain Jarry
Pierre-Yves Garceau

D-U-N-S 25-690-5522   (HQ)
MAISON DES FUTAILLES, S.E.C.
ALCOOL GLOBAL
500   Rue   D'Avaugour   Bureau   2050,
Boucherville, QC, J4B 0G6
(450) 645-9777
Emp Here 60   *Sales* 59,266,381
SIC 5182 Wine and distilled beverages
Francois Malenfant
Bernard Lavergne
Carmela De Luca

D-U-N-S 20-226-9197   (HQ)
MARCHE J.C. MESSIER INC
METRO PLUS
(*Suby of* PLACEMENTS C. D. F. G. INC)
535 Rue Samuel-De Champlain Bureau 200,
Boucherville, QC, J4B 6B6
(450) 641-3032
Emp Here 6   *Sales* 24,065,114
SIC 5411 Grocery stores
Denis Messier
France Messier

D-U-N-S 24-319-7985   (SL)
MARCHE SABREVOIS INC
535 Rue Samuel-De Champlain Bureau 2,
Boucherville, QC, J4B 6B6
(450) 655-2634
Emp Here 80   *Sales* 23,478,160
SIC 5411 Grocery stores
Gilles Messier
Jean Yves Pepin

D-U-N-S 24-799-3587   (HQ)
MATERIAUX PAYSAGERS SAVARIA LTEE
SAVARIA
950 Ch De Lorraine, Boucherville, QC, J4B
5E4
(450) 655-6147
Sales 14,850,400
SIC 5191 Farm supplies
Pierre-Yves Savaria
Steve Saravia
Steve Savaria

D-U-N-S 20-183-3493   (SL)
MECANIQUE CNC (2002) INC
1470 Rue Graham-Bell, Boucherville, QC, J4B
6H5
(450) 652-6319
Emp Here 100   *Sales* 42,273,700
SIC 1541 Industrial buildings and warehouses
Adelard Moreau
Andre Beaulieu
Daniel Sirois

D-U-N-S 24-737-1433   (HQ)
MENARD CANADA INC
GEOPAC
(*Suby of* VINCI)
1590 Rue Ampere Bureau 202, Boucherville,
QC, J4B 7L4
(450) 449-2633
Emp Here 27   *Sales* 54,793,008
SIC 1794 Excavation work
Seth Pearlman
Marie Rousseau
Dominique Jullienne
Marc Lacazedieu

D-U-N-S 24-224-3780   (SL)
MODERCO INC
115 Rue De Lauzon, Boucherville, QC, J4B
1E7
(450) 641-3150
Emp Here 110   *Sales* 16,975,420
SIC 2542 Partitions and fixtures, except wood
Stephan Julien

D-U-N-S 25-106-7542   (SL)
MONITROL R & D INC
1291 Rue Ampere, Boucherville, QC, J4B 5Z5
(450) 641-4810
Emp Here 70   *Sales* 31,302,180

SIC 5063 Electrical apparatus and equipment
Francois Routier
Gilles Routier

D-U-N-S 24-253-5243   (HQ)
MOTOVAN CORPORATION
(*Suby of* GESTION FAMILLE PALADINO INC)
1391   Rue   Gay-Lussac   Bureau   100,
Boucherville, QC, J4B 7K1
(450) 449-3903
Emp Here 100   *Sales* 36,421,500
SIC 5013 Motor vehicle supplies and new
parts
James Paladino
Carlo Paladino
Michael Paladino

D-U-N-S 25-167-3083   (BR)
NEWLY WEDS FOODS CO.
ALIMENTS NEWLY WEDS, LES
(*Suby of* NEWLY WEDS FOODS, INC.)
1381 Rue Ampere, Boucherville, QC, J4B 5Z5
(450) 641-2200
Emp Here 1,000
SIC 2099 Food preparations, nec
Martin Valois

D-U-N-S 25-150-2670   (HQ)
NORBEC ARCHITECTURAL INC
(*Suby of* CAPITAL REGIONAL ET COOPER-ATIF DESJARDINS)
97 Rue De Vaudreuil, Boucherville, QC, J4B
1K7
(450) 449-1499
Emp Here 10   *Sales* 29,772,126
SIC 3446 Architectural Metalwork
Real Menard
Jan Lembregts
Claude Vincent
Dominique Majeau
Daniel Cadoret
Pierre Grand'maison

D-U-N-S 24-891-3019   (SL)
NORCAN ALUMINUM INC
61 Ch Du Tremblay, Boucherville, QC, J4B 7L6
(450) 449-6207
Emp Here 49   *Sales* 16,039,856
SIC 2819 Industrial inorganic chemicals, nec
Ghyslain Gemme
Mathieu Boivin
Patrick Beauger

D-U-N-S 25-201-3263   (SL)
NOVALI GOURMET INC
ALIMENTS NOVALI
14 Rue De Montgolfier, Boucherville, QC, J4B
7Y4
(450) 655-7790
Emp Here 50   *Sales* 11,242,750
SIC 2045 Prepared flour mixes and doughs
Robert Leduc
Francine Theriault

D-U-N-S 20-059-9145   (BR)
OLYMEL S.E.C.
OLYMEL
(*Suby of* OLYMEL S.E.C.)
1580 Rue Eiffel, Boucherville, QC, J4B 5Y1
(514) 858-9000
Emp Here 300
SIC 5147 Meats and meat products
Leo Parent

D-U-N-S 25-173-7888   (BR)
OLYMEL S.E.C.
(*Suby of* OLYMEL S.E.C.)
1580 Rue Eiffel, Boucherville, QC, J4B 5Y1
(514) 858-9000
Emp Here 200
SIC 2011 Meat packing plants
Rejean Nadeau

D-U-N-S 25-588-1062   (SL)
PHARMAPRIX
100   Boul   De   Montarville   Unite   120,
Boucherville, QC, J4B 5M4

─────────────────────────────
▲ Public Company   ■ Public Company Family Member   **HQ** Headquarters   **BR** Branch   **SL** Single Location

(450) 655-3010
Emp Here 49   *Sales* 32,707,742
SIC 5961 Catalog and mail-order houses
Tu Le Luong

D-U-N-S 20-050-5357   (HQ)
PLASTIPAK INDUSTRIES INC
(*Suby of* GROUPE HAMRO INC)
150 Boul Industriel, Boucherville, QC, J4B
2X3
(450) 650-2200
Emp Here 21   *Sales* 71,643,600
SIC 3089 Plastics products, nec
Nadine Hamelin

D-U-N-S 20-563-3274   (HQ)
PLB INTERNATIONAL INC
(*Suby of* GESTION J. M. BRASSEUR INC)
1361 Rue Graham-Bell, Boucherville, QC, J4B
6A1
(450) 655-3155
Emp Here 25   *Sales* 34,569,000
SIC 2047 Dog and cat food
Jocelyn Brasseur
Jacinthe Brasseur
Jean Brasseur

D-U-N-S 24-148-0771   (HQ)
PNEUS UNIMAX LTEE
CENTRE DE SERVICE UNIPNEU
235 Rue J.-A.-Bombardier, Boucherville, QC,
J4B 8P1
(450) 449-0362
Sales 18,210,750
SIC 5014 Tires and tubes
Gilles C. Lachance
Bruno Leclair
Carl Patry
Claude Picard
Normand Lavoie
Denis Desharnais
Daniel Dubuc
Jocelyn Bernard
Michel La Roche
Yves Fredette

D-U-N-S 24-701-5881   (SL)
POSITOR INC.
1356 Rue Newton, Boucherville, QC, J4B 5H2
(450) 449-0327
Emp Here 26   *Sales* 12,950,028
SIC 5561 Recreational vehicle dealers
Richard Doucet

D-U-N-S 24-392-8590   (HQ)
**PPG   ARCHITECTURAL   COATINGS
CANADA INC**
BETONEL MD
(*Suby of* PPG INDUSTRIES, INC.)
500 - 1550 Rue Ampere, Boucherville, QC,
J4B 7L4
(450) 655-3121
Emp Here 150   *Sales* 805,696,740
SIC 2851 Paints and allied products
David J. Cole
Vincent Rea
Claude Brosseau
Claude St-Pierre
Daniel Archambault
Michael Mcgarry

D-U-N-S 24-740-3918   (SL)
PRESENTATION ULTIMA INC
55 Rue De Montgolfier, Boucherville, QC, J4B
8C4
(450) 641-0670
Emp Here 50   *Sales* 11,671,750
SIC 3161 Luggage
Luc Beaudry
Manon Campbell

D-U-N-S 24-836-9043   (SL)
PROCAM CONSTRUCTION INC
1220 Rue Marconi, Boucherville, QC, J4B
8G8
(450) 449-5121
Emp Here 25   *Sales* 14,258,450
SIC 1542 Nonresidential construction, nec

Remi Boutin
Yvon Caron
Annie Duhaime
Kevin Poliseno
Jonathan Boutin
Pascal Boutin

D-U-N-S 20-191-0676   (HQ)
PRODUITS CHIMIQUES MAGNUS LIMITEE
(*Suby of* GESTION MAGNUS INC)
1271 Rue Ampere, Boucherville, QC, J4B 5Z5
(450) 655-1344
Emp Here 75   *Sales* 28,402,100
SIC 2899 Chemical preparations, nec
Denis Pichet
Jacques Murray
Andre Ruel
Jean-Jacques Drieux
Mario Beaumier
Pierre Hiernaux
Daniel Rabouin
Marc Lortie
Lee Brown
Jean-Michel Arsenault

D-U-N-S 25-900-8840   (SL)
PRODUITS SAINT-HENRI INC, LES
(*Suby of* BIOLACTO INC)
91 Rue De La Barre Bureau 2, Boucherville,
QC, J4B 2X6
(450) 449-9799
Emp Here 35   *Sales* 29,245,195
SIC 5143 Dairy products, except dried or
canned
Remi Wathier
Tracey Briscoe
Robert J. Briscoe

D-U-N-S 20-709-8625   (SL)
PROMOTIONS C.D. INC
DISTRIBUTION MIRAGE PHARMA
165 Rue Jules-Leger, Boucherville, QC, J4B
7K8
(450) 641-1161
Emp Here 95   *Sales* 70,539,400
SIC 5199 Nondurable goods, nec
Fernand Collette
Jacques Collette
Michel Collette

D-U-N-S 24-813-6228   (BR)
PROVIGO DISTRIBUTION INC
*CENTRE   DISTRIBUTION   FRUITS   ET
LEGUMES*
(*Suby of* LOBLAW COMPANIES LIMITED)
180 Ch Du Tremblay, Boucherville, QC, J4B
7W3
(450) 449-8000
Emp Here 700
SIC 5148 Fresh fruits and vegetables
Michel Gaudreau

D-U-N-S 24-515-6492   (BR)
PUROLATOR INC
(*Suby of* GOVERNMENT OF CANADA)
1330 Rue Graham-Bell, Boucherville, QC, J4B
6H5
(450) 641-2430
Emp Here 298
SIC 4731 Freight transportation arrangement
Pietro Ditomasso

D-U-N-S 25-448-3191   (HQ)
RE/MAX SIGNATURE INC
130   Boul   De   Mortagne   Bureau   200,
Boucherville, QC, J4B 5M7
(450) 449-5730
Emp Here 68   *Sales* 50,266,680
SIC 6531 Real estate agents and managers
Claude Allard

D-U-N-S 24-901-5652   (SL)
REFRIGERATION ACTAIR INC
(*Suby of* GESTION ACTAIR INC)
1370   Rue   Joliot-Curie   Bureau   704,
Boucherville, QC, J4B 7L9
(450) 449-5266
Emp Here 50   *Sales* 11,653,250

SIC 1711 Plumbing, heating, air-conditioning
Michel Chagnon
Stephane Forget
Patrick Labelle

D-U-N-S 20-303-1331   (SL)
RESSOURCES GLOBALES AERO INC
MSB RESOURCES GLOBALES
333 Ch Du Tremblay Bureau J, Boucherville,
QC, J4B 7M1
(514) 667-9399
Emp Here 100   *Sales* 15,537,100
SIC 7361 Employment agencies
Marc Darolles
Mario Sevigny
Andre Begin
Philippe Robardey

D-U-N-S 20-419-7800   (HQ)
RONA INC
(*Suby of* LOWE'S COMPANIES, INC.)
220 Ch Du Tremblay, Boucherville, QC, J4B
8H7
(514) 599-5900
Emp Here 1,000   *Sales* 7,820,748,000
SIC 5072 Hardware
Sylvain Prud'homme
Ross William Mccanless
Jennifer Lynn Weber

D-U-N-S 20-181-4972   (BR)
ROTISSERIES ST-HUBERT LTEE, LES
*LA   ROTISSERIE   ST   HUBERT
BOUCHERVILLE 087*
(*Suby of* RECIPE UNLIMITED CORPORA-
TION)
500 Rue Albanel, Boucherville, QC, J4B 2Z6
(450) 449-9366
Emp Here 75
SIC 5812 Eating places
Martin Tiernan

D-U-N-S 24-406-2071   (HQ)
SANDOZ CANADA INC
SANDOZ
(*Suby of* AVARA US HOLDINGS LLC)
145 Rue Jules-Leger, Boucherville, QC, J4B
7K8
(450) 641-4903
Sales 248,695,500
SIC 2834 Pharmaceutical preparations
Michel Robidoux
Isabelle Robitaille
Martin Fournier
Tristan Imbert

D-U-N-S 20-325-0147   (SL)
SENTIMED MEDICAL CORPORATION
135 Boul De Mortagne Unit E, Boucherville,
QC, J4B 6G4

Emp Here 25   *Sales* 11,367,373
SIC 5047 Medical and hospital equipment
Jean Martimbault

D-U-N-S 24-542-0179   (SL)
**SERVICE SANTE CLAUDE GERVAIS INC,
LES**
PHARMAPRIX
520 Boul Du Fort-Saint-Louis Bureau 1,
Boucherville, QC, J4B 1S5
(450) 655-6651
Emp Here 50   *Sales* 12,647,700
SIC 5912 Drug stores and proprietary stores
Claude Gervais

D-U-N-S 25-501-1512   (HQ)
SERVICES MATREC INC
BERGERON
(*Suby of* GFL ENVIRONMENTAL INC)
4 Ch Du Tremblay Bureau 625, Boucherville,
QC, J4B 6Z5
(450) 641-3070
Emp Here 80
SIC 6712 Bank holding companies

D-U-N-S 20-381-7635   (SL)
SERVICES PHARMACEUTIQUES AVARA

BOUCHERVILLE INC
(*Suby of* AVARA PHARMA SERVICES LTD)
145 Rue Jules-Leger, Boucherville, QC, J4B
7K8
(450) 650-3050
Emp Here 525   *Sales* 174,086,850
SIC 2834 Pharmaceutical preparations
Carole Nantais

D-U-N-S 25-369-8732   (SL)
SITE INTEGRATION PLUS INC
GROUPE-SIP
1356 Rue Newton, Boucherville, QC, J4B 5H2
(450) 449-0094
Emp Here 70   *Sales* 15,248,030
SIC 1731 Electrical work
Shawn Batten

D-U-N-S 20-177-8615   (BR)
SOBEYS QUEBEC INC
1500 Boul De Montarville, Boucherville, QC,
J4B 5Y3
(514) 324-1010
Emp Here 100   *Sales* 3,342,308
SIC 5141 Groceries, general line

D-U-N-S 20-577-5591   (BR)
**SOCIETE   DES   ETABLISSEMENTS   DE
PLEIN AIR DU QUEBEC**
*PARC   NATIONAL   DES   ILES-DE-
BOUCHERVILLE*
(*Suby of* GOUVERNEMENT DE LA
PROVINCE DE QUEBEC)
55 Ile-Sainte-Marguerite, Boucherville, QC,
J4B 5J6
(450) 928-5089
Emp Here 100
SIC 7996 Amusement parks
Serge Perreault

D-U-N-S 24-051-7169   (SL)
SONIPLASTICS INC
(*Suby of* PLACEMENTS ANDRE TEASDALE
INC)
1610 Rue Eiffel, Boucherville, QC, J4B 5Y1
(450) 449-6000
Emp Here 125   *Sales* 29,851,500
SIC 3089 Plastics products, nec
Andre Teasdale
Francois Viau
Andre Sicotte-Teasdale
Bruno Lessard
Eric Drouin
Judith Simoneau

D-U-N-S 25-498-8108   (HQ)
SPB SOLUTIONS INC
(*Suby of* INVESTISSEMENTS BRASCO INC)
1350 Rue Newton, Boucherville, QC, J4B 5H2
(450) 655-3505
Emp Here 10   *Sales* 15,556,050
SIC 2048 Prepared feeds, nec
Sylvain Brasseur
Mario Couture
Gilles Thibault
Anne-Marie Renaud
Real G Menard

D-U-N-S 24-404-2495   (SL)
SYSTEMES NORBEC INC
EXSPACE
(*Suby of* CAPITAL REGIONAL ET COOPER-
ATIF DESJARDINS)
97 Rue De Vaudreuil, Boucherville, QC, J4B
1K7
(450) 449-1499
Emp Here 154   *Sales* 43,255,058
SIC 3585 Refrigeration and heating equip-
ment
Real Menard
Jan Lembregts
Claude Vincent
Dominique Majeau
Daniel Cadoret
Pierre Grand'maison

D-U-N-S 25-976-1336   (SL)
TM4 INC

(Suby of DANA INCORPORATED)
135 Rue J.-A.-Bombardier Bureau 25, Boucherville, QC, J4B 8P1
(450) 645-1444
Emp Here 100   *Sales* 19,044,200
SIC 3621 Motors and generators
Christophe Dominiak
Phillip A. Rotman Ii
Steve Demers
Seth Metzger
Brad Hargest
Jean-Hugues Lafleur
Robert Baril

D-U-N-S 24-395-2178   (BR)
TRANSPORT ROBERT (1973) LTEE
(Suby of GROUPE ROBERT INC)
65 Rue De Vaudreuil, Boucherville, QC, J4B 1K7
(514) 521-1416
Emp Here 250
SIC 4213 Trucking, except local

D-U-N-S 20-004-6600   (BR)
TREVI FABRICATION INC
TREVI
(Suby of INVESTISSEMENTS TREVI INC)
1235 Rue Ampere, Boucherville, QC, J4B 7M6
(514) 228-7384
Emp Here 200
SIC 5999 Miscellaneous retail stores, nec
Jean Francois

D-U-N-S 20-219-9493   (HQ)
TRUDEAU CORPORATION 1889 INC
HOME PRESENCE
(Suby of PLACEMENTS ROBERT TRUDEAU LTEE)
1600 Rue Eiffel, Boucherville, QC, J4B 5Y1
(450) 655-7441
Emp Here 134   *Sales* 77,674,680
SIC 5023 Homefurnishings
Anne-Marie Trudeau
Robert L. Trudeau
Lucie Brasseur

D-U-N-S 24-308-4352   (HQ)
UNI-SELECT EASTERN INC
FINISHMASTER
(Suby of UNI-SELECT INC)
170 Boul Industriel, Boucherville, QC, J4B 2X3
(450) 641-2440
Emp Here 2   *Sales* 36,421,500
SIC 5013 Motor vehicle supplies and new parts
Brent Windom
Henry Buckley
Louis Juneau
Eric Bussieres

D-U-N-S 20-578-8953   (HQ)
UNI-SELECT INC
AUTOPLUS
170 Boul Industriel, Boucherville, QC, J4B 2X3
(450) 641-2440
Emp Here 100   *Sales* 1,751,965,000
SIC 5013 Motor vehicle supplies and new parts
Brent Windom
Eric Bussieres
Melouis Juneau
Marie-Noelle Gagnon
Michelle Ann Cormier
Chris Adams
Neil Croxson
David Bibby
Stephane Gonthier
Jeffrey I Hall

D-U-N-S 25-916-0729   (HQ)
UNI-SELECT QUEBEC INC
AUTO PARTS PLUS
(Suby of UNI-SELECT INC)
170 Boul Industriel, Boucherville, QC, J4B 2X3

(450) 641-2440
Emp Here 6   *Sales* 13,946,184
SIC 5531 Auto and home supply stores
Henry Buckley
Eric Bussieres

D-U-N-S 24-061-0365   (SL)
WATERCO CANADA INC
(Suby of WATERCO LIMITED)
1380 Rue Newton Bureau 208, Boucherville, QC, J4B 5H2
(450) 748-1421
Emp Here 65   *Sales* 14,430,065
SIC 3585 Refrigeration and heating equipment
Gabrielle Brunet
Soon Sinn Goh
Soon Leong Goh
Brian Weng Keong Goh
Anthony Lawrence Fisher
Nancy Tan

D-U-N-S 24-528-8576   (SL)
WILLIAM E. BURROWES INC
BURROWES INSURANCE BROKERS
1570b Boul De Montarville, Boucherville, QC, J4B 5Y3
(450) 655-6023
Emp Here 60   *Sales* 50,883,600
SIC 6411 Insurance agents, brokers, and service
John Burrowes

Bromont, QC J2L

D-U-N-S 24-434-3166   (HQ)
ARMOIRES FABRITEC LTEE
80 Boul De L'Aeroport, Bromont, QC, J2L 1S9
(450) 534-1659
Emp Here 280   *Sales* 88,249,630
SIC 2434 Wood kitchen cabinets
Clovis Bourgeois
Jonathan Bourgeois
Nadia Bourgeois
Yvette Bourgeois

D-U-N-S 25-247-3525   (HQ)
CHATEAU BROMONT INC
AUBERGE BROMONT
90 Rue De Stanstead, Bromont, QC, J2L 1K6
(450) 534-3433
Emp Here 100   *Sales* 9,269,000
SIC 7011 Hotels and motels
Claude Boisvert
Real Martineau
Geffrey Frenette
Guy Carignan
Marie Leveille
Jaques Matte
Real Ouimet
Henry Ravary

D-U-N-S 20-400-5321   (SL)
COMPAGNIE GE AVIATION CANADA, LA
GE AVIATION
(Suby of GENERAL ELECTRIC COMPANY)
2 Boul De L'Aeroport, Bromont, QC, J2L 1S6
(450) 534-0917
Emp Here 1,000   *Sales* 197,131,000
SIC 8711 Engineering services
William G. Mateer
Bradley Smith
Helena Miller

D-U-N-S 24-708-6619   (SL)
G E MOTEURS D'AVIONS INC
2 Boul De L'Aeroport, Bromont, QC, J2L 1S6
(450) 534-0917
Emp Here 49   *Sales* 24,405,822
SIC 5599 Automotive dealers, nec
Phillipe Simonateau

D-U-N-S 24-401-1367   (BR)
GENERAL ELECTRIC CANADA COMPANY
GE AIRCRAFT ENGINES

(Suby of GENERAL ELECTRIC COMPANY)
2 Boul De L'Aeroport, Bromont, QC, J2L 1S6
(450) 534-0917
Emp Here 1,000
SIC 3625 Relays and industrial controls
Matthew Roy

D-U-N-S 25-706-5573   (BR)
GROUPE DAGENAIS M.D.C. INC
MOBILIER DAGENAIS, PHILIPPE
117 Boul De Bromont, Bromont, QC, J2L 2K7

Emp Here 100
SIC 5712 Furniture stores
Pierre St-Georges

D-U-N-S 20-634-1331   (BR)
IBM CANADA LIMITED
IBM CANADA - USINE DE BROMONT
(Suby of INTERNATIONAL BUSINESS MACHINES CORPORATION)
23 Boul De L'Aeroport, Bromont, QC, J2L 1A3
(450) 534-6000
Emp Here 1,500
SIC 3674 Semiconductors and related devices
Lois Labelle

D-U-N-S 25-738-2135   (SL)
IMMOBILIER SKI BROMONT INC
IMMOBILIER SKI BROMONT.COM
150 Rue Champlain, Bromont, QC, J2L 1A2
(450) 534-2200
Emp Here 80   *Sales* 3,429,840
SIC 5813 Drinking places
Charles Desourdy
Guy Granger

D-U-N-S 20-188-4744   (SL)
QUALI-T-GROUP ULC
QUALI-T-FAB
22 Boul De L'Aeroport, Bromont, QC, J2L 1S6
(450) 534-2032
Emp Here 50   *Sales* 10,141,500
SIC 3446 Architectural Metalwork
Giancarlo Talarico
Frank Talarico

D-U-N-S 25-974-3193   (SL)
SKI BROMONT.COM, SOCIETE EN COMMANDITE
CENTRE DE SKI BROMONT
150 Rue Champlain, Bromont, QC, J2L 1A2
(450) 534-2200
Emp Here 80   *Sales* 3,641,520
SIC 5813 Drinking places
Charles Desourdy

D-U-N-S 20-113-3282   (SL)
TELEDYNE DALSA SEMICONDUCTEUR INC
(Suby of TELEDYNE TECHNOLOGIES INC)
18 Boul De L'Aeroport, Bromont, QC, J2L 1S7
(450) 534-2321
Emp Here 250   *Sales* 70,728,750
SIC 3674 Semiconductors and related devices
Roks Edwin
Robert Mehrabian
Silvio Favrin
Melanie S. Cibik

Brossard, QC J4W

D-U-N-S 24-648-9355   (SL)
9349-6446 QUEBEC INC
EXCELTELECOM
6 Rue De La Place-Du-Commerce Bureau 100, Brossard, QC, J4W 3J9
(450) 923-3000
Emp Here 60   *Sales* 13,069,740
SIC 1731 Electrical work
Christian Hamel
Carole Zreick Hamel

D-U-N-S 25-560-8911   (BR)

CANLAN ICE SPORTS CORP
4 GLACES, LES
(Suby of CANLAN ICE SPORTS CORP)
5880 Boul Taschereau, Brossard, QC, J4W 1M6
(450) 462-2113
Emp Here 90
SIC 7999 Amusement and recreation, nec
Daniel Bourgoin

D-U-N-S 24-367-2222   (SL)
COGIR APARTMENTS REAL ESTATE INVESTMENT TRUST
BLF REIT
7250 Boul Taschereau Bureau 200, Brossard, QC, J4W 1M9
(450) 672-5090
Emp Here 2,100   *Sales* 878,966,400
SIC 6531 Real estate agents and managers
Mathieu Duguay
Moray Tawse
Richard Guay
Pierre Thabet
Guy Poulin

D-U-N-S 20-189-2808   (SL)
DECATHLON CANADA INC
2151 Boul Lapiniere, Brossard, QC, J4W 2T5
(514) 962-7545
Emp Here 170   *Sales* 41,535,760
SIC 5941 Sporting goods and bicycle shops
Nicolas Roucou
Stephane Marchioni
Guillaume Marcant

D-U-N-S 24-321-2776   (SL)
ECONOFAR (1988) INC
JEAN COUTU # 12
7400 Boul Taschereau Bureau 71, Brossard, QC, J4W 1M9

Emp Here 50   *Sales* 12,647,700
SIC 5912 Drug stores and proprietary stores
Paul St-Onge
Andre St-Onge

D-U-N-S 24-791-3929   (HQ)
ELECTRIMAT LTEE
MASKA ELECTIQUE ST-HYACINTHE
2180 Boul Lapiniere, Brossard, QC, J4W 1M2
(450) 462-2116
Sales 17,886,960
SIC 5063 Electrical apparatus and equipment
Christian Grenier
Mathieu Legris
Mario Beaudoin

D-U-N-S 25-098-2873   (SL)
FRUITS DORES INC
ALIMENTS GARNIE
1650 Rue Panama Bureau 510, Brossard, QC, J4W 2W4
(450) 923-5856
Emp Here 50   *Sales* 41,778,850
SIC 5148 Fresh fruits and vegetables
Emir Chiheb Achour

D-U-N-S 24-084-6550   (SL)
GESTION H. LEVESQUE LTEE
2180 Boul Lapiniere, Brossard, QC, J4W 1M2
(450) 462-2116
Emp Here 42   *Sales* 18,781,308
SIC 5063 Electrical apparatus and equipment
Hermel Levesque
Gilles Levesque
Lise Levesque

D-U-N-S 25-463-2540   (HQ)
GROUPE SUTTON-ACTION INC
2190 Boul Lapiniere, Brossard, QC, J4W 1M2
(450) 462-4414
Emp Here 54   *Sales* 52,361,125
SIC 6531 Real estate agents and managers
Mario Besner

D-U-N-S 20-254-5120   (HQ)
IMMOVEX INC
IMMOVEX EVALUATEURS AGREES

2210 Boul Lapiniere, Brossard, QC, J4W 1M2
(450) 671-9205
Emp Here 39   *Sales* 17,968,760
SIC 7389 Business services, nec
 Michel Audy

D-U-N-S 20-251-7850   (HQ)
MARCHE BELLEMARE INC
METRO BELLEMARE
2121 Boul Lapiniere, Brossard, QC, J4W 1L7
(450) 445-3044
Emp Here 85   *Sales* 46,956,320
SIC 5411 Grocery stores
 Claire Bellemare
 Robert Bellemare
 Rolland Bellemare

D-U-N-S 24-164-0585   (HQ)
NOXENT INC
6400 Boul Taschereau Bureau 200, Brossard,
QC, J4W 3J2
(450) 926-0662
Emp Here 20   *Sales* 11,714,400
SIC 8742 Management consulting services
 Marc-Andre Poulin
 Jean Julien
 Xavier Giraud

D-U-N-S 24-228-6094   (SL)
QUATRE GLACES (1994) INC, LES
CANLAN ICE SPORTS ET DESSIN
(*Suby of* CANLAN ICE SPORTS CORP)
5880 Boul Taschereau, Brossard, QC, J4W
1M6
(450) 462-2113
Emp Here 90   *Sales* 8,545,770
SIC 7999 Amusement and recreation, nec
 Joey St.Aubin
 F.Michael Gellard
 Grant W Ballantyne
 Jean-Francois Caudron

D-U-N-S 24-502-6992   (BR)
SANI SPORT INC
(*Suby of* GESTION SANI SPORT INC)
7777 Boul Marie-Victorin, Brossard, QC, J4W
1B3
(450) 465-7220
Emp Here 80
SIC 7991 Physical fitness facilities
 Jean Garceau

D-U-N-S 20-255-6580   (HQ)
SKYLINE (PHP) CANADA ULC
*ACIER DE FONDATIONS SKYLINE (PHP)
CANADA*
(*Suby of* NUCOR CORPORATION)
2220 Boul Lapiniere Bureau 205, Brossard,
QC, J4W 1M2
(450) 461-6366
Emp Here 5   *Sales* 268,854,300
SIC 5051 Metals service centers and offices
 Laurent De May
 Andrew Deguire
 Beth Bowers
 John Ferriola
 Robert Schmitt

D-U-N-S 20-051-6784   (HQ)
SOCIETE DE GESTION COGIR INC
APPARTEMENTS L'EXCELSIOR, LES
7250 Boul Taschereau Bureau 200, Brossard,
QC, J4W 1M9
(450) 671-6381
Emp Here 105   *Sales* 45,240,012
SIC 6531 Real estate agents and managers
 Mathieu Duguay

D-U-N-S 20-125-2686   (HQ)
SOCIETE DE GESTION COGIR S.E.N.C.
COGIR GENERAL PARTNERSHIP
7250 Boul Taschereau Bureau 200, Brossard,
QC, J4W 1M9
(450) 671-6381
Sales 25,133,340
SIC 6531 Real estate agents and managers
 Mathieu Duguay

Ehud Erez

D-U-N-S 20-715-9497   (BR)
SUPER MARCHE COLLIN INC
METRO PLUS
2004 Boul De Rome, Brossard, QC, J4W 3M7
(450) 671-8885
Emp Here 100
SIC 5411 Grocery stores
 Mathieu Tremblay

D-U-N-S 20-184-7865   (HQ)
WESTWAY HOLDINGS CANADA INC
(*Suby of* E D & F MAN DEUTSCHLAND
GMBH)
6 Rue De La Place-Du-Commerce Bureau
202, Brossard, QC, J4W 3J9
(450) 465-1715
Emp Here 40   *Sales* 37,126,000
SIC 5191 Farm supplies
 Gilbert Dagenais
 Marie-Josee Theriault
 Francine Brunet
 Arthur W Huguley Iv
 Anthony Raymond Watts

D-U-N-S 25-360-9382   (BR)
YOPLAIT LIBERTE CANADA CIE
PRODUITS DE MARQUE LIBERTE, LES
(*Suby of* YOPLAIT LIBERTE CANADA CIE)
1423 Boul Provencher, Brossard, QC, J4W
1Z3

Emp Here 150
SIC 2026 Fluid milk
 Martin Bourque

Brossard, QC J4X

D-U-N-S 24-363-9114   (SL)
9039-4735 QUEBEC INC
ACURA BROSSARD
9100 Boul Taschereau, Brossard, QC, J4X
1C3
(450) 659-1616
Emp Here 26   *Sales* 12,950,028
SIC 5511 New and used car dealers
 Jeannot Racine

D-U-N-S 20-873-2839   (SL)
9096-9080 QUEBEC INC
BROSSARD MAZDA
8450 Boul Taschereau, Brossard, QC, J4X
1C2
(450) 466-0999
Emp Here 50   *Sales* 24,903,900
SIC 5511 New and used car dealers
 Patrice Mcgrail

D-U-N-S 24-943-1040   (SL)
9119-8523 QUEBEC INC
SUBARU RIVE-SUD
9200 Boul Taschereau, Brossard, QC, J4X
1C3
(450) 465-3200
Emp Here 22   *Sales* 10,957,716
SIC 5511 New and used car dealers
 Jeannot Racine

D-U-N-S 25-257-0734   (SL)
CENTRE D'ACCUEIL MARCELLE FERRON
8600 Boul Marie-Victorin, Brossard, QC, J4X
1A1
(450) 923-1430
Emp Here 210   *Sales* 13,499,220
SIC 8361 Residential care
 Zeff Guiducci

D-U-N-S 25-233-7951   (BR)
COMMISSION SCOLAIRE MARIE-VICTORIN
ECOLE SECONDAIRE PIERRE BROSSEAU
(*Suby of* COMMISSION SCOLAIRE MARIE-VICTORIN)
8350 Boul Pelletier, Brossard, QC, J4X 1M8

(450) 465-6290
Emp Here 80
SIC 8211 Elementary and secondary schools
 Francine Charbonneau

D-U-N-S 20-357-0304   (SL)
INVESTISSEMENTS J.B. GREGOIRE INC
BARNABE MAZDA DE BROSSARD
8450 Boul Taschereau, Brossard, QC, J4X
1C2
(450) 466-0999
Emp Here 45   *Sales* 22,413,510
SIC 5511 New and used car dealers
 Joel Gregoire

D-U-N-S 24-126-1655   (SL)
LIONBRIDGE (CANADA) INC
ENTREPRISES LIONBRIDGE (CANADA)
(*Suby of* HIG CAPITAL MANAGEMENT, INC.)
7900 Boul Taschereau Bureau E204,
Brossard, QC, J4X 1C2
(514) 288-2243
Emp Here 53   *Sales* 35,452,124
SIC 7389 Business services, nec
 John Fennelly
 Robin Ayoub
 Clemente Cohen
 Brian O'donnell

D-U-N-S 24-900-4680   (SL)
RIVE SUD CHRYSLER DODGE INC
RIVE SUD CHRYSLER DODGE JEEP RAM
9400 Boul Taschereau, Brossard, QC, J4X
1C3
(450) 444-9400
Emp Here 50   *Sales* 24,903,900
SIC 5511 New and used car dealers
 Louis Dandurand
 Lucien Gendreau
 Patrick Dandurand

D-U-N-S 20-702-7785   (BR)
ST. LAWRENCE SEAWAY MANAGEMENT CORPORATION, THE
(*Suby of* ST. LAWRENCE SEAWAY MAN-AGEMENT CORPORATION, THE)
9200 Boul Marie-Victorin, Brossard, QC, J4X
1A3
(450) 672-4115
Emp Here 75
SIC 4499 Water transportation services,
 Marie Gaubreault

Brossard, QC J4Y

D-U-N-S 24-591-7047   (SL)
3764605 CANADA INC
ALIMENTS FOO LAY FOODS, LES
9600 Rue Ignace Bureau G, Brossard, QC,
J4Y 2R4
(450) 444-2956
Emp Here 25   *Sales* 20,889,425
SIC 5141 Groceries, general line
 Cheong Hung Feng

D-U-N-S 24-789-0283   (SL)
4094590 CANADA INC
SPORTS EXPERTS - ATMOSPHERE
9550 Boul Leduc Bureau 15, Brossard, QC,
J4Y 0B3

Emp Here 49   *Sales* 10,663,037
SIC 5941 Sporting goods and bicycle shops
 Yvan Briere

D-U-N-S 25-624-6471   (SL)
9039-7571 QUEBEC INC
VOLVO DE BROSSARD
9425 Boul Taschereau, Brossard, QC, J4Y
2J3
(450) 659-6688
Emp Here 100   *Sales* 62,928,000
SIC 5511 New and used car dealers
 Felix Scotti

D-U-N-S 24-935-3731   (SL)

AUTOMATIC SYSTEMES AMERIQUE INC
(*Suby of* BOLLORE PARTICIPATIONS)
4005 Boul Matte Bureau D, Brossard, QC, J4Y
2P4
(450) 659-0737
Emp Here 47   *Sales* 10,237,963
SIC 1731 Electrical work
 Massimo Boulvain
 Stephane Godin
 Luc Lissoir
 Pierre-Philippe Dube
 Massimo Boulvain

D-U-N-S 24-815-0559   (SL)
BELL FLAVORS & FRAGRANCES (CANADA) CO
ESSENCES & FRAGRANCES BELL
3800 Rue Isabelle Bureau H, Brossard, QC,
J4Y 2R3
(450) 444-3819
Emp Here 50   *Sales* 11,242,750
SIC 2087 Flavoring extracts and syrups, nec
 James Heinz
 Marina Poissant

D-U-N-S 24-363-5070   (BR)
BEST BUY CANADA LTD
BEST BUY
(*Suby of* BEST BUY CO., INC.)
8480 Boul Leduc Unit 100, Brossard, QC, J4Y
0K7
(450) 766-2300
Emp Here 100
SIC 5731 Radio, television, and electronic
stores
 Pascal Fortier

D-U-N-S 20-603-0231   (HQ)
BIRON LABORATOIRE MEDICAL INC
BIRON DIAGNOSTIC
(*Suby of* BIRON GROUPE SANTE INC)
4105 Boul Matte, Brossard, QC, J4Y 2P4
(514) 866-6146
Sales 15,141,312
SIC 8071 Medical laboratories
 Genevieve Biron
 Caroline Biron

D-U-N-S 25-066-3981   (SL)
BROSSARD CHEVROLET BUICK GMC INC
AUTOMOBILES BROSSARD BUICK
2555 Boul Matte, Brossard, QC, J4Y 2P4
(450) 619-6666
Emp Here 49   *Sales* 24,405,822
SIC 5511 New and used car dealers
 Gabriel Dallaire

D-U-N-S 20-703-5283   (BR)
CASCADES CS+ INC
(*Suby of* CASCADES INC)
9500 Av Illinois, Brossard, QC, J4Y 3B7
(450) 923-3300
Emp Here 103
SIC 8711 Engineering services
 Christian Cote

D-U-N-S 20-888-0906   (HQ)
CENTRE DE MOTOS INC
LEO HARLEY DAVIDSON
8705 Boul Taschereau, Brossard, QC, J4Y
1A4
(450) 443-4488
Sales 22,024,800
SIC 5571 Motorcycle dealers
 Eric Bouchard

D-U-N-S 20-276-6650   (BR)
CENTRE DE SANTE ET DE SERVICES SO-CIAUX CHAMPLAIN
CENTRE D'HEBERGEMENT CHAMPLAIN
5050 Place Nogent, Brossard, QC, J4Y 2K3
(450) 672-3328
Emp Here 80
SIC 8322 Individual and family services
 Christien Gilbert

D-U-N-S 20-265-5502   (SL)
CENTRE OASIS SURF INC

OASIS SURF
9520 Boul Leduc Bureau 1, Brossard, QC, J4Y 0B3
(450) 486-7873
Emp Here 50   *Sales* 13,707,600
SIC 5411 Grocery stores
Claude Coudry
Lionel Coudry
Michel Coudry

D-U-N-S 24-164-4355   (BR)
CINEPLEX ODEON CORPORATION
CINEMA CINEPLEX BROSSARD & VIP
(*Suby of* CINEPLEX INC)
9350 Boul Leduc, Brossard, QC, J4Y 0B3
(450) 678-5542
Emp Here 100
SIC 7832 Motion picture theaters, except drive-in
Tony Mathieu

D-U-N-S 20-281-4088   (SL)
CLUB VIDEO SUTTON INC
CVS PRODUCTIONS
9160 Boul Leduc Bureau 410, Brossard, QC, J4Y 0E3
(514) 251-8118
Emp Here 100   *Sales* 3,563,769
SIC 7371 Custom computer programming services
Jean Beaudry
Samuel Lepine

D-U-N-S 25-026-9636   (BR)
COMMISSION   SCOLAIRE   MARIE-VICTORIN
ECOLE   SECONDAIRE   ANTOINE BROSSARD
(*Suby of* COMMISSION SCOLAIRE MARIE-VICTORIN)
3055 Boul De Rome, Brossard, QC, J4Y 1S9
(450) 443-0010
Emp Here 150
SIC 8211 Elementary and secondary schools
Benoit Miousse

D-U-N-S 20-381-9268   (SL)
CONSTRUCTIONS 3P INC
ENTREPRISES EN PLOMBERIE PIERRE POULIN, LES
3955 Rue Isabelle, Brossard, QC, J4Y 2R2
(450) 659-6000
Emp Here 50   *Sales* 11,046,700
SIC 1711 Plumbing, heating, air-conditioning
Jonathan Senecal
Luc Charest

D-U-N-S 24-361-1428   (SL)
CORPORATION DU THEATRE L'ETOILE
ETOILE, L'
6000 Boul De Rome Bureau 240, Brossard, QC, J4Y 0B6
(450) 676-1030
Emp Here 50   *Sales* 14,221,850
SIC 6512 Nonresidential building operators
Claude Labonte
Luc Cabot
Jacques Fournier

D-U-N-S 24-189-9793   (BR)
DE LA FONTAINE & ASSOCIES INC
INTERMAT
(*Suby of* DE LA FONTAINE & ASSOCIES INC)
7503 Boul Taschereau Bureau B, Brossard, QC, J4Y 1A2
(450) 676-8335
Emp Here 90
SIC 5072 Hardware
Benoit Roy

D-U-N-S 24-358-3148   (SL)
DEVIMCO INC
6000 Boul De Rome Bureau 410, Brossard, QC, J4Y 0B6
(450) 645-2525
Emp Here 45   *Sales* 12,748,185

SIC 8741 Management services
Serge Goulet
Jean-Francois Breton

D-U-N-S 25-625-5977   (HQ)
DISTECH CONTROLES INC
(*Suby of* ACUITY BRANDS, INC.)
4205 Place Java, Brossard, QC, J4Y 0C4
(450) 444-9898
Emp Here 95   *Sales* 34,093,350
SIC 3822 Environmental controls
Martin Villeneuve
Richard K. Reece
C. Dan Smith

D-U-N-S 25-503-0017   (SL)
ENSEIGNES CMD INC
COMPUMEDIA DESIGN
(*Suby of* GSH CONSEIL INC)
3615b Rue Isabelle, Brossard, QC, J4Y 2R2
(450) 465-1100
Emp Here 25   *Sales* 13,013,550
SIC 5099 Durable goods, nec
Erik Grandjean

D-U-N-S 24-393-0174   (SL)
ENTREPRISES FRANCOIS BRIEN LTEE, LES
CANADIAN TIRE
9900 Boul Leduc Bureau 643, Brossard, QC, J4Y 0B4
(450) 443-0005
Emp Here 100   *Sales* 20,534,300
SIC 5311 Department stores
Francois Brien

D-U-N-S 24-110-3456   (HQ)
EQUIPEMENTS CONTRO VALVE INC, LES
INGENIERIE WILTECH FLOW
(*Suby of* INVESTISSEMENTS MICHAEL WILSON INC, LES)
9610 Rue Ignace Unit B, Brossard, QC, J4Y 2R4
(450) 444-5858
Sales 42,752,340
SIC 5084 Industrial machinery and equipment
Michael C. Wilson

D-U-N-S 24-395-1600   (SL)
ESSENCES ET FRAGRANCES BELL CANADA INC
3800 Rue Isabelle, Brossard, QC, J4Y 2R3
(450) 444-3819
Emp Here 40   *Sales* 33,423,080
SIC 5149 Groceries and related products, nec
Marina Poissant
James H Heinz
William H Grambrell
Paul St-Pere

D-U-N-S 25-141-3837   (HQ)
FRUITS & PASSION BOUTIQUES INC
FRUITS & PASSION
(*Suby of* THEFACESHOP CO., LTD.)
9180 Boul Leduc Bureau 280, Brossard, QC, J4Y 0N7
(450) 678-9620
Emp Here 50   *Sales* 71,830,854
SIC 5122 Drugs, proprietaries, and sundries
Jaesun Lee
Byeong Yeol Kim
Tae Hoon Kim
Tae Ock Lee

D-U-N-S 24-195-6189   (SL)
GESTION MICHEL SEGUIN INC
MARCHAND   CANADIAN   TIRE   DE BROSSARD
9900 Boul Leduc, Brossard, QC, J4Y 0B4
(450) 443-0005
Emp Here 50   *Sales* 24,903,900
SIC 5531 Auto and home supply stores
Michel Seguin

D-U-N-S 24-989-5137   (HQ)
GRIF & GRAF INC
(*Suby of* LE GRENIER D'ART (1987) INC)
9205 Boul Taschereau, Brossard, QC, J4Y

3B8
(450) 659-6999
Emp Here 200
SIC 7699 Repair services, nec
Pierre Gamache

D-U-N-S 24-614-9405   (SL)
GROUPE VETERI MEDIC INC
ANIMANIA
7415 Boul Taschereau, Brossard, QC, J4Y 1A2
(450) 656-3660
Emp Here 250   *Sales* 43,476,250
SIC 0742 Veterinary services, specialties
Sebastien Kfoury
Jerome Auger

D-U-N-S 20-277-5672   (SL)
IMAGIX IMAGERIE MEDICALE INC
GROUPE RADIOLOGIE LAVAL LAUREN-TIDES
F-4105 Boul Matte, Brossard, QC, J4Y 2P4
(514) 866-6622
Emp Here 250   *Sales* 47,551,750
SIC 8011 Offices and clinics of medical doctors
Genevieve Biron
Sylvain J. Perron
Jacques Authier
Ronald Guerin
Jean-Pierre Normand
Jean-Francois Desjardins
Yves Dansereau
Denis Filiatrault
Daniel Plante

D-U-N-S 20-308-8117   (SL)
IMMOBILIER CARBONLEO INC
INDIX30
9160 Boul Leduc Bureau 510, Brossard, QC, J4Y 0E3
(450) 550-8080
Emp Here 35   *Sales* 14,677,425
SIC 6719 Holding companies, nec
Andrew Lutfy
Nicolas Desourdy
Claude Marcotte

D-U-N-S 24-709-5953   (SL)
JCB ENTREPRENEURS GENERAUX INC
3875 Rue Isabelle, Brossard, QC, J4Y 2R2
(450) 444-8151
Emp Here 82   *Sales* 46,767,716
SIC 1542 Nonresidential construction, nec
Louis Lavigne
Benoit Labelle
Sylvie Barbe
Pascal Fortin
Francis Lavigne
Alexandre Stephane Boucher

D-U-N-S 20-248-4051   (SL)
L.A. HEBERT LTEE
9700 Place Jade, Brossard, QC, J4Y 3C1
(450) 444-4847
Emp Here 150   *Sales* 26,810,850
SIC 8711 Engineering services
Alexis Loisel
Julie Hebert

D-U-N-S 24-110-7549   (HQ)
LE GRENIER D'ART (1987) INC
PRINT MINT, THE
9205 Boul Taschereau, Brossard, QC, J4Y 3B8
(450) 659-6999
Emp Here 25   *Sales* 69,597,500
SIC 2499 Wood products, nec
Pierre Gamache

D-U-N-S 25-234-1370   (SL)
MARKETING EMS INC
SENSATION THERAPY INC
7505 Boul Taschereau Bureau 100, Brossard, QC, J4Y 1A2
(450) 443-0300
Emp Here 49   *Sales* 10,002,370
SIC 1081 Metal mining services

Heba Zilika

D-U-N-S 20-013-9884   (SL)
MONTMORENCY FORD (1997) INC
7225 Boul Taschereau, Brossard, QC, J4Y 1A1
(450) 678-9940
Emp Here 100   *Sales* 62,928,000
SIC 5511 New and used car dealers
Ray Monahan
Roger Desautels Iii
Stephane Belanger
Guy Caouette
Paul Ladouceur

D-U-N-S 20-265-5353   (SL)
PIERRE BROSSARD (1981) LTEE
(*Suby of* GESTION P.B.L. INC)
9595 Rue Ignace, Brossard, QC, J4Y 2P3
(450) 659-9641
Emp Here 75   *Sales* 16,337,175
SIC 1731 Electrical work
Bernard Brossard
Ginette Miron

D-U-N-S 24-354-3936   (SL)
PLACEMENTS HEBDEN INC
9700 Place Jade, Brossard, QC, J4Y 3C1
(450) 444-4847
Emp Here 150   *Sales* 26,810,850
SIC 8711 Engineering services
Denis Hebert

D-U-N-S 20-793-3979   (HQ)
SANTE NATURELLE A.G. LTEE
(*Suby of* SEALBOND CANADA INC)
3555 Boul Matte, Brossard, QC, J4Y 2P4
(450) 659-7723
Sales 22,721,680
SIC 2833 Medicinals and botanicals
Alan Abel Ying Choi Yu
Barbara Farina
Victor Tong
Jerry Yiu Leung Mo
Daniel Roy

D-U-N-S 20-357-0338   (SL)
SCHNEIDER ELECTRIC CANADA INC
4100 Place Java, Brossard, QC, J4Y 0C4
(450) 444-0143
Emp Here 250   *Sales* 44,684,750
SIC 8711 Engineering services
Juan Macias
Nathan Fast
Laurent Vernerey

D-U-N-S 25-242-5913   (BR)
SCHNEIDER ELECTRIC CANADA INC
SCHNEIDER ELECTRIC
(*Suby of* SCHNEIDER ELECTRIC SE)
4100 Place Java, Brossard, QC, J4Y 0C4
(450) 444-0143
Emp Here 80
SIC 3699 Electrical equipment and supplies, nec
Jean-Pierre Perreault

D-U-N-S 20-324-8203   (SL)
SKI MOJO INC
OBERSON
8025 Boul Taschereau, Brossard, QC, J4Y 1A4
(450) 462-4040
Emp Here 70   *Sales* 17,102,960
SIC 5941 Sporting goods and bicycle shops
Maurice Oberson

D-U-N-S 24-798-1280   (SL)
SPORTS DIX 30 INC
9550 Boul Leduc Bureau 15, Brossard, QC, J4Y 0B3
(450) 926-2000
Emp Here 55   *Sales* 11,293,865
SIC 5311 Department stores
Paul-Andre Trempe-Goulet

D-U-N-S 24-393-7914   (SL)
STATION SKYSPA INC

▲ Public Company   ■ Public Company Family Member   **HQ** Headquarters   **BR** Branch   **SL** Single Location

6000 Boul De Rome Bureau 400, Brossard,
QC, J4Y 0B6
(450) 462-9111
Emp Here 100   *Sales* 7,639,700
SIC 7991 Physical fitness facilities
Patrick Rake
Daniel Vincent

D-U-N-S 20-700-5419   (HQ)
STAVSTAN INC
3955 Rue De Longford, Brossard, QC, J4Y
3J6
(450) 445-7390
Sales 15,427,950
SIC 4225 General warehousing and storage
Steve Ramescu

D-U-N-S 20-187-6450   (SL)
SYSTEMES CALE INC
(*Suby of* MELLBY GARD HOLDING AB)
9005 Boul Du Quartier, Brossard, QC, J4Y
0A8
(450) 444-4484
Emp Here 26   *Sales* 11,626,524
SIC 5046 Commercial equipment, nec
Bertrand Barthelemy
Edward Olender
Anton Kaya
Benoit Reliquet

D-U-N-S 25-733-3864   (HQ)
TERRAPEX ENVIRONNEMENT LTEE
TERRAPEX
3615 Rue Isabelle Bureau A, Brossard, QC,
J4Y 2R2
(450) 444-3255
Emp Here 25   *Sales* 11,714,400
SIC 8748 Business consulting, nec
Charles Anthony Hawke

D-U-N-S 25-064-0745   (BR)
UNITED PARCEL SERVICE CANADA LTD
UPS
(*Suby of* UNITED PARCEL SERVICE, INC.)
3850 Boul Matte, Brossard, QC, J4Y 2Z2
(800) 742-5877
Emp Here 108
SIC 7389 Business services, nec
Greg Lavack

D-U-N-S 25-297-7103   (BR)
WAL-MART CANADA CORP
WALMART SUPERCENTRE
(*Suby of* WALMART INC.)
9000 Boul Leduc Unite 102, Brossard, QC,
J4Y 0E6
(450) 672-5000
Emp Here 250
SIC 5311 Department stores
Natasha Dube

Brossard, QC J4Z

D-U-N-S 24-608-2981   (SL)
9215-9516 QUEBEC INC
*MARCHE D'ALIMENTATION MARTIN
LAMARRE*
3260 Boul Lapiniere, Brossard, QC, J4Z 3L8
(450) 445-1224
Emp Here 49   *Sales* 13,433,448
SIC 5411 Grocery stores
Martin Lamarre

D-U-N-S 20-370-8409   (SL)
ACQUISIO WEB.COM, ULC
ENTREPRISES ACQUISIO WEB.COM
6300 Av Auteuil Bureau 300, Brossard, QC,
J4Z 3P2
(450) 465-2631
Emp Here 44   *Sales* 17,731,100
SIC 7371 Custom computer programming ser-
vices
David L. Brown
Kevin M. Carney
Matthew P. Mcclure

D-U-N-S 24-892-3877   (HQ)
APRIL CANADA INC
ELCO FINANCE
3250 Boul Lapiniere Bureau 100, Brossard,
QC, J4Z 3T8
(855) 745-2020
Emp Here 25   *Sales* 42,403,000
SIC 6411 Insurance agents, brokers, and ser-
vice
Sebastien Gabez
Marc-Andre Dupont
Emmanuel Morandini

D-U-N-S 20-266-1708   (SL)
APRIL MARINE CANADA INC
MARRINE EXPERT
4405 Boul Lapiniere, Brossard, QC, J4Z 3T5
(450) 671-6147
Emp Here 25   *Sales* 25,872,025
SIC 6331 Fire, marine, and casualty insurance
Nick Kidd
Lionel Boismery
Bruno Rousset
Marc-Andre Dupont

D-U-N-S 24-017-6644   (SL)
**ASSURANCES PROVENCHER VER-
REAULT & ASSOCIES INC**
7055 Boul Taschereau Bureau 620, Brossard,
QC, J4Z 1A7
(450) 676-7707
Emp Here 23   *Sales* 13,338,252
SIC 6411 Insurance agents, brokers, and ser-
vice
Real Verrault

D-U-N-S 24-842-3316   (SL)
BOULANGERIE ST-METHODE
6000 Av Auteuil, Brossard, QC, J4Z 1N3
(450) 766-0678
Emp Here 49   *Sales* 13,433,448
SIC 5461 Retail bakeries
Robert Faucher

D-U-N-S 20-297-8706   (BR)
CEGERTEC INC
GROUPEGENIE/CEGERTEC
4805 Boul Lapiniere Bureau 4300, Brossard,
QC, J4Z 0G2
(450) 656-3356
Emp Here 300   *Sales* 614,517
SIC 8621 Professional organizations
Richard Fay

D-U-N-S 24-311-9661   (SL)
DEVIMCO IMMOBILIER INC
3400 Rue De L'Eclipse Bureau 310, Brossard,
QC, J4Z 0P3
(450) 645-2525
Emp Here 100   *Sales* 20,388,300
SIC 6553 Cemetery subdividers and develop-
ers
Serge Goulet
Mathieu Jobin

D-U-N-S 20-928-8638   (SL)
ENTREPRISES MAX FRIED INC, LES
9125 Grande-Allee Bureau 1, Brossard, QC,
J4Z 3H8

Emp Here 10   *Sales* 12,103,970
SIC 5154 Livestock
Max Fried
Linda Fried

D-U-N-S 24-902-8523   (SL)
ESCOMPTE CHEZ LAFORTUNE INC
PHARMACIE JEAN-COUTU
5635 Grande-Allee Bureau 100, Brossard,
QC, J4Z 3G3
(450) 462-2120
Emp Here 65   *Sales* 15,881,320
SIC 5912 Drug stores and proprietary stores
Eugene Sabbagh
George Ibrahim

D-U-N-S 24-178-9247   (SL)
FRUITS ET LEGUMES GRANDE-ALLEE

INC
4635 Grande-Allee, Brossard, QC, J4Z 3E9
(450) 678-3167
Emp Here 47   *Sales* 13,793,419
SIC 5431 Fruit and vegetable markets
Claude Blouin
Jean-Pierre Caron
Mireille Caron

D-U-N-S 20-289-0208   (HQ)
**GE ENERGIES RENOUVELABLES
CANADA INC**
(*Suby of* GE RENEWABLE HOLDING B.V.)
5005 Boul Lapiniere Bureau 6000, Brossard,
QC, J4Z 0N5
(450) 746-6500
Emp Here 250   *Sales* 435,359,350
SIC 3511 Turbines and turbine generator sets
Pierre Marx
Helena Miller
Betty Huynh
Raghunandan Murthy

D-U-N-S 25-359-1200   (SL)
GROUPE ASSURANCE ELCO INC
(*Suby of* APRIL)
4405 Boul Lapiniere, Brossard, QC, J4Z 3T5
(450) 672-7070
Emp Here 72   *Sales* 133,037,424
SIC 6411 Insurance agents, brokers, and ser-
vice
Joseph Lanzo
Mario Lanouette

D-U-N-S 25-309-7596   (BR)
**INDUSTRIELLE ALLIANCE, ASSURANCE
ET SERVICES FINANCIERS INC**
(*Suby of* INDUSTRIELLE ALLIANCE, AS-
SURANCE ET SERVICES FINANCIERS INC)
9935 Rue De Chateauneuf Ste 230, Brossard,
QC, J4Z 3V4
(450) 672-6410
Emp Here 80
SIC 6411 Insurance agents, brokers, and ser-
vice

D-U-N-S 24-525-9218   (HQ)
MANTRA PHARMA INC
4605b Boul Lapiniere Bureau 250, Brossard,
QC, J4Z 3T5
(450) 678-7088
Sales 27,633,625
SIC 5122 Drugs, proprietaries, and sundries
Jean-Francois Letarte
Stephane B Turcotte
Normand Cantin
Pierre Cadrin

D-U-N-S 20-399-6082   (SL)
NOVACAP TMT V, S.E.C
3400 Rue De L'Eclipse Bureau 700, Brossard,
QC, J4Z 0P3
(450) 651-5000
Emp Here 60   *Sales* 13,436,460
SIC 6162 Mortgage bankers and loan corre-
spondents
Jacques Foisy

D-U-N-S 25-685-5222   (SL)
OPTIMONT INC
9995 Rue De Chateauneuf, Brossard, QC,
J4Z 3V7
(450) 465-1818
Emp Here 44   *Sales* 19,675,656
SIC 5065 Electronic parts and equipment, nec
Christian Morin

D-U-N-S 25-685-5164   (SL)
**ORGANISME D'AUTOREGLEMENTATION
DU COUTAGE IMMOBILERS DU QUEBEC,
L'**
OACIQ
4905 Boul Lapiniere Bureau 2200, Brossard,
QC, J4Z 0G2
(450) 676-4800
Emp Here 50   *Sales* 11,937,500
SIC 8611 Business associations

Nadine Lindsay

D-U-N-S 25-975-8050   (SL)
**PIERRE FABRE DERMO-COSMETIQUE
CANADA INC**
LABORATOIRES PIERRE FABRE
(*Suby of* FONDATION PIERRE FABRE)
9955 Rue De Chateauneuf Unite 115,
Brossard, QC, J4Z 3V5
(450) 676-9035
Emp Here 78   *Sales* 32,200,038
SIC 5122 Drugs, proprietaries, and sundries
Eric Ducournau
Nadine Pelletier
Linda Tibbits

D-U-N-S 20-331-4943   (SL)
ROCKWELL AUTOMATION CANADA LTD
AUTOMATISATION ROCKWELL CANADA
(*Suby of* ROCKWELL AUTOMATION
CANADA HOLDINGS INC)
9975 Rue De Chateauneuf Bureau U,
Brossard, QC, J4Z 3V6
(450) 445-3353
Emp Here 50   *Sales* 10,692,550
SIC 7372 Prepackaged software
James L Harding
Steven C Rizzo
Kathleen Donius
Steven W Etzel

D-U-N-S 20-535-2524   (BR)
ROTISSERIES ST-HUBERT LTEE, LES
(*Suby of* RECIPE UNLIMITED CORPORA-
TION)
6325 Boul Taschereau, Brossard, QC, J4Z
1A6

Emp Here 80
SIC 5812 Eating places
Martin Nadeau

D-U-N-S 24-570-1792   (HQ)
**SANEXEN SERVICES ENVIRONNEMEN-
TAUX INC**
SANEXEN - EXCAVATION, DIV OF
(*Suby of* LOGISTEC CORPORATION)
9935 Rue De Chateauneuf Unite 200,
Brossard, QC, J4Z 3V4
(450) 466-2123
Emp Here 120   *Sales* 74,590,338
SIC 4959 Sanitary services, nec
Madeleine Paquin
Alain Sauriol
Jean Paquin
Ingrid Stefancic
Rejean Loiselle
Nicole Paquin
Jean-Claude Dugas
Stephane Blanchette

D-U-N-S 24-495-8315   (BR)
TYCO SAFETY PRODUCTS CANADA LTD
SYSTEMES KANTECH
(*Suby of* JOHNSON CONTROLS INTERNA-
TIONAL PLC)
9995 Rue De Chateauneuf Unite L, Brossard,
QC, J4Z 3V7
(450) 444-2040
Emp Here 90
SIC 3699 Electrical equipment and supplies,
nec
Luc Champagne

D-U-N-S 25-324-8728   (BR)
VIGI SANTE LTEE
CHSLD VIGI BROSSARD
5955 Grande-Allee, Brossard, QC, J4Z 3S3
(450) 656-8500
Emp Here 150
SIC 8361 Residential care
Danielle Allaire

D-U-N-S 20-015-4487   (HQ)
VOITH HYDRO INC
(*Suby of* VOITH FAMILIEN VERWALTUNG
GMBH)

▲ Public Company   ■ Public Company Family Member   **HQ** Headquarters   **BR** Branch   **SL** Single Location

9955 Rue De Chateauneuf Bureau 160, Brossard, QC, J4Z 3V5
(450) 766-2100
Sales 58,877,250
SIC 1731 Electrical work
William Malus
Uwe Wehnhardt
Stephanie S. Vincent
Uwe Novak
Markus Mader

D-U-N-S 25-190-1740   (SL)
WATERS LTEE
9935 Rue De Chateauneuf Unite 330, Brossard, QC, J4Z 3V4
(450) 656-0120
Emp Here 49   *Sales* 10,796,072
SIC 8734 Testing laboratories
Richard Blais

Brownsburg-Chatham, QC J8G

D-U-N-S 24-404-4561   (SL)
GAZ COMPRIME INTERNATIONAL
1705 Rte Du Nord, Brownsburg-Chatham, QC, J8G 1E4
(450) 533-5911
Emp Here 15   *Sales* 46,587,855
SIC 4925 Gas production and/or distribution
Jean-Pierre Goulet

D-U-N-S 20-574-4274   (HQ)
JEAN JACQUES CAMPEAU INC
60 Rue Renaud, Brownsburg-Chatham, QC, J8G 2E6
(450) 562-2838
Sales 16,864,200
SIC 4151 School buses
Jacques Campeau
Martin Perreault
Muriel Mcgrath
Louis-Charles Ratelle
Rejean Fontaine

D-U-N-S 24-920-4413   (BR)
ORICA CANADA INC
(*Suby of* ORICA LIMITED)
342 Rue Mcmaster, Brownsburg-Chatham, QC, J8G 3A8
(450) 533-4201
Emp Here 400
SIC 2892 Explosives
Luc Dugas

D-U-N-S 25-527-7956   (HQ)
ORICA CANADA INC
SOUTENEMENT DU SOL MINOVA CANADA
(*Suby of* ORICA LIMITED)
301 Rue De L'Hotel-De-Ville, Brownsburg-Chatham, QC, J8G 3B5
(450) 533-4201
Emp Here 550   *Sales* 333,483,750
SIC 2892 Explosives
James K. Bonnor
Martin Briere
Suzanne R. Thigpen
Patricia Jacobs

Cabano, QC G0L

D-U-N-S 20-867-4262   (SL)
PETROLE J.M.B INC
SHELL
85 Rue Commerciale, Cabano, QC, G0L 1E0
(418) 854-2267
Emp Here 15   *Sales* 15,492,120
SIC 5172 Petroleum products, nec
Pierre Beaulieu

Candiac, QC J5R

D-U-N-S 25-699-3718   (SL)
3075109 CANADA INC
THERMOFIN
47 Boul Marie-Victorin, Candiac, QC, J5R 1B6
(450) 444-4405
Emp Here 130   *Sales* 24,971,050
SIC 3443 Fabricated plate work (boiler shop)
Louis-Charles Rondeau
Jean-Francois Roy

D-U-N-S 24-178-2929   (SL)
9123-2165 QUEBEC INC
CANDIAC TOYOTA
185 Boul De L'Industrie, Candiac, QC, J5R 1J4
(450) 659-6511
Emp Here 50   *Sales* 24,903,900
SIC 5511 New and used car dealers
Gustave M. Schlegel
Gustave Jr Schlegel
Melissa Schlegel

D-U-N-S 24-610-0353   (HQ)
9191-7906 QUEBEC INC
IGA EXTRA VALLEE
200 Rue Strasbourg, Candiac, QC, J5R 0B4
(450) 659-3434
Emp Here 15   *Sales* 15,616,260
SIC 5099 Durable goods, nec
Daniel Vallee
Jacques Vallee
Marc Vallee

D-U-N-S 24-740-9469   (SL)
9343-8919 QUEBEC INC
TECHNISEAL
(*Suby of* 9078-4349 QUEBEC INC)
300 Av Liberte, Candiac, QC, J5R 6X1
(450) 633-9303
Emp Here 60   *Sales* 17,041,260
SIC 2869 Industrial organic chemicals, nec
Robert Hattem
Alain Dorais
Claude Boivin
Bernard Casvant
Normand Chartrand
Claude Roy
Pierre Wilkie
Marc Bedard

D-U-N-S 20-856-2686   (BR)
ADM AGRI-INDUSTRIES COMPANY
COMPAGNIE ARCHER-DANIELS-MIDLAND DU CANADA
(*Suby of* ARCHER-DANIELS-MIDLAND COMPANY)
155 Av D'Iberia, Candiac, QC, J5R 3H1
(450) 659-1911
Emp Here 100
SIC 2046 Wet corn milling
Jean Pierre Paradis

D-U-N-S 20-125-2322   (HQ)
ASSURANCIA GROUPE BROSSEAU INC
ROGER OUIMET & FILS
1 Av Liberte, Candiac, QC, J5R 3X8
(450) 635-1155
Emp Here 15   *Sales* 18,657,320
SIC 6411 Insurance agents, brokers, and service
Claude Brosseau
Martine Labelle
Claude Boivin

D-U-N-S 20-265-6583   (SL)
BEAUVAIS LTEE
264 Av Liberte, Candiac, QC, J5R 6X1
(514) 871-0226
Emp Here 30   *Sales* 25,067,310
SIC 5148 Fresh fruits and vegetables
Max Dumouchel

D-U-N-S 24-524-1786   (SL)
BELCAM INC
DELAGAR DIVISION

9 Boul Montcalm N Bureau 400, Candiac, QC, J5R 3L5
(450) 619-1112
Emp Here 21   *Sales* 23,212,245
SIC 5122 Drugs, proprietaries, and sundries
John Knot

D-U-N-S 24-126-3313   (BR)
CASCADES CANADA ULC
CASCADES GROUPE TISSU-CANDIAC
(*Suby of* CASCADES INC)
75 Boul Marie-Victorin, Candiac, QC, J5R 1C2
(450) 444-6500
Emp Here 225
SIC 2621 Paper mills
Jean Fortin

D-U-N-S 24-337-2732   (BR)
CASCADES CANADA ULC
CASCADES TISSUE GROUP - CANDIAC
(*Suby of* CASCADES INC)
77 Boul Marie-Victorin, Candiac, QC, J5R 1C2
(450) 444-6400
Emp Here 210
SIC 2676 Sanitary paper products
Alain Lemaire

D-U-N-S 24-601-4021   (HQ)
CEDAROME CANADA INC
ARSENAL ART CONTEMPORAIN (MONTREAL)
21 Rue Paul-Gauguin, Candiac, QC, J5R 3X8
(450) 659-8000
Sales 40,107,696
SIC 5149 Groceries and related products, nec
Pierre Trahan
Yves Boisvert
Suzon Trahan

D-U-N-S 25-258-7936   (SL)
CENTRE LOCAL DES SERVICES COMMUNAUTAIRES KATERI INC
C L S C KATERI
90 Boul Marie-Victorin, Candiac, QC, J5R 1C1
(450) 659-7661
Emp Here 165   *Sales* 34,166,220
SIC 8399 Social services, nec
Andre Taillon
Andre Cote

D-U-N-S 20-191-5964   (HQ)
CHANEL CANADA ULC
(*Suby of* LITOR LIMITED)
55 Boul Marie-Victorin, Candiac, QC, J5R 1B6
(450) 659-1981
Emp Here 60   *Sales* 53,666,730
SIC 5122 Drugs, proprietaries, and sundries
Sachin Garg
Olivier Nicolay
Michael Rena
Guy Schreiber

D-U-N-S 25-240-2201   (BR)
COMMISSION SCOLAIRE DES GRANDES-SEIGNEURIES
ECOLE JEAN LEMAN
(*Suby of* COMMISSION SCOLAIRE DES GRANDES-SEIGNEURIES)
4 Av De Champagne, Candiac, QC, J5R 4W3
(514) 380-8899
Emp Here 80
SIC 8211 Elementary and secondary schools
Christiane Lachapelle Perron

D-U-N-S 24-354-8877   (BR)
COSTCO WHOLESALE CANADA LTD
COSTCO
(*Suby of* COSTCO WHOLESALE CORPORATION)
60 Rue Strasbourg, Candiac, QC, J5R 0B4
(450) 444-3453
Emp Here 200
SIC 5099 Durable goods, nec
Simon Pouliot

D-U-N-S 20-187-3218   (SL)
DEVELOPPEMENTS ANGELCARE INC,

LES
ANGELCARE
(*Suby of* GESTION MAURICE PINSONNAULT INC)
201 Boul De L'Industrie Bureau 104, Candiac, QC, J5R 6A6
(514) 761-0511
Emp Here 19   *Sales* 12,901,269
SIC 3443 Fabricated plate work (boiler shop)
Maurice Pinsonnault
Laura Lungu

D-U-N-S 24-922-5210   (SL)
DISTRIBUTIONS ALIMENTAIRES MANSION INC, LES
MANSION
255 Av Liberte, Candiac, QC, J5R 3X8
(450) 632-5088
Emp Here 30   *Sales* 25,067,310
SIC 5142 Packaged frozen goods
Dominic Lavergne

D-U-N-S 20-886-0601   (HQ)
ELECTROMEGA LIMITEE
105 Av Liberte, Candiac, QC, J5R 3X8
(450) 635-1020
Emp Here 39   *Sales* 19,951,092
SIC 5084 Industrial machinery and equipment
Pascal Lamoureux
Thierry Lamoureux
Michelle Allard
Jean Allard

D-U-N-S 24-355-8728   (HQ)
EMBALLAGES GAB LTEE, LES
EMBALLAGES GAB - INDUSPAC
140 Boul De L'Industrie, Candiac, QC, J5R 1J2
(450) 444-4884
Sales 18,674,800
SIC 2657 Folding paperboard boxes
Luc Guertin
Marie-Josee Renaud
Mario Latendresse

D-U-N-S 20-715-4118   (BR)
ENTREPRISES JMC (1973) LTEE, LES
MCDONALD'S CANDIAC
101 Ch Saint-Francois-Xavier, Candiac, QC, J5R 4V4
(450) 632-4723
Emp Here 100
SIC 5812 Eating places
Mike Capelli

D-U-N-S 20-014-6850   (HQ)
FENPLAST INC
160 Boul De L'Industrie, Candiac, QC, J5R 1J3
(514) 990-0012
Sales 60,807,750
SIC 3442 Metal doors, sash, and trim
Jean Marchand

D-U-N-S 20-984-5648   (SL)
FRATERNITE DES POLICIERS DE LA REGIE INTERMUNICIPALE ROUSSILLON INC
90 Ch Saint-Francois-Xavier, Candiac, QC, J5R 6M6
(450) 635-9911
Emp Here 100   *Sales* 14,287,900
SIC 8641 Civic and social associations
Stephane Thibault
Francois Michaud
Yannick Morin
Steve Gagnon
Daniel Verville

D-U-N-S 24-816-2245   (SL)
GESTION PERREAULT ET BEAULIEU INC
15 Boul Montcalm N, Candiac, QC, J5R 3L4
(450) 659-5426
Emp Here 49   *Sales* 12,394,746
SIC 5912 Drug stores and proprietary stores
Jonathan-Yan Perreault

D-U-N-S 24-458-8687   (SL)
INDUSTRIES M.K.E. (1984) INC, LES
183 Boul Montcalm N, Candiac, QC, J5R 3L6

---

(450) 659-6531
Emp Here 50   Sales 11,100,050
SIC 3589 Service industry machinery, nec
Edith Majeau

D-U-N-S 20-271-3244   (SL)
JOHNSON MATTHEY MATERIAUX POUR BATTERIES LTEE
JOHNSON MATTHEY MB
(Suby of JOHNSON MATTHEY PLC)
280 Av Liberte, Candiac, QC, J5R 6X1
(514) 906-1359
Emp Here 50   Sales 13,592,100
SIC 7699 Repair services, nec
Neil Robert Collins
Steven L. Bray
Steven Paul Robinson
Karil J. Black Wollitz

D-U-N-S 20-289-8219   (SL)
LOCWELD INC
50 Av Iberville, Candiac, QC, J5R 1J5
(450) 659-9661
Emp Here 100   Sales 19,208,500
SIC 3441 Fabricated structural Metal
Michael G. Cyr
Terry Gilliland
Maurice Brunet
Maurice J. Cyr

D-U-N-S 20-215-9471   (HQ)
MATERIAUX DE CONSTRUCTION R OLIGNY LTEE, LES
101 Boul Taschereau, Candiac, QC, J5R 1X4
(450) 659-5444
Sales 17,886,960
SIC 5031 Lumber, plywood, and millwork
Robert Oligny

D-U-N-S 20-984-5689   (SL)
METRO RICHELIEU CANDIAC INC
ALIMENTATION MARTIN CLOUTIER
50 Boul Montcalm N, Candiac, QC, J5R 3L8
(450) 444-2300
Emp Here 90   Sales 26,412,930
SIC 5411 Grocery stores
Martin Cloutier

D-U-N-S 20-187-3093   (SL)
MONITEURS ANGELCARE INC
201 Boul De L'Industrie Local 104, Candiac, QC, J5R 6A6
(450) 462-2000
Emp Here 18   Sales 10,738,897
SIC 3699 Electrical equipment and supplies, nec
Maurice Pinsonneault

D-U-N-S 24-422-8818   (SL)
NEOLECT INC
(Suby of PLACEMENTS CLAUDE GAUTHIER INC, LES)
104 Boul Montcalm N, Candiac, QC, J5R 3L8
(514) 382-1550
Emp Here 60   Sales 13,069,740
SIC 1731 Electrical work
Claude Gauthier
Sylvain Rousseau

D-U-N-S 20-191-5816   (BR)
OC CANADA HOLDINGS COMPANY
USINE DE CANDIAC
(Suby of OWENS CORNING)
131 Boul Montcalm N, Candiac, QC, J5R 3L6
(450) 619-2000
Emp Here 100
SIC 3296 Mineral wool
Pierre Charbonneau

D-U-N-S 20-363-0165   (BR)
OLDCASTLE BUILDING PRODUCTS CANADA, INC
MATERIAUX DE CONSTRUCTION OLDCASTLE CANADA INC, LES
(Suby of CRH PUBLIC LIMITED COMPANY)
2 Av D'Inverness, Candiac, QC, J5R 4W5
(450) 444-5214
Emp Here 90

SIC 5039 Construction materials, nec
Gael Argil

D-U-N-S 20-120-2772   (BR)
OLDCASTLE BUILDING PRODUCTS CANADA, INC
MATERIAUX DE CONSTRUCTION OLDCASTLE CANADA INC, LES
(Suby of CRH PUBLIC LIMITED COMPANY)
2 Av D'Inverness, Candiac, QC, J5R 4W5
(450) 444-5214
Emp Here 80
SIC 2822 Synthetic rubber
Francois Dore

D-U-N-S 25-188-3583   (SL)
OPTIMUM REASSURANCE
8 Place Avila, Candiac, QC, J5R 5R5
(450) 984-1462
Emp Here 49   Sales 90,486,291
SIC 6311 Life insurance
Serge Goulet

D-U-N-S 20-265-7094   (BR)
PHARMASCIENCE INC
(Suby of JODDES LIMITEE)
100 Boul De L'Industrie, Candiac, QC, J5R 1J1
(450) 444-9989
Emp Here 120
SIC 2834 Pharmaceutical preparations
Sylvain Duvernay

D-U-N-S 20-707-5243   (SL)
PRECIMOLD INC
PRECIMOULE
9 Boul Marie-Victorin, Candiac, QC, J5R 4S8
(450) 659-2921
Emp Here 60   Sales 28,501,560
SIC 5085 Industrial supplies
John Alvin Mcdonald

D-U-N-S 20-011-6569   (SL)
PRODUITS ZINDA CANADA INC
104 Av Liberte, Candiac, QC, J5R 6X1
(450) 635-6664
Emp Here 60   Sales 11,242,750
SIC 2041 Flour and other grain mill products
Abdelmajid Jamaleddine

D-U-N-S 20-201-3413   (HQ)
RUETGERS POLYMERES LTEE
(Suby of RAIN INDUSTRIES LIMITED)
120 Boul De L'Industrie, Candiac, QC, J5R 1J2
(450) 659-9693
Sales 28,402,100
SIC 2869 Industrial organic chemicals, nec
Gunther Weymans
Anthony Lippl
Johanne Grondin
Gerard Sweeney
Paul Francesce

D-U-N-S 20-012-0047   (BR)
TOROMONT INDUSTRIES LTD
TOROMONT CAT
(Suby of TOROMONT INDUSTRIES LTD)
350 Av Liberte, Candiac, QC, J5R 6X1
(450) 638-6091
Emp Here 100
SIC 5082 Construction and mining machinery

Cantley, QC J8V

D-U-N-S 20-552-0807   (HQ)
4094468 CANADA INC
SKI MONT-CASCADES
448 Ch Du Mont-Des-Cascades, Cantley, QC, J8V 3B2
(819) 827-0301
Sales 21,675,000
SIC 7999 Amusement and recreation, nec
Richard Hunter
Luc Desormeaux
Christine Charette
David Alexander

Pierre Bourdages

Canton Tremblay, QC G7G

D-U-N-S 24-499-1295   (SL)
CONSTRUCTION RENO-GAUTHIER ENTREPRENEUR GENERAL INC
1266 Rue De Vimy, Canton Tremblay, QC, G7G 5H8
(418) 543-8602
Emp Here 45   Sales 21,182,895
SIC 1542 Nonresidential construction, nec
Richard Gauthier
Dominic Gauthier
Patrice Gauthier

Canton-De-Hatley, QC J0B

D-U-N-S 24-547-3921   (SL)
MANOIR HOVEY (1985) INC
575 Ch Hovey, Canton-De-Hatley, QC, J0B 2C0
(819) 842-2421
Emp Here 80   Sales 7,591,920
SIC 7011 Hotels and motels
Stephen Stafford
Kathryn Stafford

D-U-N-S 20-859-7906   (BR)
SINTRA INC
ESTRIE, DIV DE
(Suby of BOUYGUES)
3600 Ch Dunant, Canton-De-Hatley, QC, J0B 2C0
(819) 346-8634
Emp Here 160
SIC 1611 Highway and street construction
Martin Cote

D-U-N-S 25-080-5892   (BR)
SODEM INC
CENTRE RECREOTOURISTIQUE MONTJOYE
(Suby of SODEM INC)
4765 Ch De Capelton, Canton-De-Hatley, QC, J0B 2C0

Emp Here 100
SIC 7299 Miscellaneous personal service
Jean Pellerin

Cap-Aux-Meules, QC G4T

D-U-N-S 24-863-6763   (SL)
C.T.M.A. TRAVERSIER LTEE
MADELEINE, LE
(Suby of COOPERATIVE DE TRANSPORT MARITIME AERIEN ASSOCIATION COOPERATIVE)
435 Ch Avila-Arseneau, Cap-Aux-Meules, QC, G4T 1J3
(418) 986-6600
Emp Here 120   Sales 47,246,880
SIC 4424 Deep sea domestic transportation of freight
Edee Chevarie
Jean-Paul Richard
Paul Delaney
Louis Hebert
Jean-Yves Miousse
Paul Duclos
Normand Lebel
Emmanuel Aucoin

D-U-N-S 20-871-7264   (HQ)
CENTRE INTEGRE DE SANTE ET DE SERVICES SOCIAUX DES ILES
CISSS DES ILES

430 Ch Principal, Cap-Aux-Meules, QC, G4T 1R9
(418) 986-2121
Emp Here 100   Sales 55,540,000
SIC 8062 General medical and surgical hospitals
Jasmine Martineau
Gaston Bourque

D-U-N-S 20-000-0594   (HQ)
COOPERATIVE DE TRANSPORT MARITIME AERIEN ASSOCIATION COOPERATIVE
CTMA
435 Ch Avila-Arseneau, Cap-Aux-Meules, QC, G4T 1J3
(418) 986-6600
Sales 102,853,000
SIC 4213 Trucking, except local

D-U-N-S 25-809-6627   (SL)
DEVELOPPEMENT CYREX INC
DOOLYS
455 Ch Principal, Cap-Aux-Meules, QC, G4T 1E4
(418) 986-2871
Emp Here 49   Sales 13,881,357
SIC 8741 Management services
Jessica Cyr

D-U-N-S 24-381-2468   (HQ)
ENTREPRISES PAUL F. DELANEY INC
SERVICE AERIEN PFD, DIV OF
165 Ch Principal, Cap-Aux-Meules, QC, G4T 1C4
(418) 986-2135
Sales 10,328,080
SIC 5172 Petroleum products, nec
Paul F Delaney

D-U-N-S 24-791-8246   (HQ)
GESTION C.T.M.A. INC
(Suby of COOPERATIVE DE TRANSPORT MARITIME AERIEN ASSOCIATION COOPERATIVE)
435 Ch Avila-Arseneau, Cap-Aux-Meules, QC, G4T 1J3
(418) 986-6600
Emp Here 150   Sales 120,111,369
SIC 6712 Bank holding companies
Edee Chevarie
Jean-Paul Richard
Paul Delaney
Louis Hebert
Jean Miousse
Paul Duclos
Jean-Yves Miousse
Normand Lebel

D-U-N-S 24-698-5329   (HQ)
NAVIGATION MADELEINE INC
C.T.M.A. VACANCIER
(Suby of COOPERATIVE DE TRANSPORT MARITIME AERIEN ASSOCIATION COOPERATIVE)
435 Ch Avila-Arseneau, Cap-Aux-Meules, QC, G4T 1J3
(418) 986-6600
Sales 19,476,368
SIC 4432 Freight transportation on the great lakes
Edee Chevarie
Jean-Paul Richard
Paul Delaney
Louis Hebert
Jean-Yves Miousse
Paul Duclos
Sylvain Miousse

Cap-D'Espoir, QC G0C

D-U-N-S 24-206-8823   (SL)
ENTREPRISES AGRICOLES & FORESTIERES DE PERCE INC, LES

884 Rue Principale, Cap-D'Espoir, QC, G0C 1G0
(418) 782-2621
Emp Here 70   *Sales* 10,910,410
SIC 2411 Logging
Michel Bouchard
Jacques Grenier
Ralph Beck
Mario Cloutier

D-U-N-S 20-244-2104   (SL)
FUMOIRS GASPE CURED INC, LES
65 Rue De La Station, Cap-D'Espoir, QC, G0C 1G0
(418) 782-5920
Emp Here 65   *Sales* 22,469,850
SIC 2091 Canned and cured fish and seafoods
Real Nicolas
Roch Lelievre

Cap-Saint-Ignace, QC G0R

D-U-N-S 24-379-7800   (SL)
PABER ALUMINIUM INC
TECHNOLOGIES DE MOULAGE
296 Ch Vincelotte, Cap-Saint-Ignace, QC, G0R 1H0
(418) 246-5626
Emp Here 70   *Sales* 12,697,160
SIC 3365 Aluminum foundries
Luc Paris
Bryan Paris
Genevieve Paris
Diane Collin

D-U-N-S 25-526-9417   (SL)
SOCIETE EN COMMANDITE PROLAM
PROLAM
439 Ch Vincelotte, Cap-Saint-Ignace, QC, G0R 1H0
(418) 246-5101
Emp Here 200   *Sales* 38,474,000
SIC 2426 Hardwood dimension and flooring mills
Benoit Risi

Cap-Sante, QC G0A

D-U-N-S 24-914-2626   (SL)
KIA CAP SANTE INC
5 Du Bois-De-L'Ail, Cap-Sante, QC, G0A 1L0
(418) 285-5555
Emp Here 45   *Sales* 28,317,600
SIC 5561 Recreational vehicle dealers

Carignan, QC J3L

D-U-N-S 25-540-7298   (BR)
RONA INC
(*Suby of* LOWE'S COMPANIES, INC.)
1458 Ch De Chambly, Carignan, QC, J3L 0J4
(450) 658-8774
Emp Here 76
SIC 5072 Hardware
Dominic Viau

D-U-N-S 20-422-1774   (SL)
TERMINAL & CABLE TC INC
TC
(*Suby of* TCP CABLE INC)
1930 Ch Bellerive, Carignan, QC, J3L 4Z4
(450) 658-1742
Emp Here 165   *Sales* 36,934,095
SIC 3714 Motor vehicle parts and accessories
Marc April
Denis Coderre

Carleton, QC G0C

D-U-N-S 20-192-2473   (HQ)
ARMAND AUTOMOBILES LTEE
LOCATION BLUE PELICAN
542 Boul Perron, Carleton, QC, G0C 1J0
(418) 364-3382
Emp Here 15   *Sales* 12,451,950
SIC 5511 New and used car dealers
Jean-Paul Guite
Raphael Guite

D-U-N-S 25-128-1742   (SL)
FABRICATION SCANDINAVE INC
CANLOG (LA MAISON DE BOIS CANADIENNE)
452 Boul Perron, Carleton, QC, G0C 1J0
(418) 364-6701
Emp Here 26   *Sales* 13,534,092
SIC 5099 Durable goods, nec
Christian Bernard

D-U-N-S 20-950-3846   (SL)
MARCHE L.V. LTEE
METRO
686 Boul Perron Gd, Carleton, QC, G0C 1J0
(418) 364-7380
Emp Here 90   *Sales* 26,412,930
SIC 5411 Grocery stores
Guy Viens
Mathieu Viens

Causapscal, QC G0J

D-U-N-S 20-212-7077   (BR)
BOIS D'OEUVRE CEDRICO INC
USINE CAUSAP
(*Suby of* BOIS D'OEUVRE CEDRICO INC)
562 Rte 132 E, Causapscal, QC, G0J 1J0
(418) 756-5727
Emp Here 100
SIC 5099 Durable goods, nec
Nancy Berube

Chambly, QC J3L

D-U-N-S 24-395-1725   (SL)
4427378 CANADA INC
CHAMBLY MAZDA
830 Boul De Perigny, Chambly, QC, J3L 1W3
(450) 658-6623
Emp Here 26   *Sales* 12,950,028
SIC 5511 New and used car dealers
Denis Morin

D-U-N-S 25-649-8254   (SL)
4486404 CANADA INC.
CHAMBLY KIA
840 Boul De Perigny, Chambly, QC, J3L 1W3
(450) 447-6699
Emp Here 25   *Sales* 12,451,950
SIC 5511 New and used car dealers
Bilodeau Charles-Andre

D-U-N-S 20-331-9140   (BR)
ANDRITZ HYDRO CANADA INC
(*Suby of* ANDRITZ AG)
7920 Rue Samuel-Hatt Bureau 7902, Chambly, QC, J3L 6W4
(450) 658-5554
Emp Here 75
SIC 8711 Engineering services
Rene Leblanc

D-U-N-S 20-126-5847   (SL)
AS DU RANGEMENT RIVE-NORD/ RIVE-SUD INC
1635 Boul Lebel Bureau 302, Chambly, QC, J3L 0R8

---

(514) 792-4036
Emp Here 70   *Sales* 17,233,020
SIC 1799 Special trade contractors, nec
Mike Huard
Myriam Huard Belanger

D-U-N-S 24-835-8509   (SL)
AUTOMOBILES LA SEIGNEURIE (1990) INC, LES
CHAMBLY HONDA
850 Boul De Perigny Bureau 112, Chambly, QC, J3L 1W3
(450) 658-6699
Emp Here 43   *Sales* 21,417,354
SIC 5511 New and used car dealers
Mario Rivest

D-U-N-S 25-391-8056   (SL)
CAISSE POPULAIRE DESJARDINS DU BASSIN-DE-CHAMBLY
CENTRE FINANCIER AUX ENTREPRISES DESJARDINS VALLEE DU RICHELIEU-YAMASKA
455 Boul Brassard, Chambly, QC, J3L 4V6
(450) 658-0691
Emp Here 50   *Sales* 11,008,876
SIC 6062 State credit unions
Sylvain Juneau
Jean-Guy Chabot
Ginette Mercier
Gerard Boisvert
Claude Corbeil
Marie-Lyne Proulx
Normand Perrault
Andree-Anne Desmeules
Michel La Barre

D-U-N-S 20-394-5741   (SL)
CANADIAN TIRE
3400 Boul Frechette, Chambly, QC, J3L 6Z6
(450) 447-8393
Emp Here 30   *Sales* 10,926,450
SIC 5014 Tires and tubes
Raymond Lewis

D-U-N-S 24-314-2523   (BR)
CARGILL LIMITED
CARGILL FOODS
(*Suby of* CARGILL, INCORPORATED)
7901 Rue Samuel-Hatt, Chambly, QC, J3L 6V7
(450) 447-4600
Emp Here 700
SIC 5153 Grain and field beans

D-U-N-S 25-627-9431   (BR)
CARTE INTERNATIONAL INC
TRANSFORMATEUR CARTE INTERNATIONAL
(*Suby of* CROCUS INVESTMENT FUND)
2032 Av Bourgogne Bureau 107, Chambly, QC, J3L 1Z6
(450) 447-5815
Emp Here 200
SIC 5065 Electronic parts and equipment, nec
Leo Guilbeault

D-U-N-S 24-869-6028   (SL)
CINTUBE LTEE
1577 Rue Watts, Chambly, QC, J3L 2Z3
(450) 658-5140
Emp Here 49   *Sales* 10,105,826
SIC 3498 Fabricated pipe and fittings
Anita L Carrier

D-U-N-S 20-026-3619   (BR)
COMMISSION SCOLAIRE DES PATRIOTES
ECOLE SECONDAIRE DE CHAMBLY
(*Suby of* COMMISSION SCOLAIRE DES PATRIOTES)
535 Boul Brassard, Chambly, QC, J3L 6H3
(450) 461-5908
Emp Here 100
SIC 8211 Elementary and secondary schools
Nicole Borremans

D-U-N-S 24-991-2432   (SL)
CONTINENTAL   BUILDING   PRODUCTS

CANADA INC
MATERIAUX DE CONSTRUCTION CANADA CONTINENTAL
(*Suby of* CONTINENTAL BUILDING PRODUCTS, INC.)
8802 Boul Industriel, Chambly, QC, J3L 4X3
(450) 447-3206
Emp Here 250   *Sales* 103,277,250
SIC 1499 Miscellaneous nonMetallic minerals, except fuels
Stephane Savard
James W. Bachman

D-U-N-S 20-554-9368   (SL)
COVANTA SOLUTIONS ENVIRONNEMENTALES INC
SORINCO
(*Suby of* COVANTA HOLDING CORPORATION)
7860 Rue Samuel-Hatt, Chambly, QC, J3L 6W4
(450) 447-1212
Emp Here 49   *Sales* 12,599,419
SIC 4953 Refuse systems
Stephen James Jones
Graham Bradley Wright
Timothy John Simpson

D-U-N-S 24-178-6560   (SL)
EBENISTERIES SAMSON SAMUEL INC, LES
EBSS
7900 Boul Industriel, Chambly, QC, J3L 4X3
(450) 447-7503
Emp Here 60   *Sales* 13,944,180
SIC 5712 Furniture stores
Denis Normand
Yves Normand

D-U-N-S 24-784-4413   (SL)
ECOLOPHARM INC
8100 Rue Samuel-Hatt, Chambly, QC, J3L 6W4
(450) 447-6307
Emp Here 26   *Sales* 28,738,970
SIC 5122 Drugs, proprietaries, and sundries
Sandrine Milante
Guy Gagnon
Gaetan Milante
Yvonne Milante

D-U-N-S 24-648-3283   (HQ)
FIBRES J. C. INC, LES
3718 Ch De La Grande-Ligne, Chambly, QC, J3L 4A7
(450) 359-4545
Sales 52,147,500
SIC 5093 Scrap and waste materials
Joseph Colubriale
Antonio (Tony) Colubriale
Frank Colubriale
Raffaela Colubriale
Cathy Colubriale
Mary Colubriale

D-U-N-S 20-961-5483   (SL)
FONDREMY INC
1465 Boul Industriel Bureau 100, Chambly, QC, J3L 4C4
(450) 658-7111
Emp Here 85   *Sales* 19,841,975
SIC 3365 Aluminum foundries
Gerard Lemair

D-U-N-S 25-672-2190   (SL)
INSTRUMENTS ISAAC INC
240 Boul Frechette, Chambly, QC, J3L 2Z5
(450) 658-7520
Emp Here 50   *Sales* 12,828,100
SIC 3823 Process control instruments
Jacques Delarochelliere

D-U-N-S 25-526-4517   (SL)
J.G. RIVE-SUD FRUITS & LEGUMES INC
SAVEUR ULTIME FLAVOUR
(*Suby of* GORDON FOOD SERVICE, INC.)
1963 Rue Patrick-Farrar, Chambly, QC, J3L

4N7
(450) 447-3092
Emp Here 75   *Sales* 53,753,700
SIC 5148 Fresh fruits and vegetables
Dean Noble
Alisha L. Cieslak
Jeffrey Maddox
Frank Geier
Richard J. Wolowski

D-U-N-S 24-610-2615   (SL)
**JEAN COUTU JEAN-PHILIPPE ROY (AFFIL-
IATED PHARMACIES)**
3300 Boul Frechette, Chambly, QC, J3L 6Z6
(450) 447-5511
Emp Here 45   *Sales* 11,382,930
SIC 5912 Drug stores and proprietary stores
Jean Roy

D-U-N-S 20-576-4249   (SL)
MAGASINS MAXI
1601 Boul De Perigny, Chambly, QC, J3L 1W9
(450) 447-7500
Emp Here 49   *Sales* 13,589,033
SIC 5411 Grocery stores
Annik Claing

D-U-N-S 20-500-4864   (SL)
OSTIGUY ET FRERES INC
BMR
1000 Boul Industriel, Chambly, QC, J3L 6Z7
(450) 658-4371
Emp Here 105   *Sales* 59,810,940
SIC 5039 Construction materials, nec
Jean-Pierre Lareau
Francois Lareau
Marc Brennan

D-U-N-S 20-192-4859   (HQ)
REMTEC INC
COLUMBIA REMTEC MANUFACTURING
(*Suby of* 128707 CANADA INC)
933 Av Simard, Chambly, QC, J3L 4B7
(450) 658-6671
Emp Here 15   *Sales* 16,327,225
SIC 3443 Fabricated plate work (boiler shop)
Anthony Roberts
David Roberts

D-U-N-S 24-569-6372   (SL)
SERAY AUTO INC
HYUNDAI
730 Boul De Perigny, Chambly, QC, J3L 1W3
(450) 658-4482
Emp Here 30   *Sales* 14,942,340
SIC 5511 New and used car dealers
Eric Bessette
Lise Bessette

D-U-N-S 20-003-9618   (SL)
SOLUTIONS INHALOSTAT INC, LES
SOLUSTAT
1697 Rue Felix-Leclerc, Chambly, QC, J3L
5Z3
(450) 447-2112
Emp Here 49   *Sales* 10,374,476
SIC 7322 Adjustment and collection services
Bruno Auclair

Chambord, QC G0W

D-U-N-S 25-380-6335   (HQ)
CENTRE DU SPORT LAC-ST-JEAN INC
CHAMBORD SPORT YAMAHA
1454 Rue Principale, Chambord, QC, G0W
1G0
(418) 342-6202
Emp Here 15   *Sales* 19,923,120
SIC 5561 Recreational vehicle dealers
Rejean Tremblay
Mathieu Tremblay
Lise Toulouse

D-U-N-S 20-192-5930   (SL)
COOPERATIVE D'APPROVISIONNEMENT

DE CHAMBORD
COOP CHAMBORD
1945 Rte 169, Chambord, QC, G0W 1G0
(418) 342-6495
Emp Here 60   *Sales* 16,449,120
SIC 5411 Grocery stores
Claude Berube
Jean-Paul Boily

D-U-N-S 20-285-8598   (SL)
**CORPORATION DU PARC REGIONAL DE
VAL-JALBERT**
*CAMPING VILLAGE HISTORIQUE DE VAL-
JALBERT*
95 Rue Saint-Georges, Chambord, QC, G0W
1G0
(418) 275-3132
Emp Here 110   *Sales* 2,880,788
SIC 8412 Museums and art galleries
Jacques Girard
Ian Lapierre
Paul Michaud
Jean Belzile
David Cleary
Catherine Imbeault
Veronique Leblanc
Steeve Gagnon
Chantale Paradis
Michele Castonguay

D-U-N-S 24-531-3887   (SL)
FERICAR INC
112 Rte 155, Chambord, QC, G0W 1G0
(418) 342-6221
Emp Here 70   *Sales* 13,532,120
SIC 3715 Truck trailers
Sabin Jean
Daniel Jean

D-U-N-S 20-698-0901   (BR)
LOUISIANA-PACIFIC CANADA LTD
*LOUISIANA-PACIFIQUE CANADA LTEE-
DIVISON QUEBEC CHAMBORD OSB*
(*Suby of* LOUISIANA-PACIFIC CORPORA-
TION)
572 155 Rte, Chambord, QC, G0W 1G0
(418) 342-6212
Emp Here 200
SIC 2611 Pulp mills
Serge Guay

D-U-N-S 24-530-4555   (SL)
SOCIETE SYLVICOLE CHAMBORD LTEE
SOCIETE SYLVICOLE
21 Rue Des Sources, Chambord, QC, G0W
1G0
(418) 342-6251
Emp Here 250   *Sales* 51,654,250
SIC 0851 Forestry services
Marcel Mailhot
Roger Allard
Benoit Boily

D-U-N-S 24-411-6526   (SL)
**UNIPRIX DANIEL GUAY & JULIE BEAUPRE
(AFFILIATED PHARMACY)**
1682 Rue Principale, Chambord, QC, G0W
1G0
(418) 342-6263
Emp Here 49   *Sales* 54,161,905
SIC 5122 Drugs, proprietaries, and sundries
Mona Fortin

Chandler, QC G0C

D-U-N-S 24-465-2277   (HQ)
AUTOMOBILES CARMER 1990 INC
GM CHEVROLET
417 Boul Rene-Levesque O, Chandler, QC,
G0C 1K0
(418) 689-4467
Sales 10,459,638
SIC 5511 New and used car dealers
Ronald Cain

Mathy Dora Kathleen Cain

D-U-N-S 25-481-2811   (SL)
MARCHE MARIO DOIRON INC
METRO
500 Av Daigneault Unite 101, Chandler, QC,
G0C 1K0
(418) 689-6999
Emp Here 50   *Sales* 13,707,600
SIC 5411 Grocery stores
Mario Doiron
Chantal Brousseau

Charette, QC G0X

D-U-N-S 20-984-6323   (HQ)
GROUPE CIRTECH INC
(*Suby of* GESTION CLAUDE BELLERIVE
INC)
660 Rue Notre-Dame Bureau 100, Charette,
QC, G0X 1E0
(819) 221-3400
Sales 34,220,280
SIC 1542 Nonresidential construction, nec
Claude Bellerive
Yvon Bellemare
Melanie Bellerive

Charlemagne, QC J5Z

D-U-N-S 24-216-3793   (SL)
9157-5548 QUEBEC INC
MARCHE CHARLEMAGNE
40 Rue Emile-Despins, Charlemagne, QC,
J5Z 3L6
(450) 581-6611
Emp Here 49   *Sales* 13,433,448
SIC 5411 Grocery stores
Peter Fogarty

Chateau-Richer, QC G0A

D-U-N-S 24-863-2221   (SL)
**CENTRE DE RENOVATION RAYMOND
BOIES INC**
8540 Boul Sainte-Anne, Chateau-Richer, QC,
G0A 1N0
(418) 824-4533
Emp Here 49   *Sales* 13,114,948
SIC 5211 Lumber and other building materials

D-U-N-S 25-383-8395   (SL)
FRERES MARISTES, LES
7141 Av Royale, Chateau-Richer, QC, G0A
1N0
(418) 824-4215
Emp Here 200   *Sales* 20,824,600
SIC 8661 Religious organizations
Gaetan Secteau
Jean-Yves Savard

D-U-N-S 24-622-8928   (BR)
PF RESOLU CANADA INC
CHATEAU RICHER MILL
(*Suby of* RESOLUTE FOREST PRODUCTS
INC)
7499 Boul Sainte-Anne, Chateau-Richer, QC,
G0A 1N0
(418) 824-4233
Emp Here 108
SIC 2421 Sawmills and planing mills, general
Christian Gauthier

D-U-N-S 25-376-7875   (SL)
ROULOTTES E. TURMEL INC
7010 Boul Sainte-Anne, Chateau-Richer, QC,
G0A 1N0
(418) 824-3401
Emp Here 33   *Sales* 16,436,574

SIC 5561 Recreational vehicle dealers
Euclide Turmel
Suzie Turmel

Chateauguay, QC J6J

D-U-N-S 24-405-9572   (SL)
133876 CANADA INC
A.D. DISPLAYS
800 Boul Ford Bureau 104, Chateauguay, QC,
J6J 4Z2
(450) 692-5570
Emp Here 60   *Sales* 19,568,160
SIC 3999 Manufacturing industries, nec
Robert Houston
Scott Jones
Glenn Emberley

D-U-N-S 20-707-7942   (SL)
141517 CANADA LTEE
CLERMONT
(*Suby of* GESTIONS PRISMES C.M. INC,
LES)
270 Boul Industriel, Chateauguay, QC, J6J
4Z2
(450) 692-5527
Emp Here 125   *Sales* 27,228,625
SIC 1761 Roofing, siding, and sheetMetal
work
Mario Levesque
Carole Dube

D-U-N-S 25-606-5194   (SL)
2948-7659 QUEBEC INC
HYUNDAI DE CHATEAUGUAY
411 Boul Saint-Francis, Chateauguay, QC, J6J
1Z6
(450) 699-8555
Emp Here 21   *Sales* 10,459,638
SIC 5511 New and used car dealers
Jean Leblanc
Dary Laflamme
Bertrand Fradet
Raymond Landry

D-U-N-S 20-407-1437   (HQ)
8061076 CANADA INC
217 Boul Industriel, Chateauguay, QC, J6J
4Z2
(514) 934-4684
Sales 20,501,250
SIC 6712 Bank holding companies
Andre Houle
Vincent Houle

D-U-N-S 24-853-9442   (SL)
9205-2976 QUEBEC INC
1200 Rue Des Cascades, Chateauguay, QC,
J6J 4Z2
(450) 699-9300
Emp Here 50   *Sales* 10,141,500
SIC 3465 Automotive stampings
Pierre Godin

D-U-N-S 24-212-5847   (SL)
9211-6409 QUEBEC INC
FICHAULT KIA
33 Boul Saint-Jean-Baptiste, Chateauguay,
QC, J6J 3H5
(450) 699-9000
Emp Here 22   *Sales* 10,957,716
SIC 5511 New and used car dealers
Benoit Fichault

D-U-N-S 20-193-1755   (SL)
**CMP SOLUTIONS MECANIQUES
AVANCEES LTEE**
(*Suby of* GESTION CMP AMS LIMITEE)
1241 Rue Des Cascades, Chateauguay, QC,
J6J 4Z2
(450) 691-5510
Emp Here 404   *Sales* 98,265,324
SIC 3499 Fabricated Metal products, nec
Steven Zimmermann
John Zimmerman

Janet Hylland

D-U-N-S 20-972-7403   (HQ)
COMMISSION SCOLAIRE NEW FRONTIER
NEW FRONTIERS SCHOOL BOARD
214 Rue Mcleod, Chateauguay, QC, J6J 2H4
(450) 691-1440
Sales 64,427,350
SIC 8211 Elementary and secondary schools
John Watson
Naila Mullahoo
Kenneth Robertson

D-U-N-S 20-712-3444   (BR)
COMMISSION SCOLAIRE NEW FRONTIER
ECOLE HOWARD S BELINGS
(*Suby of* COMMISSION SCOLAIRE NEW FRONTIER)
210 Rue Mcleod, Chateauguay, QC, J6J 2H4
(450) 691-3230
Emp Here 105
SIC 8211 Elementary and secondary schools
Gary Tennant

D-U-N-S 24-858-3833   (SL)
COMPAGNIE DE RECYCLAGE DE PAPIERS MD INC, LA
235 Boul Industriel, Chateauguay, QC, J6J 4Z2
(450) 699-3425
Emp Here 100   *Sales* 31,891,000
SIC 4953 Refuse systems
Gilbert Durocher
Pierre De Montlivault
Pierre Vandekerckhove
Anne Loussouarn
Anouk Fournier

D-U-N-S 20-815-7821   (SL)
CONSTRUCTIONS DE CASTEL INC, LES
265 Boul Industriel, Chateauguay, QC, J6J 4Z2
(450) 699-2036
Emp Here 25   *Sales* 11,768,275
SIC 1542 Nonresidential construction, nec
Stephane Lepine

D-U-N-S 24-859-8570   (SL)
EMBALLAGES SALERNO CANADA INC
SALERNO PACKAGING
(*Suby of* INTEPLAST GROUP CORPORATION)
2275 Boul Ford, Chateauguay, QC, J6J 4Z2
(450) 692-8642
Emp Here 100   *Sales* 19,476,800
SIC 2673 Bags: plastic, laminated, and coated
Joe Chen
Joseph Wang
Robert H. Wang
John Ding-E Young
Benjamin Tsao

D-U-N-S 24-711-8979   (SL)
GICLEURS ALERTE INC
1250 Rue Des Cascades, Chateauguay, QC, J6J 4Z2
(450) 692-9098
Emp Here 50   *Sales* 11,046,700
SIC 1711 Plumbing, heating, air-conditioning
Delbert Bolduc
Sandra Bolduc

D-U-N-S 20-566-2711   (HQ)
PROULX, G. INC
2800 Boul Ford, Chateauguay, QC, J6J 4Z2
(450) 691-7110
Emp Here 27   *Sales* 44,717,400
SIC 5039 Construction materials, nec
Normand Proulx

D-U-N-S 24-053-9114   (HQ)
PYRO-AIR LTEE
2575 Boul Ford, Chateauguay, QC, J6J 4Z2
(450) 691-3460
Emp Here 45   *Sales* 12,352,445
SIC 1711 Plumbing, heating, air-conditioning
Claude Lamoureux

Luc Gelinas
Yves Caron

D-U-N-S 20-233-4884   (SL)
SALERNO PELLICULE ET SACS DE PLASTIQUE (CANADA) INC
(*Suby of* INTEPLAST GROUP CORPORATION)
2275 Boul Ford, Chateauguay, QC, J6J 4Z2
(450) 692-8642
Emp Here 140   *Sales* 27,267,520
SIC 2673 Bags: plastic, laminated, and coated
Kurt Strater
Roger Sullivan
Marco Ferraresi

D-U-N-S 25-094-0152   (SL)
SERVICES EN TRANSPORT S.T.C.H. INC
GROUPE S.T.C.H.
248 Boul Industriel, Chateauguay, QC, J6J 4Z2
(450) 699-2357
Emp Here 26   *Sales* 13,519,142
SIC 4731 Freight transportation arrangement
Claude Hamel
Marc Desrosiers
Johanne Parent

D-U-N-S 24-541-3463   (SL)
TEXTILES WIN-SIR INC, LES
295 Boul Industriel Bureau A, Chateauguay, QC, J6J 4Z2
(450) 691-2747
Emp Here 100   *Sales* 13,667,400
SIC 2322 Men's and boy's underwear and nightwear
Richard Grover
Jean Duval

D-U-N-S 24-400-6052   (SL)
THERMOPOMPES N & R SOL INC
2325 Boul Ford, Chateauguay, QC, J6J 4Z2
(450) 699-3232
Emp Here 75   *Sales* 16,337,175
SIC 1731 Electrical work
Richard Pitre
Alain Parisien
Alain Laplante

D-U-N-S 20-260-9103   (SL)
THIBAULT, JACQUES ENTREPRISES INC
PHARMESCOMPTE JEAN COUTU
97 Boul D'Anjou, Chateauguay, QC, J6J 2R1
(450) 691-2622
Emp Here 60   *Sales* 14,659,680
SIC 5912 Drug stores and proprietary stores
Jacques Thibault

Chateauguay, QC J6K

D-U-N-S 24-422-9741   (SL)
4345240 CANADA INC
AUTOCAR METROPOLITAIN
147 Rue Principale, Chateauguay, QC, J6K 1G2
(450) 691-1654
Emp Here 150   *Sales* 30,855,900
SIC 4213 Trucking, except local
Yves Wininger

D-U-N-S 24-251-3141   (SL)
AMI AUTO INC
MADZA CHATEAUGUAY
191 Boul Saint-Jean-Baptiste, Chateauguay, QC, J6K 3B9
(450) 692-9600
Emp Here 25   *Sales* 12,451,950
SIC 5511 New and used car dealers
Denis Gregoire
Gilles Benoit
Claude Labreche

D-U-N-S 20-988-0066   (SL)
AUBAINERIE CONCEPT MODE, L

80 Boul D'Anjou, Chateauguay, QC, J6K 1C3
(450) 699-0444
Emp Here 60   *Sales* 10,763,760
SIC 5651 Family clothing stores
Josee Croteau

D-U-N-S 25-200-4742   (SL)
AUTOBUS AUGER METROPOLITAIN INC
147 Rue Principale, Chateauguay, QC, J6K 1G2
(450) 691-1654
Emp Here 160   *Sales* 12,043,520
SIC 4111 Local and suburban transit
Richard Auger

D-U-N-S 24-322-3385   (SL)
BARNABE NISSAN DE CHATEAUGUAY INC
CHATEAUGUAY NISSAN
(*Suby of* GESTION JOEL GREGOIRE INC)
187 Boul Saint-Jean-Baptiste, Chateauguay, QC, J6K 3B4
(450) 691-9541
Emp Here 25   *Sales* 15,732,000
SIC 5511 New and used car dealers
Joel Gregoire

D-U-N-S 20-801-9633   (BR)
CENTRE INTEGRE DE SANTE ET DE SERVICES SOCIAUX DE LA MONTEREGIE-OUEST
CENTRE D'HEBERGEMENT DE CHATEAUGUAY
(*Suby of* CENTRE INTEGRE DE SANTE ET DE SERVICES SOCIAUX DE LA MONTEREGIE-OUEST)
95 Ch De La Haute-Riviere, Chateauguay, QC, J6K 3P1
(450) 692-8231
Emp Here 205
SIC 8322 Individual and family services
Helene Lussier

D-U-N-S 24-175-0553   (SL)
DAIGNEAULT PROVOST JOLY LEBRUN INC
185 Boul Saint-Jean-Baptiste Bureau 100, Chateauguay, QC, J6K 3B4
(450) 691-9913
Emp Here 38   *Sales* 32,226,280
SIC 6411 Insurance agents, brokers, and service
Bernard Provost
Andre Daigneault
Diane Daigneault
Diane Joly
Harvey Lebrun

D-U-N-S 24-109-1339   (SL)
ENCORE AUTOMOBILE LTEE
ENCORE HONDA
266 Boul Saint-Jean-Baptiste, Chateauguay, QC, J6K 3C2
(450) 698-1060
Emp Here 28   *Sales* 13,946,184
SIC 5511 New and used car dealers
Thomas Samatas
George Guillon

D-U-N-S 20-002-1277   (BR)
FEDERATION DES CAISSES DESJARDINS DU QUEBEC
CAISSES DESJARDINS
(*Suby of* FEDERATION DES CAISSES DESJARDINS DU QUEBEC)
235 Ch De La Haute-Riviere, Chateauguay, QC, J6K 5B1
(450) 692-1000
Emp Here 75
SIC 6062 State credit unions
Lyne Vellemaire

D-U-N-S 24-251-8470   (SL)
GESTION CARBO LTEE
117 Boul Saint-Jean-Baptiste, Chateauguay, QC, J6K 3B1
(450) 691-4130
Emp Here 48   *Sales* 23,907,744

SIC 5511 New and used car dealers
Robert Leblanc

D-U-N-S 24-453-0606   (HQ)
GROUPE DPJL INC
ASSURANCE MARTIN & CYR
185 Boul Saint-Jean-Baptiste Bureau 100, Chateauguay, QC, J6K 3B4
(450) 691-9913
Emp Here 1   *Sales* 184,774,200
SIC 6411 Insurance agents, brokers, and service
Jacques Bourcier
Diane Joly
Francois Boyer
Bernard Boiteau
Bernard Provost

D-U-N-S 24-773-1735   (SL)
INSPECTEUR EN BATIMENT
110 Rue Albert-Seers, Chateauguay, QC, J6K 5E5
(514) 515-2334
Emp Here 49   *Sales* 11,350,017
SIC 8621 Professional organizations

D-U-N-S 20-474-3368   (SL)
MAISON LIANG
177a Boul Saint-Jean-Baptiste, Chateauguay, QC, J6K 3B4
(450) 692-1160
Emp Here 49   *Sales* 24,933,944
SIC 5023 Homefurnishings
Dalia Tsui San Liang

D-U-N-S 24-490-6827   (SL)
METRO PLUS
105 Rue Principale, Chateauguay, QC, J6K 1G2
(450) 699-8796
Emp Here 49   *Sales* 13,433,448
SIC 5499 Miscellaneous food stores
Daniel Creveer

D-U-N-S 25-174-7101   (BR)
METRO RICHELIEU INC
SUPER C
(*Suby of* METRO INC)
200 Boul D'Anjou Bureau 626, Chateauguay, QC, J6K 1C5
(450) 691-2880
Emp Here 105
SIC 5411 Grocery stores
Stephane Meloche

D-U-N-S 24-841-7102   (SL)
PHARMACIE MARTINE CLAVEAU ET KEVIN MARK KIRKCALDY INC
103 Rue Principale, Chateauguay, QC, J6K 1G2
(450) 691-3636
Emp Here 49   *Sales* 12,394,746
SIC 5912 Drug stores and proprietary stores
Martine Claveau

D-U-N-S 24-815-1896   (SL)
PLACEMENTS JACQUES FELIX THIBAULT INC., LES
PHARMACIE JEAN COUTU
237 Boul Saint-Jean-Baptiste Bureau 124, Chateauguay, QC, J6K 3C3
(450) 692-7981
Emp Here 70   *Sales* 17,102,960
SIC 5912 Drug stores and proprietary stores
Jacques Thibault
Line Thibault

D-U-N-S 20-107-2803   (BR)
RONA INC
RONA MARCIL & FRERES
(*Suby of* LOWE'S COMPANIES, INC.)
99 Rue Principale, Chateauguay, QC, J6K 1G2
(450) 692-9992
Emp Here 95
SIC 5072 Hardware
Julie Menard

▲ Public Company   ■ Public Company Family Member   **HQ** Headquarters   **BR** Branch   **SL** Single Location

D-U-N-S 20-646-1019   (BR)
SOBEYS CAPITAL INCORPORATED
SOBEYS # 439
(*Suby of* EMPIRE COMPANY LIMITED)
90 Boul D'Anjou, Chateauguay, QC, J6K 1C3
(450) 692-3446
Emp Here 200
SIC 5411 Grocery stores
Lina Burigon

D-U-N-S 24-589-6410   (SL)
SOLUTION FORD INC
SOLUTION OCCASION
117 Boul Saint-Jean-Baptiste, Chateauguay,
QC, J6K 3B1
(450) 691-4130
Emp Here 48   *Sales* 23,907,744
SIC 5511 New and used car dealers
Claude Jeannard
Stephanie Richard

Chelsea, QC J9B

D-U-N-S 24-347-1872   (SL)
AUBERGE & SPA LE NORDIK INC
NORDIK-SPA EN NATURE, LE
16 Ch Nordik, Chelsea, QC, J9B 2P7
(819) 484-1112
Emp Here 200   *Sales* 15,709,000
SIC 7991 Physical fitness facilities
Martin Paquette
Daniel Gingras

D-U-N-S 20-544-9767   (BR)
HYDRO-QUEBEC
(*Suby of* GOUVERNEMENT DE LA
PROVINCE DE QUEBEC)
128 Ch Mill, Chelsea, QC, J9B 1K8
(819) 827-7137
Emp Here 100
SIC 4911 Electric services
Jocelyn Pelletier

D-U-N-S 24-818-4298   (SL)
SERVICE RECREATIFS DEMSIS
75 Ch Barnes, Chelsea, QC, J9B 1H7

Emp Here 49   *Sales* 15,665,545
SIC 1389 Oil and gas field services, nec
Jean-Pierre Azzopardi

Cheneville, QC J0V

D-U-N-S 20-747-3810   (HQ)
**BOIS DE CONSTRUCTION CHENEVILLE
INC, LES**
BMR
99 Rue Albert-Ferland, Cheneville, QC, J0V
1E0
(819) 428-3903
Emp Here 1   *Sales* 12,652,950
SIC 5211 Lumber and other building materials
Yves Gagnon
Genevieve Gagnon

D-U-N-S 24-896-5675   (SL)
ENTREPRISES G.A. LEBLANC INC, LES
MARCHE METRO
45 Rue Albert-Ferland, Cheneville, QC, J0V
1E0
(819) 428-3966
Emp Here 77   *Sales* 22,597,729
SIC 5411 Grocery stores
Andre Leblanc

D-U-N-S 25-379-3434   (SL)
**FONDATION DU MOUVEMENT DU GRAAL-
CANADA INC**
MOUVEMENT DU GRAAL-CANADA
470 Ch Des Hauteurs, Cheneville, QC, J0V
1E0

(819) 428-7001
Emp Here 40   *Sales* 15,896,560
SIC 8699 Membership organizations, nec
Serge Thivierge

Chertsey, QC J0K

D-U-N-S 20-005-8688   (SL)
**FONDATION DU CARREFOUR DE LA
SANTE ET DES SERVICES SOCIAUX DE
MATAWINIE (CLSC - CHSLD)**
485 Rue Dupuis, Chertsey, QC, J0K 3K0
(450) 882-2488
Emp Here 250   *Sales* 51,767,000
SIC 8399 Social services, nec
Josee Leclair
Daien Ducharme Saint-Cyr
Christiane Gravel
Eric Tixier
Jean-Marc Hebert
Jean-Jacques Lamarche
Suzanne Provost

D-U-N-S 20-257-8951   (SL)
GROUPE CRETE CHERTSEY INC
(*Suby of* GROUPE CRETE INC)
8227 Rte 125, Chertsey, QC, J0K 3K0
(450) 882-2555
Emp Here 70   *Sales* 13,465,900
SIC 2421 Sawmills and planing mills, general
Sebastien Crete
Alain Gagnon

D-U-N-S 25-827-5627   (SL)
MARCHE ROBERT DESROCHERS INC
PROVIGO
7000 125 Rte, Chertsey, QC, J0K 3K0
(450) 882-2332
Emp Here 70   *Sales* 20,543,390
SIC 5411 Grocery stores
Robert Desrochers

D-U-N-S 25-980-5752   (HQ)
SERVICES SANITAIRES MAJ INC
COMPO RECYCLE
225 Av Du Progres, Chertsey, QC, J0K 3K0
(450) 882-9186
Sales 22,323,700
SIC 4953 Refuse systems
Michael Lafortune
Andre-Luc Lafortune
Sylvain Lafortune
Christianne Durand

Chibougamau, QC G8P

D-U-N-S 24-746-4324   (SL)
2412-8779 QUEBEC INC
LAROUCHE CONSTRUCTION
121 Rue Dubuc, Chibougamau, QC, G8P 2H4
(418) 748-4785
Emp Here 25   *Sales* 11,768,275
SIC 1542 Nonresidential construction, nec
Martin Larouche

D-U-N-S 20-822-2179   (SL)
9130-6381 QUEBEC INC
NISK CONSTRUCTION
971 3e Rue, Chibougamau, QC, G8P 1R4
(418) 748-3682
Emp Here 80   *Sales* 21,675,360
SIC 1521 Single-family housing construction
Georges Petawabano
Pierre Savage

D-U-N-S 24-592-2450   (SL)
9170-7570 QUEBEC INC
BIRON
949 3e Rue, Chibougamau, QC, G8P 1R4
(418) 748-2691
Emp Here 50   *Sales* 11,046,700

SIC 1711 Plumbing, heating, air-conditioning
Patrick Biron
Richard Biron

D-U-N-S 25-734-0414   (HQ)
**CENTRE REGIONAL DE SANTE ET DE
SERVICES SOCIAUX DE LA BAIE-JAMES**
51 3e Rue, Chibougamau, QC, G8P 1N1
(418) 748-2676
Emp Here 45   *Sales* 10,213,300
SIC 8062 General medical and surgical hospitals
Jules Pelletier

D-U-N-S 20-193-4445   (HQ)
**CHANTIERS DE CHIBOUGAMAU LTEE,
LES**
CARAVAN AVIATION
(*Suby of* 2429-3706 QUEBEC INC)
521 Ch Merrill, Chibougamau, QC, G8P 2K7
(418) 748-6481
Sales 235,043,100
SIC 2439 Structural wood members, nec
Lucien Fillion
Michel Filion
Jean-Remi Fillion
Pascal Morisette
Andreanne Filion Cloutier

D-U-N-S 20-193-4494   (SL)
CHIBOUGAMAU AUTOMOBILE INC
859 3e Rue, Chibougamau, QC, G8P 1R1
(418) 748-2634
Emp Here 21   *Sales* 10,459,638
SIC 5511 New and used car dealers
Bruno Laflamme
Guylaine Gagnon

D-U-N-S 20-859-1818   (HQ)
**COMMISSION SCOLAIRE DE LA BAIE
JAMES**
596 4e Rue, Chibougamau, QC, G8P 1S3
(418) 748-7621
Emp Here 5   *Sales* 34,691,650
SIC 8211 Elementary and secondary schools
Michel Laplace

D-U-N-S 20-591-8030   (SL)
FORAGES CHIBOUGAMAU LTEE
CHIBOUGAMAU DIAMOND DRILLING
527 Rte 167, Chibougamau, QC, G8P 2K5
(418) 748-3977
Emp Here 120   *Sales* 29,542,320
SIC 1799 Special trade contractors, nec
Serge Steve Larouche
Serge Larouche

D-U-N-S 24-174-8383   (SL)
M. A. S. CHIBOUGAMAU INC
874 3e Rue, Chibougamau, QC, G8P 1P9
(418) 748-7674
Emp Here 22   *Sales* 10,957,716
SIC 5531 Auto and home supply stores
Alain Bradette
Martin Renaud
Denise Leclerc

D-U-N-S 20-590-0715   (HQ)
METALLISATION DU NORD INC
876 Rue Perreault, Chibougamau, QC, G8P
2K3
(418) 748-6442
Emp Here 6   *Sales* 10,410,840
SIC 5093 Scrap and waste materials
Raymond Laframboise
Therese Laframboise
Michel Laframboise

D-U-N-S 25-302-7788   (SL)
MINES OPINACA LTEE, LES
333 3e Rue Bureau 2, Chibougamau, QC,
G8P 1N4
(418) 748-6449
Emp Here 49   *Sales* 11,438,315
SIC 1241 Coal mining services
Chris Woodall

Chicoutimi, QC G7G

D-U-N-S 24-237-9522   (BR)
**COMMISSION SCOLAIRE DES RIVES-DU-
SAGUENAY**
ECOLE SECONDAIRE CHARLES GRAVEL
(*Suby of* COMMISSION SCOLAIRE DES
RIVES-DU-SAGUENAY)
350 Rue Saint-Gerard, Chicoutimi, QC, G7G
1J2
(418) 541-4343
Emp Here 180
SIC 8211 Elementary and secondary schools
Joanne Allard

D-U-N-S 24-143-8779   (SL)
ENTREPRISES R.E.R. INC
*PIECES   UNIVERSELLES   AUTO
CHICOUTIMI*
1530 Boul Sainte-Genevieve, Chicoutimi, QC,
G7G 2H1

Emp Here 30   *Sales* 11,110,220
SIC 5013 Motor vehicle supplies and new
parts
Ghislain Rousseau

D-U-N-S 20-433-1961   (SL)
EQUIPEMENTS VILLENEUVE INC
1178 Boul Sainte-Genevieve, Chicoutimi, QC,
G7G 2G6
(418) 543-3600
Emp Here 29   *Sales* 14,444,262
SIC 5599 Automotive dealers, nec
Alain Bradette

Chicoutimi, QC G7H

D-U-N-S 24-125-5061   (BR)
2037247 ONTARIO LIMITED
PROVIGO MARCHE
(*Suby of* 2037247 ONTARIO LIMITED)
1155 Boul Talbot, Chicoutimi, QC, G7H 4B5
(418) 690-0063
Emp Here 200
SIC 5411 Grocery stores
Carle Pearnault

D-U-N-S 24-568-3693   (SL)
2318-7081 QUEBEC INC
1080 Boul Talbot, Chicoutimi, QC, G7H 4B6
(418) 543-1521
Emp Here 140   *Sales* 12,976,600
SIC 7011 Hotels and motels
Jean-Marc Couture

D-U-N-S 25-243-2943   (SL)
3100-2504 QUEBEC INC
SPORTS EXPERTS
1401 Boul Talbot Bureau 3, Chicoutimi, QC,
G7H 5N6
(418) 545-4945
Emp Here 65   *Sales* 15,881,320
SIC 5941 Sporting goods and bicycle shops
Roger Turcotte
Genevieve Maltais
Yvon Blackburn
Jean Maltais

D-U-N-S 25-488-3630   (SL)
3111326 CANADA INC
CAGE AUX SPORTS, LA
1611 Boul Talbot, Chicoutimi, QC, G7H 4C3
(418) 698-8611
Emp Here 75   *Sales* 3,215,475
SIC 5812 Eating places
Richard Dubuc
Gilles Lessard

D-U-N-S 24-327-1801   (BR)
3834310 CANADA INC
LE QUOTIDIEN
(*Suby of* GROUPE CAPITALES MEDIAS INC,

LE)
1051 Boul Talbot, Chicoutimi, QC, G7H 5C1
(418) 545-4474
Emp Here 200
SIC 2711 Newspapers
 Michel Simard

   D-U-N-S 24-394-2906   (SL)
9032-8402 QUEBEC INC
CANADIAN TIRE
1257 Boul Talbot Bureau 268, Chicoutimi, QC,
G7H 4C1
(418) 549-5014
Emp Here 49   *Sales* 24,405,822
SIC 5531 Auto and home supply stores
 Jean-Pierre Larochelle

   D-U-N-S 25-877-1930   (HQ)
9085-3532 QUEBEC INC
LA CAPITALE SAGUENAY LAC-ST-JEAN
1212 Boul Talbot Bureau 204, Chicoutimi, QC,
G7H 4B7
(418) 543-5511
Emp Here 72   *Sales* 31,416,675
SIC 6531 Real estate agents and managers
 Paul Legault

   D-U-N-S 24-308-7652   (SL)
9142-5454 QUEBEC INC
CORNEAU CANTIN LEBOURGNEUF
2000 Boul Talbot, Chicoutimi, QC, G7H 7Y2
(418) 698-9556
Emp Here 60   *Sales* 17,608,620
SIC 5411 Grocery stores
 Andre Michaud

   D-U-N-S 20-386-9776   (SL)
9368-9677 QUEBEC INC
545 Boul Du Royaume O, Chicoutimi, QC,
G7H 5B1
(418) 968-4343
Emp Here 26   *Sales* 10,903,230
SIC 6712 Bank holding companies
 Jean-Bernard Tremblay
 Hugues Laroche

   D-U-N-S 24-144-2763   (SL)
**ALBERT, PAUL CHEVROLET BUICK
CADILLAC GMC LTEE**
PACO
870 Boul Talbot, Chicoutimi, QC, G7H 4B4
(418) 696-4444
Emp Here 45   *Sales* 22,413,510
SIC 5511 New and used car dealers
 Paul Albert
 Jacques Dallaire
 Pierre Albert

   D-U-N-S 25-844-5386   (BR)
AMEUBLEMENTS TANGUAY INC
(*Suby of* BELANGER, A. (DETAIL) LTEE)
1990 Boul Talbot, Chicoutimi, QC, G7H 7Y3
(418) 698-4411
Emp Here 120
SIC 5712 Furniture stores
 Laval Cote

   D-U-N-S 24-378-2419   (HQ)
ARIANNE PHOSPHATE INC
ARIAN PHOSPHATE
393 Rue Racine E Bureau 200, Chicoutimi,
QC, G7H 1T2
(418) 549-7316
Sales 413,109,000
SIC 1475 Phosphate rock
 Brain Ostroff
 Daniel Boulianne
 Andrew Malashewsky
 Jean-Sebastien David
 Dominique Bouchard
 Dave Debiasio
 Marco Gagnon
 Siva Pillay
 Steven Pinney
 Jean Fontaine

   D-U-N-S 20-593-0274   (SL)
AUTO L.P. TREMBLAY, LTEE

1330 Boul Du Royaume O, Chicoutimi, QC,
G7H 5B1
(418) 549-3320
Emp Here 24   *Sales* 11,953,872
SIC 5511 New and used car dealers
 Jean-Marie Tremblay

   D-U-N-S 24-639-2559   (SL)
AUTOMOBILES CHICOUTIMI (1986) INC
AMI JUNIOR MAZDA, L'
545 Boul Du Royaume O, Chicoutimi, QC,
G7H 5B1
(418) 545-6555
Emp Here 26   *Sales* 12,950,028
SIC 5511 New and used car dealers
 Jean-Bernard Tremblay

   D-U-N-S 25-525-6075   (SL)
**AUTOMOBILES PERRON (CHICOUTIMI)
INC**
930 Boul Talbot, Chicoutimi, QC, G7H 4B4
(418) 549-7633
Emp Here 45   *Sales* 22,413,510
SIC 5511 New and used car dealers
 Andre Perron

   D-U-N-S 24-142-0459   (SL)
AUTOMOBILES ROYAUME LTEE
HYUNDAI DU ROYAUME
533 Boul Du Royaume O, Chicoutimi, QC,
G7H 5B1
(418) 543-9393
Emp Here 24   *Sales* 11,953,872
SIC 5511 New and used car dealers
 Pierre Couture
 Jean Vachon

   D-U-N-S 24-362-5634   (BR)
BEST BUY CANADA LTD
FUTURE SHOP
(*Suby of* BEST BUY CO., INC.)
1401 Boul Talbot, Chicoutimi, QC, G7H 5N6
(418) 698-6701
Emp Here 100
SIC 5731 Radio, television, and electronic
stores
 Dany Tremblay

   D-U-N-S 20-722-0518   (SL)
BLACKBURN & BLACKBURN INC
980 Boul De L'Universite E, Chicoutimi, QC,
G7H 6H1
(418) 549-4900
Emp Here 44   *Sales* 19,675,656
SIC 5044 Office equipment
 Pierre Blackburn
 Patrice Blackburn
 Denis Dufour
 Daniel Boivin

   D-U-N-S 24-759-5184   (SL)
BLACKBURN SERVICE D'INVENTAIRE INC
125 Rue Dube, Chicoutimi, QC, G7H 2V3
(418) 543-4567
Emp Here 50   *Sales* 22,460,950
SIC 7389 Business services, nec
 Andre Blackburn

   D-U-N-S 24-821-6855   (HQ)
**CAIN LAMARRE CASGRAIN WELLS,
S.E.N.C.R.L.**
CAIN LAMARRE CASGRAIN WELLS
255 Rue Racine E Bureau 600, Chicoutimi,
QC, G7H 7L2
(418) 545-4580
Emp Here 60   *Sales* 74,115,360
SIC 8111 Legal services
 Pierre Tremblay
 Guy Wells
 Francois Bouchard
 Richard Bergeron
 Yvan Bujold
 Jean Dauphinais
 Alain Letourneau
 J. Lucie Perron
 Francois G. Tremblay
 Gina Doucet

   D-U-N-S 25-001-1491   (HQ)
CAISSE DESJARDINS DE CHICOUTIMI
DESJARDINS ENTREPRISES-SAGUENAY
245 Rue Racine E, Chicoutimi, QC, G7H 1S4
(418) 549-3224
Emp Here 60   *Sales* 15,755,178
SIC 6062 State credit unions
 Denis Guay
 Robert Deschenes
 Marcel Bergeron
 Chantal Durand
 Marie-Claude Bradette
 Christian Lemieux
 Gabrielle Jacques
 Paul Lalancette
 Robert Lavoie
 Louis-Philippe Thibault

   D-U-N-S 20-538-1101   (BR)
CANADA POST CORPORATION
(*Suby of* GOVERNMENT OF CANADA)
1939 Rue Des Sapins Unite 1, Chicoutimi, QC,
G7H 0H7
(418) 690-0350
Emp Here 125
SIC 4311 U.s. postal service
 Eric Dube

   D-U-N-S 20-986-3021   (BR)
CEGERCO INC
DEMOTEC
(*Suby of* 9123-6794 QUEBEC INC)
255 Rue Racine E Bureau 595, Chicoutimi,
QC, G7H 7L2
(418) 690-3432
Emp Here 302
SIC 1522 Residential construction, nec
 Jeannot Harvey

   D-U-N-S 24-639-3268   (SL)
**CENTRE D'ENTRAINEMENT A LA VIE DE
CHICOUTIMI INC**
ATELIER DU CRAN
766 Rue Du Cenacle, Chicoutimi, QC, G7H
2J2
(418) 549-4003
Emp Here 217   *Sales* 13,949,194
SIC 8361 Residential care
 Michel Senechal

   D-U-N-S 20-030-4678   (BR)
**CENTRE DE SANTE ET DE SERVICES SO-
CIAUX DE CHICOUTIMI**
CENTRE MGR VICTOR TREMBLAY
(*Suby of* GOUVERNEMENT DE LA
PROVINCE DE QUEBEC)
1236 Rue D'Angouleme, Chicoutimi, QC, G7H
6P9
(418) 698-3907
Emp Here 100
SIC 8361 Residential care
 Benoit Duplessis

   D-U-N-S 25-047-8526   (HQ)
**CENTRE DE SANTE ET DE SERVICES SO-
CIAUX DE CHICOUTIMI**
CSSSC
(*Suby of* GOUVERNEMENT DE LA
PROVINCE DE QUEBEC)
305 Rue Saint-Vallier, Chicoutimi, QC, G7H
5H6
(418) 541-1046
Emp Here 2,200   *Sales* 608,662,400
SIC 8011 Offices and clinics of medical doc-
tors
 Richard Lemieux

   D-U-N-S 20-582-1358   (SL)
CHICOUTIMI CHRYSLER DODGE JEEP INC
CHICOUTIMI CHRYSLER
829 Boul Talbot, Chicoutimi, QC, G7H 4B5
(418) 549-2873
Emp Here 50   *Sales* 24,903,900
SIC 5511 New and used car dealers
 Jean-Patrick Tremblay
 Pierre Tremblay

   D-U-N-S 25-233-6862   (BR)

**COMMISSION SCOLAIRE DES RIVES-DU-
SAGUENAY**
ECOLE L'ODYSEE DOMINIQUE RACINE
(*Suby of* COMMISSION SCOLAIRE DES
RIVES-DU-SAGUENAY)
985 Rue Begin, Chicoutimi, QC, G7H 4P1
(418) 698-5185
Emp Here 140
SIC 8211 Elementary and secondary schools
 Carl Bouchard

   D-U-N-S 25-232-1963   (HQ)
**COMMISSION SCOLAIRE DES RIVES-DU-
SAGUENAY**
36 Rue Jacques-Cartier E, Chicoutimi, QC,
G7H 1W2
(418) 698-5000
Emp Here 100   *Sales* 198,238,000
SIC 8211 Elementary and secondary schools
 Chantale Cyr
 Jean-Francois Presse

   D-U-N-S 20-867-4171   (BR)
**COMMISSION SCOLAIRE DES RIVES-DU-
SAGUENAY**
CEA LAURE CONON
(*Suby of* COMMISSION SCOLAIRE DES
RIVES-DU-SAGUENAY)
847 Rue Georges-Vanier, Chicoutimi, QC,
G7H 4M1
(418) 698-5170
Emp Here 100
SIC 8211 Elementary and secondary schools
 Clement Pare

   D-U-N-S 24-941-1042   (SL)
CONCASSAGE T.C.G. INC
111 Rue Des Routiers, Chicoutimi, QC, G7H
5B1
(418) 698-4949
Emp Here 50   *Sales* 11,671,750
SIC 1422 Crushed and broken limestone
 Michel Gilbert
 Jean-Marc Gilbert
 Linda Gilbert
 Rejean Gilbert
 Clermont Gilbert

   D-U-N-S 25-919-1492   (BR)
**CONSEILLERS EN GESTION ET INFORMA-
TIQUE CGI INC**
CGI
(*Suby of* CGI INC)
930 Rue Jacques-Cartier E 3rd Floor,
Chicoutimi, QC, G7H 7K9
(418) 696-6789
Emp Here 425
SIC 7379 Computer related services, nec
 Daniel Bouchard

   D-U-N-S 24-750-5089   (SL)
CONSTRUCTIONS FABMEC INC
1590 Boul Du Royaume O Bureau 4,
Chicoutimi, QC, G7H 5B1
(418) 549-3636
Emp Here 49   *Sales* 14,140,567
SIC 1522 Residential construction, nec
 Michel Boivin

   D-U-N-S 25-875-3045   (SL)
CONSTRUCTIONS PLACO INC, LES
2700 Boul Talbot Bureau 41, Chicoutimi, QC,
G7H 5B1
(418) 545-3362
Emp Here 30   *Sales* 14,121,930
SIC 1542 Nonresidential construction, nec
 Denis Robitaille
 Marc Robitaille
 Mario Tremblay

   D-U-N-S 20-801-2638   (BR)
COSTCO WHOLESALE CANADA LTD
(*Suby of* COSTCO WHOLESALE CORPO-
RATION)
2500 Boul Talbot, Chicoutimi, QC, G7H 5B1
(418) 696-1112
Emp Here 200
SIC 5199 Nondurable goods, nec

▲ Public Company   ■ Public Company Family Member   **HQ** Headquarters   **BR** Branch   **SL** Single Location

Michel Perron

D-U-N-S 20-193-7448   (SL)
COUTURE, ARMAND & FILS INC
HOTEL LE MONTAGNAIS
1080 Boul Talbot, Chicoutimi, QC, G7H 4B6
(418) 543-1521
Emp Here 140   *Sales* 12,976,600
SIC 7011 Hotels and motels
Jean-Marc Couture

D-U-N-S 24-418-4649   (BR)
DELOITTE LLP
(*Suby of* DELOITTE LLP)
901 Boul Talbot Bureau 400, Chicoutimi, QC, G7H 0A1
(418) 549-6650
Emp Here 80
SIC 6733 Trusts, nec
Marc Fortin

D-U-N-S 25-542-3147   (SL)
DYNAMITAGE T.C.G. (1993) INC
CONSOLIDATION TCG
111 Rue Des Routiers, Chicoutimi, QC, G7H 5B1
(418) 698-5858
Emp Here 75   *Sales* 18,933,150
SIC 1629 Heavy construction, nec
Michel Gilbert
Jean-Marc Gilbert
Linda Gilbert
Clermont Gilbert
Rejean Gilbert

D-U-N-S 20-514-3712   (HQ)
ENTREPRISES ALFRED BOIVIN INC, LES
GROUPE ALFRED BOIVIN
2205 Rue De La Fonderie, Chicoutimi, QC, G7H 8B9
(418) 549-2457
Sales 25,244,200
SIC 1611 Highway and street construction
Rejean Boivin
Stephane Boivin

D-U-N-S 24-592-3602   (SL)
ENTREPRISES DE CONSTRUCTION GI-GARI INC, LES
766 Rue D'Alma, Chicoutimi, QC, G7H 4E6
(418) 696-1817
Emp Here 45   *Sales* 14,349,105
SIC 1521 Single-family housing construction
Sebastien Maltais
Carl Murray
Gilles Maltais

D-U-N-S 24-681-7436   (BR)
ENTREPRISES MACBAIE INC, LES
MCDONALD'S
(*Suby of* ENTREPRISES MACBAIE INC, LES)
1401 Boul Talbot Bureau 1, Chicoutimi, QC, G7H 5N6
(418) 545-3593
Emp Here 100
SIC 5812 Eating places
Patrice Gagne

D-U-N-S 24-202-8967   (HQ)
ENTREPRISES MACBAIE INC, LES
RESTAURANT MCDONALD'S
999 Boul Talbot, Chicoutimi, QC, G7H 4B5
(418) 545-3593
Emp Here 75   *Sales* 9,327,800
SIC 5812 Eating places
Daniel Bedard

D-U-N-S 24-843-3740   (HQ)
FERNAND GILBERT LTEE
1700 Boul Talbot Bureau 400, Chicoutimi, QC, G7H 7Y1
(418) 549-7705
Emp Here 100   *Sales* 31,856,400
SIC 1794 Excavation work
Jean-Marc Gilbert
Michel Gilbert
Linda Gilbert

Rejean Gilbert
Clermont Gilbert
Adam Lapointe
Eric Dufour

D-U-N-S 25-181-1980   (SL)
FOYER ST-FRANCOIS INC
912 Rue Jacques-Cartier E, Chicoutimi, QC, G7H 2A9
(418) 549-3727
Emp Here 86   *Sales* 5,596,450
SIC 8361 Residential care
Sonia Bergeron

D-U-N-S 24-863-1723   (HQ)
GAGNON FRERES INC
GALERIE DU SOMMEIL
1460 Boul Talbot, Chicoutimi, QC, G7H 4C2
(418) 690-3366
Emp Here 27   *Sales* 46,480,600
SIC 5712 Furniture stores
Frederic Gagnon
Virgine Theberge

D-U-N-S 24-148-0391   (HQ)
GAZON SAVARD (SAGUENAY) INC
BETON DUNBRICK
3478 Rang Saint-Paul, Chicoutimi, QC, G7H 0G6
(418) 543-5739
Sales 13,115,450
SIC 0181 Ornamental nursery products
Langis Savard
Carol Savard
Jules Savard
Marjolaine Savard
Gabriel Savard
Luc Savard

D-U-N-S 20-193-7141   (SL)
GESTION GEORGES ABRAHAM INC
RESTAURANT CHEZ GEORGES
433 Rue Racine E, Chicoutimi, QC, G7H 1T5
(418) 543-2875
Emp Here 80   *Sales* 3,429,840
SIC 5812 Eating places
Norma Abraham
Michel Abraham

D-U-N-S 20-193-7570   (HQ)
INTER-CITE CONSTRUCTION LTEE
205 Boul Du Royaume E, Chicoutimi, QC, G7H 5H2
(418) 549-0532
Emp Here 30   *Sales* 82,028,750
SIC 1611 Highway and street construction
Real Riverin
Nicolas Riverin

D-U-N-S 25-364-8430   (BR)
INTER-CITE CONSTRUCTION LTEE
(*Suby of* INTER-CITE CONSTRUCTION LTEE)
209 Boul Du Royaume O, Chicoutimi, QC, G7H 5C2
(418) 549-0532
Emp Here 250
SIC 1611 Highway and street construction
Marc Andre Leclerc

D-U-N-S 20-014-7481   (SL)
J. EUCLIDE PERRON LTEE
41 Rue Jacques-Cartier E, Chicoutimi, QC, G7H 5G6
(418) 543-0715
Emp Here 26   *Sales* 17,176,706
SIC 1541 Industrial buildings and warehouses
Denis Perron
Andre Perron
Gilles Perron

D-U-N-S 20-288-2924   (SL)
J.E. PERRON - INTER-CITE S.E.N.C
205 Boul Du Royaume E, Chicoutimi, QC, G7H 5H2
(418) 549-0532
Emp Here 50   *Sales* 12,517,466
SIC 1771 Concrete work

Nicolas Riverin

D-U-N-S 20-193-8008   (SL)
LEO AUTOMOBILE LTEE
1849 Boul Talbot, Chicoutimi, QC, G7H 7Y4
(418) 545-1190
Emp Here 44   *Sales* 27,688,320
SIC 5511 New and used car dealers
Dany Martin

D-U-N-S 20-986-3278   (SL)
MAISONEE D'EVELYNE, LA
546 Boul Talbot, Chicoutimi, QC, G7H 4A5
(418) 543-5822
Emp Here 30   *Sales* 13,703,230
SIC 7389 Business services, nec

D-U-N-S 24-464-8390   (SL)
MARCHE A. LAROUCHE LTEE
992 Boul Du Saguenay E, Chicoutimi, QC, G7H 1L5
(418) 543-4521
Emp Here 44   *Sales* 12,062,688
SIC 5411 Grocery stores
Donald Larouche
Claudie Larouche
Nicolas Larouche

D-U-N-S 24-763-9706   (SL)
METRO PLUS MARIO LAVOIE
1550 Boul Talbot, Chicoutimi, QC, G7H 4C2
(418) 543-7394
Emp Here 49   *Sales* 13,433,448
SIC 5411 Grocery stores
Metro Richelieu

D-U-N-S 20-795-2925   (BR)
METRO RICHELIEU INC
(*Suby of* METRO INC)
299 Rue Des Sagueneens, Chicoutimi, QC, G7H 3A5
(418) 696-4114
Emp Here 80
SIC 5411 Grocery stores
Daniel Tache

D-U-N-S 20-514-2032   (BR)
NORDA STELO INC
(*Suby of* NORDA STELO INC)
159 Rue Salaberry, Chicoutimi, QC, G7H 4K2
(418) 549-6471
Emp Here 150
SIC 8711 Engineering services
Sylvain Corneau

D-U-N-S 24-757-3418   (SL)
PACO LTEE
870 Boul Talbot, Chicoutimi, QC, G7H 4B4
(418) 696-4444
Emp Here 49   *Sales* 24,405,822
SIC 5531 Auto and home supply stores
Paul Albert

D-U-N-S 20-193-6296   (BR)
PEPSI BOTTLING GROUP (CANADA), ULC, THE
PEPSICO BEVERAGES CANADA
(*Suby of* PBG INVESTMENT (LUXEMBOURG) SARL)
1800 Boul Talbot, Chicoutimi, QC, G7H 7Y1
(418) 549-3135
Emp Here 170
SIC 5149 Groceries and related products, nec
Leo Pedneault

D-U-N-S 20-858-0936   (HQ)
PETROLES R.L. INC, LES
BELZILE
(*Suby of* ULTRAMAG CHICOUTIMI LTEE)
460 Rue Racine E, Chicoutimi, QC, G7H 1T7
(418) 543-0775
Emp Here 12   *Sales* 62,860,050
SIC 5172 Petroleum products, nec
Eric Larouche

D-U-N-S 20-870-3553   (HQ)
PRODUITS B.C.M. LTEE
340 Rue Emile-Couture, Chicoutimi, QC, G7H

8B6
(418) 545-1698
Sales 19,305,520
SIC 5198 Paints, varnishes, and supplies
Martial Bouchard
Denis Gauthier
Mireille Gauthier

D-U-N-S 24-581-1799   (HQ)
PROMOTION SAGUENAY INC
AEROGARE DE BAGOTVILLE
295 Rue Racine E, Chicoutimi, QC, G7H 1S7
(418) 698-3157
Sales 10,399,340
SIC 4725 Tour operators
Ghislain Harvey

D-U-N-S 20-202-4444   (SL)
ROCOTO LTEE
TOYOTA
1540 Boul Du Royaume O Bureau 4, Chicoutimi, QC, G7H 5B1
(418) 549-5574
Emp Here 75   *Sales* 47,196,000
SIC 5511 New and used car dealers
Guy Bergeron

D-U-N-S 24-591-6796   (HQ)
SABLIERE DRAPEAU (1986) INC
(*Suby of* INTER-CITE CONSTRUCTION LTEE)
205 Boul Du Royaume E, Chicoutimi, QC, G7H 5H2
(418) 549-0532
Emp Here 20   *Sales* 17,886,960
SIC 5032 Brick, stone, and related material
Real Riverin
Nicolas Riverin

D-U-N-S 24-170-6667   (SL)
SEMINAIRE DE CHICOUTIMI
602 Rue Racine E Bureau 102, Chicoutimi, QC, G7H 1V1
(418) 693-8448
Emp Here 30   *Sales* 11,922,420
SIC 8699 Membership organizations, nec
Robert Simard

D-U-N-S 25-484-8880   (BR)
SOBEYS QUEBEC INC
IGA YVON HACHE
1324 Boul Talbot, Chicoutimi, QC, G7H 4B8
(418) 549-9751
Emp Here 122   *Sales* 822,456
SIC 5411 Grocery stores
Yvon Hache

D-U-N-S 20-664-9373   (SL)
SOCIETE DE GESTION DE LA ZONE PORTUAIRE DE CHICOUTIMI INC
CENTRE RECREOTOURISTIQUE DE SHIP-SHAW
49 Rue La Fontaine, Chicoutimi, QC, G7H 7Y7
(418) 698-3025
Emp Here 100   *Sales* 14,287,900
SIC 8641 Civic and social associations
Rene-Philippe Harvey
Jean-Pierre Bolduc
Stephanie Larouche
Marie-Eve Gagnon
Frederic Gilbert
Hugues Lavoie
Charles Boudreault
Marc Bouchard
Simon-Olivier Cote
Fabien Hovington

D-U-N-S 20-337-9078   (BR)
STANTEC CONSULTING LTD
STANTEC EXPERTS-CONSEILS LTEE
(*Suby of* STANTEC INC)
255 Rue Racine E, Chicoutimi, QC, G7H 7L2
(418) 549-6680
Emp Here 221
SIC 8711 Engineering services
Christina Han

D-U-N-S 24-161-8706   (SL)

SYNDICAT REGIONAL DES EMPLOYES DE SOUTIEN (C S Q) ENR
895 Rue Begin, Chicoutimi, QC, G7H 4P1
(418) 698-5271
Emp Here 45   *Sales* 17,602,110
SIC 8631 Labor organizations
Eddy Foster

D-U-N-S 24-366-2728   (SL)
TRANSPORT ALFRED BOIVIN INC
2205 Rue De La Fonderie, Chicoutimi, QC, G7H 8B9
(418) 693-8681
Emp Here 115   *Sales* 23,656,190
SIC 4213 Trucking, except local
Rejean Boivin

D-U-N-S 24-908-8709   (HQ)
TRANSPORT F. GILBERT LTEE
150 Rue Des Routiers, Chicoutimi, QC, G7H 5B1
(418) 698-4848
Sales 50,016,900
SIC 4731 Freight transportation arrangement
Rejean Gilbert
Linda Gilbert
Michel Gilbert
Clermont Gilbert
Jean-Marc Gilbert

D-U-N-S 25-297-7301   (BR)
WAL-MART CANADA CORP
(*Suby of* WALMART INC.)
3017-1451 Boul Talbot, Chicoutimi, QC, G7H 5N8
(418) 693-1500
Emp Here 240
SIC 5311 Department stores
Lisette Rivard

Chicoutimi, QC G7J

D-U-N-S 24-169-4269   (SL)
AMBULANCE CHICOUTIMI INC
AMBULANCE SLN
784 Boul Barrette, Chicoutimi, QC, G7J 3Z7
(418) 543-5045
Emp Here 100   *Sales* 5,487,200
SIC 4119 Local passenger transportation, nec
Shirley Gravel

D-U-N-S 25-145-2363   (SL)
BILODEAU COUTURE ASSURANCES INC
BC ASSURES
31 Rue Racine O, Chicoutimi, QC, G7J 1E4
(418) 698-0999
Emp Here 30   *Sales* 31,046,430
SIC 6331 Fire, marine, and casualty insurance
Jean Bilodeau

D-U-N-S 20-003-5702   (SL)
CONSTRUCTIONS METHODEX INC, LES
676 Rue Des Actionnaires, Chicoutimi, QC, G7J 5A8
(418) 545-2280
Emp Here 30   *Sales* 14,121,930
SIC 1542 Nonresidential construction, nec
Louis Senechal

D-U-N-S 24-942-6966   (SL)
DEMOLITION ET EXCAVATION DEMEX INC
DEMEX
(*Suby of* 9328-9486 QUEBEC INC)
2253 Ch De La Reserve, Chicoutimi, QC, G7J 0C9
(418) 698-2222
Emp Here 75   *Sales* 31,811,017
SIC 1795 Wrecking and demolition work
Dany Tremblay
Bernard Tremblay
Yanick Tremblay
Martin Gagnon

D-U-N-S 24-490-7739   (HQ)
ELKEM METAL CANADA INC

(*Suby of* CHINA NATIONAL BLUESTAR (GROUP) CO., LTD.)
2020 Ch De La Reserve, Chicoutimi, QC, G7J 0E1
(418) 549-4171
Sales 12,697,160
SIC 3313 ElectroMetallurgical products
Jean Villeneuve
Steeve Barbeau
Eric Cantin
Jorgen Mjones
Simon Wilson
Gestur Petursson

D-U-N-S 20-193-6002   (SL)
EXCAVATION DE CHICOUTIMI INC
(*Suby of* 9001-6403 QUEBEC INC)
1201 Boul Saint-Paul, Chicoutimi, QC, G7J 3Y2
(418) 549-8343
Emp Here 100   *Sales* 24,618,600
SIC 1794 Excavation work
Jeannot Savard
Linda Savard
Therese Savard
Bruno Savard
Jeannot Savard
Martin Savard
Nancy Savard
Nancy Savard
Linda Savard
Bruno Savard

D-U-N-S 20-013-6948   (SL)
IOS SERVICES GEOSCIENTIFIQUES INC
1319 Boul Saint-Paul, Chicoutimi, QC, G7J 3Y2
(418) 698-4498
Emp Here 50   *Sales* 11,671,750
SIC 1481 NonMetallic mineral services
Rejean Girard

D-U-N-S 24-851-2951   (SL)
K.L.S (2009) INC
1615 Boul Saint-Paul, Chicoutimi, QC, G7J 3Y3
(418) 543-1515
Emp Here 150   *Sales* 27,208,200
SIC 3354 Aluminum extruded products
Remi Roy
Clement Tremblay
Mike Breed
Leslie Hammond

D-U-N-S 20-319-7202   (SL)
LAJOIE LEMIEUX NOTAIRES S.E.N.C.R.L
138 Rue Price O Bureau 208, Chicoutimi, QC, G7J 1G8
(418) 549-6464
Emp Here 25   *Sales* 11,230,475
SIC 7389 Business services, nec
Gaetan Boivin
Josee Noel
Marlene Ouellet
Martin Lajoie
Nathalie Bouchard

D-U-N-S 20-193-7844   (SL)
LAURENT LAPOINTE LTEE
1150 Boul Saint-Paul Bureau 400, Chicoutimi, QC, G7J 3C5

Emp Here 70   *Sales* 31,302,180
SIC 5039 Construction materials, nec
Lise Mercier
Guy Brisson
Richard Dionne
Sylvain Boutin
Antoine Desbiens

D-U-N-S 24-701-4975   (SL)
PNEUS UNIMAX LTEE
MEGAPNEU
255 Rue Sainte-Anne, Chicoutimi, QC, G7J 2M2
(418) 549-1210
Emp Here 28   *Sales* 10,198,020

SIC 5014 Tires and tubes
Benoit Forcier

D-U-N-S 24-791-3650   (SL)
STAS INC
SOCIETE DES TECHNOLOGIES DE L'ALUMINIUM DU SAGUENAY S.T.A.S.
622 Rue Des Actionnaires, Chicoutimi, QC, G7J 5A9
(418) 696-0074
Emp Here 100   *Sales* 22,200,100
SIC 3569 General industrial machinery, nec
Louis Bouchard
Patrice Bouchard

D-U-N-S 24-863-6243   (HQ)
VIANDES C .D .S. INC, LES
598 Boul Du Saguenay O, Chicoutimi, QC, G7J 1H4
(418) 549-9614
Emp Here 6   *Sales* 39,272,119
SIC 5147 Meats and meat products
Jean Dostie
Brigitte Boily

Chicoutimi, QC G7K

D-U-N-S 25-257-1179   (SL)
9014-5467 QUEBEC INC
2315 Boul Saint-Paul, Chicoutimi, QC, G7K 1E5
(418) 543-6477
Emp Here 25   *Sales* 12,451,950
SIC 5511 New and used car dealers

D-U-N-S 24-344-2162   (SL)
9165-8021 QUEBEC INC
FOURNITURES MARITIMES R.C.I.
1690 Rue De La Manic, Chicoutimi, QC, G7K 1J1
(418) 543-5111
Emp Here 50   *Sales* 10,131,450
SIC 7549 Automotive services, nec
Luc Gaudreault

D-U-N-S 20-400-3644   (HQ)
9372-3575 QUEBEC INC
1788 Rue Mitis, Chicoutimi, QC, G7K 1H5
(418) 543-1632
Sales 13,077,650
SIC 6712 Bank holding companies
Eloise Harvey
Robert Normandeau
Stephen Denton

D-U-N-S 24-339-7580   (SL)
ALFINITI INC
1152 Rue De La Manic, Chicoutimi, QC, G7K 1A2
(418) 696-2545
Emp Here 65   *Sales* 15,173,275
SIC 3354 Aluminum extruded products
Jean Parie

D-U-N-S 24-706-9834   (SL)
CANMEC INDUSTRIEL INC
CANMEC LAJOIE SOMEC
(*Suby of* GROUPE CANMEC INC)
1750 Rue La Grande, Chicoutimi, QC, G7K 1H7
(418) 543-9151
Emp Here 225   *Sales* 63,197,325
SIC 3569 General industrial machinery, nec
Remi Roy
Eric Vachon

D-U-N-S 20-547-5150   (HQ)
CEGERCO INC
DEMOTEC
(*Suby of* 9123-6794 QUEBEC INC)
1180 Rue Bersimis, Chicoutimi, QC, G7K 1A5
(418) 543-6159
Emp Here 50   *Sales* 114,840,250
SIC 1611 Highway and street construction
Jeannot Harvey

Jean-Francois Coude
Andre St-Cyr
Andre Salesse
Francois Caron

D-U-N-S 20-309-5823   (SL)
CERVO-POLYGAZ INC
1371 Rue De La Manic, Chicoutimi, QC, G7K 1G7
(418) 696-1212
Emp Here 26   *Sales* 18,988,970
SIC 5169 Chemicals and allied products, nec
Keiven Tremblay
Remi Pageau
Andre Barriault

D-U-N-S 24-940-9368   (SL)
CYCLE DEVINCI INC
1555 Rue De La Manic, Chicoutimi, QC, G7K 1G8
(418) 549-6218
Emp Here 60   *Sales* 13,430,580
SIC 3751 Motorcycles, bicycles and parts
Felix Gauthier
Claude Gagnon

D-U-N-S 20-193-7331   (SL)
ELECTRICITE GRIMARD INC
(*Suby of* GRIMARD.CA INC)
1235 Rue Bersimis, Chicoutimi, QC, G7K 1A4
(418) 549-6352
Emp Here 230   *Sales* 54,167,070
SIC 1731 Electrical work
Jean Grimard
Jacques Grimard
Gilbert Grimard

D-U-N-S 20-380-7164   (SL)
ENGRENAGE PROVINCIAL INC
EP SAGUENAY
1001 Rue De La Rupert, Chicoutimi, QC, G7K 0A2
(418) 693-8132
Emp Here 50   *Sales* 23,751,300
SIC 5085 Industrial supplies
Dominique Huot
Martin Grenier
Jean-Francois Carrier

D-U-N-S 20-722-9493   (HQ)
GRO-MEC INC
1911 Rue Des Outardes, Chicoutimi, QC, G7K 1C3
(418) 549-5961
Sales 10,285,002
SIC 5074 Plumbing and heating equipment and supplies (hydronics)
Claude Jacques
Eric Jacques

D-U-N-S 24-706-9990   (HQ)
GROUPE GIROUX MACONNEX INC
BRIQUE ET PAVE CHICOINE
2223 Boul Saint-Paul, Chicoutimi, QC, G7K 1E5
(418) 549-7345
Emp Here 42   *Sales* 113,925,600
SIC 5032 Brick, stone, and related material
Martin Vandry
Gerald Tremblay

D-U-N-S 20-309-5831   (SL)
GROUPE PGS 2009 INC
1371 Rue De La Manic, Chicoutimi, QC, G7K 1G7
(418) 696-1212
Emp Here 93   *Sales* 7,621,370
SIC 1711 Plumbing, heating, air-conditioning
Serge Blackburn
Remi Pageau
Keiven Tremblay
Andre Barriault
Maxime Parent

D-U-N-S 25-395-5793   (SL)
GROUPE REFRACO INC
1207 Rue Antonio-Lemaire, Chicoutimi, QC, G7K 1J2

(418) 545-4200
Emp Here 350   *Sales* 23,898,660
SIC 3297 Nonclay refractories
  Alain Pineault
  Carol Pineault
  Jean-Benoit Pineault
  Remi Pineault

D-U-N-S 24-759-1878   (SL)
MECFOR INC
MECFOR BROCHOT
(*Suby of* 9372-3575 QUEBEC INC)
1788 Rue Mitis, Chicoutimi, QC, G7K 1H5
(418) 543-1632
Emp Here 50   *Sales* 11,100,050
SIC 3569 General industrial machinery, nec
  Eloise Harvey
  Stephen Denton
  Robert Normandeau

D-U-N-S 20-193-8016   (HQ)
PRODUITS SANITAIRES LEPINE INC, LES
PRODUITS SANITAIRES LEPINE VAL-D'OR, LES
1105 Rue Bersimis, Chicoutimi, QC, G7K 1A4
(418) 545-0794
Emp Here 29   *Sales* 27,602,640
SIC 5074 Plumbing and heating equipment and supplies (hydronics)
  Gilles Dery
  Guy Cote
  Karine Turcotte
  Yves Brisson
  Jean Dostie

D-U-N-S 20-254-9838   (SL)
SOCIETE DE TRANSPORT DU SAGUENAY
1330 Rue Bersimis, Chicoutimi, QC, G7K 1A5
(418) 545-3683
Emp Here 170   *Sales* 12,796,240
SIC 4131 Intercity and rural bus transportation
  Rejean Hudon
  Luc Lalancette

D-U-N-S 25-198-0025   (SL)
SOTREM (1993) INC
CENTRE DE COULEE SHAWINIGAN A/S CLD DE SHAWINIGAN
(*Suby of* SOCCRENT 2006, SOCIETE EN COMMANDITE)
1685 Rue De La Manic, Chicoutimi, QC, G7K 1G8
(418) 696-2019
Emp Here 50   *Sales* 11,671,750
SIC 3398 Metal heat treating
  Michel Boudreault
  Jean-Philippe Harvey

D-U-N-S 24-623-5303   (HQ)
SPECTUBE INC
ALFINITI
(*Suby of* SOCCRENT 2006, SOCIETE EN COMMANDITE)
1152 Rue De La Manic, Chicoutimi, QC, G7K 1A2
(418) 696-2545
Emp Here 65   *Sales* 11,790,220
SIC 3354 Aluminum extruded products
  Jean Pare
  Bruno Gagne
  Jean-Philippe Harvey

Chisasibi, QC J0M

D-U-N-S 20-712-6603   (BR)
COMMISSION SCOLAIRE CRIE (LA)
CREE SCHOOL BOARD
(*Suby of* COMMISSION SCOLAIRE CRIE (LA))
11 Maamuu, Chisasibi, QC, J0M 1E0
(819) 855-2833
Emp Here 80
SIC 8211 Elementary and secondary schools
  Judy Deschenes

D-U-N-S 25-336-7437   (SL)
CONSEIL CRI DE LA SANTE ET DES SERVICES SOCIAUX DE LA BAIE JAMES
CCSSSBJ
Gd, Chisasibi, QC, J0M 1E0
(819) 855-9001
Emp Here 800   *Sales* 159,237,482
SIC 8062 General medical and surgical hospitals
  Mabel Herodier
  Louttit Eva
  Diamond Shirley
  Gilpin Ida
  Jonathan Sutherland
  George L. Pachanos
  Stella Moar Wapachee
  Patricia George
  Gloria Polson

D-U-N-S 24-592-3987   (SL)
CONSTRUCTION MANCHAOW INC
2 Cluster F7, Chisasibi, QC, J0M 1E0
(819) 855-2046
Emp Here 49   *Sales* 14,140,567
SIC 1522 Residential construction, nec
  Eddie Sam

D-U-N-S 24-377-8813   (HQ)
GESTION CBCC INC
3 Rue Aahppisaach, Chisasibi, QC, J0M 1E0
(819) 855-2977
Sales 18,965,940
SIC 1521 Single-family housing construction
  George Pachanos

D-U-N-S 24-177-0817   (HQ)
HOSPITAL CHISASIBI
WEESAPOU GROUPE HOME
Pr, Chisasibi, QC, J0M 1E0
(819) 855-2844
Emp Here 150   *Sales* 24,437,600
SIC 8062 General medical and surgical hospitals
  James Bobbish
  James Shecapio

Clarenceville, QC J0J

D-U-N-S 24-812-1381   (SL)
ROBITAILLE R & FILS INC
1051 Rang Victoria, Clarenceville, QC, J0J 1B0

Emp Here 49   *Sales* 17,063,117
SIC 0191 General farms, primarily crop
  Claude Robitaille

Clermont, QC G4A

D-U-N-S 24-203-4411   (SL)
MARCHE J.R. GRAVEL INC
I G A
110 Boul Notre-Dame, Clermont, QC, G4A 1G3
(418) 439-3922
Emp Here 40   *Sales* 10,966,080
SIC 5411 Grocery stores
  Real Gravel
  Michel Gravel
  Joseph Tremblay

D-U-N-S 20-194-7504   (BR)
PF RESOLU CANADA INC
(*Suby of* RESOLUTE FOREST PRODUCTS INC)
100 Rue De La Donohue, Clermont, QC, G4A 1A7
(418) 439-5300
Emp Here 213
SIC 2621 Paper mills
  Sylvain Proulx

D-U-N-S 20-525-7913   (BR)
SOCIETE DES ETABLISSEMENTS DE PLEIN AIR DU QUEBEC
PARC NATIONAL DES GRANDS JARDINS ET LE PARC NATIONAL HAUTES GORGES DE LA RIVIERE MALBAIE
(*Suby of* GOUVERNEMENT DE LA PROVINCE DE QUEBEC)
25 Boul Notre-Dame, Clermont, QC, G4A 1C2
(418) 439-1227
Emp Here 140
SIC 7999 Amusement and recreation, nec
  Claire Ducharme

Cleveland, QC J0B

D-U-N-S 25-460-9761   (SL)
9127-7509 QUEBEC INC
TOYOTA RICHMOND
151 116 Rte, Cleveland, QC, J0B 2H0
(819) 826-5923
Emp Here 28   *Sales* 13,946,184
SIC 5511 New and used car dealers
  Alain Fournier
  Peter Goorts

D-U-N-S 20-542-2595   (HQ)
GABRIEL COUTURE & FILS LTEE
PRO QUINCAILLERIE
2 Ch St-Onge, Cleveland, QC, J0B 2H0
(819) 826-3777
Sales 10,122,360
SIC 5211 Lumber and other building materials
  Marcel Couture
  Real Couture

D-U-N-S 20-762-8769   (SL)
WALES HOME, THE
RESIDENCE WALES HOME
506 Rte 243, Cleveland, QC, J0B 2H0
(819) 826-3266
Emp Here 100   *Sales* 5,924,700
SIC 8361 Residential care
  Glenn Brock

Coaticook, QC J1A

D-U-N-S 20-646-9830   (SL)
3099-3562 QUEBEC INC
FERBLANTERIE EDGAR ROY
1021 Rue Child, Coaticook, QC, J1A 2S5
(819) 849-0532
Emp Here 25   *Sales* 11,179,350
SIC 5075 Warm air heating and air conditioning
  Bruno Bouchard

D-U-N-S 24-630-6935   (BR)
9099-9012 QUEBEC INC
CODET
709 Rue Merrill, Coaticook, QC, J1A 2S2

Emp Here 90
SIC 5699 Miscellaneous apparel and accessory stores
  Fleurette Viens

D-U-N-S 24-712-6980   (SL)
ALIMENTATION COATICOOK (1986) INC
IGA
265 Rue Child, Coaticook, QC, J1A 2B5
(819) 849-6226
Emp Here 60   *Sales* 17,608,620
SIC 5411 Grocery stores
  Dominic Arsenault

D-U-N-S 20-183-1232   (HQ)
CAISSE DESJARDINS DES VERTS-SOMMETS DE L'ESTRIE
CENTRE DE SERVICE COMPTON
155 Rue Child, Coaticook, QC, J1A 2B4

(819) 849-0434
Emp Here 50   *Sales* 15,198,965
SIC 6062 State credit unions
  Pierre Langevin
  Rene Bessette
  Nadine Groulx
  Yves Bond
  Sylvie Caron
  Joelle Cote
  Sara Favreau-Perreault
  Gervais Gagnon
  Jean-Maurice Plafter
  Roxanne Provencher

D-U-N-S 20-611-4258   (SL)
CANADIAN TIRE
85 Rue Wellington, Coaticook, QC, J1A 2H6

Emp Here 30   *Sales* 10,926,450
SIC 5014 Tires and tubes
  Kelly Blair

D-U-N-S 20-194-8445   (SL)
CENTRE AGRICOLE COATICOOK INC
CHAGNON, J. M.
525 Rue Main O, Coaticook, QC, J1A 1R2
(819) 849-2663
Emp Here 25   *Sales* 11,875,650
SIC 5083 Farm and garden machinery
  Jean-Guy Rheault
  Claude Hamel

D-U-N-S 20-521-8592   (SL)
CENTRE DE SANTE ET DE SERVICES SOCIAUX DE LA MRC DE COATICOOK
138 Rue Jeanne-Mance, Coaticook, QC, J1A 1W3
(819) 849-4876
Emp Here 250   *Sales* 27,770,000
SIC 8062 General medical and surgical hospitals
  Gerard Ruest
  Donald Massicotte

D-U-N-S 20-194-8528   (HQ)
CODET INC
BIG BILL
49 Rue Maple, Coaticook, QC, J1A 1C3
(819) 849-4819
Emp Here 250   *Sales* 29,772,126
SIC 2326 Men's and boy's work clothing
  Jean-Pierre Audet
  Justin Audet
  Vincent Audet
  Jessica Audet
  Jobin Audet

D-U-N-S 20-712-1018   (BR)
COMMISSION SCOLAIRE DES HAUTS-CANTONS
ECOLE SECONDAIRE LA FRONTALIERE
(*Suby of* COMMISSION SCOLAIRE DES HAUTS-CANTONS)
311 Rue Saint-Paul E, Coaticook, QC, J1A 1G1
(819) 849-4825
Emp Here 120
SIC 8211 Elementary and secondary schools
  Caroline Champeau

D-U-N-S 20-194-9310   (HQ)
COOP DES CANTONS COOPERATIVE AGRICOLE
96 Rue Main E, Coaticook, QC, J1A 1N2
(819) 849-9833
Emp Here 20   *Sales* 73,384,600
SIC 5153 Grain and field beans
  Jean-Philippe Cote
  Mario Doyon
  Jocelyn Lachance
  Serge Boivin
  Martin Roy
  Dominique Therrien
  Eric Decubber
  Claudette Cote
  Stephane Peloquin
  Gaetan Lavigne

D-U-N-S 20-194-8593   (SL)
COUILLARD CONSTRUCTION LIMITEE
228 Rue Main E, Coaticook, QC, J1A 1N2
(819) 849-9181
Emp Here 230   *Sales* 75,466,450
SIC 1611 Highway and street construction
Daniel Cote
Marcel Pouliot
Francis Brouillard
Jerome Marion
Michel Marcoux

D-U-N-S 20-028-5778   (SL)
ENCAN SAWYERVILLE INC
ENCAN SAWYERVILLE AUCTION
512 Rue Main O, Coaticook, QC, J1A 1P9
(819) 875-3577
Emp Here 20   *Sales* 29,353,840
SIC 5154 Livestock
Daniel Lafaille
Alain Lafaille
Barry Hull
Benoit Bouffard
Claude Lafaille
Michel Lafaille

D-U-N-S 24-432-5130   (SL)
ENTREPRISES CLEMENT LAVOIE INC
92 Rue Saint-Jacques S, Coaticook, QC, J1A
2N8
(819) 849-6374
Emp Here 35   *Sales* 17,432,730
SIC 5541 Gasoline service stations
Clement Lavoie
Claudette Lavoie

D-U-N-S 25-355-9942   (SL)
GEO. SHEARD FABRICS LTD
84 Rue Merrill, Coaticook, QC, J1A 1X4
(819) 849-6311
Emp Here 103   *Sales* 25,165,784
SIC 5949 Sewing, needlework, and piece
goods
Iskender P Sheard
Perihan Sheard

D-U-N-S 20-057-0047   (HQ)
GROUPE CABICO INC
CABICO BOUTIQUE
677 Rue Akhurst, Coaticook, QC, J1A 0B4
(819) 849-7969
Emp Here 200   *Sales* 75,213,792
SIC 2434 Wood kitchen cabinets
Alain Ouzilleau
Marc Labrosse

D-U-N-S 25-670-6842   (SL)
GROUPE JLD LAGUE
544 Rue Main O, Coaticook, QC, J1A 2S5
(819) 849-0300
Emp Here 30   *Sales* 14,250,780
SIC 5084 Industrial machinery and equipment
Pierre Arsenault

D-U-N-S 20-422-1733   (SL)
LAITERIE DE COATICOOK LIMITEE
1000 Rue Child Bureau 255, Coaticook, QC,
J1A 2S5
(819) 849-2272
Emp Here 65   *Sales* 14,615,575
SIC 2024 Ice cream and frozen deserts
Jean Provencher
Johanne Provencher

D-U-N-S 24-354-7119   (SL)
MULTI X INC
60 Rue Sheard, Coaticook, QC, J1A 0B2
(819) 849-7036
Emp Here 100   *Sales* 20,189,700
SIC 3053 Gaskets; packing and sealing de-
vices
Louis Marier

D-U-N-S 25-314-0032   (SL)
NIEDNER INC
(*Suby of* LOGISTEC CORPORATION)
675 Rue Merrill, Coaticook, QC, J1A 2S2

(819) 849-2751
Emp Here 140   *Sales* 31,080,140
SIC 3569 General industrial machinery, nec
Alain Souriol
Rejean Loiselle

D-U-N-S 24-851-9238   (SL)
SUNRISE TRADEX CORP
DEFI RECUP-AIR
271 Rue Saint-Jacques S, Coaticook, QC, J1A
2P3
(819) 804-0551
Emp Here 34   *Sales* 15,203,916
SIC 5075 Warm air heating and air condition-
ing
Claude Bouthot

D-U-N-S 25-685-4100   (BR)
WATERVILLE TG INC
(*Suby of* TOYODA GOSEI CO., LTD.)
500 Rue Dionne, Coaticook, QC, J1A 2E8
(819) 849-7031
Emp Here 250
SIC 3069 Fabricated rubber products, nec

Coaticook, QC K1A

D-U-N-S 24-614-5510   (SL)
FERROTECH MENARD INC
665 Rue Akhurst, Coaticook, QC, K1A 0B4
(819) 849-9474
Emp Here 29   *Sales* 13,027,351
SIC 7389 Business services, nec
Yves Menard
Patricia Menard
Constant Perras

Compton, QC J0B

D-U-N-S 20-059-1597   (SL)
**LEBLANC, GERARD COURTIER
D'ASSURANCES LTEE**
6920 Rte Louis-S.-Saint-Laurent, Compton,
QC, J0B 1L0
(819) 823-3311
Emp Here 27   *Sales* 15,657,948
SIC 6411 Insurance agents, brokers, and ser-
vice
Olivier Leblanc

Contrecoeur, QC J0L

D-U-N-S 20-421-5453   (SL)
A. & J.L. BOURGEOIS LTEE
BETON BOURGEOIS
1745 Rte Marie-Victorin, Contrecoeur, QC,
J0L 1C0
(450) 587-2724
Emp Here 50   *Sales* 11,008,400
SIC 1794 Excavation work
Alain Bourgeois
Joanne Bourgeois
Daniel Vincent

D-U-N-S 20-323-5379   (BR)
**ARCELORMITTAL PRODUITS LONGS
CANADA S.E.N.C.**
(*Suby of* ARCELORMITTAL PRODUITS
LONGS CANADA S.E.N.C.)
2050 Rte Des Acieries, Contrecoeur, QC, J0L
1C0
(450) 587-2012
Emp Here 379
SIC 3312 Blast furnaces and steel mills

D-U-N-S 20-253-6413   (BR)
**ARCELORMITTAL PRODUITS LONGS
CANADA S.E.N.C.**
(*Suby of* ARCELORMITTAL PRODUITS

LONGS CANADA S.E.N.C.)
3900 Rte Des Acieries, Contrecoeur, QC, J0L
1C0
(450) 587-8600
Emp Here 700
SIC 3312 Blast furnaces and steel mills

D-U-N-S 20-255-1214   (HQ)
**ARCELORMITTAL PRODUITS LONGS
CANADA S.E.N.C.**
AMPLC
4000 Rte Des Acieries, Contrecoeur, QC, J0L
1C0
(450) 587-8600
Emp Here 50   *Sales* 692,195,800
SIC 3312 Blast furnaces and steel mills
Srinivas Durvasula
Nadia Thibault
Tara Macnair
Francois Perras
Rene Lopez

D-U-N-S 25-376-4716   (BR)
**CENTRE DE SANTE ET DE SERVICES SO-
CIAUX PIERRE-BOUCHER**
*CENTRE D'HEBERGEMENT DE CONTRE-
COEUR*
(*Suby of* GOUVERNEMENT DE LA
PROVINCE DE QUEBEC)
4700 Rte Marie-Victorin, Contrecoeur, QC,
J0L 1C0
(450) 468-8410
Emp Here 75
SIC 8361 Residential care
Louise Potvin

D-U-N-S 25-364-3670   (HQ)
ELEVATEUR RIVE-SUD INC
4065 Rue Industrielle, Contrecoeur, QC, J0L
1C0
(450) 587-2500
Sales 13,209,228
SIC 5153 Grain and field beans
Yann Hebert
Alain Hebert
Annie Belletete

D-U-N-S 20-793-5586   (HQ)
FORMEDICA LTEE
JD ANIMA
4859 Rue Des Ormes, Contrecoeur, QC, J0L
1C0
(450) 587-2821
Sales 14,773,785
SIC 3842 Surgical appliances and supplies
Raymond Fortin

D-U-N-S 20-195-0284   (BR)
GENFOOT INC
KAMIK
(*Suby of* 175968 CANADA INC)
4945 Rue Legendre, Contrecoeur, QC, J0L
1C0
(450) 587-2051
Emp Here 250
SIC 3143 Men's footwear, except athletic
Monique Castonguay

D-U-N-S 25-208-7247   (SL)
GROUPE TRUDO
1999 Rte Marie-Victorin, Contrecoeur, QC,
J0L 1C0
(450) 587-2098
Emp Here 49   *Sales* 11,438,315
SIC 1231 Anthracite mining
Edmond Trudeau

Cookshire-Eaton, QC J0B

D-U-N-S 25-684-9258   (SL)
3011933 CANADA INC
SOUS-TRAITANCE L.B.
80 Ch Des Etangs, Cookshire-Eaton, QC, J0B
1M0

(819) 875-5559
Emp Here 125   *Sales* 19,857,250
SIC 3069 Fabricated rubber products, nec
Louis Biron

D-U-N-S 20-370-1891   (SL)
**BOIS PRECIEUX QUEBEC CANADA 1993
INC**
3100 Rte 108 Bureau 4, Cookshire-Eaton, QC,
J0B 1M0
(866) 624-0243
Emp Here 50   *Sales* 26,027,100
SIC 5099 Durable goods, nec
Samba Kalombo
Lemuel Louis Kalombo
Okwii Maria
Guychelle Sandra Dihoulou
Casimir Pelemo Kourouma

D-U-N-S 20-370-2993   (SL)
GESTION GILLES-GENEST INC
EPICERIE IGA COOKSHIRE
35 Rue Principale E, Cookshire-Eaton, QC,
J0B 1M0
(819) 875-5455
Emp Here 50   *Sales* 13,866,360
SIC 5411 Grocery stores
Gilles Denis

D-U-N-S 20-258-9396   (SL)
MEUNERIE SAWYERVILLE INC
100 Rue De La Meunerie, Cookshire-Eaton,
QC, J0B 1M0
(819) 875-5471
Emp Here 20   *Sales* 14,850,400
SIC 5191 Farm supplies
Yves Bolduc
Lucie Lambert

D-U-N-S 20-050-7536   (BR)
PLASTIPAK INDUSTRIES INC
PLASTIPAK INDUSTRIES
(*Suby of* GROUPE HAMRO INC)
345 Rue Bibeau, Cookshire-Eaton, QC, J0B
1M0
(819) 875-3355
Emp Here 140
SIC 3089 Plastics products, nec
Robert Lafleur

D-U-N-S 20-023-0352   (SL)
VETEMENTS COOKSHIRE INC
VETEMENTS COOKSHIRE ENR
725 Rue Pope, Cookshire-Eaton, QC, J0B
1M0
(819) 875-5538
Emp Here 75   *Sales* 10,250,550
SIC 2337 Women's and misses' suits and
coats
Steve Blanchette

Cote Saint-Luc, QC H3X

D-U-N-S 20-106-3174   (BR)
**WINNERS MERCHANTS INTERNATIONAL
L.P.**
WINNERS
(*Suby of* THE TJX COMPANIES INC)
6900 Boul Decarie Bureau 3550, Cote Saint-
Luc, QC, H3X 2T8
(514) 733-4200
Emp Here 100
SIC 5651 Family clothing stores
Paul Corbeil

Cote Saint-Luc, QC H4V

D-U-N-S 24-252-5426   (SL)
**FONDATION D'AMENAGEMENT ST-
PATRICK**
ST. PATRICK SQUARE
6767 Ch De La Cote-Saint-Luc Bureau 616,

▲ Public Company   ■ Public Company Family Member   **HQ** Headquarters   **BR** Branch   **SL** Single Location

Cote Saint-Luc, QC, H4V 2Z6
(514) 481-9609
Emp Here 205   *Sales* 27,813,785
SIC 6513 Apartment building operators
Mary Mcgovern
Peter Von Ond
Beverly Rozek
Hugh Mcadam
Denis Midgley
Georgia Remond

D-U-N-S 25-212-5679   (SL)
SUPERMARCHE PAGANO ET SHNAIDMAN INC
I G A
7151 Ch De La Cote-Saint-Luc Bureau 108, Cote Saint-Luc, QC, H4V 1J2
(514) 486-3254
Emp Here 92   *Sales* 26,999,884
SIC 5411 Grocery stores
Joseph Pagano
Avi Shnaidman

D-U-N-S 24-501-2448   (SL)
YAMATECH SCIENTIFIC LTD
YAMATECH Y C S
5568 Av King-Edward, Cote Saint-Luc, QC, H4V 2K4
(514) 737-5434
Emp Here 25   *Sales* 11,179,350
SIC 5045 Computers, peripherals, and software
Jack Kincler
Dida Berku

Cote Saint-Luc, QC H4W

D-U-N-S 20-231-4993   (SL)
139273 CANADA INC
PHARMAPRIX CAVENDISH
5800 Boul Cavendish, Cote Saint-Luc, QC, H4W 2T5
(514) 482-6340
Emp Here 70   *Sales* 17,102,960
SIC 5912 Drug stores and proprietary stores
Valerie Rouimi

D-U-N-S 20-618-6681   (SL)
ALIMENTATIONS SHNAIDMAN PAGANO INC, LES
IGA 111
5800 Boul Cavendish Bureau 111, Cote Saint-Luc, QC, H4W 2T5
(514) 482-4710
Emp Here 100   *Sales* 29,347,700
SIC 5411 Grocery stores
Daniel Kraft

D-U-N-S 25-874-7500   (BR)
ALLIED SYSTEMS (CANADA) COMPANY
(*Suby of* ALLIED SYSTEMS HOLDINGS, INC.)
5901 Av Westminster, Cote Saint-Luc, QC, H4W 2J9

Emp Here 175
SIC 4213 Trucking, except local
Donald Gallant

D-U-N-S 20-296-0758   (BR)
CANADIAN PACIFIC RAILWAY COMPANY
CPR
(*Suby of* CANADIAN PACIFIC RAILWAY LIMITED)
5901 Av Westminster, Cote Saint-Luc, QC, H4W 2J9
(514) 483-7102
Emp Here 200
SIC 4011 Railroads, line-haul operating
John Ausaint

D-U-N-S 24-253-1226   (SL)
CENTRE HOSPITALIER MONT-SINAI-MONTREAL
5690 Boul Cavendish, Cote Saint-Luc, QC,

H4W 1S7
(514) 369-2222
Emp Here 250   *Sales* 27,770,000
SIC 8062 General medical and surgical hospitals
Elliot Bier
Joseph Rothbart

D-U-N-S 24-128-0572   (SL)
CSH CASTEL ROYAL INC
CASTLE ROYALE
5740 Boul Cavendish Bureau 2006, Cote Saint-Luc, QC, H4W 2T8

Emp Here 80   *Sales* 5,206,000
SIC 8361 Residential care
Zahava Grinfeld

D-U-N-S 25-246-2502   (SL)
HEBREW ACADEMY INC
ACADEMIE HEBRAIQUE
5700 Av Kellert, Cote Saint-Luc, QC, H4W 1T4
(514) 489-5321
Emp Here 100   *Sales* 10,054,800
SIC 8211 Elementary and secondary schools
Linda Lehrer
Chaya Lieberman

D-U-N-S 20-024-0344   (BR)
JEWISH PEOPLE'S SCHOOLS AND PERETZ SCHOOLS INC
BIALIK HIGH SCHOOL
(*Suby of* JEWISH PEOPLE'S SCHOOLS AND PERETZ SCHOOLS INC)
6500 Ch Kildare, Cote Saint-Luc, QC, H4W 3B8
(514) 731-3841
Emp Here 75
SIC 8211 Elementary and secondary schools
Elaine Wisenthal

D-U-N-S 20-152-5255   (HQ)
JEWISH PEOPLE'S SCHOOLS AND PERETZ SCHOOLS INC
ECOLE SECONDAIRE BIALIK
6500 Ch Kildare, Cote Saint-Luc, QC, H4W 3B8

Sales 32,642,100
SIC 8211 Elementary and secondary schools
Lee Wise
David Inzlicht
John Galambos
Warren Levine

D-U-N-S 24-338-8225   (BR)
REVERA INC
MANOIR MONTEFIORE
(*Suby of* GOVERNMENT OF CANADA)
5885 Boul Cavendish Bureau 202, Cote Saint-Luc, QC, H4W 3H4
(514) 485-5994
Emp Here 150
SIC 8051 Skilled nursing care facilities
Howard Modlin

D-U-N-S 25-201-2711   (HQ)
ULTRA ELECTRONICS FORENSIC TECHNOLOGY INC
(*Suby of* ULTRA ELECTRONICS HOLDINGS PLC)
5757 Boul Cavendish Bureau 200, Cote Saint-Luc, QC, H4W 2W8
(514) 489-4247
Emp Here 170   *Sales* 68,866,870
SIC 3821 Laboratory apparatus and furniture
Brian Sinnott
Bridget Rothwell
Mike Baptist
Michael Clayton
Gregory Field
Bridget Rothwell
Mike Baptist

D-U-N-S 24-175-5172   (BR)
UNITED CHURCH OF CANADA, THE
GRIFFITH-MCCONNELL RESIDENCE

(*Suby of* UNITED CHURCH OF CANADA, THE)
5790 Av Parkhaven, Cote Saint-Luc, QC, H4W 1X9

Emp Here 200
SIC 8051 Skilled nursing care facilities
Annette Rudy

Cote Saint-Luc, QC H7E

D-U-N-S 20-387-7621   (HQ)
MAGI-PRIX INC
VILLAGE DES MAGI-PRIX
3194 Av Des Aristocrates, Cote Saint-Luc, QC, H7E 5H8
(450) 963-0410
Emp Here 1   *Sales* 12,320,580
SIC 5331 Variety stores
Hamid Sleiman

Cote Saint-Luc, QC H7G

D-U-N-S 24-234-5549   (HQ)
9050-6015 QUEBEC INC
PETRO CANADA RELAIS
500 Boul Des Laurentides, Cote Saint-Luc, QC, H7G 2V1

Emp Here 5   *Sales* 24,903,900
SIC 5541 Gasoline service stations
Stephane Godbout

D-U-N-S 25-995-4972   (SL)
9067-6628 QUEBEC INC
RONA LE REGIONAL
164 Boul Des Laurentides, Cote Saint-Luc, QC, H7G 4P6
(450) 667-0255
Emp Here 80   *Sales* 21,412,160
SIC 5211 Lumber and other building materials
Claude Lesperance

D-U-N-S 24-161-9480   (SL)
ALUFORME LTEE
2000 Rue De Lierre, Cote Saint-Luc, QC, H7G 4Y4
(450) 669-6690
Emp Here 100   *Sales* 23,343,500
SIC 3271 Concrete block and brick
Francois Pomerleau
Audrey Pomerleau
Cristelle Pomerleau

D-U-N-S 20-927-4885   (SL)
CHARTRAND FORD (VENTES) INC
1610 Boul Saint-Martin E, Cote Saint-Luc, QC, H7G 4W6
(450) 669-6110
Emp Here 89   *Sales* 56,005,920
SIC 5511 New and used car dealers
Jean Provost
Rene Arsenault
Sylvain Hogues

D-U-N-S 25-355-9819   (SL)
COFFRAGE ALLIANCE LTEE
2000 Rue De Lierre, Cote Saint-Luc, QC, H7G 4Y4
(514) 326-5200
Emp Here 25   *Sales* 14,258,450
SIC 1542 Nonresidential construction, nec
Carolle Morin
Michel D'andre
Francois Pomerleau

D-U-N-S 20-706-6804   (SL)
CONFISERIE MONDOUX INC
DISTRIBUTIONS MONDOUX, LES
1610 Place De Lierre, Cote Saint-Luc, QC, H7G 4X7

(450) 669-1311
Emp Here 100   *Sales* 83,557,700
SIC 5145 Confectionery
Jean Mondoux
Yvan Mondoux
Rene Berichon

D-U-N-S 20-209-6624   (SL)
CORPORATION D'ACIER ALLIANCE, LA
1060 Boul Des Laurentides, Cote Saint-Luc, QC, H7G 2W1
(514) 382-5780
Emp Here 110   *Sales* 49,189,140
SIC 5051 Metals service centers and offices
Michael Deitcher
Glenda Susser

D-U-N-S 20-726-5521   (SL)
GESTION 47 LTEE
(*Suby of* GESTION 4B LTEE)
1601 Boul Saint-Martin E, Cote Saint-Luc, QC, H7G 4R4
(450) 669-7070
Emp Here 95   *Sales* 59,781,600
SIC 5511 New and used car dealers
Jean-Marc Bourassa

D-U-N-S 20-059-1662   (SL)
GROUPE MARKETING INTERNATIONAL INC
37 Boul Des Laurentides, Cote Saint-Luc, QC, H7G 2S3
(450) 972-1540
Emp Here 75   *Sales* 33,691,425
SIC 7389 Business services, nec
Micheline Durocher

D-U-N-S 25-776-0264   (SL)
INDUSTRIE DE PALETTES STANDARD (I.P.S.) INC
2400 Rue De Lierre, Cote Saint-Luc, QC, H7G 4Y4
(450) 661-4000
Emp Here 37   *Sales* 10,058,154
SIC 7699 Repair services, nec
Raed Bechara

D-U-N-S 24-253-2521   (HQ)
LESPERANCE, FRANCOIS INC
RONA LESPERANCE
164 Boul Des Laurentides, Cote Saint-Luc, QC, H7G 4P6
(450) 667-0255
Emp Here 25   *Sales* 70,262,500
SIC 5211 Lumber and other building materials
Claude Guevin
Claude Bernier
France Charlebois

D-U-N-S 20-885-7409   (HQ)
LOUIS-HEBERT UNIFORME INC
1963 Rue Notre-Dame-De-Fatima, Cote Saint-Luc, QC, H7G 4R9
(450) 668-3766
Sales 47,340,590
SIC 5136 Men's and boy's clothing
Denis Charest

D-U-N-S 25-841-0281   (BR)
MARCHE J.C. MESSIER INC
MARCHE DE LA CONCORDE
(*Suby of* PLACEMENTS C. D. F. G. INC)
155 Boul De La Concorde E, Cote Saint-Luc, QC, H7G 2C6
(450) 667-3277
Emp Here 100
SIC 5411 Grocery stores
Pierre Daneau

D-U-N-S 20-357-0395   (BR)
METRO INC
(*Suby of* METRO INC)
1600 Boul Saint-Martin E Bureau A, Cote Saint-Luc, QC, H7G 4S7
(514) 643-1000
Emp Here 100
SIC 5141 Groceries, general line

D-U-N-S 25-210-7206   (BR)

METRO RICHELIEU INC
DIVISION INFORMATIQUE
(*Suby of* METRO INC)
1600b Boul Saint-Martin E Bureau 300, Cote Saint-Luc, QC, H7G 4S7
(450) 662-3300
Emp Here 300
SIC 7374 Data processing and preparation
Jacques Couture

D-U-N-S 25-965-9415   (SL)
MP2B INC
1600a Boul Saint-Martin E Bureau 110, Cote Saint-Luc, QC, H7G 4R8
(450) 668-5555
Emp Here 60   *Sales* 50,883,600
SIC 6411 Insurance agents, brokers, and service
Pierre-Marc Brunet
Yves Brunet

D-U-N-S 24-054-0393   (SL)
OLIFRUITS LTEE
290 Boul De La Concorde E, Cote Saint-Luc, QC, H7G 2E6
(450) 667-4031
Emp Here 45   *Sales* 12,336,840
SIC 5431 Fruit and vegetable markets
Robert Zaurrini

D-U-N-S 20-369-9694   (SL)
VAN DE WATER-RAYMOND 1960 LTEE
1600a Boul Saint-Martin E Unite 680, Cote Saint-Luc, QC, H7G 4R8
(888) 597-5538
Emp Here 50   *Sales* 23,751,300
SIC 5084 Industrial machinery and equipment
Yves Raymond
Stephane Raymond
Maxine Raymond

Cote Saint-Luc, QC H7H

D-U-N-S 20-194-5102   (SL)
POLY EXCAVATION INC
295 Av Des Terrasses, Cote Saint-Luc, QC, H7H 2A7
(450) 622-4100
Emp Here 55   *Sales* 13,884,310
SIC 1623 Water, sewer, and utility lines
Louis Lefrancois

D-U-N-S 24-960-4638   (SL)
RECREGESTION LE GROUPE INC
CAMP MOTIVACTION
6010 Rue De Prince-Rupert, Cote Saint-Luc, QC, H7H 1C4
(450) 625-0196
Emp Here 160   *Sales* 14,830,400
SIC 7032 Sporting and recreational camps
Denis Caissy

Cote Saint-Luc, QC H7M

D-U-N-S 24-835-5117   (SL)
2965-6311 QUEBEC INC
PHARMACIE JEAN COUTU
2065 Boul Des Laurentides Bureau 84, Cote Saint-Luc, QC, H7M 4M2
(450) 663-0672
Emp Here 50   *Sales* 12,647,700
SIC 5912 Drug stores and proprietary stores
Richard Fournier
Luigi Villaggi

D-U-N-S 24-179-3657   (SL)
9154-4742 QUEBEC INC
PATISSERIE ST-MARTIN (2005)
2000 Boul Rene-Laennec, Cote Saint-Luc, QC, H7M 4J8
(450) 629-5115
Emp Here 50   *Sales* 13,707,600

SIC 5461 Retail bakeries
Rosario (Ross) Muro
Giuseppe (Joey) Musumeci
David Decotiis

D-U-N-S 20-290-5774   (SL)
AMERICAN TRANSPORTATION & LOGISTICS (AT&L) CANADA INC
TRANSPORTS ET LOGISTIQUES DES AMERIQUES CANADA
400 Boul Saint-Martin O Bureau 206, Cote Saint-Luc, QC, H7M 3Y8
(514) 316-6496
Emp Here 12   *Sales* 10,365,173
SIC 4731 Freight transportation arrangement
Francois Nicol
Robert Gagnon

D-U-N-S 24-018-8888   (HQ)
CENTRE DE SANTE ET DE SERVICES SOCIAUX DE LAVAL
(*Suby of* GOUVERNEMENT DE LA PROVINCE DE QUEBEC)
1755 Boul Rene-Laennec, Cote Saint-Luc, QC, H7M 3L9
(450) 668-1010
Emp Here 2,815   *Sales* 2,308,699,584
SIC 8099 Health and allied services, nec
Sylvie Bourassa
Marina Larue
Dany Aubry
Martin Delage
Julie Desjardins
Chantal Friset
Guy Germain
Genevieve Goudreault
Carol Ladouceur
Sonia Mailloux

D-U-N-S 24-213-3135   (BR)
INTERNATIONAL GRAPHICS ULC
(*Suby of* TAYLOR CORPORATION)
2135a Boul Des Laurentides, Cote Saint-Luc, QC, H7M 4M2

Emp Here 90
SIC 2678 Stationery products
Jacques Pasqualelli

D-U-N-S 24-712-5016   (SL)
POTVIN, PIERRE INC
PHARMACIE JEAN-COUTU # 237
1859 Boul Rene-Laennec Bureau 101, Cote Saint-Luc, QC, H7M 5E2
(450) 662-6064
Emp Here 64   *Sales* 12,647,700
SIC 5912 Drug stores and proprietary stores
Pierre Potvin

D-U-N-S 25-675-2973   (HQ)
PRODUITS MENAGERS FREUDENBERG INC
FHP
(*Suby of* FREUDENBERG & CO. KG)
666 Boul Saint-Martin O Bureau 220, Cote Saint-Luc, QC, H7M 5G4
(450) 975-4535
Sales 104,870,302
SIC 5199 Nondurable goods, nec

D-U-N-S 24-896-8927   (SL)
SUPERMARCHE N.G. INC
PROVIGO
1855 Boul Rene-Laennec, Cote Saint-Luc, QC, H7M 5E2
(450) 629-1850
Emp Here 90   *Sales* 26,412,930
SIC 5411 Grocery stores
Normand Girard

D-U-N-S 24-393-2501   (HQ)
SYSTEMES D'AFFAIRES POUR PUBLICATION CANADA INC
2012 Boul Rene-Laennec Bureau 275, Cote Saint-Luc, QC, H7M 4J8
(450) 902-6000
Emp Here 3   *Sales* 16,401,000

SIC 6712 Bank holding companies
Scott Roessler
Justin Cho
Rachel Arnold

Cote Saint-Luc, QC H7N

D-U-N-S 24-944-1247   (HQ)
2772981 CANADA INC
1 Place Laval Bureau 400, Cote Saint-Luc, QC, H7N 1A1
(514) 335-3246
Emp Here 2   *Sales* 53,029,900
SIC 6712 Bank holding companies
Gilles Senecal
Lucie Senecal

D-U-N-S 20-271-3012   (SL)
AGENCE DE PLACEMENT TRESOR INC
AGENCE DE PLACEMENT TRESOR
2a Rue Grenon O, Cote Saint-Luc, QC, H7N 2G6
(450) 933-7090
Emp Here 50   *Sales* 11,848,500
SIC 7361 Employment agencies
Guillermo Montiel Villalvazo

D-U-N-S 20-032-7455   (SL)
ALIMENTATION ST-DENIS INC
IGA EXTRA
307 Boul Cartier O, Cote Saint-Luc, QC, H7N 2J1
(450) 669-7501
Emp Here 49   *Sales* 13,433,448
SIC 5411 Grocery stores
Mario St-Denis

D-U-N-S 24-404-2466   (BR)
CONSULTANTS AECOM INC
AECOM TECSULT
(*Suby of* AECOM)
1 Place Laval Bureau 200, Cote Saint-Luc, QC, H7N 1A1
(450) 967-1260
Emp Here 75
SIC 8711 Engineering services
Luc Seguin

D-U-N-S 20-002-2312   (BR)
GOUVERNEMENT DE LA PROVINCE DE QUEBEC
CENTRE JEUNESSE DE LAVAL
(*Suby of* GOUVERNEMENT DE LA PROVINCE DE QUEBEC)
308 Boul Cartier O, Cote Saint-Luc, QC, H7N 2J2
(450) 975-4150
Emp Here 200
SIC 8322 Individual and family services
Daniel Euludte

D-U-N-S 24-069-5374   (HQ)
GROUPECHO CANADA INC
RAPPORTS PRE-EMPLOI GROUPECHO
1 Place Laval Bureau 400, Cote Saint-Luc, QC, H7N 1A1
(514) 335-3246
Emp Here 147   *Sales* 38,871,974
SIC 7323 Credit reporting services
Louis Senecal
Gilles Senecal

Cote Saint-Luc, QC H7S

D-U-N-S 24-548-2039   (SL)
135770 CANADA LTEE
EBENISTERIE ST-PATRICK
2037 Av Francis-Hughes, Cote Saint-Luc, QC, H7S 2G2
(450) 669-3002
Emp Here 85   *Sales* 13,117,370
SIC 2521 Wood office furniture

Ronald Amyotte
Gilles Thompson

D-U-N-S 25-448-2219   (HQ)
3717291 CANADA INC
BO-BEBE
2205 Boul Industriel, Cote Saint-Luc, QC, H7S 1P8
(450) 669-2323
Emp Here 25   *Sales* 20,916,270
SIC 5712 Furniture stores
Youssef Nassif
Charbel Nassif

D-U-N-S 20-331-8357   (HQ)
9213-0699 QUEBEC INC
BOUTIK BUZZY
2555 Boul Le Corbusier Bureau 090, Cote Saint-Luc, QC, H7S 1Z4
(450) 686-6767
Emp Here 12   *Sales* 10,464,762
SIC 5137 Women's and children's clothing
Bachir El Debs

D-U-N-S 20-292-1730   (HQ)
AGT CLIC FOODS INC
AGT FOODS
(*Suby of* AGT FOOD AND INGREDIENTS INC)
2185 Av Francis-Hughes, Cote Saint-Luc, QC, H7S 1N5
(450) 669-2663
Emp Here 5   *Sales* 26,027,100
SIC 5099 Durable goods, nec
Murad Al-Katib
Gaetan Bourassa

D-U-N-S 20-224-4554   (HQ)
ALIMENTS LESTERS LIMITEE, LES
2105 Boul Industriel, Cote Saint-Luc, QC, H7S 1P7
(450) 629-1100
Sales 69,138,000
SIC 2011 Meat packing plants
Henry Mizrahi
Bonnie Lester

D-U-N-S 24-825-8829   (SL)
ASSURANCES GROUPE VEZINA
999 Boul Saint-Martin O, Cote Saint-Luc, QC, H7S 1M5
(450) 663-6880
Emp Here 40   *Sales* 33,922,400
SIC 6411 Insurance agents, brokers, and service
Francis Vezina

D-U-N-S 20-420-3673   (SL)
BEDCO, DIVISION DE GERODON INC
(*Suby of* GERODON (CANADA) INC)
2305 Av Francis-Hughes, Cote Saint-Luc, QC, H7S 1N5
(514) 384-2820
Emp Here 115   *Sales* 27,971,565
SIC 3499 Fabricated Metal products, nec
Ronald Bedard
Alexandre Bedard
Louis Potvin
Gilles Genest
Benoit Duplessis
Marie-Claude Gevry

D-U-N-S 24-321-1190   (SL)
BEDCOLAB LTEE
(*Suby of* GERODON (CANADA) INC)
2305 Av Francis-Hughes, Cote Saint-Luc, QC, H7S 1N5
(514) 384-2820
Emp Here 100   *Sales* 53,535,200
SIC 5049 Professional equipment, nec
Ronald Bedard
Alexandre Bedard
Louis Potvin
Gilles Genest
Benoit Duplesses

D-U-N-S 25-145-3775   (BR)
BOEHRINGER INGELHEIM (CANADA) LTD

▲ Public Company   ■ Public Company Family Member   **HQ** Headquarters   **BR** Branch   **SL** Single Location

(Suby of C.H. BOEHRINGER SOHN AG & CO. KG)
2100 Rue Cunard, Cote Saint-Luc, QC, H7S 2G5

Emp Here 200
SIC 8731 Commercial physical research
Michael Cordingley

D-U-N-S 24-439-1798   (SL)
CAISSE POPULAIRE LES GRANDS BOULEVARD
1535 Boul Saint-Martin O, Cote Saint-Luc, QC, H7S 1N1
(450) 668-4000
Emp Here 26   Sales 22,049,560
SIC 6411 Insurance agents, brokers, and service
Roger Chartrand

D-U-N-S 24-315-8859   (BR)
CANADIAN TEST CASE 168 INC.
1450 Rue Cunard, Cote Saint-Luc, QC, H7S 2B7

Emp Here 4,800
SIC 3714 Motor vehicle parts and accessories

D-U-N-S 25-355-2244   (HQ)
CARISTRAP INTERNATIONAL INC
(Suby of 3165710 CANADA INC)
1760 Boul Fortin, Cote Saint-Luc, QC, H7S 1N8
(450) 667-4700
Sales 27,025,600
SIC 3199 Leather goods, nec
Audrey Karass

D-U-N-S 20-332-4561   (SL)
COENTREPRISE TRANSELEC-ARNO
2075 Boul Fortin, Cote Saint-Luc, QC, H7S 1P4
(514) 382-1550
Emp Here 100   Sales 62,661,400
SIC 4911 Electric services
Michel Matte
Louis St-Arnaud

D-U-N-S 25-904-7553   (HQ)
COMMISSION SCOLAIRE DE LAVAL
ECOLE PRIMAIRE PERE-VIMONT
955 Boul Saint-Martin O Bureau 144, Cote Saint-Luc, QC, H7S 1M5
(450) 662-7000
Emp Here 40   Sales 892,071,000
SIC 8211 Elementary and secondary schools
Louise Lortie
Robert-Andre Alexandre
Celein Blanchette
Francoise Charbonneau
Celine Clemont
Denis Comeau
Raynald Hawkins
Anthony Hemond
Lyne Lapensee
Carole Morin

D-U-N-S 20-184-6370   (SL)
DELI-PORC INC
CANAPAN MEATS
1805 Boul Industriel, Cote Saint-Luc, QC, H7S 1P5
(450) 629-0294
Emp Here 90   Sales 31,112,100
SIC 2011 Meat packing plants
Alain Tremblay
Antonio Filice

D-U-N-S 24-357-2513   (HQ)
FD ALPHA CANADA ACQUISITION INC
FORT DEARBORN
(Suby of FORT DEARBORN HOLDING COMPANY, INC.)
2277 Desste Des Laurentides (A-15) E, Cote Saint-Luc, QC, H7S 1Z6
(450) 680-5000
Emp Here 100   Sales 110,291,100
SIC 2679 Converted paper products, nec

Jeffrey L. Brezek
Chris Lumbard
Kevin Kwilinksi

D-U-N-S 24-204-5115   (HQ)
FUTURE HYDRAULIK INC
(Suby of AEA INVESTORS LP)
1597 Rue Cunard, Cote Saint-Luc, QC, H7S 2B4
(450) 687-0187
Sales 14,988,260
SIC 5084 Industrial machinery and equipment
Sam Petillo
Don Fritzinger
Craig Osborne
Otis Dufrene
Richard Payette

D-U-N-S 20-860-9680   (BR)
GREAT PACIFIC ENTERPRISES INC
GENPAK LP
(Suby of PATTISON, JIM GROUP INC)
1890 Boul Fortin, Cote Saint-Luc, QC, H7S 1N8
(450) 662-1030
Emp Here 100
SIC 3081 Unsupported plastics film and sheet

D-U-N-S 25-325-1433   (BR)
GROUPE HOTELIER GRAND CHATEAU INC
HILTON MONTREAL / LAVAL
(Suby of GROUPE HOTELIER GRAND CHATEAU INC)
2225 Des Laurentides (A-15) E, Cote Saint-Luc, QC, H7S 1Z6
(450) 682-2225
Emp Here 105
SIC 7011 Hotels and motels
Sebastien Meunier

D-U-N-S 25-780-1209   (HQ)
GROUPE VEZINA & ASSOCIES LTEE, LE
999 Boul Saint-Martin O, Cote Saint-Luc, QC, H7S 1M5
(450) 663-6880
Emp Here 94   Sales 177,383,232
SIC 6411 Insurance agents, brokers, and service
Jean Vezina
Luc Vezina

D-U-N-S 20-223-6139   (HQ)
LAROSE & FILS LTEE
KARCHER DIRECTION REGIONALE DU QUEBEC
2255 Boul Industriel, Cote Saint-Luc, QC, H7S 1P8
(514) 382-7000
Sales 11,066,400
SIC 2842 Polishes and sanitation goods
Jean Larose
Pierre Larose

D-U-N-S 20-224-4000   (SL)
LESAGE INC
(Suby of 2622-5235 QUEBEC INC)
817 Rue Salaberry, Cote Saint-Luc, QC, H7S 1H5
(514) 337-3585
Emp Here 100   Sales 23,306,500
SIC 1711 Plumbing, heating, air-conditioning
Michel Lesage
Robert Lesage
Gaetan Lesage

D-U-N-S 24-296-5879   (SL)
PLACAGE JAY GE LTEE
1800 Boul Fortin, Cote Saint-Luc, QC, H7S 1N8
(450) 663-7070
Emp Here 100   Sales 19,208,500
SIC 3471 Plating and polishing
Joseph Lastoria
Gino Lastoria
Gino Lastoria

D-U-N-S 24-248-9131   (SL)

PORTES STANDARD INC
2300 Av Francis-Hughes, Cote Saint-Luc, QC, H7S 2C1
(514) 634-8911
Emp Here 100   Sales 19,208,500
SIC 3442 Metal doors, sash, and trim
Barry Yane

D-U-N-S 20-534-2269   (HQ)
RE/MAX QUEBEC INC
(Suby of 121547 CANADA INC)
1500 Rue Cunard, Cote Saint-Luc, QC, H7S 2B7
(450) 668-7743
Emp Here 45   Sales 110,864,520
SIC 6411 Insurance agents, brokers, and service
Pierre Titley
Ginette Lambert
Sylvain Dansereau

D-U-N-S 24-050-8866   (SL)
REVETEMENTS SCELL-TECH INC, LES
SCELLTECH
1478 Rue Cunard, Cote Saint-Luc, QC, H7S 2B7
(514) 990-7886
Emp Here 65   Sales 11,001,055
SIC 1721 Painting and paper hanging
Stephane Paquette
Gyna Bonenfant

D-U-N-S 20-503-3608   (BR)
SAMUEL, SON & CO., LIMITED
(Suby of SAMUEL, SON & CO., LIMITED)
2225 Av Francis-Hughes, Cote Saint-Luc, QC, H7S 1N5
(514) 384-5220
Emp Here 200
SIC 5051 Metals service centers and offices
Dominique Vannelli

D-U-N-S 24-115-1815   (BR)
SOROC TECHNOLOGY INC
(Suby of SOROC TECHNOLOGY INC)
1800 Boul Le Corbusier Bureau 132, Cote Saint-Luc, QC, H7S 2K1
(450) 682-5029
Emp Here 200
SIC 7378 Computer maintenance and repair
Raymond Massa

D-U-N-S 20-056-9338   (HQ)
TRANSELEC/COMMON INC
(Suby of PLACEMENTS CLAUDE GAUTHIER INC, LES)
2075 Boul Fortin, Cote Saint-Luc, QC, H7S 1P4
(514) 382-1550
Emp Here 200   Sales 393,738,000
SIC 1623 Water, sewer, and utility lines
Claude Gauthier
Stephane Gauthier
Richard Lafrance

D-U-N-S 24-741-7512   (SL)
VITRECO INC
(Suby of FLYNN EQUIPMENT RENTALS LTD)
1860 Rue Cunard, Cote Saint-Luc, QC, H7S 2B2
(450) 681-0483
Emp Here 100   Sales 24,618,600
SIC 1793 Glass and glazing work
John Mcmanus
Marc Bilodeau
Sharon Sovak

D-U-N-S 25-297-6352   (BR)
WAL-MART CANADA CORP
WALMART
(Suby of WALMART INC.)
1660 Boul Le Corbusier, Cote Saint-Luc, QC, H7S 1Z2
(450) 681-1126
Emp Here 313
SIC 5311 Department stores
Karine Lussier

Cote Saint-Luc, QC H7T

D-U-N-S 25-977-2408   (SL)
2552-4018 QUEBEC INC
CHOMEDEY HYUNDAI
2480 Boul Cure-Labelle, Cote Saint-Luc, QC, H7T 1R1
(450) 682-6000
Emp Here 40   Sales 19,923,120
SIC 5511 New and used car dealers
Andre Leclair

D-U-N-S 24-544-7367   (SL)
3761045 CANADA INC
BOULANGERIE PREMIERE MOISSON
2888 Av Du Cosmodome Bureau 2, Cote Saint-Luc, QC, H7T 2X1
(450) 682-1800
Emp Here 49   Sales 13,433,448
SIC 5461 Retail bakeries
Christophe Souedet

D-U-N-S 20-702-5599   (SL)
4093640 CANADA INC
VOLVO LAVAL
2350 Boul Chomedey, Cote Saint-Luc, QC, H7T 2W3
(450) 682-3336
Emp Here 55   Sales 34,610,400
SIC 5511 New and used car dealers
Anthony Taddeo
James Taddeo

D-U-N-S 24-339-0247   (SL)
440 CHEVROLET BUICK GMC LTEE
(Suby of GROUPE AUTOMOBILES LAURUS LTEE)
3670 Sud Laval (A-440) O, Cote Saint-Luc, QC, H7T 2H6
(450) 682-3670
Emp Here 50   Sales 24,903,900
SIC 5511 New and used car dealers
Patrick Tremblay
Andre Hamel

D-U-N-S 20-780-7780   (SL)
6304966 CANADA INC
JAGUAR LAND ROVER LAVAL
3475 Boul Le Carrefour, Cote Saint-Luc, QC, H7T 3A3
(450) 688-1880
Emp Here 30   Sales 14,942,340
SIC 5511 New and used car dealers
Ercole De Coubellis
Renato De Cubellis

D-U-N-S 20-210-0772   (SL)
ARBOUR AUTOMOBILES LTEE
ARBOUR VOLKSWAGEN
2475 Boul Chomedey, Cote Saint-Luc, QC, H7T 2R2
(450) 681-8110
Emp Here 65   Sales 40,903,200
SIC 5521 Used car dealers
Andre Arbour

D-U-N-S 24-178-0373   (SL)
AUTO AMBASSADEUR INC
LEXUS LAVAL
2000 Boul Chomedey, Cote Saint-Luc, QC, H7T 2W3
(450) 686-2710
Emp Here 25   Sales 12,451,950
SIC 5511 New and used car dealers
Christian Dagenais
Louis-Carl Dagenais
Pierre Leroux

D-U-N-S 20-790-3527   (SL)
AUTO BOULEVARD SAINT-MARTIN INC
BMW LAVAL
2450 Boul Chomedey, Cote Saint-Luc, QC, H7T 2X3
(450) 682-1212
Emp Here 150   Sales 94,392,000
SIC 5511 New and used car dealers

▲ Public Company   ■ Public Company Family Member   **HQ** Headquarters   **BR** Branch   **SL** Single Location

Carmine D'argenio
Gerardo D'argenio
Eleonora D'argenio

D-U-N-S 24-337-9398   (BR)
BOSTON PIZZA INTERNATIONAL INC
(*Suby of* BOSTON PIZZA INTERNATIONAL INC)
450 Prom Du Centropolis, Cote Saint-Luc, QC, H7T 3C2
(450) 688-2229
Emp Here 80
SIC 5812 Eating places
Catherine Harton

D-U-N-S 25-359-0558   (SL)
CENTRIA COMMERCE INC
(*Suby of* FIERA CAPITAL CORPORATION)
3131 Boul Saint-Martin O Bureau 500, Cote Saint-Luc, QC, H7T 2Z5
(514) 874-0122
Emp Here 65   *Sales* 12,122,890
SIC 8742 Management consulting services
Christian Trudeau
Sylvain Brosseau
John Valentini
Raymond Laurin
Brian A. Davis
David Robinson Shaw

D-U-N-S 24-698-2383   (SL)
CHOMEDEY NISSAN INC
2465 Boul Cure-Labelle, Cote Saint-Luc, QC, H7T 1R3
(450) 682-4400
Emp Here 26   *Sales* 12,950,028
SIC 5511 New and used car dealers
Alex Riccio
Gaetano Gioia

D-U-N-S 24-576-3540   (BR)
CINEPLEX ODEON CORPORATION
CINEMA CINEPLEX LAVAL
(*Suby of* CINEPLEX INC)
2800 Av Du Cosmodome, Cote Saint-Luc, QC, H7T 2X1
(450) 978-0212
Emp Here 100
SIC 7832 Motion picture theaters, except drive-in
Genevieve Saulnier

D-U-N-S 24-336-8607   (HQ)
COLACEM CANADA INC
BERTRAND CONSTRUCTION L'ORIGNAL, UNE DIVISION DE COLACEM CANADA
(*Suby of* FINANCO SRL)
2540 Boul Daniel-Johnson Bureau 808 8e Etage, Cote Saint-Luc, QC, H7T 2S3
(450) 686-1221
Emp Here 50   *Sales* 33,782,000
SIC 1422 Crushed and broken limestone
Marco Focardi
Victorio Verdese Pier Francesco
Carlo Fanelli
Francois Gervais

D-U-N-S 25-243-3982   (SL)
COMPLEXE AUTO 440 DE LAVAL INC
LOCATION D'AUTO 440, DIV DE
3670 Sud Laval (A-440) O, Cote Saint-Luc, QC, H7T 2H6
(450) 682-3670
Emp Here 65   *Sales* 40,903,200
SIC 5511 New and used car dealers
Jean-Paul Lalonde

D-U-N-S 20-370-9899   (SL)
CONCEPTION HABITAT 2015 INC
CH 2015
2400 Boul Daniel-Johnson, Cote Saint-Luc, QC, H7T 3A4
(450) 902-2007
Emp Here 50   *Sales* 14,429,150
SIC 1522 Residential construction, nec
Yves Mongeau
Robert Laplante

Real Bouclin

D-U-N-S 20-511-7380   (BR)
CORDEE PLEIN AIR INC, LA
(*Suby of* CORDEE PLEIN AIR INC, LA)
2777 Boul Saint-Martin O, Cote Saint-Luc, QC, H7T 2Y7
(514) 524-1326
Emp Here 75
SIC 5941 Sporting goods and bicycle shops
Patrice Aylwin

D-U-N-S 24-418-4409   (SL)
CORPORATION ALLIANCE DYNAMIQUE
RONA L'ENTREPOT LAVAL
3065 Boul Le Carrefour, Cote Saint-Luc, QC, H7T 1C7
(450) 688-0688
Emp Here 49   *Sales* 12,399,891
SIC 5251 Hardware stores
Gilles Lamoureux

D-U-N-S 25-099-6402   (SL)
COSOLTEC INC
3080 Boul Le Carrefour, Cote Saint-Luc, QC, H7T 2R5
(450) 682-0000
Emp Here 30   *Sales* 14,121,930
SIC 1542 Nonresidential construction, nec
Michel Grennan

D-U-N-S 24-250-0622   (SL)
COTE, REGIS ET ASSOCIES ARCHITECTES
2990 Av Pierre-Peladeau Bureau 200, Cote Saint-Luc, QC, H7T 0B1

Emp Here 100   *Sales* 17,595,800
SIC 8712 Architectural services
Regis Cote

D-U-N-S 20-108-8536   (BR)
DELOITTE RESTRUCTURING INC
GESTION DELOITTE
(*Suby of* DELOITTE LLP)
2540 Boul Daniel-Johnson Bureau 210, Cote Saint-Luc, QC, H7T 2S3
(450) 978-3500
Emp Here 100
SIC 8721 Accounting, auditing, and bookkeeping
Audette Filion

D-U-N-S 20-533-7350   (SL)
ENSEIGNES MONTREAL NEON INC
CIE D'ENSEIGNES MONTREAL NEON
4130 Sud Laval (A-440) O, Cote Saint-Luc, QC, H7T 0H3
(450) 668-4888
Emp Here 50   *Sales* 10,941,200
SIC 3993 Signs and advertising specialties
Carlo Paolucci

D-U-N-S 24-859-8497   (SL)
FLEX EXPORT
FLEX GROUP
2525 Boul Daniel-Johnson Bureau 290, Cote Saint-Luc, QC, H7T 1S9
(450) 687-3030
Emp Here 35   *Sales* 15,522,150
SIC 7389 Business services, nec
Mostafa Chafi
Mohamed Muslam
Amena Challai

D-U-N-S 20-703-3700   (SL)
GESTION CENTRIA COMMERCE INC
3131 Boul Saint-Martin O, Cote Saint-Luc, QC, H7T 2Z5
(514) 874-0122
Emp Here 65   *Sales* 17,000,945
SIC 6712 Bank holding companies
Levis Doucet
Jean-Pierre Lambert

D-U-N-S 24-312-8738   (HQ)
GESTION RESEAU SELECTION II INC
2400 Boul Daniel-Johnson, Cote Saint-Luc,

QC, H7T 3A4
(450) 902-2000
Emp Here 15   *Sales* 10,480,995
SIC 6513 Apartment building operators
Real Bouclin
Robert Laplante

D-U-N-S 24-359-1836   (HQ)
GPL ASSURANCE INC
GPL PROULX ASSURANCE
(*Suby of* ARTHUR J. GALLAGHER & CO.)
3131 Boul Saint-Martin O Bureau 600, Cote Saint-Luc, QC, H7T 2Z5
(450) 978-5599
Emp Here 50   *Sales* 184,774,200
SIC 6411 Insurance agents, brokers, and service
Louis Thomas Labbe
Charles Proulx
Jay Glowa
Stephen J. Bryant
Phillip H. Gaunce
Greg A. Metcalfe

D-U-N-S 20-308-8703   (HQ)
GROUPE ADONIS INC
ADONIS
(*Suby of* METRO INC)
2425 Boul Cure-Labelle, Cote Saint-Luc, QC, H7T 1R3
(450) 978-2333
Emp Here 80   *Sales* 144,348,000
SIC 5411 Grocery stores
Christian Bourbonniere
Francois Thibault
Michel Cheaib
Simon Rivet

D-U-N-S 24-335-7709   (HQ)
GROUPE AUTOMOBILES LAURUS LTEE
CARREFOUR 440 CHEVROLET
3670 Sud Laval (A-440) O, Cote Saint-Luc, QC, H7T 2H6
(450) 682-3670
Sales 32,528,650
SIC 6712 Bank holding companies
Patrick Tremblay

D-U-N-S 25-359-3735   (BR)
GROUPE HOTELIER GRAND CHATEAU INC
HOTEL SHERATON LAVAL
(*Suby of* GROUPE HOTELIER GRAND CHATEAU INC)
2440 Des Laurentides (A-15) O, Cote Saint-Luc, QC, H7T 1X5
(450) 687-2440
Emp Here 200
SIC 7011 Hotels and motels
Benito Nigliorati

D-U-N-S 25-998-5471   (HQ)
GROUPE LAUZON INC
2400 Boul Chomedey Carte Des Environs, Cote Saint-Luc, QC, H7T 2W3
(450) 434-1120
Emp Here 1   *Sales* 41,002,500
SIC 6712 Bank holding companies
Francine Lauzon
Andree Lauzon

D-U-N-S 25-688-2622   (HQ)
GROUPE MULTI LUMINAIRE INC, LE
MULTI LUMINAIRE
2591 Boul Daniel-Johnson, Cote Saint-Luc, QC, H7T 1S8
(450) 681-3939
Emp Here 30   *Sales* 12,782,165
SIC 5719 Miscellaneous homefurnishings
Andre Patry
Catherine Patry
Charles Patry
Marie Claude Hinse

D-U-N-S 25-301-2983   (BR)
HUDSON'S BAY COMPANY
(*Suby of* HUDSON'S BAY COMPANY)

3045 Boul Le Carrefour, Cote Saint-Luc, QC, H7T 1C7
(450) 687-1540
Emp Here 200
SIC 5311 Department stores

D-U-N-S 24-792-1922   (SL)
INDULBEC INC
LA BONBONNICRE SWEET FACTORY
3035 Boul Le Carrefour, Cote Saint-Luc, QC, H7T 1C8
(450) 687-5083
Emp Here 26   *Sales* 21,725,002
SIC 5149 Groceries and related products, nec
Michel Jamet

D-U-N-S 25-778-8042   (SL)
INFINITI LAVAL INC
1950 Boul Chomedey, Cote Saint-Luc, QC, H7T 2W3
(514) 382-8550
Emp Here 50   *Sales* 24,903,900
SIC 5511 New and used car dealers
Louis-Carl Dagenais

D-U-N-S 20-237-1456   (BR)
INTEGRATED DISTRIBUTION SYSTEMS LIMITED PARTNERSHIP
WAJAX EQUIPMENT
(*Suby of* WAJAX CORPORATION)
2000 Rue John-Molson, Cote Saint-Luc, QC, H7T 0H4
(450) 682-3737
Emp Here 75
SIC 5084 Industrial machinery and equipment
Isabelle Morneau

D-U-N-S 25-873-9676   (BR)
INTEGRATED DISTRIBUTION SYSTEMS LIMITED PARTNERSHIP
EQUIPEMENT WAJAX
(*Suby of* WAJAX CORPORATION)
2000 Rue John-Molson, Cote Saint-Luc, QC, H7T 0H4
(450) 682-3737
Emp Here 100
SIC 5084 Industrial machinery and equipment
Sylvain Belisle

D-U-N-S 24-352-2971   (SL)
INVESSA ASSURANCES ET SERVICES FINANCIERS INC
225 Prom Du Centropolis Bureau 220, Cote Saint-Luc, QC, H7T 0B3
(450) 781-6560
Emp Here 20   *Sales* 11,598,480
SIC 6411 Insurance agents, brokers, and service
Robert Beauchamp
Jean-Francois Trudel

D-U-N-S 24-739-5023   (HQ)
IRIS, GROUPE VISUEL (1990) INC, LE
DEFI IRIS
(*Suby of* CANADIAN DEPOSITORY FOR SECURITIES LIMITED, THE)
3030 Boul Le Carrefour Bureau 1200, Cote Saint-Luc, QC, H7T 2P5
(450) 688-9060
Emp Here 35   *Sales* 228,059,952
SIC 5048 Ophthalmic goods
Eric Babin
Jason Schonfeld
Antoine Amiel
Sylvain Boucher

D-U-N-S 25-364-9099   (SL)
KENDRAKYLE INVESTMENTS INC
NORRIZON
2540 Boul Daniel-Johnson Bureau 207, Cote Saint-Luc, QC, H7T 2S3
(450) 682-6227
Emp Here 50   *Sales* 11,895,050
SIC 8742 Management consulting services
Kevin Schiissler

D-U-N-S 25-687-9222   (SL)
LAVAL AUTOS HAMEL INC

ACURA LAVAL
2500 Boul Chomedey, Cote Saint-Luc, QC, H7T 2W1
(450) 682-4050
Emp Here 30   *Sales* 14,942,340
SIC 5511 New and used car dealers
Jean-Francois Hamel
Jean-Guy Pineault

D-U-N-S 20-765-7834   (BR)
LEON'S FURNITURE LIMITED
LEON AMEUBLEMENT
(*Suby of* LEON'S FURNITURE LIMITED)
2000 Boul Daniel-Johnson, Cote Saint-Luc, QC, H7T 1A3
(450) 688-3851
Emp Here 80
SIC 5712 Furniture stores
Martin Dorion

D-U-N-S 24-208-6085   (BR)
LOBLAWS INC
MAXI & CIE
(*Suby of* LOBLAW COMPANIES LIMITED)
3500 Boul Saint-Martin O, Cote Saint-Luc, QC, H7T 2W4
(450) 688-2969
Emp Here 145
SIC 5421 Meat and fish markets
Carl Dicaire

D-U-N-S 20-305-3624   (HQ)
MASON GRAPHITE INC
3030 Boul Le Carrefour Bureau 600, Cote Saint-Luc, QC, H7T 2P5
(514) 289-3580
Emp Here 20   *Sales* 30,983,175
SIC 1499 Miscellaneous nonMetallic minerals, except fuels
Benoit Gascon
Luc Veilleux
Jean L'heureux
Mario Felicetti
Robert Allard
Andre Gagnon
Simon Marcotte
Genevieve Gauthier
Genevieve Pichet
Jacqueline Leroux

D-U-N-S 20-715-9786   (SL)
MOSAIC SALES SOLUTIONS
2500 Boul Daniel-Johnson Bureau 203, Cote Saint-Luc, QC, H7T 2P6
(450) 686-1013
Emp Here 49   *Sales* 11,480,112
SIC 8743 Public relations services
Jeff Roggers

D-U-N-S 24-074-2064   (HQ)
MS ELITE HOLDINGS INC.
1811 Boul Cure-Labelle, Cote Saint-Luc, QC, H7T 1L1
(450) 681-0060
Sales 10,462,120
SIC 6712 Bank holding companies

D-U-N-S 20-051-0134   (HQ)
NEPTUNE TECHNOLOGIES & BIORES-SOURCES INC
NEPTUNE BIOTECHNOLOGIES
545 Prom Du Centropolis Suite 100, Cote Saint-Luc, QC, H7T 0A3
(450) 687-2262
Emp Here 20   *Sales* 35,637,813
SIC 8731 Commercial physical research
James Hamilton
Michel Timperio
Marc Vaugeois
Jean-Daniel Belanger
John Moretz
Ronald Denis
Katherine Crewe
Francois R. Roy
Leendert Hendrik Staal
Richard Schottenfeld

D-U-N-S 24-650-6455   (SL)
OFFICE DU TOURISME DE LAVAL INC
TOURISME LAVAL
480 Prom Du Centropolis, Cote Saint-Luc, QC, H7T 3C2
(450) 682-5522
Emp Here 30   *Sales* 13,476,570
SIC 7389 Business services, nec
Patrice Bourbonnais
Patricia Dupuy
Raynald Adams
Charlene Baron
Marc Deblois
Genevieve Roy
Jean Lapointe
Nicole Dalpe
Pierre Desroches
Yves Legault

D-U-N-S 20-989-9520   (BR)
PACKALL PACKAGING INC
(*Suby of* PACKALL PACKAGING INC)
3470 Boul De Chenonceau, Cote Saint-Luc, QC, H7T 3B6

Emp Here 150
SIC 3089 Plastics products, nec

D-U-N-S 24-109-5439   (SL)
PORTES JPR INC, LES
4800 Sud Laval (A-440) O Unite 1, Cote Saint-Luc, QC, H7T 2Z8
(450) 661-5110
Emp Here 70   *Sales* 13,745,270
SIC 1751 Carpentry work
Pierre Gosselin

D-U-N-S 20-194-5219   (SL)
QUERIN, ARMAND AUTOMOBILES LTEE
MAZDA DE LAVAL
2385 Boul Chomedey, Cote Saint-Luc, QC, H7T 2W5
(450) 688-4787
Emp Here 57   *Sales* 35,868,960
SIC 5511 New and used car dealers
Dieter Hammer
Richard Labelle

D-U-N-S 24-205-7896   (SL)
RDP MARATHON INC
2583 Boul Chomedey, Cote Saint-Luc, QC, H7T 2R2
(450) 687-7262
Emp Here 30   *Sales* 14,250,780
SIC 5085 Industrial supplies
Eric J Short
Mahmoud Samne
Marcel Motard
Fabio Girolami

D-U-N-S 20-736-4753   (SL)
REHABILITATION DU O INC
5270 Boul Cleroux, Cote Saint-Luc, QC, H7T 2E8
(450) 682-2733
Emp Here 50   *Sales* 12,044,200
SIC 1623 Water, sewer, and utility lines
Danick Dufresne

D-U-N-S 24-339-1476   (SL)
RESIDENCES SELECTION S.E.C.- I, LES
2400 Boul Daniel-Johnson, Cote Saint-Luc, QC, H7T 3A4
(450) 902-2000
Emp Here 100   *Sales* 41,888,900
SIC 6531 Real estate agents and managers
Martin Forget
Jocelyn Trottier

D-U-N-S 20-240-3259   (HQ)
ROTISSERIES ST-HUBERT LTEE, LES
ST-HUBERT EXPRESS
(*Suby of* RECIPE UNLIMITED CORPORA-TION)
2500 Boul Daniel-Johnson Bureau 700, Cote Saint-Luc, QC, H7T 2P6
(450) 435-0674
Emp Here 135   *Sales* 2,608,161,750

SIC 6794 Patent owners and lessors
Kenneth J. Grondin
Richard Scofield
Dave Lantz

D-U-N-S 20-182-8881   (SL)
SERVICES COMERCO INC
3300 Boul Saint-Martin O Bureau 300, Cote Saint-Luc, QC, H7T 1A1
(450) 682-9900
Emp Here 160   *Sales* 197,666,880
SIC 6351 Surety insurance
Roger Bilodeau
Patricia Ocana
Jonathan Bilodeau
Daniel Quirion

D-U-N-S 25-232-8240   (BR)
SIR WILFRID LAURIER SCHOOL BOARD
LAURIER SENIOR HIGH SCHOOL
2323 Boul Daniel-Johnson, Cote Saint-Luc, QC, H7T 1H8
(450) 686-6300
Emp Here 75
SIC 8211 Elementary and secondary schools
Willy Speeckaert

D-U-N-S 25-148-0471   (HQ)
SOLUTIONS PROCESSIA INC
WWW.PROCESSIA.COM
(*Suby of* CONSULT-EXPERT 3I INC)
3131 Boul Saint-Martin O Bureau 220, Cote Saint-Luc, QC, H7T 2Z5
(450) 786-0400
Sales 13,347,760
SIC 7379 Computer related services, nec
Vincent Fraser
Marc Allard
Thomas William Emmrich

D-U-N-S 24-845-7249   (SL)
SOPLEX SOLUTIONS D'ASSURANCE INC
225 Prom Du Centropolis Bureau 215, Cote Saint-Luc, QC, H7T 0B3
(450) 781-6566
Emp Here 25   *Sales* 14,498,100
SIC 6411 Insurance agents, brokers, and ser-vice
Robert Beachamps

D-U-N-S 24-543-0384   (SL)
SPORTS 12345 INC
SPORTS EXPERTS
3035 Boul Le Carrefour Bureau T02, Cote Saint-Luc, QC, H7T 1C8
(450) 682-0032
Emp Here 60   *Sales* 14,659,680
SIC 5941 Sporting goods and bicycle shops
Pierre Dore
Therese Beaulieu
Normand Beaulieu
Jonathan Beaulieu
Serge Beaulieu

D-U-N-S 25-171-5785   (HQ)
TEAMSTERS CANADA
2540 Boul Daniel-Johnson, Cote Saint-Luc, QC, H7T 2S3
(450) 682-5521
Emp Here 21   *Sales* 23,547,000
SIC 8631 Labor organizations
Francois Laporte

D-U-N-S 24-547-9423   (SL)
TORNATECH INC
4100 Desste Sud Laval (A-440) O, Cote Saint-Luc, QC, H7T 0H3
(514) 334-2503
Emp Here 60   *Sales* 11,426,520
SIC 3625 Relays and industrial controls
Bruno Goupil
Marc Goupil

D-U-N-S 24-346-3143   (BR)
WSP CANADA INC
GENIVAR
(*Suby of* AST TRUST COMPANY (CANADA))
2525 Boul Daniel-Johnson Bureau 525, Cote

Saint-Luc, QC, H7T 1S9
(450) 686-0980
Emp Here 200
SIC 8711 Engineering services
Steven Frenza

Cote Saint-Luc, QC H7V

D-U-N-S 24-941-4694   (SL)
ASSURANCES GROUPE CONCORDE INC
3820 Boul Levesque O Bureau 101, Cote Saint-Luc, QC, H7V 1E8
(450) 973-2822
Emp Here 14   *Sales* 14,488,334
SIC 6331 Fire, marine, and casualty insurance
Jack Kusaian

D-U-N-S 25-978-4189   (HQ)
CAISSE DESJARDINS DE CHOMEDEY
CENTRE DE SERVICES SAMSON
3075 Boul Cartier O, Cote Saint-Luc, QC, H7V 1J4
(450) 688-0900
Emp Here 25   *Sales* 10,445,267
SIC 6062 State credit unions
Nathalie Charron
Diane Roy
Ronald Martineau
Robert Prud'homme
Evelyne Henry
Fawziya Maatof
Michel Gariepy

D-U-N-S 24-851-7752   (SL)
INSTITUTE NATIONAL DE LA RECHERCHE SCIENTIFIQUE
CENTRE   INRS-INSTITUT   ARMAND-FRAPPIER
531 Boul Des Prairies Bureau 26, Cote Saint-Luc, QC, H7V 1B7
(450) 687-5010
Emp Here 500   *Sales* 74,695,500
SIC 8221 Colleges and universities
Daniel Coderre
Alain Fournier

D-U-N-S 24-294-3132   (SL)
MANOIR ST-PATRICE INC
3615 Boul Perron, Cote Saint-Luc, QC, H7V 1P4
(450) 681-1621
Emp Here 125   *Sales* 7,405,875
SIC 8361 Residential care
Betty Carey
Ann Carey
Kathleen Carey
John Carey

D-U-N-S 24-853-0037   (SL)
SANOFI SANTE GRAND PUBLIC INC
(*Suby of* SANOFI)
2905 Place Louis-R.-Renaud, Cote Saint-Luc, QC, H7V 0A3
(514) 956-6200
Emp Here 50   *Sales* 55,267,250
SIC 5122 Drugs, proprietaries, and sundries
Niven Al-Khoury
Pat Papillo
Tracey Ramsay

D-U-N-S 25-104-6934   (SL)
SANOFI-AVENTIS CANADA INC
ALLEGRA
(*Suby of* SANOFI)
2905 Place Louis-R.-Renaud, Cote Saint-Luc, QC, H7V 0A3
(514) 331-9220
Emp Here 1,700   *Sales* 701,795,700
SIC 5122 Drugs, proprietaries, and sundries
Robert Quesnel
Pat Papilo
Michael Mullette

D-U-N-S 20-270-8491   (BR)

UNIVERSITE DU QUEBEC
INSTITUT NATIONALDE LA RECHERCHE SCIENTIFIQUE (INR
(*Suby of* UNIVERSITE DU QUEBEC)
531 Rue Des Prairies, Cote Saint-Luc, QC, H7V 1B7
(450) 687-5010
Emp Here 100
SIC 8221 Colleges and universities

Coteau-Du-Lac, QC J0P

D-U-N-S 20-398-5821   (HQ)
10013340 CANADA INC
GF
75 Boul Dupont, Coteau-Du-Lac, QC, J0P 1B0
(450) 455-0961
Emp Here 1   *Sales* 10,094,850
SIC 3086 Plastics foam products
Nicholas Nickoletopoulos
Pierre Archambault
Nicole Stojc
Maurice Tousignant
Derek Schaaf

D-U-N-S 24-858-2736   (SL)
ARCELORMITTAL COTEAU-DU-LAC INC
(*Suby of* ARCELORMITTAL CANADA HOLDINGS INC)
25 Rue De L'Acier, Coteau-Du-Lac, QC, J0P 1B0
(450) 763-0915
Emp Here 66   *Sales* 12,677,610
SIC 3479 Metal coating and allied services
Sylvie Menard
Lisa Marcuzzi
Todd Brien
Robert Ciancone
David Ford

D-U-N-S 20-577-5930   (SL)
ARCELORMITTAL COTEAU-DU-LAC LIMITED PARTNERSHIP
25 Rue De L'Acier, Coteau-Du-Lac, QC, J0P 1B0
(450) 763-0915
Emp Here 69   *Sales* 13,253,865
SIC 3479 Metal coating and allied services
Jack Nadeau

D-U-N-S 24-434-0907   (HQ)
C.A.T. INC
C.A.T. & DESSIN
(*Suby of* 9523383 CANADA INC)
4 Rue Du Transport, Coteau-Du-Lac, QC, J0P 1B0
(450) 763-6363
Emp Here 100   *Sales* 92,190,500
SIC 4213 Trucking, except local
Daniel Goyette
Karine Goyette
Annie Goyette
Hugo Brouillette
Frank Foscolos

D-U-N-S 24-811-0140   (SL)
EMBALLAGES MONTCORR LTEE, LES
40 Rue Industrielle, Coteau-Du-Lac, QC, J0P 1B0
(450) 763-0920
Emp Here 65   *Sales* 12,659,920
SIC 2653 Corrugated and solid fiber boxes
Andrew Beaumond
Yves Menard
Michael R. Lawson
Jason Berns
B.J. Gottlieb
Raymond Jessome

D-U-N-S 24-387-0214   (BR)
FEDEX SUPPLY CHAIN DISTRIBUTION SYSTEM OF CANADA, INC
SYSTEME DE DISTRIBUTION DE LA CHAINE D'APPROVISIONNEMENT FEDEX

DU CANADA
(*Suby of* FEDEX CORPORATION)
50 Boul Dupont, Coteau-Du-Lac, QC, J0P 1B0
(450) 763-6400
Emp Here 350
SIC 4731 Freight transportation arrangement

D-U-N-S 24-865-8510   (HQ)
HOLDING CANADIAN AMERICAN TRANSPORTATION C.A.T. INC
4 Rue Du Transport, Coteau-Du-Lac, QC, J0P 1B0
(450) 763-6363
Emp Here 10   *Sales* 92,190,500
SIC 4213 Trucking, except local
Daniel Goyette
Francois Nadeau

D-U-N-S 20-502-9655   (HQ)
RONSCO INC
75 Rue Industrielle, Coteau-Du-Lac, QC, J0P 1B0
(514) 866-1033
Emp Here 24   *Sales* 21,376,170
SIC 5088 Transportation equipment and supplies
Donald G. Regan
Domenica Francescangeli
Kent Montgomery

Cowansville, QC J2K

D-U-N-S 24-676-3197   (SL)
9122-8171 QUEBEC INC
COWANSVILLE TOYOTA
165 Rue De Salaberry, Cowansville, QC, J2K 5G9
(450) 263-8888
Emp Here 27   *Sales* 16,990,560
SIC 5511 New and used car dealers
Guy St-Louis

D-U-N-S 25-209-8579   (SL)
A.P.M. DIESEL (1992) INC.
A.P.M. DIESEL
135 Rue Miner, Cowansville, QC, J2K 3Y5
(450) 260-1999
Emp Here 55   *Sales* 12,210,055
SIC 3519 Internal combustion engines, nec
Manon Lefrancois
Jos Lefrancois
Gaetanne Lefrancois
Erick V Anistro

D-U-N-S 24-343-0282   (HQ)
ALBANY INTERNATIONAL CANADA CORP
(*Suby of* ALBANY INTERNATIONAL CORP.)
300 Rue De Westmount, Cowansville, QC, J2K 1S9
(450) 263-2880
Sales 92,236,170
SIC 2231 Broadwoven fabric mills, wool
Philip Drumelle
Joseph Gaug
Stephane Vigeant
Charles J. Silva

D-U-N-S 24-835-3872   (SL)
ANSELL CANADA INC
(*Suby of* ANSELL LIMITED)
105 Rue Lauder, Cowansville, QC, J2K 2K8
(450) 266-1850
Emp Here 35   *Sales* 38,687,075
SIC 5122 Drugs, proprietaries, and sundries
Kevin Bennett
Elaine Messier
Walter Bowen

D-U-N-S 25-743-2278   (SL)
ASSURANCE ROY YELLE INC
106 Rue Church, Cowansville, QC, J2K 1T8
(450) 263-0110
Emp Here 25   *Sales* 21,201,500
SIC 6411 Insurance agents, brokers, and service

Jacques Yelle

D-U-N-S 20-190-2611   (SL)
BESSETTE AUTOMOBILE INC
DAIMLER CHRYSLER
395 Rue De La Riviere, Cowansville, QC, J2K 1N4
(450) 263-4000
Emp Here 40   *Sales* 19,923,120
SIC 5511 New and used car dealers
Hugo Bessette
Carl Bessette

D-U-N-S 25-240-6053   (BR)
COMMISSION SCOLAIRE DU VAL-DES-CERFS
ECOLE SECONDAIRE MASSEY VANIER
(*Suby of* COMMISSION SCOLAIRE DU VAL-DES-CERFS)
222 Rue Mercier, Cowansville, QC, J2K 3R9
(450) 263-6660
Emp Here 125
SIC 8211 Elementary and secondary schools
Marie Pierre Champagne

D-U-N-S 20-576-4140   (BR)
COMMISSION SCOLAIRE EASTERN TOWNSHIPS
MASSEY VANIER HIGH SCHOOL
(*Suby of* COMMISSION SCOLAIRE EASTERN TOWNSHIPS)
224 Rue Mercier, Cowansville, QC, J2K 5C3
(450) 263-3772
Emp Here 83
SIC 8211 Elementary and secondary schools
Julie Edwards

D-U-N-S 25-365-5062   (BR)
CONSOLTEX INC
(*Suby of* GEOSAM INVESTMENTS LIMITED)
400 Rue Willard, Cowansville, QC, J2K 3A2
(514) 333-8800
Emp Here 115
SIC 2299 Textile goods, nec
Pierre Grenier

D-U-N-S 25-182-5055   (SL)
COTE, CLAUDE ASSURANCES ENR
106 Rue Church, Cowansville, QC, J2K 1T8
(450) 263-0597
Emp Here 25   *Sales* 21,201,500
SIC 6411 Insurance agents, brokers, and service
Claude Cote

D-U-N-S 20-195-2777   (SL)
DERAGON AUTO-CITE INC
DERAGON FORD
797 Boul Jean-Jacques-Bertrand, Cowansville, QC, J2K 0H9
(450) 266-0101
Emp Here 45   *Sales* 28,317,600
SIC 5511 New and used car dealers
Pierre Deragon

D-U-N-S 24-985-0504   (HQ)
EMBALLAGE PERFORMANT INC
FILMS SPECIALISES SIGMA CANADA, LES
301 Boul Grand N, Cowansville, QC, J2K 1A8
(450) 263-6363
Emp Here 70   *Sales* 12,708,640
SIC 3081 Unsupported plastics film and sheet
Alfred Teo
Robert Smith
John Reier
Vibhakar Jariwala

D-U-N-S 24-768-3527   (SL)
EXCAVATION ST-PIERRE ET TREMBLAY INC
126 Rue Dean, Cowansville, QC, J2K 3Y3
(450) 266-2100
Emp Here 80   *Sales* 15,224,180
SIC 1794 Excavation work
Dany St-Pierre
Mathieu Poulin
Jordan Lee
Rejean Demers

D-U-N-S 24-934-3534   (SL)
GROUPEMENT FORESTIER DU HAUT YA-MASKA INC
578 Rue De La Riviere, Cowansville, QC, J2K 3G6
(450) 263-7120
Emp Here 50   *Sales* 10,580,650
SIC 0851 Forestry services
Michel Barrette
Robert Savard
Gilles Charrette
Michel Gauthier

D-U-N-S 24-743-5225   (SL)
KAYTEC VINYL INC
105 Rue Des Industries, Cowansville, QC, J2K 3Y4
(450) 263-5368
Emp Here 140   *Sales* 22,240,120
SIC 3089 Plastics products, nec
Lionel Dubrofsky
Tami Dubrofsky

D-U-N-S 20-195-2728   (SL)
L. A. DAIGNEAULT & FILS LTEE
IGA EXTRA DAIGNEAULT
1531 Rue Du Sud, Cowansville, QC, J2K 2Z4
(450) 263-3686
Emp Here 125   *Sales* 36,684,625
SIC 5411 Grocery stores
Celine Daigneault

D-U-N-S 25-115-8192   (HQ)
PLANCHERS DES APPALACHES LTEE
454 Rue De La Riviere, Cowansville, QC, J2K 3G6
(450) 266-3999
Sales 19,237,000
SIC 2426 Hardwood dimension and flooring mills
Jean Leduc
Pierre Biron
Louis Bertrand
Gordon Duplain

D-U-N-S 20-195-3015   (SL)
PLOMBERIE GOYER INC
150 Rue De Sherbrooke, Cowansville, QC, J2K 3Y9
(450) 263-2226
Emp Here 60   *Sales* 13,983,900
SIC 1711 Plumbing, heating, air-conditioning
Jean-Charles Hebert
Gilles Deschamps

D-U-N-S 25-760-9537   (SL)
RESIDENCES COWANSVILLE (CRP) INC
117 Rue Principale, Cowansville, QC, J2K 1J3
(450) 266-3757
Emp Here 50   *Sales* 11,931,050
SIC 6514 Dwelling operators, except apartments
Guy Samson
Denis Robert

D-U-N-S 24-406-0351   (SL)
ROCHELEAU CHEVROLET & OLDS
434 Rue De La Riviere, Cowansville, QC, J2K 1N5
(450) 263-1541
Emp Here 22   *Sales* 10,957,716
SIC 5571 Motorcycle dealers
Jean-Pierre Rocheleau

D-U-N-S 20-332-9342   (SL)
SPIRITUEUX UNGAVA CIE LTEE, LES
291 Rue Miner, Cowansville, QC, J2K 3Y6
(450) 263-5835
Emp Here 26   *Sales* 15,285,816
SIC 5182 Wine and distilled beverages
Charles Crawford
Roland Patrick O'driscoll
Antonio Sanchez Villarreal

D-U-N-S 24-500-9402   (SL)
SUPERMARCHE A R G INC
PROVIGO GAGNON
175 Rue Principale, Cowansville, QC, J2K 3L9

Emp Here 120   Sales 35,217,240
SIC 5411 Grocery stores
Richard Gagnon
Andre Gagnon

D-U-N-S 20-855-0975   (SL)
TRAK SPORT INC
135 Rue Dean Bureau 4, Cowansville, QC,
J2K 3Y2

Emp Here 100   Sales 21,882,400
SIC 3949 Sporting and athletic goods, nec
Doug Barbor
Tucker Holland

D-U-N-S 24-207-4248   (BR)
WAL-MART CANADA CORP
WALMART
(Suby of WALMART INC.)
1770 Rue Du Sud, Cowansville, QC, J2K 3G8
(450) 263-6006
Emp Here 100
SIC 5311 Department stores
Marie Base

Crabtree, QC J0K

D-U-N-S 20-540-2126   (BR)
KRUGER PRODUCTS L.P.
(Suby of KRUGER INC)
100 1e Av, Crabtree, QC, J0K 1B0
(450) 754-2855
Emp Here 662
SIC 2676 Sanitary paper products
Stephane Lamoureux

D-U-N-S 24-178-0241   (SL)
REPITS DE GABY, LES
51 19e Rue, Crabtree, QC, J0K 1B0
(450) 754-2782
Emp Here 35   Sales 14,143,431
SIC 8699 Membership organizations, nec
Audrey Roy

D-U-N-S 24-679-4408   (SL)
TOTALE ALIMENTATION INC
130 Ch Saint-Michel Rr 3, Crabtree, QC, J0K
1B0
(450) 754-3785
Emp Here 20   Sales 10,702,480
SIC 5143 Dairy products, except dried or
canned
Denis Parent
Alain Parent

Danville, QC J0A

D-U-N-S 20-021-6765   (HQ)
MINCAVI (1986) INC
88 Ch Du Pinacle, Danville, QC, J0A 1A0
(819) 839-2747
Sales 18,943,250
SIC 8093 Specialty outpatient clinics, nec
Lyne Martineau

Daveluyville, QC G0Z

D-U-N-S 24-207-5844   (HQ)
CANLAK INC
PEINTURE CAN-LAK
674 Rue Principale Bureau 309, Daveluyville,
QC, G0Z 1C0
(819) 367-3264
Sales 25,561,890
SIC 2851 Paints and allied products
Normand Guindon
Eric Vaillancourt

D-U-N-S 20-951-4348   (SL)
DOUCET MACHINERIES INC
(Suby of GROUPE DOUCET PELLETIER
INC)
340 6e Rue, Daveluyville, QC, G0Z 1C0
(819) 367-2633
Emp Here 140   Sales 31,080,140
SIC 3553 Woodworking machinery
Gilles Doucet
Danny Pelletier

D-U-N-S 20-195-4963   (SL)
JULIEN BEAUDOIN LTEE
(Suby of 9048-6358 QUEBEC INC)
320 6e Rue, Daveluyville, QC, G0Z 1C0
(819) 367-2344
Emp Here 80   Sales 12,345,760
SIC 2514 Metal household furniture
Brian Crochetiere
Marie-Eve Crochetiere

D-U-N-S 24-792-3980   (SL)
MACHINAGE PICHE INC
414 Rue Industrielle, Daveluyville, QC, G0Z
1C0
(819) 367-3233
Emp Here 63   Sales 13,986,063
SIC 3553 Woodworking machinery
Jean-Benoit Piche

D-U-N-S 20-872-7610   (SL)
MARCHE FRECHETTE INC
BONICHOIX
276 Rue Principale, Daveluyville, QC, G0Z
1C0
(819) 367-2352
Emp Here 38   Sales 10,417,776
SIC 5411 Grocery stores
Pascal Frechette
Steve Frechette

D-U-N-S 25-077-0369   (SL)
REGIE INTERMUNICIPALE DE SECURITE
PUBLIQUE DES CHUTES
337 Rue Principale, Daveluyville, QC, G0Z
1C0
(819) 367-3395
Emp Here 25   Sales 11,230,475
SIC 7389 Business services, nec
Gaetan Legare

Degelis, QC G5T

D-U-N-S 24-942-0811   (HQ)
GROUPE DE SCIERIES G.D.S. INC
GROUPE G.D.S.
207 Rte 295, Degelis, QC, G5T 1R1
(418) 853-2566
Sales 125,275,500
SIC 2421 Sawmills and planing mills, general
Sylvain Deschenes
Frederic Lavoie
Georges Deschenes
Jacques Poitras
Sylvain Deschenes
Frederic Deschenes

D-U-N-S 24-567-8107   (HQ)
PROMOBOIS G.D.S. INC
FORESTERIE G.D.S.
207 295 Rte, Degelis, QC, G5T 1R1
(418) 853-5050
Emp Here 18   Sales 30,711,978
SIC 5099 Durable goods, nec
Guildo Deschenes
Robert Belzile
Jacques Poitras
Sylvain Deschenes

Delson, QC J5B

D-U-N-S 20-191-5766   (SL)
AUTOMOBILES CANDIAC INC, LES
30 132 Rte, Delson, QC, J5B 1H3
(450) 632-2220
Emp Here 40   Sales 19,923,120
SIC 5511 New and used car dealers
Pierre Ruel

D-U-N-S 25-822-3718   (SL)
CENTRE DE VISION DELSON INC
CENTRE DE VISION DELSON
70 132 Rte Bureau 104, Delson, QC, J5B 0A1
(450) 638-5212
Emp Here 40   Sales 14,449,480
SIC 8042 Offices and clinics of optometrists
Jean I. Cohen

D-U-N-S 25-240-5345   (BR)
COMMISSION SCOLAIRE DES GRANDES-
SEIGNEURIES
ECOLE ALTERNATIVE DES CHEMINOTS
(Suby of COMMISSION SCOLAIRE DES
GRANDES-SEIGNEURIES)
35 Rue Boardman, Delson, QC, J5B 2C3
(514) 380-8899
Emp Here 270
SIC 8211 Elementary and secondary schools
Nathalie Brault

D-U-N-S 24-870-3845   (SL)
DYFOTECH INC
120 Rue Goodfellow, Delson, QC, J5B 1V4
(450) 635-8870
Emp Here 50   Sales 12,622,100
SIC 1629 Heavy construction, nec
Sebastien Gagnon
Vincent Gagnon
Marc-Olivier Gagnon

D-U-N-S 25-592-2502   (HQ)
ENTREPOTS P C G INC, LES
121 Rue Principale N, Delson, QC, J5B 1Z2
(450) 635-8053
Emp Here 40   Sales 11,313,830
SIC 4225 General warehousing and storage
Claude Gagne
Jaques Gagne
Louise Gagne

D-U-N-S 24-958-6363   (SL)
ENTREPRISES PAUL WOODSTOCK LTEE
CANADIAN TIRE
65 132 Rte, Delson, QC, J5B 1H1
(450) 632-1700
Emp Here 90   Sales 24,088,680
SIC 5251 Hardware stores
Paul Woodstock

D-U-N-S 24-988-9494   (SL)
FORAGES C.C.L. (1993) INC, LES
237 Ch Saint-Francois-Xavier, Delson, QC,
J5B 1X8
(450) 632-3995
Emp Here 50   Sales 10,506,550
SIC 1381 Drilling oil and gas wells
Marc Andre Robichaud

D-U-N-S 20-707-0756   (HQ)
GOODFELLOW INC
225 Rue Goodfellow, Delson, QC, J5B 1V5
(450) 635-6511
Emp Here 410   Sales 365,660,382
SIC 5031 Lumber, plywood, and millwork
Patrick Goodfellow
Mary Lohmus
David Warren
Jeff Morrison
Luc Dignard
Charles Brisebois
Claude Garcia
G. Douglas Goodfellow
Normand Morin
David A. Goodfellow

D-U-N-S 24-050-3862   (SL)
H. A. VAILLANCOURT INC
30 Boul Marie-Victorin, Delson, QC, J5B 1A9

(450) 632-2109
Emp Here 30   Sales 25,067,310
SIC 5147 Meats and meat products
Andre Vaillancourt
Alain Vaillancourt
Carmen Vaillancourt

D-U-N-S 24-960-9215   (SL)
M & P DIRECTED ELECTRONICS INC
188 Ch Saint-Francois-Xavier, Delson, QC,
J5B 1X9
(450) 635-7777
Emp Here 50   Sales 22,358,700
SIC 5063 Electrical apparatus and equipment
Andre Girard
Alexandro Renaldoni

D-U-N-S 24-871-4339   (SL)
PNR RAILWORKS QUEBEC INC
(Suby of WIND POINT PARTNERS, L.P.)
100 Rue Goodfellow, Delson, QC, J5B 1V4
(450) 632-6241
Emp Here 25   Sales 12,999,175
SIC 4789 Transportation services, nec
John August
Benoit Labrosse
Kevin Riddett
John R. Brohm

D-U-N-S 25-841-0497   (BR)
PROVIGO DISTRIBUTION INC
LOBLAWS
(Suby of LOBLAW COMPANIES LIMITED)
31 Boul Georges-Gagne S, Delson, QC, J5B
2E4
(450) 638-5041
Emp Here 93
SIC 5411 Grocery stores

D-U-N-S 24-433-9974   (SL)
RESTAURATIONS DYC INC
170 Rue Brossard, Delson, QC, J5B 1X1
(450) 638-5560
Emp Here 26   Sales 12,239,006
SIC 1542 Nonresidential construction, nec
Guillaume Poirier
Chantal Brien
Gilbert Lachance

D-U-N-S 20-195-6133   (SL)
TRANSPORTS DELSON LTEE, LES
121 Rue Principale N, Delson, QC, J5B 1Z2
(450) 632-2960
Emp Here 75   Sales 15,427,950
SIC 4212 Local trucking, without storage
Claude Gagne
Jacques Gagne
Louise Gagne

D-U-N-S 25-335-5713   (SL)
VISION CHEVROLET BUICK GMC INC
30 Rte 132, Delson, QC, J5B 1H3
(450) 632-2220
Emp Here 45   Sales 22,413,510
SIC 5511 New and used car dealers
Gabriel Dallaire
Monique Bedard

D-U-N-S 24-762-8332   (HQ)
W.J. DEANS TRANSPORTATION INC
196 Rue Sutton, Delson, QC, J5B 1X3
(450) 638-5933
Emp Here 80   Sales 20,570,600
SIC 4213 Trucking, except local
Victoria Anne Deans
Valerie Deans

Deschaillons-Sur-Saint-Laurent, QC G0S

D-U-N-S 20-195-6885   (HQ)
COTE-RECO INC
CENTRE DU TRAVAIL
(Suby of GESTION LAERTECO INC)
100 12e Av, Deschaillons-Sur-Saint-Laurent,
QC, G0S 1G0

▲ Public Company   ■ Public Company Family Member   HQ Headquarters   BR Branch   SL Single Location

(819) 292-2323
Sales 108,879,290
SIC 5139 Footwear
Michel Cote
Pierre Cote
Andre Cote

Deschambault, QC G0A

D-U-N-S 20-714-9225   (BR)
ALCOA CANADA CIE
ALUMINERIE DE BAIE-COMEAU
(*Suby of* ALUMINERIE LAURALCO SARL)
1 Boul Des Sources, Deschambault, QC, G0A
1S0
(418) 286-5287
Emp Here 100
SIC 3334 Primary aluminum
Lionel Bentolila

D-U-N-S 24-422-6986   (HQ)
ALCOA DESCHAMBAULT LTEE
(*Suby of* ALUMINERIE LAURALCO SARL)
1 Boul Des Sources, Deschambault, QC, G0A
1S0
(418) 286-5287
Sales 197,479,390
SIC 3334 Primary aluminum
Martin Briere
Alain Taillefer
Jean-Francois Cyr
Diane Thumma

D-U-N-S 20-267-3133   (SL)
**ALCOA-ALUMINERIE DE DESCHAMBAULT
S.E.C.**
1 Boul Des Sources, Deschambault, QC, G0A
1S0
(418) 286-5287
Emp Here 250   *Sales* 539,049,000
SIC 3334 Primary aluminum
Jean-Yves Carrier

D-U-N-S 20-956-3084   (HQ)
**COMPAGNIE DE GESTION ALCOA-
LAURALCO**
(*Suby of* ALUMINERIE LAURALCO SARL)
1 Boul Des Sources, Deschambault, QC, G0A
1S0
(418) 286-5287
Sales 16,324,920
SIC 3354 Aluminum extruded products
Timothy D. Reyes
Jean-Francois Cyr
Amelie Moreault
Louis Langlois
Olivier Charest

D-U-N-S 24-909-4111   (SL)
PRO-METAL PLUS INC
12 Boul Des Sources, Deschambault, QC,
G0A 1S0
(418) 286-4949
Emp Here 70   *Sales* 15,540,070
SIC 3599 Industrial machinery, nec
Sylvain Deshaies
Daniel Melancon

Deux-Montagnes, QC J7R

D-U-N-S 24-785-0006   (SL)
9180-9582 QUEBEC INC
PHARMAPRIX
2500 Boul Des Promenades, Deux-
Montagnes, QC, J7R 6L2
(450) 472-6444
Emp Here 26   *Sales* 28,738,970
SIC 5122 Drugs, proprietaries, and sundries
Yanik Lapointe

D-U-N-S 20-867-3819   (BR)
SOBEYS QUEBEC INC

IGA
850 Ch D'Oka, Deux-Montagnes, QC, J7R
1L7
(450) 473-6280
Emp Here 90   *Sales* 822,456
SIC 5411 Grocery stores
Dominique Beaubien

Disraeli, QC G0N

D-U-N-S 24-420-3985   (HQ)
**CAISSE DESJARDINS DU CARREFOUR
DES LACS**
*CENTRE DE SERVICES BEAULAC-
GARTHBY*
572 Av Jacques-Cartier, Disraeli, QC, G0N
1E0
(418) 449-2652
Emp Here 20   *Sales* 10,609,270
SIC 6062 State credit unions
Guylaine Dubuc
Johanne Hamel
David Laflamme
Serge Rousseau
Ghislain Turgeon
Nicole Rouleau
Luc Beliveau
Lise Morin
Marco Sevigny
Gilles Roberge

D-U-N-S 20-995-9696   (BR)
**CENTRE DE LA PETITE ENFANCE PARC-
EN-CIEL**
(*Suby of* CENTRE DE LA PETITE ENFANCE
PARC-EN-CIEL)
888 Rue Saint-Antoine, Disraeli, QC, G0N 1E0
(418) 449-3004
Emp Here 75
SIC 8351 Child day care services
Serge Rouseau

Dolbeau-Mistassini, QC G8L

D-U-N-S 24-569-0032   (SL)
9171-1440 QUEBEC INC.
MAISON DE L'AUTO DOLBEAU-MISTASSINI
42 Boul Saint-Michel, Dolbeau-Mistassini, QC,
G8L 5J3
(418) 276-6511
Emp Here 25   *Sales* 12,451,950
SIC 5511 New and used car dealers
Luc Verreault

D-U-N-S 24-909-1158   (SL)
BLEUETS FORTIN & FILS INC
555 Rue De Quen, Dolbeau-Mistassini, QC,
G8L 5M3
(418) 276-8611
Emp Here 14   *Sales* 11,698,078
SIC 5142 Packaged frozen goods
Jean-Marie Fortin
Rejean Fortin
Daniel Fortin
Claude Fortin

D-U-N-S 24-842-3642   (HQ)
BLEUETS MISTASSINI LTEE
(*Suby of* FRUIT D'OR INC)
555 Rue De Quen, Dolbeau-Mistassini, QC,
G8L 5M3
(418) 276-8611
Sales 41,778,850
SIC 5142 Packaged frozen goods
Martin Le Moine
Rejean Fortin
Timothy K. Dohan
Carl Blouin
Sylvain Dufour

D-U-N-S 25-233-6888   (BR)

**COMMISSION SCOLAIRE DU PAYS-DES-
BLEUETS**
POLYVALENTE JEAN DOLBEAU
300 Av Jean-Dolbeau, Dolbeau-Mistassini,
QC, G8L 2T7
(418) 276-0984
Emp Here 80
SIC 8211 Elementary and secondary schools
Pierre Cote

D-U-N-S 20-195-8816   (SL)
DOLBEAU AUTOMOBILES LTEE
GM
1770 Boul Wallberg, Dolbeau-Mistassini, QC,
G8L 1H8
(418) 276-0580
Emp Here 25   *Sales* 12,451,950
SIC 5511 New and used car dealers
Michel Noel

D-U-N-S 20-195-8865   (SL)
DOLBEAU OXYGENE INC
DO2 INDUSTRIEL
303 8e Av Bureau 11, Dolbeau-Mistassini,
QC, G8L 1Z6
(418) 276-0555
Emp Here 26   *Sales* 11,626,524
SIC 5051 Metals service centers and offices
Stephane Tremblay
Frank Bernard
Sylvain Minier
Martin Perreault

D-U-N-S 24-499-9397   (SL)
**ENTREPRISE DE CONSTRUCTION GAS-
TON MORIN LTEE**
310 Rue De Quen, Dolbeau-Mistassini, QC,
G8L 5N1
(418) 276-4166
Emp Here 50   *Sales* 14,424,950
SIC 6512 Nonresidential building operators
Louise Morin
Michel Morin

D-U-N-S 24-148-2504   (SL)
**ENTREPRISES DE CONSTRUCTION BON-
NEAU, GUY LTEE, LES**
100 Rue Boulianne, Dolbeau-Mistassini, QC,
G8L 5L4
(418) 276-2301
Emp Here 30   *Sales* 14,121,930
SIC 1542 Nonresidential construction, nec
Guy Bonneau

D-U-N-S 20-517-6811   (SL)
**ENTREPRISES DE CONSTRUCTION GAS-
TON MORIN (1979) LTEE**
(*Suby of* FERME GASTON MORIN & FILS
INC)
310 Rue De Quen, Dolbeau-Mistassini, QC,
G8L 5N1
(418) 276-4166
Emp Here 100   *Sales* 25,244,200
SIC 1611 Highway and street construction
Gaston Morin
France Morin

D-U-N-S 24-393-0463   (SL)
ENTREPRISES PIERRE LAUZON LTEE
CANADIAN TIRE
1751 Boul Vezina Bureau 284, Dolbeau-
Mistassini, QC, G8L 3S4
(418) 276-2385
Emp Here 45   *Sales* 22,413,510
SIC 5531 Auto and home supply stores
Pierre Lauzon

D-U-N-S 20-183-2958   (SL)
GROUPE NOKAMIC INC
115 Rue De La Falaise, Dolbeau-Mistassini,
QC, G8L 5A6
(418) 276-0126
Emp Here 50   *Sales* 12,044,200
SIC 1629 Heavy construction, nec
Louis-Philippe Nault
Manon Poulin

D-U-N-S 25-096-5233   (SL)

MARCHE D. BOUTIN ST-FELICIEN INC
99 8e Av, Dolbeau-Mistassini, QC, G8L 1Z1
(418) 276-0361
Emp Here 50   *Sales* 13,707,600
SIC 5411 Grocery stores
Dany Boutin

D-U-N-S 24-379-5093   (HQ)
MODE CHOC (DOLBEAU) LTEE
361 Boul Vezina, Dolbeau-Mistassini, QC,
G8L 3K6
(418) 276-7189
Sales 10,763,760
SIC 5651 Family clothing stores
Raymond Roussy

D-U-N-S 25-008-6238   (BR)
PF RESOLU CANADA INC
(*Suby of* RESOLUTE FOREST PRODUCTS
INC)
1 4e Av, Dolbeau-Mistassini, QC, G8L 2R4
(418) 239-2350
Emp Here 149
SIC 2621 Paper mills

D-U-N-S 20-073-0717   (BR)
PF RESOLU CANADA INC
(*Suby of* RESOLUTE FOREST PRODUCTS
INC)
200 Rue De Quen, Dolbeau-Mistassini, QC,
G8L 5M8
(418) 679-1010
Emp Here 159
SIC 2621 Paper mills
Tony Truchon

D-U-N-S 24-465-1469   (SL)
SOCIETE SYLVICOLE MISTASSINI LTEE
245 Rue De Quen, Dolbeau-Mistassini, QC,
G8L 5M3
(418) 276-8080
Emp Here 100   *Sales* 13,675,900
SIC 0851 Forestry services
Sylvain Lalancette

D-U-N-S 24-464-2971   (SL)
**TRANSPORT DOUCET & FILS MISTASSINI
INC**
124 Rue Lavoie, Dolbeau-Mistassini, QC, G8L
4M8
(418) 276-7395
Emp Here 100   *Sales* 14,819,200
SIC 4213 Trucking, except local
Ghislain Doucet
Dave Doucet
Janick Doucet

Dollard-Des-Ormeaux, QC H8Y

D-U-N-S 24-322-0753   (SL)
DUOPHARM INC
PHARMACIE JEAN COUTU
4894 Boul Des Sources Bureau 66, Dollard-
Des-Ormeaux, QC, H8Y 3C7
(514) 684-6131
Emp Here 71   *Sales* 17,347,288
SIC 5912 Drug stores and proprietary stores
Louis Legault
Jean David

Dollard-Des-Ormeaux, QC H9A

D-U-N-S 25-240-1708   (SL)
**HEBREW FOUNDATION SCHOOL OF CON-
GREGATION BETH TIKVAH**
2 Rue Hope, Dollard-Des-Ormeaux, QC, H9A
2V5
(514) 684-6270
Emp Here 75   *Sales* 7,541,100
SIC 8211 Elementary and secondary schools
Evelyn Blanshay
Stephanie Glazer

Robyn Krane

Dollard-Des-Ormeaux, QC H9B

D-U-N-S 24-714-4157   (SL)
156861 CANADA INC
ADVANCED TECHNOLOGY & ASSEMBLY
64 Boul Brunswick, Dollard-Des-Ormeaux,
QC, H9B 2L3
(514) 421-4445
Emp Here 50   *Sales* 10,233,650
SIC 3625 Relays and industrial controls
Adel Mankoura

D-U-N-S 24-958-5456   (SL)
2758792 CANADA INC
BOUTIQUE ELECTRONIQUE, LA
3352 Boul Des Sources, Dollard-Des-Ormeaux, QC, H9B 1Z9
(514) 684-6846
Emp Here 48   *Sales* 11,727,744
SIC 5999 Miscellaneous retail stores, nec
Christopher Porteous
Scott Phelan

D-U-N-S 20-164-9477   (SL)
3081354 CANADA INC
DYNAMIC TECHNOLOGIES
2001 Rue Saint-Regis, Dollard-Des-Ormeaux,
QC, H9B 2M9

Emp Here 24   *Sales* 10,732,176
SIC 5045 Computers, peripherals, and software
George Papamikidis

D-U-N-S 25-149-1866   (HQ)
ALIMENTS VLM INC, LES
ARDO VLM
1651 Rue Saint-Regis, Dollard-Des-Ormeaux,
QC, H9B 3H7
(514) 426-4100
Sales 30,080,772
SIC 5142 Packaged frozen goods
Jeff Preston
Marcel Lessard
Philippe Haspeslagh
Jacob Rik
Roger Maes

D-U-N-S 24-668-4245   (SL)
**ATTACHES INDUSTRIELLES USCAN LTEE,
LES**
87a Boul Brunswick, Dollard-Des-Ormeaux,
QC, H9B 2J5
(514) 684-2940
Emp Here 30   *Sales* 14,250,780
SIC 5085 Industrial supplies
Alfredo Galardo
Gregg Galardo
Nicolas Meixner-Orsodi
Marie-Eve Koronkiewicz

D-U-N-S 24-815-1920   (SL)
BIOFORCE CANADA INC
AROMAFORCE
(*Suby of* ALFRED-VOGEL-STIFTUNG)
66 Boul Brunswick, Dollard-Des-Ormeaux,
QC, H9B 2L3
(514) 421-3441
Emp Here 40   *Sales* 20,966,352
SIC 5149 Groceries and related products, nec
Immacolata (Mackie) Vadcchino
Peter Gmunder

D-U-N-S 24-315-7674   (SL)
**CADILLAC CHEVROLET BUICK GMC DU
WEST ISLAND LTEE**
3650 Boul Des Sources, Dollard-Des-Ormeaux, QC, H9B 1Z9
(514) 683-6555
Emp Here 49   *Sales* 24,405,822
SIC 5511 New and used car dealers
Kapil Dilawri

Ajay Dilawri
Lalit Tony Dilawri

D-U-N-S 24-393-9613   (SL)
CANADIAN TIRE
3079 Boul Des Sources, Dollard-Des-Ormeaux, QC, H9B 1Z6
(514) 684-9750
Emp Here 40   *Sales* 19,923,120
SIC 5531 Auto and home supply stores
Alain Harvey

D-U-N-S 20-212-9227   (SL)
**CORPORATION   INTERNATIONAL
BROTHER (CANADA) LTEE, LA**
BROTHER INTERNATIONAL
(*Suby of* BROTHER INDUSTRIES, LTD.)
1 Rue Hotel-De-Ville, Dollard-Des-Ormeaux,
QC, H9B 3H6
(514) 685-0600
Emp Here 180   *Sales* 87,791,400
SIC 5084 Industrial machinery and equipment
Martin Featherston
Steven Sandler
Ishiguro Tadashi
Takeshi Yamada
Anthony J. Melfi

D-U-N-S 24-612-5314   (SL)
DES SOURCES DODGE CHRYSLER LTEE
DES SOURCES DODGE CHRYSLER JEEP
3400 Boul Des Sources, Dollard-Des-Ormeaux, QC, H9B 1Z9
(514) 685-3310
Emp Here 70   *Sales* 44,049,600
SIC 5511 New and used car dealers
Marcel J Dupont
Pierre Seguin
Rock Dupont
Pierre Desrosiers

D-U-N-S 20-177-5512   (HQ)
ELECTRONIQUES ARBELL INC
*ARBELL, DIV DE ELECTRONIQUES ACTIVE
TECH*
3633 Boul Des Sources Bureau 208, Dollard-Des-Ormeaux, QC, H9B 2K4
(514) 685-5603
Emp Here 11   *Sales* 17,135,400
SIC 4899 Communication services, nec
Lee Wise
Paul Guay
William Cleman
Harold Wise

D-U-N-S 20-794-0867   (SL)
GARAGE CIVIC LIMITEE
CIVIC HONDA D.D.O.
3650 Boul Des Sources, Dollard-Des-Ormeaux, QC, H9B 1Z9
(514) 683-5533
Emp Here 50   *Sales* 31,464,000
SIC 5511 New and used car dealers
Dieter Hammer

D-U-N-S 24-084-3946   (HQ)
GROUPE FORDIA INC
3 Rue Hotel-De-Ville, Dollard-Des-Ormeaux,
QC, H9B 3G4
(514) 336-9211
Emp Here 50   *Sales* 146,319,000
SIC 5084 Industrial machinery and equipment
Luc Paquet
Alain Paquet
Sara Paquet

D-U-N-S 25-357-0840   (SL)
**IMMOBILIER JACK ASTOR'S (DORVAL)
INC**
RESTAURANT JACK ASTOR'S BAR & GRILL
(*Suby of* SIR CORP)
3051 Boul Des Sources, Dollard-Des-Ormeaux, QC, H9B 1Z6
(514) 685-5225
Emp Here 80   *Sales* 3,641,520
SIC 5813 Drinking places
Peter Fowler

Grey Sisson

D-U-N-S 24-836-4184   (SL)
LABORATOIRES DELON (1990) INC
69 Boul Brunswick, Dollard-Des-Ormeaux,
QC, H9B 2N4
(514) 685-9966
Emp Here 100   *Sales* 27,666,000
SIC 2844 Toilet preparations
Pascale Sasson
Selim Sasson
Joseph Sasson

D-U-N-S 20-739-6391   (HQ)
PANTORAMA INDUSTRIES INC, LES
ROBERTO
2 Rue Lake, Dollard-Des-Ormeaux, QC, H9B
3H9
(514) 421-1850
Emp Here 30   *Sales* 99,804,000
SIC 5611 Men's and boys' clothing stores
Sidney Aptacker
Larry Wexler

D-U-N-S 24-317-5713   (SL)
**PHARMACIE LOUIS LEGAULT, LYETTE
BOULE, PHARMACIENS INC**
JEAN COUTU
3353 Boul Des Sources, Dollard-Des-Ormeaux, QC, H9B 1Z8
(514) 683-5460
Emp Here 40   *Sales* 10,118,160
SIC 5912 Drug stores and proprietary stores
Louis Legault
Lyette Boule

D-U-N-S 20-363-7210   (HQ)
PLATS DU CHEF ULC, LES
CUISINE ADVENTURES
(*Suby of* C.H. GUENTHER & SON LLC)
51 Rue Kesmark, Dollard-Des-Ormeaux, QC,
H9B 3J1
(514) 685-9955
Sales 34,569,000
SIC 2038 Frozen specialties, nec
Dale W. Tremblay
Gregg Thomassin
Thomas A. Mcrae
Janelle M. Sykes
Bertrand Jolicoeur
Michel Cartier
Catherine Gagnon
Marie-Josee Bisson

D-U-N-S 25-356-0692   (SL)
PRODUITS DE BEAUTE IRIS INC
69 Boul Brunswick, Dollard-Des-Ormeaux,
QC, H9B 2N4
(514) 685-9966
Emp Here 50   *Sales* 13,833,000
SIC 2844 Toilet preparations
Joseph Sasson
Mayer Sasson
Selim Sasson
Pascale Sasson

D-U-N-S 24-429-7990   (SL)
SATAU INC
71 Boul Brunswick, Dollard-Des-Ormeaux,
QC, H9B 2N4
(514) 631-5775
Emp Here 25   *Sales* 20,889,425
SIC 5149 Groceries and related products, nec
Renato Perpignani

D-U-N-S 20-181-8838   (HQ)
**SCHNEIDER   ELECTRIC   SYSTEMS
CANADA INC**
*SYSTEMES   SCHNEIDER   ELECTRIC
CANADA*
(*Suby of* SCHNEIDER ELECTRIC SE)
4 Rue Lake, Dollard-Des-Ormeaux, QC, H9B
3H9
(514) 421-4210
Sales 70,219,250
SIC 3556 Food products machinery
Jon Olson

Mary B Kibble
Patrick Ko
Annette Clayton
Ana Lurdes Dos Santos Gomes Veiga H.
Elias Matthew Panasuik

D-U-N-S 24-960-5767   (SL)
SENNHEISER (CANADA) INC
NEUMANN CANADA
(*Suby of* SENNHEISER V + V GMBH &
CO.KG)
275 Rue Kesmark, Dollard-Des-Ormeaux,
QC, H9B 3J1
(514) 426-3013
Emp Here 45   *Sales* 20,122,830
SIC 5065 Electronic parts and equipment, nec
Steffen Heise
Daniel Sennheiser
Michael Lieske

D-U-N-S 24-790-7652   (SL)
STOCKERYALE CANADA INC
275 Rue Kesmark, Dollard-Des-Ormeaux,
QC, H9B 3J1

Emp Here 120   *Sales* 22,853,040
SIC 3699 Electrical equipment and supplies,
nec
Mark Blodgett

D-U-N-S 20-271-2683   (SL)
SUPERMARCHE D.D.O. INC
IGA EXTRA
11800 Boul De Salaberry, Dollard-Des-Ormeaux, QC, H9B 2R8
(514) 685-5252
Emp Here 100   *Sales* 29,347,700
SIC 5411 Grocery stores
Enrico Lalonde
Normand Barbeau

D-U-N-S 24-385-1933   (BR)
TOP ACES INC
DISCOVERY AIR DEFENCE SERVICES INC
(*Suby of* TOP ACES HOLDINGS INC)
79b Boul Brunswick, Dollard-Des-Ormeaux,
QC, H9B 2J5
(514) 694-5565
Emp Here 130
SIC 8299 Schools and educational services,
nec
Sheila Venman

D-U-N-S 24-092-9513   (HQ)
TRANSCAT CANADA INC
CAL-MATRIX METROLOGY
(*Suby of* TRANSCAT, INC.)
90a Boul Brunswick Bureau A, Dollard-Des-Ormeaux, QC, H9B 2C5
(514) 685-9626
Sales 10,925,598
SIC 5084 Industrial machinery and equipment
Lee D. Rudow
William L. Northcote
Jennifer Nelson

Dollard-Des-Ormeaux, QC H9G

D-U-N-S 20-927-6880   (SL)
**CHENOY'S   DELICATESSEN   &   STEAK
HOUSE INC**
3616 Boul Saint-Jean, Dollard-Des-Ormeaux,
QC, H9G 1X1
(514) 620-2584
Emp Here 75   *Sales* 3,215,475
SIC 5812 Eating places
Nick Sigounis
Costa Sigounis

D-U-N-S 20-165-5854   (SL)
IMMEUBLES VILLAGE D.D.O. INC, LES
ROYAL LEPAGE VILLAGE-DOLLARD
4000 Boul Saint-Jean Bureau 2000, Dollard-Des-Ormeaux, QC, H9G 1X1

▲ Public Company   ■ Public Company Family Member   **HQ** Headquarters   **BR** Branch   **SL** Single Location

(514) 684-1141
Emp Here 45   *Sales* 14,720,715
SIC 6531 Real estate agents and managers
 Jon Engelsman
 Stewart Jones
 Gregory Clarke
 Fred Clark

D-U-N-S 24-770-1147   (SL)
LAVE AUTO A LA MAIN STEVE INC
AUTO DETAILS 1995
4216 Boul Saint-Jean, Dollard-Des-Ormeaux,
QC, H9G 1X5
(514) 696-9274
Emp Here 50   *Sales* 10,131,450
SIC 7542 Carwashes
 Stephen R Williams

Dollard-Des-Ormeaux, QC H9H

D-U-N-S 25-153-0598   (SL)
3725839 CANADA INC
HYUNDAI PRESIDENT
4600b Boul Saint-Jean, Dollard-Des-
Ormeaux, QC, H9H 2A6
(514) 624-7777
Emp Here 30   *Sales* 14,942,340
SIC 5511 New and used car dealers
 Gabriel Azouz
 Peggy Azouz

D-U-N-S 20-798-7871   (SL)
9029-0917 QUEBEC INC
PHARMAPRIX
4301 Boul Saint-Jean Bureau 77, Dollard-
Des-Ormeaux, QC, H9H 2A4
(514) 626-4477
Emp Here 50   *Sales* 12,647,700
SIC 5912 Drug stores and proprietary stores
 Faouzi Fassatoui

D-U-N-S 24-813-6525   (SL)
FADY AUTO INC
ACURA GABRIEL
4648 Boul Saint-Jean, Dollard-Des-Ormeaux,
QC, H9H 2A6
(514) 696-7777
Emp Here 34   *Sales* 16,934,652
SIC 5511 New and used car dealers
 Gabriel Azouz

Donnacona, QC G3M

D-U-N-S 24-330-1467   (SL)
9121-2936 QUEBEC INC
167 Rue Armand-Bombardier, Donnacona,
QC, G3M 1V4
(418) 285-4499
Emp Here 80   *Sales* 15,366,800
SIC 3441 Fabricated structural Metal
 Gerald Perreault

D-U-N-S 20-029-1594   (BR)
**CENTRE DE SANTE ET DE SERVICES SO-
CIAUX DE PORTNEUF**
*CENTRE HERBERGEMENT DE DONNA-
CONA*
(*Suby of* CENTRE DE SANTE ET DE SER-
VICES SOCIAUX DE PORTNEUF)
250 Boul Gaudreau Bureau 370, Donnacona,
QC, G3M 1L7
(418) 285-3025
Emp Here 115
SIC 8361 Residential care
 Chantal Simard

D-U-N-S 24-393-8961   (SL)
ENTREPRISES MICHEL HAMELIN INC, LES
CANADIAN TIRE
223 138 Rte, Donnacona, QC, G3M 1C1
(418) 285-1331
Emp Here 40   *Sales* 19,923,120

SIC 5531 Auto and home supply stores
 Michel Hamelin

D-U-N-S 25-639-1512   (SL)
LEMERVEIL, LAURA
160 Av Du Couvent, Donnacona, QC, G3M
1P5
(418) 462-3325
Emp Here 49   *Sales* 20,805,743
SIC 8999 Services, nec
 Laura Lemerveil

D-U-N-S 24-820-6088   (SL)
METAL PERREAULT INC
167 Rue Armand-Bombardier, Donnacona,
QC, G3M 1V4
(418) 285-4499
Emp Here 50   *Sales* 10,141,500
SIC 3441 Fabricated structural Metal
 Charles Carre
 Simon Harnois

D-U-N-S 24-760-0380   (SL)
TRANSPORT MATTE LTEE
*TRANSPORT DE PRODUITS FORESTIERS
C.D.L*
487 Rue Page, Donnacona, QC, G3M 1W6
(418) 285-0777
Emp Here 140   *Sales* 28,798,840
SIC 4213 Trucking, except local
 Anny Matte
 Simon Matte
 Jean Matte
 Line Matte
 Rene Matte
 Leonidas Cayer
 Melany Matte
 Keven Desroches

Dorval, QC H4S

D-U-N-S 25-999-6981   (BR)
BOMBARDIER INC
BOMBARDIER AERONAUTIQUE
(*Suby of* BOMBARDIER INC)
200 Ch De La Cote-Vertu Bureau 1110, Dor-
val, QC, H4S 2A3
(514) 420-4000
Emp Here 1,800
SIC 3721 Aircraft
 Eric Martel

Dorval, QC H4Y

D-U-N-S 24-339-6616   (SL)
3101895 NOVA SCOTIA COMPANY
AEROTERM RIVE-SUD
800 Boul Stuart-Graham S Bureau 315, Dorval, QC, H4Y 1J6
(514) 422-1000
Emp Here 40   *Sales* 10,462,120
SIC 6712 Bank holding companies
 John Cammett

D-U-N-S 20-259-6016   (SL)
3552047 CANADA INC
S.E.A. 2000 INTERNATIONAL
(*Suby of* GROUPE AERO MAG 2000 INC)
545 Boul Stuart-Graham N Bureau 201, Dor-
val, QC, H4Y 1E2
(514) 633-1118
Emp Here 225   *Sales* 71,404,200
SIC 4581 Airports, flying fields, and services
 Mario Lepine
 Pierre Lesperance

D-U-N-S 24-890-4203   (BR)
AEROPORTS DE MONTREAL
(*Suby of* AEROPORTS DE MONTREAL)
580 Boul Stuart-Graham S, Dorval, QC, H4Y
1G4

(514) 633-2811
Emp Here 500
SIC 4581 Airports, flying fields, and services
 James Cherry

D-U-N-S 24-933-6793   (HQ)
AEROPORTS DE MONTREAL
800 Place Leigh-Capreol Bureau 1000, Dor-
val, QC, H4Y 0A5
(514) 394-7200
Emp Here 100   *Sales* 389,917,175
SIC 4581 Airports, flying fields, and services
 Normand Legault
 Philippe Rainville
 Pierre Gagnon
 Robert Bouchard
 Jean-Jacques Bourgeault
 Mario Messier
 Pierre Pilote
 Jean-Pierre Desrosiers
 Danielle Poudrette
 Yves Filion

D-U-N-S 25-318-2240   (BR)
AVISCAR INC
AVIS
(*Suby of* AVIS BUDGET GROUP, INC.)
975 Boul Romeo-Vachon N Bureau 317, Dor-
val, QC, H4Y 1H2
(514) 636-1902
Emp Here 100
SIC 7514 Passenger car rental

D-U-N-S 20-184-1405   (HQ)
CAFAS FUELING, ULC
(*Suby of* ALLIED AVIATION LLC.)
780 Boul Stuart-Graham S, Dorval, QC, H4Y
1G2
(514) 636-3770
Emp Here 50   *Sales* 125,720,100
SIC 5172 Petroleum products, nec
 Brian Mcguckin
 Robert E. Rose

D-U-N-S 25-857-0977   (SL)
CARGOLUTION INC
800 Boul Stuart-Graham S Bureau 360, Dorval, QC, H4Y 1J6
(514) 636-2576
Emp Here 55   *Sales* 36,679,060
SIC 4731 Freight transportation arrangement

D-U-N-S 25-826-7454   (SL)
**ENTERPRISE   LOCATION   D'AUTOS
CANADA LIMITEE**
600 Rue Arthur-Fecteau, Dorval, QC, H4Y
1K5

Emp Here 49   *Sales* 24,405,822
SIC 5511 New and used car dealers
 William W. Snyder

D-U-N-S 20-576-6475   (BR)
**ENTERPRISE RENT-A-CAR CANADA COM-
PANY**
(*Suby of* THE CRAWFORD GROUP INC)
600 Rue Arthur-Fecteau, Dorval, QC, H4Y
1K5
(514) 422-1100
Emp Here 200
SIC 7514 Passenger car rental
 Paul Pilon

D-U-N-S 24-606-1951   (BR)
**LUXURY HOTELS INTERNATIONAL OF
CANADA ULC**
*LUXURY HOTELS INTERNATIONAL OF
CANADA, ULC*
(*Suby of* MARRIOTT INTERNATIONAL, INC.)
800 Place Leigh-Capreol, Dorval, QC, H4Y
0A5
(514) 636-6700
Emp Here 200
SIC 7011 Hotels and motels
 Brenda Rogrigue

D-U-N-S 24-800-9912   (BR)
RECIPE UNLIMITED CORPORATION

CARA OPERATIONS LIMITED
(*Suby of* RECIPE UNLIMITED CORPORA-
TION)
1185 Rue Rodolphe-Page Bureau 1, Dorval,
QC, H4Y 1H3
(514) 636-5824
Emp Here 650
SIC 5812 Eating places
 Darcy Hawkins

D-U-N-S 25-559-6087   (SL)
UPS CARTAGE SERVICES INC
750 Boul Stuart-Graham S, Dorval, QC, H4Y
1G2
(514) 636-1333
Emp Here 49   *Sales* 18,882,640
SIC 4731 Freight transportation arrangement
 David P Abney

D-U-N-S 25-297-9869   (BR)
UPS SCS, INC
UPS SUPPLY CHAIN SOLUTION
(*Suby of* UNITED PARCEL SERVICE, INC.)
800 Boul Stuart-Graham S Bureau 351, Dor-
val, QC, H4Y 1J6

Emp Here 100
SIC 4731 Freight transportation arrangement

Dorval, QC H7V

D-U-N-S 24-357-2612   (BR)
**CENTRE DE SANTE ET DE SERVICES SO-
CIAUX DE LAVAL**
(*Suby of* GOUVERNEMENT DE LA
PROVINCE DE QUEBEC)
1515 Boul Chomedey, Dorval, QC, H7V 3Y7
(450) 978-8300
Emp Here 350
SIC 8062 General medical and surgical hospi-
tals
 Jean-Francois Caron

D-U-N-S 25-974-9315   (SL)
**CENTRE HOSPITALIER AMBULATOIRE
REGIONAL DE LAVAL**
CHARL
1515 Boul Chomedey Bureau 160, Dorval,
QC, H7V 3Y7
(450) 978-8300
Emp Here 250   *Sales* 27,770,000
SIC 8062 General medical and surgical hospi-
tals
 Monique Corbeil

D-U-N-S 24-252-8610   (BR)
HOFFMANN-LA ROCHE LIMITED
ROCHE DIAGNOSTICS
(*Suby of* ROCHE HOLDING AG)
201 Boul Armand-Frappier, Dorval, QC, H7V
4A2
(450) 686-7050
Emp Here 400
SIC 5122 Drugs, proprietaries, and sundries
 Christopher Parker

Dorval, QC H9P

D-U-N-S 24-958-9946   (SL)
132405 CANADA INC
GIBBONS MAINTENANCE
1484 Boul Hymus, Dorval, QC, H9P 1J6
(514) 685-1425
Emp Here 100   *Sales* 4,020,900
SIC 7349 Building maintenance services, nec
 Harry Tossounian
 Michael Roumeliotis

D-U-N-S 24-895-9678   (SL)
148274 CANADA INC
PRIORITE EXPRESS

▲ Public Company   ■ Public Company Family Member   **HQ** Headquarters   **BR** Branch   **SL** Single Location

100 Av Jenkins Bureau 100, Dorval, QC, H9P 2R1
(514) 631-5058
Emp Here 35   *Sales* 11,366,390
SIC 4512 Air transportation, scheduled
 Sylvain Nobert
 Jean Difruscia

D-U-N-S 24-890-3452   (SL)
167986 CANADA INC
KARMIN GROUP
(*Suby of* 4269853 CANADA INC)
1901 Rte Transcanadienne, Dorval, QC, H9P 1J1
(514) 685-2202
Emp Here 100   *Sales* 69,530,000
SIC 5099 Durable goods, nec
 Lee Karls
 Johnny Karls

D-U-N-S 20-996-0033   (SL)
3174891 CANADA INC
SERVICES KD, LES
2945 Av Andre, Dorval, QC, H9P 1K7
(514) 685-9505
Emp Here 120   *Sales* 80,027,040
SIC 4783 Packing and crating
 Raymond O'farrell
 John Mcguigan
 Kristine Moses
 Carol Anne Nash

D-U-N-S 25-408-2654   (SL)
3374840 CANADA INC
565 Av Edward Vii, Dorval, QC, H9P 1E7

Emp Here 20   *Sales* 10,702,480
SIC 5141 Groceries, general line
 George Nikolopoulos

D-U-N-S 20-767-7985   (SL)
3588025 CANADA INC
SUBARU DES SOURCES
2291 Place Transcanadienne, Dorval, QC, H9P 2X7
(514) 683-3880
Emp Here 24   *Sales* 15,102,720
SIC 5511 New and used car dealers
 Kapil Dilawri

D-U-N-S 20-883-8284   (HQ)
4211677 CANADA INC
10315 Ch Cote-De-Liesse, Dorval, QC, H9P 1A6
(514) 636-8033
Emp Here 150   *Sales* 185,135,400
SIC 4212 Local trucking, without storage
 Pierre Poliquin
 Peter L. Overing

D-U-N-S 24-382-6471   (SL)
8027722 CANADA INC
SYSTEMES DE FRET MONDIAL GTI
9500 Av Ryan, Dorval, QC, H9P 3A1
(514) 634-7655
Emp Here 30   *Sales* 15,599,010
SIC 4731 Freight transportation arrangement
 Daniel Noseworthy

D-U-N-S 25-323-5121   (SL)
9015-0178 QUEBEC INC
LCI GROUP
1405 Rte Trans-Canada Bureau 100, Dorval, QC, H9P 2V9

Emp Here 10   *Sales* 17,139,393
SIC 5045 Computers, peripherals, and software

D-U-N-S 25-814-2694   (SL)
9028-7939 QUEBEC INC
DAMA CONSTRUCTION
117 Av Lindsay, Dorval, QC, H9P 2S6
(514) 636-1676
Emp Here 35   *Sales* 16,475,585
SIC 1542 Nonresidential construction, nec
 Daniel Beaulieu
 Robert Bloom

D-U-N-S 24-348-5757   (HQ)
9045-1410 QUEBEC INC
1620 Crois Newman, Dorval, QC, H9P 2R8
(514) 631-1888
Sales 63,712,800
SIC 1794 Excavation work
 Yvon Theoret
 Raynald Theoret
 Roger Theoret

D-U-N-S 20-117-7826   (HQ)
9093451 CANADA INC
CAMION VOLVO MONTREAL
10475 Ch Cote-De-Liesse, Dorval, QC, H9P 1A7
(514) 685-9444
Sales 26,126,430
SIC 5084 Industrial machinery and equipment
 Richard Noseworthy
 Daniel Deschatelets
 Luc Rivard

D-U-N-S 24-033-2127   (SL)
9119-5867 QUEBEC INC
ENTRETIEN AVANGARDISTE
657 Av Meloche, Dorval, QC, H9P 2T1
(514) 363-5115
Emp Here 85   *Sales* 2,914,270
SIC 7349 Building maintenance services, nec
 Pedro Melo

D-U-N-S 24-381-0343   (SL)
9207-4616 QUEBEC INC
SHERATON MONTREAL AIRPORT HOTEL
555 Boul Mcmillan, Dorval, QC, H9P 1B7
(514) 631-2411
Emp Here 100   *Sales* 9,489,900
SIC 7011 Hotels and motels
 Judah Bendayan
 Pierre Varadi
 Eric Aintabi

D-U-N-S 20-363-4928   (SL)
9256-8971 QUEBEC INC
LANA DISTRIBUTION
22 Av Lindsay, Dorval, QC, H9P 2T8

Emp Here 25   *Sales* 20,889,425
SIC 5149 Groceries and related products, nec
 Vijayabarat Thureswaran

D-U-N-S 24-945-0529   (BR)
ABB PRODUITS D'INSTALLATION LTEE
(*Suby of* ABB LTD)
1811 Boul Hymus, Dorval, QC, H9P 1J5
(514) 685-2277
Emp Here 100
SIC 3648 Lighting equipment, nec
 David Blier

D-U-N-S 24-835-0423   (SL)
ABRASIVE TECHNOLOGY NA, INC
(*Suby of* ABRASIVE TECHNOLOGY, INC.)
2250 Boul Hymus, Dorval, QC, H9P 1J9
(514) 421-7396
Emp Here 30   *Sales* 14,250,780
SIC 5085 Industrial supplies
 Loyal M. Jr Peterman
 Shahla Amiri

D-U-N-S 24-836-6304   (SL)
AUTO BUGATTI INC
825 Av Avoca, Dorval, QC, H9P 1G4
(514) 636-8750
Emp Here 23   *Sales* 11,455,794
SIC 5511 New and used car dealers
 Joe Visconti

D-U-N-S 24-509-7100   (SL)
AUTOMOBILES ULSAN LTEE
HYUNDAI
1625 Boul Hymus, Dorval, QC, H9P 1J5
(514) 683-5702
Emp Here 28   *Sales* 13,946,184
SIC 5511 New and used car dealers
 Robert Croft
 Claire Robert

D-U-N-S 24-402-4063   (SL)
AVIATION STARLINK INC
(*Suby of* CORPORATION STARLINK INC)
9025 Av Ryan, Dorval, QC, H9P 1A2
(514) 631-7500
Emp Here 100   *Sales* 15,242,740
SIC 4522 Air transportation, nonscheduled
 Zoran Bratuljevic
 Brian A. Cytrynbaum
 Philippe De Gaspe Beaubien Iii
 Caroline Thomassin

D-U-N-S 24-522-9724   (HQ)
BATH & BODY WORKS (CANADA) CORP
PRODUITS BATH & BODY WORKS (CANADA)
(*Suby of* CANADIAN HOLDINGS SARL)
1608 Boul Saint-Regis, Dorval, QC, H9P 1H6
(514) 684-7700
Emp Here 50   *Sales* 133,351,500
SIC 5719 Miscellaneous homefurnishings
 Timothy J. Faber
 Stuart Burgdoerfer

D-U-N-S 25-093-2451   (BR)
BOMBARDIER INC
BOMBARDIER A?RONAUTIQUE
(*Suby of* BOMBARDIER INC)
9501 Av Ryan, Dorval, QC, H9P 1A2
(514) 855-5000
Emp Here 1,200
SIC 8711 Engineering services
 Guy C. Hachey

D-U-N-S 24-856-5082   (SL)
BOURASSA WEST ISLAND INC
BMW WEST ISLAND
2000 Place Transcanadienne, Dorval, QC, H9P 2X5
(514) 683-2000
Emp Here 45   *Sales* 28,317,600
SIC 5511 New and used car dealers
 Marc Bourassa

D-U-N-S 24-712-2906   (HQ)
CENTRE DE CONFORMITE ICC INC
88 Av Lindsay, Dorval, QC, H9P 2T8
(514) 636-8146
Sales 36,383,480
SIC 5199 Nondurable goods, nec
 Michael Jeanrie
 Andrew K Li
 Norma Jeanrie
 Robert Monette

D-U-N-S 24-890-4005   (BR)
CHALLENGER MOTOR FREIGHT INC
(*Suby of* CHALLENGER INVESTMENTS II INC)
2770 Av Andre, Dorval, QC, H9P 1K6
(514) 684-2025
Emp Here 300
SIC 4213 Trucking, except local
 Laurier Bourgon

D-U-N-S 20-886-7820   (SL)
COMPAGNIE REGITAN LTEE, LA
ALLIED FOOD DISTRIBUTORS
1420 Rte Transcanadienne, Dorval, QC, H9P 1H7
(514) 685-8282
Emp Here 75   *Sales* 55,689,000
SIC 5194 Tobacco and tobacco products
 Mark Tobenstein
 Marim Tobenstein

D-U-N-S 24-603-7055   (HQ)
CONESTOGA COLD STORAGE (QUEBEC) LIMITED
(*Suby of* CONESTOGA COLD STORAGE LIMITED)
10000 Av Ryan, Dorval, QC, H9P 3A1
(514) 631-5400
Emp Here 20   *Sales* 17,073,598
SIC 4225 General warehousing and storage
 Larry Laurin
 Greg Laurin

D-U-N-S 24-362-9412   (SL)
CONVATEC CANADA LTEE
1425 Rte Transcanadienne Bureau 250, Dorval, QC, H9P 2W9
(514) 822-5985
Emp Here 75   *Sales* 33,538,050
SIC 5047 Medical and hospital equipment
 Sylvain Chiasson
 Mario Gosselin
 Nathalie Theoret
 Fabien Paquette
 Luc Massicotte
 Michael John Langford
 Bradford Carlton Barton
 Rita Guirguis

D-U-N-S 24-904-4843   (HQ)
CORPORATION SENZA, LA
LASENZA.COM
(*Suby of* REGENT, LP)
1608 Boul Saint-Regis, Dorval, QC, H9P 1H6
(514) 684-7700
Emp Here 300   *Sales* 374,265,000
SIC 5632 Women's accessory and specialty stores
 Michelle Cloutier
 Tomothy J. Faber
 Stuart Burgdoerfer

D-U-N-S 24-325-2736   (HQ)
CORPORATION STARLINK INC
9025 Av Ryan, Dorval, QC, H9P 1A2
(514) 631-7500
Emp Here 1   *Sales* 27,335,000
SIC 6712 Bank holding companies
 Philippe Iii De Gaspe Beaubien
 Brian A. Cytrynbaum

D-U-N-S 25-501-5075   (HQ)
COTY CANADA INC
(*Suby of* COTY GLOBAL HOLDINGS B.V.)
1255 Rte Transcanadienne Bureau 200, Dorval, QC, H9P 2V4
(514) 421-5050
Emp Here 120   *Sales* 99,077,040
SIC 5122 Drugs, proprietaries, and sundries
 Lori Rosario-Griffin
 Amaury De Vallois
 Robert Spensieri

D-U-N-S 20-016-1730   (SL)
DELTA PHARMA INC
1655 Rte Transcanadienne, Dorval, QC, H9P 1J1
(514) 685-7311
Emp Here 50   *Sales* 12,647,700
SIC 5912 Drug stores and proprietary stores
 Robert Fairbairn
 Kathleen Muloin
 Paul Leblanc

D-U-N-S 20-337-8922   (HQ)
DICOM TRANSPORTATION GROUP CANADA PARENT, INC
(*Suby of* ROYAL MAIL PLC)
10500 Av Ryan, Dorval, QC, H9P 2T7
(514) 636-8033
Emp Here 2   *Sales* 548,263,500
SIC 6712 Bank holding companies
 Rick Barnes

D-U-N-S 25-537-6931   (HQ)
ENTREPRISES PNH INC, LES
PHN INNOVATIONS
1985 Boul Hymus, Dorval, QC, H9P 1J8
(514) 683-3279
Emp Here 26   *Sales* 19,305,520
SIC 5199 Nondurable goods, nec
 Philip Habib
 Francois Hudon
 Alain Bertrand

D-U-N-S 24-676-5747   (HQ)
EQUIPEMENTS ARES DORVAL LTEE, LES
2000 Boul Hymus Bureau 201, Dorval, QC, H9P 1J7
(514) 683-4337
Sales 17,430,225

SIC 5719 Miscellaneous homefurnishings
David Abrams
Fouad Kejjo
Hugues Pelletier

D-U-N-S 24-516-6210   (SL)
FILS PROMPTEX YARNS INC
FILS PROMPTEX
(*Suby of* PROMPTEX INC)
30 Av Jenkins, Dorval, QC, H9P 2R1
(514) 636-9928
Emp Here 15   *Sales* 11,137,800
SIC 5199 Nondurable goods, nec
Talvinder Soor

D-U-N-S 24-353-3684   (HQ)
FLIGHTSAFETY CANADA LTD
FLIGHTSAFETY INTERNATIONAL
(*Suby of* BERKSHIRE HATHAWAY INC.)
9555 Av Ryan, Dorval, QC, H9P 1A2
(514) 631-2084
Emp Here 50   *Sales* 18,992,400
SIC 8299 Schools and educational services,
nec
Bruce Whitman
Kenneth E W Motschwiller
Doug Ware

D-U-N-S 20-869-3304   (HQ)
FRUITS DE MER STARBOARD INC
560 Av Lepine, Dorval, QC, H9P 1G2
(514) 780-1818
Sales 33,423,080
SIC 5146 Fish and seafoods
Alfred Yuk Leung Yan

D-U-N-S 24-763-1302   (HQ)
**G2S EQUIPEMENT DE FABRICATION ET
D'ENTRETIEN INC**
G2S EQUIPEMENT
1895 Ch Saint-Francois, Dorval, QC, H9P 1K3
(514) 683-8665
Emp Here 19   *Sales* 36,057,285
SIC 5013 Motor vehicle supplies and new
parts
John Leclair
Janet Zelenka
Eric A Blanchard
Paul J Barrett

D-U-N-S 24-834-4798   (SL)
GESTION CANADADIRECT INC
CANADA DIRECT
743 Av Renaud, Dorval, QC, H9P 2N1
(514) 422-8557
Emp Here 700   *Sales* 153,960,100
SIC 8732 Commercial nonphysical research
Alain Harari
Tom Taylor

D-U-N-S 24-128-4632   (BR)
GLS LOGISTICS SYSTEMS CANADA LTD
*DICOM   TRANSPORTATION   GROUP
CANADA, INC*
(*Suby of* ROYAL MAIL PLC)
10755 Ch Cote-De-Liesse, Dorval, QC, H9P
1A7
(888) 463-4266
Emp Here 800
SIC 4212 Local trucking, without storage
Pierre Poliquin

D-U-N-S 25-139-7790   (HQ)
GLS LOGISTICS SYSTEMS CANADA LTD
*DICOM   TRANSPORTATION   GROUP
CANADA*
(*Suby of* ROYAL MAIL PLC)
10500 Av Ryan, Dorval, QC, H9P 2T7
(514) 636-8033
Emp Here 750   *Sales* 593,157,000
SIC 4731 Freight transportation arrangement
Rick Barnes
Nicolas Simard
Ivan Hofmann
Kirk Serjeantson

D-U-N-S 25-211-1893   (HQ)

GRAPHIQUES MATROX INC
GMI
1055 Boul Saint-Regis, Dorval, QC, H9P 2T4
(514) 822-6000
Sales 48,248,340
SIC 8731 Commercial physical research
Lorne Trottier
Branislav Matic

D-U-N-S 20-377-4054   (SL)
**HFC PRESTIGE INTERNATIONAL CANADA
INC**
(*Suby of* COTY GLOBAL HOLDINGS B.V.)
1255 Rte Transcanadienne Bureau 200, Dor-
val, QC, H9P 2V4
(514) 421-5050
Emp Here 240   *Sales* 22,318,110
SIC 5122 Drugs, proprietaries, and sundries
Robert Spensieri
Lori Rosario-Griffin
Amaury De Vallois

D-U-N-S 25-822-9905   (SL)
HYUNDAI AUTOMOBILES ULSAN LTEE
ULSAN HYUNDAI
1625 Boul Hymus, Dorval, QC, H9P 1J5
(514) 336-4613
Emp Here 30   *Sales* 14,942,340
SIC 5511 New and used car dealers
Rejean Forget

D-U-N-S 20-112-6419   (BR)
I.M.P. GROUP LIMITED
EXECAIRE
(*Suby of* I.M.P. GROUP INTERNATIONAL IN-
CORPORATED)
10225 Av Ryan, Dorval, QC, H9P 1A2
(514) 636-7070
Emp Here 700
SIC 4581 Airports, flying fields, and services
Rob Brooks

D-U-N-S 24-525-3575   (SL)
IMPERIAL SURGICAL LTD
850 Av Halpern, Dorval, QC, H9P 1G6
(514) 631-7988
Emp Here 25   *Sales* 11,179,350
SIC 5047 Medical and hospital equipment
Mitchell Goldberg

D-U-N-S 25-526-9524   (BR)
**INFORMATION COMMUNICATION SER-
VICES (ICS) INC**
ICS SERVICE DE COURIER
(*Suby of* TFI INTERNATIONAL INC)
81 Av Lindsay, Dorval, QC, H9P 2S6
(514) 636-9744
Emp Here 200
SIC 4212 Local trucking, without storage
Soraya Masroir

D-U-N-S 20-232-2384   (HQ)
JOSEPH RIBKOFF INC
CREATIONS BRONZE
(*Suby of* NOVACAP INDUSTRIES IV, L.P.)
2375 Rue De L'Aviation, Dorval, QC, H9P 2X6
(514) 685-9191
Sales 59,700,375
SIC 2331 Women's and misses' blouses and
shirts
Domenico Mancini
John Gunn
Daniel Breault
Jacques Foisy
Anastassia Volkova
Louis Gourdeau
Joseph Ribkoff

D-U-N-S 25-368-1878   (SL)
LISI AEROSPACE CANADA CORP
2000 Place Transcanadienne, Dorval, QC,
H9P 2X5
(514) 421-4567
Emp Here 325   *Sales* 94,526,250
SIC 3721 Aircraft
Farrell Campbell
Jean-Louis Colders

Emmanuel Viellard

D-U-N-S 25-389-6278   (SL)
LIVRAISON WILLIAM LTEE
610 Av Orly, Dorval, QC, H9P 1E9
(514) 526-5901
Emp Here 50   *Sales* 12,647,700
SIC 5912 Drug stores and proprietary stores
Guy William

D-U-N-S 20-857-1042   (HQ)
LOCATION BROSSARD INC
2190 Boul Hymus, Dorval, QC, H9P 1J7
(514) 367-1343
Emp Here 100   *Sales* 58,525,610
SIC 7513 Truck rental and leasing, no drivers
Guy Brossard
Yves Carmel
Jerome Leonard
Daniel Crepeau

D-U-N-S 20-330-1593   (HQ)
LOGISTIQUE KERRY (CANADA) INC
*PARTENAIRE TOTAL LOGISTIQUES (TLP)
AIR EXPRESS*
1425 Rte Transcanadienne Bureau 150, Dor-
val, QC, H9P 2W9
(514) 420-0282
Emp Here 23   *Sales* 34,011,492
SIC 4731 Freight transportation arrangement
Peter Sancho
Alan Kam Sang Yip
Fuk Yuen Kenneth Ko

D-U-N-S 24-612-7237   (SL)
LUMIPRO INC
640 Av Lepine, Dorval, QC, H9P 1G2
(514) 633-9320
Emp Here 49   *Sales* 21,911,526
SIC 5063 Electrical apparatus and equipment
Jaddad Kallam
Guy Vallee
Alan Davis
Earl Pantel

D-U-N-S 20-317-4813   (SL)
MARCHON CANADA INC
(*Suby of* VISION SERVICE PLAN)
1975 Boul Hymus Bureau 250, Dorval, QC,
H9P 1J8
(800) 956-9290
Emp Here 87   *Sales* 46,575,624
SIC 5048 Ophthalmic goods
Alberto Zotta
Philip G. Hibbert
Andrew Skitmore

D-U-N-S 20-883-8292   (HQ)
MCCANN EQUIPMENT LTD
ETALONNAGE TECHNIQUE
10255 Ch Cote-De-Liesse, Dorval, QC, H9P
1A3
(514) 636-6344
Emp Here 35   *Sales* 38,042,940
SIC 5084 Industrial machinery and equipment
James A. Mccann
Daniel Mccann
Patricia Mccann
Kathleen Quart
Robert Mccann
Ed O'neil

D-U-N-S 25-990-3441   (SL)
METAUX PROFUSION INC
2000 Boul Hymus, Dorval, QC, H9P 1J7
(514) 822-0922
Emp Here 16   *Sales* 16,005,424
SIC 5051 Metals service centers and offices
Alain Lefebvre
Manon Morneau
Sylvie Longtin

D-U-N-S 24-226-4653   (HQ)
MICRO-ONDES APOLLO LTEE
APOLLO MICROWAVES
(*Suby of* 147780 CANADA INC)
1650 Rte Transcanadienne, Dorval, QC, H9P
1H7

(514) 421-2211
Sales 18,649,086
SIC 3663 Radio and t.v. communications
equipment
Nickolaos Vouloumanos
Vito Beato
Bill Tsounis
George Vouloumanos
Carlo Vendramin
Alina Suciu
Kelly Lavery
Frank F. Vitsentzatos

D-U-N-S 24-509-9593   (BR)
MIDLAND TRANSPORT LIMITED
(*Suby of* IRVING, J. D. LIMITED)
1560 Boul Hymus, Dorval, QC, H9P 1J6
(888) 643-5263
Emp Here 100
SIC 4212 Local trucking, without storage
Peter Legault

D-U-N-S 24-710-8111   (HQ)
MULTIBOND INC
DURAL, DIV OF
550 Av Marshall, Dorval, QC, H9P 1C9
(514) 636-6230
Sales 25,561,890
SIC 2891 Adhesives and sealants
Serge Berube
Domenic Scozzafava
Patrick Donahue

D-U-N-S 24-713-6088   (SL)
MULTIPLUS D.M. INC
10389 Ch Cote-De-Liesse, Dorval, QC, H9P
2Z3
(514) 422-8881
Emp Here 50   *Sales* 37,126,000
SIC 5199 Nondurable goods, nec
Donato (Danny) Matteo
Steven Matteo
Juan Tablo

D-U-N-S 20-652-0228   (BR)
NAV CANADA
(*Suby of* NAV CANADA)
1750 Ch Saint-Francois, Dorval, QC, H9P 2P6
(514) 633-2884
Emp Here 400
SIC 4522 Air transportation, nonscheduled
Christiane Boileau

D-U-N-S 24-800-3295   (SL)
OUTILLAGES KING CANADA INC
JEPSON
700 Av Meloche, Dorval, QC, H9P 2Y4
(514) 636-5464
Emp Here 40   *Sales* 19,001,040
SIC 5084 Industrial machinery and equipment
Howard Richman
Pauline Richman
Reuben Richman

D-U-N-S 20-859-5231   (SL)
PAVAGES D'AMOUR INC
PAVAGES D'AMOUR 2000
1635 Crois Newman, Dorval, QC, H9P 2R6
(514) 631-4570
Emp Here 40   *Sales* 11,340,960
SIC 1611 Highway and street construction
Stephane D'amour

D-U-N-S 20-191-4301   (SL)
PCC AEROSTRUCTURES DORVAL INC
AEROSTRUCTURES PCC DORVAL
(*Suby of* BERKSHIRE HATHAWAY INC.)
123 Av Avro, Dorval, QC, H9P 2Y9
(514) 421-0344
Emp Here 100   *Sales* 22,384,300
SIC 3728 Aircraft parts and equipment, nec
Joseph I Snowden
Ruth A Beyer
Shawn R. Hagel
Bonnie Moffatt

D-U-N-S 25-362-0009   (HQ)
PIVAL INTERNATIONAL INC

1600 Rte Transcanadienne Bureau 100, Dorval, QC, H9P 1H7
(514) 684-1600
Emp Here 10   *Sales* 16,456,480
SIC 4226 Special warehousing and storage, nec
Mario La Barbera
Daniel Goyette
Francois Nadeau

D-U-N-S 20-634-7577   (SL)
PLANTERRA LTEE
FOLIA 2000
2275 Ch Saint-Francois, Dorval, QC, H9P 1K3
(514) 684-0310
Emp Here 44   *Sales* 14,326,400
SIC 5992 Florists
Alastair Smith
Yves Renaud
Bernard Filiatreault

D-U-N-S 25-380-9776   (HQ)
RAIL-TERM INC
10765 Ch Cote-De-Liesse Suite 201, Dorval, QC, H9P 2R9
(514) 420-1200
Emp Here 20   *Sales* 123,445,750
SIC 4013 Switching and terminal services
Robert J Wheeler
Geoffrey Chambers
Francois Prenovost

D-U-N-S 20-646-9806   (SL)
RENOVATIONS ET RESTAURATION APRES-SINISTRE RENOVCO INC
RENOVCO
11355 Ch Cote-De-Liesse, Dorval, QC, H9P 1B2
(514) 856-9993
Emp Here 50   *Sales* 16,666,650
SIC 1541 Industrial buildings and warehouses
Walter Assi
Abboud Charbachi

D-U-N-S 20-715-2146   (BR)
ROLLS-ROYCE CANADA LIMITEE
(*Suby of* ROLLS-ROYCE HOLDINGS PLC)
9545 Ch Cote-De-Liesse Bureau 100, Dorval, QC, H9P 1A5
(514) 636-0964
Emp Here 150
SIC 4581 Airports, flying fields, and services
France Toulouse

D-U-N-S 20-962-0558   (SL)
ROXBORO EXCAVATION INC
PRECO FONDATIONS
(*Suby of* 9045-1410 QUEBEC INC)
1620 Crois Newman, Dorval, QC, H9P 2R8
(514) 631-1888
Emp Here 500   *Sales* 106,188,000
SIC 1794 Excavation work
Yvon Theoret
Raynald Theoret
Roger Theoret
Daniel Theoret
Michel Theoret

D-U-N-S 25-258-9296   (BR)
SCHENKER OF CANADA LIMITED
(*Suby of* BUNDESREPUBLIK DEUTSCHLAND)
2100 Av Reverchon Bureau 257, Dorval, QC, H9P 2S7
(514) 636-6350
Emp Here 80
SIC 4731 Freight transportation arrangement
Richard Bourke

D-U-N-S 25-337-8343   (HQ)
SDP TELECOM ULC
TELECOM SDP
1725 Rte Transcanadienne, Dorval, QC, H9P 1J1
(514) 421-5959
Sales 79,216,200
SIC 3663 Radio and t.v. communications

equipment
Yash Gupta
Ghanshyam Gupta
Sophie Gupta
Michael Clayton
Michael Miskin
Robert J. Zeitler
Keith Travis George
Deirdre Logel
Liam Mccarthy
Martin P. Slark

D-U-N-S 20-536-6784   (HQ)
SERVICES AIRBASE INC, LES
(*Suby of* AIRBASE CANADA HOLDINGS INC)
81 Av Lindsay, Dorval, QC, H9P 2S6
(514) 735-5260
Emp Here 70   *Sales* 185,007,940
SIC 6211 Security brokers and dealers
Tom Mckeown
Lloyd Anderson

D-U-N-S 20-164-9469   (SL)
SERVICES INTERNATIONALS SKYPORT INC
EXPRESS MONT-TREMBLANT
400 Av Michel-Jasmin Bureau 200, Dorval, QC, H9P 1C1
(514) 631-1155
Emp Here 110   *Sales* 8,279,920
SIC 4111 Local and suburban transit
Patrick Gilloux
Jean-Francois Bedard

D-U-N-S 20-267-0113   (BR)
SIEMENS CANADA LIMITED
AERO DERIVATIVE GAS TURBINES
(*Suby of* SIEMENS AG)
9505 Ch Cote-De-Liesse Bureau 9501, Dorval, QC, H9P 2N9
(514) 828-3400
Emp Here 310
SIC 3625 Relays and industrial controls
Tom Scarinci

D-U-N-S 20-651-9550   (BR)
SIEMENS CANADA LIMITED
(*Suby of* SIEMENS AG)
1425 Rte Transcanadienne Unite 400, Dorval, QC, H9P 2W9

Emp Here 125
SIC 3625 Relays and industrial controls
Daniel Groulx

D-U-N-S 25-674-4756   (SL)
SIMPLER NETWORKS INC
1840 Rte Transcanadienne Unite 100, Dorval, QC, H9P 1H7
(514) 684-2112
Emp Here 120   *Sales* 22,853,040
SIC 3669 Communications equipment, nec
Guillaume Rochon
Antonio Accurso
Joseph Molluso
Frank Minicucci

D-U-N-S 24-852-9419   (BR)
SKY SERVICE F.B.O. INC.
(*Suby of* SKY SERVICE F.B.O. INC.)
9785 Av Ryan, Dorval, QC, H9P 1A2
(514) 636-3300
Emp Here 200
SIC 4512 Air transportation, scheduled
Richard Mailhot

D-U-N-S 24-344-3798   (BR)
SKYSERVICE BUSINESS AVIATION INC
(*Suby of* SKYSERVICE INVESTMENTS INC)
9785 Av Ryan, Dorval, QC, H9P 1A2
(514) 636-3300
Emp Here 500
SIC 4522 Air transportation, nonscheduled
Richard Mailhot

D-U-N-S 20-955-1204   (HQ)

SMARDT INC
(*Suby of* GROUPE SMARDT REFROIDISSEURS INC)
1800 Rte Transcanadienne, Dorval, QC, H9P 1H7
(514) 426-8989
Sales 28,812,750
SIC 3443 Fabricated plate work (boiler shop)
Roger Maxwell Richmond-Smith
Lucie Roy

D-U-N-S 20-857-6991   (HQ)
SOCIETE INDUSTRIELLE JASON (CANADA) LTEE
JASON INDUSTRIAL CANADA
(*Suby of* MEGADYNE AMERICA, LLC)
9135 Ch Cote-De-Liesse, Dorval, QC, H9P 2N9
(514) 631-6781
Emp Here 20   *Sales* 18,050,988
SIC 5085 Industrial supplies
Philip Cohenca
Marco Tadolini
Georgio Tadolini

D-U-N-S 24-353-3572   (BR)
SPACEBRIDGE INC
ADVANTECH SANS FIL INC
(*Suby of* GROUPE ADVANTECH BROADBAND INC)
657 Av Orly, Dorval, QC, H9P 1G1
(514) 420-0045
Emp Here 250
SIC 3679 Electronic components, nec
Vagan Shakhgildian

D-U-N-S 24-900-0837   (HQ)
SPACEBRIDGE INC
ADVANTECHAMT
(*Suby of* GROUPE ADVANTECH BROADBAND INC)
657 Av Orly, Dorval, QC, H9P 1G1
(514) 420-0045
Emp Here 229   *Sales* 81,963,280
SIC 4899 Communication services, nec
Stella Gelerman
David Gelerman
Mary Kevork
Gutman Yevgenya

D-U-N-S 20-011-8938   (SL)
STANPRO LIGHTING SYSTEMS INC
SYSTEMES D'ECLAIRAGE STANPRO
(*Suby of* 2872404 CANADA INC)
2233 Rue De L'Aviation, Dorval, QC, H9P 2X6
(514) 739-9984
Emp Here 210   *Sales* 121,851,870
SIC 5063 Electrical apparatus and equipment
Samuel Rimoin
Victoria Nathaniel
David Nathaniel
Katy Shebath

D-U-N-S 20-330-3383   (HQ)
SUEZ CANADA INC
TRAITEMENTS DES EAUX POSEIDON, LES
(*Suby of* SUEZ)
1375 Rte Transcanadienne Bureau 400, Dorval, QC, H9P 2W8
(514) 683-1200
Sales 10,891,450
SIC 1781 Water well drilling
Mathieu Le Bourhis
Karine Rouge
Thierry Bosom
Danielle Capozzoli

D-U-N-S 20-961-1748   (HQ)
SYSTEMES ELECTRONIQUES MATROX LTEE
MATROX
1055 Boul Saint-Regis, Dorval, QC, H9P 2T4
(514) 822-6000
Emp Here 600   *Sales* 178,236,450
SIC 3674 Semiconductors and related devices
Branislav Matic
Lorne Trottier

D-U-N-S 20-114-2960   (SL)
SYSTEMES LUMINESCENT CANADA INC
ASTRONICS LSI CANADA
(*Suby of* ASTRONICS CORPORATION)
55 Av Lindsay, Dorval, QC, H9P 2S6
(514) 636-9921
Emp Here 90   *Sales* 18,513,540
SIC 4213 Trucking, except local
James S. Cramer
David Burney
Stephen Weinstein

D-U-N-S 20-107-8578   (SL)
SYSTEMES RAILTERM INC, LES
CENTRE RAIL-CONTROL
(*Suby of* RAIL-TERM INC)
10765 Ch Cote-De-Liesse Bureau 201, Dorval, QC, H9P 2R9
(514) 420-1200
Emp Here 250   *Sales* 59,262,750
SIC 8748 Business consulting, nec
Robert J. Wheeler
Geoffrey Chambers
Francois Prenovost
Gilles Richard
Jason Fries
Daniel Mongeau
Sheldon Wisson
Johanne Frappier
Bruno Houle

D-U-N-S 20-918-7033   (HQ)
TECHNOLOGIES SURFACE PRAXAIR MONTREAL S.E.C.
PRAXAIR TECHNOLOGIES DE SURFACE
10300 Av Ryan, Dorval, QC, H9P 2T7
(514) 631-2240
Emp Here 26   *Sales* 10,141,500
SIC 3479 Metal coating and allied services
Marc Emond

D-U-N-S 24-349-5392   (HQ)
TOP ACES INC
SERVICES DE DEFENSE DISCOVERY AIR
(*Suby of* TOP ACES HOLDINGS INC)
1675 Rte Transcanadienne Bureau 201, Dorval, QC, H9P 1J1
(514) 694-5565
Emp Here 150   *Sales* 61,047,000
SIC 8299 Schools and educational services, nec
Paul Bouchard
David Kleiman
Didier Toussaint

D-U-N-S 20-716-7250   (BR)
UNIVAR CANADA LTD
UNIVAR SOLUTIONS CANADA
(*Suby of* UNIVAR INC.)
2200 Ch Saint-Francois, Dorval, QC, H9P 1K2
(514) 421-0303
Emp Here 125
SIC 5169 Chemicals and allied products, nec
Jean Lessard

D-U-N-S 20-337-8539   (HQ)
VICTORIA'S SECRET (CANADA) CORP.
VICTORIA'S SECRET
(*Suby of* CANADIAN HOLDINGS SARL)
1608 Boul Saint-Regis, Dorval, QC, H9P 1H6
(514) 684-7700
Emp Here 25   *Sales* 31,188,750
SIC 5632 Women's accessory and specialty stores
Pamela Edwards
Timothy J Faber

D-U-N-S 24-225-8254   (BR)
WOOD CANADA LIMITED
AMEC EARTH & ENVIRONMENTAL DIV OF
(*Suby of* JOHN WOOD GROUP P.L.C.)
1425 Rte Transcanadienne Bureau 400, Dorval, QC, H9P 2W9
(514) 684-5555
Emp Here 150
SIC 8748 Business consulting, nec
Marlene Makhlous

D-U-N-S 20-424-0642   (BR)
YRC FREIGHT CANADA COMPANY
REIMER EXPRESS
(*Suby of* YRC WORLDWIDE INC.)
1725 Ch Saint-Francois, Dorval, QC, H9P 2S1
(514) 684-9970
Emp Here 100
SIC 4231 Trucking terminal facilities
Norman Tees

Dorval, QC H9S

D-U-N-S 24-528-5184   (SL)
127113 CANADA INC
PROVIGO
960 Ch Herron, Dorval, QC, H9S 1B3

Emp Here 90   *Sales* 26,412,930
SIC 5411 Grocery stores
Real Brouillette
Rita Brouillette

D-U-N-S 25-851-9222   (BR)
BELL EXPRESSVU INC
(*Suby of* BCE INC)
200 Boul Bouchard Bureau 72, Dorval, QC, H9S 1A8
(514) 828-6600
Emp Here 350
SIC 4833 Television broadcasting stations
Lucie Beauchamp

D-U-N-S 25-060-5037   (BR)
BELL MOBILITE INC
BELL DISTRIBUTION BUREAU DE MONTREAL
(*Suby of* BCE INC)
200 Boul Bouchard Bureau 500, Dorval, QC, H9S 5X5
(514) 333-3336
Emp Here 2,000
SIC 5999 Miscellaneous retail stores, nec
Claude Beaulieu

D-U-N-S 20-294-3952   (BR)
CHSLD LACHINE, NAZAIRE PICHE ET FOYER DORVAL, LES
CENTRE D'HERBEGREMNT DE DORVAL
225 Av De La Presentation, Dorval, QC, H9S 3L7
(514) 631-9094
Emp Here 200
SIC 8361 Residential care
Colette Parent

D-U-N-S 24-900-9762   (SL)
ELECTRICITE TRI-TECH INC
480 Boul Strathmore, Dorval, QC, H9S 2J4
(450) 420-0111
Emp Here 89   *Sales* 19,386,781
SIC 1731 Electrical work
Stephen Shepherd
Norman Bercovitch

D-U-N-S 20-564-5955   (BR)
GENERAL MOTORS ACCEPTANCE CORPORATION OF CANADA, LIMITED
GMAC
455 Boul Fenelon Bureau 310, Dorval, QC, H9S 5K1
(514) 633-6933
Emp Here 120
SIC 6153 Short-term business credit institutions, except agricultural

D-U-N-S 20-764-7637   (SL)
GESTIONS FERNANDA CIVITELLA INC, LES
PHARMAPRIX
330 Av Dorval Bureau 11, Dorval, QC, H9S 3H7
(514) 631-1827
Emp Here 40   *Sales* 10,118,160
SIC 5912 Drug stores and proprietary stores
Fernanda Civitella

D-U-N-S 20-309-3620   (SL)
PERSONNEL UNIQUE CANADA INC
ECOLE DU ROUTIER FUTUR-CAM
(*Suby of* GROUPE MANUCAM INC)
455 Boul Fenelon Bureau 210, Dorval, QC, H9S 5T8
(514) 633-6220
Emp Here 750   *Sales* 84,152,250
SIC 8741 Management services
Michael Cote Gagnon

D-U-N-S 25-240-0742   (SL)
QUEEN OF ANGELS ACADEMY INC
COLL?GE QUEEN OF ANGEL
100 Boul Bouchard, Dorval, QC, H9S 1A7
(514) 636-0900
Emp Here 85   *Sales* 7,890,210
SIC 8211 Elementary and secondary schools
Dominic Varvaro
Peggy Miller
Lynn De Grace
Joanne Dion

D-U-N-S 24-297-5068   (SL)
S.F. MARKETING INC
DIGIFLEX
(*Suby of* APVE INVESTMENTS INC)
325 Boul Bouchard, Dorval, QC, H9S 1A9
(514) 780-2070
Emp Here 135   *Sales* 78,333,345
SIC 5065 Electronic parts and equipment, nec
Solomon Fleising
Celine Fleising

D-U-N-S 20-603-8986   (HQ)
TRANSITAIRES DAVID KIRSCH LTEE
455 Boul Fenelon Bureau 130, Dorval, QC, H9S 5T8
(514) 636-0233
Emp Here 11   *Sales* 13,519,142
SIC 4731 Freight transportation arrangement
Frank Saravo
Piero Albini
Sandro Pitigliani

Drummondville, QC J2A

D-U-N-S 20-978-0865   (SL)
BROUILLETTE & FRERE INC
RENOVATEUR RONA
4500 Boul Saint-Joseph, Drummondville, QC, J2A 1A7
(819) 475-7114
Emp Here 80   *Sales* 21,412,160
SIC 5211 Lumber and other building materials
Gaston Brouillette
Marcel Brouillette
Roger Brouillette

D-U-N-S 24-740-1805   (SL)
ENTREPRISES CLEMENT RUEL (2000) INC
I G A SUPER MARCHE CLEMENT
4565 Boul Saint-Joseph, Drummondville, QC, J2A 1B4
(819) 472-1107
Emp Here 115   *Sales* 33,749,855
SIC 5411 Grocery stores
Martin Ruel

D-U-N-S 24-338-7474   (SL)
GEA FARM TECHNOLOGIES CANADA INC
DIVISION GEA HOULE
4591 Boul Saint-Joseph, Drummondville, QC, J2A 0C6
(819) 477-7444
Emp Here 325   *Sales* 91,285,025
SIC 3523 Farm machinery and equipment
Alain Courtemanche
Vern Foster
Madeleine Couture
Nathalie Courchesne

D-U-N-S 24-944-5263   (SL)
GROUPE DRUMCO CONSTRUCTION INC, LE

4825 Rte 139, Drummondville, QC, J2A 4E5
(819) 474-5035
Emp Here 25   *Sales* 14,258,450
SIC 1542 Nonresidential construction, nec
Yves Hamel
Francois Cote
Amelie Hamel
Steve Richard
Dany Chabot
Guillaume Boislard
Jacques Tanguay

D-U-N-S 24-352-4662   (SL)
LUMI-O INNOVAPLAS INC
(*Suby of* 9213-4550 QUEBEC INC)
2257 139 Rte, Drummondville, QC, J2A 2G2
(819) 850-2935
Emp Here 60   *Sales* 19,568,160
SIC 3999 Manufacturing industries, nec
Charles Goulet

D-U-N-S 20-972-6603   (SL)
PATIO DRUMMOND LTEE
LATTE DRUMMOND
8435 Boul Saint-Joseph, Drummondville, QC, J2A 3W8
(819) 394-2505
Emp Here 50   *Sales* 11,671,750
SIC 3272 Concrete products, nec
Yvan Lemaire

D-U-N-S 24-458-5550   (SL)
PLACEMENTS JULES CHAMBERLAND LTEE
2540 139 Rte, Drummondville, QC, J2A 2P9
(819) 478-4967
Emp Here 48   *Sales* 24,175,584
SIC 5113 Industrial and personal service paper
Jules Chamberland

D-U-N-S 24-344-4531   (HQ)
PLACEMENTS LUC CHAMBERLAND INC, LES
2540 139 Rte, Drummondville, QC, J2A 2P9
(819) 478-4967
Sales 13,539,230
SIC 2673 Bags: plastic, laminated, and coated
Luc Chamberland

Drummondville, QC J2B

D-U-N-S 24-864-6424   (HQ)
ABZAC CANADA INC
ABZAC AMERIQUE
2945 Boul Lemire, Drummondville, QC, J2B 6Y8
(514) 866-3488
Emp Here 100   *Sales* 55,145,550
SIC 2655 Fiber cans, drums, and similar products
Pierre Michel D'anglade
Maryse Poire
Pierre-Michel D'anglade
Luc Langevin
Eric Phaneuf

D-U-N-S 25-647-0527   (SL)
CAMIONS FREIGHTLINER STERLING DRUMMONDVILLE INC
5770 Place Kubota Bureau 4, Drummondville, QC, J2B 6V4
(819) 474-2264
Emp Here 42   *Sales* 20,919,276
SIC 5541 Gasoline service stations
Jean-Claude Beauregard
Francis Beauregard

D-U-N-S 24-342-0093   (BR)
CASCADES CANADA ULC
CASCADES INOPAK
(*Suby of* CASCADES INC)
500 Rue Lauzon, Drummondville, QC, J2B

2Z3
(819) 472-5757
Emp Here 78
SIC 3089 Plastics products, nec
Serge Blais

D-U-N-S 24-901-5959   (SL)
CENTRE DU CAMION BEAUDOIN INC
5360 Rue Saint-Roch S, Drummondville, QC, J2B 6V4
(819) 478-8186
Emp Here 100   *Sales* 62,928,000
SIC 5511 New and used car dealers
Steve Halle
Bernard Thibeault
Dominique Beauregard

D-U-N-S 24-359-5795   (BR)
CENTRE JEUNESSE DE LA MAURICIE ET DU CENTRE-DU-QUEBEC, LE
CENTRE JEUNESSE DE LA MAURICIE ET DU CENTRE-DU-QUE
(*Suby of* CENTRE JEUNESSE DE LA MAURICIE ET DU CENTRE-DU-QUEBEC, LE)
3100 Boul Lemire, Drummondville, QC, J2B 7R2
(819) 477-5115
Emp Here 120
SIC 8361 Residential care
Claude Levesque

D-U-N-S 20-979-6796   (SL)
COLLEGE SAINT-BERNARD
25 Av Des Freres-De-La-Charite, Drummondville, QC, J2B 6A2
(819) 478-3330
Emp Here 170   *Sales* 16,850,230
SIC 8211 Elementary and secondary schools
Jean Fournier
Danny Gobeil
Leo Descheneaux

D-U-N-S 24-224-5470   (HQ)
COMMISSION SCOLAIRE DES CHENES
457 Rue Des Ecoles Bureau 846, Drummondville, QC, J2B 1J3
(819) 478-6700
Emp Here 100   *Sales* 148,678,500
SIC 8211 Elementary and secondary schools
Jeanne-Mance Paul
Christiane Desbiens

D-U-N-S 20-196-4269   (SL)
CREATIONS MORIN INC, LES
2575 Boul Saint-Joseph, Drummondville, QC, J2B 7V4
(819) 474-4664
Emp Here 95   *Sales* 12,984,030
SIC 2399 Fabricated textile products, nec
Andre Morin

D-U-N-S 24-871-8751   (HQ)
DRUMMOND INFORMATIQUE LTEE
MICROAGE
412 Rue Heriot Bureau 101, Drummondville, QC, J2B 1B5
(819) 477-8886
Sales 13,944,180
SIC 5734 Computer and software stores
Martin Boisvert
Stephane Langlois
Raymond Miville Deschenes
Carl Gauvreau

D-U-N-S 24-866-2470   (SL)
FABRIMET INC
4375 Boul Saint-Joseph, Drummondville, QC, J2B 1T8
(819) 472-1164
Emp Here 90   *Sales* 17,287,650
SIC 3441 Fabricated structural Metal
Gilbert J. Guerette
Georges Guerette
Paul Guerette

D-U-N-S 24-871-2028   (SL)
FESTIVAL MONDIAL DE FOLKLORE

(DRUMMOND)

MONDIALE DES CULTURES DE DRUM-MONDVILLE
226 Rue Saint-Marcel, Drummondville, QC, J2B 2E4
(819) 472-1184
Emp Here 90   *Sales* 8,545,770
SIC 7999 Amusement and recreation, nec
  Charles Guillemette

D-U-N-S 24-374-2124   (SL)
GESTION G.G.V.M. INC
UNIPRIX
511 Rue Heriot, Drummondville, QC, J2B 7R3
(819) 477-3777
Emp Here 60   *Sales* 14,659,680
SIC 5912 Drug stores and proprietary stores
  Danny Gobeil
  Patrick Martel
  Pascal Gilbert

D-U-N-S 24-814-8108   (SL)
GESTION GUYTA INC
4275 Boul Saint-Joseph, Drummondville, QC, J2B 1T8
(819) 477-1596
Emp Here 175   *Sales* 33,614,875
SIC 3469 Metal stampings, nec
  Guy Guerette

D-U-N-S 24-760-3488   (HQ)
GROUPE TYT INC
(*Suby of* TRANSPORTS YVON TURCOTTE LTEE, LES)
675 Boul Lemire O, Drummondville, QC, J2B 8A9
(819) 474-4884
Emp Here 75   *Sales* 41,141,200
SIC 4213 Trucking, except local
  Patrick Turcotte
  Mickael Turcotte
  Rechard Guay

D-U-N-S 25-485-1868   (BR)
LOBLAWS INC
MAXI #8689
(*Suby of* LOBLAW COMPANIES LIMITED)
1850 Boul Saint-Joseph, Drummondville, QC, J2B 1R3
(819) 472-1197
Emp Here 200
SIC 5411 Grocery stores
  Caroline Lapointe

D-U-N-S 20-871-5995   (HQ)
MACHINERIES B.V. LTEE
5555 Rue Saint-Roch S, Drummondville, QC, J2B 6V4
(819) 474-4444
Sales 10,925,598
SIC 5084 Industrial machinery and equipment
  Alain Fortier
  Sebastian Bergeron
  Pierre Fortier

D-U-N-S 20-644-5327   (SL)
MARCHE CLEMENT DEFORGES INC
IGA EXTRA MARCHE
1910 Boul Saint-Joseph, Drummondville, QC, J2B 1R2
(819) 477-7700
Emp Here 49   *Sales* 13,433,448
SIC 5411 Grocery stores
  Clement Ruell

D-U-N-S 24-612-8565   (SL)
OUTILLAGE DE PRECISION DRUMMOND INC
(*Suby of* DUBOIS, ROGER INC)
5250 Rue Saint-Roch S, Drummondville, QC, J2B 6V4
(819) 474-2622
Emp Here 130   *Sales* 24,971,050
SIC 3499 Fabricated Metal products, nec
  Roger Dubois

D-U-N-S 20-698-5637   (HQ)
PORTEFEUILLE SOUCY INC

(*Suby of* SOUCY HOLDING INC)
5450 Rue Saint-Roch S, Drummondville, QC, J2B 6V4
(819) 474-6666
Sales 349,020,000
SIC 3795 Tanks and tank components
  Gilles Soucy
  Josiane Roy

D-U-N-S 24-253-3727   (HQ)
PRODUITS INDUSTRIELS DE HAUTE TEM-PERATURE PYROTEK INC
ISOMAG
(*Suby of* PYROTEK INCORPORATED)
2400 Boul Lemire, Drummondville, QC, J2B 6X9
(819) 477-0734
Emp Here 60   *Sales* 23,310,105
SIC 3569 General industrial machinery, nec
  Rejean Dault
  Don Zel Tong

D-U-N-S 24-582-0089   (SL)
RECUPERACTION CENTRE DU QUEBEC INC
5620 Rue Saint-Roch S, Drummondville, QC, J2B 6V4
(819) 477-1312
Emp Here 105   *Sales* 33,485,550
SIC 4953 Refuse systems
  Jean-Pierre Henri
  Brian Illick
  Jacques Morissette

D-U-N-S 24-327-5661   (SL)
ROSE DRUMMOND INC
ROSE DRUMMOND
210 Boul Lemire O, Drummondville, QC, J2B 8A9
(819) 474-3488
Emp Here 40   *Sales* 13,024,000
SIC 5992 Florists
  Jean-Denis Lampron
  Diane Lampron

D-U-N-S 25-899-4383   (SL)
SOCIETE SAINT-JEAN BAPTISTE DU CENTRE-DU-QUEBEC INC, LA
449 Rue Notre-Dame, Drummondville, QC, J2B 2K9
(819) 478-2519
Emp Here 22   *Sales* 40,626,498
SIC 6321 Accident and health insurance
  Francois Gardner

D-U-N-S 20-565-5699   (SL)
SOUCY BELGEN INC
(*Suby of* SOUCY HOLDING INC)
4475 Boul Saint-Joseph, Drummondville, QC, J2B 1T8
(819) 477-2434
Emp Here 72   *Sales* 13,059,936
SIC 3321 Gray and ductile iron foundries
  Gilles Soucy
  Chantal Soucy
  Josiane Roy

D-U-N-S 24-051-3358   (HQ)
SOUCY INTERNATIONAL INC
SOUCY CAOUTCHOUC
(*Suby of* SOUCY HOLDING INC)
5450 Rue Saint-Roch S, Drummondville, QC, J2B 6V4
(819) 474-6666
Emp Here 252   *Sales* 78,820,350
SIC 3714 Motor vehicle parts and accessories
  Gilles Soucy
  Josiane Roy

D-U-N-S 24-354-8211   (SL)
SOUCY PLASTIQUES INC
(*Suby of* SOUCY HOLDING INC)
5755 Place Kubota, Drummondville, QC, J2B 6V4
(819) 474-5151
Emp Here 100   *Sales* 15,885,800
SIC 3089 Plastics products, nec
  Gilles Soucy

Josiane Roy

D-U-N-S 20-196-9417   (HQ)
SPG INTERNATIONAL LTEE
WWW.RANGEMENTDOUTILS.COM
4275 Boul Saint-Joseph, Drummondville, QC, J2B 1T8
(819) 477-1596
Sales 19,208,500
SIC 3499 Fabricated Metal products, nec
  Benoit Clouatre

D-U-N-S 24-005-0802   (SL)
STRUCTURE LAFERTE INC
2300 Boul Lemire, Drummondville, QC, J2B 6X9
(819) 477-7723
Emp Here 85   *Sales* 6,656,805
SIC 2439 Structural wood members, nec
  Stephane Tourigny
  Louis-Jacques Laferte

D-U-N-S 25-356-0718   (HQ)
TEXTILES MONTEREY (1996) INC
TEXTILES LINCOLN, LES
2575 Boul Saint-Joseph, Drummondville, QC, J2B 7V4
(819) 475-4333
Sales 14,672,240
SIC 2221 Broadwoven fabric mills, manmade
  Gilles Desmarais

D-U-N-S 24-322-9028   (HQ)
TRANSPORTS YVON TURCOTTE LTEE, LES
TYT
675 Boul Lemire O, Drummondville, QC, J2B 8A9
(819) 474-4884
Sales 17,485,010
SIC 4213 Trucking, except local
  Patrick Turcotte
  Jean-Marc Turcotte
  Mickael Turcotte

Drummondville, QC J2C

D-U-N-S 20-885-4745   (HQ)
2310-3393 QUEBEC INC
PHARMACIE JEAN COUTU
520 Boul Saint-Joseph Bureau 10, Drummondville, QC, J2C 2B8
(819) 472-3003
Emp Here 1   *Sales* 14,659,680
SIC 5912 Drug stores and proprietary stores
  Danielle Gelinas

D-U-N-S 25-484-8807   (SL)
2316-7240 QUEBEC INC
HOTEL LE DAUPHIN
600 Boul Saint-Joseph, Drummondville, QC, J2C 2C1
(819) 478-4141
Emp Here 90   *Sales* 8,540,910
SIC 7011 Hotels and motels

D-U-N-S 25-466-8478   (SL)
3095-6395 QUEBEC INC
RECOLTES MARCOTTE, LES
1175 Boul Lemire, Drummondville, QC, J2C 7X8
(819) 474-7281
Emp Here 26   *Sales* 21,725,002
SIC 5148 Fresh fruits and vegetables
  Robert Brunelle
  Mario Marcotte
  Martin Brunelle
  Ghislaine Plante

D-U-N-S 25-074-5551   (SL)
9029-5015 QUEBEC INC
915 Rue Hains, Drummondville, QC, J2C 3A1
(819) 478-4971
Emp Here 49   *Sales* 20,548,395
SIC 6712 Bank holding companies

Lise Lagueux

D-U-N-S 25-904-4949   (SL)
9045-4604 QUEBEC INC
DRUMONDVILLE NISSAN
1200 Boul Rene-Levesque, Drummondville, QC, J2C 5W4
(819) 474-3930
Emp Here 35   *Sales* 17,432,730
SIC 5511 New and used car dealers
  Daniel Beaucage
  Dave Roy

D-U-N-S 20-543-5683   (SL)
9060-1899 QUEBEC INC
CENTRE ORTHOPEDIQUE CDD
126 Rue Heriot, Drummondville, QC, J2C 1J8
(819) 472-1121
Emp Here 32   *Sales* 10,419,200
SIC 5999 Miscellaneous retail stores, nec
  Jocelyne Cloutier

D-U-N-S 25-542-3386   (SL)
9067-7246 QUEBEC INC
DRUMMOND HONDA
1355 Boul Saint-Joseph, Drummondville, QC, J2C 2E4
(819) 477-1414
Emp Here 23   *Sales* 11,455,794
SIC 5521 Used car dealers
  Pierre Brunet
  Richard Chagnon

D-U-N-S 25-748-6415   (SL)
9101-7673 QUEBEC INC
L'EAU-THENTIQUE
620 Rue Cormier, Drummondville, QC, J2C 5C4
(819) 472-1180
Emp Here 55   *Sales* 15,581,500
SIC 7542 Carwashes
  Jacques Bonenfant
  Pierre Levesque

D-U-N-S 24-253-9351   (SL)
9122-4568 QUEBEC INC
TOYOTA DRUMMONDVILLE
10 Rue Cormier, Drummondville, QC, J2C 0L4
(819) 477-1777
Emp Here 40   *Sales* 19,923,120
SIC 5511 New and used car dealers
  Serge Le Roux

D-U-N-S 24-314-4800   (SL)
ACIER DRUMMOND INC
ACIER VALLEYFIELD
1750 Rue Janelle, Drummondville, QC, J2C 3E5
(819) 477-4418
Emp Here 11   *Sales* 11,003,729
SIC 5051 Metals service centers and offices
  Stephan Hamel
  Jonathan Dionne

D-U-N-S 24-349-2175   (BR)
ALIMENTS PRINCE, S.E.C.
OLYMEL
(*Suby of* ALIMENTS PRINCE, S.E.C.)
255 Rue Rocheleau, Drummondville, QC, J2C 7G2
(819) 475-3030
Emp Here 570
SIC 2013 Sausages and other prepared meats
  Francois Bessette

D-U-N-S 24-697-6963   (HQ)
ALIMENTS TRANS GRAS INC, LES
DRUMMOND EXPORT
2825 Rue Power, Drummondville, QC, J2C 6Z6
(819) 472-1125
Emp Here 50   *Sales* 51,853,500
SIC 2011 Meat packing plants
  Suzanne Gerin
  Josee Hamel

D-U-N-S 25-854-6423   (HQ)

ALPHA COMPAGNIE D'ASSURANCE INC, L'
(*Suby of* GESTIONS M. VERRIER LTEE, LES)
430 Rue Saint-Georges Unite 119, Drummondville, QC, J2C 4H4
(819) 474-7958
Sales 157,058,070
SIC 6411 Insurance agents, brokers, and service
Michel Verrier
Genevieve Verrier
Denyse Remillard
Jean-Eudes Cote
Normand Lessard

D-U-N-S 25-381-0808 (SL)
ANNABEL CANADA INC
(*Suby of* ALMON)
1645 Rue Haggerty, Drummondville, QC, J2C 5P7
(819) 472-1367
Emp Here 55 *Sales* 10,087,165
SIC 2261 Finishing plants, cotton
Nicolas Derumeaux
Sophie Derumeaux

D-U-N-S 25-747-3868 (HQ)
ANNEXAIR INC
1125 Rue Bergeron, Drummondville, QC, J2C 7V5
(819) 475-3302
Emp Here 95 *Sales* 36,186,163
SIC 3564 Blowers and fans
Francois Lemieux

D-U-N-S 20-709-9524 (SL)
AOF SERVICE ALIMENTAIRE INC
(*Suby of* ATTILA INC)
2150 Rue Sigouin, Drummondville, QC, J2C 5Z4
(819) 477-5353
Emp Here 150 *Sales* 73,159,500
SIC 5087 Service establishment equipment
Daniel Le Rossignol
Rene Fournier
Jeff York
Eric Phaneuf
Anna Martini
Marc Blanchette

D-U-N-S 25-459-9954 (SL)
AUTOMATES VEN INC
2375 Rue Power, Drummondville, QC, J2C 6Z5
(819) 477-1133
Emp Here 30 *Sales* 19,693,920
SIC 5962 Merchandising machine operators
Francois Cote

D-U-N-S 20-221-8835 (SL)
AVICOMAX INC
500 Rue Labonte, Drummondville, QC, J2C 6X9
(819) 471-5000
Emp Here 60 *Sales* 20,741,400
SIC 2015 Poultry slaughtering and processing
Bruno Ducharme

D-U-N-S 24-582-3534 (HQ)
AVJET HOLDING INC
AVJET
1525 Boul Saint-Joseph, Drummondville, QC, J2C 2E9
(819) 479-1000
Sales 62,860,050
SIC 5172 Petroleum products, nec
Denis Jacob
Sylvain Touchette
Pierre Guilbault
Glenn Kelly
Real Menard
Ross Bayus

D-U-N-S 24-354-9193 (SL)
BERNIER & CREPEAU (1988) LTEE
CHRYSLER DODGE
(*Suby of* GESTION RICHARD NADEAU INC)

160 Boul Saint-Joseph, Drummondville, QC, J2C 2A8
(819) 477-8503
Emp Here 41 *Sales* 25,800,480
SIC 5511 New and used car dealers
Richard Nadeau

D-U-N-S 20-002-9887 (BR)
CAISSE DESJARDINS DE DRUM-MONDVILLE
CENTRE DE SERVICES BOULEVARD
460 Boul Saint-Joseph, Drummondville, QC, J2C 2A8
(819) 474-2524
Emp Here 250
SIC 6062 State credit unions
Rene Lamothe

D-U-N-S 20-518-9512 (BR)
CAISSE DESJARDINS DE DRUM-MONDVILLE
CAISSE SAINT JEAN BAPTIST
460 Boul Saint-Joseph, Drummondville, QC, J2C 2A8
(819) 474-2524
Emp Here 200
SIC 6062 State credit unions
Serge Cousineau

D-U-N-S 24-403-9921 (HQ)
CANIMEX INC
COVANA
(*Suby of* DUBOIS, ROGER INC)
285 Rue Saint-Georges, Drummondville, QC, J2C 4H3
(819) 477-1335
Emp Here 400 *Sales* 121,615,500
SIC 3429 Hardware, nec
Roger Dubois
Daniel Dubois

D-U-N-S 25-871-1746 (SL)
CLUB DE HOCKEY LES VOLTIGEURS
VOLTIGEURS, LES
300 Rue Cockburn, Drummondville, QC, J2C 4L6
(819) 477-9400
Emp Here 30 *Sales* 12,711,900
SIC 7941 Sports clubs, managers, and promoters
Eric Verrier

D-U-N-S 20-909-5611 (SL)
COLLEGE D'AFFAIRES ELLIS (1974) INC
COLLEGE ELLIS CAMPUS DE DRUM-MONDVILLE
235 Rue Moisan, Drummondville, QC, J2C 1W9
(819) 477-3113
Emp Here 90 *Sales* 10,137,240
SIC 8221 Colleges and universities
Alain Scalzo
Jean-Paul Aumais
Caroline Lavallee
Michelle Bourret

D-U-N-S 20-712-0879 (BR)
COMMISSION SCOLAIRE DES CHENES
ECOLE SECONDAIRE JEAN RAIMBAULT
(*Suby of* COMMISSION SCOLAIRE DES CHENES)
175 Rue Pelletier, Drummondville, QC, J2C 2W1
(819) 474-0750
Emp Here 112
SIC 8211 Elementary and secondary schools
Denis Landry

D-U-N-S 25-232-8232 (BR)
COMMISSION SCOLAIRE DES CHENES
ECOLE POLYVALENTE MARIE RIVIER
(*Suby of* COMMISSION SCOLAIRE DES CHENES)
265 Rue Saint-Felix, Drummondville, QC, J2C 5M1
(819) 478-6600
Emp Here 100
SIC 8211 Elementary and secondary schools

Pierre Lavalle

D-U-N-S 25-885-8695 (SL)
CONSTRUCTION BERTRAND DIONNE INC
1555 Rue Janelle, Drummondville, QC, J2C 5S5
(819) 472-2559
Emp Here 40 *Sales* 18,829,240
SIC 1542 Nonresidential construction, nec
Bertrand Dionne
Yolande Labonte Dionne

D-U-N-S 20-277-8353 (BR)
CORPORATION MCKESSON CANADA, LA
AUTOMATISATION MCKESSON CANADA
(*Suby of* MCKESSON FINANCIAL HOLDINGS II UNLIMITED COMPANY)
650 Rue Bergeron, Drummondville, QC, J2C 0E2
(819) 850-5400
Emp Here 110
SIC 5122 Drugs, proprietaries, and sundries
Sonia Picard

D-U-N-S 20-265-7037 (HQ)
CVTECH INC
CVTECH R ET D
300 Rue Labonte, Drummondville, QC, J2C 6X9
(819) 477-3232
Emp Here 100 *Sales* 22,200,100
SIC 3566 Speed changers, drives, and gears
Alain Charest
Christian Mercier

D-U-N-S 24-934-0654 (BR)
DATA COMMUNICATIONS MANAGEMENT CORP
(*Suby of* DATA COMMUNICATIONS MANAGEMENT CORP)
1750 Rue Jean-Berchmans-Michaud, Drummondville, QC, J2C 7S2
(819) 472-1111
Emp Here 250
SIC 2761 Manifold business forms
Allan Reley

D-U-N-S 20-187-7628 (HQ)
DESHAIES & RAYMOND INC
650 Rue Haggerty, Drummondville, QC, J2C 3G6
(819) 472-5486
Sales 11,666,655
SIC 1541 Industrial buildings and warehouses
Jean Deshaies
Martin Ethier
Jean-Pierre Ethier

D-U-N-S 20-978-0188 (HQ)
DESSINS DRUMMOND INC, LES
DRUMMOND DESIGNS.COM
455 Boul Saint-Joseph Bureau 201, Drummondville, QC, J2C 7B5
(819) 477-3315
Sales 13,476,570
SIC 7389 Business services, nec
Yves Carignan
Marie-France Roger
Stephane Doucet

D-U-N-S 24-203-9266 (HQ)
DUBOIS, ROGER INC
GROUPE CANIMEX, LE
285 Rue Saint-Georges, Drummondville, QC, J2C 4H3
(819) 477-1335
Sales 153,513,780
SIC 6712 Bank holding companies
Roger Dubois

D-U-N-S 25-392-8758 (SL)
ENTREPRISES N.G.A. INC, LES
DISTRIBUTIONS N.G.A
(*Suby of* 9122-1994 QUEBEC INC)
350 Rue Rocheleau, Drummondville, QC, J2C 7S7
(819) 477-6891
Emp Here 45 *Sales* 25,665,210

SIC 1542 Nonresidential construction, nec
Alexandre Prince
Guylain Prince
Bernard Malo
Jean-Rene Prince
Nathalie Prince

D-U-N-S 24-776-8141 (BR)
ESSITY CANADA INC
SCA PRODUITS D'HYGIENE
(*Suby of* ESSITY CANADA INC)
999 Rue Farrell, Drummondville, QC, J2C 5P6
(819) 475-4500
Emp Here 175
SIC 5047 Medical and hospital equipment
Michelle Poirier

D-U-N-S 25-356-2201 (SL)
FEMPRO CONSUMER PRODUCTS ULC
FEMPRO
(*Suby of* FIRST QUALITY INTERNATIONAL, INC.)
1330 Rue Jean-Berchmans-Michaud, Drummondville, QC, J2C 2Z5
(819) 475-8900
Emp Here 40 *Sales* 19,476,800
SIC 2676 Sanitary paper products
James Dodge
Moshe Oppenheim
Thomas Lucarelli

D-U-N-S 24-934-5034 (SL)
GARAGE MONTPLAISIR LTEE
LAROCQUE PONTIAC BUICK GMC
875 Boul Saint-Joseph, Drummondville, QC, J2C 2C4
(819) 477-2323
Emp Here 40 *Sales* 12,636,000
SIC 7549 Automotive services, nec
Pierre Larocque

D-U-N-S 24-959-2718 (SL)
GESTION J.L.T. UNIVERSELLE INC
BEST WESTERN HOTEL UNIVERSEL
915 Rue Hains, Drummondville, QC, J2C 3A1
(819) 472-2942
Emp Here 90 *Sales* 8,540,910
SIC 7011 Hotels and motels
Jean-Louis Thiffault

D-U-N-S 20-643-5609 (SL)
GESTION RENE FORTIN INC
HYUNDAI DRUMMONDVILLE
150 Boul Saint-Joseph, Drummondville, QC, J2C 2A8
(819) 478-8148
Emp Here 24 *Sales* 11,953,872
SIC 5511 New and used car dealers
Rene Fortin

D-U-N-S 20-277-2351 (SL)
GESTION VALLIERES ET PELLETIER INC, LES
JARDINS DE LA CITE, LES
275 Rue Cockburn, Drummondville, QC, J2C 4L5
(819) 475-0545
Emp Here 100 *Sales* 6,507,500
SIC 8361 Residential care
Pascal Pelletier
Alain Vallieres
Myriam Pelletier

D-U-N-S 24-862-8104 (BR)
GOODFELLOW INC
(*Suby of* GOODFELLOW INC)
1750 Rue Haggerty, Drummondville, QC, J2C 5P8
(819) 477-6898
Emp Here 100
SIC 2426 Hardwood dimension and flooring mills
Dominique Gagne

D-U-N-S 25-732-5522 (HQ)
GROUPE D'ASSURANCES VERRIER INC
LE GROUP VERRIER COURTIERS D'ASSURANCES

430 Rue Saint-Georges Bureau 121, Drummondville, QC, J2C 4H4
(819) 477-6131
Emp Here 60   *Sales* 138,580,650
SIC 6411 Insurance agents, brokers, and service
 Michel Verrier
 Marian Jacobs

D-U-N-S 24-944-7194   (HQ)
GROUPE DE SECURITE MGM INC
975 Rue Cormier, Drummondville, QC, J2C 2N5
(819) 478-4558
Emp Here 11   *Sales* 11,525,100
SIC 3499 Fabricated Metal products, nec
 Lisa Monette
 Luc Chabot
 Mario Girard
 Yves Lussier

D-U-N-S 20-568-4020   (SL)
GUILBEAULT, R CONSTRUCTION INC
775 Boul Lemire, Drummondville, QC, J2C 7X5
(819) 474-6521
Emp Here 50   *Sales* 14,176,200
SIC 1611 Highway and street construction
 Francois Guilbeault
 Alain Guilbeault

D-U-N-S 20-309-3554   (HQ)
HOLDING SOPREMA CANADA INC
MACADEN
(*Suby of* HOLDING SOPREMA)
1688 Rue Jean-Berchmans-Michaud, Drummondville, QC, J2C 8E9
(819) 478-8163
Sales 146,203,600
SIC 6712 Bank holding companies
 Pierre-Etienne Bindschedler
 Richard Voyer
 Raymond Gauthier
 Monique Dupuis

D-U-N-S 25-672-9138   (SL)
IMMEUBLES J.C. MILOT INC, LES
HOTEL & SUITES LE DAUPHIN
600 Boul Saint-Joseph, Drummondville, QC, J2C 2C1
(819) 478-4141
Emp Here 90   *Sales* 8,540,910
SIC 7011 Hotels and motels
 Jean-Yves Milot
 France Cote

D-U-N-S 20-196-6645   (HQ)
JACQUES LAFERTE LTEE
LAFERTE
(*Suby of* GROUPE LAFERTE INC)
1650 Boul Lemire, Drummondville, QC, J2C 5A4
(819) 477-8950
Sales 40,147,800
SIC 5211 Lumber and other building materials
 Louis-Jacques Laferte

D-U-N-S 20-739-0261   (BR)
LEDVANCE LTD
(*Suby of* EUROLIGHT LUXEMBOURG HOLDINGS SARL)
1 Rue Sylvan, Drummondville, QC, J2C 2S8
(819) 478-6500
Emp Here 550
SIC 3641 Electric lamps
 Ronald Steben

D-U-N-S 24-352-2604   (SL)
LEMIRE PRECISION INC
MARTIN LEMIRE & FILS
3000 Rue Power, Drummondville, QC, J2C 6H9
(819) 475-5121
Emp Here 70   *Sales* 13,445,950
SIC 3451 Screw machine products
 Jocelyn Lemire

D-U-N-S 20-004-5891   (SL)

MAGASIN ST-JEAN, ALAIN INC
CANADIAN TIRE
715 Boul Saint-Joseph Bureau 158, Drummondville, QC, J2C 7V2
(819) 478-1471
Emp Here 100   *Sales* 62,928,000
SIC 5531 Auto and home supply stores
 Alain St-Jean

D-U-N-S 20-196-3113   (HQ)
MATECH B.T.A. INC
1570 Boul Saint-Charles, Drummondville, QC, J2C 4Z5
(819) 478-4015
Emp Here 64   *Sales* 28,044,555
SIC 5013 Motor vehicle supplies and new parts
 Serge Valois
 Rene Valois
 Martin Valois

D-U-N-S 25-808-7774   (BR)
METRO RICHELIEU INC
SUPER C
(*Suby of* METRO INC)
565 Boul Saint-Joseph Bureau 4, Drummondville, QC, J2C 2B6
(819) 474-2702
Emp Here 120
SIC 5411 Grocery stores
 Yvon Grandain

D-U-N-S 24-325-6443   (HQ)
MIDBEC LTEE
(*Suby of* GESTION G.D.J.E. INC)
1725 Boul Lemire, Drummondville, QC, J2C 5A5
(819) 477-1070
Emp Here 15   *Sales* 21,464,352
SIC 5064 Electrical appliances, television and radio
 Gerald Leveille
 Daniel Leveille
 Jocelyn Leveille
 Eric Leveille

D-U-N-S 25-103-8055   (BR)
MITCHEL-LINCOLN PACKAGING LTD
EMBALLAGES MITCHEL-LINCOLN LTEE
(*Suby of* MITCHEL-LINCOLN PACKAGING LTD)
925 Rue Rocheleau, Drummondville, QC, J2C 6L8
(819) 477-9700
Emp Here 250
SIC 2653 Corrugated and solid fiber boxes
 Normand Bonin

D-U-N-S 20-252-4021   (BR)
OLYMEL S.E.C.
OLYMEL DRUMMONDVILLE
(*Suby of* OLYMEL S.E.C.)
255 Rue Rocheleau, Drummondville, QC, J2C 7G2
(819) 475-3030
Emp Here 450
SIC 2011 Meat packing plants
 Michel Maher

D-U-N-S 25-244-7354   (SL)
PIVOT CENTRE-DU-QUEBEC
795 Rue Cormier, Drummondville, QC, J2C 6P7
(819) 478-3134
Emp Here 40   *Sales* 12,585,280
SIC 8699 Membership organizations, nec
 Christine Boisvert
 Sylvie Allard

D-U-N-S 24-836-6601   (SL)
PLACEMENTS JACQUES LAFERTE INC, LES
1650 Boul Lemire, Drummondville, QC, J2C 5A4
(819) 477-8950
Emp Here 150   *Sales* 40,147,800
SIC 5211 Lumber and other building materials
 Jacques Laferte

D-U-N-S 20-956-2540   (SL)
PLANCHERS   MERCIER   (DRUMMONDVILLE) INC, LES
1125 Rue Rocheleau, Drummondville, QC, J2C 6L8
(819) 472-1670
Emp Here 100   *Sales* 19,237,000
SIC 2426 Hardwood dimension and flooring mills
 Marielle Mercier
 Richard Mercier

D-U-N-S 24-522-5789   (BR)
PPD SOLUTION DE MOUSSE INC
PPD FOAM SOLUTION INC
(*Suby of* 148220 CANADA INC)
1275 Rue Janelle, Drummondville, QC, J2C 3E4
(819) 850-0159
Emp Here 120
SIC 2531 Public building and related furniture
 Mario Charest

D-U-N-S 25-093-4044   (BR)
RONA INC
(*Suby of* LOWE'S COMPANIES, INC.)
875 Rue Hains, Drummondville, QC, J2C 7Y8

Emp Here 80
SIC 5072 Hardware
 Selene Vachon

D-U-N-S 20-363-0991   (SL)
SCOTT BADER ATC INC
ATC POLYMERES FORMULES
(*Suby of* SCOTT BADER COMMONWEALTH LIMITED(THE))
2400 Rue Canadien Bureau 303, Drummondville, QC, J2C 7W3
(819) 477-1752
Emp Here 26   *Sales* 10,968,678
SIC 2891 Adhesives and sealants
 Jean-Claude Pierre
 Nicholas Mark Padfield
 Jean-Pascal Schroeder
 Pierre Parenteau

D-U-N-S 24-827-6110   (HQ)
SOPREMA INC
TRAXPO
(*Suby of* HOLDING SOPREMA)
1688 Rue Jean-Berchmans-Michaud, Drummondville, QC, J2C 8E9
(819) 478-8163
Emp Here 100   *Sales* 753,918,750
SIC 2952 Asphalt felts and coatings
 Pierre-Etienne Bindschedler
 Richard Voyer
 Hugo Belisle
 Monique Dupuis

D-U-N-S 25-211-0275   (SL)
SOUCY KOUTOU INC
1825 Rue Power, Drummondville, QC, J2C 5X4
(819) 478-9032
Emp Here 30   *Sales* 13,304,700
SIC 7389 Business services, nec
 Gilles Doucy
 Josiane Roy

D-U-N-S 25-107-8887   (SL)
SOUCY RIVALAIR INC
(*Suby of* SOUCY HOLDING INC)
650 Rue Rocheleau, Drummondville, QC, J2C 7R8
(819) 474-2908
Emp Here 100   *Sales* 19,208,500
SIC 3499 Fabricated Metal products, nec
 Jasmin Villeneuve
 Gilles Soucy
 Nathalie Frappier

D-U-N-S 20-322-4675   (SL)
SYNDICAT DES TRAVAILLEUSES ET TRA-VAILLEURS DE SYLVANIA
1 Rue Sylvan, Drummondville, QC, J2C 2S8

(819) 477-8541
Emp Here 240   *Sales* 68,352,480
SIC 8631 Labor organizations
 Stephane Boivert

D-U-N-S 20-016-9501   (SL)
TECHNOCELL INC
3075 Rue Kunz, Drummondville, QC, J2C 6Y4
(819) 475-0066
Emp Here 108   *Sales* 61,894,683
SIC 2621 Paper mills
 Richard Paterson-Jones
 Stephan Igel
 Georg Haggenmueller
 Roland M. Belanger

D-U-N-S 24-343-3690   (HQ)
TECHNOLOGIES HUMANWARE INC
1800 Rue Jean-Berchmans-Michaud, Drummondville, QC, J2C 7G7
(819) 471-4818
Emp Here 25   *Sales* 30,271,905
SIC 3669 Communications equipment, nec
 Gilles Pepin
 Yves Boisjoli
 Marc Tersigni
 Roy Hessel
 Francois D'alverny
 Baptiste Picquenot

D-U-N-S 20-558-0892   (SL)
TRADITION FORD (VENTES) LTEE
DRUMMONDVILLE FORD
1163 Boul Saint-Joseph, Drummondville, QC, J2C 2C8
(819) 477-3050
Emp Here 26   *Sales* 12,950,028
SIC 5511 New and used car dealers
 Michel De Lisa

D-U-N-S 20-196-3782   (HQ)
TRANSPORT BOURRET INC
(*Suby of* 9120-3752 QUEBEC INC)
375 Boul Lemire, Drummondville, QC, J2C 0C6
(819) 477-2202
Emp Here 10   *Sales* 82,971,450
SIC 4212 Local trucking, without storage
 Francois Bourret

D-U-N-S 24-712-8556   (SL)
TRANSPORT S A S DRUMMONDVILLE INC
850 Rue Labonte, Drummondville, QC, J2C 5Y4
(819) 477-6599
Emp Here 100   *Sales* 20,570,600
SIC 4213 Trucking, except local
 Marc Brouillard
 Andre Brouillette
 Donald Gauvin
 Rock Gauvin

D-U-N-S 24-863-5716   (HQ)
TRANSPORT SCOLAIRE SOGESCO INC
1125 Boul Saint-Joseph Bureau 320, Drummondville, QC, J2C 2C8
(819) 472-1991
Emp Here 16   *Sales* 621,365,300
SIC 6712 Bank holding companies
 Andre Girardin
 Dave Girardin
 Mario Provost
 Jean-Paul Provost
 Louise L'italien
 Yvon Allard
 Claude Moreau
 Marc-Olivier Beauregard
 Jean-Guy Provost
 Rhe-Jean Racine

D-U-N-S 25-335-8030   (SL)
TREMCAR DRUMMOND INC
(*Suby of* TECHNOLOGIES TREMCAR INC)
1450 Rue Hebert, Drummondville, QC, J2C 0C7
(450) 469-4840
Emp Here 80
SIC 3443 Fabricated plate work (boiler shop)

▲ Public Company   ■ Public Company Family Member   **HQ** Headquarters   **BR** Branch   **SL** Single Location

Jacques Tremblay
Jocelyne Senecal

D-U-N-S 24-176-7219   (SL)
UNION-VIE, COMPAGNIE MUTUELLE D'ASSURANCE, L'
L'UNION-VIE
142 Rue Heriot, Drummondville, QC, J2C 1J8
(819) 478-1315
Emp Here 140   *Sales* 299,175,520
SIC 6311 Life insurance
Christian Mercier
Richard Fortier
Jean Audet
Marc Boisselle
Carl Tetu
Leonard Caya

D-U-N-S 24-870-0833   (HQ)
VENMAR VENTILATION ULC
550 Boul Lemire, Drummondville, QC, J2C 7W9
(819) 477-6226
Sales 77,801,625
SIC 3634 Electric housewares and fans
Matthew Nozemack
James Slattery
Jonathon Crawford
Daniel Pellerin

D-U-N-S 24-353-2108   (SL)
VILLAGE QUEBECOIS D'ANTAN INC
1425 Rue Montplaisir, Drummondville, QC, J2C 0M2
(819) 478-1441
Emp Here 160   *Sales* 15,192,480
SIC 7999 Amusement and recreation, nec
Eric Verreault

D-U-N-S 20-163-8422   (SL)
VILLAGE QUEBECOIS D'ANTAN, LE
1425 Rue Montplaisir, Drummondville, QC, J2C 0M2
(819) 478-1441
Emp Here 250   *Sales* 26,215,000
SIC 8412 Museums and art galleries
Helene Sauvageau
Jean-Mathieu Sigouin
Viviana Magazzu
Dany Bouchard
Melanie Ayotte
Genevieve Beliveau
Erika English
Yannick Gamelin
Jean Charest
Nancy Martel

D-U-N-S 25-481-4270   (BR)
WAL-MART CANADA CORP
(*Suby of* WALMART INC.)
1205 Boul Rene-Levesque, Drummondville, QC, J2C 7V4
(819) 472-7446
Emp Here 100
SIC 5311 Department stores
Blair Lefebvre

Drummondville, QC J2E

D-U-N-S 20-249-7145   (SL)
A. GIRARDIN INC
(*Suby of* GROUPE AUTOBUS GIRARDIN LTEE)
4000 Rue Girardin, Drummondville, QC, J2E 0A1
(819) 477-3222
Emp Here 100   *Sales* 7,527,200
SIC 4151 School buses
Andre Girardin
Dave Girardin
Steve Girardin

D-U-N-S 24-600-2059   (SL)
ASSURANCES JEAN-CLAUDE LECLERC INC

LECLERC ASSURANCES ET SERVICES FINANCIERS
230 Boul Saint-Joseph O, Drummondville, QC, J2E 0G3
(819) 477-3156
Emp Here 50   *Sales* 42,403,000
SIC 6411 Insurance agents, brokers, and service
Lucie Frechette
Alain Courteau
Mcglynn Randolph B.
Thomas Reid
Stephane Roussin

D-U-N-S 25-195-8419   (SL)
CORPORATION MICRO BIRD INC
GIRARDIN MINIBUS
(*Suby of* MICRO BIRD HOLDINGS, INC)
3000 Rue Girardin, Drummondville, QC, J2E 0A1
(819) 477-8222
Emp Here 250   *Sales* 72,712,500
SIC 3713 Truck and bus bodies
Steve Girardin
Dave Girardin
Phil Horlock
Mark Ashburn Terry

D-U-N-S 24-714-1948   (SL)
FERME DES VOLTIGEURS INC
ABATTOIR DES VOLTIGEURS
2350 Boul Foucault, Drummondville, QC, J2E 0E8
(819) 478-7495
Emp Here 60   *Sales* 20,741,400
SIC 2015 Poultry slaughtering and processing
Dominique Martel
Georges Martel Jr
Bernard Martel
Georges Martel
Denise Turcotte
Nathalie Martel

D-U-N-S 24-850-2593   (HQ)
GROUPE AUTOBUS GIRARDIN LTEE
4000 Rue Girardin, Drummondville, QC, J2E 0A1
(819) 477-3222
Emp Here 2   *Sales* 109,652,700
SIC 6712 Bank holding companies
Andre Girardin
Dave Girardin
Steve Girardin

D-U-N-S 25-690-4871   (HQ)
KIMPEX INC
KIMPEX ACTION
(*Suby of* SOUCY HOLDING INC)
5355 Rue Saint-Roch S Bureau 4, Drummondville, QC, J2E 0B4
(819) 472-3326
Sales 113,718,644
SIC 5561 Recreational vehicle dealers
Gilles Soucy
Stephan Soucy
Robert Hendfield
Guy Normandin
Daniel Chandonnet
Michel Cote
Frediric Lagace

D-U-N-S 24-677-0528   (HQ)
MICRO BIRD HOLDINGS, INC
3000 Rue Girardin, Drummondville, QC, J2E 0A1
(819) 477-2012
Sales 44,768,600
SIC 3713 Truck and bus bodies
Steve Girardin
Dave Girardin
Phil Horlock
Mark Ashburn Terry

D-U-N-S 24-329-8283   (BR)
SOUCY INTERNATIONAL INC
SOUCY CAOUTCHOUC
(*Suby of* SOUCY HOLDING INC)

5195 Rue Richard, Drummondville, QC, J2E 1A7
(819) 474-4522
Emp Here 100
SIC 3795 Tanks and tank components
Yannick St-Sauveur

D-U-N-S 25-091-8187   (SL)
VOLAILLES MARTEL INC, LES
FERME DES VOLTIGEURS
2350 Boul Foucault, Drummondville, QC, J2E 0E8
(819) 478-7495
Emp Here 100   *Sales* 13,675,900
SIC 0251 Broiler, fryer, and roaster chickens
Dominique Martel
Georges Jr Martel
Bernard Martel

East Angus, QC J0B

D-U-N-S 25-543-0589   (BR)
CASCADES CANADA ULC
CACADES GROUPE CARTON PLAT EAST ANGUS
(*Suby of* CASCADES INC)
248 Rue Warner, East Angus, QC, J0B 1R0
(819) 832-5300
Emp Here 95
SIC 2631 Paperboard mills
Vincent Goulet

D-U-N-S 25-481-2803   (HQ)
COMMISSION SCOLAIRE DES HAUTS-CANTONS
308 Rue Palmer, East Angus, QC, J0B 1R0
(819) 832-4953
Emp Here 10   *Sales* 109,030,900
SIC 8211 Elementary and secondary schools
Yves Gilbert
Patricia Sevigny

D-U-N-S 20-271-4432   (SL)
GRAPHIC PACKAGING INTERNATIONAL CANADA, ULC
EMBALLAGE GRAPHIC INTERNATIONAL CANADA
(*Suby of* GRAPHIC PACKAGING HOLDING COMPANY)
2 Rue Angus N, East Angus, QC, J0B 1R0
(819) 832-5300
Emp Here 250   *Sales* 91,909,250
SIC 2621 Paper mills
Stephen R. Scherger
Michael P. Doss
Normand Laporte
Lauren S. Tashma

D-U-N-S 24-067-2811   (SL)
GROUPE EPICIERS ANGUS INC
GROUPER EPICIER ANGUS
150 Rue Angus S Bureau 10, East Angus, QC, J0B 1R0
(819) 832-2449
Emp Here 49   *Sales* 13,433,448
SIC 5411 Grocery stores
Rene Couture

D-U-N-S 24-863-4065   (BR)
HOOD PACKAGING CORPORATION
SOCIETE EMBALLAGES HOOD
(*Suby of* HOOD FLEXIBLE PACKAGING CORPORATION)
15 Rue David-Swan, East Angus, QC, J0B 1R0
(819) 832-4971
Emp Here 100
SIC 2674 Bags: uncoated paper and multiwall
Michel Bedard

Eastman, QC J0E

D-U-N-S 24-548-6402   (HQ)
CENTRE DE SANTE D'EASTMAN INC
SPA EASTMAN
895 Ch Des Diligences, Eastman, QC, J0E 1P0
(450) 297-3009
Sales 11,781,750
SIC 7991 Physical fitness facilities
Jocelyna Dubuc
Gerard Marinovich
Normand Dubuc

D-U-N-S 20-542-0185   (SL)
MARCHE J P FONTAINE INC
TRADITION
382 Rue Principale, Eastman, QC, J0E 1P0
(450) 297-2815
Emp Here 45   *Sales* 12,336,840
SIC 5411 Grocery stores
Cecile Fontaine
Bruno Fontaine

Egan, QC J9E

D-U-N-S 20-207-3136   (HQ)
AMEUBLEMENT BRANCHAUD INC
BRANCHAUD - BUCKINGHAM
52 Rte 105, Egan, QC, J9E 3A9
(819) 449-2610
Emp Here 1   *Sales* 115,073,600
SIC 5021 Furniture
Louis-Arthur Branchaud
Andre Branchaud
Joel Branchaud

Esterel, QC J0T

D-U-N-S 20-333-1822   (SL)
GESTION ESTEREL INC
HOTEL EMOTION
39 Ch Fridolin-Simard, Esterel, QC, J0T 1E0
(450) 228-2662
Emp Here 100   *Sales* 9,489,900
SIC 7011 Hotels and motels
Shawn Zarbatany
Luc Desmarteau
Donald Zarbatany
Jean Beaulieu

Fabreville, QC H7C

D-U-N-S 24-294-7117   (SL)
FRARE & GALLANT LTEE
(*Suby of* 171307 CANADA INC)
5530 Rue Maurice-Cullen, Fabreville, QC, H7C 2T3
(450) 664-4590
Emp Here 40   *Sales* 16,909,480
SIC 1541 Industrial buildings and warehouses
John Frare

Fabreville, QC H7E

D-U-N-S 24-344-9357   (HQ)
9057-4245 QUEBEC INC
3980 Boul Leman, Fabreville, QC, H7E 1A1
(450) 661-6470
Sales 27,881,700
SIC 6712 Bank holding companies
Lorenzo Borsellino

D-U-N-S 20-332-4769   (SL)
9210-7556 QUEBEC INC
INTELCO

3954d Boul Leman, Fabreville, QC, H7E 1A1

Emp Here 25   *Sales* 13,013,550
SIC 5099 Durable goods, nec
Mohammed Arich

D-U-N-S 20-356-2046   (SL)
9342-7490 QUEBEC INC
TRANSPORT FORTUNA
3980 Boul Leman, Fabreville, QC, H7E 1A1
(514) 209-1750
Emp Here 80   *Sales* 1,004,052
SIC 4212 Local trucking, without storage
Oumite Satarov

D-U-N-S 25-105-2692   (HQ)
BROUE-ALLIANCE INC
1760
(*Suby of* BROUE-ALLIANCE ARTISAN INC)
3838 Boul Leman, Fabreville, QC, H7E 1A1
(450) 661-0281
Emp Here 1   *Sales* 69,138,000
SIC 2082 Malt beverages
Antoine Geloso

D-U-N-S 20-639-8476   (SL)
CONSTRUCTION GARNIER LTEE
(*Suby of* 9057-4245 QUEBEC INC)
3980 Boul Leman, Fabreville, QC, H7E 1A1
(450) 661-6470
Emp Here 200   *Sales* 50,488,400
SIC 1623 Water, sewer, and utility lines
Lorenzo Borsellino
Lorenzo Borsellino

D-U-N-S 24-760-3103   (SL)
DISTRIBUTIONS MISSUM INC
(*Suby of* GROUPE DE COURTAGE OMNI
LTEE)
3838 Boul Leman, Fabreville, QC, H7E 1A1
(450) 661-0281
Emp Here 30   *Sales* 25,067,310
SIC 5141 Groceries, general line
Aldo Geloso

D-U-N-S 24-168-4497   (SL)
GIULIANI, G INC
3970 Boul Leman, Fabreville, QC, H7E 1A1
(450) 661-6519
Emp Here 40   *Sales* 11,340,960
SIC 1611 Highway and street construction
Isabelle Giuliani

D-U-N-S 24-835-0878   (HQ)
GROUPE DE COURTAGE OMNI LTEE
GELOSO BEVERAGE GROUP
3838 Boul Leman, Fabreville, QC, H7E 1A1
(450) 661-0281
Emp Here 1   *Sales* 83,557,700
SIC 5141 Groceries, general line
Aldo Geloso

D-U-N-S 20-590-6480   (SL)
SOCIETE DE VIN INTERNATIONALE LTEE
3838 Boul Leman, Fabreville, QC, H7E 1A1
(450) 661-0281
Emp Here 70   *Sales* 41,154,120
SIC 5182 Wine and distilled beverages
Antonio Geloso
Nicolangelo Geloso

Fabreville, QC H7L

D-U-N-S 25-779-0964   (HQ)
3100-7669 QUEBEC INC
PRO KONTROL
(*Suby of* GROUPE TECHNO DESIGN BM
LTEE, LE)
1989 Rue Michelin, Fabreville, QC, H7L 5B7
(450) 973-7765
Emp Here 20   *Sales* 20,122,830
SIC 5063 Electrical apparatus and equipment
Pierre Martin
Jonathan Lessard

D-U-N-S 24-737-1404   (SL)
ATTITUDES IMPORT INC
SNOBSHOP
3025 Boul Le Corbusier, Fabreville, QC, H7L
4C3
(450) 681-4147
Emp Here 50   *Sales* 37,126,000
SIC 5199 Nondurable goods, nec
Joel Azancot

D-U-N-S 24-946-6335   (HQ)
CAPELLA TELECOMMUNICATIONS INC
2065 Rue Michelin, Fabreville, QC, H7L 5B7
(450) 686-0033
Emp Here 25   *Sales* 14,850,680
SIC 4899 Communication services, nec
Norman Joseph Slater
Roger Gilodo
Nick Hamilton-Piercy
Wayne Rabey
Edward Chislett
Charmaine Eddy-Slater

D-U-N-S 25-390-5293   (HQ)
CONCEPT JP INC
REDKEN
2089 Rue Michelin, Fabreville, QC, H7L 5B7
(800) 795-2595
Sales 23,276,274
SIC 5087 Service establishment equipment
Jean-Pierre Perron
Sebastien Perron

D-U-N-S 24-324-4951   (SL)
**DIGICO FABRICATION ELECTRONIQUE
INC**
(*Suby of* DIGICO RESEAU GLOBAL INC)
950 Rue Bergar, Fabreville, QC, H7L 5A1
(450) 967-7100
Emp Here 85   *Sales* 15,192,815
SIC 8711 Engineering services
Jacques-Etienne Cote
Michel S Cote

D-U-N-S 24-528-5838   (HQ)
DIGICO RESEAU GLOBAL INC
950 Rue Bergar, Fabreville, QC, H7L 5A1
(450) 967-7100
Sales 16,187,570
SIC 3679 Electronic components, nec
Michel Cote
Jacques-Etienne Cote

D-U-N-S 24-458-5295   (HQ)
FABORY CANADA INC
ATTACHES METRICAN
1220 Rue Michelin, Fabreville, QC, H7L 4R3
(450) 629-6900
Emp Here 50   *Sales* 35,773,920
SIC 5072 Hardware
Sylvain Methot
Michael Setlock
Oswald Van Den Belt

D-U-N-S 20-257-2988   (SL)
**GROUPE PAQUETTE MECANIQUE DU BA-
TIMENT INC**
F. PAQUETTE & FILS
(*Suby of* 3562468 CANADA INC)
275 Boul Marc-Aurele-Fortin, Fabreville, QC,
H7L 2A2
(450) 625-2297
Emp Here 100   *Sales* 23,306,500
SIC 1711 Plumbing, heating, air-conditioning
Jean-Francois Paquette
Dominic Paquette
Dannie Clavel
Martin Gregoire

D-U-N-S 25-380-8463   (SL)
INCOSPEC COMMUNICATIONS INC
CANAVISION
(*Suby of* CAPELLA TELECOMMUNICA-
TIONS INC)
2065 Rue Michelin, Fabreville, QC, H7L 5B7
(450) 686-0033
Emp Here 26   *Sales* 11,626,524

SIC 5063 Electrical apparatus and equipment
Louis Sebastiani

D-U-N-S 20-225-4418   (SL)
REDKEN CONCEPT J P INC
2089 Rue Michelin, Fabreville, QC, H7L 5B7
(450) 687-2595
Emp Here 30   *Sales* 33,160,350
SIC 5122 Drugs, proprietaries, and sundries
Jean-Pierre Perron
Sebastien Perron

D-U-N-S 24-362-4470   (BR)
ROYAL GROUP, INC
*PROFILES POUR PORTES ET FENETRES
ROYAL*
(*Suby of* WESTLAKE CHEMICAL CORPO-
RATION)
3035 Boul Le Corbusier Bureau 7, Fabreville,
QC, H7L 4C3
(450) 687-5115
Emp Here 160
SIC 3431 Metal sanitary ware
Josee Lacroix

D-U-N-S 20-309-6375   (SL)
THERMOPLAST INC
3035 Boul Le Corbusier Bureau 7, Fabreville,
QC, H7L 4C3
(450) 687-5115
Emp Here 100   *Sales* 22,200,100
SIC 3544 Special dies, tools, jigs, and fixtures
Pierre Grandmaison
Denis Lacasse
Jean-Guy Belair
Nathalie Tremblay

Fabreville, QC H7P

D-U-N-S 20-331-5338   (SL)
9341-6246 QUEBEC INC
SUPERCLUB VIDEOTRON
523 Boul Cure-Labelle, Fabreville, QC, H7P
2P5
(450) 628-9901
Emp Here 28   *Sales* 14,575,176
SIC 5092 Toys and hobby goods and supplies
Marc Vallieres
Mathieu Hebert Vallieres
Caroline D'auteuil
Helne Hebert

D-U-N-S 20-513-6158   (SL)
GESTION GUY L'HEUREUX INC
CANADIAN TIRE 690
544 Boul Cure-Labelle Bureau 690, Fabreville,
QC, H7P 2P4
(450) 963-8686
Emp Here 70   *Sales* 44,049,600
SIC 5531 Auto and home supply stores
Guy L'heureux

D-U-N-S 24-815-0765   (HQ)
RESTAURANTS DUMAS LTEE, LES
RESTAURANT MCDONALDS
410 Boul Cure-Labelle, Fabreville, QC, H7P
2P1
(450) 628-0171
Emp Here 20   *Sales* 11,659,750
SIC 5812 Eating places
Robert Dumas

Farnham, QC J2N

D-U-N-S 24-322-1889   (SL)
9067-3385 QUEBEC INC
190 Rue Comeau, Farnham, QC, J2N 2N4
(450) 293-3106
Emp Here 200   *Sales* 69,138,000
SIC 2011 Meat packing plants
Claude Robitaille

D-U-N-S 24-337-2401   (BR)
**CENTRE DE SANTE ET DE SERVICES SO-
CIAUX LA POMMERAIE**
FOYER FARNHAM
800 Rue Saint-Paul, Farnham, QC, J2N 2K6
(450) 293-3167
Emp Here 90
SIC 8361 Residential care
Monique Boubonais

D-U-N-S 25-684-4606   (BR)
COMPAGNIE BEAULIEU CANADA
(*Suby of* BEAULIEU HOLDINGS OF
CANADA, INC.)
1144 Boul Magenta E, Farnham, QC, J2N 1C1

Emp Here 300
SIC 2273 Carpets and rugs
Serge Marceau

D-U-N-S 24-788-8894   (HQ)
DIONDE INC
1660 Boul Industriel, Farnham, QC, J2N 2X8
(450) 293-3909
Sales 24,601,500
SIC 6719 Holding companies, nec
Sylvain Dion
Patrick Dion

D-U-N-S 20-886-0247   (SL)
HARBOUR INDUSTRIES (CANADA) LTD
(*Suby of* BERKSHIRE HATHAWAY INC.)
1365 Boul Industriel, Farnham, QC, J2N 2X3
(450) 293-5304
Emp Here 58   *Sales* 10,520,504
SIC 3315 Steel wire and related products
Yannick Demers
Marc Longpre
Patricia E. Charles

D-U-N-S 20-370-9399   (SL)
**MANUFACTURIERS   D'ACCESSOIRES
MORTUAIRES LTEE**
211 Rue Berard, Farnham, QC, J2N 2L4
(450) 293-1712
Emp Here 25   *Sales* 11,179,350
SIC 5072 Hardware
Andrew Wanka

D-U-N-S 25-814-4401   (SL)
MARCHE LAPLANTE FARNHAM INC
IGA
999 Rue Principale E, Farnham, QC, J2N 1M9
(450) 293-4210
Emp Here 49   *Sales* 13,433,448
SIC 5411 Grocery stores
Ugo Gazaille

D-U-N-S 20-726-5331   (HQ)
MEUBLES DENIS RIEL INC
CLUB MEUBLES AVANTAGES
1555 Boul Industriel, Farnham, QC, J2N 2X3
(450) 293-3605
Emp Here 26   *Sales* 11,620,150
SIC 5712 Furniture stores
Denis Riel
Jean-Francois Riel
Marie-Claude Riel
Claire Riel

D-U-N-S 20-547-5473   (HQ)
TARKETT INC
AZROCK
(*Suby of* SOCIETE INVESTISSEMENT DE-
CONINCK)
1001 Rue Yamaska E, Farnham, QC, J2N 1J7
(450) 293-3173
Emp Here 230   *Sales* 1,067,148,000
SIC 2851 Paints and allied products
Andrewf Bonham
Souha Azar
Raphael Bauer
Nicolas Carre

Fassett, QC J0V

D-U-N-S 20-689-6412   (SL)
BOIS FRANCS D.V. INC, LES
131 Rue Principale, Fassett, QC, J0V 1H0
(819) 423-2338
Emp Here 30   *Sales* 68,508,810
SIC 5031 Lumber, plywood, and millwork
  Viateur Girard
  David Lauzon

Ferland-Et-Boilleau, QC G0V

D-U-N-S 20-949-5274   (SL)
COOPERATIVE FORESTIERE DE FERLAND-BOILLEAU
445 381 Rte, Ferland-Et-Boilleau, QC, G0V 1H0
(418) 676-2626
Emp Here 115   *Sales* 22,122,550
SIC 2411 Logging
  Jimmy Gagnon
  Remi Thibeault
  Luc Simard
  Gerard Poulin
  Marcus Ouellette
  Daniel Gagnon

Ferme-Neuve, QC J0W

D-U-N-S 24-355-3492   (SL)
ENTREPRISES JEAN-MAURICE PAPINEAU LTEE, LES
14 309 Rte N Bureau 100, Ferme-Neuve, QC, J0W 1C0
(819) 587-3360
Emp Here 50   *Sales* 10,580,650
SIC 0851 Forestry services
  Jean-Maurice Papineau
  Francine Meilleur

D-U-N-S 20-030-2078   (HQ)
GROUPE PICHE CONSTRUCTION INC
99 12e Rue Bureau 204, Ferme-Neuve, QC, J0W 1C0
(819) 587-3193
Emp Here 20   *Sales* 85,550,700
SIC 1542 Nonresidential construction, nec
  Yan Piche
  Yourik Piche
  Janick Piche

Fermont, QC G0G

D-U-N-S 24-146-9485   (SL)
COOPERATIVE DES CONSOMMATEURS DE FERMONT
299 Le Carrefour, Fermont, QC, G0G 1J0

Emp Here 55   *Sales* 15,078,360
SIC 5411 Grocery stores
  Claude Meilleur
  Robin Plante
  Patrick Savard

D-U-N-S 24-884-8822   (HQ)
CSSS DE L'HEMATITE
1 Rue Alexandre, Fermont, QC, G0G 1J0
(418) 287-5461
Emp Here 2   *Sales* 12,851,680
SIC 8011 Offices and clinics of medical doctors
  Normand Ducharme
  Robert Mousseau

D-U-N-S 20-318-1219   (SL)
LOCATION MONTFE
7 Rue Du Camp, Fermont, QC, G0G 1J0

(418) 287-9402
Emp Here 25   *Sales* 11,179,350
SIC 5046 Commercial equipment, nec
  Jason Rioux

D-U-N-S 20-386-8356   (BR)
MINERAI DE FER QUEBEC INC
(*Suby of* CHAMPION IRON LIMITED)
556 Rte 389, Fermont, QC, G0G 1J0
(418) 287-2000
Emp Here 500
SIC 1011 Iron ores

Fort-Coulonge, QC J0X

D-U-N-S 24-530-7082   (SL)
HABITAT METIS DU NORD INC
213 Rue Herault, Fort-Coulonge, QC, J0X 1V0
(819) 683-1344
Emp Here 49   *Sales* 16,029,223
SIC 6531 Real estate agents and managers
  Monique Bouchard

Franklin, QC J0S

D-U-N-S 24-254-8956   (SL)
VERGERS LEAHY INC
VERGERS LEAHY, LES
1772 Rte 209, Franklin, QC, J0S 1E0
(450) 827-2544
Emp Here 210   *Sales* 35,495,250
SIC 0175 Deciduous tree fruits
  James R. Leahy
  Michael Leahy

Frelighsburg, QC J0J

D-U-N-S 24-619-7131   (SL)
MAISON DE LA POMME DE FRELIGHSBURG INC
CARON
32 Rte 237 N, Frelighsburg, QC, J0J 1C0
(450) 298-5275
Emp Here 50   *Sales* 14,673,850
SIC 5431 Fruit and vegetable markets
  Real Caron
  Benoit Caron
  Jonathan Rodrigue
  Monia Caron
  Francois Jobin
  Etienne Caron
  Michel Roy
  Jean-Marc Rochon

Gaspe, QC G4X

D-U-N-S 24-097-6501   (BR)
CENTRE READAPTATION DE GASPESIE
150 Rue Mgr-Ross Bureau 550, Gaspe, QC, G4X 2R8
(418) 368-2306
Emp Here 200
SIC 8093 Specialty outpatient clinics, nec
  Nadine Francoeur

D-U-N-S 24-149-7197   (HQ)
COLLEGE D'ENSEIGNEMENT GENERALE & PROFESSIONNEL DE LA GASPESIE & DES ILES
CEGEP DE GASPE
96 Rue Jacques-Cartier, Gaspe, QC, G4X 2S8
(418) 368-2201
Sales 74,695,500
SIC 8221 Colleges and universities

  Roland Auger

D-U-N-S 25-974-6220   (SL)
COURONNES PLUS.COM INC, LES
9 Rue Des Cerisiers, Gaspe, QC, G4X 2M1
(418) 368-3670
Emp Here 160   *Sales* 52,181,760
SIC 3999 Manufacturing industries, nec
  Bruce Jones
  Brent Jones

D-U-N-S 24-203-3744   (HQ)
LA CREVETTE DU NORD ATLANTIQUE INC
139 Rue De La Reine, Gaspe, QC, G4X 1T5
(418) 368-1414
Emp Here 4   *Sales* 48,396,600
SIC 2092 Fresh or frozen packaged fish
  Gaetan Denis
  Martin Lapierre

D-U-N-S 24-423-4642   (HQ)
MENU-MER LTEE
153 Boul Renard E, Gaspe, QC, G4X 5K9
(418) 269-7714
Emp Here 6   *Sales* 25,067,310
SIC 5146 Fish and seafoods
  Jean-Yves Dumaresq
  Eric Gagne
  Tony Denis

D-U-N-S 24-327-1751   (SL)
PALES D'EOLIENNE LM (CANADA) INC
(*Suby of* GENERAL ELECTRIC COMPANY)
7 Rue Des Cerisiers, Gaspe, QC, G4X 2M1
(418) 361-3486
Emp Here 250   *Sales* 70,219,250
SIC 3523 Farm machinery and equipment
  Rodrigo Torres
  Soren Hoffer
  Alexander Boulay
  Rhonda Stewart
  Marcus Johannes Cornelis De Jong

D-U-N-S 24-942-3856   (HQ)
PECHERIES MARINARD LTEE, LES
MARINARD BIOTECH
41 Rue De L'Entrepot, Gaspe, QC, G4X 5L3
(418) 269-3381
Sales 121,846,250
SIC 2092 Fresh or frozen packaged fish
  Darrell Roche
  Pascal Noel
  Peter Buhl
  Craig Walker
  Yves Bond
  Roch Lelievre
  O'neil Bond

D-U-N-S 24-207-3641   (SL)
PHARMACIEN MARTIN GAGNON INC
ESTPHARM
39 Montee De Sandy Beach Bureau 31, Gaspe, QC, G4X 2A9
(418) 368-3341
Emp Here 70   *Sales* 17,102,960
SIC 5912 Drug stores and proprietary stores
  Martin Gagnon
  Desneiges Plourde
  Jacques Gagnon

D-U-N-S 24-893-2027   (SL)
PRODUITS SANITAIRES CLOUTIER INC
11 Boul De Gaspe, Gaspe, QC, G4X 1A1
(418) 368-7376
Emp Here 26   *Sales* 19,208,899
SIC 5169 Chemicals and allied products, nec
  Coulombe Pierrot

D-U-N-S 25-514-4818   (SL)
RES-MAR
478 Montee De Wakeham, Gaspe, QC, G4X 1Y6
(418) 368-5373
Emp Here 63   *Sales* 28,300,797
SIC 7389 Business services, nec
  Rene Landry

D-U-N-S 20-198-0026   (SL)

SIMPSON AUTOMOBILES INC
112 Boul De Gaspe, Gaspe, QC, G4X 1A9
(800) 368-2279
Emp Here 25   *Sales* 12,451,950
SIC 5511 New and used car dealers
  Brenta. Simpson
  Courtneya Simpson

Gatineau, QC J8L

D-U-N-S 24-481-9116   (SL)
AUTOBUS DU VILLAGE INC, LES
(*Suby of* TRANSPORT SCOLAIRE SO-GESCO INC)
65 Rue Thibault, Gatineau, QC, J8L 3Z1
(819) 281-9235
Emp Here 80   *Sales* 6,021,760
SIC 4151 School buses
  Robert Brazeau
  Dave Girardin
  Mario Provost

D-U-N-S 24-436-0715   (SL)
CARLE FORD INC
901 Rue Dollard, Gatineau, QC, J8L 3T4
(819) 986-3000
Emp Here 63   *Sales* 39,644,640
SIC 5511 New and used car dealers
  Louis Carle

D-U-N-S 25-495-0009   (HQ)
COMMISSION SCOLAIRE AU COEUR DES VALLEES
582 Rue Maclaren E, Gatineau, QC, J8L 2W2
(819) 986-8511
Emp Here 32   *Sales* 102,984,641
SIC 8211 Elementary and secondary schools
  Eric Antoine

D-U-N-S 24-436-7751   (SL)
PIERRE ET MAURICE DE LA FONTAINE INC
1000 Rue Dollard, Gatineau, QC, J8L 3H3
(819) 986-8601
Emp Here 40   *Sales* 17,886,960
SIC 5031 Lumber, plywood, and millwork
  Pierre Begin
  Benoit Laurent Roy
  Richard De La Fontaine

D-U-N-S 24-728-5161   (BR)
PROVIGO DISTRIBUTION INC
PROVIGO
(*Suby of* LOBLAW COMPANIES LIMITED)
130 Av Lepine, Gatineau, QC, J8L 4M4
(819) 281-5232
Emp Here 90
SIC 5411 Grocery stores
  Mario Dupuis

D-U-N-S 20-290-7994   (BR)
SUPERIOR GENERAL PARTNER INC
(*Suby of* SUPERIOR PLUS CORP)
101 Ch Donaldson, Gatineau, QC, J8L 3X3
(819) 986-1135
Emp Here 90
SIC 5169 Chemicals and allied products, nec
  Lynn Raymond

D-U-N-S 24-344-0471   (BR)
SUPERIOR PLUS LP
ERCO MONDIAL
(*Suby of* SUPERIOR PLUS CORP)
101 Ch Donaldson, Gatineau, QC, J8L 3X3
(819) 986-1135
Emp Here 75
SIC 2819 Industrial inorganic chemicals, nec
  Lyne Rmolne

D-U-N-S 24-518-6585   (SL)
SYNDICAT DES PROFESSIONNELLES DE LA SANTE DU RESEAU PAPNEAU, SPSRP-FIQ
CSSS PAPINEAU

617 Av De Buckingham, Gatineau, QC, J8L 2H4
(819) 986-3359
Emp Here 250   *Sales* 27,770,000
SIC 8062 General medical and surgical hospitals
 Stephane Bertrand
 Michael Potvin

Gatineau, QC J8M

D-U-N-S 20-109-1164   (SL)
11084836 CANADA INC.
BUCKINGHAM TOYOTA
1205 Rue Odile-Daoust, Gatineau, QC, J8M 1Y7
(819) 986-2224
Emp Here 26   *Sales* 12,950,028
SIC 5511 New and used car dealers
 Michel Kadri
 Assaad Dargham

D-U-N-S 24-393-4804   (HQ)
3120772 NOVA SCOTIA COMPANY
(*Suby of* WB ASSOCIES S.E.C.)
2 Ch De Montreal E, Gatineau, QC, J8M 1E9
(819) 986-4300
Sales 80,880,140
SIC 2621 Paper mills
 Tim Butler
 Michel Masse

D-U-N-S 20-322-9448   (SL)
7531877 CANADA LTEE
BUCKINGHAM CHRYSLER JEEP DODGE
1265 Rue Odile-Daoust, Gatineau, QC, J8M 1Y7
(819) 281-7788
Emp Here 24   *Sales* 11,953,872
SIC 5511 New and used car dealers
 Assaad Dargham

D-U-N-S 25-192-7042   (SL)
7618280 CANADA INC
DUPONT & DUPONT HONDA
1255 Rue Odile-Daoust, Gatineau, QC, J8M 1Y7
(819) 281-1110
Emp Here 25   *Sales* 12,451,950
SIC 5511 New and used car dealers
 Pascal Dupont

D-U-N-S 20-852-2594   (SL)
9084-4622 QUEBEC INC
IGA DE COTRET-BRAZEAU
1205 Rue De Neuville, Gatineau, QC, J8M 2E7
(819) 986-7579
Emp Here 49   *Sales* 13,433,448
SIC 5411 Grocery stores
 Reine-Aimee De Cotret

D-U-N-S 20-890-0167   (SL)
AUTOMOBILES BAURORE 2000 LTEE, LES
975 Ch De Masson, Gatineau, QC, J8M 1R4
(819) 986-6714
Emp Here 42   *Sales* 20,919,276
SIC 5511 New and used car dealers
 Denis Bedard
 Andre Bedard
 Andreeline Bedard

D-U-N-S 20-314-3326   (SL)
SOCIETE EN COMMANDITE PAPIER MASSON WB
SEC PAPIER MASSON WB
2 Ch De Montreal E, Gatineau, QC, J8M 1E9
(819) 986-4300
Emp Here 100   *Sales* 19,476,800
SIC 2621 Paper mills
 Carol Tremblay

D-U-N-S 20-188-6264   (HQ)
THEO MINEAULT INC
2135 Ch De Montreal O, Gatineau, QC, J8M

1P3
(819) 986-3190
Emp Here 55   *Sales* 11,542,200
SIC 2431 Millwork
 Michel Mineault
 Alain Mineault
 Nicolas Mineault
 Denis Mineault

Gatineau, QC J8P

D-U-N-S 20-506-9719   (SL)
120033 CANADA INC
HUILES A CHAUFFAGE RAYMOND, LES
581 Boul Saint-Ren? E, Gatineau, QC, J8P 8A6
(819) 663-5868
Emp Here 30   *Sales* 14,070,150
SIC 5983 Fuel oil dealers
 Raymond Sigouin
 Helene Sigouin
 Luc Sigouin
 Philippe Sigouin
 Claude Sigouin
 Marc Sigouin
 Christine Sigouin

D-U-N-S 24-102-0403   (SL)
ASSOCIATION DES RESIDENTS ET RESIDENTES DU CENTRE D'ACCEUIL DE GATINEAU, L'
CHSLD DE GATINEAU - MAISON BON SEJOUR
134 Rue Jean-Rene-Monette, Gatineau, QC, J8P 7C3
(819) 966-6450
Emp Here 150   *Sales* 9,642,300
SIC 8361 Residential care
 Helene Beauchamp
 Claudette Lepage

D-U-N-S 20-192-1009   (BR)
CIMA+ S.E.N.C.
(*Suby of* CIMA+ S.E.N.C.)
420 Boul Maloney E Bureau 201, Gatineau, QC, J8P 7N8
(819) 663-9294
Emp Here 160
SIC 8711 Engineering services
 Bernard Boileau

D-U-N-S 25-233-5443   (BR)
COMMISSION SCOLAIRE DES DRAVEURS
POLYVALENTE NICHOLAS GATINEAU
360 Boul La Verendrye E, Gatineau, QC, J8P 6K7
(819) 663-9241
Emp Here 200
SIC 8211 Elementary and secondary schools
 Claude Beaulieu

D-U-N-S 24-847-5308   (SL)
EXPERTISES SCM LES
510 Boul Maloney E Bureau 104, Gatineau, QC, J8P 1E7
(819) 663-6068
Emp Here 49   *Sales* 42,036,225
SIC 6411 Insurance agents, brokers, and service
 Larry A Shumka

D-U-N-S 25-171-5645   (BR)
HOME DEPOT OF CANADA INC
HOME DEPOT
(*Suby of* THE HOME DEPOT INC)
243 Montee Paiement, Gatineau, QC, J8P 6M7
(819) 246-4060
Emp Here 150
SIC 5231 Paint, glass, and wallpaper stores
 Daniel Pronovost

D-U-N-S 25-483-3007   (SL)
INTEGRATION RE SOURCE
ENTREPRISE ADAPTEE D'ECONOMIE SO-

CIALE ET ORGANISME A BUT NON LUCRATIF
312 Rue Saint-Louis, Gatineau, QC, J8P 8B3
(819) 770-2018
Emp Here 100   *Sales* 7,679,200
SIC 8322 Individual and family services
 Robert P. Racicot
 Jaime Paz
 Pierre Giroux
 Aurele Desjardins
 Sylvain Laflamme
 Marleen Tasse
 Louise Boudrias
 Caroline Charette

D-U-N-S 20-253-9433   (SL)
MARCHE KELLY MALONEY INC
910 Boul Maloney E, Gatineau, QC, J8P 1H5
(819) 643-2353
Emp Here 50   *Sales* 29,347,700
SIC 5411 Grocery stores
 Stephane Kelly

D-U-N-S 24-347-7598   (BR)
MARCHE LEBLANC MONTEE PAIEMENT INC
METRO PLUS
435 Montee Paiement, Gatineau, QC, J8P 0B1
(819) 561-5478
Emp Here 150
SIC 5411 Grocery stores
 Denis Ladouceur

D-U-N-S 20-422-4950   (HQ)
MATERIAUX BONHOMME INC
SHOP, LA
(*Suby of* ENTREPRISES P. BONHOMME LTEE, LES)
225 Montee Paiement, Gatineau, QC, J8P 6M7
(819) 561-5577
Emp Here 4   *Sales* 26,765,200
SIC 5211 Lumber and other building materials
 Gilles Bonhomme
 Paul Bonhomme
 Michel Charest
 Donald Marcil

D-U-N-S 24-254-6062   (BR)
PF RESOLU CANADA INC
(*Suby of* RESOLUTE FOREST PRODUCTS INC)
79 Rue Main, Gatineau, QC, J8P 4X6
(819) 643-7500
Emp Here 113
SIC 4911 Electric services

D-U-N-S 20-026-8988   (SL)
PLASTIVAL INC
MATERIAUX RE-SOURCE
312 Rue Saint-Louis, Gatineau, QC, J8P 8B3
(819) 770-2018
Emp Here 49   *Sales* 35,786,905
SIC 5162 Plastics materials and basic shapes
 Robert Riley

Gatineau, QC J8R

D-U-N-S 20-871-7392   (SL)
169727 CANADA INC
IGA EXTRA MONTEE PAIEMENT
720 Montee Paiement Bureau 100, Gatineau, QC, J8R 4A3
(819) 643-4233
Emp Here 150   *Sales* 44,021,550
SIC 5411 Grocery stores
 Christian St-Jacques

D-U-N-S 20-184-4292   (BR)
2104225 ONTARIO LTD
WESTON BAKERIES LIMITED
(*Suby of* GEORGE WESTON LIMITED)
255 Ch Industriel, Gatineau, QC, J8R 3V8

(819) 669-7246
Emp Here 81
SIC 5461 Retail bakeries
 Dave Lamoche

D-U-N-S 24-813-5667   (BR)
ALIMENTS MARTEL INC
ALI-PRET
(*Suby of* GRUPO BIMBO, S.A.B. DE C.V.)
212 Boul De L'Aeroport, Gatineau, QC, J8R 3X3
(819) 663-0835
Emp Here 200
SIC 5963 Direct selling establishments
 Serge Martel

D-U-N-S 24-383-8026   (HQ)
COOPERATIVE DES PARAMEDICS DE L'OUTAOUAIS
AMBULANCES DE LA GATINEAU, LES
505 Boul Des Affaires, Gatineau, QC, J8R 0B2
(819) 643-5005
Sales 17,011,472
SIC 4119 Local passenger transportation, nec
 Alain Gaureau
 Jonathan Cimon
 Martin Pesant
 Miles Schoenfeldt
 Marie-Ve Tremblay
 Alexandre Perreault-Nadon
 Paul Levesque
 Manon Besner
 Dominique Nadon

D-U-N-S 20-593-0428   (SL)
ENCAN OUTAOUAIS LAURENTIDES
655 Ch Industriel, Gatineau, QC, J8R 3M1
(819) 669-5775
Emp Here 10   *Sales* 12,103,970
SIC 5154 Livestock
 Andre Dumouchel

D-U-N-S 25-167-5583   (HQ)
GLATFELTER GATINEAU LTEE
1680 Rue Atmec, Gatineau, QC, J8R 7G7
(819) 669-8100
Sales 115,805,655
SIC 2621 Paper mills
 Christopher W. Astley
 Samuel Hillard
 Jill L. Urey
 Paul G. Wolfram
 Amy R. Wannemacher
 Patricia Sargeant

D-U-N-S 20-716-0958   (BR)
LOISELLE INC
EXCAVATION LOISELLE INC
(*Suby of* LOISELLE INC)
1679 Rue Jean-Louis-Malette, Gatineau, QC, J8R 0C1

Emp Here 150
SIC 1794 Excavation work
 Paul Beleuse

D-U-N-S 25-047-8125   (BR)
TRICENTRIS - TRI, TRANSFORMATION, SENSIBILISATION
TRICENTRIS
(*Suby of* TRICENTRIS - TRI, TRANSFORMATION, SENSIBILISATION)
45 Rue Pierre-Menard, Gatineau, QC, J8R 3X3
(819) 643-4448
Emp Here 75
SIC 5084 Industrial machinery and equipment
 Michel Smith

Gatineau, QC J8T

D-U-N-S 24-713-9603   (SL)
139670 CANADA LTEE
ROTISSERIES ST-HUBERT
1885 Rue Saint-Louis Bureau 100, Gatineau,

QC, J8T 6G4
(819) 568-1723
Emp Here 200   *Sales* 9,103,800
SIC 5812 Eating places
Pierre Heafey

D-U-N-S 20-577-2619   (SL)
177786 CANADA INC
TOYOTA GATINEAU
850 Boul Maloney O, Gatineau, QC, J8T 3R6
(819) 568-0066
Emp Here 80   *Sales* 50,342,400
SIC 5511 New and used car dealers
Normand Poirier
Guylaine Lapointe
Jeffrey Nicolas Montmigny
Charles Williams Montmigny

D-U-N-S 24-836-6668   (SL)
2531-7504 QUEBEC INC
850 Boul Maloney O, Gatineau, QC, J8T 3R6
(819) 568-0066
Emp Here 80   *Sales* 50,342,400
SIC 5511 New and used car dealers
Normand Poirier

D-U-N-S 24-205-0024   (SL)
2734-7681 QUEBEC INC
SOUS LE COUVERT DES ARBRES
850 Boul Maloney O, Gatineau, QC, J8T 3R6
(819) 568-0066
Emp Here 80   *Sales* 50,342,400
SIC 5511 New and used car dealers
Normand Poirier

D-U-N-S 25-973-7666   (SL)
3248224 CANADA INC
GATINEAU HONDA
1255 Boul La Verendrye O, Gatineau, QC, J8T 8K2
(819) 568-4646
Emp Here 25   *Sales* 12,451,950
SIC 5511 New and used car dealers
Pierre Grenier
Rene Dupont

D-U-N-S 20-217-2420   (SL)
3617581 CANADA INC
PROMENADE KIA
346 Boul Greber, Gatineau, QC, J8T 5R6
(819) 561-6669
Emp Here 25   *Sales* 12,451,950
SIC 5511 New and used car dealers
Vladimir Toylstoy

D-U-N-S 20-298-6261   (SL)
4544391 CANADA INC
GATINEAU NISSAN
1299 Boul La Verendrye O, Gatineau, QC, J8T 8K2
(819) 243-5454
Emp Here 32   *Sales* 15,938,496
SIC 5511 New and used car dealers
Nader Dormani

D-U-N-S 24-181-0261   (SL)
6368425 CANADA LTD
ACIER DM
47 Rue Le Baron, Gatineau, QC, J8T 4C3

Emp Here 10   *Sales* 10,003,390
SIC 5051 Metals service centers and offices
Danny Poirier

D-U-N-S 24-256-0733   (SL)
9095-1302 QUEBEC INC
CITE-JARDIN
(*Suby of* CHARTWELL MASTER CARE LP)
60 Rue De La Futaie Bureau 512, Gatineau, QC, J8T 8P5
(819) 568-2355
Emp Here 45   *Sales* 10,480,995
SIC 6513 Apartment building operators
Stephen A. Suske
Lucie St-Jacques

D-U-N-S 24-958-9920   (SL)
964211 ONTARIO LTD

MARCHE FRAIS DE GATINEAU
215 Rue Bellehumeur, Gatineau, QC, J8T 8H3

Emp Here 50   *Sales* 13,707,600
SIC 5431 Fruit and vegetable markets
Jean Luc Brazeau

D-U-N-S 25-981-3541   (SL)
ALIMENTATION FRANCIS LAMONTAGNE INC
METRO DES PROMENADES
1100 Boul Maloney O, Gatineau, QC, J8T 6G3

Emp Here 40   *Sales* 10,966,080
SIC 5411 Grocery stores
Francis Lamontagne

D-U-N-S 24-391-6579   (SL)
ALIMENTATIONS BECHAR INC
FAMILLE CHARLES IGA
455 Boul Greber, Gatineau, QC, J8T 5T7
(819) 243-0011
Emp Here 100   *Sales* 29,347,700
SIC 5411 Grocery stores
Emile Charles
Pierre Charles
Paulette Charles
Christine Charles

D-U-N-S 24-471-2217   (SL)
ATMOSPHERE
1100 Boul Maloney O, Gatineau, QC, J8T 6G3
(819) 243-3711
Emp Here 49   *Sales* 10,842,377
SIC 5941 Sporting goods and bicycle shops
Tierre Champagne

D-U-N-S 25-974-4555   (SL)
BARETTE BERNARD - ENERFLAMME INC
BARETTE BERNARD
36 Rue De Varennes Bureau 1, Gatineau, QC, J8T 0B6
(819) 243-0143
Emp Here 56   *Sales* 13,051,640
SIC 1711 Plumbing, heating, air-conditioning
Marc Racine
Eric Jomphe
Christian Vanasse
Marc Gauthier

D-U-N-S 20-921-1965   (SL)
BARETTE BERNARD - ENERFLAMME INC
37 Rue De Valcourt, Gatineau, QC, J8T 8G9
(819) 243-0143
Emp Here 49   *Sales* 20,581,869
SIC 4961 Steam and air-conditioning supply

D-U-N-S 25-080-4820   (BR)
BENSON GROUP INC
BENSON AUTO PARTS
95 Boul Greber, Gatineau, QC, J8T 3P9
(819) 669-6555
Emp Here 80
SIC 5013 Motor vehicle supplies and new parts
Josee Boucher Boucher

D-U-N-S 24-433-6681   (SL)
BROOKFIELD BRP CANADA CORP
ENTREPRISE BROOKFIELD BRP CANADA
480 Boul De La Cite Bureau 200, Gatineau, QC, J8T 8R3
(819) 561-2722
Emp Here 50   *Sales* 13,077,650
SIC 6712 Bank holding companies
Thomas Deedy
Walter Di Cesare
Dan Benoit
Bernard Cardinal
Micheline Duquette

D-U-N-S 25-974-1502   (HQ)
CENTRE DE SANTE ET DE SERVICES SO-CIAUX DE GATINEAU
(*Suby of* GOUVERNEMENT DE LA PROVINCE DE QUEBEC)
85 Rue Bellehumeur Bureau 301, Gatineau, QC, J8T 8B7

(819) 966-6016
Sales 222,160,000
SIC 8062 General medical and surgical hospitals
Louise Poirier
Charles Saucier
Roger Paradis
Sophie Lemaire
Alain Brisson
Gilles Fleury
Jean Bernier
Denis Demers
Marie-Andree Pelletier
Michele Lafontaine

D-U-N-S 25-233-5484   (BR)
COMMISSION SCOLAIRE DES DRAVEURS
ECOLE DU NOUVEAU MONDE
9 Rue Sainte-Yvonne Bureau 253, Gatineau, QC, J8T 1X6
(819) 568-0233
Emp Here 90
SIC 8211 Elementary and secondary schools
Lyne Normand

D-U-N-S 25-025-9272   (SL)
COOPERATIVE D'HABITATION LE TRAIT D'UNION DE GATINEAU
29 Rue D'Orleans Bureau 101, Gatineau, QC, J8T 5T9
(819) 561-9702
Emp Here 47   *Sales* 11,215,187
SIC 6514 Dwelling operators, except apartments
Elizabeth Bergeron
Annie Castonguay

D-U-N-S 24-354-8885   (BR)
COSTCO WHOLESALE CANADA LTD
COSTCO WHOLESALE
(*Suby of* COSTCO WHOLESALE CORPORATION)
1100 Boul Maloney O Bureau 542, Gatineau, QC, J8T 6G3
(819) 246-4005
Emp Here 400
SIC 5099 Durable goods, nec
Eric Desjardins

D-U-N-S 25-785-2355   (SL)
DILAWRI CHEVROLET BUICK GMC INC
868 Boul Maloney O, Gatineau, QC, J8T 3R6
(819) 568-5811
Emp Here 26   *Sales* 12,950,028
SIC 5511 New and used car dealers
Pawan Dilawri

D-U-N-S 20-559-3580   (BR)
ENTREPRISES JACQUES CARIGNAN LTEE, LES
CANADIAN TIRE
700 Boul Maloney O, Gatineau, QC, J8T 8K7
(819) 246-1234
Emp Here 125   *Sales* 25,667,875
SIC 5311 Department stores
Jacques Carignan
Rita Carignan

D-U-N-S 20-509-8226   (BR)
GOUVERNEMENT DE LA PROVINCE DE QUEBEC
AGENCE DE REVENU DU CANADA
(*Suby of* GOUVERNEMENT DE LA PROVINCE DE QUEBEC)
1100 Boul Maloney O Bureau 1600, Gatineau, QC, J8T 6G3
(819) 994-7739
Emp Here 110
SIC 7389 Business services, nec
Line Grondin

D-U-N-S 24-871-4396   (BR)
GROUPE BMTC INC
BRAULT & MARTINEAU
(*Suby of* BELANGER, A. (DETAIL) LTEE)
500 Boul De La Gappe, Gatineau, QC, J8T 8A8

(819) 561-5007
Emp Here 80
SIC 5712 Furniture stores
Marcel Dagenais

D-U-N-S 24-393-1909   (BR)
GROUPE DE SECURITE GARDA INC, LE
GARDA SECURITE
(*Suby of* GW INTERMEDIATE HOLDCO CORPORATION)
25 Rue De Villebois, Gatineau, QC, J8T 8J7
(819) 770-9438
Emp Here 250
SIC 7381 Detective and armored car services
Eric Simard

D-U-N-S 25-773-8526   (BR)
HUDSON'S BAY COMPANY
(*Suby of* HUDSON'S BAY COMPANY)
1100 Boul Maloney O, Gatineau, QC, J8T 6G3
(819) 243-7036
Emp Here 200
SIC 5311 Department stores
Karen Inshaw

D-U-N-S 24-988-5658   (SL)
INOVACO LTEE
RONA L'ENTREPOT GATINEAU
777 Boul De La Cite, Gatineau, QC, J8T 8J9
(819) 568-3400
Emp Here 250   *Sales* 70,262,500
SIC 5211 Lumber and other building materials
Martin Lacasse
Andre Lacasse

D-U-N-S 25-977-7944   (SL)
KOLLBEC GATINEAU CHRYSLER JEEP INC
812 Boul Maloney O, Gatineau, QC, J8T 3R6
(819) 568-1414
Emp Here 49   *Sales* 24,405,822
SIC 5511 New and used car dealers
Pawan Dilawri

D-U-N-S 20-996-2799   (SL)
LFM COURTIER IMMOBILIER AGREE INC
GROUPE SUTTON-OUTAOUAIS
130 Av Gatineau, Gatineau, QC, J8T 4J8
(819) 246-1118
Emp Here 38   *Sales* 12,430,826
SIC 6531 Real estate agents and managers
Errol Mongrain

D-U-N-S 25-026-2672   (SL)
LOEB CLUB PLUS GILLES DIONNE INC
900 Boul Maloney O, Gatineau, QC, J8T 3R6
(514) 243-5231
Emp Here 145   *Sales* 103,923,820
SIC 5141 Groceries, general line
Guy Raymond

D-U-N-S 20-249-4329   (BR)
MAGASIN LAURA (P.V.) INC
LAURA - LAURA PETITES - LAURA PLUS
(*Suby of* MAGASIN LAURA (P.V.) INC)
1076 Boul Maloney O, Gatineau, QC, J8T 3R6
(819) 561-8071
Emp Here 150
SIC 5651 Family clothing stores
Sylvie Levert

D-U-N-S 25-310-9912   (BR)
MCDONALD'S RESTAURANTS OF CANADA LIMITED
MCDONALD'S # 8114
(*Suby of* MCDONALD'S CORPORATION)
80 Boul Gr?Ber, Gatineau, QC, J8T 3P8
(819) 561-1436
Emp Here 120
SIC 5812 Eating places
Ghislain Campeau

D-U-N-S 25-812-5582   (BR)
METRO RICHELIEU INC
SUPER C
(*Suby of* METRO INC)
720 Boul Maloney O, Gatineau, QC, J8T 8K7

(819) 243-5117
Emp Here 100
SIC 5411 Grocery stores
Greg Finlay

D-U-N-S 20-254-7642   (HQ)
MOBILE SERVICE CENTER CANADA LIMITED
MOBILE KLINIK
169 Boul Greber, Gatineau, QC, J8T 3R1
(819) 568-3846
Emp Here 50   *Sales* 22,847,200
SIC 4812 Radiotelephone communication
Kenneth Campbell
Alain Adam
Naaman Zorub
Rob Bruce

D-U-N-S 20-005-2165   (SL)
PRODUITS SANITAIRES LEPINE INC, LES
LES PRODUITS SANITAIRES LEPINE VAL-D'OR
134 Av Gatineau, Gatineau, QC, J8T 4J8
(819) 205-1626
Emp Here 26   *Sales* 28,738,970
SIC 5122 Drugs, proprietaries, and sundries
Gilles Dery

D-U-N-S 24-104-0153   (SL)
PROMENADES DE L'OUTAOUAIS LTD, LES
1100 Boul Maloney O, Gatineau, QC, J8T 6G3
(819) 205-1340
Emp Here 50   *Sales* 14,424,950
SIC 6512 Nonresidential building operators
David J Azrieli

D-U-N-S 25-827-6377   (BR)
PROVIGO DISTRIBUTION INC
LOBLAW'S
(*Suby of* LOBLAW COMPANIES LIMITED)
800 Boul Maloney O, Gatineau, QC, J8T 3R6
(819) 561-9244
Emp Here 150
SIC 5411 Grocery stores
Johson Monsosem

D-U-N-S 20-288-1827   (BR)
PROVIGO DISTRIBUTION INC
MAXI & CIE
(*Suby of* LOBLAW COMPANIES LIMITED)
800 Boul Maloney O, Gatineau, QC, J8T 3R6
(819) 561-9244
Emp Here 100
SIC 5499 Miscellaneous food stores
Julie Chatlain

D-U-N-S 25-920-6662   (HQ)
RE/MAX VISION (1990) INC
225 Boul De La Gappe Bureau 102, Gatineau, QC, J8T 7Y3
(819) 243-3111
Emp Here 32   *Sales* 12,229,020
SIC 6531 Real estate agents and managers
Michel Carriere
Xavier Lecat

D-U-N-S 24-005-3418   (SL)
TREMBLAY, FRANCOIS PHARMACIE
640 Boul Maloney O, Gatineau, QC, J8T 8K7
(819) 246-9662
Emp Here 40   *Sales* 10,118,160
SIC 5912 Drug stores and proprietary stores
Francois Tremblay

D-U-N-S 20-555-7916   (BR)
WAL-MART CANADA CORP
WALMART
(*Suby of* WALMART INC.)
640 Boul Maloney O, Gatineau, QC, J8T 8K7
(819) 246-8808
Emp Here 350
SIC 5311 Department stores
Jean Francios

Gatineau, QC J8V

D-U-N-S 24-016-3308   (SL)
2875448 CANADA INC
METRO LIMBOUR
2505 Rue Saint-Louis, Gatineau, QC, J8V 1A4
(819) 561-3772
Emp Here 75   *Sales* 22,010,775
SIC 5411 Grocery stores
Sylvain Boyer
Luc Lavigueur

D-U-N-S 25-837-6276   (SL)
ANDRE, JEAN-GUY LTEE
692 Boul Greber, Gatineau, QC, J8V 3P8
(819) 243-6181
Emp Here 25   *Sales* 12,451,950
SIC 5531 Auto and home supply stores
Michel Andre

D-U-N-S 20-891-3350   (HQ)
ASSURANCES ROLAND GROULX INC, LES
ASSURANCES GROULX
540 Boul De L'Hopital Bureau 200, Gatineau, QC, J8V 3T2
(819) 243-0242
Emp Here 30   *Sales* 184,774,200
SIC 6411 Insurance agents, brokers, and service
Gerald Groulx

D-U-N-S 24-815-1540   (SL)
COLLEGE SAINT-ALEXANDRE DE LA GATINEAU
2425 Rue Saint-Louis, Gatineau, QC, J8V 1E7
(819) 561-3812
Emp Here 95   *Sales* 14,192,145
SIC 8221 Colleges and universities
Danielle Tessier
Simon Massie
Marcel Landry
Jean-Louis Giroux

D-U-N-S 20-615-8818   (SL)
GAZIFERE INC
ENBRIDGE
(*Suby of* ENBRIDGE INC)
706 Boul Greber, Gatineau, QC, J8V 3P8
(819) 771-8321
Emp Here 99   *Sales* 181,146,834
SIC 4924 Natural gas distribution
James C Grant
Glenn W. Beaumont
Jamie D Leblanc
Rodden Cameron Bassermann
William M Ramos
Malini Giridhar

D-U-N-S 25-739-3991   (SL)
TRADUCTIONS HOULE INC
540 Boul De L'Hopital Bureau 401, Gatineau, QC, J8V 3T2
(819) 568-1022
Emp Here 33   *Sales* 14,635,170
SIC 7389 Business services, nec
Robert Houle
Marc-Andre Houle

Gatineau, QC J8X

D-U-N-S 20-370-3652   (SL)
35 LAURIER LIMITED PARTNERSHIP
FOUR POINTS BY SHERATON HOTEL ET CENTRE DE CONFERENCES GATINEAU-OTTAWA
35 Rue Laurier, Gatineau, QC, J8X 4E9
(819) 778-6111
Emp Here 100   *Sales* 9,489,900
SIC 7011 Hotels and motels
John Ellen

D-U-N-S 24-421-0956   (SL)
BROOKFIELD RENEWABLE ENERGY MARKETING LP
41 Rue Victoria, Gatineau, QC, J8X 2A1
(819) 561-2722
Emp Here 100   *Sales* 67,987,400
SIC 4911 Electric services
Fabrice Iyakaremye

D-U-N-S 20-549-1512   (HQ)
BROOKFIELD RENEWABLE ENERGY PARTNERS L.P.
41 Rue Victoria, Gatineau, QC, J8X 2A1
(819) 561-2722
Sales 408,164,000
SIC 8731 Commercial physical research
Harry Goldgut
Ben Vaughan
Donald Tremblay
Sachin Shah

D-U-N-S 20-383-9956   (SL)
BROOKFIELD RENEWABLE TRADING AND MARKETING LP
41 Rue Victoria, Gatineau, QC, J8X 2A1
(819) 561-2722
Emp Here 50   *Sales* 31,330,700
SIC 4911 Electric services
Jehangir Vevaina
Karly Dyck

D-U-N-S 24-334-6553   (BR)
CENTRE DE SANTE ET DE SERVICES SOCIAUX DE GATINEAU
CENTRE D'HEBERGEMENT LA PIETA
(*Suby of* GOUVERNEMENT DE LA PROVINCE DE QUEBEC)
273 Rue Laurier, Gatineau, QC, J8X 3W8
(819) 966-6420
Emp Here 300
SIC 8062 General medical and surgical hospitals
Claire Bazinet

D-U-N-S 24-268-0080   (HQ)
CENTRES JEUNESSE DE L'OUTAOUAIS, LES
105 Boul Sacre-Coeur Bureau 1, Gatineau, QC, J8X 1C5
(819) 771-6631
Sales 35,324,320
SIC 8322 Individual and family services
Luc Cadieux

D-U-N-S 20-386-6863   (SL)
FONDATION DE L'UNIVERSITE DU QUEBEC EN OUTAOUAIS
283 Boul Alexandre-Tache Bureau F-0239, Gatineau, QC, J8X 3X7
(819) 595-3900
Emp Here 6,736   *Sales* 1,006,297,776
SIC 8221 Colleges and universities
Charles Castonguay
Chloe Berube
Marc-Andre Gervais
Andre J. Roy Roy
Nadim Ladha
Andre Larocque

D-U-N-S 25-240-1500   (BR)
FONDATION DE LA COMMISSION SCOLAIRE DES PORTAGES-DE-L'OUTAOUAIS
ECOLE SECONDAIRE DE L'ILE
255 Rue Saint-Redempteur, Gatineau, QC, J8X 2T4
(819) 771-4548
Emp Here 130
SIC 8211 Elementary and secondary schools
Michel Letang

D-U-N-S 24-845-6469   (HQ)
GINSBERG, GINGRAS & ASSOCIES INC
145 Prom Du Portage, Gatineau, QC, J8X 2K4
(819) 776-0283
Emp Here 37   *Sales* 14,082,014
SIC 8111 Legal services
Chantal Gingras
Stephan V. Moyneur
Pascal Gagnon
Richard Cadieux

Bruce Johnston
Claude B. Gingras

D-U-N-S 24-378-4233   (BR)
KRUGER PRODUCTS L.P.
PRODUITS KRUGER S.E.C.
(*Suby of* KRUGER INC)
20 Rue Laurier, Gatineau, QC, J8X 4H3
(819) 595-5302
Emp Here 480
SIC 2621 Paper mills
Stephane Lamoureux

D-U-N-S 20-174-2298   (SL)
L'ASSOCIATION TOURISTIQUE DE L'OUTAOUAIS
TOURISME OUTAOUAIS
103 Rue Laurier, Gatineau, QC, J8X 3V8
(819) 778-2222
Emp Here 25   *Sales* 11,230,475
SIC 7389 Business services, nec
Genevieve Dumas
Michele Canto

D-U-N-S 25-684-1768   (HQ)
MACADAMIAN TECHNOLOGIES INC
179 Prom Du Portage Unite 4, Gatineau, QC, J8X 2K5
(819) 772-0300
Sales 15,860,020
SIC 7371 Custom computer programming services
Frederic Boulanger
Luc Gagnon
Dinesh Kandanchatha

D-U-N-S 20-694-3537   (SL)
NORTHFORGE INNOVATIONS INC
(*Suby of* ACCESS CO.,LTD.)
72 Rue Laval, Gatineau, QC, J8X 3H3
(819) 776-6066
Emp Here 75   *Sales* 10,813,650
SIC 7371 Custom computer programming services
Brenda Pastorek
Amanda Lambert
Josef Zankowicz
Paul M. Gasparro
James Pinard
Edward J. Stewart

D-U-N-S 24-382-1246   (HQ)
RELANCE OUTAOUAIS INC, LA
SERVICE MECANESSENCE
270 Boul Des Allumettieres, Gatineau, QC, J8X 1N3
(819) 770-5325
Sales 33,130,880
SIC 8399 Social services, nec
Eric Charron
Andre Landry

D-U-N-S 24-356-8180   (BR)
RELANCE OUTAOUAIS INC, LA
(*Suby of* RELANCE OUTAOUAIS INC, LA)
45 Boul Sacre-Coeur, Gatineau, QC, J8X 1C6
(819) 776-5870
Emp Here 150
SIC 8399 Social services, nec
Jouan St-Germain

D-U-N-S 20-103-7038   (SL)
SERVICE REGIONAL D'INTERPRETATION VISUELLE DE L'OUTAOUAIS
S R I V O
115 Boul Sacre-Coeur Bureau 212, Gatineau, QC, J8X 1C5

Emp Here 25   *Sales* 11,230,475
SIC 7389 Business services, nec
Claude Carriere

D-U-N-S 24-960-7599   (SL)
TERRASSES DE LA CHAUDIERE INC, LES
25 Rue Eddy Bureau 203, Gatineau, QC, J8X 4B5
(819) 997-7129
Emp Here 44   *Sales* 11,508,332

SIC 6719 Holding companies, nec
Michael Rosenberg

Gatineau, QC J8Y

D-U-N-S 24-814-0063   (HQ)
153927 CANADA INC
PHARMACIE JEAN COUTU
15 Boul Montclair Bureau 203, Gatineau, QC,
J8Y 2E2
(819) 770-4232
Emp Here 100   *Sales* 48,865,600
SIC 5912 Drug stores and proprietary stores
Michel Quesnel

D-U-N-S 25-113-6321   (SL)
3197786 CANADA INC
ACOUSTIQUE S. MAYER
13 Rue Dumas, Gatineau, QC, J8Y 2M4
(819) 775-9844
Emp Here 150   *Sales* 40,641,300
SIC 1521 Single-family housing construction
Stephane Mayer Millette

D-U-N-S 24-712-2369   (HQ)
3223701 CANADA INC
LE GROUPE CONSTRUCTION BRIGIL
98 Rue Lois Bureau 205, Gatineau, QC, J8Y
3R7
(819) 243-7392
Sales 27,094,200
SIC 1521 Single-family housing construction
Gilles Desjardins

D-U-N-S 24-141-6655   (SL)
6358101 CANADA INC
CASINO GATINEAU ACURA
7 Boul Du Casino, Gatineau, QC, J8Y 6V7
(819) 777-1771
Emp Here 22   *Sales* 10,957,716
SIC 5511 New and used car dealers
Pawan Dilawri
Hasan Khalid

D-U-N-S 20-709-4645   (SL)
ASSURANCE ET GESTION DE RISQUES
CHARLESBOIS TREPANIER
815 Boul De La Carriere Bureau 102,
Gatineau, QC, J8Y 6T4

Emp Here 40   *Sales* 33,922,400
SIC 6411 Insurance agents, brokers, and service
Michel Drouin

D-U-N-S 24-268-0270   (HQ)
BOITE A GRAINS INC, LA
581 Boul Saint-Joseph, Gatineau, QC, J8Y
4A6
(819) 771-3000
Emp Here 27   *Sales* 10,966,080
SIC 5499 Miscellaneous food stores
Pierre Daniel Menard
Real Deslauriers

D-U-N-S 25-115-5693   (SL)
CACTUS (ISP) INTERNET INC
CACTUS COMMERCE
490 Boul Saint-Joseph Bureau 300, Gatineau,
QC, J8Y 3Y7
(819) 778-0313
Emp Here 110   *Sales* 25,554,608
SIC 4813 Telephone communication, except
radio
Antoine Normand

D-U-N-S 20-291-1756   (HQ)
CAISSE DESJARDINS DE HULL-AYLMER
DESJARDINS ENTREPRISES
250 Boul Saint-Joseph, Gatineau, QC, J8Y
3X6
(819) 776-3000
Emp Here 30   *Sales* 15,156,100
SIC 6062 State credit unions
Sylvie St-Pierre Babin

Merille Kirouac
Audrey Brousseau
Jonathan Lafreniere
Marcel Vachon
Marie-Eve Couture-Lalande
Jean-Claude Jalbert
Andre Racicot
Denis Brochu
Denis Genest

D-U-N-S 25-176-3967   (SL)
CEGEP HERITAGE COLLEGE
325 Boul De La Cite-Des-Jeunes, Gatineau,
QC, J8Y 6T3
(819) 778-2270
Emp Here 150   *Sales* 22,408,650
SIC 8221 Colleges and universities
Michael Randall

D-U-N-S 20-291-0170   (SL)
**CHARLEBOIS-TREPANIER ET ASSOCIES
2009 INC**
815 Boul De La Carriere Bureau 102,
Gatineau, QC, J8Y 6T4
(819) 777-5246
Emp Here 26   *Sales* 15,078,024
SIC 6411 Insurance agents, brokers, and service
Michel Drouin
Paul Pregent

D-U-N-S 25-023-9944   (BR)
CONSTRUCTION DJL INC
(Suby of VINCI)
20 Rue Emile-Bond, Gatineau, QC, J8Y 3M7
(819) 770-2300
Emp Here 75
SIC 1611 Highway and street construction
Martion Bouvier

D-U-N-S 24-634-0418   (SL)
DENIS CROTEAU INC
L'AUBAINERIE
9 Boul Montclair Bureau 19, Gatineau, QC,
J8Y 2E2
(819) 770-6886
Emp Here 60   *Sales* 10,763,760
SIC 5651 Family clothing stores
Denis Croteau

D-U-N-S 24-352-1189   (SL)
ED. BRUNET ET ASSOCIES CANADA INC
9 Rue Dumas, Gatineau, QC, J8Y 2M4
(819) 777-3877
Emp Here 35   *Sales* 14,677,425
SIC 6712 Bank holding companies
Raymond Brunet
James G Wilson
Philippe Houle

D-U-N-S 24-810-5785   (HQ)
**EMBALLAGES BOUDREAULT CANADA
LTEE, LES**
45 Rue Adrien-Robert, Gatineau, QC, J8Y
3S3
(819) 777-1603
Sales 25,182,900
SIC 5113 Industrial and personal service paper
Jean-Claude Boudreault
Luc Boudreault
Monique Boudreault
Josee Boudreault

D-U-N-S 25-845-7894   (SL)
**GAGNE, ISABELLE, PATRY, LAFLAMME &
ASSOCIES NOTAIRES INC**
188 Rue Montcalm Bureau 300, Gatineau,
QC, J8Y 3B5
(819) 771-3231
Emp Here 50   *Sales* 22,460,950
SIC 7389 Business services, nec
Paul Gagne

D-U-N-S 24-944-7731   (SL)
GESTION CAVEAU DES JEANS INC
84 Rue Lois, Gatineau, QC, J8Y 3R4

Emp Here 100   *Sales* 17,939,600
SIC 5651 Family clothing stores
Mario Lanthier

D-U-N-S 20-700-6610   (SL)
GESTION ROSLYN-ALVIN LTEE
PHARMAPRIX
320 Boul Saint-Joseph Bureau 221, Gatineau,
QC, J8Y 3Y8
(819) 770-6668
Emp Here 40   *Sales* 10,118,160
SIC 5912 Drug stores and proprietary stores
Fadila Benabdesiam

D-U-N-S 24-653-2394   (BR)
**GOUVERNEMENT DE LA PROVINCE DE
QUEBEC**
CENTRE READAPTATION LA RESSOURSE
*(Suby of GOUVERNEMENT DE LA
PROVINCE DE QUEBEC)*
135 Boul Saint-Raymond, Gatineau, QC, J8Y
6X7
(819) 777-6261
Emp Here 300
SIC 8011 Offices and clinics of medical doctors
Constance Vanier

D-U-N-S 20-914-7870   (BR)
**GOUVERNEMENT DE LA PROVINCE DE
QUEBEC**
CSSSG
*(Suby of GOUVERNEMENT DE LA
PROVINCE DE QUEBEC)*
116 Boul Lionel-Emond, Gatineau, QC, J8Y
1W7

Emp Here 2,000
SIC 8062 General medical and surgical hospitals

D-U-N-S 20-102-7740   (BR)
**GOUVERNEMENT DE LA PROVINCE DE
QUEBEC**
*COMISSION DE LA SANTE ET DE LA SECU-
RITE*
*(Suby of GOUVERNEMENT DE LA
PROVINCE DE QUEBEC)*
15 Rue Gamelin, Gatineau, QC, J8Y 6N5
(819) 778-8600
Emp Here 75
SIC 6331 Fire, marine, and casualty insurance

D-U-N-S 25-027-3000   (SL)
GROUPE MIOSIS, S.E.N.C.R.L.
CLINIQUE D'OPTOMETRIE MIOSIS
425 Boul Saint-Joseph, Gatineau, QC, J8Y
3Z8
(819) 771-5600
Emp Here 30   *Sales* 10,837,110
SIC 8042 Offices and clinics of optometrists
Micheline Verrette
Sheila Laplante
Marc La Salle
Sylvain Michaud

D-U-N-S 20-113-8216   (HQ)
IMEX AGRO INC
128 Boul Saint-Raymond, Gatineau, QC, J8Y
1T2
(819) 483-1515
Emp Here 6   *Sales* 71,024,045
SIC 5148 Fresh fruits and vegetables
Reynaldo Avendano

D-U-N-S 20-200-4875   (SL)
**IMMEUBLES JOSEPH PELLETIER INC,
LES**
116 Rue Lois, Gatineau, QC, J8Y 3R7
(819) 770-3038
Emp Here 34   *Sales* 14,423,206
SIC 6719 Holding companies, nec
Jacques Pelletier

D-U-N-S 20-063-2333   (SL)
JPL APRES SINISTRE INC
CONSTRUCTION J.P.L.

116 Rue Lois, Gatineau, QC, J8Y 3R7
(819) 770-3038
Emp Here 50   *Sales* 15,943,450
SIC 1521 Single-family housing construction
Marie-Andre Pelletier
Cedric Laforest

D-U-N-S 24-698-3485   (SL)
LA TRAPPE A FROMAGE DE L'OUTAOUAIS
114 Boul Saint-Raymond, Gatineau, QC, J8Y
1S9
(819) 243-6411
Emp Here 49   *Sales* 14,380,373
SIC 5451 Dairy products stores
Gilles Jr. Joanisse

D-U-N-S 20-200-3372   (HQ)
LAFLAMME, HENRI INC
IGA LAFLAMME
425 Boul Saint-Joseph, Gatineau, QC, J8Y
3Z8
(819) 770-9131
Emp Here 80   *Sales* 39,619,395
SIC 5411 Grocery stores
Jean-Pierre Laflamme
Jean-Paul Laflamme
Marius Laflamme

D-U-N-S 25-812-5574   (BR)
METRO RICHELIEU INC
SUPER C
(Suby of METRO INC)
725a Boul De La Carriere, Gatineau, QC, J8Y
6T9
(819) 595-1344
Emp Here 125
SIC 5411 Grocery stores
Daniel Barry

D-U-N-S 20-331-1550   (SL)
**ORIGINAL BAKED QUALITY PITA DIPS
INC, L'**
FRUITERIE WAKIM
320 Boul Saint-Joseph, Gatineau, QC, J8Y
3Y8
(819) 525-6555
Emp Here 100   *Sales* 34,569,000
SIC 2051 Bread, cake, and related products
Ralph Wakim

D-U-N-S 24-322-2853   (SL)
PERSONNEL OUTAOUAIS INC
92 Boul Saint-Raymond Bureau 400,
Gatineau, QC, J8Y 1S7
(819) 778-7020
Emp Here 103   *Sales* 7,693,482
SIC 7361 Employment agencies
Bernard Grenier

D-U-N-S 20-200-5047   (SL)
PILON LTEE
*(Suby of PLACEMENTS ROLAND LAVOIE
LTEE, LES)*
5 Boul Montclair, Gatineau, QC, J8Y 2E3
(819) 771-5841
Emp Here 85   *Sales* 48,418,380
SIC 5039 Construction materials, nec
Roland Lavoie

D-U-N-S 25-199-4356   (SL)
**PLACEMENTS MICHEL MAYRAND INC,
LES**
*MARCHAND CANADIAN TIRE DE SHER-
BROOKE*
355 Boul De La Carriere Bureau 176,
Gatineau, QC, J8Y 6W4
(819) 777-4381
Emp Here 110   *Sales* 22,587,730
SIC 5311 Department stores
Michel Mayrand

D-U-N-S 24-936-2583   (HQ)
PLACEMENTS ROLAND LAVOIE LTEE, LES
5 Boul Montclair, Gatineau, QC, J8Y 2E3
(819) 771-5841
Sales 23,234,750
SIC 6712 Bank holding companies
Roland Lavoie

Stephane Nadon
Pascal Manassin

D-U-N-S 25-025-8563 (BR)
PROVIGO DISTRIBUTION INC
PROVIGO MONT BLEU
(*Suby of* LOBLAW COMPANIES LIMITED)
775 Boul Saint-Joseph, Gatineau, QC, J8Y 4C1
(819) 771-7701
Emp Here 75
SIC 5411 Grocery stores
Remi Patry

D-U-N-S 20-277-7645 (BR)
RONA INC
RONA DEPOT - HULL
(*Suby of* LOWE'S COMPANIES, INC.)
95 Rue Atawe, Gatineau, QC, J8Y 6W7
(819) 770-7366
Emp Here 115
SIC 5072 Hardware
Robert Desjardins

D-U-N-S 24-676-4971 (HQ)
SERVICE DE PNEUS LAVOIE OUTAOUAIS INC
G.O. EQUIPEMENT / VENTES & SERVICE
27 Rue Mangin, Gatineau, QC, J8Y 3L8
(819) 771-2392
Emp Here 20   *Sales* 46,115,400
SIC 5014 Tires and tubes
Normand Lavoie

D-U-N-S 24-596-0760 (SL)
SPECSAUDIO 1990 INC
79 Rue Cremazie, Gatineau, QC, J8Y 3P1
(819) 777-3681
Emp Here 25   *Sales* 13,013,550
SIC 5099 Durable goods, nec
Claude Regimbald

D-U-N-S 24-666-4742 (SL)
TESSIER TRANSLATIONS CORPORATION
188 Rue Montcalm Bureau 100, Gatineau, QC, J8Y 3B5
(819) 776-6687
Emp Here 39   *Sales* 17,519,541
SIC 7389 Business services, nec
Philippe Tessier
Alain Belanger
Joanne St-Onge

Gatineau, QC J8Z

D-U-N-S 24-922-3694 (SL)
174761 CANADA INC
ARGUS MAZDA AUTO
961 Boul Saint-Joseph, Gatineau, QC, J8Z 1W8
(819) 776-6700
Emp Here 60   *Sales* 37,756,800
SIC 5511 New and used car dealers
Pierre Grenier
Rene Dupont

D-U-N-S 24-935-9076 (SL)
174762 CANADA INC
CARREFOUR NISSAN
961 Boul Saint-Joseph, Gatineau, QC, J8Z 1W8
(819) 776-6700
Emp Here 30   *Sales* 14,942,340
SIC 5511 New and used car dealers
Pierre Grenier
Rene Dupont

D-U-N-S 24-662-2252 (SL)
2088941 CANADA INC
VILLA TOYOTA
1235 Boul Saint-Joseph, Gatineau, QC, J8Z 3J6
(819) 776-0077
Emp Here 54   *Sales* 33,981,120
SIC 5511 New and used car dealers

Chantalle Lafontaine
Pierre Lafontaine

D-U-N-S 25-025-9470 (SL)
3041000 CANADA INC
CITE CHRYSLER PLYMOUTH
951 Boul Saint-Joseph, Gatineau, QC, J8Z 1S8
(819) 777-2611
Emp Here 25   *Sales* 12,451,950
SIC 5511 New and used car dealers
Helene Dupont

D-U-N-S 24-596-0091 (SL)
3595650 CANADA INC
HULL HYUNDAI
1135 Boul Saint-Joseph, Gatineau, QC, J8Z 1W8
(819) 770-7768
Emp Here 26   *Sales* 12,950,028
SIC 5511 New and used car dealers
Gilles Poirier
Robert Poirier

D-U-N-S 20-363-3552 (HQ)
8959528 CANADA INC
EXPOZONE
250 Rue Deveault Bureau A, Gatineau, QC, J8Z 1S6
(819) 778-0114
Emp Here 2   *Sales* 15,516,135
SIC 6712 Bank holding companies
Audrey Bouchard
Patrick Molla

D-U-N-S 20-787-8661 (SL)
BAILLOT, JULES & FILS LIMITEE
960 Boul Saint-Joseph, Gatineau, QC, J8Z 1T3
(819) 777-5261
Emp Here 40   *Sales* 25,171,200
SIC 5511 New and used car dealers
Michel Gauthier
Jacques Baillot
Madeleine Gauthier

D-U-N-S 20-309-5922 (SL)
BOLESS INC
15 Rue Buteau Bureau 220, Gatineau, QC, J8Z 1V4
(819) 770-3028
Emp Here 50   *Sales* 39,866,050
SIC 1542 Nonresidential construction, nec
Denis Ouellette
Jean-Marc Gerfaux
Michel Tremblay

D-U-N-S 20-331-4182 (SL)
C T M GATINEAU
73 Rue Jean-Proulx, Gatineau, QC, J8Z 1W2
(819) 777-0999
Emp Here 49   *Sales* 11,480,112
SIC 8748 Business consulting, nec
Richard Tremblay

D-U-N-S 24-435-6408 (SL)
DEMENAGEMENT OUTAOUAIS INC
150 Rue Jean-Proulx, Gatineau, QC, J8Z 1V3
(819) 771-1634
Emp Here 60   *Sales* 12,342,360
SIC 4214 Local trucking with storage
Michael Kolberg

D-U-N-S 20-889-1408 (SL)
DUPORTAGE FORD LTEE
DUPONT & DUPONT FORD
(*Suby of* ENTREPRISES D.M.V.L. LTEE, LES)
949 Boul Saint-Joseph, Gatineau, QC, J8Z 1S8
(819) 778-2751
Emp Here 50   *Sales* 24,903,900
SIC 5511 New and used car dealers
Andre Jr Dupont
J.C. Andre Dupont

D-U-N-S 20-700-6594 (HQ)
ENTREPRISES P. BONHOMME LTEE, LES
921 Boul Saint-Joseph, Gatineau, QC, J8Z 1S8

(819) 561-5577
Sales 70,262,500
SIC 5211 Lumber and other building materials
Paul Bonhomme
Michel Charest
Donald Marcil

D-U-N-S 24-532-1398 (SL)
HULL NISSAN
959 Boul Saint-Joseph, Gatineau, QC, J8Z 1W8
(819) 776-0100
Emp Here 28   *Sales* 13,946,184
SIC 5511 New and used car dealers
John Merins

D-U-N-S 20-801-5755 (HQ)
LABORATOIRES C.O.P. INC
IDEAL PROTEIN
60 Rue Jean-Proulx, Gatineau, QC, J8Z 1W1
(819) 772-4447
Sales 41,778,850
SIC 5141 Groceries, general line
Olivier Benloulou
Alain Roy

D-U-N-S 20-893-6989 (SL)
LALLIER AUTOMOBILE (HULL) INC
981 Boul Saint-Joseph, Gatineau, QC, J8Z 1W8
(819) 778-1444
Emp Here 57   *Sales* 22,864,110
SIC 5511 New and used car dealers
Jacques Gauthier
Sylvie Dagenais
Isabelle Dagenais

D-U-N-S 20-788-0485 (SL)
MAURICE SIGOUIN REPARATION DE MEUBLES LTEE
142 Ch Freeman Bureau 8, Gatineau, QC, J8Z 2B4
(819) 776-3522
Emp Here 1   *Sales* 80,247,700
SIC 7641 Reupholstery and furniture repair
Bonaventure Anagana

D-U-N-S 20-747-0477 (SL)
PLANTE, PAT AUTOS LTEE
850 Boul Saint-Joseph, Gatineau, QC, J8Z 1S9
(819) 770-0220
Emp Here 29   *Sales* 14,444,262
SIC 5511 New and used car dealers
Philippe St-Pierre
Marie-Nolle Bonicalzi

D-U-N-S 24-270-4716 (BR)
RNC MEDIA INC
CHOTV CFGSTV
(*Suby of* RNC MEDIA INC)
171a Rue Jean-Proulx Bureau 5, Gatineau, QC, J8Z 1W5
(819) 503-9711
Emp Here 80
SIC 4833 Television broadcasting stations
Robert Parent

D-U-N-S 25-685-7681 (SL)
SOLACOM TECHNOLOGIES INC
CML ATC
(*Suby of* COMTECH TELECOMMUNICATIONS CORP.)
80 Rue Jean-Proulx, Gatineau, QC, J8Z 1W1
(819) 205-8100
Emp Here 60   *Sales* 13,637,340
SIC 3812 Search and navigation equipment
Pierre Plangger
Andre Vaillant
Franz Plangger
Jocelyn Racine
Stephane Poirier Defoy
Bruce Lazenby
Donna Ronayne

D-U-N-S 25-510-2204 (SL)
SPECIALISTE DU BUREAU FREDAL INC, LE

FREDAL SOLUTIONS
186 Rue Jean-Proulx, Gatineau, QC, J8Z 1V8
(819) 205-9555
Emp Here 35   *Sales* 15,651,090
SIC 5044 Office equipment
Alain Fredette
Jocelyne Tessier-Fredette
Etienne Fredette

D-U-N-S 25-773-8880 (SL)
SURGENOR GATINEAU CHEVROLET CADILLAC LTEE
950 Boul Saint-Joseph, Gatineau, QC, J8Z 1S9
(819) 777-2731
Emp Here 50   *Sales* 24,903,900
SIC 5511 New and used car dealers
Andrew Mcgurn

D-U-N-S 24-769-8830 (HQ)
VESTA SOLUTIONS COMMUNICATIONS CORP
COMMUNICATIONS AIRBUS DS
(*Suby of* MOTOROLA SOLUTIONS, INC.)
200 Boul De La Technologie Bureau 300, Gatineau, QC, J8Z 3H6
(819) 778-2053
Sales 56,583,000
SIC 3669 Communications equipment, nec
George Krausz
Daniel G. Pekofske
Kristin L. Kruska
John Wozniak
Sue Conatser

Gatineau, QC J9A

D-U-N-S 20-309-6557 (SL)
6861083 CANADA INC
S3
53 Rue Du Blizzard, Gatineau, QC, J9A 0C8
(819) 777-2222
Emp Here 50   *Sales* 26,027,100
SIC 5091 Sporting and recreation goods
Pierre Champagne
Roch Carpentier

D-U-N-S 20-817-9999 (SL)
BRIGIL CONSTRUCTION INC
3354 Boul Des Grives Bureau 3, Gatineau, QC, J9A 0A6
(819) 243-7392
Emp Here 49   *Sales* 15,624,581
SIC 1521 Single-family housing construction
Gilles Desjardins

D-U-N-S 20-291-1731 (BR)
CAISSE DESJARDINS DE HULL-AYLMER
CENTRE DE SERVICES DU PLATEAU
(*Suby of* CAISSE DESJARDINS DE HULL-AYLMER)
219 Boul Du Plateau, Gatineau, QC, J9A 0N4
(819) 776-3000
Emp Here 225
SIC 6062 State credit unions
Stephane Miljours

D-U-N-S 20-709-4694 (SL)
GESTION VALMIRA INC
MCDONALD'S
25 Rue De L'Embellie, Gatineau, QC, J9A 3K3
(819) 595-4989
Emp Here 100   *Sales* 4,551,900
SIC 5812 Eating places
Mohamed Abouziane

D-U-N-S 20-548-3584 (BR)
PROVIGO DISTRIBUTION INC
LOBLAWS
(*Suby of* LOBLAW COMPANIES LIMITED)
1 Boul Du Plateau, Gatineau, QC, J9A 3G1
(819) 777-2747
Emp Here 170
SIC 5411 Grocery stores

Diane Nonssen

D-U-N-S 24-267-8373   (BR)
UNIVERSITE DU QUEBEC
PAVILLON ALEXANDRE TACHE
(*Suby of* UNIVERSITE DU QUEBEC)
283 Boul Alexandre-Tache, Gatineau, QC, J9A 1L8
(819) 595-3900
Emp Here 300
SIC 8221 Colleges and universities
Francis White

D-U-N-S 20-003-4770   (BR)
WAL-MART CANADA CORP
WALMART
(*Suby of* WALMART INC.)
35 Boul Du Plateau, Gatineau, QC, J9A 3G1
(819) 772-1911
Emp Here 150
SIC 5311 Department stores
Lee Tappenden

Gatineau, QC J9H

D-U-N-S 20-267-4461   (SL)
KENPIER INVESTISSEMENTS LIMITEE
DOUBLETREE BY HILTON HOTEL GATINEAU-OTTAWA
1170 Ch D'Aylmer, Gatineau, QC, J9H 7L3
(819) 778-0000
Emp Here 100   *Sales* 28,443,700
SIC 6512 Nonresidential building operators
Pierre Heafey

D-U-N-S 25-474-8650   (BR)
LOBLAWS INC
PROVIGO
(*Suby of* LOBLAW COMPANIES LIMITED)
375 Ch D'Aylmer Bureau 5, Gatineau, QC, J9H 1A5
(819) 682-4433
Emp Here 165
SIC 5411 Grocery stores
Julie Chacelain

Gatineau, QC J9J

D-U-N-S 20-013-1998   (SL)
3592898 CANADA INC
VILLA DU DECOR 1999 CANADA
1706 Ch Pink Bureau F, Gatineau, QC, J9J 3N7
(819) 771-3969
Emp Here 7   *Sales* 689,655,354
SIC 1752 Floor laying and floor work, nec
Danik Seguin
Jean-Claude Lafontaine

D-U-N-S 20-217-3154   (BR)
AUTOBUS LA QUEBECOISE INC
AUTOBUS OUTAOUAIS
(*Suby of* AUTOBUS LA QUEBECOISE INC)
545 Rue De Vernon, Gatineau, QC, J9J 3K4
(819) 770-1070
Emp Here 80
SIC 4151 School buses
Daniel Ryan

D-U-N-S 25-142-6508   (SL)
BETON AMIX LTEE
600b Rue De Vernon, Gatineau, QC, J9J 3K5
(819) 770-5092
Emp Here 45   *Sales* 10,350,855
SIC 3273 Ready-mixed concrete
Luc Danault
Michel St-Pierre
Ghislain St-Pierre

D-U-N-S 20-892-5255   (SL)
CONSTRUCTION LARIVIERE LTEE
640 Rue Auguste-Mondoux, Gatineau, QC,

J9J 3K3
(819) 770-2280
Emp Here 60   *Sales* 14,771,160
SIC 1794 Excavation work
Jean Lariviere
Pierre Lariviere
Suzanne Lariviere

D-U-N-S 24-933-8807   (SL)
ENTREPRISES D. GAUVREAU ENR
GAUVREAU TOP SOIL
930 Ch Vanier, Gatineau, QC, J9J 3J3
(819) 682-1735
Emp Here 50   *Sales* 12,044,200
SIC 1629 Heavy construction, nec
Denis Gauvreau
Eric Gauvreau

D-U-N-S 24-394-6311   (SL)
MARCHE AYLMER INC
METRO AYLMER
799 Boul Wilfrid-Lavigne Bureau 1098, Gatineau, QC, J9J 1V2
(819) 685-3490
Emp Here 50   *Sales* 13,707,600
SIC 5411 Grocery stores
Stephane Kelly

D-U-N-S 24-739-7235   (HQ)
MATERIAUX DE CONSTRUCTION D L INC
760 Rue De Vernon, Gatineau, QC, J9J 3K5
(819) 770-9974
Emp Here 40   *Sales* 22,358,700
SIC 5039 Construction materials, nec
Robert Leonard
Richard Davis

D-U-N-S 24-592-0467   (SL)
POLANE INC
621 Rue De Vernon, Gatineau, QC, J9J 3K4
(819) 772-4949
Emp Here 25   *Sales* 11,768,275
SIC 1542 Nonresidential construction, nec
Jean-Pierre Morin

D-U-N-S 25-862-4704   (SL)
SERVICE DE PNEU K & S KELLY INC
627 Rue Auguste-Mondoux, Gatineau, QC, J9J 3K2
(819) 600-1061
Emp Here 25   *Sales* 12,451,950
SIC 5531 Auto and home supply stores

D-U-N-S 20-861-2452   (HQ)
WESTERN QUEBEC SCHOOL BOARD
15 Rue Katimavik, Gatineau, QC, J9J 0E9
(819) 684-1313
Emp Here 25   *Sales* 128,854,700
SIC 8211 Elementary and secondary schools
Dan Lamoureux
Russell Copeman

Gatineau, QC K1A

D-U-N-S 24-813-5188   (BR)
GOUVERNEMENT DE LA PROVINCE DE QUEBEC
MUSEE CANADIEN DES CIVILISATIONS
(*Suby of* GOUVERNEMENT DE LA PROVINCE DE QUEBEC)
100 Rue Laurier, Gatineau, QC, K1A 0M8
(819) 776-7000
Emp Here 500
SIC 8412 Museums and art galleries
Victor Rabinovitch

D-U-N-S 25-220-5695   (HQ)
MUSEE CANADIEN DE L'HISTOIRE
THE CANADIAN WAR MUSEUM
100 Rue Laurier, Gatineau, QC, K1A 0M8
(819) 776-7000
Sales 51,695,980
SIC 8412 Museums and art galleries
Mark O'neill
David Loyer

Chrisse Unterhorrer
Stephen Quick
Jean-Marc Blais
Manon Rochon
Chantal Schryer
Megan Richardson

D-U-N-S 20-386-5980   (BR)
SODEXO QUEBEC LIMITEE
DISTINCTION BY SODEXO
(*Suby of* SODEXO)
100 Rue Laurier, Gatineau, QC, K1A 0M8
(819) 776-8391
Emp Here 90
SIC 5812 Eating places

D-U-N-S 20-386-5985   (BR)
SODEXO QUEBEC LIMITEE
DISTINCTION BY SODEXO
(*Suby of* SODEXO)
100 Rue Laurier, Gatineau, QC, K1A 0M8
(819) 776-8391
Emp Here 90
SIC 5812 Eating places

Girardville, QC G0W

D-U-N-S 20-279-1146   (BR)
PF RESOLU CANADA INC
(*Suby of* RESOLUTE FOREST PRODUCTS INC)
2250 Rang Saint-Joseph N, Girardville, QC, G0W 1R0
(418) 630-3433
Emp Here 112
SIC 2421 Sawmills and planing mills, general
Stephane Painchaud

Godmanchester, QC J0S

D-U-N-S 20-014-5431   (SL)
SUPERMARCHE BERGERON INC
IGA
2195 Ch Ridge, Godmanchester, QC, J0S 1H0
(450) 264-2909
Emp Here 49   *Sales* 13,433,448
SIC 5411 Grocery stores
Marc Andre Bergeron

Granby, QC J2G

D-U-N-S 25-105-0746   (SL)
3680258 CANADA INC
TRANSFORMATEUR DELTA
795 Boul Industriel, Granby, QC, J2G 9A1
(450) 378-3617
Emp Here 140   *Sales* 26,661,880
SIC 3612 Transformers, except electric
Roland Pelletier
Andre Pelletier

D-U-N-S 20-363-1242   (SL)
7643454 CANADA INC
C.A.H.Y.
35 Rue Dufferin Bureau 204, Granby, QC, J2G 4W5
(450) 776-3930
Emp Here 26   *Sales* 17,068,064
SIC 5963 Direct selling establishments
Alain Pouliot

D-U-N-S 24-540-7804   (HQ)
9020-5758 QUEBEC INC
AVRIL SUPERMARCHE SANTE
11 Rue Evangeline, Granby, QC, J2G 6N3
(450) 994-4794
Emp Here 25   *Sales* 29,347,700

SIC 5499 Miscellaneous food stores
Rolland Tanguay
Sylvie Senay
Francis Roy

D-U-N-S 24-335-0712   (SL)
9155-3164 QUEBEC INC
386 Rue Dorchester, Granby, QC, J2G 3Z7
(450) 372-5826
Emp Here 100   *Sales* 27,433,200
SIC 8741 Management services
Robert J. Belanger

D-U-N-S 20-332-4439   (SL)
9267-8010 QUEBEC INC
UNIPRIX ISABELLE DUPONT
338 Rue Saint-Jacques, Granby, QC, J2G 3N2
(450) 372-4447
Emp Here 60   *Sales* 14,659,680
SIC 5961 Catalog and mail-order houses
Isabelle Dupont

D-U-N-S 25-452-2894   (HQ)
A.T.L.A.S. AERONAUTIQUE INC
AIR-TERRE EQUIPEMENT
420 Rue Edouard, Granby, QC, J2G 3Z3
(450) 378-8107
Sales 47,502,600
SIC 5084 Industrial machinery and equipment
Camil Poulin
Raynald Ostiguy
Andre Bourdeau
Michel Baril

D-U-N-S 25-870-6928   (SL)
ABATTOIR DUCHARME INC
110 Rue Authier, Granby, QC, J2G 7X2
(450) 375-4620
Emp Here 50   *Sales* 11,242,750
SIC 2011 Meat packing plants
Alain Ducharme
Bruno Ducharme

D-U-N-S 24-382-9590   (BR)
AGROPUR COOPERATIVE
NARTEL
(*Suby of* AGROPUR COOPERATIVE)
510 Rue Principale, Granby, QC, J2G 2X2
(450) 375-1991
Emp Here 650
SIC 2022 Cheese; natural and processed
Louis Lefebvre

D-U-N-S 20-199-0728   (HQ)
AMENAGEMENTS RICHARD LTEE, LES
110 Rue Court, Granby, QC, J2G 4Y9
(450) 372-3019
Emp Here 2   *Sales* 10,903,230
SIC 6719 Holding companies, nec
Richard Tetreault
Louise Leduc

D-U-N-S 24-334-6900   (BR)
BOW GROUPE DE PLOMBERIE INC
DIV DE BOW PLASTIQUES
(*Suby of* BOW GROUPE DE PLOMBERIE INC)
15 Rue Vittie, Granby, QC, J2G 6N8
(450) 372-5481
Emp Here 200
SIC 3089 Plastics products, nec
Dave Barlow

D-U-N-S 24-327-1728   (HQ)
CAISSE DESJARDINS DE GRANBY-HAUTE-YAMASKA
CENTRE DE SERVICE BROMONT
450 Rue Principale, Granby, QC, J2G 2X1
(450) 777-5353
Emp Here 90   *Sales* 53,488,907
SIC 6062 State credit unions
Serge Laflamme
Andre Moise
Philippe Simonato
Josee Ouellet
Louis-Eric Bolduc
Roxana Cledon

Mathieu Couture
Normand Desloges
Michel Filion
Nicole Freniere

D-U-N-S 25-024-0926   (HQ)
CEGEP DE GRANBY HAUTE-YAMASKA
CEGEP DE GRANBY
235 Rue Saint-Jacques, Granby, QC, J2G 3N1
(450) 372-6614
Emp Here 240   *Sales* 37,347,750
SIC 8221 Colleges and universities
Robert Brodeur

D-U-N-S 20-198-5348   (SL)
CHARLAND CHEVROLET CADILLAC BUICK GMC LTEE
(*Suby of* SOCIETE DE GESTION DENIS ROBIDOUX INC)
595 Rue Boivin, Granby, QC, J2G 2M1
(450) 372-4242
Emp Here 50   *Sales* 24,903,900
SIC 5511 New and used car dealers
Denis Robidoux
Paul Balthazard

D-U-N-S 24-012-2122   (BR)
COMMISSION SCOLAIRE DU VAL-DES-CERFS
CEA CENTRE REGIONAL INTEGRE DE FORMATION
(*Suby of* COMMISSION SCOLAIRE DU VAL-DES-CERFS)
700 Rue Denison O, Granby, QC, J2G 4G3
(450) 378-8544
Emp Here 125
SIC 8249 Vocational schools, nec
Sylvain Desruisseaux

D-U-N-S 25-240-6384   (BR)
COMMISSION SCOLAIRE DU VAL-DES-CERFS
ECOLE JOSEPH-HERMAS-LECLERC
(*Suby of* COMMISSION SCOLAIRE DU VAL-DES-CERFS)
1111 Rue Simonds S, Granby, QC, J2G 9H7
(450) 378-9981
Emp Here 180
SIC 8211 Elementary and secondary schools
Christian Lacourse

D-U-N-S 24-762-7094   (HQ)
COMMISSION SCOLAIRE DU VAL-DES-CERFS
CENTR REG INTEGRE DE FORMATION
55 Rue Court, Granby, QC, J2G 9N6
(450) 372-0221
Emp Here 110   *Sales* 247,797,500
SIC 8211 Elementary and secondary schools
Paul Sarrazin
France Choiniere
Huguette Richard

D-U-N-S 24-581-6566   (SL)
CONFECTION PAGAR INC
451 Rue Edouard, Granby, QC, J2G 3Z4
(450) 375-5398
Emp Here 26   *Sales* 11,530,740
SIC 7389 Business services, nec
Pascal Larivee
Edgar Larivee

D-U-N-S 20-671-7126   (HQ)
COOP DES MONTEREGIENNES, LA
MEUNERIE SAINT-DAMASE
61 Rue Sainte-Therese, Granby, QC, J2G 7K2
(450) 378-2667
Sales 74,252,000
SIC 5191 Farm supplies
Guy Labrecque
Patrick Guillet
Benoit Labrecque
Chantal Gravel
Suzanne Ostiguy
Guy Boisvert
Denis Beaudry
Alcide Boisvert

Richard Viens
Christian Masse

D-U-N-S 20-370-5025   (HQ)
COURTIKA ASSURANCES INC
ASSURANCES MORIN ET ASSOCIES
800 Rue Principale Suite 206, Granby, QC, J2G 2Y8
(450) 372-5801
Sales 42,403,000
SIC 6411 Insurance agents, brokers, and service
David Morin

D-U-N-S 24-651-0036   (SL)
DEPANNEUR VAL MAHER INC
1000 Ch Denison E, Granby, QC, J2G 8C7
(450) 375-2041
Emp Here 45   *Sales* 12,336,840
SIC 5411 Grocery stores
Gilles Dupuis
Daniel Morin

D-U-N-S 20-792-4903   (SL)
EMBALLAGES POLIPLASTIC INC
415 Rue Saint-Vallier, Granby, QC, J2G 7Y3
(450) 378-8417
Emp Here 70   *Sales* 16,340,450
SIC 2673 Bags: plastic, laminated, and coated
Michael Friedman
Hershey Friedman
Elizabeth Friedman

D-U-N-S 20-543-6074   (HQ)
GAZ PROPANE RAINVILLE INC
BOUTIQUE FOYER PROPANE EXPRESSE
280 Rue Saint-Charles S, Granby, QC, J2G 7A9
(450) 378-4108
Emp Here 60   *Sales* 24,432,800
SIC 5984 Liquefied petroleum gas dealers
Andre Rainville
Francois Rainville
Richard Rainville

D-U-N-S 24-174-8409   (SL)
GESTION RESTO GRANBY INC
ROTISSERIE ST-HUBERT
940 Rue Principale, Granby, QC, J2G 2Z4
(450) 378-4656
Emp Here 85   *Sales* 3,869,115
SIC 5812 Eating places
Donald Trudeau

D-U-N-S 25-335-2462   (HQ)
GROUPE ESTRIE-RICHELIEU, COMPAGNIE D'ASSURANCE, LE
770 Rue Principale, Granby, QC, J2G 2Y7
(450) 378-0101
Emp Here 47   *Sales* 64,241,736
SIC 6331 Fire, marine, and casualty insurance
Michel Prevost

D-U-N-S 24-390-7107   (HQ)
INDUSTRIES CRESSWELL INC
(*Suby of* 3195538 CANADA INC)
424 Rue Saint-Vallier, Granby, QC, J2G 7Y4
(450) 378-4611
Emp Here 115   *Sales* 57,159,285
SIC 3499 Fabricated Metal products, nec
Scott B. Jones
Bryan D. Jones
Pina Santillo
Lawrence P. Cannon

D-U-N-S 24-837-2310   (SL)
INDUSTRIES DE MOULAGE POLYCELL INC, LES
(*Suby of* PLASTIQUES CELLULAIRES POLY-FORM INC)
448 Rue Edouard, Granby, QC, J2G 3Z3
(450) 378-9093
Emp Here 60   *Sales* 17,041,260
SIC 2821 Plastics materials and resins
Jean-Louis Beliveau
Danielle Beliveau

D-U-N-S 20-017-0996   (SL)
INDUSTRIES DE MOULAGE POLYMAX INC, LES
(*Suby of* PLASTIQUES CELLULAIRES POLY-FORM INC)
454 Rue Edouard, Granby, QC, J2G 3Z3
(450) 378-9093
Emp Here 100   *Sales* 15,885,800
SIC 3086 Plastics foam products
Jean-Louis Beliveau
Danielle Beliveau

D-U-N-S 20-017-0954   (SL)
INDUSTRIES DE MOULAGE POLYTECH INC, LES
(*Suby of* PLASTIQUES CELLULAIRES POLY-FORM INC)
454 Rue Edouard, Granby, QC, J2G 3Z3
(450) 378-9093
Emp Here 75   *Sales* 11,914,350
SIC 3081 Unsupported plastics film and sheet
Jean-Louis Beliveau
Danielle Beliveau
Martin Boisvert

D-U-N-S 24-402-6639   (SL)
INDUSTRIES F.M. INC
176 Rue Frontenac, Granby, QC, J2G 7R4
(450) 378-0148
Emp Here 22   *Sales* 16,335,440
SIC 5199 Nondurable goods, nec
Marc Nadeau
Diane Labelle
Alexandre Nadeau

D-U-N-S 24-032-3076   (SL)
LABELIX INC
TEKLASER
536 Rue Guy, Granby, QC, J2G 7J8
(450) 372-7777
Emp Here 25   *Sales* 11,230,475
SIC 7389 Business services, nec
Claude Bouffard
Jean-Yves Bouffard
Daniel Bouffard

D-U-N-S 20-790-6454   (HQ)
LANDES CANADA INC
ACCESSOIRES BY/PAR RAE
(*Suby of* MEDIKE INTERNATIONAL CORP)
400 Rue Saint-Vallier, Granby, QC, J2G 7Y4
(450) 378-9853
Sales 11,671,750
SIC 3199 Leather goods, nec
Jonathan Harris

D-U-N-S 20-000-2249   (SL)
MARCHE GAOUETTE INC
IGA
40 Rue Evangeline, Granby, QC, J2G 8K1
(450) 378-4447
Emp Here 100   *Sales* 29,347,700
SIC 5411 Grocery stores
Marcel Gaouette
Chantal Therrien
Jasen Gaouette

D-U-N-S 20-593-5711   (SL)
MARCHE PLOUFFE GRANBY INC
65 Rue Principale, Granby, QC, J2G 2T7
(450) 378-9926
Emp Here 49   *Sales* 13,589,033
SIC 5411 Grocery stores
Patrick Plouffe

D-U-N-S 24-812-2173   (SL)
MARTEL FILS INC
688 Rue Principale, Granby, QC, J2G 2Y4
(450) 361-6445
Emp Here 49   *Sales* 25,935,547
SIC 5099 Durable goods, nec
Michelle Martel

D-U-N-S 24-402-2521   (SL)
NSE AUTOMATECH INC
520 Rue Rutherford, Granby, QC, J2G 0B2

(450) 378-7207
Emp Here 100   *Sales* 22,200,100
SIC 3545 Machine tool accessories
Francois Lacoste
Xavier Kato
Serge Blackburn
Pierre Brouillard
Eric Ellyson
Jacques Ouellet

D-U-N-S 20-542-6505   (SL)
PATATES DINO INC
71 Rue Foch, Granby, QC, J2G 6B4
(450) 372-3373
Emp Here 26   *Sales* 21,725,002
SIC 5148 Fresh fruits and vegetables
Laurier Riendeau
Manon Riendeau
Stephane Riendeau
Pierrette Lauzon

D-U-N-S 24-355-7027   (HQ)
PETRO MONTESTRIE INC
GENDRON & LAMOUREUX
(*Suby of* GROUPE ENERGIE BDL INC)
619 Rue Laurent, Granby, QC, J2G 8Y3
(450) 378-9771
Emp Here 10   *Sales* 31,430,025
SIC 5172 Petroleum products, nec
Patrick Boule
Pierre Boule
Pierre-Marc Lamoureux
Gilbert Boule

D-U-N-S 20-198-5553   (SL)
PETROLES COULOMBE & FILS INC, LES
226 Rue Robinson S Bureau 1, Granby, QC, J2G 7M6
(450) 375-2080
Emp Here 15   *Sales* 18,858,015
SIC 5172 Petroleum products, nec
Guy Coulombe
Rene Coulombe
Raymonde Coulombe

D-U-N-S 25-380-6368   (HQ)
POLYONE DSS CANADA INC
SOCIETE POLYONE DSS CANADA
440 Rue Robinson S, Granby, QC, J2G 9R3
(450) 378-8433
Emp Here 65   *Sales* 64,479,240
SIC 3089 Plastics products, nec
Richard Altice
Robert K. James
Genevieve E. Machin
Kevin D. Jones

D-U-N-S 20-694-4493   (SL)
PRODUITS BELT-TECH INC
386 Rue Dorchester, Granby, QC, J2G 3Z7
(450) 372-5826
Emp Here 120   *Sales* 16,400,880
SIC 2399 Fabricated textile products, nec
Robert J. Belanger
Sylvie Nerbonne
Hugo Boisclair

D-U-N-S 20-198-9662   (HQ)
RAINVILLE AUTOMOBILE 1975 INC
INTERNATIONALE
15 Rue Dutilly, Granby, QC, J2G 6N6
(450) 378-3943
Emp Here 27   *Sales* 17,432,730
SIC 5511 New and used car dealers
Yves Proulx
Gilles Proulx

D-U-N-S 24-436-5073   (SL)
S.O.S. DEPANNAGE GRANBY ET REGION INC
SOS DEPANNAGE MAGASIN GENERAL
327 Rue Matton, Granby, QC, J2G 7R1
(450) 378-4208
Emp Here 49   *Sales* 11,114,817
SIC 8399 Social services, nec
Norman Dunn

D-U-N-S 24-900-3401   (SL)

SANI-ECO INC
(*Suby of GESTION SANI-ECO INC*)
530 Rue Edouard, Granby, QC, J2G 3Z6
(450) 777-4977
Emp Here 110   *Sales* 35,080,100
SIC 4953 Refuse systems
Jean-Denis Gagne
Sylvain Gagne
Juliette Gagne
Michelle Carey
Christian Gagne
Julie Gagne
Stephane Gagne

D-U-N-S 20-010-0126   (SL)
SERVICE D'ECHANGE RAPIDGAZ INC
RAPIDGAZ
241 Rue Saint-Charles S, Granby, QC, J2G
7A7
(450) 375-6644
Emp Here 50   *Sales* 62,860,050
SIC 5172 Petroleum products, nec
Andre Rainville
Francois Rainville
Richard Rainville
Raymond Beaudoin

D-U-N-S 24-865-2745   (HQ)
STEDFAST INC
AVISCEN
230 Rue Saint-Charles S, Granby, QC, J2G
3Y3
(450) 378-8441
Sales 20,174,330
SIC 2295 Coated fabrics, not rubberized
Jack Kay Jr.
Jennifer Kay Kellock

D-U-N-S 25-466-2596   (SL)
SUPER MARCHE FRONTENAC INC
PROVIGO GAGNON
320 Boul Leclerc O, Granby, QC, J2G 1V3
(450) 372-8014
Emp Here 65   *Sales* 19,076,005
SIC 5411 Grocery stores
Gilbert Ouellet
Antonio Gagnon

D-U-N-S 20-059-6703   (SL)
TERMINAL BRIGHAM INC
280 Rue Saint-Charles S, Granby, QC, J2G
7A9
(450) 378-4108
Emp Here 5   *Sales* 15,529,285
SIC 4923 Gas transmission and distribution
Richard Rainville
Andre Rainville

D-U-N-S 24-746-1585   (SL)
TRAITEURS J. D. INC, LES
635 Rue Cowie, Granby, QC, J2G 8J2

Emp Here 40   *Sales* 26,258,560
SIC 5962 Merchandising machine operators
Jeanne Jasmin

Granby, QC J2H

D-U-N-S 24-228-7985   (SL)
COLLEGE MONT SACRE-COEUR
210 Rue Denison E, Granby, QC, J2H 2R6
(450) 372-6882
Emp Here 90   *Sales* 10,137,240
SIC 8222 Junior colleges
Blanca De Gobbi
Robert Jette
Claude Lacroix

D-U-N-S 20-198-5959   (HQ)
DUBE & LOISELLE INC
583 Rue Dufferin, Granby, QC, J2H 0Y5
(450) 378-9996
Sales 93,173,080
SIC 5149 Groceries and related products, nec

Daniel Lachapelle
Gaetan Brunelle
Robert J. Briscoe

D-U-N-S 24-317-5580   (SL)
JEAN-COUTU
505 Rue Du Rubis, Granby, QC, J2H 2S3
(450) 266-3966
Emp Here 40   *Sales* 10,118,160
SIC 5912 Drug stores and proprietary stores
Julie Coderre

D-U-N-S 24-408-7313   (SL)
MARCHE ST-PIERRE ET FILS INC
585 Rue Saint-Hubert, Granby, QC, J2H 1Y5
(450) 777-0898
Emp Here 49   *Sales* 13,433,448
SIC 5411 Grocery stores
Serge Fleurent

D-U-N-S 25-407-7266   (SL)
MESSAGER RAPIDE INC
CHARBONNEAU MESSAGER RAPIDE
164 9e Rang E, Granby, QC, J2H 0T2
(450) 378-1298
Emp Here 36   *Sales* 15,965,640
SIC 7389 Business services, nec
Andre Charbonneau

D-U-N-S 25-245-0473   (SL)
ORANGE MAISON INC
904 Rue Dufferin, Granby, QC, J2H 0T8

Emp Here 49   *Sales* 40,943,273
SIC 5149 Groceries and related products, nec
Jean Gattuso

D-U-N-S 24-058-1772   (SL)
**TRANSPORTEURS EN VRAC SHEFFORD
INC, LES**
438 Rue De La Providence, Granby, QC, J2H
1H1
(450) 375-2331
Emp Here 49   *Sales* 25,478,383
SIC 4731 Freight transportation arrangement
Lucie Counoir

Granby, QC J2J

D-U-N-S 25-628-4048   (SL)
3100-8410 QUEBEC INC
LE GROUPE BERNIER DAIGLE
1165 Rue Principale, Granby, QC, J2J 0M3
(450) 994-4220
Emp Here 49   *Sales* 24,405,822
SIC 5511 New and used car dealers
Serge Bernier

D-U-N-S 25-089-0399   (SL)
9055-5749 QUEBEC INC
TRANSPORT SN
1060 Rue Andre-Line, Granby, QC, J2J 1J9
(450) 772-1112
Emp Here 125   *Sales* 25,713,250
SIC 4212 Local trucking, without storage
Sebastien Brodeur

D-U-N-S 25-488-3796   (HQ)
9106-3644 QUEBEC INC
MERCEDES-BENZ ET SMART
1289 Rue Principale, Granby, QC, J2J 0M3
(450) 372-2007
Emp Here 15   *Sales* 11,953,872
SIC 5511 New and used car dealers
Renee Thibodeau
Francois Planmondon

D-U-N-S 20-290-0965   (SL)
A7 INTEGRATION INC
884 Rue Cowie, Granby, QC, J2J 1A8
(450) 305-6218
Emp Here 70   *Sales* 13,445,950
SIC 3499 Fabricated Metal products, nec
Eric Dupere
Denis Labranche

Jean-Sebastien Pelchat
Stephane Ouellet

D-U-N-S 25-307-3548   (BR)
AGROPUR COOPERATIVE
FROMAGERIE DE GRANDBY
(*Suby of AGROPUR COOPERATIVE*)
1100 Rue Omer-Deslauriers, Granby, QC, J2J
0S7
(450) 777-5300
Emp Here 280
SIC 2022 Cheese; natural and processed
Richard Marier

D-U-N-S 24-310-6460   (BR)
ALLAN CANDY COMPANY LIMITED, THE
(*Suby of HERSHEY COMPANY*)
850 Boul Industriel, Granby, QC, J2J 1B8
(450) 372-1080
Emp Here 400
SIC 2064 Candy and other confectionery
products
Peter James

D-U-N-S 20-541-6720   (HQ)
AMADA CANADA LTD
(*Suby of AMADA HOLDINGS CO., LTD.*)
885 Rue Georges-Cros, Granby, QC, J2J 1E8
(450) 378-0111
Emp Here 30   *Sales* 23,276,274
SIC 5084 Industrial machinery and equipment
Katsumi Karimura
Louis L Gascon
Koji Yamamoto

D-U-N-S 24-954-2820   (HQ)
ARTOPEX INC
(*Suby of GROUPE PRO-PLUS INC*)
800 Rue Vadnais, Granby, QC, J2J 1A7
(450) 378-0189
Emp Here 60   *Sales* 13,888,980
SIC 2522 Office furniture, except wood
Daniel Pelletier
Martin Pelletier

D-U-N-S 24-322-9622   (SL)
AUTOBUS GRANBY INC
(*Suby of TRANSPORT SCOLAIRE SO-
GESCO INC*)
1254 Rue Principale, Granby, QC, J2J 0M2
(450) 378-9951
Emp Here 95   *Sales* 7,150,840
SIC 4142 Bus charter service, except local
Dave Girardin
Jean-Paul Provost
Louise L'italien
Mario Provost

D-U-N-S 25-023-9175   (SL)
AUTOS R. CHAGNON DE GRANBY INC
CHAGNON HONDA
1711 Rue Principale, Granby, QC, J2J 0M9
(450) 378-9963
Emp Here 40   *Sales* 19,923,120
SIC 5511 New and used car dealers
Real Chagnon
Sylvain Chagnon
Annie Chagnon

D-U-N-S 24-762-7821   (SL)
**CAOUTCHOUC ET PLASTIQUES FALPACO
INC**
825 Rue J.-A.-Bombardier, Granby, QC, J2J
1E9
(450) 378-3348
Emp Here 26   *Sales* 12,350,676
SIC 5085 Industrial supplies
Claude Robichaud

D-U-N-S 20-665-2273   (SL)
**CENTRE OPTOMETRIQUE DE GRANBY
INC**
220 Rue Saint-Jude N, Granby, QC, J2J 0C2
(450) 372-1031
Emp Here 26   *Sales* 11,626,524
SIC 5047 Medical and hospital equipment
Michelle Morin

D-U-N-S 20-033-9070   (BR)
**COMMISSION SCOLAIRE DU VAL-DES-
CERFS**
ECOLE SECONDAIRE L'ENVOLEE
(*Suby of COMMISSION SCOLAIRE DU VAL-
DES-CERFS*)
549 Rue Fournier, Granby, QC, J2J 2K5
(450) 777-7536
Emp Here 75
SIC 8211 Elementary and secondary schools
Robert Chicoine

D-U-N-S 24-768-2446   (SL)
CONSTRUCTION IDEAL DE GRANBY INC
65 Rue Saint-Jude S, Granby, QC, J2J 2N2
(450) 378-2301
Emp Here 30   *Sales* 14,121,930
SIC 1542 Nonresidential construction, nec
Daniel Grondin
Pascal Deslauriers

D-U-N-S 25-211-0630   (SL)
CONTENANTS DURABAC INC, LES
(*Suby of 9101-0538 QUEBEC INC*)
22 Ch Milton, Granby, QC, J2J 0P2
(450) 378-1723
Emp Here 70   *Sales* 13,445,950
SIC 3443 Fabricated plate work (boiler shop)
Patrick Charbonneau

D-U-N-S 20-362-7948   (SL)
COWIE INC
660 Rue Bernard, Granby, QC, J2J 0H6
(450) 375-7500
Emp Here 50   *Sales* 41,778,850
SIC 5146 Fish and seafoods
Louis Levesque

D-U-N-S 24-858-5200   (SL)
CUISINES BEAUREGARD INC
655 Rue Simonds S, Granby, QC, J2J 1C2
(450) 375-0707
Emp Here 45   *Sales* 11,387,655
SIC 5211 Lumber and other building materials
Jocelyne Giguere
Sylvain Brunelle

D-U-N-S 24-339-6590   (BR)
**DATA COMMUNICATIONS MANAGEMENT
CORP**
DATA GROUP OF COMPANIES
(*Suby of DATA COMMUNICATIONS MAN-
AGEMENT CORP*)
855 Boul Industriel, Granby, QC, J2J 1A6

Emp Here 125
SIC 2761 Manifold business forms
Luc Martel

D-U-N-S 20-289-6403   (HQ)
ELECTROGROUPE PIONEER CANADA INC
AAER
612 Ch Bernard, Granby, QC, J2J 0H6
(450) 378-9018
Sales 19,044,200
SIC 3612 Transformers, except electric
Nathan Mazurek
Raymond Haddad
Thomas Klink

D-U-N-S 25-220-0910   (SL)
EZEFLOW INC
(*Suby of EZE HOLDINGS, LLC*)
985 Rue Andre-Line, Granby, QC, J2J 1J6
(450) 375-3575
Emp Here 100   *Sales* 19,208,500
SIC 3498 Fabricated pipe and fittings
Marc Herzstein
Pierre Latendresse
Jeremy Blachman

D-U-N-S 24-510-4252   (HQ)
FIVES LINE MACHINES INC
LINE MACHINES-OUTILS
(*Suby of FIVES ORSAY*)
1000 Rue Andre-Line, Granby, QC, J2J 1E2

▲ Public Company   ■ Public Company Family Member   **HQ** Headquarters   **BR** Branch   **SL** Single Location

(450) 372-6480
Sales 22,200,100
SIC 3541 Machine tools, Metal cutting type
Denis Hugelmann
Michel Dufresne
Sylvain Dulude
Guy Lalonde

D-U-N-S 25-024-1254   (SL)
FORMULE FORD LINCOLN INC
1144 Rue Principale, Granby, QC, J2J 0M2
(450) 777-1777
Emp Here 45   *Sales* 22,413,510
SIC 5511 New and used car dealers
Guy Bissonnette

D-U-N-S 25-337-9234   (SL)
FORMULES D'AFFAIRES SUPRATECH INC
960 Rue Andre-Line, Granby, QC, J2J 1E2
(450) 777-1041
Emp Here 62   *Sales* 10,169,674
SIC 2752 Commercial printing, lithographic
Marcel Guertin
Paul Gagnon
Michel Labonte

D-U-N-S 25-194-8899   (SL)
FUSION SOLUTION INC
700 Rue Bernard, Granby, QC, J2J 0H6
(450) 372-4994
Emp Here 36   *Sales* 15,965,640
SIC 7389 Business services, nec
Carl Chausse

D-U-N-S 20-119-8095   (HQ)
GRANBY INDUSTRIES LIMITED PARTNER-SHIP
GRANBY STEEL TANKS
1020 Rue Andre-Line, Granby, QC, J2J 1J9
(450) 378-2334
Sales 41,349,270
SIC 3443 Fabricated plate work (boiler shop)
Pierre Fournier

D-U-N-S 24-022-3131   (SL)
GRAND BAZAR DE GRANBY INC, AU
GRAND BAZAR LA SOURCE DU SPORT, AU
1141 Rue Principale Bureau 378, Granby, QC, J2J 0M3
(450) 378-2022
Emp Here 80   *Sales* 19,546,240
SIC 5941 Sporting goods and bicycle shops
Mario Grondin
Pierre Grondin
Lyne Grondin

D-U-N-S 24-422-0682   (BR)
GREAT PACIFIC ENTERPRISES INC
COROPLAST DIV
(*Suby of* PATTISON, JIM GROUP INC)
700 Rue Vadnais, Granby, QC, J2J 1A7
(450) 378-3995
Emp Here 75
SIC 3081 Unsupported plastics film and sheet
Michel Loiselle

D-U-N-S 24-461-6538   (SL)
GROUPE ALLAIREGINCE INFRASTRUC-TURES INC
LES TERRASSEMENTS ALLAIRE & GINCE
70 Rue De Gatineau, Granby, QC, J2J 0P1
(450) 378-1623
Emp Here 50   *Sales* 11,008,400
SIC 1794 Excavation work
Rejean Gince
Claude Sylvain
Richard Naud

D-U-N-S 24-943-2543   (HQ)
GROUPE LCI CANADA, INC
COMPOSANTES LIPPERT
(*Suby of* LCI INDUSTRIES)
850 Rue Moeller, Granby, QC, J2J 1K7
(450) 378-6722
Sales 63,922,500
SIC 3231 Products of purchased glass
Jason D. Lippert
Andrew Namenye

Jim Menefee
Marcellus M Lebbin
Brian M. Hall

D-U-N-S 20-870-2022   (BR)
HOME DEPOT OF CANADA INC
HOME DEPOT
(*Suby of* THE HOME DEPOT INC)
165 Rue Simonds N, Granby, QC, J2J 0R7
(450) 375-5544
Emp Here 100
SIC 5251 Hardware stores

D-U-N-S 24-871-8348   (SL)
L. DAVIS TEXTILES (1991) INC
MOULAGE RANGER
780 Rue Georges-Cros, Granby, QC, J2J 1N2
(450) 375-1665
Emp Here 26   *Sales* 12,956,372
SIC 5137 Women's and children's clothing
Yvon Ranger

D-U-N-S 24-999-8923   (SL)
LASER AMP INC
770 Rue Georges-Cros, Granby, QC, J2J 1N2
(450) 776-6982
Emp Here 85   *Sales* 15,417,980
SIC 3399 Primary Metal products
Robert H. Henderson
Donald Beauregard
Alexander Lucas Henderson
Jared James Henderson

D-U-N-S 24-568-0632   (HQ)
MAPLE TREAT CORPORATION, THE
(*Suby of* ROGERS SUGAR INC)
1037 Boul Industriel, Granby, QC, J2J 2B8
(450) 777-4464
Sales 60,923,125
SIC 2099 Food preparations, nec
John Holliday
Manon Lacroix
Daniel Lafrance
Manfred Dallas H. Ross
Michael A. Heskin
Donald G. Jewell
Gary Collins

D-U-N-S 25-183-9494   (SL)
MICHEL THIBAUDEAU INC
CANADIAN TIRE 138
70 Rue Simonds N, Granby, QC, J2J 2L1
(450) 378-9884
Emp Here 50   *Sales* 12,652,950
SIC 5251 Hardware stores
Michel Thibaudeau
Mary-Judes Thibaudeau
Claude Thibaudeau

D-U-N-S 20-760-6617   (SL)
MONTESTRIE AUTORAMA INC
ESTRIE TOYOTA
6 Rue Irwin, Granby, QC, J2J 2P1
(450) 378-8404
Emp Here 26   *Sales* 12,950,028
SIC 5511 New and used car dealers
Andre Beauregard
Daniel Galipeau
Andre Jr Beauregard

D-U-N-S 20-002-8368   (BR)
PEPSICO CANADA ULC
FRITO LAY CANADA
(*Suby of* PEPSICO, INC.)
855 Rue J.-A.-Bombardier, Granby, QC, J2J 1E9
(450) 375-5555
Emp Here 125
SIC 2086 Bottled and canned soft drinks
Bernard Turgeon

D-U-N-S 24-203-6726   (SL)
PLASTUBE INC
PLASTUBE NORTH AMERICA
590 Rue Simonds S, Granby, QC, J2J 1E1
(450) 378-2633
Emp Here 140   *Sales* 39,762,940

SIC 2821 Plastics materials and resins
Christian Turgeon
Paul Matte
Nicolas Renaud
Gilles Decelles
Marc Beauchamp
Gilles Veilleux

D-U-N-S 24-528-6356   (HQ)
POISSONNERIE COWIE (1985) INC, LA
(*Suby of* 9096-5385 QUEBEC INC)
660 Rue Bernard, Granby, QC, J2J 0H6
(450) 375-7500
Emp Here 10   *Sales* 58,490,390
SIC 5142 Packaged frozen goods
Jacques Martin

D-U-N-S 24-347-5352   (BR)
POLYFORM A.G.P. INC
INDUSTRIES DE MOULAGE POLYMAX, LES
870 Boul Industriel, Granby, QC, J2J 1A4
(450) 378-9093
Emp Here 100
SIC 3081 Unsupported plastics film and sheet
Francois Dubuc

D-U-N-S 24-509-4321   (SL)
PRINCIPALE AUTOS LTEE
HYUNDAI GRANBY
1196 Rue Principale, Granby, QC, J2J 0M2
(450) 378-4666
Emp Here 22   *Sales* 10,957,716
SIC 5511 New and used car dealers
Joseph De Gobbi
Blanca De Gobbi

D-U-N-S 24-203-8383   (HQ)
PRINOTH LTD
(*Suby of* SEETECH GLOBAL INDUSTRIES SPA)
1001 Rue J.-A.-Bombardier, Granby, QC, J2J 1E9
(450) 776-3600
Emp Here 50   *Sales* 138,346,200
SIC 5013 Motor vehicle supplies and new parts
Werner Amort
Anton Seeber
Haller Horst

D-U-N-S 24-226-3705   (SL)
PRO-MEUBLES INC
800 Rue Vadnais Bureau 450, Granby, QC, J2J 1A7
(450) 378-0189
Emp Here 125   *Sales* 19,290,250
SIC 2521 Wood office furniture
Daniel Pelletier
Maurice Pelletier
Andre Pelletier

D-U-N-S 24-884-1819   (SL)
PRO-SYSTEMES APX INC
1050 Boul Industriel, Granby, QC, J2J 1A4
(450) 378-0189
Emp Here 73   *Sales* 11,265,506
SIC 2542 Partitions and fixtures, except wood
Daniel Pelletier

D-U-N-S 24-051-1873   (SL)
PUBLICITE MALGA INC
MALGA
625 Rue Georges-Cros, Granby, QC, J2J 1B4
(450) 378-4448
Emp Here 22   *Sales* 16,335,440
SIC 5199 Nondurable goods, nec
Richard Malette
Dominic Cote

D-U-N-S 24-814-6565   (HQ)
RE/MAX PROFESSIONEL INC
1050 Rue Principale, Granby, QC, J2J 2N7
(450) 378-4120
Emp Here 7   *Sales* 13,587,800
SIC 6531 Real estate agents and managers
Claude Roy
Yves Forand

Pierre Bellefleur

D-U-N-S 24-367-1612   (HQ)
REVETEMENTS AGRO INC, LES
1195 Rue Principale, Granby, QC, J2J 0M3
(450) 776-1010
Sales 11,880,320
SIC 5198 Paints, varnishes, and supplies
Michel Marcoux
Rock Marcoux

D-U-N-S 24-648-1683   (SL)
SERVICES DE MECANIQUE MOBILE B L INC
RESSORTS B L
50 Rue Saint-Jude S, Granby, QC, J2J 2N4
(450) 378-0413
Emp Here 50   *Sales* 24,903,900
SIC 5511 New and used car dealers
Daniel Lamoureux

D-U-N-S 20-005-1345   (BR)
SHERMAG IMPORT INC
BEDARD, DIV DE
(*Suby of* GROUPE BERMEX INC)
825 Boul Industriel, Granby, QC, J2J 1A5
(450) 776-6361
Emp Here 80
SIC 2511 Wood household furniture
Jean-Sebastien Beaurivage

D-U-N-S 24-619-9160   (SL)
TOPRINGS LTEE
(*Suby of* 9198-1803 QUEBEC INC)
1020 Boul Industriel, Granby, QC, J2J 1A4
(450) 375-1828
Emp Here 45   *Sales* 21,376,170
SIC 5085 Industrial supplies
Louis Menard
Alexander Menard
Frederic Theroux
Anne-Catherine Menard

D-U-N-S 24-960-0016   (HQ)
TRILLIANT NETWORKS (CANADA) INC
(*Suby of* TRILLIANT NETWORKS INC.)
610 Rue Du Luxembourg, Granby, QC, J2J 2V2
(450) 375-0556
Emp Here 60   *Sales* 55,422,740
SIC 3825 Instruments to measure electricity
Andrew C. White
Steven Muzzo
Mark Lewis

D-U-N-S 20-908-7196   (BR)
VELAN INC
(*Suby of* SOCIETE HOLDING VELAN LTEE)
1010 Rue Cowie, Granby, QC, J2J 1E7
(450) 378-2305
Emp Here 108
SIC 3494 Valves and pipe fittings, nec

D-U-N-S 25-536-1776   (SL)
VETEMENTS S P INC, LES
1237 Boul Industriel, Granby, QC, J2J 2B8
(450) 776-6111
Emp Here 110   *Sales* 15,034,140
SIC 2329 Men's and boy's clothing, nec
Serge Berard
Manon Bourget
Steve Berard

D-U-N-S 25-297-7863   (BR)
WAL-MART CANADA CORP
WAL MART GRANBY STORE- #3035
(*Suby of* WALMART INC.)
75 Rue Simonds N, Granby, QC, J2J 2S3
(450) 777-8863
Emp Here 300
SIC 5311 Department stores
Jean-Pierre Lafontaine

Grand-Mere, QC G9T

D-U-N-S 24-863-3414   (SL)
BELZILE, BEAUMIER ET BELZILE SENC
JEAN COUTU 30
765 6e Av, Grand-Mere, QC, G9T 2H8
(819) 538-8606
Emp Here 47   *Sales* 11,888,838
SIC 5912 Drug stores and proprietary stores
   Claude Belzile
   Pierre Belzile
   Marie Beaumier

D-U-N-S 20-103-5313   (SL)
HDI TECHNOLOGIES INC
200 Rue Des Batisseurs, Grand-Mere, QC,
G9T 5K5
(819) 538-3398
Emp Here 50   *Sales* 10,233,650
SIC 3679 Electronic components, nec
   Claude Rousseau
   Richard Gonneville
   Erwin Zecha

D-U-N-S 20-996-2401   (BR)
KONGSBERG INC
MEGATECH ELECTRO
(*Suby of* KONGSBERG AUTOMOTIVE ASA)
2801 3e Rue, Grand-Mere, QC, G9T 5K5
(819) 533-3202
Emp Here 125
SIC 3651 Household audio and video equipment

D-U-N-S 20-433-1979   (SL)
LIONEL VENNES & FILS INC
180 32e Av Bureau 1, Grand-Mere, QC, G9T
5K5
(819) 538-2308
Emp Here 50   *Sales* 11,046,700
SIC 1711 Plumbing, heating, air-conditioning

D-U-N-S 24-841-9236   (BR)
PMA ASSURANCES INC
(*Suby of* PMA ASSURANCES INC)
632 6e Av, Grand-Mere, QC, G9T 2H5
(819) 538-8626
Emp Here 102
SIC 6411 Insurance agents, brokers, and service
   Steve Martin

D-U-N-S 20-199-3540   (SL)
SOCIETE IMMOBILIERE LAFLECHE INC, LA
JEAN COUTU # 30
765 6e Av, Grand-Mere, QC, G9T 2H8
(819) 538-8606
Emp Here 47   *Sales* 11,888,838
SIC 5912 Drug stores and proprietary stores
   Francois Jean Coutu
   Annie Desjardins
   Eve Gauthier

D-U-N-S 20-872-7644   (SL)
VALLEE DU PARC DE SHAWINIGAN INC
VALLEE DU PARC
10000 Ch Vallee-Du-Parc, Grand-Mere, QC,
G9T 5K5
(819) 538-1639
Emp Here 85   *Sales* 11,902,465
SIC 7999 Amusement and recreation, nec
   Claude Gauthier
   Michel Matte

Grande-Riviere, QC G0C

D-U-N-S 25-092-1652   (SL)
9255-8097 QUEBEC INC.
JEAN COUTU
185 Grande Allee E, Grande-Riviere, QC,
G0C 1V0
(418) 385-2121
Emp Here 100   *Sales* 24,432,800
SIC 5912 Drug stores and proprietary stores
   Michel Whittom
   Terry Whittom

D-U-N-S 24-637-9135   (HQ)
AUTOMOBILES MAUGER FORD INC
REMORQUAGE NEW RICHMOND
119 Grande Allee E, Grande-Riviere, QC,
G0C 1V0
(418) 385-2118
Emp Here 40   *Sales* 40,903,200
SIC 5511 New and used car dealers
   Jean-Louis Mauger

D-U-N-S 20-858-0993   (SL)
POISSON SALE GASPESIEN LTEE
PSB
39 Rue Du Parc, Grande-Riviere, QC, G0C
1V0
(418) 385-2424
Emp Here 250   *Sales* 121,846,250
SIC 2091 Canned and cured fish and
seafoods
   Real Nicolas
   Serge Dube
   Paulette Methot
   Norbert Lelievre
   Sylvie Dube
   Jacques Methot

Grande-Riviere-Ouest, QC G0C

D-U-N-S 25-515-3637   (SL)
ATELIERS ACTIBEC 2000 INC, LES
508 Grande Allee O, Grande-Riviere-Ouest,
QC, G0C 1W0
(418) 385-1414
Emp Here 40   *Sales* 10,285,240
SIC 4953 Refuse systems
   Jean-Paul Leblanc
   Henri Grenier
   Gaston Roy
   Jacques Gendron
   Simon-Pierre Dube
   Rosanne Trudel
   Georges Mamelonnet
   Nathalie Drapeau

Grande-Vallee, QC G0E

D-U-N-S 20-243-4218   (SL)
COOP DE TRAVAIL EN AMENAGEMENT FORESTIER DE GRANDE-VALLEE
39c Rue Saint-Francois-Xavier E, Grande-
Vallee, QC, G0E 1K0
(418) 393-3339
Emp Here 49   *Sales* 10,369,037
SIC 0851 Forestry services
   Sylvie Langlois

Grandes-Bergeronnes, QC G0T

D-U-N-S 24-069-4724   (SL)
BERSACO, INC
717 Rue De La Montagne, Grandes-
Bergeronnes, QC, G0T 1G0
(418) 232-1100
Emp Here 70   *Sales* 13,465,900
SIC 2448 Wood pallets and skids
   Andre Gilbert
   Steeve St-Gelais
   Lucas Deschenes
   Charles Lessard
   Narcisse Morin
   Guy Deschenes

D-U-N-S 24-067-8339   (SL)
EXPLOS-NATURE
302 Rue De La Riviere, Grandes-
Bergeronnes, QC, G0T 1G0
(418) 232-6249
Emp Here 48   *Sales* 19,075,872

SIC 8699 Membership organizations, nec
   Martin Vaillancourt

Greenfield Park, QC J4V

D-U-N-S 24-858-4716   (SL)
8421722 CANADA INC
MERCEDES BENZ RIVE-SUD
(*Suby of* AUTOCANADA INC)
4844 Boul Taschereau, Greenfield Park, QC,
J4V 2J2
(450) 672-2720
Emp Here 50   *Sales* 24,903,900
SIC 5511 New and used car dealers
   Samuel Eltes
   Gerald Girouard

D-U-N-S 20-329-9938   (SL)
CONCEPT SAINT-BRUNO INC
3844 Boul Taschereau, Greenfield Park, QC,
J4V 2H9
(450) 466-0422
Emp Here 50   *Sales* 24,916,100
SIC 5137 Women's and children's clothing
   Michel Croteau

D-U-N-S 20-175-9797   (BR)
HOME DEPOT OF CANADA INC
HOME DEPOT
(*Suby of* THE HOME DEPOT INC)
500 Av Auguste, Greenfield Park, QC, J4V
3R4
(450) 462-5020
Emp Here 130
SIC 5251 Hardware stores
   Isabelle Jutras

D-U-N-S 24-509-9296   (BR)
METRO RICHELIEU INC
SUPER C
(*Suby of* METRO INC)
5012 Boul Taschereau, Greenfield Park, QC,
J4V 2J2
(450) 672-8966
Emp Here 75
SIC 5411 Grocery stores
   Stephan Duquette

D-U-N-S 20-712-3741   (BR)
RIVERSIDE SCHOOL BOARD
GREENFIELD PARK PRIMARY INTERNATIONAL SCHOOL
776 Rue Campbell, Greenfield Park, QC, J4V
1Y7
(450) 672-0042
Emp Here 88
SIC 8211 Elementary and secondary schools
   Lucie Roy

D-U-N-S 24-254-2686   (BR)
RIVERSIDE SCHOOL BOARD
CENTENNIAL REGIONAL HIGH SCHOOL
880 Rue Hudson, Greenfield Park, QC, J4V
1H1
(450) 656-6100
Emp Here 200
SIC 8211 Elementary and secondary schools
   Sherry Tite

D-U-N-S 20-655-9929   (SL)
SUPERMARCHE GEORGES BADRA INC
IGA
300 Av Auguste, Greenfield Park, QC, J4V
3R4
(450) 656-7055
Emp Here 165   *Sales* 48,423,705
SIC 5411 Grocery stores
   Georges Badra

Grenville, QC J0V

D-U-N-S 20-044-4766   (SL)

BDO CANADA LLP
289 Rue Principale, Grenville, QC, J0V 1J0

Emp Here 49   *Sales* 10,245,165
SIC 8721 Accounting, auditing, and bookkeeping
   Allen Nigel A.C.

Grenville-Sur-La-Rouge, QC J0V

D-U-N-S 25-991-8738   (HQ)
RESCO CANADA, INC
(*Suby of* THERMAL SOLUTIONS INTERMEDIATE HOLDINGS, INC.)
1330 Rte 148, Grenville-Sur-La-Rouge, QC,
J0V 1B0
(819) 242-2721
Sales 19,952,680
SIC 3312 Blast furnaces and steel mills
   Douglas G Albert
   Matthew Mastarone
   Carl M Stanton
   John E Morningstar
   Seth R Pearson
   Carole Anne Marchand

D-U-N-S 24-206-0726   (SL)
SOURCES VEO INC, LES
MONTEBELLO
1335 Ch De La Riviere-Rouge, Grenville-Sur-
La-Rouge, QC, J0V 1B0
(819) 242-2882
Emp Here 28   *Sales* 23,396,156
SIC 5149 Groceries and related products, nec
   Jean-Marc Rizk
   Georges-Vicken Patanian
   Seti K. Hamalian

D-U-N-S 20-998-0234   (HQ)
SUCCESSION FORAGE GEORGE DOWNING LTEE
410 Rue Principale, Grenville-Sur-La-Rouge,
QC, J0V 1B0
(819) 242-6469
Emp Here 20   *Sales* 191,003,920
SIC 1081 Metal mining services
   Bruce Downing
   Thomas Downing
   Stephen Downing
   Andrew Downing

Grosse-Ile, QC G4T

D-U-N-S 25-293-3890   (SL)
COOPERATIVE DES PECHEURS DE CAP DAUPHIN
51 Ch Shore, Grosse-Ile, QC, G4T 6A4
(418) 985-2321
Emp Here 50   *Sales* 13,707,600
SIC 5421 Meat and fish markets
   David Taker
   David Burke
   Murray Mckay
   Wilton Burke
   Roger Lejeune
   Ricky Burke
   Rodney Scott
   Ronald Goodwin

D-U-N-S 24-747-0412   (BR)
K+S SEL WINDSOR LTEE
MINES SELEINE
(*Suby of* K+S AG)
50 Ch Principal, Grosse-Ile, QC, G4T 6A6
(418) 985-2931
Emp Here 162
SIC 1479 Chemical and fertilizer mining

Ham-Nord, QC G0P

D-U-N-S 25-379-9282   (SL)
KHEOPS VERRE D'ART INC
KHEOPS INTERNATIONALE
(*Suby of* KHEOPS INTERNATIONAL, INC.)
541 8e Rang, Ham-Nord, QC, G0P 1A0
(819) 344-2152
Emp Here 26   *Sales* 11,626,524
SIC 5049 Professional equipment, nec
Justine Bertrand
Benoit Charbonneau
Dobrina Papillon

Hampstead, QC H3X

D-U-N-S 20-181-6332   (SL)
A.M. FISH HOLDINGS LTD
26 Rue Briardale, Hampstead, QC, H3X 3N6
(514) 788-0788
Emp Here 200   *Sales* 54,670,000
SIC 6712 Bank holding companies
Aaron M. Fish
Chiara Fish
Wally Francis Fish

Harrington Harbour, QC G0G

D-U-N-S 25-488-8670   (SL)
LOWER NORTH SHORE COMMUNITY SEAFOOD COOPERATIVE
2 Dockside Dr, Harrington Harbour, QC, G0G 1N0
(418) 795-3244
Emp Here 52   *Sales* 17,975,880
SIC 2092 Fresh or frozen packaged fish
Austin Rowsell
Winston Bobbitt
Lloyd Ransom
Gordon Ransom
Cecil Anderson

Havelock, QC J0S

D-U-N-S 20-542-3510   (SL)
CARRIERES DUCHARME INC, LES
564 Ch De Covey Hill, Havelock, QC, J0S 2C0
(450) 247-2787
Emp Here 60   *Sales* 14,006,100
SIC 3281 Cut stone and stone products
Serge Ducharme

Havre-Saint-Pierre, QC G0G

D-U-N-S 20-954-6704   (SL)
CENTRE DE SANTE ET DE SERVICES SOCIAUX DE LA MAINGANIE
1035 Prom Des Anciens, Havre-Saint-Pierre, QC, G0G 1P0
(418) 538-2212
Emp Here 250   *Sales* 18,943,250
SIC 8093 Specialty outpatient clinics, nec
Danielle Limoge

D-U-N-S 25-233-4560   (HQ)
COMMISSION SCOLAIRE DE LA MOYENNE-COTE-NORD, LA
1235 Rue De La Digue, Havre-Saint-Pierre, QC, G0G 1P0
(418) 538-3044
Sales 18,832,610
SIC 8211 Elementary and secondary schools
Marius Richard

D-U-N-S 25-488-5965   (SL)

CONSTRUCTIONS RICOR INC
1214 Rue De L'Escale, Havre-Saint-Pierre, QC, G0G 1P0
(418) 538-3201
Emp Here 45   *Sales* 21,182,895
SIC 1542 Nonresidential construction, nec
Andre Richard
Armand Richard

D-U-N-S 20-172-0559   (BR)
GOUVERNEMENT DE LA PROVINCE DE QUEBEC
COMMISSION SCOLAIRE DE LA MOYENNE-COTE-NORD
(*Suby of* GOUVERNEMENT DE LA PROVINCE DE QUEBEC)
1235 Rue De La Digue, Havre-Saint-Pierre, QC, G0G 1P0
(418) 538-2662
Emp Here 200
SIC 8211 Elementary and secondary schools
Marius Richard

D-U-N-S 24-706-3134   (SL)
POISSONNERIE DU HAVRE LTEE
968 Rue De La Berge, Havre-Saint-Pierre, QC, G0G 1P0
(418) 538-2515
Emp Here 160   *Sales* 46,956,320
SIC 5421 Meat and fish markets
Jean-Marc Marcoux
Richard Desbois
Nicol Desbois

Hebertville, QC G8N

D-U-N-S 25-418-8089   (HQ)
PROMUTUEL DU LAC AU FJORD
PROMUTUEL ASSURANCE
11 Rue Commerciale, Hebertville, QC, G8N 1N3
(418) 344-1565
Sales 133,037,424
SIC 6411 Insurance agents, brokers, and service
Omer Bouchard

D-U-N-S 20-332-7817   (SL)
PROMUTUEL DU LAC AU FLEUVE
PROMUTUEL ASSURANCE
11 Rue Commerciale, Hebertville, QC, G8N 1N3
(418) 344-1565
Emp Here 100   *Sales* 123,541,800
SIC 6331 Fire, marine, and casualty insurance
Omer Bouchard
Yvan Picard
Marco Picard
Roger Taillon
Carole Tremblay
Louise Tremblay
Martine Theriault
Guy Lapointe
Jocelyn Benoit
Yves Bouchard

Hebertville-Station, QC G0W

D-U-N-S 25-052-8965   (HQ)
SYSTEMES ADEX INC, LES
ADEXMAT
67 Rue Saint-Paul Rr 1, Hebertville-Station, QC, G0W 1T0
(418) 343-2640
Emp Here 30   *Sales* 11,671,750
SIC 3299 NonMetallic mineral products,
Rafael Bao
Simon Coutu
Andre Delisle

Hemmingford, QC J0L

D-U-N-S 24-582-2069   (SL)
AEROSPATIALE HEMMINGFORD INC
447 Rte 202 O, Hemmingford, QC, J0L 1H0
(450) 247-2722
Emp Here 94   *Sales* 9,097,224
SIC 3728 Aircraft parts and equipment, nec
Dawn-Marie Tuner
Johanah Turner
Gabias-Turner Turner

D-U-N-S 25-541-5150   (HQ)
POMMES ENDERLE INC, LES
VERGERS ENDERLE
514 Ch James-Fisher, Hemmingford, QC, J0L 1H0
(450) 247-2463
Sales 12,578,132
SIC 7389 Business services, nec
Joseph-Charles Enderle
Daniel Enderle
Glen Enderle

Henryville, QC J0J

D-U-N-S 20-199-9356   (SL)
VIATEUR PAQUETTE & FILS INC
1026 133 Rte, Henryville, QC, J0J 1E0

Emp Here 150   *Sales* 44,021,550
SIC 5411 Grocery stores
Robert Paquette
Guy Paquette
Mario Paquette
Jacques Paquette

Honfleur, QC G0R

D-U-N-S 20-431-1500   (HQ)
L. BILODEAU ET FILS LTEE
366 Rue Saint-Jean, Honfleur, QC, G0R 1N0
(418) 885-4495
Sales 26,741,780
SIC 4212 Local trucking, without storage
Isabelle Bilodeau
Gaston Bilodeau
Jerome Bilodeau

Howick, QC J0S

D-U-N-S 24-126-1911   (SL)
SOCIETE EN COMMANDITE BROSPEC 2001
13 Rue Mill, Howick, QC, J0S 1G0

Emp Here 75   *Sales* 13,604,100
SIC 3399 Primary Metal products
Mario Duhaime

Hudson, QC J0P

D-U-N-S 20-860-8398   (SL)
CLUB DE GOLF WHITLOCK
128 Cote Saint-Charles, Hudson, QC, J0P 1H0
(450) 458-5305
Emp Here 100   *Sales* 7,854,500
SIC 7997 Membership sports and recreation clubs
Wayne Baird

D-U-N-S 24-842-9586   (SL)

FONDATION DE LA MAISON DE SOINS PALLIATIFS DE VAUDREUIL-SOULANGES (FMSPVS)
F.S.S.V.S.
90 Rue Como-Gardens, Hudson, QC, J0P 1H0
(450) 202-2202
Emp Here 49   *Sales* 11,114,817
SIC 8399 Social services, nec
Jean-Marie Bourassa

D-U-N-S 20-200-0386   (HQ)
POIRIER & FILS LTEE
POIRIER IGA
484 Rue Principale, Hudson, QC, J0P 1H0
(450) 458-5573
Emp Here 60   *Sales* 51,358,475
SIC 5411 Grocery stores
Michel Poirier
Louise Poirier

Huntingdon, QC J0S

D-U-N-S 20-777-8130   (BR)
BARRIE MEMORIAL HOSPITAL FOUNDATION
C L S C HUNTINGDON
10 Rue King Bureau 200, Huntingdon, QC, J0S 1H0
(450) 829-3877
Emp Here 90
SIC 8322 Individual and family services
Yves Parent

D-U-N-S 24-312-8472   (HQ)
MAISON RUSSET INC
142 Rte 202 Bureau 103, Huntingdon, QC, J0S 1H0
(450) 264-9449
Sales 51,853,500
SIC 2037 Frozen fruits and vegetables
Leopold Moyen
Jim Brown
Luc Moyen
Hoey Graham

Ile-Aux-Noix, QC J0J

D-U-N-S 24-022-7702   (HQ)
CENTRE DU CAMION GAMACHE INC
CAMIONS RAY-LAWSON
(*Suby of* 9177-3572 QUEBEC INC)
609 Rue Principale, Ile-Aux-Noix, QC, J0J 1G0
(450) 246-3881
Emp Here 50   *Sales* 69,220,800
SIC 5521 Used car dealers
Richard Gamache
Serge Gamache
Christian Gamache

D-U-N-S 20-845-2453   (SL)
GAMEX INC
(*Suby of* 9177-3572 QUEBEC INC)
609 Rue Principale, Ile-Aux-Noix, QC, J0J 1G0
(450) 246-3881
Emp Here 29   *Sales* 18,249,120
SIC 5531 Auto and home supply stores
Christian Gamache
Serge Gamache
Richard Gamache

Inukjuak, QC J0M

D-U-N-S 25-240-6905   (BR)
COMMISSION SCOLAIRE KATIVIK
INNALIK SCHOOL

(Suby of COMMISSION SCOLAIRE KATIVIK)
Pr, Inukjuak, QC, J0M 1M0
(819) 254-8211
Emp Here 80
SIC 8211 Elementary and secondary schools
 Nathalie Mercier

Joliette, QC J6E

D-U-N-S 25-202-0052   (SL)
3100-6588 QUEBEC INC
PATRICK MORIN SUPER CENTRE
(Suby of GROUPE PATRICK MORIN INC)
920 Boul Firestone, Joliette, QC, J6E 2W5
(450) 756-4545
Emp Here 70   *Sales* 18,735,640
SIC 5251 Hardware stores
 Francois Morin
 Andre Morin
 Denis Morin
 Benoit Morin
 Michel Morin

D-U-N-S 20-309-6102   (SL)
8561567 CANADA INC
GAMME SIGNATURE PASSION
585 Rue Saint-Pierre S, Joliette, QC, J6E 8R8
(450) 759-6361
Emp Here 52   *Sales* 17,975,880
SIC 2053 Frozen bakery products, except
bread
 Marc-Andre Pouliot
 Thierry Roca
 Tom Kaneb
 Marc Gosselin

D-U-N-S 25-200-7927   (SL)
9064-4048 QUEBEC INC
DISTINCTION, LA
1505 Boul Base-De-Roc, Joliette, QC, J6E
0L1
(450) 759-6900
Emp Here 75   *Sales* 3,413,925
SIC 5812 Eating places
 Louis-Simon Denommee

D-U-N-S 25-116-9215   (SL)
**ACTION CONSTRUCTION INFRASTRUC-
TURE ACI INC**
A.C.I
1095 Rue Samuel-Racine, Joliette, QC, J6E
0E8
(450) 755-6887
Emp Here 60   *Sales* 15,146,520
SIC 1611 Highway and street construction
 Michel Bellerose

D-U-N-S 20-289-6585   (HQ)
ALIMENTS TRIOVA INC, LES
LES ALIMENTS MISS ARACHEW
696 Rue Marion, Joliette, QC, J6E 8S2
(450) 756-6322
Emp Here 1   *Sales* 24,198,300
SIC 2034 Dried and dehydrated fruits, vegeta-
bles and soup mixes
 Guy Laurendeau
 Yves Perazzelli

D-U-N-S 24-062-5249   (SL)
BISCUITERIE DOMINIC INC
285 Rue Saint-Charles-Borromee N, Joliette,
QC, J6E 4R8
(450) 756-2637
Emp Here 45   *Sales* 12,336,840
SIC 5461 Retail bakeries
 Serge Bohec

D-U-N-S 24-870-4595   (BR)
BRIDGESTONE CANADA INC
(Suby of BRIDGESTONE CORPORATION)
1200 Boul Firestone, Joliette, QC, J6E 2W5
(450) 756-1061
Emp Here 1,300
SIC 3011 Tires and inner tubes

 Daniel Deschamps

D-U-N-S 25-459-9335   (SL)
BRUNEAU ELECTRIQUE INC
GENERATRICE LANAUDIERE
527 Boul Dollard, Joliette, QC, J6E 4M5
(450) 759-6606
Emp Here 100   *Sales* 21,782,900
SIC 1731 Electrical work
 Eric Bruneau
 Patrice Bruneau

D-U-N-S 25-361-7153   (BR)
**CAISSE DESJARDINS DU NORD DE
LANAUDIERE**
*CENTRE FINANCIER AUX ENTREPRISES
JOLIETTE-DE-LANAUDIERE*
(Suby of CAISSE DESJARDINS DU NORD
DE LANAUDIERE)
275 Rue Beaudry N, Joliette, QC, J6E 6A7
(450) 756-0999
Emp Here 85
SIC 8741 Management services
 Michel Pilon

D-U-N-S 20-844-8238   (HQ)
**CENTRE DE READAPTATION EN DEFI-
CIENCE PHYSIQUE LE BOUCLIER**
1075 Boul Firestone Bureau 1000, Joliette,
QC, J6E 6X6
(450) 755-2741
Sales 117,928,340
SIC 8011 Offices and clinics of medical doc-
tors
 Marcel Lanctot

D-U-N-S 20-261-8604   (BR)
**CENTRES JEUNESSE DE LANAUDIERE,
LES**
*CENTRE DE READAPTATION POUR LES
JEUNES EN DIFFICULTE D'ADAPTATION
DE JOLIETTE*
1170 Rue Ladouceur, Joliette, QC, J6E 3W7
(450) 759-0755
Emp Here 650
SIC 8641 Civic and social associations
 Pierre Racette

D-U-N-S 25-371-5833   (BR)
**CIE MATERIAUX DE CONSTRUCTION BP
CANADA, LA**
*CIE MATERIAUX DE CONSTRUCTION BP
CANADA, LA*
(Suby of CIE MATERIAUX DE CONSTRUC-
TION BP CANADA, LA)
351 Rue Alice, Joliette, QC, J6E 8P2
(450) 682-4428
Emp Here 200
SIC 2429 Special product sawmills, nec
 Andre Roy

D-U-N-S 24-895-2207   (HQ)
COOP NOVAGO, LA
*AGRIVERT, COOPERATIVE AGRICOLE RE-
GIONALE*
839 Rue Papineau, Joliette, QC, J6E 2L6
(418) 873-2535
Sales 70,921,200
SIC 8699 Membership organizations, nec
 Jean-Nil Laganiere
 Robert Perreault
 Francois Drainville
 Valerie Ouellet
 Harry Reber
 David Mercier
 Cathy Fraser
 Benoit Massicotte
 Michel Desy
 Isabelle Bastien Barrette

D-U-N-S 20-113-8513   (HQ)
COOPERATIVE AGRICOLE PROFID'OR
COOP VAL-NORD, LA
839 Rue Papineau, Joliette, QC, J6E 2L6
(450) 759-4041
Emp Here 50   *Sales* 74,252,000
SIC 5191 Farm supplies

 Robert Perreault
 Francois Laurin
 Claude Emery
 Isabelle Bastien-Barette
 Sylvain Baril
 Simon Simard
 Isabelle Brouillette
 Claude Rivest
 Luc Forget
 Yvon Landreville

D-U-N-S 24-434-3448   (BR)
CRH CANADA GROUP INC
CIMENT ST-LAURENT
(Suby of CRH PUBLIC LIMITED COMPANY)
966 Ch Des Prairies, Joliette, QC, J6E 0L4
(450) 756-1076
Emp Here 250
SIC 3241 Cement, hydraulic
 Gilles Paquin

D-U-N-S 24-814-7100   (SL)
CROTEAU, MARCEL INC
AUBAINERIE, L'
(Suby of GESTION CROTEAU, MARCEL
INC)
990 Rue Papineau Bureau 5, Joliette, QC, J6E
2L7
(450) 756-1221
Emp Here 75   *Sales* 13,454,700
SIC 5651 Family clothing stores
 Marcel Croteau

D-U-N-S 25-494-8458   (SL)
DANFREIGHT SYSTEMS INC
1400 Ch Lasalle, Joliette, QC, J6E 0L8
(450) 755-6190
Emp Here 300   *Sales* 61,711,800
SIC 4213 Trucking, except local
 Daniel Berard

D-U-N-S 20-602-8763   (SL)
**EQUIPEMENTS INDUSTRIELS JOLIETTE
INC**
1295 Rue De Lanaudiere, Joliette, QC, J6E
3N9
(450) 756-0564
Emp Here 30   *Sales* 13,415,220
SIC 5072 Hardware
 Louis Desrochers

D-U-N-S 20-202-0590   (SL)
FILOCHROME INC
(Suby of GROUPE MALO INC, LE)
1355 Rue Lepine, Joliette, QC, J6E 4B7
(450) 759-1826
Emp Here 110   *Sales* 21,129,350
SIC 3496 Miscellaneous fabricated wire prod-
ucts
 Paul Malo
 Andre Malo

D-U-N-S 20-007-7399   (HQ)
**GAGNON, CANTIN, LACHAPELLE, SAS-
SEVILLE, ETHIER, RIOPEL, HEBERT,
LORD (SENCRL) NOTAIRES**
37 Place Bourget S Bureau 301, Joliette, QC,
J6E 5G1
(450) 755-4535
Emp Here 20   *Sales* 26,756,320
SIC 7389 Business services, nec
 Andre Lachapelle
 Guy Hebert
 Pierre Sasseville
 Adelard Ethier
 Andre Cantin
 Michel Riopel
 Robert Gagnon
 Diane Barette

D-U-N-S 20-201-8016   (SL)
GARAGE SAVIGNAC, P E LTEE
671 Rue Saint-Thomas, Joliette, QC, J6E 3R6
(450) 756-4563
Emp Here 42   *Sales* 20,919,276
SIC 5511 New and used car dealers
 Jacques Savignac

D-U-N-S 24-346-2228   (BR)
**GOUVERNEMENT DE LA PROVINCE DE
QUEBEC**
*CENTRE INTEGRE DE SANTE ET DE SER-
VICES SOCIAUX DE LANAUDIERE*
(Suby of GOUVERNEMENT DE LA
PROVINCE DE QUEBEC)
245 Rue Du Cure-Majeau, Joliette, QC, J6E
8S8
(450) 759-1157
Emp Here 200
SIC 8399 Social services, nec
 Pascale Lamy

D-U-N-S 25-412-4894   (BR)
**GOUVERNEMENT DE LA PROVINCE DE
QUEBEC**
*CENTRE LOCAL DE SANTE COMMUNAU-
TAURE DE JOLIETTE*
(Suby of GOUVERNEMENT DE LA
PROVINCE DE QUEBEC)
380 Boul Base-De-Roc, Joliette, QC, J6E 9J6
(450) 755-2111
Emp Here 150
SIC 8399 Social services, nec
 Helene Brien

D-U-N-S 24-562-7849   (BR)
GRAYMONT (QC) INC
(Suby of GRAYMONT LIMITED)
1300 Rue Notre-Dame, Joliette, QC, J6E 3Z9
(450) 759-8195
Emp Here 100
SIC 1422 Crushed and broken limestone
 Marc Lupine

D-U-N-S 20-127-1066   (HQ)
GROUPE SUTTON SYNERGIE INC
635 Rue Beaudry N Bureau 201, Joliette, QC,
J6E 8L7
(450) 585-0999
Emp Here 64   *Sales* 27,227,785
SIC 6531 Real estate agents and managers
 Fern Dontigny

D-U-N-S 24-432-3176   (SL)
JAM-BEC INC
380 Boul De L'Industrie, Joliette, QC, J6E 8V2
(450) 759-5130
Emp Here 25   *Sales* 20,889,425
SIC 5141 Groceries, general line
 Michel Berard
 Jean-Claude Berard
 Marie-Claire Vincent

D-U-N-S 24-812-3853   (SL)
JOLIETTE DODGE CHRYSLER LTEE
305 Rue Du Cure-Majeau, Joliette, QC, J6E
8S9
(450) 586-6002
Emp Here 50   *Sales* 24,903,900
SIC 5511 New and used car dealers
 Christian Le Roux
 Serge Le Roux

D-U-N-S 24-515-2285   (SL)
LIARD CONSTRUCTION INC
(Suby of GESTION DAVE-LI INC)
599 Boul Base-De-Roc, Joliette, QC, J6E 5P3

Emp Here 80
SIC 1796 Installing building equipment
 Francois Gelinas
 Luc Liard

D-U-N-S 20-376-2849   (SL)
MARTIN-PRODUITS DE BUREAU INC
BISTROPLUS MARTIN
576 Rue Saint-Viateur, Joliette, QC, J6E 3B6
(450) 757-7587
Emp Here 100   *Sales* 23,343,500
SIC 2621 Paper mills
 Stephane Bisson
 Richard Belisle
 Pierre-Hugues Laporte

D-U-N-S 20-979-0849   (SL)
OCIMAC INC

PHARMACIE JEAN COUTU
504 Boul Manseau Bureau 25, Joliette, QC, J6E 3E2
(450) 759-2560
Emp Here 50   *Sales* 12,647,700
SIC 5912 Drug stores and proprietary stores
  Vivienne Cadorette

D-U-N-S 24-945-4737   (SL)
PLASTREC INC
1461 Rue Lepine, Joliette, QC, J6E 4B7
(450) 760-3830
Emp Here 100   *Sales* 31,891,000
SIC 4953 Refuse systems
  Jean Roy
  Louis Robitaille
  Gilles Laurin
  Eric Prud'homme
  Pierre Arsenault

D-U-N-S 20-014-6020   (SL)
PRODUITS VEGKISS INC
(*Suby of* GROUPE HOLDING CONNEXION INC)
1400 Ch Lasalle, Joliette, QC, J6E 0L8
(450) 752-2250
Emp Here 26   *Sales* 21,725,002
SIC 5148 Fresh fruits and vegetables
  Daniel Berard

D-U-N-S 20-298-4126   (SL)
PROMUTUEL LANAUDIERE, SOCIETE MUTUELLE D'ASSURANCE GENERALE
PROMUTUEL ASSURANCE
1075 Boul Firestone Bureau 4100, Joliette, QC, J6E 6X6
(450) 755-5555
Emp Here 50   *Sales* 92,332,950
SIC 6331 Fire, marine, and casualty insurance
  Pierre Clermont
  Celine Lachapelle
  Renald Roy
  Anne-Marie Lacelle
  Dominique Leroux
  Jena-Luc Leblanc
  Jean-Guy Rivest
  Gilles Lacroix

D-U-N-S 25-849-3204   (BR)
PROVIGO DISTRIBUTION INC
MAXI JOLIETTE
(*Suby of* LOBLAW COMPANIES LIMITED)
909 Boul Firestone, Joliette, QC, J6E 2W4
(450) 755-2781
Emp Here 120
SIC 5411 Grocery stores
  Andre Marleaux

D-U-N-S 24-890-2744   (HQ)
SERLAN INC
957 Rue Raoul-Charette, Joliette, QC, J6E 8S4
(450) 752-0030
Emp Here 30   *Sales* 43,347,980
SIC 4783 Packing and crating
  Sylvain Thibault
  Joan Bonin

D-U-N-S 20-910-2359   (SL)
SOCIETE DE GESTION RENE RAINVILLE LTEE
PHARMAPRIX
1075 Boul Firestone Bureau 1240, Joliette, QC, J6E 6X6
(450) 759-8800
Emp Here 40   *Sales* 10,118,160
SIC 5912 Drug stores and proprietary stores
  Rene Rainville

D-U-N-S 24-943-5405   (BR)
SOEURS DE LA CONGREGATION DE NOTRE-DAME, LES
RESIDENCE   NOTRE-DAME-DE-LA-PROTECTION
(*Suby of* SOEURS DE LA CONGREGATION DE NOTRE DAME, LES)
393 Rue De Lanaudiere, Joliette, QC, J6E 3L9

(450) 752-1481
Emp Here 200
SIC 8661 Religious organizations

D-U-N-S 24-378-9992   (SL)
SYSTEMES D'ECRAN STRONG/MDI INC, LES
(*Suby of* BALLANTYNE STRONG, INC.)
1440 Rue Raoul-Charette, Joliette, QC, J6E 8S7
(450) 755-3795
Emp Here 50   *Sales* 11,364,450
SIC 3861 Photographic equipment and supplies
  Ray F. Boegner
  Lance V. Schulz
  Elise Stejkal

D-U-N-S 24-021-0856   (SL)
TECHNODIESEL INC
CHEVRETTE REPARATION
1260 Ch Des Prairies, Joliette, QC, J6E 0L4
(450) 759-3709
Emp Here 100   *Sales* 45,019,700
SIC 7538 General automotive repair shops
  Marcel Thuot
  Caroline Thuot
  Jacinte Thuot
  Andree-Anne Thuot
  Marilene Thuot

D-U-N-S 24-434-7779   (SL)
TRANSPORTS M. CHARETTE INC
635 Rue Nazaire-Laurin, Joliette, QC, J6E 0L6
(450) 760-9600
Emp Here 100   *Sales* 14,819,200
SIC 4212 Local trucking, without storage
  Mario Charette

D-U-N-S 20-056-7639   (HQ)
TRIOTECH AMUSEMENT INC
780 Rue Marion, Joliette, QC, J6E 8S2
(450) 760-9082
Sales 32,613,600
SIC 3999 Manufacturing industries, nec
  Ernest Yale
  Jacques A Drouin
  Norman Jaskolka
  Charles Sirois
  Michael E. Roach

D-U-N-S 24-860-0087   (HQ)
TRJ TELECOM INC
1355 Rue Lepine, Joliette, QC, J6E 4B7
(450) 499-1017
Sales 18,479,800
SIC 4899 Communication services, nec
  Pierre Trudel
  Louis Charles Jolicoeur
  Simon-Pierre Ratelle

D-U-N-S 25-297-6071   (BR)
WAL-MART CANADA CORP
WALMART
(*Suby of* WALMART INC.)
1505 Boul Firestone Bureau 521, Joliette, QC, J6E 9E5
(450) 752-8210
Emp Here 160
SIC 5311 Department stores
  William Ira Tofflemire

Jonquiere, QC G7S

D-U-N-S 20-124-9732   (SL)
9020-4983 QUEBEC INC
INSTITUT D' ECHAFAUDAGE-QUEBEC
2035 Rue Deschenes, Jonquiere, QC, G7S 5E3
(418) 548-5000
Emp Here 60   *Sales* 11,481,240
SIC 7353 Heavy construction equipment rental
  Richard Miousse
  Jean-Guy Miousse

D-U-N-S 20-952-4941   (SL)
ASSURANCES SAGUENAY INC
2655 Boul Du Royaume Bureau 102, Jonquiere, QC, G7S 4S9
(418) 699-1100
Emp Here 21   *Sales* 12,178,404
SIC 6411 Insurance agents, brokers, and service
  Marc Bertrand

D-U-N-S 20-711-8832   (BR)
COMMISSION SCOLAIRE DE LA JONQUIERE
E+COLE POLYVALENTE ARVIDA
2215 Boul Mellon Bureau 101, Jonquiere, QC, G7S 3G4
(418) 548-3113
Emp Here 135
SIC 8211 Elementary and secondary schools
  Fernand Tremblay

D-U-N-S 20-711-8840   (BR)
COMMISSION SCOLAIRE DE LA JONQUIERE
ECOLE POLYVALENTE JONQUIERE
3450 Boul Du Royaume, Jonquiere, QC, G7S 5T2
(418) 547-5781
Emp Here 120
SIC 8211 Elementary and secondary schools
  Jacynthe Bond

D-U-N-S 20-951-1211   (SL)
COMPAGNIE DE CHEMIN DE FER ROBERVAL-SAGUENAY INC, LA
RS
(*Suby of* RIO TINTO PLC)
1955 Boul Mellon Edifice 1001, Jonquiere, QC, G7S 4L2
(418) 699-2714
Emp Here 121   *Sales* 48,308,282
SIC 4011 Railroads, line-haul operating
  Kayam Slutsky
  Jean-Sebastien Simard
  Gervais Jacques

D-U-N-S 24-393-9464   (SL)
ENTREPRISES J.P. LAROCHELLE INC, LES
CANADIAN TIRE
2290 Boul Rene-Levesque, Jonquiere, QC, G7S 5Y5
(418) 542-3909
Emp Here 80   *Sales* 50,342,400
SIC 5531 Auto and home supply stores
  Jean-Pierre Larochelle

D-U-N-S 20-776-6924   (HQ)
GROUPE LD INC
DISTRIBUTION D.M.C.
2370 Rue Bauman, Jonquiere, QC, G7S 4S4
(418) 699-4350
Emp Here 45   *Sales* 41,457,050
SIC 5084 Industrial machinery and equipment
  Denis Jomphe
  Claude Thibeault
  Nancy Langlais
  Stephane Jomphe
  Frederick Jomphe

D-U-N-S 24-729-6239   (HQ)
INDUSTRIES GRC INC, LES
2681 Rue De La Salle, Jonquiere, QC, G7S 2A8
(418) 548-1171
Sales 18,515,465
SIC 1761 Roofing, siding, and sheetMetal work
  Helene Deschenes
  Patrick Bourgeois
  Gilles Fortin
  Jean Fortin

D-U-N-S 20-188-8344   (SL)
MEDI-PARE LTEE
FAMILI-PRIX
2075 Boul Mellon Bureau 100, Jonquiere, QC,

G7S 5Z8
(418) 548-3188
Emp Here 40   *Sales* 10,118,160
SIC 5912 Drug stores and proprietary stores
  Clement Pare
  Claire Gauthier

D-U-N-S 20-188-7726   (SL)
MERCIER, INDUSTRIES EN MECANIQUE LTEE
2035 Rue Fay, Jonquiere, QC, G7S 2N5
(418) 548-7141
Emp Here 100   *Sales* 22,200,100
SIC 3599 Industrial machinery, nec
  Sara Mercier
  Gabrielle Mercier
  Vincent Mercier

D-U-N-S 24-568-6571   (SL)
PLACEMENTS GILLES ARNOLD INC
2595 Rue Godbout, Jonquiere, QC, G7S 5S9
(418) 548-0821
Emp Here 55   *Sales* 34,610,400
SIC 5511 New and used car dealers
  Gilles Arnold Tremblay

D-U-N-S 20-323-5416   (HQ)
PROWATT INC
2361 Rue Bauman Bureau 1, Jonquiere, QC, G7S 5A9
(418) 548-1184
Sales 10,891,450
SIC 1731 Electrical work
  Sylvain Lavoie
  Martin Gravel
  Nicolas Cote
  Robert Paquet
  Remi Fournier
  Claude Ouellet

D-U-N-S 20-190-8956   (BR)
RIO TINTO ALCAN INC
(*Suby of* RIO TINTO PLC)
1955 Boul Mellon, Jonquiere, QC, G7S 0L4
(418) 699-2002
Emp Here 600
SIC 3334 Primary aluminum
  Bruce Cox

D-U-N-S 24-864-3009   (BR)
RIO TINTO ALCAN INC
ENERGIE ELECTRIQUE, DIV OF
(*Suby of* RIO TINTO PLC)
1954 Rue Davis, Jonquiere, QC, G7S 3B6

Emp Here 650
SIC 4911 Electric services
  Donald Dube

D-U-N-S 24-293-4123   (SL)
SERVICES DE SOINS DE SANTE OPTI-SOINS
2655 Boul Du Royaume Bureau 550, Jonquiere, QC, G7S 4S9
(418) 548-0010
Emp Here 25   *Sales* 46,166,475
SIC 6324 Hospital and medical service plans
  Jean Blackbern

D-U-N-S 25-783-4820   (SL)
STI MAINTENANCE INC
1946 Rue Davis, Jonquiere, QC, G7S 3B6
(418) 699-5101
Emp Here 40   *Sales* 10,973,280
SIC 8741 Management services
  Dominique Prive
  Alain Poudrier
  Claude Boily

D-U-N-S 20-526-4067   (SL)
SUPERMARCHE MELLON INC
IGA-MELLON
2085 Boul Mellon, Jonquiere, QC, G7S 3G4
(418) 548-7557
Emp Here 100   *Sales* 29,347,700
SIC 5411 Grocery stores
  Kathie St-Pierre

Dany St-Pierre
Guylaine Bouchard

D-U-N-S 20-006-4942   (SL)
**SYNDICAT NATIONAL DES EMPLOYES DE
L'ALUMINUM D'ARVIDA INC, LE**
1932 Boul Mellon, Jonquiere, QC, G7S 3H3
(418) 548-4667
Emp Here 43   *Sales* 16,819,794
SIC 8631 Labor organizations
Alain Gagnon
Rejean Savard
Louise Tremblay
Carl Dallaire

Jonquiere, QC G7X

D-U-N-S 25-244-8055   (SL)
3093-9920 QUEBEC INC
METRO P.E. PRIX
2350 Rue Saint-Hubert, Jonquiere, QC, G7X
5N4
(418) 547-6611
Emp Here 100   *Sales* 29,347,700
SIC 5411 Grocery stores
Yvon-Marie Bergeron
Sylvain Bergeron

D-U-N-S 25-093-1693   (SL)
6654100 CANADA INC
DYNAMIC EQUIPEMENT
2400 Rue Alexis-Le-Trotteur, Jonquiere, QC,
G7X 0J7
(418) 542-6164
Emp Here 29   *Sales* 13,775,754
SIC 5084 Industrial machinery and equipment
Patrice Cote
Jean-Francois Desmeules

D-U-N-S 25-134-4644   (HQ)
9007-6720 QUEBEC INC
GROUPE TRANSCOL
3495 Rue De La Recherche, Jonquiere, QC,
G7X 0H5
(418) 695-4181
Emp Here 100   *Sales* 20,570,600
SIC 4213 Trucking, except local
Claude Hubert
Germain Godin
Alain Corneau
Michel Gagnon

D-U-N-S 20-283-1587   (SL)
9105-6705 QUEBEC INC
A.R. CONSTRUCTION
2485 Rue Alexis-Le-Trotteur, Jonquiere, QC,
G7X 0E4
(418) 820-6647
Emp Here 45   *Sales* 14,349,105
SIC 1521 Single-family housing construction
Roger Dumais
Raphael Dumais
Jean-Francois Barbeau

D-U-N-S 24-137-7865   (SL)
9214-6489 QUEBEC INC
PLANCHERS EN GROS 2009
3590 Rue De L'Energie, Jonquiere, QC, G7X
9H3
(418) 695-1793
Emp Here 100   *Sales* 26,765,200
SIC 5211 Lumber and other building materials
Robert Millette
Gerard Leclerc

D-U-N-S 24-498-9455   (SL)
A.M.I. MECANIQUE INC
GROUPE INDUSTRIEL AMI
2455 Rue Cantin, Jonquiere, QC, G7X 8S7
(418) 542-3531
Emp Here 75   *Sales* 18,463,950
SIC 1796 Installing building equipment
Guy Lepine

D-U-N-S 25-046-7151   (SL)

AMIMAC (2002) LTEE
POLYMAC MAINTENANCE
3499 Rue De L'Energie, Jonquiere, QC, G7X
0C1
(418) 542-3531
Emp Here 50   *Sales* 23,751,300
SIC 5084 Industrial machinery and equipment
Martin Lepine

D-U-N-S 25-391-7546   (SL)
CAISSE DESJARDINS DE JONQUIERE
CENTRE DE SERVICE LAROUCHE
2358 Rue Saint-Dominique, Jonquiere, QC,
G7X 0M7
(418) 695-1850
Emp Here 83   *Sales* 14,593,935
SIC 6062 State credit unions
Richard Villeneuve
Regis Gaudreault
Dominic Boily
Marc-Andre Pedneault
Remi Belley
Cathy Boily
Pier-Luc Larouche
Veronique Lavoie
Christina Lavoie-Tremblay
Gabriel Plourde

D-U-N-S 24-568-0970   (HQ)
CANTIN GAGNON ASSURANCES INC
2463 Rue Saint-Dominique, Jonquiere, QC,
G7X 6K4
(418) 542-7575
Emp Here 1   *Sales* 29,682,100
SIC 6411 Insurance agents, brokers, and ser-
vice
Richard Cantin
Michel Cantin
Helene Bergeron

D-U-N-S 20-581-7448   (SL)
CENTRE DE RENOVATION F D S INC
3460 Boul Saint-Francois Unite B001, Jon-
quiere, QC, G7X 8L3
(418) 548-4676
Emp Here 40   *Sales* 10,122,360
SIC 5211 Lumber and other building materials
Luc Grenon
David Grenon

D-U-N-S 25-002-1664   (BR)
**COMMISSION SCOLAIRE DE LA JON-
QUIERE**
ECOLE SECONDAIRE KENOGAMI
1954 Rue Des Etudiants, Jonquiere, QC, G7X
4B1
(418) 542-3571
Emp Here 120
SIC 8211 Elementary and secondary schools
Sylvie Bergeron

D-U-N-S 24-907-9872   (SL)
ETOILE DODGE CHRYSLER INC, L'
3311 Boul Du Royaume, Jonquiere, QC, G7X
0C4
(418) 542-9518
Emp Here 29   *Sales* 14,444,262
SIC 5511 New and used car dealers
Paul Munger
Martin Boivin

D-U-N-S 24-499-5866   (HQ)
**EUGENE   ALLARD   PRODUITS
D'EMBALLAGE ET D'ENTRETIEN INC**
EUGENE ALLARD
2244 Rue Chapais, Jonquiere, QC, G7X 4B4
(418) 547-6654
Emp Here 35   *Sales* 22,664,610
SIC 5113 Industrial and personal service pa-
per
Jean-Denis Allard
Marc Larouche
Christine Allard
Francois Menard

D-U-N-S 25-847-6514   (SL)
FORAGE SAGUENAY INC
2370 Rue De La Metallurgie, Jonquiere, QC,

G7X 9H2
(418) 542-5059
Emp Here 50   *Sales* 12,044,200
SIC 1629 Heavy construction, nec
Conrad Bouchard
Stephane Bouchard

D-U-N-S 24-464-1890   (SL)
GALERIES FORD INC, LES
*(Suby of IMMEUBLES A & R PERRON INC,
LES)*
3443 Boul Du Royaume, Jonquiere, QC, G7X
0C5
(418) 542-9551
Emp Here 30   *Sales* 18,878,400
SIC 5511 New and used car dealers
Raoul Perron
Sylvain Tremblay
Jean-Eudes Hudon

D-U-N-S 24-325-4021   (BR)
PF RESOLU CANADA INC
*(Suby of RESOLUTE FOREST PRODUCTS
INC)*
3750 Rue De Champlain, Jonquiere, QC, G7X
1M1
(418) 695-9100
Emp Here 199
SIC 2621 Paper mills
Michel Leroux

D-U-N-S 20-951-0940   (HQ)
PHARMA-SANTE JONQUIERE INC
PHARMAPRIX
2340 Rue Saint-Hubert Bureau 23, Jonquiere,
QC, G7X 5N4
(418) 547-5795
Emp Here 80   *Sales* 21,989,520
SIC 5912 Drug stores and proprietary stores
Mario Bolduc
Jason Guillemette
Michel Plourde

D-U-N-S 24-742-5978   (BR)
PUROLATOR INC
(Suby of GOVERNMENT OF CANADA)
3479 Rue De L'Energie, Jonquiere, QC, G7X
0C1
(418) 695-1235
Emp Here 80
SIC 7389 Business services, nec
Rock Rancourt

D-U-N-S 24-051-1035   (SL)
**REMORQUAGE PROFESSIONNEL SAGUE-
NAY INC**
2386 Rue Cantin, Jonquiere, QC, G7X 8S6
(418) 695-1114
Emp Here 49   *Sales* 10,095,811
SIC 7549 Automotive services, nec
Joel Tremblay

D-U-N-S 24-498-8820   (SL)
SERVICES NOLITREX INC
*CENTRE   REGIONAL DE   TRANSBOR-
DEMENT   ET   TRAINS   ROUTIERS   DU
SAGUENAY-LAC-ST-JEAN*
3462 Rue De L'Energie, Jonquiere, QC, G7X
9H3
(418) 542-0386
Emp Here 90   *Sales* 18,513,540
SIC 4225 General warehousing and storage
Christian Ricard
Simon Ricard
Julie Tremblay
Olivier Ricard
Alexandre Dufour

D-U-N-S 20-287-9912   (BR)
SNC-LAVALIN GEM QUEBEC INC
GROUPE QUALITAS
(Suby of GROUPE SNC-LAVALIN INC)
3306 Boul Saint-Francois, Jonquiere, QC,
G7X 2W9
(418) 547-5716
Emp Here 100
SIC 8742 Management consulting services
Sylvain Goulet

D-U-N-S 20-202-4451   (SL)
TREPANIER, PHILIPPE INC
4573 Ch Saint-Isidore, Jonquiere, QC, G7X
7V5
(418) 547-4734
Emp Here 60   *Sales* 14,771,160
SIC 1791 Structural steel erection
Laurent Trepanier
Sabrina Trepanier
Veronique Trepanier

D-U-N-S 24-610-3910   (SL)
UNIPRIX PHARMACY
2095 Rue Sainte-Famille, Jonquiere, QC, G7X
4W8
(418) 547-3689
Emp Here 45   *Sales* 11,382,930
SIC 5912 Drug stores and proprietary stores
Suzanne Beauchard

D-U-N-S 24-046-6552   (SL)
VOLTAM INC
3455 Rue Du Transport, Jonquiere, QC, G7X
0B6
(418) 548-0002
Emp Here 50   *Sales* 22,358,700
SIC 5065 Electronic parts and equipment, nec
Patrice Bouchard
Louis Bouchard
Gaetan Tremblay

Jonquiere, QC G7Z

D-U-N-S 20-703-2272   (BR)
CASCADES CANADA ULC
NORAMPAC-JONQUIERE
(Suby of CASCADES INC)
4010 Ch Saint-Andre, Jonquiere, QC, G7Z
0A5

Emp Here 145
SIC 2631 Paperboard mills
Mario Nepton

Jonquiere, QC G8A

D-U-N-S 20-381-4996   (SL)
8956995 CANADA INC
ALIMENTS OATBOX
3450 Rue Saint-Dominique Bureau 100, Jon-
quiere, QC, G8A 2M3
(514) 374-1315
Emp Here 25   *Sales* 36,692,300
SIC 5153 Grain and field beans
Marc-Antoine Bovet
Pierre-Luc Lapare
Jean-Francois Kabbani
Nathalie Bourque
Martin-Pierre Roussel
Vincent Messier Lemoyne
Martin Gauthier
Sophie Roy

Kahnawake, QC J0L

D-U-N-S 20-363-7038   (SL)
CONSORTIUM PONT MOHAWK CPM
MBC
Gd, Kahnawake, QC, J0L 1B0
(450) 635-6063
Emp Here 50   *Sales* 10,580,750
SIC 1622 Bridge, tunnel, and elevated high-
way construction
Amy Rice
Sterling Deer

D-U-N-S 20-533-9505   (SL)
KAHNAWAKE FIRE BRIGADE AMBU-

LANCE SERVICE
520 Rue Old Malone, Kahnawake, QC, J0L 1B0
(450) 632-2010
Emp Here 40   *Sales* 17,968,760
SIC 7389 Business services, nec
David Scott

D-U-N-S 24-111-7746   (SL)
KATERI MEMORIAL HOSPITAL CENTRE
TEHSAKOTITSEN-THA
Gd, Kahnawake, QC, J0L 1B0
(450) 638-3930
Emp Here 150   *Sales* 16,662,000
SIC 8069 Specialty hospitals, except psychiatric
Susan Horne
Lynda Delisle

D-U-N-S 24-355-7761   (SL)
MORRIS, ALWIN
SERVICES FINANCIERS MORRIS MOHAWK
1470 Rte 138, Kahnawake, QC, J0L 1B0
(450) 633-5100
Emp Here 75   *Sales* 20,574,900
SIC 8741 Management services
Alwin Morris

Kingsey Falls, QC J0A

D-U-N-S 24-712-4027   (HQ)
BORALEX INC
BORALEX ENERGY CREATOR
36 Rue Lajeunesse, Kingsey Falls, QC, J0A 1B0
(819) 363-6363
Emp Here 100   *Sales* 363,130,858
SIC 4911 Electric services
Patrick Lemaire
Alain Rheaume
Jean-Francois Thibodeau
Patrick Decostre
Guy D'aoust
Pascal Hurtubise
Hugues Girardin
Julie Cusson
Pierre Trahan
Marie-Josse Arsenault

D-U-N-S 24-337-2724   (BR)
CASCADES CANADA ULC
CASCADES GROUPE TISSU
(*Suby of* CASCADES INC)
467 Boul Marie-Victorin, Kingsey Falls, QC, J0A 1B0
(819) 363-5600
Emp Here 167
SIC 2676 Sanitary paper products
Guillaume Bouvier

D-U-N-S 24-813-8737   (HQ)
CASCADES CANADA ULC
CASCADES
(*Suby of* CASCADES INC)
404 Boul Marie-Victorin, Kingsey Falls, QC, J0A 1B0
(819) 363-5100
Emp Here 6   *Sales* 184,582,045
SIC 6712 Bank holding companies
Mario Plourde
Alain Lemaire
Allan Hogg
Robert F. Hall

D-U-N-S 20-277-6415   (BR)
CASCADES CS+ INC
CASCADES CIP, UNE DIV DE CASCADES CANADA ULC
(*Suby of* CASCADES INC)
465 Boul Marie-Victorin, Kingsey Falls, QC, J0A 1B0
(819) 363-5920
Emp Here 113

SIC 2631 Paperboard mills
Michel Lapierre

D-U-N-S 20-288-0423   (HQ)
CASCADES CS+ INC
(*Suby of* CASCADES INC)
471 Boul Marie-Victorin, Kingsey Falls, QC, J0A 1B0
(819) 363-5700
Emp Here 9   *Sales* 28,598,240
SIC 8711 Engineering services
Mario Plourde
Jerome Nadeau
Alain Lemaire
Robert F. Hall

D-U-N-S 20-327-4956   (BR)
CASCADES CS+ INC
CASCADES GIE
(*Suby of* CASCADES INC)
15 Rue Lamontagne, Kingsey Falls, QC, J0A 1B0
(819) 363-5971
Emp Here 150
SIC 8711 Engineering services
Maxine Broderique

D-U-N-S 20-202-6399   (HQ)
CASCADES INC
404 Boul Marie-Victorin, Kingsey Falls, QC, J0A 1B0
(819) 363-5100
Emp Here 100   *Sales* 3,524,416,198
SIC 2621 Paper mills
Mario Plourde
Alain Lemaire
Thierry Trudel
Hugo D'amours
Leon Marineau
Pascal Aguettaz
Allan Hogg
Robert F. Hall
Patrick Lemaire
Martin Couture

D-U-N-S 20-689-4607   (BR)
CASCADES INC
CASCADES PLASTIQUES DIV DE
(*Suby of* CASCADES INC)
455 Boul Marie-Victorin, Kingsey Falls, QC, J0A 1B0
(819) 363-5300
Emp Here 180
SIC 3081 Unsupported plastics film and sheet
Pierre Renaud

D-U-N-S 24-821-8430   (SL)
CASCADES SONOCO INC
CASCADE SONOCO DIV KINGSEY FALLS
457 Boul Marie-Victorin, Kingsey Falls, QC, J0A 1B0
(819) 363-5400
Emp Here 100   *Sales* 19,476,800
SIC 2679 Converted paper products, nec
Luc Langevin
Jerome Nadeau
Rodger D. Fuller
Douglas Schwartz
Emilie Allen

D-U-N-S 24-395-1907   (HQ)
CASCADES TRANSPORT INC
CASCADES TRANSIT
(*Suby of* CASCADES INC)
2 Rue Parenteau, Kingsey Falls, QC, J0A 1B0
(819) 363-5800
Emp Here 100   *Sales* 68,405,351
SIC 4213 Trucking, except local
Mario Plourde
Jerome Nadeau
Alain Lemaire
Robert F. Hall

Kirkland, QC H9H

D-U-N-S 24-922-8883   (HQ)
2809664 CANADA INC
16711 Rte Transcanadienne, Kirkland, QC, H9H 3L1
(514) 343-0044
Sales 214,072,332
SIC 4731 Freight transportation arrangement
Brian Arnott

D-U-N-S 25-209-7902   (SL)
2895102 CANADA INC
LEAUTEC CRYSTAL-SOLEIL
16811 Boul Hymus, Kirkland, QC, H9H 3L4
(514) 426-1211
Emp Here 26   *Sales* 11,679,694
SIC 7389 Business services, nec
Ugo Notargiacomo

D-U-N-S 20-532-7823   (SL)
9072-3917 QUEBEC INC
PHARMAPRIX
3790 Boul Saint-Charles Bureau 69, Kirkland, QC, H9H 3C3
(514) 426-1011
Emp Here 40   *Sales* 10,118,160
SIC 5912 Drug stores and proprietary stores
Nada Nasreddine

D-U-N-S 20-381-5845   (SL)
ADVANTECH WIRELESS TECHNOLOGIES INC
ADVANTECH TECHNOLOGIES SANS FIL
(*Suby of* BAYLIN TECHNOLOGIES INC)
16715 Boul Hymus, Kirkland, QC, H9H 5M8
(514) 694-8666
Emp Here 150   *Sales* 28,566,300
SIC 3679 Electronic components, nec
Randy Dewey
Michael A. Wolfe

D-U-N-S 24-177-2057   (SL)
AGENCES D'ASSURANCE RANDLE INC
17001 Rte Transcanadienne, Kirkland, QC, H9H 0A7
(514) 694-4161
Emp Here 25   *Sales* 14,498,100
SIC 6411 Insurance agents, brokers, and service
Wildo Giardini

D-U-N-S 20-363-5024   (SL)
ALLIANCE OCCIDENTALE LOGISTIQUES INC
16766 Rte Transcanadienne Bureau 400, Kirkland, QC, H9H 4M7
(514) 534-0114
Emp Here 50   *Sales* 19,268,000
SIC 4731 Freight transportation arrangement
William Binette
Joshua Sevy

D-U-N-S 20-621-4806   (SL)
CANADIAN TIRE ASSOCIATE STORES & AUTO CENTRES
CANADIAN TIRE
16821 Rte Transcanadienne Unite 149, Kirkland, QC, H9H 5J1
(514) 697-4761
Emp Here 30   *Sales* 18,878,400
SIC 5531 Auto and home supply stores

D-U-N-S 20-212-8666   (SL)
CONSTRUCTION BROCCOLINI INC
16766 Rte Transcanadienne Unite 500, Kirkland, QC, H9H 4M7
(514) 737-0076
Emp Here 115   *Sales* 65,588,870
SIC 1542 Nonresidential construction, nec
John Broccolini
Joseph Broccolini
Paul Broccolini
Nick Iwanowski

D-U-N-S 20-050-2412   (SL)
GESTION CARRIER, ROBERT INC
73 Rue Du Chambertin, Kirkland, QC, H9H 5E3

Emp Here 75   *Sales* 9,779,325
SIC 2542 Partitions and fixtures, except wood
Robert Carrier
Lyane Voghel Carrier

D-U-N-S 25-284-6100   (HQ)
IMS SANTE CANADA INC
IQVIA
(*Suby of* IQVIA HOLDINGS INC.)
16720 Rte Transcanadienne, Kirkland, QC, H9H 5M3
(514) 428-6000
Sales 38,114,000
SIC 7363 Help supply services
Sylvia Durgerian
James Erlinger Iii
Hesler Durgerian
Eric Sherbet

D-U-N-S 24-360-4761   (HQ)
JUBILANT DRAXIMAGE INC
(*Suby of* JUBILANT LIFE SCIENCES LIMITED)
16751 Rte Transcanadienne, Kirkland, QC, H9H 4J4
(514) 694-8220
Sales 59,686,920
SIC 2834 Pharmaceutical preparations
Michael Rossi
Arpita Chatterjee
Shahir Guindi
Sanjay Bhartia
Pramod Yadav

D-U-N-S 24-676-2764   (SL)
JUBILANT HOLLISTERSTIER GENERAL PARTNERSHIP
JUBILANT HOLLISTERSTIER CONTRACT MANUFACTURING
16751 Rte Transcanadienne, Kirkland, QC, H9H 4J4
(514) 694-8220
Emp Here 410   *Sales* 135,953,540
SIC 2834 Pharmaceutical preparations
Shyam S. Bhartia

D-U-N-S 20-356-0719   (SL)
MARTINI-VISPAK INC
ACHOO TISSU
3535 Boul Saint-Charles Bureau 600, Kirkland, QC, H9H 5B9
(514) 739-4666
Emp Here 50   *Sales* 10,383,700
SIC 8743 Public relations services
Jack Dworkind
David Puterman

D-U-N-S 20-528-8215   (HQ)
MERCK CANADA INC
MERCK SHARP & DOHME
16750 Rte Transcanadienne, Kirkland, QC, H9H 4M7
(514) 428-7920
Sales 330,256,800
SIC 5122 Drugs, proprietaries, and sundries
Anna Van Acker
Bernard Houde
Daniel Simard
Jennifer Chan
Kirk Duguid

D-U-N-S 20-253-3683   (SL)
NEGOCIANTS DE GRAINS OCCIDENTAUX INC
16766 Rte Transcanadienne Bureau 400, Kirkland, QC, H9H 4M7
(514) 509-2119
Emp Here 30   *Sales* 44,030,760
SIC 5153 Grain and field beans
William Binette
Josh Sevy
Francois Binette

D-U-N-S 20-765-9186   (SL)
OSBORN & LANGE INC
AGENCE D'ASSURANCES RANDLE (2000)
17001 Rte Transcanadienne Bureau 300, Kirk-

▲ Public Company   ■ Public Company Family Member   **HQ** Headquarters   **BR** Branch   **SL** Single Location

land, QC, H9H 0A7
(514) 694-4161
Emp Here 25   *Sales* 21,201,500
SIC 6411 Insurance agents, brokers, and service
Wildo P Giardini

D-U-N-S 20-736-8192   (SL)
PROPAK PLASTICS (1979) LTD
16817 Boul Hymus, Kirkland, QC, H9H 3L4
(514) 695-9520
Emp Here 52   *Sales* 10,498,644
SIC 3081 Unsupported plastics film and sheet
Rosemary Eichholz
Andreas Nacke

D-U-N-S 20-165-5953   (SL)
RE/MAX CADIBEC INC
3535 Boul Saint-Charles Bureau 304, Kirkland, QC, H9H 5B9
(514) 694-0840
Emp Here 33   *Sales* 10,795,191
SIC 6531 Real estate agents and managers
Marc Boivin
Paul Ligeti
Michael Lapointe

D-U-N-S 20-233-7986   (HQ)
SCHERING-PLOUGH CANADA INC
MERCK
(*Suby of* MERCK & CO., INC.)
16750 Rte Transcanadienne, Kirkland, QC, H9H 4M7
(514) 426-7300
Emp Here 1,078   *Sales* 364,753,400
SIC 2834 Pharmaceutical preparations
Simard Daniel
Kirk Duguid
Bernard Houde

D-U-N-S 20-370-9001   (BR)
SINTRA INC
MELOCHE, DIVISION DE SINTRA
(*Suby of* BOUYGUES)
3125 Boul Saint-Charles, Kirkland, QC, H9H 3B9
(514) 695-3395
Emp Here 100
SIC 1611 Highway and street construction

D-U-N-S 24-739-9397   (SL)
TASK MICRO-ELECTRONICS INC
TASK MICRO-ELECTRIQUES INC
16700 Rte Transcanadienne, Kirkland, QC, H9H 4M7
(514) 697-6616
Emp Here 80   *Sales* 35,773,920
SIC 5065 Electronic parts and equipment, nec
Douglas Bellevue
Jill Mcgoldrick

D-U-N-S 20-271-3202   (SL)
TECHNOLOGIES GREAT NORTH INC
3551 Boul Saint-Charles Bureau 363, Kirkland, QC, H9H 3C4
(514) 620-3724
Emp Here 100   *Sales* 25,656,200
SIC 3844 X-ray apparatus and tubes
Irwin Lambersky
Craig Belanger

D-U-N-S 24-904-2961   (HQ)
TRAFFIC TECH INC
TRAFFIC TECH
(*Suby of* 2809664 CANADA INC)
16711 Rte Transcanadienne, Kirkland, QC, H9H 3L1
(514) 343-0044
Emp Here 645   *Sales* 365,780,150
SIC 4731 Freight transportation arrangement

D-U-N-S 20-254-3179   (SL)
TRAFFIC TECH INTERNATIONAL INC
(*Suby of* 2809664 CANADA INC)
16711 Rte Transcanadienne, Kirkland, QC, H9H 3L1
(514) 343-0044
Emp Here 96   *Sales* 64,021,632

SIC 4731 Freight transportation arrangement
Brian Arnott
Mark Schiele
Neil Arnott
Lori Posluns
Keith Winrow
David Valela

D-U-N-S 20-852-8302   (SL)
TRANSPORT DIANE PICHE INC
TIM HORTONS
3862 Boul Saint-Charles, Kirkland, QC, H9H 3C3
(514) 693-9059
Emp Here 40   *Sales* 10,966,080
SIC 5499 Miscellaneous food stores
Norman Forget

D-U-N-S 20-487-6072   (SL)
UNIPRIX PIERRE BERGERON ET MARISA SGRO (PHARMACIE AFFILIEE)
2963 Boul Saint-Charles, Kirkland, QC, H9H 3B5
(514) 694-3074
Emp Here 40   *Sales* 10,118,160
SIC 5912 Drug stores and proprietary stores
Pierre Bergeron

Kirkland, QC H9J

D-U-N-S 20-592-2342   (HQ)
CONNECTEURS ELECTRIQUES WECO INC
(*Suby of* HEINER HOLDINGS 2 INC)
18050 Rte Transcanadienne, Kirkland, QC, H9J 4A1
(514) 694-9136
Sales 10,233,650
SIC 3613 Switchgear and switchboard apparatus
Heiner Kammann
Bernard Pinet

D-U-N-S 20-725-6710   (HQ)
CONTROLES LAURENTIDE LTEE
ATLANTIC CONTROLS DIV OF
18000 Rte Transcanadienne, Kirkland, QC, H9J 4A1
(514) 697-9230
Emp Here 120   *Sales* 82,914,100
SIC 5085 Industrial supplies
Stephen Dustin
Dean Whitelaw

D-U-N-S 20-800-8982   (HQ)
CORPORATION DE SOINS DE LA SANTE HOSPIRA
(*Suby of* C.P. PHARMACEUTICALS INTERNATIONAL C.V.)
17300 Rte Transcanadienne, Kirkland, QC, H9J 2M5
(514) 695-0500
Emp Here 450   *Sales* 358,929,838
SIC 6712 Bank holding companies
Gerry Stefanatos
Serge Roussel
Vratislav Hadrava
Jonathan Cullen
John Helou

D-U-N-S 20-216-0297   (HQ)
DANESCO INC
MA MAISON
18111 Rte Transcanadienne, Kirkland, QC, H9J 3K1
(514) 694-9111
Sales 25,442,800
SIC 5023 Homefurnishings
Brigitte Roy
Robert P. Ferguson
Terrence Ferguson
Charles D'amour
William R Ferguson
Shannon Jetten

Marc Balevi
Daniel Dube

D-U-N-S 24-668-1530   (HQ)
EASTON HOCKEY CANADA, INC
BASEBALL EASTON
(*Suby of* RBG HOLDINGS CORP.)
17550 Rte Transcanadienne, Kirkland, QC, H9J 3A3
(514) 630-9669
Sales 26,027,100
SIC 5091 Sporting and recreation goods
Matt Arndt
Petar Katurich
Terence Savoie

D-U-N-S 25-498-7696   (HQ)
JOURNEY FREIGHT INTERNATIONAL INC
JOURNEY LOGISTICS
18100 Rte Transcanadienne, Kirkland, QC, H9J 4A1
(514) 344-2202
Emp Here 50   *Sales* 46,682,440
SIC 4731 Freight transportation arrangement
Brian De Filippo
Steven De Filippo
Michael De Filippo

D-U-N-S 24-815-4791   (SL)
METAL LEETWO INC
18025 Rte Transcanadienne, Kirkland, QC, H9J 3Z4
(514) 695-5911
Emp Here 75   *Sales* 7,655,130
SIC 3444 Sheet Metalwork
Michael Lee
Peter Lee

D-U-N-S 20-229-8782   (HQ)
PFIZER CANADA SRI
DIVISION MONDIALE DE RECHERCHE ET DEVELOPPEMENT DE PFIZER
(*Suby of* C.P. PHARMACEUTICALS INTERNATIONAL C.V.)
17300 Rte Transcanadienne, Kirkland, QC, H9J 2M5
(514) 695-0500
Emp Here 500   *Sales* 331,594,000
SIC 2834 Pharmaceutical preparations
John Helou
Serge Roussel
Jonathan Cullen

D-U-N-S 24-377-8474   (SL)
PHIPPS DICKSON INTEGRIA (PDI) INC
PDI
(*Suby of* GROUPE PHIPPS DICKSON INTEGRIA INC)
18103 Rte Transcanadienne, Kirkland, QC, H9J 3Z4
(514) 695-1333
Emp Here 150   *Sales* 29,066,100
SIC 2752 Commercial printing, lithographic
Gaetano Di Trapani
Jeffrey A. Mahar
Jamie Barbieri
Glenn Houston

D-U-N-S 20-702-7629   (SL)
SAFRAN CABIN CANADA CO.
CIE SAFRAN CABINE CANADA
(*Suby of* SAFRAN)
18107 Rte Transcanadienne, Kirkland, QC, H9J 3K1
(514) 697-5555
Emp Here 750   *Sales* 147,848,250
SIC 8711 Engineering services
Norman Jordan
Denis Lemelin
Jean-Yves Constantin
Laurent Tremeau
Antoine Ducros

D-U-N-S 25-356-1609   (BR)
SSH BEDDING CANADA CO
SSH BEDDING CANADA CO.
(*Suby of* SSH BEDDING CANADA CO)
17400 Rte Transcanadienne, Kirkland, QC,

H9J 2M5
(514) 694-3030
Emp Here 110
SIC 2394 Canvas and related products
Raymond Brosseau

D-U-N-S 24-851-7919   (SL)
TARGRAY AMERIQUES INC
18105 Rte Transcanadienne, Kirkland, QC, H9J 3Z4
(514) 695-8095
Emp Here 25   *Sales* 31,430,025
SIC 5172 Petroleum products, nec
Thomas A.G. Richardson
Andrew Richardson

D-U-N-S 24-857-7009   (HQ)
TARGRAY TECHNOLOGIE INTERNATIONALE INC
(*Suby of* THOMAS A.G. RICHARDSON INVESTISSEMENT INC)
18105 Rte Transcanadienne, Kirkland, QC, H9J 3Z4
(514) 695-8095
Sales 22,358,700
SIC 5063 Electrical apparatus and equipment
Andrew Richardson
Thomas A.G. Richardson

D-U-N-S 25-297-6238   (BR)
WAL-MART CANADA CORP
(*Suby of* WALMART INC.)
17000 Rte Transcanadienne, Kirkland, QC, H9J 2M5
(514) 695-3040
Emp Here 200
SIC 5311 Department stores
Kalliopi Athanasoulias

Knowlton, QC J0E

D-U-N-S 20-202-6621   (HQ)
CANARDS DU LAC BROME LTEE
CANARD LIBERE - ESPACE GOURMAND, LE
40 Ch Du Centre, Knowlton, QC, J0E 1V0
(450) 242-3825
Emp Here 1   *Sales* 58,767,300
SIC 2015 Poultry slaughtering and processing
Mario Cote
Joseph Jurgielewicz

D-U-N-S 20-332-3803   (SL)
SERVICES DAVID JONES INC, LES
29 Rue De Bondville, Knowlton, QC, J0E 1V0
(450) 955-3600
Emp Here 26   *Sales* 11,530,740
SIC 7389 Business services, nec
David Jones

Kuujjuaq, QC J0M

D-U-N-S 24-321-8880   (SL)
CENTRE DE SANTE TULATTAVIK DE L'UNGAVA
UNGAVA HOSPITAL
Gd, Kuujjuaq, QC, J0M 1C0
(819) 964-2905
Emp Here 300   *Sales* 20,497,800
SIC 8051 Skilled nursing care facilities
Madge Pomerleau

D-U-N-S 20-021-6781   (SL)
DEPANNEUR NEWVIQ'VI INC
1285 Rue Gordon, Kuujjuaq, QC, J0M 1C0
(819) 964-2228
Emp Here 40   *Sales* 10,966,080
SIC 5411 Grocery stores
Mark T Gordon
Eric Pearson
Willie Gordon

Sandy Gordon

D-U-N-S 20-114-5765   (HQ)
OFFICE MUNICIPAL D'HABITATION KA-TIVIK
1105 Rue Akianut, Kuujjuaq, QC, J0M 1C0
(819) 964-2000
Emp Here 35   *Sales* 25,133,340
SIC 6531 Real estate agents and managers
Sammy Duncan
Noah Eetook
Richard Jones
Marie-France Brisson

L'Ancienne-Lorette, QC G2E

D-U-N-S 20-188-5225   (SL)
2759-1106 QUEBEC INC
PHARMACIE JEAN COUTU
1415 Rue Notre-Dame, L'Ancienne-Lorette, QC, G2E 3A8
(418) 872-2864
Emp Here 40   *Sales* 10,118,160
SIC 5912 Drug stores and proprietary stores
Danielle Frechette

D-U-N-S 24-690-3256   (HQ)
9260-8553 QUEBEC INC
6029 Boul Wilfrid-Hamel, L'Ancienne-Lorette, QC, G2E 2H3
(418) 872-9705
Emp Here 40   *Sales* 21,412,160
SIC 5261 Retail nurseries and garden stores
Michel Cauvel De Beauville
Philippe Poullain
Benoit Jalbert

D-U-N-S 20-559-3531   (HQ)
ADRENALINE SPORTS INC
ADRENALINE SPORTS
6280 Boul Wilfrid-Hamel, L'Ancienne-Lorette, QC, G2E 2H8
(418) 687-0383
Sales 37,756,800
SIC 5571 Motorcycle dealers
Christian Moreau
Pamela Besner

D-U-N-S 25-363-1139   (HQ)
CAISSE POPULAIRE DESJARDINS DU PIEMONT LAURENTIEN
CENTRE DE SERVICES VAL-BELAIR
1638 Rue Notre-Dame, L'Ancienne-Lorette, QC, G2E 3B6
(418) 872-1445
Emp Here 50   *Sales* 16,394,971
SIC 6062 State credit unions
Renaud Audet
Claude Lefebvre
Gervais Morisette
Amelie Beauchesne
Marie-Eve Fradette
Jocelyn Ouellet
Melanie Argouin
Catherine Aubert
Francis Helie
Annie Pare

D-U-N-S 24-359-0051   (BR)
CANAC IMMOBILIER INC
(*Suby of* GESTION LABERGE INC)
6235 Boul Wilfrid-Hamel, L'Ancienne-Lorette, QC, G2E 5W2
(418) 872-2874
Emp Here 150
SIC 5211 Lumber and other building materials
Claude Boily

D-U-N-S 24-638-3095   (SL)
CONSTRUCTION DINAMO INC
6023 Boul Wilfrid-Hamel, L'Ancienne-Lorette, QC, G2E 2H3
(418) 871-6226
Emp Here 70   *Sales* 29,591,590

SIC 1541 Industrial buildings and warehouses
Jean-Yves Morissette

D-U-N-S 20-431-7499   (HQ)
EBC INC
HYDROTECH MARINE, DIV DE
1095 Rue Valets, L'Ancienne-Lorette, QC, G2E 4M7
(418) 872-0600
Emp Here 500   *Sales* 1,047,588,000
SIC 1541 Industrial buildings and warehouses
Marie-Claude Houle
Martin Houle
Francois Houle

D-U-N-S 20-309-6128   (SL)
EBC-NEILSON, ROMAINE 3 EXCAVATIONS DERIVATION (R3-06-01) S.E.N.C
EBC-NEILSON (R3-06-01)
1095 Rue Valets, L'Ancienne-Lorette, QC, G2E 4M7
(418) 872-0600
Emp Here 50   *Sales* 13,547,100
SIC 1522 Residential construction, nec
Marie-Claude Houle

D-U-N-S 20-302-4658   (SL)
EBC-POMERLEAU, PJCC 62000 S.E.N.C.
1095 Rue Valets, L'Ancienne-Lorette, QC, G2E 4M7
(418) 872-0600
Emp Here 60   *Sales* 16,256,520
SIC 1522 Residential construction, nec
Daniel Lessard

D-U-N-S 20-381-2144   (SL)
EBC-SM (NUNAVUT), S.E.N.C.
EBC-SM (GRISE FIORD), S.E.N.C.
1095 Rue Valets, L'Ancienne-Lorette, QC, G2E 4M7
(418) 872-0600
Emp Here 50   *Sales* 28,516,900
SIC 1542 Nonresidential construction, nec
Marie-Claude Houle

D-U-N-S 20-363-5313   (SL)
EDT GCV CIVIL S.E.P.
1095 Rue Valets, L'Ancienne-Lorette, QC, G2E 4M7
(418) 872-0600
Emp Here 100   *Sales* 23,428,800
SIC 8742 Management consulting services
Jean-Francois Racine

D-U-N-S 20-579-9653   (SL)
G.L.R. INC
GLR
(*Suby of* PLACEMENTS F. H. INC, LES)
1095 Rue Valets, L'Ancienne-Lorette, QC, G2E 4M7
(418) 872-3365
Emp Here 100   *Sales* 25,244,200
SIC 1623 Water, sewer, and utility lines
Martin Chagnon

D-U-N-S 25-765-9185   (HQ)
GESTION LABERGE INC
6245 Boul Wilfrid-Hamel, L'Ancienne-Lorette, QC, G2E 5W2
(418) 667-1313
Emp Here 75   *Sales* 4,751,617,000
SIC 6712 Bank holding companies
Jean Laberge
Pierre Laberge
Gilles Laberge

D-U-N-S 24-316-6712   (SL)
GLR - THIRO S.E.N.C.
1095 Rue Valets, L'Ancienne-Lorette, QC, G2E 4M7
(418) 872-3365
Emp Here 200   *Sales* 50,488,400
SIC 1623 Water, sewer, and utility lines
Louis-Andre Royer

D-U-N-S 25-765-1109   (BR)
GROUPE DE SECURITE GARDA INC, LE
GARDA DU CANADA
(*Suby of* GW INTERMEDIATE HOLDCO

CORPORATION)
1160 Rue Valets, L'Ancienne-Lorette, QC, G2E 5Y9
(418) 627-0088
Emp Here 5,000
SIC 7381 Detective and armored car services
Luc Simard

D-U-N-S 24-499-9447   (SL)
HAMEL, PLACEMENTS GAETAN INC, LES
6029 Boul Wilfrid-Hamel, L'Ancienne-Lorette, QC, G2E 2H3
(418) 871-6010
Emp Here 90   *Sales* 23,607,810
SIC 0181 Ornamental nursery products
Gaetan Hamel
Mariette Hamel

D-U-N-S 20-256-0207   (HQ)
MATERIAUX BLANCHET INC
6019 Boul Wilfrid-Hamel Bureau 200, L'Ancienne-Lorette, QC, G2E 2H3
(418) 871-2626
Emp Here 15   *Sales* 118,315,750
SIC 2421 Sawmills and planing mills, general
Jean-Paul Carrier
Timothy William Varney
John Sirois
Thomas William Gardner

D-U-N-S 25-994-9001   (SL)
PIECES D'AUTO ALAIN COTE INC
UAP NAPA
6315 Boul Wilfrid-Hamel, L'Ancienne-Lorette, QC, G2E 5W2
(418) 780-4770
Emp Here 45   *Sales* 22,413,510
SIC 5531 Auto and home supply stores
Alain Cote
Mathieu Cote
Jacques Aube
Claude Pageau

D-U-N-S 24-402-3870   (SL)
PLOMBERIE DE LA CAPITALE INC
6345 Boul Wilfrid-Hamel Unite 102, L'Ancienne-Lorette, QC, G2E 5W2
(418) 847-2818
Emp Here 49   *Sales* 10,825,766
SIC 1711 Plumbing, heating, air-conditioning
Denis Asselin

D-U-N-S 25-477-2023   (SL)
POSIMAGE INC
6285 Boul Wilfrid-Hamel, L'Ancienne-Lorette, QC, G2E 5W2
(418) 877-2775
Emp Here 60   *Sales* 19,568,160
SIC 3993 Signs and advertising specialties
Martin Boisvert

D-U-N-S 25-745-1526   (SL)
SANI-PLUS INC
GROUPE B.O.D.
1600 Rue Du Pincelier, L'Ancienne-Lorette, QC, G2E 6B7
(418) 871-4683
Emp Here 20   *Sales* 22,106,900
SIC 5122 Drugs, proprietaries, and sundries
Denis Lamoureux
Eric Lamoureux
Sophie Lamoureux
Pauline Allie

L'Ancienne-Lorette, QC G2G

D-U-N-S 20-761-1856   (SL)
CONSTRUCTION GELY INC
(*Suby of* GESTION G.A.H. INC)
1781 Rte De L'Aeroport, L'Ancienne-Lorette, QC, G2G 2P5
(418) 871-3368
Emp Here 150   *Sales* 49,217,250
SIC 1611 Highway and street construction

Henri Gelinas
Armand Gelinas
Stephane Gelinas

D-U-N-S 24-119-5531   (BR)
PROVIGO DISTRIBUTION INC
LOBLAWS
(*Suby of* LOBLAW COMPANIES LIMITED)
1201 Aut Duplessis, L'Ancienne-Lorette, QC, G2G 2B4
(418) 872-2400
Emp Here 130
SIC 5411 Grocery stores
Laurent Lindsay

D-U-N-S 24-407-6241   (SL)
TIM HORTONS RESTAURANTS
1225 Aut Duplessis, L'Ancienne-Lorette, QC, G2G 2B4
(418) 877-0989
Emp Here 48   *Sales* 13,159,296
SIC 5461 Retail bakeries
Caroline Lemieux

L'Ange Gardien, QC G0A

D-U-N-S 20-776-8359   (HQ)
9353-0251 QUEBEC INC
SOLARIS QUEBEC
6150 Boul Sainte-Anne, L'Ange Gardien, QC, G0A 2K0
(418) 822-0643
Emp Here 200   *Sales* 91,377,250
SIC 6712 Bank holding companies
Pascal Chalifour

D-U-N-S 24-370-4397   (HQ)
GAMMA MURS ET FENETRES INTERNA-TIONAL INC
GAMMA INDUSTRIES
(*Suby of* CHINA STATE CONSTRUCTION IN-TERNATIONAL HOLDINGS LIMITED)
6130 Boul Sainte-Anne, L'Ange Gardien, QC, G0A 2K0
(418) 822-1448
Sales 53,530,400
SIC 5211 Lumber and other building materials
Hai Wang
Jidong Qin
Pierre Belanger

D-U-N-S 24-424-3742   (SL)
SOLARIS INTERNATIONAL INC
(*Suby of* 9353-0251 QUEBEC INC)
6150 Boul Sainte-Anne, L'Ange Gardien, QC, G0A 2K0
(418) 822-0643
Emp Here 100   *Sales* 56,210,000
SIC 5211 Lumber and other building materials
Pascal Chalifour

D-U-N-S 20-357-2888   (SL)
SOLARIS QUEBEC PORTES ET FENETRES INC
(*Suby of* 9353-0251 QUEBEC INC)
6150 Boul Sainte-Anne, L'Ange Gardien, QC, G0A 2K0
(418) 822-0643
Emp Here 100   *Sales* 15,885,800
SIC 3089 Plastics products, nec
Pascal Chalifour
Maxime Brouillard

L'Ascension-De-Notre-Seigneur, QC G0W

D-U-N-S 25-685-2146   (BR)
PRODUITS FORESTIERS ARBEC S.E.N.C.
(*Suby of* PRODUITS FORESTIERS ARBEC S.E.N.C.)
5005 Rte Uniforet, L'Ascension-De-Notre-Seigneur, QC, G0W 1Y0

(418) 347-4900
Emp Here 200
SIC 2421 Sawmills and planing mills, general
 Alain Gauthier

L'Assomption, QC J5W

D-U-N-S 25-504-2442   (HQ)
3320235 CANADA INC
ROULOTTES R.G. GAGNON
175 Montee De Saint-Sulpice, L'Assomption,
QC, J5W 2T3
(450) 589-5718
Sales 18,878,400
SIC 5561 Recreational vehicle dealers
 Michel Blais
 Eric Lachapelle
 Marc-Andre Blais
 Marie-Pier Blais

D-U-N-S 25-846-0948   (SL)
CLOTURES ARBOIT INC, LES
230 Rue Arboit, L'Assomption, QC, J5W 4P5
(450) 589-8484
Emp Here 60   *Sales* 14,006,100
SIC 3273 Ready-mixed concrete
 Martin Verstraete
 Andre Meunier

D-U-N-S 20-888-0989   (SL)
**CORPORATION DU COLLEGE DE
L'ASSOMPTION, LA**
COLLEGE DE L'ASSOMPTION
270 Boul De L'Ange-Gardien, L'Assomption,
QC, J5W 1R7
(450) 589-5621
Emp Here 150   *Sales* 22,408,650
SIC 8221 Colleges and universities
 Jean-Pierre Bois
 Nicolas St-Cyr
 Marielle Jobin

D-U-N-S 24-515-6039   (SL)
EBENISTERIE A. BEAUCAGE INC
FIRST CHOICE CABINET
188 Ch Des Commissaires, L'Assomption,
J5W 2T7
(450) 589-6412
Emp Here 65   *Sales* 10,131,095
SIC 2434 Wood kitchen cabinets
 Alain Beaucage
 Francis Beaucage
 Genevieve Beaucage

D-U-N-S 24-337-0215   (BR)
ELECTROLUX CANADA CORP
ELECTROLUX HOME PRODUCTS
(*Suby of* AB ELECTROLUX)
802 Boul De L'Ange-Gardien, L'Assomption,
QC, J5W 1T6
(450) 589-5701
Emp Here 1,000
SIC 3634 Electric housewares and fans
 Claude Gauthier

D-U-N-S 20-333-0985   (HQ)
GROUPE AGF ACCES INC
AGF ACCES
(*Suby of* GROUPE AGF INC)
125 Rue De L'Industrie, L'Assomption, QC,
J5W 2T9
(450) 589-8100
Emp Here 100   *Sales* 105,734,000
SIC 6159 Miscellaneous business credit institutions
 Serge Gendron
 Vincent Dequoy
 Mark Clarke
 Michel Gendron
 Pierre Grand'maison

D-U-N-S 20-927-9041   (HQ)
PIECES D'AUTOS LE PORTAGE LTEE
1059 Boul De L'Ange-Gardien N,
L'Assomption, QC, J5W 1N7

---

(450) 589-5735
Emp Here 12   *Sales* 10,198,020
SIC 5013 Motor vehicle supplies and new
parts
 Maurice Marsolais
 Pierre Marsolais
 Robert Landreville
 Marie Andree Landreville

D-U-N-S 20-204-4186   (SL)
PLASTIQUES ANCHOR LTEE
730 Rue Saint-Etienne, L'Assomption, QC,
J5W 1Z1
(450) 589-5627
Emp Here 85   *Sales* 17,161,245
SIC 3089 Plastics products, nec
 Angy Potvin

D-U-N-S 24-106-7198   (HQ)
ROULOTTES R. G. GAGNON INC
RRGG
(*Suby of* 3320235 CANADA INC)
175 Montee De Saint-Sulpice, L'Assomption,
QC, J5W 2T3
(450) 589-5718
Sales 12,950,028
SIC 5561 Recreational vehicle dealers
 Michel Blais
 Eric Lachapelle

D-U-N-S 25-988-8555   (SL)
STAGELINE GROUPE INC
827 Boul De L'Ange-Gardien, L'Assomption,
QC, J5W 1T3
(450) 589-1063
Emp Here 49   *Sales* 20,548,395
SIC 6712 Bank holding companies
 Yvan Miron

D-U-N-S 24-954-8546   (SL)
STAGELINE SCENE MOBILE INC
MSR LOCATION SCENE MOBILE
(*Suby of* GROUPE STAGELINE INC)
700 Rue Marsolais, L'Assomption, QC, J5W
2G9
(450) 589-1063
Emp Here 190   *Sales* 61,965,840
SIC 3999 Manufacturing industries, nec
 Yvan Miron
 Lise Morissat

D-U-N-S 24-500-6718   (SL)
STAGELINE SCENE MOBILE INC
827 Boul De L'Ange-Gardien, L'Assomption,
QC, J5W 1T3
(450) 589-1063
Emp Here 49   *Sales* 10,722,376
SIC 3999 Manufacturing industries, nec
 Yvan Miron

D-U-N-S 24-540-9016   (SL)
**SUPERMARCHE CREVIER L'ASSOMPTION
INC**
I.G.A. EXTRA
860 Boul De L'Ange-Gardien N, L'Assomption,
QC, J5W 1P1
(450) 589-5738
Emp Here 135   *Sales* 39,619,395
SIC 5411 Grocery stores
 Micheline Papin

D-U-N-S 20-356-3192   (SL)
**SUPERMARCHE   MARQUIS
L'ASSOMPTION INC**
790 Montee De Saint-Sulpice, L'Assomption,
QC, J5W 0M6
(450) 589-0442
Emp Here 100   *Sales* 29,347,700
SIC 5411 Grocery stores
 Jessica Fouani
 Kevin Marquis

L'Epiphanie, QC J5X

D-U-N-S 20-648-9700   (SL)

GESTION MAJEAU, MARCEL INC
41 Rue Du Couvent, L'Epiphanie, QC, J5X
0B6
(450) 938-0884
Emp Here 1   *Sales* 11,073,600
SIC 6514 Dwelling operators, except apartments
 Marcel Majeau

L'Etang-Du-Nord, QC G4T

D-U-N-S 20-585-1475   (HQ)
**CAISSE POPULAIRE DESJARDINS DES
RAMEES**
*CENTRE DE SERVICE DE CAP-AUX-
MEULES*
1278 Ch De La Verniere, L'Etang-Du-Nord,
QC, G4T 3E6
(418) 986-2319
Emp Here 29   *Sales* 10,711,539
SIC 6062 State credit unions
 Lucien Presseault
 Maryse Lapierre
 Charles-Claude Dion
 Jean-Pierre Miousse
 Christian Arsenault
 Jules Arseneau
 Pascale Boudreau
 Martine Bourgeois
 Marc-Olivier Corbeil
 Michel Leblanc

D-U-N-S 20-555-4384   (HQ)
COMMISSION SCOLAIRE DES ILES
1419 Ch De L'Etang-Du-Nord, L'Etang-Du-
Nord, QC, G4T 3B9
(418) 986-5511
Emp Here 50   *Sales* 24,481,575
SIC 8211 Elementary and secondary schools
 Francine Cyr
 Diane Arsenault
 Danielle Gallant
 Brigitte Aucoin
 Marie-Josee Noel

D-U-N-S 20-886-7981   (BR)
**DEVEAU, BOURGEOIS, GAGNE, HEBERT
ET ASSOCIES S.E.N.C.R.L**
(*Suby of* DEVEAU, BOURGEOIS, GAGNE,
HEBERT ET ASSOCIES S.E.N.C.R.L)
1210 Ch De La Verniere Bureau 2, L'Etang-
Du-Nord, QC, G4T 3E6
(418) 986-4782
Emp Here 80
SIC 8111 Legal services
 Jean-Claude Gresshaber

D-U-N-S 20-393-7664   (SL)
FRUITS DE MER MADELEINE INC, LES
546 Ch Fougere, L'Etang-Du-Nord, QC, G4T
3B3
(418) 986-6016
Emp Here 50   *Sales* 41,778,850
SIC 5146 Fish and seafoods
 Claude Poirier
 Henri-Fred Poirier
 Pierre Deraspe
 Eric Poirier
 Yvon Theriault
 Denis Eloquin
 Sandro Aucoin
 Paul Chevarie
 Bruno-Pierre Bourque

D-U-N-S 20-803-0275   (SL)
FRUITS DE MER MADELEINE INC, LES
546 Ch Fougere, L'Etang-Du-Nord, QC, G4T
3B3
(418) 986-6016
Emp Here 50   *Sales* 73,530,776
SIC 5146 Fish and seafoods
 Claude Poirier
 Henri-Fred Poirier
 Pierre Deraspe

 Eric Poirier
 Yvon Theriault
 Denis Eloquin
 Sandro Aucoin
 Paul Chevarie
 Bruno-Pierre Bourque

D-U-N-S 20-289-4119   (SL)
RENAISSANCE DES ILES INC, LA
PRODUITS LA GULF QUEEN, LES
521 Ch Du Gros-Cap, L'Etang-Du-Nord, QC,
G4T 3M1
(418) 986-2710
Emp Here 250   *Sales* 121,846,250
SIC 2092 Fresh or frozen packaged fish
 Lynn Albert

L'Ile-Bizard, QC H9C

D-U-N-S 24-325-7367   (SL)
SUPER MARCHE ST-RAPHAEL INC
I G A
640 Boul Jacques-Bizard, L'Ile-Bizard, QC,
H9C 2H2
(514) 620-4443
Emp Here 60   *Sales* 17,608,620
SIC 5411 Grocery stores
 Jean Louis Lalonde

L'Ile-Perrot, QC J7V

D-U-N-S 24-836-4770   (SL)
3347818 CANADA INC
L'ILE-PERROT NISSAN
12 Boul Don-Quichotte, L'Ile-Perrot, QC, J7V
6N5
(514) 425-2255
Emp Here 26   *Sales* 12,950,028
SIC 5511 New and used car dealers
 Denis Leclerc

D-U-N-S 20-724-3403   (SL)
AUTOMOBILES ILE-PERROT INC
HONDA ILE-PERROT
40 Boul Don-Quichotte, L'Ile-Perrot, QC, J7V
6N5
(514) 453-8416
Emp Here 55   *Sales* 34,610,400
SIC 5511 New and used car dealers
 Mario Bourbonnais
 Claude Leclair

D-U-N-S 24-678-4045   (SL)
AVANTAGE FORD INC
30 Boul Don-Quichotte, L'Ile-Perrot, QC, J7V
6N5
(514) 453-5850
Emp Here 45   *Sales* 22,413,510
SIC 5511 New and used car dealers
 Micheal Iasigliola

D-U-N-S 24-635-1126   (SL)
MAGASIN FARMAJEM INC
PHARMACIE JEAN COUTU #156
405 Grand Boulevard, L'Ile-Perrot, QC, J7V
4X3
(514) 453-2896
Emp Here 55   *Sales* 13,438,040
SIC 5912 Drug stores and proprietary stores
 Richard Jolicoeur

D-U-N-S 24-516-2060   (SL)
PETROLE LEGER INC
460 Grand Boulevard, L'Ile-Perrot, QC, J7V
4X5
(514) 453-5766
Emp Here 25   *Sales* 12,451,950
SIC 5541 Gasoline service stations
 Pierre Leger

D-U-N-S 25-976-9016   (SL)
RELIANCE FOODS INTERNATIONAL INC

ALIMENTS RELIANCE INTERNATIONAL, LES
549 Grand Boulevard, L'Ile-Perrot, QC, J7V 4X4
(514) 425-1880
Emp Here 9   *Sales* 14,878,740
SIC 5142 Packaged frozen goods
 Marc Legault

        D-U-N-S 25-463-2482   (SL)
SUPERMARCHE DON QUICHOTTE INC
IGA EXTRA ROCHETTE & VEZINA
110 Boul Don-Quichotte, L'Ile-Perrot, QC, J7V 6L7
(514) 453-3027
Emp Here 200   *Sales* 58,695,400
SIC 5411 Grocery stores
 Marc Rochette
 Daniel Vezina

L'Isle-Verte, QC G0L

        D-U-N-S 24-524-8583   (SL)
9091-4532 QUEBEC INC
XMETAL
89 Rue Villeray, L'Isle-Verte, QC, G0L 1L0
(418) 898-3330
Emp Here 60   *Sales* 10,765,740
SIC 3599 Industrial machinery, nec
 Etienne Cote
 Alexandre Cote

        D-U-N-S 24-201-1617   (SL)
APRIL SUPER FLO INC
(*Suby of* 3105-4547 QUEBEC INC)
9 Rue Beland, L'Isle-Verte, QC, G0L 1K0
(418) 898-5151
Emp Here 18   *Sales* 22,629,618
SIC 5172 Petroleum products, nec
 Lucius April
 Nathaly April

L'Islet, QC G0R

        D-U-N-S 24-203-9568   (SL)
FONDERIE POITRAS LTEE
(*Suby of* CONSULTANTS SENTINEL INC)
168 Boul Nilus-Leclerc, L'Islet, QC, G0R 2C0
(418) 247-5041
Emp Here 100   *Sales* 18,138,800
SIC 3321 Gray and ductile iron foundries
 Claude Masse
 Jacques Beaudet
 Jason Robitaille
 Denis Labrecque
 Andre Nadeau
 Kamal Racine

        D-U-N-S 20-206-0810   (SL)
INDUSTRIES AMISCO LTEE, LES
33 5e Rue, L'Islet, QC, G0R 2C0
(418) 247-5025
Emp Here 288   *Sales* 64,127,520
SIC 2514 Metal household furniture
 Rejean Poitras
 Guillaume Jacques
 Nicolas Gaudreau
 Guylaine Belley
 Jacques Beaudoin

        D-U-N-S 24-366-8782   (SL)
L. & G. CLOUTIER INC
303 Boul Nilus-Leclerc, L'Islet, QC, G0R 2C0
(418) 247-5071
Emp Here 85   *Sales* 15,251,465
SIC 3599 Industrial machinery, nec
 Eric Lord
 Martin Grenier

        D-U-N-S 20-643-2247   (HQ)
OUELLET CANADA INC

CELSIAIR
(*Suby of* GROUPE OUELLET CANADA INC)
180 3e Av, L'Islet, QC, G0R 2C0
(418) 247-3947
Sales 63,197,325
SIC 3567 Industrial furnaces and ovens
 Martin Beaulieu

        D-U-N-S 24-967-5476   (SL)
UMANO MEDICAL INC
230 Boul Nilus-Leclerc, L'Islet, QC, G0R 2C0
(418) 247-3986
Emp Here 188   *Sales* 24,496,416
SIC 3841 Surgical and medical instruments
 Christian Cariou
 Ghislain Demers
 Robert Dion
 Denis Bourgault

La Baie, QC G7B

        D-U-N-S 20-183-3733   (HQ)
2737-2895 QUEBEC INC
DISTRIBUTION FROMAGERIE BOIVIN
2152 Ch Saint-Joseph, La Baie, QC, G7B 3N9
(418) 544-2622
Emp Here 40   *Sales* 66,846,160
SIC 5143 Dairy products, except dried or canned
 Luc Boivin
 Valerie Boivin
 Martin Roberge
 Eric Chabot

        D-U-N-S 24-329-6105   (SL)
6482066 CANADA INC
P.C.P. CANADA
905 Rue De L'Innovation, La Baie, QC, G7B 3N8
(418) 677-3939
Emp Here 70   *Sales* 16,340,450
SIC 3354 Aluminum extruded products
 Michel Lavoie

        D-U-N-S 20-189-2130   (HQ)
9113-0476 QUEBEC INC
FROMAGERIE BOIVIN
(*Suby of* 2737-2895 QUEBEC INC)
2152 Ch Saint-Joseph, La Baie, QC, G7B 3N9
(418) 544-2622
Emp Here 10   *Sales* 17,284,500
SIC 2022 Cheese; natural and processed
 Luc Boivin
 Valerie Boivin
 Eric Chabot
 Martin Roberge
 Pierre Otis
 Luc Simard
 Dominique Pilote
 Marc Perron
 Samuel Bouchard

        D-U-N-S 24-885-2584   (SL)
ALIMENTATION CHRISTIAN VERREAULT INC
IGA
150 6e Rue, La Baie, QC, G7B 4V9
(418) 544-8251
Emp Here 140   *Sales* 41,086,780
SIC 5411 Grocery stores
 Chantale Verreault

        D-U-N-S 20-820-2882   (SL)
AMEC CONSTRUCTION INC
312 Rue Joseph-Gagne S, La Baie, QC, G7B 3P6
(418) 544-8885
Emp Here 25   *Sales* 11,768,275
SIC 1542 Nonresidential construction, nec
 Chrystine Martel

        D-U-N-S 20-581-4551   (SL)
CANMEC LA BAIE INC
(*Suby of* GROUPE CANMEC INC)

3453 Ch Des Chutes, La Baie, QC, G7B 3N8
(418) 544-3391
Emp Here 80   *Sales* 39,018,400
SIC 5085 Industrial supplies
 Remi Roy
 Eric Vachon

        D-U-N-S 24-330-7308   (HQ)
CHARL-POL INC
(*Suby of* 8132992 CANADA INC)
4653 Ch Saint-Anicet, La Baie, QC, G7B 0J4
(418) 544-7355
Emp Here 5   *Sales* 14,364,378
SIC 3569 General industrial machinery, nec
 Gilles Leroux
 Richard Tremblay
 Catherine Frigon

        D-U-N-S 24-394-9596   (BR)
CHARL-POL INC
(*Suby of* 8132992 CANADA INC)
805 Rue De L'Innovation, La Baie, QC, G7B 3N8
(418) 677-1518
Emp Here 80
SIC 3569 General industrial machinery, nec
 Gilles Gagne

        D-U-N-S 25-233-6706   (BR)
COMMISSION SCOLAIRE DES RIVES-DU-SAGUENAY
ECOLE SECONDAIRE DES GRANDES-MAREES
(*Suby of* COMMISSION SCOLAIRE DES RIVES-DU-SAGUENAY)
1802 Av John-Kane, La Baie, QC, G7B 1K2
(418) 544-2843
Emp Here 115
SIC 8211 Elementary and secondary schools
 Luc Quenneville

        D-U-N-S 20-432-4883   (HQ)
DERY TELECOM INC
CABLEVISION HAUT ST-LAURENT
1013 Rue Bagot, La Baie, QC, G7B 2N6
(418) 544-3358
Sales 22,847,200
SIC 4841 Cable and other pay television services

        D-U-N-S 20-720-4905   (BR)
ENTREPRISES MACBAIE INC, LES
MCDONALD
(*Suby of* ENTREPRISES MACBAIE INC, LES)
1082 Rue Aime-Gravel, La Baie, QC, G7B 2M5
(418) 545-3593
Emp Here 75
SIC 5812 Eating places
 Jean-Daniel Bedard

        D-U-N-S 25-293-4583   (HQ)
FJORD-TECH INDUSTRIE INC
FJORD-TECH ROUYN-NORANDA
2760 Boul De La Grande-Baie N, La Baie, QC, G7B 3N8
(418) 544-7091
Sales 19,044,200
SIC 3625 Relays and industrial controls
 Andre Montpellier
 Josee Boudreault
 Caroline Simard
 Pierre Lavoie
 Pynthia Vignault

        D-U-N-S 25-978-0252   (SL)
J.M.Y. INC
480 Rue Joseph-Gagne S, La Baie, QC, G7B 3P6
(418) 544-8442
Emp Here 120   *Sales* 26,640,120
SIC 3599 Industrial machinery, nec
 Jean Marc Maltais
 Jean-Marc Maltais

        D-U-N-S 25-157-2124   (SL)
LIGNAREX INC

7700 Ch De La Batture, La Baie, QC, G7B 3P6
(418) 306-5049
Emp Here 49   *Sales* 23,276,274
SIC 5084 Industrial machinery and equipment
 ?ric Rousseau

        D-U-N-S 20-644-4999   (SL)
MAXI 8619
MAXI LA BAIE
2100 Rue Bagot, La Baie, QC, G7B 3Z3
(418) 544-2848
Emp Here 45   *Sales* 12,336,840
SIC 5411 Grocery stores
 Maxime Deschenes

        D-U-N-S 24-941-8476   (SL)
METATUBE (1993) INC
2713 Av Du Port, La Baie, QC, G7B 4S8
(418) 544-3303
Emp Here 130   *Sales* 24,971,050
SIC 3499 Fabricated Metal products, nec
 Francois Gagne
 Gerald Bergeron
 Johanne Toulouse

        D-U-N-S 20-643-9846   (HQ)
PRODUITS ALBA INC
300 Boul De La Grande-Baie N Bureau 3, La Baie, QC, G7B 3K3
(418) 544-3361
Emp Here 8   *Sales* 15,233,615
SIC 3251 Brick and structural clay tile
 Jean-Julien Grenon
 Gilles Grenon
 Christine Grenon

        D-U-N-S 24-109-7414   (BR)
RIO TINTO ALCAN INC
(*Suby of* RIO TINTO PLC)
262 1re Rue, La Baie, QC, G7B 3R1
(418) 544-9660
Emp Here 150
SIC 4512 Air transportation, scheduled

        D-U-N-S 20-013-9843   (BR)
RIO TINTO ALCAN INC
(*Suby of* RIO TINTO PLC)
5000 Rte Du Petit Parc, La Baie, QC, G7B 4G9
(418) 697-9600
Emp Here 800
SIC 3334 Primary aluminum
 Alf Barrios

La Corne, QC J0Y

        D-U-N-S 20-332-7379   (SL)
LITHIUM AMERIQUE DU NORD INC
500 Rte Du Lithium, La Corne, QC, J0Y 1R0
(819) 734-5000
Emp Here 60   *Sales* 14,006,100
SIC 1081 Metal mining services
 James Xiang
 Thomas Laporte Aust
 Dr. Bin Guo
 Joseph Zhen Shu

La Dore, QC G8J

        D-U-N-S 20-511-8768   (BR)
PF RESOLU CANADA INC
PRODUIT FORESTIERS RESOLU SECTEUR LA DORE
(*Suby of* RESOLUTE FOREST PRODUCTS INC)
5850 Av Des Jardins, La Dore, QC, G8J 1B4
(418) 256-3816
Emp Here 233
SIC 2421 Sawmills and planing mills, general
 Sylvain Goulet

La Durantaye, QC G0R

D-U-N-S 25-619-9568 (SL)
EQUIPEMENTS ADRIEN PHANEUF (LES)
23 Rue Olivier-Morel, La Durantaye, QC, G0R 1W0
(418) 884-2841
Emp Here 49   *Sales* 11,438,315
SIC 3131 Footwear cut stock
Yvon Phaneuf

D-U-N-S 24-791-4187 (SL)
MOBILIER M.E.Q. LTEE
(*Suby of* INVESTISSEMENT CLAUJEAN INC.)
22 Rue Olivier-Morel, La Durantaye, QC, G0R 1W0
(418) 884-3050
Emp Here 70   *Sales* 10,802,540
SIC 2511 Wood household furniture
Jean Belanger
Jean-Claude Belanger

La Guadeloupe, QC G0M

D-U-N-S 20-516-2332 (SL)
INDUSTRIES DE CIMENT LA GUADE-LOUPE INC, LES
238 14e Av, La Guadeloupe, QC, G0M 1G0
(418) 459-3542
Emp Here 60   *Sales* 10,753,140
SIC 3272 Concrete products, nec
Francine Coulombe
Virginie Gilbert
Narue-Andre Gilbert

D-U-N-S 25-382-8883 (SL)
MARCHE D'ANIMAUX VIVANTS VEILLEUX & FRERES INC
1287 14e Av, La Guadeloupe, QC, G0M 1G0
(418) 459-6832
Emp Here 10   *Sales* 12,103,970
SIC 5154 Livestock
Laurette Veilleux
Clairemont Veilleux

D-U-N-S 20-667-7668 (SL)
METAL NORGATE 2012 INC
791 8e Rue E, La Guadeloupe, QC, G0M 1G0
(418) 459-6988
Emp Here 85   *Sales* 16,327,225
SIC 3441 Fabricated structural Metal
Richard Gilbert

D-U-N-S 24-884-3864 (SL)
UNIFORMES F.O.B. (1991) LTEE
645 14e Av, La Guadeloupe, QC, G0M 1G0

Emp Here 65   *Sales* 12,948,260
SIC 2311 Men's and boy's suits and coats
Richard Bilodeau
Denise Bilodeau

La Malbaie, QC G5A

D-U-N-S 20-327-9232 (BR)
AGENCE POUR VIVRE CHEZ SOI INC
502 Rue Saint-Etienne, La Malbaie, QC, G5A 1H5
(418) 665-1067
Emp Here 120
SIC 8399 Social services, nec
Pierre Tremblay

D-U-N-S 20-203-7149 (SL)
ALIMENTATION LAPOINTE & FRERES INC
25 Boul Kane, La Malbaie, QC, G5A 1J2
(418) 665-3954
Emp Here 40   *Sales* 10,966,080

SIC 5411 Grocery stores
Pierre-Alexis Lapointe
Roger Lapointe

D-U-N-S 20-651-2787 (SL)
ALIMENTATION ROBERT DUFOUR INC
METRO LA MALBAIE
375 Boul De Comporte Bureau 129, La Malbaie, QC, G5A 1H9
(418) 665-4473
Emp Here 49   *Sales* 13,433,448
SIC 5411 Grocery stores
Robert Dufour

D-U-N-S 24-790-6118 (HQ)
ASSOCIATION TOURISTIQUE REGIONALE DE CHARLEVOIX INC
495 Boul De Comporte, La Malbaie, QC, G5A 3G3
(418) 665-4454
Emp Here 12   *Sales* 14,824,227
SIC 7389 Business services, nec
Bruno Labbe
Alyre Jomphe

D-U-N-S 24-810-8511 (SL)
AUTO FRANK MICHEL CHARLEVOIX INC
2060 Boul De Comporte, La Malbaie, QC, G5A 3C5
(418) 665-6431
Emp Here 25   *Sales* 12,451,950
SIC 5511 New and used car dealers
Eric St-Gelais

D-U-N-S 25-232-7507 (BR)
COMMISSION SCOLAIRE DE CHARLEVOIX, LA
ECOLE SECONDAIRE DU PLATEAU
(*Suby of* COMMISSION SCOLAIRE DE CHARLEVOIX, LA)
88 Rue Des Cimes, La Malbaie, QC, G5A 1T3
(418) 665-3791
Emp Here 150
SIC 8211 Elementary and secondary schools
Jocelyn Simard

D-U-N-S 24-378-8924 (SL)
DUFOUR PONTIAC CHEVROLET INC
2040 Boul De Comporte, La Malbaie, QC, G5A 3C4
(418) 665-7511
Emp Here 25   *Sales* 12,451,950
SIC 5511 New and used car dealers
Yvan Dufour

D-U-N-S 20-699-9018 (BR)
FAIRMONT HOTELS & RESORTS INC
FAIRMONT LE MANOIR RICHELIEU
(*Suby of* ACCOR)
181 Rue Richelieu Bureau 200, La Malbaie, QC, G5A 1X7
(418) 665-3703
Emp Here 600
SIC 7011 Hotels and motels
Jean-Jacques Etcheberrigaray

D-U-N-S 20-432-9510 (BR)
GENERAL CABLE COMPANY LTD
(*Suby of* PRYSMIAN SPA)
2600 Boul De Comporte, La Malbaie, QC, G5A 1N4

Emp Here 84
SIC 3357 Nonferrous wiredrawing and insulating
Charles Emond

D-U-N-S 24-393-0455 (SL)
GESTION MARIO ROY INC
CANADIAN TIRE
375 Boul De Comporte Bureau 118, La Malbaie, QC, G5A 1H9
(418) 665-6483
Emp Here 25   *Sales* 12,451,950
SIC 5531 Auto and home supply stores
Alain Belanger

D-U-N-S 25-239-1300 (SL)

HALLE COUTURE & ASSOCIES LTEE
475 Rue Saint-Etienne, La Malbaie, QC, G5A 1H5
(418) 665-3978
Emp Here 49   *Sales* 50,709,169
SIC 6311 Life insurance
Monick Tremblay

D-U-N-S 20-951-2631 (HQ)
HARVEY, AUREL & FILS INC
555 Rue Saint-Etienne, La Malbaie, QC, G5A 1J3
(418) 665-4461
Emp Here 30   *Sales* 15,669,540
SIC 4953 Refuse systems
Laurent Harvey
Bernard Harvey

D-U-N-S 25-664-5664 (SL)
PEPINIERE CHARLEVOIX INC
2375 Boul De Comporte, La Malbaie, QC, G5A 3C6
(418) 439-4646
Emp Here 100   *Sales* 26,765,200
SIC 5261 Retail nurseries and garden stores
Jean-Claude Bernier

D-U-N-S 20-609-4943 (BR)
SOCIETE DES CASINOS DU QUEBEC INC, LA
CASINO DE CHARLEVOIX, LE
(*Suby of* GOUVERNEMENT DE LA PROVINCE DE QUEBEC)
183 Rue Richelieu, La Malbaie, QC, G5A 1X8
(418) 665-5300
Emp Here 375
SIC 7032 Sporting and recreational camps
Francois Tremblay

D-U-N-S 24-942-4045 (SL)
SOCIETE EN COMMANDITE MANOIR RICHELIEU
FAIRMOUNT MANOIR RICHELIEU
181 Rue Richelieu Bureau 200, La Malbaie, QC, G5A 1X7
(418) 665-3703
Emp Here 570   *Sales* 54,530,760
SIC 7011 Hotels and motels
Louise Champagne

La Pocatiere, QC G0R

D-U-N-S 24-843-3534 (SL)
ALIMENTATION LEBEL INC
METRO LEBEL
615 Rue 1 Re, La Pocatiere, QC, G0R 1Z0
(418) 856-3827
Emp Here 120   *Sales* 35,217,240
SIC 5411 Grocery stores
Yves Lebel

D-U-N-S 24-827-1731 (BR)
BOMBARDIER TRANSPORTATION CANADA INC
BOMBARDIER TRANSPORT
(*Suby of* BOMBARDIER INC)
230 Rte O Bureau 130, La Pocatiere, QC, G0R 1Z0
(418) 856-1232
Emp Here 500
SIC 5088 Transportation equipment and supplies
Sebastien Ross

D-U-N-S 24-568-9211 (HQ)
COLLEGE D'ENSEIGNEMENT GENERAL & PROFESSIONEL DE LA POCATIERE
CEGEP DE LA POCATIERE
140 4e Av, La Pocatiere, QC, G0R 1Z0
(418) 856-1525
Emp Here 210   *Sales* 37,347,750
SIC 8221 Colleges and universities
Didier Rioux
Claude Harvey

D-U-N-S 25-242-9238 (SL)
COLLEGE STE-ANNE-DE-LA POCATIERE
100 4e Av, La Pocatiere, QC, G0R 1Z0
(418) 856-3012
Emp Here 85   *Sales* 9,574,060
SIC 8221 Colleges and universities
Richard Bernier
Martin Frenette

D-U-N-S 24-941-7221 (HQ)
GESTION BELANGER, BERNARD LTEE
1300 4e Av, La Pocatiere, QC, G0R 1Z0
(418) 856-3858
Sales 13,077,650
SIC 6712 Bank holding companies
Bernard Belanger
Jean Belanger
Germain Ouellet
Julie Belanger

D-U-N-S 24-908-8022 (SL)
KAMCO CONSTRUCTION INC
R.X. CONSTRUCTION
149 Rue Du Parc-De-L'Innovation, La Pocatiere, QC, G0R 1Z0
(418) 856-5432
Emp Here 85   *Sales* 1,556,776
SIC 1542 Nonresidential construction, nec
Daniel Dionne
Guy Malenfant
Armand Lachance

D-U-N-S 20-952-1301 (HQ)
LTG RAIL CANADA LTEE
ELECTRONIQUE S.E.M.
(*Suby of* LUMINATOR TECHNOLOGY GROUP, LLC)
151 Rue Du Parc-De-L'Innovation, La Pocatiere, QC, G0R 1Z0
(418) 856-1454
Emp Here 25   *Sales* 22,728,900
SIC 3823 Process control instruments
Roald Greboval
Richard Rosselet
Kirk Anthony Goins

La Prairie, QC J5R

D-U-N-S 25-688-1475 (SL)
2529-0032 QUEBEC INC
3005 Boul Taschereau, La Prairie, QC, J5R 5S6
(450) 444-3112
Emp Here 15   *Sales* 15,005,085
SIC 5051 Metals service centers and offices
Andre Gagnon

D-U-N-S 20-386-7874 (SL)
ACCES SERVICES SANTE GSS INC
PRAXIS SANTE
1650 Ch De Saint-Jean Bureau 101, La Prairie, QC, J5R 0J1

Emp Here 500   *Sales* 37,886,500
SIC 8093 Specialty outpatient clinics, nec
Guillaume Journel
Johanne Brien
Francisca Nol

D-U-N-S 24-590-5625 (SL)
ALIMENTATION J. G. D. INC
I G A
975 Boul Taschereau Bureau 302, La Prairie, QC, J5R 1W7
(450) 659-1611
Emp Here 115   *Sales* 33,749,855
SIC 5411 Grocery stores
Jacques Vallee
Daniel Vallee

D-U-N-S 20-237-8998 (HQ)
BOULANGERIE GADOUA LTEE
(*Suby of* GEORGE WESTON LIMITED)
170 Boul Taschereau Bureau 220, La Prairie,

QC, J5R 5H6
(450) 245-3326
Emp Here 40   *Sales* 365,538,750
SIC 2051 Bread, cake, and related products
Luc Mongeau

D-U-N-S 20-106-8090   (SL)
BRASSEUR TRANSPORT INC
1250 Rue Industrielle, La Prairie, QC, J5R 5G4
(450) 444-7079
Emp Here 100   *Sales* 14,819,200
SIC 4213 Trucking, except local
Josiane-Melanie Langlois
Chantal Martel
Martin Quesnel

D-U-N-S 24-788-7268   (HQ)
CAISSE POPULAIRE DE LA PRAIRIE
DESJARDINS ENTREPRISES- RIVE-SUD
450 Boul Taschereau, La Prairie, QC, J5R 1V1
(450) 659-5431
Emp Here 35   *Sales* 10,507,397
SIC 6062 State credit unions
Denis Senecal
Robert Clermont
Raymond Frechette
Michel Descoteaux
Georges Desilets
Michel Descoteaux
Anne-Marie Lussier
Justin Bissonnette
Luc Leveille
Isabelle Belanger

D-U-N-S 25-258-8355   (BR)
CENTRE INTEGRE DE SANTE ET DE SERVICES SOCIAUX DE LA MONTEREGIE-OUEST
CSSS JARDIN ROUSSILLON
(*Suby of* CENTRE INTEGRE DE SANTE ET DE SERVICES SOCIAUX DE LA MONTEREGIE-OUEST)
500 Av De Balmoral, La Prairie, QC, J5R 4N5
(450) 659-9148
Emp Here 200
SIC 8361 Residential care
Eric Remillard

D-U-N-S 20-102-5512   (BR)
CIMENT QUEBEC INC
UNIBETON
(*Suby of* GROUPE CIMENT QUEBEC INC)
1250 Ch Saint-Jose, La Prairie, QC, J5R 6A9
(450) 444-7942
Emp Here 170
SIC 3273 Ready-mixed concrete
Serge Fortin

D-U-N-S 24-814-9148   (SL)
COLLEGE JEAN DE LA MENNAIS
870 Ch De Saint-Jean, La Prairie, QC, J5R 2L5
(450) 659-7657
Emp Here 125   *Sales* 12,389,875
SIC 8211 Elementary and secondary schools
Stephane Guerin

D-U-N-S 25-233-6573   (BR)
COMMISSION SCOLAIRE DES GRANDES-SEIGNEURIES
ECOLE DE LA MAGDELEINE
(*Suby of* COMMISSION SCOLAIRE DES GRANDES-SEIGNEURIES)
1100 Boul Taschereau, La Prairie, QC, J5R 1W8
(514) 380-8899
Emp Here 200
SIC 8211 Elementary and secondary schools
Nathalie Berube

D-U-N-S 25-525-6265   (HQ)
COMMISSION SCOLAIRE DES GRANDES-SEIGNEURIES
50 Boul Taschereau Bureau 310, La Prairie, QC, J5R 4V3
(514) 380-8899
Emp Here 60   *Sales* 396,476,000

SIC 8211 Elementary and secondary schools
Katherine Morel
Daniel Bouthillette
Francois Jannelle
Sylvain Petit

D-U-N-S 25-362-6188   (SL)
FALCO TECHNOLOGIES INC
1245 Rue Industrielle, La Prairie, QC, J5R 2E4
(450) 444-0566
Emp Here 75   *Sales* 16,650,075
SIC 3589 Service industry machinery, nec
Marc Regnaud
Bertrand Blanchette

D-U-N-S 24-460-0714   (SL)
FRUITS ET LEGUMES TARDIF INC
559 Ch De Saint-Jean, La Prairie, QC, J5R 2L2
(450) 659-6449
Emp Here 60   *Sales* 17,608,620
SIC 5431 Fruit and vegetable markets
Jonathan Tardif

D-U-N-S 20-024-6481   (BR)
GROUPE PROMUTUEL, FEDERATION DE SOCIETE MUTUELLES D'ASSURANCES GENERALES
PROMUTUEL ASSURANCE VALLEE DU ST-LAURENT
(*Suby of* GROUPE PROMUTUEL FEDERATION DE SOCIETE MUTUELLES D'ASSURANCES GENERALES)
48 Boul Taschereau, La Prairie, QC, J5R 6C1
(450) 444-0988
Emp Here 80
SIC 6411 Insurance agents, brokers, and service
Jacinthe Phaneuf

D-U-N-S 20-375-7372   (HQ)
MECANIQUE INDUSTRIELLE FORTIER & FILS INC
MIFF
1675 Rue Industrielle, La Prairie, QC, J5R 2E4
(450) 619-9292
Emp Here 25   *Sales* 11,046,700
SIC 1711 Plumbing, heating, air-conditioning
Rene Fortier
Francois Fortier

D-U-N-S 24-373-4279   (SL)
PROFLASH TECHNOLOGIES INTERNATIONAL INC
904 Ch Saint-Jose, La Prairie, QC, J5R 6A9
(450) 444-1384
Emp Here 25   *Sales* 11,179,350
SIC 5043 Photographic equipment and supplies
Pierre Perron
Joanne Lessard

D-U-N-S 24-944-2690   (SL)
RAPIDE INVESTIGATION CANADA LTEE
114 Rue Saint-Georges, La Prairie, QC, J5R 2L9
(514) 879-1199
Emp Here 60   *Sales* 12,703,440
SIC 7323 Credit reporting services
Gilles Hubert

D-U-N-S 20-549-4599   (HQ)
RESEAU SOLUTIONS CANADA ULC
ALSTOM RESEAU CANADA
(*Suby of* GE GRID ALLIANCE B.V.)
1400 Rue Industrielle Bureau 100, La Prairie, QC, J5R 2E5
(450) 659-8921
Emp Here 200   *Sales* 105,328,875
SIC 3569 General industrial machinery, nec
Pierre Feraud
Olivier Ruiz

D-U-N-S 24-969-0264   (HQ)
RESTAURANTS P & P INC, LES
170 Boul Taschereau Bureau 300, La Prairie, QC, J5R 5H6

(450) 444-4749
Emp Here 24   *Sales* 16,723,440
SIC 6794 Patent owners and lessors
Andre Verdier
Louis Lagasse

D-U-N-S 25-248-2070   (SL)
TRANSPORT EN COMMUN LA QUEBE-COISE INC
300 Rue Des Conseillers, La Prairie, QC, J5R 2E6
(450) 659-8598
Emp Here 100   *Sales* 5,487,200
SIC 4111 Local and suburban transit
Serge Gingras

D-U-N-S 24-376-6503   (SL)
UPGI PHARMA INC
100 Boul De L'Industrie, La Prairie, QC, J5R 1J1
(514) 998-9059
Emp Here 50   *Sales* 13,833,000
SIC 2834 Pharmaceutical preparations
Benoit Lavigne
Pierre Breton

La Presentation, QC J0H

D-U-N-S 20-604-6062   (SL)
AUBIN & ST-PIERRE INC
KUBOTA
350 Rue Raygo, La Presentation, QC, J0H 1B0
(450) 796-2966
Emp Here 20   *Sales* 10,000,000
SIC 5083 Farm and garden machinery
Pierre Rathe
Jacques Rathe
Nicole Rathe

D-U-N-S 20-225-2946   (SL)
MACIOCIA MARIO & FILS LTEE
(*Suby of* 134313 CANADA LTEE)
131 Rang Des Petits-Etangs, La Presentation, QC, J0H 1B0
(450) 796-3354
Emp Here 8   *Sales* 11,741,536
SIC 5154 Livestock
Antonio Maciocia
Edouardo Maciocia

La Reine, QC J0Z

D-U-N-S 25-379-6536   (SL)
ACIERS J.P. INC, LES
15 3e Av E, La Reine, QC, J0Z 2L0
(819) 947-8291
Emp Here 30   *Sales* 14,250,780
SIC 5084 Industrial machinery and equipment
Rene Perreault

La Sarre, QC J9Z

D-U-N-S 24-401-4783   (HQ)
AUTOBUS MAHEUX LTEE, LES
156 393 Rte S, La Sarre, QC, J9Z 2X2
(819) 333-2217
Emp Here 35   *Sales* 15,054,400
SIC 4151 School buses
Claire Lemoyne Maheux
Pierre Maheux

D-U-N-S 20-204-2636   (SL)
BEAUDRY & LAPOINTE LTEE
1 111 Rte O Bureau 1110, La Sarre, QC, J9Z 1R5
(819) 333-2266
Emp Here 28   *Sales* 13,946,184
SIC 5511 New and used car dealers

Martin Langevin
Benoit Drapeau

D-U-N-S 25-240-0932   (BR)
COMMISSION SCOLAIRE ABITIBI
ECOLE DE L' ENVOL
(*Suby of* COMMISSION SCOLAIRE ABITIBI)
24 5e Av E, La Sarre, QC, J9Z 1K8
(819) 333-5591
Emp Here 85
SIC 8211 Elementary and secondary schools
Johanne Dubeau

D-U-N-S 25-766-2213   (SL)
GESTION MARC-ANDRE LORD INC
CANADIAN TIRE
91 2e Rue E Bureau 233, La Sarre, QC, J9Z 3J9

Emp Here 40   *Sales* 14,568,600
SIC 5013 Motor vehicle supplies and new parts
Marc-Andre Lord

D-U-N-S 20-544-1421   (SL)
NICOL AUTO INC
NICOL PONTIAC BUICK GMC
400 2e Rue E, La Sarre, QC, J9Z 2J1
(819) 333-5467
Emp Here 36   *Sales* 17,930,808
SIC 5511 New and used car dealers
Leandre Audet
Eric Audet

D-U-N-S 25-380-2557   (BR)
NORBORD INDUSTRIES INC
(*Suby of* NORBORD INC)
210 9e Av E, La Sarre, QC, J9Z 2L2
(819) 333-5464
Emp Here 180
SIC 2499 Wood products, nec
Claude Lebel

D-U-N-S 24-612-6668   (SL)
PETROLES CARUFEL INC, LES
PETROLE XTREME
78 8e Av O, La Sarre, QC, J9Z 1N3
(819) 762-0765
Emp Here 10   *Sales* 10,328,080
SIC 5172 Petroleum products, nec
Gilles Carufel
Josee Carufel
Juliette Carufel
Rejean Humbert

D-U-N-S 20-204-3626   (HQ)
ROBERGE ET FILS INC
RENOVATEUR RONA
45 7e Av E, La Sarre, QC, J9Z 1M5
(819) 333-5405
Emp Here 40   *Sales* 18,248,075
SIC 3442 Metal doors, sash, and trim
Jean-Guy Roberge
Pierre Roberge
Gaetan Roberge

D-U-N-S 20-546-3578   (BR)
UNIVERSITE DU QUEBEC
CENTRE DE LA SARRE
(*Suby of* UNIVERSITE DU QUEBEC)
500 Rue Principale Bureau Ar60, La Sarre, QC, J9Z 2A2
(819) 333-2624
Emp Here 100
SIC 8221 Colleges and universities
Isabelle Metivier

D-U-N-S 24-737-5020   (SL)
VARIETES LNJF INC
JEAN COUTU
84 5e Av E Bureau 73, La Sarre, QC, J9Z 1K9
(819) 333-5458
Emp Here 98   *Sales* 23,818,802
SIC 6519 Real property lessors, nec
Lise Trepanier
Jean-Francois Rondeau
Normand Gendron

La Trinite-Des-Monts, QC G0K

D-U-N-S 24-202-2697   (SL)
SOCIETE   D'EXPLOITATION   DES RESSOURCES DE LA NEIGETTE INC
1 Rue Principale O, La Trinite-Des-Monts, QC, G0K 1B0
(418) 779-2095
Emp Here 100   *Sales* 13,675,900
SIC 0851 Forestry services
 Donald Michaud
 Bernard Ouellet

La Tuque, QC G9X

D-U-N-S 20-363-6063   (HQ)
ARBEC, BOIS D'OEUVRE INC
1053 Boul Ducharme, La Tuque, QC, G9X 3C3
(819) 523-2765
Emp Here 50   *Sales* 208,792,500
SIC 2421 Sawmills and planing mills, general
 Serge Mercier
 Roger Tremblay
 Rejean Pare
 Pierre Moreau
 Joey Saputo
 Eric Bouchard

D-U-N-S 25-384-0904   (SL)
CENTRE DE BENEVOLAT DE LA TUQUE INC
497 Rue Saint-Antoine, La Tuque, QC, G9X 2Y3

Emp Here 150   *Sales* 10,435,916
SIC 8322 Individual and family services
 Brigitte Fortin

D-U-N-S 24-638-4580   (SL)
COOPERATIVE FORESTIERE DU HAUT ST-MAURICE
50 Rue Bostonnais, La Tuque, QC, G9X 2E8
(819) 523-2737
Emp Here 100   *Sales* 15,586,300
SIC 2411 Logging
 Andre Depin
 Caroline Martel
 Eric Bilodeau
 Mario Tremblay
 Daniel Desbiens
 Michel Larouche
 Carole Noreau
 Yannick Boissonneault
 Roland Caron

D-U-N-S 25-002-2647   (BR)
HYDRO-QUEBEC
(*Suby   of*   GOUVERNEMENT   DE   LA PROVINCE DE QUEBEC)
90 Rue Beaumont, La Tuque, QC, G9X 3P7
(819) 676-4280
Emp Here 150
SIC 4911 Electric services
 Jacques A Chauvette

D-U-N-S 24-146-0427   (BR)
INDUSTRIES JOHN LEWIS LTEE
INDUSTRIES JOHN LEWIS
(*Suby of* GESTION REMABEC INC)
1101 Boul Ducharme, La Tuque, QC, G9X 3C3
(819) 523-7636
Emp Here 80
SIC 2499 Wood products, nec
 Jean Boissonneault

D-U-N-S 24-736-2192   (SL)
PRODUITS FORESTIERS MAURICIE S.E.C.
2419 155 Rte S, La Tuque, QC, G9X 3N8
(819) 523-5626
Emp Here 140   *Sales* 26,931,800

SIC 2421 Sawmills and planing mills, general
 Eric Lebreux

D-U-N-S 25-258-9411   (BR)
WESTROCK COMPANY OF CANADA CORP
ROCKTENN
(*Suby of* WESTROCK COMPANY)
1000 Ch De L'Usine Bureau 2632, La Tuque, QC, G9X 3P8
(819) 676-8100
Emp Here 475
SIC 2657 Folding paperboard boxes
 Louis-Serge Gagnon

Labelle, QC J0T

D-U-N-S 25-526-9219   (HQ)
M.C. FORET INC
5946 Boul Du Cure-Labelle Rr 3, Labelle, QC, J0T 1H0
(819) 686-1464
Emp Here 80   *Sales* 13,675,900
SIC 0851 Forestry services
 Michel Caron

Lac-Au-Saumon, QC G0J

D-U-N-S 20-799-5916   (BR)
GROUPE CEDRICO INC
BOIS D' OEUVRE CEDRICO
50 Rang Didier, Lac-Au-Saumon, QC, G0J 1M0

Emp Here 80
SIC 2491 Wood preserving
 Gilles Berube

D-U-N-S 20-871-7355   (HQ)
SOCIETE   D'EXPLOITATION   DES RESSOURCES DE LA VALLEE
108 Rue Du Noviciat, Lac-Au-Saumon, QC, G0J 1M0
(418) 778-5877
Sales 11,752,155
SIC 0851 Forestry services
 Sebastien Jean
 Martin Theriault
 Mario Tremblay
 Michel Leclerc
 Roger Corbin
 Jean-Guy Rioux
 Jean-Francois Canuel
 Florent Morin
 Pierre Boudreau

Lac-Aux-Sables, QC G0X

D-U-N-S 24-690-1326   (SL)
EQUIPEMENTS GAETAN INC, LES
GROUPE LEG
320 Ch Du Lac-Huron, Lac-Aux-Sables, QC, G0X 1M0
(418) 336-2634
Emp Here 50   *Sales* 11,008,400
SIC 1794 Excavation work
 Gaetan Genest
 Denise Genest

Lac-Beauport, QC G3B

D-U-N-S 20-016-3280   (SL)
COUVRE-PLANCHER HAUTE VILLE INC
14 Ch Du Boise, Lac-Beauport, QC, G3B 2A2
(418) 841-0440
Emp Here 28   *Sales* 14,247,968

SIC 5023 Homefurnishings
 Jean-Pierre Blais

Lac-Delage, QC G3C

D-U-N-S 25-674-1505   (SL)
MANOIR DU LAC DELAGE INC
MANOIR DU LAC DELAGE, LE
40 Av Du Lac, Lac-Delage, QC, G3C 5C4
(418) 848-0691
Emp Here 90   *Sales* 8,540,910
SIC 7011 Hotels and motels
 Andre Gauthier

Lac-Des-Aigles, QC G0K

D-U-N-S 24-499-5262   (SL)
COOPERATIVE FORESTIERE HAUT PLAN VERT LAC-DES-AIGLES
109 Rue Principale, Lac-Des-Aigles, QC, G0K 1V0
(418) 779-2612
Emp Here 87   *Sales* 11,888,898
SIC 2411 Logging
 Vicky Belzile
 Claude Breault

Lac-Des-Ecorces, QC J0W

D-U-N-S 25-847-4972   (SL)
CAMION FREIGHTLINER MONT-LAURIER INC
325 Ch Du Golf, Lac-Des-Ecorces, QC, J0W 1H0
(819) 623-7177
Emp Here 28   *Sales* 13,946,184
SIC 5511 New and used car dealers
 Yves Leduc
 Nadine Osborne

D-U-N-S 24-294-0195   (HQ)
SERVICES   FORESTIERS   DE   MONT-LAURIER LTEE
EQUIPMENT LAURENTIEN
(*Suby of* 163431 CANADA INC)
327 Ch Du Golf Rr 1, Lac-Des-Ecorces, QC, J0W 1H0
(819) 623-3143
Emp Here 21   *Sales* 14,725,806
SIC 5084 Industrial machinery and equipment
 Jean-Luc Lemieux
 Denis Leduc

Lac-Des-Iles, QC J0W

D-U-N-S 20-012-0231   (BR)
IMERYS GRAPHITE & CARBON CANADA INC
(*Suby of* GROUPE BRUXELLES LAMBERT)
585 Ch Du Graphite, Lac-Des-Iles, QC, J0W 1J0
(819) 597-2911
Emp Here 75
SIC 1499 Miscellaneous nonMetallic minerals, except fuels
 Matteo Zenone

Lac-Drolet, QC G0Y

D-U-N-S 24-049-8993   (HQ)
ACIER FASTECH INC
CONSTRUCTIONN FASTECH

---

652 Rue Du Parc, Lac-Drolet, QC, G0Y 1C0
(819) 549-1010
Sales 14,795,795
SIC 1541 Industrial buildings and warehouses
 Claude Roussin
 Marco Gilbert
 Nancy Belanger
 Martin Fredette

D-U-N-S 24-202-3752   (SL)
ATTRACTION INC
PRODUCTIONS LOUNAK, LES
672 Rue Du Parc, Lac-Drolet, QC, G0Y 1C0
(819) 549-2477
Emp Here 110   *Sales* 9,482,268
SIC 5136 Men's and boy's clothing
 Julia Gagnon
 Sebastien Jacques
 Roger Charbonneau

D-U-N-S 24-863-0378   (HQ)
BOIS POULIN INC, LES
658 Rue Poulin, Lac-Drolet, QC, G0Y 1C0
(819) 549-2090
Emp Here 1   *Sales* 16,351,450
SIC 2421 Sawmills and planing mills, general
 Marco Vachon
 Vincent Roy
 David Jacques

D-U-N-S 24-821-4629   (HQ)
L.P. ROYER INC
AIRFLEX SYSTEM & DESSIN
712 Rue Principale, Lac-Drolet, QC, G0Y 1C0
(819) 549-2100
Sales 27,025,600
SIC 3143 Men's footwear, except athletic
 Yves Royer
 Simon La Rochelle

Lac-Etchemin, QC G0R

D-U-N-S 24-205-7586   (SL)
EQUIPE JUNIOR DE SKI DU MONT ORIGINAL INC
STATION DE SKI MONT-ORIGNAL
158 Rang Du Mont-Orignal, Lac-Etchemin, QC, G0R 1S0
(418) 625-1551
Emp Here 200   *Sales* 18,538,000
SIC 7011 Hotels and motels
 Michel Biron

D-U-N-S 20-202-9781   (HQ)
GARAGE FLORENT BEGIN INC
1483 277 Rte, Lac-Etchemin, QC, G0R 1S0
(418) 625-6101
Sales 10,957,716
SIC 5511 New and used car dealers
 Paul Boulanger

D-U-N-S 24-638-0679   (SL)
OFRIGIDAIRE ALIMENTATION INC
1575 Rte 277, Lac-Etchemin, QC, G0R 1S0
(418) 625-6301
Emp Here 90   *Sales* 26,412,930
SIC 5411 Grocery stores
 Georges Nadeau

D-U-N-S 24-531-3432   (HQ)
PIECES D'AUTOS G. G. M. INC
NAPA
1564 277 Rte, Lac-Etchemin, QC, G0R 1S0
(418) 625-3132
Emp Here 18   *Sales* 12,019,095
SIC 5013 Motor vehicle supplies and new parts
 Gaetan Gosselin

Lac-Megantic, QC G6B

▲ Public Company   ■ Public Company Family Member   **HQ** Headquarters   **BR** Branch   **SL** Single Location

D-U-N-S 25-179-1513   (HQ)
ASSURANCES FORTIN, GAGNON ET LE-BRUN INC
ASSURANCES DU GRANIT, LES
4138 Rue Laval, Lac-Megantic, QC, G6B 1B3
(819) 583-1208
Emp Here 13   *Sales* 19,662,739
SIC 6331 Fire, marine, and casualty insurance
  Jean Gagnon
  Michel Plante
  Annie Fortin
  Mario Morin

D-U-N-S 20-257-5643   (SL)
BESTAR INC
4220 Rue Villeneuve, Lac-Megantic, QC, G6B 2C3
(819) 583-1017
Emp Here 140   *Sales* 21,605,080
SIC 2511 Wood household furniture
  Frederick Perrault
  Mario Aube
  Alain Perreault
  Jacques Foisy
  Marc Paiement
  Marc-Antoine Lachance
  Mario Beaudoin

D-U-N-S 20-252-7677   (BR)
COMMISSION SCOLAIRE DES HAUTS-CANTONS
POLYVALENTE MONTIGNAC
(*Suby of* COMMISSION SCOLAIRE DES HAUTS-CANTONS)
3409 Rue Laval, Lac-Megantic, QC, G6B 1A5
(819) 583-3023
Emp Here 145
SIC 8211 Elementary and secondary schools
  Maryse Talbot

D-U-N-S 20-874-1165   (SL)
FROMAGE LA CHAUDIERE INC
3226 Rue Laval, Lac-Megantic, QC, G6B 1A4
(819) 583-4664
Emp Here 100   *Sales* 83,557,700
SIC 5143 Dairy products, except dried or canned
  Michel Choquette
  Mario Choquette
  Alain Choquette

D-U-N-S 24-393-9407   (SL)
GESTION STEFANO ROVER INC
CANADIAN TIRE
3642 Rue Laval, Lac-Megantic, QC, G6B 1A4
(819) 583-3332
Emp Here 40   *Sales* 19,923,120
SIC 5531 Auto and home supply stores
  Stefano Rover

D-U-N-S 24-941-3410   (HQ)
GRANULES COMBUSTIBLES ENERGEX INC
3891 Rue Du President-Kennedy, Lac-Megantic, QC, G6B 3B8
(819) 583-5131
Sales 15,389,600
SIC 2421 Sawmills and planing mills, general
  Bruce R Lisle
  Lucie Gilbert
  Joseph Breen
  Eric L. Blum

D-U-N-S 20-208-2368   (BR)
MASONITE INTERNATIONAL CORPORATION
INDUSTRIES   MANUFACTURIERES MEGANTIC DIV.
(*Suby of* MASONITE INTERNATIONAL CORPORATION)
6184 Rue Notre-Dame, Lac-Megantic, QC, G6B 3B5
(819) 583-1550
Emp Here 250
SIC 2435 Hardwood veneer and plywood
  Alain Perreault

D-U-N-S 24-208-4457   (SL)
PETROLES R.TURMEL INC, LES
PLACE DU VILLAGE
4575 Rue Latulippe, Lac-Megantic, QC, G6B 3H1
(819) 583-3838
Emp Here 22   *Sales* 27,658,422
SIC 5172 Petroleum products, nec
  Robert Turmel
  Real Turmel
  Denis Turmel
  Marc Chenel

D-U-N-S 20-030-4546   (HQ)
PROMUTUEL MONTS ET RIVES, SOCIETE MUTUELLE D'ASSURANCE GENERALE
PROMUTUEL ASSURANCE
5240 Boul Des Veterans, Lac-Megantic, QC, G6B 2G5
(819) 583-4555
Emp Here 20   *Sales* 48,041,292
SIC 6411 Insurance agents, brokers, and service
  Roger Bernier
  Georges Paradis
  Mario Quirion
  Pierre Belair
  Charles-Auguste Lafontaine
  Daniel Poirier
  Heidi Paquette
  Martine Brouard

D-U-N-S 24-023-5676   (BR)
PROVIGO DISTRIBUTION INC
MAXI #8630
(*Suby of* LOBLAW COMPANIES LIMITED)
3560 Rue Laval, Lac-Megantic, QC, G6B 2X4
(819) 583-4001
Emp Here 80
SIC 5141 Groceries, general line
  Roger Gaudreault

D-U-N-S 24-864-3900   (SL)
TAFISA CANADA INC
(*Suby of* SONAE INDUSTRIA, SGPS, S.A.)
4660 Rue Villeneuve, Lac-Megantic, QC, G6B 2C3
(819) 583-2930
Emp Here 330   *Sales* 91,868,700
SIC 2499 Wood products, nec
  George Christopher Lawrie
  Louis Brassard
  Eric Dedekam
  Robert Torralbo

D-U-N-S 20-633-8415   (BR)
TRANSPORT ROBERT (1973) LTEE
(*Suby of* GROUPE ROBERT INC)
4075 Rue Villeneuve, Lac-Megantic, QC, G6B 2C2
(819) 583-2230
Emp Here 80
SIC 4213 Trucking, except local
  Marie-Claude Sevigny

D-U-N-S 20-581-3546   (SL)
VARIETES CHARRON & LECLERC, SENC
PHARMACIE JEAN COUTU
6240 Rue Salaberry, Lac-Megantic, QC, G6B 1H8
(819) 583-2123
Emp Here 40   *Sales* 10,118,160
SIC 5912 Drug stores and proprietary stores
  Claude Charron
  Antoine Leclerc

D-U-N-S 24-319-5133   (BR)
WAL-MART CANADA CORP
WAL-MART
(*Suby of* WALMART INC.)
3130 Rue Laval, Lac-Megantic, QC, G6B 1A4
(819) 583-2882
Emp Here 120
SIC 5311 Department stores

Lachine, QC H8R

D-U-N-S 25-201-3735   (SL)
2701545 CANADA INC
PRINCE MOVING
300 Rue De La Berge-Du-Canal Bureau 312, Lachine, QC, H8R 1H3
(514) 367-0000
Emp Here 85   *Sales* 12,596,320
SIC 4213 Trucking, except local
  Claude Gizelo

D-U-N-S 24-017-8764   (HQ)
ACIER CENTURY INC
600 Rue De La Berge-Du-Canal, Lachine, QC, H8R 1H4
(514) 364-1505
Sales 13,534,092
SIC 5093 Scrap and waste materials
  Michel Chiasson
  Herbert Black
  Karl Beaudin

D-U-N-S 24-827-1384   (HQ)
ANACHEMIA CANADA CO
ANACHEMIA SCIENCE
(*Suby of* AVANTOR, INC.)
255 Rue Norman, Lachine, QC, H8R 1A3
(514) 489-5711
Emp Here 100   *Sales* 133,838,000
SIC 5049 Professional equipment, nec
  Arora Navneet
  Douglas Pitts
  Michael Kinzler
  Scott K Baker
  Gregory Blakely

D-U-N-S 24-590-8124   (HQ)
ENSEICOM INC
ENSEICOM SIGNS
(*Suby of* HI-FI + ROOM INC)
225 Rue Norman, Lachine, QC, H8R 1A3
(514) 486-2626
Sales 11,525,100
SIC 3448 Prefabricated Metal buildings and components
  Constantine Moussiss

D-U-N-S 24-740-0757   (SL)
ENTREPRISES CANBEC CONSTRUCTION INC, LES
145 Rue Richer, Lachine, QC, H8R 1R4
(514) 481-1226
Emp Here 100   *Sales* 24,618,600
SIC 1794 Excavation work
  Frank Enrico Andreoli

D-U-N-S 20-913-2328   (HQ)
ENVIRONNEMENT ROUTIER NRJ INC
GILLES COTE EXCAVATION
23 Av Milton, Lachine, QC, H8R 1K6
(514) 481-0451
Sales 12,622,100
SIC 1611 Highway and street construction
  Richard Gareau
  Nathalie Massie
  Chantal Ducharme
  Steve Bastien
  Jean Delisle

D-U-N-S 24-859-0127   (SL)
HUILES NORCO LTEE, LES
230 Rue Norman, Lachine, QC, H8R 1A1
(514) 486-9000
Emp Here 50   *Sales* 23,450,250
SIC 5983 Fuel oil dealers
  Jonathan Abracen
  Donald Gauthier

D-U-N-S 24-857-8767   (SL)
KORAB MARINE LTD
255 Rue Norman, Lachine, QC, H8R 1A3
(514) 489-5711
Emp Here 200   *Sales* 54,670,000
SIC 6712 Bank holding companies
  Ivoj K Kudrnac
  Martin Robinson

D-U-N-S 20-217-3845   (SL)
PLASTIQUES DURA (1977) LIMITEE, LES
PLASTIQUES DURA, LES
110 Rue Richer, Lachine, QC, H8R 1R2
(514) 369-8980
Emp Here 25   *Sales* 18,258,625
SIC 5162 Plastics materials and basic shapes
  Mark Rubin

D-U-N-S 24-698-1542   (SL)
REFENDOIRS C. R. LTEE, LES
300 Rue De La Berge-Du-Canal Bureau 4, Lachine, QC, H8R 1H3
(514) 366-2222
Emp Here 50   *Sales* 22,174,500
SIC 7389 Business services, nec
  Alain Duclos

Lachine, QC H8S

D-U-N-S 20-699-1668   (SL)
3401987 CANADA INC.
900 Rue Du Pacifique, Lachine, QC, H8S 1C4
(514) 367-3001
Emp Here 60   *Sales* 15,693,180
SIC 6712 Bank holding companies
  Noella Clouatre
  Clifford Herer

D-U-N-S 25-685-2047   (BR)
3539491 CANADA INC
ADF INDUSTRIES LOURDES
(*Suby of* TIL CINTREURS DE TUBES INT'L LTEE)
500 Rue Notre-Dame, Lachine, QC, H8S 2B2
(514) 634-2287
Emp Here 250
SIC 3441 Fabricated structural Metal
  Yvon Vandemale

D-U-N-S 20-545-7802   (SL)
3729451 CANADA INC
SPINELLI MAZDA
230 Boul Montreal-Toronto, Lachine, QC, H8S 1B8
(514) 637-1153
Emp Here 45   *Sales* 22,413,510
SIC 5511 New and used car dealers
  Pierre Spinelli
  Noel Spinelli

D-U-N-S 24-308-3784   (SL)
9132-1604 QUEBEC INC
STICKY MEDIA
1600 Crois Claire, Lachine, QC, H8S 1A2
(514) 485-1121
Emp Here 50   *Sales* 10,941,200
SIC 3993 Signs and advertising specialties
  Stephen Conroy
  Daniel Rosen

D-U-N-S 20-016-2191   (SL)
A.R.P. AUTO-AUXILIARIES INC
(*Suby of* 2736730 CANADA INC)
2300 Rue Victoria, Lachine, QC, H8S 1Z3
(514) 634-7000
Emp Here 20   *Sales* 13,129,280
SIC 5962 Merchandising machine operators
  Armen Kazandjian
  Kouharik Kazandjian

D-U-N-S 25-242-7109   (SL)
ACIER LACHINE INC
1520 Crois Claire, Lachine, QC, H8S 4E6
(514) 634-2252
Emp Here 15   *Sales* 15,005,085
SIC 5051 Metals service centers and offices
  Louis Ouellet
  Marc Foisy
  Richard Ouellet

D-U-N-S 25-361-8029   (BR)
ALIMENTS MARTEL INC
(*Suby of* GRUPO BIMBO, S.A.B. DE C.V.)
2387 Rue Remembrance, Lachine, QC, H8S

1X4

Emp Here 200
SIC 2099 Food preparations, nec
Simon Wookey

D-U-N-S 24-810-9811   (SL)
C L S C DU VIEUX LACHINE
1900 Rue Notre-Dame, Lachine, QC, H8S
2G2
(514) 639-0650
Emp Here 180   *Sales* 24,022,620
SIC 8399 Social services, nec
Michel Lemay
Serge Morissette

D-U-N-S 24-969-8036   (SL)
CAD INDUSTRIES FERROVIAIRES LTEE
RAILACTION
155 Boul Montreal-Toronto, Lachine, QC, H8S
1B4
(514) 634-3131
Emp Here 400   *Sales* 158,175,200
SIC 4789 Transportation services, nec
Fausto-C Levy
Lucie Dastous
Louise Martell
Masayoshi Hirose
Sebastien Nadeau
Andre Lavoie
Morita Takashi

D-U-N-S 20-652-2109   (BR)
CASCADES CANADA ULC
CASCADES RECUPERATION +
(*Suby of* CASCADES INC)
63 Boul Saint-Joseph, Lachine, QC, H8S 2K9
(514) 595-2870
Emp Here 75
SIC 4953 Refuse systems
Rejean Perron

D-U-N-S 24-294-7448   (SL)
**CENTRE D'HEBERGEMENT DE NAZAIRE
PICHE**
150 15e Av Bureau 319, Lachine, QC, H8S
3L9
(514) 637-2326
Emp Here 140   *Sales* 8,999,480
SIC 8361 Residential care
Paul Perreault

D-U-N-S 24-352-5354   (BR)
**CENTRE DE SANTE ET DE SERVICES SO-
CIAUX DE DORVAL-LACHINE-LASALLE**
CLSC DE DORVAL-LACHINE
1900 Rue Notre-Dame Bureau 262, Lachine,
QC, H8S 2G2
(514) 639-0650
Emp Here 200
SIC 7991 Physical fitness facilities
Yves Masse

D-U-N-S 24-382-9608   (BR)
**CENTRE DE SANTE ET DE SERVICES SO-
CIAUX DE DORVAL-LACHINE-LASALLE**
CENTRE D'HEBERGEMENT DE LACHINE
650 Place D'Accueil, Lachine, QC, H8S 3Z5
(514) 634-7161
Emp Here 250
SIC 8361 Residential care
Sylvie Ouellette

D-U-N-S 20-323-5528   (SL)
CENTRE DU BRICOLEUR LACHINE LTEE
650 Rue Notre-Dame Bureau 1849, Lachine,
QC, H8S 2B3
(514) 637-3767
Emp Here 25   *Sales* 11,179,350
SIC 5039 Construction materials, nec
Yves Chartier

D-U-N-S 24-054-2845   (HQ)
CINTUBE LTEE
(*Suby of* TIL CINTREURS DE TUBES INT'L
LTEE)
333 Boul Saint-Joseph Bureau 105, Lachine,
QC, H8S 2K9

(514) 634-3592
Emp Here 10   *Sales* 42,565,425
SIC 3498 Fabricated pipe and fittings
Warren G. Flowers
R.B.R. Schneider
James P. Reid
L. A. Carrier
Ann Davy
L. Michael Dyer
C.L. Volk
T. Fischer
K. A. Carrier
M. Baril

D-U-N-S 24-081-4939   (SL)
COLLEGE SAINTE-ANNE
ACADEMIE SAINTE-ANNE
1250 Boul Saint-Joseph, Lachine, QC, H8S
2M8
(514) 637-3571
Emp Here 114   *Sales* 17,030,574
SIC 8221 Colleges and universities
Ugo Cavenaghi

D-U-N-S 24-782-6972   (HQ)
CORBEC INC
1 Rue Provost Bureau 201, Lachine, QC, H8S
4H2
(514) 364-4000
Emp Here 1   *Sales* 18,138,800
SIC 3399 Primary Metal products
John R. Hall

D-U-N-S 24-407-7769   (SL)
COURRIER RAPIDE SERVICE
640 Rue Notre-Dame, Lachine, QC, H8S 2B3
(514) 866-8727
Emp Here 40   *Sales* 17,968,760
SIC 7389 Business services, nec
Richard Boudreau

D-U-N-S 20-215-6691   (HQ)
COWPER INC
677 7e Av, Lachine, QC, H8S 3A1
(514) 637-6746
Emp Here 34   *Sales* 26,126,430
SIC 5084 Industrial machinery and equipment
Grenfell Cowper

D-U-N-S 20-216-9694   (HQ)
DOMON LTEE
MEUBLES DOMON
1950 Rue Remembrance, Lachine, QC, H8S
1W9
(514) 637-5835
Sales 27,888,360
SIC 5712 Furniture stores
Marie-Heline Domon

D-U-N-S 24-646-5582   (SL)
DYNAMIC SECURITY AGENCY
2366 Rue Victoria, Lachine, QC, H8S 1Z3
(514) 898-3598
Emp Here 49   *Sales* 19,388,222
SIC 7381 Detective and armored car services
Michel Tasse

D-U-N-S 24-350-8702   (SL)
**ENCHERES D'AUTOMOBILES ST-PIERRE
(ESP) LTEE, LES**
ENCAN ESP
1600 Rue Norman, Lachine, QC, H8S 1A9
(514) 489-3131
Emp Here 50   *Sales* 18,210,750
SIC 5012 Automobiles and other motor vehi-
cles
Alain Boisvert

D-U-N-S 20-227-6648   (SL)
EQUIPEMENT D'INCENDIE GLOBE INC
590 19e Av, Lachine, QC, H8S 3S5
(514) 637-2534
Emp Here 30   *Sales* 14,250,780
SIC 5087 Service establishment equipment
Peter Lang

D-U-N-S 24-561-8715   (HQ)
EXCAVATIONS VESPO INC, LES
17 Boul Saint-Joseph, Lachine, QC, H8S 2K9

(514) 933-5057
Sales 11,008,400
SIC 1794 Excavation work
Rocco Missori
Nicola Vespoli
Renato Palmieri

D-U-N-S 24-871-2226   (SL)
GESTION PICARD-DUBUC INC
PHARMAPRIX
2880 Rue Remembrance Bureau 74, Lachine,
QC, H8S 1X8
(514) 637-3578
Emp Here 50   *Sales* 12,647,700
SIC 5912 Drug stores and proprietary stores
Normand Picard

D-U-N-S 24-369-6163   (HQ)
MAAX BATH INC
ADVANTA BY MAAX
(*Suby of* THE AMERICAN BATH GROUP)
160 Boul Saint-Joseph, Lachine, QC, H8S 2L3
(514) 844-4155
Emp Here 250   *Sales* 238,812,000
SIC 3088 Plastics plumbing fixtures
Mark A. Gold
Anthony Ricketts
Benoit Savoie Dufresne
Christopher Scott Stonecipher
Lowell F. Stonecipher

D-U-N-S 20-232-8035   (HQ)
ROSS AND ANGLIN LIMITEE
45 Boul Saint-Joseph, Lachine, QC, H8S 2K9
(514) 364-4220
Emp Here 35   *Sales* 11,543,320
SIC 1522 Residential construction, nec
Mark Thompson
Michael Thompson
Peter Thompson

D-U-N-S 20-555-0036   (SL)
SERVICES PARTAGES METSO LTEE
795 Av George-V, Lachine, QC, H8S 2R9
(877) 677-2005
Emp Here 85   *Sales* 38,183,615
SIC 7389 Business services, nec
Marisa Vandenengel
Paul J. Gannon
Todd Dillmann
Donroy Ferdinand
Bob Wissing

D-U-N-S 20-333-0345   (SL)
SIGNALISATION DE MONTREAL INC
15 Boul Saint-Joseph, Lachine, QC, H8S 2K9
(514) 821-7668
Emp Here 100   *Sales* 10,928,900
SIC 0722 Crop harvesting
Louis Thibaudeau

D-U-N-S 24-401-9212   (HQ)
**SOEURS DE SAINTE-ANNE DU QUEBEC,
LES**
SISTERS OF STE ANNE
1950 Rue Provost, Lachine, QC, H8S 1P7
(514) 637-3783
Emp Here 40   *Sales* 25,497,800
SIC 8661 Religious organizations
Claudette Archambault
Denise Pilon
Monique Pelletier
Nicole Lamontagne
Johanne Bonneau

D-U-N-S 24-916-3317   (SL)
SPINELLI HONDA
220 Boul Montreal-Toronto, Lachine, QC, H8S
1B8
(514) 637-6565
Emp Here 40   *Sales* 23,907,744
SIC 5531 Auto and home supply stores
Piere Spinelli

D-U-N-S 24-987-7739   (HQ)
SPINELLI TOYOTA (1981) INC
561 Boul Saint-Joseph, Lachine, QC, H8S
2K9

(514) 634-7171
Emp Here 40   *Sales* 10,723,673
SIC 6712 Bank holding companies
Noel Spinelli
Pierre Spenelli

Lachine, QC H8T

D-U-N-S 24-901-9076   (HQ)
115161 CANADA INC
FASHION DISTRIBUTORS, THE
5203 Rue Fairway, Lachine, QC, H8T 3K8
(514) 635-1088
Sales 20,570,600
SIC 4226 Special warehousing and storage,
nec
Randy Cohen

D-U-N-S 20-014-3514   (HQ)
1357000 ALBERTA ULC
2409 46e Av, Lachine, QC, H8T 3C9

Sales 18,277,760
SIC 4899 Communication services, nec
Jeffrey Speak
Normand Bastien
Particia Bortoluzzi
Pierre Somers

D-U-N-S 24-815-5640   (SL)
2747-6035 QUEBEC INC
SILENCIEUX FEDERAL MUFFLER
2302 52e Av, Lachine, QC, H8T 2Y3
(514) 631-1988
Emp Here 30   *Sales* 14,250,780
SIC 5084 Industrial machinery and equipment
Edmond Beauregard
Raymond Neill

D-U-N-S 20-279-3209   (BR)
3627730 CANADA INC
FREEMAN AUDIO VISUAL
(*Suby of* TFC NETHERLANDS COOPER-
ATIEF U.A.)
2056 32e Av, Lachine, QC, H8T 3H7
(514) 631-1821
Emp Here 90
SIC 7812 Motion picture and video production
Bernard Carignan

D-U-N-S 20-513-9947   (HQ)
3627730 CANADA INC
FREEMAN AUDIO VISUAL
(*Suby of* TFC NETHERLANDS COOPER-
ATIEF U.A.)
1930 Rue Onesime-Gagnon, Lachine, QC,
H8T 3M6
(514) 631-0710
Emp Here 70   *Sales* 81,833,070
SIC 7359 Equipment rental and leasing, nec
Joseph V. Popolo, Jr.
David Campbell
Victoria Prince
Carrie Freeman Parsons
Adelle Casey

D-U-N-S 24-679-1193   (SL)
4174071 CANADA INC
4905 Rue Fairway, Lachine, QC, H8T 1B7
(514) 633-7455
Emp Here 45   *Sales* 12,336,840
SIC 5499 Miscellaneous food stores
Roderick Egger

D-U-N-S 24-244-9887   (BR)
ABB INC
(*Suby of* ABB LTD)
2117 32e Av, Lachine, QC, H8T 3J1

Emp Here 100
SIC 5211 Lumber and other building materials

D-U-N-S 20-209-3076   (HQ)
ABOND CORPORATION INC
10050 Ch De La Cote-De-Liesse, Lachine,

QC, H8T 1A3
(514) 636-7979
Sales 26,027,100
SIC 5099 Durable goods, nec
Sol Schipper
Ronen Katz

D-U-N-S 24-936-0611   (SL)
ACCORD EXPOSITIONS INC
1530 46e Av, Lachine, QC, H8T 3J9
(514) 639-6998
Emp Here 42   *Sales* 18,626,580
SIC 7389 Business services, nec
Darren Pare

D-U-N-S 20-152-6808   (BR)
AMCOR PACKAGING CANADA, INC
AMCOR CANADA
(*Suby of* ORORA LIMITED)
2150 Rue Onesime-Gagnon, Lachine, QC,
H8T 3M8

Emp Here 100
SIC 2657 Folding paperboard boxes
Richard Bigrras

D-U-N-S 20-260-6059   (HQ)
ANDRITZ LTEE
ANDRITZ SEPARATION
(*Suby of* ANDRITZ AG)
2260 32e Av, Lachine, QC, H8T 3H4
(514) 631-7700
Emp Here 115   *Sales* 97,546,000
SIC 5084 Industrial machinery and equipment
Scott Ross
Liam Turner
Humbert Koefler
Thimothy J. Ryan
Carl Luhrmann

D-U-N-S 25-095-4492   (BR)
ANIXTER CANADA INC
(*Suby of* ANIXTER INTERNATIONAL INC.)
3000 Rue Louis-A.-Amos, Lachine, QC, H8T
3P8
(514) 636-3636
Emp Here 110
SIC 5063 Electrical apparatus and equipment
Donald Ducas

D-U-N-S 24-381-5326   (HQ)
ARTIKA FOR LIVING INC
ARTIKA MAISON
1756 50e Av, Lachine, QC, H8T 2V5
(514) 249-4557
Emp Here 79   *Sales* 43,398,690
SIC 3641 Electric lamps
Marc Couture
Isabelle Laforce

D-U-N-S 20-545-5418   (HQ)
BARIATRIX NUTRITION INC
SOMAPHARM
4905 Rue Fairway, Lachine, QC, H8T 1B7
(514) 633-7455
Sales 13,206,465
SIC 5499 Miscellaneous food stores
Roderick Egger
Patrick Egger
Christiane Leblanc
Robert Raich
John-Gilles Pierre
Antonia Polyderakis

D-U-N-S 24-335-6172   (SL)
BOULART INC
BAGUETTECO
1355 32e Av, Lachine, QC, H8T 3H2
(514) 631-4040
Emp Here 60   *Sales* 20,741,400
SIC 2051 Bread, cake, and related products
Michel Saillant
Marc Belanger
Claude Boivin

D-U-N-S 24-813-2342   (SL)
C.T.S. FOOD BROKERS INC
5025 Rue Francois-Cusson, Lachine, QC,

H8T 3K1
(514) 956-0356
Emp Here 20   *Sales* 10,702,480
SIC 5147 Meats and meat products
Costa Tsimiklis
Michael Vafiadis

D-U-N-S 24-525-7378   (BR)
CANADA DRAYAGE INC
4415 Rue Fairway, Lachine, QC, H8T 1B5
(514) 639-7878
Emp Here 100
SIC 4212 Local trucking, without storage
Mark Taddeo

D-U-N-S 20-764-0186   (HQ)
CANAROPA (1954) INC
1725 50e Av, Lachine, QC, H8T 3C8
(514) 636-6466
Emp Here 40   *Sales* 33,538,050
SIC 5072 Hardware
Athanasios Zissopoulos
Asimina Tsatsaronis Drimaropoulos

D-U-N-S 20-014-3472   (HQ)
CBCI TELECOM CANADA INC
CBCI TELECOM
(*Suby of* 1357000 ALBERTA ULC)
2260 46e Av, Lachine, QC, H8T 2P3
(514) 422-9333
Emp Here 40   *Sales* 16,221,512
SIC 4899 Communication services, nec
Denis Dumouchel

D-U-N-S 24-548-1494   (HQ)
CIE DANAWARES
LICENCE VINGT10, LA
1860 32e Av, Lachine, QC, H8T 3J7
(514) 342-5555
Sales 10,119,044
SIC 5092 Toys and hobby goods and supplies
Peter Gordon Lewis
Janice Howard

D-U-N-S 24-324-3367   (SL)
CLASSE AUDIO INC
5070 Rue Francois-Cusson, Lachine, QC,
H8T 1B3
(514) 636-6384
Emp Here 80   *Sales* 15,235,360
SIC 3699 Electrical equipment and supplies,
nec
Michael Viglas

D-U-N-S 24-021-2274   (SL)
COHEN, JERRY FORWARDERS LTD
ALL TYPE TRANSPORTS
5203 Rue Fairway, Lachine, QC, H8T 3K8
(514) 635-1033
Emp Here 80   *Sales* 11,855,360
SIC 4213 Trucking, except local
Randy Cohen
Jody Cohen

D-U-N-S 20-712-4178   (BR)
**COMMISSION SCOLAIRE MARGUERITE-
BOURGEOYS**
*ECOLE SECONDAIRES REGROUPEMENT
SUD COLLEGE SAINT LOUIS*
(*Suby of* COMMISSION SCOLAIRE
MARGUERITE-BOURGEOYS)
50 34e Av, Lachine, QC, H8T 1Z2
(514) 748-4662
Emp Here 80
SIC 8211 Elementary and secondary schools
Diane Laborde

D-U-N-S 25-991-2657   (SL)
COMPAGNIE U.S. COTON (CANADA), LA
2100 52e Av Bureau 100, Lachine, QC, H8T
2Y5

Emp Here 90   *Sales* 20,456,010
SIC 3842 Surgical appliances and supplies
John Nims
Quintin Shuler
Janne Ramaker
Jocelyne Massie

D-U-N-S 24-590-7019   (BR)
CONSOLIDATED FASTFRATE INC
FASTFRATE
4415 Rue Fairway, Lachine, QC, H8T 1B5
(514) 639-7747
Emp Here 100
SIC 4731 Freight transportation arrangement
Lise Para

D-U-N-S 20-231-7624   (HQ)
CONSTRUCTIONS RELIANCE INC, LES
(*Suby of* TARBRI HOLDINGS LTEE)
3285 Boul Jean-Baptiste-Deschamps, La-
chine, QC, H8T 3E4
(514) 631-7999
Sales 12,192,390
SIC 1522 Residential construction, nec
Stephen Kaplan
Steven Victor

D-U-N-S 24-354-7309   (HQ)
**CORPORATION MULTI-COLOR MON-
TREAL CANADA**
CAMEO CRAFTS
1925 32e Av, Lachine, QC, H8T 3J1
(514) 341-4850
Emp Here 82   *Sales* 23,834,202
SIC 2752 Commercial printing, lithographic
Mike Henry
Sharon E Birkett
Tanu Bhati
Ron A Vonderhaar
Shadi Abdrabo

D-U-N-S 20-011-7542   (HQ)
CORPORATION TRANSPORT VITESSE
CENTRE DE DISTRIBUTION VITESSE
1111 46e Av, Lachine, QC, H8T 3C5
(514) 631-2777
Sales 22,815,796
SIC 4213 Trucking, except local
Aldo De Carolis
Michael Scalzo
Mohamed Selim
Emidio Decarolis
Domenic Santini

D-U-N-S 24-516-9321   (SL)
**COURTIER DOUANES INTERNATIONAL
SKYWAY LTEE**
CALTEX TRANSPORT
9230 Ch De La Cote-De-Liesse, Lachine, QC,
H8T 1A1
(514) 636-0250
Emp Here 40   *Sales* 20,798,680
SIC 4731 Freight transportation arrangement
Joseph Brown Zatylny
Karen B Zatylny

D-U-N-S 20-421-7715   (HQ)
DELMAR INTERNATIONAL INC
CONSULTANTS COMMERCIAUX DELMAR
(*Suby of* DELMAR INTERNATIONAL HOLD-
INGS INC)
10636 Ch De La Cote-De-Liesse, Lachine,
QC, H8T 1A5
(514) 636-8800
Emp Here 165   *Sales* 158,175,200
SIC 4731 Freight transportation arrangement
Robert Cutler
Michael Wagen
Paul Cutler
Barclay Hurley

D-U-N-S 20-298-0421   (SL)
DISTRIBUTION EPICERIE C.T.S. INC
OROS
5025 Rue Francois-Cusson, Lachine, QC,
H8T 3K1
(514) 335-3586
Emp Here 27   *Sales* 22,560,579
SIC 5141 Groceries, general line
Costa Tsmiklis
Sarantos Erimos
Michael Vafiadis
Anastasios Erimos

D-U-N-S 24-743-1893   (SL)
**DIVERSITECH EQUIPMENT AND SALES
1984 LTD**
DIVERSITECH
1200 55e Av, Lachine, QC, H8T 3J8
(514) 631-7300
Emp Here 50   *Sales* 10,949,941
SIC 3564 Blowers and fans
Jared Simms
Marvin Simms
Andrew Simms

D-U-N-S 25-359-2380   (BR)
DOMTAR INC
ARIVA DIV OF
(*Suby of* DOMTAR LUXEMBOURG INVEST-
MENTS SARL)
2125 23e Av, Lachine, QC, H8T 1X5
(514) 635-5006
Emp Here 135
SIC 5111 Printing and writing paper
Gerry Gray

D-U-N-S 20-217-0940   (HQ)
DOVERCO INC
DEPOT ENTREPOT
2111 32e Av, Lachine, QC, H8T 3J1
(514) 420-6000
Sales 42,810,930
SIC 5113 Industrial and personal service pa-
per
Mark Dover
Nancy Fleischer
Howard Fleischer

D-U-N-S 25-633-8963   (BR)
ENTREPOTS SIMARD INC, LES
(*Suby of* ENTREPOTS SIMARD INC, LES)
2737 Rue Louis-A.-Amos, Lachine, QC, H8T
1C3
(514) 636-9411
Emp Here 200
SIC 4225 General warehousing and storage
Peter Abraham

D-U-N-S 25-149-7343   (SL)
F.P.D. EAST INC
2300 23e Av, Lachine, QC, H8T 0A3
(514) 428-0331
Emp Here 6   *Sales* 11,644,863
SIC 5148 Fresh fruits and vegetables
Paul Mahoney
Peter Martino
Sharon Mahoney

D-U-N-S 20-019-8096   (SL)
FRUITS DE MER BLUEWATER INC
(*Suby of* NIPPON SUISAN KAISHA,LTD.)
1640 Crois Brandon Bureau 201, Lachine,
QC, H8T 2N1
(514) 637-1171
Emp Here 100
SIC 2092 Fresh or frozen packaged fish
Judson Reis
Paul Coz
Steve Warhover
Joe Giannetti
Naoya Kakizoe
Akiyo Matono
Volker Kuntzsch
Hiroyuki Hamano

D-U-N-S 25-211-8120   (SL)
FRUITS DE MER LAGOON INC
1301 32e Av, Lachine, QC, H8T 3H2
(514) 383-1383
Emp Here 78   *Sales* 65,175,006
SIC 5146 Fish and seafoods
Said Cheaib

D-U-N-S 20-219-8917   (HQ)
GENFOOT INC
KAMIK
(*Suby of* 175968 CANADA INC)
1940 55e Av, Lachine, QC, H8T 3H3
(514) 341-3950
Emp Here 90   *Sales* 31,188,750

▲ Public Company   ■ Public Company Family Member   **HQ** Headquarters   **BR** Branch   **SL** Single Location

SIC 5661 Shoe stores
Richard Cook
Irwin Kastner
Norman Cook
Stephen Cook
Gardon Cook

D-U-N-S 25-244-9095 (HQ)
GRAHAM CREATIVE DECAL INC
DECALCOMANIE CREATIF GRAHAM
1790 55e Av, Lachine, QC, H8T 3J5
(514) 633-8800
Sales 12,292,991
SIC 6712 Bank holding companies
Michael Graham
Jane Graham

D-U-N-S 25-283-9980 (BR)
GRAND & TOY LIMITED
GRAND & TOY
(*Suby of* OFFICE DEPOT, INC.)
2275 52e Av, Lachine, QC, H8T 2Y8
(866) 391-8111
Emp Here 123
SIC 5943 Stationery stores
Jean Boisvert

D-U-N-S 24-865-0590 (HQ)
GROUPE CDREM INC
DISTRIBUTION B2U
10200 Ch De La Cote-De-Liesse, Lachine, QC, H8T 1A3
(514) 636-4512
Emp Here 35   *Sales* 24,432,800
SIC 5999 Miscellaneous retail stores, nec
Bertrand Bissonnette
Simon Robillard

D-U-N-S 25-337-9457 (HQ)
GROUPE DIMENSION MULTI VETERI-NAIRE INC, LE
CENTRE VETERINAIRE D.M.V.
2300 54e Av, Lachine, QC, H8T 3R2
(514) 633-8888
Sales 23,477,175
SIC 0742 Veterinary services, specialties
Michel Gosselin
Yves Tarte
Mario Comptois
Michel Gosselin
Caroline Dejaham
Yvan Dumais
Pierre Lassonde
Yvan Dumais
Caroline Dejaham

D-U-N-S 20-323-6039 (HQ)
GROUPE GRAHAM INTERNATIONAL INC
GGI INTERNATIONAL
1455 32e Av, Lachine, QC, H8T 3J1
(514) 631-6662
Sales 58,481,440
SIC 6712 Bank holding companies
Eric Saint-Jacques
Stephane Huot
Louis Belanger Martin
Marc Dufresne
Luc St-Georges
Mario Tougas
William Meder
Chantal Miklosi

D-U-N-S 20-230-9647 (HQ)
GROUPE MARCELLE INC
COSMETIQUES LISE WATIER
9200 Ch De La Cote-De-Liesse, Lachine, QC, H8T 1A1
(514) 631-7710
Emp Here 190   *Sales* 111,161,250
SIC 2844 Toilet preparations
Michael Cape
David Cape

D-U-N-S 24-353-3283 (SL)
HARCUT ENTERPRISES INC
(*Suby of* CUTBROS INC)
10636 Ch De La Cote-De-Liesse, Lachine,

QC, H8T 1A5
(514) 636-8800
Emp Here 280   *Sales* 110,722,640
SIC 4731 Freight transportation arrangement
Harrison Cutler
Robert Cutler
Paul Cutler

D-U-N-S 25-295-2353 (BR)
HONEYWELL LIMITED
(*Suby of* HONEYWELL INTERNATIONAL INC.)
2100 52e Av, Lachine, QC, H8T 2Y5
(514) 422-3400
Emp Here 190
SIC 3822 Environmental controls
Alain Lehoussel

D-U-N-S 25-524-6472 (BR)
HUDSON'S BAY COMPANY
LOGISTIQUE HBC
(*Suby of* HUDSON'S BAY COMPANY)
2105 23e Av, Lachine, QC, H8T 1X3

Emp Here 300
SIC 8742 Management consulting services
Christian Gaudreault

D-U-N-S 25-748-5177 (SL)
INSTITUT DE RECHERCHE BIOLOGIQUE YVES PONROY (CANADA) INC
YVES PONROY CANADA
(*Suby of* LILAS 2)
2035 Rue Onesime-Gagnon, Lachine, QC, H8T 3M5
(514) 448-4325
Emp Here 12   *Sales* 10,026,924
SIC 5149 Groceries and related products, nec
Francoise Garcia Gorse

D-U-N-S 24-921-8439 (HQ)
INTERTEK TESTING SERVICES NA LTD
CONTRLE TECHNIQUE APPLIQUE
(*Suby of* INTERTEK GROUP PLC)
1829 32e Av, Lachine, QC, H8T 3J1
(514) 631-3100
Emp Here 40   *Sales* 38,366,040
SIC 8734 Testing laboratories
Gregg Tiemman
Simon Knight
Anthony Mcglynn
William Joe Keating

D-U-N-S 20-888-4916 (HQ)
JEAN BLEU INC, LE
MEGA BLUES
1895 46e Av, Lachine, QC, H8T 2N9
(514) 631-3300
Emp Here 20   *Sales* 26,822,325
SIC 5611 Men's and boys' clothing stores
Allan Berlach

D-U-N-S 25-526-1265 (SL)
KOOLIAN ENTREPRISES INC, LES
AUTO-KOOL
2295 52e Av, Lachine, QC, H8T 3C3
(514) 633-9292
Emp Here 55   *Sales* 20,031,825
SIC 5013 Motor vehicle supplies and new parts
Ara Koolian
Hampartssoum Koolian
Vasken Koolian

D-U-N-S 20-234-2622 (HQ)
L. SIMARD TRANSPORT LIMITEE
(*Suby of* 124327 CANADA INC)
1212 32e Av, Lachine, QC, H8T 3K7
(514) 636-9411
Sales 20,982,012
SIC 4212 Local trucking, without storage
Ferris John Abraham
Donald Michel Abraham
Pearl Abraham

D-U-N-S 25-369-3527 (BR)
L. SIMARD TRANSPORT LIMITEE
(*Suby of* 124327 CANADA INC)

3500 Rue Fairway, Lachine, QC, H8T 1B4
(514) 636-0852
Emp Here 120
SIC 4212 Local trucking, without storage
Jessica Abraham

D-U-N-S 24-973-8600 (BR)
LESTER B. PEARSON SCHOOL BOARD
LAKESIDE ACADEMY
5050 Rue Sherbrooke, Lachine, QC, H8T 1H8
(514) 637-2505
Emp Here 75
SIC 8211 Elementary and secondary schools
John Levin

D-U-N-S 20-165-5524 (BR)
LIFTOW LIMITED
(*Suby of* LIFTOW LIMITED)
1936 32e Av, Lachine, QC, H8T 3J7
(514) 633-9360
Emp Here 100
SIC 5084 Industrial machinery and equipment
William Mc Gratten

D-U-N-S 24-811-8994 (HQ)
LOGISTIQUES TRANS-WEST INC
1900 52e Av Bureau 100, Lachine, QC, H8T 2X9
(514) 345-1090
Emp Here 245   *Sales* 46,095,250
SIC 4213 Trucking, except local
Real Gagnon

D-U-N-S 24-799-8214 (SL)
M'PLAST INC
2530 Rue Alphonse-Gariepy, Lachine, QC, H8T 3M2
(514) 633-8181
Emp Here 45   *Sales* 10,504,575
SIC 2673 Bags: plastic, laminated, and coated
Akbaraly Damdjee
Nilam Damdjee

D-U-N-S 24-461-0382 (SL)
MANUFACTURE D'EQUIPMENT HARDT INC
(*Suby of* HOLDING HARDT EQUIPEMENT INC)
1400 50e Av, Lachine, QC, H8T 2V3
(514) 631-7271
Emp Here 106   *Sales* 20,361,010
SIC 3469 Metal stampings, nec
David Friedl
Neil Creme
Marek Friedl

D-U-N-S 24-865-1143 (SL)
METAFIX INC
1925 46e Av, Lachine, QC, H8T 2P1
(514) 633-8663
Emp Here 45   *Sales* 10,228,005
SIC 3861 Photographic equipment and supplies
John L Riviere

D-U-N-S 24-491-1400 (SL)
MOULES PLASTICOR INC, LES
1170 50e Av, Lachine, QC, H8T 2V3
(514) 636-9630
Emp Here 85   *Sales* 40,377,210
SIC 5085 Industrial supplies
Giusseppe (Joseph) De Guida
Devi Di Guida

D-U-N-S 20-549-9465 (SL)
NELLSON NUTRACEUTIQUE CANADA, INC
(*Suby of* NELLSON NUTRACEUTICAL, LLC)
1125 50e Av, Lachine, QC, H8T 3P3
(514) 380-8383
Emp Here 350   *Sales* 170,584,750
SIC 2064 Candy and other confectionery products
Jamie Better
Manuel Martinez
John Fazzina
Jean Filion

D-U-N-S 24-848-8434 (SL)
OSELA INC
LASERS OSELA, LES
1869 32e Av, Lachine, QC, H8T 3J1
(514) 631-2227
Emp Here 50   *Sales* 12,828,100
SIC 3841 Surgical and medical instruments
Alain Beauregard
Nicolas Cadieux

D-U-N-S 24-541-2796 (HQ)
PNEUTECH-ROUSSEAU GROUP INC
GROUPE PNEUTECH-ROUSSEAU
1475 32e Av, Lachine, QC, H8T 3J1
(514) 635-7000
Emp Here 32   *Sales* 40,377,210
SIC 5084 Industrial machinery and equipment
Sayanthan Navaratnam
Fairy Lee

D-U-N-S 24-403-6703 (SL)
ROADRUNNER APPAREL INC
VETEMENTS ROADRUNNER, LES
2005 23e Av, Lachine, QC, H8T 1X1
(514) 631-4669
Emp Here 26   *Sales* 12,956,372
SIC 5137 Women's and children's clothing
Sheldon Bercovitch

D-U-N-S 20-220-4111 (HQ)
ROLLS-ROYCE CANADA LIMITEE
(*Suby of* ROLLS-ROYCE HOLDINGS PLC)
9500 Ch De La Cote-De-Liesse, Lachine, QC, H8T 1A2
(514) 631-3541
Emp Here 1,400   *Sales* 476,028,000
SIC 4581 Airports, flying fields, and services
Denis Giangi
Vincent Morello
Daniel Majeau
Diana Hargrave

D-U-N-S 25-037-1148 (SL)
ROUSSEAU CONTROLS INC.
1475 32e Av, Lachine, QC, H8T 3J1
(506) 859-8992
Emp Here 26   *Sales* 12,350,676
SIC 5085 Industrial supplies
Fred Goggin

D-U-N-S 24-000-9956 (SL)
SCHWAN'S CANADA CORPORATION
2900 Rue Louis-A.-Amos, Lachine, QC, H8T 3K6
(514) 631-9275
Emp Here 110   *Sales* 30,068,500
SIC 6712 Bank holding companies
Michael Aucoin
Greg Flack

D-U-N-S 24-354-6715 (SL)
SERVICE TRANS-WEST INC
LOCATION TO
1900 52e Av Bureau 100, Lachine, QC, H8T 2X9
(514) 345-1090
Emp Here 100   *Sales* 14,819,200
SIC 4213 Trucking, except local
Real Gagnon

D-U-N-S 24-386-0181 (SL)
SERVICES DE CAMIONNAGE VITESSE INC
VITESSE TRUCK REPAIR SERVICES
1111 46e Av, Lachine, QC, H8T 3C5
(514) 631-2777
Emp Here 45   *Sales* 28,396,840
SIC 4213 Trucking, except local
Aldo Decarolis
Michael Scalzo
Emidio Decarolis
Domenic Santini
Mohamed Selim

D-U-N-S 24-804-7776 (SL)
SHOPPER+ INC
123INKCARTRIDGES.CA
2210 52e Av, Lachine, QC, H8T 2Y3

(514) 631-5216
Emp Here 58   *Sales* 13,479,374
SIC 5734 Computer and software stores
Xiaobo Zhan
Fei Fei Zhan

D-U-N-S 24-419-1305   (BR)
SIGNIFY CANADA LTD
CANLYTE, DIV OF
(*Suby of* KONINKLIJKE PHILIPS N.V.)
3015 Rue Louis-A.-Amos, Lachine, QC, H8T
1C4
(514) 636-0670
Emp Here 250
SIC 3646 Commercial lighting fixtures
Michael Gentille

D-U-N-S 25-540-6282   (SL)
**SYSTEMES DE LIGNES D'EXTRUSION
FABE INC**
CDS SYSTEMS
(*Suby of* 3562603 CANADA INC)
1930 52e Av, Lachine, QC, H8T 2Y3
(514) 633-5933
Emp Here 50   *Sales* 11,100,050
SIC 3569 General industrial machinery, nec
Franco Pecora
Eksay Southidara
Antonio Pecora

D-U-N-S 25-359-4469   (SL)
TEXTILES BAKER INC, LES
1812 Rue Onesime-Gagnon, Lachine, QC,
H8T 3M6
(514) 931-0831
Emp Here 45   *Sales* 22,424,490
SIC 5131 Piece goods and notions
Harry Baker
Bernard Baker
Paul Baker

D-U-N-S 24-174-6510   (SL)
**TRANSITAIRES INTERNATIONAUX SKY-
WAY LTEE**
9262 Ch De La Cote-De-Liesse, Lachine, QC,
H8T 1A1
(514) 636-0250
Emp Here 40   *Sales* 20,798,680
SIC 4731 Freight transportation arrangement
Joseph Zatylny
Karen Zatylny
Jessica Zatylny

D-U-N-S 24-685-6637   (HQ)
TRANSPORT REMCO LIMITEE
5203 Rue Fairway, Lachine, QC, H8T 3K8
(514) 737-1900
Emp Here 105   *Sales* 133,378,400
SIC 4731 Freight transportation arrangement
Randy Cohen

D-U-N-S 24-359-0960   (BR)
UNITED PARCEL SERVICE CANADA LTD
UPS
(*Suby of* UNITED PARCEL SERVICE, INC.)
1221 32e Av Bureau 209, Lachine, QC, H8T
3H2
(514) 633-0010
Emp Here 100
SIC 7389 Business services, nec
Wesley Hay

D-U-N-S 25-125-1781   (SL)
VCS INVESTIGATION INC
SPEQ
10500 Ch De La Cote-De-Liesse Bureau 200,
Lachine, QC, H8T 1A4
(514) 737-1911
Emp Here 100   *Sales* 44,921,900
SIC 7389 Business services, nec
Patrick Prince
Pierre-Hubert Seguin

D-U-N-S 20-214-0539   (SL)
VIANDES BERNARD CENTRALE INC, LES
2001 Av 32e, Lachine, QC, H8T 3J1
(514) 780-8585
Emp Here 150   *Sales* 125,336,550

SIC 5144 Poultry and poultry products
Vasilios Billy Dedes
George Dedes

D-U-N-S 20-699-9125   (HQ)
**WAJAX INDUSTRIAL COMPONENTS LIM-
ITED PARTNERSHIP**
HY-SPEC
2200 52e Av, Lachine, QC, H8T 2Y3
(514) 636-3333
Emp Here 120   *Sales* 360,920,200
SIC 5084 Industrial machinery and equipment
Mark Foote

D-U-N-S 25-298-3689   (BR)
**WAJAX INDUSTRIAL COMPONENTS LIM-
ITED PARTNERSHIP**
WAJAX INDUSTRIAL COMPONENTS
(*Suby of* WAJAX INDUSTRIAL COMPO-
NENTS LIMITED PARTNERSHIP)
2202 52e Av, Lachine, QC, H8T 2Y3
(514) 636-3333
Emp Here 155
SIC 5084 Industrial machinery and equipment
Benoit Bazinet

D-U-N-S 24-150-6955   (SL)
WILLIAMS PHARMALOGISTICS INC
2165 Rue Onesime-Gagnon, Lachine, QC,
H8T 3M7
(514) 526-5901
Emp Here 75   *Sales* 11,114,400
SIC 4213 Trucking, except local
Jo-Ann Hayes
Michel Lunardi

Lachute, QC J8H

D-U-N-S 20-886-4488   (SL)
9175-2527 QUEBEC INC
CLUB DE GOLF DE LACHUTE (CANADA)
(*Suby of* GROUPE BEAUDET INC, LE)
355 Av Bethany, Lachute, QC, J8H 4G9
(450) 562-5228
Emp Here 140   *Sales* 10,996,300
SIC 7992 Public golf courses
Sylvain Beaudet
Regent L. Beaudet

D-U-N-S 20-363-3875   (BR)
AGROPUR COOPERATIVE
CREMES GLACEES LEBEL, LES
(*Suby of* AGROPUR COOPERATIVE)
724 Rue Principale, Lachute, QC, J8H 1Z4
(450) 562-5500
Emp Here 160
SIC 2024 Ice cream and frozen deserts

D-U-N-S 20-254-2734   (SL)
ALIMENTS LEBEL INC, LES
AGROPUR
(*Suby of* ALIMENTS BELSON INC., LES)
724 Rue Principale, Lachute, QC, J8H 1Z4
(450) 562-5500
Emp Here 50   *Sales* 11,242,750
SIC 2024 Ice cream and frozen deserts
Gaetan Lebel
Sylvie Dandurand

D-U-N-S 24-789-3522   (HQ)
ASSURANCE JONES INC
103 Av Bethany, Lachute, QC, J8H 2L2
(450) 562-8555
Emp Here 19   *Sales* 33,074,340
SIC 6411 Insurance agents, brokers, and ser-
vice
William R Jones
Robert Edouard Jones
Edith Pare Jones
Philippe Jones
Elisabeth Jones

D-U-N-S 20-978-7621   (SL)
BROWNSBURG ELECTRONIK INC

741 Rue Lowe, Lachute, QC, J8H 4N9
(450) 562-5211
Emp Here 70   *Sales* 13,330,940
SIC 3677 Electronic coils and transformers
Stephane Montreuil

D-U-N-S 20-292-3454   (SL)
CADIEUX & ASSOCIES S.E.N.C.
RONA
225 Rue Principale, Lachute, QC, J8H 2Z7
(450) 562-5285
Emp Here 26   *Sales* 11,626,524
SIC 5072 Hardware
Patrick Cadieux

D-U-N-S 24-337-2708   (BR)
CASCADES CANADA ULC
CASCADES GROUPE TISSU LACHUTE
(*Suby of* CASCADES INC)
115 Rue De La Princesse, Lachute, QC, J8H
4M3
(450) 562-8585
Emp Here 155
SIC 2676 Sanitary paper products
Regis Arsenault

D-U-N-S 25-232-8729   (BR)
**COMMISSION SCOLAIRE DE LA RIVIERE-
DU-NORD**
ECOLE POLYVALENTE LAVIGNE
452 Av D'Argenteuil Bureau 103, Lachute,
QC, J8H 1W9
(450) 562-8841
Emp Here 120
SIC 8211 Elementary and secondary schools
Alain Falardeau

D-U-N-S 24-969-5891   (SL)
CRISTINI AMERIQUE DU NORD INC
(*Suby of* S.A. GIUSEPPE CRISTINI SPA)
700 Boul Cristini, Lachute, QC, J8H 4N3
(450) 562-5511
Emp Here 55   *Sales* 10,712,240
SIC 2679 Converted paper products, nec
Vittorio Montiglio

D-U-N-S 24-150-8030   (SL)
INTERIM RESSOURCES HUMAINES INC
50 Rue Simon, Lachute, QC, J8H 3R8

Emp Here 45   *Sales* 10,663,650
SIC 7361 Employment agencies
Sylvie Desjardins

D-U-N-S 24-325-0370   (SL)
PORTES A R D INC, LES
FENETRES PRISMA
755 Boul Cristini, Lachute, QC, J8H 4N6
(450) 562-2624
Emp Here 40   *Sales* 17,886,960
SIC 5031 Lumber, plywood, and millwork
Andre Durand
Robert Durand
Louise Durand

D-U-N-S 20-420-5306   (SL)
SHOWA DENKO CARBONE CANADA INC
S SHOWA DENKO
(*Suby of* SGL CARBON SE)
505 Av Bethany Bureau 202, Lachute, QC,
J8H 4A6
(450) 409-0727
Emp Here 90   *Sales* 20,456,010
SIC 3823 Process control instruments
Carl D. Kolts
Patrice Boulanger

D-U-N-S 24-973-8188   (BR)
SIR WILFRID LAURIER SCHOOL BOARD
LAURENTIAN REGIONAL HIGH SCHOOL
448 Av D'Argenteuil, Lachute, QC, J8H 1W9
(450) 562-8571
Emp Here 80
SIC 8211 Elementary and secondary schools
Josee Cote

D-U-N-S 24-527-9070   (SL)
SUPERMARCHE LACHUTE INC

501 Av Bethany, Lachute, QC, J8H 4A6
(450) 562-7919
Emp Here 49   *Sales* 13,433,448
SIC 5411 Grocery stores
Gilles Messier
Richard Mckibbin

D-U-N-S 25-294-8856   (BR)
WAL-MART CANADA CORP
(*Suby of* WALMART INC.)
480 Av Bethany, Lachute, QC, J8H 4H5
(450) 562-0258
Emp Here 150
SIC 5311 Department stores
Sylvain Lemay

Lacolle, QC J0J

D-U-N-S 24-800-2776   (SL)
ARNEG CANADA INC
(*Suby of* ARNEG SPA)
18 Rue Richelieu, Lacolle, QC, J0J 1J0
(450) 246-3837
Emp Here 140   *Sales* 31,080,140
SIC 3585 Refrigeration and heating equip-
ment
Rejean Lalumiere
Michel Beaudry
Daniele Marzaro

Lambton, QC G0M

D-U-N-S 24-885-2444   (SL)
2843-5816 QUEBEC INC
PORTES LAMBTON
(*Suby of* GESTIONS ROGER JACQUES
LTEE, LES)
235 2e Av, Lambton, QC, G0M 1H0
(418) 486-7401
Emp Here 165   *Sales* 31,741,050
SIC 2431 Millwork
Alexandra Jacques
Michel Jacques
Marie-Pier Jacques
Marc Blain

D-U-N-S 20-203-7677   (SL)
BERNIER, A D INC
(*Suby of* GESTION YVON BERNIER INC)
229 2e Av, Lambton, QC, G0M 1H0
(418) 486-7461
Emp Here 65   *Sales* 17,397,380
SIC 5211 Lumber and other building materials
Mona Bernier

Landrienne, QC J0Y

D-U-N-S 20-203-8279   (SL)
GESTION VALBEC INC
389 Ch Du Moulin, Landrienne, QC, J0Y 1V0
(819) 732-6404
Emp Here 200   *Sales* 38,474,000
SIC 2421 Sawmills and planing mills, general
Rejean Boisvert
Luc Dufour
Benoit Cote
Yvon Lafontaine
Pierre Duhamel

Lanoraie, QC J0K

D-U-N-S 24-994-0461   (HQ)
2635-8762 QUEBEC INC
EXPRESS MONDOR
922 Grande Cote O, Lanoraie, QC, J0K 1E0

(450) 887-7446
Sales 16,456,480
SIC 4213 Trucking, except local
Eric Mondor
Dany Mondor
Billy Mondor

D-U-N-S 20-267-0550   (BR)
INTEPLAST BAGS AND FILMS CORPORATION
VIAMFILMS
(Suby of INTEPLAST GROUP CORPORATION)
1 Rue Vifan, Lanoraie, QC, J0K 1E0
(450) 887-7711
Emp Here 100
SIC 3081 Unsupported plastics film and sheet
Stephane Croteau

D-U-N-S 20-376-2893   (SL)
PEPINIERE LEMAY INC
(Suby of PEPINIERE FRANCOIS LEMAY INC)
256 Rang Saint-Henri, Lanoraie, QC, J0K 1E0
(450) 887-2761
Emp Here 100   Sales 26,230,900
SIC 0181 Ornamental nursery products
Sebastien Lemay
Francois Lemay
Carl Drouin

D-U-N-S 24-433-0445   (HQ)
PRODUITS D'ACIER HASON INC, LES
(Suby of HASON MANAGEMENT CORPORATION)
7 Rue Pinat, Lanoraie, QC, J0K 1E0
(450) 887-0800
Emp Here 170   Sales 38,417,000
SIC 3443 Fabricated plate work (boiler shop)
Denis Blain
Dang-Loc Nguyen

D-U-N-S 25-666-3142   (SL)
V.R. SOULIERE INC
179 Rue Du Parc-Industriel, Lanoraie, QC, J0K 1E0
(450) 589-1110
Emp Here 27   Sales 13,448,106
SIC 5571 Motorcycle dealers
Eric Souliere
Samuel Henault
Nancy Fortier
Danny Lane
Martine Canuel

Larouche, QC G0W

D-U-N-S 20-175-6850   (HQ)
BOIS D'INGENIERIE RESOLU-LP LAROUCHE INC
BOIS D'INGENIERIE RESOLU-LP
900 Ch Du Lac-Hippolyte, Larouche, QC, G0W 1Z0
(418) 547-2828
Sales 19,237,000
SIC 2448 Wood pallets and skids
Luc Theriault
Eric Paradis
Jason Ringblom
Travis Turner

D-U-N-S 20-126-3378   (SL)
FORESCO HOLDING INC
EQUIPE DE COURSE FORESCO
498 Boul Du Royaume, Larouche, QC, G0W 1Z0
(418) 542-8243
Emp Here 40   Sales 10,122,360
SIC 5211 Lumber and other building materials
Steeve Hobbs
Blaise Tremblay

Lasalle, QC H8N

D-U-N-S 25-095-1381   (SL)
2733-8649 QUEBEC INC
INTERPHONE MONTREAL
7351 Rue Chouinard, Lasalle, QC, H8N 2L6
(514) 768-6315
Emp Here 28   Sales 11,690,168
SIC 7382 Security systems services
Frederique Begin

D-U-N-S 20-005-3721   (SL)
9051-8051 QUEBEC INC
PHARMAPRIX
8371 Boul Newman Bureau 79, Lasalle, QC, H8N 1Y4
(514) 595-8550
Emp Here 40   Sales 10,118,160
SIC 5912 Drug stores and proprietary stores
Josee Blouin

D-U-N-S 25-222-8929   (SL)
9094-0594 QUEBEC INC
MARCHE FRUTTA SI
1255 Boul Shevchenko, Lasalle, QC, H8N 1N8
(514) 595-9111
Emp Here 80   Sales 23,478,160
SIC 5411 Grocery stores
Kim Toppetta

D-U-N-S 20-715-2591   (HQ)
ACIER NOVA INC
(Suby of 3195538 CANADA INC)
6001 Rue Irwin, Lasalle, QC, H8N 1A1
(514) 789-0511
Emp Here 77   Sales 131,439,880
SIC 5051 Metals service centers and offices
D.Bryan Jones
Scott B. Jones
Lawrence P. Cannon
Pina Santillo

D-U-N-S 20-333-0618   (SL)
ALIMENTS LEVITTS (CANADA) INC, LES
CHARCUTERIE PARISIENNE
7070 Rue Saint-Patrick, Lasalle, QC, H8N 1V2
(514) 367-1654
Emp Here 90   Sales 31,112,100
SIC 2011 Meat packing plants
Jean-Francois Desjardins

D-U-N-S 25-331-0825   (BR)
ALSCO CANADA CORPORATION
UNIFORMS & LINGE D'HOTELERIE ALSCO
(Suby of ALSCO INC.)
2500 Rue Senkus, Lasalle, QC, H8N 2X9
(514) 595-7381
Emp Here 125
SIC 7218 Industrial launderers
Alain Gauthier

D-U-N-S 24-936-2302   (HQ)
AUTOBUS TRANSCO (1988) INC
FIRST STUDENT CANADA
(Suby of FIRSTGROUP PLC)
8201 Rue Elmslie, Lasalle, QC, H8N 2W6
(514) 363-4315
Emp Here 175   Sales 26,345,200
SIC 4151 School buses
Michael Petrucci
Troy Phinney

D-U-N-S 25-060-5193   (BR)
BEST BUY CANADA LTD
GEEK SQUAD
(Suby of BEST BUY CO., INC.)
7077 Boul Newman, Lasalle, QC, H8N 1X1
(514) 368-6570
Emp Here 100
SIC 5731 Radio, television, and electronic stores
Steve Fratini

D-U-N-S 20-793-5321   (SL)
CAMPBELL & CAMERON INC
1855 Av Dollard, Lasalle, QC, H8N 1T9
(514) 762-9777
Emp Here 26   Sales 12,950,028

SIC 5511 New and used car dealers
John Raza
Linda Kay Cayford

D-U-N-S 20-213-0162   (BR)
CIE MATERIAUX DE CONSTRUCTION BP CANADA, LA
BP CANADA
(Suby of CIE MATERIAUX DE CONSTRUCTION BP CANADA, LA)
2850 Av Dollard, Lasalle, QC, H8N 2V2
(514) 364-0161
Emp Here 400
SIC 5199 Nondurable goods, nec
Marc Serre

D-U-N-S 20-963-2579   (SL)
COMPAGNIE COMMERCIALE EMEGO LTEE, LA
7373 Rue Cordner, Lasalle, QC, H8N 2R5
(514) 365-0202
Emp Here 24   Sales 11,959,728
SIC 5139 Footwear
James Chan
Enita Mann

D-U-N-S 24-869-9225   (SL)
CONCIERGERIE SPEICO INC
7651 Rue Cordner, Lasalle, QC, H8N 2X2
(514) 364-0777
Emp Here 120   Sales 3,836,160
SIC 7349 Building maintenance services, nec
Ana Luisa Gomes

D-U-N-S 20-887-0501   (SL)
CORPORATION DE CEGEP ANDRE-LAURENDEAU
1111 Rue Lapierre Bureau 300, Lasalle, QC, H8N 2J4
(514) 364-3320
Emp Here 500   Sales 74,695,500
SIC 8221 Colleges and universities
Herve Pilon

D-U-N-S 20-215-7681   (SL)
CRITES & RIDDELL INC
CRITES & RIDDELL PROMO
2695 Av Dollard, Lasalle, QC, H8N 2J8
(514) 368-8641
Emp Here 42   Sales 21,153,636
SIC 5112 Stationery and office supplies
Alain Giroux
Vincent Hayes

D-U-N-S 20-548-2099   (SL)
CRYSTAL WATER INVESTMENTS COMPANY
AQUA LEADER
7050 Rue Saint-Patrick, Lasalle, QC, H8N 1V2
(514) 363-3232
Emp Here 90   Sales 29,352,240
SIC 3949 Sporting and athletic goods, nec
Steve Cohen
William Cohen
Sylvain Charbonneau

D-U-N-S 20-115-4171   (SL)
DIRECT SOURCE INC
2695 Av Dollard, Lasalle, QC, H8N 2J8
(514) 363-8882
Emp Here 46   Sales 20,636,817
SIC 7389 Business services, nec
Bill Shannon

D-U-N-S 20-105-4959   (SL)
E.D.M. LASALLE INC
AUBAINERIE CONCEPT MODE, L'
7427 Boul Newman Bureau 36, Lasalle, QC, H8N 1X3
(514) 365-6633
Emp Here 60   Sales 12,320,580
SIC 5311 Department stores
Francois-Eric Belanger
Martyne Croteau
Danika Croteau

D-U-N-S 24-959-2296   (SL)
ECLAIRAGE AXIS INC

AXIS
2505 Rue Senkus, Lasalle, QC, H8N 2X8
(514) 948-6272
Emp Here 250   Sales 70,728,750
SIC 3648 Lighting equipment, nec
Shlomo Feldman
Gilda Feldman
Joseph Feldman

D-U-N-S 24-959-8269   (SL)
ELEMENTS CHAUFFANTS TEMPORA INC., LES
ELEMENTS CHAUFFANTS TEMPORA
2501 Av Dollard, Lasalle, QC, H8N 1S2
(514) 933-1649
Emp Here 120   Sales 26,640,120
SIC 3567 Industrial furnaces and ovens
Claire Ebrahim

D-U-N-S 20-715-0074   (BR)
ENERGIR INC
(Suby of NOVERCO INC)
2200 Rue De Cannes-Brulees, Lasalle, QC, H8N 2Z2
(514) 367-2525
Emp Here 75
SIC 4924 Natural gas distribution
Raymond Sauvageau

D-U-N-S 24-335-0340   (HQ)
ENERGY LOGISTICS INC
ENERGY TRANSPORTATION GROUP
2555 Av Dollard Edifice 8, Lasalle, QC, H8N 3A9
(514) 363-9555
Sales 40,013,520
SIC 4731 Freight transportation arrangement
Michael Cinquino
Shawn Girard

D-U-N-S 25-357-4206   (SL)
ENTREPRISES MICHEL CAPLETTE INC
PHARMACIE JEAN COUTU
(Suby of 2156-0552 QUEBEC INC)
1819 Av Dollard, Lasalle, QC, H8N 1T9
(514) 364-1644
Emp Here 120   Sales 29,319,360
SIC 5912 Drug stores and proprietary stores
Michel Caplette

D-U-N-S 24-760-3363   (HQ)
ENTREPRISES MICHEL MARCHAND INC, LES
MCDONALDS
8300 Boul Newman, Lasalle, QC, H8N 1X9
(514) 365-1223
Emp Here 170   Sales 9,327,800
SIC 5812 Eating places
Michel Marchand

D-U-N-S 20-765-8824   (SL)
EXPOSERVICE STANDARD INC
GES CANADA
(Suby of VIAD CORP)
2345 Rue Lapierre, Lasalle, QC, H8N 1B7
(514) 367-4848
Emp Here 110   Sales 36,646,280
SIC 7359 Equipment rental and leasing, nec
Jean-Marc Lefort

D-U-N-S 25-674-2800   (SL)
GESTIONS JEAN-MARC GAGNE LTEE
CANADIAN TIRE
2221 Boul Angrignon, Lasalle, QC, H8N 3E3

Emp Here 125   Sales 57,644,250
SIC 5014 Tires and tubes
Jean-Marc Gagne

D-U-N-S 24-458-9685   (SL)
GROUPE ST-HENRI INC
REMORQUES ST-HENRI
8000 Rue Saint-Patrick, Lasalle, QC, H8N 1V1
(514) 363-0000
Emp Here 70   Sales 15,669,010
SIC 3715 Truck trailers
Serge Larocque
Michel Larocque

Andre Larocque

D-U-N-S 20-926-7756   (HQ)
GUERLAIN (CANADA) LTD
12 M MOIS
(*Suby of* LVMH MOET HENNESSY LOUIS VUITTON)
2515 Rue Leger, Lasalle, QC, H8N 2V9
(514) 363-0432
Emp Here 14   *Sales* 22,106,900
SIC 5122 Drugs, proprietaries, and sundries
Jean-Francois Raymond

D-U-N-S 20-179-6393   (BR)
INTRIA ITEMS INC
INTRIA (TM)
(*Suby of* CANADIAN IMPERIAL BANK OF COMMERCE)
8301 Rue Elmslie, Lasalle, QC, H8N 3H9
(514) 368-5222
Emp Here 800
SIC 7374 Data processing and preparation
Frank Vivacqua

D-U-N-S 24-669-2586   (BR)
KRUGER INC
PACKAGING DIVISION
(*Suby of* KRUGER INC)
7474 Rue Cordner, Lasalle, QC, H8N 2W3
(514) 366-8050
Emp Here 190
SIC 2653 Corrugated and solid fiber boxes
Michel Dubuc

D-U-N-S 24-125-4783   (BR)
LABATT BREWING COMPANY LIMITED
BRASSERIE LABATT
(*Suby of* ANHEUSER-BUSCH INBEV)
2505 Rue Senkus, Lasalle, QC, H8N 2X8
(514) 595-2505
Emp Here 250
SIC 5813 Drinking places
Robert Guy

D-U-N-S 25-240-4397   (BR)
LESTER B. PEARSON SCHOOL BOARD
CHILDREN'S WORLD ACADEMY (CWA)
2241 Rue Menard, Lasalle, QC, H8N 1J4
(514) 595-2043
Emp Here 100
SIC 8211 Elementary and secondary schools
David Estok

D-U-N-S 20-271-4671   (SL)
METRO NISSAN INC
METRO HYUNDAI
8686 Boul Newman, Lasalle, QC, H8N 1Y5
(514) 366-8931
Emp Here 25   *Sales* 12,451,950
SIC 5511 New and used car dealers
Samuel Levinson

D-U-N-S 20-362-3152   (HQ)
MORGAN SCHAFFER LTEE
8300 Rue Saint-Patrick Bureau 150, Lasalle, QC, H8N 2H1
(514) 739-1967
Sales 36,767,455
SIC 8734 Testing laboratories
Mark Dunger
Gerard Joseph Giammanco Jr.
Richard Garretson
Alyson Barclay

D-U-N-S 20-265-9504   (HQ)
MORRIS NATIONAL INC
2235 Rue Lapierre, Lasalle, QC, H8N 1B7
(514) 368-1000
Sales 179,179,000
SIC 5145 Confectionery
Gerald Zubatoff
Brahm Morris Zubatoff
Jean-Pierre Lefebvre

D-U-N-S 20-067-9613   (SL)
NAPA AUTO PARTS
7214 Boul Newman, Lasalle, QC, H8N 1X2

(514) 365-5116
Emp Here 49   *Sales* 24,405,822
SIC 5531 Auto and home supply stores
Robert Hattem

D-U-N-S 20-290-1245   (SL)
PIERRE BELVEDERE INC
2555 Av Dollard, Lasalle, QC, H8N 3A9
(514) 286-2880
Emp Here 30   *Sales* 15,616,260
SIC 5092 Toys and hobby goods and supplies
Alain Savard
Stephen Petit

D-U-N-S 20-972-6900   (HQ)
PLACEMENTS SERGAKIS INC
P.J. PUB
7373 Rue Cordner, Lasalle, QC, H8N 2R5
(514) 937-0531
Sales 23,319,500
SIC 5812 Eating places
Peter Sergakis

D-U-N-S 24-373-4410   (HQ)
PRODUITS DE PISCINE TRENDIUM INC
(*Suby of* COMPAGNIE DE GESTION TRENDIUM)
7050 Rue Saint-Patrick, Lasalle, QC, H8N 1V2
(514) 363-3232
Sales 26,090,880
SIC 3949 Sporting and athletic goods, nec
Steven Cohen
Christina Cohen

D-U-N-S 20-317-7282   (BR)
PRODUITS DE PISCINE TRENDIUM INC
(*Suby of* COMPAGNIE DE GESTION TRENDIUM)
2673 Boul Angrignon, Lasalle, QC, H8N 3J3
(514) 363-7001
Emp Here 75
SIC 3949 Sporting and athletic goods, nec
Guy Parent

D-U-N-S 24-434-9361   (SL)
RECUPERACTION MARRONNIERS INC
2555 Av Dollard, Lasalle, QC, H8N 3A9
(514) 595-1212
Emp Here 120   *Sales* 58,527,600
SIC 5084 Industrial machinery and equipment
Richard Lanciault

D-U-N-S 20-232-4380   (HQ)
ROBCO INC
ANCHOR PACKING
(*Suby of* TICKERMAC INC)
7200 Rue Saint-Patrick, Lasalle, QC, H8N 2W7
(514) 367-2252
Emp Here 70   *Sales* 24,622,990
SIC 3053 Gaskets; packing and sealing devices
Barry J. Macdonald
John L. Macdonald
Donalyn Adams

D-U-N-S 25-311-2155   (HQ)
SFP CANADA LTD
CARTES CARLTON
(*Suby of* SCHURMAN FINE PAPERS)
7077 Boul Newman Bureau 15, Lasalle, QC, H8N 1X1
(514) 366-7660
Emp Here 25   *Sales* 10,880,650
SIC 5947 Gift, novelty, and souvenir shop
Dominique Andrea Schurman
Roxanne Prahser
Krista Durant

D-U-N-S 20-705-8863   (BR)
SOCIETE DE TRANSPORT DE MONTREAL
CENTRE DE TRANSPORT LASALLE
(*Suby of* SOCIETE DE TRANSPORT DE MONTREAL)
7770 Rue Saint-Patrick, Lasalle, QC, H8N 1V1
(514) 280-6382
Emp Here 600
SIC 4111 Local and suburban transit

Jean-Guy Boileau

D-U-N-S 24-319-8389   (HQ)
SUPREMEX INC
ENVELOPPE PREMIER
7213 Rue Cordner, Lasalle, QC, H8N 2J7
(514) 595-0555
Emp Here 150   *Sales* 147,896,057
SIC 2677 Envelopes
Stewart Emerson
Guy Pronovost
Dany Paradis
Robert B. Johnston
Warren J. White
Andrew I. Sullivan
Nicole Boivin
Steven P. Richardson
Georges Kobrynsky

D-U-N-S 20-514-9250   (HQ)
TRANSPORTS FUEL INC, LES
2480 Rue Senkus, Lasalle, QC, H8N 2X9
(514) 948-2225
Emp Here 145   *Sales* 76,005,300
SIC 4731 Freight transportation arrangement
Robert Piccioni

D-U-N-S 25-297-6311   (BR)
WAL-MART CANADA CORP
WALMART SUPERCENTRE
(*Suby of* WALMART INC.)
6797 Boul Newman, Lasalle, QC, H8N 3E4
(514) 368-2248
Emp Here 250
SIC 5311 Department stores

Lasalle, QC H8P

D-U-N-S 24-355-0279   (BR)
CENTRE DE SANTE ET DE SERVICES SOCIAUX DE DORVAL-LACHINE-LASALLE
CENTRE HOSPITALIER DE LACHINE DU CUSM
650 16e Av, Lasalle, QC, H8P 2S3
(514) 637-2351
Emp Here 685
SIC 8062 General medical and surgical hospitals
Daniel Petit

D-U-N-S 25-240-4231   (BR)
COMMISSION SCOLAIRE MARGUERITE-BOURGEOYS
ECOLE NOTRE DAME DES RAPIDES
(*Suby of* COMMISSION SCOLAIRE MARGUERITE-BOURGEOYS)
8585 Rue George, Lasalle, QC, H8P 1G5
(514) 595-2052
Emp Here 140
SIC 8211 Elementary and secondary schools
Carole Garand

D-U-N-S 25-060-2158   (SL)
GESTION MICHEL LANG INC
PHARMAPRIX
8096 Boul Champlain, Lasalle, QC, H8P 1B3
(514) 367-3300
Emp Here 40   *Sales* 10,118,160
SIC 5912 Drug stores and proprietary stores
Michel Lang

D-U-N-S 20-171-7845   (SL)
GESTIONS PARKER-SCOTT INC
TIM HORTONS
8080 Boul Champlain Bureau 1439, Lasalle, QC, H8P 1B3
(514) 368-2114
Emp Here 100   *Sales* 4,551,900
SIC 5812 Eating places
Louis Parker

D-U-N-S 20-712-3659   (BR)
LESTER B. PEARSON SCHOOL BOARD
FORMATION PROFESSIONNELLE

8310 Rue George, Lasalle, QC, H8P 1E5
(514) 363-6213
Emp Here 150
SIC 8211 Elementary and secondary schools
Richard Oliver

D-U-N-S 25-360-5992   (SL)
MARCHE D'ALIMENTATION BECK INC
IGA EXTRA
8130 Boul Champlain, Lasalle, QC, H8P 1B4
(514) 364-4777
Emp Here 49   *Sales* 13,433,448
SIC 5411 Grocery stores
Todd Beck

D-U-N-S 25-312-3459   (SL)
RE/MAX ACTION (1992) INC
8280 Boul Champlain, Lasalle, QC, H8P 1B5
(514) 364-3222
Emp Here 80   *Sales* 21,740,480
SIC 6531 Real estate agents and managers
Patricia Ciancotti

D-U-N-S 20-852-8237   (BR)
SOBEYS QUEBEC INC
IGA
8130 Boul Champlain, Lasalle, QC, H8P 1B4
(514) 364-4777
Emp Here 100   *Sales* 822,456
SIC 5411 Grocery stores
Todd Beck

Lasalle, QC H8R

D-U-N-S 24-347-5295   (HQ)
137882 CANADA INC
9100 Rue Elmslie, Lasalle, QC, H8R 1V6
(514) 365-1642
Sales 91,377,250
SIC 6712 Bank holding companies
Edmund W Colton

D-U-N-S 24-834-5407   (SL)
2623-4419 QUEBEC INC
IMPORT AQUATIQUES ABCEE'S
9615 Rue Clement, Lasalle, QC, H8R 4B4
(514) 363-0276
Emp Here 15   *Sales* 22,015,380
SIC 5154 Livestock
Brian Menard
Francois Archambault
Adrianna Menard
Catherine Leclaire

D-U-N-S 24-988-5492   (HQ)
2853477 CANADA INC
C.E. COPIE EXPRESS
790 Rue D'Upton, Lasalle, QC, H8R 2T9
(514) 363-5511
Emp Here 50   *Sales* 24,044,520
SIC 7334 Photocopying and duplicating services
Gerald Naimer
Usman Shaikh

D-U-N-S 20-254-9291   (SL)
4489161 CANADA INC
PAVILLONS LASALLE, LES
400 Rue Louis-Fortier Bureau 100a, Lasalle, QC, H8R 0A8
(514) 370-8000
Emp Here 100   *Sales* 6,507,500
SIC 8361 Residential care
Arik Azoulay
Georgette Azoulay
Rafael Azoulay

D-U-N-S 24-652-6859   (HQ)
AB MAURI (CANADA) LIMITEE
LEVURE FLEISCHMANN, DIV OF
(*Suby of* WITTINGTON INVESTMENTS LIMITED)
31 Rue Airlie, Lasalle, QC, H8R 1Z8
(514) 366-1053
Emp Here 115   *Sales* 48,396,600

SIC 2099 Food preparations, nec
Mark A. Prendergast
Julien Mietzitis
Daniel Kucera
Frederic Elias

D-U-N-S 24-251-6029   (SL)
C. FRAPPIER ELECTRIQUE INC
(*Suby of* 3087-6353 QUEBEC INC)
9607 Rue Clement, Lasalle, QC, H8R 4B4
(514) 363-1712
Emp Here 80   *Sales* 17,426,320
SIC 1731 Electrical work
Sylvain Frappier
Myriam Frappier

D-U-N-S 20-152-4407   (SL)
**CENTRE D'ACTION DE DEVELOPPEMENT
ET DE RECHERCHE EN EMPLOYABILITE**
CADRE LOGIS + NET
1005 Rue D'Upton, Lasalle, QC, H8R 2V2
(514) 367-3576
Emp Here 49   *Sales* 11,114,817
SIC 8399 Social services, nec
Alex Chayer

D-U-N-S 24-943-6668   (BR)
**CIE MATERIAUX DE CONSTRUCTION BP
CANADA, LA**
(*Suby of* CIE MATERIAUX DE CONSTRUC-
TION BP CANADA, LA)
9500 Rue Saint-Patrick, Lasalle, QC, H8R 1R8
(514) 364-0161
Emp Here 280
SIC 2429 Special product sawmills, nec
Marc Serre

D-U-N-S 20-297-4924   (HQ)
**CIE MATERIAUX DE CONSTRUCTION BP
CANADA, LA**
BUILDING PRODUCTS CANADA
9510 Rue Saint-Patrick, Lasalle, QC, H8R 1R9
(514) 364-0161
Emp Here 300   *Sales* 250,551,000
SIC 2493 Reconstituted wood products
Yves Gosselin
Mark F. Whitley
Keith W. Colburn

D-U-N-S 25-240-4272   (BR)
**COMMISSION SCOLAIRE MARGUERITE-
BOURGEOYS**
*ECOLE SECONDAIRE CAVELIER DE
LASALLE*
(*Suby of* COMMISSION SCOLAIRE
MARGUERITE-BOURGEOYS)
9199 Rue Centrale, Lasalle, QC, H8R 2J9
(514) 595-2044
Emp Here 150
SIC 8211 Elementary and secondary schools
Julie Lavigne

D-U-N-S 20-229-6117   (HQ)
**COMPAGNIE D'APPAREILS ELECTRIQUES
PEERLESS LTEE**
9145 Rue Boivin, Lasalle, QC, H8R 2E5
(514) 595-1671
Emp Here 110   *Sales* 32,674,350
SIC 1731 Electrical work
Rosa Samuels
Barry Fagen
Francine Samuels

D-U-N-S 24-865-7629   (SL)
CORPORATION TRIBOSPEC, LA
220 Av Lafleur, Lasalle, QC, H8R 4C9
(514) 595-7579
Emp Here 50   *Sales* 13,077,650
SIC 6712 Bank holding companies
Guiliano Cininni
Claude Gauthier

D-U-N-S 25-524-5706   (SL)
DAC AVIATION INTERNATIONAL LTEE
9371 Rue Wanklyn, Lasalle, QC, H8R 1Z2
(514) 876-0135
Emp Here 50   *Sales* 16,237,700

SIC 4581 Airports, flying fields, and services
Emmanuel Anassis

D-U-N-S 24-590-6755   (SL)
DELMAR CHEMICALS INC
(*Suby of* NINE TREES GROUP SPA)
9321 Rue Airlie, Lasalle, QC, H8R 2B2
(514) 366-7950
Emp Here 65   *Sales* 18,461,365
SIC 2833 Medicinals and botanicals
Franco Moro
Paul Legault
Luigi Erriquez

D-U-N-S 25-997-7069   (BR)
**DEPARTMENT OF NATIONAL DEFENCE
AND THE CANADIAN ARMED FORCES**
*NAVAL ENGINEERING TEST ESTABLISH-
MENT*
(*Suby of* GOVERNMENT OF CANADA)
9401 Rue Lafleur, Lasalle, QC, H8R 1Z2
(514) 366-4310
Emp Here 100
SIC 7389 Business services, nec
Mike Pittman

D-U-N-S 20-632-1812   (BR)
GCP CANADA INC
(*Suby of* W. R. GRACE & CO.)
255 Av Lafleur, Lasalle, QC, H8R 3H4
(514) 366-3362
Emp Here 100
SIC 2819 Industrial inorganic chemicals, nec

D-U-N-S 24-205-7342   (HQ)
GDI SERVICES (QUEBEC) S.E.C.
INDUSTRIES DE MAINTENANCE EMPIRE
695 90e Av, Lasalle, QC, H8R 3A4
(514) 368-1505
Sales 482,355,000
SIC 7349 Building maintenance services, nec
Claude Bigras

D-U-N-S 20-298-2757   (HQ)
GDI SERVICES AUX IMMEUBLES INC
695 90e Av, Lasalle, QC, H8R 3A4
(514) 368-1504
Emp Here 6   *Sales* 836,563,283
SIC 7349 Building maintenance services, nec
Claude Bigras
Stephane Lavigne
David Hinchey
Jocelyn Trottier
Michael Masse
Fred Edwards
David G. Samuel
Michael Boychuk
David A. Galloway
Richard G. Roy

D-U-N-S 20-298-2773   (SL)
GDI SERVICES TECHNIQUES S.E.C.
695 90e Av, Lasalle, QC, H8R 3A4
(514) 368-1504
Emp Here 100   *Sales* 4,020,900
SIC 7349 Building maintenance services, nec
Claude Bigras

D-U-N-S 24-352-1952   (HQ)
GROUPE SUTTON-CLODEM INC
(*Suby of* INVESTISSEMENTS KITZA INC)
9515 Boul Lasalle, Lasalle, QC, H8R 2M9
(514) 364-3315
Sales 58,644,460
SIC 6531 Real estate agents and managers
Christophe Folla

D-U-N-S 20-103-7764   (SL)
HATLEY - P'TITE MAISON BLEUE INC
860 90e Av, Lasalle, QC, H8R 3A2
(514) 272-8444
Emp Here 200   *Sales* 167,506,600
SIC 5137 Women's and children's clothing
Christopher Oldland
Jeremy Oldland
Nicolas Oldland
Louis Gourdeau

D-U-N-S 20-719-3371   (BR)
IMPRIMERIES TRANSCONTINENTAL INC
TRANSCONTINENTAL PRINTING INC
(*Suby of* TRANSCONTINENTAL INC)
999 Av 90e, Lasalle, QC, H8R 3A4
(514) 861-2411
Emp Here 100
SIC 2752 Commercial printing, lithographic
Brian Reid

D-U-N-S 20-542-7172   (HQ)
INDUSTRIES KINGSTON LTEE, LES
(*Suby of* 137882 CANADA INC)
9100 Rue Elmslie, Lasalle, QC, H8R 1V6
(514) 365-1642
Emp Here 2   *Sales* 28,074,600
SIC 8741 Management services
Edmund Colton
Philippe Catafago

D-U-N-S 25-548-9903   (SL)
INTERIM RESSOURCES HUMAINES INC
50 Av Labatt, Lasalle, QC, H8R 3E7

Emp Here 49   *Sales* 11,611,530
SIC 7361 Employment agencies
Sylvie Desjardins

D-U-N-S 24-988-9619   (HQ)
INVESTISSEMENTS KITZA INC
9515 Boul Lasalle, Lasalle, QC, H8R 2M9
(514) 364-3315
Emp Here 1   *Sales* 58,644,460
SIC 6531 Real estate agents and managers
Christophe Folla

D-U-N-S 20-591-9400   (HQ)
KINGSTON BYERS INC
HAUTS BOISES DU CHATEAUGUAY, LES
(*Suby of* 137882 CANADA INC)
9100 Rue Elmslie, Lasalle, QC, H8R 1V6
(514) 365-1642
Emp Here 100   *Sales* 42,273,700
SIC 1541 Industrial buildings and warehouses
Edmund W Colton
Karianne Colton
Giuliano Sanviti

D-U-N-S 25-004-2850   (BR)
LABATT BREWING COMPANY LIMITED
BRASSERIE LABATT
(*Suby of* ANHEUSER-BUSCH INBEV)
50 Av Labatt Bureau 42, Lasalle, QC, H8R
3E7
(514) 366-5050
Emp Here 1,070
SIC 2082 Malt beverages
Michel Doucet

D-U-N-S 25-196-5963   (SL)
LASALLE CENTRE RECREATIF
707 75e Av, Lasalle, QC, H8R 3Y2
(514) 367-1000
Emp Here 49   *Sales* 22,011,731
SIC 7389 Business services, nec
Benoit Gauchier

D-U-N-S 25-199-1808   (HQ)
LOGIX ITS INC
ENTREPRISES LOGIX ITS
(*Suby of* 7073241 CANADA INC)
992 Rue D'Upton, Lasalle, QC, H8R 2T9
(514) 448-9660
Sales 11,914,350
SIC 3069 Fabricated rubber products, nec
Louis Newman
Ben Z. Cohen
James Thomas Weatherall

D-U-N-S 20-544-6065   (SL)
MONTCALM SERVICES TECHNIQUES INC
695 90e Av, Lasalle, QC, H8R 3A4

Emp Here 600   *Sales* 19,503,398
SIC 7349 Building maintenance services, nec
Claude Bigras

D-U-N-S 25-410-6826   (SL)

D-U-N-S 20-253-5811   (SL)
PARQUET DE LUXE LASALLE INC
PARQUET DELUXE LASALLE
8801 Rue Elmslie, Lasalle, QC, H8R 1V4
(514) 364-9760
Emp Here 25   *Sales* 11,179,350
SIC 5031 Lumber, plywood, and millwork
Normand Amyot
Geatan Amyot

D-U-N-S 20-253-5811   (SL)
**PRODUITS DE SECURITE INDUSTRIELLE
CHECKERS CANADA INC**
990 Rue D'Upton, Lasalle, QC, H8R 2T9
(514) 366-6116
Emp Here 40   *Sales* 16,774,200
SIC 6712 Bank holding companies
Raymond Torres
James Cannon

D-U-N-S 20-423-0296   (HQ)
REN-WIL INC
(*Suby of* PLACEMENTS WILNER 2001 LTEE,
LES)
9181 Rue Boivin, Lasalle, QC, H8R 2E8
(514) 367-1741
Sales 28,855,500
SIC 2499 Wood products, nec
Jonathan Wilner
Ryan Wilner

D-U-N-S 24-355-1335   (SL)
SISCA GESTION D'AFFAIRES INC
790 Rue D'Upton, Lasalle, QC, H8R 2T9
(514) 363-5511
Emp Here 100   *Sales* 21,172,400
SIC 7334 Photocopying and duplicating ser-
vices
Usman Shaikh

D-U-N-S 24-710-9903   (SL)
**SPARTA 2002 DESIGNS & PROMOTIONS
INC**
SPARTA PEWTER
9246 Rue Boivin, Lasalle, QC, H8R 2E7
(514) 363-5674
Emp Here 37   *Sales* 27,473,240
SIC 5199 Nondurable goods, nec
Gregory Soucie
David W. Soucie
Elaine Henderson

D-U-N-S 25-683-0480   (HQ)
STOREX INDUSTRIES CORPORATION
9440 Rue Clement, Lasalle, QC, H8R 3W1
(514) 745-1234
Sales 16,405,566
SIC 3089 Plastics products, nec
Yoav Ben-Or
Aviezer Sochaczevski

D-U-N-S 24-361-3614   (SL)
TOTAL CANADA INC
TOTAL RM CANADA
(*Suby of* TOTAL SA)
220 Av Lafleur, Lasalle, QC, H8R 4C9
(514) 595-7579
Emp Here 50   *Sales* 13,512,800
SIC 2911 Petroleum refining
Ernst Wanten
Franck Bagouet
Jean-Sebastien Desroches
Herve Allibert
Christophe Charzat

D-U-N-S 20-056-6052   (HQ)
TRANSPORT DEMARK INC
9235 Rue Boivin, Lasalle, QC, H8R 2E8
(514) 365-5666
Sales 12,342,360
SIC 4212 Local trucking, without storage
Richard Tellechea

D-U-N-S 24-109-6031   (BR)
UNIFIRST CANADA LTD
UNIFORME PREMIER CHOIX
(*Suby of* UNIFIRST CORPORATION)
8951 Rue Salley, Lasalle, QC, H8R 2C8

(514) 365-8301
Emp Here 100
SIC 7218 Industrial launderers
 Annie Houle

 D-U-N-S 24-680-4058   (BR)
WEIR CANADA, INC
MARINE ENGINEERING, DIV OF
(*Suby of* WEIR GROUP PLC(THE))
9401 Rue Wanklyn, Lasalle, QC, H8R 1Z2
(514) 366-4310
Emp Here 100
SIC 5084 Industrial machinery and equipment
 Serge Lamirande

 D-U-N-S 25-672-5045   (BR)
WILSONART CANADA ULC
ARBORITE, DIV OF
(*Suby of* WILSONART CANADA ULC)
385 Av Lafleur, Lasalle, QC, H8R 3H7
(514) 366-2710
Emp Here 200
SIC 2821 Plastics materials and resins

Laterriere, QC G7N

 D-U-N-S 24-706-5261   (SL)
REBOITECH INC
112 Rue De La Pinede, Laterriere, QC, G7N 1B8
(418) 545-2893
Emp Here 225   *Sales* 39,128,625
SIC 0783 Ornamental shrub and tree services
 Rene Ouellette

 D-U-N-S 24-841-8535   (SL)
SCP 89 INC
PEDNO
3641 Rue Des Forges, Laterriere, QC, G7N 1N4
(418) 678-1506
Emp Here 75   *Sales* 14,406,375
SIC 3496 Miscellaneous fabricated wire products
 Maurice Dupere
 Denis Simard

Laurier-Station, QC G0S

 D-U-N-S 24-689-9934   (SL)
CETAL
179 Boul Laurier, Laurier-Station, QC, G0S 1N0
(418) 728-3119
Emp Here 62   *Sales* 11,926,940
SIC 2448 Wood pallets and skids
 Rene Blais
 Gino Demers
 Jean Bergeron
 Michel Martel
 Daniel Gagnon
 Guillaume Noel
 Gilles St-Onge
 Roger Bouchard

 D-U-N-S 24-318-0051   (SL)
CUISINES LAURIER INC
PORTES ET MOULURES ELEGANCE
266 Rue De La Station, Laurier-Station, QC, G0S 1N0
(418) 728-3630
Emp Here 80   *Sales* 15,389,600
SIC 2434 Wood kitchen cabinets
 Rene Pellerin
 Julien Cote
 Christian Pellerin
 Andre Talbot

 D-U-N-S 24-205-4732   (SL)
LOCATION V.A. INC
156 Boul Laurier Rr 1, Laurier-Station, QC, G0S 1N0

(418) 728-2140
Emp Here 100   *Sales* 45,019,700
SIC 7513 Truck rental and leasing, no drivers
 Jean-Francois Audet

 D-U-N-S 20-204-7759   (SL)
MIROIRS LAURIER LTEE
153 Boul Laurier Bureau 300, Laurier-Station, QC, G0S 1N0
(418) 728-2023
Emp Here 80   *Sales* 18,674,800
SIC 3231 Products of purchased glass
 Robert Mercier
 Caroline Mercier
 Melanie Mercier

 D-U-N-S 25-918-3184   (HQ)
PROMUTUEL LOTNINIERE SOCIETE MUTUELLE D'ASSURANCE GENERALE
PROMUTUEL LOTBINIERE S.M.A.G.
175 Boul Laurier Rr 1, Laurier-Station, QC, G0S 1N0
(418) 728-4110
Emp Here 20   *Sales* 38,162,700
SIC 6411 Insurance agents, brokers, and service
 Denis Dechene

 D-U-N-S 25-187-7122   (SL)
STRUCTURES ULTRATEC INC, LES
POUTRELLES MODERNES
235 Rue De La Station, Laurier-Station, QC, G0S 1N0
(418) 682-2033
Emp Here 200   *Sales* 38,474,000
SIC 2452 Prefabricated wood buildings
 Michel Beaudoin
 Andre Houle
 Maxime Beaudoin
 Philippe Beaudoin
 Samuel Beaudoin
 Luce Marois

 D-U-N-S 20-204-7718   (SL)
SUPERMARCHE LAROCHE (1991) INC
METRO
122 Boul Laurier, Laurier-Station, QC, G0S 1N0
(418) 728-2882
Emp Here 70   *Sales* 20,543,390
SIC 5411 Grocery stores
 Marcel Laroche
 Bertrand Laroche

 D-U-N-S 24-888-4772   (SL)
TEKNION LS INC
359 Rue Saint-Joseth, Laurier-Station, QC, G0S 1N0
(418) 830-0855
Emp Here 100   *Sales* 18,340,300
SIC 2211 Broadwoven fabric mills, cotton
 Jacques Alain
 Scott Bond
 David Feldberg
 Jeffrey Wilson

 D-U-N-S 24-498-9273   (HQ)
TOITURES P.L.C. INC, LES
ULTRATEC RIVE-NORD
(*Suby of* GESTION POLECO INC)
235 Rue De La Station, Laurier-Station, QC, G0S 1N0
(418) 682-2033
Sales 26,931,800
SIC 2439 Structural wood members, nec
 Michel Beaudoin
 Pierre Potvin

Laurierville, QC G0S

 D-U-N-S 25-979-5016   (SL)
COOPERATIVE AGRICOLE DES APPALACHES
303 Ch De La Grosse-?Le, Laurierville, QC, G0S 1P0

(819) 385-4272
Emp Here 49   *Sales* 11,017,895
SIC 2048 Prepared feeds, nec
 Renaud Bergeron

 D-U-N-S 24-378-9823   (HQ)
SOCIETE COOPERATIVE AGRICOLE DES APPALACHES
156 Rue Grenier, Laurierville, QC, G0S 1P0
(819) 365-4372
Emp Here 20   *Sales* 27,568,156
SIC 5251 Hardware stores
 Renaud Bergeron
 Rene Theriault
 Daniel Vigneault

Laval, QC H7C

 D-U-N-S 20-289-4820   (SL)
SERVICES INFRASPEC INC
CANALISATIONS KARIC, LES
4585 Boul Lite, Laval, QC, H7C 0B8
(450) 937-1508
Emp Here 50   *Sales* 22,174,500
SIC 7389 Business services, nec
 Eric Bellemare
 Mathieu Gagnon
 Simon Cournoyer

Laval, QC H7L

 D-U-N-S 24-800-1299   (SL)
HOWMET LAVAL CASTING LTD
4001 Aut Des Laurentides, Laval, QC, H7L 3H7
(450) 680-2500
Emp Here 300
SIC 3365 Aluminum foundries

Laval, QC H7N

 D-U-N-S 20-234-7779   (HQ)
BEAUTE STAR BEDARD INC
GROUPE TOP BEAUTE
1700 Rue Fleetwood, Laval, QC, H7N 0C6
(450) 967-7827
Emp Here 65   *Sales* 105,007,775
SIC 5122 Drugs, proprietaries, and sundries
 Marie-Christine Bourdon
 France Bourdon
 Marie-Danielle Bourdon

 D-U-N-S 24-354-3779   (SL)
BEAUTE STAR BEDARD INC
GROUPE TOP BEAUTE
1700 Rue Fleetwood, Laval, QC, H7N 0C6
(450) 967-7827
Emp Here 100   *Sales* 110,534,500
SIC 5122 Drugs, proprietaries, and sundries
 Gaetan Bourdon
 Marie-Christine Bourdon
 France Bedard Bourdon
 Marie-Danielle Bourdon

Laval, QC H7P

 D-U-N-S 20-386-9891   (SL)
3836185 CANADA INC
2850 Av Jacques-Bureau, Laval, QC, H7P 0B7
(450) 688-6264
Emp Here 1,400   *Sales* 511,712,600
SIC 6712 Bank holding companies
 Daniel Desmarais
 Dale Tschritter

 D-U-N-S 20-544-0795   (HQ)
SAIL PLEIN AIR INC
BARON SPORTS
2850 Av Jacques-Bureau, Laval, QC, H7P 0B7
(450) 688-6264
Emp Here 100   *Sales* 256,951,800
SIC 5941 Sporting goods and bicycle shops
 Norman Decarie
 Daniel Desmrais
 Dale Tschritter
 Michel Saucier
 Claude Lemieux
 Martin Fafard

Laval, QC H7T

 D-U-N-S 20-108-9112   (SL)
ACTELION PHARMACEUTIQUES CANADA INC
(*Suby of* JOHNSON & JOHNSON)
3111 Boul Saint-Martin O Bureau 300, Laval, QC, H7T 0K2
(450) 681-1664
Emp Here 11   *Sales* 12,158,795
SIC 5122 Drugs, proprietaries, and sundries
 Michael Danzl
 Chris Halyk

 D-U-N-S 24-859-0015   (SL)
BERGA RECYCLING INC
(*Suby of* SOCIETE DE GESTION GATES INC)
3055 Boul Saint-Martin O Bureau T500, Laval, QC, H7T 0J3
(514) 949-7244
Emp Here 22   *Sales* 27,291,672
SIC 5051 Metals service centers and offices
 Gaetan Dumas

 D-U-N-S 24-804-7982   (HQ)
CAISSE DESJARDINS DES GRANDS BOULEVARDS DE LAVAL
3111 Boul Saint-Martin O, Laval, QC, H7T 0K2
(450) 667-9950
Emp Here 10   *Sales* 25,471,895
SIC 6062 State credit unions
 Sylvain Courcelles
 Michel Dion
 Roger Chartrand
 Serge Vachon
 Andre Benoit
 Philippe Bougie
 Andree Brian
 Marylene Carrier
 Chantale Fontaine
 Hugo Kirallah

 D-U-N-S 20-827-2521   (SL)
CONSTRUCTION KIEWIT CIE
(*Suby of* PETER KIEWIT SONS', INC.)
3055 Boul Saint-Martin O Bureau 200, Laval, QC, H7T 0J3
(450) 435-5756
Emp Here 276   *Sales* 54,408,156
SIC 8711 Engineering services
 Christopher A. Loeffler
 Michael F. Norton
 Scott L. Cassels

 D-U-N-S 25-365-5377   (BR)
LAFARGE CANADA INC
LAFARGEHOLCIM
(*Suby of* LAFARGEHOLCIM LTD)
3055 Boul Saint-Martin O Bureau 300, Laval, QC, H7T 0J3
(438) 265-1010
Emp Here 150
SIC 1522 Residential construction, nec
 Carlos Valve

 D-U-N-S 20-332-2516   (SL)
PROTECT-YU SECURITY & TECHNOLOGIES INC

3055 Boul Saint-Martin O Bureau 5, Laval, QC, H7T 0J3
(514) 916-7280
Emp Here 14   *Sales* 467,283,600
SIC 8731 Commercial physical research
Pierre Fillion
Michel Juneau-Katsuya
Benoit Daigneault

Laval, QC H7W

D-U-N-S 25-618-7951   (BR)
2757-5158 QUEBEC INC
ARMOIRES CUISINES ACTION
(*Suby of* 2757-5158 QUEBEC INC)
4589 Aut 440 O Bureau 103, Laval, QC, H7W 0J7
(450) 688-9050
Emp Here 300
SIC 5211 Lumber and other building materials
Nathalie Laurin

Laval-Ouest, QC H7L

D-U-N-S 20-013-2772   (SL)
3427951 CANADA INC
G-TEK
180 Boul Bellerose O, Laval-Ouest, QC, H7L 6A2
(450) 628-4835
Emp Here 65   *Sales* 16,408,730
SIC 1623 Water, sewer, and utility lines
Stephane Fortin
Serge Boucher
Roger Bouliane

D-U-N-S 25-380-9875   (HQ)
AMPAK INC
4225 Des Laurentides (A-15) E, Laval-Ouest, QC, H7L 5W5
(450) 682-4141
Emp Here 21   *Sales* 21,376,170
SIC 5085 Industrial supplies
Salvatore Nicastro

D-U-N-S 20-708-6380   (SL)
ARTHUR ROGER & ASSOCIES INC
2010 Boul Dagenais O, Laval-Ouest, QC, H7L 5W2
(450) 963-5080
Emp Here 20   *Sales* 10,702,480
SIC 5141 Groceries, general line
Benoit Guglia
Daniel Parent
Roger Guglia

D-U-N-S 20-224-7284   (HQ)
BOUTIQUE LINEN CHEST (PHASE II) INC
BOUTIQUE ET MAGASIN A RAYONS LINEN CHEST
4455 Des Laurentides (A-15) E, Laval-Ouest, QC, H7L 5X8
(514) 331-5260
Emp Here 100   *Sales* 186,692,100
SIC 5719 Miscellaneous homefurnishings
Sheldon Leibner
Stanley Leibner

D-U-N-S 24-920-8554   (SL)
EQUIPMENT D'EMBALLAGE M.M.C. LTEE
(*Suby of* GESTION MCNALLY INC)
2030 Boul Dagenais O, Laval-Ouest, QC, H7L 5W2
(450) 625-4662
Emp Here 64   *Sales* 31,214,720
SIC 5084 Industrial machinery and equipment
Philippe Mcnally
John Mcnally
Marcel Belanger

D-U-N-S 20-719-1219   (BR)
FOURNITURES DE BUREAU DENIS INC

DENIS OFFICE SUPPLIES
2725 Rue Michelin, Laval-Ouest, QC, H7L 5X6
(450) 681-5300
Emp Here 80
SIC 5712 Furniture stores
Normand Latulippe

D-U-N-S 25-542-0648   (HQ)
GESTION MCNALLY INC
2030 Boul Dagenais O, Laval-Ouest, QC, H7L 5W2
(450) 625-4662
Sales 14,430,065
SIC 3556 Food products machinery
Philippe Mcnally
John Mcnally
Marcel Belanger

D-U-N-S 25-626-1330   (SL)
GROUPE MONTONI (1995) DIVISION CONSTRUCTION INC
4115 Des Laurentides (A-15) E, Laval-Ouest, QC, H7L 5W5
(450) 978-7500
Emp Here 88   *Sales* 37,200,856
SIC 1541 Industrial buildings and warehouses
Dario Montoni

D-U-N-S 20-284-5801   (SL)
IGF AXIOM INC
INSTITUT DE LA GESTION DE LA FORMATION
4125 Des Laurentides (A-15) E, Laval-Ouest, QC, H7L 5W5
(514) 645-3443
Emp Here 50   *Sales* 10,619,850
SIC 8748 Business consulting, nec
Pierre Bernier
Rodrigue Rouleau

D-U-N-S 20-253-1088   (HQ)
LEADING ENGLISH AND EDUCATION RESOURCE NETWORK (LEARN)
L.E.A.R.N
2030 Boul Dagenais O Bureau 2, Laval-Ouest, QC, H7L 5W2
(450) 622-2212
Sales 27,870,480
SIC 8733 Noncommercial research organizations
Howard Miller
Mike Dubeau

D-U-N-S 20-764-5326   (SL)
MANUFACTURE TRIPLE G. INC
BIG AL
2705 Rue Michelin, Laval-Ouest, QC, H7L 5X6
(450) 681-2700
Emp Here 21   *Sales* 10,464,762
SIC 5136 Men's and boy's clothing

D-U-N-S 20-954-5990   (HQ)
NUERA INC
HOLDING NUERA INTERNATIONAL
1980 Boul Dagenais O, Laval-Ouest, QC, H7L 5W2
(514) 955-1024
Emp Here 27   *Sales* 15,200,832
SIC 5085 Industrial supplies
Larry Mcdonald
Tom Gillespie
Howard Davidson
Susan Lecouffe
Mike Perna
Peter Webster
M.Walter Markham

D-U-N-S 25-392-2603   (HQ)
NWD SYSTEMS (MONTREAL) INC
NWD MICROAGE
4209 Des Laurentides (A-15) E, Laval-Ouest, QC, H7L 5W5
(450) 973-6678
Emp Here 63   *Sales* 18,291,288
SIC 5045 Computers, peripherals, and software

Filomeno Palmieri

D-U-N-S 25-286-9771   (SL)
PLACEMENTS ROGERCAN INC, LES
2010 Boul Dagenais O, Laval-Ouest, QC, H7L 5W2
(450) 963-5080
Emp Here 20   *Sales* 10,702,480
SIC 5149 Groceries and related products, nec
Roger Guglia

D-U-N-S 25-500-9920   (SL)
TIGER-VAC INTERNATIONAL INC
TIGER-VAC
2020 Boul Dagenais O, Laval-Ouest, QC, H7L 5W2
(450) 622-0100
Emp Here 43   *Sales* 20,426,118
SIC 5087 Service establishment equipment
Rocco Mariani
Frank Mariani
Vito Mariani

Lavaltrie, QC J5T

D-U-N-S 20-213-5682   (SL)
9006-5855 QUEBEC INC
CLINIQUE DE PHYSIOTHERAPIE LAVALTRIE ENR.
300 Rue Saint-Antoine N, Lavaltrie, QC, J5T 2G4
(450) 586-0479
Emp Here 44   *Sales* 15,894,428
SIC 8049 Offices of health practitioner
Marie-Claude Boivin

D-U-N-S 24-051-1803   (SL)
9090-5092 QUEBEC INC
COFFRAGES SYNERGY
56 Ch De Lavaltrie, Lavaltrie, QC, J5T 2H1
(450) 586-1400
Emp Here 550   *Sales* 49,386,584
SIC 3272 Concrete products, nec
Norman Turnbull
Alex Carroll
Martine Corriveau-Gougeon
Jean-Michel Fournier
Isabelle Cote
Jean-Sebastien Vaes
Maxime Champagne

D-U-N-S 24-387-7920   (HQ)
FCM RECYCLING INC
TECHNOLOGIES RECYCLAGE RE-NEWYT
91 Ch Boisjoly, Lavaltrie, QC, J5T 3L7
(450) 586-5185
Sales 12,856,550
SIC 4953 Refuse systems
Rubin Andrew
Albert Greenspoon

D-U-N-S 20-025-7330   (SL)
HALTE DU BOIS INC
ESSO
250 Aut Felix-Leclerc, Lavaltrie, QC, J5T 3K4

Emp Here 29   *Sales* 14,444,262
SIC 5541 Gasoline service stations
Richard Rompre

D-U-N-S 24-725-3482   (SL)
PLASTIQUES JOLIETTE
190 Ch Des Industries, Lavaltrie, QC, J5T 3R2

Emp Here 49   *Sales* 13,556,340
SIC 2821 Plastics materials and resins
Henri Ouellet

D-U-N-S 24-933-5886   (HQ)
VETOQUINOL N.-A. INC
VETOQUINOL PROLAB
(*Suby of* DEMABEL)
2000 Ch Georges, Lavaltrie, QC, J5T 3S5
(450) 586-2252
Emp Here 150   *Sales* 80,500,095

SIC 5122 Drugs, proprietaries, and sundries
Etienne Frechin
Diane Bourassa
Mathieu Frechin

Lawrenceville, QC J0E

D-U-N-S 20-205-3559   (SL)
MILLETTE & FILS LTEE
2105 Rue De L'Eglise, Lawrenceville, QC, J0E 1W0
(450) 535-6305
Emp Here 100   *Sales* 19,237,000
SIC 2441 Nailed wood boxes and shook
Stephane Millette
Pierre J. Tessier
Dominique Millette
Joanne Morissette
Marcelle Lemay-Millette
Robert Carignan

Lebel-Sur-Quevillon, QC J0Y

D-U-N-S 24-728-5401   (SL)
ALIMENTATION GAETAN PLANTE INC
PROVIGO
53 Place Quevillon, Lebel-Sur-Quevillon, QC, J0Y 1X0
(819) 755-4803
Emp Here 40   *Sales* 10,966,080
SIC 5411 Grocery stores
Pierre-Luc Morin

D-U-N-S 20-187-5759   (BR)
BREAKWATER RESOURCES LTD
NYRSTAR LANGLOIS
(*Suby of* NYRSTAR)
Km 42 Rte 1000, Lebel-Sur-Quevillon, QC, J0Y 1X0
(819) 755-5550
Emp Here 241
SIC 1081 Metal mining services

D-U-N-S 25-370-5438   (BR)
PF RESOLU CANADA INC
RESOLUTE FOREST PRODUCTS
(*Suby of* RESOLUTE FOREST PRODUCTS INC)
2050 Rte 805 N, Lebel-Sur-Quevillon, QC, J0Y 1X0
(819) 755-2500
Emp Here 83
SIC 2439 Structural wood members, nec

Lemoyne, QC J4P

D-U-N-S 24-801-9684   (SL)
STRATECOM INC
1940 Boul Taschereau Bureau 100a, Lemoyne, QC, J4P 3N2
(450) 466-6640
Emp Here 49   *Sales* 15,954,400
SIC 5999 Miscellaneous retail stores, nec
Sylvian Renaud

Lemoyne, QC J4R

D-U-N-S 24-795-0996   (SL)
CONSEIL SANTA MARIA 2267
173 Rue Rene-Philippe, Lemoyne, QC, J4R 2J9
(450) 671-1580
Emp Here 49   *Sales* 19,473,286
SIC 8699 Membership organizations, nec
Gerard Cartier

Lery, QC J6N

D-U-N-S 20-790-3980   (SL)
CLUB DE GOLF DE BELLE VUE (1984) INC
CLUB DE GOLF CHATEAUGUAY
880 Boul De Lery, Lery, QC, J6N 1B7
(450) 692-6793
Emp Here 100   *Sales* 7,639,700
SIC 7997 Membership sports and recreation clubs
Paul Lafleur
Marcel Pigeon

Les Cedres, QC J7T

D-U-N-S 20-201-0674   (HQ)
PEPINIERE CRAMER INC
1002 Ch Saint-Dominique, Les Cedres, QC, J7T 1P4
(450) 452-2121
Emp Here 125   *Sales* 29,579,375
SIC 0181 Ornamental nursery products
Remigio Cramerstetter
Fiorella Cramerstetter

D-U-N-S 24-351-5640   (SL)
PLASTICON CANADA INC
A.C. PLASTICS CANADA
1395 Montee Chenier, Les Cedres, QC, J7T 1L9
(450) 452-1104
Emp Here 50   *Sales* 11,671,750
SIC 3299 NonMetallic mineral products,
Martin Mossinkoff
Glenn Dedecker
Eric Lamontagne

Les Coteaux, QC J7X

D-U-N-S 20-276-8524   (SL)
PROMUTUEL VAUDREUIL-SOULANGES, SOCIETE MUTUELLE D'ASSURANCE GENERALE
245 338 Rte, Les Coteaux, QC, J7X 1A2
(450) 267-9297
Emp Here 56   *Sales* 47,491,360
SIC 6411 Insurance agents, brokers, and service
Liane Levac

Les Escoumins, QC G0T

D-U-N-S 20-431-4652   (SL)
DESMEULES AUTOMOBILES INC
FORD
182 138 Rte, Les Escoumins, QC, G0T 1K0
(418) 233-2490
Emp Here 25   *Sales* 15,732,000
SIC 5511 New and used car dealers
Guy Desmeules

D-U-N-S 24-922-2931   (SL)
LAURENTIAN PILOTAGE AUTHORITY
40 Rue Des Pilotes, Les Escoumins, QC, G0T 1K0
(418) 233-2995
Emp Here 45   *Sales* 12,129,705
SIC 4499 Water transportation services,
Rejean Lantegne

Les Mechins, QC G0J

D-U-N-S 24-942-0571   (HQ)

GROUPE MARITIME VERREAULT INC
108 Rue Du College, Les Mechins, QC, G0J 1T0
(418) 729-3030
Sales 41,822,550
SIC 6712 Bank holding companies
Denise Verreault
Richard Beaupre

D-U-N-S 20-208-1014   (HQ)
VERREAULT NAVIGATION INC
108 Rue Du College, Les Mechins, QC, G0J 1T0
(418) 729-3733
Emp Here 50   *Sales* 33,576,450
SIC 3732 Boatbuilding and repairing
Richard Beaupre
Denise Verreault
Serge Desrosiers
Bruno Fortin

Levis, QC G6C

D-U-N-S 20-191-3969   (SL)
CONCASSES DE LA RIVE-SUD INC
(*Suby of* GESTION DAMIEN MORISSETTE INC)
333 Ch Des Sables, Levis, QC, G6C 1B5
(418) 838-7444
Emp Here 80   *Sales* 21,620,480
SIC 1429 Crushed and broken stone, nec
Francois Morissette
Damien Morissette

D-U-N-S 24-907-1994   (HQ)
GESTION DAMIEN MORISSETTE INC
333 Ch Des Sables, Levis, QC, G6C 1B5
(418) 838-7444
Sales 20,501,250
SIC 6712 Bank holding companies
Francois Morissette

D-U-N-S 24-744-0105   (SL)
SYNDICAT DES SALARIES DE PINTENDRE AUTO
S S P A
914 Rte Du President-Kennedy, Levis, QC, G6C 1A5
(418) 833-8111
Emp Here 49   *Sales* 19,166,742
SIC 8631 Labor organizations
Valere Dumont

Levis, QC G6J

D-U-N-S 24-206-1182   (SL)
ALIMENTATION LAROCHE & FILS INC
MARCHE METRO PLUS
3045 Rte Lagueux Bureau 100, Levis, QC, G6J 1K6
(418) 831-7987
Emp Here 90   *Sales* 26,412,930
SIC 5411 Grocery stores
Marcel Laroche
Bertrand Laroche

D-U-N-S 25-849-9623   (SL)
CONSTRUCTIONS E. HUOT INC
CEH
15 Rue De L'Arena Bureau 400, Levis, QC, G6J 0B1
(418) 836-7310
Emp Here 26   *Sales* 12,239,006
SIC 1542 Nonresidential construction, nec
Daniel Huot
Stephane Huot
Yves Huot

D-U-N-S 20-581-7489   (SL)
ENTREPRISES LEVISIENNES INC, LES
3104 Rte Des Rivieres, Levis, QC, G6J 0B9

(418) 831-4111
Emp Here 58   *Sales* 14,641,636
SIC 1611 Highway and street construction
Jean-Guy Bergeron
Roger Bergeron
Claude Bergeron

Levis, QC G6K

D-U-N-S 20-695-3197   (SL)
CONSTRUCTION MAURICE BILODEAU INC
401 Rue Du Grand-Tronc, Levis, QC, G6K 1K8
(418) 831-4024
Emp Here 40   *Sales* 12,754,760
SIC 1521 Single-family housing construction
Jerome Cote

Levis, QC G6V

D-U-N-S 24-045-9458   (HQ)
9137-0080 QUEBEC INC
ORTHESES BIONICK
5500 Boul Guillaume-Couture Bureau 140, Levis, QC, G6V 4Z2
(418) 830-8800
Emp Here 10   *Sales* 27,274,680
SIC 3842 Surgical appliances and supplies
Nicolas Matte

D-U-N-S 24-070-8511   (SL)
ALIMENTATION ROBERT DESROCHER INC
METRO PLUS LEVIS
44 Rte Du President-Kennedy, Levis, QC, G6V 6C5
(418) 835-6313
Emp Here 49   *Sales* 13,433,448
SIC 5411 Grocery stores
Robert Desrocher

D-U-N-S 25-467-4088   (HQ)
ASSURANCES FONTAINE LEMAY & ASS INC, LES
AFL GROUP FINANCES
5331 Rue Saint-Georges, Levis, QC, G6V 4N4
(418) 835-1150
Emp Here 12   *Sales* 42,403,000
SIC 6411 Insurance agents, brokers, and service
Yan Charbonneau
Marie-Eve Fontaine
Carl Fontaine
Lyne Lapointe

D-U-N-S 20-205-9077   (SL)
AUTO METIVIER INC
LEVIS TOYOTA
160 Rte Du President-Kennedy, Levis, QC, G6V 6E1
(418) 837-4701
Emp Here 45   *Sales* 22,413,510
SIC 5511 New and used car dealers
Clement Dubois
Yvon Tardif

D-U-N-S 24-499-5171   (SL)
AUTOMOBILES LEVIKO (1991) LTEE
144 Rte Du President-Kennedy, Levis, QC, G6V 6C9
(418) 833-7140
Emp Here 25   *Sales* 12,451,950
SIC 5511 New and used car dealers
Pierre Couture

D-U-N-S 20-298-3326   (SL)
BOUVILLIONS-BELLERIVE INC
80 Rue Jacques-Nau Bureau 102, Levis, QC, G6V 9J4
(418) 838-9611
Emp Here 25   *Sales* 20,889,425
SIC 5142 Packaged frozen goods
Eric Riendeau

Daniel Proulx

D-U-N-S 25-944-8348   (SL)
CAMIONS FREIGHTLINER QUEBEC DIVISION LEVIS INC
865 Rue Archimede, Levis, QC, G6V 7M5
(418) 837-3661
Emp Here 21   *Sales* 10,459,638
SIC 5511 New and used car dealers
Paul Tremblay
Bruno De Gagne
Claude Lamontagne

D-U-N-S 24-393-9191   (SL)
CANADIAN TIRE
100 Rte Du President-Kennedy, Levis, QC, G6V 6C9
(418) 833-5525
Emp Here 30   *Sales* 14,942,340
SIC 5531 Auto and home supply stores
Gary Manks
Daniel Audet

D-U-N-S 25-190-9537   (SL)
CAPITAL DESJARDINS INC
DESJARDINS
(*Suby of* FEDERATION DES CAISSES DESJARDINS DU QUEBEC)
100 Av Des Commendeurs, Levis, QC, G6V 7N5
(418) 835-8444
Emp Here 25   *Sales* 4,417,899,585
SIC 6722 Management investment, open-end
Guy Cormier
Jean-Robert Laporte
Yvon Vinet
Chevalier Carole
Annie P. Belanger
Sylvain Dessureault
Yves Genest
Serge Rousseau
Neil Hawthorne
Louis Babineau

D-U-N-S 25-027-1160   (SL)
CENTRE D'ACCUEIL SAINT-JOSEPH DE LEVIS INC
(*Suby of* FEDERATION DES CAISSES DESJARDINS DU QUEBEC)
107 Rue Saint-Louis, Levis, QC, G6V 4G9
(418) 833-3414
Emp Here 180   *Sales* 12,298,680
SIC 8051 Skilled nursing care facilities
Michel Bedard
Christian Pouliot
Christine Malenfant
Pierre Gagnon
Andre Girard
Christine Lessard
Johanne Brien

D-U-N-S 25-488-8886   (HQ)
CENTRE DE READAPTATION EN DEFICIENCE INTELLECTUELLE ET TED
CRDITED DE CHAUDIERE-APPALACHES
55 Rue Du Mont-Marie, Levis, QC, G6V 0B8
(418) 833-3218
Emp Here 60   *Sales* 51,425,600
SIC 8361 Residential care
Corriveau Roger
Julien Andre
Dominique Paquette

D-U-N-S 20-106-9668   (SL)
CENTRE FINANCIER AUX ENTREPRISES DESJARDINS LEVIS LOTBINIERE
CFE LEVIS LOTBINIERE BELLE CHASSE
1610 Boul Alphonse-Desjardins Bureau 600, Levis, QC, G6V 0H1
(418) 834-4343
Emp Here 49   *Sales* 14,042,130
SIC 8741 Management services
Paule Desbiens
Louis Fournier

D-U-N-S 25-776-3995   (HQ)
CENTRES JEUNESSE CHAUDIERE-

APPALACHES, LES
100 Rte Monseigneur-Bourget Bureau 300, Levis, QC, G6V 2Y9
(418) 837-9331
Emp Here 80   *Sales* 42,235,600
SIC 8322 Individual and family services
Caroline Brown

D-U-N-S 20-252-5366   (SL)
CERTAS HOME AND AUTO INSURANCE COMPANY
DESJARDINS ASSURANCES
(*Suby of* FEDERATION DES CAISSES DES-JARDINS DU QUEBEC)
6300 Boul Guillaume-Couture, Levis, QC, G6V 6P9
(418) 835-4900
Emp Here 1,900   *Sales* 9,017,597,600
SIC 6411 Insurance agents, brokers, and service
Jean-Robert Laporte
Jean Royer
Helene Blackburn
Clermont Tremblay
Robert J. Boucher
Alex Johnston
Sonia Gauthier
Claude Lafleur
Michel Magnan
Pierre Reichert

D-U-N-S 24-853-6851   (SL)
CHANTIER DAVIE CANADA INC
(*Suby of* ZM INDUSTRIES LIMITED)
22 Rue George-D.-Davie, Levis, QC, G6V 0K4
(418) 837-5841
Emp Here 300   *Sales* 104,208,300
SIC 4493 Marinas
James Davies
Alex Vicefield

D-U-N-S 24-379-7693   (SL)
CITADELLE CHEVROLET CADILLAC BUICK GMC LTEE
89 Rte Du President-Kennedy, Levis, QC, G6V 6C8
(418) 835-1171
Emp Here 60   *Sales* 37,756,800
SIC 5511 New and used car dealers
Patrick Hebert
Luc Pelletier
Bertrand Hebert

D-U-N-S 24-689-8019   (SL)
COLLEGE DE LEVIS
9 Rue Monseigneur-Gosselin Bureau 109, Levis, QC, G6V 5K1
(418) 833-1249
Emp Here 100   *Sales* 11,263,600
SIC 8221 Colleges and universities
David Lehoux
Luc Paquet
Martine Gosselin
Clemence Poulin
Eric Cote
Tom Lemieux
Andre Veilleux

D-U-N-S 20-712-0259   (BR)
COMMISSION SCOLAIRE DES NAVIGA-TEURS
CENTRE DE FORMATION PROFESSION-NEL DE LEVIS
(*Suby of* COMMISSION SCOLAIRE DES NAVIGATEURS)
30 Rue Vincent-Chagnon, Levis, QC, G6V 4V6
(418) 838-8400
Emp Here 120
SIC 8221 Colleges and universities
Constance Dion

D-U-N-S 25-231-8696   (BR)
COMMISSION SCOLAIRE DES NAVIGA-TEURS
ECOLE POINTE LEVIS
(*Suby of* COMMISSION SCOLAIRE DES NAVIGATEURS)
55 Rue Des Commandeurs, Levis, QC, G6V 6P5
(418) 838-8402
Emp Here 150
SIC 8211 Elementary and secondary schools
Pierre Boulanger

D-U-N-S 25-688-2770   (BR)
COMMISSION SCOLAIRE DES NAVIGA-TEURS
ECOLE NOTRE DAME
(*Suby of* COMMISSION SCOLAIRE DES NAVIGATEURS)
6045 Rue Saint-Georges, Levis, QC, G6V 4K6
(418) 838-8548
Emp Here 250
SIC 8211 Elementary and secondary schools
Julie Gauthier

D-U-N-S 20-277-4477   (HQ)
CRT - EBC, S.E.N.C.
870 Rue Archimede, Levis, QC, G6V 7M5
(418) 833-8073
Emp Here 10   *Sales* 60,982,400
SIC 7363 Help supply services
Denis Turgeon

D-U-N-S 20-247-0456   (HQ)
CRT CONSTRUCTION INC
(*Suby of* GROUPE BE-EXC INC)
870 Rue Archimede, Levis, QC, G6V 7M5
(418) 833-8073
Emp Here 15   *Sales* 12,044,200
SIC 1622 Bridge, tunnel, and elevated highway construction
Denis Turgeon
Jean-Francois Turgeon
Maurice Leroux

D-U-N-S 24-892-3372   (SL)
CRT-HAMEL
870 Rue Archimede, Levis, QC, G6V 7M5
(418) 833-8073
Emp Here 25   *Sales* 14,258,450
SIC 1542 Nonresidential construction, nec
Denis Turgeon

D-U-N-S 24-884-5299   (HQ)
DESJARDINS ASSURANCES GENERALES INC
DESJARDINS ASSURANCES
(*Suby of* FEDERATION DES CAISSES DES-JARDINS DU QUEBEC)
6300 Boul De La Rive-Sud, Levis, QC, G6V 6P9
(418) 835-4850
Emp Here 625   *Sales* 2,136,968,000
SIC 6331 Fire, marine, and casualty insurance
Guy Cormier
Helene Blackburn
Clermont Tremblay
Robert J. Boucher
Alex Johnston
Sonia Gauthier
Henry Jr. Klecan
Claude Lafleur
Michel Magnan
Pierre Reichert

D-U-N-S 20-777-5057   (HQ)
DESJARDINS GROUPE D'ASSURANCES GENERALES INC
PELLETIER, D'AMOURS
(*Suby of* FEDERATION DES CAISSES DES-JARDINS DU QUEBEC)
6300 Boul Guillaume-Couture, Levis, QC, G6V 6P9
(418) 835-4850
Emp Here 1,500   *Sales* 21,751,394,632
SIC 6411 Insurance agents, brokers, and service
Guy Cormier
Jean Royer
Denis Dubois
Helene Blackburn
Clermont Tremblay

Robert J. Boucher
Alex Johnston
Sonia Gauthier
Henry Jr. Klecan
Claude Lafleur

D-U-N-S 20-869-0743   (HQ)
DESJARDINS SECURITE FINANCIERE, COMPAGNIE D'ASSURANCE VIE
DESJARDINS INSURANCE
(*Suby of* FEDERATION DES CAISSES DES-JARDINS DU QUEBEC)
200 Rue Des Commandeurs, Levis, QC, G6V 6R2
(418) 838-7800
Emp Here 1,950   *Sales* 11,520,394,488
SIC 6311 Life insurance
Jean-Robert Laporte
Gregory Chrispin
Francois Cholette
Jacques St-Aubin
Kathleen Bilodeau
Johanne Girard
Johanne Marceau
Francine Martel-Vaillancourt
Normand Provost
Claudia Champagne

D-U-N-S 24-863-3521   (SL)
DEVELOPPEMENT INTERNATIONAL DES-JARDINS INC
150 Rue Des Commandeurs, Levis, QC, G6V 6P8
(418) 835-2400
Emp Here 100   *Sales* 12,477,600
SIC 8741 Management services
Gerardo Almaguer
Danielle Amyot
Mario Simard
Normand De Montigny
Marcel Lauzon
Valerie Dion
Teresa Alvarez
Bernard Decaluwe
Jacques Lirette
Rejean Bellemare

D-U-N-S 25-164-6592   (BR)
ENERGIE VALERO INC
UTRAMAR RAFFINERIE JEAN GAULIN
(*Suby of* VALERO ENERGY CORPORATION)
165 Ch Des Iles, Levis, QC, G6V 7M5
(418) 837-3641
Emp Here 500
SIC 2911 Petroleum refining
Larry Werderich

D-U-N-S 20-953-2225   (HQ)
EXCAVATIONS LAFONTAINE INC, LES
GROUPE LAFONTAINE
872 Rue Archimede Bureau 92, Levis, QC, G6V 7M5
(418) 838-2121
Sales 25,244,200
SIC 1623 Water, sewer, and utility lines
Frankie Lafontaine
Mathieu Lafontaine
Francine Turgeon
Francois Lafontaine

D-U-N-S 20-247-0126   (HQ)
EXCELDOR COOPERATIVE
AVICOLE
5700 Rue J.-B.-Michaud Suite 500, Levis, QC, G6V 0B1
(418) 830-5600
Emp Here 850   *Sales* 682,339,000
SIC 2015 Poultry slaughtering and processing
Rene Proulx
Yves Cote
Francois Turcotte
Christian Jacques
Louis Ferland
Patrick Lavallee
Sebastien Charrois
Gerard Aeschlimann

D-U-N-S 20-387-1322   (SL)
EXCELDOR COOPERATIVE
5700 Rue J.-B.-Michaud Bureau 500, Levis, QC, G6V 0B1
(418) 830-5600
Emp Here 750   *Sales* 259,267,500
SIC 2015 Poultry slaughtering and processing
Yves Cote
Rene Proulx
Francois Turcotte
Louis Ferland
Patrick Lavallee
Sebastien Charrois
Gerard Aeschlimann
Christian Jacques

D-U-N-S 20-644-1842   (HQ)
FEDERATION DES CAISSES DESJARDINS DU QUEBEC
A PROPOS
100 Rue Des Commandeurs, Levis, QC, G6V 7N5
(418) 835-8444
Emp Here 1,060   *Sales* 9,691,568,435
SIC 6062 State credit unions
Guy Cormier
Serge Rousseau
Michel Tourangeau
Yvon Vinet
Carole Chevalier
Neil Hawthorn
Stephane Corbeil
Stephane Trottier
Louis Babineau
Jean-Francois Laporte

D-U-N-S 24-884-4938   (SL)
FONDS DE SECURITE DESJARDINS
DESJARDINS FONDS DE SECURITE
100 Av Des Commandeurs, Levis, QC, G6V 7N5

Emp Here 11   *Sales* 11,383,691
SIC 6351 Surety insurance
Pierre Labelle
Pierre Leblanc
Benoit Turcotte
Andre Lafortune

D-U-N-S 20-265-5064   (HQ)
GESTION N. AUGER INC
MCDONALD
5480 Rue Saint-Georges, Levis, QC, G6V 4M6
(418) 833-3241
Emp Here 100   *Sales* 4,551,900
SIC 5812 Eating places
Natalie Auger

D-U-N-S 20-386-9909   (SL)
GROUPE AUTOMOTIVE HOLAND LEVIS INC
BMW LEVIS
5303 Rue Louis-H.-La Fontaine, Levis, QC, G6V 8X4
(418) 830-5000
Emp Here 24   *Sales* 11,953,872
SIC 5521 Used car dealers
Gad Bitton
Michael Serruya
Jean-Francois Tremblay

D-U-N-S 24-863-6110   (HQ)
GROUPE BE-EXC INC
870 Rue Archimede Bureau 92, Levis, QC, G6V 7M5
(418) 833-8073
Sales 12,044,200
SIC 1622 Bridge, tunnel, and elevated highway construction
Denis Turgeon
Jean-Francois Turgeon
Maurice Leroux

D-U-N-S 20-577-1046   (SL)
JOURNAL LE PEUPLE LEVIS
5790 Boul Etienne-Dallaire, Levis, QC, G6V

8V6
(418) 833-9398
Emp Here 30   *Sales* 22,275,600
SIC 5192 Books, periodicals, and newspapers
 Bertrand Picard

D-U-N-S 25-248-2617   (SL)
LEMIEUX ASSURANCES INC
ASSURANCES FORTIN FRECHETTE
1610 Boul Alphonse-Desjardins, Levis, QC,
G6V 0H1
(418) 835-0939
Emp Here 26   *Sales* 22,049,560
SIC 6411 Insurance agents, brokers, and service
 Francois Lemieux

D-U-N-S 20-107-0427   (HQ)
LEMIEUX NOLET, COMPTABLES AGREES S.E.N.C.R.L.
LEMIEUX NOLET, CONSULTANTS
1610 Boul Alphonse-Desjardins Bureau 400,
Levis, QC, G6V 0H1
(418) 833-2114
Emp Here 60   *Sales* 20,768,500
SIC 8721 Accounting, auditing, and bookkeeping
 Eric Lachance
 Christian Guy
 Sylvain Lachance
 Martin Poirier
 Claude Moisan
 Francois Fillion
 Alain Fortier
 Stephane Dumas
 Marc-Andre Thibault
 Sylvain Moisan

D-U-N-S 25-818-6071   (BR)
MARTIN, CLAUDE & MARCEL INC
ST-HUBERT RESTAURANTS
(*Suby of* 2621-9386 QUEBEC INC)
49c Rte Du President-Kennedy, Levis, QC,
G6V 6C3
(418) 835-1234
Emp Here 150
SIC 5812 Eating places
 Salah Alazoui

D-U-N-S 20-430-8423   (SL)
P.H. TECH INC
8650 Boul Guillaume-Couture Bureau 220,
Levis, QC, G6V 9G9
(418) 833-3231
Emp Here 250   *Sales* 59,703,000
SIC 3089 Plastics products, nec
 Caroline Dallaire
 Jean-Lou Paquet
 Nicolas Renaud
 Christian Turgeon

D-U-N-S 20-205-9234   (HQ)
PAQUET & FILS LTEE
SOBEC
4 Rue Du Terroir, Levis, QC, G6V 9J3
(418) 833-9602
Sales 50,288,040
SIC 5172 Petroleum products, nec
 Jacques Paquet
 Simon Paquet
 Michel Paquet

D-U-N-S 24-941-7775   (SL)
PARE CENTRE DU CAMION WHITE GMC INC
PARE CENTRE DU CAMION VOLVO
(*Suby of* GESTION N L J M S INC)
250 Rte Du President-Kennedy, Levis, QC,
G6V 9J6
(418) 833-5333
Emp Here 45   *Sales* 28,317,600
SIC 5511 New and used car dealers
 Normand Pare

D-U-N-S 24-149-1992   (SL)
PATRO DE LEVIS INC, LE
6150 Rue Saint-Georges, Levis, QC, G6V 4J8

(418) 833-4477
Emp Here 140   *Sales* 10,750,880
SIC 8322 Individual and family services
 Daniel Dussault
 Jean Lessard

D-U-N-S 20-579-6873   (BR)
PEPSICO CANADA ULC
FRITO-LAY CANADA
(*Suby of* PEPSICO, INC.)
8450 Boul Guillaume-Couture, Levis, QC,
G6V 7L7
(418) 833-2121
Emp Here 450
SIC 2096 Potato chips and similar snacks
 France Poirier

D-U-N-S 20-763-5137   (SL)
PERSONNELLE ASSURANCES GENERALES INC, LA
LA PERSONNELLE
(*Suby of* FEDERATION DES CAISSES DESJARDINS DU QUEBEC)
6300 Boul De La Rive-Sud, Levis, QC, G6V 6P9
(418) 835-4850
Emp Here 250   *Sales* 534,242,000
SIC 6331 Fire, marine, and casualty insurance
 Guy Cormier
 Helene Blackburn
 Clermont Tremblay
 Robert J. Boucher
 Alex Johnston
 Sonia Gauthier
 Henry Jr. Klecan
 Claude Lafleur
 Michel Magnan
 Pierre Reichert

D-U-N-S 24-248-7390   (SL)
PHARMALAB INC
(*Suby of* LABORATOIRES C.O.P. INC)
8750 Boul Guillaume-Couture, Levis, QC,
G6V 9G9
(418) 833-7603
Emp Here 100   *Sales* 28,402,100
SIC 2834 Pharmaceutical preparations
 Melanie Stack
 Olivier Benloulou
 Alain Roy
 Martin Faucher

D-U-N-S 20-205-9465   (SL)
RINFRET AUTO INC
RINFRET VOLKSWAGEN
5355 Boul Guillaume-Couture, Levis, QC,
G6V 4Z3
(418) 833-2133
Emp Here 22   *Sales* 10,957,716
SIC 5511 New and used car dealers
 Denis Rinfret

D-U-N-S 24-380-0075   (SL)
SUZANNE ROY FORD INC
61 Rte Du President-Kennedy, Levis, QC, G6V 6C7
(418) 835-1915
Emp Here 30   *Sales* 14,942,340
SIC 5511 New and used car dealers

D-U-N-S 20-059-1399   (SL)
TOURNEES CLUB SELECT INC, LES
VOYAGES LA CLE DES CHAMPS
874 Rue Archimede, Levis, QC, G6V 7M5
(418) 835-3336
Emp Here 26   *Sales* 10,019,360
SIC 4725 Tour operators
 Real Boissonneault
 Paul Leblanc

D-U-N-S 25-692-0344   (SL)
TRANS BIOTECH
TRANS-TECH NETWORK
201 Mgr Bourget, Levis, QC, G6V 9V6
(418) 833-8876
Emp Here 250   *Sales* 51,020,500
SIC 8731 Commercial physical research
 Denis Beaumont

 Diane Cantin
 Marie-Helene Girard
 Suzanne Leclerc

D-U-N-S 24-689-7029   (HQ)
TRANSPORT JACQUES AUGER INC
QUEENSWAY TANK LINES
860 Rue Archimede, Levis, QC, G6V 7M5
(418) 835-9266
Emp Here 250   *Sales* 46,095,250
SIC 4212 Local trucking, without storage
 Jacques Auger

D-U-N-S 20-583-1709   (BR)
UNIVERSITE DU QUEBEC
CAMPUS DE LEVIS
(*Suby of* UNIVERSITE DU QUEBEC)
1595 Boul Alphonse-Desjardins, Levis, QC,
G6V 0A6
(418) 833-8800
Emp Here 100
SIC 8221 Colleges and universities
 Jean Nil-Theriault

D-U-N-S 20-205-9887   (HQ)
VITRERIE LEVIS INC
FEN-ESCOMPTE VL
12 Rue Du Terroir, Levis, QC, G6V 9J3
(418) 833-2161
Sales 15,651,090
SIC 5031 Lumber, plywood, and millwork
 Mario Levesque

D-U-N-S 25-498-2580   (BR)
WAL-MART CANADA CORP
WALMART DE LEVIS
(*Suby of* WALMART INC.)
5303 Rue Louis-H.-La Fontaine, Levis, QC,
G6V 8X4
(418) 833-8555
Emp Here 150
SIC 5311 Department stores
 Gilbert Roy

Levis, QC G6W

D-U-N-S 25-920-3347   (SL)
9050-7641 QUEBEC INC
RAMP-ART
4457 Boul Guillaume-Couture, Levis, QC,
G6W 6M9
(418) 838-4464
Emp Here 26   *Sales* 11,626,524
SIC 5039 Construction materials, nec
 Robert Michaud
 Yves Lacombe

D-U-N-S 25-114-6841   (HQ)
ACIER PICARD INC
3000 Rue De L'Etchemin, Levis, QC, G6W 7X6
(418) 834-8300
Emp Here 15   *Sales* 22,358,700
SIC 5051 Metals service centers and offices
 Gaetan Picard
 Genevieve Fournier-Picard
 Rejean Bacon
 Karine Fournier-Picard
 Michel Bedard
 Gino Ste-Croix
 Marc-Andre Dion

D-U-N-S 25-762-5665   (SL)
ANCIA PERSONNEL INC
ANCIA
469 Av Taniata Bureau 400, Levis, QC, G6W 5M6

Emp Here 100   *Sales* 15,537,100
SIC 7361 Employment agencies
 Francois Lefebvre
 Sophie Fortie

D-U-N-S 20-257-1089   (SL)
ARMOIRES DE CUISINE BERNIER INC

1955 3e Rue Bureau 70, Levis, QC, G6W 5M6
(418) 839-8142
Emp Here 75   *Sales* 11,689,725
SIC 2434 Wood kitchen cabinets
 Yvon Bernier

D-U-N-S 24-530-3516   (HQ)
AUTOBUS AUGER INC
880 Rue De Saint-Romuald, Levis, QC, G6W 5M6
(418) 833-2181
Sales 15,054,400
SIC 4151 School buses
 Michel Auger
 Sylvain Auger
 Marie Frederique Auger

D-U-N-S 24-637-0944   (SL)
BOIS AISE DE MONTREAL INC
(*Suby of* BOIS BONSAI INC)
1190a Rue De Courchevel Bureau 420, Levis,
QC, G6W 0M5
(418) 832-4200
Emp Here 4   *Sales* 14,134,171
SIC 5031 Lumber, plywood, and millwork
 Christian Roy
 Michel Belanger
 Philippe Lambert

D-U-N-S 24-343-8673   (HQ)
CAISSE DESJARDINS DE LA CHAUDIERE
CENTRE DE SERVICE DE SAINT-LAMBERT-DE-LAUZON
1190b Rue De Courchevel Bureau 103, Levis,
QC, G6W 0M6
(418) 839-8819
Emp Here 45   *Sales* 19,678,255
SIC 6062 State credit unions
 Louis-Marie Bissonnette
 Colin Bilodeau
 Lucie Leclerc
 Adrien Blom
 Pierre Boulanger
 Christine Caron
 Benoit Charette
 Audrey Dutilly
 Christian Giroux
 Johanne Gregoire

D-U-N-S 20-248-6874   (HQ)
COMETAL INC
2965 Boul Guillaume-Couture, Levis, QC,
G6W 6N6
(418) 839-8831
Sales 26,830,440
SIC 5075 Warm air heating and air conditioning
 Alain Poulin
 Nicolas Girard
 Jean-Michel Deblois

D-U-N-S 25-527-4391   (HQ)
COMMISSION SCOLAIRE DES NAVIGATEURS
ECOLE DU BAC
1860 1re Rue Bureau 90, Levis, QC, G6W 5M6
(418) 839-0500
Emp Here 100   *Sales* 297,357,000
SIC 8211 Elementary and secondary schools
 Leopold Castonguay
 Joanne Plourde

D-U-N-S 25-831-2776   (SL)
CONSTRUCTION RAOUL PELLETIER (1997) INC
(*Suby of* LOCATION RAOUL PELLETIER INC)
3650 Boul Guillaume-Couture, Levis, QC,
G6W 7L3
(418) 837-9833
Emp Here 100   *Sales* 24,618,600
SIC 1794 Excavation work
 Ghislain Pelletier
 Michel Pelletier
 Benjamin Pelletier

D-U-N-S 25-763-0178   (SL)

CONTROLES A.C. INC, LES
CONTROLES AC
(*Suby of* ENGIE SERVICES INC)
2185 5e Rue, Levis, QC, G6W 5M6
(418) 834-2777
Emp Here 50   *Sales* 22,358,700
SIC 5075 Warm air heating and air conditioning
Pierre Lapointe
Real Audet
Luc Duguay
Richard Pinard
Jean-Marc Therrien
John Rohde

D-U-N-S 24-746-0272   (SL)
COURTIERS EN TRANSPORT G.M.R. INC, LES
G.M.R. FREIGHT BROKERS
2111 4e Rue Bureau 100, Levis, QC, G6W 5M6
(418) 839-5768
Emp Here 22   *Sales* 11,439,274
SIC 4731 Freight transportation arrangement
Martin Tremblay

D-U-N-S 20-248-7112   (HQ)
COUVRE-PLANCHERS PELLETIER INC
COUVRE PLANCHERS MAURICE PELLETIER
4600 Boul Guillaume-Couture, Levis, QC, G6W 5N6
(418) 837-3681
Sales 16,268,210
SIC 5713 Floor covering stores
Yvan Pelletier
Sabrina Pelletier
Dominique Gagnon

D-U-N-S 20-059-0790   (HQ)
CREAFORM INC
JOURNEE DE LA METROLOGIE EN AEROSPATIALE
(*Suby of* AMETEK CREAFORM INC)
4700 Rue De La Pascaline, Levis, QC, G6W 0L9
(418) 833-4446
Sales 56,557,750
SIC 7373 Computer integrated systems design
Fanny Truchon
Bernard G. Boulet
Bruce P. Wilson

D-U-N-S 24-161-2600   (SL)
CUT TECHNOLOGIES
460 3e Av Bureau 100, Levis, QC, G6W 5M6
(418) 834-7772
Emp Here 100   *Sales* 47,502,600
SIC 5084 Industrial machinery and equipment
Mike Cloutier

D-U-N-S 20-188-6905   (HQ)
DEQ SYSTEMS CORP
(*Suby of* SCIENTIFIC GAMES CORPORATION)
1840 1re Rue Bureau 103a, Levis, QC, G6W 5M6
(418) 839-3012
Emp Here 5   *Sales* 41,297,760
SIC 6799 Investors, nec
Joseph Bertolone

D-U-N-S 24-940-5903   (SL)
DISTRIBUTIONS BEAULAC, CARL INC, LES
BEAULAC TRANSPORT
15 Rue Des Emeraudes, Levis, QC, G6W 6Y7
(418) 835-1414
Emp Here 105   *Sales* 21,599,130
SIC 4213 Trucking, except local
Carl Beaulac
Danielle Johnston

D-U-N-S 25-384-1035   (HQ)
EVIMBEC LTEE
(*Suby of* NORDA STELO INC)
1175 Boul Guillaume-Couture Bureau 200,

Levis, QC, G6W 0S2
(418) 834-7000
Sales 23,428,800
SIC 8742 Management consulting services
Serge Dussault
Pierre-Luc Dussault

D-U-N-S 20-870-5178   (SL)
GARAGE CLEMENT FOURNIER INC
VITRXPERT LEVIS
4560 Boul Guillaume-Couture, Levis, QC, G6W 6M7
(418) 837-0859
Emp Here 26   *Sales* 12,950,028
SIC 5541 Gasoline service stations
Clement Fournier

D-U-N-S 25-355-3127   (SL)
GESTION R.M.L. RODRIGUE INC
1890 1re Rue, Levis, QC, G6W 5M6
(418) 839-0671
Emp Here 120   *Sales* 26,640,120
SIC 3564 Blowers and fans
Claude Rodrigue

D-U-N-S 24-205-1563   (SL)
GESTION REJEAN LEGER INC
CANADIAN TIRE
600 Rue De La Concorde, Levis, QC, G6W 8A8
(418) 839-9797
Emp Here 90   *Sales* 24,088,680
SIC 5251 Hardware stores
Rejean Leger

D-U-N-S 25-293-2967   (BR)
GESTION TFI, SOCIETE EN COMMANDITE
TFI HOLDINGS LIMITED PARTNERSHIP
(*Suby of* GESTION TFI, SOCIETE EN COMMANDITE)
1950 3e Rue, Levis, QC, G6W 5M6

Emp Here 75
SIC 4213 Trucking, except local

D-U-N-S 24-378-8150   (SL)
GLOBCO INTERNATIONAL INC
CIBELYE IMPORT-EXPORT
(*Suby of* 9146-5047 QUEBEC INC)
1660 Boul Guillaume-Couture, Levis, QC, G6W 5M6
(418) 834-1844
Emp Here 51   *Sales* 10,491,006
SIC 4213 Trucking, except local
Alain Levasseur
Denis Harrisson

D-U-N-S 25-370-1999   (BR)
GOUVERNEMENT DE LA PROVINCE DE QUEBEC
FINANCIERE AGRICOLE DU QUEBEC
(*Suby of* GOUVERNEMENT DE LA PROVINCE DE QUEBEC)
1400 Boul Guillaume-Couture Unite Rc, Levis, QC, G6W 8K7
(418) 838-5615
Emp Here 125
SIC 8748 Business consulting, nec

D-U-N-S 24-826-8554   (HQ)
GROUPE LEVASSE INC
(*Suby of* 9146-5047 QUEBEC INC)
1660 Boul Guillaume-Couture, Levis, QC, G6W 0R5
(418) 834-1844
Emp Here 48   *Sales* 11,313,830
SIC 4213 Trucking, except local
Alain Levasseur
Denis Harrisson

D-U-N-S 20-703-2322   (HQ)
GROUPE SANFACON INC, LE
1980 5e Rue, Levis, QC, G6W 5M6
(418) 839-1370
Emp Here 4   *Sales* 27,335,000
SIC 6712 Bank holding companies
Claude Sanfacon
Richard Sanfacon

Bruno Sanfacon
Helene Sanfacon

D-U-N-S 20-430-2392   (SL)
HAMEL INC
436 Av Taniata, Levis, QC, G6W 5M6
(418) 839-4193
Emp Here 50   *Sales* 11,242,750
SIC 2038 Frozen specialties, nec
Yvon Hamel Jr

D-U-N-S 24-358-4187   (BR)
HOME DEPOT OF CANADA INC
HOME DEPOT STORE # 7189
(*Suby of* THE HOME DEPOT INC)
500 Rue De La Concorde, Levis, QC, G6W 8A8
(418) 834-7050
Emp Here 125
SIC 5251 Hardware stores
Nocolas Vanier

D-U-N-S 20-820-7147   (SL)
LOCATION RAOUL PELLETIER INC
3650 Boul Guillaume-Couture, Levis, QC, G6W 7L3
(418) 837-2147
Emp Here 49   *Sales* 13,276,158
SIC 1521 Single-family housing construction
Ghislain Pelletier
Michel Pelletier
Joel Couture
Benjamin Pelletier
Sylvie Pelletier
Eric Turcotte

D-U-N-S 24-790-9179   (HQ)
LOCATION RAOUL PELLETIER INC
3650 Boul Guillaume-Couture, Levis, QC, G6W 7L3
(418) 837-2147
Sales 25,244,200
SIC 1623 Water, sewer, and utility lines
Ghislain Pelletier
Michel Pelletier

D-U-N-S 24-940-6901   (SL)
LOGISCO INC
LOGISCO GROUPE IMMOBILIER
950 Rue De La Concorde Bureau 302, Levis, QC, G6W 8A8
(418) 834-4999
Emp Here 50   *Sales* 16,356,350
SIC 6531 Real estate agents and managers
Michel Parent
Roger Parent

D-U-N-S 20-242-1731   (HQ)
MAIBEC INC
INDUSTRIES MAIBEC
1984 5e Rue Bureau 202, Levis, QC, G6W 5M6
(418) 830-8855
Emp Here 45   *Sales* 222,712,000
SIC 2421 Sawmills and planing mills, general
Francois Tardif
Charles Tardif
Jacques Vachon
Gilbert Tardif
Patrick Labonte

D-U-N-S 20-291-2366   (HQ)
MISTRAS SERVICES INC
SPG HYDRO INTERNATIONAL
(*Suby of* MISTRAS GROUP, INC.)
765 Rue De Saint-Romuald, Levis, QC, G6W 5M6
(418) 837-4664
Emp Here 63   *Sales* 51,020,500
SIC 8734 Testing laboratories
Dennis Bertolotti
Yves Richer
Michael C. Keefe
Michael J. Lange

D-U-N-S 24-373-7124   (SL)
MTI CANADA INC
DISTRIBUTION TTI

1720 Boul Guillaume-Couture, Levis, QC, G6W 5M6
(418) 839-4127
Emp Here 50   *Sales* 23,751,300
SIC 5083 Farm and garden machinery
Jean Bacon
Joanne Lebel

D-U-N-S 24-791-7404   (SL)
OMEGACHEM INC
480 Rue Perreault, Levis, QC, G6W 7V6
(418) 837-4444
Emp Here 50   *Sales* 13,833,000
SIC 2834 Pharmaceutical preparations
Francois Laflamme
Eric Pelchat

D-U-N-S 25-459-8543   (SL)
PAQUET NISSAN INC
3580 Boul Guillaume-Couture, Levis, QC, G6W 6N7
(418) 838-3838
Emp Here 34   *Sales* 21,395,520
SIC 5511 New and used car dealers
Gratien Paquet
Yolande Alain
Stephane Paquet

D-U-N-S 25-627-9738   (SL)
QSL QUEBEC INC
(*Suby of* MISTRAS GROUP, INC.)
765 Rue De Saint-Romuald, Levis, QC, G6W 5M6
(418) 837-4664
Emp Here 150   *Sales* 47,957,550
SIC 8734 Testing laboratories
Michale J Lange
Yves Richer
Valerie Goulet
Sotirios J. Vahaviolos
Dennis Bertolotti

D-U-N-S 20-265-9355   (HQ)
RODRIGUE METAL LTEE
(*Suby of* CANERECTOR INC)
1890 1re Rue, Levis, QC, G6W 5M6
(418) 839-0400
Emp Here 60   *Sales* 17,760,080
SIC 3569 General industrial machinery, nec
Daniel Beaupre
Tim Buckland
William Nickel
Amanda Hawkins
Pierre Desormeaux

D-U-N-S 25-991-4745   (SL)
SILO SUPERIEUR (1993) INC
520 2e Av, Levis, QC, G6W 5M6
(418) 839-8808
Emp Here 45   *Sales* 10,504,575
SIC 3272 Concrete products, nec
Eric Vallieres
Dominique Vallieres
David Vallieres
Mario Lebel

D-U-N-S 20-871-7509   (BR)
SOBEYS QUEBEC INC
IGA EXTRA
1060 Boul Guillaume-Couture, Levis, QC, G6W 5M6
(418) 834-3811
Emp Here 150
SIC 5411 Grocery stores
Stephane Tardis

D-U-N-S 20-317-7704   (SL)
SUPERMETAL QUEBEC INC
(*Suby of* GESTION RELEVE SMS INC)
1955 5e Rue, Levis, QC, G6W 5M6
(418) 834-1955
Emp Here 50   *Sales* 12,309,300
SIC 1791 Structural steel erection
Jean-Francois Blouin

D-U-N-S 20-264-7731   (HQ)
SUPERMETAL STRUCTURES INC
SUPERMETAL DIVISION DE L'OUEST

▲ Public Company   ■ Public Company Family Member   **HQ** Headquarters   **BR** Branch   **SL** Single Location

(*Suby of* GESTION RELEVE SMS INC)
1955 5e Rue, Levis, QC, G6W 5M6
(418) 834-1955
Emp Here 70   *Sales* 85,130,850
SIC 3441 Fabricated structural Metal
 Jean-Francois Blouin
 Michel Marcotte
 Jacques Blouin
 Marc Robitaille
 Bruno Vien
 Jean-Francois Leclerc
 Andre Bouchard
 Andre Bougie

D-U-N-S 25-368-5457   (HQ)
TRANSPORT TFI 11 S.E.C.
TRANSPORT ST-LAMBERT
1956b 3e Rue, Levis, QC, G6W 5M6
(418) 839-6655
Sales 20,570,600
SIC 4213 Trucking, except local
 Jean-Francois Dodier

D-U-N-S 24-853-4476   (HQ)
TRANSPORT TFI 6 S.E.C.
BESNER
1950 3e Rue, Levis, QC, G6W 5M6
(418) 834-9891
Emp Here 10   *Sales* 20,570,600
SIC 4213 Trucking, except local
 Alain Bedard

D-U-N-S 24-638-9597   (SL)
TRANSPORT YN.-GONTHIER INC
2170 3e Rue, Levis, QC, G6W 6V4
(418) 839-7311
Emp Here 91   *Sales* 13,485,472
SIC 4212 Local trucking, without storage
 Yvan Gonthier
 Nancy Bolduc

D-U-N-S 25-993-0795   (SL)
VEOLIA SERVICE A L'ENVIRONNEMENT
VEOLIA SERVICE A L'ENVIRONNEMENT
2800 Rue De L'Etchemin, Levis, QC, G6W
7X6
(418) 833-6840
Emp Here 49   *Sales* 11,480,112
SIC 8748 Business consulting, nec

D-U-N-S 24-319-5075   (BR)
WAL-MART CANADA CORP
WALMART
(*Suby of* WALMART INC.)
700 Rue De La Concorde, Levis, QC, G6W
8A8
(418) 834-5115
Emp Here 120
SIC 5311 Department stores
 Phierry Roberge

Levis, QC G6X

D-U-N-S 25-822-0383   (BR)
**BLANCHETTE VACHON ET ASSOCIES CA
SENCRL**
(*Suby of* BLANCHETTE VACHON ET ASSO-
CIES CA SENCRL)
8149 Rue Du Mistral Bureau 202, Levis, QC,
G6X 1G5
(418) 387-3636
Emp Here 100
SIC 8721 Accounting, auditing, and book-
keeping
 Mario Gosselin

D-U-N-S 25-496-0495   (HQ)
CENTRE DE SANTE PAUL GILBERT
9330 Boul Du Centre-Hospitalier, Levis, QC,
G6X 1L6
(418) 380-8993
Sales 72,202,000
SIC 8069 Specialty hospitals, except psychi-
atric
 Rock Boucher

D-U-N-S 20-016-4734   (SL)
CENTRIX ENVIRONNEMENT INC
5314 Av Des Belles-Amours Bureau 104,
Levis, QC, G6X 1P2
(418) 988-3888
Emp Here 90   *Sales* 23,539,770
SIC 6712 Bank holding companies
 Joel Deschenes

D-U-N-S 24-729-4200   (SL)
COFFRAGES L.D. INC
(*Suby of* 9011-4497 QUEBEC INC)
2621 Av De La Rotonde, Levis, QC, G6X 2M2
(418) 832-7070
Emp Here 100   *Sales* 24,618,600
SIC 1799 Special trade contractors, nec
 Leandre Drouin
 Sony Petitpas
 M. Celine Drouin

D-U-N-S 25-234-0526   (BR)
**COMMISSION SCOLAIRE DES NAVIGA-
TEURS**
ECOLE SECONDAIRE LES ETCHEMINS
(*Suby of* COMMISSION SCOLAIRE DES
NAVIGATEURS)
3724 Av Des Eglises, Levis, QC, G6X 1X4
(418) 839-0500
Emp Here 190
SIC 8211 Elementary and secondary schools
 Benoit Langlois

D-U-N-S 20-580-5018   (BR)
**COMPAGNIE DES CHEMINS DE FER NA-
TIONAUX DU CANADA**
CANADIEN NATIONAL
(*Suby of* COMPAGNIE DES CHEMINS DE
FER NATIONAUX DU CANADA)
2600 Av De La Rotonde, Levis, QC, G6X 2M1

Emp Here 250
SIC 4011 Railroads, line-haul operating
 Gilbert Dunberry

D-U-N-S 20-027-6004   (SL)
DP IMMOBILIER QUEBEC INC
COMFREE
(*Suby of* PURPLEBRICKS GROUP PLC)
8389 Av Sous-Le-Vent Bureau 300, Levis, QC,
G6X 1K7
(418) 832-2222
Emp Here 100   *Sales* 22,087,100
SIC 6513 Apartment building operators
 Marco Dodier
 Marie-Christine Blain
 Ken Taylor
 David Alan Eckert
 Jean-Bruno Lessard

D-U-N-S 20-582-2661   (HQ)
MATELAS DAUPHIN INC
IMMEUBLES DAUPHIN
8124 Rue Du Blizzard, Levis, QC, G6X 1C9
(418) 832-2951
Emp Here 35   *Sales* 10,030,930
SIC 2515 Mattresses and bedsprings
 Real Theriault
 Marjolaine Theriault
 Steven Theriault

D-U-N-S 25-463-1294   (SL)
METRO CHARNY INC
8032 Av Des Eglises, Levis, QC, G6X 1X7
(418) 832-5346
Emp Here 65   *Sales* 19,076,005
SIC 5411 Grocery stores
 Jean Lebel

D-U-N-S 24-496-1160   (BR)
QUALIFAB INC
(*Suby of* 2688204 CANADA INC)
2256 Av De La Rotonde, Levis, QC, G6X 2L8
(418) 832-9193
Emp Here 100
SIC 3498 Fabricated pipe and fittings
 Frederic Halle

D-U-N-S 20-241-3951   (SL)

SANIMAX ACI INC
(*Suby of* JO-AL DISTRIBUTING LTD)
2001 Av De La Rotonde, Levis, QC, G6X 2L8
(418) 832-4645
Emp Here 90   *Sales* 31,112,100
SIC 2077 Animal and marine fats and oils
 Martin Couture
 Francois Berthiaume
 Vincent Brossard
 Andre Couture

D-U-N-S 20-381-1286   (SL)
WOOD FIBER CANADA INC
INDUSTRIELS SIMONDS, LES
2341 Av De La Rotonde, Levis, QC, G6X 2M2
(418) 832-2918
Emp Here 50   *Sales* 10,141,500
SIC 3425 Saw blades and handsaws
 Sylvain St-Hilaire
 Michael Refolo
 Henry Botticello
 John Consentino
 Michael Jackson
 Joe Neil
 Habib Y. Gorgi
 Thomas S. Bagley
 John J. Starcevich
 Craig Tompkins

Levis, QC G6Y

D-U-N-S 24-568-4022   (SL)
190937 CANADA LTEE
AUDI LEVIS
6000 Rue Des Moissons, Levis, QC, G6Y 0Z6
(418) 830-2834
Emp Here 26   *Sales* 12,950,028
SIC 5511 New and used car dealers
 Marie-Josee Begin
 Pierre Begin

D-U-N-S 20-216-9038   (SL)
9218-8069 QUEBEC INC
KIA LEVIS
5990 Boul Wilfrid-Carrier, Levis, QC, G6Y 9X9
(418) 837-9199
Emp Here 26   *Sales* 12,950,028
SIC 5511 New and used car dealers
 Marcel Lacasse
 Helene Taillefer
 Renee Savoie

D-U-N-S 20-204-8765   (HQ)
CYCLES LAMBERT INC
EVO MC
(*Suby of* BARRETT DIVERSIFIED INC)
1000 Rue Des Riveurs, Levis, QC, G6Y 9G3
(418) 835-1685
Sales 13,667,500
SIC 6712 Bank holding companies
 Edward Barett
 William Barrett
 Eric D'anjou
 Mathieu Cardinal

D-U-N-S 25-744-9025   (SL)
**FRUITS & LEGUMES ERIC FRECHETTE
INC, LES**
TASTE OF THE NORTH
750 Rue Jean-Marchand, Levis, QC, G6Y 9G6
(418) 835-6997
Emp Here 25   *Sales* 20,889,425
SIC 5148 Fresh fruits and vegetables
 Eric Frechette

D-U-N-S 24-568-8072   (BR)
MULTI-MARQUES INC
LEVIS DISTRIBUTION CENTRE
(*Suby of* GRUPO BIMBO, S.A.B. DE C.V.)
845 Rue Jean-Marchand, Levis, QC, G6Y 9G4
(418) 837-3611
Emp Here 80
SIC 5461 Retail bakeries
 Pierre Chalafour

D-U-N-S 20-431-7622   (SL)
PIECES D'AUTO TRANSIT INC, LES
TRANSIT WAREHOUSE DISTRIBUTION
1100 Rue Jean-Marchand, Levis, QC, G6Y
9G8
(866) 937-8916
Emp Here 35   *Sales* 12,747,525
SIC 5013 Motor vehicle supplies and new
parts
 Stephane Guay

D-U-N-S 20-777-3909   (SL)
SOCIETE VIA ENVIRONNEMENT
SOCIETE VIA
1200 Rue Des Riveurs, Levis, QC, G6Y 9G2
(418) 833-0421
Emp Here 49   *Sales* 14,755,958
SIC 4953 Refuse systems
 Jean-Guy Guay

D-U-N-S 20-582-1960   (SL)
STURO METAL INC
(*Suby of* GROUPE HONCO INC)
600 Rue Jean-Marchand, Levis, QC, G6Y 9G6
(418) 833-2107
Emp Here 50   *Sales* 15,764,504
SIC 3441 Fabricated structural Metal
 Francis Lacasse
 Harry Lacassa
 Carole Lacasse
 Vicky Lacasse

D-U-N-S 25-190-3522   (BR)
TEKNION LIMITED
TEKNION CONCEPT
(*Suby of* GLOBAL UPHOLSTERY CO LIM-
ITED)
975 Rue Des Calfats Bureau 45, Levis, QC,
G6Y 9E8
(418) 833-0047
Emp Here 230
SIC 2522 Office furniture, except wood
 Yves Lamontagne

D-U-N-S 20-697-3690   (SL)
TEKNION ROY & BRETON INC
*CENTRE SERVICES CLIENTS ET INNOVA-
TION*
(*Suby of* GLOBAL UPHOLSTERY CO LIM-
ITED)
975 Rue Des Calfats, Levis, QC, G6Y 9E8
(418) 884-4041
Emp Here 150   *Sales* 86,305,200
SIC 5021 Furniture
 Jacques Alain
 David Feldberg
 Scott Bond
 Danny Berube

Levis, QC G6Z

D-U-N-S 20-288-4714   (SL)
9158-9325 QUEBEC INC
SUPERMARCHE IGA PEPIN
1015 Rue Du Basilic, Levis, QC, G6Z 3K4
(418) 834-8077
Emp Here 100   *Sales* 29,347,700
SIC 5411 Grocery stores
 Jocelyn Pepin
 Tony Pepin

D-U-N-S 24-820-8571   (SL)
ECLAIRAGE CONTRASTE M.L. INC
ECLAIRAGE MIRALUX M.L.
1009 Rue Du Parc-Industriel, Levis, QC, G6Z
1C5
(418) 839-4624
Emp Here 50   *Sales* 22,358,700
SIC 5063 Electrical apparatus and equipment
 Jean Langevin
 Stephane Desmanche
 Benoit Dupuy

D-U-N-S 20-616-2497   (SL)

PETROSOL INC
GROUPE PETROSOL
(*Suby of* GESTION PETROSOL INC)
1023 Rue Renault Bureau 100, Levis, QC,
G6Z 1B6
(418) 647-3800
Emp Here 26   *Sales* 16,361,280
SIC 5541 Gasoline service stations
Louis-Gabriel Bouchard

   D-U-N-S 20-588-6331   (HQ)
**SERVICE D'ENTRETIEN CLEAN INTERNA-
TIONAL INC**
CLEAN PROPREMENT FAIT
1006 Rue Renault, Levis, QC, G6Z 2Y8
(418) 839-0928
Sales 48,235,500
SIC 7349 Building maintenance services, nec
Daniel Labrie

   D-U-N-S 24-146-7406   (BR)
SINTRA INC
CONSTRUCTION B M L, DIV.DE SINTRA
(*Suby of* BOUYGUES)
678 Av Taniata Unite 839, Levis, QC, G6Z 2C2
(418) 839-4175
Emp Here 150
SIC 1611 Highway and street construction
Maxime Mercier

   D-U-N-S 20-879-0308   (SL)
SYNERTEK INDUSTRIES INC
1044 Rue Du Parc-Industriel, Levis, QC, G6Z
1C6
(418) 835-6264
Emp Here 26   *Sales* 11,530,740
SIC 7389 Business services, nec
Cendrine Cartegnie
Philippe Jallais
Jean-Francois Boutin
Charlaine Cartegnie

Levis, QC G7A

   D-U-N-S 20-236-9356   (SL)
2637-5808 QUEBEC INC
FERME GENEST, LA
2091 Rte Marie-Victorin, Levis, QC, G7A 4H4
(418) 831-9967
Emp Here 40   *Sales* 15,896,560
SIC 8699 Membership organizations, nec
Guy Genest

   D-U-N-S 20-255-6457   (HQ)
9020-2292 QUEBEC INC
DECACER
(*Suby of* ROGERS SUGAR INC)
1060 Ch Olivier, Levis, QC, G7A 2M7
(418) 853-6265
Sales 12,099,150
SIC 2099 Food preparations, nec
John Holliday
Manon Lacroix
Daniel Lafrance
Manfred Dallas H. Ross
Michael A. Heskin
Donald G. Jewell
Gary Collins

   D-U-N-S 20-940-3059   (SL)
9123-1878 QUEBEC INC
HONCO BATIMENT D'ACIER
1190 Ch Olivier, Levis, QC, G7A 1B1
(418) 831-2245
Emp Here 50   *Sales* 16,666,650
SIC 1541 Industrial buildings and warehouses
Francis Lacasse
Carole Lacasse
Vicky Lacasse

   D-U-N-S 20-819-6332   (SL)
9124-4905 QUEBEC INC
CONSTRUCTION COUTURE & TANGUAY
1019 Ch Industriel, Levis, QC, G7A 1B3

(418) 831-1019
Emp Here 30   *Sales* 14,121,930
SIC 1542 Nonresidential construction, nec
Henri Tanguay

   D-U-N-S 24-464-8341   (HQ)
ABRASIFS J.J.S. INC
SIA
900 Ch Olivier, Levis, QC, G7A 2N1
(418) 836-0557
Emp Here 42   *Sales* 23,751,300
SIC 5085 Industrial supplies
Andree Samson

   D-U-N-S 24-146-1045   (HQ)
BAINS ULTRA INC
BAINULTRA
956 Ch Olivier, Levis, QC, G7A 2N1
(418) 831-4344
Emp Here 123   *Sales* 21,445,830
SIC 3089 Plastics products, nec
Henri Brunelle
Jean Fortin
Serge Lauzon

   D-U-N-S 24-767-9165   (BR)
BAINS ULTRA INC
(*Suby of* BAINS ULTRA INC)
1200 Ch Industriel Bureau 4, Levis, QC, G7A
1B1
(418) 831-7132
Emp Here 100
SIC 5999 Miscellaneous retail stores, nec
Daniel Gagnon

   D-U-N-S 24-325-7917   (HQ)
BOREA CONSTRUCTION ULC
CONSTRUCTION BOREA
(*Suby of* BLATTNER POMERLEAU ENERGY
ULC)
562 Rue Olivier, Levis, QC, G7A 2N6
(418) 626-2314
Emp Here 20   *Sales* 349,196,000
SIC 1541 Industrial buildings and warehouses
Jeremy James Wacker
Marc-Andre Richard
Martin Laroche
Ralph Douglas Fredrickson
Pierre Pomerleau
Jean-Philippe Towner
Scott W. Blattner

   D-U-N-S 24-206-3667   (SL)
CAM-TRAC BERNIERES INC
CAM-TRAC RIMOUSKI
830 Ch Olivier, Levis, QC, G7A 2N1
(418) 831-2324
Emp Here 33   *Sales* 10,744,800
SIC 5999 Miscellaneous retail stores, nec
Simon Laporte
Stephane Belanger

   D-U-N-S 20-235-3756   (SL)
**CONSTRUCTIONS BELAND & LAPOINTE
INC, LES**
BELAND LAPOINTE
(*Suby of* 9134867 CANADA INC)
723 Ch Industriel, Levis, QC, G7A 1B5
(418) 831-8638
Emp Here 50   *Sales* 15,162,040
SIC 1542 Nonresidential construction, nec
Pierre Boisvert
Eric Monfette
Yvon Mercier
Marc Coutellier
Kim Beland
Raphael Lapointe

   D-U-N-S 24-792-2123   (HQ)
**GROUPE ENVIRONNEMENTAL LABRIE
INC**
ENVIROQUIP
175 Rte Marie-Victorin Bureau B, Levis, QC,
G7A 2T3
(418) 831-8250
Sales 84,263,100
SIC 3531 Construction machinery
Diana Grootonk

Tom Rothenberger
Eric Gingras

   D-U-N-S 25-390-3157   (HQ)
GROUPE HONCO INC
1190 Ch Industriel, Levis, QC, G7A 1B1
(418) 831-2245
Emp Here 30   *Sales* 122,218,600
SIC 1541 Industrial buildings and warehouses
Paul Lacasse
Vicky Lacasse
Francis Lacasse
Carole Lacasse
Harry Lacasse

   D-U-N-S 24-678-2028   (HQ)
GROUPE SANI-TECH INC
1450 Rue Thomas-Powers, Levis, QC, G7A
0P9
(418) 836-0616
Emp Here 15   *Sales* 28,738,970
SIC 5122 Drugs, proprietaries, and sundries
Louis D'anjou
Simon Cote-D'anjou

   D-U-N-S 25-748-6522   (HQ)
HENRI SICOTTE INC
HS TELECOM
779 Rue De La Briqueterie, Levis, QC, G7A
2N2
(418) 836-8417
Emp Here 90   *Sales* 37,866,300
SIC 1623 Water, sewer, and utility lines
Serge Asselin
Richard Lafrance

   D-U-N-S 20-517-1119   (SL)
HOTEL BERNIERES INC
535 Rue De Bernieres, Levis, QC, G7A 1C9
(418) 831-3119
Emp Here 90   *Sales* 8,639,830
SIC 7011 Hotels and motels
Pierre Morneau
Herman Morneau
Gilbert Pelletier

   D-U-N-S 24-126-6118   (SL)
MAISON D'AFFINAGE BERGERON INC, LA
FINESSES BERGERON, LES
865 Rte Des Rivieres, Levis, QC, G7A 2V2
(418) 831-0991
Emp Here 50   *Sales* 13,707,600
SIC 5451 Dairy products stores
Mario Bergeron
Roger Bergeron

   D-U-N-S 20-618-4892   (BR)
MARTIN DESSERT INC
ST-HUBERT RESTAURANTS
(*Suby of* MARTIN DESSERT INC)
500 Rue De Bernieres, Levis, QC, G7A 1E1
(418) 836-1234
Emp Here 100
SIC 5812 Eating places
Louis Martin

   D-U-N-S 20-954-2679   (SL)
MATERIAUX BOMAT INC
BOKIT MC
(*Suby of* GROUPE GARON LTEE, LE)
1212 Ch Industriel, Levis, QC, G7A 1B1
(418) 831-4848
Emp Here 75   *Sales* 31,339,080
SIC 5039 Construction materials, nec
Emmanuel Garon
Philippe Garon
Francois Garon
David Garon

   D-U-N-S 20-255-8417   (SL)
NEILSON INC
(*Suby of* GROUPE POMERLEAU INC)
578 Ch Olivier, Levis, QC, G7A 2N6
(418) 831-2141
Emp Here 100   *Sales* 25,244,200
SIC 1622 Bridge, tunnel, and elevated high-
way construction
Martin Laroche

Pierre Pomerleau
Francis Pomerleau
Daniel Arguin

   D-U-N-S 24-522-1705   (SL)
NEILSON-EBC (7) S.E.N.C.
578 Ch Olivier, Levis, QC, G7A 2N6
(418) 831-2141
Emp Here 300   *Sales* 98,434,500
SIC 1622 Bridge, tunnel, and elevated high-
way construction
Denis Baribeau

   D-U-N-S 20-254-4417   (SL)
NEILSON-EBC (R3-01-02) S.E.N.C
578 Ch Olivier, Levis, QC, G7A 2N6
(418) 831-2141
Emp Here 100   *Sales* 25,244,200
SIC 1622 Bridge, tunnel, and elevated high-
way construction
Martin Laroche

   D-U-N-S 20-251-4352   (HQ)
NORMAND, J.R. INC
NORMAND MACHINERY
(*Suby of* GROUPE NORMAND INC)
752 Ch Olivier, Levis, QC, G7A 2N2
(418) 831-3226
Emp Here 40   *Sales* 28,501,560
SIC 5084 Industrial machinery and equipment
Andre Normand
Gaston Bilodeau
Jean-Pierre Normand

   D-U-N-S 25-401-3238   (HQ)
**PRODUCTIONS HORTICOLES DEMERS
INC, LES**
DEMERS
1196 Rue Des Carrieres, Levis, QC, G7A 0R7
(418) 831-2489
Sales 26,230,900
SIC 0171 Berry crops
Jacques Demers
Rejean Demers
Yolande Demers

   D-U-N-S 24-843-2536   (SL)
RONAM CONSTRUCTIONS INC
1085 Ch Industriel, Levis, QC, G7A 1B3
(418) 836-5569
Emp Here 60   *Sales* 34,220,280
SIC 1542 Nonresidential construction, nec
Jacques Laflamme

   D-U-N-S 20-030-4579   (SL)
SUPERMARCHE FAMILLE ROUSSEAU INC
1855 Rte Des Rivieres, Levis, QC, G7A 4X8
(418) 831-5400
Emp Here 50   *Sales* 13,707,600
SIC 5411 Grocery stores
Alain Rousseau

Longue-Pointe-De-Mingan, QC G0G

   D-U-N-S 24-792-1372   (SL)
**POSEIDON 'LES POISSONS ET CRUS-
TACES' INC**
259 Rue Du Bord-De-La-Mer, Longue-Pointe-
De-Mingan, QC, G0G 1V0
(418) 949-2331
Emp Here 100   *Sales* 29,347,700
SIC 5421 Meat and fish markets
Jean-Marc Marcoux
Richard Desbois
Nicol Desbois
Douglas Mcinnis

Longueuil, QC J4G

   D-U-N-S 24-768-1273   (SL)
128388 CANADA INC

▲ Public Company   ■ Public Company Family Member   **HQ** Headquarters   **BR** Branch   **SL** Single Location

DISTRIBUTRICES AUTOMATIQUES BEN, LES
1100 Rue Herelle Bureau 4, Longueuil, QC, J4G 2M8
(450) 646-3949
Emp Here 30   *Sales* 19,693,920
SIC 5962 Merchandising machine operators
Bernard Sauve
Ginette Sauve

D-U-N-S 24-920-8927   (HQ)
3022528 CANADA INC
DECOR EXPERT EXPO
778 Rue Jean-Neveu, Longueuil, QC, J4G 1P1
(450) 442-4087
Sales 20,214,855
SIC 7389 Business services, nec
John Bannerman
Micheline Audet
Jacques Guay

D-U-N-S 25-097-7089   (SL)
9064-3792 QUEBEC INC
2025 Rue De La Metropole, Longueuil, QC, J4G 1S9

Emp Here 100   *Sales* 26,155,300
SIC 6712 Bank holding companies
Jean Tremblay
Yves Tremblay

D-U-N-S 20-254-0621   (SL)
91933614 QUEBEC INC
JULIETTE ET CHOCOLAT
844 Rue Jean-Neveu, Longueuil, QC, J4G 2M1
(579) 721-3016
Emp Here 19   *Sales* 10,167,356
SIC 5149 Groceries and related products, nec
Juliette Brun
Lionel May

D-U-N-S 25-973-7922   (HQ)
ACIER AGF INC
ACIER ATR
(*Suby of* GROUPE AGF INC)
2270 Rue Garneau, Longueuil, QC, J4G 1E7
(450) 442-9494
Emp Here 10   *Sales* 169,900,800
SIC 1791 Structural steel erection
Serge Gendron
Mark Clarke

D-U-N-S 20-219-8586   (SL)
ACIER GENDRON LTEE
GENDRON STEEL
2270 Rue Garneau, Longueuil, QC, J4G 1E7
(450) 442-9494
Emp Here 800   *Sales* 477,963,200
SIC 5051 Metals service centers and offices
Serge Gendron
George Stougiannos

D-U-N-S 24-320-2751   (HQ)
AQUATECH SOCIETE DE GESTION DE L'EAU INC
(*Suby of* GROUPE HELIOS, GESTION D'INFRASTRUCTURES ET DE SERVICES URBAINS INC)
2099 Boul Fernand-Lafontaine, Longueuil, QC, J4G 2J4
(450) 646-5270
Sales 41,854,750
SIC 4941 Water supply
Jean-Pierre Azzopardi

D-U-N-S 20-240-8381   (HQ)
ATLANTIC PROMOTIONS INC
770 Boul Guimond, Longueuil, QC, J4G 1V6
(514) 871-1671
Emp Here 70   *Sales* 57,536,800
SIC 5023 Homefurnishings
Jacques Gatien
Gilles Gosselin
Richard Schlosberger
Eric Gatien

Philipp Park
Angelique Gatien

D-U-N-S 24-562-3004   (SL)
AUTOMOBILE G.R. COREE LONGUEUIL LTEE
HYUNDAI LONGUEUIL
1680 Boul Marie-Victorin, Longueuil, QC, J4G 1A5
(450) 670-2080
Emp Here 35   *Sales* 17,432,730
SIC 5511 New and used car dealers
Jean Rozon

D-U-N-S 20-724-9236   (HQ)
AUTRUCHE VARIETES INC
AUTRUCHE
(*Suby of* 122303 CANADA INC)
715 Rue Delage Bureau 700, Longueuil, QC, J4G 2P8
(450) 670-2323
Sales 19,305,520
SIC 5199 Nondurable goods, nec
Jurgen Strauss
Francoise Strauss
Isabelle Strauss
Gilles Strauss

D-U-N-S 24-960-7888   (SL)
CLIMAT-CONTROL SB INC
CLIMAT-CONTROL PL
800 Rue Jean-Neveu, Longueuil, QC, J4G 2M1
(514) 789-0456
Emp Here 100   *Sales* 23,306,500
SIC 1711 Plumbing, heating, air-conditioning
Serge Bastrash

D-U-N-S 25-332-2242   (SL)
CLUB PISCINE PLUS C.P.P.Q. (LONGUEUIL) INC, LE
620 Rue Jean-Neveu, Longueuil, QC, J4G 1P1
(450) 463-3112
Emp Here 65   *Sales* 15,881,320
SIC 5999 Miscellaneous retail stores, nec
Daniel Dupre
Michel Lavoie

D-U-N-S 20-188-0775   (BR)
CRH CANADA GROUP INC
DEMIX CONSTRUCTION
(*Suby of* CRH PUBLIC LIMITED COMPANY)
435 Rue Jean-Neveu, Longueuil, QC, J4G 2P9
(450) 651-1117
Emp Here 1,200
SIC 3241 Cement, hydraulic
Jean Maurice-Forget

D-U-N-S 20-738-0577   (BR)
CRH CANADA GROUP INC
DEMIX BETON
(*Suby of* CRH PUBLIC LIMITED COMPANY)
435 Rue Jean-Neveu, Longueuil, QC, J4G 2P9
(450) 651-1117
Emp Here 250
SIC 3273 Ready-mixed concrete

D-U-N-S 25-390-5137   (HQ)
D-BOX TECHNOLOGIES INC
D-BOX
2172 Rue De La Province, Longueuil, QC, J4G 1R7
(450) 442-3003
Sales 28,241,020
SIC 3625 Relays and industrial controls
Claude Mc Master
Sebastien Mailhot
Robert Desautels
Elaine C. Phenix
Jean-Francois Lacroix
Philippe Roy
Jean Rene Halde
Kit Dalaroy
Louis Bernier
Sylvain Lafrance

D-U-N-S 24-769-2775   (HQ)
DAIKIN APPLIED CANADA INC
DAIKIN (MC)
(*Suby of* DAIKIN INDUSTRIES, LTD.)
603 Rue Beriault, Longueuil, QC, J4G 1Z1
(450) 674-2442
Emp Here 12   *Sales* 18,781,308
SIC 5075 Warm air heating and air conditioning
Michael Schwartz
Pierre Boyer
Creg Parlee

D-U-N-S 24-933-5878   (HQ)
DANACA TRANSPORT MONTREAL LTEE
(*Suby of* GESTION REAL GRONDIN INC)
2555 Rue Jean-Desy, Longueuil, QC, J4G 1G6
(450) 463-0020
Emp Here 54   *Sales* 12,342,360
SIC 4212 Local trucking, without storage
Real Jr Grondin
Steeve Jutras
Tommy St-Arnaud

D-U-N-S 24-340-5425   (BR)
DH CORPORATION
DAVIS HENDERSON INTERCHEQUES
(*Suby of* VISTA EQUITY PARTNERS MANAGEMENT, LLC)
830 Rue Delage, Longueuil, QC, J4G 2V4
(450) 463-6372
Emp Here 200
SIC 6211 Security brokers and dealers
Jacques Mercier

D-U-N-S 24-741-6456   (SL)
EQUIPEMENT D'ESSAI AEROSPATIAL C.E.L LTEE
715 Rue Delage Bureau 400, Longueuil, QC, J4G 2P8
(450) 442-9994
Emp Here 100   *Sales* 48,773,000
SIC 5088 Transportation equipment and supplies
Charles Lussier
Annie Desaulniers

D-U-N-S 24-516-1351   (HQ)
FONDATION DU CENTRE JEUNESSE DE LA MONTEREGIE
575 Rue Adoncour, Longueuil, QC, J4G 2M6
(450) 679-0140
Emp Here 100   *Sales* 153,584,000
SIC 8322 Individual and family services
Robert Lacoste
Martin Belanger
Eliane Martel-Roy
Dominique Dubois
Marie-Claude Esprimont
Martin Hebert
Catherine Lemay
Alain St-Pierre
Hubert Gagnier
Suzanne Lepage

D-U-N-S 25-172-2427   (HQ)
FORTIN, JEAN & ASSOCIES SYNDICS INC
2360 Boul Marie-Victorin, Longueuil, QC, J4G 1B5
(450) 442-3260
Emp Here 40   *Sales* 10,010,715
SIC 8111 Legal services
Jean Fortin
Jean Fortin Jr

D-U-N-S 25-152-0623   (SL)
GONDERFLEX INTERNATIONAL INC
530 Boul Guimond, Longueuil, QC, J4G 1P8
(450) 651-2224
Emp Here 25   *Sales* 11,875,650
SIC 5084 Industrial machinery and equipment
Mete Gonder

D-U-N-S 24-677-0379   (HQ)
GROUPE AGF INC
2270 Rue Garneau, Longueuil, QC, J4G 1E7

(450) 442-9494
Sales 783,276,000
SIC 7353 Heavy construction equipment rental
Pierre Grand'maison
Serge Gendron
Vanessa Jodoin
Julie Proulx
Maxime Gendron
Gary Early Mintz
Philippe Duval
Christiane Bergevin

D-U-N-S 24-357-4555   (HQ)
GROUPE CD BEDARD INC
753 Rue Beriault, Longueuil, QC, J4G 1X7
(450) 679-7704
Sales 10,462,120
SIC 6712 Bank holding companies
Jarame Tremblay

D-U-N-S 25-534-9516   (HQ)
GROUPE HELIOS, GESTION D'INFRASTRUCTURES ET DE SERVICES URBAINS INC
2099 Boul Fernand-Lafontaine, Longueuil, QC, J4G 2J4
(450) 646-1903
Emp Here 10   *Sales* 24,689,880
SIC 8741 Management services
Jean-Pierre Azzopardi
Alain Gauthier
Rejean Goulet

D-U-N-S 20-251-8353   (HQ)
GROUPE LMT INC
METAUX TREMBLAY, LES
2025 Rue De La Metropole, Longueuil, QC, J4G 1S9
(450) 640-8700
Sales 19,208,500
SIC 3442 Metal doors, sash, and trim
Jean Tremblay
Yves Tremblay
Alain Dumont
Stephane Richard
Dominic Simard

D-U-N-S 20-363-7793   (HQ)
GROUPE LUMENPULSE INC
LUMENPULSE
(*Suby of* POWER CORPORATION DU CANADA)
1220 Boul Marie-Victorin, Longueuil, QC, J4G 2H9
(514) 937-3003
Sales 70,728,750
SIC 3646 Commercial lighting fixtures
Francois-Xavier Souvay
Pierre Larochelle
Peter Timothaetos
Marilyn Mauricio
Nicolas Belanger
Michel Ringuet
Claude Genereux
Olivier Desmarais

D-U-N-S 20-523-6131   (BR)
GROUPE SOGIDES INC
MESSAGERIES ADP
(*Suby of* QUEBECOR MEDIA INC)
2315 Rue De La Province, Longueuil, QC, J4G 1G4
(450) 640-1237
Emp Here 200
SIC 2731 Book publishing
Pierre Lesperance

D-U-N-S 20-303-1265   (BR)
GROUPE TYT INC
(*Suby of* TRANSPORTS YVON TURCOTTE LTEE, LES)
454 Rue Jean-Neveu, Longueuil, QC, J4G 1N8
(819) 474-4884
Emp Here 150
SIC 4213 Trucking, except local
Michel Tobrin

D-U-N-S 25-285-5127   (SL)
MANAGEMENT SIMO INC
(*Suby of* GROUPE HELIOS, GESTION D'INFRASTRUCTURES ET DE SERVICES URBAINS INC)
2099 Boul Fernand-Lafontaine, Longueuil, QC, J4G 2J4
(514) 281-6525
Emp Here 125   *Sales* 70,636,875
SIC 4971 Irrigation systems
Jean-Pierre Azzopardi

D-U-N-S 24-799-5157   (SL)
MAXI CRISP INC
2066 Rue De La Province, Longueuil, QC, J4G 1R7
(450) 670-4256
Emp Here 30   *Sales* 13,415,220
SIC 5046 Commercial equipment, nec

D-U-N-S 20-309-3208   (SL)
MECANO-SOUDURE DRUMMOND INC
(*Suby of* CANERECTOR INC)
700 Rue Talon, Longueuil, QC, J4G 1P7
(514) 526-4411
Emp Here 60   *Sales* 10,883,280
SIC 3399 Primary Metal products
Tim Buckland
Amanda Hawkins
William Nickel

D-U-N-S 20-420-5579   (HQ)
NAVADA LTEE
EXP-AIR CLIMATISATION-REFRIGERATION
675 Rue Herelle, Longueuil, QC, J4G 2M8
(450) 679-3370
Emp Here 180   *Sales* 30,485,480
SIC 1711 Plumbing, heating, air-conditioning
Luc Bergeron
Robert Laberge
Mathieu Georges
Francis Ranaud

D-U-N-S 20-010-7576   (SL)
OPSIS GESTION D'INFRASTRUCTURES INC
(*Suby of* GROUPE HELIOS, GESTION D'INFRASTRUCTURES ET DE SERVICES URBAINS INC)
2099 Boul Fernand-Lafontaine, Longueuil, QC, J4G 2J4
(514) 982-6774
Emp Here 80   *Sales* 9,982,080
SIC 8741 Management services
Jean-Pierre Azzopardi

D-U-N-S 20-201-5897   (HQ)
PRATT & WHITNEY CANADA CIE
P & WC
(*Suby of* PRATT AERO LIMITED PARTNERSHIP)
1000 Boul Marie-Victorin, Longueuil, QC, J4G 1A1
(450) 677-9411
Emp Here 5,000   *Sales* 1,783,568,950
SIC 3519 Internal combustion engines, nec
Maria Della Posta
Nicolas Amyot
Theodore Adams
Patrick Bertrand

D-U-N-S 24-432-3739   (SL)
PRODUITS GRISSPASTA LTEE
805 Boul Guimond, Longueuil, QC, J4G 1M1
(450) 651-4150
Emp Here 140   *Sales* 48,396,600
SIC 2098 Macaroni and spaghetti
Licio Petaccia
Eddy Petaccia
Willy Petaccia
Ettore Petaccia

D-U-N-S 20-235-9592   (SL)
PUBL TRANS CANADA ADVERTISING (QUEBEC) LTD
625 Boul Guimond, Longueuil, QC, J4G 1L9

Emp Here 21   *Sales* 15,592,920
SIC 5199 Nondurable goods, nec
Jean Payot
Monique Lamarre

D-U-N-S 20-574-0371   (BR)
QUINCAILLERIE RICHELIEU LTEE
QUINCAILLERIE RICHELIEU LTEE
(*Suby of* QUINCAILLERIE RICHELIEU LTEE)
800 Rue Beriault, Longueuil, QC, J4G 1R8
(514) 259-3737
Emp Here 80
SIC 5072 Hardware
Mark Daubois

D-U-N-S 24-675-3644   (SL)
REFRIGERATION, PLOMBERIE & CHAUFFAGE LONGUEUIL INC
R.P.C. LONGUEUIL
(*Suby of* GESTION JESSYCAN INC)
800 Rue Jean-Neveu, Longueuil, QC, J4G 2M1
(514) 789-0456
Emp Here 70   *Sales* 13,462,960
SIC 7623 Refrigeration service and repair
Serge Bastrash

D-U-N-S 20-796-9192   (BR)
RESEAU DE TRANSPORT DE LONGUEUIL
1150 Boul Marie-Victorin, Longueuil, QC, J4G 2M4
(450) 442-8600
Emp Here 900
SIC 4111 Local and suburban transit
Helene Thebodeau

D-U-N-S 24-935-4994   (SL)
RODI DESIGN INC
ARTEMANO
1100 Boul Marie-Victorin, Longueuil, QC, J4G 2H9
(450) 679-7755
Emp Here 100   *Sales* 15,432,200
SIC 2512 Upholstered household furniture
Bruno Rodi

D-U-N-S 25-408-4916   (SL)
SECURO VISION INC
(*Suby of* SERVICES OPTOMETRIQUES (OPT) INC)
2285 Rue De La Metropole, Longueuil, QC, J4G 1E5
(450) 679-2330
Emp Here 30   *Sales* 15,616,260
SIC 5099 Durable goods, nec
Jean Frederick Bouchard
Patrice Lacoste

D-U-N-S 25-355-8084   (SL)
SENTERRE ENTREPRENEUR GENERAL INC
SENTERRE ENTREPRENEUR ELECTRICIEN
550 Boul Guimond, Longueuil, QC, J4G 1P8
(450) 655-9301
Emp Here 25   *Sales* 11,768,275
SIC 1542 Nonresidential construction, nec
Guy Senterre
Sylvie Desrochers
Marc-Andre Senterre
Patrick Senterre

D-U-N-S 24-953-6496   (SL)
SOGEP INC
ARENA CHENIER
(*Suby of* GROUPE HELIOS, GESTION D'INFRASTRUCTURES ET DE SERVICES URBAINS INC)
2099 Boul Fernand-Lafontaine, Longueuil, QC, J4G 2J4
(514) 527-9546
Emp Here 100   *Sales* 12,477,600
SIC 8741 Management services
Jean-Pierre Azzopardi

D-U-N-S 20-719-3439   (SL)
SOLUTIONS MAGNETIQUES TRANSFAB

INC
2315 Rue De La Metropole, Longueuil, QC, J4G 1E5
(450) 449-0412
Emp Here 30   *Sales* 13,415,220
SIC 5063 Electrical apparatus and equipment
Frank Falvo
Paul Cmikiewicz

D-U-N-S 24-890-7883   (SL)
SUPERMARCH DJS COUSINEAU INC
I.G.A. COUSINEAU
455 Boul Jean-Paul-Vincent, Longueuil, QC, J4G 1R3
(450) 646-4302
Emp Here 100   *Sales* 29,347,700
SIC 5411 Grocery stores
Jean Cousineau

D-U-N-S 24-800-8849   (SL)
TALON SEBEQ INC
(*Suby of* MILLER GROUP INC)
555 Boul Guimond, Longueuil, QC, J4G 1L9
(450) 677-7449
Emp Here 60   *Sales* 15,146,520
SIC 1611 Highway and street construction
Pierre Morgan
Jean-Yves Llenas
Frederic Roussel
Francois Vachon
Steven Moote

D-U-N-S 24-386-3227   (SL)
VIZIMAX INC
ENTREPRISES VIZIMAX, LES
2284 Rue De La Province, Longueuil, QC, J4G 1G1
(450) 679-0003
Emp Here 40   *Sales* 17,886,960
SIC 5065 Electronic parts and equipment, nec
Jean-Guy Lacombe
Salil Munjal
Tony Van Bommel
Gary Clifford
Daniel Peloquin
Isabelle Mayrand
Eric Bolduc

D-U-N-S 20-182-6448   (HQ)
YVES ROCHER AMERIQUE DU NORD INC
EXPERTS DE LA COSMETIQUE VEGETALE, LES
(*Suby of* ROCHER PARTICIPATIONS)
2199 Boul Fernand-Lafontaine, Longueuil, QC, J4G 2V7
(450) 442-9555
Emp Here 40   *Sales* 91,768,500
SIC 5999 Miscellaneous retail stores, nec
Jean-David Schwartz
Chantal Lavallee

Longueuil, QC J4H

D-U-N-S 25-026-0411   (SL)
2938286 CANADA INC
LONGUEUIL MAZDA
60 Boul Roland-Therrien, Longueuil, QC, J4H 3V8
(450) 928-2000
Emp Here 26   *Sales* 12,950,028
SIC 5511 New and used car dealers
Serge Minguy

D-U-N-S 25-201-3016   (SL)
9003-7755 QUEBEC INC
HOLIDAY INN MONTREAL LONGUEUIL
900 Rue Saint-Charles E, Longueuil, QC, J4H 3Y2
(450) 646-8100
Emp Here 85   *Sales* 8,066,415
SIC 7011 Hotels and motels
Ghislain Lacelle

D-U-N-S 24-204-0512   (SL)
9102-7045 QUEBEC INC

GLM
(*Suby of* R.R. FINANCE CORPORATION INC)
365 Rue Saint-Jean Bureau 212, Longueuil, QC, J4H 2X7
(450) 465-0441
Emp Here 85
SIC 8611 Business associations
Louis-Luc Roy
Louis-Francois Pothier-Roy

D-U-N-S 20-376-1684   (SL)
ALIMENTATION RAYMOND DROUIN INC
369 Rue Saint-Jean O, Longueuil, QC, J4H 2X7
(450) 679-4570
Emp Here 50   *Sales* 13,707,600
SIC 5411 Grocery stores
Raymond Drouin
Sebastien Drouin
Marie-Josee Drouin

D-U-N-S 20-881-7069   (SL)
ASSOCIATION SOGERIVE INC
MARINA PORT DE PLAISANCE REAL BOUVIER
101 Ch De La Rive, Longueuil, QC, J4H 4C9
(450) 442-9575
Emp Here 49   *Sales* 13,207,901
SIC 4493 Marinas
Daniel Beauchesne
Sylvie Parent
Micheline Dube

D-U-N-S 25-065-3565   (BR)
ATLIFIC INC
HOLIDAY INN LONGUEUIL
900 Rue Saint-Charles E, Longueuil, QC, J4H 3Y2
(450) 646-8100
Emp Here 75
SIC 7011 Hotels and motels
Jhislain Lacelle

D-U-N-S 20-072-3538   (SL)
CANADA BETON ET DECORATIONS INC
BATIMENTS CANADA
777 Rue D'Auvergne, Longueuil, QC, J4H 3T9
(450) 463-7084
Emp Here 49   *Sales* 13,892,676
SIC 1611 Highway and street construction
Said Chohra

D-U-N-S 25-210-6463   (HQ)
CENTRE COMMUNAUTAIRE JURIDIQUE DE LA RIVE-SUD
BUREAU AIDE JURIDIQUE
101 Boul Roland-Therrien Bureau 301, Longueuil, QC, J4H 4B9
(450) 928-7655
Emp Here 6   *Sales* 11,088,200
SIC 8111 Legal services
Yvan Niquette

D-U-N-S 24-107-3154   (BR)
CENTRE SPORTIF PALADIUM INC
PALADIUM
475 Boul Roland-Therrien, Longueuil, QC, J4H 4A6
(450) 646-9995
Emp Here 90
SIC 7999 Amusement and recreation, nec
Richard Gauvin

D-U-N-S 25-986-0229   (HQ)
CENTRES DENTAIRES LAPOINTE INC
(*Suby of* 9152-2177 QUEBEC INC)
116 Rue Guilbault, Longueuil, QC, J4H 2T2
(450) 679-2300
Emp Here 48   *Sales* 15,063,264
SIC 8021 Offices and clinics of dentists
Larry Lapointe
Yves Lapointe

D-U-N-S 20-998-9755   (SL)
CHOCOLAT PERFECTION INC
570 Boul Roland-Therrien Bureau 217, Longueuil, QC, J4H 3V9

▲ Public Company   ■ Public Company Family Member   **HQ** Headquarters   **BR** Branch   **SL** Single Location

(450) 674-4546
Emp Here 25   *Sales* 20,889,425
SIC 5149 Groceries and related products, nec
Gilles Jr Parazelli
Daniel Parazelli

D-U-N-S 20-254-9895   (HQ)
**COLLEGE D'ENSEIGNEMENT GEN-
ERAL ET PROFESSIONNEL EDOUARD-
MONTPETIT**
COLLEGE EDOUARD-MONTEPTIT
945 Ch De Chambly, Longueuil, QC, J4H 3M6
(450) 679-2631
Sales 20,146,500
SIC 8222 Junior colleges
Jean-Paul Gagne
Annie Rivard
Pierre Chasse
Linda Dorval
Jacques Archambault
Mimose Constant
Josee Mercier
Patrick Monarque
Charles Fortin
Margot Pfeiffer Page

D-U-N-S 24-895-6880   (BR)
**COMMISSION SCOLAIRE MARIE-
VICTORIN**
*ECOLE SECONDAIRE JACQUES
ROUSSEAU*
(*Suby of* COMMISSION SCOLAIRE MARIE-
VICTORIN)
444 Rue De Gentilly E, Longueuil, QC, J4H
3X7
(450) 651-6800
Emp Here 200
SIC 8211 Elementary and secondary schools
Nancy Brisson

D-U-N-S 24-434-0170   (HQ)
**COMMISSION SCOLAIRE MARIE-
VICTORIN**
13 Rue Saint-Laurent E, Longueuil, QC, J4H
4B7
(450) 670-0730
Emp Here 200   *Sales* 328,480,366
SIC 8211 Elementary and secondary schools
Serge Lefebvre
Lucie Desilets
Colette Larosse

D-U-N-S 20-734-4755   (HQ)
**CORPORATION DE DEVELOPPEMENT
CUIRS BENTLEY INC, LA**
375 Boul Roland-Therrien Bureau 210,
Longueuil, QC, J4H 4A6
(450) 651-5000
Emp Here 3   *Sales* 569,097,513
SIC 6712 Bank holding companies
Walter Lamothe
Jacques Foisy
Frederick Perrault
Philippe Martin

D-U-N-S 24-654-1432   (SL)
ELEVEURS DE PORCS DU QUEBEC LES
COMITE CONJOINT ACPQ FPPQ SEPQ
555 Boul Roland-Therrien Bureau 120,
Longueuil, QC, J4H 4E9
(450) 679-0540
Emp Here 49   *Sales* 13,556,340
SIC 2879 Agricultural chemicals, nec
David Boissonneault

D-U-N-S 20-192-0563   (HQ)
ELEVEURS DE PORCS DU QUEBEC, LES
555 Boul Roland-Therrien Bureau 120,
Longueuil, QC, J4H 4E9
(450) 679-0540
Sales 16,423,020
SIC 8621 Professional organizations
David Duval
Yvan Frechette
Louis-Philippe Roy
Jean Larose

D-U-N-S 24-562-1958   (SL)

**FEDERATION DES PRODUCTEURS DE
CULTURES COMMERCIALES DU QUEBEC**
FPCCQ
555 Boul Roland-Therrien Bureau 505,
Longueuil, QC, J4H 4G4
(450) 679-0530
Emp Here 45   *Sales* 10,113,480
SIC 6111 Federal and federally sponsored
credit agencies
Christian Overbeek
Benoit Legault
Marc Labelle

D-U-N-S 20-920-0463   (SL)
GROUPE SUTTON - ACTUEL INC
GROUPE SUTTON - AVANTAGE PLUS
115 Rue Saint-Charles O, Longueuil, QC, J4H
1C7
(450) 651-1079
Emp Here 45   *Sales* 14,720,715
SIC 6531 Real estate agents and managers
Vincent Ladouceur
Nicole Cyr

D-U-N-S 20-928-0320   (SL)
GROUPE VIAU INC
550 Ch De Chambly Bureau 300, Longueuil,
QC, J4H 3L8

Emp Here 23   *Sales* 13,562,585
SIC 6411 Insurance agents, brokers, and ser-
vice
Robert Viau
Rodolphe Dupere
Nicole L Machabee

D-U-N-S 25-908-7497   (SL)
GUY HUBERT ET ASSOCIES INC
80 Rue Saint-Laurent O Bureau 210,
Longueuil, QC, J4H 1L8
(579) 721-3252
Emp Here 49   *Sales* 11,017,895
SIC 2023 Dry, condensed and evaporated
dairy products
Philippe Hubert

D-U-N-S 25-090-5122   (BR)
HEROUX-DEVTEK INC
LANDING GEAR, DIV
(*Suby of* HEROUX-DEVTEK INC)
755 Rue Thurber, Longueuil, QC, J4H 3N2
(450) 679-5450
Emp Here 480
SIC 3728 Aircraft parts and equipment, nec
Brent Kozar

D-U-N-S 24-314-4586   (HQ)
**KNOWLTON DEVELOPMENT CORPORA-
TION INC**
KDC
255 Boul Roland-Therrien Bureau 100,
Longueuil, QC, J4H 4A6
(450) 243-2000
Emp Here 3   *Sales* 603,015,342
SIC 6712 Bank holding companies
Nicholas Whitley
Pierre Prud'homme
Justine Cheng

D-U-N-S 24-933-8856   (SL)
LONGUEUIL NISSAN INC
760 Rue Saint-Charles E, Longueuil, QC, J4H
1C3
(450) 442-2000
Emp Here 37   *Sales* 18,428,886
SIC 5511 New and used car dealers
Serge Minguy

D-U-N-S 25-485-1074   (HQ)
**PRODUCTEURS DE LAIT DU QUEBEC,
LES**
PRODUCTEUR DE LAIT QUEBECOIS, LE
555 Boul Roland-Therrien Bureau 415,
Longueuil, QC, J4H 4G3
(450) 679-0530
Sales 10,203,700
SIC 8631 Labor organizations

Alain Bourbeau
Denis Morin
Pierre Lampron
Noramand Barriault
Gilbrt Perreault
Gabriel Rancourt
Richard Bouchard
Daniel Cote
Real Gauthier
Pierre Thibault

D-U-N-S 24-461-2438   (SL)
RE/MAX LONGUEUIL INC
50 Rue Saint-Charles O Bureau 100,
Longueuil, QC, J4H 1C6
(450) 651-8331
Emp Here 51   *Sales* 13,859,556
SIC 6531 Real estate agents and managers
Serge Lacaille

D-U-N-S 25-500-5654   (HQ)
RESTAURANTS T.S.N.A. INC
MCDONALD'S
365 Rue Saint-Jean, Longueuil, QC, J4H 2X7
(450) 670-5609
Emp Here 100   *Sales* 10,726,970
SIC 5812 Eating places
Gilbert Christidis

D-U-N-S 25-355-8738   (SL)
RIVE SUD PONTIAC BUICK GMC INC
GM
395 Rue Saint-Charles O, Longueuil, QC, J4H
1G1

Emp Here 40   *Sales* 19,923,120
SIC 5511 New and used car dealers
Rene Legrand
Jean-Rene Forte
Rene Forte

D-U-N-S 20-954-8523   (SL)
**SOEURS DES SAINTS NOMS DE JESUS ET
DE MARIE DU QUEBEC, LES**
MAISON JESUS MARIE
86 Rue Saint-Charles E, Longueuil, QC, J4H
1A9
(450) 651-0179
Emp Here 115   *Sales* 11,974,145
SIC 8661 Religious organizations
Denise Riel

D-U-N-S 24-515-3341   (HQ)
**SOEURS DES SAINTS NOMS DE JESUS ET
DE MARIE DU QUEBEC, LES**
PENSIONAT ST NOM DE MARIE
82 Rue Saint-Charles E, Longueuil, QC, J4H
1A9
(450) 651-3744
Emp Here 140
SIC 8661 Religious organizations
Denise Riel

D-U-N-S 20-165-1799   (SL)
SPB ORGANIZATIONNAL PSYCHOLOGY
GRISVERT
555 Boul Roland-Therrien Unite 300,
Longueuil, QC, J4H 4E7
(450) 646-1022
Emp Here 50   *Sales* 18,061,850
SIC 8049 Offices of health practitioner
Alain Reid
Julie Carignan
Alain Dumas
Etienne Beaulieu

D-U-N-S 24-502-2702   (HQ)
**SPB PSYCHOLOGIE ORGANISATION-
NELLE INC.**
SPB DIMENSIONS
555 Boul Roland-Therrien Bureau 300,
Longueuil, QC, J4H 4E7
(450) 646-1022
Emp Here 40   *Sales* 15,274,000
SIC 8999 Services, nec
Pierre Gauthier
Alain Reid

D-U-N-S 24-432-5791   (HQ)
UNION DES PRODUCTEURS AGRICOLE, L'
UPA
555 Boul Roland-Therrien Bureau 100,
Longueuil, QC, J4H 3Y9
(450) 679-0530
Sales 31,328,220
SIC 8631 Labor organizations
Marcel Groleau
Paul Doyon
Denis Roy
Charles-Felix Ross

Longueuil, QC J4J

D-U-N-S 24-427-9845   (SL)
2759-9687 QUEBEC INC.
VOYAGES FUNTASTIQUE LONGUEUIL
1516 Ch De Chambly, Longueuil, QC, J4J 3X5
(450) 670-1235
Emp Here 25   *Sales* 12,999,175
SIC 4724 Travel agencies
Claudette Aube

D-U-N-S 20-181-0160   (SL)
DTS PHARMA INC
PHARMACIE JEAN COUTU
1049 Boul Roland-Therrien Bureau 236,
Longueuil, QC, J4J 4L3
(450) 928-0030
Emp Here 40   *Sales* 10,118,160
SIC 5912 Drug stores and proprietary stores
Paul St-Onge
Charles Rivest

D-U-N-S 20-380-8555   (SL)
GROUPE ALERTE SANTE INC
440 Boul Sainte-Foy, Longueuil, QC, J4J 5G5
(450) 670-0911
Emp Here 50   *Sales* 13,716,600
SIC 8741 Management services
Claude Lemay
Stephane Demers
Jean Murray
Jean-Charles Boily
Marc Desrosiers
Jean Rodrigue
Eric Tremblay
Martin Rousseau
Dave Ross
Claude Girard

D-U-N-S 20-465-3422   (SL)
GROUPE CONSEIL FXINNOVATION INC
FX INNOVATION
125 Boul Sainte-Foy, Longueuil, QC, J4J 1W7

Emp Here 49   *Sales* 11,673,194
SIC 8748 Business consulting, nec
David Marotte

D-U-N-S 20-368-8523   (SL)
IGA MARCHE LACOSTE HEBERT
1401 Ch De Chambly, Longueuil, QC, J4J 3X6
(450) 677-2869
Emp Here 49   *Sales* 14,380,373
SIC 5411 Grocery stores

D-U-N-S 25-627-7005   (SL)
OPTIONS NON TRADITIONNELLES INC.
125 Boul Sainte-Foy Bureau 300, Longueuil,
QC, J4J 1W7
(450) 646-1030
Emp Here 49   *Sales* 10,542,960
SIC 8748 Business consulting, nec
Josee Jutras

D-U-N-S 20-120-0072   (SL)
SYM-CRC INC
*SYMBIOSE CUSTOMER CONTACT CEN-
TER*
174 Boul Sainte-Foy Bureau 101, Longueuil,
QC, J4J 1W9

(877) 565-6777
Emp Here 100   *Sales* 45,442,182
SIC 7389 Business services, nec
  Sylvain Lapointe

D-U-N-S 20-201-6036   (SL)
VITRERIE LONGUEUIL INC
BATTERIES EXPERT LONGUEUIL
241 Boul Sainte-Foy, Longueuil, QC, J4J 1X1
(450) 651-0900
Emp Here 27   *Sales* 12,073,698
SIC 5039 Construction materials, nec
  Luc Robert
  Benoit Robert
  Yvon Robert
  Daniel Robert

Longueuil, QC J4K

D-U-N-S 24-813-9669   (HQ)
141793 CANADA INC
869 Boul Cure-Poirier O, Longueuil, QC, J4K
2C3
(450) 674-1521
Sales 15,651,090
SIC 5063 Electrical apparatus and equipment
  Roger Thibault

D-U-N-S 24-955-1698   (SL)
2972344 CANADA INC
LONGUEUIL TOYOTA
900 Rue Saint-Laurent O, Longueuil, QC, J4K
1C5
(450) 674-7474
Emp Here 58   *Sales* 36,498,240
SIC 5511 New and used car dealers
  Jacques Lalonde
  Marc Daigle

D-U-N-S 25-126-6636   (SL)
**ALLIANCE DU PERSONNEL PROFESSION-
NEL ET TECHNIQUE DE LA SANTE ET DES
SERVICES SOCIAUX**
APTS
1111 Rue Saint-Charles O Bureau 1050,
Longueuil, QC, J4K 5G4
(450) 670-2411
Emp Here 100   *Sales* 22,087,100
SIC 6513 Apartment building operators
  Carolle Dube

D-U-N-S 20-314-3821   (SL)
**ARCELORMITTAL   EXPLOITATION
MINIERE CANADA S.E.N.C.**
1010 Rue De Serigny, Longueuil, QC, J4K
5G7
(418) 766-2000
Emp Here 1,000   *Sales* 255,774,000
SIC 1011 Iron ores
  Pierre Lapointe

D-U-N-S 20-376-3409   (SL)
ATIS S.E.C.
1111 Rue Saint-Charles O, Longueuil, QC,
J4K 5G4
(450) 928-0101
Emp Here 100   *Sales* 19,237,000
SIC 2431 Millwork
  Robert Doyon

D-U-N-S 24-502-6104   (SL)
BEIGNES M.W.M. INC., LES
TIM HORTONS
895 Rue Saint-Laurent O, Longueuil, QC, J4K
2V1
(450) 677-6363
Emp Here 49   *Sales* 13,433,448
SIC 5461 Retail bakeries
  Charles Marcotte

D-U-N-S 24-322-2325   (HQ)
CARTIER ENERGIE EOLIENNE INC
(*Suby of* INNERGEX II INC)
1111 Rue Saint-Charles O Bureau 1155e,
Longueuil, QC, J4K 5G4

(450) 928-0426
Emp Here 30   *Sales* 23,184,718
SIC 4911 Electric services
  Michel Letellier
  Nathalie Theberge
  Jean Perron

D-U-N-S 24-084-4266   (HQ)
CHAUSSURES BO-PIEDS INC
CHAUSSURES TENDANCE
2626 Rue Papineau, Longueuil, QC, J4K 3M4
(450) 651-9222
Emp Here 5   *Sales* 19,733,560
SIC 5661 Shoe stores
  Richard Rivest

D-U-N-S 25-232-9990   (BR)
**COLLEGE   CHARLES-LEMOYNE   DE
LONGUEUIL INC**
PAVILLON LE CLASSIQUE
(*Suby of* COLLEGE CHARLES-LEMOYNE
DE LONGUEUIL INC)
1430 Rue Patenaude, Longueuil, QC, J4K
5H4
(450) 463-1592
Emp Here 230
SIC 8211 Elementary and secondary schools
  Rejean Palardy

D-U-N-S 25-233-0311   (BR)
COLLEGE FRANCAIS (1965) INC
*COLLEGE FRANCAIS ANNEXE RIVE SUD
PRIMAIRE*
1391 Rue Beauregard, Longueuil, QC, J4K
2M3
(450) 670-7391
Emp Here 150
SIC 8211 Elementary and secondary schools

D-U-N-S 25-243-2679   (SL)
CONSTRUCTION GILLES LANTHIER INC
2119 Rue Sainte-Helene, Longueuil, QC, J4K
3T5
(450) 670-8238
Emp Here 30   *Sales* 14,121,930
SIC 1542 Nonresidential construction, nec
  Gilles Lanthier

D-U-N-S 24-900-5828   (SL)
CRC SOGEMA INC
(*Suby of* COWATERSOGEMA INTERNA-
TIONAL INC)
1111 Rue Saint-Charles O Bureau 454,
Longueuil, QC, J4K 5G4
(450) 651-2800
Emp Here 90
SIC 8742 Management consulting services

D-U-N-S 20-501-8963   (SL)
ENTREPRISES C. & R. MENARD INC
2711 Rue Papineau, Longueuil, QC, J4K 3M6
(450) 679-3131
Emp Here 50   *Sales* 12,044,200
SIC 1629 Heavy construction, nec
  Jean-Claude Menard
  Rene Menard

D-U-N-S 24-681-7733   (BR)
EQUIPE PCJ INC
MCDONALD'S
(*Suby of* EQUIPE PCJ INC)
822 Rue Saint-Laurent O, Longueuil, QC, J4K
1C3
(450) 651-1154
Emp Here 200
SIC 5812 Eating places
  Andre Clavel

D-U-N-S 24-765-4762   (SL)
EXTERNAT SAINT-JEAN-EUDES
*ASSOCIATION   DES   PARENTS   DE
L'EXTERNAT SAINT-JEAN-EUDES*
2151 Rue Saint-Georges, Longueuil, QC, J4K
4A7
(450) 677-2184
Emp Here 49   *Sales* 22,381,941
SIC 7389 Business services, nec
  Louis Trudelle

D-U-N-S 20-855-7843   (HQ)
**GEOPHYSIQUE G.P.R. INTERNATIONAL
INC**
GEOPHYSICS G.P.R. INTERNATIONAL
2545 Rue De Lorimier Bureau 100, Longueuil,
QC, J4K 3P7
(450) 679-2400
Emp Here 21   *Sales* 10,615,175
SIC 8999 Services, nec
  Rejean Paul

D-U-N-S 25-523-1342   (SL)
GESTION TERMICO INC
120 Place Charles-Le Moyne Bureau 300,
Longueuil, QC, J4K 2T4
(450) 670-3422
Emp Here 250   *Sales* 166,723,000
SIC 4729 Passenger transportation arrange-
ment
  Michael Genereux

D-U-N-S 20-555-5837   (BR)
**GOUVERNEMENT DE LA PROVINCE DE
QUEBEC**
*AGENCE DE SANTE ET DES SEVICES SO-
CIAUX DE LA MONTEREGIE*
(*Suby of* GOUVERNEMENT DE LA
PROVINCE DE QUEBEC)
1255 Rue Beauregard, Longueuil, QC, J4K
2M3
(450) 928-6777
Emp Here 460
SIC 8399 Social services, nec
  Daniele Moore

D-U-N-S 20-188-5980   (HQ)
GROUPE ATIS INC
FOCUS PORTES & FENETRES
1111 Rue Saint-Charles O Bureau 952,
Longueuil, QC, J4K 5G4
(450) 928-0101
Sales 75,706,100
SIC 2591 Drapery hardware and window
blinds and shades
  Benoit Alain
  Andre Parent
  Gerard Geoffrion
  Suzanne Blanchet
  Guy Leblanc
  Michel Lanctot
  Melanie Kau

D-U-N-S 20-011-5520   (HQ)
**GROUPE TABAC SCANDINAVE CANADA
INC**
COLTS AND OLD PORT CIGAR COMPANY
(*Suby of* SCANDINAVIAN TOBACCO
GROUP A/S)
1000 Rue De Serigny Bureau 600, Longueuil,
QC, J4K 5B1
(450) 677-1807
Sales 64,218,331
SIC 5194 Tobacco and tobacco products
  Sylvain Laporte
  Eric Vincent
  Marc Rheaume
  Sophie-Anne Brodeur

D-U-N-S 20-738-9032   (HQ)
HEROUX-DEVTEK INC
1111 Rue Saint-Charles O Bureau 600,
Longueuil, QC, J4K 5G4
(450) 679-3330
Emp Here 17   *Sales* 365,874,400
SIC 3593 Fluid power cylinders and actuators
  Gilles Labbe
  Martin Brassard
  Real Belanger
  Stephane Rainville
  Annie Goudreault
  Jean Gravel
  Remy Langelier
  Patrick Gagnon
  Jean-Philippe Sanche
  Eric Sauvageau

D-U-N-S 20-289-8037   (SL)

HIGHLAND COPPER COMPANY INC
COMPAGNIE DE CUIVRE HIGHLAND
1111 Rue Saint-Charles O Bureau 101,
Longueuil, QC, J4K 5G4
(450) 677-2455
Emp Here 6   *Sales* 14,325,294
SIC 1021 Copper ores
  Denis Miville-Deschenes
  Carole Plante
  Alain Krushnisky
  David Fennell
  John L. Johnson
  Jo Mark Zurel
  Allen Winters
  Luc Lessard
  Jean Desrosiers

D-U-N-S 24-872-1409   (HQ)
INNERGEX INC
(*Suby of* INNERGEX RENEWABLE ENERGY
INC)
1225 Rue Saint-Charles O 10e Etage,
Longueuil, QC, J4K 0B9
(450) 928-2550
Sales 84,764,250
SIC 4931 Electric and other services com-
bined
  Michel Letellier
  Nathalie Theberge
  Jean Perron

D-U-N-S 20-698-5751   (HQ)
INNERGEX RENEWABLE ENERGY INC
*INNERGEX ENERGIE RENOUVELABEL DE-
VELOPPEMENT DURABLE*
1225 Rue Saint-Charles O Bureau 10,
Longueuil, QC, J4K 0B9
(450) 928-2550
Emp Here 75   *Sales* 437,133,743
SIC 4931 Electric and other services com-
bined
  Michel Letellier
  Jean La Couture
  Renaud De Batz
  Peter Grover
  Francois Hebert
  Yves Baribeault
  Anne Cliche
  Colleen Giroux-Schmidt
  Robert Guillemette
  Matt Kennedy

D-U-N-S 24-053-8009   (SL)
INSTITUT NAZARETH ET LOUIS-BRAILLE
1111 Rue Saint-Charles O Bureau 200,
Longueuil, QC, J4K 5G4
(450) 463-1710
Emp Here 130   *Sales* 9,850,490
SIC 8093 Specialty outpatient clinics, nec
  Jacques Doyon
  Line Ampleman

D-U-N-S 24-861-1147   (SL)
**JACQUES CARTIER AND CHAMPLAIN
BRIDGES INCORPORATED, THE**
(*Suby of* GOVERNMENT OF CANADA)
1225 Rue Saint-Charles O Unite 500,
Longueuil, QC, J4K 0B9
(450) 651-8771
Emp Here 180   *Sales* 59,060,700
SIC 1622 Bridge, tunnel, and elevated high-
way construction
  Sandra Martel
  Paul T. Kefalas
  Richard Cacchione
  Catherine Lavoie
  Sylvain Villiard
  Dale Williams
  Henri-Jean Bonnis

D-U-N-S 20-504-3029   (HQ)
LOCATION RADIO TAXI UNION LTEE
1605 Rue Vercheres, Longueuil, QC, J4K 2Z6
(450) 679-6262
Emp Here 103   *Sales* 8,204,648
SIC 4121 Taxicabs

▲ Public Company   ■ Public Company Family Member   **HQ** Headquarters   **BR** Branch   **SL** Single Location

Romeo Cyr
Serge Rivest
Pierre Poupart

D-U-N-S 24-562-7393   (SL)
PERM-A-TEM INC
45 Place Charles-Le Moyne Bureau 100,
Longueuil, QC, J4K 5G5

Emp Here 50   *Sales* 12,047,777
SIC 7361 Employment agencies
 Sebastien Cicchillitti
 Lauretta Leblanc

D-U-N-S 20-717-3886   (HQ)
PNEUS CHARTRAND DISTRIBUTION INC
PNEU ACTION
1060 Boul La Fayette, Longueuil, QC, J4K 3B1
(450) 670-1585
Sales 57,644,250
SIC 5014 Tires and tubes
 Robert Chartrand

D-U-N-S 20-795-6157   (SL)
REGIE DU BATIMENT DU QUEBEC
201 Place Charles-Le Moyne Bureau 310,
Longueuil, QC, J4K 2T5
(450) 928-7603
Emp Here 50   *Sales* 22,460,950
SIC 7389 Business services, nec
 Roger Morin

D-U-N-S 24-528-6943   (SL)
SANTINEL INC
1061 Boul Sainte-Foy, Longueuil, QC, J4K
1W5
(450) 679-7801
Emp Here 50   *Sales* 11,714,400
SIC 8748 Business consulting, nec
 Maxime St-Jean
 Rivard Viviane
 Vincent Cote

D-U-N-S 20-087-0157   (BR)
SOCIETE DE GESTION COGIR S.E.N.C.
HABITATS LAFAYETTE, LES
(*Suby of* SOCIETE DE GESTION COGIR
S.E.N.C.)
100 Boul La Fayette Unite 426, Longueuil, QC,
J4K 5H6
(450) 674-8111
Emp Here 100
SIC 6513 Apartment building operators
 Yves Malette

D-U-N-S 20-378-9284   (SL)
SOGEMA TECHNOLOGIES INC
STRATEGIS TECHNOLOGIES
1111 Rue Saint-Charles O Bureau 700,
Longueuil, QC, J4K 5G4
(450) 651-2800
Emp Here 50   *Sales* 11,734,800
SIC 8731 Commercial physical research
 David Baron
 Philippe Lecoq

D-U-N-S 24-725-4501   (HQ)
STORNOWAY DIAMOND CORPORATION
SOCIETE DE DIAMANT STORNOWAY
111 Rue Saint-Charles O Bureau 400,
Longueuil, QC, J4K 5G4
(450) 616-5555
Emp Here 25   *Sales* 125,456,026
SIC 1499 Miscellaneous nonMetallic minerals,
except fuels
 Mattew L. Manson
 Eberhard Scherkus
 Patrick Godin
 Yves Perron
 Ian Holl
 Robin Hopkins
 Sylvie Gervais
 Brian Glover
 Martin Boucher
 Annie Torkia-Lagace

D-U-N-S 25-209-9239   (SL)

SUPERMARCHE SARAZIN, GILLES INC
I G A
825 Rue Saint-Laurent O, Longueuil, QC, J4K
2V1
(450) 677-5237
Emp Here 125   *Sales* 36,684,625
SIC 5411 Grocery stores
 Gilles Sarazin

D-U-N-S 25-739-3801   (HQ)
TECHNOLOGIES INTERACTIVES MEDIA-GRIF INC
1111 Rue Saint-Charles O Bureau 255,
Longueuil, QC, J4K 5G4
(450) 449-0102
Emp Here 250   *Sales* 64,427,066
SIC 7372 Prepackaged software
 Claude Roy
 Paul Bourque
 Helene Hallak
 Mark Eigenbauer
 Andre Leblanc
 Suzanne Moquin
 Jean-Michel Stam
 Camil Rousseau
 Stephane Anglaret
 Philippe Duval

D-U-N-S 20-056-6912   (HQ)
TECHNOLOGY EVALUATION CENTERS INC
CONNECTIVIA
1000 Rue De Serigny Bureau 300, Longueuil,
QC, J4K 5B1
(514) 954-3665
Sales 21,627,300
SIC 7371 Custom computer programming ser-
vices
 Yves Payette
 Francois Achim
 Lucie St-Georges
 Steve Saviuk

D-U-N-S 24-345-0793   (BR)
UNIVERSITE DE SHERBROOKE
CAMPUS LONGUEUIL
(*Suby of* UNIVERSITE DE SHERBROOKE)
150 Place Charles-Le Moyne Bureau 200,
Longueuil, QC, J4K 0A8
(450) 463-1835
Emp Here 150
SIC 8221 Colleges and universities
 Francois Gravel

D-U-N-S 20-333-0642   (HQ)
VAC OXYGENE ULC
LOCATION D'EQUIPEMENTS GUS
(*Suby of* MAINE OXY-ACETYLENE SUPPLY
COMPANY)
1733 Boul Taschereau, Longueuil, QC, J4K
2X9
(450) 679-3406
Emp Here 8   *Sales* 14,606,900
SIC 5169 Chemicals and allied products, nec
 Daniel Guerin
 Martin I. Eisenstein
 Patrick Heffernan
 Bryan Gentry

Longueuil, QC J4L

D-U-N-S 25-611-1691   (SL)
3116506 CANADA INC
BOULANGERIE PREMIERE MOISSON
2479 Ch De Chambly, Longueuil, QC, J4L
1M2
(450) 468-4406
Emp Here 72   *Sales* 21,130,344
SIC 5461 Retail bakeries
 Alain Merlin
 Liliane Colpron

D-U-N-S 24-978-1514   (SL)
CONSULTATION EN TECHNOLOGIE DE

L'INFORMATION ET DES COMUNICATIONS DACSYS INC
DACSYS
612 Rue Du Capricorne, Longueuil, QC, J4L
4X2
(514) 260-1616
Emp Here 150   *Sales* 18,716,400
SIC 8741 Management services
 Djalil Abdoul Assouma

D-U-N-S 20-201-4213   (SL)
MARCHE CENTRAL C.J.C. LTEE
MARCHE METRO
(*Suby of* PLACEMENTS C. D. F. G. INC)
2642 Ch De Chambly, Longueuil, QC, J4L
1M5
(450) 651-4123
Emp Here 82   *Sales* 24,065,114
SIC 5411 Grocery stores
 Denis Messier
 France Messier

D-U-N-S 24-509-1681   (BR)
METRO RICHELIEU INC
SUPER C, DIV DE
(*Suby of* METRO INC)
2901 Ch De Chambly, Longueuil, QC, J4L
1M7
(450) 651-6886
Emp Here 125
SIC 5411 Grocery stores
 Louis Cantin

D-U-N-S 25-219-6527   (SL)
PHARMACIE JEAN-MICHEL COUTU ET TRISTAN GIGUERE INC
JEAN COUTU #035 - #305
3245 Ch De Chambly Bureau 305, Longueuil,
QC, J4L 4K5
(450) 670-2496
Emp Here 49   *Sales* 12,394,746
SIC 5912 Drug stores and proprietary stores
 Jean-Michel Coutu

D-U-N-S 25-740-6116   (SL)
SANTEREGIE INC
3645 Ch De Chambly, Longueuil, QC, J4L 1N9

Emp Here 100   *Sales* 15,537,100
SIC 7361 Employment agencies
 Isabelle Choquette
 Jean Emmanuel Cesar

D-U-N-S 24-253-6878   (SL)
VERCHERES AUTO INC
LONGUEUIL HONDA
3551 Ch De Chambly, Longueuil, QC, J4L 4E2
(450) 679-4710
Emp Here 50   *Sales* 31,464,000
SIC 5511 New and used car dealers
 Chantale Morin

Longueuil, QC J4M

D-U-N-S 24-405-7527   (HQ)
CENTRE DE SANTE ET DE SERVICES SO-CIAUX PIERRE-BOUCHER
(*Suby of* GOUVERNEMENT DE LA
PROVINCE DE QUEBEC)
1333 Boul Jacques-Cartier E, Longueuil, QC,
J4M 2A5
(450) 468-8410
Sales 422,104,000
SIC 8062 General medical and surgical hospi-
tals
 Claude Bouchard
 Louise Potvin

D-U-N-S 25-291-3876   (SL)
CLSC SIMONNE-MONET-CHARTRAND
1303 Boul Jacques-Cartier E, Longueuil, QC,
J4M 2Y8
(450) 463-2850
Emp Here 150   *Sales* 31,060,200
SIC 8399 Social services, nec

Marc Lachance
Martine Lelerc
Robert Lauzon
Fleurette Vermette

Longueuil, QC J4N

D-U-N-S 24-104-6072   (BR)
2104225 ONTARIO LTD
WESTON BAKERIES LIMITED
(*Suby of* GEORGE WESTON LIMITED)
2700 Boul Jacques-Cartier E Bureau 67,
Longueuil, QC, J4N 1L5
(450) 448-7246
Emp Here 325
SIC 2051 Bread, cake, and related products
 Bertrand Dube

D-U-N-S 20-528-6904   (HQ)
9071-2670 QUEBEC INC
HYDRAULIQUES R.N.P
2400 Ch Du Lac, Longueuil, QC, J4N 1G8
(450) 670-5445
Sales 13,300,728
SIC 5084 Industrial machinery and equipment
 Nathalie Proulx

D-U-N-S 24-203-9035   (SL)
9119-6188 QUEBEC INC
EMPIRE SPORT
2786 Ch Du Lac Bureau 1, Longueuil, QC,
J4N 1B8
(450) 646-2888
Emp Here 300   *Sales* 37,426,500
SIC 5699 Miscellaneous apparel and acces-
sory stores
 Philippe Grise
 Patrick Byarelle
 Pierre-Antoine Fredercik

D-U-N-S 24-934-8020   (SL)
ACEMA IMPORTATIONS INC
2616 Boul Jacques-Cartier E, Longueuil, QC,
J4N 1P8
(450) 646-2591
Emp Here 20   *Sales* 10,702,480
SIC 5141 Groceries, general line
 Marc Fortin
 Francois Bibeau

D-U-N-S 24-167-7160   (BR)
ARCELORMITTAL PRODUITS LONGS CANADA S.E.N.C.
MITTAL CANADA
(*Suby of* ARCELORMITTAL PRODUITS
LONGS CANADA S.E.N.C.)
2555 Ch Du Lac, Longueuil, QC, J4N 1C1
(450) 442-7700
Emp Here 150
SIC 3316 Cold finishing of steel shapes
 Robert Beauden

D-U-N-S 24-103-7972   (HQ)
BOULANGERIES WESTON QUEBEC LIMI-TEE
(*Suby of* GEORGE WESTON LIMITED)
2700 Boul Jacques-Cartier E, Longueuil, QC,
J4N 1L5
(450) 448-7246
Emp Here 245   *Sales* 121,846,250
SIC 2051 Bread, cake, and related products
 Ralph Robinson
 Robert Balcon
 Robert Vaux

D-U-N-S 24-124-7845   (HQ)
CAISSE DESJARDINS PIERRE-BOUCHER
DESJARDINS ENTREPRISESRIVE-SUD
2401 Boul Roland-Therrien, Longueuil, QC,
J4N 1C5
(450) 468-7411
Emp Here 100   *Sales* 19,876,480
SIC 6062 State credit unions
 Normand Besner

Pierre Gagnon
Martine Lapointe
Alain Dery
Andre Gascon
Phuong-Minh Phan
Marie-Michele Drolet
Kim Demontignac
Johanne Dube
Gaetan Beliveau

D-U-N-S 20-293-7285   (BR)
CANADIAN TIRE REAL ESTATE LIMITED
INVESTISSEMENTS RAYMOND GAGNE, LES
(*Suby of* CANADIAN TIRE CORPORATION, LIMITED)
2211 Boul Roland-Therrien Bureau 256, Longueuil, QC, J4N 1P2
(450) 448-1177
Emp Here 150
SIC 6531 Real estate agents and managers
Raymond Gagne

D-U-N-S 25-233-4859   (SL)
CENTRE DE FORMATION PROFESSION-NELLE PIERRE DUPUY
1150 Ch Du Tremblay, Longueuil, QC, J4N 1A2
(450) 468-4000
Emp Here 300   *Sales* 29,735,700
SIC 8211 Elementary and secondary schools
Michel Lapierre
Richard Charest

D-U-N-S 25-233-1640   (BR)
COMMISSION SCOLAIRE MARIE-VICTORIN
ECOLE BEL ESSOR
(*Suby of* COMMISSION SCOLAIRE MARIE-VICTORIN)
1250 Ch Du Tremblay, Longueuil, QC, J4N 1A2
(450) 468-0833
Emp Here 80
SIC 8211 Elementary and secondary schools
Chantal Sauve

D-U-N-S 25-081-6097   (HQ)
EMPIRE SPORTS INC
2786 Ch Du Lac Bureau 1, Longueuil, QC, J4N 1B8
(450) 646-2888
Emp Here 50   *Sales* 36,649,200
SIC 5941 Sporting goods and bicycle shops
Philippe Grise
Frederic Pierre-Antoine
Patrick Byarelle

D-U-N-S 25-027-3349   (BR)
PROVIGO DISTRIBUTION INC
PROVIGO LE MARCHE LONGUEUIL
(*Suby of* LOBLAW COMPANIES LIMITED)
1150 Rue King-George, Longueuil, QC, J4N 1P3
(450) 647-1717
Emp Here 120
SIC 5411 Grocery stores
Reginald Morneau

D-U-N-S 24-066-9122   (BR)
SOCIETE EN COMMANDITE LES PROME-NADES DU PARC
PROMENADES DU PARC, LES
1910 Rue Adoncour Bureau 500, Longueuil, QC, J4N 1T3
(450) 448-3448
Emp Here 100
SIC 3993 Signs and advertising specialties
Jean-Denis Parent

D-U-N-S 24-648-9462   (SL)
VIBROSYSTM INC
ZOOM
2727 Boul Jacques-Cartier E, Longueuil, QC, J4N 1L7
(450) 646-2157
Emp Here 90   *Sales* 20,456,010
SIC 3823 Process control instruments

Marius Cloutier
Mathieu Cloutier
Pierre Favreau

D-U-N-S 25-294-7536   (BR)
WAL-MART CANADA CORP
(*Suby of* WALMART INC.)
1999 Boul Roland-Therrien, Longueuil, QC, J4N 1A3
(450) 448-2688
Emp Here 300
SIC 5311 Department stores
Eric Roy

D-U-N-S 25-411-1495   (HQ)
WM QUEBEC INC
CANADIAN WASTE
(*Suby of* WASTE MANAGEMENT, INC.)
2457 Ch Du Lac, Longueuil, QC, J4N 1P1
(450) 646-7870
Emp Here 50   *Sales* 81,430,500
SIC 4953 Refuse systems
Aaron Joseph Johnson
Donald P Wright
Courtney Alison Tippy
Leslie K Nagy
David Reed

Longueuil, QC J4P

D-U-N-S 20-909-2998   (HQ)
COLLEGE CHARLES-LEMOYNE DE LONGUEUIL INC
ACADEMIE INTERNATIONALE CHARLES-LEMOYNE
901 Ch Tiffin, Longueuil, QC, J4P 3G6
(514) 875-0505
Emp Here 85   *Sales* 23,902,560
SIC 8221 Colleges and universities
Claude Paul-Hus
Sylvain Larocque
Michel Rocheleau
Laury-Ann C.Paulin
David Bowles
Francois La Roche
Nicolas Beylich

D-U-N-S 25-242-9196   (SL)
COLLEGE NOTRE-DAME-DE-LOURDES
845 Ch Tiffin, Longueuil, QC, J4P 3G5
(450) 670-4740
Emp Here 100   *Sales* 9,282,600
SIC 8211 Elementary and secondary schools
Remi Poliquin

Lorrainville, QC J0Z

D-U-N-S 20-726-6768   (SL)
CLEMENT, CHRYSLER DODGE LTEE
EQUIPEMENT CLEMENT
77 Rue De L'Eglise N, Lorrainville, QC, J0Z 2R0
(819) 625-2187
Emp Here 26   *Sales* 12,950,028
SIC 5511 New and used car dealers
Normand Clement
Michelyne Clement

Louiseville, QC J5V

D-U-N-S 24-421-3216   (SL)
9107-7081 QUEBEC INC
351 Rue Notre-Dame N, Louiseville, QC, J5V 1X9
(819) 228-9497
Emp Here 75   *Sales* 19,616,475
SIC 6712 Bank holding companies
Monia Lacasse

D-U-N-S 25-497-9578   (SL)
ALIMENTS SERVAL CANADA LTEE, LES
(*Suby of* FINANCIERE SERVAL CANADA INC)
303 Rue Saint-Marc, Louiseville, QC, J5V 2G2
(819) 228-5551
Emp Here 24   *Sales* 11,400,624
SIC 5085 Industrial supplies
Fabien Fontaine
Michel Bach
Beatrice Lemaitre
Robert Wynands
Rene Demers

D-U-N-S 20-795-7759   (HQ)
CAISSE DESJARDINS DE L'OUEST DE LA MAURICIE
CENTRE DE SERVICES SAINT-BARNABE
75 Av Saint-Laurent Bureau 300, Louiseville, QC, J5V 1J6
(819) 228-9422
Emp Here 50   *Sales* 17,094,675
SIC 6062 State credit unions
Jacques Duranleau
Luc Pombert
Johanne Beaulieu Sylvestre
Annie Plante
Rene J. Lemire
Jean Boisvert
Karine Arseneault
Monique Bellemare
Jules Berneche
Michel Bournival

D-U-N-S 24-401-9915   (HQ)
CANADEL INC
CANADEL FURNITURE
700 Rue Canadel, Louiseville, QC, J5V 3A4
(819) 228-8471
Sales 211,531,750
SIC 2511 Wood household furniture
Guy Deveault
Michel Deveault

D-U-N-S 24-314-7498   (BR)
CANADEL INC
(*Suby of* CANADEL INC)
700 Rue Canadel, Louiseville, QC, J5V 3A4
(819) 228-8471
Emp Here 500
SIC 2511 Wood household furniture
Guy Deveault

D-U-N-S 24-759-3650   (SL)
CENTRE D'HEBERGEMENT SOIN LONGUE DUREE MRC DE MASKINONGE, LE
181 6e Av, Louiseville, QC, J5V 1V2
(819) 228-2706
Emp Here 1   *Sales* 15,813,372
SIC 8361 Residential care
Therese Globensky

D-U-N-S 20-206-6635   (SL)
CHEMISE EMPIRE LTEE
451 Av Saint-Laurent, Louiseville, QC, J5V 1K4
(819) 228-2821
Emp Here 140   *Sales* 19,134,360
SIC 2321 Men's and boy's furnishings
Rene St-Amant
Helene Beland
Marie-Josee Bergeron

D-U-N-S 24-667-4998   (SL)
COLORIDE INC
80 Av Saint-Martin, Louiseville, QC, J5V 1B4
(819) 228-5553
Emp Here 100   *Sales* 32,613,600
SIC 3999 Manufacturing industries, nec
Nicolas Leclabart
Oliver Mathai
Guylaine Millette

D-U-N-S 20-859-5249   (SL)
CYRILLE FRIGON (1996) INC
CFI
1351 Boul Saint-Laurent O, Louiseville, QC,

J5V 2L4
(819) 228-9491
Emp Here 35   *Sales* 21,527,667
SIC 5153 Grain and field beans
Remi Frigon

D-U-N-S 24-120-7930   (BR)
GOUVERNEMENT DE LA PROVINCE DE QUEBEC
RESIDENCE AVELLIN DALCOURT
(*Suby of* GOUVERNEMENT DE LA PROVINCE DE QUEBEC)
450 2e Rue, Louiseville, QC, J5V 1V3
(819) 228-2700
Emp Here 300
SIC 8361 Residential care
Yves Martin

D-U-N-S 24-337-3664   (BR)
IMPRIMERIES TRANSCONTINENTAL 2005 S.E.N.C
TRANSCONTINENTAL GAGNE
(*Suby of* IMPRIMERIES TRANSCONTINENTAL 2005 S.E.N.C.)
750 Rue Deveault, Louiseville, QC, J5V 3C2
(819) 228-2766
Emp Here 325
SIC 7389 Business services, nec
Stephane Gadbois

D-U-N-S 20-206-6916   (HQ)
LABORATOIRES CHOISY LTEE
390 Boul Saint-Laurent E, Louiseville, QC, J5V 2L7
(819) 228-5564
Emp Here 100   *Sales* 56,804,200
SIC 2842 Polishes and sanitation goods
Guy L. Trudeau
Francine Noel Trudeau
Pierre Simard
Jean-Francois Trudeau

D-U-N-S 20-206-7161   (SL)
LOUISEVILLE AUTOMOBILE LTEE
871 Boul Saint-Laurent O, Louiseville, QC, J5V 1L3

Emp Here 45   *Sales* 22,413,510
SIC 5511 New and used car dealers
Normand Lessard
Patrick Lessard

D-U-N-S 25-373-7381   (SL)
MARCHE D'ALIMENTATION DIANE RO-DRIGUE INC
I G A
714 Boul Saint-Laurent O, Louiseville, QC, J5V 1K7
(819) 228-5818
Emp Here 50   *Sales* 13,707,600
SIC 5411 Grocery stores
Diane Rodrigue

D-U-N-S 20-248-6569   (SL)
MARCHE EMERY & FILS INC
METRO PLUS EMERY LOUISEVILLE
80 Rue Saint-Marc, Louiseville, QC, J5V 2E6
(819) 228-2764
Emp Here 95   *Sales* 27,880,315
SIC 5411 Grocery stores
Richard Emery
Madeleine Morin

D-U-N-S 24-664-2102   (BR)
MARQUIS IMPRIMEUR INC
MARQUIS GAGNE
(*Suby of* MARQUIS IMPRIMEUR INC)
750 Rue Deveault, Louiseville, QC, J5V 3C2
(819) 228-2766
Emp Here 100
SIC 2732 Book printing
Martin Lacharite

D-U-N-S 24-434-7126   (HQ)
PANNEAUX MASKI INC
MASKI
(*Suby of* 9015-3065 QUEBEC INC)
50 10e Av, Louiseville, QC, J5V 0A5

(819) 228-8461
Sales 16,351,450
SIC 2421 Sawmills and planing mills, general
Michel Gervais
Serge Gervais
Daniel Pellerin

D-U-N-S 20-695-0318   (HQ)
PLANCHERS GROLEAU INC
541 Av Dalcourt, Louiseville, QC, J5V 2Z7
(819) 228-4446
Emp Here 45   *Sales* 20,546,568
SIC 3996 Hard surface floor coverings, nec
Louise Groleau
Sebastien Tremblay
Patrick Tremblay

Lourdes-De-Blanc-Sablon, QC G0G

D-U-N-S 24-200-4471   (HQ)
CENTRE DE LA SANTE ET DU SERVICES SOCIAUX DE LA BASSE COTE-NORD
CSSS DE LA BASE COTE-NORD
1070   Boul   Docteur-Camille-Marcoux,
Lourdes-De-Blanc-Sablon, QC, G0G 1W0
(418) 461-2144
Sales 27,770,000
SIC 8062 General medical and surgical hospitals
Marc Fortin

Lourdes-De-Joliette, QC J0K

D-U-N-S 20-370-1347   (SL)
GREGOIRE SPORT INC
MAGASIN EN LIGNE DIRTNROAD.COM, LE
2061 Boul Barrette, Lourdes-De-Joliette, QC,
J0K 1K0
(450) 752-2201
Emp Here 26   *Sales* 12,950,028
SIC 5599 Automotive dealers, nec
Gaby Gregoire
Serge Gregoire
Marie-Josee Gregoire
David Gregoire

Lyster, QC G0S

D-U-N-S 20-799-5957   (SL)
COOPERATIVE AGRICOLE-APPALACHE
120 Rue Saint-Pierre, Lyster, QC, G0S 1V0
(819) 389-5553
Emp Here 49   *Sales* 19,698,824
SIC 8699 Membership organizations, nec
Marcel Nadeau

D-U-N-S 20-206-8680   (SL)
INDUSTRIES LYSTER INC
2555 Rue Becancour, Lyster, QC, G0S 1V0

Emp Here 100   *Sales* 23,343,500
SIC 3369 Nonferrous foundries, nec
Claude Fournier

Macamic, QC J0Z

D-U-N-S 24-842-2545   (SL)
D.M.C. SOUDURE INC
DMC SOUDURE
1816 Rte 111 E, Macamic, QC, J0Z 2S0
(819) 782-2514
Emp Here 120   *Sales* 29,542,320
SIC 1799 Special trade contractors, nec
Denis Marion

Magog, QC J1X

D-U-N-S 25-464-8827   (SL)
2709970 CANADA INC
TOYOTA MAGOG
2500 Rue Sherbrooke, Magog, QC, J1X 4E8
(819) 843-9883
Emp Here 26   *Sales* 12,950,028
SIC 5511 New and used car dealers
Roland Gaudreau
Jean-Philippe Gaudreau

D-U-N-S 20-333-0352   (SL)
4361806 CANADA INC
DISTRIBUTION MMO
(*Suby of* SHERGROUP INC)
205 Rue Du Centre, Magog, QC, J1X 5B6
(819) 843-4441
Emp Here 100   *Sales* 44,717,400
SIC 5072 Hardware
Jocelyn Anctil
Francine Anctil

D-U-N-S 24-904-1401   (HQ)
9128-3820 QUEBEC INC
IGA GAZAILLE
1526 Rue Sherbrooke, Magog, QC, J1X 2T3
(819) 868-1122
Emp Here 50   *Sales* 32,282,470
SIC 5411 Grocery stores
Michel Gazaille

D-U-N-S 20-356-0388   (SL)
9192-2773 QUEBEC INC
INTER-PROVINCIAL MECANIQUE MAINTE-NANCE
2620 Rue Macpherson, Magog, QC, J1X 0E6
(819) 868-4215
Emp Here 26   *Sales* 12,350,676
SIC 5084 Industrial machinery and equipment
Steve Malenfant
Patrick Malenfant
Yves Bolland

D-U-N-S 24-357-7884   (HQ)
ARJOHUNTLEIGH MAGOG INC
BHM MEDICAL
2001 Rue Tanguay, Magog, QC, J1X 5Y5
(819) 868-0441
Sales 42,048,465
SIC 3841 Surgical and medical instruments
Mickael Persson
C. Paul W. Smith
Niklas Blomstedt
Julien Bouchard

D-U-N-S 20-191-2933   (HQ)
CAISSE   DESJARDINS   DU   LAC-MEMPHREMAGOG
CENTRE DE SERVICE D'EASTMAN
230 Rue Principale O, Magog, QC, J1X 2A5

Emp Here 60   *Sales* 17,677,516
SIC 6062 State credit unions
Margerie Legare
Danielle Bolduc
Maxime Ferland
Maxime Langlois
Christine Allard
Laurent Auger
Louise Cote
Georgianne Gagnon
Gaetan Giguere
Charles Guay

D-U-N-S 20-885-2871   (HQ)
CAMSO INC
CAMOPLAST SOLIDEAL - CENTRE TECH-NIQUE
(*Suby of* COMPAGNIE GENERALE DES ETABLISSEMENTS MICHELIN)
2633 Rue Macpherson, Magog, QC, J1X 0E6
(819) 868-1500
Emp Here 75   *Sales* 1,791,090,000

SIC 3011 Tires and inner tubes
Thomas Bottcher
Catherine Conides
Kent Carson
Ronald Jeffrey Maclean
Stephen Legault
Luc Minguet
Joan Ekins Martin

D-U-N-S 24-352-2898   (BR)
CAMSO INC
SYSTEMES DE CHENILLES CTC DIV OF
(*Suby of* COMPAGNIE GENERALE DES ETABLISSEMENTS MICHELIN)
2675 Rue Macpherson, Magog, QC, J1X 0E6
(819) 868-1500
Emp Here 85
SIC 8731 Commercial physical research
Rui Carreira

D-U-N-S 20-909-3905   (HQ)
COMMISSION   SCOLAIRE   EASTERN TOWNSHIPS
EASTERN TOWNSHIPS SCHOOL BOARD
340 Rue Saint-Jean-Bosco, Magog, QC, J1X 1K9
(819) 868-3100
Sales 109,030,900
SIC 8211 Elementary and secondary schools
Mike Murray
Joy Humenuik
Kandy Mackey
Michel Soucy

D-U-N-S 20-381-4892   (SL)
CONCEPTROMEC EXPORTATION INC
1780 Boul Industriel, Magog, QC, J1X 4V9
(819) 847-3627
Emp Here 70   *Sales* 12,317,060
SIC 8711 Engineering services
Stephane Begin
Roger Gamelin

D-U-N-S 24-792-6280   (SL)
CONCEPTROMEC INC
CONCEPTROMEC 2001
(*Suby of* INVESTISSEMENTS KREATOR INC)
1782 Boul Industriel, Magog, QC, J1X 4V9
(819) 847-3627
Emp Here 62   *Sales* 13,764,062
SIC 3559 Special industry machinery, nec
Stephane Begin
Roger Gamelin

D-U-N-S 24-680-6066   (BR)
DIFCO, TISSUS DE PERFORMANCE INC
(*Suby of* BERRY GLOBAL GROUP, INC.)
160 Rue Principale E, Magog, QC, J1X 4X5

Emp Here 200
SIC 2299 Textile goods, nec
Ioannis Pananis

D-U-N-S 20-548-3816   (SL)
G-SPEK INC
2039 Rue Rene-Patenaude, Magog, QC, J1X 7J2
(819) 868-7655
Emp Here 90   *Sales* 18,170,730
SIC 3089 Plastics products, nec
Eric Graveson

D-U-N-S 20-118-8195   (SL)
GESTION SOLUTIONS PLASTIK INC
2123 Boul Industriel, Magog, QC, J1X 7J7
(819) 847-2466
Emp Here 70   *Sales* 14,132,790
SIC 3089 Plastics products, nec
Yvan Lavigne
Yvon Bisaillon
Guy Beland

D-U-N-S 25-259-9139   (BR)
GOUVERNEMENT DE LA PROVINCE DE QUEBEC
CENTRE DE SANTE ET DE SERVICES SO-

CIAUX DE MEMPHREMAGOG
(*Suby of* GOUVERNEMENT   DE   LA PROVINCE DE QUEBEC)
50 Rue Saint-Patrice E, Magog, QC, J1X 3X3
(819) 843-2572
Emp Here 900
SIC 8062 General medical and surgical hospitals
Sylvie Moreau

D-U-N-S 20-013-8373   (HQ)
GROUPE KANWAL INC
GESTION S.P.S.
1426 Boul Industriel, Magog, QC, J1X 4V9
(819) 868-4156
Emp Here 1   *Sales* 77,122,399
SIC 6712 Bank holding companies
Sutinderpaul Kanwal Singh

D-U-N-S 20-543-5071   (SL)
GURIT AMERICAS INC
555 Boul Poirier, Magog, QC, J1X 7L1
(819) 847-2182
Emp Here 250   *Sales* 111,161,250
SIC 2899 Chemical preparations, nec
Stefan Gautschi
Marc-Andre Watson
Rudolf Hadorn

D-U-N-S 24-760-3848   (SL)
INVESTISSEMENTS JEAN C. LAPIERRE LTEE
CANADIAN TIRE
2135 Rue Sherbrooke, Magog, QC, J1X 2T5
(819) 843-3939
Emp Here 80   *Sales* 29,137,200
SIC 5014 Tires and tubes
Jean-Claude Lapierre

D-U-N-S 25-366-8883   (SL)
KANWAL INC
INDUSTRIEL RPT
(*Suby of* GROUPE KANWAL INC)
1426 Boul Industriel, Magog, QC, J1X 4V9
(819) 868-5152
Emp Here 160   *Sales* 25,417,280
SIC 3089 Plastics products, nec
Sutinderpaul Singh Kanwal

D-U-N-S 24-355-7287   (HQ)
LAPALME, GERMAIN & FILS INC
2972 Ch Milletta, Magog, QC, J1X 0R4
(819) 843-2367
Sales 12,309,300
SIC 1794 Excavation work
Jacques Lapalme
Pierre Lapalme
Gerald Lapalme
Gerald Lapalme
Guillaume Lapalme
Vincent Lapalme

D-U-N-S 25-012-1493   (SL)
LE HAVRE DES CANTONS
231 Dollard, Magog, QC, J1X 2M5
(819) 868-1010
Emp Here 46   *Sales* 12,726,360
SIC 2869 Industrial organic chemicals, nec
Xrox Aane Bourgaunt

D-U-N-S 20-207-0652   (SL)
LEFKO PRODUITS DE PLASTIQUE INC
(*Suby of* PLACEMENTS SCANS INC, LES)
1700 Boul Industriel, Magog, QC, J1X 4V9
(819) 843-9237
Emp Here 60   *Sales* 17,041,260
SIC 2821 Plastics materials and resins
Serge Lamoureux
Christian Lamoureux
Normand Lamoureux
Alain Lamoureux

D-U-N-S 24-126-2174   (SL)
MAGOG FORD (2000) INC
2000 Rue Sherbrooke, Magog, QC, J1X 2T3
(819) 843-3673
Emp Here 25   *Sales* 12,451,950

▲ Public Company   ■ Public Company Family Member   **HQ** Headquarters   **BR** Branch   **SL** Single Location

SIC 5531 Auto and home supply stores
Gilles Beaucage

D-U-N-S 25-970-0318　　(SL)
MAGOG TOYOTA INC
2500 Rue Sherbrooke, Magog, QC, J1X 4E8
(819) 843-9883
Emp Here 25　　*Sales* 12,451,950
SIC 5511 New and used car dealers
Roland Gadreu

D-U-N-S 25-355-3630　　(SL)
MAGOTTEAUX LTEE
(*Suby of* SIGDO KOPPERS S.A.)
601 Rue Champlain, Magog, QC, J1X 2N1
(819) 843-0443
Emp Here 100　　*Sales* 18,138,800
SIC 3325 Steel foundries, nec
Sebastien Dossogne
Raphael Delhaye
Jean-Marc Xhenseval
Marc Babineau
Fabrice Heughebaert
Alan Greer

D-U-N-S 24-107-1687　　(HQ)
**NOURYON PATE ET PERFORMANCE
CANADA INC**
(*Suby of* NOURYON COOPERATIEF U.A.)
1900 Rue Saint-Patrice E Bureau 25, Magog,
QC, J1X 3W5
(819) 843-8942
Emp Here 65　　*Sales* 34,934,583
SIC 2899 Chemical preparations, nec
Gilles Villeneuve
Tift Shepherd
Pierre Marchand
Mathieu Hade
Sebastien Maurice

D-U-N-S 25-027-3919　　(HQ)
PEINTURE & PIECES D.R. INC
AUTO VALUE
2509 Rue Sherbrooke, Magog, QC, J1X 4E7
(819) 843-0550
Emp Here 12　　*Sales* 13,448,106
SIC 5531 Auto and home supply stores
Dany Robert

D-U-N-S 24-190-5657　　(BR)
PROVIGO DISTRIBUTION INC
LOBLAWS
(*Suby of* LOBLAW COMPANIES LIMITED)
1350 Rue Sherbrooke, Magog, QC, J1X 2T3
(819) 868-8630
Emp Here 100
SIC 5411 Grocery stores
Liette Fauteux

D-U-N-S 25-876-5254　　(BR)
PYRO-AIR LTEE
(*Suby of* PYRO-AIR LTEE)
2301 Rue Principale O, Magog, QC, J1X 0J4
(819) 847-2014
Emp Here 75
SIC 1711 Plumbing, heating, air-conditioning
Guy Renaud

D-U-N-S 24-132-0782　　(SL)
QUALITE PERFORMANCE MAGOG INC
MAGOG HONDA
2400 Rue Sherbrooke, Magog, QC, J1X 4E6
(819) 843-0099
Emp Here 28　　*Sales* 13,300,728
SIC 5088 Transportation equipment and sup-
plies
Christian Saint-Pierre

D-U-N-S 20-107-9501　　(SL)
QUINCO & CIE INC
STICS DECO
2035 Rue Rene-Patenaude, Magog, QC, J1X
7J2
(819) 847-4001
Emp Here 110　　*Sales* 9,963,366
SIC 2679 Converted paper products, nec
Elaine Paquin

Ginette Pouliot
Rejean Galvin

D-U-N-S 24-890-1043　　(SL)
R-MAG 118 INC
ROTISSERIE ST-HUBERT
1615 Ch De La Riviere-Aux-Cerises Bureau 2,
Magog, QC, J1X 3W3
(819) 847-3366
Emp Here 80　　*Sales* 3,641,520
SIC 5812 Eating places
Jocelyn Proulx

D-U-N-S 24-345-9273　　(HQ)
SHERGROUP INC
205 Rue Du Centre, Magog, QC, J1X 5B6
(819) 843-4441
Sales 30,888,550
SIC 6712 Bank holding companies
Jocelyn Anctil
Renelle Anctil
Francine Anctil

D-U-N-S 20-996-1226　　(SL)
SUPERMARCHE J.P.V. PLOUFFE INC
METRO PLOUFFE
460 Rue Saint-Patrice O, Magog, QC, J1X
1W9
(819) 843-9202
Emp Here 100　　*Sales* 29,347,700
SIC 5411 Grocery stores
Daniel Plouffe
Patrick Plouffe

D-U-N-S 25-361-2691　　(SL)
TORA MAGOG LIMITEE
TIGRE GEANT
(*Suby of* GIANT TIGER STORES LIMITED)
1730 Rue Sherbrooke, Magog, QC, J1X 2T3
(819) 843-3043
Emp Here 50　　*Sales* 10,267,150
SIC 5399 Miscellaneous general merchandise
Paul Goudreau

D-U-N-S 20-271-0513　　(SL)
USIHOME INC
(*Suby of* SHERGROUP INC)
1455 Boul Industriel, Magog, QC, J1X 4P2
(819) 847-0666
Emp Here 100　　*Sales* 19,636,100
SIC 1752 Floor laying and floor work, nec
Jocelyn Anctil
Gesner Blenkhorn
David Anctil
Stephane Cote
Francine Rouleau Anctil

D-U-N-S 24-356-8131　　(BR)
WAL-MART CANADA CORP
ACCES PHARMA CHEZ WALMART
(*Suby of* WALMART INC.)
1935 Rue Sherbrooke, Magog, QC, J1X 2T5
(819) 868-9775
Emp Here 80
SIC 5311 Department stores

Malartic, QC J0Y

D-U-N-S 20-381-8240　　(SL)
9222-0201 QUEBEC INC
LOCATION DUMCO
890 Rue La Salle, Malartic, QC, J0Y 1Z0
(819) 757-4868
Emp Here 50　　*Sales* 11,008,400
SIC 1794 Excavation work
Michel Lefebvre
Sylvain Goulet
Lucie Mailhot

D-U-N-S 24-858-0065　　(HQ)
ASDR CANADA INC
ASDR
691 Rue Royale, Malartic, QC, J0Y 1Z0
(819) 757-3039
Emp Here 80　　*Sales* 43,861,080

SIC 6712 Bank holding companies
Stephen Authier
Philippe Authier
Carl Dufour
Marc Turcotte
Pierre Fillion

D-U-N-S 20-290-2821　　(HQ)
CANADIAN MALARTIC GP
MINE CANADIAN MALARTIC
100 Ch Du Lac Mourier, Malartic, QC, J0Y 1Z0
(819) 757-2225
Sales 173,926,320
SIC 1041 Gold ores
Eric Tremblay

D-U-N-S 20-574-5941　　(BR)
**CENTRE DE SANTE ET DE SERVICES SO-
CIAUX DE LA VALLEE-DE-L'OR**
HOPITAL PSYCHIATRIQUE DE MALARTIC
(*Suby of* CENTRE DE SANTE ET DE SER-
VICES SOCIAUX DE LA VALLEE-DE-L'OR)
1141 Rue Royale, Malartic, QC, J0Y 1Z0
(819) 825-5858
Emp Here 110
SIC 8062 General medical and surgical hospi-
tals
Simone Plourde

Maniwaki, QC J9E

D-U-N-S 20-327-9448　　(HQ)
**FONDATION SANTE VALLEE-DE-LA-
GATINEAU**
CSSS DE LA VALLEE-DE-LA-GATINEAU , LE
309 Boul Desjardins, Maniwaki, QC, J9E 2E7
(819) 449-4690
Sales 82,591,300
SIC 8062 General medical and surgical hospi-
tals
Andre Benoit
Michel Gauthier
Sylvie Martin
Muriel Bainbridge
Chantal Chartrand
Bernard Dumont

D-U-N-S 24-341-2470　　(BR)
**FONDATION SANTE VALLEE-DE-LA-
GATINEAU**
*CENTRE DE SANTE ET DE SERVICES SO-
CIAUX DE LA VALLEE-DE-LA-GATINEAU*
(*Suby of* FONDATION SANTE VALLEE-DE-
LA-GATINEAU)
177 Rue Des Oblats, Maniwaki, QC, J9E 1G5
(819) 449-2513
Emp Here 100
SIC 8361 Residential care
Sylvie Martin

D-U-N-S 25-626-2705　　(SL)
GENDRON CHRYSLER JEEP DODGE
259 Boul Desjardins, Maniwaki, QC, J9E 2E4
(819) 449-1611
Emp Here 32　　*Sales* 15,938,496
SIC 5511 New and used car dealers
Robert D Gendron

D-U-N-S 20-207-3573　　(HQ)
GERARD HUBERT AUTOMOBILES LTEE
HUBERT AUTO
241 Boul Desjardins, Maniwaki, QC, J9E 2E3
(819) 449-2266
Sales 36,498,240
SIC 5511 New and used car dealers
Gerard Hubert

D-U-N-S 25-201-9989　　(SL)
**LAUZON-RESSOURCES FORESTIERES
INC**
(*Suby of* PLACEMENTS LAUZON INC)
77 Rue Commerciale, Maniwaki, QC, J9E 1N8
(819) 449-3636
Emp Here 70　　*Sales* 13,465,900

SIC 2411 Logging
David Lauzon

D-U-N-S 20-718-0378　　(SL)
MAXI MANIWAKI INC
MAXI
170 Rue Principale S, Maniwaki, QC, J9E 1Z7
(819) 449-6822
Emp Here 49　　*Sales* 13,433,448
SIC 5411 Grocery stores
Martin Dupuis

D-U-N-S 25-150-0278　　(BR)
PF RESOLU CANADA INC
ABITIBIBOWATER
(*Suby of* RESOLUTE FOREST PRODUCTS
INC)
200 Ch De Montcerf, Maniwaki, QC, J9E 1A1
(819) 449-2100
Emp Here 98
SIC 2421 Sawmills and planing mills, general
Paul Grondin

D-U-N-S 25-201-0108　　(SL)
REXFORET INC
248 Rue Cartier, Maniwaki, QC, J9E 3P5
(819) 449-6088
Emp Here 100　　*Sales* 13,675,900
SIC 0851 Forestry services
Yves Lamarre
Carol Turgeon

Manouane, QC J0K

D-U-N-S 20-367-3574　　(SL)
**SERVICES FORESTIERS ET TERRITORI-
AUX DE MANAWAN (SFTM) INC**
180 Rue Amiskw, Manouane, QC, J0K 1M0

Emp Here 80　　*Sales* 11,202,320
SIC 7999 Amusement and recreation, nec
Yann Flamand
Vincent Flamand
Jacques Habel

Manseau, QC G0X

D-U-N-S 20-313-9845　　(SL)
CANNEBERGES ATOKA INC
3025 Rte 218, Manseau, QC, G0X 1V0
(819) 356-2001
Emp Here 100　　*Sales* 16,902,500
SIC 0171 Berry crops
Marc Bieler
Earl Larson
Sami Doucet
Richard A. Stamm
Jon Cowell
Derek May

Mansonville, QC J0E

D-U-N-S 20-921-0991　　(BR)
**CAISSE DESJARDINS DU LAC-
MEMPHREMAGOG**
CENTRE DE SERVICE
(*Suby of* CAISSE DESJARDINS DU LAC-
MEMPHREMAGOG)
342 Rue Principale, Mansonville, QC, J0E 1X0
(819) 843-3328
Emp Here 111
SIC 6036 Savings institutions, except federal
Jean Dupont

Maria, QC G0C

D-U-N-S 20-207-5198   (SL)
MAGASIN COOP DE MARIA IGA
IGA
524 Boul Perron, Maria, QC, G0C 1Y0
(418) 759-3440
Emp Here 50   *Sales* 16,148,450
SIC 5411 Grocery stores
 Martin Deraiche

D-U-N-S 20-288-3831   (SL)
VENT DE L'EST INC
711 Boul Perron, Maria, QC, G0C 1Y0
(418) 759-3054
Emp Here 65   *Sales* 12,378,730
SIC 3621 Motors and generators
 Luc Boudreau
 Luc Lafontaine
 Steven Fugere
 Mitchell Fournier

Marieville, QC J3M

D-U-N-S 20-033-9211   (BR)
COMMISSION SCOLAIRE DES HAUTES-RIVIERES
ECOLE MGR EUCLIDE THEBERGE
(*Suby of* COMMISSION SCOLAIRE DES HAUTES-RIVIERES)
677 Rue Desjardins, Marieville, QC, J3M 1R1
(450) 460-4491
Emp Here 120
SIC 8211 Elementary and secondary schools
 Magalie Petelle

D-U-N-S 25-684-9167   (SL)
CONSTRUCTION MARIEVILLE INC
MCI ENTREPRENEUR GENERAL
2010 Rue Du Pont, Marieville, QC, J3M 1J9
(450) 460-7955
Emp Here 65   *Sales* 11,768,275
SIC 1542 Nonresidential construction, nec
 Normand Blanchard

D-U-N-S 20-207-6154   (HQ)
GELPAC ROUVILLE SOLUTIONS EMBALLAGE INC
PAPIER ROUVILLE
(*Suby of* GELPAC INC)
400 Rue Henri-Bourassa, Marieville, QC, J3M 1R9
(450) 460-4466
Sales 19,476,800
SIC 2674 Bags: uncoated paper and multiwall
 Paul Gelinas
 Jocelyne Gelinas Laurin

D-U-N-S 20-291-1996   (HQ)
GESTION D'ACTIFS GLADU INC
NAP GLADU
2115 Rue Saint-Cesaire, Marieville, QC, J3M 1E5
(450) 460-4481
Emp Here 75   *Sales* 19,208,500
SIC 3423 Hand and edge tools, nec
 Gregory Webb
 Timothy Rash
 Jeannot Perron

D-U-N-S 25-360-2692   (HQ)
IFASTGROUPE 2004 L.P.
INFASCO DISTRIBUTION
700 Rue Ouellette, Marieville, QC, J3M 1P6
(450) 658-8741
Emp Here 370   *Sales* 109,453,950
SIC 3452 Bolts, nuts, rivets, and washers
 Benoit Beaulieu

D-U-N-S 24-651-3639   (SL)
L'EQUIPOULE INC
2010 Av Industrielle, Marieville, QC, J3M 1J5
(450) 730-0336
Emp Here 49   *Sales* 18,890,431
SIC 0259 Poultry and eggs, nec

 Danielle Simard

D-U-N-S 24-434-4552   (BR)
PARMALAT CANADA INC
(*Suby of* PARMALAT SPA)
2350 Rue Saint-Cesaire, Marieville, QC, J3M 1E1

Emp Here 90
SIC 2022 Cheese; natural and processed
 Jean Francois Gagne

D-U-N-S 20-308-9743   (HQ)
SIVACO WIRE GROUP 2004 L.P.
SIVACO QUEBEC
800 Rue Ouellette, Marieville, QC, J3M 1P5
(450) 658-8741
Emp Here 325   *Sales* 103,373,175
SIC 3496 Miscellaneous fabricated wire products
 Denis Peloquin

Marsoui, QC G0E

D-U-N-S 24-942-9259   (SL)
BOIS MARSOUI G.D.S. INC
BOIS ROCHER PERCE G.D.S.
2 Rte De La Mine Candego, Marsoui, QC, G0E 1S0
(418) 288-5635
Emp Here 78   *Sales* 15,004,860
SIC 2421 Sawmills and planing mills, general
 Guildo Deschenes
 Jacques Poitras
 Sebastien Lavoie
 Georges Deschenes
 Sylvain Deschenes
 Deschenes Deschenes

Mascouche, QC J7K

D-U-N-S 25-543-3435   (SL)
9027-0653 QUEBEC INC
RONA L'ENTREPOT MASCOUCHE
175 Montee Masson, Mascouche, QC, J7K 3B4
(450) 474-6181
Emp Here 225   *Sales* 63,236,250
SIC 5251 Hardware stores
 Jean-Marc Brien

D-U-N-S 25-901-5621   (SL)
9240-9770 QUEBEC INC
500 PLANCHERS DESIGN
500 Rue Sicard, Mascouche, QC, J7K 3G5
(450) 474-5002
Emp Here 49   *Sales* 11,286,660
SIC 5713 Floor covering stores
 Rosa Caccarello

D-U-N-S 24-933-8989   (HQ)
ALBI LE GEANT INC
ALBI
3550 Av De La Gare, Mascouche, QC, J7K 3C1
(450) 474-7000
Sales 62,928,000
SIC 5511 New and used car dealers
 Denis Leclerc

D-U-N-S 20-873-2730   (SL)
ALBI LE GEANT INC
ALBI
3550 Av De La Gare, Mascouche, QC, J7K 3C1
(450) 474-5555
Emp Here 200   *Sales* 125,856,000
SIC 5511 New and used car dealers
 Denis Leclerc

D-U-N-S 24-385-2923   (SL)
AUTOMOBILES L F B INC, LES

GRENIER VOLKSWAGEN
118 Montee Masson, Mascouche, QC, J7K 3B5
(450) 474-2428
Emp Here 25   *Sales* 12,451,950
SIC 5511 New and used car dealers
 Louis Grenier

D-U-N-S 25-016-0652   (HQ)
CAISSE POPULAIRE DESJARDINS LE MANOIR
CENTRE DE SERVICES LA PLAINE
820 Montee Masson, Mascouche, QC, J7K 3B6
(450) 474-2474
Emp Here 59   *Sales* 13,682,693
SIC 6062 State credit unions
 Martin Leveille
 Line Lemelin
 Caroline Normand
 Lyne Chauvette
 Richard Blais
 Robert Bonin
 Jean-Marc Brien
 Raymond Lamarche
 Patricia Lebel
 Benjamin Alarie

D-U-N-S 25-965-9068   (BR)
CENTRE DE READAPTATION LA MYRIADE, LE
1280 Ch Saint-Henri, Mascouche, QC, J7K 2N1
(450) 474-4175
Emp Here 80
SIC 8361 Residential care
 Robert Lasalle

D-U-N-S 20-014-3688   (SL)
CONCEPT MASCOUCHE INC
AUBAINERIE MASCOUCHE
161 Montee Masson Bureau 44, Mascouche, QC, J7K 3B4
(450) 474-3315
Emp Here 85   *Sales* 15,248,660
SIC 5651 Family clothing stores
 Yanik Dessureault

D-U-N-S 25-201-5631   (SL)
CULASSES DU FUTUR L. R. INC, LES
1390 Av De La Gare, Mascouche, QC, J7K 2Z2
(514) 966-3450
Emp Here 60   *Sales* 13,430,580
SIC 3714 Motor vehicle parts and accessories
 Rene Labrecque
 Line Lehoux

D-U-N-S 20-357-0593   (SL)
ENTREPRISES LISE LAVOIE INC, LES
1407 Av De La Gare, Mascouche, QC, J7K 3G6
(450) 474-0404
Emp Here 30   *Sales* 13,415,220
SIC 5039 Construction materials, nec
 Lise Lavoie

D-U-N-S 20-115-0567   (HQ)
EQUIPEMENTS SPM INC
1290 Av De La Gare, Mascouche, QC, J7K 2Z2
(450) 966-6616
Emp Here 5   *Sales* 82,428,150
SIC 1771 Concrete work
 Sylvain Cote
 Martin Cote
 Pierre Cote

D-U-N-S 20-234-1939   (SL)
FORTERRA PIPE & PRECAST BC, ULC
FORTERRA TUYAUX ET PREFABRIQUES C-B
(*Suby of* CONSTRUCTIONS LOUISBOURG LTEE)
1331 Av De La Gare, Mascouche, QC, J7K 3G6

Emp Here 50   *Sales* 11,671,750

SIC 3272 Concrete products, nec
 Jeffery K. Bradley
 William M. Brown
 Lori Browne

D-U-N-S 20-390-5784   (HQ)
GESTION RAPID INC.
321 Montee Masson Bureau 301, Mascouche, QC, J7K 2L6

Sales 12,344,940
SIC 8741 Management services
 David Brochu

D-U-N-S 24-834-6058   (SL)
HOULE & FRERES GARAGE (TERREBONNE) LTEE
HOULE ET FRERES (HYUNDAY)
290 Montee Masson, Mascouche, QC, J7K 3B5
(450) 474-1110
Emp Here 44   *Sales* 21,915,432
SIC 5511 New and used car dealers
 Yves Houle
 Serge Houle

D-U-N-S 24-362-1690   (HQ)
IMPORT EXPORT SEAPASS INC
(*Suby of* GESTION RAPID INC.)
321 Montee Masson Bureau 301, Mascouche, QC, J7K 2L6
(450) 918-4300
Emp Here 9   *Sales* 75,810,200
SIC 6799 Investors, nec
 David Brochu
 Daniel Delisle

D-U-N-S 25-457-8230   (HQ)
INTER PROPANE INC
LAVE CAMION INTER
460 Rue Sicard, Mascouche, QC, J7K 3G5
(450) 474-4000
Sales 12,415,865
SIC 5169 Chemicals and allied products, nec
 Carmelo Letizia
 Giovanni (Johnny) Letizia

D-U-N-S 20-033-9708   (BR)
MARCHE J.C. MESSIER INC
SUPER MARCH? MASCOUCHE
(*Suby of* PLACEMENTS C. D. F. G. INC)
875 Mont?E Masson, Mascouche, QC, J7K 3T3
(450) 966-9996
Emp Here 100
SIC 5411 Grocery stores
 Richard Lamonte

D-U-N-S 24-920-5329   (SL)
RESERVOIRS GIL-FAB INTERNATIONAL INC, LES
AT&S (ADVANCE TANKS & SYSTEMS)
(*Suby of* GESTION JERICO INC)
1429 Av De La Gare, Mascouche, QC, J7K 3G6
(450) 474-7400
Emp Here 80   *Sales* 15,366,800
SIC 3443 Fabricated plate work (boiler shop)
 Pierre Fournier

D-U-N-S 20-978-6656   (SL)
RONPIEN INC
PHARMACIE JEAN-COUTU 163
3131 Boul De Mascouche, Mascouche, QC, J7K 3B7
(450) 474-6171
Emp Here 50   *Sales* 12,647,700
SIC 5912 Drug stores and proprietary stores
 Martin D'amours

D-U-N-S 24-065-7937   (BR)
SOBEYS QUEBEC INC
I G A EXTRA MASCOUCHE
65 Montee Masson, Mascouche, QC, J7K 3B4
(450) 474-2444
Emp Here 120   *Sales* 822,456
SIC 5411 Grocery stores
 Lina Durigon

D-U-N-S 25-199-1154 (BR)
VIGI SANTE LTEE
CHSLD VIGI ET BLAIS
2893 Av Des Ancetres, Mascouche, QC, J7K 1X6
(450) 474-6991
Emp Here 150
SIC 8051 Skilled nursing care facilities
Vincent Simonetta

D-U-N-S 25-498-2903 (BR)
WAL-MART CANADA CORP
WAL-MART
(*Suby of* WALMART INC.)
155 Montee Masson Bureau 3149, Mascouche, QC, J7K 3B4
(450) 474-2679
Emp Here 225
SIC 5311 Department stores
Denis Gosselin

Mascouche, QC J7L

D-U-N-S 24-889-9866 (HQ)
AUTOBUS TERREMONT LTEE
343 Ch Des Anglais, Mascouche, QC, J7L 3P8
(450) 477-1500
Emp Here 105 *Sales* 10,538,080
SIC 4151 School buses
Jean-Louis Tasse
Denis Cyr

D-U-N-S 24-548-3862 (SL)
TROIS DIAMANTS AUTOS (1987) LTEE
DODGE CHRYSLER JEEP
3035 Ch Gascon, Mascouche, QC, J7L 3X7
(450) 477-6348
Emp Here 32 *Sales* 20,136,960
SIC 5511 New and used car dealers
Francois Bonin

Mashteuiatsh, QC G0W

D-U-N-S 24-128-3196 (SL)
DEVELOPPEMENT PIEKUAKAMI ILNU-ATSH
1425 Rue Ouiatchouan, Mashteuiatsh, QC, G0W 2H0
(418) 275-8181
Emp Here 100 *Sales* 27,433,200
SIC 8741 Management services
Alain Paul
Sylvie Launiere
Colette Robertson

D-U-N-S 24-943-0612 (SL)
GESTION A.D.L. SENC
A.D.L. TOBACO
1665 Rue Nishk, Mashteuiatsh, QC, G0W 2H0
(418) 275-6161
Emp Here 80 *Sales* 14,672,240
SIC 2131 Chewing and smoking tobacco
Alain Paul
Donald Paul
Luc Paul
Guy Boulianne

D-U-N-S 25-834-5888 (SL)
PEKUAKAMIULNUATSH TAKUHIKAN
65 Rue Uapakalu, Mashteuiatsh, QC, G0W 2H0
(418) 275-2473
Emp Here 49 *Sales* 13,937,413
SIC 6512 Nonresidential building operators
Jilbert Dominique

Maskinonge, QC J0K

D-U-N-S 20-302-2975 (SL)
BERMEX INTERNATIONAL INC
(*Suby of* GROUPE BERMEX INC)
215 Boul Ouest, Maskinonge, QC, J0K 1N0
(819) 601-8702
Emp Here 100
SIC 2511 Wood household furniture
Richard Darveau
Daniel Walker
Gaetan Bellemare
Maurice Lafreniere

D-U-N-S 24-341-1969 (HQ)
MEUBLES BDM + INC
BERMEX
(*Suby of* GROUPE BERMEX INC)
215 Boul Ouest, Maskinonge, QC, J0K 1N0
(819) 227-2284
Emp Here 20 *Sales* 111,332,500
SIC 2511 Wood household furniture
Richard Darveau
Alex Adimari
Philippe Darveau
Gaetan Bellemare
Maurice Darveau
Rene Darveau
Denis Darveau
Christian Roy
Laura Amelia Carlucci

Massueville, QC J0G

D-U-N-S 24-636-3949 (SL)
VIANDE RICHELIEU INC
(*Suby of* BOUVRY EXPORTS CALGARY LTD)
595 Rue Royale, Massueville, QC, J0G 1K0
(450) 788-2667
Emp Here 90 *Sales* 31,112,100
SIC 2011 Meat packing plants
Marc Bouvry

Matagami, QC J0Y

D-U-N-S 24-608-2718 (SL)
9223-3196 QUEBEC INC
C. CARON
9 Rue Nottaway, Matagami, QC, J0Y 2A0

Emp Here 26 *Sales* 11,626,524
SIC 5039 Construction materials, nec
Amelie Bechard
Marie-Helene Duval
Maxime Bellier
Herve Leblanc

D-U-N-S 20-604-2293 (HQ)
CARON, CAMILLE INC
RENOVATEUR RONA, LE
9 Rue Nottaway, Matagami, QC, J0Y 2A0

Sales 10,375,419
SIC 5211 Lumber and other building materials
Camille Caron

D-U-N-S 25-240-9131 (SL)
HARNOIS ENERGIES INC
LE PETROLES LANAUDIERE
1640 Boul Industriel, Matagami, QC, J0Y 2A0
(819) 739-2563
Emp Here 500 *Sales* 591,136,500
SIC 5172 Petroleum products, nec
Serge Harnois
Luc Harnois
Claudinw Harnois

Matane, QC G4W

D-U-N-S 25-243-3016 (SL)
6318703 CANADA INC
MERIDIEN MARITIME REPARATION
1460 Rue De Matane-Sur-Mer, Matane, QC, G4W 3M6
(418) 562-0911
Emp Here 100 *Sales* 22,384,300
SIC 3731 Shipbuilding and repairing
Angello Marcotte
Mathias Marcotte

D-U-N-S 20-052-3525 (SL)
9029-2970 QUEBEC INC
VETEMENTS B.D.
135 Boul Dion, Matane, QC, G4W 3L8
(418) 562-3751
Emp Here 80 *Sales* 35,937,520
SIC 7389 Business services, nec
Benoit Desjardins

D-U-N-S 24-379-1720 (SL)
ATELIERS LEOPOLD DESROSIERS INC
60 Rue Brillant, Matane, QC, G4W 0J9
(418) 562-2640
Emp Here 150 *Sales* 100,336,200
SIC 7389 Business services, nec
Lucie Lapointe
Jean-Marie Doiron

D-U-N-S 20-313-9696 (HQ)
BETON PROVINCIAL FINANCE LTEE
1825 Av Du Phare O, Matane, QC, G4W 3M6
(418) 562-0074
Emp Here 1 *Sales* 274,497,259
SIC 6712 Bank holding companies
Andre Belanger
Nicole Belanger
Alain Bisson

D-U-N-S 20-207-7988 (HQ)
BETON PROVINCIAL LTEE
BETON ALLIANCE
(*Suby of* BETON PROVINCIAL FINANCE LTEE)
1825 Av Du Phare O, Matane, QC, G4W 3M6
(418) 562-0074
Emp Here 50 *Sales* 274,131,750
SIC 6712 Bank holding companies
Andre Belanger
Nicole Belanger
Alain Bisson

D-U-N-S 24-378-2943 (SL)
BOUFFARD SANITAIRE INC
GROUPE BOUFFARD, DIV DE
75 Rue Savard, Matane, QC, G4W 0H9
(418) 562-5116
Emp Here 50 *Sales* 12,856,550
SIC 4953 Refuse systems
Dominique Bouffard

D-U-N-S 20-053-3556 (SL)
CANADIAN TIRE
145 Rue Piuze, Matane, QC, G4W 0H7
(418) 562-5144
Emp Here 30 *Sales* 10,926,450
SIC 5014 Tires and tubes
Michel Hamelin

D-U-N-S 25-517-3239 (SL)
CENTRE DE SANTE & DE SERVICES SOCI-AUX DE MATANE
349 Av Saint-Jerome, Matane, QC, G4W 3A8
(418) 562-5741
Emp Here 1 *Sales* 25,723,380
SIC 8611 Business associations
Clement Gauthier

D-U-N-S 24-464-2518 (SL)
COLLEGE D'ENSEIGNEMENT GENERAL & PROFESSIONNEL DE MATANE
CEGEP DE MATANE
616 Av Saint-Redempteur, Matane, QC, G4W 1L1
(418) 562-1240
Emp Here 215 *Sales* 32,119,065
SIC 8221 Colleges and universities

Jean-Pierre Clermont
Viateur De Champlain

D-U-N-S 20-871-3933 (SL)
CONCEPT MAT INC
41 Rue Brillant, Matane, QC, G4W 0J7
(418) 562-6680
Emp Here 25 *Sales* 11,179,350
SIC 5031 Lumber, plywood, and millwork
Charles-Eric Gauthier

D-U-N-S 24-204-7587 (SL)
CUISINES GASPESIENNES MATANE LTEE, LES
CUISINES GASPESIENNES
85 Rue Du Port Bureau 1, Matane, QC, G4W 3M6
(418) 562-5757
Emp Here 110 *Sales* 38,025,900
SIC 2013 Sausages and other prepared meats
Enrico Carpinteri
Tony Carpinteri

D-U-N-S 20-431-3761 (SL)
EASTERN QUEBEC SEAFOODS (1998) LTD
(*Suby of* FORMANDENS DEPARTEMENT)
1600 Rue De Matane-Sur-Mer, Matane, QC, G4W 3M6
(418) 562-1273
Emp Here 100 *Sales* 34,569,000
SIC 2092 Fresh or frozen packaged fish
Jean-Pierre Chamberland
Lars Peterson

D-U-N-S 20-949-9060 (SL)
ENTREPRISES D'ELECTRICITE J.M.N. INC
19 Rue Durette, Matane, QC, G4W 0J5
(418) 562-4009
Emp Here 100 *Sales* 21,782,900
SIC 1731 Electrical work
Paul-Andre Dion
Eric Mcneil
Martin Beland

D-U-N-S 24-991-9358 (SL)
GESTION D. PRESSAULT INC
MARCHAND CANADIAN TIRE DE LA SARRE
145 Rue Piuze, Matane, QC, G4W 0H7
(418) 562-5144
Emp Here 40 *Sales* 19,923,120
SIC 5531 Auto and home supply stores
Dominique Pressault

D-U-N-S 24-308-9211 (SL)
MARMEN ENERGIE INC
(*Suby of* GESTION MARMEN INC)
1905 Av Du Phare O, Matane, QC, G4W 3M6
(418) 562-4569
Emp Here 100 *Sales* 22,200,100
SIC 3569 General industrial machinery, nec
Fernand Pellerin
Patrick Pellerin
Linda Pellerin
Annie Pellerin

D-U-N-S 24-145-8652 (SL)
MARQUIS AUTOMOBILES INC
1065 Av Du Phare O, Matane, QC, G4W 3M6
(418) 562-3333
Emp Here 35 *Sales* 22,024,800
SIC 5511 New and used car dealers
Daniel Marquis
Daniel Bouffard
Helene Dufour
Yves Durette

D-U-N-S 20-297-7625 (HQ)
PAVAGES DES MONTS INC, LES
PAVAGE DE LA VALLEE
(*Suby of* BETON PROVINCIAL FINANCE LTEE)
2245 Rue Du Phare O, Matane, QC, G4W 3N1
(418) 562-4343
Emp Here 1 *Sales* 11,671,750
SIC 3273 Ready-mixed concrete
Andre Belanger

Nicole Belanger
Alain Bisson

D-U-N-S 24-622-9058   (HQ)
PETROLES J.D. INC
60 Rue Du Port, Matane, QC, G4W 3M6
(418) 562-0969
Emp Here 6   *Sales* 12,393,696
SIC 5172 Petroleum products, nec
  Richard Dionne

D-U-N-S 25-514-9999   (SL)
PRODUCTIONS VIC PELLETIER INC, LES
GROUPE PVP
296 Rue Saint-Pierre, Matane, QC, G4W 2B9
(514) 667-0787
Emp Here 80   *Sales* 7,522,960
SIC 7812 Motion picture and video production
  Victorien Pelletier
  Vincent Leroux
  Robert Tremblay

D-U-N-S 25-146-3394   (BR)
RAYONIER A.M. CANADA G.P.
TEMBEC
(*Suby of* RAYONIER A.M. CANADA G.P.)
400 Rue Du Port, Matane, QC, G4W 3M6
(418) 794-2001
Emp Here 148
SIC 2611 Pulp mills
  Joseph Pitre

D-U-N-S 20-207-9273   (BR)
SUPERMARCHES GP INC, LES
METRO G P
750 Av Du Phare O Bureau 4415, Matane,
QC, G4W 3W8
(418) 562-4434
Emp Here 75
SIC 5411 Grocery stores
  Marien Boulianne

D-U-N-S 24-706-3480   (HQ)
TELECOMMUNICATIONS DENIS GIGNAC INC
TELECOMMUNICATIONS DE L'EST
(*Suby of* IRIS TECHNOLOGIES INC)
143 Boul Dion, Matane, QC, G4W 3L8
(418) 562-9000
Emp Here 14   *Sales* 12,565,960
SIC 4899 Communication services, nec
  Samer Bishay
  Magdi Wanis
  Hing Sang Hum
  Daniel Gignac

D-U-N-S 24-319-5026   (BR)
WAL-MART CANADA CORP
WAL MART 1025
(*Suby of* WALMART INC.)
150 Rue Piuze, Matane, QC, G4W 4T2
(418) 566-4779
Emp Here 120
SIC 5311 Department stores

D-U-N-S 24-420-9933   (HQ)
WEC TOURS QUEBEC INC
(*Suby of* ALOYS WOBBEN STIFTUNG)
300 Rue Du Port, Matane, QC, G4W 3M6
(514) 363-7266
Sales 24,748,300
SIC 1771 Concrete work
  Hans-Dieter Kettwig
  Norbert Hoelscher

Matapedia, QC G0J

D-U-N-S 25-090-7441   (BR)
GOUVERNEMENT DE LA PROVINCE DE QUEBEC
C.L.S.C. MALAUZE
(*Suby of* GOUVERNEMENT DE LA
PROVINCE DE QUEBEC)
14 Boul Perron E, Matapedia, QC, G0J 1V0

Emp Here 125
SIC 8399 Social services, nec
  Charles Guerette

Mcmasterville, QC J3G

D-U-N-S 25-611-0941   (HQ)
CENTRE DE L'AUTO BLAIN, MARIO INC, LE
KIA MARIO BLAIN
545 Boul Laurier, Mcmasterville, QC, J3G 6P2
(450) 464-4551
Sales 12,950,028
SIC 5511 New and used car dealers
  Mario Blain

D-U-N-S 24-079-8830   (BR)
SOCIETE DE GESTION COGIR INC
RESIDENCES RICHELOISES, LES
(*Suby of* SOCIETE DE GESTION COGIR
INC)
701 Ch Du Richelieu Bureau 139, Mcmaster-
ville, QC, J3G 6T5
(450) 467-7667
Emp Here 100
SIC 6513 Apartment building operators
  Roger Migneault

Melbourne, QC J0B

D-U-N-S 24-649-1591   (HQ)
USINATECH INC
USINATECH CANADA
1099 Ch D'Ely, Melbourne, QC, J0B 2B0
(819) 826-3774
Sales 70,219,250
SIC 3599 Industrial machinery, nec
  Rudy Pelletier
  Patrick M. Cote
  Normand Pelletier

Mercier, QC J6R

D-U-N-S 20-356-9199   (SL)
9264-1711 QUEBEC INC
DUCLOS CHRYSLER MERCIER
179 Boul Saint-Jean-Baptiste, Mercier, QC,
J6R 2C1
(450) 844-7888
Emp Here 23   *Sales* 11,455,794
SIC 5511 New and used car dealers
  Marcel Duclos
  Louis-Philippe Duclos

D-U-N-S 24-335-7477   (HQ)
CAISSE DESJARDINS DE L'OUEST DE LA MONTEREGIE
CENTRE DE SERVICES SAINTE-MARTINE
724 Boul Saint-Jean-Baptiste, Mercier, QC,
J6R 0B2
(450) 698-2204
Emp Here 32   *Sales* 13,099,853
SIC 6062 State credit unions
  Maxime Lavoie
  Pierre Bergevin
  Luc Pouliot
  Richard Bergevin
  Karen Gearey
  Rejean Julien
  William Mcdiarmid
  Roxanne Hebert
  Normand Vigneault
  Louise Poirier

D-U-N-S 24-228-4883   (HQ)
ENTREPRISE ROBERT THIBERT INC
DEXTRAIL
200 Boul Saint-Jean-Baptiste Bureau 212,

Mercier, QC, J6R 2L2
(450) 699-0560
Sales 115,288,500
SIC 5013 Motor vehicle supplies and new
parts
  Robert Thibert
  Christian Thibert

D-U-N-S 24-945-6195   (SL)
MARCHE DUCHEMIN ET LACAS INC
IGA
927 Boul Saint-Jean-Baptiste, Mercier, QC,
J6R 2K8
(450) 691-7647
Emp Here 93   *Sales* 27,293,361
SIC 5411 Grocery stores
  Normand Duchemin
  Jacques Lacas

D-U-N-S 24-823-0075   (SL)
PLACEMENTS JACQUES FELIX THIBEAULT INC, LES
JEAN COUTU
777 Boul Saint-Jean-Baptiste, Mercier, QC,
J6R 1G1
(450) 692-5990
Emp Here 49   *Sales* 12,394,746
SIC 5912 Drug stores and proprietary stores
  Jacques Felix Thibeault

D-U-N-S 20-187-8720   (SL)
PRODUCTIONS MARAICHERES BOURGET & FRERES INC, LES
410 Boul Sainte-Marguerite, Mercier, QC, J6R
2L1
(450) 691-0468
Emp Here 45   *Sales* 15,411,015
SIC 0139 Field crops, except cash grain
  Pierre-Andre Bourget
  Eric Bourget
  Benoit Bourget

D-U-N-S 20-127-1371   (SL)
ROBERT TRANS GAZ ENR
15 Rue Giroux, Mercier, QC, J6R 2P3

Emp Here 17   *Sales* 52,799,569
SIC 4925 Gas production and/or distribution
  Robert Nathalie

Messines, QC J0X

D-U-N-S 25-285-9046   (BR)
SOCIETE DE PROTECTION DES FORETS CONTRE LE FEU (SOPFEU)
*SOCIETE DE PROTECTION DES FORETS
CONTRE LE FEU (SO*
(*Suby of* SOCIETE DE PROTECTION DES
FORETS CONTRE LE FEU (SOPFEU))
175 105 Rte, Messines, QC, J0X 2J0
(819) 449-4271
Emp Here 80
SIC 0851 Forestry services
  Ken Berube

Metabetchouan-Lac-A-La-Croix, QC G8G

D-U-N-S 24-439-1715   (SL)
ASSURANCE 5000 INC
ASSURANCE TREMBLAY
89 Rue Saint-Andre, Metabetchouan-Lac-A-
La-Croix, QC, G8G 1V5
(418) 349-5000
Emp Here 49   *Sales* 28,416,276
SIC 6411 Insurance agents, brokers, and ser-
vice
  Rachelle Maltais

D-U-N-S 24-381-1262   (SL)
LAR MACHINERIE INC
(*Suby of* GROUPE LAR INC)

1760 169 Rte, Metabetchouan-Lac-A-La-
Croix, QC, G8G 1B1
(418) 349-2875
Emp Here 200   *Sales* 44,400,200
SIC 3599 Industrial machinery, nec
  Yvon Levesque
  Jacques Villeneuve
  Marc Gravel

D-U-N-S 24-730-0825   (HQ)
TRANSPORTS J.M. BERNIER INC
75 Rue Des Erables, Metabetchouan-A-
La-Croix, QC, G8G 1P9
(418) 349-3496
Emp Here 93   *Sales* 19,747,776
SIC 4213 Trucking, except local
  Jean-Marie Bernier
  Claude Bernier

D-U-N-S 20-006-3159   (SL)
TREMBLAY ASSURANCE LTEE
15 Rue Saint-Antoine, Metabetchouan-Lac-A-
La-Croix, QC, G8G 1H2
(418) 349-2841
Emp Here 28   *Sales* 23,745,680
SIC 6411 Insurance agents, brokers, and ser-
vice
  Rachelle Maltais

Milan, QC G0Y

D-U-N-S 24-360-5032   (HQ)
MAISON USINEX INC
INNOVATION CLIMAT
114 Rte 214, Milan, QC, G0Y 1E0
(819) 657-4268
Sales 17,611,230
SIC 1521 Single-family housing construction
  Raymond Morin
  Christian Morin
  Luc Morin
  Guy Morin
  Rejean Morin

Mirabel, QC J7J

D-U-N-S 24-698-7820   (SL)
156023 CANADA INC
PLANETE MAZDA
20900 Ch De La Cote N, Mirabel, QC, J7J 0E5
(450) 437-8000
Emp Here 40   *Sales* 19,923,120
SIC 5511 New and used car dealers
  Yvon Loiselle
  Sylvain Loiselle

D-U-N-S 25-200-7216   (HQ)
2962-9060 QUEBEC INC
BOULONS PLUS
12770 Rue Brault, Mirabel, QC, J7J 0W3
(450) 420-1839
Emp Here 28   *Sales* 12,736,240
SIC 5085 Industrial supplies
  Maxime Cousineau
  Isabelle Cousineau
  Jean Cousineau

D-U-N-S 20-298-6642   (SL)
9091-9101 QUEBEC INC
SYSTEMES PAUL DAVIS RIVE-NORD
14495 Rue Joseph-Marc-Vermette, Mirabel,
QC, J7J 1X2
(450) 434-5858
Emp Here 53   *Sales* 14,359,926
SIC 1522 Residential construction, nec
  Eric Melancon

D-U-N-S 24-318-5126   (HQ)
9111-7523 QUEBEC INC
12500 Rue De L'Avenir, Mirabel, QC, J7J 2K3
(450) 435-9995
Sales 16,401,000

SIC 6712 Bank holding companies
Karl Mongrain

D-U-N-S 25-280-5242 (SL)
9173-1307 QUEBEC INC
CERAMIQUES B.G.
(*Suby of* GESTION BASLER ET FILS INC)
13448 Boul Du Cure-Labelle, Mirabel, QC, J7J
1G9
(450) 939-3255
Emp Here 26 *Sales* 11,626,524
SIC 5032 Brick, stone, and related material
Frederic Basler

D-U-N-S 20-563-2128 (HQ)
AGENCES KYOTO LTEE, LES
ST-JEROME TOYOTA
(*Suby of* GROUPE AUTOMOBILES KYOTO
LTEE)
16500 Montee Guenette, Mirabel, QC, J7J
2E2
(450) 438-1255
Emp Here 50 *Sales* 56,635,200
SIC 5511 New and used car dealers
Aime Vialle
Jean–Louis Vialle

D-U-N-S 20-120-8266 (HQ)
**BELL HELICOPTER TEXTRON CANADA
LIMITEE**
BELL HELICOPTERE TEXTRON
(*Suby of* TEXTRON INC.)
12800 Rue De L'Avenir, Mirabel, QC, J7J 1R4
(450) 971-6500
Emp Here 1,000 *Sales* 290,850,000
SIC 3721 Aircraft
Mitch Snyder
Cynthia Garneau
Felipe Gumucio
Al Vetere

D-U-N-S 20-370-8342 (BR)
BID GROUP TECHNOLOGIES LTD
*EQUIPEMENTS COMACT UNE DIVISION
DE BID GROUP TECHNOLOGIES*
(*Suby of* BID GROUP TECHNOLOGIES LTD)
18095 Rue Lapointe, Mirabel, QC, J7J 1E3
(450) 435-2121
Emp Here 350
SIC 3553 Woodworking machinery

D-U-N-S 24-989-6010 (SL)
BIESSE CANADA INC
(*Suby of* BI.FIN. SRL)
18005 Rue Lapointe, Mirabel, QC, J7J 0G2
(450) 437-5534
Emp Here 35 *Sales* 16,625,910
SIC 5084 Industrial machinery and equipment
Cristian Berardi
Federico Broccoli
Roberto Selci

D-U-N-S 20-547-6844 (HQ)
**CAISSE POPULAIRE DESJARDINS DE
L'ENVOLEE**
CENTRE DE SERVICE BLAINVILLE
13845 Boul Du Cure-Labelle, Mirabel, QC, J7J
1A1
(450) 430-4603
Emp Here 50 *Sales* 21,810,433
SIC 6062 State credit unions
Alain Martineau
Audrey Laurin
Yvon Fournier
Jean-Frederic Martin
Rejean Bouchard
Jonathan Clement
Sandra Drouin
Gilles Daviault
Claude Forest
Ghislain Hogue

D-U-N-S 20-882-3302 (HQ)
CENTRE DE LOCATION G.M. INC
LOCATION GM
12075 Rue Arthur-Sicard Bureau 101,
Mirabel, QC, J7J 0E9

(450) 434-0505
Emp Here 20 *Sales* 14,351,550
SIC 7359 Equipment rental and leasing, nec
Alexandre Cantin
Jean-Francois Cantain
Mathieu Kingsbury

D-U-N-S 25-836-8968 (BR)
CENTRE DU GOLF U.F.O. INC
CLUB DE GOLF GLENDALE
9500 Rang Sainte-Henriette, Mirabel, QC, J7J
2A1
(514) 990-8392
Emp Here 100
SIC 7997 Membership sports and recreation
clubs
Normand St-Germain

D-U-N-S 25-233-0139 (BR)
**COMMISSION SCOLAIRE DE LA RIVIERE-
DU-NORD**
*CENTRE FORMATION DU TRANSPORT
ROUTIER*
17000 Rue Aubin, Mirabel, QC, J7J 1B1
(450) 435-0167
Emp Here 100
SIC 8299 Schools and educational services,
nec
Danielle Leblanc

D-U-N-S 24-177-2367 (HQ)
CONSORTIUM M.R. CANADA LTEE
(*Suby of* CORPORATION
D'INVESTISSEMENT MICHEL RAYMOND
INC, LA)
14243 Boul Du Cure-Labelle, Mirabel, QC, J7J
1M2
(514) 328-6060
Sales 27,477,905
SIC 1541 Industrial buildings and warehouses
Michel Raymond
Pascal Raymond

D-U-N-S 20-791-4883 (SL)
**CONSTRUCTION RAYMOND ET FILS INC,
LES**
14243 Boul Du Cure-Labelle, Mirabel, QC, J7J
1M2
(450) 979-4847
Emp Here 60 *Sales* 16,256,520
SIC 1521 Single-family housing construction
Michel Raymond
Pascal Raymond
Diane Dumouchel Raymond

D-U-N-S 25-825-4689 (SL)
FONDREC INC
14078 Rue De La Chapelle, Mirabel, QC, J7J
2C8
(450) 432-2688
Emp Here 100 *Sales* 23,343,500
SIC 3365 Aluminum foundries
Jean-Francois Simard

D-U-N-S 24-710-9945 (SL)
GARIER INC
(*Suby of* 2967-3142 QUEBEC INC)
13050 Rue Brault Unite 123, Mirabel, QC, J7J
0W4
(450) 437-7852
Emp Here 90 *Sales* 19,980,090
SIC 3569 General industrial machinery, nec
Rosaire Gariepy
Michel Gariepy

D-U-N-S 25-410-8004 (HQ)
GESTION RACAN INC
(*Suby of* 8389616 CANADA INC)
18101 Rue J.A.Bombardier, Mirabel, QC, J7J
2H8
(450) 979-1212
Emp Here 1 *Sales* 17,767,750
SIC 6712 Bank holding companies
Giuseppe J Racanelli

D-U-N-S 20-252-6695 (HQ)
GROUPE ETHIER INC
16800 Ch Charles Unite 123, Mirabel, QC, J7J
0V9

(450) 435-9581
Sales 29,245,195
SIC 5148 Fresh fruits and vegetables
Denis Bissonnette
Pascal Ethier
Jacelyn Ethier
Ginette Ethier

D-U-N-S 24-231-1043 (HQ)
GROUPE PROCAN EQUIPEMENT INC
GPE EQUIPEMENT DE MINE ET SERVICES
11700 Rue De L'Avenir Bureau 204, Mirabel,
QC, J7J 0G7
(450) 420-1119
Emp Here 5 *Sales* 11,875,650
SIC 5082 Construction and mining machinery
Mohamed El Hariri
Luc Tessier

D-U-N-S 25-092-8632 (SL)
HALO PHARMACEUTICAL CANADA INC
AUREOLE PHARMACEUTIQUE CANADA
(*Suby of* CAMBREX CORPORATION)
17800 Rue La Lapointe, Mirabel, QC, J7J 0W8
(450) 433-7673
Emp Here 250 *Sales* 82,898,500
SIC 2834 Pharmaceutical preparations
Lee Karras
Samantha Hanley
Gregory P. Sargen
Barry Lederman
Maryse Laliberte

D-U-N-S 20-291-9056 (SL)
HAMEL AUTOS DE MIRABEL INC
MERCEDES-BENZ BLAINVILLE
10000 Rue Du Plein-Air, Mirabel, QC, J7J 1S5
(450) 435-1313
Emp Here 26 *Sales* 12,950,028
SIC 5511 New and used car dealers
Jean-Francois Hamel
Yvan Boucher
Pascal Landry
Daniel Bourgon
Corrado Vindigni
Dominic Vallee
Martin Cote

D-U-N-S 20-370-6460 (SL)
**IMPRIMERIE QUEBECOR MEDIA (2015)
INC**
IMPRIMERIE MIRABEL
(*Suby of* QUEBECOR MEDIA INC)
12800 Rue Brault, Mirabel, QC, J7J 0W4
(514) 380-3600
Emp Here 100 *Sales* 16,402,700
SIC 2731 Book publishing
Pierre Karl Peladeau
Marc M. Tremblay
Jean-Francois Pruneau

D-U-N-S 20-560-5228 (SL)
INGENIA TECHNOLOGIES INC
(*Suby of* 8389616 CANADA INC)
18101 Rue J.A.Bombardier, Mirabel, QC, J7J
2H8
(450) 979-1212
Emp Here 65 *Sales* 14,430,065
SIC 3585 Refrigeration and heating equip-
ment
Giuseppe J Racanelli
Lise Daigle

D-U-N-S 20-370-4226 (SL)
INVENTAIRES LAPARE INC
11329 Montee Sainte-Marianne, Mirabel, QC,
J7J 2B2
(450) 435-2997
Emp Here 100 *Sales* 44,921,900
SIC 7389 Business services, nec
Gaston Jr Lapare

D-U-N-S 20-302-5796 (HQ)
INVESTISSEMENTS TREVI INC
TREVI
12775 Rue Brault, Mirabel, QC, J7J 0C4
(450) 973-1249
Emp Here 1 *Sales* 91,377,250

SIC 6712 Bank holding companies
Clement Hudon
Gisele Desrochers
Chantal Bourdon
John Leboutillier
Stephan Cloutier
Benoit Hudon
Michel Bernard
Jacques Dorion
Robert Cloutier

D-U-N-S 20-297-8656 (HQ)
LALLEMAND SOLUTIONS SANTE INC
NICAR INTERNATIONAL
(*Suby of* PLACEMENTS LALLEMAND INC)
17975 Rue Des Gouverneurs, Mirabel, QC,
J7J 2K7
(450) 433-9139
Emp Here 100 *Sales* 28,402,100
SIC 2836 Biological products, except diagnos-
tic
Jerome Panes
Tatiana Mikhailova
Francois Leblanc
Francine Mondou
Antoine Chagnon
William Nankervis
Kevin Ouellette

D-U-N-S 20-253-4368 (SL)
M.I. VIAU & FILS LIMITEE
14311 Rte Sir-Wilfrid-Laurier, Mirabel, QC,
J7J 2G4
(450) 436-8221
Emp Here 25 *Sales* 11,179,350
SIC 5074 Plumbing and heating equipment
and supplies (hydronics)
Jean-Claude Lariviere
Daniel Lariviere

D-U-N-S 20-689-6396 (HQ)
MAGASINS TREVI INC
PISCINES TREVI
(*Suby of* INVESTISSEMENTS TREVI INC)
12775 Rue Brault, Mirabel, QC, J7J 0C4
(450) 973-1249
Emp Here 180 *Sales* 45,884,250
SIC 5999 Miscellaneous retail stores, nec
Clement Hudon
Chantal Bourdon
John Leboutillier
Michel Bernard
Benoit Hudon
Stephan Cloutier

D-U-N-S 20-330-4456 (SL)
MARCHE ST-JANVIER INC
13380 Boul Du Cure-Labelle, Mirabel, QC, J7J
1G9
(450) 971-7881
Emp Here 100 *Sales* 29,347,700
SIC 5411 Grocery stores
Serge Girard
Julie Girard
Isabelle Girard

D-U-N-S 20-370-8255 (SL)
METAUX ABSOLUS INC
ABSOLUTE METALS
17550 Rue Charles, Mirabel, QC, J7J 1X9
(450) 437-1777
Emp Here 10 *Sales* 10,003,390
SIC 5051 Metals service centers and offices
Eric Dube

D-U-N-S 24-390-2413 (SL)
METAUX M.P.I. INC
DISTRIBUTION JOCA
12695 Rue Du Parc, Mirabel, QC, J7J 0W5
(450) 420-0858
Emp Here 26 *Sales* 11,626,524
SIC 5051 Metals service centers and offices
William Harrisson

D-U-N-S 25-817-0278 (SL)
ORANGE TRAFFIC INC
(*Suby of* 3929761 CANADA INC)

18195 Rue J.A.Bombardier, Mirabel, QC, J7J 0E7
(800) 363-5913
Emp Here 26   *Sales* 11,626,524
SIC 5046 Commercial equipment, nec
Roger Jr. Fugere
Philippe Fugere

D-U-N-S 24-541-4453   (SL)
PAQUETTE, GERALD ENTREPRENEUR ELECTRICIEN ET ASSOCIES INC
17820 Rue Charles, Mirabel, QC, J7J 1J5
(450) 430-9323
Emp Here 60   *Sales* 13,069,740
SIC 1731 Electrical work
Gerald Paquette
Danielle Lajeunesse
Claude Couture

D-U-N-S 25-293-1555   (BR)
QUEBECOR MEDIA INC
QUEBECOR MEDIA INC
(*Suby of* QUEBECOR MEDIA INC)
12800 Rue Brault, Mirabel, QC, J7J 0W4
(450) 663-9000
Emp Here 100
SIC 5994 News dealers and newsstands
Mario Gouin

D-U-N-S 24-000-6846   (HQ)
ROBOTSHOP INC
LYNXMOTION
(*Suby of* GESTION MS 3000 INC)
18005 Rue Lapointe Bureau 305, Mirabel, QC, J7J 0G2
(450) 420-1446
Sales 27,551,508
SIC 5084 Industrial machinery and equipment
Mario Tremblay
Sandra Fradet

D-U-N-S 24-870-7341   (BR)
SAFRAN LANDING SYSTEMS CANADA INC
MESSIER-DOWTY
(*Suby of* SAFRAN)
13000 Rue Du Parc, Mirabel, QC, J7J 0W6
(450) 434-3400
Emp Here 200
SIC 3728 Aircraft parts and equipment, nec
Jean Blondin

D-U-N-S 20-549-2635   (SL)
SONACA MONTREAL INC
SONACA NMF CANADA
(*Suby of* SOCIETE NATIONALE DE CONSTRUCTION AEROSPATIALE)
13075 Rue Brault, Mirabel, QC, J7J 0W2
(450) 434-6114
Emp Here 300   *Sales* 87,255,000
SIC 3728 Aircraft parts and equipment, nec
Bernard Delvaux
Roger Simard
Erik Van Ockenburg
Pierre Sonveaux

D-U-N-S 24-365-2083   (SL)
TECHNILAB PHARMA INC
17800 Rue Lapointe, Mirabel, QC, J7J 0W8
(450) 433-7673
Emp Here 400   *Sales* 146,203,600
SIC 6712 Bank holding companies
Jean-Guy Goulet
Matthias Eschrichts
Walter Buhl
Gerd Lehmann
Joel Belanger

D-U-N-S 24-804-8097   (BR)
TEVA CANADA LIMITED
(*Suby of* TEVA PHARMACEUTICAL INDUSTRIES LIMITED)
17800 Rue Lapointe Bureau 123, Mirabel, QC, J7J 0W8
(450) 433-7673
Emp Here 250
SIC 2834 Pharmaceutical preparations

Mario Malaborza

D-U-N-S 20-793-4357   (HQ)
TREVI FABRICATION INC
CORNELIUS
(*Suby of* INVESTISSEMENTS TREVI INC)
12775 Rue Brault, Mirabel, QC, J7J 0C4
(514) 228-7384
Sales 32,613,600
SIC 3949 Sporting and athletic goods, nec
Benoit Hudon
Chantal Bourdon
Gisele Desrochers

Mirabel, QC J7N

D-U-N-S 24-381-2901   (SL)
4224795 CANADA INC
9200 Rue Desvoyaux, Mirabel, QC, J7N 2H4
(450) 475-7924
Emp Here 125   *Sales* 34,168,750
SIC 6712 Bank holding companies
Sylvain Terrault

D-U-N-S 25-287-1371   (BR)
AEROPORTS DE MONTREAL
(*Suby of* AEROPORTS DE MONTREAL)
12655 Boul Henri-Fabre O Unite A4, Mirabel, QC, J7N 1E1
(514) 394-7377
Emp Here 185
SIC 4581 Airports, flying fields, and services
Yves Provancher

D-U-N-S 20-552-6168   (HQ)
ASPHALTE, BETON, CARRIERES RIVE-NORD INC
5605 Rte Arthur-Sauve, Mirabel, QC, J7N 2W4
(450) 258-4242
Sales 50,488,400
SIC 1611 Highway and street construction
Alain Bisson
Gilles Desrosiers

D-U-N-S 25-355-6757   (HQ)
AVIANOR INC
(*Suby of* 2842441 CANADA INC)
12405 Rue Service A-2, Mirabel, QC, J7N 1E4

Emp Here 10   *Sales* 72,712,500
SIC 3728 Aircraft parts and equipment, nec
Earl Diamond
Sylvain Savard

D-U-N-S 24-125-0815   (BR)
CENTRE INTEGRE DE SANTE ET DE SERVICES SOCIAUX DES LAURENTIDES
CENTRE D'HEBERGEMENT DE SAINT-BENOIT
(*Suby of* CENTRE INTEGRE DE SANTE ET DE SERVICES SOCIAUX DES LAURENTIDES)
9100 Rue Dumouchel, Mirabel, QC, J7N 5A1
(450) 258-2481
Emp Here 100
SIC 7041 Membership-basis organization hotels
Andre Desautels

D-U-N-S 20-292-4049   (SL)
CENTRE INTERNATIONAL DE COURSE AUTOMOBILE (ICAR) INC
CIRCUIT ICAR
12800 Boul Henri-Fabre, Mirabel, QC, J7N 0A6
(514) 955-4227
Emp Here 35   *Sales* 11,012,120
SIC 8699 Membership organizations, nec
Marc Arseneau
Mirelle Baida

D-U-N-S 24-886-2752   (SL)
CHAREX INC
14940 Rue Louis-M.-Taillon, Mirabel, QC, J7N

2K4
(450) 475-1135
Emp Here 50   *Sales* 14,429,150
SIC 1522 Residential construction, nec
Stephane Charette
Yvon Theoret
Nicolas Charette

D-U-N-S 20-380-8246   (SL)
COVIA CANADA LTEE
11974 Rte Sir-Wilfrid-Laurier, Mirabel, QC, J7N 1P5
(450) 438-1238
Emp Here 50   *Sales* 10,206,500
SIC 1481 NonMetallic mineral services
Kevin F. Crawford
Warren Grover
Louis R Mastandrea

D-U-N-S 25-232-6293   (SL)
HYDROSERRE INC
HYDROSERRE MIRABEL
9200 Rue Desvoyaux, Mirabel, QC, J7N 2H4
(450) 475-7924
Emp Here 50   *Sales* 15,048,060
SIC 0161 Vegetables and melons
Sylvain Terrault
Daniel Terrault
Chantal Desjardins

D-U-N-S 20-018-9918   (SL)
IGA ST-AUGUSTIN
14995 Rue Des Saules, Mirabel, QC, J7N 2A3
(450) 475-1118
Emp Here 30   *Sales* 25,067,310
SIC 5149 Groceries and related products, nec
Serge Girard

D-U-N-S 25-907-1256   (SL)
INVESTISSEMENTS NOLINOR INC, LES
NOLINOR AVIATION
(*Suby of* 2621-7067 QUEBEC INC)
11600 Rue Louis-Bisson, Mirabel, QC, J7N 1G9
(450) 476-0018
Emp Here 260   *Sales* 82,511,520
SIC 4512 Air transportation, scheduled
Jacques Prud'homme
Marco Prud'homme
Linda Gravel
Dominique Prud'homme

D-U-N-S 20-188-3845   (HQ)
L3 TECHNOLOGIES MAS INC
(*Suby of* L3HARRIS TECHNOLOGIES, INC.)
10000 Rue Helen-Bristol, Mirabel, QC, J7N 1H3
(450) 476-4000
Emp Here 800   *Sales* 89,696,000
SIC 7699 Repair services, nec
Nick Farah
Bruce R Latimer
Dan Azmon
Jacques Comtois

D-U-N-S 20-251-4972   (SL)
LAFOND, J.-RENE INC
3203 Ch Charles-Leonard, Mirabel, QC, J7N 2Y7
(450) 258-2448
Emp Here 23   *Sales* 10,925,598
SIC 5083 Farm and garden machinery
Jean Rene Lafond
Murielle Gagne-Lafond
Alexandre Lafond
Simon Daoust

D-U-N-S 20-247-5190   (SL)
MARCHE L. ETHIER & FILS INC
MARCHE DE LA PLACE (2000), LE
9300 Rue Saint-Etienne, Mirabel, QC, J7N 2N2
(450) 258-2084
Emp Here 50   *Sales* 13,707,600
SIC 5411 Grocery stores
Serge Ethier

D-U-N-S 20-706-9613   (SL)

MARCHE ST-CANUT INC
IGA
9600 Rue Henri-Piche, Mirabel, QC, J7N 0T4
(450) 431-3244
Emp Here 49   *Sales* 13,433,448
SIC 5411 Grocery stores
Normand D'amours

D-U-N-S 20-560-8511   (HQ)
MECACHROME CANADA INC
(*Suby of* MECA DEV)
11100 Rue Julien-Audette, Mirabel, QC, J7N 3L3
(450) 476-3939
Sales 41,695,610
SIC 3728 Aircraft parts and equipment, nec
Jean-Charles Raillat
Jocelyn Cote

D-U-N-S 20-247-2833   (SL)
MONDOU, REAL INC
BOUTIQUE AGRICOLE LE CAMPAGNARD
(*Suby of* GESTION M.R. MONDOU INC)
12429 Rte Arthur-Sauve, Mirabel, QC, J7N 2C2
(450) 258-2817
Emp Here 40   *Sales* 13,827,600
SIC 2048 Prepared feeds, nec
Michel Mondou

D-U-N-S 25-181-8725   (BR)
PRATT & WHITNEY CANADA CIE
MIRABEL AEROSPACE CENTRE
(*Suby of* PRATT AERO LIMITED PARTNERSHIP)
11155 Rue Julien-Audette, Mirabel, QC, J7N 0G6
(450) 476-0049
Emp Here 175
SIC 3519 Internal combustion engines, nec
Rany Issa

D-U-N-S 24-858-6315   (SL)
PRO-AMINO INTERNATIONAL INC
(*Suby of* 8825122 CANADA INC)
12700 Boul Henri-Fabre E, Mirabel, QC, J7N 0A6
(800) 555-2170
Emp Here 50   *Sales* 17,284,500
SIC 2032 Canned specialties
Jean Bourassa-Marineau

D-U-N-S 20-183-2362   (SL)
SAFRAN MOTEURS D'HELICOPTERES CANADA INC
TURBOMECA CANADA
(*Suby of* SAFRAN)
11800 Rue Helen-Bristol, Mirabel, QC, J7N 3G8
(450) 476-2550
Emp Here 50   *Sales* 14,165,000
SIC 7538 General automotive repair shops
Thierry Derrien
Cedric Jochum
Olivier Le-Merrer

D-U-N-S 20-332-5071   (SL)
SOCIETE EN COMMANDITE AIRBUS CANADA
13100 Boul Henri-Fabre E, Mirabel, QC, J7N 3C6
(514) 855-7110
Emp Here 1,000   *Sales* 290,850,000
SIC 3721 Aircraft
Philippe Balducchi

D-U-N-S 24-978-2041   (SL)
STELIA AERONAUTIQUE CANADA INC
STELIA AMERIQUE DU NORD
(*Suby of* AIRBUS SE)
12000 Rue Henry-Giffard, Mirabel, QC, J7N 1H4
(450) 595-8300
Emp Here 100   *Sales* 22,384,300
SIC 3721 Aircraft
Christophe Henno
Jean-Pierre Cousserans
Jean Thibodeau

▲ Public Company   ■ Public Company Family Member   **HQ** Headquarters   **BR** Branch   **SL** Single Location

Dominique Salliot
Guillaume Vuillermoz
Jean-Luc Toqueboeuf
Didier Bonnin
Laurent Defever

D-U-N-S 24-225-5545 (SL)
UNIROC INC
5605 Rte Arthur-Sauve, Mirabel, QC, J7N 2W4
(450) 258-4242
Emp Here 50 *Sales* 14,176,200
SIC 1611 Highway and street construction
Andre Belanger
Gilles Desrosiers
David Whissell
Alain Bisson

D-U-N-S 24-785-4354 (SL)
VOLAILLES MIRABEL LTEE
(Suby of 153641 CANADA INC)
9051 Rte Sir-Wilfrid-Laurier, Mirabel, QC, J7N 1L6
(450) 258-0444
Emp Here 20 *Sales* 13,936,200
SIC 6799 Investors, nec
Elias Simitsakos
Emmanuel Simitsakos

D-U-N-S 20-284-9196 (BR)
WORLDWIDE FLIGHT SERVICES LTD
(Suby of WORLDWIDE FLIGHT SERVICES, INC.)
11955 Rue Henry-Giffard Suite 200, Mirabel, QC, J7N 1G3
(450) 476-9248
Emp Here 80
SIC 4731 Freight transportation arrangement
Maurice Euter

Mistissini, QC G0W

D-U-N-S 24-051-6294 (HQ)
COMMISSION SCOLAIRE CRIE (LA)
203 Main St, Mistissini, QC, G0W 1C0
(418) 923-2764
Emp Here 47 *Sales* 72,900,690
SIC 8211 Elementary and secondary schools
Kathleen Wootton
Bella Mianscum
Abraham Jolly
Serge Beliveau
Caroline Mark
Kimberly Quinn
Pierre Desjardins
Jane Blacksmith
Matthew Rabbitskin
Natalie Petawabano

Mont-Joli, QC G5H

D-U-N-S 25-484-8963 (SL)
ALIMENTATION DE LA MITIS INC
IGA
1330 Boul Benoit-Gaboury, Mont-Joli, QC, G5H 4B2
(418) 775-8915
Emp Here 80 *Sales* 23,478,160
SIC 5411 Grocery stores
Carl Desjardins

D-U-N-S 25-001-9056 (BR)
ARMOIRES FABRITEC LTEE
ARMOIRES CAMBOARD
(Suby of ARMOIRES FABRITEC LTEE)
1230 Rue Industrielle, Mont-Joli, QC, G5H 3S2
(418) 775-7010
Emp Here 85
SIC 2434 Wood kitchen cabinets
Nicole Cemelis

D-U-N-S 20-954-7793 (SL)
AROMATHEQUE INC
UNIPRIX
26 Av Du Docteur-Rene-A.-Lepage, Mont-Joli, QC, G5H 1R2
(418) 775-8841
Emp Here 50 *Sales* 12,647,700
SIC 5912 Drug stores and proprietary stores
Henry Paradis
Guy Bergeron
Raymonde F Forbes Raiche
Richard Gendron

D-U-N-S 20-208-5775 (SL)
AUTOMOBILES BOUCHARD & FILS INC
FORD
1800 Boul Jacques-Cartier, Mont-Joli, QC, G5H 2W8
(418) 775-4378
Emp Here 28 *Sales* 13,946,184
SIC 5511 New and used car dealers
Andre Roussel

D-U-N-S 24-341-3965 (HQ)
BOIS BSL INC
BOIS B.S.L MATANE
(Suby of GESTION FAMILLE G. OUELLET INC)
1081 Boul Industriel, Mont-Joli, QC, G5H 3K8
(418) 775-5360
Emp Here 145 *Sales* 143,842,000
SIC 5023 Homefurnishings
Gino Ouellet

D-U-N-S 20-208-6658 (BR)
BRADKEN CANADA MANUFACTURED PRODUCTS LTD
FONDERIE NORCAST
(Suby of HITACHI, LTD.)
105 Av De La Fonderie, Mont-Joli, QC, G5H 1W2
(418) 775-4358
Emp Here 200
SIC 3321 Gray and ductile iron foundries
Steven Ian

D-U-N-S 20-592-6157 (SL)
CENTRAP INC
1111 Rue Industrielle, Mont-Joli, QC, G5H 3T9
(418) 775-7202
Emp Here 125 *Sales* 24,046,250
SIC 2431 Millwork
Charles Blais
Rene Lavoie
Michel Gosselin
Georges Coulombe
Patrice Fournier
Yvan Gagnon
Jean Ross

D-U-N-S 20-955-1167 (SL)
PERREAULT, YVAN & FILS INC
ENTREPOT
235 Av Perreault, Mont-Joli, QC, G5H 3K6
(418) 775-7743
Emp Here 85 *Sales* 71,024,045
SIC 5142 Packaged frozen goods
Sabin Perreault
Eric Perreault
Nicole Perreault
Rolande Perreault

D-U-N-S 25-307-3183 (BR)
SUPERMARCHES GP INC, LES
METRO G P
40 Av Doucet, Mont-Joli, QC, G5H 0B8
(418) 775-8848
Emp Here 80
SIC 5411 Grocery stores
Claude Roy

D-U-N-S 24-913-8384 (SL)
TRANSPORT DP INC
1213 Rue Industrielle, Mont-Joli, QC, G5H 3T9
(418) 775-1311
Emp Here 20 *Sales* 10,702,480

SIC 5143 Dairy products, except dried or canned
Claude Deschenes

Mont-Laurier, QC J9L

D-U-N-S 20-290-5634 (SL)
9144-8720 QUEBEC INC
GROUPE KTG
1092 Rue Lachapelle, Mont-Laurier, QC, J9L 3T9
(819) 623-6745
Emp Here 70 *Sales* 17,233,020
SIC 1799 Special trade contractors, nec
Gaetan Gagne

D-U-N-S 20-297-7419 (HQ)
9168-1924 QUEBEC INC
F. DAUDELIN ET FILS
1351 Boul Albiny-Paquette, Mont-Laurier, QC, J9L 1M8
(819) 623-1767
Emp Here 80 *Sales* 71,203,500
SIC 5039 Construction materials, nec
Eric Deslongchamps
Lorraine Deslongchamps
Roger Deslongchamps

D-U-N-S 24-206-0304 (SL)
9181-2958 QUEBEC INC
FERME LA ROSE DES VENTS
2443 Ch Du 5e-Rang S, Mont-Laurier, QC, J9L 3G7
(819) 623-5672
Emp Here 24 *Sales* 20,053,848
SIC 5144 Poultry and poultry products
Jean-Guy Lacelle
Diane Aubin

D-U-N-S 20-308-8158 (SL)
9196-5905 QUEBEC INC
395 Boul Des Ruisseaux, Mont-Laurier, QC, J9L 0H6
(819) 623-4422
Emp Here 250 *Sales* 69,597,500
SIC 2411 Logging
Daniel Morin
Norman Paquette
Lysette Gagnon
Michel Lagace
Jean-Francois Belzile
Mario Gauthier

D-U-N-S 24-612-9795 (SL)
AUTO MONT CHEVROLET BUICK GMC LTEE
1300 Boul Albiny-Paquette, Mont-Laurier, QC, J9L 1M7
(819) 623-1122
Emp Here 23 *Sales* 11,455,794
SIC 5511 New and used car dealers
Richard Valiquette
Jacques Lafleur

D-U-N-S 24-747-3341 (SL)
AUTOMOBILES BELLEM INC, LES
HONDA DE MONT-LAURIER
2050 Boul Albiny-Paquette Bureau 3, Mont-Laurier, QC, J9L 3G5
(819) 623-7341
Emp Here 21 *Sales* 10,459,638
SIC 5511 New and used car dealers
Guy Crevier
Isabelle Goyer

D-U-N-S 24-676-5593 (SL)
BOIS NOBLES KA'N'ENDA LTEE
701 Rue Iberville, Mont-Laurier, QC, J9L 3W7
(819) 623-2445
Emp Here 100 *Sales* 15,586,300
SIC 2421 Sawmills and planing mills, general
Pierre Grand'maison

D-U-N-S 24-941-2891 (SL)
CENTRE DU CAMION MONT-LAURIER INC,

LE
3763 Ch De La Lievre N, Mont-Laurier, QC, J9L 3G4
(819) 623-3433
Emp Here 24 *Sales* 11,953,872
SIC 5531 Auto and home supply stores
Serge Brisebois

D-U-N-S 24-345-6279 (BR)
CENTRE HOSPITALIER ET CENTRE DE READAPTATION ANTOINE-LABELLE
CENTRE D HEBERGEMENT SAINTE-ANNE
411 Rue De La Madone, Mont-Laurier, QC, J9L 1S1
(819) 623-5940
Emp Here 150
SIC 8361 Residential care
Pierre Urbain

D-U-N-S 20-415-6590 (SL)
CLAUDE AUTO (1984) INC
TOYOTA
330 Boul Albiny-Paquette, Mont-Laurier, QC, J9L 1J9
(819) 623-3511
Emp Here 25 *Sales* 12,451,950
SIC 5511 New and used car dealers
Michel Benoit
Gaston Benoit

D-U-N-S 25-233-5849 (HQ)
COMMISSION SCOLAIRE PIERRE-NEVEU, LA
525 Rue De La Madone, Mont-Laurier, QC, J9L 1S4
(819) 623-4310
Emp Here 50 *Sales* 79,295,200
SIC 8211 Elementary and secondary schools
Claudine Millaire

D-U-N-S 25-337-7543 (SL)
LOCATION LOUIS ANDRE PELLETIER LTEE
233 Boul Albiny-Paquette, Mont-Laurier, QC, J9L 1K2
(819) 623-4015
Emp Here 17 *Sales* 21,372,417
SIC 5172 Petroleum products, nec
Louis Andre Pelletier
Mathieu Pelletier
Ginette Pelletier
Mathieu Pelletier
Jean-Francois Choquette

D-U-N-S 24-820-3887 (SL)
MARCHE DORE & FILS INC
METRO
939 Boul Albiny-Paquette Bureau 1, Mont-Laurier, QC, J9L 3J1
(819) 623-6984
Emp Here 80 *Sales* 23,478,160
SIC 5431 Fruit and vegetable markets
Ronald Dore
Patrick Dore

D-U-N-S 20-208-8274 (SL)
MARCHE LEBLANC INC
IGA
101 Rue Hebert, Mont-Laurier, QC, J9L 3H9
(819) 623-3200
Emp Here 24 *Sales* 29,934,654
SIC 5411 Grocery stores
Marcel Leblanc
Anne Leblanc
Alain Leblanc
Luc Leblanc

D-U-N-S 25-496-1303 (SL)
METAL GOSSELIN LTEE
1591 Boul Albiny-Paquette, Mont-Laurier, QC, J9L 1M8
(819) 623-3369
Emp Here 23 *Sales* 10,285,002
SIC 5051 Metals service centers and offices
Mario Gosselin
Denis Gosselin

D-U-N-S 24-759-4005 (SL)

ORDRE FRATERNEL DES AIGLES DE MONT-LAURIER INC
742 Rue De La Madone, Mont-Laurier, QC, J9L 1S9

Emp Here 200   *Sales* 26,303,000
SIC 8641 Civic and social associations
Bernard Filion
Laurier Alarie
Raymond Lacelle

D-U-N-S 24-459-5161   (SL)
PERFORMANCE LAURENTIDES INC
PERFORMANCE LOCATION
1435 Boul Albiny-Paquette, Mont-Laurier, QC, J9L 1M8
(819) 623-6331
Emp Here 62   *Sales* 39,015,360
SIC 5511 New and used car dealers
Claude Forget

D-U-N-S 20-208-7839   (SL)
PIECES D'AUTO LEON GRENIER (1987) INC, LES
AUTO PARTS PLUS
1260 Boul Albiny-Paquette, Mont-Laurier, QC, J9L 1M7
(819) 623-3740
Emp Here 45   *Sales* 16,389,675
SIC 5013 Motor vehicle supplies and new parts
Sylvain Piche

D-U-N-S 20-208-8738   (SL)
ST-PIERRE, JULES LTEE
1054 Boul Albiny-Paquette, Mont-Laurier, QC, J9L 1M1

Emp Here 35   *Sales* 29,245,195
SIC 5149 Groceries and related products, nec
Jacques St-Pierre

D-U-N-S 24-687-8883   (SL)
SUPERIEUR PROPANE
252 Av Du Moulin, Mont-Laurier, QC, J9L 3W1

Emp Here 25   *Sales* 11,922,328
SIC 5984 Liquefied petroleum gas dealers
Christian Germain

D-U-N-S 25-683-9564   (BR)
UNIBOARD CANADA INC
(*Suby of* UNIBOARD CANADA INC)
845 Rue Jean-Baptiste-Reid, Mont-Laurier, QC, J9L 3W3
(819) 623-7133
Emp Here 105
SIC 2493 Reconstituted wood products
Sylvain Cote

Mont-Royal, QC H3P

D-U-N-S 24-678-1608   (SL)
9223-0846 QUEBEC INC
JEAN COUTU
1365 Av Beaumont, Mont-Royal, QC, H3P 2H7
(514) 738-2401
Emp Here 50   *Sales* 12,647,700
SIC 5912 Drug stores and proprietary stores
Francois Jean Coutu
Jihad Kahwati

D-U-N-S 20-202-4472   (BR)
ALTASCIENCES COMPAGNIE INC
ALGORITHME PHARMA
(*Suby of* ALTASCIENCES ACQUISITION HOLDINGS, LP)
1200 Av Beaumont, Mont-Royal, QC, H3P 3P1
(514) 858-6077
Emp Here 200
SIC 8731 Commercial physical research
Christopher Perkin

D-U-N-S 25-097-8301   (BR)
BOUTIQUE LINEN CHEST (PHASE II) INC
LINEN CHEST
(*Suby of* BOUTIQUE LINEN CHEST (PHASE II) INC)
2305 Ch Rockland Bureau 500, Mont-Royal, QC, H3P 3E9
(514) 341-7810
Emp Here 79
SIC 5714 Drapery and upholstery stores
Hourig Tanachian

D-U-N-S 25-240-3621   (BR)
COMMISSION SCOLAIRE MARGUERITE-BOURGEOYS
ECOLE SECONDAIRE PIERRE LAPORTE
(*Suby of* COMMISSION SCOLAIRE MARGUERITE-BOURGEOYS)
1101 Ch Rockland, Mont-Royal, QC, H3P 2X8
(514) 739-6311
Emp Here 125
SIC 8211 Elementary and secondary schools
Jean-Guy Perras

D-U-N-S 24-635-3312   (SL)
DIVERSION P.L. SPORTS INC
SPORTS EXPERTS
2305 Ch Rockland Bureau 320, Mont-Royal, QC, H3P 3E9
(514) 735-4751
Emp Here 100   *Sales* 24,432,800
SIC 5941 Sporting goods and bicycle shops
Marc-Antoine Papineau
Vincent Papineau

D-U-N-S 20-551-2697   (SL)
FLOGEN TECHNOLOGIES INC
FLOGEN
1255 Boul Laird Bureau 388, Mont-Royal, QC, H3P 2T1
(514) 344-8786
Emp Here 200   *Sales* 28,836,400
SIC 7371 Custom computer programming services
Florian Kongoli
Shpetime Llubani

D-U-N-S 20-800-7570   (SL)
GESTION SARMASO INC
PHARMAPRIX
2305 Ch Rockland Bureau 191, Mont-Royal, QC, H3P 3E9
(514) 739-5551
Emp Here 50   *Sales* 12,647,700
SIC 5912 Drug stores and proprietary stores
Mario Zerbe

D-U-N-S 25-665-0706   (BR)
HUDSON'S BAY COMPANY
BAY, THE
(*Suby of* HUDSON'S BAY COMPANY)
2435 Ch Rockland, Mont-Royal, QC, H3P 2Z3
(514) 739-5521
Emp Here 200
SIC 5331 Variety stores
Anick Saldivar

D-U-N-S 20-765-6125   (HQ)
IMMEUBLES TURRET INC
1320 Boul Graham Bureau 330, Mont-Royal, QC, H3P 3C8
(514) 737-7132
Sales 12,152,450
SIC 6514 Dwelling operators, except apartments
Herbert S Lang

D-U-N-S 20-765-2251   (SL)
ROYAL LEPAGE (1598)
1301 Ch Canora, Mont-Royal, QC, H3P 2J5
(514) 735-2281
Emp Here 50   *Sales* 13,587,800
SIC 6531 Real estate agents and managers
Louis Cahier

D-U-N-S 24-056-8626   (HQ)
SAJO INC

1320 Boul Graham Bureau 129, Mont-Royal, QC, H3P 3C8
(514) 385-0333
Sales 83,807,040
SIC 1542 Nonresidential construction, nec
Salvatore Guerrera
Nick Tedeschi
Franca Tedeschi

D-U-N-S 20-332-8117   (HQ)
SAMA RESOURCES INC
1320 Boul Graham Bureau 132, Mont-Royal, QC, H3P 3C8
(514) 747-4653
Emp Here 5   *Sales* 20,865,294
SIC 6799 Investors, nec
Marc-Antoine Audet
Benoit La Salle
Kathleen Jones-Bartels
Isabelle Gauthier
Raphael Beaudoin
Marcel Aubut
Richard Quesnel
Eric Finlayson
Govind Friedland
Ousmane Paye

D-U-N-S 24-709-9468   (HQ)
SERVICES COMMEMORATIFS CELEBRIS INC
BOURGIE URGEL
160 Boul Graham, Mont-Royal, QC, H3P 3H9
(514) 735-2025
Emp Here 100   *Sales* 22,424,000
SIC 7261 Funeral service and crematories
Richard Balwdin Jr
Yvan Rodrigue
Jacques Cossette

D-U-N-S 24-400-7530   (SL)
SUPER MARCHE RACICOT (1980) INC
METRO RACICOT
1280 Av Beaumont, Mont-Royal, QC, H3P 3E5
(514) 737-3511
Emp Here 150   *Sales* 44,021,550
SIC 5411 Grocery stores
Jean-Guy Racicot
Lyette Racicot
Stephanie Racicot

D-U-N-S 24-680-6546   (HQ)
T.A.C. CORROSION-RESISTANT TECHNOLOGY INC
1255 Boul Laird Bureau 240, Mont-Royal, QC, H3P 2T1
(514) 737-8566
Sales 11,671,750
SIC 3272 Concrete products, nec
Michel Girard
Robert Gallant
Andrew Baird

D-U-N-S 25-307-2748   (BR)
VIGI SANTE LTEE
CENTRE D'HEBERGEMENT ET DE SOINS DE LONGUE DUREE MONT-ROYAL
275 Av Brittany, Mont-Royal, QC, H3P 3C2
(514) 739-5593
Emp Here 350
SIC 8361 Residential care
Louise Lecuyer

Mont-Royal, QC H3R

D-U-N-S 25-298-6468   (BR)
COMMISSION SCOLAIRE MARGUERITE-BOURGEOYS
ECOLE SECONDAIRE MONT-ROYAL
(*Suby of* COMMISSION SCOLAIRE MARGUERITE-BOURGEOYS)
50 Av Montgomery, Mont-Royal, QC, H3R 2B3
(514) 731-2761
Emp Here 80

SIC 8211 Elementary and secondary schools
Marc-Philippe Vincent

D-U-N-S 24-344-1644   (SL)
CYTRONICS HOLDING CORPORATION LTD
3333 Boul Graham Bureau 101, Mont-Royal, QC, H3R 3L5
(514) 382-0820
Emp Here 25   *Sales* 10,483,875
SIC 6719 Holding companies, nec
Sydney Cohen

D-U-N-S 24-773-2931   (SL)
L'EDIFICE 3333 BOUL GRAHAM
3333 Boul Graham Bureau 100, Mont-Royal, QC, H3R 3L5
(514) 341-8182
Emp Here 49   *Sales* 13,316,044
SIC 6531 Real estate agents and managers
Giannandr Dario

D-U-N-S 24-835-5781   (SL)
MONT-ROYAL DEVELOPPEMENT
20 Av Roosevelt, Mont-Royal, QC, H3R 1Z4
(514) 734-3034
Emp Here 49   *Sales* 11,480,112
SIC 8748 Business consulting, nec
Philippe Roy

D-U-N-S 24-676-6034   (SL)
PSB BOISJOLI S.E.N.R.C.L
3333 Boul Graham Bureau 400, Mont-Royal, QC, H3R 3L5
(514) 341-5511
Emp Here 65   *Sales* 13,499,525
SIC 8721 Accounting, auditing, and bookkeeping
Ellis Basevitz
Michael Fogel
Andree Guy

D-U-N-S 24-394-8614   (SL)
THOMSON REUTERS DT IMPOT ET COMPTABILITE INC
DR TAX SOFTWARE
(*Suby of* THOMSON COMPANY INC, THE)
3333 Boul Graham Bureau 222, Mont-Royal, QC, H3R 3L5
(514) 733-8355
Emp Here 50   *Sales* 10,692,550
SIC 7372 Prepackaged software
Eric Neveu
Terra Rebick
Heather O'hagan
Paula R Monaghan
Peter A Aziz

Mont-Royal, QC H4N

D-U-N-S 24-870-9289   (HQ)
157503 CANADA INC
MANTEAUX MANTEAUX
4360 Ch De La Cote-De-Liesse, Mont-Royal, QC, H4N 2P7
(514) 344-5140
Emp Here 20   *Sales* 37,426,500
SIC 5621 Women's clothing stores
Harold Perlman
Monte Perlman
Mary Rinaldi

D-U-N-S 20-212-0262   (HQ)
SONOVISION CANADA INC
4480 Ch De La Cote-De-Liesse Bureau 215, Mont-Royal, QC, H4N 2R1
(514) 344-5008
Emp Here 15   *Sales* 16,402,700
SIC 2741 Miscellaneous publishing
Laurent Gautret

▲ Public Company   ■ Public Company Family Member   **HQ** Headquarters   **BR** Branch   **SL** Single Location

Mont-Royal, QC H4P

D-U-N-S 24-054-0229 (SL)
109578 CANADA LTEE
INTERNATIONAL NEON
5790 Rue Ferrier, Mont-Royal, QC, H4P 1M7
(514) 937-0044
Emp Here 48   *Sales* 10,503,552
SIC 3993 Signs and advertising specialties
Albert Baudi
Amerigo Baudi

D-U-N-S 25-851-5287 (SL)
152163 CANADA INC
ACC S COMMUNICATION
5591 Rue Pare, Mont-Royal, QC, H4P 1P7
(514) 735-5248
Emp Here 32   *Sales* 13,419,360
SIC 6719 Holding companies, nec
Richard Blatt
Lisa Blatt Alexander

D-U-N-S 24-969-1601 (HQ)
2920654 CANADA INC
HANDEE PRODUCTS
5785 Rue Pare, Mont-Royal, QC, H4P 1S1
(514) 736-0810
Sales 29,700,800
SIC 5199 Nondurable goods, nec
Susan B Gardyn

D-U-N-S 20-266-7390 (SL)
9168-8820 QUEBEC INC
VETEMENTS WET DOG
5771 Rue Ferrier, Mont-Royal, QC, H4P 1N3
(514) 735-6622
Emp Here 26   *Sales* 12,956,372
SIC 5136 Men's and boy's clothing
Andy Kastner

D-U-N-S 24-321-7494 (SL)
97971 CANADA INC
5405 Av Royalmount, Mont-Royal, QC, H4P 1H6
(514) 731-7736
Emp Here 50   *Sales* 15,943,450
SIC 1521 Single-family housing construction
Joel Rosen

D-U-N-S 20-791-7006 (SL)
ALPER, SEYMOUR INC
5520 Rue Pare Bureau 1, Mont-Royal, QC, H4P 2M1
(514) 737-3434
Emp Here 45   *Sales* 26,096,580
SIC 6411 Insurance agents, brokers, and service
Elliott Alper
Seymour Alper

D-U-N-S 20-794-3036 (SL)
ASSURANCES MICHEL BROSSEAU LTEE
5665 Av Royalmount Bureau 200, Mont-Royal, QC, H4P 2P9
(514) 288-9141
Emp Here 31   *Sales* 17,977,644
SIC 6411 Insurance agents, brokers, and service
Michel Brosseau
Vincent Frechette

D-U-N-S 24-205-9611 (SL)
BASQ INTERNATIONAL INC
(*Suby of* 3343103 CANADA INC)
8515 Place Devonshire Bureau 214, Mont-Royal, QC, H4P 2K1
(514) 733-0066
Emp Here 50   *Sales* 22,460,950
SIC 7389 Business services, nec
Neil Weinman
Robert Lavoie

D-U-N-S 20-706-9774 (SL)
BONAVISTA BOVI HOME/MAISON INC
BONAVISTA FABRICS
8515 Place Devonshire Bureau 100, Mont-Royal, QC, H4P 2K1

(514) 273-6300
Emp Here 60   *Sales* 30,531,360
SIC 5023 Homefurnishings
Michael Darwish

D-U-N-S 20-211-5692 (SL)
CESIUM TELECOM INCORPORATED
CESIUM
5798 Rue Ferrier, Mont-Royal, QC, H4P 1M7
(514) 798-8686
Emp Here 58   *Sales* 25,936,092
SIC 5065 Electronic parts and equipment, nec
Sanjay Bakshani
Vicken Kanadjian

D-U-N-S 20-212-8468 (SL)
CIE ELECTRIQUE BRITTON LTEE, LA
ELECTRIQUE BRITTON
8555 Ch Devonshire Bureau 213, Mont-Royal, QC, H4P 2L3
(514) 342-5520
Emp Here 200   *Sales* 43,565,800
SIC 1731 Electrical work
Perry Britton
Paul Tassone Rocco
Michel Lafontaine

D-U-N-S 25-475-0060 (SL)
CORPORATION COMMERCIALE CRESCENT
5430 Av Royalmount, Mont-Royal, QC, H4P 1H7
(514) 739-3355
Emp Here 35   *Sales* 15,522,150
SIC 7389 Business services, nec
Stephen Kisber

D-U-N-S 24-420-7747 (HQ)
DAVIDSTEA INC
THES DAVIDSTEA, LES
5430 Rue Ferrier, Mont-Royal, QC, H4P 1M2
(514) 739-0006
Emp Here 26   *Sales* 160,075,995
SIC 5499 Miscellaneous food stores
Herschel Segal
Frank Zitella
Dominique Choquette
Sarah Segal
Martin Hillcoat
Nathalie Binda
Damon Sloane
Julie Laurin
Emilia Di Raddo
Max Ludwig Fischer

D-U-N-S 20-235-9253 (SL)
DISTRIBUTEURS TOWN LTEE
5473 Rue Pare, Mont-Royal, QC, H4P 1P7
(514) 735-4555
Emp Here 35   *Sales* 38,687,075
SIC 5122 Drugs, proprietaries, and sundries
Robert Schachter

D-U-N-S 24-420-2078 (HQ)
DOLLARAMA INC
5805 Av Royalmount, Mont-Royal, QC, H4P 0A1
(514) 737-1006
Emp Here 12,764   *Sales* 2,542,285,263
SIC 5999 Miscellaneous retail stores, nec
Neil Rossy
Geoffrey Robillard
Josee Kouri
Michael Ross
Stephen Gunn
Joshua Bekenstein
Nicholas Nomicos
Gregory David
John J. Swidler
Huw Thomas

D-U-N-S 20-232-8282 (HQ)
DOLLARAMA L.P.
5805 Av Royalmount, Mont-Royal, QC, H4P 0A1
(514) 737-1006
Emp Here 245   *Sales* 2,737,944,000
SIC 5331 Variety stores

Neil Rossy

D-U-N-S 24-788-7342 (SL)
EDILIVRE INC
5740 Rue Ferrier, Mont-Royal, QC, H4P 1M7
(514) 738-0202
Emp Here 40   *Sales* 29,700,800
SIC 5192 Books, periodicals, and newspapers
Albert Soussan
Perla Bensimon Soussan
Chantal Daoust

D-U-N-S 24-526-8354 (SL)
EMBALLAGES STUART INC
(*Suby of* SUPREMEX INC)
5454 Ch De La Cote-De-Liesse, Mont-Royal, QC, H4P 1A5
(514) 344-5000
Emp Here 75
SIC 2657 Folding paperboard boxes

D-U-N-S 25-997-7861 (SL)
ENTREPRISES DE CONSTRUCTION DAWCO INC
CONSTRUCTION SOLIMEC
(*Suby of* DCM GROUP INDUSTRIAL CONTRACTORS INC)
8315 Ch Devonshire, Mont-Royal, QC, H4P 2L1
(514) 738-3033
Emp Here 100   *Sales* 21,782,900
SIC 1731 Electrical work
Serge Tousignant
Neil Macrae
Richard Gadoury
Stephane Tousignant
Claude Thibault

D-U-N-S 20-399-4611 (SL)
ENTREPRISES LA CANADIENNE INC
C LA CANADIENNE
5745 Rue Pare, Mont-Royal, QC, H4P 1S1
(514) 731-2112
Emp Here 50   *Sales* 11,671,750
SIC 3143 Men's footwear, except athletic
Nicolas Topiol
Nicholas Martire
Scott Jackson
Pinetta Shuster
Robert Hamel
Marc Benoit

D-U-N-S 20-956-3365 (BR)
ERICSSON CANADA INC
RECHERCHE ERICSSON CANADA
(*Suby of* TELEFON AB LM ERICSSON)
8400 Boul Decarie, Mont-Royal, QC, H4P 2N2
(514) 345-7900
Emp Here 1,550
SIC 5065 Electronic parts and equipment, nec
Romi Roy

D-U-N-S 24-351-9758 (HQ)
EXCEL AUTOMOBILES MONTREAL LTEE
EXCEL HONDA
(*Suby of* GESTION CORPORATIVE TLS LTEE)
5400 Rue Pare, Mont-Royal, QC, H4P 1R3
(514) 342-6360
Sales 62,928,000
SIC 5511 New and used car dealers
Tomas Samatas
Melissa Ann Chipman Samatas
Vanessa Lynn Samatas
Jessica Laura Samatas

D-U-N-S 20-219-1128 (SL)
FRABELS INC
(*Suby of* 119460 CANADA INC)
5580 Rue Pare, Mont-Royal, QC, H4P 2M1
(514) 842-8561
Emp Here 26   *Sales* 10,410,840
SIC 5094 Jewelry and precious stones
George Stern

D-U-N-S 20-355-7608 (SL)
FREEMARK APPAREL BRANDS RETAIL

BE INC
5640 Rue Pare, Mont-Royal, QC, H4P 2M1
(514) 341-7333
Emp Here 450   *Sales* 27,301,610
SIC 5651 Family clothing stores
Mark Routtenberg
Lawrence Routtenberg
Michael Routtenberg
Howard Schnider

D-U-N-S 24-870-6145 (SL)
GROUPE ASPEX INC
(*Suby of* GESTION OPTIFER INC)
5440 Rue Pare, Mont-Royal, QC, H4P 1R3
(514) 938-2020
Emp Here 225   *Sales* 120,454,200
SIC 5049 Professional equipment, nec
Nonu Ifergan
Karen Ifergan

D-U-N-S 24-970-9353 (HQ)
GROUPE DYNAMITE INC
CHADO
(*Suby of* 3752372 CANADA INC)
5592 Rue Ferrier, Mont-Royal, QC, H4P 1M2
(514) 733-3962
Emp Here 300   *Sales* 235,163,175
SIC 5621 Women's clothing stores
Andrew Lutfy
Chistian Roy

D-U-N-S 24-251-0720 (SL)
HB CONNECTIONS INC
GROUPE HB
8190 Ch Royden, Mont-Royal, QC, H4P 2T2
(514) 340-4414
Emp Here 36   *Sales* 43,890,043
SIC 3171 Women's handbags and purses
David Sachs
Gaby Berelovich
Denise Sachs

D-U-N-S 20-214-1446 (SL)
INDUSTRIES CENTURY INC, LES
CENTURYAMADEUS
5645 Av Royalmount, Mont-Royal, QC, H4P 2P9
(514) 842-3933
Emp Here 65   *Sales* 12,378,730
SIC 3645 Residential lighting fixtures
Ivan Levine
Sheldon Abramovitch

D-U-N-S 20-236-0053 (SL)
INDUSTRIES DE PLASTIQUE TRANSCO LTEE, LES
FLEXOPACK
8096 Ch Montview, Mont-Royal, QC, H4P 2L7
(514) 733-9951
Emp Here 100   *Sales* 20,189,700
SIC 3081 Unsupported plastics film and sheet
Mitch Herman
Stephen Lash
Sandra Lash

D-U-N-S 20-220-6942 (SL)
INDUSTRIES GARANTIES LIMITEE, LES
5420 Rue Pare, Mont-Royal, QC, H4P 1R3
(514) 342-3400
Emp Here 75   *Sales* 17,479,875
SIC 1711 Plumbing, heating, air-conditioning
Jeffrey N. Shapiro
Gary Shapiro

D-U-N-S 20-220-3154 (HQ)
KOMBI SPORTS INC
KOMBI
5711 Rue Ferrier, Mont-Royal, QC, H4P 1N3
(514) 341-4321
Sales 19,932,880
SIC 5137 Women's and children's clothing
Edward Pascal
Mark Pascal

D-U-N-S 24-890-3841 (BR)
KRAFT HEINZ CANADA ULC
(*Suby of* THE KRAFT HEINZ COMPANY)

8600 Ch Devonshire, Mont-Royal, QC, H4P 2K9
(514) 343-3300
Emp Here 1,000
SIC 2022 Cheese; natural and processed
Sylvie Goudet

D-U-N-S 24-417-6405   (SL)
MARKETING MANN, ALBERT INC
MANN MARKETING
8191 Ch Montview, Mont-Royal, QC, H4P 2P2
(514) 800-6266
Emp Here 40   *Sales* 20,354,240
SIC 5023 Homefurnishings
Albert Mann

D-U-N-S 20-549-6727   (SL)
MARQUES DE VETEMENTS FREEMARK INC
5640 Rue Pare, Mont-Royal, QC, H4P 2M1
(514) 341-7333
Emp Here 80   *Sales* 67,002,640
SIC 5136 Men's and boy's clothing
Mark Routtenberg
Michael Routtenberg
Howard Schnider
Lawrence Routtenberg

D-U-N-S 20-332-4368   (HQ)
MARQUES DE VETEMENTS FREEMARK TEC INC
BENCH
5640 Rue Pare, Mont-Royal, QC, H4P 2M1
(514) 341-7333
Sales 85,581,930
SIC 5611 Men's and boys' clothing stores
Mark Routtenberg
Lawrence Routtenberg
Howard Schnider
Michael Routtenberg

D-U-N-S 25-401-2594   (SL)
MOMENTIS INFORMATIQUE INC
5500 Av Royalmount Bureau 250, Mont-Royal, QC, H4P 1H7
(514) 939-2306
Emp Here 50   *Sales* 10,692,550
SIC 7372 Prepackaged software
Jeffrey Payne
Howard Stotland
Stanley Zack
Ketty Munk
William Lassner
Pierre Renaud
Frank M Schlesinger

D-U-N-S 24-804-5556   (SL)
MOROCCANOIL CANADA INC
(*Suby of* MOROCCANOIL ISRAEL LTD)
5742 Rue Ferrier, Mont-Royal, QC, H4P 1M7
(514) 448-8967
Emp Here 60   *Sales* 24,769,260
SIC 5122 Drugs, proprietaries, and sundries
Jonathan Dahan
Ron Erenreich

D-U-N-S 24-330-7373   (SL)
OPTICASET INC
5440 Rue Pare Bureau 101, Mont-Royal, QC, H4P 1R3
(514) 739-6993
Emp Here 25   *Sales* 11,179,350
SIC 5049 Professional equipment, nec
David Ifrah
Nonu Ifergan
Karen Ifergan

D-U-N-S 24-934-6917   (SL)
PERRIN INC
SNO-BALL
(*Suby of* KOMBI SPORTS INC)
5711 Rue Ferrier, Mont-Royal, QC, H4P 1N3
(514) 341-4321
Emp Here 21   *Sales* 10,464,762
SIC 5136 Men's and boy's clothing
Mark Richman
Philippe Martin

Edward Pascal

D-U-N-S 25-211-1729   (SL)
PRESENTOIRS POINT 1 INC
8479 Place Devonshire Bureau 100, Mont-Royal, QC, H4P 2K1
(514) 344-4888
Emp Here 100   *Sales* 23,343,500
SIC 2653 Corrugated and solid fiber boxes
Bruce Gornitsky

D-U-N-S 20-330-8473   (SL)
RAYMARK ULC
MI9 RETAIL
5460 Ch De La Cote-De-Liesse, Mont-Royal, QC, H4P 1A5
(514) 737-0941
Emp Here 86   *Sales* 15,248,746
SIC 7371 Custom computer programming services
James Zubok

D-U-N-S 20-693-8925   (SL)
S. ROSSY INC
DOLLARAMA
5805 Av Royalmount, Mont-Royal, QC, H4P 0A1
(514) 737-1006
Emp Here 200   *Sales* 44,174,200
SIC 6514 Dwelling operators, except apartments
Lawrence Rossy

D-U-N-S 20-233-1120   (HQ)
SAFDIE & CO. INC
ELEGANCE
(*Suby of* 8967776 CANADA INC)
8191 Ch Montview, Mont-Royal, QC, H4P 2P2
(514) 344-7599
Sales 24,916,100
SIC 5131 Piece goods and notions
Jeffrey Kirstein
Gary Wechsler

D-U-N-S 24-158-7588   (SL)
SERVICES INDUSTRIELS SYSTEMEX (S.I.S.) INC
8260 Ch Devonshire Unite 240, Mont-Royal, QC, H4P 2P7
(514) 738-6323
Emp Here 50   *Sales* 16,280,000
SIC 5999 Miscellaneous retail stores, nec
Louis Soucy

D-U-N-S 24-903-2343   (HQ)
STOKES CANADA INC
(*Suby of* MOVEX INC)
5660 Rue Ferrier, Mont-Royal, QC, H4P 1M7
(514) 341-4334
Sales 169,889,811
SIC 5719 Miscellaneous homefurnishings
Morris Shiveck
Jordan Shiveck
Stuart Shiveck

D-U-N-S 20-234-9080   (HQ)
STOKES INC
ARTICLES INTERNATIONAUX
(*Suby of* MOVEX INC)
5660 Rue Ferrier, Mont-Royal, QC, H4P 1M7
(514) 341-4334
Emp Here 100   *Sales* 169,889,811
SIC 5719 Miscellaneous homefurnishings
Jordan Shiveck
Stuart Shiveck
Morris Shiveck

D-U-N-S 20-213-9387   (BR)
UNILEVER CANADA INC
UNILEVER BESTFOODS
(*Suby of* UNILEVER PLC)
5430 Ch De La Cote-De-Liesse, Mont-Royal, QC, H4P 1A5

Emp Here 80
SIC 2086 Bottled and canned soft drinks
Denis Labattaglia

D-U-N-S 20-236-4501   (SL)
UPTOWN AUTOMOBILES INC
UPTOWN VOLVO
(*Suby of* 3406032 CANADA INC)
8665 Boul Decarie, Mont-Royal, QC, H4P 2T9
(514) 737-6666
Emp Here 50   *Sales* 24,903,900
SIC 5511 New and used car dealers
Charles Hammer
Pietro D'alessandro

D-U-N-S 24-793-7738   (SL)
VOYAGE GARTH ALLEN MARKSTED INC
8260 Ch Devonshire Bureau 210, Mont-Royal, QC, H4P 2P7
(514) 344-8888
Emp Here 30   *Sales* 11,560,800
SIC 4724 Travel agencies
Eli Cohen
Gregory Respitz

D-U-N-S 24-489-4499   (BR)
WAWANESA MUTUAL INSURANCE COMPANY, THE
COMPAGNIE D'ASSURANCE WAWANESA
(*Suby of* WAWANESA MUTUAL INSURANCE COMPANY, THE)
8585 Boul Decarie, Mont-Royal, QC, H4P 2J4
(514) 342-2211
Emp Here 150
SIC 6331 Fire, marine, and casualty insurance
Claude Auclair

D-U-N-S 20-552-3637   (BR)
WESTROCK COMPANY OF CANADA CORP
(*Suby of* WESTROCK COMPANY)
5550 Av Royalmount, Mont-Royal, QC, H4P 1H7
(514) 736-6889
Emp Here 225
SIC 4225 General warehousing and storage
Peter Boyne

Mont-Royal, QC H4T

D-U-N-S 24-164-1187   (SL)
3645118 CANADA INC
U.T.V. INTERNATIONAL
8650 Ch Darnley, Mont-Royal, QC, H4T 1M4
(514) 345-0990
Emp Here 25   *Sales* 10,483,875
SIC 6712 Bank holding companies
Andrzej Sztorc

D-U-N-S 24-171-1725   (SL)
3762530 CANADA INC
MANSFIELD MEDICAL DIST
5775 Av Andover, Mont-Royal, QC, H4T 1H6
(514) 739-3633
Emp Here 50   *Sales* 55,267,250
SIC 5122 Drugs, proprietaries, and sundries
Irwin Braude

D-U-N-S 20-215-3714   (HQ)
9256-5589 QUEBEC INC
CACHERE CLASSIQUE
8593 Ch Delmeade, Mont-Royal, QC, H4T 1M1
(514) 522-1196
Sales 12,533,655
SIC 5147 Meats and meat products
Shlome Rotter

D-U-N-S 20-737-2814   (HQ)
A.M.G. MEDICALE INC
A. M. G. MEDICAL
8505 Ch Dalton, Mont-Royal, QC, H4T 1V5
(514) 737-5251
Sales 22,358,700
SIC 5047 Medical and hospital equipment
Philip Delbuey
Allan Goldenberg
Ben Topor
Robert Oringer

D-U-N-S 24-324-7553   (HQ)
BOW GROUPE DE PLOMBERIE INC
BOW METALLICS
5700 Ch De La Cote-De-Liesse, Mont-Royal, QC, H4T 1B1
(514) 735-5551
Emp Here 97   *Sales* 71,643,600
SIC 3089 Plastics products, nec
Gilles Cyr
Michel Berger
Simon Robillard

D-U-N-S 24-799-4155   (SL)
C S G BRODERIE & SOIE INTERNATIONALE INC
8660 Ch Darnley Bureau 102, Mont-Royal, QC, H4T 1M4
(514) 738-3899
Emp Here 70   *Sales* 46,823,560
SIC 7389 Business services, nec
Mark Stefanopoulos
John Calderone

D-U-N-S 25-059-4546   (SL)
DISTRIBUTIONS MONTREX INC, LES
5934 Ch De La Cote-De-Liesse, Mont-Royal, QC, H4T 2A5
(514) 737-8929
Emp Here 50   *Sales* 12,216,400
SIC 5961 Catalog and mail-order houses
Denis Benoit

D-U-N-S 24-582-6446   (HQ)
EMBALLAGES CRE-O-PACK CANADA INC
GROUPE CREOPACK
8420 Ch Darnley, Mont-Royal, QC, H4T 1M4
(514) 343-9666
Sales 22,200,100
SIC 3565 Packaging machinery
Michel Champoux
Jean Sebastien Comtois

D-U-N-S 24-434-3828   (HQ)
ENTREPRISES ELECTRIQUES NADCO INC
MARINDUSTRIEL
8550 Ch Delmeade, Mont-Royal, QC, H4T 1L7
(514) 342-2748
Sales 10,925,598
SIC 5085 Industrial supplies
Normand R. Nadeau
Eric Nadeau
Michael Nadeau
Jonathan Nadeau

D-U-N-S 24-902-7939   (HQ)
FRANKLIN EMPIRE INC
CAPEL ELECTRIQUE
8421 Ch Darnley, Mont-Royal, QC, H4T 2B2
(514) 341-3720
Emp Here 100   *Sales* 261,111,150
SIC 5063 Electrical apparatus and equipment
Robert Shapiro
Bernard Backman
Clifford Backman

D-U-N-S 24-203-4374   (SL)
FRUIT DOME INC
5975 Av Andover, Mont-Royal, QC, H4T 1H8
(514) 664-4470
Emp Here 50   *Sales* 14,441,007
SIC 5149 Groceries and related products, nec
Johnny Borsellino
Anthony Borsellino
Vittoria Borsellino

D-U-N-S 25-232-5832   (SL)
GROUPE GESTION NOR INC
8550 Ch Delmeade, Mont-Royal, QC, H4T 1L7
(514) 342-2744
Emp Here 42   *Sales* 10,985,226
SIC 6712 Bank holding companies
Normand Nadeau

D-U-N-S 20-330-8655   (BR)
GROUPE MARCELLE INC
LISE WATIER COSMETIQUES, DIV
(*Suby of* GROUPE MARCELLE INC)

5600 Ch De La Cote-De-Liesse, Mont-Royal, QC, H4T 4L1
(514) 735-2309
Emp Here 150
SIC 2844 Toilet preparations
David Cape

D-U-N-S 20-543-3881   (HQ)
MAISON JOSEPH BATTAT LTEE
(*Suby of* BATTAT INC)
8440 Ch Darnley, Mont-Royal, QC, H4T 1M4
(866) 665-5524
Sales 48,671,000
SIC 5092 Toys and hobby goods and supplies
Isaac Battat
Joseph Battat
Yvette Battat
Dany Battat

D-U-N-S 20-225-6863   (SL)
MANSFIELD MEDICAL DISTRIBUTORS LTD
5775 Av Andover, Mont-Royal, QC, H4T 1H6
(514) 739-3633
Emp Here 50   *Sales* 55,267,250
SIC 5122 Drugs, proprietaries, and sundries
Irwin Braude
Vince Iannotti
Marvin Braude

D-U-N-S 24-904-5899   (SL)
OUTIL-PAC INC
OUTIL-PAC (ESTRIE)
(*Suby of* DESCOURS ET CABAUD SA)
5895 Av Andover, Mont-Royal, QC, H4T 1H8
(514) 733-3555
Emp Here 26   *Sales* 12,350,676
SIC 5084 Industrial machinery and equipment
Philippe Legris
Robert Lafreniere
Alain Morvand
Francois Heraud
Philippe Legris

D-U-N-S 24-155-5098   (BR)
SCHINDLER ELEVATOR CORPORATION
(*Suby of* SCHINDLER HOLDING AG)
8577 Ch Dalton, Mont-Royal, QC, H4T 1V5
(514) 737-5507
Emp Here 100
SIC 3534 Elevators and moving stairways
Nathalie Boulianne

D-U-N-S 24-769-3500   (SL)
SIGVARIS CORPORATION
CORPORATION SIGVARIS
(*Suby of* SIGVARIS HOLDING AG)
8423 Ch Dalton, Mont-Royal, QC, H4T 1V5
(514) 336-2362
Emp Here 28   *Sales* 12,520,872
SIC 5047 Medical and hospital equipment
Scot J. Dube
Craig Miller
Christopher Deehy
Daniel Straub
Andreas Schonenberger

D-U-N-S 20-119-8418   (HQ)
SUPERTEK CANADA INC
PRODUITS DIVINE
8605 Ch Darnley, Mont-Royal, QC, H4T 1X2
(514) 737-8354
Emp Here 46   *Sales* 26,027,100
SIC 5099 Durable goods, nec
Denis Benoit
Pierre Benoit

D-U-N-S 20-419-4062   (HQ)
TISSUS RENTEX INC., LES
8650 Ch Delmeade, Mont-Royal, QC, H4T 1L6
(514) 735-2641
Sales 27,510,450
SIC 2258 Lace and warp knit fabric mills
Jay Derstenfeld

D-U-N-S 20-118-7445   (HQ)
ULTRA ELECTRONICS TCS INC

SYSTEMES DE COMMUNICATION TAC-TIQUES ULTRA ELECTRONICS
(*Suby of* ULTRA ELECTRONICS HOLDINGS PLC)
5990 Ch De La Cote-De-Liesse, Mont-Royal, QC, H4T 1V7
(514) 855-6363
Emp Here 150   *Sales* 70,728,750
SIC 3679 Electronic components, nec
Iwan Jemczyk
Frank Furfaro
Bridget Rothwell
Mike Baptist

Mont-Saint-Gregoire, QC J0J

D-U-N-S 24-297-3618   (SL)
ALIMENTS LA BROCHETTE INC, LES
(*Suby of* 2945-8619 QUEBEC INC)
404 Rte 104, Mont-Saint-Gregoire, QC, J0J 1K0
(450) 346-4144
Emp Here 40   *Sales* 33,423,080
SIC 5144 Poultry and poultry products
Francois Tarte
Ariste Tarte

D-U-N-S 24-902-7392   (HQ)
COUVOIR UNIK INC
222 104 Rte, Mont-Saint-Gregoire, QC, J0J 1K0
(450) 347-0126
Emp Here 15   *Sales* 17,348,355
SIC 0254 Poultry hatcheries
Rolland Robitaille
Denis Robitaille

D-U-N-S 24-218-5051   (SL)
ROBITAILLE R & FILS INC
522 Rang De Versailles, Mont-Saint-Gregoire, QC, J0J 1K0
(450) 358-1355
Emp Here 49   *Sales* 18,890,431
SIC 0213 Hogs
Claude Robitaille

D-U-N-S 25-475-2421   (SL)
TRANSPORT A. LABERGE ET FILS INC
CAMIONNAGE TOWTAL
(*Suby of* GESTION TRANSPORT A. LABERGE ET FILS INC)
255 104 Rte, Mont-Saint-Gregoire, QC, J0J 1K0
(450) 347-4336
Emp Here 14   *Sales* 20,570,600
SIC 4212 Local trucking, without storage
Richard Laberge
Andre Sabourin

Mont-Saint-Hilaire, QC J3G

D-U-N-S 20-533-0009   (SL)
CENTRE DE LA NATURE DU MONT-SAINT-HILAIRE
422 Ch Des Moulins, Mont-Saint-Hilaire, QC, J3G 4S6
(450) 467-1755
Emp Here 27   *Sales* 11,464,389
SIC 8999 Services, nec
Bernard Lefebvre

Mont-Saint-Hilaire, QC J3H

D-U-N-S 20-271-2352   (SL)
ADARE PHARMACEUTICALS, ULC
ADARE PHARMATECH CANADA
(*Suby of* PHARMATECH LUX HOLDCO II, SARL)

597 Boul Sir-Wilfrid-Laurier, Mont-Saint-Hilaire, QC, J3H 6C4
(514) 774-2973
Emp Here 50   *Sales* 13,833,000
SIC 2834 Pharmaceutical preparations
John Fraher
Daniel Belanger

D-U-N-S 24-709-7470   (HQ)
APTALIS PHARMA CANADA ULC
ACCURETTE DESSIN
597 Boul Sir-Wilfrid-Laurier, Mont-Saint-Hilaire, QC, J3H 6C4
(450) 467-5138
Emp Here 70   *Sales* 198,154,080
SIC 5122 Drugs, proprietaries, and sundries
Edward Perier Jr.
Edward Gudaitis
Mauro Naddeo
A. Robert D. Bailey
Kira M. Schwartz

D-U-N-S 24-364-7836   (HQ)
BBA INC
BBA-TOP CONTROL
(*Suby of* GROUPE BBA INC)
375 Boul Sir-Wilfrid-Laurier, Mont-Saint-Hilaire, QC, J3H 6C3
(450) 464-2111
Emp Here 100   *Sales* 78,852,400
SIC 8711 Engineering services
Mathieu Riedl
Andre Allaire
Normand Girard
Frederic Didier
Stephan Landry
Guy Janneteau
Martin Milot

D-U-N-S 25-240-5519   (BR)
COMMISSION SCOLAIRE DES PATRIOTES
ECOLES SECONDAIRES - MONT-SAINT-HILAIRE - OZIAS-LEDUC
(*Suby of* COMMISSION SCOLAIRE DES PA-TRIOTES)
525 Rue Jolliet, Mont-Saint-Hilaire, QC, J3H 3N2
(450) 467-0261
Emp Here 140
SIC 8211 Elementary and secondary schools
Daniel Deangelis

D-U-N-S 24-110-7841   (BR)
EMERGIS INC
ENTREPRISE TELLUS, DE
(*Suby of* TELUS CORPORATION)
505 Boul Sir-Wilfrid-Laurier, Mont-Saint-Hilaire, QC, J3H 4X7
(800) 363-9398
Emp Here 105
SIC 7371 Custom computer programming ser-vices

D-U-N-S 24-083-5843   (SL)
ENTREPRISES MICHAUDVILLE INC, LES
(*Suby of* PLACEMENTS ROBERT PHANEUF INC)
270 Rue Brunet, Mont-Saint-Hilaire, QC, J3H 0M6
(450) 446-9933
Emp Here 26   *Sales* 71,026,978
SIC 8711 Engineering services
Robert Phaneuf
Sylvain Phaneuf

D-U-N-S 25-705-6754   (SL)
FORACTION INC
(*Suby of* PLACEMENTS ROBERT PHANEUF INC)
270 Rue Brunet, Mont-Saint-Hilaire, QC, J3H 0M6
(450) 446-8144
Emp Here 26   *Sales* 13,208,799
SIC 1629 Heavy construction, nec
Robert Phaneuf

D-U-N-S 20-277-5003   (HQ)

GROUPE BBA INC
375 Boul Sir-Wilfrid-Laurier, Mont-Saint-Hilaire, QC, J3H 6C3
(450) 464-2111
Emp Here 1   *Sales* 100,142,548
SIC 8711 Engineering services
Andre Allaire
Normand Girard
Pierre Girard
Serge Benoit
Guy Janneteau
Stephan Landry
Mathieu Riedl
Frederic Didier

D-U-N-S 25-359-6654   (HQ)
GROUPE MICHAUDVILLE INC
(*Suby of* PLACEMENTS ROBERT PHANEUF INC)
270 Rue Brunet, Mont-Saint-Hilaire, QC, J3H 0M6
(450) 446-9933
Sales 78,227,523
SIC 6712 Bank holding companies
Robert Phaneuf
Sylvain Phaneuf
Jacques Gaumond
Sylvie Laquerre
Claude Lussier
Daniel Dichiaro
Jocelyn St-Louis
Leandre Phaneuf

D-U-N-S 24-340-6662   (HQ)
MINES ABCOURT INC
ABCOURT SILVER MINE
506 Rue Des Falaises, Mont-Saint-Hilaire, QC, J3H 5R7
(450) 446-5511
Sales 16,554,052
SIC 1081 Metal mining services
Renaud Hinse
Julie Godard
Andre De Guise
Jean-Guy Courtois
Normand Hinse
Francois Mestrallet
Claude Ferland
Christine Lefebvre

D-U-N-S 24-864-9717   (HQ)
PLACEMENTS ROBERT PHANEUF INC
270 Rue Brunet, Mont-Saint-Hilaire, QC, J3H 0M6
(450) 446-9933
Sales 20,967,750
SIC 6712 Bank holding companies
Robert Phaneuf
Sylvain Phaneuf

D-U-N-S 20-033-9187   (SL)
SUPERMARCHE MONT ST-HILAIRE
345 Boul Honorius-Charbonneau, Mont-Saint-Hilaire, QC, J3H 5H6
(450) 467-8977
Emp Here 49   *Sales* 13,433,448
SIC 5411 Grocery stores
Gaetan Reindeau
Louise Riendeau

Mont-Tremblant, QC J8E

D-U-N-S 25-047-1559   (SL)
9268-8241 QUEBEC INC
PIECES D'AUTO P. & B. GAREAU (2012)
230 Rue De Saint-Jovite Bureau 229, Mont-Tremblant, QC, J8E 2Z9
(819) 425-3711
Emp Here 40   *Sales* 19,923,120
SIC 5511 New and used car dealers
Martin Lacelle
Sylvain Gauthier
Melanie Dufour

▲ Public Company   ■ Public Company Family Member   **HQ** Headquarters   **BR** Branch   **SL** Single Location

D-U-N-S 20-324-3378　(SL)
ALUMINIUM J CLEMENT INC
1535 117 Rte, Mont-Tremblant, QC, J8E 2X9
(819) 425-7122
Emp Here 50　　*Sales* 12,622,100
SIC 1629 Heavy construction, nec
Jeannot Clement
Johanne Clement

D-U-N-S 24-634-3867　(HQ)
APOTRES DE L'AMOUR INFINI CANADA, LES
APOTRES DE L'AMOUR INFINI LES EDITIONS MAGNIFICAT, LES
290 7e Rang, Mont-Tremblant, QC, J8E 1Y4
(819) 425-7257
Emp Here 100　　*Sales* 20,824,600
SIC 8661 Religious organizations
Michel Lavallee
Jacques Garand
Timothy Boyle
Micheline Daoust
Patricia Lofquist
Renald Morel
Pere Michel Boulanger

D-U-N-S 25-356-6061　(SL)
CHATEAU M.T. INC
FAIRMONT TREMBLANT
3045 Ch De La Chapelle, Mont-Tremblant, QC, J8E 1E1
(819) 681-7000
Emp Here 300　　*Sales* 28,700,400
SIC 7011 Hotels and motels
Patrice Malo
Thierry Brossard
Louis Aubuchon
Terence P. Badour
Matthew Blackmore

D-U-N-S 24-729-6999　(SL)
CLUB TREMBLANT INC
121 Rue Cuttle, Mont-Tremblant, QC, J8E 1B9

Emp Here 80　　*Sales* 7,591,920
SIC 7011 Hotels and motels
Richard De Warren Rosanbo

D-U-N-S 25-541-6588　(BR)
COMMISSION SCOLAIRE DES LAURENTIDES
ECOLE POLYVALENTE CURE MERCURE
(*Suby of* COMMISSION SCOLAIRE DES LAURENTIDES)
700 Boul Du Docteur-Gervais, Mont-Tremblant, QC, J8E 2T3
(819) 425-3743
Emp Here 120
SIC 8211 Elementary and secondary schools
Johanne Vallancourt

D-U-N-S 25-537-1478　(SL)
COMPAGNIE DE VILLEGIATURE ET DE DEVELOPEMENT GRAND LODGE INC, LA
GRAND LODGE DU MONT TREMBLANT, LE
2396 Rue Labelle, Mont-Tremblant, QC, J8E 1T8
(819) 425-2734
Emp Here 110　　*Sales* 10,195,900
SIC 7011 Hotels and motels
Daniel Hanley
Michel Garnier

D-U-N-S 24-360-3805　(HQ)
COUPAL & FILS INC
GROUPE YVES GAGNON MONT-TREMBLANT
(*Suby of* 168566 CANADA INC)
349 117 Rte, Mont-Tremblant, QC, J8E 2X4
(819) 425-8771
Emp Here 1　　*Sales* 18,735,640
SIC 5211 Lumber and other building materials
Yves Gagnon
Genevieve Gagnon

D-U-N-S 25-001-2721　(HQ)
DUBE COOKE PEDICELLI INC

ASSURANCES DCPA
370 Rue De Saint-Jovite Bureau 202, Mont-Tremblant, QC, J8E 2Z9
(450) 537-3646
Emp Here 26　　*Sales* 22,049,560
SIC 6411 Insurance agents, brokers, and service
Mark Pedicelli
Jonathan Dubee

D-U-N-S 24-500-8321　(SL)
EXCAVATION R.B. GAUTHIER INC
246 Rte 117, Mont-Tremblant, QC, J8E 2X1
(819) 425-2074
Emp Here 100　　*Sales* 24,618,600
SIC 1794 Excavation work
Benoit Gauthier
Ronald Gauthier

D-U-N-S 24-978-6596　(SL)
GESTION GCL INC
PISCINES JOVITEL
1595 Rte 117, Mont-Tremblant, QC, J8E 2X9
(819) 425-2711
Emp Here 49　　*Sales* 15,954,400
SIC 5999 Miscellaneous retail stores, nec
Catherine Larin

D-U-N-S 20-574-0918　(HQ)
GROUPE BARBE & ROBIDOUX.SAT INC
991 Rue De Saint-Jovite Rm 201, Mont-Tremblant, QC, J8E 3J8
(819) 425-2777
Emp Here 24　　*Sales* 12,500,895
SIC 3829 Measuring and controlling devices, nec
Daniel Robidoux

D-U-N-S 24-679-3082　(SL)
INVESTISSEMENTS MICHEL DESLAURIERS INC, LES
CANADIAN TIRE
370 117 Rte, Mont-Tremblant, QC, J8E 2X3
(819) 425-1110
Emp Here 40　　*Sales* 19,923,120
SIC 5531 Auto and home supply stores
Michel Deslauriers

D-U-N-S 20-955-3499　(SL)
LGL RESORTS COMPANY
COMPAGNIE DE VILLEGIATURE LGL
2396 Rue Labelle, Mont-Tremblant, QC, J8E 1T8
(819) 425-2734
Emp Here 100　　*Sales* 9,489,900
SIC 7011 Hotels and motels
Charles Robert Iii Hanley

D-U-N-S 24-940-7883　(SL)
LOCATION JEAN MILLER INC
169 117 Rte, Mont-Tremblant, QC, J8E 2X2
(819) 425-3797
Emp Here 70　　*Sales* 13,394,780
SIC 7353 Heavy construction equipment rental
Jean Miller

D-U-N-S 20-254-2569　(SL)
MACHINERIES ST-JOVITE INC., LES
MACHINERIES ST-JOVITE, LES
1313 Rue De Saint-Jovite, Mont-Tremblant, QC, J8E 3J9
(819) 425-3737
Emp Here 25　　*Sales* 11,875,650
SIC 5084 Industrial machinery and equipment
Luc Forget
Alban Forget

D-U-N-S 20-649-2063　(SL)
METRO MARCHE CHEVREFILS MT-TREMBLANT
1011 Rue De Saint-Jovite, Mont-Tremblant, QC, J8E 3J9
(819) 425-3381
Emp Here 49　　*Sales* 13,433,448
SIC 5411 Grocery stores
Stephane Demers

D-U-N-S 24-356-9931　(HQ)
NORDMEC CONSTRUCTION INC
GROUPE NORDMEC, LE
390 Rue Simeon Bureau 3, Mont-Tremblant, QC, J8E 2R2
(819) 429-5555
Sales 23,536,550
SIC 1542 Nonresidential construction, nec
Joel Prud'homme
Michel Labelle

D-U-N-S 25-359-2109　(SL)
STATION MONT TREMBLANT INC
(*Suby of* HAWK HOLDING COMPANY, LLC)
1000 Ch Des Voyageurs, Mont-Tremblant, QC, J8E 1T1
(819) 681-3000
Emp Here 2,000　　*Sales* 191,336,000
SIC 7011 Hotels and motels
Patrice Malo
Thierry Brossard
David Perry
Julie Bodden
Karen Sanford

D-U-N-S 24-528-2082　(SL)
STATION MONT-TREMBLANT SOCIETE EN COMMANDITE
BAR CAPPUCINO
1000 Ch Des Voyageurs, Mont-Tremblant, QC, J8E 1T1
(819) 681-2000
Emp Here 2,000　　*Sales* 191,336,000
SIC 7011 Hotels and motels
Patrice Malo

Montebello, QC J0V

D-U-N-S 24-698-8778　(BR)
FAIRMONT HOTELS & RESORTS INC
FAIRMONT LE CHATEAU MONTEBELLO
(*Suby of* ACCOR)
392 Rue Notre-Dame, Montebello, QC, J0V 1L0
(819) 423-6341
Emp Here 175
SIC 7011 Hotels and motels
Werner Sapp

Montmagny, QC G5V

D-U-N-S 24-394-7889　(SL)
9050-4283 QUEBEC INC
CANADIAN TIRE
488 Av Saint-David, Montmagny, QC, G5V 4P9
(418) 248-2602
Emp Here 49　　*Sales* 24,405,822
SIC 5531 Auto and home supply stores
Patrick Venne

D-U-N-S 20-386-7416　(SL)
9262-4261 QUEBEC INC
175 4e Rue, Montmagny, QC, G5V 3L6
(418) 248-3089
Emp Here 35　　*Sales* 14,677,425
SIC 6712 Bank holding companies
Patrick Clavet

D-U-N-S 25-543-3005　(SL)
ARMANEAU AUTOS INC
MONTMAGNY TOYOTA
140 Boul Tache O, Montmagny, QC, G5V 3A5
(418) 248-2323
Emp Here 26　　*Sales* 12,950,028
SIC 5511 New and used car dealers
Carl Martineau

D-U-N-S 20-265-5569　(HQ)
BUREAUTIQUE COTE-SUD INC
MONBURO

49 Rue Saint-Jean-Baptiste E, Montmagny, QC, G5V 1J6
(418) 248-4949
Emp Here 51　　*Sales* 89,616,031
SIC 5112 Stationery and office supplies
Remi Faucher

D-U-N-S 24-879-6554　(SL)
CARON AUTOMOBILES INC
MONTMAGNY HYUNDAI
75 Boul Tache E, Montmagny, QC, G5V 1B6
(418) 248-7877
Emp Here 26　　*Sales* 12,950,028
SIC 5511 New and used car dealers
Michel Caron
Hans Jenkins

D-U-N-S 20-295-8513　(BR)
CENTRE DE READAPTATION EN DEFICIENCE INTELLECTUELLE ET TED
CRDI CHAUDIERE-APPALACHES
(*Suby of* CENTRE DE READAPTATION EN DEFICIENCE INTELLECTUELLE ET TED)
20 Av Cote, Montmagny, QC, G5V 1Z9
(418) 248-4970
Emp Here 150
SIC 8361 Residential care
Michel Langlais

D-U-N-S 25-915-9143　(HQ)
CENTRE DE SANTE ET SERVICES SOCIAUX DE MONTMAGNY - L'ISLET
CSSS
(*Suby of* GOUVERNEMENT DE LA PROVINCE DE QUEBEC)
22 Av Cote, Montmagny, QC, G5V 1Z9
(418) 248-0639
Sales 133,296,000
SIC 8062 General medical and surgical hospitals
Patricia Pouliot
Johannie Morin
Marie-Helene Caron
Josee Anctil
Pauline Jean

D-U-N-S 25-066-3317　(SL)
CHABOT CARROSSERIE INC
264 Ch Des Poirier, Montmagny, QC, G5V 4S5
(418) 234-1525
Emp Here 50　　*Sales* 10,131,450
SIC 7532 Top and body repair and paint shops
Normand Morin

D-U-N-S 20-711-9962　(BR)
COMMISSION SCOLAIRE DE LA COTE-DU-SUD, LA
ECOLE SECONDAIRE LOUIS-JACQUES-CASAULT
141 Boul Tache E, Montmagny, QC, G5V 1B9
(418) 248-2370
Emp Here 112
SIC 8211 Elementary and secondary schools
Sabine Prevost

D-U-N-S 20-721-9619　(HQ)
DIFFUSION ARTEQ INC
10 St-Jean-Baptiste E, Montmagny, QC, G5V 1J7
(418) 248-3332
Emp Here 10　　*Sales* 74,252,000
SIC 5199 Nondurable goods, nec
Jean Alart
Denis Jean

D-U-N-S 25-911-2006　(SL)
GESTION POMERLEAU PAGE INC
ROTISSERIE ST-HUBERT EXPRESS MONTMAGNY
205 Ch Des Poirier, Montmagny, QC, G5V 3X7
(418) 241-2102
Emp Here 26　　*Sales* 10,903,230
SIC 6712 Bank holding companies
Charles Pomerleau
Martin Page

D-U-N-S 25-372-5246　(SL)

GILMYR TRANSPORT INC
315 Ch Du Coteau, Montmagny, QC, G5V 3R8
(418) 241-5747
Emp Here 100   *Sales* 14,819,200
SIC 4213 Trucking, except local
Gilbert Thibault
Myrtha D'amours

D-U-N-S 24-376-8715   (HQ)
GROUPE MONTEL INC
225 4e Av, Montmagny, QC, G5V 4N9
(418) 248-0235
Sales 54,123,300
SIC 6712 Bank holding companies
Michel Doucet
Claire Brunelle
Jerome Doucet

D-U-N-S 25-368-1506   (SL)
HABITAFLEX CONCEPT INC
240 Av Des Ateliers, Montmagny, QC, G5V 4G4
(418) 248-8886
Emp Here 49   *Sales* 12,399,891
SIC 5211 Lumber and other building materials
Daniel Laprise

D-U-N-S 20-728-8924   (SL)
IMPORTATIONS NOSTALGIA MARKETING & DESIGN LTEE
20 Av De La Cour, Montmagny, QC, G5V 2V9
(418) 248-2600
Emp Here 25   *Sales* 18,777,995
SIC 5199 Nondurable goods, nec
Philippe Jacques

D-U-N-S 24-465-9751   (SL)
INDUSTRIES CARON (MEUBLES) INC, LES
45 4e Rue, Montmagny, QC, G5V 3K8
(418) 248-0255
Emp Here 125   *Sales* 24,046,250
SIC 2434 Wood kitchen cabinets
Michel Caron
Claude Caron

D-U-N-S 20-872-9900   (SL)
LAPOINTE AUTOMOBILES INC
160 Boul Tache O, Montmagny, QC, G5V 3A5
(418) 248-8899
Emp Here 19   *Sales* 13,129,916
SIC 5511 New and used car dealers
Martin Godbout
Jean Godbout
Louis-Pierre Godbout
Francesca Maulu

D-U-N-S 20-320-5153   (BR)
LEMIEUX NOLET COMPTABLES AGREES S.E.N.C.R.L.
(*Suby of* LEMIEUX NOLET, COMPTABLES AGREES S.E.N.C.R.L.)
25 Boul Tache O Bureau 205, Montmagny, QC, G5V 2Z9
(418) 248-1910
Emp Here 130
SIC 3578 Calculating and accounting equipment
Stephane Dumas

D-U-N-S 20-209-0858   (SL)
LEMIEUX, JACQUES (GROSSISTE) INC
MEILLEUR, LE
179 Rue Des Industries, Montmagny, QC, G5V 4G2
(418) 248-8117
Emp Here 50   *Sales* 41,778,850
SIC 5141 Groceries, general line
Jacques Lemieux

D-U-N-S 20-209-0932   (SL)
MAGASIN CO-OP DE MONTMAGNY
IGA
70 Boul Tache O, Montmagny, QC, G5V 3A4
(418) 248-1230
Emp Here 125   *Sales* 36,684,625
SIC 5411 Grocery stores
Clement Asselin

Bertrand Proulx
Vicky Vesina

D-U-N-S 24-821-6152   (HQ)
MAISONS LAPRISE INC
LAPRISE
166 4e Rue, Montmagny, QC, G5V 3L5
(418) 248-0401
Sales 19,237,000
SIC 2452 Prefabricated wood buildings
Daniel Laprise

D-U-N-S 24-202-8850   (HQ)
MARQUIS IMPRIMEUR INC
IMPRIMERIE LE LAURENTIEN
350 Rue Des Entrepreneurs, Montmagny, QC, G5V 4T1
(418) 246-5666
Emp Here 200   *Sales* 48,443,500
SIC 2732 Book printing
Serge Loubier
Marc Delisle
Pierre Frechette
Jacques Lefebvre
Nicolas Savoie
Jacques Mallette
Jacques Rochefort

D-U-N-S 20-209-1104   (SL)
MONTEL INC
(*Suby of* GROUPE MONTEL INC)
225 4e Av, Montmagny, QC, G5V 4N9
(418) 248-0235
Emp Here 195   *Sales* 30,092,790
SIC 2542 Partitions and fixtures, except wood
Michel Doucet
Claire Brunelle
Jerome Doucet

D-U-N-S 20-208-9314   (SL)
PLANCHERS MERCIER INC, LES
330 Rue Des Entrepreneurs, Montmagny, QC, G5V 4T1
(418) 248-1785
Emp Here 75   *Sales* 32,009,754
SIC 2426 Hardwood dimension and flooring mills
Marielle Mercier
Richard Mercier

D-U-N-S 20-271-3715   (HQ)
PROMUTUEL MONTMAGNY-L'ISLET, SO-CIETE MUTUELLE D'ASSURANCE GEN-ERALE
PROMUTUEL ASSURANCE
124 Boul Tache O, Montmagny, QC, G5V 3A5
(418) 248-7940
Emp Here 26   *Sales* 48,041,292
SIC 6411 Insurance agents, brokers, and service
Laurent Deladurantaye
Annie Gagnon
Julie Belanger
Gilles Ouellet
Pierre Beauregard
Andre Richard
Andre Chouinard
Nicole Beland
Odette Caron
Alain Talbot

D-U-N-S 24-638-5033   (SL)
RESSORTS LIBERTE INC
LIBERTY SPRING
173 Rue Des Industries, Montmagny, QC, G5V 4G2
(418) 248-8871
Emp Here 600   *Sales* 145,938,600
SIC 3495 Wire springs
Mathieu Ouellet

D-U-N-S 20-290-8315   (SL)
RESSORTS LIBERTE MEXIQUE INC
173 Rue Des Industries, Montmagny, QC, G5V 4G2
(418) 248-8871
Emp Here 140   *Sales* 31,338,020

SIC 3714 Motor vehicle parts and accessories
Richard Guimont
Mathieu Ouellet

D-U-N-S 24-638-7054   (SL)
RESTAURANT A LA RIVE INC
153 Rue Saint-Louis, Montmagny, QC, G5V 1N4
(418) 248-3494
Emp Here 80   *Sales* 3,641,520
SIC 5812 Eating places
Martin Brandl

D-U-N-S 20-113-1294   (BR)
TEKNION LIMITED
TEKNION QUEBEC
(*Suby of* GLOBAL UPHOLSTERY CO LIM-ITED)
45 Ch Des Cascades, Montmagny, QC, G5V 3M6
(418) 248-5711
Emp Here 175
SIC 2522 Office furniture, except wood
Andre Dufresne

D-U-N-S 25-509-9079   (SL)
TRANSPORT GILMYR INC
315 Ch Du Coteau, Montmagny, QC, G5V 3R8
(418) 241-5747
Emp Here 245   *Sales* 50,397,970
SIC 4213 Trucking, except local
Gilbert Thibault
Myrtha D'amours
Marcus Deschenes

Montreal, QC H1A

D-U-N-S 20-978-8397   (SL)
AXIA SERVICES
AXIA SECURITE
13025 Rue Jean-Grou, Montreal, QC, H1A 3N6
(514) 642-3250
Emp Here 175   *Sales* 5,594,400
SIC 7349 Building maintenance services, nec
Eric Degrave
Marc Antoine Flot

D-U-N-S 20-216-3614   (HQ)
DELOM SERVICES INC
DELOM SOLUTIONS
13065 Rue Jean-Grou, Montreal, QC, H1A 3N6
(514) 642-8220
Emp Here 150   *Sales* 37,888,616
SIC 7694 Armature rewinding shops
Mario Montpetit
Marc Sarazin

D-U-N-S 20-558-7509   (SL)
DELSTAR ENERGIE INC
12885 Rue Jean-Grou, Montreal, QC, H1A 3N6
(514) 642-8222
Emp Here 100   *Sales* 19,232,800
SIC 7699 Repair services, nec
Marc Sarazin
Jean-Yves Sarazin
Mario Montpetit

D-U-N-S 24-410-7384   (SL)
IMPORTATIONS & DISTRIBUTIONS B.H. INC
BULK SISTERS
12880 Rue Jean-Grou, Montreal, QC, H1A 3N5
(514) 356-1276
Emp Here 22   *Sales* 18,382,694
SIC 5141 Groceries, general line
Natalie-Catherine Provost
Claudine Provost
Stephane Provost
Claudette Hebert Provost

Montreal, QC H1B

D-U-N-S 24-324-5792   (HQ)
ELEGANCE COLONIAL INC
(*Suby of* GESTION ANDRE WAECHTER INC)
3800 Boul Du Tricentaire, Montreal, QC, H1B 5T8
(514) 640-1212
Sales 14,427,750
SIC 2431 Millwork
Luc Desrosiers
Claude Jutras
Andre Waechter

D-U-N-S 25-476-7650   (SL)
GESTION ANDRE R. VAILLANCOURT LTEE
CANADIAN TIRE
3500 Boul Du Tricentaire Bureau 303, Mon-treal, QC, H1B 0A3
(514) 645-2761
Emp Here 80   *Sales* 16,427,440
SIC 5399 Miscellaneous general merchandise
Andre Vaillancourt

D-U-N-S 20-226-3653   (SL)
HUTCHINSON AERONAUTIQUE & INDUS-TRIE LIMITEE
MARQUEZ TRANSTECH
(*Suby of* TOTAL SA)
3650 Boul Du Tricentaire, Montreal, QC, H1B 5M8
(514) 640-9006
Emp Here 119   *Sales* 18,904,102
SIC 3089 Plastics products, nec
Cedric Duclos
Eric Faucher
Patricia Fauconnier
Jean-Francois Simonnet

D-U-N-S 24-522-9054   (SL)
TEKALIA AERONAUTIK (2010) INC
3900 Boul Du Tricentaire, Montreal, QC, H1B 5L6
(514) 640-2411
Emp Here 135   *Sales* 12,108,960
SIC 7629 Electrical repair shops
Dominique Dallaire
Stephane Arsenault
Jean-Philippe Sanche
Gilles Labbe
Martin Brassard
Martin Perreault

Montreal, QC H1C

D-U-N-S 24-388-8174   (HQ)
6894658 CANADA INC
ZOHAR PLASTIQUE GROUP
10660 Boul Henri-Bourassa E, Montreal, QC, H1C 1G9
(514) 881-1234
Sales 15,142,275
SIC 3081 Unsupported plastics film and sheet
Serge Aflalo
Jean-Mark Aflalo
Michel Alfalo

D-U-N-S 20-533-3961   (SL)
ATPAC INC
10700 Boul Henri-Bourassa E, Montreal, QC, H1C 1G9
(514) 881-8888
Emp Here 70   *Sales* 25,495,050
SIC 5013 Motor vehicle supplies and new parts
Dolores Richardson

D-U-N-S 25-905-5481   (SL)
BERGER BLANC INC, LE
9825 Boul Henri-Bourassa E, Montreal, QC, H1C 1G5

(514) 494-2002
Emp Here 50   Sales 15,731,600
SIC 8699 Membership organizations, nec
Pierre Couture

D-U-N-S 25-097-9465   (SL)
CUISINE CROTONE INC
9800 Boul Maurice-Duplessis, Montreal, QC,
H1C 1G1
(514) 648-3553
Emp Here 130   Sales 25,008,100
SIC 2434 Wood kitchen cabinets
Amodio Cerrelli
Concetta Cerrelli
Michele Primerano
Francesco Comito

D-U-N-S 20-280-6951   (HQ)
DEMOSPEC DECONSTRUCTION INC
DEMO SPECIALISTE
10000 Boul Henri-Bourassa E, Montreal, QC,
H1C 1T1
(514) 648-6366
Sales 24,618,600
SIC 1795 Wrecking and demolition work
Sylvain Vallee
Simon Lacasse
Yannick Dagenais

D-U-N-S 24-362-4397   (SL)
G.T. SERVICE DE CONTENEURS INC
G.T. ENTREPOSAGE
10000 Boul Maurice-Duplessis, Montreal, QC,
H1C 2A2
(514) 648-4848
Emp Here 65   Sales 17,669,730
SIC 7692 Welding repair
Gisueppe Terrigno
Donato Terringo

D-U-N-S 24-822-2163   (SL)
GROUPE MULTI-PAVAGE INC.
9855 Boul Henri-Bourassa E, Montreal, QC,
H1C 1G5
(514) 723-3000
Emp Here 40   Sales 11,531,701
SIC 1611 Highway and street construction
Raymond Trembly

D-U-N-S 24-770-1071   (HQ)
INDUSTRIES SANIMAX INC
(Suby of JO-AL DISTRIBUTING LTD)
9900 Boul Maurice-Duplessis, Montreal, QC,
H1C 1G1
(514) 648-3000
Sales 544,871,600
SIC 6712 Bank holding companies
Andre Couture
Martin Couture
Vincent Brossard
Julie Couture
John M. Jr Mayer
Benn Mikula
Hani Basile
Genevieve Fortier
Bertrand Jolicoeur

D-U-N-S 24-679-1185   (HQ)
JO-AL DISTRIBUTING LTD
DISTRIBUTION JO-AL
9900 6e Rue, Montreal, QC, H1C 1G2
(514) 643-3391
Sales 409,370,080
SIC 6712 Bank holding companies
Martin Couture
Andre Couture

D-U-N-S 20-226-1939   (HQ)
METRO INC
11011 Boul Maurice-Duplessis, Montreal, QC,
H1C 1V6
(514) 643-1000
Emp Here 250   Sales 10,504,943,371
SIC 5141 Groceries, general line
Eric R. La Fleche
Simon Rivet
Francois Thibault
Christian Bourbonniere

Carmen Fortino
Serge Boulanger
Marie-Claude Bacon
Genevieve Bich
Mireille Desjarlais
Martin Allaire

D-U-N-S 24-852-8320   (BR)
METRO RICHELIEU INC
(Suby of METRO INC)
11555 Boul Maurice-Duplessis Bureau 1,
Montreal, QC, H1C 2A1
(514) 643-1000
Emp Here 250
SIC 4225 General warehousing and storage
Yves Vegina

D-U-N-S 24-257-1065   (HQ)
METRO RICHELIEU INC
AUX P'TITS SOINS
(Suby of METRO INC)
11011 Boul Maurice-Duplessis, Montreal, QC,
H1C 1V6
(514) 643-1000
Emp Here 450   Sales 7,525,518,000
SIC 5141 Groceries, general line
Eric R. Lafleche
Francois Thibault
Simon Rivet

D-U-N-S 24-509-0121   (HQ)
PIECES D'AUTO AT-PAC INC
(Suby of P.H. VITRES D'AUTOS INC)
10700 Boul Henri-Bourassa E, Montreal, QC,
H1C 1G9
(514) 881-8888
Emp Here 40   Sales 18,210,750
SIC 5013 Motor vehicle supplies and new
parts
Mario Jutras
Marc Desmarais
Christian Bergeron
Maxime Dumas

D-U-N-S 25-286-9490   (HQ)
SANIMAX ABP INC
(Suby of JO-AL DISTRIBUTING LTD)
9900 6e Rue, Montreal, QC, H1C 1G2
(514) 643-3391
Emp Here 1   Sales 10,285,240
SIC 4953 Refuse systems
Andre Couture
Martin Couture
Vincent Brossard

D-U-N-S 24-837-6456   (HQ)
SANIMAX EEI INC
(Suby of JO-AL DISTRIBUTING LTD)
9900 Boul Maurice-Duplessis, Montreal, QC,
H1C 1G1
(514) 648-3000
Sales 15,427,950
SIC 4212 Local trucking, without storage
Martin Couture
Francois Berthiaume
Vincent Brossard
Andre Couture

D-U-N-S 20-224-9975   (HQ)
SANIMAX LOM INC
(Suby of JO-AL DISTRIBUTING LTD)
9900 Boul Maurice-Duplessis, Montreal, QC,
H1C 1G1
(514) 648-3000
Emp Here 110   Sales 78,468,985
SIC 2077 Animal and marine fats and oils
Martin Couture
Antonio Galasso
Andre Couture
Vincent Brossard

D-U-N-S 24-378-4311   (HQ)
SANIMAX SAN INC
(Suby of JO-AL DISTRIBUTING LTD)
9900 Boul Maurice-Duplessis, Montreal, QC,
H1C 1G1
(514) 648-6001
Emp Here 300   Sales 477,637,300

SIC 2077 Animal and marine fats and oils
Martin Couture
Francois Berthiaume
Vincent Brossard
Ande Couture
Julie Couture

D-U-N-S 20-236-1259   (SL)
TRIPAR INC
TRIPAR ENOVA, DIV OF
9750 Boul Maurice-Duplessis, Montreal, QC,
H1C 1G1
(514) 648-7471
Emp Here 50   Sales 10,141,500
SIC 3469 Metal stampings, nec
Ben Sevack
Lloyd Sevack

D-U-N-S 20-517-4977   (BR)
VILLE DE MONTREAL
STATION D'EPURATION DES EAU USE, LA
JEAN-R-MARCOTTE
(Suby of VILLE DE MONTREAL)
12001 Boul Maurice-Duplessis, Montreal, QC,
H1C 1V3
(514) 280-4400
Emp Here 300
SIC 4971 Irrigation systems
Richard Fontaine

D-U-N-S 20-707-5867   (BR)
VILLE DE MONTREAL
STATION D'EPURATION
(Suby of VILLE DE MONTREAL)
12001 Boul Maurice-Duplessis, Montreal, QC,
H1C 1V3
(514) 280-4359
Emp Here 300
SIC 7389 Business services, nec
Caroline Lapage

Montreal, QC H1E

D-U-N-S 24-871-2978   (HQ)
174664 CANADA LTEE
JUNON
7900 Av Marco-Polo, Montreal, QC, H1E 2S5
(514) 648-1015
Sales 10,903,230
SIC 6712 Bank holding companies
Gerlando Argento
Alfonso Argento

D-U-N-S 24-901-4762   (SL)
2704242 CANADA INC
INTERMARCH LAGORIA, L'
9025 Boul Maurice-Duplessis, Montreal, QC,
H1E 6M3
(514) 648-1883
Emp Here 120   Sales 35,217,240
SIC 5411 Grocery stores
Luisa Longo Chimienti

D-U-N-S 20-559-9892   (SL)
9080-0822 QUEBEC INC
PHARMAPRIX
8222 Boul Maurice-Duplessis, Montreal, QC,
H1E 2Y5
(514) 494-8888
Emp Here 45   Sales 11,382,930
SIC 5912 Drug stores and proprietary stores
Andre Lauzon
Lyselle Cloutier

D-U-N-S 20-549-1454   (HQ)
9097-4775 QUEBEC INC
IMPORTATION J & F
9100 Boul Maurice-Duplessis, Montreal, QC,
H1E 7C2
(514) 494-4798
Sales 28,629,810
SIC 5099 Durable goods, nec
Bruno Morabito

D-U-N-S 24-377-0836   (SL)

9180-2710 QUEBEC INC
UNIGAZ
7364 Boul Henri-Bourassa E, Montreal, QC,
H1E 1P2
(514) 351-4000
Emp Here 7   Sales 21,740,999
SIC 4924 Natural gas distribution
Robert Varnaitis
Sylvain Marcotte

D-U-N-S 25-355-9090   (SL)
ALIMENTATION L'EPICIER INC
CONCEPT ALIMENTAIRE L'EPICIER
11460 Boul Armand-Bombardier, Montreal,
QC, H1E 2W9
(514) 351-1991
Emp Here 50   Sales 13,707,600
SIC 5411 Grocery stores
Carl Lefebvre
Claude Descoteaux

D-U-N-S 24-728-9015   (SL)
ATTACHES ET SUSPENSION MONTREAL-NORD
8065 Boul Henri-Bourassa E, Montreal, QC,
H1E 2Z3
(514) 643-4106
Emp Here 35   Sales 17,432,730
SIC 5531 Auto and home supply stores
Claude Berthiaume

D-U-N-S 24-669-1588   (BR)
AUTOBUS TRANSCO (1988) INC
AUTOBUS TRANSCO
(Suby of FIRSTGROUP PLC)
7975 Boul Henri-Bourassa E, Montreal, QC,
H1E 1N9
(514) 648-8625
Emp Here 100
SIC 4151 School buses
Jean Bourdon

D-U-N-S 20-231-5784   (HQ)
BOISERIES RAYMOND INC
BOISERIES MILLE ILES
(Suby of GESTION ANDRE WAECHTER
INC)
11880 56e Av, Montreal, QC, H1E 2L6
(514) 494-1141
Emp Here 202   Sales 69,597,500
SIC 2431 Millwork
Joel Roussin
Dominique Santoire

D-U-N-S 24-387-9785   (SL)
COMMERCE JARDINO FRESH INC
8145 Av Marco-Polo, Montreal, QC, H1E 5Y8
(514) 664-5566
Emp Here 12   Sales 10,026,924
SIC 5148 Fresh fruits and vegetables
Salvatore Urso

D-U-N-S 20-228-2612   (HQ)
COMPAGNIE D'ECHANTILLONS NA-TIONAL LIMITEE
COMPAGNIE U.S. SAMPLE
11500 Boul Armand-Bombardier, Montreal,
QC, H1E 2W9
(514) 648-4000
Emp Here 250   Sales 116,264,400
SIC 2782 Blankbooks and looseleaf binders
Marilyn Kader
Randi Kader

D-U-N-S 20-886-7135   (HQ)
CONSTRUCTION BAO INC
GROUPE BAO, LE
7875 Av Marco-Polo, Montreal, QC, H1E 1N8
(514) 648-2272
Sales 19,798,640
SIC 1771 Concrete work
Alberto Bao
Marco Bao
Rafael Bao

D-U-N-S 24-859-9313   (SL)
CONSTRUCTION DIMCO INC.
9221-7017 QUEBEC INC.

8601 Boul Henri-Bourassa E Bureau 100, Montreal, QC, H1E 1P4
(514) 494-1001
Emp Here 50   Sales 14,176,200
SIC 1611 Highway and street construction
Franco Di Martino

D-U-N-S 24-548-1387   (SL)
COUVERTURES ST-LEONARD INC, LES
11365 55e Av, Montreal, QC, H1E 2R2
(514) 648-1118
Emp Here 60   Sales 13,069,740
SIC 1761 Roofing, siding, and sheetMetal work
Sylvain Sansregret
Stephane Sansregret

D-U-N-S 20-376-3185   (SL)
DIMCO DL INC
8601 Boul Henri-Bourassa E, Montreal, QC, H1E 1P4
(514) 494-1001
Emp Here 50   Sales 14,176,200
SIC 1611 Highway and street construction
Franco Di Martino
Luc La Haye

D-U-N-S 24-742-6349   (SL)
EMBALLAGE D'ALIMENTS LATINA INC
DISTRIBUTION BEN-MAR '90'
9200 Rue Robert-Armour Bureau 1, Montreal, QC, H1E 2H1
(514) 643-0784
Emp Here 26   Sales 13,534,092
SIC 5099 Durable goods, nec
Domenico Pampena
Giuseppe Pampena

D-U-N-S 20-230-6452   (HQ)
EMBALLAGES POLYSTAR INC
GROUPE POLYSTAR
7975 Av Marco-Polo, Montreal, QC, H1E 1N8
(514) 648-8171
Emp Here 72   Sales 12,708,640
SIC 3081 Unsupported plastics film and sheet
Hershey Friedman
Rita Friedman

D-U-N-S 24-174-1008   (SL)
ENTREPOSEURS DE FIBRES R & F LTEE
7975 Av Marco-Polo, Montreal, QC, H1E 1N8
(514) 648-8171
Emp Here 100   Sales 20,189,700
SIC 3081 Unsupported plastics film and sheet
Hershey Friedman

D-U-N-S 24-190-7513   (SL)
ENTREPRISES ROLAND DOYON
CANADIAN TIRE
7555 Boul Maurice-Duplessis Bureau 454, Montreal, QC, H1E 7N2
(514) 643-2232
Emp Here 55   Sales 14,720,860
SIC 5251 Hardware stores
Roland Doyon

D-U-N-S 25-038-6344   (SL)
FABRICATION RAMPES ET ESCALIERS PRESTIGE INC
F.A.B. RAMPES ECS. PRESTIGE
11750 Av J.-J.-Joubert, Montreal, QC, H1E 7E7
(514) 324-2107
Emp Here 50   Sales 10,141,500
SIC 3446 Architectural Metalwork
Vincent De Luca

D-U-N-S 24-364-1813   (SL)
FRUITS DE MER LIBERIO INC
(Suby of GORDON FOOD SERVICE, INC.)
7337 Av Jean-Valets, Montreal, QC, H1E 3H4
(514) 750-4022
Emp Here 31   Sales 25,902,887
SIC 5142 Packaged frozen goods
Dean Noble
Alisha L. Cieslak
Jeffrey Maddox
Frank Geier

Richard J. Wolowski

D-U-N-S 24-500-8438   (HQ)
GROUPE ARTITALIA INC
FABRICATION DE MEUBLE HEMSLEY
11755 Boul Rodolphe-Forget, Montreal, QC, H1E 7J8
(514) 643-0114
Emp Here 250   Sales 111,332,500
SIC 2542 Partitions and fixtures, except wood
Antonio Vardaro
Enzo Vardaro
Nicola Vardaro
Giosue Vardaro

D-U-N-S 25-411-3947   (HQ)
GROUPE G3 INC, LE
G3 TRANSPORT
(Suby of SEABOARD LIQUID CARRIERS LIMITED)
9135 Boul Henri-Bourassa E, Montreal, QC, H1E 1P4
(514) 648-8522
Sales 30,855,900
SIC 4213 Trucking, except local
Joseph Shannon
Mark Shannon

D-U-N-S 20-056-3315   (HQ)
GROUPE J.S.V. INC, LE
ACIER METOSTEEL
(Suby of GROUPE MAV INC., LE)
8015 Av Marco-Polo, Montreal, QC, H1E 5Y8
(514) 842-8351
Emp Here 45   Sales 33,251,820
SIC 5085 Industrial supplies
Marc Viau

D-U-N-S 24-371-0600   (BR)
IMPRIMERIES TRANSCONTINENTAL 2005 S.E.N.C
TRANSCONTINENTAL O'KEEFE MONTREAL
(Suby of IMPRIMERIES TRANSCONTINENTAL 2005 S.E.N.C.)
8000 Av Blaise-Pascal, Montreal, QC, H1E 2S7

Emp Here 250
SIC 2752 Commercial printing, lithographic

D-U-N-S 24-814-9254   (SL)
INDUSTRIES CENDREX INC, LES
CENDREX-ARCO METAL
11303 26e Av, Montreal, QC, H1E 6N6
(514) 493-1489
Emp Here 50   Sales 10,141,500
SIC 3442 Metal doors, sash, and trim
Christian Turgeon
Paul Matte

D-U-N-S 24-762-3911   (SL)
INDUSTRIES FORESTEEL INC, LES
9225 Boul Henri-Bourassa E, Montreal, QC, H1E 1P6
(514) 645-9251
Emp Here 150   Sales 13,454,400
SIC 7692 Welding repair
Pierre Lefebvre
Francois Gamache
Michel Roy

D-U-N-S 20-419-7255   (HQ)
JPMA GLOBAL INC
ENTREPRISE JPMA GLOBAL
7335 Boul Henri-Bourassa E, Montreal, QC, H1E 3T5
(514) 648-1042
Sales 89,066,000
SIC 2542 Partitions and fixtures, except wood
Giuseppe Paventi
Martino Paventi
Virginio Basile
Joseph Belli
Roberto Ciricilo
Antonietta E Paventi
Giuseppina Paventi
Maria Paventi

D-U-N-S 25-323-5246   (SL)
LUC CHARBONNEAU FRUITS & LEGUMES INC
L C FRUITS & LEGUMES
8135 Av Marco-Polo, Montreal, QC, H1E 5Y8
(514) 337-3955
Emp Here 20   Sales 10,702,480
SIC 5148 Fresh fruits and vegetables
Luc Charbonneau
Pierre Charbonneau

D-U-N-S 24-637-1322   (SL)
METOPOXY INC
(Suby of 2800420 CANADA INC)
7335 Boul Henri-Bourassa E, Montreal, QC, H1E 3T5
(514) 648-1042
Emp Here 80   Sales 15,366,800
SIC 3479 Metal coating and allied services
Giuseppe Paventi
Virginio Basile
Martino Paventi
Antonietta E Paventi
Joseph Belli
Roberto Circillo
Antonella Paventi
Giuseppina Paventi
Giuseppe Paventi
Maria Paventi

D-U-N-S 20-210-4766   (SL)
PAPIERS ATLAS INC, LES
9000 Rue Pierre-Bonne, Montreal, QC, H1E 6W5
(514) 494-1931
Emp Here 50   Sales 11,671,750
SIC 2657 Folding paperboard boxes
Mala Balshine
Edward Birenbaum

D-U-N-S 24-403-7172   (HQ)
PAPIERS ET EMBALLAGES ARTEAU INC
CONVERTISSEUR DE PAPIERS ARTEAU, DIVISION DE PAPIERS ET EMBALLAGES ARTEAU
11420 Boul Armand-Bombardier, Montreal, QC, H1E 2W9
(514) 494-2222
Sales 25,182,900
SIC 5113 Industrial and personal service paper
Alain Arteau
France Arteau

D-U-N-S 20-229-6257   (SL)
PEINTURES PROLUX INC
11430 56e Av, Montreal, QC, H1E 2L5
(514) 648-4911
Emp Here 20   Sales 14,850,400
SIC 5198 Paints, varnishes, and supplies
Henri Ades
David Ades

D-U-N-S 24-501-3586   (HQ)
PORTES DUSCO LTEE, LES
STANLEY DOOR SYSTEMS
11825 Av J.-J.-Joubert, Montreal, QC, H1E 7J5
(514) 355-4877
Sales 10,753,140
SIC 3231 Products of purchased glass
Harvey Dubrofsky

D-U-N-S 20-298-1312   (HQ)
PRODUITS AUTOMOBILES LAURENTIDE INC
SOLVA-NET
(Suby of HIG CAPITAL MANAGEMENT, INC.)
9355 Boul Henri-Bourassa E, Montreal, QC, H1E 1P4
(514) 643-1917
Sales 10,094,850
SIC 3089 Plastics products, nec
Richard Boudreaux
Spiros Kondonis

D-U-N-S 20-229-0433   (SL)
PRODUITS DE VIANDE PAC-RITE INC, LES

9090 Rue Pierre-Bonne, Montreal, QC, H1E 6W5
(514) 524-3557
Emp Here 25   Sales 20,889,425
SIC 5147 Meats and meat products
Luis Miguel Sanchez
Robert Larin
Harry Sterner

D-U-N-S 20-295-6090   (SL)
PRODUITS ORAPI-DRY SHINE INC., LES
7521 Boul Henri-Bourassa E, Montreal, QC, H1E 1N9
(514) 735-3272
Emp Here 15   Sales 15,492,120
SIC 5172 Petroleum products, nec
Guy Chifflot

D-U-N-S 24-903-6294   (SL)
R.D.-PHAR INC
PHARMACIE JEAN COUTU
8315 Boul Maurice-Duplessis, Montreal, QC, H1E 3B5
(514) 643-2808
Emp Here 55   Sales 13,438,040
SIC 5912 Drug stores and proprietary stores
Yves Pichette
Paule Langlois

D-U-N-S 24-103-0209   (SL)
SEPT FRERES CONSTRUCTION INC
(Suby of 174664 CANADA LTEE)
7910 Av Marco-Polo, Montreal, QC, H1E 2S5
(514) 648-0935
Emp Here 30   Sales 12,682,110
SIC 1541 Industrial buildings and warehouses
Alfonso Argento

D-U-N-S 25-501-0191   (SL)
SERVICE & MAINTENANCE DE CASTEL (1997) INC
11650 Av J.-J.-Joubert, Montreal, QC, H1E 7E7
(514) 648-5166
Emp Here 35   Sales 16,625,910
SIC 5087 Service establishment equipment
Charles Bauer
Patrick Bauer
Cecile Bauer
Alain Bauer

D-U-N-S 20-227-7133   (HQ)
SERVICE DE FREINS MONTREAL LTEE
FRENO
11650 6e Av Bureau 151, Montreal, QC, H1E 1S1
(514) 648-7403
Sales 29,137,200
SIC 5013 Motor vehicle supplies and new parts
Stephane Faust
Marie-Claude Aubut

D-U-N-S 20-101-1280   (HQ)
SERVICES ENVIRONNEMENTAUX DELSAN-A.I.M. INC, LES
AIM DELSAN
(Suby of COMPAGNIE AMERICAINE DE FER & METAUX INC, LA)
7825 Boul Henri-Bourassa E, Montreal, QC, H1E 1N9
(514) 494-9898
Emp Here 200   Sales 90,259,800
SIC 1795 Wrecking and demolition work
Herbert Black
Ronald Black

D-U-N-S 20-214-4155   (BR)
SYSCO CANADA, INC
SYSCO QUEBEC
(Suby of SYSCO CORPORATION)
11625 Av 55e Bureau 864, Montreal, QC, H1E 2K2
(514) 494-5200
Emp Here 260
SIC 5141 Groceries, general line
Francz Roc

D-U-N-S 20-961-9576   (SL)
TECHNIPRODEC LTEE
11865 Av Adolphe-Caron, Montreal, QC, H1E
6J8
(514) 648-5423
Emp Here 55   *Sales* 12,311,365
SIC 3728 Aircraft parts and equipment, nec
Sebastien Farkas
Pierrette Mercure Farkas
Andre Bernard Farkas
Daniel Fillaudeau
Marc Jobin
Clarence Desrosiers

D-U-N-S 20-996-8957   (SL)
TRIDENT INDUSTRIES INC, LES
8277 Boul Henri-Bourassa E, Montreal, QC,
H1E 1P4
(514) 648-0285
Emp Here 50   *Sales* 11,192,150
SIC 3728 Aircraft parts and equipment, nec
Osvaldo Baccalaro
Candida Mancini

D-U-N-S 24-510-4369   (SL)
TU-MEC INC
(Suby of GESTION RELEVE SMS INC)
11700 Av Lucien-Gendron, Montreal, QC,
H1E 7J7
(514) 881-1801
Emp Here 60   *Sales* 13,983,900
SIC 1711 Plumbing, heating, air-conditioning
Edward Lenard
Daniel Rocheleau

D-U-N-S 24-460-6869   (HQ)
VENTILATION MAXIMUM LTEE
9229 Rue Pierre-Bonne, Montreal, QC, H1E
7J6
(514) 648-8011
Sales 16,650,075
SIC 3564 Blowers and fans
Serge Ramsay
Linda Ramsay

Montreal, QC H1G

D-U-N-S 24-959-0712   (HQ)
**COLLEGE D'ENSEIGNEMENT GENERAL
ET PROFESSIONEL MARIE-VICTORIN**
CEGEP MARIE-VICTORIN
7000 Rue Marie-Victorin, Montreal, QC, H1G
2J6
(514) 325-0150
Sales 74,695,500
SIC 8221 Colleges and universities
Serge Foucher
Stephane Lavallee
Normand Blanchard

Montreal, QC H1J

D-U-N-S 20-381-1468   (SL)
IMPORTATIONS KROPS INC
ENTREPRISE AGRI-MONDO
(Suby of MICHAL INC)
9761 Boul Des Sciences, Montreal, QC, H1J
0A6
(514) 525-6464
Emp Here 20   *Sales* 52,161,005
SIC 5148 Fresh fruits and vegetables
Joseph Borsellino
Francis Routhier
Michel Routhier
Ian Routhier

D-U-N-S 20-998-9631   (HQ)
ROPACK INC
ROPACK PHARMA SOLUTIONS
10801 Rue Mirabeau, Montreal, QC, H1J 1T7
(514) 353-7000
Emp Here 250   *Sales* 116,057,900

SIC 2834 Pharmaceutical preparations
Yves Massicotte
Paul Dupont

Montreal, QC H1K

D-U-N-S 24-326-8443   (BR)
**CENTRE DE SANTE ET DE SERVICES SO-
CIAUX DE LA POINTE-DE-L'ILE**
4900 Boul Lapointe, Montreal, QC, H1K 4W9
(514) 353-1227
Emp Here 350
SIC 8361 Residential care

D-U-N-S 25-240-0965   (BR)
**COMMISSION SCOLAIRE DE LA POINTE-
DE-L'ILE**
ECOLE SECONDAIRE ANJOU
(Suby of COMMISSION SCOLAIRE DE LA
POINTE-DE-L'ILE)
8205 Rue Fonteneau, Montreal, QC, H1K 4E1
(514) 353-9970
Emp Here 150
SIC 8211 Elementary and secondary schools
Lily Carignan

Montreal, QC H1L

D-U-N-S 25-647-9973   (SL)
**ALIMENTATION   BLANCHETTE   &
CYRENNE INC**
TRADITION
9280 Rue Sherbrooke E, Montreal, QC, H1L
1E5
(514) 351-1252
Emp Here 40   *Sales* 10,966,080
SIC 5411 Grocery stores
Michel Cyrenne

D-U-N-S 25-458-3107   (SL)
ALIMENTATION HOCHELAGA G.S. INC
IGA
7975 Rue Hochelaga, Montreal, QC, H1L 2K9
(514) 351-7340
Emp Here 65   *Sales* 19,076,005
SIC 5411 Grocery stores
Serge Godin
Louisa Silvestrie

D-U-N-S 24-669-2214   (HQ)
**CENTRALE DES SYNDICATS DU QUEBEC
(CSQ), LA**
9405 Rue Sherbrooke E, Montreal, QC, H1L
6P3
(514) 356-8888
Emp Here 100   *Sales* 62,656,440
SIC 8631 Labor organizations
Louis Chabot
Gabriel Marchand
Daniel B. Lafreniare

D-U-N-S 25-449-7027   (BR)
**CENTRE INTEGRE UNIVERSITAIRE SANTE
ET SERVICES SOCIAUX DU CENTRE-SUD-
DE-L'ILE-DE-MONTREAL**
*CENTRE JEUNESSE DE MONTREAL MONT
ST-ANTOINE*
(Suby of CENTRE INTEGRE UNIVERSI-
TAIRE SANTE ET SERVICES SOCIAUX DU
CENTRE-SUD-DE-L'ILE-DE-MONTREAL)
8147 Rue Sherbrooke E, Montreal, QC, H1L
1A7
(514) 356-4500
Emp Here 100
SIC 8322 Individual and family services
Jean Premont

D-U-N-S 24-944-2237   (SL)
COLLEGE DE MONT-ROYAL
COLLEGE MONT-ROYAL
2165 Rue Baldwin, Montreal, QC, H1L 5A7

---

(514) 351-7851
Emp Here 200   *Sales* 29,878,200
SIC 8221 Colleges and universities
Anne-Marie Blais

D-U-N-S 25-240-7366   (BR)
COMMISSION SCOLAIRE DE MONTREAL
ECOLE SECONDAIRE LOUISE TRICHET
(Suby of COMMISSION SCOLAIRE DE
MONTREAL)
2800 Boul Lapointe, Montreal, QC, H1L 5M1
(514) 596-5035
Emp Here 108
SIC 8211 Elementary and secondary schools
Jean-Francois Gagnon

D-U-N-S 24-792-5097   (SL)
CONSTRUCTION LANOUE, PASCAL INC
8400 Rue Sherbrooke E, Montreal, QC, H1L
1B2
(514) 544-8999
Emp Here 49   *Sales* 14,140,567
SIC 1522 Residential construction, nec
Pascal Lanoue

D-U-N-S 24-529-7486   (SL)
DUPUIS, PIERRE ET CAMILLE INC
2150 Boul Pierre-Bernard, Montreal, QC, H1L
4P4
(514) 351-9950
Emp Here 14   *Sales* 14,459,312
SIC 5172 Petroleum products, nec
Pierre Dupuis
Ginette Dupuis

D-U-N-S 20-221-4524   (SL)
HOULE AUTOMOBILE LTEE
HOULE TOYOTA
9080 Rue Hochelaga, Montreal, QC, H1L 2N9
(514) 351-5010
Emp Here 40   *Sales* 19,923,120
SIC 5511 New and used car dealers
Andre Houle
Guy Houle
Yvon Houle
Louis Houle
Michel Houle
Yves Houle

D-U-N-S 24-326-2644   (SL)
**MONTREAL GATEWAY TERMINALS PART-
NERSHIP**
MGTP
305 Rue Curatteau, Montreal, QC, H1L 6R6
(514) 257-3040
Emp Here 700   *Sales* 243,152,700
SIC 4491 Marine cargo handling
Kevin Doherty

D-U-N-S 20-223-8960   (SL)
PIECES D'AUTOS PAUL LAVIGNE INC, LES
PIECES D'AUTO LAVIGNE
3087 Rue Des Ormeaux, Montreal, QC, H1L
4Y1
(514) 351-4210
Emp Here 75   *Sales* 27,316,125
SIC 5013 Motor vehicle supplies and new
parts
Stephane Lavigne
Pierrette Lavigne-Rocheleau

D-U-N-S 20-175-9763   (SL)
**REPIT-RESSOURCE DE L'EST DE MON-
TREAL**
7707 Rue Hochelaga Bureau 100, Montreal,
QC, H1L 2K4
(514) 353-1479
Emp Here 100   *Sales* 6,842,200
SIC 8322 Individual and family services
Serge Forget
Benoit Cantin
Mario Dalpe
Judy Bambach

Montreal, QC H1M

D-U-N-S 25-233-7761   (BR)
COMMISSION SCOLAIRE DE MONTREAL
ECOLE SECONDAIRE LOUIS-RIEL
(Suby of COMMISSION SCOLAIRE DE
MONTREAL)
5850 Av De Carignan, Montreal, QC, H1M
2V4
(514) 596-4134
Emp Here 140
SIC 8211 Elementary and secondary schools
Sabine Posso

D-U-N-S 25-331-3605   (SL)
GROUPE D.R.I. INC
5125 Rue Du Trianon Bureau 510, Montreal,
QC, H1M 2S5

Emp Here 100
SIC 8742 Management consulting services

D-U-N-S 24-204-7962   (SL)
MARCHE BEAUBIEN INC
6333 Rue Beaubien E, Montreal, QC, H1M
3E6
(514) 254-6081
Emp Here 50   *Sales* 13,707,600
SIC 5411 Grocery stores
Bernard Lemay

D-U-N-S 25-605-3067   (SL)
**MULTI-CAISSES ET MULTI-RESOURCES
INC**
M C M R PERSONNEL
(Suby of GESTION BOYER ET LAROCQUE
INC)
5125 Rue Du Trianon Bureau 560, Montreal,
QC, H1M 2S5
(514) 848-1845
Emp Here 200   *Sales* 14,938,800
SIC 7363 Help supply services
Daniel Boyer
Christian Larocque

Montreal, QC H1N

D-U-N-S 24-057-1724   (SL)
ACME AWNINGS PRESTIGE
AUVENTS PRESTIGE
5598 Rue Hochelaga Bureau 101, Montreal,
QC, H1N 3L7
(514) 252-1998
Emp Here 50   *Sales* 22,358,700
SIC 5039 Construction materials, nec
Carole Prudeau

D-U-N-S 20-000-1209   (SL)
ALIMENTATION DOMINIC POTVIN INC
METRO PLUS
6550 Rue Sherbrooke E, Montreal, QC, H1N
1C6
(514) 259-8403
Emp Here 112   *Sales* 32,869,424
SIC 5411 Grocery stores
Dominique Potvin

D-U-N-S 24-366-2744   (BR)
BLINDS TO GO INC
(Suby of BLINDS TO GO INC)
3100 Boul De L'Assomption, Montreal, QC,
H1N 3S4
(514) 259-9955
Emp Here 200
SIC 2591 Drapery hardware and window
blinds and shades
Roberto Delgadillo

D-U-N-S 24-250-9172   (SL)
**BUANDERIE CENTRALE DE MONTREAL
INC**
7250 Rue Joseph-Daoust, Montreal, QC, H1N
3N9
(514) 253-1635
Emp Here 100   *Sales* 10,678,200
SIC 7218 Industrial launderers

▲ Public Company   ■ Public Company Family Member   **HQ** Headquarters   **BR** Branch   **SL** Single Location

Andre Lemieux
Ginette Proulx
Francois Leroux
Raymond Morel
Martin Ouellet
Patricia Mcdougall
Georges Bendavid
Paul Harmat
Yves Amyot

D-U-N-S 24-667-4667   (SL)
C L S C OLIVIER-GUIMOND
5810 Rue Sherbrooke E, Montreal, QC, H1N
1B2
(514) 255-2365
Emp Here 140   *Sales* 10,738,140
SIC 8082 Home health care services
Lyne Lacasse

D-U-N-S 20-215-1262   (HQ)
CADRES COLUMBIA INC
6251 Rue Notre-Dame E, Montreal, QC, H1N
2E9
(514) 253-2999
Sales 38,474,000
SIC 2499 Wood products, nec
Neil Mintz
Joseph (Joe) Antonucci

D-U-N-S 20-572-9887   (BR)
CANADA POST CORPORATION
DEPOT K
(*Suby of* GOVERNMENT OF CANADA)
6700 Rue Sherbrooke E, Montreal, QC, H1N
1C9
(514) 259-3233
Emp Here 80
SIC 4311 U.s. postal service
Larbi Brouri

D-U-N-S 24-935-7831   (BR)
CATELLI FOODS CORPORATION
RONZONI FOODS CANADA
(*Suby of* EBRO FOODS, SA)
6890 Rue Notre-Dame E, Montreal, QC, H1N
2E5
(514) 256-1601
Emp Here 140
SIC 2098 Macaroni and spaghetti
Sylvain Allie

D-U-N-S 24-345-6204   (BR)
**CENTRE DE SANTE ET DE SERVICES SO-
CIAUX LUCILLE-TEASDALE**
CENTRE HEBERGEMENT JEANNE-LEBER
(*Suby of* CENTRE DE SANTE ET DE SER-
VICES SOCIAUX LUCILLE-TEASDALE)
7445 Rue Hochelaga, Montreal, QC, H1N 3V2
(514) 251-6000
Emp Here 200
SIC 8322 Individual and family services
Francois Gagnon Clouatre

D-U-N-S 24-345-6196   (BR)
**CENTRE DE SANTE ET DE SERVICES SO-
CIAUX LUCILLE-TEASDALE**
SITE OLIVIER GUIMOND
(*Suby of* CENTRE DE SANTE ET DE SER-
VICES SOCIAUX LUCILLE-TEASDALE)
5810 Rue Sherbrooke E, Montreal, QC, H1N
1B2
(514) 255-2365
Emp Here 220
SIC 8322 Individual and family services
Johanne Lemire

D-U-N-S 24-788-2624   (BR)
CGC INC
(*Suby of* USG NETHERLANDS GLOBAL
HOLDINGS B.V.)
7200 Rue Notre-Dame E, Montreal, QC, H1N
3L6
(514) 255-4061
Emp Here 125
SIC 3275 Gypsum products
Richard Lalonde

D-U-N-S 24-109-6841   (BR)

**COCA-COLA REFRESHMENTS CANADA
COMPANY**
(*Suby of* THE COCA-COLA COMPANY)
2750 Boul De L'Assomption, Montreal, QC,
H1N 2G9
(514) 254-9411
Emp Here 400
SIC 2086 Bottled and canned soft drinks

D-U-N-S 25-232-9651   (BR)
COMMISSION SCOLAIRE DE MONTREAL
*ECOLE SECONDAIRE ECOLE EDOUARD-
MONTPETIT*
(*Suby of* COMMISSION SCOLAIRE DE
MONTREAL)
6200 Av Pierre-De Coubertin, Montreal, QC,
H1N 1S4
(514) 596-4140
Emp Here 100
SIC 8211 Elementary and secondary schools
Mario Heroux

D-U-N-S 25-240-7374   (BR)
COMMISSION SCOLAIRE DE MONTREAL
ECOLE MARGUERITE DE LAJEMMERAIS
(*Suby of* COMMISSION SCOLAIRE DE
MONTREAL)
5555 Rue Sherbrooke E, Montreal, QC, H1N
1A2
(514) 596-5100
Emp Here 100
SIC 8211 Elementary and secondary schools
Alain Guillemette

D-U-N-S 20-997-2512   (HQ)
DUBO ELECTRIQUE LTEE
DUBO DEPOT
(*Suby of* ADMINISTRATION J.B. LTEE)
5780 Rue Ontario E, Montreal, QC, H1N 0A2
(514) 255-7711
Emp Here 105   *Sales* 72,530,875
SIC 5063 Electrical apparatus and equipment
Sylvie Boileau
Mireille Perrault Boileau
Ann Mc Loughlan
Francois Veilleux

D-U-N-S 24-945-0438   (HQ)
ENTREPOTS LAFRANCE INC
GROUPE LAFRANCE
(*Suby of* ENTREPRISES DENIS BINEAU
INC, LES)
7055 Rue Notre-Dame E, Montreal, QC, H1N
3R8
(514) 254-6688
Emp Here 40   *Sales* 11,313,830
SIC 4225 General warehousing and storage
Daniel Bineau
Claudine Bineau

D-U-N-S 25-990-1304   (HQ)
**EXPERTECH BATISSEUR DE RESEAUX
INC**
EXPERTECH
(*Suby of* BCE INC)
2555 Boul De L'Assomption, Montreal, QC,
H1N 2G8
(866) 616-8459
Emp Here 200   *Sales* 117,754,500
SIC 1731 Electrical work
Stephane Martel
Michel Lalande
Stephen G Howe
Bernard Le Duc

D-U-N-S 25-335-3916   (BR)
**FEDERATION DES CAISSES DESJARDINS
DU QUEBEC**
CCPEDQ
(*Suby of* FEDERATION DES CAISSES DES-
JARDINS DU QUEBEC)
3155 Boul De L'Assomption, Montreal, QC,
H1N 3S8
(514) 253-7300
Emp Here 800
SIC 4899 Communication services, nec

D-U-N-S 20-562-9512   (SL)

FILLION, LOUIS ELECTRONIQUE INC
5690 Rue Sherbrooke E, Montreal, QC, H1N
1A1
(514) 254-6041
Emp Here 54   *Sales* 12,549,762
SIC 5731 Radio, television, and electronic
stores
Bernard Fillion
Sylvie Thibault

D-U-N-S 20-860-0684   (HQ)
**FONDATION DE L'INSTITUT UNIVERSI-
TAIRE EN SANTE MENTALE DE MON-
TREAL**
*CENTRE DE RECHERCHE FERNAD
SEGUIN*
7401 Rue Hochelaga, Montreal, QC, H1N 3M5
(514) 251-4000
Sales 215,700,300
SIC 8063 Psychiatric hospitals
Francois Castonguay
Michel Tourangeau
Pierre Miron
Andre Guay
Sonia Lupien
Michel Lesage
Denise Fortin
Richard Ardouin
Guylaine Marcotte
Carole Morin

D-U-N-S 24-434-1012   (HQ)
FRIGOVIANDE INC
FRIGO
6065 Rue Hochelaga, Montreal, QC, H1N 1X7
(514) 256-0400
Emp Here 35   *Sales* 13,707,600
SIC 5421 Meat and fish markets
Paul Bougard
Gilles Vincent
Pierre Bougard

D-U-N-S 20-313-9753   (SL)
GMS CAPITAL CORP
3055 Boul De L'Assomption, Montreal, QC,
H1N 2H1

Emp Here 10   *Sales* 11,053,450
SIC 5122 Drugs, proprietaries, and sundries
Martial Rolland
Caroline Coulombe
Serge Lebel
Bernard Canneva
Claude Pellerin
Gerard Dad

D-U-N-S 24-943-7716   (HQ)
GROUPE ARCHAMBAULT INC
ARCHAMBAULT
5655 Av Pierre-De Coubertin, Montreal, QC,
H1N 1R2
(514) 272-4049
Emp Here 90   *Sales* 155,221,146
SIC 5736 Musical instrument stores
Blaise Renaud

D-U-N-S 25-984-8211   (SL)
GROUPE S S E
5948 Rue Hochelaga, Montreal, QC, H1N 1X1
(514) 254-9492
Emp Here 49   *Sales* 19,388,222
SIC 7381 Detective and armored car services

D-U-N-S 20-309-3042   (SL)
GRUES J.M. FRANCOEUR INC
6155 Rue La Fontaine, Montreal, QC, H1N
2B8
(514) 747-5700
Emp Here 60   *Sales* 26,953,140
SIC 7389 Business services, nec
Stephane Francoeur
Pascal Francoeur

D-U-N-S 24-858-9913   (SL)
HOMEOCAN INC
3025 Boul De L'Assomption, Montreal, QC,
H1N 2H2

(514) 256-6303
Emp Here 50   *Sales* 13,833,000
SIC 2834 Pharmaceutical preparations
Michele B. Boisvert

D-U-N-S 24-562-6692   (HQ)
HUNT REFRIGERATION (CANADA) INC
(*Suby of* GROUPE FINANCIER SCORPIO
INC)
6360 Rue Notre-Dame E, Montreal, QC, H1N
2E1
(514) 259-9041
Sales 10,873,680
SIC 7623 Refrigeration service and repair
Allan Espy
Robert Nadeau
Helene Newsbury

D-U-N-S 24-320-9475   (SL)
L.J.M. MARKETING INC
JEAN COUTU #55
6420 Rue Sherbrooke E Bureau 55, Montreal,
QC, H1N 3P6
(514) 259-6991
Emp Here 62   *Sales* 14,351,778
SIC 5912 Drug stores and proprietary stores

D-U-N-S 24-678-1038   (BR)
LALLEMAND INC
LALLEMAND BIO-INGREDIENTS
(*Suby of* PLACEMENTS LALLEMAND INC)
5494 Rue Notre-Dame E, Montreal, QC, H1N
2C4
(514) 255-4887
Emp Here 80
SIC 2099 Food preparations, nec
Martin Trottier

D-U-N-S 25-990-9273   (HQ)
LIBRAIRIE RENAUD-BRAY INC
FOIRE DU LIVRE
5655 Av Pierre-De Coubertin, Montreal, QC,
H1N 1R2
(514) 272-4049
Emp Here 100   *Sales* 88,281,297
SIC 5942 Book stores
Blaise Renaud

D-U-N-S 20-230-8821   (HQ)
LITERIE PRIMO INC
PRIMO INTERNATIONAL
(*Suby of* 2739941 CANADA INC)
7000 Rue Hochelaga, Montreal, QC, H1N 1Y7
(514) 256-7543
Emp Here 15   *Sales* 13,230,256
SIC 5021 Furniture
George Itzkovitz
Hyman Itzkovitz
David Itzkovitz
Robert Itzkovitz
Marlene Itzkovitz

D-U-N-S 25-361-4432   (BR)
MAISON DES FUTAILLES, S.E.C.
ALCOOL GLOBAL (MC)
(*Suby of* MAISON DES FUTAILLES, S.E.C.)
2021 Rue Des Futailles, Montreal, QC, H1N
3M7
(450) 645-9777
Emp Here 200
SIC 2084 Wines, brandy, and brandy spirits

D-U-N-S 25-356-9867   (BR)
METRO RICHELIEU INC
JARDIN MERITE MONTREAL, DIV OF
(*Suby of* METRO INC)
5400 Av Pierre-De Coubertin, Montreal, QC,
H1N 1P7

Emp Here 150
SIC 5148 Fresh fruits and vegetables
Christian Bourbonniere

D-U-N-S 24-890-3411   (SL)
MORIN, JEAN-GUY INC
AU BON SOIN
5955 Rue Sherbrooke E, Montreal, QC, H1N
1B7

(514) 254-7513
Emp Here 62   *Sales* 15,148,336
SIC 5912 Drug stores and proprietary stores
Jean-Guy Morin
Jean-Francois Morin
Benoit Morin

D-U-N-S 20-289-8607   (SL)
MURAFLEX INC
5502 Rue Notre-Dame E, Montreal, QC, H1N 2C4
(450) 462-3632
Emp Here 120   *Sales* 18,518,640
SIC 2522 Office furniture, except wood
Fernando Petreccia
Paolo Righetto
Paolo Galloti
Niccolo Fischer

D-U-N-S 24-228-4271   (SL)
PHARMACIE MORIN INC
5955 Rue Sherbrooke E, Montreal, QC, H1N 1B7
(514) 254-7513
Emp Here 100   *Sales* 24,432,800
SIC 5912 Drug stores and proprietary stores
Benoit Morin
Jean-Francois Morin

D-U-N-S 20-632-3651   (HQ)
PROCECO LTEE
7300 Rue Tellier, Montreal, QC, H1N 3T7
(514) 254-8494
Sales 33,300,150
SIC 3569 General industrial machinery, nec
Helmut Schauer
Robert J. Burns

D-U-N-S 20-541-1580   (SL)
PRODUITS DE PLASTIQUE AGE INC, LES
PLASTIQUE AGE
7295 Rue Tellier, Montreal, QC, H1N 3S9
(514) 251-9550
Emp Here 250   *Sales* 39,714,500
SIC 3089 Plastics products, nec
Mark Smolka
Adam Murawski

D-U-N-S 24-803-5300   (SL)
PRODUITS PETROLIERS NORCAN S.E.N.C., LES
6370 Rue Notre-Dame E, Montreal, QC, H1N 2E1
(514) 253-2222
Emp Here 30   *Sales* 37,716,030
SIC 5172 Petroleum products, nec
Garcin Garry

D-U-N-S 24-707-0456   (SL)
PROFESSIONNEL(LE)S EN SOINS DE SANTE UNIS LES
5630 Rue Hochelaga, Montreal, QC, H1N 3L7
(514) 932-4417
Emp Here 49   *Sales* 11,451,055
SIC 8621 Professional organizations
Michel T Leger

D-U-N-S 20-805-5272   (BR)
PROVIGO DISTRIBUTION INC
LOBLAWS
(*Suby of* LOBLAW COMPANIES LIMITED)
7600 Rue Sherbrooke E, Montreal, QC, H1N 3W1
(514) 257-4511
Emp Here 140
SIC 5411 Grocery stores
Dominique Tremblay

D-U-N-S 20-908-7071   (BR)
ROTISSERIES ST-HUBERT LTEE, LES
ST HUBERT CADILLAC
(*Suby of* RECIPE UNLIMITED CORPORATION)
6225 Rue Sherbrooke E, Montreal, QC, H1N 1C3
(514) 259-6939
Emp Here 80
SIC 5812 Eating places
Sylvain Vezina

D-U-N-S 20-760-9058   (HQ)
SOCIETE DES ALCOOLS DU QUEBEC
(*Suby of* GOUVERNEMENT DE LA PROVINCE DE QUEBEC)
7500 Rue Tellier, Montreal, QC, H1N 3W5
(514) 254-6000
Emp Here 100   *Sales* 1,284,759,000
SIC 5921 Liquor stores
Alain Brunet
Johanne Brunet
Martine Comtois
Nicole Diamond-Gelinas
Lucie Martel
Lyne Bouchard
Marc Bruneau
Helene Levesque
Nora Arzoumanain
Michael Stephen Pesner

D-U-N-S 24-323-5376   (BR)
SOCIETE DES ALCOOLS DU QUEBEC
S.A.Q.
(*Suby of* GOUVERNEMENT DE LA PROVINCE DE QUEBEC)
560 Rue Hector-Barsalou, Montreal, QC, H1N 3T2
(514) 254-6000
Emp Here 300
SIC 5921 Liquor stores
Michele Thivierge

D-U-N-S 24-357-6845   (HQ)
SOGEFI AIR & COOLING CANADA CORP
(*Suby of* CIR SPA COMPAGNIE INDUSTRI-ALI RIUNITE)
1500 Rue De Boucherville, Montreal, QC, H1N 3V3
(514) 764-8806
Sales 109,542,030
SIC 3599 Industrial machinery, nec
Frederic Sipahi
Cedric Fournier
Pierre Dufflot

D-U-N-S 25-156-7822   (SL)
TRANSPORTS LACOMBE INC, LES
5644 Rue Hochelaga, Montreal, QC, H1N 3L7
(514) 256-0050
Emp Here 70   *Sales* 10,373,440
SIC 4212 Local trucking, without storage
Nathalie Chapados

D-U-N-S 20-236-2737   (HQ)
UAP INC
UAP PIECES D'AUTO
(*Suby of* GENUINE PARTS COMPANY)
7025 Rue Ontario E, Montreal, QC, H1N 2B3
(514) 251-6565
Emp Here 350   *Sales* 739,468,600
SIC 5013 Motor vehicle supplies and new parts
Alain Masse
Frank Pipito
Martin Rolland
Paul Donahue
Scott Leprohon
Kevin Herron

D-U-N-S 24-796-9251   (BR)
UAP INC
NAPA PIECES D'AUTO
(*Suby of* GENUINE PARTS COMPANY)
2095 Av Haig, Montreal, QC, H1N 3E2
(514) 251-7638
Emp Here 300
SIC 5013 Motor vehicle supplies and new parts

D-U-N-S 24-050-0632   (BR)
WINNERS MERCHANTS INTERNATIONAL L.P.
WINNERS
(*Suby of* THE TJX COMPANIES INC)
7275 Rue Sherbrooke E Bureau 2000, Montreal, QC, H1N 1E9
(514) 798-1908
Emp Here 100

SIC 5651 Family clothing stores
Steve Gandron

Montreal, QC H1P

D-U-N-S 24-425-3683   (HQ)
ALIMENTS ALASKO INC
FOODELICIOUS
6810 Boul Des Grandes-Prairies, Montreal, QC, H1P 3P3
(514) 328-6661
Emp Here 36   *Sales* 34,258,657
SIC 5142 Packaged frozen goods
Steven Leakos
Bruno Masson
David Gisborne
Morten Steen-Jorgensen

D-U-N-S 20-550-7523   (HQ)
SAPUTO PRODUITS LAITIERS CANADA S.E.N.C.
FROMA-DAR
6869 Boul Metropolitain, Montreal, QC, H1P 1X8
(514) 328-6662
Emp Here 150   *Sales* 2,201,518,045
SIC 2022 Cheese; natural and processed
Emmanuel Saputo

D-U-N-S 25-900-3023   (SL)
URGENCES-SANTE
6700 Rue Jarry E, Montreal, QC, H1P 0A4
(514) 723-5600
Emp Here 1,426   *Sales* 93,853,709
SIC 4119 Local passenger transportation, nec
Nicola D'ulisse
Arianne Trudeau
Louis Poirier
Claude Belisle
Gilles Bourgeois
Anie Samson

Montreal, QC H1R

D-U-N-S 20-331-1261   (SL)
TP-HOLIDAY GROUP LIMITED
HOLIDAY GROUP
(*Suby of* TRAVELPRO GROUP HOLDINGS, INC.)
4875 Boul Des Grandes-Prairies, Montreal, QC, H1R 1X4
(514) 325-0660
Emp Here 123   *Sales* 62,678,160
SIC 5099 Durable goods, nec
Raymond Durocher
Daniel Penn
Blake Lipham
Leanne Narwani

Montreal, QC H1T

D-U-N-S 20-421-1858   (SL)
BRUNELLE, GUY INC
4450 Rue Belanger, Montreal, QC, H1T 1B5
(514) 729-0008
Emp Here 75   *Sales* 12,693,525
SIC 1721 Painting and paper hanging
Francis Brunelle
Colette Boismenu

D-U-N-S 24-405-6503   (BR)
CANADIAN CANCER SOCIETY
SOCIETE CANADIENNE DE MONTREAL
(*Suby of* CANADIAN CANCER SOCIETY)
5151 Boul De L'Assomption, Montreal, QC, H1T 4A9
(514) 255-5151
Emp Here 201

SIC 8399 Social services, nec
Suzanne Dubois

D-U-N-S 24-562-0703   (SL)
CENTRE D'HEBERGEMENT ET DE SOINS DE LONGUE DUREE PROVIDENCE SAINT-JOSEPH INC
MAISON ST-JOSEPH
5605 Rue Beaubien E Bureau 114, Montreal, QC, H1T 1X4
(514) 254-4991
Emp Here 115   *Sales* 11,974,145
SIC 8661 Religious organizations
Claire Houde
Danielle Gaboury

D-U-N-S 24-354-8422   (BR)
CENTRE HOSPITALIER UNIVERSITAIRE SAINTE-JUSTINE
CENTRE DE READAPTATION MARIE EN-FANT DU CHU SAINTE-JUSTINE
(*Suby of* CENTRE HOSPITALIER UNIVERSITAIRE SAINTE-JUSTINE)
5200 Rue Belanger, Montreal, QC, H1T 1C9
(514) 374-1710
Emp Here 450
SIC 8093 Specialty outpatient clinics, nec
Fabrice Brunet

D-U-N-S 20-333-1269   (BR)
CENTRE INTEGRE UNIVERSITAIRE SANTE ET SERVICES SOCIAUX DU CENTRE-SUD-DE-L'ILE-DE-MONTREAL
LE CENTRE JEUNESSE DE MONTREAL - INSTITUT UNIVERSITAIRE
(*Suby of* CENTRE INTEGRE UNIVERSITAIRE SANTE ET SERVICES SOCIAUX DU CENTRE-SUD-DE-L'ILE-DE-MONTREAL)
4675 Rue Belanger, Montreal, QC, H1T 1C2
(514) 593-3979
Emp Here 200
SIC 8011 Offices and clinics of medical doctors

D-U-N-S 25-501-8996   (SL)
FONDATION D'INSTITUT CANADIEN-POLONAIS DU BIEN-ETRE INC
5655 Rue Belanger, Montreal, QC, H1T 1G2
(514) 259-2551
Emp Here 130   *Sales* 8,210,670
SIC 8052 Intermediate care facilities
Frances Sztuka

D-U-N-S 20-978-2366   (SL)
HOPITAL SANTA CABRINI
CENTRE D'ACCEUIL DANTE
5655 Rue Saint-Zotique E, Montreal, QC, H1T 1P7
(514) 252-1535
Emp Here 1,500   *Sales* 166,620,000
SIC 8062 General medical and surgical hospitals
Michel Trozzo
Vincent Gagliardi
Irene Giannetti
Vincent Radino
Emilio B Imbriglio
Pasquale Artuso
Mario Discepola
Giuseppe Di Battista
David De Sanctis
Nathalie Demers

D-U-N-S 20-542-1118   (SL)
INSTITUT DE CARDIOLOGIE DE MONTREAL
CENTRE DE RECHERCHE DE L'INSTITUT DE CARDIOLOGIE DE MONTREAL
5000 Rue Belanger, Montreal, QC, H1T 1C8
(514) 376-3330
Emp Here 2,000   *Sales* 222,160,000
SIC 8069 Specialty hospitals, except psychiatric
Pierre Anctil
Eric Bedard
Melanie La Couture
Manon Leveille

Isabelle Perras
Christian Baron
Valerie Hurteloup
Henri-Paul Rousseau
Lucie Verret
Isabelle Viger

D-U-N-S 20-370-1144 (SL)
MAGIC TECHNOLOGY
6635 39e Av, Montreal, QC, H1T 2W9
(438) 388-6512
Emp Here 80 *Sales* 18,029,316
SIC 7378 Computer maintenance and repair
R.Richard Drif

D-U-N-S 24-859-0226 (SL)
PHARMACIE CAROLINE MILETTE
5700 Rue Saint-Zotique E Bureau 100, Montreal, QC, H1T 3Y7
(514) 255-5797
Emp Here 60 *Sales* 14,659,680
SIC 5912 Drug stores and proprietary stores
Caroline Milette

D-U-N-S 25-410-6388 (HQ)
PLACEMENTS ROBERT SIMARD INC
JEAN COUTU
4466 Rue Beaubien E, Montreal, QC, H1T 3Y8
(514) 728-3674
Sales 13,438,040
SIC 5912 Drug stores and proprietary stores
Robert Simard

D-U-N-S 24-430-7880 (SL)
RE-MAX MONTREAL METRO INC
5136 Rue De Bellechasse, Montreal, QC, H1T 2A4
(514) 251-9000
Emp Here 35 *Sales* 11,449,445
SIC 6531 Real estate agents and managers
Andre Theoret

Montreal, QC H1V

D-U-N-S 25-243-7439 (SL)
2990181 CANADA INC
HOTEL AUBERGE UNIVERSEL MONTREAL
5000 Rue Sherbrooke E, Montreal, QC, H1V 1A1
(514) 253-3365
Emp Here 80 *Sales* 7,591,920
SIC 7011 Hotels and motels
Anthony Frattaroli
Giovanni Santonianni

D-U-N-S 25-411-3533 (SL)
3122298 CANADA INC
BOULANGERIE PREMIERE MOISSON
4445 Rue Ontario E Bureau 4, Montreal, QC, H1V 3V3
(514) 259-5929
Emp Here 40 *Sales* 10,966,080
SIC 5461 Retail bakeries
Albert Alarcon

D-U-N-S 25-485-1959 (SL)
ALIMENTATION DENIS GODIN INC
METRO MORGAN 2024
4405 Rue Sainte-Catherine E, Montreal, QC, H1V 1Y4
(514) 254-0126
Emp Here 45 *Sales* 12,336,840
SIC 5411 Grocery stores
Denis Godin

D-U-N-S 25-245-9532 (SL)
ALUMICO ARCHITECTURAL INC
(*Suby of* ENTREPRISES HENMIT INC, LES)
4343 Rue Hochelaga Bureau 100, Montreal, QC, H1V 1C2
(514) 255-4343
Emp Here 60 *Sales* 34,177,680
SIC 5031 Lumber, plywood, and millwork
Regent Labrosse

Mathieu Beland
Pierre Mc Nicoll

D-U-N-S 24-054-5954 (HQ)
ALUMICO METAL & OXIDATION INC
(*Suby of* ENTREPRISES HENMIT INC, LES)
4343 Rue Hochelaga Bureau 100, Montreal, QC, H1V 1C2
(514) 255-4343
Sales 38,417,000
SIC 3471 Plating and polishing
Rejean Labrosse
Mathieu Beland
Pierre Mc Nicoll

D-U-N-S 25-248-3698 (HQ)
ASSOCIATION PARITAIRE POUR LA SANTE ET LA SECURITE DU TRAVAIL DU SECTEUR AFFAIRES SOCIALES
5100 Rue Sherbrooke E Bureau 950, Montreal, QC, H1V 3R9
(514) 253-6871
Sales 10,203,700
SIC 8631 Labor organizations
Eric Bonneau
Mona Landry
Chantal Schmidt
Philippe Crevier
Mona Landry
Noella Tremblay
Donald L. Gilbert
Richard Despres
Ingrid Tremblay
Maude Pelletier

D-U-N-S 24-516-4785 (SL)
BOULOT VERS..., LE
4447 Rue De Rouen, Montreal, QC, H1V 1H1
(514) 259-2312
Emp Here 28 *Sales* 11,127,592
SIC 8699 Membership organizations, nec
Jeanne Dore
Michel Gendron
Pierre Legault
Mario Longpre

D-U-N-S 20-056-5773 (HQ)
BOUTIQUE LA VIE EN ROSE INC
BIKINI VILLAGE
4320 Av Pierre-De Coubertin, Montreal, QC, H1V 1A6
(514) 256-9446
Emp Here 230 *Sales* 324,363,000
SIC 5632 Women's accessory and specialty stores
Francois Roberge

D-U-N-S 20-791-2742 (SL)
BUANDERIE VILLERAY LTEE
4740 Rue De Rouen, Montreal, QC, H1V 3T7
(514) 259-4531
Emp Here 100 *Sales* 8,962,900
SIC 7218 Industrial launderers
Benoit Laurent

D-U-N-S 24-658-1750 (BR)
CASCADES CANADA ULC
CASCADES EMBALLAGE CARTON-CAISSE
(*Suby of* CASCADES INC)
2755 Rue Viau, Montreal, QC, H1V 3J4
(514) 251-3800
Emp Here 250
SIC 2631 Paperboard mills

D-U-N-S 25-365-0493 (BR)
CASCADES CANADA ULC
NORAMPAC-SPB
(*Suby of* CASCADES INC)
2755 Rue Viau, Montreal, QC, H1V 3J4
(514) 251-3800
Emp Here 500
SIC 2652 Setup paperboard boxes
Marco Daoust

D-U-N-S 24-712-1841 (SL)
CHSLD PROVIDENCE NOTRE-DAME DE LOURDES INC
1870 Boul Pie-Ix, Montreal, QC, H1V 2C6

(514) 527-4595
Emp Here 200 *Sales* 13,713,200
SIC 8051 Skilled nursing care facilities
Claire Houde
Claudette Leroux

D-U-N-S 25-240-6731 (BR)
COMMISSION SCOLAIRE DE MONTREAL
ECOLE SECONDAIRE EULALIE DUROCHER
(*Suby of* COMMISSION SCOLAIRE DE MONTREAL)
2455 Av Letourneux, Montreal, QC, H1V 2N9
(514) 596-4949
Emp Here 80
SIC 8211 Elementary and secondary schools
Amelie Girard

D-U-N-S 25-240-3712 (BR)
COMMISSION SCOLAIRE DE MONTREAL
ECOLE CHOMEDEY-DE-MAISONNEUVE
(*Suby of* COMMISSION SCOLAIRE DE MONTREAL)
1860 Av Morgan, Montreal, QC, H1V 2R2
(514) 596-4844
Emp Here 87
SIC 8211 Elementary and secondary schools
Eric Sirois

D-U-N-S 20-298-3169 (HQ)
DENTAL WINGS INC
PAVILLON DENTAIRE
(*Suby of* STRAUMANN HOLDING AG)
2251 Av Letourneux, Montreal, QC, H1V 2N9
(514) 807-8485
Sales 18,022,750
SIC 7371 Custom computer programming services
Michael Rynerson
Seti Hamalian
Robin Provost

D-U-N-S 20-527-9164 (HQ)
EAUX NAYA INC, LES
(*Suby of* NAYA LUXCO SARL)
2030 Boul Pie-Ix Bureau 214.4, Montreal, QC, H1V 2C8
(514) 525-6292
Emp Here 10 *Sales* 58,053,996
SIC 5149 Groceries and related products, nec
Marc-David Bismuth
Daniel Cote
Daniel Cotte
Philippe-Loic Jacob
David Heidecorn

D-U-N-S 20-503-7328 (SL)
ENTREPRISES MARSOLAIS INC, LES
5045 Rue Ontario, Montreal, QC, H1V 1M7
(514) 254-7171
Emp Here 35 *Sales* 25,988,200
SIC 5193 Flowers and florists supplies
Hugo Grenon
Nicolas Lussier

D-U-N-S 24-405-3492 (SL)
FRANCE DELICES INC
SUPER FINE
(*Suby of* 2987953 CANADA INC)
5065 Rue Ontario E, Montreal, QC, H1V 3V2
(514) 259-2291
Emp Here 185 *Sales* 90,166,225
SIC 2051 Bread, cake, and related products
Colette Faletto-Durot
Laurent Durot
Jacques Durot
Ghislaine Durot

D-U-N-S 20-777-8747 (HQ)
HENAULT & GOSSELIN INC
4100 Rue Notre-Dame E, Montreal, QC, H1V 3T5
(514) 522-0909
Emp Here 35 *Sales* 17,233,020
SIC 1794 Excavation work
Conrad Gosselin
Francois Ethier
Manon Gosselin

Jocelyn Martin
Sophie Gagnon
Jean-Marc Cyr
Joel Briand
Joel Robitaille-Legare
Hugh Shepherd

D-U-N-S 24-669-1877 (BR)
KRAFT HEINZ CANADA ULC
CHRISTIE BROWN & CO BAKERY
(*Suby of* THE KRAFT HEINZ COMPANY)
3055 Rue Viau Bureau 4, Montreal, QC, H1V 3J5
(514) 259-6921
Emp Here 636
SIC 2051 Bread, cake, and related products

D-U-N-S 24-117-9014 (SL)
LABORATOIRES BUG TRACKER INC
(*Suby of* TECHNOLOGIES GLOBALSTEP INC)
2030 Boul Pie-Ix Bureau 307, Montreal, QC, H1V 2C8
(514) 496-0093
Emp Here 140 *Sales* 26,110,840
SIC 8742 Management consulting services
Gagan Ahluwalia
Mike Forni
Sanjiv Ahluwalia

D-U-N-S 20-363-7645 (BR)
MMCC SOLUTIONS CANADA COMPANY
TELEPERFORMANCE CANADA
(*Suby of* TELEPERFORMANCE SE)
2030 Boul Pie-Ix Bureau 330, Montreal, QC, H1V 2C8
(514) 287-1717
Emp Here 500
SIC 7389 Business services, nec

D-U-N-S 25-864-7155 (BR)
MULTI-MARQUES INC
BOULANGERIE MULTI-MARQUES
(*Suby of* GRUPO BIMBO, S.A.B. DE C.V.)
3265 Rue Viau, Montreal, QC, H1V 3J5
(514) 255-9492
Emp Here 200
SIC 2051 Bread, cake, and related products
Patrick Dionne

D-U-N-S 25-148-0018 (HQ)
OBJECTIF LUNE INC
BGL SOFT
(*Suby of* JALAK RECREATIE B.V.)
2030 Boul Pie-Ix Bureau 500, Montreal, QC, H1V 2C8
(514) 875-5863
Sales 60,302,376
SIC 5112 Stationery and office supplies
Didier Gombert
Martin Dallaire
Peter Van Schaick

D-U-N-S 25-209-9031 (SL)
QUALI DESSERTS INC
5067 Rue Ontario E, Montreal, QC, H1V 3V2
(514) 259-2415
Emp Here 55 *Sales* 19,012,950
SIC 2051 Bread, cake, and related products
Jacques Durot

D-U-N-S 20-213-5505 (HQ)
QUEBEC LINGE CO
QUEBEC LINGE
4375 Rue De Rouen, Montreal, QC, H1V 1H2
(514) 670-2005
Emp Here 422 *Sales* 48,435,840
SIC 7213 Linen supply
William Evans
Theresa Schulz
Dan Lagermeier

D-U-N-S 20-887-3778 (SL)
REGROUPEMENT DES ORGANISMES NATIONAUX DE LOISIRS DU QUEBEC
REGROUPEMENT LOISIR QUEBEC
4545 Av Pierre-De Coubertin, Montreal, QC, H1V 0B2

---

(514) 252-3126
Emp Here 50   *Sales* 19,870,700
SIC 8699 Membership organizations, nec
 Sylvain Lalonde
 Jean-Pierre Leroux
 Simon Tanguay

D-U-N-S 24-676-4518   (SL)
SOCIETE DE GESTION DU RESEAU IN-
FORMATIQUE DES COMMISSIONS SCO-
LAIRES
SOCIETE GRICS
5100 Rue Sherbrooke E Bureau 300, Mon-
treal, QC, H1V 3R9
(514) 251-3700
Emp Here 330   *Sales* 74,656,230
SIC 7376 Computer facilities management
 Jean-Francois Lachance
 Christiane Barbe
 Sebastien Gougeon
 Marius Richard
 Pierre Boulay
 Julie Laberge
 Andre Lamarche
 Caroline Dupre
 Lorraine Mayer
 Joanne Simoneau-Polenz

D-U-N-S 20-909-2063   (SL)
SOCIETE EN COMMANDITE FREE 2 PLAY
4750 Rue Sherbrooke E, Montreal, QC, H1V
3S8
(514) 328-3668
Emp Here 150   *Sales* 12,509,250
SIC 7941 Sports clubs, managers, and promoters
 Lino Anthony Saputo

D-U-N-S 24-654-3933   (HQ)
SOLOTECH INC
DARPEX
(*Suby of* GROUPE SOLOTECH INC)
5200 Rue Hochelaga Bureau 100, Montreal,
QC, H1V 1G3
(514) 526-3094
Sales 70,728,750
SIC 3645 Residential lighting fixtures
 Martin Tremblay
 Nicolas Lavoie

D-U-N-S 20-370-9865   (HQ)
TECHNOLOGIES GLOBALSTEP INC
2030 Boul Pie-Ix Bureau 307, Montreal, QC,
H1V 2C8
(514) 496-0093
Sales 23,428,800
SIC 8742 Management consulting services
 Gagan Ahluwalia
 Mike Forni
 Sanjiv Ahluwalia

D-U-N-S 24-362-8752   (BR)
TETRA TECH INDUSTRIES INC
BPR
(*Suby of* TETRA TECH, INC.)
5100 Rue Sherbrooke E Bureau 400, Mon-
treal, QC, H1V 3R9
(514) 257-0707
Emp Here 175
SIC 8711 Engineering services
 Celine Bellavance

D-U-N-S 20-181-9930   (HQ)
TETRA TECH INDUSTRIES INC
INDUSTRIES TETRA TECH
(*Suby of* TETRA TECH, INC.)
5100 Rue Sherbrooke E, Montreal, QC, H1V
3R9
(514) 257-1112
Emp Here 250   *Sales* 68,995,850
SIC 8711 Engineering services
 Denis Harvie
 Francois Morin
 Dan L. Batrack
 Steven Burdick

D-U-N-S 20-329-9458   (HQ)
TETRA TECH QE INC

(*Suby of* TETRA TECH, INC.)
5100 Rue Sherbrooke E Bureau 900, Mon-
treal, QC, H1V 3R9
(514) 257-0707
Emp Here 602   *Sales* 61,241,117
SIC 8711 Engineering services
 Stephane D'amours
 Sylvain Lavoie
 Bernie Teufele
 Richard A Lemmon
 Steven M Burdick

D-U-N-S 20-884-5586   (SL)
THEATRE DENISE PELLETIER INC
SALLE FRED BARRY, LA
4353 Rue Sainte-Catherine E, Montreal, QC,
H1V 1Y2
(514) 253-8974
Emp Here 200   *Sales* 21,196,800
SIC 7922 Theatrical producers and services
 Michel Blais
 Remi Brousseau

D-U-N-S 24-081-4962   (SL)
VEZINA ASSURANCES INC
VEZINA DUFAULT
(*Suby of* MARSH & MCLENNAN COMPA-
NIES, INC.)
4374 Av Pierre-De Coubertin Bureau 220,
Montreal, QC, H1V 1A6
(514) 253-5221
Emp Here 70   *Sales* 129,341,940
SIC 6411 Insurance agents, brokers, and ser-
vice

D-U-N-S 24-355-4008   (BR)
VILLE DE MONTREAL
CENTRE DE SERVICES PARTAGES-
MATERIEL ROULANT ET ATELIERS, LE
(*Suby of* VILLE DE MONTREAL)
2269 Rue Viau, Montreal, QC, H1V 3H8
(514) 872-4303
Emp Here 450
SIC 7538 General automotive repair shops
 Guy Charbonneau

Montreal, QC H1W

D-U-N-S 24-327-2775   (SL)
9026-2437 QUEBEC INC
PHARMAPRIX
3845 Rue Ontario E, Montreal, QC, H1W 1S5
(514) 524-7727
Emp Here 50   *Sales* 12,647,700
SIC 5912 Drug stores and proprietary stores
 Francois Lalande

D-U-N-S 25-980-5237   (SL)
AGENCE   D'ASSURANCES   ANDRE
DUFRESNE
4061 Rue Hochelaga, Montreal, QC, H1W
1K4
(514) 256-3626
Emp Here 25   *Sales* 21,201,500
SIC 6411 Insurance agents, brokers, and ser-
vice
 Andre Dufresne

D-U-N-S 24-701-1997   (SL)
ALIMENTATION ERIC DA PONTE INC
METRO ONTARIO
3800 Rue Ontario E, Montreal, QC, H1W 1S4
(514) 524-8850
Emp Here 78   *Sales* 22,891,206
SIC 5411 Grocery stores
 Eric Da Ponte

D-U-N-S 20-270-8723   (SL)
BD APD INC
AU PAIN DORE
3075 Rue De Rouen, Montreal, QC, H1W 3Z2
(514) 528-8877
Emp Here 140   *Sales* 100,340,240
SIC 5149 Groceries and related products, nec

 Lionel Ladouceur
 Pascale Closson-Duquette
 Andrew Johnston

D-U-N-S 20-961-2357   (HQ)
C.E.V. INC
CEV
3055 Rue Adam, Montreal, QC, H1W 3Y7
(514) 521-8253
Emp Here 49   *Sales* 29,066,310
SIC 5065 Electronic parts and equipment, nec
 Jean Jr. Meunier
 Justin Meunier
 Linda Meunier

D-U-N-S 25-973-4994   (HQ)
CENTRE DE SANTE ET DE SERVICES SO-
CIAUX LUCILLE-TEASDALE
PAVILLON J HENRI-CHARBONNEAU
3095 Rue Sherbrooke E, Montreal, QC, H1W
1B2
(514) 523-0991
Sales 115,325,450
SIC 6513 Apartment building operators
 Marc Rochefort
 Maurice Thibeault

D-U-N-S 24-667-4626   (SL)
CHIC RESTO-POP INC, LE
1500 Av D'Orleans, Montreal, QC, H1W 3R1
(514) 521-4089
Emp Here 137   *Sales* 6,389,543
SIC 5812 Eating places
 Jacynthe Ouellette
 Rene-Phillippe Bertrand
 Suzane Boudrias

D-U-N-S 25-173-0594   (SL)
COOPERATIVE DES TRAVAILLEUSES ET
TRAVAILLEURS EN RESTAURATION LA
DEMOCRATE
ROTISSERIE ST-HUBERT
2901 Rue Sherbrooke E, Montreal, QC, H1W
1B2

Emp Here 100   *Sales* 4,551,900
SIC 5812 Eating places
 Michel Maurais

D-U-N-S 24-470-4115   (SL)
DUFRESNE, ANDRE INSURANCE
4061 Rue Hochelaga, Montreal, QC, H1W
1K4
(514) 256-3626
Emp Here 23   *Sales* 19,505,380
SIC 6411 Insurance agents, brokers, and service
 Andre Dufresne

D-U-N-S 20-223-3748   (SL)
ENTREPRISES ELECTRIQUES L.M. INC,
LES
C.R. COMPREF
3006 Rue Sainte-Catherine E, Montreal, QC,
H1W 2B8
(514) 523-2831
Emp Here 100   *Sales* 21,782,900
SIC 1731 Electrical work
 Robert Lamarre
 Alexandre Fortin
 Marc Evangeliste
 Jean-Philippe Lamarre
 Martin Charbonneau

D-U-N-S 24-742-1233   (SL)
ENTREPRISES HENRI RAVARY LTEE, LES
CANADIAN TIRE
3025 Rue Sherbrooke E Bureau 400, Mon-
treal, QC, H1W 1B2
(514) 521-8888
Emp Here 120   *Sales* 24,641,160
SIC 5399 Miscellaneous general merchandise
 Henri Ravary

D-U-N-S 24-935-8920   (SL)
GROUPE L.E.D. LAMARRE, EVANGE-
LISTE, DELISLE INC
3006 Rue Sainte-Catherine E, Montreal, QC,

H1W 2B8
(514) 523-2831
Emp Here 54   *Sales* 14,760,900
SIC 6712 Bank holding companies
 Robert Lamarre
 Marc Evangeliste
 Gilles Delisle
 Paul Evangeliste

D-U-N-S 24-945-0750   (SL)
JODOIN   LAMARRE   PRATTE   ARCHI-
TECTES INC
3200 Rue Rachel E, Montreal, QC, H1W 1A4
(514) 527-8821
Emp Here 83   *Sales* 14,835,337
SIC 8712 Architectural services
 Maurice Cabana
 Masrc Rendeau
 Michel Bourassa
 Jean Martin
 Michel Broz

D-U-N-S 20-223-3300   (HQ)
LALLEMAND INC
BIOFORET
(*Suby of* PLACEMENTS LALLEMAND INC)
1620 Rue Prefontaine, Montreal, QC, H1W
2N8
(514) 522-2131
Emp Here 20   *Sales* 34,569,000
SIC 2099 Food preparations, nec
 Antoine Chagnon
 Francois Chagnon
 Paul S Echenberg
 Jean Chagnon
 Jacques Chaize
 Merrill Eastman
 Bryan Kent
 Alfred Oetsch
 David Morris
 Michelle Samson-Doel

D-U-N-S 24-365-0434   (HQ)
LANTIC INC
(*Suby of* ROGERS SUGAR INC)
4026 Rue Notre-Dame E, Montreal, QC, H1W
2K3
(514) 527-8686
Emp Here 300   *Sales* 268,061,750
SIC 2062 Cane sugar refining
 John Holliday
 Manon Lacroix
 Michel P. Desbiens
 Michael A. Heskin
 Stuart A. Belkin
 Ross H. Dallas
 Donald G. Jewell
 Daniel Lafrance

D-U-N-S 20-642-1856   (BR)
LOBLAWS SUPERMARKETS LIMITED
PROVIGO
(*Suby of* LOBLAW COMPANIES LIMITED)
2925 Rue Rachel E, Montreal, QC, H1W 3Z8
(514) 522-4442
Emp Here 200
SIC 5411 Grocery stores
 Patrick Auclair

D-U-N-S 20-739-6185   (HQ)
LOCATION JEAN LEGARE LTEE
LEGARE LOCATION D'AUTO
3035 Rue Hochelaga, Montreal, QC, H1W
1G1
(514) 522-6466
Emp Here 20   *Sales* 12,950,028
SIC 5511 New and used car dealers
 Nathalie Legare
 Kevin Voyer

D-U-N-S 24-607-9367   (SL)
MAXI PREFONTAINE
2925 Rue Sherbrooke E, Montreal, QC, H1W
1B2
(514) 521-0660
Emp Here 49   *Sales* 13,433,448
SIC 5411 Grocery stores

▲ Public Company   ■ Public Company Family Member   **HQ** Headquarters   **BR** Branch   **SL** Single Location

Claude Sonny

D-U-N-S 25-976-2805   (SL)
OCTASIC INC
OCTASIC SEMICONDUCTOR
2901 Rue Rachel E Bureau 30, Montreal, QC,
H1W 4A4
(514) 282-8858
Emp Here 90   *Sales* 17,139,780
SIC 3679 Electronic components, nec
Michel Laurence
Lucie Gelinas
Michel Brule
Kenneth Burkhardt
Jacques Foisy
Thomas Awad
Martin Laurence
Charles Sylvestre
Pierre Daigle

D-U-N-S 25-390-1797   (SL)
**PHARMACIE   RAYMOND   BEAUCAIRE
PHARMACIEN INC**
PHARMACIE JEAN COUTU
3452 Rue Ontario E, Montreal, QC, H1W 1R2
(514) 522-1126
Emp Here 40   *Sales* 10,118,160
SIC 5912 Drug stores and proprietary stores
Raymond Beaucaire

D-U-N-S 24-418-4250   (HQ)
PLACEMENTS LALLEMAND INC
1620 Rue Prefontaine, Montreal, QC, H1W
2N8
(514) 522-2133
Emp Here 12   *Sales* 34,569,000
SIC 2099 Food preparations, nec
Robert Briscoe
Arthur R.A. Scace
Bryan Kent
James Fisher
Jacques Chaize
Robert W Murdoch
Alfred Oetsch
Merrill Eastman
Paul S Echenberg
Francoise Chagnon

D-U-N-S 20-101-1819   (SL)
RE/MAX HARMONIE INC
3550 Rue Rachel E Bureau 201, Montreal,
QC, H1W 1A7
(514) 259-8884
Emp Here 45   *Sales* 14,720,715
SIC 6531 Real estate agents and managers
Pierre Lafond

D-U-N-S 25-533-9723   (HQ)
ROGERS SUGAR INC
4026 Rue Notre-Dame E, Montreal, QC, H1W
2K3
(514) 940-4350
Emp Here 1   *Sales* 544,185,137
SIC 6726 Investment offices, nec
John Holliday
Manon Lacroix
Patrick Dionne
Jean-Francois Khalil
Mike Walton
Daniel L. Lafrance
Michael A Heskin
A Stuart Belkin
Dallas H Ross
Donald G Jewell

D-U-N-S 20-416-4800   (HQ)
ROTISSERIES AU COQ LTEE, LES
3060 Rue Hochelaga, Montreal, QC, H1W
1G2
(514) 527-8833
Sales 32,802,000
SIC 6712 Bank holding companies
Elise Benny
Stephane St-Hilaire

D-U-N-S 25-832-1512   (BR)
TRANSPORT CANADA
MONTREAL PORT ADMINISTRATION

(Suby of GOVERNMENT OF CANADA)
3400 Rue Notre-Dame E, Montreal, QC, H1W
2J2
(514) 283-7020
Emp Here 250
SIC 4111 Local and suburban transit
Daniel Dagenais

D-U-N-S 24-763-3902   (SL)
VILLE MARIE SUZUKI AUTOMOBILE INC
2995 Rue Hochelaga, Montreal, QC, H1W
1G1
(514) 598-8666
Emp Here 53   *Sales* 33,351,840
SIC 5511 New and used car dealers
Anthony Pietrantonio

Montreal, QC H1X

D-U-N-S 25-332-2200   (HQ)
BLINDS TO GO INC
AU BON MARCHE
3510 Boul Saint-Joseph E, Montreal, QC, H1X
1W6
(514) 255-4000
Emp Here 50   *Sales* 266,703,000
SIC 5719 Miscellaneous homefurnishings
Stephen J. Shiller
Nkere Udofia
Richard Shiller

D-U-N-S 20-181-2547   (SL)
CANADIENNE DE CROISSANCE
3795 Rue Masson Bureau 108, Montreal, QC,
H1X 1S7

Emp Here 1   *Sales* 14,539,596
SIC 8741 Management services
Philippe (Filit) Walesa

D-U-N-S 25-479-6709   (SL)
COLLEGE DE ROSEMONT
6400 16e Av, Montreal, QC, H1X 2S9
(514) 376-1620
Emp Here 450   *Sales* 44,603,550
SIC 8222 Junior colleges
Stephane Godbout

D-U-N-S 20-884-3698   (SL)
COLLEGE JEAN-EUDES INC
3535 Boul Rosemont, Montreal, QC, H1X 1K7
(514) 376-5740
Emp Here 100   *Sales* 10,054,800
SIC 8211 Elementary and secondary schools
Nancy Desbiens
Helene Gaudet Chandler

D-U-N-S 25-240-7069   (BR)
COMMISSION SCOLAIRE DE MONTREAL
*ECOLE   SAINTE-BERNADETTE-
SOUBIROUS*
(Suby of COMMISSION SCOLAIRE DE
MONTREAL)
6855 16e Av, Montreal, QC, H1X 2T5
(514) 596-4166
Emp Here 80
SIC 8211 Elementary and secondary schools
Diane Paquette

D-U-N-S 25-690-4137   (HQ)
COMMISSION SCOLAIRE DE MONTREAL
CSDM
3737 Rue Sherbrooke E, Montreal, QC, H1X
3B3
(514) 596-6000
Emp Here 367   *Sales* 809,009,278
SIC 8211 Elementary and secondary schools
Catherine Harel Bourdon
Marie-Jose Mastromonaco

D-U-N-S 20-301-1379   (BR)
**GOUVERNEMENT DE LA PROVINCE DE
QUEBEC**
*CHSLD   CENTRE   D'HEBERGEMENT
ROBERT CLICHE*

(Suby of GOUVERNEMENT   DE   LA
PROVINCE DE QUEBEC)
3730 Rue De Bellechasse, Montreal, QC, H1X
3E5
(514) 374-8665
Emp Here 125
SIC 8361 Residential care
Renee Pettigrew

D-U-N-S 25-456-9130   (BR)
MARCHE J.C. MESSIER INC
METRO ST-JOSEPH
(Suby of PLACEMENTS C. D. F. G. INC)
3600 Boul Saint-Joseph E, Montreal, QC, H1X
1W6
(514) 254-2950
Emp Here 100
SIC 5411 Grocery stores
Gilles Messier

D-U-N-S 20-960-5120   (HQ)
**SOEURS DE LA PRESENTATION DE MARIE
DU QUEBEC**
3600 Rue Belanger, Montreal, QC, H1X 1B1
(514) 721-4979
Emp Here 2   *Sales* 10,772,700
SIC 8661 Religious organizations
Clemence Moreau
Gisele Patenaude

D-U-N-S 20-762-3521   (HQ)
**UNIVESTA ASSURANCES & SERVICES FI-
NANCIERS INC**
3925 Rue Rachel E Bureau 100, Montreal,
QC, H1X 3G8
(514) 899-5377
Emp Here 65   *Sales* 129,341,940
SIC 6411 Insurance agents, brokers, and ser-
vice
Bernard Chagnon
Bruno Simard

D-U-N-S 20-503-6551   (SL)
VOYAGES MALAVOY INC
CLUB VOYAGE MALAVOY
3425 Rue Beaubien E, Montreal, QC, H1X
1G8
(514) 286-7559
Emp Here 26   *Sales* 10,019,360
SIC 4724 Travel agencies
Odette Thomas

Montreal, QC H1Y

D-U-N-S 20-051-6479   (HQ)
2330-2029 QUEBEC INC
MEDICUS
(Suby of INDUSTRIES J C BLEAU LTEE)
5135 10e Av, Montreal, QC, H1Y 2G5
(514) 525-3757
Emp Here 50   *Sales* 30,296,672
SIC 5999 Miscellaneous retail stores, nec
Jacinte Bleau
Michel Coutu
Normand Messier
Michel Lanctot

D-U-N-S 24-991-0683   (SL)
9138-1616 QUEBEC INC
MITO SUSHI
4600 Rue Molson, Montreal, QC, H1Y 0A3
(514) 223-2600
Emp Here 160   *Sales* 25,681,190
SIC 5149 Groceries and related products, nec
Serge Mboumtcho
Ngoc Vu Nguyen

D-U-N-S 25-680-1635   (SL)
ALIMENTATION MARC BOUGIE INC
PROVIGO MARC BOUGIE
3185 Rue Beaubien E, Montreal, QC, H1Y
1H5
(514) 721-2433
Emp Here 75   *Sales* 22,010,775
SIC 5411 Grocery stores

Marc Bougie

D-U-N-S 24-390-0730   (SL)
**ALIMENTATION POIVRE ET SEL LA CHAR-
CUTIERE INC**
*ALIMENTATION   POIVRE   ET   SEL   LA
PATISSIERE*
3245 Rue Masson, Montreal, QC, H1Y 1Y4
(514) 374-3611
Emp Here 26   *Sales* 21,725,002
SIC 5149 Groceries and related products, nec
Ivan Cote
Robert Sauro
Pasquale Casale

D-U-N-S 25-244-1423   (HQ)
ALIMENTATION TRACY INC
NEPCO
4900 Rue Molson, Montreal, QC, H1Y 3J8
(450) 743-0644
Emp Here 2   *Sales* 41,778,850
SIC 5146 Fish and seafoods
Gilles Ferron

D-U-N-S 25-537-4977   (SL)
ALTO DESIGN INC
2600 Rue William-Tremblay Bureau 220, Mon-
treal, QC, H1Y 3J2
(514) 278-3050
Emp Here 24   *Sales* 10,781,256
SIC 7389 Business services, nec
Mario Gagnon

D-U-N-S 20-326-4028   (SL)
**ASSOCIATION DES POMPIERS DE MON-
TREAL INC**
ADPM
2655 Place Chasse 2e Etage, Montreal, QC,
H1Y 2C3
(514) 527-9691
Emp Here 1,000   *Sales* 284,802,000
SIC 8631 Labor organizations
Christopher Ross
Richard Lafortune
Luc Boisvert
Francois Rosa

D-U-N-S 20-574-0090   (SL)
ASSURANCE BURROWES INC
2600 Boul Saint-Joseph E Bureau 206, Montreal, QC, H1Y 2A4
(514) 522-2661
Emp Here 30   *Sales* 17,397,720
SIC 6411 Insurance agents, brokers, and service
Louise Piche

D-U-N-S 25-140-9587   (SL)
BURROWES COURTIERS D'ASSURANCES
2647 Place Chasse, Montreal, QC, H1Y 2C3
(514) 522-2661
Emp Here 49   *Sales* 41,554,940
SIC 6411 Insurance agents, brokers, and ser-
vice
John Burrowes

D-U-N-S 24-085-0099   (SL)
**CENTRE D'ETUDE ET DE COOPERATION
INTERNATIONALE**
C E C I
3000 Rue Omer-Lavallee, Montreal, QC, H1Y
3R8
(514) 875-9911
Emp Here 200   *Sales* 15,358,400
SIC 8322 Individual and family services
Danielle Lamy
Jean-Francois Michaud
Michelle Bussieres
Yves Alavo

D-U-N-S 25-979-8812   (HQ)
**CORPORATION COMPAGNONS DE MON-
TREAL**
2602 Beaubien E, Montreal, QC, H1Y 1G5
(514) 727-4444
Emp Here 40   *Sales* 10,207,485
SIC 8399 Social services, nec
Louis Lelievre

▲ Public Company   ■ Public Company Family Member   **HQ** Headquarters   **BR** Branch   **SL** Single Location

D-U-N-S 25-210-7669   (SL)
EFFIGIS GEO SOLUTIONS INC
VGI SOLUTIONS
(*Suby of* GROUPE VIASAT INC)
4101 Rue Molson Bureau 400, Montreal, QC, H1Y 3L1
(514) 495-6500
Emp Here 145   *Sales* 20,906,390
SIC 7371 Custom computer programming services
Lovett Lewis
Pierre Vincent
Magella Bouchard
Claude Levasseur
Michel Rheault

D-U-N-S 24-636-9318   (SL)
GESTION QUADRIVIUM LTEE
RACHELLE-BERY PRODUITS NATURELS
2506 Rue Beaubien E, Montreal, QC, H1Y 1G2

Emp Here 100   *Sales* 29,347,700
SIC 5411 Grocery stores
Jacques Van Geenhoven

D-U-N-S 20-363-4923   (HQ)
GRIMARD OPTIQUE INC
3108 Rue Beaubien E, Montreal, QC, H1Y 1H3
(514) 439-0602
Emp Here 6   *Sales* 36,649,200
SIC 5995 Optical goods stores
Robert Grimard

D-U-N-S 20-289-8730   (SL)
INVESTISSEMENT IMMOBILIER CCSM LTEE
APPARTEMENTS DU SQUARE ANGUS, LES
3200 Rue Omer-Lavallee, Montreal, QC, H1Y 3P5
(514) 523-1160
Emp Here 100   *Sales* 22,087,100
SIC 6513 Apartment building operators
Daniel Lussier
Raymond Simard
Raymond Lafond
Robert Lafreniere
Greg Doyle

D-U-N-S 24-698-5188   (HQ)
PECHERIES NORREF QUEBEC INC, LES
NORREF FISHERIES QUEBEC
(*Suby of* GROUPE COLABOR INC)
4900 Rue Molson, Montreal, QC, H1Y 3J8
(514) 593-9999
Sales 107,507,400
SIC 5146 Fish and seafoods
Lionel Ettedgui
Josee Gagnon

D-U-N-S 24-593-8449   (SL)
PROLUXON INC
5549 Boul Saint-Michel, Montreal, QC, H1Y 2C9
(514) 374-4993
Emp Here 55   *Sales* 11,980,595
SIC 1731 Electrical work
Valy Tremblay

D-U-N-S 20-253-3980   (SL)
QUINCAILLERIE BEAUBIEN INC
CLIMATISATION BEAUBIEN
3194 Rue Beaubien E, Montreal, QC, H1Y 1H4
(514) 727-0525
Emp Here 30   *Sales* 13,415,220
SIC 5072 Hardware
Serge Blain
Pauline Blain
Andre Blain

D-U-N-S 25-918-5361   (BR)
RESEARCH HOUSE INC
QUEBEC RECHERCHES
(*Suby of* RESEARCH HOUSE INC)
2953 Rue Belanger Bureau 214, Montreal, QC, H1Y 3G4

Emp Here 80
SIC 8732 Commercial nonphysical research
Mau Lao

D-U-N-S 20-236-9450   (SL)
SAFILO CANADA INC
4800 Rue Molson, Montreal, QC, H1Y 3J8
(514) 521-2555
Emp Here 40   *Sales* 17,886,960
SIC 5049 Professional equipment, nec
Giannino Lorenzon
Claudio Gottardi
Vittorio Tabacchi

D-U-N-S 25-467-2173   (HQ)
TRANSPLANT QUEBEC
4100 Rue Molson Bureau 200, Montreal, QC, H1Y 3N1
(514) 286-1414
Sales 11,714,400
SIC 8742 Management consulting services
Jean Gravel
Louis Beaulieu

Montreal, QC H1Z

D-U-N-S 24-970-9015   (HQ)
2920409 CANADA INC
BOULANGERIE BON MARCHE CANTOR
8575 8e Av, Montreal, QC, H1Z 2X2
(514) 374-2700
Sales 58,490,390
SIC 5149 Groceries and related products, nec
Maxwell Cantor

D-U-N-S 20-305-3439   (SL)
3727513 CANADA INC
PLATINUM FASHIONS
8920 Boul Pie-Ix Bureau 300, Montreal, QC, H1Z 4H9
(514) 328-7212
Emp Here 20   *Sales* 10,122,394
SIC 5131 Piece goods and notions
Pat Polifroni
Pina Polifroni

D-U-N-S 25-686-1337   (SL)
3727513 CANADA INC
PLATINUM FASHIONS 2000
8920 Boul Pie-Ix Bureau 300, Montreal, QC, H1Z 4H9
(514) 328-9220
Emp Here 30   *Sales* 14,949,660
SIC 5136 Men's and boy's clothing
Pat Polifroni
Angelo Verelli
Pina Polifroni

D-U-N-S 20-309-0642   (SL)
4019636 CANADA INC
ALIMENTS KIM PHAT (JARRY), LES
(*Suby of* EMPIRE COMPANY LIMITED)
3733 Rue Jarry E Bureau A, Montreal, QC, H1Z 2G1
(514) 727-8919
Emp Here 26   *Sales* 21,725,002
SIC 5141 Groceries, general line
Kok Chang Yip
Alex Yip
Sebastien Bellehumeur
Yvan Ouellet
Alain Menard

D-U-N-S 25-894-5708   (SL)
9013-6573 QUEBEC INC
S I R SOLUTIONS
3565 Rue Jarry E Bureau 650, Montreal, QC, H1Z 4K6
(514) 593-5012
Emp Here 70   *Sales* 10,092,740
SIC 7371 Custom computer programming services
Gilles Beauchamp

D-U-N-S 20-031-4255   (SL)

9058-7239 QUEBEC INC
PAYSANNE FRUITS & LEGUMES, LA
9250 Boul Pie-Ix, Montreal, QC, H1Z 4H7
(514) 850-0020
Emp Here 42   *Sales* 35,094,234
SIC 5148 Fresh fruits and vegetables
Eric Bergeron

D-U-N-S 24-363-6979   (SL)
9117-4227 QUEBEC INC
ELECTRONIQUE ADDISON
8018 20e Av, Montreal, QC, H1Z 3S7
(514) 376-1740
Emp Here 50   *Sales* 22,358,700
SIC 5065 Electronic parts and equipment, nec
Christian Labreche
Yves Labreche

D-U-N-S 20-412-6516   (HQ)
9790446 CANADA INC
9455 Rue J.-J.-Gagnier, Montreal, QC, H1Z 3C8
(514) 384-0660
Sales 41,002,500
SIC 6712 Bank holding companies
Andre Lessard
Richard Lessard

D-U-N-S 24-363-8793   (SL)
ALIMENTS BERCY INC, LES
(*Suby of* MICHAL INC)
9210 Boul Pie-Ix, Montreal, QC, H1Z 4H7
(514) 528-6262
Emp Here 120   *Sales* 20,868,600
SIC 0723 Crop preparation services for market
Michel Routhier
Alain Routhier

D-U-N-S 20-547-7495   (SL)
ALTERNATURE INC
9210 Boul Pie-Ix, Montreal, QC, H1Z 4H7
(514) 382-7520
Emp Here 100   *Sales* 44,921,900
SIC 7389 Business services, nec
Jean-Francois Laverdure

D-U-N-S 25-489-4710   (SL)
BEAVER FASHIONS LIMITED
3565 Rue Jarry E Bureau 109, Montreal, QC, H1Z 4K6
(514) 721-1180
Emp Here 30   *Sales* 13,304,700
SIC 7389 Business services, nec
Frank Marzoli

D-U-N-S 20-223-9604   (HQ)
BELRON CANADA INCORPOREE
(*Suby of* D'IETEREN)
8288 Boul Pie-Ix, Montreal, QC, H1Z 3T6
(514) 593-7000
Emp Here 250   *Sales* 152,483,200
SIC 7536 Automotive glass replacement shops
Claude Lalonde
David Miller
Gary Lubner
Robert Harritt

D-U-N-S 20-211-7651   (SL)
BERWIL LTEE
8651 9e Av Bureau 1, Montreal, QC, H1Z 3A1
(514) 376-0121
Emp Here 50   *Sales* 11,653,250
SIC 1711 Plumbing, heating, air-conditioning
Brian Bergeron
Edouard Bergeron Jr
Edouard Bergeron Sr

D-U-N-S 20-887-1053   (SL)
BOUTRY CANADA LTEE
2170 Av Charland, Montreal, QC, H1Z 1B1

Emp Here 22   *Sales* 10,450,572
SIC 5087 Service establishment equipment
Yvon Tessier

D-U-N-S 25-479-5388   (HQ)

CENTRE DE PIECES ET SERVICES EXPERT INC
ELECTRO EXPERTS
8260 Boul Pie-Ix, Montreal, QC, H1Z 3T6
(514) 943-5755
Emp Here 15   *Sales* 72,530,875
SIC 5064 Electrical appliances, television and radio
Normand Brasseur
Karl Brasseur

D-U-N-S 20-331-4294   (HQ)
CIRQUE DU SOLEIL CANADA INC
EDITIONS GROMMELOT
8400 2e Av, Montreal, QC, H1Z 4M6
(514) 722-2324
Sales 86,700,000
SIC 7999 Amusement and recreation, nec
Daniel Lamarre
Jonathan Tetrault
Jocelyn Cote
Stephane Lefebvre
David Trujillo

D-U-N-S 24-970-5229   (HQ)
CIRQUE DU SOLEIL INC
GROUPE CIRQUE DU SOLEIL
(*Suby of* CIRQUE DU SOLEIL CANADA INC)
Cirque Du Soleil, Montreal, QC, H1Z 4M6
(514) 722-2324
Emp Here 2,560   *Sales* 346,800,000
SIC 7999 Amusement and recreation, nec

D-U-N-S 25-257-4348   (SL)
CLSC DE SAINT-MICHEL
3355 Rue Jarry E, Montreal, QC, H1Z 2E5
(514) 374-8223
Emp Here 150   *Sales* 31,060,200
SIC 8399 Social services, nec
Pierre Durocher

D-U-N-S 20-024-6564   (BR)
COMMISSION SCOLAIRE DE MONTREAL
ECOLE POLYVALENTE LOUIS JOSEPH PAPINEAU
(*Suby of* COMMISSION SCOLAIRE DE MONTREAL)
2901 Rue De Louvain E, Montreal, QC, H1Z 1J7
(514) 596-5353
Emp Here 180
SIC 8211 Elementary and secondary schools
Pierre Gagnon

D-U-N-S 24-527-1523   (SL)
CONFECTIONS STROMA INC., LES
3565 Rue Jarry E Bureau 501, Montreal, QC, H1Z 4K6
(514) 381-8422
Emp Here 30   *Sales* 13,304,700
SIC 7389 Business services, nec
Maria De Palma

D-U-N-S 24-959-1140   (BR)
CORPORATION MCKESSON CANADA, LA
MCKESSON SERVICES PHARMACEUTIQUES
(*Suby of* MCKESSON FINANCIAL HOLDINGS II UNLIMITED COMPANY)
8290 Boul Pie-Ix Bureau 1, Montreal, QC, H1Z 4E8
(514) 593-4531
Emp Here 250
SIC 5122 Drugs, proprietaries, and sundries
Dominic Pilla

D-U-N-S 24-739-7672   (SL)
CREATIONS SERGIO CANUTO INC
3637 Boul Cremazie, Montreal, QC, H1Z 2J4
(514) 729-1116
Emp Here 24   *Sales* 10,643,760
SIC 7389 Business services, nec
Gino Canuto

D-U-N-S 20-215-1940   (HQ)
DECORS DE MAISON COMMONWEALTH INC

ART LINEN MANUFACTURING
8800 Boul Pie-Ix, Montreal, QC, H1Z 3V1
(514) 384-8290
Sales 39,865,760
SIC 5131 Piece goods and notions
Harvey Levenson
David Levenson

D-U-N-S 24-254-5085   (HQ)
DESCAIR INC
AIRCO
(*Suby of* ENTREPRISES MIRCA INC, LES)
8335 Boul Saint-Michel, Montreal, QC, H1Z
3E6
(514) 744-6751
Emp Here 40   *Sales* 22,358,700
SIC 5078 Refrigeration equipment and sup-
plies
Francois Deschenes
Jacques Deschenes
Martin Deschenes
Marc Lapierre

D-U-N-S 20-793-4605   (HQ)
DESCHENES & FILS LTEE
BALISCUS L'ESPACE EAU ET PLOMBERIE
(*Suby of* ENTREPRISES MIRCA INC, LES)
3901 Rue Jarry E Bureau 100, Montreal, QC,
H1Z 2G1
(514) 374-3110
Emp Here 140   *Sales* 115,011,000
SIC 5074 Plumbing and heating equipment
and supplies (hydronics)
Martin Deschenes
Francois Deschenes
Jacques Deschenes
Marc Lapierre

D-U-N-S 20-216-8241   (SL)
DIVCO LIMITEE
(*Suby of* IMMEUBLES SINGLE TROIS LIMI-
TEE, LES)
8300 Boul Pie-Ix, Montreal, QC, H1Z 4E8
(514) 593-8888
Emp Here 40   *Sales* 16,909,480
SIC 1541 Industrial buildings and warehouses
Adam Turner
Bruno Guerrera
Jocelyn Gagnon
Jordan Aberman

D-U-N-S 25-233-9577   (SL)
ECOLE NATIONALE DE CIRQUE
8181 2e Av, Montreal, QC, H1Z 4N9
(514) 982-0859
Emp Here 100   *Sales* 9,282,600
SIC 8211 Elementary and secondary schools
Sebastien Guenette
Jocelyn Beaudoin
Marc Gagnon
Stephane Achard
Pierre Carrier
Marc Lalonde
Claude Bedard
Luc Filiatreault
David J. Forest
Normand Legault

D-U-N-S 20-530-9912   (HQ)
ENTREPOT DE MONTREAL 1470 INC
ATELIER M.C AUTO XPERT
(*Suby of* GROUPE MONACO AUTOMOTIVE
INC)
3455 Rue Jarry E, Montreal, QC, H1Z 2G1
(514) 374-9880
Sales 92,230,800
SIC 5013 Motor vehicle supplies and new
parts
Domenico Monaco

D-U-N-S 24-434-7225   (HQ)
ENTREPRISES MIRCA INC, LES
3901 Rue Jarry E Bureau 250, Montreal, QC,
H1Z 2G1
(514) 253-3110
Sales 490,513,078
SIC 6712 Bank holding companies

Jacques Deschenes
Monique Champagne
Eric Deschenes
Francois Deschenes
Martin Deschenes

D-U-N-S 24-322-2788   (SL)
**FEDERATION   AUTONOME   DE
L'ENSEIGNEMENT**
400-8550 Boul Pie-Ix, Montreal, QC, H1Z 4G2
(514) 666-7763
Emp Here 26   *Sales* 10,170,108
SIC 8631 Labor organizations
Sylvain Malette

D-U-N-S 20-309-4024   (BR)
G&K SERVICES CANADA INC
(*Suby of* CINTAS CORPORATION)
8400 19e Av, Montreal, QC, H1Z 4J3
(514) 723-7666
Emp Here 300
SIC 7213 Linen supply
Jean-Francois Gravel

D-U-N-S 25-400-8485   (HQ)
GESTION FETIA INC
8400 2e Av, Montreal, QC, H1Z 4M6
(514) 722-2324
Sales 73,101,800
SIC 6712 Bank holding companies

D-U-N-S 24-393-0315   (SL)
GESTION RENE J. BEAUDOIN INC
CANADIAN TIRE
2225 Boul Cremazie E, Montreal, QC, H1Z
4N4
(514) 729-1861
Emp Here 90   *Sales* 18,480,870
SIC 5311 Department stores
Rene J Beaudoin

D-U-N-S 20-290-5071   (SL)
GILDAN APPAREL (CANADA) LP
3701 Rue Jarry E, Montreal, QC, H1Z 2G1
(514) 376-3000
Emp Here 300   *Sales* 70,950,900
SIC 2252 Hosiery, nec
Glenn Chamandy

D-U-N-S 24-823-7997   (SL)
GLOBAL RESSOURCES HUMAINES INC
3737 Boul Cremazie E Bureau 400, Montreal,
QC, H1Z 2K4
(514) 788-0599
Emp Here 100   *Sales* 26,155,300
SIC 6712 Bank holding companies
Marc-Andre Robert
Richard Dufour

D-U-N-S 24-224-2147   (SL)
GRAND PRIX IMPORT INC
8275 17e Av, Montreal, QC, H1Z 4J9
(514) 328-2300
Emp Here 29   *Sales* 10,562,235
SIC 5013 Motor vehicle supplies and new
parts
Raphael Iovannone
Domenic Iovannone
Fabio Iovannone
Marie Iovannone

D-U-N-S 24-858-1258   (HQ)
GROUPE DESCHENES INC
LES GROSSISTES P & H
(*Suby of* ENTREPRISES MIRCA INC, LES)
3901 Rue Jarry E Bureau 250, Montreal, QC,
H1Z 2G1
(514) 253-3110
Emp Here 49   *Sales* 604,917,395
SIC 6712 Bank holding companies
Francois Deschenes
Martin Deschenes
Marc Lapierre
Jacques Deschenes
Gilles Leroux
Richard Lord
John Le Boutillier
Andrew T. Molson

Eric Deschenes

D-U-N-S 25-286-9854   (HQ)
GROUPE MEQUALTECH INC
8740 Boul Pie-Ix, Montreal, QC, H1Z 3V1
(514) 593-5755
Sales 10,462,120
SIC 6712 Bank holding companies
Robert Desautels
Alexandre Desautels
Nathalie Desautels
Paulette Lussie

D-U-N-S 24-814-5963   (HQ)
GUESS? CANADA CORPORATION
GUESS? CANADA DETAIL
(*Suby of* GUESS? EUROPE, B.V.)
8275 19e Av, Montreal, QC, H1Z 4K2
(514) 593-4107
Emp Here 58   *Sales* 1,005,039,600
SIC 5136 Men's and boy's clothing
Victor Herrero
Teri Manby
Jason Miller

D-U-N-S 20-220-9029   (SL)
HAMILTON LINGERIE (1978) LTD
BELLINA LINGERIE
3565 Rue Jarry E Bureau 600, Montreal, QC,
H1Z 4K6
(514) 721-2151
Emp Here 120   *Sales* 16,400,880
SIC 2341 Women's and children's underwear
Sylvie Messina

D-U-N-S 20-227-1235   (HQ)
INDUSTRIES MIDWAY LTEE
AERO
8270 Boul Pie-Ix, Montreal, QC, H1Z 3T6
(514) 722-1122
Emp Here 1   *Sales* 16,593,969
SIC 5136 Men's and boy's clothing
Craig Bromberg
Franco Messina

D-U-N-S 20-234-6557   (SL)
INDUSTRIES SPLEND'OR LTEE, LES
8660 8e Av, Montreal, QC, H1Z 2W8

Emp Here 80   *Sales* 14,672,240
SIC 2253 Knit outerwear mills
John Caporicci
Paolo Caporicci
Alessio Caporicci

D-U-N-S 24-762-2558   (HQ)
J.P. LESSARD CANADA INC
(*Suby of* 9790446 CANADA INC)
9455 Rue J.-J.-Gagnier, Montreal, QC, H1Z
3C8
(514) 384-0660
Sales 34,959,750
SIC 1711 Plumbing, heating, air-conditioning
Andre Lessard
Richard Lessard

D-U-N-S 24-886-9641   (HQ)
KEURIG CANADA INC
VKI TECHNOLOGIES
(*Suby of* KEURIG DR PEPPER INC.)
3700 Rue Jean-Rivard Bureau 1, Montreal,
QC, H1Z 4K3
(514) 593-7711
Emp Here 25   *Sales* 17,284,500
SIC 2095 Roasted coffee
Stephane Glorieux
Mike Degnan
Peter G. Leemputte
Ozan Dokmemecioglu
Alberto Mouron
Jean-Daniel Gervais
Chris Mcmahon
Caroline Losson
Jean-Olivier Boucher
Eric Brassard

D-U-N-S 24-404-4426   (SL)
LABORATOIRE D'ESSAIS MEQUALTECH

INC
(*Suby of* GROUPE MEQUALTECH INC)
8740 Boul Pie-Ix, Montreal, QC, H1Z 3V1
(514) 593-5755
Emp Here 90   *Sales* 60,201,720
SIC 7389 Business services, nec
Robert Desautels
Nathalie Desautels

D-U-N-S 24-180-0184   (SL)
LANGEVIN & FOREST LTEE
CONNAISSEURS DE BOIS
9995 Boul Pie-Ix, Montreal, QC, H1Z 3X1
(514) 322-9330
Emp Here 55   *Sales* 14,720,860
SIC 5211 Lumber and other building materials
Henri Turcot

D-U-N-S 25-201-5201   (SL)
MEMTRONIK INNOVATIONS INC
CLAVIERS MEMTRONIK, LES
8648 Boul Pie-Ix, Montreal, QC, H1Z 4G2
(514) 374-1010
Emp Here 80   *Sales* 15,235,360
SIC 3613 Switchgear and switchboard appa-
ratus
Stephane Forget

D-U-N-S 20-357-3605   (SL)
METAL ARTECH INC
9455 Rue J.-J.-Gagnier, Montreal, QC, H1Z
3C8
(514) 384-0660
Emp Here 200   *Sales* 38,417,000
SIC 3444 Sheet Metalwork
Andre Lessard
Richard Lessard

D-U-N-S 24-648-2665   (SL)
PIE IX DODGE CHRYSLER 2000 INC
CARROSSIER PROCOLOR PIE IX
9350 Boul Pie-Ix, Montreal, QC, H1Z 4E9
(514) 342-8500
Emp Here 80   *Sales* 50,342,400
SIC 5511 New and used car dealers
Claude Leclair
Caroline Mcfarlane-Leclair
Marc Champagne

D-U-N-S 24-082-2148   (SL)
RACINE & CHAMBERLAND INC
ASSURANCE DECENNALE
4001 Boul Cremazie E Bureau 100, Montreal,
QC, H1Z 2L2
(514) 722-3501
Emp Here 25   *Sales* 14,498,100
SIC 6411 Insurance agents, brokers, and ser-
vice
Sylvain Racine

D-U-N-S 20-796-0050   (BR)
REBUTS SOLIDES CANADIENS INC
GROUPE TIRU
2240 Rue Michel-Jurdant, Montreal, QC, H1Z
4N7
(514) 593-9211
Emp Here 100
SIC 7389 Business services, nec
Marc Andre Gouin

D-U-N-S 24-356-9469   (HQ)
SERVICES DE CAFE VAN HOUTTE INC
CAFE SELENA
(*Suby of* KEURIG DR PEPPER INC.)
3700 Rue Jean-Rivard, Montreal, QC, H1Z
4K3
(514) 593-7711
Emp Here 1   *Sales* 695,957,600
SIC 5046 Commercial equipment, nec
Sylvain Toutant
Michel Slight
Jean-Olivier Boucher
Robert Valcourt

D-U-N-S 25-483-7339   (BR)
SERVICES DE CAFE VAN HOUTTE INC
VAN HOUTTE
(*Suby of* KEURIG DR PEPPER INC.)

8215 17e Av, Montreal, QC, H1Z 4J9
(514) 728-2233
Emp Here 100
SIC 7389 Business services, nec
Denis Sarranin

D-U-N-S 20-706-9266   (BR)
SIEMENS CANADA LIMITED
SIEMENS TECHNOLOGIES DU BATIMENT
(*Suby of* SIEMENS AG)
8455 19e Av, Montreal, QC, H1Z 4J2

Emp Here 125
SIC 5999 Miscellaneous retail stores, nec
Marcel Laflamme

D-U-N-S 25-361-6437   (BR)
SIEMENS CANADA LIMITED
SIEMENS PROTECTION INCENDIE
(*Suby of* SIEMENS AG)
8455 19e Av, Montreal, QC, H1Z 4J2

Emp Here 130
SIC 5063 Electrical apparatus and equipment
Marcel Laflamme

D-U-N-S 20-229-6133   (HQ)
VETEMENTS PEERLESS INC
(*Suby of* PLACEMENTS BAREJO SRI, LES)
8888 Boul Pie-Ix, Montreal, QC, H1Z 4J5
(514) 593-9300
Sales 291,868,500
SIC 2311 Men's and boy's suits and coats
Alvin Segal
Joel Segal
Barbara Segal
Renee Segal

Montreal, QC H2A

D-U-N-S 20-165-7702   (HQ)
3225518 CANADA INC
VOYAGES JET-SET
2590 Rue Jean-Talon E, Montreal, QC, H2A
1T9
(514) 847-1287
Emp Here 6   *Sales* 12,999,175
SIC 4724 Travel agencies
Malik Hadid

D-U-N-S 25-362-1908   (SL)
**ALIMENTS ESPOSITO (ST-MICHEL) LTEE,
LES**
7030 Boul Saint-Michel, Montreal, QC, H2A
2Z4
(514) 722-1069
Emp Here 40   *Sales* 10,966,080
SIC 5411 Grocery stores
Angelo Esposito
Antonio Esposito
Johnny Esposito

Montreal, QC H2B

D-U-N-S 25-756-2975   (SL)
PHARMACIE RENE RIVARD
2330 Rue Fleury E, Montreal, QC, H2B 1K9
(514) 387-7102
Emp Here 71   *Sales* 17,347,288
SIC 5912 Drug stores and proprietary stores
Rene Rivard

D-U-N-S 25-757-0812   (SL)
**SERVICES DE SANTE LES RAYONS DE
SOLEIL INC**
2055 Rue Sauve E Bureau 100, Montreal, QC,
H2B 1A8
(514) 383-7555
Emp Here 70   *Sales* 10,875,970
SIC 7363 Help supply services
Gabrielle Simic

D-U-N-S 20-714-9399   (SL)
**SYNDICAT DES TRAVAILLEUSES & TRA-
VAILLEURS DE LA CSN DU CSSS DU AM-N**
2180 Rue Fleury E, Montreal, QC, H2B 1K3
(514) 383-5054
Emp Here 49   *Sales* 19,166,742
SIC 8631 Labor organizations
Robert Poisson

Montreal, QC H2C

D-U-N-S 20-124-5086   (SL)
**CENTRE DE RESSOURCES EDUCATIVES
ET COMMUNAUTAIRES POUR ADULTES**
CRECA
10770 Rue Chambord, Montreal, QC, H2C
2R8
(514) 596-7629
Emp Here 27   *Sales* 12,128,913
SIC 7389 Business services, nec
Claude Ampleman
Danielle Prince
Max De La Huerta
Diane Mayer
Denise Brunelle
Mina Islahen
Francoise Dube
Amutan Subashini
Luigi Amari

D-U-N-S 20-972-4418   (SL)
COLLEGE MONT-SAINT-LOUIS
1700 Boul Henri-Bourassa E, Montreal, QC,
H2C 1J3
(514) 382-1560
Emp Here 120   *Sales* 11,894,280
SIC 8211 Elementary and secondary schools
Michel Gigon
Andre Lacroix

D-U-N-S 20-979-6879   (SL)
COLLEGE REGINA ASSUMPTA (1995)
*CENTRE CULTUREL & SPORTIF REGINA
ASSUMPTA*
1750 Rue Sauriol E, Montreal, QC, H2C 1X4
(514) 382-9998
Emp Here 250   *Sales* 24,779,750
SIC 8211 Elementary and secondary schools
Nicole Brodeue
Ida Teoli
Jacqueline Villeneuve
Michel Guindon
Ann-Marie Colizza
Marc Lamirande
Josee Provost
Veronique Boussion
Carole Gaudin
Michel Laplante

D-U-N-S 20-482-4531   (SL)
**JEAN COUTU ANNIE LAROCHE & MICHEL
ST-GEORGES (AFFILIATED PHARMACIES)**
1221 Rue Fleury E, Montreal, QC, H2C 1R2

Emp Here 49   *Sales* 12,394,746
SIC 5912 Drug stores and proprietary stores
Michel St-Georges

D-U-N-S 20-856-7529   (SL)
RESIDENCE BERTHIAUME-DU TREMBLAY
1635 Rue Gouin E, Montreal, QC, H2C 1C2
(514) 381-1841
Emp Here 310   *Sales* 21,181,060
SIC 8051 Skilled nursing care facilities
Nicole Ouellet
Mario Lariviere
Chantal Bernatchez
Sylvie St-Hilaire
Pierrette Rolland
Roger Bergeron
Lydia Ingenito

D-U-N-S 24-000-2662   (HQ)
UNION DES EMPLOYES ET EMPLOYEES

DE SERVICE, SECTION LOCALE 800
920 Rue De Port-Royal E, Montreal, QC, H2C
2B3
(514) 385-1717
Emp Here 25   *Sales* 19,557,900
SIC 8631 Labor organizations
Raymond Larcher
Claude St-Marseille
Cristina Cabral

Montreal, QC H2E

D-U-N-S 20-819-6555   (SL)
2313-3606 QUEBEC INC
CONSTRUCTION NCL
2251 Rue Jean-Talon E, Montreal, QC, H2E
1V6
(514) 325-0966
Emp Here 50   *Sales* 15,943,450
SIC 1521 Single-family housing construction
Benito Mariano
Luigi Mariano
Carla Mariana

D-U-N-S 24-650-9509   (HQ)
CAFE DEPOT INC, LE
2464 Rue Jean-Talon E, Montreal, QC, H2E
1W2
(514) 281-2067
Emp Here 8   *Sales* 87,757,740
SIC 6794 Patent owners and lessors
Antonio Elisii

D-U-N-S 25-500-0820   (HQ)
CENTRE LA TRAVERSEE
1460 Boul Cremazie E, Montreal, QC, H2E
1A2
(514) 321-4984
Emp Here 130   *Sales* 8,356,660
SIC 8361 Residential care
Joanne Pratte
Ghislaine Brosseau
Michel Lavallee
Ginette Magnan

D-U-N-S 20-031-3901   (BR)
COMMISSION SCOLAIRE DE MONTREAL
ECOLE VICTOR DORE
(*Suby of* COMMISSION SCOLAIRE DE
MONTREAL)
1350 Boul Cremazie E, Montreal, QC, H2E
1A1
(514) 596-4300
Emp Here 100
SIC 8211 Elementary and secondary schools
Anne Alexandre

D-U-N-S 25-233-8009   (BR)
COMMISSION SCOLAIRE DE MONTREAL
*ECOLE SECONDAIRE JOSEPH CHARBON-
NEAU*
(*Suby of* COMMISSION SCOLAIRE DE
MONTREAL)
8200 Rue Rousselot, Montreal, QC, H2E 1Z6
(514) 596-4350
Emp Here 100
SIC 8211 Elementary and secondary schools
Louise Paquette

D-U-N-S 20-655-9655   (SL)
DAMSAR INC
TIM HORTONS
8115 Av Papineau, Montreal, QC, H2E 2H7
(514) 374-0177
Emp Here 50   *Sales* 13,707,600
SIC 5499 Miscellaneous food stores
Nader Azrak

D-U-N-S 20-126-0978   (SL)
**RIVET, PATRICE & MANON ST-JEAN PHAR-
MACIENS SENC**
PHARMACIE JEAN-COUTU
1465 Rue Jean-Talon E Bureau 282, Montreal,
QC, H2E 1S8

(514) 270-2151
Emp Here 100   *Sales* 24,432,800
SIC 5912 Drug stores and proprietary stores
Patrice Rivet
Manon St-Jean

D-U-N-S 20-888-3223   (HQ)
**SYNDICAT DES PROFESSIONNELLES EN
SOINS DU CENTRE DE SANTE ET SER-
VICES SOCIAUX DU COEUR DE**
(*Suby of* GOUVERNEMENT DE LA
PROVINCE DE QUEBEC)
1385 Rue Jean-Talon E, Montreal, QC, H2E
1S6
(514) 495-6767
Emp Here 1,300   *Sales* 222,160,000
SIC 8062 General medical and surgical hospi-
tals
Daniel Gagne
Menad Aba
Pacheco Gonzales
Anny Carpentier
Martine Plante

Montreal, QC H2G

D-U-N-S 20-377-7268   (SL)
9270-6258 QUEBEC INC
TITAN SECURITE
5446 Rue Chapleau Bureau 201, Montreal,
QC, H2G 2E4
(514) 444-9999
Emp Here 50   *Sales* 28,163,298
SIC 7381 Detective and armored car services
Ghenadie Odobescu

D-U-N-S 24-161-5009   (SL)
AVANTAGE PLUS INC
A+ ENTREPRENEURS GENERAUX
5420 Rue Chapleau, Montreal, QC, H2G 2E4
(514) 525-2000
Emp Here 22   *Sales* 10,356,082
SIC 1542 Nonresidential construction, nec
Louis Lachapelle

D-U-N-S 20-158-8618   (SL)
**BOULANGERIE ET FROMENT ET DE SEVE
INC**
2355 Rue Beaubien E, Montreal, QC, H2G
1N3
(514) 722-4301
Emp Here 45   *Sales* 10,118,475
SIC 2051 Bread, cake, and related products
Rene Sicard

D-U-N-S 20-253-1398   (HQ)
**CAISSE DESJARDINS DE LORIMIER-
VILLERAY**
CENTRE DE SERVICE LOISIRS QUEBEC
2050 Boul Rosemont, Montreal, QC, H2G 1T1
(514) 376-7676
Emp Here 10   *Sales* 15,156,100
SIC 6062 State credit unions
Laurent Bourdon
Zoe Berthiaume-Dutrisac
Jean-Pierre Cantin
Michel Richer
Lucille Ouimet
Michel Belisle
Clement Chaput
Nicole Clouatre
Guy Cousineau
Raymond Gagnon

D-U-N-S 20-362-3012   (HQ)
CAISSE DESJARDINS DU COEUR-DE-L'ILE
CENTRE DE SERVICES ANGUS
2050 Boul Rosemont, Montreal, QC, H2G 1T1
(514) 376-7676
Emp Here 50   *Sales* 15,156,100
SIC 6062 State credit unions
Jean-Pierre Cantin
Catherine Bureau-Lavallee
Nicole Clouatre

Guy Cousineau
Michel Richer
Manon Landry
Lucille Ouimet
Isabelle Bernard
Pierre Paul Boucher
Laurent Bourdon

D-U-N-S 24-739-5783   (SL)
CONSTRUCTION IRENEE PAQUET & FILS INC
1300 Rue Saint-Zotique E, Montreal, QC, H2G 1G5
(514) 273-3910
Emp Here 25   *Sales* 11,768,275
SIC 1542 Nonresidential construction, nec
Irenee Paquet
Daniel Paquet
Mario Paquet

D-U-N-S 24-033-8546   (SL)
COURTIER MULTI PLUS INC
5650 Rue D'Iberville Bureau 630, Montreal, QC, H2G 2B3
(514) 376-0313
Emp Here 40   *Sales* 33,922,400
SIC 6411 Insurance agents, brokers, and service
Benoit Despres

D-U-N-S 20-332-5345   (SL)
EKUMEN
6616 Av Des Erables, Montreal, QC, H2G 2N1
(438) 764-7433
Emp Here 1   *Sales* 15,567,760
SIC 7922 Theatrical producers and services
Jacques Poulin-Denis
Olivier Girouard
Eve Garnier
Genadi Voinerchuk
Marie-Christine Girouard

D-U-N-S 20-113-6053   (SL)
GESTION SUMMIT STEPS INC
5700 Rue Fullum, Montreal, QC, H2G 2H7
(514) 271-2358
Emp Here 100   *Sales* 13,667,400
SIC 2387 Apparel belts
Milton Lackman

D-U-N-S 20-104-7854   (HQ)
GROUPE ALIMENTAIRE NORDIQUE INC, LE
NORDIQUE FOOD GROUP
6569 Av Papineau Bureau 100, Montreal, QC, H2G 2X3
(514) 419-3510
Emp Here 2   *Sales* 18,321,570
SIC 2091 Canned and cured fish and seafoods
Gilles Ferron
Stephane Ferron
Marco Ferron

D-U-N-S 25-200-1664   (SL)
MARCHE D'ALIMENTATION MARCANIO & FILS INC
METRO
1550 Rue Belanger, Montreal, QC, H2G 1A8
(514) 729-1866
Emp Here 95   *Sales* 27,880,315
SIC 5411 Grocery stores
Frank Marcanio
Sabatino Marcanio

D-U-N-S 24-607-9110   (SL)
MARCHE MARCANIO ET FILS INC
METRO
1550 Rue Belanger, Montreal, QC, H2G 1A8
(514) 729-1866
Emp Here 49   *Sales* 13,433,448
SIC 5411 Grocery stores
Frank Marcanio

D-U-N-S 25-263-9393   (SL)
MECANICAM AUTO
5612 Rue Cartier, Montreal, QC, H2G 2T9

(514) 495-1007
Emp Here 28   *Sales* 13,946,184
SIC 5511 New and used car dealers
Mario Phenoeu

D-U-N-S 24-047-9639   (SL)
NEPCO INC
ALIMENTATION TRACY
6569 Av Papineau, Montreal, QC, H2G 2X3
(514) 729-0404
Emp Here 26   *Sales* 21,725,002
SIC 5144 Poultry and poultry products
Gilles Ferron
Stephane Ferron
Marco Ferron
Karina Ferron

D-U-N-S 24-728-6011   (SL)
POISSONERIE ODESSA INC., LES
ODESSA
6569 Av Papineau Bureau 100, Montreal, QC, H2G 2X3
(450) 743-9999
Emp Here 49   *Sales* 13,433,448
SIC 5421 Meat and fish markets
Gilles Ferron

D-U-N-S 20-232-9579   (SL)
ROYAL PHOTO INC
2106 Boul Rosemont, Montreal, QC, H2G 1T4
(514) 273-1723
Emp Here 26   *Sales* 11,626,524
SIC 5043 Photographic equipment and supplies
Felix Morin
Denis Morin

D-U-N-S 20-926-6600   (SL)
SERVICES DOCUMENTAIRES MULTIMEDIA (S.D.M) INC
SDM
5650 Rue D'Iberville Bureau 620, Montreal, QC, H2G 2B3
(514) 382-0895
Emp Here 60   *Sales* 12,342,360
SIC 4226 Special warehousing and storage, nec
Louis Cabral
Jocelyne Dion
Marcel Forest
Lise Gosselin
Francine Bergeron
Martine Simard
Sylvie Thibault
Phillippe Sauvageau

D-U-N-S 24-249-8892   (SL)
XYZ TECHNOLOGIE CULTURELLE INC
ACTO
5700 Rue Fullum, Montreal, QC, H2G 2H7
(514) 340-7717
Emp Here 70   *Sales* 34,118,420
SIC 8999 Services, nec
Eric Cyr
Jacques Larue
Dildel Lavoie
Simon Terriar
Joel Beauchamp

Montreal, QC H2H

D-U-N-S 24-834-3006   (SL)
157971 CANADA INC
SIGNATURE SERVICE D'ENTRETIEN
4315 Rue Frontenac Bureau 200, Montreal, QC, H2H 2M4
(514) 527-1146
Emp Here 200   *Sales* 6,393,600
SIC 7349 Building maintenance services, nec
Robert Barbeau
Jacques Marion

D-U-N-S 20-290-5733   (SL)
8782601 CANADA INC
ECHAFAUDAGE IMPACT

4293 Rue Hogan, Montreal, QC, H2H 2N2
(514) 931-7228
Emp Here 50   *Sales* 23,751,300
SIC 5082 Construction and mining machinery
Steve White

D-U-N-S 24-177-7820   (SL)
ALIMEX INC
4425 Rue D'Iberville, Montreal, QC, H2H 2L7
(514) 522-5700
Emp Here 26   *Sales* 11,626,524
SIC 5046 Commercial equipment, nec
Marcel Castonguay
Pierre Castonguay

D-U-N-S 24-667-8395   (SL)
C L S C PLATEAU MONT-ROYAL
4689 Av Papineau, Montreal, QC, H2H 1V4
(514) 521-7663
Emp Here 160   *Sales* 12,286,720
SIC 8322 Individual and family services
Daniel Leblanc

D-U-N-S 20-370-4965   (BR)
CENTRE INTEGRE UNIVERSITAIRE SANTE ET SERVICES SOCIAUX DU CENTRE-SUD-DE-L'ILE-DE-MONTREAL
CENTRE DE READAPTATION LUCIE-BRUNEAU
(*Suby of* CENTRE INTEGRE UNIVERSITAIRE SANTE ET SERVICES SOCIAUX DU CENTRE-SUD-DE-L'ILE-DE-MONTREAL)
2275 Av Laurier E, Montreal, QC, H2H 2N8
(514) 527-4527
Emp Here 500
SIC 8011 Offices and clinics of medical doctors

D-U-N-S 24-346-5312   (BR)
CENTRE INTEGRE UNIVERSITAIRE SANTE ET SERVICES SOCIAUX DU CENTRE-SUD-DE-L'ILE-DE-MONTREAL
CENTRE DE READAPTATION LUCIE-BRUNEAU
(*Suby of* CENTRE INTEGRE UNIVERSITAIRE SANTE ET SERVICES SOCIAUX DU CENTRE-SUD-DE-L'ILE-DE-MONTREAL)
2222 Av Laurier E, Montreal, QC, H2H 1C4
(514) 527-4527
Emp Here 200
SIC 8011 Offices and clinics of medical doctors
Mario Carpentier

D-U-N-S 20-545-6424   (SL)
CENTRE PERE SABLON
CAMP DE JOUR DU CENTRE DE LOISIRS IMMACULEE-CONCEPTION
4265 Av Papineau, Montreal, QC, H2H 1T3
(514) 527-1256
Emp Here 100   *Sales* 7,854,500
SIC 7997 Membership sports and recreation clubs
Hubert Sibre
Isabelle Theroux
Francois Godbout
Celine Carriere
Felix Furst
Martine Quintal
Andre Charon
Laurent Godbout
Angele Martineau
Joel Therriault

D-U-N-S 20-031-3976   (BR)
COMMISSION DES SERVICES ELECTRIQUES DE MONTREAL
COMMISSION DES SERVICES ELECTRIQUES DE LA VILLE DE MONTREAL
(*Suby of* COMMISSION DES SERVICES ELECTRIQUES DE MONTREAL)
4305 Rue Hogan, Montreal, QC, H2H 2N2
(514) 868-3111
Emp Here 100
SIC 1799 Special trade contractors, nec
Denis Leblanc

D-U-N-S 25-240-0817   (BR)
COMMISSION SCOLAIRE DE MONTREAL
ECOLE SAINT PIERRE CLAVER
(*Suby of* COMMISSION SCOLAIRE DE MONTREAL)
2110 Boul Saint-Joseph E, Montreal, QC, H2H 1E7
(514) 596-5700
Emp Here 150
SIC 8211 Elementary and secondary schools
Lucie Terelman

D-U-N-S 20-357-3894   (SL)
CORSIM CONSTRUCTION INC
(*Suby of* P.G.C. (S.M.) INC)
2003 Rue Gilford, Montreal, QC, H2H 1H2
(514) 345-9320
Emp Here 20   *Sales* 38,919,400
SIC 1522 Residential construction, nec
Sebastien Mathieu

D-U-N-S 25-245-5324   (HQ)
EDITIONS NOVALIS INC, LES
OWL
4475 Rue Frontenac, Montreal, QC, H2H 2S2

Emp Here 50   *Sales* 13,122,160
SIC 2721 Periodicals
Gilles Blouin
Suzanne Spino

D-U-N-S 24-253-5391   (SL)
ETUIS BOBLEN CASES INC
BOBLEN CASES
(*Suby of* PLACEMENTS FRAINE INC)
4455 Rue Frontenac, Montreal, QC, H2H 2S2
(514) 523-8163
Emp Here 100   *Sales* 27,025,600
SIC 3161 Luggage
Leandro Delli Fraine
Marissa Delli Fraine
Sabrina Delli Fraine

D-U-N-S 24-240-2464   (SL)
FRUITERIE VAL-MONT INC, LA
2147 Av Du Mont-Royal E, Montreal, QC, H2H 1J9
(514) 523-8212
Emp Here 49   *Sales* 13,433,448
SIC 5431 Fruit and vegetable markets
Artenio Checchin

D-U-N-S 20-004-1809   (HQ)
GROUPE COMPTANT QUEBEC INC
COMPTANT.COM
2024 Av Du Mont-Royal E, Montreal, QC, H2H 1J6
(514) 527-6023
Emp Here 4   *Sales* 24,432,800
SIC 5932 Used merchandise stores
Steve Pare

D-U-N-S 25-502-0638   (SL)
GROUPE SCABRINI INC
2700 Rue Rachel E, Montreal, QC, H2H 1S7

Emp Here 100   *Sales* 16,402,700
SIC 2732 Book printing
Pierre Goulet

D-U-N-S 24-698-4116   (HQ)
INVESTISSEMENTS SYLNIC INC, LES
4351 Rue D'Iberville, Montreal, QC, H2H 2L7
(514) 598-8130
Sales 54,826,350
SIC 6712 Bank holding companies
Claude Desrochers

D-U-N-S 24-711-5587   (SL)
MAISONNEUVE ALUMINIUM INC
5477 Rue Chabot Bureau 100, Montreal, QC, H2H 1Z1
(514) 523-1155
Emp Here 26   *Sales* 10,991,162
SIC 1541 Industrial buildings and warehouses
Steve Lempert

D-U-N-S 24-901-8615   (HQ)

OPTIQUE NIKON CANADA INC
LABORATOIRES TECH-CITE
(*Suby* of NIKON-ESSILOR CO., LTD.)
5075 Rue Fullum Bureau 100, Montreal, QC, H2H 2K3
(514) 521-6565
Emp Here 132   *Sales* 59,812,660
SIC 3851 Ophthalmic goods
Isabelle Mongeau
Charlotte Louet
Nicolas Barbier
Masahiro Horie

D-U-N-S 20-214-0836   (SL)
PAPIER REBUT CENTRAL INC
4270 Rue Hogan, Montreal, QC, H2H 2N4
(514) 526-4965
Emp Here 25   *Sales* 13,013,550
SIC 5093 Scrap and waste materials
Steven Toulch
Jo-Ann Toulch

D-U-N-S 24-083-0398   (SL)
REGROUPEMENT DES CENTRE DE LA PETITE ENFANCE DE L'
RCPEIM
4321 Av Papineau, Montreal, QC, H2H 1T3
(514) 528-1442
Emp Here 180   *Sales* 45,394,200
SIC 8611 Business associations
Gina Gasparrini
Celine Marchand

D-U-N-S 24-768-4087   (HQ)
RENOVATIONS MARTIN MARTIN INC
BAIN MAGIQUE
5187 Av Papineau, Montreal, QC, H2H 1W1
(514) 270-6599
Emp Here 45   *Sales* 70,262,500
SIC 5211 Lumber and other building materials
Martin Martin
Eric Martin
Eric Charest

D-U-N-S 20-911-3174   (SL)
SALAISON LA MAISON DU ROTI INC
1969 Av Du Mont-Royal E, Montreal, QC, H2H 1J5
(514) 521-2448
Emp Here 100   *Sales* 83,557,700
SIC 5147 Meats and meat products
Michel Legrand
Philippe Legrand

D-U-N-S 25-046-7912   (SL)
SOCIETE BIBLIQUE CANADIEN
2700 Rue Rachel E Bureau 100, Montreal, QC, H2H 1S7
(514) 524-7873
Emp Here 49   *Sales* 11,972,072
SIC 5942 Book stores

D-U-N-S 20-165-8932   (SL)
STAFF PERSONNEL EVENEMENTIEL INC
STAFF
5000 Rue D'Iberville Bureau 239, Montreal, QC, H2H 2S6
(514) 899-8776
Emp Here 26   *Sales* 11,530,740
SIC 7389 Business services, nec
Josee Rousseau

D-U-N-S 24-405-3484   (SL)
SUPER MARCHE MONT-ROYAL (1988) INC
SUPER MARCHE METRO #1571
2185 Av Du Mont-Royal E, Montreal, QC, H2H 1K2
(514) 522-5146
Emp Here 70   *Sales* 20,543,390
SIC 5411 Grocery stores
Jean-Yves Lebel
Gaston Marquis

D-U-N-S 24-811-6071   (HQ)
SUPERCLUB VIDEOTRON LTEE, LE
ACCES JEUX
(*Suby* of QUEBECOR MEDIA INC)
4545 Rue Frontenac Bureau 101, Montreal,

QC, H2H 2R7
(514) 259-6000
Emp Here 60   *Sales* 2,086,529,400
SIC 6794 Patent owners and lessors
Jean Novak
Marc M. Tremblay
Jean-Francois Pruneau

D-U-N-S 25-685-7111   (HQ)
VENTES RUDOLPH 2000 INC, LES
4625 Rue D'Iberville, Montreal, QC, H2H 2L9
(514) 596-1998
Emp Here 46   *Sales* 41,778,850
SIC 5149 Groceries and related products, nec
Ronald Letourneau

Montreal, QC H2J

D-U-N-S 24-747-4273   (HQ)
150147 CANADA INC
GASPE CURED
4284 Rue De La Roche Bureau 220, Montreal, QC, H2J 3H9
(438) 380-3516
Sales 23,554,451
SIC 4731 Freight transportation arrangement
Luc Reeves
Real Nicolas
Roch Lelievre
Robert Langlois
Benoit Reeves

D-U-N-S 24-337-6923   (SL)
4048873 CANADA INC
BOULANGERIE PREMIERE MOISSON
860 Av Du Mont-Royal E, Montreal, QC, H2J 1X1
(514) 523-2751
Emp Here 45   *Sales* 12,336,840
SIC 5461 Retail bakeries
Liliane Colpron
Marie-Odette Charbonneau

D-U-N-S 20-929-1194   (SL)
ASSOCIATION DE BIENFAISSANCE ET DE RETRAITE DES POLICIERS DE LA VILLE DE MONTREAL
ABRPPVM
480 Rue Gilford Bureau 200, Montreal, QC, H2J 1N3
(514) 527-8061
Emp Here 50   *Sales* 92,332,950
SIC 6371 Pension, health, and welfare funds
Louis Monette

D-U-N-S 20-523-4722   (SL)
AUTISME ET TROUBLES ENVAHISSANTS DU DEVELOPPEMENT MONTR AL
ATEDM
4450 Rue Saint-Hubert Bureau 320, Montreal, QC, H2J 2W9
(514) 524-6114
Emp Here 45   *Sales* 10,743,750
SIC 8611 Business associations
Carmen Lahaie

D-U-N-S 20-230-6742   (SL)
AUTOMOBILES POPULAR INC, LES
VOLKSWAGEN
5441 Rue Saint-Hubert, Montreal, QC, H2J 2Y4
(514) 274-5471
Emp Here 80   *Sales* 50,342,400
SIC 5511 New and used car dealers
Antoine Bassili

D-U-N-S 24-742-7388   (HQ)
BRASSEURS GMT INC, LES
BELLE GUEULE & DESSIN
(*Suby* of BRASSEURS RJ INC, LES)
5585 Rue De La Roche, Montreal, QC, H2J 3K3
(514) 274-4941
Sales 48,396,600
SIC 2082 Malt beverages

Roger Jaar
Philippe Jaar
Armida Jaar

D-U-N-S 25-998-5042   (HQ)
BRASSEURS RJ INC, LES
5585 Rue De La Roche, Montreal, QC, H2J 3K3
(514) 274-4941
Sales 28,692,270
SIC 2082 Malt beverages
Roger Jaar
Raymond Jaar
Armida Jaar
Philippe Jaar

D-U-N-S 24-437-9850   (SL)
CAISSE DESJARDINS - CENTREDE SERVICE
1685 Rue Rachel E, Montreal, QC, H2J 2K6
(514) 524-3551
Emp Here 49   *Sales* 11,012,456
SIC 6159 Miscellaneous business credit institutions
Richard Beaulieu

D-U-N-S 25-244-5721   (HQ)
CAISSE DESJARDINS DES POLICIERS ET POLICIERES
CENTRE DE SERVICE DES POLICIERS ET POLICIERES MUNICIPAUX DU QUEBEC
460 Rue Gilford, Montreal, QC, H2J 1N3
(514) 847-1004
Sales 10,609,270
SIC 6062 State credit unions
Normand Prevost
Andre Bouchard
Francois Lemay
Stephane Laroche
Jacques Dextradeur
Guy Cote
Robert St-Jean
Jean Beaudoin
Michel Thomassin
Richard Nardozza

D-U-N-S 24-321-0747   (HQ)
CONCEPTS ZONE INC, LES
ZONE
(*Suby* of GESTION MADELEINE DE VILLERS INC)
4246 Rue Saint-Denis, Montreal, QC, H2J 2K8
(514) 845-3530
Emp Here 20   *Sales* 23,240,300
SIC 5719 Miscellaneous homefurnishings
Madeleine Devillers

D-U-N-S 20-252-0292   (SL)
CROTEAU, PIERRE INC
AUBAINERIE, L'
(*Suby* of GESTION JOCELYNE CROTEAU INC)
1490 Av Du Mont-Royal E Bureau 3, Montreal, QC, H2J 1Y9
(514) 521-0059
Emp Here 125   *Sales* 22,424,500
SIC 5621 Women's clothing stores
Jocelyne Croteau

D-U-N-S 24-074-7134   (SL)
FRATERNITE DES POLICIERS ET POLICIERES DE MONTREAL INC
F.P.P.M.
480 Rue Gilford Bureau 300, Montreal, QC, H2J 1N3
(514) 527-4161
Emp Here 26   *Sales* 10,203,700
SIC 8631 Labor organizations
Yves Francoeur
Mario Lanoie
Andre Gendron
Yves Gendron
Pascal Poirier
Jean-Francois Potvin
Kathie Boutin

D-U-N-S 25-285-8840   (HQ)

GESTION MADELEINE DE VILLERS INC
4246 Rue Saint-Denis, Montreal, QC, H2J 2K8
(514) 845-4090
Emp Here 1   *Sales* 23,240,300
SIC 5719 Miscellaneous homefurnishings
Madeleine Devilleres

D-U-N-S 20-219-5681   (SL)
GROUPE CHASSE INC
CHASSE TOYOTA
819 Rue Rachel E, Montreal, QC, H2J 2H7
(514) 527-3411
Emp Here 50   *Sales* 24,903,900
SIC 5511 New and used car dealers
Claude Chasse
Maxime Chasse

D-U-N-S 24-050-3185   (SL)
KANUK INC
485 Rue Rachel E, Montreal, QC, H2J 2H1
(514) 284-4494
Emp Here 100   *Sales* 13,667,400
SIC 2311 Men's and boy's suits and coats
Scott Jackson

D-U-N-S 20-519-0064   (HQ)
MARCHES D'ALIMENTS NATURELS TAU INC, LES
LES MARCHES TAU
4238 Rue Saint-Denis, Montreal, QC, H2J 2K8
(514) 843-4420
Emp Here 10   *Sales* 13,433,448
SIC 5411 Grocery stores
Gary Brown
Doris Brown

D-U-N-S 25-634-5054   (SL)
RUDSACK
829 Av Du Mont-Royal E, Montreal, QC, H2J 1W9
(514) 508-4100
Emp Here 49   *Sales* 24,417,778
SIC 5136 Men's and boy's clothing
Evik Asatoorian

D-U-N-S 24-154-1163   (SL)
S.R.E.P.E. INC
4837 Rue Boyer Bureau 240, Montreal, QC, H2J 3E6
(514) 525-3447
Emp Here 50   *Sales* 33,946,150
SIC 6211 Security brokers and dealers
Guillaume Drapeau

D-U-N-S 24-474-6272   (SL)
VIA CAPITALE DU MONT ROYAL
1152 Av Du Mont-Royal E, Montreal, QC, H2J 1X8
(514) 597-2121
Emp Here 49   *Sales* 13,316,044
SIC 6531 Real estate agents and managers

Montreal, QC H2K

D-U-N-S 20-860-2714   (SL)
AGENCE DE SECURITE D'INVESTIGATION EXPO INC
2335 Rue Ontario E, Montreal, QC, H2K 1W2
(514) 523-5333
Emp Here 75   *Sales* 30,019,553
SIC 7381 Detective and armored car services
Dannie Gaudreault
Jacques Lessard

D-U-N-S 25-757-5209   (SL)
ALIMENTATION DANIEL BRUYERE INC
METRO AU PIEDS DU POND
1955 Rue Sainte-Catherine E, Montreal, QC, H2K 2H6
(514) 525-5090
Emp Here 100   *Sales* 29,347,700
SIC 5411 Grocery stores
Daniel Bruyere

D-U-N-S 24-057-3613   (SL)

ALLO PROF
FONDATION ALLO PROF
1000 Rue Fullum, Montreal, QC, H2K 3L7
(514) 509-2025
Emp Here 100   *Sales* 21,994,300
SIC 8732 Commercial nonphysical research
Jacynthe Cote
Brigitte Hebert
Lorraine Normand-Charbonneau
Michelle Adams
Pierre Boucher
Andre Lachapelle
Isabelle Gadbois

    D-U-N-S 24-241-1481   (SL)
ATELIER KOLLONTAI INC
KOLLONTAI
2065 Rue Parthenais Bureau 389, Montreal,
QC, H2K 3T1
(514) 223-4899
Emp Here 22   *Sales* 14,442,208
SIC 5961 Catalog and mail-order houses
Gabrielle Tousignant

    D-U-N-S 20-052-9050   (BR)
BELL MEDIA INC
CTV
(*Suby of* BCE INC)
1205 Av Papineau, Montreal, QC, H2K 4R2
(514) 273-6311
Emp Here 130
SIC 4833 Television broadcasting stations
Donald Bastien

    D-U-N-S 24-344-2659   (BR)
CENTRE DE SANTE ET DE SERVICES SO-CIAUX JEANNE-MANCE
CENTRE D'EBERGEMENT GAMELIN LAVERGNE
1440 Rue Dufresne, Montreal, QC, H2K 3J3
(514) 527-8921
Emp Here 500
SIC 8361 Residential care
Chantale Lapointe

    D-U-N-S 20-118-8914   (HQ)
CONALJAN INC
4045 Rue Parthenais, Montreal, QC, H2K 3T8
(514) 522-2121
Emp Here 75
SIC 6719 Holding companies, nec
Pierre Jean
Patricia Jean
Pierre-Albert Jean
Sebastien Jean

    D-U-N-S 20-744-2554   (BR)
CONFEDERATION DES SYNDICATS NA-TIONAUX (C.S.N.)
SYNDICAT DES TRAVAILLEUSES ET DES TRAVAILLEURS DE LA CSN
1601 Av De Lorimier, Montreal, QC, H2K 4M5
(514) 529-4993
Emp Here 600
SIC 8631 Labor organizations
Julie Dion

    D-U-N-S 24-762-8977   (SL)
CONSTRUCTION ALBERT JEAN LTEE
(*Suby of* CONALJAN INC)
4045 Rue Parthenais, Montreal, QC, H2K 3T8
(514) 522-2121
Emp Here 50   *Sales* 28,516,900
SIC 1542 Nonresidential construction, nec
Pierre-Albert Jean
Jean Patricia
Sebastien Jean

    D-U-N-S 20-215-4449   (HQ)
CORDEE PLEIN AIR INC, LA
CLUB PLEIN AIR LA CORDEE
2159 Rue Sainte-Catherine E, Montreal, QC,
H2K 2H9
(514) 524-1326
Emp Here 125   *Sales* 45,884,250
SIC 5941 Sporting goods and bicycle shops
Pierre Deslongchamps

Louise Bernard
Rene Lamoureux
Danielle Charron
Joanne Labrecque
Francois Deschenes

    D-U-N-S 24-850-0019   (SL)
CORPORATION CHAMPION PIPE LINE LIMITEE
(*Suby of* ENERGIR, S.E.C.)
1717 Rue Du Havre, Montreal, QC, H2K 2X3
(514) 598-3444
Emp Here 5   *Sales* 15,529,285
SIC 4922 Natural gas transmission
Stephane Santerre
Nathalie Longval
Pierre Despars
Sophie Brochu

    D-U-N-S 20-216-3226   (SL)
DELISLE AUTO LTEE
2815 Rue Sherbrooke E, Montreal, QC, H2K
1H2
(514) 523-1122
Emp Here 50   *Sales* 24,903,900
SIC 5511 New and used car dealers
Marcel Delisle
Daniel Delisle
Gilles Delisle
Jean-Pierre Delisle

    D-U-N-S 24-522-9542   (HQ)
DISTRIBUTION HMH INC
1815 Av De Lorimier, Montreal, QC, H2K 3W6
(514) 523-1523
Sales 19,305,520
SIC 5192 Books, periodicals, and newspapers
Herve Foulon
Arnaud Foulon
Alexandrine Foulon

    D-U-N-S 20-860-2797   (SL)
EDITIONS HURTUBISE INC
1815 Av De Lorimier, Montreal, QC, H2K 3W6
(514) 523-1523
Emp Here 35   *Sales* 25,988,200
SIC 5192 Books, periodicals, and newspapers
Herve Foulon
Arnault Foulon

    D-U-N-S 25-623-4766   (BR)
EMONDAGE ST-GERMAIN ET FRERES LTEE
(*Suby of* EMONDAGE ST-GERMAIN ET FR-ERES LTEE)
4032 Av De Lorimier, Montreal, QC, H2K 3X7
(514) 525-7485
Emp Here 75
SIC 0721 Crop planting and protection
Jean St-Germain

    D-U-N-S 20-231-1981   (HQ)
ENERGIR INC
ECOLE DE TECHNOLOGIE GAZIERE
(*Suby of* NOVERCO INC)
1717 Rue Du Havre, Montreal, QC, H2K 2X3
(514) 598-3444
Emp Here 300   *Sales* 2,018,274,851
SIC 4924 Natural gas distribution
Sophie Brochu
Jean Houde
Nathalie Longval
Francois Gervais
Pierre Monahan
Ghislain Gauthier
Mary-Ann Bell
Marie Deschamps
Renaud Faucher
Jean-Luc Gravel

    D-U-N-S 24-904-1245   (HQ)
ENERGIR, S.E.C.
ECOLE DE TECHNOLOGIE GAZIERE
1717 Rue Du Havre, Montreal, QC, H2K 2X3
(514) 598-3444
Emp Here 917   *Sales* 1,522,883,188
SIC 4924 Natural gas distribution

Sophie Brochu

    D-U-N-S 24-630-9426   (SL)
EXPO SECURITE INVESTIGATIONS INC
1600 Av De Lorimier Bureau 140, Montreal,
QC, H2K 3W5

Emp Here 40   *Sales* 17,739,600
SIC 7389 Business services, nec
Dannie Gaudreault

    D-U-N-S 24-252-7646   (HQ)
FEDERATION DES EMPLOYES ET EM-PLOYEES DE SERVICES PUBLICS (CSN) INC
FEESP
1601 Av De Lorimier Bureau 150, Montreal,
QC, H2K 4M5
(514) 598-2360
Emp Here 27   *Sales* 19,557,900
SIC 8631 Labor organizations
Ginette Guerin

    D-U-N-S 25-500-3014   (HQ)
FONDACTION, LE FONDS DE DEVEL-OPPEMENT DE LA CSN POUR LA COOP-ERATION ET L'EMPLOI
CARREFOUR FINANCIER SOLIDAIRE
2175 Boul De Maisonneuve E Bureau 103,
Montreal, QC, H2K 4S3
(514) 525-5505
Emp Here 72   *Sales* 103,244,400
SIC 6799 Investors, nec
Leopold Beaulieu
Diane Beaudry
Michel Tetreault
Marc Picard
Claude Demers
Pierre B. Lafreniere
Thierry C. Pauchant
Jasmine Hinse
Jacques Letourneau
Clement Guimond

    D-U-N-S 24-933-5621   (SL)
GAZ METRO INC
1717 Rue Du Havre, Montreal, QC, H2K 2X3
(514) 598-3444
Emp Here 4   *Sales* 12,423,428
SIC 4922 Natural gas transmission
Lyne Burelle

    D-U-N-S 24-061-5539   (BR)
GOUVERNEMENT DE LA PROVINCE DE QUEBEC
TELE-QUEBEC
(*Suby of* GOUVERNEMENT DE LA PROVINCE DE QUEBEC)
1000 Rue Fullum, Montreal, QC, H2K 3L7
(514) 521-2424
Emp Here 275
SIC 4833 Television broadcasting stations
Michele Fortin

    D-U-N-S 20-223-5834   (SL)
HECTOR LARIVEE INC
D.G.B. FRUITERIE
1755 Rue Bercy, Montreal, QC, H2K 2T9
(514) 521-8331
Emp Here 100   *Sales* 83,557,700
SIC 5148 Fresh fruits and vegetables
Guy Larivee
Michel Larivee
Daniel Larivee

    D-U-N-S 20-190-4633   (SL)
INNOVADERM RECHERCHES INC
INNOVADERM RECHERCHES LAVAL
1851 Rue Sherbrooke E Unite 502, Montreal,
QC, H2K 4L5
(514) 521-3111
Emp Here 65   *Sales* 11,726,975
SIC 8731 Commercial physical research
Robert Bissonnette

    D-U-N-S 20-222-4432   (SL)
JOLICOEUR LTEE

(*Suby of* SERVICE INDUSTRIEL JOLI-COEUR LTEE)
4132 Rue Parthenais, Montreal, QC, H2K 3T9
(514) 526-4444
Emp Here 100   *Sales* 10,678,200
SIC 7218 Industrial launderers
Andre Jolicoeur

    D-U-N-S 24-083-6288   (BR)
JTI-MACDONALD CORP
(*Suby of* JAPAN TOBACCO INC.)
2455 Rue Ontario E Bureau 4, Montreal, QC,
H2K 1W3
(514) 598-2525
Emp Here 500
SIC 2111 Cigarettes
Mike Beasson

    D-U-N-S 20-715-7137   (BR)
PELMOREX WEATHER NETWORKS (TELE-VISION) INC
WEATHER NETWORK
(*Suby of* PELMOREX CORP)
1205 Av Papineau Bureau 251, Montreal, QC,
H2K 4R2
(514) 597-0232
Emp Here 120
SIC 8999 Services, nec
Souad Gara

    D-U-N-S 24-970-8355   (BR)
PELMOREX WEATHER NETWORKS (TELE-VISION) INC
METEO MEDIA
(*Suby of* PELMOREX CORP)
1755 Boul Rene-Levesque E Bureau 251,
Montreal, QC, H2K 4P6
(514) 597-1700
Emp Here 133
SIC 4833 Television broadcasting stations
Maureen Rogers

    D-U-N-S 24-801-1413   (SL)
RESEAU DES SPORTS (RDS) INC, LE
RDS
(*Suby of* BCE INC)
1755 Boul Rene-Levesque E Bureau 300,
Montreal, QC, H2K 4P6
(514) 599-2244
Emp Here 250   *Sales* 83,636,000
SIC 4841 Cable and other pay television ser-vices
Gerald Frappier
Kevin Assaf

    D-U-N-S 24-811-6907   (SL)
SOCIETE DE GESTION REJEAN & SERGE AUCOIN INTERNATIONAL INC
CIMENTERIE PORT-DANIEL
2359 Rue Frontenac, Montreal, QC, H2K 2Z8
(514) 356-3545
Emp Here 12   *Sales* 12,393,696
SIC 5172 Petroleum products, nec
Rejean Aucoin
Serge Aucoin

    D-U-N-S 20-737-1829   (SL)
SYNDICAT DES EMPLOYES EN RADIO TELEDIFFUSION DE TELE-QUEBEC
1000 Rue Fullum Bureau 231, Montreal, QC,
H2K 3L7
(514) 529-2805
Emp Here 49   *Sales* 19,489,104
SIC 8631 Labor organizations
Sylvain Leboeuf

    D-U-N-S 24-425-3618   (SL)
VALENER INC
1717 Rue Du Havre, Montreal, QC, H2K 2X3
(514) 598-6220
Emp Here 4   *Sales* 55,671,344
SIC 6712 Bank holding companies
Pierre Monahan
Serge Regnier
Mary-Ann Bell
Francois Gervais
Gwen Klees

Montreal, QC H2L

D-U-N-S 24-828-7005   (SL)
127901 CANADA INC
955 Rue Amherst, Montreal, QC, H2L 3K4
(514) 523-1182
Emp Here 75   *Sales* 19,616,475
SIC 6712 Bank holding companies
Pierre L'esperance

D-U-N-S 24-055-2146   (SL)
ALLIANCE QUEBECOISE DES TECHNI-CIENS DE L'IMAGE ET DU SON (AQTIS)
533 Rue Ontario E Bureau 300, Montreal, QC, H2L 1N8
(514) 844-2113
Emp Here 47   *Sales* 18,445,150
SIC 8631 Labor organizations
Alexandre Curzi
Dominique Fortin
Alexis Duceppe
Eric Charles Lapointe
Francesca Waltzing
Gilles Charland
Michel Arcand
Jean-Francois Forget
Jose Poulin
Maurice Roy

D-U-N-S 25-658-5951   (HQ)
ARO INC
1001 Rue Sherbrooke E Bureau 700, Montreal, QC, H2L 1L3
(514) 322-1414
Sales 65,120,575
SIC 7322 Adjustment and collection services
Michael Ogilvie

D-U-N-S 25-590-3478   (BR)
BELL MEDIA INC
VIRGIN RADIO
(*Suby of* BCE INC)
1717 Boul Rene-Levesque E, Montreal, QC, H2L 4T9
(514) 529-3200
Emp Here 100
SIC 4832 Radio broadcasting stations

D-U-N-S 20-533-4654   (BR)
BELL MEDIA INC
ENERGIE 94.3 FM
(*Suby of* BCE INC)
1717 Boul Rene-Levesque E Bureau 120, Montreal, QC, H2L 4T9
(514) 529-3200
Emp Here 400
SIC 4832 Radio broadcasting stations
Jacques Parisien

D-U-N-S 20-265-8886   (HQ)
BIBLIOTHEQUE ET ARCHIVES NA-TIONALES DU QUEBEC
BANQ
(*Suby of* GOUVERNEMENT DE LA PROVINCE DE QUEBEC)
475 Boul De Maisonneuve E, Montreal, QC, H2L 5C4
(514) 873-1100
Emp Here 75   *Sales* 60,002,091
SIC 8231 Libraries
Jean-Louis Roy
Gaston Bellemare

D-U-N-S 25-906-0515   (SL)
CAMPUS
1111 Rue Sainte-Catherine E, Montreal, QC, H2L 2G6
(514) 526-9867
Emp Here 200   *Sales* 9,103,800
SIC 5813 Drinking places
Luc Marchand

D-U-N-S 20-213-4441   (BR)
CANADIAN BROADCASTING CORPORA-TION
CBC

(*Suby of* GOVERNMENT OF CANADA)
1400 Boul Rene-Levesque E, Montreal, QC, H2L 2M2
(514) 597-6000
Emp Here 3,000
SIC 4833 Television broadcasting stations
Hubert Lacroix

D-U-N-S 25-091-0296   (BR)
CENTRE HOSPITALIER DE L'UNIVERSITE DE MONTREAL
CENTRE HOSPITALIER DE L'UNIVERSITE DE MONTREAL
(*Suby of* CENTRE HOSPITALIER DE L'UNIVERSITE DE MONTREAL)
1560 Rue Sherbrooke E, Montreal, QC, H2L 4M1
(800) 224-7737
Emp Here 2,000
SIC 8062 General medical and surgical hospitals
Bourgon Carole

D-U-N-S 25-736-7276   (SL)
CINEGROUPE INTERACTIF INC
1010 Rue Sainte-Catherine E, Montreal, QC, H2L 2G3
(514) 524-7567
Emp Here 47   *Sales* 10,050,997
SIC 7372 Prepackaged software
Ernest Godin

D-U-N-S 25-995-2641   (SL)
CLINIQUE SANTE VOYAGE SAINT-LUC
1560 Rue Sherbrooke E, Montreal, QC, H2L 4M1
(514) 890-8332
Emp Here 26   *Sales* 13,519,142
SIC 4724 Travel agencies
Luce Moreau

D-U-N-S 20-790-4749   (HQ)
COMPAGNIE FRANCE FILM INC
THEATRE SAINT-DENIS
505 Rue Sherbrooke E Bureau 2401, Montreal, QC, H2L 4N3
(514) 844-0680
Emp Here 20   *Sales* 12,799,665
SIC 6512 Nonresidential building operators
Pierre Rene
Gilles Vinet
Roland Giguere
Robert Trudeau
Gilles Loslier

D-U-N-S 25-192-1912   (SL)
FABRIQUE ARHOMA INC, LA
1700 Rue Ontario E, Montreal, QC, H2L 1S7
(514) 598-1700
Emp Here 26   *Sales* 21,725,002
SIC 5149 Groceries and related products, nec
Jerome Couture

D-U-N-S 25-244-0771   (SL)
FONDATION DE L'UNIVERSITE DU QUE-BEC A MONTREAL
FONDATION UQAM
405 Boul De Maisonneuve E Bureau 2300, Montreal, QC, H2L 4J5
(514) 987-3030
Emp Here 26   *Sales* 11,679,694
SIC 7389 Business services, nec
Jean-Marc Eustache
Jean Laurin

D-U-N-S 20-024-0757   (BR)
FONDATION DE LA MAISON DU PERE
LA RESIDENCE GIA DE SEVE
(*Suby of* FONDATION DE LA MAISON DU PERE)
545 Rue De La Gauchetiere E Bureau 296, Montreal, QC, H2L 5E1
(514) 843-3739
Emp Here 75
SIC 8361 Residential care
France Desjardins

D-U-N-S 24-904-0353   (BR)

FONDATION UNIVERSITE DU QUEBEC
UNIVERSITE DU QUEBEC
(*Suby of* UNIVERSITE DU QUEBEC)
405 Rue Sainte-Catherine E, Montreal, QC, H2L 2C4

Emp Here 4,000
SIC 8221 Colleges and universities
Jacques Larose

D-U-N-S 24-394-9182   (HQ)
GESTION MARC DESERRES INC
1265 Rue Berri Bureau 1000, Montreal, QC, H2L 4X4
(514) 842-6695
Sales 82,591,650
SIC 5999 Miscellaneous retail stores, nec
Marc Deserres

D-U-N-S 24-320-3176   (SL)
GESTIONS FORTIER-ALLAN 29 INC
PHARMAPRIX
901 Rue Sainte-Catherine E Bureau 29, Montreal, QC, H2L 2E5
(514) 842-4915
Emp Here 50   *Sales* 12,647,700
SIC 5912 Drug stores and proprietary stores
Pierre-Benoit Tremblay
Eric Van Hoenacker

D-U-N-S 24-475-6987   (BR)
GOUVERNEMENT DE LA PROVINCE DE QUEBEC
BIBLIOTHEQUE ET ARCHIVES NA-TIONALES DU QUEBEC
(*Suby of* GOUVERNEMENT DE LA PROVINCE DE QUEBEC)
475 Boul De Maisonneuve E, Montreal, QC, H2L 5C4
(514) 873-1100
Emp Here 600
SIC 8231 Libraries
Lise Bissonnette

D-U-N-S 25-325-1557   (BR)
GOUVERNEUR INC
HOTEL GOUVERNEUR
(*Suby of* GOUVERNEUR INC)
1415 Rue Saint-Hubert, Montreal, QC, H2L 3Y9
(514) 842-4881
Emp Here 145
SIC 7011 Hotels and motels
Carlo D Orazi

D-U-N-S 24-751-9296   (SL)
GROUP VOYAGES VP INC
1259 Rue Berri Bureau 600, Montreal, QC, H2L 4C7
(514) 939-9999
Emp Here 40   *Sales* 15,414,400
SIC 4724 Travel agencies
Paul Lariviere

D-U-N-S 25-469-6321   (BR)
GROUPE ARCHAMBAULT INC
500 Rue Sainte-Catherine E, Montreal, QC, H2L 2C6
(514) 849-6201
Emp Here 100
SIC 5735 Record and prerecorded tape stores
Michel Moreau

D-U-N-S 20-418-0871   (HQ)
GROUPE SOGIDES INC
CHARRON EDITEUR
(*Suby of* QUEBECOR MEDIA INC)
955 Rue Amherst, Montreal, QC, H2L 3K4
(514) 523-1182
Emp Here 60   *Sales* 58,132,200
SIC 2731 Book publishing
Pierre Karl Peladeau
Jean-Francois Pruneau
Marc M. Tremblay

D-U-N-S 20-235-4718   (HQ)
GROUPE TVA INC
ADDIK.TV

(*Suby of* QUEBECOR MEDIA INC)
1600 Boul De Maisonneuve E, Montreal, QC, H2L 4P2
(514) 526-9251
Emp Here 100   *Sales* 418,635,296
SIC 4833 Television broadcasting stations
France Lauziere
Martin Picard
Anick Dubois
Denis Rozon
Serge Fortin
Jean-Francois Reid
Veronique Mercier
Claude Foisy
Lyne Robitaille
Marc M. Tremblay

D-U-N-S 20-178-1999   (BR)
GROUPE TVA INC
(*Suby of* QUEBECOR MEDIA INC)
1475 Rue Alexandre-Deseve, Montreal, QC, H2L 2V4
(514) 526-9251
Emp Here 800
SIC 1799 Special trade contractors, nec
Camille Couture

D-U-N-S 20-573-7260   (BR)
HYDRO-QUEBEC
SOCIETE D'ENERGIE DE LA BAIE JAMES
(*Suby of* GOUVERNEMENT DE LA PROVINCE DE QUEBEC)
888 Boul De Maisonneuve E, Montreal, QC, H2L 4S8
(514) 286-2020
Emp Here 100
SIC 4911 Electric services

D-U-N-S 24-815-1474   (SL)
INSTITUT RAYMOND-DEWAR
CENTRE DE READAPTATION SPECIALISE EN SURDITE ET EN COMMUNICATION
3600 Rue Berri Bureau 469, Montreal, QC, H2L 4G9
(514) 284-2214
Emp Here 230   *Sales* 14,784,860
SIC 8361 Residential care
Luc M. Malo
Julie Blanchet
Ursula Dumon
Jean-Paul W. Tremblay
Dominique Lemay
Patrick Levesque
Sylvie Lemay
Sandra Mac Leod
Maxim Mainville
Natacha Trudeau

D-U-N-S 25-973-4846   (SL)
INTERFORUM CANADA INC
EDITIS
(*Suby of* VIVENDI)
1001 Boul De Maisonneuve E Bureau 1001, Montreal, QC, H2L 4P9
(514) 281-1050
Emp Here 14   *Sales* 10,395,280
SIC 5192 Books, periodicals, and newspapers
Eric Levy
Kevin Leonard
Walter Dellazoppa
Nycole Desjardins

D-U-N-S 25-461-3169   (SL)
LEBLANC & DAVID MARKETING INC
RABAIS CAMPUS
425 Rue Sherbrooke E Bureau 12, Montreal, QC, H2L 1J9
(514) 982-0180
Emp Here 25   *Sales* 18,563,000
SIC 5192 Books, periodicals, and newspapers
Roland David

D-U-N-S 25-173-1162   (SL)
MARKO AUDIO POST PRODUCTION INC
STUDIOS MARKO
910 Rue De La Gauchetiere E Bureau Entree, Montreal, QC, H2L 2N4

(514) 282-0961
Emp Here 25   *Sales* 11,087,250
SIC 7389 Business services, nec
  Norman Lloyd

D-U-N-S 20-760-9280   (SL)
MESSAGERIES A.D.P. INC
MESSAGERIES ADP
(*Suby of* QUEBECOR MEDIA INC)
955 Rue Amherst, Montreal, QC, H2L 3K4
(514) 523-1182
Emp Here 150   *Sales* 88,373,850
SIC 5192 Books, periodicals, and newspapers
  Lyne Robitaille
  Jean-Francois Pruneau
  Marc M. Tremblay

D-U-N-S 24-350-5828   (HQ)
MOLSON INC
(*Suby of* MOLSON COORS BREWING COM-
PANY)
1555 Rue Notre-Dame E, Montreal, QC, H2L
2R5
(514) 521-1786
Sales 2,512,599,000
SIC 5181 Beer and ale
  Stewart Glendinning
  Lori A. Ball
  Kelly L. Brown
  Wouter Vosmeer

D-U-N-S 24-943-2824   (HQ)
OMER DESERRES INC
DESERRES OMER
(*Suby of* GESTION MARC DESERRES INC)
1265 Rue Berri Bureau 1000, Montreal, QC,
H2L 4X4
(514) 842-6695
Emp Here 70   *Sales* 82,591,650
SIC 5999 Miscellaneous retail stores, nec
  Marc Deserres

D-U-N-S 20-736-6139   (SL)
SOCIETE D'ENERGIE DE LA BAIE JAMES
SEBJ
(*Suby of* GOUVERNEMENT DE LA
PROVINCE DE QUEBEC)
800 Boul De Maisonneuve E Bureau 1100,
Montreal, QC, H2L 4L8
(514) 286-2020
Emp Here 300   *Sales* 33,660,900
SIC 8741 Management services
  Eric Martel
  Real Laporte
  Pierre Gagnon
  David Murray
  Jean-Hugues Lafleur

D-U-N-S 24-974-1489   (HQ)
**SOCIETE DE SAINT-VINCENT DE PAUL DE
MONTREAL, LA**
1930 Rue De Champlain, Montreal, QC, H2L
2S8
(514) 526-5937
Emp Here 25   *Sales* 19,870,700
SIC 8699 Membership organizations, nec
  Pierre Pratte
  Madeleine Lafrance

D-U-N-S 20-706-6478   (BR)
SOCIETE DE TRANSPORT DE MONTREAL
(*Suby of* SOCIETE DE TRANSPORT DE
MONTREAL)
2000 Rue Berri, Montreal, QC, H2L 4V7
(514) 786-6876
Emp Here 200
SIC 4111 Local and suburban transit
  Carole Legault

D-U-N-S 20-960-1673   (HQ)
**SOCIETE DES MISSIONAIRES D'AFRIQUE
(PERES   BLANCS)   PROVINCE   DE
L'AMERIQUE DU NORD**
PERES BLANCS, LES
1640 Rue Saint-Hubert, Montreal, QC, H2L
3Z3
(514) 849-1167
Emp Here 23   *Sales* 21,865,830

SIC 8661 Religious organizations
  Jacques Charron
  Andre Bilodeau

D-U-N-S 20-127-1595   (SL)
**SYNDICAT DE PROFESSIONNELLES ET
PROFESSIONNELS DU GOUVERNEMENT
DU QUEBEC**
1001 Rue Sherbrooke E Bureau 300, Mon-
treal, QC, H2L 1L3
(514) 849-1103
Emp Here 45   *Sales* 17,660,250
SIC 8631 Labor organizations
  Gilles Dussault
  Michael Isaacs
  Luc Bruneau
  Luce Bernier
  Jeanne Bouchard
  Patrick Albert
  Carole Letendre

D-U-N-S 20-113-8695   (HQ)
**SYSTEMES MEDICAUX INTELERAD IN-
CORPOREE, LES**
INTELERAD
800 Boul De Maisonneuve E 12eme Etage,
Montreal, QC, H2L 4L8
(514) 931-6222
Emp Here 250   *Sales* 51,680,440
SIC 7371 Custom computer programming ser-
vices
  Paul Lepage
  Francois Laflamme
  Randall I. Oka
  Pascal Tremblay
  Richard K. Rubin
  David Brassard
  Brian Cosgrove

D-U-N-S 24-020-8702   (HQ)
TVA VENTES ET MARKETING INC
TVA INTERACTIF
(*Suby of* QUEBECOR MEDIA INC)
1600 Boul De Maisonneuve E, Montreal, QC,
H2L 4P2
(514) 526-9251
Emp Here 1   *Sales* 20,037,100
SIC 7319 Advertising, nec
  France Lauziere
  Denis Rozon
  Marc M. Tremblay
  Donald Lizotte

D-U-N-S 20-137-3151   (SL)
ZONE3 INC
ZONE3 SPECTACLES
1055 Boul Rene-Levesque E Bureau 300,
Montreal, QC, H2L 4S5
(514) 284-5555
Emp Here 500   *Sales* 44,848,000
SIC 7812 Motion picture and video production
  Andre Larin
  Luc Benoit
  Michel Bissonnette
  Pierre Guilbault
  Valier Boivin

Montreal, QC H2M

D-U-N-S 24-649-1948   (HQ)
**ASSOCIATION DES MANOEUVRES INTER-
PROVINCIAUX (AMI), L'**
565 Boul Cremazie E Bureau 3800, Montreal,
QC, H2M 2V6
(514) 381-8780
Sales 10,561,266
SIC 8631 Labor organizations
  Alain Lussier
  John Jocelyn
  Francois John

D-U-N-S 20-294-3499   (BR)
C.L.S.C. MONTREAL-NORD
1615 Av Emile-Journault, Montreal, QC, H2M

2G3
(514) 384-2000
Emp Here 120
SIC 8361 Residential care
  Martine Fortin

D-U-N-S 20-300-7265   (HQ)
CENTRE DE SERVICES DE PAIE CGI INC
(*Suby of* CGI INC)
1611 Boul Cremazie E 7th Floor, Montreal,
QC, H2M 2P2
(514) 850-6300
Emp Here 200   *Sales* 44,364,720
SIC 8721 Accounting, auditing, and book-
keeping
  Francois Boulanger
  Benoit Dube
  Kevin Linder
  Max Rogan

D-U-N-S 20-387-3539   (SL)
COLLEGE AHUNTSIC
CEGEP D'AHUNTSIC
9155 Rue Saint Hubert, Montreal, QC, H2M
1Y8
(514) 389-5921
Emp Here 1,000   *Sales* 149,391,000
SIC 8221 Colleges and universities
  Nathalie Vallee

D-U-N-S 20-764-5318   (HQ)
**COMMISSION DE LA CONSTRUCTION DU
QUEBEC**
CCQ
8485 Av Christophe-Colomb, Montreal, QC,
H2M 0A7
(514) 341-7740
Emp Here 400   *Sales* 252,190,000
SIC 8611 Business associations
  Andre Menard
  Michel Mclaughlin

D-U-N-S 25-144-7132   (BR)
**COMMISSION DE LA CONSTRUCTION DU
QUEBEC**
(*Suby of* COMMISSION DE LA CONSTRUC-
TION DU QUEBEC)
1201 Boul Cremazie E, Montreal, QC, H2M
0A6
(514) 593-3121
Emp Here 175
SIC 8611 Business associations
  Hugo Napper

D-U-N-S 20-555-8914   (BR)
**CONSEILLERS EN GESTION ET INFORMA-
TIQUE CGI INC**
CGI
(*Suby of* CGI INC)
9555 Av Christophe-Colomb, Montreal, QC,
H2M 2E3
(514) 374-7777
Emp Here 150
SIC 4899 Communication services, nec
  Sylvain Dupras

D-U-N-S 24-737-4924   (SL)
CORPORATION STELLAR CANADA INC
255 Boul Cremazie E Bureau 400, Montreal,
QC, H2M 1L5
(514) 850-6900
Emp Here 250   *Sales* 83,636,000
SIC 4813 Telephone communication, except
radio
  Robert Raymond
  Steve Morphett
  Raymonde Robert
  Scott Letier
  Jeffrey Jensen

D-U-N-S 20-417-5764   (SL)
**EDITIONS   DU   RENOUVEAU   PEDA-
GOGIQUE INC**
ERPI
(*Suby of* PEARSON PLC)
1611 Boul Cremazie E Etage 10, Montreal,
QC, H2M 2P2

(514) 334-2690
Emp Here 100   *Sales* 16,402,700
SIC 2731 Book publishing
  Normand Cleroux
  Tony Seebalack
  James Reeve

D-U-N-S 24-225-3250   (HQ)
**ESTIMATEURS PROFESSIONELS LER-
OUX, BEAUDRY, PICARD & ASSOCIES
INC, LES**
GROUPE LEROUX, LE
255 Boul Cremazie E Bureau 9e, Montreal,
QC, H2M 1L5
(514) 384-4220
Emp Here 90   *Sales* 41,888,900
SIC 6531 Real estate agents and managers
  Jos Leroux
  Jean Leroux
  Michele Leroux

D-U-N-S 20-883-0687   (SL)
**EXCELLENCE LIFE INSURANCE COM-
PANY, THE**
IA EXCELLENCE
(*Suby of* INDUSTRIELLE ALLIANCE, AS-
SURANCE ET SERVICES FINANCIERS INC)
1611 Boul Cremazie E Bureau 900, Montreal,
QC, H2M 2P2
(514) 327-0020
Emp Here 125   *Sales* 267,121,000
SIC 6311 Life insurance
  Pierre Vincent
  Jennifer Dibblee
  Jocelyne Bourgon
  Pierre Brodeur
  Yvon Charest
  Denyse Chicoyne
  Robert Coallier
  Claude Lamoureux
  John A. Leboutillier
  Jacques Martin

D-U-N-S 20-845-1570   (BR)
**FEDERATION DES CAISSES DESJARDINS
DU QUEBEC**
SERVICES DE PAIE
(*Suby of* FEDERATION DES CAISSES DES-
JARDINS DU QUEBEC)
1611 Boul Cremazie E Bureau 300, Montreal,
QC, H2M 2P2
(514) 356-5000
Emp Here 400
SIC 8721 Accounting, auditing, and book-
keeping

D-U-N-S 24-460-3817   (HQ)
**FEDERATION DES TRAVAILLEURS ET
TRAVAILLEUSES DU QUEBEC (FTQ)**
F T Q
565 Boul Cremazie E Bureau 12100, Mon-
treal, QC, H2M 2W3
(514) 383-8000
Emp Here 10   *Sales* 29,433,750
SIC 8631 Labor organizations
  Henri Masse
  Rene Roy

D-U-N-S 25-822-5143   (BR)
**FONDS DE SOLIDARITE DES TRA-
VAILLEURS DU QUEBEC (F.T.Q.)**
FONDS DE SOLIDARITE FTQ
(*Suby of* FONDS DE SOLIDARITE DES TRA-
VAILLEURS DU QUEBEC (F.T.Q.))
8717 Rue Berri, Montreal, QC, H2M 2T9
(514) 383-3663
Emp Here 100
SIC 6722 Management investment, open-end
  Gaetan Morin

D-U-N-S 24-501-4543   (HQ)
**FONDS DE SOLIDARITE DES TRA-
VAILLEURS DU QUEBEC (F.T.Q.)**
FSTQ
545 Boul Cremazie E Bureau 200, Montreal,
QC, H2M 2W4
(514) 383-8383
Emp Here 450   *Sales* 366,038,820

SIC 6722 Management investment, open-end
Gaetan Morin
Robert Parizeau
Daniel Boyer
Pierre-Maurice Vachon
Serge Cadieux
Sylvie Des Roches
Christine Beaubien
Gerry Boutin
Louise Chabot
Anouk Collet

D-U-N-S 24-116-9338   (BR)
GOUVERNEMENT DE LA PROVINCE DE QUEBEC
CENTRE DOLLARD CORMIER
(*Suby of* GOUVERNEMENT DE LA PROVINCE DE QUEBEC)
950 Rue De Louvain E, Montreal, QC, H2M 2E8
(514) 385-1232
Emp Here 403
SIC 8093 Specialty outpatient clinics, nec
Madelaine Roy

D-U-N-S 20-725-3980   (SL)
LE RELAIS CHEVROLET CADILLAC BUICK GMC LTEE
9411 Av Papineau, Montreal, QC, H2M 2G5
(514) 384-6380
Emp Here 85   *Sales* 53,488,800
SIC 5521 Used car dealers
Francois Verdy
Pascal Verdy

D-U-N-S 24-056-6273   (HQ)
METALLURGISTES UNIS D'AMERIQUE
LE SYNDICAT DE METALLOS
565 Boul Cremazie E Bureau 5100, Montreal, QC, H2M 2V8
(514) 599-2000
Sales 92,332,950
SIC 6371 Pension, health, and welfare funds
Michel Arsenault

D-U-N-S 20-715-7368   (BR)
NORDIA INC
(*Suby of* PLATINUM EQUITY, LLC)
255 Boul Cremazie E, Montreal, QC, H2M 1L5
(514) 387-1285
Emp Here 200
SIC 7389 Business services, nec

D-U-N-S 20-961-9972   (SL)
ORDRE DES TRAVAILLEURS SOCIAUX ET DES THERAPEUTES CONJUGAUX ET FAMILIAUX DU QUEBEC
OTSTCFQ
255 Boul Cremazie E Bureau 520, Montreal, QC, H2M 1L5
(514) 731-3925
Emp Here 50   *Sales* 12,075,750
SIC 8621 Professional organizations
Guylaine Ouimette
Sonia Cisternas
Pierre-Paul Malenfant
Serge Turcotte
Sylvio Rioux

D-U-N-S 24-352-9963   (SL)
PETRIE RAYMOND S.E.N.C.R.L
255 Boul Cremazie E Bureau 1000, Montreal, QC, H2M 1L5
(514) 342-4740
Emp Here 80   *Sales* 16,614,800
SIC 8721 Accounting, auditing, and book-keeping
Marcel Pilon
France Gagnon
Chantal Robidas
Guy Lapointe
Andre Bernier
Alexandre Roy
Guylaine Lemay
Jean-Guy Dumas
Yvan Martin
Jean-Pierre Raby

D-U-N-S 25-827-6294   (BR)
PROVIGO DISTRIBUTION INC
MAXI
(*Suby of* LOBLAW COMPANIES LIMITED)
8305 Av Papineau, Montreal, QC, H2M 2G2
(514) 376-6457
Emp Here 150
SIC 5411 Grocery stores
Richard Riendeau

D-U-N-S 24-051-3572   (SL)
RHEAUME, MICHEL & ASSOCIES LTEE
800-1611 Boul Cremazie E, Montreal, QC, H2M 2P2
(514) 329-3333
Emp Here 60   *Sales* 50,883,600
SIC 6411 Insurance agents, brokers, and service
Dominique Laberge

D-U-N-S 24-021-3066   (BR)
SCM INSURANCE SERVICES INC
SCM CANADA
(*Suby of* SCM INSURANCE SERVICES INC)
255 Boul Cremazie E Bureau 1070, Montreal, QC, H2M 1L5
(514) 331-1030
Emp Here 150
SIC 6411 Insurance agents, brokers, and service
Richard Berreault

D-U-N-S 20-706-4929   (SL)
SPORTS MONTREAL INC
CENTRE DE CONDITIONNEMENT PHYSIQUE L'OPTION SANTE
1000 Av Emile-Journault, Montreal, QC, H2M 2E7
(514) 872-7177
Emp Here 250   *Sales* 23,917,000
SIC 7032 Sporting and recreational camps
Michel Martin
Roger Domingue
Chantal Robidas
Raymond Labrosse
Vincent Destouches
Yoann David Gauthier
Jean-Guy Rochon
Caroline Pujol

D-U-N-S 24-650-0151   (SL)
SUPERMARCHE ANDRE GRASSET INC
8935 Av Andre-Grasset, Montreal, QC, H2M 2E9
(514) 382-1465
Emp Here 115   *Sales* 33,749,855
SIC 5411 Grocery stores
Gilles Messier
Denis Messier

D-U-N-S 25-485-3195   (SL)
SYNDICAT DES EMPLOYEES ET EMPLOYES PROFESIONNELS-LES ET DE BUREAU-QUEBEC (SEPB-QUEBEC)
565 Boul Cremazie E Bureau 11100, Montreal, QC, H2M 2W2
(514) 522-6511
Emp Here 38   *Sales* 14,913,100
SIC 8631 Labor organizations
Maurice Laplante
Pierre Gerin-Roze
Claude Picotte
Jack Fitch
Dumoulin Chantal
Daniel Gamelin
Gisele Dupuis
Francois Leduc
Daniel Larose
Pierre Tourville

D-U-N-S 25-624-6331   (HQ)
SYNDICAT QUEBECOIS DES EMPLOYEES & EMPLOYES DE SERVICE SECTION LOCAL 298 (FTQ)
565 Boul Cremazie E Bureau 4300, Montreal, QC, H2M 2V6

(514) 727-1696
Emp Here 48   *Sales* 21,192,300
SIC 8631 Labor organizations
Raymond Forget
Daniel Boyer

D-U-N-S 20-592-3720   (BR)
VILLE DE MONTREAL
DIRECTION DES RESSOURCES HUMAINES
(*Suby of* VILLE DE MONTREAL)
9335 Rue Saint-Hubert, Montreal, QC, H2M 1Y7
(514) 385-2893
Emp Here 300
SIC 8322 Individual and family services
Julie Morin

Montreal, QC H2N

D-U-N-S 20-616-0579   (SL)
152258 CANADA INC
AGENCE IMPORT ET EXPORT
555 Rue Chabanel O Bureau M53b, Montreal, QC, H2N 2H7
Emp Here 25   *Sales* 12,667,579
SIC 5137 Women's and children's clothing
Stamatios Vasilantonopoulos

D-U-N-S 24-872-1664   (HQ)
163972 CANADA INC
JUDITH & CHARLES
(*Suby of* 3378683 CANADA INC)
9600 Rue Meilleur Bureau 730, Montreal, QC, H2N 2E3
(514) 385-3629
Emp Here 39   *Sales* 12,557,720
SIC 5621 Women's clothing stores
Charles Le Pierres

D-U-N-S 25-356-5188   (HQ)
168662 CANADA INC
LILIANNE LINGERIE
333 Rue Chabanel O Bureau 800, Montreal, QC, H2N 2E7
(514) 384-7691
Emp Here 8   *Sales* 17,939,600
SIC 5632 Women's accessory and specialty stores
Francois Lapierre
Michel Lapierre
Anny-Claude Lapierre
Norman Lutfy

D-U-N-S 20-738-0254   (HQ)
190712 CANADA INC
270 Rue De Louvain O, Montreal, QC, H2N 1B6
(514) 389-8221
Sales 22,008,360
SIC 2297 Nonwoven fabrics
Stuart K Zuckerman
Alison R Rudson
Richard W. Zuckerman
Alan Zuckerman

D-U-N-S 24-960-3101   (SL)
2810221 CANADA INC
VETEMENT CLOTHESLINE
9500 Rue Meilleur Bureau 800, Montreal, QC, H2N 2B7
(514) 388-0284
Emp Here 30   *Sales* 14,949,660
SIC 5136 Men's and boy's clothing
Joelle Berdugo

D-U-N-S 24-335-7733   (SL)
2854-5150 QUEBEC INC
DU+ CONSEILS
9601 Boul Saint-Laurent, Montreal, QC, H2N 1P6
(514) 385-1762
Emp Here 70   *Sales* 19,910,590
SIC 6512 Nonresidential building operators

Benoit Duplessis

D-U-N-S 20-118-0820   (HQ)
3378683 CANADA INC
9600 Rue Meilleur Bureau 630, Montreal, QC, H2N 2E3
(514) 385-3629
Sales 19,134,500
SIC 6712 Bank holding companies
Charles Le Pierres

D-U-N-S 20-718-9148   (SL)
4113993 CANADA INC
ALISON SHERI
555 Rue Chabanel O Bureau 707, Montreal, QC, H2N 2H8
(514) 382-7066
Emp Here 20   *Sales* 10,006,500
SIC 5137 Women's and children's clothing
Sheldon Mazoff
Lei Wang

D-U-N-S 24-357-0665   (HQ)
6938001 CANADA INC
ZACKS
(*Suby of* FIXCO HOLDINGS INC)
433 Rue Chabanel O Unite 801, Montreal, QC, H2N 2J7
(514) 383-0026
Emp Here 105
SIC 5621 Women's clothing stores
Jeffrey Fixman

D-U-N-S 25-381-1004   (SL)
9076-5223 QUEBEC INC
CIE. MYLES INTERNATIONAL
9200 Rue Meilleur Ste 501, Montreal, QC, H2N 2A5
(514) 274-5677
Emp Here 39   *Sales* 19,845,384
SIC 5023 Homefurnishings
Jeffrey Lann

D-U-N-S 20-691-6129   (SL)
9149-5077 QUEBEC INC
RUNNERS CLOTHING INTERNATIONAL
333 Rue Chabanel O Bureau 504, Montreal, QC, H2N 2E7
(514) 381-2886
Emp Here 19   *Sales* 14,886,063
SIC 5137 Women's and children's clothing
Ron Kaminski

D-U-N-S 24-351-8839   (SL)
9189-8718 QUEBEC INC
ACADEX IMPORTS
350 Rue De Louvain O Bureau 310, Montreal, QC, H2N 2E8
(514) 389-7297
Emp Here 120   *Sales* 100,503,960
SIC 5137 Women's and children's clothing
Brian Stott

D-U-N-S 20-209-3340   (HQ)
ACCESSOIRES OUTILLAGE LIMITEE
8755 Boul Saint-Laurent, Montreal, QC, H2N 1M2
(514) 387-6466
Sales 11,875,650
SIC 5082 Construction and mining machinery
Jean-Claude Mallette
Sylvain Mallette
Manon Girouard
Stephanie Mallette
Gisele Mallette

D-U-N-S 20-644-2142   (SL)
AGENCES LISETTE LIMOGES INC, LES
LISETTE L MONTREAL
9250 Av Du Parc Bureau 300, Montreal, QC, H2N 1Z2
(514) 385-1222
Emp Here 50   *Sales* 24,916,100
SIC 5137 Women's and children's clothing
Lisette Limoges

D-U-N-S 25-368-2058   (BR)
AVIVA CANADA INC

AVIVA
(Suby of GENERAL ACCIDENT PLC)
555 Rue Chabanel O Bureau 900, Montreal,
QC, H2N 2H8
(514) 850-4100
Emp Here 170
SIC 6411 Insurance agents, brokers, and service

D-U-N-S 25-502-4499   (SL)
B.L. INTIMATE APPAREL CANADA INC
LINGERIE ZEBRA - CENTRE DE LIQUIDATION
(Suby of BERKSHIRE HATHAWAY INC.)
9500 Rue Meilleur Bureau 111, Montreal, QC,
H2N 2B7
(514) 858-9254
Emp Here 35   *Sales* 17,441,270
SIC 5137 Women's and children's clothing
 Christopher Mark Champion
 Ben Lieberman
 Martin Lieberman
 Richard Carlson Price

D-U-N-S 20-211-2637   (SL)
BEAUMARCHE INC
B.I. GROUP
9124 Boul Saint-Laurent, Montreal, QC, H2N
1M9
(514) 382-4062
Emp Here 27   *Sales* 13,454,694
SIC 5137 Women's and children's clothing
 Rose Svarc
 Allan Svarc
 Paul Svarc

D-U-N-S 24-958-7031   (HQ)
BIJOUTIERS DOUCET 1993 INC, LES
BIJOUTERIE LATENDRESSE
9250 Rue Meilleur Bureau 201, Montreal, QC,
H2N 2A5
(514) 385-4500
Emp Here 20   *Sales* 45,884,250
SIC 5944 Jewelry stores
 Carlos Charles Benezra

D-U-N-S 20-220-9144   (SL)
CABRELLI INC
C DESIGN
9200 Rue Meilleur Bureau 300, Montreal, QC,
H2N 2A9
(514) 384-4750
Emp Here 25   *Sales* 12,458,050
SIC 5137 Women's and children's clothing
 Mark Golfman

D-U-N-S 20-213-6172   (HQ)
CANSEW INC
CS DESIGN
111 Rue Chabanel O Bureau 101, Montreal,
QC, H2N 1C9
(514) 382-2807
Sales 22,008,360
SIC 2284 Thread mills
 Hershie Schachter
 Jack Schachter
 Mark Schachter

D-U-N-S 24-684-2160   (HQ)
CAPITAL STIKLY INC
MANTEAUX MOOSE
225 Rue Chabanel O Bureau 200, Montreal,
QC, H2N 2C9
(514) 381-5393
Sales 12,956,372
SIC 5136 Men's and boy's clothing
 Noah Stern
 Ayal Twik
 Donald Levy

D-U-N-S 24-179-8479   (SL)
**CENTRE SOCIAL DES FONCTIONNAIRES
MUNICIPAUX DE MONTREAL**
*CENTRE SOCIAL DES COLS BLANCS DE
L'ILE DE MONTREAL*
8790 Av Du Parc, Montreal, QC, H2N 1Y6
(514) 842-9463
Emp Here 499   *Sales* 65,625,985

SIC 8641 Civic and social associations
 Francine Bouliane
 Patrick Dubois
 Benoit Audette
 Jonathan Arsenault
 Johanne Joly
 Maryse Chretien
 Lyne Lachapelle
 Gilles Maheu

D-U-N-S 20-270-5133   (SL)
CHAPELLERIE JEAN MYRIAM INC, LA
CHAPELLERIE, LA
555 Rue Chabanel O Unite 303, Montreal, QC,
H2N 2H8
(514) 383-0549
Emp Here 40   *Sales* 19,932,880
SIC 5137 Women's and children's clothing
 Christian Hamelin
 Pascal Pelletier
 Richard Pelletier

D-U-N-S 24-370-6556   (HQ)
CIOT INC
CIOT CANADA
(Suby of CIOT MT INC)
9151 Boul Saint-Laurent, Montreal, QC, H2N
1N2
(514) 382-5180
Emp Here 185   *Sales* 113,925,600
SIC 5032 Brick, stone, and related material
 Giuseppe Panzera
 Michael Panzera
 Fernando Mammoliti
 Kristina Panzera
 Rocco Matteo

D-U-N-S 24-741-2943   (SL)
COLLECTION CONRAD C INC
PROPORTION PETITE
9320 Boul Saint-Laurent Bureau 200, Montreal, QC, H2N 1N7
(514) 385-9599
Emp Here 120   *Sales* 16,400,880
SIC 2337 Women's and misses' suits and
coats
 Jeffrey Cape
 Michael Cape

D-U-N-S 20-291-2689   (SL)
CREATIONS CLAIRE BELL INC
8955 Boul Saint-Laurent Bureau 301, Montreal, QC, H2N 1M5
(514) 270-1477
Emp Here 26   *Sales* 12,956,372
SIC 5137 Women's and children's clothing
 Ronnie Gottlieb

D-U-N-S 24-970-9346   (SL)
CREATIONS G.S.L. INC
CREATIONS NATHALIE BARBARA
(Suby of SUPPORTS SPENCER CANADA
LIMITEE)
9494 Boul Saint-Laurent Bureau 800, Montreal, QC, H2N 1P4
(514) 273-0422
Emp Here 45   *Sales* 22,424,490
SIC 5137 Women's and children's clothing
 Jurgen Bauer
 Markus Haug
 France Beauregard

D-U-N-S 24-615-0866   (SL)
CREATIONS NOC NOC INC
BALI
9600 Rue Meilleur Bureau 750, Montreal, QC,
H2N 2E3
(514) 381-2554
Emp Here 24   *Sales* 11,959,728
SIC 5137 Women's and children's clothing
 Camille Chahine

D-U-N-S 20-761-7648   (HQ)
DECOLIN INC
(Suby of NOVACAP INDUSTRIES IV, L.P.)
9150 Av Du Parc, Montreal, QC, H2N 1Z2
(514) 384-2910
Emp Here 50   *Sales* 57,536,800

SIC 5023 Homefurnishings
 Michel Mendel
 Marc Mactavish
 Mark Gordon
 Wole James
 Alissa Rappaport
 Barry Steinberg

D-U-N-S 20-071-0402   (SL)
ENERGY MASTER
9150 Rue Meilleur, Montreal, QC, H2N 2A5
(514) 433-6487
Emp Here 5   *Sales* 15,529,285
SIC 4924 Natural gas distribution

D-U-N-S 24-169-0726   (HQ)
ENTREPRISES ERNEST (MTL) LTEE, LES
ANTHONY
9200 Rue Meilleur Bureau 101, Montreal, QC,
H2N 2A9
(514) 858-5258
Emp Here 30   *Sales* 43,664,250
SIC 5611 Men's and boys' clothing stores
 Mark Iarrera
 Carolyn Iarrera

D-U-N-S 24-667-9195   (HQ)
FABTRENDS INTERNATIONAL INC
9350 Av De L'Esplanade, Montreal, QC, H2N
1V6
(514) 382-2210
Sales 19,932,880
SIC 5131 Piece goods and notions
 Loren Litwin
 Neil Dick
 Charles Cohen

D-U-N-S 24-364-4239   (SL)
FDJ FRENCH DRESSING INC
225 Rue Chabanel O Bureau 200, Montreal,
QC, H2N 2C9
(514) 333-7171
Emp Here 20   *Sales* 10,006,500
SIC 5137 Women's and children's clothing
 Noah Stern
 Ayal Twik

D-U-N-S 24-433-5071   (HQ)
FLAMCAN TEXTILES INC
EEJAY TEXTILES
9600 Rue Meilleur Bureau 101, Montreal, QC,
H2N 2E3

Sales 10,963,084
SIC 5131 Piece goods and notions
 Louis Flamenbaum
 Edward Jakubiak

D-U-N-S 24-870-1872   (SL)
GESTIONS ARDOVA LTEE, LES
433 Rue Chabanel O Bureau 1000, Montreal,
QC, H2N 2J8
(514) 381-5941
Emp Here 35   *Sales* 14,677,425
SIC 6712 Bank holding companies
 Robert Cohen

D-U-N-S 25-495-4563   (BR)
GROUPE ALGO INC
(Suby of GROUPE ALGO INC)
225 Rue Chabanel O, Montreal, QC, H2N 2C9
(514) 384-3551
Emp Here 75
SIC 2335 Women's, junior's, and misses'
dresses

D-U-N-S 24-922-2043   (HQ)
GROUPE APP (CANADA) INC
MACKAGE
600 Rue Chabanel O, Montreal, QC, H2N 2K6
(514) 388-5287
Sales 17,939,600
SIC 5699 Miscellaneous apparel and accessory stores
 Patrick Elfassy
 Ilan Elfassy
 Benjamin Hochberg
 Collins Ward

 Meir Elfassy
 Jason Kim
 Eran Elfassy
 Gary Wassner
 Elisa Dahan

D-U-N-S 20-610-6374   (HQ)
GROUPE ATALLAH INC
SSENSE
(Suby of ATALLAH INTERNATIONAL INC)
333 Rue Chabanel O Bureau 900, Montreal,
QC, H2N 2E7
(514) 600-5818
Emp Here 1   *Sales* 18,713,250
SIC 5632 Women's accessory and specialty
stores
 Rami Atallah
 Bassel Atallah
 Firas Atallah
 Samih Attalah
 Fadia Suckarieh

D-U-N-S 20-330-3656   (SL)
GROUPE CABRELLI INC
CABRELLI DESIGN
9200 Rue Meilleur Bureau 300, Montreal, QC,
H2N 2A9
(514) 384-4750
Emp Here 25   *Sales* 12,458,050
SIC 5137 Women's and children's clothing
 Mark Golfman

D-U-N-S 25-286-5183   (SL)
**GROUPE DE TISSUS NINO MARCELLO
INC, LE**
ROUTE 97
555 Rue Chabanel O Unite 902, Montreal, QC,
H2N 2H7
(514) 441-3555
Emp Here 25   *Sales* 12,458,050
SIC 5137 Women's and children's clothing
 Jamal Abdul Rashid

D-U-N-S 24-502-5531   (SL)
GROUPE MINIMOME INC
DEUX PAR DEUX
(Suby of 2689316 CANADA INC)
225 Rue Chabanel O Bureau 800, Montreal,
QC, H2N 2C9
(514) 383-3408
Emp Here 40   *Sales* 19,932,880
SIC 5137 Women's and children's clothing
 Claude Diwan
 Zacharie Elmaleh
 Maurice Elmaleh

D-U-N-S 20-761-9156   (HQ)
GROUPE S.M. INC, LE
GROUPE S.M.
(Suby of GROUPE SMI INC, LE)
433 Rue Chabanel O 12e Etage, Montreal,
QC, H2N 2J8
(514) 982-6001
Emp Here 148
SIC 8711 Engineering services

D-U-N-S 24-890-1431   (HQ)
GROUPE S.M. INTERNATIONAL INC, LE
TRC SMI
(Suby of LE GROUPE S.M. INTERNATIONAL
S.E.C.)
433 Rue Chabanel O Bureau 1200, Montreal,
QC, H2N 2J8
(514) 982-6001
Emp Here 148   *Sales* 87,526,164
SIC 8711 Engineering services
 Francois Gaudreau
 Richard Helie
 Pirre-Yves Methot

D-U-N-S 20-551-5286   (SL)
GROUPE STERLING INTIMITE INC, LE
9600 Rue Meilleur Bureau 930, Montreal, QC,
H2N 2E3
(514) 385-0500
Emp Here 26   *Sales* 12,956,372
SIC 5137 Women's and children's clothing

▲ Public Company   ■ Public Company Family Member   **HQ** Headquarters   **BR** Branch   **SL** Single Location

Elliot Berzan

D-U-N-S 20-531-6578   (HQ)
GROUPE TOUCHETTE INC
AAAAAA S.P. RADIAL SERVICE
9000 Boul Saint-Laurent, Montreal, QC, H2N 1M7
(514) 381-1888
Emp Here 300   *Sales* 230,577,000
SIC 5014 Tires and tubes
Nicolas Touchette
Frederic Bouthiller
Andre Touchette

D-U-N-S 25-186-7628   (SL)
GROUPE TRIUM INC
9031 Av Du Parc, Montreal, QC, H2N 1Z1
(514) 355-1625
Emp Here 45   *Sales* 33,413,400
SIC 5199 Nondurable goods, nec
Pierre Gendron
Pierre Bellemare

D-U-N-S 24-858-9400   (SL)
HAPPY KIDS CANADA INC
KIDS CLOTHING WAREHOUSE
8955 Boul Saint-Laurent Bureau 301, Montreal, QC, H2N 1M5
(514) 270-1477
Emp Here 75   *Sales* 37,374,150
SIC 5137 Women's and children's clothing
Ronnie Gottlieb

D-U-N-S 24-110-4090   (SL)
IMPORTATIONS JEREMY D. LIMITED
LUCIEN DAUNOIS
9333 Boul Saint-Laurent Bureau 200, Montreal, QC, H2N 1P6
(514) 385-3898
Emp Here 226   *Sales* 59,965,710
SIC 2335 Women's, junior's, and misses' dresses
Patrick Elhadad
Valerie Elhadad

D-U-N-S 24-111-7829   (HQ)
IMPORTATIONS RALLYE INC
433 Rue Chabanel O Bureau 1000, Montreal, QC, H2N 2J8
(514) 381-5941
Sales 17,441,270
SIC 5136 Men's and boy's clothing
Dov Cohen
Josiane Benchimol

D-U-N-S 25-298-4331   (SL)
IMPORTATIONS S.M.D. LTEE, LES
555 Rue Chabanel O, Montreal, QC, H2N 2H7
(514) 389-3474
Emp Here 23   *Sales* 11,461,406
SIC 5137 Women's and children's clothing
Moise Derhy
Guy Derhy
Alice Derhy

D-U-N-S 24-424-8238   (SL)
KIM-LAUREN & CIE INC
KIM & CO
(*Suby of* 7919042 CANADA INC)
9400 Boul Saint-Laurent Bureau 402, Montreal, QC, H2N 1P3
(514) 385-3582
Emp Here 26   *Sales* 12,956,372
SIC 5137 Women's and children's clothing
Kim Mendelson

D-U-N-S 24-418-5513   (SL)
LEVY CANADA FASHION COMPANY
MODE LEVY CANADA
225 Rue Chabanel O Bureau 200, Montreal, QC, H2N 2C9
(514) 908-0104
Emp Here 20   *Sales* 10,006,500
SIC 5136 Men's and boy's clothing
Noah Stern
Gary Levy
Donald Levy

D-U-N-S 20-879-0852   (HQ)
MANUFACTURE DE BAS CULOTTES LAMOUR INC
AMOUR HOSIERY, L'
55 Rue De Louvain O Bureau 200, Montreal, QC, H2N 1A4
(514) 381-7687
Sales 18,340,300
SIC 2251 Women's hosiery, except socks
Benjamin Lieberman
Martin Lieberman
Michael Lieberman

D-U-N-S 20-234-6532   (SL)
MANUFACTURIER DE BAS DE NYLON SPLENDID INC
55 Rue De Louvain O Bureau 200, Montreal, QC, H2N 1A4
(514) 381-7687
Emp Here 200   *Sales* 167,506,600
SIC 5137 Women's and children's clothing
Aron Liberman
Frieda Lieberman
Sam Lieberman

D-U-N-S 20-370-3418   (SL)
MODE RVING INC
METARA
555 Rue Chabanel O Bureau M42b, Montreal, QC, H2N 2J2
(514) 577-2172
Emp Here 1   *Sales* 10,387,224
SIC 2389 Apparel and accessories, nec
Goutam Mitra

D-U-N-S 24-581-6111   (HQ)
MODES CAZZA INC
CAZZA PETITE
(*Suby of* FIXCO HOLDINGS INC)
433 Rue Chabanel O Unite 801, Montreal, QC, H2N 2J7
(514) 383-0026
Emp Here 10   *Sales* 16,504,432
SIC 5621 Women's clothing stores
Jeffrey Fixman

D-U-N-S 24-051-1683   (SL)
MODES CORWIK INC
COTON EN FLEUR
(*Suby of* 9184-3706 QUEBEC INC)
225 Rue Chabanel O Bureau 200, Montreal, QC, H2N 2C9
(514) 381-5393
Emp Here 100   *Sales* 83,753,300
SIC 5137 Women's and children's clothing
Freddy Twik
Hezi Twik
Shai Twik
Ayal Twik
Shelley Twik

D-U-N-S 24-422-6168   (SL)
MODES KNIT SET (2010) LTEE, LES
9500 Rue Meilleur Bureau 510, Montreal, QC, H2N 2B7

Emp Here 23   *Sales* 11,461,406
SIC 5137 Women's and children's clothing
Steve Pearson
Anna Lapointe
Michel Harouche

D-U-N-S 20-227-8925   (SL)
MODES MORSAM INC
350 Rue De Louvain O Bureau 101, Montreal, QC, H2N 2E8
(514) 383-0033
Emp Here 20   *Sales* 10,006,500
SIC 5137 Women's and children's clothing
Steven Lupovich
Ginette Wood

D-U-N-S 24-343-5315   (SL)
MODES ZERO II 60 INC
9400 Boul Saint-Laurent Bureau 200, Montreal, QC, H2N 1P3
(514) 383-3580
Emp Here 20   *Sales* 10,006,500

SIC 5137 Women's and children's clothing
Michael Shapiro
Susan Krane

D-U-N-S 20-566-3391   (SL)
NOXS INC
AUBAINES LEE
(*Suby of* 4392256 CANADA INC)
9500 Rue Meilleur Bureau 200, Montreal, QC, H2N 2B7
(514) 385-0636
Emp Here 40   *Sales* 19,932,880
SIC 5136 Men's and boy's clothing
George Botchoun

D-U-N-S 24-349-4577   (SL)
RAND ACCESSORIES INC
CONCESSIONNAIRE DCK CANADA
(*Suby of* RAND FRERES)
9350 Av De L'Esplanade Bureau 222, Montreal, QC, H2N 1V6
(514) 385-3482
Emp Here 20   *Sales* 10,410,840
SIC 5094 Jewelry and precious stones
Michael Ziegler
Adam Goldberg
Bernard Perez

D-U-N-S 25-247-3640   (HQ)
RUDSAK INC
2XPOSE
(*Suby of* 6317120 CANADA INC)
9160 Boul Saint-Laurent Bureau 400, Montreal, QC, H2N 1M9
(514) 389-9661
Emp Here 75   *Sales* 79,600,500
SIC 2386 Leather and sheep-lined clothing
Evik Asatoorian

D-U-N-S 20-216-9041   (SL)
SERVICE DE COUPAGE DOMINION INC
99 Rue Chabanel O Bureau 104, Montreal, QC, H2N 1C3
(514) 270-4118
Emp Here 30   *Sales* 15,265,680
SIC 5023 Homefurnishings
Murraya. Cuttler

D-U-N-S 20-386-2859   (SL)
SERVICES DE PERSONNEL S.M. INC.
433, Rue Chabanel Ouest 12e Etage, Montreal, QC, H2N 2J9
(514) 982-6001
Emp Here 500   *Sales* 37,347,000
SIC 7361 Employment agencies
Martin Franco

D-U-N-S 24-676-0235   (HQ)
SISTEMALUX INC
9320 Boul Saint-Laurent Bureau 100, Montreal, QC, H2N 1N7
(514) 523-1339
Sales 58,024,700
SIC 5063 Electrical apparatus and equipment
Salvatore Folisi
Massimiliano Guzzini
Andrea Sasso
Antoine Dufresne Folisi
Alessandro Folisi
Marie-Josee Dufresne
Cristiano Venturini
Matteo Mengoni

D-U-N-S 24-834-9557   (SL)
SOCIETE DE COMMERCE ACADEX INC
CLUB SNOB
350 Rue De Louvain O Bureau 310, Montreal, QC, H2N 2E8
(514) 389-7297
Emp Here 120   *Sales* 100,503,960
SIC 5137 Women's and children's clothing
Joseph Khouri
Michael Khouri
Nathali Khouri

D-U-N-S 20-236-2851   (SL)
SOUS-VETEMENTS U.M. INC, LES
(*Suby of* 136482 CANADA INC)

9200 Boul Saint-Laurent, Montreal, QC, H2N 1M9
(514) 387-3791
Emp Here 150   *Sales* 20,501,100
SIC 2321 Men's and boy's furnishings
Carl Grekin

D-U-N-S 24-683-6816   (SL)
TEMPLE LIFESTYLE INCORPORATED
9600 Rue Meilleur Bureau 932, Montreal, QC, H2N 2E3
(514) 382-3805
Emp Here 15   *Sales* 12,533,655
SIC 5149 Groceries and related products, nec
Christopher Magnone
Michael Magnone
Kaila Magnone
Mark Cigos

D-U-N-S 20-760-2939   (SL)
TRICOT IDEAL INC
9494 Boul Saint-Laurent Bureau 400, Montreal, QC, H2N 1P4
(514) 381-4496
Emp Here 80   *Sales* 14,672,240
SIC 2253 Knit outerwear mills
Edward Binet

D-U-N-S 25-976-9446   (SL)
TXT CARBON FASHIONS INC
433 Rue Chabanel O Bureau 400, Montreal, QC, H2N 2J4
(514) 382-8271
Emp Here 60   *Sales* 29,899,320
SIC 5136 Men's and boy's clothing
Tony Simoes
Frank Nicodemo

D-U-N-S 24-529-1208   (SL)
UGO-SAC IMPORTS LTD
9500 Rue Meilleur Bureau 600, Montreal, QC, H2N 2B7
(514) 382-4271
Emp Here 20   *Sales* 10,006,500
SIC 5137 Women's and children's clothing
Louis Stern
Morton Stern

D-U-N-S 25-524-7439   (SL)
VETEMENTS URBAN RAGS INC
9130 Av Du Parc, Montreal, QC, H2N 1Z2
(514) 384-6922
Emp Here 35   *Sales* 17,441,270
SIC 5137 Women's and children's clothing
Vant Tashdjian
Parsegh Vahe Tashdjian

Montreal, QC H2P

D-U-N-S 24-896-7465   (SL)
4453760 CANADA INC
EUREKA LIGHTING
225 Rue De Liege O Bureau 200, Montreal, QC, H2P 1H4
(514) 385-3515
Emp Here 100   *Sales* 19,044,200
SIC 3645 Residential lighting fixtures
Patrick Foley
Christian B. Fabi
Guy St-Pierre
Serge Lambert

D-U-N-S 20-117-3403   (SL)
9108-1950 QUEBEC INC
VIA TRANS INTERNATIONAL
8355 Rue Jeanne-Mance, Montreal, QC, H2P 2Y1

Emp Here 35   *Sales* 18,198,845
SIC 4731 Freight transportation arrangement
Peter Panagiotis Kalaganis

D-U-N-S 20-270-9440   (HQ)
9292-1394 QUEBEC INC
VERO MODA

(Suby of HEARTLAND A/S)
225 Rue De Liege O Bureau A, Montreal, QC,
H2P 1H4
(514) 381-4392
Sales 24,916,100
SIC 5136 Men's and boy's clothing
Martha Arnadottir
Thomas Borglum Jensen
Grimur Gararsson

D-U-N-S 20-178-7657   (SL)
AGENCES WANT INC, LES
ESSENTIELS DE VIE WANT, LES
8480 Rue Jeanne-Mance, Montreal, QC, H2P
2S3
(514) 868-9268
Emp Here 30   *Sales* 14,949,660
SIC 5137 Women's and children's clothing
Jacqueline Gelber
Mark Wiltzer

D-U-N-S 20-253-6272   (SL)
**BESTSELLER VENTES EN GROS CANADA
INC**
BESTSELLER
(Suby of HEARTLAND A/S)
225 Rue De Liege O, Montreal, QC, H2P 1H4
(514) 381-4392
Emp Here 120   *Sales* 100,503,960
SIC 5136 Men's and boy's clothing
Anders Holch Povlsen
Dominique Belisle
Thomas Brglum Jensen

D-U-N-S 24-988-5674   (SL)
CHENAIL FRUITS ET LEGUMES INC
CHENAIL IMPORT-EXPORT
340 Rue Bellarmin, Montreal, QC, H2P 1G5
(514) 858-7540
Emp Here 50   *Sales* 41,778,850
SIC 5148 Fresh fruits and vegetables
Jean-Francois Chenail
Antonio Bono

D-U-N-S 24-121-5396   (BR)
COMMISSION SCOLAIRE DE MONTREAL
ECOLE SECONDAIRE LUCIEN PAGE
(Suby of COMMISSION SCOLAIRE DE
MONTREAL)
8200 Boul Saint-Laurent, Montreal, QC, H2P
2L8
(514) 596-5400
Emp Here 250
SIC 8211 Elementary and secondary schools
Louis Bienvenue

D-U-N-S 25-240-2789   (BR)
COMMISSION SCOLAIRE DE MONTREAL
ECOLE SECONDAIRE GEORGES VANIER
(Suby of COMMISSION SCOLAIRE DE
MONTREAL)
1205 Rue Jarry E, Montreal, QC, H2P 1W9
(514) 596-4160
Emp Here 125
SIC 8211 Elementary and secondary schools
Mathieu Desjardins

D-U-N-S 20-053-3086   (HQ)
**COMPAGNIE   D'ASSURANCES   GEN-
ERALES TD**
AVANTAGE BUREAU CHEZ SOI
(Suby of TORONTO-DOMINION BANK, THE)
50 Boul Cremazie O Bureau 1200, Montreal,
QC, H2P 1B6
(514) 382-6060
Emp Here 1   *Sales* 7,913,192,504
SIC 6311 Life insurance
Kenneth W. Lalonde
Antonietta Di Girolamo
Riaz Ahmed
Susan Anne Cummings
Philip C. Moore
John W. Thompson
John Capozzolo
Andrew Pilkington
Elaine Lajeunesse

D-U-N-S 24-635-9707   (SL)
**CORPORATION DES MAITRES MECANI-
CIENS EN TUYAUTERIE DU QUEBEC**
C M M T Q
8175 Boul Saint-Laurent, Montreal, QC, H2P
2M1
(514) 382-2668
Emp Here 55   *Sales* 13,283,325
SIC 8621 Professional organizations
Robert Brown

D-U-N-S 24-851-6861   (SL)
DISTRIBUTIONS BELLUCCI LTEE, LES
BELLUCCI
8145 Boul Saint-Laurent, Montreal, QC, H2P
2M1
(514) 388-1555
Emp Here 26   *Sales* 11,626,524
SIC 5046 Commercial equipment, nec
Stephane Bellucci
Yann Bellucci

D-U-N-S 20-324-4512   (SL)
FATIMA AIT ADDI
PHARMACIE FATIMA AIT ADDI
370 Rue Jarry E, Montreal, QC, H2P 1T9
(514) 382-4730
Emp Here 50   *Sales* 12,647,700
SIC 5912 Drug stores and proprietary stores
Fatima Ait Addi

D-U-N-S 25-334-2810   (SL)
**FAUTEUX, BRUNO, BUSSIERE, LEEWAR-
DEN, CPA, S.E.N.C.R.L.**
F.B.B.L.
1100 Boul Cremazie E Bureau 805, Montreal,
QC, H2P 2X2
(514) 729-3221
Emp Here 110   *Sales* 22,845,350
SIC 8721 Accounting, auditing, and book-
keeping
Gilles Bussiere
Scott Grafton
Robert Leewarden
Michel Trudel
Anne-Marie Desloges

D-U-N-S 25-355-6252   (SL)
GLOBAL M.J.L. LTEE
8355 Rue Jeanne-Mance, Montreal, QC, H2P
2Y1
(514) 858-5566
Emp Here 70   *Sales* 43,852,655
SIC 5148 Fresh fruits and vegetables
Sylvain Mayrand
Alain Jacques
Lina Mayrand

D-U-N-S 20-331-8308   (HQ)
GROUPE LUMINAIRES INC, LE
EUREKA
225 Rue De Liege O Bureau 200, Montreal,
QC, H2P 1H4
(514) 385-3515
Emp Here 1   *Sales* 19,044,200
SIC 3648 Lighting equipment, nec
Christian B. Fabi
Marc Buan
Patrick Foley
Eric Bommer
Hugo Larouche

D-U-N-S 25-334-5565   (BR)
HYDRO-QUEBEC
(Suby of GOUVERNEMENT DE LA
PROVINCE DE QUEBEC)
140 Boul Cremazie O, Montreal, QC, H2P 1C3
(514) 858-8000
Emp Here 821
SIC 8731 Commercial physical research
Rino Ouellette

D-U-N-S 20-221-6651   (SL)
IMPENCO LTEE
240 Rue Guizot O, Montreal, QC, H2P 1L5
(514) 383-1200
Emp Here 100   *Sales* 23,343,500

SIC 3172 Personal leather goods, nec
Jack Herzog

D-U-N-S 20-802-2991   (SL)
IRWIN TOGS INC
ELLABEE INTERNATIONAL
8484 Av De L'Esplanade, Montreal, QC, H2P
2R7
(514) 384-7760
Emp Here 50   *Sales* 24,916,100
SIC 5137 Women's and children's clothing
Edward Binet

D-U-N-S 24-509-5435   (SL)
ITALBEC INTERNATIONAL INC
375 Rue De Liege O, Montreal, QC, H2P 1H6
(514) 383-0668
Emp Here 44   *Sales* 10,271,140
SIC 3281 Cut stone and stone products
Olimpia Testa
Giovanni Testa
Michael Panzera
Giuseppe Panzera

D-U-N-S 20-223-8754   (SL)
J.B. LAVERDURE INC
JBL INTERNATIONAL
400 Boul Cremazie O, Montreal, QC, H2P 1C7
(514) 382-7520
Emp Here 90   *Sales* 75,201,930
SIC 5148 Fresh fruits and vegetables
Jean-Francois Laverdure
Michel Routhier

D-U-N-S 24-390-8238   (HQ)
MEDISOLUTION (2009) INC
SOFTINPG
(Suby of CONSTELLATION SOFTWARE
INC)
110 Boul Cremazie O Bureau 1200, Montreal,
QC, H2P 1B9
(514) 850-5000
Emp Here 60   *Sales* 44,717,400
SIC 5045 Computers, peripherals, and soft-
ware
Jeff Bender
John Billowits
Mark H Leonard

D-U-N-S 24-828-6411   (HQ)
MELOCHE MONNEX INC
(Suby of TORONTO-DOMINION BANK, THE)
50 Boul Cremazie O Bureau 1200, Montreal,
QC, H2P 1B6
(514) 382-6060
Emp Here 700   *Sales* 2,596,575,936
SIC 6712 Bank holding companies
Kenneth W. Lalonde
Tonny Menon
Raymond C.H. Chun
James V. Russell
Monica C. Kowal
Antonietta Di Girolamo

D-U-N-S 25-151-9724   (HQ)
PAGEAU MOREL INC
210 Boul Cremazie O Bureau 110, Montreal,
QC, H2P 1C6
(514) 382-5150
Sales 51,171,260
SIC 6712 Bank holding companies
Rejean Berthiaume
Jacques De Grace
Claude Giguere
Francois Laframboise
Nicole Vachon
Michel Carpentier
Roland Charneux
Luc Ste-Marie
Sylvain Lavoie

D-U-N-S 20-229-8667   (HQ)
**PETRIFOND   FONDATION   COMPAGNIE
LIMITEE**
8320 Boul Saint-Laurent, Montreal, QC, H2P
2M3
(514) 387-2838
Emp Here 12   *Sales* 12,309,300

SIC 1794 Excavation work
Vincent Luongo
Christian Lemieux
Guiseppe Salvo
Daniel Vadeboncoeur

D-U-N-S 20-979-9225   (BR)
PHARMASCIENCE INC
PENDOPHARM
(Suby of JODDES LIMITEE)
8580 Av De L'Esplanade, Montreal, QC, H2P
2R8
(514) 384-6516
Emp Here 250
SIC 2834 Pharmaceutical preparations

D-U-N-S 24-873-7504   (HQ)
PRIMMUM INSURANCE COMPANY
AVANTAGE 2 MILLIONS
(Suby of TORONTO-DOMINION BANK, THE)
50 Boul Cremazie O Bureau 1200, Montreal,
QC, H2P 1B6
(514) 382-6060
Emp Here 260   *Sales* 718,021,248
SIC 6331 Fire, marine, and casualty insurance
Kenneth W. Lalonde
Riaz Ahmed
Susan Anne Cummings
Philip C. Moore
John W. Thompson
John Capozzolo
Andrew C. Pilkington
Elaine Lajeunesse
Antonietta Di Girolamo

D-U-N-S 24-305-2040   (HQ)
**SECURITE   NATIONALE   COMPAGNIE
D'ASSURANCE**
(Suby of TORONTO-DOMINION BANK, THE)
50 Boul Cremazie O Bureau 1200, Montreal,
QC, H2P 1B6
(514) 382-6060
Emp Here 1,500   *Sales* 2,061,105,251
SIC 6712 Bank holding companies
Kenneth W. Lalonde
Antonietta Di Girolamo
Riaz Ahmed
Susan Anne Cummings
Philip C. Moore
John W. Thompson
John Capozzolo
Andrew C. Pilkington
Elaine Lajeunesse

D-U-N-S 20-706-6833   (SL)
SUPERMARCHE DEZIEL INC
IGA
1155 Rue Jarry E, Montreal, QC, H2P 1W9
(514) 725-9323
Emp Here 50   *Sales* 13,707,600
SIC 5411 Grocery stores
Alain Deziel

D-U-N-S 20-521-9467   (HQ)
**SYNDICAT DES EMPLOYE-E-S DE TECH-
NIQUES PROFFESSION**
*SETPBHQ SECTION LOCALE 2000, SYN-
DICAT CANADIEN DE LA FONCTION
PUBLIQUE (F.T.Q.)*
2e Etage 1010, Rue De Liege E, Montreal,
QC, H2P 1L2
(514) 381-2000
Emp Here 27   *Sales* 11,734,740
SIC 8631 Labor organizations
Luc-Andre Faubert

D-U-N-S 25-522-8074   (HQ)
**SYNDICAT EMPLOYEE-ES DE METIERS
D'HYDRO-QUEBEC SECTION LOCALE
1500 SCFP (F.T.Q.)**
SCFP (F.T.Q.)
1010 Rue De Liege E Bureau 1500, Montreal,
QC, H2P 1L2
(514) 387-1500
Sales 12,125,898
SIC 8631 Labor organizations
Richard Perrault

Sylvain Dubreuil

D-U-N-S 24-458-5352   (SL)
TRAVAILLEURS ET TRAVAILLEUSES UNIS DE L'ALIMENTATION ET DU COMMERCE LOCAL-500
1200 Boul Cremazie E Bureau 100, Montreal, QC, H2P 3A7
(514) 332-5825
Emp Here 60   *Sales* 23,547,000
SIC 8631 Labor organizations
Antonio Filato
Robert Armstrong

D-U-N-S 24-205-0719   (HQ)
VENTE AU DETAIL BESTSELLER CANADA INC
BESTSELLER FASHION
(*Suby of* HEARTLAND A/S)
225a Rue De Liege O, Montreal, QC, H2P 1H4
(514) 381-4392
Sales 418,766,500
SIC 5136 Men's and boy's clothing
Anders Holch Povlsen
Dominique Belisle
Thomas Brglum Jensen

D-U-N-S 25-245-5894   (HQ)
VETEMENTS MARK-EDWARDS INC
RILEY AND JAMES; DIV OF
8480 Rue Jeanne-Mance Bureau 201, Montreal, QC, H2P 2S3
(514) 388-2353
Emp Here 30   *Sales* 19,932,880
SIC 5137 Women's and children's clothing
Mark Wiltzer
Jacqueline Gelber

D-U-N-S 20-765-2397   (SL)
VIAU, ROGER & FILS INC
1100 Boul Cremazie E Bureau 500, Montreal, QC, H2P 2X2
(514) 374-9345
Emp Here 29   *Sales* 16,817,796
SIC 6411 Insurance agents, brokers, and service
Robert Viau
Yves Brassard
Jean Viau

Montreal, QC H2R

D-U-N-S 24-969-1783   (HQ)
157341 CANADA INC
7236 Rue Marconi, Montreal, QC, H2R 2Z5
(514) 844-5050
Sales 16,401,000
SIC 6712 Bank holding companies
Mark Sherman

D-U-N-S 25-144-7009   (BR)
168662 CANADA INC
LINGERIE LILIANNE
(*Suby of* 168662 CANADA INC)
260 Rue Gary-Carter, Montreal, QC, H2R 2V7
(514) 384-7691
Emp Here 100
SIC 5632 Women's accessory and specialty stores
Sandra Janeiro

D-U-N-S 24-922-8529   (SL)
2618-1833 QUEBEC INC
274 Rue Jean-Talon E, Montreal, QC, H2R 1S7
(514) 273-3224
Emp Here 60   *Sales* 16,401,000
SIC 6712 Bank holding companies
Flavio Zeffiro

D-U-N-S 24-325-9769   (HQ)
ACT3 M.H.S. INC
ACTE3 M.H.S.
(*Suby of* 157341 CANADA INC)

7236 Rue Marconi, Montreal, QC, H2R 2Z5
(514) 844-5050
Emp Here 75   *Sales* 25,046,375
SIC 7319 Advertising, nec
Mark Sherman
Robert Jenkyn
Chris Marcolefas
Lisa Di Marco
Vasso Fragos
Patricia Gray

D-U-N-S 24-053-0501   (SL)
BOURDON, EDOUARD & FILS INC
METRO
760 Rue Jean-Talon E, Montreal, QC, H2R 1V1
(514) 270-5226
Emp Here 80   *Sales* 23,478,160
SIC 5411 Grocery stores
Jean-Guy Bourdon
Sylvie Bourdon

D-U-N-S 20-213-1744   (SL)
C & M TEXTILES INC
C & M
7500 Rue Saint-Hubert, Montreal, QC, H2R 2N6
(514) 272-0247
Emp Here 50   *Sales* 10,880,650
SIC 5949 Sewing, needlework, and piece goods
Peter Auger
Andrew Auger

D-U-N-S 25-167-7522   (SL)
DIVERTISSEMENTS GAMELOFT INC
(*Suby of* VIVENDI)
7250 Rue Marconi, Montreal, QC, H2R 2Z5
(514) 798-1700
Emp Here 310   *Sales* 57,217,630
SIC 7371 Custom computer programming services
Alexandre De Rochefort
Mario Poulin

D-U-N-S 24-164-3720   (SL)
DOCUMENS TRADUCTION INC
DOCUMENS
(*Suby of* VERSALYS INC)
7245 Rue Alexandra Bureau 301, Montreal, QC, H2R 2Y9
(514) 868-9899
Emp Here 500
SIC 7389 Business services, nec
Olivier Lenormand
Marie-France Deschamps
Francois De Laubier

D-U-N-S 20-996-6084   (HQ)
EDITIONS QUEBEC-AMERIQUE INC, LES
QUEBEC AMERIQUE
(*Suby of* GROUPE QUEBEC AMERIQUE INC, LE)
7240 Rue Saint-Hubert, Montreal, QC, H2R 2N1
(514) 499-3000
Sales 10,661,755
SIC 2741 Miscellaneous publishing
Jacques Fortin
Gisele Fortin
Caroline Fortin

D-U-N-S 24-528-3817   (HQ)
FROMAGERIES PIMAR INC, LES
FROMAGERIE HAMEL
220 Rue Jean-Talon E, Montreal, QC, H2R 1S7
(514) 272-1161
Emp Here 40   *Sales* 21,130,344
SIC 5451 Dairy products stores
Marc Picard
Ian Picard
Murielle Chaput

D-U-N-S 24-357-7629   (BR)
GOLDER ASSOCIATES LTD
GOLDER ASSOCIES
(*Suby of* GOLDER ASSOCIATES CORPO-

RATION)
7250 Rue Du Mile End 3e Etage, Montreal, QC, H2R 3A4
(514) 383-0990
Emp Here 200
SIC 8748 Business consulting, nec
Robert Ferri

D-U-N-S 20-009-5425   (HQ)
GROUPE JOHANNE VERDON INC
ESPACE SANTE BEAUTE JOHANNE VERDON
1274 Rue Jean-Talon E Bureau 200, Montreal, QC, H2R 1W3
(514) 272-0018
Sales 13,707,600
SIC 5499 Miscellaneous food stores
Johanne Verdon
Daniel Grenon

D-U-N-S 25-973-6981   (HQ)
INDUSTRIES GOODWILL RENAISSANCE MONTREAL INC
BOUTIQUE COMMUNAUTAIRE FRIPE-PRIX RENAISSANCE
7250 Boul Saint-Laurent, Montreal, QC, H2R 2X9
(514) 276-3626
Emp Here 50   *Sales* 98,870,200
SIC 5399 Miscellaneous general merchandise
Yvon Arseneault
Janine Desrosiers-Choquette
Yves Prevost
Chantal Clouatre
Pierre Legault
Daniel Binette
Sheila Murphy
Robert Potvin
Paul-Andre Lazure

D-U-N-S 20-364-0651   (SL)
LXRANDCO INC
40 Jean-Talon St W 17th Fl Suite 34, Montreal, QC, H2R 2W5
(514) 623-2052
Emp Here 7   *Sales* 29,042,816
SIC 5963 Direct selling establishments
Stephen Goldsmith
Camillo Di Prata
Luc Mannella
Frederick Mannella
Stephane Guerin
Audrey Lara
Kei Izawa

D-U-N-S 20-372-9236   (SL)
LXRANDCO, INC
LXR & CO
7399 Boul Saint-Laurent, Montreal, QC, H2R 1W7
(514) 654-9993
Emp Here 381   *Sales* 29,042,816
SIC 5632 Women's accessory and specialty stores
Steven David Goldsmith
Luc Mannella
Camillo Di Prata
Kei Izawa
Joseph Mimran
Javier San Juan
Frederick Mannella

D-U-N-S 25-287-0928   (SL)
PATRO LE PREVOST INC
7355 Av Christophe-Colomb, Montreal, QC, H2R 2S5
(514) 273-8535
Emp Here 83   *Sales* 7,691,195
SIC 8322 Individual and family services
Manon Ethier-Rollin

D-U-N-S 20-263-5926   (HQ)
PROMARK-TELECON INC
(*Suby of* CAPITAL REGIONAL ET COOPER-ATIF DESJARDINS)
7450 Rue Du Mile End, Montreal, QC, H2R 2Z6

(514) 644-2214
Emp Here 60   *Sales* 59,631,192
SIC 4899 Communication services, nec
Andre Heroux

D-U-N-S 20-289-6148   (SL)
TELECON DESIGN INC
(*Suby of* CAPITAL REGIONAL ET COOPER-ATIF DESJARDINS)
7450 Rue Du Mile End, Montreal, QC, H2R 2Z6
(514) 644-2333
Emp Here 150   *Sales* 26,810,850
SIC 8711 Engineering services
Andre Heroux

D-U-N-S 24-387-5783   (HQ)
TELECON INC
GROUPE TELECON
(*Suby of* CAPITAL REGIONAL ET COOPER-ATIF DESJARDINS)
7450 Rue Du Mile End, Montreal, QC, H2R 2Z6
(514) 644-2333
Emp Here 1,200   *Sales* 715,301,113
SIC 6712 Bank holding companies
Andre Heroux
Christian Paupe
Pierre Belanger
Mario Bouchard
Guy Marier
Yves Devin
Annie Hotte

D-U-N-S 25-284-8114   (SL)
TOUCHTUNES DIGITAL JUKEBOX INC
(*Suby of* SEARCHLIGHT CAPITAL PART-NERS, L.P.)
7250 Rue Du Mile End Bureau 202, Montreal, QC, H2R 3A4
(514) 762-6244
Emp Here 100   *Sales* 32,613,600
SIC 3931 Musical instruments
W. Ross Honey
Pamela Schoenfeld
Patrick Barry
Phillip Bacal

D-U-N-S 24-976-5004   (SL)
VICONICS TECHNOLOGIES INC
TECHNOLOGIES VICONICS
(*Suby of* SCHNEIDER ELECTRIC SE)
7262 Rue Marconi, Montreal, QC, H2R 2Z5
(514) 321-5660
Emp Here 70   *Sales* 15,910,230
SIC 3822 Environmental controls
Laurent Bataille
Jean-Yves Mouttet
Adrian Davis Thomas
Mary Kibble
Patrick Ok

D-U-N-S 25-978-2659   (SL)
VOS VACATION
8060 Rue Saint-Hubert, Montreal, QC, H2R 2P3
(514) 270-3186
Emp Here 23   *Sales* 11,959,241
SIC 4724 Travel agencies
Dominique Continelli

D-U-N-S 20-503-7641   (HQ)
VOYAGES BERGERON INC
7725 Rue Saint-Denis, Montreal, QC, H2R 2E9
(514) 273-3301
Emp Here 12   *Sales* 12,479,208
SIC 4724 Travel agencies
Lyne Rose

Montreal, QC H2S

D-U-N-S 24-524-2099   (SL)
125382 CANADA INC
5800 Rue Saint-Denis Bureau 402, Montreal,

QC, H2S 3L5
(514) 274-2407
Emp Here 25   *Sales* 12,458,050
SIC 5137 Women's and children's clothing

D-U-N-S 24-387-8209   (SL)
3838731 CANADA INC
GROUPE BUONANOTTE
6885 Boul Saint-Laurent, Montreal, QC, H2S
3C9
(514) 284-4988
Emp Here 80   *Sales* 20,924,240
SIC 6712 Bank holding companies
Massimo Lecas
Roberto Pesut
Angelo Leone

D-U-N-S 20-270-8590   (SL)
7979134 CANADA INC
BOULANGERIE PREMIERE MOISSON
7075 Av Casgrain, Montreal, QC, H2S 3A3

Emp Here 50   *Sales* 11,242,750
SIC 2051 Bread, cake, and related products
Mario Boulanger
Josee Fiset

D-U-N-S 24-761-6324   (SL)
BEHAVIOUR INTERACTIF INC
A2M
6666 Rue Saint-Urbain, Montreal, QC, H2S
3H1
(514) 843-4484
Emp Here 250   *Sales* 46,143,250
SIC 7371 Custom computer programming ser-
vices
Remi Racine
Roland Ribotti

D-U-N-S 24-322-4573   (SL)
BRUNO & NICK INC
*ALIMENTS FINS DE L'USINE DE LA
FOURCHETTE GRASSE, LES*
6766 Rue Marconi, Montreal, QC, H2S 3J7
(514) 272-8998
Emp Here 35   *Sales* 29,245,195
SIC 5141 Groceries, general line
Bruno Cestra

D-U-N-S 24-667-4709   (SL)
C L S C LA PETITE PATRIE
6520 Rue De Saint-Vallier, Montreal, QC, H2S
2P7
(514) 273-4508
Emp Here 150   *Sales* 31,060,200
SIC 8399 Social services, nec
Yves Poirier
St-Jean Bolduc

D-U-N-S 20-926-4720   (HQ)
**CAISSE POPULAIRE DESJARDINS CANA-
DIENNE ITALIENNE**
CENTRE DE SERVICE FLEURY
6999 Boul Saint-Laurent, Montreal, QC, H2S
3E1
(514) 270-4124
Emp Here 14   *Sales* 17,787,723
SIC 6062 State credit unions
Mariano De Carolis
Robert Guerriero
Elio Cerundolo
Paul Dell'aniello
Carole Gagliardi
Raffaele Di Lillo
Serge Branconnier
Anna Cortina
Pierre Gebran
Claude Gobeil

D-U-N-S 20-544-7667   (SL)
**COMITE PARITAIRE DE L'INDUSTRIE DES
SERVICES AUTOMOBILES DE LA REGION
DE MONTREAL**
CPA MONTREAL
509 Rue Belanger Bureau 165, Montreal, QC,
H2S 1G5
(514) 288-3003
Emp Here 45   *Sales* 10,516,275

SIC 8621 Professional organizations
Roger Goudreau

D-U-N-S 24-805-2529   (BR)
COMMISSION SCOLAIRE DE MONTREAL
ECOLE ST-AMBROISE
(*Suby of* COMMISSION SCOLAIRE DE
MONTREAL)
6555 Rue De Normanville, Montreal, QC, H2S
2B8
(514) 596-4940
Emp Here 100
SIC 8211 Elementary and secondary schools
Johanne Levesque

D-U-N-S 20-386-8112   (BR)
**CRANBROOK GLEN ENTERPRISES LIM-
ITED**
L.L. LOZEAU
(*Suby of* GILAMY HOLDINGS INC)
6229 Rue Saint-Hubert, Montreal, QC, H2S
2L9
(514) 274-6577
Emp Here 100
SIC 5946 Camera and photographic supply
stores

D-U-N-S 24-232-5969   (SL)
ECLAIRAGE DIMENSION PLUS INC
ECLAIRAGE DIMENSION PLUS
6666 Rue Saint-Urbain Bureau 320, Montreal,
QC, H2S 3H1
(514) 332-9966
Emp Here 26   *Sales* 11,626,524
SIC 5063 Electrical apparatus and equipment
Serge Le Myre
Benoit Martin

D-U-N-S 20-332-9974   (HQ)
ELEMENT AI INC
6650 Rue Saint-Urbain Bureau 500, Montreal,
QC, H2S 3G9
(514) 379-3568
Sales 73,829,200
SIC 7371 Custom computer programming ser-
vices
Jean-Francois Gagne
Anne Martel
Jean-Sebastien Cournoyer
Yoshua Bengio
Matt Ocko

D-U-N-S 24-516-5311   (SL)
GESTION L.L. LOZEAU LTEE
6229 Rue Saint-Hubert, Montreal, QC, H2S
2L9
(514) 274-6577
Emp Here 127   *Sales* 34,715,450
SIC 6719 Holding companies, nec
Lise L Simard
Jean Simard

D-U-N-S 24-678-8132   (SL)
GESTION REJEAN TROTTIER INC
MARCHAND CANADIAN TIRE DE VERDUN
6275 Boul Saint-Laurent Bureau 343, Mon-
treal, QC, H2S 3C3
(514) 273-2428
Emp Here 30   *Sales* 14,942,340
SIC 5531 Auto and home supply stores
Rejean Trottier

D-U-N-S 20-259-5711   (SL)
GFP LES HOTES DE MONTREAL INC
HM SECURITE
6983 Rue De La Roche, Montreal, QC, H2S
2E6
(514) 274-6837
Emp Here 400   *Sales* 10,621,610
SIC 7381 Detective and armored car services
Pierre Touzin

D-U-N-S 20-553-4360   (BR)
HOME DEPOT OF CANADA INC
HOME DEPOT
(*Suby of* THE HOME DEPOT INC)
100 Rue Beaubien O, Montreal, QC, H2S 3S1

(514) 490-8030
Emp Here 175
SIC 5211 Lumber and other building materials
Max-Alix Bosse

D-U-N-S 24-953-6546   (HQ)
HOPPER INC
TECHNOLOGIES HOPPER, LES
5795 Av De Gaspe Bureau 100, Montreal, QC,
H2S 2X3
(514) 276-0760
Sales 10,048,397
SIC 7371 Custom computer programming ser-
vices
Frederic Lalonde
Sophie Forest
Philip C. Wolf
Jeff Fagnan
Damien Steel
Normand Chartrand

D-U-N-S 24-348-3919   (SL)
INDUSTRIES CAPITOL INC, LES
5795 Av De Gaspe, Montreal, QC, H2S 2X3
(514) 273-0451
Emp Here 150   *Sales* 27,208,200
SIC 3364 Nonferrous die-castings except alu-
minum
Yahia Reguieg
Hernan Ciecha
Arron Fish
Michael Kincaid
Eddy Rosenberg
Ron Domachevsky
Peter Blaikie

D-U-N-S 20-064-4505   (SL)
JEAN-FRANCOIS ROCHEFORT INC
6600 Rue Saint-Urbain Bureau 440, Montreal,
QC, H2S 3G8
(514) 273-7256
Emp Here 100   *Sales* 13,667,400
SIC 2389 Apparel and accessories, nec
Jean-Francois Rochefort

D-U-N-S 20-562-0792   (SL)
LINGERIE HAGO INC
(*Suby of* SCHLAGER HOLDING LTD)
7070 Rue Saint-Urbain, Montreal, QC, H2S
3H6
(514) 276-2518
Emp Here 30   *Sales* 14,949,660
SIC 5137 Women's and children's clothing
Aaron Sander
Hilda Feldman

D-U-N-S 20-217-9164   (SL)
**MANUFACTURE DE VETEMENTS EMPIRE
INC**
(*Suby of* 9014-1805 QUEBEC INC)
5800 Rue Saint-Denis Bureau 302, Montreal,
QC, H2S 3L5
(514) 279-7341
Emp Here 185   *Sales* 25,284,690
SIC 2311 Men's and boy's suits and coats
Ronald E. Leibovitch

D-U-N-S 24-353-8993   (HQ)
MODES HOW INTERNATIONAL INC, LES
6595 Rue Saint-Urbain, Montreal, QC, H2S
3G6
(514) 904-0055
Sales 12,458,050
SIC 5137 Women's and children's clothing
Steven Shein
Howard Codas

D-U-N-S 25-244-5937   (SL)
**PHARMACIEN A. LAJEUNESSE & ASSO-
CIES**
PHARMACIE JEAN COUTU
6461 Av Christophe-Colomb, Montreal, QC,
H2S 2G5
(514) 273-7373
Emp Here 45   *Sales* 11,382,930
SIC 5912 Drug stores and proprietary stores
Andre Lajeunesse

D-U-N-S 24-902-8531   (HQ)
PLACEMENTS A. LAJEUNESSE INC
6500 Rue Saint-Hubert, Montreal, QC, H2S
2M3
(514) 272-8233
Sales 27,335,000
SIC 6712 Bank holding companies
Andre Lajeunesse

D-U-N-S 20-585-2234   (SL)
PROS DE LA PHOTO (QUEBEC) INC, LES
STUDIO NANC
90 Rue Beaubien O Bureau 101, Montreal,
QC, H2S 1V6
(514) 322-7476
Emp Here 49   *Sales* 10,374,476
SIC 7335 Commercial photography
Michel Labadie

D-U-N-S 20-215-1759   (SL)
PROS DE LA PHOTO (QUEBEC) INC, LES
BLACKS PHOTO
90 Rue Beaubien O Bureau 201, Montreal,
QC, H2S 1V6
(514) 273-1588
Emp Here 100   *Sales* 48,074,500
SIC 7384 Photofinish laboratories
Michel Labadie
Alain Garnier
Marc Sauvageau

D-U-N-S 24-768-2909   (SL)
RAMVAL INC
PHARMACIE JEAN COUTU
(*Suby of* PLACEMENTS A. LAJEUNESSE
INC)
6500 Rue Saint-Hubert, Montreal, QC, H2S
2M3
(514) 272-8233
Emp Here 100   *Sales* 24,432,800
SIC 5912 Drug stores and proprietary stores
Andre Lajeunesse
Valerie Lajeunesse
Gabriel Baddour

D-U-N-S 20-590-3474   (SL)
REMAX DU CARTIER INC
7085 Boul Saint-Laurent, Montreal, QC, H2S
3E3
(514) 278-7170
Emp Here 40   *Sales* 13,085,080
SIC 6531 Real estate agents and managers
Lyne Benoit

D-U-N-S 24-707-2721   (HQ)
SCHLAGER HOLDING LTD
HAGO
7070 Rue Saint-Urbain, Montreal, QC, H2S
3H6
(514) 276-2518
Sales 16,401,000
SIC 6712 Bank holding companies
Sara Schlager

D-U-N-S 20-565-6218   (HQ)
**SOLUTIONS DE MAINTENANCE AP-
PLIQUEES (AMS) INC**
7075 Rue Marconi, Montreal, QC, H2S 3K4
(514) 272-8400
Emp Here 250   *Sales* 23,976,000
SIC 7349 Building maintenance services, nec
Eliot Supino
Louisa Supino

D-U-N-S 20-800-1854   (BR)
**SYNDICAT DES PROFESSIONNELLES EN
SOINS DU CENTRE DE SANTE ET SER-
VICES SOCIAUX DU COEUR DE**
*CENTRE DE SANTE ET DE SERVICES SO-
CIAUX DU COEUR-DE-L'ILE*
(*Suby of* GOUVERNEMENT DE LA
PROVINCE DE QUEBEC)
6910 Rue Boyer, Montreal, QC, H2S 2J7
(514) 272-3011
Emp Here 100
SIC 8322 Individual and family services
Lise Boutet

▲ Public Company   ■ Public Company Family Member   **HQ** Headquarters   **BR** Branch   **SL** Single Location

Montreal, QC H2T

D-U-N-S 20-715-4431 (SL)
ATTRACTION IMAGES PRODUCTIONS INC
5455 Av De Gaspe Bureau 804, Montreal, QC,
H2T 3B3
(514) 285-7001
Emp Here 1,000   Sales 149,813,000
SIC 7922 Theatrical producers and services
Marleen Beaulieu
Richard Speer

D-U-N-S 20-561-4089 (SL)
CAPT-AIR INC
5860 Boul Saint-Laurent, Montreal, QC, H2T
1T3
(514) 273-4331
Emp Here 25   Sales 11,875,650
SIC 5087 Service establishment equipment
Andre Rouette
Daniel Rouette
Julien Rouette

D-U-N-S 20-370-0604 (SL)
CARTOUCHES CERTIFIEES INC
NEEDEMPTY
160 Rue Saint-Viateur E Bureau 411, Montreal, QC, H2T 1A8
(888) 573-6787
Emp Here 26   Sales 12,350,676
SIC 5085 Industrial supplies

D-U-N-S 20-267-0154 (HQ)
**CENTRE INTEGRE UNIVERSITAIRE SANTE
ET SERVICES SOCIAUX DU CENTRE-SUD-
DE-L'ILE-DE-MONTREAL**
CIUSSS DU CENTRE-SUD-DE-L'ILE-DE-
MONTREAL
155 Boul Saint-Joseph E, Montreal, QC, H2T
1H4
(514) 593-2044
Emp Here 50   Sales 2,161,560,000
SIC 8011 Offices and clinics of medical doctors
Sonia Belanger
Jean-Marc Potvin
Pierre-Paul Milette
Jacques Couillard
Celine Roy
Annie-Kim Gilbert
Marie-Claude Levesque
Julie D'entremont
Francois Leroux
Renald Breton

D-U-N-S 20-712-4616 (BR)
COMMISSION SCOLAIRE DE MONTREAL
ECOLE DE L'ETINCELLE
(Suby of COMMISSION SCOLAIRE DE
MONTREAL)
6080 Av De L'Esplanade, Montreal, QC, H2T
3A3
(514) 596-4800
Emp Here 85
SIC 8211 Elementary and secondary schools
Pascal Gallant

D-U-N-S 20-277-7918 (SL)
DISTRICT M INC
5455 Av De Gaspe Bureau 730, Montreal, QC,
H2T 3B3
(888) 881-6930
Emp Here 90   Sales 76,765,353
SIC 7311 Advertising agencies
Jean-Francois Cote
Patrice Marin
Sebastien Filion
Serge Michaud

D-U-N-S 20-214-8268 (HQ)
EDITEUR GUERIN LTEE
LIBRAIRIE GUERIN
(Suby of INVESTISSEMENTS REICHENBACH INC, LES)
4501 Rue Drolet, Montreal, QC, H2T 2G2

(514) 842-3481
Emp Here 15   Sales 16,402,700
SIC 2731 Book publishing
Marc-Aime Guerin

D-U-N-S 24-944-1965 (SL)
EMBALLAGE CADEAU NOBLE INC
CHATEAUGUAY PACKAGING
5623 Av Casgrain, Montreal, QC, H2T 1Y1
(514) 278-8500
Emp Here 40   Sales 29,700,800
SIC 5199 Nondurable goods, nec
Samuel Herzog
Mordechai Weber
Eliezer Herzog

D-U-N-S 25-860-9937 (SL)
ENTREPRISES PANTHERE VERTE INC
PANTHERE VERTE, LA
160 Rue Saint-Viateur E Bureau 101, Montreal, QC, H2T 1A8
(514) 507-2620
Emp Here 120   Sales 5,462,280
SIC 5812 Eating places
Moshe Chaim Shoham
David Ben-David
Eric Gross

D-U-N-S 24-978-3700 (SL)
GROUPE ALPHARD INC
5570 Av Casgrain Bureau 101, Montreal, QC,
H2T 1X9
(514) 543-6580
Emp Here 75   Sales 13,196,850
SIC 8711 Engineering services
Thierry Jacquelin
Claude Bissonnette
Francis Gagnon

D-U-N-S 20-290-8885 (BR)
GROUPE YELLOW INC
ARTICLES DE CUIR J E FOURNIER
(Suby of PLACEMENTS YELLOW INC, LES)
5665 Boul Saint-Laurent, Montreal, QC, H2T
1S9
(514) 273-0424
Emp Here 100
SIC 5661 Shoe stores
Susanne Yvon

D-U-N-S 20-237-6463 (HQ)
GROUPE YELLOW INC
AERO
(Suby of PLACEMENTS YELLOW INC, LES)
5665 Boul Saint-Laurent, Montreal, QC, H2T
1S9
(514) 273-0424
Emp Here 70   Sales 124,755,000
SIC 5661 Shoe stores
Douglas Avrith

D-U-N-S 24-295-6886 (SL)
JIMMISS CANADA INC
INTIMODE
5425 Av Casgrain Bureau 502, Montreal, QC,
H2T 1X6
(514) 271-3133
Emp Here 75   Sales 10,250,550
SIC 2322 Men's and boy's underwear and
nightwear
Alphonse Battah
Allan Battah
Robert Battah
Larry Dorais

D-U-N-S 20-236-4154 (SL)
MANUFACTURE UNIVERSELLE S.B. INC
5555 Av Casgrain Bureau 300, Montreal, QC,
H2T 1Y1
(514) 271-1177
Emp Here 100   Sales 13,667,400
SIC 2341 Women's and children's underwear
Stephen Brownstein
Harold Brownstein

D-U-N-S 24-680-1430 (SL)
MODASUITE INC
CORPORATION MODASUITE

160 Rue Saint-Viateur E Bureau 610, Montreal, QC, H2T 1A8
(438) 384-0824
Emp Here 50   Sales 24,916,100
SIC 5136 Men's and boy's clothing
Yifeng Song
Hicham Ratnani
Eric Kim
John Stokes
Marc Baillargeon
Joanne Nemeroff
Eric D'anjou
Eric Simon

D-U-N-S 24-768-6595 (SL)
MODE PETIT BOUFFON INC, LA
5425 Av Casgrain Bureau 401, Montreal, QC,
H2T 1X6
(514) 276-9828
Emp Here 20   Sales 10,006,500
SIC 5137 Women's and children's clothing
David Rosenberg
Glick Pesya Rosenberg

D-U-N-S 25-022-0282 (SL)
ORDRE PROFESSIONEL DES TECHNOLOGISTES MEDICAUX DU QUEBEC, L'
OPTMQ
281 Av Laurier E Bureau 162, Montreal, QC,
H2T 1G2
(514) 527-9811
Emp Here 30   Sales 11,734,740
SIC 8631 Labor organizations
Alain Collette

D-U-N-S 20-857-3402 (HQ)
PAJAR DISTRIBUTION LTD
BLUE PLANET BY PAJAR
(Suby of PAJAR HOLDINGS INC)
4509 Av Coloniale, Montreal, QC, H2T 1V8
(514) 844-3067
Sales 34,882,540
SIC 5139 Footwear
Jacques Golbert
Rachel Golbert
Paul Golbert

D-U-N-S 24-475-0402 (HQ)
PAJAR HOLDINGS INC
4509 Av Coloniale, Montreal, QC, H2T 1V8
(514) 844-3067
Sales 10,462,120
SIC 6712 Bank holding companies
Paul Golbert
Rachel Golbert
Jacques Golbert

D-U-N-S 24-760-1102 (SL)
PRODUCTION PAJAR LTEE
(Suby of PAJAR HOLDINGS INC)
4509 Av Coloniale, Montreal, QC, H2T 1V8
(514) 844-3067
Emp Here 26   Sales 12,956,372
SIC 5139 Footwear
Paul Golbert
Jacques Golbert

D-U-N-S 20-301-9203 (HQ)
PRODUITS BREATHER INC
BREATHER
5605 Av De Gaspe Bureau 610, Montreal, QC,
H2T 2A4
(514) 574-8059
Sales 37,700,010
SIC 6531 Real estate agents and managers
Julien Smith
Aja Baxter
James Fitzgerald
Venky Ganesan
William D. Porteous
Jonathan H. Pearce

D-U-N-S 24-433-8083 (HQ)
SODEM INC
4750 Av Henri-Julien Bureau Rc 050, Montreal, QC, H2T 2C8
(514) 527-9546
Emp Here 50   Sales 24,955,200

SIC 8741 Management services
Jean-Pierre Azzopardi

D-U-N-S 24-970-9866 (HQ)
SOFTVOYAGE INC
201 Av Laurier E Bureau 630, Montreal, QC,
H2T 3E6
(514) 273-0008
Sales 20,122,830
SIC 5045 Computers, peripherals, and software
Moise Levy

D-U-N-S 25-859-7645 (SL)
STUDIOS FRAMESTORE INC
FRAMESTORE
(Suby of BEIJING XINGWU CULTURE DEVELOPMENT CO.,LTD.)
5455 Av De Gaspe Bureau 900, Montreal, QC,
H2T 3B3
(514) 277-0004
Emp Here 550   Sales 49,332,800
SIC 7812 Motion picture and video production
William Sargent
Andre Ryan
Mel Sullivan
Michel Fournier

D-U-N-S 20-224-2202 (SL)
TRICOTS LELA INC, LES
ARAIGNEE
5425 Av Casgrain Bureau 601, Montreal, QC,
H2T 1X6
(514) 271-3102
Emp Here 110   Sales 92,128,630
SIC 5137 Women's and children's clothing
Charles Binet
Dora Binet
George Binet

D-U-N-S 24-374-4575 (SL)
UBISOFT ARTS NUMERIQUES INC
(Suby of UBISOFT ENTERTAINMENT)
5505 Boul Saint-Laurent Bureau 2000, Montreal, QC, H2T 1S6
(514) 490-2000
Emp Here 100   Sales 20,037,100
SIC 7336 Commercial art and graphic design
Yannis Mallat
Yves Guillemot
Claude Guillemot

D-U-N-S 25-849-6041 (HQ)
UBISOFT DIVERTISSEMENTS INC
ATELIER UBI, L'
(Suby of UBISOFT ENTERTAINMENT)
5505 Boul Saint-Laurent Bureau 5000, Montreal, QC, H2T 1S6
(514) 490-2000
Emp Here 1,600   Sales 553,719,000
SIC 7371 Custom computer programming services
Yves Guillemot
Claude Guillemot

Montreal, QC H2V

D-U-N-S 24-490-2169 (SL)
116278 CANADA INC
ALIMENTS MOUKAS
365 Rue Beaubien O, Montreal, QC, H2V 1C8
(514) 495-2435
Emp Here 19   Sales 10,167,356
SIC 5144 Poultry and poultry products
Eftimios Moukas

D-U-N-S 20-229-0078 (SL)
167395 CANADA INC
SUPERMARCHE PA
5242 Av Du Parc, Montreal, QC, H2V 4G7
(514) 273-8782
Emp Here 70   Sales 20,543,390
SIC 5411 Grocery stores
Sarantos Erimos

Anastasios Erimos
Constantinos Moumouris
Parhas Nikos

D-U-N-S 24-815-2662 (SL)
2741-3327 QUEBEC INC
PHARMACIE JEAN COUTU
5692 Av Du Parc, Montreal, QC, H2V 4H1
(514) 270-6500
Emp Here 40   *Sales* 10,118,160
SIC 5912 Drug stores and proprietary stores
Robert Cotchikian

D-U-N-S 20-955-7318 (HQ)
3855155 CANADA INC
SUPERMARCHE P.A.
5029 Av Du Parc, Montreal, QC, H2V 4E9
(514) 271-8788
Sales 58,695,400
SIC 5411 Grocery stores
Sarantos Erimos
Anastasios Erimos
Nikos Parhas
George Foustoukos

D-U-N-S 20-912-5020 (SL)
9191-0174 QUEBEC INC
SUPERMARCHES QUATRE FRERES ENR
5600 Av Du Parc, Montreal, QC, H2V 4H1
(514) 272-5258
Emp Here 49   *Sales* 13,433,448
SIC 5411 Grocery stores

D-U-N-S 24-082-5844 (HQ)
CENTRE DU PIN LIMITEE, LE
225 Rue Joseph-Tison, Montreal, QC, H2V 4S5
(514) 278-5551
Emp Here 20   *Sales* 17,077,960
SIC 5193 Flowers and florists supplies
Jean-Pierre Fournier
Jean Fournier

D-U-N-S 20-534-3655 (BR)
CSG SECURITY CORPORATION
CHUBB EDWARDS
(*Suby of* UNITED TECHNOLOGIES CORPORATION)
6680 Av Du Parc, Montreal, QC, H2V 4H9
(514) 272-7700
Emp Here 220
SIC 1731 Electrical work
Benoit Martin

D-U-N-S 20-500-7883 (HQ)
ENTREPRISES LEZNOFF LTEE, LES
6525 Rue Waverly, Montreal, QC, H2V 4M2
(514) 273-7207
Sales 15,265,680
SIC 5023 Homefurnishings
Louis Leznoff
Seth Leznoff
Aaron Leznoff
Dale Leznoff
Joseph Leznoff

D-U-N-S 20-624-4282 (SL)
ENTRETIEN 4M INC
4-M MAINTENANCE
6300 Av Du Parc Bureau 202, Montreal, QC, H2V 4H8
(514) 274-9933
Emp Here 100   *Sales* 4,020,900
SIC 7349 Building maintenance services, nec
Stavros (Steve) Mitropoulos

D-U-N-S 20-380-8790 (SL)
FRIENDEFI INC
QARROT
6750 Av De L'Esplanade Bureau 320, Montreal, QC, H2V 4M1
(514) 397-0415
Emp Here 100   *Sales* 17,595,800
SIC 8711 Engineering services
Aaron Carr
Francis Fontaine

D-U-N-S 20-210-9039 (HQ)

MAISON DU BAGEL INC
ST-VIATEUR BAGEL
263 Rue Saint-Viateur O, Montreal, QC, H2V 1Y1
(514) 276-8044
Emp Here 50   *Sales* 13,707,600
SIC 5461 Retail bakeries
Jiuseppe Morena
Marco Sblano

D-U-N-S 20-214-4275 (HQ)
MANUFACTURE DE LINGERIE CHATEAU INC
GUY LAROCHE
215 Rue Saint-Zotique O, Montreal, QC, H2V 1A2
(514) 274-7505
Emp Here 20   *Sales* 24,916,100
SIC 5136 Men's and boy's clothing
Michael Jr Khoury
Jefferson Khoury
Daniel Khoury
Kenneth Khoury
Lawrence Khoury

D-U-N-S 20-417-5285 (SL)
MONAS & CIE LTEE
4575 Av Du Parc, Montreal, QC, H2V 4E4
(514) 842-1421
Emp Here 25   *Sales* 11,179,350
SIC 5046 Commercial equipment, nec
Antonios Anthony Moshonas
Maria Stella Marika Moshonas
Robert Moshonas

D-U-N-S 24-592-1309 (HQ)
NURUN INC
NURUN SERVICES CONSEILS
(*Suby of* PUBLICIS GROUPE HOLDINGS B.V.)
358 Rue Beaubien O, Montreal, QC, H2V 4S6
(514) 392-1900
Emp Here 120   *Sales* 147,658,400
SIC 7371 Custom computer programming services
Claude Renaud
Ariel Marciano
Duncan Bruce

D-U-N-S 25-514-1301 (HQ)
PUBLICIS CANADA INC
BCP
(*Suby of* PUBLICIS GROUPE HOLDINGS B.V.)
358 Rue Beaubien O Bureau 500, Montreal, QC, H2V 4S6
(514) 285-1414
Emp Here 75   *Sales* 97,381,365
SIC 7311 Advertising agencies
Duncan Bruce
Yves Gougoux
Claude Renaud
Andrew Bruce
Arthur Sadoun
Ann Garreaud

D-U-N-S 24-400-8884 (SL)
RADIATEURS MONTREAL INC
RADIATEUR MONTREAL RADIATOR
270 Rue Beaubien O, Montreal, QC, H2V 1C4
(514) 276-8521
Emp Here 80   *Sales* 17,907,440
SIC 3714 Motor vehicle parts and accessories
Stephane Joly

D-U-N-S 20-724-6711 (SL)
SERVICES D'ENTRETIEN D'EDIFICES ALLIED (QUEBEC) INC
ALLIED BUILDING SERVICES
6585 Rue Jeanne-Mance, Montreal, QC, H2V 4L1
(514) 272-1137
Emp Here 250   *Sales* 7,992,000
SIC 7349 Building maintenance services, nec
Costas Scoufaras
Peter Scoufaras

D-U-N-S 24-336-1826 (HQ)
SOLUTIONS INFORMATIQUES INSO INC
BOUTIQUE WEB INSO
6615 Av Du Parc, Montreal, QC, H2V 4J1
(514) 270-4477
Emp Here 120   *Sales* 29,050,375
SIC 5734 Computer and software stores
Dimo Tsakpinoglou
Phrixo Tsakpinoglou
Eric Massenavette

D-U-N-S 24-804-8048 (SL)
STUDIOS MOMENT FACTORY INC, LES
MOMENT FACTORY
6250 Av Du Parc, Montreal, QC, H2V 4H8
(514) 843-8433
Emp Here 320   *Sales* 64,118,720
SIC 7336 Commercial art and graphic design
Eric Fournier
Dominic Bessette
Dominic Audet

D-U-N-S 20-517-4204 (SL)
UNIPRIX LAURENT TETREAULT & ASSOCIATE (AFFILIATED PHARMACY)
5647 Av Du Parc, Montreal, QC, H2V 4H2
(514) 276-9353
Emp Here 49   *Sales* 13,556,340
SIC 2834 Pharmaceutical preparations
Laurent Tetreault

D-U-N-S 25-446-8788 (BR)
YMCA DU QUEBEC, LES
CENTRE Y DU PARC, LE
(*Suby of* YMCA DU QUEBEC, LES)
5550 Av Du Parc, Montreal, QC, H2V 4H1
(514) 271-3437
Emp Here 130
SIC 7991 Physical fitness facilities
Marie Claude Leblanc

Montreal, QC H2W

D-U-N-S 25-248-2989 (SL)
ASSOCIATION D'ENTRAIDE LE CHAINON INC, L'
CHAINON, LE
4373 Av De L'Esplanade, Montreal, QC, H2W 1T2
(514) 845-0151
Emp Here 105   *Sales* 8,063,160
SIC 8322 Individual and family services
Marie-Helene Houle

D-U-N-S 25-366-6945 (BR)
CARAT CANADA INC
(*Suby of* DENTSU INC.)
4446 Boul Saint-Laurent Bureau 500, Montreal, QC, H2W 1Z5
(514) 287-2555
Emp Here 75
SIC 7311 Advertising agencies
Nigel Morris

D-U-N-S 24-869-9514 (SL)
GROUPE HEXAVOGUE INC, LE
4200 Boul Saint-Laurent Bureau 200, Montreal, QC, H2W 2R2
(514) 286-4392
Emp Here 25   *Sales* 12,458,050
SIC 5137 Women's and children's clothing
Ernest Battah
Elaine Battah
Diane Battah
Kathleen Battah

D-U-N-S 20-137-3169 (SL)
INSTITUT DE RECHERCHES CLINIQUES DE MONTREAL
I.R.C.M.
110 Av Des Pins O, Montreal, QC, H2W 1R7
(514) 987-5500
Emp Here 250   *Sales* 51,020,500
SIC 8733 Noncommercial research organiza-

tions
Louise-Lambert Lagace
Christine Le Jeune
Robert Laurier
Breton Guy
Helene Robitaille
Brian Z. Gelfand
Monique Jerome-Forget
Michel Lesperance
Luc Boileau
Andre Couillard

D-U-N-S 25-197-5389 (HQ)
LACOSTE CANADA INC
LACOSTE
(*Suby of* MAUS FRERES SA)
4200 Boul Saint-Laurent Bureau 901, Montreal, QC, H2W 2R2
(514) 286-1212
Sales 49,832,200
SIC 5136 Men's and boy's clothing
Joelle Grunberg
Gregoire Brasset
Karine Sansot-Vincent

D-U-N-S 20-714-6635 (SL)
MAKWA AVENTURES INC, LES
CAMP USA-MONDE
4079 Rue Saint-Denis, Montreal, QC, H2W 2M7
(514) 285-2583
Emp Here 88   *Sales* 39,531,272
SIC 7389 Business services, nec
Carl Boudreault

D-U-N-S 25-508-5169 (HQ)
NEWAD MEDIA INC
MEDIA NEWAD
4200 Boul Saint-Laurent Bureau 1440, Montreal, QC, H2W 2R2
(514) 278-3222
Emp Here 65   *Sales* 24,244,891
SIC 7312 Outdoor advertising services
Michael Reha
Phillip Marchessault
Brian Wyatt
Michel Labadie

D-U-N-S 20-363-3891 (SL)
SONDER CANADA INC
COLLECTION SONDER
15 Rue Marie-Anne O Bureau 201, Montreal, QC, H2W 1B6
(800) 657-9859
Emp Here 50   *Sales* 13,587,800
SIC 6531 Real estate agents and managers
Francis Davidson Tanguay
Phil Rothenberg
Lucas Pellan
Nabeel Hyatt
Neil Mehta
Vivek Pattipati

D-U-N-S 20-514-9672 (SL)
SPERIAN VETEMENTS DE PROTECTION LTEE
(*Suby of* HONEYWELL INTERNATIONAL INC.)
4200 Boul Saint-Laurent, Montreal, QC, H2W 2R2
Emp Here 100
SIC 3842 Surgical appliances and supplies
Brice De La Morandiere
Ruben A Dos Reis
Winfield W Major
Henri-Dominique Petit

D-U-N-S 20-918-7371 (SL)
TOON BOOM ANIMATION INC
CORUS ENTERTAINMENT, DIV OF
(*Suby of* CORUS ENTERTAINMENT INC)
4200 Boul Saint-Laurent Bureau 1020, Montreal, QC, H2W 2R2
(514) 278-8666
Emp Here 70   *Sales* 16,268,210
SIC 5734 Computer and software stores

Doug Murphy
Christine Nalborczyk

D-U-N-S 24-065-7374   (SL)
TRIBAL NOVA INC
TRIBAL NOVA KIDS
(*Suby of* HOUGHTON MIFFLIN HARCOURT COMPANY)
4200 Boul Saint-Laurent Bureau 1203, Montreal, QC, H2W 2R2
(514) 598-0444
Emp Here 25   *Sales* 13,013,550
SIC 5092 Toys and hobby goods and supplies
John J. Lynch Jr
William F. Bayers
Joseph Abbott

Montreal, QC H2X

D-U-N-S 25-018-7549   (SL)
6038263 CANADA INC
CLUB LA CITE
3575 Av Du Parc, Montreal, QC, H2X 3P9
(514) 288-8221
Emp Here 40   *Sales* 12,585,280
SIC 8699 Membership organizations, nec
Lee Gilbert

D-U-N-S 20-322-3297   (HQ)
9104-7332 QUEBEC INC
MAISON DE THE CAMELLIA SINENSIS
351 Rue Emery, Montreal, QC, H2X 1J2
(514) 286-4002
Emp Here 10   *Sales* 21,725,002
SIC 5149 Groceries and related products, nec
Hugo Americi
Jasmin Desharnais
Francois Marchand
Kevin Gascoyne

D-U-N-S 24-811-8259   (HQ)
ASSOCIATION ECHEC ET MATHEMATIQUES
ECHEC & MATH
3423 Rue Saint-Denis Bureau 400, Montreal, QC, H2X 3L2
(514) 845-8352
Emp Here 15   *Sales* 10,410,840
SIC 5092 Toys and hobby goods and supplies
Guy Laurain
Larry Bevand

D-U-N-S 20-716-9819   (SL)
ASSOCIATION INTERNATIONALE DES ETUDIANTS EN SCIENCES ECONOMIQUES ET COMMERCIALES
AIESEC
315 Rue Sainte-Catherine E Bureau 213, Montreal, QC, H2X 3X2
(514) 987-3288
Emp Here 49   *Sales* 11,451,055
SIC 8621 Professional organizations
Lloyd Tenj

D-U-N-S 20-051-6552   (SL)
AVID TECHNOLOGY CANADA CORP
TECHNOLOGIE AVID CANADA
(*Suby of* AVID TECHNOLOGY, INC.)
3510 Boul Saint-Laurent Bureau 300, Montreal, QC, H2X 2V2
(514) 845-1636
Emp Here 100   *Sales* 14,418,200
SIC 7371 Custom computer programming services
Brian E Agle
Alessandra C Melloni
Ryan H Murray

D-U-N-S 24-085-5585   (SL)
BCP LTEE
BCP REPUTATION
3530 Boul Saint-Laurent Bureau 300, Montreal, QC, H2X 2V1

(514) 285-0077
Emp Here 70   *Sales* 14,025,970
SIC 7311 Advertising agencies
Yves Gougoux
Alain Bergeron
Andrew Bruce
Claude Renaud
Arthur Sadoun
Ann Garreaud

D-U-N-S 25-306-2244   (HQ)
BGIS O&M SOLUTIONS INC
NEXACOR
(*Suby of* BGIS GLOBAL INTEGRATED SOLUTIONS CANADA LP*)
87 Rue Ontario O Bureau 200, Montreal, QC, H2X 0A7
(514) 840-8660
Emp Here 120   *Sales* 135,225,600
SIC 6531 Real estate agents and managers
Gordon Ian Hicks
Jim Arthur Neal
Andrew Mclachin
Peter Papagiammis

D-U-N-S 20-713-7675   (SL)
BISHARA PHARMA INC
UNIPRIX
3575 Av Du Parc Bureau 5602, Montreal, QC, H2X 3P9
(514) 849-6176
Emp Here 60   *Sales* 14,659,680
SIC 5912 Drug stores and proprietary stores
Marc Bishara
Carl Bishara

D-U-N-S 20-331-4893   (HQ)
CAPRION BIOSCIENCES INC
CAPRION PROTEOME
201 Av Du President-Kennedy Bureau 3900, Montreal, QC, H2X 3Y7
(514) 360-3600
Sales 13,833,000
SIC 2834 Pharmaceutical preparations
Martin Leblanc
Janine Nicholls
Andrea Ponti
Michael Irvine Mortimer
Normand Rivard

D-U-N-S 24-362-4355   (BR)
CENTRE HOSPITALIER DE L'UNIVERSITE DE MONTREAL
CENTRE HOSPITALIER DE L'UNIVERSITE DE MONTREAL
(*Suby of* CENTRE HOSPITALIER DE L'UNIVERSITE DE MONTREAL)
1058 Rue Saint-Denis, Montreal, QC, H2X 3J4
(514) 890-8000
Emp Here 1,000
SIC 8062 General medical and surgical hospitals

D-U-N-S 20-883-1198   (HQ)
CENTRE HOSPITALIER DE L'UNIVERSITE DE MONTREAL
CHUM, LE
850 Rue Saint-Denis, Montreal, QC, H2X 0A9
(514) 890-8000
Emp Here 8,000   *Sales* 1,110,800,000
SIC 8062 General medical and surgical hospitals
Jean-Claude Deschenes
Michel Baron
Christian Paire
Alain Cousineau
Serge Aubry

D-U-N-S 20-363-0640   (BR)
CENTRE INTEGRE UNIVERSITAIRE SANTE ET SERVICES SOCIAUX DU CENTRE-SUD-DE-L'ILE-DE-MONTREAL
HOPITAL DE LA MISERICORDE
(*Suby of* CENTRE INTEGRE UNIVERSITAIRE SANTE ET SERVICES SOCIAUX DU CENTRE-SUD-DE-L'ILE-DE-MONTREAL)
3430 Rue Jeanne-Mance, Montreal, QC, H2X

2J9
(514) 842-1147
Emp Here 190
SIC 8011 Offices and clinics of medical doctors
Leon Lafleur

D-U-N-S 24-545-8075   (SL)
CHAMBRE DE LA SECURITE FINANCIERE
300 Rue Leo-Pariseau Bureau 2600, Montreal, QC, H2X 4B8
(514) 282-5777
Emp Here 26   *Sales* 48,013,134
SIC 6351 Surety insurance
Luc Labelle

D-U-N-S 24-073-3159   (SL)
COMPAGNIE INTERNATIONALE DE PRODUITS ALIMENTAIRES ET COMMERCE DE DETAIL INC
JC JULIETTE & CHOCOLAT
1615 Rue Saint-Denis, Montreal, QC, H2X 3K3
(514) 287-3555
Emp Here 35   *Sales* 29,245,195
SIC 5149 Groceries and related products, nec
Juliette Brun

D-U-N-S 24-812-2988   (HQ)
CONSULTANTS AECOM INC
TECSULT INTERNATIONAL
(*Suby of* AECOM)
85 Rue Sainte-Catherine O, Montreal, QC, H2X 3P4
(514) 287-8500
Emp Here 600   *Sales* 197,131,000
SIC 8711 Engineering services
Doug Allingham
Jean Nehme
Stephan Trudeau
Nathan Schauerte

D-U-N-S 20-713-8384   (SL)
CORPORATION D'HABITATION JEANNE-MANCE, LA
150 Rue Ontario E Bureau 1, Montreal, QC, H2X 1H1
(514) 872-1221
Emp Here 26   *Sales* 11,530,740
SIC 7389 Business services, nec
Robert Labelle

D-U-N-S 20-593-2119   (HQ)
FESTIVAL JUSTE POUR RIRE
CHAOS FESTIVAL
2101 Boul Saint-Laurent, Montreal, QC, H2X 2T5
(514) 845-3155
Sales 13,005,000
SIC 7999 Amusement and recreation, nec
Curtis Millen
Richard B Levy
Chris Silbermann
Steve Stanford
Jacques Andre-Dupont
Geoff Molson

D-U-N-S 24-677-2842   (HQ)
FONDATION DU CEGEP DU VIEUX MONTREAL, LA
CEGEP DU VIEUX MONTREAL
255 Rue Ontario E, Montreal, QC, H2X 1X6
(514) 982-3437
Sales 141,013,000
SIC 8221 Colleges and universities
Michel Couillard
Mylene Boisclair
Martine Lapointe
Michel Boisvert
Jacques Desautels
Nancy Duncan
Marc Deserres
Jean M. Gagne
Philippe Molitor
Caroline Roy

D-U-N-S 24-811-3987   (SL)
GALLIMARD LTEE

EDITO
3700a Boul Saint-Laurent, Montreal, QC, H2X 2V4
(514) 499-0072
Emp Here 25   *Sales* 18,563,000
SIC 5192 Books, periodicals, and newspapers
Florence Noyer
Mathieu Cosson
Elisabeth Borouchaki

D-U-N-S 20-524-1446   (HQ)
GESTION JUSTE POUR RIRE INC
EDITIONS ROZON CANADA
2101 Boul Saint-Laurent, Montreal, QC, H2X 2T5
(514) 845-3155
Sales 10,404,000
SIC 7999 Amusement and recreation, nec
Curtis Millen
Richard B. Levy
Jacques Aube
Chris Silbermann
Steve Stanford
Geoff Molson
Anna Martini

D-U-N-S 24-346-4349   (BR)
GOUVERNEMENT DE LA PROVINCE DE QUEBEC
INSTITUT DE TOURISME ET D'HOTELLERIE DU QUEBEC, L'
(*Suby of* GOUVERNEMENT DE LA PROVINCE DE QUEBEC)
3535 Rue Saint-Denis, Montreal, QC, H2X 3P1
(514) 282-5111
Emp Here 200
SIC 8249 Vocational schools, nec
Lucille Daoust

D-U-N-S 24-107-1836   (SL)
HOPITAL CHINOIS DE MONTREAL (1963) INC, L'
189 Av Viger E, Montreal, QC, H2X 3Y9
(514) 875-9120
Emp Here 225   *Sales* 15,373,350
SIC 8051 Skilled nursing care facilities
Lorenza Feng
Sangian Zhang
Nguu Tu Tran
Felix Ma
Mo Ling Wong
John Tam
Kim Uyen Tran
Celerina Wan
Susan Maruay
Robin Tom

D-U-N-S 25-525-0334   (SL)
IC AXON INC
(*Suby of* GP STRATEGIES CORPORATION)
3575 Boul Saint-Laurent Bureau 650, Montreal, QC, H2X 2T7
(514) 940-1142
Emp Here 65   *Sales* 12,122,890
SIC 8742 Management consulting services
Carole Gins

D-U-N-S 24-994-1964   (SL)
IMPORTATIONS EXPORTATIONS LAM INC
LAM IMPORT
2115 Boul Saint-Laurent, Montreal, QC, H2X 2T5
(514) 843-3030
Emp Here 23   *Sales* 17,077,960
SIC 5199 Nondurable goods, nec
Dai Tong Lam
Sai Hung Tran

D-U-N-S 24-502-6190   (BR)
KUEHNE + NAGEL LTD
KUEHNE + NAGEL
(*Suby of* KUHNE HOLDING AG)
3510 Boul Saint-Laurent Bureau 400, Montreal, QC, H2X 2V2
(514) 397-9900
Emp Here 100

SIC 4731 Freight transportation arrangement
John Stoppenbrink

D-U-N-S 25-074-5452 (SL)
LA SALLE STEEL CORPORATION
180 Boul Rene-Levesque E Bureau 500, Montreal, QC, H2X 1N6
(514) 933-8899
Emp Here 15   Sales 15,005,085
SIC 5051 Metals service centers and offices
Robert Naggiar

D-U-N-S 25-332-0451 (HQ)
LABARRE GAUTHIER INC
LG2
3575 Boul Saint-Laurent Bureau 900, Montreal, QC, H2X 2T7
(514) 281-8901
Emp Here 30   Sales 10,586,200
SIC 7311 Advertising agencies
Sylvain Labarre
Paul Gauthier

D-U-N-S 25-486-8938 (SL)
MEDLEY, LE
1170 Rue Saint-Denis, Montreal, QC, H2X 3J5

Emp Here 25   Sales 11,230,475
SIC 7389 Business services, nec
Denis Peroux
Mark Bolay
Paul Matt

D-U-N-S 24-178-5760 (SL)
METROPOLIS
59 Rue Sainte-Catherine E, Montreal, QC, H2X 1K5
(514) 844-3500
Emp Here 48   Sales 13,652,976
SIC 6512 Nonresidential building operators
Stephane Bougie

D-U-N-S 24-509-0451 (SL)
MUSEE D'ART CONTEMPORAIN DE MONTREAL
185 Rue Sainte-Catherine O, Montreal, QC, H2X 3X5
(514) 847-6226
Emp Here 100   Sales 9,136,900
SIC 8412 Museums and art galleries
Marcel Brisebois
Pierre Bourgie
Serge Guerin

D-U-N-S 20-885-1365 (SL)
NEURORX RESEARCH INC
RECHERCHE NEURORX
3575 Av Du Parc Bureau 5322, Montreal, QC, H2X 3P9
(514) 906-0062
Emp Here 50   Sales 11,734,800
SIC 8731 Commercial physical research
Arnold Douglas

D-U-N-S 20-764-9807 (SL)
ORCHESTRE SYMPHONIQUE DE MONTREAL
1600 Rue Saint-Urbain, Montreal, QC, H2X 0S1
(514) 842-9951
Emp Here 130   Sales 19,475,690
SIC 7929 Entertainers and entertainment groups
Madeleine Careau
Lucien Bouchard
Stephen Rosenhek
Mathieu L'allier
Norman Steinberg
Helene Desmarais
Marie-Josee Nadeau
Thierry Dorval
L. Jacques Menard
Jean-Andre Elie

D-U-N-S 20-363-2489 (SL)
POLISH WAR VETERAN'S SOCIETY
63 Rue Prince-Arthur E, Montreal, QC, H2X 1B4

(514) 842-7551
Emp Here 100   Sales 14,287,900
SIC 8641 Civic and social associations
Edouard Rolicz

D-U-N-S 24-197-3010 (SL)
PROACTION GROUPE CONSEILS INC
257 Rue Sherbrooke E Bureau 100, Montreal, QC, H2X 1E3
(514) 284-7447
Emp Here 70   Sales 14,820,680
SIC 7311 Advertising agencies
Denis Lefebevre
Antoine Drapeau-Perreault
Jean-Philippe Raiche

D-U-N-S 25-543-6396 (SL)
PROPERTIES TERRA INCOGNITA INC
TERRW INCONNUE
3530 Boul Saint-Laurent Bureau 500, Montreal, QC, H2X 2V1
(514) 847-3536
Emp Here 50   Sales 16,356,350
SIC 6531 Real estate agents and managers
Daniel Langlois

D-U-N-S 25-526-4772 (BR)
PROVIGO DISTRIBUTION INC
(Suby of LOBLAW COMPANIES LIMITED)
3421 Av Du Parc, Montreal, QC, H2X 2H6
(514) 281-0488
Emp Here 75
SIC 5411 Grocery stores
Michel Lefebvre

D-U-N-S 24-760-7729 (SL)
SANTE MONTREAL COLLECTIF CJV, S.E.C.
CONSTRUCTION SANTE MONTREAL
1031 Rue Saint-Denis, Montreal, QC, H2X 3H9
(514) 394-1440
Emp Here 50   Sales 28,516,900
SIC 1542 Nonresidential construction, nec
John Hewson

D-U-N-S 20-165-7447 (SL)
SAT SOCIETE DES ARTS TECHNOLOGIES
SAT, LA
1201 Boul Saint-Laurent, Montreal, QC, H2X 2S6
(514) 844-2033
Emp Here 115   Sales 165,439,115
SIC 8699 Membership organizations, nec
Monique Savoie
Ghyslain Boileau

D-U-N-S 20-856-3304 (SL)
SOCIETE DE LA PLACE DES ARTS DE MONTREAL
PLACE DES ARTS
(Suby of GOUVERNEMENT DE LA PROVINCE DE QUEBEC)
260 Boul De Maisonneuve O, Montreal, QC, H2X 1Y9
(514) 285-4200
Emp Here 600   Sales 28,002,954
SIC 6512 Nonresidential building operators
Marc Blondeau
Jean Laurin
Michel Tourangeau
Genevieve Pichet
Monique Lacas
Denise Melillo
Michel Gagnon
Isabelle Marier
Esther Carrier
Frederique Cardinal

D-U-N-S 24-220-5727 (HQ)
SYSTEMES D'ENERGIE RENOUVELABLE CANADA INC
RES CANADA
(Suby of RENEWABLE ENERGY SYSTEMS HOLDINGS LIMITED)
300 Rue Leo-Pariseau Bureau 2516, Montreal, QC, H2X 4B3

(514) 525-2113
Sales 27,194,960
SIC 4911 Electric services
Graham Reid
Marcia Emmons
Christopher Howson
Donald Joyce
Ivor Catto
Gavin Mcalpine
Douglas Mcalpine
Brian R.L. Evans

D-U-N-S 20-112-7003 (HQ)
TELEBEC, SOCIETE EN COMMANDITE
TELEBEC INTERNET
87 Rue Ontario O 200, Montreal, QC, H2X 0A7
(514) 493-5300
Emp Here 100   Sales 267,635,200
SIC 4813 Telephone communication, except radio
Roch Dube

D-U-N-S 24-677-1869 (HQ)
TRANSAT A.T. INC
300 Rue Leo-Pariseau Bureau 600, Montreal, QC, H2X 4C2
(514) 987-1616
Emp Here 120   Sales 2,311,314,723
SIC 6712 Bank holding companies
Jean-Marc Eustahe
Bernard Bussieres
Daniel Godbout
Denis Petrin
Bruno Leclaire
Christophe Hennebelle
Annick Guerard
Lina De Cesare
Jacques Simoneau
Philippe Sureau

D-U-N-S 24-431-3482 (HQ)
TRANSAT DISTRIBUTION CANADA INC
A LA CARTE REWARDS TRAVEL
(Suby of TRANSAT A.T. INC)
300 Rue Leo-Pariseau Bureau 600, Montreal, QC, H2X 4C2
(514) 987-1616
Emp Here 50   Sales 170,433,778
SIC 4725 Tour operators
Joseph Adamo
Bernard Bussieres
Jean-Marc Eustache
Nathalie Boyer

D-U-N-S 24-801-0969 (HQ)
TRANSAT TOURS CANADA INC
AIR TRANSAT
(Suby of TRANSAT A.T. INC)
300 Rue Leo-Pariseau Bureau 500, Montreal, QC, H2X 4B3
(514) 987-1616
Emp Here 170   Sales 92,532,492
SIC 4725 Tour operators
Annick Guerard
Bernard Bussieres
Jean-Marc Eustache
Denis Petrin
Andre De Montigny

D-U-N-S 20-288-3567 (SL)
UNITE DE SANTE INTERNATIONALE
CENTRE HOSTIPALIER DE L'UNIVERSITE DE MONTREAL (CHUM)
850 Rue Saint-Denis Bureau S03, Montreal, QC, H2X 0A9
(514) 890-8156
Emp Here 50   Sales 11,714,400
SIC 8742 Management consulting services
Albert Lucien

D-U-N-S 20-581-9928 (BR)
UNIVERSITE DU QUEBEC
(Suby of UNIVERSITE DU QUEBEC)
315 Rue Sainte-Catherine E Bureau 3570, Montreal, QC, H2X 3X2
(514) 987-3000
Emp Here 250

SIC 8221 Colleges and universities

D-U-N-S 25-541-1282 (SL)
VIDEOTRON SERVICE INFORMATIQUE LTEE
300 Av Viger E Bureau 6, Montreal, QC, H2X 3W4
(514) 281-1232
Emp Here 4,000   Sales 667,388,000
SIC 7374 Data processing and preparation
Claude Chagnon

D-U-N-S 20-960-6854 (SL)
VILLA MEDICA INC
HOPITAL DE READAPTATION VILLA MEDICA
225 Rue Sherbrooke E, Montreal, QC, H2X 1C9
(514) 288-8201
Emp Here 350   Sales 22,046,337
SIC 8069 Specialty hospitals, except psychiatric
Guillaume Journel
Anne Beauchamp
Johanne Brien

D-U-N-S 25-355-6211 (SL)
XLR8 MEDIA INC
PHD MONTREAL
(Suby of OMNICOM GROUP INC.)
3575 Boul Saint-Laurent Bureau 400, Montreal, QC, H2X 2T7
(514) 286-9000
Emp Here 132   Sales 26,448,972
SIC 7311 Advertising agencies
Alain Desormiers
Cam Reston
Fred Forster

Montreal, QC H2Y

D-U-N-S 20-692-3950 (SL)
/N SPRO INC
(Suby of BUNKER HILL CAPITAL, L.P.)
465 Rue Saint-Jean Bureau 601, Montreal, QC, H2Y 2R6
(514) 907-2505
Emp Here 100   Sales 12,477,600
SIC 8741 Management services
Luc Hedou
Mark H. Hurd
Jason H. Hurd
Robert L. Jr. Clark

D-U-N-S 20-558-1049 (SL)
2040830 ONTARIO INC
ARAGON MARKETING GROUP
460 Rue Saint-Paul E Suite 330, Montreal, QC, H2Y 3V1

Emp Here 60   Sales 14,057,280
SIC 8743 Public relations services
Darryl Hicks
Kurt Klischuk

D-U-N-S 24-368-6313 (BR)
9071-3975 QUEBEC INC
ALIMENTS LUCYPORC
(Suby of 9071-3975 QUEBEC INC)
410 Rue Saint-Nicolas Bureau 5, Montreal, QC, H2Y 2P5
(514) 286-1754
Emp Here 225
SIC 2011 Meat packing plants
Denis Levasseur

D-U-N-S 20-332-9438 (SL)
9310-8405 QUEBEC INC
ZONE EN SECURITE
239 Rue Du Saint-Sacrement Bureau 304, Montreal, QC, H2Y 1W9
(514) 251-5050
Emp Here 100   Sales 39,567,800
SIC 7381 Detective and armored car services

Danya Archambault

D-U-N-S 20-381-0424   (SL)
9342-6484 QUEBEC INC
MANDY'S
425 Rue Saint-Nicolas, Montreal, QC, H2Y 2P4
(514) 619-9649
Emp Here 240   *Sales* 11,193,360
SIC 5812 Eating places
Amanda Wolfe
Rebecca Wolfe
Lou Carrier

D-U-N-S 24-174-8375   (SL)
ACCEUIL BONNEAU INC
427 Rue De La Commune E, Montreal, QC, H2Y 1J4
(514) 845-3906
Emp Here 26   *Sales* 10,332,764
SIC 8699 Membership organizations, nec
Nicole Fournier

D-U-N-S 20-266-6269   (HQ)
AGENCE MIRUM CANADA INC
IMAGE TWIST
(*Suby of* RUSSELL SQUARE HOLDING B.V.)
500 Rue Saint-Jacques Bureau 1420, Montreal, QC, H2Y 1S1
(514) 987-9992
Emp Here 45   *Sales* 17,031,535
SIC 7311 Advertising agencies
Brian Fraser
Tom Lobene
Kevin Farewell
Eric Gross

D-U-N-S 24-814-5336   (SL)
ALES GROUPE CANADA INC
420 Rue Notre-Dame O Bureau 500, Montreal, QC, H2Y 1V3
(514) 932-3636
Emp Here 26   *Sales* 12,956,372
SIC 5131 Piece goods and notions
Rachid Yousri
Abdel Oudghiri
Raphael Desrues

D-U-N-S 24-500-7166   (HQ)
ALFID SERVICES IMMOBILIERS LTEE
GROUPE ALFID, LE
500 Place D'Armes Suite 1500, Montreal, QC, H2Y 2W2
(514) 282-7654
Emp Here 50   *Sales* 41,888,900
SIC 6531 Real estate agents and managers
Jean-Jacques Laurans
Jean-Luc Binette
Oscar Tagliabue

D-U-N-S 24-231-4875   (SL)
AQUILINI PROPERTIES LIMITED PARTNERSHIP
HOTEL EMBASSY SUITES
215 Rue Saint-Jacques Unite 120, Montreal, QC, H2Y 1M6
(514) 847-9547
Emp Here 49   *Sales* 13,937,413
SIC 6512 Nonresidential building operators
Jocelyn Lafond

D-U-N-S 24-376-1165   (SL)
ARTIFACT LOGICIEL INC
ARTIFACT ACCELERATED LEARNING
300 Rue Du Saint-Sacrement Bureau 223, Montreal, QC, H2Y 1X4
(514) 286-6665
Emp Here 55   *Sales* 17,937,480
SIC 3999 Manufacturing industries, nec
Jacques Hamel
Ronald Wheeler

D-U-N-S 20-418-6985   (HQ)
ATLIFIC INC
ATLIFIC HOTELS
250 Rue Saint-Antoine O Bureau 400, Montreal, QC, H2Y 0A3

(514) 509-5500
Emp Here 25   *Sales* 13,725,360
SIC 8741 Management services
Richard Ade
Bonnie Ng
Robert Chartrand
Raymond St-Pierre
Christine Kennedey

D-U-N-S 24-842-7465   (SL)
AUBERGE SUR LA ROUTE, L'
426 Rue Saint-Gabriel, Montreal, QC, H2Y 2Z9
(514) 954-1041
Emp Here 21   *Sales* 38,779,839
SIC 6311 Life insurance
Marc Tolay

D-U-N-S 24-240-6416   (SL)
AUDIO ZONE INC
444 Rue Saint-Paul E, Montreal, QC, H2Y 3V1
(514) 931-9466
Emp Here 25   *Sales* 11,087,250
SIC 7389 Business services, nec
Patrice Gill

D-U-N-S 25-095-6638   (HQ)
AXXESS INTERNATIONAL COURTIERS EN DOUANES INC
360 Rue Saint-Jacques Bureau 1200, Montreal, QC, H2Y 1P5
(514) 849-9377
Emp Here 65   *Sales* 65,355,416
SIC 4731 Freight transportation arrangement
Richard Gervais
Anthony J. Yakubosky

D-U-N-S 20-269-1093   (HQ)
BANK OF MONTREAL
BMO NESBITT BURNS
119 Rue Saint-Jacques, Montreal, QC, H2Y 1L6
(514) 877-7373
Emp Here 3,000   *Sales* 17,792,580,876
SIC 6021 National commercial banks
Darryl White
Thomas E. Flynn
Jean-Michel Ares
J Robert S Prichard
Don M. Wilson Iii
Jan Babiak
Sophie Brochu
George A Cope
Christine A Edwards
Ronald H. Farmer

D-U-N-S 20-715-6899   (BR)
BANQUE NATIONALE DU CANADA
(*Suby of* BANQUE NATIONALE DU CANADA)
500 Place D'Armes Bureau 500, Montreal, QC, H2Y 2W3
(514) 394-6642
Emp Here 80
SIC 6021 National commercial banks
Winston Chin

D-U-N-S 20-979-4916   (HQ)
BARREAU DU QUEBEC, LE
445 Boul Saint-Laurent Bureau 100, Montreal, QC, H2Y 3T8
(514) 954-3400
Emp Here 134   *Sales* 36,287,205
SIC 8621 Professional organizations
Lise Tremblay

D-U-N-S 24-426-5299   (HQ)
BC2 GROUPE CONSEIL INC
GROUPE BC2
85 Rue Saint-Paul O Bureau 300, Montreal, QC, H2Y 3V4
(514) 507-3600
Emp Here 2   *Sales* 13,941,950
SIC 8748 Business consulting, nec
Michel Collins
Olivier Perron-Collins
Yves Perron
Kristopher Parent

Veronique Alepin
Dany Tremblay
Francois Fortin

D-U-N-S 20-858-2130   (BR)
CANADIAN PRESS, THE
(*Suby of* CANADIAN PRESS, THE)
215 Rue Saint-Jacques Unite 100, Montreal, QC, H2Y 1M6
(514) 849-3212
Emp Here 75
SIC 7383 News syndicates
Jean Roy

D-U-N-S 20-421-5834   (HQ)
CHAMBRE DE COMMERCE DU MONTREAL METROPOLITAIN
380 Rue Saint-Antoine O Bureau 6000, Montreal, QC, H2Y 3X7
(514) 871-4000
Sales 10,982,500
SIC 8611 Business associations
Michel Leblanc

D-U-N-S 24-837-0546   (SL)
CIME DECOR INC
C D I MOBILIER DE BUREAU
420 Rue Mcgill Bureau 100, Montreal, QC, H2Y 2G1
(514) 842-2463
Emp Here 23   *Sales* 11,703,688
SIC 5021 Furniture
Marisa Delbello
Sebastien Plantevin
Francois Tetreault

D-U-N-S 24-800-4426   (SL)
COALISION INC
LOLE
700 Rue Saint-Antoine E Bureau 110, Montreal, QC, H2Y 1A6
(514) 798-3534
Emp Here 100   *Sales* 13,667,400
SIC 2339 Women's and misses' outerwear, nec
Todd Steele
Francois Plamondon
Olaf Guerrand Hermes
Eric D'anjou
Pierre Servan-Schreiber
Jimmy Argyropolous
Stephen H. Simon
Anthony Sigel

D-U-N-S 20-187-2376   (HQ)
COLT RESOURCES INC
500 Place D'Armes Bureau 1800, Montreal, QC, H2Y 2W2
(438) 259-3315
Sales 119,377,450
SIC 1081 Metal mining services
John Gravelle
Filipe Faria
Luis Martins
Jorge Valente
Paul Yeou
Joe Kin Foo Tai
Hans H. Hertell

D-U-N-S 20-286-3606   (SL)
COMMISSION FOR ENVIRONMENTAL CO-OPERATION
CEC
393 Rue Saint-Jacques Bureau 200, Montreal, QC, H2Y 1N9
(514) 350-4300
Emp Here 60   *Sales* 15,209,400
SIC 8748 Business consulting, nec
Cesar Rafael Chavez
Riccardo Embriaco

D-U-N-S 20-103-3664   (BR)
COMMUNICATION DEMO INC
(*Suby of* COMMUNICATION DEMO INC)
407 Rue Mcgill Bureau 311, Montreal, QC, H2Y 2G3
(514) 985-2523
Emp Here 75

SIC 7389 Business services, nec
Yves Aganier

D-U-N-S 20-564-5146   (HQ)
COMPAGNIE D'ARRIMAGE EMPIRE LTEE
500 Place D'Armes Bureau 2800, Montreal, QC, H2Y 2W2
(514) 288-2221
Emp Here 10   *Sales* 25,998,350
SIC 4731 Freight transportation arrangement
Andrew Chodos
Roberta Bonnie Chodos

D-U-N-S 25-598-1839   (HQ)
CORPORATION COMPUWARE DU CANADA
500 Place D'Armes Bureau 1800, Montreal, QC, H2Y 2W2
(438) 259-3300
Sales 107,070,400
SIC 5045 Computers, peripherals, and software
Joseph Hagen Aho
Christopher Hollo

D-U-N-S 24-896-1419   (SL)
CORPORATION DES HOTELS INTER-CONTINENTAL (MONTREAL), LA
HOTEL INTER-CONTINENTAL (MONTREAL)
(*Suby of* INTERCONTINENTAL HOTELS GROUP PLC)
360 Rue Saint-Antoine O, Montreal, QC, H2Y 3X4
(514) 987-9900
Emp Here 300   *Sales* 28,700,400
SIC 7011 Hotels and motels
Lewis N. Fader
Hammer Randall S.
Frank Guarascio

D-U-N-S 24-057-0804   (HQ)
COURTAGE BGL LTEE
300 Rue Du Saint-Sacrement Bureau 123, Montreal, QC, H2Y 1X4
(514) 288-8111
Emp Here 36   *Sales* 41,347,304
SIC 4731 Freight transportation arrangement
James Barriere

D-U-N-S 20-563-4819   (HQ)
COURTIERS EN DOUANES GENERAL INC, LES
GCB LOGISTICS
112 Rue Mcgill Bureau 200, Montreal, QC, H2Y 2E5
(514) 876-1704
Emp Here 16   *Sales* 10,399,340
SIC 4731 Freight transportation arrangement
William Gartner
Alan Gartner
Lisa Gartner
Sidney (Sid) Gartner

D-U-N-S 20-288-4185   (SL)
CW PROFESSIONAL SERVICES (CANADA) ULC
LOCHBRIDGE
(*Suby of* M4 GLOBAL SOLUTIONS HOLDING COOPERATIEF U.A.)
500 Rue Saint-Jacques, Montreal, QC, H2Y 1S1
(514) 281-1888
Emp Here 200   *Sales* 33,369,400
SIC 7379 Computer related services, nec
Robb Curtis Warwick
James Anthony Byrnes
Robin Le Penderson

D-U-N-S 20-298-4183   (SL)
CWP INDUSTRIEL INC
(*Suby of* MCGILL ST-LAURENT INC)
407 Rue Mcgill Bureau 315, Montreal, QC, H2Y 2G3
(514) 871-2120
Emp Here 10   *Sales* 36,744,624
SIC 5031 Lumber, plywood, and millwork
Philippe Boisclair
Christian L'abbe

Julien Prince

D-U-N-S 24-518-8698   (SL)
CYGNUS MARKETING INC
507 Place D'Armes Bureau 1519, Montreal, QC, H2Y 2W8
(514) 284-5569
Emp Here 49   *Sales* 11,480,112
SIC 8742 Management consulting services
Sebastien Webb

D-U-N-S 20-016-4809   (SL)
DASSAULT SYSTEMES CANADA INC
DASSAULT SYSTEMES CANADA INNOVA-TION TECHNOLOGIES
(*Suby of* DASSAULT SYSTEMES)
393 Rue Saint-Jacques Bureau 300, Montreal, QC, H2Y 1N9
(514) 940-2949
Emp Here 250   *Sales* 56,557,750
SIC 7373 Computer integrated systems design
Frederic Tardif

D-U-N-S 24-479-7200   (SL)
E F VOYAGES CULTURELS
E F EDUCATION FIRST
407 Rue Mcgill Bureau 400, Montreal, QC, H2Y 2G3
(800) 387-7708
Emp Here 31   *Sales* 16,118,977
SIC 4724 Travel agencies
Vincent White

D-U-N-S 25-982-3024   (SL)
EF EDUCATION
407 Rue Mcgill Bureau 400, Montreal, QC, H2Y 2G3
(514) 904-0180
Emp Here 49   *Sales* 25,478,383
SIC 4724 Travel agencies
Matthew Noble

D-U-N-S 25-370-2070   (BR)
EXPEDIA CANADA CORP
(*Suby of* LIBERTY EXPEDIA HOLDINGS, INC.)
63 Rue De Bresoles Bureau 100, Montreal, QC, H2Y 1V7
(514) 286-8180
Emp Here 80
SIC 3823 Process control instruments

D-U-N-S 25-462-5890   (SL)
FABRIQUE DE LA PAROISSE NOTRE-DAME DE MONTREAL, LA
BASILIQUE NOTRE-DAME DE MONTREAL
424 Rue Saint-Sulpice, Montreal, QC, H2Y 2V5
(514) 842-2925
Emp Here 230   *Sales* 23,948,290
SIC 8661 Religious organizations
Robert Gagne
Yoland Tremblay
Pierre L Gravel
Guy Chamberland
Michel St-Pierre
Nicole Ouellet

D-U-N-S 20-280-8051   (HQ)
FICODIS INC
465 Rue Saint-Jean Bureau 708, Montreal, QC, H2Y 2R6
(514) 360-4007
Sales 14,250,780
SIC 5084 Industrial machinery and equipment
Christophe Bevillard
Rene Carron
Sernin Marichal
Laurent Fillion
Michel Vezina
Aurelien Chaufour
Ginette Miron
Ian Moffatt

D-U-N-S 20-329-9284   (SL)
FONDS D'ASSURANCE RESPONSABILITE PROFESSIONNELLE DU BARREAU DU

QUEBEC
445 Boul Saint-Laurent Bureau 300, Montreal, QC, H2Y 3T8
(514) 954-3452
Emp Here 17   *Sales* 12,332,463
SIC 6351 Surety insurance
Maria De Michele

D-U-N-S 20-856-9723   (SL)
FOR. PAR SODEPLAN INC
FOR
388 Rue Saint-Jacques Bureau 900, Montreal, QC, H2Y 1S1
(514) 871-8833
Emp Here 26   *Sales* 11,530,740
SIC 7389 Business services, nec
Andre Davignon

D-U-N-S 24-978-3056   (SL)
FUSION BPO SERVICES LIMITED
SERVICES FUSION BPO
(*Suby of* XPLORE-TECH SERVICES PRIVATE LIMITED)
507 Place D'Armes Bureau 1000, Montreal, QC, H2Y 2W8
(514) 227-3126
Emp Here 450   *Sales* 137,286,450
SIC 7389 Business services, nec
Kishore Saraogi
Lalita Sinha

D-U-N-S 20-760-5361   (HQ)
GESCA LTEE
750 Boul Saint-Laurent, Montreal, QC, H2Y 2Z4
(514) 285-7000
Emp Here 20   *Sales* 193,774,000
SIC 2711 Newspapers
Pierre-Elliott Levasseur
Guy Crevier
Patrick Buchholz
Andre Desmarais
Desmarais Paul Jr.
Michel Plessis-Belair
Jacques Parisien

D-U-N-S 20-330-9182   (SL)
GESCA NUMERIQUE INC
(*Suby of* PRESSE (2018) INC, LA)
750 Boul Saint-Laurent, Montreal, QC, H2Y 2Z4
(514) 285-7000
Emp Here 85   *Sales* 12,255,470
SIC 7371 Custom computer programming services
Pierre-Elliott Levasseur
Patrick Buchholz
Guy Crevier

D-U-N-S 24-073-2631   (SL)
GESTION 357 DE LA COMMUNE INC
357C, LE
357 Rue De La Commune O, Montreal, QC, H2Y 2E2
(514) 499-0357
Emp Here 50   *Sales* 22,174,500
SIC 7389 Business services, nec
Daniel Langlois

D-U-N-S 20-521-6968   (SL)
GESTION D'ETUDE PPKF (1984) INC
LEROUX COTE & BURROGANO
507 Place D'Armes Bureau 1300, Montreal, QC, H2Y 2W8
(514) 282-1287
Emp Here 30   *Sales* 13,304,700
SIC 7389 Business services, nec
Bruno Burrogano

D-U-N-S 24-635-4450   (SL)
GESTION LJT INC
380 Rue Saint-Antoine O Bureau 7100, Montreal, QC, H2Y 3X7
(514) 842-8891
Emp Here 55   *Sales* 15,088,260
SIC 8741 Management services
Robert B Legault
Pierre Savoie

Christian Joly
Robert Thiffault

D-U-N-S 24-345-6212   (BR)
GEXEL TELECOM INTERNATIONAL INC
(*Suby of* ARTHUR J. GALLAGHER & CO.)
507 Place D'Armes Bureau 1503, Montreal, QC, H2Y 2W8
(514) 935-9300
Emp Here 200
SIC 8732 Commercial nonphysical research

D-U-N-S 20-856-3643   (HQ)
GIBBYS RESTAURANT INC
GIBBYS
(*Suby of* GIBBY'S HOLDINGS INC)
298 Place D'Youville, Montreal, QC, H2Y 2B6
(514) 282-1837
Emp Here 95   *Sales* 4,551,900
SIC 5812 Eating places
Morris Levis
Claudia Folkard
George Chiotis
Gilbert Rosenberg

D-U-N-S 20-798-9752   (BR)
GOUVERNEMENT DE LA PROVINCE DE QUEBEC
DIRECTION REGIONAL EMPLOI QUEBEC
(*Suby of* GOUVERNEMENT DE LA PROVINCE DE QUEBEC)
276 Rue Saint-Jacques, Montreal, QC, H2Y 1N3
(514) 725-5221
Emp Here 85
SIC 8331 Job training and related services
Normand Clavel

D-U-N-S 20-124-3545   (BR)
GOUVERNEMENT DE LA PROVINCE DE QUEBEC
DIRECTEUR DE POURSUITES CRIM-INELLES ET PENALES
(*Suby of* GOUVERNEMENT DE LA PROVINCE DE QUEBEC)
1 Rue Notre-Dame E Bureau 4.100, Montreal, QC, H2Y 1B6
(514) 393-2703
Emp Here 150
SIC 8111 Legal services
Diane Laniel

D-U-N-S 20-333-1566   (SL)
GRAIN ST-LAURENT INC
(*Suby of* MCGILL ST-LAURENT INC)
407 Rue Mcgill Bureau 315, Montreal, QC, H2Y 2G3
(514) 871-2037
Emp Here 18   *Sales* 26,418,456
SIC 5153 Grain and field beans
Philippe Boisclair
Christian L'abbe

D-U-N-S 20-576-5584   (SL)
GROUPE ASKIDA INC
AXON INTEGRATION & DEVELOPPEMENT
410 Rue Saint-Nicolas Bureau 101, Montreal, QC, H2Y 2P5
(514) 286-9366
Emp Here 89   *Sales* 15,780,679
SIC 7371 Custom computer programming services
Steeve Duchesne
Yvan Bolduc
Francois Bonetto
Serge Thiboutot
Michel Lacasse
Paul Martineau

D-U-N-S 20-566-6100   (HQ)
GROUPE CSL INC
CANADA STEAMSHIP LINES
759 Rue Du Square-Victoria Bureau 600, Montreal, QC, H2Y 2K3
(514) 982-3800
Sales 519,905,747
SIC 4424 Deep sea domestic transportation of

freight
Louis Martel
John Sypnowich
Meredith H. Hayes
Greg Maddison
R. James E. Martin
David P.A. Martin
Paul W.J. Martin
Jacques Bougie
Lone Fonss Schroder
William Linton

D-U-N-S 20-290-5097   (SL)
GROUPE IN-RGY CONSULTATION INC
GROUPE SAPERGY CONSULTATION
390 Rue Le Moyne, Montreal, QC, H2Y 1Y3
(514) 906-7767
Emp Here 50   *Sales* 10,590,200
SIC 7373 Computer integrated systems design
Thierry Bodson
Sebastien Massicotte

D-U-N-S 24-712-7236   (HQ)
GROUPE PIXCOM INC
PIXINTER
444 Rue Saint-Paul E, Montreal, QC, H2Y 3V1
(514) 931-1188
Emp Here 11   *Sales* 91,377,250
SIC 6712 Bank holding companies
Jacquelin Bouchard
Sylvie Desrochers
Michael Ross
Marc Cantin
Robert Charpentier

D-U-N-S 20-370-8235   (SL)
HOTELLUS CANADA HOLDINGS INC
GESTION HOTELLUS CANADA
360 Rue Saint-Antoine O, Montreal, QC, H2Y 3X4
(514) 987-9900
Emp Here 220   *Sales* 21,046,960
SIC 7011 Hotels and motels
Lars Haggstrorm
Liia Nou
Nils Lindberg
Dominic Deangelis
Bernard Chenevert

D-U-N-S 24-742-8782   (BR)
INVESTISSEMENT QUEBEC
(*Suby of* INVESTISSEMENT QUEBEC)
413 Rue Saint-Jacques Bureau 500, Montreal, QC, H2Y 1N9
(514) 873-4375
Emp Here 100
SIC 8748 Business consulting, nec
Mario Albert

D-U-N-S 20-504-0611   (SL)
J. RENE HEBERT LTEE
300 Rue Du Saint-Sacrement Bureau 28, Montreal, QC, H2Y 1X4
(514) 281-0112
Emp Here 30   *Sales* 15,599,010
SIC 4731 Freight transportation arrangement
Francois Dupuis
Lucie Dupuis
Gilles Dupuis
Jeannine Dupuis

D-U-N-S 20-221-4318   (SL)
JARDINS NELSON INC
407 Place Jacques-Cartier, Montreal, QC, H2Y 3B1
(514) 861-5731
Emp Here 100   *Sales* 4,551,900
SIC 5812 Eating places
Robert Ruel

D-U-N-S 20-175-3444   (SL)
JESTA I.S. INC
JESTA
755 Rue Berri Bureau 200, Montreal, QC, H2Y 3E5
(514) 925-5100
Emp Here 90   *Sales* 12,976,380

SIC 7371 Custom computer programming services
 Moris Chemtov
 Eric Aintabi
 Stephanie Aintabi
 Judah Bendayan

   D-U-N-S 20-181-5243   (SL)
JITNEYTRADE INC
DIVISION CLIENTS PROFESSIONNELS
360 Rue Saint-Jacques, Montreal, QC, H2Y
1P5
(514) 985-8080
Emp Here 26   *Sales* 13,811,382
SIC 6231 Security and commodity exchanges
 Eric Cote
 Jean-Francois Sabourin
 Pierre-Yves Courgeon
 Alain Miquelon
 Rene Perreault

   D-U-N-S 20-738-4694   (SL)
KENAR CONSULTANTS INC
(*Suby of* NFOE INC)
511 Place D'Armes Bureau 100, Montreal,
QC, H2Y 2W7
(514) 397-2616
Emp Here 60   *Sales* 10,724,340
SIC 8712 Architectural services
 Alan E. Orton
 Michael B.H. Sullivan
 Rafie Sossantour
 Victor Marques

   D-U-N-S 20-559-8225   (SL)
KEYRUS CANADA INC
KEYRUS
759 Rue Du Square-Victoria Unit 420, Montreal, QC, H2Y 2J7
(514) 989-2000
Emp Here 70   *Sales* 11,380,880
SIC 7379 Computer related services, nec
 Eric Cohen
 Eric Blanchet
 Rebecca Meimoun
 Laetitia Adjadj

   D-U-N-S 24-920-9404   (HQ)
LEGER MARKETING INC
VILLAGE 360
507 Place D'Armes Bureau 700, Montreal,
QC, H2Y 2W8
(514) 845-5660
Emp Here 425   *Sales* 163,265,600
SIC 8732 Commercial nonphysical research
 Jean-Marc Leger
 Bertrand Hebert
 Anne-Marie Marois
 Benoit Leroux
 Jacques Nantel
 Chuck Chakrapani
 Bruce Shandler
 Pierre Weill

   D-U-N-S 24-761-9799   (HQ)
LIGHTSPEED POS INC
LIGHTSPEED
700 Rue Saint-Antoine E Bureau 300, Montreal, QC, H2Y 1A6
(514) 907-1801
Sales 33,369,400
SIC 7372 Prepackaged software
 Dax Dasilva
 Dave Sherry
 Jean Paul Chauvet
 Chris Arsenault
 Normand Chartrand
 Thomas Birch
 Michael Mcgraw

   D-U-N-S 24-813-8323   (HQ)
LOGISTEC ARRIMAGE INC
*CANADA ENTERPRISES STEVEDORING
AND TERMINALS*
(*Suby of* LOGISTEC CORPORATION)
360 Rue Saint-Jacques Bureau 1500, Montreal, QC, H2Y 3X1

(514) 844-9381
Emp Here 75   *Sales* 138,944,400
SIC 4491 Marine cargo handling
 Madelaine Paquin
 Jean-Claude Dugas
 Ingrid Stefancic
 Nicole Paquin
 Rodney Corrigan

   D-U-N-S 20-634-6454   (HQ)
LOGISTEC CORPORATION
360 Rue Saint-Jacques Bureau 1500, Montreal, QC, H2Y 3X1
(514) 844-9381
Emp Here 75   *Sales* 443,397,182
SIC 4491 Marine cargo handling
 Madeleine Paquin
 Frank Vannelli
 Ingrid Stefancic
 Alain Pilotte
 George Di Sante
 Kevin Bourbonnais
 Michel Miron
 Stephane Blanchette
 Trip Bailey
 Marie-Chantal Savoy

   D-U-N-S 24-865-2117   (HQ)
LOGISTIQUE TRANS-PRO INC
(*Suby of* PLACEMENTS MAPEBO INC)
407 Rue Mcgill Bureau 910, Montreal, QC,
H2Y 2G3
(514) 858-6482
Sales 46,682,440
SIC 4731 Freight transportation arrangement
 Peter Boyko
 Rola Eldik
 Eric Boyko

   D-U-N-S 20-192-6594   (HQ)
LOUISIANA-PACIFIC CANADA LTD
(*Suby of* LOUISIANA-PACIFIC CORPORATION)
507 Place D'Armes Bureau 400, Montreal,
QC, H2Y 2W8
(514) 861-4724
Emp Here 22   *Sales* 139,195,000
SIC 2431 Millwork
 William B. Southern
 Sallie B. Bailey
 Peter H Finley

   D-U-N-S 24-361-6146   (SL)
LUDIA INC
410 Rue Saint-Nicolas Bureau 400, Montreal,
QC, H2Y 2P5
(514) 313-3370
Emp Here 250   *Sales* 173,825,000
SIC 5092 Toys and hobby goods and supplies
 Jean-Francois Marcoux
 Alexandre Thabet
 Robert Bradley Martin
 Cecile Frot-Coutaz
 Keith Hindle

   D-U-N-S 20-547-6190   (SL)
MARKETEL COMMUNICATIONS INC
413 Rue Saint-Jacques 10e Etage, Montreal,
QC, H2Y 1N9
(514) 935-9445
Emp Here 140   *Sales* 28,051,940
SIC 7311 Advertising agencies
 Jacques L. Duval

   D-U-N-S 24-019-2914   (SL)
MARKETEL/MCCANN-ERICKSON LTEE
GROUPE TACTIQUE
(*Suby of* THE INTERPUBLIC GROUP OF
COMPANIES INC)
413 Rue Saint-Jacques Bureau 10e, Montreal,
QC, H2Y 1N9
(514) 935-9445
Emp Here 140   *Sales* 28,051,940
SIC 7311 Advertising agencies
 Jacques L Duval
 Conrad Gagnon

   D-U-N-S 24-354-6215   (SL)

MAZARS HAREL DROUIN, S.E.N.C.R.L.
HAREL DROUIN GESTION CONSEILS
215 Rue Saint-Jacques Bureau 1200, Montreal, QC, H2Y 1M6
(514) 845-9253
Emp Here 85   *Sales* 17,653,225
SIC 8721 Accounting, auditing, and bookkeeping
 Michel Brousseau
 Donald Gauthier
 Serge Principe
 Sylvie Garon
 Louise Papin
 Louise Roby
 Martin Cloutier
 Annick Morneau-Montreuil
 Lucette Poliquin
 Lino Delarosbil

   D-U-N-S 20-028-1723   (SL)
MAZARS, S.E.N.C.R.L.
215 Rue Saint-Jacques, Bureau 1200, Montreal, QC, H2Y 1M6
(514) 878-2600
Emp Here 50   *Sales* 10,454,250
SIC 8721 Accounting, auditing, and bookkeeping
 Johanne Fortier
 Serge Principe
 Sylvie Garon
 Louise Papin
 Louise Roby
 Martin Cloutier
 Annick Morneau-Montreuil
 Lucette Poliquin
 Lino Delarosbil
 Lucie Lavoie

   D-U-N-S 25-311-0464   (BR)
**MCDONALD'S   RESTAURANTS   OF
CANADA LIMITED**
MCDONALD'S
(*Suby of* MCDONALD'S CORPORATION)
1 Rue Notre-Dame E, Montreal, QC, H2Y 1B6
(514) 285-8720
Emp Here 75
SIC 5812 Eating places
 Anna Macuso

   D-U-N-S 24-375-7254   (HQ)
MCGILL ST-LAURENT INC
407 Rue Mcgill Bureau 315, Montreal, QC,
H2Y 2G3
(514) 871-2120
Sales 20,122,830
SIC 5031 Lumber, plywood, and millwork
 Philippe Boisclair
 Christian L'abbe

   D-U-N-S 20-564-4701   (HQ)
MCLEAN KENNEDY INC
(*Suby of* GESTION KENMONT INC)
368 Rue Notre-Dame O Bureau 100, Montreal, QC, H2Y 1T9
(514) 849-6111
Emp Here 18   *Sales* 20,798,680
SIC 4731 Freight transportation arrangement
 Robert G Mcboyle
 William R S Eakin
 John Langlais

   D-U-N-S 20-960-9510   (SL)
**MEDITERRANEAN SHIPPING COMPANY
(CANADA) INC**
*COMPAGNIE   MARITIME   MEDITERRA-
NEENNE (CANADA)*
(*Suby of* UNITED AGENCIES LIMITED SA)
7 Rue Saint-Jacques, Montreal, QC, H2Y 1K9
(514) 844-3711
Emp Here 181   *Sales* 120,707,452
SIC 4731 Freight transportation arrangement
 Sokat Shaikh
 Norman Tam
 Bourquin Elvio
 Eduard O Sigrist

   D-U-N-S 25-173-0156   (SL)

MONTREAL INTERNATIONAL
380 Rue Saint-Antoine O Bureau 8000, Montreal, QC, H2Y 3X7
(514) 987-8191
Emp Here 85   *Sales* 21,546,650
SIC 8748 Business consulting, nec
 L. Jacques Menard
 Harout Chitilian
 Manon Gauthier
 Tony Loffreda
 Virginie Dufour
 Marie-Chantal Girard
 Peter Kruyt
 John Parisella
 Hubert Bolduc
 Valerie Vezina

   D-U-N-S 20-022-7619   (SL)
MONTRIUM HOSTED SOLUTIONS INC
SOLUTIONS HEBERGEES MONTRIUM
507 Place D'Armes Bureau 1050, Montreal,
QC, H2Y 2W8
(514) 223-9153
Emp Here 48   *Sales* 11,419,248
SIC 8742 Management consulting services
 Paul Keith Fenton
 Michael Zwetkow

   D-U-N-S 20-227-7554   (HQ)
MONTSHIP INC
(*Suby of* TREALMONT TRANSPORT INC)
360 Rue Saint-Jacques Bureau 1000, Montreal, QC, H2Y 1R2
(514) 286-4646
Emp Here 44   *Sales* 68,410,774
SIC 4731 Freight transportation arrangement
 D. Brian Mcdonald
 Domenic Bravi
 Brent M. Coulthard
 Robert Rabnett
 Scott Pichette
 Gracinda Pires
 Michel Sellitto

   D-U-N-S 24-800-4673   (SL)
N F O E & ASSOCIES ARCHITECTS
KENAR CONSULTANTS
511 Place D'Armes Bureau 100, Montreal,
QC, H2Y 2W7
(514) 397-2616
Emp Here 75   *Sales* 13,405,425
SIC 8712 Architectural services
 Masharu Fukushima
 Alan Orton
 Rafie Sossanpour
 Michael Sullivan
 Patricia L. Hurley

   D-U-N-S 25-107-5271   (SL)
**NAVIGATION DES ETATS INDEPENDANTS
DU COMMONWEALTH INC**
CIS NAVIGATION
478 Rue Mcgill, Montreal, QC, H2Y 2H2
(514) 499-1999
Emp Here 25   *Sales* 12,999,175
SIC 4731 Freight transportation arrangement
 Alexandre A Maistrenko
 Andrei B Smirnov

   D-U-N-S 20-370-2613   (HQ)
NFOE INC
511 Place D'Armes Bureau 100, Montreal,
QC, H2Y 2W7
(514) 397-2616
Emp Here 49   *Sales* 14,299,120
SIC 8712 Architectural services
 Alan Orton
 Rafie Sossanpour
 Michael Sullivan
 Victor Marques
 Hicham Marquoum

   D-U-N-S 20-298-6352   (BR)
NORDA STELO INC
(*Suby of* NORDA STELO INC)
33 Rue Saint-Jacques Bureau 400, Montreal,
QC, H2Y 1K9

(514) 282-4181
Emp Here 85
SIC 8711 Engineering services
Martin Choiniere

D-U-N-S 25-308-6557 (SL)
NORTEC MARINE AGENCIES INC
MARCH SHIPPING (DIV OF)
465 Rue Saint-Jean Bureau 708, Montreal,
QC, H2Y 2R6
(514) 985-2329
Emp Here 80 *Sales* 41,597,360
SIC 4731 Freight transportation arrangement
Jim Surphlis
Jacques Richard
Ralph Fabrizio

D-U-N-S 25-686-1824 (HQ)
**NOTARIUS - TECHNOLGIES ET SYSTEMES
D'INFORMATION NOTARIALE INC**
NOTARIUS
465 Rue Mcgill Bureau 300, Montreal, QC,
H2Y 2H1
(514) 281-1577
Sales 22,460,950
SIC 7389 Business services, nec
Jean Lambert
Maurice Piette
Nathalie Denis
Daniel Pinard
Louise Archambault
Charlaine Bouchard
Claude Charpentier

D-U-N-S 20-303-1133 (SL)
NVENTIVE INC
AGENCE MEDIA EQUATION HUMAINE
215 Rue Saint-Jacques Bureau 500, Montreal,
QC, H2Y 1M6
(514) 312-4969
Emp Here 80 *Sales* 14,184,880
SIC 7371 Custom computer programming ser-
vices
Francois Tanguay

D-U-N-S 24-084-9117 (SL)
OGILVY MONTREAL INC
COMMUNICATIONA ID EST
215 Rue Saint-Jacques Bureau 333, Montreal,
QC, H2Y 1M6
(514) 861-1811
Emp Here 50 *Sales* 10,586,200
SIC 7311 Advertising agencies
Daniel Demers
Martin Gosselin
Steven Goldstein
Tro Piliguian
Andy Watson
Denis Piquette
John Seifert
David Aubert

D-U-N-S 25-503-9232 (BR)
ONE10 CANADA HOLDINGS ULC
CARLSON MARKETING
(*Suby of* ONE10 LLC)
759 Rue Du Square-Victoria Bureau 105,
Montreal, QC, H2Y 2J7
(514) 288-9889
Emp Here 120
SIC 8732 Commercial nonphysical research

D-U-N-S 24-591-0633 (SL)
**PAQUETTE ET ASSOCIES HUISSIERS DE
JUSTICE S.E.N.C.R.L.**
511 Place D'Armes Bureau 800, Montreal,
QC, H2Y 2W7
(514) 937-5500
Emp Here 110 *Sales* 12,197,020
SIC 8111 Legal services
Michel Lachance
Jean-Guy Lachance

D-U-N-S 20-059-6646 (HQ)
PCO INNOVATION CANADA INC
IDCAD SERVICES CONSEILS
(*Suby of* ACCENTURE INC)
384 Rue Saint-Jacques, Montreal, QC, H2Y

1S1
(514) 866-3000
Sales 36,641,495
SIC 8711 Engineering services
William F. Morris
Darrin M. Meehan

D-U-N-S 20-230-2519 (SL)
PHOTO SERVICE LTEE
FOTO SOURCE PHOTO SERVICE
222 Rue Notre-Dame O, Montreal, QC, H2Y
1T3
(514) 849-2291
Emp Here 30 *Sales* 13,415,220
SIC 5043 Photographic equipment and sup-
plies
Jean-Charles Savard
Louise Durante

D-U-N-S 24-554-6606 (SL)
PLANET GASTRONOMIE
465 Rue Saint-Jean, Montreal, QC, H2Y 2R6

Emp Here 49 *Sales* 25,935,547
SIC 5099 Durable goods, nec
Vincent Mahe

D-U-N-S 20-230-7443 (HQ)
POWER CORPORATION DU CANADA
SQUARE VICTORIA IMMOBILIER
751 Rue Du Square-Victoria, Montreal, QC,
H2Y 2J3
(514) 286-7400
Emp Here 100 *Sales* 36,463,189,996
SIC 6211 Security brokers and dealers
Paul Jr. Desmarais
Andre Desmarais
Gregory D. Tretiak
Claude Genereux
Olivier Desmarais
Paul Desmarais Iii
Paul C. Genest
Arnaud Bellens
Denis Le Vasseur
Yuhong Liu

D-U-N-S 24-676-4799 (HQ)
POWER FINANCIAL CORPORATION
(*Suby of* POWER CORPORATION DU
CANADA)
751 Rue Du Square-Victoria, Montreal, QC,
H2Y 2J3
(514) 286-7400
Emp Here 1,000 *Sales* 35,649,746,550
SIC 6712 Bank holding companies
R. Jeffrey Orr
Paul Desmarais Jr
Andre Desmarais
Michel Plessis-Belair
Amaury De Seze
Gregory D Tretik
Claude Genereux
Olivier Desmarais
Paul Desmarais Iii
Paul C Genest

D-U-N-S 20-215-2138 (HQ)
PRESSE (2018) INC, LA
AUTO LOISIRS
750 Boul Saint-Laurent, Montreal, QC, H2Y
2Z4
(514) 285-7000
Sales 96,887,000
SIC 2711 Newspapers
Pierre-Elliott Levasseur
Patrick Buchholz
Alain Gignac
Claire Bara
Nathalie Fagnan
Pierre Lapointe
Martin Gourdeau
Sophie Cousineau
Guy Crevier
Patrick Clouatre

D-U-N-S 20-357-5980 (HQ)
PRODUITS DE BOIS CANADIENS - MON-

TREAL INC
PRODUITS FORESTIERS DU CANADA
(*Suby of* MCGILL ST-LAURENT INC)
407 Rue Mcgill Bureau 315, Montreal, QC,
H2Y 2G3
(514) 871-2120
Sales 22,358,700
SIC 5031 Lumber, plywood, and millwork
Philippe Boisclair
Christian L'abbe

D-U-N-S 20-314-2583 (SL)
**PROVENCHER ROY + ASSOCIES ARCHI-
TECTES INC**
PROVENCHER ROY
276 Rue Saint-Jacques Bureau 700, Montreal,
QC, H2Y 1N3
(514) 844-3938
Emp Here 100 *Sales* 24,151,500
SIC 8621 Professional organizations
Claude Provencher
Alain Compera
Line Belhumeur
Claude Bourbeau

D-U-N-S 25-684-9001 (HQ)
R3D CONSEIL INC
R3D
485 Rue Mcgill Bureau 1110, Montreal, QC,
H2Y 2H4
(514) 879-9000
Emp Here 10 *Sales* 63,348,549
SIC 8742 Management consulting services
Marc-Andre Roy

D-U-N-S 20-924-8371 (SL)
RESTAURANT AIX INC
BAR SUITE 701
711 Cote De La Place-D'Armes, Montreal,
QC, H2Y 2X6
(514) 904-1201
Emp Here 100 *Sales* 4,551,900
SIC 5812 Eating places
Dimitrios C. Antonopoulos

D-U-N-S 24-515-2582 (SL)
RESTAURANT DU VIEUX PORT INC
39 Rue Saint-Paul E, Montreal, QC, H2Y 1G2
(514) 866-3175
Emp Here 80 *Sales* 3,429,840
SIC 5812 Eating places
Anthony Antonopoulos
Costas Antonopoulos

D-U-N-S 24-296-5101 (SL)
**RESTAURANT SAINT-PAUL (MONTREAL)
LTEE**
KEG STEAKHOUSE & BAR
(*Suby of* RECIPE UNLIMITED CORPORA-
TION)
25 Rue Saint-Paul E, Montreal, QC, H2Y 1G2
(514) 871-9093
Emp Here 200 *Sales* 9,327,800
SIC 5812 Eating places
Kevin Major

D-U-N-S 25-324-1202 (BR)
SAP CANADA INC
(*Suby of* SAP SE)
380 Rue Saint-Antoine O Bureau 2000, Mon-
treal, QC, H2Y 3X7
(514) 350-7300
Emp Here 90
SIC 7372 Prepackaged software
Renee Giguere

D-U-N-S 20-548-9318 (SL)
**SECRETARIAT DE LA CONVENTION SUR
LA DIVERSITE BIOLOGIQUE**
SCBD
413 Rue Saint-Jacques Bureau 500, Montreal,
QC, H2Y 1N9
(514) 288-2220
Emp Here 75 *Sales* 10,715,925
SIC 8641 Civic and social associations
Ahmed Bjooghlas

D-U-N-S 24-311-6915 (SL)

TREAL INC (continued — header)

**SERVICES D'IMPRESSION ESSENCE DU
PAPIER INC**
127 Rue Saint-Pierre Bureau 200, Montreal,
QC, H2Y 2L6
(514) 286-2880
Emp Here 175 *Sales* 47,836,250
SIC 6712 Bank holding companies
Guy Belanger

D-U-N-S 25-108-1022 (SL)
**SERVICES FINANCIERS PENSON CANADA
INC**
(*Suby of* PENSON WORLDWIDE INC)
360 Rue Saint-Jacques Bureau 1201, Mon-
treal, QC, H2Y 1P5

Emp Here 140
SIC 6289 Security and commodity service
Richard Ness
Liam Cheung
Francois Gervais

D-U-N-S 25-991-3929 (SL)
SNC-LAVALIN GTS INC
360 Rue Saint-Jacques Bureau 1600, Mon-
treal, QC, H2Y 1P5
(514) 393-1000
Emp Here 80 *Sales* 20,924,240
SIC 6712 Bank holding companies
Jean Nehme
Yves Laverdiere

D-U-N-S 24-871-7084 (HQ)
**SOCIETE DU VIEUX-PORT DE MONTREAL
INC**
CAFE DES ECLUSIERS
(*Suby of* GOVERNMENT OF CANADA)
333 Rue De La Commune O, Montreal, QC,
H2Y 2E2
(514) 283-5256
Sales 59,165,625
SIC 8743 Public relations services
Grant Walsh
John Mcbain
Robert Howald
Greg Barker
Clint Hames
Barbara Sutherland
Nicholas Macos
Toby Jenkins
Jocelyne Houle

D-U-N-S 24-253-0947 (SL)
**SOCIETE QUEBECOISE D'INFORMATION
JURIDIQUE**
SOQUIJ
715 Rue Du Square-Victoria Bureau 600,
Montreal, QC, H2Y 2H7
(514) 842-8741
Emp Here 120 *Sales* 19,683,240
SIC 2759 Commercial printing, nec
Claude Paul-Hus
Guy Mercier
Estelle Tremblay

D-U-N-S 24-542-0344 (HQ)
**SOEURS DE LA CHARITE (SOEURS
GRISES) DE MONTREAL, LES**
MAISON DE MERE D'YOUVILLE
138 Rue Saint-Pierre, Montreal, QC, H2Y 2L7
(514) 842-9411
Emp Here 20 *Sales* 20,824,600
SIC 8661 Religious organizations
Faye Wylie

D-U-N-S 24-050-6113 (HQ)
SOGELCO INTERNATIONAL INC
SOGEL
(*Suby of* CONSULTRANS INTERNATIONAL
LTEE)
715 Rue Du Square-Victoria Bureau 400,
Montreal, QC, H2Y 2H7
(514) 849-2414
Emp Here 10 *Sales* 33,423,080
SIC 5146 Fish and seafoods
Gabriel Elbaz

▲ Public Company ■ Public Company Family Member **HQ** Headquarters **BR** Branch **SL** Single Location

D-U-N-S 20-718-0030   (SL)
SOLUTIONS CONTACT PHOCUS INC
507 Place D'Armes Bureau 800, Montreal,
QC, H2Y 2W8
(514) 788-5650
Emp Here 200   *Sales* 133,781,600
SIC 7389 Business services, nec

D-U-N-S 24-173-6776   (SL)
TOURS CHANTECLERC INC
(*Suby of* GROUPE HOLDING QUEBECOIS
(G.H.Q.) INC)
152 Rue Notre-Dame E, Montreal, QC, H2Y
3P6
(514) 398-9535
Emp Here 50   *Sales* 25,998,350
SIC 4725 Tour operators
 Bernard Beauchamp
 Claude St-Pierre

D-U-N-S 24-763-6590   (SL)
TRADUCTIONS SERGE BELAIR INC
276 Rue Saint-Jacques Bureau 900, Montreal,
QC, H2Y 1N3
(514) 844-4682
Emp Here 200   *Sales* 18,418,217
SIC 7389 Business services, nec
 Serge Belair

D-U-N-S 25-813-6878   (SL)
TRANS CANADA TRAIL
321 Rue De La Commune O Bureau 300,
Montreal, QC, H2Y 2E1
(514) 485-3959
Emp Here 25   *Sales* 11,230,475
SIC 7389 Business services, nec
 Deborah Apps
 Paul Labarge
 Cameron Clark
 James Bishop
 Rick Morgan
 Ruth Marr
 Lori Spence
 Ron Hicks
 Jazmine Brown
 Carolyn Mackay

D-U-N-S 20-381-6400   (BR)
UBISOFT DIVERTISSEMENTS INC
STUDIO UBISOFT SAINT-ANTOINE
(*Suby of* UBISOFT ENTERTAINMENT)
250 Rue Saint-Antoine O Bureau 700, Mon-
treal, QC, H2Y 0A3
(514) 908-8100
Emp Here 140
SIC 7371 Custom computer programming ser-
vices

Montreal, QC H2Z

D-U-N-S 24-836-2592   (SL)
162013 CANADA INC
IBD
1080 Cote Du Beaver Hall, Montreal, QC, H2Z
1S8

Emp Here 100
SIC 7389 Business services, nec

D-U-N-S 24-363-2937   (HQ)
AIMIA INC
525 Av Viger O Bureau 1000, Montreal, QC,
H2Z 0B2
(514) 897-6800
Emp Here 39   *Sales* 126,678,844
SIC 8732 Commercial nonphysical research
 Jeremy Rabe
 William (Bill) Mcewan
 Edouard Vo-Quang
 W. Brian Edwards
 Thomas D. Gardner
 Emma Griffin
 Robert (Chris) Kreidler
 Philip Mittleman

Steve Leonard
Linda Kuga Pikulin

D-U-N-S 20-715-3185   (BR)
ALSTOM CANADA INC
ALSTOM TELECITE MONTREAL
(*Suby of* GE RENEWABLE HOLDING B.V.)
1050 Cote Du Beaver Hall, Montreal, QC, H2Z
0A5
(514) 333-0888
Emp Here 100
SIC 7311 Advertising agencies
 Angelo Guercioni

D-U-N-S 20-277-4576   (SL)
ALSTOM TRANSPORT CANADA INC
ALSTOM
1050 Cote Du Beaver Hall Bureau 1840, Mon-
treal, QC, H2Z 0A5
(514) 333-0888
Emp Here 250   *Sales* 72,712,500
SIC 3743 Railroad equipment
 Angelo Guercioni
 Jerome Wallut
 Michael Blankenship
 Michael Carrato

D-U-N-S 24-350-2429   (SL)
AUTOMOBILES ROCHMAT INC
HONDA DE SIGL
1124 Rue De Bleury, Montreal, QC, H2Z 1N4
(514) 879-1550
Emp Here 40   *Sales* 19,923,120
SIC 5511 New and used car dealers
 Jean-Claude Gravel
 Dennis Gendron
 Vincent Chiara

D-U-N-S 20-114-5153   (SL)
CAPITAL D'AMERIQUE CDPQ INC
CDP CAPITAL - AMERIQUE
(*Suby of* GOUVERNEMENT DE LA
PROVINCE DE QUEBEC)
1000 Place Jean-Paul-Riopelle Bureau 12e,
Montreal, QC, H2Z 2B3
(514) 842-3261
Emp Here 900   *Sales* 1,923,271,200
SIC 6371 Pension, health, and welfare funds
 Kim Thomassin
 Christian Dube
 Melanie Julien

D-U-N-S 24-241-3255   (SL)
CAPITAL TRAITEUR MONTREAL INC
CAPITAL TRAITEUR
159 Rue Saint-Antoine O Bureau 400, Mon-
treal, QC, H2Z 2A7
(514) 875-1897
Emp Here 150   *Sales* 6,827,850
SIC 5812 Eating places
 Nick Tsatas

D-U-N-S 24-988-1020   (SL)
CAPITAL TRAITEUR MONTREAL INC
201 Av Viger O, Montreal, QC, H2Z 1X7
(514) 871-3111
Emp Here 98   *Sales* 4,460,862
SIC 5812 Eating places
 Steve Tsatas

D-U-N-S 20-649-0430   (SL)
CDP CAPITAL-CONSEIL IMMOBILIER INC
CDP CAPITAL-CI
(*Suby of* GOUVERNEMENT DE LA
PROVINCE DE QUEBEC)
1000 Place Jean-Paul-Riopelle Bureau A 300,
Montreal, QC, H2Z 2B3
(514) 875-3360
Emp Here 100   *Sales* 147,406,100
SIC 6722 Management investment, open-end
 William Tresham
 Louiselle Paquin
 Yves Andre Godon

D-U-N-S 25-147-9010   (HQ)
**CIM-CONSEIL EN IMMOBILISATION ET
MANAGEMENT INC**

440 Boul Rene-Levesque O Bureau 1700,
Montreal, QC, H2Z 1V7
(514) 393-4563
Sales 12,748,185
SIC 8741 Management services
 Mario St-Cyr
 Raymond Harvey

D-U-N-S 25-672-1812   (BR)
**FEDERATION DES CAISSES DESJARDINS
DU QUEBEC**
SERVICES DE CARTES DESJARDINS
(*Suby of* FEDERATION DES CAISSES DES-
JARDINS DU QUEBEC)
425 Av Viger O Bureau 900, Montreal, QC,
H2Z 1W5
(514) 397-4789
Emp Here 300
SIC 6062 State credit unions
 Yves Genest

D-U-N-S 20-562-5072   (HQ)
**FONDS SOCIAL DES EMPLOYES DE LA
CAISSE DE DEPOT ET PLACEMENT DU
QUEBEC**
CENTRE CDP CAPITAL
1000 Place Jean-Paul-Riopelle Bureau A12,
Montreal, QC, H2Z 2B3
(514) 842-3261
Emp Here 800   *Sales* 764,164,450
SIC 6399 Insurance carriers, nec
 Julie Robitaille
 Camille O'carroll
 Marie-Eve Desjardins
 Martine Lalonde
 Yann Langlais Plante

D-U-N-S 24-815-3579   (SL)
GESTION SINOMONDE INC
HOLIDAY INN MONTREAL CENTRE-VILLE
99 Av Viger O, Montreal, QC, H2Z 1E9
(514) 878-9888
Emp Here 100   *Sales* 27,335,000
SIC 6712 Bank holding companies
 Kin Chung Cheung
 Wei Qing (Alice) Xiao
 Baojun Wang
 Antonio Yuk Lum Chui
 Chi Fai Tsang
 Zhong He Shui
 Yan Huang
 Zhen Hua Wu

D-U-N-S 20-137-2757   (BR)
**GOUVERNEMENT DE LA PROVINCE DE
QUEBEC**
PROTECTEUR DU CITOYEN
(*Suby of* GOUVERNEMENT DE LA
PROVINCE DE QUEBEC)
1080 Cote Du Beaver Hall Bureau 1000, Mon-
treal, QC, H2Z 1S8
(514) 873-2032
Emp Here 132
SIC 8322 Individual and family services
 Raymonde Saint-Germain

D-U-N-S 25-362-0371   (BR)
**GOUVERNEMENT DE LA PROVINCE DE
QUEBEC**
MONTREAL CONVENTION CENTRE
(*Suby of* GOUVERNEMENT DE LA
PROVINCE DE QUEBEC)
159 Rue Saint-Antoine O Bureau 900, Mon-
treal, QC, H2Z 1H2
(514) 871-8122
Emp Here 222
SIC 7389 Business services, nec
 Raymond Larivee

D-U-N-S 20-176-6172   (BR)
**GOUVERNEMENT DE LA PROVINCE DE
QUEBEC**
*SOCIETE DU PALAIS DES CONGRES DE
MONTREAL*
(*Suby of* GOUVERNEMENT DE LA
PROVINCE DE QUEBEC)
159 Rue Saint-Antoine O Bureau 900, Mon-

treal, QC, H2Z 1H2
(514) 871-8122
Emp Here 125
SIC 7389 Business services, nec
 Remo Larive

D-U-N-S 24-239-5460   (SL)
GRANDE EPOQUE INC, LA
EPOCH TIMES
1099 Rue Clark Bureau 3, Montreal, QC, H2Z
1K3
(514) 954-0756
Emp Here 20   *Sales* 13,350,098
SIC 5963 Direct selling establishments
 Xiaoe Hu

D-U-N-S 20-589-9920   (SL)
GROUPE SECOR INC
555 Boul Rene-Levesque O Bureau 900, Montreal, QC, H2Z 1B1

Emp Here 75   *Sales* 16,001,850
SIC 8732 Commercial nonphysical research
 Madeleine Chenette
 Jocelyn Leclerc

D-U-N-S 20-542-9533   (HQ)
GROUPE SNC-LAVALIN INC
455 Boul Rene-Levesque O Bureau 202, Mon-
treal, QC, H2Z 1Z3
(514) 393-1000
Emp Here 50   *Sales* 7,644,705,117
SIC 8711 Engineering services
 Neil A. Bruce
 James Cullens
 Sylvain Girard
 Hartland J. A. Paterson
 Erik J. Ryan
 Chantal Sorel
 Marie-Claude Dumas
 Jonathan Wilkinson
 Alexander Taylor
 Jose J. Surez

D-U-N-S 24-167-6154   (HQ)
HYDRO-QUEBEC INTERNATIONAL INC
(*Suby of* GOUVERNEMENT DE LA
PROVINCE DE QUEBEC)
75 Boul Rene-Levesque O Bureau 101, Mon-
treal, QC, H2Z 1A4
(514) 289-2211
Emp Here 100   *Sales* 55,191,859
SIC 6719 Holding companies, nec
 Eric Martel
 Steve Demers
 Pierre Gagnon
 Jean-Hugues Lafleur
 Real Laporte

D-U-N-S 25-093-3269   (SL)
IVANHOE CAMBRIDGE I INC.
IVANHOE CAMBRIDGE
(*Suby of* GOUVERNEMENT DE LA
PROVINCE DE QUEBEC)
1001 Rue Du Square-Victoria Bureau 500,
Montreal, QC, H2Z 2B5
(514) 841-7600
Emp Here 150   *Sales* 20,351,550
SIC 6512 Nonresidential building operators
 Lorna Telfer
 Robert Coallier
 Marie-France Soucy
 Vincent Filion
 Claude Caty
 Karen Laflamme
 David Peterson
 John Riordan
 Frederick Castonguay
 Sylvain Gareau

D-U-N-S 20-544-5356   (HQ)
IVANHOE CAMBRIDGE INC
1000 DE LA GAUCHETIERE
(*Suby of* GOUVERNEMENT DE LA
PROVINCE DE QUEBEC)
1001 Rue Du Square-Victoria Bureau 500,
Montreal, QC, H2Z 2B5

(514) 841-7600
Emp Here 500   *Sales* 203,515,500
SIC 6512 Nonresidential building operators
  Daniel Fournier
  Denis Boulianne
  Sylvain Gareau
  Gilles Horrobin
  David R. Peterson
  Line Rivard
  Pierre Seccareccia
  Real Brunet
  Martin Roy
  Jamie Forster

   D-U-N-S 20-547-8832   (SL)
KPMG-SECOUR
555 Boul Rene-Levesque O Bureau 1700,
Montreal, QC, H2Z 1B1

Emp Here 49   *Sales* 10,417,476
SIC 8721 Accounting, auditing, and book-
keeping
  Langloir Guy

   D-U-N-S 20-234-8926   (HQ)
MAGASIN DE MUSIQUE STEVE INC
MUSIQUE STEVE
51 Rue Saint-Antoine O, Montreal, QC, H2Z
1G9
(514) 878-2216
Emp Here 100   *Sales* 163,395,500
SIC 5099 Durable goods, nec
  Lea Kirman
  Michael Kirman
  William Kirman

   D-U-N-S 20-007-2655   (SL)
MCA VALEURS MOBILIERES INC
555 Boul Rene-Levesque O Bureau 140, Montreal, QC, H2Z 1B1

Emp Here 40   *Sales* 27,156,920
SIC 6211 Security brokers and dealers
  Michel Cousineau
  Gilles Beauregard

   D-U-N-S 20-884-2641   (HQ)
MISSION OLD BREWERY
902 Boul Saint-Laurent, Montreal, QC, H2Z
1J2
(514) 866-6591
Sales 10,927,940
SIC 8361 Residential care
  Matthew Pearce
  Mathiew Pierce

   D-U-N-S 20-243-6650   (SL)
MP REPRODUCTIONS INC
1030 Rue Chenneville, Montreal, QC, H2Z
1V8
(514) 861-8541
Emp Here 49   *Sales* 20,457,794
SIC 7384 Photofinish laboratories
  Maria Carmela Martinez

   D-U-N-S 24-901-1578   (HQ)
NOVERCO INC
1000 Place Jean-Paul-Riopelle Bureau A12,
Montreal, QC, H2Z 2B3
(514) 847-2126
Sales 731,018,000
SIC 6712 Bank holding companies
  Renaud Faucher
  Eric Cantin
  Eve Giard
  Francois Duquette
  Vern Yu
  David Robottom
  Richard Dinneny

   D-U-N-S 20-972-2560   (HQ)
**OFFICE MUNICIPAL D'HABITATION DE
MONTREAL**
O.M.H.M.
415 Rue Saint-Antoine O 2e Etage, Montreal,
QC, H2Z 2B9
(514) 872-6442
Emp Here 5   *Sales* 130,600,800

SIC 6531 Real estate agents and managers
  Robert Labelle
  Danielle Fournier
  Ghislaine Laramee
  Sylvain Labrecque
  Johanne Goulet
  Christian Champagne
  Sylvie Crispo
  Lise Guillemette
  Marie-France Raynault
  Danielle Cecile

   D-U-N-S 24-542-8446   (SL)
PELLEMON INC
(*Suby of* GROUPE SNC-LAVALIN INC)
455 Boul Rene-Levesque O, Montreal, QC,
H2Z 1Z3
(514) 735-5651
Emp Here 250   *Sales* 49,282,750
SIC 8711 Engineering services
  Terry Lefebvre
  Arden R. Furlotte
  Richard Fecteau
  Normand Dubuc

   D-U-N-S 20-890-9478   (SL)
PRESIMA INC
(*Suby of* NAB ASSET MANAGEMENT LIM-
ITED)
1000 Place Jean-Paul-Riopelle Unite 400,
Montreal, QC, H2Z 2B6
(514) 673-1375
Emp Here 16   *Sales* 13,244,432
SIC 6722 Management investment, open-end
  Jean-Guy Talbot

   D-U-N-S 20-380-8100   (SL)
SINORAMA CORPORATION
998 Blvd Saint-Laurent Office 518, Montreal,
QC, H2Z 9Y9
(514) 866-6888
Emp Here 3   *Sales* 98,277,721
SIC 4724 Travel agencies
  Qian Hong
  Jing Wenjia
  Zhao Hongxi

   D-U-N-S 24-204-9851   (HQ)
SITQ INTERNATIONAL INC
SITQ
(*Suby of* GOUVERNEMENT DE LA
PROVINCE DE QUEBEC)
1001 Rue Du Square-Victoria Bureau 500,
Montreal, QC, H2Z 2B5
(514) 287-1852
Sales 49,910,400
SIC 8741 Management services
  Nathalie Palladitcheff
  Nathalie Gravel
  Denis Boulianne
  Lisette Roy

   D-U-N-S 20-050-4541   (SL)
SITQ NATIONAL INC
(*Suby of* GOUVERNEMENT DE LA
PROVINCE DE QUEBEC)
1001 Rue Du Square-Victoria Bureau C 200,
Montreal, QC, H2Z 2B1
(514) 287-1852
Emp Here 210   *Sales* 730,285,290
SIC 6798 Real estate investment trusts
  Nathalie Gravel
  Denis Boulianne

   D-U-N-S 24-903-2327   (SL)
SNC-LAVALIN CONSTRUCTION INC
(*Suby of* GROUPE SNC-LAVALIN INC)
455 Boul Rene-Levesque O Bureau 202, Mon-
treal, QC, H2Z 1Z3
(514) 393-1000
Emp Here 4,154   *Sales* 2,901,120,368
SIC 1542 Nonresidential construction, nec
  Terry Lefebvre
  Stephanie Vaillancourt
  Arden R. Furlotte

   D-U-N-S 20-329-9466   (HQ)

SNC-LAVALIN GEM QUEBEC INC
GROUPE QUALITAS
(*Suby of* GROUPE SNC-LAVALIN INC)
455 Boul Rene-Levesque O, Montreal, QC,
H2Z 1Z3
(514) 393-8000
Emp Here 100   *Sales* 96,488,000
SIC 8742 Management consulting services
  Robert Landry
  Arden R. Furlotte
  Terry Lefebvre

   D-U-N-S 24-895-5288   (HQ)
SNC-LAVALIN INC
ENERGIE/POWER, DIV OF
(*Suby of* GROUPE SNC-LAVALIN INC)
455 Boul Rene-Levesque O, Montreal, QC,
H2Z 1Z3
(514) 393-1000
Emp Here 3,000   *Sales* 5,125,406,000
SIC 8711 Engineering services
  Neil Bruce
  Arden R. Furlotte
  Jose J. Suarez
  Hartland J.A. Paterson
  Alexander S Taylor
  Ian L. Edwards
  Sylvain Girard

   D-U-N-S 20-713-6545   (SL)
**SOCIETE EN COMMANDITE 901 SQUARE
VICTORIA**
HOTEL W MONTREAL
901 Rue Du Square-Victoria Bureau 1471,
Montreal, QC, H2Z 1R1
(514) 395-3100
Emp Here 80   *Sales* 7,591,920
SIC 7011 Hotels and motels
  Jean-Francois Pouliot

   D-U-N-S 25-357-0568   (SL)
TELE-SONDAGES PLUS INC
TELE-SURVEYS PLUS
505 Boul Rene-Levesque O Bureau 1400,
Montreal, QC, H2Z 1Y7
(514) 392-4702
Emp Here 50   *Sales* 10,667,900
SIC 8732 Commercial nonphysical research
  Marouchka Cidroff

   D-U-N-S 25-150-2795   (SL)
TEVA CANADA INNOVATION G.P. -S.E.N.C.
1080 Cote Du Beaver Hall, Montreal, QC, H2Z
1S8
(514) 878-0095
Emp Here 65   *Sales* 71,847,425
SIC 5122 Drugs, proprietaries, and sundries
  Jean Godin
  Jean Francois Boily

   D-U-N-S 25-876-8514   (SL)
UNIKTOUR INC
ALLIBERT-TREKKING
(*Suby of* AVANTAGE)
555 Boul Rene-Levesque O Bureau 3, Mon-
treal, QC, H2Z 1B1
(514) 722-0909
Emp Here 26   *Sales* 17,339,192
SIC 4724 Travel agencies
  Philippe Bergeron
  Alain Capestan
  Lionel Habasque
  Frederic Giroir
  Richard Remy

   D-U-N-S 24-600-3917   (BR)
VERREAULT INC
(*Suby of* GROUPE DESSAU INC)
1080 Cote Du Beaver Hall Bureau 800, Mon-
treal, QC, H2Z 1S8
(514) 845-4104
Emp Here 76
SIC 1541 Industrial buildings and warehouses
  Marc Verreault

   D-U-N-S 25-360-1223   (HQ)
VIDEOGLOBE 1 INC

(*Suby of* ENTERTAINMENT ONE LIMITED
PARTNERSHIP)
455 Rue Saint-Antoine O Bureau 300, Mon-
treal, QC, H2Z 1J1
(514) 738-6665
Sales 58,024,700
SIC 5065 Electronic parts and equipment, nec
  Karim Trottier
  Patrick Roy
  Yvonne Molleur

Montreal, QC H3A

   D-U-N-S 20-362-9860   (SL)
10393266 CANADA INC
ADAM INTERNATIONAL
925 Boul De Maisonneuve O Bureau 247,
Montreal, QC, H3A 0A5

Emp Here 240   *Sales* 54,338,389
SIC 2521 Wood office furniture
  Lutfu Kirkan
  Belkiz Kirkan
  Turan Unlu
  Esther Lucia Chavaleh Nuesi Lebon

   D-U-N-S 24-944-4209   (HQ)
158473 CANADA INC
1555 Rue Peel Bureau 1100, Montreal, QC,
H3A 3L8
(514) 846-4000
Sales 139,258,929
SIC 6712 Bank holding companies
  Yvan Dupont

   D-U-N-S 25-211-9458   (SL)
2985420 CANADA INC
HOLIDAY INN MONTREAL MIDTOWN
420 Rue Sherbrooke O, Montreal, QC, H3A
1B2

Emp Here 150   *Sales* 18,716,400
SIC 8741 Management services
  Michael Rosenberg

   D-U-N-S 20-105-5923   (SL)
3025235 NOVA SCOTIA ULC
HOTEL OMNI MONT-ROYAL
(*Suby of* TRT HOLDINGS, INC)
1050 Rue Sherbrooke O, Montreal, QC, H3A
2R6
(514) 985-6225
Emp Here 200   *Sales* 19,133,600
SIC 7011 Hotels and motels
  James Caldwell
  Jean-Francois Pouliot
  David G Adams
  Paul A Jorge

   D-U-N-S 20-124-2984   (SL)
3619842 CANADA INC
NATIONAL INFO-TECH CENTRE
666 Rue Sherbrooke O Ste 801, Montreal,
QC, H3A 1E7

Emp Here 80
SIC 5961 Catalog and mail-order houses

   D-U-N-S 24-386-2492   (SL)
3958230 CANADA INC
600 Boul De Maisonneuve O Bureau 2200,
Montreal, QC, H3A 3J2
(450) 646-9760
Emp Here 1,966   *Sales* 718,590,694
SIC 6712 Bank holding companies
  Jean Coutu
  Francois J. Coutu

   D-U-N-S 20-550-9438   (HQ)
4207602 CANADA INC
CAMEO KNITTING
2024 Rue Peel Bureau 400, Montreal, QC,
H3A 1W5
(514) 881-2525
Sales 24,916,100

SIC 5136 Men's and boy's clothing
William Cleman, M.

D-U-N-S 20-298-0165   (HQ)
7503083 CANADA INC
JOMEDIA
2000 Rue Peel Bureau 400, Montreal, QC,
H3A 2W5
(514) 384-1570
Sales 24,633,616
SIC 8732 Commercial nonphysical research
Kenneth Helal
Philip J. Keezer

D-U-N-S 20-332-9370   (SL)
9191-1404 QUEBEC INC
BUFFET LA PLAZA
420 Rue Sherbrooke O, Montreal, QC, H3A
1B2
(514) 499-7777
Emp Here 50   *Sales* 14,956,500
SIC 5921 Liquor stores
Vincent Morena
Antonio Amicone

D-U-N-S 25-400-7974   (BR)
ACCENTURE INC
(*Suby of* ACCENTURE INC)
1800 Av Mcgill College Bureau 800, Montreal,
QC, H3A 3J6
(514) 848-1648
Emp Here 250
SIC 8741 Management services
Andre Telmosse

D-U-N-S 25-541-0078   (SL)
ACE COM CANADA CORPORATION
1981 Av Mcgill College Bureau 500, Montreal,
QC, H3A 2X1

Emp Here 174
SIC 4899 Communication services, nec

D-U-N-S 24-866-0268   (SL)
AD HOC RECHERCHE INC
AD HOC MARKETING
400 Boul De Maisonneuve O Bureau 1200,
Montreal, QC, H3A 1L4
(514) 937-4040
Emp Here 150   *Sales* 32,991,450
SIC 8732 Commercial nonphysical research
Stephane Harris
Michel Berne

D-U-N-S 20-856-6349   (BR)
AIG INSURANCE COMPANY OF CANADA
CHARTIS
(*Suby of* AMERICAN INTERNATIONAL
GROUP, INC.)
2000 Av Mcgill College Bureau 1200, Mon-
treal, QC, H3A 3H3
(514) 842-0603
Emp Here 100
SIC 6411 Insurance agents, brokers, and ser-
vice
Rita Moretta

D-U-N-S 25-837-8855   (SL)
ALIA CONSEIL INC
ALIA CONSULTING
550 Rue Sherbrooke O, Montreal, QC, H3A
1B9
(418) 652-1737
Emp Here 49   *Sales* 28,894,203
SIC 6411 Insurance agents, brokers, and ser-
vice
Catherine Prive

D-U-N-S 24-959-4268   (HQ)
ALSTOM CANADA INC
GE GRID SOLUTIONS
(*Suby of* GE RENEWABLE HOLDING B.V.)
1010 Rue Sherbrooke O Bureau 2320, Mon-
treal, QC, H3A 2R7
(514) 281-6200
Emp Here 5   *Sales* 365,140,100
SIC 3511 Turbines and turbine generator sets
Betty Huynk

Helena Miller
Angelo Guercioni
Robert Richard

D-U-N-S 25-362-1817   (HQ)
AMENAGEMENT GRANRIVE INC
PLACE DU CENTRE
600 Boul De Maisonneuve O Bureau 2600,
Montreal, QC, H3A 3J2
(514) 499-8300
Emp Here 5   *Sales* 13,044,288
SIC 6531 Real estate agents and managers
Alan Marcovitz
William Pencer
Michael Feil

D-U-N-S 20-254-5430   (SL)
APPDIRECTE CANADA INC
APPAIDE
(*Suby of* APPDIRECT, INC.)
2050 Rue De Bleury, Montreal, QC, H3A 2J5
(514) 876-4449
Emp Here 100   *Sales* 14,418,200
SIC 7371 Custom computer programming ser-
vices
Nicolas Desmarais
Daniel Saks
Lennart Lepner

D-U-N-S 20-794-1469   (HQ)
**ASSOCIATION   D'HOSPITALISATION
CANASSURANCE**
CROIX BLEUE DU QUEBEC (LA)
550 Rue Sherbrooke O, Montreal, QC, H3A
1B9
(514) 286-7658
Emp Here 250   *Sales* 453,803,700
SIC 6321 Accident and health insurance
Guy Tremblay
Michel Robillard
Francoise Chagnon
Nelson Ward
Mormand Laurin
Louis Gosselin
Andr St-Onge
Suzanne Landry
Louise Proulx

D-U-N-S 20-370-1581   (SL)
**ASSOCIATION   ETUDIANTE   DE
L'UNIVERSITE MCGILL**
3600 Rue Mctavish Bureau 1200, Montreal,
QC, H3A 0G3
(514) 398-6800
Emp Here 100   *Sales* 24,151,500
SIC 8621 Professional organizations
Muna Tojiboeva
Madeleine Kausel
Vivian Campbell
Moshkforoush Mana
Maya Koparkar
Lejean Jemark Earle
Connor Spencer
Noah Lew
Alexander Scheffel
Jessica Rau

D-U-N-S 24-103-9101   (SL)
**ASSOCIATION   QUEBECOISE
D'ETABLISSEMENT DE SANTE & DES
SERVICES SOCIAUX**
SERVICES CLSC
505 Boul De Maisonneuve O Bureau 400,
Montreal, QC, H3A 3C2
(514) 842-4861
Emp Here 90   *Sales* 20,414,970
SIC 8399 Social services, nec
Lise Denis

D-U-N-S 25-244-2215   (HQ)
ASTRAL MEDIA AFFICHAGE, S.E.C.
AEROTV & DESSIN
1800 Av Mcgill College Bureau 2700, Mon-
treal, QC, H3A 3J6
(514) 939-5000
Emp Here 41   *Sales* 10,586,200
SIC 7312 Outdoor advertising services

Jacques Parisien
Luc Sabbatini

D-U-N-S 20-290-3530   (SL)
ATOMIC FICTION CANADA, INC
METHOD STUDIOS
(*Suby of* MACANDREWS & FORBES INCOR-
PORATED)
2050 Rue De Bleury Bureau 800, Montreal,
QC, H3A 2J5
(514) 600-0399
Emp Here 300   *Sales* 26,908,800
SIC 7819 Services allied to motion pictures
John Wallace
Stefanie Liquori Digrigoli
John Eric Cummins
Julie Brocklehurst
Guillaume Massy

D-U-N-S 24-685-1294   (SL)
AXA ASSISTANCE CANADA INC
(*Suby of* AXA)
2001 Boul Robert-Bourassa Bureau 1850,
Montreal, QC, H3A 2L8
(514) 285-9053
Emp Here 50   *Sales* 92,387,100
SIC 6411 Insurance agents, brokers, and ser-
vice
Isabelle Cerf
Riccardo Iacovino
Mathieu Labouree
Serge Henri Rene Morelli
Franz Regimbeau

D-U-N-S 20-764-9591   (HQ)
AXA ASSURANCES INC
AXA GENERAL INSURANCE
2020 Boul Robert-Bourassa Bureau 100,
Montreal, QC, H3A 2A5
(514) 282-1914
Emp Here 400   *Sales* 4,273,936,000
SIC 6311 Life insurance
Charles Brindamour
Claude Dussault
Yves Brouillette
Louise Roy
Eileen Mercier
Timothy H. Penner
Claude Desilets

D-U-N-S 24-944-4639   (HQ)
AXOR CONSTRUCTION CANADA INC
(*Suby of* 158473 CANADA INC)
1555 Rue Peel Bureau 1100, Montreal, QC,
H3A 3L8
(514) 846-4000
Sales 57,033,800
SIC 1542 Nonresidential construction, nec
Yvan Dupont
Maurice Choquette

D-U-N-S 24-104-6437   (BR)
BANK OF NOVA SCOTIA, THE
SCOTIABANK
(*Suby of* BANK OF NOVA SCOTIA, THE)
1002 Rue Sherbrooke O Bureau 200, Mon-
treal, QC, H3A 3L6
(514) 499-5432
Emp Here 90
SIC 6021 National commercial banks

D-U-N-S 24-365-1713   (BR)
BANK OF NOVA SCOTIA, THE
SCOTIAMCLEOD
(*Suby of* BANK OF NOVA SCOTIA, THE)
1002 Rue Sherbrooke O Bureau 600, Mon-
treal, QC, H3A 3L6
(514) 287-3600
Emp Here 200
SIC 6021 National commercial banks
Andre Bourret

D-U-N-S 24-375-7528   (BR)
BBA INC
BBA-TOP CONTROL
(*Suby of* GROUPE BBA INC)
2020 Boul Robert-Bourassa, Montreal, QC,

H3A 2A5
(514) 866-2111
Emp Here 100
SIC 8711 Engineering services
Yves Betournay

D-U-N-S 24-177-7101   (HQ)
BCA RESEARCH INC
RECHERCHE BCA
(*Suby of* EUROMONEY INSTITUTIONAL IN-
VESTOR PLC)
1002 Rue Sherbrooke O Bureau 1600, Mon-
treal, QC, H3A 3L6
(514) 499-9550
Sales 142,313,800
SIC 6282 Investment advice
Bashar Al-Rehany
Nicoletta Manoleas
Derek Valente
Anastasios Avgeriou
Garry Evans
Marko Papic
Martin H. Barnes
Dhaval Joshi
Doug Peta
Fordham Christopher

D-U-N-S 25-843-6633   (HQ)
BEAUFIELD RESOURCES INC
1801 Mcgill College Ave Bureau 950, Mon-
treal, QC, H3A 2N4
(514) 842-3443
Emp Here 5   *Sales* 11,937,745
SIC 1041 Gold ores
Ronald W. Stewart
George N. Mannard
Mathieu Stephens
Vatche Tchakmakian
Herve Thiboutot
Robert Wares
Donald R. Siemens

D-U-N-S 20-858-2940   (SL)
BECHTEL QUEBEC LIMITEE
1500 Boul Robert-Bourassa Bureau 910,
Montreal, QC, H3A 3S7

Emp Here 200   *Sales* 36,161,827
SIC 8711 Engineering services
Andrew C. Greig
Victor Tom
Russell J. Barretta

D-U-N-S 25-733-8228   (SL)
BELL MEDIA RADIO S.E.N.C.
CHOM 97.7
1800 Av Mcgill College Unite 1600, Montreal,
QC, H3A 3K9
(514) 939-5000
Emp Here 100   *Sales* 22,847,200
SIC 4832 Radio broadcasting stations
Ian Greenberg

D-U-N-S 24-709-8841   (HQ)
**BFL CANADA RISQUES ET ASSURANCES
INC**
BFL CANADA
(*Suby of* FIRST LION HOLDINGS INC)
2001 Av Mcgill College Bureau 2200, Mon-
treal, QC, H3A 1G1
(514) 843-3632
Emp Here 110   *Sales* 177,166,545
SIC 6411 Insurance agents, brokers, and ser-
vice
Barry F. Lorenzetti
Jacques Dufresne
Daniel Binette
Bertrand Lauzon
Guylaine Dechaine
Lisa Giannone
Peter Perdikis
Ciro Cucciniello

D-U-N-S 24-508-9891   (SL)
**BUREAU DES INTERVIEWEURS PROFES-
SIONNELS (B.I.P.) (1988) INC**
2021 Av Union Bureau 1221, Montreal, QC,

H3A 2S9
(514) 288-1980
Emp Here 100   *Sales* 21,335,800
SIC 8732 Commercial nonphysical research
Lucie Leclerc
Robert Leblanc

D-U-N-S 20-852-9995   (BR)
BURGUNDY ASSET MANAGEMENT LTD
GESTION D' ACTIF BURGUNDY
(*Suby of* BURGUNDY ASSET MANAGE-
MENT LTD)
1501 Av Mcgill College Bureau 2090, Mon-
treal, QC, H3A 3M8
(514) 844-8091
Emp Here 80
SIC 8741 Management services
Claude Bedard

D-U-N-S 20-176-2163   (SL)
**CANADA   MILLENNIUM   SCHOLARSHIP
FOUNDATION**
1000 Rue Sherbrooke O Unite 800, Montreal,
QC, H3A 3G4

Emp Here 40   *Sales* 15,896,560
SIC 8699 Membership organizations, nec
Norman Riddell
Paul Bourque

D-U-N-S 24-101-8725   (SL)
CANADIAN TEST CASE 158
505 Boul De Maisonneuve O Bureau 906,
Montreal, QC, H3A 3C2
(514) 904-1496
Emp Here 158   *Sales* 46,369,366
SIC 5499 Miscellaneous food stores

D-U-N-S 20-387-4409   (SL)
CANASSISTANCE INC
1-800-USEBLUE
550 Rue Sherbrooke O, Montreal, QC, H3A
3S3
(800) 264-1852
Emp Here 50   *Sales* 14,164,650
SIC 8741 Management services
Guy Tremblay
Louis Gosselin
Michel Robillard
Yvan Fortin

D-U-N-S 20-884-9182   (SL)
**CANASSURANCE   COMPAGNIE
D'ASSURANCE INC**
(*Suby   of   ASSOCIATION
D'HOSPITALISATION CANASSURANCE)
550 Rue Sherbrooke O Bureau B9, Montreal,
QC, H3A 3S3
(514) 286-8400
Emp Here 350
SIC 6321 Accident and health insurance
Claude Boivin
Richard Lachance
Gilles Drapeau

D-U-N-S 24-648-0909   (SL)
CARAT STRATEGEM INC
CARAT COMMANDITE
(*Suby of* DENTSU INC.)
400 Boul De Maisonneuve O Bureau 250,
Montreal, QC, H3A 1L4
(514) 284-4446
Emp Here 80   *Sales* 16,029,680
SIC 7311 Advertising agencies
Nigel Morris
Louise Gauthier
Scott Hughes
Dave Wein

D-U-N-S 20-764-5458   (SL)
CENTRAIDE DU GRAND MONTREAL
CENTRAIDE MONTREAL
493 Rue Sherbrooke O, Montreal, QC, H3A
1B6
(514) 288-1261
Emp Here 100   *Sales* 13,345,900
SIC 8399 Social services, nec

Nathalie Bernier
Robert Dumas
David Goodman
Michel C. Lauzon
Frederic Legault
Thi Be Nguyen
Nandini Ramanujam
Kim Thomassin
Sandy Vassiadis
Caroline Bougie

D-U-N-S 24-085-2301   (HQ)
**CENTRE COMMUNAUTAIRE JURIDIQUE
DE MONTREAL**
AIDE JURIDIQUE
425 Boul De Maisonneuve O Bureau 600,
Montreal, QC, H3A 3K5
(514) 864-2111
Emp Here 20   *Sales* 51,469,000
SIC 8111 Legal services
Claude Hargreaves
Lise Lestage

D-U-N-S 25-672-2398   (SL)
**CENTRE DES RECOLLETS-FOUCHER SO-
CIETE EN COMMANDITE**
1555 Rue Peel Bureau 700, Montreal, QC,
H3A 3L8
(514) 940-1555
Emp Here 41   *Sales* 17,193,555
SIC 6719 Holding companies, nec
Norman G Spencer

D-U-N-S 25-138-8716   (HQ)
**CHRIS DANIELLE MICRO SOLUTIONS
(CDMS) INC**
C.D.M.S
550 Rue Sherbrooke O Bureau 250, Montreal,
QC, H3A 1B9
(514) 286-2367
Emp Here 1   *Sales* 14,632,560
SIC 7379 Computer related services, nec
Symeon Chrisanthos
Danielle Lafleur

D-U-N-S 20-112-3960   (SL)
CIBC ASSET MANAGEMENT INC
RENAISSANCE INVESTMENTS
(*Suby of* CANADIAN IMPERIAL BANK OF
COMMERCE)
1500 Boul Robert-Bourassa Bureau 800,
Montreal, QC, H3A 3S6
(514) 875-7040
Emp Here 100   *Sales* 93,917,700
SIC 6282 Investment advice
David Scandiffio
Jon Hountalas
Peter H Lee
John Braive
Doris Mariga
Lester G Cheng
Frank Vivacqua
Steven Meston
Tracy Best
Stephen Gittens

D-U-N-S 20-591-0847   (BR)
CIBC WORLD MARKETS INC
CIBC WOOD GUNDY
(*Suby of* CANADIAN IMPERIAL BANK OF
COMMERCE)
600 Boul De Maisonneuve O Bureau 3050,
Montreal, QC, H3A 3J2
(514) 847-6300
Emp Here 200
SIC 6211 Security brokers and dealers

D-U-N-S 25-200-9402   (BR)
CISCO SYSTEMS CANADA CO
SYSTEMS CISCO CANADA
(*Suby of* CISCO SYSTEMS, INC.)
1800 Av Mcgill College Bureau 700, Montreal,
QC, H3A 3J6
(514) 847-6800
Emp Here 80
SIC 5999 Miscellaneous retail stores, nec
Jean-Claude Ouellet

D-U-N-S 20-763-0260   (SL)
CLUB MAA INC
2070 Rue Peel, Montreal, QC, H3A 1W6
(514) 845-2233
Emp Here 100   *Sales* 7,854,500
SIC 7997 Membership sports and recreation
clubs
Wayne Heuff
Louise Kierans
Kavanagh Judith
Kelly W. Randall
Pierre Blanchet
Claude Belanger
Elizabeth Bitar
Keith Eaman
Stephen Weir
Jan Edwards Peeters

D-U-N-S 24-599-9792   (SL)
**COLLIERS   INTERNATIONAL   (QUEBEC)
INC**
COLLIERS INTERNATIONAL
(*Suby of* COLLIERS INTERNATIONAL
GROUP INC)
1800 Av Mcgill College Bureau 400, Montreal,
QC, H3A 3J6
(514) 866-1900
Emp Here 60   *Sales* 25,133,340
SIC 6531 Real estate agents and managers
David Bowden
Andrew Maravita
Dylan Taylor
Robert Hemming

D-U-N-S 20-297-9894   (SL)
COMMANDITE FPI PRO INC
FPI PRO
2000 Rue Mansfield Bureau 920, Montreal,
QC, H3A 2Z6
(514) 933-9552
Emp Here 6   *Sales* 30,998,033
SIC 6153 Short-term business credit institu-
tions, except agricultural
James W. Beckerleg
Gordon G. Lawlor
Mark O'brien
Alison Schafer

D-U-N-S 24-799-2154   (SL)
COMMUNICATIONS LMT INC
OPTIMA CELL
1500 Av Mcgill College, Montreal, QC, H3A
3J5
(514) 285-9263
Emp Here 26   *Sales* 11,626,524
SIC 5065 Electronic parts and equipment, nec

D-U-N-S 25-401-7403   (SL)
COMMUNICATIONS TRANSCRIPT INC
625 Av Du President-Kennedy Bureau 800,
Montreal, QC, H3A 1K2
(514) 874-9134
Emp Here 37   *Sales* 16,409,130
SIC 7389 Business services, nec
Wilma Scappaticci
Joanne Saint-Denis

D-U-N-S 20-340-0754   (SL)
COMPAGNIE D'ASSURANCE DU QUEBEC
(*Suby of* RSA INSURANCE GROUP PLC)
1001 Boul De Maisonneuve O Bureau 1400,
Montreal, QC, H3A 3C8
(514) 844-1116
Emp Here 90   *Sales* 192,327,120
SIC 6331 Fire, marine, and casualty insurance
Rowan Saunders
Marcel J Bundock
George Anderson
Robert Mcfarlane
Simon Lee
Guy Dufresne
Charles White
Nick Creatura
Marie Claude Desroches
Robin G Richardson

D-U-N-S 24-375-0119   (BR)

**COMPUTERSHARE TRUST COMPANY OF
CANADA**
COMPUTERSHARE
(*Suby of* COMPUTERSHARE LIMITED)
1500 Boul Robert-Bourassa Bureau 700,
Montreal, QC, H3A 3S8
(514) 982-7888
Emp Here 450
SIC 6733 Trusts, nec
David Nugent

D-U-N-S 20-763-3413   (HQ)
CORPORATION BNP PARIBAS CANADA
(*Suby of* BNP PARIBAS)
1981 Av Mcgill College Bureau 515, Montreal,
QC, H3A 2W8
(514) 285-6000
Emp Here 200   *Sales* 68,331,600
SIC 6021 National commercial banks
Catherine Magnier
Andre Tetreault
Ivan Saldanha
Sonja Volpe
Pierre Bouchara

D-U-N-S 24-052-8364   (HQ)
**CORPORATION DE SERVICE DE LA CHAM-
BRE DES NOTAIRES DU QUEBEC, LA**
*CORPORATION DE SERVICE DES NO-
TAIRES DU QUEBEC*
1801 Av Mcgill College Bureau 600, Montreal,
QC, H3A 0A7
(514) 879-1793
Sales 30,434,430
SIC 8621 Professional organizations
Maurice Piette
Hugues Poulin
Michel Y. Gaudreau

D-U-N-S 25-285-4351   (SL)
CORPORATION FINANCIERE BROME INC
CREDIT COMMERCIALE C.C.F.M.
550 Rue Sherbrooke O Bureau 700, Montreal,
QC, H3A 1B9
(514) 842-2975
Emp Here 45   *Sales* 83,099,655
SIC 6351 Surety insurance
Pierre Therrien
Bernard Deschamps
Germain Benoit
Jocelyn Moreau
Johanne Vezina
Sylvain Labarre

D-U-N-S 24-381-1945   (SL)
CORPORATION INTERACTIVE EIDOS
EIDOS-MONTREAL
(*Suby of* SQUARE ENIX HOLDINGS CO.,
LTD.)
400 Boul De Maisonneuve O 6e Etage, Mon-
treal, QC, H3A 1L4
(514) 670-6300
Emp Here 250   *Sales* 46,143,250
SIC 7371 Custom computer programming ser-
vices
Phil Rogers
Koichiro Hayashi
David Anfossi

D-U-N-S 20-380-8022   (SL)
**CORPORATION   INTERNATIONALE   MA-
SONITE**
BELHUMEUR DOORS
1501 Av Mcgill College Suite 26e, Montreal,
QC, H3A 3N9
(514) 841-6400
Emp Here 750   *Sales* 208,792,500
SIC 2431 Millwork
Frederick J. Lynch
Russell T Tiejema
Robert Lewis
William Oesterle
Daphne Jones
Thomas Greene
Jody L. Bilney
Peter R. Dachowski

George Lorch
Jonathan Foster

D-U-N-S 24-865-1481   (HQ)
CORPORATION OPTIMUM
(*Suby of* OPTIGAM INC)
425 Boul De Maisonneuve O Bureau 1700,
Montreal, QC, H3A 3G5
(514) 288-2010
Emp Here 3   *Sales* 182,754,500
SIC 6712 Bank holding companies
Anabelle Blondeau
Henri Joli-Coeur
Louis Fontaine
Nathalie Blondeau

D-U-N-S 25-195-6504   (SL)
COVERDELL CANADA CORPORATION
1801 Av Mcgill College Bureau 800, Montreal,
QC, H3A 2N4
(514) 847-7800
Emp Here 341   *Sales* 228,097,628
SIC 7389 Business services, nec
Vincent Dibenedetto
Gary A Johnson

D-U-N-S 20-764-8445   (SL)
CROP INC
550 Rue Sherbrooke O Bureau 900, Montreal,
QC, H3A 1B9
(514) 807-9431
Emp Here 50   *Sales* 11,734,800
SIC 8732 Commercial nonphysical research
Elyse Turmel
Alain Giguere

D-U-N-S 25-993-4342   (SL)
CUSHMAN & WAKEFIELD LTEE
999 Boul De Maisonneuve O Bureau 1500,
Montreal, QC, H3A 3L4
(514) 841-5011
Emp Here 49   *Sales* 13,316,044
SIC 6531 Real estate agents and managers

D-U-N-S 25-195-5928   (BR)
DAVIES WARD PHILLIPS & VINEBERG LLP
DAVIES
(*Suby of* DAVIES WARD PHILLIPS &
VINEBERG LLP)
1501 Av Mcgill College Bureau 2600, Mon-
treal, QC, H3A 3N9
(514) 841-6400
Emp Here 200
SIC 8111 Legal services
Richard Cherney

D-U-N-S 25-245-9466   (SL)
DEMERS BEAULNE S.E.N.C.R.L.
1800 Av Mcgill College Bureau 600, Montreal,
QC, H3A 3J6
(514) 878-9631
Emp Here 160   *Sales* 33,229,600
SIC 8721 Accounting, auditing, and book-
keeping
Paul Beaulne
Stephane Lachance
Andre Hebert
Martin Fagnan
Natalie Beaudoin
Raymond Martel
Michel Hamelin
Patrick Beaudet
Robert St-Aubin
Dominique Tran

D-U-N-S 20-281-5411   (HQ)
DENTSU AEGIS NETWORK CANADA INC
(*Suby of* DENTSU INC.)
400 Boul De Maisonneuve O Bureau 250,
Montreal, QC, H3A 1L4
(514) 284-4446
Emp Here 5   *Sales* 58,481,440
SIC 6712 Bank holding companies
Dave Wein
Scott Hughes
Philip Filippopoulos

D-U-N-S 25-494-7708   (SL)

DESTINATIONS ETC INC
VOYAGE 2040
1470 Rue Peel Bureau 110, Montreal, QC,
H3A 1T1
(514) 849-0707
Emp Here 60   *Sales* 31,198,020
SIC 4724 Travel agencies
Jacob Lazare

D-U-N-S 24-959-1298   (HQ)
DEVOIR INC, LE
JOURNAL LE DEVOIR
(*Suby of* IMPRIMERIE POPULAIRE LIMITEE,
L')
2050 Rue De Bleury, Montreal, QC, H3A 2J5
(514) 985-3333
Sales 27,128,360
SIC 2711 Newspapers
Andre Ryan
Michel Rioux
Denis Sirois
Fortin Michele
Alain Saulnier
Anne Joli-Coeur
Eric Desrosiers
Brian Myles
Suzanne Moquin
Lucie Remillard

D-U-N-S 25-541-1159   (HQ)
DIFCO, TISSUS DE PERFORMANCE INC
DIFCO
(*Suby of* BERRY GLOBAL GROUP, INC.)
1411 Rue Peel Bureau 505, Montreal, QC,
H3A 1S5
(819) 434-2159
Sales 70,950,900
SIC 2299 Textile goods, nec
Ioannis Pananis
Dennis Norman
Eric Henderson

D-U-N-S 24-329-4209   (HQ)
DOMTAR CORPORATION
395 Boul De Maisonneuve O Bureau 200,
Montreal, QC, H3A 1L6
(514) 848-5555
Emp Here 400   *Sales* 5,098,000,000
SIC 2611 Pulp mills
John D. Williams
Razvan Theodoru
David G. Maffucci
Robert E. Apple
David J. Illingworth
Giannella Alvarez
Denis Turcotte
Pamela B. Strobel
Brian M. Levitt
Mary Winston

D-U-N-S 20-216-9744   (HQ)
DOMTAR INC
BG DESIGN
(*Suby of* DOMTAR LUXEMBOURG INVEST-
MENTS SARL)
395 Boul De Maisonneuve O Bureau 200,
Montreal, QC, H3A 1L6
(514) 848-5555
Emp Here 500   *Sales* 1,643,705,027
SIC 2611 Pulp mills
Michael Garcia
Daniel Buron
Razvan L. Theodoru
Patrick Loulou
John D. Williams

D-U-N-S 24-885-8511   (SL)
ELEKTA LTEE
(*Suby of* ELEKTA AB (PUBL))
2050 Rue De Bleury Bureau 200, Montreal,
QC, H3A 2J5
(514) 840-9600
Emp Here 26   *Sales* 11,626,524
SIC 5047 Medical and hospital equipment
Peter Gaccione
Michael J Hartman
Alfred L.J. Page

Michael J. Hartman

D-U-N-S 24-312-6989   (BR)
ENERGIE VALERO INC
ULTRACONFORT
(*Suby of* VALERO ENERGY CORPORATION)
2200 Av Mcgill College Unite 400, Montreal,
QC, H3A 3P8
(514) 493-5201
Emp Here 100
SIC 5983 Fuel oil dealers

D-U-N-S 20-409-2654   (HQ)
ENERGIE VALERO INC
ULTRAMAR
(*Suby of* VALERO ENERGY CORPORATION)
1801 Av Mcgill College Bureau 1300, Mon-
treal, QC, H3A 2N4
(514) 982-8200
Emp Here 425   *Sales* 4,137,955,500
SIC 5172 Petroleum products, nec
Martine Peloquin
Julie Normand
Bruce Macdonald
Donna M. Titzman

D-U-N-S 24-364-7992   (HQ)
ENERKEM INC
1130 Rue Sherbrooke O Bureau 1500, Mon-
treal, QC, H3A 2M8
(514) 875-0284
Emp Here 60   *Sales* 56,804,200
SIC 2869 Industrial organic chemicals, nec
Vincent Chornet
Emilie Christiansen
Neil S. Suslak
Joshua Ruch
Anne Gerritt De Vries
Lawrence Allan Macdonald
Michael Dennis
Andree-Lise Methot
Dominique Boies

D-U-N-S 25-201-1705   (HQ)
ENGIE SERVICES INC
1001 Boul De Maisonneuve O Bureau 1000,
Montreal, QC, H3A 3C8
(514) 876-8748
Sales 53,355,371
SIC 8742 Management consulting services
Jean-Luc Billiani
Jean-Marc Therrien
Luc Duguay
John S. Sullivan

D-U-N-S 24-343-8715   (HQ)
ENTREPRISES CANDEREL INC
2000 Rue Peel Bureau 900, Montreal, QC,
H3A 2W5
(514) 842-8636
Emp Here 85   *Sales* 27,335,000
SIC 6712 Bank holding companies
Jonathan Wener
David Hawrysh

D-U-N-S 24-960-9264   (SL)
EQUIPE SPECTRA INC, L'
PROMOTIONS AZUR, LES
(*Suby of* SOCIETE SPECTRA SCENE INC,
LA)
400 Boul De Maisonneuve O 9eme Etage,
Montreal, QC, H3A 1L4
(514) 525-7732
Emp Here 200   *Sales* 29,962,600
SIC 7922 Theatrical producers and services
Alain Simard
Jacques-Andre Dupont
Jacques Aube
Geoffrey E. Molson
France Margaret Belanger

D-U-N-S 25-297-1593   (BR)
ERNST & YOUNG INC
(*Suby of* ERNST & YOUNG INC)
900 Boul De Maisonneuve O, Montreal, QC,
H3A 0A8
(514) 875-6060
Emp Here 200

SIC 8721 Accounting, auditing, and bookkeeping
Guy Frechette

D-U-N-S 25-244-9616   (HQ)
**ESI TECHNOLOGIES DE L'INFORMATION
INC**
1550 Rue Metcalfe Bureau 1100, Montreal,
QC, H3A 1X6
(514) 745-3311
Emp Here 140   *Sales* 26,695,520
SIC 7379 Computer related services, nec
Greg Rokos
Pierre Courchesne
Patrick Naoum

D-U-N-S 24-522-5037   (SL)
**EVO MERCHANT SERVICES CORP.
CANADA**
EVO CANADA
505 Boul De Maisonneuve O Bureau 150,
Montreal, QC, H3A 3C2

Emp Here 100   *Sales* 44,717,400
SIC 5046 Commercial equipment, nec
Mark Lachance
Alon Kindler
Ayman Ibrahim
Kevin Lambrix
Kevin Lavigne

D-U-N-S 24-851-8073   (BR)
EXP SERVICES INC
EXP GLOBAL
(*Suby of* EXP GLOBAL INC)
1001 Boul De Maisonneuve O Bureau 800b,
Montreal, QC, H3A 3C8
(514) 788-6158
Emp Here 100
SIC 8711 Engineering services
Marc Tremblay

D-U-N-S 24-051-4005   (HQ)
EXPLORANCE INC
EXPLORANCE BLUE
1470 Rue Peel Bureau 500, Montreal, QC,
H3A 1T1
(514) 938-2111
Sales 16,684,700
SIC 7372 Prepackaged software
Samer Bekai-Saab
Enzo Blasi
Marc Lamy
Tanios Bekai-Saab

D-U-N-S 24-711-0554   (HQ)
**FEDERATION INTERPROFESSIONNELLE
DE LA SANTE DU QUEBEC-FIQ**
2050 Rue De Bleury, Montreal, QC, H3A 2J5
(514) 987-1141
Emp Here 100   *Sales* 46,133,780
SIC 8631 Labor organizations
Lina Bonamie
Daniel Gilbert
Sylvie Savard
Michele Boisclair
Birgitte Fauteux
Monique Leroux
Elaine Trottier
Suzanne Lavoie
Lise Martel

D-U-N-S 20-819-7889   (HQ)
FIERA CAPITAL CORPORATION
FIERA CAPITAL GESTION PRIVEE
1981 Mcgill College Ave Suite 1500, Montreal,
QC, H3A 0H5
(514) 954-3300
Emp Here 75   *Sales* 409,591,139
SIC 6282 Investment advice
Jean-Guy Desjardins
Vincent Duhamel
Jean-Philippe Lemay
Martin Dufresne
Julie Lalonde
Ted Eccleston
Lucas Pontillo

▲ Public Company   ■ Public Company Family Member   **HQ** Headquarters   **BR** Branch   **SL** Single Location

Dominic Grimard
Nancy Cloutier
Nicolas Papageorgiou

D-U-N-S 24-373-2471   (HQ)
FIRST LION HOLDINGS INC
GESTIONS PREMIER LION
2001 Av Mcgill College Bureau 2200, Montreal, QC, H3A 1G1
(514) 843-3632
Sales 1,352,639,640
SIC 6411 Insurance agents, brokers, and service
Barry F. Lorenzetti
Bertrand Lauzon
Bradley G. Potter
Daniel Binette
Jacques Dufresne
John Wright
Jeffrey Roth
Ciro Cucciniello
Penny Dyte
Norman M. Steinberg

D-U-N-S 24-402-7934   (HQ)
FIVES SOLIOS INC
FIVES SOLIOS ENVIRONNEMENT
(*Suby of* FIVES ORSAY)
625 Av Du President-Kennedy, Montreal, QC, H3A 1K2
(514) 284-0341
Sales 12,350,676
SIC 5084 Industrial machinery and equipment
Sylvain Dulude
Aurelie Filion
Hugues Vincent
Thierry Allegrucci

D-U-N-S 20-633-7474   (SL)
FONDATION CENTRAIDE DU GRAND MONTREAL
493 Rue Sherbrooke O, Montreal, QC, H3A 1B6
(514) 288-1261
Emp Here 49   *Sales* 19,473,286
SIC 8699 Membership organizations, nec
Pierre Monahan

D-U-N-S 20-107-0245   (HQ)
FONDATION LUCIE & ANDRE CHAGNON
OBSERVATOIRE DES TOUT-PETITS
2001 Av Mcgill College Bureau 1000, Montreal, QC, H3A 1G1
(514) 380-2001
Sales 79,123,055
SIC 8699 Membership organizations, nec
Andre Chagnon
Claude Chagnon
Christian Chagnon
Alban D'amours
Martine Vallee
Nathalie Fortin
Eve-Isabelle Chevrier
Marc-Andre Chagnon

D-U-N-S 20-381-8229   (SL)
FONDS D'ASSURANCE RESPONSABILITE PROFESSIONNELLE DE L'ORDRE DES PHARMACIENS DU QUEBEC
FARPOPQ
2020 Boul Robert-Bourassa Bureau 2160, Montreal, QC, H3A 2A5
(514) 281-0300
Emp Here 50   *Sales* 92,387,100
SIC 6411 Insurance agents, brokers, and service
Stephane Plante
Claude Gagnon
Gerard Guilbault
Stephane Lavallee
Jean-Michel Lavoie
Louise Sanscartier
Caroline Thomassin
Jean Vaillancourt
Brigitte Corbeil

D-U-N-S 20-792-7823   (HQ)

FORMULA GROWTH LIMITED
1010 Rue Sherbrooke O Bureau 2300, Montreal, QC, H3A 2R7
(514) 288-5136
Emp Here 13   *Sales* 10,862,768
SIC 6282 Investment advice
John W Dobson
Randy Kelly
Rosana Vitale

D-U-N-S 24-646-6663   (SL)
FRANCO FOLIES DE MONTREAL
400 Boul De Maisonneuve O, Montreal, QC, H3A 1L4
(514) 288-1040
Emp Here 49   *Sales* 11,480,112
SIC 8742 Management consulting services
Alain Simard

D-U-N-S 24-256-3708   (SL)
GEMME CANADIENNE P.A. INC
1002 Rue Sherbrooke O Bureau 2525, Montreal, QC, H3A 3L6
(514) 287-1951
Emp Here 25   *Sales* 13,013,550
SIC 5094 Jewelry and precious stones
Pierre Akkelian
Papken Akkelian

D-U-N-S 25-106-6957   (HQ)
GEMPERLE INC
1002 Rue Sherbrooke O Bureau 2525, Montreal, QC, H3A 3L6
(514) 287-9017
Sales 10,410,840
SIC 5094 Jewelry and precious stones
Karnig Akkelian
Pierre Akkelian
Papken Akkelian

D-U-N-S 24-569-3122   (HQ)
GESTION CANDEREL INC
(*Suby of* ENTREPRISES CANDEREL INC)
2000 Rue Peel Bureau 900, Montreal, QC, H3A 2W5
(514) 842-8636
Emp Here 30   *Sales* 15,817,200
SIC 6553 Cemetery subdividers and developers
Jonathan Wener
David Hawrysh

D-U-N-S 25-108-4307   (SL)
GESTION D'ACTIFS SECTORIELS INC
1000 Rue Sherbrooke O Bureau 2120, Montreal, QC, H3A 3G4
(514) 849-8777
Emp Here 26   *Sales* 13,811,382
SIC 6282 Investment advice
Jerome Pfund
Michael Sjostrom
Vihang Errunza
Laurent Chaix
Winnie Pao
Brett Goodin
Marilina Mastronardi
Jill Mavro

D-U-N-S 20-897-2807   (SL)
GESTION DE FONDS SENTIENT CANADA LTEE
1010 Rue Sherbrooke O Bureau 1512, Montreal, QC, H3A 2R7

Emp Here 50   *Sales* 41,388,850
SIC 6722 Management investment, open-end
Bonita Chan
Michel Marier
Charles Riopel
John Mears
Natalia Katherine Maclean
D'arcy Pierson Doherty
Gilbert Percy Clark
Nicholas Mead
Wayne Richardson
Andrew Pullar

D-U-N-S 25-672-5888   (HQ)
GESTION DU GROUPE REDBOURNE INC
1555 Rue Peel Bureau 700, Montreal, QC, H3A 3L8
(514) 940-1555
Emp Here 34   *Sales* 20,967,750
SIC 6719 Holding companies, nec
Peter Francis Coughlin
Norman George Spencer

D-U-N-S 24-119-4344   (SL)
GESTION SIERA CAPITAL INC
SIERA YNG CAPITAL
1501 Av Mcgill College Bureau 800, Montreal, QC, H3A 3M8
(514) 954-3300
Emp Here 49   *Sales* 20,548,395
SIC 6712 Bank holding companies
Pierre Blanchette

D-U-N-S 24-529-0549   (HQ)
GILDAN ACTIVEWEAR INC
GILDAN
600 Boul De Maisonneuve O 33eme Etage, Montreal, QC, H3A 3J2
(514) 735-2023
Emp Here 125   *Sales* 2,908,565,000
SIC 2259 Knitting mills, nec
Glenn J. Chamandy
Michael R. Hoffman
Rhodri J. Harries
Benito A. Masi
William D. Anderson
George Heller
Gonzalo F. Valdes-Fauli
Russell Goodman
Donald C. Berg
Anne Martin-Vachon

D-U-N-S 24-062-7625   (BR)
GLOBAL CREDIT & COLLECTION INC
(*Suby of* GLOBAL CREDIT & COLLECTION INC)
2055 Rue Peel Bureau 100, Montreal, QC, H3A 1V4
(514) 284-5533
Emp Here 200
SIC 7322 Adjustment and collection services
Dianne Bouchard

D-U-N-S 24-460-8535   (SL)
GLOBAL FURS INC
400 Boul De Maisonneuve O Bureau 100, Montreal, QC, H3A 1L4
(514) 288-6644
Emp Here 35   *Sales* 17,441,270
SIC 5137 Women's and children's clothing
Thomas Nacos

D-U-N-S 25-365-2713   (HQ)
GLOBALEX GESTION DE RISQUES INC
GLOBAL EXPERT GESTION DE RISQUES
1130 Rue Sherbrooke O, Montreal, QC, H3A 2M8
(514) 382-9625
Emp Here 50   *Sales* 42,403,000
SIC 6411 Insurance agents, brokers, and service
Jacques L Brouillette

D-U-N-S 25-739-4213   (SL)
GLOBALEX GESTION DE RISQUES INC
999 Boul De Maisonneuve O, Montreal, QC, H3A 3L4
(514) 382-6674
Emp Here 60   *Sales* 50,883,600
SIC 6411 Insurance agents, brokers, and service
Jacques L. Brouillette
Helene Ouellet

D-U-N-S 24-380-6353   (HQ)
GOUVERNEUR INC
HOTEL DES GOUVERNEURS
1000 Rue Sherbrooke O Bureau 2300, Montreal, QC, H3A 3R3
(514) 875-8822
Emp Here 25   *Sales* 114,801,600

SIC 7011 Hotels and motels
Claude Jacques Goupil

D-U-N-S 20-212-9305   (BR)
GREAT-WEST LIFE ASSURANCE COMPANY, THE
GREAT WEST MARKETING & PENSION DEPARTMENT
(*Suby of* POWER CORPORATION DU CANADA)
2001 Boul Robert-Bourassa Unite 1000, Montreal, QC, H3A 2A6
(514) 350-7975
Emp Here 400
SIC 6411 Insurance agents, brokers, and service
Jean-Pierre Beaudet

D-U-N-S 24-382-9574   (SL)
GROUPE AECON QUEBEC LTEE
AECON
(*Suby of* AECON GROUP INC)
2015 Rue Peel Bureau 600, Montreal, QC, H3A 1T8
(514) 388-8928
Emp Here 100   *Sales* 42,273,700
SIC 1541 Industrial buildings and warehouses
Roger Arsenault
John M. Beck

D-U-N-S 24-960-5684   (SL)
GROUPE AXOR INC
(*Suby of* 158473 CANADA INC)
1555 Rue Peel Bureau 1100, Montreal, QC, H3A 3L8
(514) 846-4000
Emp Here 151   *Sales* 86,121,038
SIC 1542 Nonresidential construction, nec
Yvan Dupont
Maurice Choquette

D-U-N-S 24-959-6685   (HQ)
GROUPE BIRKS INC
BRINKHAUS FACTORY
2020 Boul Robert-Bourassa Bureau 200, Montreal, QC, H3A 2A5
(514) 397-2501
Emp Here 250   *Sales* 91,046,604
SIC 5944 Jewelry stores
Jean-Christophe Bedos
Niccolo Rossi Di Montelera
Miranda Melfi
Shirley A. Dawe
Emily Berlin
Frank Di Tomas
Louis L. Roquet
Davide Barberis Canonico
Joseph F.X. Zahra

D-U-N-S 20-716-6435   (SL)
GROUPE CONSEIL FXINNOVATION INC
FX INNOVATION
400 Boul De Maisonneuve O Bureau 1100, Montreal, QC, H3A 1L4
(514) 525-5777
Emp Here 100   *Sales* 23,428,800
SIC 8742 Management consulting services
David Marotte
Georges Riachy
Guillaume Bazinet

D-U-N-S 20-113-8711   (SL)
GROUPE NEXIO INC
NEXIO.COM
2050 Rue De Bleury Bureau 500, Montreal, QC, H3A 2J5
(514) 798-3707
Emp Here 200   *Sales* 33,369,400
SIC 7379 Computer related services, nec
Martial Rivard
Francois Dansereau
Gerard Chagnon
Claude Mcmaster
Natalie Lariviere

D-U-N-S 24-256-3641   (HQ)
GROUPE OPTIMUM INC

AN OPTIMUM PARTNER
(Suby of OPTIGAM INC)
425 Boul De Maisonneuve O Bureau 1700,
Montreal, QC, H3A 3G5
(514) 288-2010
Emp Here 25   Sales 67,838,500
SIC 6514 Dwelling operators, except apart-
ments
  Gilles Blondeau
  Jean-Claude Page
  Louis Fontaine
  Claude Lamonde
  Anabelle Blondeau
  Pierre Bienvenu
  Pierre Comtois
  Jacques M. Gagnon
  Nathalie Blondeau
  Michel Theroux

    D-U-N-S 24-698-4041   (HQ)
GROUPE SANTE MEDISYS INC
SERVICE CONCIERGE MEDISYS
(Suby of TELUS CORPORATION)
600 Boul De Maisonneuve O 22e Etage, Mon-
treal, QC, H3A 3J2
(514) 845-1211
Emp Here 185   Sales 53,041,100
SIC 8093 Specialty outpatient clinics, nec
  Josh Blair
  Andrea Wood
  Doug French

    D-U-N-S 25-991-3051   (HQ)
GROUPE ZOOM MEDIA INC
ZOOM MARKETING ACTIF
(Suby of FRANBEAU INC)
999 Boul De Maisonneuve O Bureau 1000,
Montreal, QC, H3A 3L4
(514) 842-1155
Emp Here 7   Sales 29,240,720
SIC 6712 Bank holding companies
  Francois De Gaspe-Beaubien
  Philippe De Gaspe-Beaubien
  Charles H Hantho
  John Galantic
  Frederic Emry
  Peggy Green
  James Warner

    D-U-N-S 20-762-5203   (SL)
H.W. HOLLINGER (CANADA) INC
550 Rue Sherbrooke O Bureau 2070, Mon-
treal, QC, H3A 1B9
(514) 842-8421
Emp Here 25   Sales 14,498,100
SIC 6411 Insurance agents, brokers, and ser-
vice
  Michael Hollinger
  Sarah Hollinger

    D-U-N-S 20-234-3757   (BR)
HOGG ROBINSON CANADA INC
HRG AMERIQUE DU NORD
(Suby of HOGG ROBINSON GROUP LIM-
ITED)
1550 Rue Metcalfe Bureau 700, Montreal, QC,
H3A 1X6
(514) 286-6300
Emp Here 200
SIC 4725 Tour operators

    D-U-N-S 20-118-5183   (SL)
HOTELS CANPRO INC, LES
SOFITEL HOTEL & RESORTS
1155 Rue Sherbrooke O, Montreal, QC, H3A
2N3
(514) 285-9000
Emp Here 100   Sales 9,489,900
SIC 7011 Hotels and motels
  Naomi Azrieli

    D-U-N-S 20-386-6650   (SL)
HUB INTERNATIONAL
1010 Sherbrooke St W Ste 2510, Montreal,
QC, H3A 2R7
(514) 787-7200
Emp Here 30   Sales 25,441,800

SIC 6411 Insurance agents, brokers, and service
  Robert Dunn

    D-U-N-S 25-469-8830   (SL)
HYDRO ALUMINIUM CANADA INC
(Suby of NORSK HYDRO ASA)
2000 Av Mcgill College Bureau 2310, Mon-
treal, QC, H3A 3H3
(514) 840-9110
Emp Here 902
SIC 3334 Primary aluminum
  Patrice Wache
  Terrance Conley
  Knut Meel
  Einar Glomnes

    D-U-N-S 24-710-9002   (HQ)
IMMEUBLES CARREFOUR RICHELIEU
LTEE, LES
CARREFOUR RICHELIEU
600 Boul De Maisonneuve O Bureau 2600,
Montreal, QC, H3A 3J2
(514) 499-8300
Emp Here 78   Sales 17,669,680
SIC 6512 Nonresidential building operators
  Irwin Adelson
  William Pencer
  Brian Whibbs
  Kenneth Nixon

    D-U-N-S 20-707-3560   (HQ)
IMMEUBLES YALE LIMITEE, LES
2015 Rue Peel Bureau 1200, Montreal, QC,
H3A 1T8
(514) 845-2265
Emp Here 20   Sales 10,462,120
SIC 6719 Holding companies, nec
  Morris Mashaal
  Victor Mashaal
  David M Mashaal
  Emile Mashaal
  Albert Mashaal
  Ronald Mashaal

    D-U-N-S 24-128-1612   (HQ)
INDUSTRIELLE ALLIANCE VALEURS MO-
BILIERES INC
IA VALEURS MOBILIERES
(Suby of INDUSTRIELLE ALLIANCE, AS-
SURANCE ET SERVICES FINANCIERS INC)
2200 Av Mcgill College Bureau 350, Montreal,
QC, H3A 3P8
(514) 499-1066
Emp Here 20   Sales 26,560,350
SIC 6211 Security brokers and dealers
  Richard Legault
  Caroline Labrecque
  Mark Arthur
  I. David Bird
  Lise Douville
  Andre Dubuc
  Marc-Andre Elie
  Donald Mcfarlane
  Normand Pepin

    D-U-N-S 20-175-1273   (HQ)
INFOROUTE SANTE DU CANADA INC
1000 Rue Sherbrooke O Bureau 1200, Mon-
treal, QC, H3A 3G4
(514) 868-0550
Emp Here 60   Sales 40,074,200
SIC 7338 Secretarial and court reporting
  Michael Green

    D-U-N-S 24-802-3736   (SL)
INGENIO, FILALE DE LOTO-QUEBEC INC
(Suby of GOUVERNEMENT DE LA
PROVINCE DE QUEBEC)
500 Rue Sherbrooke O Bureau 2000, Mon-
treal, QC, H3A 3G6
(514) 282-0210
Emp Here 50   Sales 10,667,900
SIC 8732 Commercial nonphysical research
  Nathalie Rajotte

    D-U-N-S 24-326-8745   (SL)

INSTITUT DE RECHERCHE ROBERT
SAUVE EN SANTE ET EN SECURITE
DU TRAVAIL
IRSST
505 Boul De Maisonneuve O, Montreal, QC,
H3A 3C2
(514) 288-1551
Emp Here 131   Sales 30,097,774
SIC 8731 Commercial physical research
  Diane Gaudet

    D-U-N-S 20-174-7883   (SL)
INTERDIGITAL CANADA LTEE
INTERDIGITAL
(Suby of INTERDIGITAL, INC.)
1000 Rue Sherbrooke O Bureau 1000, Mon-
treal, QC, H3A 3G4
(514) 904-6300
Emp Here 54   Sales 12,337,488
SIC 4812 Radiotelephone communication
  Robert A. Difazio

    D-U-N-S 25-467-5507   (HQ)
INVESTISSEMENTS   IMMOBILIERS
KEVLAR INC
KEVLAR - COMPLEXE DE VILLE
(Suby of GROUPE KEVLAR INC)
1800 Av Mcgill College Bureau 1900, Mon-
treal, QC, H3A 3J6
(514) 393-8858
Emp Here 16   Sales 41,888,900
SIC 6531 Real estate agents and managers
  Rene Bellerive
  Philippe Morin

    D-U-N-S 24-387-1626   (SL)
INVESTISSEMENTS MONIT INC, LES
1000 RUE SHERBROOKE OUEST
1000 Rue Sherbrooke O Unite 1800, Montreal,
QC, H3A 3G4
(514) 933-3000
Emp Here 49   Sales 13,316,044
SIC 6531 Real estate agents and managers
  Barry Kotler
  Leah Kotler
  Eliasz Kotler

    D-U-N-S 25-308-6136   (SL)
INVESTISSEMENTS RAMAN 'S.E.N.C.',
LES
CATLIE SUITES HOTEL, LE
1110 Rue Sherbrooke O Bureau 301, Mon-
treal, QC, H3A 1G8
(514) 844-3951
Emp Here 100   Sales 9,489,900
SIC 7011 Hotels and motels
  Douglas Cohen
  Jonathan Cohen

    D-U-N-S 20-856-9103   (HQ)
JARISLOWSKY, FRASER LIMITEE
(Suby of BANK OF NOVA SCOTIA, THE)
1010 Rue Sherbrooke O Bureau 2005, Mon-
treal, QC, H3A 2R7
(514) 842-2727
Emp Here 60   Sales 179,315,388
SIC 6282 Investment advice
  Maxime Menard
  Pierre Lapointe
  Alexandra Jarislowsky
  Glen Gowland
  Charles Emond
  Jane Craighead
  Caroline Bell-Ritchie

    D-U-N-S 24-581-8828   (HQ)
JPDL MULTI MANAGEMENT INC
JPDL
1555 Rue Peel Bureau 500, Montreal, QC,
H3A 3L8
(514) 287-1070
Emp Here 24   Sales 35,452,124
SIC 7389 Business services, nec
  Jean-Paul De Lavison

    D-U-N-S 20-882-2981   (BR)
KPMG LLP

(Suby of KPMG LLP)
600 Boul De Maisonneuve O Unite1500, Montreal, QC, H3A 0A3
(514) 840-2100
Emp Here 750
SIC 8721 Accounting, auditing, and bookkeeping

    D-U-N-S 20-215-5537   (HQ)
L'OREAL CANADA INC
BIOTHERM CANADA
(Suby of L'OREAL)
1500 Boul Robert-Bourassa Bureau 600,
Montreal, QC, H3A 3S7
(514) 287-4800
Emp Here 250   Sales 533,574,000
SIC 2844 Toilet preparations
  Frank Kollmar
  Frederic Roze
  Philippe Dalle
  Serge L. Brodeur
  Frank Kollmar

    D-U-N-S 24-500-7463   (SL)
LANGLOIS GAUDREAU S.E.N.C.
1002 Rue Sherbrooke O Bureau 27, Montreal,
QC, H3A 3L6
(514) 842-9512
Emp Here 100   Sales 11,088,200
SIC 8111 Legal services
  Raynold Langlois
  Laurent Trudeau
  Pierre Tourigny
  France Simard

    D-U-N-S 24-863-0634   (HQ)
LANGLOIS KRONSTROM DESJARDINS
S.E.N.C.
1002 Rue Sherbrooke O Bureau 2800, Mon-
treal, QC, H3A 3L6
(514) 842-9512
Emp Here 70   Sales 22,176,400
SIC 8111 Legal services
  Raynold Langlois
  Richard Ramsay
  Jean-Francois Gagnon

    D-U-N-S 20-791-7670   (SL)
LEXUS TRAVEL INC
UNIGLOBE VOYAGE LEXUS
1411 Rue Peel Bureau 403, Montreal, QC,
H3A 1S5
(514) 397-9221
Emp Here 52   Sales 27,038,284
SIC 4724 Travel agencies
  Samir Hanna
  Margrit Shakir

    D-U-N-S 25-357-2143   (HQ)
LOGICIELS DTI INC
DEN-O-TECH INTERNATIONAL
1800 Av Mcgill College Unite 1800, Montreal,
QC, H3A 3J6
(514) 499-0910
Sales 17,731,100
SIC 7371 Custom computer programming ser-
vices
  Anthony Turcotte
  Kim Nakamaru

    D-U-N-S 20-165-9054   (BR)
LONDON   LIFE,   COMPAGNIE
D'ASSURANCE-VIE
LONDON LIFE INSURANCE COMPANY
(Suby of POWER CORPORATION DU
CANADA)
1800 Av Mcgill College Unite 1100, Montreal,
QC, H3A 3J6
(514) 931-4242
Emp Here 100
SIC 6311 Life insurance

    D-U-N-S 24-121-4527   (BR)
LONDON   LIFE,   COMPAGNIE
D'ASSURANCE-VIE
LONDON LIFE INSURANCE COMPANY
(Suby of POWER CORPORATION DU

CANADA)
2001 Boul Robert-Bourassa Unite 800, Montreal, QC, H3A 2A6
(514) 350-5500
Emp Here 400
SIC 6411 Insurance agents, brokers, and service
  Phil Slomimsky

D-U-N-S 24-354-5993   (BR)
MANUFACTURERS LIFE INSURANCE COMPANY, THE
FINANCIERE MANUVIE
(*Suby of* MANULIFE FINANCIAL CORPORATION)
2000 Rue Mansfield Unite 300, Montreal, QC, H3A 2Z4
(514) 288-6268
Emp Here 800
SIC 6311 Life insurance
  Celine Laforce

D-U-N-S 20-914-8514   (BR)
MANULIFE CANADA LTD
MANULIFE FINANCIAL 1182
(*Suby of* MANULIFE FINANCIAL CORPORATION)
2000 Rue Mansfield Unite 200, Montreal, QC, H3A 2Z4
(514) 845-1612
Emp Here 750
SIC 8742 Management consulting services

D-U-N-S 20-553-6688   (BR)
MARSH CANADA LIMITED
(*Suby of* MARSH & MCLENNAN COMPANIES, INC.)
1981 Av Mcgill College Bureau 820, Montreal, QC, H3A 3T4
(514) 285-4700
Emp Here 250
SIC 6411 Insurance agents, brokers, and service
  Rony Rokach

D-U-N-S 24-885-4973   (SL)
MBA RECHERCHE INC
1470 Rue Peel Bureau 800, Montreal, QC, H3A 1T1
(514) 284-9644
Emp Here 50   *Sales* 10,667,900
SIC 8732 Commercial nonphysical research
  Maxime Bourbonnais

D-U-N-S 25-039-9102   (BR)
MCGILL UNIVERSITY HEALTH CENTRE
MCGILL HOPITAL NEUROLOGIQUE DE MONTREAL
(*Suby of* MCGILL UNIVERSITY HEALTH CENTRE)
3801 Rue University Bureau 548, Montreal, QC, H3A 2B4
(514) 398-6644
Emp Here 2,000
SIC 8062 General medical and surgical hospitals
  Guy Rouleau

D-U-N-S 24-342-6454   (BR)
MCGILL UNIVERSITY HEALTH CENTRE
ROYAL VICTORIA HOSPITAL
(*Suby of* MCGILL UNIVERSITY HEALTH CENTRE)
687 Av Des Pins O Bureau 1408, Montreal, QC, H3A 1A1
(514) 934-1934
Emp Here 3,000
SIC 8062 General medical and surgical hospitals
  Arthur Porter

D-U-N-S 24-425-1364   (BR)
MCMILLAN LLP
(*Suby of* MCMILLAN LLP)
1000 Rue Sherbrooke O Bureau 2700, Montreal, QC, H3A 3G4
(514) 987-5000
Emp Here 100

SIC 8111 Legal services
  Ron Johnson

D-U-N-S 20-308-9073   (BR)
MEDAVIE INC
CROIX BLEUE MEDAVIE
(*Suby of* MEDAVIE INC)
550 Rue Sherbrooke O Bureau 1200, Montreal, QC, H3A 1B9
(514) 286-7778
Emp Here 300
SIC 6321 Accident and health insurance
  Eric Laberge

D-U-N-S 25-189-7737   (SL)
MEDISYS CORPORATE HEALTH LP
SERVICES DE SANTE MEDISYS
500 Rue Sherbrooke O Bureau 1100, Montreal, QC, H3A 3C6
(514) 499-2778
Emp Here 100   *Sales* 7,512,900
SIC 8093 Specialty outpatient clinics, nec
  Sheldon Elman

D-U-N-S 20-179-0271   (SL)
MEGALEXIS COMMUNICATION INC
666 Rue Sherbrooke O Bureau 602, Montreal, QC, H3A 1E7
(514) 861-4999
Emp Here 36   *Sales* 15,965,640
SIC 7389 Business services, nec
  Ann Rutledge

D-U-N-S 24-460-7578   (BR)
MERCER (CANADA) LIMITED
MERCER INVESTMENT CONSULTING
(*Suby of* MARSH & MCLENNAN COMPANIES, INC.)
1981 Av Mcgill College Bureau 800, Montreal, QC, H3A 3T5
(514) 285-1802
Emp Here 500
SIC 8999 Services, nec

D-U-N-S 25-243-5177   (HQ)
METRO LOGISTIQUE INC
(*Suby of* GROUPE DE CHAINE D'APPROVISIONNEMENT METRO INC)
1002 Rue Sherbrooke O Bureau 2000, Montreal, QC, H3A 3L6
(514) 333-5500
Emp Here 10   *Sales* 36,225,759
SIC 6512 Nonresidential building operators
  Hanif Nanji
  Marc D'amour

D-U-N-S 24-053-0998   (HQ)
MONSTER WORLDWIDE CANADA INC
COMMUNICATIONS TMP WORLDWIDE
(*Suby of* RANDSTAD N.V.)
2020 Boul Robert-Bourassa Bureau 2000, Montreal, QC, H3A 2A5
(514) 284-0231
Sales 27,335,000
SIC 6712 Bank holding companies
  Peter Gilfillan
  Evan K. Kornrich

D-U-N-S 24-018-8656   (SL)
OKA COMPUTER SYSTEMS LTD
2075 Rue University Bureau 750, Montreal, QC, H3A 2L1

Emp Here 114   *Sales* 6,740,091
SIC 7379 Computer related services, nec

D-U-N-S 25-689-9857   (HQ)
OLAMETER INC
2000 Av Mcgill College Bureau 500, Montreal, QC, H3A 3H3
(514) 982-6664
Emp Here 10   *Sales* 183,048,600
SIC 7389 Business services, nec
  Jan Peeters
  Jean-Pierre Carette
  Byron L. Knief
  Shawn Abbott
  Susan Burkman

Judith Kavanagh

D-U-N-S 24-803-5334   (HQ)
OLIN CANADA ULC
PRODUITS OLIN CHLOR ALKALI
2020 Boul Robert-Bourassa Bureau 2190, Montreal, QC, H3A 2A5
(514) 397-6100
Emp Here 50   *Sales* 56,804,200
SIC 2819 Industrial inorganic chemicals, nec
  James A Varilek
  Eric A. Blanchard
  Teresa Vermillion
  Todd A. Slater
  John L Mcintosh

D-U-N-S 20-534-1162   (BR)
OPINION SEARCH INC
NIELSEN
1080 Rue Beaverhall Bureau 400, Montreal, QC, H3A 1E4
(514) 288-0199
Emp Here 460
SIC 8732 Commercial nonphysical research
  Steve Mcdonald

D-U-N-S 20-296-2044   (SL)
OPTIMUM ACTUAIRES & CONSEILLERS INC
OPTIMUM GESTION DE RISQUES
(*Suby of* OPTIGAM INC)
425 Boul De Maisonneuve O Bureau 1120, Montreal, QC, H3A 3G5
(514) 288-1620
Emp Here 30   *Sales* 14,622,180
SIC 8999 Services, nec
  Anabelle Blondeau
  Claude Lamonde
  Natalie Colpron
  Louis Seguin
  Patrick Lamontagne
  Anne Jolicoeur
  Andre Gaudreault
  Marcel Le Houillier
  Louis Fontaine

D-U-N-S 24-763-5626   (HQ)
OPTIMUM GENERAL INC
(*Suby of* OPTIGAM INC)
425 Boul De Maisonneuve O Bureau 1500, Montreal, QC, H3A 3G5
(514) 288-8725
Sales 380,380,304
SIC 6331 Fire, marine, and casualty insurance
  Jean-Claude Page
  Gilles Blondeau
  Henri Joli-Coeur
  Paul Tremblay
  Louis Fontaine
  Pierre St-Laurent

D-U-N-S 24-934-1132   (SL)
OPTIMUM GESTION DE PLACEMENTS INC
OPTIMUM PLACEMENTS
(*Suby of* OPTIGAM INC)
425 Boul De Maisonneuve O Bureau 1620, Montreal, QC, H3A 3G5
(514) 288-7545
Emp Here 24   *Sales* 22,540,248
SIC 6282 Investment advice
  Jean-Claude Page
  Claude Lamonde
  Pierre Comtois
  Anabelle Blondeau
  Louis Seguin
  Louis Fontaine
  Patrick Lamontagne

D-U-N-S 20-911-4412   (HQ)
OPTIMUM REASSURANCE INC
(*Suby of* OPTIGAM INC)
425 Boul De Maisonneuve O Bureau 1200, Montreal, QC, H3A 3G5
(514) 288-1900
Sales 114,449,670
SIC 6411 Insurance agents, brokers, and service

Jean-Claude Page
Serge Goulet
Anabelle Blondeau
Charles Belzil
Jacques M. Gagnon
Mark J. Oppenheim
Anne Joli-Coeur
Rita Dionne-Marsolais
Denis Latulippe
Jean-Marc Fortier

D-U-N-S 20-762-1954   (HQ)
OPTIMUM SOCIETE D'ASSURANCE INC
(*Suby of* OPTIGAM INC)
425 Boul De Maisonneuve O Bureau 1500, Montreal, QC, H3A 3G5
(514) 288-8711
Emp Here 80   *Sales* 184,774,200
SIC 6411 Insurance agents, brokers, and service
  Noella Anthony
  Jacques Auger

D-U-N-S 24-713-7755   (BR)
ORACLE CANADA ULC
(*Suby of* ORACLE CORPORATION)
600 Boul De Maisonneuve O Bureau 1900, Montreal, QC, H3A 3J2
(514) 843-6762
Emp Here 200
SIC 7372 Prepackaged software
  Rene Giguere

D-U-N-S 24-892-6870   (SL)
ORDRE DES DENTISTES DU QUEBEC
FONDS D'ASSURANCE-RESPONSABILITE PROFESSIONNELLE DE L'ORDRE DES DENTISTES DU QUEBEC
2020 Boul Robert-Bourassa Bureau 2160, Montreal, QC, H3A 2A5
(514) 281-0300
Emp Here 49   *Sales* 90,486,291
SIC 6324 Hospital and medical service plans
  Barry Dolman

D-U-N-S 24-363-2887   (HQ)
OVIVO INC
(*Suby of* SKION GMBH)
1010 Rue Sherbrooke O Bureau 1700, Montreal, QC, H3A 2R7
(514) 284-2224
Emp Here 30   *Sales* 238,404,500
SIC 3569 General industrial machinery, nec
  Marc Barbeau
  Pierre-Marc Sarrazin
  Charles Taillon
  David Mcausland
  Justin Methot
  Reinhard Hubner
  Raphael Simon
  Jurgen Giebmann

D-U-N-S 24-319-4276   (HQ)
PAPIER DOMTAR (CANADA) INC
(*Suby of* DOMTAR LUXEMBOURG INVESTMENTS SARL)
395 Boul De Maisonneuve O Bureau 200, Montreal, QC, H3A 1L6
(514) 848-5555
Emp Here 30   *Sales* 1,655,101,774
SIC 2611 Pulp mills
  John D Williams
  Razven Theodoru

D-U-N-S 24-382-3536   (HQ)
PEDS LEGWEAR INC
PEDS CHAUSSETTES & CIE
(*Suby of* GILDAN ACTIVEWEAR INC)
1501 Av Mcgill College Bureau 914, Montreal, QC, H3A 3M8
(514) 875-5575
Emp Here 20   *Sales* 146,568,275
SIC 5136 Men's and boy's clothing
  Warren Chisling
  Nicolas Lavoie
  Lindsay Matthews

D-U-N-S 25-674-4541 (HQ)
PLACEMENTS MONTRUSCO BOLTON INC
1501 Av Mcgill College Bureau 1200, Montreal, QC, H3A 3M8
(514) 842-6464
Sales 75,134,160
SIC 6282 Investment advice
James Carmody
Sylvain Boule
Benoit Leroux
Sylvain Boule
Josee Lachapelle
Bernard Tanguay
Christian Godin
Umesh Vallipuram
Jennifer Borggaard

D-U-N-S 20-379-3034 (HQ)
PLASTIQUES IPL INC
IPL
1000 Sherbrooke W St Suite 700, Montreal, QC, H3A 3G4
(438) 320-6188
Emp Here 2,000 *Sales* 573,148,800
SIC 3089 Plastics products, nec
Alan Walsh
Susan Holburn
Pat Dalton
David L. Mcausland
Rose Bridget Hynes
Hugh Mccutcheon
Geoffrey Meagher
Sharon Pel
Linda Kuga Pikulin
Mary Ritchie

D-U-N-S 24-342-1349 (BR)
RGA LIFE REINSURANCE COMPANY OF CANADA
(*Suby of* REINSURANCE GROUP OF AMERICA, INCORPORATED)
1981 Av Mcgill College Unite 1300, Montreal, QC, H3A 3A8
(514) 985-5260
Emp Here 130
SIC 6311 Life insurance

D-U-N-S 20-791-9002 (SL)
RICHTER S.E.N.C.R.L.
CONSEILLERS, FISCALITE AMERICAINE
1981 Av Mcgill College Suite 11e, Montreal, QC, H3A 2W9
(514) 934-3400
Emp Here 250 *Sales* 46,213,250
SIC 8721 Accounting, auditing, and bookkeeping
Robert Zittrer
John Swidler
Stephen Rosenhek
Yves Vincent
Howard Gross

D-U-N-S 20-716-0040 (BR)
ROYAL & SUN ALLIANCE INSURANCE COMPANY OF CANADA
(*Suby of* RSA INSURANCE GROUP PLC)
1001 Boul De Maisonneuve O Bureau 1004, Montreal, QC, H3A 3C8
(514) 844-1116
Emp Here 80
SIC 6411 Insurance agents, brokers, and service
Marie-Claude Desroche

D-U-N-S 20-566-7090 (HQ)
ROYAL INSTITUTE FOR ADVANCEMENT OF LEARNING MCGILL
845 Sherbrooke Street West, Montreal, QC, H3A 0G4
(514) 398-8120
Emp Here 500 *Sales* 907,318,348
SIC 8221 Colleges and universities
Stuart Cobett

D-U-N-S 20-800-9683 (BR)
ROYAL INSTITUTE FOR ADVANCEMENT OF LEARNING MCGILL

FACULTY OF BIOLOGICAL & BIOMEDICAL ENGINEERING
(*Suby of* ROYAL INSTITUTE FOR ADVANCEMENT OF LEARNING MCGILL)
817 Rue Sherbrooke O Bureau 382, Montreal, QC, H3A 0C3
(514) 398-7251
Emp Here 150
SIC 8221 Colleges and universities
Jim A Nicell

D-U-N-S 20-540-8503 (HQ)
ROYNAT INC
ROYNAT CAPITAL
(*Suby of* BANK OF NOVA SCOTIA, THE)
1002 Rue Sherbrooke O Bureau 1100, Montreal, QC, H3A 3L6
(514) 987-4947
Emp Here 40 *Sales* 11,197,050
SIC 6159 Miscellaneous business credit institutions
David Daum
Gillian Riley
Abdurrehman Muhammadi
Glenda Caratao
Laurie Stang

D-U-N-S 25-501-5125 (SL)
RPSC HOLDINGS LTD
SOCIETE A PORTEFEUILLE RPSC
2050 Rue De Bleury Bureau 300, Montreal, QC, H3A 2J5
(514) 286-2636
Emp Here 130 *Sales* 29,701,360
SIC 4813 Telephone communication, except radio
Hamnett P Hill Jr
Shahir Guindi
Hamnett P Hill Sr.

D-U-N-S 20-564-0725 (BR)
SCOTIA CAPITAL INC
SCOTIAMCLEOD
(*Suby of* BANK OF NOVA SCOTIA, THE)
1002 Rue Sherbrooke O Bureau 600, Montreal, QC, H3A 3L6
(514) 287-3600
Emp Here 180
SIC 6211 Security brokers and dealers
Andre Bourret

D-U-N-S 20-340-0481 (SL)
SECURIGLOBE INC
ECONOGLOBE
1450 Rue City Councillors Bureau 1000, Montreal, QC, H3A 2E6
(450) 462-2444
Emp Here 16 *Sales* 11,607,024
SIC 6321 Accident and health insurance
Johanne Murphy

D-U-N-S 20-791-6925 (HQ)
SENVEST CAPITAL INC
1000 Rue Sherbrooke O Bureau 2400, Montreal, QC, H3A 3G4
(514) 281-8082
Sales 21,223,824
SIC 6211 Security brokers and dealers
Victor Mashaal
Richard Mashaal
George Malikotsis
Frank Daniel
Ronald G Assaf
David Basner
Jeffrey L. Jonas

D-U-N-S 20-762-9643 (HQ)
SERVICES DE GESTION QUANTUM LIMITEE, LES
2000 Av Mcgill College Bureau 1800, Montreal, QC, H3A 3H3
(514) 842-5555
Emp Here 125 *Sales* 44,881,200
SIC 8741 Management services
Lyon M. Gould
Cynthia Feigin
Brian M. Schneiderman

D-U-N-S 25-848-8584 (SL)
SERVICES DE PLACEMENT DE PERSONNEL DURAND & PRATT INC, LES
DURAND & PRATT
666 Rue Sherbrooke O Bureau 800, Montreal, QC, H3A 1E7
(514) 987-1815
Emp Here 200 *Sales* 14,938,800
SIC 7361 Employment agencies
Doris Durand
Louise Pratt

D-U-N-S 20-691-0767 (SL)
SERVICES FINANCIERS XN (CANADA) INC
XN RISK
600 Boul De Maisonneuve O Bureau 2310, Montreal, QC, H3A 3J2
(514) 908-1835
Emp Here 26 *Sales* 48,041,292
SIC 6411 Insurance agents, brokers, and service
Charles Robinet-Duffo
Cesar Moufarrege
Benoit Audet
Charles-Henri Bujard

D-U-N-S 20-015-9676 (SL)
SERVICES LINGUISTIQUES VERSACOM INC
VERSACOM
(*Suby of* 9058-8138 QUEBEC INC)
1501 Av Mcgill College 6e Etage, Montreal, QC, H3A 3M8
(514) 397-1950
Emp Here 180 *Sales* 120,403,440
SIC 7389 Business services, nec
Benoit Le Blanc
Odile Poliquin
Claudette Monty
Charlotte Leclercq
Nathalie Nicol
Greta Sterle

D-U-N-S 25-076-7258 (SL)
SKYLINK VOYAGES INC
DESTIGO (TM)
1450 Rue City Councillors Bureau 110, Montreal, QC, H3A 2E6
(514) 842-6344
Emp Here 65 *Sales* 33,797,855
SIC 4729 Passenger transportation arrangement
Joane Tetreault
Walter Arbib
Surget Babra

D-U-N-S 24-821-2375 (SL)
SOCIETE D'ELECTROLYSE ET DE CHIMIE ALCAN LIMITEE
1188 Rue Sherbrooke O, Montreal, QC, H3A 3G2

Emp Here 100
SIC 3334 Primary aluminum

D-U-N-S 20-024-7125 (SL)
SOCIETE DE SERVICES DENTAIRES (A.C.D.Q.) INC
CENTRE DENTAIDE
425 Boul De Maisonneuve O Bureau 1450, Montreal, QC, H3A 3G5
(514) 282-1425
Emp Here 20 *Sales* 14,508,780
SIC 6324 Hospital and medical service plans
Stephane Guoyette

D-U-N-S 24-942-2437 (HQ)
SOCIETE DES CASINOS DU QUEBEC INC, LA
CASINO DE MONTREAL
(*Suby of* GOUVERNEMENT DE LA PROVINCE DE QUEBEC)
500 Rue Sherbrooke O Bureau 1500, Montreal, QC, H3A 3C6
(514) 282-8000
Emp Here 769 *Sales* 464,625,300
SIC 7999 Amusement and recreation, nec

Claude Poisson
Lynne Roiter
Alain Cousineau

D-U-N-S 20-860-1161 (HQ)
SOCIETE DES LOTERIES DU QUEBEC
(*Suby of* GOUVERNEMENT DE LA PROVINCE DE QUEBEC)
500 Rue Sherbrooke O, Montreal, QC, H3A 3C6
(514) 282-8000
Emp Here 300 *Sales* 595,108,800
SIC 7999 Amusement and recreation, nec
Lynne Roiter
Helene Fortin
Alain Albert
Lynda Durand
Jean-Andre Eli
Nathalie Goodwin

D-U-N-S 20-882-8855 (HQ)
SOCIETE GENERALE (CANADA)
SOCIETE GENERALE CORPORATE INVESTMENT
(*Suby of* SOCIETE GENERALE)
1501 Av Mcgill College Bureau 1800, Montreal, QC, H3A 3M8
(514) 841-6000
Emp Here 115 *Sales* 35,030,700
SIC 6081 Foreign bank and branches and agencies
Diletta Prando
Alain Lellouche
Didier Varlet
Pierre Matuszewski
Maria Patsios

D-U-N-S 24-813-8869 (HQ)
SOCIETE SPECTRA SCENE INC, LA
400 Boul De Maisonneuve O Bureau 800, Montreal, QC, H3A 1L4
(514) 523-3378
Sales 37,453,250
SIC 7922 Theatrical producers and services
Alain Simard
Jacques-Andre Dupont
Jacques Aube
Geoffrey E. Molson
France Margaret Belanger

D-U-N-S 20-177-8094 (SL)
SODRAC (2003) INC
SOCIETE DU DROIT DE REPRODUCTION DES AUTEURS COMPOSITEURS ET EDITEURS AU CANADA
1470 Rue Peel Bureau 1010, Montreal, QC, H3A 1T1
(514) 845-3268
Emp Here 32 *Sales* 12,528,064
SIC 6794 Patent owners and lessors
Frederic Weber
Alain Lauzon

D-U-N-S 20-559-6955 (HQ)
SOLUTIONS ABILIS INC
1010 Rue Sherbrooke O Bureau 1900, Montreal, QC, H3A 2R7
(514) 844-4888
Sales 18,110,755
SIC 7379 Computer related services, nec
Eric Le Goff
Alain Elbaz
Jean Parisien
Pierre Shedleur
Robert A. Proulx
Philippe Labelle

D-U-N-S 20-414-7983 (SL)
SOLUTIONS MUNVO INC
MUNVO
1400 Rue Metcalfe Suite 300, Montreal, QC, H3A 1X2
(514) 392-9822
Emp Here 100 *Sales* 18,041,500
SIC 8731 Commercial physical research
Mathieu Sabourin

▲ Public Company ■ Public Company Family Member **HQ** Headquarters **BR** Branch **SL** Single Location

D-U-N-S 20-553-9294 (HQ)
SOLUTIONS VICTRIX INC, LES
630 Rue Sherbrooke O Bureau 1100, Montreal, QC, H3A 1E4
(514) 879-1919
Emp Here 150 *Sales* 33,369,400
SIC 7379 Computer related services, nec
Marc-Andre Poulin
Stephane Gariepy
Xavier Giraud
Jean Mathieu

D-U-N-S 25-673-6463 (SL)
SPEQ LE DEVOIR INC
2050 Rue De Bleury Bureau 900, Montreal, QC, H3A 3M9
(514) 985-3333
Emp Here 125 *Sales* 34,168,750
SIC 6712 Bank holding companies
Yves L Ducharme
Clement Richard

D-U-N-S 24-366-8675 (SL)
STRADIGI INC
LABORATOIRES STRADIGI
1470 Rue Peel Bureau A1050, Montreal, QC, H3A 1T1
(514) 395-9018
Emp Here 60 *Sales* 10,638,660
SIC 7371 Custom computer programming services
Basil Bouraropoulos
Curtis Gavura

D-U-N-S 24-978-0326 (SL)
TAMAGGO INC
2001 Av Mcgill College Bureau 700, Montreal, QC, H3A 1G1

Emp Here 50 *Sales* 10,233,650
SIC 3651 Household audio and video equipment
Jean-Claude Artonne
Bukhard Vetsch
Marie-Christine Laroque

D-U-N-S 20-852-6876 (BR)
TAXI CANADA LTD
TAXI L'AGENCE DE PUBLICITE
(*Suby of* WPP PLC)
1435 Rue Saint-Alexandre Bureau 620, Montreal, QC, H3A 2G4
(514) 842-8294
Emp Here 80
SIC 7311 Advertising agencies
Paul Lavoie

D-U-N-S 24-301-3315 (HQ)
TECHNIGLOBE INC
666 Rue Sherbrooke O Unite 800, Montreal, QC, H3A 1E7
(514) 987-1815
Sales 11,621,518
SIC 7322 Adjustment and collection services
Louise Pratt

D-U-N-S 25-957-1883 (HQ)
TECHNOMEDIA FORMATION INC
APPRENTISSAGE EN LIGNE BRIDGE
(*Suby of* CLAUDIUS FINANCE SARL)
1001 Boul De Maisonneuve O, Montreal, QC, H3A 3C8
(514) 287-1561
Sales 10,813,650
SIC 7371 Custom computer programming services
Alain Latry
Sylvain Jauze
Marcel Messier
Dwaine Maltais
Gerard Duval
Shawna Berthold
Thierry Luthi
Patrick Bertrand
Alexandre Gonthier

D-U-N-S 20-292-0872 (SL)

TELECOMMUNICATIONS GLOBAL CROSSING-CANADA LTEE
1140 Boul De Maisonneuve O, Montreal, QC, H3A 1M8
(800) 668-4210
Emp Here 100 *Sales* 18,479,800
SIC 4899 Communication services, nec
Jeff K Storey
John M Ryan
Linda Diadori
Katia Desilles-Lemieux

D-U-N-S 20-784-7489 (SL)
TELECONFERENCE GLOBAL CROSSING-CANADA LTEE
1140 Boul De Maisonneuve O, Montreal, QC, H3A 1M8

Emp Here 200 *Sales* 45,694,400
SIC 4899 Communication services, nec
Katia Desilles-Lemieux

D-U-N-S 25-201-7520 (HQ)
THERATECHNOLOGIES INC
EXOPEP
2015 Rue Peel Suite 1100, Montreal, QC, H3A 1T8
(514) 336-7800
Emp Here 25 *Sales* 45,055,128
SIC 8731 Commercial physical research
Luc Tanguay
Philippe Dubuc
Marie-Noel Colussi
Christian Marsolais
Lyne Fortin
Boucher Denis
Jocelyn Lafond
Dawn Svoronos
Paul Pommier
Jean-Denis Talon

D-U-N-S 20-584-4157 (SL)
TICKETPRO INC
1981 Av Mcgill College Bureau 1600, Montreal, QC, H3A 2Y1
(514) 849-0237
Emp Here 70 *Sales* 10,595,830
SIC 7922 Theatrical producers and services
Mathieu Dupuis
Vitalie Sanduta
Guy Dufort
Michel Goulet

D-U-N-S 20-998-3386 (HQ)
TIDAN INC
666 Rue Sherbrooke O Bureau 2300, Montreal, QC, H3A 1E7
(514) 845-6393
Sales 16,565,325
SIC 6513 Apartment building operators
Jack Sofer
Michael Yuval

D-U-N-S 20-298-4469 (SL)
TIGERTEL COMMUNICATIONS INC
CENTRE D'APPELS TIGERTEL
550 Rue Sherbrooke O Bureau 1650, Montreal, QC, H3A 1B9
(514) 843-4313
Emp Here 30 *Sales* 13,476,570
SIC 7389 Business services, nec
Doug Swift

D-U-N-S 24-473-9793 (HQ)
TOURS NEW YORK INC
ALIO
1410 Rue Stanley Bureau 1015, Montreal, QC, H3A 1P8
(514) 287-1066
Emp Here 32 *Sales* 38,012,844
SIC 4725 Tour operators
Jason Roussakis
Khalid Somra
Carmine Domenicucci

D-U-N-S 24-176-8902 (SL)
TOWER ARCTIC LTD

2055 Rue Peel Bureau 960, Montreal, QC, H3A 1V4

Emp Here 25 *Sales* 11,768,275
SIC 1542 Nonresidential construction, nec
John Jacobsen
Eric Jacobsen
Daniel Kadlak

D-U-N-S 20-126-5043 (BR)
TOWERS WATSON CANADA INC
WILLIS TOWERS WATSON(MC)
(*Suby of* WILLIS TOWERS WATSON PUBLIC LIMITED COMPANY)
1800 Av Mcgill College Bureau 2200, Montreal, QC, H3A 3J6
(514) 982-9411
Emp Here 130
SIC 8999 Services, nec
Michel Tougas

D-U-N-S 24-432-9017 (BR)
TOWERS WATSON ULC
(*Suby of* WILLIS TOWERS WATSON PUBLIC LIMITED COMPANY)
600 Boul De Maisonneuve O Bureau 2400, Montreal, QC, H3A 3J2

Emp Here 85
SIC 8741 Management services
Michel Tougas

D-U-N-S 25-756-9509 (BR)
TRANSCONTINENTAL INC
MEDIAS TRANSCONTINENTAL
(*Suby of* TRANSCONTINENTAL INC)
2001 Boul Robert-Bourassa Unite 900, Montreal, QC, H3A 2A6
(514) 499-0491
Emp Here 110
SIC 2721 Periodicals
Jules Poitras

D-U-N-S 24-250-4335 (SL)
TRANSPERFECT TRANSLATION INC
(*Suby of* TRANSPERFECT GLOBAL, INC.)
1010 Rue Sherbrooke O Bureau 811, Montreal, QC, H3A 2R7
(514) 861-5177
Emp Here 50 *Sales* 22,460,950
SIC 7389 Business services, nec
Elizabeth Elting
Philip R. Shawe
Judith Lass Elting
Lawrence Shawe

D-U-N-S 20-290-1039 (HQ)
UNIVERSITE MCGILL
845 Rue Sherbrooke O Bureau 310, Montreal, QC, H3A 0G4
(514) 398-4455
Emp Here 100 *Sales* 746,955,000
SIC 8221 Colleges and universities
Suzanne Fortier
Stephen Strople
David Noble Harpp
Stuart Cobbett
Thierry Vandal
Claude Genereux
Gerald Butts
Peter Coughlin
Samuel Minzberg
Michael Boychuk

D-U-N-S 24-352-0731 (HQ)
WESTCLIFF MANAGEMENT LTD
GALERIES DE GRANBY
600 Boul De Maisonneuve O Bureau 2600, Montreal, QC, H3A 3J2
(514) 499-8300
Emp Here 150 *Sales* 33,130,650
SIC 6512 Nonresidential building operators
Alan Marcovitz
William Pencer
Keith Jones

D-U-N-S 20-184-3294 (BR)

WINNERS MERCHANTS INTERNATIONAL L.P.
WINNERS
(*Suby of* THE TJX COMPANIES INC)
1500 Av Mcgill College, Montreal, QC, H3A 3J5
(514) 788-4949
Emp Here 120
SIC 5651 Family clothing stores
Christine Fenton

Montreal, QC H3B

D-U-N-S 20-362-8359 (SL)
10087408 CANADA INC
RESTO BAR 1909
1280 Ave Des Canadiens-De-Montreal, Montreal, QC, H3B 3B3
(514) 261-7661
Emp Here 100 *Sales* 4,551,900
SIC 5812 Eating places
Grant Cobb
France Margaret Belanger
Geoff Molson
Ken Grondin
William Gregson

D-U-N-S 20-309-5930 (SL)
111616 OPERATIONS (CANADA) INC
(*Suby of* KPP (NO. 2) TRUSTEES LIMITED)
1 Place Ville-Marie Unite 3900, Montreal, QC, H3B 4M7
(800) 465-6325
Emp Here 54 *Sales* 12,273,606
SIC 3861 Photographic equipment and supplies
Steven Ross
Phillip Gibbons

D-U-N-S 24-106-7797 (SL)
123179 CANADA INC
RESTER MANAGEMENT HERMES EDIFICE
1117 Rue Sainte-Catherine O Bureau 303, Montreal, QC, H3B 1H9
(514) 844-2612
Emp Here 100 *Sales* 24,304,900
SIC 6519 Real property lessors, nec
Joseph Drazin

D-U-N-S 25-413-0446 (SL)
3169693 CANADA INC
BOULANG PREMIERE MOISSON GARS
895 Rue De La Gauchetiere O Bureau 401, Montreal, QC, H3B 4G1
(514) 393-1247
Emp Here 50 *Sales* 13,707,600
SIC 5461 Retail bakeries
Bertrand Labelle
Benoit Nolin

D-U-N-S 20-524-1214 (HQ)
3887804 CANADA INC
1250 Boul Rene-Levesque O, Montreal, QC, H3B 4W8
(514) 845-1515
Sales 57,062,100
SIC 8011 Offices and clinics of medical doctors
Mark J. Cohen
Avraham Wallerstein

D-U-N-S 24-999-9020 (HQ)
9152-2458 QUEBEC INC
LGM SOLUTION
1000 Rue De La Gauchetiere O Bureau 2400, Montreal, QC, H3B 4W5
(514) 209-2665
Emp Here 70 *Sales* 13,347,760
SIC 7379 Computer related services, nec
Martin Delarosbil

D-U-N-S 24-848-9366 (BR)
A.S.A.P. SECURED INC
1255 Rue Peel Bureau 1101, Montreal, QC,

H3B 2T9
(514) 868-0202
Emp Here 200
SIC 7381 Detective and armored car services
Louis-Philippe Bourdon

D-U-N-S 20-234-4672   (BR)
ACCOR MANAGEMENT CANADA INC
FAIRMONT HOTELS INC
(*Suby of* ACCOR MANAGEMENT CANADA INC)
900 Boul Rene-Levesque O, Montreal, QC, H3B 4A5
(514) 861-3511
Emp Here 800
SIC 7011 Hotels and motels
Nathalie Gallant

D-U-N-S 25-688-2424   (HQ)
ADACEL INC
ADACEL TECHNOLOGIES
(*Suby of* ADACEL TECHNOLOGIES LIMITED)
895 Rue De La Gauchetiere O Bureau 300, Montreal, QC, H3B 4G1
(450) 444-2687
Sales 22,728,900
SIC 3812 Search and navigation equipment
Gary Pearson
Daniel Verret
William Lang

D-U-N-S 20-024-0450   (HQ)
ADDENDA CAPITAL INC
(*Suby of* CO-OPERATORS GROUP LIMITED, THE)
800 Boul Rene-Levesque O Bureau 2750, Montreal, QC, H3B 1X9
(514) 287-0223
Emp Here 25   *Sales* 21,248,280
SIC 6282 Investment advice
Michael White
Carmand Normand
Kathy Bardswick
Daniel Burns
Ann Marshal
Roland Courtois
Michel Therien
Bruce West

D-U-N-S 25-737-2540   (SL)
AEDIFICA INC
606 Rue Cathcart Bureau 800, Montreal, QC, H3B 1K9
(514) 844-6611
Emp Here 120   *Sales* 21,448,680
SIC 8712 Architectural services
Michel Dubuc
Suzanne Brouillard
Guy Favreau

D-U-N-S 20-213-5513   (HQ)
AIR LIQUIDE CANADA INC
ACCESS
1250 Boul Rene-Levesque O Bureau 1700, Montreal, QC, H3B 5E6
(514) 933-0303
Emp Here 200   *Sales* 1,156,077,000
SIC 2813 Industrial gases
Bertrand Masselot
Marie-Josee Guerin
Jerome Pelletan
Michael J. Graff

D-U-N-S 20-503-8771   (HQ)
ALCOA CANADA CIE
ALUMINERIE DE BAIE-COMEAU
(*Suby of* ALUMINERIE LAURALCO SARL)
1 Place Ville-Marie Bureau 2310, Montreal, QC, H3B 3M5
(514) 904-5030
Emp Here 100   *Sales* 916,955,848
SIC 3334 Primary aluminum
Timothy D. Reyes
Jean-Francois Cyr
Amelie Moreault
Louis Langlois

Nicklaus A. Oliver
Olivier Charest

D-U-N-S 25-210-0060   (HQ)
ALITHYA CANADA INC
6I SOLUTION
(*Suby of* AST TRUST COMPANY (CANADA))
700 Rue De La Gauchetiere O Bureau 2400, Montreal, QC, H3B 5M2
(514) 285-5552
Emp Here 250   *Sales* 433,240,000
SIC 7379 Computer related services, nec
Paul Raymond
Pierre Turcotte
Claude Thibault
Robert Lamarre
Natalie Piccinin
Eric Banville
Nigel Fonseca
Bertrand Gonthier
Margot Loren
Franck Benhamou

D-U-N-S 25-887-0534   (HQ)
ALLIANCE POUR LA SANTE ETUDIANTE AU QUEBEC INC
ASEQ
1200 Av Mcgill College Bureau 2200, Montreal, QC, H3B 4G7
(514) 844-4423
Sales 92,332,950
SIC 6324 Hospital and medical service plans
Lev Bukhman
Lyudmila Bukhman

D-U-N-S 20-317-5575   (BR)
ALTUS GROUP LIMITED
(*Suby of* ALTUS GROUP LIMITED)
1100 Boul Rene-Levesque O Bureau 1600, Montreal, QC, H3B 4N4
(514) 392-7700
Emp Here 100
SIC 6531 Real estate agents and managers
Jean Guy Bernard

D-U-N-S 24-870-3944   (BR)
AON CANADA INC
(*Suby of* AON PLC)
700 Rue De La Gauchetiere O Unite 1800, Montreal, QC, H3B 0A5
(514) 842-5000
Emp Here 225
SIC 6411 Insurance agents, brokers, and service

D-U-N-S 20-563-2990   (BR)
AON HEWITT INC
GROUPE CONSEIL AON
(*Suby of* AON PLC)
700 Rue De La Gauchetiere O Bureau 1900, Montreal, QC, H3B 0A7
(514) 845-6231
Emp Here 500
SIC 8999 Services, nec
Rejean Tremblay

D-U-N-S 25-496-6245   (HQ)
AON PARIZEAU INC
(*Suby of* AON PLC)
700 Rue De La Gauchetiere O Bureau 1700, Montreal, QC, H3B 0A4
(514) 842-5000
Emp Here 200   *Sales* 977,697,424
SIC 6411 Insurance agents, brokers, and service
Johanne Lepine
Vanessa Bonomo
Daniel Green
Christine Lithgow
Stephane Lesperance

D-U-N-S 24-449-5771   (BR)
AON REED STENHOUSE INC
(*Suby of* AON PLC)
700 De La Gauchetiere O Bureau 1800, Montreal, QC, H3B 0A4

(514) 842-5000
Emp Here 650
SIC 6411 Insurance agents, brokers, and service
Daniel Green

D-U-N-S 20-523-9101   (SL)
ASSOCIATION QUEBECOISE DES TRANSPORTS
AQTR
1255 Rue University Bureau 200, Montreal, QC, H3B 3X4
(514) 523-6444
Emp Here 58   *Sales* 14,007,870
SIC 8621 Professional organizations
Dominique Lacoste
Sandra Martel
Julie Morin
Martin Thibault
Chantal Aylwin
Michel Veilleux
Nicolas Theberge
Daniel Dagenais
Catherine Morency
Carl Robitaille

D-U-N-S 20-294-3556   (SL)
ASSURANCES GENERALES BANQUE NATIONAL INC
1100 Boul Robert-Bourassa Unite 11, Montreal, QC, H3B 3A5
(514) 871-7507
Emp Here 200   *Sales* 247,083,600
SIC 6331 Fire, marine, and casualty insurance
Denis Blackburn

D-U-N-S 25-060-1007   (SL)
AURAY CAPITAL CANADA INC
(*Suby of* RAYMOND CHABOT GRANT THORNTON S.E.N.C.R.L.)
600 Rue De La Gauchetiere O Bureau 2740, Montreal, QC, H3B 4L8
(514) 499-8440
Emp Here 15   *Sales* 12,416,655
SIC 6726 Investment offices, nec
Marc Audet
Jean Gosselin
Pierre Lapointe
Jean Chiasson
Louis Roy

D-U-N-S 24-206-6756   (BR)
AVIVA CANADA INC
AVIVA TRADERS
(*Suby of* GENERAL ACCIDENT PLC)
630 Boul Rene-Levesque O Bureau 900, Montreal, QC, H3B 1S6
(514) 876-5029
Emp Here 300
SIC 6331 Fire, marine, and casualty insurance
Martin Eric Tremblay

D-U-N-S 24-168-3804   (BR)
AVIVA INSURANCE COMPANY OF CANADA
AVIVA COMPAGNIE D'ASSURANCE DU CANADA
(*Suby of* GENERAL ACCIDENT PLC)
630 Boul Rene-Levesque O Bureau 700, Montreal, QC, H3B 1S6
(514) 399-1200
Emp Here 300
SIC 6331 Fire, marine, and casualty insurance
Normand Brunet

D-U-N-S 24-936-0918   (SL)
AVOGESCO INC
1 Place Ville-Marie Bureau 1300, Montreal, QC, H3B 0E6
(514) 925-6300
Emp Here 75   *Sales* 20,574,900
SIC 8741 Management services
Luc Mailhot
Bruno Floriani
Jacques Rossignal
Norman A Rishikof

D-U-N-S 20-882-6339   (HQ)

BANQUE DE DEVELOPPEMENT DU CANADA
BDC
(*Suby of* GOVERNMENT OF CANADA)
5 Place Ville-Marie Bureau 400, Montreal, QC, H3B 5E7
(514) 283-5904
Emp Here 750   *Sales* 777,423,156
SIC 6141 Personal credit institutions
Jean-Rene Halde
Paul Buron
Pierre Dubreuil
Paul Kirkconnell
Jerome Nycz
Chantal Belzie
Michel Bergeron
Louise Paradis
Thomas R. Spencer
Eric Boyko

D-U-N-S 20-837-2453   (BR)
BANQUE NATIONALE DU CANADA
ALTANIRA SECURITIES
(*Suby of* BANQUE NATIONALE DU CANADA)
1100 Boul Robert-Bourassa Bureau 12e, Montreal, QC, H3B 3A5
(514) 866-6755
Emp Here 180
SIC 6531 Real estate agents and managers

D-U-N-S 24-358-1639   (HQ)
BANQUE NATIONALE DU CANADA
BANQUE NATIONALE ASSURANCES
600 Rue De La Gauchetiere O Bureau 4e, Montreal, QC, H3B 4L3
(514) 394-4385
Emp Here 5,000   *Sales* 5,334,573,312
SIC 6021 National commercial banks
Louis Vachon
Stephane Achard
Lucie Blanchet
William Bonnell
Dominique Fagnoule
Martin Gagnon
Denis Girouard
Brigitte Hebert
Ghislain Parent
Ricardo Pascoe

D-U-N-S 25-610-3540   (HQ)
BCF CAPITAL S.E.N.C
1100 Boul Rene-Levesque O Bureau 2500, Montreal, QC, H3B 5C9
(514) 397-8500
Sales 72,056,600
SIC 8111 Legal services
Mario P Charpentier
Richard Epstein
Serge Fournier
Nathalie Gagnon
Serge Lebel
Francois Lefebvre
Eric Ouimet
Gaetan Prince
Andre Ryan
Jules Turcotte

D-U-N-S 20-517-6782   (BR)
BDO CANADA LLP
MONTREAL ACCOUNTING
(*Suby of* BDO CANADA LLP)
1000 Rue De La Gauchetiere O Bureau 200, Montreal, QC, H3B 4W5
(514) 931-0841
Emp Here 125
SIC 8721 Accounting, auditing, and bookkeeping
Pierre Lucien

D-U-N-S 24-815-4957   (HQ)
BELANGER SAUVE S.E.N.C.R.L.
5 Place Ville-Marie Bureau 900, Montreal, QC, H3B 2G2
(514) 878-3081
Sales 13,860,250
SIC 8111 Legal services

Pierre Sauve
Alain-Claude Desforge
Michel Dupuy

D-U-N-S 24-101-7354   (SL)
BESSEMER AND LAKE ERIE RAILROAD COMPANY
(Suby of COMPAGNIE DES CHEMINS DE FER NATIONAUX DU CANADA)
935 Rue De La Gauchetiere O Bureau 11, Montreal, QC, H3B 2M9
(514) 399-4536
Emp Here 502   *Sales* 247,879,066
SIC 4011 Railroads, line-haul operating
Hans Burkhard

D-U-N-S 24-547-7906   (HQ)
BIMCOR INC
(Suby of BCE INC)
1000 Rue De La Gauchetiere O Bureau 1300, Montreal, QC, H3B 5A7
(514) 394-4750
Sales 26,560,350
SIC 6282 Investment advice
Curtis J.E Millen
Remy Orsoli
Michel Lalande
Bernard Le Duc
Michael Keenan

D-U-N-S 20-549-7329   (BR)
BLAKE, CASSELS & GRAYDON LLP
(Suby of BLAKE, CASSELS & GRAYDON LLP)
1 Place Ville-Marie Bureau 3000, Montreal, QC, H3B 4N8
(514) 982-4000
Emp Here 120
SIC 8111 Legal services
Alex Chan

D-U-N-S 20-227-6952   (HQ)
BOMBARDIER INC
BOMBARDIER AERONAUTIQUE
800 Boul Rene-Levesque O 29e Etage, Montreal, QC, H3B 1Y8
(514) 861-9481
Emp Here 4,500   *Sales* 16,236,000,000
SIC 3743 Railroad equipment
Alain Bellemare
Pierre Beaudoin
J.R. Andre Bombardier
Jean-Louis Fontaine
John Di Bert
Daniel Brennan
Francois Caza
Mtre Daniel Desjardins
Mike Nadolski
Louis G. Veronneau

D-U-N-S 25-498-7142   (BR)
BORDEN LADNER GERVAIS LLP
BLG
(Suby of BORDEN LADNER GERVAIS LLP)
1000 Rue De La Gauchetiere O Bureau 900, Montreal, QC, H3B 5H4
(514) 879-1212
Emp Here 300
SIC 8111 Legal services
Richard Carl

D-U-N-S 25-201-7496   (SL)
BOWATER PRODUITS FORESTIERS DU CANADA ULC
1155 Metcalfe Rue Bureau 800, Montreal, QC, H3B 5H2

Emp Here 4,280   *Sales* 783,949,000
SIC 2621 Paper mills

D-U-N-S 20-175-6132   (HQ)
CABINET DE RELATIONS PUBLIQUES NATIONAL INC, LE
AD-LIB FORMATION
(Suby of GROUPE CONSEIL RES PUBLICA INC)
1155 Rue Metcalfe Suite 800, Montreal, QC,

H3B 0C1
(514) 843-7171
Emp Here 70   *Sales* 20,515,660
SIC 8743 Public relations services
Luc Ouelette
Raplh Sutton
Serge Paquette
Zdenka Buric
Andrew T. Molson
John Crean
Royal Poulin
Jean-Pierre Vasseur
Valerie Beauregard
Sarah Elizabeth Diamond

D-U-N-S 20-052-4267   (BR)
CAIN LAMARRE CASGRAIN WELLS, S.E.N.C.R.L.
(Suby of CAIN LAMARRE CASGRAIN WELLS, S.E.N.C.R.L.)
630 Boul Rene-Levesque O Bureau 2780, Montreal, QC, H3B 1S6
(514) 393-4580
Emp Here 80
SIC 8111 Legal services
Stephane Lamarre

D-U-N-S 20-715-6741   (BR)
CALIAN LTD
SED SYSTEMS ENGINEER, A DIV OF
(Suby of CALIAN GROUP LTD)
700 Rue De La Gauchetiere O Bureau 26e, Montreal, QC, H3B 5M2

Emp Here 300
SIC 7361 Employment agencies
Natalie Tremblay

D-U-N-S 25-108-4034   (BR)
CANACCORD GENUITY CORP
(Suby of CANACCORD GENUITY GROUP INC)
1250 Boul Rene-Levesque O Bureau 2000, Montreal, QC, H3B 4W8

Emp Here 100
SIC 6211 Security brokers and dealers
Guy Brunet

D-U-N-S 24-801-0464   (HQ)
CANADIAN NATIONAL RAILWAYS PENSION TRUST FUND
CN INVESTMENT, DIV OF
(Suby of COMPAGNIE DES CHEMINS DE FER NATIONAUX DU CANADA)
5 Place Ville-Marie Bureau 1100, Montreal, QC, H3B 2G2
(514) 399-5963
Sales 89,917,721
SIC 6726 Investment offices, nec
Tullio Cedraschi

D-U-N-S 25-992-2375   (HQ)
CANADIAN ROYALTIES INC
NUNAVIK NICKEL PROJECT
(Suby of JILIN JIEN NICKEL INDUSTRY CO., LTD.)
800 Boul Rene-Levesque O Bureau 410, Montreal, QC, H3B 1X9
(514) 879-1688
Emp Here 65   *Sales* 63,943,500
SIC 1081 Metal mining services
Parviz Farsangi
Denis Doucet
Louiza Benzekri
Marc-Andre De Seve
James Xiang
Ruobing Wang
Qin Hongwei

D-U-N-S 20-178-1833   (BR)
CARTHOS SERVICES LP
OSLER HOSKIN & HARCOURT
(Suby of CARTHOS SERVICES LP)
1000 Rue De La Gauchetiere O Bureau 2100, Montreal, QC, H3B 4W5

(514) 904-8100
Emp Here 150
SIC 8111 Legal services
Marc Boulet

D-U-N-S 20-302-9244   (SL)
CENTRE SHERATON LIMITED PARTNERSHIP, LE
1201 Boul Rene-Levesque O Bureau 217, Montreal, QC, H3B 2L7
(514) 878-2000
Emp Here 250   *Sales* 23,917,000
SIC 7011 Hotels and motels
Stephen P. Foster

D-U-N-S 20-381-1398   (SL)
CHATEAU CHAMPLAIN LIMITED PARTNERSHIP
CHATEAU CHAMPLAIN
1050 Rue De La Gauchetiere O, Montreal, QC, H3B 4C9
(514) 878-9000
Emp Here 250   *Sales* 23,917,000
SIC 7011 Hotels and motels
Jacob Sofer

D-U-N-S 24-101-7552   (SL)
CHICAGO, CENTRAL & PACIFIC RAILROAD COMPANY
(Suby of COMPAGNIE DES CHEMINS DE FER NATIONAUX DU CANADA)
935 Rue De La Gauchetiere O, Montreal, QC, H3B 2M9
(514) 399-4536
Emp Here 3,218   *Sales* 1,588,993,694
SIC 4011 Railroads, line-haul operating
Hans Burkhard

D-U-N-S 24-324-7681   (BR)
CHUBB INSURANCE COMPANY OF CANADA
CHUBB DU CANADA COMPANY D'ASSURANCE
(Suby of CHUBB LIMITED)
1250 Boul Rene-Levesque O Bureau 2700, Montreal, QC, H3B 4W8
(514) 938-4000
Emp Here 75
SIC 6331 Fire, marine, and casualty insurance
Brent Mcallister

D-U-N-S 20-714-3681   (BR)
CIBC INVESTOR SERVICES INC
CIBC INVESTORS EDGE
(Suby of CANADIAN IMPERIAL BANK OF COMMERCE)
1155 Boul Rene-Levesque O Bureau 1501, Montreal, QC, H3B 2J6
(514) 876-3343
Emp Here 85
SIC 6282 Investment advice
Jean-Marc Farley

D-U-N-S 25-293-8881   (BR)
CIBC WORLD MARKETS INC
CIBC WOOD GUNDY
(Suby of CANADIAN IMPERIAL BANK OF COMMERCE)
1 Place Ville-Marie Bureau 4125, Montreal, QC, H3B 3P9
(514) 392-7600
Emp Here 80
SIC 6211 Security brokers and dealers
Charles Martel

D-U-N-S 20-107-3496   (BR)
CINEPLEX ODEON CORPORATION
CINEMA BANQUE SCOTIA MONTREAL
(Suby of CINEPLEX INC)
977 Rue Sainte-Catherine O, Montreal, QC, H3B 4W3
(514) 842-0549
Emp Here 200
SIC 7832 Motion picture theaters, except drive-in
Joe De Luca

D-U-N-S 25-759-5579   (SL)

COFOMO INC
1000 Rue De La Gauchetiere O Unite 1500, Montreal, QC, H3B 4X5
(514) 866-0039
Emp Here 450   *Sales* 75,081,150
SIC 7379 Computer related services, nec
Regis Desjardins

D-U-N-S 24-909-2206   (HQ)
COGECO COMMUNICATIONS INC
(Suby of GESTION AUDEM INC)
5 Place Ville-Marie Bureau 1700, Montreal, QC, H3B 0B3
(514) 874-2600
Emp Here 400   *Sales* 1,842,025,688
SIC 4841 Cable and other pay television services
Jan Peeters
Louis Audet
Christian Jolivet
David Mcausland
Patricia Curadeau-Grou
Joanne Ferstman
Lib Gibson
Carole J. Salomon
Colleen Abdoulah
James C. Cherry

D-U-N-S 20-332-5121   (SL)
COGECO CONNEXION INC
(Suby of GESTION AUDEM INC)
5 Place Ville-Marie Bureau 1700, Montreal, QC, H3B 0B3
(514) 764-4700
Emp Here 1,000   *Sales* 334,544,000
SIC 4841 Cable and other pay television services
Ken Smithard
Caroline Dignard
Louis Audet
Jan Peeters
Christian Jolivet
Patrice Ouimet

D-U-N-S 24-050-4050   (HQ)
COGECO INC
COGECO & DESSIN
(Suby of GESTION AUDEM INC)
5 Place Ville-Marie Bureau 1700, Montreal, QC, H3B 0B3
(514) 764-4700
Emp Here 497   *Sales* 1,929,147,523
SIC 4832 Radio broadcasting stations
Philippe Jette
Christian Jolivet
Marie-Helene Labrie
Luc Noiseux
Diane Nyisztor
Patrice Ouimet
Elizabeth Alves
Philippe Bonin
Nathalie Dorval
Martin Grenier

D-U-N-S 20-309-3794   (HQ)
COGECO MEDIA ACQUISITIONS INC
CHMP
(Suby of GESTION AUDEM INC)
5 Place Ville-Marie Bureau 1700, Montreal, QC, H3B 0B3
(514) 764-4700
Emp Here 1   *Sales* 294,965,763
SIC 6712 Bank holding companies
Richard Lachance
Marie-Claude Laroche
Louis Audet
Jan Peeters
Christian Jolivet
Patrice Ouimet

D-U-N-S 20-887-5484   (SL)
COLLEGE DES MEDECINS DU QUEBEC
1250 Boul Rene-Levesque O Bureau 3500, Montreal, QC, H3B 0G2
(514) 933-4441
Emp Here 90   *Sales* 21,736,350

SIC 8621 Professional organizations
Charles Bernard
Josee Dubois
Jean-Pierre Boucher
Yves Robert
Yves Langlois
Suzanne Lalonde
Nicole Vallieres
Armand Aalamian
Jean-Pierre Dubeau
Richard Essiambre

D-U-N-S 24-251-5476   (SL)
COLLINS BARROW MONTREAL
625 Boul Rene-Levesque O Bureau 1100,
Montreal, QC, H3B 1R2
(514) 866-8553
Emp Here 60   Sales 12,461,100
SIC 8721 Accounting, auditing, and book-
keeping
Joseph Schlesinger
Lionel Goldman
Lorne Richter
Abe Zylberlight
Sonia Medvescek
Howard Berish
Jeffrey Greenberg
Stuart Ladd
Antoinette Coluni
Florentyna Jallet

D-U-N-S 20-106-9817   (HQ)
COMMUNAUTO INC
ASSOCIATION NORD-AMERICAINE DE
SERVICE DE PARTAGE DE VEHICULES
1117 Rue Sainte-Catherine O Bureau 806,
Montreal, QC, H3B 1H9
(514) 842-4545
Emp Here 20   Sales 14,165,000
SIC 7515 Passenger car leasing
Benoit Robert
Marco Viviani
Jean-Francois Charette
Antonio Occhionero
Brigitte Courtehoux

D-U-N-S 20-370-9860   (SL)
COMPAGNIE BROADSIGN CANADA
1100 Boul Robert-Bourassa 12e Etage, Mon-
treal, QC, H3B 3A5
(514) 399-1184
Emp Here 90   Sales 15,957,990
SIC 7371 Custom computer programming ser-
vices
Burr Smith
Dana Tunks
Jean Beaudry

D-U-N-S 20-882-7139   (SL)
**COMPAGNIE D'ASSURANCE MISSISQUOI,
LA**
(Suby of ECONOMICAL MUTUAL INSUR-
ANCE COMPANY)
5 Place Ville-Marie Unite 1400, Montreal, QC,
H3B 2G2
(514) 875-5790
Emp Here 205   Sales 438,078,440
SIC 6331 Fire, marine, and casualty insurance
Rowan Saunders
Barbara Fraser
Dan J. Fortin
Micheal J. Kelly
Michael Padfield
Philip Mather
Gerald A. Hopper
Michael P. Stramaglia
John H. Bowey
Richard M. Freeborough

D-U-N-S 20-883-5231   (HQ)
COMPAGNIE D'ASSURANCE SONNET
(Suby of ECONOMICAL MUTUAL INSUR-
ANCE COMPANY)
5 Place Ville-Marie Bureau 1400, Montreal,
QC, H3B 0A8
(514) 875-5790
Emp Here 210   Sales 662,460,080

SIC 6331 Fire, marine, and casualty insurance
Rowan Saunders
Michael Padfield
Philip Mather
Gerard A. Hooper
Michael P. Stramaglia
John H. Bowey
Richard M. Freebrough
W. David Wilson
Elizabeth Delbianco
Barbara Fraser

D-U-N-S 20-581-4861   (BR)
**COMPAGNIE DES CHEMINS DE FER NA-
TIONAUX DU CANADA**
CN INVESTMENT, DIV
(Suby of COMPAGNIE DES CHEMINS DE
FER NATIONAUX DU CANADA)
5 Place Ville-Marie Bureau 1100, Montreal,
QC, H3B 2G2
(514) 399-4811
Emp Here 75
SIC 4011 Railroads, line-haul operating
Russell J Hiscock

D-U-N-S 20-213-5729   (HQ)
**COMPAGNIE DES CHEMINS DE FER NA-
TIONAUX DU CANADA**
CANADIAN NATIONAL RAILWAY
935 Rue De La Gauchetiere 16e Etage O,
Montreal, QC, H3B 2M9
(514) 399-5430
Emp Here 1,000   Sales 10,856,778,742
SIC 4011 Railroads, line-haul operating
Jean-Jacques Ruest
Mike Cory
Sean Finn
Ghislain Houle
Kimberly A. Madigan
Michael Foster
Doug Macdonald
Keith Reardon
Mitch Beekman
Bernd Beyer

D-U-N-S 20-432-9882   (HQ)
COMPAGNIE MINIERE IOC INC
(Suby of RIO TINTO PLC)
1190 Av Des Canadiens-De-Montreal Bureau
400, Montreal, QC, H3B 0E3
(418) 968-7400
Emp Here 25   Sales 511,548,000
SIC 1011 Iron ores
Clayton Walker
Thierry Martel
Maurice Mcclure
Maxime Savignac
Marie-Christine Dupont
Mark Fuller
Yasutaku Okamoto
Kenji Nakamura
William Mcneil

D-U-N-S 25-275-0042   (SL)
CONWAY JACQUES COURTIERS
1250 Boul Rene-Levesque O, Montreal, QC,
H3B 4W8
(514) 935-4242
Emp Here 49   Sales 90,486,291
SIC 6311 Life insurance
Andre Deschambault

D-U-N-S 25-973-3269   (SL)
DANA LOGIC INC
1155 Boul Rene-Levesque O Bureau 2500,
Montreal, QC, H3B 2K4
(514) 845-5326
Emp Here 65   Sales 13,900,315
SIC 7372 Prepackaged software
Lam Vien Nguyen

D-U-N-S 20-883-5264   (SL)
DE GRANDPRE CHAIT S.E.N.C.R.L.
1000 Rue De La Gauchetiere O Bureau 2900,
Montreal, QC, H3B 4W5
(514) 878-4311
Emp Here 100   Sales 11,088,200

SIC 8111 Legal services
Eric David
Jonathan Maxime Fecteau
Martin Delisle
Stephen Solomon
Philipp Duffy
Stephane Lalande
Sylvain Belair
Martin Raymond
Eric Lasry
Stephanie La Rocque

D-U-N-S 24-989-1268   (SL)
DENAULT, BERGERON & ASSOCIES INC
1100 Boul Rene-Levesque O Bureau 1520,
Montreal, QC, H3B 4N4
Emp Here 140   Sales 10,457,160
SIC 7363 Help supply services
Guy Denault

D-U-N-S 24-226-7180   (BR)
DENTONS CANADA LLP
SERVICES FMC
(Suby of DENTONS CANADA LLP)
1 Place Ville-Marie Bureau 3900, Montreal,
QC, H3B 4M7
(514) 878-8800
Emp Here 300
SIC 8111 Legal services
Claude Morency

D-U-N-S 25-275-6247   (SL)
**DEVELOPPEMENT EDF RENOUVE-
LABLES INC**
DEVELOPPEMENT EDF EN CANADA
1134 Rue Sainte-Catherine O Bureau 910,
Montreal, QC, H3B 1H4
(514) 397-9997
Emp Here 304   Sales 82,337,792
SIC 1711 Plumbing, heating, air-conditioning
Alfred Kurzenhauser
Cory Basil
Robin Deveaux
Marc Mcclean

D-U-N-S 20-793-1106   (HQ)
DEVENCORE INVESTMENTS INC
DEVENCORE - NKF
800 Boul Rene-Levesque O Bureau 900, Mon-
treal, QC, H3B 1X9
(514) 392-1330
Sales 29,322,230
SIC 6531 Real estate agents and managers
Jacques Gagnier
Susan Tutt
Jean Laurin
Stephen Cheasley
John T Bishop
David Fullerton

D-U-N-S 24-529-6876   (HQ)
DEVENCORE LTEE
NEWMARK KNIGHT FRANK - DEVENCORE
(Suby of DEVENCORE INVESTMENTS INC)
800 Boul Rene-Levesque O Bureau 900, Mon-
treal, QC, H3B 1X9
(514) 392-1330
Emp Here 5   Sales 41,888,900
SIC 6531 Real estate agents and managers
Jean Laurin
Susan Tutt
Stephen Cheasley
Jacques Gagnier

D-U-N-S 24-435-1466   (HQ)
DIAMANTS BASAL INC
PRINCEBELLA
1255 Boul Robert-Bourassa Bureau 460,
Montreal, QC, H3B 3B6
(514) 861-6675
Sales 10,410,840
SIC 5094 Jewelry and precious stones
Karen Segalovith

D-U-N-S 20-596-8878   (SL)
DIVISION DES INVESTISSEMENTS DU CN

5 Place Ville-Marie Bureau 101, Montreal, QC,
H3B 2G2
(514) 399-4811
Emp Here 49   Sales 40,561,073
SIC 6726 Investment offices, nec

D-U-N-S 24-101-7396   (SL)
**DULUTH, MISSABE AND IRON RANGE
RAILWAY COMPANY**
(Suby of COMPAGNIE DES CHEMINS DE
FER NATIONAUX DU CANADA)
935 Rue De La Gauchetiere O Bureau 4e,
Montreal, QC, H3B 2M9
(514) 399-4536
Emp Here 502
SIC 4011 Railroads, line-haul operating
Hans Burkhard

D-U-N-S 24-958-2313   (HQ)
EACOM TIMBER CORPORATION
(Suby of KELSO & COMPANY, L.P.)
1100 Boul Rene-Levesque O Bureau 2110,
Montreal, QC, H3B 4N4
(514) 848-6815
Emp Here 15   Sales 278,390,000
SIC 2426 Hardwood dimension and flooring
mills
Kevin Edgson
Jeff Webber
Patrick Belisle
Joseph Jay Gurandiano
Christopher D Hodgson
Philip E. Berney
George E. Matelich
Matthew S. Edgerton

D-U-N-S 24-356-9386   (BR)
**ECONOMICAL MUTUAL INSURANCE COM-
PANY**
COMPAGNIE D'ASSURANCE MISSISQUOI,
LA
(Suby of ECONOMICAL MUTUAL INSUR-
ANCE COMPANY)
5 Place Ville-Marie Unite 1400, Montreal, QC,
H3B 2G2
(514) 875-5790
Emp Here 300
SIC 6331 Fire, marine, and casualty insurance
Ronald Pavelack

D-U-N-S 20-271-4531   (HQ)
EGR INC
ASSURACTION
(Suby of GROUPE FINANCIER ESSOR INC)
1100 Boul Robert-Bourassa 6e Etage, Mon-
treal, QC, H3B 3A5
(514) 370-4800
Emp Here 20   Sales 897,013,656
SIC 6411 Insurance agents, brokers, and ser-
vice
Richard Drouin
Michel Duval
Francois Boyer
Simon Marchand-Fortier
Serge Boucher
Jocelyn Tessier
Antoine Leblanc

D-U-N-S 24-205-8415   (BR)
ELECTRONIC ARTS (CANADA) INC
EA SPORTS
(Suby of ELECTRONIC ARTS INC.)
3 Place Ville-Marie Bureau 12350, Montreal,
QC, H3B 0E7
(514) 448-8800
Emp Here 500
SIC 7371 Custom computer programming ser-
vices
Alain Tascan

D-U-N-S 20-182-7966   (HQ)
ELITE GROUP INC
1175 Place Du Frere-Andre, Montreal, QC,
H3B 3X9
(514) 383-4720
Sales 22,358,700
SIC 5064 Electrical appliances, television and

radio
Danny Lavy
Marie-Michele Normandeau
Marla Ruttenberg

D-U-N-S 24-393-5074   (SL)
ENERCON CANADA INC
(Suby of ALOYS WOBBEN STIFTUNG)
700 Rue De La Gauchetiere O Bureau 1200,
Montreal, QC, H3B 5M2
(514) 363-7266
Emp Here 100   Sales 25,349,000
SIC 8748 Business consulting, nec
Hans-Dieter Kettwig
Meinhard Stelte
Michael Weidemann

D-U-N-S 20-363-0751   (SL)
ENERGERE INC
(Suby of GESTION E.C.I. INC)
1200 Av Mcgill College Bureau 700, Montreal,
QC, H3B 4G7
(514) 848-9199
Emp Here 50   Sales 13,077,650
SIC 6712 Bank holding companies
Frederic Gaulin

D-U-N-S 20-104-2129   (HQ)
EQUISOFT INC
1250 Boul Rene-Levesque O 33e Etage, Mon-
treal, QC, H3B 4W8
(514) 989-3141
Sales 18,353,170
SIC 7379 Computer related services, nec
Luis Romero
Sylvain Brosseau
Fulvo Bussandri
Stephane Gilker
Paul Villemaire
Laird Elliott
Daniel O'hara
Nicolas Ledoux
Steeve Michaud

D-U-N-S 24-174-2662   (BR)
ERNST & YOUNG LLP
(Suby of ERNST & YOUNG LLP)
1 Place Ville-Marie Bureau 1900, Montreal,
QC, H3B 1X9
(514) 875-6060
Emp Here 700
SIC 8721 Accounting, auditing, and book-
keeping
Guy Flechette

D-U-N-S 20-265-5049   (HQ)
**ESSOR ASSURANCES PLACEMENTS
CONSEILS INC**
ESSOR ASSURANCES
(Suby of GROUPE FINANCIER ESSOR INC)
1100 Boul Robert-Bourassa, Montreal, QC,
H3B 3A5
(514) 878-9373
Emp Here 10   Sales 1,423,831,200
SIC 6411 Insurance agents, brokers, and ser-
vice
Michel Duval

D-U-N-S 20-303-6694   (SL)
EVOLOCITY FINANCIAL GROUP INC
AVANCE MERCANTILE
(Suby of ON DECK CAPITAL, INC.)
1100 Boul Rene-Levesque O Bureau 1825,
Montreal, QC, H3B 4N4
(877) 781-0148
Emp Here 49   Sales 11,480,112
SIC 8742 Management consulting services
Greenspoon Harley
David Souaid
Neil Wechsler

D-U-N-S 25-308-3950   (HQ)
FACILITE INFORMATIQUE CANADA INC
FACILITE INFORMATIQUE
(Suby of CGI INC)
5 Place Ville-Marie Bureau 1045, Montreal,
QC, H3B 2G2

(514) 284-5636
Emp Here 120
SIC 7379 Computer related services, nec
Francois Boulanger
Benoit Dube
Kevin Linder
Max Rogan

D-U-N-S 24-632-8517   (SL)
FAGEN & FILS
625 Rue Belmont, Montreal, QC, H3B 2M1

Emp Here 26   Sales 13,534,092
SIC 5093 Scrap and waste materials
Lesly Fagen

D-U-N-S 24-890-4237   (BR)
FAIRMONT HOTELS & RESORTS INC
FAIRMONT HOTEL LE REINE ELIZABETH
(Suby of ACCOR)
900 Boul Rene-Levesque O, Montreal, QC,
H3B 4A5
(514) 861-3511
Emp Here 700
SIC 7011 Hotels and motels
Martin Leclair

D-U-N-S 20-356-5601   (HQ)
FAIRSTONE FINANCIERE INC
FAIRSTONE SALES SOLUTIONS
630 Boul Rene-Levesque O Bureau 1400,
Montreal, QC, H3B 1S6
(800) 995-2274
Emp Here 50   Sales 687,271,000
SIC 6141 Personal credit institutions
Scott Wood
Carol A. Bell
Patricia Curadeau-Grou
Aneek Mamik
Thomas Harding
R. Alexander Mills
John Oros

D-U-N-S 24-970-6052   (HQ)
FEDNAV INTERNATIONAL LTEE
FEDERAL ATLANTIC LAKES LINE (FALL
LINE)
1000 Rue De La Gauchetiere O Bureau 3500,
Montreal, QC, H3B 4W5
(514) 878-6500
Emp Here 55   Sales 23,623,440
SIC 4412 Deep sea foreign transportation of
freight
Paul M. Pathy
Paul A. Gourdeau
David Grieve
James E. Cobb
Wojtek Hryckowian
Andrew Mallalieu
John M.B Williams
Christopher D. De Caires
Peter N. Boos

D-U-N-S 20-218-5476   (HQ)
FEDNAV LIMITEE
CANARCTIC
(Suby of OCEANPATH INC)
1000 Rue De La Gauchetiere O Bureau 3500,
Montreal, QC, H3B 4W5
(514) 878-6500
Emp Here 125   Sales 83,366,640
SIC 4412 Deep sea foreign transportation of
freight

D-U-N-S 20-422-3044   (HQ)
FINANCIERE BANQUE NATIONALE INC
NATIONAL BANK INDEPENDENT NET-
WORK DIV.
5e Etage 1155, Rue Metcalfe, Montreal, QC,
H3B 2V6
(514) 879-2222
Emp Here 700   Sales 572,515,922
SIC 6021 National commercial banks
Davis Brian
Martin Lavigne
Martin Theriault
Alain Legris

Martin Gagnon
Denis Brind'amour
Denis Girouard

D-U-N-S 25-200-2134   (SL)
**FOND D'ASSURANCE RESPONSABILITE
PROFESSIONNELLE DE LA CHAMBRE
DES NOTAIRES DU QUEBEC**
FARPCNQ
1200 Av Mcgill College Bureau 1500, Mon-
treal, QC, H3B 4G7
(514) 871-4999
Emp Here 20   Sales 20,697,620
SIC 6351 Surety insurance
Marlene Ouellet

D-U-N-S 24-852-8577   (HQ)
FOREX INC
BOIS NOBLES KA'N'ENDA
1250 Boul Rene-Levesque O Bureau 3930,
Montreal, QC, H3B 4W8
(514) 935-0702
Emp Here 10   Sales 20,661,700
SIC 0851 Forestry services
Jean-Jacques Cossette
Alain Cossette

D-U-N-S 24-141-4486   (SL)
FULLER LANDAU SENCRL
1010 Rue De La Gauchetiere O Bureau 200,
Montreal, QC, H3B 2S1
(514) 875-2865
Emp Here 70   Sales 14,537,950
SIC 8721 Accounting, auditing, and book-
keeping
Melvin Greene
Nick Moraitis
Myer Spivak
Gilles Marleau
Rejean Roy
Patrick Sullivan
Ernest Furt
Frank Fiorino
Edward Prorok
Joshua Miller

D-U-N-S 20-551-4644   (SL)
GASTEM INC
1155 Boul Robert-Bourassa Unite 1215, Montreal, QC, H3B 3A7

Emp Here 10   Sales 46,637,547
SIC 1382 Oil and gas exploration services
Raymond Savoie
Regent Watier
Zoran Arnadjelovic
Murray Rodgers
Jonathan Kelafant
Paul Glover
Michel Lemoine

D-U-N-S 20-104-3499   (SL)
GENOME QUEBEC
BIO BANQUE GENIZON
630 Boul Rene-Levesque O Bureau 2660,
Montreal, QC, H3B 1S6
(514) 398-0668
Emp Here 100   Sales 22,975,400
SIC 8731 Commercial physical research
Martin Godbout
Marie-Lucie Morin
Suzanne Vinet
Brian White-Guay
Francois R. Roy
Anie Perrault
Sophie D'amours
Jean Brunet
Helene Desmarais
Paule Tetu

D-U-N-S 25-258-1368   (HQ)
GESTION ALCOA CANADA CIE
(Suby of ALUMINERIE LAURALCO SARL)
1 Place Ville-Marie Bureau 2310, Montreal,
QC, H3B 3M5
(514) 904-5030
Sales 1,425,109,000

SIC 3334 Primary aluminum
Martin Briere
Louis Langlois
Amelie Moreault
Agnello Borim
Jean-Francois Cyr
Alain Taillefer
Nicklaus A. Oliver

D-U-N-S 24-836-1248   (HQ)
GESTION AUDEM INC
5 Place Ville-Marie Bureau 915, Montreal, QC,
H3B 2G2
(514) 874-2600
Emp Here 5   Sales 917,772,024
SIC 4833 Television broadcasting stations
Louis Audet
Louis Caouette
Francois Audet

D-U-N-S 20-886-7507   (HQ)
GESTION D'ACTIFS CIBC INC
(Suby of CANADIAN IMPERIAL BANK OF
COMMERCE)
1000 Rue De La Gauchetiere O Bureau 3100,
Montreal, QC, H3B 4W5
(514) 875-7040
Sales 1,167,385,000
SIC 6726 Investment offices, nec
David Scandiffio
Jon Hountalas
Doris Mariga
Frank Vivacqua
Steven Meston
Stephen Gittens
Lee Bennett
Edward Dodig
Jessica Childs

D-U-N-S 25-211-1950   (SL)
GESTION DE PORTEFEUILLE NATCAN INC
1100 Boul Robert-Bourassa Unite 400, Montreal, QC, H3B 3A5

Emp Here 110   Sales 30,068,500
SIC 6719 Holding companies, nec
Melanie Frappier
Eric Bujold
Brian Davis
Martin Gagnon

D-U-N-S 24-131-1369   (SL)
GESTION FERIQUE
FERIQUE GESTION DE FONDS
1010 Rue De La Gauchetiere O, Montreal,
QC, H3B 2N2
(514) 840-9206
Emp Here 25   Sales 20,694,425
SIC 6722 Management investment, open-end

D-U-N-S 20-897-3037   (SL)
GESTION MD MANAGEMENT
1000 Rue De La Gauchetiere O Bureau 650,
Montreal, QC, H3B 4W5
(514) 392-1434
Emp Here 45   Sales 12,344,940
SIC 8741 Management services

D-U-N-S 20-317-5778   (SL)
GESTION NEUF ASSOCIES INC
NEUF ARCHITECTS
630 Boul Rene-Levesque O Bureau 3200,
Montreal, QC, H3B 1S6
(514) 847-1117
Emp Here 84   Sales 15,014,076
SIC 8712 Architectural services
Andre Cousineau
Bruno St-Jean
Antoine Cousineau
Anh Le Quang
Azad Chichmanian
Jean-Francois Trahan
Guy Caron

D-U-N-S 24-904-2003   (SL)
GESTIONS DOROTHEE MINVILLE INC
PHARMAPRIX

390 Rue Sainte-Catherine O, Montreal, QC,
H3B 1A1
(514) 875-7070
Emp Here 60   *Sales* 14,659,680
SIC 5912 Drug stores and proprietary stores
  Dorothee Minville

D-U-N-S 20-211-8746   (BR)
GESTIONS MONIT LTEE, LES
(*Suby of* GESTIONS MONIT LTEE, LES)
1255 Rue University, Montreal, QC, H3B 3X4
(514) 861-9772
Emp Here 200
SIC 6531 Real estate agents and managers
  Pierre Cuccioletta

D-U-N-S 24-676-6682   (HQ)
GOOGLE CANADA CORPORATION
(*Suby of* ALPHABET INC.)
1253 Av Mcgill College Bureau 150, Montreal,
QC, H3B 2Y5
(514) 670-8700
Sales 17,731,100
SIC 7375 Information retrieval services
  Kathryn W. Hall
  Robert Andreatta

D-U-N-S 20-057-0450   (BR)
GOWLING WLG (CANADA) LLP
(*Suby of* GOWLING WLG (CANADA) LLP)
1 Place Ville-Marie Bureau 3700, Montreal,
QC, H3B 3P4
(514) 878-9641
Emp Here 200
SIC 8111 Legal services

D-U-N-S 20-912-5678   (BR)
GOWLINGS CANADA INC
(*Suby of* GOWLINGS CANADA INC)
1 Place Ville-Marie Bureau 3700, Montreal,
QC, H3B 3P4
(514) 878-9641
Emp Here 150
SIC 8111 Legal services
  Sharon Mitchell

D-U-N-S 24-101-7479   (SL)
**GRAND TRUNK WESTERN RAILROAD IN-
CORPORATED**
(*Suby of* COMPAGNIE DES CHEMINS DE
FER NATIONAUX DU CANADA)
935 Rue De La Gauchetiere O Bureau 14,
Montreal, QC, H3B 2M9
(514) 399-4536
Emp Here 1,400   *Sales* 553,613,200
SIC 4731 Freight transportation arrangement
  Hans Burkhard

D-U-N-S 25-080-3228   (SL)
GROUPE ALTUS
1100 Boul Rene-Levesque O Bureau 1600,
Montreal, QC, H3B 4N4

Emp Here 40   *Sales* 16,755,560
SIC 6531 Real estate agents and managers
  Jean-Guy Bernard
  Michel Bouchard
  Josee Derepentigny
  Pierre Laliberte
  Mario Picard
  Sylvain Leclair
  Jean-Francois Rioux

D-U-N-S 24-020-7712   (HQ)
GROUPE CONSEIL RES PUBLICA INC
RES PUBLICA
1155 Rue Metcalfe Bureau 800, Montreal, QC,
H3B 0C1
(514) 843-2343
Emp Here 100   *Sales* 91,377,250
SIC 6712 Bank holding companies
  Andrew T. Molson
  Jean-Pierre Vasseur
  Valerie Beauregard
  Royal Poulin
  Pat Przybyski
  Gary R. Koops

Doris Juergens

D-U-N-S 25-286-0630   (HQ)
**GROUPE FACILITE INFORMATIQUE (GFI)
INC**
(*Suby of* 3330559 CANADA INC)
5 Place Ville-Marie Bureau 1045, Montreal,
QC, H3B 2G2
(514) 284-5636
Emp Here 100
SIC 7371 Custom computer programming ser-
vices
  Gary Butler

D-U-N-S 20-714-6346   (BR)
GROUPE SPORTSCENE INC
CAGE AU SPORT, LA
(*Suby of* GROUPE SPORTSCENE INC)
1212 Rue De La Gauchetiere O, Montreal,
QC, H3B 2S2
(514) 925-2255
Emp Here 80
SIC 5812 Eating places
  Benoit Gaulin

D-U-N-S 24-759-7008   (HQ)
GROUPE VISION NEW LOOK INC
BOUTIQUE NEW LOOK SIGNATURE
(*Suby of* CANADIAN DEPOSITORY FOR SE-
CURITIES LIMITED, THE)
1 Place Ville-Marie Suite 3670, Montreal, QC,
H3B 3P2
(514) 877-4119
Emp Here 27   *Sales* 220,631,941
SIC 5995 Optical goods stores
  W John Bennett
  Antoine Amiel
  Tania Clarke
  Richard Cherney
  Emmett C. Pearson
  Paul S Echenberg
  William M. Cleman
  Denyse Chicoine
  Pierre Matuszewski

D-U-N-S 20-858-1710   (SL)
GSMPRJCT CREATION INC
GSM PROJECT
355 Rue Sainte-Catherine O Bureau 500,
Montreal, QC, H3B 1A5
(514) 288-4233
Emp Here 70   *Sales* 46,823,560
SIC 7389 Business services, nec
  Yves Mayrand
  Alexandre Taillefer
  Annie Derome

D-U-N-S 24-803-2133   (BR)
H&M HENNES & MAURITZ INC
H & M
(*Suby of* RAMSBURY INVEST AB)
1100 Rue Sainte-Catherine O, Montreal, QC,
H3B 1H4
(514) 788-4590
Emp Here 100
SIC 5651 Family clothing stores
  Veronique Perrom

D-U-N-S 25-393-1471   (BR)
HATCH CORPORATION
(*Suby of* HATCH CORPORATION)
5 Place Ville-Marie Bureau 1400, Montreal,
QC, H3B 2G2
(514) 861-0583
Emp Here 600
SIC 8711 Engineering services
  Rop Metka

D-U-N-S 20-193-6601   (BR)
HATCH LTD
(*Suby of* HATCHCOS HOLDINGS LTD)
5 Place Ville-Marie Bureau 1400, Montreal,
QC, H3B 2G2
(514) 861-0583
Emp Here 600
SIC 8711 Engineering services
  Rob Metka

D-U-N-S 25-364-7044   (SL)
HEXAVEST INC
(*Suby of* 9264-7064 QUEBEC INC)
1250 Boul Rene-Levesque O Bureau 4200,
Montreal, QC, H3B 4W8
(514) 390-8484
Emp Here 46   *Sales* 10,777,248
SIC 8742 Management consulting services
  Marc Christopher Lavoie
  Denis Rivest
  Vital Proulx
  Robert Brunelle
  Thomas E. Jr. Faust

D-U-N-S 24-101-7511   (SL)
ILLINOIS CENTRAL RAILROAD COMPANY
(*Suby of* COMPAGNIE DES CHEMINS DE
FER NATIONAUX DU CANADA)
935 Rue De La Gauchetiere O Bureau 11,
Montreal, QC, H3B 2M9
(514) 399-4536
Emp Here 3,218   *Sales* 1,588,993,694
SIC 4011 Railroads, line-haul operating
  Hans Burkhard

D-U-N-S 25-990-2328   (SL)
IMAGE HOME PRODUCTS INC, L'
MIGHTY ELECTRIC
1175 Place Du Frere-Andre, Montreal, QC,
H3B 3X9
(514) 383-4720
Emp Here 50   *Sales* 84,260,085
SIC 5063 Electrical apparatus and equipment
  Michael Prazoff
  Marie-Michele Normandeau
  Susan Hodon
  Ian Mendez
  Marla Ruttenberg

D-U-N-S 20-019-8377   (HQ)
**IMPRIMERIES TRANSCONTINENTAL 2005
S.E.N.C.**
ACTIVATION MARKETING
1 Place Ville-Marie Bureau 3240, Montreal,
QC, H3B 0G1
(514) 954-4000
Emp Here 100   *Sales* 1,550,192,000
SIC 2752 Commercial printing, lithographic
  Brian Reid

D-U-N-S 20-763-4510   (HQ)
IMPRIMERIES TRANSCONTINENTAL INC
ABONNEMENT QUEBEC & DESSIN
(*Suby of* TRANSCONTINENTAL INC)
1 Place Ville-Marie Unite 3240, Montreal, QC,
H3B 3Y2
(514) 954-4000
Emp Here 160   *Sales* 762,113,142
SIC 2752 Commercial printing, lithographic
  Brian Reid
  Christine Desaulniers
  Francois Olivier
  Donald Lecavalier

D-U-N-S 25-319-1894   (BR)
INDIGO BOOKS & MUSIC INC
CHAPTERS
(*Suby of* INDIGO BOOKS & MUSIC INC)
1171 Rue Sainte-Catherine O Bureau 777,
Montreal, QC, H3B 1K4

Emp Here 100
SIC 5942 Book stores

D-U-N-S 20-010-8525   (HQ)
INDIGO PARC CANADA INC
GESTIPARC
1 Place Ville-Marie Bureau 1130, Montreal,
QC, H3B 2A7
(514) 874-1208
Emp Here 40   *Sales* 62,787,200
SIC 7299 Miscellaneous personal service
  Wilfried Thierry
  Louis Jacob
  Serge Clemente

D-U-N-S 24-324-8999   (HQ)

D-U-N-S 24-073-0783   (SL)
INFRA-PSP CANADA INC
(*Suby of* GOVERNMENT OF CANADA)
1250 Boul Rene-Levesque O Bureau 1400,
Montreal, QC, H3B 4W8
(514) 937-2772
Emp Here 65   *Sales* 569,255,200
SIC 6282 Investment advice
  Neil Cunningham
  Darren Baccus
  Marie-Claude Cardin
  Alison Breen

D-U-N-S 24-073-0783   (SL)
INVESTISSEMENTS RAYPAUL LTEE, LES
1258 Rue Stanley, Montreal, QC, H3B 2S7
(514) 871-0057
Emp Here 41   *Sales* 13,412,207
SIC 6531 Real estate agents and managers
  Ray Monahan

D-U-N-S 24-051-5023   (HQ)
IOU FINANCIAL INC
1 Place Ville-Marie Bureau 1670, Montreal,
QC, H3B 2B6
(514) 789-0694
Sales 14,531,336
SIC 6712 Bank holding companies
  Philippe Marleau
  Robert Gloer
  Madeline Wade
  Jeff Turner
  Christophe Choquart
  David Kennedy
  Evan Price
  Serguei Kouzmine
  Wayne Pommen
  Yves Roy

D-U-N-S 24-334-0366   (HQ)
IPERCEPTIONS INC
ANALYTIQUE IPERCEPTIONS
606 Rue Cathcart Suite 1007, Montreal, QC,
H3B 1K9
(514) 488-3600
Sales 13,196,580
SIC 8732 Commercial nonphysical research
  Pascal Cardinal
  Martin Le Sauteur
  Dufour Phillippe
  Alexandre Taillefer
  Dominic Becotte
  Denis M Sirois
  Francois-Charles Sirois
  Jerry Tarasofsky

D-U-N-S 20-236-8742   (HQ)
JACK VICTOR LIMITED
1250 Rue Saint-Alexandre Bureau 100, Mon-
treal, QC, H3B 3H6
(514) 866-4891
Emp Here 997   *Sales* 265,335,000
SIC 2311 Men's and boy's suits and coats
  Alan Victor
  Christine Victor

D-U-N-S 20-213-6420   (HQ)
KRONOS CANADA INC
(*Suby of* KRONOS WORLDWIDE, INC.)
1255 Boul Robert-Bourassa Bureau 1102,
Montreal, QC, H3B 3W7
(514) 397-3501
Emp Here 1   *Sales* 207,649,215
SIC 2816 Inorganic pigments
  Robert D Graham
  Antoine B. Doan
  Gregory M. Swalwell
  Frederic Boisselle

D-U-N-S 24-340-0178   (SL)
LAROCHELLE GROUPE CONSEIL INC
1010 Rue De La Gauchetiere O Bureau 650,
Montreal, QC, H3B 2N2
(514) 848-1881
Emp Here 49   *Sales* 11,657,149
SIC 8742 Management consulting services
  Eric Larochelle

D-U-N-S 24-490-2656 (HQ)
LAVERY DE BILLY, SOCIETE EN NOM COL-LECTIF A RESPONSABILITE LIMITEE
1 Place Ville-Marie Bureau 4000, Montreal, QC, H3B 4M4
(514) 871-1522
Emp Here 150 *Sales* 102,938,000
SIC 8111 Legal services
Pierre L. Baribeau
Daniel Bouchard
Rene Branchaud
Andre Champagne
Pierre Denis
Michel Desrosiers
Philippe Frere
Nicolas Gagnon
Catherine Maheu
Elisabeth Pinard

D-U-N-S 20-290-0957 (HQ)
LORD'STACE INC
GEGL
1155 Boul Rene-Levesque O Unite 4000, Montreal, QC, H3B 3V2
(418) 575-4942
Sales 22,358,700
SIC 5063 Electrical apparatus and equipment
Normand Lord

D-U-N-S 20-417-0120 (HQ)
MACDOUGALL, MACDOUGALL & MAC-TIER INC
1010 Rue De La Gauchetiere O Bureau 2000, Montreal, QC, H3B 4J1
(514) 394-3000
Emp Here 100
SIC 6211 Security brokers and dealers

D-U-N-S 25-466-4998 (SL)
MALAGA INC
1 Place Ville-Marie Bureau 4000, Montreal, QC, H3B 4M4
(514) 393-9000
Emp Here 100 *Sales* 23,343,500
SIC 1081 Metal mining services
Jean Martineau
Pierre Monet
Rene Branchaud

D-U-N-S 24-568-1858 (SL)
MASS INSURANCE BROKER
630 Boul Rene-Levesque O Bureau 2500, Montreal, QC, H3B 1S6
(514) 925-3222
Emp Here 49 *Sales* 28,416,276
SIC 6411 Insurance agents, brokers, and service
Andre Morneau

D-U-N-S 24-380-3306 (HQ)
MAYA GOLD & SILVER INC
1 Place Ville-Marie Bureau 2901, Montreal, QC, H3B 0E9
(514) 866-2008
Sales 11,937,745
SIC 1081 Metal mining services
Noureddine Mokaddem
Rene Branchaud
R. Martin Wong
Nikolaos Sofronis
Robert Taub
Elena Clarici

D-U-N-S 20-576-4322 (BR)
MCCARTHY TETRAULT LLP
(*Suby of* MCCARTHY TETRAULT LLP)
1000 Rue De La Gauchetiere O Bureau 2500, Montreal, QC, H3B 0A2

Emp Here 200
SIC 8111 Legal services
Karl Tabbakh

D-U-N-S 25-357-8686 (BR)
MEDIAS TRANSCONTINENTAL INC
SODEMA
(*Suby of* TRANSCONTINENTAL INC)

1155 Boul Rene-Levesque O Unite 100, Montreal, QC, H3B 4R1
(514) 287-1717
Emp Here 400
SIC 7389 Business services, nec

D-U-N-S 24-252-3231 (HQ)
MEDIAS TRANSCONTINENTAL INC
MOOSE JAW TIMES HERALD
(*Suby of* TRANSCONTINENTAL INC)
1 Place Ville Marie Bureau 3240, Montreal, QC, H3B 0G1
(514) 954-4000
Emp Here 200 *Sales* 205,400,440
SIC 2721 Periodicals
Olivier Francois
Christine Desaulniers
Nelson Gentiletti
Donald Lecavalier

D-U-N-S 24-343-2262 (HQ)
MEDIAS TRANSCONTINENTAL S.E.N.C.
AD-BAG
1 Place Ville-Marie Bureau 3315, Montreal, QC, H3B 3N2
(514) 392-9000
Emp Here 200 *Sales* 387,548,000
SIC 2721 Periodicals
Natalie Lariviere

D-U-N-S 25-315-8489 (BR)
MERRILL LYNCH CANADA INC
(*Suby of* BANK OF AMERICA CORPORATION)
1250 Boul Rene-Levesque O Bureau 3100, Montreal, QC, H3B 4W8
(514) 846-1050
Emp Here 100
SIC 6211 Security brokers and dealers

D-U-N-S 20-698-5587 (BR)
MILLER THOMSON LLP
(*Suby of* MILLER THOMSON LLP)
1000 Rue De La Gauchetiere O Bureau 3700, Montreal, QC, H3B 4W5
(514) 875-5210
Emp Here 100
SIC 8111 Legal services
Louis Michel Tremblay

D-U-N-S 20-332-7887 (HQ)
MINERAI DE FER QUEBEC INC
(*Suby of* CHAMPION IRON LIMITED)
1100 Boul Rene-Levesque O Bureau 610, Montreal, QC, H3B 4N4
(514) 316-4858
Emp Here 26 *Sales* 11,671,750
SIC 1011 Iron ores
William Michael O'keeffe
Jorge Estepa
Natacha Garoute
Andrew John Love
Michelle Cormier
Amyot Choquette
Gaston Morin

D-U-N-S 24-357-5011 (SL)
MINES D'OR DYNACOR INC
625 Rene-Levesque Boul O Bureau 1105, Montreal, QC, H3B 1R2
(514) 393-9000
Emp Here 168 *Sales* 104,649,558
SIC 1041 Gold ores
Jean Martineau
Leonard Teoli
Jorge Luis Crdenas
Pierre Lepine
Rene Branchaud
Marc Duchesne
Roger Demers
Eddy Canova
Rejean Gourde
Isabelle Rocha

D-U-N-S 20-790-6793 (SL)
MINET INC
AON GLOBAL PROFESSIONS PRACTICE

(*Suby of* AON SPECIAL RISK RESOURCES, INC.)
700 Rue De La Gauchetiere O Bureau 1800, Montreal, QC, H3B 0A5
(514) 288-2273
Emp Here 79 *Sales* 145,971,618
SIC 6411 Insurance agents, brokers, and service
Barry Mathews
John Gower Carr
Christine Lithgow

D-U-N-S 20-276-7802 (BR)
MNP LLP
MNP S.E.N.C.R.L., S.R.L.
(*Suby of* MNP LLP)
1155 Boul Rene-Levesque O Bureau 2300, Montreal, QC, H3B 2K2
(514) 932-4115
Emp Here 225
SIC 8721 Accounting, auditing, and bookkeeping
Rasik Greiss

D-U-N-S 25-997-3832 (SL)
MOHAWK INTERNET TECHNOLOGIES
TECHNOLOGIES MOHAWK D'INTERNET
1250 Boul Rene-Levesque O Bureau 4100, Montreal, QC, H3B 4W8
(450) 638-4007
Emp Here 70 *Sales* 15,993,040
SIC 4899 Communication services, nec
Tewatohnhi Saktha

D-U-N-S 24-431-4456 (SL)
MONTREAL CENTRE SPORTS INC
SPORTS EXPERTS
930 Rue Sainte-Catherine O, Montreal, QC, H3B 1E2
(514) 866-1914
Emp Here 70 *Sales* 17,102,960
SIC 5941 Sporting goods and bicycle shops
Alain Goulet

D-U-N-S 24-057-2797 (SL)
MUNICH COMPAGNIE DE REASSURANCE, LA
630 Boul Rene-Levesque O Bureau 2630, Montreal, QC, H3B 1S6
(514) 866-6825
Emp Here 20 *Sales* 11,598,480
SIC 6411 Insurance agents, brokers, and service
Richard Letarte

D-U-N-S 24-895-5965 (SL)
MUSIQUEPLUS INC
COMBAT DES CLIPS (MC)
355 Rue Sainte-Catherine O, Montreal, QC, H3B 1A5
(514) 284-7587
Emp Here 185 *Sales* 42,267,320
SIC 4833 Television broadcasting stations
Maxime Remillard

D-U-N-S 20-015-8587 (HQ)
NAKISA INC
(*Suby of* 4538081 CANADA INC)
733 Rue Cathcart, Montreal, QC, H3B 1M6
(514) 228-2000
Emp Here 113 *Sales* 18,743,660
SIC 7371 Custom computer programming services
Babak Varjavandi

D-U-N-S 24-131-4512 (SL)
NATIONAL BANK SECURITIES INC.
NATIONAL BANK QUEBEC GROWTH FUND
1100 Boul Robert-Bourassa Unite 10 E, Montreal, QC, H3B 3A5
(514) 394-6282
Emp Here 29 *Sales* 24,409,277
SIC 6722 Management investment, open-end

D-U-N-S 20-765-0094 (HQ)
NATIONAL BANK TRUST INC
A-LA-CARTE ESTATES
(*Suby of* BANQUE NATIONALE DU

CANADA)
600 Rue De La Gauchetiere O Bureau 2800, Montreal, QC, H3B 4L2
(514) 871-7100
Emp Here 60 *Sales* 27,096,583
SIC 6021 National commercial banks
Nicolas Milette
Martin Gagnon
Cynthia Lepage
Frank Di Tomaso
Germain Carriere
Maryse Bertrand
Caroline Biron
France David
Sebastien Rene

D-U-N-S 20-202-4613 (BR)
NORDA STELO INC
(*Suby of* NORDA STELO INC)
630 Boul Rene-Levesque O Bureau 1500, Montreal, QC, H3B 1S6
(800) 463-2839
Emp Here 100
SIC 7363 Help supply services
Martin Choiniere

D-U-N-S 25-456-4339 (SL)
NORMANDIN BEAUDRY, ACTUAIRES CONSEIL INC
NORMANDIN BEAUDRY
630 Boul Rene-Levesque O Suite 30e, Montreal, QC, H3B 1S6
(514) 285-1122
Emp Here 110 *Sales* 53,614,660
SIC 8999 Services, nec
Rene Beaudry
Eric Montminy
Pierre Parent
Nathalie Gingras

D-U-N-S 24-489-7203 (BR)
NORTHBRIDGE FINANCIAL CORPORATION
(*Suby of* FAIRFAX FINANCIAL HOLDINGS LIMITED)
1000 Rue De La Gauchetiere O, Montreal, QC, H3B 4W5
(514) 843-1111
Emp Here 120
SIC 6411 Insurance agents, brokers, and service
Jean Francois

D-U-N-S 20-856-7495 (HQ)
NORTON ROSE FULBRIGHT CANADA S.E.N.C.R.L., S.R.L.
1 Place Ville-Marie Bureau 2500, Montreal, QC, H3B 4S2
(514) 847-4747
Emp Here 500 *Sales* 288,226,400
SIC 8111 Legal services
Jean Bertrand
Pierre Bienvenu
Robert Borduas
Daniele Boutet
Claude Brunet
James R. Cade
Michel G. Carle
Mario Caron
Jane E. Caskey
Jules Charette

D-U-N-S 25-658-3816 (HQ)
NOVIPRO INC
NOVIPRO EST DU CANADA
1010 Rue De La Gauchetiere O Bureau 1900, Montreal, QC, H3B 2N2
(514) 744-5353
Sales 16,268,210
SIC 5734 Computer and software stores
Yves Paquette
Pierre Lanthier

D-U-N-S 24-677-5857 (BR)
OCEANEX INC
OCEANEX GLOBAL LOGISTICS
(*Suby of* OCEANEX INC)

630 Boul Rene-Levesque O Bureau 2550, Montreal, QC, H3B 1S6

Emp Here 100
SIC 4424 Deep sea domestic transportation of freight
Steve Bilas

D-U-N-S 20-533-9232   (HQ)
OFFICE D'INVESTISSEMENT DES REGIMES DE PÉNSIONS DU SECTEUR PUBLIC
INVESTISSEMENTS PSP
(*Suby of* GOVERNMENT OF CANADA)
1250 Boul Rene-Levesque O Bureau 900, Montreal, QC, H3B 4W8
(514) 937-2772
Emp Here 100   *Sales* 142,354,873
SIC 6411 Insurance agents, brokers, and service
Neil Cunningham
Alison Breen
Leon Courville
William A. Mackinnon
Lynn Haight
Micheline Bouchard
Garnet Garven
Timothy Hodgson
Martin Glynn

D-U-N-S 24-668-4013   (SL)
OFFICE DES CONGRES ET DU TOURISME DU GRAND MONTREAL INC, L'
ASSOCIATION TOURISTIQUE REGIONALE DE MONTREAL, L'
800 Boul Rene-Levesque O Bureau 2450, Montreal, QC, H3B 1X9
(514) 844-5400
Emp Here 70   *Sales* 13,055,420
SIC 8743 Public relations services
Raymond Bachand
Bernard Chenevert
Bastien Biron
J. D. Miller
Chantal Fontaine
Claude Gilbert
Anne-Marie Jean
Raymond Larivee
David Rheault
Dominique Lapointe

D-U-N-S 24-320-6385   (SL)
ONEPOINT CANADA INC
TECHNOLOGIE S-ONE CANADA
606 Rue Cathcart Bureau 400, Montreal, QC, H3B 1K9
(514) 989-3116
Emp Here 70   *Sales* 11,380,880
SIC 7379 Computer related services, nec
Pierre-Paul Melanson
David Layani

D-U-N-S 20-376-2992   (SL)
ORDRE DES DENTISTES DU QUEBEC
FONDS D'ASSURANCE-RESPONSABILITE PROFESSIONNELLE DE L'ORDRE DES DENTISTES DU QUEBEC(F.A.R.
800 Boul Rene-Levesque O Bureau 1640, Montreal, QC, H3B 1X9
(514) 281-0300
Emp Here 50   *Sales* 42,403,000
SIC 6411 Insurance agents, brokers, and service
Barry Dolman
Veronique Gagnon
Veronic Deschenes
Eric Normandeau
Louis Flamand

D-U-N-S 20-884-1098   (SL)
ORDRE DES INGENIEURS DU QUEBEC
1100 Av Des Canadiens-De-Montreal Bureau 350, Montreal, QC, H3B 2S2
(514) 845-6141
Emp Here 142   *Sales* 16,715,551
SIC 8621 Professional organizations

Lorraine Gotin
Anita Khouah
Chantal Michaud

D-U-N-S 20-289-9829   (HQ)
OSISKO GOLD ROYALTIES LTD
1100 Av Des Canadiens-De-Montreal Bureau 300, Montreal, QC, H3B 2S2
(514) 940-0670
Sales 371,827,804
SIC 6282 Investment advice
Sean Roosen
Bryan A. Coates
Elif Levesque
Luc Lessard
Andre Le Bel
Joseph De La Plante
Frederic Ruel
Francois Vezina
Michael Spencer
Joanne Ferstman

D-U-N-S 25-809-9738   (HQ)
OSISKO METALS INCORPORATED
EXPLORATION BOWMORE
1100 Av Des Canadiens-De-Montreal Bureau 300, Montreal, QC, H3B 2S2
(514) 861-4441
Sales 31,038,137
SIC 1081 Metal mining services
Jeff Hussey
Killian Charles
Robin Adair
Paul A. Dumas
Lili Mance
Christina Lalli
Anthony Glavac
Robert Wares
John Burzynski
Amy Satov

D-U-N-S 24-680-6033   (BR)
OSLER, HOSKIN & HARCOURT LLP
(*Suby of* OSLER, HOSKIN & HARCOURT LLP)
1000 Rue De La Gauchetiere O Bureau 2100, Montreal, QC, H3B 4W5
(514) 904-8100
Emp Here 100
SIC 8111 Legal services
Shahir Guindi

D-U-N-S 24-204-9810   (SL)
PALM COMMUNICATION MARKETING INC
COMMUNICATION MARKETING PALM
(*Suby of* VIVENDI)
1253 Av Mcgill College, Montreal, QC, H3B 2Y5
(514) 845-7256
Emp Here 70   *Sales* 14,025,970
SIC 7311 Advertising agencies
Thomas Olesinski

D-U-N-S 20-562-7859   (SL)
PCM VENTES CANADA INC
1100 Boul Robert-Bourassa, Montreal, QC, H3B 3A5
(514) 373-8700
Emp Here 50   *Sales* 11,517,000
SIC 5734 Computer and software stores
Simon Abuyounes
Sean Lefebvre

D-U-N-S 20-961-4460   (HQ)
PICTET CANADA S.E.C.
1000 Rue De La Gauchetiere O Bureau 3100, Montreal, QC, H3B 4W5
(514) 288-8161
Sales 37,567,080
SIC 6211 Security brokers and dealers
Pictet Nicolas
Renaud De Planta
Remy Best

D-U-N-S 24-799-4056   (SL)
PLACEMENTS MONTEVA INC
MONTEVA AVIATION

1134 Rue Sainte-Catherine O Bureau 800, Montreal, QC, H3B 1H4
(438) 796-8990
Emp Here 50   *Sales* 20,967,750
SIC 6719 Holding companies, nec
Rafid Louis
Lewis Shwan

D-U-N-S 25-534-1166   (BR)
POSTMEDIA NETWORK INC
GAZETTE, LA
(*Suby of* POSTMEDIA NETWORK CANADA CORP)
1010 Rue Sainte-Catherine O Bureau 200, Montreal, QC, H3B 5L1
(514) 284-0040
Emp Here 100
SIC 2711 Newspapers

D-U-N-S 20-309-5716   (BR)
PRICEWATERHOUSECOOPERS LLP
(*Suby of* PRICEWATERHOUSECOOPERS LLP)
1250 Boul Rene-Levesque O Bureau 2800, Montreal, QC, H3B 4W8
(514) 866-8409
Emp Here 750
SIC 8721 Accounting, auditing, and bookkeeping
Guy Leblanc

D-U-N-S 25-683-6032   (SL)
QUANTUM CAPITAL CORPORATION
615 Boul Rene Levesque, Ste 460, Montreal, QC, H3B 1P5

Emp Here 50   *Sales* 10,311,680
SIC 5045 Computers, peripherals, and software

D-U-N-S 20-356-6336   (BR)
QUEBECOR MEDIA INC
QUEBECOR NUMERIQUE
(*Suby of* QUEBECOR MEDIA INC)
1100 Boul Rene-Levesque O Suite 20e, Montreal, QC, H3B 4N4
(514) 380-1999
Emp Here 75
SIC 7311 Advertising agencies

D-U-N-S 20-856-3932   (HQ)
RAYMOND CHABOT GRANT THORNTON S.E.N.C.R.L.
RAYMOND CHABOT GRANT THORNTON RCGT
600 Rue De La Gauchetiere O Bureau 2000, Montreal, QC, H3B 4L8
(514) 878-2691
Emp Here 600   *Sales* 465,090,148
SIC 8721 Accounting, auditing, and bookkeeping
Marc Bergeron
Eric Bergeron
Pierre Bernard
Jean Bernier
Michel Bernier
Daniel Berthelot
Louise Bilodeau
Donald Boucher
Alain Briere
Andre Champagne

D-U-N-S 24-667-6258   (HQ)
RAYMOND CHABOT INC
(*Suby of* RAYMOND CHABOT GRANT THORNTON S.E.N.C.R.L.)
600 Rue De La Gauchetiere O Bureau 2000, Montreal, QC, H3B 4L8
(514) 879-1385
Emp Here 25   *Sales* 13,305,840
SIC 8111 Legal services
Jean Gagnon

D-U-N-S 20-175-8596   (HQ)
RAYONIER A.M. CANADA ENTERPRISES INC
ENTREPRISES TEMBEC, LES

(*Suby of* RAYONIER A.M. GLOBAL HOLDINGS LUXEMBOURG SCS)
4 Place Ville-Marie Bureau 100, Montreal, QC, H3B 2E7
(514) 871-0137
Sales 1,102,911,000
SIC 2611 Pulp mills
Paul Dottori
Patrick Lebel
Lynn Poirier
William R. Manzer
Frank A. Ruperto
Michael R. Herman

D-U-N-S 20-376-2757   (HQ)
RAYONIER A.M. CANADA G.P.
TEMBEC
4 Place Ville-Marie Bureau 100, Montreal, QC, H3B 2E7
(514) 871-0137
Sales 257,345,900
SIC 2611 Pulp mills
Paul Dottori

D-U-N-S 20-755-0344   (HQ)
RAYONIER A.M. CANADA INDUSTRIES INC
TEMBEC INDUSTRIES
(*Suby of* RAYONIER A.M. GLOBAL HOLDINGS LUXEMBOURG SCS)
4 Place Ville-Marie Bureau 100, Montreal, QC, H3B 2E7
(514) 871-0137
Emp Here 33   *Sales* 1,113,560,000
SIC 2421 Sawmills and planing mills, general
Chris Black
Patrick Lebel
Lynn Poirier
Paul G. Boynton
Frank A. Ruperto
Michael R. Herman

D-U-N-S 25-200-4429   (SL)
RAYONIER A.M. COMPAGNIE DE CONSTRUCTION INC
CONSTRUCTION TEMBEC
(*Suby of* RAYONIER A.M. GLOBAL HOLDINGS LUXEMBOURG SCS)
4 Place Ville-Marie Bureau 100, Montreal, QC, H3B 2E7
(514) 871-0137
Emp Here 50   *Sales* 21,136,850
SIC 1541 Industrial buildings and warehouses
Paul Cousineau
Paolo G. Dottori
Patrick Lebel
Lynn Poirier
Dany Gagnon

D-U-N-S 24-233-9354   (HQ)
RED ISLE PRIVATE INVESTMENTS INC
1250 Boul Rene-Levesque O, Montreal, QC, H3B 4W8

Sales 313,090,360
SIC 6282 Investment advice
Guthrie Stewart
Marie-Claude Cardin
Darren Baccus

D-U-N-S 24-761-6118   (HQ)
RESSOURCES FALCO LTEE
1100 Av Des Canadiens-De-Montreal Bureau 300, Montreal, QC, H3B 2S2
(514) 905-3162
Emp Here 16   *Sales* 59,118,333
SIC 6799 Investors, nec
Luc Lessard
Sean Roosen
Ronald Bougie
Helene Cartier
Anthony Glavac
Christian Laroche
Andre Le Bel
Claude Leveillee
Francois Vezina
Vincent Metcalfe

D-U-N-S 25-360-8574   (SL)
RESSOURCES MSV INC
1155 Boul Robert-Bourassa Unite 1405, Montreal, QC, H3B 3A7
(418) 748-7691
Emp Here 75   *Sales* 18,228,675
SIC 6519 Real property lessors, nec
Andre Y. Fortier
Alain Blais
Real Savoie

D-U-N-S 25-361-3194   (BR)
RGA LIFE REINSURANCE COMPANY OF CANADA
(*Suby of* REINSURANCE GROUP OF AMERICA, INCORPORATED)
1255 Rue Peel Bureau 1000, Montreal, QC, H3B 2T9
(514) 985-5502
Emp Here 78
SIC 6311 Life insurance
Josee Malboeuf

D-U-N-S 24-346-9298   (HQ)
RIO TINTO ALCAN INC
ALCAN AUTOMOTIVE STRUCTURES
(*Suby of* RIO TINTO PLC)
1190 Av Des Canadiens-De-Montreal Bureau 400, Montreal, QC, H3B 0E3
(514) 848-8000
Emp Here 600   *Sales* 9,772,176,000
SIC 3334 Primary aluminum
Alf Barrios
Julie Parent
Gervais Jacques
Marie-Christine Dupont
Bruce Cox
Jocelin Paradis

D-U-N-S 20-763-3694   (SL)
RIO TINTO ALCAN INTERNATIONAL LTEE
RTA INTERNATIONAL
(*Suby of* RIO TINTO PLC)
1190 Av Des Canadiens-De-Montreal Bureau 400, Montreal, QC, H3B 0E3
(514) 848-8000
Emp Here 500   *Sales* 102,041,000
SIC 8731 Commercial physical research
Alf Barrios
Timothy Gillett Bradley
Jocelin Paradis
Jean-Francois Couture
Matt Halliday

D-U-N-S 25-358-3074   (HQ)
RIO TINTO GESTION CANADA INC
RIO TINTO
(*Suby of* RIO TINTO PLC)
1190 Av Des Canadiens-De-Montreal Bureau 400, Montreal, QC, H3B 0E3
(514) 288-8400
Sales 222,322,500
SIC 2816 Inorganic pigments
Jocelin Paradis
Julie Parent
Danielle Ethier

D-U-N-S 24-713-7342   (HQ)
ROBIC, S.E.N.C.R.L.
COPYRIGHTER
630 Boul Rene-Levesque O 20e Etage, Montreal, QC, H3B 1S6
(514) 987-6242
Emp Here 1   *Sales* 16,632,300
SIC 8111 Legal services
Laurent Carriere

D-U-N-S 24-346-3093   (BR)
ROTISSERIES ST-HUBERT LTEE, LES
(*Suby of* RECIPE UNLIMITED CORPORATION)
1180 Av Des Canadiens-De-Montreal, Montreal, QC, H3B 2S2
(514) 866-0500
Emp Here 90
SIC 5812 Eating places
Audrey Lachance

D-U-N-S 20-203-2558   (HQ)
RSW INC
RSW-LMB
(*Suby of* AECOM)
1010 Rue De La Gauchetiere O Bureau 1400, Montreal, QC, H3B 2N2
(514) 287-8500
Emp Here 3   *Sales* 44,354,475
SIC 8711 Engineering services
Joseph Salim

D-U-N-S 24-353-1209   (SL)
SDL INTERNATIONAL (CANADA) INC
ALPNET CANADA
1155 Rue Metcalfe Bureau 1200, Montreal, QC, H3B 2V6
(514) 844-2577
Emp Here 200   *Sales* 133,781,600
SIC 7389 Business services, nec
Frank Raco
Kevin J. Keating
Dominic Lavelle

D-U-N-S 20-904-3392   (SL)
SERVICES DE LOCALISATION GAT INTERNATIONAL INC
1100 Av Des Canadiens-De-Montreal Bureau C25, Montreal, QC, H3B 2S2
(514) 288-7818
Emp Here 40   *Sales* 17,739,600
SIC 7389 Business services, nec
Johanne Plante

D-U-N-S 24-522-8320   (SL)
SERVICES OR LP/SEC
SERVICES OR LP
1 Place Ville-Marie Unite 2500, Montreal, QC, H3B 1R1
(514) 847-4747
Emp Here 800   *Sales* 99,820,800
SIC 8741 Management services
Susan Da Silva

D-U-N-S 20-333-0105   (SL)
SERVICES S & E SOCIETE EN COMMANDITE
1155 Boul Rene-Levesque O Bureau 4100, Montreal, QC, H3B 3V2
(514) 397-3318
Emp Here 250   *Sales* 46,626,500
SIC 8742 Management consulting services
Stikeman Elliott

D-U-N-S 25-978-5657   (SL)
SHAWA ENTERPRISES CORP
SHAWA ENTERPRISES CANADA
1250 Boul Robert-Bourassa Unite 921, Montreal, QC, H3B 3B8

Emp Here 55   *Sales* 12,352,218
SIC 6512 Nonresidential building operators
Hasan Shawa
Hazem Shawa

D-U-N-S 24-182-8693   (SL)
SIGMA ASSISTEL INC
1100 Boul Rene-Levesque O Bureau 514, Montreal, QC, H3B 4N4
(514) 875-9170
Emp Here 60   *Sales* 26,953,140
SIC 7389 Business services, nec
Louise Des Ormeaux
Stephane Fiset
Louise Tourgeon
Jean-Francois Chalifoux
Andre Girard
Colette Pierrot
Normand Desautels

D-U-N-S 24-178-5666   (HQ)
SOCIETE CONSEIL GROUPE LGS
SERVICES-CONSEILS EN AFFAIRES IBM
(*Suby of* INTERNATIONAL BUSINESS MACHINES CORPORATION)
1 Place Ville-Marie Bureau 2200, Montreal, QC, H3B 2B2
(514) 964-0939
Emp Here 300   *Sales* 89,762,400

SIC 8741 Management services
Bernard Roy
Matthew R. Snell
Daniel Renaud
Claude Guay

D-U-N-S 20-699-8481   (HQ)
SOCIETE DE FIDUCIE BMO
ADVISOR'S ADVANTAGE TRUST
(*Suby of* BANK OF MONTREAL)
1250 Boul Rene-Levesque O Unite 4600, Montreal, QC, H3B 5J5
(514) 877-7373
Sales 93,917,700
SIC 6211 Security brokers and dealers
Elizabeth Dorsch
Myra Cridland
Paul Dubal
Thomas Burian
Edgar N. Legzdins
Rebecca Tascona
Caroline Dabu
Lisa Milburn
Sai Cherla
Sam Jeries

D-U-N-S 24-310-7815   (HQ)
SOCIETE DE PORTEFEUILLE ET D'ACQUISITION BANQUE NATIONAL INC
(*Suby of* BANQUE NATIONALE DU CANADA)
600 Rue De La Gauchetiere O Bureau 11e, Montreal, QC, H3B 4L2
(514) 394-4385
Emp Here 500   *Sales* 992,722,444
SIC 6712 Bank holding companies
Louis Vachon
Jean Dagenais
Melanie Frappier
Ghislain Parent

D-U-N-S 24-675-7686   (SL)
SPIEGEL SOHMER INC
SPIEGEL SOHMER AVOCATS
1255 Rue Peel Bureau 1000, Montreal, QC, H3B 2T9
(514) 875-2100
Emp Here 115   *Sales* 12,751,430
SIC 8111 Legal services
Alwynn Gillett

D-U-N-S 25-801-0842   (BR)
STANTEC CONSULTING LTD
(*Suby of* STANTEC INC)
1060 Boul Robert-Bourassa Unite 600, Montreal, QC, H3B 4V3
(514) 281-1033
Emp Here 800
SIC 8711 Engineering services
Jean Tousignant

D-U-N-S 20-183-0416   (BR)
STARWOOD HOTELS & RESORTS, INC
SHERATON MONTREAL, LE
(*Suby of* MARRIOTT INTERNATIONAL, INC.)
1201 Boul Rene-Levesque O Bureau 217, Montreal, QC, H3B 2L7
(514) 878-2046
Emp Here 375
SIC 7011 Hotels and motels
Michel G Giguere

D-U-N-S 24-358-3866   (BR)
STIKEMAN ELLIOTT LLP
(*Suby of* STIKEMAN ELLIOTT LLP)
1155 Boul Rene-Levesque O Bureau B01, Montreal, QC, H3B 4R1
(514) 397-3000
Emp Here 501
SIC 8111 Legal services
Lucia Pollice

D-U-N-S 24-865-9633   (HQ)
STUDIOS DESIGN GHA INC
GHA DESIGN
1100 Av Des Canadiens-De-Montreal Bureau 130, Montreal, QC, H3B 2S2

(514) 843-5812
Sales 22,460,950
SIC 7389 Business services, nec
Steve Sutton
Paola Marques
Frank Di Niro

D-U-N-S 24-974-0150   (BR)
SUN LIFE ASSURANCE COMPANY OF CANADA
(*Suby of* SUN LIFE FINANCIAL INC)
1001 Rue Du Square-Dorchester Bureau 600, Montreal, QC, H3B 1N1
(514) 731-7961
Emp Here 100
SIC 6311 Life insurance
Claude Cote

D-U-N-S 24-108-3161   (BR)
SUN LIFE ASSURANCE COMPANY OF CANADA
(*Suby of* SUN LIFE FINANCIAL INC)
1155 Rue Metcalfe Bureau 20, Montreal, QC, H3B 2V9
(514) 866-6411
Emp Here 2,500
SIC 6311 Life insurance
Robert Allard

D-U-N-S 20-577-6961   (SL)
SUN LIFE ASSURANCES (CANADA) LIMITEE
SUN LIFE FINANCIAL
(*Suby of* SUN LIFE FINANCIAL INC)
1155 Rue Metcalfe Bureau 1024, Montreal, QC, H3B 2V9
(514) 866-6411
Emp Here 50   *Sales* 92,387,100
SIC 6411 Insurance agents, brokers, and service
Natalie Michele Brady
Katherine Ann Cunningham
Brigitte Catellier
Paul K. Fryer
David J. Hayes
John Thomas Donnelly
Michael Christopher Van Alphen
Sloane Fayth Litchen
Suzanne Morin

D-U-N-S 20-356-2905   (SL)
SUN LIFE DU CANADA, COMPAGNIE D'ASSURANCE-VIE
FINANCIERE SUN LIFE
1155 Rue Metcalfe Bureau 1410, Montreal, QC, H3B 2V9
(514) 393-8820
Emp Here 1,000   *Sales* 2,136,968,000
SIC 6311 Life insurance
Dean A Connor
Michael Ronald Troy Krushel
Hugh D. Segal
William Anderson
Martin J.G Glynn
Barbara G. Stymiest
Marianne Harris
Sara Grootwassink Lewis
Scott Francis Powers
Stephanie Lynne Coyles

D-U-N-S 24-826-4744   (SL)
SYNCHRONICA INC
(*Suby of* MYRIAD GROUP AG)
1100 Av Des Canadiens-De-Montreal, Montreal, QC, H3B 2S2
(514) 390-1333
Emp Here 100   *Sales* 25,349,000
SIC 8748 Business consulting, nec
Carsten Brinkschulte
Anthony Decristofaro
Angus Dent
David Berman

D-U-N-S 24-082-1728   (HQ)
SYSTEMATIX TECHNOLOGIES DE L'INFORMATION INC
SYSTEMATIX

1 Place Ville-Marie Unite 1601, Montreal, QC, H3B 3Y2
(514) 393-1313
Emp Here 140   *Sales* 33,369,400
SIC 7379 Computer related services, nec
Daniel Deschenes
Norbert Rozko

D-U-N-S 24-900-9374   (SL)
SYSTRA CANADA INC
CANARAIL
(*Suby of* SYSTRA)
1100 Boul Rene-Levesque O Etage 10e, Montreal, QC, H3B 4N4
(514) 985-0930
Emp Here 100   *Sales* 17,873,900
SIC 8711 Engineering services
Pierre Verzat
Dave Spagnolo
Donald Gillstrom
Joseph Sarkis
Linda Belanger
Olivier Dezorme
Andrew Mcnaughton

D-U-N-S 20-253-9912   (HQ)
TAXELCO INC
355 Rue Sainte-Catherine O Bureau 500, Montreal, QC, H3B 1A5
(514) 504-8293
Sales 17,500,666
SIC 4119 Local passenger transportation, nec
Dominic Becotte
Normand Chartrand
Nataly-Claude Simard
Jocelyn Moreau
Ariane Cloutier

D-U-N-S 20-555-8856   (BR)
TELUS COMMUNICATIONS (QUEBEC) INC
(*Suby of* TELUS CORPORATION)
630 Boul Rene-Levesque O Bureau 2200, Montreal, QC, H3B 1S6
(514) 242-8870
Emp Here 200
SIC 4899 Communication services, nec
Louis Morin

D-U-N-S 24-423-0517   (HQ)
TELUS SOLUTIONS EN SANTE INC
TELUS HEALTH WOLF EMR
(*Suby of* TELUS CORPORATION)
22e Etage 630, Boul Rene-Levesque O, Montreal, QC, H3B 1S6
(514) 665-3050
Emp Here 50   *Sales* 266,955,200
SIC 7372 Prepackaged software
Josh Blair
Paul Lepage
Monique Mercier

D-U-N-S 24-458-4397   (HQ)
TRANSCONTINENTAL INC
ACTIVATION MARKETING
1 Place Ville-Marie Bureau 3240, Montreal, QC, H3B 0G1
(514) 954-4000
Emp Here 269   *Sales* 1,620,147,610
SIC 6712 Bank holding companies
Francois Olivier
Christine Desaulniers
Pierre Marcoux
Francois R. Roy
Anna Martini
Nathalie Marcoux
Remi Marcoux
Isabelle Marcoux
Mario Plourde
Annie Thabet

D-U-N-S 24-523-4369   (HQ)
TRANSCONTINENTAL INTERACTIF INC
ACTIVATION MARKETING
(*Suby of* TRANSCONTINENTAL INC)
1 Place Ville-Marie Bureau 3240, Montreal, QC, H3B 0G1

(514) 954-4000
Sales 10,586,200
SIC 7311 Advertising agencies
Francois Olivier
Christine Desaulniers
Donald Lecavalier
Nelson Gentiletti

D-U-N-S 24-422-8362   (SL)
TRANSDEV CANADA INC
VEOLIA TRANSDEV CANADA
(*Suby of* CAISSE DES DEPOTS ET CONSIGNATIONS)
1100 Boul Rene-Levesque O Bureau 1305, Montreal, QC, H3B 4N4
(450) 970-8899
Emp Here 65   *Sales* 23,758,085
SIC 6712 Bank holding companies
Dominique Lemay
Nicole Dutilly
Jennifer Coyne
Jacques Laherre
Yann Leriche

D-U-N-S 20-577-8363   (HQ)
V INTERACTIONS INC
ACTION TQS
(*Suby of* GROUPE V MEDIA INC)
355 Rue Sainte-Catherine O, Montreal, QC, H3B 1A5
(514) 390-6100
Emp Here 120   *Sales* 45,694,400
SIC 4833 Television broadcasting stations
Maxime Remillard
Tony Porrello

D-U-N-S 24-822-0998   (HQ)
VALEURS MOBILIERES DESJARDINS INC
COURTAGE EN LIGNE DISNAT
(*Suby of* FEDERATION DES CAISSES DESJARDINS DU QUEBEC)
1170 Rue Peel Bureau 300, Montreal, QC, H3B 0A9
(514) 987-1749
Emp Here 200   *Sales* 1,041,737,016
SIC 6211 Security brokers and dealers
Kristen Zimakas
Francois Drouin
Radek Loudin
Jean-Yves Bourgeois
Luc Papineau
Alain Pineau

D-U-N-S 24-019-7160   (HQ)
VIA RAIL CANADA INC
VIA RAIL CANAADA, CENTRE DE MAINTENANCE DE MONTREAL BUREAU DE VENTES DE TELEPHONE
(*Suby of* GOVERNMENT OF CANADA)
3 Place Ville-Marie Bureau 500, Montreal, QC, H3B 2C9
(514) 871-6000
Emp Here 270   *Sales* 163,020,600
SIC 4111 Local and suburban transit
Yves Desjardins-Siciliano
Jean-Francois Legault
Ramona Rosanne Materi
Jane Mowat
Francoise Bertrand
Kathy Baig
Daniel F. Gallivan
Jonathan Goldbloom
Stanley Ross Goldsworthy
Glenn Rainbird

D-U-N-S 20-179-5148   (BR)
VIA RAIL CANADA INC
(*Suby of* GOVERNMENT OF CANADA)
895 Rue De La Gauchetiere O Bureau 429, Montreal, QC, H3B 4G1
(514) 989-2626
Emp Here 100
SIC 4111 Local and suburban transit
David Hoff

D-U-N-S 24-342-2339   (BR)
VOLT CANADA INC
VMC GAME LABS

(*Suby of* VOLT INFORMATION SCIENCES INC)
1155 Rue Metcalfe Bureau 2002, Montreal, QC, H3B 2V6
(514) 787-3175
Emp Here 200
SIC 8734 Testing laboratories
Olivier Desrosiers

D-U-N-S 24-677-0478   (HQ)
VOXDATA SOLUTIONS INC
VOXDATA TELECOM
1155 Rue Metcalfe Bureau 1860, Montreal, QC, H3B 2V6
(514) 871-1920
Emp Here 400   *Sales* 234,180,800
SIC 4899 Communication services, nec
France Couture

D-U-N-S 24-421-8975   (SL)
W.B.C. CORPORATION
CONSULTANTS RELLIM
1000 Rue De La Gauchetiere O, Montreal, QC, H3B 4W5

Emp Here 25   *Sales* 10,615,175
SIC 8999 Services, nec
Martin Lavoie
John Thibeau
Francois Morin

D-U-N-S 25-973-6791   (HQ)
ZARA CANADA INC
ZARA
(*Suby of* PONTEGADEA INVERSIONES SL)
1200 Av Mcgill College Bureau 1550, Montreal, QC, H3B 4G7
(514) 868-1516
Emp Here 10   *Sales* 81,090,750
SIC 5651 Family clothing stores
Alfonso Vazquez Bergantinos
Antonio Abril Abadin
Jose Manuel Romay De La Colina

D-U-N-S 20-908-8517   (HQ)
ZIM CIE DE SERVICES DE NAVIGATION INTEGREE (CANADA) LTEE
ZIM CONTAINER SERVICE
(*Suby of* ZIM INTEGRATED SHIPPING SERVICES LTD)
1155 Boul Rene-Levesque O Bureau 400, Montreal, QC, H3B 4R1
(844) 454-5072
Emp Here 35   *Sales* 31,497,920
SIC 4491 Marine cargo handling
Volker Kluge
Asad Amath
Rafael Ben Ari

Montreal, QC H3C

D-U-N-S 25-081-6121   (SL)
9069-5057 QUEBEC INC
PUBLICATIONS HANSON
1000 Rue Saint-Antoine O Ste 509, Montreal, QC, H3C 3R7

Emp Here 350
SIC 2711 Newspapers

D-U-N-S 24-646-7067   (SL)
9182-9978 QUEBEC INC
KLIENTEL
774 Rue Saint Paul O, Montreal, QC, H3C 1M4
(514) 876-4101
Emp Here 100   *Sales* 21,335,800
SIC 8732 Commercial nonphysical research
Raynald Harvey
Alajarin Pierre
Daniel Hebert

D-U-N-S 20-370-6721   (HQ)
ABITIBIBOWATER CANADA INC

COMPAGNIE ABITIBIBOWATER DU CANADA
(*Suby of* RESOLUTE FOREST PRODUCTS INC)
111 Rue Duke Bureau 5000, Montreal, QC, H3C 2M1
(514) 875-2160
Emp Here 4   *Sales* 1,735,071,223
SIC 6712 Bank holding companies
Yves Laflamme
Jacques P. Vachon
Jo-Ann Longworth

D-U-N-S 24-713-3044   (HQ)
ACCEO SOLUTIONS INC
(*Suby of* CONSTELLATION SOFTWARE INC)
75 Rue Queen Bureau 5200, Montreal, QC, H3C 2N6
(514) 868-0333
Emp Here 200   *Sales* 92,286,500
SIC 7371 Custom computer programming services
Jeff Bender
Todd Richardson

D-U-N-S 25-393-7791   (SL)
AGENCE INTERNATIONALE TRADEBRIDGE INC
620 Rue Saint-Jacques Bureau 500, Montreal, QC, H3C 1C7
(514) 393-9100
Emp Here 45   *Sales* 23,398,515
SIC 4731 Freight transportation arrangement
Richard H. Francis
Luigi Colizza
John Sims

D-U-N-S 24-922-1946   (SL)
ALIZENT CANADA INC
KEOPS TECHNOLOGIES
740 Rue Notre-Dame O Bureau 600, Montreal, QC, H3C 3X6
(514) 876-2855
Emp Here 50   *Sales* 11,714,400
SIC 8742 Management consulting services
Gonzalo Garcia
Cedric Guidi
Ole Hoefelmann
Alexis Duret
Olivier Delabroy
Stephane Rousseau
Luc Doyon
Marc Fortier
Krystal Staniforth

D-U-N-S 20-289-6643   (SL)
APPROVISIONNEMENT DE NAVIRES CLIPPER INC
770 Rue Mill, Montreal, QC, H3C 1Y3
(514) 937-9561
Emp Here 24   *Sales* 11,400,624
SIC 5088 Transportation equipment and supplies
Keith Bishop
Mark Bishop
David Bishop

D-U-N-S 24-976-3418   (HQ)
ARENA DES CANADIENS INC, L'
EVENKO
1275 Rue Saint-Antoine O, Montreal, QC, H3C 5L2
(514) 932-2582
Sales 90,768,700
SIC 7941 Sports clubs, managers, and promoters
Luc Bertrand
Geoffrey E Molson
France Margaret Belanger
Andrew T Molson
Anna Martini

D-U-N-S 20-790-7650   (HQ)
ASSOCIATION DES EMPLOYEURS MARITIME, L'
2100 Av Pierre-Dupuy, Montreal, QC, H3C

3R5
(514) 878-3721
Emp Here 40   *Sales* 16,037,478
SIC 8631 Labor organizations
Bryan Mackasey
Brian Michael Craig

D-U-N-S 24-837-1023   (HQ)
AUTOCARS ORLEANS EXPRESS INC
740 Rue Notre-Dame O Bureau 1000, Montreal, QC, H3C 3X6
(514) 395-4000
Emp Here 35   *Sales* 18,818,000
SIC 4131 Intercity and rural bus transportation
Jean-Francois Bedard
Clement Michel
Patrick Gilloux

D-U-N-S 24-901-5827   (HQ)
AUTODESK CANADA CIE
(*Suby of* AUTODESK, INC.)
10 Rue Duke, Montreal, QC, H3C 2L7
(514) 393-1616
Emp Here 325   *Sales* 123,663,910
SIC 7371 Custom computer programming services
Deborah Lynn Clifford
Kristen Marie Nordlof
Susan Marie Savage

D-U-N-S 20-852-3527   (HQ)
AV & R VISION & ROBOTIQUES INC
269 Rue Prince, Montreal, QC, H3C 2N4
(514) 788-1420
Emp Here 25   *Sales* 10,542,960
SIC 8742 Management consulting services
Jean-Francois Dupont
Pierre Racine
Denis Williams
Yves Deom
Louis-Joseph Cliche
Philippe Simonato

D-U-N-S 20-574-0611   (HQ)
AVERNA TECHNOLOGIES INC
87 Rue Prince Bureau 510, Montreal, QC, H3C 2M7
(514) 842-7577
Emp Here 248   *Sales* 68,592,500
SIC 3825 Instruments to measure electricity
Francois Rainville
Andre Gareau
Marieve Carrier
Lori Seidman
Andre Gauthier
David Bernardi
Andre Thompson
Marc Baillargeon
Maurice Beausejour
Marinella Ermacora

D-U-N-S 24-786-5249   (HQ)
BOWATER CANADIAN LIMITED
(*Suby of* RESOLUTE FOREST PRODUCTS INC)
111 Boul Robert-Bourassa Unite 5000, Montreal, QC, H3C 2M1
(514) 875-2160
Sales 202,200,350
SIC 2621 Paper mills
Yves Laflamme
Jacques P. Vachon
Jo-Ann Longworth

D-U-N-S 20-421-6303   (HQ)
C.H. ROBINSON MONDIAL CANADA, LTEE
(*Suby of* C.H. ROBINSON INVESTMENTS SARL)
645 Rue Wellington Bureau 400, Montreal, QC, H3C 0L1
(514) 288-2161
Emp Here 250   *Sales* 132,471,730
SIC 4731 Freight transportation arrangement
Ben G. Campbell
Gerran Ferrey
Mina La Rocca

D-U-N-S 20-117-2298   (HQ)
CAFES VIENNE PRESS INC, LES
1422 Rue Notre-Dame O, Montreal, QC, H3C 1K9
(514) 935-5553
Emp Here 2   *Sales* 16,401,000
SIC 6712 Bank holding companies
Marcel Hachem

D-U-N-S 24-896-7234   (BR)
CANADIAN PACIFIC RAILWAY COMPANY
CPR
(*Suby of* CANADIAN PACIFIC RAILWAY LIMITED)
1100 Rue De La Gauchetiere, Montreal, QC, H3C 3E4
(514) 395-5151
Emp Here 500
SIC 4111 Local and suburban transit
Fred Green

D-U-N-S 24-346-9210   (SL)
CENTRES D'EVALUATION DE LA TECHNOLOGIE INC
CONNECTIVIA
740 Rue Saint-Maurice, Montreal, QC, H3C 1L5
(514) 954-3665
Emp Here 49   *Sales* 19,166,742
SIC 8631 Labor organizations
Lorne Goloff

D-U-N-S 20-519-1179   (BR)
CIMA+ S.E.N.C.
(*Suby of* CIMA+ S.E.N.C.)
740 Rue Notre-Dame O Unite 900, Montreal, QC, H3C 3X6
(514) 337-2462
Emp Here 200
SIC 8711 Engineering services
Jean-Pierre Normand

D-U-N-S 24-054-8743   (SL)
CLUB DE HOCKEY CANADIEN, INC
ARENA DU ROCKET, L'
(*Suby of* ARENA DES CANADIENS INC, L')
1275 Rue Saint-Antoine O, Montreal, QC, H3C 5L2
(514) 932-2582
Emp Here 110   *Sales* 9,076,870
SIC 7941 Sports clubs, managers, and promoters
Andrew T. Molson
Geoffrey E Molson
France Margaret Belanger
Luc Bertrand
Anna Martini

D-U-N-S 20-553-5219   (HQ)
CMA CGM (CANADA) INC
DELMAS
(*Suby of* MERIT CORPORATION SAL)
740 Rue Notre-Dame O Bureau 1330, Montreal, QC, H3C 3X6
(514) 908-7001
Emp Here 78   *Sales* 35,828,884
SIC 4412 Deep sea foreign transportation of freight
Mathieu Friedberg
Jean-Baptiste Longin
Michel Sawaya

D-U-N-S 25-526-2354   (HQ)
CNIM CANADA INC
(*Suby of* ARNINA SARL)
1499 Rue William, Montreal, QC, H3C 1R4
(514) 932-1220
Emp Here 51   *Sales* 16,872,076
SIC 3534 Elevators and moving stairways
Jacques Rompre
Philipe Demigne
Jean-Luc Chauveau
Bernard Dabezies

D-U-N-S 20-552-0906   (HQ)
CORPORATION DE SECURITE GARDA WORLD
GW HONOS SECURITY

(*Suby of* GW INTERMEDIATE HOLDCO CORPORATION)
1390 Rue Barre, Montreal, QC, H3C 5X9
(514) 281-2811
Emp Here 1,000   *Sales* 3,771,411,322
SIC 7381 Detective and armored car services
Stephan Cretier
Pierre-Hubert Seguin
Jean-Luc Landry
Francois Plamondon
Helene Desmarais
Patrick Prince

D-U-N-S 24-102-0770   (SL)
CORPORATION EFUNDRAISING.COM INC
FUNDRAISING.COM
33 Rue Prince Bureau 200, Montreal, QC, H3C 2M7

Emp Here 110   *Sales* 73,579,880
SIC 7389 Business services, nec
Marc Alcindor

D-U-N-S 24-411-9710   (SL)
DELOITTE ERS INC
DELOITTE E.R.S.
1190 Av Des Canadiens-De-Montreal Bureau 500, Montreal, QC, H3C 0M7
(514) 393-7115
Emp Here 49   *Sales* 10,245,165
SIC 8721 Accounting, auditing, and bookkeeping
Chantale Viau

D-U-N-S 20-015-9098   (HQ)
DEMENAGEMENT KING'S TRANSFER INTERNATIONAL INC
287 Rue Eleanor, Montreal, QC, H3C 2C1
(514) 932-2957
Emp Here 95   *Sales* 20,570,600
SIC 4213 Trucking, except local
William E O'donnell

D-U-N-S 24-964-8978   (HQ)
DISTILLERIES SAZERAC DU CANADA INC, LES
950 Ch Des Moulins, Montreal, QC, H3C 3W5
(514) 395-3200
Sales 82,915,767
SIC 5182 Wine and distilled beverages
Mark Brown
Chris Ritchie
Joe Bongiovi
Chris Skinger
Gerry Christiano

D-U-N-S 24-520-3489   (SL)
DOCU PLUS
980 Rue Saint-Antoine O Bureau 615, Montreal, QC, H3C 1A8
(514) 875-1616
Emp Here 49   *Sales* 10,374,476
SIC 7334 Photocopying and duplicating services
Malcolm Desouza

D-U-N-S 20-188-2979   (SL)
DONOHUE MALBAIE INC
(*Suby of* RESOLUTE FOREST PRODUCTS INC)
111 Boul Robert-Bourassa Unite 5000, Montreal, QC, H3C 2M1
(514) 875-2160
Emp Here 420   *Sales* 154,407,540
SIC 2621 Paper mills
Yves Laflamme
Jo-Ann Longworth
Jacques P. Vachon

D-U-N-S 24-253-8841   (HQ)
EDITIONS BLAIS, YVON INC, LES
EDITIONS DROIT ET ENTREPRISE, LES
(*Suby of* THOMSON COMPANY INC, THE)
75 Rue Queen Bureau 4700, Montreal, QC, H3C 2N6
(514) 842-3937
Sales 38,992,480

SIC 8999 Services, nec
Neil Sternthal
Heather O'hagan
Terra Rebick
Paula R Monaghan
Stewart Katz

D-U-N-S 24-351-9704   (HQ)
ENTREPRISE DE COMMUNICATIONS TANK INC
55 Rue Prince, Montreal, QC, H3C 2M7
(514) 373-3333
Emp Here 100   *Sales* 18,803,448
SIC 7311 Advertising agencies
Marc Lanouette
Mathieu Cloutier
John Grudzina
Robert Oates
Chris Esposito
Eric Gross

D-U-N-S 24-156-8257   (SL)
ENTREPRISES QMD INC, LES
990 Rue Notre-Dame O Bureau 200, Montreal, QC, H3C 1K1
(514) 875-4356
Emp Here 50   *Sales* 15,943,450
SIC 1521 Single-family housing construction
Luc Quenneville
Jean Morissette
Jean Philippe Le Guerrier

D-U-N-S 24-636-7619   (SL)
GESTION ACCEO INC
75 Rue Queen Bureau 4700, Montreal, QC, H3C 2N6
(514) 288-7161
Emp Here 140   *Sales* 23,358,580
SIC 7379 Computer related services, nec
Gilles Letourneau

D-U-N-S 24-365-4881   (SL)
GESTION SOROMA (MONT ORFORD) INC
640 Rue Saint-Paul O, Montreal, QC, H3C 1L9
(514) 527-9546
Emp Here 100   *Sales* 23,428,800
SIC 8742 Management consulting services
Vincent Renaud
Michel Collins

D-U-N-S 20-501-6413   (HQ)
GILLESPIE-MUNRO INC
NAVIGATION GILLSHIP
740 Rue Notre-Dame O Bureau 1120, Montreal, QC, H3C 3X6
(514) 871-1033
Emp Here 57   *Sales* 66,022,308
SIC 4731 Freight transportation arrangement
Christopher J. Gillespie
Maurice Vezina
Garry Mooney
P. Jeremy Bolger

D-U-N-S 20-117-1126   (HQ)
GROUPE CAFE VIENNE 1998 INC, LE
CAFE VIENNE
(*Suby of* CAFES VIENNE PRESS INC, LES)
1422 Rue Notre-Dame O, Montreal, QC, H3C 1K9
(514) 935-5553
Emp Here 56   *Sales* 61,946,640
SIC 6794 Patent owners and lessors
Marcel Hachem

D-U-N-S 25-746-6862   (HQ)
GROUPE COTE REGIS INC
REGIS COTE ET ASSOCIES, ARCHITECTES
682 Rue William Bureau 200, Montreal, QC, H3C 1N9
(514) 871-8595
Emp Here 52   *Sales* 22,342,375
SIC 8712 Architectural services
Regis Cote
Jocelyn Boilard
Jerome Cote

D-U-N-S 24-322-9648   (HQ)

GROUPE DE SECURITE GARDA INC, LE
AGENCE DE SECURITE BELLEY
(*Suby of* GW INTERMEDIATE HOLDCO CORPORATION)
1390 Rue Barre, Montreal, QC, H3C 5X9
(514) 281-2811
Emp Here 700   *Sales* 3,480,974,210
SIC 7381 Detective and armored car services
Stephane Cretier
Jean-Luc Meunier
Pierre-Hubert Seguin
Patrick Prince

D-U-N-S 24-355-6888   (HQ)
GROUPE IBI/DAA INC
HUARDIERE, LA
(*Suby of* IBI GROUP)
100 Rue Peel 4e Etage, Montreal, QC, H3C 0L8
(514) 316-1010
Sales 38,023,500
SIC 8748 Business consulting, nec
Scotte E. Stewart
Daniel Arbour
David M. Thom
Stephen Taylor
Philip H. Beinhaker

D-U-N-S 24-836-8565   (SL)
GROUPE MTA CONSEILS EN GESTION D'EVENEMENTS PUBLIQUES INC, LE
80 Rue Queen Bureau 601, Montreal, QC, H3C 2N5
(514) 982-0835
Emp Here 200   *Sales* 37,301,200
SIC 8742 Management consulting services
Richard Therien

D-U-N-S 24-419-0653   (HQ)
GROUPE STINGRAY INC
STINGRAY DIGITAL GROUP
730 Rue Wellington, Montreal, QC, H3C 1T4
(514) 664-1244
Emp Here 50   *Sales* 101,056,492
SIC 5045 Computers, peripherals, and software
Eric Boyko
Mark Pathy
Lloyd Perry Feldman
Francois-Charles Sirois
Pascal Tremblay
Jacques Parisien
Gary S. Rich
Robert G. Steele
Claudine Blondin-Bronfman
David Purdy

D-U-N-S 24-057-3191   (BR)
IMPERIAL PARKING CANADA CORPORATION
STATIONNEMENT IMPERIAL
(*Suby of* GATES GROUP CAPITAL PARTNERS, LLC)
640 Rue Saint-Paul O Bureau 106, Montreal, QC, H3C 1L9
(514) 875-5626
Emp Here 100
SIC 7521 Automobile parking
Allan Copping

D-U-N-S 20-233-8810   (HQ)
INDUSTRIES MARINE SEAGULF INC
815 Rue Mill, Montreal, QC, H3C 1Y5
(514) 935-6933
Emp Here 10   *Sales* 17,100,936
SIC 5088 Transportation equipment and supplies
Robert Zeagman
Donald Keays
Lorraine Z. Keays
Stephen Scholes

D-U-N-S 24-711-8441   (HQ)
INTELCOM COURRIER CANADA INC
INTELCOM EXPRESS
1380 Rue William Bureau 200, Montreal, QC, H3C 1R5

(514) 937-0430
Emp Here 12   *Sales* 22,460,950
SIC 7389 Business services, nec
Jean-Sebastien Joly
David Letourneau
Donald Jean
Bernard Langevin

D-U-N-S 25-615-2187   (SL)
INTELCOM COURRIER CANADA INC
COLITREX
1380 Rue William, Montreal, QC, H3C 1R5
(514) 875-2778
Emp Here 50   *Sales* 22,460,950
SIC 7389 Business services, nec
Jean-Sebastien Joly
David Letourneau
Maxime Tourangeau
Rick Gaetz
Yvon Roy

D-U-N-S 20-298-2864   (HQ)
KEOLIS CANADA INC
GROUPE ORLEANS
740 Rue Notre-Dame O Bureau 1000, Montreal, QC, H3C 3X6
(514) 395-4000
Sales 27,335,000
SIC 6712 Bank holding companies
Patrick Gilloux
Clement Michel
Jean-Francois Bedard
Yves Devin

D-U-N-S 20-222-8029   (HQ)
KING'S TRANSFER VAN LINES INC
KING'S TRANSFER INTERNATIONAL
287 Rue Eleanor, Montreal, QC, H3C 2C1
(514) 932-2957
Emp Here 55   *Sales* 11,114,400
SIC 4212 Local trucking, without storage
William O'donnell
Charles O'donnell

D-U-N-S 20-320-1368   (SL)
L'ARENA DES CANADIENS INC
ATLAS ARTISTES
1275 Rue Saint-Antoine O, Montreal, QC, H3C 5L2
(514) 989-2814
Emp Here 100   *Sales* 8,712,800
SIC 7941 Sports clubs, managers, and promoters
Luc Bertrand
Geoffrey E. Molson
Andrew T. Molson

D-U-N-S 24-433-8505   (HQ)
LOGIBEC INC
LOGIBES GROUPE INFORMATIQUE
700 Rue Wellington Bureau 1500, Montreal, QC, H3C 3S4
(514) 766-0134
Emp Here 80   *Sales* 61,894,080
SIC 7372 Prepackaged software
Marc Brunet
David Smolen
Howard Park
Dave Kreter
Travis Pearson
Patrick Hampson

D-U-N-S 20-851-5549   (HQ)
MAGENTA STUDIO PHOTO INC
300 Rue De La Montagne, Montreal, QC, H3C 2B1
(514) 935-2225
Sales 21,172,400
SIC 7335 Commercial photography
Magda Slezak

D-U-N-S 20-253-3444   (SL)
MEDIAQMI INC
24 HEURES
(*Suby of* QUEBECOR MEDIA INC)
612 Rue Saint-Jacques, Montreal, QC, H3C 4M8

(514) 380-6400
Emp Here 250   *Sales* 48,443,500
SIC 2711 Newspapers
Pierre Karl Peladeau
Marc M Tremblay
Hugues Simard

D-U-N-S 20-363-8663   (SL)
MINTZ GLOBAL SCREENING INC
8313784 CANADA
1303 Rue William Bureau 200, Montreal, QC, H3C 1R4
(514) 587-6200
Emp Here 50   *Sales* 10,667,900
SIC 8732 Commercial nonphysical research
Jim Mintz
Tim Whipple
Robert Lynch

D-U-N-S 24-881-4824   (SL)
MONTREAL PORT ADMINISTRATION
MONTREAL PORT AUTHORITY
(*Suby of* GOVERNMENT OF CANADA)
2100 Av Pierre-Dupuy Bureau 1, Montreal, QC, H3C 3R5
(514) 283-7011
Emp Here 226   *Sales* 78,503,586
SIC 4491 Marine cargo handling
Sylvie Vachon
Marie-Claude Boisvert
Real Couture
Daniel Dagenais
Tony Boemi
Marie-Claude Leroux
Serge Auclair
Sophie Roux
Marc Y. Bruneau
Eric Simard

D-U-N-S 20-271-4499   (SL)
MONTREAL STUDIOS ET EQUIPMENTS S.E.N.C
1777 Rue Carrie-Derick, Montreal, QC, H3C 6G2
(514) 866-2170
Emp Here 250   *Sales* 22,424,000
SIC 7812 Motion picture and video production
Michel Trudel

D-U-N-S 20-332-9081   (HQ)
MUSIQUE SELECT INC
ALLIANCE
(*Suby of* QUEBECOR MEDIA INC)
612 Rue Saint-Jacques, Montreal, QC, H3C 4M8
(514) 380-1999
Emp Here 1   *Sales* 11,364,450
SIC 3861 Photographic equipment and supplies
Anne Vivien
Marc M. Tremblay
Hugues Simard
Pierre Karl Peladeau
Martin Tremblay

D-U-N-S 20-381-5779   (SL)
NETGOVERN INC
ARCHITECTES DE MESSAGERIE
180 Rue Peel Bureau 333, Montreal, QC, H3C 2G7
(514) 392-9220
Emp Here 55   *Sales* 11,761,805
SIC 7372 Prepackaged software
Pierre Chamberland
Andre Thauvette
Nicolae Nicolae
Frederic Bourget
Jocelyn Auger

D-U-N-S 20-107-8313   (SL)
NETGOVERN INC
NETMAIL
180 Rue Peel Bureau 333, Montreal, QC, H3C 2G7
(514) 392-9220
Emp Here 50   *Sales* 10,692,550
SIC 7372 Prepackaged software
Pierre Chamberland

Frederic Bourget
Andrey Thauvette
Nicolae Stefan
Jocelyn Auger

D-U-N-S 20-381-7952   (SL)
NUMERIQ INC
GOJI
(*Suby of* QUEBECOR MEDIA INC)
612 Rue Saint-Jacques, Montreal, QC, H3C 4M8
(514) 380-1827
Emp Here 235   *Sales* 78,617,840
SIC 4899 Communication services, nec
Pierre Karl Peladeau
Marc M. Tremblay
Jean-Francois Pruneau

D-U-N-S 25-190-1401   (SL)
PARC SIX FLAGS MONTREAL S.E.C.
RONDE, LA
22 Ch Macdonald, Montreal, QC, H3C 6A3
(514) 397-0402
Emp Here 200   *Sales* 15,709,000
SIC 7996 Amusement parks
Len Turtora
Andre Goulet

D-U-N-S 24-988-8900   (HQ)
PF RESOLU CANADA INC
SOCIETE ABITIBI-CONSOLIDATED
(*Suby of* RESOLUTE FOREST PRODUCTS INC)
111 Boul Robert-Bourassa Unite 5000, Montreal, QC, H3C 2M1
(514) 875-2160
Emp Here 150   *Sales* 979,984,431
SIC 0831 Forest products
Yves Laflamme
Jo-Ann Longworth
Jacques P. Vachon

D-U-N-S 25-502-8326   (SL)
PHEROMONE INTERACTIF INC
75 Rue Queen Bureau 3100, Montreal, QC, H3C 2N6

Emp Here 55   *Sales* 10,163,890
SIC 4899 Communication services, nec
Philippe Le Roux
Yves Lapierre
Andre Belanger

D-U-N-S 25-091-7494   (SL)
PREMIER CHOIX SOLUTIONS DE PAIEMENT S.E.N.C.
SEKURE CARD SERVICES
1000 Rue Saint-Antoine O Bureau 333, Montreal, QC, H3C 3R7
(866) 437-3189
Emp Here 150   *Sales* 100,336,200
SIC 7389 Business services, nec
Eyal Artzy

D-U-N-S 24-501-1853   (HQ)
PURKINJE INC
614 Rue Saint-Jacques Bureau 200, Montreal, QC, H3C 1E2
(514) 355-0888
Emp Here 50   *Sales* 22,358,700
SIC 5045 Computers, peripherals, and software
Mary-Anne Carignan
Francois Carignan

D-U-N-S 20-419-7701   (HQ)
QUEBECOR INC
EDIFICE 612 ST-JACQUES
(*Suby of* PLACEMENTS PELADEAU INC, LES)
612 Rue Saint-Jacques Bureau 700, Montreal, QC, H3C 4M8
(514) 380-1999
Emp Here 166   *Sales* 3,169,624,462
SIC 6712 Bank holding companies
Pierre Karl Peladeau
J.Serge Sasseville

Lyne Robitaille
Mathieu Turbide
Marc M. Tremblay
Christian Jette
Hugues Simard
Martin Tremblay
Brian Mulroney
Sylvie Lalande

D-U-N-S 20-356-6781   (HQ)
QUEBECOR MEDIA INC
AGENCE QMI
612 Rue Saint-Jacques, Montreal, QC, H3C
4M8
(514) 380-1999
Emp Here 25   *Sales* 16,402,700
SIC 2711 Newspapers
Pierre Karl Peladeau
Marc M. Tremblay
Brian Mulroney
Normand Provost
Sylvie Lalande
Robert Pare
Erik Peladeau
Andre P. Brosseau
Christian Dube
Andrea Czapary Martin

D-U-N-S 24-347-8828   (HQ)
RESOLUTE FOREST PRODUCTS INC
PRODUITS FORESTIERS RESOLU
111 Boul Robert-Bourassa Bureau 5000,
Montreal, QC, H3C 2M1
(514) 875-2160
Sales 3,756,000,000
SIC 2621 Paper mills
Yves Laflamme
Bradley P. Martin
Patrice Minguez
Steve Boniferro
John Lafave
Jo-Ann Longworth
Richard Tremblay
Jacques P. Vachon
Hugues Dorban
Silvana Travaglini

D-U-N-S 24-500-7257   (HQ)
SECURITE KOLOSSAL INC
AGENCE DE SECURITE REGIONALE
(*Suby of* GW INTERMEDIATE HOLDCO
CORPORATION)
1390 Rue Barre, Montreal, QC, H3C 1N4
(514) 253-4021
Emp Here 50   *Sales* 2,060,457,097
SIC 5065 Electronic parts and equipment, nec
Stephan Cretier
Jean-Luc Meunier
Pierre-Hubert Seguin
Patrick Prince

D-U-N-S 24-324-8580   (SL)
**SERVICE D'ENTRETIEN DES PLANTES AL-
PHA INC**
ALPHA PLANTES
230 Rue Peel, Montreal, QC, H3C 2G7
(514) 935-1812
Emp Here 55   *Sales* 24,707,045
SIC 7389 Business services, nec
Georges Liby
Sonia Liby
Sacha Liby
Monique Soucy

D-U-N-S 25-323-8935   (HQ)
SID LEE INC
DIESEL MARKETING
(*Suby of* GESTION SID LEE CANADA INC)
75 Rue Queen Bureau 1400, Montreal, QC,
H3C 2N6
(514) 282-2200
Sales 90,547,585
SIC 7311 Advertising agencies
Bertrand Cesvet
Gerard Tardif
Jean-Francois Bouchard
Adam John Hughes

Michael Birkin

D-U-N-S 20-051-6065   (SL)
SIMULATIONS CMLABS INC
LABOS CM
645 Rue Wellington Bureau 301, Montreal,
QC, H3C 1T2
(514) 287-1166
Emp Here 95   *Sales* 13,697,290
SIC 7371 Custom computer programming ser-
vices
Robert J. Weldon
Marek Teichmann
Robert Beauchemin
Luc Filiatreault
Guillaume Herve
Arnold Free

D-U-N-S 20-760-5015   (SL)
**SOCIETE D'HYPOTHEQUE DE LA BANQUE
ROYALE**
(*Suby of* ROYAL BANK OF CANADA)
1 Place Ville-Marie, Montreal, QC, H3C 3A9
(514) 874-7222
Emp Here 700   *Sales* 279,190,800
SIC 6162 Mortgage bankers and loan corre-
spondents
Jessica Clinton
Laguine Denis
Alanna Scott
Matthew Varey
Kim Mason
Katherine Gibson
Leanne Kaufman
Anthony Maiorino
Wayne E. Bossert
David John Agnew

D-U-N-S 24-326-7312   (BR)
**SOCIETE DES CASINOS DU QUEBEC INC,
LA**
CASINO DE MONTREAL
(*Suby of* GOUVERNEMENT DE LA
PROVINCE DE QUEBEC)
1 Av Du Casino, Montreal, QC, H3C 4W7
(514) 392-2756
Emp Here 3,500
SIC 7999 Amusement and recreation, nec

D-U-N-S 24-522-5979   (SL)
**SOLUTIONS   BEYOND   TECHNOLOGIES
INC**
BEYOND TECHNOLOGIES
111 Boul Robert-Bourassa Bureau 3600,
Montreal, QC, H3C 2M1
(514) 227-7323
Emp Here 100   *Sales* 16,684,700
SIC 7379 Computer related services, nec
Luc Dubois
Leonardo De Araujo
Francois Potier
Alain Dupont
Sebastien Tessier
Alain Dubois
Sebastien Caron

D-U-N-S 20-277-2513   (SL)
SOLUTIONS MEDIAS 360 INC
CONSULTANT AUTO 360
355 Rue Peel Bureau 901, Montreal, QC, H3C
2G9
(514) 717-9812
Emp Here 135   *Sales* 19,464,570
SIC 7371 Custom computer programming ser-
vices
Daniel Martin
Louis-Yves Cloutier
Mark Vallee
Marc-Andre Allaire
Normand Martin

D-U-N-S 20-693-8073   (SL)
SOSEN INC
JOUVIANCE
(*Suby of* FUNCTIONALAB INC)
995 Rue Wellington Bureau 210, Montreal,
QC, H3C 1V3

(514) 789-1255
Emp Here 26   *Sales* 28,738,970
SIC 5122 Drugs, proprietaries, and sundries
Roger Southin
Francis S. Maheu
Erick Geoffrion

D-U-N-S 24-835-2494   (SL)
**STATIONNEMENT & DEVELOPPEMENT IN-
TERNATIONAL INC**
PARCOBEC
544 Rue De L'Inspecteur Bureau 200, Mon-
treal, QC, H3C 2K9
(514) 396-6421
Emp Here 75   *Sales* 21,247,500
SIC 7521 Automobile parking
Eric Kushner

D-U-N-S 24-933-5423   (SL)
TAMEC INC
L'ANNUAIRE DU TELECOPIEUR
980 Rue Saint-Antoine O Bureau 400, Montreal, QC, H3C 1A8

Emp Here 80   *Sales* 10,830,880
SIC 2741 Miscellaneous publishing
Eric Vaillancourt
Michel Lafontaine
Yves St-Sauveur

D-U-N-S 20-189-7886   (HQ)
TATA COMMUNICATIONS (CANADA) LTD
(*Suby of* TATA COMMUNICATIONS LIMITED)
1441 Rue Carrie-Derick, Montreal, QC, H3C
4S9
(514) 868-7272
Emp Here 400   *Sales* 379,222,000
SIC 4899 Communication services, nec
John Hayduk
David M. Ryan
Patrick Bibeau
John Randall Freeman
Ilangovan Gnanaprakasam

D-U-N-S 24-125-6879   (BR)
TELUS COMMUNICATIONS INC
TELUS SOLUTIONS D'AFFAIRES
(*Suby of* TELUS CORPORATION)
111 Boul Robert-Bourassa Unite 4200, Mon-
treal, QC, H3C 2M1
(514) 392-0373
Emp Here 90
SIC 4899 Communication services, nec
Roberto Depani

D-U-N-S 25-739-2696   (SL)
TINK PROFITABILITE NUMERIQUE INC
CONCEPT S21
87 Rue Prince Bureau 140, Montreal, QC,
H3C 2M7
(514) 866-0995
Emp Here 115   *Sales* 16,580,930
SIC 7371 Custom computer programming ser-
vices
Jocelyn Couture
Marcel Tremblay

D-U-N-S 20-534-4091   (BR)
UNIVERSITE DU QUEBEC
UNIVERSITE DU QUEBEC A MONTREAL
(*Suby of* UNIVERSITE DU QUEBEC)
1440 Rue Saint-Denis, Montreal, QC, H3C
3P8
(514) 987-3092
Emp Here 3,500
SIC 8221 Colleges and universities
Jean Pellerin

D-U-N-S 20-909-4234   (HQ)
VIDEOTRON LTEE
BEAUCE DISTRIBUTION T.V.
(*Suby of* QUEBECOR MEDIA INC)
612 Rue Saint-Jacques Bureau 700, Montreal,
QC, H3C 4M8
(514) 281-1232
Emp Here 150   *Sales* 1,170,904,000
SIC 4841 Cable and other pay television ser-
vices

Jean-Francois Pruneau
Emilie Duguay
Brian Mulroney
Normand Provost
Sylvie Lalande
Andre P. Brosseau
Chantal Belanger

D-U-N-S 24-944-1262   (HQ)
VISION GLOBALE A.R. LTEE
VISION GLOBAL
80 Rue Queen Bureau 201, Montreal, QC,
H3C 2N5
(514) 879-0020
Emp Here 100   *Sales* 31,393,600
SIC 7812 Motion picture and video production
Mathieu Lefebvre
Pierre Guerin
Daniel Byette
Samuel Lalo

Montreal, QC H3G

D-U-N-S 20-387-3976   (SL)
10643645 CANADA INC
FOUR SEASONS HOTEL MONTREAL
1440 Rue De La Montagne, Montreal, QC,
H3G 1Z5
(514) 843-2500
Emp Here 300   *Sales* 28,700,400
SIC 7011 Hotels and motels
Andrew Lutfy
Goncalo Monteiro

D-U-N-S 24-351-1305   (SL)
4256344 CANADA INC
(*Suby of* MANULIFE FINANCIAL CORPORA-
TION)
1245 Rue Sherbrooke O Bureau 2100, Mon-
treal, QC, H3G 1G3
(877) 499-9555
Emp Here 2,400   *Sales* 5,128,723,200
SIC 6311 Life insurance
Svetlana Radan
Mario Vertolli
Eddy Mezzetta

D-U-N-S 20-288-6099   (BR)
7660715 CANADA INC
COSSETTE
(*Suby of* VISION 7 INTERNATIONAL INC)
2100 Drummond St, Montreal, QC, H3G 1X1
(514) 845-2727
Emp Here 94
SIC 4899 Communication services, nec
Nathalie Bernier

D-U-N-S 20-180-1813   (SL)
9010-5826 QUEBEC INC
SIR WINSTON CHURCHILL PUB
1459 Rue Crescent, Montreal, QC, H3G 2B2
(514) 288-3814
Emp Here 100   *Sales* 4,551,900
SIC 5812 Eating places
Paul Nakis

D-U-N-S 20-762-6276   (SL)
ACADEMIE MICHELE-PROVOST INC
1517 Av Des Pins O, Montreal, QC, H3G 1B3
(514) 935-2344
Emp Here 95   *Sales* 9,552,060
SIC 8211 Elementary and secondary schools
Michele Provost
Franco Baschiera

D-U-N-S 20-211-7565   (BR)
ALITHYA CANADA INC
C.I.A
(*Suby of* AST TRUST COMPANY (CANADA))
1350 Boul Rene-Levesque O Bureau 200,
Montreal, QC, H3G 1T4
(514) 285-5552
Emp Here 131
SIC 7379 Computer related services, nec

D-U-N-S 20-925-2246   (SL)
ASSOCIATION CHRETIENNE DES JEUNES FEMMES DE MONTREAL
Y DES FEMMES
1355 Boul Rene-Levesque O Bureau 208, Montreal, QC, H3G 1T3
(514) 866-9941
Emp Here 250   *Sales* 23,917,000
SIC 7032 Sporting and recreational camps
Genevieve Gregoire
Sylvie Mercier
Jocelyne Boivin
Brigitte Simard
Marie-Josee Neveu
Miriam Pozza

D-U-N-S 20-774-8864   (HQ)
BANQUE LAURENTIENNE DU CANADA
10 X LESS MORTGAGE (MC)
1360 Boul Rene-Levesque O Bureau 600, Montreal, QC, H3G 0E5
(514) 284-4500
Emp Here 500   *Sales* 805,875,627
SIC 6712 Bank holding companies
Francois Desjardins
Francois Laurin
Deborah Rose
Craig Backman
William Mason
Stephane Therrien
Isabelle Courville
Michael Mueller
Lise Bastarache
Sonia Baxendale

D-U-N-S 25-675-6974   (BR)
CANADIAN AUTOMOBILE ASSOCIATION
CAA-QUEBEC
(*Suby of* CANADIAN AUTOMOBILE ASSOCIATION)
1180 Rue Drummond Bureau 610, Montreal, QC, H3G 2S1
(855) 861-5750
Emp Here 150
SIC 1541 Industrial buildings and warehouses
Paul Pelletier

D-U-N-S 24-851-3116   (HQ)
CGI INC
BANKING TRANSFORMED
1350 Boul Rene-Levesque O Suite 25e, Montreal, QC, H3G 1T4
(514) 841-3200
Emp Here 1,200   *Sales* 8,808,624,126
SIC 7371 Custom computer programming services
George D. Schindler
Serge Godin
Benoit Dube
Stuart A. Forman
Mike Keating
Guy Vigeant
Bernard Labelle
Lorne Gorber
Daniel Rocheleau
Francois Boulanger

D-U-N-S 20-252-7065   (HQ)
CIMENT MCINNIS INC
1350 Boul Rene-Levesque O Bureau 205, Montreal, QC, H3G 2W2
(438) 382-3331
Emp Here 75   *Sales* 28,402,100
SIC 2891 Adhesives and sealants
Louis Laporte
Jean Moreau
Andre Racine
Gilles Poulain
Robert Raven
David L Mcausland
Justin Methot
Marcel Dutil

D-U-N-S 20-790-8310   (SL)
COLLEGE O'SULLIVAN DE MONTREAL INC
1191 Rue De La Montagne, Montreal, QC, H3G 1Z2
(514) 866-4622
Emp Here 70   *Sales* 10,864,840
SIC 8244 Business and secretarial schools
Joanne Rousseau
Jacques Rousseau
Suzanne Drouin
Robin Mayers
Isabel Schurman

D-U-N-S 20-010-3310   (BR)
COMPUTER SCIENCES CANADA INC
C S C
(*Suby of* DXC TECHNOLOGY COMPANY)
1360 Boul Rene-Levesque O Bureau 300, Montreal, QC, H3G 2W7

Emp Here 700
SIC 7379 Computer related services, nec
Costa Petroutsas

D-U-N-S 24-895-5924   (HQ)
CONSEILLERS EN GESTION ET INFORMATIQUE CGI INC
CGI
(*Suby of* CGI INC)
1350 Boul Rene-Levesque O 15e Etage, Montreal, QC, H3G 1T4
(514) 841-3200
Emp Here 500   *Sales* 1,340,321,503
SIC 6712 Bank holding companies
Benoit Dube
Facois Boulanger
Kevin Linder
Max Rogan

D-U-N-S 24-958-8476   (SL)
CONSEILLERS LOGISIL INC, LES
LOGISIL
1440 Rue Sainte-Catherine O Bureau 400, Montreal, QC, H3G 1R8

Emp Here 90   *Sales* 14,632,560
SIC 7379 Computer related services, nec
Denis D'ambroise

D-U-N-S 24-240-2068   (SL)
DRW CANADA CO
TECHNOLOGIES VIGILANT
1360 Boul Rene-Levesque O Bureau 1700, Montreal, QC, H3G 2W4
(514) 940-4040
Emp Here 100   *Sales* 23,428,800
SIC 8742 Management consulting services
Arvind Ramanathan
Joshua Felker

D-U-N-S 25-437-0781   (SL)
EDITION JEUX INFINIS INC
JEUX INFINIS
2110 Rue Drummond Bureau 200, Montreal, QC, H3G 1W9

Emp Here 50   *Sales* 26,027,100
SIC 5092 Toys and hobby goods and supplies
Martin Pinard
Serge Michaud
Nick Foster
Paul Mari
Anthony Brown
David Dreger
Richard Waller

D-U-N-S 24-871-7217   (SL)
FEDERATION   MONDIALE   DE L'HEMOPHILIE
FEDERACION MUNDIAL DE LA HEMOFILIA
1425 Boul Rene-Levesque O Bureau 1010, Montreal, QC, H3G 1T7
(514) 875-7944
Emp Here 30   *Sales* 11,922,420
SIC 8699 Membership organizations, nec
Claudia Black

D-U-N-S 24-359-1984   (HQ)
FONDS DE PLACEMENT IMMOBILIER BTB

BTB REIT
1411 Rue Crescent Bureau 300, Montreal, QC, H3G 2B3
(514) 286-0188
Emp Here 25   *Sales* 66,275,551
SIC 6798 Real estate investment trusts
Michel Leonard
Benoit Cyr
Sylvie Laporte
Paolo Valente
Jocelyn Proteau
Jean-Pierre Janson
Luc Martin
Fernand Perreault
Lucie Ducharme
Luc Lachapelle

D-U-N-S 20-004-7061   (SL)
GESTIONS LUCAP INC
PHARMAPRIX
1500 Rue Sainte-Catherine O, Montreal, QC, H3G 1S8
(514) 933-4744
Emp Here 100   *Sales* 24,432,800
SIC 5912 Drug stores and proprietary stores
Daniel Mongrain

D-U-N-S 20-602-1545   (HQ)
GROUPE ARCOP S.E.N.C., LE
LE GROUPE ARCOP
1244 Rue Sainte-Catherine O Bureau 3e, Montreal, QC, H3G 1P1
(514) 878-3941
Emp Here 55   *Sales* 11,439,296
SIC 8712 Architectural services
Ramesh Khosla
Bruce Allan
Allan Thomas
Norman Glouberman
Edward Hercun
Bruno Verenini
John Cowle
Robert Lapierre
Stephen Propst

D-U-N-S 25-393-0572   (HQ)
GROUPE HAMELIN INC
ENTREPRISES HAMELIN
(*Suby of* GROUPE HAMRO INC)
1328 Redpath Cres, Montreal, QC, H3G 2K2
(514) 934-5577
Emp Here 2   *Sales* 20,449,512
SIC 2821 Plastics materials and resins
Robert Hamelin
Roland Sauvageau

D-U-N-S 24-669-1679   (BR)
HOLT, RENFREW & CIE, LIMITEE
HOLT RENFREW
1300 Rue Sherbrooke O, Montreal, QC, H3G 1H9
(514) 842-5111
Emp Here 200
SIC 5651 Family clothing stores
Michel Jalbert

D-U-N-S 25-825-9977   (BR)
HRC CANADA INC
HARD ROCK CAFE MONTREAL
(*Suby of* THE SEMINOLE TRIBE OF FLORIDA INC)
1458 Rue Crescent, Montreal, QC, H3G 2B6

Emp Here 80
SIC 5812 Eating places
Pascal Coeurdassier

D-U-N-S 24-385-4622   (BR)
IBM CANADA LIMITED
(*Suby of* INTERNATIONAL BUSINESS MACHINES CORPORATION)
1360 Boul Rene-Levesque O Bureau 400, Montreal, QC, H3G 2W6
(888) 245-5572
Emp Here 150
SIC 7372 Prepackaged software
Oliver Paul

D-U-N-S 25-762-8060   (SL)
LA PANTHERE VERTE
2153 Rue Mackay, Montreal, QC, H3G 2J2
(514) 903-4744
Emp Here 49   *Sales* 35,786,905
SIC 5169 Chemicals and allied products, nec
Moshe Chaim Shoham

D-U-N-S 20-852-3014   (HQ)
LIQUID NUTRITION INC
2007 Rue Bishop, Montreal, QC, H3G 2E8

Emp Here 10   *Sales* 27,880,315
SIC 5499 Miscellaneous food stores
Christian Jammal

D-U-N-S 25-243-8239   (SL)
LJC DEVELOPMENT CORPORATION
LOEWS HOTEL VOGUE
(*Suby of* LOEWS CORPORATION)
1425 Rue De La Montagne, Montreal, QC, H3G 1Z3
(514) 285-5555
Emp Here 115   *Sales* 11,001,820
SIC 7011 Hotels and motels
Paul W. Whetsell
Jonathan M Tisch
John J Kenny
Vince Dunleavy

D-U-N-S 24-131-9578   (SL)
MANULIFE TRUST SERVICES LIMITED
1245 Rue Sherbrooke O Bureau 1500, Montreal, QC, H3G 1G3
(514) 499-7999
Emp Here 49   *Sales* 40,561,073
SIC 6722 Management investment, open-end
Charles Guay

D-U-N-S 20-763-6036   (HQ)
MCGILL UNIVERSITY HEALTH CENTRE
MUHC
1650 Av Cedar, Montreal, QC, H3G 1A4
(514) 934-1934
Emp Here 200   *Sales* 1,444,040,000
SIC 8062 General medical and surgical hospitals
Pierre Gfeller
Peter Kruyt
Sarah Prichard
Andre Bonnici
Suzanne Fortier
Dale Maccandlish-Weil
Deep Khosla
James Cherry
Kevin O'farrell
Mary-Anne Carignan

D-U-N-S 20-254-9499   (HQ)
MICHAEL KORS (CANADA) CO
(*Suby of* CAPRI HOLDINGS LIMITED)
3424 Rue Simpson, Montreal, QC, H3G 2J3
(514) 737-5677
Sales 17,939,600
SIC 5632 Women's accessory and specialty stores
John D. Idol
Debra Margles
Krista A. Mcdonough

D-U-N-S 25-371-0768   (HQ)
MICHAEL KORS (CANADA) HOLDINGS LTD
GESTION MICHAEL KORS (CANADA)
(*Suby of* CAPRI HOLDINGS LIMITED)
3424 Rue Simpson, Montreal, QC, H3G 2J3
(514) 737-5677
Emp Here 100   *Sales* 74,853,000
SIC 5632 Women's accessory and specialty stores
John D. Idol
Debra Margles
Thomas J. Edwards, Jr.
Krista A. Mcdonough
Rosina Silla

D-U-N-S 20-856-9343   (HQ)

MUSEE DES BEAUX-ARTS DE MONTREAL
BOUTIQUE M
1380 Rue Sherbrooke O, Montreal, QC, H3G
1J5
(514) 285-2000
Sales 19,923,400
SIC 8412 Museums and art galleries
Jacques Parisien
Julia Reitman
Michel De La Cheneliere
Nadia Hammadi
Alix D'anglejan-Chatillon
Rene Malo
Serge Joyal
Joe Battat
Roger Fournelle
Bruce Mcniven

D-U-N-S 20-588-6984   (BR)
MUSEE DES BEAUX-ARTS DE MONTREAL
(*Suby of* MUSEE DES BEAUX-ARTS DE
MONTREAL)
1379 Rue Sherbrooke O, Montreal, QC, H3G
1J5
(514) 285-1600
Emp Here 200
SIC 8412 Museums and art galleries
Serge Joyal

D-U-N-S 20-288-0902   (BR)
NESTLE CANADA INC
NESPRESSO CANADA
(*Suby of* NESTLE S.A.)
2060 Rue De La Montagne Bureau 304, Mon-
treal, QC, H3G 1Z7
(514) 350-5754
Emp Here 100
SIC 3634 Electric housewares and fans
Peter Brabeck-Letmathe

D-U-N-S 25-541-2280   (SL)
OASIS ESTHETIQUE DISTRIBUTION INC
DR. HAUSCHKA CANADA
1231 Rue Sainte-Catherine O Bureau 303,
Montreal, QC, H3G 1P5
(514) 286-9148
Emp Here 25   *Sales* 27,633,625
SIC 5122 Drugs, proprietaries, and sundries
Andreas Ernst
Enaam Takla

D-U-N-S 20-858-6164   (HQ)
**ORGANISATION CATHOLIQUE CANADI-
ENNE POUR LE DEVELOPPEMENT ET LA
PAIX**
DEVELOPPEMENT ET PAIX
1425 Boul Rene-Levesque O Bureau 300,
Montreal, QC, H3G 1T7
(514) 257-8711
Emp Here 60   *Sales* 56,736,960
SIC 8699 Membership organizations, nec
David Leduc

D-U-N-S 25-194-3080   (SL)
RESTAURANT NEWTOWN INC
NEWTOWN
1476 Rue Crescent, Montreal, QC, H3G 2B6
(514) 284-6555
Emp Here 100   *Sales* 4,551,900
SIC 5812 Eating places
Christopher Nacos

D-U-N-S 20-762-3190   (HQ)
SCDA (2015) INC
(*Suby of* MANULIFE FINANCIAL CORPORA-
TION)
1245 Rue Sherbrooke O Bureau 2100, Mon-
treal, QC, H3G 1G3
(514) 499-8855
Emp Here 1,600   *Sales* 4,273,936,000
SIC 6311 Life insurance

D-U-N-S 20-320-7225   (SL)
SOINS DIRECT INC
1414 Rue Drummond Bureau 620, Montreal,
QC, H3G 1W1
(514) 739-1919
Emp Here 125   *Sales* 9,444,888

SIC 7361 Employment agencies
Pierre Lefort
Chantal Bourgeois

D-U-N-S 24-327-8202   (HQ)
TOURAM LIMITED PARTNERSHIP
AIR CANADA VACATIONS
1440 Rue Sainte-Catherine O Bureau 600,
Montreal, QC, H3G 1R8
(514) 876-0700
Sales 166,723,000
SIC 4724 Travel agencies
Robert Milton

D-U-N-S 24-326-4368   (HQ)
TRITON DIGITAL CANADA INC
1440 Rue Sainte-Catherine O Bureau 1200,
Montreal, QC, H3G 1R8
(514) 448-4037
Sales 22,847,200
SIC 4899 Communication services, nec
Neal Schore

D-U-N-S 24-106-9806   (HQ)
UNION DES ARTISTES
CSA
1441 Boul Rene-Levesque O Bureau 400,
Montreal, QC, H3G 1T7
(514) 288-6682
Emp Here 70   *Sales* 18,355,140
SIC 8621 Professional organizations
Sophie Pregent
Jack Robitaille
Marie-Claude Arpin
Ghyslain Dufresne

D-U-N-S 20-632-7637   (HQ)
UNIVERSITE CONCORDIA
1455 Boul De Maisonneuve O, Montreal, QC,
H3G 1M8
(514) 848-2424
Emp Here 1,000   *Sales* 373,477,500
SIC 8221 Colleges and universities
Alan Shepard
Hebert Jr Norman
Danielle Tessier
Kate Melissa Wheeler
Suzanne Sauvage
Maria E Peluso
Georges M Paulez
Edward Dr.Little
Melanie Hotchkiss
Sandra Dr.Betton

D-U-N-S 24-345-5313   (BR)
UNIVERSITE CONCORDIA
CENTRE FOR CONTINUING EDUCATION
(*Suby of* UNIVERSITE CONCORDIA)
1600 Rue Sainte-Catherine O 1er Etage Fb-
117, Montreal, QC, H3G 1M8
(514) 848-3600
Emp Here 175
SIC 8221 Colleges and universities
Murray Sang

D-U-N-S 20-112-2806   (HQ)
**VALEURS MOBILIERES BANQUE LAU-
RENTIENNE INC**
*COURTAGE ESCOMPTE BANQUE LAU-
RENTIENNE*
(*Suby of* BANQUE LAURENTIENNE DU
CANADA)
1360 Boul Rene-Levesque O Bureau 620,
Montreal, QC, H3G 0E8
(514) 350-2800
Emp Here 20   *Sales* 341,553,120
SIC 6211 Security brokers and dealers
Michel C. Trudeau
Francois Desjardins
Sophie Lapierre
Genevieve Drouin
Patrick F.J. Sheils
Benedetto Vendittelli
Riccardo Magini
Pierre Godbout
Francois Laurin
Susan Kudzman

D-U-N-S 20-939-6253   (BR)
VISION 7 COMMUNICATIONS INC
BLITZ DIRECT, DATA & PROMOTION
(*Suby of* VISION 7 INTERNATIONAL INC)
2100 Rue Drummond, Montreal, QC, H3G
1X1
(514) 845-2727
Emp Here 400
SIC 8743 Public relations services
Benoit Bessette

D-U-N-S 20-703-5622   (BR)
VISION 7 COMMUNICATIONS INC
SIMPLESTRATUS
(*Suby of* VISION 7 INTERNATIONAL INC)
2100 Rue Drummond, Montreal, QC, H3G
1X1
(514) 282-4709
Emp Here 300
SIC 4899 Communication services, nec

D-U-N-S 20-534-8910   (BR)
VISION 7 COMMUNICATIONS INC
COSSETTE COMMUNICATION
(*Suby of* VISION 7 INTERNATIONAL INC)
2100 Rue Drummond, Montreal, QC, H3G
1X1
(514) 845-4040
Emp Here 350
SIC 8743 Public relations services
Melanie Dunn

D-U-N-S 20-765-0813   (HQ)
YMCA DU QUEBEC, LES
GARDERIE DU CENTRE Y CARTIERVILLE
1435 Rue Drummond Bureau 4e, Montreal,
QC, H3G 1W4
(514) 849-5331
Emp Here 250   *Sales* 207,068,000
SIC 8399 Social services, nec
Stephane Vaillancourt
Nancy Audette
Yves Mehe
Jean Ouellet

Montreal, QC H3H

D-U-N-S 24-934-5695   (HQ)
131427 CANADA INC
COLLEGE LASALLE INDUSTRIE
2000 Rue Sainte-Catherine O Bureau 2, Mon-
treal, QC, H3H 2T2
(514) 939-4444
Emp Here 180   *Sales* 29,878,200
SIC 8221 Colleges and universities
Jacques Marchand
Elie Halwagi
Andre Lefebvre

D-U-N-S 25-099-8622   (SL)
3566072 CANADA INC
LOCATION AUTOMAX
1920 Rue Sainte-Catherine O, Montreal, QC,
H3H 1M4
(514) 937-7777
Emp Here 50   *Sales* 24,903,900
SIC 5511 New and used car dealers
Gabriel Azouz
Pierre Salah

D-U-N-S 24-320-2574   (HQ)
3731537 CANADA INC
G.C.L.
2000 Rue Sainte-Catherine O Bureau 9000,
Montreal, QC, H3H 2T2
(514) 939-4442
Sales 27,335,000
SIC 6712 Bank holding companies
Claude Marchand
Piero Greco
Remi Marchand

D-U-N-S 20-703-6620   (BR)
3855155 CANADA INC
SUPERMARCHE P.A.

(*Suby of* 3855155 CANADA INC)
1420 Rue Du Fort, Montreal, QC, H3H 2C4

Emp Here 100
SIC 5411 Grocery stores
Anastasios Erimos

D-U-N-S 24-312-4133   (SL)
9145-1971 QUEBEC INC
MERIDIEN VERSAILLES- MONTREAL, LE
1808 Rue Sherbrooke O, Montreal, QC, H3H
1E5
(514) 933-8111
Emp Here 100   *Sales* 9,489,900
SIC 7011 Hotels and motels
Mike Yuval
Jack Sofer

D-U-N-S 24-204-9406   (BR)
ASTRAL BROADCASTING GROUP INC
CHAINES TELE ASTRAL
1616 Boul Rene-Levesque O Bureau 300,
Montreal, QC, H3H 1P8
(514) 939-3150
Emp Here 100
SIC 4833 Television broadcasting stations

D-U-N-S 24-000-7497   (HQ)
ASTRAL MEDIA RADIO INC
ENERGIE
2100 Rue Sainte-Catherine O Bureau 1000,
Montreal, QC, H3H 2T3
(514) 529-3200
Emp Here 50   *Sales* 261,613,408
SIC 4832 Radio broadcasting stations
Jacques Parisien
Claude Gagnon
Ian Greenberg
Andre Bureau

D-U-N-S 20-178-0363   (BR)
BANK OF NOVA SCOTIA, THE
SCOTIABANK
(*Suby of* BANK OF NOVA SCOTIA, THE)
1922 Rue Sainte-Catherine O Bureau 300,
Montreal, QC, H3H 1M4

Emp Here 100
SIC 6021 National commercial banks
Jentsch Dieter W.

D-U-N-S 24-061-5943   (BR)
BEST BUY CANADA LTD
FUTURE SHOP
(*Suby of* BEST BUY CO., INC.)
2313 Rue Sainte-Catherine O Bureau 108,
Montreal, QC, H3H 1N2

Emp Here 100
SIC 5731 Radio, television, and electronic
stores

D-U-N-S 24-590-0170   (SL)
CENTRE CANADIEN D'ARCHITECURE
1920 Rue Baile, Montreal, QC, H3H 2S6
(514) 939-7028
Emp Here 110   *Sales* 11,534,600
SIC 8412 Museums and art galleries
Phyllis Lambert

D-U-N-S 24-490-4710   (SL)
COLLEGE DE MONTREAL
1931 Rue Sherbrooke O, Montreal, QC, H3H
1E3
(514) 933-7397
Emp Here 90   *Sales* 10,137,240
SIC 8221 Colleges and universities
Guy Lefebvre
Paul Villemaire
Luc Edith
Jacques Giguere
Serge Gatineau
Michel St-Germain
Regent Gagnon
Pauline Langlois
Hugo Lambert
Pierre Bournaki

▲ Public Company   ■ Public Company Family Member   **HQ** Headquarters   **BR** Branch   **SL** Single Location

D-U-N-S 20-962-9245   (HQ)
COLLEGE LASALLE
GARDERIE LASALLE DES PETITS
2120 Rue Sainte-Catherine O, Montreal, QC,
H3H 1M7
(514) 939-2006
Sales 39,410,800
SIC 8249 Vocational schools, nec
Jacques Marchand
Elie Halwagi
Marie-Christine Tremblay
Alain Barette
Jean-Yves Marquis

D-U-N-S 20-924-9747   (HQ)
**CORPORATION   ARCHIEPISCOPALE
CATHOLIQUE ROMAINE DE MONTREAL,
LA**
*CATHEDRALE (BASILIQUE) MARIE-REINE-
DU- MONDE ET SAINT-JACQUES*
2000 Rue Sherbrooke O, Montreal, QC, H3H
1G4
(514) 931-7311
Emp Here 1   *Sales* 10,412,300
SIC 8661 Religious organizations
Christian Lepine
Francois Sarrazin
Jean-Jacques Martin
Claire Houde
Thomas Dowd
Alain Faubert

D-U-N-S 24-936-0850   (SL)
GENIVAR INC
Edifice Northern 1600 Rene-Levesque Blvd
W, Montreal, QC, H3H 1P9
(514) 340-0046
Emp Here 5,500   *Sales* 641,324,463
SIC 8711 Engineering services

D-U-N-S 20-298-3805   (HQ)
GROUPE WSP GLOBAL INC
(*Suby of* AST TRUST COMPANY (CANADA))
1600 Boul Rene-Levesque O Bureau 16, Mon-
treal, QC, H3H 1P9
(514) 340-0046
Emp Here 7,900   *Sales* 5,995,146,426
SIC 8741 Management services
Alexandre L'heureux
Isabelle Adjahi
Alain Michaud
Albert Aubry
Suzanne Gendron
Andre-Martin Bouchard
Bruno Roy
Paul Dollin
Robert Ouellette
Jenny Dho

D-U-N-S 24-715-1041   (SL)
**INSTITUT DE RECHERCHE DU CENTRE
UNIVERSITAIRE DE SANTE MCGILL, L'**
2155 Rue Guy Bureau 500, Montreal, QC,
H3H 2R9
(514) 934-8354
Emp Here 750   *Sales* 244,478,250
SIC 8071 Medical laboratories
Cinzia Raponi
Pierre Lortie
Graham Bagnall
David Eidelman
Raymond Royer
Daniel Gagnier
Bruze Mazer
Mary-Anne Carignan
Pierre Gfeller

D-U-N-S 24-865-1515   (HQ)
INVESTISSEMENTS PROSPA INC
1262 Rue Saint-Mathieu, Montreal, QC, H3H
2H8

Sales 18,382,694
SIC 5149 Groceries and related products, nec
Philip Charles Hirst

D-U-N-S 24-345-2880   (BR)

MCGILL UNIVERSITY HEALTH CENTRE
*HOPITAL DE MONTREAL POUR ENFANTS,
L'*
(*Suby of* MCGILL UNIVERSITY HEALTH
CENTRE)
2300 Rue Tupper Bureau F372, Montreal, QC,
H3H 1P3
(514) 412-4307
Emp Here 2,000
SIC 8069 Specialty hospitals, except psychi-
atric
Martin Alfonso

D-U-N-S 20-649-3954   (SL)
PUBLICITE TAXI MONTREAL INC
MEC MONTREAL
1600 Boul Rene-Levesque O Bureau 1200,
Montreal, QC, H3H 1P9
(514) 935-6375
Emp Here 60   *Sales* 12,703,440
SIC 7311 Advertising agencies
Jacques Labelle
Robert Guenette
Thomas D. Cook

D-U-N-S 25-632-5416   (HQ)
REBUTS SOLIDES CANADIENS INC
1635 Rue Sherbrooke O Bureau 300, Mon-
treal, QC, H3H 1E2
(514) 987-5151
Emp Here 15   *Sales* 81,430,500
SIC 4953 Refuse systems
Gilbert Durocher
Anouk Fournier
Pierre De Montlivault
Anne Loussouarn
Pierre Vandekerckhove

D-U-N-S 24-570-5397   (SL)
SAINE MARKETING INC
2222 Boul Rene-Levesque O Bureau 220,
Montreal, QC, H3H 1R6
(514) 931-8233
Emp Here 900   *Sales* 197,948,700
SIC 8732 Commercial nonphysical research
Jean Saine

D-U-N-S 20-979-3538   (HQ)
SCHWARTZ LEVITSKY FELDMAN LLP
SLF
1980 Rue Sherbrooke O Etage 10, Montreal,
QC, H3H 1E8
(514) 937-6392
Emp Here 40   *Sales* 24,922,200
SIC 8721 Accounting, auditing, and book-
keeping
Morty Lober
Luciano D'ignazio
Jonathan Ragnauth
Jeffrey Feldman
Ralph Ginzburg
Gerald Goldberg
Brian Mozessohn
Stacy Mitchell
Kai Chang
Bernard Jeanty

D-U-N-S 20-032-6994   (BR)
SECURITAS CANADA LIMITED
(*Suby of* SECURITAS AB)
1980 Rue Sherbrooke O Bureau 300, Mon-
treal, QC, H3H 1E8
(514) 935-2533
Emp Here 1,500
SIC 7381 Detective and armored car services
Jean Ruel

D-U-N-S 24-542-8834   (HQ)
**SOEURS DE LA CONGREGATION DE
NOTRE-DAME, LES**
2330 Rue Sherbrooke O, Montreal, QC, H3H
1G8
(514) 931-5891
Sales 10,772,700
SIC 8661 Religious organizations
Ona Bessette
Agnes Campbell

D-U-N-S 20-101-0662   (SL)
SOEURS GRISES DE MONTREAL, LES
*MAISON MERE DES SOEURS GRISES DE
MONTREAL*
1190 Rue Guy, Montreal, QC, H3H 2L4

Emp Here 130   *Sales* 13,535,990
SIC 8661 Religious organizations

D-U-N-S 25-307-2870   (BR)
**STANDARD BROADCAST PRODUCTIONS
LTD**
C J A D
1411 Rue Du Fort Unite 300, Montreal, QC,
H3H 2N7
(514) 989-2523
Emp Here 150
SIC 4832 Radio broadcasting stations
Brett Dakin

D-U-N-S 24-383-8690   (BR)
TRADER CORPORATION
(*Suby of* APAX PARTNERS LLP)
1600 Boul Rene-Levesque O Bureau 140,
Montreal, QC, H3H 1P9
(514) 764-4000
Emp Here 200
SIC 2721 Periodicals
Luc Morin

D-U-N-S 24-791-0854   (HQ)
WSP CANADA INC
AQUAPRAXIS
(*Suby of* AST TRUST COMPANY (CANADA))
1600 Boul Rene-Levesque O 16e Etage, Mon-
treal, QC, H3H 1P9
(514) 340-0046
Emp Here 800   *Sales* 1,604,219,001
SIC 6712 Bank holding companies
Hugo Blasutta
Andre Desautels
Josee Gagnon
Victoria Trim

Montreal, QC H3J

D-U-N-S 24-205-5536   (SL)
ALERTPAY INCORPORATED
PAIEMENTS ALERTES
1610 Rue Notre-Dame O Suite 175, Montreal,
QC, H3J 1M1
(514) 748-5774
Emp Here 100   *Sales* 16,258,400
SIC 7379 Computer related services, nec
Firoz Patel
Ferhan Patel

D-U-N-S 24-226-7057   (BR)
ARDENT MILLS ULC
(*Suby of* CHS INC.)
2110 Rue Notre-Dame O, Montreal, QC, H3J
1N2
(514) 939-8051
Emp Here 80
SIC 2041 Flour and other grain mill products
Jean-Pierre Roy

D-U-N-S 24-083-6338   (HQ)
CANADA WORLD YOUTH INC
2330 Rue Notre-Dame O Bureau 300, Mon-
treal, QC, H3J 1N4
(514) 931-3526
Emp Here 30   *Sales* 16,439,375
SIC 8641 Civic and social associations
Susan Handrigan
Mathieu Pearce
John Cawley

D-U-N-S 24-887-2801   (SL)
GASTRONOMIA ALIMENTS FINS INC
1619b Rue William, Montreal, QC, H3J 1R1
(514) 281-6400
Emp Here 25   *Sales* 14,808,772
SIC 5142 Packaged frozen goods

Vincent Mahe
Jean-Philippe Brouillet

D-U-N-S 24-208-5616   (BR)
PROGRAM DE PORTAGE INC, LE
*PROGRAM FOR MENTALLY ILL CHEMICAL
ABUSERS (MICA)*
(*Suby of* PROGRAM DE PORTAGE INC, LE)
2455 Av Lionel-Groulx, Montreal, QC, H3J 1J6
(514) 935-3431
Emp Here 300
SIC 8322 Individual and family services

D-U-N-S 24-541-8371   (HQ)
**PROGRAMME DE PORTAGE RELATIF A LA
DEPENDENCE DE LA DROGUE INC, LE**
865 Place Richmond, Montreal, QC, H3J 1V8
(514) 939-0202
Sales 14,440,400
SIC 8069 Specialty hospitals, except psychi-
atric
Peter Howlett
Tricia L. Kuhl

D-U-N-S 20-228-6803   (HQ)
**QUINCAILLERIE NOTRE-DAME DE ST-
HENRI INC**
RONA
2371 Rue Notre-Dame O Bureau 1, Montreal,
QC, H3J 1N3
(514) 932-5616
Emp Here 65   *Sales* 22,750,420
SIC 5251 Hardware stores
Georges Lanouette
Jean Lanouette
Marc Lanouette

D-U-N-S 25-156-0934   (SL)
**SERVICES DE CALECHES & TRAINEAUX
LUCKY LUC ENR, LES**
1810 Rue Basin, Montreal, QC, H3J 1S3
(514) 934-6105
Emp Here 30   *Sales* 15,599,010
SIC 4789 Transportation services, nec
Luc Desparois

Montreal, QC H3K

D-U-N-S 20-223-8408   (SL)
9278-3455 QUEBEC INC
GROUPE LAUZON
(*Suby of* GROUPE LAUZON INC)
2715 Rue De Reading, Montreal, QC, H3K
1P7
(514) 937-8571
Emp Here 200   *Sales* 143,343,200
SIC 5147 Meats and meat products
Francine Lauzon
Andree Lauzon
Felix Des Ruisseaux

D-U-N-S 20-762-7811   (HQ)
BOUTIQUE TRISTAN & ISEUT INC
TRISTAN
(*Suby of* 2324-3637 QUEBEC INC)
20 Rue Des Seigneurs, Montreal, QC, H3K
3K3
(514) 937-4601
Emp Here 105   *Sales* 87,328,500
SIC 5621 Women's clothing stores
Lili Fortin
Gilles R Fortin
Denise Deslauriers
Charles Fortin
Laurence Fortin
Caroline Deslauriers

D-U-N-S 20-303-5399   (SL)
CDA-TEQ QUEBEC INC
1201 Rue De Conde, Montreal, QC, H3K 2E4
(514) 789-0529
Emp Here 20   *Sales* 10,702,480
SIC 5142 Packaged frozen goods
Jerome Ferrer

Patrice De Felice

D-U-N-S 25-259-2696   (HQ)
CLAN PANNETON (1993) INC, LE
DEMENAGEMENT LE CLAN PANNETON
(*Suby of* 3092-2926 QUEBEC INC)
2660 Rue Mullins, Montreal, QC, H3K 1P4
(514) 937-0707
Emp Here 50   *Sales* 11,114,400
SIC 4214 Local trucking with storage
 Daniel Moshutz
 Pierre-Olivier Cyr
 Lise Panneton

D-U-N-S 24-019-2542   (SL)
CLINIQUE COMMUNAUTAIRE POINTE-ST-CHARLES
500 Av Ash, Montreal, QC, H3K 2R4
(514) 937-9251
Emp Here 120   *Sales* 22,824,840
SIC 8011 Offices and clinics of medical doctors
 Luc Leblanc

D-U-N-S 24-958-9789   (SL)
COMPAGNIE DE POISSONS DE MONTREAL LTEE, LA
1647 Rue Saint-Patrick, Montreal, QC, H3K 3G9
(514) 486-9537
Emp Here 10   *Sales* 104,266,980
SIC 5146 Fish and seafoods
 Maxim Beaudry
 Gabrielle Beaudry
 Martin Beaudry

D-U-N-S 25-832-1876   (BR)
COSTCO WHOLESALE CANADA LTD
COSTCO MONTREAL
(*Suby of* COSTCO WHOLESALE CORPORATION)
300 Rue Bridge, Montreal, QC, H3K 2C3
(514) 938-5170
Emp Here 200
SIC 5399 Miscellaneous general merchandise
 Max Inporneri

D-U-N-S 24-679-5850   (SL)
DISTRIBUTIONS MAROLINE INC
MAROLINE
751 Rue Richardson Bureau 4600, Montreal, QC, H3K 1G6
(514) 343-0448
Emp Here 40   *Sales* 17,886,960
SIC 5064 Electrical appliances, television and radio
 Henri Amiel
 David Amiel
 Jonathan Amiel
 Marilyn Dalton

D-U-N-S 20-400-5586   (SL)
EMBALLAGE CANFAB INC
(*Suby of* INVESTISSEMENTS CANFAB INC., LES)
2740 Rue Saint-Patrick, Montreal, QC, H3K 1B8
(514) 935-5265
Emp Here 80   *Sales* 15,581,440
SIC 2655 Fiber cans, drums, and similar products
 Thomas Klein

D-U-N-S 25-140-6828   (HQ)
GROUP GSOFT INC
1751 Rue Richardson Bureau 5400, Montreal, QC, H3K 1G6
(514) 303-8203
Sales 11,190,360
SIC 8742 Management consulting services
 Simon De Baene
 Guillaume Roy
 Sebastien Leduc
 Maxime Boissonneault
 Christian Merat

D-U-N-S 20-213-3716   (HQ)
INVESTISSEMENTS CANFAB INC., LES

2740 Rue Saint-Patrick, Montreal, QC, H3K 1B8
(514) 935-5265
Emp Here 53   *Sales* 12,659,920
SIC 2655 Fiber cans, drums, and similar products
 Thomas Klein

D-U-N-S 20-651-0427   (BR)
MOORE CANADA CORPORATION
R.R. DONNELLEY
(*Suby of* R. R. DONNELLEY & SONS COMPANY)
1500 Rue Saint-Patrick, Montreal, QC, H3K 0A3
(514) 415-7300
Emp Here 100
SIC 2759 Commercial printing, nec
 Pierre Dallaen

D-U-N-S 25-739-3561   (HQ)
OPAL-RT TECHNOLOGIES INC
1751 Rue Richardson Bureau 2525, Montreal, QC, H3K 1G6
(514) 935-2323
Sales 18,743,660
SIC 7371 Custom computer programming services
 Jean Belanger
 Lise Laforce
 Vincent Lapointe

D-U-N-S 20-309-4297   (HQ)
PAGES JAUNES LIMITEE
YELLOW MEDIA
1751 Rue Richardson Bureau 2300, Montreal, QC, H3K 1G6
(514) 934-2611
Emp Here 900   *Sales* 437,572,684
SIC 2741 Miscellaneous publishing
 David A. Eckert
 John R. Ireland
 Dany Paradis
 Stephen K. Smith
 Franco Sciannamblo
 Treena Cooper
 Susan Kudzman
 Donald Hunter Morrison
 Kalpana Raina
 Craig Forman

D-U-N-S 24-902-8358   (SL)
PRODUCTIONS PIXCOM INC
(*Suby of* GROUPE PIXCOM INC)
1720 Rue Du Canal, Montreal, QC, H3K 3E6
(514) 931-1188
Emp Here 100   *Sales* 8,916,300
SIC 7812 Motion picture and video production
 Jacquelin Bouchard
 Nicola Merola
 Sylvie Desrochers

D-U-N-S 25-746-6102   (SL)
PRODUCTIONS VENDOME II INC, LES
VENDOME TELE
1751 Rue Richardson Bureau 5 105, Montreal, QC, H3K 1G6
(514) 369-4834
Emp Here 150   *Sales* 15,897,600
SIC 7922 Theatrical producers and services
 Andre Dubois

D-U-N-S 25-389-6377   (HQ)
RAY-MONT LOGISTIQUES CANADA INC
1751 Rue Richardson Bureau 4504, Montreal, QC, H3K 1G6
(514) 933-4449
Emp Here 50   *Sales* 66,689,200
SIC 4731 Freight transportation arrangement
 Charles Raymond

D-U-N-S 24-311-7103   (SL)
REVE ALCHIMIQUE INC
CASTEL ROC
1751 Rue Richardson, Montreal, QC, H3K 1G6
(514) 904-3700
Emp Here 100   *Sales* 52,054,200

SIC 5092 Toys and hobby goods and supplies
 Andrew Day
 Giacomo Duranti

D-U-N-S 20-694-7900   (SL)
SERVICES DE JEUX BABEL INC
BABEL
(*Suby of* KEYWORDS STUDIOS PLC)
1751 Rue Richardson Bureau 8400, Montreal, QC, H3K 1G6
(514) 904-3700
Emp Here 500   *Sales* 92,286,500
SIC 7371 Custom computer programming services
 Andrew Day
 Giacomo Duranti
 Nicolas Liorzou
 David Lawson

D-U-N-S 20-567-8969   (BR)
SOCIETE DES CASINOS DU QUEBEC INC, LA
(*Suby of* GOUVERNEMENT DE LA PROVINCE DE QUEBEC)
325 Rue Bridge Bureau 1178, Montreal, QC, H3K 2C7
(514) 409-3111
Emp Here 350
SIC 7311 Advertising agencies

D-U-N-S 24-098-7896   (BR)
SYMCOR INC
(*Suby of* SYMCOR INC)
650 Rue Bridge, Montreal, QC, H3K 3K9
(514) 787-4325
Emp Here 400
SIC 2621 Paper mills
 Francois Siarx

D-U-N-S 20-286-1923   (SL)
THEATRIXX TECHNOLOGIES INC
1655 Rue Richardson, Montreal, QC, H3K 3J7
(514) 939-3077
Emp Here 50   *Sales* 10,233,650
SIC 3613 Switchgear and switchboard apparatus
 Jr. Jacques Tessier
 Francois Levasseur
 Gabriel Duschinsky

D-U-N-S 24-712-7046   (SL)
TRIUM MOBILIER DE BUREAU INC
ESPACE SANTE
3200 Rue Saint-Patrick, Montreal, QC, H3K 3H5
(514) 878-8000
Emp Here 50   *Sales* 25,442,800
SIC 5021 Furniture
 Daniel Perreault

Montreal, QC H3L

D-U-N-S 20-632-5011   (HQ)
2164-1204 QUEBEC INC
MAISON DU PEINTRE, LA
9795 Rue Waverly, Montreal, QC, H3L 2V7
(514) 381-8524
Emp Here 4   *Sales* 28,958,280
SIC 5198 Paints, varnishes, and supplies
 Lionel Rodgers
 Daniel Rodgers
 Jacinthe Morin
 Vincent Ferrara

D-U-N-S 25-672-9153   (SL)
3469051 CANADA INC
GROUPE AXXYS
9680 Boul Saint-Laurent, Montreal, QC, H3L 2M9
(514) 388-8080
Emp Here 45   *Sales* 21,182,895
SIC 1542 Nonresidential construction, nec
 Yohan Ohayon
 Ilan Reich

D-U-N-S 20-288-1173   (HQ)
4423038 CANADA INC
SOGO
9850 Rue Meilleur, Montreal, QC, H3L 3J4
(514) 385-5568
Emp Here 2   *Sales* 13,077,650
SIC 6712 Bank holding companies
 Nathan Saleh

D-U-N-S 20-008-8891   (SL)
9046-6483 QUEBEC INC
RE/MAX PRO-COMMERCIAL
10314 Boul Saint-Laurent, Montreal, QC, H3L 2P2
(514) 382-6789
Emp Here 49   *Sales* 16,029,223
SIC 6531 Real estate agents and managers
 Ginette Cholette

D-U-N-S 24-226-8753   (HQ)
BOIS EXPANSION INC
9750 Boul Saint-Laurent, Montreal, QC, H3L 2N3
(514) 381-5626
Emp Here 38   *Sales* 39,798,486
SIC 5031 Lumber, plywood, and millwork
 Jacques Bergevin
 Eric Bergevin
 Louise Bergevin
 Edith Bergevin

D-U-N-S 24-541-9437   (HQ)
BOUTHILLETTE PARIZEAU INC
CBA EXPERTS-CONSEILS
9825 Rue Verville, Montreal, QC, H3L 3E1
(514) 383-3747
Sales 17,873,900
SIC 8711 Engineering services
 Pierre Hebert
 Claude Decary
 Patrick St-Onge
 Dominic Latour
 Jean Pierre

D-U-N-S 20-323-5791   (HQ)
BUFFALO INTERNATIONAL INC
BUFFALO INTERNATIONAL
(*Suby of* LOTUS INTERNATIONAL INC)
400 Rue Sauve O, Montreal, QC, H3L 1Z8
(514) 388-3551
Sales 18,340,300
SIC 2211 Broadwoven fabric mills, cotton
 Gabriel Bitton
 Michel Bitton
 David Bitton
 Charles Bitton

D-U-N-S 25-182-2821   (SL)
CENTRE DE PSYCHOLOGIE GOUIN INC
39 Boul Gouin O, Montreal, QC, H3L 1H9
(514) 331-5530
Emp Here 45   *Sales* 16,255,665
SIC 8049 Offices of health practitioner
 Yohan Emond

D-U-N-S 24-359-5019   (SL)
COMPAGNIE DE COMMERCE A.S. & F. LTEE
9850 Rue Meilleur, Montreal, QC, H3L 3J4
(514) 385-5568
Emp Here 50   *Sales* 24,916,100
SIC 5136 Men's and boy's clothing
 Elie Saleh
 Nathan Saleh
 Marguerite Saleh

D-U-N-S 24-934-7329   (HQ)
CONSOLTEX INC
FUTURA
(*Suby of* GEOSAM INVESTMENTS LIMITED)
560 Boul Henri-Bourassa O Bureau 302, Montreal, QC, H3L 1P4
(514) 333-8800
Emp Here 19   *Sales* 22,008,360
SIC 2299 Textile goods, nec
 George Armoyan
 Robert Jeffery

Hripsime Armoyan

D-U-N-S 24-679-4309   (HQ)
DISTRIBUTION AD WATERS (CAN) INC
9805 Rue Clark, Montreal, QC, H3L 2R5
(514) 381-4141
Emp Here 1   *Sales* 22,358,700
SIC 5074 Plumbing and heating equipment
and supplies (hydronics)
David Ross
Antonio Masecchia
Michael Panzera
Giuseppe Panzera

D-U-N-S 25-362-0702   (BR)
DOUBLETEX
(*Suby of* DOUBLETEX)
9785 Rue Jeanne-Mance, Montreal, QC, H3L
3B6
(514) 382-1770
Emp Here 175
SIC 2211 Broadwoven fabric mills, cotton
Richard Zuckerman

D-U-N-S 20-822-2914   (SL)
**ESTIMATIONS DE CONSTRUCTION DU
QUEBEC INC**
CONSTRUCTIONS EMBEC
78 Rue De Port-Royal E, Montreal, QC, H3L
1H7 .

Emp Here 30   *Sales* 14,121,930
SIC 1542 Nonresidential construction, nec
Emilio Fernandez
Silvan Alfredo

D-U-N-S 24-351-0807   (SL)
GIRO INC
*GROUPE   EN   INFORMATIQUE   ET
RECHERCHE OPERATIONNELLE, LE*
(*Suby of* ENTREPRISES GIRO INC, LES)
75 Rue De Port-Royal E Bureau 500, Mon-
treal, QC, H3L 3T1
(514) 383-0404
Emp Here 330   *Sales* 60,909,090
SIC 7371 Custom computer programming ser-
vices
Jean Aubin
Jean-Marc Rousseau
Joanne Blais
Daniel Dubuc
Jean-Yves Blais
Jean Boisvert
Lise Seguin
Marc Dupont
Nigel Hamer
Huguette Benoit

D-U-N-S 25-847-3466   (SL)
GROUPE SOLUTION COLLECT SOLU INC
560 Boul Henri-Bourassa O Bureau 202, Mon-
treal, QC, H3L 1P4
(514) 331-1074
Emp Here 49   *Sales* 12,363,239
SIC 7322 Adjustment and collection services
Ghislain Rheaume
Andre Pitoscia

D-U-N-S 20-226-3802   (HQ)
J. J. MARSHALL INC
J J M
9780 Rue Waverly, Montreal, QC, H3L 2V5
(514) 381-5647
Sales 10,504,575
SIC 2657 Folding paperboard boxes
Michael Glynn
Fouad Khoury
Glynn Margaret

D-U-N-S 20-231-7319   (HQ)
REITMANS (CANADA) LIMITEE
ADDITION ELLE
250 Rue Sauve O, Montreal, QC, H3L 1Z2
(514) 384-1140
Sales 694,481,512
SIC 5621 Women's clothing stores
Jeremy H. Reitman

Stephen F. Reitman
Richard Wait
Alain Murad
Diane Archibald
Aldo Battista
Julie Blanchet
Leta Bridgeman
Domenic Carbone
Nicolas Gaudreau

D-U-N-S 20-849-6729   (HQ)
SERVICES FINANCIERS NCO, INC
AGENCE DE RECOUVREMENT NCO
(*Suby of* GATESTONE & CO. INC)
75 Rue De Port-Royal E Bureau 240, Mon-
treal, QC, H3L 3T1
(514) 385-4444
Emp Here 1,000   *Sales* 601,113,000
SIC 7322 Adjustment and collection services
Pasquale Di Franco
Maria A. Albino
Irving Shapiro

Montreal, QC H3M

D-U-N-S 25-245-5233   (BR)
BONDUELLE CANADA INC
(*Suby of* BONDUELLE)
600 Rue Henri Bourassa O Bureau 630, Mon-
treal, QC, H3M 3E2
(514) 384-4281
Emp Here 250
SIC 2037 Frozen fruits and vegetables

D-U-N-S 25-240-6699   (BR)
COMMISSION SCOLAIRE DE MONTREAL
ECOLE EVANGELINE
(*Suby of* COMMISSION SCOLAIRE DE
MONTREAL)
11845 Boul De L'Acadie Bureau 281, Mon-
treal, QC, H3M 2T4
(514) 596-5280
Emp Here 100
SIC 8211 Elementary and secondary schools
Pierre Simard

D-U-N-S 20-228-8346   (HQ)
LABORATOIRES OMEGA LIMITEE
(*Suby of* NICHI-IKO PHARMACEUTICAL
CO.,LTD.)
11177 Rue Hamon, Montreal, QC, H3M 3E4
(514) 335-0310
Emp Here 100   *Sales* 28,402,100
SIC 2834 Pharmaceutical preparations
Bruce W. Levins
Tamura Yuichi
Jeffrey Greve
Mikhail Eydelman
Peter Kaemmerer

D-U-N-S 20-591-3577   (HQ)
PATTERSON DENTAIRE CANADA INC
1205 Boul Henri-Bourassa O, Montreal, QC,
H3M 3E6
(514) 745-4040
Emp Here 200   *Sales* 279,989,096
SIC 5047 Medical and hospital equipment
James G. Ryan
Gugino Ann B.
Scott P Anderson
Alain Dumais

D-U-N-S 24-226-7172   (SL)
SUPERMARCHE PIERRE M LEDUC INC
*SUPERMARCHE   PIERRE   LEDUC   ET
FILLES*
2820 Rue De Salaberry, Montreal, QC, H3M
1L3
(514) 745-1640
Emp Here 45   *Sales* 12,336,840
SIC 5411 Grocery stores
Pierre M Leduc

Montreal, QC H3N

D-U-N-S 24-600-2646   (SL)
138984 CANADA LTEE
KILO GATEAUX
6744 Rue Hutchison, Montreal, QC, H3N 1Y4
(514) 270-3024
Emp Here 60   *Sales* 13,491,300
SIC 2051 Bread, cake, and related products
Robert Bennett
Malcolm Bennett

D-U-N-S 24-683-5917   (SL)
176061 CANADA INC
NEW HOMEMANDE KOSHER BAKERY, THE
6915 Av Querbes, Montreal, QC, H3N 2B3
(514) 270-5567
Emp Here 45   *Sales* 10,118,475
SIC 2051 Bread, cake, and related products
Pinchos Freund
Hanna Felsen Freund

D-U-N-S 24-978-2223   (SL)
9191-1263 QUEBEC INC
RESSOURCE DE LA MONTAGNE
7001 Av Du Parc, Montreal, QC, H3N 1X7
(514) 316-7457
Emp Here 100   *Sales* 28,443,700
SIC 6512 Nonresidential building operators
Michael Lapenna
Vincent Chiara

D-U-N-S 20-212-7353   (HQ)
BRAULT & BOUTHILLIER LTEE
BB EDUCATION
700 Av Beaumont, Montreal, QC, H3N 1V5
(514) 273-9186
Sales 22,358,700
SIC 5049 Professional equipment, nec
Marc Vaugeois
Paul Le Brun
Jean-Stephane Yansouni
Yves Brault
Michael Derai
Philippe St-Cyr Adam
Catherine Parent

D-U-N-S 20-363-1288   (SL)
CAPITAL ONE BANK (CANADA BRANCH)
*BANQUE   CAPITAL   ONE   (SUCCURSALE
CANADIENNE)*
(*Suby of* CAPITAL ONE FINANCIAL CORPO-
RATION)
950 Av Beaumont, Montreal, QC, H3N 1V5
(800) 481-3239
Emp Here 100   *Sales* 22,394,100
SIC 6153 Short-term business credit institu-
tions, except agricultural
Richard D. Fairbank
Shane T Holdaway
Michael I. Wassmer
R. Scott Blackley
John G. Finneran Jr.
Bradford H. Warner
Catherine G West
Pierre E. Leroy
Peter E. Raskind
Parna Chennapragada

D-U-N-S 24-562-3103   (SL)
**CENTRE DE RECHERCHE INFORMATIQUE
DE MONTREAL INC**
*COMPUTER   RESEARCH   INSTITUTE   OF
MONTREAL*
405 Av Ogilvy Bureau 101, Montreal, QC, H3N
1M3
(514) 840-1234
Emp Here 60   *Sales* 13,785,240
SIC 8731 Commercial physical research
Francoys Labonte
Steven Chamberland
Andre Manseau
Julie Insley
Pierre Dumouchel

Pierre Courchesne
Daniel Granger
Guillaume Bazinet
Claude Vigeant
Jean Talbot

D-U-N-S 20-223-7319   (SL)
**ENTREPRISES   LAURENTIEN   ELEC-
TRIQUE INC, LES**
890 Boul Cremazie O, Montreal, QC, H3N 1A4
(514) 276-8551
Emp Here 80   *Sales* 17,426,320
SIC 1731 Electrical work
Marco Tozzi
Ronaldo Tozzi
Marco Tozzi
Michel Tozzi

D-U-N-S 20-363-7947   (SL)
ENTRETIEN P.E.A.C.E. PLUS INC
ECOLIGHTING SOLUTIONS
950 Av Ogilvy Bureau 200, Montreal, QC, H3N
1P4
(514) 273-9764
Emp Here 100   *Sales* 4,020,900
SIC 7349 Building maintenance services, nec
Nicholas Lazaris
Theodore Lazaris
Menashi Mashaal
Danielle Benchimol

D-U-N-S 24-678-7654   (SL)
FIBRENOIRE INC
FIBRE NOIRE INTERNET
(*Suby of* QUEBECOR MEDIA INC)
550 Av Beaumont Bureau 320, Montreal, QC,
H3N 1V1
(514) 907-3002
Emp Here 48   *Sales* 10,966,656
SIC 4813 Telephone communication, except
radio
Philippe Cloutier
Marc M. Tremblay
Manon Brouillette
Jean-Francois Pruneau
Jean-Philippe Gagnon

D-U-N-S 20-737-7086   (HQ)
FUJITSU CONSEIL (CANADA) INC
DMR
(*Suby of* FUJITSU CONSULTING (CANADA)
HOLDINGS, INC.)
7101 Av Du Parc Bureau 102, Montreal, QC,
H3N 1X9
(514) 877-3301
Emp Here 350   *Sales* 216,620,000
SIC 7379 Computer related services, nec
David Shearer
Jeremy Barry
Perry Tenser
Robert Pryor

D-U-N-S 24-052-6264   (SL)
GLACIER BILBOQUET INC, LE
6833 Av Du Parc, Montreal, QC, H3N 1W8

Emp Here 20   *Sales* 10,702,480
SIC 5143 Dairy products, except dried or
canned
Pierre Morin

D-U-N-S 24-922-8693   (SL)
INVESTISSEMENTS PELLERIN INC, LES
8600 Av De L'Epee, Montreal, QC, H3N 2G6
(514) 273-8855
Emp Here 250   *Sales* 91,377,250
SIC 6712 Bank holding companies
Daniel Pellerin

D-U-N-S 20-221-8058   (SL)
KILO GATEAUX LTEE
6744 Rue Hutchison, Montreal, QC, H3N 1Y4
(514) 270-3024
Emp Here 40   *Sales* 33,423,080
SIC 5149 Groceries and related products, nec
Robert Benette

D-U-N-S 24-320-9558   (SL)

MODES J & X LTEE, LES
7101 Av Du Parc Bureau 301, Montreal, QC, H3N 1X9

Emp Here 40   Sales 17,739,600
SIC 7389 Business services, nec
John Papamakarios

D-U-N-S 24-460-4062   (SL)
MONTREAL PITA INC
ORIGINAL RNW
654 Av Beaumont, Montreal, QC, H3N 1V5
(514) 495-4513
Emp Here 40   Sales 10,966,080
SIC 5461 Retail bakeries
Nabil Bachour
Roxanne Asfour
Molhem Sabbageh

D-U-N-S 24-376-1009   (HQ)
NERON INC
550 Av Beaumont Bureau 500, Montreal, QC, H3N 1V1
(514) 759-8672
Sales 10,941,200
SIC 3961 Costume jewelry
Caroline Neron

D-U-N-S 24-177-5902   (BR)
PROVIGO DISTRIBUTION INC
LOBLAWS
(Suby of LOBLAW COMPANIES LIMITED)
375 Rue Jean-Talon O, Montreal, QC, H3N 2Y8
(514) 948-2600
Emp Here 350
SIC 5411 Grocery stores
Marcilino Nagozi

D-U-N-S 20-233-4470   (SL)
SALAISON LEVESQUE INC
500 Av Beaumont, Montreal, QC, H3N 1T7
(514) 273-1702
Emp Here 30   Sales 25,067,310
SIC 5147 Meats and meat products
Regis Levesque
Annie Levesque

D-U-N-S 20-233-5915   (HQ)
SAMUELSOHN LIMITEE
GOOD SUITS DON'T JUST HAPPEN
(Suby of GRANO RETAIL INVESTMENTS INC)
6930 Av Du Parc, Montreal, QC, H3N 1W9
(514) 273-7741
Sales 66,333,750
SIC 2311 Men's and boy's suits and coats
Stephan Granovsky
Alan R Peck

Montreal, QC H3R

D-U-N-S 24-321-0705   (SL)
105262 CANADA INC
CITE NISSAN
3500 Rue Jean-Talon O, Montreal, QC, H3R 2E8
(514) 739-3175
Emp Here 60   Sales 37,756,800
SIC 5511 New and used car dealers
Sarkis Liberian
Haroutian Liberian

D-U-N-S 20-426-4435   (HQ)
191837 CANADA INC
SECUR-ASSURE
3901 Rue Jean-Talon O Bureau 301, Montreal, QC, H3R 2G4
(514) 373-3131
Emp Here 90   Sales 2,653,357
SIC 5999 Miscellaneous retail stores, nec
Zev Laine

D-U-N-S 24-254-3338   (SL)
COMMUNICATIONS   METRO-MONTREAL

INC
I24 CALL MANAGEMENT SOLUTIONS
3901 Rue Jean-Talon O Bureau 200, Montreal, QC, H3R 2G4
(514) 736-6767
Emp Here 40   Sales 17,739,600
SIC 7389 Business services, nec
Gary Blair

D-U-N-S 24-423-1887   (SL)
SECURASSURE CANADA INC
3901 Rue Jean-Talon O Bureau 301, Montreal, QC, H3R 2G4
(514) 373-3131
Emp Here 90   Sales 3,790,510
SIC 5999 Miscellaneous retail stores, nec
Zevi Laine

Montreal, QC H3S

D-U-N-S 25-076-3901   (SL)
9070-4701 QUEBEC INC
PHARMAPRIX
2635 Av Van Horne, Montreal, QC, H3S 1P6
(514) 731-3366
Emp Here 50   Sales 12,647,700
SIC 5912 Drug stores and proprietary stores
Samir Djaoued

D-U-N-S 24-712-9554   (SL)
ASSOCIES SPORTIFS DE MONTREAL, SOCIETE EN COMMANDITE, LES
RESTAURANT LES JARDINS DU BOISE
6105 Av Du Boise, Montreal, QC, H3S 2V9
(514) 737-0000
Emp Here 205   Sales 15,425,225
SIC 7991 Physical fitness facilities
Francois Leduc

D-U-N-S 25-687-6640   (HQ)
CARMICHAEL ENGINEERING LTD
C.M.A REFRIGERATION
3822 Av De Courtrai, Montreal, QC, H3S 1C1
(514) 735-4361
Emp Here 36   Sales 106,450,740
SIC 8711 Engineering services
Miller Carmichael

D-U-N-S 24-815-2225   (SL)
CENTRE D'ACCUEIL FATHER DOWD
6565 Ch Hudson Bureau 217, Montreal, QC, H3S 2T7

Emp Here 77   Sales 4,562,019
SIC 8361 Residential care
Fergus Growndwater
Helene Mckay

D-U-N-S 20-370-8610   (SL)
COMMANDITE KRUGER BROMPTON INC
3285 Ch De Bedford, Montreal, QC, H3S 1G5
(514) 737-1131
Emp Here 1   Sales 77,907,200
SIC 2621 Paper mills
Joseph Kruger
David Spraley
David Angel
Janet Shulist

D-U-N-S 20-337-3159   (HQ)
EMBALLAGES KRUGER S.E.C.
3285 Ch De Bedford, Montreal, QC, H3S 1G5
(514) 737-1131
Emp Here 50   Sales 183,818,500
SIC 2671 Paper; coated and laminated packaging
Joseph Kruger Ii

D-U-N-S 20-217-8935   (SL)
EMBIX COMPAGNIE D'IMPORTATIONS DE MONTRES LTEE
ATRONIC
2550 Ch Bates Bureau 301, Montreal, QC, H3S 1A7

---

(514) 731-3978
Emp Here 28   Sales 14,575,176
SIC 5094 Jewelry and precious stones
Robert Bixenspanner
Raphael Bixenspanner

D-U-N-S 20-416-6565   (HQ)
F. D. L. COMPAGNIE LTEE
3600 Av Barclay Bureau 200, Montreal, QC, H3S 1K5
(514) 737-2268
Sales 27,135,400
SIC 6513 Apartment building operators
Roger Fournelle
Pierre Fournelle
Jean-Rene Fournelle
Michel Fournelle
Marie-Annick Fournelle
Michel-Erik Fournelle

D-U-N-S 24-811-1080   (HQ)
GESTION QUADRATEL INC
6000 Ch Deacon, Montreal, QC, H3S 2T9
(514) 731-5298
Sales 20,501,250
SIC 6712 Bank holding companies
Gilles Chatel
Claude Chatel

D-U-N-S 20-302-6778   (SL)
GESTIONS MILLER CARMICHAEL INC
3822 Av De Courtrai, Montreal, QC, H3S 1C1
(514) 735-4361
Emp Here 540   Sales 197,374,860
SIC 6712 Bank holding companies
Miller Carmichael

D-U-N-S 24-861-1378   (HQ)
IMMEUBLES FAIRWAY INC, LES
FAIRWAY REALTIES
5858 Ch De La Cote-Des-Neiges Unite 612, Montreal, QC, H3S 2S1
(514) 342-2791
Sales 13,559,453
SIC 6512 Nonresidential building operators
Aaron Gelber
Norman Sternthal

D-U-N-S 20-370-8607   (HQ)
KRUGER BROMPTON S.E.C
3285 Ch De Bedford, Montreal, QC, H3S 1G5
(819) 846-2721
Sales 19,476,800
SIC 2621 Paper mills
Janet Shulist

D-U-N-S 20-222-9431   (HQ)
KRUGER INC
KRUGER RECYCLAGE
3285 Ch De Bedford, Montreal, QC, H3S 1G5
(514) 343-3100
Emp Here 120   Sales 1,231,399,821
SIC 6712 Bank holding companies
Joseph Kruger Ii
David Angel
Donald Cayouette
David Spraley
Carmela De Luca
Sarah Kruger
Gene Kruger
George Bunze

D-U-N-S 24-827-7134   (SL)
KRUGER IPI INC
(Suby of KRUGER INC)
3285 Ch De Bedford, Montreal, QC, H3S 1G5
(514) 343-3100
Emp Here 89
SIC 2421 Sawmills and planing mills, general
David Spraley
Angel David
Carmela De Luca

D-U-N-S 20-370-8086   (HQ)
KRUGER WAYAGAMACK S.E.C.
3285 Ch De Bedford, Montreal, QC, H3S 1G5
(514) 343-3100
Sales 91,909,250

SIC 2621 Paper mills
Joseph Kruger

D-U-N-S 20-763-8420   (HQ)
L'INSTITUT DE READAPTATION GINGRAS-LINDSAY-DE-MONTREAL
IRGLM
6300 Av De Darlington, Montreal, QC, H3S 2J4
(514) 340-2085
Emp Here 250   Sales 53,318,400
SIC 8069 Specialty hospitals, except psychiatric
Fernand Lafleur
Jacques R Nolet

D-U-N-S 20-216-8530   (HQ)
MODES DO-GREE LTEE, LES
AARDVARK
3205 Ch De Bedford, Montreal, QC, H3S 1G3
(514) 904-2109
Sales 12,956,372
SIC 5136 Men's and boy's clothing
Richard Tock
David Tock

D-U-N-S 24-389-0782   (HQ)
PAPIERS DE PUBLICATION KRUGER INC
(Suby of KRUGER INC)
3285 Ch De Bedford, Montreal, QC, H3S 1G5
(514) 737-1131
Emp Here 10   Sales 275,727,750
SIC 2611 Pulp mills
Joseph Kruger
David Spraley
George J. Bunze
David Angel
Carmela De Luca

D-U-N-S 20-387-6644   (SL)
PRODUITS KRUGER SHERBROOKE INC
3285 Ch De Bedford, Montreal, QC, H3S 1G5
(514) 737-1131
Emp Here 100   Sales 18,340,300
SIC 2221 Broadwoven fabric mills, manmade
Dino Joe Bianco
Francois Paroyan
David Alexander Spraley
David Angel

D-U-N-S 20-320-7142   (SL)
SERVICES DE SOINS A DOMICILE ROYAL TREATMENT INC
REM-MEDI HEALTH CARE SERVICES
5757 Av Decelles, Montreal, QC, H3S 2C3
(514) 342-8293
Emp Here 150   Sales 11,204,100
SIC 7361 Employment agencies
David Diner
Shlomo Razin

D-U-N-S 24-475-8595   (SL)
SYSCOR
6600 Ch De La Cote-Des-Neiges Bureau 600, Montreal, QC, H3S 2A9
(514) 737-3201
Emp Here 115   Sales 16,580,930
SIC 7371 Custom computer programming services
Martine Alfonse
Stephane Beaudry
Pierre Brunet
Normand Rinfret
Jeff Barkun
Peter Abraham

Montreal, QC H3T

D-U-N-S 24-945-3184   (SL)
2739-9708 QUEBEC INC
EXO-FRUITS
5192 Ch De La Cote-Des-Neiges, Montreal, QC, H3T 1X8
(514) 738-1384
Emp Here 50   Sales 13,707,600

▲ Public Company   ■ Public Company Family Member   **HQ** Headquarters   **BR** Branch   **SL** Single Location

SIC 5431 Fruit and vegetable markets
Amjad Ansari

D-U-N-S 24-082-8319   (HQ)
AGENCE UNIVERSITAIRE DE LA FRANCO-PHONIE
AUF
3034 Boul Edouard-Montpetit, Montreal, QC,
H3T 1J7
(514) 343-6630
Emp Here 1   *Sales* 20,985,500
SIC 8641 Civic and social associations
Sorin Mihai Cimpeanu
Khaled Bouabdallah
Jacques Comby
Salim Daccache
Sackona Phoeurng
Alain Verhaagen
Christina Vigna
Caroline Malaussena
Fadia Kiwan
Hong Phan Le

D-U-N-S 25-246-1058   (SL)
ALIMENTATION DUPLESSIS, MARTIN INC
5150 Ch De La Cote-Des-Neiges, Montreal,
QC, H3T 1X8
(514) 738-7377
Emp Here 100   *Sales* 29,347,700
SIC 5411 Grocery stores
Martin Duplessis

D-U-N-S 24-022-6951   (SL)
**AUXILIAIRE DE L'HOPITAL GENERAL JUIF
SIR MORTIMER B. DAVIS INC, LES**
3755 Ch De La Cote-Sainte-Catherine Bureau
A018, Montreal, QC, H3T 1E2
(514) 340-8216
Emp Here 23   *Sales* 10,332,037
SIC 7389 Business services, nec
Eileen Fleischer
Hela Boro

D-U-N-S 24-405-6289   (SL)
CAROPHIL INC
PHARMAPRIX
5122 Ch De La Cote-Des-Neiges Bureau 2,
Montreal, QC, H3T 1X8
(514) 738-8464
Emp Here 100   *Sales* 24,432,800
SIC 5912 Drug stores and proprietary stores
Nabil Chikh

D-U-N-S 20-355-5347   (SL)
**CENTRE COMMUNAUTAIRE DE LOISIR DE
LA COTE-DES-NEIGES**
5347 Ch De La Cote-Des-Neiges, Montreal,
QC, H3T 1Y4
(514) 733-1478
Emp Here 100   *Sales* 6,842,200
SIC 8322 Individual and family services
Josee Belanger
Annie Corriveau
Marc Saint-Cyr
Artem Chinkarouk
Francois Larochelle
Genevieve Plouffe
Colette Oger
Glenn Subad
Emilie Dufour-Lauzon

D-U-N-S 20-763-7646   .(HQ)
CENTRE HOSPITALIER DE ST. MARY'S
3830 Av Lacombe, Montreal, QC, H3T 1M5
(514) 345-3511
Sales 255,282,200
SIC 8062 General medical and surgical hospi-
tals
James Cherry
Jean Aucoin
Rachel Renaud
Cynda Heward
Joseph Adamo
Terrence Didus

D-U-N-S 25-426-5820   (HQ)
CENTRE HOSPITALIER UNIVERSITAIRE

SAINTE-JUSTINE
*CENTRE DE READAPTATION MARIE EN-
FANT*
3175 Ch De La Cote-Sainte-Catherine, Mon-
treal, QC, H3T 1C5
(514) 345-4931
Emp Here 4,000   *Sales* 499,860,000
SIC 8069 Specialty hospitals, except psychi-
atric
Ann Macdonald
Andre Roy
Caroline Barbir
Helene Boisjoly
Louise Champoux-Paille
Champoux-Paille Bastien
Marie-Josee Hebert
Frederick Perrault
Annie Lemieux
Guillaume Gfeller

D-U-N-S 24-634-6605   (HQ)
**COOPERATIVE DE L'ECOLE DES HAUTES
ETUDES COMMERCIALES**
COOP HEC MONTREAL
5255 Av Decelles Bureau 2340, Montreal, QC,
H3T 2B1
(514) 340-6396
Emp Here 90   *Sales* 34,205,920
SIC 5942 Book stores
Daniel Cote
Lucas Maniere-Despert
Patrice-Damien Perret
Denis Pageau

D-U-N-S 20-858-3054   (HQ)
**CORPORATION DE L'ECOLE DES HAUTES
ETUDES COMMERCIALES DE MONTREAL**
HSC MONTREAL
3000 Ch De La Cote-Sainte-Catherine, Mon-
treal, QC, H3T 2A7
(514) 340-6000
Sales 141,013,000
SIC 8221 Colleges and universities
Helene Desmarais
Federico Pasin
Michel Patry
Claude Seguin
Jean-Guy Desjardin
Jacynthe Cote
Stephane Pitre
Guy Breton
Jean Talbot
Suzanne Rivard

D-U-N-S 25-022-8046   (SL)
**CORPORATION DE L'ECOLE POLYTECH-
NIQUE DE MONTREAL**
ECOLE POLYTECHNIQUE DE MONTREAL
2900 Boul Edouard-Montpetit, Montreal, QC,
H3T 1J4
(514) 340-4711
Emp Here 1,000   *Sales* 141,013,000
SIC 8221 Colleges and universities

D-U-N-S 24-317-5663   (SL)
DOLARIAN, STEPHAN
PHARMACIE JEAN COUTU M C
5510 Ch De La Cote-Des-Neiges Bureau 215,
Montreal, QC, H3T 1Y9
(514) 344-8338
Emp Here 40   *Sales* 10,118,160
SIC 5912 Drug stores and proprietary stores
Stephan Dolarian

D-U-N-S 20-857-2446   (SL)
**FONDATION DE L'HOPITAL GENERAL JUIF
SIR MORTIMER B. DAVIS**
3755 Ch De La Cote-Sainte-Catherine Bureau
A104, Montreal, QC, H3T 1E2
(514) 340-8251
Emp Here 4,869   *Sales* 1,008,214,092
SIC 8399 Social services, nec
Howard Dermer
Sheldon Elman
Edward Wiltzer
Bernard Poulin
Irwin Kramer

Joel Segal
Bernard Stotland
Richard Dubrovsky
Miles Leutner
Tony Loffreda

D-U-N-S 20-125-5929   (BR)
ROTISSERIES ST-HUBERT LTEE, LES
RESTAURANT ST HUBERT
(*Suby of* RECIPE UNLIMITED CORPORA-
TION)
5235 Ch De La Cote-Des-Neiges, Montreal,
QC, H3T 1Y1
(514) 342-9495
Emp Here 135
SIC 6794 Patent owners and lessors
Eric Catubal

D-U-N-S 20-762-2838   (HQ)
UNIVERSITE DE MONTREAL
2900 Boul Edouard-Montpetit, Montreal, QC,
H3T 1J4
(514) 343-6111
Emp Here 400   *Sales* 1,128,104,000
SIC 8221 Colleges and universities
Alexandre Chabot
Marc Gold
Louise Roy
Claude Benoit
Michel Patry
Therese Cabana
Guy Breton
Sylvainne Chaput
Maurice Charlebois
Frencoise Guenette

D-U-N-S 25-764-7792   (BR)
UNIVERSITE DE MONTREAL
UNIVERSITE DE MONTREAL, L'
(*Suby of* UNIVERSITE DE MONTREAL)
3744 Rue Jean-Brillant, Montreal, QC, H3T
1P1
(514) 343-6090
Emp Here 125
SIC 8221 Colleges and universities
Raymond Lalande

Montreal, QC H3V

D-U-N-S 24-224-9795   (SL)
**L'ORATOIRE SAINT-JOSEPH DU MONT-
ROYAL**
*ORATOIRE SAINT-JOSEPH DU MONT-
ROYAL*
3800 Ch Queen-Mary, Montreal, QC, H3V 1H6
(514) 733-8211
Emp Here 175   *Sales* 18,221,525
SIC 8661 Religious organizations
Louis Trempe
Alain Pare
Nicole Beaudoin
Gilles Labelle

D-U-N-S 24-107-4756   (SL)
PLACEMENTS ROCKHILL LTEE, LES
ROCKHILL APARTMENTS
(*Suby of* COMPAGNIE DES CHEMINS DE
FER NATIONAUX DU CANADA)
4858 Ch De La Cote-Des-Neiges Bureau 503,
Montreal, QC, H3V 1G8
(514) 738-4704
Emp Here 45   *Sales* 10,480,995
SIC 6513 Apartment building operators
Russell J. Hiscock
Serge Riopel

D-U-N-S 24-377-4416   (HQ)
SYSTEMES CANADIEN KRONOS INC
(*Suby of* KRONOS PARENT CORPORA-
TION)
3535 Ch Queen-Mary Bureau 500, Montreal,
QC, H3V 1H8
(514) 345-0580
Emp Here 182   *Sales* 49,834,710

SIC 7371 Custom computer programming ser-
vices
Christopher Russell Todd
Spiros Paleologos
John Arthur Butler

Montreal, QC H3W

D-U-N-S 24-355-7738   (SL)
CENTRE SEGAL DES ARTS DE LA SCENE
5170 Ch De La Cote-Sainte-Catherine, Mon-
treal, QC, H3W 1M7
(514) 739-7944
Emp Here 160   *Sales* 16,957,440
SIC 7922 Theatrical producers and services
Alvin Segal
Joel Segal

D-U-N-S 20-972-5167   (SL)
**COLLEGE INTERNATIONAL MARIE DE
FRANCE**
4635 Ch Queen-Mary, Montreal, QC, H3W
1W3
(514) 737-1177
Emp Here 125   *Sales* 12,389,875
SIC 8211 Elementary and secondary schools
Brigitte Peytier
Jean Guilbaur
Ingrid Moise
Karima Tidjani
Catherine Mounier
Caroline Codsi
Laurent Marchal
Bernard Laporte
Anne Duprat
Bruno Lafeytaud

D-U-N-S 20-764-9823   (SL)
FEDERATION CJA
*FEDERATION DES SERVICES COMMU-
NAUTAIRES*
5151 Ch De La Cote-Sainte-Catherine, Mon-
treal, QC, H3W 1M6
(514) 735-3541
Emp Here 100   *Sales* 6,842,200
SIC 8322 Individual and family services
Deborah Corber
Susan Laxer
Justin Vineberg
Kathy Lempert
Yair Szlak
Susan Szalpeter
David Cape
Evan Feldman
Dean Mendel
Martin Schartz

D-U-N-S 20-715-9562   (HQ)
FEDERATION CJA
CENTRE ETUDIANTS HILLEL
5151 Ch De La Cote-Sainte-Catherine, Mon-
treal, QC, H3W 1M6
(514) 345-2645
Emp Here 150   *Sales* 11,595,592
SIC 8322 Individual and family services
Deborah Corber
Yair Szlak
Audrey Hadida
Susan Laxer
Pascale Hasen
David Amiel
Evan Feldman
Mitchell Shiller
Justin Vineberg
Gilbert Tordjman

D-U-N-S 24-860-7145   (HQ)
GESTION BRINEKY INC
5035 Ch Mira, Montreal, QC, H3W 2B9
(514) 282-3300
Sales 27,666,000
SIC 2842 Polishes and sanitation goods
Avrum Morrow

▲ Public Company   ■ Public Company Family Member   **HQ** Headquarters   **BR** Branch   **SL** Single Location

D-U-N-S 20-230-5587 (SL)
GESTION LISE HAMEL-CHARTRAND INC
PHARMAPRIX
4815 Av Van Horne, Montreal, QC, H3W 1J2
(514) 739-1758
Emp Here 88   *Sales* 21,500,864
SIC 5912 Drug stores and proprietary stores
  Lise Hamel

D-U-N-S 24-900-3617 (SL)
ISRA-GUARD (I.G.S.) SECURITE INC
I.G.S. SECURITY
5165 Ch Queen-Mary Bureau 512, Montreal,
QC, H3W 1X7
(514) 489-6336
Emp Here 250   *Sales* 6,562,500
SIC 7381 Detective and armored car services
  Jacob Haimovici
  Isaac Bettan

D-U-N-S 25-463-4447 (SL)
**JEWISH COMMUNITY COUNCIL OF MON-
TREAL**
6819 Boul Decarie, Montreal, QC, H3W 3E4
(514) 739-6363
Emp Here 80   *Sales* 8,618,160
SIC 8661 Religious organizations
  Yochanan Kuhnreich
  Jack Lehrer
  Y.L. Pal
  M. Labow
  F Pfeiffer
  S Deitcher

D-U-N-S 20-211-5507 (SL)
LOCATION BENCH & TABLE INC
PARTY TIME RENTS, DIV OF
6999 Av Victoria, Montreal, QC, H3W 3E9
(514) 738-4755
Emp Here 50   *Sales* 14,608,450
SIC 7359 Equipment rental and leasing, nec
  Allan Vosko

D-U-N-S 24-833-2348 (BR)
SOBEYS QUEBEC INC
4885 Av Van Horne, Montreal, QC, H3W 1J2
(514) 731-8336
Emp Here 80
SIC 5141 Groceries, general line

D-U-N-S 25-456-7548 (SL)
SUPERMARCHE ORNAWKA INC
I.G.A.
4885 Av Van Horne, Montreal, QC, H3W 1J2
(514) 731-8336
Emp Here 70   *Sales* 20,543,390
SIC 5411 Grocery stores
  Steve Ornawka

D-U-N-S 24-108-6263 (HQ)
**TALMUD TORAHS UNIS DE MONTREAL
INC**
HERZLIAH HIGH SCHOOL
4840 Av Saint-Kevin Bureau 210, Montreal,
QC, H3W 1P2
(514) 739-2294
Emp Here 10   *Sales* 13,535,990
SIC 8661 Religious organizations
  Sidney Benudiz
  Alexandra Obadia
  Steeve Azoulay
  Isabelle Danino
  Lionel Soussan
  Isaac Bendayan
  Howard Liebman
  Michael Mire

Montreal, QC H3X

D-U-N-S 25-418-7115 (SL)
405-4547 CANADA INC
DECARIE SATURN SAAB
6100 Boul Decarie, Montreal, QC, H3X 2J8
(514) 342-2222
Emp Here 45   *Sales* 22,413,510

SIC 5511 New and used car dealers
  Jean-Claude Gravel

D-U-N-S 20-109-5911 (BR)
COMMISSION SCOLAIRE DE MONTREAL
ECOLE SAINT-LUC
(*Suby of* COMMISSION SCOLAIRE DE
MONTREAL)
6300 Ch De La Cote-Saint-Luc, Montreal, QC,
H3X 2H4
(514) 596-5920
Emp Here 150
SIC 8211 Elementary and secondary schools
  Maryse Tremblay

D-U-N-S 20-884-4951 (HQ)
FONDATION CANADIENNE DU REIN, LA
5160 Boul Decarie Bureau 310, Montreal, QC,
H3X 2H9
(514) 369-4806
Emp Here 25   *Sales* 36,236,900
SIC 8399 Social services, nec
  Paul Kidston
  Christopher Gobeil
  Julian Midgley
  Anne Schultz
  Terrance Tomkins
  David Stack
  Gregory Robbins
  Mary-Pat Shaw
  Tahir Shafiq
  Ferdinand Tchounkeu

D-U-N-S 24-322-7626 (HQ)
**FONDATION EDUCATIVE DE LA COMMIS-
SION SCOLAIRE ENGLISH-MONTREAL,
LA**
6000 Av Fielding, Montreal, QC, H3X 1T4
(514) 483-7200
Emp Here 250   *Sales* 246,579,061
SIC 8211 Elementary and secondary schools
  Dominic Spiridigliozzi
  John A Simms
  Viky Keller
  Andre Michaels
  Michael Bucci
  Dennis Kounadis
  Antonio Lacroce
  Nickolas Katalifos

D-U-N-S 25-975-6997 (HQ)
GEXEL TELECOM INTERNATIONAL INC
INVESTISSEMENT LC
(*Suby of* ARTHUR J. GALLAGHER & CO.)
5250 Boul Decarie Bureau 100, Montreal, QC,
H3X 2H9
(514) 935-9300
Emp Here 400   *Sales* 234,180,800
SIC 4899 Communication services, nec
  Eric Mestdagh
  Roberto Depani
  Elizabeth Fontaine
  Stan Tyo

D-U-N-S 25-503-4118 (HQ)
INSIGHT CANADA INC
LOGICIELS INSIGHT CANADA
(*Suby of* INSIGHT ENTERPRISES, INC.)
5410 Boul Decarie, Montreal, QC, H3X 4B2
(514) 344-3500
Emp Here 50   *Sales* 106,681,200
SIC 5734 Computer and software stores
  Kenneth T. Lamneck
  Carmella Orlando
  Glynis A. Bryan

D-U-N-S 20-108-8189 (SL)
INSIGHT DIRECT CANADA, INC
INFORMATIQUE INSIGHT DIRECT
(*Suby of* INSIGHT ENTERPRISES, INC.)
5410 Boul Decarie, Montreal, QC, H3X 4B2
(514) 344-3500
Emp Here 400   *Sales* 77,190,400
SIC 8742 Management consulting services
  Kenneth T. Lamneck
  Michael Walker
  Glynis A Bryan

D-U-N-S 24-126-4600 (SL)
LEVY PILOTTE S.E.N.C.R.L.
DSK
5250 Boul Decarie Bureau 700, Montreal, QC,
H3X 3Z6
(514) 487-1566
Emp Here 50   *Sales* 10,454,250
SIC 8721 Accounting, auditing, and book-
keeping
  Nick Vanelli
  Aaron Chazan
  Mohammed Shakibnia
  Ather Kandella
  Alex Brzezinski
  Joseph Khoury
  Jean Pilotte
  Raouf Guirguis
  Stephen Coplain
  Johnny Colonna

D-U-N-S 24-354-6772 (SL)
**RESIDENCE SEPHARADE SALOMON
(COMMUNAUTE SEPHARADE UNIFIEE DU
QUEBEC)**
5900 Boul Decarie, Montreal, QC, H3X 2J7
(514) 733-2157
Emp Here 100   *Sales* 5,924,700
SIC 8361 Residential care
  Marc Karon
  Armond Afilalo
  Sylvain Abitbol
  Joelle Khalfa
  Ralph Benatar
  Michel Abitbol
  Michel Bitton
  Salomon Oziel

D-U-N-S 20-764-5912 (SL)
SCHECHTER, SOLOMON ACADEMY INC
5555 Ch De La Cote-Saint-Luc, Montreal, QC,
H3X 2C9
(514) 485-0866
Emp Here 100   *Sales* 9,282,600
SIC 8211 Elementary and secondary schools
  Shimshon Hamerman
  Gerry Kesselman

D-U-N-S 20-236-4642 (SL)
UDISCO LTEE
(*Suby of* 95237 CANADA INC)
4660 Boul Decarie, Montreal, QC, H3X 2H5
(514) 481-8107
Emp Here 23   *Sales* 11,972,466
SIC 5092 Toys and hobby goods and supplies
  Lyon Kunin
  Doron Kunin

Montreal, QC H3Y

D-U-N-S 20-314-0918 (SL)
SPIVO CANADA INC
3150 Place De Ramezay Bureau 202, Mon-
treal, QC, H3Y 0A3
(514) 726-1749
Emp Here 50   *Sales* 10,941,200
SIC 3949 Sporting and athletic goods, nec
  Sandra Hutchinson

Montreal, QC H3Z

D-U-N-S 20-764-6837 (HQ)
COLLEGE DAWSON
3040 Rue Sherbrooke O, Montreal, QC, H3Z
1A4
(514) 931-8731
Sales 99,119,000
SIC 8222 Junior colleges
  Richard Filion

D-U-N-S 24-524-1588 (HQ)
CORPORATION FINANCIERE THINKING

CAPITAL
4200 Boul Dorchester O Bureau 300, Mon-
treal, QC, H3Z 1V2
(866) 889-9412
Emp Here 1   *Sales* 93,917,700
SIC 6211 Security brokers and dealers
  Jeffrey Mitelman
  Som Seif

D-U-N-S 25-857-2791 (SL)
**FONDATION DE L'HOPITAL DE MONTREAL
POUR ENFANTS, LA**
HOPITAL POUR ENFANTS DE MONTREAL
3400 Boul De Maisonneuve O Bureau 1420,
Montreal, QC, H3Z 3B8
(514) 934-4846
Emp Here 25   *Sales* 11,230,475
SIC 7389 Business services, nec
  Louise Dery Goldberg
  Maryse Ulrich
  Nicholas Steinmetz
  Greg Rokos
  Marie-Josee Gariepy
  Timothy Price

D-U-N-S 20-911-0626 (SL)
GESTION RITEAL INC
PHARMA PRIX
1500 Av Atwater, Montreal, QC, H3Z 1X5
(514) 931-4283
Emp Here 88   *Sales* 21,500,864
SIC 5912 Drug stores and proprietary stores
  Dominique Voyer

D-U-N-S 24-433-3100 (HQ)
GROUPE FINANCIER FORT INC
FORT ASSURANCE
3400 Boul De Maisonneuve O Bureau 1115,
Montreal, QC, H3Z 3B8
(514) 288-6161
Sales 38,162,700
SIC 6411 Insurance agents, brokers, and ser-
vice
  Stephan Bernatchez

D-U-N-S 25-380-7606 (HQ)
HAPAG-LLOYD (CANADA) INC
(*Suby of* HAPAG-LLOYD AG)
3400 Boul De Maisonneuve O Bureau 1200,
Montreal, QC, H3Z 3E7
(514) 934-5133
Emp Here 250   *Sales* 130,494,540
SIC 4731 Freight transportation arrangement
  Uffe Ostergaard
  Tim Whittaker
  Wolfgang Schoch

D-U-N-S 24-174-1115 (SL)
KSH SOLUTIONS INC
KSH
3400 Boul De Maisonneuve O Bureau 1600,
Montreal, QC, H3Z 3B8
(514) 932-4611
Emp Here 210   *Sales* 37,535,190
SIC 8711 Engineering services
  Martin Pereira
  Marc Rowan
  Christian Brisebois
  Giuseppe Masella

D-U-N-S 25-257-4413 (SL)
LEROUX, SYLVAIN M. ENTREPRISES LTD
CANADIAN TIRE
1500 Av Atwater Bureau G, Montreal, QC,
H3Z 1X5
(514) 939-1820
Emp Here 70   *Sales* 18,735,640
SIC 5251 Hardware stores
  Sylvain Leroux

D-U-N-S 24-359-5878 (SL)
NAVIGATION CP LIMITEE
(*Suby of* TUI AG)
3400 Boul De Maisonneuve O Bureau 1200,
Montreal, QC, H3Z 3E7
(514) 934-5133
Emp Here 130   *Sales* 86,695,960

▲ Public Company   ■ Public Company Family Member   **HQ** Headquarters   **BR** Branch   **SL** Single Location

SIC 4731 Freight transportation arrangement
Deiter Brettshneider
Tim Whittaker
Wilfred Rau
Holger G. Oetjen

D-U-N-S 20-265-8902 (SL)
OCEANWIDE CANADA INC
CARGO COVER
(Suby of INSURITY, INC.)
3400 Boul De Maisonneuve O Bureau 1450,
Montreal, QC, H3Z 3B8
(514) 289-9090
Emp Here 200   Sales 28,836,400
SIC 7371 Custom computer programming services
Mark Adessky
Robert Charles Larew
Jeffrey Julius Glazer

D-U-N-S 24-346-3085 (BR)
**REGIE REGIONALE DE LA SANTE ET DES
SERVICES SOCIAUX NUNAVIK**
MODULE DU NORD QUEBECOIS
*(Suby of REGIE REGIONALE DE LA SANTE
ET DES SERVICES SOCIAUX NUNAVIK)*
4039 Rue Tupper Bureau 7, Montreal, QC,
H3Z 1T5
(514) 932-9047
Emp Here 100
SIC 8059 Nursing and personal care, nec
Marie-Pierre Bergeron

D-U-N-S 25-173-6526 (SL)
**SUPERMARCHE LEFEBVRE ET FILLES
INC**
IGA
1500 Av Atwater, Montreal, QC, H3Z 1X5
(514) 933-0995
Emp Here 49   Sales 13,433,448
SIC 5411 Grocery stores
Jacques Lefebvre

D-U-N-S 24-527-1648 (HQ)
TECSYS INC
ENTERPRISE SUPPLY CHAIN GROUP
1 Place Alexis Nihon Bureau 800, Montreal,
QC, H3Z 3B8
(514) 866-0001
Emp Here 240   Sales 51,390,487
SIC 6712 Bank holding companies
Peter Brereton
Dave Brereton
Berty Ho-Wo-Cheong
Greg Macneill
Vito Calabretta
Catherine Sigmar
Randy Trimm
Yan Charbonneau
Dimitrios Argitis
Jason Mcdermott

D-U-N-S 20-253-0622 (SL)
THERAPEUTIQUE KNIGHT INC
3400 Boul De Maisonneuve O Bureau 1055,
Montreal, QC, H3Z 3B8
(514) 484-4483
Emp Here 48   Sales 15,916,512
SIC 2834 Pharmaceutical preparations
Jonathan Ross Goodman
Samira Sakhia
Amal Khouri
James C. Gale
Meir Jakobsohn
Robert N. Lande
Sylvie Tendler
Nancy Harrison

D-U-N-S 24-527-8205 (BR)
XEROX CANADA LTD
(Suby of XEROX CORPORATION)
3400 Boul De Maisonneuve O Bureau 900,
Montreal, QC, H3Z 3G1
(514) 939-3769
Emp Here 150
SIC 5044 Office equipment
Martin Vachant

D-U-N-S 20-292-5806 (SL)
Z-SC1 CORP
Z-SC1 BIOMEDICAL
4148a Rue Sainte-Catherine O Bureau 337,
Montreal, QC, H3Z 0A2
(877) 381-5500
Emp Here 89   Sales 22,834,018
SIC 3821 Laboratory apparatus and furniture
Jean Fallacara
Helene Spidgel

Montreal, QC H4A

D-U-N-S 24-772-5570 (SL)
9264 0085 QUEBEC INC
HYDROMAX
6080 Rue Sherbrooke O, Montreal, QC, H4A
1Y1

Emp Here 49   Sales 13,556,340
SIC 2879 Agricultural chemicals, nec
Paolo Correia

D-U-N-S 24-175-1213 (HQ)
BESCO BEAUTE (1980) LTEE
VENTES LIFE TIME, LES
(Suby of 124839 CANADA INC)
5770 Ch Upper-Lachine, Montreal, QC, H4A
2B3
(514) 481-1115
Emp Here 9   Sales 15,474,830
SIC 5122 Drugs, proprietaries, and sundries
Howard Cohen
Heidi Moscovitch Cohen

D-U-N-S 20-033-2011 (SL)
**CENTRE UNIVERSITAIRE DE SANTE
MCGILL**
CUSM
1001 Boul Decarie, Montreal, QC, H4A 3J1
(514) 934-1934
Emp Here 17,437   Sales 1,936,901,960
SIC 8062 General medical and surgical hospitals
Normand Rinfret
Claudio Bussandri
Robert Rabinovitch
David H Laidley
Ann Lynch
Ewa Sidorowicz
Guy Rouleau
Martine Alfonso
Vassilios Papadopoulos
Joanne Brodeur

D-U-N-S 25-817-5991 (SL)
CENTURY 21 VISION LTD
5517 Av De Monkland, Montreal, QC, H4A
1C8
(514) 481-2126
Emp Here 80   Sales 21,740,480
SIC 6531 Real estate agents and managers
Jeff Adessky

D-U-N-S 24-815-4882 (SL)
**CORPORATION DE GESTION E.A. MICHOT,
LA**
PHARMAPRIX
5038 Rue Sherbrooke O, Montreal, QC, H4A
1S7
(514) 484-3531
Emp Here 75   Sales 18,324,600
SIC 5912 Drug stores and proprietary stores
Leonardo Panunto
Joe Cacciatore

D-U-N-S 20-331-6489 (SL)
**ENTREPRENEURS ELECTRICIENS SIMP-
KIN LTEE**
5800 Rue Saint-Jacques, Montreal, QC, H4A
2E9
(514) 481-0125
Emp Here 50   Sales 12,309,300
SIC 1799 Special trade contractors, nec

Robert Larson
Richard Larsen
Daniel Rouleau

D-U-N-S 24-582-5844 (SL)
**FOURNITURES DE PLOMBERIE ET
CHAUFFAGE SUTTON LTEE**
PLOMBERIE SUTTON
2174 Av De Clifton, Montreal, QC, H4A 2N6
(514) 488-2581
Emp Here 45   Sales 20,122,830
SIC 5074 Plumbing and heating equipment
and supplies (hydronics)
Brian Sutton
Greg Boyd

D-U-N-S 20-220-9284 (HQ)
HANGER, J. E. OF MONTREAL INC
*ORTHOPEDIC SPORTS & MEDICINE OF
WEST ISLAND*
5545 Rue Saint-Jacques, Montreal, QC, H4A
2E3
(514) 489-8213
Sales 12,273,606
SIC 3842 Surgical appliances and supplies
Gino Berretta
Carlo Berretta

D-U-N-S 25-998-2916 (SL)
INTER.NET CANADA LTEE
INTER.NET
*(Suby of UNISERVE COMMUNICATIONS
CORPORATION)*
5252 Boul De Maisonneuve O Bureau 200,
Montreal, QC, H4A 3S5
(514) 481-2585
Emp Here 100
SIC 4813 Telephone communication, except
radio
Michael Eric Schmidt

D-U-N-S 20-962-9435 (SL)
LOWER CANADA COLLEGE
COLLEGE LOWER CANADA, LE
4090 Av Royal, Montreal, QC, H4A 2M5
(514) 482-9916
Emp Here 130   Sales 12,885,470
SIC 8211 Elementary and secondary schools
Doug Lewin
Teresa Calandriello Fata
Rob Velan
Nicole Simard-Laurin
Christopher Shannon
David Schwartz
Marc Tellier
Anne-Marie Boucher
Doug Lewin
Priscilla Whitehead

D-U-N-S 25-448-9461 (SL)
MAISON ELIZABETH INC
2131 Av De Marlowe, Montreal, QC, H4A 3L4
(514) 482-2488
Emp Here 30   Sales 11,922,420
SIC 8699 Membership organizations, nec
Linda Schachtler
Cerise Morris
Howard Nadler
Jane Bracewell

D-U-N-S 20-228-3123 (SL)
NELCO INC
5510 Rue Saint-Jacques, Montreal, QC, H4A
2E2
(514) 481-5614
Emp Here 27   Sales 12,073,698
SIC 5074 Plumbing and heating equipment
and supplies (hydronics)
Peter Malo

D-U-N-S 20-633-0383 (BR)
OTIS CANADA, INC
*(Suby of UNITED TECHNOLOGIES CORPO-
RATION)*
5311 Boul De Maisonneuve O, Montreal, QC,
H4A 1Z5
(514) 489-9781
Emp Here 80

SIC 7699 Repair services, nec
Jean Piuze

D-U-N-S 24-943-5694 (BR)
**SOEURS DE LA CONGREGATION DE
NOTRE-DAME, LES**
*INFIRMERIE NOTRE DAME DE BON SEC-
OURS*
*(Suby of SOEURS DE LA CONGREGATION
DE NOTRE-DAME, LES)*
5015 Av Notre-Dame-De-Grace, Montreal,
QC, H4A 1K2
(514) 485-1461
Emp Here 150
SIC 8661 Religious organizations
Myriam Boutot

D-U-N-S 24-870-3662 (BR)
VIGI SANTE LTEE
CHSLD VIGI REINE ELIZABETH
2055 Av Northcliffe Bureau 412, Montreal, QC,
H4A 3K6
(514) 788-2085
Emp Here 200
SIC 8361 Residential care
Guylaine Lavoie

D-U-N-S 24-175-3409 (SL)
VILLA-MARIA
4245 Boul Decarie, Montreal, QC, H4A 3K4
(514) 484-4950
Emp Here 160   Sales 15,859,040
SIC 8222 Junior colleges
Giovanni Barberio

Montreal, QC H4B

D-U-N-S 24-958-9078 (HQ)
136562 CANADA INC
MOTO INTERNATIONAL
6695 Rue Saint-Jacques Bureau 514, Montreal, QC, H4B 1V3
(514) 483-6686
Sales 24,903,900
SIC 5571 Motorcycle dealers
Charles Gref

D-U-N-S 24-904-3217 (SL)
160276 CANADA INC
6865 Boul De Maisonneuve O, Montreal, QC,
H4B 1T1

Emp Here 40   Sales 16,774,200
SIC 6712 Bank holding companies
Irene Woods
Irene Woods

D-U-N-S 24-081-1406 (SL)
188461 CANADA INC
FORD LINCOLN
7100 Rue Saint-Jacques, Montreal, QC, H4B
1V2
(514) 487-7777
Emp Here 42   Sales 20,919,276
SIC 5511 New and used car dealers
Gabriel Azouz

D-U-N-S 20-325-0212 (SL)
9013-5617 QUEBEC INC
PHARMAPRIX
6411 Rue Sherbrooke O, Montreal, QC, H4B
1N3
(819) 823-2295
Emp Here 50   Sales 12,647,700
SIC 5912 Drug stores and proprietary stores
Ann Labrecque

D-U-N-S 20-791-9796 (SL)
**CENTRE DE READAPTATION CONSTANCE
LETHBRIDGE, LE**
7005 Boul De Maisonneuve O, Montreal, QC,
H4B 1T3
(514) 487-1770
Emp Here 200   Sales 15,154,600
SIC 8093 Specialty outpatient clinics, nec

▲ Public Company   ■ Public Company Family Member   **HQ** Headquarters   **BR** Branch   **SL** Single Location

Patrick Merci-Lavalle

D-U-N-S 24-420-3969   (SL)
CENTRE DE READAPTATION MAB-MACKAY
7000 Rue Sherbrooke O, Montreal, QC, H4B 1R3
(514) 489-8201
Emp Here 100   *Sales* 7,512,900
SIC 8093 Specialty outpatient clinics, nec
Thomas M Davis
Patricia O'connor
Lucia Capozzo
Martin Graham
Stanley Vincelli
Michael Di Grappa
Malik Rejesh
Camillio Zacchia
Allan Aitken
Valerie Shannon

D-U-N-S 25-684-4648   (SL)
DI-TECH INC
2125 Rue Lily-Simon, Montreal, QC, H4B 3A1

Emp Here 85   *Sales* 15,657,765
SIC 2269 Finishing plants, nec
Abie Sterner
Penina Helwani
Claude Helwani

D-U-N-S 25-467-5770   (SL)
ECOLE SECONDAIRE LOYOLA
7272 Rue Sherbrooke O, Montreal, QC, H4B 1R2
(514) 486-1101
Emp Here 85   *Sales* 7,890,210
SIC 8211 Elementary and secondary schools
Paul Donovan
Gerald Mathieu
Robert C. Brennan
Donald V. Flynn

D-U-N-S 20-387-1608   (SL)
FORD LINCOLN GABRIEL, S.E.C.
FORD GABRIEL
7100 Rue Saint-Jacques, Montreal, QC, H4B 1V2
(514) 487-7777
Emp Here 50   *Sales* 24,903,900
SIC 5511 New and used car dealers
Gabriel Azouz

D-U-N-S 25-746-1855   (BR)
GOUVERNEMENT DE LA PROVINCE DE QUEBEC
CENTRE DE READAPTATION CONSTANCE LETHBRIDGE
(*Suby of* GOUVERNEMENT DE LA PROVINCE DE QUEBEC)
7005 Boul De Maisonneuve O Bureau 620, Montreal, QC, H4B 1T3
(514) 487-1770
Emp Here 205
SIC 7352 Medical equipment rental
Patrick Murphy-Lavalee

D-U-N-S 20-226-7845   (SL)
MELDRUM THE MOVER INC
DEMENAGEURS MELDRUM, LES
6645 Rue Sherbrooke O, Montreal, QC, H4B 1N4
(514) 400-0182
Emp Here 100   *Sales* 14,819,200
SIC 4213 Trucking, except local
Thomas Q (Tom) Filgiano

D-U-N-S 24-501-4261   (HQ)
MOTO M.T.L. INTERNATIONAL INC
MOTO DAYTONA
(*Suby of* 136562 CANADA INC)
6695 Rue Saint-Jacques, Montreal, QC, H4B 1V3
(514) 483-6686
Sales 47,196,000
SIC 5571 Motorcycle dealers
Charles Gref
Sylvain Lamanque

Raymond Gref

D-U-N-S 20-512-3651   (SL)
MOTOS DAYTONA INC
(*Suby of* 136562 CANADA INC)
6695 Rue Saint-Jacques, Montreal, QC, H4B 1V3
(514) 483-6686
Emp Here 45   *Sales* 28,317,600
SIC 5571 Motorcycle dealers
Gabriel Azouz
Raymond Gref
Sylvain Lamanque

D-U-N-S 24-541-4867   (BR)
PARMALAT CANADA INC
PARMALAT DAIRY & BAKERY
(*Suby of* PARMALAT SPA)
7470 Rue Saint-Jacques, Montreal, QC, H4B 1W4
(514) 484-8401
Emp Here 300
SIC 2026 Fluid milk
Josee Charbonneau

D-U-N-S 24-099-2425   (BR)
PARMALAT CANADA INC
(*Suby of* PARMALAT SPA)
1900 Av Westmore, Montreal, QC, H4B 1Z3
(514) 369-3534
Emp Here 250
SIC 5143 Dairy products, except dried or canned
Pierre Samoisette

D-U-N-S 24-709-7066   (SL)
PROTEC INVESTIGATION AND SECURITY INC
CELLPAGE
3333 Boul Cavendish Bureau 200, Montreal, QC, H4B 2M5
(514) 485-3255
Emp Here 100   *Sales* 39,567,800
SIC 7381 Detective and armored car services
Steven Moscovitch

D-U-N-S 24-288-2371   (SL)
RTG PROTECH INC
3333 Boul Cavendish Bureau 270, Montreal, QC, H4B 2M5
(514) 868-1919
Emp Here 30   *Sales* 13,528,469
SIC 7389 Business services, nec
Tony Gentile

D-U-N-S 24-461-3188   (HQ)
TRICOTS LIESSE (1983) INC
JASCO JERSEY
(*Suby of* 126217 CANADA INC)
2125 Rue Lily-Simon, Montreal, QC, H4B 3A1
(514) 342-0685
Sales 54,395,690
SIC 2257 Weft knit fabric mills
Claude Helwani

D-U-N-S 20-220-3956   (SL)
W. GORDON INC
GORDONS PNEUS MECANIQUE
2125 Boul Cavendish, Montreal, QC, H4B 2Y2
(514) 481-7771
Emp Here 40   *Sales* 19,923,120
SIC 5531 Auto and home supply stores
Bruce Gordon
Heather Gordon

Montreal, QC H4C

D-U-N-S 24-945-6948   (SL)
2865-8169 QUEBEC INC
RESEAU BUREAUTIQUE
4700 Rue Saint-Ambroise Bureau 100, Montreal, QC, H4C 2C7
(514) 937-1117
Emp Here 50   *Sales* 25,442,800
SIC 5021 Furniture

Pierre Roy
Veronique Feat
Nicolas St-Germain

D-U-N-S 20-254-1587   (SL)
2956-1198 QUEBEC INC
DEFLECTEUR AIRFLOW
3974 Rue Notre-Dame O Bureau 101, Montreal, QC, H4C 1R1
(514) 573-2850
Emp Here 21   *Sales* 10,931,382
SIC 5099 Durable goods, nec
Robert Martineau

D-U-N-S 24-350-8129   (HQ)
3762971 CANADA INC
(*Suby of* BRASSEURS RJ INC, LES)
5080 Rue Saint-Ambroise, Montreal, QC, H4C 2G1
(514) 939-3060
Emp Here 1   *Sales* 27,335,000
SIC 6712 Bank holding companies
Roger Jaar
Philippe Jaar
Armida Jaar

D-U-N-S 20-332-7747   (SL)
7818696 CANADA INC
TRENDINNOVATIONS
642 Rue De Courcelle Bureau 101, Montreal, QC, H4C 3C5
(514) 659-1681
Emp Here 26   *Sales* 15,446,960
SIC 5912 Drug stores and proprietary stores
Jean-Francois Gauthier
Jelena Neylan

D-U-N-S 20-115-8313   (SL)
9015-9492 QUEBEC INC
BOULANGERIE PREMIERE MOISSON
3025 Rue Saint-Ambroise, Montreal, QC, H4C 2C2
(514) 932-0328
Emp Here 75   *Sales* 22,010,775
SIC 5461 Retail bakeries
Bertrand Labelle
Liliane Colpron

D-U-N-S 25-849-3949   (SL)
A LA CARTE EXPRESS INC
ALCE
4700 Rue Saint-Ambroise Bureau 44, Montreal, QC, H4C 2C7
(514) 933-7000
Emp Here 70   *Sales* 10,373,440
SIC 4212 Local trucking, without storage
Michel Lepine

D-U-N-S 24-684-4968   (SL)
AAA CANADA INC
780 Av Brewster Bureau 03-200, Montreal, QC, H4C 2K1
(514) 733-6655
Emp Here 750   *Sales* 238,014,000
SIC 4581 Airports, flying fields, and services
Denis Deschamps
Benoit Hudon
Gilles Chauby
Cedric Nouvelot
Stephanie Fafard
Michel Blaquiere

D-U-N-S 24-954-1913   (SL)
ALLAN RAMSAY ET COMPAGNIE LIMITEE
(*Suby of* IMPERIAL TOBACCO CANADA LIMITEE)
3711 Rue Saint-Antoine O, Montreal, QC, H4C 3P6
(514) 932-6161
Emp Here 100   *Sales* 18,340,300
SIC 2111 Cigarettes
Marie Polet

D-U-N-S 25-492-6566   (SL)
BONLOOK INC
BON REGARD
4020 Rue Saint-Ambroise Bureau 489, Montreal, QC, H4C 2C7

(855) 943-5566
Emp Here 100   *Sales* 24,432,800
SIC 5995 Optical goods stores
Sophie Boulanger
Louis-Felix Boulanger
Andre Boulanger
Andre Forest
Elana Gorbatyuk
Anna Martini
Josee Perreault
Eric Phaneuf
Pierre Fitzgibbon

D-U-N-S 24-812-2624   (SL)
BRASSERIE MCAUSLAN INC, LA
ST-AMBROISE
(*Suby of* BRASSEURS RJ INC, LES)
5080 Rue Saint-Ambroise, Montreal, QC, H4C 2G1
(514) 939-3060
Emp Here 100   *Sales* 34,569,000
SIC 2082 Malt beverages
Roger Jaar
Philippe Jaar
Armida Jaar

D-U-N-S 24-865-9989   (SL)
CITERNES BEDARD INC
5785 Place Turcot, Montreal, QC, H4C 1V9
(514) 937-1670
Emp Here 82   *Sales* 15,750,970
SIC 3443 Fabricated plate work (boiler shop)
Nabil Attirgi

D-U-N-S 20-852-8799   (BR)
COMMISSION SCOLAIRE DE MONTREAL
ECOLE DES METIERS DU SUD OUEST DE MONTREAL
(*Suby of* COMMISSION SCOLAIRE DE MONTREAL)
717 Rue Saint-Ferdinand, Montreal, QC, H4C 2T3
(514) 596-5960
Emp Here 85
SIC 8211 Elementary and secondary schools
Michel Lachapelle

D-U-N-S 20-215-4126   (HQ)
CORPORATION COPNICK, LA
6198 Rue Notre-Dame O, Montreal, QC, H4C 1V4
(514) 937-9306
Emp Here 20   *Sales* 18,218,970
SIC 5093 Scrap and waste materials
Micheal Etcovitch
Ruth Etcovitch

D-U-N-S 20-289-6734   (BR)
DAN AGENCY INC
DENTSUBOS INC
(*Suby of* DENTSU INC.)
3970 Rue Saint-Ambroise, Montreal, QC, H4C 2C7
(514) 848-0010
Emp Here 100
SIC 7311 Advertising agencies
Michel Ostugey

D-U-N-S 24-944-1080   (HQ)
DRAKKAR & ASSOCIES INC
DRAKKAR RESSOURCES HUMAINES
780 Av Brewster Bureau 200, Montreal, QC, H4C 2K1
(514) 733-6655
Emp Here 80   *Sales* 112,203,000
SIC 8741 Management services
Denis Deschamps
Michel Blaquiere
Stephanie Fafard

D-U-N-S 24-954-1632   (SL)
DU MAURIER LTEE
3711 Rue Saint-Antoine O, Montreal, QC, H4C 3P6
(514) 932-6161
Emp Here 635   *Sales* 116,460,905
SIC 2111 Cigarettes
Alexandre Jalleau

▲ Public Company   ■ Public Company Family Member   **HQ** Headquarters   **BR** Branch   **SL** Single Location

Donald Mccarty

D-U-N-S 24-348-4784 (SL)
ENTREPRISE DE CONSTRUCTION T.E.Q. INC
780 Av Brewster Bureau 3-300, Montreal, QC, H4C 2K1
(514) 933-3838
Emp Here 50 *Sales* 21,136,850
SIC 1541 Industrial buildings and warehouses
 Emmanuel Triassi
 Francesco Maria Rotundi
 Stephane Coudry
 Luisa Biasutti
 Fabrizio Tonucci
 Roberto Bianchini

D-U-N-S 20-555-9941 (SL)
GAZ NATUREL WESTMOUNT
325 Rue Saint-Augustin, Montreal, QC, H4C 2N7
(514) 564-1189
Emp Here 5 *Sales* 15,529,285
SIC 4924 Natural gas distribution
 Claude Charbonneau

D-U-N-S 25-408-1813 (SL)
H.C. VIDAL LTEE
ENTREPRISE J.M. VIDAL ET ASSOCIES
5700 Rue Philippe-Turcot, Montreal, QC, H4C 1V6
(514) 937-6187
Emp Here 70 *Sales* 13,462,960
SIC 7699 Repair services, nec
 Jean-Marc Vidal
 Christian Vidal
 Rejean Dumont
 Francois Renaud
 Jan Bystrzycki

D-U-N-S 20-553-4527 (BR)
HOME DEPOT OF CANADA INC
HOME DEPOT
(*Suby of* THE HOME DEPOT INC)
4625 Rue Saint-Antoine O, Montreal, QC, H4C 1E2
(514) 846-4770
Emp Here 200
SIC 5039 Construction materials, nec
 Jules Ratelle

D-U-N-S 24-903-5940 (HQ)
IMAFLEX INC
CANSIT
5710 Rue Notre-Dame O, Montreal, QC, H4C 1V2
(514) 935-5710
Emp Here 85 *Sales* 65,448,532
SIC 3081 Unsupported plastics film and sheet
 Joseph Abbandonato
 Tony Abbandonato
 Ralf Dujardin
 Gerry Phelps
 John Ripplinger
 Giancarlo Santella
 Philip Nolan
 Michel Baril
 Consolato Gattuso
 Mario Settino

D-U-N-S 20-221-6990 (HQ)
IMPERIAL TOBACCO CANADA LIMITEE
BAT CANADA
3711 Rue Saint-Antoine O, Montreal, QC, H4C 3P6
(514) 932-6161
Emp Here 304 *Sales* 289,481,500
SIC 2111 Cigarettes
 Jorge Araya
 Eric Thauvette
 Tamara Gitto

D-U-N-S 20-420-3491 (HQ)
IMPERIAL TOBACCO COMPAGNIE LIMITEE
(*Suby of* IMPERIAL TOBACCO CANADA LIMITEE)
3711 Rue Saint-Antoine O, Montreal, QC,

H4C 3P6
(514) 932-6161
Sales 176,747,700
SIC 5194 Tobacco and tobacco products

D-U-N-S 24-167-4480 (SL)
IMPORTATIONS MIRDO CANADA INC., LES
6312 Rue Notre-Dame O, Montreal, QC, H4C 1V4
(514) 932-1523
Emp Here 55 *Sales* 40,838,600
SIC 5199 Nondurable goods, nec
 Hayk Bosnakyan
 Nurhan Papucyan
 Hrayr Comlekcioglu

D-U-N-S 24-377-7708 (HQ)
IPROSPECT CANADA INC
NVI
(*Suby of* DENTSU INC.)
3970 Rue Saint-Ambroise, Montreal, QC, H4C 2C7
(514) 524-7149
Sales 11,621,518
SIC 7311 Advertising agencies
 Guillaume Bouchard
 Louise Gauthier
 Scott Hughes
 Dave Wein

D-U-N-S 24-895-8423 (HQ)
JOHN PLAYER & FILS LTEE
(*Suby of* IMPERIAL TOBACCO CANADA LIMITEE)
3711 Rue Saint-Antoine O, Montreal, QC, H4C 3P6
(514) 932-6161
Sales 11,137,800
SIC 5194 Tobacco and tobacco products
 Christoph Blattier
 Pierre Leclerc
 Caroline Ferland

D-U-N-S 25-217-4206 (BR)
KRUGER INC
(*Suby of* KRUGER INC)
5845 Place Turcot, Montreal, QC, H4C 1V9
(514) 934-0600
Emp Here 140
SIC 2631 Paperboard mills
 Steve Hicknell

D-U-N-S 24-317-6356 (HQ)
LEMAY CO INC
LEMAY ARCHITECTURE + DESIGN
3500 Rue Saint-Jacques, Montreal, QC, H4C 1H2
(514) 932-5101
Emp Here 50 *Sales* 137,286,450
SIC 7389 Business services, nec
 Louis T. Lemay
 Pierre Larouche
 Marc Bouchard
 Andre Cardinal

D-U-N-S 20-228-7587 (SL)
O'CONNELL, THOMAS INC
5700 Rue Notre-Dame O, Montreal, QC, H4C 1V1
(514) 932-2145
Emp Here 50 *Sales* 11,046,700
SIC 1711 Plumbing, heating, air-conditioning
 Claude Gosselin
 Eric Bergeron
 Michel Trolio

D-U-N-S 24-697-1386 (SL)
PLASTIQUE CADUNA INC
(*Suby of* BATTAT INC)
5655 Rue Philippe-Turcot, Montreal, QC, H4C 3K8
(514) 932-7821
Emp Here 100 *Sales* 15,885,800
SIC 3089 Plastics products, nec
 John Chamberland
 Joseph Battat

D-U-N-S 20-377-7128 (SL)

PRODUCTIONS TMV INC
642 Rue De Courcelle Bureau 209, Montreal, QC, H4C 3C5
(514) 228-8740
Emp Here 100 *Sales* 17,731,100
SIC 7374 Data processing and preparation
 Jean-Noel Sciretta

D-U-N-S 25-502-9803 (HQ)
PRODUITS MURPHCO LTEE, LES
METAL EN FEUILLES MURPHCO
5363 Rue Notre-Dame O Bureau 117, Montreal, QC, H4C 1T7
(514) 937-3275
Emp Here 1 *Sales* 11,179,350
SIC 5033 Roofing, siding, and insulation
 Murphy Savoie

D-U-N-S 20-227-6895 (SL)
PRODUITS POLYWRAP DU CANADA LTEE, LES
5590 Boul Monk, Montreal, QC, H4C 3R8
(514) 933-2121
Emp Here 50 *Sales* 11,671,750
SIC 2673 Bags: plastic, laminated, and coated
 Gilbert Guigui

D-U-N-S 24-710-2247 (SL)
SERVICE DE MANUTENTION D.B. INC
SERVICE D B
3971 Rue Notre-Dame O, Montreal, QC, H4C 1R2
(514) 934-5681
Emp Here 200 *Sales* 14,938,800
SIC 7363 Help supply services
 Francois Brind'amour
 Daniel Durocher

D-U-N-S 24-784-1542 (SL)
SOCIETE DE GESTION DU FONDS POUR LE DEVELOPPEMENT DES JEUNES ENFANTS
AVENIR D'ENFANTS
4720 Rue Dagenais Bureau 117, Montreal, QC, H4C 1L7
(514) 526-2187
Emp Here 49 *Sales* 11,114,817
SIC 8399 Social services, nec
 Jean-Pierre Hotte
 Jean-Marc Chouinard
 Julie Meloche
 Julie Dostaler

D-U-N-S 25-463-4793 (SL)
TOURS JUMPSTREET TOURS INC, LES
EDUCATOURS
(*Suby of* TUI AG)
780 Av Brewster Suite 02-300, Montreal, QC, H4C 2K1
(514) 843-3311
Emp Here 28 *Sales* 12,358,476
SIC 4724 Travel agencies
 Mark Clarke
 Tom Clarke
 Bill Irwin
 Brendan Jones

D-U-N-S 20-298-2799 (HQ)
VIZEUM CANADA INC
VIZEUM
(*Suby of* DENTSU INC.)
3970 Rue Saint-Ambroise, Montreal, QC, H4C 2C7
(514) 270-1010
Emp Here 5 *Sales* 10,586,200
SIC 7311 Advertising agencies
 Dave Wein
 Louise Gauthier
 Scott Hughes

Montreal, QC H4E

D-U-N-S 24-490-0411 (SL)

132087 CANADA INC
SUPER MARCHE CLAUDE ST-PIERRE IGA
6675 Boul Monk, Montreal, QC, H4E 3J2
(514) 767-5323
Emp Here 52 *Sales* 15,260,804
SIC 5411 Grocery stores
 Claude St Pierre

D-U-N-S 20-591-0623 (SL)
ALIMENTS DA VINCI LTEE, LES
5655 Rue Beaulieu, Montreal, QC, H4E 3E4
(514) 769-1234
Emp Here 120 *Sales* 41,482,800
SIC 2045 Prepared flour mixes and doughs
 Michael Mazzaferro
 Claudia Russo

D-U-N-S 20-566-9617 (SL)
ALLIED TEXTILES & REFUSE INC
3700 Rue Saint-Patrick Bureau 200, Montreal, QC, H4E 1A2
(514) 932-5962
Emp Here 46 *Sales* 23,944,932
SIC 5093 Scrap and waste materials
 Mark Kaufman

D-U-N-S 25-331-0338 (BR)
ARCELORMITTAL PRODUITS LONGS CANADA S.E.N.C.
(*Suby of* ARCELORMITTAL PRODUITS LONGS CANADA S.E.N.C.)
5900 Rue Saint-Patrick, Montreal, QC, H4E 1B3
(514) 762-5260
Emp Here 140
SIC 3312 Blast furnaces and steel mills

D-U-N-S 24-815-3595 (SL)
BENEVOLES DE LA RESIDENCE YVON-BRUNET INC, LES
6250 Av Newman, Montreal, QC, H4E 4K4
(514) 765-8000
Emp Here 178 *Sales* 11,442,196
SIC 8361 Residential care
 Huguette Couture
 Jacqueline Lacombe

D-U-N-S 24-346-5585 (HQ)
CENTRE DE SANTE ET DE SERVICES SOCIAUX DU SUD-OUEST-VERDUN
HOPITAL DE VERDUN
(*Suby of* GOUVERNEMENT DE LA PROVINCE DE QUEBEC)
6161 Rue Laurendeau, Montreal, QC, H4E 3X6
(514) 762-2777
Emp Here 20 *Sales* 422,104,000
SIC 8062 General medical and surgical hospitals
 Lorraine Duchesne-Noiseux
 Gilles Beaudry
 Sonia Belanger
 Pascale Bedard
 Andreia Bittencourt
 Patrice Catoir
 Bernard Circe
 Gaetan Couture
 Jennifer De Combe
 Robert Degray

D-U-N-S 20-294-2996 (SL)
COMMUNICATIONS MEDPLAN INC
COMMUNICATIONS MEDIA GO DESIGN
2077 Rue Cabot, Montreal, QC, H4E 1E2
(514) 767-6166
Emp Here 50 *Sales* 11,714,400
SIC 8748 Business consulting, nec
 Isabelle Halle

D-U-N-S 25-099-1965 (BR)
CONSTRUCTION DJL INC
(*Suby of* VINCI)
6200 Rue Saint-Patrick, Montreal, QC, H4E 1B3
(514) 766-8256
Emp Here 100
SIC 1611 Highway and street construction

Pierre Aube

D-U-N-S 25-335-9202   (SL)
CONSTRUCTIONS QUORUM INC
5200 Rue Saint-Patrick Bureau 200, Montreal,
QC, H4E 4N9
(514) 822-2882
Emp Here 51   *Sales* 13,818,042
SIC 1522 Residential construction, nec
Peter Cosentini
Guy Laporte

D-U-N-S 20-602-7286   (SL)
ENTREPRISES LARRY INC
4200 Rue Saint-Patrick, Montreal, QC, H4E
1A5
(514) 767-5363
Emp Here 60   *Sales* 28,501,560
SIC 5084 Industrial machinery and equipment
Sylvain Gervais
Martin Caron
Cynthia Servat-Gervais

D-U-N-S 20-265-6203   (BR)
EUROVIA QUEBEC CONSTRUCTION INC
(Suby of VINCI)
6200 Rue Saint-Patrick, Montreal, QC, H4E
1B3
(514) 766-8256
Emp Here 100
SIC 1611 Highway and street construction
Maxime Lebeau

D-U-N-S 20-883-5827   (SL)
INVESTIGATIONS RK INC
2100 Av De L'Eglise, Montreal, QC, H4E 1H4
(514) 761-7121
Emp Here 100   *Sales* 39,567,800
SIC 7381 Detective and armored car services
Pierre C. Ricard

D-U-N-S 20-214-2790   (SL)
LUCIEN CHARBONNEAU LIMITEE
(Suby of GROUPE CHARBONNEAU INC)
1955 Rue Cabot, Montreal, QC, H4E 1E2
(514) 336-2500
Emp Here 70   *Sales* 16,314,550
SIC 1711 Plumbing, heating, air-conditioning
Jean Charbonneau
Dany Litwin
Eric Moreau
Eric Loiselle

D-U-N-S 20-370-2451   (SL)
LUXURY RETREATS INTERNATIONAL ULC
VILLAS PRIVEES DE LUXE
5530 Rue Saint-Patrick Bureau 2210, Mon-
treal, QC, H4E 1A8
(514) 400-5109
Emp Here 250   *Sales* 31,194,000
SIC 8741 Management services
Garth Ernest Bossow
Jeff Mullen
David Charles Bernstein

D-U-N-S 24-955-0773   (SL)
NOVA TUBE INC
(Suby of 3195538 CANADA INC)
5870 Rue Saint-Patrick, Montreal, QC, H4E
1B3
(514) 762-5220
Emp Here 60   *Sales* 11,525,100
SIC 3441 Fabricated structural Metal
Scott B. Jones
D. Brian Jones
Pina Santillo
Lawrence P. Cannon

D-U-N-S 24-763-6087   (SL)
P.J. IMPEX INC
5532 Rue Saint-Patrick Bureau 300, Montreal,
QC, H4E 1A8
(514) 369-2035
Emp Here 22   *Sales* 18,382,694
SIC 5141 Groceries, general line
Chad Coleman

D-U-N-S 20-234-7753   (SL)

PRODUITS STAR APPETIZING INC, LES
1685 Rue Cabot, Montreal, QC, H4E 1C9
(514) 765-0614
Emp Here 20   *Sales* 10,006,500
SIC 5181 Beer and ale
Howard Saskin
Samuel Saskin
Sally Saskin

D-U-N-S 20-531-7576   (HQ)
REVISION MILITAIRE INC
3800 Rue Saint-Patrick Bureau 200, Montreal,
QC, H4E 1A4
(514) 739-4444
Sales 17,273,964
SIC 3851 Ophthalmic goods
Jonathan Blanshay
Linda Watson
Charles Dollimore
Jeffrey Drummond
Neil Murdoch

D-U-N-S 24-477-4121   (HQ)
STAR SALT INC
SEL PLUS, DIV. OF
3351 Rue Saint-Patrick, Montreal, QC, H4E
1A1
(514) 933-1117
Emp Here 3   *Sales* 12,533,655
SIC 5149 Groceries and related products, nec
Clinton Henderson

D-U-N-S 24-614-5288   (HQ)
**UNITES MOBILES DE COIFFURE DE MON-
TREAL INC, LES**
COIFFURE BEL-AGE QUEBEC
6226 Boul Monk, Montreal, QC, H4E 3H7
(514) 766-3553
Emp Here 10   *Sales* 16,017,300
SIC 7231 Beauty shops
Claude Tailleur

Montreal, QC H4G

D-U-N-S 20-387-6099   (SL)
GESTIONS GILBERT ROY INC
MARCHAND CANADIAN TIRE DE VERDUN
3180 Rue Wellington, Montreal, QC, H4G 1T3
(514) 766-8561
Emp Here 50   *Sales* 24,903,900
SIC 5531 Auto and home supply stores
Gilbert Roy

Montreal, QC H4J

D-U-N-S 24-318-2503   (SL)
3965546 CANADA LIMITEE
*NOVATEK INTERNATIONAL PHARMACEU-
TICAL SOFTWARE*
5995 Boul Gouin O Bureau 308, Montreal, QC,
H4J 2P8
(514) 337-7337
Emp Here 250   *Sales* 46,143,250
SIC 7371 Custom computer programming ser-
vices
Parsa Famili
Aram Montazami
Dierdre Burnett
Mazda Famili
Payam Montazami

D-U-N-S 25-240-2581   (BR)
COMMISSION SCOLAIRE DE MONTREAL
ECOLE STE-ODILE
(Suby of COMMISSION SCOLAIRE DE
MONTREAL)
12055 Rue Depatie, Montreal, QC, H4J 1W9
(514) 596-5565
Emp Here 75
SIC 8211 Elementary and secondary schools
Line Galiichand

D-U-N-S 25-357-1962   (SL)
**CORBEILLE - BORDEAUX -
CARTIERVILLE, LA**
RESTAURANT FESTIGOUT
5080 Rue Dudemaine, Montreal, QC, H4J 1N6
(514) 856-0838
Emp Here 30   *Sales* 12,738,210
SIC 8999 Services, nec
Sonia Demers
Georges Fournier
Yves Provost
John Roumeliotis
Claude Lamoureux
Jean-Yves Laverdure
Jean Paul Simard
Gisele Renaud
Therese Milot
Romeo Ditommaso

D-U-N-S 25-233-5989   (SL)
ECOLE ARMENIENNE SOURP HAGOP, L'
ECOLE SECONDAIRE PASDERMAJIAN
3400 Rue Nadon, Montreal, QC, H4J 1P5
(514) 332-1373
Emp Here 85   *Sales* 7,890,210
SIC 8211 Elementary and secondary schools
Jean Arakelian
Hagop Boulgarian

D-U-N-S 24-406-5090   (SL)
EPICERIE SALTARELLI ET FILS INC
EUROMARCHE LATINA (1980)
11847 Boul Laurentien, Montreal, QC, H4J
2M1
(514) 331-5879
Emp Here 55   *Sales* 16,141,235
SIC 5411 Grocery stores
Arturo Saltarelli
Antonio Saltarelli
Cecilia Saltarelli

D-U-N-S 25-830-4476   (SL)
GESTION KM INC
JEAN COUTU 065
5855 Boul Gouin O, Montreal, QC, H4J 1E5
(514) 334-8641
Emp Here 49   *Sales* 12,394,746
SIC 5912 Drug stores and proprietary stores
Nelly Kanou
Tanya Kanou
Sita Marachian

D-U-N-S 20-032-6820   (SL)
**MAISON DES PARENTS DE BORDEAUX-
CARTIERVILLE INC**
5680 Rue De Salaberry, Montreal, QC, H4J
1J7
(514) 745-1144
Emp Here 28   *Sales* 11,127,592
SIC 8699 Membership organizations, nec
Sophie Deleuil Millette

Montreal, QC H4K

D-U-N-S 20-792-6387   (SL)
COLLEGE SAINTE MARCELLAINE
9155 Boul Gouin O, Montreal, QC, H4K 1C3
(514) 334-9651
Emp Here 100   *Sales* 9,282,600
SIC 8211 Elementary and secondary schools
Mylene Nault

D-U-N-S 24-345-5933   (BR)
FONDATION LE PILIER
MAISON ST DENIS BOURGET, LA
(Suby of FONDATION LE PILIER)
23 Av Du Ruisseau, Montreal, QC, H4K 2C8
(450) 624-9922
Emp Here 150
SIC 8361 Residential care

D-U-N-S 20-859-5199   (SL)
LALLIER AUTOMOBILE (MONTREAL) INC
HONDA

12435 Boul Laurentien, Montreal, QC, H4K
2J2
(514) 337-2330
Emp Here 48   *Sales* 23,907,744
SIC 5511 New and used car dealers
Michel Dagenais
Denise Dagenais

Montreal, QC H4M

D-U-N-S 20-883-6866   (SL)
DUO COMMUNICATIONS OF CANADA LTD
DUOCOM CANADA
10000 Boul Cavendish, Montreal, QC, H4M
2V1

Emp Here 70   *Sales* 32,669,775
SIC 5099 Durable goods, nec

Montreal, QC H4N

D-U-N-S 20-381-2227   (SL)
10684210 CANADA INC
METRO MEDIA
101 Boul Marcel-Laurin Bureau 320, Montreal,
QC, H4N 2M3
(514) 286-1066
Emp Here 140   *Sales* 22,963,780
SIC 2721 Periodicals
Michael Raffoul
Andrew Mule

D-U-N-S 24-922-6556   (HQ)
162583 CANADA INC
1625 Rue Chabanel O Bureau 801, Montreal,
QC, H4N 2S7
(514) 384-4776
Emp Here 2   *Sales* 10,483,875
SIC 6712 Bank holding companies
David Schnapp
Steve Wexler

D-U-N-S 24-858-9590   (SL)
2842-3861 QUEBEC INC
PROMOTIONS V P S
1201 Rue De Louvain O, Montreal, QC, H4N
1G6
(514) 858-0066
Emp Here 49   *Sales* 11,480,112
SIC 8743 Public relations services
Robert Gagnon

D-U-N-S 24-990-4855   (SL)
2944715 CANADA INC
THOMAS FRUITS ET LEGUMES
9150 Rue Charles-De La Tour, Montreal, QC,
H4N 1M2
(514) 389-3815
Emp Here 45   *Sales* 37,600,965
SIC 5148 Fresh fruits and vegetables
Nick Argiris
Mario Argiris
Nikolaos Argiris

D-U-N-S 24-357-7728   (SL)
3310485 CANADA INC
1625 Rue Chabanel O Bureau 201, Montreal,
QC, H4N 2S7
(514) 388-1700
Emp Here 45   *Sales* 18,870,975
SIC 6712 Bank holding companies
Sheldon Lewis
Benton Lewis

D-U-N-S 20-386-7411   (HQ)
3379710 CANADA INC
1450 Rue De Louvain O, Montreal, QC, H4N
1G5
(514) 495-1531
Sales 12,816,097
SIC 6712 Bank holding companies
Jeffrey Ayoub

D-U-N-S 20-317-4941 (SL)
8268533 CANADA INC
VAPEUR EXPRESS, LE
155 Boul Montpellier, Montreal, QC, H4N 2G3
(514) 385-2509
Emp Here 50 *Sales* 37,126,000
SIC 5194 Tobacco and tobacco products
Peter Raimondo
Antonio Raimondo
Rosie Zappitelli

D-U-N-S 20-558-8176 (SL)
9127-2021 QUEBEC INC
BLUE SPIKE BEVERAGES
1350 Rue Mazurette Bureau 314, Montreal, QC, H4N 1H2
(514) 739-9112
Emp Here 50 *Sales* 29,395,800
SIC 5182 Wine and distilled beverages
Nicolas Gagnon-Oosterwaal
Mathieu Gagnon-Oosterwaal
Jeff Wright

D-U-N-S 20-289-1651 (SL)
9199-4467 QUEBEC INC
EARTH RATED
(*Suby of* 9252-8595 QUEBEC INC)
1350 Rue Mazurette Bureau 228, Montreal, QC, H4N 1H2
(514) 316-2404
Emp Here 20 *Sales* 14,850,400
SIC 5199 Nondurable goods, nec
Abaragidan Gnanendran
David Ngo
Monica Sposato

D-U-N-S 20-395-6685 (SL)
9356-1405 QUEBEC INC.
COWIE
9050, Rue Charles-De La Tour, Montreal, QC, H4N 1M2

Emp Here 50 *Sales* 19,275,950
SIC 0273 Animal aquaculture
Louis Levesque

D-U-N-S 24-837-0363 (HQ)
ALIMENTS IMEX INC
1605 Rue De Beauharnois O Bureau 100, Montreal, QC, H4N 1J6

Emp Here 10 *Sales* 12,533,655
SIC 5141 Groceries, general line
Suzanne Britten

D-U-N-S 20-267-3356 (SL)
ALTA CONSTRUCTION (2011) LTEE
ALTA - OCI CONSTRUCTION
1655 Rue De Beauharnois O, Montreal, QC, H4N 1J6
(514) 748-8881
Emp Here 40 *Sales* 11,340,960
SIC 1611 Highway and street construction
Alain Gauvin
Hugues Fastrel
Bruno Fayolle

D-U-N-S 20-267-4024 (SL)
BELLA HOSIERY MILLS INC
SUPERFIT
1401 Rue Legendre O Bureau 200, Montreal, QC, H4N 2R9
(514) 274-6500
Emp Here 50 *Sales* 12,828,100
SIC 3842 Surgical appliances and supplies
Susan Werner
Barry William Werner
Albert Werner

D-U-N-S 20-271-1925 (SL)
BENISTI USA LLC
1650 Rue Chabanel O, Montreal, QC, H4N 3M8
(514) 384-0140
Emp Here 48 *Sales* 24,196,489
SIC 5136 Men's and boy's clothing
Maurice Benisti

D-U-N-S 24-857-9898 (HQ)
BEXEL INC
ALIMENTS FLAMINGO
(*Suby of* COOP FEDEREE, LA)
9001 Boul De L'Acadie Bureau 200, Montreal, QC, H4N 3H7
(514) 858-2222
Emp Here 100
SIC 0251 Broiler, fryer, and roaster chickens
Jean-Francois Harel
Luc Forget
Muriel Dubois
Mathieu Couture
Rejean Nadeau

D-U-N-S 24-760-9592 (BR)
BONNETERIE BELLA INC.
SUPER FIX
(*Suby of* BONNETERIE BELLA INC.)
1401 Rue Legendre O, Montreal, QC, H4N 2R9
(514) 381-8519
Emp Here 120
SIC 2251 Women's hosiery, except socks
Samuel Scharf

D-U-N-S 24-475-7415 (HQ)
CANADAWIDE FRUIT WHOLESALERS INC
(*Suby of* 3123472 CANADA INC)
1370 Rue De Beauharnois O Bureau 200, Montreal, QC, H4N 1J5
(514) 382-3232
Emp Here 145 *Sales* 107,507,400
SIC 5148 Fresh fruits and vegetables
George Pitsikoulis
Michael Pitsikoulis
Nick Pitsikoulis

D-U-N-S 25-502-3269 (HQ)
CHEMINS DE FER QUEBEC-GATINEAU INC
(*Suby of* GENESEE & WYOMING INC.)
9001 Boul De L'Acadie Bureau 600, Montreal, QC, H4N 3H5
(514) 948-6999
Emp Here 20 *Sales* 10,538,080
SIC 4111 Local and suburban transit
Louis Gravel
Harold Perrault
Thomas D. Savage
Matthew O. Walsh
Caroline Healey

D-U-N-S 20-235-0898 (SL)
COLLECTION ARIANNE INC
1655 Rue De Louvain O, Montreal, QC, H4N 1G6
(514) 385-9393
Emp Here 125 *Sales* 17,084,250
SIC 2341 Women's and children's underwear
Norman Rossy

D-U-N-S 24-889-7951 (SL)
CONSENSO CREATIONS INC
1565 Rue Chabanel O, Montreal, QC, H4N 2W3

Emp Here 30 *Sales* 14,949,660
SIC 5136 Men's and boy's clothing
Simon Cohen

D-U-N-S 20-215-4050 (HQ)
COOP FEDEREE, LA
FLAMINGO
9001 Boul De L'Acadie Bureau 200, Montreal, QC, H4N 3H7
(514) 858-2222
Emp Here 1,000 *Sales* 5,062,373,662
SIC 5191 Farm supplies
Ghislain Gervais
Muriel Dubois
Mathieu Couture
Jean-Francois Harel
Normand Marcil
Benoit Massicotte
Richard Ferland
Cathy Fraser
Patrick Soucy

Francois Drainville

D-U-N-S 25-470-8667 (SL)
COOP FEDEREE, LA
9001 Boul De L'Acadie, Montreal, QC, H4N 3H7
(514) 384-6450
Emp Here 49 *Sales* 11,909,401
SIC 6519 Real property lessors, nec
Denis Richard

D-U-N-S 25-541-1951 (SL)
CORPORATION MAGIL CONSTRUCTION
1655 Rue De Beauharnois O Bureau 16, Montreal, QC, H4N 1J6
(514) 341-9899
Emp Here 50 *Sales* 13,716,600
SIC 8741 Management services
Alain Gauvin
Hughes Fastrel
Giovanni Marcovecchio
Bruno Fayolle
Francis Fayolle

D-U-N-S 24-369-9746 (BR)
COSTCO WHOLESALE CANADA LTD
COSTCO
(*Suby of* COSTCO WHOLESALE CORPORATION)
1015 Rue Du Marche-Central, Montreal, QC, H4N 3J8
(514) 381-1251
Emp Here 150
SIC 5399 Miscellaneous general merchandise
Eric Caissy

D-U-N-S 24-902-8184 (SL)
CREATIONS ROBO INC
COCCOLI
1205 Rue De Louvain O, Montreal, QC, H4N 1G6
(514) 382-6501
Emp Here 20 *Sales* 10,006,500
SIC 5137 Women's and children's clothing
Marian Spino Vachon

D-U-N-S 24-800-3592 (SL)
CROTEAU, J. A. (1989) INC
AUBAINERIE JEAN TALON
1001 Rue Du Marche-Central Local A11, Montreal, QC, H4N 1J8
(514) 382-3403
Emp Here 60 *Sales* 10,763,760
SIC 5651 Family clothing stores
Jonathan Robert
Johanne Croteau

D-U-N-S 24-697-9140 (HQ)
DISTRIBUTEURS ESSEX CONTINENTALE INC, LES
985 Rue Du Marche-Central, Montreal, QC, H4N 1K2
(514) 745-1222
Sales 16,711,540
SIC 5148 Fresh fruits and vegetables
Francesco Ferrarelli
Ronald Christopher Wilson
Robert George Graham

D-U-N-S 20-362-2451 (HQ)
DISTRIBUTION MFG INC
DISTRIBUTEUR H. MIRON
(*Suby of* 7339101 CANADA INC)
387 Rue Deslauriers, Montreal, QC, H4N 1W2
(514) 344-5558
Sales 10,745,288
SIC 5143 Dairy products, except dried or canned
Dimitrios Nikolidakis
Constantinos Mastrantonis
George Michopoulos
Charalambos Nikolidakis

D-U-N-S 24-896-8018 (SL)
DISTRIBUTIONS AGRI-SOL INC
1509 Rue Antonio-Barbeau, Montreal, QC, H4N 2R5

(514) 381-4804
Emp Here 25 *Sales* 20,889,425
SIC 5148 Fresh fruits and vegetables
Murray O'neil
Harry Enns

D-U-N-S 25-683-6354 (HQ)
DONATO FRUITS ET LEGUMES INC
1605 Rue De Beauharnois O, Montreal, QC, H4N 1J6
(514) 388-1622
Sales 10,026,924
SIC 5148 Fresh fruits and vegetables
Concettina (Connie) Gallucci

D-U-N-S 24-254-2215 (SL)
ENTREPRISES TZANET INC, LES
1375 Rue De Louvain O Bureau 71, Montreal, QC, H4N 1G6
(514) 383-0030
Emp Here 26 *Sales* 11,626,524
SIC 5046 Commercial equipment, nec
Sotirios Tzanetatos
Angelo Tzanetatos
Odyssefs Tzanetatos

D-U-N-S 20-626-6124 (HQ)
FABRICVILLE CO. INC
9195 Rue Charles-De La Tour, Montreal, QC, H4N 1M3
(514) 383-3942
Sales 73,414,800
SIC 5949 Sewing, needlework, and piece goods

D-U-N-S 24-421-9098 (HQ)
FAYOLLE CANADA INC
1655 Rue De Beauharnois O, Montreal, QC, H4N 1J6
(514) 381-6970
Emp Here 1 *Sales* 20,967,750
SIC 6712 Bank holding companies
Bruno Fayolle
Hugues Fastrel

D-U-N-S 24-805-3766 (SL)
FERMES LUFA INC, LES
LES ALIMENTS LUFA
1400 Rue Antonio-Barbeau Bureau 201, Montreal, QC, H4N 1H5
(514) 669-3559
Emp Here 15 *Sales* 12,533,655
SIC 5148 Fresh fruits and vegetables
Dave Furneaux
Mohamed Hage
Andrew Ferrier
Remy Kosseim
Pascal Drouin

D-U-N-S 25-742-9514 (HQ)
FRANCIS INTERNATIONAL TRADING (CANADA) INC
1605 Rue Chabanel O Bureau 300, Montreal, QC, H4N 2T7
(514) 858-1088
Emp Here 1 *Sales* 22,994,501
SIC 2389 Apparel and accessories, nec
Yan Lin

D-U-N-S 24-943-1404 (HQ)
FRUITS & LEGUMES GAETAN BONO INC
995 Rue Du Marche-Central, Montreal, QC, H4N 1K2
(514) 381-1387
Sales 138,148,816
SIC 5148 Fresh fruits and vegetables
Giuseppe Lavorato
Michel Lavorato
Salvatore Lavorato

D-U-N-S 20-241-7846 (HQ)
G2MC INC
GALERIE DU MEUBLE, LA
1215 Boul Cremazie O, Montreal, QC, H4N 2W1
(514) 382-1443
Emp Here 41 *Sales* 23,240,300
SIC 5712 Furniture stores
Pierre Simard

Stephane Corbeil
Jean-Stephane Yansouni
Louis Jean
Christian Rousseau
Terry Enepekides
Eric Corbeil
Marc Benoit
Johanne Bourque

D-U-N-S 25-690-3808 (HQ)
GENESEE & WYOMING CANADA INC
(*Suby of* GENESEE & WYOMING INC.)
9001 Boul De L'Acadie Bureau 904, Montreal,
QC, H4N 3H5
(514) 948-6999
Emp Here 17   *Sales* 113,570,090
SIC 4011 Railroads, line-haul operating
Louis Gravel
Harold Perrault
Caroline Healey
Christopher Liucci
John C Hellmann
David A Brown
Ricky Mclellan
Allison M. Fergus
Michael O. Miller

D-U-N-S 25-973-5033 (SL)
GESTION GUY GERVAIS INC
(*Suby of* GROUPE CARREAUX CERAGRES
INC)
1370 Rue Chabanel O, Montreal, QC, H4N
1H4
(514) 384-5590
Emp Here 100   *Sales* 44,717,400
SIC 5032 Brick, stone, and related material
Guy Gervais
Sylvain Albert

D-U-N-S 25-835-9207 (SL)
GOLDER CONSTRUCTION INC
CONSTRUCTION GOLDER
(*Suby of* GOLDER ASSOCIATES CORPO-
RATION)
9200 Boul De L'Acadie Bureau 10, Montreal,
QC, H4N 2T2
(514) 389-1631
Emp Here 70   *Sales* 12,511,730
SIC 8711 Engineering services
Ateesh Roop
Jill Lepage
Jean-Francois Bolduc

D-U-N-S 24-073-3787 (HQ)
GRAINS ELITE S.E.C.
9001 Boul De L'Acadie Bureau 200, Montreal,
QC, H4N 3H7

Sales 22,015,380
SIC 5153 Grain and field beans
Denis Richard
Luc Forget

D-U-N-S 20-289-4895 (BR)
GROUPE ADONIS INC
ADONIS
(*Suby of* METRO INC)
2001 Rue Sauve O, Montreal, QC, H4N 3L6
(514) 382-8606
Emp Here 600
SIC 5411 Grocery stores
Naaman Abboud

D-U-N-S 24-294-9220 (SL)
HACHETTE CANADA INC
(*Suby of* LAGARDERE SCA)
9001 Boul De L'Acadie Bureau 1002, Mon-
treal, QC, H4N 3H5
(514) 382-3034
Emp Here 19   *Sales* 14,107,880
SIC 5192 Books, periodicals, and newspapers
Christian Chevrier
Luc Pariseau
Stephanie Ferran

D-U-N-S 20-514-1794 (BR)
HOME DEPOT OF CANADA INC

D-U-N-S 24-256-2643 (SL)
HOME DEPOT 7146 L'ACADIE
(*Suby of* THE HOME DEPOT INC)
1000 Rue Sauve O Bureau 1000, Montreal,
QC, H4N 3L5
(514) 333-6868
Emp Here 117
SIC 5251 Hardware stores
Francois Lemieux

D-U-N-S 24-256-2643 (SL)
**IMPORTATIONS-EXPORTATIONS BENISTI
INC**
BENISTI IMPORTATION ET EXPORTATION
(*Suby of* MANIOLI INVESTMENTS INC)
1650 Rue Chabanel O, Montreal, QC, H4N
3M8
(514) 384-0140
Emp Here 100   *Sales* 83,753,300
SIC 5136 Men's and boy's clothing
Maurice Benisti

D-U-N-S 25-674-7882 (SL)
INDUSTRIES CANZIP (2000) INC, LES
1615 Rue Chabanel O, Montreal, QC, H4N
2T7
(514) 934-0331
Emp Here 75   *Sales* 16,411,800
SIC 3965 Fasteners, buttons, needles, and
pins
Sylvie St-Louis
Albert Tsau

D-U-N-S 20-860-1062 (SL)
L.O.D.A INC
1200 Rue De Louvain O, Montreal, QC, H4N
1G5
(514) 382-0571
Emp Here 25   *Sales* 11,087,250
SIC 7389 Business services, nec
Mario Fasciano
Taras M. Iwanycki

D-U-N-S 24-328-4275 (SL)
MAGASIN MYRLANIE INC
*MARCHAND CANADIAN TIRE DE MON-
TREAL*
9050 Boul De L'Acadie, Montreal, QC, H4N
2S5
(514) 388-6464
Emp Here 50   *Sales* 24,903,900
SIC 5531 Auto and home supply stores
Alain Harvey
Johanne Noel

D-U-N-S 24-226-1410 (HQ)
MAISON SAMI T.A. FRUITS INC, LA
SAMI FRUITS
1505 Rue Legendre O, Montreal, QC, H4N
1H6
(514) 858-6363
Emp Here 30   *Sales* 29,347,700
SIC 5431 Fruit and vegetable markets
Sami Al Asmar
Taleb Al Asmar
Anastasia Al Asmar
Lilia Al Asmar
Nadia Al Asmar
Flavio Condo

D-U-N-S 24-945-5429 (HQ)
MANIOLI INVESTMENTS INC
INVESTISSEMENTS MANIOLI, LES
1650 Rue Chabanel O Bureau 1205, Mon-
treal, QC, H4N 3M8
(514) 384-0140
Sales 27,335,000
SIC 6712 Bank holding companies
Maurice Benisti

D-U-N-S 20-017-4857 (HQ)
MONTRES BIG TIME INC
9250 Boul De L'Acadie Bureau 340, Montreal,
QC, H4N 3C5
(514) 384-6464
Emp Here 47   *Sales* 10,880,650
SIC 5944 Jewelry stores
Elie Dayan

D-U-N-S 25-198-6451 (SL)
NCH CANADA INC
BIOAMP
9001 Boul De L'Acadie Bureau 800, Montreal,
QC, H4N 3H5
(514) 733-4572
Emp Here 26   *Sales* 18,988,970
SIC 5169 Chemicals and allied products, nec
James Edward Bird

D-U-N-S 20-534-1709 (HQ)
PHARMAPRIX INC
(*Suby of* LOBLAW COMPANIES LIMITED)
400 Av Saite-Croix Bureau 200, Montreal, QC,
H4N 3L4
(514) 933-9331
Sales 34,840,500
SIC 6794 Patent owners and lessors
Jeffrey Leger
George Hamam
Anthony Spina
Eric Bouchard
Adam Grabowski

D-U-N-S 24-810-9167 (SL)
POINT ZERO GIRLS CLUB INC
POINT ZERO
1650 Rue Chabanel O, Montreal, QC, H4N
3M8
(514) 384-0140
Emp Here 40   *Sales* 19,932,880
SIC 5137 Women's and children's clothing
Nicole Benisti

D-U-N-S 24-667-9245 (SL)
PRODUCTION ACYPOL INC
(*Suby of* 9331611 CANADA INC)
1350 Rue Mazurette Bureau 409, Montreal,
QC, H4N 1H2
(514) 388-8888
Emp Here 100
SIC 5136 Men's and boy's clothing
Bessy Argiropoulos

D-U-N-S 20-011-0976 (SL)
REPERAGE BOOMERANG INC
(*Suby of* CALAMP CORP.)
9280 Boul De L'Acadie, Montreal, QC, H4N
3C5
(514) 234-8722
Emp Here 150   *Sales* 87,037,050
SIC 5065 Electronic parts and equipment, nec
Richard T. Riley
Thomas Wooters
Claude Iunno
Frederic Poitras

D-U-N-S 20-225-2490 (HQ)
REPRODUCTIONS-PHOTOS M.P. LTEE
222 Boul Lebeau, Montreal, QC, H4N 1R4
(514) 383-4313
Sales 15,597,000
SIC 8741 Management services
Carmela Maria Martinez
Giovanna Martinez

D-U-N-S 20-277-8932 (HQ)
RESEAU SANS FIL OTODATA INC
9280 Boul De L'Acadie, Montreal, QC, H4N
3C5
(514) 673-0244
Sales 10,028,977
SIC 3663 Radio and t.v. communications
equipment
Andre Boulay
Federico Marcantonio
Jason Gallovich

D-U-N-S 24-555-7538 (SL)
ROBOCUTS INC
1625 Rue Chabanel O Bureau 729, Montreal,
QC, H4N 2S7
(514) 388-8001
Emp Here 25   *Sales* 11,087,250
SIC 7389 Business services, nec
Dave Fernandes

D-U-N-S 25-286-1935 (BR)

D-U-N-S 25-198-6451 (SL)
RONA INC
RENO-DEPOT DE MARCHE CENTRAL
(*Suby of* LOWE'S COMPANIES, INC.)
1011 Rue Du Marche-Central, Montreal, QC,
H4N 3J6
(514) 385-6888
Emp Here 220
SIC 5251 Hardware stores
Dominic Meiser

D-U-N-S 20-237-7453 (SL)
TEXTILES D. ZINMAN LTEE
459 Rue Deslauriers, Montreal, QC, H4N 1W2
(514) 276-2597
Emp Here 20   *Sales* 10,006,500
SIC 5131 Piece goods and notions
Ronald Chorlton
Alfredo Enbom

D-U-N-S 20-357-0544 (SL)
UNIVINS ET SPIRITUEUX (CANADA) INC
SELECTIONS TANDEM
(*Suby of* INVESTISSEMENTS VINI-QUATRO
INC, LES)
1350 Rue Mazurette Bureau 326, Montreal,
QC, H4N 1H2
(514) 522-9339
Emp Here 45   *Sales* 26,456,220
SIC 5182 Wine and distilled beverages
Daniel Richard
Gianmaria Cesari

D-U-N-S 20-370-4564 (SL)
VOYAGES VISION DT QUEBEC-EST INC
ENTREPOT CROISIERE
(*Suby of* DIRECT TRAVEL INC.)
400 Av Sainte-Croix 100 O, Montreal, QC,
H4N 3L4
(514) 748-2522
Emp Here 100   *Sales* 66,689,200
SIC 4724 Travel agencies
Edward Adams
Joel Ostrov
Azra Kanji
Michael Yirilli

Montreal, QC H4P

D-U-N-S 25-200-9022 (HQ)
3096-3227 QUEBEC INC
*CENTRE DE TECHNOLOGIES INFORMA-
TIQUES GROUPE ACCESS*
8270 Rue Mayrand, Montreal, QC, H4P 2C5
(514) 288-6000
Emp Here 25   *Sales* 14,309,568
SIC 5045 Computers, peripherals, and soft-
ware
Elie Douglas
Habib Malik
Joy Stephens

D-U-N-S 20-560-3785 (SL)
6091636 CANADA INC
MARKET ENGINES
4700 Rue De La Savane Bureau 310, Mon-
treal, QC, H4P 1T7
(514) 448-6931
Emp Here 90   *Sales* 40,429,710
SIC 7389 Business services, nec
Daniel Assouline
Michael Dadoun

D-U-N-S 20-277-7017 (SL)
9155-8593 QUEBEC INC
LOCATION AUTOLUXE
5015 Rue Buchan, Montreal, QC, H4P 1S4

Emp Here 11   *Sales* 29,112,224
SIC 5012 Automobiles and other motor vehi-
cles
Charles Morris
Benjamin Daniels
Bernard David

D-U-N-S 24-249-9486   (SL)
9156-4302 QUEBEC INC
DM INFOTECH
7881 Boul Decarie Bureau 300, Montreal, QC, H4P 2H2
(514) 733-5828
Emp Here 14   *Sales* 12,020,472
SIC 5045 Computers, peripherals, and software
Derek George
Marc Bailey
Karl Martin

D-U-N-S 20-470-2551   (SL)
9186-5758 QUEBEC INC
CENTRE IOS
5000 Rue Buchan Bureau 1000, Montreal, QC, H4P 1T2
(514) 342-4151
Emp Here 500   *Sales* 93,253,000
SIC 8742 Management consulting services
Mona Eid Chebli
Jade Chebli
Elie Chebli

D-U-N-S 20-381-0395   (SL)
9195-4750 QUEBEC INC
GROUPE NORDIA
8255 Av Mountain Sights Bureau 408, Montreal, QC, H4P 2B5
(514) 340-7737
Emp Here 37   *Sales* 30,916,349
SIC 5149 Groceries and related products, nec
Arda Saglam
Jean-Francois Hamel

D-U-N-S 24-418-0548   (SL)
9209-5256 QUEBEC INC
LINKNOW MEDIA
4700 Rue De La Savane Bureau 210, Montreal, QC, H4P 1T7
(514) 906-4713
Emp Here 60   *Sales* 10,638,660
SIC 7374 Data processing and preparation
Wesley Mendelovitch

D-U-N-S 24-828-8677   (SL)
9219-1568 QUEBEC INC
ENTREPRISE MINDGEEK CANADA
7777 Boul Decarie Bureau 300, Montreal, QC, H4P 2H2
(514) 359-3555
Emp Here 750   *Sales* 108,136,500
SIC 7371 Custom computer programming services
Antoon Feras
David Tassilo

D-U-N-S 20-309-0089   (SL)
A.X.C. CONSTRUCTION INC
(Suby of AXOR EXPERTS-CONSEILS INC)
5101 Rue Buchan Bureau 400, Montreal, QC, H4P 1S4
(514) 937-3737
Emp Here 150   *Sales* 27,975,900
SIC 8742 Management consulting services
Denis Cadoret
Francois Lussier
Jacques Grenier
Marc-Andre Desjardins
Denis Courchesne

D-U-N-S 25-209-9346   (HQ)
ACP MARKETING CANADA INC
ACP RAIL INTERNATIONAL
8375 Rue Bougainville Bureau 100, Montreal, QC, H4P 2G5
(514) 733-5247
Sales 36,679,060
SIC 4725 Tour operators
Alexander C. Popescu
Diane Popescu
Denis Grenier

D-U-N-S 24-935-1511   (HQ)
AGENCES D'ASSURANCE COPOLOFF INC, LES

5500 Av Royalmount Bureau 325, Montreal, QC, H4P 1H7
(514) 731-9605
Emp Here 42   *Sales* 81,252,996
SIC 6351 Surety insurance
Sidney Copoloff
Lottie Copoloff
Shelly Copoloff

D-U-N-S 24-761-7389   (SL)
ALERT SERVICES INC
ALERT PAY
8255 Av Mountain Sights Bureau 100, Montreal, QC, H4P 2B5

Emp Here 140   *Sales* 31,986,080
SIC 4813 Telephone communication, except radio
Nazlin Patel
Firoz Patel

D-U-N-S 20-731-4084   (SL)
ARTICLES EN CUIR C.B.M. INC
8370 Rue Labarre, Montreal, QC, H4P 2E7
(514) 738-5858
Emp Here 50   *Sales* 37,126,000
SIC 5199 Nondurable goods, nec
Sam Gestetner
Aaron Gestetner

D-U-N-S 20-318-8388   (SL)
AUTO MODENA INC.
FERRARI DU QUEBEC
3980 Rue Jean-Talon O, Montreal, QC, H4P 1V6
(514) 337-7274
Emp Here 30   *Sales* 10,926,450
SIC 5012 Automobiles and other motor vehicles
Umberto Bonfa

D-U-N-S 25-394-5000   (SL)
AUTOMOBILES SILVER STAR (MONTREAL) INC
SILVER STAR
7800 Boul Decarie, Montreal, QC, H4P 2H4
(514) 735-5501
Emp Here 100   *Sales* 62,928,000
SIC 5511 New and used car dealers
Samuel Eltes
Jeff Budning

D-U-N-S 20-332-2425   (SL)
BONBONS OINK OINK INC, LES
SQUISHCANDY
4810 Rue Jean-Talon O, Montreal, QC, H4P 2N5
(514) 731-4555
Emp Here 250   *Sales* 121,846,250
SIC 2064 Candy and other confectionery products
Sarah Segal

D-U-N-S 20-997-8667   (HQ)
BOULANGERIE CASCHER DE MONTREAL LTEE
7005 Av Victoria, Montreal, QC, H4P 2N9
(514) 739-3651
Emp Here 10   *Sales* 20,889,425
SIC 5149 Groceries and related products, nec
Sholomo Bineth
Michael Bineth

D-U-N-S 20-565-5558   (SL)
CANBEC AUTOMOBILE INC
BMW CANBEC
(Suby of AUTOCANADA INC)
4070 Rue Jean-Talon O, Montreal, QC, H4P 1V5
(514) 289-6464
Emp Here 100   *Sales* 62,928,000
SIC 5511 New and used car dealers
Paul Antony
Raj Juneja

D-U-N-S 25-242-0088   (SL)
CARPETTE MULTI DESIGN C.M.D. INC
BOUTIQUE ORIGINE

8134 Boul Decarie Bureau A, Montreal, QC, H4P 2S8
(514) 344-8877
Emp Here 25   *Sales* 12,721,400
SIC 5023 Homefurnishings
Benoit Bouchard
Sylvain Bouchard
Jacques Bouchard

D-U-N-S 20-213-5810   (SL)
CIE CANADIENNE DE PRODUITS OPTIQUES LTEE, LA
COS
8360 Rue Mayrand, Montreal, QC, H4P 2C9
(514) 737-6777
Emp Here 65   *Sales* 29,066,310
SIC 5049 Professional equipment, nec
Fred Hochsteadter
Robert Hochsteadter
Judith Hochsteadter

D-U-N-S 24-954-6896   (HQ)
CIE D'ECLAIRAGE UNION LTEE, LA
UNION LUMINAIRE & DECOR
8150 Boul Decarie, Montreal, QC, H4P 2S8
(514) 340-5000
Emp Here 62   *Sales* 29,960,658
SIC 5063 Electrical apparatus and equipment
Bram Naimer
Clifford Naimer
Darren Naimer

D-U-N-S 24-351-0286   (HQ)
COLLECTIONS DE STYLE R.D. INTERNATIONALES LTEE, LES
(Suby of 6479987 CANADA INC)
5275 Rue Ferrier Bureau 200, Montreal, QC, H4P 1L7
(514) 342-1222
Emp Here 20   *Sales* 32,390,930
SIC 5137 Women's and children's clothing
Kenneth Hollinger

D-U-N-S 20-565-7310   (HQ)
CORPORATION DE GESTION POSITRON CANADA
5101 Rue Buchan Suite 220, Montreal, QC, H4P 2R9
(514) 345-2220
Emp Here 1   *Sales* 54,826,350
SIC 6712 Bank holding companies
Reginald Weiser

D-U-N-S 24-320-1293   (HQ)
DORMAKABA CANADA INC
(Suby of DORMAKABA HOLDING AG)
7301 Boul Decarie, Montreal, QC, H4P 2G7
(514) 735-5410
Sales 84,874,500
SIC 3699 Electrical equipment and supplies, nec
Sandra Heller
Michael Kincaid
Kurt Niederhause

D-U-N-S 20-290-3951   (SL)
ERFA CANADA 2012 INC
8250 Boul Decarie Bureau 110, Montreal, QC, H4P 2P5
(514) 931-3133
Emp Here 23   *Sales* 25,422,935
SIC 5122 Drugs, proprietaries, and sundries
Simon Soucy
Marielle Ethier

D-U-N-S 25-392-8576   (HQ)
GROUPE MAD SCIENCE INC
GROUPE SCIENCE EN FOLIE
8360 Rue Bougainville Bureau 201, Montreal, QC, H4P 2G1
(514) 344-4181
Sales 20,904,300
SIC 6794 Patent owners and lessors
Ariel Shlien
Shafik Mina

D-U-N-S 25-945-6171   (BR)
GROUPE SPORTSCENE INC

CAGE AUX SPORTS, LA
(Suby of GROUPE SPORTSCENE INC)
5485 Rue Des Jockeys, Montreal, QC, H4P 2T7
(514) 731-2020
Emp Here 100
SIC 5812 Eating places
Emile Haykal

D-U-N-S 24-954-8462   (SL)
HOPITEL INC
RESEAUX DE SANTE MEDITEL
(Suby of 97875 CANADA INC)
8225 Rue Labarre, Montreal, QC, H4P 2E6
(514) 739-2525
Emp Here 100   *Sales* 33,314,800
SIC 7359 Equipment rental and leasing, nec
Harold Schneider
Gary Schneider

D-U-N-S 20-764-7207   (HQ)
HUB INTERNATIONAL QUEBEC LIMITEE
ASSURANCE MURDOCH, CREVIER
(Suby of HELLMAN & FRIEDMAN LLC)
8500 Boul Decarie, Montreal, QC, H4P 2N2
(514) 374-9600
Emp Here 50   *Sales* 640,724,040
SIC 6411 Insurance agents, brokers, and service
Stephen Blais
Martin P Hughes
Jeff Botosan
John M. Albright

D-U-N-S 24-320-6120   (BR)
INVESTORS GROUP FINANCIAL SERVICES INC
(Suby of POWER CORPORATION DU CANADA)
8250 Boul Decarie Bureau 200, Montreal, QC, H4P 2P5
(514) 733-3950
Emp Here 80
SIC 8742 Management consulting services
Satou Mata Kamara

D-U-N-S 24-508-9008   (HQ)
JODDES LIMITEE
6111 Av Royalmount Bureau 100, Montreal, QC, H4P 2T4
(514) 340-1114
Emp Here 4   *Sales* 365,509,000
SIC 6719 Holding companies, nec
Morris Goodman
Samuel Altman
David Goodman
Shawna Goodman
Deborah Goodman Davis

D-U-N-S 24-528-2868   (SL)
LUCIANI AUTOMOBILES INC
4040 Rue Jean-Talon O, Montreal, QC, H4P 1V5
(514) 340-1344
Emp Here 40   *Sales* 19,923,120
SIC 5511 New and used car dealers
Camilo Luciani

D-U-N-S 20-696-2719   (SL)
MEADE RAY INTERNATIONAL INC
ENTREPRISES MEADE RAY INTERNATIONAL
8370 Rue Labarre, Montreal, QC, H4P 2E7
(514) 738-5858
Emp Here 22   *Sales* 16,335,440
SIC 5199 Nondurable goods, nec
Shula Ungar

D-U-N-S 20-228-9849   (HQ)
MODES MAISON HERITAGE INC
5000 Rue Jean-Talon O Bureau 150, Montreal, QC, H4P 1W9
(514) 341-1311
Sales 13,230,256
SIC 5023 Homefurnishings
Sassoon S Khazzam

D-U-N-S 20-216-2376   (SL)

MOTEURS DECARIE INC, LES
BENTLEY MONTREAL
8255 Rue Bougainville, Montreal, QC, H4P 2T3
(514) 334-9910
Emp Here 45   *Sales* 22,413,510
SIC 5511 New and used car dealers
Joel Segal

D-U-N-S 24-763-2417   (SL)
NEXIA FRIEDMAN S.E.N.C.R.L.
8000 Boul Decarie Bureau 500, Montreal, QC, H4P 2S4
(514) 731-7901
Emp Here 75   *Sales* 15,576,375
SIC 8721 Accounting, auditing, and book-keeping
Joel Engel
Michel Mercure
Jerry Grossman
Lawrence Chandler
Marven Minkoff
David Rak
Steve Harrar
Sherri Lemcovitz
Stephen Shecter
Johanthan Bicher

D-U-N-S 20-961-1052   (HQ)
OMNITRANS INC
4300 Rue Jean-Talon O, Montreal, QC, H4P 1W3
(514) 288-6664
Emp Here 152   *Sales* 108,036,504
SIC 4731 Freight transportation arrangement
Stephen Segal
Martin J Goldenberg

D-U-N-S 25-355-4737   (HQ)
ONESPAN CANADA INC
ESIGNLIVE
(*Suby of* ONESPAN INC.)
8200 Boul Decarie Bureau 300, Montreal, QC, H4P 2P5
(514) 337-5255
Emp Here 93   *Sales* 18,022,750
SIC 7371 Custom computer programming services
Scott Clements
Tommy Petrogiannis
Mark S. Hoyt

D-U-N-S 24-459-6946   (HQ)
PHARMASCIENCE INC
ROYALMOUNT PHARMACEUTICALS
(*Suby of* JODDES LIMITEE)
6111 Av Royalmount Bureau 100, Montreal, QC, H4P 2T4
(514) 340-1114
Emp Here 650   *Sales* 497,391,000
SIC 2834 Pharmaceutical preparations
David Goodman
Morris Goodman
Gregory M.C. Orleski
Sonia Girolamo
Jean-Guy Goulet

D-U-N-S 20-726-9200   (HQ)
POSITRON INC
(*Suby of* CORPORATION DE GESTION POSITRON CANADA)
5101 Rue Buchan Suite 220, Montreal, QC, H4P 2R9
(514) 345-2220
Sales 20,948,620
SIC 3661 Telephone and telegraph apparatus
Reginald Weiser

D-U-N-S 24-321-4454   (SL)
POYRY (MONTREAL) INC
(*Suby of* POYRY OYJ)
5250 Rue Ferrier Bureau 700, Montreal, QC, H4P 1L4
(514) 341-3221
Emp Here 100   *Sales* 17,873,900
SIC 8711 Engineering services
Vilho Salovaara

Peter Morel
Carl Gagnon
Bruno Floriani
Anne Viitala
Juuso Pajunen

D-U-N-S 24-678-9937   (HQ)
PRESAGIS CANADA INC
(*Suby of* CAE INC)
4700 Rue De La Savane Bureau 300, Montreal, QC, H4P 1T7
(514) 341-3874
Sales 42,828,160
SIC 5045 Computers, peripherals, and software
Jean-Michel Briere
Mark Hounsell
Sonya Branco

D-U-N-S 24-403-2140   (SL)
RESTAURANT MACGEORGES INC
HARVEY'S
7475 Boul Decarie, Montreal, QC, H4P 2G9
(514) 738-3588
Emp Here 75   *Sales* 3,413,925
SIC 5812 Eating places
Marco Voutsinos

D-U-N-S 24-362-9479   (BR)
RGIS CANADA ULC
RGIS SPECIALISTES EN INVENTAIRE
(*Suby of* THE BLACKSTONE GROUP L P)
8300 Rue Bougainville, Montreal, QC, H4P 2G1
(514) 521-5258
Emp Here 150
SIC 7389 Business services, nec
Sylvie Bouchard

D-U-N-S 20-793-5743   (HQ)
SINTRA INC
EMULSIONS & BITUMES S.T.E.B.
(*Suby of* BOUYGUES)
4984 Place De La Savane, Montreal, QC, H4P 2M9
(514) 341-5331
Emp Here 25   *Sales* 557,795,500
SIC 1611 Highway and street construction
Francois Vachon
Germain Perron
Louis R Gabanna
Jean-Yves Llenas
Frederic Roussel

D-U-N-S 20-557-6619   (SL)
SNC-LAVALIN PHARMA INC
(*Suby of* GROUPE SNC-LAVALIN INC)
8000 Boul Decarie 3eme Etage, Montreal, QC, H4P 2S4
(514) 735-5651
Emp Here 160
SIC 8711 Engineering services
Arden R. Furlotte
Narsain Jaipersaud
Normand Dubuc
Terry Lefebvre

D-U-N-S 24-020-1913   (HQ)
SOCIETE POUR LA PREVENTION DE LA CRUAUTE ENVERS LES ANIMAUX (CANA-DIENNE), LA
S.P.C.A. DE MONTREAL, LA
5215 Rue Jean-Talon O, Montreal, QC, H4P 1X4
(514) 735-2711
Emp Here 10   *Sales* 100,702,070
SIC 8699 Membership organizations, nec
Samira Sakhia
Lucy Modesti
Marc-Andre Saucier-Nadeau
Isabelle Brodeur
Louise Cantin
Marie-Claude St-Amant
Elise Desaulniers

D-U-N-S 24-108-8350   (HQ)
SYSTEMES SYNTAX LTEE
SYNTAX.NET

8000 Boul Decarie Bureau 300, Montreal, QC, H4P 2S4
(514) 733-7777
Emp Here 43   *Sales* 10,121,379
SIC 7372 Prepackaged software
Ryan Etinson
Ted Mocarski
Michael Etinson
Kristian Valenta
Stephane Tremblay
Tony Veilleux
Christian Primeau

D-U-N-S 20-928-4132   (SL)
TECHNOLOGIE DE PENSEE LTEE
5250 Rue Ferrier Bureau 812, Montreal, QC, H4P 1L4
(514) 489-8251
Emp Here 65   *Sales* 14,773,785
SIC 3841 Surgical and medical instruments
Harold K. Myers
Lawrence Klein

D-U-N-S 20-572-9168   (BR)
WAL-MART CANADA CORP
WALMART
(*Suby of* WALMART INC.)
5400 Rue Jean-Talon O, Montreal, QC, H4P 2T5
(514) 735-0913
Emp Here 250
SIC 5311 Department stores
Jean-Francois Boisvert

Montreal, QC H4R

D-U-N-S 20-267-4339   (HQ)
CHAUSSURES L'INTERVALLE INC
4345 Boul Poirier, Montreal, QC, H4R 2A4
(438) 386-4555
Emp Here 6   *Sales* 24,916,100
SIC 5139 Footwear
Vita Scalia

D-U-N-S 24-320-2525   (HQ)
SUEZ TREATMENT SOLUTIONS CANADA L.P.
SUEZ SOLUTIONS DE TRAITEMENT CANADA
5490 Boul Thimens Bureau 100, Montreal, QC, H4R 2K9
(514) 683-1200
Emp Here 1   *Sales* 10,891,450
SIC 1781 Water well drilling
Nadine Leslie

Montreal, QC H4S

D-U-N-S 20-046-1684   (HQ)
GENETEC INC
2280 Alfred-Nobel Blvd, Montreal, QC, H4S 2A4
(514) 332-4000
Sales 36,045,500
SIC 7371 Custom computer programming services
Pierre Racz
Alain Cote

D-U-N-S 20-417-5046   (HQ)
GROUPE RESTAURANTS IMVESCOR INC
BATON ROUGE STEAKHOUSE & BAR
(*Suby of* GROUPE D'ALIMENTATION MTY INC)
8150 Rte Transcanadienne Bureau 310, Montreal, QC, H4S 1M5
(514) 341-5544
Emp Here 30   *Sales* 2,037,843,714
SIC 6794 Patent owners and lessors
Stanley Ma
Eric Lefebvre

Claude St-Pierre

D-U-N-S 25-380-8885   (SL)
LUNDBECK CANADA INC
(*Suby of* LUNDBECKFONDEN)
2600 Boul Alfred-Nobel Bureau 400, Montreal, QC, H4S 0A9
(514) 844-8515
Emp Here 94   *Sales* 38,805,174
SIC 5122 Drugs, proprietaries, and sundries
Panayiotes Anastasiou
Thomas D. Forrester
Lucie Dufour

D-U-N-S 25-707-3804   (HQ)
PARAZA PHARMA INC
2525 Av Marie-Curie, Montreal, QC, H4S 2E1
(514) 337-7200
Sales 77,374,150
SIC 5122 Drugs, proprietaries, and sundries
Arshad Siddiqui
Fakeha Ahmad
Ajay Gupta
Sultan Ahmad

D-U-N-S 20-555-6657   (HQ)
RICHELIEU HARDWARE CANADA LTD
(*Suby of* QUINCAILLERIE RICHELIEU LTEE)
7900 Boul Henri-Bourassa O, Montreal, QC, H4S 1V4
(514) 336-4144
Emp Here 10   *Sales* 29,902,860
SIC 5072 Hardware
Richard Lord
Antoine Aucliar
Guy Grenier
Craig Ratchford
Helene Levesque
John Statton

D-U-N-S 20-369-9470   (SL)
SOLUTIONS D'AIR DESHUMIDIFIE INC
TECHNOLOGIES SERESCO
(*Suby of* MADISON INDUSTRIES HOLD-INGS LLC)
5685 Rue Cypihot, Montreal, QC, H4S 1R3
(514) 336-3330
Emp Here 100   *Sales* 44,717,400
SIC 5078 Refrigeration equipment and supplies
Rex E. Lane
Dave Janicek

D-U-N-S 20-554-1092   (HQ)
SYSTEMES HAIVISION INC
HAIVISION NETWORK VIDEO
2600 Boul Alfred-Nobel 5eme Etage, Montreal, QC, H4S 0A9
(514) 334-5445
Sales 42,437,250
SIC 3669 Communications equipment, nec
Miroslav Wicha
Thomas O Hecht
Philippe Mailfait
Neil Hindle
Glenn E. Duval
Robin M. Rush

D-U-N-S 20-730-1375   (HQ)
WEIGH-TRONIX CANADA, ULC
AVERY WEIGH-TRONIX TM
(*Suby of* ILLINOIS TOOL WORKS INC.)
6429 Rue Abrams, Montreal, QC, H4S 1X9
(514) 695-0380
Sales 19,092,086
SIC 3596 Scales and balances, except laboratory
Maryann Spiegel
Mark Ristow
Steven L. Martindale

D-U-N-S 24-648-5189   (SL)
WIPECO INDUSTRIES INC, LES
WIPECO
3333 Rue Douglas-B.-Floreani, Montreal, QC, H4S 1Y6
(514) 935-2551
Emp Here 45   *Sales* 23,424,390

▲ Public Company   ■ Public Company Family Member   **HQ** Headquarters   **BR** Branch   **SL** Single Location

SIC 5093 Scrap and waste materials
Jonathan Kaufman
Mark Babin
Stephen Rees

Montreal, QC H4T

D-U-N-S 20-735-8417   (SL)
GETRACAN INC
130 Montee De Liesse, Montreal, QC, H4T 1N4
(514) 382-4860
Emp Here 25   *Sales* 12,458,050
SIC 5136 Men's and boy's clothing
Earl Green

D-U-N-S 24-814-6037   (HQ)
LITERIES UNIVERSELLES PAGA INC
MAISON CONDELLE
6395 Ch De La Cote-De-Liesse, Montreal, QC, H4T 1E5
(514) 376-7882
Emp Here 50   *Sales* 365,509,000
SIC 6712 Bank holding companies
Paul Nassar
Christine Valleaux

D-U-N-S 24-431-0095   (SL)
MARTINI-VISPAK INC
ACHOO TISSU
174 Rue Merizzi, Montreal, QC, H4T 1S4
(514) 344-1551
Emp Here 49   *Sales* 10,374,476
SIC 7311 Advertising agencies

Montreal, QC H4V

D-U-N-S 25-245-6983   (SL)
ALIMENTATIONS GOVANNI ROUSSO 2004 INC
MARCHE METRO
6645 Av Somerled, Montreal, QC, H4V 1T3
(514) 486-3042
Emp Here 50   *Sales* 13,707,600
SIC 5411 Grocery stores
Govanni Rousso

D-U-N-S 20-714-5702   (SL)
COOPERATION ECHANGE CANADA INC
ICE CURRENCY SERVICE
975 Boul Romeo-Vachon-Aeroport N, Montreal, QC, H4V 1H1
(514) 828-0068
Emp Here 30   *Sales* 20,367,690
SIC 6231 Security and commodity exchanges
Marie Lenna

D-U-N-S 25-198-6022   (SL)
INSTITUT CANADIEN POUR DEVELOPPEMENT NEURO-INTEGRATIF, L
GIANT STEP SCHOOL
5460 Av Connaught, Montreal, QC, H4V 1X7
(514) 935-1911
Emp Here 110   *Sales* 10,903,090
SIC 8211 Elementary and secondary schools
Jocelyne Lecompte

D-U-N-S 24-896-5840   (SL)
MAGASINS D'ESCOMPTE ALMICO INC, LES
JEAN COUTU 258
6624 Av Somerled, Montreal, QC, H4V 1T2
(514) 487-6530
Emp Here 50   *Sales* 12,647,700
SIC 5912 Drug stores and proprietary stores
Quoc Huy Hoang

D-U-N-S 24-324-9674   (SL)
PHARMACIE QUOC HUY HOANG INC
PHARMACIE JEAN COUTU
6624 Av Somerled Bureau 258, Montreal, QC, H4V 1T2

---

(514) 487-6530
Emp Here 50   *Sales* 12,647,700
SIC 5912 Drug stores and proprietary stores
Quoc Huy Hoang
Michel Bougie
Allan Schmeltzer

Montreal, QC H4Y

D-U-N-S 20-698-8490   (BR)
AIR CANADA
AIR CANADA CARGO
(*Suby of* AIR CANADA)
735 Stuart Graham N, Montreal, QC, H4Y 1C3

Emp Here 125
SIC 4512 Air transportation, scheduled

Montreal, QC H4Z

D-U-N-S 20-762-9684   (HQ)
ASSOCIATION DU TRANSPORT AERIEN INTERNATIONAL (IATA)
IATA
800 Rue Du Square-Victoria Bureau 1538, Montreal, QC, H4Z 1A1
(514) 874-0202
Emp Here 380   *Sales* 302,628,000
SIC 8611 Business associations
Akbar Al Baker
Paul Steele
Enrique Cueto
David Bronczek
Yang Ho Cho
Naresh Goyal
Harry Hohmeister
Alan Joyce
Liu Shaoyong
Calin Rovinescu

D-U-N-S 20-792-8888   (HQ)
BOURSE DE MONTREAL INC
BOURSE CANADIENNE DE PRODUITS DE-RIVES
(*Suby of* TMX GROUP LIMITED)
800 Rue Du Square-Victoria 4e Etage, Montreal, QC, H4Z 1A1
(514) 871-2424
Sales 142,313,800
SIC 6231 Security and commodity exchanges
Charles Martin Winograd
Luc Bertrand
Jean Martel
Harry A Jaako
Gerri B Sinclair
Marie Giguere
William Warwick Linton
Kevin Sullivan
Anthony Walsh

D-U-N-S 24-901-3061   (SL)
CENTRE INFORMATIQUE DNB LIMITEE
ELECTRONIQUE DNB
800 Place Victoria Bureau 2700, Montreal, QC, H4Z 1B7

Emp Here 75
SIC 5045 Computers, peripherals, and software

D-U-N-S 20-363-3227   (SL)
CENTRES DE DONNEES ESTRUXTURE INC
800 Rue Du Square-Victoria Bureau 1, Montreal, QC, H4Z 1B7
(514) 369-2209
Emp Here 42   *Sales* 12,830,160
SIC 8999 Services, nec
Todd Coleman
Nicolas Vanasse
Annie Corbeil

Lyne Rousseau

D-U-N-S 25-092-8616   (HQ)
CONSEIL INTERNATIONAL DES AERO-PORTS
PROGRAMME D'ACCREDITATION PROFESSIONNELLE DE GESTION D'AEROPORT
800 Rue Sq Victoria Bureau 1810, Montreal, QC, H4Z 1G8
(514) 373-1224
Sales 13,348,900
SIC 4581 Airports, flying fields, and services
Bongani Maseko
Martin Eurnekian
Rina Arlegui
Arnaud Feist
Seiw Hiang Lee
Tom Ruth
Sani Sener
Ps Nair
Emmanuel Menanteau
Martin Eurnekian

D-U-N-S 24-890-3676   (HQ)
DUNTON RAINVILLE SENC
800 Rue Du Square-Victoria Bureau 43, Montreal, QC, H4Z 1A1
(514) 866-6743
Sales 16,632,300
SIC 8111 Legal services
Jean-Jacques Rainville
Louis-Philippe Bourgeois
Alain Chevrier
Sebastien Dorion
Paul-Andre Martel

D-U-N-S 24-590-5203   (BR)
FASKEN MARTINEAU DUMOULIN LLP
(*Suby of* FASKEN MARTINEAU DUMOULIN LLP)
800 Rue Du Square-Victoria Bureau 3700, Montreal, QC, H4Z 1A1
(514) 397-7400
Emp Here 175
SIC 8111 Legal services
Eric Bedard

D-U-N-S 20-909-0646   (SL)
GESTION ORION LTEE
800 Rue Du Square-Victoria Bureau 3700, Montreal, QC, H4Z 1A1
(514) 871-9167
Emp Here 85   *Sales* 23,318,220
SIC 8741 Management services
Charles E. Flam
Barry H. Shapiro
Yves Cousineau

D-U-N-S 24-255-6868   (SL)
GESTION PLACE VICTORIA INC
800 Rue Du Square-Victoria Bureau 4120, Montreal, QC, H4Z 1A1
(514) 875-6010
Emp Here 40   *Sales* 11,331,720
SIC 8741 Management services
Sol J Polachek
Gary Polachek

D-U-N-S 24-045-8146   (HQ)
GESTOLEX, SOCIETE EN COMMANDITE
800 Rue Du Square-Victoria Bureau 4300, Montreal, QC, H4Z 1H1
(450) 686-8683
Sales 27,335,000
SIC 6712 Bank holding companies
Jean-Jacques Rainville

D-U-N-S 20-554-2884   (BR)
GOUVERNEMENT DE LA PROVINCE DE QUEBEC
AUTORITE DES MARCHES FINANCIERS
(*Suby of* GOUVERNEMENT DE LA PROVINCE DE QUEBEC)
800 Sq Victoria 22e Etage, Montreal, QC, H4Z 1G3
(514) 395-0337
Emp Here 520

SIC 8741 Management services
Jean St -Gelis

D-U-N-S 24-081-4707   (SL)
GROUPEMENT DES ASSUREURS AUTO-MOBILES
800 Place-Victoria Bureau 2410, Montreal, QC, H4Z 0A2
(514) 288-1537
Emp Here 55   *Sales* 101,625,810
SIC 6411 Insurance agents, brokers, and service
Johanne Lamanque
Martin Beaulieu
Jean Vincent
Jean Bertrand

D-U-N-S 24-125-0534   (BR)
INSURANCE BUREAU OF CANADA
GROUPEMENT DES ASSUREURS AUTO-MOBILES (GAA)
(*Suby of* INSURANCE BUREAU OF CANADA)
800 Rue Du Square-Victoria Bureau 2410, Montreal, QC, H4Z 0A2
(514) 288-4321
Emp Here 75
SIC 6411 Insurance agents, brokers, and service
Marc-Andre Gagnon

D-U-N-S 20-393-6886   (HQ)
INTERTAPE POLYMER INC.
800 Rue Du Square-Victoria, Montreal, QC, H4Z 1A1

Sales 15,956,061
SIC 2295 Coated fabrics, not rubberized
Melbourne Yull

D-U-N-S 24-903-6948   (HQ)
MAGIL LAURENTIENNE GESTION IMMO-BILIERE INC
MAGIL LAURENTIENNE GESTION IMMO-BILLIERE/TERRAINS ST-JACQUES
800 Rue Du Square-Victoria Bureau 4120, Montreal, QC, H4Z 1A1
(514) 875-6010
Emp Here 47   *Sales* 14,221,850
SIC 6512 Nonresidential building operators
Christian Couture
Gary E. Polachek
Michel Bedard

D-U-N-S 25-528-6064   (BR)
MORNEAU SHEPELL LTD
SHEPPELL FGI, DIV OF
(*Suby of* MORNEAU SHEPELL INC)
800 Square Victoria Bureau 4000, Montreal, QC, H4Z 0A4
(514) 878-9090
Emp Here 50
SIC 8999 Services, nec
Pierre Chamberland

D-U-N-S 24-491-3125   (SL)
PLACEMENTS PLACEVIC LTEE, LES
800 Rue Du Square-Victoria Bureau 4120, Montreal, QC, H4Z 1A1
(514) 875-6010
Emp Here 30   *Sales* 12,580,650
SIC 6712 Bank holding companies
Gary E Polachek
Vincent Chiara
Joe Marsilii

D-U-N-S 20-909-0588   (SL)
ROBINSON, SHEPPARD, SHAPIRO, S.E.N.C.R.L.
800 Rue Du Square-Victoria Bureau 4600, Montreal, QC, H4Z 1H6
(514) 878-2631
Emp Here 165   *Sales* 18,295,530
SIC 8111 Legal services
Charles E Flam
Nicholas Kernjevic
Jean-Pierre Sheppard

▲ Public Company   ■ Public Company Family Member   **HQ** Headquarters   **BR** Branch   **SL** Single Location

France Dulude
Jean-Francois Bilodeau
Normand Laurendeau
Mariella Destefano
Francois Druprat
Gilbert Hourani
Michel Green

Montreal, QC H5A

D-U-N-S 20-230-3996   (SL)
9161-5781 QUEBEC INC
PLACE BONAVENTURE
800 Rue De La Gauchetiere O Bureau 1100,
Montreal, QC, H5A 1M1
(514) 397-2222
Emp Here 110   *Sales* 24,295,810
SIC 6512 Nonresidential building operators
Marcel Joly
Aaron Wetherhill
Brahm Cramer

D-U-N-S 24-246-2799   (BR)
CORUS ENTERTAINMENT INC
(*Suby of* CORUS ENTERTAINMENT INC)
800 Rue De La Gauchetiere O Bureau 1100,
Montreal, QC, H5A 1M1
(514) 767-9250
Emp Here 500
SIC 7922 Theatrical producers and services
Martin Fournier

D-U-N-S 25-094-8296   (HQ)
FIDO SOLUTIONS INC
FIDO
(*Suby of* ROGERS COMMUNICATIONS INC)
800 Rue De La Gauchetiere O Bureau 4000,
Montreal, QC, H5A 1K3
(514) 937-2121
Emp Here 300   *Sales* 669,088,000
SIC 4899 Communication services, nec
Graeme H. Mcphail
David P. Miller
Anthony Staffieri

D-U-N-S 24-356-2555   (HQ)
RIMANESA PROPERTIES INC
KEVRIC
(*Suby of* HOLDING MIRANESA INC)
800 Rue De La Gauchetiere O Bureau 240,
Montreal, QC, H5A 1K6
(514) 397-2211
Sales 16,459,920
SIC 8741 Management services
Richard Hylands

D-U-N-S 20-227-7778   (HQ)
SOCIETE DE TRANSPORT DE MONTREAL
800 Rue De La Gauchetiere O Bureau 8420,
Montreal, QC, H5A 1J6
(514) 786-4636
Emp Here 700   *Sales* 1,117,325,951
SIC 4111 Local and suburban transit
Philippe Schnobb
Marvin Rotrand
Linda Lebrun
Marie-Claude Leonard
Francois Chamberland
Luc Lamontagne
Michel Lafrance
Renee Amilcar
Alain Briere
Luc Tremblay

Montreal, QC H5B

D-U-N-S 20-112-2988   (HQ)
CAPITAL REGIONAL ET COOPERATIF DESJARDINS
CAPITAL REGIONAL
2 Complexe Desjardins O Bureau 1717, Mon-

treal, QC, H5B 1B8
(514) 281-2322
Sales 115,902,103
SIC 6719 Holding companies, nec
Sylvie Lalande
Chantal Belanger
Jacques Jobin
Louis-Regis Tremblay
Marlene Deveaux
Bruno Morin
Charles Auger
Jean-Claude Gagnon
Marcel Ostiguy
Marc Barbeau

D-U-N-S 25-397-2244   (HQ)
DESJARDINS GESTION INTERNATIONALE D'ACTIFS INC
DESJARDINS ASSET MANAGEMENT
(*Suby of* FEDERATION DES CAISSES DES-JARDINS DU QUEBEC)
1 Complexe Desjardins, Montreal, QC, H5B 1B3
(514) 281-2859
Emp Here 3   *Sales* 13,716,600
SIC 8741 Management services
Nicolas Richard
Stephane Fiset
Sylvie Pinard
Christian Duceppe
Marc Provost

D-U-N-S 24-082-3914   (BR)
DESJARDINS GROUPE D'ASSURANCES GENERALES INC
(*Suby of* FEDERATION DES CAISSES DES-JARDINS DU QUEBEC)
1 Complexe Desjardins Bureau 1, Montreal,
QC, H5B 1B1
(514) 350-8300
Emp Here 200
SIC 6411 Insurance agents, brokers, and service
Jean-Francois Caron

D-U-N-S 24-987-7804   (HQ)
DESJARDINS HOLDING FINANCIER INC
(*Suby of* FEDERATION DES CAISSES DES-JARDINS DU QUEBEC)
1 Rue Complexe Desjardins S 40e Etage,
Montreal, QC, H5B 1J1
(418) 838-7870
Emp Here 100   *Sales* 48,671,296,520
SIC 6411 Insurance agents, brokers, and service
Renaud Coulombe
Real Bellemare

D-U-N-S 25-190-7978   (BR)
DESJARDINS SECURITE FINANCIERE, COMPAGNIE D'ASSURANCE VIE
DESJARDINS FINANCIAL SECURITIES, LIFE INSURANCE COMPANY
(*Suby of* FEDERATION DES CAISSES DES-JARDINS DU QUEBEC)
1 Complexe Desjardins, Montreal, QC, H5B 1E2
(514) 285-3000
Emp Here 500
SIC 6311 Life insurance
Richard Fortier

D-U-N-S 25-108-9967   (BR)
DESJARDINS SECURITE FINANCIERE, COMPAGNIE D'ASSURANCE VIE
(*Suby of* FEDERATION DES CAISSES DES-JARDINS DU QUEBEC)
2 Complexe Desjardins Tour E, Montreal, QC,
H5B 1E2
(514) 350-8700
Emp Here 500
SIC 6311 Life insurance
Ginette Savard

D-U-N-S 20-290-8810   (SL)
DESJARDINS SOCIETE DE PLACEMENT INC

DESJARDINS
(*Suby of* FEDERATION DES CAISSES DES-JARDINS DU QUEBEC)
2 Complexe Desjardins, Montreal, QC, H5B 1H5
(866) 666-1280
Emp Here 50   *Sales* 46,958,850
SIC 6211 Security brokers and dealers
Eric Landry
Stephane Fiset
Sylvie Pinard
Sebastien Vallee
Roger Tessier
Francois Chaput

D-U-N-S 20-356-1006   (HQ)
DESJARDINS SOCIETE FINANCIERE INC
(*Suby of* FEDERATION DES CAISSES DES-JARDINS DU QUEBEC)
1 Complexe Desjardins, Montreal, QC, H5B 1J1
(418) 838-7870
Emp Here 1   *Sales* 3,681,772,157
SIC 6712 Bank holding companies
Guy Cormier
Yvon Vinet
Renaud Coulombe
Jean-Robert Laporte
Annie P. Belanger
Yves Genest
Serge Rousseau
Carole Chevalier
Louis Babineau

D-U-N-S 25-334-5227   (BR)
FEDERATION DES CAISSES DESJARDINS DU QUEBEC
(*Suby of* FEDERATION DES CAISSES DES-JARDINS DU QUEBEC)
1 Complex Desjardins, Montreal, QC, H5B 1B2
(514) 281-7000
Emp Here 500
SIC 6062 State credit unions
Monique Lerouq

D-U-N-S 20-909-2360   (HQ)
FEDERATION DES MEDECINS SPECIAL-ISTES DU QUEBEC
2 Complexe Desjardins Bureau 3000, Mon-treal, QC, H5B 1G8
(514) 350-5000
Sales 16,387,770
SIC 8621 Professional organizations
Diane Francoeur
Raynald Ferland
J. Marc Girard
Karine Tousignant
Roger C. Gregoire
Sylviane Forget
Gilles O'hara
Chantal Bolduc
Joffre-Claude Allard

D-U-N-S 20-857-0440   (HQ)
FIDUCIE DESJARDINS INC
DESJARDINS
(*Suby of* FEDERATION DES CAISSES DES-JARDINS DU QUEBEC)
1 Complexe Desjardins Tour S, Montreal, QC,
H5B 1E4
(514) 286-9441
Emp Here 700   *Sales* 3,402,722,880
SIC 6733 Trusts, nec
Guy Cormier
Yvon Vinet
Renaud Coulombe
Carole Chevalier
Annie P. Belanger
Sylvain Dessureault
Yves Genest
Serge Rousseau
Neil Hawthorn
Louis Babineau

D-U-N-S 24-131-6699   (SL)
FINANCIERE DES PROFESSIONNELS INC

2 Complexe Desjardins E Bureau 31, Mon-treal, QC, H5B 1C2
(514) 350-5054
Emp Here 26   *Sales* 19,069,752
SIC 6722 Management investment, open-end
Andre Sirard

D-U-N-S 20-792-9910   (HQ)
GESTION DESJARDINS CAPITAL INC
CAPITAL F
(*Suby of* FEDERATION DES CAISSES DES-JARDINS DU QUEBEC)
2 Complexe Desjardins Bureau 1717, Mon-treal, QC, H5B 1B8
(514) 281-7131
Sales 13,077,650
SIC 6719 Holding companies, nec
Hubert Thibault
Brigitte Dupuis
Benoit Lefebvre
Martin Brunelle
Nicolas Richard
Luc Menard

D-U-N-S 24-851-9501   (HQ)
GROUPE TECHNOLOGIES DESJARDINS INC
GTD
(*Suby of* FEDERATION DES CAISSES DES-JARDINS DU QUEBEC)
Etage Cp 1 Succ Pl-Desjardins, Montreal, QC,
H5B 1B2
(514) 281-7000
Emp Here 100   *Sales* 226,231,000
SIC 7376 Computer facilities management
Guy Cormier
Serge Rousseau
Jean-Robert Laporte
Pauline D'amboise
Yvon Vinet
Louis Babineau
Annie P. Belanger
Benoit Belanger
Claude Chapdelaine
Carole Chevalier

D-U-N-S 24-851-7216   (SL)
PROFESSIONALS' FINANCIAL INC.
2 Complexe Desjardins E, Montreal, QC, H5B 1C2
(514) 350-5075
Emp Here 70   *Sales* 37,184,490
SIC 6282 Investment advice
Andre Sirard
Francois Landry

D-U-N-S 25-142-8033   (BR)
VALEURS MOBILIERES DESJARDINS INC
DESJARDINS SECURITIES
(*Suby of* FEDERATION DES CAISSES DES-JARDINS DU QUEBEC)
2 Complexe Desjardins Tour E 15 +Tage, Mon-treal, QC, H5B 1J2
(514) 286-3180
Emp Here 1,200
SIC 6211 Security brokers and dealers
Yves Neron

Montreal, QC H7B

D-U-N-S 20-363-8221   (SL)
GROUPE CONTANT INC
CONTANT
(*Suby of* CONTANT, GASTON INC)
6310 Boul Des Mille-Iles, Montreal, QC, H7B 1B3
(450) 666-6676
Emp Here 180   *Sales* 103,905,360
SIC 5599 Automotive dealers, nec
Chantal Contant
Arnaud Bernard
Isabelle Contant
Jean-Luc Contant
Simon Contant

▲ Public Company   ■ Public Company Family Member   **HQ** Headquarters   **BR** Branch   **SL** Single Location

Vincent Contant
Patrick Gaston Contant

Montreal, QC H7C

D-U-N-S 24-902-8598   (SL)
2321-1998 QUEBEC INC
MONTREAL BRIQUE ET PIERRE
1070 Montee Masson, Montreal, QC, H7C
2R2
(450) 661-1515
Emp Here 60   *Sales* 16,059,120
SIC 5211 Lumber and other building materials
Guy Locas
Laure Bissonnette

D-U-N-S 24-802-2191   (HQ)
2971038 CANADA INC
5535 Rue Ernest-Cormier, Montreal, QC, H7C
2S9
(450) 665-8780
Sales 11,875,650
SIC 5084 Industrial machinery and equipment
Roland Nadeau

D-U-N-S 20-210-5094   (HQ)
9273-9127 QUEBEC INC
ALIMENTS CHATEL, LES
(*Suby of* GESTION QUADRATEL INC)
575 Montee Saint-Francois, Montreal, QC,
H7C 2S8
(514) 935-5446
Emp Here 45   *Sales* 53,753,700
SIC 5147 Meats and meat products
Claude Chatel
Gilles Chatel
Laurence Letourneau

D-U-N-S 20-962-6738   (HQ)
AIREX INDUSTRIES INC
AIREX CONTROLE
2500 Rue Bernard-Lefebvre, Montreal, QC,
H7C 0A5
(514) 351-2303
Emp Here 50   *Sales* 13,320,060
SIC 3564 Blowers and fans
Guy Prud'homme
Pierre Rancourt
Antonio Vasilakos

D-U-N-S 20-288-2791   (SL)
ALIMENTS CHATEL INC, LES
575 Montee St Francois, Montreal, QC, H7C
2S8
(514) 935-5446
Emp Here 26   *Sales* 21,725,002
SIC 5147 Meats and meat products
Eric Riendeau
Daniel Proulx

D-U-N-S 20-280-5987   (SL)
BRAGO CONSTRUCTION INC
EDITH BOUCHARD DESIGNER
5535 Rue Maurice-Cullen, Montreal, QC, H7C
2T8
(450) 661-1121
Emp Here 50   *Sales* 15,943,450
SIC 1521 Single-family housing construction
Yves D'astous
Jean-Francois D'astous
Philippe D'astous

D-U-N-S 20-258-7473   (HQ)
BRIQUE ET PIERRE MONTREAL INC
1070 Montee Masson, Montreal, QC, H7C
2R2
(514) 321-8402
Emp Here 53   *Sales* 31,302,180
SIC 5032 Brick, stone, and related material
Guy Locas
Edouard Amborski
Laure Bissonnette
Michel Deraiche

D-U-N-S 20-190-8451   (HQ)

CAISSE POPULAIRE DESJARDINS DES MILLE-ILES
CENTRE DE SERVICE DUVERNAY
4433 Boul De La Concorde E, Montreal, QC,
H7C 1M4
(450) 661-7274
Emp Here 40   *Sales* 16,184,912
SIC 6062 State credit unions
Sylvain Filion
Normand De Montigny
Martine Lafrance
Guy Villeneuve
Anne-Catherine Farley
Marie-Helene Forget
Michel Gingras
Bilal Khoder
Chilandre Patry
Jessica Pilon

D-U-N-S 25-783-3590   (SL)
CENTRE DE CONDITIONNEMENT PHYSIQUE ATLANTIS INC.
ATLANTIS
4745 Av Des Industries, Montreal, QC, H7C
1A1
(450) 664-2285
Emp Here 55   *Sales* 17,937,480
SIC 3949 Sporting and athletic goods, nec
Raymond Sansoucy

D-U-N-S 24-346-3358   (BR)
CENTRE DE SANTE ET DE SERVICES SO-CIAUX DE LAVAL
CENTRE D'HEBERGEMENT DE LA PINIERE
(*Suby of* GOUVERNEMENT DE LA PROVINCE DE QUEBEC)
4895 Rue Saint-Joseph, Montreal, QC, H7C
1H6
(450) 661-3305
Emp Here 100
SIC 8361 Residential care
Francine Therrien

D-U-N-S 24-351-8644   (HQ)
CITERNES EXPERTS INC
TANKMART INTERNATIONAL
4545 Av Des Industries, Montreal, QC, H7C
1A1
(514) 323-5510
Emp Here 70   *Sales* 33,251,820
SIC 5085 Industrial supplies
Ronald Laberge
Robert Kavanagh

D-U-N-S 24-803-9302   (SL)
COFFRAGE MAGMA (10 ANS) INC
1500 Rue Marcel-Benoit, Montreal, QC, H7C
0A9
(450) 664-4989
Emp Here 70   *Sales* 17,233,020
SIC 1799 Special trade contractors, nec
Yan Le Houillier

D-U-N-S 24-357-8049   (SL)
COLLECTIONS UNIMAGE INC
COLLECTIONS PIACENTE
5620 Rue Ernest-Cormier, Montreal, QC, H7C
2T5
(450) 661-6444
Emp Here 100   *Sales* 17,939,600
SIC 5699 Miscellaneous apparel and acces-sory stores
Enzo Mancini
Sabrina Piacente

D-U-N-S 24-570-8193   (SL)
COLLEGE LAVAL
1275 Av Du College, Montreal, QC, H7C 1W8
(450) 661-7714
Emp Here 180   *Sales* 17,841,420
SIC 8211 Elementary and secondary schools
Jacques B Geoffroy
Antonine Boily Bousquet
Michel Baillargeon
Jean-Marc Cardinal
Stephanie Houle

Guy Boissoneau
Pierre Lafrance
Real Sauvageau
Marie-Helene Beaulac

D-U-N-S 20-215-6303   (HQ)
COUREY, GEORGE INC
COURTEX
(*Suby of* GESTION COUREY INC)
6620 Rue Ernest-Cormier, Montreal, QC, H7C
2T5
(450) 661-6620
Sales 45,797,040
SIC 5023 Homefurnishings
Ronald Courey
Gerald Courey
Michael Courey

D-U-N-S 24-548-3128   (SL)
DISTRIBUTIONS B.M.B. (1985) S.E.C. , LES
BMB GLOBAL SOURCING
4500 Rue Bernard-Lefebvre, Montreal, QC,
H7C 0A5
(514) 382-6520
Emp Here 50   *Sales* 22,358,700
SIC 5039 Construction materials, nec
Andre Lefebvre

D-U-N-S 25-243-8650   (SL)
ENTREPRISE SANITAIRE F.A. LTEE
ENVIRO CONNEXIONS
(*Suby of* WASTE CONNECTIONS, INC)
4799 Rue Bernard-Lefebvre, Montreal, QC,
H7C 0A5
(450) 661-5080
Emp Here 112   *Sales* 23,039,072
SIC 4212 Local trucking, without storage
Ronald J. Mittelstadt
Domenico (Dan) Pio
Worthing F. Jackman
Patrick J. Shea
Steven F. Bouck

D-U-N-S 20-280-7496   (SL)
ENTREPRISES PEP (2000) INC, LES
3000 Rue Bernard-Lefebvre, Montreal, QC,
H7C 0A5
(450) 661-5050
Emp Here 100   *Sales* 24,618,600
SIC 1794 Excavation work
Davio Pallotta

D-U-N-S 20-752-3929   (HQ)
EQUIPEMENT COMAIRCO LTEE
(*Suby of* 2971038 CANADA INC)
5535 Rue Ernest-Cormier, Montreal, QC, H7C
2S9
(450) 665-8780
Emp Here 25   *Sales* 48,773,000
SIC 5084 Industrial machinery and equipment
Roland Y. Nadeau
Eddy Nadeau
Caroline Filion
Felix Nadeau
Daniel Nadeau
David Nadeau
Gilles Desrosiers

D-U-N-S 24-676-9533   (HQ)
GROUPE CT INC
MONTREAL PHOTOCOPIEUR
5545 Rue Maurice-Cullen, Montreal, QC, H7C
2T8
(450) 967-3142
Emp Here 15   *Sales* 11,626,524
SIC 5044 Office equipment
Tomy Belanger
Pinto Nicolas

D-U-N-S 25-152-0185   (SL)
INDUSTRIES SHOW CANADA INC, LES
SHOW CANADA PRODUCTIONS
5555 Rue Maurice-Cullen, Montreal, QC, H7C
2T8
(450) 664-5155
Emp Here 350   *Sales* 62,558,650
SIC 8712 Architectural services
Jean Labadie

D-U-N-S 24-419-8862   (HQ)
LEFEBVRE & BENOIT S.E.C.
MATERIAUX DE CONSTRUCTION L&B
4500 Rue Bernard-Lefebvre, Montreal, QC,
H7C 0A5
(450) 667-6000
Sales 44,717,400
SIC 5039 Construction materials, nec
Caroline Lefebvre

D-U-N-S 24-515-3648   (HQ)
MAGASINS HART INC
BARGAIN GIANT STORES
(*Suby of* LITERIES UNIVERSELLES PAGA INC)
900 Place Paul-Kane, Montreal, QC, H7C 2T2
(450) 661-4155
Emp Here 60   *Sales* 136,897,200
SIC 5311 Department stores
Paul Nassar

D-U-N-S 24-082-8277   (HQ)
NOVEXCO INC
HAMSTER
950 Place Paul-Kane, Montreal, QC, H7C 2T2
(450) 686-1212
Emp Here 100   *Sales* 110,817,864
SIC 5044 Office equipment
Eric Brassard
Denis Mathieu
Jean-Yves Grenier
Claude A. Picard
Guy Bergeron
Marc Crevier
Gilles C. Lachance
Robert Cloutier
Martin Labrecque
Dominic Legare

D-U-N-S 20-415-3803   (HQ)
PELICAN INTERNATIONAL INC
1000 Place Paul-Kane, Montreal, QC, H7C
2T2
(450) 664-1222
Emp Here 360   *Sales* 138,153,750
SIC 3732 Boatbuilding and repairing
Antoine Elie
Christian Elie
Marie-Christine Piedboeuf
Martin Deschenes
Louis Duchesne
Gilles Dulude
Pierre Prud'homme

D-U-N-S 20-181-1275   (BR)
PEPSICO CANADA ULC
FRITO-LAY CANADA
(*Suby of* PEPSICO, INC.)
6755 Rue Ernest-Cormier, Montreal, QC, H7C
2T4
(450) 664-5800
Emp Here 250
SIC 2096 Potato chips and similar snacks
David Laurie

D-U-N-S 24-251-6888   (SL)
PIECES D'AUTOS TRANSBEC INC, LES
ATLAS ACCESSOIRES D'AUTOS
5505 Rue Ernest-Cormier, Montreal, QC, H7C
0A1
(450) 665-4440
Emp Here 100   *Sales* 62,928,000
SIC 5531 Auto and home supply stores
Pierre Deaudelin
Dominic Deaudelin

D-U-N-S 20-317-4545   (SL)
PRODUITS DE BATIMENT FUSION BUILD-ING PRODUCTS INC
4500 Rue Bernard-Lefebvre, Montreal, QC,
H7C 0A5
(514) 381-7456
Emp Here 55   *Sales* 10,564,675
SIC 3441 Fabricated structural Metal
Alexandre Lefebvre
Mario Caissie
Caroline Lefebvre

Andree Caissie-Savoie

D-U-N-S 20-214-9019   (SL)
RTI-CLARO INC
CLAIRO PRECISION
(*Suby of* ARCONIC INC.)
5515 Rue Ernest-Cormier, Montreal, QC, H7C
2S9
(450) 786-2001
Emp Here 285   *Sales* 80,049,945
SIC 3599 Industrial machinery, nec
Christian Ouimet
Jeremy Halford
Marilyn Fayock
Pedro Rosas

D-U-N-S 24-683-7673   (SL)
**SYSTEMES INTERIEURS BERNARD MNJ &
ASSOCIES INC**
5000 Rue Bernard-Lefebvre, Montreal, QC,
H7C 0A5
(450) 665-1335
Emp Here 250   *Sales* 45,797,750
SIC 1742 Plastering, drywall, and insulation
Hugo Bernard
Nick Bernard
Daniel Courchesne
Jean-Luc Villette

D-U-N-S 24-740-3926   (HQ)
UNIBOARD CANADA INC
FORPAN
5555 Rue Ernest-Cormier, Montreal, QC, H7C
2S9
(450) 664-6000
Emp Here 75   *Sales* 236,631,500
SIC 2493 Reconstituted wood products
James N Hogg
Yvon Rousseau
Lionel Dubrofsky
Tami Dubrofsky
Richard Cherney
Andrew Dubrofsky

D-U-N-S 24-343-9515   (BR)
UNIBOARD CANADA INC
UNIBOARD SURFACES
(*Suby of* UNIBOARD CANADA INC)
5555 Rue Ernest-Cormier, Montreal, QC, H7C
2S9
(450) 661-7122
Emp Here 100
SIC 2426 Hardwood dimension and flooring
mills
Pascal Labrie

Montreal, QC H7E

D-U-N-S 20-503-9068   (SL)
125173 CANADA INC
ALCO SPORTS
2380 Montee Masson, Montreal, QC, H7E 4P2
(450) 666-2444
Emp Here 25   *Sales* 12,451,950
SIC 5561 Recreational vehicle dealers
Alden Kowarsky
Gerald Kowarsky

D-U-N-S 20-370-7187   (HQ)
9462287 CANADA INC
2000 Rue Leopold-Hamelin, Montreal, QC,
H7E 4P2
(450) 720-1331
Emp Here 1   *Sales* 14,511,040
SIC 3341 Secondary nonferrous Metals
Pierre Sylvestre
Michel Fortier
Jean-Guy Hamelin
Bertin Castonguay
Antoine De Mortemart
Daniel Labrecque
Michel Levesque
Cyril Wolkonsky

D-U-N-S 24-667-7215   (SL)

AUTOBUS RIVE-NORD LTEE
1325 Montee Masson, Montreal, QC, H7E 4P2
(450) 661-7140
Emp Here 80   *Sales* 6,021,760
SIC 4151 School buses
Eric Chartrand

D-U-N-S 20-709-8088   (HQ)
CENTRE AGRICOLE J.L.D. INC
GROUPE J.L.D. LAGUE
3900 Sud Laval (A-440) E, Montreal, QC, H7E
5N2
(514) 373-4899
Sales 121,932,500
SIC 5083 Farm and garden machinery
Terry Enepekides
Pierre Simard
Catherine Parent
Simon Dumais
Jean-Stephane Yansouni
Marc Benoit
Daniel Dion
Jean-Yves Dion
Scott Jackson
Andre Lague

D-U-N-S 25-847-3818   (BR)
**CHARTWELL QUEBEC (MEL) HOLDINGS
INC**
LOGGIAS VILLA VAL DES ARBRES, LES
(*Suby of* CHARTWELL MASTER CARE LP)
3245 Boul Saint-Martin E, Montreal, QC, H7E
4T6
(450) 661-0911
Emp Here 149
SIC 8361 Residential care
Melanye Sagala

D-U-N-S 24-420-9040   (SL)
COFFRAGE MEGAFORME INC
2500 Montee Saint-Francois, Montreal, QC,
H7E 4P2

Emp Here 60   *Sales* 14,942,238
SIC 1799 Special trade contractors, nec
Steven Unsworth
Real Pomerleau

D-U-N-S 24-893-3483   (BR)
COMMISSION SCOLAIRE DE LAVAL
*INSTITUT DE PROTECTION CONTRE LES
INCENDIES DU QUEBEC (IPIQ), L'*
(*Suby of* COMMISSION SCOLAIRE DE
LAVAL)
1740 Montee Masson, Montreal, QC, H7E 4P2
(450) 662-7000
Emp Here 75
SIC 8331 Job training and related services
Guy Dussault

D-U-N-S 24-052-6814   (HQ)
**COMPAGNIE DE CONSTRUCTION ET DE
DEVELOPPEMENT CRIE LTEE, LA**
3983 Boul Lite, Montreal, QC, H7E 1A3
(450) 661-1102
Emp Here 35   *Sales* 162,321,600
SIC 1522 Residential construction, nec
Robert Baribeau
Tanya Pash
Randy Bosum
Jackie Blacksmith
Emily Whiskeychan Gilpin
James Bobbish
Clarence Sr. Joly
Rusty Cheezo
Derrick Neeposh
George Sandy

D-U-N-S 24-801-0530   (SL)
CONSTRUCTION SOTER INC
4085 Rang Saint-Elzear E, Montreal, QC, H7E
4P2
(450) 664-2818
Emp Here 75   *Sales* 18,933,150
SIC 1611 Highway and street construction
Eric Giguere
Joseph Giguere

Jocelyn Giguere

D-U-N-S 24-650-5606   (SL)
DONCAR CONSTRUCTION INC
4085 Rang Saint-Elzear E, Montreal, QC, H7E
4P2

Emp Here 70   *Sales* 17,670,940
SIC 1623 Water, sewer, and utility lines
Jocelyn Giguere
Eric Giguere
Joseph Giguere

D-U-N-S 24-969-9141   (SL)
**ENTREPRISES LA CHARCUTIERE LAVAL
INC**
PATISSIERE, LA
3315 Boul De La Concorde E, Montreal, QC,
H7E 2C3

Emp Here 50   *Sales* 13,707,600
SIC 5411 Grocery stores
Vincent Camerota

D-U-N-S 24-327-2882   (SL)
GESTION CHRISTIAN DUGUAY INC
PHARMAPRIX
3100 Boul De La Concorde E Bureau 50d,
Montreal, QC, H7E 2B8
(450) 661-7748
Emp Here 45   *Sales* 11,382,930
SIC 5912 Drug stores and proprietary stores
Christian Duguay

D-U-N-S 24-353-9848   (SL)
GESTION JACQUES BOURGET INC
JEAN COUTU
2955 Boul De La Concorde E Bureau 76, Mon-
treal, QC, H7E 2B5
(450) 661-6921
Emp Here 60   *Sales* 14,659,680
SIC 5912 Drug stores and proprietary stores
Jacques Bourget

D-U-N-S 24-393-9217   (SL)
GESTIONS REJEAN SAVARD LTEE
CANADIAN TIRE
4975 Boul Robert-Bourassa Bureau 231,
Montreal, QC, H7E 0A4
(450) 665-4747
Emp Here 40   *Sales* 19,923,120
SIC 5531 Auto and home supply stores
Rejean Savard

D-U-N-S 24-813-3233   (SL)
ICANDA CORPORATION
(*Suby of* GESTION IMMOBILIERE M.S.E.
INC)
3131 Boul De La Concorde E Bureau 306,
Montreal, QC, H7E 4W4
(450) 661-2972
Emp Here 50   *Sales* 12,309,300
SIC 1794 Excavation work
Raoul Altable
Stephane Lessard
Eric Lessard
Marco Lessard

D-U-N-S 24-195-0190   (SL)
MARCHE HEBERT SENECAL INC
IGA EXTRA
5805 Boul Robert-Bourassa, Montreal, QC,
H7E 0A4
(450) 665-4441
Emp Here 109   *Sales* 31,988,993
SIC 5411 Grocery stores
Eric Hebert
Sonia Senecal

D-U-N-S 25-494-7674   (HQ)
MULTI RECYCLAGE S.D. INC
3030 Montee Saint-Francois, Montreal, QC,
H7E 4P2
(450) 625-9191
Emp Here 12   *Sales* 10,373,440
SIC 4212 Local trucking, without storage
Martin Cloutier

D-U-N-S 24-570-2733   (SL)
RE-MAX IMMO-CONTACT INC
2820 Boul Saint-Martin E Bureau 201, Mon-
treal, QC, H7E 5A1
(450) 661-6810
Emp Here 33   *Sales* 10,795,191
SIC 6531 Real estate agents and managers
Alain M Chaput

D-U-N-S 24-797-8211   (SL)
SALVEX INC
2450 Montee Saint-Francois Bureau 2, Mon-
treal, QC, H7E 4P2
(450) 664-4335
Emp Here 30   *Sales* 14,121,930
SIC 1542 Nonresidential construction, nec
Domenico Salvo

D-U-N-S 20-715-0892   (SL)
**SERVICES TECHNIQUES LAURENTIDES
INC**
3131 Boul De La Concorde E Bureau 410,
Montreal, QC, H7E 4W4

Emp Here 30   *Sales* 13,304,700
SIC 7389 Business services, nec
Marc Jobin

D-U-N-S 24-922-3579   (HQ)
SIMARD-BEAUDRY CONSTRUCTION INC
BANISTER PIPELINE CONSTRUCTION
4230 Rang Saint-Elzear E, Montreal, QC, H7E
4P2
(450) 664-5700
Emp Here 50   *Sales* 50,488,400
SIC 1622 Bridge, tunnel, and elevated high-
way construction
Lisa Accurso

D-U-N-S 20-331-5007   (HQ)
TOTAL METAL RECUPERATION (TMR) INC
(*Suby of* 9462287 CANADA INC)
2000 Rue Leopold-Hamelin, Montreal, QC,
H7E 4P2
(450) 720-1331
Sales 14,511,040
SIC 3341 Secondary nonferrous Metals
Jean-Guy Hamelin
Louis-David Sansoucy
Paul-Emile Tremblay
Marcel Francoeur
Marie-Christine Tessier
Bertrand Masse

Montreal, QC H7K

D-U-N-S 24-369-1792   (BR)
**CAISSE   DESJARDINS   DE   VIMONT-
AUTEUIL**
CENTRE DE SERVICE AUTEUIL
(*Suby of* CAISSE DESJARDINS DE VIMONT-
AUTEUIL)
5350 Boul Des Laurentides, Montreal, QC,
H7K 2J8
(450) 669-2694
Emp Here 75
SIC 6062 State credit unions
Michel Bouroz

D-U-N-S 25-983-9970   (SL)
FONDATION LE PILIER
FONDATION INTEGRACTION DU QUEBEC
5273 Rue Thibault, Montreal, QC, H7K 3R5
(450) 963-3751
Emp Here 49   *Sales* 11,114,817
SIC 8399 Social services, nec
Sylvain Fontaine

D-U-N-S 25-536-1198   (SL)
**ORCHIDEE   BLANCHE   CENTRE
D'HEBERGEMENT   SOINS   LONGUE
DUREE INC, L**
CHSLD L'ORCHIDEE BLANCHE
2577 Boul Rene-Laennec, Montreal, QC, H7K

3V4
(450) 629-1200
Emp Here 165   *Sales* 9,775,755
SIC 8361 Residential care
Normand Goyette

Montreal, QC H7L

D-U-N-S 24-697-3192   (HQ)
149942 CANADA INC
DISTRIBUTIONS ALIMENTAIRES B.L.P.
1955 Rue Monterey, Montreal, QC, H7L 3T6
(450) 688-7660
Sales 37,600,965
SIC 5144 Poultry and poultry products
Peter Berlemis
Louis Berlemis
Bobby Bousioutis

D-U-N-S 24-399-1036   (SL)
156560 CANADA INC
WEED MAN
1123 Nord Laval (A-440) O, Montreal, QC,
H7L 3W3
(514) 337-1222
Emp Here 250   *Sales* 38,916,250
SIC 0782 Lawn and garden services
Roger Mongeon
Marise Auray
Pierre Garant
James Trow
Brenda Rice
Donal W. Dankowich
Terry Kurth

D-U-N-S 25-674-4442   (SL)
2525-7577 QUEBEC INC.
3050 Boul Industriel, Montreal, QC, H7L 4P7

Emp Here 150   *Sales* 42,603,150
SIC 2821 Plastics materials and resins
Guy David
James Quinn
Richard Maille

D-U-N-S 25-242-7315   (HQ)
2982897 CANADA INC
EPM MECANIC
2425 Rue Michelin, Montreal, QC, H7L 5B9
(514) 332-4830
Sales 11,653,250
SIC 1711 Plumbing, heating, air-conditioning
Carlos Le Houx
Yannick Gauthier
Ernest Trainor
Claude Moreau

D-U-N-S 25-257-9339   (SL)
3093-6975 QUEBEC INC
CIE D'ENSEIGNES MONTREAL NEON
1780 Place Martenot Bureau 17, Montreal,
QC, H7L 5B5
(450) 668-4888
Emp Here 50   *Sales* 10,941,200
SIC 3993 Signs and advertising specialties
Linda Dupre

D-U-N-S 24-349-4379   (SL)
6669409 CANADA INC
FIRST AID CENTRAL
3504 Av Francis-Hughes, Montreal, QC, H7L
5A9
(450) 696-1090
Emp Here 28   *Sales* 20,790,560
SIC 5199 Nondurable goods, nec
Emmanuel Tzortzis
Antonios Kourebeles

D-U-N-S 24-055-9984   (SL)
9022-5814 QUEBEC INC
LOGICIELS LOC
1867 Rue Berlier, Montreal, QC, H7L 3S4
(450) 663-6327
Emp Here 70   *Sales* 12,411,770

SIC 7371 Custom computer programming services
Stephan Mercier
Yvan Boutin
Sylvain Fournier
Andre Paradis

D-U-N-S 20-400-5941   (SL)
9149-8980 QUEBEC INC
MAZAYA CONSTRUCTION
1683 Rue Taillefer, Montreal, QC, H7L 1T9
(514) 467-9555
Emp Here 24   *Sales* 11,297,544
SIC 1542 Nonresidential construction, nec
Collette Imad

D-U-N-S 20-331-8373   (SL)
9227-6898 QUEBEC INC
BOUTIQUE BUZZY
1527 Nord Laval (A-440) O Bureau 230, Montreal, QC, H7L 3W3

Emp Here 22   *Sales* 11,090,057
SIC 5136 Men's and boy's clothing
Bachir El-Debs

D-U-N-S 24-791-4570   (SL)
AJPRO DISTRIBUTION INC
?ROS & COMPAGNIE
2047 Nord Laval (A-440) O, Montreal, QC,
H7L 3W3
(450) 681-0666
Emp Here 30   *Sales* 14,949,660
SIC 5137 Women's and children's clothing
Andre Provost

D-U-N-S 24-335-6560   (BR)
ALCOA CANADA CIE
DIV HOWMET LAVAL CASTING
(*Suby of* ALUMINERIE LAURALCO SARL)
4001 Des Laurentides (A-15) E, Montreal, QC,
H7L 3H7
(450) 680-2500
Emp Here 273
SIC 3334 Primary aluminum
John Pellegrino

D-U-N-S 24-743-0150   (HQ)
ALIMENTATION COUCHE-TARD INC
CIRCLE K
4204 Boul Industriel, Montreal, QC, H7L 0E3
(450) 662-3272
Emp Here 200   *Sales* 51,394,400,000
SIC 5411 Grocery stores
Brian Hannasch
Alain Bouchard
Jacob Schram
Hans-Olav Hoidahl
Jorn Madsen
Alex Miller
Dennis Tewell
Darrell Davis
Kathleen K. Cunnington
Stephane Trudel

D-U-N-S 20-257-2731   (HQ)
ALIMENTS WHYTE'S INC, LES
MRS. WHYTE'S PRODUCTS
(*Suby of* EJJ HOLDINGS INC)
1540 Rue Des Patriotes, Montreal, QC, H7L
2N6
(450) 625-1976
Emp Here 25   *Sales* 83,557,700
SIC 5141 Groceries, general line
Paul Kawaja
Elisabeth Kawaja
Andrew Anderson

D-U-N-S 24-811-6246   (HQ)
ALTEL INC
ALARME ALTEC
(*Suby of* CONVERGINT TECHNOLOGIES
LLC)
3150 Boul Le Corbusier, Montreal, QC, H7L
4S8
(450) 682-9788
Emp Here 1   *Sales* 12,216,400
SIC 5999 Miscellaneous retail stores, nec

Alan Bergschneider
Jim Boutwell
Brian Haw
Walter W. Winkel Iii
Ken Lochiatto
Alain Deschamps

D-U-N-S 24-174-4762   (SL)
ALUMINIUM B. BOUCHARD INC
125 Rue De La Pointe-Langlois, Montreal, QC,
H7L 3J4
(450) 622-9543
Emp Here 60   *Sales* 13,069,740
SIC 1761 Roofing, siding, and sheetMetal
work
Benoit Bouchard
Serge Bouchard
Juliette Labelle Bouchard

D-U-N-S 24-768-4392   (SL)
AQUAREHAB EAU POTABLE INC
2145 Rue Michelin, Montreal, QC, H7L 5B8
(450) 687-3472
Emp Here 132   *Sales* 43,311,180
SIC 1623 Water, sewer, and utility lines
Claudio Grilli

D-U-N-S 24-207-5021   (HQ)
AQUAREHAB INC
2145 Rue Michelin, Montreal, QC, H7L 5B8
(450) 687-3472
Emp Here 24   *Sales* 25,244,200
SIC 1623 Water, sewer, and utility lines
Christophe Ashkar
Gaetan Turbide
Luc Danis

D-U-N-S 25-244-1100   (BR)
ARTOPEX INC
(*Suby of* GROUPE PRO-PLUS INC)
2129 Rue Berlier, Montreal, QC, H7L 3M9
(450) 973-9655
Emp Here 100
SIC 2522 Office furniture, except wood
Daniel Pelletier

D-U-N-S 25-794-8729   (SL)
ATELIER DE TRI DES MATIERES PLASTIQUES RECYCLABLES DU QUEBEC INC
ATMPRQ
3405 Boul Industriel, Montreal, QC, H7L 4S3
(450) 667-5347
Emp Here 46   *Sales* 12,726,360
SIC 2821 Plastics materials and resins
Allan Bilodeau

D-U-N-S 20-210-7827   (SL)
AVMOR LTEE
ECOPURE
(*Suby of* GESTION BRINEKY INC)
950 Rue Michelin, Montreal, QC, H7L 5C1
(450) 629-8074
Emp Here 100   *Sales* 28,402,100
SIC 2842 Polishes and sanitation goods
Avrum Morrow
Mattie Chinks
Juli Morrow

D-U-N-S 20-738-0809   (HQ)
CAMFIL CANADA INC
ENTREPRISE CAMFIL FARR POWER SYSTEMS N A
(*Suby of* CAMFIL AB)
2785 Av Francis-Hughes, Montreal, QC, H7L
3J6
(450) 629-3030
Emp Here 50   *Sales* 60,966,250
SIC 5085 Industrial supplies
Armando Brunetti
Darrell Cain
Carl Larochelle
Per Carlsson

D-U-N-S 20-888-0708   (HQ)
CAN-AQUA INTERNATIONAL LTEE
2250 Boul Dagenais O, Montreal, QC, H7L
5Y2

(450) 625-3088
Emp Here 21   *Sales* 10,732,176
SIC 5074 Plumbing and heating equipment
and supplies (hydronics)
Jean Beaudoin

D-U-N-S 25-358-9717   (SL)
**CHEMINEES SECURITE INTERNATIONAL
LTEE**
(*Suby of* DURAVENT HOLDING B.V.)
2125 Rue Monterey, Montreal, QC, H7L 3T6
(450) 973-9999
Emp Here 220   *Sales* 18,491,125
SIC 3317 Steel pipe and tubes
Simon Davis
Brian Pesola
Coen Rooijmans
Cary B. Wood
Piet Veenema
Alexander Van Wassenaer

D-U-N-S 25-361-8912   (SL)
CIRION BIOPHARMA RECHERCHE INC
3150 Rue Delaunay, Montreal, QC, H7L 5E1
(450) 688-6445
Emp Here 26   *Sales* 10,903,230
SIC 6712 Bank holding companies
Sylvain Desrochers
Lise Dallaire

D-U-N-S 20-323-5275   (HQ)
COMPAGNIE 2 AMERIKS INC, LA
GOGO QUINOA
2300 Rue Michelin, Montreal, QC, H7L 5C3
(438) 380-3330
Sales 21,725,002
SIC 5149 Groceries and related products, nec
Martin Bilodeau
Clara Cohen

D-U-N-S 24-859-5527   (HQ)
CONFISERIES REGAL INC
EURO-EXCELLENCE
1625 Boul Dagenais O, Montreal, QC, H7L
5A3
(450) 628-6700
Emp Here 95   *Sales* 178,462,284
SIC 5145 Confectionery
Hani Basile
Barry Mintz
Joseph Neufeld

D-U-N-S 24-648-3374   (SL)
CONSTRUCTION SOCAM LTEE
3300 Av Francis-Hughes, Montreal, QC, H7L
5A7
(450) 662-9000
Emp Here 40   *Sales* 18,829,240
SIC 1542 Nonresidential construction, nec
Francois Chevrier

D-U-N-S 24-422-4924   (HQ)
COUCHE-TARD INC
BANNIERE ESSO
(*Suby of* ALIMENTATION COUCHE-TARD
INC)
4204 Boul Industriel, Montreal, QC, H7L 0E3
(450) 662-6632
Emp Here 50   *Sales* 2,738,483,488
SIC 5541 Gasoline service stations
Stephane Trudel
Claude Tessier
Christine Anagnostou

D-U-N-S 20-197-4292   (SL)
DENIS, MAURICE ET FILS INC
1745 Rue Guillet, Montreal, QC, H7L 5B1
(450) 687-3840
Emp Here 50   *Sales* 11,046,700
SIC 1711 Plumbing, heating, air-conditioning
Stephan Heris
Karine Chabot Denis
Maxime Bourassa-Leduc
Luc Denis

D-U-N-S 25-357-6409   (BR)
DEVTEK AEROSPACE INC
DEVTEK AEROSPACE INC.

▲ Public Company   ■ Public Company Family Member   **HQ** Headquarters   **BR** Branch   **SL** Single Location

(Suby of HEROUX-DEVTEK INC)
3675 Boul Industriel, Montreal, QC, H7L 4S3
(450) 629-3454
Emp Here 180
SIC 3599 Industrial machinery, nec

D-U-N-S 20-118-5852   (HQ)
DISTRIBUTION COUCHE-TARD INC
CENTRE DE DISTRIBUTION COUCHE-TARD
(Suby of ALIMENTATION COUCHE-TARD INC)
4204 Boul Industriel, Montreal, QC, H7L 0E3
(450) 662-6632
Emp Here 65   *Sales* 74,252,000
SIC 5199 Nondurable goods, nec
Stephane Trudel
Christine Anagnostou
Claude Tessier

D-U-N-S 24-475-2168   (HQ)
ENTREPRISES DE REFRIGERATION L.S. INC, LES
1610 Rue Guillet, Montreal, QC, H7L 5B2
(450) 682-8105
Emp Here 50   *Sales* 46,613,000
SIC 1711 Plumbing, heating, air-conditioning
Sylvain Sergerie
Maurice Peladeau

D-U-N-S 24-776-2250   (SL)
EXCEL PRIX GROSSISTE EN ALIMENTA-TION INC
LE GROUPE MARTEL
1225 Rue Bergar, Montreal, QC, H7L 4Z7
(450) 967-0076
Emp Here 100   *Sales* 29,347,700
SIC 5411 Grocery stores
Serge Martel

D-U-N-S 20-632-9708   (HQ)
FOURNITURES DE BUREAU DENIS INC
2990 Boul Le Corbusier, Montreal, QC, H7L 3M2
(450) 687-8682
Emp Here 150   *Sales* 251,259,900
SIC 5112 Stationery and office supplies
Normand Latulippe
Jean-Luc Latulippe
Stephane Latulippe
Benoit Latulippe

D-U-N-S 20-024-9399   (SL)
GEEP CANADA INC
GEEP ECOSYS
2995 Boul Le Corbusier, Montreal, QC, H7L 3M3
(450) 506-0220
Emp Here 50   *Sales* 11,517,000
SIC 5734 Computer and software stores
Jeffrey Jermyn
Joe Caruso

D-U-N-S 24-377-2980   (HQ)
GEEP ECOSYS INC
SOCIETE GEEP CANADA
2995 Boul Le Corbusier, Montreal, QC, H7L 3M3
(450) 506-0220
Emp Here 35   *Sales* 61,565,480
SIC 5045 Computers, peripherals, and soft-ware
Jeffrey Jermyn
Joe Caruso

D-U-N-S 24-363-3307   (SL)
GESTION RONALD HERTELEER INC
3985 Boul Industriel, Montreal, QC, H7L 4S3
(514) 384-8300
Emp Here 60   *Sales* 15,693,180
SIC 6712 Bank holding companies
Ronald Herteleer

D-U-N-S 20-420-8847   (SL)
GROUPE EDUCALIVRES INC
EDITIONS GRAND DUC, DIV
955 Rue Bergar, Montreal, QC, H7L 4Z6

(514) 334-8466
Emp Here 100   *Sales* 13,538,600
SIC 2731 Book publishing
Jean-Guy Blanchette
Joseph Cristofaro
Louis Martin

D-U-N-S 24-763-5337   (HQ)
GROUPE F.G.B. 2000 INC, LE
1225 Rue Bergar, Montreal, QC, H7L 4Z7
(450) 967-0076
Emp Here 80
SIC 5141 Groceries, general line
Sylva Belanger

D-U-N-S 24-068-7504   (SL)
GROUPE TOMAPURE INC
1790 Place Martenot, Montreal, QC, H7L 5B5
(450) 663-6444
Emp Here 21   *Sales* 17,547,117
SIC 5148 Fresh fruits and vegetables
Daniel Larivee
Michel Larivee
Guy Larivee

D-U-N-S 25-781-0085   (SL)
GYMN-EAU LAVAL
2465 Rue Honore-Mercier, Montreal, QC, H7L 2S9
(450) 625-2674
Emp Here 30   *Sales* 11,922,420
SIC 8699 Membership organizations, nec
Francine Lariviere

D-U-N-S 20-332-5493   (BR)
HOWMET CANADA COMPANY
COMPAGNIE HOWMET CANADA
(Suby of HOWMET CANADA COMPANY)
4001 Des Laurentides (A-15) E, Montreal, QC, H7L 3H7
(450) 680-2500
Emp Here 230
SIC 3365 Aluminum foundries
John Pellegrino

D-U-N-S 24-050-5404   (SL)
HVAC INC
2185 Rue Le Chatelier, Montreal, QC, H7L 5B3
(514) 748-4822
Emp Here 75   *Sales* 17,479,875
SIC 1711 Plumbing, heating, air-conditioning
Martin Lesiege
Stephane Robert
Pierre Levesque

D-U-N-S 24-709-6746   (SL)
IMPRIMERIE L'EMPREINTE INC
L'EMPREINTE
4177 Boul Industriel, Montreal, QC, H7L 0G7
(514) 331-0741
Emp Here 100   *Sales* 16,402,700
SIC 2752 Commercial printing, lithographic
Francois Chartrand
Yves Beauchamp
Luc Janson
Sebastien Chartrand
Marjolaine Beaule

D-U-N-S 20-999-6289   (SL)
INSTALLATIONS   ELECTRIQUES PICHETTE INC, LES
(Suby of PLACEMENTS FRANCOIS PICHETTE LTEE, LES)
3080 Rue Peugeot, Montreal, QC, H7L 5C5
(450) 682-4411
Emp Here 50   *Sales* 10,891,450
SIC 1731 Electrical work
Francois Pichette
Paul Pichette

D-U-N-S 24-742-4369   (SL)
JUNISE VENTES INC
JUNISE PLASTIQUE
4001 Boul Industriel, Montreal, QC, H7L 4S3
(514) 858-7777
Emp Here 22   *Sales* 11,080,476
SIC 5113 Industrial and personal service pa-

per
Nissim Amar
Judah Amar

D-U-N-S 20-222-8763   (HQ)
KOLOSTAT INC
KOLOFIS
(Suby of HOLDING KOLOSTAT ESOP INC)
2005 Rue Le Chatelier, Montreal, QC, H7L 5B3
(514) 333-7333
Emp Here 195   *Sales* 46,613,000
SIC 1711 Plumbing, heating, air-conditioning
Stanley H. Segal
John P. Billick

D-U-N-S 25-780-3379   (SL)
LAVAL CABLE ET GRANULATIONS INC
270 Boul Saint-Elzear O, Montreal, QC, H7L 3P2
(450) 668-8100
Emp Here 10   *Sales* 10,003,390
SIC 5051 Metals service centers and offices
Franco Di Menna

D-U-N-S 20-223-7186   (HQ)
MAGASIN LAURA (P.V.) INC
COMBO PETITES
3000 Boul Le Corbusier, Montreal, QC, H7L 3W2
(450) 973-6090
Emp Here 3   *Sales* 132,614,565
SIC 5621 Women's clothing stores
Kalman Fisher
Melanie Fisher

D-U-N-S 20-226-9254   (HQ)
MEP TECHNOLOGIES INC
3100 Rue Peugeot, Montreal, QC, H7L 5C6
(450) 682-0804
Emp Here 164   *Sales* 85,130,850
SIC 3444 Sheet Metalwork
Armand Afilalo
Joseph Sassano
Kathy Afilalo

D-U-N-S 24-842-7734   (HQ)
METALIUM INC
RAPIDE METAL
4020 Rue Garand, Montreal, QC, H7L 5C9
(450) 963-0411
Emp Here 12   *Sales* 44,717,400
SIC 5051 Metals service centers and offices
Donald Albert
Catherine Frigon
Gilles Leroux
Simon Albert

D-U-N-S 20-376-2435   (HQ)
MOULAGE D'ALUMINIUM HOWMET LTEE
(Suby of ARCONIC INC.)
4001 Desste Des Laurentides (A-15) E, Mon-treal, QC, H7L 3H7
(450) 680-2500
Sales 101,793,500
SIC 3355 Aluminum rolling and drawing, nec
Gary J Warness
Dolores A Yura
Martin Pinel
Mario Longhi

D-U-N-S 25-098-9647   (SL)
MSC REHABILITATION INC
2145 Rue Michelin, Montreal, QC, H7L 5B8
(450) 687-5610
Emp Here 25   *Sales* 11,087,250
SIC 7389 Business services, nec
Sylvain Comeau
Michel Champagne

D-U-N-S 20-402-1257   (SL)
NAPA AUTO PARTS
2999 Boul Le Corbusier, Montreal, QC, H7L 3M3
(450) 681-6495
Emp Here 49   *Sales* 24,405,822
SIC 5531 Auto and home supply stores
Robert Hattem

D-U-N-S 24-697-4414   (SL)
PARIS LADOUCEUR & ASSOCIES INC
63 Rue De La Pointe-Langlois, Montreal, QC, H7L 3J4
(450) 963-2777
Emp Here 35   *Sales* 11,449,445
SIC 6531 Real estate agents and managers
Vincent Ladouceur

D-U-N-S 20-300-7711   (BR)
PARKER HANNIFIN CANADA
PARKER FILTERATION CANADA DIV OF
(Suby of PARKER-HANNIFIN CORPORA-TION)
2785 Av Francis-Hughes, Montreal, QC, H7L 3J6
(450) 629-3030
Emp Here 90
SIC 3569 General industrial machinery, nec
Lynn Moline

D-U-N-S 20-417-0062   (SL)
PEINTURES M.F. INC
1605 Boul Dagenais O, Montreal, QC, H7L 5A3
(450) 628-3831
Emp Here 45   *Sales* 12,449,700
SIC 2851 Paints and allied products
Emanuele Morello
Pierre Chapdelaine

D-U-N-S 24-836-0406   (HQ)
PLACEMENTS   FRANCOIS   PICHETTE LTEE, LES
3080 Rue Peugeot, Montreal, QC, H7L 5C5
(450) 682-4411
Sales 13,505,398
SIC 1731 Electrical work
Francois Pichette

D-U-N-S 24-591-1128   (HQ)
PLANTES D'INTERIEUR VERONNEAU INC, LES
PLANTES ET DECORS VERONNEAU, LES
2965 Boul Le Corbusier, Montreal, QC, H7L 3M3
(450) 680-1989
Sales 22,275,600
SIC 5193 Flowers and florists supplies
Guy Veronneau

D-U-N-S 25-690-2230   (SL)
PLASTIQUES MULTICAP INC, LES
3232 Rue Delaunay, Montreal, QC, H7L 5E1
(450) 681-1661
Emp Here 40   *Sales* 11,066,400
SIC 2821 Plastics materials and resins
Salvatore Nicastro

D-U-N-S 24-401-3751   (SL)
PLOMBERIE DANIEL COTE INC
3000 Montee Saint-Aubin, Montreal, QC, H7L 3N8
(450) 973-2545
Emp Here 133   *Sales* 30,997,645
SIC 1711 Plumbing, heating, air-conditioning
Daniel Cote
Benoit Malouin
Marie-Claude Lebeuf
Cote Jeremie

D-U-N-S 20-363-1049   (SL)
PRESTILUX INC
3537 Boul Le Corbusier, Montreal, QC, H7L 4Z4
(450) 963-5096
Emp Here 50   *Sales* 55,267,250
SIC 5122 Drugs, proprietaries, and sundries
Francois Carlier

D-U-N-S 20-230-9340   (SL)
PRODUITS ALIMENTAIRES BERTHELET INC
1805 Rue Berlier, Montreal, QC, H7L 3S4
(514) 334-5503
Emp Here 100   *Sales* 34,569,000
SIC 2034 Dried and dehydrated fruits, vegeta-bles and soup mixes

Guy Berthelet
Serge Racette
Danny Berthelet
Dominique Berthelet
Marcel Ostiguy
Pierre Berthelet

D-U-N-S 20-107-2407   (HQ)
PRODUITS INTEGRES AVIOR INC
1001 Nord Laval (A-440) O Bureau 200, Montreal, QC, H7L 3W3
(450) 629-6200
Emp Here 40   *Sales* 72,712,500
SIC 3728 Aircraft parts and equipment, nec
Stephen Kearns
Karanjit S. Dulat
Alexander Smirnow
Pierre Racine
Cynthia Z Brighton
Howard L. Romanow
Guy Boutin

D-U-N-S 20-988-0702   (SL)
PROGESYS INC
4020 Boul Le Corbusier Bureau 201, Montreal, QC, H7L 5R2
(450) 667-7646
Emp Here 50   *Sales* 11,895,050
SIC 8742 Management consulting services
Riad Faour
Joel Gaudreault

D-U-N-S 20-886-4520   (HQ)
REGULVAR INC
3985 Boul Industriel, Montreal, QC, H7L 4S3
(450) 629-0435
Emp Here 40   *Sales* 168,266,850
SIC 5084 Industrial machinery and equipment
Yves Harel
Marc Dugre
Benoit Gohier
Michel Harel
Andre Harel
Johanne Quevillon

D-U-N-S 20-544-1827   (HQ)
SERVICE & CONSTRUCTION MOBILE LTEE
MOBILE SERVICE & CONSTRUCTION
1820 Place Martenot Bureau 383, Montreal, QC, H7L 5B5
(514) 383-5752
Sales 24,618,600
SIC 1799 Special trade contractors, nec
Reginald Tremblay

D-U-N-S 20-316-3514   (SL)
SERVICES BIOANALYTIQUES BIOTRIAL INC
(*Suby of* BIOTRIAL RESEARCH)
3885 Boul Industriel, Montreal, QC, H7L 4S3
(450) 663-6724
Emp Here 60   *Sales* 13,785,240
SIC 8731 Commercial physical research
Jean-Marc Gandon

D-U-N-S 24-422-9261   (SL)
SIGNA + INC
975 Rue Bergar, Montreal, QC, H7L 4Z6
(450) 668-0047
Emp Here 45   *Sales* 20,214,855
SIC 7389 Business services, nec
Francis Jeannotte
Domenico Cammaleri
Judith Dagenais

D-U-N-S 24-179-4429   (HQ)
SILHOUET-TONE CORPORATION
DISTRIBUTION SOMAK
1985 Rue Monterey, Montreal, QC, H7L 3T6
(450) 688-0123
Emp Here 40   *Sales* 35,874,960
SIC 3999 Manufacturing industries, nec
Eric Ghedin
Alphonse Ghedin

D-U-N-S 25-504-1329   (SL)

SOMAK INTERNATIONAL INC
1985 Rue Monterey, Montreal, QC, H7L 3T6
(450) 688-0123
Emp Here 30   *Sales* 33,160,350
SIC 5122 Drugs, proprietaries, and sundries
Eric Ghedin

D-U-N-S 24-402-8395   (SL)
VIANDES BOVITENDRES INC
95 Rue De La Pointe-Langlois, Montreal, QC, H7L 3J4
(450) 663-4375
Emp Here 18   *Sales* 15,040,386
SIC 5147 Meats and meat products
Denis Ardouin

D-U-N-S 24-338-0875   (SL)
VIANDES OR-FIL INTERNATIONAL INC, LES
(*Suby of* 9153-9460 QUEBEC INC)
2080 Rue Monterey, Montreal, QC, H7L 3S3
(450) 687-5664
Emp Here 500   *Sales* 41,778,850
SIC 5147 Meats and meat products
Antonio Filice
Bernard Paquette
Mario Cote
Daniel Daigle

Montreal, QC H7M

D-U-N-S 25-966-5099   (SL)
AUTO SENATEUR INC
VIMONT TOYOTA LAVAL
255 Boul Saint-Martin E, Montreal, QC, H7M 1Z1
(450) 663-2020
Emp Here 70   *Sales* 44,049,600
SIC 5511 New and used car dealers
Christian Dagenais
Louis-Carl Dagenais

D-U-N-S 20-215-8820   (HQ)
CYRS LTEE
1789 Boul Des Laurentides, Montreal, QC, H7M 2P7

Emp Here 50   *Sales* 12,557,720
SIC 5621 Women's clothing stores
Esther Avrith

D-U-N-S 25-779-5203   (SL)
D B D AUTO INC
DESMEULES HUYNDAI
1215 Boul Des Laurentides, Montreal, QC, H7M 2Y1
(450) 668-6393
Emp Here 26   *Sales* 12,950,028
SIC 5511 New and used car dealers
Claude Desmeules

D-U-N-S 20-910-4736   (SL)
ENTREPRISES J.G GUIMOND INC, LES
143 Rue De La Station, Montreal, QC, H7M 3W1
(450) 663-7155
Emp Here 50   *Sales* 23,536,550
SIC 1542 Nonresidential construction, nec
Jean-Guy Guimond

Montreal, QC H7N

D-U-N-S 24-325-2780   (SL)
ALIMENTATION R DENIS INC
MAGASIN PROVIGO
255 Boul De La Concorde O, Montreal, QC, H7N 5T1
(450) 668-0793
Emp Here 75   *Sales* 22,010,775
SIC 5411 Grocery stores
Robert Denis

D-U-N-S 24-321-9540   (SL)
CANTIN, DENIS R LTEE
CANADIAN TIRE #300
1450 Boul Le Corbusier, Montreal, QC, H7N 6J5
(450) 682-9922
Emp Here 150   *Sales* 30,801,450
SIC 5311 Department stores
Denis Cantin

D-U-N-S 20-534-6500   (SL)
COLLEGE LETENDRE
1000 Boul De L'Avenir, Montreal, QC, H7N 6J6
(450) 688-9933
Emp Here 100   *Sales* 11,263,600
SIC 8221 Colleges and universities
Yves Legault
Andre Pelletier
Liette Gadbois

D-U-N-S 24-249-9973   (SL)
GROUPE PREMIER MEDICAL INC
2 Place Laval Bureau 250, Montreal, QC, H7N 5N6
(450) 667-7737
Emp Here 26   *Sales* 15,078,024
SIC 6411 Insurance agents, brokers, and service
Frank Devito
Mario Gosselin

D-U-N-S 20-003-8862   (BR)
HOME DEPOT OF CANADA INC
HOME DEPOT
(*Suby of* THE HOME DEPOT INC)
1400 Boul Le Corbusier, Montreal, QC, H7N 6J5
(450) 680-2225
Emp Here 100
SIC 5251 Hardware stores
Michel Cote

Montreal, QC H7P

D-U-N-S 20-164-6119   (SL)
2747-8353 QUEBEC INC
DISTRIBUTIONS CHRISTIAN DUGAS
530 Place Forand, Montreal, QC, H7P 5L9
(450) 622-0070
Emp Here 50   *Sales* 41,778,850
SIC 5143 Dairy products, except dried or canned
Christian Dugas

D-U-N-S 25-826-1155   (SL)
3097-8217 QUEBEC INC
PHARMACIE JEAN COUTU
3475 Boul Dagenais O Bureau 119, Montreal, QC, H7P 4V9
(450) 963-0846
Emp Here 50   *Sales* 12,647,700
SIC 5912 Drug stores and proprietary stores
Nicolas Rompre

D-U-N-S 24-853-4831   (SL)
3609022 CANADA INC
4155 Chomedey (A-13) E, Montreal, QC, H7P 0A8
(450) 628-4488
Emp Here 75   *Sales* 38,164,200
SIC 5021 Furniture
David Berger
Ronald Leader

D-U-N-S 20-015-3174   (SL)
4069838 CANADA INC
SEGUIN NAUD VENTES & MARKETING
2750 Av Jacques-Bureau, Montreal, QC, H7P 6B3
(450) 681-0400
Emp Here 26   *Sales* 21,725,002
SIC 5141 Groceries, general line
Robert Naud
Andre Seguin

D-U-N-S 20-267-2911   (SL)
9273743 CANADA INC
CONSULTANTS A.G.I.R.
(*Suby of* CAPITAL REGIONAL ET COOPERATIF DESJARDINS)
4141 Nord Laval (A-440) O Bureau 200, Montreal, QC, H7P 4W6
(450) 973-8808
Emp Here 95   *Sales* 21,704,840
SIC 4899 Communication services, nec
Andre Heroux
Christian Paupe

D-U-N-S 24-020-4867   (SL)
9314-0887 QUEBEC INC
(*Suby of* SIMARD-BEAUDRY CONSTRUCTION INC)
4300 Boul Saint-Elzear O, Montreal, QC, H7P 4J4
(450) 622-5448
Emp Here 425
SIC 6712 Bank holding companies
Antonio Accurso

D-U-N-S 20-277-9153   (SL)
BASSE FRERES ALIMENTATION ORIENTALE (2013) INC
BASSE NUTS
4555 Nord Laval (A-440) O, Montreal, QC, H7P 4W6
(450) 781-1255
Emp Here 26   *Sales* 21,725,002
SIC 5145 Confectionery
Maurice Benisti
Nicole Benisti

D-U-N-S 25-364-8216   (HQ)
BSN MEDICAL INC
(*Suby of* ESSITY AB (PUBL))
4455 Nord Laval (A-440) O Unite 255, Montreal, QC, H7P 4W6
(450) 978-0738
Emp Here 38   *Sales* 61,565,480
SIC 5047 Medical and hospital equipment
Sylvie Bertrand
Joseph Carpinelli
Todd Healy

D-U-N-S 20-197-4839   (SL)
C.A. SPENCER INC
(*Suby of* CASLUMBER INC)
2930 Boul Dagenais O, Montreal, QC, H7P 1T1
(450) 622-2420
Emp Here 125   *Sales* 71,203,500
SIC 5031 Lumber, plywood, and millwork
Claude Cadrin
Michel Ferron
Pierre Cadrin

D-U-N-S 24-569-5671   (HQ)
CASLUMBER INC
C.A. SPENCER
2885 Boul Dagenais O, Montreal, QC, H7P 1T2
(450) 622-2420
Sales 45,688,625
SIC 6712 Bank holding companies
Claude Cadrin
Michel Ferron
Pierre Cadrin

D-U-N-S 24-741-2653   (SL)
CENTRE D'EVALUATION & READAPTION PHYSIQUE C.E.R.P. INC
CENTRE DE MEDECINE SPORTIVE DE LAVAL ET PHYSIO PLUS
3095 Nord Laval (A-440) O, Montreal, QC, H7P 4W5
(450) 688-0445
Emp Here 45   *Sales* 16,255,665
SIC 8049 Offices of health practitioner
Josee Morin

D-U-N-S 20-266-1435   (SL)
CHOMEDEY/DESLAURIERS FORD LINCOLN INC
440 FORD LINCOLN

(*Suby of* GESTION SYLVAIN HOGUES LTEE)
2705 Boul Chomedey, Montreal, QC, H7P 0C2
(450) 666-3673
Emp Here 110   *Sales* 69,220,800
SIC 5511 New and used car dealers
Sylvain Hogues
Serge Boucher

   D-U-N-S 25-999-7237   (SL)
CONSTRUCTION G-NESIS INC
4915 Rue Louis-B.-Mayer, Montreal, QC, H7P 0E5
(514) 370-8303
Emp Here 49   *Sales* 11,803,316
SIC 1623 Water, sewer, and utility lines
Stephane Chaumont
Sabrina Giguere
Marcel Fortier

   D-U-N-S 25-103-6067   (SL)
CONSTRUCTION SOTER INC
EQUIPEMENTS SOTER
4915 Rue Louis-B.-Mayer, Montreal, QC, H7P 0E5
(450) 664-2818
Emp Here 49   *Sales* 15,624,581
SIC 1521 Single-family housing construction
Patrick Francoeur

   D-U-N-S 20-533-1775   (BR)
COSTCO WHOLESALE CANADA LTD
(*Suby of* COSTCO WHOLESALE CORPORATION)
2999 Nord Laval A-440 O, Montreal, QC, H7P 5P4
(450) 686-7420
Emp Here 150
SIC 5099 Durable goods, nec
Louis Samtillo

   D-U-N-S 25-780-8865   (SL)
ENTREPRISES LAMCOIL INC, LES
2748 Boul Daniel-Johnson, Montreal, QC, H7P 5Z7
(450) 682-4444
Emp Here 29   *Sales* 12,861,210
SIC 7389 Business services, nec
Patrick L'Ecuyer
Patrick Robillard

   D-U-N-S 24-373-2422   (BR)
FGL SPORTS LTD
(*Suby of* CANADIAN TIRE CORPORATION, LIMITED)
4855 Rue Louis-B.-Mayer, Montreal, QC, H7P 6C8
(450) 687-5200
Emp Here 187
SIC 5941 Sporting goods and bicycle shops
Jean-Stephane Tremblay

   D-U-N-S 25-509-6877   (HQ)
FROMAGERIE DES NATIONS INC
3535 Nord Laval (A-440) O Unite 440, Montreal, QC, H7P 5G9
(450) 682-3862
Emp Here 25   *Sales* 41,778,850
SIC 5143 Dairy products, except dried or canned
Jeff Joly

   D-U-N-S 20-294-1873   (HQ)
GA INTERNATIONAL INC
LABTAG
3208 Av Jacques-Bureau, Montreal, QC, H7P 0A9
(450) 973-9420
Emp Here 28   *Sales* 14,949,660
SIC 5131 Piece goods and notions
Gourgen Ambartsoumian

   D-U-N-S 24-858-0698   (SL)
GARANTIES NATIONALES MRWV LIMITEE, LES
GARANTIE NATIONALE
4605 Rue Louis-B.-Mayer, Montreal, QC, H7P 6G5
(450) 688-9496
Emp Here 15   *Sales* 10,881,585

SIC 6399 Insurance carriers, nec
Gregory Veilleux
Amelie Cantin
Jennifer Dibblee
Denis Picard

   D-U-N-S 24-510-1407   (HQ)
GEROQUIP INC
4795 Rue Louis-B.-Mayer, Montreal, QC, H7P 6G5
(450) 978-0200
Emp Here 34   *Sales* 16,545,438
SIC 5039 Construction materials, nec
Alain Dion
Wayne Murray

   D-U-N-S 20-549-2486   (SL)
GRAND MARCHE COL-FAX INC
COL-FAX
3699 Nord Laval (A-440) O, Montreal, QC, H7P 5P6
(450) 688-7773
Emp Here 60   *Sales* 17,608,620
SIC 5411 Grocery stores
Dimitrios Tsiolis
Anastasios Tsiolis
Konstandina Moutsos

   D-U-N-S 20-737-6591   (HQ)
GSF CANADA INC
(*Suby of* GROUPE SERVICES FRANCE)
4705 Rue Louis-B.-Mayer, Montreal, QC, H7P 6G5
(450) 686-0555
Sales 59,136,723
SIC 7349 Building maintenance services, nec
Marcel Langelier
Francois Leforestier
Christophe Cognee
Jean-Louis Noisiez

   D-U-N-S 25-106-8607   (HQ)
INDULBEC INC
CONFISERIE SWEET FACTORY, LA
(*Suby of* FRANCHISES I.C.I. INC, LES)
3625 Boul Cure-Labelle Bureau 100, Montreal, QC, H7P 0A5
(450) 689-5726
Emp Here 5   *Sales* 20,889,425
SIC 5145 Confectionery
Michele Jamet

   D-U-N-S 20-240-3044   (SL)
MOTOCYCLETTES & ARTICLES DE SPORTS PONT-VIAU INC
HARLEY-DAVIDSON LAVAL
4501 Nord Laval (A-440) O, Montreal, QC, H7P 4W6
(450) 973-4501
Emp Here 25   *Sales* 15,732,000
SIC 5571 Motorcycle dealers
Jean Guy Groulx

   D-U-N-S 25-686-7995   (HQ)
NORDIA INC
(*Suby of* PLATINUM EQUITY, LLC)
3020 Av Jacques-Bureau 2e Etage, Montreal, QC, H7P 6G2
(514) 415-7088
Emp Here 35   *Sales* 1,471,597,600
SIC 7389 Business services, nec
John Di Nardo
Guy Neveu
Paul R. Henry
Lucio Milanovich

   D-U-N-S 24-826-3357   (SL)
NORSECO INC
HORTICLUB
2914 Boul Cure-Labelle, Montreal, QC, H7P 5R9
(514) 332-2275
Emp Here 30   *Sales* 15,960,420
SIC 5191 Farm supplies
Bruno Dubuc
Christian Chartrand
Marie-Claude Caron
Ruckstuhl Christine

   D-U-N-S 25-896-2922   (SL)
PROAX TECHNOLOGIES LTEE
3505 Rue John-Pratt, Montreal, QC, H7P 0C9
(450) 902-5900
Emp Here 35   *Sales* 15,722,665
SIC 7389 Business services, nec
Stephen Murray Daub

   D-U-N-S 25-428-7654   (SL)
SERVICES EXP INC, LES
(*Suby of* EXP GLOBAL INC)
4500 Rue Louis-B.-Mayer, Montreal, QC, H7P 6E4
(450) 682-8013
Emp Here 49   *Sales* 10,796,072
SIC 8734 Testing laboratories
Jean Bellesleur

   D-U-N-S 24-138-8870   (SL)
SIMPLE CONCEPT INC
BONE STRUCTURE MD
2812 Rue Joseph-A.-Bombardier, Montreal, QC, H7P 6E2
(450) 978-0602
Emp Here 50   *Sales* 11,369,150
SIC 1751 Carpentry work
Marc-Andre Bovet
Michelle Tremblay

   D-U-N-S 20-253-5217   (BR)
SONEPAR CANADA INC
LUMEN
(*Suby of* SOCIETE DE NEGOCE ET DE PARTICIPATION)
4655 Nord Laval (A-440) O, Montreal, QC, H7P 5P9
(450) 688-9249
Emp Here 210
SIC 5063 Electrical apparatus and equipment
Roland Cadieux

   D-U-N-S 20-501-6942   (HQ)
SPECIALITES MONARCH INC, LES
4155 Chomedey (A-13) E, Montreal, QC, H7P 0A8
(450) 628-4488
Sales 38,164,200
SIC 5021 Furniture
David Berger

   D-U-N-S 20-999-9887   (SL)
SUGI CANADA LTEE
FAIRWAY GOLF
3255 Rue Jules-Brillant, Montreal, QC, H7P 6C9
Emp Here 35   *Sales* 17,441,270
SIC 5139 Footwear
Yves Pare

   D-U-N-S 20-915-3175   (BR)
WOLSELEY CANADA INC
(*Suby of* FERGUSON PLC)
4200 Rue Louis-B.-Mayer, Montreal, QC, H7P 0G1
(450) 680-4040
Emp Here 220
SIC 5075 Warm air heating and air conditioning
Sebastien Laforge

Montreal, QC H7R

   D-U-N-S 25-284-5508   (SL)
CLUB LAVAL-SUR-LE-LAC, LE
150 Rue Les Peupliers, Montreal, QC, H7R 1G4
(450) 627-2643
Emp Here 100   *Sales* 7,854,500
SIC 7992 Public golf courses
Remi Racine
Luc Martin
Luc Lapointe
Francois Tellier

   D-U-N-S 25-823-0606   (SL)
PHARMACIE NICOLAS CARBONNEAU INC
JEAN COUTU
4515 Boul Arthur-Sauve, Montreal, QC, H7R 5P8
(450) 962-7455
Emp Here 49   *Sales* 12,394,746
SIC 5912 Drug stores and proprietary stores
Nicolas Carbonneau

Montreal, QC H7S

   D-U-N-S 20-125-2926   (SL)
2945-9609 QUEBEC INC
CENTURY 21 MAX-IMMO
1850 Boul Le Corbusier 200, Montreal, QC, H7S 2N5
(450) 682-4666
Emp Here 120   *Sales* 50,266,680
SIC 6531 Real estate agents and managers
Andre Charbonneau

   D-U-N-S 20-554-7474   (HQ)
ALLIANCE DE L'INDUSTRIE TOURISTIQUE DU QUEBEC
ALLIANCE
1575 Boul De L'Avenir Bureau 330, Montreal, QC, H7S 2N5
(450) 686-8358
Emp Here 10   *Sales* 11,679,694
SIC 7389 Business services, nec
Eric Larouche
Randa Napky
Priscilla Nemey
Andre Nollet
Marc Plourde
Jean-Michel Ryan
Benoit Sirard
Manuela Teixeira
Martin Soucy
Patrice Malo

   D-U-N-S 20-320-1681   (HQ)
CAPITAL DESSAU INC
(*Suby of* GROUPE DESSAU INC)
1200 Boul Saint-Martin O Bureau 300, Montreal, QC, H7S 2E4
(514) 281-1010
Emp Here 7   *Sales* 279,759,000
SIC 8742 Management consulting services
Marc Verreault
Jacques Chouinard
Nancy Cournoyer

   D-U-N-S 24-337-2716   (BR)
CASCADES CANADA ULC
CASCADES GROUPE TISSUS LAVAL
(*Suby of* CASCADES INC)
2345 Des Laurentides (A-15) E, Montreal, QC, H7S 1Z7
(450) 688-1152
Emp Here 75
SIC 2676 Sanitary paper products
Mate Mevica

   D-U-N-S 20-214-9480   (SL)
CLERMONT, MARIETTE INC
MARIETTE CLERMONT MEUBLE
2300 Boul Le Corbusier, Montreal, QC, H7S 2C9
(450) 934-7502
Emp Here 45   *Sales* 10,365,300
SIC 5712 Furniture stores
Jean-Francois Clermont

   D-U-N-S 24-523-3841   (BR)
CORPORATION A.U.B. INC
AUBAINERIE CONCEPT MODE GALERIES LAVAL
(*Suby of* CORPORATION A.U.B. INC)
1605 Boul Le Corbusier, Montreal, QC, H7S 1Z3
(450) 681-3317
Emp Here 90

▲ Public Company   ■ Public Company Family Member   **HQ** Headquarters   **BR** Branch   **SL** Single Location

SIC 5651 Family clothing stores
Lime Boulanger

D-U-N-S 24-092-3466   (HQ)
CORPORATION DES ALIMENTS I-D
1800 Sud Laval (A-440) O, Montreal, QC, H7S 2E7
(450) 687-2680
Emp Here 200   *Sales* 197,096,900
SIC 5141 Groceries, general line
Philip Issenman
Bernard Issenman
Robert Issenman

D-U-N-S 24-429-6398   (HQ)
DESSAU INC
(Suby of GROUPE DESSAU INC)
1200 Boul Saint-Martin O Bureau 300, Montreal, QC, H7S 2E4
(514) 281-1010
Emp Here 150   *Sales* 876,578,200
SIC 8742 Management consulting services
Marc Verreault
Jacques Chouinard
Nancy Cournoyer

D-U-N-S 25-845-3232   (HQ)
DISTINCTIVE APPLIANCES INC
ELECTRO-MENAGERS DISTINCTIVE
2025 Rue Cunard, Montreal, QC, H7S 2N1
(450) 687-6311
Sales 45,112,800
SIC 5064 Electrical appliances, television and radio
Jacques Amiel
Pierre Mailloux

D-U-N-S 24-092-8031   (BR)
ELECTRO SAGUENAY INC
(Suby of ELECTRO SAGUENAY LTEE)
1555 Boul De L'Avenir Bureau 306, Montreal, QC, H7S 2N5

Emp Here 75
SIC 4899 Communication services, nec
Jean-Pierre Fleury

D-U-N-S 20-193-6056   (HQ)
ERGORECHERCHE LTEE
2101 Boul Le Carrefour Bureau 200, Montreal, QC, H7S 2J7
(450) 973-6700
Sales 10,435,964
SIC 3842 Surgical appliances and supplies
Sylvain Boucher
Danielle Boucher
Frederic Petit
Louis Desrosiers
Michel Pierron
Francois Tellier
Catherine Chamouton
Gilles Laporte

D-U-N-S 24-676-0375   (BR)
G2MC INC
LA MAISON DU MEUBLE CORBEIL
(Suby of G2MC INC)
2323 Des Laurentides (A-15) E, Montreal, QC, H7S 1Z7
(450) 682-3022
Emp Here 100
SIC 5712 Furniture stores
Mathieu Desjardins

D-U-N-S 25-976-1377   (HQ)
GROUPE DESSAU INC
1200 Boul Saint-Martin O Bureau 300, Montreal, QC, H7S 2E4
(514) 281-1010
Emp Here 500   *Sales* 2,193,054,000
SIC 6712 Bank holding companies
Marc Verreault
Jacques Chouinard
Paul Lefrancois
Francois Dionne
Nancy Cournoyer

D-U-N-S 20-125-0441   (HQ)

GROUPE SUTTON EXCELLENCE INC
1555 Boul De L'Avenir Bureau 100, Montreal, QC, H7S 2N5
(450) 662-3036
Sales 62,833,350
SIC 6531 Real estate agents and managers
Julie Gaucher

D-U-N-S 20-917-8800   (SL)
GTC (MEDIA)-HEBDO COURRIER LAVAL
2700 Av Francis-Hughes Bureau 200, Montreal, QC, H7S 2B9
(450) 667-4360
Emp Here 60   *Sales* 44,551,200
SIC 5192 Books, periodicals, and newspapers
Rejean Monette

D-U-N-S 24-311-4183   (SL)
I-D BEVERAGES INC
1800 Sud Laval (A-440) O, Montreal, QC, H7S 2E7
(450) 687-2680
Emp Here 49   *Sales* 23,276,274
SIC 5084 Industrial machinery and equipment
Philip Issenman

D-U-N-S 20-540-4684   (SL)
LABORATOIRE COULEUR UNIVERSEL INC
810 Rue Salaberry, Montreal, QC, H7S 1H3
(514) 384-2251
Emp Here 30   *Sales* 12,525,180
SIC 7384 Photofinish laboratories
Martin Wirshofter

D-U-N-S 24-274-5615   (HQ)
LABORATOIRE VICTHOM INC
CLINIQUE DU PIED EQUILIBRE
(Suby of ERGORECHERCHE LTEE)
2101 Boul Le Carrefour Bureau 102, Montreal, QC, H7S 2J7
(450) 239-6162
Sales 17,772,800
SIC 8069 Specialty hospitals, except psychiatric
Sylvain Boucher
Danielle Boucher
Gilles Laporte

D-U-N-S 25-194-5150   (HQ)
LVM INC
CPI CORROSION
(Suby of GROUPE DESSAU INC)
1200 Boul Saint-Martin O Bureau 300, Montreal, QC, H7S 2E4
(514) 281-1010
Emp Here 75   *Sales* 279,759,000
SIC 8742 Management consulting services
Marc Verreault
Jacques Chouinard
Nancy Cournoyer

D-U-N-S 25-212-6107   (HQ)
METRA ALUMINIUM INC
METRA SYSTEMS
(Suby of METRA HOLDING SPA)
2000 Boul Fortin, Montreal, QC, H7S 1P3
(450) 629-4260
Sales 18,138,800
SIC 3355 Aluminum rolling and drawing, nec
Mario Bertoli
Richard Laramee
Alessandro Biava Giacomelli
Enrico Zampedri

D-U-N-S 20-332-7093   (SL)
MONTAGE SAINT-LAURENT INC
807 Rue Marshall, Montreal, QC, H7S 1J9
(450) 786-1792
Emp Here 100   *Sales* 24,618,600
SIC 1791 Structural steel erection
Benoit Drouin
Jean-Rene Drouin
Marc O'connor
Rene Guizzetti
Louis Guertin
Marcel Dutil

D-U-N-S 20-194-2869   (SL)

OIL-DRI CANADA ULC
COMPAGNIE DE PRODUITS FAVORITE, LA
(Suby of OIL-DRI CORPORATION OF AMERICA)
730 Rue Salaberry, Montreal, QC, H7S 1H3
(450) 663-5750
Emp Here 60   *Sales* 29,263,800
SIC 5085 Industrial supplies
Daniel S. Jaffee
Richard M. Jaffee
Daniel T Smith
Douglas A Graham
Laura G. Scheland
Jeffrey M Libert
Daniel J Jones

D-U-N-S 24-812-1709   (SL)
PRODUITS PLASTITEL INC, LES
GROUPE PLASTITEL
2604 Rue Debray, Montreal, QC, H7S 2J8
(450) 687-0060
Emp Here 50   *Sales* 10,094,850
SIC 3089 Plastics products, nec
Denis Deshaies
Stephane Poirier
Michael Pouliot

D-U-N-S 24-762-9975   (BR)
PROVIGO DISTRIBUTION INC
(Suby of LOBLAW COMPANIES LIMITED)
2700 Av Francis-Hughes Bureau 2172, Montreal, QC, H7S 2B9
(514) 383-8800
Emp Here 350
SIC 4225 General warehousing and storage

D-U-N-S 24-363-0907   (BR)
RGIS CANADA ULC
(Suby of THE BLACKSTONE GROUP L P)
1882 Boul Saint-Martin O Bureau 200, Montreal, QC, H7S 1M9

Emp Here 100
SIC 7389 Business services, nec
Nicole Marcheterre

D-U-N-S 25-286-1943   (BR)
RONA INC
RENO-DEPOT DE LAVAL
(Suby of LOWE'S COMPANIES, INC.)
1505 Boul Le Corbusier, Montreal, QC, H7S 1Z3
(450) 682-2220
Emp Here 100
SIC 5251 Hardware stores
Luc Guteau

D-U-N-S 20-033-6665   (SL)
TRIMAX SECURITE INC
1965 Boul Industriel Bureau 200, Montreal, QC, H7S 1P6
(450) 934-5200
Emp Here 50   *Sales* 22,174,500
SIC 7389 Business services, nec
Daniel Filteau
Ezio Turrin
Frederico Ramos

D-U-N-S 20-243-5244   (HQ)
VERREAULT INC
CONSORTIUM POMERLEAU VERREAULT ACCIONA
(Suby of GROUPE DESSAU INC)
1200 Boul Saint-Martin O Bureau 300, Montreal, QC, H7S 2E4
(514) 845-4104
Sales 83,269,348
SIC 1542 Nonresidential construction, nec
Marc Verreault
Jacques Chouinard
Nancy Cournoyer

D-U-N-S 25-308-0519   (BR)
VILLE DE LAVAL
TRAVAUX PUBLICS
(Suby of VILLE DE LAVAL)
2550 Boul Industriel, Montreal, QC, H7S 2G7

(450) 662-4600
Emp Here 300
SIC 4953 Refuse systems

D-U-N-S 24-005-1339   (SL)
VOYAGES TRADITOURS INC
TRADITOURS
1575 Boul De L'Avenir Bureau 100, Montreal, QC, H7S 2N5
(514) 907-7712
Emp Here 70   *Sales* 46,682,440
SIC 4724 Travel agencies
Eric Doyon
Sebastien Forest
Guy Bessette
Jacques Rodier
Gilles Genest
Mathieu Cloutier
Stephane Gagne

Montreal, QC H7W

D-U-N-S 24-371-6342   (SL)
4128001 CANADA INC
MOURELATOS SUPERMAKET
4919 Boul Notre-Dame, Montreal, QC, H7W 1V3
(450) 681-4300
Emp Here 50   *Sales* 13,707,600
SIC 5411 Grocery stores
Efthymios Mourelatos

D-U-N-S 24-346-6070   (SL)
9168-9406 QUEBEC INC
AMIR KITCHEN
1033 Chomedey (A-13) E, Montreal, QC, H7W 4V3
(450) 668-5888
Emp Here 29   *Sales* 24,231,733
SIC 5147 Meats and meat products
Nicole Zreik
Leila Zreik

D-U-N-S 25-794-7291   (SL)
CORPORATION DU CENTRE DU SABLON INC
CENTRE DU SABLON
755 Ch Du Sablon, Montreal, QC, H7W 4H5
(450) 688-8961
Emp Here 75   *Sales* 5,131,650
SIC 8322 Individual and family services
Pierre Fontaine
Brian Tracey

D-U-N-S 25-984-3790   (SL)
GENSCI OCF INC
1105 Chomedey (A-13) E, Montreal, QC, H7W 5J8
(450) 688-8699
Emp Here 25   *Sales* 11,179,350
SIC 5047 Medical and hospital equipment
Uwe Tritthardt

D-U-N-S 24-697-4364   (HQ)
GLORY GLOBAL SOLUTIONS (CANADA) INC
GLORY SOLUTIONS GLOBALES CANADA
(Suby of GLORY LTD.)
1111 Chomedey (A-13) E Unite 200, Montreal, QC, H7W 5J8
(450) 686-8800
Emp Here 40   *Sales* 33,090,876
SIC 5044 Office equipment
Chris Reagan
Michael R. Henry

D-U-N-S 20-418-3966   (SL)
HUILES BERTRAND INC, LES
(Suby of 9026-1231 QUEBEC INC)
4949 Boul Levesque O, Montreal, QC, H7W 2R8
(450) 682-2845
Emp Here 10   *Sales* 12,572,010
SIC 5172 Petroleum products, nec
Robert Bertrand

▲ Public Company   ■ Public Company Family Member   **HQ** Headquarters   **BR** Branch   **SL** Single Location

D-U-N-S 25-095-0102   (SL)
ORUS INTEGRATION INC
AGT
1109 Chomedey (A-13) E, Montreal, QC, H7W 5J8

Emp Here 50   *Sales* 12,828,100
SIC 3823 Process control instruments
Francois Simard
Louis Dicaire

D-U-N-S 25-494-9787   (SL)
SIDEL CANADA INC
CERMEX CANADA
(*Suby of* TETRA LAVAL HOLDINGS B.V.)
1045 Chomedey (A-13) E, Montreal, QC, H7W 4V3
(450) 973-3337
Emp Here 210   *Sales* 58,984,170
SIC 3535 Conveyors and conveying equipment
Marc Aury
Stephane Banville
Mike Decotiis

Montreal, QC H7X

D-U-N-S 24-834-2602   (HQ)
BETAPLEX INC
132 Rue Principale, Montreal, QC, H7X 3V2
(450) 969-3300
Sales 14,664,600
SIC 1521 Single-family housing construction
Nazir Aridi

D-U-N-S 24-677-4616   (SL)
CENTRE DE LA PETITE ENFANCE LA GI-BOULEE
531 Rue Huberdeau, Montreal, QC, H7X 1P6
(450) 689-6442
Emp Here 75   *Sales* 4,580,175
SIC 8351 Child day care services
Sylvie Pilon

D-U-N-S 24-389-5252   (BR)
CENTRE DE SANTE ET DE SERVICES SOCIAUX DE LAVAL
CENTRE D'HEBERGEMENT SAINTE-DOROTHEE
(*Suby of* GOUVERNEMENT DE LA PROVINCE DE QUEBEC)
350 Boul Samson O, Montreal, QC, H7X 1J4
(450) 689-0933
Emp Here 300
SIC 8361 Residential care
Monique Menard

Montreal, QC H9P

D-U-N-S 25-244-9079   (SL)
HOMME ET SA MAISON LTEE, L'
SENTINEL ALARM
605 Av Marshall, Montreal, QC, H9P 1E1
(514) 737-1010
Emp Here 40   *Sales* 15,827,120
SIC 7382 Security systems services
Ivan Spector
Selma Spector
Norman Spector

Montreal-Est, QC H1B

D-U-N-S 20-420-9225   (SL)
3323501 CANADA INC
GALVAN METAL
8201 Place Marien, Montreal-Est, QC, H1B 5W6

(514) 322-9120
Emp Here 50   *Sales* 10,141,500
SIC 3479 Metal coating and allied services
John Mancuso
John Jr Mancuso
Joseph Mancuso

D-U-N-S 24-107-2107   (HQ)
BITUMAR INC
(*Suby of* PLACEMENTS BITUMAR INC, LES)
11155 Rue Sainte-Catherine E, Montreal-Est, QC, H1B 0A4
(514) 645-4561
Emp Here 35   *Sales* 49,997,360
SIC 2911 Petroleum refining
Jean Lussier
Daniel Theriault
Marc Theriault
Sylvain Ouellette

D-U-N-S 20-105-7952   (SL)
CHIMIE PARACHEM INC
3500 Av Broadway, Montreal-Est, QC, H1B 5B4
(514) 640-2200
Emp Here 65   *Sales* 43,724,135
SIC 1311 Crude petroleum and natural gas
Andre Brunelle
Dan Sorochan
Luc Seguin
Charles Boulanger
Denis Roy
Jean-Jacques Carrier
Myriam Murray-Levasseur

D-U-N-S 20-309-6735   (SL)
CHIMIE PARACHEM S.E.C.
CHIMIE PARACHEM
3500 Av Broadway, Montreal-Est, QC, H1B 5B4
(514) 640-2200
Emp Here 50   *Sales* 15,985,250
SIC 1311 Crude petroleum and natural gas
Pierre Barnes

D-U-N-S 20-216-3879   (HQ)
DE LUXE PRODUITS DE PAPIER INC
COFLEX PACKAGING DIV OF DLP
(*Suby of* OAK HILL CAPITAL PARTNERS, L.P.)
200 Av Marien, Montreal-Est, QC, H1B 4V2
(514) 645-4571
Emp Here 180   *Sales* 91,909,250
SIC 2671 Paper; coated and laminated packaging
Stan Bikulege
Alex E Washington
Robert Cummings
Paul Palmisano

D-U-N-S 20-217-2557   (HQ)
DUFORT ET LAVIGNE LTEE
(*Suby of* MEDLINE INDUSTRIES, INC.)
8581 Place Marien, Montreal-Est, QC, H1B 5W6
(514) 527-9381
Emp Here 94   *Sales* 44,717,400
SIC 5047 Medical and hospital equipment
Ernie Philip
Diane Reid
Antoine Chulia

D-U-N-S 20-013-7961   (SL)
ENTREPRISE INDORAMA PTA MONTREAL S.E.C
10200 Rue Sherbrooke E, Montreal-Est, QC, H1B 1B4
(514) 645-7887
Emp Here 145   *Sales* 41,183,045
SIC 2821 Plastics materials and resins
Michel Douville

D-U-N-S 24-581-9164   (HQ)
G.C.L. EQUIPEMENTS INC
PAYSAGES LAGAN
35 Av Laganiere, Montreal-Est, QC, H1B 5T1
(514) 640-0840
Sales 11,008,400

SIC 1794 Excavation work
Guy Laganiere
Denis Laganiere
Guylaine Laganiere

D-U-N-S 24-828-5538   (HQ)
GROUPE BMTC INC
BRAULT ET MARTINEAU
(*Suby of* BELANGER, A. (DETAIL) LTEE)
8500 Place Marien, Montreal-Est, QC, H1B 5W8
(514) 648-5757
Emp Here 10   *Sales* 552,706,117
SIC 6712 Bank holding companies
Yves Des Groseillers
Marie-Berthe Des Groseillers
Michele Des Groseillers
Tony Fionda
Gabriel Castiglio
Anne-Marie Leclair
Lucien Bouchard
Andre Berard
Charles Des Groseillers

D-U-N-S 24-896-4132   (BR)
NEXANS CANADA INC
(*Suby of* NEXANS)
460 Av Durocher, Montreal-Est, QC, H1B 5H6
(514) 645-2301
Emp Here 135
SIC 3366 Copper foundries
Carlos Sanchez

D-U-N-S 20-598-1363   (HQ)
PAPERCON CANADA HOLDING CORP
(*Suby of* OAK HILL CAPITAL PARTNERS, L.P.)
200 Av Marien, Montreal-Est, QC, H1B 4V2
(514) 645-4571
Emp Here 1   *Sales* 73,101,800
SIC 6712 Bank holding companies
Stan Bikulege

D-U-N-S 20-227-7323   (HQ)
PIPE-LINES MONTREAL LIMITEE, LES
10803 Rue Sherbrooke E, Montreal-Est, QC, H1B 1B3
(514) 645-8797
Emp Here 8   *Sales* 43,220,034
SIC 4612 Crude petroleum pipelines
Thomas A. Hardison
John Gillies
Daniel P. Sorochan
Myriam Murphy-Levasseur
John Doll
Glenn Peterson
Dietmar Kohlmann
William A. Jr. Sawyer
James B. Rose
Allen Mcintyre

D-U-N-S 24-353-0615   (HQ)
PLACEMENTS BITUMAR INC, LES
11155 Rue Sainte-Catherine E, Montreal-Est, QC, H1B 0A4
(514) 645-4561
Sales 11,671,750
SIC 2911 Petroleum refining
Jean Lussier
Sylvain Ouellette
Daniel Theriault
Marc Theriault

D-U-N-S 24-668-5861   (SL)
PLIMETAL INC
(*Suby of* ADOLFO PALUMBO INC)
8555 Place Marien, Montreal-Est, QC, H1B 5W6
(514) 648-2260
Emp Here 69   *Sales* 13,253,865
SIC 3469 Metal stampings, nec
Adolfo Palumbo
Michael Palumbo
Jonathan Palumbo
Christian Soucy

D-U-N-S 20-737-2251   (BR)

SHELL CANADA LIMITED
PRODUITS SHELL CANADA
(*Suby of* ROYAL DUTCH SHELL PLC)
10501 Rue Sherbrooke E, Montreal-Est, QC, H1B 1B3
(514) 645-1661
Emp Here 450
SIC 2911 Petroleum refining
Bob Berrd

D-U-N-S 24-760-2829   (SL)
SOCIETE EN COMMANDITE USINE DE SOUFRE SUNCOR MONTREAL
11450 Rue Cherrier, Montreal-Est, QC, H1B 1A6
(514) 645-1636
Emp Here 41   *Sales* 29,944,145
SIC 5169 Chemicals and allied products, nec
France Belanger

D-U-N-S 25-080-5850   (BR)
SODEM INC
CENTRE RECREATIF EDOUARD RIVET
(*Suby of* SODEM INC)
11111 Rue Notre-Dame E, Montreal-Est, QC, H1B 2V7
(514) 640-2737
Emp Here 75
SIC 7999 Amusement and recreation, nec
Helene Michau

D-U-N-S 20-220-0598   (HQ)
USINES GIANT INC
11021 Rue Notre-Dame E, Montreal-Est, QC, H1B 2V5
(514) 645-8893
Sales 66,485,025
SIC 3639 Household appliances, nec
Claude Lesage
Lise Lesage
Jean-Claude Lesage

Montreal-Est, QC H1E

D-U-N-S 25-661-7817   (SL)
A I M QUEBEC
9100 Boul Henri-Bourassa E, Montreal-Est, QC, H1E 2S4
(514) 648-3883
Emp Here 49   *Sales* 10,105,826
SIC 3471 Plating and polishing
Hurbert Black

D-U-N-S 24-417-0747   (HQ)
AIM METAUX & ALLIAGES INC
9100 Boul Henri-Bourassa E, Montreal-Est, QC, H1E 2S4
(514) 494-2000
Sales 187,113,219
SIC 6712 Bank holding companies
Richard Black
Ronald Black
Herbert Black

D-U-N-S 24-354-1468   (HQ)
AIM METAUX & ALLIAGES S.E.C.
9100 Boul Henri-Bourassa E, Montreal-Est, QC, H1E 2S4
(514) 494-2000
Sales 84,638,298
SIC 3399 Primary Metal products
Richard Black

D-U-N-S 20-209-7986   (HQ)
COMPAGNIE AMERICAINE DE FER & METAUX INC, LA
AIM RECYCLAGE
9100 Boul Henri-Bourassa E, Montreal-Est, QC, H1E 2S4
(514) 494-2000
Emp Here 450   *Sales* 814,348,000
SIC 3341 Secondary nonferrous Metals
Herbert Black
Ronald Black
Zannella Lucianna

Montreal-Est, QC H1L

D-U-N-S 24-580-4885   (HQ)
GROUPE PETROLIER OLCO ULC
GROUPE PETROLIER OLCO, LE
(*Suby of* ARCLIGHT CAPITAL HOLDINGS, LLC)
2775 Av Georges-V, Montreal-Est, QC, H1L 6J7
(514) 645-6526
Emp Here 85   *Sales* 290,839,158
SIC 5172 Petroleum products, nec
Jack Trykoski
Richard Pouliot
Georges Karawani
Kamil Khan
Erik B Carlson
Randall O'connor

D-U-N-S 24-894-0231   (HQ)
INTERTEK TESTING SERVICES (ITS) CANADA LTD
(*Suby of* INTERTEK GROUP PLC)
2561 Av Georges-V, Montreal-Est, QC, H1L 6S4
(514) 640-6332
Emp Here 25   *Sales* 71,428,700
SIC 8731 Commercial physical research
Andre Lacroix
Joe Keating
Anthony Mcglynn
Gregg Tiemann

D-U-N-S 20-693-5632   (HQ)
MANASTE INSPECTION QUALITY QUANTITY (CANADA) INC
BUREAU VERITAS - INSPECTORATE
9756 Rue Notre-Dame E, Montreal-Est, QC, H1L 3R4
(514) 645-5554
Sales 10,399,340
SIC 4785 Inspection and fixed facilities
Kevin Somers
Laurence Hayden
Barry Benton
Robert Squires
Joe Gravino

D-U-N-S 24-970-9528   (SL)
TRANSPORT LYON INC
A AB ACTION ADMINISTRATION
9999 Rue Notre-Dame E, Montreal-Est, QC, H1L 3R5
(514) 322-4422
Emp Here 80   *Sales* 11,855,360
SIC 4214 Local trucking with storage
Jean Choquette
Simon Choquette
Jean Choquette

D-U-N-S 25-150-5426   (HQ)
VOPAK TERMINALS OF CANADA INC
TRANSIT MONTANK
(*Suby of* KONINKLIJKE VOPAK N.V.)
2775 Av Georges-V, Montreal-Est, QC, H1L 6J7
(514) 687-3193
Emp Here 16   *Sales* 23,371,040
SIC 5169 Chemicals and allied products, nec
Boudewijn Siemons
Nevin Ata Alla
Wim Samlal

D-U-N-S 20-289-5546   (HQ)
VOPAK TERMINAUX DE L'EST DU CANADA INC
VOPAK TERMINAL MONTREAL-EST
(*Suby of* KONINKLIJKE VOPAK N.V.)
2775 Av Georges-V, Montreal-Est, QC, H1L 6J7
(514) 687-3193
Sales 18,988,970
SIC 5169 Chemicals and allied products, nec
Boudewijn Siemons
Nevin Ata Alla

Wim Samlal

Montreal-Nord, QC H1G

D-U-N-S 24-943-7047   (SL)
119678 CANADA INC
TERTAC
11600 Boul Albert-Hudon, Montreal-Nord, QC, H1G 3K2
(514) 328-4230
Emp Here 100   *Sales* 20,189,700
SIC 3089 Plastics products, nec
Robert Giustini

D-U-N-S 25-244-2793   (SL)
160841 CANADA INC
NEO CAFE
10671 Av Brunet, Montreal-Nord, QC, H1G 5E1
(514) 325-3680
Emp Here 20   *Sales* 10,702,480
SIC 5149 Groceries and related products, nec
George Bourhas
John S Roditis

D-U-N-S 24-837-2500   (SL)
9020-2516 QUEBEC INC
MARVID POULTRY CANADA
5671 Boul Industriel, Montreal-Nord, QC, H1G 3Z9
(514) 321-8376
Emp Here 85   *Sales* 29,383,650
SIC 2015 Poultry slaughtering and processing
Moishe Friedman

D-U-N-S 25-896-2794   (SL)
9080-3404 QUEBEC INC
KIA SAINT-LEONARD
6464 Boul Henri-Bourassa E, Montreal-Nord, QC, H1G 5W9
(514) 256-1010
Emp Here 35   *Sales* 17,432,730
SIC 5511 New and used car dealers
Giancarlo Di Marco

D-U-N-S 25-394-7816   (SL)
ALIMENTS PASTA ROMANA INC
11430 Boul Albert-Hudon, Montreal-Nord, QC, H1G 3J8
(514) 494-4767
Emp Here 50   *Sales* 11,242,750
SIC 2098 Macaroni and spaghetti
Bernard Filippone
Michael Filippone
Patrick Filippone
Egidio Filippone

D-U-N-S 24-667-4352   (HQ)
ALUMINIUM CARUSO & FILS INC
5528 Rue De Castille, Montreal-Nord, QC, H1G 3E5
(514) 326-2274
Sales 10,141,500
SIC 3442 Metal doors, sash, and trim
Calogero Caruso

D-U-N-S 24-355-8475   (SL)
ARMATURE DNS 2000 INC
11001 Av Jean-Meunier, Montreal-Nord, QC, H1G 4S7
(514) 324-1141
Emp Here 140   *Sales* 26,661,880
SIC 3625 Relays and industrial controls
Giuseppe Rinaldi
Tullio Lattanzio

D-U-N-S 25-248-1189   (SL)
AUTOBUS IDEAL INC
5101 Boul Industriel, Montreal-Nord, QC, H1G 3H1
(514) 323-2355
Emp Here 88   *Sales* 4,828,736
SIC 4151 School buses
Pierre Deschenes
Ronald Deschenes

Nancy Trudeau

D-U-N-S 20-212-9151   (SL)
BROSSARD FRERES INC
BROPAC
10848 Av Moisan, Montreal-Nord, QC, H1G 4N7
(514) 321-4121
Emp Here 50   *Sales* 41,778,850
SIC 5149 Groceries and related products, nec
Louis Brossard
Jean Brossard
Sylvie Brossard
Michel Brossard

D-U-N-S 24-226-2400   (SL)
CAPMATIC LTEE
(*Suby of* ALLOWORLD INC)
12180 Boul Albert-Hudon, Montreal-Nord, QC, H1G 3K7
(514) 322-0062
Emp Here 80   *Sales* 17,760,080
SIC 3565 Packaging machinery
Alioscia Bassani
Loris Bassani
Claudia Bassani

D-U-N-S 25-240-3555   (BR)
COMMISSION SCOLAIRE DE LA POINTE-DE-L'ILE
ECOLE LE CARIGNAN
(*Suby of* COMMISSION SCOLAIRE DE LA POINTE-DE-L'ILE)
11480 Boul Rolland, Montreal-Nord, QC, H1G 3T9
(514) 328-3570
Emp Here 85
SIC 8211 Elementary and secondary schools
Alain Gascon

D-U-N-S 25-240-2342   (BR)
COMMISSION SCOLAIRE DE LA POINTE-DE-L'ILE
ECOLE SECONDAIRE HENRI BOURASSA
(*Suby of* COMMISSION SCOLAIRE DE LA POINTE-DE-L'ILE)
6051 Boul Maurice-Duplessis, Montreal-Nord, QC, H1G 1Y6
(514) 328-3200
Emp Here 200
SIC 8211 Elementary and secondary schools
Jean-Francois Bouchard

D-U-N-S 24-311-7632   (SL)
CTM INTERNATIONAL GIFTWARE INC
(*Suby of* PLACEMENTS ELISII INC, LES)
11420 Boul Albert-Hudon, Montreal-Nord, QC, H1G 3J6
(514) 324-4200
Emp Here 35   *Sales* 25,988,200
SIC 5199 Nondurable goods, nec
Carlo Elisii
Antonio Elisii

D-U-N-S 25-733-4136   (HQ)
DIMA IMPORT-EXPORT INC
MERCI ALIMENTS EN VRAC
12020 Boul Albert-Hudon, Montreal-Nord, QC, H1G 3K7
(514) 955-7295
Emp Here 34   *Sales* 41,778,850
SIC 5149 Groceries and related products, nec
Johnny Daou

D-U-N-S 20-913-7186   (BR)
FONDATION EDUCATIVE DE LA COMMISSION SCOLAIRE ENGLISH-MONTREAL, LA
COMMISSION SCOLAIRE ENGLISH-MONTREAL
(*Suby of* FONDATION EDUCATIVE DE LA COMMISSION SCOLAIRE ENGLISH-MONTREAL, LA)
11575 Av P.-M.-Favier, Montreal-Nord, QC, H1G 6E5
(514) 328-4442
Emp Here 150

SIC 8211 Elementary and secondary schools
Robert Stocker

D-U-N-S 20-604-7839   (SL)
FONDERIES SHELLCAST INC
10645 Av Lamoureux, Montreal-Nord, QC, H1G 5L4
(514) 322-3760
Emp Here 100   *Sales* 23,343,500
SIC 3365 Aluminum foundries
Bodo Morgenstern

D-U-N-S 20-363-9427   (SL)
GABRIEL MONTREAL-NORD, S.E.C.
GABRIEL KIA
6464 Boul Henri-Bourassa E, Montreal-Nord, QC, H1G 5W9
(514) 323-7777
Emp Here 25   *Sales* 12,451,950
SIC 5511 New and used car dealers
Roch Sinclair

D-U-N-S 24-363-8330   (SL)
GESTION JEAN LAFRAMBOISE INC
11450 Boul Albert-Hudon, Montreal-Nord, QC, H1G 3J9

Emp Here 70   *Sales* 13,944,280
SIC 2326 Men's and boy's work clothing
Richard Laframboise
Serge Laframboise

D-U-N-S 20-977-9388   (SL)
GESTION MAGDI TEBECHRANI INC., LES
PHARMAPRIX
6000 Boul Henri-Bourassa E, Montreal-Nord, QC, H1G 2T6
(514) 323-5010
Emp Here 50   *Sales* 12,647,700
SIC 5912 Drug stores and proprietary stores
Magdi Tebechrani

D-U-N-S 24-801-1744   (SL)
HANI AUTO INC
GABRIEL HONDA
7000 Boul Henri-Bourassa E, Montreal-Nord, QC, H1G 6C4
(514) 327-7777
Emp Here 45   *Sales* 22,413,510
SIC 5511 New and used car dealers
Gabriel Azouz

D-U-N-S 25-685-0793   (BR)
INDUSTRIES DOREL INC, LES
DOREL INDUSTRIES INC
(*Suby of* INDUSTRIES DOREL INC, LES)
12345 Boul Albert-Hudon Bureau 100, Montreal-Nord, QC, H1G 3L1
(514) 323-1247
Emp Here 325
SIC 2511 Wood household furniture
Ira Goldstein

D-U-N-S 24-312-0305   (HQ)
INVESTISSEMENTS PENTABEL LIMITEE, LES
6868 Boul Maurice-Duplessis, Montreal-Nord, QC, H1G 1Z6
(514) 327-2800
Sales 19,134,500
SIC 6712 Bank holding companies
Real Belanger
Normand Belanger
Denis Belanger

D-U-N-S 24-214-8000   (SL)
MARCHE C.D.L. TELLIER INC
IGA
6190 Boul Henri-Bourassa E, Montreal-Nord, QC, H1G 5X3
(514) 321-0120
Emp Here 100   *Sales* 29,347,700
SIC 5411 Grocery stores
Danielle Tellier
Chantal Tellier
Lise Tellier

D-U-N-S 24-871-4990   (SL)

MEGASTAR ELECTRONIQUES INC.
5061 Rue D'Amiens, Montreal-Nord, QC, H1G
3G2
(514) 329-0042
Emp Here 26   *Sales* 11,626,524
SIC 5065 Electronic parts and equipment, nec
  Bruno Pietrantonio
  Franco Pietrantonio

        D-U-N-S 20-709-3944   (BR)
METRO RICHELIEU INC
SUPER C
(*Suby of* METRO INC)
6000 Boul Henri-Bourassa E, Montreal-Nord,
QC, H1G 2T6
(514) 323-4370
Emp Here 98
SIC 5411 Grocery stores
  Claude Gagnon

        D-U-N-S 20-696-3352   (SL)
PHARMACIE KANOU & YOUSSEF S.E.N.C.
PHARMACIE JEAN COUTU
6405 Boul Leger Bureau 38, Montreal-Nord,
QC, H1G 1L4
(514) 323-6270
Emp Here 40   *Sales* 10,118,160
SIC 5912 Drug stores and proprietary stores
  Marc Kanou
  Roba Youssef

        D-U-N-S 20-964-3634   (SL)
PIE IX TOYOTA INC
TOYOTA MONTREAL NORD
6767 Boul Henri-Bourassa E, Montreal-Nord,
QC, H1G 2V6
(514) 329-0909
Emp Here 30   *Sales* 14,942,340
SIC 5511 New and used car dealers
  Jean Alloul

        D-U-N-S 20-230-9365   (HQ)
PRODUITS BEL INC
(*Suby of* INVESTISSEMENTS PENTABEL
LIMITEE, LES)
6868 Boul Maurice-Duplessis, Montreal-Nord,
QC, H1G 1Z6
(514) 327-2800
Emp Here 61   *Sales* 12,378,730
SIC 3644 Noncurrent-carrying wiring devices
  Real Belanger
  Catherine Belanger
  Denis Belanger
  Eric Belanger

        D-U-N-S 25-525-5903   (BR)
SOBEYS CAPITAL INCORPORATED
SOBEYS QUEBEC
(*Suby of* EMPIRE COMPANY LIMITED)
11281 Boul Albert-Hudon, Montreal-Nord,
QC, H1G 3J5
(514) 324-1010
Emp Here 150
SIC 5141 Groceries, general line
  Marc Poulin

        D-U-N-S 20-251-8254   (BR)
SOBEYS CAPITAL INCORPORATED
SOBEYS
(*Suby of* EMPIRE COMPANY LIMITED)
11281 Boul Albert-Hudon, Montreal-Nord,
QC, H1G 3J5
(514) 324-1010
Emp Here 800
SIC 5141 Groceries, general line

        D-U-N-S 20-651-3629   (BR)
SOBEYS CAPITAL INCORPORATED
SOBEYS
(*Suby of* EMPIRE COMPANY LIMITED)
11281 Boul Albert-Hudon, Montreal-Nord,
QC, H1G 3J5
(514) 324-1010
Emp Here 150
SIC 5411 Grocery stores

        D-U-N-S 24-525-3823   (BR)
TELECON INC

(*Suby of* CAPITAL REGIONAL ET COOPER-
ATIF DESJARDINS)
6789 Boul Leger, Montreal-Nord, QC, H1G
6H8

Emp Here 120
SIC 4899 Communication services, nec
  Normand Lemyre

        D-U-N-S 24-319-5224   (BR)
WAL-MART CANADA CORP
WALMART
(*Suby of* WALMART INC.)
6140 Boul Henri-Bourassa E, Montreal-Nord,
QC, H1G 5X3
(514) 324-7853
Emp Here 200
SIC 5311 Department stores
  Jean-Francois Boisvert

Montreal-Nord, QC H1H

        D-U-N-S 20-165-6704   (SL)
2969-9899 QUEBEC INC
S.I.R.C.O.
3905 Boul Industriel, Montreal-Nord, QC, H1H
2Z2
(514) 744-1010
Emp Here 60   *Sales* 23,740,680
SIC 7381 Detective and armored car services
  Claude Sarrazin

        D-U-N-S 20-309-3489   (SL)
9208-3179 QUEBEC INC
MNM HOCKEY
10240 Av Armand-Lavergne, Montreal-Nord,
QC, H1H 3N4
(514) 664-4646
Emp Here 23   *Sales* 15,098,672
SIC 5961 Catalog and mail-order houses
  Marc Mackarous

        D-U-N-S 24-322-1327   (BR)
9387-0616 QUEBEC INC
PRODUITS ALIMENTAIRES VIAU INC, LES
(*Suby of* MAPLE LEAF FOODS INC)
10035 Av Plaza, Montreal-Nord, QC, H1H 4L5
(514) 321-8260
Emp Here 230
SIC 5147 Meats and meat products
  Joe Reda

        D-U-N-S 24-325-1733   (SL)
BONUS METAL CANADA INC
10171 Av Pelletier, Montreal-Nord, QC, H1H
3R2
(514) 321-4820
Emp Here 24   *Sales* 11,400,624
SIC 5084 Industrial machinery and equipment
  David Newman

        D-U-N-S 20-355-9877   (HQ)
**CAISSE DESJARDINS DE SAULT-AU-
RECOLLET-MONTREAL-NORD**
CENTRE DE SERVICES FLEURY
10205 Boul Pie-Ix, Montreal-Nord, QC, H1H
3Z4
(514) 322-9310
Emp Here 85   *Sales* 15,156,100
SIC 6062 State credit unions
  Robert Richard
  Sergio Gutierrez
  Benoit Jacques
  Francine Legrand
  Helene Robitaille
  Angelo Rubino
  Jean-Marc Simard
  Janny Gaspard
  Marianne Dessureault
  Andre J. Belanger

        D-U-N-S 20-216-3739   (SL)
CHAUSSURES DE LUCA MONTREAL INC
BELUGA
9999 Boul Saint-Michel, Montreal-Nord, QC,

H1H 5G7
(514) 279-4541
Emp Here 45   *Sales* 10,504,575
SIC 3144 Women's footwear, except athletic
  Vincenzo Passarelli
  Antonio Santella
  Giuseppina Passarelli
  Franco Rota
  Anna Gianfriddo In Passarelli

        D-U-N-S 20-999-4540   (SL)
CHSLD MARIE-CLARET INC
3345 Boul Henri-Bourassa E, Montreal-Nord,
QC, H1H 1H6
(514) 322-4380
Emp Here 100   *Sales* 6,507,500
SIC 8361 Residential care
  Jean-Guy Laplante
  Christianne Hubert

        D-U-N-S 20-910-6251   (BR)
**COMMISSION SCOLAIRE DE LA POINTE-
DE-L'ILE**
ECOLE SECONDAIRE CALIXA LAVALEE
(*Suby of* COMMISSION SCOLAIRE DE LA
POINTE-DE-L'ILE)
11411 Av Pelletier, Montreal-Nord, QC, H1H
3S3
(514) 328-3250
Emp Here 220
SIC 8211 Elementary and secondary schools
  Dominic Blanchette

        D-U-N-S 20-030-5139   (BR)
**COMMISSION SCOLAIRE DE LA POINTE-
DE-L'ILE**
ECOLE CENTRE AMOS
(*Suby of* COMMISSION SCOLAIRE DE LA
POINTE-DE-L'ILE)
10748 Boul Saint-Vital, Montreal-Nord, QC,
H1H 4T3
(514) 328-3272
Emp Here 100
SIC 8211 Elementary and secondary schools
  Nathalie Labelle

        D-U-N-S 20-216-4620   (SL)
ENTREPRISES DERO INC
(*Suby of* 9056-1820 QUEBEC INC)
9960 Av Plaza, Montreal-Nord, QC, H1H 4L6
(514) 327-1108
Emp Here 65   *Sales* 10,325,770
SIC 3089 Plastics products, nec
  Damiano Di Liello
  Joseph Paventi

        D-U-N-S 24-902-8697   (SL)
ENTREPRISES KIM LUU INC, LES
PHARMAPRIX
10551 Boul Pie-Ix, Montreal-Nord, QC, H1H
4A3
(514) 321-1230
Emp Here 40   *Sales* 10,118,160
SIC 5912 Drug stores and proprietary stores
  David Fortin

        D-U-N-S 24-460-5127   (SL)
GASTON OUELLETTE & FILS INC
9960 Boul Saint-Vital, Montreal-Nord, QC,
H1H 4S6
(514) 388-3927
Emp Here 80   *Sales* 17,426,320
SIC 1731 Electrical work
  Sebastien Ouellette

        D-U-N-S 24-815-1995   (SL)
**HOPITAL MARIE-CLARAC DES SOEURS
DE CHARITE DE STE-MARIE (1995) INC**
(*Suby of* SOEURS DE LA CHARITE STE-
MARIE)
3530 Boul Gouin E, Montreal-Nord, QC, H1H
1B7
(514) 321-8800
Emp Here 300   *Sales* 45,049,800
SIC 8069 Specialty hospitals, except psychi-
atric
  Martine Cote
  Samir Naoum

  Pierre-Anne Mandato
  Claire Croteau
  Marie-Helene Sirois
  Marie-Helene Desrosiers

        D-U-N-S 20-230-7971   (SL)
**INDUSTRIES DE FIBRE DE VERRE PRE-
MIER INC, LES**
3390 Rue De Mont-Joli, Montreal-Nord, QC,
H1H 2X8
(514) 321-6410
Emp Here 70   *Sales* 18,965,940
SIC 1522 Residential construction, nec
  Paul Belanger
  Guy Felton
  Raymond Chevalier
  Denis Desjardins
  Rollande Moreau
  Lise Belanger

        D-U-N-S 20-642-7671   (BR)
LOBLAWS INC
MAXI
(*Suby of* LOBLAW COMPANIES LIMITED)
10200 Boul Pie-Ix, Montreal-Nord, QC, H1H
3Z1
(514) 321-3111
Emp Here 120
SIC 5411 Grocery stores
  Stephan Seguin

        D-U-N-S 24-426-4268   (SL)
NORDEST VOLKSWAGEN INC
10395 Boul Pie-Ix, Montreal-Nord, QC, H1H
3Z7
(514) 325-3422
Emp Here 50   *Sales* 24,903,900
SIC 5511 New and used car dealers
  Andre Arbour
  Stephanie Arbour
  Sebastien Arbour

        D-U-N-S 24-677-4913   (SL)
PRIMO INSTRUMENT INC
MTP INSTRUMENT, LES
(*Suby of* ARDIAN HOLDING)
4407 Rue De Charleroi, Montreal-Nord, QC,
H1H 1T6
(514) 329-3242
Emp Here 30   *Sales* 14,250,780
SIC 5084 Industrial machinery and equipment
  Pierre Tetrault
  Thomas Peretti
  Francois Prospert
  Olivier Delrieu
  Jean-Philippe Gelbert Maury

        D-U-N-S 20-236-8072   (SL)
VESTSHELL INC
G.S.L. MOULD & DIE
10378 Av Pelletier, Montreal-Nord, QC, H1H
3R3
(514) 326-1280
Emp Here 100   *Sales* 18,138,800
SIC 3324 Steel investment foundries
  Joseph K. Laflamme

Montreal-Ouest, QC H4X

        D-U-N-S 24-740-0187   (SL)
2900319 CANADA INC
ENCORE INDUSTRIES
146 Prom Ronald, Montreal-Ouest, QC, H4X
1M8
(514) 489-9159
Emp Here 20   *Sales* 10,006,500
SIC 5137 Women's and children's clothing
  Hyman-Marc Percher

        D-U-N-S 20-856-7925   (SL)
CIMTEL (QUEBEC) INC
AMEUBLEMENT DE BUREAU AMBIANCE
71 Av Westminster N, Montreal-Ouest, QC,
H4X 1Y8

(514) 481-4344
Emp Here 26   Sales 11,626,524
SIC 5065 Electronic parts and equipment, nec
Paul Choquette
Robert Choquette

D-U-N-S 20-765-6398   (HQ)
COMPAGNIE DIVERSIFIEE EDELSTEIN LTEE, LA
ECHOTAPE
(Suby of 2927179 CANADA INC)
9001 Ch Avon Bureau 100, Montreal-Ouest, QC, H4X 2G8
(514) 489-8689
Sales 35,256,060
SIC 5113 Industrial and personal service paper
Marilyn Edelstein
Cherie Edelstein

D-U-N-S 24-370-4371   (SL)
ENTREPRISES B. DURAND INC, LES
48 Av Wolseley N, Montreal-Ouest, QC, H4X 1V5
(514) 481-0368
Emp Here 2   Sales 10,483,875
SIC 6719 Holding companies, nec
Rollande Durand
Daniel Durand

D-U-N-S 20-751-7793   (SL)
SUNFORCE PRODUCTS INC
9015 Ch Avon Bureau 2017, Montreal-Ouest, QC, H4X 2G8
(514) 989-2100
Emp Here 35   Sales 12,747,525
SIC 5013 Motor vehicle supplies and new parts
Micheal Dahan
Leslie Wexelman

Montreal-Ouest, QC H7H

D-U-N-S 24-697-7904   (SL)
ECOLE HORIZON JEUNESSE
155 Boul Sainte-Rose E, Montreal-Ouest, QC, H7H 1P2
(450) 662-6720
Emp Here 114   Sales 11,299,566
SIC 8211 Elementary and secondary schools
Raymond Gagnon

Montreal-Ouest, QC H7N

D-U-N-S 25-362-6683   (BR)
IRON MOUNTAIN CANADA OPERATIONS ULC
ARCHIVE IRON MOUNTAIN
(Suby of IRON MOUNTAIN INCORPORATED)
1655 Rue Fleetwood, Montreal-Ouest, QC, H7N 4B2
(450) 667-5960
Emp Here 100
SIC 4226 Special warehousing and storage, nec
Ted Maclean

D-U-N-S 24-799-2860   (SL)
SKI MOJO INC
OBERSON
(Suby of 156946 CANADA INC)
1355 Boul Des Laurentides, Montreal-Ouest, QC, H7N 4Y5
(450) 669-5123
Emp Here 45   Sales 12,216,400
SIC 5941 Sporting goods and bicycle shops
Maurice Oberson
Joanne Oberson
Alexandra Oberson
Daniel L'ecuyer

Montreal-Ouest, QC H7V

D-U-N-S 24-601-5416   (HQ)
137448 CANADA INC
BIJOUTERIE EDOUARD
734 Boul Cure-Labelle, Montreal-Ouest, QC, H7V 2T9
(450) 978-5638
Emp Here 10   Sales 39,092,480
SIC 5944 Jewelry stores
Edouard Sebag

D-U-N-S 20-529-8826   (SL)
3474534 CANADA INC
UNIPRIX ST PHANE SANSREGRET
800 Boul Chomedey Bureau 160, Montreal-Ouest, QC, H7V 3Y4
(450) 682-7711
Emp Here 100   Sales 24,432,800
SIC 5999 Miscellaneous retail stores, nec
Stephane Sansregret

D-U-N-S 20-702-8601   (SL)
4129849 CANADA INC
807 Boul Cure-Labelle, Montreal-Ouest, QC, H7V 2V2
(450) 781-8800
Emp Here 1   Sales 13,000,005
SIC 6712 Bank holding companies

D-U-N-S 24-000-2985   (SL)
4335325 CANADA INC
CHOMEDEY KIA
1530 Boul Chomedey, Montreal-Ouest, QC, H7V 3N8
(450) 680-1000
Emp Here 24   Sales 11,953,872
SIC 5511 New and used car dealers
Mike Gergian

D-U-N-S 24-385-2501   (SL)
6423264 CANADA INC
BOISE NOTRE DAME, LES RESIDENCES
3055 Boul Notre-Dame Bureau 1700, Montreal-Ouest, QC, H7V 4C6
(450) 681-3055
Emp Here 100   Sales 6,507,500
SIC 8361 Residential care
Yvon Joyal
Michele Lanteigne

D-U-N-S 24-373-4709   (HQ)
ALTASCIENCES COMPAGNIE INC
ALGORITHME PHARMA
(Suby of ALTASCIENCES ACQUISITION HOLDINGS, LP)
575 Boul Armand-Frappier, Montreal-Ouest, QC, H7V 4B3
(450) 973-6077
Emp Here 350   Sales 122,449,200
SIC 8731 Commercial physical research
Christopher Perkin
Yves Glaude

D-U-N-S 20-033-5102   (BR)
CENTRE DE SANTE ET DE SERVICES SOCIAUX DE LAVAL
CLSC-CHSLD DU RUISSEAU-PAPINEAU
(Suby of GOUVERNEMENT DE LA PROVINCE DE QUEBEC)
800 Boul Chomedey Bureau 200, Montreal-Ouest, QC, H7V 3Y4
(450) 682-2952
Emp Here 600
SIC 8399 Social services, nec
Guy Lepage

D-U-N-S 24-737-0864   (SL)
CITOXLAB AMERIQUE DU NORD INC
(Suby of CHARLES RIVER LABORATORIES INTERNATIONAL, INC.)
445 Boul Armand-Frappier, Montreal-Ouest, QC, H7V 4B3
(450) 973-2240
Emp Here 250   Sales 51,020,500

SIC 8731 Commercial physical research
Glenn Washer
David P. Johst
Birgit Girshick

D-U-N-S 20-010-1769   (SL)
CORPORATION XPRIMA.COM
RESULTATS SUR TOUTE LA LIGNE, EN LIGNE
420 Boul Armand-Frappier Bureau 200, Montreal-Ouest, QC, H7V 4B4
(450) 681-5868
Emp Here 103   Sales 10,050,928
SIC 7374 Data processing and preparation
Jean-Philippe Paquin

D-U-N-S 24-429-7057   (SL)
CREATIONS MALO INC
750 Boul Cure-Labelle Bureau 200, Montreal-Ouest, QC, H7V 2T9
(450) 682-6561
Emp Here 45   Sales 14,676,120
SIC 3911 Jewelry, precious Metal
Habib Malo
Joseph Malo
Antoine Malo
Elie Malo

D-U-N-S 20-211-5023   (HQ)
CROESUS FINANSOFT INC
600 Boul Armand-Frappier Bureau 200, Montreal-Ouest, QC, H7V 4B4
(450) 662-6101
Emp Here 50   Sales 16,580,930
SIC 7371 Custom computer programming services
Remy Therrien
Sylvian Simpson
Jacques Gelinas
Guy Sirois
Denys L'archeveque
Vincent Guyaux
Lucie Laiberte

D-U-N-S 25-411-5041   (SL)
GROUPE CENSEO INC
SERVICES FINANCIERS PAQUETTE DUBEAU
1200 Boul Chomedey Bureau 1050, Montreal-Ouest, QC, H7V 3Z3
(450) 973-8000
Emp Here 22   Sales 12,758,328
SIC 6411 Insurance agents, brokers, and service
Gad Attias
Jacques Paquette

D-U-N-S 20-422-2012   (HQ)
INDUSTRIES MONDIALES ARMSTRONG CANADA LTEE, LES
SONOBOARD TMA 26598
(Suby of ARMSTRONG WORLD INDUSTRIES, INC.)
1595 Boul Daniel-Johnson Bureau 300, Montreal-Ouest, QC, H7V 4C2
(450) 902-3900
Sales 63,496,320
SIC 3996 Hard surface floor coverings, nec
Benoit Paquette
Victor Grizzle
David Cookson
Lingling Stewart
Bryan Y.M. Tham

D-U-N-S 24-019-2377   (SL)
PLACEMENTS RABPHAR INC
JEAN COUTU (MARQUE DE COMMERCE)
610 Boul Cure-Labelle, Montreal-Ouest, QC, H7V 2T7
(450) 687-5910
Emp Here 100   Sales 24,432,800
SIC 5912 Drug stores and proprietary stores
Benoit Latreille
Jean Thiffault

D-U-N-S 20-625-4711   (HQ)
PROMETIC BIOSCIENCES INC

(Suby of PROMETIC SCIENCES DE LA VIE INC)
500 Boul Cartier O Bureau 150, Montreal-Ouest, QC, H7V 5B7
(450) 781-0115
Sales 13,833,000
SIC 2834 Pharmaceutical preparations
Pierre Laurin
Patrick Sartore
Bruce Pritchard

D-U-N-S 25-355-2681   (HQ)
PROMETIC SCIENCES DE LA VIE INC
PROMETIC
440 Boul Armand-Frappier Bureau 300, Montreal-Ouest, QC, H7V 4B4
(450) 781-0115
Emp Here 25   Sales 35,914,324
SIC 2834 Pharmaceutical preparations
Kenneth Galbraith
Bruce Pritchard
Patrick Sartore
John Moran
Martin Leclerc
Stefan V. Clulow
Simon Best
Zachary J. Newton
Gary J. Bridger
Neil A. Klompas

D-U-N-S 20-253-1216   (HQ)
PROTECH BUSINESS SOLUTIONS INC
PROTECH SOLUTIONS
1200 Boul Chomedey Bureau 720, Montreal-Ouest, QC, H7V 3Z3
(450) 934-9800
Emp Here 8   Sales 19,586,925
SIC 7361 Employment agencies
Jean Doucet
Ron Stevens
Angela Caldwell

D-U-N-S 25-473-8883   (HQ)
RE/MAX 2001 INC
RE/MAX DU SECTEUR
360 Boul Cure-Labelle, Montreal-Ouest, QC, H7V 2S1
(450) 625-2001
Sales 50,266,680
SIC 6531 Real estate agents and managers
Jocelyne Harton

D-U-N-S 24-676-8717   (SL)
RESIDENCE RIVIERA INC
2999 Boul Notre-Dame, Montreal-Ouest, QC, H7V 4C4
(450) 682-0111
Emp Here 160   Sales 17,772,800
SIC 8069 Specialty hospitals, except psychiatric
Marilyn Nadon
Perry Nadon
Andre Nadon
Jean Nadon

D-U-N-S 20-194-5458   (HQ)
ROUSSEAU, MARC LTEE
520 Boul Cure-Labelle, Montreal-Ouest, QC, H7V 2T2
(450) 688-1170
Emp Here 25   Sales 11,387,655
SIC 5211 Lumber and other building materials
Serge Rousseau

D-U-N-S 24-619-7123   (SL)
SILVER STAR MANUFACTURING CO INC
MANUFACTURE DE BIJOUX ETOILES D'ARGENT
750 Boul Cure-Labelle Bureau 205, Montreal-Ouest, QC, H7V 2T9
(450) 682-3381
Emp Here 60   Sales 19,568,160
SIC 3911 Jewelry, precious Metal
Habib Malo
Elye Malo
Fulda Yildirmaz

▲ Public Company   ■ Public Company Family Member   **HQ** Headquarters   **BR** Branch   **SL** Single Location

D-U-N-S 24-812-3788   (HQ)
TECHNOLOGIES 20-20 INC
2020 MC
400 Boul Armand-Frappier Bureau 2020, Montreal-Ouest, QC, H7V 4B4
(514) 332-4110
Sales 16,684,700
SIC 7372 Prepackaged software
  Mark Stoever
  Kevin F Collins
  Rishi Chandna
  Bernhard Nann
  Mark C. Goldstein

D-U-N-S 24-710-0290   (HQ)
TECHNOLOGIES ORBITE INC
ORBITE
500 Boul Cartier O Bureau 249, Montreal-Ouest, QC, H7V 5B7
(450) 680-3341
Emp Here 26   *Sales* 10,230,960
SIC 1081 Metal mining services
  Glenn R. Kelly
  Charles Taschereau
  Jacques Bedard
  Genevieve Marchand
  Philippe Levesque-Groleau
  Hubert Dumont
  Claude Lamoureux
  Pierre B Meunier
  Stephane Bertrand
  Pascal Decary

Morin-Heights, QC J0R

D-U-N-S 24-205-1196   (SL)
3522920 CANADA INC
80 Rue Campbell Rr 2, Morin-Heights, QC, J0R 1H0
(450) 226-2314
Emp Here 2   *Sales* 17,988,400
SIC 2032 Canned specialties
  Michael Tott
  Michael Tott

D-U-N-S 24-855-1074   (SL)
9181-8153 QUEBEC INC
IGA MARCHE MORIN-HEIGHTS
680 Ch Du Village, Morin-Heights, QC, J0R 1H0
(450) 226-5769
Emp Here 70   *Sales* 20,543,390
SIC 5411 Grocery stores
  Pierre Desmanches

D-U-N-S 20-370-1078   (SL)
CONCEPT GOURMET DU VILLAGE ULC
CONCEPT GOURMET DU VILLAGE
539 Ch Du Village, Morin-Heights, QC, J0R 1H0
(800) 668-2314
Emp Here 53   *Sales* 44,285,581
SIC 5149 Groceries and related products, nec
  Jeffrey Reich
  Gregory Reich
  David Reich

Murdochville, QC G0E

D-U-N-S 24-866-9405   (SL)
ENERGIE EOLIENNE DU MONT COPPER INC
1500 198 Rte, Murdochville, QC, G0E 1W0
(418) 784-2800
Emp Here 20   *Sales* 10,393,100
SIC 4911 Electric services
  Erich Ossowski

Namur, QC J0V

D-U-N-S 20-237-8816   (SL)
LEGGETT, H. & FILS INC
904 Rue Du Centenaire, Namur, QC, J0V 1N0
(819) 426-2176
Emp Here 50   *Sales* 20,967,750
SIC 6712 Bank holding companies
  Thomas Leggett
  Peter Leggett

Napierville, QC J0J

D-U-N-S 20-252-3247   (BR)
2104225 ONTARIO LTD
WESTON BAKERIES LIMITED
(*Suby of* GEORGE WESTON LIMITED)
150 Boul Industriel, Napierville, QC, J0J 1L0
(450) 245-7542
Emp Here 200
SIC 2051 Bread, cake, and related products
  Yvan Dufour

D-U-N-S 24-420-3894   (HQ)
CAISSE DESJARDINS DES SEIGNEURIES DE LA FRONTIERE
CENTRE DE SERVICES LACOLLE
373 Rue Saint-Jacques, Napierville, QC, J0J 1L0
(450) 245-3391
Emp Here 30   *Sales* 12,193,787
SIC 6062 State credit unions
  Pierre Savard
  Isabelle Bourgeois
  Victor Legault
  Jean-Francois Bousquet
  Yvon Fournier
  Diane Latour
  Isabelle Guay
  Valerie Leclair
  Charles Patenaude
  Guy Trudeau

D-U-N-S 24-176-7151   (HQ)
LAREAU - COURTIERS D'ASSURANCES INC
ASSURANCES LAREAU ROUSSILLON
4 Rte 219 Bureau 707, Napierville, QC, J0J 1L0
(450) 245-3322
Emp Here 17   *Sales* 42,403,000
SIC 6411 Insurance agents, brokers, and service
  Philippe Lareau
  Matthieu Seguin

D-U-N-S 24-959-8988   (SL)
NORMANDIN TRANSIT INC
151 Boul Industriel, Napierville, QC, J0J 1L0
(450) 245-0445
Emp Here 550   *Sales* 113,138,300
SIC 4213 Trucking, except local
  Andre Normandin
  Danielle Normandin

New Carlisle, QC G0C

D-U-N-S 25-514-6151   (HQ)
EASTERN SHORES SCHOOL BOARD
40 Rue Mount-Sorrel, New Carlisle, QC, G0C 1Z0
(418) 752-2247
Emp Here 15   *Sales* 34,691,650
SIC 8211 Elementary and secondary schools
  Donna Bisson
  Michael Chesser

New Richmond, QC G0C

D-U-N-S 24-226-4880   (SL)
9125-9051 QUEBEC INC.
MARCHE D'ALIMENTATION MARTIN DUGUAY
120 Boul Perron O, New Richmond, QC, G0C 2B0
(418) 392-4237
Emp Here 50   *Sales* 13,707,600
SIC 5411 Grocery stores
  Martin Duguay

D-U-N-S 24-436-7608   (SL)
A & R DECORATIONS
166 Rte 299, New Richmond, QC, G0C 2B0
(418) 392-4686
Emp Here 49   *Sales* 36,383,480
SIC 5199 Nondurable goods, nec
  Russell Campbell

D-U-N-S 25-244-1803   (SL)
CLEMENT GAGNON ET JACINTHE DES-JARDINS, PHARMACIENS (S.E.N.C.)
JEAN COUTU
145 Ch Cyr, New Richmond, QC, G0C 2B0
(418) 392-4451
Emp Here 40   *Sales* 10,118,160
SIC 5912 Drug stores and proprietary stores
  Jacinthe Desjardins
  Clement Gagnon

D-U-N-S 24-730-7184   (SL)
FABRICATION DELTA INC
154 Ch Saint-Edgar, New Richmond, QC, G0C 2B0
(418) 392-2624
Emp Here 100   *Sales* 19,044,200
SIC 3621 Motors and generators
  Francois Arsenault
  Benoit Gascon
  Rene Ricard

Nicolet, QC J3T

D-U-N-S 20-400-5375   (SL)
AGROCENTRE TECHNOVA INC
AGROCENTRE ST-PIE
(*Suby of* COOP FEDEREE, LA)
515 Rue De Monseigneur-Courchesne, Nicolet, QC, J3T 1C8
(819) 293-5851
Emp Here 50   *Sales* 37,126,000
SIC 5191 Farm supplies
  Stephane Chaume
  France Beliveau
  Marika Trepanier
  Benoit Brunelle
  Carle-Sebastien Perron

D-U-N-S 24-176-8233   (SL)
ATELIER PEPIN INC
1369 Boul Louis-Frechette, Nicolet, QC, J3T 1M3
(819) 293-5584
Emp Here 45   *Sales* 19,957,050
SIC 7389 Business services, nec
  Bernadette Pepin
  Robert Balit
  Laurent Balit
  Marjolaine Pepin

D-U-N-S 20-909-6965   (HQ)
CENTRE AGRICOLE NICOLET-YAMASKA INC
2025 Boul Louis-Frechette, Nicolet, QC, J3T 1M4
(819) 293-4441
Sales 11,875,650
SIC 5083 Farm and garden machinery
  Michel Rheault

D-U-N-S 24-355-6722   (HQ)
COMMISSION SCOLAIRE DE LA RIVERAINE
375 Rue De Monseigneur-Brunault, Nicolet,

QC, J3T 1Y6
(819) 293-5821
Emp Here 100   *Sales* 69,383,300
SIC 8211 Elementary and secondary schools
  Johane Croteau
  Pascal Blondin
  Johanne Jacques

D-U-N-S 20-978-2374   (SL)
CONSTRUCTION G. THERRIEN 2010 INC
THERRIEN ENTREPRENEUR GENERAL
3885 Boul Louis-Frechette, Nicolet, QC, J3T 1T7
(819) 293-6921
Emp Here 50   *Sales* 23,536,550
SIC 1542 Nonresidential construction, nec
  Paul Cusson
  Denis Leclerc
  Normand Hamelin
  Sebastien Couture

D-U-N-S 24-177-8083   (SL)
LABRADOR LAURENTIENNE INC
2540 Boul Louis-Frechette, Nicolet, QC, J3T 1N1
(819) 293-4555
Emp Here 25   *Sales* 20,889,425
SIC 5149 Groceries and related products, nec
  Pierre Rivard

D-U-N-S 24-403-6505   (SL)
NITEK LASER INC
305 Rte Du Port, Nicolet, QC, J3T 1R7
(819) 293-4887
Emp Here 50   *Sales* 11,671,750
SIC 3398 Metal heat treating
  Francois Dubuc

D-U-N-S 24-225-0454   (SL)
PHARMACIE CHRISTINE LEGER & MARTIN COTE INC
PHARMACIE JEAN COUTU
1693 Boul Louis-Frechette, Nicolet, QC, J3T 1Z6
(819) 293-6111
Emp Here 45   *Sales* 11,382,930
SIC 5912 Drug stores and proprietary stores
  Christine Leger
  Martin Cote

D-U-N-S 20-238-1935   (HQ)
SOGETEL INC
DIMENSION HUMAINE
111 Rue Du 12-Novembre, Nicolet, QC, J3T 1S3
(819) 293-6125
Emp Here 80   *Sales* 22,847,200
SIC 4813 Telephone communication, except radio
  Michel Biron
  Jean-Philippe Saia
  Michel Pettigrew
  Thiago De Souza Isis
  Richard Biron
  Isabelle Biron
  Georges Biron
  Louise Begin
  Sylvain Bellerive
  Sophie Houde

D-U-N-S 25-973-8938   (SL)
SUPER MARCHE CLEMENT NICOLET INC
I G A
2000 Boul Louis-Frechette Unite 100, Nicolet, QC, J3T 1M9
(819) 293-6937
Emp Here 62   *Sales* 18,195,574
SIC 5411 Grocery stores
  Martin Auger
  Francois Arseneault

D-U-N-S 25-286-0044   (SL)
THERMOFORME D'AMERIQUE INC
THERMOFORM OF AMERICA
970 Rue Theophile-Saint-Laurent, Nicolet, QC, J3T 1B4
(819) 293-8899
Emp Here 50   *Sales* 10,094,850

SIC 3089 Plastics products, nec
Colette Leblanc

D-U-N-S 25-911-9329   (SL)
U P A CENTRE DU QUEBEC
1940 Rue Des Pins, Nicolet, QC, J3T 1Z9
(819) 293-5838
Emp Here 56   *Sales* 13,120,128
SIC 8748 Business consulting, nec
Denis Bilodeau
Louise Couture
Jean-Pierre Belisle

Normandin, QC G8M

D-U-N-S 20-321-7208   (SL)
9051-8127 QUEBEC INC
J.A. MECANIQUE
1144 Rue Lydoric-Doucet, Normandin, QC,
G8M 5A6
(418) 274-5525
Emp Here 75   *Sales* 13,196,850
SIC 8711 Engineering services
Eric Cloutier

D-U-N-S 20-238-4228   (HQ)
CO-OP DES DEUX RIVES
1455 Av Du Rocher Bureau 102, Normandin,
QC, G8M 3X5
(418) 274-2910
Emp Here 20   *Sales* 11,387,655
SIC 5211 Lumber and other building materials
Gervais Laprise

D-U-N-S 20-954-5839   (SL)
**ENCANS D'ANIMAUX DU LAC ST-JEAN
INC, LES**
1360 Rang Nord, Normandin, QC, G8M 4P5
(418) 274-2233
Emp Here 32   *Sales* 46,966,144
SIC 5154 Livestock
Andre Bussiere
Roger Bussiere
Johanne Bussieres
Jean-Francois Bussiere
Daniel Bussiere
Mario Bussiere

D-U-N-S 20-721-1947   (SL)
GESTION TREMBLAY LEBOEUF INC
SUPER MARCHE IGA
1130 Rue Saint-Cyrille, Normandin, QC, G8M
4J7
(418) 274-2009
Emp Here 50   *Sales* 13,707,600
SIC 5411 Grocery stores
Denis Cloutier

D-U-N-S 24-381-5859   (SL)
M.C.T. PNEUS INC
M.C.T. FORESTIER
1293 Rue Du Parc-Industriel, Normandin, QC,
G8M 4C6
(418) 274-3765
Emp Here 26   *Sales* 12,950,028
SIC 5531 Auto and home supply stores
Robin Tremblay
Marc Tremblay

D-U-N-S 20-104-9595   (HQ)
NATURE 3M INC
BILODEAU
943 Rue Saint-Cyrille, Normandin, QC, G8M
4H9
(418) 274-2511
Emp Here 20   *Sales* 37,126,000
SIC 5199 Nondurable goods, nec
Mario Bilodeau

North Hatley, QC J0B

D-U-N-S 24-056-8485   (SL)

**MAISON BLANCHE DE NORTH HATLEY
INC, LA**
977 Rue Massawippi, North Hatley, QC, J0B
2C0
(450) 666-1567
Emp Here 82   *Sales* 7,781,718
SIC 7021 Rooming and boarding houses
Serge Croteau

Notre-Dame-De-L'Ile-Perrot, QC J7V

D-U-N-S 24-217-3941   (SL)
9171-2802 QUEBEC INC
METRO NOTRE DAME DU ILE-PERROT
450 Boul Don-Quichotte, Notre-Dame-De-
L'Ile-Perrot, QC, J7V 0J9
(514) 425-6111
Emp Here 100   *Sales* 29,347,700
SIC 5411 Grocery stores
Bernard Lemay

D-U-N-S 20-370-3673   (SL)
9363-9888 QUEBEC INC
SANIVAC
100 Rue Huot, Notre-Dame-De-L'Ile-Perrot,
QC, J7V 7Z8
(514) 700-5319
Emp Here 50   *Sales* 14,608,450
SIC 7359 Equipment rental and leasing, nec
Vincent Kelly
David Kelly
Carole-Ann Kelly
Francois Beaulieu-Lauzon

D-U-N-S 24-580-7698   (SL)
TECHNOLOGIES K.K. INC, LES
64 Rue Huot, Notre-Dame-De-L'Ile-Perrot,
QC, J7V 7Z8
(514) 453-6732
Emp Here 57   *Sales* 12,654,057
SIC 3599 Industrial machinery, nec
Kipling Crooks

Notre-Dame-Des-Pins, QC G0M

D-U-N-S 24-105-7152   (SL)
AUTOMOBILES DU BOULEVARD 2000 INC
3260 Rte Du President-Kennedy, Notre-
Dame-Des-Pins, QC, G0M 1K0
(418) 774-4100
Emp Here 25   *Sales* 12,451,950
SIC 5521 Used car dealers
Marc Lessard

D-U-N-S 25-393-0549   (SL)
GESTION L. FECTEAU LTEE
3150 Ch Royal, Notre-Dame-Des-Pins, QC,
G0M 1K0
(418) 774-3324
Emp Here 80   *Sales* 20,924,240
SIC 6712 Bank holding companies
Marc Fecteau

D-U-N-S 24-489-7414   (SL)
MANOIR DE LA ROSELIERE
3055 1e Av Bureau 259, Notre-Dame-Des-
Pins, QC, G0M 1K0
(418) 774-6700
Emp Here 49   *Sales* 13,442,268
SIC 8741 Management services
Gil Gilbert

D-U-N-S 24-498-9703   (HQ)
MENUISERIE DES PINS LTEE
QUINCAILLERIE FUTURA, DIV DE
(*Suby of* QUINCAILLERIE RICHELIEU LTEE)
3150 Ch Royal, Notre-Dame-Des-Pins, QC,
G0M 1K0
(418) 774-3324
Emp Here 80   *Sales* 16,351,450
SIC 2431 Millwork

Richard Lord
Antoine Auclair
Yannick Godeau
Serge Labbe
Marc Fecteau

Notre-Dame-Des-Prairies, QC J6E

D-U-N-S 20-108-6597   (SL)
9003-2723 QUEBEC INC
LAPOINTE SPORTS
576 131 Rte, Notre-Dame-Des-Prairies, QC,
J6E 0M2
(450) 752-1224
Emp Here 28   *Sales* 13,946,184
SIC 5551 Boat dealers
Jean Gariepy

D-U-N-S 25-762-0059   (SL)
ALBI FORD LINCOLN JOLIETTE INC
525 131 Rte, Notre-Dame-Des-Prairies, QC,
J6E 0M1
(450) 759-7750
Emp Here 50   *Sales* 24,903,900
SIC 5511 New and used car dealers
Denis Leclerc

D-U-N-S 24-326-5220   (SL)
AUTOMOBILES AUMONT (1977) INC, LES
JOLIETTE TOYOTA
357 Boul Antonio-Barrette, Notre-Dame-Des-
Prairies, QC, J6E 1G1
(450) 759-3449
Emp Here 40   *Sales* 19,923,120
SIC 5511 New and used car dealers
Natalie Aumont
Gilles Aumont
Paula Aumont

D-U-N-S 25-200-8081   (SL)
**AUTOMOBILES FRANCOIS ST-JEAN INC,
LES**
MAZDA JOLIETTE
560 131 Rte, Notre-Dame-Des-Prairies, QC,
J6E 0M2
(450) 752-1212
Emp Here 30   *Sales* 14,942,340
SIC 5521 Used car dealers
Francois St-Jean

D-U-N-S 25-107-0595   (SL)
**AUTOMOBILES VILLENEUVE JOLIETTE
(1996) INC**
VILLENEUVE HONDA
570 131 Rte, Notre-Dame-Des-Prairies, QC,
J6E 0M2
(450) 759-8155
Emp Here 26   *Sales* 12,950,028
SIC 5511 New and used car dealers
Francois St-Jean

D-U-N-S 20-202-0236   (SL)
CHALUT, A . AUTO LTEE
250 Boul Antonio-Barrette, Notre-Dame-Des-
Prairies, QC, J6E 6J5
(450) 756-1638
Emp Here 26   *Sales* 12,950,028
SIC 5511 New and used car dealers
Alain Chalut

D-U-N-S 20-201-8800   (SL)
**ENTREPRISES ANTONIO LAPORTE & FILS
INC, LES**
501 Rte 131, Notre-Dame-Des-Prairies, QC,
J6E 0M1
(450) 756-1779
Emp Here 45   *Sales* 21,376,170
SIC 5083 Farm and garden machinery
Simon Laporte

D-U-N-S 20-255-5389   (SL)
MALO, GILLES INC
100 Rue Des Entreprises, Notre-Dame-Des-
Prairies, QC, J6E 0L9

(450) 757-2424
Emp Here 35   *Sales* 19,961,830
SIC 1542 Nonresidential construction, nec
Alain Malo
Patrice Laporte

D-U-N-S 25-837-1749   (SL)
MARCHE CREVIER IGA INC
IGA CREVIER JOLIETTE
17 Rue Gauthier N, Notre-Dame-Des-Prairies,
QC, J6E 1T7
(450) 759-2554
Emp Here 133   *Sales* 39,032,441
SIC 5411 Grocery stores
George Pilon

D-U-N-S 24-857-6951   (HQ)
**TURQUOISE, CABINET EN ASSURANCE
DE DOMMAGES INC, LA**
INOVESCO
481 131 Rte, Notre-Dame-Des-Prairies, QC,
J6E 0M1
(450) 759-6265
Emp Here 10   *Sales* 240,206,460
SIC 6411 Insurance agents, brokers, and ser-
vice
Ginette Mailhot
Pierre Lambert

Notre-Dame-Du-Mont-Carmel, QC G0X

D-U-N-S 25-684-0067   (SL)
RENE ST-CYR (1996) INC
RENE ST-CYR PLANCHERS ET ESCALIERS
3330 Rte 157, Notre-Dame-Du-Mont-Carmel,
QC, G0X 3J0
(819) 379-2202
Emp Here 40   *Sales* 17,886,960
SIC 5031 Lumber, plywood, and millwork
Guylaine St-Cyr
Claude St-Cyr

Notre-Dame-Du-Nord, QC J0Z

D-U-N-S 24-842-0671   (SL)
KING CONSTRUCTION ENR
84 Rue Ontario, Notre-Dame-Du-Nord, QC,
J0Z 3B0

Emp Here 40   *Sales* 12,754,760
SIC 1521 Single-family housing construction
Steve King

D-U-N-S 20-415-7739   (SL)
TEMISKO (1983) INC
TEMISKO
91 Rue Ontario, Notre-Dame-Du-Nord, QC,
J0Z 3B0
(819) 723-2416
Emp Here 90   *Sales* 1,923,690
SIC 3715 Truck trailers
Nelson Pouliot
Richard Cyrenne
Dany Roy
Frederic Dumont

Notre-Dame-Du-Portage, QC G0L

D-U-N-S 20-579-6543   (SL)
AUBERGE DU PORTAGE LTEE
671 Rte Du Fleuve, Notre-Dame-Du-Portage,
QC, G0L 1Y0
(418) 862-3601
Emp Here 100   *Sales* 9,489,900
SIC 7011 Hotels and motels
Ginette Toussaint
Alexandre Defoy

Nouvelle, QC G0C

D-U-N-S 20-693-3199 (SL)
CONSTRUCTION MICHEL MALTAIS INC
CENTRE DE PORTES ET FENETRES NOU-VELLE
775 Rte 132 E, Nouvelle, QC, G0C 2E0
(418) 794-2605
Emp Here 40   *Sales* 12,754,760
SIC 1521 Single-family housing construction
Michel Maltais
Mathieu Caissy
Karine Maltais

Nouvelle-Ouest, QC G0C

D-U-N-S 20-174-5424 (SL)
PRODUITS FORESTIERS TEMREX, SOCI-ETE EN COMMANDITE
PRODUITS FORESTIER TEMREX USINE NOUVELLE
521 Rte 132 O, Nouvelle-Ouest, QC, G0C 2G0
(418) 794-2211
Emp Here 100   *Sales* 19,237,000
SIC 2421 Sawmills and planing mills, general
Claudine Chan Weng

Obedjiwan, QC G0W

D-U-N-S 25-672-1036 (SL)
SOCIETE EN COMMANDITE SCIERIE OPIT-CIWAN
De La Pointe, Obedjiwan, QC, G0W 3B0
(819) 974-1116
Emp Here 65   *Sales* 12,504,050
SIC 2421 Sawmills and planing mills, general
Louis-Marie Bouchard

Oka, QC J0N

D-U-N-S 20-252-3429 (BR)
AGROPUR COOPERATIVE
AGROPUR COOPERATIVE
(*Suby of* AGROPUR COOPERATIVE)
1400 Ch D'Oka, Oka, QC, J0N 1E0
(450) 479-6396
Emp Here 150
SIC 2022 Cheese; natural and processed
Roger Massicotte

D-U-N-S 25-485-2122 (BR)
GOUVERNEMENT DE LA PROVINCE DE QUEBEC
PARK NATIONAL D'OKA
(*Suby of* GOUVERNEMENT DE LA PROVINCE DE QUEBEC)
2020 Ch D'Oka, Oka, QC, J0N 1E0
(450) 479-8365
Emp Here 200
SIC 7996 Amusement parks
Richard Rozon

D-U-N-S 24-377-0752 (SL)
JARDINS VEGIBEC INC, LES
MARACIHER
171 Rang Sainte-Sophie, Oka, QC, J0N 1E0
(450) 496-0566
Emp Here 230   *Sales* 38,875,750
SIC 0191 General farms, primarily crop
Pascal Lecault
Chantal Legault
Berchmans Lecault
Christine Seguin

Orford, QC J1X

D-U-N-S 25-683-1280 (SL)
HOTEL CHERIBOURG INC
2603 Ch Du Parc, Orford, QC, J1X 8C8
(819) 843-3308
Emp Here 120   *Sales* 11,122,800
SIC 7011 Hotels and motels
George Marois

D-U-N-S 24-110-6673 (SL)
JOUVENCE, BASE DE PLEIN AIR INC
JOUVENCE L'AUBERGE
131 Ch De Jouvence, Orford, QC, J1X 6R2
(450) 532-3134
Emp Here 125   *Sales* 11,958,500
SIC 7011 Hotels and motels
Claude Carriere
Francois Leduc
Philippe Gaudet
Yves Bergeron
Yanick Alarie
Emile Grieco
Suzane Brouillette
Josee Carrriere
Jean Bibeau
Sebastien Rodrigue

D-U-N-S 25-210-0821 (SL)
MANOIR DES SABLES INC
90 Av Des Jardins, Orford, QC, J1X 6M6
(819) 847-4747
Emp Here 120   *Sales* 11,122,800
SIC 7011 Hotels and motels
Georges Marois
Michel Joncas

Ormstown, QC J0S

D-U-N-S 20-171-8926 (SL)
CENTRE D'ACCUEIL DU HAUT-ST LAU-RENT (CHSLD)
65 Rue Hector, Ormstown, QC, J0S 1K0
(450) 829-2346
Emp Here 120   *Sales* 7,713,840
SIC 8361 Residential care
Francine Lortie

D-U-N-S 24-224-6486 (HQ)
EQUIPEMENTS LAPLANTE & LEVESQUE LTEE, LES
EQUIPEMENTS L & L, LES
780 Rte 201, Ormstown, QC, J0S 1K0
(450) 829-3516
Sales 17,575,962
SIC 5083 Farm and garden machinery
Michel Laplante
Pierre Laplante
Charles Laplante
Jocelyn Hart

Otterburn Park, QC J3G

D-U-N-S 24-872-0484 (SL)
CHOCOLATERIE LA CABOSSE D'OR INC
973 Ch Ozias-Leduc, Otterburn Park, QC, J3G 4S6
(450) 464-6937
Emp Here 45   *Sales* 15,556,050
SIC 2064 Candy and other confectionery products
Jean-Paul Crowin
Martine Crowin

Outremont, QC H2V

D-U-N-S 24-295-2232 (SL)

163288 CANADA INC
ROLLS RUFINA LINGERIE
47 Av Courcelette, Outremont, QC, H2V 3A5
(514) 277-0880
Emp Here 50   *Sales* 24,916,100
SIC 5137 Women's and children's clothing
Joseph Zardouk

D-U-N-S 20-123-7147 (SL)
BOUCHARD PARENT ASSOCIES INC
ADRESSE IMMOBILIERE HOMA
1185 Av Bernard, Outremont, QC, H2V 1V5
(514) 271-4820
Emp Here 70   *Sales* 19,243,242
SIC 6531 Real estate agents and managers

D-U-N-S 24-871-2382 (HQ)
CEDROM-SNI INC
(*Suby of* CISION LTD.)
825 Av Querbes Bureau 200, Outremont, QC, H2V 3X1
(514) 278-6060
Emp Here 60   *Sales* 20,562,480
SIC 4899 Communication services, nec
Nicole Guillot
Steve Solomon
Jason Edelboim
Jack Pearlstein
Kevin Akeroyd

D-U-N-S 20-793-6097 (HQ)
COLLEGE STANISLAS INCORPORE
780 Boul Dollard, Outremont, QC, H2V 3G5
(514) 273-9521
Emp Here 15   *Sales* 16,850,230
SIC 8211 Elementary and secondary schools
Guy Le Clair
Francois Choquette
Olivier Pratt
Rene Malo
Guy Le Clair
Magali Jalabert
Philippe Mora
Herve Tison
Gilles Bulota
Marie-Christine Auboug

D-U-N-S 24-055-1739 (SL)
ECOLE BETH JACOB DE RAV HIRSCH-PRUNG
1750 Av Glendale, Outremont, QC, H2V 1B3
(514) 731-6607
Emp Here 100   *Sales* 9,282,600
SIC 8211 Elementary and secondary schools
Tzeduck Mandelcorn
Joseph Drazin
Herschel Schecter

D-U-N-S 24-502-2363 (SL)
FONDATION JULES & PAUL-EMILE LEGER
EDITIONS DES PARTENAIRES
130 Av De L'Epee, Outremont, QC, H2V 3T2
(514) 495-2409
Emp Here 27   *Sales* 19,148,724
SIC 8699 Membership organizations, nec
Andre Dostie
Louis Roberge
Maurice Cote
Pierre Langlois
Andree Guy
Norman Macissac

D-U-N-S 24-206-5865 (HQ)
NATIONAL MERCHANDISING CORPORA-TION
400 Av Atlantic Bureau 705, Outremont, QC, H2V 1A5
(514) 764-0141
Emp Here 12   *Sales* 23,428,800
SIC 8748 Business consulting, nec
Martin Beland

D-U-N-S 20-229-7354 (HQ)
OPTIQUE PERFECT INC
1265 Av Ducharme, Outremont, QC, H2V 1E6
(514) 274-9407
Emp Here 20   *Sales* 11,179,350

SIC 5049 Professional equipment, nec
Jacques Benguigui

D-U-N-S 24-828-3459 (SL)
PERFECT OPTICAL HOLDINGS LTD
(*Suby of* 138457 CANADA INC)
1265 Av Ducharme, Outremont, QC, H2V 1E6
(514) 274-9407
Emp Here 25   *Sales* 11,179,350
SIC 5049 Professional equipment, nec
Isaac Benguigui

D-U-N-S 24-326-4801 (SL)
STEINER & ALEXANDERS INC
INTER-CONTINENTAL MERCANTILE
45 Ch Bates Bureau 200, Outremont, QC, H2V 1A6
(514) 271-1101
Emp Here 24   *Sales* 12,212,544
SIC 5023 Homefurnishings
Alexander Schwartz

D-U-N-S 24-713-1816 (HQ)
TVA PUBLICATIONS INC
100 PLANS
(*Suby of* QUEBECOR MEDIA INC)
7 Ch Bates, Outremont, QC, H2V 4V7
(514) 848-7000
Emp Here 230   *Sales* 48,443,500
SIC 2759 Commercial printing, nec
France Lauziere
Marc M. Tremblay
Denis Rozon
Marie-Pierre Simard

D-U-N-S 20-852-1695 (HQ)
WINDIGO AVENTURE INC
AVENTURIA TOURS
400 Av Atlantic Bureau 802, Outremont, QC, H2V 1A5
(514) 948-4145
Sales 16,691,388
SIC 8699 Membership organizations, nec
Charles Frobisher
Jean-Christophe Viard

Pabos, QC G0C

D-U-N-S 20-579-7434 (SL)
MARCHE BLAIS INC
204 Boul Pabos, Pabos, QC, G0C 2H0
(418) 689-3564
Emp Here 20   *Sales* 16,711,540
SIC 5146 Fish and seafoods
Jean-Paul Blais
Roland Blais
Joseph Albert Blais
Roland Jr. Blais

Pabos Mills, QC G0C

D-U-N-S 24-940-9038 (SL)
CONSTRUCTION J.C. LEPAGE LTEE
254 132 Rte, Pabos Mills, QC, G0C 2J0
(418) 689-0568
Emp Here 49   *Sales* 13,316,044
SIC 6531 Real estate agents and managers
Michel Lepage

Papineauville, QC J0V

D-U-N-S 24-589-0512 (HQ)
LAUZON - PLANCHERS DE BOIS EX-CLUSIFS INC
BUTTERFLY
(*Suby of* PLACEMENTS LAUZON INC)
2101 Cote Des Cascades, Papineauville, QC, J0V 1R0

(819) 427-5144
Emp Here 250   *Sales* 199,369,800
SIC 5031 Lumber, plywood, and millwork
David Lauzon

D-U-N-S 25-355-7821   (HQ)
PLACEMENTS LAUZON INC
LAUZON
2101 Cote Des Cascades, Papineauville, QC,
J0V 1R0
(819) 427-5144
Emp Here 1   *Sales* 208,340,130
SIC 6712 Bank holding companies
David Lauzon

Paspebiac, QC G0C

D-U-N-S 24-253-9923   (SL)
UNIPECHE M.D.M. LTEE
(Suby of GESTION UNIPECHE M.D.M. LTEE)
66 Av Du Quai, Paspebiac, QC, G0C 2K0
(418) 752-6700
Emp Here 100   *Sales* 34,569,000
SIC 2092 Fresh or frozen packaged fish
Jean-Marc Marcoux
Richard Desbois
Nicol Desbois
Douglas Mc Innis
Roger Pinel

Perce, QC G0C

D-U-N-S 20-322-8957   (BR)
VIA RAIL CANADA INC
(Suby of GOVERNMENT OF CANADA)
44 132 Rte O Bureau Lb1, Perce, QC, G0C
2L0
(418) 782-2747
Emp Here 200
SIC 4111 Local and suburban transit

Petit-Saguenay, QC G0V

D-U-N-S 25-995-7624   (SL)
DOMAINE LAFOREST
485 170 Rte, Petit-Saguenay, QC, G0V 1N0
(418) 638-5408
Emp Here 49   *Sales* 11,012,456
SIC 6159 Miscellaneous business credit insti-
tutions
Andre Desmarais

Petite-Riviere-Saint-Francois, QC G0A

D-U-N-S 24-356-4288   (SL)
MASSIF INC, LE
1350 Rue Principale, Petite-Riviere-Saint-
Francois, QC, G0A 2L0
(877) 536-2774
Emp Here 250   *Sales* 23,917,000
SIC 7011 Hotels and motels
Claude Choquette
Daniel Gauthier

Philipsburg, QC J0J

D-U-N-S 24-516-3597   (SL)
EMPAQUETAGES MESSIER INC
1050 Rte 133, Philipsburg, QC, J0J 1N0
(450) 248-3921
Emp Here 30   *Sales* 15,109,740
SIC 5113 Industrial and personal service pa-

per
Denis Messier
Ginette Messier

Piedmont, QC J0R

D-U-N-S 24-978-2686   (HQ)
CERAMIQUE ITAL-NORD LTEE
ITALNORD
569 Boul Des Laurentides Bureau 117, Pied-
mont, QC, J0R 1K0
(450) 227-8866
Sales 11,179,350
SIC 5032 Brick, stone, and related material
Bruno Pandin
Sotiria Petropoulos

Pierrefonds, QC H8Y

D-U-N-S 24-864-6671   (HQ)
175246 CANADA INC
RESTAURANT MCDONALD'S
4928 Boul Des Sources Bureau 2545, Pierrefonds, QC, H8Y 3E1
(514) 684-0779
Emp Here 250   *Sales* 13,991,700
SIC 5812 Eating places
Frederic Cassir

D-U-N-S 20-855-7231   (SL)
COLLEGE BEAUBOIS
4901 Rue Du College-Beaubois, Pierrefonds,
QC, H8Y 3T4
(514) 684-7642
Emp Here 106   *Sales* 10,506,614
SIC 8211 Elementary and secondary schools
Jean-Francois Albert

D-U-N-S 25-298-5650   (BR)
LESTER B. PEARSON SCHOOL BOARD
RIVERDALE HIGH SCHOOL
5060 Boul Des Sources, Pierrefonds, QC, H8Y
3E4
(514) 684-2337
Emp Here 80
SIC 8211 Elementary and secondary schools
Roger Rampersad

D-U-N-S 25-474-1168   (SL)
**MARCHE FLORAL INTER-PROVINCIAL
LTEE**
3600 Boul Pitfield, Pierrefonds, QC, H8Y 3L4
(514) 334-7733
Emp Here 25   *Sales* 11,230,475
SIC 7389 Business services, nec
Francois Caron

D-U-N-S 24-356-2030   (SL)
MEDIA CASH REGISTER INC
9580 Boul Gouin O, Pierrefonds, QC, H8Y
1R3
(514) 685-3630
Emp Here 25   *Sales* 12,591,450
SIC 5112 Stationery and office supplies
Eric Bernard

Pierrefonds, QC H8Z

D-U-N-S 25-474-4790   (SL)
ALIMENTATION DANIEL INC
METRO
13057 Boul Gouin O, Pierrefonds, QC, H8Z
1X1
(514) 620-7370
Emp Here 45   *Sales* 12,336,840
SIC 5411 Grocery stores
Daniel Audet

Pierrefonds, QC H9H

D-U-N-S 25-390-4775   (SL)
3183441 CANADA INC
*SUPERMARCHE MOURELATOS (PIERRE-
FONDS)*
4957 Boul Saint-Jean, Pierrefonds, QC, H9H
2A9
Emp Here 90   *Sales* 26,412,930
SIC 5411 Grocery stores
Eftymios Mourelatos
Christos Mourelatos
Peter Mourelatos
Hercules Tzougrakis
Larry Steinberg

D-U-N-S 25-990-7111   (SL)
**CLUB PISCINE PLUS C.P.P.Q. (WEST IS-
LAND) INC, LE**
CLUB PISCINE
14920 Boul De Pierrefonds, Pierrefonds, QC,
H9H 4G2
(514) 696-2582
Emp Here 40   *Sales* 13,024,000
SIC 5999 Miscellaneous retail stores, nec
Yvon Lemire
Matthew Lemire
Annie-France Chavy

D-U-N-S 24-803-2083   (BR)
RONA INC
RONA L'ENTREPOT
(Suby of LOWE'S COMPANIES, INC.)
3933 Boul Saint-Charles, Pierrefonds, QC,
H9H 3C7
(514) 624-2332
Emp Here 150
SIC 5072 Hardware

D-U-N-S 20-581-8110   (SL)
VALERIO, TOMASELLI
PHARMACIE JEAN COUTU
4930 Boul Saint-Jean, Pierrefonds, QC, H9H
4B2
(514) 620-7920
Emp Here 50   *Sales* 12,647,700
SIC 5912 Drug stores and proprietary stores
Tomaselli Valerio

D-U-N-S 25-258-8454   (BR)
VIGI SANTE LTEE
*CENTRE D'HEBERGEMENT ET DE SOINS
DE LONGUE DUREE PIERREFONDS*
14775 Boul De Pierrefonds Bureau 229, Pier-
refonds, QC, H9H 4Y1
(514) 620-1220
Emp Here 80
SIC 8361 Residential care
Caroline Habib

Pierrefonds, QC H9K

D-U-N-S 20-928-1708   (SL)
COLLEGE CHARLEMAGNE INC
COLLEGE CHARLEMAGNE
5000 Rue Pilon, Pierrefonds, QC, H9K 1G4
(514) 626-7060
Emp Here 160   *Sales* 23,902,560
SIC 8221 Colleges and universities
Brian Dempsey

Pierreville, QC J0G

D-U-N-S 25-463-3308   (SL)
ROUILLARD & FRERES INC
21 Rue Georges, Pierreville, QC, J0G 1J0
(450) 568-3510
Emp Here 49   *Sales* 13,433,448

SIC 5411 Grocery stores
Frederick Rouillard

Pincourt, QC J7W

D-U-N-S 24-713-9256   (HQ)
AQUA DATA INC
AQUA CAD
95 5e Av, Pincourt, QC, J7W 5K8
(514) 425-1010
Emp Here 100   *Sales* 27,789,520
SIC 7373 Computer integrated systems de-
sign
Francis Lebuis

D-U-N-S 20-928-0692   (HQ)
PIECES D'AUTO PINCOURT INC, LES
AUTOPLUS
35 Ch Duhamel, Pincourt, QC, J7W 4C6
(514) 453-5610
Emp Here 17   *Sales* 12,747,525
SIC 5013 Motor vehicle supplies and new
parts
Richard Larente
Andre Larente
Suzanne Larente

Plaisance, QC J0V

D-U-N-S 20-891-7401   (SL)
**CHARLEBOIS, MAURICE ALIMENTATION
LTEE**
267 Rue Marie-Claude, Plaisance, QC, J0V
1S0
Emp Here 35   *Sales* 29,245,195
SIC 5142 Packaged frozen goods
Sylvain Charlebois
Christiane Charlebois
Stephane Charlebois

Plessisville, QC G6L

D-U-N-S 20-550-3068   (SL)
4170083 CANADA INC
CARBOTECH INTERNATIONAL
2250 Rue Saint-Jean, Plessisville, QC, G6L
2Y4
(819) 362-6317
Emp Here 75   *Sales* 16,650,075
SIC 3553 Woodworking machinery
Dary Laflamme
Luc Houde
Raymond Landry
Christian Provost

D-U-N-S 25-366-6952   (HQ)
9187-2853 QUEBEC INC
2299 Av Vallee, Plessisville, QC, G6L 2Y6
(819) 252-6315
Sales 13,077,650
SIC 6712 Bank holding companies
Jennifer Poire

D-U-N-S 24-200-7037   (BR)
AGROPUR COOPERATIVE
AGROPUR
(Suby of AGROPUR COOPERATIVE)
2400 Rue De La Cooperative, Plessisville, QC,
G6L 3G8
(819) 362-7338
Emp Here 85
SIC 2023 Dry, condensed and evaporated
dairy products

D-U-N-S 20-363-6287   (SL)
ATOCAS DE L'ERABLE INC, LES
CONGELATEUR DE L'ERABLE

2249 Rue Garneau, Plessisville, QC, G6L 2Y7
(819) 621-7166
Emp Here 50   *Sales* 17,321,671
SIC 0171 Berry crops
Pierre Fortier
Josee Poisson

D-U-N-S 20-239-6560   (HQ)
BOUTIN, V. EXPRESS INC
1397 Rue Savoie, Plessisville, QC, G6L 1J8
(819) 362-7333
Emp Here 70   *Sales* 41,141,200
SIC 4213 Trucking, except local
Bernard Boutin
Marc Binette

D-U-N-S 25-501-6321   (HQ)
C.B.R. LASER INC
FABRI METAL
(*Suby of* GESTION C.B.R. LASER INC)
340 Rte 116, Plessisville, QC, G6L 2Y2
(819) 362-9339
Emp Here 50   *Sales* 152,540,500
SIC 7389 Business services, nec
Claude Beauvillier

D-U-N-S 25-363-1550   (HQ)
CAISSE DESJARDINS DE L'ERABLE
CENTRE DE SERVICE DE LOURDES
1658 Rue Saint-Calixte, Plessisville, QC, G6L
1P9
(819) 362-3236
Emp Here 54   *Sales* 19,322,486
SIC 6062 State credit unions
Paul Gagne
Andre Grenier
Yvon Jr Fiset
Valerye Bedard
Danis Beauvillier
Jean-Philippe Boutin
Richard Cote
Edith Laliberte
Noel Lemieux
Genevieve Manseau

D-U-N-S 20-205-9341   (HQ)
**CITADELLE COOPERATIVE DE PRODUC-
TEURS DE SIROP D'ERABLE**
SHADY MAPLE FARMS PRODUCTION
2100 Av Saint-Laurent, Plessisville, QC, G6L
2R3
(819) 362-3241
Emp Here 70   *Sales* 34,569,000
SIC 2099 Food preparations, nec
Michel Labbe
Laurent Cloutier
Jean-Marie Chouinard
Simon Deschenes
Paul Beauregard
Michel Belanger
Laurier Gauthier
Jean-Claude Brochu
Denis Pellerin
Pierre Fortier

D-U-N-S 25-232-8547   (BR)
**COMMISSION SCOLAIRE DES BOIS-
FRANCS**
ECOLE POLYVALENTE LA SAMARE
(*Suby of* COMMISSION SCOLAIRE DES
BOIS-FRANCS)
1159 Rue Saint-Jean, Plessisville, QC, G6L
1E1
(819) 362-3226
Emp Here 130
SIC 8211 Elementary and secondary schools
Danielle Beliveau

D-U-N-S 20-239-7477   (HQ)
COMPAGNIE MOTOPARTS INC
1124 Rue Saint-Calixte, Plessisville, QC, G6L
1N8
(819) 362-7373
Emp Here 57   *Sales* 29,263,800
SIC 5085 Industrial supplies
Jean-Guy Cote

D-U-N-S 20-239-6776   (SL)

DUBOIS & FRERES LIMITEE
637 Av Saint-Louis, Plessisville, QC, G6L 2L9
(819) 362-7377
Emp Here 30   *Sales* 14,942,340
SIC 5511 New and used car dealers
Jean-Francois Dubois
Marie-Helene Binette
Nathacha Methot

D-U-N-S 25-479-5875   (SL)
**EQUIPEMENTS A. PROVENCHER & FILS
INC, LES**
2175 Rue Saint-Jean, Plessisville, QC, G6L
2Y4
(819) 225-0225
Emp Here 29   *Sales* 13,775,754
SIC 5083 Farm and garden machinery
Michel Provencher

D-U-N-S 20-381-4715   (SL)
**FOURNITURES INDUSTRIELLES PASCO
INC, LES**
1124 Rue Saint-Calixte, Plessisville, QC, G6L
1N8
(819) 362-7345
Emp Here 55   *Sales* 15,034,250
SIC 6712 Bank holding companies
Jean-Guy Cote

D-U-N-S 24-384-9358   (HQ)
GESTION C.B.R. LASER INC
340 Rte 116, Plessisville, QC, G6L 2Y2
(819) 362-2095
Sales 100,514,975
SIC 6712 Bank holding companies
Claude Beauvillier

D-U-N-S 24-426-8723   (SL)
GESTION M.E.W. INC
2255 Av Vallee, Plessisville, QC, G6L 3P8
(819) 362-6315
Emp Here 60   *Sales* 13,320,060
SIC 3599 Industrial machinery, nec
Jennifer Poire
Allen Poire

D-U-N-S 24-377-8362   (HQ)
GROUPE BOUTIN INC
1397 Rue Savoie, Plessisville, QC, G6L 1J8
(819) 362-7333
Sales 182,754,500
SIC 6712 Bank holding companies
Bernard Boutin
Jean-Philippe Boutin

D-U-N-S 24-940-6935   (HQ)
GROUPE MACHINEX INC
(*Suby of* 9045-1691 QUEBEC INC)
2121 Rue Olivier, Plessisville, QC, G6L 3G9
(819) 362-3281
Emp Here 3   *Sales* 24,601,500
SIC 6712 Bank holding companies
Pierre Pare

D-U-N-S 20-582-0285   (SL)
INDUSTRIES MACHINEX INC
MACHINEX
(*Suby of* 9045-1691 QUEBEC INC)
2121 Rue Olivier, Plessisville, QC, G6L 3G9
(819) 362-3281
Emp Here 350   *Sales* 98,306,950
SIC 3559 Special industry machinery, nec
Pierre Pare

D-U-N-S 20-592-5795   (HQ)
LOCATION HEBERT 2000 LTEE
BUDGET LOCATION
750 Av Saint-Louis, Plessisville, QC, G6L 2M1
(819) 362-8816
Emp Here 7   *Sales* 14,942,340
SIC 5511 New and used car dealers
Andre Hebert

D-U-N-S 20-239-7360   (SL)
MAGASIN CO-OP DE PLESSISVILLE
IGA EXTRA
1971 Rue Bilodeau, Plessisville, QC, G6L 3J1
(819) 362-6357
Emp Here 110   *Sales* 32,282,470

SIC 5411 Grocery stores
Jacques Labreque
Gilles Dion
Gaston Nadeau

D-U-N-S 24-202-9312   (SL)
PLESSITECH INC
(*Suby of* 9187-2853 QUEBEC INC)
2250 Av Vallee, Plessisville, QC, G6L 2Y6
(819) 362-6315
Emp Here 50   *Sales* 13,592,100
SIC 7692 Welding repair
Allen Poire
Jennifer Poire

D-U-N-S 24-102-8567   (BR)
**SAPUTO PRODUITS LAITIERS CANADA
S.E.N.C.**
(*Suby of* SAPUTO PRODUITS LAITIERS
CANADA S.E.N.C.)
1245 Av Forand, Plessisville, QC, G6L 1X5
(819) 362-6378
Emp Here 140
SIC 2022 Cheese; natural and processed
Jean-Claude Couture

D-U-N-S 24-820-7698   (HQ)
SEMICAN ATLANTIC INC
366 10e Rang, Plessisville, QC, G6L 2Y2
(819) 362-6759
Sales 37,126,000
SIC 5191 Farm supplies
Jacques Beauchesne
France Gingras

D-U-N-S 25-976-3217   (HQ)
SEMICAN INTERNATIONAL INC
SEMICAN
(*Suby of* SEMICAN ATLANTIC INC)
366 10e Rang, Plessisville, QC, G6L 2Y2
(819) 362-6759
Sales 29,353,840
SIC 5153 Grain and field beans
Jacques Beauchesne

D-U-N-S 24-568-1879   (HQ)
TRANSNAT EXPRESS INC
TRANSNAT LOGISTIQUE
1397 Rue Savoie, Plessisville, QC, G6L 1J8
(819) 362-7333
Emp Here 300   *Sales* 73,752,400
SIC 4213 Trucking, except local
Bernard Boutin
Pierre Lefebvre

D-U-N-S 20-017-1283   (SL)
USNR/KOCKUMS CANCAR COMPANY
U.S.N.R.
(*Suby of* USNR, LLC)
1600 Rue Saint-Paul, Plessisville, QC, G6L
1C1
(819) 362-7362
Emp Here 80   *Sales* 17,760,080
SIC 3553 Woodworking machinery
George Van Hoomissen
Richard H. Ward
Ronald W. Giesbers

Pohenegamook, QC G0L

D-U-N-S 24-759-6216   (SL)
MEUBLES REAL LEVASSEUR & FILS INC
1907 Rue Principale, Pohenegamook, QC,
G0L 1J0
(418) 859-3159
Emp Here 50   *Sales* 11,517,000
SIC 5712 Furniture stores
Lyne Cote-Levasseur
Laury Levasseur

D-U-N-S 25-331-5105   (HQ)
POUTRELLES INTERNATIONALES INC
480 Rue Jocelyn-Bastille, Pohenegamook,
QC, G0L 1J0

(418) 893-1515
Sales 11,542,200
SIC 2448 Wood pallets and skids
Bruno Lebel

D-U-N-S 24-147-0079   (SL)
TRANSPORT GUY LEVASSEUR INC
876 Rue Principale, Pohenegamook, QC, G0L
1J0
(418) 859-2294
Emp Here 70   *Sales* 10,373,440
SIC 4213 Trucking, except local
Guy Levasseur

Pointe-Aux-Outardes, QC G5C

D-U-N-S 20-561-1044   (HQ)
SANI-MANIC COTE-NORD INC
37 Ch De La Scierie, Pointe-Aux-Outardes,
QC, G5C 0B7
(418) 589-2376
Emp Here 35   *Sales* 10,185,800
SIC 7699 Repair services, nec
Arnold Gauthier

Pointe-Aux-Trembles, QC H1A

D-U-N-S 24-890-1860   (SL)
2968-4305 QUEBEC INC
PHARMAPRIX
12800 Rue Sherbrooke E Bureau 61, Pointe-
Aux-Trembles, QC, H1A 4Y3
(514) 498-4840
Emp Here 65   *Sales* 15,881,320
SIC 5912 Drug stores and proprietary stores
Marc Champagne

D-U-N-S 25-998-7977   (SL)
4501403 CANADA INC
DEPANNEUR BELANGER XL
3478 32e Av, Pointe-Aux-Trembles, QC, H1A
3M1
(514) 498-7227
Emp Here 49   *Sales* 13,433,448
SIC 5411 Grocery stores
Yan Besner

D-U-N-S 20-763-8441   (SL)
9093-6907 QUEBEC INC
IGA LEBLANC
13155 Rue Sherbrooke E, Pointe-Aux-
Trembles, QC, H1A 1B9
(514) 498-2220
Emp Here 150   *Sales* 44,021,550
SIC 5411 Grocery stores
Gerard Leblanc

D-U-N-S 25-242-7158   (SL)
**ABEILLES SERVICES DE CONDITION-
NEMENT INC, LES**
ABEILLES BUSY BEES
12910 Boul Metropolitain E, Pointe-Aux-
Trembles, QC, H1A 4A7
(514) 640-6941
Emp Here 45   *Sales* 20,214,855
SIC 7389 Business services, nec
Patrick Paradis

D-U-N-S 20-021-4901   (SL)
ALIMENTATION ANDREA JOLICOEUR INC
METRO DE LA ROUSSELLIERE
3000 Boul De La Rousseliere, Pointe-Aux-
Trembles, QC, H1A 4G3
(514) 498-7117
Emp Here 100   *Sales* 29,347,700
SIC 5411 Grocery stores
Marc Landry

D-U-N-S 24-590-3323   (HQ)
ANJINNOV CONSTRUCTION INC
13550 Boul Henri-Bourassa E, Pointe-Aux-
Trembles, QC, H1A 0A4

▲ Public Company   ■ Public Company Family Member   **HQ** Headquarters   **BR** Branch   **SL** Single Location

(514) 353-3000
Emp Here 20   *Sales* 16,475,585
SIC 1542 Nonresidential construction, nec
Pierre Monty
Pascal Michaud
Robert Lacroix

D-U-N-S 20-016-8768   (HQ)
BEACON ROOFING SUPPLY CANADA COMPANY
GROUPE BEDARD
(*Suby of* BEACON ROOFING SUPPLY, INC.)
13145 Rue Prince-Arthur, Pointe-Aux-Trembles, QC, H1A 1A9
(514) 642-8998
Emp Here 45   *Sales* 68,355,360
SIC 5039 Construction materials, nec
John C. Smith Jr.
Cooper Ross D.
Buck Robert R.

D-U-N-S 20-857-7023   (SL)
BROADWAY PAVING LTD, THE
3620 39e Av, Pointe-Aux-Trembles, QC, H1A 3V1
(514) 642-5811
Emp Here 40   *Sales* 11,340,960
SIC 1611 Highway and street construction
Robert D'Errico
Matthieu D'Errico

D-U-N-S 20-859-6742   (SL)
CENTRE LE CARDINAL INC
12900 Rue Notre-Dame E, Pointe-Aux-Trembles, QC, H1A 1R9
(514) 645-0095
Emp Here 225   *Sales* 33,787,350
SIC 8069 Specialty hospitals, except psychiatric
Andre Groulx
Betty G. Carey
John Carey
Ann Carey
Kathleen Carey

D-U-N-S 20-882-0845   (HQ)
COMMISSION SCOLAIRE DE LA POINTE-DE-L'ILE
550 53e Av, Pointe-Aux-Trembles, QC, H1A 2T7
(514) 642-9520
Emp Here 170   *Sales* 288,238,052
SIC 8211 Elementary and secondary schools
Miville Boudreault
Pierre Boulay

D-U-N-S 24-743-6660   (SL)
GESTION HEROUX ET SAUCIER INC
JEAN COUTU
12675 Rue Sherbrooke E, Pointe-Aux-Trembles, QC, H1A 3W7
(514) 642-2251
Emp Here 40   *Sales* 10,118,160
SIC 5912 Drug stores and proprietary stores
Claude Saucier
Nicole Heroux
Catherine Bertrand
Jonathan Rouisse

D-U-N-S 20-225-6827   (SL)
INDUSTRIES APRIL INC, LES
12755 Boul Industriel, Pointe-Aux-Trembles, QC, H1A 4Z6
(514) 640-5355
Emp Here 150   *Sales* 26,882,850
SIC 3231 Products of purchased glass
Robert Beaudre

D-U-N-S 20-107-4957   (SL)
MACNO TELECOM INC
12655 Boul Industriel, Pointe-Aux-Trembles, QC, H1A 4Z6
(514) 498-1555
Emp Here 60   *Sales* 11,087,880
SIC 4899 Communication services, nec
Sylvain Dufour

D-U-N-S 24-204-7921   (SL)

MARCHE DE LA ROUSSELIERE INC
3000 Boul De La Rousseliere, Pointe-Aux-Trembles, QC, H1A 4G3
(514) 498-7117
Emp Here 50   *Sales* 13,707,600
SIC 5411 Grocery stores
Bernard Lemay

D-U-N-S 25-827-6351   (BR)
PROVIGO DISTRIBUTION INC
MAXI
(*Suby of* LOBLAW COMPANIES LIMITED)
12780 Rue Sherbrooke E, Pointe-Aux-Trembles, QC, H1A 4Y3
(514) 498-2675
Emp Here 100
SIC 5411 Grocery stores
Daniel Dupont

D-U-N-S 25-108-0169   (SL)
RE MAX CITE INC
13150 Rue Sherbrooke E, Pointe-Aux-Trembles, QC, H1A 4B1
(514) 644-0000
Emp Here 42   *Sales* 11,413,752
SIC 6531 Real estate agents and managers
Andre Mandanica

D-U-N-S 20-022-1526   (SL)
RE/MAX DE LA POINTE INC
RE/MAX DE LA POINTE
13150 Rue Sherbrooke E Bureau 201, Pointe-Aux-Trembles, QC, H1A 4B1
(514) 644-0000
Emp Here 60   *Sales* 16,305,360
SIC 6531 Real estate agents and managers
Andre Theoret

D-U-N-S 24-509-3984   (SL)
SERVICE REMTEC INC
TANKMART PARTS & SERVICES
3560 39e Av, Pointe-Aux-Trembles, QC, H1A 3V1
(514) 642-6020
Emp Here 35   *Sales* 12,747,525
SIC 5013 Motor vehicle supplies and new parts
Ronald Laberge

D-U-N-S 20-266-3191   (HQ)
WESTROCK COMPANY OF CANADA CORP
PRESENTOIRS ROCKTENN
(*Suby of* WESTROCK COMPANY)
15400 Rue Sherbrooke E Bureau A-15, Pointe-Aux-Trembles, QC, H1A 3S2
(514) 642-9251
Emp Here 300   *Sales* 294,109,600
SIC 2657 Folding paperboard boxes
Steven C Voorhees
Ward H Dickson
Robert B. Mcintosh

Pointe-Aux-Trembles, QC H1B

D-U-N-S 20-332-8919   (SL)
8863377 CANADA INC
MAZDA POINTE-AUX-TREMBLES
12277 Boul Metropolitain E, Pointe-Aux-Trembles, QC, H1B 5R3
(514) 645-1694
Emp Here 40   *Sales* 19,923,120
SIC 5511 New and used car dealers
Gabriel Gennarelli

D-U-N-S 25-400-4864   (SL)
9039-8082 QUEBEC INC
DOMAINE HONDA POINTE-AUX-TREMBLES
12150 Rue Sherbrooke E, Pointe-Aux-Trembles, QC, H1B 1C7
(514) 645-6700
Emp Here 25   *Sales* 12,451,950
SIC 5511 New and used car dealers
Pierre Deveault

D-U-N-S 20-649-1904   (BR)
9327-0197 QUEBEC INC
(*Suby of* TFI INTERNATIONAL INC)
12321 Boul Metropolitain E, Pointe-Aux-Trembles, QC, H1B 5R3
(514) 645-7184
Emp Here 100
SIC 4213 Trucking, except local
Jacques Tremblay

D-U-N-S 20-270-9168   (HQ)
BEAUDRY & CADRIN INC
GROUPE A PLUS
12225 Boul Metropolitain E, Pointe-Aux-Trembles, QC, H1B 5R3
(514) 352-5620
Emp Here 50   *Sales* 83,557,700
SIC 5149 Groceries and related products, nec
Francois Beaudry
Jean-Philippe Beaudry

D-U-N-S 20-211-2314   (SL)
BEAUDRY, JEAN-PAUL LTEE
12225 Boul Metropolitain E, Pointe-Aux-Trembles, QC, H1B 5R3
(514) 352-5620
Emp Here 65   *Sales* 54,312,505
SIC 5141 Groceries, general line
Jean-Philippe Beaudry
Francois Beaudry
Jean-Philippe Beaudry

D-U-N-S 25-198-6808   (SL)
CENTRE D'HEBERGEMENT ET DE SOINS DE LONGUE DUREE BOURGET INC
CENTRE BOURGET
11570 Rue Notre-Dame E, Pointe-Aux-Trembles, QC, H1B 2X4
(514) 645-1673
Emp Here 140   *Sales* 9,599,240
SIC 8051 Skilled nursing care facilities
Yvan Girard
Jean-Francois Girard
Diane Girard
Claire Cauchon Girard

D-U-N-S 24-073-4603   (SL)
CHAPITEAUX CLASSIC INC, LES
LOCATION DE TENTE ACME
12301 Boul Metropolitain E, Pointe-Aux-Trembles, QC, H1B 5R3
(514) 645-4555
Emp Here 35   *Sales* 11,396,000
SIC 5999 Miscellaneous retail stores, nec
Sylvain Menard
Alan Gauthier

D-U-N-S 24-415-6845   (SL)
FISHER AND LUDLOW
12450 Boul Industriel, Pointe-Aux-Trembles, QC, H1B 5M5

Emp Here 25   *Sales* 11,875,650
SIC 5084 Industrial machinery and equipment
Michel Gagne

D-U-N-S 24-253-4170   (HQ)
GANOTEC INC
3777 Rue Dollard-Desjardins, Pointe-Aux-Trembles, QC, H1B 5W9
(819) 377-5533
Sales 349,196,000
SIC 1541 Industrial buildings and warehouses
Sebastien Larivee
Dean J. Kampschneider
Michael F. Norton
Thomas S. Shelby

D-U-N-S 24-935-5819   (SL)
GESTION MARIO CHRISTIN INC
12011 Rue Sherbrooke E, Pointe-Aux-Trembles, QC, H1B 1C6
(514) 640-1050
Emp Here 106   *Sales* 28,975,100
SIC 6712 Bank holding companies
Mario Christin

D-U-N-S 24-329-8465   (BR)

GROUPE PATRICK MORIN INC
PATRICK MORIN INC
(*Suby of* GROUPE PATRICK MORIN INC)
11850 Rue Sherbrooke E, Pointe-Aux-Trembles, QC, H1B 1C4
(514) 645-1115
Emp Here 92
SIC 5211 Lumber and other building materials
Mario Laprise

D-U-N-S 20-217-1299   (SL)
HOULE TOYOTA LTEE
12305 Rue Sherbrooke E, Pointe-Aux-Trembles, QC, H1B 1C8
(514) 640-5010
Emp Here 50   *Sales* 24,903,900
SIC 5511 New and used car dealers
Michel Houle

D-U-N-S 25-337-3898   (SL)
INDUSTRIES D'EMBALLAGES STARPAC LTEE, LES
12105 Boul Industriel, Pointe-Aux-Trembles, QC, H1B 5W4
(514) 645-5895
Emp Here 75   *Sales* 11,914,350
SIC 3081 Unsupported plastics film and sheet
Hershey Friedman
Rita Friedman

D-U-N-S 24-351-6713   (SL)
INDUSTRIES DE LAVAGE DENTEX INC, LES
12480 Rue April, Pointe-Aux-Trembles, QC, H1B 5N5

Emp Here 125   *Sales* 13,347,750
SIC 7218 Industrial launderers
Daniel Terrault

D-U-N-S 25-690-3071   (SL)
INDUSTRIES RONDI INC, LES
12425 Boul Industriel, Pointe-Aux-Trembles, QC, H1B 5M7
(514) 640-0888
Emp Here 60   *Sales* 12,113,820
SIC 3089 Plastics products, nec
Francois Morin
Mimmo Pasqua

D-U-N-S 20-996-0285   (HQ)
MCMAHON DISTRIBUTEUR PHARMACEUTIQUE INC
BRUNET
(*Suby of* METRO INC)
12225 Boul Industriel Bureau 100, Pointe-Aux-Trembles, QC, H1B 5M7
(514) 355-8350
Sales 167,192,505
SIC 5122 Drugs, proprietaries, and sundries
Eric R. La Fleche
Simon Rivet
Francois Thibault

D-U-N-S 24-226-5663   (BR)
METRO RICHELIEU INC
MCMAHON DISTRIBUTEUR PHARMACEUTIQUE
(*Suby of* METRO INC)
12225 Boul Industriel Bureau 100, Pointe-Aux-Trembles, QC, H1B 5M7
(514) 355-8350
Emp Here 200
SIC 5122 Drugs, proprietaries, and sundries

D-U-N-S 20-381-1208   (SL)
PG4 CONSTRUCTION CORP.
CONSTRUCTION PG4
(*Suby of* GANOTEC INC)
3777 Rue Dollard-Desjardins, Pointe-Aux-Trembles, QC, H1B 5W9
(514) 354-5533
Emp Here 50   *Sales* 21,136,850
SIC 1541 Industrial buildings and warehouses
Sebastien Larivee
Michael F. Norton
Walter L. Bentley

Thomas S. Shelby
Alessandro Saltarelli

D-U-N-S 24-908-2496   (SL)
PLACEMENTS JEAN BEAUDRY INC, LES
GROUPE PRO-JEAN, LE
12305 Boul Metropolitain E, Pointe-Aux-Trembles, QC, H1B 5R3
(514) 640-4440
Emp Here 700   *Sales* 255,856,300
SIC 6712 Bank holding companies
Jean Beaudry

D-U-N-S 20-715-0314   (BR)
PRESSE (2018) INC, LA
PRESSE, LTEE, LA
(*Suby of* PRESSE (2018) INC, LA)
12300 Boul Metropolitain E, Pointe-Aux-Trembles, QC, H1B 5Y2
(514) 640-1840
Emp Here 300
SIC 7319 Advertising, nec
Alain Marcoux

D-U-N-S 25-673-7719   (SL)
PRODUITS NON FERREUX GAUTHIER INC, LES
12355 Rue April, Pointe-Aux-Trembles, QC, H1B 5L8
(514) 642-4090
Emp Here 70   *Sales* 16,340,450
SIC 3356 Nonferrous rolling and drawing, nec
Robert Gauthier
Judith Gauthier

D-U-N-S 24-896-3654   (BR)
SUNCOR ENERGY INC
(*Suby of* SUNCOR ENERGY INC)
11701 Rue Sherbrooke E, Pointe-Aux-Trembles, QC, H1B 1C3
(514) 640-8000
Emp Here 600
SIC 2911 Petroleum refining
Bruno Francoeur

D-U-N-S 25-101-7893   (SL)
TECHNI-DATA PERFORMANCE INC
12305 Boul Metropolitain E, Pointe-Aux-Trembles, QC, H1B 5R3
(514) 640-1666
Emp Here 50   *Sales* 11,895,050
SIC 8742 Management consulting services
Jean Beaudry
Michel Crepeau

D-U-N-S 24-730-1559   (SL)
TECNICKROME AERONAUTIQUE INC
(*Suby of* SPP CANADA AIRCRAFT, INC)
12264 Rue April Bureau 1, Pointe-Aux-Trembles, QC, H1B 5N5
(514) 640-0333
Emp Here 80   *Sales* 15,366,800
SIC 3471 Plating and polishing
Masatoshi Yamabayashi
Natsuo Hashimoto
Gilles Demers
Eli Brigler
Andrew Morrow

D-U-N-S 20-541-4121   (SL)
TRANSFORMATEUR FEDERAL LTEE
GROUPE FEDERAL, LE
5059 Boul Saint-Jean-Baptiste, Pointe-Aux-Trembles, QC, H1B 5V3
(514) 640-5059
Emp Here 25   *Sales* 13,013,550
SIC 5099 Durable goods, nec
Julien Gagnon
Francine Larose
Lucie Gagnon

D-U-N-S 25-837-5286   (BR)
TRANSPORT JACQUES AUGER INC
12305 Boul Metropolitain E, Pointe-Aux-Trembles, QC, H1B 5R3
(514) 493-3835
Emp Here 150
SIC 4212 Local trucking, without storage

Anne Marree

D-U-N-S 24-835-4367   (HQ)
VEOLIA ES CANADA SERVICES INDUS-TRIELS INC
DRAINAMAR
(*Suby of* VEOLIA ENVIRONNEMENT)
1705 3e Av, Pointe-Aux-Trembles, QC, H1B 5M9
(514) 645-1621
Emp Here 200   *Sales* 211,719,300
SIC 4953 Refuse systems
William Dicroce
Jason Salgo
Mireille Dufresne

D-U-N-S 20-928-3100   (SL)
VIBAC CANADA INC
SEALAST
(*Suby of* VIBAC SPA)
12250 Boul Industriel, Pointe-Aux-Trembles, QC, H1B 5M5
(514) 640-0250
Emp Here 100   *Sales* 19,476,800
SIC 2672 Paper; coated and laminated, nec
Anna Luigia Gentile
Pietro Battista
Alberto Depaoli
Jocelyne Rodrigue
Rino Petrella
Georges Mouannes

Pointe-Aux-Trembles, QC H1C

D-U-N-S 25-965-4903   (SL)
F.X. LANGE INC
10550 Boul Henri-Bourassa E, Pointe-Aux-Trembles, QC, H1C 1G6
(514) 648-7445
Emp Here 10   *Sales* 10,003,390
SIC 5051 Metals service centers and offices
Adelard Lange

Pointe-Aux-Trembles, QC H3C

D-U-N-S 20-289-1602   (SL)
CORPORATION GARDAWORLD SERVICES TRANSPORT DE VALEURS CANADA
G4S SOLUTION VALEURS
1390 Rue Barre, Pointe-Aux-Trembles, QC, H3C 5X9
(514) 281-2811
Emp Here 100   *Sales* 53,120,700
SIC 6211 Security brokers and dealers
Stephan Cretier
Patrick Prince
Pierre-Hubert Seguin

Pointe-Claire, QC H7X

D-U-N-S 20-860-4434   (BR)
WINNERS MERCHANTS INTERNATIONAL L.P.
HOMESENSE
(*Suby of* THE TJX COMPANIES INC)
1050 Chomedey (A-13) O, Pointe-Claire, QC, H7X 4C9
(450) 969-2007
Emp Here 105
SIC 5651 Family clothing stores
Teressa Lutzac

Pointe-Claire, QC H7Y

D-U-N-S 24-364-2357   (BR)

CLUBLINK CORPORATION ULC
CLUB DE GOLF ISLESMERE
(*Suby of* TWC ENTERPRISES LIMITED)
1199 Ch Du Bord-De-L'Eau, Pointe-Claire, QC, H7Y 1A9
(450) 689-4130
Emp Here 120
SIC 7992 Public golf courses
Eric Lamarre

Pointe-Claire, QC H9P

D-U-N-S 25-688-0576   (HQ)
AMD MEDICOM INC
A.M.D. RITMED
(*Suby of* 7593759 CANADA INC)
2555 Ch De L'Aviation, Pointe-Claire, QC, H9P 2Z2
(514) 633-1111
Emp Here 20   *Sales* 13,637,340
SIC 3842 Surgical appliances and supplies
Ronald Reuben
Annie Corbeil
Guillaume Laverdure
Ian Levine
David Goodman

D-U-N-S 25-291-9014   (SL)
GLOBOCAM (MONTREAL) INC
155 Av Reverchon, Pointe-Claire, QC, H9P 1K1
(514) 344-4000
Emp Here 125   *Sales* 72,156,500
SIC 5511 New and used car dealers
Serge Boyer
Gilles Francois Guy Beaudoin Giguere Landry

D-U-N-S 24-787-6295   (HQ)
MEDICOM GROUP INC
GROUPE MEDICOM
(*Suby of* 7593759 CANADA INC)
2555 Ch De L'Aviation, Pointe-Claire, QC, H9P 2Z2
(514) 636-6262
Emp Here 40   *Sales* 14,773,785
SIC 3843 Dental equipment and supplies
Ronald Reuben
David Goodman
Guillaume Laverdure

Pointe-Claire, QC H9R

D-U-N-S 24-668-8592   (HQ)
144503 CANADA INC
NATURE PET CENTER
(*Suby of* INVESTISSEMENTS HOHAG INC)
6361 Rte Transcanadienne Bureau 119, Pointe-Claire, QC, H9R 5A5
(514) 694-6843
Emp Here 5   *Sales* 31,762,640
SIC 5999 Miscellaneous retail stores, nec
Stephane Rolf Hagen

D-U-N-S 24-920-5998   (SL)
163453 CANADA INC
VIDEO MAISON CMR
6800 Rte Transcanadienne, Pointe-Claire, QC, H9R 1C2
(514) 956-7482
Emp Here 45   *Sales* 23,424,390
SIC 5099 Durable goods, nec
Richard Brotto
Jeannie Ali Zorina

D-U-N-S 20-237-1878   (HQ)
190394 CANADA INC
WALTER TECHNOLOGIES POUR SUR-FACES
(*Suby of* ONCAP MANAGEMENT PART-NERS LP)
5977 Rte Transcanadienne, Pointe-Claire, QC,

H9R 1C1
(514) 630-2800
Emp Here 50   *Sales* 85,352,750
SIC 5085 Industrial supplies
Pierre Somers
Haisook Somers
Franco Vitale

D-U-N-S 25-149-9372   (SL)
3330389 CANADA INC
SMT-ASSY ELECTRONIQUE
125 Boul Hymus, Pointe-Claire, QC, H9R 1E6
(514) 428-8898
Emp Here 50   *Sales* 10,233,650
SIC 3679 Electronic components, nec
Mario Lapointe
Leyanis Guevara Canete

D-U-N-S 24-380-2787   (HQ)
4271815 CANADA INC
61 Boul Hymus, Pointe-Claire, QC, H9R 1E2
(514) 428-0848
Sales 18,218,970
SIC 5093 Scrap and waste materials
Alvin Zoltan
Charles Rozansky

D-U-N-S 24-793-4164   (SL)
4501403 CANADA INC
DEPANNEUR BELANGER XI
230 Boul Hymus, Pointe-Claire, QC, H9R 5P5
(514) 694-3747
Emp Here 49   *Sales* 13,433,448
SIC 5411 Grocery stores
Yan Besner

D-U-N-S 20-370-7161   (SL)
8885168 CANADA INC
INSULFLEX ELECTRONICS
215 Rue Voyageur, Pointe-Claire, QC, H9R 6B2
(819) 294-4484
Emp Here 250   *Sales* 53,094,000
SIC 1799 Special trade contractors, nec
Sydney Knecht

D-U-N-S 20-288-4607   (SL)
9121-1128 QUEBEC INC
188 Av Oneida, Pointe-Claire, QC, H9R 1A8
(514) 694-3439
Emp Here 57   *Sales* 15,081,190
SIC 6712 Bank holding companies
Daniel Lachapelle

D-U-N-S 20-295-7460   (SL)
9156-0763 QUEBEC INC
DISTRIBUTION SINOMEX
6500 Rte Transcanadienne Unite 400, Pointe-Claire, QC, H9R 0A5
(514) 695-9192
Emp Here 26   *Sales* 11,626,524
SIC 5065 Electronic parts and equipment, nec
Derek George

D-U-N-S 24-458-0973   (SL)
9159-9159 QUEBEC INC
PHARMAPRIX
6815 Rte Transcanadienne, Pointe-Claire, QC, H9R 5J1
(514) 695-4211
Emp Here 40   *Sales* 10,118,160
SIC 5912 Drug stores and proprietary stores
Nora Al-Khoury

D-U-N-S 24-709-9257   (BR)
ABB PRODUITS D'INSTALLATION LTEE
T & B COMMANDER
(*Suby of* ABB LTD)
4025 Rte Transcanadienne, Pointe-Claire, QC, H9R 1B4
(514) 694-6800
Emp Here 75
SIC 3699 Electrical equipment and supplies, nec
Sophie Dewez

D-U-N-S 25-998-4284   (BR)
ABB PRODUITS D'INSTALLATION LTEE

GFI
(*Suby of* ABB LTD)
180 Av Labrosse, Pointe-Claire, QC, H9R 1A1
(514) 630-4877
Emp Here 194
SIC 3699 Electrical equipment and supplies, nec
Slobodin Todorovic

D-U-N-S 24-739-3309   (SL)
ACCORD INTERNATIONAL LEAF INC
193 Av Labrosse, Pointe-Claire, QC, H9R 1A3

Emp Here 16   *Sales* 19,366,352
SIC 5159 Farm-product raw materials, nec
Louis Lapointe

D-U-N-S 20-217-9206   (SL)
ALIMENTS LUDA FOODS INC
ALIMENTS E.D.
6200 Rte Transcanadienne, Pointe-Claire, QC, H9R 1B9
(514) 695-3333
Emp Here 60   *Sales* 20,741,400
SIC 2034 Dried and dehydrated fruits, vegetables and soup mixes
Victor Eiser
Robert Eiser
Leslie Eiser

D-U-N-S 20-233-1047   (SL)
ALIMENTS NOBLE INC
250 Av Avro, Pointe-Claire, QC, H9R 6B1
(514) 426-0680
Emp Here 50   *Sales* 11,242,750
SIC 2064 Candy and other confectionery products
Lee Shulkin
Stephane Blanchet

D-U-N-S 20-217-8786   (HQ)
AMEUBLEMENTS EL RAN LTEE
ACCENT
2751 Rte Transcanadienne, Pointe-Claire, QC, H9R 1B4
(514) 630-5656
Emp Here 460   *Sales* 102,648,565
SIC 2512 Upholstered household furniture
Sheldon Lubin
Eric Abecassis

D-U-N-S 20-285-9195   (HQ)
ANDRITZ HYDRO CANADA INC
(*Suby of* ANDRITZ AG)
6100 Rte Transcanadienne, Pointe-Claire, QC, H9R 1B9
(514) 428-6700
Sales 68,995,850
SIC 8711 Engineering services
Daniel Carrier
Liam Turner
Timothy J. Ryan
Didier Dechaud
Wolfgang Semper
Martin Schoeberl
Frederic Sauze
Stephen Schmidt
Christian Lenzin

D-U-N-S 24-086-9540   (SL)
ANODIZING & PAINT T.N.M INC
21 Ch De L'Aviation, Pointe-Claire, QC, H9R 4Z2
(514) 335-7001
Emp Here 50   *Sales* 10,141,500
SIC 3471 Plating and polishing
Tanweer Naqvi

D-U-N-S 24-460-8469   (SL)
ARSLAN AUTOMOTIVE CANADA LTEE
FABRICATION STRAIN TEC
84 Av Leacock, Pointe-Claire, QC, H9R 1H1
(514) 694-1113
Emp Here 30   *Sales* 14,942,340
SIC 5511 New and used car dealers
Arman Gurarslan
Savars Gurarslan

D-U-N-S 20-514-1083   (BR)
ASSOCIATED MATERIALS CANADA LIMITED
PRODUITS DE BATIMENT GENTEK
(*Suby of* ASSOCIATED MATERIALS GROUP, INC.)
2501 Aut Transcanadienne, Pointe-Claire, QC, H9R 1B3
(514) 426-7801
Emp Here 125
SIC 3444 Sheet Metalwork
John Umiastoski

D-U-N-S 25-060-5540   (SL)
AUTOMOBILES FAIRVIEW INC
VOLVO POINTE-CLAIRE
15 Av Auto Plaza, Pointe-Claire, QC, H9R 5Z7
(514) 630-3666
Emp Here 33   *Sales* 16,436,574
SIC 5511 New and used car dealers
Charles Hammer

D-U-N-S 24-025-7857   (SL)
AUTOMOBILES MET-HAM INC
FAIRVIEW MAZDA
575 Boul Saint-Jean, Pointe-Claire, QC, H9R 3K1
(514) 685-5555
Emp Here 26   *Sales* 16,361,280
SIC 5511 New and used car dealers
Kapil Dilawri
Ajay Dilawri
Lalit Tony Dilawri

D-U-N-S 20-210-7850   (HQ)
AVON CANADA INC
AVON CANADA
(*Suby of* CERBERUS CAPITAL MANAGEMENT, L.P.)
5500 Rte Transcanadienne, Pointe-Claire, QC, H9R 1B6
(514) 695-3371
Sales 103,205,250
SIC 5122 Drugs, proprietaries, and sundries
Goran Petrovic
Colleen Leithman
Luigi Del Vecchio
Matt Prevost

D-U-N-S 24-782-6212   (SL)
AVOTUS INC
116 Av Pendennis, Pointe-Claire, QC, H9R 1H6

Emp Here 49   *Sales* 22,096,499
SIC 7389 Business services, nec
James Martino

D-U-N-S 20-370-3413   (SL)
BELCAN CANADA INC
(*Suby of* BELCAN, LLC)
1000 Boul Saint-Jean Bureau 715, Pointe-Claire, QC, H9R 5P1
(514) 697-9212
Emp Here 250   *Sales* 49,282,750
SIC 8711 Engineering services
Lance Kwasniewski
Kim White
Elizabeth Ferris

D-U-N-S 20-172-0625   (BR)
BEST BUY CANADA LTD
GEEK SQUAD
(*Suby of* BEST BUY CO., INC.)
6321 Rte Transcanadienne Unite 121, Pointe-Claire, QC, H9R 5A5
(514) 428-1999
Emp Here 100
SIC 5999 Miscellaneous retail stores, nec
Ron Wilson

D-U-N-S 20-564-0683   (HQ)
BIRD ENTREPRENEURS GENERAUX LTEE
(*Suby of* BIRD CONSTRUCTION INC)
1870 Boul Des Sources Bureau 200, Pointe-Claire, QC, H9R 5N4
(514) 426-1333
Sales 25,244,200

SIC 1611 Highway and street construction
Ian J. Boyd
Nolan B. Jenkins
Wayne R. Gingrich

D-U-N-S 24-352-0335   (HQ)
BOSCUS CANADA INC
900 Av Selkirk, Pointe-Claire, QC, H9R 3S3
(514) 694-9805
Sales 17,886,960
SIC 5031 Lumber, plywood, and millwork
Dary Laflamme
Christian Provost
Raymond Landry

D-U-N-S 20-590-7587   (HQ)
BOUCLAIR INC
BOUCLAIR HOME
(*Suby of* INVESTISSEMENTS ALJUSA INC)
152 Av Alston, Pointe-Claire, QC, H9R 6B4
(514) 426-0115
Emp Here 90   *Sales* 266,703,000
SIC 5719 Miscellaneous homefurnishings
Jeff York
Peter Goldberg
Lionel Trombert
Eric Boyko
Frederic Vitre

D-U-N-S 24-836-2741   (HQ)
BRECON FOODS INC
189 Boul Hymus Bureau 406, Pointe-Claire, QC, H9R 1E9
(514) 426-8140
Sales 16,711,540
SIC 5142 Packaged frozen goods
Richard Morgan
Suzan Morgan
Rachel Morgan

D-U-N-S 24-081-0718   (SL)
CANPEPTIDE INC
265 Boul Hymus Bureau 1500, Pointe-Claire, QC, H9R 1G6
(514) 697-2168
Emp Here 49   *Sales* 13,556,340
SIC 2834 Pharmaceutical preparations
Yaode Riu

D-U-N-S 20-860-3035   (HQ)
CENTRE DE SANTE ET DE SERVICES SOCIAUX DE L'OUEST-DE-L'ILE
HOPITAL GENERAL DU LAKESHORE
160 Av Stillview, Pointe-Claire, QC, H9R 2Y2
(514) 630-2225
Sales 133,296,000
SIC 8062 General medical and surgical hospitals
Robert Bedard
Nick Ditomaso
Renee Soumis
Luc Lepage
Roch Carron

D-U-N-S 20-720-0085   (HQ)
CHANDELLES ET CREATIONS ROBIN INC
ARTIZAN
151 Av Alston, Pointe-Claire, QC, H9R 5V9
(514) 426-5999
Emp Here 36   *Sales* 20,929,524
SIC 5137 Women's and children's clothing
Robin Valliear

D-U-N-S 24-546-0659   (SL)
CLAUDE NEON LIMITEE
1868 Boul Des Sources Bureau 200, Pointe-Claire, QC, H9R 5R2
(514) 693-9436
Emp Here 49   *Sales* 10,902,713
SIC 3993 Signs and advertising specialties
Ryan Barrington-Foote

D-U-N-S 25-240-3878   (BR)
COMMISSION SCOLAIRE MARGUERITE-BOURGEOYS
ECOLE FELIX LECLERC
(*Suby of* COMMISSION SCOLAIRE MARGUERITE-BOURGEOYS)

311 Av Inglewood, Pointe-Claire, QC, H9R 2Z8
(514) 855-4225
Emp Here 120
SIC 8211 Elementary and secondary schools
Jean-Pierre Bernard

D-U-N-S 20-884-6501   (SL)
COMPAGNIE DIVERSIFIEE DE L'EST LTEE
EDCO DU CANADA
131 Boul Hymus, Pointe-Claire, QC, H9R 1E7
(514) 694-5353
Emp Here 100   *Sales* 19,208,500
SIC 3497 Metal foil and leaf
Sylvia Freyer

D-U-N-S 25-671-3991   (SL)
COMPAGNIE WW HOTELS (POINTE-CLAIRE)
HOLIDAY INN MONTREAL AEROPORT OUEST
6700 Rte Transcanadienne, Pointe-Claire, QC, H9R 1C2
(514) 697-7110
Emp Here 168   *Sales* 15,571,920
SIC 7011 Hotels and motels
A. Majid Mangalji
Fereed Mangalji

D-U-N-S 20-548-4202   (SL)
CONFORTCHEM INC
76 Boul Hymus, Pointe-Claire, QC, H9R 1E3
(514) 332-1140
Emp Here 16   *Sales* 94,808,626
SIC 5169 Chemicals and allied products, nec
Rawi Kayal
Patrick Arrata
Philippe Kayal
Bashir Labat

D-U-N-S 25-973-4432   (HQ)
COPAP COMMERCE INC
(*Suby of* SELA INDUSTRIES INC)
755 Boul Saint-Jean Bureau 305, Pointe-Claire, QC, H9R 5M9
(514) 693-9150
Sales 166,445,138
SIC 5111 Printing and writing paper
David Sela
Laurent Barbe
Denys Lamarre

D-U-N-S 24-813-0429   (SL)
COPAP INC
ENTREPRISES COPAP
(*Suby of* SELA INDUSTRIES INC)
755 Boul Saint-Jean Bureau 305, Pointe-Claire, QC, H9R 5M9
(514) 693-9150
Emp Here 24   *Sales* 83,391,220
SIC 2295 Coated fabrics, not rubberized
David Sela
Laurent Barbe
Denys Lamarre

D-U-N-S 24-969-4993   (HQ)
CORPORATION D'ECLAIRAGE GREENLITE, LA
GREENLITE
(*Suby of* GREENLITE GLOBAL INC)
115 Boul Brunswick Bureau 102, Pointe-Claire, QC, H9R 5N2
(514) 695-9090
Sales 13,415,220
SIC 5063 Electrical apparatus and equipment
Tarana Nina Gupta

D-U-N-S 24-354-8893   (BR)
COSTCO WHOLESALE CANADA LTD
COSTCO
(*Suby of* COSTCO WHOLESALE CORPORATION)
5701 Rte Transcanadienne, Pointe-Claire, QC, H9R 1B7
(514) 426-5052
Emp Here 100
SIC 5099 Durable goods, nec

Eric Caissy

D-U-N-S 24-357-5284   (SL)
COUPE LASER ULTRA INC
(*Suby of* GROUPE ULTRA (2001) INC)
205 Boul Brunswick Bureau 400, Pointe-Claire, QC, H9R 1A5
(514) 333-8156
Emp Here 25   *Sales* 11,230,475
SIC 7389 Business services, nec
Sebastien Charest
Gilles Gauthier
Stephen Demers

D-U-N-S 20-016-5632   (HQ)
CUMMINS EST DU CANADA SEC
VENTES ET SERVICE CUMMINS
7200 Rte Transcanadienne, Pointe-Claire, QC, H9R 1C2
(514) 695-8410
Emp Here 85   *Sales* 95,107,350
SIC 5084 Industrial machinery and equipment
Michael Christodoulou

D-U-N-S 20-015-2671   (HQ)
DESIGN FRANK LYMAN INC
2500 Boul Des Sources, Pointe-Claire, QC, H9R 0B3
(514) 695-1719
Sales 13,667,400
SIC 2335 Women's, junior's, and misses' dresses
Frank Lyman

D-U-N-S 24-324-9039   (SL)
DIABSOLUT INC
GROUPE RHWIZE
181 Boul Hymus Bureau 100, Pointe-Claire, QC, H9R 5P4
(514) 461-3314
Emp Here 80   *Sales* 18,743,040
SIC 8748 Business consulting, nec
Joseph Diab

D-U-N-S 24-179-2274   (HQ)
DIAMANT ELINOR INC.
BIJORKA
987 Boul Saint-Jean, Pointe-Claire, QC, H9R 5M3
(450) 688-6288
Emp Here 9   *Sales* 24,432,800
SIC 5944 Jewelry stores
Joseph Sebag
Shirit Shebag
Elinor Shebag

D-U-N-S 24-788-2046   (HQ)
ELECTRONIQUES PROMARK INC
215 Rue Voyageur, Pointe-Claire, QC, H9R 6B2
(514) 426-4104
Sales 282,915,000
SIC 3679 Electronic components, nec
Sydney Knecht

D-U-N-S 20-333-1769   (SL)
EMBALLAGES SXP INC
DURABOX
(*Suby of* SUPREMEX INC)
269 Boul Saint Jean Ste 211b, Pointe-Claire, QC, H9R 3J1
(514) 364-3269
Emp Here 50   *Sales* 11,671,750
SIC 2631 Paperboard mills
Emerson Stewart
Lyne Begin

D-U-N-S 24-858-6117   (SL)
ENTREPRISES IMPORTFAB INC
50 Boul Hymus, Pointe-Claire, QC, H9R 1C9
(514) 694-0721
Emp Here 60   *Sales* 16,599,600
SIC 2834 Pharmaceutical preparations
Sylvain Renzi
Paolo Renzi

D-U-N-S 20-123-0385   (SL)
ERICKSON, DARYL HOLDINGS INC

263 Av Labrosse, Pointe-Claire, QC, H9R 1A3
(514) 630-7484
Emp Here 30   *Sales* 12,792,241
SIC 6712 Bank holding companies
Daryl Erickson

D-U-N-S 25-108-4505   (HQ)
EVEREST AUTOMATION INC
227d Boul Brunswick, Pointe-Claire, QC, H9R 4X5
(514) 630-9290
Emp Here 18   *Sales* 16,625,910
SIC 5084 Industrial machinery and equipment
Marc Cote
Eric Maier

D-U-N-S 24-936-0827   (SL)
EXOVA
121 Boul Hymus, Pointe-Claire, QC, H9R 1E6
(514) 697-3400
Emp Here 100   *Sales* 23,469,600
SIC 8734 Testing laboratories
Harry Baikowitz

D-U-N-S 20-764-0921   (SL)
FAIRVIEW NISSAN LIMITEE
SPINELLI NISSAN
345 Boul Brunswick, Pointe-Claire, QC, H9R 4S1
(514) 697-5222
Emp Here 85   *Sales* 53,488,800
SIC 5511 New and used car dealers
Pierre Spinelli
Noel Spinelli

D-U-N-S 20-356-5379   (SL)
FAMAR MONTREAL INC
(*Suby of* NERINE FOUNDATION)
3535 Rte Transcanadienne, Pointe-Claire, QC, H9R 1B4
(514) 428-7488
Emp Here 150   *Sales* 42,603,150
SIC 2834 Pharmaceutical preparations
Markus Hoelzl
Catherine Kalopissis
Friedrich Sernetz

D-U-N-S 20-214-7666   (BR)
FCA CANADA INC
CHRYSLER CANADA
(*Suby of* FIAT CHRYSLER AUTOMOBILES N.V.)
3000 Rte Transcanadienne, Pointe-Claire, QC, H9R 1B1
(514) 630-2500
Emp Here 120
SIC 5012 Automobiles and other motor vehicles
Eric Corso

D-U-N-S 24-570-8086   (HQ)
FOURNITURES DE MEUBLES ET DE LITERIE SINCA INC
DESIGN STIL
(*Suby of* 3060802 CANADA INC)
870 Av Ellingham, Pointe-Claire, QC, H9R 3S4
(514) 697-0101
Emp Here 10   *Sales* 13,862,394
SIC 5072 Hardware
Richard Morsink

D-U-N-S 24-346-6179   (BR)
FPINNOVATIONS
PAPRICAN
(*Suby of* FPINNOVATIONS)
570 Boul Saint-Jean, Pointe-Claire, QC, H9R 3J9
(514) 630-4100
Emp Here 280
SIC 8733 Noncommercial research organizations
Alan Potter

D-U-N-S 24-340-8866   (HQ)
FPINNOVATIONS
FERIC EASTERN, DIV OF
570 Boul Saint-Jean, Pointe-Claire, QC, H9R

3J9
(514) 630-4100
Emp Here 250   *Sales* 74,258,215
SIC 8731 Commercial physical research
Pierre Lapointe
Yvon Pelletier
Norine Young
Charles Tardif
Al Ward
Bruce Mayer
Catherine Cobden
Daniel Archambault
Mark Feldinger
Pierre Lapointe

D-U-N-S 20-541-5573   (HQ)
FUTURE ELECTRONICS (CDA) LTD
(*Suby of* INVESTISSEMENTS ALONIM INC, LES)
237 Boul Hymus, Pointe-Claire, QC, H9R 5C7
(514) 694-7710
Emp Here 1,500   *Sales* 4,637,914,271
SIC 5065 Electronic parts and equipment, nec
Robert G. Miller
Pierre Guilbault
Frank Bilotta

D-U-N-S 20-267-3745   (HQ)
FUTURE ELECTRONIQUE INC
(*Suby of* INVESTISSEMENTS ALONIM INC, LES)
237 Boul Hymus, Pointe-Claire, QC, H9R 5C7
(514) 694-7710
Emp Here 30   *Sales* 580,247,000
SIC 5065 Electronic parts and equipment, nec
Robert G. Miller
Rodney Miller
Pierre Guilbault

D-U-N-S 20-219-9089   (BR)
GENERAL MOTORS OF CANADA COMPANY
PARTS DISTRIBUTION CENTRE
(*Suby of* GENERAL MOTORS COMPANY)
5000 Rte Transcanadienne, Pointe-Claire, QC, H9R 1B6
(514) 630-6209
Emp Here 200
SIC 5012 Automobiles and other motor vehicles
Josephine Primiani

D-U-N-S 24-364-8586   (SL)
GLOBAL-SKY LOGISTICS INC
81 Boul Hymus, Pointe-Claire, QC, H9R 1E2
(514) 223-3399
Emp Here 185   *Sales* 60,335,160
SIC 3944 Games, toys, and children's vehicles
Theodore Frank
Sheryl Fremeth

D-U-N-S 20-220-2586   (SL)
GLOBE ELECTRIC COMPANY INC
(*Suby of* W4 INTERNATIONAL INC)
150 Av Oneida, Pointe-Claire, QC, H9R 1A8
(888) 543-1388
Emp Here 93   *Sales* 53,962,971
SIC 5063 Electrical apparatus and equipment
Edward Glen Weinstein

D-U-N-S 24-053-5211   (HQ)
GRAVELUNI INC
PHARMACIE PIERRE GRAVEL
277 Boul Saint-Jean, Pointe-Claire, QC, H9R 3J1
(514) 695-1122
Sales 12,647,700
SIC 5912 Drug stores and proprietary stores
Pierre Gravel

D-U-N-S 24-375-1372   (HQ)
GROUPE EMBALLAGE SPECIALISE S.E.C.
IVEX
3300 Rte Transcanadienne, Pointe-Claire, QC, H9R 1B1
(514) 636-7951
Emp Here 25   *Sales* 119,406,000

SIC 3089 Plastics products, nec
Paul Gaulin

D-U-N-S 20-333-1830   (BR)
GROUPE LUMINAIRES INC, LE
LUMINIS
(*Suby of* GROUPE LUMINAIRES INC, LE)
260 Av Labrosse, Pointe-Claire, QC, H9R 5L5
(514) 683-3883
Emp Here 100
SIC 5719 Miscellaneous homefurnishings
Nicolas Cohen

D-U-N-S 20-297-8909   (SL)
GROUPE MINT GREEN INC, LE
(*Suby of* PLACEMENTS E.M. FLETCHER INC)
6900 Rte Transcanadienne, Pointe-Claire, QC, H9R 1C2
(514) 333-4461
Emp Here 30   *Sales* 14,949,660
SIC 5136 Men's and boy's clothing
Edward M. Fletcher
James A Macphee
J. Robert Cote

D-U-N-S 24-022-8684   (SL)
HIBON INC
(*Suby of* IR CANADA SALES & SERVICE ULC)
100 Rue Voyageur, Pointe-Claire, QC, H9R 6A8
(514) 631-3501
Emp Here 24   *Sales* 11,400,624
SIC 5084 Industrial machinery and equipment
Yves Tranzeat
Shawn White
Barbara Santoro

D-U-N-S 24-361-7276   (BR)
HOME DEPOT OF CANADA INC
HOME DEPOT
(*Suby of* THE HOME DEPOT INC)
185 Boul Hymus, Pointe-Claire, QC, H9R 1E9
(514) 630-8631
Emp Here 100
SIC 5251 Hardware stores
Eric Berthiaume

D-U-N-S 25-301-3023   (BR)
HUDSON'S BAY COMPANY
BAY, THE
(*Suby of* HUDSON'S BAY COMPANY)
6790 Aut Transcanadienne, Pointe-Claire, QC, H9R 1C5
(514) 697-4870
Emp Here 300
SIC 5311 Department stores
Mario Lacroix

D-U-N-S 24-385-0448   (HQ)
HYDRO EXTRUSION CANADA INC
SAPA EXTRUSION AMERIQUE DU NORD
(*Suby of* NORSK HYDRO ASA)
325 Av Avro, Pointe-Claire, QC, H9R 5W3
(514) 697-5120
Emp Here 150   *Sales* 36,277,600
SIC 3354 Aluminum extruded products
Charles J. Straface
Jacquelyne Belcastro
Robert Kavanaugh
Paul Amirault

D-U-N-S 20-005-3275   (SL)
I.E.I. INC
39 Boul Hymus, Pointe-Claire, QC, H9R 4T2
(514) 630-8149
Emp Here 20   *Sales* 10,006,500
SIC 5137 Women's and children's clothing
Karsten E. Schmid
Amelie Leibl

D-U-N-S 25-258-2424   (HQ)
IMMEUBLES VILLAGE POINTE-CLAIRE INC
ROYAL LEPAGE VILLAGE
263 Boul Saint-Jean, Pointe-Claire, QC, H9R 3J1

(514) 694-2121
Sales 12,229,020
SIC 6531 Real estate agents and managers
Jon Engelsman
Stewart Jones

D-U-N-S 20-213-6008   (SL)
INDUSTRIES C.P.S. INC, LES
30 Ch De L'Aviation, Pointe-Claire, QC, H9R 5M6
(514) 695-0400
Emp Here 100   *Sales* 22,384,300
SIC 3728 Aircraft parts and equipment, nec
Herman Schaubhut
Peter Wiedemann

D-U-N-S 20-237-5218   (SL)
INDUSTRIES DE CABLES D'ACIER LTEE
BRIDON BEKAERT LE GROUPE CABLES
(*Suby of* NV BEKAERT SA)
5501 Rte Transcanadienne, Pointe-Claire, QC, H9R 1B7
(800) 565-5501
Emp Here 200   *Sales* 38,417,000
SIC 3496 Miscellaneous fabricated wire products
Steeve Bonome
Steeven Saules

D-U-N-S 20-203-4690   (SL)
INDUSTRIES LEESTA LTEE, LES
6 Av Du Plateau, Pointe-Claire, QC, H9R 5W2
(514) 694-3930
Emp Here 135   *Sales* 30,218,805
SIC 3728 Aircraft parts and equipment, nec
Ernest Henri Staub Sr.
Ernest Anton Staub Jr.
Elizabeth Gabriele Staub
Felicia Katharina Staub

D-U-N-S 24-922-5475   (HQ)
INNOVAK GROUP INC, THE
INNOVAK DIRECT
62 Boul Hymus, Pointe-Claire, QC, H9R 1E1
(514) 695-7221
Sales 16,650,075
SIC 3546 Power-driven handtools
Robert M Davis
Andre Hudon
Rona Davis
Julia Sax
Michael Sax

D-U-N-S 20-736-1775   (HQ)
INTERIEURS MOBILIA INC, LES
AMEUBLEMENTS THOMASVILLE
2525 Boul Des Sources, Pointe-Claire, QC, H9R 5Z9
(514) 685-7557
Emp Here 50   *Sales* 37,184,480
SIC 5712 Furniture stores
Johannes J. Kau
Melanie Kau
Johann M. Kau

D-U-N-S 20-557-5611   (HQ)
INVESTISSEMENTS ALONIM INC, LES
237 Boul Hymus, Pointe-Claire, QC, H9R 5C7
(514) 694-7710
Emp Here 1   *Sales* 3,147,032,490
SIC 6712 Bank holding companies
Robert G. Miller
Rodney Miller
Pierre Guilbault

D-U-N-S 25-315-8794   (BR)
INVESTORS GROUP FINANCIAL SERVICES INC
INVESTORS SALES & SERVICES WEST ISLAND
(*Suby of* POWER CORPORATION DU CANADA)
6500 Rte Transcanadienne Unite 600, Pointe-Claire, QC, H9R 0A5
(514) 426-0886
Emp Here 60
SIC 8741 Management services
Raymond Massa

D-U-N-S 25-996-6430   (SL)
ISC APPLIED SYSTEMS CORP
SYSTEMES APPLIQUES ISC
290 Av Labrosse, Pointe-Claire, QC, H9R 5L8
(514) 782-1400
Emp Here 50   *Sales* 10,233,650
SIC 3699 Electrical equipment and supplies, nec
Christopher Catterall
Eric Garzon
Younes El Asrany
Sharon Peck

D-U-N-S 24-527-4899   (HQ)
JASZTEX FIBRES INC
JUPITER JUVENILE
61 Boul Hymus, Pointe-Claire, QC, H9R 1E2
(514) 697-3096
Sales 22,008,360
SIC 2297 Nonwoven fabrics
Alvin Zoltan

D-U-N-S 20-213-6149   (HQ)
K+S SEL WINDSOR LTEE
WINDSOR SALT
(*Suby of* K+S AG)
755 Boul Saint-Jean Bureau 700, Pointe-Claire, QC, H9R 5M9
(514) 630-0900
Emp Here 35   *Sales* 357,339,285
SIC 1479 Chemical and fertilizer mining
Christian H Herrmann
Francois G. Allard
Timothy A. Mckean

D-U-N-S 25-405-0784   (HQ)
KAMINS DERMATOLOGIQUE, INC
B. KAMINS-CHEMIST
325 Av Stillview, Pointe-Claire, QC, H9R 2Y6
(514) 428-1628
Sales 12,158,795
SIC 5122 Drugs, proprietaries, and sundries
Ben Kaminsky
Howard Kaminsky
Mildred Kaminsky

D-U-N-S 24-365-2091   (HQ)
KAR INDUSTRIEL INC
FOURNITURES INDUSTRIELLES DU-RAMILL
100 Av Columbus, Pointe-Claire, QC, H9R 4K4
(514) 694-4711
Emp Here 10   *Sales* 33,251,820
SIC 5084 Industrial machinery and equipment
Meek Ward
Yvonne Karijo
Karijo-Benedik Magda

D-U-N-S 20-192-3005   (BR)
KAYCAN LTEE
(*Suby of* KAYCAN LTEE)
160 Av Oneida, Pointe-Claire, QC, H9R 1A8
(514) 694-7200
Emp Here 100
SIC 5039 Construction materials, nec
Patrick Gilfillan

D-U-N-S 20-909-0349   (HQ)
KAYCAN LTEE
3075 Rte Transcanadienne, Pointe-Claire, QC, H9R 1B4
(514) 694-5855
Emp Here 100   *Sales* 537,728,832
SIC 5033 Roofing, siding, and insulation
Lionel Dubrofsky
Tami Dubrofsky
Ruben Dubrofsky

D-U-N-S 20-727-0331   (HQ)
L.B. FOSTER TECHNOLOGIES FERROVIAIRES CANADA LTEE
(*Suby of* L. B. FOSTER COMPANY)
172 Boul Brunswick, Pointe-Claire, QC, H9R 5P9
(514) 695-8500
Emp Here 21   *Sales* 23,276,274

SIC 5088 Transportation equipment and supplies
Steven R Fletcher
Robert Ness
Patrick J Guinee
Robert P Bauer
John F Kasel

D-U-N-S 20-858-5604   (SL)
LABORATOIRES ODAN LTEE, LES
ACETAMINOPHENE-ODAN 325 MG COMPRIMES
(*Suby of* GESTION DYNUS LTEE)
325 Av Stillview, Pointe-Claire, QC, H9R 2Y6
(514) 428-1628
Emp Here 120   *Sales* 28,402,100
SIC 2834 Pharmaceutical preparations
Howard Kaminsky

D-U-N-S 24-176-1584   (SL)
LEADER AUTO RESSOURCES LAR INC
2525 Aut Transcanadienne Bureau 937, Pointe-Claire, QC, H9R 4V6
(514) 694-6880
Emp Here 80   *Sales* 100,576,080
SIC 5172 Petroleum products, nec
Robert B. Issenman
Jean-Marc Bourassa
Allen F. Macphee
Andre Dorais
Louis Dandurand
Jean-Guy Thibault
Jean Sauvageau
Carl Sytema
Douglas R. Mac Donald
Carl Keegan

D-U-N-S 25-240-8711   (BR)
LESTER B. PEARSON SCHOOL BOARD
JOHN RENNIE HIGH SCHOOL
501 Boul Saint-Jean, Pointe-Claire, QC, H9R 3J5
(514) 697-3210
Emp Here 100
SIC 8211 Elementary and secondary schools
Cristina Prata

D-U-N-S 25-241-0253   (BR)
LESTER B. PEARSON SCHOOL BOARD
LINDSAY PLACE HIGH SCHOOL
111 Av Broadview, Pointe-Claire, QC, H9R 3Z3
(514) 694-2760
Emp Here 120
SIC 8211 Elementary and secondary schools
Dona Bianchi

D-U-N-S 25-240-3985   (BR)
LESTER B. PEARSON SCHOOL BOARD
ST THOMAS HIGH SCHOOL
120 Av Ambassador, Pointe-Claire, QC, H9R 1S8
(514) 694-3770
Emp Here 90
SIC 8211 Elementary and secondary schools
David Abracen

D-U-N-S 20-224-5114   (HQ)
MANUFACTURE LEVITON DU CANADA LTEE
(*Suby of* LEVITON MANUFACTURING CO., INC.)
165 Boul Hymus, Pointe-Claire, QC, H9R 1E9
(514) 954-1840
Emp Here 1   *Sales* 58,024,700
SIC 5063 Electrical apparatus and equipment
Jean Belhumeur
David Shaanan
Mark Baydarian
Stephan Sokolow
Donald J. Hendler
Bruce Brown

D-U-N-S 24-372-0468   (SL)
MANUTENTION QUEBEC INC
COENTREPRISE MANUTENTION QUEBEC ET GAUTHIER INTERLIFT

100a Boul Hymus, Pointe-Claire, QC, H9R 1E4
(514) 694-4223
Emp Here 30   *Sales* 14,250,780
SIC 5084 Industrial machinery and equipment
Frederic Chatel
Jean-Louis Lapointe

D-U-N-S 24-860-2583   (HQ)
MATERIAUX DE CONSTRUCTION KP LTEE
(*Suby of* KAYCAN LTEE)
3075 Aut Transcanadienne, Pointe-Claire, QC, H9R 1B4
(514) 694-5855
Emp Here 65   *Sales* 79,046,772
SIC 3089 Plastics products, nec
Lionel Dubrofsky
Tami Dubrofsky

D-U-N-S 24-489-7773   (SL)
MEDICAL PLASTIC DEVICES M.P.D. INC
MEDICAL PLASTIC DEVICES
161 Av Oneida, Pointe-Claire, QC, H9R 1A9
(514) 694-9835
Emp Here 40   *Sales* 10,262,480
SIC 3841 Surgical and medical instruments
William A Lloyd

D-U-N-S 24-382-9566   (SL)
MEDTRONIC CRYOCATH LP
CRYOCATH TECHNOLOGY
9000 Rte Transcanadienne, Pointe-Claire, QC, H9R 5Z8
(514) 694-1212
Emp Here 250   *Sales* 133,838,000
SIC 5047 Medical and hospital equipment
Michael Bridges

D-U-N-S 25-990-1445   (SL)
MEDXL INC
285 Av Labrosse, Pointe-Claire, QC, H9R 1A3
(514) 695-7474
Emp Here 100   *Sales* 44,717,400
SIC 5047 Medical and hospital equipment
Paul Parisien

D-U-N-S 20-024-6325   (BR)
METRO RICHELIEU INC
METRO POINTE CLAIRE
(*Suby of* METRO INC)
325 Boul Saint-Jean, Pointe-Claire, QC, H9R 3J1
(514) 697-6520
Emp Here 120
SIC 5411 Grocery stores
Phillip Birjandi

D-U-N-S 20-231-2807   (HQ)
MINTECH CANADA INC
MINTEQ INTERNATIONAL DIV OF
(*Suby of* MINERALS TECHNOLOGIES INC.)
1870 Boul Des Sources Bureau 100, Pointe-Claire, QC, H9R 5N4
(514) 697-8260
Emp Here 8   *Sales* 16,059,120
SIC 5211 Lumber and other building materials
Kenneth Massimine
Daniel J. Monagle
Lynne Daley
Yves Dube

D-U-N-S 25-195-8773   (SL)
MPB COMMUNICATIONS INC
(*Suby of* TECHNOLOGIES MPB INC, LES)
147 Boul Hymus, Pointe-Claire, QC, H9R 1E9
(514) 694-8751
Emp Here 50   *Sales* 11,487,700
SIC 8731 Commercial physical research

D-U-N-S 20-730-6171   (SL)
ORDINATEURS EN GROS MICROBYTES INC, LES
MICROBYTES
940 Boul Saint-Jean Bureau 15, Pointe-Claire, QC, H9R 5N8
(514) 426-2586
Emp Here 30   *Sales* 13,415,220
SIC 5045 Computers, peripherals, and soft-

ware
Corey Grauer

D-U-N-S 20-999-4771 (HQ)
PACE INVESTCO LTD
GESTION PACE INVESTCO
193 Boul Brunswick, Pointe-Claire, QC, H9R
5N2
(514) 630-6820
Emp Here 20 *Sales* 19,001,040
SIC 5085 Industrial supplies
Cosmo Pace
Brian Pace
Susan Pace
Nancy Pace

D-U-N-S 20-928-9735 (SL)
PENTAGON GRAPHICS LTD
CARTEL PACKAGING
271 Av Labrosse, Pointe-Claire, QC, H9R 1A3
(514) 339-5995
Emp Here 90 *Sales* 14,762,430
SIC 2752 Commercial printing, lithographic
Issie Caron
Glenn Caron
Felice Caron
Benjamin Caron

D-U-N-S 25-476-5787 (SL)
PLACEMENT POTENTIEL INC
111 Av Donegani, Pointe-Claire, QC, H9R
2W3
(514) 694-0315
Emp Here 100 *Sales* 7,469,400
SIC 7361 Employment agencies
Ken Francis
James Smith
Marjorie Rutherford
Kattackal Ligeo
Ray O'farrel
Heather Green
Noel Burke
Louis Gascon

D-U-N-S 20-794-2868 (SL)
PLACEMENTS CAMBRIDGE INC
CAMBRIDGE, LE
340 Boul Hymus Bureau 640, Pointe-Claire,
QC, H9R 6B3
(514) 694-8383
Emp Here 50 *Sales* 16,356,350
SIC 6531 Real estate agents and managers
Jonathan Sigler
Normand Belanger
Linda Simard
Jacques Vincent

D-U-N-S 24-516-4967 (SL)
**PLAN DE PROTECTION MECANIQUE
P.P.M. INC**
2525 Aut Transcanadienne, Pointe-Claire, QC,
H9R 4V6

Emp Here 17 *Sales* 12,332,463
SIC 6351 Surety insurance
Herb Stein
Jean-Marc Bourassa
Robert Issenman

D-U-N-S 24-175-6477 (HQ)
POMPACTION INC
119 Boul Hymus, Pointe-Claire, QC, H9R 1E5
(514) 697-8600
Sales 29,263,800
SIC 5084 Industrial machinery and equipment
Sylvain Gagnier
Francis Gagnier
Bernard Santerre
Pierre Mc Cann
Pierre Rinfret
Michel Laporte

D-U-N-S 24-896-7960 (SL)
POWER TRADING INC
2555 Boul Des Sources, Pointe-Claire, QC,
H9R 5Z3
(514) 421-2225
Emp Here 24 *Sales* 12,493,008

SIC 5099 Durable goods, nec
Barry Abugov
Ara Soukiassian

D-U-N-S 24-052-2268 (HQ)
PRETIUM CANADA COMPANY
DUOPAC PACKAGING
3300 Rte Transcanadienne, Pointe-Claire, QC,
H9R 1B1
(514) 428-0002
Emp Here 150 *Sales* 53,732,700
SIC 3089 Plastics products, nec
George A. Abd

D-U-N-S 20-763-5434 (HQ)
**PRODUITS CHIMIQUES AMPLEX LTEE,
LES**
600 Av Delmar, Pointe-Claire, QC, H9R 4A8
(514) 630-3309
Sales 14,606,900
SIC 5169 Chemicals and allied products, nec
Nicole C. Belanger
Caroline Belanger
Nathalie Belanger

D-U-N-S 20-232-4778 (SL)
PROTECTION INCENDIE ROBERTS LTEE
26a Boul Hymus Bureau 49, Pointe-Claire,
QC, H9R 1C9
(514) 695-7070
Emp Here 70 *Sales* 33,251,820
SIC 5084 Industrial machinery and equipment
Bernard M Beliveau
Paul Donnelly

D-U-N-S 24-990-4392 (HQ)
PSI PROLEW INC
SCOTT INDUSTRIAL, DIV DE
975 Av Selkirk, Pointe-Claire, QC, H9R 4S4
(514) 697-7867
Emp Here 25 *Sales* 23,276,274
SIC 5084 Industrial machinery and equipment
Gordon Yapp

D-U-N-S 24-458-2235 (HQ)
R.O.E. LOGISTICS INC
R.O.E. LOGISTIQUES
195 Rue Voyageur, Pointe-Claire, QC, H9R
6B2
(514) 396-0000
Emp Here 90 *Sales* 86,695,960
SIC 4731 Freight transportation arrangement
Alan J. Barbner

D-U-N-S 20-151-9506 (BR)
SCHNEIDER ELECTRIC CANADA INC
SCHNEIDER ELECTRIC
(*Suby of* SCHNEIDER ELECTRIC SE)
825 Av Bancroft, Pointe-Claire, QC, H9R 4L6

Emp Here 85
SIC 3699 Electrical equipment and supplies,
nec
Luc Belanger

D-U-N-S 24-802-1888 (HQ)
SELA INDUSTRIES INC
755 Boul Saint-Jean Bureau 305, Pointe-
Claire, QC, H9R 5M9
(514) 693-9150
Sales 110,117,590
SIC 6712 Bank holding companies
David B. Sela
Denys Lamarre

D-U-N-S 24-168-9835 (HQ)
SERIGRAPHIE RICHFORD INC
2001 Boul Des Sources Bureau 101, Pointe-
Claire, QC, H9R 5Z4
(514) 426-8700
Sales 22,963,780
SIC 2759 Commercial printing, nec
Jean-Charles Briere
Rishee Behl
Dave Campbell

D-U-N-S 20-234-2200 (HQ)
SIKA CANADA INC

SIKA SARNAFIL
(*Suby of* SIKA AG)
601 Av Delmar, Pointe-Claire, QC, H9R 4A9
(514) 697-2610
Emp Here 57 *Sales* 28,402,100
SIC 2891 Adhesives and sealants
Christoph Alexander Ganz
Richard Aubertin
Anne Seebode
Puneet Gupta
Stephen Lysik

D-U-N-S 25-201-7488 (SL)
SIMEX DEFENCE INC
EQUIPEMENTS SIMEX
216 Boul Brunswick, Pointe-Claire, QC, H9R
1A6
(514) 697-7655
Emp Here 30 *Sales* 14,250,780
SIC 5088 Transportation equipment and sup-
plies
Sam Mouallem

D-U-N-S 24-337-6352 (HQ)
SOCIETE XYLEM CANADA
XYLEM APPLIED WATER SYSTEMS
300 Av Labrosse, Pointe-Claire, QC, H9R 4V5
(514) 695-0133
Emp Here 10 *Sales* 41,888,900
SIC 6531 Real estate agents and managers
Kelley Caldarelli
Marc Blais
Derrick Chaulk
Chris Hartwick

D-U-N-S 20-720-3501 (BR)
SONEPAR CANADA INC
LUMEN
(*Suby of* SOCIETE DE NEGOCE ET DE PAR-
TICIPATION)
117 Boul Hymus Bureau 17, Pointe-Claire,
QC, H9R 1E5
(514) 426-0629
Emp Here 210
SIC 5063 Electrical apparatus and equipment
Lyette Chartrand

D-U-N-S 20-567-4281 (SL)
SOURCES 40 WESTT INC
2305 Rte Transcanadienne, Pointe-Claire, QC,
H9R 5Z5
(514) 428-9378
Emp Here 80 *Sales* 3,641,520
SIC 5812 Eating places
Terry Morentzos
Lise Drancontaidis
Stephano Grigoropoulos

D-U-N-S 24-635-4302 (SL)
SOUVENIRS AVANTI INC
OCEAN STATE EMBLEM
116 Av Leacock, Pointe-Claire, QC, H9R 1H1
(514) 694-0707
Emp Here 180 *Sales* 58,704,480
SIC 3993 Signs and advertising specialties
Anthony Jr. Ronci
Jean-Ann Ronci

D-U-N-S 20-003-0240 (BR)
SPINELLI TOYOTA (1981) INC
SPINELLI FAIRVIEW TOYOTA
(*Suby of* SPINELLI TOYOTA (1981) INC)
10 Av Auto Plaza, Pointe-Claire, QC, H9R 3H9
(514) 694-1510
Emp Here 90
SIC 5511 New and used car dealers
Francois Houle

D-U-N-S 20-873-4355 (BR)
SPINELLI TOYOTA (1981) INC
SPINELLI TOYOTA POINTE CLAIRE
(*Suby of* SPINELLI TOYOTA (1981) INC)
10 Av Auto Plaza, Pointe-Claire, QC, H9R 3H9
(514) 694-1510
Emp Here 100
SIC 5511 New and used car dealers
Erik Lockwood

D-U-N-S 20-622-7337 (BR)
SPINELLI TOYOTA (1981) INC
SPINELLI TOYOTA POINTE CLAIRE
(*Suby of* SPINELLI TOYOTA (1981) INC)
12 Av Auto Plaza, Pointe-Claire, QC, H9R
4W6
(514) 694-1510
Emp Here 100
SIC 5511 New and used car dealers
Pierre Spinelli

D-U-N-S 20-693-2589 (SL)
SYSTEMES D'EMBALLAGE AESUS INC
SYSTEMES D'ETIQUETAGE AESUS, LES
188 Av Oneida, Pointe-Claire, QC, H9R 1A8
(514) 694-3439
Emp Here 57 *Sales* 12,654,057
SIC 3565 Packaging machinery
Samantha Lewis
Stephen Mons
Patrick Wilson
Daniel Lachapelle
Graham Lewis

D-U-N-S 20-381-2755 (SL)
TECHNI-AIR 2000 INC
97 Boul Hymus, Pointe-Claire, QC, H9R 1E2
(514) 918-0299
Emp Here 75 *Sales* 13,196,850
SIC 8711 Engineering services
Gilles Valiquette
Jose Lozano

D-U-N-S 20-996-2059 (HQ)
TECHNOLOGIES MPB INC, LES
CENTRE DE TESTS ELECTRONIQUES
151 Boul Hymus, Pointe-Claire, QC, H9R 1E9
(514) 694-8751
Emp Here 132 *Sales* 47,957,550
SIC 8734 Testing laboratories
Jane Bachynski
Asoke Ghosh
Wrl Clements

D-U-N-S 24-677-2987 (HQ)
THORBURN FLEX INC
173 Av Oneida, Pointe-Claire, QC, H9R 1A9
(514) 695-8710
Sales 13,382,600
SIC 5251 Hardware stores
Charles Zuckerman
Robert Thornburn
Alon S. Ossip
Jeff O. Palmer
Simon Rosen

D-U-N-S 24-343-8681 (SL)
THORBURN INTERNATIONAL INC
173 Av Oneida, Pointe-Claire, QC, H9R 1A9
(514) 695-8710
Emp Here 145 *Sales* 52,998,805
SIC 6712 Bank holding companies
Robert Thornburn

D-U-N-S 24-944-8218 (BR)
TOROMONT INDUSTRIES LTD
*TOROMONT CAT - MATERIAL HANDLING
DIVISION*
(*Suby of* TOROMONT INDUSTRIES LTD)
4000 Aut Transcanadienne, Pointe-Claire, QC,
H9R 1B2
(514) 426-6700
Emp Here 120
SIC 5082 Construction and mining machinery

D-U-N-S 25-501-5588 (HQ)
**VORTEX STRUCTURES AQUATIQUES IN-
TERNATIONALES INC**
(*Suby of* GESTION STELLA HAMELIN INC)
328 Av Avro, Pointe-Claire, QC, H9R 5W5
(514) 694-3868
Sales 32,613,600
SIC 3949 Sporting and athletic goods, nec
Stephen Hamelin
Stephan Gradek
Virginie Guilbeault

D-U-N-S 24-892-2689 (SL)

WEST ISLAND HOTELS INC
HOTEL HOLIDAY INN POINTE-CLAIRE
6700 Rte Transcanadienne, Pointe-Claire, QC, H9R 1C2
(514) 697-7110
Emp Here 100   *Sales* 9,489,900
SIC 7011 Hotels and motels
Steve Gupta

D-U-N-S 20-025-4212   (BR)
YMCA DU QUEBEC, LES
YMCA POINTE CLAIRE
(*Suby of* YMCA DU QUEBEC, LES)
230 Boul Brunswick, Pointe-Claire, QC, H9R 5N5
(514) 630-9622
Emp Here 135
SIC 8399 Social services, nec
Mario Durso

Pointe-Claire, QC H9S

D-U-N-S 24-813-6434   (SL)
C.H.S.L.D. BAYVIEW INC
27 Ch Du Bord-Du-Lac Lakeshore, Pointe-Claire, QC, H9S 4H1
(514) 695-9384
Emp Here 150   *Sales* 10,284,900
SIC 8051 Skilled nursing care facilities
Thomas Samatas
Laura Samatas
Barbara Samatas
Geroge Guillon

D-U-N-S 25-240-4025   (BR)
COMMISSION SCOLAIRE MARGUERITE-BOURGEOYS
ECOLE MARGUERITE BOURGEOYS
(*Suby of* COMMISSION SCOLAIRE MARGUERITE-BOURGEOYS)
3 Av Sainte-Anne, Pointe-Claire, QC, H9S 4P6
(514) 855-4236
Emp Here 80
SIC 8211 Elementary and secondary schools
Michele Prince Seguin

D-U-N-S 24-323-8201   (SL)
OSMOCO LABORATORIES INC
OSMOCO EMERGENCY TEAM
260 Ch Du Bord-Du-Lac Lakeshore, Pointe-Claire, QC, H9S 4K9
(514) 694-4567
Emp Here 67   *Sales* 34,876,314
SIC 5099 Durable goods, nec
Paul Chamberland

D-U-N-S 20-026-3890   (SL)
PANIER & CADEAU INC, LE
BEAU CADEAU & PANIER PANACHE
274 Ch Du Bord-Du-Lac Lakeshore, Pointe-Claire, QC, H9S 4K9
(514) 695-7038
Emp Here 87   *Sales* 21,256,536
SIC 5947 Gift, novelty, and souvenir shop
Toni Cohcand
John Angus

D-U-N-S 25-867-9737   (HQ)
RE/MAX ROYAL (JORDAN) INC
201 Av Cartier, Pointe-Claire, QC, H9S 4S2
(514) 694-6900
Sales 10,870,240
SIC 6531 Real estate agents and managers
Arvin Thomas
Caroline Salette

Pointe-Lebel, QC G0H

D-U-N-S 24-204-9245   (SL)
ENTREPRISES JULIEN BERNIER INC, LES
46 Ch De La Scierie Rr 1, Pointe-Lebel, QC,

G0H 1N0
Emp Here 86   *Sales* 12,744,512
SIC 4212 Local trucking, without storage
Julien Bernier
Martin Bernier
Louise Bernier

Pont-Rouge, QC G3H

D-U-N-S 25-489-1294   (SL)
GOLF DU GRAND PORTNEUF INC, LE
BOUTIQUE DE GOLF LE GRAND PORTNEUF
2 Rte 365, Pont-Rouge, QC, G3H 3R4
(418) 329-2238
Emp Here 80   *Sales* 6,111,760
SIC 7992 Public golf courses
Raymond Carpentier
Jean-Marc Carpentier
Simon Carpentier
Michel Noel

D-U-N-S 20-721-1707   (SL)
SUPER MARCHE J.C. BEDARD LTEE
169 Rue Dupont, Pont-Rouge, QC, G3H 1N3
(418) 873-2415
Emp Here 50   *Sales* 13,707,600
SIC 5411 Grocery stores
Jean-Claude Bedard
Armand Bedard
Lise Bedard

Port-Cartier, QC G5B

D-U-N-S 24-864-7815   (SL)
IGA ALIMENTATION COOP POR
26 Boul Des Iles, Port-Cartier, QC, G5B 0A4
(418) 766-0008
Emp Here 49   *Sales* 14,622,233
SIC 5411 Grocery stores

D-U-N-S 20-955-5473   (HQ)
PASCAL CHEVROLET LTEE
80 Boul Du Portage-Des-Mousses, Port-Cartier, QC, G5B 1E1
(418) 766-4343
Emp Here 24   *Sales* 17,930,808
SIC 5511 New and used car dealers
Pascal Gaudet

D-U-N-S 25-212-3583   (BR)
PRODUITS FORESTIERS ARBEC S.E.N.C.
(*Suby of* PRODUITS FORESTIERS ARBEC S.E.N.C.)
175 Boul Portage Des Mousses, Port-Cartier, QC, G5B 2V9
(418) 766-2299
Emp Here 450
SIC 2421 Sawmills and planing mills, general
Mario Belanger

Portneuf, QC G0A

D-U-N-S 25-170-3310   (BR)
AGC FLAT GLASS NORTH AMERICA LTD
AFG GLASS
(*Suby of* AGC INC.)
250 Rue De Copenhague, Portneuf, QC, G0A 2Y0
Emp Here 250
SIC 3211 Flat glass

D-U-N-S 24-394-8861   (BR)
CHARL-POL INC
(*Suby of* 8132992 CANADA INC)
440 Rue Lucien-Thibodeau, Portneuf, QC,

G0A 2Y0
(418) 286-4881
Emp Here 80
SIC 3569 General industrial machinery, nec
Denis Dubois

D-U-N-S 20-240-5635   (HQ)
FRENECO LTEE
261 Rue Saint-Charles, Portneuf, QC, G0A 2Y0
(418) 286-3341
Sales 14,427,750
SIC 2439 Structural wood members, nec
Jean Frenette
Gerald Frenette

D-U-N-S 25-368-2504   (SL)
MPI MOULIN A PAPIER DE PORTNEUF, INC
200 Rue Du Moulin, Portneuf, QC, G0A 2Y0
(418) 286-3461
Emp Here 50   *Sales* 10,094,850
SIC 3089 Plastics products, nec
Karim N. Jadavji

D-U-N-S 25-167-2804   (SL)
PHARMACIE GAETAN, JACQUES ET MARCOT, JULIE
196 1re Av, Portneuf, QC, G0A 2Y0
(418) 286-3301
Emp Here 30   *Sales* 33,160,350
SIC 5122 Drugs, proprietaries, and sundries
Gaetan Jacques
Julie Marcotte

D-U-N-S 24-907-4493   (SL)
SELECTION DU PATISSIER INC
PASTRY SELECTIONS
450 2e Av, Portneuf, QC, G0A 2Y0
(418) 286-3400
Emp Here 100   *Sales* 8,562,268
SIC 2052 Cookies and crackers
Mario Audet
Yvon Hardy
Michel Baribeau
Rejean Proulx

D-U-N-S 20-271-2501   (SL)
SERRES SAVOURA ST-ETIENNE INC, LES
SAVOURA
(*Suby of* SERRES SAGAMI INC, LES)
700 Rue Lucien-Thibodeau, Portneuf, QC, G0A 2Y0
(418) 286-6681
Emp Here 80   *Sales* 20,984,720
SIC 0161 Vegetables and melons
Stephane Roy
Caroline Dalpe

Portneuf-Sur-Mer, QC G0T

D-U-N-S 20-006-0486   (SL)
CRABIERS DU NORD INC, LES
428 Rue Principale, Portneuf-Sur-Mer, QC, G0T 1P0
(418) 238-2132
Emp Here 100   *Sales* 34,569,000
SIC 2091 Canned and cured fish and seafoods
Raymond Morneau
Yan Riverin
Marie-Helene Morneau
Gerard Ross
Norbert Fontaine
Gilles Gagnon
Marc Genest
Darry Noel
Aime Tremblay
Mario Tremblay

Prevost, QC J0R

D-U-N-S 25-857-1231   (BR)

CENTRES DE LA JEUNESSE ET DE LA FAMILLE BATSHAW, L
LES CENTRES DE LA JEUNESSE ET DE LA FAMILLE BATSHAW
(*Suby of* CENTRES DE LA JEUNESSE ET DE LA FAMILLE BATSHAW, L)
3065 Boul Du Cure-Labelle, Prevost, QC, J0R 1T0
(450) 224-8234
Emp Here 150
SIC 8322 Individual and family services
Wayne Adams

D-U-N-S 24-904-1526   (SL)
MARCHE DOMINIC PICHE INC
AXEP PLUS
3023 Boul Labelle, Prevost, QC, J0R 1T0
Emp Here 45   *Sales* 12,544,331
SIC 5411 Grocery stores
Dominic Piche

D-U-N-S 20-793-3441   (HQ)
PETROLE PAGE INC
2899 Boul Du Cure-Labelle Bureau 100, Prevost, QC, J0R 1T0
(450) 224-1795
Sales 13,132,140
SIC 5983 Fuel oil dealers
Roger Page
Claude Page

Price, QC G0J

D-U-N-S 20-430-0149   (HQ)
BOIS D'OEUVRE CEDRICO INC
BUREAU ADMINISTRATIF
39 Rue Saint-Jean-Baptiste, Price, QC, G0J 1Z0
(418) 775-7516
Emp Here 45   *Sales* 69,597,500
SIC 2431 Millwork
Denis Berube
Nancy Berube

Princeville, QC G6L

D-U-N-S 24-747-1360   (SL)
ALIMENTS VERMONT FOODS INC
210 Rue Saint-Jean-Baptiste N, Princeville, QC, G6L 5E1
Emp Here 175   *Sales* 60,495,750
SIC 2011 Meat packing plants
Marcel Heroux

D-U-N-S 20-778-2822   (SL)
BATEAUX PRINCECRAFT INC
(*Suby of* BRUNSWICK INTERNATIONAL GROUP SARL)
725 Rue Saint-Henri, Princeville, QC, G6L 5C2
(819) 364-5581
Emp Here 310   *Sales* 90,163,500
SIC 3732 Boatbuilding and repairing
Steve Langlais
Judith P. Zelisko
Christopher F. Dekker
Claude Lebel

D-U-N-S 20-314-0330   (HQ)
DEMTEC INC
50 Boul Industriel, Princeville, QC, G6L 4P2
(819) 364-2043
Sales 14,429,150
SIC 1522 Residential construction, nec
Philippe Picory
Sebastien Neault

D-U-N-S 25-257-8760   (SL)
FONDERIE LEMOLTECH INC

30 Rue Saint-Pierre, Princeville, QC, G6L 5A9
(819) 364-7616
Emp Here 80   *Sales* 7,264,512
SIC 3365 Aluminum foundries
  Bertrand Doucet
  Melanie Mailhot
  Nicolas Gagnon

  D-U-N-S 20-297-9159   (SL)
GALVANISATION QUEBEC INC
225 Rue Jeremie-Pacaud, Princeville, QC,
G6L 0A1
(819) 505-4440
Emp Here 50   *Sales* 10,141,500
SIC 3479 Metal coating and allied services
  Claude Beauvillier
  John R. Hall

  D-U-N-S 24-380-5868   (SL)
JARDINERIE FERNAND FORTIER INC, LA
99 116 Rte E, Princeville, QC, G6L 4K6
(819) 364-5009
Emp Here 70   *Sales* 18,735,640
SIC 5261 Retail nurseries and garden stores
  Fernand Fortier

  D-U-N-S 25-075-3829   (SL)
NATART JUVENILE INC
TULIPE JUVENILE
289 Boul Baril O, Princeville, QC, G6L 3V8

Emp Here 26   *Sales* 13,230,256
SIC 5021 Furniture
  Antonio De Bonis
  Michel De Bonis
  Jean-Marie Rancourt

  D-U-N-S 25-010-4882   (BR)
OLYMEL S.E.C.
FLAMINGO
(*Suby of* OLYMEL S.E.C.)
155 Rue Saint-Jean-Baptiste N, Princeville,
QC, G6L 5C9
(819) 364-5501
Emp Here 350
SIC 2011 Meat packing plants
  Martin Croteau

  D-U-N-S 24-066-0469   (SL)
REMBOURRAGE ANP INC
105 Rue Beaudet, Princeville, QC, G6L 4L3
(819) 364-2645
Emp Here 60   *Sales* 13,430,580
SIC 3732 Boatbuilding and repairing
  Sebastien Noreau

  D-U-N-S 24-633-4960   (SL)
REMBOURRAGE PRINCEVILLE TECH
105 Rue Beaudet, Princeville, QC, G6L 4L3
(819) 364-2645
Emp Here 26   *Sales* 12,950,028
SIC 5551 Boat dealers
  Patrice Ledu

  D-U-N-S 20-721-2952   (SL)
REMEQ INC
391 Rue Saint-Jean-Baptiste N, Princeville,
QC, G6L 5G3
(819) 364-5400
Emp Here 65   *Sales* 14,549,795
SIC 3715 Truck trailers
  Bernard Cormier

  D-U-N-S 20-777-5735   (SL)
RENOVATION EXPO INC
40 Rue Saint-Pierre, Princeville, QC, G6L 5A9
(819) 364-2616
Emp Here 66   *Sales* 15,338,598
SIC 5712 Furniture stores
  Gerald Simoneau
  Gilles Cote

  D-U-N-S 20-240-6633   (SL)
TRICOTS DUVAL & RAYMOND LTEE, LES
DURAY
11 Rue Saint-Jacques O, Princeville, QC, G6L
5E6

(819) 364-2927
Emp Here 95   *Sales* 17,423,285
SIC 2252 Hosiery, nec
  Yan Raymond
  Samuel Raymond
  Dany Legare

Puvirnituq, QC J0M

  D-U-N-S 25-330-8506   (HQ)
CENTRE DE SANTE INUULITSIVIK
Gd, Puvirnituq, QC, J0M 1P0
(819) 988-2957
Sales 16,662,000
SIC 8062 General medical and surgical hospitals
  Paelussie Anjiyou

  D-U-N-S 25-325-1367   (BR)
COMMISSION SCOLAIRE KATIVIK
ECOLE IGUARSIVIK
(*Suby of* COMMISSION SCOLAIRE KATIVIK)
Gd, Puvirnituq, QC, J0M 1P0
(819) 988-2960
Emp Here 90
SIC 8211 Elementary and secondary schools
  Lousemier Han

Quebec, QC G1B

  D-U-N-S 20-029-9589   (BR)
COURTIERS INTER-QUEBEC INC, LES
(*Suby of* COURTIERS INTER-QUEBEC INC,
LES)
900 Boul Raymond, Quebec, QC, G1B 3G3

Emp Here 150
SIC 6531 Real estate agents and managers
  Danielle Lamontagne

  D-U-N-S 24-249-1871   (SL)
OUELLET, PATRICK 1843 INC
PHARMAPRIX
1 Rue Guyon Bureau 1843, Quebec, QC, G1B
1T1
(418) 666-1410
Emp Here 45   *Sales* 11,382,930
SIC 5912 Drug stores and proprietary stores
  Patrick Ouellet

Quebec, QC G1C

  D-U-N-S 24-249-0881   (SL)
9084-2733 QUEBEC INC
COMMUNICATION PL
2650 Ch Du Petit-Village, Quebec, QC, G1C
1V9
(418) 624-1301
Emp Here 100   *Sales* 18,479,800
SIC 4841 Cable and other pay television services
  Pierre Lepine

  D-U-N-S 20-526-7052   (SL)
9118-8706 QUEBEC INC
BEAUPORT MAZDA
585 Rue Clemenceau, Quebec, QC, G1C 7Z9
(418) 667-3131
Emp Here 49   *Sales* 24,405,822
SIC 5511 New and used car dealers
  Paul Daigle
  Dany Gosselin

  D-U-N-S 25-625-9615   (HQ)
ANIMALERIE DYNO INC
2377 Boul Louis-Xiv, Quebec, QC, G1C 1B2
(418) 661-7128
Emp Here 119   *Sales* 30,541,000
SIC 5999 Miscellaneous retail stores, nec

  Andre Rodrigue
  Simon Rodrigue

  D-U-N-S 20-204-9383   (SL)
AUTOBUS LAVAL LTEE
ECOBUS, L'
445 Rue Des Alleghanys Bureau 201, Quebec, QC, G1C 4N4
(418) 667-3265
Emp Here 175   *Sales* 13,172,600
SIC 4151 School buses
  Louise Giroux
  Jacques Langlois
  Gilles St-Cyr
  Romain Girard

  D-U-N-S 25-081-1353   (SL)
AUTOMOBILES ROBERGE LTEE
BEAUPORT HYUNDAI
545 Rue Clemenceau, Quebec, QC, G1C 7B6
(418) 666-2000
Emp Here 60   *Sales* 37,756,800
SIC 5511 New and used car dealers
  Paul Daigle

  D-U-N-S 25-170-0688   (HQ)
CAISSE DESJARDINS DE BEAUPORT
CAISSE DE BEAUPORT
799 Rue Clemenceau, Quebec, QC, G1C 8J7
(418) 660-3119
Emp Here 65   *Sales* 16,491,407
SIC 6062 State credit unions
  Joanne Richard
  Lise Malouin
  Frederick Desjardins
  Jacques Auger
  Jean Beaupre
  Cimon Boily
  Joelle Boisvert
  Stephane Chum-Chhin
  Murielle Drapeau
  Gilles Fortin

  D-U-N-S 20-919-1290   (HQ)
**CENTRE DE SANTE ET DE SERVICES SO-
CIAUX DE QUEBEC-NORD**
LE CSSS DE QUEBEC-NORD
(*Suby of* GOUVERNEMENT DE LA
PROVINCE DE QUEBEC)
4e Etage 2915, Av Du Bourg-Royal, Quebec,
QC, G1C 3S2
(418) 661-5666
Emp Here 100   *Sales* 570,621,000
SIC 8011 Offices and clinics of medical doctors
  Pierre Leveille
  Christine Verner
  Lucie Lacroix
  Jean-Louis Lapointe

  D-U-N-S 25-257-4546   (BR)
**CENTRE DE SANTE ET DE SERVICES SO-
CIAUX DU PONTIAC**
CENTRE ST-AUGUSTIN
(*Suby of* GOUVERNEMENT DE LA
PROVINCE DE QUEBEC)
2135 Rue De La Terrasse-Cadieux, Quebec,
QC, G1C 1Z2
(418) 667-3910
Emp Here 500
SIC 8051 Skilled nursing care facilities
  Bernard Bouchard

  D-U-N-S 20-106-9866   (SL)
**CENTRE FINANCIER AUX ENTREPRISES -
QUEBEC-CAPITALE**
DESJARDINS
3333 Rue Du Carrefour Bureau 280, Quebec,
QC, G1C 5R9
(418) 660-2229
Emp Here 49   *Sales* 13,442,268
SIC 8741 Management services
  Michel Bureau

  D-U-N-S 20-648-3018   (SL)
CHARLES-AUGUSTE FORTIER INC
C.A.F.

424 Boul Raymond, Quebec, QC, G1C 8K9
(418) 661-0043
Emp Here 100   *Sales* 24,618,600
SIC 1794 Excavation work
  Julie Coallier
  Florent Fortier
  Mario Fortier
  Edith Fortier

  D-U-N-S 25-234-0047   (BR)
**COMMISSION   SCOLAIRE   DES
PREMIERES-SEIGNEURIES**
*COMMISSION   SCOLAIRE   DES
PREMIERES-SEIGNEURIES*
(*Suby of* COMMISSION SCOLAIRE DES
PREMIERES-SEIGNEURIES)
2233 Av Royale, Quebec, QC, G1C 1P3
(418) 821-8988
Emp Here 130
SIC 8211 Elementary and secondary schools
  Nathalie Vezina

  D-U-N-S 20-711-9905   (BR)
**COMMISSION   SCOLAIRE   DES
PREMIERES-SEIGNEURIES**
*COMMISSION   SCOLAIRE   DES
PREMIERES-SEIGNEURIES*
(*Suby of* COMMISSION SCOLAIRE DES
PREMIERES-SEIGNEURIES)
2265 Av Larue, Quebec, QC, G1C 1J9
(418) 821-4220
Emp Here 120
SIC 8211 Elementary and secondary schools
  Christian Couture

  D-U-N-S 24-892-0253   (SL)
**COMPTOIRS MOULES RIVE-NORD INC,
LES**
414 Boul Raymond, Quebec, QC, G1C 0L6
(418) 667-8814
Emp Here 30   *Sales* 13,415,220
SIC 5039 Construction materials, nec
  Diane Beland

  D-U-N-S 25-743-2682   (SL)
CONNEXION TECHNIC INC
(*Suby of* INVESTISSEMENTS LS3M INC)
989 Av Nordique Bureau 100, Quebec, QC.
G1C 0C7
(418) 660-6276
Emp Here 65   *Sales* 16,002,090
SIC 1799 Special trade contractors, nec
  Michel Brouillette

  D-U-N-S 24-208-4192   (SL)
CONSTRUCTION CITADELLE INC
419 Rue Des Monteregiennes, Quebec, QC,
G1C 7J7
(418) 661-9351
Emp Here 35   *Sales* 16,475,585
SIC 1542 Nonresidential construction, nec
  Gilles Lemelin
  Luc Lemire

  D-U-N-S 20-516-9980   (SL)
**ENTREPRISES ANTONIO BARRETTE INC,
LES**
LEAB MECANIQUE DE PROCEDE
437 Rue Des Monteregiennes, Quebec, QC,
G1C 7J7
(418) 686-6455
Emp Here 49   *Sales* 12,599,419
SIC 4959 Sanitary services, nec
  Rejean Thibodeau
  Gilles Thibodeau
  Ian Thibodeau

  D-U-N-S 24-673-2791   (SL)
**ENTREPRISES BOULOS,PIERRE L INC,
LES**
*MARCHAND CANADIAN TIRE DE BEAU-
PORT*
705 Rue Clemenceau, Quebec, QC, G1C 7T9
(418) 663-4334
Emp Here 49   *Sales* 24,405,822
SIC 5531 Auto and home supply stores
  Pierre Boulos

▲ Public Company   ■ Public Company Family Member   **HQ** Headquarters   **BR** Branch   **SL** Single Location

D-U-N-S 20-643-4102 (SL)
ENTREPRISES L.T. LTEE, LES
BETON LAGACE
1209 Rue Wilbrod-Robert, Quebec, QC, G1C
0L1
(418) 663-0555
Emp Here 70   *Sales* 17,999,170
SIC 4959 Sanitary services, nec
Pierre Lagace
Michel Lagace
Carol Lagace

D-U-N-S 24-250-4962 (HQ)
EPSYLON CONCEPT INC
1010 Av Nordique, Quebec, QC, G1C 0H9
(418) 661-6262
Sales 12,485,525
SIC 3449 Miscellaneous Metalwork
Alain Lefrancois
Jean Lefrancois

D-U-N-S 24-096-9225 (BR)
**FEDERATION DES CAISSES DESJARDINS
DU QUEBEC**
*CENTRE FINANCIER AUX ENTREPRISES
DE LA CAPITALE*
(*Suby of* FEDERATION DES CAISSES DES-
JARDINS DU QUEBEC)
3333 Rue Du Carrefour Bureau 280, Quebec,
QC, G1C 5R9
(418) 660-2229
Emp Here 136
SIC 6159 Miscellaneous business credit insti-
tutions
Michel Bureau

D-U-N-S 20-222-8933 (SL)
FRUITS ET LEGUMES BEAUPORT INC
FLB SOLUTIONS
275 Av Du Semoir, Quebec, QC, G1C 7V5
(418) 661-6938
Emp Here 80   *Sales* 66,846,160
SIC 5148 Fresh fruits and vegetables
Philippe Vennes
Eric Drouin
Carl Drouin

D-U-N-S 20-704-8963 (HQ)
GESTION CHRISTIAN J. OUELLET INC
JEAN COUTU
3333 Rue Du Carrefour, Quebec, QC, G1C
5R9
(418) 667-7534
Emp Here 20   *Sales* 10,118,160
SIC 5912 Drug stores and proprietary stores
Christian Ouellet

D-U-N-S 25-292-9906 (SL)
GESTION JEAN PAQUETTE INC
CANADIAN TIRE 184
705 Rue Clemenceau Bureau 184, Quebec,
QC, G1C 7T9
(418) 663-4334
Emp Here 118   *Sales* 24,230,474
SIC 5311 Department stores
Jean Paquette

D-U-N-S 25-672-6134 (HQ)
GROUPE MACADAM INC
GROUPE CONFORT GLOBAL
4550 Boul Sainte-Anne, Quebec, QC, G1C
2H9
(418) 661-2400
Emp Here 45   *Sales* 12,044,200
SIC 1622 Bridge, tunnel, and elevated high-
way construction
Gilles Pilote

D-U-N-S 25-484-9169 (BR)
LOBLAWS INC
MAXI BEAUPORT
(*Suby of* LOBLAW COMPANIES LIMITED)
699 Rue Clemenceau, Quebec, QC, G1C 4N6
(418) 666-0155
Emp Here 90
SIC 5411 Grocery stores
Sebastien Tesser

D-U-N-S 24-689-5965 (SL)
LOCATION 18E RUE INC
BEAUPORT NISSAN
455 Rue Clemenceau, Quebec, QC, G1C 7B6
(418) 647-1822
Emp Here 47   *Sales* 23,409,666
SIC 5511 New and used car dealers
Luc Beaudoin
Prime Roberge

D-U-N-S 24-205-3965 (SL)
METRO EXCAVATION INC
2144 Boul Louis-Xiv, Quebec, QC, G1C 1A2
(418) 661-5771
Emp Here 5   *Sales* 19,053,425
SIC 1794 Excavation work
Rene Lagace
Richard Lagace

D-U-N-S 20-120-1220 (SL)
NOVA CONSTRUCTION C.P. INC
NOVA CONSTRUCTION
1259 Rue Paul-Emile-Giroux, Quebec, QC,
G1C 0K9
(418) 660-8111
Emp Here 40   *Sales* 10,837,680
SIC 1521 Single-family housing construction
Cyrille Parent
Marcel Parent

D-U-N-S 25-744-8753 (SL)
PARADIS AMENAGEMENT URBAIN INC
436 Rue Des Adirondacks, Quebec, QC, G1C
7E8
(418) 660-4060
Emp Here 60   *Sales* 11,969,100
SIC 4959 Sanitary services, nec
Francois Paradis

D-U-N-S 20-432-5591 (SL)
PARTAGEC INC
1299 Rue Paul-Emile-Giroux, Quebec, QC,
G1C 0K9
(418) 647-1428
Emp Here 200   *Sales* 17,939,200
SIC 7218 Industrial launderers
Georges Smith
Guy Thibodeau
Georges Smith
Daniel Bernard
Pierre-Andre Tremblay
Marc Thibeault
Denis Potvin
Francois Latreille
Caroline Imbeau
Guy Gignac

D-U-N-S 20-202-5438 (SL)
PROMETEK INC
1005 Av Nordique, Quebec, QC, G1C 0C7
(418) 527-4445
Emp Here 50   *Sales* 13,379,430
SIC 3441 Fabricated structural Metal
Jean Pouliot
Sebastien Noel
Jocelyn Gamache
Andre Cote
Sylvain St-Pierre
Sonia Ouellette

D-U-N-S 24-500-5301 (SL)
S.T.R. ELECTRONIQUE INC
610 Rue Ardouin, Quebec, QC, G1C 7J8
(418) 660-8899
Emp Here 26   *Sales* 11,626,524
SIC 5045 Computers, peripherals, and soft-
ware
Julie Sirois

D-U-N-S 20-376-2732 (SL)
SG TRANSPORT ENERGIE INC
520 Rue Adanac, Quebec, QC, G1C 7B7
(418) 660-8888
Emp Here 50   *Sales* 13,077,650
SIC 6712 Bank holding companies
Denis Giguere

D-U-N-S 20-298-1556 (BR)

SOBEYS CAPITAL INCORPORATED
BANIERE IGA EXTRA, LA
(*Suby of* EMPIRE COMPANY LIMITED)
969 Av Nordique Bureau 458, Quebec, QC,
G1C 7S8
(418) 667-5700
Emp Here 150
SIC 5411 Grocery stores
Richard Plante

D-U-N-S 20-265-9140 (SL)
STERIS CANADA ULC
CORPORATION STERIS CANADA
(*Suby of* STERIS LIMITED)
490 Boul Armand-Paris, Quebec, QC, G1C
8A3
(418) 664-1549
Emp Here 230   *Sales* 55,943,130
SIC 3431 Metal sanitary ware
Michael J. Tokich
Ronald E. Snyder
Michael Pace
Karen L. Burton

D-U-N-S 24-207-5513 (SL)
VITRERIE LABERGE (1988) INC
415 Rue Des Alleghanys, Quebec, QC, G1C
4N4
(418) 663-6363
Emp Here 80   *Sales* 21,412,160
SIC 5231 Paint, glass, and wallpaper stores
Gilles Laberge
Pierre Laberge
Marc Laberge
Jean Lagerge

Quebec, QC G1E

D-U-N-S 24-354-2177 (HQ)
9109-5521 QUEBEC INC
3261 Rue Loyola, Quebec, QC, G1E 2R9
(418) 660-2037
Emp Here 4   *Sales* 16,774,200
SIC 6712 Bank holding companies
Robert Desautels
Martin Tremblay

D-U-N-S 20-198-2154 (SL)
**ALIMENTS ORIGINAL, DIVISION CANTIN
INC**
1910 Av Du Sanctuaire, Quebec, QC, G1E
3L2
(418) 663-3523
Emp Here 65   *Sales* 22,469,850
SIC 2033 Canned fruits and specialties
Steeve Tremblay

D-U-N-S 24-101-3452 (BR)
CANAC IMMOBILIER INC
(*Suby of* GESTION LABERGE INC)
947 Av Royale, Quebec, QC, G1E 1Z9
(418) 667-1729
Emp Here 1,000
SIC 5039 Construction materials, nec
Jacques Gregoire

D-U-N-S 24-336-4259 (BR)
**CENTRE DE SANTE ET DE SERVICES SO-
CIAUX DE QUEBEC-NORD**
*CENTRE D'HEBERGEMENT YVONNE-
SYLVAIN*
(*Suby of* GOUVERNEMENT DE LA
PROVINCE DE QUEBEC)
3365 Rue Guimont, Quebec, QC, G1E 2H1
(418) 663-8171
Emp Here 250
SIC 8361 Residential care
Bernard Bouchard

D-U-N-S 20-003-5397 (BR)
**CENTRE INTEGRE UNIVERSITAIRE DE
SANTE ET DE SERVICES SOCIAUX DE LA
CAPITALE-NATIONALE, LE**
CENTRE D'HEBERGEMENT DU FARGY

(*Suby of* GOUVERNEMENT DE LA
PROVINCE DE QUEBEC)
700 Boul Des Chutes, Quebec, QC, G1E 2B7
(418) 663-9934
Emp Here 88
SIC 8361 Residential care
Louise Hamel

D-U-N-S 20-711-9756 (BR)
**COMMISSION   SCOLAIRE   DES
PREMIERES-SEIGNEURIES**
*COMMISSION   SCOLAIRE   DES
PREMIERES-SEIGNEURIES*
(*Suby of* COMMISSION SCOLAIRE DES
PREMIERES-SEIGNEURIES)
645 Av Du Cenacle, Quebec, QC, G1E 1B3
(418) 666-4666
Emp Here 100
SIC 8211 Elementary and secondary schools
Gilles Tetraut

D-U-N-S 25-232-7077 (HQ)
**COMMISSION   SCOLAIRE   DES
PREMIERES-SEIGNEURIES**
643 Av Du Cenacle, Quebec, QC, G1E 1B3
(418) 666-4666
Emp Here 150   *Sales* 276,145,534
SIC 8211 Elementary and secondary schools
Clement Turcotte
Marie-France Painchaud
Jean-Francois Parent
Paule Pouliot
Louis Dandurand
Marie-Claude Asselin

D-U-N-S 25-232-7358 (BR)
**COMMISSION   SCOLAIRE   DES
PREMIERES-SEIGNEURIES**
*COMMISSION   SCOLAIRE   DES
PREMIERES-SEIGNEURIES*
(*Suby of* COMMISSION SCOLAIRE DES
PREMIERES-SEIGNEURIES)
2740 Av Saint-David, Quebec, QC, G1E 4K7
(418) 666-4500
Emp Here 155
SIC 8211 Elementary and secondary schools
Isabelle Tremblay

D-U-N-S 24-908-5937 (HQ)
**CORPORATION FINANCIERE J. DE-
SCHAMPS INC**
755 Boul Des Chutes, Quebec, QC, G1E 2C2
(418) 667-3322
Sales 63,964,075
SIC 6712 Bank holding companies
Jean Deschamps

D-U-N-S 20-189-9846 (HQ)
DESCHAMPS IMPRESSION INC
755 Boul Des Chutes, Quebec, QC, G1E 2C2
(418) 667-3322
Sales 32,805,400
SIC 2759 Commercial printing, nec
Jean Deschamps
Christian Deschamps
Francis Deschamps

D-U-N-S 20-327-2351 (SL)
ENTRAIDE AGAPE
TRESORS D'AGAPE, AUX
3148 Ch Royal, Quebec, QC, G1E 1V2
(418) 661-7485
Emp Here 26   *Sales* 10,332,764
SIC 8699 Membership organizations, nec
Alexi Roger

D-U-N-S 25-500-5746 (HQ)
**FONDATION DES SOURDS DU QUEBEC
(F.S.Q.) INC, LA**
3348 Boul Monseigneur-Gauthier, Quebec,
QC, G1E 2W2
(418) 660-6800
Emp Here 115   *Sales* 23,812,820
SIC 8399 Social services, nec
Gaston Forgues
Daniel Forgues

▲ Public Company   ■ Public Company Family Member   **HQ** Headquarters   **BR** Branch   **SL** Single Location

D-U-N-S 24-340-7066   (BR)
FONDATION DU CENTRE JEUNESSE DE QUEBEC
CENTRE DE READAPTATION LE GOUVERNAIL
3510 Rue Cambronne, Quebec, QC, G1E 7H2
(418) 661-3700
Emp Here 150
SIC 8322 Individual and family services
Louis Mcclish

D-U-N-S 20-869-7466   (HQ)
GAROY CONSTRUCTION INC
(*Suby of* GROUPE GAROY INC)
4000 Boul Sainte-Anne, Quebec, QC, G1E 3M5
(418) 661-1754
Sales 18,829,240
SIC 1542 Nonresidential construction, nec
Jean-Francois Roy
Dominique Roy

D-U-N-S 20-596-0805   (BR)
GOUVERNEMENT DE LA PROVINCE DE QUEBEC
CENTRE JEUNESSE DE QUEBEC SERVICE D'URGENCE SOCIALE
(*Suby of* GOUVERNEMENT DE LA PROVINCE DE QUEBEC)
3510 Rue Cambronne, Quebec, QC, G1E 7H2
(418) 661-3700
Emp Here 1,200
SIC 8399 Social services, nec
Michele Sylvestre

D-U-N-S 25-765-2719   (SL)
HABITATIONS CONSULTANTS H.L. INC
104 Rue Seigneuriale, Quebec, QC, G1E 4Y5
(418) 666-1324
Emp Here 40   *Sales* 18,829,240
SIC 1542 Nonresidential construction, nec
Frank Hayes
Jean-Francois Hayes
Lisette Hayes

D-U-N-S 20-297-9308   (SL)
LE SYNDICAT DE LA COPROPRIETE LES JARDINS DU HAVRE
25 Rue Des Mouettes Bureau 431, Quebec, QC, G1E 7G1
(418) 660-6599
Emp Here 50   *Sales* 13,587,800
SIC 6531 Real estate agents and managers
Alain Tremblay
Daniel Bouchard
Nicole Turcotte
Francine Chabot
Andre Laroche
Pierre Nolet
Francine Laflamme
Mariette Bujold
Willie St-Laurent

D-U-N-S 25-983-3937   (SL)
MARCHE DU VIEUX BEAUPORT INC
IGA VIEUX BEAUPORT
771 Av Royale, Quebec, QC, G1E 1Z1
(418) 661-9181
Emp Here 49   *Sales* 13,433,448
SIC 5411 Grocery stores
Michel Laflamme

D-U-N-S 25-768-2070   (BR)
MARTIN, CLAUDE & MARCEL INC
ROTISSERIE ST-HUBERT
(*Suby of* 2621-9386 QUEBEC INC)
3410 Boul Sainte-Anne, Quebec, QC, G1E 3L7
(418) 663-1234
Emp Here 100
SIC 5812 Eating places
Pierre Martin

D-U-N-S 20-803-4988   (BR)
METRO RICHELIEU INC
(*Suby of* METRO INC)
2968 Boul Sainte-Anne, Quebec, QC, G1E

3J3

Emp Here 125
SIC 5431 Fruit and vegetable markets
Jacques Laplante

D-U-N-S 24-201-8661   (BR)
MULTI-MARQUES INC
USINE GAILURON
(*Suby of* GRUPO BIMBO, S.A.B. DE C.V.)
553 Av Royale, Quebec, QC, G1E 1Y4
(418) 661-4400
Emp Here 130
SIC 2051 Bread, cake, and related products
Same Doucet

D-U-N-S 20-564-8541   (SL)
SECURITE SIROIS EVENEMENTS SPECIAUX INC
SECURITE AVANT-SCENE
104 Rue Seigneuriale, Quebec, QC, G1E 4Y5
(418) 692-4137
Emp Here 500   *Sales* 13,125,000
SIC 7381 Detective and armored car services
Martin Sirois

D-U-N-S 25-762-2332   (SL)
SOCIETE EN COMMENDITE PLACE ALEXANDRA
2475 Rue Alexandra, Quebec, QC, G1E 7A8
(418) 666-7636
Emp Here 45   *Sales* 10,480,995
SIC 6513 Apartment building operators
Rene Belsile

Quebec, QC G1G

D-U-N-S 20-192-8462   (SL)
BOURBEAU, GERARD & FILS INC
CENTRE JARDIN BOURBEAU
8285 1re Av, Quebec, QC, G1G 4C1
(418) 623-5401
Emp Here 30   *Sales* 22,275,600
SIC 5193 Flowers and florists supplies
Andre Bourbeau
Martin Bourbeau
Denise Bourbeau

D-U-N-S 20-192-8603   (SL)
CHARLESBOURG AUTOMOBILES LTEE
CHARLESBOURG TOYOTA
16070 Boul Henri-Bourassa, Quebec, QC, G1G 3Z8
(418) 623-9843
Emp Here 60   *Sales* 37,756,800
SIC 5511 New and used car dealers
Marc Tardif
Marc-Andre Tardif

D-U-N-S 20-006-7473   (SL)
FOND SRS DE L'ETABLISSEMENT DE DETENTION DE QUEBEC, LE
ATELIERS D'ELLE, LES
500 Rue De La Faune, Quebec, QC, G1G 0G9
(418) 622-7100
Emp Here 150   *Sales* 24,604,050
SIC 2752 Commercial printing, lithographic
Simon Potvin
Ginette Guilbault-Baril
Claude Ouellet
Marie-Josee Gagnon
Jean-Louis Brochu
Rita Biron
Jean Paul Careau
Kathleen Carroll
Paul Dery

D-U-N-S 20-717-1963   (BR)
GOUVERNEMENT DE LA PROVINCE DE QUEBEC
CRDI DE QUEBEC
(*Suby of* GOUVERNEMENT DE LA PROVINCE DE QUEBEC)
7843 Rue Des Santolines, Quebec, QC, G1G

0G3
(418) 683-2511
Emp Here 741
SIC 8361 Residential care

D-U-N-S 20-777-3896   (BR)
GROUPE NORMANDIN INC
NORMANDIN BDJ
(*Suby of* GROUPE NORMANDIN INC)
15021 Boul Henri-Bourassa, Quebec, QC, G1G 3Z2
(418) 626-7216
Emp Here 78
SIC 5812 Eating places
Andre Lacombe

D-U-N-S 20-959-6787   (SL)
HOTEL & GOLF MARIGOT INC
FOUR POINTS BY SHERATON
7900 Rue Du Marigot, Quebec, QC, G1G 6T8
(418) 627-8008
Emp Here 100   *Sales* 9,489,900
SIC 7011 Hotels and motels
Guy St-Gelais
Daniel Plante

D-U-N-S 24-499-2806   (SL)
MAISON CHRYSLER DE CHARLESBOURG LTEE, LA
(*Suby of* GESTION PAUL DAIGLE INC)
15070 Boul Henri-Bourassa, Quebec, QC, G1G 3Z4
(418) 622-4700
Emp Here 50   *Sales* 24,903,900
SIC 5511 New and used car dealers
Paul Daigle
Mario Goupil

Quebec, QC G1H

D-U-N-S 25-258-6490   (SL)
2954-8682 QUEBEC INC
MAISON DE JADE
475 Boul De L'Atrium Bureau 104, Quebec, QC, G1H 7H9

Emp Here 180   *Sales* 8,193,420
SIC 5812 Eating places
Kenneth Ing
Kung King Ng
Diane Vachon

D-U-N-S 20-554-1159   (SL)
9120-9734 QUEBEC INC
I G A DES SOURCES
4250 1re Av Bureau 95, Quebec, QC, G1H 2S5
(418) 627-0660
Emp Here 200   *Sales* 58,695,400
SIC 5411 Grocery stores
Alain Gagne

D-U-N-S 24-890-1670   (SL)
BRASSELER CANADA INC
(*Suby of* BRASSELER U.S.A., INC.)
4500 Boul Henri-Bourassa Bureau 230, Quebec, QC, G1H 3A5
(418) 622-1195
Emp Here 23   *Sales* 10,285,002
SIC 5047 Medical and hospital equipment
Brigitte Ouimet

D-U-N-S 24-363-8777   (HQ)
CAISSE POPULAIRE DESJARDINS DE CHARLESBOURG
CENTRE DE SERVICES DE LAC-SAINT-CHARLES
155 76e Rue E, Quebec, QC, G1H 1G4
(418) 626-1146
Emp Here 50   *Sales* 44,643,493
SIC 6062 State credit unions
Francois Bergeron
Frederic Arteau
Denis Rheaume
Jacques Lagace

Chloe Brault Lampron
Sylvie Couillard
Marc Giguere
Ghislain Gosselin
Raymond Gouge
Bryan Labrecque

D-U-N-S 25-258-8744   (SL)
CENTRE D'HEBERGEMENT ST-JEAN-EUDES INC
6000 3e Av O, Quebec, QC, G1H 7J5
(418) 627-1124
Emp Here 240   *Sales* 16,398,240
SIC 8051 Skilled nursing care facilities
Nicolas Labreche

D-U-N-S 24-346-4364   (BR)
CENTRE DE SANTE ET DE SERVICES SOCIAUX DE QUEBEC-NORD
CLSC LA SOURCE
(*Suby of* GOUVERNEMENT DE LA PROVINCE DE QUEBEC)
190 76e Rue E, Quebec, QC, G1H 7K4
(418) 628-6808
Emp Here 3,000
SIC 8011 Offices and clinics of medical doctors

D-U-N-S 24-326-2164   (BR)
COMMISSION SCOLAIRE DES PREMIERES-SEIGNEURIES
COMMISSION SCOLAIRE DES PREMIERES-SEIGNEURIES
(*Suby of* COMMISSION SCOLAIRE DES PREMIERES-SEIGNEURIES)
800 Rue De La Sorbonne, Quebec, QC, G1H 1H1
(418) 622-7821
Emp Here 200
SIC 8331 Job training and related services
Celine Genest

D-U-N-S 25-746-8629   (HQ)
COURTIERS INTER-QUEBEC INC, LES
ROYAL LEPAGE
805 Rue De Nemours, Quebec, QC, G1H 6Z5
(418) 622-7537
Emp Here 63   *Sales* 50,266,680
SIC 6531 Real estate agents and managers
Paul H. Everell

D-U-N-S 24-378-8122   (HQ)
DEVELOPPEMENTS GERARD BROUSSEAU INC
7609 Av Grignon, Quebec, QC, G1H 6V7
(418) 626-6712
Emp Here 2   *Sales* 12,368,776
SIC 6512 Nonresidential building operators
Gerard Brousseau

D-U-N-S 24-895-7219   (SL)
FOYER DE CHARLESBOURG INC
7150 Boul Cloutier, Quebec, QC, G1H 5V5
(418) 628-0456
Emp Here 125   *Sales* 8,035,250
SIC 8361 Residential care
Gratien Tardif

D-U-N-S 24-820-9132   (SL)
LALLIER AUTOMOBILE (CHARLESBOURG) INC
4650 3e Av O, Quebec, QC, G1H 6E7
(418) 627-1010
Emp Here 47   *Sales* 23,409,666
SIC 5511 New and used car dealers
Jean-Louis Duplessis

D-U-N-S 25-743-5081   (SL)
MANOIR ET COURS DE L'ATRIUM INC
545 Rue Francis-Byrne, Quebec, QC, G1H 7L3
(418) 626-6060
Emp Here 90   *Sales* 5,856,750
SIC 8361 Residential care
Pierre Ferland
Michel Joncas

D-U-N-S 24-202-3265   (BR)

MARTIN, CLAUDE & MARCEL INC
ST-HUBERT BAR-B-Q
(*Suby of* 2621-9386 QUEBEC INC)
7352 Boul Henri-Bourassa, Quebec, QC, G1H
3E4
(418) 622-0220
Emp Here 80
SIC 5812 Eating places

D-U-N-S 25-526-6496 (SL)
PRESENCE INFORMATIQUE INC
PRESENCE
4600 Boul Henri-Bourassa Local 130, Quebec, QC, G1H 3A5
(418) 681-2470
Emp Here 25 *Sales* 13,013,550
SIC 5099 Durable goods, nec
Jean-Luc Carmichael

D-U-N-S 24-730-4652 (SL)
RE/MAX CAPITALE (1983) INC
RE/MAX CAPITALE
7385 Boul Henri-Bourassa, Quebec, QC, G1H
3E5
(418) 627-3120
Emp Here 60 *Sales* 16,305,360
SIC 6531 Real estate agents and managers
Charles Rodrigue
Oona Rodrigue

D-U-N-S 24-637-8079 (SL)
**SOEURS DE SAINT-FRANCOIS D'ASSISE,
LES**
LA MAISON SAINTE-MARIE DES ANGES
600 60e Rue E, Quebec, QC, G1H 3A9
(418) 623-1515
Emp Here 95 *Sales* 10,234,065
SIC 8661 Religious organizations
Marguerite Turcotte
Louise Coveney

Quebec, QC G1J

D-U-N-S 24-890-8048 (SL)
BOUCHERIE DENIS COUTURE INC
I G A
825 4e Av, Quebec, QC, G1J 3A6
(418) 648-2633
Emp Here 60 *Sales* 17,608,620
SIC 5411 Grocery stores
Denis Couture
Diane Pouliot

D-U-N-S 24-109-7349 (SL)
**CLUB NAUTIQUE DE LA BAIE DE BEAU-
PORT**
BAIE DE BEAUPORT
1 Boul Henri-Bourassa, Quebec, QC, G1J
1W8
(418) 266-0722
Emp Here 49 *Sales* 11,643,648
SIC 8621 Professional organizations

D-U-N-S 25-232-0692 (BR)
**COMMISSION SCOLAIRE DE LA CAPI-
TALE, LA**
ECOLE SECONDAIRE JEAN DE BREBEUF
1640 8e Av, Quebec, QC, G1J 3N5
(418) 686-4040
Emp Here 82
SIC 8211 Elementary and secondary schools
Lucie Bertrand-Bisson

D-U-N-S 25-371-3119 (BR)
**COMPAGNIE AMERICAINE DE FER &
METAUX INC, LA**
AIM
(*Suby of* COMPAGNIE AMERICAINE DE FER
& METAUX INC, LA)
999 Boul Montmorency, Quebec, QC, G1J
3W1
(418) 649-1000
Emp Here 155
SIC 3341 Secondary nonferrous Metals

D-U-N-S 20-557-5116 (HQ)
**COMPAGNIE DE PAPIERS WHITE BIRCH
CANADA**
FF SOUCY
(*Suby of* WHITE BIRCH LUXEMBOURG
HOLDING SARL)
10 Boul Des Capucins, Quebec, QC, G1J 0G9
(418) 525-2500
Emp Here 50 *Sales* 735,274,000
SIC 2621 Paper mills
Peter Brant
Christopher Brant
Thimothy J Butler

D-U-N-S 24-530-5727 (SL)
**GAGNON SENECHAL COULOMBE & AS-
SOCIES**
800 Boul Des Capucins, Quebec, QC, G1J
3R8
(418) 648-1717
Emp Here 31 *Sales* 13,925,789
SIC 7389 Business services, nec
Andre Senechal
Louis Coulombe
Marc Gagnon

D-U-N-S 20-241-1872 (HQ)
GLASSINE CANADA INC
(*Suby of* SIMKINS INDUSTRIES, INC.)
1245 Boul Montmorency, Quebec, QC, G1J
5L6
(418) 522-8262
Sales 17,529,120
SIC 2621 Paper mills
Claude Jean
Ronald Hermus
Michelle Simkins-Rubell
Barbara Camera

D-U-N-S 20-555-5175 (BR)
**GOUVERNEMENT DE LA PROVINCE DE
QUEBEC**
*DIRECTION DE LA MAINTENANCE DES
AERONEFS DU SERVICE AERIEN*
(*Suby of* GOUVERNEMENT DE LA
PROVINCE DE QUEBEC)
700 Rue 7e, Quebec, QC, G1J 2S1
(418) 528-8350
Emp Here 185
SIC 4581 Airports, flying fields, and services
Robert Charbonneau

D-U-N-S 25-020-8204 (SL)
**REGIE DES CLUBS D'EXCELLENCE COL-
LEGE D'ENSEIGNEMENT GENERAL ET
PROFESSIONNEL DE LIMOILOU**
CEGEP LIMOILOU
1300 8e Av Bureau 1400, Quebec, QC, G1J
5L5
(418) 647-6600
Emp Here 600 *Sales* 89,634,600
SIC 8221 Colleges and universities
Kevin Therrien
Mivhel Saucier
Francois Godbout
Jean-Pierre Lacasse
Nancy Dumont
Hanh Phan

D-U-N-S 25-195-3642 (HQ)
**SOCIETE EN COMMANDITE STADACONA
WB**
SCIERIE LEDUC
10 Boul Des Capucins, Quebec, QC, G1J 0G9
(418) 842-8405
Sales 69,597,500
SIC 2421 Sawmills and planing mills, general
Peter M. Brant

D-U-N-S 25-503-9695 (SL)
TIRU (CANADA) INC
1210 Boul Montmorency, Quebec, QC, G1J
3V9
(418) 648-8818
Emp Here 50 *Sales* 12,856,550
SIC 4953 Refuse systems
Gilbert Durocher

Pierre Vandekerckhove
Pierre De Montlivault
Fabrice Grasset

Quebec, QC G1K

D-U-N-S 20-721-0923 (HQ)
**(T.P.Q.) TERMINAUX PORTUAIRES DU
QUEBEC INC**
T.P.Q.
(*Suby of* QUEBEC STEVEDORING COM-
PANY LTD)
961 Boul Champlain, Quebec, QC, G1K 4J9
(418) 529-6521
Emp Here 60 *Sales* 52,104,150
SIC 4491 Marine cargo handling
Denis Dupuis
Yvon Dupuis
Jean Gaudreau
Andrew Chodos
Jean-Francois Dupuis
Alphonse Belanger

D-U-N-S 20-182-7305 (SL)
3072930 NOVA SCOTIA COMPANY
HOTEL PUR
395 Rue De La Couronne, Quebec, QC, G1K
7X4
(418) 647-2611
Emp Here 90 *Sales* 8,540,910
SIC 7011 Hotels and motels
John Yoon

D-U-N-S 20-523-8251 (HQ)
3834310 CANADA INC
EDIMEDIA
(*Suby of* GROUPE CAPITALES MEDIAS INC,
LE)
410 Boul Charest E Bureau 300, Quebec, QC,
G1K 8G3
(418) 686-3233
Emp Here 3 *Sales* 88,360,944
SIC 2711 Newspapers
Martin Cauchon

D-U-N-S 20-322-8655 (SL)
4355768 CANADA INC
CRAKMEDIA NETWORK
410 Boul Charest E Bureau 500, Quebec, QC,
G1K 8G3
(418) 977-3169
Emp Here 50 *Sales* 10,941,200
SIC 3993 Signs and advertising specialties
Nicolas Chretien

D-U-N-S 20-566-5289 (SL)
6143580 CANADA INC.
RESTAURANT PANACHE
10 Rue Saint-Antoine, Quebec, QC, G1K 4C9
(418) 692-1022
Emp Here 100 *Sales* 4,287,300
SIC 5812 Eating places
Evan Price
Alexendra Lucy Price

D-U-N-S 25-542-9631 (SL)
9070-5245 QUEBEC INC
INTERMARCHE ST-ROCH
272 Rue Saint-Joseph E, Quebec, QC, G1K
3A9
(418) 648-2805
Emp Here 44 *Sales* 12,062,688
SIC 5411 Grocery stores
Eric Courtemanche Baril
Rejean Perron

D-U-N-S 20-136-0870 (SL)
9277-8091 QUEBEC INC
DESTINATION CANADA 2000
105 Cote De La Montagne Suite 105, Quebec,
QC, G1K 4E4
(418) 692-3621
Emp Here 26 *Sales* 13,519,142
SIC 4724 Travel agencies
Manon Vigneux

John K. Matte
Paul Matte
Richard Kirouac

D-U-N-S 24-805-7031 (BR)
ABB INC
(*Suby of* ABB LTD)
585 Boul Charest E Bureau 300, Quebec, QC,
G1K 9H4
(418) 877-2944
Emp Here 200
SIC 3823 Process control instruments
Marc Corriveau

D-U-N-S 24-354-0056 (SL)
**ABCP ARCHITECTURE ET URBANISME
LTEE**
300 Rue Saint-Paul Bureau 412, Quebec, QC,
G1K 7R1
(418) 649-7369
Emp Here 60 *Sales* 10,724,340
SIC 8712 Architectural services
Francois Moreau
Bernard-Serge Gagne
Vadim Siegel
Dany Blackburn
Pierre Guimont
Cathy Dumas
Michel Veilleux

D-U-N-S 24-568-7322 (HQ)
**ADMINISTRATION PORTUAIRE DU QUE-
BEC**
PORT DE QUEBEC
150 Rue Dalhousie Bureau 2268, Quebec,
QC, G1K 4C4
(418) 648-3640
Sales 23,623,440
SIC 4491 Marine cargo handling
Mario Girard
Marie-France Poulin
Claude Rousseau
Joli-Coeur Jacques
Denis Bernier
Marie-Soleil Tremblay

D-U-N-S 25-782-8202 (SL)
ANGLOCOM INC
ON TRADUIT A QUEBEC
300 Rue Saint-Paul Bureau 210, Quebec, QC,
G1K 7R1
(418) 529-6928
Emp Here 27 *Sales* 11,974,230
SIC 7389 Business services, nec
Grant Hamilton
Gregory Avenet

D-U-N-S 20-298-2120 (SL)
ANIMATION SQUEEZE STUDIO INC
STUDIO SQUEEZE
520 Boul Charest E Bureau 340, Quebec, QC,
G1K 3J3
(418) 476-1786
Emp Here 85 *Sales* 2,367,278
SIC 7336 Commercial art and graphic design
Denis Dore
Patrick Beaulieu
Francois Houde

D-U-N-S 25-247-0737 (SL)
AUBERGE SAINT-ANTOINE INC
10 Rue Saint-Antoine, Quebec, QC, G1K 4C9
(418) 692-2211
Emp Here 100 *Sales* 9,489,900
SIC 7011 Hotels and motels
Evan Price
Eric Llewellyn Price

D-U-N-S 20-699-9000 (SL)
BEENOX INC
305 Boul Charest E Bureau 700, Quebec, QC,
G1K 3H3
(418) 522-2468
Emp Here 260 *Sales* 47,988,980
SIC 7371 Custom computer programming ser-
vices
Eric Hirshberg
Jeffrey A. Brown

▲ Public Company ■ Public Company Family Member **HQ** Headquarters **BR** Branch **SL** Single Location

Denis Durkin
Chris B. Walther
Robert A. Kotick

D-U-N-S 20-512-4188   (HQ)
BENJO INC
BEDONDAINE
(*Suby of* GM DEVELOPPEMENT INC)
520 Boul Charest E Bureau 233, Quebec, QC,
G1K 3J3
(418) 640-0001
Emp Here 30   *Sales* 14,659,680
SIC 5945 Hobby, toy, and game shops
Genevieve Marcon

D-U-N-S 25-732-8120   (HQ)
BGLA INC
BRIERE GILBERT + ASSOCIES ARCHI-TECTES
50 Cote Dinan, Quebec, QC, G1K 8N6
(418) 694-9041
Emp Here 35   *Sales* 12,511,730
SIC 8712 Architectural services
Stephane Gilbert
Martin Briere
Stephane Lefebvre
Yvon Lachance
Pierre-Andre Levesque
Nadine Poitras
Caroline Girard

D-U-N-S 24-080-0743   (SL)
BOULANGERIE ARTISANALE LA BOITE A PAIN INC
BOITE A PAIN CAFE NAPOLI
289 Rue Saint-Joseph E, Quebec, QC, G1K
3B1
(418) 647-3666
Emp Here 49   *Sales* 13,433,448
SIC 5461 Retail bakeries
Patrick Nisot

D-U-N-S 24-381-5487   (SL)
BOULET LEMELIN YACHT INC
1125 Boul Champlain, Quebec, QC, G1K 0A2
(418) 681-5655
Emp Here 30   *Sales* 14,942,340
SIC 5551 Boat dealers
Richard Boulet
Francois Lemelin
Patrice Lemelin

D-U-N-S 20-429-9689   (SL)
BUNGE DU CANADA LTEE
(*Suby of* BUNGE LIMITED)
300 Rue Dalhousie, Quebec, QC, G1K 8M8
(418) 692-3761
Emp Here 50   *Sales* 11,100,050
SIC 3523 Farm machinery and equipment
Todd A. Bastean
Geralyn F. Hayes
David Kabbes
Aaron L. Elliott
Gregory Thebeau
John E. Sabourin
Karl J. Gerrand
Gino Becerra
W.D. Mooney
Georges P. li Allard

D-U-N-S 25-391-4998   (HQ)
CAISSE D'ECONOMIE SOLIDAIRE DES-JARDINS
CENTRE DE SERVICES MONTREAL
155 Boul Charest E Bureau 500, Quebec, QC,
G1K 3G6
(418) 647-1527
Emp Here 53   *Sales* 18,100,592
SIC 6062 State credit unions
Paul Ouellet
Gerald Larose
Leopold Beaulieu
Hubert Fortin
Christiane Fradette
Brigitte Duchesneau
Therese Chaput
Sokchiveneath Taing Chhoan

Louise Pettigrew
Josee Montpetit

D-U-N-S 20-917-9477   (BR)
CAISSE DESJARDINS DE QUEBEC
CAISSE DESJARDINS DU CENTRE-VILLE DE QUEBEC
(*Suby of* CAISSE DESJARDINS DE QUE-BEC)
135 Rue Saint-Vallier O, Quebec, QC, G1K
1J9
(418) 687-2810
Emp Here 150
SIC 6062 State credit unions

D-U-N-S 24-915-6410   (SL)
CANADA ADMINISTRATION
271 Rue De L'Estuaire, Quebec, QC, G1K 8S8
(418) 648-3645
Emp Here 49   *Sales* 25,478,383
SIC 4731 Freight transportation arrangement
Mario Girard

D-U-N-S 24-256-7393   (SL)
CEB CANADA INC
400 Boulevard Jean-Lesage Unite 500, Que-bec, QC, G1K 8W1
(418) 523-6663
Emp Here 50   *Sales* 11,517,000
SIC 5734 Computer and software stores
Warren Thune
Barron Anschutz

D-U-N-S 24-639-2880   (BR)
CENTRALE DES SYNDICATS DU QUEBEC (CSQ), LA
CSQ
(*Suby of* CENTRALE DES SYNDICATS DU QUEBEC (CSQ), LA)
320 Rue Saint-Joseph E Bureau 100, Quebec,
QC, G1K 9E7
(514) 356-8888
Emp Here 90
SIC 8631 Labor organizations

D-U-N-S 25-291-4692   (BR)
CENTRE DE SANTE ET DE SERVICES SO-CIAUX DE LA VIEILLE-CAPITALE
CLSC BASSE-VILLE LIMOILOU VANIER
50 Rue Saint-Joseph E, Quebec, QC, G1K
3A5
(418) 529-2572
Emp Here 1,300
SIC 8322 Individual and family services
Andre Metivier

D-U-N-S 20-288-6107   (SL)
CITOYEN OPTIMUM S.E.C.
CITIZEN RELATIONS
300 Rue Saint-Paul Bureau 300, Quebec, QC,
G1K 7R1
(418) 647-2727
Emp Here 200   *Sales* 45,694,400
SIC 4899 Communication services, nec
Daryl Mccullough

D-U-N-S 20-288-5992   (HQ)
CITOYEN RELATIONS INC
(*Suby of* VISION 7 INTERNATIONAL INC)
300 Rue Saint-Paul Bureau 300, Quebec, QC,
G1K 7R1
(418) 521-3744
Emp Here 5   *Sales* 21,704,840
SIC 4899 Communication services, nec
Daryl Mccullough
Sandra Giguere
Michael Girard

D-U-N-S 20-363-5263   (HQ)
COMMISSION DES NORMES, DE L'EQUITE, DE LA SANTE ET DE LA SECURITE DU TRAVAIL, LA
CNESST
524 Rue Bourdages Bureau 370, Quebec,
QC, G1K 7E2
(877) 639-0744
Emp Here 1,000   *Sales* 6,410,904,000
SIC 6331 Fire, marine, and casualty insurance

Manuelle Oudar
Martine Begin
Michel Beaudoin
Josee Dupont
Claude Sicard
Bruno Labrecque
Carl Gauthier

D-U-N-S 25-240-4686   (BR)
COMMISSION SCOLAIRE DE LA CAPI-TALE, LA
ECOLE SECONDAIRE CARDINAL ROY
50 Rue Du Cardinal-Maurice-Roy, Quebec,
QC, G1K 8S9
(418) 686-4040
Emp Here 80
SIC 8211 Elementary and secondary schools
Elizabeth Fortin

D-U-N-S 20-574-8150   (BR)
COMMISSION SCOLAIRE DE LA CAPI-TALE, LA
COMMISSION SCOLAIRE DE LA CAPITALE, LA
125 Rue Des Commissaires O Bureau 210,
Quebec, QC, G1K 1M7
(418) 686-4040
Emp Here 80
SIC 5049 Professional equipment, nec
Luc Galvani

D-U-N-S 24-758-8866   (SL)
CONFEDERATION DES ASSOCIATIONS D'ETUDIANTS ET D'ETUDIANTES DE L'UNIVERSITE LAVAL (CADEU
CADEUL
Pavillon Maurice-Pollack Bureau 2265, Que-bec, QC, G1K 7P4
(418) 656-7931
Emp Here 100   *Sales* 14,287,900
SIC 8641 Civic and social associations
Cedric Williams
Jasmin Roy

D-U-N-S 24-592-8833   (BR)
CONSEILLERS EN GESTION ET INFORMA-TIQUE CGI INC
CGI
(*Suby of* CGI INC)
410 Boul Charest E Bureau 700, Quebec, QC,
G1K 8G3
(418) 623-0101
Emp Here 1,200
SIC 7379 Computer related services, nec

D-U-N-S 24-610-7494   (HQ)
COPERNIC INC
MOMMA.COM
(*Suby of* CONSTELLATION SOFTWARE INC)
400 Boul Jean-Lesage Bureau 345, Quebec,
QC, G1K 8W1
(418) 524-4661
Sales 20,185,480
SIC 7371 Custom computer programming services
Jeff Bender
Mark H Leonard

D-U-N-S 24-530-8770   (SL)
COPIES DE LA CAPITALE INC, LES
CENTRE NUMERIQUE DE LA CAPITALE
235 Boul Charest E, Quebec, QC, G1K 3G8
(418) 648-1911
Emp Here 100   *Sales* 13,538,600
SIC 2752 Commercial printing, lithographic
Daniel Linteau
Helen Rowan

D-U-N-S 24-863-4891   (SL)
CORPORATION DES PILOTES DU BAS SAINT-LAURENT INC
240 Rue Dalhousie, Quebec, QC, G1K 8M8
(418) 692-0444
Emp Here 85   *Sales* 18,138,320
SIC 4499 Water transportation services,
Carl Robitaille

Robert Pouliot
Jean D'aquila
Simon Mercier
Nicolas Gouin
Andre Boudreault
Nicolas St-Arnaud
Pierre Vezina

D-U-N-S 20-288-5877   (SL)
COSSETTE DIGITAL INC
(*Suby of* COSSETTE COMMUNICATION INC)
300 Rue Saint-Paul Bureau 300, Quebec, QC,
G1K 7R1
(418) 647-2727
Emp Here 200   *Sales* 45,694,400
SIC 4899 Communication services, nec
Brett Marchand

D-U-N-S 20-355-5180   (SL)
CROISIERES AML INC
CROISIERES DU PORT DE MONTREAL
(*Suby of* GROUPE A M L INC)
124 Rue Saint-Pierre, Quebec, QC, G1K 4A7
(866) 856-6668
Emp Here 100   *Sales* 39,372,400
SIC 4424 Deep sea domestic transportation of
freight
Yan Hamel

D-U-N-S 20-363-6212   (SL)
DESGAGNES MARINE CARGO INC
(*Suby of* GROUPE DESGAGNES INC)
21 Rue Du Marche-Champlain Bureau 100,
Quebec, QC, G1K 8Z8
(418) 692-1000
Emp Here 250
SIC 4412 Deep sea foreign transportation of
freight
Louis-Marie Beaulieu
Michel Denis
Francoys Royer

D-U-N-S 20-363-6220   (SL)
DESGAGNES MARINE PETRO INC
(*Suby of* GROUPE DESGAGNES INC)
21 Rue Du Marche-Champlain Bureau 100,
Quebec, QC, G1K 8Z8
(418) 692-1000
Emp Here 250
SIC 4412 Deep sea foreign transportation of
freight
Louis-Marie Beaulieu
Michel Denis
Francoys Royer

D-U-N-S 20-314-2013   (SL)
DRAGAGE OCEAN DM INC
105 Rue Abraham-Martin Unite 500, Quebec.
QC, G1K 8N1
(418) 694-1414
Emp Here 50   *Sales* 12,044,200
SIC 1629 Heavy construction, nec
Jacques Tanguay
Gordon Bain
Jean-Philippe Brunet

D-U-N-S 25-173-1816   (HQ)
ECONOLER INC
CENTRE DE FORMATION ECONOLER
160 Rue Saint-Paul Bureau 200, Quebec, QC,
G1K 3W1
(418) 692-2592
Emp Here 39   *Sales* 10,542,960
SIC 8748 Business consulting, nec
Pierre Langlois
Pierre Baillargeon
Danielle Dorion
Normand Michaud

D-U-N-S 24-818-9016   (SL)
EVOLUTION MOBILE
305 Boul Charest E, Quebec, QC, G1K 3H3
(418) 524-3436
Emp Here 49   *Sales* 21,911,526
SIC 5065 Electronic parts and equipment, nec
Claude Hamel

D-U-N-S 25-893-6350   (BR)
FONDATION DU CENTRE JEUNESSE DE QUEBEC
SOUS-REGION QUEBEC-SUD
540 Boul Charest E, Quebec, QC, G1K 8L1
(418) 529-7351
Emp Here 140
SIC 8322 Individual and family services

D-U-N-S 24-164-4991   (SL)
FRIMA STUDIO INC
HUMAGADE
395 Rue Victor-Revillon, Quebec, QC, G1K 3M8
(418) 529-9697
Emp Here 100   *Sales* 21,172,400
SIC 7336 Commercial art and graphic design
Christian Diagle
Begin Phillipe
Francois Macerola

D-U-N-S 20-174-8659   (SL)
G.D.G. INFORMATIQUE ET GESTION INC
330 Rue De Saint-Vallier E Bureau 23, Quebec, QC, G1K 9C5
(418) 647-0006
Emp Here 200   *Sales* 28,836,400
SIC 7371 Custom computer programming services
Gaetan Duchesne

D-U-N-S 24-498-2138   (HQ)
GENEX COMMUNICATIONS INC
AGENCE NEWS
410 Boul Charest E, Quebec, QC, G1K 8G3
(418) 266-6166
Emp Here 26   *Sales* 17,135,400
SIC 4832 Radio broadcasting stations
Patrice Demers

D-U-N-S 20-319-8747   (HQ)
GM DEVELOPPEMENT INC
520 Boul Charest E Bureau 233, Quebec, QC, G1K 3J3
(418) 692-7470
Sales 11,449,445
SIC 6531 Real estate agents and managers
Genevieve Marcon
Jean Campeau

D-U-N-S 24-345-8630   (BR)
GOUVERNEMENT DE LA PROVINCE DE QUEBEC
CENTRE D'HEBERGEMENT NOTRE DAME DE LOURDES & SAINT CHARLES
(*Suby of* GOUVERNEMENT DE LA PROVINCE DE QUEBEC)
105 Rue Hermine, Quebec, QC, G1K 1Y5
(418) 529-2501
Emp Here 350
SIC 8051 Skilled nursing care facilities

D-U-N-S 24-203-5772   (HQ)
GROUPE DESGAGNES INC
21 Rue Du Marche-Champlain Bureau 100, Quebec, QC, G1K 8Z8
(418) 692-1000
Emp Here 65   *Sales* 219,305,400
SIC 6719 Holding companies, nec
Louis-Marie Beaulieu
Francoys Royer

D-U-N-S 25-072-1008   (HQ)
GROUPE OCEAN INC, LE
(*Suby of* 9215-7064 QUEBEC INC)
105 Rue Abraham-Martin Bureau 500, Quebec, QC, G1K 8N1
(418) 694-1414
Emp Here 50   *Sales* 261,765,000
SIC 3731 Shipbuilding and repairing
Jacques Tanguay
Jean-Philipp Brunet

D-U-N-S 20-194-2872   (BR)
GROUPE RESTOS PLAISIRS INC, LE
CAFE DU MONDE
(*Suby of* GROUPE RESTOS PLAISIRS INC, LE)

84 Rue Dalhousie Bureau 140, Quebec, QC, G1K 8M5
(418) 692-4455
Emp Here 80
SIC 5812 Eating places
Marie Simard

D-U-N-S 25-762-8594   (BR)
GROUPE RESTOS PLAISIRS INC, LE
COCHON DINGUE, LE
(*Suby of* GROUPE RESTOS PLAISIRS INC, LE)
46 Boul Champlain, Quebec, QC, G1K 4H7
(418) 694-0303
Emp Here 100
SIC 5812 Eating places
Alexandre Paradis

D-U-N-S 25-674-0531   (HQ)
H2O INNOVATION INC
H2O INNOVATION USA
(*Suby of* CANADIAN DEPOSITORY FOR SECURITIES LIMITED, THE)
330 Rue De Saint-Vallier E Bureau 340, Quebec, QC, G1K 9C5
(418) 688-0170
Emp Here 25   *Sales* 61,571,580
SIC 3589 Service industry machinery, nec
Frederic Dugre
William Douglass,
Rock Gaulin,
Denis Guibert,
Gregory Madden,
Marc Blanchet
Guillaume Clairet,
Philippe Gervais
Stephen A Davis
Elaine C. Phenix

D-U-N-S 24-204-5474   (SL)
IDEE PRO INC
54 Rue De La Pointe-Aux-Lievres, Quebec, QC, G1K 5Y3
(418) 522-4455
Emp Here 85   *Sales* 13,942,295
SIC 2759 Commercial printing, nec
Benoit Robichaud

D-U-N-S 24-821-2144   (HQ)
IMPACT RESEARCH INC
(*Suby of* VISION 7 INTERNATIONAL INC)
300 Rue Saint-Paul Bureau 300, Quebec, QC, G1K 7R1
(418) 647-2727
Emp Here 45   *Sales* 39,589,740
SIC 8732 Commercial nonphysical research
Joseph Leon
Sandra Giguere
Michael Girard

D-U-N-S 24-051-6943   (BR)
INDUSTRIES GRC INC, LES
(*Suby of* INDUSTRIES GRC INC, LES)
10c Cote De La Canoterie Bureau 7, Quebec, QC, G1K 3X4
(418) 692-1112
Emp Here 125
SIC 3444 Sheet Metalwork
Andre Fournier

D-U-N-S 24-203-5673   (SL)
INDUSTRIES OCEAN INC
(*Suby of* 9215-7064 QUEBEC INC)
105 Rue Abraham-Martin Bureau 500, Quebec, QC, G1K 8N1
(418) 438-2745
Emp Here 100   *Sales* 22,384,300
SIC 3731 Shipbuilding and repairing
Jacques Tanguay
Jean-Philippe Brunet

D-U-N-S 24-531-6146   (HQ)
INSTITUT CANADIEN DE QUEBEC, L'
BIBLIOTHEQUE GABRIELLE ROY
350 Rue Saint-Joseph E 4e Etage, Quebec, QC, G1K 3B2
(418) 529-0924
Sales 11,096,820

SIC 8231 Libraries
Roland Villeneuve

D-U-N-S 20-253-3667   (HQ)
INSTITUT NATIONAL DE LA RECHERCHE SCIENTIFIQUE
INRS
490 Rue De La Couronne, Quebec, QC, G1K 9A9
(418) 654-4677
Sales 124,081,856
SIC 8733 Noncommercial research organizations
Daniel Coderre
Yves Begin
Claude Arbour
Lana Fiset
Jean-Francois Blais
Frederico Rosei
Charles Dozois
Claire Poitras
Nadine Blackburn
Jean Morin

D-U-N-S 24-820-4588   (SL)
L'AVIATIC CLUB INC
LE CHARBON
450 Rue De La Gare-Du-Palais Bureau 104, Quebec, QC, G1K 3X2
(418) 522-3555
Emp Here 85   *Sales* 3,869,115
SIC 5812 Eating places
Richard Demers
Martin Girard
Jean-Francois Houde

D-U-N-S 25-480-1111   (HQ)
LEPINE-CLOUTIER LTEE
ATHOS
(*Suby of* SERVICE CORPORATION INTERNATIONAL)
715 Rue De Saint-Vallier E, Quebec, QC, G1K 3P9
(418) 529-3371
Sales 18,152,940
SIC 7261 Funeral service and crematories
Michel Boutin
Sylvain Trottier

D-U-N-S 24-706-2870   (HQ)
LOCATION OCEAN INC
(*Suby of* 9215-7064 QUEBEC INC)
105 Rue Abraham-Martin Bureau 500, Quebec, QC, G1K 8N1
(418) 694-1414
Sales 208,416,600
SIC 4492 Towing and tugboat service
Gordon Bain
Jacques Tangauy

D-U-N-S 24-864-1052   (SL)
MOBILIER DE BUREAU MBH INC
MBH AMENAGEMENT + MOBILIER DE BUREAU
25 Rue Saint-Joseph E, Quebec, QC, G1K 3A6
(418) 647-1332
Emp Here 36   *Sales* 18,318,816
SIC 5021 Furniture
Gilles Tanguay
Francois Tanguay

D-U-N-S 25-824-0928   (HQ)
MUSEE DE LA CIVILISATION
85 Rue Dalhousie, Quebec, QC, G1K 8R2
(418) 643-2158
Sales 20,972,000
SIC 8412 Museums and art galleries
Margaret Delisle
Michel Cote

D-U-N-S 24-391-1356   (HQ)
NEMASKA LITHIUM INC
NEMASKA LITHIUM SHAWINIGAN TRANSFORMATION
450 Rue De La Gare-Du-Palais, Quebec, QC, G1K 3X2

(418) 704-6038
Sales 30,983,175
SIC 1479 Chemical and fertilizer mining
Guy Bourassa
Marc Dagenais
Steve Nadeau
Rene Lessard
Michel Baril
Paul-Henri Couture
Francois Biron
Patrick Godin
Shigeki Miwa

D-U-N-S 20-281-4500   (BR)
NURUN INC
(*Suby of* PUBLICIS GROUPE HOLDINGS B.V.)
330 Rue De Saint-Vallier E Bureau 120, Quebec, QC, G1K 9C5
(418) 627-2001
Emp Here 250
SIC 7371 Custom computer programming services
Jacques Malo

D-U-N-S 24-638-3335   (SL)
ORBITOUR LTEE
OMNITOUR
105 Cote De La Montagne Bureau 601, Quebec, QC, G1K 4E4
(418) 692-1223
Emp Here 26   *Sales* 10,019,360
SIC 4724 Travel agencies
Jacques Morissette

D-U-N-S 25-765-3840   (SL)
PAQUET, CHRISTINE ET CHARLES BOISVERT, PHARMACIENS S.E.N.C.
JEAN COUTU
138 Rue Saint-Vallier O Bureau 175, Quebec, QC, G1K 1K1
(418) 525-4981
Emp Here 44   *Sales* 11,129,976
SIC 5912 Drug stores and proprietary stores
Christine Paquet
Charles Boisvert

D-U-N-S 25-413-4059   (HQ)
POLYCOR INC
TUILES POLYCOR
76 Rue Saint-Paul Bureau 100, Quebec, QC, G1K 3V9
(418) 692-4695
Emp Here 20   *Sales* 206,554,500
SIC 1423 Crushed and broken granite
Patrick Perus
Terence Mathieu
Francois Darmayan
Hugues Jacquin

D-U-N-S 20-387-4958   (SL)
QSL CANADA INC
(T.P.Q.) TERMINAUX PORTUAIRES DU QUEBEC
(*Suby of* QUEBEC STEVEDORING COMPANY LTD)
961 Boul Champlain, Quebec, QC, G1K 4J9
(418) 522-4701
Emp Here 100   *Sales* 39,372,400
SIC 4491 Marine cargo handling
Denis Dupuis

D-U-N-S 24-199-9127   (HQ)
QUEBEC STEVEDORING COMPANY LTD
ARRIMAGE DU SAINT-LAURENT, DIV DE
961 Boul Champlain, Quebec, QC, G1K 4J9
(418) 522-4701
Sales 33,466,540
SIC 4491 Marine cargo handling
Robert Bellisle
Jean-Francois Dupuis
Andrew Chodos
Bonnie Chodos
Denis Dupuis

D-U-N-S 24-638-0109   (HQ)
RELAIS NORDIK INC
(*Suby of* GROUPE DESGAGNES INC)

21 Rue Du Marche-Champlain Bureau 100, Quebec, QC, G1K 8Z8
(418) 692-1000
Sales 39,372,400
SIC 4424 Deep sea domestic transportation of freight
  Louis-Marie Beaulieu
  Michel Denis
  Francois Royar

D-U-N-S 25-266-5034   (SL)
SERVICE DU DEVELOPPEMENT ECONOMIQUE
295 Boul Charest E, Quebec, QC, G1K 3G8
(418) 641-6186
Emp Here 49   Sales 22,011,731
SIC 7389 Business services, nec
  Sonia Rate

D-U-N-S 24-781-9972   (SL)
SKIRON INC
ENTREPRISE SKIRON
56 Rue Saint-Pierre Bureau 101, Quebec, QC, G1K 4A1
(418) 694-0114
Emp Here 152   Sales 30,456,392
SIC 7311 Advertising agencies
  Andreas Rauch
  Sophie Tremblay

D-U-N-S 20-073-8552   (SL)
SOCIETE D'EXPLORATION MINIERE VIO
116 Rue Saint-Pierre Bureau 200, Quebec, QC, G1K 4A7
(418) 692-2678
Emp Here 180   Sales 429,758,820
SIC 1081 Metal mining services
  Hugues Belzile

D-U-N-S 20-873-6900   (HQ)
SOCIETE DES TRAVERSIERS DU QUEBEC
STQ
(Suby of GOUVERNEMENT DE LA PROVINCE DE QUEBEC)
250 Rue Saint-Paul, Quebec, QC, G1K 9K9
(418) 643-2019
Emp Here 320   Sales 225,784,650
SIC 4482 Ferries
  Jocelyn Fortier
  Lise Breton
  Danielle Amyot
  Julie Coulombe-Godbout
  Fabienne Desrochers
  Annie Fournier
  Richard Michaud

D-U-N-S 20-297-6804   (SL)
SOCIETE GESTION LIBRAIRIE INC
LIBRAIRIE PANPOUPE
286 Rue Saint-Joseph E, Quebec, QC, G1K 3A9
(418) 692-1175
Emp Here 25   Sales 10,483,875
SIC 6712 Bank holding companies
  Denis Lebrun

D-U-N-S 24-346-4182   (SL)
STEIN MONAST S.E.N.C.R.L.
70 Rue Dalhousie Bureau 300, Quebec, QC, G1K 4B2
(418) 529-6531
Emp Here 100   Sales 15,401,100
SIC 8111 Legal services
  Catherine Cloutier
  Jean Brunet
  Marie-Helene Betournay

D-U-N-S 20-363-6246   (BR)
TESSIER LTEE
MTTL COENTREPRISE
(Suby of GROUPE DESGAGNES INC)
21 Rue Du Marche-Champlain, Quebec, QC, G1K 8Z8
(418) 569-3739
Emp Here 100
SIC 7353 Heavy construction equipment rental

D-U-N-S 24-843-5281   (SL)
TRAVAUX MARITIMES OCEAN INC
105 Rue Abraham-Martin Bureau 500, Quebec, QC, G1K 8N1
(418) 694-1414
Emp Here 50   Sales 12,044,200
SIC 1629 Heavy construction, nec
  Jacques Tanguay
  Jean-Philippe Brunet

D-U-N-S 24-056-4828   (BR)
UBISOFT DIVERTISSEMENTS INC
UBISOFT DIVERTISSEMENTS
(Suby of UBISOFT ENTERTAINMENT)
390 Boul Charest E Bureau 600, Quebec, QC, G1K 3H4
(418) 524-1222
Emp Here 300
SIC 3944 Games, toys, and children's vehicles
  Nicolas Rioux

D-U-N-S 24-500-0468   (HQ)
UNIQUE ASSURANCES GENERALES INC, L'
MULTI-CHOIX
(Suby of LA CAPITALE PARTICIPATIONS INC)
625 Rue Saint Amable, Quebec, QC, G1K 0E1
(418) 683-2711
Emp Here 105   Sales 532,105,032
SIC 6331 Fire, marine, and casualty insurance
  Jean St-Gelais
  Yves Gagnon
  Jacques Cotton
  Pierre Marc Bellavance
  Dominique Dubuc
  Richard Fiset
  Marie-Josee Linteau
  Carl Gauthier
  Dominique Salvy

D-U-N-S 20-293-6519   (BR)
UNIVERSITE DU QUEBEC
INRS ETE INSTITUT NATIONALE DE LA RECHECHE SCIENTIFIQUE
(Suby of UNIVERSITE DU QUEBEC)
490 Rue De La Couronne, Quebec, QC, G1K 9A9
(418) 654-2665
Emp Here 350
SIC 8732 Commercial nonphysical research
  Yves Begin

D-U-N-S 24-853-4799   (BR)
UNIVERSITE DU QUEBEC
TELUQ
(Suby of UNIVERSITE DU QUEBEC)
455 Rue Du Parvis Bureau 2140, Quebec, QC, G1K 9H6
(418) 657-2262
Emp Here 200
SIC 8221 Colleges and universities
  Pierre Le Gallais

D-U-N-S 20-873-2354   (HQ)
UNIVERSITE DU QUEBEC
UNIVERSITE DU QUEBEC A MONTREAL (UQAM)
475 Rue Du Parvis, Quebec, QC, G1K 9H7
(418) 657-3551
Emp Here 135   Sales 2,790,325,098
SIC 8221 Colleges and universities
  Jean Johanne
  Annie Bergeron
  Marie-Jose Fortin

D-U-N-S 24-888-3840   (BR)
UNIVERSITE DU QUEBEC
CENTRE UBANISATION CULTURE ET SOCIETE
(Suby of UNIVERSITE DU QUEBEC)
490 Rue De La Couronne, Quebec, QC, G1K 9A9
(418) 687-6400
Emp Here 175
SIC 8221 Colleges and universities
  Daniel Coderre

D-U-N-S 24-522-6407   (HQ)
VISION 7 COMMUNICATIONS INC
SIMPLESTRATUS
(Suby of VISION 7 INTERNATIONAL INC)
300 Rue Saint-Paul Bureau 300, Quebec, QC, G1K 7R1
(418) 647-2727
Emp Here 27   Sales 794,251,057
SIC 6712 Bank holding companies
  Brett Marchand
  Sandra Giguere
  Michael Girard

D-U-N-S 20-252-6570   (HQ)
VISION 7 INTERNATIONAL INC
300 Rue Saint-Paul Bureau 300, Quebec, QC, G1K 7R1
(418) 647-2727
Sales 794,616,566
SIC 6712 Bank holding companies
  Brett Marchand
  Sandra Giguere
  He Shen
  Mimi Wuensch
  Hong Zheng

Quebec, QC G1L

D-U-N-S 24-841-9574   (SL)
2737-1822 QUEBEC INC
JEAN COUTU
3417 1re Av, Quebec, QC, G1L 3R4
(418) 622-1237
Emp Here 50   Sales 12,647,700
SIC 5912 Drug stores and proprietary stores
  Claude Lachance

D-U-N-S 24-146-2795   (HQ)
9022-9097 QUEBEC INC
PNEUS RATTE
103 3e Av, Quebec, QC, G1L 2V3
(418) 529-5378
Emp Here 30   Sales 59,950,020
SIC 5014 Tires and tubes
  Stephane Ratte
  Charlyne Ratte

D-U-N-S 24-863-0493   (BR)
AGROPUR COOPERATIVE
AGROPUR DIVISION NATREL
(Suby of AGROPUR COOPERATIVE)
2465 1re Av, Quebec, QC, G1L 3M9
(418) 641-0857
Emp Here 215
SIC 2026 Fluid milk
  Jerry Verhoef

D-U-N-S 20-277-2968   (SL)
CARNAVAL DE QUEBEC INC
FABRIQUE DU CARNAVAL, LA
205 Boul Des Cedres, Quebec, QC, G1L 1N8
(418) 626-7173
Emp Here 100   Sales 14,002,900
SIC 7999 Amusement and recreation, nec
  Alain April
  William C.Gobeil

D-U-N-S 25-042-7663   (BR)
CENTRE HOSPITALIER UNIVERSITAIRE DE QUEBEC
HOPITAL SAINT FRANCOIS D'ASSISE
(Suby of CENTRE HOSPITALIER UNIVERSITAIRE DE QUEBEC)
10 Rue De L'Espinay Bureau 520, Quebec, QC, G1L 3L5
(418) 525-4444
Emp Here 8,964
SIC 8062 General medical and surgical hospitals
  Gertrude Bourdon

D-U-N-S 20-914-4851   (BR)
COMMISSION SCOLAIRE DE LA CAPI-TALE, LA

CENTRE LOUIS-JOLLIET
1201 Rue De La Pointe-Aux-Lievres, Quebec, QC, G1L 4M1
(418) 686-4040
Emp Here 100
SIC 8211 Elementary and secondary schools
  Alain Blais

D-U-N-S 20-712-0515   (BR)
COMMISSION SCOLAIRE DE LA CAPI-TALE, LA
ECOLE SECONDAIRE NOTRE DAME DE ROC AMADOUR
1625 Boul Benoit-Xv, Quebec, QC, G1L 2Z3
(418) 686-4040
Emp Here 80
SIC 8211 Elementary and secondary schools
  Danielle Boucher

D-U-N-S 20-560-5657   (SL)
DSL LOGIC
75 Rue Des Epinettes, Quebec, QC, G1L 1N6

Emp Here 40   Sales 17,028,000
SIC 5065 Electronic parts and equipment, nec

D-U-N-S 20-240-8654   (HQ)
DU-SO / JAC-SIL INC
DU-SO PIECES D'AUTO
377 Rue Dupuy, Quebec, QC, G1L 1P2
(418) 626-5276
Emp Here 40   Sales 30,229,845
SIC 5013 Motor vehicle supplies and new parts
  Gaetan Dussault
  Claude Dussault
  Jacques Dussault

D-U-N-S 20-581-4593   (HQ)
ENGRENAGE PROVINCIAL INC
HYDRAULIQUE EP
165 Boul Des Cedres, Quebec, QC, G1L 1M8
(418) 683-2745
Emp Here 12   Sales 47,502,600
SIC 5085 Industrial supplies
  Dominique Huot
  Martin Grenier
  Jean-Francois Carrier
  Jean-Marc Huot

D-U-N-S 24-736-6300   (HQ)
ENTREPRISES ELAINE ROY INC, LES
PETRO CANADA
2600 Rue De La Concorde, Quebec, QC, G1L 6A5
(418) 621-9802
Emp Here 26   Sales 62,928,000
SIC 5541 Gasoline service stations
  Elaine Roy

D-U-N-S 20-515-1350   (BR)
FOR-NET INC
GROUPE FORTIN, LE
1875 Av De La Normandie, Quebec, QC, G1L 3Y8
(418) 529-6103
Emp Here 100
SIC 7349 Building maintenance services, nec
  Claude Bore

D-U-N-S 24-335-7766   (SL)
GROUPE COTE-HUOT INC
LES ENTREPRISES ROBERT COTE
165 Boul Des Cedres, Quebec, QC, G1L 1M8
(418) 626-1142
Emp Here 42   Sales 18,781,308
SIC 5063 Electrical apparatus and equipment
  Jean-Robert Cote

D-U-N-S 20-381-4603   (HQ)
GROUPE RATTE INC
103 3e Av, Quebec, QC, G1L 2V3
(418) 683-1518
Sales 91,377,250
SIC 6712 Bank holding companies
  Stephane Ratte
  Charlyne Ratte

D-U-N-S 25-989-1869   (SL)
MAISON BERGEVIN INC, LA
199 Rue Joly, Quebec, QC, G1L 1N7

Emp Here 35   Sales 29,245,195
SIC 5149 Groceries and related products, nec
Marie-Claude Bergevin

D-U-N-S 20-270-8749   (HQ)
PNEUS RATTE INC
AUTOPNEU
(Suby of GROUPE RATTE INC)
103 3e Av, Quebec, QC, G1L 2V3
(418) 529-5378
Emp Here 45   Sales 144,313,000
SIC 5531 Auto and home supply stores
Stephane Ratte
Charlyne Ratte

D-U-N-S 20-243-3710   (SL)
TAXI COOP QUEBEC 525-5191
MESSAGERIE PAR TAXI
496 2e Av, Quebec, QC, G1L 3B1
(418) 525-4953
Emp Here 50   Sales 24,903,900
SIC 5541 Gasoline service stations
Abdallah Homsy
Kamal Chergui
Nancy Drolet
Yahya Adda
Sadi Fateh
Mohamed Dardari
Alain Beaulieu

D-U-N-S 24-308-3644   (HQ)
VIANDEX INC
GROSSISTE LE FRIGO
199 Rue Joly, Quebec, QC, G1L 1N7
(418) 780-3211
Sales 107,507,400
SIC 5143 Dairy products, except dried or canned
Pierre Gagne
Christian Vignola
Pierre-Benoit Lessard

Quebec, QC G1M

D-U-N-S 25-401-0150   (SL)
2961-4765 QUEBEC INC
SCOLART
595 Boul Pierre-Bertrand Bureau 125, Quebec, QC, G1M 3T8
(418) 622-5126
Emp Here 26   Sales 13,534,092
SIC 5092 Toys and hobby goods and supplies
Marcel Gagne

D-U-N-S 20-439-2759   (SL)
4488601 CANADA INC
BOULEVARD TOYOTA
120 Rue Du Marais, Quebec, QC, G1M 3G2
(418) 683-6565
Emp Here 50   Sales 18,210,750
SIC 5012 Automobiles and other motor vehicles
Mario Masayuki Toyotoshi
Naoyuki Toyotoshi
Marcelo Hiroyuki Toyotoshi
Emilie Brassard

D-U-N-S 25-359-4493   (HQ)
4542410 CANADA INC
LAURA SECORD
550 Av Godin, Quebec, QC, G1M 2K2
(418) 687-5320
Emp Here 10   Sales 96,809,392
SIC 5441 Candy, nut, and confectionery stores
Jean Leclerc
Nicolas Leclerc

D-U-N-S 20-707-5552   (SL)
9049-8049 QUEBEC INC

CAPITALE QUEBEC CHAMPLAIN, LA
850 Boul Pierre-Bertrand Bureau 230, Quebec, QC, G1M 3K8
(418) 628-2223
Emp Here 40   Sales 13,085,080
SIC 6531 Real estate agents and managers
Jean-Denis Morin
Richard Paradis

D-U-N-S 20-872-6018   (SL)
9085-1379 QUEBEC INC
IGA
1035 Boul Wilfrid-Hamel, Quebec, QC, G1M 2R7
(418) 683-4775
Emp Here 85   Sales 24,945,545
SIC 5411 Grocery stores
Patrick Poulin

D-U-N-S 24-343-7832   (SL)
9182-2452 QUEBEC INC
BMW VILLE DE QUEBEC
215 Rue Etienne-Dubreuil, Quebec, QC, G1M 4A6
(418) 681-5000
Emp Here 40   Sales 19,923,120
SIC 5511 New and used car dealers
Bertrand Roberge

D-U-N-S 20-266-2904   (SL)
9258-0547 QUEBEC INC
BMW VILLE DE QUEBEC
215 Rue Etienne-Dubreuil, Quebec, QC, G1M 4A6
(418) 681-5000
Emp Here 90   Sales 56,635,200
SIC 5599 Automotive dealers, nec
Bertrand Roberge

D-U-N-S 24-337-7665   (HQ)
9378-7471 QUEBEC INC
AQUA PLEASURE
(Suby of INVESTISSEMENTS TREVI INC)
909 Boul Pierre-Bertrand Bureau 150, Quebec, QC, G1M 3R8
(418) 687-1988
Sales 24,432,800
SIC 5999 Miscellaneous retail stores, nec
Benoit Hudon

D-U-N-S 20-984-4294   (BR)
9378-7471 QUEBEC INC
PISCINES PRO ET PATIOS N.V. INC
(Suby of INVESTISSEMENTS TREVI INC)
945 Av Godin, Quebec, QC, G1M 2X5
(418) 687-1988
Emp Here 125
SIC 7999 Amusement and recreation, nec

D-U-N-S 24-807-6767   (SL)
ALIMENTS PROLIMER INC
650 Boul Pere-Lelievre Bureau 200, Quebec, QC, G1M 3T2

Emp Here 50   Sales 41,778,850
SIC 5141 Groceries, general line
Michel St-Supery

D-U-N-S 20-952-3893   (HQ)
ASHTON CASSE-CROUTE INC
CHEZ ASHTON
(Suby of PLACEMENTS ASHTON LEBLOND INC, LES)
1100 Av Galibois Bureau 250, Quebec, QC, G1M 3M7
(418) 682-2288
Emp Here 10   Sales 11,659,750
SIC 5812 Eating places
Ashton Leblond

D-U-N-S 20-241-2789   (SL)
AUTOMOBILES MAURICE PARENT INC
MAZDA CHATEL
205 Rue Etienne-Dubreuil, Quebec, QC, G1M 4A6
(418) 627-4601
Emp Here 43   Sales 21,417,354
SIC 5511 New and used car dealers

Jean-Maurice Blais
Pierre Rheaume

D-U-N-S 24-363-7324   (SL)
AVENTECH INTERNATIONAL INC
850 Boul Pierre-Bertrand Bureau 185, Quebec, QC, G1M 3K8
(418) 843-8966
Emp Here 10   Sales 10,003,390
SIC 5051 Metals service centers and offices
Pierre Rancourt
Marc Leblanc

D-U-N-S 20-051-1108   (SL)
BEAUPRE CAPITALE CHRYSLER INC
225 Rue Du Marais, Quebec, QC, G1M 3C8
(418) 687-2604
Emp Here 70   Sales 44,049,600
SIC 5511 New and used car dealers
Andre Voyer
Jean-Pierre Voyer
Matthieu Laplante
Raynald Tremblay

D-U-N-S 25-247-2337   (SL)
BOUCHER, MARC PHARMACIEN
PHARMACIE JEAN COUTU
5 Rue Marie-De-L'Incarnation, Quebec, QC, G1M 3J4

Emp Here 40   Sales 10,118,160
SIC 5912 Drug stores and proprietary stores
Marc Boucher

D-U-N-S 20-869-7698   (HQ)
BUREAU D'EVALUATION DE QUEBEC INC
CENTRE D'ESTIMATION LA CAPITALE QUEBEC
275 Rue Metivier Bureau 170, Quebec, QC, G1M 3X8
(418) 871-6777
Emp Here 20   Sales 11,087,250
SIC 7389 Business services, nec
Jean-Pierre Turcotte
Emile Cote

D-U-N-S 24-378-0624   (SL)
CAMIONS INTERNATIONAL ELITE LTEE
265 Rue Etienne-Dubreuil, Quebec, QC, G1M 4A6
(418) 687-9510
Emp Here 80   Sales 50,342,400
SIC 5511 New and used car dealers
Steve Halle
Claude Brousseau

D-U-N-S 25-883-2914   (BR)
CARON & GUAY INC
(Suby of CARON & GUAY INC)
615 Boul Pierre-Bertrand, Quebec, QC, G1M 3J3
(418) 683-7534
Emp Here 200
SIC 5211 Lumber and other building materials
Alain Guay

D-U-N-S 20-912-1925   (BR)
CENTRE DE SANTE ET DE SERVICES SO-CIAUX DE LA VIEILLE-CAPITALE
RESIDENCE ST ANTOINE
1451 Boul Pere-Lelievre Bureau 363, Quebec, QC, G1M 1N8
(418) 683-2516
Emp Here 200
SIC 8361 Residential care
Claude Gagne

D-U-N-S 24-464-8713   (HQ)
CENTRE MASSICOTTE INC
CLUB PISCINE
687 Boul Pierre-Bertrand, Quebec, QC, G1M 2E4
(418) 687-4340
Emp Here 50   Sales 16,268,210
SIC 5712 Furniture stores
Richard Massicotte
Martin Perreault

D-U-N-S 24-192-1787   (BR)
CHARCUTERIE LA TOUR EIFFEL INC
(Suby of MCCAIN FOODS GROUP INC)
485 Rue Des Entrepreneurs, Quebec, QC, G1M 2V2
(418) 687-2840
Emp Here 100
SIC 5147 Meats and meat products
Melissa Latifi

D-U-N-S 24-498-3680   (BR)
COCA-COLA REFRESHMENTS CANADA COMPANY
EMBOUTEILLAGE COCA COLA
(Suby of THE COCA-COLA COMPANY)
990 Av Godin, Quebec, QC, G1M 2X9
(418) 686-4884
Emp Here 80
SIC 5149 Groceries and related products, nec
Stephane Goudreau

D-U-N-S 25-411-3574   (HQ)
CONGEBEC INC
(Suby of CONGEBEC LOGISTIQUE INC)
810 Av Godin, Quebec, QC, G1M 2X9
(418) 683-3491
Emp Here 15   Sales 25,713,250
SIC 4222 Refrigerated warehousing and storage
Nicholas-Paul Pedneault
Vicky Trepanier

D-U-N-S 24-334-0689   (HQ)
CONGEBEC LOGISTIQUE INC
810 Av Godin, Quebec, QC, G1M 2X9
(418) 683-3491
Emp Here 1   Sales 34,168,750
SIC 6712 Bank holding companies
Christian Roy

D-U-N-S 24-869-5346   (SL)
DOLBEC Y. LOGISTIQUE/LOGISTICS IN-TERNATIONAL INC.
361 Rue Des Entrepreneurs, Quebec, QC, G1M 1B4
(418) 688-9115
Emp Here 21   Sales 10,919,307
SIC 4731 Freight transportation arrangement
Pierre Dolbec
Raymonde Begin
Ginette Blouin
Denis Gendron

D-U-N-S 20-241-5626   (HQ)
DUFRESNE, FERNAND INC
EKO
455 Rue Des Entrepreneurs Bureau 513, Quebec, QC, G1M 2V2
(418) 688-1820
Emp Here 35   Sales 45,884,250
SIC 5983 Fuel oil dealers
Pierre Dufresne
Jacques Dufresne
Francis Dufresne
Jean-Claude Gadras
Ross Bayus
Gilles Cossette
Jerome Dufresne
Pierre-Olivier Dufresne
Richard Labadie

D-U-N-S 24-208-4796   (SL)
ENTREPRISES LITEL INC, LES
(Suby of BOUYGUES)
465 Rue Metivier, Quebec, QC, G1M 2X2
(418) 527-5643
Emp Here 250   Sales 82,028,750
SIC 1623 Water, sewer, and utility lines
Francois Vachon
Germain Perron

D-U-N-S 25-875-4514   (HQ)
EXCELLENTE GESTION INC
ECOLE DE CONDUITE TECNIC
550 Boul Pere-Lelievre Bureau 100, Quebec, QC, G1M 3R2
(418) 529-3868
Sales 12,012,900

SIC 8299 Schools and educational services, nec
Stephane Santerre
Sebastien Riou Ouellet

D-U-N-S 24-226-5614　　(BR)
EXFO INC
EXFO 2 PRODUCTION
(*Suby of* EXFO INC)
436 Rue Nolin, Quebec, QC, G1M 1E7
(418) 683-0211
Emp Here 200
SIC 3827 Optical instruments and lenses
Germain Lamonde

D-U-N-S 24-591-8966　　(HQ)
EXFO INC
400 Av Godin, Quebec, QC, G1M 2K2
(418) 683-0211
Emp Here 640　　*Sales* 269,546,000
SIC 3827 Optical instruments and lenses
Philippe Morin
Germain Lamonde
Stephen Bull
Luc Gagnon
Claudio Mazzuca
Abdelkrim Benamar
Julie Lamontagne
Pierre Plamondon
Michael Scheppke
Wim Te Niet

D-U-N-S 24-581-2230　　(SL)
F. DUFRESNE INC
455 Rue Des Entrepreneurs, Quebec, QC, G1M 2V2
(418) 688-1820
Emp Here 49　　*Sales* 10,296,419
SIC 1311 Crude petroleum and natural gas
Pierre Dufresne

D-U-N-S 24-208-4382　　(HQ)
FILTRUM INC
FILTRUM CONSTRUCTION
430 Rue Des Entrepreneurs, Quebec, QC, G1M 1B3
(418) 687-0628
Sales 12,622,100
SIC 1629 Heavy construction, nec
Francois Noel
Serge Poirier
Yves Langevin
Simon Lejeune
Louis Boulanger

D-U-N-S 24-498-7616　　(SL)
FOURNIER CHEVROLET OLDSMOBILE INC
305 Rue Du Marais, Quebec, QC, G1M 3C8
(418) 687-5200
Emp Here 60　　*Sales* 37,756,800
SIC 5511 New and used car dealers
Gaston Fournier
Yvon Fournier
Pascal Fournier

D-U-N-S 25-155-7062　　(BR)
FRANKLIN EMPIRE INC
ELECTRO MECANIK PLAYFORD
(*Suby of* FRANKLIN EMPIRE INC)
215 Rue Fortin, Quebec, QC, G1M 3M2
(418) 683-1724
Emp Here 98
SIC 1531 Operative builders
Guillaume Begin

D-U-N-S 20-387-0159　　(HQ)
FYI SERVICES ET PRODUITS QUEBEC INC
GROUPE MARCHAND GIGUERE
(*Suby of* FYI EYE CARE SERVICES AND PRODUCTS INC)
1100 Av Galibois Bureau A200, Quebec, QC, G1M 3M7
(418) 527-6682
Emp Here 100　　*Sales* 45,884,250
SIC 5995 Optical goods stores
Alan Ulsifer

Frederic Marchand
Michael Naugle

D-U-N-S 25-198-1346　　(SL)
GESTION J. M. LEROUX LTEE
CANADIAN TIRE
30 Boul Wilfrid-Hamel, Quebec, QC, G1M 2P7
(418) 687-2111
Emp Here 100　　*Sales* 26,765,200
SIC 5251 Hardware stores
Jean Marc Leroux

D-U-N-S 25-358-6010　　(HQ)
GESTION MARC NADEAU INC
625 Rue Du Marais, Quebec, QC, G1M 2Y2
(418) 681-0696
Sales 11,242,750
SIC 2095 Roasted coffee
Marc Nadeau

D-U-N-S 20-713-7048　　(BR)
GOUVERNEMENT DE LA PROVINCE DE QUEBEC
INSTITUT DE READAPATION EN DEFICIENCE PHYSIQUE DE QUEBEC
(*Suby of* GOUVERNEMENT DE LA PROVINCE DE QUEBEC)
525 Boul Wilfrid-Hamel, Quebec, QC, G1M 2S8
(418) 649-3700
Emp Here 1,300
SIC 8093 Specialty outpatient clinics, nec
Louise Lavergne

D-U-N-S 25-765-2081　　(SL)
GRAPHISCAN QUEBEC INC
GRAPHISCAN IMPRIMEUR
210 Rue Fortin Bureau 100, Quebec, QC, G1M 0A4
(418) 266-0707
Emp Here 35　　*Sales* 15,722,665
SIC 7389 Business services, nec
Denis Gagnon
Conrad Allard

D-U-N-S 20-588-6661　　(HQ)
GROUPE EDGENDA INC
AFI
1751 Rue Du Marais Bureau 300, Quebec, QC, G1M 0A2
(418) 626-2344
Emp Here 2　　*Sales* 19,751,904
SIC 8741 Management services
Marie-Pier St-Hilaire
Patrick St-Hilaire

D-U-N-S 24-464-1320　　(HQ)
GROUPE MARCHAND RENE INC
GESTION CENTREVISION
1100 Av Galibois Bureau A200, Quebec, QC, G1M 3M7
(418) 527-6682
Emp Here 34　　*Sales* 40,378,140
SIC 5995 Optical goods stores
Frederick Marchand

D-U-N-S 20-553-6233　　(BR)
GROUPE TVA INC
TELE 4
(*Suby of* QUEBECOR MEDIA INC)
450 Av Bechard, Quebec, QC, G1M 2E9
(418) 688-9330
Emp Here 150
SIC 4833 Television broadcasting stations
Nathalie Langevin

D-U-N-S 20-873-1539　　(HQ)
INSTITUT DE READAPTATION EN DEFICIENCE PHYSIQUE DE QUEBEC
525 Boul Wilfrid-Hamel, Quebec, QC, G1M 2S8
(418) 529-9141
Emp Here 98,504,900
SIC 8093 Specialty outpatient clinics, nec
Louise Lavergne
Claude Lafrance
Luc Malo

D-U-N-S 24-706-9925　　(SL)
ISOLATION AIR-PLUS INC
THERMO-PROTEC
560 Av Bechard, Quebec, QC, G1M 2E9
(418) 683-2999
Emp Here 70　　*Sales* 11,366,670
SIC 1742 Plastering, drywall, and insulation
Alain Baron
Jacques Bedard
Guillaume Bouchard

D-U-N-S 24-933-8401　　(SL)
JL DESJARDINS AUTO COLLECTION INC
DESJARDINS AUTO COLLECTION
175 Rue Du Marais, Quebec, QC, G1M 3C8
(418) 683-4450
Emp Here 200　　*Sales* 125,856,000
SIC 5511 New and used car dealers
Jean-Luc Desjardins

D-U-N-S 20-870-2654　　(SL)
LA-BIL INC
ARMAND GENEST & FILS
895 Av Godin, Quebec, QC, G1M 2X5
(418) 842-3216
Emp Here 60　　*Sales* 13,983,900
SIC 1711 Plumbing, heating, air-conditioning
Nicolas Bourgoin

D-U-N-S 24-690-0211　　(SL)
LEGUBEC INC
905 Rue Fernand-Dufour, Quebec, QC, G1M 3B2
(418) 681-3531
Emp Here 26　　*Sales* 21,725,002
SIC 5148 Fresh fruits and vegetables
Martin Ostiguy

D-U-N-S 24-204-1049　　(HQ)
MULTIVER LTEE
ISOVER
436 Rue Berube, Quebec, QC, G1M 1C8
(418) 687-0770
Emp Here 150　　*Sales* 83,099,250
SIC 3231 Products of purchased glass
Edgar Cormier
Caroline Moisan
Denis Cormier
Luc Cormier
Edgar Cormier
Marco Clavet
Nikolas Lachance

D-U-N-S 24-942-1264　　(BR)
NEXANS CANADA INC
(*Suby of* NEXANS)
1081 Boul Pierre-Bertrand, Quebec, QC, G1M 2E8

Emp Here 120
SIC 3643 Current-carrying wiring devices
Gaetan Ducharme

D-U-N-S 24-390-8220　　(SL)
NUTRIART INC
550 Av Godin, Quebec, QC, G1M 2K2
(418) 687-5320
Emp Here 60　　*Sales* 20,741,400
SIC 2066 Chocolate and cocoa products
Jean Leclerc

D-U-N-S 25-775-6395　　(SL)
ORICOM INTERNET INC
SERKO.CA
(*Suby of* 9313-8816 QUEBEC INC)
400 Rue Nolin Bureau 150, Quebec, QC, G1M 1E7
(418) 683-4557
Emp Here 75　　*Sales* 7,439,370
SIC 4813 Telephone communication, except radio
Alain Bergeron
Bernard Lepine
Mikael Bilodeau
Sylvie Pearson
Marcel Leblanc
Maxime Vallieres

D-U-N-S 20-242-6383　　(SL)
P.E. PAGEAU INC
460 Rue Metivier, Quebec, QC, G1M 2T8
(418) 681-8080
Emp Here 75　　*Sales* 18,933,150
SIC 1611 Highway and street construction
Michel Pageau
Steve Senechal

D-U-N-S 25-878-8348　　(HQ)
PETROLES CADEKO INC
DEPANNEUR PETRO-CANADA
455 Rue Des Entrepreneurs Bureau 652, Quebec, QC, G1M 2V2
(418) 688-9188
Emp Here 1　　*Sales* 31,430,025
SIC 5172 Petroleum products, nec
Pierre Dufresne
Jacques Dufresne
Alain Bibeau
Stephane Gobeil

D-U-N-S 24-126-5011　　(HQ)
PMT ROY ASSURANCE ET SERVICES FINANCIERS INC
955 Boul Pierre-Bertrand Bureau 140, Quebec, QC, G1M 2E8
(418) 780-0808
Sales 184,774,200
SIC 6411 Insurance agents, brokers, and service
Pierre Smith
Andre Roy
Andre Phan
Francois Boyer
Jean Martin
Cinthia Nadeau

D-U-N-S 20-645-1283　　(BR)
PROVIGO DISTRIBUTION INC
MAXI FLEUR DE LYS
(*Suby of* LOBLAW COMPANIES LIMITED)
552 Boul Wilfrid-Hamel, Quebec, QC, G1M 3E5
(418) 640-1700
Emp Here 100
SIC 5411 Grocery stores
Gaetan Larouche

D-U-N-S 24-942-5679　　(HQ)
QUEBEC MULTIPLANTS
TOMATES BONBON
755 Rue Du Marais, Quebec, QC, G1M 3R7
(418) 687-1616
Sales 37,126,000
SIC 5193 Flowers and florists supplies
Jean-Denis Boulet

D-U-N-S 24-759-6430　　(SL)
RAPIDO EQUIPEMENT INC
735 Av Pruneau Bureau 100, Quebec, QC, G1M 2J9
(418) 684-9000
Emp Here 21　　*Sales* 10,685,976
SIC 5021 Furniture
Come Veilleux

D-U-N-S 25-286-1893　　(BR)
RONA INC
RENO DEPOT
(*Suby of* LOWE'S COMPANIES, INC.)
999 Rue Du Marais, Quebec, QC, G1M 3T9
(418) 688-2220
Emp Here 125
SIC 5251 Hardware stores
Steve Michaud

D-U-N-S 24-758-6241　　(BR)
SECURITE KOLOSSAL INC
(*Suby of* GW INTERMEDIATE HOLDCO CORPORATION)
325 Rue Du Marais Bureau 220, Quebec, QC, G1M 3R3
(418) 683-1713
Emp Here 3,500
SIC 7381 Detective and armored car services
Jocelyn Beaulieu

D-U-N-S 20-579-6683   (SL)
SOVEA AUTOS LTEE
CAPITALE NISSAN
125 Rue Du Marais, Quebec, QC, G1M 3C8
(418) 681-0011
Emp Here 35   *Sales* 22,024,800
SIC 5511 New and used car dealers
  Jean Fortier

D-U-N-S 24-804-6505   (SL)
SUPERMARCHE CLAKA INC
SUPERMARCHE METRO FERLAND
1625 Rue Du Marais, Quebec, QC, G1M 0A2
(418) 688-1441
Emp Here 50   *Sales* 13,707,600
SIC 5411 Grocery stores
  Serge Ferland

D-U-N-S 20-639-2974   (SL)
SYMCO 2015 INC
SYMCO CONSTRUCTION
320 Boul Pierre-Bertrand Bureau 106, Quebec, QC, G1M 2C8
(581) 981-4774
Emp Here 30   *Sales* 14,121,930
SIC 1542 Nonresidential construction, nec
  Jeremie Toupin
  Mario Toupin
  Raphael Toupin

D-U-N-S 20-266-7523   (HQ)
TBC CONSTRUCTIONS INC
760 Av Godin, Quebec, QC, G1M 2K4
(418) 681-0671
Emp Here 250   *Sales* 135,424,000
SIC 1711 Plumbing, heating, air-conditioning
  Sebastien Pelletier
  Remy Martineau
  Mathieu St-Gelais
  Vincent Croteau

Quebec, QC G1N

D-U-N-S 24-532-1153   (SL)
129157 CANADA INC
ACCESSOIRES DE MOTOS A. D. M.
1831 Boul Wilfrid-Hamel, Quebec, QC, G1N 3Z1
(418) 527-4489
Emp Here 40   *Sales* 19,923,120
SIC 5571 Motorcycle dealers
  Michel Matton

D-U-N-S 25-469-4086   (HQ)
2972-6924 QUEBEC INC
PORTES ET CADRES METALEC
(*Suby of* GROUPE HONCO INC)
2150 Rue Leon-Harmel, Quebec, QC, G1N 4L2
(418) 683-2431
Emp Here 30   *Sales* 11,525,100
SIC 3442 Metal doors, sash, and trim
  Francis Lacasse
  Vicky Lacasse
  Harry Lacasse
  Carole Lacasse

D-U-N-S 20-558-3193   (SL)
3089554 NOVA SCOTIA ULC
ZETEC
(*Suby of* ROPER TECHNOLOGIES, INC.)
875 Boul Charest O Bureau 100, Quebec, QC, G1N 2C9
(418) 266-3020
Emp Here 73   *Sales* 16,592,097
SIC 3829 Measuring and controlling devices, nec
  Wayne Wilkinson
  David B. Liner
  Paul J. Soni

D-U-N-S 20-799-8464   (SL)
9153-7639 QUEBEC INC
KIA STE-FOY
1600 Rue Cyrille-Duquet, Quebec, QC, G1N 2E5
(418) 654-2929
Emp Here 26   *Sales* 12,950,028
SIC 5511 New and used car dealers
  Serge Beaudoin
  Steeve Michel

D-U-N-S 24-366-6133   (SL)
9190-5730 QUEBEC INC
ARCOTEC QUEBEC
1175 Rue Lomer-Gouin, Quebec, QC, G1N 1T3
(418) 687-4711
Emp Here 25   *Sales* 11,179,350
SIC 5031 Lumber, plywood, and millwork
  Gilles Drouin
  Karene Drouin
  Helene Drouin
  Manon Drouin

D-U-N-S 20-297-8107   (SL)
9217-5041 QUEBEC INC
DISTRIBUTIONS FRANCO
1095 Rue Eugene-Chinic, Quebec, QC, G1N 4N2
(581) 741-3233
Emp Here 38   *Sales* 19,780,596
SIC 5094 Jewelry and precious stones
  Francis Cote
  Annie Racicot
  Jahel Cote

D-U-N-S 20-381-3589   (SL)
9300-4901 QUEBEC INC
MCKINNON MULTI-SERVICES
356 Rue Jackson, Quebec, QC, G1N 4C5
(581) 742-1222
Emp Here 50   *Sales* 44,921,900
SIC 7389 Business services, nec
  Simon Mckinnon
  Felix-Antoine Bourdeau

D-U-N-S 24-392-0340   (SL)
AGENCE COMEDIHAU INC
HUMOUR DU MONDE
214 Av Saint-Sacrement Bureau 130, Quebec, QC, G1N 3X6
(418) 647-2525
Emp Here 50   *Sales* 13,077,650
SIC 6712 Bank holding companies
  Sylvain Parent-Bedard
  Francois Macerola
  Francois Lapointe
  Robert Charpentier
  Pierre Roy
  Robert Dutton
  Yves Lagace

D-U-N-S 24-205-4187   (SL)
ALIMENTATION SERRO INC
METRO FERLAND
707 Boul Charest O, Quebec, QC, G1N 4P6
(418) 681-7385
Emp Here 70   *Sales* 20,543,390
SIC 5411 Grocery stores
  Serge Ferland

D-U-N-S 20-058-4311   (HQ)
ASCENSEURS DESIGN INC
1865 Rue A.-R.-Decary, Quebec, QC, G1N 3Z8
(418) 681-2023
Emp Here 29   *Sales* 20,426,118
SIC 5084 Industrial machinery and equipment
  Richard Savard
  Alain Dupont
  Venise Soucy

D-U-N-S 20-722-3470   (HQ)
ATLANTIS POMPE STE-FOY INC
(*Suby of* GRO-MEC INC)
1844 Boul Wilfrid-Hamel, Quebec, QC, G1N 3Z2
(418) 681-7301
Emp Here 40   *Sales* 25,651,404
SIC 5084 Industrial machinery and equipment
  Claude Jacques

  Josee Godbout

D-U-N-S 24-206-6330   (HQ)
AV-TECH INC
2300 Rue Leon-Harmel Bureau 101, Quebec, QC, G1N 4L2
(418) 686-2300
Emp Here 125   *Sales* 16,004,877
SIC 1711 Plumbing, heating, air-conditioning
  Gilles Shooner

D-U-N-S 24-639-2187   (SL)
BEAUVAIS & VERRET INC
2181 Rue Leon-Harmel, Quebec, QC, G1N 4N5
(418) 688-1336
Emp Here 25   *Sales* 11,768,275
SIC 1542 Nonresidential construction, nec
  Louis E Beauvais
  Jacques Verret
  Jean-Pierre Brisson
  Claire Giroux

D-U-N-S 25-285-9897   (SL)
C.P.U. DESIGN INC
(*Suby of* CPU SERVICE D'ORDINATEUR INC)
2323 Boul Du Versant-Nord Bureau 100, Quebec, QC, G1N 4P4
(418) 681-6974
Emp Here 30   *Sales* 13,415,220
SIC 5045 Computers, peripherals, and software
  Lofti Ghattas
  Marleen Giroux

D-U-N-S 20-363-6634   (HQ)
CAISSE DESJARDINS DE QUEBEC
150 Rue Marie-De-L'Incarnation, Quebec, QC, G1N 4G8
(418) 687-2810
Emp Here 100   *Sales* 42,700,250
SIC 6062 State credit unions
  Robert Bouchard
  Danielle Beriau
  Andree Fontaine
  Michel Bonnette
  Anne Mckenna
  Marcel Veilleux
  Elisabeth Bussieres

D-U-N-S 20-540-6312   (BR)
CANADA POST CORPORATION
(*Suby of* GOVERNMENT OF CANADA)
660 Rue Graham-Bell, Quebec, QC, G1N 0B2
(418) 847-2160
Emp Here 100
SIC 4311 U.s. postal service
  Claude Allard

D-U-N-S 20-363-7223   (SL)
CANAM PONTS CANADA INC
CANAM-BRIDGES
(*Suby of* CANAM LUX PARENT COMPANY SARL)
1445 Rue Du Grand-Tronc, Quebec, QC, G1N 4G1
(418) 683-2561
Emp Here 250   *Sales* 82,028,750
SIC 1622 Bridge, tunnel, and elevated highway construction
  Marcel Dutil
  Rene Guizzetti
  Robert Dutil
  Robin Lapointe
  Louis Guertin
  Marc Dutil
  Monica Dugas

D-U-N-S 24-384-6024   (HQ)
CAPITAL TRANSIT INC
IMMEUBLES TANDEM
(*Suby of* GESTION ACAP INC)
2035 Rue Du Haut-Bord Bureau 300, Quebec, QC, G1N 4R7
(418) 914-0777
Emp Here 6   *Sales* 11,237,200

SIC 6159 Miscellaneous business credit institutions
  Pierre Papillon
  Hadge Sall

D-U-N-S 20-188-3852   (HQ)
CERATEC INC
(*Suby of* GESTION CERATEC INC)
414 Av Saint-Sacrement, Quebec, QC, G1N 3Y3
(418) 681-0101
Emp Here 28   *Sales* 44,717,400
SIC 5032 Brick, stone, and related material
  Paul Raiche
  Kenneth Raiche
  Curtis Raiche
  Christian Houle

D-U-N-S 25-662-4599   (SL)
CGI POSTES CANADA
1940 Rue Leon-Harmel, Quebec, QC, G1N 4K3
(418) 682-8663
Emp Here 49   *Sales* 13,207,901
SIC 4311 U.s. postal service
  Luc Bard

D-U-N-S 24-402-0090   (SL)
CLIVENCO INC
1185 Rue Philippe-Paradis Bureau 200, Quebec, QC, G1N 4E2
(418) 682-6373
Emp Here 50   *Sales* 11,046,700
SIC 1711 Plumbing, heating, air-conditioning
  Michel Blanchette

D-U-N-S 25-019-6052   (BR)
COMMISSION SCOLAIRE DE LA CAPITALE, LA
ECOLE DES METIERS ET OCCUPATIONS DE L'INDUSTRIE DE LA CONSTRUCTION DE QUEBEC
1060 Rue Borne, Quebec, QC, G1N 1L9
(418) 686-4040
Emp Here 80
SIC 8331 Job training and related services
  Martin Durocher

D-U-N-S 25-243-1523   (HQ)
CONSTRUCTION MICHEL GAGNON LTEE
2250 Rue Leon-Harmel Bureau 200, Quebec, QC, G1N 4L2
(418) 687-3824
Sales 24,357,150
SIC 1742 Plastering, drywall, and insulation
  Luc Gagnon
  Dany Carriere
  Jean-Philippe Hamel

D-U-N-S 20-381-1240   (HQ)
CONSULAIR INC
CONSULAIR GASTON BOULANGER
2022 Rue Lavoisier Bureau 125, Quebec, QC, G1N 4L5
(418) 650-5960
Sales 11,530,740
SIC 7389 Business services, nec
  Christian Gagnon
  Carl Jackson

D-U-N-S 25-072-8995   (SL)
COREM
1180 Rue De La Mineralogie, Quebec, QC, G1N 1X7
(418) 527-8211
Emp Here 88   *Sales* 19,354,984
SIC 8732 Commercial nonphysical research
  Paul Cousin
  Jean-Francois Leroux
  Jean Ouellet
  Annie Lessard
  John Mullally
  Francis Fournier
  Frederic Cormier
  Andre Morneau
  Stephane Rivard
  Catherine Cobden

D-U-N-S 20-429-8830 (HQ)
COULOMBE QUEBEC LIMITEE
(*Suby of* ENTREPRISES COUREM (1988) LTEE)
2300 Rue Cyrille-Duquet, Quebec, QC, G1N 2G5
(418) 687-2700
Emp Here 84 *Sales* 175,458,600
SIC 2086 Bottled and canned soft drinks
Marc Coulombe

D-U-N-S 24-499-0370 (SL)
COUMELIE INC
2300 Rue Cyrille-Duquet, Quebec, QC, G1N 2G5
(418) 687-2700
Emp Here 200 *Sales* 54,670,000
SIC 6712 Bank holding companies
Rene Coulombe

D-U-N-S 24-623-0460 (HQ)
CPU SERVICE D'ORDINATEUR INC
CPU
2323 Boul Du Versant-Nord Bureau 100, Quebec, QC, G1N 4P4
(418) 681-1234
Emp Here 60 *Sales* 23,358,580
SIC 7378 Computer maintenance and repair
Lotfi Ghattas

D-U-N-S 24-340-8189 (SL)
DISTRI-CARR LTEE
214 Av Saint-Sacrement Bureau 130, Quebec, QC, G1N 3X6

Emp Here 126 *Sales* 35,021,375
SIC 6712 Bank holding companies
Viateur Gagnon

D-U-N-S 24-377-7810 (SL)
ELECTROMIKE INC
1375 Rue Frank-Carrel Bureau 2, Quebec, QC, G1N 2E7
(418) 681-4138
Emp Here 40 *Sales* 17,886,960
SIC 5065 Electronic parts and equipment, nec
Marc Page

D-U-N-S 20-639-8328 (SL)
EMBALLAGE AVICO INC
DISTRIBUTION AVICO
1460 Rue Provinciale, Quebec, QC, G1N 4A2
(418) 682-5024
Emp Here 250 *Sales* 86,422,500
SIC 2015 Poultry slaughtering and processing
Jean Gagne
Pierre Gagne
Christian Vignola

D-U-N-S 20-120-4364 (SL)
EMBALLAGES L.P. AUBUT INC
1135 Rue Taillon, Quebec, QC, G1N 4G7
(418) 523-2956
Emp Here 21 *Sales* 15,592,920
SIC 5199 Nondurable goods, nec
Judith Beaulieu
Mathieu Blouin

D-U-N-S 24-377-3702 (SL)
ENTREPRISES DE NETTOYAGE MARCEL LABBE INC
ML ENTRETIEN MULTI SERVICES
340 Rue Jackson, Quebec, QC, G1N 4C5
(418) 523-9411
Emp Here 120 *Sales* 3,836,160
SIC 7349 Building maintenance services, nec
Alain Arsenault
Michel Arseneault

D-U-N-S 25-148-6668 (HQ)
FIVES SERVICES INC
ECL-CDG SERVICES
(*Suby of* FIVES ORSAY)
1580 Rue Provinciale, Quebec, QC, G1N 4A2
(418) 656-9140
Emp Here 5 *Sales* 11,539,680
SIC 7699 Repair services, nec
Sylvain Dulude

Edgard Caillier
Aurelie Fillon
Fabrice Baran
Hugues Vincent

D-U-N-S 25-222-9703 (BR)
FPINNOVATIONS
PMP SOLUTIONS
(*Suby of* FPINNOVATIONS)
300 Rue De Dieppe, Quebec, QC, G1N 3M8
(418) 659-2647
Emp Here 100
SIC 8731 Commercial physical research
Francois Leger

D-U-N-S 20-013-8449 (HQ)
FUTURA MANUFACTURIER DE PORTES ET FENETRES INC
FUTURA PORTES ET FENETRES
1451 Rue Frank-Carrel, Quebec, QC, G1N 4N7
(418) 681-7272
Emp Here 50 *Sales* 11,437,776
SIC 3089 Plastics products, nec
Jean-Pierre Gaulin
Doris Gaulin
Guy Morin
Claude Gaulin

D-U-N-S 20-242-5195 (SL)
GABRIEL MILLER INC
1850 Rue Provinciale, Quebec, QC, G1N 4A2
(418) 628-5550
Emp Here 23 *Sales* 10,826,813
SIC 1542 Nonresidential construction, nec
Guy Miller
Francis Miller
David Miller

D-U-N-S 20-241-1864 (BR)
GENERAL ELECTRIC CANADA COMPANY
GE
(*Suby of* GENERAL ELECTRIC COMPANY)
1130 Boul Charest O, Quebec, QC, G1N 2E2
(418) 682-8500
Emp Here 125
SIC 3625 Relays and industrial controls

D-U-N-S 20-243-1573 (HQ)
GESTION CERATEC INC
414 Av Saint-Sacrement, Quebec, QC, G1N 3Y3
(418) 681-0101
Emp Here 50 *Sales* 131,014,440
SIC 5032 Brick, stone, and related material
Paul Raiche
Curtis Raiche
Kenneth Raiche
Christian Houle

D-U-N-S 24-201-8414 (SL)
GESTION LITTLE MOUSE INC
1350 Rue Cyrille-Duquet, Quebec, QC, G1N 2E5
(418) 681-6381
Emp Here 140 *Sales* 34,205,920
SIC 5999 Miscellaneous retail stores, nec
Stephane Savard

D-U-N-S 24-790-7504 (HQ)
GESTION QUEMAR INC
AUDIO VIDEO D.G.
194 Av Saint-Sacrement, Quebec, QC, G1N 3X6
(418) 681-5088
Emp Here 18 *Sales* 41,643,360
SIC 5099 Durable goods, nec
Denis Gagne
Sylvie Gagne

D-U-N-S 20-702-9633 (BR)
GROUPE CANAM INC
CANAM BRIDGES
(*Suby of* CANAM LUX PARENT COMPANY SARL)
1445 Rue Du Grand-Tronc, Quebec, QC, G1N 4G1

(418) 683-2561
Emp Here 160
SIC 3443 Fabricated plate work (boiler shop)
Robin Lapointe

D-U-N-S 24-204-5847 (HQ)
GROUPE GUILBAULT LTEE
435 Rue Faraday, Quebec, QC, G1N 4G6
(418) 681-0575
Sales 46,095,250
SIC 4213 Trucking, except local
Eric Gignac
Nadine Guilbault
Daniel Gariepy
Guylaine Ouellet

D-U-N-S 24-529-9839 (HQ)
GROUPE SPORTS-INTER PLUS INC, LE
ATLANTIC GYM & SPORTS
420 Rue Faraday, Quebec, QC, G1N 4E5
(418) 527-0244
Sales 13,013,550
SIC 5091 Sporting and recreation goods
Christian De Muy
Pauline Guimond

D-U-N-S 20-250-1318 (BR)
HONEYWELL LIMITED
(*Suby of* HONEYWELL INTERNATIONAL INC.)
2366 Rue Galvani Bureau 4, Quebec, QC, G1N 4G4
(418) 688-8320
Emp Here 80
SIC 3822 Environmental controls
Leandre Rousseau

D-U-N-S 25-352-9879 (SL)
INFODEV ELECTRONIC DESIGNERS INTERNATIONAL INC
INFODEV
1995 Rue Frank-Carrel Bureau 202, Quebec, QC, G1N 4H9
(418) 681-3539
Emp Here 60 *Sales* 13,320,060
SIC 3571 Electronic computers
Pierre Deslauriers

D-U-N-S 25-337-6305 (HQ)
INNOVMETRIC LOGICIELS INC
IMALIGN
(*Suby of* 3584585 CANADA INC)
2014 Rue Cyrille-Duquet Bureau 310, Quebec, QC, G1N 4N6
(418) 688-2061
Sales 16,684,700
SIC 7372 Prepackaged software
Marc Soucy
Esther Bouliane

D-U-N-S 20-551-5369 (HQ)
JAN-PRO CANADA EST INC
JAN-PRO DES MARITIMES
2323 Boul Du Versant-Nord Bureau 114, Quebec, QC, G1N 4P4
(418) 527-1400
Emp Here 11 *Sales* 18,813,870
SIC 6794 Patent owners and lessors
Jean Roberge
Francois Carmichael
Sylvain Primeau
Eric Lapointe

D-U-N-S 25-198-7608 (HQ)
JAN-PRO CANADA INC
JAN-PRO
2323 Boul Du Versant-Nord Bureau 114, Quebec, QC, G1N 4P4
(418) 527-1400
Emp Here 5 *Sales* 18,813,870
SIC 6794 Patent owners and lessors
Jean Roberge

D-U-N-S 24-117-8636 (SL)
LABORATOIRE DE CANALISATIONS SOUTERRAINES (LCS) INC
255 Av Saint-Sacrement, Quebec, QC, G1N 3X9

(418) 651-9306
Emp Here 40 *Sales* 17,739,600
SIC 7389 Business services, nec
Lynda Landry
Richard Thibault
Daniel Cantin

D-U-N-S 24-204-0152 (SL)
LALLIER AUTOMOBILE (QUEBEC) INC
LALLIER SAINTE-FOY
(*Suby of* 2543-3533 QUEBEC INC)
2000 Rue Cyrille-Duquet, Quebec, QC, G1N 2E8
(418) 687-2525
Emp Here 100 *Sales* 62,928,000
SIC 5511 New and used car dealers
Guy Duplessis

D-U-N-S 24-841-6273 (HQ)
LAMBERT SOMEC INC
1505 Rue Des Tanneurs, Quebec, QC, G1N 4S7
(418) 687-1640
Emp Here 230 *Sales* 70,652,700
SIC 1731 Electrical work
Michel Boutin
Philippe Pelletier
Pierre-Luc Montminy
Yvan Laroche
Nicolas Rouleau
Guy Frappier
Jean-Francois Lapointe

D-U-N-S 20-429-9440 (SL)
LAVAL VOLKSWAGEN LTEE
777 Boul Charest O, Quebec, QC, G1N 2C6
(418) 687-4451
Emp Here 62 *Sales* 39,015,360
SIC 5511 New and used car dealers
Raymond Ouellet
Olivier Fleury-Bellavance
Pascal Ouellet

D-U-N-S 20-308-4421 (SL)
LEPAGE SIGNATURE INC
LEPAGESIGNATURE.COM
(*Suby of* TELWEB CAPITAL INC)
960 Rue Raoul-Jobin Bureau D, Quebec, QC, G1N 1S9
(418) 476-1678
Emp Here 6 *Sales* 401,238,500
SIC 1793 Glass and glazing work
Stephan Lepage

D-U-N-S 20-330-6063 (SL)
LEVIO CONSEILS INC
LEVIO
1995 Rue Frank-Carrel Bureau 219, Quebec, QC, G1N 4H9
(418) 914-3623
Emp Here 104 *Sales* 17,352,088
SIC 7379 Computer related services, nec
Francois Dion
Neil Meagher
Stephane Boudreault

D-U-N-S 24-570-3715 (HQ)
LOGIC-CONTROLE INC
AV-TECH
2300 Rue Leon-Harmel Bureau 101, Quebec, QC, G1N 4L2
(418) 686-2300
Sales 12,073,698
SIC 5065 Electronic parts and equipment, nec
Gilles Shooner

D-U-N-S 24-200-3986 (HQ)
LUMISOLUTION INC
162 Av Du Sacre-Coeur, Quebec, QC, G1N 2W2
(418) 522-5693
Sales 14,441,007
SIC 5063 Electrical apparatus and equipment
Georges Tremblay
Christine Tremblay

D-U-N-S 20-242-2358 (SL)
MAGASIN LATULIPPE INC

▲ Public Company ■ Public Company Family Member **HQ** Headquarters **BR** Branch **SL** Single Location

NEGOCIANT CHASSE & PECHE DUPONT
637 Rue Saint-Vallier O, Quebec, QC, G1N 1C6
(418) 529-0024
Emp Here 150   *Sales* 30,801,450
SIC 5311 Department stores
Francois Latulippe
Louis Latulippe

D-U-N-S 20-253-7007   (SL)
MARLIN CHEVROLET BUICK GMC INC
2145 Rue Frank-Carrel, Quebec, QC, G1N 2G2
(418) 688-1212
Emp Here 50   *Sales* 18,210,750
SIC 5012 Automobiles and other motor vehicles
Gabriel Dallaire
Monique Bedard

D-U-N-S 20-186-4471   (SL)
MATH SPORT INC
1130 Boul Charest O Bureau 7, Quebec, QC, G1N 2E2
(581) 999-7707
Emp Here 22   *Sales* 13,932,178
SIC 3149 Footwear, except rubber, nec
Mathieu Raymond
Pierre-Hugo Vigneux

D-U-N-S 20-912-1933   (BR)
MULTIVER LTEE
MULTIVER DIVISION ISOVER
(*Suby of* MULTIVER LTEE)
1950 Rue Leon-Harmel, Quebec, QC, G1N 4K3
(418) 687-0770
Emp Here 100
SIC 3211 Flat glass
Jean-Luc Vinette

D-U-N-S 20-381-0952   (HQ)
NURAN WIRELESS INC
2150 Cyrille-Duquet, Quebec, QC, G1N 2G3
(418) 914-7484
Emp Here 4   *Sales* 11,052,342
SIC 3679 Electronic components, nec
Martin Bedard
Maxime Dumas
Francis Letourneau
Thierry Cases

D-U-N-S 20-039-0634   (SL)
OFFICE MUNICIPAL D'HABITATION DE QUEBEC
110 Rue De Courcelette, Quebec, QC, G1N 4T4
(418) 780-5200
Emp Here 49   *Sales* 19,166,742
SIC 8631 Labor organizations
Sonia Bilodeau

D-U-N-S 24-907-5987   (SL)
OUTILLAGE INDUSTRIEL QUEBEC LTEE
FOURNITURES INDUSTRIELLES DU QUEBEC
395 Av Marconi, Quebec, QC, G1N 4A5
(418) 683-2527
Emp Here 25   *Sales* 11,875,650
SIC 5084 Industrial machinery and equipment
Sylvain Lortie
Denis Legere

D-U-N-S 20-325-4607   (SL)
PANTHERA DENTAL INC
2035 Rue Du Haut-Bord, Quebec, QC, G1N 4R7
(418) 527-0388
Emp Here 110   *Sales* 25,001,790
SIC 3843 Dental equipment and supplies
Jean-Pierre Desmarais
Gabriel Robichaud
Luc Marengere
Diane Robichaud
Nicola Urbani

D-U-N-S 20-515-9056   (SL)
PARA-NET BUANDERIE & NETTOYAGE A

SEC INC
PARATEX
1105 Rue Vincent-Massey, Quebec, QC, G1N 1N2
(418) 688-0889
Emp Here 85   *Sales* 7,618,465
SIC 7219 Laundry and garment services, nec
Dominic Parent

D-U-N-S 24-206-1638   (HQ)
PETITS DELICES G.T. INC, AUX
2022 Rue Lavoisier Bureau 198, Quebec, QC, G1N 4L5
(418) 683-8099
Emp Here 10   *Sales* 10,565,172
SIC 5451 Dairy products stores
Paul Giroux

D-U-N-S 20-363-2120   (SL)
POKA INC
POKA TECHNOLOGIES
214 Av Saint-Sacrement Bureau 240, Quebec, QC, G1N 3X6
(418) 476-2188
Emp Here 50   *Sales* 10,692,550
SIC 7372 Prepackaged software
Alexandre Leclerc
Antoine Bisson
Chris Arsenault
Mathieu Provost

D-U-N-S 20-309-2093   (SL)
QUALTECH INC
PCM FABRICATING
(*Suby of* GESTION QUALTECH INC)
1880 Rue Leon-Harmel, Quebec, QC, G1N 4K3
(418) 686-3802
Emp Here 135   *Sales* 10,159,292
SIC 7373 Computer integrated systems design
Nicolas Giguere
Andre Giguere

D-U-N-S 24-207-9960   (SL)
REFRIGERATION NOEL INC
(*Suby of* 2422-8827 QUEBEC INC)
1700 Rue Leon-Harmel, Quebec, QC, G1N 4R9
(418) 663-0879
Emp Here 100   *Sales* 19,232,800
SIC 7623 Refrigeration service and repair
Jean-Paul Alexandre

D-U-N-S 24-790-5979   (SL)
REVENCO (1991) INC
1755 Rue Provinciale, Quebec, QC, G1N 4S9
(418) 682-5993
Emp Here 50   *Sales* 10,891,450
SIC 1731 Electrical work
Alain Drolet
Alain Boivin
Mario Landry
Marc Pednaud
Sebastien Ouellet

D-U-N-S 24-324-2513   (SL)
ROBOVER INC
BALIVERNES BOUTIQUE
(*Suby of* TARDIF, PIERRE INC)
1595 Boul Wilfrid-Hamel, Quebec, QC, G1N 3Y7
(418) 682-3580
Emp Here 150   *Sales* 26,882,850
SIC 3231 Products of purchased glass
Anne Tardif
Gilles Tardif
Yan Arsenault
Jean Tardif

D-U-N-S 20-242-0147   (SL)
S. HUOT INC
1000 Rue Raoul-Jobin, Quebec, QC, G1N 4N3
(418) 681-0291
Emp Here 130   *Sales* 28,860,130
SIC 3535 Conveyors and conveying equipment

Michel Huot
Jean-Marc Huot
Tien Huynh Thien

D-U-N-S 24-792-4756   (HQ)
SAVARD ORTHO CONFORT INC
DEPANAGO VENTES INSTITUTIONNELLES, DIV DE
1350 Rue Cyrille-Duquet, Quebec, QC, G1N 2E5
(418) 681-6381
Emp Here 120   *Sales* 34,205,920
SIC 5999 Miscellaneous retail stores, nec
Stephane Savard
Alain Simard

D-U-N-S 25-365-8066   (BR)
SERVICES DE PNEUS DESHARNAIS INC
DESHARNAIS PNEUS & MECANIQUE
710 Boul Charest O, Quebec, QC, G1N 2C1
(418) 681-6041
Emp Here 150   *Sales* 1,494,234
SIC 5531 Auto and home supply stores
Denis Desharnais

D-U-N-S 25-888-3537   (SL)
SOCIETE DE PROTECTION DES FORETS CONTRE LES INSECTES ET MALADIES
SOPFIM
1780 Rue Semple, Quebec, QC, G1N 4B8
(418) 681-3381
Emp Here 108   *Sales* 22,314,636
SIC 0851 Forestry services
Raynald Arial
Pierre-Maurice Gagnon
Andre Tremblay
Richard Caissy
Jean-Francois Desbiens
Jimmy Pronovost
Deni Villeneuve
Nathalie Morin
Jean-Pierre Gagne
Jacob Martin-Malus

D-U-N-S 20-703-1936   (HQ)
TARDIF, PIERRE INC
1595 Boul Wilfrid-Hamel, Quebec, QC, G1N 3Y7
(418) 655-1521
Emp Here 3   *Sales* 41,002,500
SIC 6719 Holding companies, nec
Anne Tardif
Gilles Tardif
Yan Arsenault

D-U-N-S 24-379-2785   (HQ)
TRANSPORT BERNIERES INC
1721 Rue A.-R.-Decary, Quebec, QC, G1N 3Z7
(418) 684-2421
Emp Here 170   *Sales* 38,720,010
SIC 4213 Trucking, except local
Daniel Bouchard

D-U-N-S 24-941-0606   (HQ)
TRANSPORT GUILBAULT CANADA INC
(*Suby of* GROUPE GUILBAULT LTEE)
435 Rue Faraday, Quebec, QC, G1N 4G6
(418) 681-5272
Emp Here 200   *Sales* 147,504,800
SIC 4213 Trucking, except local
Eric Gignac
Nadine Guilbault
Daniel Gariepy

D-U-N-S 20-199-6253   (HQ)
TRANSPORT GUILBAULT INC
(*Suby of* GROUPE GUILBAULT LTEE)
435 Rue Faraday, Quebec, QC, G1N 4G6
(418) 681-0575
Emp Here 140   *Sales* 129,066,700
SIC 4213 Trucking, except local
Eric Gignac
Nadine Guilbault
Daniel Gariepy

D-U-N-S 24-380-5835   (SL)
TRANSPORT GUILBAULT INTERNA-

TIONAL INC
(*Suby of* GROUPE GUILBAULT LTEE)
435 Rue Faraday, Quebec, QC, G1N 4G6
(418) 681-0575
Emp Here 251   *Sales* 46,279,631
SIC 4213 Trucking, except local
Eric Gignac
Nadine Guilbault
Daniel Garieby

D-U-N-S 20-178-2971   (SL)
TRANSPORT GUILBAULT LONGUE DISTANCE INC
(*Suby of* GROUPE GUILBAULT LTEE)
435 Rue Faraday, Quebec, QC, G1N 4G6
(418) 681-0575
Emp Here 25   *Sales* 12,999,175
SIC 4731 Freight transportation arrangement
Eric Gignac
Nadine Guibault
Daniel Gariepy

Quebec, QC G1P

D-U-N-S 24-591-9832   (SL)
2333-2224 QUEBEC INC
STE-FOY HYUNDAI
2400 Av Dalton, Quebec, QC, G1P 3X1
(418) 654-9292
Emp Here 50   *Sales* 24,903,900
SIC 5511 New and used car dealers
Pierre Racine

D-U-N-S 24-630-7388   (SL)
24184863 QUEBEC INC
COPIEXPRESS
2717 Av Watt Bureau 150, Quebec, QC, G1P 3X3
(418) 659-1560
Emp Here 30   *Sales* 12,525,180
SIC 7384 Photofinish laboratories
Helene Guernault
Guy Stapelton

D-U-N-S 24-863-9387   (HQ)
2846-4436 QUEBEC INC
2440 Av Dalton, Quebec, QC, G1P 3X1
(418) 266-6600
Emp Here 1   *Sales* 13,940,850
SIC 6712 Bank holding companies
Normand Hinse

D-U-N-S 20-320-0022   (HQ)
9056-6696 QUEBEC INC
FIX AUTO SAINTE-FOY
2700 Av Watt, Quebec, QC, G1P 3T6
(418) 654-1414
Sales 15,298,200
SIC 7538 General automotive repair shops
Eric Poulin

D-U-N-S 24-381-0772   (SL)
9184-2518 QUEBEC INC
INDUSTRIES ROCAND, LES
2511 Boul Du Parc-Technologique, Quebec, QC, G1P 4S5
(418) 656-9917
Emp Here 60   *Sales* 13,320,060
SIC 3544 Special dies, tools, jigs, and fixtures
Andre Rochette

D-U-N-S 24-896-4454   (HQ)
9381-0596 QUEBEC INC
SOURIS MINI
2530 Boul Wilfrid-Hamel Bureau 101, Quebec, QC, G1P 2J1
(418) 524-6464
Sales 37,426,500
SIC 5651 Family clothing stores
Steeve Beaudet
Annie Bellavance

D-U-N-S 20-286-2707   (BR)
ACIER AGF INC
ACIER ECAN

(*Suby of* GROUPE AGF INC)
595 Av Newton, Quebec, QC, G1P 4C4
(418) 877-7715
Emp Here 100
SIC 2499 Wood products, nec
Gabriel Bonin

D-U-N-S 24-804-1522   (HQ)
ADDENERGIE TECHNOLOGIES INC
ADDENERGIE
2800 Rue Louis-Lumiere Ste 100, Quebec,
QC, G1P 0A4
(877) 505-2674
Emp Here 34   *Sales* 10,028,977
SIC 3629 Electrical industrial apparatus, nec
Louis Tremblay
Daniel Mailloux
Michel Alain
Pierre Nelis
Robert Benoit
Magaly Charbonneau
Norman Hebert

D-U-N-S 24-391-4921   (BR)
AECOM CANADA LTD
AECOM CONSULTANTS
(*Suby of* AECOM)
4700 Boul Wilfrid-Hamel, Quebec, QC, G1P
2J9
(418) 871-2444
Emp Here 100
SIC 8742 Management consulting services
Joane St-Onge

D-U-N-S 20-242-1293   (HQ)
ALIMENTS KRISPY KERNELS INC
AUTOMOBILES JALBERT
(*Suby of* DISTRIBUTION DENIS JALBERT
INC)
2620 Av Watt, Quebec, QC, G1P 3T5
(418) 658-4640
Emp Here 100   *Sales* 109,652,700
SIC 6712 Bank holding companies
Denis Jalbert

D-U-N-S 20-792-0625   (SL)
ATELIER DE MECANIQUE PREMONT INC
PREMONT HARLEY DAVIDSON
2495 Boul Wilfrid-Hamel, Quebec, QC, G1P
2H9
(418) 683-0563
Emp Here 40   *Sales* 14,568,600
SIC 5012 Automobiles and other motor vehicles
Laurent Premont

D-U-N-S 24-464-3003   (SL)
AUTOMATISATION JRT INC
405 Av Galilee, Quebec, QC, G1P 4M6
(418) 871-6016
Emp Here 80   *Sales* 15,235,360
SIC 3613 Switchgear and switchboard apparatus
St Tremblay
Luc Hebert
Stephan Cote
Remi Rodrigue
Stephan Cote

D-U-N-S 24-884-6503   (SL)
BOULANGERIE PATISSERIE DUMAS INC
CROISSANTS DE BERCY
2391 Av Watt, Quebec, QC, G1P 3X2
(418) 658-2037
Emp Here 45   *Sales* 10,118,475
SIC 2051 Bread, cake, and related products
Jean-Guy Dumas
Francois Dumas

D-U-N-S 25-285-7578   (HQ)
BPR INC
ASSEAU-BPR
(*Suby of* TETRA TECH, INC.)
4655 Boul Wilfrid-Hamel, Quebec, QC, G1P
2J7
(418) 871-8151
Emp Here 300   *Sales* 344,979,250

SIC 8711 Engineering services
Denis Harvie
Dan L. Batrack
Richard A. Lemmon
Francois Morin
Steven M. Burdick

D-U-N-S 20-722-9659   (HQ)
BRASSARD BURO INC
2747 Av Watt, Quebec, QC, G1P 3X3
(418) 657-5500
Emp Here 47   *Sales* 25,182,900
SIC 5112 Stationery and office supplies
Eric Brassard

D-U-N-S 24-639-3383   (SL)
CAMIONS FREIGHTLINER QUEBEC INC
2380 Av Dalton, Quebec, QC, G1P 3X1
(418) 657-2425
Emp Here 62   *Sales* 39,015,360
SIC 5511 New and used car dealers
Serge Boyer

D-U-N-S 20-578-6668   (HQ)
CANTIN BEAUTE LTEE
2495 Av Dalton, Quebec, QC, G1P 3S5
(418) 654-0444
Emp Here 35   *Sales* 45,602,496
SIC 5087 Service establishment equipment
Raynald Bouchard
Eric Bouchard

D-U-N-S 24-623-7143   (HQ)
CAPILEX-BEAUTE LTEE
CAPILEX-BEAUTE MONTREAL
2670 Av Dalton, Quebec, QC, G1P 3S4
(418) 653-2500
Sales 12,350,676
SIC 5087 Service establishment equipment
Pierre Leroux
Guy Leroux
Jean Marier

D-U-N-S 20-870-4429   (HQ)
CENTRE DE RECHERCHE INDUSTRIELLE DU QUEBEC
BUREAU DE NORMALISATION DU QUEBEC (BNQ)
333 Rue Franquet, Quebec, QC, G1P 4C7
(418) 659-1550
Emp Here 51   *Sales* 45,918,450
SIC 8731 Commercial physical research
Sophie D'amours
Yves Larocque
Denis Hardy
Sylvie Cloutier
Luc Langevin
Pierre Talbot
Thu Ha To
Chantal Trepanier
Robert Teasdale

D-U-N-S 25-690-3758   (HQ)
CERAMIQUE DECORS M.S.F. INC
SOLIGO GRUPPO
2750 Av Dalton, Quebec, QC, G1P 3S4
(418) 781-0955
Emp Here 51   *Sales* 15,338,598
SIC 5713 Floor covering stores
Joseph Soligo
David Soligo
Raphael Soligo

D-U-N-S 25-842-1148   (HQ)
COMMUNICATION DEMO INC
925 Av Newton Bureau 220, Quebec, QC,
G1P 4M2
(418) 877-0704
Emp Here 30   *Sales* 40,134,480
SIC 7389 Business services, nec
Andre Desjardins
Mario Morissette
Mario Lafrance

D-U-N-S 20-284-6601   (BR)
CONSULTANTS AECOM INC
AECOM TECSULT
(*Suby of* AECOM)

4700 Boul Wilfrid-Hamel, Quebec, QC, G1P
2J9
(418) 871-2444
Emp Here 80
SIC 8711 Engineering services
Luc Benoit

D-U-N-S 24-623-7945   (HQ)
DECTRONIQUE (1984) INC
DECTRO INTERNATIONAL
1000 Boul Du Parc-Technologique, Quebec,
QC, G1P 4S3
(418) 650-0303
Sales 10,941,200
SIC 3999 Manufacturing industries, nec
Clement Beaumont
Karine Beaumont

D-U-N-S 25-361-0026   (HQ)
DENMAR INC
2365 Av Watt, Quebec, QC, G1P 3X2
(418) 654-2888
Sales 16,774,200
SIC 6712 Bank holding companies
Denis Plamondon
Mario Martel

D-U-N-S 25-991-3762   (HQ)
DISTRIBUTION DENIS JALBERT INC
ALIMENTS KRISPY KERNELS
2620 Av Watt, Quebec, QC, G1P 3T5
(418) 658-4640
Emp Here 1   *Sales* 182,754,500
SIC 6712 Bank holding companies
Denis Jalbert

D-U-N-S 20-954-4873   (SL)
DISTRIBUTION STE-FOY (1982) LTEE
DSF
(*Suby of* PLACEMENTS ROBERT LEONARD
LTEE, LES)
685 Av Newton, Quebec, QC, G1P 4C4
(418) 871-8133
Emp Here 30   *Sales* 13,415,220
SIC 5039 Construction materials, nec
Robert Leonard
Jean Blain

D-U-N-S 24-597-6845   (HQ)
EDDYFI NDT INC
AILE D'ARGENT MOYEN ORIENT
3425 Rue Pierre-Ardouin, Quebec, QC, G1P
0B3
(418) 780-1565
Sales 56,088,950
SIC 5084 Industrial machinery and equipment
Martin Theriault
Louis-Georges Gauvin
Jim Costain
Jean-Francois Grenon
Mario Bouchard

D-U-N-S 20-722-9352   (SL)
EDITION LE TELEPHONE ROUGE INC
GROUPE ETR
2555 Av Watt Bureau 6, Quebec, QC, G1P
3T2
(418) 658-8122
Emp Here 80   *Sales* 16,937,920
SIC 7331 Direct mail advertising services
Guy Lafond
Sonia Labonte

D-U-N-S 20-192-8447   (SL)
EMBALLAGES L. BOUCHER INC, LES
(*Suby of* 2168-3321 QUEBEC INC)
1360 Av Galilee, Quebec, QC, G1P 4E3
(418) 681-2320
Emp Here 50   *Sales* 25,182,900
SIC 5113 Industrial and personal service paper
Andre Boucher
Claire Martel Boucher
Helene Boucher

D-U-N-S 25-690-5266   (HQ)
ENGLOBE CORP
COENTREPRISE LVM - INSPEC-SOL

(*Suby of* ONCAP II L.P.)
505 Boul Du Parc-Technologique Suite 200,
Quebec, QC, G1P 4S9
(418) 781-0191
Emp Here 150   *Sales* 155,665,000
SIC 0711 Soil preparation services
Robert Youden
Stephen Montminy
Linda Beaudin
Michael Lay
Gregory Baylin
Aly Hadibhai
Xavier Dennery

D-U-N-S 25-335-5291   (SL)
ENTREPRISES CAFECTION INC
(*Suby of* LONE STAR INTERNATIONAL FINANCE HOLDINGS (IRELAND) UNLIMITED COMPANY)
2355 Av Dalton, Quebec, QC, G1P 3S3
(418) 650-6162
Emp Here 100   *Sales* 22,200,100
SIC 3589 Service industry machinery, nec
Andrea Zocchi
Francois Baron
Hendrikus Van Gorp

D-U-N-S 24-465-5171   (SL)
ENTREPRISES P.P. HALLE LTEE
SERVICES ALIMENTAIRE HALLE
2610 Boul Wilfrid-Hamel, Quebec, QC, G1P
2J1
(418) 687-4740
Emp Here 25   *Sales* 20,889,425
SIC 5142 Packaged frozen goods
Danny Halle
Gilles Halle

D-U-N-S 24-758-6068   (SL)
FLEURIGROS 1995 INC
(*Suby of* DENMAR INC)
2365 Av Watt Bureau 1, Quebec, QC, G1P
3X2
(418) 654-2888
Emp Here 40   *Sales* 29,700,800
SIC 5193 Flowers and florists supplies
Denis Plamondon
Mario Martel

D-U-N-S 24-389-5765   (SL)
GELLULE INC
2300 Boul Pere-Lelievre, Quebec, QC, G1P
2X5
(418) 681-6351
Emp Here 26   *Sales* 10,903,230
SIC 6712 Bank holding companies
Mathieu Labonte

D-U-N-S 25-543-8483   (SL)
GENEOHM SCIENCES CANADA INC
BD DIAGNOSTIC
(*Suby of* BECTON, DICKINSON AND COMPANY)
2555 Boul Du Parc-Technologique, Quebec,
QC, G1P 4S5
(418) 780-5800
Emp Here 300   *Sales* 99,478,200
SIC 2835 Diagnostic substances
Gary M Defazio
Jamie Condie

D-U-N-S 20-267-2846   (HQ)
GENEPOC INC
(*Suby of* MERIDIAN BIOSCIENCE, INC.)
360 Rue Franquet Bureau 100, Quebec, QC,
G1P 4N3
(418) 650-3535
Sales 13,833,000
SIC 2835 Diagnostic substances
Tanja Dowe
Patrice Allibert
Marie-Josee Pare
Michel G. Bergeron
Jeremy Bridge-Cook
Denis Robichon
J. Chuck Morrison

D-U-N-S 20-517-0293   (HQ)

GENTEC INC
2625 Av Dalton, Quebec, QC, G1P 3S9
(418) 651-8000
Sales 28,566,300
SIC 3625 Relays and industrial controls
Francois Giroux
Michel Giroux

D-U-N-S 20-179-5346   (BR)
GOUVERNEMENT DE LA PROVINCE DE QUEBEC
DIRECTION DES LABORATOIRES D'EXPERTISES ET D'ANALYSES ALIMEN-TAIRES
(*Suby of* GOUVERNEMENT DE LA PROVINCE DE QUEBEC)
2700 Rue Einstein Bureau C2105, Quebec, QC, G1P 3W8
(418) 643-1632
Emp Here 75
SIC 8731 Commercial physical research
Jacques Menard

D-U-N-S 24-277-4172   (SL)
GROUPE TRANSTECK INC
GROUPE TRAFIC
2797 Av Watt, Quebec, QC, G1P 3X3
(418) 651-9595
Emp Here 100   *Sales* 14,819,200
SIC 4213 Trucking, except local
David Hains

D-U-N-S 25-903-0930   (BR)
GSI ENVIRONNEMENT INC
(*Suby of* ONCAP II L.P.)
4495 Boul Wilfrid-Hamel Bureau 100, Quebec, QC, G1P 2J7
(418) 872-4227
Emp Here 200
SIC 8748 Business consulting, nec
Nathalie Duchesne

D-U-N-S 20-778-3374   (SL)
GUAY BUSSIERES & ASSOCIES INC
3405 Boul Wilfrid-Hamel Bureau 200, Quebec, QC, G1P 2J3

Emp Here 21   *Sales* 12,178,404
SIC 6411 Insurance agents, brokers, and service
Sylvain Jacques
Florian Vallee

D-U-N-S 20-432-2564   (SL)
HICHAUD INC
2485 Boul Neuville, Quebec, QC, G1P 3A6
(418) 682-0782
Emp Here 60   *Sales* 16,215,360
SIC 3149 Footwear, except rubber, nec
Pierre Thibodeau

D-U-N-S 24-614-8790   (SL)
HOPITAL VETERINAIRE DAUBIGNY
BUREAU VETERINAIRE DE LA RIVWE SUD
3349 Boul Wilfrid-Hamel, Quebec, QC, G1P 2J3
(418) 872-5355
Emp Here 100   *Sales* 10,928,900
SIC 0742 Veterinary services, specialties
Michelle Cutler
Steve Quon
Martin Godbout
Orin Litman

D-U-N-S 24-145-0949   (HQ)
HUOT, REAL INC
HUOT
(*Suby of* ENTREPRISES MIRCA INC, LES)
2550 Av Dalton, Quebec, QC, G1P 3S4
(418) 634-5967
Emp Here 24   *Sales* 23,751,300
SIC 5085 Industrial supplies
Francois Deschenes
Jacques Deschenes
Martin Deschenes
Marc Lapierre

D-U-N-S 25-526-0184   (HQ)

ID BIOMEDICAL CORPORATION OF QUEBEC
GLAXOSMITHKLINE BIOLOGICALS NORTH AMERICA
(*Suby of* GLAXOSMITHKLINE PLC)
2323 Boul Du Parc-Technologique, Quebec, QC, G1P 4R8
(450) 978-4599
Emp Here 1,000   *Sales* 344,631,000
SIC 8731 Commercial physical research
Eric Moreau
Vincent Moline
Renee Langlois
Loren Cooper

D-U-N-S 24-865-2468   (SL)
INFECTIO DIAGNOSTIC INC
BD DIAGNOSTICS
2555 Boul Du Parc-Technologique, Quebec, QC, G1P 4S5
(418) 681-4343
Emp Here 45   *Sales* 11,545,290
SIC 3842 Surgical appliances and supplies
Nancy Peche

D-U-N-S 25-685-1981   (HQ)
INSTITUT DE RECHERCHE ET DEVELOPPEMENT EN AGROENVIRONEMENT INC
I.R.D.A.
2700 Rue Einstein Bureau D1110, Quebec, QC, G1P 3W8
(418) 643-2380
Sales 27,800,234
SIC 8731 Commercial physical research
Georges Archambault
Julie Bilodeau
Andre Martin
Pascal Van Nieuwenhuyse
Richard Dion
Francis Desrochers
Denis Audet
Julie Bilodeau
Isabelle Rivard
Richard Lehoux

D-U-N-S 24-638-5470   (HQ)
INSTITUT NATIONAL D'OPTIQUE
INO
2740 Rue Einstein, Quebec, QC, G1P 4S4
(418) 657-7006
Emp Here 100   *Sales* 40,816,400
SIC 8731 Commercial physical research
Alain Chandonnet
Jacques Topping
Philippe Boivin
Normand R Bourque
Francois Giroux
Jean-Guy Paquet
Hugues St-Pierre
Jean-Marie Toulouse
Guy Laberge
Monique Begin L

D-U-N-S 20-776-5132   (HQ)
JULIEN INC
AC CUISINES
(*Suby of* 9129-3605 QUEBEC INC)
955 Rue Lachance, Quebec, QC, G1P 2H3
(418) 687-3630
Sales 92,598,800
SIC 3914 Silverware and plated ware
Gilles St-Pierre
Michel-Luc St-Pierre
Carl-David Belley

D-U-N-S 24-392-3039   (SL)
LEDDARTECH INC
4535 Boul Wilfrid-Hamel Bureau 240, Quebec, QC, G1P 2J7
(418) 653-9000
Emp Here 26   *Sales* 11,679,694
SIC 7389 Business services, nec
Michel Brule
Charles Boulanger
Claude Dore

Fabio Gamacorta
Simon Morris
Nicolas Landrin
Robert Baumann
Peter Marks

D-U-N-S 20-297-7224   (HQ)
LOAD SYSTEMS INTERNATIONAL INC
DIVISION RADIO TRANSMETTEURS
2666 Boul Du Parc-Technologique Bureau 190, Quebec, QC, G1P 4S6
(418) 650-2330
Sales 10,233,650
SIC 3625 Relays and industrial controls
Steven W. Berglund
John E. Huey Iii
James A. Kirkland
Stephen Wolven

D-U-N-S 24-531-5734   (SL)
MACK STE-FOY INC
2550 Av Watt, Quebec, QC, G1P 3T4
(418) 651-9397
Emp Here 49   *Sales* 17,846,535
SIC 5012 Automobiles and other motor vehicles
Simon Poire
Eric Poire

D-U-N-S 20-198-2261   (BR)
METRO RICHELIEU INC
EPICERIE QUEBEC
(*Suby of* METRO INC)
635 Av Newton, Quebec, QC, G1P 4C4
(418) 871-7101
Emp Here 225
SIC 5141 Groceries, general line
Marc Cassidy

D-U-N-S 24-684-8241   (HQ)
MICROCOM 'M' INC
ALARME MICROCOM
(*Suby of* GW INTERMEDIATE HOLDCO CORPORATION)
3710 Boul Wilfrid-Hamel, Quebec, QC, G1P 2J2
(418) 871-7676
Emp Here 1   *Sales* 19,783,900
SIC 7382 Security systems services
Daniel Demers
Patrick Prince
Pierre-Hubert Seguin

D-U-N-S 20-590-3615   (BR)
NORDIA INC
(*Suby of* PLATINUM EQUITY, LLC)
5200 Boul De L'Ormiere, Quebec, QC, G1P 1K7
(418) 864-7359
Emp Here 400
SIC 4899 Communication services, nec
Gaston Sevigny

D-U-N-S 24-820-7599   (HQ)
OLYMPUS NDT CANADA INC
(*Suby of* OLYMPUS CORPORATION)
3415 Rue Pierre-Ardouin, Quebec, QC, G1P 0B3
(418) 872-1155
Sales 96,029,500
SIC 3829 Measuring and controlling devices, nec
Fabrice Cancre
Stephen G. Froehle
Lisa Kerr
Pierre Lacroix
William Collins

D-U-N-S 25-371-7946   (HQ)
OPSENS INC
INFLO SOLUTIONS
750 Boul Du Parc-Technologique, Quebec, QC, G1P 4S3
(418) 781-0333
Sales 14,166,466
SIC 3827 Optical instruments and lenses
Louis Laflamme

Claude Belleville
Tony Gibbons
Gaetan Duplain
Robin Villeneuve
Denis Sirois
Jean Lavigueur
Denis Harrington
Pat Mackin

D-U-N-S 25-779-0998   (HQ)
OPTEL VISION INC
GROUPE OPTEL
2680 Boul Du Parc-Technologique, Quebec, QC, G1P 4S6
(418) 688-0334
Sales 67,429,419
SIC 5044 Office equipment
Louis Roy

D-U-N-S 25-470-7086   (SL)
PISCINES SOUCY INC
ENTRETIEN DE PISCINES SOUCY
3605 Boul Wilfrid-Hamel, Quebec, QC, G1P 2J4
(418) 872-4440
Emp Here 60   *Sales* 14,771,160
SIC 1799 Special trade contractors, nec
Stephane Drouin

D-U-N-S 20-202-4340   (SL)
POSTE EXPRESS INC
2659 Av Watt Bureau 5, Quebec, QC, G1P 3T2
(418) 653-1045
Emp Here 25   *Sales* 11,215,661
SIC 7389 Business services, nec
Richard Emond

D-U-N-S 20-515-0899   (HQ)
PREMOULE INC
CENTRE DE COUPE PREMOULE DE QUEBEC
2375 Av Dalton Bureau 200, Quebec, QC, G1P 3S3
(418) 652-7777
Emp Here 250   *Sales* 78,807,960
SIC 3083 Laminated plastics plate and sheet
Louis Deslauriers
Jean Houde
Yves P. Gosselin
Francois Baron
Charles Roberge
Yvan Gaudreau
Francois Giroux

D-U-N-S 20-120-9934   (BR)
PREMOULE INC
2375 Av Dalton Unite 200, Quebec, QC, G1P 3S3
(418) 652-1422
Emp Here 250
SIC 2434 Wood kitchen cabinets
Anne Deslauriers

D-U-N-S 25-402-1348   (SL)
PROMOTION LEPINE INC
2800 Boul Wilfrid-Hamel, Quebec, QC, G1P 2J1
(418) 687-0084
Emp Here 25   *Sales* 18,258,625
SIC 5169 Chemicals and allied products, nec
Francine Genois

D-U-N-S 25-857-5893   (BR)
PROVIGO DISTRIBUTION INC
MAXI LES SAULES
(*Suby of* LOBLAW COMPANIES LIMITED)
5150 Boul De L'Ormiere, Quebec, QC, G1P 4B2
(418) 872-3866
Emp Here 75
SIC 5411 Grocery stores
Luc Boucher

D-U-N-S 20-119-2096   (HQ)
SADE CANADA INC
(*Suby of* VEOLIA ENVIRONNEMENT)
1564 Av Ampere, Quebec, QC, G1P 4B9

(581) 300-7233
Emp Here 20   *Sales* 12,622,100
SIC 1623 Water, sewer, and utility lines
Philippe Voisin
Didier Hermand

D-U-N-S 24-464-9372   (HQ)
SERVICE DE PNEUS AUCLAIR INC
AUTOPNEU AUCLAIR
3755 Boul Wilfrid-Hamel, Quebec, QC, G1P
2J4
(418) 871-6740
Emp Here 25   *Sales* 49,713,120
SIC 5531 Auto and home supply stores
Michel Auclair
Benoit Auclair
Normand Cote

D-U-N-S 25-494-4416   (SL)
SILICYCLE INC
SILICA SERVING CHEMISTRY
2500 Boul Du Parc-Technologique, Quebec,
QC, G1P 4S6
(418) 874-0054
Emp Here 50   *Sales* 13,833,000
SIC 2819 Industrial inorganic chemicals, nec
Hugo St-Laurent
Johane Boucher-Champagne
Luc Fortier
Serge Olivier
Emile Langlois
Pierre Plante
Francois Morissette
Louis Laflamme

D-U-N-S 25-475-1290   (BR)
SOBEYS CAPITAL INCORPORATED
IGA EXTRA
(*Suby of* EMPIRE COMPANY LIMITED)
5005 Boul De L'Ormiere Bureau 445, Quebec,
QC, G1P 1K6
(418) 877-3922
Emp Here 130
SIC 5411 Grocery stores
Nancy Godbout

D-U-N-S 24-821-3977   (BR)
SOBEYS CAPITAL INCORPORATED
SOBEYS QUEBEC
(*Suby of* EMPIRE COMPANY LIMITED)
950 Av Galilee Bureau 2008, Quebec, QC,
G1P 4B7
(418) 681-1922
Emp Here 400
SIC 5141 Groceries, general line

D-U-N-S 24-344-2261   (SL)
**SOCIETE DE QUEBEC POUR PREVENIR
LES CRUAUTES CONTRE LES ANIMAUX,
LA**
S.P.A. DE QUEBEC
1130 Av Galilee Bureau 487, Quebec, QC,
G1P 4B7
(418) 527-9104
Emp Here 26   *Sales* 10,332,764
SIC 8699 Membership organizations, nec
Denys Pelletier

D-U-N-S 25-914-1047   (BR)
SOLOTECH INC
(*Suby of* GROUPE SOLOTECH INC)
935 Rue Lachance Bureau 200, Quebec, QC,
G1P 2H3
(418) 683-5553
Emp Here 100
SIC 3645 Residential lighting fixtures
Martin Chouimard

D-U-N-S 20-362-6119   (BR)
SPECTRIS CANADA INC
*CORPORATION SCIENTIFIQUE CLAISSE,
LA*
(*Suby of* SPECTRIS PLC)
350 Rue Franquet Bureau 45, Quebec, QC,
G1P 4P3
(418) 656-6453
Emp Here 80
SIC 5049 Professional equipment, nec

Christian Marcoux

D-U-N-S 24-895-2454   (SL)
SUPERMARCHE BELSERA INC
2300 Boul Pere-Lelievre, Quebec, QC, G1P
2X5
(418) 682-4197
Emp Here 49   *Sales* 13,433,448
SIC 5411 Grocery stores
Serge Denis

D-U-N-S 20-387-2304   (HQ)
SYNEOS HEALTH CLINIQUE INC
SYNEOS HEALTH
(*Suby of* SYNEOS HEALTH HOLDINGS UK
LIMITED)
2500 Rue Einstein, Quebec, QC, G1P 0A2
(418) 527-4000
Emp Here 375   *Sales* 37,905,100
SIC 8071 Medical laboratories
Riaz Bandali
Michael Donovan
Jonathan Olefson
Thomas Edward Zajkowski
Brandon Anthony Cormier

D-U-N-S 24-804-9376   (SL)
TECHSOL MARINE INC
(*Suby of* 9215-7064 QUEBEC INC)
4800 Rue Rideau, Quebec, QC, G1P 4P4
(418) 688-2230
Emp Here 70   *Sales* 13,330,940
SIC 3625 Relays and industrial controls
Edwin Van Ierland
Francois Lessard
Patrick Lebeau
Martin Roberge
Eric Trambley

D-U-N-S 25-105-6792   (SL)
TERAXION INC
2716 Rue Einstein, Quebec, QC, G1P 4S8
(418) 658-9500
Emp Here 100   *Sales* 19,044,200
SIC 3661 Telephone and telegraph apparatus
Alain-Jacques Simard
Richard Kirouac

D-U-N-S 25-690-0895   (SL)
TSO3 INC
2505 Av Dalton, Quebec, QC, G1P 3S5
(418) 651-0003
Emp Here 80   *Sales* 2,532,000
SIC 3842 Surgical appliances and supplies
Richard M. Rumble
Josianne Beaudry
Steven West
Jean-Pierre Robert
Martin Madden
Jeffrey Pompeo
Linda Rosenstock
Sara Elford
Glen Kayll

D-U-N-S 20-592-2610   (SL)
VIANDES P.P. HALLE LTEE, LES
HALLE SERVICES ALIMENTAIRES
2610 Boul Wilfrid-Hamel, Quebec, QC, G1P
2J1
(418) 687-4740
Emp Here 50   *Sales* 41,778,850
SIC 5147 Meats and meat products
Liliane Vigneault-Halle
Danny Halle

Quebec, QC G1R

D-U-N-S 24-821-7994   (SL)
AUBERGE DU TRESOR INC
(*Suby of* 161734 CANADA INC)
20 Rue Sainte-Anne, Quebec, QC, G1R 3X2
(418) 694-1876
Emp Here 100   *Sales* 9,269,000
SIC 7011 Hotels and motels

Nicole Plante

D-U-N-S 20-520-2901   (BR)
BANQUE NATIONALE DU CANADA
*EPARGNE PLACEMENTS QUEBEC
BANQUE NATIONAL*
(*Suby of* BANQUE NATIONALE DU
CANADA)
333 Grande Allee E Bureau 400, Quebec, QC,
G1R 5W3
(418) 521-6400
Emp Here 75
SIC 6021 National commercial banks
Jocelyn Malo

D-U-N-S 24-942-2692   (HQ)
BIOREX INC
295 Ch Sainte-Foy, Quebec, QC, G1R 1T5
(418) 522-4945
Emp Here 7   *Sales* 23,428,800
SIC 8748 Business consulting, nec
Marc Gagnon
Esther Ruelland

D-U-N-S 20-950-5973   (SL)
BOURGABEC INC
CHEZ DAGOBERT
600 Grande Allee E, Quebec, QC, G1R 2K5
(418) 522-0393
Emp Here 75   *Sales* 3,215,475
SIC 5813 Drinking places
Gilles Laberge
Giovani Maur

D-U-N-S 20-298-2021   (SL)
**BRASSARD GOULET YARGEAU SER-
VICES FINANCIERS INTEGRES INC**
BRASSARD GOULET YARGEAU
686 Grande Allee E Bureau 100, Quebec, QC,
G1R 2K5
(418) 682-5853
Emp Here 43   *Sales* 12,181,599
SIC 8741 Management services
Eric Brassard
Miguel Yargeau
Jean-Raymond Castelli
David Poliquin

D-U-N-S 20-581-6549   (BR)
**CANADIAN BROADCASTING CORPORA-
TION**
RADIO CANADA
(*Suby of* GOVERNMENT OF CANADA)
888 Rue Saint-Jean Unite 224, Quebec, QC,
G1R 5H6
(418) 656-8206
Emp Here 250
SIC 4832 Radio broadcasting stations
Louise Cordeau

D-U-N-S 20-874-2932   (HQ)
**CAPITALE ASSURANCES GENERALES
INC, LA**
ASSURANCE BEAULIEU
(*Suby of* LA CAPITALE PARTICIPATIONS
INC)
625 Rue Jacques-Parizeau, Quebec, QC,
G1R 2G5
(418) 781-1618
Emp Here 250   *Sales* 1,602,726,000
SIC 6321 Accident and health insurance
Rene Rouleau
Dominique Dubuc
Pierre Marc Bellavance
Normand Rinfret
Denis Briere
Robert St-Denis
Patrice Forget
Dominique Salvy
Francois Turenne
Yvan Gendron

D-U-N-S 20-777-7749   (HQ)
**CAPITALE ASSUREUR DE
L'ADMINISTRATION PUBLIQUE INC, LA**
CAPITALE CARD
(*Suby of* CAPITALE MUTUELLE DE

L'ADMINISTRATION PUBLIQUE, LA)
625 Rue Jacques-Parizeau, Quebec, QC,
G1R 2G5
(418) 644-4106
Emp Here 400   *Sales* 6,280,548,952
SIC 6311 Life insurance
Jean St-Gelais
Jacques Cotton
Pierre Marc Bellavance
Dominique Dubuc
Francois Latreille
Richard Fiset
Danielle Chevrette
Alain Briere
Josee Germain
Jacques Cotton

D-U-N-S 24-942-3401   (HQ)
CAPITALE GROUPE FINANCIER INC, LA
(*Suby of* CAPITALE MUTUELLE DE
L'ADMINISTRATION PUBLIQUE, LA)
625 Rue Jacques-Parizeau, Quebec, QC,
G1R 2G5
(418) 644-4229
Sales 15,034,250
SIC 6712 Bank holding companies
Jean St-Gelais
Jacques Cotton
Pierrce Marc Bellavance

D-U-N-S 24-381-4431   (HQ)
CAPITALE IMMOBILIERE MFQ INC, LA
(*Suby of* CAPITALE MUTUELLE DE
L'ADMINISTRATION PUBLIQUE, LA)
625 Rue Jacques-Parizeau, Quebec, QC,
G1R 2G5
(418) 644-4267
Emp Here 12   *Sales* 23,038,895
SIC 6531 Real estate agents and managers
Jean St-Gelais
Pierre Marc Bellavance

D-U-N-S 24-942-3369   (HQ)
**CAPITALE MUTUELLE DE
L'ADMINISTRATION PUBLIQUE, LA**
625 Rue Jacques-Parizeau, Quebec, QC,
G1R 2G5
(418) 644-4229
Emp Here 11   *Sales* 1,458,736,674
SIC 6311 Life insurance
Jean St-Gelais
Jacques Cotton
Pierre Marc Bellavance
Dominique Dubuc
Francois Latreille
Richard Fiset
Danielle Chevrette
Alain Briere
Josee Germain
Hubert Bolduc

D-U-N-S 25-433-5771   (BR)
**CENTRE DE SANTE ET DE SERVICES SO-
CIAUX DE LA VIEILLE-CAPITALE**
55 Ch Sainte-Foy, Quebec, QC, G1R 1S9
(418) 641-2572
Emp Here 95
SIC 8011 Offices and clinics of medical doc-
tors
Gaetan Garon

D-U-N-S 24-045-4251   (BR)
**CENTRE HOSPITALIER UNIVERSITAIRE
DE QUEBEC**
CHUQ
(*Suby of* CENTRE HOSPITALIER UNIVERSI-
TAIRE DE QUEBEC)
11 Cote Du Palais Bureau 3431, Quebec, QC,
G1R 2J6
(418) 525-4444
Emp Here 400
SIC 8062 General medical and surgical hospi-
tals

D-U-N-S 25-356-7275   (HQ)
**CENTRE HOSPITALIER UNIVERSITAIRE
DE QUEBEC**

CHUQ
11 Cote Du Palais, Quebec, QC, G1R 2J6
(418) 525-4444
Emp Here 1,500   *Sales* 1,555,120,000
SIC 8062 General medical and surgical hospitals
Martin Beaumont
Lucie Grenier
Caroline Imbeault
Daniel La Roche
Stephane Tremblay
Maryse Turcotte
Brigitte Martel
Andre Garon
Marie-Frederique Fournier
Martine Lachance

D-U-N-S 20-294-1519   (BR)
CENTRE HOSPITALIER UNIVERSITAIRE DE QUEBEC
CHUQ PAVILLON HOTEL DIEU DE QUEBEC
(*Suby of* CENTRE HOSPITALIER UNIVERSITAIRE DE QUEBEC)
9 Rue Mcmahon, Quebec, QC, G1R 3S3
(418) 691-5281
Emp Here 300
SIC 8732 Commercial nonphysical research
Luc Belanger

D-U-N-S 20-290-9479   (HQ)
CHU DE QUEBEC - UNIVERSITE LAVAL
APR-CHU DE QUEBEC
11 Cote Du Palais, Quebec, QC, G1R 2J6
(418) 525-4444
Sales 2,755,107,000
SIC 8733 Noncommercial research organizations
Gertrude Bourdon
Gaston Bedard
Katia Boivin
Serge Genest
Maryse Laurendeau
Sophie Lefrancois
Patrice Montminy
Steven Ross
Jean Beaupre
Michel Bergeron

D-U-N-S 20-241-9909   (SL)
COGIRES INC
HOTEL CHATEAU LAURIER QUEBEC
1220 Place George-V O, Quebec, QC, G1R 5B8
(418) 522-3848
Emp Here 100   *Sales* 9,269,000
SIC 7011 Hotels and motels
Alain Girard
Guylaine Girard
Robert Girard
Chantal Girard
Michel Girard

D-U-N-S 25-002-5186   (SL)
COLLEGE FRANCOIS-DE-LAVAL
6 Rue De La Vieille-Universite Bureau 70, Quebec, QC, G1R 5X8
(418) 694-1020
Emp Here 100   *Sales* 9,282,600
SIC 8211 Elementary and secondary schools
Philippe Leclerc
Marc Ballaire

D-U-N-S 20-298-8239   (SL)
COMMISSION DE LA CAPITALE NATIONALE DU QUEBEC
CCNQ
525 Boul Rene-Levesque E Bureau Rc, Quebec, QC, G1R 5S9
(418) 528-0773
Emp Here 50   *Sales* 11,714,400
SIC 8743 Public relations services
Marie Claire Ouellet
Brigitte Vachon
Helene Corriveau
Juan Vargas
Etienne Talbot

Elisabeth Corneau

D-U-N-S 24-380-9881   (HQ)
DESJARDINS SECURITE FINANCIERE INVESTISSEMENTS INC
DESJARDINS FINANCIAL SECURITY INVESTMENTS
(*Suby of* FEDERATION DES CAISSES DESJARDINS DU QUEBEC)
1150 Rue De Claire-Fontaine, Quebec, QC, G1R 5G4
(877) 647-5435
Emp Here 6   *Sales* 26,029,143
SIC 6282 Investment advice
Andre Langlois
Francois Cholette
Andre Girard
Michael Rogers

D-U-N-S 25-258-6318   (BR)
ERNST & YOUNG LLP
(*Suby of* ERNST & YOUNG LLP)
90 Rue De Maisonneuve, Quebec, QC, G1R 2C3
(514) 875-6060
Emp Here 800
SIC 8721 Accounting, auditing, and bookkeeping
Roger Bou

D-U-N-S 24-335-7717   (BR)
FASKEN MARTINEAU DUMOULIN LLP
(*Suby of* FASKEN MARTINEAU DUMOULIN LLP)
140 Grande Allee E Bureau 800, Quebec, QC, G1R 5M8
(418) 640-2000
Emp Here 100
SIC 8111 Legal services
Guy Dion

D-U-N-S 25-359-4790   (BR)
FRONTENAC HOTEL GP INC
FAIRMONT LE CHATEAU FRONTENAC
(*Suby of* FRONTENAC HOTEL GP INC)
1 Rue Des Carrieres, Quebec, QC, G1R 5J5
(418) 692-3861
Emp Here 600
SIC 7011 Hotels and motels
Robert Mercure

D-U-N-S 20-642-0890   (BR)
GOUVERNEMENT DE LA PROVINCE DE QUEBEC
PROTECTEUR DU CITOYEN, LE
(*Suby of* GOUVERNEMENT DE LA PROVINCE DE QUEBEC)
525 Boul Rene-Levesque E Bureau 125, Quebec, QC, G1R 5Y4
(418) 643-2688
Emp Here 150
SIC 8111 Legal services
Raymonde Saint-Germain

D-U-N-S 20-332-9672   (BR)
GOUVERNEMENT DE LA PROVINCE DE QUEBEC
MUSEE NATIONAL DES BEAUX ARTS DU QUEBEC
(*Suby of* GOUVERNEMENT DE LA PROVINCE DE QUEBEC)
179 Rue Grande Allee O, Quebec, QC, G1R 2H1
(418) 643-2150
Emp Here 100
SIC 8412 Museums and art galleries
Line Ouellet

D-U-N-S 24-386-8358   (BR)
GOUVERNEMENT DE LA PROVINCE DE QUEBEC
CSPQ
(*Suby of* GOUVERNEMENT DE LA PROVINCE DE QUEBEC)
150 Boul Rene-Levesque E, Quebec, QC, G1R 2B2
(418) 646-4646
Emp Here 450

SIC 8742 Management consulting services
Claude Blais

D-U-N-S 25-335-3445   (BR)
GOUVERNEMENT DE LA PROVINCE DE QUEBEC
INSTITUT DE LA STATISTIQUE DE QUEBEC
(*Suby of* GOUVERNEMENT DE LA PROVINCE DE QUEBEC)
200 Ch Sainte-Foy 3e Etage Bureau 300, Quebec, QC, G1R 5T4
(418) 691-2401
Emp Here 250
SIC 2721 Periodicals
Stephane Mercier

D-U-N-S 24-813-9016   (HQ)
GROUPE LES MANOIRS DU QUEBEC INC, LES
MANOIR ST-SAUVEUR
44 Cote Du Palais, Quebec, QC, G1R 4H8
(418) 692-1030
Emp Here 15   *Sales* 18,538,000
SIC 7011 Hotels and motels
Diane Boutin
Sandra Varin

D-U-N-S 24-730-2854   (HQ)
GROUPE RESTOS PLAISIRS INC, LE
BISTRO DU BOUCHER
1225 Cours Du General-De Montcalm Bureau 419, Quebec, QC, G1R 4W6
(418) 694-9222
Emp Here 25   *Sales* 23,319,500
SIC 5812 Eating places
Pierre Moreau
Jacques Gauthier

D-U-N-S 25-983-7250   (HQ)
GROUPE SOMITEL INC
ABONNEMENT CANADA
1026 Rue Saint-Jean Bureau 400, Quebec, QC, G1R 1R7
(418) 692-5892
Emp Here 25   *Sales* 22,847,200
SIC 4899 Communication services, nec
Dominique Labrousse

D-U-N-S 25-405-7169   (HQ)
GROUPE VOYAGES QUEBEC INC
GROUPE VOYAGE SUD
(*Suby of* 3099-0907 QUEBEC INC)
174 Grande Allee O, Quebec, QC, G1R 2G9
(418) 525-4585
Emp Here 32   *Sales* 51,996,700
SIC 4725 Tour operators
Paul Plourde

D-U-N-S 20-776-8805   (BR)
HILTON CANADA CO.
HILTON
(*Suby of* HILTON WORLDWIDE HOLDING LLP)
1100 Boul Rene-Levesque E Bureau 1797, Quebec, QC, G1R 5V2
(418) 647-2411
Emp Here 350
SIC 7011 Hotels and motels
Dany Thebeaut

D-U-N-S 24-367-2206   (BR)
HOTEL PALACE ROYAL INC
775 Av Honore-Mercier, Quebec, QC, G1R 6A5
(418) 694-2000
Emp Here 90
SIC 7011 Hotels and motels
Jacques Robitialle

D-U-N-S 24-551-5858   (SL)
LA CAPITALE - COMPAGNIE D'ASSURANCE
525 Boul Rene-Levesque E, Quebec, QC, G1R 5S9
(418) 266-1700
Emp Here 48   *Sales* 27,836,352
SIC 6411 Insurance agents, brokers, and service

Jean-Yves Dupere

D-U-N-S 20-714-3699   (HQ)
LA CAPITALE SERVICES CONSEILS INC
LA CAPITALE ASSURANCE ET SERVICES FINANCIERS
625 Rue Jacques-Parizeau, Quebec, QC, G1R 2G5
(418) 747-7600
Emp Here 10   *Sales* 48,013,134
SIC 6311 Life insurance
Steven Ross
Monique L Begin
Pierre Marc Bellavance
Danielle Poire
Eli Pichelli
Guy Chouinard
Julie Levesque
Roland Guerin
Julie Faucher

D-U-N-S 20-537-3306   (SL)
LUSSIER DALE PARIZEAU INC
DALE PARIZEAU MORRIS MACKENZIE
900 Boul Rene-Levesque E Bureau 700, Quebec, QC, G1R 2B5
(418) 647-1111
Emp Here 40   *Sales* 33,922,400
SIC 6411 Insurance agents, brokers, and service
Solange Trepanier

D-U-N-S 20-722-1698   (HQ)
MAISON SIMONS INC, LA
DJAB
20 Cote De La Fabrique, Quebec, QC, G1R 3V9
(418) 692-3630
Emp Here 225   *Sales* 389,194,000
SIC 5651 Family clothing stores
Peter D. Simons
Richard J. Simons
James Haberlin

D-U-N-S 24-205-0110   (SL)
ORCHESTRE SYMPHONIQUE DE QUEBEC, L'
O S Q
437 Grande Allee E Bureau 250, Quebec, QC, G1R 2J5
(418) 643-8486
Emp Here 85   *Sales* 9,008,640
SIC 7929 Entertainers and entertainment groups
Michel Letourneau
Pierre Boucher

D-U-N-S 20-254-2627   (SL)
PLACE MONTCALM HOTEL INC
HOTEL LOEWS LE CONCORDE
(*Suby of* LOEWS CORPORATION)
1225 Cours Du General-De Montcalm, Quebec, QC, G1R 4W6
(418) 647-2222
Emp Here 250   *Sales* 23,917,000
SIC 7011 Hotels and motels
Jonathan M Tisch
Paul W Whetsell

D-U-N-S 24-820-6302   (SL)
RESSOURCES ROBEX INC
437 Grande Allee E Bureau 100, Quebec, QC, G1R 2J5
(581) 741-7421
Emp Here 9   *Sales* 44,777,622
SIC 1081 Metal mining services
Georges Cohen
Benjamin Cohen
Augustin Rousselet
Richard Faucher
Christian Marti
Claude Goulet
Michel Doyon
Julien Cohen
Simon Boudreau

D-U-N-S 20-242-9981   (SL)
RESTAURANT CONTINENTAL INC

26 Rue Saint-Louis, Quebec, QC, G1R 3Y9
(418) 694-9995
Emp Here 75   *Sales* 3,413,925
SIC 5812 Eating places
  Mathieu Pettigrew
  Sylvain Pageauv
  Nicolas Rousseau

D-U-N-S 20-649-0224   (BR)
SOBEYS CAPITAL INCORPORATED
IGA
(*Suby of* EMPIRE COMPANY LIMITED)
255 Ch Sainte-Foy, Quebec, QC, G1R 1T5
(418) 524-9890
Emp Here 85
SIC 5411 Grocery stores
  Sandra Deschaine

D-U-N-S 24-530-9976   (SL)
SOCIETE DE GESTION CAP-AUX-PIERRES INC
HOTEL CLARENDON
(*Suby of* GROUPE DUFOUR INC)
57 Rue Sainte-Anne, Quebec, QC, G1R 3X4
(418) 692-2480
Emp Here 100   *Sales* 9,269,000
SIC 7011 Hotels and motels
  Robert Pilleniere
  Jean-Francois Duclos

D-U-N-S 20-574-5826   (BR)
SOCIETE DU CENTRE DES CONGRES DE QUEBEC
CENTRE DES CONGRES DE QUEBEC
(*Suby of* SOCIETE DU CENTRE DES CONGRES DE QUEBEC)
1000 Boul Rene-Levesque E, Quebec, QC, G1R 5T8
(418) 644-4000
Emp Here 75
SIC 7389 Business services, nec
  Pierre-Michel Bouchard

D-U-N-S 25-122-8235   (SL)
SOCIETE DU GRAND THEATRE DE QUEBEC, LA
269 Boul Rene-Levesque E, Quebec, QC, G1R 2B3
(418) 643-8111
Emp Here 200   *Sales* 21,196,800
SIC 7922 Theatrical producers and services
  Nathalie Belanger

D-U-N-S 24-075-1060   (BR)
SOCIETE PARC-AUTO DU QUEBEC
SPAQ
965 Place D'Youville, Quebec, QC, G1R 3P1
(418) 694-9662
Emp Here 220
SIC 7521 Automobile parking
  Andr Grondines

D-U-N-S 24-499-6989   (HQ)
SOCIETE QUEBECOISE DES INFRAS-TRUCTURES
(*Suby of* GOUVERNEMENT DE LA PROVINCE DE QUEBEC)
1075 Rue De L'Amerique-Francaise, Quebec, QC, G1R 5P8
(418) 646-1766
Emp Here 344   *Sales* 270,451,200
SIC 6531 Real estate agents and managers
  Luc Meunier
  Jonatan Julien
  Eric Thibault
  Daniel Primeau
  Pierre Babineau
  Claude Dube
  Daniel Archambault

D-U-N-S 24-842-8096   (SL)
TALBOT, JOHANNE PHARMACIENNE
PHARMACIE JEAN COUTU
110 Boul Rene-Levesque O Bureau 118, Quebec, QC, G1R 2A5
(418) 522-1235
Emp Here 42   *Sales* 10,624,068

SIC 5912 Drug stores and proprietary stores
  Carine Turcotte

Quebec, QC G1S

D-U-N-S 24-908-0813   (SL)
ALIMENTATION RAYMOND ROUSSEAU INC
ALIMENTATION IGA
1580 Ch Saint-Louis, Quebec, QC, G1S 1G6
(418) 527-7758
Emp Here 50   *Sales* 13,707,600
SIC 5411 Grocery stores
  Raymond Rousseau

D-U-N-S 25-244-5473   (HQ)
ARCHEVEQUE CATHOLIQUE ROMAIN DE QUEBEC, L'
CAMPAGNE MAJEURE 2014-2019
1073 Boul Rene-Levesque O, Quebec, QC, G1S 4R5
(418) 688-1211
Emp Here 150   *Sales* 16,867,926
SIC 8661 Religious organizations
  Gerald Cyprien Lacroix
  Jean Tailleur
  Claude Laliberte
  Alain Pouliot
  Gaetan Proulx
  Denis Grondin

D-U-N-S 20-872-1910   (SL)
ASSOCIATION YWCA DE QUEBEC, L'
Y.W.C.A QUEBEC
855 Av Holland, Quebec, QC, G1S 3S5
(418) 683-2155
Emp Here 60   *Sales* 42,552,720
SIC 8699 Membership organizations, nec
  Ginette Defoy

D-U-N-S 20-519-5360   (SL)
ASSURANCES ETERNA INC
SERVICES FINANCIERS ETERNA
1134 Grande Allee O Bureau 400, Quebec, QC, G1S 1E5
(418) 266-1000
Emp Here 25   *Sales* 16,973,075
SIC 6282 Investment advice
  Paul Tardif

D-U-N-S 25-016-0397   (SL)
COLLEGE D'ENSEIGNEMENT GENERAL ET PROFESSIONEL FRANCOIS-XAVIER-GARNEAU
CEGEP FRANCOIS-XAVIER-GARNEAU
1640 Boul De L'Entente, Quebec, QC, G1S 4S7
(418) 688-8310
Emp Here 100   *Sales* 11,263,600
SIC 8222 Junior colleges
  Yves Blouin

D-U-N-S 25-240-1666   (SL)
COLLEGE MERICI
755 Grande Allee O Bureau 683, Quebec, QC, G1S 1C1
(418) 683-1591
Emp Here 170   *Sales* 25,396,470
SIC 8221 Colleges and universities
  Jacques Desbois
  Pierre Marc Bellavance
  Johanne Decoste
  Nicole Bilodeau
  Pierre Jolin
  Patrick Lemieux
  Marguerite Chenard
  Cecile Cantin
  Jacques Desbois
  Jacques Plamondon

D-U-N-S 25-767-1222   (SL)
COLLEGE SAINT-CHARLES-GARNIER, LE
SALLE JEAN-PAUL TARDIF
1150 Boul Rene-Levesque O, Quebec, QC,

G1S 1V7
(418) 681-0107
Emp Here 100   *Sales* 11,263,600
SIC 8221 Colleges and universities
  Henriette Dumont
  Jean-Paul Rouleau
  Claude Robert
  Fabien Gabillet
  Patrice Royer
  David Cloute Cote
  Claude Letarte
  Mario Gagnon
  Francine Giguere
  Jean Robitaille

D-U-N-S 25-298-8464   (BR)
COMMISSION SCOLAIRE DE LA CAPI-TALE, LA
ECOLE ANNE HEBERT
555 Ch Sainte-Foy, Quebec, QC, G1S 2J9
(418) 686-4040
Emp Here 80
SIC 8211 Elementary and secondary schools
  Annie Gosselin

D-U-N-S 20-704-8708   (BR)
COMMISSION SCOLAIRE DES DECOU-VREURS
ECOLE SAINT MICHEL SECTEUR AUTISME
(*Suby of* COMMISSION SCOLAIRE DES DE-COUVREURS)
1255 Av Du Chanoine-Morel, Quebec, QC, G1S 4B1
(418) 684-0064
Emp Here 90
SIC 8211 Elementary and secondary schools
  Nicole Mailloux

D-U-N-S 20-273-3825   (SL)
CORPORATION NOTRE-DAME DE BON-SECOURS, LA
CHANMPENOISE, LA
990 Rue Gerard-Morisset, Quebec, QC, G1S 1X6
(418) 681-4637
Emp Here 75   *Sales* 4,443,525
SIC 8361 Residential care
  Georges Smith
  Sylvain Cote
  Christian Auger
  Aubert Belzile
  Carol Dacres
  Louise Montreuil
  Steve Gilbert
  Sylvain Gagnon

D-U-N-S 24-821-4546   (SL)
COTE TASCHEREAU SAMSON DEMERS S.E.N.C.R.L
CTSD
871 Grande Allee O Bureau 100, Quebec, QC, G1S 2L1
(418) 688-9375
Emp Here 30   *Sales* 13,476,570
SIC 7389 Business services, nec
  Claude Robitaille
  Louis-Phillip Baillargeon
  Nicole Morneau
  Claude Samson
  Francois Rainville
  Doris Couture
  Denis Duguay
  Christine Gagnon
  Louis Martel

D-U-N-S 24-592-6696   (BR)
DELOITTE RESTRUCTURING INC
DELOITTE
(*Suby of* DELOITTE LLP)
925 Grande Allee O Bureau 400, Quebec, QC, G1S 4Z4
(418) 624-3333
Emp Here 150
SIC 8721 Accounting, auditing, and book-keeping
  Gilles Cossette

D-U-N-S 24-759-0615   (HQ)
GROUPE GERMAIN INC
HOTEL LE GERMAIN
1200 Rue Des Soeurs-Du-Bon-Pasteur Bureau 500, Quebec, QC, G1S 0B1
(418) 687-1123
Emp Here 40   *Sales* 12,436,840
SIC 7011 Hotels and motels
  Jean-Yves Germain
  Christiane Germain
  Claude Choquette
  Henrick Simard
  Anne Darche
  Michel Cyr

D-U-N-S 25-776-3920   (SL)
HOPITAL DU ST-SACREMENT DU CENTRE HOSPITALIER AFFILIE UQ
C H A
(*Suby of* CENTRE HOSPITALIER UNIVERSI-TAIRE DE QUEBEC)
1050 Ch Sainte-Foy, Quebec, QC, G1S 4L8
(418) 682-7511
Emp Here 200   *Sales* 22,216,000
SIC 8062 General medical and surgical hospi-tals
  Marie Girard
  Pierre Halle

D-U-N-S 24-884-1660   (HQ)
INDUSTRIELLE ALLIANCE, ASSURANCE AUTO ET HABITATION INC
IA AUTO AND HOME INSURANCE
(*Suby of* INDUSTRIELLE ALLIANCE, AS-SURANCE ET SERVICES FINANCIERS INC)
925 Grande Allee O Bureau 230, Quebec, QC, G1S 1C1
(418) 650-4600
Sales 812,047,840
SIC 6331 Fire, marine, and casualty insurance
  Michel Laurin
  Karine Hebert
  Normand Pepin
  Yvon Charest
  Yvon Trepanie
  Francois Giroux
  Gilles Bernier
  Michel Bougie
  Edmee Metivier
  Andre Pouliot

D-U-N-S 24-637-9895   (HQ)
INDUSTRIELLE ALLIANCE, ASSURANCE ET SERVICES FINANCIERS INC
FINANCE SAL
1080 Grande Allee O, Quebec, QC, G1S 1C7
(418) 684-5000
Emp Here 700   *Sales* 5,950,342,598
SIC 6311 Life insurance
  Denis Ricard
  Jennifer Dibblee
  Mary C. Ritchie
  Robert Coallier
  Claude Lamoureux
  Jacques Martin
  Danielle Morin
  Michael Sean Hanley
  Agathe Cote
  Louis Tetu

D-U-N-S 24-383-6207   (BR)
INDUSTRIELLE ALLIANCE, ASSURANCE ET SERVICES FINANCIERS INC
(*Suby of* INDUSTRIELLE ALLIANCE, AS-SURANCE ET SERVICES FINANCIERS INC)
925 Grande Allee O Bureau 200, Quebec, QC, G1S 4Z4
(418) 686-7738
Emp Here 500
SIC 6411 Insurance agents, brokers, and ser-vice
  Bruno Turcotte

D-U-N-S 24-821-6426   (HQ)
JOLI-COEUR LACASSE S.E.N.C.R.L
JOLICOEUR LACASSE AVOCATS
1134 Grande Allee O Bureau 600, Quebec,

QC, G1S 1E5
(418) 681-7007
Sales 36,028,300
SIC 8111 Legal services
Pierre Bolduc
Marie-Jose Cote
Francois Barbeau
Jean Beaupre
Jacques Cantin

D-U-N-S 25-835-5056   (SL)
PAVILLON SAINT-DOMINIQUE
1045 Boul Rene-Levesque O, Quebec, QC, G1S 1V3
(418) 681-3561
Emp Here 115   *Sales* 8,831,080
SIC 8322 Individual and family services
Marie Line Curadeau

D-U-N-S 24-346-3499   (BR)
RESIDENCE COTE JARDINS INC
880 Av Painchaud, Quebec, QC, G1S 0A3
(418) 688-1221
Emp Here 100
SIC 8361 Residential care
Jean Dostert

D-U-N-S 25-658-3605   (BR)
RESIDENCE LE GIBRALTAR INC
(*Suby of* RESIDENCE LE GIBRALTAR INC)
1300 Ch Sainte-Foy Bureau 610, Quebec, QC, G1S 0A6
(418) 681-2777
Emp Here 75
SIC 8361 Residential care
Claude Boulianne

D-U-N-S 24-900-6321   (SL)
SAINT BRIGID'S HOME INC
1645 Ch Saint-Louis, Quebec, QC, G1S 4M3
(418) 681-4687
Emp Here 200   *Sales* 12,856,400
SIC 8361 Residential care
Louis Hanrahan

Quebec, QC G1T

D-U-N-S 24-316-1820   (HQ)
CAISSE DESJARDINS DE SILLERY–SAINT-LOUIS-DE-FRANCE
CENTRE DE SERVICE FINANCIER AUX ENTREPRISES CAISSES DESJARDINS DES HAUTES-MAREES
1444 Av Maguire, Quebec, QC, G1T 1Z3
(418) 681-3566
Emp Here 60   *Sales* 14,152,367
SIC 6062 State credit unions
Kathleen Bilodeau
Louis Roy
Nicole Bilodeau
Celine Plante
Patricia Blanchet Maheux
Renaud Gilbert
Jean-Claude Gagnon
Gilles Jobin
Viateur Laplante
Cecile Larouche

D-U-N-S 25-002-1458   (SL)
COLLEGE JESUS MARIE DE SILLERY
(*Suby of* RELIGIEUSES DE JESUS-MARIE, LES)
2047 Ch Saint-Louis, Quebec, QC, G1T 1P3
(418) 687-9250
Emp Here 140   *Sales* 13,876,660
SIC 8211 Elementary and secondary schools
Marc Choquette
Julie Pelletier
Dorval Genevieves
Claude Beaumont

D-U-N-S 25-785-1733   (SL)
ENTREPRISES PIERRE PICARD INC, LES
1350 Av Maguire Bureau 103, Quebec, QC,

G1T 1Z3
(418) 683-4492
Emp Here 75   *Sales* 3,015,675
SIC 7349 Building maintenance services, nec
Pierre Picard

D-U-N-S 25-785-3275   (SL)
PRODUCTIONS ARCHY'S INC, LES
ANIMATIONS ARCHY
1457 Av Oak, Quebec, QC, G1T 1Z5
(418) 688-3553
Emp Here 36   *Sales* 15,965,640
SIC 7389 Business services, nec
Elyse Bastarache

D-U-N-S 24-730-5766   (HQ)
RELIGIEUSES DE JESUS-MARIE, LES
LES RELIGIEUSES DE JESUS-MARIE RESIDENCE SOUS-LES-BOIS
2049 Ch Saint-Louis, Quebec, QC, G1T 1P2
(418) 687-9260
Sales 11,453,530
SIC 8661 Religious organizations
Celine Poulin
Lorraine Maheu
Celine Latulippe

D-U-N-S 20-340-0747   (BR)
ROYAL & SUN ALLIANCE INSURANCE COMPANY OF CANADA
RSA
(*Suby of* RSA INSURANCE GROUP PLC)
2475 Boul Laurier, Quebec, QC, G1T 1C4
(418) 622-2040
Emp Here 200
SIC 6411 Insurance agents, brokers, and service
Nathalie Cloutier

D-U-N-S 20-400-3615   (SL)
TERREAU BIOGAS, LIMITED PARTNERSHIP
1327 Av Maguire Bureau 100, Quebec, QC, G1T 1Z2
(418) 476-1686
Emp Here 6   *Sales* 18,635,142
SIC 4922 Natural gas transmission
Rino Dumont

Quebec, QC G1V

D-U-N-S 25-665-7222   (SL)
3089-3242 QUEBEC INC
HOTEL PLAZA
3031 Boul Laurier, Quebec, QC, G1V 2M2
(418) 658-2727
Emp Here 100   *Sales* 9,489,900
SIC 7011 Hotels and motels
Jacques Robitaille

D-U-N-S 20-174-9939   (HQ)
9023-4436 QUEBEC INC
ATMOSPHERE
(*Suby of* 9023-4451 QUEBEC INC)
2700 Boul Laurier, Quebec, QC, G1V 2L8
(418) 658-1820
Sales 15,148,336
SIC 5941 Sporting goods and bicycle shops
Martin Boucher

D-U-N-S 25-400-9509   (HQ)
9023-4451 QUEBEC INC
GROUPE BOUCHER SPORT
2700 Boul Laurier Unite 3000, Quebec, QC, G1V 2L8
(418) 658-1820
Sales 219,305,400
SIC 6712 Bank holding companies
Martin Boucher

D-U-N-S 24-630-4930   (HQ)
9130-1093 QUEBEC INC
CARREFOUR SAINT-GEORGES
(*Suby of* FONDS DE PLACEMENT IMMOBILIER COMINAR)

2820 Boul Laurier Bureau 850, Quebec, QC, G1V 0C1
(418) 681-8151
Emp Here 26   *Sales* 44,174,200
SIC 6512 Nonresidential building operators
Michel Dallaire
Manon Deslauriers

D-U-N-S 25-474-0442   (SL)
ALIMENTATION MARIE GIGNAC INC
METRO PLACE SAINTE-FOY
2450 Boul Laurier Bureau 418, Quebec, QC, G1V 2L1
(418) 651-8150
Emp Here 45   *Sales* 12,336,840
SIC 5411 Grocery stores
Marie Gignac

D-U-N-S 20-590-8221   (SL)
ALIMENTATION THOMASSIN, STEPHANE INC
PROVIGO THOMASSIN, STEPHANE
815 Av Myrand, Quebec, QC, G1V 2V7
(418) 683-1981
Emp Here 49   *Sales* 13,433,448
SIC 5411 Grocery stores
Stephane Thomassin

D-U-N-S 25-542-7239   (BR)
AON HEWITT INC
GROUPE CONSEIL AON
(*Suby of* AON PLC)
2600 Boul Laurier Bureau 750, Quebec, QC, G1V 4W2
(418) 650-1119
Emp Here 85
SIC 8999 Services, nec
Claude Plamondon

D-U-N-S 20-029-9753   (BR)
ASSOCIATION DES ETUDIANTS DU COLLEGE REGIONAL CHAMPLAIN L'
CEGEP CHAMPLAIN ST LAWRENCE
790 Av Neree-Tremblay, Quebec, QC, G1V 4K2
(418) 656-6921
Emp Here 110
SIC 8211 Elementary and secondary schools
Edward Edouard

D-U-N-S 20-777-9638   (BR)
AXA ASSURANCES INC
(*Suby of* AXA ASSURANCES INC)
2640 Boul Laurier Bureau 900, Quebec, QC, G1V 5C2

Emp Here 150
SIC 6311 Life insurance

D-U-N-S 20-936-4145   (SL)
BEAUGARTE (QUEBEC INC)
2590 Boul Laurier Unite 150, Quebec, QC, G1V 4M6

Emp Here 100   *Sales* 4,551,900
SIC 5812 Eating places
Jean-Pierre Goulet

D-U-N-S 25-846-7919   (SL)
BEAUGARTE (QUEBEC) INC
2600 Boul Laurier, Quebec, QC, G1V 4W1

Emp Here 85   *Sales* 3,869,115
SIC 5812 Eating places
Jean-Pierre Goulet

D-U-N-S 25-331-3415   (BR)
BOIS DAAQUAM INC
(*Suby of* GROUPE LEBEL INC)
2590 Boul Laurier Bureau 740, Quebec, QC, G1V 4M6

Emp Here 250
SIC 2421 Sawmills and planing mills, general
Francois Seguin

D-U-N-S 25-256-7870   (SL)
BOIS INDIFOR INC, LES
2590 Boul Laurier Bureau 1040, Quebec, QC,

G1V 4M6
(418) 877-2294
Emp Here 6   *Sales* 35,296,906
SIC 5031 Lumber, plywood, and millwork
Yves Careau
Carmin Hamel

D-U-N-S 20-867-5020   (BR)
CAPITALE GESTION FINANCIERE INC, LA
CAPITALE, LA
650-2875 Boul Laurier, Quebec, QC, G1V 5B1
(418) 644-0038
Emp Here 300   *Sales* 1,108,209
SIC 6411 Insurance agents, brokers, and service
Mario Cusson

D-U-N-S 20-189-8132   (SL)
CARTES, TIMBRES ET MONNAIE STE-FOY INC
CARTES, TIMBRES & MONNAIES STE-FOY
(*Suby of* GESTION BENDOY INC)
2740 Boul Laurier, Quebec, QC, G1V 4P7
(418) 658-5639
Emp Here 26   *Sales* 11,679,694
SIC 7389 Business services, nec
Benoit Doyon
Mireille Bergeron
Dave Doyon
Anthony Doyon

D-U-N-S 24-329-8572   (SL)
CENTRE DE RECHERCHE EN INFECTIOLOGIE (CRI)
2705 Boul Laurier Bureau Rc 709, Quebec, QC, G1V 4G2
(418) 654-2705
Emp Here 49   *Sales* 10,407,453
SIC 8748 Business consulting, nec
Michel G. Bergeron

D-U-N-S 25-762-9808   (SL)
CENTRE DE REFERENCE EN AGRICULTURE ET AGROALIMENTAIRE DU QUEBEC
CRAAQ
2875 Boul Laurier Unite 900, Quebec, QC, G1V 5B1
(418) 523-5411
Emp Here 30   *Sales* 11,922,420
SIC 8699 Membership organizations, nec
Brigitte Dumont

D-U-N-S 20-386-7119   (BR)
CENTRE HOSPITALIER UNIVERSITAIRE DE QUEBEC
CENTRE HOSPITALIER UNIVERSITAIRE DE QUEBEC
(*Suby of* CENTRE HOSPITALIER UNIVERSITAIRE DE QUEBEC)
2705 Boul Laurier Bureau 2211, Quebec, QC, G1V 4G2
(418) 525-4444
Emp Here 100
SIC 8062 General medical and surgical hospitals

D-U-N-S 20-387-6073   (HQ)
COMINAR CONSTRUCTION S.E.C.
2820 Boul Laurier Bureau 850, Quebec, QC, G1V 0C1
(418) 681-8151
Sales 57,033,800
SIC 1542 Nonresidential construction, nec
Alban D'amours

D-U-N-S 20-955-5689   (HQ)
COMMISSION SCOLAIRE DES DECOUVREURS
945 Av Wolfe Bureau 100, Quebec, QC, G1V 4E2
(418) 652-2121
Emp Here 100   *Sales* 247,797,500
SIC 8211 Elementary and secondary schools
Alain Fortier

D-U-N-S 20-712-0416   (BR)
COMMISSION SCOLAIRE DES DECOUVREURS

CENTRE DE FORMATION PROFESSION-NELLE MARIE ROLLET
(*Suby of* COMMISSION SCOLAIRE DES DE-COUVREURS)
3000 Boul Hochelaga, Quebec, QC, G1V 3Y4
(418) 652-2159
Emp Here 90
SIC 8211 Elementary and secondary schools
 Normand Lacasse

D-U-N-S 20-544-9460   (BR)
COMPAGNIE DE TELEPHONE BELL DU CANADA OU BELL CANADA, LA
(*Suby of* BCE INC)
2715 Boul Du Versant-Nord, Quebec, QC, G1V 1A3
(418) 691-1080
Emp Here 85
SIC 4899 Communication services, nec
 Odette Caroline Bosse

D-U-N-S 24-309-5093   (HQ)
COOPERATIVE DE L'UNIVERSITE LAVAL
COOP DU CEGEP DE LIMOILOU
2305 Rue De L'Universite Bureau 1100, Quebec, QC, G1V 0B4
(418) 656-2600
Emp Here 250   *Sales* 164,479,050
SIC 6712 Bank holding companies
 Christian Djoko Kamgain
 Laurent Aubin
 Delphine Talamona
 Jean-Francois Forgues
 Bernard Garnier
 Paul Michaud
 Elizabeth Coulombe
 Francois Godbout
 Yan Cimon
 Simon Laberge

D-U-N-S 24-539-2803   (SL)
COOPSCO SAINTE-FOY
COLLEGE D'ENSEIGNEMENT GENERAL ET PROFESSIONNEL DE SAINTE-FOY
2410 Ch Sainte-Foy, Quebec, QC, G1V 1T3
(418) 659-6600
Emp Here 50   *Sales* 10,880,650
SIC 5942 Book stores
 Marie-Elyse Desjardins
 Myriam Arseneault
 Sabrina Harvey
 Francois Drouin
 Carol Arseneault
 Audrey Tardif
 Charles Doucet
 Florence Claveau-Roy
 Guillaume Morin
 Danny Dubois

D-U-N-S 24-707-0550   (SL)
CORPORATION DE LA SALLE ALBERT-ROUSSEAU, LA
SALLE ALBERT-ROUSSEAU
2410 Ch Sainte-Foy, Quebec, QC, G1V 1T3
(418) 659-6629
Emp Here 150   *Sales* 33,130,650
SIC 6512 Nonresidential building operators
 Carl Laflamme
 Alain Brochier
 Sylvie Robitaille

D-U-N-S 20-692-9759   (HQ)
CORPORATION EPIDERMA INC
EPIDERMA
2590 Boul Laurier Bureau 330, Quebec, QC, G1V 4M6
(418) 651-8678
Sales 12,557,440
SIC 7231 Beauty shops
 Pierre Montminy
 Christine Vezina
 Carl Tremblay
 Jean Lavigueur
 Eve-Lyne Biron
 Philippe Huneault
 Lise Lapierre

D-U-N-S 20-778-4158   (HQ)
DALCON INC
DALCON CONSTRUCTION
2820 Boul Laurier Bureau 1050, Quebec, QC, G1V 0C1
(418) 781-6300
Emp Here 50   *Sales* 349,196,000
SIC 1542 Nonresidential construction, nec
 Michel Dallaire
 Michel Paquet

D-U-N-S 25-285-9384   (SL)
DALLAIRE FOREST KIROUAC, COMPT-ABLES PROFESSIONNELS AGRES, S.E.N.C.R.L.
1175 Av Lavigerie Bureau 580, Quebec, QC, G1V 4P1
(418) 650-2266
Emp Here 50   *Sales* 10,454,250
SIC 8721 Accounting, auditing, and book-keeping
 Michel Dallaire
 Yvon Dolbec
 Sylvie Belliveau
 Sophie Rochefort
 Josee Olivery

D-U-N-S 24-313-8844   (HQ)
ENDOCEUTICS INC
CLINIQUE DE RECHERCHE DES TRAITE-MENTS HORMONAUX
(*Suby of* ENDORECHERCHE INC)
2795 Boul Laurier Bureau 500, Quebec, QC, G1V 4M7
(418) 653-0033
Sales 34,463,100
SIC 8731 Commercial physical research
 Dennis Turpin
 Claude Labrie
 Celine Martel

D-U-N-S 20-716-5817   (HQ)
EPIDERMA QUEBEC INC
(*Suby of* CORPORATION EPIDERMA INC)
2590 Boul Laurier Bureau 330, Quebec, QC, G1V 4M6
(418) 266-2027
Emp Here 43   *Sales* 13,347,750
SIC 7231 Beauty shops
 Pierre Montminy

D-U-N-S 24-945-9546   (BR)
ERNST & YOUNG LLP
(*Suby of* ERNST & YOUNG LLP)
2875 Boul Laurier Unite 410, Quebec, QC, G1V 0C7
(418) 524-5151
Emp Here 100
SIC 8721 Accounting, auditing, and book-keeping
 Maurice Tremblay

D-U-N-S 25-148-0620   (HQ)
FONDS DE PLACEMENT IMMOBILIER COMINAR
CARREFOUR CHAREST
2820 Boul Laurier Bureau 850, Quebec, QC, G1V 0C1
(418) 681-8151
Emp Here 5   *Sales* 556,939,634
SIC 6799 Investors, nec
 Sylvain Cossette
 Alain Dallaire
 Heather C. Kirk
 Marie-Andree Boutin
 Wally Commisso
 Jean Laramee
 Michael Racine
 Richard Fortin
 Caroline Lacroix
 Johanne Leclerc

D-U-N-S 24-689-6955   (BR)
FUJITSU CONSEIL (CANADA) INC
DMR
(*Suby of* FUJITSU CONSULTING (CANADA) HOLDINGS, INC.)

2960 Boul Laurier Bureau 400, Quebec, QC, G1V 4S1
Emp Here 600
SIC 7379 Computer related services, nec

D-U-N-S 20-567-4836   (SL)
GESTION FRP INC
FRP CONSULTING GROUP
2960 Boul Laurier Bureau 214, Quebec, QC, G1V 4S1
(418) 652-1737
Emp Here 50   *Sales* 11,895,050
SIC 8742 Management consulting services
 Patrick Rivard
 Hugo Prive
 Catherine Prive

D-U-N-S 25-172-7475   (SL)
GESTION LEGALIS INC
1195 Av Lavigerie Bureau 200, Quebec, QC, G1V 4N3
(418) 658-9966
Emp Here 49   *Sales* 50,709,169
SIC 6311 Life insurance
 Suzanne Fortin

D-U-N-S 25-168-8057   (SL)
GESTION VINNY INC
MCDONALD'S
2950 Boul Laurier, Quebec, QC, G1V 2M4
(418) 659-4484
Emp Here 100   *Sales* 4,551,900
SIC 5812 Eating places
 Richard Berube

D-U-N-S 20-648-1756   (SL)
GROUPE AUTO STE-FOY INC
STE-FOY TOYOTA
2777 Boul Du Versant-Nord, Quebec, QC, G1V 1A4
(418) 658-1340
Emp Here 100   *Sales* 62,928,000
SIC 5511 New and used car dealers
 Jacques Saillant
 Charles Saillant
 Alexandre Saillant

D-U-N-S 20-704-8641   (SL)
GROUPE CONSEIL DFM INC, LE
1175 Av Lavigerie Bureau 580, Quebec, QC, G1V 4P1
(418) 650-2266
Emp Here 49   *Sales* 20,548,395
SIC 6712 Bank holding companies
 Michel Dallaire

D-U-N-S 20-277-7488   (BR)
GROUPE FACILITE INFORMATIQUE (GFI) INC
(*Suby of* 3330559 CANADA INC)
1100-2875 Boul Laurier, Quebec, QC, G1V 5B1
(418) 780-3950
Emp Here 90
SIC 7371 Custom computer programming services

D-U-N-S 24-169-4277   (HQ)
GROUPE LE MASSIF INC
SENS LE MASSIF DE CHARLEVOIX MAGAZINE
2505 Boul Laurier Bureau 200, Quebec, QC, G1V 2L2
(418) 948-1725
Sales 10,150,284
SIC 8741 Management services
 Daniel Gauthier
 Claude Choquette
 Jean Leclerc
 Claude Desjardins
 Dominique Brown
 Dany Renauld
 Christiane Germain
 Jean-Paul L'allier
 Michel Audet
 Diane Lanctot

D-U-N-S 20-785-0884   (SL)
GROUPE MDMP INC
2960 Boul Laurier Bureau 380, Quebec, QC, G1V 4S1
(418) 657-4444
Emp Here 15   *Sales* 12,533,655
SIC 5146 Fish and seafoods
 Jean-Marc Marcoux
 Richard Desbois
 Nicol Desbois
 Douglas Mcinnis
 Roger Pinel

D-U-N-S 24-758-5862   (BR)
HEMA-QUEBEC
(*Suby of* HEMA-QUEBEC)
1070 Av Des Sciences-De-La-Vie, Quebec, QC, G1V 5C3
(418) 780-4362
Emp Here 414
SIC 8099 Health and allied services, nec

D-U-N-S 25-318-4675   (BR)
HOLT, RENFREW & CIE, LIMITEE
HOLT RENFREW CANADA
2452 Boul Laurier, Quebec, QC, G1V 2L1
(514) 842-5111
Emp Here 106
SIC 5611 Men's and boys' clothing stores
 Carl Desruisseaux

D-U-N-S 25-991-8761   (HQ)
INSTITUT NATIONALE DE SANTE PUBLIQUE DU QUEBEC
CENTRE DE TOXICOLOGIE DU QUEBEC
945 Av Wolfe Bureau 4, Quebec, QC, G1V 5B3
(418) 650-5115
Emp Here 150   *Sales* 91,901,600
SIC 8731 Commercial physical research
 Luc Boileau
 Jean-Louis Coulombe

D-U-N-S 20-522-1570   (SL)
INTER-GROUPE ASSURANCES INC
1175 Av Lavigerie Bureau 475, Quebec, QC, G1V 4P1
(418) 682-5666
Emp Here 30   *Sales* 17,397,720
SIC 6411 Insurance agents, brokers, and service
 Bernard Laporte
 Sylvain Racine
 Christian Foisy

D-U-N-S 24-148-0961   (HQ)
IQ SOQUIA INC
SOCIETE QUEBECOISE D'INITIATIVES AGRO-ALIMENTAIRES
(*Suby of* INVESTISSEMENT QUEBEC)
1195 Av Lavigerie Bureau 060, Quebec, QC, G1V 4N3
(418) 643-5172
Emp Here 90
SIC 6719 Holding companies, nec
 Andre Petitclerc
 Marc Paquet
 Christian Settano

D-U-N-S 24-148-6059   (HQ)
LABORATOIRE POULIOT INC
POULIOT - ORTHESE - CHAUSSURE
2815 Ch Des Quatre-Bourgeois, Quebec, QC, G1V 1X8
(418) 652-0100
Emp Here 26   *Sales* 10,261,776
SIC 5999 Miscellaneous retail stores, nec
 Helene Bisson
 Marc-Andre Bisson
 Jean Bertin Gingras
 Jean-Claude Grondin
 Serge Olivier

D-U-N-S 20-309-0899   (SL)
LANGLOIS AVOCATS S.E.N.C.R.L.
LANGLOIS GAUDREAU O'CONNOR
2820 Boul Laurier Bureau 1300, Quebec, QC, G1V 0C1

▲ Public Company   ■ Public Company Family Member   **HQ** Headquarters   **BR** Branch   **SL** Single Location

(418) 650-7000
Emp Here 435   *Sales* 89,556,060
SIC 8111 Legal services
Gerry Apostolatos
Bernard Cliche
Rene Paquette
Jean Gregoire
Valerie Lemaire
Francois Vallieres
Louise Boutin
Hubert Camirand
Pierre Galardo
Chantal Chatelain

D-U-N-S 25-526-8419   (SL)
LE PUB UNIVERSITAIRE INC
LE PUB
2325 Rue De L'Universite Bureau 1312, Quebec, QC, G1V 0B3
(418) 656-7075
Emp Here 80   *Sales* 3,641,520
SIC 5812 Eating places
Thomas Pouliot

D-U-N-S 20-853-4995   (SL)
LIQUOR STORE CABARET
2600 Boul Laurier Bureau 180, Quebec, QC, G1V 4T3

Emp Here 49   *Sales* 14,657,370
SIC 5921 Liquor stores
Alain Marceau

D-U-N-S 25-767-4648   (BR)
MAISONS LAPRISE INC
(*Suby of* MAISONS LAPRISE INC)
2700 Boul Laurier Unite 2540, Quebec, QC, G1V 2L8
(418) 683-3343
Emp Here 200
SIC 2452 Prefabricated wood buildings
Daniel Laprise

D-U-N-S 24-379-6174   (SL)
MALENFANT DALLAIRE, S.E.N.C.R.L.
2600 Boul Laurier Bureau 872, Quebec, QC, G1V 4W2
(418) 654-0636
Emp Here 50   *Sales* 10,454,250
SIC 8721 Accounting, auditing, and bookkeeping
Claude Dontigny
Frederic Pouliot
Julie Perreault
Nathalie Robitaille
Caroline Ferland
Richard Pelchat
Denis Cote

D-U-N-S 25-674-3006   (HQ)
MEDICAGO INC
(*Suby of* MITSUBISHI CHEMICAL HOLDINGS CORPORATION)
1020 Rte De L'Eglise Bureau 600, Quebec, QC, G1V 3V9
(418) 658-9393
Emp Here 42   *Sales* 10,568,684
SIC 8731 Commercial physical research
Bruce Clark
Michael Schunk
Nathalie Landry
Marc-Andre D'aoust
Todd Talarico
Yatika Kohli
Jean-Luc Martre
Mike Wanner

D-U-N-S 20-363-1007   (SL)
MEDICAGO R&D INC
(*Suby of* MITSUBISHI CHEMICAL HOLDINGS CORPORATION)
1020 Rte De L'Eglise Bureau 600, Quebec, QC, G1V 3V9
(418) 658-9393
Emp Here 100   *Sales* 22,975,400
SIC 8731 Commercial physical research
Bruce D. Clark
Michael Wanner

D-U-N-S 24-464-8069   (HQ)
MICRO LOGIC SAINTE-FOY LTEE
MICRO LOGIC CENTRE DE SERVICE
2786 Ch Sainte-Foy, Quebec, QC, G1V 1V8
(418) 658-6624
Emp Here 120   *Sales* 84,070,580
SIC 5045 Computers, peripherals, and software
Stephane Garneau
Guy Gagnon
Julien Dernaucourt
Mario Cote
Benoit Herard
Marie-Helene Plamondon
Estelle Azemard

D-U-N-S 24-593-2603   (SL)
MICROFLEX 2001 LLC
2505 Boul Laurier Bureau 300, Quebec, QC, G1V 2L2
(418) 694-2300
Emp Here 70   *Sales* 12,411,770
SIC 7371 Custom computer programming services
Kathy Willard

D-U-N-S 20-273-4070   (SL)
MISSISQUOI COMPAGNIE D'ASSURANCE, LA
1175 Av Lavigerie Bureau 30, Quebec, QC, G1V 4P1

Emp Here 25   *Sales* 21,201,500
SIC 6411 Insurance agents, brokers, and service
Therese Bergeron

D-U-N-S 24-999-9277   (HQ)
MULTIFORCE TECHNOLOGIES INC
MULTIFORCE
(*Suby of* ESI TECHNOLOGIES DE L'INFORMATION INC)
2954 Boul Laurier Unite 320, Quebec, QC, G1V 4T2
(418) 780-8020
Sales 107,070,400
SIC 5045 Computers, peripherals, and software
Greg Rokos
Pierre Courchesne
Marc Veilleux

D-U-N-S 25-281-3444   (HQ)
NORTON ROSE FULBRIGHT CANADA S.E.N.C.R.L. S.R.L.
OGILVY RENAULT
2828 Boul Laurier Bureau 1500, Quebec, QC, G1V 0B9
(418) 640-7414
Emp Here 5   *Sales* 102,938,000
SIC 8111 Legal services
Jean Bertrand

D-U-N-S 25-456-9064   (BR)
NORTON ROSE FULBRIGHT CANADA S.E.N.C.R.L., S.R.L.
NORTON ROSE FULBRIGHT
(*Suby of* NORTON ROSE FULBRIGHT CANADA S.E.N.C.R.L., S.R.L.)
2828 Boul Laurier Bureau 1500, Quebec, QC, G1V 0B9
(418) 640-5000
Emp Here 150
SIC 8111 Legal services
Rachel Dussault

D-U-N-S 24-380-3426   (HQ)
PATES A TOUT INC
2500 Ch Des Quatre-Bourgeois, Quebec, QC, G1V 4P9
(418) 651-8284
Emp Here 46   *Sales* 11,242,750
SIC 2098 Macaroni and spaghetti
Alain Villeneuve
Pauline Kaine

D-U-N-S 24-317-5531   (SL)
PHARMACIE S GAGNON & L MARMEN

S.E.N.C
2766 Ch Sainte-Foy, Quebec, QC, G1V 1V5
(418) 657-2956
Emp Here 40   *Sales* 10,118,160
SIC 5912 Drug stores and proprietary stores
Luc Marmen

D-U-N-S 25-782-9291   (HQ)
POISSONNERIE UNIMER INC
2500 Ch Des Quatre-Bourgeois, Quebec, QC, G1V 4P9
(418) 654-1880
Emp Here 15   *Sales* 25,067,310
SIC 5146 Fish and seafoods
Jocelyn Fortier

D-U-N-S 24-378-8312   (BR)
PRICEWATERHOUSECOOPERS LLP
(*Suby of* PRICEWATERHOUSECOOPERS LLP)
2640 Boul Laurier Bureau 1700, Quebec, QC, G1V 5C2
(418) 522-7001
Emp Here 700
SIC 8721 Accounting, auditing, and bookkeeping
Zicat Yannick

D-U-N-S 24-864-0229   (HQ)
PRODUITS FORESTIERS D&G LTEE, LES
JACOMAU
2590 Boul Laurier Bureau 500, Quebec, QC, G1V 4M6
(418) 657-6505
Emp Here 10   *Sales* 57,069,950
SIC 2421 Sawmills and planing mills, general
Maurice Grondin
Jacques Bussieres

D-U-N-S 24-707-1194   (HQ)
SERVICES CONSEILS ARBITREX INC, LES
ARBITREX
2875 Boul Laurier Unite 200, Quebec, QC, G1V 5B1
(418) 651-9900
Sales 13,860,250
SIC 8111 Legal services
Martin Bouffard

D-U-N-S 24-499-5510   (SL)
SERVICES CONSEILS SYSTEMATIX INC, LES
2600 Boul Laurier Bureau 128, Quebec, QC, G1V 4Y4
(418) 681-0151
Emp Here 144   *Sales* 24,025,968
SIC 7379 Computer related services, nec
Jean Gagne
Daniel Deschenes
Norbert Rozko

D-U-N-S 20-794-4310   (SL)
SERVICES DE SECRETARIAT INTEGRALE ENR, LES
SECRETARIAT INTEGRALE CAPITALE RESSOURCES HUMAINES
2590 Boul Laurier Bureau 1020, Quebec, QC, G1V 4M6
(418) 624-4989
Emp Here 100   *Sales* 15,537,100
SIC 7361 Employment agencies
Helene Couture

D-U-N-S 25-098-0786   (HQ)
SERVICES ENERGETIQUES ECOSYSTEM INC, LES
ECOSYSTEM
2875 Boul Laurier Bureau 950 Edifice Delta 3, Quebec, QC, G1V 2M2
(418) 651-1257
Emp Here 50   *Sales* 30,496,060
SIC 1731 Electrical work
Andre Rochette

D-U-N-S 25-210-4070   (SL)
SERVICES INFIRMIERS PRO-SOIN INC
PRO-SOIN
2750 Ch Sainte-Foy Bureau 240, Quebec, QC,

G1V 1V6
(418) 653-4471
Emp Here 100   *Sales* 27,433,200
SIC 8741 Management services
Luc Bastien
Barbara Watts

D-U-N-S 20-386-9438   (SL)
SOCIETE DE DEVELOPPEMENT INTERNATIONAL (SDI) INC
2006 Rue Richer, Quebec, QC, G1V 1P1
(418) 264-8188
Emp Here 100   *Sales* 25,349,000
SIC 8748 Business consulting, nec
Kotchikpa Gabriel Lawin

D-U-N-S 20-400-6741   (SL)
SSQ DISTRIBUTION INC
ASSURANCE VOYAGES COMPARAISON
(*Suby of* FONDS DE SOLIDARITE DES TRAVAILLEURS DU QUEBEC (F.T.Q.))
2525 Boul Laurier, Quebec, QC, G1V 4Z6
(418) 682-1245
Emp Here 26   *Sales* 10,891,114
SIC 6531 Real estate agents and managers
Elise Poulin
Carl Cleary
Patrick Cyr
Eric Trudel
David Fortier
Marie-Claude Harvey
Genevieve Fortier

D-U-N-S 20-778-0917   (HQ)
SSQ SOCIETE D'ASSURANCE-VIE INC
SSQ GROUPE FINANCIER
(*Suby of* FONDS DE SOLIDARITE DES TRAVAILLEURS DU QUEBEC (F.T.Q.))
2525 Boul Laurier, Quebec, QC, G1V 4Z6
(418) 651-7000
Emp Here 650   *Sales* 2,805,838,984
SIC 6311 Life insurance
Jean-Francois Chalifoux
Pierre Genest
Emile Vallee
Helene Plante
Eddy Jomphe
Andrew Macdougall
Normand Brouillet
Sylvain Picard
Normand A. Turnbull
Denyse Paradis

D-U-N-S 25-366-0278   (SL)
SSQ SOCIETE D'ASSURANCES GENERALES INC
SSQ ASSURANCES GENERALES
(*Suby of* FONDS DE SOLIDARITE DES TRAVAILLEURS DU QUEBEC (F.T.Q.))
2515 Boul Laurier, Quebec, QC, G1V 2L2
(819) 538-4610
Emp Here 300   *Sales* 1,423,831,200
SIC 6411 Insurance agents, brokers, and service
Germain Menard
Yves Demers
Eve Girard
Jacques Rochefort
Andre L'Ecuyer
Richard Bell
Michel Lessard
Johanne Goulet
Kathleen Grant
Pierre Vaillancourt

D-U-N-S 20-290-3316   (HQ)
SSQ, SOCIETE D'ASSURANCE INC
SSQ ASSURANCE
(*Suby of* FONDS DE SOLIDARITE DES TRAVAILLEURS DU QUEBEC (F.T.Q.))
2525 Boul Laurier, Quebec, QC, G1V 2L2
(418) 651-7000
Emp Here 10   *Sales* 123,541,800
SIC 6311 Life insurance
Jean-Francois Chalifoux
Emile Vallee

Rene Hamel
Elise Poulin
Normand Brouillet
Claude Choquette
Carolle Dube
Eddy Jomphe
Jude Martineau
Gaetan Morin

D-U-N-S 24-523-3908 (BR)
TICKETMASTER CANADA LP
(*Suby of* LIVE NATION ENTERTAINMENT, INC.)
2505 Boul Laurier Bureau 300, Quebec, QC, G1V 2L2
(418) 694-2300
Emp Here 100
SIC 7922 Theatrical producers and services
Omar Bennis

D-U-N-S 25-284-2992 (SL)
TREMBLAY BOIS MIGNAULT LEMAY & ASSOCIES INC
1195 Av Lavigerie Bureau 200, Quebec, QC, G1V 4N3
(418) 658-9966
Emp Here 70   *Sales* 10,780,770
SIC 8111 Legal services
Celine Beaudry

D-U-N-S 25-999-9142 (BR)
UNIVERSITE LAVAL
CENTRE COPL
(*Suby of* UNIVERSITE LAVAL)
2375 Rue De La Terrasse, Quebec, QC, G1V 0A6
(418) 656-2454
Emp Here 200
SIC 3851 Ophthalmic goods
Real Vallee

D-U-N-S 20-870-4593 (HQ)
UNIVERSITE LAVAL
2345 Allee Des Bibliotheques, Quebec, QC, G1V 0A6
(418) 656-3530
Emp Here 10   *Sales* 352,532,500
SIC 8221 Colleges and universities
Marie-France Poulin
Sophie D'amours
Monique Richer
Sophie D'amours
Luc Brouillette
Claude Tessier
Loubna Ghaouti
Sylvie Dillard
Barbara Poirier
Najat Aattouri

D-U-N-S 24-685-4942 (BR)
UNIVERSITE LAVAL
CENTRE D'ETUDES INTERAMERICAINES
(*Suby of* UNIVERSITE LAVAL)
1030 Av Des Sciences Humaines, Quebec, QC, G1V 0A6
(418) 656-2131
Emp Here 4,000
SIC 8221 Colleges and universities
Gabriel Coulombe

D-U-N-S 24-851-7125 (BR)
UNIVERSITE LAVAL
DEPARTEMENT DE GENIE MECANIQUE
(*Suby of* UNIVERSITE LAVAL)
1065 Av De La Medecine Pavillon Adrien-Pouliot, Quebec, QC, G1V 0A6
(418) 656-3474
Emp Here 2,000
SIC 8221 Colleges and universities
Clement Gosselin

D-U-N-S 20-869-5353 (HQ)
VOYAGES LAURIER DU VALLON INC, LES
2450 Boul Laurier Bureau 10, Quebec, QC, G1V 2L1
(418) 653-1882
Emp Here 25   *Sales* 20,798,680
SIC 4724 Travel agencies

Nicole Laroche
Mark Wilkie
John Beauvais

Quebec, QC G1W

D-U-N-S 24-355-0246 (HQ)
2153-1090 QUEBEC INC
3690 Boul Neilson, Quebec, QC, G1W 0A9
(418) 781-0471
Sales 27,335,000
SIC 6712 Bank holding companies
Andree Pichette
Stephane Pichette
Doris Pichette

D-U-N-S 20-137-5081 (HQ)
9065-0805 QUEBEC INC
SUTTON GROUP
3075 Ch Des Quatre-Bourgeois Bureau 430, Quebec, QC, G1W 4Y5
(418) 657-6060
Emp Here 100   *Sales* 62,833,350
SIC 6531 Real estate agents and managers
Robert D'aoust

D-U-N-S 24-993-9471 (SL)
9187-7571 QUEBEC INC
CLARION HOTEL QUEBEC
3125 Boul Hochelaga, Quebec, QC, G1W 2P9
(418) 653-7267
Emp Here 90   *Sales* 8,540,910
SIC 7011 Hotels and motels
Mike Yuval
Jack Sofer

D-U-N-S 25-672-6704 (HQ)
CAISSE DESJARDINS DE SAINTE-FOY
DESJARDINS ENTREPRISES–QUEBEC-PORTNEUF
990 Av De Bourgogne Bureau 200, Quebec, QC, G1W 0E8
(418) 653-0515
Emp Here 16   *Sales* 31,184,912
SIC 6062 State credit unions
Louis Babineau
Pierre R. Tremblay
Chanele Morel-Lebrun
Philippe Beaulieu
Marie Caron
Yves Michaud
Remi Grenier
Michel Laferriere
Pierrick Lafreniere
Evelyne Moreau

D-U-N-S 24-592-8007 (HQ)
CENTRALE DES SYNDICATS DEMOCRATIQUES
CSD
990 Av De Bourgogne Bureau 600, Quebec, QC, G1W 0E8
(418) 529-2956
Emp Here 20   *Sales* 22,784,160
SIC 8631 Labor organizations
Francois Vaudreuil
Martin L'abbee
Jean-Claude Dufresne
Serge Tremblay
Charles Rouleau

D-U-N-S 24-689-6518 (SL)
CENTRE D'HEBERGEMENT DU BOISE LTEE
(*Suby of* 2153-1090 QUEBEC INC)
3690 Boul Neilson, Quebec, QC, G1W 0A9
(418) 781-0471
Emp Here 100   *Sales* 5,924,700
SIC 8361 Residential care
Stephane Pichette
Andree Pichette

D-U-N-S 24-423-0418 (SL)
CONCEPT MODE STE-FOY INC

999 Av De Bourgogne Bureau A1, Quebec, QC, G1W 4S6
(418) 653-3214
Emp Here 60   *Sales* 10,763,760
SIC 5621 Women's clothing stores
Patricia Croteau
Dave King
Normand Decarie

D-U-N-S 24-380-7872 (HQ)
COOPERATIVE DES CONSOMMATEURS DE STE-FOY
999 Av De Bourgogne, Quebec, QC, G1W 4S6
(418) 658-6472
Sales 63,391,032
SIC 5411 Grocery stores
Huguette Lamontagne
Denis Laprise

D-U-N-S 25-368-6836 (HQ)
COVEO SOLUTIONS INC
3175 Ch Des Quatre-Bourgeois Bureau 200, Quebec, QC, G1W 2K7
(418) 263-1111
Sales 28,836,400
SIC 7371 Custom computer programming services
Louis Tetu
Laurent Simoneau
Jean Lavigueur
Gwin Howard
Alberto Yepez
Lawrence Pentland
Leo Annab

D-U-N-S 20-953-1334 (SL)
DENDROTIK INC
3083 Ch Des Quatre-Bourgeois Bureau 100, Quebec, QC, G1W 2K6
(418) 653-7066
Emp Here 30   *Sales* 14,250,780
SIC 5082 Construction and mining machinery
Johanne Mcneil
Andre Mcneil

D-U-N-S 24-956-1155 (SL)
FONDATION UNIVERSITAS DU CANADA
FONDS UNIVERSITAS, LES
1035 Av Wilfrid-Pelletier Bureau 500, Quebec, QC, G1W 0C5
(877) 410-7333
Emp Here 24   *Sales* 16,723,440
SIC 6732 Trusts: educational, religious, etc.
Jean Marchand
Gaston Roy

D-U-N-S 20-952-0758 (SL)
GESTION UNIVERSITAS INC
3005 Av Maricourt Bureau 250, Quebec, QC, G1W 4T8
(418) 651-8975
Emp Here 65   *Sales* 95,813,965
SIC 6722 Management investment, open-end
Gaston Roy
Jean Marchand
Isabelle Grenier
Josiane Rivard
Sonia Dupere
Pascal Gilbert
Christian Lebeuf

D-U-N-S 24-908-3429 (HQ)
GROUPE JACOBUS INC
BIJOUTERIE JACOBUS
3175 Ch Des Quatre-Bourgeois Bureau 35, Quebec, QC, G1W 2K7
(418) 658-7373
Emp Here 5   *Sales* 13,438,040
SIC 5944 Jewelry stores
Jacques Labrecque

D-U-N-S 24-730-1765 (HQ)
MALLETTE S.E.N.C.R.L.
3075 Ch Des Quatre-Bourgeois Bureau 200, Quebec, QC, G1W 5C4
(418) 653-4431
Emp Here 40   *Sales* 83,183,850

SIC 8721 Accounting, auditing, and bookkeeping
Gabriel Gagnon
Lucie Couturier
Remi Vachon
Paul Gilbert
Marc Dagenais
Andre Rioux
Claude Jacques
Jose Arsenault
Robert Fortier
Guy Chabot

D-U-N-S 24-637-5240 (HQ)
NORDA STELO INC
1015 Av Wilfrid-Pelletier, Quebec, QC, G1W 0C4
(418) 654-9600
Emp Here 325   *Sales* 209,747,384
SIC 8711 Engineering services
Patrick Quigley
Alex Brisson
Christian Berube
Jean-Pierre Caron

D-U-N-S 20-914-4299 (BR)
NORTHERN MICRO INC
(*Suby of* CONVERGE TECHNOLOGY SOLUTIONS CORP.)
3107 Av Des Hotels Bureau 2, Quebec, QC, G1W 4W5
(418) 654-1733
Emp Here 75
SIC 5734 Computer and software stores
Gervais Pherrien

D-U-N-S 24-942-6149 (SL)
OGESCO CONSTRUCTION INC
(*Suby of* 9094-7474 QUEBEC INC)
3070 Ch Des Quatre-Bourgeois, Quebec, QC, G1W 2K4
(418) 651-8774
Emp Here 43   *Sales* 24,524,534
SIC 1542 Nonresidential construction, nec
Louis Martin

D-U-N-S 20-002-8426 (BR)
PROVIGO DISTRIBUTION INC
PROVIGO
(*Suby of* LOBLAW COMPANIES LIMITED)
3440 Ch Des Quatre-Bourgeois Bureau 8143, Quebec, QC, G1W 4T3
(418) 653-6241
Emp Here 90
SIC 5411 Grocery stores
Helene Lalonde

D-U-N-S 20-870-0112 (SL)
RE/MAX FORTIN, DELAGE INC
3175 Ch Des Quatre-Bourgeois Bureau 120, Quebec, QC, G1W 2K7
(418) 653-5353
Emp Here 52   *Sales* 14,131,312
SIC 6531 Real estate agents and managers
Jean Gravel
Gilles Delage
Jacqueline Houle

Quebec, QC G1X

D-U-N-S 24-202-7456 (BR)
4211677 CANADA INC
GOJIT
5150 Rue John-Molson, Quebec, QC, G1X 3X4
(514) 761-2345
Emp Here 100
SIC 7389 Business services, nec
Daniel Therrien

D-U-N-S 20-309-3695 (SL)
9274-4531 QUEBEC INC
LAURIER MAZDA
3000 Av Watt Bureau 1, Quebec, QC, G1X 3Y8

(418) 659-9000
Emp Here 26   *Sales* 11,530,740
SIC 7389 Business services, nec
Jacques Saillant
Charles Saillant
Alexandre Saillant

D-U-N-S 24-129-5810   (BR)
CAISSE DESJARDINS DE SAINTE-FOY
CENTRE DE SERVICE DE LA COLLINE
(*Suby of* CAISSE DESJARDINS DE SAINTE-FOY)
3211 Ch Sainte-Foy, Quebec, QC, G1X 1R3
(418) 653-0515
Emp Here 85
SIC 6062 State credit unions
Andre Champagne

D-U-N-S 20-016-8461   (SL)
CHATEAU BONNE ENTENTE INC
RESTAURANT MONTE CRISTO
3400 Ch Sainte-Foy, Quebec, QC, G1X 1S6
(418) 650-4550
Emp Here 150   *Sales* 13,903,500
SIC 7011 Hotels and motels
Pierre Pomerleau
Jacques Tanguay
Alain April
Daniel Arguin
Michel Cloutier

D-U-N-S 25-918-3291   (BR)
COMMISSION SCOLAIRE DES DECOUVREURS
ECOLE SECONDAIRE LES COMPAGNONS DE QUARTIER
(*Suby of* COMMISSION SCOLAIRE DES DECOUVREURS)
3643 Av Des Compagnons, Quebec, QC, G1X 3Z6
(418) 652-2170
Emp Here 140
SIC 8211 Elementary and secondary schools
Danielle Grenier

D-U-N-S 20-801-2612   (BR)
COSTCO WHOLESALE CANADA LTD
COSTCO
(*Suby of* COSTCO WHOLESALE CORPORATION)
3233 Av Watt, Quebec, QC, G1X 4W2
(418) 656-0666
Emp Here 200
SIC 5099 Durable goods, nec
Alain Ouellet

D-U-N-S 25-170-2718   (BR)
FEDERATION QUEBECOISE DES COOPERATIVES EN MILIEU SCOLAIRE
(*Suby of* FEDERATION QUEBECOISE DES COOPERATIVES EN MILIEU SCOLAIRE)
3188 Ch Sainte-Foy Bureau 200, Quebec, QC, G1X 1R4
(418) 650-3333
Emp Here 105
SIC 8621 Professional organizations
Danis Gauthier

D-U-N-S 24-638-8151   (SL)
GESTION BBFD INC
BRUNET
3730 Rue Du Campanile, Quebec, QC, G1X 4G6
(418) 658-1337
Emp Here 50   *Sales* 12,647,700
SIC 5912 Drug stores and proprietary stores
Richard Blais

D-U-N-S 25-401-0416   (SL)
GESTION ST-H. INC
1294 Rue Roland-Desmeules, Quebec, QC, G1X 4Y3
(450) 836-7201
Emp Here 31   *Sales* 13,000,005
SIC 6712 Bank holding companies
Denis St-Louis

D-U-N-S 20-059-8766   (SL)

INFINITI QUEBEC INC
2766 Rue Einstein, Quebec, QC, G1X 4N8
(418) 658-3535
Emp Here 26   *Sales* 16,361,280
SIC 5511 New and used car dealers
Michel Potvin

D-U-N-S 20-764-0124   (BR)
INTEGRATED DISTRIBUTION SYSTEMS LIMITED PARTNERSHIP
WAJAX POWER SYSTEMS
(*Suby of* WAJAX CORPORATION)
2997 Av Watt, Quebec, QC, G1X 3W1
(418) 651-4236
Emp Here 85
SIC 5084 Industrial machinery and equipment
Gilbert Dumas

D-U-N-S 20-858-0092   (HQ)
J.A. LARUE INC
3003 Av Watt, Quebec, QC, G1X 3W2
(418) 658-3003
Emp Here 65   *Sales* 15,540,070
SIC 3569 General industrial machinery, nec
Denis Larue
Andre Larue
Louis Larue

D-U-N-S 25-092-6842   (SL)
J.L. DESJARDINS AUTO COLLECTION INC
3330 Av Watt, Quebec, QC, G1X 4S6
(418) 650-0063
Emp Here 22   *Sales* 11,142,012
SIC 5511 New and used car dealers
Jennifer Demers

D-U-N-S 20-482-9345   (SL)
JEAN COUTU MARIE-CLAUDE OUELLET & ANNIE SANFACON
1221 Rue Charles-Albanel, Quebec, QC, G1X 4Y5
(418) 874-0275
Emp Here 49   *Sales* 12,394,746
SIC 5912 Drug stores and proprietary stores

D-U-N-S 20-298-3706   (SL)
L'INDUSTRIELLE-ALLIANCE SERVICES IMMOBILIERS INC
INDUSTRIAL-ALLIANCE LIFE REAL ESTATE SERVICES
(*Suby of* INDUSTRIELLE ALLIANCE, ASSURANCE ET SERVICES FINANCIERS INC)
3810 Rue De Marly, Quebec, QC, G1X 4B1
(418) 651-7308
Emp Here 700   *Sales* 94,973,900
SIC 6513 Apartment building operators
Mario Bedard
Amelie Cantin

D-U-N-S 25-484-9144   (BR)
LEON'S FURNITURE LIMITED
MEUBLES LEON
(*Suby of* LEON'S FURNITURE LIMITED)
2840 Rue Einstein, Quebec, QC, G1X 5H3
(418) 683-9600
Emp Here 90
SIC 5712 Furniture stores
Eric Dernier

D-U-N-S 20-857-8559   (HQ)
MACPEK INC
RSSW & DESIGN (MC)
2970 Av Watt, Quebec, QC, G1X 4P7
(418) 659-1144
Sales 108,371,190
SIC 5013 Motor vehicle supplies and new parts
Jean-Francois Pouliot
Claude-Andre Pouliot

D-U-N-S 20-267-0006   (SL)
TOUT-PRET INC
2950 Av Watt Bureau 12, Quebec, QC, G1X 4A8
(418) 527-5557
Emp Here 25   *Sales* 20,889,425
SIC 5149 Groceries and related products, nec
Jean-Patrice Fournier

Cindy Parent-Tremblay
Martin Gagne
Maxine Poulut

D-U-N-S 20-952-0881   (HQ)
TRANSDIFF INC
TRANSDIFF PETERBILT DE QUEBEC
2901 Av Watt, Quebec, QC, G1X 3W1
(418) 653-3422
Sales 44,049,600
SIC 5511 New and used car dealers
Pierre Pouliot

Quebec, QC G1Y

D-U-N-S 20-253-4236   (SL)
9381-0455 QUEBEC INC
SOURIS MINI
(*Suby of* 9381-0596 QUEBEC INC)
1450 Rue Esther-Blondin Bureau 100, Quebec, QC, G1Y 3N7
(418) 254-6464
Emp Here 250   *Sales* 209,383,250
SIC 5137 Women's and children's clothing
Steeve Beaudet
Annie Bellavance

D-U-N-S 20-029-9787   (BR)
COMMISSION SCOLAIRE DES DECOUVREURS
ECOLE PRIMAIRE SECONDAIRE DES GRANDES MAREES
(*Suby of* COMMISSION SCOLAIRE DES DECOUVREURS)
1505 Rue Des Grandes-Marees, Quebec, QC, G1Y 2T3
(418) 652-2196
Emp Here 90
SIC 8211 Elementary and secondary schools
Eric Beaupre

Quebec, QC G2A

D-U-N-S 24-345-5651   (BR)
CENTRE DE SANTE ET DE SERVICES SOCIAUX DE QUEBEC-NORD
CENTRE DE SANTE DE LA HAUT ST CHARLES
(*Suby of* GOUVERNEMENT DE LA PROVINCE DE QUEBEC)
11999 Rue De L'Hopital Bureau 217, Quebec, QC, G2A 2T7
(418) 843-2572
Emp Here 500
SIC 8399 Social services, nec
Lucie Lacroix

D-U-N-S 24-345-6295   (BR)
COMMISSION SCOLAIRE DE LA CAPITALE, LA
ECOLE SECONDAIRE ROGER COMTOIS
158 Boul Des Etudiants, Quebec, QC, G2A 1N8
(418) 686-4040
Emp Here 146
SIC 8211 Elementary and secondary schools
Pierre Lapointe

D-U-N-S 20-308-8161   (SL)
SPORT S.M. INC
11337 Boul Valcartier, Quebec, QC, G2A 2M4
(418) 842-2703
Emp Here 40   *Sales* 19,923,120
SIC 5571 Motorcycle dealers
Robert Begin
Yves Matteau
Dave Marcotte
Michel Paradis

Quebec, QC G2B

D-U-N-S 20-400-6964   (HQ)
9003-9306 QUEBEC INC
GESTION AFINITI
9115 Boul De L'Ormiere, Quebec, QC, G2B 3K2
(418) 407-4400
Emp Here 11   *Sales* 17,571,600
SIC 8742 Management consulting services
Julie Serre
Denis Serre
Marc Serre

D-U-N-S 20-553-8932   (SL)
BOUVIER INC, LE
RESTAURANT NORMANDIN
(*Suby of* GROUPE NORMANDIN INC)
2335 Boul Bastien, Quebec, QC, G2B 1B3
(418) 842-9160
Emp Here 100
SIC 5812 Eating places
Denis Pigeon
Martin Duval

D-U-N-S 20-206-4903   (HQ)
COOPERATIVE DES CONSOMMATEURS DE LORETTEVILLE
IGA
250 Rue Louis-Ix, Quebec, QC, G2B 1L4
(418) 842-2341
Emp Here 86   *Sales* 48,423,705
SIC 5411 Grocery stores
Yvan Pageau
Michel Bouchard

D-U-N-S 25-944-7977   (SL)
GESTION DOMINIQUE BOND INC
JEAN COUTU
2160 Boul Bastien, Quebec, QC, G2B 1B7
(418) 842-3648
Emp Here 50   *Sales* 12,647,700
SIC 5912 Drug stores and proprietary stores
Dominique Bond

D-U-N-S 24-730-6137   (HQ)
GROUPE NORMANDIN INC
2335 Boul Bastien, Quebec, QC, G2B 1B3
(418) 842-9160
Sales 477,675,500
SIC 8721 Accounting, auditing, and bookkeeping
Normand Bries
Martin Duval
Denis Pigeon

D-U-N-S 24-706-9974   (SL)
PROVINCE DU QUEBEC DE L'UNION CANADIENNE DES MONIALES DE L'ORDRE DE SAINTE-URSULE
CENTRE DE SPIRITUALITE DES URSULINES
20 Rue Des Dames-Ursulines, Quebec, QC, G2B 2V1
(418) 692-2523
Emp Here 250   *Sales* 26,030,750
SIC 8661 Religious organizations
Monique Pelletier

D-U-N-S 20-370-9670   (HQ)
RESTAURANT NORMANDIN (2014) INC
RESTAURANT NORMANDIN
(*Suby of* GROUPE NORMANDIN INC)
2335 Boul Bastien, Quebec, QC, G2B 1B3
(418) 842-9160
Emp Here 25   *Sales* 11,659,750
SIC 5812 Eating places
Denis Pigeon
Martin Duval

D-U-N-S 25-767-3566   (SL)
SERVICE REGIONAL D'INTERPRETARIAT DE L'EST DU QUEBEC INC
SRIEQ: SERVICE D'AIDE A LA COMMUNICATION / BAS ST-LAURENT
9885 Boul De L'Ormiere, Quebec, QC, G2B

3K9
(418) 622-1037
Emp Here 50   *Sales* 22,460,950
SIC 7389 Business services, nec
  Manon Desharnais
  Yves Dube
  Charles Wilson
  Gilles Nolet

Quebec, QC G2C

D-U-N-S 20-700-5849   (SL)
9075-6602 QUEBEC INC
6275 Boul De L'Ormiere, Quebec, QC, G2C
1B9
(418) 842-3232
Emp Here 50   *Sales* 16,666,650
SIC 1541 Industrial buildings and warehouses
  Guy J Gaudet

D-U-N-S 20-362-3538   (SL)
9230-9970 QUEBEC INC
IGA EXTRA CONVIVIO
(*Suby of* COOPERATIVE DES CONSOMMA-
TEURS DE LORETTEVILLE)
2295 Av Chauveau Bureau 200, Quebec, QC,
G2C 0G7
(418) 842-3381
Emp Here 175   *Sales* 51,358,475
SIC 5411 Grocery stores
  Yanic Drouin

D-U-N-S 20-205-7345   (HQ)
AMEUBLEMENTS TANGUAY INC
SIGNATURE MAURICE TANGUAY
(*Suby of* BELANGER, A. (DETAIL) LTEE)
7200 Rue Armand-Viau, Quebec, QC, G2C
2A7
(800) 826-4829
Emp Here 200   *Sales* 213,362,400
SIC 5712 Furniture stores
  Maurice Tanguay
  Jacques Tanguay
  Yves Des Groseillers

D-U-N-S 24-380-7950   (HQ)
**CAISSE DESJARDINS DES RIVIERES DE
QUEBEC**
CENTRE DE SERVICES SAINT-EMILE
2287 Av Chauveau, Quebec, QC, G2C 0G7
(418) 842-1214
Emp Here 75   *Sales* 46,999,218
SIC 6062 State credit unions
  Suzanne Canac-Marquis
  Christian Lavoie
  Claude Lantier
  Marie-Catherine Paquet
  Jean-Yves Parent
  Murielle Foucault
  Paul Gardon
  Nathalie Godin
  Jean-Louis Duchesne
  Julie Masse

D-U-N-S 24-200-1519   (HQ)
CHOCOLATS FAVORIS INC, LES
CHOCOLATS FAVORIS
4355 Rue Jean-Marchand Bureau 101, Que-
bec, QC, G2C 0N2
(418) 915-9311
Emp Here 10   *Sales* 121,846,250
SIC 2026 Fluid milk
  Dominique Brown
  Charles Auger
  Virginie Faucher
  Claude Choquette
  Luc Dupont
  Marc Poulin
  Sylvain Toutant

D-U-N-S 24-239-8886   (BR)
**COMMISSION SCOLAIRE DE LA CAPI-
TALE, LA**
ECOLE SECONDAIRE DE NEUFCHATEL

3600 Av Chauveau, Quebec, QC, G2C 1A1
(418) 686-4040
Emp Here 150
SIC 8211 Elementary and secondary schools

D-U-N-S 20-712-0614   (BR)
**COMMISSION SCOLAIRE DE LA CAPI-
TALE, LA**
*CENTRE FORMATION PROFESSIONNELLE
DE NEUFCHATEL*
3400 Av Chauveau, Quebec, QC, G2C 1A1
(418) 686-4040
Emp Here 90
SIC 8331 Job training and related services
  Christiane Samson

D-U-N-S 24-842-3238   (BR)
CORPORATION MCKESSON CANADA, LA
(*Suby of* MCKESSON FINANCIAL HOLD-
INGS II UNLIMITED COMPANY)
2655 Rue De Celles, Quebec, QC, G2C 1K7
(418) 845-3061
Emp Here 150
SIC 5122 Drugs, proprietaries, and sundries
  Beaunoit Savoir

D-U-N-S 20-558-8531   (HQ)
DISTRIBUTION PHARMAPLUS INC
GROUPE LAVOIE PHARMACY
2905 Rue De Celles Bureau 102, Quebec,
QC, G2C 1W7
(418) 667-5499
Sales 12,158,795
SIC 5122 Drugs, proprietaries, and sundries
  Laurier Lavoie
  Jerome-Henri Lavoie
  Laurie-Eve Lavoie

D-U-N-S 24-465-5254   (SL)
EQUIPEMENTS E.M.U. LTEE
E.M.U./RYDER
3975 Rue Jean-Marchand, Quebec, QC, G2C
2J2
(418) 767-2277
Emp Here 60   *Sales* 28,501,560
SIC 5084 Industrial machinery and equipment
  Rejean Potvin
  Nicolas Potvin
  Marc Potvin
  Dave Potvin

D-U-N-S 24-820-1154   (HQ)
FAMILIPRIX INC
BIOMEDIC
6000 Rue Armand-Viau Bureau 418, Quebec,
QC, G2C 2C5
(418) 847-3311
Emp Here 250   *Sales* 478,872,360
SIC 5122 Drugs, proprietaries, and sundries
  Albert Falardeau
  Gerald Cloutier
  Regis Tremblay
  Louis-Marie Garant
  Richard Lord
  Jocelyn Proteau
  Chantal Gaboury
  Joanne Mailloux
  Stephane Ruest

D-U-N-S 20-234-5513   (SL)
GENIARP INC
RESIDENCE
4650 Boul De L'Auvergne, Quebec, QC, G2C
2B5
(418) 847-3333
Emp Here 35   *Sales* 11,189,675
SIC 1389 Oil and gas field services, nec
  Jean-Luc Bedard

D-U-N-S 25-978-2282   (SL)
GROUPE EQUICONCEPT INC
2160 Rue De Celles, Quebec, QC, G2C 1X8
(418) 847-1480
Emp Here 80   *Sales* 20,924,240
SIC 6712 Bank holding companies
  Marc Vaugeois

D-U-N-S 24-404-0270   (HQ)

GROUPE POLYALTO INC
PLASTIQUE ALTO
3825 Rue Jean-Marchand, Quebec, QC, G2C
2J2
(418) 847-8311
Sales 19,180,215
SIC 3089 Plastics products, nec
  Marc Lewis
  Marc Savard
  Eric Toutant

D-U-N-S 24-392-7113   (SL)
GUILBAULT LOGISTIQUE INC
IDEAL CENTRE LOGISTIQUE QUEBEC
(*Suby of* GROUPE GUILBAULT LTEE)
8000 Rue Armand-Viau Bureau 300, Quebec,
QC, G2C 2E2
(418) 843-5587
Emp Here 26   *Sales* 13,519,142
SIC 4731 Freight transportation arrangement
  Eric Gignac
  Nadine Guilbault

D-U-N-S 20-872-2405   (SL)
GUILLEMETTE, JEAN-PAUL INC
CANADIAN TIRE 342
4500 Rue Armand-Viau Bureau 342, Quebec,
QC, G2C 2B9
(418) 872-6221
Emp Here 75   *Sales* 20,073,900
SIC 5251 Hardware stores
  Jean-Paul Guillemette

D-U-N-S 24-638-4077   (HQ)
HMI CONSTRUCTION INC
(*Suby of* ANDRITZ AG)
6275 Boul De L'Ormiere, Quebec, QC, G2C
1B9
(418) 842-3232
Sales 42,273,700
SIC 1541 Industrial buildings and warehouses
  Daniel Carrier
  Liam Turner
  Guy J. Gaudet
  Timothy Joseph Ryan
  Christian Stoebich
  Jean-Francois Lemay

D-U-N-S 20-511-6937   (BR)
HYDRO-QUEBEC
*HYDRO QUEBEC HYDRODIRECT SIEGE
REGIONAL TERRITOIRE MONTMORENCY*
(*Suby of* GOUVERNEMENT DE LA
PROVINCE DE QUEBEC)
2625 Boul Lebourgneuf Bureau 14, Quebec,
QC, G2C 1P1
(888) 385-7252
Emp Here 2,200
SIC 4911 Electric services
  Andre Cailla

D-U-N-S 24-204-3834   (HQ)
INFORMATIQUE COTE, COULOMBE INC
ICC TECHNOLOGIES
3770 Rue Jean-Marchand, Quebec, QC, G2C
1Y6
(418) 628-2100
Emp Here 48   *Sales* 15,957,990
SIC 7371 Custom computer programming ser-
vices
  Louis-Phillipe Cote
  Sonya Cote

D-U-N-S 20-241-7234   (HQ)
JEAN-PAUL FORTIN (1997) INC
CHAUSSURES GILBERT
2050 Rue De Celles, Quebec, QC, G2C 1X8
(418) 845-5369
Emp Here 22   *Sales* 30,497,320
SIC 5661 Shoe stores
  Francois Monat
  Lina Gilbert

D-U-N-S 24-730-5048   (SL)
JOUET K.I.D. INC
AGENCE DE PUBLICITE D.I.K.
4000 Rue Jean-Marchand Bureau 120, Que-

---

bec, QC, G2C 1Y6
(418) 627-0101
Emp Here 50   *Sales* 26,027,100
SIC 5092 Toys and hobby goods and supplies
  Andre Kirouac

D-U-N-S 24-842-1067   (SL)
M. LEMIEUX INC
5005 Rue Hugues-Randin, Quebec, QC, G2C
0G5
(418) 688-5050
Emp Here 40   *Sales* 19,001,040
SIC 5085 Industrial supplies
  Andre Bilodeau

D-U-N-S 20-016-6606   (SL)
M2S ELECTRONIQUE LTEE
(*Suby of* GESTION M2S LTEE)
2855 Rue De Celles, Quebec, QC, G2C 1K7
(418) 842-1717
Emp Here 90   *Sales* 17,139,780
SIC 3669 Communications equipment, nec
  Bertrand Saucier
  Mario Marcotte

D-U-N-S 24-908-7784   (HQ)
MAB PROFIL INC
*GSP GESTION STRATEGIQUE DE PRO-
JETS*
2800 Rue Jean-Perrin Bureau 200, Quebec,
QC, G2C 1T3
(418) 842-4100
Emp Here 55   *Sales* 30,531,360
SIC 5021 Furniture
  Patrick Morissette

D-U-N-S 24-348-0733   (BR)
MEDIAS TRANSCONTINENTAL S.E.N.C.
(*Suby of* MEDIAS TRANSCONTINENTAL
S.E.N.C.)
2850 Rue Jean-Perrin, Quebec, QC, G2C 2C8

Emp Here 165
SIC 2752 Commercial printing, lithographic

D-U-N-S 25-924-1362   (SL)
MULTI-METAL G. BOUTIN INC
6500 Rue Roland-Bedard, Quebec, QC, G2C
0J2
(418) 842-5888
Emp Here 50   *Sales* 10,141,500
SIC 3446 Architectural Metalwork
  Stephane Boutin
  Dany Bourassa
  Michel Boutin

D-U-N-S 24-791-0367   (HQ)
ORTHOFAB INC
(*Suby of* GESTION ORTHOFAB INC)
2160 Rue De Celles, Quebec, QC, G2C 1X8
(418) 847-5225
Emp Here 50   *Sales* 18,183,120
SIC 3842 Surgical appliances and supplies
  Richard Lapierre
  Jean Painchaud
  Pierre Simard
  Denis Carbonneau
  Daniel Belanger

D-U-N-S 20-871-1705   (HQ)
P.R. DISTRIBUTIONS INC
FASBEC
6500 Rue Zephirin-Paquet, Quebec, QC, G2C
0M3
(418) 872-6018
Emp Here 20   *Sales* 28,501,560
SIC 5084 Industrial machinery and equipment
  Guy Lord
  Rolande Lapointe
  Claire Lord

D-U-N-S 20-330-0066   (SL)
PREMIER AVIATION QUEBEC INC
800 8e Rue De L'Aeroport, Quebec, QC, G2C
2S6
(418) 800-1325
Emp Here 100   *Sales* 32,475,400
SIC 4581 Airports, flying fields, and services

Renato Di Bartolo
Franco Di Bartolo

D-U-N-S 25-281-7556   (BR)
PUROLATOR INC
(*Suby of* GOVERNMENT OF CANADA)
7000 Rue Armand-Viau, Quebec, QC, G2C
2C4
(888) 744-7123
Emp Here 300
SIC 4731 Freight transportation arrangement
Richard Badeau

D-U-N-S 25-165-0602   (BR)
REGULVAR INC
(*Suby of* REGULVAR INC)
2800 Rue Jean-Perrin Bureau 100, Quebec,
QC, G2C 1T3
(418) 842-5114
Emp Here 300
SIC 1796 Installing building equipment
Michel Cochrane

Quebec, QC G2E

D-U-N-S 20-703-8097   (SL)
9100-9647 QUEBEC INC
NOVA PERMIS & ESCORTES ROUTIERES
2800 Av Saint-Jean-Baptiste Bureau 235,
Quebec, QC, G2E 6J5
(418) 527-7775
Emp Here 26   *Sales* 10,179,052
SIC 6794 Patent owners and lessors
Louis Juneau
Monique Comeau

D-U-N-S 25-197-1693   (SL)
ASSUREXPERTS INC
540 Rue Michel-Fragasso, Quebec, QC, G2E
5N4
(418) 871-2289
Emp Here 30   *Sales* 17,397,720
SIC 6411 Insurance agents, brokers, and ser-
vice
Pierre Boisvert
Real Breton

D-U-N-S 24-380-9340   (SL)
ATELIERS T.A.Q. INC
GROUPE TAQ
5255 Rue Rideau, Quebec, QC, G2E 5H5
(418) 871-4912
Emp Here 185   *Sales* 123,747,980
SIC 7389 Business services, nec
Andre Desrochers
Richard Emond
Luc Paris
Jean Page
Roch Laflamme
Marcel Malouin
Alain Berube
Stephane Fortier
Jacques Simard

D-U-N-S 25-744-7755   (SL)
CLEF DE SOL INC, LA
445 Av Saint-Jean-Baptiste Bureau 220, Que-
bec, QC, G2E 5N7
(418) 627-0840
Emp Here 50   *Sales* 16,280,000
SIC 5999 Miscellaneous retail stores, nec
Bertrand Bergeron

D-U-N-S 20-298-1791   (SL)
CONSTRUCTION DERIC INC
(*Suby of* GROUPE DERIC INC)
5145 Rue Rideau, Quebec, QC, G2E 5H5
(418) 781-2228
Emp Here 45   *Sales* 19,023,165
SIC 1541 Industrial buildings and warehouses
Eric Desbiens

D-U-N-S 24-941-0986   (SL)
CONSTRUCTION DROLET, MARC INC
DROLET ENTREPENEUR GENERAL

5475 Rue Rideau, Quebec, QC, G2E 5V9
(418) 871-7574
Emp Here 40   *Sales* 10,837,680
SIC 1521 Single-family housing construction
Marc Drolet

D-U-N-S 20-776-5926   (SL)
CRIBTEC INC
(*Suby of* GROUPE DERIC INC)
5145 Rue Rideau, Quebec, QC, G2E 5H5
(418) 622-5992
Emp Here 50   *Sales* 10,891,450
SIC 1731 Electrical work
Eric Desbiens

D-U-N-S 20-250-2191   (HQ)
ENTREPRISES POL R INC
GEORGES NADEAU
5085 Rue Rideau, Quebec, QC, G2E 5H5
(418) 872-0000
Emp Here 130   *Sales* 113,925,600
SIC 5033 Roofing, siding, and insulation

D-U-N-S 25-484-8633   (HQ)
ESKIMO EXPRESS INC
MORNEAU ESKIMO
(*Suby of* GESTION DENIS MORNEAU (1993)
INC)
5055 Rue Rideau Bureau 500, Quebec, QC,
G2E 5H5
(418) 681-1212
Emp Here 75   *Sales* 21,501,015
SIC 4213 Trucking, except local
Andre Morneau
Micheline Morneau

D-U-N-S 20-129-2696   (SL)
**FEDERATION DE L'UPA DE LA CAPITALE-
NATIONALE-COTE-NORD**
5185 Rue Rideau, Quebec, QC, G2E 5S2
(418) 872-0770
Emp Here 49   *Sales* 16,780,883
SIC 0181 Ornamental nursery products
Denis Villeneuve

D-U-N-S 24-868-2861   (SL)
FINANCES & INDEMNISATIONS INC
540 Rue Michel-Fragasso, Quebec, QC, G2E
5N4
(418) 861-9506
Emp Here 35   *Sales* 10,082,018
SIC 8741 Management services
Pierre Boisvert

D-U-N-S 24-936-0942   (HQ)
FISO TECHNOLOGIES INC
(*Suby of* ROCTEST LTEE)
500 Av Saint-Jean-Baptiste Bureau 195, Que-
bec, QC, G2E 5R9
(418) 688-8065
Emp Here 40   *Sales* 13,637,340
SIC 3827 Optical instruments and lenses
Joss Cohen

D-U-N-S 24-322-0568   (HQ)
GECKO ALLIANCE GROUP INC
450 Rue Des Canetons, Quebec, QC, G2E
5W6
(418) 872-4411
Sales 19,044,200
SIC 3625 Relays and industrial controls
Michel Authier
Luc St-Georges
Benoit Laflamme
Ghislain Lacroix
Jean Gaudreault
Katya Laviolette

D-U-N-S 20-555-0069   (BR)
GECKO ALLIANCE GROUP INC
(*Suby of* GECKO ALLIANCE GROUP INC)
450 Av Saint-Jean-Baptiste Bureau 200, Que-
bec, QC, G2E 6H5
(418) 872-4411
Emp Here 208
SIC 3625 Relays and industrial controls
Michel Authier

D-U-N-S 25-999-0539   (HQ)
GENTEC ELECTRO-OPTIQUE INC
445 Av Saint-Jean-Baptiste Bureau 160, Que-
bec, QC, G2E 5N7
(418) 651-8003
Sales 12,828,100
SIC 3826 Analytical instruments
Michel Giroux
Francois Giroux

D-U-N-S 25-198-7681   (BR)
GHD CONSULTANTS LTEE
INSPEC-SOL
(*Suby of* GHD GROUP LIMITED)
445 Av Saint-Jean-Baptiste Bureau 390, Que-
bec, QC, G2E 5N7
(418) 658-0112
Emp Here 500
SIC 8621 Professional organizations
Yves Tessier

D-U-N-S 20-278-9421   (SL)
GROUPE ACCISST INC, LE
5232 Boul Wilfrid-Hamel, Quebec, QC, G2E
2G9
(418) 864-7432
Emp Here 35   *Sales* 28,972,195
SIC 6722 Management investment, open-end
Serge Gagne
Eric Gagne
Jean-Yves Gagne

D-U-N-S 20-298-2906   (HQ)
GROUPE DERIC INC
5145 Rue Rideau, Quebec, QC, G2E 5H5
(418) 781-2228
Emp Here 15   *Sales* 27,335,000
SIC 6712 Bank holding companies
Eric Desbiens

D-U-N-S 24-191-8197   (BR)
GROUPE LUMENPULSE INC
(*Suby of* POWER CORPORATION DU
CANADA)
445 Av Saint-Jean-Baptiste Bureau 120, Que-
bec, QC, G2E 5N7
(418) 871-8039
Emp Here 300
SIC 3646 Commercial lighting fixtures
Patrick Robitaille

D-U-N-S 24-907-5169   (HQ)
INFORMATIQUE PRO-CONTACT INC
PROCONTACT STRATEGIES CONSEILS
1000 Av Saint-Jean-Baptiste Bureau 111,
Quebec, QC, G2E 5G5
(418) 871-1622
Emp Here 80   *Sales* 107,070,400
SIC 5045 Computers, peripherals, and soft-
ware
Jonathan Legault
Jean-Francois Welch
Christian Desrochers
Jean-Philippe Couture

D-U-N-S 24-228-8988   (SL)
JES CONSTRUCTION INC
EXCAVATION GERVAIS DUCLOS 2008
5145 Rue Rideau Bureau 200, Quebec, QC,
G2E 5H5
(418) 874-0007
Emp Here 40   *Sales* 18,829,240
SIC 1542 Nonresidential construction, nec
Eric Blanchette
Jean Chouinard
Stephane Soucy

D-U-N-S 24-909-4020   (SL)
LABOPRO P.S. INC
PHOTO DE LA CAPITALE
1405 Av Saint-Jean-Baptiste Bureau 115,
Quebec, QC, G2E 5K2
(418) 681-6128
Emp Here 40   *Sales* 16,700,240
SIC 7384 Photofinish laboratories
Michel Plante

D-U-N-S 20-180-6598   (SL)

**LEVESQUE & ASSOCIES CONSTRUCTION
INC**
475 Rue Des Canetons, Quebec, QC, G2E
5X6
(418) 263-0982
Emp Here 60   *Sales* 25,364,220
SIC 1541 Industrial buildings and warehouses
Jacques Levesque
Marc Levesque

D-U-N-S 24-378-5656   (HQ)
MANUGYPSE INC
(*Suby of* GESTION LABERGE INC)
5385 Rue Rideau Bureau 871, Quebec, QC,
G2E 5V9
(418) 871-8088
Sales 17,886,960
SIC 5039 Construction materials, nec
Jean Laberge
Pierre Laberge
Gilles Laberge

D-U-N-S 24-864-4502   (SL)
PROPUR INC
5185 Rue Rideau, Quebec, QC, G2E 5S2
(418) 862-7739
Emp Here 3   *Sales* 12,920,901
SIC 5148 Fresh fruits and vegetables
Luc Garon
Rejean Dube

D-U-N-S 24-531-2343   (HQ)
SANI METAL LTEE
SML STAINLESS STEEL GROUP
5170 Rue Rideau, Quebec, QC, G2E 5S4
(418) 872-5170
Sales 24,691,520
SIC 2514 Metal household furniture
Michel Pelletier
Simon Pelletier
Luc Vezina

D-U-N-S 25-297-6675   (BR)
SIEMENS CANADA LIMITED
(*Suby of* SIEMENS AG)
2800 Av Saint-Jean-Baptiste Bureau 190,
Quebec, QC, G2E 6J5
(418) 687-4524
Emp Here 130
SIC 3625 Relays and industrial controls
Stephane Chayer

D-U-N-S 25-980-3765   (BR)
UNITED PARCEL SERVICE CANADA LTD
UPS
(*Suby of* UNITED PARCEL SERVICE, INC.)
625 Rue Des Canetons, Quebec, QC, G2E
5X6
(418) 872-2686
Emp Here 80
SIC 7389 Business services, nec
Cyril Craig

Quebec, QC G2G

D-U-N-S 24-759-5838   (HQ)
2553-4330 QUEBEC INC
AEROPRO
714 7e Avenue De L'Aeroport, Quebec, QC,
G2G 2T6
(418) 877-2808
Sales 15,751,702
SIC 4512 Air transportation, scheduled
Aurele Labbe

D-U-N-S 20-649-1727   (BR)
ACCEO SOLUTIONS INC
(*Suby of* CONSTELLATION SOFTWARE
INC)
7710 Boul Wilfrid-Hamel, Quebec, QC, G2G
2J5
(418) 877-0088
Emp Here 960
SIC 7372 Prepackaged software
Denis Carrier

▲ Public Company   ■ Public Company Family Member   **HQ** Headquarters   **BR** Branch   **SL** Single Location

D-U-N-S 25-330-8340   (HQ)
AEROPORT DE QUEBEC INC
AEROPORT INTERNATIONALE JEAN LESAGE DE QUEBEC
505 Rue Principale, Quebec, QC, G2G 0J4
(418) 640-2700
Emp Here 1   *Sales* 47,419,016
SIC 4581 Airports, flying fields, and services
 Andre Fortin
 Jean-Claude L'abbe
 Gaetan Gagne
 Liliane Laverdiere
 Denis Therrien
 Alain April
 Jean-Guy Paquet
 Lise Lapierre
 Andre Lortie
 Pierre Pelletier

D-U-N-S 24-348-1681   (BR)
ALLSTATE INSURANCE COMPANY OF CANADA
(*Suby of* THE ALLSTATE CORPORATION)
1150 Aut Duplessis Unit 600, Quebec, QC, G2G 2B5
(819) 569-5911
Emp Here 100
SIC 6411 Insurance agents, brokers, and service
 Robert Laplante

D-U-N-S 20-868-6832   (HQ)
AUTOBUS LA QUEBECOISE INC
LIGNE D'AUTOBUS DECOUVERTE
607 6e Avenue De L'Aeroport, Quebec, QC, G2G 2T4
(418) 872-5525
Emp Here 100   *Sales* 8,430,464
SIC 4151 School buses
 Mathieu Gingras

D-U-N-S 24-232-1458   (BR)
GOUVERNEMENT DE LA PROVINCE DE QUEBEC
SERVICE AERIEN GOUVERNEMENTAL
(*Suby of* GOUVERNEMENT DE LA PROVINCE DE QUEBEC)
700 7e Rue De L'Aeroport, Quebec, QC, G2G 2S8
(418) 528-8686
Emp Here 190
SIC 8711 Engineering services
 Benoit Carrier

D-U-N-S 20-179-6120   (BR)
HOME DEPOT OF CANADA INC
(*Suby of* THE HOME DEPOT INC)
1516 Av Jules-Verne, Quebec, QC, G2G 2R5
(418) 872-8007
Emp Here 125
SIC 5211 Lumber and other building materials
 Nicolas Vallieres

D-U-N-S 20-576-6590   (BR)
NAV CANADA
(*Suby of* NAV CANADA)
515 Rue Principale, Quebec, QC, G2G 2T8
(418) 871-7032
Emp Here 110
SIC 4899 Communication services, nec
 Benoit Bannon

D-U-N-S 20-726-2986   (HQ)
SIGNALISATION VER-MAC INC
PANNEX
1781 Rue Bresse, Quebec, QC, G2G 2V2
(418) 654-1303
Sales 33,327,350
SIC 3669 Communications equipment, nec
 Whitney Richardson
 Sandra-Lee Mcbain

D-U-N-S 25-258-6862   (HQ)
SOCIETE DE PROTECTION DES FORETS CONTRE LE FEU (SOPFEU)
715 7e Rue De L'Aeroport, Quebec, QC, G2G 2S7

(418) 871-3341
Sales 75,147,600
SIC 0851 Forestry services
 Genevieve Labrecque
 Pierre Cormier
 Chantal Savoie
 Michel Deshaies
 Simon Beaudoin
 Maryse Belanger
 Richard Caissy
 Gaetan Vallee
 Julie Fortin
 Marc Lauzon

D-U-N-S 24-216-0153   (HQ)
TRANS-SOL AVIATION SERVICE INC
FBO-MONTREAL (YUL)
(*Suby of* AVJET HOLDING INC)
230 2e Av De L'Aeroport, Quebec, QC, G2G 2T2
(418) 877-6708
Emp Here 1   *Sales* 48,443,500
SIC 2759 Commercial printing, nec
 Denis Jacob

D-U-N-S 25-498-2549   (BR)
WAL-MART CANADA CORP
WALMART
(*Suby of* WALMART INC.)
1470 Av Jules-Verne Bureau 3146, Quebec, QC, G2G 2R5
(418) 874-6068
Emp Here 160
SIC 5311 Department stores
 Daniel Pellerin

Quebec, QC G2J

D-U-N-S 20-377-7193   (SL)
10684651 CANADA INC
STUDIOS BKOM
825 Boul Lebourgneuf Bureau 130, Quebec, QC, G2J 0B9
(888) 523-1883
Emp Here 80   *Sales* 14,184,880
SIC 7371 Custom computer programming services
 Frederic Martin
 Marie-Helene Boivin

D-U-N-S 20-526-4786   (SL)
4094590 CANADA INC
SPORT EXPERT ATMOSPHERE
200 Rue Bouvier Unite 100, Quebec, QC, G2J 1R8
(418) 627-6665
Emp Here 60   *Sales* 14,659,680
SIC 5941 Sporting goods and bicycle shops
 Yvan Briere

D-U-N-S 20-952-7498   (HQ)
AGENCE DE VOYAGES D'AUTOMOBILE ET TOURING CLUB DU QUEBEC INC
ACCES VACANCES
(*Suby of* AUTOMOBILE ET TOURING CLUB DU QUEBEC (A.T.C.Q.))
444 Rue Bouvier, Quebec, QC, G2J 1E3
(418) 624-8222
Emp Here 25   *Sales* 54,826,350
SIC 6712 Bank holding companies
 Richard Lachance
 Elisabeth Larochelle-Lachance
 Stephane Pare
 Rene Proulx
 Benoit Bessette

D-U-N-S 20-400-6329   (HQ)
AGENCE DE VOYAGES DE L'AUTOMOBILE ET TOURING CLUB DU QUEBEC INC
(*Suby of* AUTOMOBILE ET TOURING CLUB DU QUEBEC (A.T.C.Q.))
444 Rue Bouvier, Quebec, QC, G2J 1E3
(418) 624-2424
Emp Here 1   *Sales* 98,859,500

SIC 4724 Travel agencies
 Richard Lachance
 Sophie Gagne
 Stephane Pare
 Rene Proulx
 Benoit Bessette

D-U-N-S 24-907-3586   (HQ)
AUTOMOBILE ET TOURING CLUB DU QUE-BEC (A.T.C.Q.)
CAA QUEBEC
444 Rue Bouvier, Quebec, QC, G2J 1E3
(418) 624-2424
Emp Here 400   *Sales* 147,921,000
SIC 8699 Membership organizations, nec
 Richard Lachance
 Rene Proulx
 Benoit Bessette
 Sophie Gagne
 Richard Lachance
 Michel Sanschagrin
 Diane Bourdeau
 Paul Pelletier
 Jean-Pierre Drewitt
 William Betournay

D-U-N-S 24-381-3128   (SL)
BOUCHER LORTIE INC
850 Rue Des Rocailles Bureau 1124, Quebec, QC, G2J 1A5
(418) 623-2323
Emp Here 75   *Sales* 17,479,875
SIC 1711 Plumbing, heating, air-conditioning
 Marco Boucher
 Stephane Boucher

D-U-N-S 24-206-1687   (HQ)
CANAC IMMOBILIER INC
(*Suby of* GESTION LABERGE INC)
5355 Boul Des Gradins, Quebec, QC, G2J 1C8
(418) 667-1313
Sales 22,358,700
SIC 5039 Construction materials, nec
 Jean Laberge
 Pierre Laberge
 Gilles Laberge

D-U-N-S 20-363-5214   (HQ)
CANAC-MARQUIS GRENIER LTEE
CANAC
(*Suby of* GESTION LABERGE INC)
5355 Boul Des Gradins, Quebec, QC, G2J 1C8
(418) 667-1313
Emp Here 100   *Sales* 365,509,000
SIC 6719 Holding companies, nec
 Jean Laberge
 Pierre Laberge
 Gilles Laberge

D-U-N-S 20-530-0366   (BR)
CANADA POST CORPORATION
(*Suby of* CANADA POST CORPORATION)
6700 Boul Pierre-Bertrand Bureau 200, Quebec, QC, G2J 0B6

Emp Here 100
SIC 4311 U.s. postal service

D-U-N-S 20-288-9945   (SL)
CHRONO AVIATION INC
706a 7e Av De L'Aeroport, Quebec, QC, G2J 2T6
(418) 529-4444
Emp Here 52   *Sales* 16,887,208
SIC 4522 Air transportation, nonscheduled
 Vincent Gagnon-Pouliot
 Dany Gagnon

D-U-N-S 24-987-8711   (SL)
CONSTRUCTION POLARIS INC
DYNAMITAGE DU QUEBEC
500 -797 Boul Lebourgneuf, Quebec, QC, G2J 0B5
(418) 861-9877
Emp Here 100   *Sales* 24,618,600
SIC 1794 Excavation work

 Robert Phaneuf
 Michel Poisson
 Serge Roy
 Jacques Gaumond
 Jocelyn St-Louis

D-U-N-S 25-832-1835   (BR)
COSTCO WHOLESALE CANADA LTD
COSTCO
(*Suby of* COSTCO WHOLESALE CORPORATION)
440 Rue Bouvier, Quebec, QC, G2J 1E3
(418) 627-5100
Emp Here 200
SIC 5099 Durable goods, nec
 Luc Lelievre

D-U-N-S 24-746-8713   (SL)
GESTION GERALD SAVARD INC
CANADIAN TIRE #405
5500 Boul Des Gradins Bureau 405, Quebec, QC, G2J 1A1
(418) 622-7333
Emp Here 80   *Sales* 19,546,240
SIC 5941 Sporting goods and bicycle shops
 Gerald Savard

D-U-N-S 24-499-4596   (HQ)
GESTION J.M.CLEMENT LTEE
5830 Boul Pierre-Bertrand Bureau 400, Quebec, QC, G2J 1B7
(418) 626-0006
Emp Here 2   *Sales* 182,754,500
SIC 6712 Bank holding companies
 Charles Clement
 Jean Clement

D-U-N-S 25-118-9606   (HQ)
GROUPE D'APPROVISIONNEMENT EN COMMUN DE L'EST DU QUEBEC
GACEQ
710 Rue Bouvier Bureau 296, Quebec, QC, G2J 1C2
(418) 780-8111
Emp Here 15   *Sales* 24,418,602
SIC 6221 Commodity contracts brokers, dealers
 Francois Latreille
 Raymond Coulombe
 Gaetan Lamy
 Marie Caron
 Francine Dube
 Mario Morand
 Nicole Morin
 Lucie Letendre
 Nathalie Boisvert
 Jean-Philippe Legault

D-U-N-S 25-155-9829   (SL)
GROUPE INCURSION INC
INCURSION VOYAGE
815 Boul Lebourgneuf Bureau 202, Quebec, QC, G2J 0C1
(418) 687-2400
Emp Here 25   *Sales* 12,999,175
SIC 4724 Travel agencies
 Liroy Haddad
 Dan Chetrit
 George Levesquelevesque
 David Gatteaugatteau

D-U-N-S 24-852-8676   (HQ)
HOLLIS INSURANCE INC
AGENCE D'ASSURANCE NFIA
(*Suby of* INDUSTRIELLE ALLIANCE, ASSURANCE ET SERVICES FINANCIERS INC)
6700 Boul Pierre-Bertrand Bureau 300, Quebec, QC, G2J 0B4
(418) 623-4330
Emp Here 15   *Sales* 36,933,180
SIC 6311 Life insurance
 John Hopkin
 Manon Gauthier
 Caroline Labrecque
 Stephane Blanchette
 Paul Grimes
 Pepin Normand

Andre Dubuc
Gerald Bouwers
Mustos Carl
Andrew H. Dalglish

D-U-N-S 20-179-6088   (BR)
HOME DEPOT OF CANADA INC
HOME DEPOT
(*Suby of* THE HOME DEPOT INC)
300 Rue Bouvier, Quebec, QC, G2J 1R8
(418) 634-8880
Emp Here 130
SIC 5211 Lumber and other building materials
Pierre Longchamps

D-U-N-S 24-051-6810   (BR)
HYDRO-QUEBEC
SYNDICAT EMPLOYES DE METIERS HYDRO-QUEBEC
(*Suby of* GOUVERNEMENT DE LA PROVINCE DE QUEBEC)
5050 Boul Des Gradins Bureau 200, Quebec, QC, G2J 1P8
(418) 624-2811
Emp Here 600
SIC 8631 Labor organizations
Guy Bureau

D-U-N-S 20-289-8755   (BR)
IMMEUBLES ROUSSIN LTEE, LES
LES JARDINS LEBOURGNEUF
(*Suby of* GESTION MAURICE ROUSSIN LTEE)
780 Boul Lebourgneuf, Quebec, QC, G2J 1S1
(418) 623-5333
Emp Here 180
SIC 6512 Nonresidential building operators
Jocelin Cloutier

D-U-N-S 24-884-1629   (HQ)
INVESTIA SERVICES FINANCIERS INC
(*Suby of* INDUSTRIELLE ALLIANCE, ASSURANCE ET SERVICES FINANCIERS INC)
6700 Boul Pierre-Bertrand Bureau 300, Quebec, QC, G2J 0B4
(418) 684-5548
Emp Here 2   *Sales* 46,958,850
SIC 6282 Investment advice
Louis H. Deconinck
Karine Hebert
Paul Grimes
Normand Pepin
Bruno Michaud
Andre Dubuc
Gerald Bouwers
Carl Mustos

D-U-N-S 20-250-0211   (HQ)
J.M. CLEMENT LTEE
BEBE CONFORT
(*Suby of* GESTION J.M.CLEMENT LTEE)
5830 Boul Pierre-Bertrand Bureau 400, Quebec, QC, G2J 1B7
(418) 626-0006
Emp Here 85   *Sales* 61,129,950
SIC 5641 Children's and infants' wear stores
Charles Clement
France Clement
Caroline Clement
Jean Clement
Marie Clement

D-U-N-S 25-849-1570   (BR)
LOBLAWS INC
MAXI # 8649
(*Suby of* LOBLAW COMPANIES LIMITED)
350 Rue Bouvier, Quebec, QC, G2J 1R8
(418) 623-5475
Emp Here 90
SIC 5411 Grocery stores
Stephane Cote

D-U-N-S 25-542-4194   (HQ)
MARTIN DESSERT INC
TADAM
665 Rue Des Rocailles, Quebec, QC, G2J 1A9

(418) 622-0220
Sales 34,569,000
SIC 2051 Bread, cake, and related products
Denis Martin

D-U-N-S 20-581-2019   (HQ)
MARTIN, CLAUDE & MARCEL INC
ST-HUBERT BAR-B-Q
(*Suby of* 2621-9386 QUEBEC INC)
701 Rue Des Rocailles, Quebec, QC, G2J 1A9
(418) 622-0220
Sales 37,311,200
SIC 5812 Eating places
Pierre Martin
Louis Martin
Jean Martin
Marcel Martin

D-U-N-S 20-234-6016   (BR)
SOBEYS CAPITAL INCORPORATED
I G A EXTRA LEBOURGNEUF
(*Suby of* EMPIRE COMPANY LIMITED)
5555 Boul Des Gradins, Quebec, QC, G2J 1C8
(418) 622-5262
Emp Here 140
SIC 5411 Grocery stores
Stephane Tardis

D-U-N-S 20-873-1661   (HQ)
SYNDICAT DE LA FONCTION PUBLIQUE ET PARAPUBLIQUE DU QUEBEC INC
101 - TRANSPORTS - REGION DE LA CAPITALE
5100 Boul Des Gradins, Quebec, QC, G2J 1N4
(418) 623-2424
Sales 28,480,200
SIC 8631 Labor organizations
Christian Daigle
Patrick Audy
Maryse Rousseau
Melanie Deziel
Lina Chiasson
Carl Ouellet
Yvon Brault

D-U-N-S 20-776-5983   (SL)
SYNDICAT DES INSPECTEURS ET DES REPARTITEURS DU RESEAU DE TRANSPORT DE LA CAPITALE (FISA)
REPARTITEURS DU RESEAU DE TRANSPORT DE LA CAPITALE
720 Rue Des Rocailles, Quebec, QC, G2J 1A5
(418) 627-2351
Emp Here 1,200   *Sales* 67,456,800
SIC 4111 Local and suburban transit
Eric Poirier
Jean Cote
Luc-Andre Roy
Diane Beaumont
Montminy Joanne

D-U-N-S 24-759-5861   (SL)
SYSTEMES TECHNO-POMPES INC, LES
6055 Rue Des Tournelles, Quebec, QC, G2J 1P7
(418) 623-2022
Emp Here 70   *Sales* 16,314,550
SIC 1711 Plumbing, heating, air-conditioning
Roger Fortin
Pierre Fortin
Renold Asselin

Quebec, QC G2K

D-U-N-S 24-863-6987   (HQ)
2427-9028 QUEBEC INC
SPORTS EXPERTS
5401 Boul Des Galeries Bureau 240, Quebec, QC, G2K 1N4
(418) 627-0062
Sales 10,880,650
SIC 5941 Sporting goods and bicycle shops
Yvan Briere

Marthe Auger
Philippe Briere
Many Briere

D-U-N-S 24-707-3356   (SL)
9220-3785 QUEBEC INC
CIRCUIT ACURA
4901 Boul Des Galeries, Quebec, QC, G2K 1X1
(418) 622-8180
Emp Here 25   *Sales* 12,451,950
SIC 5511 New and used car dealers
Benoit Theetge
Donald Theetge

D-U-N-S 20-326-6221   (SL)
ALLIANCE PERSONNELLE PROFESSIONELLE ET TECHNIQUE DE LA SANTE ET DES SERVICES SOCIAUX
APTS
1305 Boul Lebourgneuf Bureau 200, Quebec, QC, G2K 2E4
(418) 622-2541
Emp Here 49   *Sales* 19,166,742
SIC 8631 Labor organizations
Andree Sylvain

D-U-N-S 20-721-1012   (BR)
CIMA+ S.E.N.C.
(*Suby of* CIMA+ S.E.N.C.)
1145 Boul Lebourgneuf Bureau 300, Quebec, QC, G2K 2K8
(418) 623-3373
Emp Here 80
SIC 8711 Engineering services

D-U-N-S 25-487-6931   (BR)
COFFRAGES DOMINIC LTEE, LES
COFFRAGE CCC
(*Suby of* 110507 CANADA INC)
6921 Boul Pierre-Bertrand, Quebec, QC, G2K 1M1
(418) 626-3271
Emp Here 100
SIC 1799 Special trade contractors, nec
Brian Angers

D-U-N-S 25-244-7446   (BR)
COMPAGNIE D'ASSURANCE BELAIR INC, LA
BELAIR DIRECT
(*Suby of* INTACT FINANCIAL CORPORATION)
5400 Boul Des Galeries Bureau 500, Quebec, QC, G2K 2B4
(418) 877-1199
Emp Here 110
SIC 6331 Fire, marine, and casualty insurance

D-U-N-S 24-378-1424   (HQ)
CONSTRUCTIONS BE-CON INC, LES
1054 Boul Bastien Bureau 418, Quebec, QC, G2K 1E6
(418) 626-3583
Sales 23,536,550
SIC 1542 Nonresidential construction, nec
Patrick Pilote
Dominic Vezina
Miguel Tardif

D-U-N-S 24-820-9785   (BR)
DESCHENES & FILS LTEE
LACROIX DECOR
(*Suby of* ENTREPRISES MIRCA INC, LES)
1105 Rue Des Rocailles, Quebec, QC, G2K 2K6
(418) 627-4711
Emp Here 125
SIC 5074 Plumbing and heating equipment and supplies (hydronics)
Eric Patry

D-U-N-S 25-456-1764   (BR)
DESSAU INC
(*Suby of* GROUPE DESSAU INC)
1260 Boul Lebourgneuf Bureau 250, Quebec, QC, G2K 2G2

(418) 626-1688
Emp Here 120
SIC 8711 Engineering services
Olivier Rochette

D-U-N-S 25-748-2414   (BR)
ESSOR ASSURANCES PLACEMENTS CONSEILS INC
(*Suby of* GROUPE FINANCIER ESSOR INC)
5600 Boul Des Galeries Bureau 600, Quebec, QC, G2K 2H6
(418) 692-0660
Emp Here 100
SIC 6411 Insurance agents, brokers, and service
Michel Duval

D-U-N-S 25-459-6950   (HQ)
FLAGEC INC
GROUPE FLEURY & ASSOCIES
1220 Boul Lebourgneuf Bureau 200, Quebec, QC, G2K 2G4
(418) 523-7015
Emp Here 7   *Sales* 14,659,680
SIC 5912 Drug stores and proprietary stores
Gilles Fleury

D-U-N-S 20-241-7994   (HQ)
GARAGE DESHARNAIS & FILS LTEE
DESHARNAIS PNEUS ET MECANIQUE
6055 Boul Pierre-Bertrand, Quebec, QC, G2K 1M1
(418) 628-0203
Emp Here 50   *Sales* 78,784,475
SIC 7538 General automotive repair shops
Fernand Desharnais
Denis Desharnais

D-U-N-S 24-391-8161   (SL)
GESTION F.D. DESHARNAIS INC
6055 Boul Pierre-Bertrand, Quebec, QC, G2K 1M1
(418) 628-0203
Emp Here 175   *Sales* 78,784,475
SIC 7538 General automotive repair shops
Denis Desharnais

D-U-N-S 24-371-9213   (HQ)
GROUPE PPP LTEE, LE
GROUPE PPP
(*Suby of* INDUSTRIELLE ALLIANCE, ASSURANCE ET SERVICES FINANCIERS INC)
1165 Boul Lebourgneuf Bureau 250, Quebec, QC, G2K 2C9
(418) 623-8155
Emp Here 100   *Sales* 320,545,200
SIC 6351 Surety insurance
Michel Laurin
Alnoor R. Jiwani
Amelie Cantin
Denis Ricard
Sean O'brien

D-U-N-S 24-821-6384   (HQ)
GROUPE PROMUTUEL FEDERATION DE SOCIETE MUTUELLES D'ASSURANCES GENERALES
GROUPE PROMUTUEL
2000 Boul Lebourgneuf Bureau 400, Quebec, QC, G2K 0B6
(418) 840-1313
Emp Here 200   *Sales* 3,205,452,000
SIC 6311 Life insurance
Omer Bouchard
Laurent De Ladurantaye
Roger Brouard
Yvon Belaira
Guy Lapointe
Yvan Rose
Michel Gauthier
Rene Berube
Fernand Timmons
Jean Bussieres

D-U-N-S 24-802-2167   (BR)
GROUPE RESTAURANTS IMVESCOR INC
RESTAURANT SCORES BATON ROUGE
(*Suby of* GROUPE D'ALIMENTATION MTY

INC)
1875 Rue Bouvier, Quebec, QC, G2K 0B5
(418) 624-2525
Emp Here 100
SIC 6794 Patent owners and lessors
 David Bazinet

D-U-N-S 20-262-4149   (SL)
GROUPE SANTE PHYSIMED
1300 Boul Lebourgneuf Bureau 300, Quebec,
QC, G2K 2N1
(418) 624-2001
Emp Here 30   *Sales* 17,397,720
SIC 6411 Insurance agents, brokers, and ser-
vice
 Eric Caron

D-U-N-S 20-432-6276   (HQ)
GUAY INC
ARMAND GUAY
1160 Rue Bouvier, Quebec, QC, G2K 1L9
(418) 628-8460
Emp Here 75   *Sales* 164,241,964
SIC 7353 Heavy construction equipment
rental
 Jean-Marc Baronet
 Guillaume Gagnon

D-U-N-S 24-207-0142   (BR)
HUDSON'S BAY COMPANY
LA BAIE
(*Suby of* HUDSON'S BAY COMPANY)
5401 Boul Des Galeries, Quebec, QC, G2K
1N4
(418) 627-5922
Emp Here 150
SIC 5311 Department stores
 Corinne Claveau

D-U-N-S 20-592-7841   (SL)
LESSARD, M LTEE
LESSARD HYUNDAI
300 Boul Louis-Xiv, Quebec, QC, G2K 1W7
(418) 623-5471
Emp Here 40   *Sales* 19,923,120
SIC 5511 New and used car dealers
 Gilles Lessard
 Charles Lessard

D-U-N-S 24-147-2682   (SL)
LIBEO INC
SYS-TECH
5700 Boul Des Galeries Bureau 300, Quebec,
QC, G2K 0H5
(418) 520-0739
Emp Here 65   *Sales* 11,525,215
SIC 7374 Data processing and preparation
 Jean-Francois Rousseau

D-U-N-S 24-820-4968   (HQ)
LNLC INC
LUNETTERIE NEW LOOK (CANADA)
1100 Rue Bouvier Bureau 100, Quebec, QC,
G2K 1L9
(418) 624-6100
Emp Here 12   *Sales* 74,699,559
SIC 5995 Optical goods stores
 Michel Laurendeau

D-U-N-S 24-591-3009   (SL)
MACHINERIE P.W. INC
ATELIER D'USINAGE
151 Boul Louis-Xiv, Quebec, QC, G2K 1W6
(418) 622-5155
Emp Here 70   *Sales* 15,540,070
SIC 3599 Industrial machinery, nec
 Andre Wagner
 Denis Wagner

D-U-N-S 20-242-3570   (SL)
MACHINERIES PROVINCIALES INC
1160 Rue Bouvier, Quebec, QC, G2K 1L9
(418) 628-8460
Emp Here 130
SIC 7699 Repair services, nec
 Jean-Marc Baronet

D-U-N-S 25-623-1361   (SL)

OLYMPE CONSULTANTS
1500 Rue Migneron, Quebec, QC, G2K 1X5

Emp Here 49   *Sales* 11,480,112
SIC 8748 Business consulting, nec
 Pierre Audet

D-U-N-S 24-942-9911   (SL)
PREMIER QUEBEC INC
6655 Boul Pierre-Bertrand Bureau 101, Que-
bec, QC, G2K 1M1
(418) 681-4733
Emp Here 25   *Sales* 11,179,350
SIC 5072 Hardware
 Pierre Cartier
 Liette Dubois

D-U-N-S 24-391-5233   (HQ)
**PROMUTUEL CAPITAL, SOCIETE DE
FIDUCIE INC**
2000 Boul Lebourgneuf Bureau 400, Quebec,
QC, G2K 0B6

Sales 12,416,655
SIC 6722 Management investment, open-end
 Omer Bouchard
 Frenand Timmons
 Jean Bussieres
 Michel Gauthier
 Yvon Belair
 Rene Berube
 Roger Brouard
 Laurent De Ladurantaye
 Guy Lapointe
 Yvan Rose

D-U-N-S 24-864-2910   (HQ)
RADIO-ONDE INC
AMOS 3601
6655 Boul Pierre-Bertrand Bureau 643, Que-
bec, QC, G2K 1M1
(418) 527-1602
Emp Here 42   *Sales* 28,559,000
SIC 4899 Communication services, nec
 Gaetan Normandin
 Daniel Gagnon
 Roch Charbonneau
 Jean Laporte
 Gerald Guerin
 Luc St-Georges

D-U-N-S 25-466-1002   (SL)
RDL LEGARE MC NICOLL INC
1305 Boul Lebourgneuf Bureau 401, Quebec,
QC, G2K 2E4
(418) 622-6666
Emp Here 50   *Sales* 10,454,250
SIC 8721 Accounting, auditing, and book-
keeping
 Pierre Legare
 Yvon Lavoie
 Gilles Vendal

D-U-N-S 24-339-9081   (BR)
SNC-LAVALIN INC
PELLEMON
(*Suby of* GROUPE SNC-LAVALIN INC)
5500 Boul Des Galeries Bureau 200, Quebec,
QC, G2K 2E2
(418) 621-5500
Emp Here 250
SIC 8711 Engineering services
 Michel L'abbe

Quebec, QC G2L

D-U-N-S 25-412-7533   (BR)
**CENTRE HOSPITALIER UNIVERSITAIRE
DE QUEBEC**
SERVICES FINANCIERS DU CHUQ
(*Suby of* CENTRE HOSPITALIER UNIVERSI-
TAIRE DE QUEBEC)
775 Rue Saint-Viateur Unite 130a, Quebec,
QC, G2L 2Z3

Emp Here 3,000
SIC 8062 General medical and surgical hospi-
tals
 Claude Roy

D-U-N-S 20-845-2271   (SL)
**COOPERATIVE DES CONSOMATEURS DE
CHARLESBOURG**
IGA EXTRA
1233 Boul Louis-Xiv, Quebec, QC, G2L 1L9
(418) 628-2525
Emp Here 40   *Sales* 11,093,088
SIC 5411 Grocery stores
 Jean-Pierre D'arcy

Quebec, QC G2M

D-U-N-S 24-690-4452   (SL)
9089-3470 QUEBEC INC
PAGE, MARCEL ELECTRICIEN
290 Rue Bernier E, Quebec, QC, G2M 1K7
(418) 849-6246
Emp Here 100   *Sales* 21,782,900
SIC 1731 Electrical work
 Marcel Page
 Eric Tanguay

D-U-N-S 24-890-5226   (SL)
ALIMENTATION A.D.R. INC
I G A
795 Boul Du Lac Bureau 264, Quebec, QC,
G2M 0E4
(418) 849-3674
Emp Here 48   *Sales* 13,159,296
SIC 5411 Grocery stores
 Denis Rousseau

Quebec, QC G2N

D-U-N-S 20-175-2768   (SL)
9231-4897 QUEBEC INC
LES ENTREPRISES GAEVAN
625 Rue De L'Argon, Quebec, QC, G2N 2G7
(418) 841-2001
Emp Here 26   *Sales* 12,350,676
SIC 5082 Construction and mining machinery
 Gaetan Couture

D-U-N-S 24-146-4346   (HQ)
CHAUSSURES REGENCE INC
REGENCE
(*Suby of* PLACEMENTS CHRISTIAN BERG-
ERON INC)
655 Rue De L'Argon, Quebec, QC, G2N 2G7
(418) 849-7997
Sales 119,910,750
SIC 3144 Women's footwear, except athletic
 Christian Bergeron

D-U-N-S 20-711-9913   (BR)
**COMMISSION   SCOLAIRE   DES
PREMIERES-SEIGNEURIES**
*COMMISSION   SCOLAIRE   DES
PREMIERES-SEIGNEURIES*
(*Suby of* COMMISSION SCOLAIRE DES
PREMIERES-SEIGNEURIES)
700 Rue De L'Argon, Quebec, QC, G2N 2G5
(418) 634-5580
Emp Here 135
SIC 8299 Schools and educational services,
nec
 Eddy Vallieres

D-U-N-S 25-371-5445   (SL)
EDITIONS PRATICO-PRATIQUES INC
1685 Boul Talbot, Quebec, QC, G2N 0C6
(418) 877-0259
Emp Here 85   *Sales* 13,942,295
SIC 2721 Periodicals
 Caty Berube

D-U-N-S 20-544-7808   (HQ)
FESTO DIDACTIQUE LTEE
LAB-VOLT
(*Suby of* FESTO BETEILIGUNGEN GMBH &
CO. KG)
675 Rue Du Carbone, Quebec, QC, G2N 2K7
(418) 849-1000
Sales 66,142,000
SIC 3999 Manufacturing industries, nec
 Michel Lessard
 Michel Fortier
 Christian Engau
 Thomas Lichtenberger
 Enrico Ruhle

D-U-N-S 20-852-9987   (SL)
GESTION GAEVAN INC
DELTA NATIONAL
625 Rue De L'Argon, Quebec, QC, G2N 2G7
(418) 841-2001
Emp Here 40   *Sales* 19,923,120
SIC 5511 New and used car dealers
 Gaetan Couture

D-U-N-S 25-258-7704   (BR)
GROUPE CHAMPLAIN INC
*CENTRE D'HEBERGEMENT CHAMPLAIN-
DES-MONTAGNES*
791 Rue De Sherwood, Quebec, QC, G2N
1X7
(418) 849-1891
Emp Here 100
SIC 8361 Residential care
 Andre Brunelle

D-U-N-S 24-531-2350   (HQ)
MAISON DU GIBIER INC, LA
(*Suby of* VIANDEX INC)
585 Rue De L'Argon, Quebec, QC, G2N 2G7
(418) 849-8427
Sales 40,107,696
SIC 5147 Meats and meat products
 Pierre Gagne
 Christian Vignola

D-U-N-S 20-181-8130   (HQ)
**PLACEMENTS CHRISTIAN BERGERON
INC**
655 Rue De L'Argon, Quebec, QC, G2N 2G7
(418) 849-7997
Sales 16,401,000
SIC 6712 Bank holding companies
 Christian Bergeron

Quebec, QC G3A

D-U-N-S 20-553-9187   (SL)
9020-7424 QUEBEC INC
IGA DES SOURCES
3373 Rue De L'Hetriere, Quebec, QC, G3A
0M2
(418) 872-4113
Emp Here 225   *Sales* 43,304,400
SIC 5411 Grocery stores
 Alain Gagne
 Gaetan Quirion

Quebec, QC G3E

D-U-N-S 24-820-8506   (HQ)
ALFRED CLOUTIER LIMITEE
BARBO, DIV DE
1737 Rue William-Marsh, Quebec, QC, G3E
1K9
(418) 842-4390
Sales 11,671,750
SIC 3144 Women's footwear, except athletic
 Serge Brie

D-U-N-S 20-249-1106   (SL)
AUCLAIR & MARTINEAU INC

AMIMOC
(*Suby of* TT GROUP LIMITED)
2277 Rue De La Faune, Quebec, QC, G3E
1S9
(418) 842-1943
Emp Here 90   *Sales* 24,323,040
SIC 3144 Women's footwear, except athletic
Xavier Leclercq
Jonathan Leclercq

D-U-N-S 20-249-1205   (SL)
CLOUTIER, EUGENE INC
1659 Rue Des Roselins, Quebec, QC, G3E
1G2
(418) 842-2087
Emp Here 80   *Sales* 21,620,480
SIC 3131 Footwear cut stock
Guillaume Deschenes
Luc Lauzon

D-U-N-S 20-925-6929   (BR)
RESTAURANTS MIKA INC, LES
RESTAURANT MCDONALD'S
(*Suby of* RESTAURANTS MIKA INC, LES)
1154 Rue De La Faune, Quebec, QC, G3E
1T2
(418) 845-6323
Emp Here 150
SIC 5812 Eating places
Stan O'neil

D-U-N-S 24-380-1263   (BR)
**SOCIETE EN COMMANDITE STADACONA
WB**
SCIERIE LEDUC, DIV OF
(*Suby of* SOCIETE EN COMMANDITE
STADACONA WB)
1092 Av Lapierre Bureau 220, Quebec, QC,
G3E 1Z3

Emp Here 75
SIC 2421 Sawmills and planing mills, general
Paul Baillargeon

D-U-N-S 25-332-0654   (SL)
**SYSTEME DE SECURITE A C DE QUEBEC
INC**
1394 Rue De Fronsac, Quebec, QC, G3E 1A3
(418) 842-7440
Emp Here 105   *Sales* 22,872,045
SIC 1731 Electrical work
Michel Boily

Quebec, QC G3G

D-U-N-S 20-203-6091   (SL)
ENTREPRISES P.E.B. LTEE, LES
1190 Av Du Lac-Saint-Charles, Quebec, QC,
G3G 2S9
(418) 849-2841
Emp Here 100   *Sales* 25,244,200
SIC 1623 Water, sewer, and utility lines
David Beaulieu
Sophie Beaulieu

D-U-N-S 24-941-9847   (HQ)
GROUPE S.M. TARDIF INC
15971 Boul De La Colline, Quebec, QC, G3G
3A7
(418) 849-7104
Emp Here 1   *Sales* 43,736,000
SIC 6712 Bank holding companies
Serge Tardif

D-U-N-S 20-203-6182   (SL)
MARCHE RHEAUME INC
SUPERMARCHE I G A
1501 Rue Jacques-Bedard, Quebec, QC,
G3G 1P9
(418) 849-4416
Emp Here 45   *Sales* 12,336,840
SIC 5411 Grocery stores
Michel Rheaume

D-U-N-S 20-870-3991   (SL)

PAGUI INC
(*Suby of* GROUPE S.M. TARDIF INC)
15971 Boul De La Colline, Quebec, QC, G3G
3A7
(418) 849-1832
Emp Here 75   *Sales* 16,337,175
SIC 1731 Electrical work
Serge Tardif
Genevieve Tardif
Claire Renaud Tardif

D-U-N-S 24-149-5399   (SL)
SM CONSTRUCTION INC
MORELCO
(*Suby of* GROUPE S.M. TARDIF INC)
15971 Boul De La Colline, Quebec, QC, G3G
3A7
(418) 849-7104
Emp Here 50   *Sales* 28,516,900
SIC 1542 Nonresidential construction, nec
Serge Tardif
Genevieve Tardif
Claire Renaud Tardif
Claude Faucher

Quebec, QC G3J

D-U-N-S 24-706-6616   (HQ)
CLUB VIDEO ECLAIR INC
1889 Boul Pie-Xi N, Quebec, QC, G3J 1P4
(418) 845-1212
Emp Here 14   *Sales* 20,181,600
SIC 7841 Video tape rental
Richard Boivin

D-U-N-S 25-356-3175   (SL)
PRODUITS DE PATISSERIE MICHAUD INC
EL DIVINO PECADO
1520 Av Des Affaires, Quebec, QC, G3J 1Y8
(418) 843-3712
Emp Here 25   *Sales* 20,889,425
SIC 5149 Groceries and related products, nec
Mario Michaud

D-U-N-S 20-224-3312   (SL)
SOYLUTIONS INC
(*Suby of* EARTH'S OWN FOOD COMPANY
INC)
1629 Av Des Affaires, Quebec, QC, G3J 1Y7
(418) 845-9888
Emp Here 50   *Sales* 17,284,500
SIC 2035 Pickles, sauces, and salad dress-
ings
Maheb Nathoo
Sandeep Cheema

Quebec, QC G3K

D-U-N-S 24-386-0041   (SL)
9180-6166 QUEBEC INC
HONDA DE LA CAPITALE
1507 Boul Pie-Xi S, Quebec, QC, G3K 1Y1
(418) 845-6060
Emp Here 26   *Sales* 12,950,028
SIC 5511 New and used car dealers
Denis Michel

D-U-N-S 20-317-7696   (SL)
9223-4202 QUEBEC INC
OPTIMUM SOLUTIONS
15369 Rue Du Petit-Vallon, Quebec, QC, G3K
0E6
(418) 840-2406
Emp Here 40   *Sales* 31,899,602
SIC 2038 Frozen specialties, nec
Christine Cote

D-U-N-S 20-363-4431   (SL)
9311-9089 QUEBEC INC
HYUNDAI VAL-BELAIR
1459 Boul Pie-Xi S, Quebec, QC, G3K 0P8

(418) 767-2500
Emp Here 31   *Sales* 15,440,418
SIC 5511 New and used car dealers
Denis Michel
Michel Dionne

D-U-N-S 24-821-4538   (SL)
CARTIER CHEVROLET BUICK GMC LTEE
1475 Boul Pie-Xi S, Quebec, QC, G3K 1H1
(418) 847-6000
Emp Here 90   *Sales* 24,903,900
SIC 5511 New and used car dealers
Bertrand Hebert
Luc Cote

D-U-N-S 20-293-7277   (SL)
**CENTRE DE SANTE ET DE SERVICES SO-
CIAUX DE QUEBEC-NORD-CLSC DE LA
JACQUES-CARTIER -VAL-BELA**
*CENTRE DE SANTE DE LA HAUT ST
CHARLES*
1465 Rue De L'Etna, Quebec, QC, G3K 2S2
(418) 843-2572
Emp Here 200   *Sales* 287,720,200
SIC 8699 Membership organizations, nec
Lucie Lacroix

D-U-N-S 25-823-0721   (SL)
DEFFOSSES ET VALLEE S.E.N.C
JEAN COUTU
1065 Boul Pie-Xi N Bureau 263, Quebec, QC,
G3K 2S5
(418) 840-0337
Emp Here 40   *Sales* 10,118,160
SIC 5912 Drug stores and proprietary stores
Marie-Michelle Deffosses

Quyon, QC J0X

D-U-N-S 24-179-4911   (SL)
MOUNTAINVIEW TURF FARM LTD
MOUNTAINVIEW TURF
4790 5e Conc, Quyon, QC, J0X 2V0
(819) 458-2632
Emp Here 40   *Sales* 10,122,360
SIC 5261 Retail nurseries and garden stores
William Hamilton
Susan Hamilton
Jared Hamilton
Lindsay Hamilton

Rawdon, QC J0K

D-U-N-S 25-200-6762   (SL)
ALIMENTATIONS GAREAU INC
IGA
3450 Rue Queen, Rawdon, QC, J0K 1S0
(450) 834-2633
Emp Here 60   *Sales* 17,608,620
SIC 5411 Grocery stores
Denis Guilbault
Jocelyne Gareau
Sylvain Guilbault

D-U-N-S 24-890-7909   (SL)
**CENTRE D' HEBERGEMENT ET DE SOINS
DE LONGUE DUREE HEATHER INC**
CHSLD
(*Suby of* ARBEC, PAUL INC)
3931 Rue Lakeshore Drive, Rawdon, QC, J0K
1S0
(450) 834-3070
Emp Here 100   *Sales* 5,924,700
SIC 8361 Residential care
Paul Arbec

D-U-N-S 20-171-7464   (BR)
COMMISSION SCOLAIRE DES SAMARES
ECOLE SECONDAIRE DES CHUTES
(*Suby of* COMMISSION SCOLAIRE DES
SAMARES)
3144 18e Av Bureau 760, Rawdon, QC, J0K

1S0
(450) 758-3749
Emp Here 75
SIC 8211 Elementary and secondary schools
Nancy Delisle

D-U-N-S 24-106-7362   (SL)
DISTRIBUTIONS JOSEE PERRAULT INC
JEAN COUTU
3285 1e Av Bureau 100, Rawdon, QC, J0K
1S0
(450) 834-2582
Emp Here 60   *Sales* 14,659,680
SIC 5912 Drug stores and proprietary stores
Josee Perreault

D-U-N-S 25-481-5236   (SL)
SUPERMARCHE BOUCHER INC
METRO
3528 Rue Metcalfe, Rawdon, QC, J0K 1S0
(450) 834-2561
Emp Here 80   *Sales* 23,478,160
SIC 5411 Grocery stores
Jean-Pierre Boucher

D-U-N-S 24-102-9771   (SL)
TRAVAIL ADAPTE DE LANAUDIERE
3131 5e Av, Rawdon, QC, J0K 1S0
(450) 834-7678
Emp Here 85   *Sales* 18,870,085
SIC 3549 Metalworking machinery, nec
Claude Levac

Repentigny, QC J5Y

D-U-N-S 24-835-0076   (SL)
168360 CANADA INC
HYUNDAI REPENTIGNY
845 Rue Notre-Dame Bureau 1989, Repentigny, QC, J5Y 1C4
(450) 582-3182
Emp Here 60   *Sales* 37,756,800
SIC 5511 New and used car dealers
Gabriel Gennarelli

D-U-N-S 20-621-4467   (SL)
3370160 CANADA INC
MAZDA REPENTIGNY
839 Rue Notre-Dame, Repentigny, QC, J5Y
1C4
(450) 654-7111
Emp Here 45   *Sales* 22,413,510
SIC 5511 New and used car dealers
Guylaine Caron

D-U-N-S 20-435-3072   (SL)
BLACKBURN + H.P.
21 Rue Rollet, Repentigny, QC, J5Y 3R3

Emp Here 4   *Sales* 12,423,428
SIC 4924 Natural gas distribution
Alain Blackburn

D-U-N-S 20-033-9435   (BR)
**COMMISSION SCOLAIRE DES AFFLU-
ENTS**
ECOLE SECONDAIRE FELIX LECLERC
(*Suby of* COMMISSION SCOLAIRE DES AF-
FLUENTS)
250 Boul Louis-Philippe-Picard, Repentigny,
QC, J5Y 3W9
(450) 492-3578
Emp Here 125
SIC 8211 Elementary and secondary schools
Pierre Bouchard

D-U-N-S 24-434-0746   (HQ)
ENTREPRISES CD VARIN INC, LES
PETRO CANADA
285 Rue Valmont, Repentigny, QC, J5Y 3H6
(450) 654-9253
Emp Here 5   *Sales* 13,707,600
SIC 5411 Grocery stores
Daniel Varin
Celine Varin

▲ Public Company   ■ Public Company Family Member   **HQ** Headquarters   **BR** Branch   **SL** Single Location

D-U-N-S 20-007-9171 (HQ)
FONDATION DU CEGEP REGIONAL DE LANAUDIERE
781 Rue Notre-Dame, Repentigny, QC, J5Y 1B4
(450) 470-0911
Emp Here 200   *Sales* 89,634,600
SIC 8221 Colleges and universities
 Marcel Cote
 Alain Lamarre
 Helene Bailleu

D-U-N-S 20-726-5984 (SL)
GIRARD AUTOMOBILE INC
REPENTIGNY FIAT
283 Rue Valmont, Repentigny, QC, J5Y 3H5
(450) 581-1490
Emp Here 45   *Sales* 22,413,510
SIC 5511 New and used car dealers
 Pierre Girard

D-U-N-S 25-995-7306 (SL)
GROUPE GAUDREAULT INC, LE
1500 Rue Raymond-Gaudreault, Repentigny, QC, J5Y 4E3
(450) 585-1210
Emp Here 705   *Sales* 257,683,845
SIC 6712 Bank holding companies
 Martin Gaudreault
 Manon Gaudreault

D-U-N-S 20-543-4376 (SL)
SABEM, SEC
AUTOBUS LACHENAIE
1500 Rue Raymond-Gaudreault, Repentigny, QC, J5Y 4E3
(450) 585-1210
Emp Here 250   *Sales* 14,053,500
SIC 4151 School buses
 Clement Michel

D-U-N-S 24-935-6296 (SL)
SUPERMARCHE CREVIER (IBERVILLE) INC
MARCHE CREVIER
(*Suby of* GESTION CREVIER, JEAN-CLAUDE INC)
1124 Boul Iberville Bureau 110, Repentigny, QC, J5Y 3M6
(450) 704-4750
Emp Here 70   *Sales* 17,102,960
SIC 5999 Miscellaneous retail stores, nec
 Georges Pilon
 Francis Pilon

D-U-N-S 24-612-0500 (SL)
SUPERMARCHE CREVIER (VALMONT) INC
I.G.A.
315 Rue Valmont, Repentigny, QC, J5Y 0Y5
(450) 657-5082
Emp Here 49   *Sales* 13,433,448
SIC 5411 Grocery stores
 Jean-Claude Crevier

Repentigny, QC J5Z

D-U-N-S 24-129-6990 (SL)
3496252 CANADA INC
MOBILIER BOOMRANG
340 Rue Saint-Paul, Repentigny, QC, J5Z 4H9
(450) 585-0308
Emp Here 24   *Sales* 12,212,544
SIC 5021 Furniture
 Mario Aube
 Gilles Pansera

D-U-N-S 24-339-0031 (SL)
6535577 CANADA INC
VISION HARLEY DAVIDSON
47 Rue De Lyon, Repentigny, QC, J5Z 4Z3
(450) 582-2442
Emp Here 25   *Sales* 12,451,950
SIC 5571 Motorcycle dealers
 Claude Comeau

D-U-N-S 24-385-4499 (HQ)
9210-7580 QUEBEC INC
LIBRAIRIE RAFFIN
29 Rue De Lyon, Repentigny, QC, J5Z 4Z3
(450) 585-9909
Emp Here 4   *Sales* 17,102,960
SIC 5942 Book stores
 Martin Granger
 Chantale Michel

D-U-N-S 20-308-6348 (SL)
EQUIPEMENTS DE SUPERMARCHES CONCEPT INTERNATIONAL INC
CSF INTERNATIONAL
429 Rue Des Industries, Repentigny, QC, J5Z 4Y8
(450) 582-3017
Emp Here 50   *Sales* 22,358,700
SIC 5078 Refrigeration equipment and supplies
 Mathieu Grenier
 Jeff Glazer

D-U-N-S 24-821-3899 (SL)
EXCAVATION NORMAND MAJEAU INC
337 Rue Charles-Marchand, Repentigny, QC, J5Z 4N8
(450) 581-8248
Emp Here 49   *Sales* 10,969,677
SIC 1794 Excavation work
 Michel Majeau

D-U-N-S 25-463-3357 (SL)
GEDILEX INC
JEAN COUTU
515 Boul Lacombe Bureau 255, Repentigny, QC, J5Z 1P5
(450) 581-6545
Emp Here 65   *Sales* 15,881,320
SIC 5912 Drug stores and proprietary stores
 Claude Coltron
 Maryse Rivest

D-U-N-S 24-697-4182 (HQ)
GENERAL DYNAMICS PRODUITS DE DEFENSE ET SYSTEMES TACTIQUES-CANADA INC
SIMUNITION
(*Suby of* GENERAL DYNAMICS CORPORATION)
5 Montee Des Arsenaux, Repentigny, QC, J5Z 2P4
(450) 581-3080
Emp Here 790   *Sales* 243,231,000
SIC 3483 Ammunition, except for small arms, nec
 Rene Blouin
 Del S. Dameron
 Alain Boisvert
 Mark C. Roualet
 Firath H Gezen

D-U-N-S 25-365-2127 (BR)
GROUPE PATRICK MORIN INC
PATRICK MORIN INC
(*Suby of* GROUPE PATRICK MORIN INC)
567 Boul Pierre-Le Gardeur, Repentigny, QC, J5Z 5H1
(450) 585-8564
Emp Here 100
SIC 5211 Lumber and other building materials
 Michelle Morin

D-U-N-S 24-350-2312 (HQ)
GROUPE TELTECH INC
GROUPE TEL-TECH
345d Rue Marion, Repentigny, QC, J5Z 4W8
(450) 657-2000
Sales 14,783,840
SIC 4899 Communication services, nec
 Francois Tessier

D-U-N-S 25-965-9147 (SL)
PHARMACIE JEAN COUTU
155 Boul Lacombe Unite 160, Repentigny, QC, J5Z 3C4
(450) 654-6747
Emp Here 49   *Sales* 12,394,746

SIC 5912 Drug stores and proprietary stores
 Marc Airoldi

D-U-N-S 25-408-2787 (SL)
PLOMBERIE & CHAUFFAGE ALAIN DAIGLE INC
310 Rue Charles-Marchand, Repentigny, QC, J5Z 4P1
(450) 657-1499
Emp Here 80   *Sales* 18,645,200
SIC 1711 Plumbing, heating, air-conditioning
 Alain Daigle
 Alexandre Caty
 Serge Dupuis

D-U-N-S 24-711-1768 (SL)
SYNCA MARKETING INC
SYNCA DIRECT
337 Rue Marion, Repentigny, QC, J5Z 4W8
(450) 582-1093
Emp Here 35   *Sales* 15,651,090
SIC 5047 Medical and hospital equipment
 Raymond Monette

D-U-N-S 25-389-4158 (HQ)
VIANDES RIENDEAU LTEE
399 Rue Des Industries, Repentigny, QC, J5Z 4Y8
(450) 654-6262
Sales 29,245,195
SIC 5147 Meats and meat products
 Eric Riendeau

D-U-N-S 24-227-8208 (HQ)
VINCENT S. VARIETE LIMITEE
VINCENT SELECTION 1971
433 Rue Saint-Paul, Repentigny, QC, J5Z 0C9
(450) 585-1687
Emp Here 18   *Sales* 16,711,540
SIC 5149 Groceries and related products, nec
 Sylvie Stortini
 Jocelyn Hamel-Stortini
 Steve Hamel-Stortini

Repentigny, QC J6A

D-U-N-S 24-402-6274 (SL)
2437-0223 QUEBEC INC
MARINA DE REPENTIGNY, LA
364 Rue Notre-Dame, Repentigny, QC, J6A 2S5
(450) 581-7071
Emp Here 50   *Sales* 10,669,600
SIC 4493 Marinas
 Nicolas Papadakis

D-U-N-S 24-896-0999 (SL)
2858-6691 QUEBEC INC
SUPERMARCHE IBERVILLE
305 Boul Iberville, Repentigny, QC, J6A 2A6
(450) 581-2630
Emp Here 65   *Sales* 19,076,005
SIC 5411 Grocery stores
 Bernard Lemay
 Denis Gagne

D-U-N-S 24-167-8333 (SL)
9085327 CANADA INC
ALBI NISSAN DE REPENTIGNY
225 Boul Brien, Repentigny, QC, J6A 6M4
(450) 585-5824
Emp Here 65   *Sales* 22,024,800
SIC 5511 New and used car dealers
 Denis Leclerc

D-U-N-S 25-851-5311 (SL)
ACOUSTIQUE ISOLATION QUATRE SAISONS INC
ISOLATION QUATRE SAISONS
525 Rue Lanaudiere, Repentigny, QC, J6A 7N1
(450) 657-5000
Emp Here 27   *Sales* 12,073,698
SIC 5033 Roofing, siding, and insulation
 Jean Fortin

D-U-N-S 20-243-7786 (SL)
ARCHEVEQUE & RIVEST LTEE, L'
96 Boul Industriel, Repentigny, QC, J6A 4X6
(450) 581-4480
Emp Here 35   *Sales* 16,475,585
SIC 1542 Nonresidential construction, nec
 Charles-Emile Rivest
 Sylvain Rivest
 Jean Rivest

D-U-N-S 24-108-1298 (HQ)
ATELIERS G. PAQUETTE INC
104 Rue Laroche, Repentigny, QC, J6A 7M5
(450) 654-6744
Emp Here 37   *Sales* 10,185,800
SIC 7629 Electrical repair shops
 Daniel Picotte
 Benoit Picotte
 Francois Paquette

D-U-N-S 25-650-5751 (HQ)
BUANDERIE BLANCHELLE INC, LA
94 Rue De Normandie, Repentigny, QC, J6A 4W2
(450) 585-1218
Emp Here 140   *Sales* 23,320,960
SIC 7218 Industrial launderers
 Pierre Ferron
 Robert Ferron

D-U-N-S 20-725-8302 (HQ)
C. CROTEAU INC
L'AUBAINERIE 14
(*Suby of* GESTION DESSUREAULT INC)
220 Boul Brien, Repentigny, QC, J6A 7E9
(450) 581-7373
Sales 17,939,600
SIC 5651 Family clothing stores
 Sophie Dessureault
 Michel Dessureault

D-U-N-S 24-680-6124 (HQ)
CAISSE DESJARDINS PIERRE-LE GARDEUR
CENTRE DE SERVICE CHARLEMAGNE
477 Rue Notre-Dame, Repentigny, QC, J6A 2T6
(450) 585-5555
Emp Here 10   *Sales* 50,250,002
SIC 6062 State credit unions
 Alain Reche
 Robert St-Aubin
 Stephanie Pilon
 Eric Coiteux
 Dion Michel
 Isabelle Payette
 Michel Perreault
 Sebastien Senechal
 Guillaume Simoneau

D-U-N-S 20-726-0803 (HQ)
CHAMARD, JACQUES & FILS INC
619 Boul Iberville, Repentigny, QC, J6A 2C5
(450) 581-0101
Emp Here 10   *Sales* 13,707,600
SIC 5411 Grocery stores
 Jacques Chamard

D-U-N-S 20-243-7620 (SL)
CLIMATISATION VALLEE & FILS INC
83 Rue Laroche, Repentigny, QC, J6A 7M3
(450) 581-4360
Emp Here 50   *Sales* 11,653,250
SIC 1711 Plumbing, heating, air-conditioning
 Guy Lagace
 Jacques Vallee
 Daniel Vallee
 Pierre Vallee
 Jean-Francois Lagace

D-U-N-S 20-725-3311 (SL)
FRENETTE, GEFFREY LTEE
CANADIAN TIRE
115 Boul Brien, Repentigny, QC, J6A 8J3
(450) 585-9840
Emp Here 75   *Sales* 15,400,725
SIC 5311 Department stores

Geffrey Frenette

D-U-N-S 20-243-8396   (SL)
GARAGE P VENNE INC
94 Rue Notre-Dame, Repentigny, QC, J6A
2P3
(514) 343-3428
Emp Here 21   *Sales* 10,459,638
SIC 5511 New and used car dealers
Luc Venne

D-U-N-S 24-527-2802   (SL)
GESTION G.S.F. INC
581 Rue Notre-Dame Bureau 302, Re-
pentigny, QC, J6A 2V1
(450) 654-5226
Emp Here 60   *Sales* 16,459,920
SIC 8741 Management services
Rejean Labre
Ginette Daneau

D-U-N-S 24-835-1470   (HQ)
GESTION JOCELYNE CROTEAU INC
91 Rue Ouimet, Repentigny, QC, J6A 1E1
(450) 581-2092
Sales 22,424,500
SIC 5621 Women's clothing stores
Jocelyne Croteau

D-U-N-S 25-012-0487   (SL)
GESTION RENE J. BEAUDOIN INC
*MARCHAND CANADIAN TIRE DE RE-
PENTIGNY*
115 Boul Brien, Repentigny, QC, J6A 8J3
(450) 585-9840
Emp Here 49   *Sales* 13,433,448
SIC 5411 Grocery stores
Rene Beaudoin

D-U-N-S 20-594-2530   (SL)
IMMEUBLES CJS RIVEST INC
96 Boul Industriel, Repentigny, QC, J6A 4X6
(450) 581-4480
Emp Here 50   *Sales* 16,128,106
SIC 1521 Single-family housing construction
Charles-Emile Rivest
Sylvain Rivest

D-U-N-S 24-125-5004   (BR)
LOBLAWS INC
LOBLAWS
(Suby of LOBLAW COMPANIES LIMITED)
86 Boul Brien, Repentigny, QC, J6A 5K7
(450) 581-8866
Emp Here 100
SIC 5411 Grocery stores
Claude Brodeur

D-U-N-S 20-765-7479   (BR)
**MCDONALD'S   RESTAURANTS   OF
CANADA LIMITED**
MCDONALD'S
(Suby of MCDONALD'S CORPORATION)
185 Rue Notre-Dame, Repentigny, QC, J6A
2R3
(450) 581-8520
Emp Here 80
SIC 5812 Eating places
Marc Couteau

D-U-N-S 25-448-3852   (BR)
METRO RICHELIEU INC
SUPER C REPENTIGNY
(Suby of METRO INC)
85 Boul Brien Bureau 101, Repentigny, QC,
J6A 8B6
(450) 581-3072
Emp Here 120
SIC 5141 Groceries, general line
Donald Houle

D-U-N-S 20-831-4018   (SL)
PORTES DE GARAGE CEDO INC
605 Boul Iberville Bureau 2061, Repentigny,
QC, J6A 5H9
(450) 585-4224
Emp Here 40   *Sales* 10,292,606
SIC 5211 Lumber and other building materials

Pierre Guneau
Richard Poirier

D-U-N-S 20-591-6901   (SL)
**REPENTIGNY CHEVROLET BUICK GMC
INC**
612 Rue Notre-Dame, Repentigny, QC, J6A
2T9
(450) 581-9500
Emp Here 40   *Sales* 25,171,200
SIC 5511 New and used car dealers
Mariette Rioux

D-U-N-S 24-609-1958   (HQ)
RESEAU GLP & CIE INC
PETRO CANADA
95 Boul Brien, Repentigny, QC, J6A 8B6
(450) 654-8787
Emp Here 5   *Sales* 24,903,900
SIC 5541 Gasoline service stations
Pascal Laporte

D-U-N-S 24-250-6264   (SL)
SERVICES PROFESSIONNELS INC
SPA
529 Rue Notre-Dame Bureau 300, Repentigny, QC, J6A 2T6

Emp Here 30   *Sales* 17,397,720
SIC 6411 Insurance agents, brokers, and ser-
vice
Maurice Poirier

D-U-N-S 25-837-3893   (SL)
SUPER MARCHE IBERVILLE INC
305 Boul Iberville, Repentigny, QC, J6A 2A6
(450) 581-2630
Emp Here 49   *Sales* 13,433,448
SIC 5411 Grocery stores
Denis Gagne

D-U-N-S 24-527-1184   (SL)
**SUPERMARCHE CREVIER (REPENTIGNY)
INC**
(Suby of GESTION CREVIER, JEAN-
CLAUDE INC)
180 Boul Brien, Repentigny, QC, J6A 7E9
(450) 582-0201
Emp Here 140   *Sales* 41,086,780
SIC 5411 Grocery stores
Jean-Claude Crevier
Georges Pilon

D-U-N-S 25-526-0408   (SL)
**SUPERMARCHE MARQUIS REPENTIGNY
INC**
METRO MARQUIS REPENTIGNY
150 Rue Louvain, Repentigny, QC, J6A 8J7
(450) 585-1445
Emp Here 170   *Sales* 49,891,090
SIC 5411 Grocery stores
Jean-Paul Marquis
Maryline Marquis

D-U-N-S 25-963-6124   (SL)
SUZUKI SUBARU REPENTIGNY INC
575 Rue Notre-Dame, Repentigny, QC, J6A
2T6
(514) 891-9950
Emp Here 30   *Sales* 14,942,340
SIC 5511 New and used car dealers
Michel Auger

D-U-N-S 24-082-8256   (SL)
TRANSPORT MICHEL GASSE ET FILS INC
TRANSPORT S. & M. GASS
219 Rue De Capri, Repentigny, QC, J6A 5L1
(450) 657-4667
Emp Here 25   *Sales* 11,768,275
SIC 1542 Nonresidential construction, nec
Michel Gasse
Sebastien Gasse
Louise Piette

D-U-N-S 25-294-7742   (BR)
WAL-MART CANADA CORP
WAL MART
(Suby of WALMART INC.)

100 Boul Brien Bureau 66, Repentigny, QC,
J6A 5N4
(450) 654-8886
Emp Here 200
SIC 5311 Department stores

Richelieu, QC J3L

D-U-N-S 20-243-8701   (SL)
A. & D. PREVOST INC
PREVOST ALUMINIUM ARCHITECTURAL
(Suby of CAPITAL REGIONAL ET COOPER-
ATIF DESJARDINS)
305 12e Av, Richelieu, QC, J3L 3T2
(450) 658-8771
Emp Here 100   *Sales* 19,208,500
SIC 3449 Miscellaneous Metalwork
Claude Cardin
Celine Letarte
Paul Laurin
Pierre Guilbault
Camille Thibodeau
Jean-Luc Meunier

D-U-N-S 25-363-0925   (HQ)
**CAISSE POPULAIRE DESJARDINS DE
RICHELIEU-SAINT-MATHIAS**
*DESJARDINS ENTREPRISESVALLEE DU
RICHELIEU-YAMASKA*
1111 3e Rue, Richelieu, QC, J3L 3Z2
(450) 658-0649
Emp Here 70   *Sales* 11,819,527
SIC 6062 State credit unions
Sylvain Lessard
Joanne Desjardins
Simon Leblanc
Louise Loiselle
Lucie Desgreniers
Nathalie Tremblay
Raynald Cornellier
Maxime Elsek Gaudreault
Robert Bleau
Nathalie Croteau

D-U-N-S 25-731-5846   (SL)
HICAT CORPORATION INC
640 14e Av Bureau 102, Richelieu, QC, J3L
5R5
(450) 982-1494
Emp Here 350   *Sales* 101,797,500
SIC 3732 Boatbuilding and repairing
Albert B. Beauchamps

D-U-N-S 25-334-4949   (SL)
MARCHE MICHEL LEMIEUX INC
IGA
450 Ch Richelieu, Richelieu, QC, J3L 3R8
(450) 658-1831
Emp Here 100   *Sales* 29,347,700
SIC 5411 Grocery stores
Michel Lemieux

D-U-N-S 25-190-5212   (SL)
**PIECES D'AUTOS CHAMBLY RICHELIEU
INC**
NAPA PIECES D'AUTO
2000 Ch Des Patriotes Bureau 299, Richelieu,
QC, J3L 6M1
(450) 658-7474
Emp Here 26   *Sales* 12,950,028
SIC 5531 Auto and home supply stores
Alain Brunelle
Yves Pelletier
Pierre Lefebvre
Robert Hattem

D-U-N-S 20-415-7077   (SL)
TRANSPORTS R.M.T. INC
400 Boul Richelieu, Richelieu, QC, J3L 3R8
(450) 658-1795
Emp Here 100   *Sales* 20,570,600
SIC 4212 Local trucking, without storage
Pierre Ostiguy

Richmond, QC J0B

D-U-N-S 20-243-9022   (SL)
DYSON & ARMSTRONG INC
555 Rue Craig, Richmond, QC, J0B 2H0
(819) 826-3306
Emp Here 40   *Sales* 19,923,120
SIC 5511 New and used car dealers
William Stevens
David Stevens
Joyce Stevens

D-U-N-S 24-390-3940   (SL)
ENGRENAGES SPECIALISES INC
(Suby of 9209-2600 QUEBEC INC)
620 Rue Desmarais, Richmond, QC, J0B 2H0
(819) 826-3379
Emp Here 26   *Sales* 12,350,676
SIC 5085 Industrial supplies
Christian Noel

D-U-N-S 24-319-8058   (BR)
EXO-S INC
(Suby of CAPITAL REGIONAL ET COOPER-
ATIF DESJARDINS)
425 10e Av, Richmond, QC, J0B 2H0
(819) 826-5911
Emp Here 200
SIC 3089 Plastics products, nec
Jose Verrier

D-U-N-S 24-865-0624   (HQ)
GESTRUDO INC
34 Rue Belmont, Richmond, QC, J0B 2H0
(819) 826-5941
Emp Here 25   *Sales* 16,401,000
SIC 6712 Bank holding companies
Edmond Trudeau
Suzanne Trudeau
Nathalie Trudeau

D-U-N-S 25-683-5380   (SL)
INNOTEX INC
275 Rue Gouin Bureau 1010, Richmond, QC,
J0B 2H0
(819) 826-5971
Emp Here 75   *Sales* 10,250,550
SIC 2311 Men's and boy's suits and coats
Louis Carpentier
Roger Yergeau
Guy Couture
Bruno Yergeau

Rigaud, QC J0P

D-U-N-S 24-675-8734   (SL)
2735-3861 QUEBEC INC
CENTRE DE SKI MONT-RIGAUD
(Suby of 9105-1755 QUEBEC INC)
321 Ch Des Erables, Rigaud, QC, J0P 1P0
(450) 451-0000
Emp Here 180   *Sales* 16,684,200
SIC 7011 Hotels and motels
Luc Elie
Stephane Elie
Karine Labbe

D-U-N-S 24-376-5877   (SL)
ASMODEE CANADA INC
(Suby of PAI PARTNERS)
31 Rue De La Cooperative, Rigaud, QC, J0P
1P0
(450) 424-0655
Emp Here 26   *Sales* 13,534,092
SIC 5092 Toys and hobby goods and supplies
Jayson Pickford
David B. Modica
Patricia Mainville
Christian T. Petersen

D-U-N-S 20-927-9421   (SL)
COLLEGE BOURGET

ARENA BOURGET
65 Rue Saint-Pierre, Rigaud, QC, J0P 1P0
(450) 451-0815
Emp Here 200   *Sales* 29,878,200
SIC 8221 Colleges and universities
  Jean-Marc St-Jacques
  Yves Cossette

D-U-N-S 24-021-7612   (SL)
EPICERIE R. CADIEUX & FILS INC
IGA
461 Ch De La Grande-Ligne, Rigaud, QC, J0P
1P0
(450) 451-5318
Emp Here 66   *Sales* 19,369,482
SIC 5411 Grocery stores
  Eric Faubert
  Caroline Faubert

D-U-N-S 20-243-9865   (HQ)
MAXRELCO INC
(*Suby of* GESTION CLAUDE JACQUES
GOUPIL INC)
90 201 Rte, Rigaud, QC, J0P 1P0
(450) 458-5375
Emp Here 5   *Sales* 37,448,950
SIC 6712 Bank holding companies
  Jacques Goupil

D-U-N-S 24-834-9508   (SL)
**SERVICES ALIMENTAIRES DELTA DAILY-
FOOD (CANADA) INC, LES**
FLEURY MICHON
(*Suby of* FLEURY MICHON)
26 Rue J.-Marc-Seguin, Rigaud, QC, J0P 1P0
(450) 451-6761
Emp Here 400   *Sales* 37,210,444
SIC 2038 Frozen specialties, nec
  Claude Bergeron
  Jean-Louis Roy
  Regis Lebrun

Rimouski, QC G0L

D-U-N-S 25-941-0587   (SL)
**COOPERATIVE DES ENCANS D'ANIMAUX
DU BAS-SAINT-LAURENT**
3229 132 Rte O, Rimouski, QC, G0L 1B0
(418) 736-5788
Emp Here 20   *Sales* 24,207,940
SIC 5154 Livestock
  Rene Gagnon

Rimouski, QC G5L

D-U-N-S 20-919-1514   (SL)
168287 CANADA INC
CONSTRUCTION TECHNIPRO BSL
217 Av Leonidas S Bureau 3b, Rimouski, QC,
G5L 2T5
(418) 722-9257
Emp Here 60   *Sales* 25,364,220
SIC 1541 Industrial buildings and warehouses
  Marc Pigeon

D-U-N-S 24-863-5955   (SL)
2846-3826 QUEBEC INC
DESROSIERS TOYOTA
210 Av Leonidas S, Rimouski, QC, G5L 2T2
(418) 722-6633
Emp Here 25   *Sales* 12,451,950
SIC 5511 New and used car dealers
  Carl Doucet
  Jean Doucet
  Line Marcoux

D-U-N-S 20-560-6911   (SL)
9144-1923 QUEBEC INC
CLUB PAPETIER, LE
192 Rue Saint-Germain E, Rimouski, QC, G5L
1A8

(418) 723-0606
Emp Here 25   *Sales* 11,179,350
SIC 5045 Computers, peripherals, and soft-
ware
  Remi Faucher

D-U-N-S 25-072-1912   (SL)
9183-9530 QUEBEC INC
PIECES D'AUTOS SELECT
401 Rue Saint-Jean-Baptiste E, Rimouski,
QC, G5L 1Z2
(418) 723-1156
Emp Here 26   *Sales* 12,950,028
SIC 5531 Auto and home supply stores
  Marco Lauzier
  Daniel Theriault
  Marco Desjardins
  Patrick Gagne

D-U-N-S 20-288-3138   (SL)
9275-0181 QUEBEC INC
CONSTRUCTION TECHNIPRO BSL
290 Rue Michaud Unite 101, Rimouski, QC,
G5L 6A4
(418) 722-9257
Emp Here 60   *Sales* 34,220,280
SIC 1542 Nonresidential construction, nec
  Marc Pigeon
  Harold D'astous

D-U-N-S 24-146-9840   (SL)
AMH CANADA LTEE
ULTAMIG
391 Rue Saint-Jean-Baptiste E, Rimouski,
QC, G5L 1Z2
(418) 724-4105
Emp Here 60   *Sales* 13,320,060
SIC 3548 Welding apparatus
  Ali Osmani

D-U-N-S 20-244-0376   (HQ)
AMIOT, MARIUS INC
350 2e Rue E, Rimouski, QC, G5L 7J4
(418) 723-1155
Emp Here 5   *Sales* 10,926,450
SIC 5013 Motor vehicle supplies and new
parts
  Roch Amiot

D-U-N-S 20-330-3193   (HQ)
ARMOIRES DISTINCTION INC
180 Av Leonidas S, Rimouski, QC, G5L 2T2
(418) 723-6857
Emp Here 46   *Sales* 13,382,600
SIC 5211 Lumber and other building materials
  Benoit Beaulieu

D-U-N-S 24-181-9387   (SL)
**ASSOCIATION DES CROISIERES DU
SAINT-LAURENT**
84 Rue Saint-Germain E Bureau 206, Ri-
mouski, QC, G5L 1A6
(418) 725-0135
Emp Here 17   *Sales* 17,592,977
SIC 6331 Fire, marine, and casualty insurance
  Priscilla Nemey

D-U-N-S 20-951-5659   (SL)
**BEAULIEU DECOR D'ASTOUS & FRERES
INC**
BEAULIEU DECOR
385 2e Rue E, Rimouski, QC, G5L 2G4
(418) 723-9487
Emp Here 51   *Sales* 11,852,553
SIC 5713 Floor covering stores
  Martin D'astous

D-U-N-S 24-638-1818   (SL)
BENOIT JOBIN INC
CONSTRUCTION JOBIN, BENOIT
25 Rue Saint-Germain E, Rimouski, QC, G5L
1A3
(418) 725-0742
Emp Here 26   *Sales* 12,239,006
SIC 1542 Nonresidential construction, nec
  Dany Levasseur
  Robin Huet

D-U-N-S 20-715-9638   (BR)

BIBLIOTHEQUE ET ARCHIVES NA-
TIONALES DU QUEBEC
BANQ
(*Suby of* GOUVERNEMENT DE LA
PROVINCE DE QUEBEC)
337 Rue Moreault, Rimouski, QC, G5L 1P4
(418) 727-3500
Emp Here 100
SIC 8231 Libraries
  Christine Durant

D-U-N-S 25-016-1601   (HQ)
CAISSE DESJARDINS DE RIMOUSKI
*DESJARDINS ENTREPRISESBAS-SAINT-
LAURENT*
100 Rue Julien-Rehel, Rimouski, QC, G5L
0G6
(418) 723-3368
Emp Here 70   *Sales* 21,292,161
SIC 6062 State credit unions
  Martin Desrosiers
  Michel Emond
  Stephane Plante
  Gilles Langelier
  Alain Beaulieu
  Real Chapados
  Melina De Champlain
  Richard Gauthier
  Gabrielle Langlais
  Jean-Francois Marquis

D-U-N-S 24-407-6027   (HQ)
**CENTRE INTEGRE DE SANTE ET DE SER-
VICES SOCIAUX DU BAS-SAINT-LAURENT**
CISSS DU BAS-SAINT-LAURENT
355 Boul Saint-Germain, Rimouski, QC, G5L
3N2
(418) 724-3000
Emp Here 200   *Sales* 1,656,544,000
SIC 8399 Social services, nec
  Hugues St-Pierre
  Isabelle Malo
  Jean-Claude Babin
  Gilbert Beaupre
  Kathleen Bouffrard
  Yves Boulianne
  Francois Deschenes
  Daniel Dionne
  Marcelle Dube
  Nathalie Dube

D-U-N-S 25-232-3647   (BR)
COMMISSION SCOLAIRE DES PHARES
ECOLE PAUL-HUBERT
250 Boul Arthur-Buies O, Rimouski, QC, G5L
7A7
(418) 724-3439
Emp Here 200
SIC 8211 Elementary and secondary schools
  Jean-Francois Parent

D-U-N-S 20-871-2174   (SL)
CONSTRUCTION J.C. LEPAGE LTEE
569 Rue De Lausanne, Rimouski, QC, G5L
4A7
(418) 724-4239
Emp Here 25   *Sales* 11,768,275
SIC 1542 Nonresidential construction, nec
  Michel Lepage
  Jean-Claude Lepage

D-U-N-S 20-190-6294   (HQ)
COOP PURDEL, LA
155 Rue Saint-Jean-Baptiste E, Rimouski,
QC, G5L 1Y7
(418) 736-4363
Emp Here 10   *Sales* 64,128,510
SIC 5083 Farm and garden machinery
  Jean-Paul Theriault
  Victor Carrier
  Laurent Proulx

D-U-N-S 20-244-1341   (HQ)
DICKNER INC
*PRODUITS INDUSTRIELS DE BEAUCE
(2013)*
559 Rue De Lausanne, Rimouski, QC, G5L

4A7
(418) 723-7936
Emp Here 28   *Sales* 16,625,910
SIC 5084 Industrial machinery and equipment
  Remi Thibeault
  Richard Fournier
  Serge Barriault

D-U-N-S 24-568-0780   (SL)
ENTREPRISES GHISLAIN G FORTIN LTEE
CANADIAN TIRE #320
419 Boul Jessop Bureau 320, Rimouski, QC,
G5L 7Y5
(418) 722-8426
Emp Here 47   *Sales* 23,409,666
SIC 5531 Auto and home supply stores
  Ghislain Fortin

D-U-N-S 20-366-5497   (SL)
**FEDERATION DE L'UPA DU BAS-SAINT-
LAURENT**
284 Rue Potvin, Rimouski, QC, G5L 7P5
(418) 723-2424
Emp Here 71   *Sales* 27,863,950
SIC 8631 Labor organizations
  Gilbert Marquis

D-U-N-S 24-638-9100   (SL)
FILLES DE JESUS, (RIMOUKI)
949 Boul Saint-Germain, Rimouski, QC, G5L
8Y9
(418) 723-4346
Emp Here 92   *Sales* 9,910,884
SIC 8661 Religious organizations
  Solange Mailloux
  Monique Denis

D-U-N-S 20-873-6579   (SL)
**FONDATION DU CENTRE REGIONALE DE
SANTE ET DE SERVICES SOCIAUX RI-
MOUSKI INC**
*FONDATION DU CENTRE HOSPITALIER
REGIONAL DE RIMOUSKI*
(*Suby of* GOUVERNEMENT DE LA
PROVINCE DE QUEBEC)
150 Av Rouleau, Rimouski, QC, G5L 5T1
(418) 724-8580
Emp Here 78   *Sales* 8,664,240
SIC 8062 General medical and surgical hospi-
tals
  Francois Seguin
  Stephanie Boulianne
  Jacques Lebrun
  Maude Bernier
  Carl Berube
  Nathalie Babin
  Valmond Santerre
  Marc Cote
  Olivier Hebert
  Marie-Pierre Blouin

D-U-N-S 24-639-2070   (HQ)
GESTION H. DICKNER LTEE
559 Rue De Lausanne, Rimouski, QC, G5L
4A7
(418) 723-7936
Sales 10,808,606
SIC 6512 Nonresidential building operators
  Benoit Dickner
  Serge Barriault
  Louise Dickner
  Denis Dickner

D-U-N-S 20-104-9793   (SL)
INNOVATION MARITIME
53 Rue Saint-Germain O, Rimouski, QC, G5L
4B4
(418) 725-3525
Emp Here 25   *Sales* 11,230,475
SIC 7389 Business services, nec
  Daniel Dion
  Guy Fortin
  Eric Hudier
  Louis Morin
  Pierre Parent
  Christian Cote
  Jean Brousseau

▲ Public Company   ■ Public Company Family Member   **HQ** Headquarters   **BR** Branch   **SL** Single Location

D-U-N-S 20-325-3521   (SL)
LA FONDATION DE L'INSTITUT MARITIME DU QUEBEC INC
53 Rue Saint-Germain O, Rimouski, QC, G5L 4B4
(418) 724-2822
Emp Here 100   *Sales* 12,012,900
SIC 8299 Schools and educational services, nec
Peggy Swan Berube
Louis Hebert
Guylaine Saint-Laurent
Serge Guay
Alain Richard
Gaston Fortin
Daniel Dion
Jerry Young
Stephane Arsenault

D-U-N-S 20-939-6758   (SL)
PEPSI COLA CANADA LTEE
SOCIETE DU GROUPE D'EMBOUTEILLAGE PEPSI
401 Boul De La Riviere, Rimouski, QC, G5L 7R1
(418) 722-8080
Emp Here 45   *Sales* 37,600,965
SIC 5149 Groceries and related products, nec
Sean Bousada

D-U-N-S 24-378-6456   (HQ)
PG SOLUTIONS INC
(*Suby of* CONSTELLATION SOFTWARE INC)
217 Av Leonidas S Bureau 13, Rimouski, QC, G5L 2T5
(418) 724-5037
Emp Here 60   *Sales* 20,185,480
SIC 7371 Custom computer programming services
Jeff Bender

D-U-N-S 24-531-2392   (HQ)
PURIBEC INC
177 Rue De L'Eveche O, Rimouski, QC, G5L 4H8
(418) 722-7326
Emp Here 24   *Sales* 11,626,524
SIC 5074 Plumbing and heating equipment and supplies (hydronics)
Stephane Giasson
Serge Giasson
Jasmin Giasson

D-U-N-S 24-402-2000   (HQ)
R. CROTEAU RIMOUSKI INC
AUBAINERIE, L'
(*Suby of* GESTION ALAIN HEBERT INC)
400 Boul Jessop, Rimouski, QC, G5L 1N1
(418) 723-1614
Sales 10,763,760
SIC 5651 Family clothing stores
Alain Hebert
Jean-Philippe Hebert
Francois Hebert

D-U-N-S 25-309-1557   (BR)
SOBEYS CAPITAL INCORPORATED
IGA EXTRA
(*Suby of* EMPIRE COMPANY LIMITED)
395 Av Sirois, Rimouski, QC, G5L 8R2
(418) 724-2244
Emp Here 110
SIC 5411 Grocery stores

D-U-N-S 24-532-0239   (SL)
SUPER MARCHE SIROIS INC
METRO SIROIS
465 Boul Saint-Germain, Rimouski, QC, G5L 3P2
(418) 722-0722
Emp Here 45   *Sales* 12,336,840
SIC 5411 Grocery stores
Bruno Sirois
Nelson Sirois
Gaston Sirois
Valmont Sirois

D-U-N-S 20-244-3370   (HQ)
TELUS COMMUNICATIONS (QUEBEC) INC
(*Suby of* TELUS CORPORATION)
6 Rue Jules-A.-Brillant Bureau 20602, Rimouski, QC, G5L 1W8
(418) 723-2271
Emp Here 100   *Sales* 731,018,000
SIC 6712 Bank holding companies
Francois Cote
Isabelle Plante
Monique Mercier

D-U-N-S 25-019-6565   (BR)
TELUS COMMUNICATIONS INC
TELUS COMMUNICATIONS INC
(*Suby of* TELUS CORPORATION)
6 Rue Jules-A.-Brillant Bureau 20602, Rimouski, QC, G5L 1W8
(418) 310-1212
Emp Here 200
SIC 4899 Communication services, nec
Jean Pascal Fournier

D-U-N-S 24-758-9476   (BR)
UNIVERSITE DU QUEBEC
UNIVERSITE DU QUEBEC A RIMOUSKI
(*Suby of* UNIVERSITE DU QUEBEC)
300 Allee Des Ursulines, Rimouski, QC, G5L 3A1
(418) 723-1986
Emp Here 650
SIC 8221 Colleges and universities
Michel Ringuet

Rimouski, QC G5M

D-U-N-S 24-403-8647   (SL)
4134320 CANADA INC
VOLKSWAGEN RIMOUSKI
379 Boul Arthur-Buies E, Rimouski, QC, G5M 0C7
(418) 724-5180
Emp Here 25   *Sales* 12,451,950
SIC 5511 New and used car dealers
Serge Harvey

D-U-N-S 25-209-9700   (SL)
9003-4406 QUEBEC INC
FORMULE MAZDA
169 Boul Sainte-Anne, Rimouski, QC, G5M 1C3
(418) 725-0911
Emp Here 25   *Sales* 12,451,950
SIC 5511 New and used car dealers
Andre Simard
Diane Defoy

D-U-N-S 25-993-3500   (SL)
AUTOMOBILES BOUCHARD & FILS INC
BOUCHARD FORD
401 Av Leonidas S, Rimouski, QC, G5M 1A1
(418) 722-4388
Emp Here 26   *Sales* 12,950,028
SIC 5511 New and used car dealers
Frederick Poirier

D-U-N-S 20-569-5138   (SL)
AVENUE PONTIAC BUICK GMC INC
140 Montee Industrielle-Et-Commerciale, Rimouski, QC, G5M 1B1
(418) 725-2001
Emp Here 22   *Sales* 10,957,716
SIC 5511 New and used car dealers
Daniel Caron
Wilbert Bechard

D-U-N-S 20-244-0665   (SL)
BOULEVARD CHEVROLET INC
GM
374 Montee Industrielle-Et-Commerciale, Rimouski, QC, G5M 1X1
(888) 844-5489
Emp Here 62   *Sales* 39,015,360
SIC 5511 New and used car dealers

Daniel Caron
Wiebert Decharb
Pierre Robichaud

D-U-N-S 25-323-4046   (BR)
CANAC IMMOBILIER INC
(*Suby of* GESTION LABERGE INC)
228 Rue Des Negociants, Rimouski, QC, G5M 1B6
(418) 723-0007
Emp Here 85
SIC 5211 Lumber and other building materials
Denis Faber

D-U-N-S 24-907-2828   (SL)
CENTRE TECHNO-PNEU INC
MOLDEX
445 Rue De L'Expansion, Rimouski, QC, G5M 1B4
(418) 724-4104
Emp Here 60   *Sales* 37,756,800
SIC 5531 Auto and home supply stores
Marcel Marquis
Jean-Francois Marquis
Eric Marquis

D-U-N-S 20-290-7200   (SL)
DATRAN BAS ST-LAURENT INC
290 Av De L'Industrie, Rimouski, QC, G5M 1W4
Emp Here 50   *Sales* 37,750,415
SIC 5198 Paints, varnishes, and supplies
Joel Brossard

D-U-N-S 24-143-8340   (HQ)
ENTREPRISES VAGABOND INC, LES
ZABE JEANS
(*Suby of* GESTION A.J.L.R. INC)
451 Rue De L'Expansion, Rimouski, QC, G5M 1B4
(418) 724-2243
Emp Here 15   *Sales* 62,377,500
SIC 5621 Women's clothing stores
Andre Racine

D-U-N-S 20-695-0003   (HQ)
GAGNON IMAGE INC
ENSEIGNES BELANGER
70 Montee Industrielle-Et-Commerciale Bureau F, Rimouski, QC, G5M 1B1
(418) 723-2394
Emp Here 20   *Sales* 15,616,260
SIC 5099 Durable goods, nec
Nick Gagnon
Dave Gagnon

D-U-N-S 20-056-5856   (HQ)
GESTION A.J.L.R. INC
451 Rue De L'Expansion, Rimouski, QC, G5M 1B4
(418) 724-2243
Emp Here 1   *Sales* 183,120,009
SIC 6712 Bank holding companies
Andre Racine

D-U-N-S 24-490-5019   (SL)
MEGA FORMULE D'OCCASION
169 Boul Sainte-Anne, Rimouski, QC, G5M 1C3
(418) 723-5955
Emp Here 25   *Sales* 12,451,950
SIC 5521 Used car dealers
Andre Simard

D-U-N-S 20-244-3305   (SL)
PRODUITS METALLIQUES POULIOT MACHINERIE INC
PRODUITS METALIQUES PMI
261 Av Du Havre, Rimouski, QC, G5M 0B3
(418) 723-2610
Emp Here 50   *Sales* 16,666,650
SIC 1541 Industrial buildings and warehouses
Jean Pouliot
Sebastien Noel
Gino Picard

D-U-N-S 24-145-6763   (SL)
STRUCTURES G.B. LTEE, LES

105 Montee Industrielle-Et-Commerciale, Rimouski, QC, G5M 1A8
(418) 724-9433
Emp Here 150   *Sales* 27,208,200
SIC 3312 Blast furnaces and steel mills
Andre Collin
Gino Roy
Jean-Philippe Leblanc
Pascal Chouinard
Raymond Garon

D-U-N-S 24-895-3254   (SL)
VILLE DE RIMOUSKI
475 2e Rue E, Rimouski, QC, G5M 0A1
(418) 724-3142
Emp Here 49   *Sales* 11,480,112
SIC 8743 Public relations services
Claude Perinet

D-U-N-S 24-207-4206   (BR)
WAL-MART CANADA CORP
WALMART
(*Suby of* WALMART INC.)
415 Montee Industrielle-Et-Commerciale Bureau 3198, Rimouski, QC, G5M 1Y1
(418) 722-1990
Emp Here 200
SIC 5311 Department stores
Chris Cyrenne

Riviere-Du-Loup, QC G5R

D-U-N-S 25-258-8405   (BR)
9130-1168 QUEBEC INC
IVANHOE CAMBRIDGE S
(*Suby of* FONDS DE PLACEMENT IMMOBILIER COMINAR)
298 Boul Armand-Theriault Bureau 2, Riviere-Du-Loup, QC, G5R 4C2
(418) 862-7848
Emp Here 926
SIC 6512 Nonresidential building operators

D-U-N-S 20-298-3185   (SL)
ACIER QUEBEC-MARITIMES INC
396 Rue Temiscouata, Riviere-Du-Loup, QC, G5R 2Z2
(418) 862-1320
Emp Here 20   *Sales* 20,006,780
SIC 5051 Metals service centers and offices
Jean-Claude Chouinard

D-U-N-S 25-471-1104   (SL)
ADELARD SOUCY (1975) INC
SOUCY INDUSTRIEL
217 Rue Temiscouata, Riviere-Du-Loup, QC, G5R 2Y6
(418) 862-2355
Emp Here 175   *Sales* 31,279,325
SIC 8711 Engineering services
Frederick Soucy

D-U-N-S 20-244-5995   (SL)
AUBERGE DE LA POINTE INC
RESTAURANT L'ESPADON
10 Boul Cartier, Riviere-Du-Loup, QC, G5R 6A1
(418) 862-3514
Emp Here 80   *Sales* 7,591,920
SIC 7011 Hotels and motels
Jean Cote

D-U-N-S 20-244-6035   (HQ)
BASTILLE, J. M. INC
396 Rue Temiscouata Bureau 744, Riviere-Du-Loup, QC, G5R 2Z2
(418) 862-3346
Sales 26,027,100
SIC 5093 Scrap and waste materials
Jean-Pierre Bastille
Pierre-Luc Bastille
Michael Bastille

D-U-N-S 25-107-7533   (SL)
BASTILLE, MARTIN INC

ACIER MARTIN BASTILLE
227 Rte De L'Anse-Au-Persil, Riviere-Du-Loup, QC, G5R 5Z5
(418) 862-1705
Emp Here 10   *Sales* 10,003,390
SIC 5051 Metals service centers and offices
 Martin Bastille

 D-U-N-S 24-746-4308   (SL)
BERUBE CHEVROLET CADILLAC BUICK GMC LTEE
(*Suby of* SERVICE BERUBE LTEE)
101 Boul Cartier, Riviere-Du-Loup, QC, G5R 2N3
(418) 862-6324
Emp Here 26   *Sales* 12,950,028
SIC 5511 New and used car dealers
 Patrick Berube
 Gaston Berube

 D-U-N-S 24-820-5205   (SL)
CAMIONS FREIGHTLINER RIVIERE-DU-LOUP INC
CARREFOUR DU CAMION R.D.L.
100 Boul Industriel, Riviere-Du-Loup, QC, G5R 0K5
(418) 862-3192
Emp Here 52   *Sales* 18,939,180
SIC 5012 Automobiles and other motor vehicles
 Denis Morin
 Gabriel Morin
 Jacques Roy

 D-U-N-S 24-378-5347   (SL)
CAMPOR ENVIRONNEMENT INC
98 Rue Des Equipements, Riviere-Du-Loup, QC, G5R 5W9
(418) 867-8577
Emp Here 40   *Sales* 12,045,680
SIC 4953 Refuse systems
 Laurent Gagnon
 Michael Levesque

 D-U-N-S 24-326-8476   (BR)
CENTRE DE SANTE ET DE SERVICES SOCIAUX DE RIVIERE-DU-LOUP
RESIDENCE SAINT-JOSEPH, LA
(*Suby of* GOUVERNEMENT DE LA PROVINCE DE QUEBEC)
28 Rue Joly, Riviere-Du-Loup, QC, G5R 3H2
(418) 862-6385
Emp Here 155
SIC 8059 Nursing and personal care, nec
 Raymond April

 D-U-N-S 25-888-3438   (SL)
CENTRE FINANCIER S.F.L. DU LITTORAL INC
SERVICES FINANCIERS LA LAURENTIENNE
290 Boul De L'Hotel-De-Ville Bureau 200, Riviere-Du-Loup, QC, G5R 5C6
(418) 862-4980
Emp Here 20   *Sales* 14,508,780
SIC 6311 Life insurance
 Frederic Deschamps
 Jean-Marie Deschamps
 Serge Basque

 D-U-N-S 24-131-9974   (SL)
CHAUFFAGE RDL PG INC
160 Rue Louis-Philippe-Lebrun, Riviere-Du-Loup, QC, G5R 5W8
(418) 862-5351
Emp Here 12   *Sales* 12,393,696
SIC 5172 Petroleum products, nec
 Jacques Dube

 D-U-N-S 20-954-8080   (HQ)
COLLEGE D'ENSEIGNEMENT GENERAL ET PROFESSIONNEL DE RIVIERE-DU-LOUP
CEGEP DE RIVIERE-DU-LOUP
80 Rue Frontenac, Riviere-Du-Loup, QC, G5R 1R1
(418) 862-6903
Sales 15,363,863

SIC 8221 Colleges and universities
 Mario Landry
 Martine Ouellet
 Dominic Theriault
 Leonard Dube
 Benoit Plante
 Martin Pelletier
 Sylvie Rossignol
 Marilyne D'amours
 Guillaume Castonguay
 Stephane Boudreau

 D-U-N-S 25-233-7738   (BR)
COMMISSION SCOLAIRE DE KAMOURASKA RIVIERE-DU-LOUP
ECOLE SECONDAIRE RIVIERE DU LOUP
320 Rue Saint-Pierre, Riviere-Du-Loup, QC, G5R 3V3
(418) 862-8203
Emp Here 160
SIC 8211 Elementary and secondary schools
 Sylvie Soucy

 D-U-N-S 20-577-7910   (SL)
COTE OUELLET THIVIERGE NOTAIRES INC
646 Rue Lafontaine Bureau 100, Riviere-Du-Loup, QC, G5R 3C8
(418) 863-5050
Emp Here 30   *Sales* 13,304,700
SIC 7389 Business services, nec
 Nadine Lavoie

 D-U-N-S 24-311-5867   (SL)
ECCO INVESTISSEMENT INC
54 Rue Amyot, Riviere-Du-Loup, QC, G5R 3E9
(418) 867-1695
Emp Here 250   *Sales* 91,377,250
SIC 6712 Bank holding companies
 Louis-Frederic Lebel

 D-U-N-S 20-244-7066   (SL)
GARAGE WINDSOR LTEE
(*Suby of* SERVICE RIOUX INC)
287 Rue Temiscouata, Riviere-Du-Loup, QC, G5R 2Y7
(418) 862-3586
Emp Here 30   *Sales* 18,878,400
SIC 5511 New and used car dealers
 Jean Pomerleau
 Yves Pomerleau
 Nicholas Leblond

 D-U-N-S 24-814-0498   (SL)
GRAND-PORTAGE VOLKSWAGEN INC
GRAND-PORTAGE AUTOMOBILES
157 Rue Fraser, Riviere-Du-Loup, QC, G5R 1C9
(418) 862-3490
Emp Here 25   *Sales* 12,451,950
SIC 5511 New and used car dealers
 Martin Pomerleau

 D-U-N-S 20-559-9876   (HQ)
GROUPE LEBEL INC
GROUPE LEBEL (2004)
54 Rue Amyot, Riviere-Du-Loup, QC, G5R 3E9
(877) 567-5910
Emp Here 10   *Sales* 118,315,750
SIC 2421 Sawmills and planing mills, general
 Louis-Frederic Lebel

 D-U-N-S 20-794-3577   (BR)
GROUPE NORMANDIN INC
(*Suby of* GROUPE NORMANDIN INC)
83 Boul Cartier, Riviere-Du-Loup, QC, G5R 2N1
(418) 867-1366
Emp Here 75
SIC 5812 Eating places
 Remy Lavoie

 D-U-N-S 20-873-2016   (SL)
HOPITAL ST-JOSEPH
28 Rue Joly, Riviere-Du-Loup, QC, G5R 3H2

(418) 862-6385
Emp Here 244   *Sales* 27,103,520
SIC 8069 Specialty hospitals, except psychiatric
 Gilles Paradis

 D-U-N-S 20-438-1150   (SL)
INFIRMIERES DE L'HUMANITE
4 Rue Des Ormes, Riviere-Du-Loup, QC, G5R 4W7

Emp Here 150   *Sales* 16,662,000
SIC 8062 General medical and surgical hospitals
 Andreanne Turgeon

 D-U-N-S 20-012-1213   (SL)
J.M. BASTILLE ACIER INC
(*Suby of* BASTILLE, J. M. INC)
396 Rue Temiscouata, Riviere-Du-Loup, QC, G5R 2Z2
(418) 862-3346
Emp Here 100   *Sales* 52,054,200
SIC 5093 Scrap and waste materials
 Jean-Pierre Bastille
 Pierre-Luc Bastille
 Michaael Bastille

 D-U-N-S 24-942-9614   (SL)
LE CENTRE ROUTIER (1994) INC
INTERNATIONAL NAVISTAR
375 Rue Temiscouata Bureau 998, Riviere-Du-Loup, QC, G5R 2Y9

Emp Here 50   *Sales* 24,903,900
SIC 5511 New and used car dealers
 Steve Halle
 Jacinthe Levesque
 Jean Fraser
 Yannick Bourdages
 Serge Boucher
 Kevin Michaud
 Diego Michaud
 Serge Deschamps

 D-U-N-S 20-244-7454   (HQ)
LEPAGE, ALPHONSE INC
LEPAGE MILWORK
141 Ch Des Raymond, Riviere-Du-Loup, QC, G5R 5X9
(418) 862-2611
Sales 15,885,800
SIC 3089 Plastics products, nec
 Guy Bonneville

 D-U-N-S 20-244-7561   (SL)
MAGASIN COOP DE RIVIERE-DU-LOUP
METRO
298 Boul Armand-Theriault Bureau 60, Riviere-Du-Loup, QC, G5R 4C2
(418) 862-3590
Emp Here 65   *Sales* 19,076,005
SIC 5411 Grocery stores
 Jacques Boucher
 Rejean Boucher
 Marcel Brouillette
 Michel Caron
 Edith Tremblay
 Claude Levesque
 Rejean Banville
 Normand Provencal
 Gilles Gosselin
 Sylvie Cyr

 D-U-N-S 20-925-6325   (BR)
MCDONALD'S RESTAURANTS OF CANADA LIMITED
RESTAURANT MCDONALD'S
(*Suby of* MCDONALD'S CORPORATION)
100 Rue Des Cerisiers, Riviere-Du-Loup, QC, G5R 6E8
(418) 863-4242
Emp Here 80
SIC 5812 Eating places
 Richard Juneau

 D-U-N-S 24-499-1238   (SL)
MOTEL BOULEVARD CARTIER INC

ROTISSERIE ST-HUBERT
80 Boul Cartier, Riviere-Du-Loup, QC, G5R 2M9
(418) 867-1830
Emp Here 100   *Sales* 4,551,900
SIC 5812 Eating places
 Charles Pomerleau
 Denise Laforest
 Yves Pomerleau

 D-U-N-S 25-359-0038   (SL)
PLACEMENTS BERIVES INC, LES
4 SAISONS CHEVROLET OLDSMOBILE (1988)
101 Boul Cartier, Riviere-Du-Loup, QC, G5R 2N3
(418) 862-6324
Emp Here 29   *Sales* 14,444,262
SIC 5511 New and used car dealers
 Yves Masse

 D-U-N-S 24-758-7363   (HQ)
PRELCO INC
VARALEX
94 Boul Cartier, Riviere-Du-Loup, QC, G5R 2M9
(418) 862-2274
Emp Here 350   *Sales* 127,845,000
SIC 3211 Flat glass
 Roger Lavoie
 Richard Langlais
 Nicole Goulet
 Yvan Thibault
 Dominic Lavoie

 D-U-N-S 24-638-5330   (HQ)
PRELSECUR INC
94 Boul Cartier, Riviere-Du-Loup, QC, G5R 2M9
(418) 862-2274
Sales 71,081,820
SIC 3211 Flat glass
 Roger Lavoie
 Dominic Lavoie
 Nicole Goulet
 Yvon Theriault
 Richard Langlais

 D-U-N-S 24-821-6590   (HQ)
PREMIER HORTICULTURE LTEE
TOURBIERE MALPEC
(*Suby of* GESTION BELANGER, BERNARD LTEE)
1 Av Premier Bureau 101, Riviere-Du-Loup, QC, G5R 6C1
(418) 862-6356
Emp Here 100   *Sales* 123,932,700
SIC 1499 Miscellaneous nonMetallic minerals, except fuels
 Bernard Belanger
 Jean Belanger
 Martin Noel
 Germain Ouellet

 D-U-N-S 24-706-9966   (HQ)
PREMIER TECH LTEE
(*Suby of* GESTION BELANGER, BERNARD LTEE)
1 Av Premier Bureau 101, Riviere-Du-Loup, QC, G5R 6C1
(418) 867-8883
Emp Here 150   *Sales* 768,303,000
SIC 6712 Bank holding companies
 Bernard Belanger
 Germain Ouellet
 Gilles Laurin
 Jean-Yves Leblanc
 Jean Belanger
 Martin Cauchon
 Pierre Racine
 Martin Noel

 D-U-N-S 24-821-0627   (HQ)
PREMIER TECH TECHNOLOGIES LIMITEE
PREMIER TECH SYSTEMS
(*Suby of* GESTION BELANGER, BERNARD LTEE)

▲ Public Company   ■ Public Company Family Member   **HQ** Headquarters   **BR** Branch   **SL** Single Location

1 Av Premier, Riviere-Du-Loup, QC, G5R 6C1
(418) 867-8883
Emp Here 499   *Sales* 168,526,200
SIC 3565 Packaging machinery

D-U-N-S 20-256-0900   (SL)
PRIMA AUTOMOBILES INC
136 Ch Des Raymond, Riviere-Du-Loup, QC,
G5R 5X6
(418) 867-1420
Emp Here 24   *Sales* 11,953,872
SIC 5511 New and used car dealers
Luc Robitaille

D-U-N-S 24-729-7336   (BR)
SINTRA INC
CONSTRUCTION BML
(*Suby of* BOUYGUES)
105 Rue Louis-Philippe-Lebrun, Riviere-Du-
Loup, QC, G5R 5W5
(418) 862-0000
Emp Here 250
SIC 1611 Highway and street construction
Maxime Mercier

D-U-N-S 25-309-1599   (BR)
SOBEYS CAPITAL INCORPORATED
IGA EXTRA
(*Suby of* EMPIRE COMPANY LIMITED)
254 Boul De L'Hotel-De-Ville Bureau 451,
Riviere-Du-Loup, QC, G5R 1M4
(418) 862-7861
Emp Here 150
SIC 5411 Grocery stores

D-U-N-S 20-298-5875   (SL)
SOCIETE EN COMMANDITE FF SOUCY WB
F.F SOUCY
191 Rue Delage, Riviere-Du-Loup, QC, G5R
6E2
(418) 862-6941
Emp Here 100   *Sales* 19,476,800
SIC 2621 Paper mills
Nicolas Cloutier

D-U-N-S 24-159-7272   (SL)
SYNDICAT SCFP DU CSSSRDL
28 Rue Joly, Riviere-Du-Loup, QC, G5R 3H2

Emp Here 120   *Sales* 47,886,064
SIC 8631 Labor organizations
Daniel Fournier

D-U-N-S 24-531-6161   (SL)
TOURBES NIROM PEAT MOSS INC, LES
315 Ch Des Raymond, Riviere-Du-Loup, QC,
G5R 5Y5
(418) 862-0075
Emp Here 10   *Sales* 14,676,920
SIC 5159 Farm-product raw materials, nec
Marcel Levesque
Christian Levesque

D-U-N-S 24-144-7440   (SL)
VIANDES DU BRETON INC, LES
OEUFS BRETON, LES
(*Suby of* BRETON TRADITION 1944 INC)
150 Ch Des Raymond, Riviere-Du-Loup, QC,
G5R 5X8
(418) 863-6711
Emp Here 540   *Sales* 263,187,900
SIC 2011 Meat packing plants
Vincent Breton
Lucien Breton
Marie-Josee Landry

D-U-N-S 24-207-4230   (BR)
WAL-MART CANADA CORP
(*Suby of* WALMART INC.)
100 Rue Des Cerisiers, Riviere-Du-Loup, QC,
G5R 6E8
(418) 862-3003
Emp Here 120
SIC 5311 Department stores
Pierre Graveline

Riviere-Ouelle, QC G0L

D-U-N-S 20-244-9740   (HQ)
TOURBIERES LAMBERT INC
(*Suby of* GESTION GABERT INC)
106 Ch Lambert, Riviere-Ouelle, QC, G0L
2C0
(418) 852-2885
Emp Here 75   *Sales* 40,435,230
SIC 1499 Miscellaneous nonMetallic minerals,
except fuels
Gabriel Lambert
Francois Lambert
Jerome Lambert

Riviere-Rouge, QC J0T

D-U-N-S 20-633-9488   (SL)
9222-0524 QUEBEC INC
MARCHE RAYMOND ET FILS
1395 Rue L'Annonciation S, Riviere-Rouge,
QC, J0T 1T0

Emp Here 49   *Sales* 13,433,448
SIC 5411 Grocery stores
Yvon Raymond

D-U-N-S 24-126-1473   (BR)
**CENTRE HOSPITALIER ET CENTRE DE
READAPTATION ANTOINE-LABELLE**
*CENTRE HOSPITALIER ET CENTRE DE
READAPTATION ANTOINE-LABELLE*
1525 Rue L'Annonciation N, Riviere-Rouge,
QC, J0T 1T0
(819) 275-2411
Emp Here 700
SIC 8062 General medical and surgical hospi-
tals
Jean-Pierre Urbain

D-U-N-S 24-180-1794   (SL)
SERRES FRANK ZYRONSKI INC, LES
1853 Ch Laliberte, Riviere-Rouge, QC, J0T
1T0
(819) 275-5156
Emp Here 30   *Sales* 10,274,010
SIC 0181 Ornamental nursery products
Frank Zyronski
Louise Saint-Arnaud

Riviere-Saint-Paul, QC G0G

D-U-N-S 20-400-5581   (SL)
9036-4514 QUEBEC INC
I & S SEAFOODS
45 Rue Whiteley, Riviere-Saint-Paul, QC, G0G
2P0
(418) 379-2087
Emp Here 70   *Sales* 58,490,390
SIC 5146 Fish and seafoods
Irving Roberts

Roberval, QC G8H

D-U-N-S 24-689-7524   (SL)
9071- 0575 QUEBEC INC
GARAGE GHISLAIN LECLERC
1638 Boul Marcotte, Roberval, QC, G8H 2P2
(418) 275-2724
Emp Here 89   *Sales* 25,213,700
SIC 7532 Top and body repair and paint shops
Martin Leclerc
Julien Cote

D-U-N-S 24-388-5436   (HQ)
9206-5580 QUEBEC INC
UNIPRIX GUAY ET BEAUPRE

1221 Boul Marcotte, Roberval, QC, G8H 3B8
(418) 275-5288
Emp Here 10   *Sales* 12,647,700
SIC 5912 Drug stores and proprietary stores
Daniel Guay
Julie Beaupre

D-U-N-S 20-938-8383   (BR)
**COMMISSION SCOLAIRE DU PAYS-DES-
BLEUETS**
ECOLE CITE ETUDIANTE
171 Boul De La Jeunesse, Roberval, QC, G8H
2N9
(418) 275-3110
Emp Here 90
SIC 8211 Elementary and secondary schools
Sylvain Bouchard

D-U-N-S 25-842-3099   (SL)
F D D C H DE JONQUIERE
989 Rue Collard, Roberval, QC, G8H 1X9
(418) 765-3444
Emp Here 11   *Sales* 11,383,691
SIC 6321 Accident and health insurance

D-U-N-S 20-649-4069   (SL)
MAXI ROBERVAL
150 Av Saint-Alphonse, Roberval, QC, G8H
3P8
(418) 275-4471
Emp Here 90   *Sales* 13,938,146
SIC 5411 Grocery stores
Jarvais Bouchard

D-U-N-S 24-707-3091   (SL)
PRODUITS GILBERT INC, LES
GILBERT EQUIMENTS DE SCIERIES
1840 Boul Marcotte, Roberval, QC, G8H 2P2
(418) 275-5041
Emp Here 125   *Sales* 27,750,125
SIC 3553 Woodworking machinery
Sylvain Gilbert

D-U-N-S 25-299-0197   (BR)
**SOCIETE DE PROTECTION DES FORETS
CONTRE LE FEU (SOPFEU)**
(*Suby of* SOCIETE DE PROTECTION DES
FORETS CONTRE LE FEU (SOPFEU))
1230 Rte De L'Aeroport, Roberval, QC, G8H
2M9
(418) 275-6400
Emp Here 100
SIC 0851 Forestry services
Sylvain Tremblay

D-U-N-S 20-642-1799   (SL)
**STAGEM   DIVISION   ENTREPRISE
D'INSERTION INC**
150 Rte De Sainte-Hedwidge, Roberval, QC,
G8H 2M9
(418) 275-7241
Emp Here 52   *Sales* 10,003,240
SIC 2421 Sawmills and planing mills, general
Gagnon Jean
Michel De Champlain
Steeve Martel

D-U-N-S 20-245-1662   (SL)
SUPER MARCHE ROBERVAL INC
IGA
1221 Boul Marcotte Bureau 1, Roberval, QC,
G8H 3B8
(418) 275-4692
Emp Here 100   *Sales* 29,347,700
SIC 5411 Grocery stores
Michel Gravel

Rosemere, QC J7A

D-U-N-S 20-928-6608   (SL)
9067-3476 QUEBEC INC
METRO ROSEMERE
348 Ch De La Grande-Cote, Rosemere, QC,
J7A 1K3
(450) 621-3510
Emp Here 50   *Sales* 13,707,600

SIC 5411 Grocery stores
Rejean Lemay

D-U-N-S 20-798-7848   (SL)
9141-9721 QUEBEC INC
PHARMAPRIX
401 Boul Labelle, Rosemere, QC, J7A 3T2
(450) 971-4664
Emp Here 40   *Sales* 10,118,160
SIC 5912 Drug stores and proprietary stores
Oana Bugnariu

D-U-N-S 24-346-3168   (BR)
ACADEMIE STE-THERESE INC, L'
1 Ch Des Ecoliers, Rosemere, QC, J7A 4Y1
(450) 434-1130
Emp Here 90
SIC 8211 Elementary and secondary schools

D-U-N-S 25-647-7951   (BR)
CLSC-CHSLD THERESE DE BLAINVILLE
*CENTRE D'HEBERGEMENT HUBERT MAI-
SON NEUVE*
365 Ch De La Grande-Cote, Rosemere, QC,
J7A 1K4
(450) 621-3760
Emp Here 200
SIC 8361 Residential care
Robert Bedard

D-U-N-S 20-971-7644   (SL)
CLUB DE GOLF DE ROSEMERE
282 Boul Labelle, Rosemere, QC, J7A 2H6
(450) 437-7555
Emp Here 80   *Sales* 6,283,600
SIC 7997 Membership sports and recreation
clubs
Rejean Berthiaume
Michel Larose
Claude Bourdin
Robert Lalonde
Daniel Randall
Helene Paradis
Marcel Carriere
Lester Raymond
Marc Gagnon
Andre C. Vaillancourt

D-U-N-S 24-053-4529   (SL)
EXTERNAT SACRE-COEUR
535 Rue Lefrancois, Rosemere, QC, J7A 4R5
(450) 621-6720
Emp Here 75   *Sales* 6,961,950
SIC 8211 Elementary and secondary schools
Sylvie Levesque
Jean Drouin
Christian Beauregard
Suzanne Demers
Raymond Filteau
Charles-Alain Carriere
Andre Brodeur
Pierre Boutet

D-U-N-S 25-301-2942   (BR)
HUDSON'S BAY COMPANY
BAIE, LA
(*Suby of* HUDSON'S BAY COMPANY)
401 Boul Labelle, Rosemere, QC, J7A 3T2
(450) 433-6991
Emp Here 100
SIC 5311 Department stores
Jeff Shields

D-U-N-S 25-475-5739   (SL)
**JEAN COUTU JACQUES BOUILLON (AF-
FILIATED PHARMACIES**
PHARMACIE JEAN COUTU
253b Boul Labelle, Rosemere, QC, J7A 2H3
(450) 437-9151
Emp Here 40   *Sales* 10,118,160
SIC 5912 Drug stores and proprietary stores
Jacques Bouillon

D-U-N-S 25-293-0813   (SL)
MARTINEAU, REAL INC
CANADIAN TIRE ROSEMERE
10 Boul Bouthillier, Rosemere, QC, J7A 4B4

(450) 437-2007
Emp Here 120   *Sales* 32,118,240
SIC 5251 Hardware stores
  Real Martineau

D-U-N-S 24-800-1265   (SL)
ODEM INTERNATIONAL INC
(*Suby of* EXPORT PACKERS COMPANY IN-
CORPORATED)
483 Ch De La Grande-Cote, Rosemere, QC,
J7A 1M1
(450) 965-1412
Emp Here 12   *Sales* 10,026,924
SIC 5149 Groceries and related products, nec
  Elise Gagnon
  Daniel A. Leblanc
  Normand Bernier
  Werter Mior
  Brian Lampert
  Francis Dalpe

D-U-N-S 20-024-5137   (BR)
PROVIGO DISTRIBUTION INC
MAXI
(*Suby of* LOBLAW COMPANIES LIMITED)
339 Boul Labelle, Rosemere, QC, J7A 2H7
(450) 437-0471
Emp Here 150
SIC 5411 Grocery stores
  Patrick Boucher

D-U-N-S 25-222-5933   (BR)
SIR WILFRID LAURIER SCHOOL BOARD
ROSEMERE HIGH SCHOOL
530 Rue Northcote, Rosemere, QC, J7A 1Y2
(450) 621-5900
Emp Here 110
SIC 8211 Elementary and secondary schools
  Karen Lorenz

D-U-N-S 24-018-9423   (BR)
WAL-MART CANADA CORP
(*Suby of* WALMART INC.)
401 Boul Labelle Bureau 3080, Rosemere,
QC, J7A 3T2
(450) 435-2982
Emp Here 200
SIC 5311 Department stores
  Denis Gosselin

Rougemont, QC J0L

D-U-N-S 24-468-5595   (HQ)
3346625 CANADA INC
54 Rang De La Montagne, Rougemont, QC,
J0L 1M0
(450) 469-2912
Emp Here 2   *Sales* 402,059,900
SIC 6712 Bank holding companies
  Pierre-Paul Lassonde
  Nathalie Lassonde

D-U-N-S 20-245-3635   (HQ)
A. LASSONDE INC
LASSONDE SERVICES
(*Suby of* 3346625 CANADA INC)
170 5e Av, Rougemont, QC, J0L 1M0
(450) 469-4926
Emp Here 300   *Sales* 536,123,500
SIC 2033 Canned fruits and specialties
  Jean Gattuso
  Yves Toupin
  Caroline Lemoine
  Pierre-Paul Lassonde
  Nathalie Lassonde

D-U-N-S 25-304-9290   (BR)
ARTERRA WINES CANADA, INC
VINCOR QUEBEC
(*Suby of* ONTARIO TEACHERS' PENSION
PLAN BOARD)
175 Ch De Marieville, Rougemont, QC, J0L
1M0
(450) 469-3104
Emp Here 120

SIC 5182 Wine and distilled beverages
  Normand Leroux

D-U-N-S 20-181-9971   (HQ)
**ENTREPRISES BERNARD SORNIN INC,
LES**
MATERIELLES INDUSTRIELLES, LES
325 La Grande-Caroline, Rougemont, QC,
J0L 1M0
(450) 469-4934
Sales 19,016,415
SIC 3444 Sheet Metalwork
  Michel Sornin
  Daniel Matte

D-U-N-S 24-857-6795   (SL)
ENTREPRISES S.M.T.R. INC
500 Rte 112, Rougemont, QC, J0L 1M0
(450) 469-3153
Emp Here 135   *Sales* 60,776,595
SIC 7538 General automotive repair shops
  Claude Robert
  Michel Robert

D-U-N-S 24-316-3651   (SL)
FERME C.M.J.I. ROBERT INC
AUBERGE DU COTEAU
1105 La Petite-Caroline, Rougemont, QC, J0L
1M0
(450) 469-3090
Emp Here 65   *Sales* 17,050,085
SIC 0172 Grapes
  Claude Robert
  Michel Robert

D-U-N-S 24-458-4413   (HQ)
GROUPE ROBERT INC
500 Rte 112, Rougemont, QC, J0L 1M0
(450) 460-1112
Emp Here 150   *Sales* 424,076,300
SIC 4213 Trucking, except local
  Claude Robert
  Michel Robert
  Jacques Gregoire
  Marcel Ostiguy
  Sylvain Langis
  Pierre Patry

D-U-N-S 24-019-5297   (SL)
IMMEUBLES RB LTEE
(*Suby of* GROUPE ROBERT INC)
500 Rte 112, Rougemont, QC, J0L 1M0
(450) 469-3153
Emp Here 250   *Sales* 46,095,250
SIC 4225 General warehousing and storage
  Claude Robert
  Gerard Bernard

D-U-N-S 24-475-2903   (HQ)
INDUSTRIES LASSONDE INC
.(*Suby of* 3346625 CANADA INC)
755 Rue Principale, Rougemont, QC, J0L 1M0
(450) 469-4926
Emp Here 10   *Sales* 1,208,411,556
SIC 6712 Bank holding companies
  Pierre-Paul Lassonde
  Jean Gattuso
  Guy Blanchette
  Stefano Bertolli
  Peter Mattson
  Yves Toupin
  Pierre Turner
  Seth French
  Chantal Belanger
  Denis Boudreault

D-U-N-S 20-515-5018   (BR)
INDUSTRIES LASSONDE INC
LASSONDE, A.
(*Suby of* 3346625 CANADA INC)
705 Rue Principale, Rougemont, QC, J0L 1M0
(450) 469-4926
Emp Here 250
SIC 2033 Canned fruits and specialties
  Jean Gattuso

D-U-N-S 20-761-8778   (SL)

INDUSTRIES PAULYMARK INC
340 La Grande-Caroline, Rougemont, QC,
J0L 1M0
(514) 861-0180
Emp Here 60   *Sales* 14,006,100
SIC 2679 Converted paper products, nec
  Mario Marcil
  Jean-Guy Marcil
  Annie Marcil

D-U-N-S 20-245-3593   (SL)
MATERIEL INDUSTRIEL LTEE, LE
CONSTANT AIR-FLO
(*Suby of* ENTREPRISES BERNARD SORNIN
INC, LES)
325 La Grande-Caroline Rr 5, Rougemont,
QC, J0L 1M0
(450) 469-4934
Emp Here 90   *Sales* 17,287,650
SIC 3444 Sheet Metalwork
  Michel Sornin

D-U-N-S 20-319-8452   (HQ)
ROBERT TRANSPORT SPECIALIZED INC
DCR EXPRESS
500 Rte 112, Rougemont, QC, J0L 1M0
(450) 460-1112
Emp Here 20   *Sales* 25,998,350
SIC 4731 Freight transportation arrangement
  Claude Robert
  Michel Robert

D-U-N-S 24-944-8416   (HQ)
SPECIALITES LASSONDE INC
ENTREPOSAGE SUPERVISION
(*Suby of* 3346625 CANADA INC)
170 5e Av, Rougemont, QC, J0L 1M0
(450) 469-0856
Sales 13,827,600
SIC 2033 Canned fruits and specialties
  Jean Gattuso
  Nathalie St-Yves
  Caroline Lamoine
  Pierre-Paul Lassonde
  Nathalie Lassonde

D-U-N-S 20-245-3759   (HQ)
TRANSPORT ROBERT (1973) LTEE
ROBERT MEDIA
(*Suby of* GROUPE ROBERT INC)
500 Rte 112, Rougemont, QC, J0L 1M0
(450) 469-3153
Emp Here 200   *Sales* 46,095,250
SIC 4213 Trucking, except local
  Claude Robert
  Michel Robert

D-U-N-S 25-992-5592   (SL)
**VINS ARTERRA CANADA, DIVISION QUE-
BEC, INC**
MASSON
(*Suby of* ONTARIO TEACHERS' PENSION
PLAN BOARD)
175 Ch De Marieville, Rougemont, QC, J0L
1M0
(514) 861-2404
Emp Here 126   *Sales* 43,556,940
SIC 2084 Wines, brandy, and brandy spirits
  John Wright
  Donald Dychuk
  James Verdoni

Rouyn-Noranda, QC J0Y

D-U-N-S 24-864-0914   (BR)
AGNICO EAGLE MINES LIMITED
*AGNICO EAGLE MINES, DIVISION
LARONDE*
(*Suby of* AGNICO EAGLE MINES LIMITED)
10200 Rte De Preissac, Rouyn-Noranda, QC,
J0Y 1C0
(819) 759-3700
Emp Here 650
SIC 1041 Gold ores

  Michel Leclerc

D-U-N-S 25-106-5728   (SL)
MINES AGNICO EAGLE LIMITEE
10200 Rte De Preissac, Rouyn-Noranda, QC,
J0Y 1C0
(819) 759-3644
Emp Here 9,188   *Sales* 2,242,604,000
SIC 1241 Coal mining services
  Sean Boyd
  James D. Nasso
  Ammar Al-Joundi
  David Smith
  R. Gregory Laing
  Leanne M. Baker
  Mel Leiderman
  J. Marfyn Roberts
  Robert Joseph Gemmell
  Sean Emmet Riley

Rouyn-Noranda, QC J0Z

D-U-N-S 24-899-4790   (HQ)
BREAKWATER RESOURCES LTD
MINE BOUCHARD-HEBERT
(*Suby of* NYRSTAR)
8900 Rang Des Ponts, Rouyn-Noranda, QC,
J0Z 1P0
(819) 637-2075
Emp Here 9   *Sales* 63,943,500
SIC 1081 Metal mining services
  Larry Giegerich
  Cintia Zanellato
  Roman Matej
  Maciej Sciasko

D-U-N-S 25-284-3842   (SL)
PLASTIQUES G PLUS INC
180 Rue D'Evain, Rouyn-Noranda, QC, J0Z
1Y0
(819) 768-8888
Emp Here 54   *Sales* 10,902,438
SIC 3089 Plastics products, nec
  Dan Gagnon
  Nina Dion
  Pierre Trudel

Rouyn-Noranda, QC J9X

D-U-N-S 24-758-7629   (HQ)
121352 CANADA INC
TECHNOSUB
(*Suby of* GROUPE TECHNOSUB INC)
1156 Av Lariviere, Rouyn-Noranda, QC, J9X
4K8
(819) 797-3300
Emp Here 110   *Sales* 43,091,235
SIC 5084 Industrial machinery and equipment
  Yvan Blais
  Eric Beaupre
  Sonia Leveque
  Gaetan Langlois
  Patrick Martel
  Benoit Desormeaux
  Bryan Coates
  Martine Paiement

D-U-N-S 24-712-2450   (SL)
2242974 CANADA INC
CONSTRUCTION PROMEC
1300 Rue Saguenay, Rouyn-Noranda, QC,
J9X 7C3
(819) 797-7500
Emp Here 249   *Sales* 58,641,741
SIC 1731 Electrical work
  Denis Rene

D-U-N-S 24-842-5068   (SL)
2732-2304 QUEBEC INC
AMI HONDA, L'
1225 Av Lariviere, Rouyn-Noranda, QC, J9X

6M6
(819) 762-6565
Emp Here 35　　　　*Sales* 17,432,730
SIC 5511 New and used car dealers
Pierre Cloutier
Jean Dion

D-U-N-S 20-291-0154　　　(HQ)
2950-0519 QUEBEC INC
MOREAU INDUSTRIEL
(*Suby of* GESTION WM S.E.N.C.)
160 Boul Industriel, Rouyn-Noranda, QC, J9X
6T3
(819) 797-0088
Sales 73,171,422
SIC 1731 Electrical work
Morty White
Chantal Cadieux
Jean-Yves Moreau

D-U-N-S 20-266-6694　　　(HQ)
9064-4287 QUEBEC INC
MRT
543 Boul Temiscamingue, Rouyn-Noranda,
QC, J9X 7C8
(819) 762-2620
Emp Here 5　　　　*Sales* 20,570,600
SIC 4212 Local trucking, without storage
Martin Roy

D-U-N-S 25-223-0149　　　(SL)
9085-7160 QUEBEC INC
CLINIQUE D'OPTOMETRIE IRIS
75 Rue Monseigneur-Tessier O, Rouyn-
Noranda, QC, J9X 2S5
(819) 764-4747
Emp Here 31　　　*Sales* 10,093,600
SIC 5995 Optical goods stores
Lucie Dube
Normand Turcotte

D-U-N-S 20-552-6499　　　(SL)
**AGENCES DE SECURITE MIRADO 2002
INC**
AGENCE DE SECURITE MIRADO 2002, LES
121 8e Rue, Rouyn-Noranda, QC, J9X 2A5
(819) 797-5184
Emp Here 200　　　*Sales* 5,250,000
SIC 7381 Detective and armored car services
Caroline Lemire

D-U-N-S 24-629-5260　　　(HQ)
AMNOR INDUSTRIES INC
8 Rue Doyon, Rouyn-Noranda, QC, J9X 7B4
(819) 762-9044
Emp Here 25　　　*Sales* 16,582,362
SIC 7699 Repair services, nec
Richard Gaudreau
Christopher M Scaringe
Francis S Zilka

D-U-N-S 25-797-9682　　　(SL)
ATELIERS MANUTEX INC, LES
230 Av Marcel-Baril, Rouyn-Noranda, QC,
J9X 7C1
(819) 764-4415
Emp Here 80　　　*Sales* 39,865,760
SIC 5136 Men's and boy's clothing
Cecile Grenier
Francine Seguin
Charles Cloutier
Johanne Lacasse
Marc-Andre Matte
Brigitte Gagnon
Diane Bedard
Helene Piuze
Cecile Montemurro

D-U-N-S 25-246-2866　　　(HQ)
AU CARROSSIER INC
ACCES TOYOTA
1355 Av Lariviere, Rouyn-Noranda, QC, J9X
6M6
(819) 762-5000
Emp Here 33　　　*Sales* 22,413,510
SIC 5511 New and used car dealers
Dominque Perigny

Joel Meilleur
Jean Dion

D-U-N-S 24-835-2643　　　(SL)
BRETON & THIBAULT LTEE
HOME HARDWARE
(*Suby of* 9166-0688 QUEBEC INC)
333 Boul Rideau, Rouyn-Noranda, QC, J9X
5Y6
(819) 797-4949
Emp Here 75　　　*Sales* 20,073,900
SIC 5251 Hardware stores
Michel Mathieu
Pierre Tardif
Monique Harvey

D-U-N-S 24-489-6817　　　(HQ)
CENTRE DE READAPTATION LA MAISON
ORTHAIDE
7 9e Rue, Rouyn-Noranda, QC, J9X 2A9
(819) 762-6592
Emp Here 120　　　*Sales* 39,943,470
SIC 8011 Offices and clinics of medical doc-
tors
Line St-Amour
Clement Bernier

D-U-N-S 24-459-7423　　　(HQ)
**COMMISSION SCOLAIRE DE ROUYN-
NORANDA**
70 Rue Des Oblats E, Rouyn-Noranda, QC,
J9X 3N6
(819) 762-8161
Sales 79,295,200
SIC 8211 Elementary and secondary schools
Richard Gauthier

D-U-N-S 25-237-3357　　　(SL)
**CONSTRUCTION　　　LA-RAY　　DIVISION
ROUYN-NORANDA**
950 Rue Saguenay, Rouyn-Noranda, QC, J9X
7B6
(819) 762-9345
Emp Here 49　　　*Sales* 15,624,581
SIC 1521 Single-family housing construction
Rene Laroche

D-U-N-S 20-565-5392　　　(SL)
CONSTRUCTION TALBON INC
203 Boul Industriel, Rouyn-Noranda, QC, J9X
6P2
(819) 797-0122
Emp Here 60　　　*Sales* 25,364,220
SIC 1541 Industrial buildings and warehouses
Paul Bernier
Michel Belanger

D-U-N-S 25-365-2549　　　(SL)
DCR LOGISTICS INC
150 Av Marcel-Baril, Rouyn-Noranda, QC,
J9X 7C1
(819) 764-4944
Emp Here 40　　　*Sales* 15,414,400
SIC 4731 Freight transportation arrangement
Gilbert Dusseault
Jean Dion
Marcel Coulombe

D-U-N-S 20-245-6414　　　(SL)
DELICANA NORD-OUEST INC
680 Av Chausse, Rouyn-Noranda, QC, J9X
4B9
(819) 762-3555
Emp Here 100　　　*Sales* 83,557,700
SIC 5147 Meats and meat products
Joe Montemurro
Jocelyne Trudel
Robert Cloutier

D-U-N-S 24-916-3523　　　(SL)
DION SERVICES FINANCIERS
1380 Av Lariviere, Rouyn-Noranda, QC, J9X
4L1
(819) 797-4400
Emp Here 18　　　*Sales* 18,627,858
SIC 6351 Surety insurance
Jean Dion

D-U-N-S 24-866-8779　　　(SL)

FORAGE CHIBOUGAMAU LTEE
180 Boul Industriel, Rouyn-Noranda, QC, J9X
6T3
(819) 797-9144
Emp Here 49　　　*Sales* 10,170,597
SIC 1481 NonMetallic mineral services
Serge Larouche

D-U-N-S 24-820-3275　　　(SL)
GESTION GILLES ST-MICHEL INC
CANADIAN TIRE #089
245 Boul Rideau, Rouyn-Noranda, QC, J9X
5Y6
(819) 762-4375
Emp Here 65　　　*Sales* 13,347,295
SIC 5399 Miscellaneous general merchandise
Gilles St-Michel
Lise Mongeau

D-U-N-S 20-972-6249　　　(BR)
**GOUVERNEMENT DE LA PROVINCE DE
QUEBEC**
MINISTERE DES TRANSPORT DU QUEBEC
(*Suby of* GOUVERNEMENT DE LA
PROVINCE DE QUEBEC)
80 Av Quebec, Rouyn-Noranda, QC, J9X 6R1
(819) 763-3237
Emp Here 100
SIC 1611 Highway and street construction
Jaclin Begin

D-U-N-S 25-746-0956　　　(BR)
GOUVERNEUR INC
HOTEL GOUVERNEUR LE NORANDA
(*Suby of* GOUVERNEUR INC)
41 6e Rue, Rouyn-Noranda, QC, J9X 1Y8
(819) 762-2341
Emp Here 80
SIC 7011 Hotels and motels
Marc Brule

D-U-N-S 20-356-1147　　　(SL)
GROUPE PROMEC INC
1300 Rue Saguenay, Rouyn-Noranda, QC,
J9X 7C3
(819) 797-7500
Emp Here 50　　　*Sales* 10,891,450
SIC 1731 Electrical work
Peter Capkun
Benoit Lessard
Denis Rene
Eric Poulin
Stephane Lacroix

D-U-N-S 20-550-5246　　　(SL)
INDUSTRIES BLAIS INC, LES
CONSTRUCTION IB MAURITANIE
(*Suby of* PLACEMENTS JACQUES BLAIS
INC, LES)
155 Boul Industriel, Rouyn-Noranda, QC, J9X
6P2
(819) 764-3284
Emp Here 40　　　*Sales* 22,813,520
SIC 1542 Nonresidential construction, nec
Jacques Blais

D-U-N-S 24-296-8733　　　(SL)
**INTREPIDES DE ROUYN-NORANDA INC.,
LES**
INTREPIDES A DOMICILE, LES
380 Av Richard Bureau 203, Rouyn-Noranda,
QC, J9X 4L3
(819) 762-7217
Emp Here 125　　　*Sales* 8,540,750
SIC 8059 Nursing and personal care, nec
Suzanne Jodouin

D-U-N-S 24-019-5495　　　(SL)
J.Y. MOREAU ELECTRIQUE INC
1
(*Suby of* GESTION WM S.E.N.C.)
160 Boul Industriel, Rouyn-Noranda, QC, J9X
6T3
(819) 797-0088
Emp Here 250　　　*Sales* 57,129,599
SIC 1799 Special trade contractors, nec
Jean-Francois Moreau
Jean-Yves Moreau

Chantal Cadieux
Morton Jay White
John A. Hatherly
Michelle Cormier
Neelan Krishna Mayenkar

D-U-N-S 24-489-5330　　　(HQ)
LOCATION BLAIS INC
BLAIS RECREATIF
792 Av Quebec, Rouyn-Noranda, QC, J9X
7B1
(819) 797-9292
Sales 17,100,936
SIC 5082 Construction and mining machinery
Marc Blais
Serge Junior Blais

D-U-N-S 20-204-2594　　　(HQ)
MARCEL BARIL LTEE
DISTRIBUTEURS PAPINEAU
101 Av Marcel-Baril, Rouyn-Noranda, QC,
J9X 5P5
(819) 764-3211
Emp Here 62　　　*Sales* 40,245,660
SIC 5074 Plumbing and heating equipment
and supplies (hydronics)
Jean-Yves Baril
Michel Baril
Guy Baril
Marie-Josee Baril

D-U-N-S 20-019-7796　　　(SL)
MARCHE BELANGER INC
IGA EXTRA 8533
680 Av Chausse, Rouyn-Noranda, QC, J9X
4B9
(819) 762-2992
Emp Here 160　　　*Sales* 46,956,320
SIC 5411 Grocery stores
Marc Belanger

D-U-N-S 25-407-5690　　　(SL)
PAQUIN FORD LTEE
PAQUIN MAZDA
1155 Av Lariviere, Rouyn-Noranda, QC, J9X
4K9
(819) 797-3673
Emp Here 40　　　*Sales* 19,923,120
SIC 5511 New and used car dealers
Stephane Paquin
Patrick Paquin
Guy Paquin Jr
Chantal Paquin
Guy Paquin

D-U-N-S 20-028-5588　　　(HQ)
PNEUS G.B.M., S.E.N.C.
PNEUS G.B.M.
1000 Rue Saguenay, Rouyn-Noranda, QC,
J9X 7B6
(819) 762-0854
Emp Here 13　　　*Sales* 18,210,750
SIC 5014 Tires and tubes
Maurice Boivin
Noel Bertrand
Gerald Genesse

D-U-N-S 20-314-0173　　　(SL)
POIRIER CHRYSLER JEEP DODGE LTEE
1265 Av Lariviere, Rouyn-Noranda, QC, J9X
6M6
(819) 764-7437
Emp Here 25　　　*Sales* 12,451,950
SIC 5511 New and used car dealers
Yvon Poirier
Mario Poirier

D-U-N-S 20-632-1671　　　(HQ)
PRODUITS SANITAIRES NORFIL INC
ASPIRATEUR EN GROS
320 Av Turpin, Rouyn-Noranda, QC, J9X 7E1
(819) 762-8129
Emp Here 12　　　*Sales* 12,415,865
SIC 5169 Chemicals and allied products, nec
Denis Pilon
France Pilon

D-U-N-S 20-228-6514　　　(HQ)

RNC MEDIA INC
CKRN (RADIO)
380 Av Murdoch, Rouyn-Noranda, QC, J9X
1G5
(819) 762-0741
Emp Here 85   *Sales* 51,406,200
SIC 4832 Radio broadcasting stations
Pierre Brousseau

D-U-N-S 24-942-8970   (SL)
ROTISSERIE ROUYN-NORANDA INC
ROTISSERIE ST-HUBERT
60 Av Quebec, Rouyn-Noranda, QC, J9X 6P9
(819) 797-2151
Emp Here 75   *Sales* 3,413,925
SIC 5812 Eating places
Claude Cossette
Chantale Theoret
Jean-Yves Cossette

D-U-N-S 24-571-3800   (SL)
S. C. F P SECTION LOCALE 1500
75 Av Quebec, Rouyn-Noranda, QC, J9X 7A2
(819) 762-4422
Emp Here 26   *Sales* 10,341,157
SIC 8631 Labor organizations
Richard Perreault,

D-U-N-S 25-683-2403   (HQ)
**SERVICES D'ENTRETIEN MINIERS INDUS-
TRIELS R.N. 2000 INC**
155 Boul Industriel, Rouyn-Noranda, QC, J9X
6P2
(819) 797-4387
Emp Here 118   *Sales* 45,403,008
SIC 1241 Coal mining services
Jocelyne Blais
Jean-Francois Blais

D-U-N-S 25-783-5546   (SL)
SHELL O'TRENTE ENR
630 Boul Rideau, Rouyn-Noranda, QC, J9X
7G1
(819) 764-3530
Emp Here 50   *Sales* 24,903,900
SIC 5541 Gasoline service stations
Yvon Martin

D-U-N-S 20-113-8240   (BR)
SINTRA INC
LAMOTHE, DIV DE
(*Suby of* BOUYGUES)
240 Av Marcel-Baril, Rouyn-Noranda, QC,
J9X 7C1
(819) 762-6505
Emp Here 95
SIC 8711 Engineering services
Denis Laporte

D-U-N-S 20-314-3300   (BR)
SNC-LAVALIN STAVIBEL INC
GROUPE STAVIBEL INC
(*Suby of* GROUPE SNC-LAVALIN INC)
1375 Av Lariviere, Rouyn-Noranda, QC, J9X
6M6
(819) 764-5181
Emp Here 230
SIC 8711 Engineering services

D-U-N-S 24-885-0039   (BR)
SOBEYS CAPITAL INCORPORATED
SOBEYS
(*Suby of* EMPIRE COMPANY LIMITED)
333 Av Montemurro, Rouyn-Noranda, QC,
J9X 7C6
(819) 797-1900
Emp Here 200
SIC 5141 Groceries, general line
Karine Chasle

D-U-N-S 20-245-6539   (SL)
SUPER MARCHE ROY INC
METRO
240 Av Lariviere, Rouyn-Noranda, QC, J9X
4G8
(819) 762-5783
Emp Here 72   *Sales* 21,130,344
SIC 5411 Grocery stores

Pierre Duplain

D-U-N-S 25-134-9416   (SL)
SUPERMARCHE ROY INC
IGA ROY
240 Av Lariviere Bureau 550, Rouyn-Noranda,
QC, J9X 4G8
(819) 762-7739
Emp Here 49   *Sales* 13,433,448
SIC 5411 Grocery stores
Pierre Duplain

D-U-N-S 20-245-4963   (HQ)
**THIBAULT CHEVROLET CADILLAC BUICK
GMC DE ROUYN-NORANDA LTEE**
CENTRE DU CAMION THIBAULT
375 Boul Rideau, Rouyn-Noranda, QC, J9X
5Y7
(819) 762-1751
Emp Here 28   *Sales* 56,635,200
SIC 5511 New and used car dealers
Alain Thibault
Jacinthe Corriveau
Marc-Andre Thibault

D-U-N-S 24-669-2107   (BR)
UNIVERSITE DU QUEBEC
(*Suby of* UNIVERSITE DU QUEBEC)
445 Boul De L'Universite, Rouyn-Noranda,
QC, J9X 5E4
(819) 762-0971
Emp Here 500
SIC 8221 Colleges and universities
Jules Arsenault

D-U-N-S 25-498-3067   (BR)
WAL-MART CANADA CORP
WALMART
(*Suby of* WALMART INC.)
275 Boul Rideau Bureau 3136, Rouyn-
Noranda, QC, J9X 5Y6
(819) 762-0619
Emp Here 200
SIC 5311 Department stores
Yves Theriault

Rouyn-Noranda, QC J9Y

D-U-N-S 25-374-6713   (SL)
9015-6472 QUEBEC INC
CONSTRUCTION AUDET & KNIGHT
140 Rue Jacques-Bibeau, Rouyn-Noranda,
QC, J9Y 0A3
(819) 764-4666
Emp Here 60   *Sales* 15,146,520
SIC 1629 Heavy construction, nec
Martin Knight
Sylvain Dallaire
Guylain Audet
Julie Samuel

D-U-N-S 24-915-3573   (SL)
**AEROPORT REGIONAL DE ROUYN NO-
RANDA**
80 Av De L'Aeroport Bureau 82, Rouyn-
Noranda, QC, J9Y 0G1
(819) 762-8171
Emp Here 49   *Sales* 15,912,946
SIC 4581 Airports, flying fields, and services
Marie-Reine Robert

D-U-N-S 24-085-8134   (SL)
MANSEAU & PERRON INC
(*Suby of* 9049-6035 QUEBEC INC)
701 Av Davy, Rouyn-Noranda, QC, J9Y 0A8
(819) 762-2818
Emp Here 65   *Sales* 14,158,885
SIC 1761 Roofing, siding, and sheetMetal
work
Julie Lariviere
Alain Racette
Lorrain Marteln
Donald Dionne

D-U-N-S 24-908-2868   (HQ)

MATERIAUX CAMPAGNA (2003) INC
RONA
1200 Rue Mantha, Rouyn-Noranda, QC, J9Y
0G2
(819) 797-1200
Emp Here 30   *Sales* 10,122,360
SIC 5211 Lumber and other building materials
Denis Campagna
Pierre Campagna

D-U-N-S 24-826-7333   (SL)
MBI DRILLING PRODUCTS INC
MBI MANUFACTURE
110 Rue Jacques-Bibeau, Rouyn-Noranda,
QC, J9Y 0A3
(819) 762-9645
Emp Here 50   *Sales* 22,743,060
SIC 5084 Industrial machinery and equipment
Daniel Misiano
Gaetan Langlois
Guillaume Lemire
Dany Laliberte
Maurice Boutin
Michel Gilbert
Martine Paiement
Steven Breint

D-U-N-S 24-339-6517   (SL)
MINES OPINACA LTEE, LES
(*Suby of* NEWMONT GOLDCORP CORPO-
RATION)
853 Boul Rideau Bureau 764, Rouyn-
Noranda, QC, J9Y 0G3
(819) 764-6400
Emp Here 100   *Sales* 12,477,600
SIC 8741 Management services
Patrick Merrin
Lincoln Schreiner
Anna M Tudela
Jason Attew
Todd White

D-U-N-S 20-416-0642   (SL)
PROPAIR INC
20 Rue Pronovost, Rouyn-Noranda, QC, J9Y
0G1
(819) 762-0811
Emp Here 100   *Sales* 12,194,192
SIC 4512 Air transportation, scheduled
Etienne Lambert
Pierre Fillion

D-U-N-S 25-212-2127   (SL)
**SECURITAS TRANSPORT AVIATION SECU-
RITY LTD**
*SURETE DU TRANSPORT AERIEN SECU-
RITAS*
(*Suby of* SECURITAS AB)
100 Av De L'Aeroport Unite 17, Rouyn-
Noranda, QC, J9Y 0G1
(819) 764-3507
Emp Here 750   *Sales* 228,810,750
SIC 7389 Business services, nec
Richard Marinos
Alois Seliner
Johan Gordts

Roxboro, QC H8Y

D-U-N-S 24-570-1854   (BR)
GROUPE ADONIS INC
MARCHE ADONIS
(*Suby of* METRO INC)
4601 Boul Des Sources, Roxboro, QC, H8Y
3C5
(514) 685-5050
Emp Here 85
SIC 5411 Grocery stores
Pierre Cheaid

D-U-N-S 20-501-0226   (HQ)
PEPINIERE PIERREFONDS INC
11409 Boul Gouin O, Roxboro, QC, H8Y 1X7

(514) 684-5051
Emp Here 30   *Sales* 12,652,950
SIC 5261 Retail nurseries and garden stores
Michelina Di Marco
Riccardo Di Marco

Roxton Falls, QC J0H

D-U-N-S 25-979-1890   (SL)
CHEVRIER LAPORTE & ASSOCIES INC
319 Rue Notre-Dame, Roxton Falls, QC, J0H
1E0

Emp Here 49   *Sales* 50,709,169
SIC 6311 Life insurance
Louis Gendron

D-U-N-S 20-302-8220   (SL)
ROSKI COMPOSITES INC
ROSKI
130 Rue De L'Eglise Bureau 3, Roxton Falls,
QC, J0H 1E0
(450) 548-5821
Emp Here 100   *Sales* 62,928,000
SIC 5561 Recreational vehicle dealers
Yves Carbonneau
Janick Beauregard
Estelle Brouillard

Roxton Pond, QC J0E

D-U-N-S 24-254-2076   (SL)
ENVIRO 5 INC
1101 139 Rte, Roxton Pond, QC, J0E 1Z0
(450) 777-2551
Emp Here 50   *Sales* 11,046,700
SIC 1711 Plumbing, heating, air-conditioning
Frederick Cote
Isabelle Valcourt

Sacre-Coeur-Saguenay, QC G0T

D-U-N-S 24-530-5503   (HQ)
BOISACO INC
648 Ch Du Moulin Bureau 250, Sacre-Coeur-
Saguenay, QC, G0T 1Y0
(418) 236-4633
Sales 19,237,000
SIC 2421 Sawmills and planing mills, general
Steeve St-Gelais
Joe Marsili
Karl Gauthier
Benjamin Dufour
Sylvain Boily
Martin Simard
Jeannot Simard
Tommy Gauthier
Serge Mercier
Joey Saputo

D-U-N-S 25-108-0206   (SL)
SACOPAN INC
(*Suby of* MASONITE INTERNATIONAL COR-
PORATION)
652 Ch Du Moulin, Sacre-Coeur-Saguenay,
QC, G0T 1Y0
(418) 236-1414
Emp Here 50   *Sales* 11,100,050
SIC 3544 Special dies, tools, jigs, and fixtures
Guy Deschenes
Jim Kingry
Chris Virostek
Denis Turcotte
Jim Morrison
Dan Ellis
Richard Belanger
Richard Drouin
Steeve St-Gelais

Richard Drouin

Saint-Adalbert, QC G0R

D-U-N-S 25-090-1113   (SL)
2621-9634 QUEBEC INC
LES BOIS STE-GAU
37 204 Rte E, Saint-Adalbert, QC, G0R 2M0
(418) 356-5591
Emp Here 65   *Sales* 10,131,095
SIC 2491 Wood preserving
Stephane Gauvin
Martin Gauvin

Saint-Agapit, QC G0S

D-U-N-S 25-233-1517   (BR)
COMMISSION SCOLAIRE DES NAVIGA-TEURS
ECOLE SECONDAIRE BEAURIVAGE
(*Suby of* COMMISSION SCOLAIRE DES NAVIGATEURS)
1134 Rue Du Centenaire, Saint-Agapit, QC, G0S 1Z0
(418) 888-3961
Emp Here 93
SIC 8211 Elementary and secondary schools
Christiane Guay

Saint-Alexandre-D'Iberville, QC J0J

D-U-N-S 20-246-3683   (SL)
FREGEAU, B. & FILS INC
402 Rue Saint-Denis, Saint-Alexandre-D'Iberville, QC, J0J 1S0
(450) 346-3487
Emp Here 70   *Sales* 10,373,440
SIC 4212 Local trucking, without storage
Serge Fregeau
Michel Fregeau
Louise Fregeau
Marie-Jeanne Fregeau

Saint-Alexandre-De-Kamouraska, QC G0L

D-U-N-S 24-206-7262   (SL)
ALIMENTS ASTA INC
ASTA FOOD
767   Rte   289,   Saint-Alexandre-De-Kamouraska, QC, G0L 2G0
(418) 495-2728
Emp Here 435   *Sales* 212,012,475
SIC 2011 Meat packing plants
Jacques Poitras

D-U-N-S 24-464-4027   (SL)
GROUPEMENT   FORESTIER   DE KAMOURASKA INC
605   289   Rte,   Saint-Alexandre-De-Kamouraska, QC, G0L 2G0
(418) 495-2054
Emp Here 90   *Sales* 12,308,310
SIC 0851 Forestry services
Raymond Boucher
France Gagnon Rioux
Renald Bernier
Sarah Belanger
Gerald Landry

Saint-Alexis-Des-Monts, QC J0K

D-U-N-S 20-234-4482   (SL)

AUBERGE DU LAC SACACOMIE INC
HOTEL SACACOMIE
4000   Ch   Yvon-Plante,   Saint-Alexis-Des-Monts, QC, J0K 1V0
(819) 265-4444
Emp Here 100   *Sales* 9,599,811
SIC 7011 Hotels and motels
Joyce Plante

D-U-N-S 25-674-5290   (SL)
SIMDAR INC
AUBERGE LAC-A-L'EAU-CLAIRE
500 Ch Du Lac-A-L'Eau-Claire, Saint-Alexis-Des-Monts, QC, J0K 1V0
(819) 265-3185
Emp Here 125   *Sales* 11,586,250
SIC 7011 Hotels and motels
Pierre Simard

Saint-Alphonse-De-Granby, QC J0E

D-U-N-S 24-325-8972   (BR)
CONTITECH CANADA, INC
(*Suby of* CONTINENTAL AG)
127 Rang Parent, Saint-Alphonse-De-Granby, QC, J0E 2A0
(450) 375-5050
Emp Here 220
SIC 3069 Fabricated rubber products, nec
Gilles Bilodeau

D-U-N-S 20-554-0490   (SL)
LAGUE ET GOYETTE LTEE
S.G. SPORT MARINE
124 Rue Authier, Saint-Alphonse-De-Granby, QC, J0E 2A0
(450) 777-1101
Emp Here 26   *Sales* 12,350,676
SIC 5088 Transportation equipment and supplies
Simon Goyette
Marc-Aubre Paquette

D-U-N-S 24-848-6362   (BR)
SINTRA INC
(*Suby of* BOUYGUES)
101 Rue De La Sintra, Saint-Alphonse-De-Granby, QC, J0E 2A0
(450) 375-4471
Emp Here 100
SIC 1611 Highway and street construction
Guylaine Boutin

Saint-Alphonse-Rodriguez, QC J0K

D-U-N-S 20-246-4426   (SL)
9069-7897 QUEBEC INC
MARCHE ST-ALPHONSE
790 343 Rte, Saint-Alphonse-Rodriguez, QC, J0K 1W0
(450) 883-2963
Emp Here 40   *Sales* 10,966,080
SIC 5411 Grocery stores
Dany Flamand
Patricia Girard

D-U-N-S 25-968-9586   (BR)
SOCIETE POUR LES ENFANTS HANDI-CAPES DU QUEBEC
CAMP PAPILLON
(*Suby of* SOCIETE POUR LES ENFANTS HANDICAPES DU QUEBEC)
210 Rue Papillon, Saint-Alphonse-Rodriguez, QC, J0K 1W0
(450) 883-2915
Emp Here 150
SIC 7032 Sporting and recreational camps
Sylvianne Renaud

Saint-Ambroise, QC G7P

D-U-N-S 25-323-5899   (SL)
GEANT MOTORISE INC, LE
(*Suby of* SURPLUS DE MANUFACTURE PHILIPPE BOUCHARD & FILS INC)
173 Rte 172, Saint-Ambroise, QC, G7P 2N5
(418) 672-4744
Emp Here 80   *Sales* 34,472,988
SIC 5561 Recreational vehicle dealers
Andre Bouchard

D-U-N-S 20-266-8307   (SL)
LEGUPRO INC
DISTRIBUTION PROPUR
1424 Rang Des Chutes, Saint-Ambroise, QC, G7P 2V4
(418) 672-4717
Emp Here 26   *Sales* 21,725,002
SIC 5142 Packaged frozen goods
Martin Brassard
Serge Vachon
Mathieu Bouchard
Mario Dallaire
Julien Rivard

D-U-N-S 20-253-8062   (SL)
PEPINIERE BOUCHER DIVISION PLANTS FORESTIERS INC
(*Suby of* 2730-9277 QUEBEC INC)
94 Rang Des Aulnaies, Saint-Ambroise, QC, G7P 2B4
(418) 672-4779
Emp Here 50   *Sales* 13,115,450
SIC 0181 Ornamental nursery products
Stephane Boucher

Saint-Anaclet, QC G0K

D-U-N-S 20-244-0434   (SL)
MIRALIS INC
ARMOIRES MIRALIS
200 Rue Des Fabricants, Saint-Anaclet, QC, G0K 1H0
(418) 723-6686
Emp Here 180   *Sales* 34,626,600
SIC 2434 Wood kitchen cabinets
Daniel Drapeau
Harold Belanger

Saint-Andre-Avellin, QC J0V

D-U-N-S 24-363-8355   (BR)
CENTRE DE SANTE ET SERVICES SOCI-AUX DE PAPINEAU
CLSC ET CENTRE D'HEBERGEMENT PETITE-NATION
(*Suby of* CENTRE DE SANTE ET SERVICES SOCIAUX DE PAPINEAU)
14 Rue Saint-Andre, Saint-Andre-Avellin, QC, J0V 1W0
(819) 983-7341
Emp Here 240
SIC 8361 Residential care
Rejeanne Pilotte

D-U-N-S 24-662-2559   (HQ)
PROMUTUEL   L'OUTAOUAIS   SOCIETE MUTUELLE D'ASSURANCE GENERALE
PROMUTUEL L'OUTAOUAIS
629 321 Rte N Rr 3, Saint-Andre-Avellin, QC, J0V 1W0
(819) 983-6141
Emp Here 20   *Sales* 10,343,284
SIC 6411 Insurance agents, brokers, and service
Gary Thompson

Saint-Andre-D'Argenteuil, QC J0V

D-U-N-S 24-156-7994   (BR)
ASPHALTE, BETON, CARRIERES RIVE-NORD INC
ABC
134   Rte   Du   Long-Sault,   Saint-Andre-D'Argenteuil, QC, J0V 1X0
(450) 258-4242
Emp Here 130
SIC 5082 Construction and mining machinery
Francine Vaillancourt

Saint-Anicet, QC J0S

D-U-N-S 20-192-3984   (SL)
J.R. CAZA & FRERE INC
3755 Rte 132, Saint-Anicet, QC, J0S 1M0
(450) 264-2300
Emp Here 20   *Sales* 10,000,000
SIC 5083 Farm and garden machinery
William Caza
Lambert Caza

D-U-N-S 20-264-5511   (SL)
SOUDURES J.M. TREMBLAY (1987) INC, LES
GROUPE TREMBLAY
1303 Rte 132, Saint-Anicet, QC, J0S 1M0
(450) 264-5690
Emp Here 50   *Sales* 11,671,750
SIC 3312 Blast furnaces and steel mills
Pierre Tremblay
Guy Clermont

Saint-Anselme, QC G0R

D-U-N-S 24-761-5623   (HQ)
CAISSE DESJARDINS DU COEUR DE BEL-LECHASSE
CENTRE DE SERVICES SAINTE-CLAIRE
730 Rte Begin, Saint-Anselme, QC, G0R 2N0
(418) 885-4421
Emp Here 10   *Sales* 13,224,113
SIC 6062 State credit unions
Marc Bouchard
Mario Cloutier
Clement Pouliot
Nathalie Dumont
Paule Baillargeon
Robert Bolduc
Evelyne Brochu
Sylvie Fortier
Annik Godbout
Alain Larochelle

D-U-N-S 20-296-5229   (BR)
COMMISSION SCOLAIRE DE LA COTE-DU-SUD, LA
ECOLE SECONDAIRE DE SAINT ANSELME
825 Rte Begin, Saint-Anselme, QC, G0R 2N0
(418) 885-4431
Emp Here 135
SIC 8211 Elementary and secondary schools
Mari-Andre Gilbert

D-U-N-S 20-247-0159   (HQ)
COUTURE, ALFRED LIMITEE
MARCHE COUTURE
420 Rue Principale, Saint-Anselme, QC, G0R 2N0
(418) 885-4425
Emp Here 150   *Sales* 26,955,275
SIC 0723 Crop preparation services for market
Bernard Couture
Laurence Couture

D-U-N-S 20-247-0282   (SL)
EQUIPEMENTS FRONTMATEC INC

---

51 Rte Morissette, Saint-Anselme, QC, G0R 2N0
(418) 885-4493
Emp Here 300   *Sales* 84,263,100
SIC 3569 General industrial machinery, nec
Henrik Andersen
Marcel Couture

D-U-N-S 24-345-5586   (BR)
EXCELDOR COOPERATIVE
PRODUITS EXCELDOR, LES
(*Suby of* EXCELDOR COOPERATIVE)
1000 Rte Begin, Saint-Anselme, QC, G0R 2N0
(418) 885-4451
Emp Here 200
SIC 2015 Poultry slaughtering and processing
Michel Leclerc

D-U-N-S 25-716-6785   (SL)
GROUPE SINOX INC
SINOX CONCEPT
16 Rue Turgeon, Saint-Anselme, QC, G0R 2N0
(418) 885-8276
Emp Here 75   *Sales* 5,318,747
SIC 3556 Food products machinery
Gaston Lacasse
Sonia Bilodeau
Remi Gagne
Steve Lavoie

D-U-N-S 20-247-0290   (SL)
MAGASIN COOP DE ST-ANSELME
I G A
70 Rue Principale, Saint-Anselme, QC, G0R 2N0
(418) 885-4461
Emp Here 40   *Sales* 12,918,760
SIC 5411 Grocery stores
Gaetan Leblond

D-U-N-S 24-591-4858   (BR)
MAPLE LEAF FOODS INC
(*Suby of* MAPLE LEAF FOODS INC)
254 Rue Principale, Saint-Anselme, QC, G0R 2N0

Emp Here 120
SIC 5411 Grocery stores
Marie-Claude Lamontagne

D-U-N-S 24-207-9416   (SL)
PARE CHEVROLET OLDSMOBILE INC
1239 Rte Begin, Saint-Anselme, QC, G0R 2N0

Emp Here 22   *Sales* 10,957,716
SIC 5511 New and used car dealers
Normand Pare
Rejean Pare
Gilles Pare
Claudette Pare

D-U-N-S 24-376-5950   (SL)
PLATE 2000 INC
GROUPE P.BOLDUC
1239 Rte Begin, Saint-Anselme, QC, G0R 2N0
(418) 885-0085
Emp Here 26   *Sales* 12,350,676
SIC 5082 Construction and mining machinery
Patrick Bolduc

Saint-Antoine-De-Tilly, QC G0S

D-U-N-S 24-792-5225   (SL)
FROMAGERIE BERGERON INC
BAGELCHESSE
3837 Rte Marie-Victorin, Saint-Antoine-De-Tilly, QC, G0S 2C0
(418) 886-2234
Emp Here 110   *Sales* 38,025,900
SIC 2022 Cheese; natural and processed
Roger Bergeron

Sylvain Bergeron
Mario Bergeron

D-U-N-S 24-820-7458   (SL)
GROUPE J.L. LECLERC INC
LECLERC LEVAGE INDUSTRIEL
4919 Rte Marie-Victorin, Saint-Antoine-De-Tilly, QC, G0S 2C0
(418) 886-2474
Emp Here 115   *Sales* 25,530,115
SIC 3599 Industrial machinery, nec
Jerome Leclerc
Julie Leclerc
Gilles Leclerc
Michel Leclerc
Dany Imbeault

Saint-Apollinaire, QC G0S

D-U-N-S 24-464-5644   (SL)
BANLIEUE FORD INC
344 Rue Laurier, Saint-Apollinaire, QC, G0S 2E0
(418) 881-2323
Emp Here 21   *Sales* 10,459,638
SIC 5511 New and used car dealers
Pierre Bergeron

D-U-N-S 25-484-8955   (SL)
GESTION GAETAN BOUCHER
MARCHE IGA
405 273 Rte, Saint-Apollinaire, QC, G0S 2E0
(418) 881-3112
Emp Here 40   *Sales* 10,966,080
SIC 5411 Grocery stores
Gaetan Boucher

D-U-N-S 24-390-1092   (HQ)
GROUPE PRO-FAB INC
RESIDENCE P.F, LES
294 Rue Laurier Bureau 881, Saint-Apollinaire, QC, G0S 2E0
(418) 881-2288
Emp Here 1   *Sales* 19,237,000
SIC 2452 Prefabricated wood buildings
Martin Roy
Martin Boulet
Michelle Cormier
Frank G Hayes
Greg Gleason

D-U-N-S 20-016-5715   (BR)
JELD-WEN OF CANADA LTD
JELD-WEN OF CANADA, LTD
(*Suby of* JELD-WEN HOLDING, INC.)
90 Rue Industrielle Bureau 200, Saint-Apollinaire, QC, G0S 2E0
(418) 881-3974
Emp Here 300
SIC 2431 Millwork

D-U-N-S 20-247-1983   (SL)
LAFLAMME PORTES ET FENETRES CORP
A.B.P. & DEESIN
(*Suby of* GROUPE ATIS INC)
39 Rue Industrielle, Saint-Apollinaire, QC, G0S 2E0
(418) 881-3950
Emp Here 300   *Sales* 83,517,000
SIC 2431 Millwork
Robert Doyon
Andre Parent
Mathieu Lalonde
Gabriel Belanger

Saint-Arsene, QC G0L

D-U-N-S 20-191-4975   (HQ)
TRANSPORT MORNEAU INC
MORNEAU TRANSPORT
(*Suby of* GESTION DENIS MORNEAU (1993)

INC)
40 Rue Principale, Saint-Arsene, QC, G0L 2K0
(418) 862-2727
Emp Here 125   *Sales* 64,829,158
SIC 4213 Trucking, except local
Andre Morneau
Micheline Morneau

Saint-Augustin-De-Desmaures, QC G3A

D-U-N-S 20-330-0301   (SL)
6702601 CANADA INC
TROPBON
4919 Rue Saint-Felix, Saint-Augustin-De-Desmaures, QC, G3A 1B4
(418) 571-0705
Emp Here 21   *Sales* 17,547,117
SIC 5149 Groceries and related products, nec
Guylaine Blondeau

D-U-N-S 25-355-3747   (SL)
9001-6262 QUEBEC INC
30 Rue Des Grands-Lacs, Saint-Augustin-De-Desmaures, QC, G3A 2E6
(418) 878-4135
Emp Here 300   *Sales* 109,652,700
SIC 6712 Bank holding companies
Louis Garneau

D-U-N-S 20-051-2411   (SL)
9099-7768 QUEBEC INC
E.B.M LASER
109 Rue Des Grands-Lacs, Saint-Augustin-De-Desmaures, QC, G3A 1V9
(418) 878-3616
Emp Here 50   *Sales* 10,141,500
SIC 3444 Sheet Metalwork
Gaetan St-Jean
Rodrigue Major
Michel N. Dugal
Daniel Potvin

D-U-N-S 20-013-1345   (SL)
A. BEAUMONT TRANSPORT INC
280 Rte De Fossambault, Saint-Augustin-De-Desmaures, QC, G3A 2P9
(418) 878-4888
Emp Here 120   *Sales* 9,411,600
SIC 4213 Trucking, except local
Andre Beaumont
Linda Laperriere

D-U-N-S 20-127-2080   (SL)
ACIER HYDRAULIQUE INC
173 Rue De Liverpool, Saint-Augustin-De-Desmaures, QC, G3A 2C8
(418) 878-5711
Emp Here 11   *Sales* 11,003,729
SIC 5051 Metals service centers and offices
Donald Tardis

D-U-N-S 24-214-8281   (SL)
ALIMENTATION OLIVIER,GUY INC
3525 Rue De L'Hetriere, Saint-Augustin-De-Desmaures, QC, G3A 0C1
(418) 872-4444
Emp Here 49   *Sales* 13,433,448
SIC 5411 Grocery stores
Guy Olivier

D-U-N-S 25-335-8386   (SL)
AMEC USINAGE INC
110 Rue Des Grands-Lacs, Saint-Augustin-De-Desmaures, QC, G3A 2K1
(418) 878-4133
Emp Here 55   *Sales* 12,210,055
SIC 3599 Industrial machinery, nec
Francois Doyon
Christian Beaulieu

D-U-N-S 20-581-4320   (HQ)
BISCUITS LECLERC LTEE
ALIMENTS F. LECLERC
(*Suby of* GROUPE BISCUITS LECLERC INC)

91 Rue De Rotterdam, Saint-Augustin-De-Desmaures, QC, G3A 1T1
(418) 878-2601
Emp Here 50   *Sales* 243,692,500
SIC 2052 Cookies and crackers
Denis Leclerc

D-U-N-S 25-369-5738   (BR)
BISCUITS LECLERC LTEE
(*Suby of* GROUPE BISCUITS LECLERC INC)
70 Rue De Rotterdam, Saint-Augustin-De-Desmaures, QC, G3A 1S9
(418) 878-2601
Emp Here 400
SIC 2052 Cookies and crackers
Jean Leclerc

D-U-N-S 20-721-7100   (HQ)
BREMO INC
JOINTEMENT INTER
(*Suby of* MANTIS INVESTMENTS, INC.)
214 138 Rte, Saint-Augustin-De-Desmaures, QC, G3A 2X9
(418) 878-4070
Emp Here 80   *Sales* 22,240,120
SIC 3052 Rubber and plastics hose and beltings
Andre Morin
Marc-Andre Allard
Pierre Sylvain

D-U-N-S 25-021-6421   (SL)
CAMPUS NOTRE-DAME-DE-FOY
SERVICES ALIMENTAIRES CAMPUS NOTRE-DAME-DE-FOY
5000 Rue Clement-Lockquell, Saint-Augustin-De-Desmaures, QC, G3A 1B3
(418) 872-8041
Emp Here 200   *Sales* 29,878,200
SIC 8221 Colleges and universities
Marie-Helene Riverin
Michel Levesque
Guy Dufour
Pierre-Henri Robitaille
Raymond Boutin
Odette Nappert
Dominique Veilleux
Anne Douville
Lea Racine
Guillaume Crochetiere

D-U-N-S 20-440-1120   (HQ)
CONSTRUCTION BSL INC
BSL ENTREPRENEUR GENERAL
315 Rue De Rotterdam, Saint-Augustin-De-Desmaures, QC, G3A 2E5
(418) 878-4448
Emp Here 15   *Sales* 45,627,040
SIC 1542 Nonresidential construction, nec
Rosaire Tanguay

D-U-N-S 24-850-4706   (SL)
E B M LASER INC
109 Rue Des Grands-Lacs, Saint-Augustin-De-Desmaures, QC, G3A 1V9
(418) 878-3616
Emp Here 49   *Sales* 21,731,010
SIC 7389 Business services, nec
Gaetan St-Jean

D-U-N-S 20-308-9800   (SL)
ECHAFAUDAGE PLUS (QUEBEC) INC
148 Rue D'Amsterdam, Saint-Augustin-De-Desmaures, QC, G3A 2R1
(418) 878-3885
Emp Here 78   *Sales* 19,202,508
SIC 1799 Special trade contractors, nec
Bruno Tasse
Jean-Marc Champigny
Renaud St-Germain
Jonathan Burns

D-U-N-S 25-246-3179   (SL)
ENTREPOTS E.F.C. INC, LES
COOL
50 Rue Des Grands-Lacs, Saint-Augustin-De-Desmaures, QC, G3A 2E6

---

(418) 878-5660
Emp Here 35   *Sales* 11,666,655
SIC 1541 Industrial buildings and warehouses
Mario Guerin

D-U-N-S 25-501-9176   (HQ)
ENTREPRISES MICROTEC INC, LES
ALARMCAP
(*Suby of* STANLEY BLACK & DECKER, INC.)
4780 Rue Saint-Felix, Saint-Augustin-De-Desmaures, QC, G3A 2J9
(418) 864-7924
Emp Here 98   *Sales* 87,037,050
SIC 5063 Electrical apparatus and equipment
Fred Fong

D-U-N-S 24-820-5932   (SL)
EQUIPEMENTS PLANNORD LTEE
TRANSPORT CARLANN
70 Rue D'Anvers, Saint-Augustin-De-Desmaures, QC, G3A 1S4
(418) 878-4007
Emp Here 22   *Sales* 10,450,572
SIC 5084 Industrial machinery and equipment
Simon Paquet
Maxime Jutras
Jacques Paquet
Michel Paquet

D-U-N-S 25-358-8982   (HQ)
FABRICANT DE POELES INTERNATIONAL INC
SBI
250 Rue De Copenhague Bureau 1, Saint-Augustin-De-Desmaures, QC, G3A 2H3
(418) 878-3040
Emp Here 170   *Sales* 54,726,975
SIC 3433 Heating equipment, except electric
Gilles Cantin
Jean-Francois Cantin

D-U-N-S 24-884-0514   (SL)
FUMOIR GRIZZLY INC
GRIZZLY
(*Suby of* PLACEMENTS GRIZZLY INC)
159 Rue D'Amsterdam, Saint-Augustin-De-Desmaures, QC, G3A 2V5
(418) 878-8941
Emp Here 63   *Sales* 21,778,470
SIC 2091 Canned and cured fish and seafoods
Laura Boivin
Richard Guay

D-U-N-S 24-870-3753   (HQ)
GIBIERS CANABEC INC, LES
115 Rue Des Grands-Lacs, Saint-Augustin-De-Desmaures, QC, G3A 2T9
(418) 843-0782
Sales 37,600,965
SIC 5147 Meats and meat products
Alexandre Therrien

D-U-N-S 24-381-3151   (HQ)
GRANICOR INC
300 Rue De Rotterdam Bureau 21, Saint-Augustin-De-Desmaures, QC, G3A 1T4
(418) 878-3530
Emp Here 75   *Sales* 14,337,520
SIC 3281 Cut stone and stone products
Alain Robitaille
Paul Jr Robitaille
Georges Robitaille

D-U-N-S 25-094-1614   (SL)
GROUPE C.D.J. INC
4740 Rue Saint-Felix, Saint-Augustin-De-Desmaures, QC, G3A 1B1

Emp Here 120   *Sales* 3,836,160
SIC 7349 Building maintenance services, nec
Alain Alzas

D-U-N-S 25-367-7314   (SL)
GROUPE MANUFACTURIER D'ASCENSEURS GLOBAL TARDIF INC, LE
(*Suby of* GROUPE TARDIF GLF INC, LE)

120 Rue De Naples, Saint-Augustin-De-Desmaures, QC, G3A 2Y2
(418) 878-4116
Emp Here 150   *Sales* 26,810,850
SIC 8711 Engineering services
Francois Tardif

D-U-N-S 20-700-8645   (HQ)
GROUPE TARDIF GLF INC, LE
GLOBAL TARDIF
120 Rue De Naples, Saint-Augustin-De-Desmaures, QC, G3A 2Y2
(418) 878-4116
Emp Here 1   *Sales* 44,400,200
SIC 3534 Elevators and moving stairways
Francois Tardif

D-U-N-S 20-297-8305   (SL)
IMPORTATIONS N & N INC, LES
PELUCHE ET TARTINE
109 Rue D'Amsterdam, Saint-Augustin-De-Desmaures, QC, G3A 2V5
(418) 878-9555
Emp Here 23   *Sales* 11,461,406
SIC 5137 Women's and children's clothing
Noel Bedard
Chantal Forcier
Nancy Bedard

D-U-N-S 25-198-7525   (SL)
INVESTISSEMENTS DU HAUT-ST-LAURENT INC, LES
JARDINS DU HAUT ST-LAURENT 1990
4770 Rue Saint-Felix, Saint-Augustin-De-Desmaures, QC, G3A 0K9
(418) 872-4936
Emp Here 150   *Sales* 8,887,050
SIC 8361 Residential care
Hyman Polanski

D-U-N-S 24-380-9063   (HQ)
LOBE RESEAU INC
LOBE
3520 Rue De L'Hetriere Bureau 103, Saint-Augustin-De-Desmaures, QC, G3A 0B4
(418) 877-7222
Emp Here 35   *Sales* 17,048,925
SIC 8093 Specialty outpatient clinics, nec
Martin Cousineau

D-U-N-S 25-076-0972   (HQ)
LOUIS GARNEAU SPORTS INC
AIRDRY
30 Rue Des Grands-Lacs, Saint-Augustin-De-Desmaures, QC, G3A 2E6
(418) 878-4135
Emp Here 25   *Sales* 79,600,500
SIC 2329 Men's and boy's clothing, nec
Louis Garneau

D-U-N-S 24-940-8253   (HQ)
MANULIFT E.M.I. LTEE
MANULIFT
100 Rue D'Anvers, Saint-Augustin-De-Desmaures, QC, G3A 1S4
(418) 878-5424
Emp Here 1   *Sales* 17,575,962
SIC 5084 Industrial machinery and equipment
Jean-Yves Drolet
Martin Drolet

D-U-N-S 20-861-3604   (SL)
MECART INC
(*Suby of* ENTREPRISES POL R INC)
110 Rue De Rotterdam, Saint-Augustin-De-Desmaures, QC, G3A 1T3
(418) 880-7000
Emp Here 45   *Sales* 10,504,575
SIC 3296 Mineral wool
Benoit Poupart
Daniel Desbiens

D-U-N-S 20-716-3416   (BR)
METRO RICHELIEU INC
JARDIN MERITE DE QUEBEC
(*Suby of* METRO INC)
60 Rue D'Anvers, Saint-Augustin-De-

Desmaures, QC, G3A 1S4

Emp Here 100
SIC 5431 Fruit and vegetable markets
Jacques Laplante

D-U-N-S 20-362-3970   (SL)
PLACEMENTS BOIVAIN INC
DMB DISTRIBUTION
149 Rue D'Amsterdam, Saint-Augustin-De-Desmaures, QC, G3A 2V5
(418) 878-3373
Emp Here 100   *Sales* 83,557,700
SIC 5142 Packaged frozen goods
Sylvain Laroche
Conrad Boivin

D-U-N-S 24-325-1456   (SL)
PORTES ET FENETRES M.P.M. INC
VITRERIE M.P.M.
167 Rue D'Amsterdam, Saint-Augustin-De-Desmaures, QC, G3A 2V5
(418) 870-1544
Emp Here 29   *Sales* 12,968,046
SIC 5031 Lumber, plywood, and millwork
Paul-Omer Begin
Michel Pageau
Martin Duchesneau

D-U-N-S 24-342-2594   (SL)
PREMIERE SOCIETE EN COMMANDITE NATIONALE ALARMCAP
A.T.S. SECURITE
4780 Rue Saint-Felix, Saint-Augustin-De-Desmaures, QC, G3A 2J9
(418) 864-7924
Emp Here 190   *Sales* 91,341,550
SIC 7382 Security systems services
Len Sudermann

D-U-N-S 20-330-2633   (BR)
PREMOULE INC
PREMOULE COMPTOIRS
270 Rue Des Grands-Lacs, Saint-Augustin-De-Desmaures, QC, G3A 2K1
(418) 878-5384
Emp Here 200
SIC 3083 Laminated plastics plate and sheet
Yvan Gaudreau

D-U-N-S 24-908-9871   (HQ)
PREVERCO INC
BFS 2002
285 Rue De Rotterdam, Saint-Augustin-De-Desmaures, QC, G3A 2E5
(800) 667-2725
Emp Here 195   *Sales* 55,678,000
SIC 2426 Hardwood dimension and flooring mills
Fernand Dufresne
Julien Dufresne
Bruno Dufresne
Marie-Claude Perreault
Jean-Francois Dufresne
Michel Gariepy

D-U-N-S 25-842-1155   (SL)
PRO AUTOMATION INC
243 Rue De Bordeaux, Saint-Augustin-De-Desmaures, QC, G3A 2M8
(418) 878-4500
Emp Here 28   *Sales* 18,380,992
SIC 5962 Merchandising machine operators
Pierre Gagnon
Danny Hebert
Luc Deschenes

D-U-N-S 25-673-0433   (SL)
PRODUCTIONS ATLAN INC., LES
120 Rue De Rotterdam, Saint-Augustin-De-Desmaures, QC, G3A 1T3
(418) 878-5881
Emp Here 60   *Sales* 12,113,820
SIC 3069 Fabricated rubber products, nec
Cecil Sebastian
Diane Guay

D-U-N-S 25-149-1692   (HQ)

PRODUITS DE CONSTRUCTION DERBY INC
MATERIAUX DE CONSTRUCTION DERBY
160 Rue Des Grands-Lacs, Saint-Augustin-De-Desmaures, QC, G3A 2K1
(418) 878-6161
Sales 28,402,100
SIC 2822 Synthetic rubber
Ralph Bruno
Francois Giroux
James G. Andersen
Matt Rumilly
Isabel Boivin

D-U-N-S 24-582-5372   (SL)
QUALITE CONSTRUCTION (CDN) LTEE
155 Rue D'Amsterdam, Saint-Augustin-De-Desmaures, QC, G3A 2V5
(418) 878-4044
Emp Here 25   *Sales* 10,944,105
SIC 1542 Nonresidential construction, nec
Sebastien Pelletier
Vincent Grenier
Nicolas Duguay

D-U-N-S 25-106-6858   (SL)
R M H INDUSTRIE INC
130 Rue De Rotterdam, Saint-Augustin-De-Desmaures, QC, G3A 1T3
(418) 878-0875
Emp Here 60   *Sales* 13,320,060
SIC 3599 Industrial machinery, nec
Pierre Juneau
Claude Regnier

D-U-N-S 20-266-1039   (HQ)
SAINT-AUGUSTIN CANADA ELECTRIQUE INC
STACE
(*Suby of* LORD'STACE INC)
75 Rue D'Anvers, Saint-Augustin-De-Desmaures, QC, G3A 1S5
(418) 878-6900
Sales 20,975,850
SIC 1711 Plumbing, heating, air-conditioning
Normand Lord

D-U-N-S 24-637-5729   (SL)
SEMINAIRE SAINT-FRANCOIS
4900 Rue Saint-Felix, Saint-Augustin-De-Desmaures, QC, G3A 0L4
(418) 872-0611
Emp Here 120   *Sales* 11,894,280
SIC 8211 Elementary and secondary schools
Jean-Marc Boule

D-U-N-S 20-512-3255   (SL)
SERVICE D'EQUIPEMENT G.D. INC
104 Rue D'Anvers, Saint-Augustin-De-Desmaures, QC, G3A 1S4
(418) 681-0080
Emp Here 26   *Sales* 12,350,676
SIC 5082 Construction and mining machinery
Guy Deschenes

D-U-N-S 24-419-0216   (BR)
TELECON INC
(*Suby of* CAPITAL REGIONAL ET COOPER-ATIF DESJARDINS)
104 Rue D'Anvers, Saint-Augustin-De-Desmaures, QC, G3A 1S4
(418) 878-9595
Emp Here 125
SIC 4899 Communication services, nec
Francois Houde

D-U-N-S 20-431-9347   (BR)
TOROMONT INDUSTRIES LTD
TOROMONT CAT
(*Suby of* TOROMONT INDUSTRIES LTD)
100 Rue De Rotterdam, Saint-Augustin-De-Desmaures, QC, G3A 1T2
(418) 878-3000
Emp Here 190
SIC 5082 Construction and mining machinery

D-U-N-S 24-884-8017   (HQ)
TRANSPORT TFI 4, S.E.C.

KINGSWAY VRAC
140 Rue Des Grands-Lacs, Saint-Augustin-De-Desmaures, QC, G3A 2K1
(418) 870-5454
Emp Here 25   *Sales* 20,570,600
SIC 4213 Trucking, except local
Chantal Martel

D-U-N-S 24-790-7678   (BR)
VIGI SANTE LTEE
C H S L D VIGI SAINT AUGUSTIN
4954 Rue Clement-Lockquell, Saint-Augustin-De-Desmaures, QC, G3A 1V5
(418) 871-1232
Emp Here 130
SIC 8361 Residential care
Mario Soucy

Saint-Barthelemy, QC J0K

D-U-N-S 24-082-2262   (HQ)
MACHINERIES NORDTRAC LTEE
1060 Montee Saint-Laurent, Saint-Barthelemy, QC, J0K 1X0
(450) 885-3202
Sales 26,825,150
SIC 5083 Farm and garden machinery
Michel Noel
Eric Caumartin
Denis Villemure
Jean Pesant
Paul Morin
Normand Picotte
Eric St-Georges
Alain Dugre

Saint-Basile, QC G0A

D-U-N-S 20-247-4029   (HQ)
CIMENT QUEBEC INC
UNIBETON
(*Suby of* GROUPE CIMENT QUEBEC INC)
145 Boul Du Centenaire, Saint-Basile, QC, G0A 3G0
(418) 329-2100
Emp Here 180   *Sales* 140,629,500
SIC 3241 Cement, hydraulic
Luc Papillon
Jon Morrish
Francois Proulx
Michel Demers
Andre Morissette
Francois Perrin
Bertrand Morin
Henner Boettcher
Arnaldo Bertola

D-U-N-S 24-969-1734   (HQ)
GROUPE CIMENT QUEBEC INC
145 Boul Du Centenaire, Saint-Basile, QC, G0A 3G0
(418) 329-2100
Sales 127,845,000
SIC 3241 Cement, hydraulic
Luc Papillon
Francois Proulx
Jon Morrish
Andre Morissette
Francois Perrin

D-U-N-S 20-574-0173   (HQ)
PROMUTUEL PORTNEUF-CHAMPLAIN SOCIETE, MUTUAL D'ASSURANCE GENERALE
ASSURANCE PROMUTUEL PORTNEUF-CHAMPLAIN
257 Boul Du Centenaire Rr 1, Saint-Basile, QC, G0A 3G0
(418) 329-3330
Emp Here 15   *Sales* 42,403,000
SIC 6411 Insurance agents, brokers, and ser-

vice
Michel Gauthier
Jean-Paul Rousseau
Jean Mottard
Richard Audet

Saint-Basile-Le-Grand, QC J3N

D-U-N-S 20-791-9270   (SL)
132082 CANADA INC
SIROTIERE DU SOMMET YAMASKA
250 Ch Bella-Vista, Saint-Basile-Le-Grand, QC, J3N 1L1
(450) 461-1988
Emp Here 40   *Sales* 13,698,680
SIC 0161 Vegetables and melons
Normand Saurette

D-U-N-S 24-319-9044   (SL)
9151-8100 QUEBEC INC
ST-BASILE TOYOTA
141 Boul Sir-Wilfrid-Laurier, Saint-Basile-Le-Grand, QC, J3N 1M2
(450) 653-1003
Emp Here 35   *Sales* 17,432,730
SIC 5511 New and used car dealers
Robert Mercil

D-U-N-S 20-978-1301   (HQ)
BEAULIEU & LAMOUREUX INC
LUMI-AIR DORION
283 Boul Sir-Wilfrid-Laurier, Saint-Basile-Le-Grand, QC, J3N 1M2
(450) 653-1752
Emp Here 30   *Sales* 17,886,960
SIC 5063 Electrical apparatus and equipment
Claude Blanchard

D-U-N-S 24-810-7971   (SL)
CONSTRUCTIONS FGP INC, LES
33 Montee Robert, Saint-Basile-Le-Grand, QC, J3N 1L7
(450) 441-2727
Emp Here 40   *Sales* 18,829,240
SIC 1542 Nonresidential construction, nec
Francois Godmer
Gaston Patry

D-U-N-S 24-434-7084   (SL)
GARAGE DODGE CHRYSLER DE SAINT-BASILE INC
DODGE CHRYSLER DE SAINT-BASILE
225 Boul Sir-Wilfrid-Laurier, Saint-Basile-Le-Grand, QC, J3N 1M2
(450) 653-0114
Emp Here 25   *Sales* 12,451,950
SIC 5511 New and used car dealers
Heinz Schlegel

D-U-N-S 20-332-7416   (HQ)
GESTION MAISON ETHIER INC
267 Boul Sir-Wilfrid-Laurier, Saint-Basile-Le-Grand, QC, J3N 1M8
(450) 653-1556
Sales 23,240,300
SIC 5712 Furniture stores
Francois Ethier
Sylvain Bonneau
Pierre Ethier

D-U-N-S 24-849-9092   (SL)
GROUPE C. & G. BEAULIEU INC
(*Suby of* 3228835 CANADA INC)
368 Boul Grand E, Saint-Basile-Le-Grand, QC, J3N 1M4
(450) 653-9581
Emp Here 150   *Sales* 104,758,800
SIC 1542 Nonresidential construction, nec
Valerie Beaulieu

D-U-N-S 20-871-7418   (HQ)
MARCHE LAMBERT ET FRERES INC
2400 Boul Du Millenaire, Saint-Basile-Le-Grand, QC, J3N 1T8

(450) 441-3800
Sales 28,869,600
SIC 5411 Grocery stores
Bruno Lambert
Ivan Lambert
Luc Lambert
Renaud Lambert
Thierry Lambert

D-U-N-S 20-798-4456   (SL)
PHARMACIE SONIA GUIMONT PHARMACIENNE INC
JEAN COUTU
275 Boul Sir-Wilfrid-Laurier Bureau 100, Saint-Basile-Le-Grand, QC, J3N 1V6
(450) 441-1944
Emp Here 45   *Sales* 11,382,930
SIC 5912 Drug stores and proprietary stores
Sonia Guimont

Saint-Benoit-Labre, QC G0M

D-U-N-S 25-089-2353   (SL)
9048-9493 QUEBEC INC
COUTURE VOIE EXPRESS
(*Suby of* 9094-1253 QUEBEC INC)
27 Rue Industrielle, Saint-Benoit-Labre, QC, G0M 1P0
(418) 228-6979
Emp Here 70   *Sales* 14,399,420
SIC 4213 Trucking, except local
Sylvain Couture
Vincent Couture

D-U-N-S 24-639-2229   (HQ)
CONSTRUCTIONS BINET INC, LES
(*Suby of* GESTION MARTIN BINET INC)
227 Rte 271, Saint-Benoit-Labre, QC, G0M 1P0
(418) 228-1578
Emp Here 25   *Sales* 23,536,550
SIC 1542 Nonresidential construction, nec
Martin Binet
Nadia Binet
Louis-David Poirier
Francine Binet

D-U-N-S 20-013-1220   (SL)
R.C.M. MODULAIRE INC
CUISINES VALENCIA
28 Rue Industrielle, Saint-Benoit-Labre, QC, G0M 1P0
(418) 227-4044
Emp Here 200   *Sales* 38,474,000
SIC 2452 Prefabricated wood buildings

D-U-N-S 20-517-1259   (SL)
TOITURES FECTEAU INC
320 Rte 271, Saint-Benoit-Labre, QC, G0M 1P0
(418) 228-9651
Emp Here 55   *Sales* 10,580,350
SIC 2439 Structural wood members, nec
Kathy Poulin
Jean-Paul Grondin
Steeve Grondin
Jean-Pierre Chabot

Saint-Bernard, QC G0S

D-U-N-S 20-247-5646   (HQ)
ALIMENTS BRETON INC
FERME BSL
1312 Rue Saint-Georges, Saint-Bernard, QC, G0S 2G0
(418) 475-6601
Emp Here 25   *Sales* 41,778,850
SIC 5149 Groceries and related products, nec
Lucien Breton
Claude Jacques
Gilles L'ecuyer

D-U-N-S 25-380-6665   (SL)
BRETON AGRI-MANAGEMENT INC
1312 Rue Saint-Georges, Saint-Bernard, QC, G0S 2G0
(418) 475-6601
Emp Here 50   *Sales* 13,716,600
SIC 8741 Management services
Magella Breton

D-U-N-S 20-251-2208   (HQ)
BRETON TRADITION 1944 INC
CUISIVIANDES
1312 Rue Saint-Georges, Saint-Bernard, QC, G0S 2G0
(418) 475-6601
Emp Here 225   *Sales* 536,123,500
SIC 2011 Meat packing plants
Lucien Breton
Vincent Breton
Magella Breton
Nathalie Breton
Line Breton
Serge Breton
Claude Jacques

Saint-Bernard-De-Lacolle, QC J0J

D-U-N-S 20-203-3049   (HQ)
FORTIN, J E INC
116 Boul Fortin, Saint-Bernard-De-Lacolle, QC, J0J 1V0
(450) 246-3867
Sales 21,599,130
SIC 4213 Trucking, except local
J Eugene Fortin
Jean-Claude Fortin
Annie Fortin

D-U-N-S 24-858-3742   (SL)
UFP CANADA INC
PRODUITS FORESTIERS UNIVERSELLES DU CANADA
(*Suby of* UNIVERSAL FOREST PRODUCTS, INC.)
110 Montee Guay, Saint-Bernard-De-Lacolle, QC, J0J 1V0
(450) 246-3829
Emp Here 80   *Sales* 15,389,600
SIC 2499 Wood products, nec
Michael F. Mordell
David A. Tutas
Michael R. Cole
Michel Guilbeault

Saint-Bonaventure, QC J0C

D-U-N-S 25-469-6404   (SL)
9310-6607 QUEBEC INC
771 Rue Principale Bureau 396, Saint-Bonaventure, QC, J0C 1C0
(819) 396-2293
Emp Here 50   *Sales* 13,833,000
SIC 2875 Fertilizers, mixing only
Marcel Fafard
Martin Fafard
Claude Fafard

Saint-Boniface-De-Shawinigan, QC G0X

D-U-N-S 24-100-1770   (SL)
COOPERATIVE FORESTIERE DU BAS ST-MAURICE
1410 Boul Trudel E, Saint-Boniface-De-Shawinigan, QC, G0X 2L0
(819) 535-6262
Emp Here 40   *Sales* 15,896,560
SIC 8699 Membership organizations, nec
Luc Frigon

D-U-N-S 20-247-6370   (SL)
PORTES MILETTE INC
100 Av Industrielle, Saint-Boniface-De-Shawinigan, QC, G0X 2L0
(819) 535-5588
Emp Here 150   *Sales* 28,855,500
SIC 2431 Millwork
Gerard Millette
Guy Roy
Sophie Milette
Chantal Frigon
Fortin Coulombe
Mario Millette
Michel Millette
Andre Fortin

D-U-N-S 24-766-2120   (SL)
ST-BONIFACE MUNICIPAL GARAGE
500 Municipale Pl, Saint-Boniface-De-Shawinigan, QC, G0X 2L0
(819) 535-5443
Emp Here 49   *Sales* 14,115,174
SIC 7538 General automotive repair shops

Saint-Bruno, QC J3V

D-U-N-S 24-379-2335   (SL)
175784 CANADA INC
PANZINI DEMOLITION
585 Rue Sagard, Saint-Bruno, QC, J3V 6C1
(450) 461-3310
Emp Here 150   *Sales* 30,855,900
SIC 4212 Local trucking, without storage
Jean-Philippe Brissette
Guillaume Brissette

D-U-N-S 20-700-5682   (HQ)
3728099 CANADA INC
1370 Rue Hocquart, Saint-Bruno, QC, J3V 6E1
(450) 653-7868
Emp Here 2   *Sales* 18,870,975
SIC 6712 Bank holding companies

D-U-N-S 24-311-5586   (HQ)
4366492 CANADA INC
1360 Rue Montarville, Saint-Bruno, QC, J3V 3T5
(514) 498-7777
Sales 16,774,200
SIC 6712 Bank holding companies
Michel Dufresne
Nicolas Dufresne

D-U-N-S 24-108-4052   (HQ)
9351-8371 QUEBEC INC
1905 Boul Sir-Wilfrid-Laurier, Saint-Bruno, QC, J3V 0G8
(450) 653-1553
Emp Here 30   *Sales* 37,756,800
SIC 5511 New and used car dealers
Sylvie Niquet

D-U-N-S 20-400-2497   (SL)
9458778 CANADA LIMITED
AUDI ST-BRUNO
1917 Boul Sir-Wilfrid-Laurier, Saint-Bruno, QC, J3V 0G8
(514) 443-5648
Emp Here 150   *Sales* 6,827,850
SIC 5812 Eating places
Kapil Dilawri
Ajay Dilawri
Lalit Tony Dilawri
Bryan Czinkan

D-U-N-S 20-327-3198   (SL)
ALIMENTS EXCEL S.E.C., LES
1081 Rue Parent, Saint-Bruno, QC, J3V 6L7
(450) 441-6111
Emp Here 250   *Sales* 121,846,250
SIC 2015 Poultry slaughtering and processing
Jean-Pierre Dube

D-U-N-S 25-244-4898   (SL)

ARCHAMBAULT, J. L. PHARMACIEN
PHARMACIE JEAN-COUTU
12 Boul Clairevue O Bureau 39, Saint-Bruno, QC, J3V 1P8
(450) 653-1528
Emp Here 45   *Sales* 11,382,930
SIC 5912 Drug stores and proprietary stores
Jean L Archambault

D-U-N-S 20-254-4722   (SL)
B. K. FER OUVRE INC
BK INDUSTRIES
1800 Rue Marie-Victorin, Saint-Bruno, QC, J3V 6B9
(514) 820-7423
Emp Here 60   *Sales* 11,525,100
SIC 3441 Fabricated structural Metal
Gregory Kornek

D-U-N-S 24-512-4024   (SL)
BOIRON CANADA INC
BOIRON DOLISOS
(*Suby of* BOIRON)
1300 Rue Rene-Descartes, Saint-Bruno, QC, J3V 0B7
(450) 723-2066
Emp Here 26   *Sales* 28,738,970
SIC 5122 Drugs, proprietaries, and sundries
Janick Boudazin
Lucie Clement
Maurice Clermont
Valerie Poinsot

D-U-N-S 20-179-0420   (BR)
BOMBARDIER INC
BOMBARDIER TRANSPORTATION
(*Suby of* BOMBARDIER INC)
1101 Rue Parent, Saint-Bruno, QC, J3V 6E6
(450) 441-2020
Emp Here 800
SIC 4111 Local and suburban transit
Joanne Bissonnette

D-U-N-S 24-389-1442   (HQ)
BOMBARDIER TRANSPORTATION CANADA HOLDING INC
BOMBARDIER
(*Suby of* BOMBARDIER INC)
1101 Rue Parent, Saint-Bruno, QC, J3V 6E6
(450) 441-2020
Emp Here 3   *Sales* 503,671,402
SIC 6712 Bank holding companies
Benoit Brossoit
Julie Turgeon
Richard Coulombe

D-U-N-S 24-368-4458   (HQ)
BOMBARDIER TRANSPORTATION CANADA INC
BOMBARDIER TRANSPORT
(*Suby of* BOMBARDIER INC)
1101 Rue Parent, Saint-Bruno, QC, J3V 6E6
(450) 441-3193
Emp Here 200   *Sales* 152,456,000
SIC 7363 Help supply services
Benoit Brossoit
Julie Turgeon
Richard Coulombe

D-U-N-S 24-335-7485   (HQ)
CAISSE DESJARDINS DU MONT-SAINT-BRUNO
CENTRE DE SERVICE SAINT-BASILE-LE-GRAND
1649 Rue Montarville, Saint-Bruno, QC, J3V 3T8
(450) 653-3646
Emp Here 63   *Sales* 10,723,373
SIC 6062 State credit unions
Sylvain Dessureault
Linda Lamarre
Martin Richard
Gerald Jenkins
Nathalie Berzosa
Robert Mignault
Florent Fortier
Marc-Andre Lehoux

Sandrine Bedard
Myriam Lagueux

D-U-N-S 20-332-1492   (BR)
CASCADES CANADA ULC
CASCADES EMBALLAGE CARTON-CAISSE, UNE DIVISION DE CASCADES CANADA ULC
(*Suby of* CASCADES INC)
1061 Rue Parent, Saint-Bruno, QC, J3V 6R7
(450) 461-8600
Emp Here 250
SIC 2631 Paperboard mills
Allan Hogg

D-U-N-S 20-331-0479   (BR)
CCL INDUSTRIES INC
ETIQUETTES CCL MONTREAL
(*Suby of* CCL INDUSTRIES INC)
1315 Rue Rene-Descartes, Saint-Bruno, QC, J3V 0B7
(450) 653-3071
Emp Here 150
SIC 2679 Converted paper products, nec
Pierre Dery

D-U-N-S 25-233-7068   (BR)
COMMISSION SCOLAIRE DES PATRIOTES
ECOLE SECONDAIRE DU MONT-BRUNO
(*Suby of* COMMISSION SCOLAIRE DES PATRIOTES)
221 Boul Clairevue E, Saint-Bruno, QC, J3V 5J3
(450) 653-1541
Emp Here 60
SIC 8211 Elementary and secondary schools
Marc Courtemanche

D-U-N-S 20-309-4750   (HQ)
COMMISSION SCOLAIRE DES PATRIOTES
1740 Rue Roberval, Saint-Bruno, QC, J3V 3R3
(450) 441-2919
Emp Here 1   *Sales* 227,577,224
SIC 8211 Elementary and secondary schools
Joseph Atalla
Luc Lapointe
Patrick Mendes
Linda Fortin

D-U-N-S 20-419-9509   (SL)
COMPAGNIE DE DYNAMIQUE AVANCEE LTEE, LA
(*Suby of* 7667213 CANADA INC)
1700 Rue Marie-Victorin, Saint-Bruno, QC, J3V 6B9
(450) 653-7220
Emp Here 120   *Sales* 33,705,240
SIC 3535 Conveyors and conveying equipment
Peter Hanna
Kevin Williams
Naji Elabiad
Peter Sakaitis

D-U-N-S 24-890-4435   (BR)
CONSTRUCTION DJL INC
(*Suby of* VINCI)
580 Rang Des Vingt-Cinq E, Saint-Bruno, QC, J3V 0G6
(450) 653-2423
Emp Here 100
SIC 1422 Crushed and broken limestone
Norman Scully

D-U-N-S 24-835-4565   (SL)
CONSTRUCTIONS BRI INC, LES
CARON CONTRUCTION
585 Rue Sagard, Saint-Bruno, QC, J3V 6C1
(450) 461-3310
Emp Here 300   *Sales* 63,712,800
SIC 1794 Excavation work
Jean Brissette

D-U-N-S 20-955-0263   (HQ)
CYME INTERNATIONAL T & D INC
(*Suby of* EATON CORPORATION PUBLIC LIMITED COMPANY)

1485 Rue Roberval Bureau 104, Saint-Bruno, QC, J3V 3P8
(450) 461-3655
Sales 10,092,740
SIC 7371 Custom computer programming services
Richard M. Eubanks
Roger W. Shea
Lizbeth L. Wright

D-U-N-S 20-540-8131   (HQ)
DEMENAGEMENT MONT-BRUNO/LAKESHORE INC
1900 Rue Marie-Victorin, Saint-Bruno, QC, J3V 6B9
(450) 653-7891
Emp Here 40   *Sales* 10,373,440
SIC 4213 Trucking, except local
Martin Forget

D-U-N-S 24-256-1744   (HQ)
DENSI CORPORATION
DENSIGRAPHIX KOPI
(*Suby of* DENSI HOLDING INC)
1100 Rue Parent, Saint-Bruno, QC, J3V 6L8
(450) 441-1300
Sales 14,676,120
SIC 3955 Carbon paper and inked ribbons
Eric Melka

D-U-N-S 24-788-3739   (SL)
DOMAINE DU SKI MONT BRUNO INC
SKI MONT SAINT-BRUNO
(*Suby of* 164457 CANADA INC)
550 Rang Des Vingt-Cinq E, Saint-Bruno, QC, J3V 0G6
(450) 653-3441
Emp Here 500   *Sales* 47,834,000
SIC 7011 Hotels and motels
Serge Couture
Pauline Huot Couture
Michel Couture
Tony Dinielli

D-U-N-S 24-551-9041   (SL)
ENTREPRISES A & R BROCHU CONSTRUCTION INC , LES
1505 Rue Marie-Victorin, Saint-Bruno, QC, J3V 6B7
(450) 441-7444
Emp Here 49   *Sales* 13,320,258
SIC 7699 Repair services, nec

D-U-N-S 24-050-2831   (SL)
ENTREPRISES DUPONT 1972 INC, LES
SERVICE MECANIQUE EXPRESS JOLIETTE
(*Suby of* TFI INTERNATIONAL INC)
601 Rue Sagard, Saint-Bruno, QC, J3V 6C1
(450) 653-9362
Emp Here 110   *Sales* 22,627,660
SIC 4212 Local trucking, without storage
Josiane-Melanie Langlois
Chantal Martel

D-U-N-S 20-859-0521   (HQ)
EQUIPEMENT BONI INC
BONI DESIGN
1299 Rue Marie-Victorin, Saint-Bruno, QC, J3V 6B7
(450) 653-1299
Sales 30,864,400
SIC 2542 Partitions and fixtures, except wood
Jacinthe Majeau

D-U-N-S 20-381-7101   (BR)
EUROFINS ENVIRONMENT TESTING CANADA, INC
EUROFINS ESSAIS ENVIRONNEMENTAUX
(*Suby of* EUROFINS ENVIRONMENT TESTING CANADA, INC)
1390 Rue Hocquart, Saint-Bruno, QC, J3V 6E1
(450) 441-5880
Emp Here 100
SIC 8734 Testing laboratories

D-U-N-S 20-177-5637   (BR)

HOME DEPOT OF CANADA INC
(*Suby of* THE HOME DEPOT INC)
901 Rue De L'Etang, Saint-Bruno, QC, J3V
6N8
(450) 461-2000
Emp Here 100
SIC 5251 Hardware stores
 Gerard Brehin

 D-U-N-S 24-654-9641   (BR)
HUDSON'S BAY COMPANY
(*Suby of* HUDSON'S BAY COMPANY)
800 Boul Des Promenades, Saint-Bruno, QC,
J3V 5J9
(450) 653-4455
Emp Here 130
SIC 5311 Department stores
 Marie Latroix

 D-U-N-S 24-787-8275   (SL)
INSTEAD ROBOTIC CORP
1370 Rue Hocquart, Saint-Bruno, QC, J3V
6E1
(450) 653-7868
Emp Here 50   *Sales* 11,714,400
SIC 8748 Business consulting, nec
 Jean-Paul Boillot
 Andre Galibois
 Martine Boillot

 D-U-N-S 24-840-8598   (SL)
INSTITUTION QUEBEC
1395 Rue Marie-Victorin, Saint-Bruno, QC,
J3V 6B7
(450) 482-0724
Emp Here 25   *Sales* 12,075,384
SIC 5087 Service establishment equipment

 D-U-N-S 24-762-5692   (SL)
**INVESTISSEMENT PIERRE MARCOTTE
LIMITEE, LES**
CANADIAN TIRE
900 Rue De L'Etang, Saint-Bruno, QC, J3V
6K8
(450) 653-0222
Emp Here 100   *Sales* 20,534,300
SIC 5311 Department stores
 Pierre Marcotte
 Stephane Marcotte

 D-U-N-S 20-296-8298   (BR)
MAISON SIMONS INC, LA
(*Suby of* MAISON SIMONS INC, LA)
600 Boul Des Promenades, Saint-Bruno, QC,
J3V 6L9
(514) 282-1840
Emp Here 200
SIC 5311 Department stores
 Peter Simons

 D-U-N-S 20-034-1506   (BR)
MARCHE LAMBERT ET FRERES INC
IGA EXTRA
23 Boul Seigneurial O, Saint-Bruno, QC, J3V
2G9
(450) 653-4466
Emp Here 200
SIC 5411 Grocery stores
 Bruno Lambert

 D-U-N-S 24-490-6954   (SL)
MECAR METAL INC
1560 Rue Marie-Victorin, Saint-Bruno, QC,
J3V 6B9
(450) 653-1002
Emp Here 98   *Sales* 21,756,098
SIC 3585 Refrigeration and heating equipment
 Michael Gallagher
 Sean Gallagher
 Mireille Ouellette

 D-U-N-S 20-928-6582   (HQ)
NTP/STAG CANADA INC
COAST DISTRIBUTION SYSTEM, THE
(*Suby of* KEYSTONE AUTOMOTIVE OPERATIONS INC)
1545 Rue Marie-Victorin, Saint-Bruno, QC,

J3V 6B7
(450) 441-2707   .
Emp Here 83   *Sales* 20,570,600
SIC 4213 Trucking, except local
 Dominick Zarcone
 Derek Willshire
 Varun Laroyia
 Matthew Mckay
 Johanne Massey

 D-U-N-S 24-109-6718   (HQ)
PORTES ET FENETRES VERDUN LTEE
GROUPE VERDUN
1305 Rue Marie-Victorin Bureau 300, Saint-
Bruno, QC, J3V 6B7
(450) 441-0472
Sales 11,179,350
SIC 5039 Construction materials, nec
 Alain Pion
 Dominic Pion

 D-U-N-S 24-547-9449   (HQ)
PRODUITS FORESTIERS M.E.S. INC, LES
590 Rue Sagard, Saint-Bruno, QC, J3V 6C2
(450) 461-1767
Sales 22,358,700
SIC 5031 Lumber, plywood, and millwork
 Michel Caux
 Stephane Caux
 Johanne Caux

 D-U-N-S 25-199-4786   (SL)
REMAX ACTIF INC
1592 Rue Montarville Bureau 102, Saint-
Bruno, QC, J3V 3T7
(450) 461-1708
Emp Here 40   *Sales* 13,085,080
SIC 6531 Real estate agents and managers
 Micheline Beaugrand

 D-U-N-S 24-582-1905   (SL)
ST-BRUNO MODES ET SPORTS INC
SPORTS EXPERTS #526
750 Boul Des Promenades, Saint-Bruno, QC,
J3V 6A8
(450) 372-0368
Emp Here 100   *Sales* 17,939,600
SIC 5699 Miscellaneous apparel and accessory stores
 Marie-Claude Heroux

 D-U-N-S 20-050-2370   (SL)
STELPRO DESIGN INC
CHALAIR ELECTRIK
1041 Rue Parent, Saint-Bruno, QC, J3V 6L7
(450) 441-0101
Emp Here 400   *Sales* 97,292,400
SIC 3433 Heating equipment, except electric
 Yves Chabot
 Francois Seguin
 Connie Chabot
 Etienne Guay

 D-U-N-S 24-812-4158   (HQ)
STRUCTURES BRETON INC, LES
ACIER BRETON
(*Suby of* GESTION BRETON INC)
500 Rue Sagard, Saint-Bruno, QC, J3V 6C2
(450) 653-9999
Sales 34,755,660
SIC 1791 Structural steel erection
 Ray Kazemi
 Danoit Massicotte

 D-U-N-S 24-870-9149   (SL)
SUPERMARCHE ST-BRUNO INC
750 Montee Montarville, Saint-Bruno, QC, J3V
6B1
(450) 461-0792
Emp Here 50   *Sales* 13,707,600
SIC 5411 Grocery stores
 Gaetan Riendeau

 D-U-N-S 24-083-9381   (SL)
SYSTEMES B.M.H. INC, LES
1395 Rue Rene-Descartes, Saint-Bruno, QC,
J3V 0B7

(450) 441-1770
Emp Here 50   *Sales* 21,052,964
SIC 3559 Special industry machinery, nec
 Michel Blais
 Marie-Claude Blias

 D-U-N-S 24-920-5204   (SL)
TRANS-HERB E INC
1090 Rue Parent, Saint-Bruno, QC, J3V 6L8
(450) 441-0779
Emp Here 110   *Sales* 38,025,900
SIC 2099 Food preparations, nec
 Johanne Dion
 Paul Higgins Jr

 D-U-N-S 25-498-3331   (BR)
WAL-MART CANADA CORP
(*Suby of* WALMART INC.)
1475 Boul Saint-Bruno, Saint-Bruno, QC, J3V
6J1
(450) 653-9996
Emp Here 200
SIC 5311 Department stores
 Eric Laplante

Saint-Bruno-De-Guigues, QC J0Z

 D-U-N-S 20-247-7949   (HQ)
AUTOMOBILE PAQUIN LTEE
17 Rue Principale N, Saint-Bruno-De-
Guigues, QC, J0Z 2G0
(819) 728-2289
Emp Here 25   *Sales* 15,440,418
SIC 5511 New and used car dealers
 Christien Paquin
 Serge Paquin
 Daniel Paquin

Saint-Bruno-Lac-Saint-Jean, QC G0W

 D-U-N-S 24-941-3139   (SL)
**BLEUETS SAUVAGES DU QUEBEC INC,
LES**
(*Suby of* USINE DE CONGELATION DE ST-
BRUNO INC)
698 Rue Melancon Bureau 160, Saint-Bruno-
Lac-Saint-Jean, QC, G0W 2L0
(418) 343-2410
Emp Here 600   *Sales* 430,029,600
SIC 5142 Packaged frozen goods
 Jean-Pierre Senneville
 Dominique Larouche
 Remi Dufresne
 Jean-Eudes Senneville
 Jean-Philippe Harvey

 D-U-N-S 24-530-8184   (SL)
FRUITS BLEUS INC, LES
698 Rue Melancon, Saint-Bruno-Lac-Saint-
Jean, QC, G0W 2L0
(418) 343-2206
Emp Here 40   *Sales* 13,698,680
SIC 0171 Berry crops
 Jean-Eudes Senneville
 Remi Defresne

 D-U-N-S 24-821-0775   (HQ)
NUTRINOR COOPERATIVE
AGRINOR
425 Rue Melancon, Saint-Bruno-Lac-Saint-
Jean, QC, G0W 2L0
(418) 343-3636
Emp Here 30   *Sales* 109,652,700
SIC 6712 Bank holding companies
 Jean Lavoie
 Dominic Perron
 Gerald Rousseau
 Steve Gagnon
 Normand Marcil
 David Hossay
 Pierre Murray

 Mario Dallaire
 Marilyn Cote
 Normand Lapointe

 D-U-N-S 24-148-1027   (HQ)
**USINE DE CONGELATION DE ST-BRUNO
INC**
USINE DE CONGELATION
698 Rue Melancon, Saint-Bruno-Lac-Saint-
Jean, QC, G0W 2L0
(418) 343-2206
Emp Here 50   *Sales* 110,628,600
SIC 4222 Refrigerated warehousing and storage
 Dominique Larouche
 Jean-Philippe Harvey
 Remi Dufresne
 Jean-Eudes Senneville
 Jean-Pierre Senneville
 Maurice St-Pierre
 Clement Tremblay
 Dany Gaudreault

Saint-Casimir, QC G0A

 D-U-N-S 20-514-7853   (SL)
CONTRE-PLAQUE ST-CASIMIR INC
(*Suby of* COLUMBIA FOREST PRODUCTS,
INC.)
420 Rte Guilbault, Saint-Casimir, QC, G0A
3L0
(418) 339-2313
Emp Here 500   *Sales* 19,237,000
SIC 2435 Hardwood veneer and plywood
 Bradley L Thompson
 Ron Jorde
 Robert Picard

Saint-Celestin, QC J0C

 D-U-N-S 20-362-2717   (HQ)
GROUPE AGRITEX INC, LE
AGRICOTECH
230 Rue Marquis, Saint-Celestin, QC, J0C
1G0
(819) 229-3686
Emp Here 25   *Sales* 45,884,250
SIC 5999 Miscellaneous retail stores, nec
 Roy Louis
 Patrick Allard
 Simon Gauthier

 D-U-N-S 25-400-9202   (SL)
INDUSTRIES PRO-TAC INC, LES
445 Rue Jean-Clermont, Saint-Celestin, QC,
J0C 1G0
(819) 229-1288
Emp Here 90   *Sales* 18,170,730
SIC 3053 Gaskets; packing and sealing devices
 Francine Clermont
 Lucie Bourque

 D-U-N-S 24-404-2909   (SL)
TRANSPORT SAF (1994) INC
TRANSPORT S.A.F. 1994
(*Suby of* TFI INTERNATIONAL INC)
1227 Rang Saint-Joseph, Saint-Celestin, QC,
J0C 1G0
(819) 229-3638
Emp Here 30   *Sales* 15,599,010
SIC 4731 Freight transportation arrangement
 Jules Soucy
 Josiane M Langlois
 Chantal Martel
 Martin Quesnel

Saint-Cesaire, QC J0L

D-U-N-S 20-997-3403   (BR)
BALLIN INC
(Suby of GESTIONS JOSEPH BALINSKY INC, LES)
2100 Av De L'Union, Saint-Cesaire, QC, J0L 1T0
(450) 469-4957
Emp Here 120
SIC 2339 Women's and misses' outerwear, nec
  Daniel Lemgloes

D-U-N-S 24-512-4693   (BR)
BONDUELLE CANADA INC
BONDUELLE AMERIQUE DU NORD
(Suby of BONDUELLE)
1055 Rte 112, Saint-Cesaire, QC, J0L 1T0
(450) 469-3159
Emp Here 200
SIC 5149 Groceries and related products, nec
  Marco St-Amand

D-U-N-S 24-902-7210   (SL)
CAPSULES AMCOR FLEXIBLES CANADA INC
(Suby of AMCOR LTD)
2301 Rte 112, Saint-Cesaire, QC, J0L 1T0
(450) 469-0777
Emp Here 130   *Sales* 24,971,050
SIC 3466 Crowns and closures
  Jean De Guerry
  David Andison
  David Andison

D-U-N-S 24-679-5699   (HQ)
CARGESCO (2002) INC
2325 Boul Industriel, Saint-Cesaire, QC, J0L 1T0
(450) 469-3168
Sales 42,752,340
SIC 5084 Industrial machinery and equipment
  Lise Meunier
  David Cartier
  Josee Cartier

D-U-N-S 20-545-9766   (BR)
COMMISSION SCOLAIRE DES HAUTES-RIVIERES
ECOLE SECONDAIRE PAUL GERMAIN OS-TIGUY
(Suby of COMMISSION SCOLAIRE DES HAUTES-RIVIERES)
1881 Av Saint-Paul, Saint-Cesaire, QC, J0L 1T0
(450) 469-3187
Emp Here 75
SIC 8211 Elementary and secondary schools
  Serge Gobat

D-U-N-S 24-667-9427   (SL)
EMBALLAGES JEAN CARTIER INC
CARTIER
(Suby of CARGESCO (2002) INC)
2325 Boul Industriel, Saint-Cesaire, QC, J0L 1T0
(450) 469-3168
Emp Here 50   *Sales* 23,751,300
SIC 5084 Industrial machinery and equipment
  David Cartier

D-U-N-S 24-372-5491   (SL)
LUDIK DESIGNER CONFISEUR INC
BONNIE & CLYDE
660 Rte 112, Saint-Cesaire, QC, J0L 1T0
(450) 469-0514
Emp Here 25   *Sales* 20,889,425
SIC 5145 Confectionery
  Francois St-Laurent
  Marie-Eve Gladu

D-U-N-S 24-914-2402   (SL)
RESIDENCE DU COLLEGE CRP (2014) INC
1390 Rue Notre-Dame, Saint-Cesaire, QC, J0L 1T0
(450) 816-1390
Emp Here 49   *Sales* 41,554,940
SIC 6411 Insurance agents, brokers, and ser-

vice
  Guy Samson

D-U-N-S 24-434-6995   (SL)
SEMENCES PROGRAIN INC
PROGRAIN
145 Rang Du Bas-De-La-Riviere N, Saint-Cesaire, QC, J0L 1T0
(450) 469-5744
Emp Here 55   *Sales* 17,937,480
SIC 3999 Manufacturing industries, nec
  Alain Letourneau
  Marc-Oliver Gerant

Saint-Charles-Borromee, QC J6E

D-U-N-S 20-202-0434   (SL)
CHEZ HENRI MAJEAU ET FILS INC
RESTAURANT CHEZ HENRI
30 Rue De La Visitation, Saint-Charles-Borromee, QC, J6E 4M8
(450) 759-1113
Emp Here 100   *Sales* 4,551,900
SIC 5812 Eating places
  Martin Majeau

D-U-N-S 24-328-6957   (SL)
CONSTRUCTION BERNARD BORDELEAU INC.
HABITATIONS BORDELEAU, LES
100 Rue Romeo-Gaudreault, Saint-Charles-Borromee, QC, J6E 0A1
(450) 752-2660
Emp Here 49   *Sales* 14,140,567
SIC 1522 Residential construction, nec
  Bernard Bordeleau

D-U-N-S 24-812-4810   (SL)
KARAM FRUITS ET LEGUMES INC
KARAM FRUITS ET LEGUMES L'ENTREPOT
700 Rue De La Visitation, Saint-Charles-Borromee, QC, J6E 7S3
(450) 753-5881
Emp Here 26   *Sales* 21,725,002
SIC 5148 Fresh fruits and vegetables
  Robin Rivest
  Andre Rivest

D-U-N-S 24-063-9489   (SL)
MARCHE CREVIER IGA (S.C.B) INC
655 Rue De La Visitation, Saint-Charles-Borromee, QC, J6E 4P9
(450) 752-1441
Emp Here 49   *Sales* 13,433,448
SIC 5411 Grocery stores
  Serge St-Onge

D-U-N-S 25-361-2899   (SL)
TORA SAINT-CHARLES-BORROMEE LIMI-TEE
TIGRE GEANT
(Suby of GIANT TIGER STORES LIMITED)
197 Rue De La Visitation Bureau 109, Saint-Charles-Borromee, QC, J6E 4N6
(450) 760-3568
Emp Here 50   *Sales* 10,267,150
SIC 5311 Department stores
  Jean-Guy Boucher

Saint-Charles-De-Bellechasse, QC G0R

D-U-N-S 24-367-6512   (HQ)
CAISSE DESJARDINS DES SEIGNEURIES DE BELLECHASE
CENTRE DE SERVICES BEAUMONT
2807 Av Royale, Saint-Charles-De-Bellechasse, QC, G0R 2T0
(418) 887-3337
Emp Here 12   *Sales* 10,856,509
SIC 6062 State credit unions

Guy Desrosiers
Robert Carriere
Pierre Bouchard
Jacques Lefebvre
Jocelyne Roy
Laval Larouche
Stephane Bilodeau
Edith Bneton
Lucie Labrecque
Stephanie Laliberte

D-U-N-S 25-210-7651   (HQ)
LAFLAMME, GEORGES INC
HOME HARDWARE
2609 Av Royale O Rr 1, Saint-Charles-De-Bellechasse, QC, G0R 2T0
(418) 887-3347
Sales 20,122,830
SIC 5072 Hardware
  Roger Laflamme
  Pierre Laflamme

D-U-N-S 20-248-1461   (SL)
MEUBLE IDEAL LTEE
(Suby of INVESTISSEMENT CLAUJEAN INC.)
6 Rue Saint-Thomas, Saint-Charles-De-Bellechasse, QC, G0R 2T0
(418) 887-3331
Emp Here 200   *Sales* 30,864,400
SIC 2511 Wood household furniture
  Claude Belanger
  Jean Belanger

D-U-N-S 20-593-5117   (HQ)
SPECIALITES PRODAL (1975) LTEE, LES
SPECIALITES PRODAL
(Suby of BRETON TRADITION 1944 INC)
251 Av Boyer, Saint-Charles-De-Bellechasse, QC, G0R 2T0
(418) 887-3301
Sales 11,242,750
SIC 2013 Sausages and other prepared meats
  Serge Breton

Saint-Christophe-D'Arthabask, QC G6R

D-U-N-S 20-381-7754   (SL)
GROUPE GAGNE CONSTRUCTION INC
22 Rue Des Affaires, Saint-Christophe-D'Arthabask, QC, G6R 0B2
(819) 809-2270
Emp Here 40   *Sales* 19,106,950
SIC 1541 Industrial buildings and warehouses
  Joel Gagne
  Christian Gagnon
  Guillaume Pouliot

D-U-N-S 25-009-1886   (SL)
PLOMBERIE PHCB INC
4 Rue Des Affaires, Saint-Christophe-D'Arthabask, QC, G6R 0B2
(819) 260-4422
Emp Here 49   *Sales* 10,825,766
SIC 1711 Plumbing, heating, air-conditioning
  Denis Houle

Saint-Clement, QC G0L

D-U-N-S 20-430-1907   (HQ)
SERVICE AGROMECANIQUE INC
SERVICE AGRO MECANIQUE
24 Rue Principale O, Saint-Clement, QC, G0L 2N0
(418) 963-2177
Emp Here 15   *Sales* 19,001,040
SIC 5083 Farm and garden machinery
  Monique Roy
  Pierre Tremblay
  Michel Tremblay

Claude Tremblay

Saint-Colomban, QC J5K

D-U-N-S 24-578-4546   (SL)
SOURCE SANTE ACTION INC
100 Rue Johanne, Saint-Colomban, QC, J5K 2A5
(450) 560-4980
Emp Here 49   *Sales* 13,881,357
SIC 8741 Management services
  Jimmy Doyle
  Josee Rivest

Saint-Come-Liniere, QC G0M

D-U-N-S 24-379-4542   (BR)
MULTI-MARQUES INC
(Suby of GRUPO BIMBO, S.A.B. DE C.V.)
1295 1e Av O, Saint-Come-Liniere, QC, G0M 1J0
(418) 685-3351
Emp Here 80
SIC 2051 Bread, cake, and related products
  Alain Bedard

Saint-Constant, QC J5A

D-U-N-S 24-736-7324   (HQ)
AUTOMOBILE EN DIRECT.COM INC
AUTO USA
360 Rte 132, Saint-Constant, QC, J5A 1M3
(450) 638-6664
Emp Here 20   *Sales* 24,903,900
SIC 5511 New and used car dealers
  Sebastien Bisaillon

D-U-N-S 24-189-0578   (HQ)
CAISSES DESJARDINS DES BERGES DE ROUSSILLON
CENTRE DE SERVICE CANDIAC
296 Voie De La Desserte, Saint-Constant, QC, J5A 2C9
(450) 632-2820
Emp Here 80   *Sales* 15,384,616
SIC 6062 State credit unions
  Yves Bisson
  Michel Dupuis
  Keven Blondin
  Ginette Laurencelle
  Janie Fradette
  Helene Gingras
  Eric Bachand
  France Lariviere

D-U-N-S 25-973-4291   (SL)
CALIFORNIA L.I.N.E. INC
(Suby of 2743221 CANADA INC)
701 Rang Saint-Pierre N Unit? 1, Saint-Constant, QC, J5A 0R2
(450) 632-9000
Emp Here 60   *Sales* 12,342,360
SIC 4212 Local trucking, without storage
  Francois Cousineau

D-U-N-S 20-248-4267   (SL)
DESSUREAULT, JEAN-CLAUDE PHARMA-CIEN
UNIPRIX
113 Rue Saint-Pierre Unite 101, Saint-Constant, QC, J5A 0M3
(450) 632-2730
Emp Here 44   *Sales* 11,129,976
SIC 5912 Drug stores and proprietary stores
  Jean-Claude Dessurault

D-U-N-S 20-294-1808   (SL)
ENTOUR AUTOMOBILES INC

ST-CONSTANT HONDA
270 Rte 132, Saint-Constant, QC, J5A 2C9
(450) 632-7155
Emp Here 26   *Sales* 12,950,028
SIC 5511 New and used car dealers
Tom Samatas
Melissa Ann Chipman Samatas
Jessica Laura Samatas
Vanessa Lynn Samatas

D-U-N-S 24-421-3265   (BR)
GROUPE CHAMPLAIN INC
CENTRE D'HEBERGEMENT CHAMPLAIN-JEAN-LOUIS-LAPIERRE
199 Rue Saint-Pierre, Saint-Constant, QC, J5A 2N8
(450) 632-4451
Emp Here 75
SIC 8361 Residential care
Jean-Pierre Paquette

D-U-N-S 25-368-1589   (BR)
HOME DEPOT OF CANADA INC
HOME DEPOT
(*Suby of* THE HOME DEPOT INC)
490 Voie De La Desserte, Saint-Constant, QC, J5A 2S6
(450) 633-2030
Emp Here 100
SIC 5251 Hardware stores
Francois Lemieux

D-U-N-S 24-510-3072   (SL)
JARDINS PAUL COUSINEAU & FILS INC, LES
COUSINEAU FARMS
701 Rang Saint-Pierre N, Saint-Constant, QC, J5A 0R2
(450) 635-9000
Emp Here 175   *Sales* 29,579,375
SIC 0161 Vegetables and melons
Jean-Marie Cousineau
Vincent Cousineau
Pascal Cousineau
Laurent Cousineau
Martin Cousineau
Veronique Cousineau
Jeanne-D'arc Cousineau

D-U-N-S 20-503-6585   (SL)
LABORATOIRES CHARLES RIVER SAINT-CONSTANT S.A.
(*Suby of* CHARLES RIVER LABORATORIES INTERNATIONAL, INC.)
324 Rang Saint-Regis N, Saint-Constant, QC, J5A 2E7
(450) 638-1571
Emp Here 110   *Sales* 22,727,870
SIC 0279 Animal specialties, nec
David Leroux-Petersen
Davide-Andrea Molho
David Johst

D-U-N-S 20-258-7890   (HQ)
MAILLOUX BAILLARGEON INC
222 Rue Saint-Pierre, Saint-Constant, QC, J5A 2A2
(514) 861-8417
Emp Here 59   *Sales* 19,568,160
SIC 3999 Manufacturing industries, nec
Raynald Ostiguy

D-U-N-S 24-346-3184   (BR)
MARCHE LAMBERT ET FRERES INC
IGA
400 132 Rte, Saint-Constant, QC, J5A 2J8

Emp Here 100
SIC 5411 Grocery stores

D-U-N-S 24-542-2415   (SL)
SAINT-CONSTANT AUTO 2010 INC
SAINT-CONSTANT MAZDA
48 Rue Saint-Pierre, Saint-Constant, QC, J5A 1B9
(450) 632-0700
Emp Here 45   *Sales* 22,413,510
SIC 5511 New and used car dealers

Paul Hayes

D-U-N-S 24-207-4214   (BR)
WAL-MART CANADA CORP
WALMART
(*Suby of* WALMART INC.)
500 Voie De La Desserte Unite 132, Saint-Constant, QC, J5A 2S5
(450) 632-2192
Emp Here 100
SIC 5311 Department stores
Armand Collard

Saint-Cuthbert, QC J0K

D-U-N-S 24-051-8803   (SL)
AMARO INC
(*Suby of* H. COLPRON INC)
4061 Grand Rang Sainte-Catherine, Saint-Cuthbert, QC, J0K 2C0
(514) 593-5144
Emp Here 58   *Sales* 41,569,528
SIC 5149 Groceries and related products, nec
Daniel Colpron

D-U-N-S 24-836-5132   (HQ)
H. COLPRON INC
4061 Grand Rang Sainte-Catherine, Saint-Cuthbert, QC, J0K 2C0
(514) 593-5144
Emp Here 5   *Sales* 16,401,000
SIC 6712 Bank holding companies
Daniel Colpron
Paul Juneau
Jean-Pierre Lebel
Pascal Alenti
Daniel Luquette

D-U-N-S 24-256-9119   (SL)
VOLAILLE GIANNONE INC
(*Suby of* 4285905 CANADA INC)
2320 Rue Principale, Saint-Cuthbert, QC, J0K 2C0
(450) 836-3063
Emp Here 90   *Sales* 31,112,100
SIC 2011 Meat packing plants
Rejean Nadeau
Rene Proulx
Paul Beauchamp
Eric Cadoret
Carole Potvin
Christian Jacques

Saint-Cyprien, QC G0L

D-U-N-S 20-248-5157   (SL)
MOULAGE SOUS PRESSION A.M.T. INC
DARONA
106 Rue Cote, Saint-Cyprien, QC, G0L 2P0
(418) 963-3227
Emp Here 100   *Sales* 23,343,500
SIC 3365 Aluminum foundries
Felix Jean

Saint-Cyprien-De-Napierville, QC J0J

D-U-N-S 20-362-4622   (SL)
COOP UNIFRONTIERES, LA
COOP UNIFRONTIERES - SECTEUR AGRICOLE/CENTRE DE MELANGE - NAPIERVILLE, LA
4 Rang Saint-Andre, Saint-Cyprien-De-Napierville, QC, J0J 1L0
(450) 245-3308
Emp Here 110   *Sales* 117,738,161
SIC 5153 Grain and field beans
Sylvain Brault
Daniel Guerin

Louise Isabelle
Bruno Dubuc
Karen Hogue
Chantal Agnew
Bruno Castagnier
Luc Leroux
Hugo Landry
Andre Giroux

D-U-N-S 24-330-9650   (SL)
FERMES HOTTE ET VAN WINDEN INC, LES
316 Rang Saint-Andre, Saint-Cyprien-De-Napierville, QC, J0J 1L0
(450) 245-3433
Emp Here 65   *Sales* 17,050,085
SIC 0161 Vegetables and melons
Jean-Bernard Van-Winden
Yvan Hotte
Lucille Lessard
Nicole Guerin

Saint-Cyrille-De-Wendover, QC J1Z

D-U-N-S 24-987-8026   (BR)
ABATTOIR COLBEX INC
455 4e Rang De Simpson, Saint-Cyrille-De-Wendover, QC, J1Z 1T8

Emp Here 80
SIC 2011 Meat packing plants

D-U-N-S 25-978-8529   (SL)
CONDOR CHIMIQUES INC
SEALFLEX
2645 Boul Terra-Jet Bureau B, Saint-Cyrille-De-Wendover, QC, J1Z 1B3
(819) 474-6661
Emp Here 50   *Sales* 10,206,500
SIC 2911 Petroleum refining
Louis Lepage
Louis-A Jr Lepage

D-U-N-S 24-003-6413   (SL)
ROULOTTES LUPIEN (2000) INC
2700 Rte 122, Saint-Cyrille-De-Wendover, QC, J1Z 1C1
(819) 397-4949
Emp Here 26   *Sales* 16,361,280
SIC 5571 Motorcycle dealers
Benoit Levesque
Michael Levesque
Maxime Levesque

Saint-Damase, QC J0H

D-U-N-S 20-109-6059   (BR)
COOP FEDEREE, LA
OLYMEL
(*Suby of* COOP FEDEREE, LA)
249 Rue Principale, Saint-Damase, QC, J0H 1J0
(450) 797-2691
Emp Here 350
SIC 5191 Farm supplies
Claude Chapdelaine

D-U-N-S 24-529-3733   (SL)
DEVELOPPEMENT BONNET INC
DAMAFRUIT
(*Suby of* GROUPE BONNET INC)
54 Rue Principale, Saint-Damase, QC, J0H 1J0
(450) 797-3301
Emp Here 45   *Sales* 37,600,965
SIC 5143 Dairy products, except dried or canned
Philippe Bonnet
Claude Bonnet
Michel Bonnet

D-U-N-S 25-705-8826   (BR)

EXCELDOR COOPERATIVE
PRODUITS EXCELDOR, LES
(*Suby of* EXCELDOR COOPERATIVE)
125 Rue Sainte-Anne Gd, Saint-Damase, QC, J0H 1J0
(450) 797-3331
Emp Here 250
SIC 2011 Meat packing plants
Daniel Vienvenue

D-U-N-S 24-526-8859   (SL)
FINANCIERE BONNET INC
(*Suby of* GROUPE BONNET INC)
54 Rue Principale, Saint-Damase, QC, J0H 1J0
(450) 797-3301
Emp Here 140
SIC 2022 Cheese; natural and processed
Michel Bonnet
Philippe Bonnet
Claude Bonnet

D-U-N-S 24-904-5089   (HQ)
GROUPE BONNET INC
54 Rue Principale, Saint-Damase, QC, J0H 1J0
(450) 797-3301
Emp Here 3   *Sales* 51,389,800
SIC 6712 Bank holding companies
Philippe Bonnet
Claude Bonnet
Michel Bonnet

D-U-N-S 20-212-1542   (BR)
OLYMEL S.E.C.
OLYMEL FLAMINGO SAINT DAMASE
(*Suby of* OLYMEL S.E.C.)
249 Rue Principale, Saint-Damase, QC, J0H 1J0
(450) 797-2691
Emp Here 355
SIC 2015 Poultry slaughtering and processing
Claude Chapdelaine

Saint-Damase-Des-Aulnaies, QC G0R

D-U-N-S 24-792-6645   (SL)
COUTURE C G H INC
12 Rue Belanger, Saint-Damase-Des-Aulnaies, QC, G0R 2X0
(418) 598-3208
Emp Here 80   *Sales* 15,936,320
SIC 2339 Women's and misses' outerwear, nec
Marthe Paradis
Richard Delisle
Madeleine Paradis

D-U-N-S 25-310-0945   (HQ)
TRANSPORTS DUCAMPRO INC
GLOBEHAUL TRANSPORTATION
229 Rte 204, Saint-Damase-Des-Aulnaies, QC, G0R 2X0
(418) 598-9319
Emp Here 50   *Sales* 20,570,600
SIC 4213 Trucking, except local
Alain Dube
Isabelle Robichaud

Saint-Damien, QC J0K

D-U-N-S 25-543-6461   (SL)
MANUTENTIONS MARSOLAIS BRENDON INC
7255 Ch De Sainte-?M?Lie, Saint-Damien, QC, J0K 2E0

Emp Here 27   *Sales* 14,039,109
SIC 4789 Transportation services, nec
Fernand Marsolais
Eric Marsolais

Luc Marsolais
Nancy Marsolais

Saint-Damien-De-Buckland, QC G0R

D-U-N-S 25-233-7654   (BR)
COMMISSION SCOLAIRE DE LA COTE-DU-SUD, LA
ECOLE SECONDAIRE DE SAINT-DAMIEN
70 Rte Saint-Gerard, Saint-Damien-De-Buckland, QC, G0R 2Y0
(418) 789-1001
Emp Here 75
SIC 8211 Elementary and secondary schools

D-U-N-S 25-488-8621   (SL)
CONGREGATION DES SOEURS DE NOTRE-DAME DU PERPETUEL SECOURS
159 Rue Commerciale, Saint-Damien-De-Buckland, QC, G0R 2Y0
(418) 789-2112
Emp Here 103   *Sales* 10,724,669
SIC 8661 Religious organizations
Pierrette Leblanc

D-U-N-S 20-430-9124   (SL)
I. THIBAULT INC
TIBO
(*Suby of* GESTION THIBAULT INC)
26 Rue De L'Entreprise, Saint-Damien-De-Buckland, QC, G0R 2Y0
(418) 789-2891
Emp Here 75   *Sales* 16,650,075
SIC 3544 Special dies, tools, jigs, and fixtures
Marc Thibault
Denis Thibault

D-U-N-S 20-332-4350   (HQ)
IPL INC
(*Suby of* PLASTIQUES IPL INC)
140 Rue Commerciale, Saint-Damien-De-Buckland, QC, G0R 2Y0
(418) 789-2880
Emp Here 600   *Sales* 200,602,080
SIC 3089 Plastics products, nec
Alan Walsh
John Hannigan
Pat Dalton

Saint-Denis-De-Brompton, QC J0B

D-U-N-S 20-059-1506   (HQ)
ANCTIL, J. INC
ANCTIL, DIVISION ENVIRONNEMENT
3110 Rte 222, Saint-Denis-De-Brompton, QC, J0B 2P0
(819) 846-2747
Sales 13,114,948
SIC 5211 Lumber and other building materials
Jocelyn Anctil
Francine Anctil
Vincent Anctil
David Anctil
Caroline Anctil

Saint-Denis-Sur-Richelieu, QC J0H

D-U-N-S 20-213-9101   (HQ)
BONDUELLE CANADA INC
BONDUELLE AMERIQUE DE NORD
(*Suby of* BONDUELLE)
540 Ch Des Patriotes, Saint-Denis-Sur-Richelieu, QC, J0H 1K0
(450) 787-3411
Emp Here 125   *Sales* 292,431,000
SIC 2033 Canned fruits and specialties
Christophe Bonduelle
Daniel Vielfaure

Daniel Caumartin

Saint-Dominique, QC J0H

D-U-N-S 20-248-7906   (HQ)
CARRIERES DE ST-DOMINIQUE LTEE, LES
BETON GRANBY
700 Rue Principale, Saint-Dominique, QC, J0H 1L0
(450) 774-2591
Sales 35,843,800
SIC 3273 Ready-mixed concrete
Jacques Sylvestre
Pierrette Sylvestre
Jacques Sylvestre Jr.
Claude Jr. Sylvestre

D-U-N-S 25-100-2531   (SL)
METALLURGIE SYCA INC
500 Rue Principale, Saint-Dominique, QC, J0H 1L0
(450) 261-0853
Emp Here 38   *Sales* 10,513,080
SIC 2819 Industrial inorganic chemicals, nec
Marc Grenier

Saint-Dominique-Du-Rosaire, QC J0Y

D-U-N-S 24-941-5647   (HQ)
COOPERATIVE FORESTIERE ST-DOMINIQUE
289 Rue Principale, Saint-Dominique-Du-Rosaire, QC, J0Y 2K0
(819) 732-5723
Emp Here 94   *Sales* 21,161,300
SIC 0851 Forestry services
Jacques Martel
Marcel Binette

Saint-Donat-De-Montcalm, QC J0T

D-U-N-S 20-248-8193   (SL)
2318-4211 QUEBEC INC
BOULANGERIE SAINT-DONAT ENR
413 Rue Principale, Saint-Donat-De-Montcalm, QC, J0T 2C0
(819) 424-2220
Emp Here 40   *Sales* 10,966,080
SIC 5461 Retail bakeries
Guillaume St-Amour

D-U-N-S 25-200-7265   (SL)
COMPAGNIE IMMOBILIERE GUEYMARD & ASSOCIES LTEE
CENTRE DE SKI MONT LA RESERVE
251 Ch Fusey, Saint-Donat-De-Montcalm, QC, J0T 2C0
(819) 424-1373
Emp Here 30   *Sales* 12,580,650
SIC 6719 Holding companies, nec
Herve Gueymard
Andree Mongeon Gueymard
Vianney Belanger
Carole Bouchard

Saint-Edouard-De-Lotbiniere, QC G0S

D-U-N-S 24-149-0937   (SL)
BOIS DE PLANCHER P.G. INC, LES
BOIS FRANC MODEL
2424 Rue Principale, Saint-Edouard-De-Lotbiniere, QC, G0S 1Y0
(418) 796-2328
Emp Here 100   *Sales* 21,794,864
SIC 2426 Hardwood dimension and flooring

---

mills
Claude Garneau
Helene Garneau
Anne-Marie Faucher
Robert Rousseau
Jean-Francois Dion
Oliver Garneau
Vincent Blanchet
Carl Gilbert

D-U-N-S 25-684-4481   (HQ)
HAMEL CONSTRUCTION INC
ENTREPRISES PO BO HA ENR, LES
(*Suby of* GESTION G A J HAMEL INC)
2106 Rue Principale, Saint-Edouard-De-Lotbiniere, QC, G0S 1Y0
(418) 796-2074
Sales 17,873,900
SIC 8711 Engineering services
Guy Hamel
Michel Hamel
Yvon Hamel
Pierre Hamel
Nicole Hamel
Stephane Dusablon

D-U-N-S 24-965-5718   (SL)
HAMEL-CRT S.E.N.C.
CENTRALE - HAMEL-CRT, DIV OF
2106 Rte Principale, Saint-Edouard-De-Lotbiniere, QC, G0S 1Y0
(418) 796-2074
Emp Here 50   *Sales* 12,622,100
SIC 1611 Highway and street construction
Guy Hamel

Saint-Elzear, QC G0S

D-U-N-S 20-949-7676   (HQ)
ESCALIERS GRENIER, GILLES INC
BOIS CINTRE MSGB
586 Av Texel, Saint-Elzear, QC, G0S 2J2
(418) 387-6317
Emp Here 69   *Sales* 13,465,900
SIC 2431 Millwork
Gilles Grenier
Marco Grenier
Steven Grenier

D-U-N-S 20-331-7628   (HQ)
TEXEL MATERIAUX TECHNIQUES INC
485 Rue Des Erables, Saint-Elzear, QC, G0S 2J0
(418) 387-5910
Emp Here 250   *Sales* 59,125,750
SIC 2297 Nonwoven fabrics
Guy Berube
Chad A. Mcdaniel
Randall Gonzales
Andre Rheaume

Saint-Elzear-De-Bonaventure, QC G0C

D-U-N-S 20-249-0736   (HQ)
ASSOCIATION COOPERATIVE FORESTIERE DE ST-ELZEAR
215 Rte De L'Eglise, Saint-Elzear-De-Bonaventure, QC, G0C 2W0
(418) 534-2596
Emp Here 150   *Sales* 29,240,240
SIC 2421 Sawmills and planing mills, general
Christian Bourdages
Patrick Lebrasseur
John Lapoint

D-U-N-S 25-195-2008   (SL)
SCIERIE ST-ELZEAR INC
(*Suby of* ASSOCIATION COOPERATIVE FORESTIERE DE ST-ELZEAR)
215 Rte De L'Eglise, Saint-Elzear-De-Bonaventure, QC, G0C 2W0

---

(418) 534-2596
Emp Here 150   *Sales* 28,855,500
SIC 2421 Sawmills and planing mills, general
Christian Bourdages
Jonathan Calpetard
Hugo Chicoine
Patrick Lebrasseur
John Lapointe
Jonathan Synnott

Saint-Ephrem-De-Beauce, QC G0M

D-U-N-S 20-249-1684   (SL)
CLERMOND HAMEL LTEE
BOIS HAMEL
(*Suby of* 166826 CANADA INC)
25 7e Rang S, Saint-Ephrem-De-Beauce, QC, G0M 1R0
(418) 484-2888
Emp Here 63   *Sales* 12,119,310
SIC 2421 Sawmills and planing mills, general
Carmin Hamel
Lucie Hamel

D-U-N-S 24-229-2584   (SL)
CONSTRUCTION M.G.P. INC
140 Rte 271 S, Saint-Ephrem-De-Beauce, QC, G0M 1R0
(418) 484-5740
Emp Here 140   *Sales* 37,931,880
SIC 1522 Residential construction, nec
Martin Plante
Charles Fortin

D-U-N-S 20-430-4943   (SL)
FILATURE LEMIEUX INC
(*Suby of* GESTION J P LEMIEUX INC)
125 108 Rte E, Saint-Ephrem-De-Beauce, QC, G0M 1R0
(418) 484-2169
Emp Here 87   *Sales* 15,956,061
SIC 2281 Yarn spinning mills
Marc Lemieux
Serge Lemieux
Gaetane Pouliot

D-U-N-S 25-362-6055   (SL)
GESTIONS BAILLARGEON & OUELLET INC
430 108 Rte O, Saint-Ephrem-De-Beauce, QC, G0M 1R0
(418) 484-5666
Emp Here 105   *Sales* 28,701,750
SIC 6712 Bank holding companies
Bruno Baillargeon

D-U-N-S 20-516-3439   (SL)
INDUSTRIES LONGCHAMPS LTEE, LES
25 Boul Saint-Joseph, Saint-Ephrem-De-Beauce, QC, G0M 1R0
(418) 484-2080
Emp Here 60   *Sales* 26,953,140
SIC 7389 Business services, nec
Jean-Marie Longchamps
Claude Longchamps
Manon Longchamps

D-U-N-S 24-904-1740   (SL)
MARCHE ROMEO ROY & FILS INC
MARCHES TRADITION, LES
108 Rte 108 E, Saint-Ephrem-De-Beauce, QC, G0M 1R0
(418) 484-2085
Emp Here 50   *Sales* 13,707,600
SIC 5411 Grocery stores
Denis Roy
Pauline Turcotte

D-U-N-S 20-266-0700   (BR)
MASONITE INTERNATIONAL CORPORATION
PORTES BAILLARGEON, LES
(*Suby of* MASONITE INTERNATIONAL CORPORATION)
430 Rte 108 O Bureau 489, Saint-Ephrem-De-

Beauce, QC, G0M 1R0
(418) 484-5666
Emp Here 110
SIC 2431 Millwork
Jonathan Turcotte

D-U-N-S 24-145-7902   (HQ)
RENE MATERIAUX COMPOSITES LTEE
(*Suby of* NANOXPLORE INC)
55 Rte 271 S, Saint-Ephrem-De-Beauce, QC,
G0M 1R0
(418) 484-5282
Emp Here 150   *Sales* 79,983,750
SIC 3714 Motor vehicle parts and accessories
Denis Bertrand
Pierre Massicotte

D-U-N-S 24-318-0390   (HQ)
SIGMA INDUSTRIES INC
(*Suby of* NANOXPLORE INC)
55 Rte 271 S, Saint-Ephrem-De-Beauce, QC,
G0M 1R0
(418) 484-5282
Sales 45,056,951
SIC 3089 Plastics products, nec
Denis Bertrand
Jean-Francois Dore
Bruno Doyon
Pierre Massicotte
Gerald Desourdy
Claude Dupuis
Neman Malek
Roger Demers

D-U-N-S 20-579-0785   (SL)
TRANSPORT COUTURE & FILS LTEE
(*Suby of* TFI INTERNATIONAL INC)
99 Rte 271 S, Saint-Ephrem-De-Beauce, QC,
G0M 1R0
(418) 484-2104
Emp Here 180   *Sales* 37,027,080
SIC 4213 Trucking, except local
Chantal Martel
Josiane-Melanie Langlois

Saint-Esprit, QC J0K

D-U-N-S 20-249-1809   (HQ)
GARAGE VILLEMAIRE & FILS INC
CENTRE DU PNEUS VILLEMAIRE
55 Rue Gregoire, Saint-Esprit, QC, J0K 2L0
(450) 839-7777
Sales 29,137,200
SIC 5014 Tires and tubes
Benoit Villemaire
Dany Villemaire

D-U-N-S 25-010-4908   (BR)
OLYMEL S.E.C.
TRANSPORT TRANSBO
(*Suby of* OLYMEL S.E.C.)
57 125 Rte, Saint-Esprit, QC, J0K 2L0
(450) 839-7258
Emp Here 80
SIC 4212 Local trucking, without storage
Carole Grenier

D-U-N-S 24-125-2787   (BR)
OLYMEL S.E.C.
FLAMINGO
(*Suby of* OLYMEL S.E.C.)
125 Rue Saint-Isidore, Saint-Esprit, QC, J0K
2L0
(450) 839-7258
Emp Here 700
SIC 2011 Meat packing plants

D-U-N-S 24-327-7584   (BR)
OLYMEL S.E.C.
OLYMEL SAINT-ESPRIT
(*Suby of* OLYMEL S.E.C.)
25 Rte 125 E, Saint-Esprit, QC, J0K 2L0
(450) 839-7258
Emp Here 700

SIC 2011 Meat packing plants
Richard Tremblay

D-U-N-S 24-764-0985   (BR)
SUPRALIMENT S.E.C.
(*Suby of* SUPRALIMENT S.E.C.)
25 125 Rte E, Saint-Esprit, QC, J0K 2L0
(450) 839-7258
Emp Here 800
SIC 2011 Meat packing plants
Richard Tremblay

Saint-Etienne-Des-Gres, QC G0X

D-U-N-S 20-255-0729   (SL)
**CONSTRUCTION ET PAVAGE BOISVERT
INC**
180 Boul De La Gabelle, Saint-Etienne-Des-
Gres, QC, G0X 2P0
(819) 374-7277
Emp Here 50   *Sales* 11,008,400
SIC 1794 Excavation work
Carl Poulin
Mario Parenteau

D-U-N-S 24-168-6708   (SL)
CONSTRUCTION YVAN BOISVERT INC
180 Boul De La Gabelle, Saint-Etienne-Des-
Gres, QC, G0X 2P0
(819) 374-7277
Emp Here 180   *Sales* 44,313,480
SIC 1794 Excavation work
Yvan Boisvert

D-U-N-S 20-283-2353   (SL)
PAVAGE BOISVERT INC
180 Boul De La Gabelle, Saint-Etienne-Des-
Gres, QC, G0X 2P0
(819) 374-8277
Emp Here 100   *Sales* 23,343,500
SIC 2951 Asphalt paving mixtures and blocks
Yvan Boisvert

D-U-N-S 24-057-0171   (SL)
**RECUPERATION MAURICIE, SOCIETE EN
NOM COLLECTIF**
400 Boul La Gabelle Bureau 23, Saint-
Etienne-Des-Gres, QC, G0X 2P0
(819) 372-5125
Emp Here 80   *Sales* 25,512,800
SIC 4953 Refuse systems
Michel Camiran

D-U-N-S 25-995-6725   (SL)
SERRES DU ST-LAURENT (LES)
360 Boul De La Gabelle, Saint-Etienne-Des-
Gres, QC, G0X 2P0
(819) 694-6944
Emp Here 49   *Sales* 16,780,883
SIC 0181 Ornamental nursery products
Yvan Gauvin

Saint-Eustache, QC J7P

D-U-N-S 25-448-3340   (SL)
2846-6589 QUEBEC INC
UNIPRIX
509 Boul Arthur-Sauve, Saint-Eustache, QC,
J7P 4X4
(450) 473-4169
Emp Here 75   *Sales* 18,324,600
SIC 5912 Drug stores and proprietary stores
Marc-Andre Pinel
Stephane Granger
Matthieu Leduc
Martin Halley

D-U-N-S 20-620-3940   (HQ)
2970-7528 QUEBEC INC
H. GREGOIRE
625 Rue Dubois, Saint-Eustache, QC, J7P
3W1

---

(450) 472-7272
Emp Here 175   *Sales* 262,782,450
SIC 5511 New and used car dealers
Krikor Hairabedian

D-U-N-S 24-379-1220   (SL)
4486404 CANADA INC
VOLKSWAGEN LAUZON SAINT-EUSTACHE
312 Rue Dubois, Saint-Eustache, QC, J7P
4W9
(450) 623-8977
Emp Here 45   *Sales* 22,413,510
SIC 5511 New and used car dealers
Charles-Andre Bilodeau

D-U-N-S 25-701-3102   (SL)
9038-7200 QUEBEC INC
TIM HORTONS
255 25e Av Bureau 926, Saint-Eustache, QC,
J7P 4Y1
(450) 974-3493
Emp Here 50   *Sales* 13,707,600
SIC 5461 Retail bakeries
Graham Black

D-U-N-S 20-767-8066   (SL)
9060-5015 QUEBEC INC
440 Rue Dubois, Saint-Eustache, QC, J7P
4W9
(450) 623-1438
Emp Here 100   *Sales* 26,765,200
SIC 5211 Lumber and other building materials
Gilles Lamoureux
Jean-Francois Fiset
Jean-Marc Legault
Francois Bertrand
Serge Legault
Guy Perron

D-U-N-S 20-007-2853   (SL)
9064-6795 QUEBEC INC
CLUB VOYAGES SOLERAMA
497 Ch De La Grande-Cote, Saint-Eustache,
QC, J7P 1K3
(450) 473-2934
Emp Here 30   *Sales* 11,560,800
SIC 4724 Travel agencies
Diane Tanguay

D-U-N-S 20-370-6643   (SL)
9368-7952 QUEBEC INC
CLUB VOYAGES SOLERAMA
497 Ch De La Grande-Cote, Saint-Eustache,
QC, J7P 1K3
(450) 473-2934
Emp Here 26   *Sales* 10,019,360
SIC 4724 Travel agencies
Manon Doucet

D-U-N-S 24-324-9802   (SL)
AUTOS JEAN-FRANCOIS HAMEL LTEE
HAMEL HONDA
332 Rue Dubois, Saint-Eustache, QC, J7P
4W9
(450) 491-0440
Emp Here 90   *Sales* 56,635,200
SIC 5511 New and used car dealers
Jean-Francois Hamel
Gilles Lachepelle

D-U-N-S 24-890-2520   (SL)
BRETON, DENIS CHEVROLET LTEE
364 Rue Dubois, Saint-Eustache, QC, J7P
4W9
(450) 472-3200
Emp Here 40   *Sales* 19,923,120
SIC 5511 New and used car dealers
Denis Breton

D-U-N-S 20-249-4530   (SL)
CARRIERE ST-EUSTACHE LTEE
(*Suby of* GROUPE MATHERS INC)
555 Av Mathers, Saint-Eustache, QC, J7P
4C1
(450) 430-9090
Emp Here 50   *Sales* 11,671,750
SIC 1422 Crushed and broken limestone
Brigitte Mathers

D-U-N-S 20-763-6671   (SL)
CINE-PARC ST-EUSTACHE INC
*MARCHE AUX PUCES CINE-PARC ST-
EUSTACHE*
(*Suby of* GROUPE MATHERS INC)
555 Av Mathers, Saint-Eustache, QC, J7P
4C1
(514) 879-1707
Emp Here 200   *Sales* 17,832,600
SIC 7833 Drive-in motion picture theaters
Brigitte Mathers

D-U-N-S 25-074-3853   (SL)
CONSULTANTS S.P.I. INC
*SECURITE PROFESSIONNELLE DU QUE-
BEC*
136c Rue Saint-Laurent, Saint-Eustache, QC,
J7P 5G1
(514) 288-8868
Emp Here 100   *Sales* 39,567,800
SIC 7381 Detective and armored car services
Dany Laflamme

D-U-N-S 20-434-2224   (SL)
ESPACE HOUBLON INC
ESPACE HOUBLON EPICERIE FINE
180 25e Av, Saint-Eustache, QC, J7P 2V2
(450) 983-7122
Emp Here 19   *Sales* 10,167,356
SIC 5141 Groceries, general line
Francis Corbeil
Frederic Poitras
Martin Bisson
Sebastien Lalande

D-U-N-S 24-742-6281   (SL)
EXCELLENCE DODGE CHRYSLER INC
EXCELLENCE FIAT
250 Rue Dubois, Saint-Eustache, QC, J7P
4W9
(450) 491-5555
Emp Here 35   *Sales* 17,432,730
SIC 5511 New and used car dealers
Serge Bourdeau
Yannick Bourdeau

D-U-N-S 20-302-4757   (SL)
GESTION MAHEL INC
HAMEL AUTO DIRECT
130 Rue Dubois, Saint-Eustache, QC, J7P
4W9
(450) 974-0440
Emp Here 78   *Sales* 3,550,482
SIC 5812 Eating places
Jean-Francois Hamel

D-U-N-S 25-024-2013   (SL)
**GRENIER POPULAIRE DES BASSES LAU-
RENTIDES**
BUR-CYCLE
217 Rue Saint-Laurent, Saint-Eustache, QC,
J7P 4W4
(450) 623-5891
Emp Here 49   *Sales* 11,286,660
SIC 5712 Furniture stores
Andre Rioux

D-U-N-S 25-027-6730   (SL)
HAMEL HYUNDAI INC
130 Rue Dubois, Saint-Eustache, QC, J7P
4W9
(450) 974-0440
Emp Here 45   *Sales* 22,413,510
SIC 5511 New and used car dealers
Jean-Francois Hamel
Linda Labrie

D-U-N-S 24-326-1182   (SL)
LOUKIL, SAID
ESPUMA
247 Rue Isabelle, Saint-Eustache, QC, J7P
4E9
(450) 491-3366
Emp Here 20   *Sales* 10,073,160
SIC 5111 Printing and writing paper
Said Loukil
Simha Loukil
Anissalah Loukil

▲ Public Company   ■ Public Company Family Member   **HQ** Headquarters   **BR** Branch   **SL** Single Location

Misie-Sandra Loukil

D-U-N-S 24-326-1450   (SL)
MARCHE ANDRE MARTEL INC
METRO
219 Rue Saint-Laurent, Saint-Eustache, QC,
J7P 4W4
(450) 472-7720
Emp Here 90   *Sales* 26,412,930
SIC 5411 Grocery stores
Andre Martel
Lucie Martel

D-U-N-S 20-357-3381   (SL)
NADON SPORT SAINT-EUSTACHE INC
NADON SPORT
645 Rue Dubois, Saint-Eustache, QC, J7P
3W1
(450) 473-2381
Emp Here 35   *Sales* 17,432,730
SIC 5571 Motorcycle dealers
Gerald Nadon
Martin Nadon
Nathalie Nadon

D-U-N-S 24-811-1478   (SL)
PAQUETTE, ROBERT AUTOBUS & FILS INC
222 25e Av, Saint-Eustache, QC, J7P 4Z8
(450) 473-4526
Emp Here 120   *Sales* 9,032,640
SIC 4151 School buses
Martin Paquette

D-U-N-S 24-439-1665   (SL)
**PROMUTUEL DEUX-MONTAGNES, SO-
CIETE MUTUELLE D'ASSURANCE GEN-
ERALE**
PROMUTUEL ASSURANCE
200 Rue Dubois, Saint-Eustache, QC, J7P
4W9
(450) 623-5774
Emp Here 26   *Sales* 15,078,024
SIC 6411 Insurance agents, brokers, and ser-
vice
Chantal Ladouceur
Daniel Campeau
Richard Pilon
Luc Gregoire

D-U-N-S 24-168-4216   (SL)
RENOVAPRIX INC
BMR
226 25e Av, Saint-Eustache, QC, J7P 4Z8
(450) 472-3000
Emp Here 40   *Sales* 10,122,360
SIC 5211 Lumber and other building materials
Yves Gariepy

D-U-N-S 25-027-6771   (BR)
SOBEYS QUEBEC INC
IGA
299 Boul Arthur-Sauve, Saint-Eustache, QC,
J7P 2B1
(450) 472-1558
Emp Here 75   *Sales* 822,456
SIC 5411 Grocery stores
Erick Hebert

D-U-N-S 20-332-9821   (SL)
SURETE CAVALERIE INC
GROUPE PRODUCTION JL
193a Boul Arthur-Sauve, Saint-Eustache, QC,
J7P 2A7
(450) 983-7070
Emp Here 145   *Sales* 3,806,250
SIC 7381 Detective and armored car services

D-U-N-S 20-249-3730   (SL)
VENTES FORD BRUNELLE LTEE, LES
(Suby of GESTION ANDRE BRUNELLE INC)
500 Rue Dubois, Saint-Eustache, QC, J7P
4W9
(450) 491-1110
Emp Here 40   *Sales* 25,171,200
SIC 5511 New and used car dealers
Pierre Brunelle

Saint-Eustache, QC J7R

D-U-N-S 24-581-9529   (HQ)
130355 CANADA INC
BAIN MAGIQUE
225 Rue Roy, Saint-Eustache, QC, J7R 5R5
(450) 472-0024
Sales 23,828,700
SIC 3088 Plastics plumbing fixtures
Glenn Cotton
Brian Cotton
Raffi Apanian

D-U-N-S 24-902-4456   (SL)
2436-3392 QUEBEC INC
MAISON DES FLEURS VIVACES, LA
807 Boul Arthur-Sauve, Saint-Eustache, QC,
J7R 4K3
(450) 472-8400
Emp Here 25   *Sales* 18,563,000
SIC 5193 Flowers and florists supplies
Michel Corbeil

D-U-N-S 24-667-7434   (SL)
4397291 CANADA INC
AUTODROME ST-EUSTACHE
1016 Boul Arthur-Sauve, Saint-Eustache, QC,
J7R 4K3
(450) 472-6222
Emp Here 25   *Sales* 10,593,250
SIC 7948 Racing, including track operation
Alan Labrosse

D-U-N-S 24-423-7124   (HQ)
ADESA MONTREAL CORPORATION
ADESA MONTREAL
(Suby of KAR AUCTION SERVICES, INC.)
300 Boul Albert-Mondou, Saint-Eustache, QC,
J7R 7A7
(450) 472-4400
Sales 288,626,000
SIC 5511 New and used car dealers
John Hammer
Sheryl Watson
Trevor Henderson

D-U-N-S 24-373-5425   (HQ)
B3CG INTERCONNECT INC
B3CG INTERCONNEXION
(Suby of AQ GROUP AB)
310 Boul Industriel, Saint-Eustache, QC, J7R
5R4
(450) 491-4040
Sales 36,555,520
SIC 4899 Communication services, nec
Francois Demers
Celine Brunet

D-U-N-S 20-857-7049   (HQ)
BEAUWARD SHOPPING CENTRES LTD
430 Boul Arthur-Sauve Bureau 6010, Saint-
Eustache, QC, J7R 6V7
(450) 473-6831
Emp Here 30   *Sales* 16,281,240
SIC 6512 Nonresidential building operators
Marc Bibeau
Michel Cloutier
Richard Hamelin
Fernand Bibeau

D-U-N-S 24-226-1535   (SL)
**CABANE A SUCRE CONSTANTIN (1992)
INC**
MAGASIN GENERAL.CA, LE
(Suby of IMMEUBLE M. & A. CONSTANTIN
INC)
1054 Boul Arthur-Sauve, Saint-Eustache, QC,
J7R 4K3
(450) 473-2374
Emp Here 100   *Sales* 34,569,000
SIC 2099 Food preparations, nec
Andre Constantin
Michel Constantin
Danny Constantin
Gaby Constantin
Michael Constantin

Maxime Constantin

D-U-N-S 24-851-7844   (BR)
**CENTRE INTEGRE DE SANTE ET DE SER-
VICES SOCIAUX DES LAURENTIDES**
CLSC JEAN-OLIVIER-CHENIER
(Suby of CENTRE INTEGRE DE SANTE
ET DE SERVICES SOCIAUX DES LAUREN-
TIDES)
29 Ch D'Oka, Saint-Eustache, QC, J7R 1K6
(450) 491-1233
Emp Here 300
SIC 8062 General medical and surgical hospi-
tals
Laurianne O'brien

D-U-N-S 20-634-4731   (HQ)
CHRISTIE INNOMED INC
(Suby of GROUPE CHRISTIE INC)
516 Rue Dufour, Saint-Eustache, QC, J7R
0C3
(450) 472-9120
Emp Here 80   *Sales* 82,979,560
SIC 5047 Medical and hospital equipment
Erik Grandjean
Martin Roy
Michel Vachon
Leonard Aucoin
Marcel Ostiguy
Josee Morin

D-U-N-S 25-541-4732   (HQ)
**COMMISSION   SCOLAIRE   DE   LA
SEIGNEURIE-DES-MILLE-ILES**
430 Boul Arthur-Sauve Bureau 3050, Saint-
Eustache, QC, J7R 6V7
(450) 974-7000
Emp Here 175   *Sales* 327,786,533
SIC 8211 Elementary and secondary schools
Jean-Francois Lachance
Daniel Trempe

D-U-N-S 20-330-6535   (BR)
CONCORD PREMIUM MEATS LTD
VIANDES CONCORD, LES
(Suby of CONCORD PREMIUM MEATS LTD)
160 Rue Williams, Saint-Eustache, QC, J7R
0A4
(450) 623-7676
Emp Here 100
SIC 5147 Meats and meat products
Joseph Mannara

D-U-N-S 20-258-1054   (HQ)
CONSTRUCTIONS LOUISBOURG LTEE
BAR BLACK JACK
699 Boul Industriel, Saint-Eustache, QC, J7R
6C3
(450) 623-7100
Emp Here 215   *Sales* 43,791,055
SIC 8711 Engineering services
Lisa Accurso

D-U-N-S 20-180-0989   (HQ)
DISTRIBUTION BATH FITTER INC
BAIN MAGIQUE
(Suby of BATH FITTER TENNESSEE, INC.)
225 Rue Roy, Saint-Eustache, QC, J7R 5R5
(450) 472-0024
Emp Here 100   *Sales* 26,765,200
SIC 5211 Lumber and other building materials
Glenn Cotton
Brian Cotton
Raffi Apanian

D-U-N-S 20-603-6733   (HQ)
**EDITIONS   BLAINVILLE-DEUX-
MONTAGNES INC, LES**
JOURNAL L'EVEIL
53 Rue Saint-Eustache, Saint-Eustache, QC,
J7R 2L2
(450) 473-1700
Emp Here 55   *Sales* 12,302,025
SIC 2711 Newspapers
Jean-Claude Langlois
Michel Langlois

D-U-N-S 24-377-2113   (SL)

EMD TECHNOLOGIES INCORPORATED
HEICO LIGHTING
(Suby of HEICO CORPORATION)
400 Rue Du Parc, Saint-Eustache, QC, J7R
0A1
(450) 491-2100
Emp Here 85   *Sales* 19,319,565
SIC 3844 X-ray apparatus and tubes
Nadim Bakhache
Judith Vetter
Elizabeth R. Letendre
Carlos L. Macau, Jr.
Victor H. Mendelson

D-U-N-S 20-252-6505   (SL)
ENTREPRISE T.R.A. (2011) INC
145 Rue Daoust Bureau 101, Saint-Eustache,
QC, J7R 6P4
(450) 491-2940
Emp Here 50   *Sales* 26,027,100
SIC 5099 Durable goods, nec
Serge Daignault

D-U-N-S 24-600-9344   (SL)
FERMES SERBI INC, LES
841 25e Av, Saint-Eustache, QC, J7R 4K3
(450) 623-2369
Emp Here 40   *Sales* 13,698,680
SIC 0161 Vegetables and melons
Suzanne Lavallee Bigras

D-U-N-S 24-352-3615   (HQ)
FORTERRA PRESSURE PIPE, ULC
FORTERRA CONDUITE SOUS PRESSION
699 Boul Industriel, Saint-Eustache, QC, J7R
6C3
(450) 623-2200
Sales 17,921,900
SIC 3272 Concrete products, nec
Mark D Carpenter
Charles R Brown
Lori Browne
Jeffery K Bradley

D-U-N-S 20-197-6238   (HQ)
GESTION GEORGES SZARAZ INC.
311 Rue Boileau, Saint-Eustache, QC, J7R
2V5

Sales 12,344,940
SIC 8741 Management services
Georges Szaraz

D-U-N-S 24-483-4300   (SL)
GOYER PETROLE HUILE A CHAUFFGE
794 Boul Arthur-Sauv?, Saint-Eustache, QC,
J7R 4K3
(450) 473-4794
Emp Here 15   *Sales* 15,492,120
SIC 5172 Petroleum products, nec
Diane Goyer

D-U-N-S 24-502-1118   (SL)
GROUPE LEFEBVRE M.R.P INC, LE
210 Rue Roy, Saint-Eustache, QC, J7R 5R6
(450) 491-6444
Emp Here 125   *Sales* 21,399,784
SIC 1799 Special trade contractors, nec
Richard Lefebvre
Patrice Lefebvre
Philippe Lefebvre

D-U-N-S 20-387-1660   (BR)
GROUPE SANTE VALEO INC
RESIDENCE L'ARTISAN
495 Rue Bibeau, Saint-Eustache, QC, J7R
0B9
(450) 472-6115
Emp Here 140
SIC 8361 Residential care
Yves Parent

D-U-N-S 24-351-2451   (HQ)
GROUPE VOLVO CANADA INC
PREVOST
(Suby of AB VOLVO)
1000 Boul Industriel Bureau 1160, Saint-
Eustache, QC, J7R 5A5

---

(450) 472-6410
Emp Here 950   *Sales* 1,383,462,000
SIC 5012 Automobiles and other motor vehicles
 Ralph Acs
 Emmanuelle Toussaint
 Krzysztof Trembecki
 W. Macdonal Macintosh

D-U-N-S 20-370-6684   (HQ)
IMMEUBLE M. & A. CONSTANTIN INC
1054 Boul Arthur-Sauve, Saint-Eustache, QC, J7R 4K3
(450) 473-2374
Emp Here 6   *Sales* 38,743,954
SIC 6712 Bank holding companies
 Andre Constantin
 Michel Constantin
 Maxime Constantin
 Danny Constantin
 Gaby Constantin
 Michael Constantin

D-U-N-S 24-394-7897   (SL)
J.M. DUBRIS LTEE
CANADIAN TIRE
500 Boul Arthur-Sauve, Saint-Eustache, QC, J7R 4Z3
(450) 472-2270
Emp Here 45   *Sales* 22,413,510
SIC 5531 Auto and home supply stores
 Norman Ducharme

D-U-N-S 24-799-9782   (SL)
LOGITRANS INC
440 Rue Du Parc, Saint-Eustache, QC, J7R 7G6
(450) 565-8900
Emp Here 2   *Sales* 16,638,944
SIC 4731 Freight transportation arrangement
 Normand Guindon

D-U-N-S 20-249-4050   (HQ)
LUSSIER, BERNARD INC
PHARM ESCOMPTE JEAN COUTU
378 Boul Arthur-Sauve, Saint-Eustache, QC, J7R 2J4
(450) 473-3911
Emp Here 5   *Sales* 30,541,000
SIC 5912 Drug stores and proprietary stores
 Angelo Zaccara
 Jean-Maurice Vandargoten

D-U-N-S 25-650-6387   (SL)
MANUFACTURIERS D'ALUMINIUM OTTAWA INC, LES
GOUTTIERES DES LAURENTIDES, LES
439 Boul Industriel, Saint-Eustache, QC, J7R 5R3
(450) 983-3766
Emp Here 10   *Sales* 10,003,390
SIC 5051 Metals service centers and offices
 Louis Maisonneuve
 Jocelyn Maisonneuve

D-U-N-S 20-249-4191   (HQ)
NADON SPORT INC
62 Rue Saint-Louis, Saint-Eustache, QC, J7R 1X7
(450) 473-2381
Emp Here 15   *Sales* 11,455,794
SIC 5571 Motorcycle dealers
 Maurice Nadon
 Claude Nadon
 Gerald Nadon
 Nathalie Nadon

D-U-N-S 20-249-4001   (HQ)
PIECES D'AUTO LACROIX INC
825 Boul Arthur-Sauve, Saint-Eustache, QC, J7R 4K3
(450) 473-0661
Emp Here 28   *Sales* 18,939,180
SIC 5013 Motor vehicle supplies and new parts
 Jean-Guy Lacroix
 Sylvain Lacroix
 Denis Lacroix

 Denise Goyer Lacroix

D-U-N-S 24-228-9791   (SL)
POWERCAST INC
CASTFORGE
540 Boul Industriel, Saint-Eustache, QC, J7R 5V3
(450) 473-1517
Emp Here 70   *Sales* 16,340,450
SIC 3365 Aluminum foundries
 Krishan K Gupta
 Gilles Seguin
 Ravi K Gupta

D-U-N-S 20-370-3129   (SL)
QUADCO INC
EQUIPEMENT QUADCO
(*Suby of* KOMATSU AMERICA CORP)
30 Boul Industriel, Saint-Eustache, QC, J7R 5C1
(450) 623-3340
Emp Here 160   *Sales* 76,120,900
SIC 5082 Construction and mining machinery
 Mitsuru Ueno
 Christopher Schafer
 Stephane Chartier

D-U-N-S 25-814-1183   (HQ)
SAULNIER AUTOMOBILES INC
REMORQUAGE GOYER
445 Boul Industriel, Saint-Eustache, QC, J7R 5R3
(450) 623-7446
Sales 37,756,800
SIC 5511 New and used car dealers
 Andre Hebert
 Chantale Tremblay

D-U-N-S 20-249-4597   (HQ)
SCHOKBETON QUEBEC INC
PERFORMANCE DE L'EXTRA-PORTEE, LA
430 Boul Arthur-Sauve Bureau 6030, Saint-Eustache, QC, J7R 6V7
(450) 473-6831
Sales 12,545,330
SIC 3272 Concrete products, nec
 Robert Bibeau
 Fernand R Bibeau
 Nathalie Parent

D-U-N-S 20-280-7041   (BR)
SIMARD-BEAUDRY CONSTRUCTION INC
(*Suby of* SIMARD-BEAUDRY CONSTRUCTION INC)
699 Boul Industriel, Saint-Eustache, QC, J7R 6C3

Emp Here 100
SIC 1442 Construction sand and gravel
 Yves Blanchard

D-U-N-S 24-374-2199   (HQ)
SOCIETE DE GESTION B3CG INTERCONNECT INC
(*Suby of* AQ GROUP AB)
310 Boul Industriel, Saint-Eustache, QC, J7R 5R4
(450) 491-4040
Emp Here 3   *Sales* 58,481,440
SIC 6712 Bank holding companies
 Francois Demers
 Celine Brunet
 Nerijus Olsauskas
 Per Lindblad

D-U-N-S 20-370-8771   (HQ)
SYSTEMES DE SECURITE PARADOX LTEE
(*Suby of* 9065-1498 QUEBEC INC)
780 Boul Industriel, Saint-Eustache, QC, J7R 5V3
(450) 491-7444
Sales 70,445,835
SIC 3669 Communications equipment, nec
 Shmuel Hershkovitz
 Tomer Hershkovitz
 Ali Kobeissi

D-U-N-S 25-285-8097   (SL)

TRI-TEXCO INC
BARTEX
1001 Boul Industriel, Saint-Eustache, QC, J7R 6C3
(450) 974-1001
Emp Here 100   *Sales* 28,402,100
SIC 2865 Cyclic crudes and intermediates
 Aaron Davenport
 Natalie Laham
 Barry Penney
 Julian Steinberg

D-U-N-S 24-742-7750   (SL)
VENTILEX INC
(*Suby of* 3141781 CANADA INC)
348 Boul Industriel, Saint-Eustache, QC, J7R 5R4
(450) 473-9843
Emp Here 65   *Sales* 15,149,225
SIC 1711 Plumbing, heating, air-conditioning
 Yves Rousseau
 Hughes Vallee

D-U-N-S 20-651-6739   (BR)
WAL-MART CANADA CORP
(*Suby of* WALMART INC.)
764 Boul Arthur-Sauve Bureau 3089, Saint-Eustache, QC, J7R 4K3
(450) 491-6922
Emp Here 200
SIC 5311 Department stores
 Diane Hervieux

Saint-Evariste-De-Forsyth, QC G0M

D-U-N-S 20-761-5626   (SL)
DELOUPE INC
102 Rue Du Parc-Industriel, Saint-Evariste-De-Forsyth, QC, G0M 1S0
(418) 459-6443
Emp Here 80   *Sales* 17,907,440
SIC 3715 Truck trailers
 Dominic Drapeau
 Isabelle Morin
 Steve Gaudreau

D-U-N-S 24-531-8399   (SL)
ESTAMPRO INC
LIFCO
104 Rue Du Parc-Industriel, Saint-Evariste-De-Forsyth, QC, G0M 1S0
(418) 459-3423
Emp Here 100   *Sales* 24,259,264
SIC 3599 Industrial machinery, nec
 Dominic Fortin
 Sebastien Fortin
 Caroline Fortin

Saint-Fabien-De-Panet, QC G0R

D-U-N-S 24-389-5716   (BR)
CENTRE DE SANTE ET SERVICES SOCIAUX DE MONTMAGNY - L'ISLET
CLSC DE SAINT-FABIEN-DE-PANET
(*Suby of* GOUVERNEMENT DE LA PROVINCE DE QUEBEC)
10 Rue Alphonse, Saint-Fabien-De-Panet, QC, G0R 2J0
(418) 249-2572
Emp Here 1,000
SIC 8062 General medical and surgical hospitals
 Celine Lemelin

Saint-Faustin-Lac-Carre, QC J0T

D-U-N-S 24-388-6913   (SL)
CONSTRUCTION VP INC

1450 Rte 117, Saint-Faustin-Lac-Carre, QC, J0T 1J2
Emp Here 35   *Sales* 11,160,415
SIC 1521 Single-family housing construction
 Donald Provost

D-U-N-S 20-254-1975   (HQ)
GROUPE CRETE DIVISION ST-FAUSTIN INC
(*Suby of* GROUPE CRETE INC)
1617 Rte 117, Saint-Faustin-Lac-Carre, QC, J0T 1J2
(819) 688-5550
Sales 33,538,050
SIC 5031 Lumber, plywood, and millwork
 Sebastien Crete
 Jean-Rene Jacob

D-U-N-S 24-826-3365   (HQ)
GROUPE CRETE INC
1617 Rte 117, Saint-Faustin-Lac-Carre, QC, J0T 1J2
(418) 365-4457
Emp Here 4   *Sales* 85,444,200
SIC 5031 Lumber, plywood, and millwork
 Martin Crete
 Sebastien Crete
 Jean-Rene Jacob

Saint-Felicien, QC G8K

D-U-N-S 20-050-3683   (SL)
3105-4521 QUEBEC INC
METRO DES BOUTIN
1200 Boul Saint-Felicien, Saint-Felicien, QC, G8K 2N6
(418) 679-1431
Emp Here 60   *Sales* 17,608,620
SIC 5411 Grocery stores
 Marc Boutin
 Boutin Normand

D-U-N-S 24-381-5383   (SL)
9195-7639 QUEBEC INC
780 Boul Hamel, Saint-Felicien, QC, G8K 1X9
(418) 679-4533
Emp Here 85   *Sales* 19,841,975
SIC 1422 Crushed and broken limestone
 Michel Paradis
 Sandra Paradis

D-U-N-S 20-580-5153   (SL)
BLEUETIERES SENCO INC, LES
1459 Boul Du Sacre-Coeur, Saint-Felicien, QC, G8K 1B3
(418) 679-1472
Emp Here 150   *Sales* 107,507,400
SIC 5142 Packaged frozen goods
 Jean-Eudes Senneville
 Madeleine Perron
 Jean-Pierre Senneville

D-U-N-S 24-851-9212   (SL)
ENEL GREEN POWER CANADA INC
SOCIETE DE COGENERATION
1250 Rue De L'Energie, Saint-Felicien, QC, G8K 3J2
(418) 630-3800
Emp Here 30   *Sales* 15,589,650
SIC 4911 Electric services
 Pascal Turcotte

D-U-N-S 24-591-3546   (HQ)
EXCAVATION PARADIS, MICHEL INC
FELCO
1270 Rue Nelligan, Saint-Felicien, QC, G8K 1N1
(418) 679-4533
Emp Here 28   *Sales* 20,195,360
SIC 1611 Highway and street construction
 Michel Paradis
 Luc Perron
 Maxime St-Gelais

D-U-N-S 20-253-4983   (BR)
EXCAVATION PARADIS, MICHEL INC
EXCAVATION MICHEL PARADIS INC
(*Suby of* EXCAVATION PARADIS, MICHEL INC)
780 Boul Hamel, Saint-Felicien, QC, G8K 1X9
(418) 679-4533
Emp Here 80
SIC 1794 Excavation work
Michel Paradis

D-U-N-S 20-723-5904   (HQ)
FERLAC INC
1039 Rue De Carillon, Saint-Felicien, QC, G8K 2A2
(418) 679-1676
Emp Here 12   *Sales* 68,014,100
SIC 5251 Hardware stores
Caroline Fradet
Bertrand Fradet
Jean Lepage

D-U-N-S 20-118-4913   (HQ)
FIBREK S.E.N.C.
4000 Ch Saint Eusebe, Saint-Felicien, QC, G8K 2R6
(418) 679-8585
Sales 119,482,025
SIC 2611 Pulp mills
Richard Garneau

D-U-N-S 20-592-8021   (SL)
GIRARD, B & FILS INC
I G A
1199 Boul Saint-Felicien, Saint-Felicien, QC, G8K 3J1
(418) 679-1304
Emp Here 75   *Sales* 22,010,775
SIC 5411 Grocery stores
Bruno Girard

D-U-N-S 20-249-5982   (SL)
L.D. AUTO (1986) INC
854 Boul Du Sacre-Coeur, Saint-Felicien, QC, G8K 1S2
(418) 679-1546
Emp Here 32   *Sales* 15,938,496
SIC 5511 New and used car dealers
Jean Dumas

D-U-N-S 20-270-8772   (SL)
LABORATOIRES CHEZ-NOUS INC., LES
606 Boul Du Sacre-Coeur, Saint-Felicien, QC, G8K 1T5
(418) 679-2694
Emp Here 11   *Sales* 12,158,795
SIC 5122 Drugs, proprietaries, and sundries
Guy Laurent Trudeau
Paul Lescadres
Roger Lessard
Pierre Simard
Francyne Noel Trudeau

D-U-N-S 25-201-7579   (BR)
PF RESOLU CANADA INC
(*Suby of* RESOLUTE FOREST PRODUCTS INC)
900 Boul Hamel, Saint-Felicien, QC, G8K 2X4
(418) 679-0552
Emp Here 97
SIC 2421 Sawmills and planing mills, general
Pierre-Luc Bluteau

D-U-N-S 20-331-4992   (SL)
SERRES TOUNDRA INC
4190 Rte Saint-Eusebe, Saint-Felicien, QC, G8K 2N9
(418) 679-1834
Emp Here 250   *Sales* 42,256,250
SIC 0182 Food crops grown under cover
Eric Dube
Caroline Fradet
Bertrand Fradet
Yves Laflamme
Richard Garneau

D-U-N-S 20-182-6901   (SL)
SOCIETE DE COGENERATION DE ST-

FELICIEN, SOCIETE EN COMMANDITE
1250 Rue De L'Energie, Saint-Felicien, QC, G8K 3J2
(418) 630-3800
Emp Here 30   *Sales* 12,456,870
SIC 4931 Electric and other services combined
Stephanie Gagnon
Pascal Brun

D-U-N-S 24-790-7884   (HQ)
ST-FELICIEN DIESEL (1988) INC
981 Boul Hamel, Saint-Felicien, QC, G8K 2E3
(418) 679-2474
Emp Here 45   *Sales* 16,310,520
SIC 7699 Repair services, nec
Marjolaine Auclair

Saint-Felix-De-Kingsey, QC J0B

D-U-N-S 20-337-8877   (SL)
GESTION MARTIN BOUTET INC
1180 Rte 243, Saint-Felix-De-Kingsey, QC, J0B 2T0
(819) 848-2521
Emp Here 1   *Sales* 19,134,500
SIC 6712 Bank holding companies
Martin Boutet

D-U-N-S 24-253-3933   (SL)
GIGUERE & MORIN INC
1175 Rte 243, Saint-Felix-De-Kingsey, QC, J0B 2T0
(819) 848-2525
Emp Here 95   *Sales* 14,806,985
SIC 2426 Hardwood dimension and flooring mills
Clement Morin
Guy Morin
Marco Morin

D-U-N-S 24-362-4496   (SL)
TRANSPORT TFI 19, S.E.C.
DUROCHER INTERNATIONAL
1214 Rte 255, Saint-Felix-De-Kingsey, QC, J0B 2T0
(819) 848-2042
Emp Here 100   *Sales* 20,570,600
SIC 4213 Trucking, except local
Steve Lamontagne

Saint-Felix-De-Valois, QC J0K

D-U-N-S 25-173-1287   (SL)
ASSURANCES ROBILLARD & ASSOCIES INC, LES
ASSURANCES ROBILLARD
461 Ch De Joliette Bureau 100, Saint-Felix-De-Valois, QC, J0K 2M0
(450) 889-5557
Emp Here 15   *Sales* 10,881,585
SIC 6311 Life insurance
Michel Robillard

D-U-N-S 20-249-7269   (HQ)
BELL-GAZ LTEE
RB PROPANE
5300 Ch De Saint-Gabriel, Saint-Felix-De-Valois, QC, J0K 2M0
(450) 889-5944
Emp Here 33   *Sales* 17,822,190
SIC 5984 Liquefied petroleum gas dealers
Michel Lehoux

D-U-N-S 25-503-9315   (HQ)
COMMISSION SCOLAIRE DES SAMARES
POLYVALENTE L'ACHIGAN
4671 Rue Principale Bureau 190, Saint-Felix-De-Valois, QC, J0K 2M0
(450) 439-6046
Emp Here 50   *Sales* 322,136,750
SIC 8211 Elementary and secondary schools

Michel Forget
Jean-Guy Chartier Jr
France Trudel Lanoue

D-U-N-S 24-316-3917   (SL)
GROUPE BIBEAU INC
(*Suby of* USINES D'AUTRAY LTEE, LES)
4581 Rang Castle-D'Autray, Saint-Felix-De-Valois, QC, J0K 2M0
(450) 889-5505
Emp Here 50   *Sales* 11,192,150
SIC 3713 Truck and bus bodies
Nathalie Bibeau

D-U-N-S 24-650-3890   (SL)
PLASTIQUES G.P.R. INC
LORD PLASTIQUE
5200 Ch De Saint-Gabriel, Saint-Felix-De-Valois, QC, J0K 2M0
(450) 889-7277
Emp Here 100   *Sales* 20,189,700
SIC 3089 Plastics products, nec
Gino Belleville
Dany Belleville

D-U-N-S 20-051-7477   (HQ)
POIRIER-BERARD LTEE
COUVOIR RAMSAY
4401 Rue Crepeau, Saint-Felix-De-Valois, QC, J0K 2M0
(450) 889-5541
Emp Here 50   *Sales* 24,794,040
SIC 0259 Poultry and eggs, nec
Jacques Leclerc
Pierre Houde
Stephane Ethier

D-U-N-S 20-540-2860   (SL)
RAINVILLE, ROGER & FILS INC
IGA 8196
3100 Rue Henri-L.-Chevrette, Saint-Felix-De-Valois, QC, J0K 2M0
(450) 889-4747
Emp Here 50   *Sales* 13,707,600
SIC 5411 Grocery stores
Mario Rainville
Ginette Robillard Rainville

D-U-N-S 20-725-0697   (HQ)
USINES D'AUTRAY LTEE, LES
BIBEAU
4581 Rang Castle-D'Autray, Saint-Felix-De-Valois, QC, J0K 2M0
(450) 889-5505
Sales 43,736,000
SIC 6712 Bank holding companies
Nathalie Bibeau

Saint-Francois-Du-Lac, QC J0G

D-U-N-S 20-978-7571   (SL)
DUPUIS MAGNA COSMETIQUES INTERNATIONAL INC
(*Suby of* GESTION J. LESSARD INC)
191 Rue Leveille, Saint-Francois-Du-Lac, QC, J0G 1M0
(450) 568-3517
Emp Here 19   *Sales* 21,001,555
SIC 5122 Drugs, proprietaries, and sundries
Johanne Lessard

D-U-N-S 24-943-3210   (BR)
GROUPE VOLVO CANADA INC
NOVA BUS
(*Suby of* AB VOLVO)
155 Rte Marie-Victorin, Saint-Francois-Du-Lac, QC, J0G 1M0
(450) 568-3335
Emp Here 130
SIC 3711 Motor vehicles and car bodies
Jean- Francois Nadeau

D-U-N-S 25-074-6336   (SL)
SYNDICAT NATIONAL TCA
NOVABUS

155 Rte Marie-Victorin, Saint-Francois-Du-Lac, QC, J0G 1M0
(514) 531-5362
Emp Here 45   *Sales* 17,602,110
SIC 8631 Labor organizations
Yves Daunais

Saint-Frederic, QC G0N

D-U-N-S 25-974-8721   (SL)
PAR NADO INC
SAFARI CONDO
821 Rue Du Parc, Saint-Frederic, QC, G0N 1P0
(418) 426-3666
Emp Here 100   *Sales* 22,384,300
SIC 3799 Transportation equipment, nec
Daniel Nadeau
Stephane Nadeau
Johanne Nadeau
Dominique Nadeau
Frederic Pratte

Saint-Fulgence, QC G0V

D-U-N-S 20-955-3189   (SL)
OUELLET & JOBIN INC
SAGAMIE LE DEPANNEUR PLUS
50 Rte De Tadoussac Bureau 2, Saint-Fulgence, QC, G0V 1S0
(418) 674-2811
Emp Here 25   *Sales* 12,451,950
SIC 5541 Gasoline service stations
Nevil Gagnon

Saint-Gabriel-De-Brandon, QC J0K

D-U-N-S 25-089-8327   (HQ)
113514 CANADA INC
FABRIQUE JML
262 Rue Marcel Rr 2, Saint-Gabriel-De-Brandon, QC, J0K 2N0
(450) 835-2066
Sales 13,415,220
SIC 5031 Lumber, plywood, and millwork
Jean-Marie Pichette
Lise Pichette

D-U-N-S 24-636-3741   (SL)
ENTREPRISES ROBERT CHARETTE INC, LES
1003 3e Rang, Saint-Gabriel-De-Brandon, QC, J0K 2N0
(450) 835-7988
Emp Here 20   *Sales* 10,702,480
SIC 5144 Poultry and poultry products
Robert Charette

D-U-N-S 20-250-5855   (SL)
MARCHE BOURGEAULT INC
MARCHE METRO
160 Rue Saint-Gabriel, Saint-Gabriel-De-Brandon, QC, J0K 2N0
(450) 835-4794
Emp Here 50   *Sales* 13,707,600
SIC 5411 Grocery stores
Serge Bourgeault
Roger Bourgeault
Marguerite Bourgeault

Saint-Gedeon-De-Beauce, QC G0M

D-U-N-S 24-499-9157   (BR)
GROUPE CANAM INC
CANAM

(Suby of CANAM LUX PARENT COMPANY SARL)
115 Boul Canam N, Saint-Gedeon-De-Beauce, QC, G0M 1T0
(418) 582-3331
Emp Here 700
SIC 3441 Fabricated structural Metal
Andre Clemrmont

D-U-N-S 20-250-6812 (SL)
MAGASIN COOP ST-GEDEON
105 Boul Canam S, Saint-Gedeon-De-Beauce, QC, G0M 1T0
(418) 582-3977
Emp Here 36 *Sales* 11,626,884
SIC 5411 Grocery stores
Stanley Olscamp
Martin Moreau

Saint-Georges, QC G5Y

D-U-N-S 24-941-7650 (SL)
119759 CANADA LTEE
8850 35e Av, Saint-Georges, QC, G5Y 5C2
(418) 459-3423
Emp Here 40 *Sales* 16,774,200
SIC 6712 Bank holding companies
Gaetan Fortin

D-U-N-S 24-707-1517 (HQ)
131519 CANADA INC
4100 10e Av, Saint-Georges, QC, G5Y 7S3
(418) 228-9458
Emp Here 1 *Sales* 13,077,650
SIC 6712 Bank holding companies
Roland Veilleux

D-U-N-S 24-760-2089 (SL)
2625-8368 QUEBEC INC
MARCHE LAVAL VEILLEUX & FILS
16850 Boul Lacroix, Saint-Georges, QC, G5Y 8G9
(418) 228-8661
Emp Here 52 *Sales* 15,260,804
SIC 5411 Grocery stores
Laval Veilleux

D-U-N-S 24-216-4163 (SL)
9155- 5714 QUEBEC INC
MARCHE LAVAL VEILLEUX & FILS
17850 Boul Lacroix, Saint-Georges, QC, G5Y 5B8
(418) 228-8661
Emp Here 101 *Sales* 84,393,277
SIC 5141 Groceries, general line
Joel Veilleux
Noel Gilbert

D-U-N-S 24-820-5148 (SL)
AUTHENTIQUE POSE CAFE INC, L'
BIOSPHERA
9555 10e Av, Saint-Georges, QC, G5Y 8J8
(418) 228-3191
Emp Here 55 *Sales* 10,669,918
SIC 5046 Commercial equipment, nec
Michel Blais
Pierre Ouellet
Francois De L'Etoile
Turcot Sylvain
Pascal Theriault

D-U-N-S 24-466-0759 (SL)
AUTOMOBILE NATIONAL (1999) INC
585 90e Rue, Saint-Georges, QC, G5Y 3L1
(418) 228-8838
Emp Here 30 *Sales* 14,942,340
SIC 5511 New and used car dealers
Pierre Couture

D-U-N-S 24-637-4730 (SL)
AUTOMOBILES B. G. P. INC
8800 Boul Lacroix, Saint-Georges, QC, G5Y 2B5
(418) 228-5825
Emp Here 30 *Sales* 14,942,340

SIC 5511 New and used car dealers
Gilles Bernard

D-U-N-S 20-252-7719 (HQ)
BEAUBOIS GROUP INC
(Suby of GROUPE POMERLEAU INC)
521 6e Av N, Saint-Georges, QC, G5Y 0H1
(418) 228-5104
Sales 69,597,500
SIC 2431 Millwork
Pierre Pomerleau
Francis Pomerleau
Daniel Arguin
Eric Doyon

D-U-N-S 20-776-6197 (SL)
BEAUCE CARNAVAL INC
1340 Boul Dionne, Saint-Georges, QC, G5Y 3V6
(418) 228-8008
Emp Here 75 *Sales* 10,502,175
SIC 7999 Amusement and recreation, nec
Jaques Vallee
Paul Vallee

D-U-N-S 20-250-7679 (SL)
BEAUCE METAL INC
11855 35e Av, Saint-Georges, QC, G5Y 5B9
(418) 228-5566
Emp Here 20 *Sales* 20,006,780
SIC 5051 Metals service centers and offices
Richard Sirois
Bernard Sirois

D-U-N-S 20-289-3046 (BR)
BID GROUP TECHNOLOGIES LTD
(Suby of BID GROUP TECHNOLOGIES LTD)
4000 40e Rue, Saint-Georges, QC, G5Y 8G4
(418) 228-8911
Emp Here 250
SIC 3553 Woodworking machinery
Simon Grondin

D-U-N-S 25-983-6166 (BR)
BIZOU INTERNATIONAL INC
(Suby of BIZOU INTERNATIONAL INC)
8585 Boul Lacroix, Saint-Georges, QC, G5Y 5L6
(418) 227-0424
Emp Here 250
SIC 5944 Jewelry stores
Yvan Fecteau

D-U-N-S 24-200-2251 (SL)
BOA-FRANC INC
MIRAGE
1255 98e Rue, Saint-Georges, QC, G5Y 8J5
(418) 227-1181
Emp Here 300 *Sales* 57,711,000
SIC 2426 Hardwood dimension and flooring mills
Pierre Thabet
Andre Poirier
Marco Gagne

D-U-N-S 24-335-1272 (HQ)
BOA-FRANC, S.E.N.C.
MUSKOKA
1255 98e Rue, Saint-Georges, QC, G5Y 8J5
(418) 227-1181
Emp Here 1 *Sales* 90,476,750
SIC 2426 Hardwood dimension and flooring mills
Pierre Thabet

D-U-N-S 24-390-8378 (HQ)
CAISSE DESJARDINS DU SUD DE LA CHAUDIERE
CENTRE DE SERVICES BEAUCEVILLE
10555 Boul Lacroix, Saint-Georges, QC, G5Y 1K2
(418) 228-8824
Emp Here 80 *Sales* 24,561,760
SIC 6062 State credit unions
Donald Paquet
Robert Baril
Christine Caron
Pierre Couillard

Hugo Poulin
Karine Veilleux
Marc Grenier
Claude Loignon
Roger Longchamps
Germain Nadeau

D-U-N-S 20-174-1951 (BR)
CAISSE DESJARDINS DU SUD DE LA CHAUDIERE
CENTRE FINANCIER AUX ENTREPRISES DES CAISSES DESJARDINS CHAUDIERE-SUD
(Suby of CAISSE DESJARDINS DU SUD DE LA CHAUDIERE)
1275 Boul Dionne, Saint-Georges, QC, G5Y 0R4
(418) 227-7000
Emp Here 142
SIC 8741 Management services

D-U-N-S 20-363-8452 (HQ)
CANAM BATIMENTS ET STRUCTURES INC
CANAM
(Suby of CANAM LUX PARENT COMPANY SARL)
11505 1re Av Bureau 500, Saint-Georges, QC, G5Y 7X3
(418) 582-3331
Emp Here 10 *Sales* 52,294,665
SIC 3441 Fabricated structural Metal
Marc Dutil
Marcel Dutil
Louis Guertin
Rene Guizzetti

D-U-N-S 20-296-5534 (BR)
CENTRE DE SANTE ET DE SERVICES SO-CIAUX DE BEAUCE
12523 25e Av, Saint-Georges, QC, G5Y 5N6
(418) 228-2244
Emp Here 150
SIC 8399 Social services, nec
Denis Lafontain

D-U-N-S 24-568-1150 (HQ)
CLYVANOR LTEE
2125 95e Rue Bureau 1, Saint-Georges, QC, G5Y 8J1
(418) 228-7690
Sales 11,542,200
SIC 2439 Structural wood members, nec
Stephane Blanchette
Marie-Lou Blouin

D-U-N-S 20-530-7247 (BR)
COMMISSION SCOLAIRE DE LA BEAUCE-ETCHEMIN
CENTRE INTEGRE DE MECANIQUE IN-DUSTRIELLE DE LA CHAUDIERE CIMIC
(Suby of COMMISSION SCOLAIRE DE LA BEAUCE-ETCHEMIN)
11700 25e Av, Saint-Georges, QC, G5Y 8B8
(418) 228-1993
Emp Here 75
SIC 8211 Elementary and secondary schools
Chantale Doyon

D-U-N-S 25-232-7598 (BR)
COMMISSION SCOLAIRE DE LA BEAUCE-ETCHEMIN
ECOLE POLYVALENTE DE ST GEORGES
(Suby of COMMISSION SCOLAIRE DE LA BEAUCE-ETCHEMIN)
2121 119e Rue, Saint-Georges, QC, G5Y 5S1
(418) 228-8964
Emp Here 140
SIC 8211 Elementary and secondary schools
Germain Ouellet

D-U-N-S 24-637-9614 (HQ)
COMMISSION SCOLAIRE DE LA BEAUCE-ETCHEMIN
1925 118e Rue, Saint-Georges, QC, G5Y 7R7
(418) 228-5541
Emp Here 75 *Sales* 200,914,213
SIC 8211 Elementary and secondary schools

Charles-Henri Lecours
Normand Lessard
Fabien Giguere
Suzie Lucas

D-U-N-S 24-317-5465 (SL)
DANIEL LAVOIE PHARMACIEN INC
JEAN COUTU
11400 1re Ave, Saint-Georges, QC, G5Y 5S4
(418) 227-1515
Emp Here 40 *Sales* 10,118,160
SIC 5912 Drug stores and proprietary stores
Daniel Lavoie

D-U-N-S 25-213-3033 (SL)
DESJARDINS GROUPE D'ASSURANCES GENERALES INC
15590 8e Av, Saint-Georges, QC, G5Y 7X6
Emp Here 49 *Sales* 28,416,276
SIC 6411 Insurance agents, brokers, and service
Sylvie Paquette

D-U-N-S 20-250-9584 (SL)
EBI ELECTRIC INC
EBI
(Suby of GESTION 2250 90 INC)
2250 90e Rue, Saint-Georges, QC, G5Y 7J7
(418) 228-5505
Emp Here 80 *Sales* 17,426,320
SIC 1731 Electrical work
Serge Martel

D-U-N-S 20-950-2699 (SL)
ENTREPRISES J.C. LEVESQUE INC, LES
MARCHAND CANADIAN TIRE DE SAINT-GEROGES
500 107e Rue, Saint-Georges, QC, G5Y 8K1
(418) 228-8843
Emp Here 50 *Sales* 18,210,750
SIC 5014 Tires and tubes
Jean-Claude Levesque
Diane Chiasson

D-U-N-S 25-859-5136 (SL)
FAMILIPRIX-ROY ET LEBLOND INC
899 17e Rue, Saint-Georges, QC, G5Y 4W1
(418) 228-1017
Emp Here 48 *Sales* 12,141,792
SIC 5912 Drug stores and proprietary stores
Denis Roy

D-U-N-S 25-096-2037 (SL)
GESTION ROCECO INC
2685 121e Rue, Saint-Georges, QC, G5Y 5G2
(418) 227-4402
Emp Here 25 *Sales* 10,483,875
SIC 6712 Bank holding companies
Robert Couture

D-U-N-S 24-759-8170 (SL)
GESTIONS G H P (1986) INC, LES
521 6e Av N, Saint-Georges, QC, G5Y 0H1
(418) 228-6688
Emp Here 120 *Sales* 14,973,120
SIC 8741 Management services
Bernard St-Louis
Normand Pomerleau
Jean-Pierre Begin
Francois Fecteau

D-U-N-S 20-250-7943 (HQ)
GROUPE CANAM INC
BUILDMASTER
(Suby of CANAM LUX PARENT COMPANY SARL)
11505 1re Av Bureau 500, Saint-Georges, QC, G5Y 7H5
(418) 228-8031
Emp Here 100 *Sales* 1,038,353,139
SIC 3441 Fabricated structural Metal
Marc Dutil
Marcel Dutil
Rene Guizzetti
Louis Guertin
Paul Bamatter

Joel Rotroff
Joel Stanwood
Randall Swift
Zachary Carson
Julie Proulx

D-U-N-S 24-821-6467   (HQ)
GROUPE POMERLEAU INC
521 6e Av N, Saint-Georges, QC, G5Y 0H1
(418) 228-6688
Emp Here 1   *Sales* 1,096,527,000
SIC 6712 Bank holding companies
Pierre Pomerleau
Francis Pomerleau

D-U-N-S 24-908-9715   (HQ)
IMAGES TURBO INC, LES
1225 107e Rue, Saint-Georges, QC, G5Y 8C3
(418) 227-8872
Sales 36,015,760
SIC 7532 Top and body repair and paint shops
Pier Veilleux

D-U-N-S 24-464-5842   (SL)
IMPORTATIONS JACQUES FOURNIER LTEE, LES
2525 127e Rue, Saint-Georges, QC, G5Y 5G4
(418) 228-8594
Emp Here 40   *Sales* 29,700,800
SIC 5199 Nondurable goods, nec
Jacques Fournier

D-U-N-S 20-966-8651   (SL)
KENNEBEC DODGE CHRYSLER INC
10240 Boul Lacroix, Saint-Georges, QC, G5Y 1K1
(418) 228-5575
Emp Here 26   *Sales* 12,950,028
SIC 5511 New and used car dealers
Richard Poulin

D-U-N-S 24-890-2004   (SL)
L'USINE TAC TIC INC
MERECO
2030 127e Rue, Saint-Georges, QC, G5Y 2W8
(418) 227-4279
Emp Here 80   *Sales* 6,859,233
SIC 7389 Business services, nec
Marco Trudel
Anthony James Lynch
Dean Justin Treister

D-U-N-S 20-528-1483   (HQ)
MANAC INC
COMBOPLATE
2275 107e Rue, Saint-Georges, QC, G5Y 8G6
(418) 228-2018
Emp Here 550   *Sales* 279,216,000
SIC 3715 Truck trailers
Charles Dutil
Stephane Vachon
Me Julie Demers
Gilles Poulin
Marcel Dutil
Alain Tremblay
Annie Thabet
Pierre Grand'maison

D-U-N-S 20-331-3606   (BR)
MODE CHOC (ALMA) LTEE
MODE CHOC
(*Suby of* MODE CHOC (ALMA) LTEE)
610 Rue 90e, Saint-Georges, QC, G5Y 3L2
(418) 221-6850
Emp Here 100
SIC 5651 Family clothing stores
Richard Paquet

D-U-N-S 20-579-9315   (SL)
PAVAGE SARTIGAN LTEE
2125 98e Rue, Saint-Georges, QC, G5Y 8J5
(418) 228-3875
Emp Here 49   *Sales* 13,892,676
SIC 1611 Highway and street construction
Renald Savard
Julien Savard

D-U-N-S 20-250-9428   (HQ)
PAVAGES ABENAKIS LTEE
11380 79e Av, Saint-Georges, QC, G5Y 5B9
(418) 228-8116
Sales 16,408,730
SIC 1611 Highway and street construction
Yves Pouliot
Jacinthe Mathieu

D-U-N-S 24-689-5403   (HQ)
PERES NATURE INC, LES
P'TIT GRAND CAFE, LE
10735 1re Av, Saint-Georges, QC, G5Y 2B8
(418) 227-4444
Emp Here 95   *Sales* 35,217,240
SIC 5431 Fruit and vegetable markets
Clement Bedard
Saphir Veilleux-Bedard
Ulyss Giroux-Bedard
Mareva-Luna Giroux-Bedard

D-U-N-S 24-377-3975   (SL)
PLACEMENTS M DROUIN INC, LES
DEPANNEUR LE FRIGO
14920 Boul Lacroix, Saint-Georges, QC, G5Y 1R6
(418) 228-0051
Emp Here 21   *Sales* 10,459,638
SIC 5541 Gasoline service stations
Daniel Drouin

D-U-N-S 20-251-0715   (HQ)
POMERLEAU INC
EKI RENTAL
(*Suby of* GROUPE POMERLEAU INC)
521 6e Av N, Saint-Georges, QC, G5Y 0H1
(418) 228-6688
Emp Here 125   *Sales* 1,027,565,073
SIC 1542 Nonresidential construction, nec
Pierre Pomerleau
Francis Pomerleau
Jean-Philippe Towner
Jean Lacouture
Jean-Yves Leblanc
Michael Fortier
Patricia Curadeau-Grou
Dalton Mcguinty
Charles Guay
Alain Tremblay

D-U-N-S 24-638-8656   (SL)
PORTES & FENETRES ABRITEK INC
5195 127e Rue, Saint-Georges, QC, G5Y 5B9
(418) 228-3293
Emp Here 50   *Sales* 10,094,850
SIC 3089 Plastics products, nec
Josee Bilodeau

D-U-N-S 25-501-9473   (SL)
POULIN, NIKOL INC
NPI GROUP
3100 Boul Dionne, Saint-Georges, QC, G5Y 3Y4
(418) 228-3267
Emp Here 37   *Sales* 30,916,349
SIC 5141 Groceries, general line
Nikol Poulin
Dave Poulin
Karine Poulin

D-U-N-S 24-349-5921   (SL)
ST-GEORGES CHEVROLET PONTIAC BUICK CADILLAC GMC INC
520 87e Rue, Saint-Georges, QC, G5Y 7L9
(418) 228-8801
Emp Here 40   *Sales* 19,923,120
SIC 5511 New and used car dealers
Pierre Couture

D-U-N-S 25-698-0277   (SL)
SYNDICAT DES METALLOS SECTION LOCAL 9153
11780 1re Av Bureau 204, Saint-Georges, QC, G5Y 2C8

Emp Here 49   *Sales* 19,166,742
SIC 8631 Labor organizations

Philips Dore

D-U-N-S 25-527-1272   (HQ)
TAPIS VENTURE INC
GESTION CLUDE THIBAUDEAU
700 120e Rue, Saint-Georges, QC, G5Y 6R6
(418) 227-5955
Sales 27,510,450
SIC 2273 Carpets and rugs
Richard Duval
Alexandre Lacroix
Stephan Guindon

D-U-N-S 20-333-0709   (SL)
TECFAB INTERNATIONAL INC
TECFAB METAL EXPERT
11535 1re Av Bureau 500, Saint-Georges, QC, G5Y 7H5
(418) 228-8031
Emp Here 50   *Sales* 10,378,161
SIC 3312 Blast furnaces and steel mills

D-U-N-S 20-115-7794   (SL)
USINE TAC TIC INC, L'
MERECO
2030 127e Rue, Saint-Georges, QC, G5Y 2W8
(418) 227-4279
Emp Here 70   *Sales* 11,481,890
SIC 2789 Bookbinding and related work
Marco Trudel
Anthony James Lynch
Dean Justin Treister

D-U-N-S 20-869-1220   (HQ)
VETEMENTS DE SPORT R.G.R. INC
(*Suby of* 131519 CANADA INC)
4100 10e Av, Saint-Georges, QC, G5Y 7S3
(418) 228-9458
Sales 12,458,050
SIC 5136 Men's and boy's clothing
Rolland Veilleux

D-U-N-S 24-319-5067   (BR)
WAL-MART CANADA CORP
WALMART
(*Suby of* WALMART INC.)
750 107e Rue, Saint-Georges, QC, G5Y 0A1
(418) 220-0010
Emp Here 170
SIC 5311 Department stores

Saint-Georges, QC G5Z

D-U-N-S 20-251-0392   (SL)
CHAREST, F. LTEE
1085 42e Rue N, Saint-Georges, QC, G5Z 0T9
(418) 228-9747
Emp Here 40   *Sales* 29,700,800
SIC 5194 Tobacco and tobacco products
Francois Beaudry
Jean-Philippe Beaudry
Alain Rheaume
Serge Nadeau

Saint-Georges, QC G6A

D-U-N-S 24-908-7313   (SL)
BOIS KENNEBEC LTEE
BOIS KENNEBEC - USINE 001
(*Suby of* CANADEL INC)
8475 25e Av, Saint-Georges, QC, G6A 1M8
(418) 228-1414
Emp Here 115   *Sales* 22,122,550
SIC 2431 Millwork
Guy Deveault
Michel Deveault

D-U-N-S 20-250-8412   (SL)
CENTRE DU CAMION (BEAUCE) INC, LE

8900 25e Av, Saint-Georges, QC, G6A 1K5
(418) 228-8005
Emp Here 40   *Sales* 14,568,600
SIC 5012 Automobiles and other motor vehicles
Jean-Francois Poulin
Steve Halle

D-U-N-S 25-697-7661   (HQ)
DIMENSION COMPOSITE INC
2530 95e Rue, Saint-Georges, QC, G6A 1E3
(418) 228-0212
Sales 11,671,750
SIC 3296 Mineral wool
Jean-Pierre Tremblay

D-U-N-S 24-942-0456   (HQ)
DUVALTEX (CANADA) INC
VICTOR GROUP
2805 90e Rue, Saint-Georges, QC, G6A 1K1
(418) 227-9897
Emp Here 140   *Sales* 34,846,570
SIC 2221 Broadwoven fabric mills, manmade
Alain Duval

D-U-N-S 24-941-8591   (HQ)
DUVALTEX INC
2805 90e Rue, Saint-Georges, QC, G6A 1K1
(418) 227-9897
Sales 13,077,650
SIC 6712 Bank holding companies
Alain Duval
Francois Chevarie

D-U-N-S 24-464-8812   (HQ)
GARAGA INC
8500 25e Av, Saint-Georges, QC, G6A 1K5
(418) 227-2828
Emp Here 125   *Sales* 38,417,000
SIC 3442 Metal doors, sash, and trim
Michel Gendreau
Maxime Gendreau
Martin Gendreau

D-U-N-S 20-362-7245   (HQ)
GESTION INDUSTRIES INC
9095 25e Av, Saint-Georges, QC, G6A 1A1
(418) 228-8934
Emp Here 1   *Sales* 38,269,000
SIC 6712 Bank holding companies
Raymond Dutil

D-U-N-S 25-291-9279   (HQ)
GROUPE CONTROLE INC
MATISS
8800 25e Av, Saint-Georges, QC, G6A 1K5
(418) 227-9141
Sales 20,967,750
SIC 6712 Bank holding companies
Jacques Martel
Pierre Martel

D-U-N-S 25-286-1109   (SL)
MATISS INC
(*Suby of* GROUPE CONTROLE INC)
8800 25e Av, Saint-Georges, QC, G6A 1K5
(418) 227-9141
Emp Here 50   *Sales* 11,100,050
SIC 3569 General industrial machinery, nec
Jacques Martel
Marc Dutil

D-U-N-S 20-721-6151   (SL)
MAXI-METAL INC
9345 25e Av, Saint-Georges, QC, G6A 1L1
(418) 228-6637
Emp Here 65   *Sales* 14,549,795
SIC 3713 Truck and bus bodies
Danny Dufour

D-U-N-S 24-746-3300   (SL)
O.S.I. MACHINERIE INC
OSI MACHINERIE
(*Suby of* IMMOBILISATION 2010 INC)
2510 98e Rue, Saint-Georges, QC, G6A 1E4
(418) 228-6868
Emp Here 60   *Sales* 13,320,060

SIC 3553 Woodworking machinery
Andre Lapointe

D-U-N-S 24-343-0266   (SL)
PORTES GARAGA: STANDARD + INC
8500 25e Av, Saint-Georges, QC, G6A 1K5
(418) 227-2828
Emp Here 200   *Sales* 54,670,000
SIC 6712 Bank holding companies
Michel Gendreau

Saint-Georges-De-Champlain, QC G9T

D-U-N-S 20-259-7050   (SL)
2788331 CANADA INC
MARCH? TRADITION ST-GEORGES
701 Av Saint-Georges, Saint-Georges-De-
Champlain, QC, G9T 5K4
(819) 533-5445
Emp Here 49   *Sales* 13,433,448
SIC 5411 Grocery stores
Paul Sills
Daniel Sills

Saint-Georges-De-Windsor, QC J0A

D-U-N-S 25-250-6683   (SL)
CANARD IMPERIAL DE BROME LTEE
*CANARD LIBERE - ESPACE GOURMAAD,
LE*
243 Rte 249, Saint-Georges-De-Windsor, QC,
J0A 1J0
(819) 828-2219
Emp Here 100
SIC 0259 Poultry and eggs, nec
Mario Cote
Joseph Jr Jurgielewicz

Saint-Germain-De-Grantham, QC J0C

D-U-N-S 20-290-9784   (SL)
ADVANCE DRAINAGE SYSTEM INC
(*Suby of* ADVANCED DRAINAGE SYSTEMS,
INC.)
250a Boul Industriel, Saint-Germain-De-
Grantham, QC, J0C 1K0
(800) 733-7473
Emp Here 49   *Sales* 11,420,185
SIC 1711 Plumbing, heating, air-conditioning
Joseph A. Chlapaty
Thomas Fussner
Mark B. Sturgeon

D-U-N-S 20-640-4126   (SL)
CISOLIFT DISTRIBUTION INC
192 Rue Sylvestre, Saint-Germain-De-
Grantham, QC, J0C 1K0
(819) 395-3838
Emp Here 22   *Sales* 10,450,572
SIC 5084 Industrial machinery and equipment
Guy Therrien
Yan Leblanc
Stephane Plante

D-U-N-S 20-415-9495   (SL)
EMBALLAGE CODERRE PACKAGING INC
413 Rte 122, Saint-Germain-De-Grantham,
QC, J0C 1K0
(819) 395-4223
Emp Here 45   *Sales* 10,504,575
SIC 2674 Bags: uncoated paper and multiwall
Simon Coderre

D-U-N-S 20-321-6635   (BR)
**INTEGRATED DISTRIBUTION SYSTEMS
LIMITED PARTNERSHIP**
WAJAX POWER SYSTEMS
(*Suby of* WAJAX CORPORATION)

243 Rue Des Artisans, Saint-Germain-De-
Grantham, QC, J0C 1K0
(819) 472-4076
Emp Here 100
SIC 5084 Industrial machinery and equipment
Roland Barde

D-U-N-S 24-414-8123   (BR)
**INTEGRATED DISTRIBUTION SYSTEMS
LIMITED PARTNERSHIP**
GENERATRICE DRUMMOND
(*Suby of* WAJAX CORPORATION)
243 Rue Des Artisans, Saint-Germain-De-
Grantham, QC, J0C 1K0
(819) 472-4076
Emp Here 105
SIC 5063 Electrical apparatus and equipment
Roland Barbe

D-U-N-S 24-635-5077   (HQ)
RASAKTI INC
(*Suby of* GESTION SYNERRA INC)
148 Rue Sylvestre, Saint-Germain-De-
Grantham, QC, J0C 1K0
(819) 395-1111
Emp Here 91   *Sales* 11,062,646
SIC 3812 Search and navigation equipment
Andre Roseberry

D-U-N-S 24-758-9757   (HQ)
S.G.T. 2000 INC
SGT TRANSPORT
354 Ch Yamaska, Saint-Germain-De-
Grantham, QC, J0C 1K0
(819) 395-4213
Emp Here 300   *Sales* 38,617,400
SIC 4213 Trucking, except local
Denis Coderre
Jean-Pierre Rabbath

D-U-N-S 20-542-3841   (SL)
SAC DRUMMOND INC
192 Ch De La Station, Saint-Germain-De-
Grantham, QC, J0C 1K0
(819) 395-4286
Emp Here 45   *Sales* 22,413,510
SIC 5541 Gasoline service stations
Denis Beaudoin
Jean Bousada
Gilles St-Pierre

D-U-N-S 20-196-9904   (SL)
VAILLANCOURT INC
VAILLANCOURT PORTES ET FENETRES
252 Boul Industriel, Saint-Germain-De-
Grantham, QC, J0C 1K0
(819) 395-4484
Emp Here 180   *Sales* 28,594,440
SIC 3089 Plastics products, nec
Pierre Vaillancourt
Carl Vaillancourt

D-U-N-S 24-108-1025   (HQ)
VALMETAL INC
230 Boul Industriel, Saint-Germain-De-
Grantham, QC, J0C 1K0
(819) 395-4282
Sales 19,980,090
SIC 3523 Farm machinery and equipment
Yvon Vallieres
Lise Lehoullier Vallieres
Eric Vallieres
Dominic Vallieres
David Vallieres

Saint-Gilbert, QC G0A

D-U-N-S 20-251-2331   (SL)
MOISAN, ELOI INC
20 354 Rte, Saint-Gilbert, QC, G0A 3T0
(418) 268-3232
Emp Here 50   *Sales* 12,652,950
SIC 5211 Lumber and other building materials
Pierre-Paul Moisan

Francois Moisan
Olivier Moisan

Saint-Gilles, QC G0S

D-U-N-S 24-143-8589   (SL)
FENETRES ELITE INC, LES
264 Rue Demers, Saint-Gilles, QC, G0S 2P0
(418) 888-4342
Emp Here 150   *Sales* 40,147,800
SIC 5211 Lumber and other building materials
Renald Montminy

Saint-Godefroi, QC G0C

D-U-N-S 24-689-4752   (SL)
PRODUITS MARINS ST-GODEFROI INC
157 Rue Principale, Saint-Godefroi, QC, G0C
3C0
(418) 752-5578
Emp Here 35   *Sales* 29,245,195
SIC 5146 Fish and seafoods
Guy Aubut
Janick Aubut

Saint-Guillaume, QC J0C

D-U-N-S 20-251-3602   (SL)
AGRILAIT, COOPERATIVE AGRICOLE
CENTRE DE MELANGE D'ENGRAIS
83 Rang De L'Eglise, Saint-Guillaume, QC,
J0C 1L0
(819) 396-2022
Emp Here 145   *Sales* 50,125,050
SIC 2022 Cheese; natural and processed
Yvon Cyr
Ghyslain Gervais
Nathalie Frenette
Michel Brouillard
Andre Labonte
Marc Tessier
Alexandre Lavoie
Denis Denoncourt

D-U-N-S 20-251-3420   (HQ)
JOYAL, CLAUDE INC
1 Rue Principale, Saint-Guillaume, QC, J0C
1L0
(819) 396-2161
Emp Here 15   *Sales* 26,126,430
SIC 5083 Farm and garden machinery
Claude Joyal
Ghislain Joyal
Nathalie Joyal

D-U-N-S 24-804-4849   (HQ)
MACHINERIE C. & H. INC
MACHINERIE CH WOTTON
12 Rte 122, Saint-Guillaume, QC, J0C 1L0
(819) 396-2185
Emp Here 25   *Sales* 23,751,300
SIC 5083 Farm and garden machinery
Gervais Laroche
Daniel Riendeau
Gerry Mcneil
Gilles Denette

Saint-Henri-De-Levis, QC G0R

D-U-N-S 20-761-3084   (SL)
ALLEN ENTREPRENEUR GENERAL INC
CWA MECANIQUE DE PROCEDE
118 Rue De La Gare, Saint-Henri-De-Levis,
QC, G0R 3E0

(418) 882-2277
Emp Here 150   *Sales* 37,866,300
SIC 1611 Highway and street construction
Annie Allen
Christian Provencal
Allen Maxime

D-U-N-S 25-526-9136   (SL)
FORTIER 2000 LTEE
146 Rue Commerciale, Saint-Henri-De-Levis,
QC, G0R 3E0
(418) 882-2205
Emp Here 55   *Sales* 12,838,925
SIC 3273 Ready-mixed concrete
Real Riverin

D-U-N-S 20-016-5756   (BR)
JELD-WEN OF CANADA LTD
JELD-WEN OF CANADA, LTD
(*Suby of* JELD-WEN HOLDING, INC.)
115 Rue De La Gare, Saint-Henri-De-Levis,
QC, G0R 3E0
(418) 882-2223
Emp Here 150
SIC 2431 Millwork
Gilles Bouchard

D-U-N-S 24-379-1076   (SL)
LEMIEUX ASSURANCES INC
ASSURANCES FORTIN FRECHETTE
186 Rue Commerciale, Saint-Henri-De-Levis,
QC, G0R 3E0
(418) 882-0801
Emp Here 26   *Sales* 15,078,024
SIC 6411 Insurance agents, brokers, and ser-
vice
Francois Lemieux

D-U-N-S 20-803-4954   (SL)
MARCHE IGA ST-HENRI DE LEVIS INC
59 Rte Campagna, Saint-Henri-De-Levis, QC,
G0R 3E0
(418) 882-5375
Emp Here 60   *Sales* 17,608,620
SIC 5411 Grocery stores
Louis Lapointe

D-U-N-S 20-263-4861   (SL)
**PHOENIX SERVICES ENVIRONNEMEN-
TAUX INC.**
144 Rte Du President-Kennedy, Saint-Henri-
De-Levis, QC, G0R 3E0
(418) 882-0014
Emp Here 100
SIC 7389 Business services, nec
Herman Savard
Philippe Savard

D-U-N-S 20-778-4901   (HQ)
PRESTOLAM INC
2766 Rte Du President-Kennedy, Saint-Henri-
De-Levis, QC, G0R 3E0
(418) 882-2242
Sales 11,574,150
SIC 2541 Wood partitions and fixtures
Yvon Tremblay
Normand Beausoleil
Martin Tremblay

D-U-N-S 24-376-8699   (BR)
SUPRALIMENT S.E.C.
(*Suby of* SUPRALIMENT S.E.C.)
183 Rte Du President-Kennedy, Saint-Henri-
De-Levis, QC, G0R 3E0
(418) 882-2282
Emp Here 617
SIC 2011 Meat packing plants
Normand Valliere

D-U-N-S 24-388-4116   (SL)
T.M.S. SYSTEME INC
POUTRELLES VESCOM CANADA
170 Rte Du President-Kennedy, Saint-Henri-
De-Levis, QC, G0R 3E0
(418) 895-6877
Emp Here 100   *Sales* 23,343,500
SIC 3272 Concrete products, nec
Gilbert Roy

▲ Public Company   ■ Public Company Family Member   **HQ** Headquarters   **BR** Branch   **SL** Single Location

Saint-Hippolyte, QC J8A

D-U-N-S 24-890-5408   (SL)
ALIMENTATION ST-ONGE INC
I G A
972 Ch Des Hauteurs, Saint-Hippolyte, QC, J8A 1L2
(450) 224-5179
Emp Here 55   *Sales* 16,141,235
SIC 5411 Grocery stores
Yves St-Onge
Denise St-Onge

D-U-N-S 24-382-6166   (SL)
EXCAVATIONS GILLES ST-ONGE INC, LES
GROUPE ST-ONGE, LE
1075 Crois Des Hauteurs, Saint-Hippolyte, QC, J8A 0A5
(450) 224-0555
Emp Here 41   *Sales* 10,093,626
SIC 1794 Excavation work
Guylaine St-Onge

D-U-N-S 24-561-8822   (SL)
PLEIN AIR BRUCHESI INC
CAMPS BRUCHESI
50 365e Av, Saint-Hippolyte, QC, J8A 2Y6
(450) 563-3056
Emp Here 80   *Sales* 7,415,200
SIC 7032 Sporting and recreational camps
Luc Jarry
Fernand Simoneau
Claude Jette
Marc-Antoine De Lorimier

Saint-Honore-De-Chicoutimi, QC G0V

D-U-N-S 24-205-1456   (HQ)
CONSTRUCTION J. & R. SAVARD LTEE
1201 Boul Martel, Saint-Honore-De-Chicoutimi, QC, G0V 1L0
(418) 543-5933
Sales 11,008,400
SIC 1794 Excavation work
Rock Savard
Diane Tremblay

D-U-N-S 24-887-9053   (BR)
IAMGOLD CORPORATION
IAMGOLD CORPORATION
(*Suby of* IAMGOLD CORPORATION)
3400 Ch Du Columbium, Saint-Honore-De-Chicoutimi, QC, G0V 1L0
(418) 673-4694
Emp Here 400
SIC 1081 Metal mining services
Gilles Ferlatte

D-U-N-S 20-058-9799   (BR)
NIOBEC INC
MINE NIOBEC, LA
(*Suby of* MAGRIS RESOURCES INC)
3400 Ch Du Columbium, Saint-Honore-De-Chicoutimi, QC, G0V 1L0
(418) 673-4694
Emp Here 400
SIC 1081 Metal mining services
Gilles Farlatte

Saint-Honore-De-Shenley, QC G0M

D-U-N-S 24-759-6380   (SL)
USINE SARTIGAN INC
888 Rte 269, Saint-Honore-De-Shenley, QC, G0M 1V0
(418) 485-6797
Emp Here 75   *Sales* 11,689,725
SIC 2421 Sawmills and planing mills, general
Steeve Roy

Keaven Roy

Saint-Hubert, QC J3Y

D-U-N-S 24-836-2048   (HQ)
131638 CANADA INC
MICHEL ST ARNEAULT
4605 Av Thibault, Saint-Hubert, QC, J3Y 3S8
(450) 445-0550
Sales 19,134,500
SIC 6712 Bank holding companies
Michel St Arneault

D-U-N-S 20-540-4163   (SL)
1638-2723 QUEBEC INC.
PREVENTION INCENDIE SAFETY FIRST QUEBEC
(*Suby of* PLACEMENTS SAFETY FIRST INC)
2805 Boul Losch, Saint-Hubert, QC, J3Y 3V6
(514) 866-8683
Emp Here 35   *Sales* 16,625,910
SIC 5087 Service establishment equipment
Alain Perusse
Patrick Masse
Eric Beaudry

D-U-N-S 25-502-0752   (HQ)
2425-1761 QUEBEC INC
4355 Boul Sir-Wilfrid-Laurier, Saint-Hubert, QC, J3Y 3X3
(450) 443-6666
Sales 51,389,800
SIC 6712 Bank holding companies
Guy Lamarre

D-U-N-S 25-674-5399   (HQ)
3523462 CANADA INC
DELICES DE LA FORET - VALLI
3400 Boul Losch Bureau 35, Saint-Hubert, QC, J3Y 5T6
(450) 443-0060
Sales 33,423,080
SIC 5141 Groceries, general line
Eric Fortin
Roberto Trunzo
Claire Montambault

D-U-N-S 25-976-4090   (HQ)
3611981 CANADA INC
6200 Rte De L'A?Roport, Saint-Hubert, QC, J3Y 8Y9
(450) 443-0000
Sales 85,432,960
SIC 4512 Air transportation, scheduled
Julien Robert

D-U-N-S 25-502-4036   (HQ)
9051-4076 QUEBEC INC
GROUPE CHAGNON
3500 Boul Sir-Wilfrid-Laurier, Saint-Hubert, QC, J3Y 6T1
(450) 321-2446
Sales 37,866,300
SIC 1622 Bridge, tunnel, and elevated highway construction
Jean Chagnon
Michael Richard
Claude Chagnon

D-U-N-S 24-381-6779   (SL)
9136-3283 QUEBEC INC
FORMINTEK
5335 Rue Albert-Millichamp Bureau 1, Saint-Hubert, QC, J3Y 8Z8
(450) 350-0420
Emp Here 32   *Sales* 14,309,568
SIC 5045 Computers, peripherals, and software
Stephane Charbonneau
Marc-Andre Poirier

D-U-N-S 20-883-7609   (SL)
9338-4337 QUEBEC INC
BETON METROPOLITAIN
6600 Grande Allee, Saint-Hubert, QC, J3Y

1B7
(450) 656-5121
Emp Here 60   *Sales* 14,006,100
SIC 3273 Ready-mixed concrete
Dany Laflamme

D-U-N-S 20-357-0932   (SL)
9736140 CANADA INC
PASCAN
(*Suby of* 9736093 CANADA INC)
6200 Rte De L'Aeroport, Saint-Hubert, QC, J3Y 8Y9
(450) 443-0500
Emp Here 50   *Sales* 16,237,700
SIC 4512 Air transportation, scheduled
Julian Roberts
Yani Gagnon

D-U-N-S 24-800-7189   (SL)
ACTION CHEVROLET INC
7955 Ch De Chambly, Saint-Hubert, QC, J3Y 5K2
(450) 445-7333
Emp Here 45   *Sales* 28,317,600
SIC 5511 New and used car dealers
Stephane Guilbault

D-U-N-S 20-951-8729   (SL)
AIRMEDIC INC
AIRMEDIC AMBULANCE AERIENNE
4980 Rte De L'Aeroport, Saint-Hubert, QC, J3Y 8Y9
(450) 766-0770
Emp Here 100   *Sales* 32,475,400
SIC 4522 Air transportation, nonscheduled
Stephan Huot

D-U-N-S 20-236-5532   (SL)
ALIMENTS VALLI INC., LES
ALIMENTS VIVI
(*Suby of* 3523462 CANADA INC)
3400 Boul Losch Bureau 35, Saint-Hubert, QC, J3Y 5T6
(450) 443-0060
Emp Here 25   *Sales* 20,889,425
SIC 5141 Groceries, general line
Eric Fortin

D-U-N-S 24-339-8448   (HQ)
AMCAN-JUMAX INC
ANCRAGES CANADIENS
(*Suby of* PLACEMENTS MECYVA INC)
3300 2e Rue, Saint-Hubert, QC, J3Y 8Y7
(450) 445-8888
Sales 22,801,248
SIC 5085 Industrial supplies
Max Latifi

D-U-N-S 20-793-8960   (HQ)
ATELIER LA FLECHE DE FER INC, L'
AFFI
3800 Rue Richelieu, Saint-Hubert, QC, J3Y 7B1
(450) 656-9150
Emp Here 16   *Sales* 38,428,194
SIC 7629 Electrical repair shops
Daniel Perreault
Roger Pedneault
Jean-Charles Dagenais
Pierre Bariteau
Fernand R. Plante
Pierre Hebert
Mireille Berichon
Denis Roy
Sylvie L'ecuyer

D-U-N-S 24-332-7470   (SL)
AUTO MSHOP
4535 Av Thibault Bureau 1, Saint-Hubert, QC, J3Y 7N1
(579) 720-7747
Emp Here 25   *Sales* 12,451,950
SIC 5511 New and used car dealers
Sostas Wong

D-U-N-S 24-226-2082   (BR)
BELL TECHNICAL SOLUTIONS INC
BELL SOLUTIONS TECHNIQUES

(*Suby of* BCE INC)
6396 Grande Allee, Saint-Hubert, QC, J3Y 8J8
(450) 678-0100
Emp Here 150
SIC 4899 Communication services, nec
Yvon Hebert

D-U-N-S 25-391-4238   (HQ)
CAISSE DESJARDINS DE SAINT-HUBERT
CENTRE DE SERVICE BERNARD-RACICOT
2400 Boul Gaetan-Boucher, Saint-Hubert, QC, J3Y 5B7
(450) 443-0047
Emp Here 40   *Sales* 11,608,728
SIC 6062 State credit unions
Stephane Boismenu
Michel Adam
Vanessa Sylvestre
Caroline Fortier
Jean-Pierre Proulx
Francois Beauchemin
Alexandre Bouffard
Nicole Breton
Julie Gosselin
Louisette Trahan

D-U-N-S 20-860-8406   (HQ)
CARGAIR LTEE
6100 Rte De L'Aeroport, Saint-Hubert, QC, J3Y 8Y9
(450) 656-4783
Emp Here 50   *Sales* 14,683,790
SIC 4522 Air transportation, nonscheduled
Josee Prud'homme
Louis-Martin Roy
O. Guy Prud'homme

D-U-N-S 20-231-4860   (BR)
CARGILL LIMITED
CARGILL ANIMAL NUTRITION DIV
(*Suby of* CARGILL, INCORPORATED)
5928 Boul Cousineau Bureau 300, Saint-Hubert, QC, J3Y 7R9
(450) 676-8607
Emp Here 200
SIC 5191 Farm supplies
Charles Lateinte

D-U-N-S 24-527-9294   (SL)
CENTRE ACCEUIL HENRIETTE CERE
6435 Ch De Chambly, Saint-Hubert, QC, J3Y 3R6
(450) 678-3291
Emp Here 100   *Sales* 5,924,700
SIC 8361 Residential care
Gisele Lacoste

D-U-N-S 25-145-2835   (HQ)
CENTRE MONTEREGIEN DE READAPTATION
5300 Ch De Chambly, Saint-Hubert, QC, J3Y 3N7
(450) 676-7447
Emp Here 200   *Sales* 30,098,000
SIC 7991 Physical fitness facilities
Francois Blais

D-U-N-S 25-737-7465   (SL)
CERTEX-CENTRE DE RECUPERATION ET DE RECYCLAGE DU TEXTILE INC
CERTEX-20-ANS
7500 Grande Allee, Saint-Hubert, QC, J3Y 0V7
(450) 926-1733
Emp Here 140   *Sales* 44,647,400
SIC 4953 Refuse systems
Jean-Sylvain Pelletier

D-U-N-S 24-710-6834   (HQ)
COLISPRO INC
NATIONEX
3505 Boul Losch, Saint-Hubert, QC, J3Y 5T7
(450) 445-7171
Emp Here 100   *Sales* 100,336,200
SIC 7389 Business services, nec
Catryn Pinard
Raymond Fortier

Jocelyne Pinard

D-U-N-S 20-712-2735   (BR)
COMMISSION SCOLAIRE MARIE-VICTORIN
ECOLE SECONDAIRE ANDRE LAUREN-DEAU
(*Suby of* COMMISSION SCOLAIRE MARIE-VICTORIN)
7450 Boul Cousineau, Saint-Hubert, QC, J3Y 3L4
(450) 678-2080
Emp Here 200
SIC 8211 Elementary and secondary schools
Marie Taillon

D-U-N-S 25-233-1111   (BR)
COMMISSION SCOLAIRE MARIE-VICTORIN
ECOLE D'IBERVILLE
(*Suby of* COMMISSION SCOLAIRE MARIE-VICTORIN)
5095 Rue Aurele, Saint-Hubert, QC, J3Y 2E6
(450) 678-0145
Emp Here 110
SIC 8211 Elementary and secondary schools
Pierre Vocino

D-U-N-S 20-602-1370   (SL)
COMPAGNIE D'ACIER ARCHIDROME DU CANADA LTEE, LA
3100 Boul Losch, Saint-Hubert, QC, J3Y 3V8
(450) 678-4444
Emp Here 15   *Sales* 15,005,085
SIC 5051 Metals service centers and offices
Rolande Ouellette

D-U-N-S 24-964-6212   (SL)
COMPOUNDS FELIX INC, LES
3455 Rue Richelieu, Saint-Hubert, QC, J3Y 7P9
(450) 443-6888
Emp Here 50   *Sales* 16,346,148
SIC 2672 Paper; coated and laminated, nec
Pierre Giguere
Jean Giguere
Marie Audet Giguere

D-U-N-S 25-284-4519   (BR)
COSTCO WHOLESALE CANADA LTD
COSTCO
(*Suby of* COSTCO WHOLESALE CORPORATION)
5025 Boul Cousineau, Saint-Hubert, QC, J3Y 3K7
(450) 443-3618
Emp Here 200
SIC 5099 Durable goods, nec
Richard Stamand

D-U-N-S 24-740-4551   (SL)
DISTRIBUTION CLUB TISSUS (1994) INC
TEXLIMA
(*Suby of* GESTION TEXLIMA INC)
1651 Boul Des Promenades Bureau 676, Saint-Hubert, QC, J3Y 5K2
(450) 462-1717
Emp Here 60   *Sales* 14,659,680
SIC 5949 Sewing, needlework, and piece goods
Mario Petit
Linda Guerin

D-U-N-S 20-927-7466   (SL)
DUCLOS LONGUEUIL CHRYSLER DODGE JEEP RAM INC
AUTOMOBILES DUCLOS LONGUEUIL
(*Suby of* GROUPE MONARD LTEE, LE)
5055 Boul Cousineau, Saint-Hubert, QC, J3Y 3K7
(450) 656-4110
Emp Here 70   *Sales* 44,049,600
SIC 5511 New and used car dealers
Marcel Duclos
Louis-Philippe Duclos

D-U-N-S 20-633-8394   (HQ)
ECOLE DE CONDUITE TECNIC RIVE SUD

INC
3285 Montee Saint-Hubert, Saint-Hubert, QC, J3Y 4J4
(450) 443-4104
Emp Here 8   *Sales* 12,012,900
SIC 8299 Schools and educational services, nec
Yves Aube
Bernard Aube
Roland Aube

D-U-N-S 25-275-0828   (SL)
ENTREPRISE CLAUDE CHAGNON INC
3500 Boul Sir-Wilfrid-Laurier, Saint-Hubert, QC, J3Y 6T1
(450) 321-2446
Emp Here 49   *Sales* 10,788,232
SIC 1794 Excavation work

D-U-N-S 20-887-7761   (HQ)
ENTREPRISES CLAUDE CHAGNON INC, LES
(*Suby of* 9051-4076 QUEBEC INC)
3500 Boul Sir-Wilfrid-Laurier, Saint-Hubert, QC, J3Y 6T1
(450) 321-2446
Sales 12,044,200
SIC 1629 Heavy construction, nec
Jean Chagnon
Michael Richard
Michael Richard

D-U-N-S 24-174-0380   (HQ)
ESCOPHAR INC
PHARMACIE JEAN COUTU
5245 Boul Cousineau Bureau 149, Saint-Hubert, QC, J3Y 6J8
(450) 462-2200
Emp Here 30   *Sales* 10,118,160
SIC 5912 Drug stores and proprietary stores
Andre St-Onge
Ghislaine Vidal St-Onge

D-U-N-S 25-380-7192   (SL)
EXCEL CLIMATISATION INC
PLOMBERIE C.A. BOUCLIN
4915 Boul Sir-Wilfrid-Laurier Bureau 1, Saint-Hubert, QC, J3Y 3X5
(450) 676-1944
Emp Here 100   *Sales* 23,306,500
SIC 1711 Plumbing, heating, air-conditioning
Francois Lanthier

D-U-N-S 20-690-1568   (SL)
GALA SYSTEMES INC
3185 1re Rue, Saint-Hubert, QC, J3Y 8Y6
(450) 678-7226
Emp Here 80   *Sales* 15,366,800
SIC 3423 Hand and edge tools, nec
Philippe Laforest

D-U-N-S 24-736-4198   (SL)
GESTION S. BISAILLON INC
4645 Ch De Chambly, Saint-Hubert, QC, J3Y 3M9
(450) 462-2828
Emp Here 80   *Sales* 24,903,900
SIC 5511 New and used car dealers
Sebastien Bisaillon

D-U-N-S 24-826-3316   (HQ)
GROUPE VARITRON INC
VARITRON
4811 Ch De La Savane, Saint-Hubert, QC, J3Y 9G1
(450) 926-1778
Emp Here 30   *Sales* 87,037,050
SIC 5065 Electronic parts and equipment, nec
Michel Farley
John Vincent
Denis Chabot
Ramon Galvan

D-U-N-S 24-811-9422   (SL)
KOPEL INC
3360 2e Rue, Saint-Hubert, QC, J3Y 8Y7
(514) 398-9595
Emp Here 60   *Sales* 26,830,440

SIC 5065 Electronic parts and equipment, nec
Christian Gauthier
Jean-Pierre Biron
Andre Globensky
Bernard Nolet

D-U-N-S 24-175-4217   (SL)
LABORATOIRES CONFAB INC
(*Suby of* RENAISSANCE ACQUISITION HOLDINGS, LLC)
4355 Boul Sir-Wilfrid-Laurier, Saint-Hubert, QC, J3Y 3X3
(450) 443-6666
Emp Here 400   *Sales* 132,637,600
SIC 2834 Pharmaceutical preparations
David J Koo
Carlyn Solomon

D-U-N-S 25-394-0472   (SL)
LABORATOIRES KABS INC
KABS PHARMACEUTICAL SERVICES
4500 Rue De Tonnancour, Saint-Hubert, QC, J3Y 9G2
(450) 656-4404
Emp Here 95   *Sales* 17,139,425
SIC 8731 Commercial physical research
Jean-Simon Blais
Gerard Akinocho

D-U-N-S 20-998-0010   (HQ)
LOCATION D'OUTILS BROSSARD INC
LOU-TEC
3905 Montee Saint-Hubert, Saint-Hubert, QC, J3Y 4K2
(450) 678-3385
Emp Here 10   *Sales* 33,314,800
SIC 7359 Equipment rental and leasing, nec
Jean-Claude Hetu
Christian Hetu
Alain Hetu

D-U-N-S 25-841-0166   (BR)
MARCHE BELLEMARE INC
(*Suby of* MARCHE BELLEMARE INC)
5350 Grande Allee Bureau 1353, Saint-Hubert, QC, J3Y 1A3
(450) 676-0220
Emp Here 90
SIC 5411 Grocery stores
Robert Bellemare

D-U-N-S 25-894-5443   (SL)
MARCHE DUBREUIL VEILLETTE INC
IGA
6250 Boul Cousineau Bureau 100, Saint-Hubert, QC, J3Y 8X9
(450) 462-4420
Emp Here 60   *Sales* 17,608,620
SIC 5411 Grocery stores
Daniel Veillette
Chantal Dubreuil

D-U-N-S 25-080-2352   (SL)
MAX AVIATION INC
CARGAIR
6100 Rte De L'Aeroport, Saint-Hubert, QC, J3Y 8Y9
(450) 462-8511
Emp Here 50   *Sales* 16,237,700
SIC 4512 Air transportation, scheduled
Josee Prud'homme

D-U-N-S 24-860-4725   (HQ)
METROBEC INC
ACIER METROPOLITAN
(*Suby of* 102492 CANADA LTEE)
5055 Rue Ramsay, Saint-Hubert, QC, J3Y 2S3
(450) 656-6666
Emp Here 110   *Sales* 41,458,300
SIC 4953 Refuse systems
Richard Leibov
Mark Leibov

D-U-N-S 24-106-9384   (SL)
MICHEL ST-ARNEAULT INC
4605 Av Thibault, Saint-Hubert, QC, J3Y 3S8

(450) 445-0550
Emp Here 80   *Sales* 27,655,200
SIC 2037 Frozen fruits and vegetables
Michel St-Arneault
Remy St-Arneault

D-U-N-S 24-325-3635   (SL)
MICRO-CLAIR INTERNATIONAL INC
3050 2e Rue, Saint-Hubert, QC, J3Y 8Y7
(438) 796-5712
Emp Here 41   *Sales* 11,343,060
SIC 2842 Polishes and sanitation goods
Leila Fakhouri

D-U-N-S 25-543-6602   (HQ)
MIRAZED INC
3715 Boul Losch, Saint-Hubert, QC, J3Y 5T7
(450) 656-6320
Sales 16,402,700
SIC 2759 Commercial printing, nec
Claude St-Martin

D-U-N-S 24-322-1822   (HQ)
NATIONEX INC
(*Suby of* COLISPRO INC)
3505 Boul Losch, Saint-Hubert, QC, J3Y 5T7
(450) 445-7171
Emp Here 10   *Sales* 23,359,388
SIC 7389 Business services, nec
Catryn Pinard

D-U-N-S 24-589-2997   (HQ)
NAUTILUS PLUS INC
KINEQUIP
3550 1re Rue, Saint-Hubert, QC, J3Y 8Y5
(514) 666-5814
Emp Here 50   *Sales* 156,006,450
SIC 5941 Sporting goods and bicycle shops
Richard Blais
Jacques Foisy

D-U-N-S 24-589-7251   (SL)
OLIVIER, JACQUES FORD INC
OLIVIER FORD
4405 Ch De Chambly, Saint-Hubert, QC, J3Y 3M7
(450) 445-3673
Emp Here 70   *Sales* 44,049,600
SIC 5511 New and used car dealers
Jacques Jr Olivier

D-U-N-S 20-210-5086   (SL)
OMNIPLAST INC
5350 Rue Ramsay, Saint-Hubert, QC, J3Y 2S4
(450) 656-9272
Emp Here 90   *Sales* 17,529,120
SIC 2673 Bags: plastic, laminated, and coated
Marc Robitaille
Eric Robitaille
Elie Nawar

D-U-N-S 24-489-4747   (SL)
PIECES D'AUTO SUPER INC
AUTO PARTS PLUS
7803 Ch De Chambly, Saint-Hubert, QC, J3Y 5K2
(450) 676-1850
Emp Here 28   *Sales* 13,946,184
SIC 5531 Auto and home supply stores
Andre Gamelin

D-U-N-S 24-710-2072   (HQ)
RE/MAX PRIVILEGE INC
5920 Boul Cousineau, Saint-Hubert, QC, J3Y 7R9
(450) 678-3150
Sales 23,038,895
SIC 6531 Real estate agents and managers
Serge Lacaille

D-U-N-S 20-712-3774   (BR)
RIVERSIDE SCHOOL BOARD
ECOLE SECONDAIRE MACDONALD-CARTIER, L'
7445 Ch De Chambly, Saint-Hubert, QC, J3Y 3S3

(450) 678-1070
Emp Here 100
SIC 8211 Elementary and secondary schools
Lyse Brodeur

D-U-N-S 20-375-3207   (SL)
ROGER BISSON INC
BISSON EXPERT
5450 Rue Ramsay, Saint-Hubert, QC, J3Y 2S4
(514) 990-2519
Emp Here 50   *Sales* 14,429,150
SIC 1522 Residential construction, nec
Raymond Bisson
Luc Blanchet
Alain Gagnon
Normand Grondin

D-U-N-S 24-334-7510   (BR)
RONA INC
RENO-DEPOT
(*Suby of* LOWE'S COMPANIES, INC.)
5035 Boul Cousineau, Saint-Hubert, QC, J3Y 3K7
(450) 656-4422
Emp Here 100
SIC 5211 Lumber and other building materials
Christian Drouin

D-U-N-S 25-672-9427   (SL)
ST-GERMAIN EGOUTS & AQUEDUCS INC
3800 Boul Sir-Wilfrid-Laurier, Saint-Hubert, QC, J3Y 6T1
(450) 671-6171
Emp Here 30   *Sales* 13,415,220
SIC 5032 Brick, stone, and related material
Daniel Berthiaume
Rene Berthiaume

D-U-N-S 20-562-0842   (SL)
STE-MARIE, CLAUDE SPORT INC
5925 Ch De Chambly, Saint-Hubert, QC, J3Y 3R4
(450) 678-4700
Emp Here 30   *Sales* 14,942,340
SIC 5571 Motorcycle dealers
Luc Marchand

D-U-N-S 24-799-5301   (HQ)
SUMMUM BEAUTE INTERNATIONAL INC
SUMMUM BEAUTE INTERNATIONAL (DISTRIBUTION)
(*Suby of* SOCIETE FINANCIERE GRENCO INC)
4400 Boul Kimber, Saint-Hubert, QC, J3Y 8L4
(450) 678-3231
Emp Here 45   *Sales* 55,267,250
SIC 5122 Drugs, proprietaries, and sundries
Paul-Emile Grenier
Jean-Yves Grenier
Stephan Grenier
Renaud Grenier
Diane Grenier

D-U-N-S 24-834-8013   (HQ)
TECHO-BLOC INC
PIERRES STONEDGE, LES
5255 Rue Albert-Millichamp, Saint-Hubert, QC, J3Y 8Z8
(877) 832-4625
Emp Here 90   *Sales* 63,922,500
SIC 3272 Concrete products, nec
Calogero Ciccarello
Nancy Larocca

D-U-N-S 24-346-8811   (SL)
TOITURES COUTURE & ASSOCIES INC
(*Suby of* COUTURE, LAURENT & ASSOCIES INC)
6565 Boul Maricourt, Saint-Hubert, QC, J3Y 1S8
(450) 678-2562
Emp Here 150   *Sales* 28,953,150
SIC 1761 Roofing, siding, and sheetMetal work
Laurent Couture
Maryse Couture
Pierre Bernard

Lionel Alladio
Andre Couture

D-U-N-S 20-201-4916   (HQ)
TUYAUX ET MATERIEL DE FONDATION LTEE
ACIERS DYMIN ALBERTA, LES
(*Suby of* PLACEMENTS MIKE DYM LTEE, LES)
5025 Rue Ramsay, Saint-Hubert, QC, J3Y 2S3
(450) 445-0050
Sales 11,179,350
SIC 5051 Metals service centers and offices
Jack Dym

Saint-Hubert, QC J3Z

D-U-N-S 24-386-2427   (BR)
AGROPUR COOPERATIVE
AGROPUR FINE CHEESE DIVISION
(*Suby of* AGROPUR COOPERATIVE)
4700 Rue Armand-Frappier, Saint-Hubert, QC, J3Z 1G5
(450) 443-5662
Emp Here 75
SIC 8741 Management services
Robert Goul

D-U-N-S 20-198-5504   (HQ)
AGROPUR COOPERATIVE
AGROPUR DIVISION NATREL
4600 Rue Armand-Frappier, Saint-Hubert, QC, J3Z 1G5
(450) 878-2333
Emp Here 150   *Sales* 4,572,975,989
SIC 5143 Dairy products, except dried or canned
Rene Moreau
Roger Massicotte
Jeannie Van Dyk
Lorraine Bedard
Michel Couture
Jean-Pierre Lacombe
Celine Delhaes
Valere Lieutenant
Alain Forget
Roger Beaulieu

D-U-N-S 24-958-6686   (HQ)
ALIMENTS ULTIMA INC
ALIMENTS ULTIMA FOODS & DESSIN
(*Suby of* AGROPUR COOPERATIVE)
4600 Rue Armand-Frappier, Saint-Hubert, QC, J3Z 1G5
(450) 651-3737
Emp Here 300   *Sales* 341,169,500
SIC 2026 Fluid milk
Roger Massicote
Alain Forget
Marie-France Veilleux
Robert Coallier

D-U-N-S 20-856-1514   (HQ)
AREO-FEU LTEE
CONSULTANTS ATHENA
5205 Rue J.-A.-Bombardier, Saint-Hubert, QC, J3Z 1G4
(450) 651-2240
Sales 16,625,910
SIC 5087 Service establishment equipment
Helene Picard
Josee Guillemette

D-U-N-S 24-852-5839   (HQ)
AXSUN INC
ADT
(*Suby of* STAVSTAN INC)
4900 Rue Armand-Frappier Bureau 450, Saint-Hubert, QC, J3Z 1G5
(450) 445-3003
Emp Here 85   *Sales* 60,020,280
SIC 4731 Freight transportation arrangement
Steve Ramescu

Francis Longpre
Bruce R Hague

D-U-N-S 25-149-8374   (SL)
CAPOL INC
COLAROME
5132 Rue J.-A.-Bombardier, Saint-Hubert, QC, J3Z 1H1
(450) 766-8707
Emp Here 17   *Sales* 14,204,809
SIC 5141 Groceries, general line
Marc Beaudoin
Marc Beaudoin
Robert G. Evans
Bernd Strack
Christian Hauk

D-U-N-S 25-098-1396   (SL)
CICAME ENERGIE INC
POLTEC
(*Suby of* SOC INDUST CONSTR APPAREI MATERIEL ELECT)
5400 Rue J.-A.-Bombardier, Saint-Hubert, QC, J3Z 1G8
(450) 679-7778
Emp Here 44   *Sales* 19,044,200
SIC 3643 Current-carrying wiring devices
Vincent Roy
Franck Willier
Pierre Lachaud

D-U-N-S 20-286-1261   (BR)
COMMISSION SCOLAIRE MARIE-VICTORIN
ECOLE DES MILLE-FLEURES
(*Suby of* COMMISSION SCOLAIRE MARIE-VICTORIN)
1600 Rue De Monaco, Saint-Hubert, QC, J3Z 1B7
(450) 462-3844
Emp Here 75
SIC 8211 Elementary and secondary schools
Christian Godin

D-U-N-S 24-859-0754   (SL)
ENGRENAGES POWER-LINK2 INC, LES
POWER LINK
5405 Rue J.-A.-Bombardier, Saint-Hubert, QC, J3Z 1K3
(450) 678-0588
Emp Here 24   *Sales* 11,400,624
SIC 5085 Industrial supplies
Michael Preziuso
Serge Cote
Modestino Preziuso
Gerald William Preziuso
Ginette Cote
Gerard John Preziuso
Gilles Faucher

D-U-N-S 25-308-3620   (SL)
ETIQUETTES PROFECTA INC
5050 Rue Armand-Frappier, Saint-Hubert, QC, J3Z 1G5
(450) 676-0000
Emp Here 75   *Sales* 17,507,625
SIC 2672 Paper; coated and laminated, nec
Pierre Roberge

D-U-N-S 24-424-8766   (BR)
FEDERAL EXPRESS CANADA CORPORATION
FEDEX SHIP CENTRE
(*Suby of* FEDEX CORPORATION)
5005 Rue J.-A.-Bombardier Bureau A, Saint-Hubert, QC, J3Z 1G4
(800) 463-3339
Emp Here 100
SIC 7389 Business services, nec

D-U-N-S 24-242-3973   (HQ)
GROUPE FOODAROM INC
FOODRAM MC
5400 Rue Armand-Frappier, Saint-Hubert, QC, J3Z 1G5
(450) 443-3113
Sales 21,725,002

SIC 5149 Groceries and related products, nec
Pierre Miclette
John Murphy
Jean Leclerc

D-U-N-S 20-381-9271   (SL)
GROUPE LEXIS MEDIA INC
ACTION D'AUTRAY
7750 Boul Cousineau Bureau 103, Saint-Hubert, QC, J3Z 0C8
(514) 394-7156
Emp Here 130   *Sales* 21,323,510
SIC 2711 Newspapers
Frederic Couture
Elie Akoury

D-U-N-S 24-771-1856   (HQ)
LIBERTE NATURAL FOODS INC
(*Suby of* YOPLAIT LIBERTE CANADA CIE)
5000 Rue J.-A.-Bombardier, Saint-Hubert, QC, J3Z 1H1
(450) 926-5222
Emp Here 115   *Sales* 44,021,550
SIC 5499 Miscellaneous food stores
Paul Roach

D-U-N-S 20-381-3779   (SL)
PRO INGREDIENTS INC
INGREDIENTS PROFESSIONNELS
7750 Boul Cousineau Bureau 402, Saint-Hubert, QC, J3Z 0C8
(450) 632-1199
Emp Here 8   *Sales* 11,959,815
SIC 5159 Farm-product raw materials, nec
Richard Gaudet

D-U-N-S 24-392-8483   (BR)
PRODUITS ALIMENTAIRES ANCO LTEE, LES
AGROPUR
(*Suby of* AGROPUR COOPERATIVE)
4700 Rue Armand-Frappier, Saint-Hubert, QC, J3Z 1G5
(450) 443-4838
Emp Here 110
SIC 5143 Dairy products, except dried or canned
Emile Cordeau

D-U-N-S 20-265-8555   (HQ)
PRODUITS DE PAPIER LAPACO LTEE, LES
(*Suby of* WELLSPRING CAPITAL MANAGEMENT LLC)
5200 Rue J.-A.-Bombardier, Saint-Hubert, QC, J3Z 1H1
(450) 632-5140
Emp Here 25   *Sales* 16,555,280
SIC 2679 Converted paper products, nec
Roderick Leyden
David Walkowski
Russell Snow

D-U-N-S 24-851-7166   (HQ)
SERVICES RICOVA INC
SERVICE DE RECYCLAGE GW, LES
(*Suby of* GROUPE RICOVA INC)
5000 Rue Armand-Frappier, Saint-Hubert, QC, J3Z 1G5
(450) 466-6688
Sales 12,227,616
SIC 4953 Refuse systems
Dominic Colubriale

D-U-N-S 20-697-0720   (SL)
SYSTEMS VIC INC
EQUIPEMENT VICTORIA
5200 Rue Armand-Frappier, Saint-Hubert, QC, J3Z 1G5
(450) 926-3164
Emp Here 30   *Sales* 13,415,220
SIC 5075 Warm air heating and air conditioning
Nizar Barrou
Helene Bouchard

D-U-N-S 24-871-6029   (SL)
THEVCO ELECTRONIQUE INC
5200 Rue Armand-Frappier, Saint-Hubert,

QC, J3Z 1G5
(450) 926-2777
Emp Here 150   *Sales* 34,093,350
SIC 3822 Environmental controls
Nizar Barrou
Helene Bouchard

D-U-N-S 20-416-8926   (HQ)
YOPLAIT LIBERTE CANADA CIE
A TASTE OF MONTREAL SINCE 1928
5000 Rue J.-A.-Bombardier, Saint-Hubert,
QC, J3Z 1H1
(450) 926-5222
Emp Here 175   *Sales* 121,358,865
SIC 2022 Cheese; natural and processed
Benjamin John Pearman
Charles Brent Robbins
Mark Beakhouse
Alice Lee
Olivier Faujour
S. Dale Storey

Saint-Hubert, QC J4T

D-U-N-S 24-958-6934   (HQ)
ADJUVANTS EUCLID CANADA INC
ENTREPRISE FLOWCRETE
(*Suby of* RPM INTERNATIONAL INC.)
2835 Grande Allee Bureau 300, Saint-Hubert,
QC, J4T 3K3
(450) 465-2233
Sales 27,022,765
SIC 5169 Chemicals and allied products, nec
Moorman Scott
Claude Bedard
Edward Bedard
David Reif

D-U-N-S 20-858-8236   (HQ)
BIJOUTERIE LAVIGUEUR LTEE
LAVIGUEUR
3981 Rue De Mont-Royal Bureau 100, Saint-
Hubert, QC, J4T 2H4
(450) 672-3233
Emp Here 12   *Sales* 28,097,720
SIC 5944 Jewelry stores
Jean-Louis Lavigueur
Charles Lavigueur

D-U-N-S 20-712-2743   (BR)
**COMMISSION SCOLAIRE MARIE-
VICTORIN**
ECOLE MONSEIGNEUR PARENT
(*Suby of* COMMISSION SCOLAIRE MARIE-
VICTORIN)
3875 Grande Allee, Saint-Hubert, QC, J4T
2V8
(450) 676-0261
Emp Here 228
SIC 8211 Elementary and secondary schools
Gerard Tricoche

D-U-N-S 25-233-1277   (BR)
**COMMISSION SCOLAIRE MARIE-
VICTORIN**
ECOLE ST JOSEPH
(*Suby of* COMMISSION SCOLAIRE MARIE-
VICTORIN)
3855 Grande Allee, Saint-Hubert, QC, J4T
2V8
(450) 678-2781
Emp Here 201
SIC 8211 Elementary and secondary schools
Helene Trudeau

D-U-N-S 25-211-1174   (HQ)
MOMENTUM DISTRIBUTION INC
F3 DISTRIBUTION
(*Suby of* 9045-2582 QUEBEC INC)
2045 Rue Francis Bureau 200, Saint-Hubert,
QC, J4T 0A6
(450) 466-5115
Emp Here 35   *Sales* 41,718,000
SIC 5091 Sporting and recreation goods

Claude Roy
Claude Penneton
Normand Chartrand
Claude Beaulieu
Bertin Castonguay
Louis Fortier

D-U-N-S 20-996-5297   (HQ)
REFPLUS INC
(*Suby of* 9261-6614 QUEBEC INC)
2777 Grande Allee, Saint-Hubert, QC, J4T
2R4
(450) 641-2665
Emp Here 150   *Sales* 47,749,090
SIC 3585 Refrigeration and heating equip-
ment
Mathieu Cardinal
Francois Fauteux
Gilles Cyr
Michel Lecompte
Eric D'anjou
Ness Lakdawala
Aurele Cardinal

D-U-N-S 25-157-6260   (BR)
VIGI SANTE LTEE
CHSLD VIGI MONTEREGIE
2042 Boul Marie, Saint-Hubert, QC, J4T 2B4
(450) 671-5596
Emp Here 120
SIC 8051 Skilled nursing care facilities
Sylvie Aubry

Saint-Hugues, QC J0H

D-U-N-S 20-057-9212   (SL)
ISOPORC INC
652 Rte Du Moulin, Saint-Hugues, QC, J0H
1N0
(450) 794-2555
Emp Here 50   *Sales* 19,275,950
SIC 0213 Hogs
Mario Cote
Bernard Paquette
Micheline Rondeau

Saint-Hyacinthe, QC J2R

D-U-N-S 20-309-4800   (SL)
BUNGE GRAIN DU CANADA INC
CAM-RAIL
6120 Rue Des Seigneurs E, Saint-Hyacinthe,
QC, J2R 1Z9

Emp Here 26   *Sales* 38,159,992
SIC 5153 Grain and field beans
Todd A Bastean
Larry Clarke
James Marks
Soren Schroder

D-U-N-S 25-258-7852   (SL)
CENTRE DU CAMION STE-MARIE INC, LE
5400 Rue Martineau, Saint-Hyacinthe, QC,
J2R 1T8
(450) 796-4004
Emp Here 44   *Sales* 21,915,432
SIC 5511 New and used car dealers
Marc Tardif

D-U-N-S 20-257-1915   (HQ)
COMAX, COOPERATIVE AGRICOLE
COOP COMAX, LA
4880 Rue Des Seigneurs E, Saint-Hyacinthe,
QC, J2R 1Z5
(450) 799-3211
Emp Here 125   *Sales* 121,846,250
SIC 2048 Prepared feeds, nec
Michel Gauvin
Guy Crepeau
Martin Brodeur-Choquette

Laurent Bousquet
Alain Desautels
Guy Tessier
Patrice Gagnon
Benoit Chaput
Francois Jodoin
Samuel Benoit

D-U-N-S 20-566-2018   (BR)
COOP FEDEREE, LA
OLYMEL FLAMINGO, DIV OF
(*Suby of* COOP FEDEREE, LA)
3250 Boul Laurier E, Saint-Hyacinthe, QC,
J2R 2B6
(450) 773-6661
Emp Here 500
SIC 5144 Poultry and poultry products
Michel Blouin

D-U-N-S 24-108-9879   (SL)
EMBALLAGES MASKA INC
7450 Av Pion, Saint-Hyacinthe, QC, J2R 1R9
(450) 796-2040
Emp Here 42   *Sales* 21,153,636
SIC 5113 Industrial and personal service pa-
per
Patrick L. Larmon
John A. Howlett
Daniel J. Lett

D-U-N-S 24-116-5120   (SL)
**ENTREPRISES ELECTRIQUES A. & R.
LTEE, LES**
5655 Rue Lamoureux, Saint-Hyacinthe, QC,
J2R 1S3
(450) 253-8690
Emp Here 50   *Sales* 12,044,200
SIC 1623 Water, sewer, and utility lines
Mathieu St-Onge
David Brodeur
Ginette Touchette
Normand St-Onge

D-U-N-S 25-146-2453   (SL)
**ENTREPRISES PIERRE L BOULOS INC,
LES**
CANADIAN TIRE
5930 Rue Martineau, Saint-Hyacinthe, QC,
J2R 2H6
(450) 796-4226
Emp Here 86   *Sales* 31,322,490
SIC 5014 Tires and tubes
Pierre L Boulos

D-U-N-S 20-257-1741   (HQ)
GERMAIN LARIVIERE (1970) LTEE
ELECTRO-SOLDE
(*Suby of* GERMAIN LARIVIERE INC)
4370 Boul Laurier E, Saint-Hyacinthe, QC,
J2R 2C1
(450) 799-5522
Emp Here 80   *Sales* 46,480,600
SIC 5712 Furniture stores
Jean Lariviere
David Lariviere

D-U-N-S 24-313-9719   (HQ)
GERMAIN LARIVIERE INC
4370 Boul Laurier E, Saint-Hyacinthe, QC,
J2R 2C1
(450) 799-5522
Emp Here 25   *Sales* 34,860,450
SIC 5722 Household appliance stores
Jean Lariviere
David Lariviere

D-U-N-S 24-763-1542   (HQ)
GESTION M A S INC
2890 Boul Laurier E, Saint-Hyacinthe, QC,
J2R 1P8
(450) 774-7511
Emp Here 1   *Sales* 25,694,900
SIC 6712 Bank holding companies
Pierre Letendre

D-U-N-S 20-000-0750   (SL)
JEFO NUTRITION INC
CENTRE   INTERNATIONAL   DE

*RECHERCHE EN ALIMENTATION ANIMALE
DE ST-HYACINTHE*
4900 Rue Martineau, Saint-Hyacinthe, QC,
J2R 1K3
(450) 799-4454
Emp Here 26   *Sales* 21,725,002
SIC 5141 Groceries, general line
Jean Fontaine

D-U-N-S 24-402-7926   (SL)
JEFO NUTRITION INC
*CENTRE   INTERNATIONAL   DE
RECHERCHE EN ALIMENTATION ANIMALE
DE ST-HYACINTHE*
5020 Av Jefo, Saint-Hyacinthe, QC, J2R 2E7
(450) 799-2000
Emp Here 95   *Sales* 70,539,400
SIC 5191 Farm supplies
Jean Fontaine
Guy Talbot
Gilles Beaupre

D-U-N-S 24-402-7769   (SL)
LABORATOIRES G.M.F. (1983) INC
7485 Av Duplessis, Saint-Hyacinthe, QC, J2R
1S5
(450) 796-4772
Emp Here 10   *Sales* 11,053,450
SIC 5122 Drugs, proprietaries, and sundries
Maurice Bissette
Ghislain Benoit
Yves Sarrazin

D-U-N-S 24-015-8969   (HQ)
RESEAU ENCANS QUEBEC (S.E.C)
5110 Rue Martineau, Saint-Hyacinthe, QC,
J2R 1T9
(450) 796-2612
Sales 22,460,950
SIC 7389 Business services, nec
Sonia Roy

D-U-N-S 20-252-2868   (SL)
RESSORTS MASKA INC
(*Suby of* GESTION M A S INC)
2890 Boul Laurier E, Saint-Hyacinthe, QC,
J2R 1P8
(450) 774-7511
Emp Here 40   *Sales* 11,332,000
SIC 7539 Automotive repair shops, nec
Pierre Letendre
Samuel Letendre
Nicolas Letendre
Sebastien Letendre

D-U-N-S 20-505-0024   (SL)
SOUDURE M. COUTURE & FILS INC
SOUDURE COUTURE
8020 Av Duplessis, Saint-Hyacinthe, QC, J2R
1S6
(450) 796-1617
Emp Here 50   *Sales* 10,141,500
SIC 3446 Architectural Metalwork
Jean-Paul Couture
France Jodoin

D-U-N-S 25-846-0690   (HQ)
SYNAGRI S.E.C.
ENGRAIS FERTICO, LES
5175 Boul Laurier E, Saint-Hyacinthe, QC,
J2R 2B4
(450) 799-3225
Emp Here 30   *Sales* 34,393,840
SIC 3999 Manufacturing industries, nec
Jean-Claude Brulotte

D-U-N-S 20-355-5594   (BR)
TROUW NUTRITION CANADA INC
SHUR-GAIN
4780 Rue Martineau, Saint-Hyacinthe, QC,
J2R 1V1
(450) 799-5011
Emp Here 80
SIC 2048 Prepared feeds, nec
Jacques Leclerc

D-U-N-S 20-292-3629   (BR)
VEOLIA ES CANADA SERVICES INDUS-

TRIELS INC
(*Suby of* VEOLIA ENVIRONNEMENT)
7950 Av Pion, Saint-Hyacinthe, QC, J2R 1R9
(450) 796-6060
Emp Here 1,000
SIC 4953 Refuse systems

D-U-N-S 25-377-6009   (BR)
WAL-MART CANADA CORP
WALMART
(*Suby of* WALMART INC.)
5950 Rue Martineau, Saint-Hyacinthe, QC, J2R 2H6
(450) 796-4001
Emp Here 200
SIC 5311 Department stores
Sylvain Rhainds

Saint-Hyacinthe, QC J2S

D-U-N-S 20-266-8505   (SL)
3095-0497 QUEBEC INC
MARCHE DESSAULLES
1340 Boul Choquette, Saint-Hyacinthe, QC, J2S 6G1
(450) 778-5558
Emp Here 60   *Sales* 17,608,620
SIC 5411 Grocery stores
Jean Allaire
Gilles Allaire

D-U-N-S 25-410-6180   (SL)
3286509 CANADA INC
LES GALERIES NISSAN
450 Rue Daniel-Johnson E, Saint-Hyacinthe, QC, J2S 8W5
(450) 774-1679
Emp Here 30   *Sales* 14,942,340
SIC 5511 New and used car dealers
Daniel Beaucage

D-U-N-S 20-181-6530   (SL)
3652548 CANADA INC
ST-HYACINTHE SUZUKI
3400 Av Cusson, Saint-Hyacinthe, QC, J2S 8N9
(450) 774-1332
Emp Here 25   *Sales* 12,451,950
SIC 5511 New and used car dealers
Michel Gagne
Marc Perras

D-U-N-S 20-558-7301   (HQ)
4223373 CANADA INC
ACCESSOIRES DE MOTO ADM
3003 Rue Picard, Saint-Hyacinthe, QC, J2S 1H2
(450) 252-4488
Emp Here 1   *Sales* 12,451,950
SIC 5571 Motorcycle dealers
Michel Matton
Karine Matton

D-U-N-S 24-103-1546   (SL)
9165-1588 QUEBEC INC
IGA
5445 Boul Laurier O, Saint-Hyacinthe, QC, J2S 3V6
(450) 773-0333
Emp Here 90   *Sales* 26,412,930
SIC 5411 Grocery stores
Guy Jodoin

D-U-N-S 20-356-5221   (SL)
9343-0114 QUEBEC INC
CENTRE DE CONGRES DE SAINT-HYACINTHE
1325 Rue Daniel-Johnson O, Saint-Hyacinthe, QC, J2S 8S4
(450) 252-7988
Emp Here 75   *Sales* 21,332,775
SIC 6512 Nonresidential building operators
Michel Douville

D-U-N-S 24-420-4744   (BR)

AGROPUR COOPERATIVE
AGROPUR, DIV FROMAGES FIN
(*Suby of* AGROPUR COOPERATIVE)
995 Rue Daniel-Johnson E, Saint-Hyacinthe, QC, J2S 7V6
(450) 773-6493
Emp Here 150
SIC 5143 Dairy products, except dried or canned
Sylvain Tourcotte

D-U-N-S 24-958-6470   (SL)
ALIMENTATION SOGESCO INC
I G A
(*Suby of* SOGESCO PLANNING INC)
3000 Boul Laframboise, Saint-Hyacinthe, QC, J2S 4Z4
(450) 773-7582
Emp Here 152   *Sales* 44,608,504
SIC 5411 Grocery stores
Dany Benoit

D-U-N-S 20-996-4402   (HQ)
ALIMENTS BCI INC, LES
4800 Av Pinard, Saint-Hyacinthe, QC, J2S 8E1
(888) 797-3210
Emp Here 15   *Sales* 58,767,300
SIC 2032 Canned specialties
Jean-Stephane Yansouni

D-U-N-S 24-347-3514   (HQ)
ALIMENTS PRINCE, S.E.C.
BACON AMERICA
2200 Av Pratte Bureau 400, Saint-Hyacinthe, QC, J2S 4B6
(450) 771-7060
Emp Here 343   *Sales* 170,584,750
SIC 2013 Sausages and other prepared meats
Sylvain Fournaise

D-U-N-S 25-837-6797   (SL)
ATELIERS TRANSITION INC, LES
1255 Rue Delorme Bureau 103, Saint-Hyacinthe, QC, J2S 2J3
(450) 771-2747
Emp Here 60   *Sales* 40,134,480
SIC 7389 Business services, nec
Michel Guevin
Serge Ouimet
Michel Morin

D-U-N-S 24-921-7407   (SL)
AUTOMOBILES F.M. INC
VOLKSWAGEN ST-HYACINTHE
5705 Av Trudeau, Saint-Hyacinthe, QC, J2S 1H5
(450) 773-4736
Emp Here 27   *Sales* 11,322,585
SIC 6712 Bank holding companies
Marie-Josee Fafard
Sylvie Fafard
Annie Fafard

D-U-N-S 25-874-1461   (SL)
AUTOMOBILES J. D. A. INC
ANGERS TOYOTA
3395 Boul Laframboise, Saint-Hyacinthe, QC, J2S 4Z7
(450) 774-9191
Emp Here 38   *Sales* 18,926,964
SIC 5511 New and used car dealers
Jacques Angers

D-U-N-S 20-014-3712   (SL)
AUTOS ECONOMIQUES CASAVANT INC, LES
HONDA CASAVANT
350 Rue Daniel-Johnson E, Saint-Hyacinthe, QC, J2S 8W5
(450) 774-1724
Emp Here 35   *Sales* 17,432,730
SIC 5511 New and used car dealers
Felix Lambert
Alexandre Lambert

D-U-N-S 24-901-9308   (SL)

BARIL FORD LINCOLN INC
6875 Boul Laurier O, Saint-Hyacinthe, QC, J2S 9A5
(514) 454-7070
Emp Here 50   *Sales* 24,903,900
SIC 5511 New and used car dealers
Michel Baril
Eric Dumouchel
Marie-Claude Baril

D-U-N-S 20-760-8753   (HQ)
BARRY CALLEBAUT CANADA INC
BOUCHEES D'AMOUR
2950 Rue Nelson, Saint-Hyacinthe, QC, J2S 1Y7
(450) 774-9131
Sales 243,692,500
SIC 2066 Chocolate and cocoa products
Peter Boone
Darko Suman
Etienne Blais
Remco J. Steenbergen

D-U-N-S 25-837-0493   (BR)
BEAUWARD SHOPPING CENTRES LTD
GALERIES ST HYACINTHE, LES
(*Suby of* BEAUWARD SHOPPING CENTRES LTD)
3200 Boul Laframboise Bureau 1009, Saint-Hyacinthe, QC, J2S 4Z5
(450) 773-8282
Emp Here 1,200
SIC 6512 Nonresidential building operators
Andre Brochu

D-U-N-S 24-085-0354   (SL)
BECTROL INC
4550 Av Beaudry, Saint-Hyacinthe, QC, J2S 8A5
(450) 774-1330
Emp Here 30   *Sales* 13,415,220
SIC 5063 Electrical apparatus and equipment
Sylvain Benoit
Stefan Benoit

D-U-N-S 20-125-3650   (SL)
BIENA INC
2955 Rue Cartier, Saint-Hyacinthe, QC, J2S 1L4
(450) 778-5505
Emp Here 75   *Sales* 25,926,750
SIC 2023 Dry, condensed and evaporated dairy products
Gulshan Arora
Monica Daga

D-U-N-S 25-392-1035   (SL)
BIO BISCUIT INC
5505 Av Trudeau Bureau 15, Saint-Hyacinthe, QC, J2S 1H5
(450) 778-1349
Emp Here 100   *Sales* 34,569,000
SIC 2047 Dog and cat food
Pierre Lemieux
David Gaucher
Royal Lemieux

D-U-N-S 20-381-2425   (SL)
BIO BISCUIT INC
5505 Av Trudeau Bureau 15, Saint-Hyacinthe, QC, J2S 1H5
(450) 778-1349
Emp Here 100   *Sales* 22,485,500
SIC 2047 Dog and cat food
Pierre Lemieux
David Gaucher
Royal Lemieux

D-U-N-S 24-684-7839   (SL)
BRASSEURS DU MONDE INC
PICOLEUR, LE
3755 Rue Picard Porte 2, Saint-Hyacinthe, QC, J2S 1H3
(450) 250-2611
Emp Here 26   *Sales* 15,285,816
SIC 5181 Beer and ale
Gilles Dube
Dominic Charbonneau

Christine Barre
Yvan Charbonneau
Daniel Choquette
Andre Cournoyer
Philippe Bonnet

D-U-N-S 20-251-9666   (SL)
BROUILLETTE AUTOMOBILE INC
2750 Rue Lafontaine, Saint-Hyacinthe, QC, J2S 2N6
(450) 773-8551
Emp Here 41   *Sales* 20,421,198
SIC 5511 New and used car dealers
Richard Chagnon

D-U-N-S 20-859-8607   (HQ)
C.D.M.V. INC
(*Suby of* INVESTISSEMENT QUEBEC)
2999 Boul Choquette, Saint-Hyacinthe, QC, J2S 6H5
(450) 771-2368
Emp Here 180   *Sales* 155,252,080
SIC 5047 Medical and hospital equipment
Lucia Pollice
Marc Paquet
Mario Vinet
Ernest Desrosiers
Lucie Henault
Sylvain Raymond
Caron Martin
Sylvie Pinsonnault
Lucie Chabot
Jean Gaudreault

D-U-N-S 20-363-6639   (HQ)
CAISSE DESJARDINS DE LA REGION DE SAINT-HYACINTHE
CENTRE DE SERVICES LA PRESENTATION
1697 Rue Girouard O, Saint-Hyacinthe, QC, J2S 2Z9
(450) 768-3030
Emp Here 50   *Sales* 15,156,100
SIC 6062 State credit unions
Serge Bosse
Mario Dussault
Luc Gravel
Celine Bernard
Jean-Paul Poirier
Genevieve Blain
Real Brodeur
Cynthia Brunelle
Marc-Antoine Gaucher

D-U-N-S 20-860-5501   (SL)
CANTINE LUCIE INC
5825 Av Desjardins, Saint-Hyacinthe, QC, J2S 1A4
(450) 774-8585
Emp Here 40   *Sales* 26,258,560
SIC 5963 Direct selling establishments
Jean-Guy Brillon

D-U-N-S 24-591-0450   (SL)
CARREFOUR DE LA VOITURE IMPORTEE INC
HYUNDAI CASAVANT
200 Rue Daniel-Johnson E, Saint-Hyacinthe, QC, J2S 8W5
(514) 856-7878
Emp Here 24   *Sales* 11,953,872
SIC 5511 New and used car dealers
Felix Lambert

D-U-N-S 20-271-0414   (SL)
CASAVANT FRERES S.E.C
900 Rue Girouard E, Saint-Hyacinthe, QC, J2S 2Y2
(450) 773-5001
Emp Here 50   *Sales* 10,941,200
SIC 3931 Musical instruments
Remi Dor

D-U-N-S 24-432-0560   (HQ)
CENTRE D'INSEMINATION ARTIFICIELLE DU QUEBEC (C.I.A.Q.) SOCIETE EN COMMANDITE
C.I.A.Q.
3450 Rue Sicotte, Saint-Hyacinthe, QC, J2S

2M2
(450) 774-1141
Sales 22,731,900
SIC 8093 Specialty outpatient clinics, nec
Martin Caron

D-U-N-S 20-649-4028   (SL)
COLLEGE ANTOINE-GIROUARD
700 Rue Girouard E, Saint-Hyacinthe, QC,
J2S 2Y2

Emp Here 90   *Sales* 10,137,240
SIC 8221 Colleges and universities
Doninique Lestage
Benoit Gingras
Andre Leblanc
Alain Rivard
Benoit Lucie
Bernard Nander
Sylvain Giard
Louis-Francois Langelier
Stephane Bourgeois
Claude Corbeil

D-U-N-S 24-326-5634   (SL)
**COLLEGE D'ENSEIGNEMENT GENERAL
ET PROFESSIONEL DE SAINT-HYACINTHE**
CEGEP DE SAINT-HYACINTHE
3000 Av Boulle, Saint-Hyacinthe, QC, J2S
1H9
(450) 773-6800
Emp Here 400   *Sales* 39,647,600
SIC 8222 Junior colleges
Emmanuel Montini

D-U-N-S 24-812-9132   (SL)
COLLEGE SAINT-MAURICE
630 Rue Girouard O, Saint-Hyacinthe, QC,
J2S 2Y3
(450) 773-7478
Emp Here 100   *Sales* 11,263,600
SIC 8221 Colleges and universities
Louise Cordeau
Edith Lavoie
Therese Doyon
Fernande Viens
Andre D'aragon
Luc Langelier
Jean-Pierre Jeannotte
Daniel Paradis

D-U-N-S 25-240-5675   (BR)
COMMISSION SCOLAIRE DE SAINT-HYACINTHE, LA
POLYVALENTE HYACINTHE-DELORME
(*Suby of* COMMISSION SCOLAIRE DE
SAINT-HYACINTHE, LA)
2700 Av T.-D.-Bouchard, Saint-Hyacinthe, QC,
J2S 7G2
(450) 773-8408
Emp Here 160
SIC 8211 Elementary and secondary schools
Nancy Prevereault

D-U-N-S 24-177-0999   (HQ)
COMMISSION SCOLAIRE DE SAINT-HYACINTHE, LA
2255 Av Sainte-Anne, Saint-Hyacinthe, QC,
J2S 5H7
(450) 773-8401
Emp Here 50   *Sales* 198,238,000
SIC 8211 Elementary and secondary schools
Richard Flibotte
France Martin
Yvan Gauthier

D-U-N-S 20-543-7403   (SL)
CONCORDE AUTOMOBILE (1990) LTEE
3003 Rue Picard, Saint-Hyacinthe, QC, J2S
1H2
(450) 774-5336
Emp Here 40   *Sales* 19,923,120
SIC 5511 New and used car dealers
Marc Charest
Guy Lincourt
Carole Morrisseau
Gabriel Bessette

D-U-N-S 25-099-1890   (SL)
**CONSTRUCTIONS DANIEL LOISELLE INC,
LES**
1350 Av St-Jacques, Saint-Hyacinthe, QC,
J2S 6M6

Emp Here 50   *Sales* 23,536,550
SIC 1542 Nonresidential construction, nec
Daniel Loiselle
Josee Loiselle

D-U-N-S 20-886-5196   (BR)
COOPSCO SAINT-HYACINTHE
INSTITUT DE TECHNOLOGIE AGRO-ALIMENTAIRE
(*Suby of* COOPSCO SAINT-HYACINTHE)
3230 Rue Sicotte, Saint-Hyacinthe, QC, J2S
2M2
(450) 778-6504
Emp Here 200
SIC 8222 Junior colleges
Dominique Viaud

D-U-N-S 20-050-4848   (HQ)
COOPSCO SAINT-HYACINTHE
3000 Av Boulle, Saint-Hyacinthe, QC, J2S
1H9
(450) 774-2727
Emp Here 26   *Sales* 11,517,000
SIC 5734 Computer and software stores
Louis Samson
Paul Gauthier
Genevieve Despars
Frederic Roby
Alexandre St-Onge
Annie Prevost

D-U-N-S 20-009-4907   (BR)
**CSSS RICHELIEU-YAMASKA CH DE LA
MRC D'ACTON**
CENTRE D'EBERGEMENT ANDREE PER-RAULT
(*Suby of* CSSS RICHELIEU-YAMASKA CH
DE LA MRC D'ACTON)
1955 Av Pratte, Saint-Hyacinthe, QC, J2S
7W5
(450) 771-4536
Emp Here 95
SIC 7021 Rooming and boarding houses
Louise Laliberte

D-U-N-S 20-252-0078   (HQ)
DBC COMMUNICATIONS INC
COURRIER DE ST-HYACINTHE
655 Av Sainte-Anne, Saint-Hyacinthe, QC,
J2S 5G4
(450) 773-3190
Emp Here 55   *Sales* 16,631,820
SIC 4899 Communication services, nec
Benoit Chartier

D-U-N-S 24-346-5569   (BR)
DELTA HOTELS NO. 12 LIMITED PARTNER-SHIP
HOTEL DES SEIGNEURS
1200 Rue Johnson O, Saint-Hyacinthe, QC,
J2S 7K7

Emp Here 200
SIC 7011 Hotels and motels

D-U-N-S 20-294-8431   (BR)
DESSERCOM INC
AMBULANCES SAINT HYACINTHE
592 Av Sainte-Marie, Saint-Hyacinthe, QC,
J2S 4R5
(450) 773-5223
Emp Here 100
SIC 4119 Local passenger transportation, nec
Lyne Dubois

D-U-N-S 25-240-3084   (SL)
**ECOLE SECONDAIRE SAINT-JOSEPH DE
ST-HYACINTHE**
2875 Av Bourdages N, Saint-Hyacinthe, QC,
J2S 5S3
(450) 774-7087
Emp Here 100   *Sales* 9,282,600

SIC 8211 Elementary and secondary schools
Robert Blanchette
Monique Mathieu
Jean-Carol Fournier
Lise Berger
Louisette Guertin
Lise Flibotte
Andre Dufault
Pierre Duclos
Robertine Roy
Herve Gagnon

D-U-N-S 20-123-0542   (HQ)
ENTREPOSAGE MASKA LTEE
2825 Boul Casavant O, Saint-Hyacinthe, QC,
J2S 7Y4
(450) 773-9615
Emp Here 24   *Sales* 22,627,660
SIC 4225 General warehousing and storage
Alain Caron
Benoit Martel
Anne Roger

D-U-N-S 20-737-5143   (SL)
FEDERATION DE LA CSN-CONSTRUCTION
MONTEREGIE ST-HYACINTHE CSN- CON-STRUCTION
2000 Rue Girouard O Bureau 201, Saint-Hyacinthe, QC, J2S 3A6
(450) 261-8053
Emp Here 49   *Sales* 19,166,742
SIC 8631 Labor organizations
Pierre Brassard

D-U-N-S 25-501-7717   (SL)
GALENOVA INC
4555 Av Beaudry, Saint-Hyacinthe, QC, J2S
8W2
(450) 778-2837
Emp Here 50   *Sales* 55,267,250
SIC 5122 Drugs, proprietaries, and sundries
Jean-Philippe Gentes
Bertrand Bolduc

D-U-N-S 24-317-1985   (SL)
**GENTES ET BOLDUC PHARMACIENS
S.E.N.C.**
4555 Av Beaudry, Saint-Hyacinthe, QC, J2S
8W2
(450) 778-2837
Emp Here 50   *Sales* 12,647,700
SIC 5912 Drug stores and proprietary stores
Jean Philippe Gentes

D-U-N-S 25-445-3900   (SL)
GESTION DELOITTE S.E.C
850 Boul Casavant O, Saint-Hyacinthe, QC,
J2S 7S3
(450) 774-4000
Emp Here 49   *Sales* 11,657,149
SIC 8742 Management consulting services
Francois Lanoue

D-U-N-S 24-256-0407   (SL)
GESTION RESTO ST-HYACINTHE INC
ROTISSERIE ST-HUBERT
1315 Rue Daniel-Johnson O, Saint-Hyacinthe,
QC, J2S 8S4
(450) 774-7770
Emp Here 80   *Sales* 3,429,840
SIC 5812 Eating places
Bernard Labbe
Steve Deslauriers

D-U-N-S 24-085-8501   (SL)
GESTION THERRIEN COUTURE INC
1200 Rue Daniel-Johnson O Unite 7000,
Saint-Hyacinthe, QC, J2S 7K7
(450) 773-6326
Emp Here 50   *Sales* 14,164,650
SIC 8741 Management services
Normand Therrien
Jean-Luc Couture

D-U-N-S 20-017-8580   (SL)
GROUPE CHINOOK AVENTURE INC
SIROCCO COMMUNICATION
990 Av De L'H?Tel-De-Ville, Saint-Hyacinthe,

QC, J2S 5B2
(514) 773-1911
Emp Here 26   *Sales* 10,332,764
SIC 8699 Membership organizations, nec
Yan Loiselle-Blanchard

D-U-N-S 24-703-3504   (SL)
**GROUPE DESMARAIS PINSONNEAULT &
AVARD INC**
DPA ASSURANCES
3395 Rue Picard, Saint-Hyacinthe, QC, J2S
1H3
(450) 250-3321
Emp Here 50   *Sales* 28,996,200
SIC 6411 Insurance agents, brokers, and ser-vice
Yvon Pinsonneault
Jean-Philip Pinsonneault
Marc Ayotte

D-U-N-S 20-362-7021   (HQ)
GROUPE GOYETTE INC
(*Suby of* GESTION NIALA INC)
2825 Boul Casavant O, Saint-Hyacinthe, QC,
J2S 7Y4
(450) 773-9615
Emp Here 1   *Sales* 127,928,150
SIC 6712 Bank holding companies
Alain Caron

D-U-N-S 20-252-2850   (HQ)
GROUPE MASKA INC
BATTERIES ELECTRIQUES QUEBEC
(*Suby of* GESTION M. A. E. INC)
550 Av Vaudreuil, Saint-Hyacinthe, QC, J2S
4H2
(450) 372-1676
Emp Here 110   *Sales* 72,184,040
SIC 5084 Industrial machinery and equipment
Roger Letendre
Simon Letendre
Martin Letendre

D-U-N-S 24-800-0283   (HQ)
GROUPE NUTRI INC
MONKLAND EGG GRADING, DIV OF
6655 Rue Picard, Saint-Hyacinthe, QC, J2S
1H3
(514) 745-1045
Emp Here 50   *Sales* 136,176,040
SIC 5144 Poultry and poultry products
Michel Gauvin
Robert Desilets
Bruno Leclerc
Luc Morin
Gilles Bilodeau
Richard Decelles
Mathieu Poirier
Jean-Francois Allie
Serge Lefebvre

D-U-N-S 20-925-9290   (SL)
GROUPE VIF INC
PLASTIQUES VIF
(*Suby of* 10849715 CANADA INC)
4000 Boul Casavant O, Saint-Hyacinthe, QC.
J2S 9E3
(450) 774-6953
Emp Here 45   *Sales* 21,376,170
SIC 5085 Industrial supplies
Thierry Carriere

D-U-N-S 20-927-7805   (HQ)
HUMANIA ASSURANCE INC
1555 Rue Girouard O Bureau 201, Saint-Hyacinthe, QC, J2S 2Z6
(514) 866-6051
Sales 224,381,640
SIC 6311 Life insurance
Richard Gagnon
Jacques Desmeules
Michel Cote
Gaetan Couture
Jacques Martineau
Rene Deslane
Joanne Vezina
Johanne Cassis

Guylaine Leclerc

D-U-N-S 24-475-2820   (HQ)
IMMEUBLES GOYETTE INC, LES
ENTREPOSAGE MASKA DIVISION DE GROUPE GOYETTE
(*Suby of* GESTION NIALA INC)
2825 Boul Casavant O, Saint-Hyacinthe, QC, J2S 7Y4
(450) 773-9615
Emp Here 250   *Sales* 47,486,950
SIC 6512 Nonresidential building operators
Alain Caron

D-U-N-S 24-954-7092   (SL)
IMPRIMERIE DUMAINE INC
5350 Av Trudeau, Saint-Hyacinthe, QC, J2S 7Y8
(450) 774-3536
Emp Here 100   *Sales* 16,402,700
SIC 2752 Commercial printing, lithographic
Marc Dumaine
Mario Hainault

D-U-N-S 24-179-4700   (BR)
IMPRIMERIES TRANSCONTINENTAL INC
TRANSCONTINENTAL PRINTING INC
(*Suby of* TRANSCONTINENTAL INC)
2700 Boul Casavant O, Saint-Hyacinthe, QC, J2S 7S4
(450) 773-0289
Emp Here 260
SIC 2752 Commercial printing, lithographic
Jacques Meunier

D-U-N-S 20-176-5620   (HQ)
INDECK COMBUSTION CORPORATION
(*Suby of* INDECK POWER EQUIPMENT CO.)
4300 Av Beaudry, Saint-Hyacinthe, QC, J2S 8A5
(450) 774-5326
Emp Here 20   *Sales* 23,306,500
SIC 1711 Plumbing, heating, air-conditioning
Marsha Forsythe-Fournier
Thomas W Mcparlan
Steven Page

D-U-N-S 20-963-0284   (HQ)
LANGELIER ASSURANCES INC
2500 Boul Casavant O, Saint-Hyacinthe, QC, J2S 7R8
(514) 745-8435
Emp Here 20   *Sales* 33,922,400
SIC 6411 Insurance agents, brokers, and service
Luc Langelier
Louis-Francois Jr Langelier

D-U-N-S 24-044-8741   (BR)
LOBLAW COMPANIES LIMITED
LOBLAWS
(*Suby of* LOBLAW COMPANIES LIMITED)
2000 Boul Casavant O, Saint-Hyacinthe, QC, J2S 7K2
(450) 771-6601
Emp Here 150
SIC 5411 Grocery stores
Ernesto Perrrota

D-U-N-S 24-490-6988   (HQ)
LUSSIER PONTIAC BUICK G M C LTEE
3000 Rue Dessaulles, Saint-Hyacinthe, QC, J2S 2V8
(450) 778-1112
Sales 18,926,964
SIC 5511 New and used car dealers
Guy Lussier

D-U-N-S 20-000-5366   (BR)
METRO RICHELIEU INC
SUPER C ST HYACINTHE
(*Suby of* METRO INC)
3800 Av Cusson, Saint-Hyacinthe, QC, J2S 8V6
(450) 771-1651
Emp Here 90
SIC 5141 Groceries, general line
Philippe Belanger

D-U-N-S 20-331-4372   (SL)
NATUR+L XTD INC
NATUREL HPP
2905 Av Jose-Maria-Rosell, Saint-Hyacinthe, QC, J2S 0J9
(450) 250-4981
Emp Here 50   *Sales* 11,734,800
SIC 8731 Commercial physical research
Stephane Carrier
Philippe Bonnet

D-U-N-S 25-683-4847   (SL)
OLIGEL DISTRIBUTION INC
2775 Av Bourdages N, Saint-Hyacinthe, QC, J2S 5S3

Emp Here 23   *Sales* 19,218,271
SIC 5142 Packaged frozen goods
Jean-Pierre Savard
Andree Sansoucy-Savard

D-U-N-S 24-896-4322   (HQ)
OLYMEL S.E.C.
FLAMINGO
2200 Av Pratte Bureau 400, Saint-Hyacinthe, QC, J2S 4B6
(450) 771-0400
Emp Here 100   *Sales* 5,260,346,305
SIC 2011 Meat packing plants
Rejean Nadeau

D-U-N-S 25-105-4284   (BR)
OLYMEL S.E.C.
(*Suby of* OLYMEL S.E.C.)
1425 Av St-Jacques, Saint-Hyacinthe, QC, J2S 6M7
(450) 778-2211
Emp Here 450
SIC 7299 Miscellaneous personal service
Michele Oliver

D-U-N-S 20-248-8086   (HQ)
PAVAGES MASKA INC
USINE BEDFORD
3450 Boul Choquette, Saint-Hyacinthe, QC, J2S 8V9
(450) 773-2591
Emp Here 30   *Sales* 50,488,400
SIC 1611 Highway and street construction
Jean Chagnon
Nancy Gaudette
Michael Richard

D-U-N-S 20-278-9686   (SL)
PP DESLANDES INC
(*Suby of* GESTION REAL DESLANDES INC)
4775 Av Trudeau, Saint-Hyacinthe, QC, J2S 7W9
(450) 778-2426
Emp Here 50   *Sales* 10,891,450
SIC 1731 Electrical work
Real Deslandes
France Gonthier

D-U-N-S 25-978-2258   (SL)
PRODUITS FORESTIERS AMPRO INC
AMPRO
3025 Rue Cartier, Saint-Hyacinthe, QC, J2S 1L4
(450) 250-7888
Emp Here 51   *Sales* 22,805,874
SIC 5031 Lumber, plywood, and millwork
Alain Messier

D-U-N-S 25-542-7080   (SL)
PRODUITS NEPTUNE INC, LES
NEPTUNE INTERNATIONAL
6835 Rue Picard, Saint-Hyacinthe, QC, J2S 1H3
(450) 773-7058
Emp Here 230   *Sales* 55,943,130
SIC 3431 Metal sanitary ware
Jean Rochette

D-U-N-S 24-871-2622   (SL)
PRODUITS POUR ANIMAUX YAMAS INC
3175 Boul Choquette, Saint-Hyacinthe, QC, J2S 7Z8

(418) 771-4622
Emp Here 25   *Sales* 11,179,350
SIC 5033 Roofing, siding, and insulation
Michel Trottier

D-U-N-S 24-346-3119   (BR)
RESTAURANTS MAC-VIC INC, LES
MCDONALD' S
3005 Boul Laframboise, Saint-Hyacinthe, QC, J2S 4Z6
(450) 774-5955
Emp Here 100
SIC 5812 Eating places
Isabelle Desneir

D-U-N-S 24-440-5101   (BR)
RESTAURANTS MAC-VIC INC, LES
MC DONALDS
3200 Boul Laframboise, Saint-Hyacinthe, QC, J2S 4Z5
(450) 261-8880
Emp Here 80
SIC 5812 Eating places
Isabelle Besmair

D-U-N-S 24-392-4029   (BR)
SAINT-HYACINTHE, VILLE DE
SERVICE INCENDIE SAINT-HYACINTHE
(*Suby of* SAINT-HYACINTHE, VILLE DE)
935 Rue Dessaulles, Saint-Hyacinthe, QC, J2S 3C4
(450) 778-8550
Emp Here 80
SIC 7389 Business services, nec
Daniel Dubois

D-U-N-S 24-541-1368   (BR)
SAPUTO PRODUITS LAITIERS CANADA S.E.N.C.
SAPUTO SAINT-HYACINTHE
(*Suby of* SAPUTO PRODUITS LAITIERS CANADA S.E.N.C.)
1195 Rue Daniel-Johnson E Unite 117, Saint-Hyacinthe, QC, J2S 7Y6
(450) 773-1004
Emp Here 100
SIC 2023 Dry, condensed and evaporated dairy products
Jacques Bettez

D-U-N-S 24-430-9498   (SL)
SERRES PION, ROSAIRE & FILS INC, LES
8185 Grand Rang, Saint-Hyacinthe, QC, J2S 9A8
(450) 796-3193
Emp Here 100   *Sales* 26,230,900
SIC 0181 Ornamental nursery products
Dominic Pion
Caroline Pion

D-U-N-S 20-176-5588   (SL)
SOCIETE DE CHAUDIERES INDECK
(*Suby of* INDECK POWER EQUIPMENT CO.)
4300 Av Beaudry, Saint-Hyacinthe, QC, J2S 8A5
(450) 774-5326
Emp Here 80   *Sales* 15,366,800
SIC 3443 Fabricated plate work (boiler shop)
Andre Granger
Marsha Forsythe-Fournier
Gerald Forsythe

D-U-N-S 20-120-5858   (SL)
SPECIALITES M.B. INC
(*Suby of* 131638 CANADA INC)
5450 Av Trudeau, Saint-Hyacinthe, QC, J2S 7Y8
(450) 771-1415
Emp Here 50   *Sales* 17,284,500
SIC 2013 Sausages and other prepared meats
Michel Saint-Arneault

D-U-N-S 24-557-2057   (SL)
ST-HYACINTHE CHRYSLER JEEP DODGE INC
BROUILLETTE AUTOMOBILE
1155 Boul Choquette, Saint-Hyacinthe, QC, J2S 0C4

(450) 924-0568
Emp Here 26   *Sales* 12,950,028
SIC 5531 Auto and home supply stores
Richard Chagnon

D-U-N-S 24-859-9412   (SL)
STERINOVA INC
ENTREPRISES STERINOVA, LES
3005 Av Jose-Maria-Rosell, Saint-Hyacinthe, QC, J2S 0J9
(450) 252-2520
Emp Here 49   *Sales* 13,556,340
SIC 2834 Pharmaceutical preparations
Jean-Phillipe Gentes
Bertrand Bolduc
Alex Berube
Bruce Heusgel
Michael Pietsch
Rob Albert

D-U-N-S 24-101-1910   (HQ)
SUPRALIMENT S.E.C.
ALIMENTS DELIHAM
2200 Av Pratte Bureau 400, Saint-Hyacinthe, QC, J2S 4B6
(450) 771-0400
Emp Here 150   *Sales* 731,077,500
SIC 2011 Meat packing plants
Denis Richard

D-U-N-S 25-475-0904   (SL)
THERRIEN COUTURE AVOCATS S.E.N.C.R.L.
1200 Rue Daniel-Johnson O # 7000, Saint-Hyacinthe, QC, J2S 7K7
(450) 773-6326
Emp Here 100   *Sales* 11,088,200
SIC 8111 Legal services
Normand Therrien
Jean-Philippe Turgeon
Francois Montfils
Jean-Luc Couture

D-U-N-S 25-222-9778   (SL)
VIANDES LACROIX INC, LES
LACROIX MEATS
4120 Boul Casavant O, Saint-Hyacinthe, QC, J2S 8E3
(450) 778-0188
Emp Here 350   *Sales* 170,584,750
SIC 2011 Meat packing plants
Michel Lacroix
Maxime Lacroix

Saint-Hyacinthe, QC J2T

D-U-N-S 20-415-9750   (SL)
9026-4979 QUEBEC INC
IGA JODOIN, GUY
2260 Rue Saint-Charles, Saint-Hyacinthe, QC, J2T 1V5
(450) 774-4189
Emp Here 95   *Sales* 27,880,315
SIC 5411 Grocery stores
Guy Jodoin

D-U-N-S 24-945-2129   (HQ)
CABLES BEN-MOR INC, LES
BEN-MOR
1105 Rue Lemire, Saint-Hyacinthe, QC, J2T 1L8
(450) 778-0022
Sales 44,717,400
SIC 5051 Metals service centers and offices
Benoit Frappier
Lyne-Mireille Leduc
Richard Plante
Eric Rompre

D-U-N-S 24-933-4699   (SL)
COMPTOIR AGRICOLE DE ST-HYACINTHE
4420 Rue Saint-Pierre O, Saint-Hyacinthe, QC, J2T 5G8

Emp Here 25   *Sales* 11,875,650

▲ Public Company   ■ Public Company Family Member   **HQ** Headquarters   **BR** Branch   **SL** Single Location

SIC 5083 Farm and garden machinery
Patrice Gagnon

D-U-N-S 20-000-1407   (SL)
DISTRIBUTION LE PERCO INC
16535 Av Petit, Saint-Hyacinthe, QC, J2T 3J5
(450) 773-7146
Emp Here 50   Sales 32,823,200
SIC 5962 Merchandising machine operators
Patrick St-Onge
Barbara Bouchard

D-U-N-S 20-363-0074   (SL)
INVESTISSEURS 3 B INC
3B HOCKEY
15855 Av Hubert, Saint-Hyacinthe, QC, J2T 4C9
(450) 773-5258
Emp Here 150   Sales 10,415,920
SIC 2329 Men's and boy's clothing, nec
Steve Berard
Manon Bourget

D-U-N-S 25-298-7920   (HQ)
LAW-MAROT-MILPRO INC
LAW-MAROT
1150 Rue Brouillette, Saint-Hyacinthe, QC, J2T 2G8
(450) 771-6262
Sales 18,870,085
SIC 3535 Conveyors and conveying equipment
Yves Labelle
Rejean Lussier
Real Blackburn
Robin Bousque

D-U-N-S 24-431-4548   (SL)
ORGUES LETOURNEAU LTEE
16355 Av Savoie, Saint-Hyacinthe, QC, J2T 3N1
(450) 774-2698
Emp Here 65   Sales 15,106,195
SIC 5736 Musical instrument stores
Fernand Letourneau
Antonia Letourneau

D-U-N-S 20-882-3542   (SL)
PRODUITS CHIMIQUES G.H. LTEE
GHC
(Suby of LUXEMBOURG INVESTMENT COMPANY 149 SARL)
1550 Rue Brouillette, Saint-Hyacinthe, QC, J2T 2G8
(450) 774-9151
Emp Here 43   Sales 11,896,380
SIC 2816 Inorganic pigments
Andrew Kaveh Nikou
Shahram Haghighi
Janathan Sassoon

D-U-N-S 20-330-1866   (SL)
PRODUITS MICROZINC INC, LES
1375 Rue Brouillette, Saint-Hyacinthe, QC, J2T 2G7
(450) 774-9151
Emp Here 15   Sales 10,225,608
SIC 3339 Primary nonferrous Metals, nec
Philippe Bailet
Stephan Tabah

D-U-N-S 24-352-4691   (SL)
RIENDEAU, GAETAN INC
METRO
(Suby of ENTREPRISES GAETAN RIENDEAU INC, LES)
2030 Boul Laurier E, Saint-Hyacinthe, QC, J2T 1K7
(450) 774-2311
Emp Here 90   Sales 26,412,930
SIC 5411 Grocery stores
Gaetan Riendeau

D-U-N-S 24-394-3060   (SL)
SNOC INC
17200 Av Centrale, Saint-Hyacinthe, QC, J2T 4J7
(450) 774-5238
Emp Here 70   Sales 13,330,940

SIC 3648 Lighting equipment, nec
Richard Circe
Robert Bachand
Richard Morin

D-U-N-S 24-021-7133   (HQ)
SOEURS DE CHARITE DE SAINT-HYACINTHE, LES
MAISON STE-ANNE
16470 Av Bourdages S, Saint-Hyacinthe, QC, J2T 4J8
(450) 773-9785
Emp Here 140   Sales 14,993,712
SIC 8661 Religious organizations
Diane Beaudoin

D-U-N-S 25-258-3620   (BR)
SPORT MASKA INC
REEBOK-CCM
(Suby of SPORT MASKA INC)
15855 Av Hubert, Saint-Hyacinthe, QC, J2T 4C9
(450) 773-5258
Emp Here 160
SIC 2329 Men's and boy's clothing, nec
Mac O'cpoole

D-U-N-S 25-114-8599   (SL)
SYSTEMES DE DIFFUSION SPRAYLOGIK INC, LES
17420 Av Centrale, Saint-Hyacinthe, QC, J2T 3L7
(450) 778-1850
Emp Here 35   Sales 15,651,090
SIC 5047 Medical and hospital equipment
Richard Garon
Johanne Lacroix
Mark Garon
Michel Garon
Roger Garon
Therese Morin

Saint-Hyacinthe, QC J4T

D-U-N-S 20-216-8857   (SL)
CORPORATIF RENAUD INC
3445 Boul Laframboise, Saint-Hyacinthe, QC, J4T 2G1
(450) 462-9991
Emp Here 40   Sales 19,923,120
SIC 5521 Used car dealers
Michel Renaud

Saint-Isidore, QC G0S

D-U-N-S 20-251-4527   (HQ)
AGRI-MARCHE INC
236 Rue Sainte-Genevieve, Saint-Isidore, QC, G0S 2S0
(418) 882-5656
Sales 34,569,000
SIC 2041 Flour and other grain mill products
Patrice Brochu
Guylaine Brochu
Denis Guay
Jean-Pierre Brochu

D-U-N-S 24-915-3532   (SL)
BRIQUE & PAVE DONAT FORTIER
2036 Rang De La Riviere, Saint-Isidore, QC, G0S 2S0
(418) 882-5879
Emp Here 49   Sales 11,438,315
SIC 3241 Cement, hydraulic
Pierre Arseneau

D-U-N-S 20-640-3953   (SL)
MARCHE D'ANIMAUX DE L'EST
2020 Rang De La Riviere, Saint-Isidore, QC, G0S 2S0
(418) 882-6301
Emp Here 20   Sales 24,207,940

SIC 5154 Livestock
Edoardo Macciocia

D-U-N-S 24-419-7682   (HQ)
OUTILLEUR S.E.C., L'
OUTILLEUR AGRICOLE, L'
236 Rue Sainte-Genevieve, Saint-Isidore, QC, G0S 2S0
(418) 882-5656
Sales 13,382,600
SIC 5251 Hardware stores
Patrice Brochu

D-U-N-S 24-220-5701   (SL)
STEEGRAIN INC
103 Rue Sainte-Genevieve, Saint-Isidore, QC, G0S 2S0
(418) 882-3731
Emp Here 12   Sales 14,524,764
SIC 5153 Grain and field beans
Steeven Lagrange

Saint-Isidore-De-Laprairie, QC J0L

D-U-N-S 20-265-9280   (SL)
FORAGE ANDRE ROY INC
186 Rue Boyer, Saint-Isidore-De-Laprairie, QC, J0L 2A0
(450) 454-1244
Emp Here 40   Sales 11,340,960
SIC 1611 Highway and street construction
Andre Roy

D-U-N-S 20-540-8081   (SL)
GUINOIS & FRERES LTEE
1365 Rue Saint-Regis, Saint-Isidore-De-Laprairie, QC, J0L 2A0
(450) 454-3196
Emp Here 40   Sales 10,492,360
SIC 0181 Ornamental nursery products
Gaston Guinois
Jean-Luc Guinois
Sylvain Guinois
Marie-Jeanne Guinois
Mary Jane Guinois

D-U-N-S 20-888-4890   (SL)
KEFOR LTEE
175 Rue Boyer, Saint-Isidore-De-Laprairie, QC, J0L 2A0
(450) 454-4636
Emp Here 100   Sales 19,237,000
SIC 2439 Structural wood members, nec
Daniel Devaux
Michel Trudeau
Gerard Robitaille

D-U-N-S 20-500-6125   (HQ)
LANCTOT, J.C. INC
LANCTOT COUVRE-SOL DESIGN
(Suby of 9108-5605 QUEBEC INC)
148 Rue Boyer, Saint-Isidore-De-Laprairie, QC, J0L 2A0
(450) 692-4655
Emp Here 44   Sales 11,517,000
SIC 5713 Floor covering stores
Denis Lanctot

D-U-N-S 24-022-0319   (BR)
SINTRA INC
(Suby of BOUYGUES)
7 Rang Saint-Regis S, Saint-Isidore-De-Laprairie, QC, J0L 2A0
(450) 638-0172
Emp Here 100
SIC 1611 Highway and street construction
Francis Mondor

Saint-Jacques, QC J0K

D-U-N-S 24-541-7019   (SL)
COLLEGE ESTHER-BLONDIN

101 Rue Sainte-Anne, Saint-Jacques, QC, J0K 2R0
(450) 839-7652
Emp Here 85   Sales 7,890,210
SIC 8211 Elementary and secondary schools
Anne Turcotte

D-U-N-S 24-355-3237   (HQ)
GROUPE JETTE ASSURANCES INC
153 Rue Saint-Jacques, Saint-Jacques, QC, J0K 2R0
(450) 839-3911
Sales 22,049,560
SIC 6411 Insurance agents, brokers, and service
Yannick Jette
Michel Jette
Martin Jette
Pierre Jette
Paul Jette

D-U-N-S 24-073-9909   (BR)
INDUSTRIES MAILHOT INC
(Suby of GROUPE MAILHOT INC)
2721 Rang Saint-Jacques, Saint-Jacques, QC, J0K 2R0
(450) 839-3663
Emp Here 200
SIC 3569 General industrial machinery, nec
Yvan Morin

D-U-N-S 20-252-6224   (HQ)
INDUSTRIES MAILHOT INC
(Suby of GROUPE MAILHOT INC)
2721 Rang Saint-Jacques, Saint-Jacques, QC, J0K 2R0
(450) 477-6222
Emp Here 20   Sales 63,197,325
SIC 3569 General industrial machinery, nec
Charles Massicotte

D-U-N-S 20-212-8943   (BR)
IPEX INC
IPEX MANAGEMENT
(Suby of ALIAXIS)
247 Rue Principale, Saint-Jacques, QC, J0K 2R0
(450) 839-2655
Emp Here 75
SIC 3088 Plastics plumbing fixtures
Sylvain Turbide

Saint-Jacques-Le-Mineur, QC J0J

D-U-N-S 24-601-6745   (SL)
FERME MARAICHERE A. GUINOIS & FILS INC
50 Rang Saint-Philippe N, Saint-Jacques-Le-Mineur, QC, J0J 1Z0
(450) 515-5212
Emp Here 35   Sales 11,986,345
SIC 0161 Vegetables and melons
Alain Guinois
Anick Guinois-Cote

Saint-Jean-Baptiste, QC J0L

D-U-N-S 25-697-4544   (SL)
CAMIONS A & R DUBOIS INC
DUBOIS, CAMIONS ALAIN REGIS
2745 Rue Principale, Saint-Jean-Baptiste, QC, J0L 2B0
(450) 464-4631
Emp Here 40   Sales 19,923,120
SIC 5531 Auto and home supply stores
Regis Dubois
Alain Dubois

D-U-N-S 20-109-5861   (BR)
COOP FEDEREE, LA
UNIDINDON

▲ Public Company   ■ Public Company Family Member   **HQ** Headquarters   **BR** Branch   **SL** Single Location

(Suby of COOP FEDEREE, LA)
3380 Rue Principale Bureau 430, Saint-Jean-Baptiste, QC, J0L 2B0
(450) 467-2875
Emp Here 450
SIC 2015 Poultry slaughtering and processing
Rejean Nadeau

D-U-N-S 20-252-7081   (SL)
COOPERATIVE REGIONALE D'ELECTRICITE DE ST-JEAN-BAPTISTE-DE-ROUVILLE
COOP D'ELECTRICITE
3113 Rue Principale, Saint-Jean-Baptiste, QC, J0L 2B0
(450) 467-5583
Emp Here 14   Sales 14,583,387
SIC 4911 Electric services
Eric Durand
Johanne Van Rossum
Stephane Surprenant
Yves Barre
Jean Messier
Robert Dion
Luc Beaudoin

D-U-N-S 25-245-9433   (BR)
OLYMEL S.E.C.
UNIDINDON
(Suby of OLYMEL S.E.C.)
3380 Rue Principale, Saint-Jean-Baptiste, QC, J0L 2B0
(450) 467-2875
Emp Here 450
SIC 2015 Poultry slaughtering and processing
Pierre Poissant

D-U-N-S 20-005-2009   (SL)
R ROBITAILLE ET FILS INC
4000 Ch Benoit, Saint-Jean-Baptiste, QC, J0L 2B0
(450) 795-3915
Emp Here 49   Sales 16,780,883
SIC 0119 Cash grains, nec
Claude Robitaille

D-U-N-S 24-788-5536   (SL)
VERGERS PAUL JODOIN INC
JUS TRADITION, LES
3333 Rang Du Cordon, Saint-Jean-Baptiste, QC, J0L 2B0
(450) 467-4744
Emp Here 60   Sales 15,738,540
SIC 0175 Deciduous tree fruits
Francois Jodoin
Pierre Jodoin
Sylvain Jodoin

Saint-Jean-D'Orleans, QC G0A

D-U-N-S 20-107-7018   (SL)
FERME ONESIME POULIOT INC
5354 Ch Royal, Saint-Jean-D'Orleans, QC, G0A 3W0
(418) 829-2801
Emp Here 50   Sales 17,123,350
SIC 0171 Berry crops
Daniel Pouliot
Guy Pouliot

Saint-Jean-De-Matha, QC J0K

D-U-N-S 20-296-9361   (HQ)
SUPERMARCHE BOUCHER INC
METRO BOUCHER
841 Rte Louis-Cyr, Saint-Jean-De-Matha, QC, J0K 2S0
(450) 886-1010
Emp Here 25   Sales 22,010,775
SIC 5411 Grocery stores
Jean-Pierre Boucher

Saint-Jean-Port-Joli, QC G0R

D-U-N-S 24-531-6435   (SL)
'HORISOL', COOPERATIVE DE TRAVAILLEURS
HORISOL, COOP DE TRAVAIL
18 Rue Des Societaires, Saint-Jean-Port-Joli, QC, G0R 3G0
(418) 598-3048
Emp Here 90   Sales 14,027,670
SIC 2421 Sawmills and planing mills, general
Lise Bernier
Gaetan Labonte
Edith Caron
Simon Pelletier
Daniel St-Pierre
Jean Fournier
Yves Pelletier
Marielyne Michaud

D-U-N-S 20-252-9558   (SL)
MAGASIN COOP LA PAIX
321 Rte De L'Eglise, Saint-Jean-Port-Joli, QC, G0R 3G0
(418) 598-3385
Emp Here 62   Sales 16,997,424
SIC 5411 Grocery stores
Denis Lavoie

D-U-N-S 25-500-1661   (BR)
METRO RICHELIEU INC
(Suby of METRO INC)
61 2e Rang E, Saint-Jean-Port-Joli, QC, G0R 3G0
(418) 598-3371
Emp Here 80
SIC 5411 Grocery stores
Josee Caron

D-U-N-S 20-252-9137   (SL)
PLASTIQUES GAGNON INC
117 Av De Gaspe O, Saint-Jean-Port-Joli, QC, G0R 3G0
(418) 598-3361
Emp Here 135   Sales 12,107,520
SIC 3089 Plastics products, nec
Francois Gagnon
Monika Gagnon
Jean Gagnon

D-U-N-S 24-820-6062   (SL)
ROUSSEAU METAL INC
105 Av De Gaspe O, Saint-Jean-Port-Joli, QC, G0R 3G0
(418) 598-3381
Emp Here 250   Sales 60,807,750
SIC 3499 Fabricated Metal products, nec
Simon-Pierre Pare
Michael Lacombe
Charles-Alexandre Pare
Sbastien Lavoie
Roger L'esperance
Guy Gendron

Saint-Jean-Sur-Richelieu, QC J2W

D-U-N-S 24-800-2065   (HQ)
2732-3930 QUEBEC INC
GROUPE YVES GAGNON
950 Rue Bernier, Saint-Jean-Sur-Richelieu, QC, J2W 2H1
(450) 359-1311
Sales 15,651,090
SIC 5039 Construction materials, nec
Yves Gagnon
Genevieve Gagnon

D-U-N-S 20-916-0964   (SL)
6138144 CANADA LTEE
HABITATIONS QUALIPRO
60 Rue Des Geais-Bleus, Saint-Jean-Sur-Richelieu, QC, J2W 3E5

Emp Here 45   Sales 14,349,105
SIC 1521 Single-family housing construction
Marko Savor

D-U-N-S 24-369-4754   (BR)
CAISSE DESJARDINS DU HAUT-RICHELIEU
CENTRE GESTION DES AVOIRS
(Suby of CAISSE DESJARDINS DU HAUT-RICHELIEU)
175 Boul Omer-Marcil, Saint-Jean-Sur-Richelieu, QC, J2W 0A3
(450) 359-5933
Emp Here 250
SIC 6062 State credit unions

D-U-N-S 24-180-5287   (SL)
DERY TOYOTA LTEE
250 Rue Moreau, Saint-Jean-Sur-Richelieu, QC, J2W 0E9
(450) 359-9000
Emp Here 49   Sales 24,405,822
SIC 5511 New and used car dealers
Francois Dery

D-U-N-S 25-408-4270   (SL)
DUPONT FORD LTEE
190 Rue Moreau, Saint-Jean-Sur-Richelieu, QC, J2W 2M4
(450) 359-3673
Emp Here 38   Sales 18,926,964
SIC 5511 New and used car dealers
Olivier Dupont
Catherine Dupont

D-U-N-S 20-253-9441   (HQ)
EMBALLAGE ST-JEAN LTEE
FLEXGRAPH
(Suby of INVESTISSEMENTS CHAMBERMONT INC)
80 Rue Moreau, Saint-Jean-Sur-Richelieu, QC, J2W 2M4
(450) 349-5871
Emp Here 110   Sales 91,909,250
SIC 2673 Bags: plastic, laminated, and coated
Marc Leclair
Frederic Houle
Gilles Veilleux
Jean Chagnon
Jean-Yves Leblanc

D-U-N-S 24-227-8810   (SL)
FERMES PROLIX INC
705 Boul Saint-Luc, Saint-Jean-Sur-Richelieu, QC, J2W 2G6
(450) 348-9436
Emp Here 9   Sales 10,893,573
SIC 5153 Grain and field beans
Pierre Alix
Michel Alix
Jean-Philippe Alix
Guillaume Alix
Yvan Alix
Jacques Alix

D-U-N-S 20-357-0270   (SL)
GESTION GREGOIRE INC
BARNABE KIA
210 Rue Moreau, Saint-Jean-Sur-Richelieu, QC, J2W 0E9
(450) 347-2835
Emp Here 25   Sales 12,451,950
SIC 5511 New and used car dealers
Barnabe Gregoire

D-U-N-S 20-357-0288   (SL)
GESTIONS J.B. GREGOIRE INC
BARNABE MAZDA
96 Rue Moreau, Saint-Jean-Sur-Richelieu, QC, J2W 2M4
(450) 348-6835
Emp Here 25   Sales 12,451,950
SIC 5511 New and used car dealers
Joel Gregoire

D-U-N-S 25-393-3709   (HQ)

LOGISTIK UNICORP INC
LOGISTIQUE UNICORP
820 Ch Du Grand-Bernier N, Saint-Jean-Sur-Richelieu, QC, J2W 0A6
(450) 349-9700
Sales 180,112,127
SIC 7213 Linen supply
Louis Bibeau
Erin Murphy
Michelle Cormier
John A. Hatherly
Michel Mercure
Morty White

D-U-N-S 24-896-6707   (SL)
MARCHE PERREAULT & GELINAS INC
IGA SAINT-LUC
318 Boul Saint-Luc, Saint-Jean-Sur-Richelieu, QC, J2W 2A3
(450) 359-4110
Emp Here 49   Sales 13,433,448
SIC 5411 Grocery stores
Alain Perreault

D-U-N-S 25-193-3768   (BR)
PROVIGO DISTRIBUTION INC
MAXI
(Suby of LOBLAW COMPANIES LIMITED)
200 Boul Omer-Marcil, Saint-Jean-Sur-Richelieu, QC, J2W 2V1
(450) 348-0998
Emp Here 135
SIC 5411 Grocery stores
Nathalie Lefebvre

D-U-N-S 20-253-7528   (SL)
RONDEAU CHRYSLER JEEP DODGE INC
180 Rue Moreau, Saint-Jean-Sur-Richelieu, QC, J2W 2M4
(450) 359-7333
Emp Here 50   Sales 24,903,900
SIC 5511 New and used car dealers
Michel Rondeau
Robert Rondeau

D-U-N-S 25-244-1431   (SL)
SOCIETE EN COMMANDITE PASQUIER
PASQUIER
87 Boul Saint-Luc Bureau A, Saint-Jean-Sur-Richelieu, QC, J2W 1E2
(450) 299-9999
Emp Here 20   Sales 16,711,540
SIC 5141 Groceries, general line
Robert Paquette
Mario Paquette
Guy Paquette
Jacques Paquette

D-U-N-S 24-227-0544   (SL)
TCED INTL INC
TRANS-CANADA ENERGIE
700 Ch Du Grand-Bernier N, Saint-Jean-Sur-Richelieu, QC, J2W 2H1
(450) 348-8720
Emp Here 65   Sales 23,673,975
SIC 5013 Motor vehicle supplies and new parts
Elise Rozon
Joel Rozon
Sara Rozon
Louise Rozon

D-U-N-S 24-207-4198   (BR)
WAL-MART CANADA CORP
WALMART SUPERCENTRE
(Suby of WALMART INC.)
100 Boul Omer-Marcil, Saint-Jean-Sur-Richelieu, QC, J2W 2X2
(450) 349-0666
Emp Here 100
SIC 5311 Department stores

Saint-Jean-Sur-Richelieu, QC J2X

D-U-N-S 24-858-0714   (SL)
9215-5936 QUEBEC INC
860 Rue Lucien-Beaudin, Saint-Jean-Sur-Richelieu, QC, J2X 5V5
(450) 346-6363
Emp Here 72   *Sales* 13,711,824
SIC 3612 Transformers, except electric
Bernard Duvoisin
Robert Isbister

D-U-N-S 20-200-9064   (HQ)
ABB PRODUITS D'INSTALLATION LTEE
GFI
(*Suby of* ABB LTD)
700 Av Thomas, Saint-Jean-Sur-Richelieu, QC, J2X 2M9
(450) 347-5318
Emp Here 374   *Sales* 282,915,000
SIC 3699 Electrical equipment and supplies, nec
Nathalie Pilon
Vince Pesce
Sylvie Bergeron
Guy Dionne
Guido Mussehl

D-U-N-S 24-804-7974   (BR)
AP INFRASTRUCTURE SOLUTIONS LP
(*Suby of* TREVLUC HOLDINGS LTD)
800 Boul Pierre-Tremblay, Saint-Jean-Sur-Richelieu, QC, J2X 4W8
(450) 346-4481
Emp Here 150
SIC 3312 Blast furnaces and steel mills
Eric Caron

D-U-N-S 24-874-8795   (BR)
BUANDERIE BLANCHELLE INC, LA
(*Suby of* BUANDERIE BLANCHELLE INC, LA)
825 Av Montrichard, Saint-Jean-Sur-Richelieu, QC, J2X 5K8
(450) 347-4390
Emp Here 120
SIC 7218 Industrial launderers
Pierre Chabot

D-U-N-S 25-257-4942   (SL)
CADEX INC
755 Av Montrichard, Saint-Jean-Sur-Richelieu, QC, J2X 5K8
(450) 348-6774
Emp Here 77   *Sales* 17,501,253
SIC 3821 Laboratory apparatus and furniture
Serge Dextraze

D-U-N-S 20-289-0794   (HQ)
CAISSE DESJARDINS DU HAUT-RICHELIEU
730 Boul D'Iberville, Saint-Jean-Sur-Richelieu, QC, J2X 3Z9
(450) 357-5000
Emp Here 30   *Sales* 17,080,100
SIC 6062 State credit unions
Luc Bazinet
Manon Bertrand
Bernard Alix
Catherine Boucher
Francois-Luc Dallaire
Yves Delorme
Rejean Messier
Jacinthe Surprenant
Julie Levesque
Audrey Archambault

D-U-N-S 25-234-2092   (BR)
COMMISSION SCOLAIRE DES HAUTES-RIVIERES
POLYVALENTE MARCEL LANDRY
(*Suby of* COMMISSION SCOLAIRE DES HAUTES-RIVIERES)
365 Av Landry, Saint-Jean-Sur-Richelieu, QC, J2X 2P6
(450) 347-1225
Emp Here 180
SIC 8211 Elementary and secondary schools
Jocelyne Tremblay

D-U-N-S 25-233-6912   (SL)
ECOLE SECONDAIRE MARCELLIN-CHAMPAGNAT
14 Ch Des Patriotes E, Saint-Jean-Sur-Richelieu, QC, J2X 5P9
(450) 347-5343
Emp Here 121   *Sales* 11,993,399
SIC 8211 Elementary and secondary schools
Jacques Belisle
Rejeanne Dupuis-Gauthier
Monique Lapierre
Francois Martel
Alain Lamontagne

D-U-N-S 24-811-6568   (HQ)
GESTION SOLENO INC
1160 Rte 133, Saint-Jean-Sur-Richelieu, QC, J2X 4J5
(450) 347-7855
Emp Here 10   *Sales* 19,208,500
SIC 3498 Fabricated pipe and fittings
Alain Poirier
Normand Poirier
Gaston Blais
Marcel Lacaille
Real Laflamme

D-U-N-S 24-561-7360   (HQ)
GROUPE CARON & CARON INC
(*Suby of* CORPORATION DE CAPITAL CARON & CARON)
800 Boul Pierre-Tremblay, Saint-Jean-Sur-Richelieu, QC, J2X 4W8
(450) 545-7174
Sales 21,506,280
SIC 3272 Concrete products, nec
Eric Caron
Michel Caron

D-U-N-S 24-607-9003   (SL)
IGA #8113
435 9e Av, Saint-Jean-Sur-Richelieu, QC, J2X 1K5
(450) 358-2804
Emp Here 49   *Sales* 13,433,448
SIC 5411 Grocery stores
Denis Rene

D-U-N-S 20-500-9087   (SL)
INDUSTRIES RAINVILLE INC
175 Rte 104, Saint-Jean-Sur-Richelieu, QC, J2X 5T7
(450) 347-5521
Emp Here 45   *Sales* 21,376,170
SIC 5084 Industrial machinery and equipment
Ghislain Sabourin

D-U-N-S 20-955-3978   (SL)
METAL SIGMA INC
PEINTURE EN POUDRE MONTEREGIE (PPM)
750 Rue Lucien-Beaudin, Saint-Jean-Sur-Richelieu, QC, J2X 5M3
(450) 348-7333
Emp Here 110   *Sales* 21,129,350
SIC 3499 Fabricated Metal products, nec
Richard Houle
Michel Oligny

D-U-N-S 20-200-8652   (SL)
MONDOR LTEE
785 Rue Honore-Mercier, Saint-Jean-Sur-Richelieu, QC, J2X 3S2
(450) 347-5321
Emp Here 95   *Sales* 12,984,030
SIC 2339 Women's and misses' outerwear, nec
Denis Beaudoin
Daniel Rochefort

D-U-N-S 24-865-1846   (SL)
PETROLES C.L. INC, LES
DEPANNEUR LUCAR NAPIERVILLE
25 104 Rte, Saint-Jean-Sur-Richelieu, QC, J2X 1H2
(450) 346-7555
Emp Here 33   *Sales* 16,436,574
SIC 5541 Gasoline service stations

Luc Trudeau

D-U-N-S 20-200-8769   (SL)
PHARLEM INC
795 Boul D'Iberville, Saint-Jean-Sur-Richelieu, QC, J2X 4S7
(450) 347-2000
Emp Here 48   *Sales* 12,141,792
SIC 5912 Drug stores and proprietary stores
Jocelyn Ferland
Serge Parent

D-U-N-S 20-563-9768   (HQ)
SUPER MARCHE LAPLANTE INC
IGA
420 2e Av Bureau 171, Saint-Jean-Sur-Richelieu, QC, J2X 2B8
(450) 357-1258
Sales 29,347,700
SIC 5411 Grocery stores
Germain Laplante

D-U-N-S 20-254-3674   (SL)
TRANSFORMATEURS DELTA STAR INC
DELTA STAR
(*Suby of* DELTA STAR, INC.)
860 Rue Lucien-Beaudin, Saint-Jean-Sur-Richelieu, QC, J2X 5V5
(450) 346-6622
Emp Here 130   *Sales* 36,778,950
SIC 3612 Transformers, except electric
Ivan Tepper
Stephen Newman
Steven Jones
Theodore Segal
Janet Collins
Jane Horne
Jason Greene
Alex Nemorin

D-U-N-S 20-200-9114   (HQ)
TREMCAR INC
(*Suby of* TECHNOLOGIES TREMCAR INC)
790 Av Montrichard, Saint-Jean-Sur-Richelieu, QC, J2X 5G4
(450) 347-7822
Sales 76,120,900
SIC 3443 Fabricated plate work (boiler shop)
Daniel Tremblay
Jacques Tremblay
Martin Lussier

Saint-Jean-Sur-Richelieu, QC J2Y

D-U-N-S 20-253-5647   (SL)
CARRIERE BERNIER LTEE
25 Ch Du Petit-Bernier, Saint-Jean-Sur-Richelieu, QC, J2Y 1B8
(514) 875-2841
Emp Here 200   *Sales* 54,051,200
SIC 1422 Crushed and broken limestone
Luc Ouimet
Jean-Guy Ouimet

D-U-N-S 25-872-8666   (BR)
TRANSPORTS DUCAMPRO INC
(*Suby of* TRANSPORTS DUCAMPRO INC)
1200 Boul Saint-Luc, Saint-Jean-Sur-Richelieu, QC, J2Y 1A5
(450) 348-4400
Emp Here 100
SIC 4213 Trucking, except local
Daniel Roy

Saint-Jean-Sur-Richelieu, QC J3A

D-U-N-S 25-023-9274   (SL)
2550-7856 QUEBEC INC
COMPLEXE OASIS ST-JEAN
1050 Rue Stefoni, Saint-Jean-Sur-Richelieu, QC, J3A 1T5

(450) 349-5861
Emp Here 100   *Sales* 6,507,500
SIC 8361 Residential care
Brown Binion

D-U-N-S 25-188-2163   (BR)
2757-5158 QUEBEC INC
ARMOIRES CUISINES ACTION
(*Suby of* 2757-5158 QUEBEC INC)
1050 Boul Du Seminaire N Bureau 210, Saint-Jean-Sur-Richelieu, QC, J3A 1S7
(450) 359-7980
Emp Here 100
SIC 2434 Wood kitchen cabinets
Christian Vangent

D-U-N-S 24-407-8015   (SL)
9185-9322 QUEBEC INC
SAINT-JEAN HYUNDAI
1000 Rue Douglas, Saint-Jean-Sur-Richelieu, QC, J3A 1V1
(450) 348-6816
Emp Here 26   *Sales* 12,950,028
SIC 5571 Motorcycle dealers
Francois Duquette

D-U-N-S 20-033-9120   (BR)
COMMISSION SCOLAIRE DES HAUTES-RIVIERES
ECOLE MARIE RIVIER
(*Suby of* COMMISSION SCOLAIRE DES HAUTES-RIVIERES)
511 Rue Pierre-Caisse, Saint-Jean-Sur-Richelieu, QC, J3A 1N5
(450) 348-0958
Emp Here 100
SIC 8211 Elementary and secondary schools
Chantal Boutet

D-U-N-S 25-233-9205   (BR)
COMMISSION SCOLAIRE DES HAUTES-RIVIERES
POLYVALENTE CHAMOINE ARMAND RACI-COT
(*Suby of* COMMISSION SCOLAIRE DES HAUTES-RIVIERES)
940 Boul De Normandie, Saint-Jean-Sur-Richelieu, QC, J3A 1A7
(450) 348-0413
Emp Here 100
SIC 8211 Elementary and secondary schools
Manon Ouellet

D-U-N-S 24-630-7164   (SL)
CONCESSIONNAIRE HONDA DE
400 Rue Laberge, Saint-Jean-Sur-Richelieu, QC, J3A 1G5
(450) 347-7567
Emp Here 30   *Sales* 14,942,340
SIC 5511 New and used car dealers
Dieter Hammer

D-U-N-S 24-857-4071   (SL)
CSH L'OASIS ST. JEAN INC
CHARTWELL OASIS ST-JEAN, RESIDENCE POUR RETRAITES
1050 Rue Stefoni, Saint-Jean-Sur-Richelieu, QC, J3A 1T5
(450) 349-5861
Emp Here 100   *Sales* 6,507,500
SIC 8361 Residential care
Vlad Volodarski

D-U-N-S 20-253-6074   (HQ)
DAIGNEAULT & FRERE (1966) INC
HONDA DE SAINT-JEAN
400 Rue Laberge, Saint-Jean-Sur-Richelieu, QC, J3A 1G5
(450) 347-7567
Sales 20,136,960
SIC 5511 New and used car dealers
Armando Betti

D-U-N-S 20-603-4910   (SL)
DERY AUTOMOBILE LTEE
TOYOTA
1055 Boul Du Seminaire N, Saint-Jean-Sur-Richelieu, QC, J3A 1R7

▲ Public Company   ■ Public Company Family Member   **HQ** Headquarters   **BR** Branch   **SL** Single Location

(450) 359-9000
Emp Here 45   Sales 22,413,510
SIC 5511 New and used car dealers
Francois B. Dery
Francois-Martin Dery

D-U-N-S 25-172-8226   (SL)
ENTREPRISES RAYMOND LEWIS INC, LES
CANADIAN TIRE
855 Boul Du Seminaire N Bureau 153, Saint-Jean-Sur-Richelieu, QC, J3A 1J2
(450) 348-3851
Emp Here 125   Sales 78,660,000
SIC 5531 Auto and home supply stores
Raymond Lewis

D-U-N-S 24-351-1680   (SL)
ESCOMPTES FERNAND LACHANCE INC.
PHARMACIE JEAN COUTU #62 (PJC)
947 Boul Du Seminaire N, Saint-Jean-Sur-Richelieu, QC, J3A 1K1
(450) 348-9251
Emp Here 65   Sales 15,881,320
SIC 5912 Drug stores and proprietary stores
Fernand Lachance

D-U-N-S 20-859-4796   (SL)
GESTION CLAUDIUS INC
PHARMAPRIX
1000 Boul Du Seminaire N Bureau 4, Saint-Jean-Sur-Richelieu, QC, J3A 1E5
(450) 348-6813
Emp Here 55   Sales 13,438,040
SIC 5912 Drug stores and proprietary stores
Karyne Lacasse

D-U-N-S 25-448-1617   (BR)
METRO RICHELIEU INC
SUPER C
(Suby of METRO INC)
600 Rue Pierre-Caisse Bureau 2000, Saint-Jean-Sur-Richelieu, QC, J3A 1M1
(450) 348-0927
Emp Here 80
SIC 5411 Grocery stores
Marc Beaule

D-U-N-S 25-147-6461   (SL)
MULTI-PORTIONS INC
DALISA
(Suby of 177150 CANADA INC)
815 Rue Plante, Saint-Jean-Sur-Richelieu, QC, J3A 1M8
(450) 347-6152
Emp Here 80   Sales 27,655,200
SIC 2011 Meat packing plants
Fernand Pascoal

D-U-N-S 25-209-8595   (SL)
RACINE CHEVROLET BUICK GMC LTEE
1080 Rue Douglas, Saint-Jean-Sur-Richelieu, QC, J3A 0A2
(450) 359-5900
Emp Here 48   Sales 23,907,744
SIC 5511 New and used car dealers
Marcel Racine
Florian Boire

D-U-N-S 24-176-6989   (SL)
ROMEO BESSETTE & FILS INC
815 Rue Plante, Saint-Jean-Sur-Richelieu, QC, J3A 1M8
(450) 359-1471
Emp Here 20   Sales 11,598,480
SIC 6411 Insurance agents, brokers, and service
Jean-Francois Bessette

D-U-N-S 24-174-1792   (SL)
ROTISSERIES DU HAUT RICHELIEU LTEE, LES
ROTISSERIE ST HUBERT
960 Boul Du Seminaire N, Saint-Jean-Sur-Richelieu, QC, J3A 1L2
(450) 348-6876
Emp Here 80   Sales 3,429,840
SIC 5812 Eating places
Daniel Toupin

Jean-Pierre Leger

Saint-Jean-Sur-Richelieu, QC J3B

D-U-N-S 20-715-8895   (SL)
2747-6761 QUEBEC INC
IGA EXTRA GLADU
400 Boul Du Seminaire N Bureau 2747, Saint-Jean-Sur-Richelieu, QC, J3B 5L2
(450) 349-2878
Emp Here 160   Sales 46,956,320
SIC 5411 Grocery stores
Michel Gladu

D-U-N-S 25-211-4749   (BR)
ABB PRODUITS D'INSTALLATION LTEE
(Suby of ABB LTD)
100 Rue Longtin, Saint-Jean-Sur-Richelieu, QC, J3B 3G5
(450) 347-2304
Emp Here 375
SIC 3644 Noncurrent-carrying wiring devices
Pierre Paul Riopel

D-U-N-S 24-051-4455   (HQ)
ACIERS H & H INC, LES
ACIER VALLEYFIELD
920 Rue Pierre-Caisse, Saint-Jean-Sur-Richelieu, QC, J3B 7Y5
(450) 349-5801
Sales 20,006,780
SIC 5051 Metals service centers and offices
Yvon Guillotte

D-U-N-S 24-401-0273   (SL)
AXIM CONSTRUCTION INC
650 Rue Boucher Bureau 106, Saint-Jean-Sur-Richelieu, QC, J3B 7Z8
(450) 358-3885
Emp Here 50   Sales 28,516,900
SIC 1542 Nonresidential construction, nec
Maxime Pepin
Patrice Pepin

D-U-N-S 20-362-6056   (HQ)
BAILLARGEON - MSA INC
800 Rue Des Carrieres, Saint-Jean-Sur-Richelieu, QC, J3B 2P2
(450) 346-4441
Emp Here 4   Sales 13,077,650
SIC 6712 Bank holding companies
Nancy Ferland
Edith Montplaisir
Philippe-Antoine Baillargeon
Pascale Baillargeon

D-U-N-S 20-963-5366   (HQ)
BARRETTE-CHAPAIS LTEE
(Suby of GESTION YVES BARRETTE INC)
583 Ch Du Grand-Bernier N, Saint-Jean-Sur-Richelieu, QC, J3B 8K1
(450) 357-7000
Sales 173,993,750
SIC 2421 Sawmills and planing mills, general
Benoit Barrete
Yves Barrette

D-U-N-S 24-365-5490   (SL)
BARRETTEBOIS INC
BARRETTE REMAN
(Suby of GESTION YVES BARRETTE INC)
583 Ch Du Grand-Bernier N, Saint-Jean-Sur-Richelieu, QC, J3B 8K1
(450) 357-7000
Emp Here 275   Sales 61,232,875
SIC 2511 Wood household furniture
Hugues Simon
Martin Blais
Yves Barrette
Benoit Barrette
Luc Dufour

D-U-N-S 24-570-6809   (SL)
BRAULT, OMER INC
865 Rue Aubry, Saint-Jean-Sur-Richelieu,

QC, J3B 7R4
(450) 347-3342
Emp Here 49   Sales 10,673,621
SIC 1761 Roofing, siding, and sheetMetal work
Marc Brault
Nick Vallieres
Fernand Brault
Ronald Durand
Lorenzo Pietrantonio

D-U-N-S 24-763-2292   (HQ)
CARPETTES LANART INC
300 Rue Saint-Louis, Saint-Jean-Richelieu, QC, J3B 1Y4
(450) 348-4843
Sales 25,442,800
SIC 5023 Homefurnishings
Derek Galbraith

D-U-N-S 20-882-2049   (BR)
CENTRE INTEGRE DE SANTE ET DE SERVICES SOCIAUX DE LA MONTEREGIE-OUEST
SERVICES DE READAPTATION DU SUD-OUEST ET DU RENFORT, LES
(Suby of CENTRE INTEGRE DE SANTE ET DE SERVICES SOCIAUX DE LA MONTEREGIE-OUEST)
315 Rue Macdonald Bureau 105, Saint-Jean-Sur-Richelieu, QC, J3B 8J3
(450) 348-6121
Emp Here 200
SIC 8361 Residential care
Gilles Bertrand

D-U-N-S 25-233-4644   (HQ)
COMMISSION SCOLAIRE DES HAUTES-RIVIERES
210 Rue Notre-Dame, Saint-Jean-Richelieu, QC, J3B 6N3
(450) 359-6411
Emp Here 75   Sales 202,202,760
SIC 8211 Elementary and secondary schools
Andree Bouchard
Natasha Galloy
Magda Fares
Luc Mercier
Erminia Merlo
Claude Monty
Johanne Ouellette Langlois
Yvon Pineault
Sylvie Rousselle
Lise Soutiere

D-U-N-S 25-240-0882   (BR)
COMMISSION SCOLAIRE DES HAUTES-RIVIERES
ECOLE JOSEPH AMEDEE BELANGER
(Suby of COMMISSION SCOLAIRE DES HAUTES-RIVIERES)
151 Rue Notre-Dame, Saint-Jean-Richelieu, QC, J3B 6M9
(450) 348-4747
Emp Here 300
SIC 8211 Elementary and secondary schools
Denis Plante

D-U-N-S 24-257-2667   (HQ)
COPICOM INC
50 Rue Saint-Jacques, Saint-Jean-Richelieu, QC, J3B 2J9
(450) 347-8252
Sales 11,626,524
SIC 5044 Office equipment
Pierre Normand
Robert Masse
Claude Masse

D-U-N-S 24-593-6849   (SL)
CORPORATION DE FESTIVAL DE MONT-GOLFIERES DE SAINT-JEAN-SUR-RICHELIEU INC
ECOLE DE PILOTAGE DE MONT-GOLFIERES DU QUEBEC
5 Ch De L'Aeroport, Saint-Jean-Sur-Richelieu, QC, J3B 7B5

(450) 346-6000
Emp Here 250   Sales 21,675,000
SIC 7999 Amusement and recreation, nec
Michel Fecteau
Patricia Poissant
Andree Senneville
Pierre Beauvais
Stephane Beaudin
Benoit Fortin
Jean Fortine

D-U-N-S 25-063-3864   (SL)
CORPORATION DU FORT ST-JEAN
CAMPUS DU FORT SAINT-JEAN
15 Rue Jacques-Cartier N, Saint-Jean-Richelieu, QC, J3B 8R8
(450) 358-6900
Emp Here 100   Sales 41,888,900
SIC 6531 Real estate agents and managers
Alain Beauchamp
Christiane Marcoux
Fernand Pascoal
Mario Heroux
Carolyn Hug
Fernand Croisetiere
Alain Laplante
Stephane Legrand
Veronique Tougas
Steve Hetu

D-U-N-S 20-376-6167   (SL)
CUNNINGHAM LINDSEY CANADA LIMITED
523 Boul Du Seminaire N Bureau 103, Saint-Jean-Sur-Richelieu, QC, J3B 5L8

Emp Here 49   Sales 28,894,203
SIC 6411 Insurance agents, brokers, and service

D-U-N-S 25-332-0097   (SL)
DISTRIBUTION LAURENT LEBLANC INC
DLL
370 Rue Saint-Louis, Saint-Jean-Sur-Richelieu, QC, J3B 1Y4
(450) 346-7044
Emp Here 26   Sales 12,350,676
SIC 5088 Transportation equipment and supplies
Lyne Leblanc
Annie Leblanc
Michel Mailloux

D-U-N-S 20-793-2088   (HQ)
ENTREPRISES BARRETTE LTEE, LES
(Suby of GESTION YVES BARRETTE INC)
583 Ch Du Grand-Bernier N, Saint-Jean-Sur-Richelieu, QC, J3B 8K1
(450) 357-7000
Emp Here 100   Sales 486,462,000
SIC 3496 Miscellaneous fabricated wire products
Luc Dufour
Yves Barrette
Martin Blais

D-U-N-S 20-253-6231   (HQ)
ENTREPRISES DOMINION BLUELINE INC, LES
230 Rue Foch Bureau 450, Saint-Jean-Sur-Richelieu, QC, J3B 2B2
(450) 346-6827
Emp Here 250   Sales 234,509,240
SIC 5112 Stationery and office supplies
George M Savoy
Harolde M Savoy
Robert Lepine
Hugues Richard
Nicolas Savoie

D-U-N-S 20-764-5938   (SL)
EQUIPEMENT MAX-ATLAS INTERNATIONAL INC
(Suby of GESTIONS MOVAR INC, LES)
371 Ch Du Grand-Bernier N, Saint-Jean-Sur-Richelieu, QC, J3B 4S2
(450) 346-8848
Emp Here 150   Sales 30,855,900

SIC 4212 Local trucking, without storage
Tibor Varga
Andrew Morena

D-U-N-S 20-253-8252   (SL)
FABRICATION METELEC LTEE
300 Rue Carreau, Saint-Jean-Sur-Richelieu,
QC, J3B 2G4
(450) 346-6363
Emp Here 51   *Sales* 11,109,279
SIC 1761 Roofing, siding, and sheetMetal
work
Michel Paquette
Roger Huber
Doris Huber
Peter Huber

D-U-N-S 25-972-1777   (BR)
**FONDATION DU CENTRE JEUNESSE DE
LA MONTEREGIE**
*FONDATION DU CENTRE JEUNESSE DE LA
MONTEREGIE*
(*Suby of* FONDATION DU CENTRE JE-
UNESSE DE LA MONTEREGIE)
145 Boul Saint-Joseph Bureau 200, Saint-
Jean-Sur-Richelieu, QC, J3B 1W5
(450) 359-7525
Emp Here 80
SIC 8322 Individual and family services
Camil Picard

D-U-N-S 20-564-6185   (SL)
FORMICA CANADA INC
FORMICA
(*Suby of* HAL TRUST)
25 Rue Mercier, Saint-Jean-Sur-Richelieu,
QC, J3B 6E9
(450) 347-7541
Emp Here 250   *Sales* 59,703,000
SIC 3089 Plastics products, nec
Mitchell P. Quint
Brent Strobel
Raul Jr. Rosado
Leigh Box
Claude Sarrazin

D-U-N-S 24-742-5820   (SL)
GESTION YVON GUILLOTTE INC
920 Rue Pierre-Caisse, Saint-Jean-Sur-
Richelieu, QC, J3B 7Y5
(450) 349-5801
Emp Here 20   *Sales* 20,006,780
SIC 5051 Metals service centers and offices

D-U-N-S 20-302-8857   (SL)
GROUPE CAMBLI INC
CAMBLI INTERNATIONAL
555 Rue Saint-Louis, Saint-Jean-Sur-
Richelieu, QC, J3B 8X7
(450) 358-4920
Emp Here 275   *Sales* 7,218,750
SIC 7381 Detective and armored car services
Veronique Tougas
Martin Cousineau

D-U-N-S 20-999-2155   (SL)
GROUPE G.L.P. HI-TECH INC
PROTOTYPES STEPONE
440 Rue Saint-Michel, Saint-Jean-Sur-
Richelieu, QC, J3B 1T4
(450) 348-4918
Emp Here 90   *Sales* 14,297,220
SIC 3089 Plastics products, nec
Serge Gagne
Christian Boudreau
Nathalie Gagne

D-U-N-S 20-297-8458   (SL)
GROUPE LML LTEE, LE
L.M.L. AUTOMATISATION
360 Boul Du Seminaire N Bureau 22, Saint-
Jean-Sur-Richelieu, QC, J3B 5L1
(450) 347-1996
Emp Here 80   *Sales* 17,426,320
SIC 1731 Electrical work
Rejean Quintal

D-U-N-S 20-200-9098   (SL)

HUILES THUOT ET BEAUCHEMIN INC, LES
MAZOUT PROPANE BEAUCHEMIN
775 Rue Gaudette, Saint-Jean-Sur-Richelieu,
QC, J3B 7S7
(450) 359-4440
Emp Here 25   *Sales* 11,725,125
SIC 5983 Fuel oil dealers
Dominic Beauchemin
Mario Beauchemin
Mathieu Beauchemin

D-U-N-S 25-448-2540   (SL)
**IMMEUBLES RICHELIEU N. REON INC,
LES**
ROYAL LEPAGE HAUT-RICHELIEU
550 Boul Du Seminaire N, Saint-Jean-Sur-
Richelieu, QC, J3B 5L6
(450) 349-5883
Emp Here 55   *Sales* 14,946,580
SIC 6531 Real estate agents and managers
Rene Brouillette

D-U-N-S 20-928-0098   (SL)
LEFEBVRE, PAYETTE ET ASSOCIES INC
170 Rue Saint-Jacques, Saint-Jean-Sur-
Richelieu, QC, J3B 2K5
(514) 856-7751
Emp Here 25   *Sales* 14,498,100
SIC 6411 Insurance agents, brokers, and ser-
vice
Jean Payette
Francois Payette
Louis Lefebvre
Louise Lefebvre

D-U-N-S 20-253-8120   (SL)
MARTIN INC
SUEDART
285 Rue Saint-Jacques Bureau 2, Saint-Jean-
Sur-Richelieu, QC, J3B 2L1
(450) 347-2373
Emp Here 90   *Sales* 8,066,610
SIC 7219 Laundry and garment services, nec
Alain Martin
Luc Martin
Daniel Martin
Michel Martin

D-U-N-S 24-224-4135   (SL)
MOULES MIRPLEX INC, LES
765 Rue Pierre-Caisse, Saint-Jean-Sur-
Richelieu, QC, J3B 8C6
(450) 348-6611
Emp Here 30   *Sales* 14,250,780
SIC 5085 Industrial supplies
Marc Bertrand
Michel Denicourt
Gaetan Robert
Sylvain Aubut

D-U-N-S 24-612-5991   (SL)
MSA INFRASTRUCTURES INC
BETON MOBILE ST-ALPHONSE
(*Suby of* BAILLARGEON - MSA INC)
800 Rue Des Carrieres, Saint-Jean-Sur-
Richelieu, QC, J3B 2P2
(450) 346-4441
Emp Here 50   *Sales* 11,671,750
SIC 3273 Ready-mixed concrete
Guy Lefebvre
Melanie Gagnon
Paul Juneau

D-U-N-S 25-540-7504   (SL)
NOVA GRAIN INC
(*Suby of* 3410935 CANADA INC)
800 Rue Boucher, Saint-Jean-Sur-Richelieu,
QC, J3B 7Z8
(450) 348-0976
Emp Here 11   *Sales* 16,144,612
SIC 5153 Grain and field beans
Guylaine Brochu
Patrice Brochu

D-U-N-S 24-330-9163   (SL)
NYACK TECHNOLOGY INC
160 Rue Vanier, Saint-Jean-Sur-Richelieu,

QC, J3B 3R4
(450) 245-0373
Emp Here 100   *Sales* 27,666,000
SIC 2821 Plastics materials and resins
Andree Sebbag

D-U-N-S 20-007-1012   (BR)
OLYMEL S.E.C.
FLAMINGO
(*Suby of* OLYMEL S.E.C.)
770 Rue Claude, Saint-Jean-Sur-Richelieu,
QC, J3B 2W5
(450) 347-2241
Emp Here 100
SIC 2011 Meat packing plants
Michel Blouin

D-U-N-S 20-200-7548   (SL)
P. BAILLARGEON LTEE
(*Suby of* BAILLARGEON - MSA INC)
800 Rue Des Carrieres, Saint-Jean-Sur-
Richelieu, QC, J3B 2P2
(514) 866-8333
Emp Here 140   *Sales* 45,936,100
SIC 1611 Highway and street construction
Josee De La Durantaye
Pascale Baillargeon
Phillippe Antoine Baillargeon
Annik Bussieres

D-U-N-S 24-901-7955   (HQ)
PCAS CANADA INC
ST-JEAN PHOTOCHIMIE
(*Suby of* EURAZEO)
725 Rue Trotter, Saint-Jean-Sur-Richelieu,
QC, J3B 8J8
(450) 348-0901
Sales 14,201,050
SIC 2899 Chemical preparations, nec
Pierre Schreiner
Seon Kang
Didier Schneider
Eric Moissenot
Vincent Touraille
Maxime Garayt

D-U-N-S 20-253-9326   (HQ)
PIECES D'AUTO ST-JEAN INC
PIECES D'AUTO DE BEDFORD
650 Rue De Dijon, Saint-Jean-Sur-Richelieu,
QC, J3B 8G3
(450) 348-3871
Sales 10,926,450
SIC 5013 Motor vehicle supplies and new
parts
Daniel Dulac
Eric Brissette

D-U-N-S 24-387-5973   (SL)
**PRODUITS RECREATIFS FUTURE BEACH
INC**
160 Rue Vanier, Saint-Jean-Sur-Richelieu,
QC, J3B 3R4
(450) 245-0373
Emp Here 100   *Sales* 22,384,300
SIC 3732 Boatbuilding and repairing
Rober Farber

D-U-N-S 25-525-1548   (SL)
PRODUITS THERMOVISION INC
COMPOSANTES THERMOVISION
680 Boul Industriel, Saint-Jean-Sur-Richelieu,
QC, J3B 7X4
(450) 348-4970
Emp Here 100   *Sales* 20,189,700
SIC 3083 Laminated plastics plate and sheet
Jean-Guy Surprenant
Paule Gagnon

D-U-N-S 24-535-6899   (SL)
R. ROBITAILLE & FILS INC
486 Rue De Versailles, Saint-Jean-Sur-
Richelieu, QC, J3B 4H3
(450) 347-7494
Emp Here 49   *Sales* 16,780,883
SIC 0191 General farms, primarily crop
Denis Robitaille

Claude Robitaille

D-U-N-S 25-494-9381   (SL)
REVETEMENT R.H.R. INC
755 Rue Boucher, Saint-Jean-Sur-Richelieu,
QC, J3B 8P4
(450) 359-7868
Emp Here 50   *Sales* 12,652,950
SIC 5211 Lumber and other building materials
Claude Doucet
Karl Doucet
Stephan Doucet
Marco Doucet

D-U-N-S 24-636-6306   (HQ)
RHEINMETALL CANADA INC
(*Suby of* RHEINMETALL AG)
225 Boul Du Seminaire S, Saint-Jean-Sur-
Richelieu, QC, J3B 8E9
(450) 358-2000
Emp Here 250   *Sales* 72,426,240
SIC 3669 Communications equipment, nec
Stephane Oehrli
Robert Montcalm
Ernst Fuerst
Alexander Sagel

D-U-N-S 20-858-3732   (HQ)
**SERVICES DE READAPTATION SUD
OUEST ET DU RENFORT, LES**
315 Rue Macdonald Bureau 105, Saint-Jean-
Sur-Richelieu, QC, J3B 8J3
(450) 348-6121
Emp Here 20   *Sales* 16,070,500
SIC 8361 Residential care
Gilles Bertrand

D-U-N-S 20-356-1600   (SL)
TECHNOLOGIES GSC INC
(*Suby of* GESTION TECHNOLOGIES GSC
INC)
160 Rue Vanier, Saint-Jean-Sur-Richelieu,
QC, J3B 3R4
(450) 245-0373
Emp Here 40   *Sales* 78,399,303
SIC 2821 Plastics materials and resins
Anuj Singh
Brian Mcgee
Jason Neimark

D-U-N-S 20-253-7130   (HQ)
TERMACO LTEE
325 Boul Industriel, Saint-Jean-Sur-Richelieu,
QC, J3B 7M3
(450) 346-6871
Sales 51,078,510
SIC 3444 Sheet Metalwork
Stephane Huot
Nicolas Belanger
Patrick Dussault
Etienne-Antoine Veilleux
Normand Tanguay

D-U-N-S 24-667-3701   (HQ)
TRANSDEV QUEBEC INC
LIMOCAR
(*Suby of* TRANSDEV CANADA INC)
720 Rue Trotter, Saint-Jean-Sur-Richelieu,
QC, J3B 8T2
(514) 787-1998
Emp Here 1   *Sales* 56,214,000
SIC 4151 School buses
Nicole Dutilly
Jennifer Coyne
Jacques Laherre
Yann Leriche

D-U-N-S 24-019-9661   (SL)
TRANSPORT BOURASSA INC
TRANSPORT GUY BOURASSA
800 Rue De Dijon, Saint-Jean-Sur-Richelieu,
QC, J3B 8G3
(450) 346-5313
Emp Here 350   *Sales* 71,997,100
SIC 4212 Local trucking, without storage
Jean Bourassa
Sylvie Bourassa

Saint-Jerome, QC J5L

D-U-N-S 24-712-5883   (SL)
AUTOBUS BRUNET INC, LES
BRUNET ET CLOUTIER
986 Rue Des Lacs, Saint-Jerome, QC, J5L
1T4
(450) 438-8363
Emp Here 103   *Sales* 7,753,016
SIC 4151 School buses
Jean-Pierre Brunet

D-U-N-S 20-564-0626   (SL)
CENTRE DE PLOMBERIE ST-JEROME INC
BALISCUS
1075 Boul Du Grand-Heron, Saint-Jerome,
QC, J5L 1G2
(450) 436-2318
Emp Here 150   *Sales* 34,959,750
SIC 1711 Plumbing, heating, air-conditioning
Sylvain Allaire
Claudette Allaire

D-U-N-S 24-904-1708   (SL)
MARCHE ROBERT TELLIER (1990) INC
IGA
872 Montee Sainte-Therese, Saint-Jerome,
QC, J5L 2L1
(450) 565-5977
Emp Here 100   *Sales* 29,347,700
SIC 5411 Grocery stores
Robert Tellier

D-U-N-S 25-389-8563   (SL)
TRANSPORTS INTER-NORD INC, LES
LOCAVAN
455 Boul Lajeunesse O, Saint-Jerome, QC,
J5L 2P7
(450) 438-7133
Emp Here 96   *Sales* 14,226,432
SIC 4212 Local trucking, without storage
Steve Mclaughlin
Dave Mclaughlin

Saint-Jerome, QC J7Y

D-U-N-S 24-828-4960   (HQ)
123273 CANADA INC
PHARMACIE JEAN COUTU
298 Rue De Martigny O Unite 101, Saint-
Jerome, QC, J7Y 4C9
(450) 436-1022
Emp Here 7   *Sales* 45,884,250
SIC 5912 Drug stores and proprietary stores
Yves Tremblay
Jean Provost

D-U-N-S 24-920-4173   (HQ)
152429 CANADA INC
C.D.E
298 Rue De Martigny O Bureau 10, Saint-
Jerome, QC, J7Y 4C9
(450) 438-1263
Sales 24,594,570
SIC 5063 Electrical apparatus and equipment
Francois Pageau

D-U-N-S 25-381-2929   (SL)
2969-9477 QUEBEC INC
CLOUMATIC
11 Rue John-F.-Kennedy Bureau 2, Saint-
Jerome, QC, J7Y 4B4
(450) 436-9390
Emp Here 11   *Sales* 11,003,729
SIC 5051 Metals service centers and offices
Jacques Garon
Jean-Philippe Garon

D-U-N-S 25-475-2314   (SL)
9023-4683 QUEBEC INC
MARCHE LORD DE LAFONTAINE
2012 Rue Saint-Georges, Saint-Jerome, QC,

J7Y 1M8
(450) 565-8890
Emp Here 150   *Sales* 44,021,550
SIC 5411 Grocery stores
Monique Lord

D-U-N-S 25-527-3336   (SL)
9030-5418 QUEBEC INC
ALIMENTS G DION, LES
801 Montee Saint-Nicolas, Saint-Jerome, QC,
J7Y 4C7
(450) 569-8001
Emp Here 50   *Sales* 11,242,750
SIC 2099 Food preparations, nec
Gaston Dion
Louiselle Morin

D-U-N-S 24-177-1885   (SL)
9098-2067 QUEBEC INC
TIM HORTONS
1 Rue John-F.-Kennedy, Saint-Jerome, QC,
J7Y 4B4
(450) 660-6200
Emp Here 150   *Sales* 6,827,850
SIC 5812 Eating places
Jean-Pierre Germain
Line Aubin-Germain

D-U-N-S 20-102-5504   (SL)
9098-2067 QUEBEC INC
TIM HORTONS
2001 Boul Du Cure-Labelle, Saint-Jerome,
QC, J7Y 1S2
(450) 431-6411
Emp Here 150   *Sales* 6,827,850
SIC 5812 Eating places
Jean-Pierre Germain
Line Aubin-Germain

D-U-N-S 24-208-4916   (SL)
9158-9093 QUEBEC INC
MARCHE LORD & ASSOCIES IGA
1005 Boul Du Grand-Heron, Saint-Jerome,
QC, J7Y 3P2
(450) 438-5214
Emp Here 49   *Sales* 13,433,448
SIC 5411 Grocery stores
Monique Lord

D-U-N-S 25-335-3411   (SL)
ACADEMIE LAFONTAINE INC
2171 Boul Maurice, Saint-Jerome, QC, J7Y
4M7
(450) 431-3733
Emp Here 200   *Sales* 19,823,800
SIC 8211 Elementary and secondary schools
Marie-Josee Boulianne
Veronique Guerin
Thierry Lefebvre
Martin Carmel
Melanie Mondou
Luc Landry
Pascal St-Onge
Theleme Domon
Francois Cholette
Alexandre Guay

D-U-N-S 20-252-9699   (SL)
ACIER OUELLETTE INC
ACIER OUELLETTE SAINT-JEROME
(*Suby of* DESCOURS ET CABAUD SA)
22 Rue John-F.-Kennedy, Saint-Jerome, QC,
J7Y 4B6
(514) 876-1414
Emp Here 50   *Sales* 22,358,700
SIC 5051 Metals service centers and offices
Paul C. Shaw
Linda Shaw
Francois Heraud
Philippe Legris

D-U-N-S 25-766-1249   (SL)
AGENCE DE PLACEMENT SELECT INC
96 Rue De Martigny O, Saint-Jerome, QC, J7Y
2G1
(450) 431-6292
Emp Here 50   *Sales* 11,848,500
SIC 7361 Employment agencies

Louise Lavigne

D-U-N-S 24-901-4283   (BR)
AKZO NOBEL COATINGS LTD
AKZO NOBEL PEINTURES
(*Suby of* AKZO NOBEL N.V.)
1001 Boul Roland-Godard, Saint-Jerome, QC,
J7Y 4C2
(*phone*)
Emp Here 100
SIC 2851 Paints and allied products
Denis Berthiaume

D-U-N-S 25-763-7751   (SL)
AUTOBUS TRANSCOBEC (1987) INC, LES
21 Rue John-F.-Kennedy, Saint-Jerome, QC,
J7Y 4B4
(450) 432-9748
Emp Here 150   *Sales* 11,290,800
SIC 4151 School buses
Jean-Pierre Brunet
Martin Paquette
Yves Seguin

D-U-N-S 20-375-3710   (SL)
**CENTRE D'HEBERGEMENT ET DE SOINS
DE LONGUE DUREE LOUISE-FAUBERT
INC**
CHSLD LOUISE-FAUBERT
300 Rue Du Docteur-Charles-Leonard, Saint-
Jerome, QC, J7Y 0N2
(450) 710-1770
Emp Here 100   *Sales* 6,456,000
SIC 8059 Nursing and personal care, nec
Paul Jr Arbec
Martin St-Jean

D-U-N-S 20-253-0408   (HQ)
**CENTRE DE DISTRIBUTION ELECTRIQUE
LIMITEE**
CDE ELECTRIQUE
(*Suby of* 152429 CANADA INC)
298 Rue De Martigny O, Saint-Jerome, QC,
J7Y 4C9
(450) 438-1263
Sales 24,594,570
SIC 5063 Electrical apparatus and equipment
Francois Pageau

D-U-N-S 25-758-6859   (BR)
CENTRE JEUNESSE DES LAURENTIDES
PROTECTION DE LA JEUNESSE
358 Rue Laviolette, Saint-Jerome, QC, J7Y
2T1
(450) 432-9753
Emp Here 80
SIC 8322 Individual and family services
Bernard Fortin

D-U-N-S 24-527-1606   (SL)
COMPAGNIE DU BOIS FRANC DZD INC, LA
PLANCHERS BELLEFEUILLE
450 Boul Roland-Godard, Saint-Jerome, QC,
J7Y 4G8
(450) 431-1643
Emp Here 50   *Sales* 16,323,580
SIC 5031 Lumber, plywood, and millwork
Sefi Dollinger
Guy Dollinger
Heinz Leeb

D-U-N-S 25-684-8805   (HQ)
**CONSTRUCTION DEMATHIEU & BARD
(CDB) INC**
CDB CONSTRUCTION
170 Boul Roland-Godard, Saint-Jerome, QC,
J7Y 4P7
(450) 569-8043
Sales 12,622,100
SIC 1622 Bridge, tunnel, and elevated high-
way construction
Rene Simon
Brice Charlier
Ilies Amami
Louis Charette

D-U-N-S 20-330-1424   (SL)
DB-AECON PONT ST-JACQUES S.E.P

170 Boul Roland-Godard, Saint-Jerome, QC,
J7Y 4P7
(450) 569-8043
Emp Here 100   *Sales* 24,088,400
SIC 1622 Bridge, tunnel, and elevated high-
way construction
Rene Simon

D-U-N-S 20-253-4962   (SL)
DBC S.E.P.
170 Boul Roland-Godard, Saint-Jerome, QC,
J7Y 4P7
(450) 569-8043
Emp Here 100   *Sales* 12,622,100
SIC 1629 Heavy construction, nec
Rene Simon

D-U-N-S 24-109-7559   (SL)
DOPPELMAYR CANADA LTEE
DOPPELMAYR CTEC
(*Suby of* AMD PRIVATSTIFTUNG)
800 Montee Saint-Nicolas, Saint-Jerome, QC,
J7Y 4C8
(450) 432-1128
Emp Here 100   *Sales* 22,384,300
SIC 3799 Transportation equipment, nec
Andre Lamoureux
Jim Anderson
Mark Bee

D-U-N-S 24-923-0509   (SL)
**ENTREPRISES ISABELLE DESJARDINS
INC, LES**
PHARMAPRIX
900 Boul Grignon Bureau 116, Saint-Jerome,
QC, J7Y 3S7
(450) 438-1293
Emp Here 45   *Sales* 11,382,930
SIC 5912 Drug stores and proprietary stores
Isabelle Desjardins

D-U-N-S 20-290-1732   (HQ)
ENTREPRISES ROLLAND INC, LES
BOLSHOI
256 Boul Jean-Baptiste-Rolland O, Saint-
Jerome, QC, J7Y 0L6
(450) 569-3951
Emp Here 150   *Sales* 147,054,800
SIC 2621 Paper mills
Philip Rundle
Fabian De Armas
Richard Stokes
Matt Kever
Anthony Chambers

D-U-N-S 25-362-6451   (BR)
ENTREPRISES ROLLAND INC, LES
*CASCADES CENTRE DE TRANSFORMA-
TION*
(*Suby of* ENTREPRISES ROLLAND INC,
LES)
980 Rue De L'Industrie, Saint-Jerome, QC,
J7Y 4B8
(450) 569-0040
Emp Here 130
SIC 5111 Printing and writing paper
Mario Plourde

D-U-N-S 20-610-7109   (SL)
ENZYME TESTING LABS INC
(*Suby of* KEYWORDS STUDIOS PLC)
2031 Boul Du Cure-Labelle, Saint-Jerome,
QC, J7Y 1S5
(450) 995-2000
Emp Here 250   *Sales* 46,143,250
SIC 7371 Custom computer programming ser-
vices
Andrew Day
Giacomo Duranti
Nicolas Liorzou

D-U-N-S 20-253-0895   (SL)
**EQUIPEMENT DE BUREAU ROBERT
LEGARE LTEE**
411 Rue John-F.-Kennedy, Saint-Jerome, QC,
J7Y 4B5
(450) 438-3894
Emp Here 26   *Sales* 11,626,524

▲ Public Company   ■ Public Company Family Member   **HQ** Headquarters   **BR** Branch   **SL** Single Location

SIC 5044 Office equipment
Dominic Legare
Etienne Legare
Suzette Legare
Robert Legare

D-U-N-S 24-250-2565   (BR)
GENERAL CABLE COMPANY LTD
(Suby of PRYSMIAN SPA)
800 Ch De La Riviere-Du-Nord, Saint-Jerome,
QC, J7Y 5G2
(450) 436-1450
Emp Here 100
SIC 3357 Nonferrous wiredrawing and insulating
Robert Clement

D-U-N-S 24-637-2353   (SL)
GIRALDEAU INTER-AUTO INC
BUDGET LOCATION D'AUTOS
2180 Boul Du Cure-Labelle, Saint-Jerome,
QC, J7Y 1T3
(450) 476-0720
Emp Here 33   Sales 16,436,574
SIC 5511 New and used car dealers
Krikor Hairabedian

D-U-N-S 20-704-8930   (BR)
GOUVERNEMENT DE LA PROVINCE DE QUEBEC
MINISTERE DE LA JUSTICE DIRECTION REGIONAL DES LAURENTIDES
(Suby of GOUVERNEMENT DE LA PROVINCE DE QUEBEC)
25 Rue De Martigny O, Saint-Jerome, QC, J7Y 4Z1
(450) 431-4406
Emp Here 100
SIC 8111 Legal services
Michel Caouette

D-U-N-S 24-372-6036   (SL)
GROUPE LEV-FAB INC
ATELIER TAC
640 Boul Monseigneur-Dubois, Saint-Jerome,
QC, J7Y 3L8
(450) 438-7164
Emp Here 65   Sales 14,430,065
SIC 3599 Industrial machinery, nec
Luc Levasseur

D-U-N-S 20-567-9210   (HQ)
H. CHALUT LTEE
BOUTIQUE BOUCHERVILLE
2172 Boul Du Cure-Labelle, Saint-Jerome,
QC, J7Y 1T3
(450) 438-4153
Sales 47,502,600
SIC 5087 Service establishment equipment
Alain Jacquaz
Jean-Luc Sabourin

D-U-N-S 25-365-4719   (BR)
HOME DEPOT OF CANADA INC
HOME DEPOT
(Suby of THE HOME DEPOT INC)
1045 Boul Du Grand-Heron, Saint-Jerome,
QC, J7Y 3P2
(450) 565-6020
Emp Here 150
SIC 5251 Hardware stores
Sylvio Pintal

D-U-N-S 24-922-2969   (SL)
I.C.C. COMPAGNIE DE CHEMINEES INDUS-TRIELLES INC
400 Rue John-F.-Kennedy, Saint-Jerome,
J7Y 4B7
(450) 565-6336
Emp Here 200   Sales 38,417,000
SIC 3443 Fabricated plate work (boiler shop)
Douglas Singer
Raymond B. Bonar
Andre Bibaud
Lesley Fournier

D-U-N-S 25-232-3977   (HQ)
ICON DU CANADA INC

(Suby of BAIN CAPITAL, LP)
900 Rue De L'Industrie, Saint-Jerome, QC,
J7Y 4B8
(450) 565-2955
Emp Here 14   Sales 11,972,466
SIC 5091 Sporting and recreation goods
Richard Hebert
Everett Smith

D-U-N-S 20-363-1452   (HQ)
INDUSTRIES J. HAMELIN INC, LES
(Suby of CARRIS FINANCIAL CORP.)
690 Boul Roland-Godard, Saint-Jerome, QC,
J7Y 4C5
(450) 431-3221
Sales 28,860,130
SIC 3553 Woodworking machinery
David Ferraro
David Fitz-Gerald

D-U-N-S 24-679-7166   (SL)
LUMI-O INTERNATIONAL INC
SPA-O
370 Boul Lajeunesse O, Saint-Jerome, QC,
J7Y 4E5
(450) 565-5544
Emp Here 65   Sales 21,198,840
SIC 3949 Sporting and athletic goods, nec
Charles Goulet

D-U-N-S 25-256-9843   (SL)
MAGASIN POULIN INC
MARCHAND CANADIAN TIRE DE ST-JEROME
700 Boul Monseigneur-Dubois, Saint-Jerome,
QC, J7Y 4Y9
(450) 438-3506
Emp Here 80   Sales 29,137,200
SIC 5014 Tires and tubes
Jean Guy Poulin

D-U-N-S 24-433-0940   (SL)
MARCHE ELITE ST-JEROME INC
METRO FAMILLE THIBEAULT ST-JEROME
430 Boul Monseigneur-Dubois, Saint-Jerome,
QC, J7Y 3L8
(450) 432-3433
Emp Here 100   Sales 29,347,700
SIC 5411 Grocery stores
Nelson Thibeault
Louise Marquis

D-U-N-S 24-081-7072   (HQ)
MATERIAUX LAURENTIENS INC
ACCESSOIRES DE JARDIN
(Suby of 3151263 CANADA INC)
2159 Boul Du Cure-Labelle, Saint-Jerome,
QC, J7Y 1T1
(450) 438-9780
Emp Here 25   Sales 70,262,500
SIC 5211 Lumber and other building materials
Denis Warnett

D-U-N-S 24-054-9142   (SL)
MAURICE FOUCAULT INC
TRANSPORT ES FOUCAULT
260 Boul Roland-Godard, Saint-Jerome, QC,
J7Y 4P7
(450) 530-3420
Emp Here 10   Sales 31,058,570
SIC 4924 Natural gas distribution
Eric Foucault
Stephane Foucault

D-U-N-S 25-362-1080   (HQ)
MEUBLES FOLIOT INC
721 Boul Roland-Godard, Saint-Jerome, QC,
J7Y 4C1
(450) 565-9166
Sales 30,864,400
SIC 2531 Public building and related furniture
Daniel Foliot
Stephane Belisle
Marie-Eve Foliot

D-U-N-S 20-725-9466   (BR)
MUELLER CANADA LTD
(Suby of MUELLER WATER PRODUCTS,

INC.)
230 Rue Castonguay, Saint-Jerome, QC, J7Y
2J7
Emp Here 110
SIC 5999 Miscellaneous retail stores, nec
Alain Couture

D-U-N-S 24-340-3867   (HQ)
PAPINEAU INT, S.E.C.
LOGISTIQUE MIRABEL
851 Boul Roland-Godard, Saint-Jerome, QC,
J7Y 4C2
(450) 432-7555
Emp Here 25   Sales 46,095,250
SIC 4213 Trucking, except local
Chantal Martel

D-U-N-S 20-253-4384   (SL)
PRODUITS DE METAL VULCAIN INC
31 Rue John-F.-Kennedy, Saint-Jerome, QC,
J7Y 4B4
(450) 436-5355
Emp Here 210   Sales 51,078,510
SIC 3469 Metal stampings, nec
Serge Desjardins
Luc Lusignan

D-U-N-S 25-853-2654   (BR)
PROVIGO DISTRIBUTION INC
MAXI COMPAGNIE
(Suby of LOBLAW COMPANIES LIMITED)
900 Boul Grignon, Saint-Jerome, QC, J7Y 3S7
(450) 436-3824
Emp Here 110
SIC 5411 Grocery stores
Mark Bonville

D-U-N-S 20-253-3543   (SL)
RAYONESE TEXTILE INC
(Suby of CULP, INC.)
500 Boul Monseigneur-Dubois, Saint-Jerome,
QC, J7Y 3L8
(450) 476-1991
Emp Here 160   Sales 37,840,480
SIC 2221 Broadwoven fabric mills, manmade
Robert G. Culp Iv
Blair C. Barwick
Kenneth R. Bowling
Eric Stevens
Patrick Deschenes

D-U-N-S 24-641-5645   (SL)
RENOVATEUR REGIONAL
1025 Boul Jean-Baptiste-Rolland O, Saint-
Jerome, QC, J7Y 4Y7
(450) 560-3979
Emp Here 100   Sales 26,765,200
SIC 5211 Lumber and other building materials
Andre Dagenais

D-U-N-S 25-332-0519   (SL)
SOUCY BARON INC
(Suby of SOUCY HOLDING INC)
851 Rue Baron, Saint-Jerome, QC, J7Y 4E1
(450) 436-2433
Emp Here 100   Sales 15,885,800
SIC 3069 Fabricated rubber products, nec
Gilles Soucy

D-U-N-S 20-052-0695   (HQ)
ST-JEROME CHEVROLET BUICK GMC INC
GROUPE CARBUR ST-JEROME AUTO DE-
POT
265 Rue John-F.-Kennedy, Saint-Jerome, QC,
J7Y 4B5
(450) 438-1203
Sales 19,923,120
SIC 5511 New and used car dealers
Daniel Jarry
Jean-Sebastien Martin

D-U-N-S 24-698-4801   (SL)
TRANSCOBEC (1987) INC
AUTOBUS C MONGEAU
21 Rue John-F.-Kennedy, Saint-Jerome, QC,
J7Y 4B4

(450) 432-9748
Emp Here 120   Sales 9,032,640
SIC 4151 School buses
Jean-Pierre Brunet
Martin Paquette
Yves Seguin

D-U-N-S 20-739-0501   (SL)
VARIETES PIERRE PRUD'HOMME INC, LES
801 Rue Price, Saint-Jerome, QC, J7Y 4E2
(450) 438-2977
Emp Here 50   Sales 26,027,100
SIC 5099 Durable goods, nec
Pierre Prud'homme
Marc Prud'homme
Martin Prud'homme
Huguette Prud'homme

D-U-N-S 20-247-0944   (SL)
VENTES FORD ELITE (1978) INC
2171 Boul Du Cure-Labelle, Saint-Jerome,
QC, J7Y 1T1
(450) 436-3142
Emp Here 55   Sales 34,610,400
SIC 5511 New and used car dealers
Michel Audette

D-U-N-S 24-099-9909   (BR)
WAL-MART CANADA CORP
(Suby of WALMART INC.)
1030 Boul Du Grand-Heron, Saint-Jerome,
QC, J7Y 5K8
(450) 438-6776
Emp Here 200
SIC 5311 Department stores
Eric Theriault

Saint-Jerome, QC J7Z

D-U-N-S 25-758-7709   (SL)
AGENCE DE LA SANTE ET DES SERVICES SOCIAUX DES LAURENTIDES, L'
500 Boul Des Laurentides Bureau 1010,
Saint-Jerome, QC, J7Z 4M2
(450) 436-8622
Emp Here 180   Sales 24,022,620
SIC 8399 Social services, nec
Micheline Valliere Joly

D-U-N-S 20-253-0192   (HQ)
BOUCHERIE COTE INC
952a Rue Labelle, Saint-Jerome, QC, J7Z
5M8
(450) 438-4159
Emp Here 4   Sales 17,669,680
SIC 6512 Nonresidential building operators
Francois Cote
Bernard Cote

D-U-N-S 20-513-6778   (HQ)
CAISSE DESJARDINS DE SAINT-ANTOINE-DES-LAURENTIDES
DESJARDINS   ENTREPRISES-
LAURENTIDES
663 Boul Saint-Antoine, Saint-Jerome, QC,
J7Z 3B8
(450) 436-5331
Emp Here 45   Sales 14,213,758
SIC 6062 State credit unions
Sylvie Tremblay
Eric Gagnon
Marc-Antoine Lachance
Nathalie Proulx
Marie-Claude Bergeron
Lise Gendron
Ronald Gill
Pierre A. Giroux
Caroline Lavoie
Suzanne Leduc

D-U-N-S 20-844-8253   (BR)
CENTRE DE READAPTATION EN DEFI-CIENCE PHYSIQUE LE BOUCLIER
CENTRE DE READAPTATION LE BOUCLIER

(Suby of CENTRE DE READAPTATION EN DEFICIENCE PHYSIQUE LE BOUCLIER)
225 Rue Du Palais, Saint-Jerome, QC, J7Z 1X7
(450) 560-9898
Emp Here 350
SIC 8011 Offices and clinics of medical doctors
Lise Bolduc

D-U-N-S 20-602-2212   (SL)
CENTRE DU SPORT ALARY INC
1324 Boul Saint-Antoine, Saint-Jerome, QC, J7Z 7M2
(450) 436-2242
Emp Here 35   *Sales* 17,432,730
SIC 5571 Motorcycle dealers
Richard Alary
Pierre Alary
Stephane Alary

D-U-N-S 25-766-1439   (BR)
CENTRE INTEGRE DE SANTE ET DE SERVICES SOCIAUX DE LANAUDIERE
CISSS DE LANAUDIERE - LE BOUCLIER
(Suby of CENTRE INTEGRE DE SANTE ET DE SERVICES SOCIAUX DE LANAUDIERE)
11 Rue Boyer, Saint-Jerome, QC, J7Z 2K5
(450) 432-7588
Emp Here 87
SIC 8049 Offices of health practitioner
Lise Bolduc

D-U-N-S 20-363-0637   (BR)
CENTRE INTEGRE DE SANTE ET DE SERVICES SOCIAUX DES LAURENTIDES
CISSS DE LAURENTIDES, LE
(Suby of CENTRE INTEGRE DE SANTE ET DE SERVICES SOCIAUX DES LAURENTIDES)
500 Boul Des Laurentides Bureau 1010, Saint-Jerome, QC, J7Z 4M2
(450) 436-8622
Emp Here 180
SIC 8011 Offices and clinics of medical doctors
Jean-Francois Foisy

D-U-N-S 25-424-1615   (HQ)
CENTRE INTEGRE DE SANTE ET DE SERVICES SOCIAUX DES LAURENTIDES
CISSS DE LAURENTIDES, LE
290 Rue De Montigny, Saint-Jerome, QC, J7Z 5T3
(450) 432-2777
Emp Here 100   *Sales* 684,745,200
SIC 8011 Offices and clinics of medical doctors
Roger Gibb
Florian Brissette
Diane Rioux

D-U-N-S 20-100-4053   (BR)
COMMISSION SCOLAIRE DE LA RIVIERE-DU-NORD
ECOLE DE L'HORIZON SOLEIL
1155 Av Du Parc, Saint-Jerome, QC, J7Z 6X6
(450) 438-1296
Emp Here 110
SIC 8211 Elementary and secondary schools
Nicole Leblanc

D-U-N-S 24-012-1652   (BR)
COMMISSION SCOLAIRE DE LA RIVIERE-DU-NORD
ECOLE SECONDAIRE CAP JEUNESSE
600 36e Av, Saint-Jerome, QC, J7Z 5W2
(450) 436-1858
Emp Here 120
SIC 8211 Elementary and secondary schools
Jean Vaillancourt

D-U-N-S 25-232-8844   (BR)
COMMISSION SCOLAIRE DE LA RIVIERE-DU-NORD
ECOLE POLYVALENTE ST JEROME
535 Rue Filion, Saint-Jerome, QC, J7Z 1J6

(450) 436-1560
Emp Here 240
SIC 8211 Elementary and secondary schools

D-U-N-S 20-217-5188   (SL)
COMPAGNIE EAGLE LUMBER LIMITEE, LA
BOCAN MATERIAUX
435 Boul Jean-Baptiste-Rolland E, Saint-Jerome, QC, J7Z 4J4
(450) 432-4004
Emp Here 60   *Sales* 16,059,120
SIC 5211 Lumber and other building materials
Michel Bock
Joanne Bock
Michel Jr. Bock
Marie-Josee Bock
Stephane Bock

D-U-N-S 25-285-4104   (SL)
CONCEPTION GENIK INC
GENIK AUTOMATION
715 Rue Nobel Bureau 108, Saint-Jerome, QC, J7Z 7A3
(450) 436-7706
Emp Here 70   *Sales* 33,251,820
SIC 5084 Industrial machinery and equipment
Donald Turcotte
Marc Bergeron
Marc Lussier
Daniel Lemay
Patrick Gariepy

D-U-N-S 24-896-7135   (SL)
CUISINES NUTRI-DELI INC, LES
535 Rue Filion, Saint-Jerome, QC, J7Z 1J6
(450) 438-5278
Emp Here 100   *Sales* 4,551,900
SIC 5812 Eating places
Benoit Belisle

D-U-N-S 24-362-8687   (SL)
ELECTRO COMPOSITES (2008) ULC
(Suby of HUBBELL LUXEMBOURG, SARL)
325 Rue Scott, Saint-Jerome, QC, J7Z 1H3
(450) 431-2777
Emp Here 55   *Sales* 10,474,310
SIC 3644 Noncurrent-carrying wiring devices
Gerben Baker
Kevin Potts
Maria R. Lee
Patricia B Morrison
Wayne Cable
Megan Preneta
Joseph A. Capozzoli

D-U-N-S 25-291-4874   (BR)
GOUVERNEMENT DE LA PROVINCE DE QUEBEC
CLSC DE SAINT JEROME
(Suby of GOUVERNEMENT DE LA PROVINCE DE QUEBEC)
430 Rue Labelle, Saint-Jerome, QC, J7Z 5L3
(450) 431-2221
Emp Here 260
SIC 8399 Social services, nec
Chantale Fortin

D-U-N-S 24-259-1505   (SL)
INDUSTRIES THERMOPLUS AIR INC, LES
262 Rue Scott, Saint-Jerome, QC, J7Z 1H1
(450) 436-7555
Emp Here 26   *Sales* 11,626,524
SIC 5075 Warm air heating and air conditioning
Pat Occhicone

D-U-N-S 20-609-4273   (SL)
LUNETTERIE BRANCHES INC., LES
BRANCHERS, LES
509 Rue Saint-Georges, Saint-Jerome, QC, J7Z 5B6
(450) 432-3914
Emp Here 49   *Sales* 15,954,400
SIC 5995 Optical goods stores
Patrick Bolduc

D-U-N-S 25-784-8655   (SL)
MARCHE ELITE ST-ANTOINE INC

MARCHE METRO ELITE ST-ANTOINE
633 Boul Des Laurentides, Saint-Jerome, QC, J7Z 4M4
(450) 432-3433
Emp Here 160   *Sales* 46,956,320
SIC 5411 Grocery stores
Louise Marquis
Nelson Thibault

D-U-N-S 25-096-4827   (SL)
OUTILLAGE SUMMIT
803 Rue Saint-Georges, Saint-Jerome, QC, J7Z 5E1
(450) 592-0747
Emp Here 25   *Sales* 11,179,350
SIC 5072 Hardware
Shamsherali Punjani

D-U-N-S 20-416-1483   (HQ)
PAUL GRAND'MAISON INC
GRAND'MAISON HEATING-AIR CONDITIONNING
200 Boul Lachapelle, Saint-Jerome, QC, J7Z 7L2
(450) 438-1266
Emp Here 21   *Sales* 12,194,130
SIC 5983 Fuel oil dealers
Marc Grand'maison
Pascal Grand'maison
Lyne Grand'maison

D-U-N-S 25-783-5389   (SL)
PRESENTOIR FILOTECH INC
234 Rue De Sainte-Paule, Saint-Jerome, QC, J7Z 1A8
(450) 432-2266
Emp Here 50   *Sales* 10,941,200
SIC 3993 Signs and advertising specialties
Sylvain Danylo

D-U-N-S 25-466-3040   (SL)
PRODUITS JUPITER INC, LES
BAR SPECTACLE LE VIEUX SHACK
338 Rue Saint-Georges, Saint-Jerome, QC, J7Z 5A5
(450) 436-7500
Emp Here 50   *Sales* 11,242,750
SIC 2082 Malt beverages
Gaetan Lapointe

D-U-N-S 25-394-4490   (SL)
RBF INTERNATIONAL LTEE
AQUA SOLUTIONS
(Suby of 2427-2791 QUEBEC INC)
780 Rue Nobel, Saint-Jerome, QC, J7Z 7A3
(450) 438-4416
Emp Here 50   *Sales* 36,517,250
SIC 5169 Chemicals and allied products, nec
Claude Carriere
Dominic Carriere
Stephane Arsenault
Stephane Cyr

D-U-N-S 20-007-2366   (SL)
RUEL VENNE LEONARD ASSOCIES
PME INTER NOTAIRES
100 Rue De La Gare, Saint-Jerome, QC, J7Z 2C1
(450) 432-2661
Emp Here 40   *Sales* 17,968,760
SIC 7389 Business services, nec
Francois Venne

D-U-N-S 20-177-1214   (SL)
SERRES ROYALES INC, LES
1954 Boul Saint-Antoine, Saint-Jerome, QC, J7Z 7M2
(450) 438-1334
Emp Here 20   *Sales* 10,702,480
SIC 5148 Fresh fruits and vegetables
Gilles Lemieux

D-U-N-S 24-837-1049   (SL)
TRICA INC
800 Rue Pasteur, Saint-Jerome, QC, J7Z 7K9
(450) 431-4897
Emp Here 100   *Sales* 15,432,200
SIC 2519 Household furniture, nec

Francois Caron
Alexandre Paquette

D-U-N-S 20-792-0302   (SL)
VOIE RAPIDE DES LAURENTIDES
DES LAURENTIDES FORD
155 Boul Lachapelle Bureau 158, Saint-Jerome, QC, J7Z 7L2
(450) 436-2264
Emp Here 45   *Sales* 22,413,510
SIC 5511 New and used car dealers
Marie-Josee Aube
Samuel Leveille

Saint-Joseph-De-Beauce, QC G0S

D-U-N-S 20-873-3642   (HQ)
ATELIER DE READAPTATION AU TRAVAIL DE BEAUCE INC, L'
A.R.T.B.
1280 Av Du Palais, Saint-Joseph-De-Beauce, QC, G0S 2V0
(418) 397-4341
Sales 16,400,070
SIC 7349 Building maintenance services, nec
Pierre Thibodeau
Pierre Cloutier
Denis Marcoux
Jules Caron
Manon Tousignant
Maryse Fecteau
Charles Laflamme
Guy Chabot
Louis Tremblay
Harold Vachon

D-U-N-S 24-916-2764   (SL)
CENTRE DE MATERIAUX COMPOSITES
170 Rue Du Parc, Saint-Joseph-De-Beauce, QC, G0S 2V0
(418) 397-6514
Emp Here 31   *Sales* 12,125,898
SIC 8631 Labor organizations

D-U-N-S 24-465-1238   (SL)
CHEMISES L. L. LESSARD INC
1195 Av Du Palais, Saint-Joseph-De-Beauce, QC, G0S 2V0
(418) 397-5665
Emp Here 45   *Sales* 19,957,050
SIC 7389 Business services, nec
Laurier Lessard
Lisette Lessard

D-U-N-S 20-711-9251   (BR)
COMMISSION SCOLAIRE DE LA BEAUCE-ETCHEMIN
ECOLE SECONDAIRE VEILLEUX
(Suby of COMMISSION SCOLAIRE DE LA BEAUCE-ETCHEMIN)
695 Av Robert-Cliche, Saint-Joseph-De-Beauce, QC, G0S 2V0
(418) 397-6841
Emp Here 102
SIC 8211 Elementary and secondary schools
Jean-Francois Giguere

D-U-N-S 20-777-1713   (SL)
COOPERATIVE DE SERVICES A DOMICILE BEAUCE-NORD
700 Av Robert-Cliche, Saint-Joseph-De-Beauce, QC, G0S 2V0
(418) 397-8283
Emp Here 49   *Sales* 11,114,817
SIC 8399 Social services, nec
Alain Goulet

D-U-N-S 20-951-5782   (HQ)
CUISITEC LTEE
175 Rue Michener, Saint-Joseph-De-Beauce, QC, G0S 2V0
(418) 397-5432
Emp Here 2   *Sales* 12,652,950
SIC 5211 Lumber and other building materials

Normand Cloutier
Jhislaine Felardeau

D-U-N-S 20-582-4055   (SL)
MANUFACTURE FRAMECO LTEE
230 Rue Du Parc, Saint-Joseph-De-Beauce,
QC, G0S 2V0
(418) 397-6895
Emp Here 50   *Sales* 10,141,500
SIC 3443 Fabricated plate work (boiler shop)
Andree Cloutier
Jeannine Cloutier

D-U-N-S 24-226-2322   (SL)
MARCHE PIERRE JOBIDON INC
IGA
1021 Av Du Palais, Saint-Joseph-De-Beauce,
QC, G0S 2V0
(418) 397-5213
Emp Here 49   *Sales* 13,433,448
SIC 5411 Grocery stores
Pierre Jobidon

D-U-N-S 20-331-6708   (HQ)
MBI PLASTIQUE INC
MOULEURS DE BEAUCE
1335 Av Du Palais, Saint-Joseph-De-Beauce,
QC, G0S 2V0
(418) 397-8088
Sales 14,297,220
SIC 3089 Plastics products, nec
Eric Veilleux
Nicolas Jacques

D-U-N-S 24-202-2382   (SL)
**PLACEMENTS JACQUES GOULET LTEE,
LES**
830 Av Beland, Saint-Joseph-De-Beauce, QC,
G0S 2V0

Emp Here 100   *Sales* 15,586,300
SIC 2431 Millwork
Jacques Goulet

D-U-N-S 20-777-1697   (SL)
RECYCLAGE DE PAPIER HANNA LTEE
760 Av Guy-Poulin, Saint-Joseph-De-Beauce,
QC, G0S 2V0
(418) 397-5859
Emp Here 26   *Sales* 13,534,092
SIC 5093 Scrap and waste materials
Michael Thomas Knox

D-U-N-S 25-542-8773   (HQ)
REGITEX INC
745 Av Guy-Poulin, Saint-Joseph-De-Beauce,
QC, G0S 2V0
(418) 397-5775
Sales 18,340,300
SIC 2282 Throwing and winding mills
Lisa Fecteau

D-U-N-S 20-578-8508   (SL)
STRUCTURES ST-JOSEPH LTEE
200 Rue Du Parc, Saint-Joseph-De-Beauce,
QC, G0S 2V0
(418) 397-5712
Emp Here 100   *Sales* 19,237,000
SIC 2439 Structural wood members, nec
Pierre Andre Begin
Yvan Begin
Jean-Philippe Begin

Saint-Joseph-De-Sorel, QC J3R

D-U-N-S 24-355-5369   (SL)
ALLIAGES ZABO INC
201 Rue Montcalm Bureau 213, Saint-Joseph-
De-Sorel, QC, J3R 1B9
(450) 746-1126
Emp Here 10   *Sales* 10,003,390
SIC 5051 Metals service centers and offices
Michel Beaudoin
Christiane St-Germain

D-U-N-S 20-551-5260   (HQ)
FORGES DE SOREL CIE, LES
FINKL STEEL - SOREL
100 Rue Mccarthy, Saint-Joseph-De-Sorel,
QC, J3R 3M8
(450) 746-4030
Emp Here 350   *Sales* 146,582,640
SIC 3312 Blast furnaces and steel mills
Richard Lahaye
Mark Shirley
Mathieu Bourgeois
Richard Godin

D-U-N-S 25-007-7674   (SL)
FORGES DE SOREL CIE, LES
FINKL STEEL - SOREL
100 Rue Mccarthy, Saint-Joseph-De-Sorel,
QC, J3R 3M8
(450) 746-4030
Emp Here 1   *Sales* 44,804,750
SIC 3291 Abrasive products
Richard Lahaye
Mathieu Bourgeois
Richard Godin
Mark Shirley

D-U-N-S 20-261-4343   (HQ)
J. FAGEN & FILS INC
*FAGEN INTERNATIONAL FREIGHT SER-
VICES*
201 Rue Montcalm Bureau 100, Saint-Joseph-
De-Sorel, QC, J3R 1B9
(450) 742-8880
Emp Here 16   *Sales* 18,218,970
SIC 5093 Scrap and waste materials
Lesly Fagen
Leonard Fagen

D-U-N-S 24-098-8704   (HQ)
MINERAUX MART INC
(Suby of GESTION MCMARLAND INC)
201 Rue Montcalm Bureau 213, Saint-Joseph-
De-Sorel, QC, J3R 1B9
(450) 746-1126
Emp Here 40   *Sales* 22,358,700
SIC 5051 Metals service centers and offices
Michel Beaudoin

Saint-Joseph-Du-Lac, QC J0N

D-U-N-S 20-871-7103   (SL)
9139-6317 QUEBEC INC
IGA LAMOUREUX
3765 Ch D'Oka, Saint-Joseph-Du-Lac, QC,
J0N 1M0
(450) 413-2789
Emp Here 160   *Sales* 46,956,320
SIC 5411 Grocery stores
Yves Lamoureux

D-U-N-S 24-212-7855   (SL)
VERGER LACROIX INC
649 Ch Principal, Saint-Joseph-Du-Lac, QC,
J0N 1M0
(450) 623-4888
Emp Here 26   *Sales* 21,725,002
SIC 5148 Fresh fruits and vegetables
Pascal Lacroix
Danielle Marceau

Saint-Jules, QC G0N

D-U-N-S 24-320-4885   (SL)
IMPRIMERIE NORECOB INC
NORECOB IMPRIMEUR
(Suby of GROUPE VALLIERES INC)
340 Rue Principale, Saint-Jules, QC, G0N
1R0
(418) 397-2233
Emp Here 75   *Sales* 12,302,025
SIC 2731 Book publishing

Pierre Mccann
Celine Vallieres
Marc Vallieres

Saint-Just-De-Bretenieres, QC G0R

D-U-N-S 20-256-1692   (HQ)
BOIS DAAQUAM INC
(Suby of GROUPE LEBEL INC)
370 Rte 204, Saint-Just-De-Bretenieres, QC,
G0R 3H0
(418) 244-3601
Sales 33,664,750
SIC 2421 Sawmills and planing mills, general
Louis-Frederic Lebel

Saint-Lambert, QC H2H

D-U-N-S 20-271-2170   (SL)
POST-PROD CMJ TECH INC
5000 Rue D'Iberville Bureau 332, Saint-
Lambert, QC, H2H 2S6
(514) 731-4242
Emp Here 49   *Sales* 20,457,794
SIC 7384 Photofinish laboratories
John Kuyk

Saint-Lambert, QC J4P

D-U-N-S 25-391-6936   (HQ)
**CAISSE   DESJARDINS   CHARLES-
LEMOYNE**
DESJARDINS ENTREPRISESRIVE-SUD
477 Av Victoria, Saint-Lambert, QC, J4P 2J1
(450) 671-3733
Emp Here 28   *Sales* 10,678,255
SIC 6062 State credit unions
Lorne Bouchard
Rollande Girard Dilalla
Lisa Baillargeon
Danielle Latour
Loic Blancquaert
Andree Grimard
Audree Lirette
Claude Panneton
Roger Riverin
Antonin Roy

D-U-N-S 25-176-8784   (BR)
DARE FOODS LIMITED
ALIMENTS DARE
(Suby of DARE FOODS LIMITED)
845 Av Saint-Charles, Saint-Lambert, QC,
J4P 2A2
(450) 671-6121
Emp Here 280
SIC 2051 Bread, cake, and related products
Nadya St-Gelais

D-U-N-S 24-943-7385   (SL)
GESTION ROBERT M. HARVEY INC
210 Boul Desaulniers, Saint-Lambert, QC,
J4P 1M6
(450) 658-8771
Emp Here 175   *Sales* 33,614,875
SIC 3449 Miscellaneous Metalwork
Robert M. Harvey
Therese Harvey
Bernard Harvey

D-U-N-S 25-064-0323   (BR)
MAGASINS J.L. TAYLOR INC, LES
TAYLOR'S
(Suby of MAGASINS J.L. TAYLOR INC, LES)
556 Av Victoria, Saint-Lambert, QC, J4P 2J5
(450) 672-9722
Emp Here 100
SIC 5651 Family clothing stores

Linda St-Onge

D-U-N-S 20-254-6032   (HQ)
MAGASINS J.L. TAYLOR INC, LES
PASSEPORTAYLOR
525 Av Notre-Dame Bureau 672, Saint-
Lambert, QC, J4P 2K6
(450) 672-9722
Emp Here 15   *Sales* 18,836,580
SIC 5651 Family clothing stores
Robert Taylor
Charles-James Taylor

D-U-N-S 25-980-4201   (SL)
**MARCHE IGA LOUISE MENARD ST-
LAMBERT INC**
371 Av Victoria, Saint-Lambert, QC, J4P 2H7
(450) 466-3880
Emp Here 75   *Sales* 22,010,775
SIC 5411 Grocery stores
Louise Menard

D-U-N-S 24-052-5209   (HQ)
MARCHES LOUISE MENARD INC, LES
*MARCHES LOUISE MENARD (ILE-DES-
SOEURS), LES*
34 Av Argyle, Saint-Lambert, QC, J4P 2H4
(514) 843-6116
Sales 48,116,000
SIC 5411 Grocery stores
Louise Menard
Bruno Menard

D-U-N-S 20-254-5695   (SL)
**PHARMACIE BEDARD LYNE PHARMACI-
ENNE INC**
PROXIN
490 Av Victoria, Saint-Lambert, QC, J4P 2J4
(450) 671-5563
Emp Here 42   *Sales* 10,624,068
SIC 5912 Drug stores and proprietary stores
Lyne Bedard

D-U-N-S 25-663-7997   (SL)
QUEBEC EN FORME
668 Av Victoria, Saint-Lambert, QC, J4P 2J6

Emp Here 49   *Sales* 11,114,817
SIC 8399 Social services, nec
Claude Chagnon

D-U-N-S 25-665-3239   (HQ)
RE/MAX PERFORMANCE INC
RE/MAX
15 Rue Du Prince-Arthur, Saint-Lambert, QC,
J4P 1X1
(450) 466-4000
Emp Here 25   *Sales* 13,587,800
SIC 6531 Real estate agents and managers
Jacques Trembley

D-U-N-S 25-321-4001   (BR)
REVERA INC
RESIDENCE DU PARC
(Suby of GOVERNMENT OF CANADA)
33 Av Argyle, Saint-Lambert, QC, J4P 3P5
(450) 465-1401
Emp Here 100
SIC 8051 Skilled nursing care facilities

D-U-N-S 20-302-3023   (HQ)
ROCTEST LTEE
CORPORATION D'ACQUISITION ROLL
680 Av Birch, Saint-Lambert, QC, J4P 2N3
(450) 465-1113
Sales 17,873,900
SIC 8711 Engineering services
Frederic Borne
Janet Barbookles
Michael Larkin

Saint-Lambert, QC J4R

D-U-N-S 20-319-9617   (SL)
ALIMENTATION RICHARD GAGNON S C

INC
1461 Av Victoria, Saint-Lambert, QC, J4R 1R5
(450) 671-6205
Emp Here 49   *Sales* 13,433,448
SIC 5411 Grocery stores
 Richard Gagnon

 D-U-N-S 20-926-2385   (HQ)
INDUSTRIES LYNX INC
175 Rue Upper Edison, Saint-Lambert, QC,
J4R 2R3
(514) 866-1068
Sales 15,366,800
SIC 3442 Metal doors, sash, and trim
 Doris T. Schram
 Robert G Schram Jr

 D-U-N-S 25-665-4443   (SL)
**JARDINS INTERIEURS DE SAINT-
LAMBERT INC, LES**
(*Suby of* 9108-9458 QUEBEC INC)
1705 Av Victoria Bureau 904, Saint-Lambert,
QC, J4R 2T7
(450) 671-1314
Emp Here 100
SIC 6513 Apartment building operators
 Christian B. Sweetser
 Jeffrey H. Miller
 Frank Cerrone

 D-U-N-S 25-495-4548   (SL)
**MARCHES LOUISE MENARD (PREVILLE)
INC, LES**
IGA #8215
299 Boul Sir-Wilfrid-Laurier Bureau 201,
Saint-Lambert, QC, J4R 2L1
(450) 923-9399
Emp Here 100   *Sales* 29,347,700
SIC 5411 Grocery stores
 Louise Menard

 D-U-N-S 24-251-8699   (SL)
PHARMAPRIX CLAUDINE LOUBERT INC
LOUBERT, CLAUDINE
1031 Av Victoria, Saint-Lambert, QC, J4R 1P6
(450) 671-8367
Emp Here 45   *Sales* 11,382,930
SIC 5912 Drug stores and proprietary stores
 Claudine Loubert

 D-U-N-S 24-766-2575   (HQ)
RICARDO MEDIA INC
ESCAPES RICARDO
300 Rue D'Arran, Saint-Lambert, QC, J4R
1K5
(450) 465-4500
Emp Here 50   *Sales* 24,604,050
SIC 2721 Periodicals
 Denis Chamberland
 Ricardo Larrivee
 Brigitte Coutu

Saint-Lambert, QC J4S

 D-U-N-S 20-961-9790   (SL)
COUNTRY CLUB DE MONTREAL, LE
5 Rue Riverside, Saint-Lambert, QC, J4S 1B7
(450) 671-6181
Emp Here 100   *Sales* 7,854,500
SIC 7997 Membership sports and recreation
clubs
 Robert Gour

Saint-Lambert-De-Lauzon, QC G0S

 D-U-N-S 20-055-6087   (SL)
EPICERIE CENTRE-MATIC INC
1233 Rue Des Erables, Saint-Lambert-De-
Lauzon, QC, G0S 2W0
(418) 889-9723
Emp Here 80   *Sales* 23,478,160

SIC 5411 Grocery stores
 Leon Buteau
 Nicolas Buteau

 D-U-N-S 24-205-1154   (HQ)
GROUPE MUNDIAL INC
12 Rue Napoleon-Couture, Saint-Lambert-
De-Lauzon, QC, G0S 2W0
(418) 889-0502
Sales 27,335,000
SIC 6712 Bank holding companies
 Louis Veilleux

 D-U-N-S 24-202-6094   (SL)
METAL BERNARD INC
(*Suby of* GROUPE MUNDIAL INC)
12 Rue Napoleon-Couture, Saint-Lambert-
De-Lauzon, QC, G0S 2W0
(418) 889-0502
Emp Here 100   *Sales* 66,890,800
SIC 7389 Business services, nec
 Louis Veilleux
 Claude Beauviller
 Rene Tremblay

 D-U-N-S 20-531-0282   (SL)
METEO FENETRES ET PORTES INC
FENETRES METEO
132c Rue Leon-Vachon, Saint-Lambert-De-
Lauzon, QC, G0S 2W0

Emp Here 26   *Sales* 11,626,524
SIC 5031 Lumber, plywood, and millwork
 Jean Morin

 D-U-N-S 24-326-2669   (SL)
OEUFS OVALE S.E.C., LES
205 Rue Damase-Breton, Saint-Lambert-De-
Lauzon, QC, G0S 2W0
(418) 889-8088
Emp Here 50   *Sales* 41,778,850
SIC 5144 Poultry and poultry products
 Daniel Lavoie

 D-U-N-S 25-880-0692   (SL)
OUTILLEURS, S.E.C., L'
RONA
1325 Rue Du Pont, Saint-Lambert-De-
Lauzon, QC, G0S 2W0
(418) 889-9521
Emp Here 50   *Sales* 22,358,700
SIC 5072 Hardware
 Patrice Brochu

 D-U-N-S 20-184-9101   (SL)
OVALE SEC
205 Rue Damase-Breton, Saint-Lambert-De-
Lauzon, QC, G0S 2W0
(418) 889-8088
Emp Here 65   *Sales* 54,312,505
SIC 5144 Poultry and poultry products
 Daniel Lavoie

 D-U-N-S 24-706-2136   (SL)
RESTAURANT-BAR LA ROCHELIERE INC
DEPANNEUR LA ROCHELIERE
1370 Rue Du Pont, Saint-Lambert-De-
Lauzon, QC, G0S 2W0
(418) 889-0183
Emp Here 31   *Sales* 15,440,418
SIC 5541 Gasoline service stations
 Denis Larochelle

 D-U-N-S 20-860-9818   (SL)
REVETEMENTS ALNORDICA INC
1230 Rue Des Erables, Saint-Lambert-De-
Lauzon, QC, G0S 2W0
(418) 889-9761
Emp Here 60   *Sales* 13,069,740
SIC 1761 Roofing, siding, and sheetMetal
work
 Rejean Dufour
 Gerald Fontaine
 Francois Gagnon

 D-U-N-S 20-181-8254   (BR)
ROYAL GROUP, INC
PRODUITS DE BATIMENT RESIDENTIEL

(*Suby of* WESTLAKE CHEMICAL CORPO-
RATION)
1401 Rue Bellevue, Saint-Lambert-De-
Lauzon, QC, G0S 2W0

Emp Here 130
SIC 3089 Plastics products, nec
 Gilles Lemay

Saint-Laurent, QC H4K

 D-U-N-S 24-302-5679   (SL)
11375644 CANADA INC
ALIMENTS KIM PHAT (ST-LAURENT), LES
(*Suby of* EMPIRE COMPANY LIMITED)
1935 Boul Keller, Saint-Laurent, QC, H4K 2V6
(514) 727-9999
Emp Here 50   *Sales* 14,673,850
SIC 5411 Grocery stores
 Kok Chang Yip
 Alex Yip
 Sebastien Bellehumeur
 Yvan Ouellet
 Alain Menard

 D-U-N-S 20-649-1235   (SL)
FABRICATIONS DOR-VAL LTEE, LES
11800 Boul Laurentien, Saint-Laurent, QC,
H4K 2E1
(514) 336-7780
Emp Here 80   *Sales* 12,345,760
SIC 2531 Public building and related furniture
 Ronald Goldsmith
 Fred Goldsmith

 D-U-N-S 24-491-1301   (SL)
MARCHE DUCHEMIN ET FRERES INC
IGA
1947 Boul Keller, Saint-Laurent, QC, H4K 2V6
(514) 336-8085
Emp Here 105   *Sales* 30,815,085
SIC 5411 Grocery stores
 Normand Duchemin

Saint-Laurent, QC H4L

 D-U-N-S 24-970-8975   (SL)
2970-9177 QUEBEC INC
PHARMAPRIX
1051 Rue Decarie, Saint-Laurent, QC, H4L
3M8
(514) 748-7725
Emp Here 94   *Sales* 22,966,832
SIC 5912 Drug stores and proprietary stores
 Donald Newhook
 Salvatore Coppa

 D-U-N-S 25-525-9939   (SL)
3424626 CANADA INC
SUPERMARCHE MOURELATOS
1855 Av O'Brien, Saint-Laurent, QC, H4L 3W6
(450) 681-4100
Emp Here 94   *Sales* 13,707,600
SIC 5411 Grocery stores
 Efthymios Mourelatos
 Christos Mourelatos

 D-U-N-S 20-605-0650   (SL)
**ASSOCIATION DES ETUDIANTS DU
CEGEP ST-LAURENT INC**
LIBRAIRIE LAURENTIENNE
625 Av Sainte-Croix, Saint-Laurent, QC, H4L
3X7
(514) 747-4026
Emp Here 35   *Sales* 11,012,120
SIC 8699 Membership organizations, nec
 Genevieve Solomon

 D-U-N-S 24-321-1349   (HQ)
**CAISSE POPULAIRE DESJARDINS DE
SAINT-LAURENT, LA**

CENTRE DE SERVICE MONTPELLIER
1460 Rue De L'Eglise, Saint-Laurent, QC, H4L
2H6
(514) 748-8821
Emp Here 30   *Sales* 10,789,202
SIC 6062 State credit unions
 Yves Gibeau
 Gilles Deslauriers
 Jerome Youmani Lankoande
 Pierre Bergeron
 Martine Melancon
 Jacques Primeau
 Arielle Rakoto
 Suzanne Lalonde
 Karim Abdel-Sheheid
 Christian Belanger

 D-U-N-S 24-081-0150   (SL)
**CENTRE D'HEBERGEMENT ST-VINCENT
DE MARIE INC**
1175 Boul De La Cote-Vertu, Saint-Laurent,
QC, H4L 5J1
(514) 744-1175
Emp Here 105   *Sales* 7,199,430
SIC 8051 Skilled nursing care facilities
 Danny Macdonald

 D-U-N-S 25-973-8276   (HQ)
**COMMISSION SCOLAIRE MARGUERITE-
BOURGEOYS**
*CENTRE INTEGRE DE MECANIQUE, DE
METALLURGIE ET D'ELECTRICITE CIMME*
1100 Boul De La Cote-Vertu, Saint-Laurent,
QC, H4L 4V1
(514) 855-4500
Emp Here 200   *Sales* 320,649,965
SIC 8211 Elementary and secondary schools
 Dominic Bertrand

 D-U-N-S 20-298-2294   (SL)
ENTREPRISES D'ELECTRICITE E.G. LTEE
1753 Rue Grenet, Saint-Laurent, QC, H4L
2R6
(514) 748-0505
Emp Here 94   *Sales* 21,782,900
SIC 1731 Electrical work
 Robert Drapeau
 Claude Drapeau
 Vincent-Rivard Drapeau
 John Panagiotopoulos

 D-U-N-S 20-534-1634   (HQ)
PHARMA NTK INC
GROUPE JEAN COUTU
740 Boul De La Cote-Vertu, Saint-Laurent,
QC, H4L 5C8
(514) 744-2555
Sales 25,654,440
SIC 5912 Drug stores and proprietary stores
 Nelly Kanou
 Tania Kanou

 D-U-N-S 20-227-3413   (HQ)
ROBERT MITCHELL INC
PRODUITS INDUSTRIELS MITCHELL
(*Suby of* CANERECTOR INC)
350 Boul Decarie, Saint-Laurent, QC, H4L
3K5
(514) 747-2471
Emp Here 6   *Sales* 137,425,515
SIC 3498 Fabricated pipe and fittings
 Richard Belanger
 Tim Buckland
 Amanda Hawkins
 William Nickel
 Pierre Desormeaux

 D-U-N-S 20-532-6908   (BR)
SOEURS DE SAINTE-CROIX
(*Suby of* SOEURS DE SAINTE-CROIX)
900 Boul De La Cote-Vertu, Saint-Laurent,
QC, H4L 4T9

Emp Here 80
SIC 8661 Religious organizations
 Claire Vanier

▲ Public Company   ■ Public Company Family Member   **HQ** Headquarters   **BR** Branch   **SL** Single Location

D-U-N-S 20-855-9369   (HQ)
VANIER COLLEGE OF GENERAL AND VO-CATIONAL EDUCATION
CEGEP VANIER COLLEGE
821 Av Sainte-Croix, Saint-Laurent, QC, H4L 3X9
(514) 744-7500
Sales 26,190,450
SIC 8222 Junior colleges
Jean-Francois Parent
Andrew Mackay
Lise Begin
Darren Becker
Magnan Monique
John Mcmahon

Saint-Laurent, QC H4M

D-U-N-S 20-764-9281   (SL)
3653340 CANADA INC
BERKSHIRE GROUP
9800 Boul Cavendish Bureau 200, Saint-Laurent, QC, H4M 2V9

Emp Here 49   *Sales* 33,267,227
SIC 6211 Security brokers and dealers
Eyal Amon
Michael Faracino

D-U-N-S 20-059-4757   (HQ)
BREVILLE CANADA S.E.C.
BREVILLE
9800 Cavendish Blvd Ste 250, Saint-Laurent, QC, H4M 2V9
(514) 683-3535
Sales 15,651,090
SIC 5064 Electrical appliances, television and radio
Stephen Krauss

D-U-N-S 20-213-5604   (HQ)
CMC ELECTRONIQUE INC
(*Suby of* TRANSDIGM GROUP INCORPORATED)
600 Boul Dr.-Frederik-Philips, Saint-Laurent, QC, H4M 2S9
(514) 748-3148
Emp Here 800   *Sales* 197,131,000
SIC 8711 Engineering services
Robin St-Arnaud
Jonathan David Crandall
Sarah Louise Wynne

D-U-N-S 24-589-8275   (HQ)
COMMISSION SCOLAIRE KATIVIK
9800 Boul Cavendish Bureau 400, Saint-Laurent, QC, H4M 2V9
(514) 482-8220
Emp Here 100   *Sales* 102,751,566
SIC 8211 Elementary and secondary schools
Annie Grenier

D-U-N-S 20-056-5450   (HQ)
CRISTOMEL INC
100 Boul Alexis-Nihon Bureau 105, Saint-Laurent, QC, H4M 2N6
(514) 747-1575
Emp Here 75   *Sales* 80,302,800
SIC 5045 Computers, peripherals, and software
Antoine Nohra

D-U-N-S 24-517-0519   (HQ)
DIALOGIC CORPORATION
DIALOGIC
(*Suby of* NOVACAP TMT IV, S.E.C.)
9800 Cavendish 5e Etage, Saint-Laurent, QC, H4M 2V9
(514) 745-5500
Emp Here 30   *Sales* 138,429,750
SIC 7371 Custom computer programming services
Bill Crank
Stephane Tremblay

Gary Morrison
Yvonne Daniels

D-U-N-S 25-390-0872   (HQ)
FAMIC TECHNOLOGIES INC
(*Suby of* 3338959 CANADA INC)
9999 Boul Cavendish Bureau 350, Saint-Laurent, QC, H4M 2X5
(514) 748-8050
Sales 22,358,700
SIC 5045 Computers, peripherals, and software
Charbel Nasr
Philippe Beland
Yves Pigeon

D-U-N-S 24-773-7427   (BR)
FEDEX TRADE NETWORKS TRANSPORT & BROKERAGE (CANADA), INC
FEDEX TRADE NETWORKS
(*Suby of* FEDEX CORPORATION)
9800 Cavendish Blvd 3rd Fl, Saint-Laurent, QC, H4M 2V9
(514) 845-3171
Emp Here 100
SIC 4731 Freight transportation arrangement

D-U-N-S 24-860-4444   (HQ)
GROUPE CANTREX NATIONWIDE INC
GROUPE VOLUMAX
9900 Boul Cavendish Bureau 400, Saint-Laurent, QC, H4M 2V2
(514) 335-0260
Emp Here 66   *Sales* 56,857,180
SIC 7389 Business services, nec
Jeannine Ghaleb
Owen Tharrington
Leslie Kirk
Sean Crane

D-U-N-S 24-902-5305   (HQ)
GROUPE INTERTAPE POLYMER INC, LE
ENGINEERED COATED PRODUCTS
9999 Boul Cavendish Bureau 200, Saint-Laurent, QC, H4M 2X5
(514) 731-7591
Emp Here 150   *Sales* 1,053,019,000
SIC 2672 Paper; coated and laminated, nec
Gregory A.C. Yull
Jeffrey Crystal
Douglas Nalette
Shawn Nelson
Joseph Tocci
Randi Booth
Mary Beth Thompson
James Pantelidis
Melbourne F. Yull
Robert J. Foster

D-U-N-S 25-389-7474   (HQ)
IQVIA RDS CANADA ULC
INNOVEX CANADA
(*Suby of* IQVIA HOLDINGS INC.)
100 Boul Alexis-Nihon 8e Etage, Saint-Laurent, QC, H4M 2P4
(514) 855-0888
Sales 47,329,324
SIC 8731 Commercial physical research
Eric Mitchell Sherbet
Debra Giroux

D-U-N-S 24-357-3297   (SL)
LANTHEUS MI CANADA INC
LANTHEUS MEDICAL IMAGING
(*Suby of* LANTHEUS HOLDINGS, INC.)
1111 Boul Dr.-Frederik-Philips Bureau 100, Saint-Laurent, QC, H4M 2X6
(514) 333-1003
Emp Here 15   *Sales* 19,586,925
SIC 3845 Electromedical equipment
Mary Anne Heino
Frederick Genzardi
Michael P. Duffy
John Crowley
Pierre Tardif

D-U-N-S 25-475-2660   (SL)

LOGICIELS TANGERINE INC
555 Boul Dr.-Frederik-Philips Bureau 450, Saint-Laurent, QC, H4M 2X4
(514) 748-9309
Emp Here 50   *Sales* 11,714,400
SIC 8742 Management consulting services
Greg Brown
Benoit Trottier

D-U-N-S 24-963-4734   (HQ)
PALADIN LABS INC
ISODIAGNOSTIKA, DIV OF
(*Suby of* ENDO INTERNATIONAL PUBLIC LIMITED COMPANY)
100 Boul Alexis-Nihon Bureau 600, Saint-Laurent, QC, H4M 2P2
(514) 340-1112
Sales 28,402,100
SIC 2834 Pharmaceutical preparations
Livio Di Francesco
Deanna Voss
Daniel Vas

D-U-N-S 20-997-0458   (SL)
PARTENAIRES EN VOYAGES INC
100 Boul Alexis-Nihon, Ste 110, Saint-Laurent, QC, H4M 2N6

Emp Here 4   *Sales* 16,250,025
SIC 4724 Travel agencies

D-U-N-S 24-994-1352   (SL)
SEMAFO INC
SOCIETE D'EXPLORATION MINIERE D'AFRIQUE DE L'OUEST
100 Boul Alexis-Nihon Bureau 700, Saint-Laurent, QC, H4M 2P3
(514) 744-4408
Emp Here 1,034   *Sales* 296,679,000
SIC 1081 Metal mining services
Benoit Desormeaux
Eric Paul-Hus
Sylvain Duchesne
John Jentz
Alain Melanson
Patrick Moryoussef
Richard Roy
Martin Milette
John Leboutillier
Terence F. Bowles

D-U-N-S 24-725-8119   (SL)
SILONEX INC
2150 Rue Ward, Saint-Laurent, QC, H4M 1T7

Emp Here 49   *Sales* 10,028,977
SIC 3674 Semiconductors and related devices
Fred Rohrbacher

D-U-N-S 20-794-0610   (HQ)
SOCIETE MAKIVIK
1111 Boul Dr.-Frederik-Philips 3e Etage, Saint-Laurent, QC, H4M 2X6
(514) 745-8880
Emp Here 70   *Sales* 441,119,280
SIC 4512 Air transportation, scheduled
Charlie Watt
Andrew Moorhouse
Adamie Padlayat
Andy Pirti
Muncy Novalinga
Etua Kaukai
Noah Ningiuruvik
Maggie Akapahatak
Rhoda Kokiapik
Eli Aullaluk

D-U-N-S 20-327-4584   (SL)
STANTEC ARCHITECTURE QUEBEC LTD
100 Boul Alexis-Nihon Bureau 110, Saint-Laurent, QC, H4M 2N6
(514) 739-0708
Emp Here 61   *Sales* 10,733,438
SIC 8712 Architectural services
Robert J Gomes

D-U-N-S 20-500-1340   (HQ)

SWISSPORT CANADA INC
SERVISAIR
100 Boul Alexis-Nihon Unite 400, Saint-Laurent, QC, H4M 2N8
(514) 748-2277
Emp Here 25   *Sales* 400,467,000
SIC 4581 Airports, flying fields, and services
Michael La Salle
Rodrigue Levesque

D-U-N-S 24-763-1315   (SL)
THINKMAX CONSULTING INC
1111 Boul Dr.-Frederik-Philips Bureau 500, Saint-Laurent, QC, H4M 2X6
(514) 316-8959
Emp Here 49   *Sales* 13,881,357
SIC 8741 Management services
Marc P. Belliveau
Yves Giguere

D-U-N-S 24-812-4906   (SL)
TORCE FINANCIAL GROUPE INC
575 Rue Dorais, Saint-Laurent, QC, H4M 1Z7

Emp Here 40   *Sales* 11,331,720
SIC 8741 Management services
David Ho

D-U-N-S 20-555-5274   (BR)
VELAN INC
(*Suby of* SOCIETE HOLDING VELAN LTEE)
2125 Rue Ward, Saint-Laurent, QC, H4M 1T6
(514) 748-7743
Emp Here 149
SIC 3494 Valves and pipe fittings, nec
I Velan

D-U-N-S 24-392-6859   (SL)
VOTI INC
VOTI DETECTION
790 Rue Begin, Saint-Laurent, QC, H4M 2N5
(514) 782-1566
Emp Here 52   *Sales* 11,819,028
SIC 3845 Electromedical equipment
Rory Olson
Karna Gupta
Stuart Campbell
James Fleck
Neil Hindle
Joel King
David Crevier

D-U-N-S 25-247-3236   (SL)
WABTEC CANADA INC
VAPOR RAIL
10000 Boul Cavendish, Saint-Laurent, QC, H4M 2V1
(514) 335-4200
Emp Here 300   *Sales* 179,236,200
SIC 5051 Metals service centers and offices
David M Seitz
Greg C. Lewis

Saint-Laurent, QC H4N

D-U-N-S 25-202-3767   (SL)
166606 CANADA INC
LEXUS-TOYOTA GABRIEL
3333 Ch De La Cote-De-Liesse, Saint-Laurent, QC, H4N 3C2
(514) 748-7777
Emp Here 105   *Sales* 66,074,400
SIC 5511 New and used car dealers
Gabriel Azouz

D-U-N-S 25-200-6978   (SL)
2946-4617 QUEBEC INC
CENTURY PRODUCTS
393a Av Sainte-Croix, Saint-Laurent, QC, H4N 2L3

Emp Here 75   *Sales* 20,749,500
SIC 2816 Inorganic pigments
William F Servay

D-U-N-S 20-265-8514   (SL)
6202667 CANADA INC
PORSCHE PRESTIGE
3535 Ch De La Cote-De-Liesse, Saint-Laurent, QC, H4N 2N5
(514) 356-7777
Emp Here 85   *Sales* 22,232,005
SIC 6712 Bank holding companies
  Gabriel Azouz

D-U-N-S 20-695-0599   (SL)
6356036 CANADA INC
12 OUNCES
590 Rue Hodge, Saint-Laurent, QC, H4N 2A4
(514) 389-8885
Emp Here 26   *Sales* 12,956,372
SIC 5137 Women's and children's clothing
  Marc Regenstreif

D-U-N-S 20-411-1054   (HQ)
7339101 CANADA INC
7 DAYS GROUP
387 Rue Deslauriers, Saint-Laurent, QC, H4N 1W2
(514) 344-5558
Sales 11,769,885
SIC 6712 Bank holding companies
  Dimitrios Nikolidakis
  Michail Mastronikolas
  Charalambos Nikolidakis

D-U-N-S 20-266-1856   (SL)
8756074 CANADA INC
TRICOTS MAXIME
828 Rue Deslauriers, Saint-Laurent, QC, H4N 1X1
(514) 336-0445
Emp Here 150   *Sales* 27,510,450
SIC 2258 Lace and warp knit fabric mills
  Maxime Theriault

D-U-N-S 25-081-0355   (HQ)
9071-7851 QUEBEC INC
O.K. KIDS
200 Boul Lebeau, Saint-Laurent, QC, H4N 1R4
(514) 332-5437
Emp Here 15   *Sales* 125,629,950
SIC 5137 Women's and children's clothing
  Nemer Batchoun

D-U-N-S 20-229-6604   (HQ)
AGENCES W PELLETIER (1980) INC
A.P.A
(*Suby of* INVESTISSEMENTS SYLNIC INC, LES)
1400 Boul Jules-Poitras, Saint-Laurent, QC, H4N 1X7
(514) 276-6700
Emp Here 61   *Sales* 54,625,760
SIC 5087 Service establishment equipment
  Claude Desrochers
  Andre Cheply

D-U-N-S 24-052-0705   (BR)
AGROPUR COOPERATIVE
NARTEL
(*Suby of* AGROPUR COOPERATIVE)
333 Boul Lebeau, Saint-Laurent, QC, H4N 1S3
(800) 501-1150
Emp Here 400
SIC 3556 Food products machinery
  Pierre Lemieux

D-U-N-S 24-871-5815   (HQ)
ALIMENTS FONTAINE SANTE INC
FONTAINE SANTE
(*Suby of* PLACEMENTS MECYVA INC)
450 Rue Deslauriers, Saint-Laurent, QC, H4N 1V8
(514) 745-3085
Emp Here 130   *Sales* 55,310,400
SIC 2099 Food preparations, nec
  Max Latifi
  Melissa Latifi

D-U-N-S 25-498-8017   (SL)

ALIMENTS ROMA LTEE, LES
(*Suby of* GROUPE RAMACIERI INC)
660 Rue Wright, Saint-Laurent, QC, H4N 1M6
(514) 332-0340
Emp Here 80   *Sales* 27,655,200
SIC 2032 Canned specialties
  Pascal Ramacieri
  Sylvia Ramacieri

D-U-N-S 24-813-9461   (SL)
ALIMENTS TOUSAIN INC
95 Rue Stinson, Saint-Laurent, QC, H4N 2E1
(514) 748-7353
Emp Here 38   *Sales* 31,751,926
SIC 5141 Groceries, general line
  Dikran Markarian

D-U-N-S 24-895-4414   (SL)
ALPHACASTING INC
391 Av Sainte-Croix, Saint-Laurent, QC, H4N 2L3
(514) 748-7511
Emp Here 100   *Sales* 18,138,800
SIC 3324 Steel investment foundries
  Arduino Centazzo
  Frederik-Pierre Centazzo
  William Szabo
  Jean Bergeron
  Athanasios Polyzos

D-U-N-S 20-927-2822   (SL)
BERARDINI, FERNANDO INC
LAITERIE BERARDINI
80 Rue Stinson, Saint-Laurent, QC, H4N 2E7
(514) 744-9412
Emp Here 24   *Sales* 20,053,848
SIC 5143 Dairy products, except dried or canned
  Fernando Berardini

D-U-N-S 20-213-8582   (SL)
BIJOUTERIE CARMEN INC
CARMEN WATCHES DIV OF CARMEN JEWELLERY
(*Suby of* 116842 CANADA INC)
700 Rue Hodge Ave Suite 200, Saint-Laurent, QC, H4N 2V2
(514) 273-1718
Emp Here 26   *Sales* 13,534,092
SIC 5094 Jewelry and precious stones
  Marvin Feiler Meyer

D-U-N-S 24-922-2654   (SL)
BOULANGERIE ANDALOS INC
ANDALOS BAKERY AND PASTRY
350 Boul Lebeau, Saint-Laurent, QC, H4N 1R5
(514) 856-0983
Emp Here 40   *Sales* 13,827,600
SIC 2051 Bread, cake, and related products
  Elie Cheaib
  Roger Cheaib
  Pascale Cheaib

D-U-N-S 24-352-0512   (SL)
BOULANGERIE GONDOLE INC
225 Rue Benjamin-Hudon, Saint-Laurent, QC, H4N 1J1
(514) 956-5555
Emp Here 20   *Sales* 10,702,480
SIC 5149 Groceries and related products, nec
  Cheaib Faten Akl

D-U-N-S 20-212-4335   (HQ)
BOULEVARD DODGE CHRYSLER JEEP (2000) INC
2955 Ch De La Cote-De-Liesse, Saint-Laurent, QC, H4N 2N3
(514) 748-2955
Emp Here 1   *Sales* 37,756,800
SIC 5511 New and used car dealers
  Ray Monahan
  Roger Desautels Iii
  Paul Ladouceur
  Guy Caouette

D-U-N-S 24-797-7882   (SL)
BOULEVARD METROPOLITAIN AUTOMO-

BILE INC
HYUNDAI SAINT-LAURENT
100 Boul Montpellier, Saint-Laurent, QC, H4N 0H8
(514) 748-0100
Emp Here 49   *Sales* 24,405,822
SIC 5511 New and used car dealers
  Roger Desautels Iii

D-U-N-S 24-295-6472   (HQ)
BOUTIQUE COLORI INC
COLORI
2255 Ch De La Cote-De-Liesse, Saint-Laurent, QC, H4N 2M6
(514) 858-7494
Emp Here 100   *Sales* 30,564,975
SIC 5621 Women's clothing stores
  Matt D'andrea
  Markus D'andrea

D-U-N-S 25-247-1792   (SL)
BUSREL INC
200 Rue Deslauriers, Saint-Laurent, QC, H4N 1V8
(514) 336-0000
Emp Here 100   *Sales* 20,037,100
SIC 7311 Advertising agencies
  Raymond Brodeur

D-U-N-S 20-634-5373   (BR)
CERATEC INC
CERATEC VAUDREUIL
(*Suby of* GESTION CERATEC INC)
1620 Boul Jules-Poitras, Saint-Laurent, QC, H4N 1Z3
(514) 956-0341
Emp Here 75
SIC 5032 Brick, stone, and related material
  Curtis Raiche

D-U-N-S 20-762-6201   (HQ)
CHATEAU INC, LE
CHATEAUWORKS & DESIGN
105 Boul Marcel-Laurin, Saint-Laurent, QC, H4N 2M3
(514) 738-7000
Emp Here 300   *Sales* 142,542,621
SIC 5621 Women's clothing stores

D-U-N-S 20-234-8413   (HQ)
CIE D'IMPORTATION DE NOUVEAUTES STEIN INC, LA
ALTA MODA TM
865 Rue Deslauriers, Saint-Laurent, QC, H4N 1X3
(514) 334-3366
Emp Here 34   *Sales* 17,441,270
SIC 5137 Women's and children's clothing
  Percy Stein

D-U-N-S 25-240-3464   (BR)
COMMISSION SCOLAIRE MARGUERITE-BOURGEOYS
ECOLE HENRI BEAULIEU
(*Suby of* COMMISSION SCOLAIRE MARGUERITE-BOURGEOYS)
235 Rue Bleignier, Saint-Laurent, QC, H4N 1B1
(514) 332-0742
Emp Here 75
SIC 8211 Elementary and secondary schools
  Samir Nicolas

D-U-N-S 24-360-9778   (HQ)
COMO DIFFUSION INC
COMO
(*Suby of* 8053537 CANADA INC)
103 Boul Marcel-Laurin, Saint-Laurent, QC, H4N 2M3
(514) 286-2666
Sales 42,357,370
SIC 5137 Women's and children's clothing
  Anthony Kirstein
  Paul Ostrov

D-U-N-S 20-213-6388   (HQ)
COMPAGNIE CANADIAN TECHNICAL TAPE LTEE

(*Suby of* GROUPE INTERTAPE POLYMER INC, LE)
455 Boul De La Cote-Vertu, Saint-Laurent, QC, H4N 1E8
(514) 334-1510
Emp Here 26   *Sales* 34,279,168
SIC 2672 Paper; coated and laminated, nec
  Howard Cohen
  Paul Cohen

D-U-N-S 24-848-3773   (SL)
COMPAGNIE MEXX CANADA
MEXX
(*Suby of* EROGLU GIYIM SANAYI TICARET ANONIM SIRKETI)
905 Rue Hodge, Saint-Laurent, QC, H4N 2B3
(514) 383-5555
Emp Here 750   *Sales* 628,149,750
SIC 5137 Women's and children's clothing
  Robbie Reynders
  Kurt Hans
  Steve Eisner

D-U-N-S 24-426-7386   (SL)
CONTINU-GRAPH INC
409 Boul Lebeau, Saint-Laurent, QC, H4N 1S2
(514) 331-0741
Emp Here 100   *Sales* 16,402,700
SIC 2752 Commercial printing, lithographic
  Francois Chartrand

D-U-N-S 24-474-3258   (SL)
COPISCOPE INC
DELCOM BUSINESS SOLUTIONS
460 Boul Montpellier Bureau 267, Saint-Laurent, QC, H4N 2G7
(514) 744-3610
Emp Here 50   *Sales* 22,358,700
SIC 5065 Electronic parts and equipment, nec
  Antonio Del Signore
  Rocco Del Duca

D-U-N-S 20-309-4313   (HQ)
DEVELOPPEMENT OLYMBEC INC
(*Suby of* INVESTISSEMENTS OLYMBEC INC)
333 Boul Decarie Bureau 500, Saint-Laurent, QC, H4N 3M9
(514) 344-3334
Emp Here 36   *Sales* 14,221,850
SIC 6512 Nonresidential building operators
  Richard Stern
  Derek Stern
  Brian Glasberg

D-U-N-S 25-526-2347   (SL)
DEVELOPPEMENTS REKERN INC, LES
OLYMBEC
333 Boul Decarie 5e Etage, Saint-Laurent, QC, H4N 3M9
(514) 344-3334
Emp Here 50   *Sales* 20,967,750
SIC 6719 Holding companies, nec
  Derek Stern

D-U-N-S 25-200-4098   (HQ)
DEX BROS. CIE DE VETEMENTS LTEE
DEX
(*Suby of* 3494926 CANADA INC)
390 Rue Deslauriers, Saint-Laurent, QC, H4N 1V8
(514) 383-2474
Emp Here 60   *Sales* 65,327,574
SIC 5137 Women's and children's clothing
  Jacky Alloul

D-U-N-S 20-926-4399   (SL)
DIFFUSION DIMEDIA INC
539 Boul Lebeau, Saint-Laurent, QC, H4N 1S2
(514) 336-3941
Emp Here 90   *Sales* 66,826,800
SIC 5192 Books, periodicals, and newspapers
  Pascal Assathiany
  Serge Theroux

D-U-N-S 20-792-8136   (HQ)

ESSILOR GROUPE CANADA INC
CANOPTEC
(*Suby of* ESSILORLUXOTTICA)
371 Rue Deslauriers, Saint-Laurent, QC, H4N
1W2
(514) 337-2211
Sales 135,444,056
SIC 5049 Professional equipment, nec
Arnaud Bussieres
Barbara Heffez-Piper
Marc Tirapelle
Jean Carrier Guillomet
Christophe Perreault
Pascal Bouchard

D-U-N-S 20-288-4854   (HQ)
F.W. WARD & SONS INC
515 Deslauriers St, Saint-Laurent, QC, H4N
1W2
(514) 858-9331
Emp Here 10   *Sales* 11,698,078
SIC 5148 Fresh fruits and vegetables
Mike Sangiorgio
Alfonso Morelli

D-U-N-S 20-032-6929   (BR)
**FIRST CANADIAN TITLE COMPANY LIM-
ITED**
FIRST CANADIAN TITLE
(*Suby of* FIRST AMERICAN FINANCIAL
CORPORATION)
333 Boul Decarie Bureau 200, Saint-Laurent,
QC, H4N 3M9
(514) 744-1210
Emp Here 130
SIC 6361 Title insurance
Laurent Nadeau

D-U-N-S 20-330-5722   (HQ)
FLS INTERMEDIATE 2 ULC
400 Av Sainte-Croix, Saint-Laurent, QC, H4N
3L4
(514) 739-0939
Emp Here 5   *Sales* 109,652,700
SIC 6719 Holding companies, nec
Michael Yirilli
Azra Kanji
John Leach
Greg Sheldon

D-U-N-S 24-739-4257   (HQ)
**FLS TRANSPORTATION SERVICES LIM-
ITED**
SERVICES DE TRANSPORT FLS, LES
(*Suby of* FLS INTERMEDIATE 2 ULC)
400 Av Sainte-Croix, Saint-Laurent, QC, H4N
3L4
(514) 739-0939
Emp Here 100   *Sales* 118,631,400
SIC 4731 Freight transportation arrangement
John Leach
Azra Kanji
Greg Sheldon
Michael Yirilli
Pierre Gagne

D-U-N-S 24-802-7752   (SL)
FRUITS ET LEGUMES BOTSIS INC, LES
140 Rue Stinson, Saint-Laurent, QC, H4N 2E7
(514) 389-7676
Emp Here 55   *Sales* 16,104,183
SIC 5148 Fresh fruits and vegetables
Christos Botsis

D-U-N-S 20-500-1449   (SL)
GENIE AUDIO INC
(*Suby of* NATUS MEDICAL INCORPO-
RATED)
125 Rue Gagnon Bureau 102, Saint-Laurent,
QC, H4N 1T1
(514) 856-9212
Emp Here 26   *Sales* 11,626,524
SIC 5047 Medical and hospital equipment
Jonathan A. Kennedy
Dan Mcnaulty
William B. Hill

D-U-N-S 25-365-0428   (HQ)

GESTION MICHAEL ROSSY LTEE
450 Boul Lebeau, Saint-Laurent, QC, H4N
1R7
(514) 335-6255
Emp Here 1   *Sales* 114,081,000
SIC 5311 Department stores
Michael Ditullio
Douglas Khoury
Michael Jr. Rossy

D-U-N-S 25-503-2674   (SL)
GESTIONS LENALCO (CANADA) LTEE
455 Boul De La Cote-Vertu, Saint-Laurent,
QC, H4N 1E8
(514) 334-1510
Emp Here 3   *Sales* 22,688,050
SIC 6712 Bank holding companies
Howard Cohen
Alice Cohen
Paul Cohen

D-U-N-S 24-835-2247   (HQ)
GROUPE CARREAUX CERAGRES INC
CERAGRES LES-BAINS
825 Rue Deslauriers, Saint-Laurent, QC, H4N
1X3
(514) 384-5590
Emp Here 75   *Sales* 79,747,920
SIC 5032 Brick, stone, and related material
Guy Gervais

D-U-N-S 24-990-4285   (SL)
GROUPE LEMUR INC, LE
PETIT LEM
275 Rue Stinson Bureau 201, Saint-Laurent,
QC, H4N 2E1
(514) 748-6234
Emp Here 60   *Sales* 29,899,320
SIC 5137 Women's and children's clothing
Gabriel Di Miele

D-U-N-S 20-232-6666   (HQ)
GROUPE RAMACIERI INC
660 Rue Wright, Saint-Laurent, QC, H4N 1M6
(514) 332-0340
Sales 11,242,750
SIC 2032 Canned specialties
Domenico Ramacieri
Pascal Ramacieri
Diuseppe Ramacieri
Sylvia Ramacieri

D-U-N-S 20-792-5587   (SL)
HEINEMANN ELECTRIC CANADA LIMITEE
343 Rue Deslauriers, Saint-Laurent, QC, H4N
1W2
(514) 332-1163
Emp Here 60   *Sales* 34,814,820
SIC 5065 Electronic parts and equipment, nec
Graham Shaw
Julie Shaw

D-U-N-S 25-739-3165   (SL)
HYMOPACK LTD
1225 Rue Hodge, Saint-Laurent, QC, H4N
2B5

Emp Here 100
SIC 2673 Bags: plastic, laminated, and
coated

D-U-N-S 24-033-2085   (SL)
INSERCO-QUEBEC INC
674 Rue Deslauriers, Saint-Laurent, QC, H4N
1W5
(514) 523-1551
Emp Here 47   *Sales* 20,844,030
SIC 7389 Business services, nec
Mohamed Pememe

D-U-N-S 20-309-4300   (HQ)
INVESTISSEMENTS OLYMBEC INC
GROUPE CORPORATIF OLYMBEC
333 Boul Decarie Etage 5e, Saint-Laurent,
QC, H4N 3M9
(514) 344-3334
Emp Here 25   *Sales* 21,868,000
SIC 6719 Holding companies, nec

Richard Stern
Derek Stern

D-U-N-S 20-222-2469   (HQ)
JCORP INC
JONATHAN G
95 Rue Gince, Saint-Laurent, QC, H4N 1J7
(514) 384-3872
Sales 37,374,150
SIC 5136 Men's and boy's clothing
Jonathan Gurman
Marvin Gurman

D-U-N-S 20-222-4176   (BR)
**JOHNSON CONTROLS NOVA SCOTIA
U.L.C.**
SOCIETE DE CONTROLE JOHNSON
(*Suby of* JOHNSON CONTROLS INTERNA-
TIONAL PUBLIC LIMITED COMPANY)
395 Av Sainte-Croix Bureau 100, Saint-
Laurent, QC, H4N 2L3
(514) 747-2580
Emp Here 135
SIC 1711 Plumbing, heating, air-conditioning
Isabelle Lavoie

D-U-N-S 24-933-5480   (HQ)
LABORATOIRES DERMO-COSMETIK INC
PHYTOBIOMARIN
68 Rue Stinson, Saint-Laurent, QC, H4N 2E7
(514) 735-1531
Sales 11,066,400
SIC 2844 Toilet preparations
Marc Sayer
Naoum Araj
Katia Kossa
Gilles Thibault

D-U-N-S 20-032-6218   (HQ)
LGV QUEBEC INC
400 Av Sainte-Croix Bureau 110, Saint-
Laurent, QC, H4N 3L4
(514) 748-2522
Emp Here 150   *Sales* 118,631,400
SIC 4724 Travel agencies
Joel Ostrov
Jacob Lazare
Brain Robertson
Arend Roos
William Brock

D-U-N-S 20-290-7168   (BR)
LGV QUEBEC INC
VISION TRAVEL
(*Suby of* LGV QUEBEC INC)
400 Av Sainte-Croix Bureau 100, Saint-
Laurent, QC, H4N 3L4
(514) 748-2522
Emp Here 100
SIC 4724 Travel agencies
Joel Ostrov

D-U-N-S 24-054-8560   (SL)
LIEBERMAN-TRANCHEMONTAGNE INC
653 Rue Hodge, Saint-Laurent, QC, H4N 2A3
(514) 747-5510
Emp Here 20   *Sales* 10,177,120
SIC 5023 Homefurnishings
Andre L'africain

D-U-N-S 20-376-1361   (SL)
LOBLAW QUEBEC LIMITEE
(*Suby of* LOBLAW COMPANIES LIMITED)
330 Av Sainte-Croix, Saint-Laurent, QC, H4N
3K4
(514) 747-0606
Emp Here 500
SIC 5411 Grocery stores
Claude Gariepy
Pierre Poirier
Bernard J. Mcdonell
Donald G. Reid

D-U-N-S 20-291-0147   (SL)
LUMENWERX ULC
SERVICES LUMENWERX
B-393 Rue Sainte-Croix, Saint-Laurent, QC,
H4N 2L3

(514) 225-4304
Emp Here 49   *Sales* 10,028,977
SIC 3645 Residential lighting fixtures
Moses Feldman
Morris Feldman

D-U-N-S 20-232-8266   (HQ)
MICHAEL ROSSY LTEE
MAGAUBAINES
(*Suby of* GESTION MICHAEL ROSSY LTEE)
450 Boul Lebeau, Saint-Laurent, QC, H4N
1R7
(514) 335-6255
Emp Here 65   *Sales* 76,054,000
SIC 5311 Department stores
Michael Ditullio
Douglas Khoury

D-U-N-S 24-424-8410   (HQ)
MODE CAPITAL INC, LA
CLUB NUAGE
1200 Boul Jules-Poitras Bureau 200, Saint-
Laurent, QC, H4N 1X7
(514) 337-4444
Sales 12,458,050
SIC 5137 Women's and children's clothing
Arie Dahan

D-U-N-S 20-016-2464   (BR)
MOORE CANADA CORPORATION
R.R. DONNELLEY
(*Suby of* R. R. DONNELLEY & SONS COM-
PANY)
395 Av Sainte-Croix Bureau 100, Saint-
Laurent, QC, H4N 2L3

Emp Here 100
SIC 2731 Book publishing
Luc Gauthier

D-U-N-S 25-210-0250   (SL)
NASRI INTERNATIONAL INC
DIDI
500 Boul Lebeau, Saint-Laurent, QC, H4N
1R5
(514) 334-8282
Emp Here 26   *Sales* 12,956,372
SIC 5137 Women's and children's clothing
Paul Nasri

D-U-N-S 24-106-9038   (HQ)
**NATIONAL ENVIRONMENTAL PRODUCTS
LTD**
NEPTRONIC
(*Suby of* 9150-6675 QUEBEC INC)
400 Boul Lebeau, Saint-Laurent, QC, H4N
1R6
(514) 333-1433
Sales 70,219,250
SIC 3585 Refrigeration and heating equip-
ment
Zev Kopel
Luis I. Melgares
Biagio Di Lorenzo
Louis Strauss
Yves Cyr
Jason Strauss

D-U-N-S 20-764-5425   (HQ)
NATIONAL FILM BOARD OF CANADA
ONF
(*Suby of* GOVERNMENT OF CANADA)
3155 Ch De La Cote-De-Liesse, Saint-
Laurent, QC, H4N 2N4
(514) 283-9000
Emp Here 350   *Sales* 44,848,000
SIC 7812 Motion picture and video production
Tom Perlmutter
Luisa Frate
Keith Clarkson
Eric Dubeau
Nancy Juneau
Betsy Chaly
Charles Vallerand

D-U-N-S 24-325-0458   (SL)
PNB NATION LLC
(*Suby of* JCORP INC)

95 Rue Gince, Saint-Laurent, QC, H4N 1J7
(514) 384-3872
Emp Here 100   *Sales* 17,939,600
SIC 5651 Family clothing stores
Jonathan Burman

D-U-N-S 24-251-2221   (SL)
PRANA BIOVEGETALIENS INC
1440 Boul Jules-Poitras, Saint-Laurent, QC,
H4N 1X7
(514) 276-4864
Emp Here 52   *Sales* 43,450,004
SIC 5149 Groceries and related products, nec
Alon Farber
Marie-Josee Richer
Ken Messick
Paul Richardson
Elizabeth Frank

D-U-N-S 20-106-3968   (HQ)
PRODUITS ANDALOS INC
230 Boul Lebeau, Saint-Laurent, QC, H4N
1R4
(514) 832-1000
Sales 21,725,002
SIC 5149 Groceries and related products, nec
Elie Cheaib
Roger Cheaib
Pascale Cheaib

D-U-N-S 24-803-2968   (SL)
**PRODUITS DE PREMIERS SOINS EMER-
GENCY (2011) INC**
700 Boul Lebeau, Saint-Laurent, QC, H4N
1R5

Emp Here 35   *Sales* 25,988,200
SIC 5199 Nondurable goods, nec
Bachir Azbaty
Simon Shatzky

D-U-N-S 24-679-0133   (HQ)
PROSOL INC
CENTRE DU POSEUR PROFESSIONNEL
(*Suby of* FASCO FLOORING ACCESSORIES
SYSTEM CORP)
165 Rue Deslauriers Bureau 254, Saint-
Laurent, QC, H4N 2S4
(514) 745-1212
Emp Here 25   *Sales* 51,124,150
SIC 5169 Chemicals and allied products, nec
Leon Simon
Leo Van Vugt

D-U-N-S 24-054-8057   (HQ)
PROVIGO DISTRIBUTION INC
PROVIGO
(*Suby of* LOBLAW COMPANIES LIMITED)
400 Av Sainte-Croix, Saint-Laurent, QC, H4N
3L4
(514) 383-3000
Emp Here 800   *Sales* 17,917,900,000
SIC 5141 Groceries, general line
Jocyanne Bourdeau
Robert Balcom
Pierre Dandoy

D-U-N-S 24-226-7664   (HQ)
QUEBEC LOISIRS ULC
(*Suby of* INTERNATIONAL TECHNOLOGY
SOLUTIONS SARL)
253 Boul Decarie, Saint-Laurent, QC, H4N
2L7
(514) 340-2932
Sales 88,373,850
SIC 5192 Books, periodicals, and newspapers
Nicolas Lebeau
Jean-Guy Brault
Dany Combelles
Joel Le Bihan

D-U-N-S 20-330-2674   (SL)
RENOVATIONS OLYMBEC INC
333 Boul Decarie 5e Etage, Saint-Laurent,
QC, H4N 3M9
(514) 344-3334
Emp Here 26   *Sales* 12,380,757
SIC 1542 Nonresidential construction, nec

Derek Stern

D-U-N-S 20-232-7821   (HQ)
ROSENBLOOM GROUPE INC
(*Suby of* GESTIONS ROPAL-ROJAK INC)
1225 Rue Hodge, Saint-Laurent, QC, H4N
2B5
(514) 748-7711
Sales 75,377,970
SIC 5113 Industrial and personal service paper

D-U-N-S 24-374-8675   (BR)
**SAPUTO PRODUITS LAITIERS CANADA
S.E.N.C.**
SAPUTO DAIRY PRODUCTS CANADA GP
(*Suby of* SAPUTO PRODUITS LAITIERS
CANADA S.E.N.C.)
2365 Ch De La Cote-De-Liesse, Saint-
Laurent, QC, H4N 2M7
(514) 328-6663
Emp Here 225
SIC 5143 Dairy products, except dried or
canned

D-U-N-S 25-501-3468   (BR)
**SAPUTO PRODUITS LAITIERS CANADA
S.E.N.C.**
(*Suby of* SAPUTO PRODUITS LAITIERS
CANADA S.E.N.C.)
100 Rue Stinson, Saint-Laurent, QC, H4N 2E7
(514) 328-3312
Emp Here 90
SIC 5143 Dairy products, except dried or
canned

D-U-N-S 20-707-0137   (SL)
SOCADIS INC
420 Rue Stinson, Saint-Laurent, QC, H4N 3L7
(514) 331-3300
Emp Here 180   *Sales* 106,048,620
SIC 5192 Books, periodicals, and newspapers
Nicole Haguelon
Genevieve Castonguay

D-U-N-S 24-108-8053   (HQ)
SOINS ESTHETIQUES PHYTODERM INC
PHYTODERM
68 Rue Stinson, Saint-Laurent, QC, H4N 2E7
(514) 735-1531
Sales 82,900,875
SIC 5122 Drugs, proprietaries, and sundries
Marc Sayer

D-U-N-S 24-035-1528   (SL)
SOL-R PRODUITS DE FENETRES
50 Rue Benjamin-Hudon, Saint-Laurent, QC,
H4N 1H8

Emp Here 25   *Sales* 12,721,400
SIC 5023 Homefurnishings
Jean-Sebastien Binette

D-U-N-S 24-402-5011   (HQ)
**SOLUTIONS   DE   RECONNAISSANCE
RIDEAU INC**
*RIDEAU ORDERS, MEDALS AND DECORA-
TIONS*
473 Rue Deslauriers, Saint-Laurent, QC, H4N
1W2
(514) 336-9200
Sales 50,965,965
SIC 8748 Business consulting, nec
Peter Hart
Jean-Francois Grou
Patrick Elalouf
Gordon J. Feeney
Stephan Morency
Jean Marcotte
Melissa Sonberg
Lester J. Fernandes

D-U-N-S 24-933-7049   (SL)
SPIKE MARKS INC
CASA CUBANA
(*Suby of* 115772 CANADA LTEE)
275 Rue Stinson, Saint-Laurent, QC, H4N 2E1

(514) 737-0066
Emp Here 115   *Sales* 67,753,285
SIC 5194 Tobacco and tobacco products
Andre Dunn
Gilda Estrella

D-U-N-S 24-365-9906   (BR)
SUPREMEX INC
ENVELOPPE MONTREAL
(*Suby of* SUPREMEX INC)
645 Rue Stinson, Saint-Laurent, QC, H4N 2E6
(514) 331-7110
Emp Here 88
SIC 2677 Envelopes

D-U-N-S 25-097-8848   (HQ)
TECHNOLOGIES ITF INC
GROUPE 3SP - AVENSYS
400 Boul Montpellier, Saint-Laurent, QC, H4N
2G7
(514) 748-4848
Sales 44,400,200
SIC 3545 Machine tool accessories
Fotis Konstantinidis
Nizar Tabet

D-U-N-S 24-107-6041   (HQ)
TELIO & CIE INC
TELIO
(*Suby of* GESTION TELIO INC)
625 Rue Deslauriers, Saint-Laurent, QC, H4N
1W8
(514) 271-4607
Emp Here 50   *Sales* 34,882,540
SIC 5131 Piece goods and notions
Andre Telio
Raymond Telio

D-U-N-S 20-271-3210   (SL)
THINADDICTIVES INC
ALIMENTATION NONNI'S
(*Suby of* NONNI''S FOODS LLC)
258 Boul Lebeau, Saint-Laurent, QC, H4N
1R4
(514) 484-4321
Emp Here 100   *Sales* 34,569,000
SIC 2052 Cookies and crackers
Robert Sigler
Mark R. Burgett
Konrad A. Salaber
Brian Hansberry

D-U-N-S 20-882-2304   (SL)
TRICOT MONDIAL INC
BULLETIN
(*Suby of* 119826 CANADA INC)
490 Boul Montpellier, Saint-Laurent, QC, H4N
2G7
(514) 279-9333
Emp Here 25   *Sales* 13,013,550
SIC 5091 Sporting and recreation goods
Nadeem Zakem
Waleed Zakem
Naif Zakem

D-U-N-S 20-188-6772   (BR)
UPS SCS INC
UPS SCS, INC
(*Suby of* UNITED PARCEL SERVICE, INC.)
101 Boul Marcel-Laurin, Saint-Laurent, QC,
H4N 2M3
(514) 285-1500
Emp Here 250
SIC 4731 Freight transportation arrangement
Michel Vallee

D-U-N-S 24-946-9420   (SL)
VETEMENTS MAJCO INC
ANTISTAR CLOTHING
(*Suby of* 4145593 CANADA INC)
1200 Boul Jules-Poitras Bureau 100, Saint-
Laurent, QC, H4N 1X7
(514) 956-0322
Emp Here 30   *Sales* 14,949,660
SIC 5137 Women's and children's clothing
Judson James Majdell

D-U-N-S 24-084-8101   (SL)
VETEMENTS VA-YOLA LTEE, LES

550 Rue Deslauriers, Saint-Laurent, QC, H4N
1V8
(514) 337-4175
Emp Here 30   *Sales* 14,949,660
SIC 5137 Women's and children's clothing
Samir Kersheh
Yola Kersheh
Theo Kersheh

D-U-N-S 24-357-0160   (SL)
VISCOFAN CANADA INC
(*Suby of* VISCOFAN SA)
290 Rue Benjamin-Hudon Bureau 2, Saint-
Laurent, QC, H4N 1J4
(514) 333-1700
Emp Here 20   *Sales* 16,711,540
SIC 5149 Groceries and related products, nec
David Flomen

D-U-N-S 24-110-4918   (SL)
VOYAGES ENCORE TRAVEL INC
GROUPE ENCORE
1285 Rue Hodge Bureau 101, Saint-Laurent,
QC, H4N 2B6
(514) 738-7171
Emp Here 50   *Sales* 19,268,000
SIC 4724 Travel agencies
Monique Mardinian

D-U-N-S 20-237-2470   (HQ)
WEBSTER & FILS LIMITEE
WEBSTER & SONS
2585 Ch De La Cote-De-Liesse, Saint-
Laurent, QC, H4N 2M8
(514) 332-4541
Emp Here 15   *Sales* 13,415,220
SIC 5032 Brick, stone, and related material
William D Webster
Pierre Paradis
Andrew D Webster
Robert N. Wilson

Saint-Laurent, QC H4P

D-U-N-S 24-835-3385   (HQ)
ELECTRONIQUE ABRA CORPORATION
5465 Ch De La Cote-De-Liesse, Saint-
Laurent, QC, H4P 1A1
(514) 731-0117
Sales 11,179,350
SIC 5065 Electronic parts and equipment, nec
Morley Lonn
Frank Lombardi

Saint-Laurent, QC H4R

D-U-N-S 20-356-6492   (SL)
10079952 CANADA INC
COMPRESSEURS QUEBEC
(*Suby of* CBENG GROUP LTD)
2431 Rue Guenette, Saint-Laurent, QC, H4R
2E9
(514) 337-0566
Emp Here 60   *Sales* 29,263,800
SIC 5084 Industrial machinery and equipment
Fares Kabbani
Barbara L. Burns
David Patterson
Tim Whelan
Baron Carlson
Mark Linville

D-U-N-S 24-508-8406   (HQ)
1092072 ONTARIO INC
ELFE JUVENILE PRODUCTS
4500 Boul Thimens, Saint-Laurent, QC, H4R
2P2
(514) 344-3533
Sales 25,442,800
SIC 5021 Furniture

D-U-N-S 24-600-9104   (SL)
150157 CANADA INC
EMPIRE CANADA
2320 Rue Cohen, Saint-Laurent, QC, H4R
2N8
(514) 745-1080
Emp Here 24   *Sales* 10,732,176
SIC 5074 Plumbing and heating equipment
and supplies (hydronics)
Jean-Marc Beaudin

D-U-N-S 20-422-0859   (SL)
1506369 ALBERTA ULC
TRANS CANADERM, DIV OF
(*Suby of* GLAXOSMITHKLINE PLC)
6635 Boul Henri-Bourassa O, Saint-Laurent,
QC, H4R 1E1

Emp Here 90   *Sales* 37,153,890
SIC 5122 Drugs, proprietaries, and sundries
Richard J Mackay
Madeleine Saumur

D-U-N-S 24-393-9209   (SL)
4178963 CANADA INC
CANADIAN TIRE MAGASINS ASSOCIES
#318 ET #099
11200 Boul Cavendish, Saint-Laurent, QC,
H4R 2J7
(514) 337-4862
Emp Here 50   *Sales* 24,903,900
SIC 5531 Auto and home supply stores
Stephane Lorrin

D-U-N-S 24-370-1575   (SL)
4453166 CANADA INC
DIVISION JEANS W. GREEN
1420 Rue Beaulac, Saint-Laurent, QC, H4R
1R7
(514) 744-5559
Emp Here 25   *Sales* 12,458,050
SIC 5136 Men's and boy's clothing
Warren Green
Mei Aiping
Marvin Pascal

D-U-N-S 25-105-6875   (HQ)
5N PLUS INC
4385 Rue Garand, Saint-Laurent, QC, H4R
2B4
(514) 856-0644
Emp Here 75   *Sales* 217,995,000
SIC 3339 Primary nonferrous Metals, nec
Arjang Roshan
Nicholas Audet
Paul Tancell
Pascal Coursol
Evelyne Bundock
Richard Perron
Luc Bertrand
Jean-Marie Bourassa
Jennie S. Hwang
James T. Fahey

D-U-N-S 20-325-3711   (SL)
7513283 CANADA INC
MOMENTUM TRAVEL GROUP
3333 Boul De La Cote-Vertu Bureau 600,
Saint-Laurent, QC, H4R 2N1
(514) 570-7741
Emp Here 280   *Sales* 29,230,589
SIC 4813 Telephone communication, except
radio
Ryan Branston
Matthew Keezer
Eric Parent
Marc-Andre Laporte
Nick Hart

D-U-N-S 24-959-1496   (HQ)
90401 CANADA LTEE
2255 Rue Cohen, Saint-Laurent, QC, H4R
2N7
(514) 334-5000
Emp Here 5   *Sales* 255,856,300
SIC 6712 Bank holding companies
Michael Brownstein

Andre Lescarveau
Robert Laufer
Morton Brownstein
Cheryl Brownstein
Janis Brownstein
Andre Lescarbeau

D-U-N-S 24-819-0683   (HQ)
AAF CANADA INC
AAF INTERNATIONAL
(*Suby of* DAIKIN INDUSTRIES, LTD.)
3233 Rue Sartelon, Saint-Laurent, QC, H4R
1E6
(514) 333-9048
Emp Here 14   *Sales* 10,732,176
SIC 5075 Warm air heating and air condition-
ing
Philip Whitaker
Ryan C Mcgary

D-U-N-S 24-057-1729   (HQ)
**AGENCE D'ASSURANCE VIE MANUEL
SMITH LTEE**
FINANCIERE MSA, LA
3333 Boul De La Cote-Vertu Ste 450, Saint-
Laurent, QC, H4R 2N1
(514) 343-0200
Sales 11,383,691
SIC 6311 Life insurance
Stephen Smith
Lily Kornik
Andre Azzi

D-U-N-S 20-302-8139   (HQ)
ALLIANCE HANGER INC
GROUPE POLINEX ERA
2500 Rue Guenette, Saint-Laurent, QC, H4R
2H2
(514) 339-9600
Emp Here 3   *Sales* 17,287,650
SIC 3496 Miscellaneous fabricated wire prod-
ucts
Jean-Luc Lavergne
Mark Schneiderman

D-U-N-S 25-688-3422   (SL)
ANALOGIC CANADA CORPORATION
CORPORATION ANRAD
(*Suby of* ANLG HOLDING COMPANY, INC.)
4950 Rue Levy, Saint-Laurent, QC, H4R 2P1
(514) 856-6920
Emp Here 115   *Sales* 26,421,710
SIC 8731 Commercial physical research
Fred B. Parks
William P. Rousmaniere
David J. Flanagan

D-U-N-S 24-569-2918   (HQ)
ARGUS TELECOM INTERNATIONAL INC
(*Suby of* ENTREPRISES ARGUS TELECOM
INC)
2505 Rue Guenette, Saint-Laurent, QC, H4R
2E9
(514) 331-0840
Emp Here 29   *Sales* 35,773,920
SIC 5065 Electronic parts and equipment, nec
John Mccabe

D-U-N-S 24-834-3295   (SL)
ARTMETCO INC
2375 Rue Cohen, Saint-Laurent, QC, H4R
2N5
(514) 339-2707
Emp Here 130   *Sales* 24,971,050
SIC 3444 Sheet Metalwork
Daniel Kucer
Armand Afilalo

D-U-N-S 20-519-9396   (BR)
BANQUE NATIONALE DU CANADA
(*Suby of* BANQUE NATIONALE DU
CANADA)
1130 Boul Marcel-Laurin, Saint-Laurent, QC,
H4R 1J7
(514) 332-4220
Emp Here 79
SIC 6021 National commercial banks

D-U-N-S 20-419-4708   (HQ)
BLAKE, A. E. VENTES LTEE
3588 Boul Poirier, Saint-Laurent, QC, H4R 2J5
(514) 332-4214
Emp Here 10   *Sales* 10,955,175
SIC 5169 Chemicals and allied products, nec
Karen Blake
Debra Blake

D-U-N-S 25-540-9823   (BR)
BOMBARDIER INC
BOMBARDIER AERONAUTIQUE
(*Suby of* BOMBARDIER INC)
1800 Boul Marcel-Laurin, Saint-Laurent, QC,
H4R 1K2
(514) 855-5000
Emp Here 1,100
SIC 3812 Search and navigation equipment
Guy C. Hachey

D-U-N-S 24-254-4799   (HQ)
BOUTIQUE UNISEXE JOVEN INC
QUELS SONT VOS GOUTS
3616 Boul Poirier, Saint-Laurent, QC, H4R 2J5
(514) 382-5940
Sales 12,557,720
SIC 5611 Men's and boys' clothing stores
Richard Papazian

D-U-N-S 24-678-5588   (HQ)
CANADO/NACAN EQUIPEMENT INC
GROUPE CANADO/NACAN
5782 Boul Thimens, Saint-Laurent, QC, H4R
2K9
(514) 333-0077
Sales 11,875,650
SIC 5084 Industrial machinery and equipment
Daniel Juneau

D-U-N-S 20-212-9581   (HQ)
CHAUSSURES BROWNS INC
BROWNS
(*Suby of* 90401 CANADA LTEE)
2255 Rue Cohen, Saint-Laurent, QC, H4R
2N7
(514) 334-5000
Emp Here 80   *Sales* 118,517,250
SIC 5661 Shoe stores
Michael Brownstein
Andre Lescarbeau
Robert Laufer
David Brownstein
Cheryl Brownstein Stein
Janis Brownstein

D-U-N-S 20-633-5499   (SL)
CHAUSSURES M & M INC
BABY LOVE - TRADE MARK
(*Suby of* 4345614 CANADA INC)
4350 Boul Thimens, Saint-Laurent, QC, H4R
2P2
(514) 738-8210
Emp Here 35   *Sales* 17,441,270
SIC 5139 Footwear
Joerg Peschlow
Claude Potvin
Cliffert Peschlow
Keir Peschlow

D-U-N-S 20-237-6083   (HQ)
CIRCUL-AIRE INC
(*Suby of* 4489705 CANADA INC)
3999 Boul De La Cote-Vertu, Saint-Laurent,
QC, H4R 1R2
(514) 337-3331
Emp Here 65   *Sales* 15,318,069
SIC 3564 Blowers and fans
Ness Lakdawala
David Johnson

D-U-N-S 25-240-3308   (BR)
**COMMISSION SCOLAIRE MARGUERITE-
BOURGEOYS**
ECOLE SECONDAIRE SAINT LAURENT
(*Suby of* COMMISSION SCOLAIRE
MARGUERITE-BOURGEOYS)
2395 Boul Thimens, Saint-Laurent, QC, H4R
1T4

(514) 332-3190
Emp Here 110
SIC 8211 Elementary and secondary schools
Louise Chenard

D-U-N-S 25-748-1853   (SL)
COMPRESSEURS QUEBEC A K ENR
INTER-POWER, DIV DE
2431 Rue Guenette, Saint-Laurent, QC, H4R
2E9
(514) 337-0566
Emp Here 30   *Sales* 14,250,780
SIC 5084 Industrial machinery and equipment
Fares Kabbani

D-U-N-S 20-271-4705   (BR)
CONFISERIES REGAL INC
CHOCOLAT JEAN-TALON
(*Suby of* CONFISERIES REGAL INC)
4620 Boul Thimens, Saint-Laurent, QC, H4R
2B2
(514) 333-8540
Emp Here 110
SIC 5145 Confectionery
Marc Plante

D-U-N-S 25-688-8306   (BR)
CONGLOM INC
(*Suby of* CONGLOM INC)
4600 Boul Poirier, Saint-Laurent, QC, H4R
2C5
(514) 333-6666
Emp Here 100
SIC 5122 Drugs, proprietaries, and sundries
T Kostelidis

D-U-N-S 20-228-2158   (HQ)
CORPORATION MCKESSON CANADA, LA
ADJUVANTZ
(*Suby of* MCKESSON FINANCIAL HOLD-
INGS II UNLIMITED COMPANY)
4705 Rue Dobrin, Saint-Laurent, QC, H4R
2P7
(514) 745-2100
Emp Here 225   *Sales* 258,013,125
SIC 5122 Drugs, proprietaries, and sundries
Paula Keays
Loris Zancan
Jennifer Zerczy

D-U-N-S 20-309-0477   (SL)
CP TECH CORPORATION
CP TECH
2300 Rue Cohen, Saint-Laurent, QC, H4R
2N8
(514) 333-0030
Emp Here 100   *Sales* 19,208,500
SIC 3479 Metal coating and allied services
Cynthia Z. Brighton
Helen Z. Benjamin
William T Ziegler
Peter M. Ziegler
Karl H. Ziegler

D-U-N-S 24-888-9214   (HQ)
CREDIT VW CANADA, INC
VOLKSWAGEN FINANCE
(*Suby of* VOLKSWAGEN AG)
4865 Rue Marc-Blain Bureau 300, Saint-
Laurent, QC, H4R 3B2
(514) 332-4333
Sales 11,197,050
SIC 6159 Miscellaneous business credit insti-
tutions
Maloney Darren
Meima Horst
Patrick Lefebvre
Scott Mitchell
Daniel Weissland

D-U-N-S 20-178-4217   (SL)
D2 TECHNOLOGIE INC
2119 Boul Marcel-Laurin, Saint-Laurent, QC,
H4R 1K4
(514) 904-5888
Emp Here 100   *Sales* 24,432,800
SIC 5999 Miscellaneous retail stores, nec
Eric Barbeau

D-U-N-S 24-415-3339   (SL)
DANKA MDS
5924 Boul Henri-Bourassa O, Saint-Laurent, QC, H4R 1V9
(514) 339-5000
Emp Here 46   *Sales* 20,570,004
SIC 5044 Office equipment
Guy Boucher

D-U-N-S 20-585-9635   (BR)
DECISIONONE CORPORATION
(*Suby of* D1 HOLDINGS, LLC)
2505 Rue Cohen, Saint-Laurent, QC, H4R 2N5
(514) 338-1927
Emp Here 80
SIC 7378 Computer maintenance and repair
Normand Robichaud

D-U-N-S 24-294-8594   (HQ)
DECTRON INC
(*Suby of* MADISON INDUSTRIES HOLDINGS LLC)
3999 Boul De La Cote-Vertu, Saint-Laurent, QC, H4R 1R2
(514) 336-3330
Sales 27,750,125
SIC 3585 Refrigeration and heating equipment
Ness Lakdawala
Roxanne Lakdawala
David Johnson

D-U-N-S 25-675-0639   (HQ)
DECTRON INTERNATIONALE INC
(*Suby of* MADISON INDUSTRIES HOLDINGS LLC)
3999 Boul De La Cote-Vertu, Saint-Laurent, QC, H4R 1R2
(514) 336-3330
Emp Here 100   *Sales* 120,777,110
SIC 3585 Refrigeration and heating equipment
Ness Lakdawala
David Johnson
Claude Proulx
Leonard B.C. Schlemm
Roshan Katrak

D-U-N-S 20-633-0078   (SL)
DESJARDINS FORD LTEE
ENTREPRISE PLUS
1150 Boul Marcel-Laurin, Saint-Laurent, QC, H4R 1J7
(514) 332-3850
Emp Here 50   *Sales* 24,903,900
SIC 5511 New and used car dealers
Jean-Luc Desjardins

D-U-N-S 20-217-0320   (HQ)
DORFIN INC
EMBALLAGES KUSH-PACK, DIVISION DE DORFIN
5757 Boul Thimens, Saint-Laurent, QC, H4R 2H6
(514) 335-0333
Emp Here 55   *Sales* 30,219,480
SIC 5113 Industrial and personal service paper
Stanley Aranoff
Beryl Aranoff

D-U-N-S 20-856-5713   (SL)
DUBORD & RAINVILLE INC
(*Suby of* PEKELES HOLDINGS INC)
4045 Boul Poirier, Saint-Laurent, QC, H4R 2G9
(514) 735-6111
Emp Here 150   *Sales* 104,295,000
SIC 5099 Durable goods, nec
Gerald Pekeles

D-U-N-S 25-502-0794   (SL)
EMBALLAGES   TRANSCONTINENTAL FLEXIPAK INC
(*Suby of* TRANSCONTINENTAL INC)
5020 Boul Thimens, Saint-Laurent, QC, H4R 2B2

(514) 335-0001
Emp Here 45   *Sales* 10,504,575
SIC 2673 Bags: plastic, laminated, and coated
Brian Reid
Karl Boustany
Nelson Gentiletti

D-U-N-S 20-735-9589   (HQ)
ENTREPRISES AMIRA INC, LES
5375 Boul Henri-Bourassa O, Saint-Laurent, QC, H4R 1C1
(514) 382-9823
Sales 50,134,620
SIC 5149 Groceries and related products, nec
Sabry Boulos
Ragaa Boulos
Adel Boulos

D-U-N-S 24-435-2688   (HQ)
ENTREPRISES EMILE CREVIER INC
2025 Rue Lucien-Thimens, Saint-Laurent, QC, H4R 1K8
(514) 331-2951
Sales 50,288,040
SIC 5172 Petroleum products, nec
Pierre Crevier
Jean-Francois Crevier
Vincent Desquirez
Louis-Philippe Crevier
Mathieu St-Louis
Helene Crevier
Lorraine Crevier

D-U-N-S 25-209-8629   (HQ)
EXPERTS EN MEMOIRE INTERNATIONALE INC, LES
CANRAM
2321 Rue Cohen, Saint-Laurent, QC, H4R 2N7
(514) 333-5010
Sales 35,773,920
SIC 5044 Office equipment
Gerard Reusing
Guadalupe Reusing
Lawrence Reusing

D-U-N-S 25-536-1560   (SL)
FERSTEN WORLDWIDE INC
FW
4600 Boul Poirier, Saint-Laurent, QC, H4R 2C5
(514) 739-1644
Emp Here 100   *Sales* 13,667,400
SIC 2353 Hats, caps, and millinery
Mitchell Fersten

D-U-N-S 20-918-6639   (BR)
FONDATION EDUCATIVE DE LA COMMISSION SCOLAIRE ENGLISH-MONTREAL, LA
COMMISSION   SCOLAIRE   ENGLISH-MONTREAL
(*Suby of* FONDATION EDUCATIVE DE LA COMMISSION SCOLAIRE ENGLISH-MONTREAL, LA)
2505 Boul De La Cote-Vertu, Saint-Laurent, QC, H4R 1P3
(514) 331-8781
Emp Here 80
SIC 8211 Elementary and secondary schools
Claude Dansereau

D-U-N-S 20-183-1133   (HQ)
FORGET & SAUVE, AUDIOPROTHESISTES S.E.N.C.
GROUPE FORGET, LE
5255 Boul Henri-Bourassa O Bureau 410, Saint-Laurent, QC, H4R 2M6
(514) 353-0001
Emp Here 10   *Sales* 30,541,000
SIC 5999 Miscellaneous retail stores, nec
Steve Forget
Magella Sauve

D-U-N-S 20-882-5984   (BR)
G.N. JOHNSTON EQUIPMENT CO. LTD.
G.N. JOHNSTON EQUIPMENT CO. LTD

(*Suby of* TOYOTA INDUSTRIES CORPORATION)
5000 Rue Levy, Saint-Laurent, QC, H4R 2P1
(514) 956-0020
Emp Here 275
SIC 5084 Industrial machinery and equipment
Luc Beauchemin

D-U-N-S 24-697-2137   (HQ)
GANT PARIS DU CANADA LTEE, LE
AQUA STOP
(*Suby of* TORSTEN JANSSON HOLDING AB)
2315 Rue Cohen, Saint-Laurent, QC, H4R 2N7
(514) 345-0135
Emp Here 70   *Sales* 100,503,960
SIC 5136 Men's and boy's clothing
Ernest R Johnson
Guy Darveau
William Wong
Torsten Jansson
Jens I. Petersson

D-U-N-S 24-323-0948   (HQ)
GESTION D'INVESTISSEMENT 2300 INC
(*Suby of* GESTION TREE ROOTS INC)
2300 Rue Emile-Belanger, Saint-Laurent, QC, H4R 3J4
(514) 747-2536
Emp Here 2   *Sales* 2,071,705,012
SIC 6712 Bank holding companies
Aldo Bensadoun
Peter Mendell

D-U-N-S 20-558-6147   (HQ)
GESTION   IMMOBILIERE   LUC   MAURICE INC
2400 Rue Des Nations Bureau 137, Saint-Laurent, QC, H4R 3G4
(514) 331-2788
Sales 32,802,000
SIC 6719 Holding companies, nec
Luc Maurice

D-U-N-S 24-323-0955   (HQ)
GESTION TREE ROOTS INC
2300 Rue Emile-Belanger, Saint-Laurent, QC, H4R 3J4
(514) 747-2536
Emp Here 6   *Sales* 709,356,930
SIC 5661 Shoe stores
Aldo Bensadoun
Peter Mendell
David Bensadoun
Douglas Bensadoun
Samuel Minzberg
Dianne Bibeau

D-U-N-S 20-719-4809   (HQ)
GLOBEX COURRIER EXPRESS INTERNATIONAL INC
2267 Rue Guenette, Saint-Laurent, QC, H4R 2E9
(514) 739-7977
Emp Here 60   *Sales* 18,688,460
SIC 4512 Air transportation, scheduled
Arie Bettan
Charles Fortin

D-U-N-S 24-351-1735   (HQ)
GROUPE ACCENT-FAIRCHILD INC
ACCENT HOME PRODUCTS
5151 Boul Thimens, Saint-Laurent, QC, H4R 2C8
(514) 748-6721
Sales 35,619,920
SIC 5023 Homefurnishings
Evan Feldman
Solly Feldman

D-U-N-S 20-707-9179   (HQ)
GROUPE ALDO INC, LE
ACCESS
(*Suby of* GESTION TREE ROOTS INC)
2300 Rue Emile-Belanger, Saint-Laurent, QC, H4R 3J4

(514) 747-2536
Emp Here 750   *Sales* 706,861,830
SIC 5661 Shoe stores
David Bensadoun
Norman Jaskolka
Catherine Ross
Peter Mendell
Douglas Bensadoun
Samuel Minzberg
Dianne Bibeau
Aldo Bensadoun
Marie-Josee Lamothe
Farah Ramzan Golant

D-U-N-S 24-347-8380   (BR)
GROUPE ALDO INC, LE
CENTRE DE DISTRIBUTION GROUPE ALDO
(*Suby of* GESTION TREE ROOTS INC)
3665 Boul Poirier, Saint-Laurent, QC, H4R 3J2
(514) 747-5892
Emp Here 100
SIC 5139 Footwear

D-U-N-S 24-371-8306   (SL)
GROUPE ERA INC
2500 Rue Guenette, Saint-Laurent, QC, H4R 2H2
(514) 335-0550
Emp Here 100   *Sales* 15,885,800
SIC 3083 Laminated plastics plate and sheet
Jean-Luc Lavergne
Gerry Shapiro
Mark Schneiderman
Marc Tremblay

D-U-N-S 20-252-1956   (SL)
GROUPE MAURICE INC, LE
2400 Rue Des Nations Bureau 137, Saint-Laurent, QC, H4R 3G4
(514) 331-2788
Emp Here 40   *Sales* 11,543,320
SIC 1522 Residential construction, nec
Luc Maurice

D-U-N-S 25-540-6472   (HQ)
HEMA-QUEBEC
4045 Boul De La Cote-Vertu, Saint-Laurent, QC, H4R 2W7
(514) 832-5000
Emp Here 600   *Sales* 266,156,928
SIC 8099 Health and allied services, nec
Nathalie Fagnan
Martine Carre
Michele Beaupre Beriau
Smaranda Ghibu
Patricia Pelletier
Christine Beaubien
Jean-Marie Leclerc
Daniel Beaupre
Jean-Frederic Lafontaine
Wilson Sanon

D-U-N-S 20-876-7264   (BR)
IAN MARTIN LIMITED
(*Suby of* MARTIN, IAN TECHNOLOGY STAFFING LIMITED)
3333 Boul De La Cote-Vertu Bureau 202, Saint-Laurent, QC, H4R 2N1
(514) 338-3800
Emp Here 100
SIC 7361 Employment agencies

D-U-N-S 24-801-1512   (SL)
INDUSTRIES LECO INC
3235 Rue Sartelon, Saint-Laurent, QC, H4R 1E9
(514) 332-0535
Emp Here 50   *Sales* 13,833,000
SIC 2821 Plastics materials and resins
Roger Prunier

D-U-N-S 24-349-8230   (SL)
INVESTISSEMENT IMMOBILIER GROUPE MAURICE INC
2400 Rue Des Nations Bureau 137, Saint-Laurent, QC, H4R 3G4

(514) 331-2788
Emp Here 50   *Sales* 20,967,750
SIC 6719 Holding companies, nec
Luc Maurice

D-U-N-S 25-689-9360   (HQ)
INVESTISSEMENTS ISAAM INC, LES
3100 Boul De La Cote-Vertu Bureau 210,
Saint-Laurent, QC, H4R 2J8
(514) 335-6606
Emp Here 1   *Sales* 13,077,650
SIC 6712 Bank holding companies
Irving Choran

D-U-N-S 24-836-2089   (SL)
LICAPLAST INDUSTRIES EMBALLAGES INC
2835 Rue Duchesne, Saint-Laurent, QC, H4R 1J2
(514) 335-4091
Emp Here 80   *Sales* 18,674,800
SIC 2673 Bags: plastic, laminated, and coated
Raymond Nawar
Joseph Nawar

D-U-N-S 25-303-9697   (BR)
LONDON LIFE, COMPAGNIE D'ASSURANCE-VIE
LONDON LIFE INSURANCE COMPANY
(*Suby of* POWER CORPORATION DU CANADA)
3773 Boul De La Cote-Vertu Bureau 200,
Saint-Laurent, QC, H4R 2M3

Emp Here 80
SIC 6311 Life insurance

D-U-N-S 24-864-7802   (SL)
MATCO PACKAGING INC
MPI MATCO
2519 Rue Cohen, Saint-Laurent, QC, H4R 2N5
(514) 337-6050
Emp Here 24   *Sales* 17,528,280
SIC 5169 Chemicals and allied products, nec
Daniel David
David Mucciarone

D-U-N-S 24-508-7895   (HQ)
MATHESON VALVES & FITTINGS LTD
4060 Boul Poirier, Saint-Laurent, QC, H4R 2A5
(514) 337-1106
Emp Here 12   *Sales* 11,875,650
SIC 5085 Industrial supplies
Arthur Matheson
Edrina Black

D-U-N-S 20-534-1659   (SL)
MAY BALIAN & EMAD GABRA S.E.N.C.R.L.
PJC JEAN COUTU
2085 Boul Marcel-Laurin, Saint-Laurent, QC, H4R 1K4
(514) 334-1823
Emp Here 40   *Sales* 10,118,160
SIC 5912 Drug stores and proprietary stores
May Balian

D-U-N-S 24-890-5473   (SL)
MCCOPIER (CANADA) INC
4430 Rue Garand, Saint-Laurent, QC, H4R 2A3
(514) 344-1515
Emp Here 24   *Sales* 10,732,176
SIC 5044 Office equipment
Robert Auerbach

D-U-N-S 20-226-7621   (SL)
MEDICANA INC
2261 Rue Guenette, Saint-Laurent, QC, H4R 2E9
(514) 335-2677
Emp Here 24   *Sales* 10,285,002
SIC 5047 Medical and hospital equipment
Christian Chammas
Roland Chammas

D-U-N-S 25-380-6251   (HQ)

MEDISCA PHARMACEUTIQUE INC
6090 Boul Henri-Bourassa O, Saint-Laurent, QC, H4R 3A6
(800) 932-1039
Emp Here 73   *Sales* 82,564,200
SIC 5122 Drugs, proprietaries, and sundries
Antonio Dos Santos

D-U-N-S 24-770-4398   (HQ)
METSO FLOW CONTROL CANADA LTD
AUTOMATION METSO CANADA
(*Suby of* METSO OYJ)
4716 Boul Thimens, Saint-Laurent, QC, H4R 2B2
(514) 908-7045
Emp Here 14   *Sales* 35,151,924
SIC 5084 Industrial machinery and equipment
Eeva-Liisa Virkkunen
Carrol Lamarche
Donroy Ferdinand

D-U-N-S 24-372-1490   (BR)
METSO MINERALS CANADA INC
(*Suby of* METSO OYJ)
4900 Boul Thimens, Saint-Laurent, QC, H4R 2B2
(514) 335-5426
Emp Here 80
SIC 5084 Industrial machinery and equipment
Lee Bartholomew

D-U-N-S 20-227-3348   (HQ)
MITCHEL-LINCOLN PACKAGING LTD
BONCOR CONTAINERS
3737 Boul Thimens, Saint-Laurent, QC, H4R 1V1
(514) 332-3480
Emp Here 325   *Sales* 238,964,050
SIC 2653 Corrugated and solid fiber boxes
James Garfinkle
David Garfinkle
Irving Granovsky
John Cherry

D-U-N-S 20-544-9267   (HQ)
NATURISTE INC
(*Suby of* 4190637 CANADA INC)
5900 Boul Henri-Bourassa O, Saint-Laurent, QC, H4R 1V9
(514) 336-2244
Emp Here 30   *Sales* 13,718,466
SIC 5149 Groceries and related products, nec
Stephen Rosenhek

D-U-N-S 24-528-2124   (HQ)
NITREX METAL INC
(*Suby of* CORPORATION DE DEVELOPPE-MENT NITREX INC)
3474 Boul Poirier, Saint-Laurent, QC, H4R 2J5
(514) 335-7191
Emp Here 26   *Sales* 56,583,000
SIC 3625 Relays and industrial controls
Michel J Korwin
Stephane Tremblay
Etienne Antoine Veilleux
David Brassard
Christopher Morawski

D-U-N-S 20-216-5627   (HQ)
P. & R. DESJARDINS CONSTRUCTION INC
1777 Rue Begin, Saint-Laurent, QC, H4R 2B5
(514) 748-1234
Sales 23,536,550
SIC 1542 Nonresidential construction, nec
Marc-Antoine Desjardins
Marc Desjardins

D-U-N-S 24-327-7592   (HQ)
PEKELES HOLDINGS INC
4045 Boul Poirier, Saint-Laurent, QC, H4R 2G9
(514) 735-6111
Emp Here 2   *Sales* 41,002,500
SIC 6712 Bank holding companies
Gerald Pekeles

D-U-N-S 25-658-1729   (BR)
PEPSI BOTTLING GROUP (CANADA), ULC,

THE
PEPSICO BEVERAGES CANADA
(*Suby of* PBG INVESTMENT (LUXEM-BOURG) SARL)
3700 Boul Thimens, Saint-Laurent, QC, H4R 1T8
(514) 332-3770
Emp Here 600
SIC 2086 Bottled and canned soft drinks
Sylvain Charbonneau

D-U-N-S 20-927-3820   (HQ)
PETROLES CREVIER INC
LE GROUPE DES MARCHANDS DE PETROLES DU QUEBEC
(*Suby of* ENTREPRISES EMILE CREVIER INC)
2025 Rue Lucien-Thimens, Saint-Laurent, QC, H4R 1K8
(514) 331-2951
Emp Here 45   *Sales* 74,174,859
SIC 5172 Petroleum products, nec
Jean-Francois Crevier
Crevier Louis Philippe
Jacques Crevier

D-U-N-S 20-381-2479   (SL)
PF CONSUMER HEALTHCARE CANADA ULC
(*Suby of* C.P. PHARMACEUTICALS INTER-NATIONAL C.V.)
1025 Boul Marcel-Laurin, Saint-Laurent, QC, H4R 1J6
(514) 695-0500
Emp Here 829   *Sales* 274,891,426
SIC 2834 Pharmaceutical preparations
John Helou
Serge Roussel

D-U-N-S 24-677-0197   (BR)
PFIZER CANADA SRI
PFIZER CANADA INC
(*Suby of* C.P. PHARMACEUTICALS INTER-NATIONAL C.V.)
1025 Boul Marcel-Laurin, Saint-Laurent, QC, H4R 1J6
(514) 744-6771
Emp Here 150
SIC 2834 Pharmaceutical preparations

D-U-N-S 20-623-3467   (SL)
PHARMACIE JEAN COUTU
2085 Boul Marcel-Laurin, Saint-Laurent, QC, H4R 1K4
(514) 745-3003
Emp Here 40   *Sales* 10,118,160
SIC 5912 Drug stores and proprietary stores

D-U-N-S 20-230-3566   (HQ)
PINKHAM & SONS BUILDING MAINTE-NANCE INC
2449 Rue Guenette, Saint-Laurent, QC, H4R 2E9
(514) 332-4522
Emp Here 130   *Sales* 4,795,200
SIC 7349 Building maintenance services, nec
Jerry Pinkham
Carl Pinkham
Michael Pinkham

D-U-N-S 24-433-3332   (SL)
PRODUITS ALIMENTAIRES SA-GER INC, LES
PRODUITS ALIMENTAIRES SAGER, LES
(*Suby of* FATA INDUSTRIES INC, LES)
6755 Boul Henri-Bourassa O, Saint-Laurent, QC, H4R 1E1
(514) 643-4887
Emp Here 62   *Sales* 21,432,780
SIC 2079 Edible fats and oils
Anthony M Fata
Santo John Fata
Santo Fata
Amelia Fata

D-U-N-S 25-291-8719   (SL)
PRODUITS FLEURCO INC, LES
4575 Boul Poirier, Saint-Laurent, QC, H4R

2A4
(514) 326-2222
Emp Here 55   *Sales* 14,720,860
SIC 5211 Lumber and other building materials
Robert Schachter
Mark Reinish
Michael Salamon

D-U-N-S 25-170-1785   (BR)
PROVIGO DISTRIBUTION INC
MAXI
(*Suby of* LOBLAW COMPANIES LIMITED)
1757 Boul Marcel-Laurin, Saint-Laurent, QC, H4R 1J5
(514) 747-2203
Emp Here 145
SIC 5411 Grocery stores
Pierre Mignault

D-U-N-S 20-882-8129   (BR)
PUROLATOR INC
COURRIER PUROLATOR
(*Suby of* GOVERNMENT OF CANADA)
1305 Rue Tees, Saint-Laurent, QC, H4R 2A7
(514) 337-6710
Emp Here 250
SIC 4731 Freight transportation arrangement

D-U-N-S 24-322-6339   (HQ)
RAYMOND LANCTOT LTEE
LANCTOT
5290 Boul Thimens, Saint-Laurent, QC, H4R 2B2
(514) 731-6841
Sales 41,643,360
SIC 5091 Sporting and recreation goods
Diane Lanctot

D-U-N-S 20-021-2612   (SL)
RECYCAN INC
(*Suby of* ANHEUSER-BUSCH INBEV)
3555 Rue Ashby, Saint-Laurent, QC, H4R 2K3
(514) 379-1006
Emp Here 50   *Sales* 12,856,550
SIC 4953 Refuse systems
Maxime Couture
Philippe Cote
Jean Robitaille

D-U-N-S 25-995-6837   (SL)
SERVICES J. SONIC INC
BOITEOUVERTE.CA
6869 Boul Henri-Bourassa O, Saint-Laurent, QC, H4R 1E1
(514) 341-5789
Emp Here 72   *Sales* 32,196,528
SIC 5031 Lumber, plywood, and millwork
Jean Aucoin

D-U-N-S 20-051-5612   (HQ)
SERVOMAX INC
1790 Rue Beaulac, Saint-Laurent, QC, H4R 1W8
(514) 745-5757
Sales 15,722,665
SIC 7389 Business services, nec
Arie Koifman

D-U-N-S 24-855-9317   (SL)
SIVEM PHARMACEUTICALS ULC
(*Suby of* MCKESSON FINANCIAL HOLD-INGS II UNLIMITED COMPANY)
4800 Rue Levy, Saint-Laurent, QC, H4R 2P1
(514) 832-1290
Emp Here 10   *Sales* 11,053,450
SIC 5122 Drugs, proprietaries, and sundries
Paula Keays
Loris Zancan
Michele Lau
Ivan Elias
Mai Anh Tran

D-U-N-S 25-357-1673   (BR)
SLH TRANSPORT INC
(*Suby of* HOLDING CANADIAN AMERICAN TRANSPORTATION C.A.T. INC)
3075 Boul Thimens, Saint-Laurent, QC, H4R 1Y3

(514) 335-4990
Emp Here 100
SIC 4213 Trucking, except local
Denis Mcmahon

D-U-N-S 20-287-9854   (HQ)
SML CANADA ACQUISITION CORP
BLONDO CANADA
(*Suby of* STEVEN MADDEN, LTD.)
2328 Rue Cohen, Saint-Laurent, QC, H4R
2N8
(514) 858-7272
Sales 24,916,100
SIC 5136 Men's and boy's clothing
Thomas Alberga
Awadhesh Sinha
Edward Rosenfeld

D-U-N-S 20-277-3925   (HQ)
SPECTRIS CANADA INC
ARBRE BLEU DONNEES CELLULAIRES
(*Suby of* SPECTRIS PLC)
4921 Place Olivia, Saint-Laurent, QC, H4R
2V6
(514) 956-2132
Emp Here 15   *Sales* 34,023,670
SIC 5049 Professional equipment, nec
Clive Graeme Watson
Daniel Raymond
Oscar Enrique Almeida
Nicholas John Popper

D-U-N-S 25-673-8725   (BR)
SPORT MASKA INC
(*Suby of* SPORT MASKA INC)
3400 Rue Raymond-Lasnier, Saint-Laurent,
QC, H4R 3L3
(514) 461-8000
Emp Here 200
SIC 3949 Sporting and athletic goods, nec
Rene Habal

D-U-N-S 20-252-1043   (HQ)
SPORT MASKA INC
CCM HOCKEY
3400 Rue Raymond-Lasnier, Saint-Laurent,
QC, H4R 3L3
(514) 461-8000
Emp Here 550   *Sales* 250,016,760
SIC 3949 Sporting and athletic goods, nec
Richard J. Blackshaw
Laurent Gauthier
Patrick Duncan
Joanne Aucoin
Matt Kunica
John Macintyre

D-U-N-S 20-910-4843   (SL)
STANEX INC
SERCAB
2437 Rue Guenette, Saint-Laurent, QC, H4R
2E9
(514) 333-5280
Emp Here 40   *Sales* 17,886,960
SIC 5065 Electronic parts and equipment, nec
Demetre Alexopoulos
Duarte Velosa
Pierre Gagnon
Jimmy Hatzis

D-U-N-S 24-959-2270   (HQ)
STELLA-JONES INC
SJ & DESIGN
3100 Boul De La Cote-Vertu Bureau 300,
Saint-Laurent, QC, H4R 2J8
(514) 934-8666
Emp Here 5   *Sales* 1,610,127,531
SIC 2491 Wood preserving
Brian Mcmanus
Katherine A Lehman
Eric Vachon
Marla Eichenbaum
Ian Jones
Gordon Murray
Andre Daigle
George J. Bunze
Nycol Pageau-Goyette
Karen Laflamme

D-U-N-S 25-501-1785   (HQ)
**SYSTEMES D'ENTRAINEMENT MEGGITT
(QUEBEC) INC**
*SYSTEMES DE DETECTION MEGGITT
CANADA*
(*Suby of* MEGGITT PLC)
6140 Boul Henri-Bourassa O, Saint-Laurent,
QC, H4R 3A6
(514) 339-9938
Emp Here 25   *Sales* 11,426,520
SIC 3699 Electrical equipment and supplies,
nec
Edward Duckless
Jeff Murphy
Marina Thomas
Tayeb Ghilanie

D-U-N-S 20-331-4877   (BR)
**TECHNOLOGIES SURFACE PRAXAIR
MONTREAL S.E.C.**
*PRAXAIR SURFACE TECHNOLOGIES
MONTREAL L.P.*
(*Suby of* TECHNOLOGIES SURFACE PRAX-
AIR MONTREAL S.E.C.)
2300 Rue Cohen, Saint-Laurent, QC, H4R
2N8
(514) 333-0030
Emp Here 85
SIC 1721 Painting and paper hanging
Ken Miura

D-U-N-S 20-302-6174   (SL)
THALES OPTRONIQUE CANADA INC
4868 Rue Levy, Saint-Laurent, QC, H4R 2P1
(514) 337-7878
Emp Here 55   *Sales* 12,500,895
SIC 3827 Optical instruments and lenses
Michel Lamarche

D-U-N-S 20-856-0870   (SL)
TI TITANIUM LTEE
(*Suby of* AMERICAN INDUSTRIAL ACQUISI-
TION CORPORATION)
5055 Rue Levy, Saint-Laurent, QC, H4R 2N9
(514) 334-5781
Emp Here 75   *Sales* 14,406,375
SIC 3443 Fabricated plate work (boiler shop)
Daniel Lefebvre
Brent Willey

D-U-N-S 20-553-3784   (BR)
**TYCO INTEGRATED FIRE & SECURITY
CANADA, INC**
SIMPLEX GRINNELL
(*Suby of* JOHNSON CONTROLS INTERNA-
TIONAL PUBLIC LIMITED COMPANY)
5800 Boul Henri-Bourassa O, Saint-Laurent,
QC, H4R 1V9
(514) 737-5505
Emp Here 108
SIC 7389 Business services, nec
Nicolas Zigayer

D-U-N-S 20-573-6403   (BR)
**TYCO INTEGRATED FIRE & SECURITY
CANADA, INC**
SIMPLEXGRINNELL
(*Suby of* JOHNSON CONTROLS INTERNA-
TIONAL PUBLIC LIMITED COMPANY)
5700 Boul Henri-Bourassa O, Saint-Laurent,
QC, H4R 1V9
(514) 737-5505
Emp Here 150
SIC 7382 Security systems services
Danny Tosques

D-U-N-S 25-540-6522   (SL)
**USACAN MEDIA DISTRIBUTION SERVICE
INC**
SERVICE USACAN
1459 Rue Begin, Saint-Laurent, QC, H4R 1V8

Emp Here 125   *Sales* 92,815,000
SIC 5199 Nondurable goods, nec
Jacques Bourbigot
Roger Forget

D-U-N-S 24-475-2853   (HQ)
VALMET LTEE
(*Suby of* VALMET OYJ)
4900 Boul Thimens, Saint-Laurent, QC, H4R
2B2
(514) 335-5426
Sales 55,613,646
SIC 3554 Paper industries machinery
David H. King
Emily Rogers
Rasmus Oksala
Kristen Wald
Nick Colledanchise

D-U-N-S 24-052-2854   (HQ)
VIANDES AGRO INC
(*Suby of* INVESTISSEMENTS ISAAM INC,
LES)
3100 Boul De La Cote-Vertu Bureau 210,
Saint-Laurent, QC, H4R 2J8
(514) 335-6606
Sales 20,889,425
SIC 5147 Meats and meat products
Pat Giordano
Anna Choran
Irving Choran

D-U-N-S 20-231-4878   (HQ)
W. RALSTON (CANADA) INC
(*Suby of* INTEPLAST GROUP CORPORA-
TION)
3300 Boul De La Cote-Vertu Bureau 200,
Saint-Laurent, QC, H4R 2B7
(514) 334-5656
Emp Here 15   *Sales* 38,953,600
SIC 2673 Bags: plastic, laminated, and
coated
Joe Chan
Ronnie Chang
Joseph Wang
Robert Wang
Herman Sterling
John Young

D-U-N-S 20-237-2926   (SL)
WENGER LTEE
MONTRES ORA, LES
(*Suby of* 3368556 CANADA INC)
3521 Boul Thimens, Saint-Laurent, QC, H4R
1V5
(514) 337-4455
Emp Here 100   *Sales* 69,530,000
SIC 5094 Jewelry and precious stones
Harold Wenger
Alan Wenger
Frederick Wenger
David Wenger

D-U-N-S 20-418-3974   (HQ)
YKK CANADA INC
(*Suby of* YKK CORPORATION)
3939 Boul Thimens, Saint-Laurent, QC, H4R
1X3
(514) 332-3350
Emp Here 95   *Sales* 32,613,600
SIC 3965 Fasteners, buttons, needles, and
pins
James Maguire
Yvan Jutras
Kenji Miyamoto
James K. Reed

Saint-Laurent, QC H4S

D-U-N-S 20-237-3510   (SL)
108786 CANADA INC
OPTIQUE WESTERN
4775 Rue Cousens, Saint-Laurent, QC, H4S
1X5
(514) 383-0042
Emp Here 63   *Sales* 28,171,962
SIC 5049 Professional equipment, nec
Radu Suliteanu
Michael Suliteanu

D-U-N-S 20-370-8057   (SL)
1092072 ONTARIO INC
DUEDATE LOGISTICS
2520 Av Marie-Curie, Saint-Laurent, QC, H4S
1N1
(800) 511-1100
Emp Here 26   *Sales* 10,019,360
SIC 4731 Freight transportation arrangement
Sheldon Bern
Ivan Bern

D-U-N-S 24-676-2269   (SL)
120348 CANADA INC
4600 Ch Du Bois-Franc, Saint-Laurent, QC,
H4S 1A7
(514) 331-3130
Emp Here 110   *Sales* 64,807,490
SIC 5199 Nondurable goods, nec
Bruce Shadeed

D-U-N-S 24-762-5353   (SL)
166260 CANADA INC
4747 Boul De La Cote-Vertu, Saint-Laurent,
QC, H4S 1C9
(514) 336-8780
Emp Here 75   *Sales* 20,501,250
SIC 6712 Bank holding companies
Mac Moyse

D-U-N-S 20-856-9632   (SL)
191017 CANADA INC
4747 Boul De La Cote-Vertu, Saint-Laurent,
QC, H4S 1C9
(514) 336-8780
Emp Here 90   *Sales* 45,797,040
SIC 5023 Homefurnishings
David Moyse
Mac Moyse
Kenneth Moyse

D-U-N-S 25-404-8762   (SL)
2931028 CANADA INC
APPELEZ MAURICE COURRIER
6405 Rue Vanden-Abeele, Saint-Laurent, QC,
H4S 1S1
(514) 335-6161
Emp Here 92   *Sales* 21,019,424
SIC 4813 Telephone communication, except
radio
Robert Aboud

D-U-N-S 25-475-6091   (SL)
2946-5440 QUEBEC INC
ULTIDENT
4850 Ch Du Bois-Franc Bureau 100, Saint-
Laurent, QC, H4S 1A7
(514) 335-3433
Emp Here 26   *Sales* 11,626,524
SIC 5047 Medical and hospital equipment
Nadine Jachimowicz
Gilles Cohen

D-U-N-S 24-827-0998   (SL)
4233964 CANADA INC
2575 Boul Pitfield, Saint-Laurent, QC, H4S
1T2
(514) 383-4442
Emp Here 614   *Sales* 76,599,570
SIC 5621 Women's clothing stores
Arden Dervishian

D-U-N-S 24-235-3096   (SL)
9162-7331 QUEBEC INC
TRANSPORT SGH
7420 Rue Verite, Saint-Laurent, QC, H4S 1C5
(877) 353-7683
Emp Here 30   *Sales* 11,560,800
SIC 4731 Freight transportation arrangement
Sharnjit Kaur Nakhanj

D-U-N-S 20-240-5577   (HQ)
9327-0197 QUEBEC INC
MARCAN TRANSPORT
(*Suby of* TFI INTERNATIONAL INC)
8801 Rte Transcanadienne Bureau 500, Saint-
Laurent, QC, H4S 1Z6
(514) 331-4000
Emp Here 50   *Sales* 55,314,300

SIC 4213 Trucking, except local
Josiane-M. Langlois
Chantal Martel
Josiane-Melanie Langlois

D-U-N-S 25-242-8024   (BR)
ABB INC
(Suby of ABB LTD)
800 Boul Hymus, Saint-Laurent, QC, H4S 0B5
(514) 710-1203
Emp Here 250
SIC 3612 Transformers, except electric

D-U-N-S 20-213-4326   (HQ)
ABB INC
ABB BOMEM
(Suby of ABB LTD)
800 Boul Hymus, Saint-Laurent, QC, H4S 0B5
(438) 843-6000
Emp Here 100   Sales 633,729,600
SIC 3621 Motors and generators
Nathalie Pilon
Sylvie Bergeron
Guy Dionne
Guido Mussehl

D-U-N-S 20-381-5100   (SL)
ABB   SOLUTIONS   INDUSTRIELLES (CANADA) INC
(Suby of ABB LTD)
800 Boul Hymus, Saint-Laurent, QC, H4S 0B5
(450) 688-8690
Emp Here 200   Sales 135,974,800
SIC 4911 Electric services
Nathalie Pilon
Sylvie Bergeron
Guy Dionne
Guido Mussehl

D-U-N-S 24-111-9148   (HQ)
ACCESSOIRES POUR VELOS O.G.D. LTEE
OUTDOOR GEAR CANADA
10555 Boul Henri-Bourassa O, Saint-Laurent, QC, H4S 1A1
(514) 332-1320
Emp Here 74   Sales 16,937,920
SIC 7312 Outdoor advertising services
David Bowman
James Buckingham

D-U-N-S 20-329-9651   (SL)
ACHAT SURPLUS MONTREAL INC
2800 Rue De Miniac, Saint-Laurent, QC, H4S 1K9
(438) 995-2650
Emp Here 6   Sales 11,832,085
SIC 5065 Electronic parts and equipment, nec
Serguei Boborykine
Garri Evdosin

D-U-N-S 25-331-3951   (SL)
ACIERS   INOXYDABLES   C.F.F.   (QUEBEC) INC
ACIERS INOXYDABLES
(Suby of C.F.F. HOLDINGS INC)
4900 Ch Du Bois-Franc, Saint-Laurent, QC, H4S 1A7
(514) 337-7700
Emp Here 35   Sales 16,625,910
SIC 5085 Industrial supplies
Brian Mccomb

D-U-N-S 24-057-8166   (SL)
AERO MAG 2000 (YUL) INC
(Suby of GROUPE AERO MAG 2000 INC)
8181 Rue Herve-Saint-Martin, Saint-Laurent, QC, H4S 2A5
(514) 636-1930
Emp Here 75   Sales 16,788,225
SIC 3728 Aircraft parts and equipment, nec
Mario Lepine
Martin Lepine
Pierre Lesperance

D-U-N-S 25-542-5241   (HQ)
AERRIANTA INTERNATIONAL (AMERIQUE DU NORD) INC
(Suby of DAA PUBLIC LIMITED COMPANY)

6400 Rue Abrams, Saint-Laurent, QC, H4S 1Y2
(514) 335-0254
Emp Here 20   Sales 30,421,600
SIC 5399 Miscellaneous general merchandise
Anthony Kenny
Mario M. Caron
Jacques Dagenais
Gerard Crawford
Jacqueline Mcdonagh

D-U-N-S 20-209-5022   (HQ)
AIR CANADA
AIR CANADA CARGO
7373 Boul De La Cote-Vertu Bureau 1290, Saint-Laurent, QC, H4S 1Z3
(514) 393-3333
Emp Here 1,000   Sales 13,695,112,630
SIC 4512 Air transportation, scheduled
Calin Rovinescu
Michael Rousseau
Richard Steer
Catherine Dyer
Duncan Bureau
Lucie Guillemette
Ferio Pugliese
Kevin C. Howlett
Amos Kazzaz
Craig Landry

D-U-N-S 24-402-4733   (HQ)
AIR INUIT LTEE
AIR INUIT SERVICE D'ENTRETIEN
(Suby of SOCIETE MAKIVIK)
6005 Boul De La Cote-Vertu, Saint-Laurent, QC, H4S 0B1
(514) 905-9445
Emp Here 600   Sales 193,584,720
SIC 4512 Air transportation, scheduled
Pita Aatami
Noah Tayara
Patricia Mcleod
Paul Brotto
Johnny May
Tommy Palliser
Hani Ackad
Johnny Adams
Christian Busch

D-U-N-S 24-676-9129   (HQ)
AIR TRANSAT A.T. INC
AIR TRANSAT CARGO
(Suby of TRANSAT A.T. INC)
5959 Boul De La Cote-Vertu, Saint-Laurent, QC, H4S 2E6
(514) 906-0330
Emp Here 6   Sales 317,352,000
SIC 4512 Air transportation, scheduled
Jean-Francois Lemay
Denis Petrin
Agnieszka Charysz
Jean-Marc Eustache
Annick Guerard
Bernard Bussieres

D-U-N-S 20-314-3060   (SL)
AJW TECHNIQUE INC
(Suby of AJW INTERNATIONAL LIMITED)
7055 Rue Alexander-Fleming Bureau 100, Saint-Laurent, QC, H4S 2B7
(514) 339-5100
Emp Here 100   Sales 26,697,800
SIC 4581 Airports, flying fields, and services
Christopher Whiteside
Gavin Simmonds
Ian Malin
Allan Pennycuick

D-U-N-S 25-392-6356   (HQ)
ALFAGOMMA CANADA INC
AG ALFAGOMMA DESIGN
(Suby of ALFA GOMMA SPA)
6550 Rue Abrams Bureau 6540, Saint-Laurent, QC, H4S 1Y2
(514) 333-5577
Emp Here 25   Sales 17,100,936

SIC 5085 Industrial supplies
Gennasio Enrico
Sandra Rollin
Massimo Eritale
Giacinto Bei

D-U-N-S 24-987-9222   (SL)
ALIMENTS CONAN INC, LES
7007 Boul Henri-Bourassa O, Saint-Laurent, QC, H4S 2E2
(514) 334-7977
Emp Here 45   Sales 37,600,965
SIC 5141 Groceries, general line
Randy White
Russell T Libby
Thomas P Kurz
Kimberly A Freeburn
Curtis Cusinato

D-U-N-S 20-330-3177   (SL)
ALIMENTS EXPRESCO INC
EXPRESCO
(Suby of PREMIUM BRANDS HOLDINGS CORPORATION)
8205 Rte Transcanadienne, Saint-Laurent, QC, H4S 1S4
(514) 344-9499
Emp Here 500   Sales 243,692,500
SIC 2013 Sausages and other prepared meats
Dennis Papakostas
George Tiritidis
William D. Kalutycz
Wilhelm Huber Jr.
George Paleologou

D-U-N-S 24-698-4520   (SL)
ALIMENTS ROSEHILL INC, LES
EPICES ROSE VALLEY SPICES
7171 Boul Thimens, Saint-Laurent, QC, H4S 2A2
(514) 745-1153
Emp Here 50   Sales 41,778,850
SIC 5149 Groceries and related products, nec
Georges Sarbanis
Costas Sarbanis

D-U-N-S 20-719-2753   (BR)
AMDOCS   CANADIAN   MANAGED   SERVICES INC
(Suby of AMDOCS LIMITED)
2351 Boul Alfred-Nobel Bureau 200, Saint-Laurent, QC, H4S 0B2
(514) 338-3100
Emp Here 400
SIC 7371 Custom computer programming services
Zeev Berkowitz

D-U-N-S 24-458-0064   (SL)
AMEUBLEMENTS GILBERT LTEE, LES
8855 Boul Henri-Bourassa O, Saint-Laurent, QC, H4S 1P7

Emp Here 80   Sales 12,345,760
SIC 2542 Partitions and fixtures, except wood
Marie L Gilbert
Ian Gilbert

D-U-N-S 20-253-1919   (SL)
APTOS CANADA INC
SOLUTIONS APTOS CANADA
(Suby of APTOS UK HOLDING LIMITED)
9300 Rte Transcanadienne Bureau 300, Saint-Laurent, QC, H4S 1K5
(514) 426-0822
Emp Here 250   Sales 46,143,250
SIC 7371 Custom computer programming services
Noel Goggin
David Baum
Mark Bentler
Jason Wright
Umang Kajaria
Seth Brody

D-U-N-S 25-007-3827   (HQ)

ARLBERG HOLDINGS INC
4505 Rue Cousens, Saint-Laurent, QC, H4S 1X5

Sales 10,462,120
SIC 6712 Bank holding companies
Stephen Courey

D-U-N-S 20-210-9518   (HQ)
BALLIN INC
BERTINI MODA
(Suby of GESTIONS JOSEPH BALINSKY INC, LES)
2825 Rue Brabant-Marineau, Saint-Laurent, QC, H4S 1R8
(514) 333-5501
Emp Here 150   Sales 132,667,500
SIC 2325 Men's and boys' trousers and slacks
Joseph Balinsky
Ronald Balinsky
Susan Balinsky

D-U-N-S 20-043-1427   (HQ)
BEIERSDORF CANADA INC
(Suby of MAXINGVEST AG)
2344 Boul Alfred-Nobel Bureau 100a, Saint-Laurent, QC, H4S 0A4
(514) 956-4330
Sales 28,738,970
SIC 5122 Drugs, proprietaries, and sundries
Graeme Fleckney
Mathieu Levasseur
Pierre Locas

D-U-N-S 24-313-9388   (HQ)
BELDEN CANADA INC
BELDEN
(Suby of BELDEN INC.)
2310 Boul Alfred-Nobel, Saint-Laurent, QC, H4S 2B4
(514) 822-2345
Sales 11,671,750
SIC 3315 Steel wire and related products
Alec Lappe
Henk Derksen
Guylaine Branchaud
John S. Stroup

D-U-N-S 25-476-9425   (SL)
BIOMERIEUX CANADA, INC
(Suby of COMPAGNIE MERIEUX ALLIANCE)
7815 Boul Henri-Bourassa O, Saint-Laurent, QC, H4S 1P7
(514) 336-7321
Emp Here 60   Sales 32,121,120
SIC 5047 Medical and hospital equipment
Stefan Willemsen
Brian Amrstrong
Gino Martel
Mark O'driscoll
Xavier Nouvelot

D-U-N-S 20-971-8527   (HQ)
BOLLORE LOGISTIQUES CANADA INC
TTA
(Suby of BOLLORE PARTICIPATIONS)
3400 Rue Douglas-B.-Floreani, Saint-Laurent, QC, H4S 1V2
(514) 956-7870
Emp Here 200   Sales 139,260,020
SIC 4731 Freight transportation arrangement
Thierry Ehrenbogen
Antonio Rodrigues
Frederic Fontan

D-U-N-S 20-399-7163   (SL)
BRENNTAG CANADA INC
9999 Rte Transcanadienne, Saint-Laurent, QC, H4S 1V1
(514) 333-7820
Emp Here 50   Sales 36,517,250
SIC 5169 Chemicals and allied products, nec
Lars Schneider

D-U-N-S 24-083-4036   (HQ)
BULA CANADA INC
BLACK CANYON

4005 Rue Sartelon, Saint-Laurent, QC, H4S 2A6
(514) 270-4222
Sales 125,629,950
SIC 5136 Men's and boy's clothing
Leonard Marcovitch

D-U-N-S 24-325-7677   (SL)
CAMIONS INTERNATIONAL WEST ISLAND INC
6100 Ch Saint-Francois, Saint-Laurent, QC, H4S 1B7
(514) 333-4412
Emp Here 60   *Sales* 37,756,800
SIC 5521 Used car dealers
Luc Paquin

D-U-N-S 20-697-3468   (BR)
CERIDIAN CANADA LTD
(*Suby of* FOUNDATION HOLDINGS, INC.)
8777 Rte Transcanadienne, Saint-Laurent, QC, H4S 1Z6
(514) 908-3000
Emp Here 100
SIC 8721 Accounting, auditing, and book-keeping
Helene Bedard

D-U-N-S 24-944-1031   (SL)
CERIKO ASSELIN LOMBARDI INC
CONSTRUCTION C.A.L.
3005 Rue Halpern, Saint-Laurent, QC, H4S 1P5
(514) 956-5511
Emp Here 30   *Sales* 14,121,930
SIC 1542 Nonresidential construction, nec
Peter Lombardi

D-U-N-S 20-317-4719   (HQ)
CHARLES LAPIERRE INC
NJM CLI
5600 Rue Kieran, Saint-Laurent, QC, H4S 2B5
(514) 337-6990
Sales 23,751,300
SIC 5084 Industrial machinery and equipment
Michel Lapierre
Daniel Lapierre
Marc Lapierre

D-U-N-S 20-209-5410   (HQ)
CIE CANADIENNE DE PAPIER & D'EMBALLAGE LTEE
CPP
3001 Rue Brabant-Marineau, Saint-Laurent, QC, H4S 1V5
(514) 333-4040
Sales 22,664,610
SIC 5113 Industrial and personal service paper
Louis Appel
John Taylor
Brian Charney

D-U-N-S 25-308-7233   (HQ)
CLARIANT (CANADA) INC
MASTERBATCHES DIV DE
(*Suby of* CLARIANT AG)
4600 Rue Cousens, Saint-Laurent, QC, H4S 1X3
(514) 334-1117
Sales 18,988,970
SIC 5169 Chemicals and allied products, nec
Kenneth L. Golder
Christopher S. Barnard
Michael P. Whitcombe

D-U-N-S 24-709-6449   (HQ)
CONGLOM INC
BELLE
2600 Av Marie-Curie, Saint-Laurent, QC, H4S 2C3
(514) 333-6666
Emp Here 40   *Sales* 87,037,050
SIC 5063 Electrical apparatus and equipment
Tasso Kostelidis
Litsa Papaevangelou
Dimitrios (Jimmy) Kostelidis
Petros Kostelidis

D-U-N-S 25-286-4608   (SL)
CONSTRUCTIONS CONCREATE LTEE
5840 Rue Donahue, Saint-Laurent, QC, H4S 1C1
(514) 335-0412
Emp Here 50   *Sales* 12,044,200
SIC 1622 Bridge, tunnel, and elevated highway construction
Walter Smirnow
Francis Dextraze
Antonio La Corte
Asessandro Pelle

D-U-N-S 24-590-0857   (HQ)
CONSTRUCTIONS DE MAUSOLEES CARRIER INC, LES
CMC
7575 Boul Thimens, Saint-Laurent, QC, H4S 2A2
(514) 832-3733
Sales 15,399,126
SIC 1542 Nonresidential construction, nec
Louis-Philippe Carrier

D-U-N-S 25-991-6955   (SL)
CONTRACTEURS ARMSERV INC
6400 Rue Vanden-Abeele, Saint-Laurent, QC, H4S 1R9
(514) 333-5340
Emp Here 25   *Sales* 11,179,350
SIC 5074 Plumbing and heating equipment and supplies (hydronics)
Sylvain Lewis
Joseph John Paulin

D-U-N-S 25-308-7803   (HQ)
CONTROLES I.S.I. INC, LES
4030 Ch Du Bois-Franc, Saint-Laurent, QC, H4S 1A7
(514) 338-1562
Sales 11,245,824
SIC 8748 Business consulting, nec
Philippe Doucas
Ian Seivwright
Shaun Cuggy

D-U-N-S 20-999-6131   (SL)
CONTROLES PROVAN ASSOCIES INC, LES
2315 Rue Halpern, Saint-Laurent, QC, H4S 1S3
(514) 332-3230
Emp Here 27   *Sales* 12,825,702
SIC 5084 Industrial machinery and equipment

D-U-N-S 20-322-9489   (HQ)
CORPORATION ABBVIE
(*Suby of* ABBVIE INC.)
8401 Rte Transcanadienne, Saint-Laurent, QC, H4S 1Z1
(514) 906-9700
Sales 132,637,600
SIC 2834 Pharmaceutical preparations
Steven G. Ramage
William Chase
Stephane Lassignardie

D-U-N-S 24-816-7983   (HQ)
CORPORATION ADFAST
(*Suby of* DAVID & CLAUDE HOLDINGS CANADA INC)
2685 Rue Diab, Saint-Laurent, QC, H4S 1E7
(514) 337-7307
Emp Here 50   *Sales* 21,868,000
SIC 6712 Bank holding companies
Yves Dandurand
Lucie Gautier
Claude Dandurand
Denis Perron

D-U-N-S 24-204-9984   (BR)
COVIDIEN CANADA ULC
COVIDIEN MANUFACTURING
8455 Rte Transcanadienne, Saint-Laurent, QC, H4S 1Z1
(514) 332-1220
Emp Here 400
SIC 2834 Pharmaceutical preparations

D-U-N-S 25-688-9338   (HQ)
COVIDIEN CANADA ULC
AUTO SUTURE
8455 Rte Transcanadienne, Saint-Laurent, QC, H4S 1Z1
(877) 664-8926
Emp Here 50   *Sales* 44,717,400
SIC 5047 Medical and hospital equipment
Neil Fraser
Olaf Felske
Jason Caron

D-U-N-S 25-300-8809   (BR)
CROWN METAL PACKAGING CANADA LP
(*Suby of* CROWN HOLDINGS INC.)
5789 Rue Cypihot, Saint-Laurent, QC, H4S 1R3
(514) 956-8900
Emp Here 100
SIC 3411 Metal cans
Michel Ste-Marie

D-U-N-S 20-216-0024   (HQ)
DANSON DECOR INC
(*Suby of* RICMARAL INC)
3425 Rue Douglas-B.-Floreani, Saint-Laurent, QC, H4S 1Y6
(514) 335-2435
Emp Here 87   *Sales* 66,826,800
SIC 5199 Nondurable goods, nec
Mark Aziz
Richard Aziz

D-U-N-S 25-087-3564   (HQ)
DOMGEN INVESTMENTS INC
9500 Boul Henri-Bourassa O, Saint-Laurent, QC, H4S 1N8

Sales 20,904,300
SIC 6799 Investors, nec
Constantino Carrara

D-U-N-S 20-119-2593   (SL)
DSI DISPENSING SYSTEMS INTERNATIONAL INC
5800 Boul Thimens, Saint-Laurent, QC, H4S 1S5
(514) 433-4562
Emp Here 65   *Sales* 14,430,065
SIC 3585 Refrigeration and heating equipment
Michael Bertone

D-U-N-S 24-320-9673   (SL)
EDICIBLE LTEE
NOBEL DIRECT
2825 Rue Brabant-Marineau, Saint-Laurent, QC, H4S 1R8
(514) 336-0710
Emp Here 250   *Sales* 48,443,500
SIC 2789 Bookbinding and related work
Max Dahan
Roben Dahan

D-U-N-S 24-047-3418   (SL)
EI BRAND MANAGEMENT INC
2520 Av Marie-Curie, Saint-Laurent, QC, H4S 1N1
(514) 344-3533
Emp Here 40   *Sales* 19,932,880
SIC 5137 Women's and children's clothing
Shell Bern
Ivan Bern

D-U-N-S 24-251-9494   (SL)
ELIMETAL INC
(*Suby of* HOLDECOM INC)
1515 Boul Pitfield, Saint-Laurent, QC, H4S 1G3
(514) 956-7400
Emp Here 110   *Sales* 19,952,680
SIC 3324 Steel investment foundries
Eli Kedem

D-U-N-S 20-882-2767   (HQ)
ENTREPRISE COMMERCIALE SHAH LIMITEE, L'
ALL SEASONS

(*Suby of* GROUPE SOMCHAND KASTUR LIMITEE)
3401 Rue Douglas-B.-Floreani, Saint-Laurent, QC, H4S 1Y6
(514) 336-2462
Emp Here 40   *Sales* 62,224,200
SIC 2068 Salted and roasted nuts and seeds
Kirit Shah
Kamal Shah
Sanjeev Shah

D-U-N-S 24-611-8046   (SL)
ENTREPRISES D'ALIMENTATION POUR ANIMAUX FAMILIER (A.P.A.F) INC, LES
APAF
(*Suby of* HELUCA)
4850 Ch Du Bois-Franc Bureau 200, Saint-Laurent, QC, H4S 1A7
(514) 745-1262
Emp Here 20   *Sales* 14,850,400
SIC 5191 Farm supplies
Valerie Cauvin

D-U-N-S 25-543-9408   (HQ)
ENTREPRISES MTY TIKI MING INC, LES
AU VIEUX DULUTH EXPRESS (MD)
(*Suby of* GROUPE D'ALIMENTATION MTY INC)
8210 Rte Transcanadienne, Saint-Laurent, QC, H4S 1M5
(514) 336-8885
Emp Here 120   *Sales* 1,262,350,287
SIC 6794 Patent owners and lessors
Stanley Ma
Marc Benzacar
Claude St-Pierre

D-U-N-S 20-227-8057   (HQ)
EQUIPEMENT MOORE LTEE
DICKIE MOORE RENTAL
(*Suby of* PLACEMENTS R.J.L. LTEE, LES)
4955 Ch Saint-Francois, Saint-Laurent, QC, H4S 1P3
(514) 333-1212
Emp Here 85   *Sales* 63,404,900
SIC 5084 Industrial machinery and equipment
John R. Moore

D-U-N-S 20-540-1912   (HQ)
EQUIPEMENTS RAPCO INC, LES
5510 Rue Vanden-Abeele, Saint-Laurent, QC, H4S 1P9
(514) 332-6562
Emp Here 20   *Sales* 11,179,350
SIC 5072 Hardware
Leslie Enberg
Jean Plourde
Steven Enberg

D-U-N-S 20-218-1491   (HQ)
ERICSSON CANADA INC
RECHERCHE ERICSSON CANADA
(*Suby of* TELEFON AB LM ERICSSON)
8275 Rte Transcanadienne, Saint-Laurent, QC, H4S 0B6
(514) 738-8300
Emp Here 200   *Sales* 1,073,456,950
SIC 5065 Electronic parts and equipment, nec
Graham Osborne
Roy Lizzi
Jaco Pretorius
Mike Sisto

D-U-N-S 20-218-2143   (SL)
EUGENE TEXTILES (2003) INC
TEXTILES CAMELOT
1391 Rue Saint-Amour, Saint-Laurent, QC, H4S 1T4
(514) 382-2400
Emp Here 24   *Sales* 13,535,942
SIC 5131 Piece goods and notions
Max Haupt
Steven Haupt

D-U-N-S 24-799-7976   (SL)
G.T.C.A. MET-ALL INC
1215 Montee De Liesse, Saint-Laurent, QC,

H4S 1J7
(514) 334-2801
Emp Here 53   *Sales* 10,180,505
SIC 3444 Sheet Metalwork
  Daniel Nimijean
  Arpad Danny Toth

D-U-N-S 20-253-4566   (HQ)
GHD CONSULTANTS LTEE
INSPEC-SOL
(*Suby of* GHD GROUP LIMITED)
4600 Boul De La Cote-Vertu Bureau 200,
Saint-Laurent, QC, H4S 1C7
(514) 333-5151
Emp Here 100   *Sales* 117,055,500
SIC 8621 Professional organizations
  Steve Lecuyer
  Stephen M. Quigley
  Eric Boulanger
  Elizabeth Dias
  Elias Massad

D-U-N-S 24-878-1502   (SL)
GI-OCEAN INTERNATIONAL LTEE
9899 Rte Transcanadienne, Saint-Laurent,
QC, H4S 1V1
(514) 339-9994
Emp Here 50   *Sales* 41,778,850
SIC 5146 Fish and seafoods
  Sok Chea Taing

D-U-N-S 20-220-2354   (HQ)
GLAZERS INC
7800 Boul Henri-Bourassa O, Saint-Laurent,
QC, H4S 1P4
(514) 335-1500
Emp Here 26   *Sales* 15,616,260
SIC 5099 Durable goods, nec
  Irwin Glazer
  Charles Kotler
  Amanda Jayne Kotler

D-U-N-S 25-148-7815   (HQ)
GLOBE UNION (CANADA) INC
(*Suby of* GLOBE UNION INDUSTRIAL
CORP.)
4610 Ch Du Bois-Franc, Saint-Laurent, QC,
H4S 1A7
(514) 907-8000
Sales 37,562,616
SIC 5074 Plumbing and heating equipment
and supplies (hydronics)
  Scott Ouyoung
  Charles Frankel
  Daniel Mercier

D-U-N-S 24-870-5873   (HQ)
GRASS VALLEY CANADA
*GRASS VALLEY, UNE MARQUE DE
BELDEN*
3499 Rue Douglas-B.-Floreani, Saint-Laurent,
QC, H4S 2C6
(514) 333-1772
Sales 127,311,750
SIC 3679 Electronic components, nec
  Marco Lopez

D-U-N-S 20-266-2946   (SL)
**GREEN CROSS BIOTHERAPEUTIQUES
INC**
GREEN CROSS (MD)
2911 Av Marie-Curie, Saint-Laurent, QC, H4S
0B7
(514) 375-5800
Emp Here 50   *Sales* 13,833,000
SIC 2834 Pharmaceutical preparations
  Min Taek Lee
  Jin Sung Huh
  John Christopher Shambleau
  Gee-Hun Kim

D-U-N-S 24-206-6855   (SL)
**GREENVISION TECHNOLOGIES CORPO-
RATION**
7809 Rte Transcanadienne, Saint-Laurent,
QC, H4S 1L3
(514) 745-0310
Emp Here 25   *Sales* 11,179,350

SIC 5065 Electronic parts and equipment, nec
  Fred Jalbout
  Bassam Dib-Jalbout

D-U-N-S 20-209-6129   (HQ)
GROUPE ALGO INC
A2Z
5555 Rue Cypihot, Saint-Laurent, QC, H4S
1R3
(514) 388-8888
Emp Here 120
SIC 2335 Women's, junior's, and misses'
dresses
  Marc Kakon
  Dan Elituv
  Raymond Gagnon
  Jeffrey Mandel
  Sol Chankowsky

D-U-N-S 24-980-1465   (HQ)
GROUPE D'ALIMENTATION MTY INC
8210 Rte Transcanadienne, Saint-Laurent,
QC, H4S 1M5
(514) 336-8885
Emp Here 120   *Sales* 194,910,579
SIC 6794 Patent owners and lessors
  Stanley Ma
  Claude St-Pierre
  Dickie Orr
  David Wong
  Stephen Stone A
  Murat Amutlu
  Gary Oconnor
  Eric Lefebvre

D-U-N-S 24-812-0503   (HQ)
**GROUPE INTERNATIONAL TRAVELWAY
INC**
JETSTREAM
4600 Ch Du Bois-Franc, Saint-Laurent, QC,
H4S 1A7
(514) 331-3130
Emp Here 48   *Sales* 64,807,490
SIC 5199 Nondurable goods, nec
  Bruce Shadeed
  Gerry Shadeed
  Maureen Shadeed

D-U-N-S 25-243-7850   (SL)
GROUPE PARIMA INC
4450 Rue Cousens, Saint-Laurent, QC, H4S
1X6
(514) 338-3780
Emp Here 75   *Sales* 20,749,500
SIC 2834 Pharmaceutical preparations
  Claude Mongrain
  Louis David Cantin

D-U-N-S 24-135-9897   (HQ)
GROUPE PHOENICIA INC
PRODUITS PHOENICIA
(*Suby of* METRO INC)
2605 Boul Pitfield, Saint-Laurent, QC, H4S
1T2
(514) 389-6363
Emp Here 10   *Sales* 66,846,160
SIC 5149 Groceries and related products, nec
  Christian Bourbonniere
  Francois Thibault
  Sherif El Gharbawy
  Simon Rivet

D-U-N-S 24-386-8382   (HQ)
GSM (CANADA) PTY LTD
BILLABONG
(*Suby of* OAKTREE CAPITAL GROUP, LLC)
5900 Rue Kieran, Saint-Laurent, QC, H4S 2B5
(514) 336-6382
Sales 26,027,100
SIC 5091 Sporting and recreation goods
  David Tanner
  Gregory William Healy
  Andrew Bruenjes

D-U-N-S 24-934-7766   (HQ)
HOLDECOM INC
ELIMETAL
1515 Boul Pitfield, Saint-Laurent, QC, H4S

1G3
(514) 956-7400
Sales 30,068,500
SIC 6712 Bank holding companies
  Eli Kedem
  Cipora Kedem

D-U-N-S 24-713-9694   (HQ)
HYPERTEC SYSTEMES INC
GROUPE HYPERTEC
9300 Rte Transcanadienne, Saint-Laurent,
QC, H4S 1K5
(514) 745-4540
Sales 27,750,125
SIC 3571 Electronic computers
  Robert Ahdoot
  Eliot Ahdoot
  Mark Girgis
  Sergei Nikolaev

D-U-N-S 20-370-6759   (SL)
ICU MEDICAL CANADA INC
ICU
2600 Boul Alfred-Nobel Bureau 100, Saint-
Laurent, QC, H4S 0A9
(514) 905-2600
Emp Here 65   *Sales* 29,066,310
SIC 5047 Medical and hospital equipment
  Vivek Jain
  Scott E. Lamb
  Ramon De Ridder
  Cornelis De Rooij
  Christian Voigtlander
  Anthony Milano

D-U-N-S 20-763-5939   (HQ)
IDENTIFICATION MULTI SOLUTIONS INC
IMS
9000 Boul Henri-Bourassa O, Saint-Laurent,
QC, H4S 1L5
(514) 336-3213
Emp Here 28   *Sales* 28,501,560
SIC 5084 Industrial machinery and equipment
  Jean Ethier
  Louise Baillargeon
  Pierre Levesque

D-U-N-S 24-532-5985   (SL)
IMPORTATIONS CACHERES INC.
6600 Boul Thimens, Saint-Laurent, QC, H4S
1S5

Emp Here 49   *Sales* 41,631,889
SIC 5141 Groceries, general line
  Mark E. Shamber

D-U-N-S 24-083-5033   (SL)
IMPORTATIONS VENETO LIMITEE
PRIMA MODA
2569 Rue De Miniac, Saint-Laurent, QC, H4S
1E5
(514) 735-1898
Emp Here 25   *Sales* 12,458,050
SIC 5137 Women's and children's clothing
  Sheldon Schlimper
  Philip Schlimper
  Rona Light

D-U-N-S 24-904-0643   (HQ)
IMPRESSION PARAGRAPH INC
GROUPE LAURIER
8150 Rte Transcanadienne Bureau 100, Saint-
Laurent, QC, H4S 1M5
(514) 735-7770
Emp Here 60   *Sales* 11,481,890
SIC 2752 Commercial printing, lithographic
  Martin Lepine
  Luc Boileau

D-U-N-S 24-256-4771   (SL)
INDUSTRIES GENO INC, LES
5750 Ch Saint-Francois, Saint-Laurent, QC,
H4S 1B7
(514) 331-4915
Emp Here 33   *Sales* 15,675,858
SIC 5085 Industrial supplies
  Jean-Yves Gregoire

D-U-N-S 20-210-4436   (SL)
INDUSTRIES HAGEN LTEE
3235 Rue Guenette, Saint-Laurent, QC, H4S
1N2
(514) 331-2818
Emp Here 50   *Sales* 13,833,000
SIC 2819 Industrial inorganic chemicals, nec

D-U-N-S 20-225-5840   (HQ)
**INDUSTRIES MAJESTIC (CANADA) LTEE,
LES**
INTERNATIONAL MAJESTIC
5905 Rue Kieran, Saint-Laurent, QC, H4S 0A3
(514) 727-2000
Sales 24,916,100
SIC 5136 Men's and boy's clothing
  Sam Landsman
  Esther Landsman

D-U-N-S 24-741-1481   (SL)
INDUSTRIES POLYKAR INC, LES
5637 Rue Kieran, Saint-Laurent, QC, H4S 0A3
(514) 335-0059
Emp Here 50   *Sales* 11,671,750
SIC 2673 Bags: plastic, laminated, and
coated
  Elyse Damdjee
  Aziz Karim

D-U-N-S 24-323-8029   (HQ)
INFLIGHT CANADA INC
4650 Boul De La Cote-Vertu Bureau 200,
Saint-Laurent, QC, H4S 1C7
(514) 331-9771
Sales 15,263,532
SIC 1799 Special trade contractors, nec
  George Smallhorn

D-U-N-S 25-653-2920   (HQ)
INSTITUT NEOMED
7171 Rue Frederick-Banting, Saint-Laurent,
QC, H4S 1Z9
(514) 367-1212
Sales 27,633,625
SIC 5122 Drugs, proprietaries, and sundries
  Max Fehlmann
  Francois Painchaud
  Pierre-Yves Desbien
  Donald Olds
  Michael Berendt
  Jacques Gagne
  Roderick Budd
  Michelle Savoie
  Patricia Gauthier
  Laurence Rulleau

D-U-N-S 25-999-8334   (BR)
IPEX INC
IPEX MANAGEMENT
(*Suby of* ALIAXIS)
6665 Ch Saint-Francois, Saint-Laurent, QC,
H4S 1B6
(514) 337-2624
Emp Here 120
SIC 3089 Plastics products, nec
  Claude Jean

D-U-N-S 24-355-7915   (HQ)
JOINTS ETANCHES R.B. INC, LES
8585 Boul Henri-Bourassa O, Saint-Laurent,
QC, H4S 1P7
(514) 334-2220
Emp Here 44   *Sales* 23,751,300
SIC 5085 Industrial supplies
  Dollard Leblanc
  Andre Huot
  Robert Weber
  Melissa Leblanc

D-U-N-S 24-419-6403   (BR)
**KONICA MINOLTA BUSINESS SOLUTIONS
(CANADA) LTD**
KONICA MINOLTA
(*Suby of* KONICA MINOLTA, INC.)
8555 Rte Transcanadienne, Saint-Laurent,
QC, H4S 1Z6
(514) 335-2157
Emp Here 80

SIC 5044 Office equipment
Mai Do

D-U-N-S 24-044-8816   (SL)
KUEHNE + NAGEL LOGISTICS INC
(Suby of KUHNE HOLDING AG)
2500 Av Marie-Curie, Saint-Laurent, QC, H4S 1N1
(514) 683-9630
Emp Here 100   Sales 66,689,200
SIC 4731 Freight transportation arrangement
Peter Messerli
Donald Edward

D-U-N-S 24-836-3772   (SL)
L.E.S. MECANIQUE INC
1200 Rue Saint-Amour, Saint-Laurent, QC, H4S 1J2
(514) 333-6968
Emp Here 50   Sales 10,131,450
SIC 7538 General automotive repair shops
Steven Larocque
Karl Klein
Edmond Larocque

D-U-N-S 20-209-2896   (HQ)
LABORATOIRES ABBOTT, LIMITEE
GROUPE CANALAC LABORATOIRES AB-BOTT
(Suby of ABBOTT LABORATORIES)
8625 Rte Transcanadienne, Saint-Laurent, QC, H4S 1Z6
(514) 832-7000
Emp Here 300   Sales 497,391,000
SIC 2834 Pharmaceutical preparations
Jorge Sacco
Elizabeth Onwudiwe
Brian B. Yoor
Matt Harris
Brigitte Pomerleau

D-U-N-S 20-317-5752   (BR)
LOCKHEED MARTIN CANADA INC
LOCKHEED MARTIN COMMERCIAL EN-GINE SOLUTIONS
(Suby of LOCKHEED MARTIN CORPORA-TION)
7171 Boul De La Cote-Vertu, Saint-Laurent, QC, H4S 1Z3
(514) 340-8400
Emp Here 150
SIC 4581 Airports, flying fields, and services
Raymond Piselli

D-U-N-S 24-525-0506   (SL)
MACDONALD MAINTENANCE INC
GROUPE MMI
6037 Ch Saint-Francois, Saint-Laurent, QC, H4S 1B6
(514) 637-6453
Emp Here 101   Sales 12,602,376
SIC 8741 Management services
Annie Laplante

D-U-N-S 20-719-0807   (HQ)
MEMOTEC INC
(Suby of COMTECH TELECOMMUNICA-TIONS CORP.)
7755 Boul Henri-Bourassa O, Saint-Laurent, QC, H4S 1P7
(514) 738-4781
Sales 15,993,040
SIC 4899 Communication services, nec
Yves Hupe
Michael D. Porcelain
Francois St-Pierre
Nancy Stallone
John Branscum

D-U-N-S 24-101-6880   (HQ)
MERCEDES TEXTILES LIMITED
5838 Rue Cypihot, Saint-Laurent, QC, H4S 1Y5
(514) 335-4337
Emp Here 70   Sales 23,050,200
SIC 3429 Hardware, nec
Robert Richardson
Victor Melo

Elizabeth Richardson

D-U-N-S 24-796-2157   (SL)
METRO NORAMCO INC
5855 Rue Kieran, Saint-Laurent, QC, H4S 0A3
(514) 595-9595
Emp Here 25   Sales 11,179,350
SIC 5063 Electrical apparatus and equipment
Michel Bejin

D-U-N-S 24-461-1513   (SL)
MICRO ELECTRONIQUES G.B. INC
6620 Rue Abrams, Saint-Laurent, QC, H4S 1Y1
(514) 333-7373
Emp Here 30   Sales 13,415,220
SIC 5045 Computers, peripherals, and software
Solange Dugas
Allan Pangborn

D-U-N-S 25-978-5467   (HQ)
NEXT SUCCESS INC
CHAMPIONCASES.COM
8086 Rte Transcanadienne, Saint-Laurent, QC, H4S 1M5
(514) 343-5544
Emp Here 1   Sales 11,179,350
SIC 5065 Electronic parts and equipment, nec
Jeffrey Thaw

D-U-N-S 20-356-4745   (SL)
NJM PACKAGING INC
NJM EMBALLAGE
(Suby of PRO MACH, INC.)
5600 Rue Kieran, Saint-Laurent, QC, H4S 2B5
(514) 337-6990
Emp Here 100   Sales 47,502,600
SIC 5084 Industrial machinery and equipment
Mark Anderson
Andrew W. Moeder
Michel Lapierre

D-U-N-S 20-073-0676   (SL)
OLD DUTCH FOODS LTD
ADAM'S
6525 Rue Abrams, Saint-Laurent, QC, H4S 1X9
(514) 745-4449
Emp Here 250   Sales 121,846,250
SIC 2096 Potato chips and similar snacks
Steven C. Aanenson
Eric E. Aanenson
Bonna Jean Bateman
Iris Treichel

D-U-N-S 24-560-0283   (SL)
OTSUKA CANADA PHARMACEUTICAL INC
(Suby of OTSUKA HOLDINGS CO.,LTD.)
2250 Boul Alfred-Nobel Bureau 301, Saint-Laurent, QC, H4S 2C9
(514) 332-3001
Emp Here 55   Sales 13,438,040
SIC 5912 Drug stores and proprietary stores
Allison Rosenthal

D-U-N-S 24-460-7156   (BR)
PANALPINA INC
(Suby of PANALPINA WELTTRANSPORT (HOLDING) AG)
2520 Av Marie-Curie, Saint-Laurent, QC, H4S 1N1
(514) 421-7444
Emp Here 120
SIC 4731 Freight transportation arrangement
Patrick Manning

D-U-N-S 25-541-0904   (BR)
PENSKE TRUCK LEASING CANADA INC
LOCATION DE CAMIONS PENSKE
(Suby of PENSKE TRUCK LEASING CO., L.P.)
2500 Boul Pitfield, Saint-Laurent, QC, H4S 1Z7
(514) 333-4080
Emp Here 15,000
SIC 7513 Truck rental and leasing, no drivers
Alessio D'alleva

D-U-N-S 24-678-9895   (HQ)
PLACEMENTS ARDEN INC, LES
ARDENE
2575 Boul Pitfield, Saint-Laurent, QC, H4S 1T2
(514) 383-4442
Emp Here 70   Sales 75,975,795
SIC 5621 Women's clothing stores
Arden Dervishian
Mark Dervishian
Jerry Dervishian
Dorine Dervishian

D-U-N-S 24-352-5131   (SL)
PLACEMENTS BARAKAT INC, LES
5637 Rue Kieran, Saint-Laurent, QC, H4S 0A3
(514) 335-0059
Emp Here 50   Sales 20,967,750
SIC 6712 Bank holding companies
Elyse Damdjee
Aziz Karim

D-U-N-S 24-889-9130   (SL)
PLACEMENTS E.G.B. INC., LES
9000 Boul Henri-Bourassa O, Saint-Laurent, QC, H4S 1L5
(514) 336-3213
Emp Here 60   Sales 15,693,180
SIC 6712 Bank holding companies
Gilles Baillargeon
Lise David

D-U-N-S 24-362-5576   (SL)
PLACEMENTS RRJ INC, LES
5800 Rue Kieran, Saint-Laurent, QC, H4S 2B5

Emp Here 200   Sales 117,831,800
SIC 5191 Farm supplies
Rene Modugno

D-U-N-S 24-433-8786   (SL)
PLAZA CHEVROLET HUMMER CADILLAC INC
10480 Boul Henri-Bourassa O, Saint-Laurent, QC, H4S 1N6
(514) 332-1673
Emp Here 125
SIC 5511 New and used car dealers
Pierre Cloutier
Alain Cloutier

D-U-N-S 24-402-4159   (SL)
PLOMBERIE RICHARD JUBINVILLE INC
PLOMBERIE JUBINVILLE
5600 Ch Du Bois-Franc, Saint-Laurent, QC, H4S 1A9
(514) 333-0856
Emp Here 60   Sales 11,046,700
SIC 1711 Plumbing, heating, air-conditioning
Sandra Jubinville
Marc Darsigny
Marc-Andre Sauriol

D-U-N-S 20-230-8383   (HQ)
PRESTON PHIPPS INC
6400 Rue Vanden-Abeele, Saint-Laurent, QC, H4S 1R9
(514) 333-5340
Emp Here 25   Sales 38,009,790
SIC 5074 Plumbing and heating equipment and supplies (hydronics)
Mark J. Paulin
Rino Forgione
Richard Cyr

D-U-N-S 20-114-4057   (BR)
PRETIUM CANADA COMPANY
PRETIUM PACKAGING
(Suby of PRETIUM CANADA COMPANY)
2800 Rue Halpern, Saint-Laurent, QC, H4S 1R2
(514) 336-8210
Emp Here 100
SIC 3089 Plastics products, nec
Martin Roy

D-U-N-S 25-243-0491   (SL)
PRODUCTIONS MIGHTY MAC CANADA

INC, LES
5555 Rue Cypihot, Saint-Laurent, QC, H4S 1R3
(514) 388-8888
Emp Here 20   Sales 10,006,500
SIC 5137 Women's and children's clothing
Dan Elituv
Bessy Argiropoulos

D-U-N-S 25-782-3179   (SL)
PRODUITS & BASES DE SOUPE MAJOR DU CANADA INC, LES
ALIMENTS ROSE HILL
7171 Boul Thimens, Saint-Laurent, QC, H4S 2A2
(514) 745-1163
Emp Here 40   Sales 33,423,080
SIC 5149 Groceries and related products, nec
Georges Sarbanis
Spiro Raptis

D-U-N-S 20-998-4129   (HQ)
PROTECH CHIMIE LTEE
(Suby of 2885425 CANADA INC)
7600 Boul Henri-Bourassa O, Saint-Laurent, QC, H4S 1W3
(514) 745-0200
Emp Here 180   Sales 122,277,375
SIC 2851 Paints and allied products
David Ades

D-U-N-S 24-367-6439   (BR)
PROTECTION INCENDIE VIKING INC
(Suby of SECURITE POLYGON INC)
3005 Boul Pitfield, Saint-Laurent, QC, H4S 1H4
(514) 332-5110
Emp Here 95
SIC 5063 Electrical apparatus and equipment
Robert Lapierre

D-U-N-S 20-250-4395   (SL)
QSG INC
(Suby of BARCODES LLC)
8102 Rte Transcanadienne, Saint-Laurent, QC, H4S 1M5
(514) 744-1000
Emp Here 70   Sales 11,481,890
SIC 2759 Commercial printing, nec
Gilles Gaudreault

D-U-N-S 24-907-5128   (HQ)
QUICKSTYLE INDUSTRIES INC
INFINIUM DEZINE
(Suby of ARLBERG HOLDINGS INC)
4505 Rue Cousens, Saint-Laurent, QC, H4S 1X5
(514) 956-9711
Emp Here 50   Sales 38,164,200
SIC 5023 Homefurnishings
Stephen Courey

D-U-N-S 20-541-8411   (HQ)
QUINCAILLERIE RICHELIEU LTEE
BOISERIES LUSSIER, DIV DE QUINCAIL-LERIE RICHELIEU
7900 Boul Henri-Bourassa O Bureau 200, Saint-Laurent, QC, H4S 1V4
(514) 336-4144
Emp Here 200   Sales 772,861,694
SIC 5072 Hardware
Antoine Auclair
Lord Richard
Guy Grenier
Genevieve Quevillon
Jeff Crews
Marjolaine Plante
Craig Ratchford
Yannick Godeau
Eric Daignault
Marion Kloibhofer

D-U-N-S 25-210-7974   (SL)
REMATEK INC
REMATEK-ENERGIE
8975 Boul Henri-Bourassa O, Saint-Laurent, QC, H4S 1P7

(514) 333-6414
Emp Here 56   *Sales* 12,432,056
SIC 3544 Special dies, tools, jigs, and fixtures
Marco Deblois

D-U-N-S 24-016-0072   (HQ)
RESEAUX ACCEDIAN INC, LES
SYSTEMES PERFORMANTS, LES
2351 Boul Alfred-Nobel Suite N-410, Saint-Laurent, QC, H4S 0B2
(514) 331-6181
Sales 25,349,000
SIC 8748 Business consulting, nec
Patrick Ostiguy
Tom Manley
Francois Marineau
Dough Smidl
David Dial
Carlo Fidanza
Peter Newcombe
Martin Lebeau
Shahir Guindi
Antoine Paquin

D-U-N-S 25-973-3491   (SL)
RF-MTL ELECTRONIQUE INC
1415 Rue Saint-Amour, Saint-Laurent, QC, H4S 1T4
(514) 332-9998
Emp Here 30   *Sales* 13,415,220
SIC 5065 Electronic parts and equipment, nec
Eugen Budileanu
Tatiana Vlat Budileanu

D-U-N-S 20-298-4647   (HQ)
RICHELIEU FINANCES LTEE
(*Suby of* QUINCAILLERIE RICHELIEU LTEE)
7900 Boul Henri-Bourassa O Bureau 200, Saint-Laurent, QC, H4S 1V4
(514) 336-4144
Emp Here 2   *Sales* 18,314,450
SIC 6719 Holding companies, nec
Richard Lord
Antoine Auclair
Yannick Godeau

D-U-N-S 20-059-6372   (BR)
ROLF C. HAGEN INC
2450 Av Marie-Curie, Saint-Laurent, QC, H4S 1N1

Emp Here 75
SIC 5199 Nondurable goods, nec
Christine Kuras

D-U-N-S 24-736-3356   (HQ)
SC 360 INC
2425 Boul Pitfield, Saint-Laurent, QC, H4S 1W8
(514) 735-8557
Sales 11,714,400
SIC 8748 Business consulting, nec
Francois Gaudreau

D-U-N-S 20-266-6744   (HQ)
SERVICES DE FRET PATRIOT INC
(*Suby of* TFI INTERNATIONAL INC)
6800 Ch Saint-Francois, Saint-Laurent, QC, H4S 1B7
(514) 631-2900
Emp Here 29   *Sales* 18,718,812
SIC 4731 Freight transportation arrangement
Chantal Martel
Josiane-Melanie Langlois

D-U-N-S 24-865-6100   (HQ)
SERVICES HEALTHMARK LTEE, LES
(*Suby of* RICHARDS PACKAGING INCOME FUND)
8827 Boul Henri-Bourassa O, Saint-Laurent, QC, H4S 1P7
(514) 336-0012
Sales 34,265,695
SIC 5122 Drugs, proprietaries, and sundries
Gerry Glynn
William D. Fletcher
Enzio Di Gennaro

D-U-N-S 20-363-8390   (HQ)
SINOBEC TRADING INC
(*Suby of* SINOBEC GROUP INC)
4455 Rue Cousens, Saint-Laurent, QC, H4S 1X5
(514) 339-9333
Sales 11,620,150
SIC 5719 Miscellaneous homefurnishings
Zhong Li

D-U-N-S 20-234-4065   (HQ)
SMITH & NEPHEW INC
(*Suby of* SMITH & NEPHEW PLC)
2250 Boul Alfred-Nobel Bureau 300, Saint-Laurent, QC, H4S 2C9
(514) 956-1010
Emp Here 60   *Sales* 71,737,168
SIC 5047 Medical and hospital equipment
Jon Thomas Olsen
Ingeborg Oie

D-U-N-S 20-412-2998   (HQ)
SOCIETE   BRISTOL-MYERS   SQUIBB CANADA, LA
BMS CANADA
(*Suby of* BRISTOL-MYERS SQUIBB COMPANY)
2344 Boul Alfred-Nobel Bureau 300, Saint-Laurent, QC, H4S 0A4
(514) 333-3200
Sales 82,898,500
SIC 2834 Pharmaceutical preparations
Jeffrey Galik
Michael Rea
Alan Reba
Katherine R. Kelly
Joanie Schwartz

D-U-N-S 20-297-7356   (SL)
SOCIETE D'ASSURANCES AUTOMOBILES DE QUEBEC
CONTROLE ROUTIER QUEBEC
7575 Boul Henri-Bourassa O Bureau 66, Saint-Laurent, QC, H4S 1Z2
(514) 873-7620
Emp Here 35   *Sales* 15,522,150
SIC 7389 Business services, nec
Bernard Denis

D-U-N-S 20-725-0390   (SL)
SOCIETE D'OUTILLAGE M.R. LTEE
S.O.M.R.
8500 Boul Henri-Bourassa O, Saint-Laurent, QC, H4S 1P4
(514) 336-5182
Emp Here 72   *Sales* 12,918,888
SIC 3599 Industrial machinery, nec
Bruno Floriant
Stephane Floriant

D-U-N-S 20-182-4906   (HQ)
SOLID XPERTS INC
ENTREPRISES SOLID XPERTS
2650 Av Marie-Curie, Saint-Laurent, QC, H4S 2C3
(514) 343-9111
Emp Here 75   *Sales* 13,347,760
SIC 7372 Prepackaged software
Jean-Francois Niaison
Susie Go
Alex P. Habrich

D-U-N-S 25-104-8385   (SL)
SOLINE TRADING LTD
9899 Rte Transcanadienne, Saint-Laurent, QC, H4S 1V1
(514) 339-1818
Emp Here 50   *Sales* 41,778,850
SIC 5146 Fish and seafoods
David Ho

D-U-N-S 20-113-5980   (SL)
SOLUTIONS MECANICA INC, LES
COURANT MECANICA
10000 Boul Henri-Bourassa O, Saint-Laurent, QC, H4S 1R5
(514) 340-1818
Emp Here 70   *Sales* 10,092,740

SIC 7371 Custom computer programming services
Alex P Habrich
Emmanuel Maes
Eric Bille

D-U-N-S 20-370-0088   (SL)
SPECTOR & CO. INC
SPECTOR & COMPAGNIE
(*Suby of* BLUE POINT CAPITAL PARTNERS LLC)
5700 Rue Kieran, Saint-Laurent, QC, H4S 2B5
(514) 337-7721
Emp Here 26   *Sales* 13,095,108
SIC 5112 Stationery and office supplies
Robert Spector
Charles Mark Chaikin
Jeffrey Robich
Graham Lloyd

D-U-N-S 24-896-3894   (SL)
SUBLIME DESSERT INC
7777 Boul Thimens, Saint-Laurent, QC, H4S 2A2
(514) 333-0338
Emp Here 55   *Sales* 19,012,950
SIC 2024 Ice cream and frozen deserts
George Michael

D-U-N-S 24-902-7509   (HQ)
SYSTEMES FONEX DATA INC, LES
5400 Ch Saint-Francois, Saint-Laurent, QC, H4S 1P6
(514) 333-6639
Emp Here 50   *Sales* 26,830,440
SIC 5065 Electronic parts and equipment, nec
Pasquale Dipierro

D-U-N-S 24-934-5455   (HQ)
SYSTEMES TESTFORCE INC
TESTFORCE
9450 Rte Transcanadienne, Saint-Laurent, QC, H4S 1R7
(514) 856-0970
Emp Here 1   *Sales* 17,886,960
SIC 5065 Electronic parts and equipment, nec
Sami Stephan
Tony Tirelli

D-U-N-S 20-106-1335   (SL)
TECHNOPARC MONTREAL
CENTRE D'INITIATIVE TECHNOLOGIQUE DE MONTREAL (CITEC)
7150 Rue Albert-Einstein Bureau 200, Saint-Laurent, QC, H4S 2C1
(514) 956-2525
Emp Here 25   *Sales* 10,472,225
SIC 6531 Real estate agents and managers
Jean-Luc Landry
Andre Labrie
Mario Monette
Michel Clair
Alan Desousa
Paul Saint-Jacques
Peter R O'brien
Manon L'archeveque
Michel Desbiens
Marcel Valois

D-U-N-S 20-519-4306   (BR)
TELE-MOBILE COMPANY
TELUS MOBILITY
(*Suby of* TELE-MOBILE COMPANY)
8851 Rte Transcanadienne Bureau 1, Saint-Laurent, QC, H4S 1Z6
(514) 832-2000
Emp Here 700
SIC 4899 Communication services, nec
Julie Latulippe

D-U-N-S 25-690-6124   (HQ)
TELESTA THERAPEUTICS INC
(*Suby of* PROMETIC SCIENCES DE LA VIE INC)
2600 Boul Alfred-Nobel Bureau 301, Saint-Laurent, QC, H4S 0A9
(514) 697-6636
Emp Here 110   *Sales* 10,301,946

SIC 2834 Pharmaceutical preparations
Pierre Laurin
Patrick Sartore

D-U-N-S 24-367-1588   (HQ)
TFI INTERNATIONAL INC
TRANSFORCE
8801 Rte Transcanadienne Bureau 500, Saint-Laurent, QC, H4S 1Z6
(514) 331-4113
Emp Here 1,800   *Sales* 3,883,914,231
SIC 4213 Trucking, except local
Alain Bedard
Gregory Rumble
Rick Hashie
Brian Kohut
Leslie Abi-Karam
Andre Berard
Lucien Bouchard
Diane Giard
Richard Guay
Debra Kelly-Ennis

D-U-N-S 24-892-1772   (SL)
TFI TRANSPORT 12 L.P. / TRANSPORT TFI 12, S.E.C.
8801 Rte Transcanadienne Unit? 500, Saint-Laurent, QC, H4S 1Z6 .
(514) 331-4000
Emp Here 120   *Sales* 24,684,720
SIC 4213 Trucking, except local
Alain Bedard

D-U-N-S 24-344-2691   (HQ)
TFORCE HOLDINGS INC
(*Suby of* TFI INTERNATIONAL INC)
8801 Rte Transcanadienne Bureau 500, Saint-Laurent, QC, H4S 1Z6
(514) 331-4000
Emp Here 3   *Sales* 5,080,940,609
SIC 6719 Holding companies, nec
Chantal Martel
Josiane-Melanie Langlois

D-U-N-S 20-229-5945   (BR)
THYSSENKRUPP MATERIALS CA, LTD
VIMETAL, DIV OF
(*Suby of* THYSSENKRUPP AG)
4700 Ch Du Bois-Franc, Saint-Laurent, QC, H4S 1A7
(514) 337-0161
Emp Here 83
SIC 5093 Scrap and waste materials
Mike Laroche

D-U-N-S 24-680-3969   (HQ)
TOOTSI IMPEX INC
MELANGE DES BOIS
8800 Boul Henri-Bourassa O, Saint-Laurent, QC, H4S 1P4
(514) 381-9790
Sales 41,778,850
SIC 5145 Confectionery
Ali Shayesteh
Kayvan Shayesteh
Farhad Shayesteh

D-U-N-S 24-959-3211   (HQ)
TRANS-PLUS V.M. INC
2400 Rue Halpern, Saint-Laurent, QC, H4S 1S8
(514) 332-5020
Sales 12,999,175
SIC 4731 Freight transportation arrangement
Vincenzo Mazzei
Michel Paquette

D-U-N-S 25-243-6563   (SL)
TRANSPORT   ECOLE-BEC   MONTREAL (EBM) INC
8835 Boul Henri-Bourassa O, Saint-Laurent, QC, H4S 1P7
(514) 595-5609
Emp Here 100   *Sales* 14,819,200
SIC 4212 Local trucking, without storage
Michel Paquette

D-U-N-S 20-224-2590   (HQ)

TRANSPORT LEMIEUX, HERVE (1975) INC
TRANSPORT TRANS-ACTION
6500 Ch Saint-Francois, Saint-Laurent, QC,
H4S 1B7
(514) 337-2203
Sales 64,533,350
SIC 4212 Local trucking, without storage
Guy Lemieux
Jean-Francois Page

D-U-N-S 25-362-7376   (HQ)
TRANSPORT TFI 1, S.E.C.
TRANSPORT J.C. GERMAIN
8801 Rte Transcanadienne Bureau 500, Saint-
Laurent, QC, H4S 1Z6
(514) 331-4000
Emp Here 200   *Sales* 103,205,250
SIC 5122 Drugs, proprietaries, and sundries
Nelly Kanau

D-U-N-S 24-422-8685   (SL)
TRANSPORT TFI 14 S.E.C.
MANUTEX
8801 Rte Transcanadienne Bureau 500, Saint-
Laurent, QC, H4S 1Z6
(514) 331-4000
Emp Here 111   *Sales* 22,833,366
SIC 4213 Trucking, except local
Philippe Papineau

D-U-N-S 24-374-2579   (HQ)
TRANSPORT TFI 15 S.E.C.
TRANSPORT GREGOIRE
8801 Rte Transcanadienne Bureau 500, Saint-
Laurent, QC, H4S 1Z6
(514) 331-4000
Emp Here 5   *Sales* 41,141,200
SIC 4213 Trucking, except local
Josiane-Melanie Langlois

D-U-N-S 20-112-2111   (HQ)
TRANSPORT TFI 2, S.E.C.
IMMEUBLES TRANSFORCE
8801 Rte Transcanadienne Bureau 500, Saint-
Laurent, QC, H4S 1Z6
(514) 331-4000
Emp Here 20   *Sales* 184,381,000
SIC 4213 Trucking, except local
Alain Bedard

D-U-N-S 24-375-5266   (HQ)
TRANSPORT TFI 21, S.E.C.
MCARTHUR EXPRESS
8801 Rte Transcanadienne Bureau 500, Saint-
Laurent, QC, H4S 1Z6
(514) 856-7500
Emp Here 50   `Sales* 2,013,788,000
SIC 5021 Furniture
Alain Bedard

D-U-N-S 24-761-6571   (HQ)
TRANSPORT TFI 22 S.E.C.
LOOMIS EXPRESS
8801 Rte Transcanadienne Bureau 500, Saint-
Laurent, QC, H4S 1Z6
(514) 331-4000
Emp Here 10   *Sales* 41,141,200
SIC 4212 Local trucking, without storage
Josiane-Melanie Langlois

D-U-N-S 20-112-3432   (HQ)
TRANSPORT TFI 5, S.E.C.
KINGSWAY TRANSPORT OF AMERICA
6700 Ch Saint-Francois, Saint-Laurent, QC,
H4S 1B7
(514) 856-5559
Emp Here 200   *Sales* 368,762,000
SIC 4213 Trucking, except local
Alain Bedard

D-U-N-S 20-564-5018   (HQ)
TRANSPORT TFI 7 S.E.C
CANADIAN FREIGHTWAYS
8801 Rte Transcanadienne Bureau 500, Saint-
Laurent, QC, H4S 1Z6
(514) 331-4000
Emp Here 100   *Sales* 106,203,456
SIC 4213 Trucking, except local

Alain Bedard

D-U-N-S 24-612-2790   (SL)
ULTRASPEC FINISHING INC
(*Suby of* MONTREAL AEROSPACE GROUP
INC)
2600 Rue De Miniac, Saint-Laurent, QC, H4S
1L7
(514) 337-1782
Emp Here 93   *Sales* 4,228,014
SIC 3479 Metal coating and allied services
Nicolas Nassr

D-U-N-S 20-223-7491   (SL)
**VANNES ET RACCORDS LAURENTIEN
LTEE**
GROUPE SWAGELOK QUEBEC
2425 Rue Halpern, Saint-Laurent, QC, H4S
1S3
(418) 872-3622
Emp Here 26   *Sales* 12,350,676
SIC 5085 Industrial supplies
Andre Ouellet

D-U-N-S 20-253-2651   (BR)
**VEOLIA EAU TECHNOLOGIES CANADA
INC**
(*Suby of* VEOLIA ENVIRONNEMENT)
3901 Rue Sartelon, Saint-Laurent, QC, H4S
2A6
(514) 334-7230
Emp Here 300
SIC 1629 Heavy construction, nec
Benoit Gagne

D-U-N-S 20-227-0518   (HQ)
**VEOLIA EAU TECHNOLOGIES CANADA
INC**
GROUPE JMI
(*Suby of* VEOLIA ENVIRONNEMENT)
4105 Rue Sartelon, Saint-Laurent, QC, H4S
2B3
(514) 334-7230
Emp Here 168   *Sales* 59,060,700
SIC 1629 Heavy construction, nec
Benoit Gagne
Olivier Marcadet
Gilles Filion
Klaus Andresen
John Santelli

D-U-N-S 24-354-1406   (HQ)
VETEMENTS EFG INC
DISTRIBUTION EURO STYLE
3335 Boul Pitfield, Saint-Laurent, QC, H4S
1H3
(514) 333-9119
Emp Here 11   *Sales* 12,557,720
SIC 5621 Women's clothing stores
Daniel Gaudreau

D-U-N-S 24-812-7912   (SL)
VIMETAL INC
4700 Ch Du Bois-Franc, Saint-Laurent, QC,
H4S 1A7
(514) 336-6824
Emp Here 40   *Sales* 17,886,960
SIC 5051 Metals service centers and offices
Haim Kotler

D-U-N-S 20-504-0595   (SL)
VOLAILLES ET VIANDE AMGA LTEE
9555 Rte Transcanadienne, Saint-Laurent,
QC, H4S 1V3
(514) 273-8848
Emp Here 50   *Sales* 41,778,850
SIC 5144 Poultry and poultry products
Angelo Mardas
Peter Mardas
Clara Mardas
Despina Mardas

D-U-N-S 24-382-3585   (BR)
WABTEC CANADA INC
VAPOR RAIL DIV OF
(*Suby of* WESTINGHOUSE AIR BRAKE
TECHNOLOGIES CORPORATION)
10655 Boul Henri-Bourassa O, Saint-Laurent,

QC, H4S 1A1
(514) 335-4200
Emp Here 275
SIC 3743 Railroad equipment
James Watson

D-U-N-S 25-529-6683   (SL)
WEST SAFETY SERVICES CANADA INC
(*Suby of* MOUNT OLYMPUS HOLDINGS,
INC.)
7150 Rue Alexander-Fleming, Saint-Laurent,
QC, H4S 2C8
(514) 340-3300
Emp Here 230   *Sales* 76,945,120
SIC 4899 Communication services, nec
Thomas B Barker
Ronald Beaumont
David C. Mussman
Jan Dutton Madsen
Nancee R Berger
Mark A Schimdt

Saint-Laurent, QC H4T

D-U-N-S 20-370-3397   (SL)
10033618 CANADA INC
DESSIN SHELLY
(*Suby of* 3361781 CANADA INC)
4930 Rue Courval, Saint-Laurent, QC, H4T
1L1
(514) 343-0220
Emp Here 32   *Sales* 16,283,392
SIC 5021 Furniture
Samuel S Drazin
Ami Drazin

D-U-N-S 24-325-0883   (SL)
109652 CANADA LTD/LTEE
RUBY INTERNATIONAL
8750 Ch De La Cote-De-Liesse Bureau 100,
Saint-Laurent, QC, H4T 1H2
(514) 344-9660
Emp Here 40   *Sales* 19,932,880
SIC 5136 Men's and boy's clothing
Robert Choueke

D-U-N-S 24-377-6007   (SL)
1801794 ONTARIO INC
DISTRIBUTION FLORALE SIERRA
(*Suby of* FLORAL GROUP LTD, THE)
935 Rue Reverchon, Saint-Laurent, QC, H4T
4L2
(514) 733-3515
Emp Here 100   *Sales* 24,432,800
SIC 5992 Florists
Peter John Vermeer
Ian Jeffrey Vermeer
Charles Vermeer
Arthur Anthony Vermeer
David John Vermeer

D-U-N-S 20-210-8163   (HQ)
191609 CANADA INC
4125 Rue Griffith, Saint-Laurent, QC, H4T
1A9
(514) 731-9466
Emp Here 100   *Sales* 29,215,200
SIC 2673 Bags: plastic, laminated, and
coated
Leonard C. Carpenter
Bonita Joan Carpenter

D-U-N-S 25-245-9722   (HQ)
2904357 CANADA INC
ACF/TRANSPORTAIDE
615 Rue Mccaffrey, Saint-Laurent, QC, H4T
1N3
(514) 340-2844
Sales 11,204,100
SIC 7361 Employment agencies
Jody Foster

D-U-N-S 24-944-1759   (SL)
2960-2778 QUEBEC INC
SIGNATURE TEXTILE PAR VAL-ABEL

7300 Rte Transcanadienne, Saint-Laurent,
QC, H4T 1A3
(514) 448-9455
Emp Here 45   *Sales* 22,424,490
SIC 5131 Piece goods and notions
Jonathan Abelson

D-U-N-S 24-322-2721   (HQ)
3294269 CANADA INC
CELLULAR SOLUTION
7020 Ch De La C?Te-De-Liesse, Saint-
Laurent, QC, H4T 1E7
(514) 344-8883
Emp Here 7   *Sales* 24,432,800
SIC 5999 Miscellaneous retail stores, nec
Nisso Ifrah
Gary Katsof

D-U-N-S 24-319-1488   (SL)
3522997 CANADA INC
180 Montee De Liesse, Saint-Laurent, QC,
H4T 1N7
(450) 455-3963
Emp Here 4,000   *Sales* 1,486,625,672
SIC 6712 Bank holding companies
Mario Levasseur

D-U-N-S 20-381-7700   (SL)
4520556 CANADA INC
180 Montee De Liesse, Saint-Laurent, QC,
H4T 1N7
(514) 904-1216
Emp Here 650   *Sales* 20,779,200
SIC 7349 Building maintenance services, nec
Helena Correia

D-U-N-S 24-384-6776   (HQ)
7098961 CANADA INC
BEYOND THE RACK
4600 Rue Hickmore, Saint-Laurent, QC, H4T
1K2
(514) 733-4666
Sales 50,026,755
SIC 5621 Women's clothing stores
Nonu Ifergan

D-U-N-S 20-297-9233   (SL)
7190891 CANADA INC
CONSTRUCTION MARATHON
4200 Rue Hickmore, Saint-Laurent, QC, H4T
1K2
(514) 488-2525
Emp Here 50   *Sales* 12,044,200
SIC 1623 Water, sewer, and utility lines
Lee Lalli

D-U-N-S 25-688-8710   (SL)
9052-9025 QUEBEC INC
DISTRIBUTION VTL
(*Suby of* GESTION BURCASS LTEE)
700 Montee De Liesse, Saint-Laurent, QC,
H4T 1N8
(514) 631-6669
Emp Here 200   *Sales* 41,141,200
SIC 4213 Trucking, except local
Larry Burn
Claude Guillemette

D-U-N-S 25-886-8819   (SL)
9052-9975 QUEBEC INC
PLAZA VOLARE
6600 Ch De La Cote-De-Liesse, Saint-
Laurent, QC, H4T 1E3
(514) 735-5150
Emp Here 80   *Sales* 7,170,320
SIC 7299 Miscellaneous personal service
Vincent Morena

D-U-N-S 20-288-4664   (SL)
9248-5523 QUEBEC INC
DISTRIBUTION DIRECTE
4575 Rue Hickmore, Saint-Laurent, QC, H4T
1S5
(514) 934-4545
Emp Here 50   *Sales* 22,460,950
SIC 7389 Business services, nec
Felice Terriaca

D-U-N-S 20-330-2914   (SL)

▲ Public Company   ■ Public Company Family Member   **HQ** Headquarters   **BR** Branch   **SL** Single Location

9248-9202 QUEBEC INC
VINYL VVID
235 Rue Ness, Saint-Laurent, QC, H4T 1S1
(514) 508-2529
Emp Here 35   *Sales* 22,976,240
SIC 5963 Direct selling establishments
Abraham Zrihan
Shimon Zrihan

D-U-N-S 25-392-2652   (HQ)
9297-6232 QUEBEC INC
361 Rue Locke, Saint-Laurent, QC, H4T 1X7
(514) 389-5757
Sales 64,237,950
SIC 5947 Gift, novelty, and souvenir shop
Albert Levy
Jimmy Levy

D-U-N-S 24-529-7585   (HQ)
A.J.M. PROMOTIONS SPORTIVES INTER-NATIONALES LTEE
350 Rue Mccaffrey, Saint-Laurent, QC, H4T 1N1
(514) 344-6767
Sales 80,403,168
SIC 5136 Men's and boy's clothing
Alastair Macrae
Lianne Macrae
Baik Sung Soo
B.S Baik
Evan Macrae

D-U-N-S 24-354-5324   (HQ)
ALIMENTS KOYO INC
4605 Rue Hickmore, Saint-Laurent, QC, H4T 1S5
(514) 744-1299
Emp Here 30   *Sales* 25,067,310
SIC 5149 Groceries and related products, nec
Toshifumi Kagemori
Hitomi Kagemori
Teruha Kagemori

D-U-N-S 20-794-2392   (HQ)
ALIMENTS UNI INC, LES
6100 Ch De La Cote-De-Liesse Bureau 200, Saint-Laurent, QC, H4T 1E3
(514) 731-3401
Emp Here 11   *Sales* 10,026,924
SIC 5147 Meats and meat products
Steven Mintz
Roberto Pietrovito

D-U-N-S 24-082-9200   (HQ)
ARAMARK QUEBEC INC
(Suby of ARAMARK)
4900 Rue Fisher, Saint-Laurent, QC, H4T 1J6
(514) 341-7770
Emp Here 75   *Sales* 116,597,500
SIC 5812 Eating places
Andy Siklos
Nicolas Seguier
Doug Weatherbee

D-U-N-S 20-290-9289   (HQ)
AVENSYS SOLUTIONS INC
178 Rue Merizzi, Saint-Laurent, QC, H4T 1S4
(514) 738-6766
Sales 12,350,676
SIC 5084 Industrial machinery and equipment
Martin D'amours
Pierre Michaud

D-U-N-S 24-922-5954   (HQ)
BAYLIS MEDICALE CIE INC
(Suby of GESTION BMC-DORIAN INC)
5959 Rte Transcanadienne, Saint-Laurent, QC, H4T 1A1
(514) 488-9801
Emp Here 40   *Sales* 60,254,560
SIC 5047 Medical and hospital equipment
Frank Baylis
Shan Krishna
Vafa Jamali
Brendan R. Cunneen
Karna Gupta

D-U-N-S 24-944-0843   (BR)

BOMBARDIER INC
BOMBARDIER AERONAUTIQUE
(Suby of BOMBARDIER INC)
8575 Ch De La Cote-De-Liesse, Saint-Laurent, QC, H4T 1G5
(514) 344-6620
Emp Here 230
SIC 8249 Vocational schools, nec
Hank Blasiak

D-U-N-S 24-366-0680   (BR)
BUREAU VERITAS CANADA (2019) INC
MAXXAM ANALYTICS INTERNATIONAL CORPORATION
(Suby of BUREAU VERITAS)
889 Montee De Liesse, Saint-Laurent, QC, H4T 1P5
(514) 448-9001
Emp Here 180
SIC 8748 Business consulting, nec

D-U-N-S 20-213-1454   (HQ)
CAE INC
8585 Ch De La Cote-De-Liesse, Saint-Laurent, QC, H4T 1G6
(514) 341-6780
Emp Here 250   *Sales* 2,252,722,450
SIC 3699 Electrical equipment and supplies, nec
Marc Parent
Pascal Grenier
Helene V. Gagnon
Dan Sharkey
Sonya Branco
Andrew Arnovitz
Mark Hounsell
John Manley
Michael E. Roach
Margaret S. Billson

D-U-N-S 24-828-2568   (HQ)
CAE INTERNATIONAL HOLDINGS LIMITED
GESTION CAE INTERNATIONAL
(Suby of CAE INC)
8585 Ch De La Cote-De-Liesse, Saint-Laurent, QC, H4T 1G6
(514) 341-6780
Emp Here 1   *Sales* 198,836,896
SIC 6712 Bank holding companies
Sonya Branco
Mark Hounsell
Constantino Malatesta

D-U-N-S 24-390-6554   (HQ)
CAE SANTE CANADA INC
(Suby of CAE INC)
8585 Ch De La Cote-De-Liesse, Saint-Laurent, QC, H4T 1G6
(514) 341-6780
Sales 10,233,650
SIC 3699 Electrical equipment and supplies, nec
Robert Amyot
Jennifer Jula
Sonya Branco
Mark Hounsell

D-U-N-S 25-201-6662   (HQ)
CALEGO INTERNATIONAL INC
6265 Ch De La Cote-De-Liesse Bureau 200, Saint-Laurent, QC, H4T 1C3
(514) 334-2117
Sales 13,013,550
SIC 5099 Durable goods, nec
Stephen Rapps
Irwin Ludmer

D-U-N-S 20-796-8798   (BR)
CANADA POST CORPORATION
DEPARTEMENT DES COMMUNICATIONS
(Suby of GOVERNMENT OF CANADA)
555 Rue Mcarthur Bureau 1506, Saint-Laurent, QC, H4T 1T4
(514) 345-4571
Emp Here 3,500
SIC 4311 U.s. postal service
Line Brien

D-U-N-S 20-010-3039   (HQ)
CAPESPAN NORTH AMERICA INC
CAPESPAN AMERIQUE DU NORD
(Suby of INVESTISSEMENTS CAPESPAN CANADA INC, LES)
6700 Ch De La Cote-De-Liesse Bureau 301, Saint-Laurent, QC, H4T 2B5
(514) 739-9181
Sales 20,889,425
SIC 5148 Fresh fruits and vegetables
Mark Greenberg
Paul Marier
Marc Solomon
Howard Freeman

D-U-N-S 24-339-0478   (SL)
CAPESPAN NORTH AMERICA INC
(Suby of INVESTISSEMENTS CAPESPAN CANADA INC, LES)
6700 Ch De La Cote-De-Liesse Bureau 301, Saint-Laurent, QC, H4T 2B5
(514) 739-9181
Emp Here 25   *Sales* 32,742,500
SIC 5148 Fresh fruits and vegetables
Mark Greenberg
Paul Marier
Howard Freeman

D-U-N-S 20-738-6202   (HQ)
CENTURA QUEBEC LTEE
(Suby of CENTURA LIMITED)
5885 Ch De La Cote-De-Liesse, Saint-Laurent, QC, H4T 1C3
(514) 336-4311
Emp Here 1   *Sales* 74,051,640
SIC 5032 Brick, stone, and related material
Brian Cowie
Adam Poyntz
Claude Digneault
Lucie Desjardins

D-U-N-S 24-529-5456   (SL)
CENTURY INTERNATIONAL ARMS LTD
INTERNATIONAL FIREARMS
353 Rue Isabey, Saint-Laurent, QC, H4T 1Y2
(514) 731-8883
Emp Here 55   *Sales* 28,629,810
SIC 5091 Sporting and recreation goods
Michael Sucher

D-U-N-S 25-528-0265   (HQ)
CIE D'HABILLEMENT SE CE LTEE, LA
SE CE DISTRIBUTION
(Suby of PLACEMENTS ZZACC INC, LES)
6445 Ch De La Cote-De-Liesse, Saint-Laurent, QC, H4T 1S9
(514) 341-4440
Emp Here 40   *Sales* 113,066,955
SIC 5137 Women's and children's clothing
Catherine Claman

D-U-N-S 25-392-7529   (SL)
COHENDAV INC
153 Rue Graveline, Saint-Laurent, QC, H4T 1R4
(514) 342-6700
Emp Here 42   *Sales* 17,612,910
SIC 6712 Bank holding companies
Peter Cohen

D-U-N-S 24-835-3328   (SL)
COMMERCE INTERNATIONAL MANHAT-TAN INC
MODES I AM JE SUIS
6150 Rte Transcanadienne, Saint-Laurent, QC, H4T 1X5
(514) 388-5588
Emp Here 45   *Sales* 22,424,490
SIC 5136 Men's and boy's clothing
Ted Rozenwald
Maria Alter

D-U-N-S 24-994-0396   (SL)
COMMERCE KOLTECH LTEE
943 Rue Reverchon, Saint-Laurent, QC, H4T 4L2
(514) 739-4111
Emp Here 22   *Sales* 16,067,590

SIC 5169 Chemicals and allied products, nec
Alexey Ziskin

D-U-N-S 24-678-8595   (HQ)
COMPAGNIE DE VETEMENTS C-IN2 INC
8750 Ch De La Cote-De-Liesse Bureau 100, Saint-Laurent, QC, H4T 1H2
(514) 344-9660
Sales 24,417,778
SIC 5136 Men's and boy's clothing
Gregory Sovell

D-U-N-S 24-342-7429   (BR)
COMPAGNIE DES CHEMINS DE FER NA-TIONAUX DU CANADA
CN INTERMODAL
(Suby of COMPAGNIE DES CHEMINS DE FER NATIONAUX DU CANADA)
4500 Rue Hickmore, Saint-Laurent, QC, H4T 1K2
(514) 734-2288
Emp Here 130
SIC 4013 Switching and terminal services
Michel Vachon

D-U-N-S 20-820-9135   (SL)
CONSTRUCTION CYBCO INC
7089 Rte Transcanadienne, Saint-Laurent, QC, H4T 1A2
(514) 284-2228
Emp Here 22   *Sales* 10,356,082
SIC 1542 Nonresidential construction, nec
Patrick Bellemare
Serge Chiasson
Benoit Herard

D-U-N-S 20-289-6049   (SL)
CONTINENTAL INVESTISSEMENTS CAPI-TAL INC
CONTINENTAL CAPITAL
7575 Rte Transcanadienne Ste 100, Saint-Laurent, QC, H4T 1V6
(514) 875-6661
Emp Here 220   *Sales* 147,159,760
SIC 7389 Business services, nec
Andrew Chelminski
Muriel Kunzli

D-U-N-S 24-890-5887   (HQ)
CORPORATION PRESSE COMMERCE D'ARTAGNAN
3339 Rue Griffith Bureau 4, Saint-Laurent, QC, H4T 1W5
(514) 333-5041
Emp Here 35   *Sales* 23,859,810
SIC 5994 News dealers and newsstands
Richard Repper
Kathy Blais
Eva Bonneau-Goyer
Jeffrey Mcnulty
Danielle Aquin
Eric Bilodeau

D-U-N-S 24-977-3292   (HQ)
CORPORATION SERVICES MONERIS
(Suby of MONERIS SOLUTIONS CORPORA-TION)
7350 Rte Transcanadienne, Saint-Laurent, QC, H4T 1A3
(514) 733-0443
Sales 66,890,800
SIC 7389 Business services, nec
Wayne Griffiths
Fern Glowinsky
Jeff Guthrie
James Baumgartner

D-U-N-S 24-429-6729   (SL)
COSBEC INC
699 Rue Gougeon, Saint-Laurent, QC, H4T 2B4
(514) 336-2411
Emp Here 49   *Sales* 23,276,274
SIC 5087 Service establishment equipment
Jacques Proulx
Martin Pressault
Lise V. Ward

▲ Public Company   ■ Public Company Family Member   **HQ** Headquarters   **BR** Branch   **SL** Single Location

D-U-N-S 24-698-1963   (HQ)
CUIRS BENTLEY INC
ACCESS
(*Suby of* CORPORATION DE DEVELOPPE-
MENT CUIRS BENTLEY INC, LA)
6125 Ch De La Cote-De-Liesse, Saint-
Laurent, QC, H4T 1C8
(514) 341-9333
Emp Here 100   *Sales* 285,216,498
SIC 5948 Luggage and leather goods stores
 Walter Lamothe
 Jacques Foisy
 Frederick Perrault
 Joanne Nemeroff
 Philippe Martin
 Eric Cadorette

D-U-N-S 24-990-4244   (SL)
DECOUPAGE M.P.S. INC
123 Montee De Liesse, Saint-Laurent, QC,
H4T 1S6
(514) 744-8291
Emp Here 50   *Sales* 23,751,300
SIC 5084 Industrial machinery and equipment
 Yvon Dagenais

D-U-N-S 24-205-7201   (BR)
**DHL GLOBAL FORWARDING (CANADA)
INC**
(*Suby of* DEUTSCHE POST AG)
555 Montee De Liesse, Saint-Laurent, QC,
H4T 1P5
(514) 344-3447
Emp Here 150
SIC 4731 Freight transportation arrangement
 Richard Courchesne

D-U-N-S 24-542-6788   (SL)
DISTRIBUTEURS JARDEL INC, LES
ARROW FASTENER CANADA
7575 Rte Transcanadienne Bureau 405, Saint-
Laurent, QC, H4T 1V6
(514) 321-3983
Emp Here 25   *Sales* 12,591,450
SIC 5112 Stationery and office supplies
 Eugene Gargaro
 John Sznewags
 Irwin A Frankel
 Sheldon Betsalel
 Gary Duboff

D-U-N-S 24-764-0506   (SL)
**DISTRIBUTION FISHER CAPESPAN
CANADA**
6700 Ch De La Cote-De-Liesse Bureau 301,
Saint-Laurent, QC, H4T 2B5
(514) 739-9181
Emp Here 25   *Sales* 20,889,425
SIC 5148 Fresh fruits and vegetables
 Mark Greenberg

D-U-N-S 20-218-6065   (SL)
ECLAIRAGE UNILIGHT LIMITEE
4400 Rue Hickmore, Saint-Laurent, QC, H4T
1K2
(514) 769-1533
Emp Here 100
SIC 3645 Residential lighting fixtures
 Michael Holy
 James R Johnston

D-U-N-S 20-237-5929   (SL)
EMBALLAGE WORKMAN INC
MULTISAC
(*Suby of* PUYOUNG INDUSTRIAL CO., LTD.)
345 Montee De Liesse, Saint-Laurent, QC,
H4T 1P5
(514) 344-7227
Emp Here 100   *Sales* 19,476,800
SIC 2671 Paper; coated and laminated pack-
aging
 Koh Youngjin
 Mark Kraminer
 Myoungjo Kim

D-U-N-S 25-134-6995   (HQ)
EMBALLAGES FESTIVAL INC
(*Suby of* MITCHEL-LINCOLN PACKAGING

LTD)
8286 Ch De La Cote-De-Liesse, Saint-
Laurent, QC, H4T 1G7
(514) 731-3713
Sales 55,689,000
SIC 5199 Nondurable goods, nec
 James Garfinkel
 Normand Boivin
 Michael Goriani

D-U-N-S 25-904-5003   (SL)
EPS LANTRIC INC
7750 Rte Transcanadienne, Saint-Laurent,
QC, H4T 1A5
(514) 735-4561
Emp Here 18   *Sales* 18,006,102
SIC 5051 Metals service centers and offices
 Denis Langevin

D-U-N-S 20-851-8907   (SL)
EQUIPEMENT D'INCENDIE PRIORITE INC
7528 Ch De La Cote-De-Liesse, Saint-
Laurent, QC, H4T 1E7
(514) 636-2431
Emp Here 45   *Sales* 23,424,390
SIC 5099 Durable goods, nec
 Elias Khury
 Lisa Gregory

D-U-N-S 20-230-7468   (HQ)
**EQUIPEMENTS POWER SURVEY LTEE,
LES**
*EQUIPEMENTS POWER SURVEY INTER-
NATIONAL, LES*
7880 Rte Transcanadienne, Saint-Laurent,
QC, H4T 1A5
(514) 333-8392
Sales 15,235,360
SIC 3625 Relays and industrial controls
 Chris Hutter
 Mario Laflamme
 Sylvain Lanoue
 Scott B. Ungerer
 Michael J.S. Edmonds
 Amitabh Srivastava
 Melanie Kfoury
 Pierre-Andre Meunier

D-U-N-S 25-297-5594   (BR)
**FEDERAL EXPRESS CANADA CORPORA-
TION**
FEDEX SHIP CENTRE
(*Suby of* FEDEX CORPORATION)
4041 Rue Sere, Saint-Laurent, QC, H4T 2A3
(800) 463-3339
Emp Here 200
SIC 7389 Business services, nec

D-U-N-S 20-562-1964   (HQ)
FERRO TECHNIQUE LTEE
DYNASTY MACHINERY
819 Rue Mccaffrey, Saint-Laurent, QC, H4T
1N3
(514) 341-3450
Emp Here 15   *Sales* 21,376,170
SIC 5084 Industrial machinery and equipment
 Stephen Stein
 Jeffrey Veldhoen
 Brian Donnelly
 George Miechowsky

D-U-N-S 20-424-0212   (BR)
**FORD MOTOR COMPANY OF CANADA,
LIMITED**
(*Suby of* FORD MOTOR COMPANY)
6505 Rte Transcanadienne Bureau 200, Saint-
Laurent, QC, H4T 1S3
(514) 744-1800
Emp Here 150
SIC 5012 Automobiles and other motor vehi-
cles
 Francois Trudeau

D-U-N-S 25-356-9396   (HQ)
FUTECH HITECH INC
352 Rue Mcarthur, Saint-Laurent, QC, H4T
1X8

(514) 351-1495
Emp Here 14   *Sales* 17,886,960
SIC 5063 Electrical apparatus and equipment
 Pierre Fournier
 Michel Beaudoin
 Jacques Lafleur
 Richard Comeau
 Mario Lantagne

D-U-N-S 25-672-0301   (SL)
G.D. NIRVANA INC
DELICES DE DAWN, LES
955 Rue Mccaffrey, Saint-Laurent, QC, H4T
1N3
(514) 739-9111
Emp Here 30   *Sales* 25,067,310
SIC 5149 Groceries and related products, nec
 Dawn Hodes
 Gavin Grant
 Andrew Hodes

D-U-N-S 25-150-8974   (SL)
GENATEC INC
5929 Rte Transcanadienne Bureau 240, Saint-
Laurent, QC, H4T 1Z6
(514) 855-1223
Emp Here 35   *Sales* 15,651,090
SIC 5045 Computers, peripherals, and soft-
ware
 Abi Nader Nagib

D-U-N-S 24-235-1275   (HQ)
GESTION MAJERO INC
8180 Cote-De-Liesse Road, Saint-Laurent,
QC, H4T 1G8

Sales 12,344,940
SIC 8741 Management services
 Robert Briscoe

D-U-N-S 24-860-6493   (SL)
GESTIONS MONK HERITAGE INC
255 Montee De Liesse, Saint-Laurent, QC,
H4T 1P5
(514) 345-0135
Emp Here 65   *Sales* 17,000,945
SIC 6712 Bank holding companies
 Peter Monk

D-U-N-S 20-363-3800   (SL)
GOODFOOD MARKET CORP
MARCHE GOODFOOD
4600 Rue Hickmore, Saint-Laurent, QC, H4T
1K2
(514) 730-9530
Emp Here 800   *Sales* 53,585,072
SIC 8322 Individual and family services
 Jonathan Ferrari
 Neil Cuggy
 Philippe Adam
 Hamnett Hill
 Donald Olds
 Terry Yanofsky

D-U-N-S 20-908-9648   (SL)
GROUPE BBH INC
ECONO
4400 Rue Hickmore, Saint-Laurent, QC, H4T
1K2
(514) 633-6765
Emp Here 45   *Sales* 33,978,127
SIC 5136 Men's and boy's clothing
 Claude Lampron

D-U-N-S 24-934-6958   (SL)
GROUPE JACOB INC
6125 Ch De La Cote-De-Liesse, Saint-
Laurent, QC, H4T 1C8
(514) 731-8877
Emp Here 1   *Sales* 87,328,500
SIC 5621 Women's clothing stores
 Joseph Basmaji

D-U-N-S 24-367-4087   (HQ)
GROUPE LINENCORP INC
6435 Ch De La Cote-De-Liesse, Saint-
Laurent, QC, H4T 1E5
(514) 335-2120
Sales 15,265,680

SIC 5023 Homefurnishings
 Gary Shinder

D-U-N-S 24-335-5554   (BR)
GROUPE POLYALTO INC
(*Suby of* GROUPE POLYALTO INC)
4105 Rue Hickmore, Saint-Laurent, QC, H4T
1S5
(514) 738-6817
Emp Here 100
SIC 5162 Plastics materials and basic shapes
 Gilles Hudon

D-U-N-S 24-834-5035   (SL)
GROUPE SANTE PHYSIMED INC
CENTRE MEDICAL PHYSIMED
6363 Rte Transcanadienne Bureau 121, Saint-
Laurent, QC, H4T 1Z9
(514) 747-8888
Emp Here 100   *Sales* 16,064,600
SIC 8011 Offices and clinics of medical doc-
tors
 Albert Benhaim
 Gilles Racine

D-U-N-S 20-370-1177   (SL)
GURIT OUTILLAGE (AMERICAS) INC
7562 Ch De La Cote-De-Liesse, Saint-
Laurent, QC, H4T 1E7
(514) 522-6329
Emp Here 66   *Sales* 13,320,060
SIC 3523 Farm machinery and equipment
 Rudolf Hadorn
 Binjiang Chen
 Angelo Quabba
 Marc Robitaille

D-U-N-S 20-210-3081   (BR)
HENRY SCHEIN CANADA, INC
(*Suby of* HENRY SCHEIN, INC.)
3403 Rue Griffith, Saint-Laurent, QC, H4T
1W5
(800) 668-5558
Emp Here 91
SIC 5047 Medical and hospital equipment
 Philippe Dacher

D-U-N-S 24-387-7644   (HQ)
**HETTICH CANADA LIMITED PARTNER-
SHIP**
140 Rue Barr, Saint-Laurent, QC, H4T 1Y4
(514) 333-3952
Emp Here 26   *Sales* 22,358,700
SIC 5072 Hardware
 Mike Squizzato

D-U-N-S 20-338-4532   (SL)
HOTELS COTE-DE-LIESSE INC
HOLIDAY INN MONTREAL AEROPORT
6500 Ch De La Cote-De-Liesse, Saint-
Laurent, QC, H4T 1E3
(514) 739-6440
Emp Here 200   *Sales* 18,538,000
SIC 7011 Hotels and motels
 Michael Rosenberg
 Martin Rosenberg
 Herman Luger
 Chanie Rosenberg

D-U-N-S 20-424-2648   (SL)
IEC HOLDEN INC
ENTREPRISE IEC HOLDEN
(*Suby of* GESTION MAJERO INC)
8180 Ch De La Cote-De-Liesse, Saint-
Laurent, QC, H4T 1G8
(514) 735-4371
Emp Here 350   *Sales* 99,020,250
SIC 3621 Motors and generators
 Robert J. Briscoe
 Robert G. Briscoe
 Carolyn Gass

D-U-N-S 24-214-7713   (BR)
IKEA CANADA LIMITED PARTNERSHIP
IKEA DIRECT
(*Suby of* QINGDAO HONGYISEN CON-
STRUCTION ENGINEERING SERVICE CO.,
LTD.)

▲ Public Company   ■ Public Company Family Member   **HQ** Headquarters   **BR** Branch   **SL** Single Location

9090 Boul Cavendish, Saint-Laurent, QC, H4T 1Z8
(514) 904-8619
Emp Here 200
SIC 5712 Furniture stores
Elaine Thomas

D-U-N-S 24-522-3958   (HQ)
IMMEUBLES STRUC-TUBE LTEE
6000 Rte Transcanadienne, Saint-Laurent, QC, H4T 1X9
(514) 333-9747
Sales 19,754,255
SIC 5712 Furniture stores
Marcel Knafo
Emile Knafo

D-U-N-S 24-474-8521   (SL)
IMPORTATIONS INTERNATIONALES BO-CHITEX INC, LES
ACCESSOIRES CAPELLI
225 Montee De Liesse, Saint-Laurent, QC, H4T 1P5
(514) 381-3310
Emp Here 32   *Sales* 15,946,304
SIC 5137 Women's and children's clothing
Abe (Abbouo) Bochi
Pierre (Peter) Bochi

D-U-N-S 24-527-2646   (SL)
INDUSTRIES CHEMI-3 INC
346 Rue Isabey, Saint-Laurent, QC, H4T 1W1
(514) 365-0050
Emp Here 15   *Sales* 10,955,175
SIC 5169 Chemicals and allied products, nec
Jay Saks
Robert Saks
Warren Saks

D-U-N-S 20-257-3275   (SL)
INDUSTRIES SEFINA LTEE, LES
(*Suby of* 115588 CANADA INC)
750 Rue Mcarthur, Saint-Laurent, QC, H4T 1W2
(514) 735-5911
Emp Here 80   *Sales* 15,389,600
SIC 2431 Millwork
Andre Levy

D-U-N-S 25-996-6000   (SL)
INFYNIA.COM INC
170 Montee De Liesse, Saint-Laurent, QC, H4T 1N6
(514) 332-1999
Emp Here 80   *Sales* 14,184,880
SIC 7371 Custom computer programming services
Jean-Pierre Reid
Marc Michielli

D-U-N-S 25-286-1026   (HQ)
INTELLICO - IDS INC
BLUESTAR CANADA
(*Suby of* UNITED RADIO INCORPORATED)
6830 Ch De La Cote-De-Liesse, Saint-Laurent, QC, H4T 2A1
(800) 317-2323
Sales 22,358,700
SIC 5045 Computers, peripherals, and software
Michel Sirois
Doug Jr Bivins
Stephen G Cuntz

D-U-N-S 20-883-7039   (SL)
INTERPAC CORPORATION INC
6855 Ch De La Cote-De-Liesse, Saint-Laurent, QC, H4T 1E5
(514) 340-9440
Emp Here 50   *Sales* 11,671,750
SIC 2673 Bags: plastic, laminated, and coated
Barry Zryl

D-U-N-S 25-359-8049   (HQ)
INVESTISSEMENTS CAPESPAN CANADA INC, LES
6700 Ch De La Cote-De-Liesse Bureau 301,

Saint-Laurent, QC, H4T 2B5
(514) 739-9181
Emp Here 2   *Sales* 33,423,080
SIC 5148 Fresh fruits and vegetables
Andrew De Haast
Howard Freedman

D-U-N-S 20-290-4488   (SL)
JACK COOPER CANADA 2 LIMITED PARTNERSHIP
(*Suby of* JACK COOPER ENTERPRISES, INC.)
8050 Boul Cavendish, Saint-Laurent, QC, H4T 1T1
(514) 731-3016
Emp Here 100   *Sales* 20,570,600
SIC 4213 Trucking, except local
Don Gallant

D-U-N-S 24-327-3484   (SL)
JOYLYPSO INC
(*Suby of* RENNAT INC)
4850 Rue Bourg, Saint-Laurent, QC, H4T 1J2
(514) 735-4255
Emp Here 140   *Sales* 68,282,200
SIC 5087 Service establishment equipment
Marvin Tanner

D-U-N-S 20-248-6770   (BR)
KONTRON CANADA INC
KONTRON COMMUNICATIONS
(*Suby of* S&T AG)
600 Rue Mccaffrey, Saint-Laurent, QC, H4T 1N1
(450) 437-4661
Emp Here 125
SIC 4899 Communication services, nec
Robert Courteau

D-U-N-S 20-330-3318   (SL)
KOYO FOODS QUEBEC INC
4605 Rue Hickmore, Saint-Laurent, QC, H4T 1S5
(514) 744-1299
Emp Here 35   *Sales* 29,245,195
SIC 5149 Groceries and related products, nec
Toshifumi Kagemori

D-U-N-S 20-555-1851   (SL)
L3 MAPPS INC
AUTOMATISATION MARINE ET SIMULATION POUR CENTRALES L-3
(*Suby of* L3HARRIS TECHNOLOGIES, INC.)
8565 Ch De La Cote-De-Liesse, Saint-Laurent, QC, H4T 1G5
(514) 787-5000
Emp Here 227   *Sales* 53,810,577
SIC 8748 Business consulting, nec
Rangesh Kasturi
Bruce Latimer

D-U-N-S 25-969-2960   (BR)
LAFARGE CANADA INC
(*Suby of* LAFARGEHOLCIM LTD)
4000 Rue Hickmore, Saint-Laurent, QC, H4T 1K2
(514) 344-1788
Emp Here 80
SIC 5032 Brick, stone, and related material
Francois Legault

D-U-N-S 24-072-6658   (SL)
LAIRD CONTROLS CANADA LIMITED
BELTPACK
3950 Rue Hickmore, Saint-Laurent, QC, H4T 1K2
(514) 908-1659
Emp Here 100   *Sales* 19,044,200
SIC 3663 Radio and t.v. communications equipment
Richard Morse
Julien Chouinard
Jacquelyn Kauffman

D-U-N-S 20-223-4944   (HQ)
LANIEL (CANADA) INC
AUTOMEX
(*Suby of* BROKERHOUSE DISTRIBUTORS

INC)
7101 Rte Transcanadienne, Saint-Laurent, QC, H4T 1A2
(514) 331-3031
Emp Here 54   *Sales* 26,830,440
SIC 5044 Office equipment
Jean-Marc Laniel

D-U-N-S 20-298-0637   (SL)
LE BIFTHEQUE INC
BOUCHERIE LE BIFTHEQUE
6705 Ch De La Cote-De-Liesse, Saint-Laurent, QC, H4T 1E5

Emp Here 100   *Sales* 4,551,900
SIC 5812 Eating places
Michael Solzer

D-U-N-S 24-860-3438   (HQ)
LOVEPAC INC
140 Rue Barr, Saint-Laurent, QC, H4T 1Y4
(514) 904-4300
Sales 13,476,570
SIC 7389 Business services, nec
Robert Sibthorpe

D-U-N-S 20-254-2106   (SL)
MANHATTAN INTERNATIONAL CONCEPTS INC
CONCEPTS MANHATTAN INTERNATIONAL
6150 Rte Transcanadienne, Saint-Laurent, QC, H4T 1X5
(514) 388-5588
Emp Here 26   *Sales* 12,956,372
SIC 5136 Men's and boy's clothing
Ted Rozenwald

D-U-N-S 20-226-2713   (HQ)
MARIMAC INC
UNIVERSAL LINENS
6395 Ch De La Cote-De-Liesse, Saint-Laurent, QC, H4T 1E5
(514) 725-7600
Emp Here 40   *Sales* 27,334,800
SIC 2392 Household furnishings, nec
Paul Nassar

D-U-N-S 24-834-1992   (HQ)
MEGA BRANDS INC
BILLY BEATS
4505 Rue Hickmore, Saint-Laurent, QC, H4T 1K4
(514) 333-5555
Emp Here 1,100   *Sales* 75,810,200
SIC 3944 Games, toys, and children's vehicles
Angela Lam
Bisma Ansari

D-U-N-S 24-619-3098   (HQ)
MEGATEL INFORMATION SYSTEMS INC
MEGATEL
3930 Rue Griffith, Saint-Laurent, QC, H4T 1A7
(514) 333-0717
Emp Here 35   *Sales* 18,050,988
SIC 5084 Industrial machinery and equipment
Moise Hasrouny
Souad Hasrouny
Marc Hasrouny

D-U-N-S 20-038-7727   (SL)
MISSFRESH INC
EAT LOVE FRESH
(*Suby of* METRO INC)
4220 Rue Griffith, Saint-Laurent, QC, H4T 4L6
(844) 647-7373
Emp Here 165   *Sales* 31,756,560
SIC 5421 Meat and fish markets
Marie-Eve Prevost
Simon Rivet
Bernard Prevost
Christian Bourbonniere
Marc Giroux
Francois Thibault

D-U-N-S 24-203-1321   (HQ)
NATURE'S TOUCH FROZEN FOODS INC
ALIMENTS ORGANIQUES NATURE'S

TOUCH
5105-M Rue Fisher, Saint-Laurent, QC, H4T 1J8
(514) 737-7790
Sales 30,080,772
SIC 5142 Packaged frozen goods
John Tentomas
Theo Prokos
Marc Poulin

D-U-N-S 20-421-5792   (SL)
NIVEL INC
MARKETING TANBORE
(*Suby of* RENNAT INC)
4850 Rue Bourg, Saint-Laurent, QC, H4T 1J2
(514) 735-4251
Emp Here 220   *Sales* 117,777,440
SIC 5046 Commercial equipment, nec
Marvin Tanner
Munawer Chattoo
Joyce Tanner

D-U-N-S 25-245-5621   (SL)
OEC GROUPAGE OUTREMER EXPRESS (MONTREAL) INC
OEC GROUP
(*Suby of* OVERSEAS EXPRESS CONSOLIDATORS (CANADA) INC)
725 Montee De Liesse, Saint-Laurent, QC, H4T 1P5
(514) 633-1246
Emp Here 50   *Sales* 25,998,350
SIC 4731 Freight transportation arrangement
Marc Bibeau

D-U-N-S 20-514-2412   (HQ)
OVERSEAS EXPRESS CONSOLIDATORS (CANADA) INC
OEC CANADA/GOE CANADA
725 Montee De Liesse, Saint-Laurent, QC, H4T 1P5
(514) 905-1246
Emp Here 50   *Sales* 80,027,040
SIC 4731 Freight transportation arrangement
Marc Bibeau

D-U-N-S 24-896-4371   (BR)
PACCAR OF CANADA LTD
PACCAR LEASING
(*Suby of* PACCAR INC)
7500 Rte Transcanadienne, Saint-Laurent, QC, H4T 1A5
(514) 735-2581
Emp Here 150
SIC 5511 New and used car dealers
Jean Robitaille

D-U-N-S 24-020-8223   (SL)
PORTES GENSTEEL INC
4950 Rue Hickmore, Saint-Laurent, QC, H4T 1K6
(514) 733-3562
Emp Here 50   *Sales* 10,141,500
SIC 3442 Metal doors, sash, and trim
Antonio Gervasi
Bruno Gervasi
Vince Giannini
Concetta Gervasi
Anna-Maria Montesano

D-U-N-S 20-277-2828   (SL)
PRODUITS CLAIR DE LUNE INC
CLAIR DE LUNE
361 Rue Locke, Saint-Laurent, QC, H4T 1X7
(514) 389-5757
Emp Here 200   *Sales* 46,480,600
SIC 5719 Miscellaneous homefurnishings
Albert Levy
Jimmy Levy

D-U-N-S 24-988-6441   (SL)
PRODUITS SEATPLY INC
SEATPLY
(*Suby of* GESTIONS DARIUS INC)
150 Rue Merizzi, Saint-Laurent, QC, H4T 1S4
(514) 340-1513
Emp Here 80   *Sales* 15,389,600
SIC 2426 Hardwood dimension and flooring

mills
Levon Afeyan
Eddy Yazadjian

D-U-N-S 20-417-6838   (HQ)
PRODUITS STANDARD INC
5905 Ch De La Cote-De-Liesse, Saint-Laurent, QC, H4T 1C3
(514) 342-1199
Emp Here 150   *Sales* 113,148,165
SIC 5063 Electrical apparatus and equipment
David B. Nathaniel
Kelly Hanson
Jason Prevost
Daniela Di Pietro
Marie-Josee Garneau
Ovi Shebath
Ileana Stinghe
Pascal Auger
Victoria Nathaniel

D-U-N-S 20-032-7208   (SL)
PROPRIETES BELCOURT INC, LES
6500 Rte Transcanadienne Bureau 210, Saint-Laurent, QC, H4T 1X4
(514) 344-1300
Emp Here 40   *Sales* 15,451,720
SIC 1531 Operative builders
Michael Zunenshine

D-U-N-S 24-144-2131   (BR)
PSION INC
(*Suby of* MOTOROLA SOLUTIONS, INC.)
7575 Rte Transcanadienne Bureau 500, Saint-Laurent, QC, H4T 1V6

Emp Here 250
SIC 3571 Electronic computers
Bertrand Martelle

D-U-N-S 20-297-9902   (BR)
PVH CANADA, INC
CALVIN KLEVIN
(*Suby of* PVH CORP.)
7445 Ch De La Cote-De-Liesse, Saint-Laurent, QC, H4T 1G2
(514) 278-6000
Emp Here 200
SIC 5136 Men's and boy's clothing
Emanuel Chirico

D-U-N-S 20-703-0151   (HQ)
REBOX CORP
CORPORATION REBOX
(*Suby of* YOUNGEAU INC)
7500 Ch De La Cote-De-Liesse, Saint-Laurent, QC, H4T 1E7
(514) 335-1717
Emp Here 35   *Sales* 18,131,688
SIC 5113 Industrial and personal service paper
Mark Young
Keith Primeau
Brian Young

D-U-N-S 24-294-5830   (HQ)
RECOCHEM INC
ENTREPRISES RECOCHEM, LES
(*Suby of* HIG CAPITAL MANAGEMENT, INC.)
850 Montee De Liesse, Saint-Laurent, QC, H4T 1P4
(514) 341-3550
Emp Here 225   *Sales* 104,803,914
SIC 2899 Chemical preparations, nec
Richard Boudreaux
Keval Patel
Peter Gudwin
Alain Tanguay
Rahul Ketkar

D-U-N-S 20-702-8973   (HQ)
RENNAT INC
4850 Rue Bourg, Saint-Laurent, QC, H4T 1J2
(514) 735-4255
Emp Here 1   *Sales* 81,508,507
SIC 6712 Bank holding companies
Marvin Tanner

D-U-N-S 24-206-3084   (SL)
REVISION SECURITY INC
DIRECT ALERT
460 Rue Isabey, Saint-Laurent, QC, H4T 1V3
(514) 448-6285
Emp Here 27   *Sales* 12,073,698
SIC 5065 Electronic parts and equipment, nec
Gregory Kis
Laurence Paperman

D-U-N-S 24-740-8495   (HQ)
REXEL AMERIQUE DU NORD INC
(*Suby of* REXEL)
505 Rue Locke Bureau 202, Saint-Laurent, QC, H4T 1X7
(514) 332-5331
Emp Here 3   *Sales* 840,670,700
SIC 6712 Bank holding companies
Roger Little
Rene Merat
Patrick Berard

D-U-N-S 25-975-9843   (HQ)
ROTALEC CANADA INC
ROTLEC AUTOMATION
900 Rue Mccaffrey, Saint-Laurent, QC, H4T 2C7
(514) 341-3685
Emp Here 25   *Sales* 23,751,300
SIC 5084 Industrial machinery and equipment
Robert Tayler
Francine Fauteux

D-U-N-S 24-323-2428   (HQ)
ROTALEC INTERNATIONAL INC
900 Rue Mccaffrey, Saint-Laurent, QC, H4T 2C7
(514) 341-3685
Emp Here 1   *Sales* 22,358,700
SIC 5065 Electronic parts and equipment, nec
Farhat Bichh

D-U-N-S 20-215-0454   (SL)
S. COHEN INC
153 Rue Graveline, Saint-Laurent, QC, H4T 1R4
(514) 342-6700
Emp Here 200   *Sales* 27,334,800
SIC 2326 Men's and boy's work clothing
Benjamin Cohen

D-U-N-S 20-252-7651   (SL)
SAVAGE CANAC INTERNATIONAL INC
6505 Rte Transcanadienne Bureau 405, Saint-Laurent, QC, H4T 1S3
(514) 734-4700
Emp Here 100   *Sales* 23,700,150
SIC 8742 Management consulting services
Alen B Alexander
Michel Martineau
Gennaro Patella
Kelly J Flint

D-U-N-S 24-809-3796   (BR)
SECURITAS CANADA LIMITED
(*Suby of* SECURITAS AB)
817 Rue Mccaffrey, Saint-Laurent, QC, H4T 1N3
(514) 938-3433
Emp Here 90
SIC 7381 Detective and armored car services
Bruce Grozelle

D-U-N-S 20-911-0204   (HQ)
SERVICES FERROVIAIRES CANAC INC
(*Suby of* SAVAGE ENTERPRISES HOLDINGS, LLC)
6505 Rte Transcanadienne Bureau 405, Saint-Laurent, QC, H4T 1S3
(514) 734-4700
Emp Here 125   *Sales* 56,101,500
SIC 8741 Management services
Kirk W Aubry
Gennaro Patella
Isaac Haboucha
Lewis Benson
Curtis Dowd

D-U-N-S 24-569-6000   (SL)
SGS SPORTS INC
BODY GLOVE
6400 Ch De La Cote-De-Liesse, Saint-Laurent, QC, H4T 1E3
(514) 737-5665
Emp Here 34   *Sales* 16,942,948
SIC 5137 Women's and children's clothing
Steven Gellis

D-U-N-S 20-315-9272   (HQ)
SMITH QUALITY MEAT & POULTRY INC
125 Rue Barr, Saint-Laurent, QC, H4T 1W6
(514) 735-2100
Emp Here 9   *Sales* 10,862,501
SIC 5147 Meats and meat products
Reuf Bektasevic

D-U-N-S 24-902-5099   (HQ)
SOCIETE HOLDING VELAN LTEE
7007 Ch De La Cote-De-Liesse, Saint-Laurent, QC, H4T 1G2
(514) 748-7743
Emp Here 3   *Sales* 437,815,800
SIC 3494 Valves and pipe fittings, nec
A.K. Velan
Peter O. Velan
Ivan C. Velan
Tom Velan

D-U-N-S 20-289-1537   (SL)
SPCRC HOLDINGS INC
GESTION SPCRC
850 Mont?E De Liesse, Saint-Laurent, QC, H4T 1P4
(514) 341-3550
Emp Here 681   *Sales* 248,911,629
SIC 6712 Bank holding companies
Robert F. Desmarais
Alain Tanguay
Tyler Matlock

D-U-N-S 20-603-1478   (SL)
STANLEY SECURITY SOLUTIONS CANADA INC
INTIVID SOLUTIONS
160 Rue Graveline, Saint-Laurent, QC, H4T 1R7

Emp Here 90
SIC 5065 Electronic parts and equipment, nec

D-U-N-S 20-856-5960   (HQ)
STRUC-TUBE LTEE
(*Suby of* IMMEUBLES STRUC-TUBE LTEE)
6000 Rte Transcanadienne, Saint-Laurent, QC, H4T 1X9
(514) 333-9747
Emp Here 20   *Sales* 19,754,255
SIC 5712 Furniture stores
Marcel Knafo
Marcel Knafo
Julien Knafo

D-U-N-S 20-298-1999   (SL)
SUNICE INC
850 Rue Mccaffrey, Saint-Laurent, QC, H4T 1N1
(514) 341-6767
Emp Here 26   *Sales* 12,956,372
SIC 5136 Men's and boy's clothing
Alen Brandman
Conrad Tappert
Jacques Bohbot

D-U-N-S 25-400-8105   (HQ)
SUSTEMA INC
IN TEGRATION
3590 Rue Griffith, Saint-Laurent, QC, H4T 1A7
(514) 744-5499
Sales 13,739,112
SIC 5021 Furniture
Guy Boudreault

D-U-N-S 24-402-9492   (SL)
SYSTEMES INFORMATIQUES O.G.C. INC, LES

7575 Rte Transcanadienne Bureau 403, Saint-Laurent, QC, H4T 1V6
(514) 331-7873
Emp Here 30   *Sales* 13,415,220
SIC 5045 Computers, peripherals, and software
Olivier Du Paul
Christian St-Pierre
Luc Chantelain
Tina Gauthier

D-U-N-S 20-691-7804   (HQ)
TARKETT SPORTS CANADA INC
PRODUIT FIELDTURF
(*Suby of* SOCIETE INVESTISSEMENT DE-CONINCK)
7445 Ch De La Cote-De-Liesse Bureau 200, Saint-Laurent, QC, H4T 1G2
(514) 340-9311
Sales 13,320,060
SIC 3523 Farm machinery and equipment
Eric Daliere
Pedro Azevedo
Souha Azar
Marie-France Nantel

D-U-N-S 24-903-4612   (HQ)
TEXTILES J.P. DOUMAK INC
855 Rue Mccaffrey, Saint-Laurent, QC, H4T 1N3
(514) 342-9397
Sales 19,932,880
SIC 5131 Piece goods and notions
Martin Smith
Irving Maklan
Marc Chevrier

D-U-N-S 20-962-5169   (SL)
THREAD COLLECTIVE INC
HOTEL DOGGY
850 Rue Mccaffrey, Saint-Laurent, QC, H4T 1N1
(514) 345-1777
Emp Here 105   *Sales* 87,940,965
SIC 5136 Men's and boy's clothing
Alen Brandman
Jacques Bohbot

D-U-N-S 24-296-6208   (SL)
TRIO-SELECTION INC
CREAM SODA
8305 Ch De La C?Te-De-Liesse, Saint-Laurent, QC, H4T 1G5
(514) 387-2591
Emp Here 30   *Sales* 14,949,660
SIC 5137 Women's and children's clothing
Darshan Khurana
Lloyd Prizant
Subhash Khanna

D-U-N-S 24-978-3536   (SL)
TRU SIMULATION + TRAINING CANADA INC
TRU SIMULATION + FORMATION
(*Suby of* TEXTRON INC.)
6767 Ch De La Cote-De-Liesse, Saint-Laurent, QC, H4T 1E5
(514) 342-0800
Emp Here 200   *Sales* 56,583,000
SIC 3699 Electrical equipment and supplies, nec
James Takats
Mary Fraser Lovejoy
George Karam
Ann T. Willaman
Robert E. Lupone
John Curran R.

D-U-N-S 20-765-4021   (SL)
UNITED ACOUSTIQUE & PARTITIONS CO INC
645 Rue Mccaffrey, Saint-Laurent, QC, H4T 1N3
(514) 737-8337
Emp Here 65   *Sales* 10,554,765
SIC 1742 Plastering, drywall, and insulation
James J Heaslip

D-U-N-S 24-330-9288   (SL)
VAN ACTION (2005) INC
VAN ACTION SAVARIA
(*Suby of* CORPORATION SAVARIA)
4870 Rue Courval, Saint-Laurent, QC, H4T 1L1
(514) 342-5000
Emp Here 65   *Sales* 14,549,795
SIC 3716 Motor homes
  Marcel Bourrassa
  Jean-Marie Bourassa

D-U-N-S 20-236-7033   (HQ)
VELAN INC
(*Suby of* SOCIETE HOLDING VELAN LTEE)
7007 Ch De La Cote-De-Liesse, Saint-Laurent, QC, H4T 1G2
(514) 748-7743
Emp Here 416   *Sales* 366,865,000
SIC 3494 Valves and pipe fittings, nec
  Yves Leduc
  Tom Velan
  Rob Velan
  William Sheffield
  James A Mannebach
  Cheryl Hooper
  Jacques Latendresse

D-U-N-S 25-258-4677   (BR)
VELAN INC
(*Suby of* SOCIETE HOLDING VELAN LTEE)
550 Rue Mcarthur, Saint-Laurent, QC, H4T 1X8
(514) 748-7743
Emp Here 230
SIC 3494 Valves and pipe fittings, nec

D-U-N-S 24-783-8709   (HQ)
VERITIV CANADA, INC
ADELCO
(*Suby of* VERITIV CORPORATION)
4300 Rue Hickmore, Saint-Laurent, QC, H4T 1K2
(514) 367-3111
Emp Here 69   *Sales* 1,192,646,992
SIC 5111 Printing and writing paper
  Mark W. Hianik
  Daniel Rowntree
  Erminia Shulak

D-U-N-S 25-400-8626   (SL)
VETEMENTS NTD INC, LES
ADMIT ONE
700 Rue Mccaffrey, Saint-Laurent, QC, H4T 1N1
(514) 341-8330
Emp Here 100   *Sales* 49,832,200
SIC 5136 Men's and boy's clothing
  Michael Eliesen

D-U-N-S 25-229-7031   (SL)
WARCO EQUIPMENT LTD
364 Rue Mcarthur, Saint-Laurent, QC, H4T 1X8
(514) 685-7878
Emp Here 25   *Sales* 10,483,875
SIC 6712 Bank holding companies
  Dan Levine
  Jeffrey Steinberg

D-U-N-S 20-010-8038   (BR)
WOLSELEY CANADA INC
(*Suby of* FERGUSON PLC)
4200 Rue Hickmore, Saint-Laurent, QC, H4T 1K2
(514) 344-9378
Emp Here 100
SIC 5074 Plumbing and heating equipment and supplies (hydronics)
  Pierre Quilliam

D-U-N-S 25-672-6365   (HQ)
WORLEE INTERNATIONAL INC
VAN EEGHEN
750 Rue Gougeon, Saint-Laurent, QC, H4T 4L5
(514) 332-6455
Sales 25,902,887

SIC 5149 Groceries and related products, nec
  Arthur Sousa
  Michiel Blijdenstein

Saint-Laurent, QC H7B

D-U-N-S 20-370-7570   (HQ)
6368174 CANADA INC
6165 Rue Dessureaux, Saint-Laurent, QC, H7B 1B1
(450) 968-0880
Sales 27,335,000
SIC 6712 Bank holding companies
  Gaetan Alepins

Saint-Laurent, QC H7C

D-U-N-S 24-380-5855   (SL)
MONTPAK INTERNATIONAL INC
5730 Rue Maurice-Cullen, Saint-Laurent, QC, H7C 2V1
(450) 665-9524
Emp Here 100   *Sales* 34,569,000
SIC 2011 Meat packing plants
  Alexandre Fontaine
  Fontaine Donald
  Fabien Fontaine

Saint-Laurent, QC H7L

D-U-N-S 25-173-0800   (SL)
SERVICES ALIMENTAIRES WOLFE INC
2624 Boul Des Oiseaux, Saint-Laurent, QC, H7L 4N9
(450) 628-5760
Emp Here 70   *Sales* 58,490,390
SIC 5149 Groceries and related products, nec
  Ghislain Wolfe

Saint-Laurent, QC H7M

D-U-N-S 24-101-6430   (BR)
MULTI RECYCLE S.D. INC
(*Suby of* MULTI RECYCLE S.D. INC)
140 Rue Saulnier, Saint-Laurent, QC, H7M 1S8
(450) 975-9952
Emp Here 104
SIC 4953 Refuse systems
  Pierre Noel

D-U-N-S 24-570-2964   (HQ)
S. BOUDRIAS HORTICOLE INC
APPALACHE VALLEY
29 Rue Saulnier, Saint-Laurent, QC, H7M 1S7
(450) 663-4245
Sales 11,066,400
SIC 2875 Fertilizers, mixing only
  Stephane Boudrias

Saint-Laurent, QC H7N

D-U-N-S 25-091-4736   (SL)
COOPERATIVE DES TRAVAILLEURS ET TRAVAILLEUSES PREMIER DEFI LAVAL
ROTISSERIES ST-HUBERT # 19
1111 Boul Des Laurentides, Saint-Laurent, QC, H7N 5B5
(450) 668-7085
Emp Here 115   *Sales* 5,234,685
SIC 5812 Eating places
  Sylvie Tremblay

  Joanne Guimond
  Nicole St-Pierre

Saint-Laurent, QC H7P

D-U-N-S 20-561-1127   (HQ)
TECHNOLOGIES SYNERGX INC
2912 Rue Joseph-A.-Bombardier, Saint-Laurent, QC, H7P 6E3
(450) 978-1240
Sales 18,867,198
SIC 7389 Business services, nec
  Stephane Lemieux
  Samuel Nasso
  Francois Carriere
  Marc Beauchemin
  Kenneth Wawrew
  Stephane Tremblay

Saint-Laurent, QC H7R

D-U-N-S 20-124-1655   (SL)
BLEU TECH MONTREAL INC
BLEU TECH
(*Suby of* LIXIL GROUP CORPORATION)
4150 Chomedey (A-13) O, Saint-Laurent, QC, H7R 6E9
(450) 767-2890
Emp Here 100   *Sales* 17,873,900
SIC 8712 Architectural services
  John Fasanella
  Thomas Gannon
  Johannes Prinsloo

D-U-N-S 20-188-2185   (HQ)
CORPORATION SAVARIA
SILVER CROSS
4350 Desste Chomedey (A-13) O, Saint-Laurent, QC, H7R 6E9
(450) 681-5655
Emp Here 1,035   *Sales* 216,842,947
SIC 3999 Manufacturing industries, nec
  Marcel Bourassa
  Sebastien Bourassa
  Alexandre Bourassa
  Helene Bernier
  Vince Sciamanna
  Mauro Ferrara
  Peter Drutz
  Jean-Louis Chapdelaine
  Sylvain Dumoulin
  Alain Tremblay

D-U-N-S 24-323-7013   (SL)
EPICERIE QUINTAL & FRERES 1978 INC
I G A
4805 Boul Arthur-Sauve, Saint-Laurent, QC, H7R 3X2
(450) 627-3123
Emp Here 90   *Sales* 26,412,930
SIC 5411 Grocery stores
  Henri Quintal
  Yvon Quintal

D-U-N-S 24-014-1614   (HQ)
GESTIONS AZURE INC., LES
7909 Boul Arthur-Sauve, Saint-Laurent, QC, H7R 3X8
(450) 969-0150
Sales 10,462,120
SIC 6712 Bank holding companies
  Jean Parenteau

D-U-N-S 25-138-9128   (HQ)
NORTRAX QUEBEC INC
NORTRAX
(*Suby of* DEERE & COMPANY)
4500 Desste Chomedey (A-13) O, Saint-Laurent, QC, H7R 6E9
(450) 625-3221
Emp Here 40   *Sales* 48,773,000

SIC 5084 Industrial machinery and equipment
  Chris Holmes
  James Fodi
  Michael Rugeroni
  Gail E. Mccombs
  David F. Thorne
  Francois Richard

D-U-N-S 25-258-7811   (SL)
SANTE COURVILLE INC
CENTRE GERIATRIQUE DE BEL AGE
5200 80e Rue, Saint-Laurent, QC, H7R 5T6
(450) 627-7990
Emp Here 101   *Sales* 5,983,947
SIC 8361 Residential care
  Kenneth Courville
  Christine Durocher

D-U-N-S 20-764-7272   (HQ)
SERUM INTERNATIONAL INC
4400 Desste Chomedey (A-13) O, Saint-Laurent, QC, H7R 6E9
(450) 625-8511
Sales 13,953,016
SIC 5139 Footwear
  Josef Kanner
  Helga Kanner

D-U-N-S 24-163-1592   (SL)
SUPERMARCHE PERRIER ET MARTEL INC
MARCHE METRO PERRIER ET MARTEL
6155 Boul Arthur-Sauve, Saint-Laurent, QC, H7R 3X8
(450) 627-4496
Emp Here 78   *Sales* 17,354,103
SIC 5411 Grocery stores
  Michel Perrier
  Lyse Perrier

Saint-Laurent, QC H7S

D-U-N-S 25-167-9130   (SL)
3254160 CANADA INC
850 Av Munck, Saint-Laurent, QC, H7S 1B1
(514) 384-5060
Emp Here 150   *Sales* 41,002,500
SIC 6712 Bank holding companies
  Gilles Plante

D-U-N-S 20-229-0359   (HQ)
ACIER PACIFIQUE INC
845 Av Munck, Saint-Laurent, QC, H7S 1A9
(514) 384-4690
Emp Here 39   *Sales* 22,358,700
SIC 5051 Metals service centers and offices
  Joseph Antebi
  Anthony Andreoli

D-U-N-S 24-581-4397   (SL)
COMMODITY IMPORT INC
845 Av Munck, Saint-Laurent, QC, H7S 1A9
(514) 384-4690
Emp Here 35   *Sales* 14,677,425
SIC 6719 Holding companies, nec
  Joseph Antebi
  Roger Antebi

D-U-N-S 20-215-8531   (SL)
CUSTOM DIAMOND INTERNATIONAL INC
CUISINES CUSTOM DIAMOND INTERNATIONAL
895 Av Munck, Saint-Laurent, QC, H7S 1A9
(450) 668-0330
Emp Here 50   *Sales* 10,141,500
SIC 3469 Metal stampings, nec
  Ronald Diamond
  Ron Tepper

D-U-N-S 24-168-7748   (SL)
POLYEXPERT INC
(*Suby of* FONDS POLYCO INC)
850 Av Munck, Saint-Laurent, QC, H7S 1B1
(514) 384-5060
Emp Here 80   *Sales* 12,708,640
SIC 3081 Unsupported plastics film and sheet

Gilles Plante
Lise Plante

Saint-Laurent, QC H7V

D-U-N-S 25-190-1083 (HQ)
CIMA CANADA INC
CIMA +
3400 Boul Du Souvenir Suite 600, Saint-Laurent, QC, H7V 3Z2
(514) 337-2462
Emp Here 250 *Sales* 31,416,840
SIC 8741 Management services
Francois Plourde
Andre Couturier
Andre Desjardins
Jean-Pierre Normand
Marc Cantin
Andre Chaumont
Luc Jolicoeur

D-U-N-S 24-517-1293 (HQ)
CIMA+ S.E.N.C.
AUDY FARLEY LALANDE LA BERGE ET AS-SOCIES
3400 Boul Du Souvenir Bureau 600, Saint-Laurent, QC, H7V 3Z2
(514) 337-2462
Emp Here 200 *Sales* 492,827,500
SIC 8711 Engineering services
Francois Plourde

D-U-N-S 24-019-1783 (SL)
SERVIER CANADA INC
INSTITUT SERVIER DU DIABETE
(*Suby of* STICHTING FIRS)
235 Boul Armand-Frappier, Saint-Laurent, QC, H7V 4A7
(450) 978-9700
Emp Here 163 *Sales* 67,289,823
SIC 5122 Drugs, proprietaries, and sundries
Antoine Beillevaire
Frederic Fasano
Dominique Gervais

D-U-N-S 25-497-0858 (HQ)
UPLAND SOFTWARE INC
TENROX ENTREPRISES, LES
(*Suby of* UPLAND SOFTWARE, INC.)
275 Boul Armand-Frappier Bureau 531, Saint-Laurent, QC, H7V 4A7
(450) 688-3444
Emp Here 96 *Sales* 17,731,100
SIC 7371 Custom computer programming services
Jay A. Lefton
John T. Mcdonald

Saint-Laurent-Ile-D'Orleans, QC G0A

D-U-N-S 25-152-2892 (SL)
FERME MAURICE ET PHILIPPE VAILLAN-COURT INC
6678 Ch Royal, Saint-Laurent-Ile-D'Orleans, QC, G0A 3Z0
(418) 828-9374
Emp Here 72 *Sales* 18,886,248
SIC 0171 Berry crops
Philippe Vailllancourt
Josianne Girard

Saint-Lazare, QC J7T

D-U-N-S 20-381-4769 (SL)
GESTION FAMILLE DEZIEL INC
1869 Ch Sainte-Angelique, Saint-Lazare, QC, J7T 2X9

(450) 455-6165
Emp Here 100 *Sales* 29,347,700
SIC 5411 Grocery stores
Richard Deziel
Anthony Deziel
Ryan Deziel
Annie Filion

D-U-N-S 24-942-2726 (BR)
POIRIER & FILS LTEE
IGA FAMILLE RICK DEZIEL.
(*Suby of* POIRIER & FILS LTEE)
1869 Ch Sainte-Angelique, Saint-Lazare, QC, J7T 2X9
(450) 455-6165
Emp Here 150
SIC 5411 Grocery stores
Rick Deziel

Saint-Lazare-De-Bellechasse, QC G0R

D-U-N-S 24-456-1879 (SL)
CLSC DE BELLECHASSE SOCIAL
100a Rue Monseigneur-Bilodeau, Saint-Lazare-De-Bellechasse, QC, G0R 3J0
(418) 883-2227
Emp Here 45 *Sales* 10,207,485
SIC 8399 Social services, nec
Michele Collard

D-U-N-S 24-884-3872 (HQ)
EQUIPEMENTS D'ERABLIERE C.D.L. INC, LES
257 Rte 279, Saint-Lazare-De-Bellechasse, QC, G0R 3J0
(418) 883-5158
Emp Here 1 *Sales* 26,027,100
SIC 5099 Durable goods, nec
Jean -Marie Chabot
Vallier Chabot
Marc-Andre Chabot
Pascal Houle
Martin Juneau
Martin Chabot

Saint-Leon, QC J0K

D-U-N-S 25-256-5619 (SL)
GERARD BERGERON & FILS INC
1486 Rang Barthelemy, Saint-Leon, QC, J0K 2W0
(819) 228-3936
Emp Here 30 *Sales* 10,274,010
SIC 0134 Irish potatoes
Sylvain Bergeron
Isabelle Bergeron

Saint-Leonard, QC H1P

D-U-N-S 20-115-6739 (SL)
2618-7922 QUEBEC INC
PENNZOIL ST-LEONARD
8055 Boul Langelier, Saint-Leonard, QC, H1P 2B7
(514) 852-9181
Emp Here 1 *Sales* 11,360,888
SIC 5172 Petroleum products, nec
Andre Piche

D-U-N-S 20-012-4266 (SL)
3680215 CANADA INC
6660 Rue P.-E.-Lamarche, Saint-Leonard, QC, H1P 1J7
(514) 325-4488
Emp Here 50 *Sales* 11,671,750
SIC 3312 Blast furnaces and steel mills
Sylvain Pelletier

D-U-N-S 24-361-0719 (HQ)

4372727 CANADA INC
DUCHARME SEATING
9275 Rue Le Royer, Saint-Leonard, QC, H1P 3H7
(514) 328-2772
Emp Here 2 *Sales* 16,774,200
SIC 6712 Bank holding companies
Eric Rocheleau
Frederic Dionne

D-U-N-S 24-383-5860 (SL)
4507525 CANADA INC
CORSINI INTERNATIONAL
8755 Boul Langelier, Saint-Leonard, QC, H1P 2C6
(514) 356-0677
Emp Here 50 *Sales* 11,517,000
SIC 5712 Furniture stores
Davide Cinelli

D-U-N-S 25-243-9146 (SL)
9042-0209 QUEBEC INC
LES GALLERIES ACURA
5625 Boul Metropolitain E, Saint-Leonard, QC, H1P 1X3
(514) 362-2872
Emp Here 25 *Sales* 12,451,950
SIC 5511 New and used car dealers
Jacques Breton
Allain Berthiaume

D-U-N-S 20-012-0850 (BR)
A. LASSONDE INC
ORANGE MAISON, DIV DE
(*Suby of* 3346625 CANADA INC)
9420 Boul Langelier, Saint-Leonard, QC, H1P 3H8
(514) 351-4010
Emp Here 300
SIC 5499 Miscellaneous food stores
Martin Laliberte

D-U-N-S 20-050-2958 (HQ)
ADT CANADA INC
ALARME DIGITECH
8481 Boul Langelier, Saint-Leonard, QC, H1P 2C3
(514) 323-5000
Emp Here 50 *Sales* 164,856,300
SIC 1731 Electrical work
Andrea Czapary-Martin
Antonio Cioffi
Michelle H. Miranda
Lee David Jackson

D-U-N-S 24-420-5535 (SL)
ALIMENTS CONGELES MOOV INC
6810 Boul Des Grandes-Prairies, Saint-Leonard, QC, H1P 3P3
(514) 328-6661
Emp Here 20 *Sales* 10,702,480
SIC 5142 Packaged frozen goods
Platon Gavrielatos

D-U-N-S 24-678-3682 (SL)
ALIMENTS FIDAS LTEE, LES
6575 Boul Des Grandes-Prairies, Saint-Leonard, QC, H1P 3G8
(514) 322-7575
Emp Here 108 *Sales* 77,405,328
SIC 5146 Fish and seafoods
Maurice Racine

D-U-N-S 24-083-9142 (HQ)
ALIMENTS SAPUTO LIMITEE
LANDMARK
(*Suby of* JOLINA CAPITAL INC)
6869 Boul Metropolitain E, Saint-Leonard, QC, H1P 1X8
(514) 328-6662
Emp Here 70 *Sales* 518,902,384
SIC 5141 Groceries, general line
Lino Anthony Jr. Saputo
Emanuele Saputo
Louis-Phillipe Carriere

D-U-N-S 20-568-7429 (SL)
BINGO VEZINA INC

6125 Boul Metropolitain E, Saint-Leonard, QC, H1P 1X7
(514) 321-5555
Emp Here 70 *Sales* 36,437,940
SIC 5092 Toys and hobby goods and supplies
Claudette Vezina
Stephane Robitaille
Eric Robitaille
Pascale Robitaille
Patrick Robitaille

D-U-N-S 24-889-7738 (HQ)
BOULANGERIE VACHON INC
(*Suby of* GRUPO BIMBO, S.A.B. DE C.V.)
8770 Boul Langelier Bureau 230, Saint-Leonard, QC, H1P 3C6
(514) 326-5084
Emp Here 50 *Sales* 860,059,200
SIC 5149 Groceries and related products, nec
Joseph Mccarthy
Christine Labelle
Darrell Miller

D-U-N-S 24-509-6359 (SL)
BOULANGERIES COMAS INC, LES
COPENHAGEN DANISH
6325 Boul Des Grandes-Prairies Bureau 5, Saint-Leonard, QC, H1P 1A5
(514) 323-1880
Emp Here 100 *Sales* 83,557,700
SIC 5142 Packaged frozen goods
Christian Comas
Charles Comas

D-U-N-S 24-650-4328 (HQ)
BURO DESIGN INTERNATIONAL A.Q. INC
BURO DESIGN INTERNATIONAL
5715 Boul Metropolitain E, Saint-Leonard, QC, H1P 1X3
(514) 955-6644
Sales 13,888,980
SIC 2521 Wood office furniture
Alain Quintal

D-U-N-S 24-648-5429 (SL)
C L S C SAINT-LEONARD
5540 Rue Jarry E, Saint-Leonard, QC, H1P 1T9
(514) 328-3460
Emp Here 200 *Sales* 15,025,800
SIC 8093 Specialty outpatient clinics, nec
Suzanne Hebert

D-U-N-S 20-379-9411 (HQ)
C&C PACKING LIMITED PARTNERSHIP
EMBALLAGES C&C
6800 Boul Des Grandes-Prairies, Saint-Leonard, QC, H1P 3P3
(514) 939-2273
Emp Here 70 *Sales* 68,233,900
SIC 2011 Meat packing plants
George Paleologou
William D. Kalutycz
Robert Bianconi

D-U-N-S 24-769-4433 (SL)
CERAMIQUES ROYAL LTEE, LES
CUISINE ROYAL
8845 Rue Pascal-Gagnon, Saint-Leonard, QC, H1P 1Z4
(514) 324-0002
Emp Here 26 *Sales* 11,626,524
SIC 5032 Brick, stone, and related material
Giuseppe Lucia
Francesco Lucia
Crispino Lucia
Antonina Lucia

D-U-N-S 24-864-6523 (HQ)
CHAUSSURES RUBINO INC, LES
9300 Rue Du Prado, Saint-Leonard, QC, H1P 3B4
(514) 326-0566
Emp Here 15 *Sales* 24,647,139
SIC 5661 Shoe stores
Vincenzo Rubino
Carlo Ferrare

D-U-N-S 24-479-9909 (BR)
COMMISSION SCOLAIRE DE LA POINTE-DE-L'ILE
ECOLE PRIMAIRE GABRIELLE ROY
(Suby of COMMISSION SCOLAIRE DE LA POINTE-DE-L'ILE)
5950 Rue Honore-Mercier, Saint-Leonard, QC, H1P 3E4
(514) 321-8475
Emp Here 100
SIC 8211 Elementary and secondary schools
Jos- Luis Requena

D-U-N-S 24-404-5472 (HQ)
COMMUNICATIONS TRISPEC INC, LES
8500 Rue Pascal-Gagnon, Saint-Leonard, QC, H1P 1Y4
(514) 328-2025
Emp Here 27 *Sales* 17,886,960
SIC 5065 Electronic parts and equipment, nec
Nino Cesta
Vincent Cesta

D-U-N-S 24-403-5002 (HQ)
CONSCORP INC
CORPORATION CONS
6800 Boul Des Grandes-Prairies, Saint-Leonard, QC, H1P 3P3
(514) 939-2273
Emp Here 35 *Sales* 11,242,750
SIC 2011 Meat packing plants
Stanley Cons
Ronald Cons
Michael Cons

D-U-N-S 20-227-7158 (SL)
COUVERTURE MONTREAL-NORD LTEE
8200 Rue Lafrenaie, Saint-Leonard, QC, H1P 2A9
(514) 324-8300
Emp Here 80 *Sales* 17,426,320
SIC 1761 Roofing, siding, and sheetMetal work
Richard Nadeau
Marc Nadeau
Louise Nadeau
Nicole Nadeau

D-U-N-S 20-216-1428 (HQ)
DAUBOIS INC
6155 Boul Des Grandes-Prairies, Saint-Leonard, QC, H1P 1A5
(514) 328-1253
Emp Here 70 *Sales* 40,245,660
SIC 5032 Brick, stone, and related material
Philippe Daubois
Louis Daubois

D-U-N-S 24-053-4214 (HQ)
DISTRIBUTIONS MULTI-PRO INC
8480 Rue Champ D'Eau, Saint-Leonard, QC, H1P 1Y3
(514) 955-1128
Sales 10,006,500
SIC 5169 Chemicals and allied products, nec
Jacques Boucher
Gilles Durocher

D-U-N-S 20-323-4880 (HQ)
DOMFOAM INC
DOMFOAM INTERNATIONAL
(Suby of PLACEMENTS S.P. CANADA INC, LES)
8785 Boul Langelier, Saint-Leonard, QC, H1P 2C9
(514) 325-8120
Emp Here 10 *Sales* 20,189,700
SIC 3083 Laminated plastics plate and sheet
Terry Pomerantz

D-U-N-S 20-323-4997 (BR)
DOMFOAM INC
DOMFOAM INTERNATIONAL
(Suby of PLACEMENTS S.P. CANADA INC, LES)
6675 Rue Bombardier, Saint-Leonard, QC, H1P 2W2

(514) 852-3959
Emp Here 250
SIC 3086 Plastics foam products
Jhon Havard

D-U-N-S 20-330-7769 (SL)
DOMFOAM INTERNATIONAL INC
MANUFACTURE DOMFOAM INTERNA-TIONAL
(Suby of GLOBAL UPHOLSTERY CO LIMITED)
8785 Boul Langelier, Saint-Leonard, QC, H1P 2C9
(514) 325-8120
Emp Here 100 *Sales* 15,885,800
SIC 3086 Plastics foam products
Tony Vallecoccia
Saul Feldberg
David Feldberg
Dale Mcneil

D-U-N-S 20-292-3090 (SL)
ECO-LOGIXX - GROSSISTE ALIMENTAIRE ET PRODUITS D'EMBALLAGES INC
MORENCY
9209 Boul Langelier, Saint-Leonard, QC, H1P 3K9
(514) 351-3031
Emp Here 26 *Sales* 11,626,524
SIC 5074 Plumbing and heating equipment and supplies (hydronics)
Daniel Lacombe

D-U-N-S 20-058-1796 (SL)
ELECTRIQUE PERFECTION INC
8685 Rue Pascal-Gagnon, Saint-Leonard, QC, H1P 1Y5
(514) 376-0100
Emp Here 60 *Sales* 13,069,740
SIC 1731 Electrical work
Raffaele Sabatino
Mauro Maurizio
Giuseppe Randisi

D-U-N-S 24-325-1030 (SL)
EMPAQUETEURS UNIS DE FRUITS DE MER LTEE, LES
UNITED EXPRESS
6575 Boul Des Grandes-Prairies, Saint-Leonard, QC, H1P 3G8
(514) 322-5888
Emp Here 35 *Sales* 29,245,195
SIC 5146 Fish and seafoods
Maurice Recine
Adriana Recine

D-U-N-S 24-061-0829 (HQ)
ENTREPRISES DORO J.C.S. INC, LES
6050 Boul Des Grandes-Prairies Bureau 204, Saint-Leonard, QC, H1P 1A2
(514) 722-3676
Emp Here 60 *Sales* 11,659,750
SIC 5812 Eating places

D-U-N-S 25-825-4341 (SL)
EURO-PHARM INTERNATIONAL CANADA INC
CCREST LABORATORIES
9400 Boul Langelier, Saint-Leonard, QC, H1P 3H8
(514) 324-1073
Emp Here 36 *Sales* 39,792,420
SIC 5122 Drugs, proprietaries, and sundries
Emanuele Caltagirone
Antoinette Trocchia
Giovani Caltagirone
Giuseppe Caltagirone

D-U-N-S 24-357-2307 (SL)
FANA SPORTS INC
DISTRIBUTION FANA SPORTS
6140 Rue Marivaux, Saint-Leonard, QC, H1P 3K3
(514) 648-8888
Emp Here 25 *Sales* 12,458,050
SIC 5136 Men's and boy's clothing
Antonio Baranello
Giovani Sansalone

D-U-N-S 24-694-4933 (SL)
FESTIVAL JUSTE POUR RIRE
FESTIVAL DE FILMS JUSTE POUR RIRE
8375 Rue Pascal-Gagnon, Saint-Leonard, QC, H1P 1Y5
Emp Here 26 *Sales* 11,039,782
SIC 8999 Services, nec
Gilbert Rozon

D-U-N-S 24-862-6660 (SL)
FRATUM PHARMA INC
9380 Boul Langelier, Saint-Leonard, QC, H1P 3H8
(514) 322-6111
Emp Here 49 *Sales* 12,394,746
SIC 5912 Drug stores and proprietary stores
Emanuele Caltagirone

D-U-N-S 25-989-1380 (HQ)
GENERAL NOLI CANADA INC
(Suby of GENERAL NOLI SPEDIZIONI INTERNAZIONALI SPA)
8000 Boul Langelier Bureau 514, Saint-Leonard, QC, H1P 3K2
(514) 852-6262
Emp Here 8 *Sales* 17,158,911
SIC 4731 Freight transportation arrangement
Kevin Coates
Gianluca Pirrotta
Gianni Bachini

D-U-N-S 24-167-5990 (HQ)
GIVESCO INC
BRIQUES & PIERRE NADON
(Suby of PLACEMENTS MECYVA INC)
9495 Rue Pascal-Gagnon, Saint-Leonard, QC, H1P 1Z4
(514) 327-7175
Emp Here 125 *Sales* 113,925,600
SIC 5039 Construction materials, nec
Max Latifi
Melissa Latifi

D-U-N-S 24-402-8861 (SL)
GROUPE ADF INC
AU DRAGON FORGE
8788 Rue Aeterna, Saint-Leonard, QC, H1P 2R9
(514) 327-5383
Emp Here 49 *Sales* 21,911,526
SIC 5039 Construction materials, nec
Pierre Paschini

D-U-N-S 20-234-5591 (SL)
GROUPE G & G LTEE
6245 Boul Des Grandes-Prairies, Saint-Leonard, QC, H1P 1A5
(514) 325-3711
Emp Here 45 *Sales* 12,232,890
SIC 7692 Welding repair
Shant Imamedjian
Arto Imamedjian

D-U-N-S 20-209-6731 (HQ)
GUILLEVIN INTERNATIONAL CIE
GUILLEVIN SANTE-SECURITE
(Suby of GII HOLDINGS CORP)
6555 Boul Metropolitain E Bureau 301, Saint-Leonard, QC, H1P 3H3
(514) 329-2100
Emp Here 40 *Sales* 638,271,700
SIC 5063 Electrical apparatus and equipment
Robert J. Bouchard
Keith Colburn
Alain Fontaine

D-U-N-S 24-176-0768 (HQ)
HEBDRAULIQUE INC
BOYAUX MULTIFLEX
8410 Rue Champ D'Eau, Saint-Leonard, QC, H1P 1Y3
(514) 327-5966
Emp Here 20 *Sales* 11,525,100
SIC 3492 Fluid power valves and hose fittings
Rene Hebert
Louis Tremblay

Louis-Rene Hebert
Alexandre Hebert

D-U-N-S 24-988-8249 (SL)
IMPORTATION BERCHICCI LTEE
6205 Boul Couture, Saint-Leonard, QC, H1P 3G7
(514) 325-2020
Emp Here 20 *Sales* 16,711,540
SIC 5143 Dairy products, except dried or canned
Joe Occhiuto
Giuseppe Occhiuto
Maria Occhiuto
Giovanni Occhiuto

D-U-N-S 25-309-7091 (BR)
INDUSTRIELLE ALLIANCE, ASSURANCE ET SERVICES FINANCIERS INC
INDUSTRIELLE ALLIANCE ASSURANCE ET SERVICES FINANCE
(Suby of INDUSTRIELLE ALLIANCE, ASSURANCE ET SERVICES FINANCIERS INC)
6555 Boul Metropolitain E Bureau 403, Saint-Leonard, QC, H1P 3H3
(514) 324-3811
Emp Here 80
SIC 6411 Insurance agents, brokers, and service
Rodolphe St-Pierre

D-U-N-S 24-226-9074 (SL)
INDUSTRIES BONIMETAL INC, LES
9225 Rue Le Royer, Saint-Leonard, QC, H1P 3H7
(514) 325-6151
Emp Here 23 *Sales* 10,332,037
SIC 7389 Business services, nec
John Deprosperis

D-U-N-S 20-542-7966 (SL)
INDUSTRIES DESORMEAU INC
8195 Rue Pascal-Gagnon, Saint-Leonard, QC, H1P 1Y5
(514) 321-2432
Emp Here 75 *Sales* 33,538,050
SIC 5072 Hardware
Simon Desormeau

D-U-N-S 20-722-0583 (HQ)
INDUSTRIES RAD INC
FAUCHER INDUSTRIES
(Suby of GESTION INDUSTRIES INC)
6363 Boul Des Grandes-Prairies, Saint-Leonard, QC, H1P 1A5
(418) 228-8934
Sales 31,338,020
SIC 3751 Motorcycles, bicycles and parts
Raymond Dutil

D-U-N-S 20-253-0457 (HQ)
INGREDIENTS ALIMENTAIRES BSA INC, LES
BSA
(Suby of FRUTAROM (UK) HOLDINGS LIMITED)
6005 Boul Couture, Saint-Leonard, QC, H1P 3E1
(514) 852-2719
Emp Here 143 *Sales* 39,173,850
SIC 2099 Food preparations, nec
Alon Granot
Amos Anatot

D-U-N-S 24-321-1042 (HQ)
JOLINA CAPITAL INC
8000 Boul Langelier Bureau 200, Saint-Leonard, QC, H1P 3K2
(514) 328-3541
Emp Here 1 *Sales* 3,785,576,713
SIC 6712 Bank holding companies
Emanuele Lino Saputo
Joe Marsilii
Joey Saputo

D-U-N-S 20-416-4560 (HQ)
MAISON AMI-CO (1981) INC, LA
AMI-CO

8455 Boul Langelier, Saint-Leonard, QC, H1P 2C5
(514) 351-7520
Emp Here 25   *Sales* 33,251,820
SIC 5087 Service establishment equipment
Sophie Ouellette
Gilbert Ouellette
Bruno Rochette

D-U-N-S 24-849-8045   (SL)
MECANICACTION INC
6660 Rue P.-E.-Lamarche, Saint-Leonard, QC, H1P 1J7
(514) 666-9770
Emp Here 105   *Sales* 10,511,298
SIC 1711 Plumbing, heating, air-conditioning
Sylvain Pelletier
Jean-Yves St-Louis
Pierre Lemire

D-U-N-S 20-422-5205   (SL)
PLACE TEVERE INC
RESTAURANT TEVERE
(Suby of 154181 CANADA INC)
8610 Rue Du Creusot, Saint-Leonard, QC, H1P 2A7
(514) 322-9762
Emp Here 140   *Sales* 6,529,460
SIC 5812 Eating places
Oreste Pulice
Guiseppe Reda
Raphael Pulice

D-U-N-S 24-525-1322   (HQ)
PRODUITS FORESTIERS ARBEC INC
8000 Boul Langelier Bureau 210, Saint-Leonard, QC, H1P 3K2
(514) 327-3350
Sales 91,377,250
SIC 6712 Bank holding companies
Joey Saputo
Serge Mercier
Joe Marsilii

D-U-N-S 24-322-1897   (HQ)
PRODUITS FORESTIERS ARBEC S.E.N.C.
8770 Boul Langelier Bureau 216, Saint-Leonard, QC, H1P 3C6
(514) 327-3350
Sales 173,158,580
SIC 2421 Sawmills and planing mills, general
Karine Girard

D-U-N-S 20-222-2402   (SL)
PRODUITS PLASTIQUES JAY INC
8875 Boul Langelier, Saint-Leonard, QC, H1P 2C8
(514) 321-7272
Emp Here 80   *Sales* 16,151,760
SIC 3089 Plastics products, nec
Larry Pollock
Nicole Pollock

D-U-N-S 24-891-3027   (SL)
PROVENT HCE INC
6150 Boul Des Grandes-Prairies, Saint-Leonard, QC, H1P 1A2
(514) 643-0642
Emp Here 40   *Sales* 17,886,960
SIC 5064 Electrical appliances, television and radio
Eugenio Masciotra

D-U-N-S 20-884-0199   (HQ)
ROXON MEDI-TECH LTEE
9400 Rue Pascal-Gagnon, Saint-Leonard, QC, H1P 1Z7
(514) 326-7780
Emp Here 18   *Sales* 17,886,960
SIC 5047 Medical and hospital equipment
Michael Solomita
Franca Solomita
Micheal Solomita

D-U-N-S 24-946-2144   (HQ)
SAPUTO INC
(Suby of JOLINA CAPITAL INC)
6869 Boul Metropolitain E, Saint-Leonard, QC,

H1P 1X8
(514) 328-6662
Emp Here 135   *Sales* 9,188,003,138
SIC 2022 Cheese; natural and processed
Lino A. Saputo Jr
Carl Colizza
Gaetane Wagner
Maxime Therrien
Anthony M. Fata
Tony Meti
Annalisa King
Henry E. Demone
Annette Verschuren
Karen Kinsley

D-U-N-S 25-308-3513   (BR)
SAPUTO PRODUITS LAITIERS CANADA S.E.N.C.
(Suby of SAPUTO PRODUITS LAITIERS CANADA S.E.N.C.)
7750 Rue Pascal-Gagnon, Saint-Leonard, QC, H1P 3L1
(514) 328-6662
Emp Here 150
SIC 2022 Cheese; natural and processed

D-U-N-S 20-332-9425   (SL)
SYSTEMES URBAINS INC
(Suby of ENVIRONNEMENT ROUTIER NRJ INC)
8345 Rue Pascal-Gagnon, Saint-Leonard, QC, H1P 1Y5
(514) 321-5205
Emp Here 50   *Sales* 10,891,450
SIC 1731 Electrical work
Richard Gareau
Nathalie Massie
Chantal Ducharme
Steve Bastien

D-U-N-S 24-870-8448   (SL)
VETEMENTS PRESTIGIO INC, LES
6370 Boul Des Grandes-Prairies, Saint-Leonard, QC, H1P 1A2
(514) 955-7131
Emp Here 80   *Sales* 35,937,520
SIC 7389 Business services, nec
Leonardo Bonadonna

D-U-N-S 25-542-5811   (SL)
VISUASCAN INC
(Suby of SUPPLY CHAIN SERVICES, LLC)
9066 Rue Pascal-Gagnon, Saint-Leonard, QC, H1P 2X4
(514) 322-2725
Emp Here 24   *Sales* 11,400,624
SIC 5084 Industrial machinery and equipment
Sidney W. Jr. Emery
Gilles Seguin

Saint-Leonard, QC H1R

D-U-N-S 24-870-8604   (SL)
173532 CANADA INC
7870 Rue Fleuricourt, Saint-Leonard, QC, H1R 2L3
(514) 274-2870
Emp Here 80   *Sales* 20,924,240
SIC 6712 Bank holding companies
Alain Delisle
Benoit Delisle

D-U-N-S 24-324-5391   (SL)
3812073 CANADA INC
I G P SPECIALISTES D'INVENTAIRE
4929 Rue Jarry E Bureau 208, Saint-Leonard, QC, H1R 1Y1
(514) 324-1024
Emp Here 60   *Sales* 26,953,140
SIC 7389 Business services, nec
Jean-Claude Giroux

D-U-N-S 20-555-0051   (SL)
9141-1967 QUEBEC INC

DISTRIBUTION HORIZON NATURE
4815 Boul Couture, Saint-Leonard, QC, H1R 3H7
(514) 326-0185
Emp Here 45   *Sales* 37,600,965
SIC 5149 Groceries and related products, nec
Daniel Dubuc

D-U-N-S 20-270-9911   (SL)
9312-5581 QUEBEC INC
HOTEL BONAVENTURE
5250 Rue Jarry E, Saint-Leonard, QC, H1R 3A9
(514) 878-2332
Emp Here 250   *Sales* 23,917,000
SIC 7011 Hotels and motels
Kuen Chan Tai Kong

D-U-N-S 24-256-8855   (SL)
AGENCE ANDRE BEAULNE LTEE
BEAULNE & RHEAUME
5055 Boul Metropolitain E Bureau 200, Saint-Leonard, QC, H1R 1Z7
(514) 329-3333
Emp Here 50   *Sales* 28,996,200
SIC 6411 Insurance agents, brokers, and service
Andre Beaulne

D-U-N-S 24-189-4562   (SL)
ALIMENTS S.R.C. INC, LES
(Suby of 9220-3298 QUEBEC INC)
4617 Boul Des Grandes-Prairies, Saint-Leonard, QC, H1R 1A5
(514) 721-2421
Emp Here 50   *Sales* 13,707,600
SIC 5411 Grocery stores
Remi Gagnon
Jessica Dupuis

D-U-N-S 25-501-6354   (SL)
BAS A.Y.K. INC, LES
5505 Boul Des Grandes-Prairies, Saint-Leonard, QC, H1R 1B3
(514) 279-4648
Emp Here 225   *Sales* 53,213,175
SIC 2252 Hosiery, nec
Asher Krausz

D-U-N-S 24-067-7976   (SL)
CENTRE COMMUNAUTAIRE LEONARDO DA VINCI
8370 Boul Lacordaire, Saint-Leonard, QC, H1R 3Y6
(514) 955-8350
Emp Here 100   *Sales* 6,842,200
SIC 8322 Individual and family services
Pat Buttino

D-U-N-S 25-201-3503   (SL)
CENTRE DE RECEPTION LE MADISON INC
MADISON, LE
8750 Boul Provencher, Saint-Leonard, QC, H1R 3N7
(514) 374-7428
Emp Here 100   *Sales* 8,962,900
SIC 7299 Miscellaneous personal service
Stefano Gentile
Liborio Gentile
Giuseppe Gentile

D-U-N-S 25-324-3760   (HQ)
COMPLEXE DE L'AUTO PARK AVENUE INC
PARK AVENUE TOYOTA
4505 Boul Metropolitain E Bureau 201, Saint-Leonard, QC, H1R 1Z4
(514) 899-9000
Emp Here 5   *Sales* 216,469,500
SIC 5511 New and used car dealers
Norman E Hebert
Diane Dunlop
Bernard Le Blanc
Norman John Hebert
Normand Barabe

D-U-N-S 20-330-0538   (SL)
DELICOUKI INC
CROUTE DOREE, LA

(Suby of GAUBERY INC)
5695 Boul Des Grandes-Prairies Bureau 118, Saint-Leonard, QC, H1R 1B3
(514) 731-2705
Emp Here 25   *Sales* 20,889,425
SIC 5149 Groceries and related products, nec
Godefroy Aubery
Jean-Louis Aubery
Edouard Aubery

D-U-N-S 25-542-2685   (SL)
GESTION PHARMASSO INC
UNIPRIX
9235 Boul Lacordaire, Saint-Leonard, QC, H1R 2B6
(514) 324-2600
Emp Here 45   *Sales* 11,382,930
SIC 5912 Drug stores and proprietary stores
Pierre Corbeil
Stephane Morin

D-U-N-S 24-675-4907   (SL)
HAMEL CHEVROLET BUICK GMC LTEE
9455 Boul Lacordaire, Saint-Leonard, QC, H1R 3E8
(514) 327-3540
Emp Here 50   *Sales* 24,903,900
SIC 5511 New and used car dealers
Andre Hamel

D-U-N-S 24-334-0028   (BR)
HOOD PACKAGING CORPORATION
GLOPAK
(Suby of HOOD FLEXIBLE PACKAGING CORPORATION)
4755 Boul Des Grandes-Prairies, Saint-Leonard, QC, H1R 1A6
(514) 323-4517
Emp Here 150
SIC 2673 Bags: plastic, laminated, and coated
Yves Quintin

D-U-N-S 20-217-1885   (HQ)
JOHN SCOTTI AUTOMOTIVE LTEE
4315 Boul Metropolitain E, Saint-Leonard, QC, H1R 1Z4
(514) 725-9394
Emp Here 50   *Sales* 92,504,160
SIC 5521 Used car dealers
John Scotti

D-U-N-S 20-210-9427   (HQ)
PLASTIQUES BALCAN LIMITEE, LES
PLOYMAX
(Suby of GESTIONS GUILKOHN INC)
9340 Rue De Meaux, Saint-Leonard, QC, H1R 3H2
(514) 326-0200
Emp Here 190   *Sales* 31,771,600
SIC 3081 Unsupported plastics film and sheet
Marcos Kohn

D-U-N-S 24-136-0226   (SL)
SADERCOM INC
GROUPE CMA
4875 Boul Metropolitain E Bureau 100, Saint-Leonard, QC, H1R 3J2
(514) 326-4100
Emp Here 30   *Sales* 17,397,720
SIC 6411 Insurance agents, brokers, and service
Norman Caty

D-U-N-S 25-872-7882   (SL)
SIGNALISATION COMO INC
4325 Rue J.-B.-Martineau, Saint-Leonard, QC, H1R 3W9
(514) 327-2875
Emp Here 40   *Sales* 11,686,760
SIC 7359 Equipment rental and leasing, nec
Lidia Forcillo

D-U-N-S 20-418-2760   (HQ)
SOCIETE EN COMMANDITE CANADELLE
BIKY
4405 Boul Metropolitain E, Saint-Leonard, QC, H1R 1Z4

(514) 376-6240
Sales 24,916,100
SIC 5137 Women's and children's clothing
Joia M Johnson

D-U-N-S 20-928-3761   (HQ)
VAST-AUTO DISTRIBUTION LTEE
AUTO MAXIMUM
4840 Boul Des Grandes-Prairies, Saint-
Leonard, QC, H1R 1A1
(514) 955-3188
Emp Here 1   *Sales* 57,644,250
SIC 5013 Motor vehicle supplies and new
parts
Giuseppe Del Vasto
Gilles Morneau

Saint-Leonard, QC H1S

D-U-N-S 24-676-2462   (HQ)
149667 CANADA INC
CENTRE HI-FI
6925 Rue Jean-Talon E, Saint-Leonard, QC,
H1S 1N2
(514) 254-2153
Emp Here 4   *Sales* 11,517,000
SIC 5731 Radio, television, and electronic
stores
Silvia D'alimonte
Danile D'alimonte
Mike Sciscente

D-U-N-S 24-970-8942   (SL)
2739-0988 QUEBEC INC
UNIPRIX
4675 Rue Jean-Talon E, Saint-Leonard, QC,
H1S 1K3
(514) 722-4664
Emp Here 40   *Sales* 10,118,160
SIC 5912 Drug stores and proprietary stores
Maher Mahrouse
Bassam Chalati

D-U-N-S 25-502-4937   (SL)
2941902 CANADA INC
BONANZA LALUMIERE
6852a Rue Jean-Talon E, Saint-Leonard, QC,
H1S 1N1
(514) 252-8277
Emp Here 200   *Sales* 58,695,400
SIC 5411 Grocery stores
Daniele Lalumiere

D-U-N-S 24-321-5266   (SL)
AUTOMOBILES RIMAR INC
RIMAR VOLKSWAGON
5500 Boul Metropolitain E, Saint-Leonard, QC,
H1S 1A6
(514) 253-4888
Emp Here 26   *Sales* 12,950,028
SIC 5511 New and used car dealers
Modesto Di Tommaso
Silvie Di Tommaso

D-U-N-S 24-128-4426   (HQ)
**CAISSE DESJARDINS DE MERCIER-
ROSEMONT**
CENTRE DE SERVICE BEAUBIEN
6955 Rue Jean-Talon E, Saint-Leonard, QC,
H1S 1N2
(514) 254-7878
Emp Here 60   *Sales* 16,886,210
SIC 6062 State credit unions
Marc Pominville
Ginette Lefebvre
Robert Lizotte
Gilles Marette
Real Martin
Emilie Moreau
Michel Tourangeau
Louisette Deneault Abran
Sophie Primeau
Real Charest

D-U-N-S 24-393-2246   (SL)

CANADIAN TIRE
6565 Rue Jean-Talon E, Saint-Leonard, QC,
H1S 1N2
(514) 257-9350
Emp Here 49   *Sales* 24,405,822
SIC 5531 Auto and home supply stores

D-U-N-S 20-107-8396   (BR)
CONSTRUCTIONS MAXERA INC, LES
RESIDENCE LE CITADIN
7675 Rue Lespinay, Saint-Leonard, QC, H1S
3C6
(514) 254-9002
Emp Here 148
SIC 8361 Residential care
Berlyne Nelson

D-U-N-S 20-693-0344   (HQ)
CORPORATION GROUPE PHARMESSOR
PROXIMED
(*Suby of* MCKESSON FINANCIAL HOLD-
INGS II UNLIMITED COMPANY)
5000 Boul Metropolitain E, Saint-Leonard, QC,
H1S 3G7
(514) 725-1212
Sales 66,320,700
SIC 5122 Drugs, proprietaries, and sundries
Paula Keays
Todd E. Baldanzi
John G. Saia
Mai Anh Tran
Carlo D'amico

D-U-N-S 24-800-7114   (SL)
FELBER INC
JEAN COUTU
7275 Boul Langelier, Saint-Leonard, QC, H1S
1V6
(514) 259-4614
Emp Here 65   *Sales* 15,881,320
SIC 5912 Drug stores and proprietary stores
Robert Felber

D-U-N-S 25-240-4306   (BR)
**FONDATION EDUCATIVE DE LA COMMIS-
SION SCOLAIRE ENGLISH-MONTREAL,
LA**
*COMMISSION   SCOLAIRE   ENGLISH-
MONTREAL*
(*Suby of* FONDATION EDUCATIVE DE
LA COMMISSION SCOLAIRE ENGLISH-
MONTREAL, LA)
7355 Boul Viau, Saint-Leonard, QC, H1S 3C2
(514) 374-6000
Emp Here 85
SIC 8211 Elementary and secondary schools
Eileen Kelly

D-U-N-S 20-972-0135   (SL)
JOSEPH D'ONOFRIO ET ASSOCIES INC
GROUPE D'ONOFRIO
5045 Rue Jean-Talon E Bureau 201, Saint-
Leonard, QC, H1S 0B6
(514) 328-2555
Emp Here 37   *Sales* 21,457,188
SIC 6411 Insurance agents, brokers, and ser-
vice
Lina D'onofrio
Zinaida Bauza D'onofrio

D-U-N-S 24-394-2922   (SL)
LEGARE, DUPERRE INC
CANADIAN TIRE
4250 Rue Jean-Talon E, Saint-Leonard, QC,
H1S 1J7
(514) 723-2233
Emp Here 49   *Sales* 24,405,822
SIC 5531 Auto and home supply stores
Daniel Legare

D-U-N-S 20-224-9645   (SL)
LOMBARDI AUTO LTEE
LOMBARDI HONDA
4356 Boul Metropolitain E, Saint-Leonard, QC,
H1S 1A2
(514) 728-2222
Emp Here 49   *Sales* 24,405,822
SIC 5511 New and used car dealers

Marcel Agarand
Julia Lombardi
Maria Lombardi
Andre Jobin
Patrice Aceto

D-U-N-S 20-224-9959   (SL)
**LONGUE POINTE CHRYSLER DODGE
(1987) LTEE**
6200 Boul Metropolitain E, Saint-Leonard, QC,
H1S 1A9
(514) 256-5092
Emp Here 125   *Sales* 78,660,000
SIC 5511 New and used car dealers
Gilles Ferland

D-U-N-S 20-421-5024   (HQ)
MAGNUS POIRIER INC
7388 Boul Viau, Saint-Leonard, QC, H1S 2N9
(514) 727-2847
Emp Here 28   *Sales* 16,978,338
SIC 7261 Funeral service and crematories
Jacques Poirier
Claude Poirier
Marc Poirier

D-U-N-S 20-890-9494   (SL)
MARCHE TELLIER JEAN-TALON INC
IGA TELLIER
5000 Rue Jean-Talon E, Saint-Leonard, QC,
H1S 1K6
(514) 728-3535
Emp Here 96   *Sales* 28,173,792
SIC 5411 Grocery stores
Michel Tellier

D-U-N-S 24-138-2188   (BR)
**MCDONALD'S   RESTAURANTS   OF
CANADA LIMITED**
RESTAURANTS MCDONALD'S
(*Suby of* MCDONALD'S CORPORATION)
7445 Boul Langelier, Saint-Leonard, QC, H1S
1V6
(514) 252-1105
Emp Here 80
SIC 5812 Eating places
Joe Pistilli

D-U-N-S 24-502-5960   (BR)
METRO RICHELIEU INC
SUPER C
(*Suby of* METRO INC)
6775 Rue Jean-Talon E, Saint-Leonard, QC,
H1S 1N2
(514) 252-0230
Emp Here 100
SIC 5411 Grocery stores
Gilles Sarazin

D-U-N-S 25-755-6910   (HQ)
MONTREAL AUTO PRIX INC
4900 Boul Metropolitain E, Saint-Leonard, QC,
H1S 3A4
(514) 593-9020
Emp Here 70   *Sales* 44,049,600
SIC 5521 Used car dealers
Richard Martin
Richard Martin
Sylvain Lamoureux

D-U-N-S 24-203-3582   (SL)
PECB GROUP INC
ENTREPRISES PECB, LES
6683 Rue Jean-Talon E Bureau 336, Saint-
Leonard, QC, H1S 0A5
(514) 814-2548
Emp Here 82   *Sales* 13,331,888
SIC 7379 Computer related services, nec

D-U-N-S 24-327-2759   (SL)
PHARMAPRIX
4420 Rue Jean-Talon E, Saint-Leonard, QC,
H1S 1J7
(514) 723-1000
Emp Here 40   *Sales* 10,118,160
SIC 5912 Drug stores and proprietary stores
Katia Sajous

D-U-N-S 25-210-3197   (HQ)

**PIECES POUR AUTOMOBILE JEAN-TALON
(1993) LTEE**
7655 Boul Viau, Saint-Leonard, QC, H1S 2P4
(514) 374-2113
Emp Here 29   *Sales* 21,852,900
SIC 5013 Motor vehicle supplies and new
parts
Matteo Del Vasto

D-U-N-S 20-323-6393   (BR)
SOBEYS CAPITAL INCORPORATED
IGA EXTRA
(*Suby of* EMPIRE COMPANY LIMITED)
7150 Boul Langelier, Saint-Leonard, QC, H1S
2X6
(514) 254-5454
Emp Here 150
SIC 5141 Groceries, general line
Pierre Guy

D-U-N-S 20-517-2880   (SL)
ST-LEONARD NISSAN INC
NISSAN
4400 Boul Metropolitain E, Saint-Leonard, QC,
H1S 1A2
(514) 365-7777
Emp Here 44   *Sales* 21,915,432
SIC 5511 New and used car dealers
Maurice Roy

D-U-N-S 24-460-4765   (HQ)
**TRAVAILLEURS & TRAVAILLEUSES UNIS
DE L'ALIMENTATION ET DU COMMERCE T
U A C LOCAL 501**
T U A C LOCAL 501
4850 Boul Metropolitain E Bureau 501, Saint-
Leonard, QC, H1S 2Z7
(514) 725-9525
Emp Here 42   *Sales* 17,602,110
SIC 8631 Labor organizations
Yvon Bellemare

D-U-N-S 24-085-6286   (HQ)
UNIPRIX INC
UNIPRIX SANTE
(*Suby of* MCKESSON FINANCIAL HOLD-
INGS II UNLIMITED COMPANY)
5000 Boul Metropolitain E Bureau 100, Saint-
Leonard, QC, H1S 3G7
(514) 725-1212
Emp Here 110   *Sales* 586,217,178
SIC 5912 Drug stores and proprietary stores
Alain Arel

D-U-N-S 25-294-8500   (BR)
WAL-MART CANADA CORP
WALMART SUPERCENTRE
(*Suby of* WALMART INC.)
7445 Boul Langelier, Saint-Leonard, QC, H1S
1V6
(514) 899-1889
Emp Here 300
SIC 5311 Department stores

Saint-Leonard, QC H1T

D-U-N-S 24-383-2537   (SL)
4259238 CANADA INC
INTERMARCHE LAGORIA (BELANGER),L'
5915 Rue Belanger, Saint-Leonard, QC, H1T
1G8
(514) 259-4216
Emp Here 55   *Sales* 16,141,235
SIC 5411 Grocery stores
Cosimo Chimienti
Rocco Chimienti
Antonio Longo
Michael Mule
Domenico Melfi

Saint-Leonard-D'Aston, QC J0C

D-U-N-S 25-095-9749   (SL)
9228-5329 QUEBEC INC
ALDES CANADA
(*Suby of* ALDES INTERNATIONAL)
100 Rue Carter, Saint-Leonard-D'Aston, QC,
J0C 1M0
(819) 399-3400
Emp Here 75   *Sales* 16,650,075
SIC 3564 Blowers and fans
Stanislas Lacroix
Etienne Gendreau

D-U-N-S 24-843-2254   (SL)
ALIMENTS BARI INC, LES
297 155 Rte, Saint-Leonard-D'Aston, QC, J0C
1M0
(819) 399-2277
Emp Here 55   *Sales* 19,012,950
SIC 2099 Food preparations, nec
Francois Baril
Marc Baril

D-U-N-S 24-383-0473   (SL)
BEAUDRY MORIN INC
BEAUDRY EQUIPEMENTS LAITIERS
565 Rue Principale, Saint-Leonard-D'Aston,
QC, J0C 1M0
(819) 399-2403
Emp Here 30   *Sales* 14,250,780
SIC 5084 Industrial machinery and equipment
Yvan Beaudry
Nicole Duval

D-U-N-S 25-021-5696   (BR)
**COMMISSION   SCOLAIRE   DE   LA
RIVERAINE**
ECOLE SECONDAIRE LA DECOUVERTE
(*Suby of* COMMISSION SCOLAIRE DE LA
RIVERAINE)
401 Rue Germain, Saint-Leonard-D'Aston,
QC, J0C 1M0
(819) 399-2122
Emp Here 86
SIC 8211 Elementary and secondary schools
Annie Tourigny

D-U-N-S 20-184-2163   (BR)
NORTEK AIR SOLUTIONS CANADA, INC
(*Suby of* VENMAR VENTILATION ULC)
200 Rue Carter, Saint-Leonard-D'Aston, QC,
J0C 1M0
(819) 399-2175
Emp Here 230
SIC 1711 Plumbing, heating, air-conditioning
Silvain Lauziere

Saint-Liguori, QC J0K

D-U-N-S 24-713-2152   (HQ)
FILTRATION L.A.B. INC
193 Rang De L'Eglise, Saint-Liguori, QC, J0K
2X0
(450) 754-4222
Emp Here 50   *Sales* 17,760,080
SIC 3564 Blowers and fans
Claude Bedard
Caroline Bedard
Marc-Andre Bedard
Louise Drolet
Antonio Lastarza

Saint-Lin-Laurentides, QC J5M

D-U-N-S 24-969-1858   (HQ)
2950-4602 QUEBEC INC
MOREL ET FILS
435 Rue Saint-Isidore, Saint-Lin-Laurentides,
QC, J5M 2V1
(450) 439-2000
Emp Here 30   *Sales* 14,720,860
SIC 5251 Hardware stores

Yves Morel
Gilles Morel

D-U-N-S 24-527-0145   (SL)
ALUMINIUM ANDRE GAGNON INC
1225 Rang De La Riviere N, Saint-Lin-
Laurentides, QC, J5M 1Y7
(450) 439-3324
Emp Here 50   *Sales* 12,044,200
SIC 1629 Heavy construction, nec
Andre Gagnon

D-U-N-S 20-512-9690   (BR)
BURO DESIGN INTERNATIONAL A.Q. INC
(*Suby of* BURO DESIGN INTERNATIONAL
A.Q. INC)
125 Rue Quintal, Saint-Lin-Laurentides, QC,
J5M 2S8
(450) 439-8554
Emp Here 180
SIC 2521 Wood office furniture
Marcel Guilbault

D-U-N-S 20-557-8581   (SL)
COMPOSITES VCI INC
(*Suby of* GROUPE COMPOSITES VCI INC)
830   12e Av Bureau 915,   Saint-Lin-
Laurentides, QC, J5M 2V9
(450) 302-4646
Emp Here 110   *Sales* 31,120,650
SIC 3699 Electrical equipment and supplies,
nec
Yves Hamelin
Sylvain Rivard
Sylvain Bulota
Andre Scaini
Sylvain Bulota

D-U-N-S 24-346-4505   (BR)
**GOUVERNEMENT DE LA PROVINCE DE
QUEBEC**
*CENTRE D' HEBERGEMENT ST-ANTOINE-
DE-PADOUE*
(*Suby   of*   GOUVERNEMENT   DE   LA
PROVINCE DE QUEBEC)
521 Rue Saint-Antoine, Saint-Lin-Laurentides,
QC, J5M 3A3
(450) 439-2609
Emp Here 125
SIC 8361 Residential care

D-U-N-S 24-547-7195   (SL)
JARDINS G & R LTEE, LES
1043 Rue Gariepy, Saint-Lin-Laurentides, QC,
J5M 2N1
(450) 439-3425
Emp Here 45   *Sales* 37,600,965
SIC 5148 Fresh fruits and vegetables
Rene Berard

D-U-N-S 24-815-0625   (SL)
MAISONS USINEES COTE INC
388 Rue Saint-Isidore, Saint-Lin-Laurentides,
QC, J5M 2V1
(450) 439-8737
Emp Here 85   *Sales* 13,248,355
SIC 2452 Prefabricated wood buildings
Rejean Cote
Virginie Cote
Raphael Cote

D-U-N-S 20-632-2513   (SL)
MAXI CANADA INC
COMPAGNIE DE VOLAILLES MAXI, LA
688 Rue Du Parc, Saint-Lin-Laurentides, QC,
J5M 3B4
(450) 439-2500
Emp Here 175   *Sales* 60,495,750
SIC 2015 Poultry slaughtering and processing
Hugo Boisvert
John Koufis
Eric Bannon
Casey Lynch
Iain Bridges
David Harding
Tony Faulkner
Tim Shanley

Kabir Mundkur

D-U-N-S 24-573-4863   (SL)
NAPA PIECES D'AUTO
557 Rue Saint-Louis, Saint-Lin-Laurentides,
QC, J5M 2X2
(450) 439-2006
Emp Here 26   *Sales* 12,950,028
SIC 5531 Auto and home supply stores
Daniel Bouaechant

D-U-N-S 20-737-8654   (HQ)
RACETTE, J. P. INC
557 Rue Saint-Louis, Saint-Lin-Laurentides,
QC, J5M 2X2
(450) 439-2006
Emp Here 17   *Sales* 11,455,794
SIC 5531 Auto and home supply stores
Daniel Beauchamp
Jocelyn Deschenes
Sylvie Poulin

Saint-Louis-De-Blandford, QC G0Z

D-U-N-S 20-103-4217   (SL)
**CANNEBERGES BECANCOUR MANAGE-
MENT INC**
PRODUITS CANNEBERGES BECANCOUR
94   Rang   Saint-Francois,   Saint-Louis-De-
Blandford, QC, G0Z 1B0
(819) 364-3853
Emp Here 20   *Sales* 10,702,480
SIC 5148 Fresh fruits and vegetables
Jonathan Deccubber

Saint-Louis-De-Gonzague, QC J0S

D-U-N-S 24-326-4264   (HQ)
EBENISTERIE ST-URBAIN LTEE
EBSU
226   Rue   Principale,   Saint-Louis-De-
Gonzague, QC, J0S 1T0
(450) 427-2687
Sales 17,313,300
SIC 2431 Millwork
Napoleon Boucher
Jeremie Boucher

D-U-N-S 20-331-6500   (SL)
HUDSON VALLEY FARMS (CA) ULC
HUDSON VALLEY PRODUITS DE CANARD
228   Rue   Principale,   Saint-Louis-De-
Gonzague, QC, J0S 1T0
(450) 377-8766
Emp Here 26   *Sales* 10,023,494
SIC 0259 Poultry and eggs, nec
Marcus Henley
Izzy Yanay
Michael Ginor
Laurie Ginor

D-U-N-S 20-254-9176   (SL)
MAHEU, GERARD INC
DUNDEE FEEDS
289 5e Rang, Saint-Louis-De-Gonzague, QC,
J0S 1T0
(450) 377-1420
Emp Here 25   *Sales* 18,563,000
SIC 5191 Farm supplies
Richard Maheu
Laurent Blier
Andre Brisson
Patrick Mcdonald
Marc Leduc
Huguette Maheu Leduc

Saint-Louis-Du-Ha-Ha, QC G0L

D-U-N-S 24-146-3389   (HQ)
V T L LOCATION INC
Cp 99, Saint-Louis-Du-Ha-Ha, QC, G0L 3S0
(418) 854-7383
Sales 12,747,525
SIC 5012 Automobiles and other motor vehi-
cles
Donald Viel

Saint-Ludger, QC G0M

D-U-N-S 20-955-0185   (HQ)
EQUIPEMENTS LAPIERRE INC, LES
EXTRUSIONS LAPIERRE
99 Rue De L'Escale, Saint-Ludger, QC, G0M
1W0
(819) 548-5454
Sales 36,630,165
SIC 3569 General industrial machinery, nec
Donald Lapierre
Carl Lapierre
Chantal Lapierre
Anick Lapierre

Saint-Ludger-De-Milot, QC G0W

D-U-N-S 20-433-6226   (SL)
**COOPERATIVE FORESTIERE DE PETIT-
PARIS**
576 Rue Gaudreault, Saint-Ludger-De-Milot,
QC, G0W 2B0
(418) 373-2575
Emp Here 250   *Sales* 48,092,500
SIC 2411 Logging
Claude Kenty
Stephan Caouette
Claudie Tremblay
Alain Paradis

D-U-N-S 24-213-2129   (SL)
GEO-FOR INC
633 Av Gagnon, Saint-Ludger-De-Milot, QC,
G0W 2B0

Emp Here 49   *Sales* 10,369,037
SIC 0851 Forestry services
Yves Mercier

D-U-N-S 24-760-3970   (SL)
PRODUITS FORESTIERS PETIT PARIS INC
75 Ch De Chutes-Des-Passes, Saint-Ludger-
De-Milot, QC, G0W 2B0
(418) 373-2801
Emp Here 125   *Sales* 24,046,250
SIC 2491 Wood preserving
Claude Kenty
Roger Tremblay

Saint-Malo, QC J0B

D-U-N-S 20-500-1985   (HQ)
J.M. CHAMPEAU INC
ENTREPRISES J.M. CHAMPEAU, LES
491 Rte 253, Saint-Malo, QC, J0B 2Y0
(819) 658-2245
Sales 30,779,200
SIC 2421 Sawmills and planing mills, general
Pierre Champeau
Rejeanne Champeau

Saint-Marc-Des-Carrieres, QC G0A

D-U-N-S 20-029-1651   (BR)
**CENTRE DE SANTE ET DE SERVICES SO-
CIAUX DE PORTNEUF**

CENTRE D' HEBERGEMENT ST MARC DES CARRIERES
(Suby of CENTRE DE SANTE ET DE SER-VICES SOCIAUX DE PORTNEUF)
444 Rue Beauchamp, Saint-Marc-Des-Carriere, QC, G0A 4B0
(418) 268-3511
Emp Here 95
SIC 8361 Residential care
Nathalie Grondines

D-U-N-S 24-890-7933   (HQ)
CENTRE DE SANTE ET DE SERVICES SO-CIAUX DE PORTNEUF
CSSS DE PORTNEUF
1045 Boul Bona-Dussault, Saint-Marc-Des-Carriere, QC, G0A 4B0
(418) 268-3571
Emp Here 40   *Sales* 63,958,250
SIC 7991 Physical fitness facilities
Philippe Leboeuf
Julien Simon
Chantale Simard

D-U-N-S 20-255-1990   (HQ)
CONSTRUCTION ET PAVAGE PORTNEUF INC
PAVAGE ROUTEK, DIV OF
599 Boul Bona-Dussault, Saint-Marc-Des-Carriere, QC, G0A 4B0
(418) 268-3558
Emp Here 20   *Sales* 18,933,150
SIC 1611 Highway and street construction
Julien Savard
Renald Savard
Alain Savard
David Marcotte

D-U-N-S 25-479-9950   (SL)
GRAYMONT (PORTNEUF) INC
BETON ST-MARC
(Suby of GRAYMONT LIMITED)
595 Boul Bona-Dussault, Saint-Marc-Des-Carriere, QC, G0A 4B0
(418) 268-3501
Emp Here 80   *Sales* 21,620,480
SIC 1481 NonMetallic mineral services
Stephane Godin
Celia Helen Johnson
Steve Boulay

D-U-N-S 24-232-7351   (HQ)
MATERIAUX AUDET INC
CENTRE DE RENOVATION G. HARVEY
294 Boul Bona-Dussault, Saint-Marc-Des-Carriere, QC, G0A 4B0
(418) 268-3525
Emp Here 70   *Sales* 19,053,425
SIC 5039 Construction materials, nec
Mario Audet
Marie-Claude Audet
Onil Audet

Saint-Marc-Du-Lac-Long, QC G0L

D-U-N-S 24-524-1521   (SL)
GLENDYNE INC
396 Rue Principale, Saint-Marc-Du-Lac-Long, QC, G0L 1T0
(418) 893-7221
Emp Here 225   *Sales* 57,530,250
SIC 3281 Cut stone and stone products
Irenee Bouchard
Marie-Pier Baril
Michel Fauconnier
Dany Pelletier
Jacques Poitras
Luc Pelletier
Jean-Claude Tisseyre
Gaetan Langlois
Alain Pelletier

Saint-Martin, QC G0M

D-U-N-S 25-232-7580   (BR)
COMMISSION SCOLAIRE DE LA BEAUCE-ETCHEMIN
POLYVALENTE BELANGER
(Suby of COMMISSION SCOLAIRE DE LA BEAUCE-ETCHEMIN)
30a Ch De La Polyvalente Bureau 3033, Saint-Martin, QC, G0M 1B0
(418) 228-5541
Emp Here 85
SIC 8211 Elementary and secondary schools
Daniel Bolduc

D-U-N-S 24-941-9250   (SL)
DESIGN FRANC ART INC
(Suby of S.P.F.C. INC)
29 7e Rue O, Saint-Martin, QC, G0M 1B0
(418) 382-3122
Emp Here 100   *Sales* 32,613,600
SIC 3993 Signs and advertising specialties
Francis Carrier

D-U-N-S 20-643-6396   (HQ)
GESTION BC-A INC
ALTRUM
38 Av Du Pont O, Saint-Martin, QC, G0M 1B0
(418) 382-3930
Sales 19,857,250
SIC 3089 Plastics products, nec
Bernard Bolduc

D-U-N-S 20-581-2274   (SL)
MOBILIER RUSTIQUE (BEAUCE) INC
(Suby of J.F.S.R. INC)
50 1e Rue O, Saint-Martin, QC, G0M 1B0
(418) 382-5987
Emp Here 96   *Sales* 14,814,912
SIC 2511 Wood household furniture
Jean-Francois Rancourt
Camil Rancourt

D-U-N-S 20-052-5561   (SL)
PRODUITS MATRA INC
21 11e Rue O, Saint-Martin, QC, G0M 1B0
(418) 382-5151
Emp Here 175   *Sales* 33,664,750
SIC 2431 Millwork
Nicolas Drouin
Jean-Francois Drouin
Steeve Grondin

Saint-Mathias-Sur-Richelieu, QC J3L

D-U-N-S 20-255-4895   (SL)
BELISLE SOLUTION-NUTRITION INC
BELISLE
196 Ch Des Patriotes, Saint-Mathias-Sur-Richelieu, QC, J3L 6A7
(450) 658-8733
Emp Here 55   *Sales* 19,012,950
SIC 2048 Prepared feeds, nec
Yan Turmine

D-U-N-S 24-958-5639   (HQ)
PRODUITS FRACO LTEE, LES
FRACO
(Suby of HOLDING RAINVILLE INC)
91 Ch Des Patriotes, Saint-Mathias-Sur-Richelieu, QC, J3L 6B6
(514) 990-7750
Emp Here 60   *Sales* 19,208,500
SIC 3446 Architectural Metalwork
Emmanuelle Rainville
Armand Rainville
Marc Dufresne
Jean Jr. Gladu
Claude Courvette
Julie Rainville
Benjamin Garant
Joel Bardier

Saint-Mathieu-De-Beloeil, QC J3G

D-U-N-S 24-969-7525   (SL)
7853807 CANADA INC
TRANSPORT WATSON MONTREAL
3126 Rue Bernard-Pilon, Saint-Mathieu-De-Beloeil, QC, J3G 4S5
(450) 467-7352
Emp Here 100   *Sales* 20,570,600
SIC 4213 Trucking, except local
Michel Robert
Robert Bellisle
Dominic Picard
Claude Robert

D-U-N-S 25-106-1511   (SL)
9095-6988 QUEBEC INC
INTER-MEUBLE
3120 Rue Bernard-Pilon, Saint-Mathieu-De-Beloeil, QC, J3G 4S5
(450) 467-8181
Emp Here 40   *Sales* 10,122,360
SIC 5211 Lumber and other building materials
Rejean Drapeau

D-U-N-S 20-254-2924   (HQ)
BEAUCHESNE, EDOUARD (1985) INC
(Suby of PLACEMENTS ROBERT LEONARD LTEE, LES)
3211 Rue De L'Industrie, Saint-Mathieu-De-Beloeil, QC, J3G 4S5
(450) 467-8776
Emp Here 100   *Sales* 44,717,400
SIC 5039 Construction materials, nec
Robert Leonard

D-U-N-S 24-352-4931   (SL)
CONSULTANTS F. DRAPEAU INC
DRAPEAU
2005 Ch De L'Industrie, Saint-Mathieu-De-Beloeil, QC, J3G 0S4
(450) 467-2642
Emp Here 50   *Sales* 13,592,100
SIC 7699 Repair services, nec
Daniel Drapeau
Sylvain Drapeau
Francois Drapeau
Nathalie Drapeau
Sonya Fortiea

D-U-N-S 24-740-1003   (SL)
FINES HERBES DE CHEZ NOUS INC, LES
FINES HERBES AROMATIQUES FRAICHES
116 Ch Trudeau, Saint-Mathieu-De-Beloeil, QC, J3G 0E3
(450) 464-2969
Emp Here 50   *Sales* 13,707,600
SIC 5431 Fruit and vegetable markets
Gerard Trudeau
Francoise St-Onge
Vincent Trudeau

D-U-N-S 24-326-6947   (SL)
KEYSTONE AUTOMOTIVE INDUSTRIES ON INC
KEYSTONE AUTOMOTIVE INDUSTRIES
2095 Rue De L'Industrie, Saint-Mathieu-De-Beloeil, QC, J3G 4S5
(450) 464-2511
Emp Here 60   *Sales* 21,852,900
SIC 5013 Motor vehicle supplies and new parts
Matthew J. Mckay
Robert Wagman
Dominick Zarcone

D-U-N-S 24-418-5521   (SL)
SIMPORT SCIENTIFIQUE INC
(Suby of 3088081 CANADA INC)
2588 Rue Bernard-Pilon Bureau 1, Saint-Mathieu-De-Beloeil, QC, J3G 4S5
(450) 464-1723
Emp Here 50   *Sales* 10,094,850
SIC 3089 Plastics products, nec
Andre Lafond

Huguette Lafond

D-U-N-S 24-989-0138   (SL)
SUNRISE TRADEX CORPORATION
IMPORTATIONS SUNRISE TRADEX, LES
3122 Rue Bernard-Pilon, Saint-Mathieu-De-Beloeil, QC, J3G 4S5
(450) 536-2175
Emp Here 27   *Sales* 12,073,698
SIC 5075 Warm air heating and air conditioning
Shirley Chang
Paul Gemme

D-U-N-S 20-117-4062   (SL)
VR ST-CYR INC
CAMPING MART
3465 Ch De L'Industrie, Saint-Mathieu-De-Beloeil, QC, J3G 0R9
(450) 446-3660
Emp Here 50   *Sales* 24,903,900
SIC 5571 Motorcycle dealers
Pierre St-Cyr
Valerie St-Cyr
Dominic St-Cyr

Saint-Mathieu-De-Laprairie, QC J0L

D-U-N-S 24-314-8926   (SL)
CAMIONS MASKA INC
KENWORTH MASKA
690 Mont?E Monette, Saint-Mathieu-De-Laprairie, QC, J0L 2H0
(450) 444-5600
Emp Here 49   *Sales* 17,846,535
SIC 5012 Automobiles and other motor vehicles
Pierre Letendre

D-U-N-S 20-276-2543   (SL)
SIGNALISATION SIGNA PRO INC
700 Montee Monette, Saint-Mathieu-De-Laprairie, QC, J0L 2H0
(450) 444-0006
Emp Here 70   *Sales* 31,302,180
SIC 5063 Electrical apparatus and equipment
Sylvain Gauthier

D-U-N-S 20-308-8653   (SL)
SIGNEL SERVICES INC
700 Montee Monette, Saint-Mathieu-De-Laprairie, QC, J0L 2H0
(450) 444-0006
Emp Here 90   *Sales* 29,352,240
SIC 3993 Signs and advertising specialties
Sylvian Gauthier
Martine Dionne

Saint-Michel, QC J0L

D-U-N-S 24-510-1613   (SL)
CLOVIS ISABELLE ET FILS INC.
2420 Rue Principale, Saint-Michel, QC, J0L 2J0
(450) 454-7200
Emp Here 46   *Sales* 12,066,214
SIC 0161 Vegetables and melons
Clovis Isabelle
Roger Isabelle
Michel Isabelle
Mario Isabelle
Daniel Isabelle
Louise Isabelle

D-U-N-S 24-739-4414   (HQ)
FERTI TECHNOLOGIES INC
ENVIROSOL
560 Ch Rheaume, Saint-Michel, QC, J0L 2J0
(450) 454-5367
Emp Here 10   *Sales* 13,833,000
SIC 2874 Phosphatic fertilizers

Marc Vaillancourt
Daniel Dancause
Hugo Provencher
Claudie Vaillancourt

D-U-N-S 24-110-5600   (SL)
MARAICHER A. BARBEAU & FILS INC, LE
2430 Rue Principale, Saint-Michel, QC, J0L
2J0
(450) 454-2555
Emp Here 60   *Sales* 15,738,540
SIC 0182 Food crops grown under cover
Andre Barbeau
Jean-Pierre Barbeau
Francine Barbeau
Emile Monchamp

D-U-N-S 24-525-2593   (HQ)
REMORQUAGE ST-MICHEL INC
GROUPE TRANSPORT ST-MICHEL
340 Ch Pigeon, Saint-Michel, QC, J0L 2J0
(450) 454-9973
Emp Here 128   *Sales* 58,525,610
SIC 7549 Automotive services, nec
Sylvain Oligny

Saint-Michel-Des-Saints, QC J0K

D-U-N-S 20-015-2358   (SL)
ALIMENTATION D.M. ST-GEORGES INC
PROVIGO
110 Rue Brassard, Saint-Michel-Des-Saints,
QC, J0K 3B0
(450) 833-1313
Emp Here 40   *Sales* 10,966,080
SIC 5411 Grocery stores
Danielle St-Georges

Saint-Modeste, QC G0L

D-U-N-S 24-500-2043   (HQ)
TOURBIERES BERGER LTEE, LES
121 1er Rang, Saint-Modeste, QC, G0L 3W0
(418) 862-4462
Emp Here 130   *Sales* 512,841,560
SIC 5159 Farm-product raw materials, nec
Marc Bourgoin
Melissa Berger
Valerie Berger
Diane Marchand
Caroline Mailloux
Alain Pelletier
Marie Belanger Joseeb
Claudin Berger
Regis Berger
Rejean Dancause

Saint-Narcisse, QC G0X

D-U-N-S 20-696-8997   (SL)
9132-8997 QUEBEC INC
LOCUSI
700 Rue Notre-Dame, Saint-Narcisse, QC,
G0X 2Y0
(418) 328-3200
Emp Here 38   *Sales* 12,117,022
SIC 1521 Single-family housing construction
Rejean Kean
Stephanie Lemay

D-U-N-S 24-434-6854   (SL)
GESTION CENTURION INC
(*Suby of* TEMPUR SEALY INTERNATIONAL,
INC.)
555 Rue Panneton, Saint-Narcisse, QC, G0X
2Y0
(418) 328-3361
Emp Here 115   *Sales* 17,747,030

SIC 2515 Mattresses and bedsprings
Lawrence Rogers

Saint-Narcisse-De-Beaurivage, QC G0S

D-U-N-S 20-237-9848   (HQ)
**SOCIETE COOPERATIVE AGRICOLE LA
SEIGNEURIE**
404 Rue Saint-Francois, Saint-Narcisse-De-
Beaurivage, QC, G0S 1W0
(418) 475-6645
Emp Here 88   *Sales* 38,025,900
SIC 2041 Flour and other grain mill products
Frederic Martineau

Saint-Nicolas, QC G7A

D-U-N-S 24-205-2744   (SL)
BONNES GATERIES 2007 INC
PATISSERIE L'ARC-EN-CIEL
710 Rte Lagueux, Saint-Nicolas, QC, G7A
1A7
(418) 831-4948
Emp Here 20   *Sales* 10,702,480
SIC 5149 Groceries and related products, nec
Mario Cloutier

D-U-N-S 25-233-6920   (BR)
**COMMISSION SCOLAIRE DES NAVIGA-
TEURS**
ECOLE SECONDAIRE DE L'ENVOL
(*Suby of* COMMISSION SCOLAIRE DES
NAVIGATEURS)
368 Rte Du Pont, Saint-Nicolas, QC, G7A 2V3
(418) 834-2461
Emp Here 75
SIC 8211 Elementary and secondary schools
Lyne Martel

D-U-N-S 20-716-1212   (BR)
RESTAURANT NORMANDIN (2014) INC
(*Suby of* GROUPE NORMANDIN INC)
530 Rte Du Pont, Saint-Nicolas, QC, G7A 2N9
(418) 831-1991
Emp Here 80
SIC 5812 Eating places

Saint-Norbert, QC J0K

D-U-N-S 20-255-8599   (SL)
**AUTOMOBILES LAPORTE, REJEAN & FILS
LTEE**
1881 Rue Principale, Saint-Norbert, QC, J0K
3C0
(450) 836-3783
Emp Here 24   *Sales* 11,953,872
SIC 5511 New and used car dealers
Martin Laporte
Dominique Laporte
Simon Laporte

D-U-N-S 20-700-6201   (SL)
ENTREPRISES DAVID LAUZON, LES
1680 Rue Principale Rr 5, Saint-Norbert, QC,
J0K 3C0
(819) 427-5144
Emp Here 200   *Sales* 38,474,000
SIC 2426 Hardwood dimension and flooring
mills
David Lauzon

D-U-N-S 24-352-2500   (BR)
**LAUZON - PLANCHERS DE BOIS EX-
CLUSIFS INC**
(*Suby of* PLACEMENTS LAUZON INC)
1680 Rue Principale Rr 5, Saint-Norbert, QC,
J0K 3C0
(450) 836-4405
Emp Here 100

SIC 2426 Hardwood dimension and flooring
mills
Michelle Fouli

Saint-Odilon, QC G0S

D-U-N-S 24-820-2269   (SL)
STRUCTURES DE BEAUCE INC, LES
305 Rue Du Parc Rr 1, Saint-Odilon, QC, G0S
3A0
(418) 464-2000
Emp Here 50   *Sales* 12,309,300
SIC 1791 Structural steel erection
Benoit Drouin

Saint-Omer, QC G0C

D-U-N-S 24-783-4281   (SL)
**CONSTRUCTION ENERGIE RENOUVE-
LABLE S.E.N.C.**
C.E.R.
178 132 Rte E, Saint-Omer, QC, G0C 2Z0
(418) 364-6027
Emp Here 300   *Sales* 84,874,500
SIC 3621 Motors and generators
Claude Lapointe

D-U-N-S 24-149-8708   (SL)
CONSTRUCTION L.F.G. INC
178 Rte 132 E, Saint-Omer, QC, G0C 2Z0
(418) 364-7082
Emp Here 100   *Sales* 42,273,700
SIC 1541 Industrial buildings and warehouses
Claude Lapointe
Harold Berube

Saint-Ours, QC J0G

D-U-N-S 24-970-5500   (BR)
CANADA PIPE COMPANY ULC
FONDERIE LAPERLE, DIV DE
(*Suby of* MCWANE (GIBRALTAR) LIMITED
LUXEMBOURG SCS)
106 Montee Basse, Saint-Ours, QC, J0G 1P0
(450) 785-2205
Emp Here 100
SIC 3322 Malleable iron foundries
Mathieu Frechette

D-U-N-S 24-743-3691   (SL)
FERME ST-OURS INC
8 Rue Bourgeois, Saint-Ours, QC, J0G 1P0
(450) 785-2148
Emp Here 40   *Sales* 33,423,080
SIC 5144 Poultry and poultry products
Serge Lefebvre
Martine Bourgeois
Chantal Bourgeois

Saint-Pacome, QC G0L

D-U-N-S 20-255-9662   (SL)
ROLAND & FRERES LIMITEE
*ACADEMIE CULINAIRE ROLAND & FR-
ERES*
(*Suby of* BEAUDRY & CADRIN INC)
22 Rue Fortier, Saint-Pacome, QC, G0L 3X0
(418) 852-2191
Emp Here 30   *Sales* 25,067,310
SIC 5141 Groceries, general line
Francois Beaudry
Jean-Philippe Beaudry

Saint-Pamphile, QC G0R

D-U-N-S 20-578-6445   (BR)
MAIBEC INC
(*Suby of* MAIBEC INC)
24 6e Rang Bureau 6, Saint-Pamphile, QC,
G0R 3X0
(418) 356-3331
Emp Here 800
SIC 2421 Sawmills and planing mills, general
Andre Pilon

D-U-N-S 24-377-9576   (BR)
MATERIAUX BLANCHET INC
(*Suby of* MATERIAUX BLANCHET INC)
1030 Rte Elgin S, Saint-Pamphile, QC, G0R
3X0
(418) 356-3344
Emp Here 260
SIC 2421 Sawmills and planing mills, general
Emmanuel Forget

D-U-N-S 20-643-8830   (SL)
TRANSBOIS (CANADA) LTEE
631 Rue Principale N, Saint-Pamphile, QC,
G0R 3X0
(418) 356-3371
Emp Here 70   *Sales* 10,373,440
SIC 4212 Local trucking, without storage
Laurent Jalbert

Saint-Pascal, QC G0L

D-U-N-S 20-580-3455   (SL)
9190-4144 QUEBEC INC.
IGA SAINT-PASCAL & IGA
400 Av Chapleau, Saint-Pascal, QC, G0L 3Y0
(418) 492-2902
Emp Here 50   *Sales* 13,707,600
SIC 5411 Grocery stores
Andre Tanguay

D-U-N-S 20-256-0652   (SL)
AUTOMOBILE KAMOURASKA (1992) INC
*OLIVIER   KAMOURASKA   CHRYSLER
DODGE JEEP RAM*
255 Av Patry, Saint-Pascal, QC, G0L 3Y0
(418) 492-3432
Emp Here 30   *Sales* 18,224,899
SIC 5511 New and used car dealers
Jacques Jr Olivier
Daniel Fox

D-U-N-S 25-232-7770   (BR)
**COMMISSION   SCOLAIRE   DE
KAMOURASKA RIVIERE-DU-LOUP**
*ECOLE   SECONDAIRE   CHANOINE
BEAUDET*
525 Av De L'Eglise, Saint-Pascal, QC, G0L
3Y0
(418) 856-7030
Emp Here 75
SIC 8211 Elementary and secondary schools

D-U-N-S 20-256-0520   (SL)
COMPAGNIE NORMAND LTEE, LA
340 Rue Tache, Saint-Pascal, QC, G0L 3Y0
(418) 492-2712
Emp Here 80   *Sales* 17,760,080
SIC 3524 Lawn and garden equipment
Alain Normand
Marc Normand
Louis Normand

D-U-N-S 24-144-5931   (SL)
MARCEL CHAREST ET FILS INC
997 Rte 230 E, Saint-Pascal, QC, G0L 3Y0
(418) 492-5911
Emp Here 25   *Sales* 11,768,275
SIC 1542 Nonresidential construction, nec
Guy Charest
Marc Charest
Rachel Dumais

▲ Public Company   ■ Public Company Family Member   **HQ** Headquarters   **BR** Branch   **SL** Single Location

D-U-N-S 24-395-1394   (SL)
PETERBILT QUEBEC EAST LTD
195 Av Du Parc, Saint-Pascal, QC, G0L 3Y0
(418) 492-7383
Emp Here 30   *Sales* 14,942,340
SIC 5511 New and used car dealers
Tim Hawkins
Richard Hawkins

Saint-Paul, QC J0K

D-U-N-S 24-849-6148   (SL)
DE CHAMPLAIN DESIGN INC
812 Boul De L'Industrie, Saint-Paul, QC, J0K 3E0
(450) 760-2098
Emp Here 26   *Sales* 12,956,372
SIC 5136 Men's and boy's clothing
Michel Sansregret

D-U-N-S 20-255-2311   (HQ)
GROUPE PATRICK MORIN INC
PATRICK MORIN
620 Boul De L'Industrie, Saint-Paul, QC, J0K 3E0
(450) 752-4774
Emp Here 70   *Sales* 569,628,000
SIC 5039 Construction materials, nec
Denis Morin
Benoit Morin
Michel Morin
Francois Morin
Andre Morin
Colette Morin
Madeleine Morin

Saint-Paul, QC J6E

D-U-N-S 20-885-9066   (SL)
MALO TRANSPORT (1971) INC
23 Ch Saint-Jacques, Saint-Paul, QC, J6E 3H2
(450) 756-8008
Emp Here 75   *Sales* 15,427,950
SIC 4213 Trucking, except local
Alain Chalut

D-U-N-S 24-547-4697   (SL)
VIANDES PERREAULT PELLERIN INC
11 Rue Du Cure-Valois, Saint-Paul, QC, J6E 7L8
(450) 759-8023
Emp Here 20   *Sales* 10,702,480
SIC 5147 Meats and meat products
Serge Perreault
Mario Pellerin

Saint-Paul-D'Abbotsford, QC J0E

D-U-N-S 25-389-6344   (HQ)
CAN-BEC IMMOBILIER INC
1260 Rue Principale E, Saint-Paul-D'Abbotsford, QC, J0E 1A0
(450) 379-2088
Emp Here 30   *Sales* 12,682,110
SIC 1541 Industrial buildings and warehouses
Jacques Viens

D-U-N-S 20-859-4085   (SL)
INDUSTRIES N.R.C. INC
2430 Rue Principale E Bureau 160, Saint-Paul-D'Abbotsford, QC, J0E 1A0
(450) 379-5796
Emp Here 100   *Sales* 22,384,300
SIC 3799 Transportation equipment, nec
Norbert Pigeon
Sylvain Pigeon
Stephane Pigeon

Colette Menard Pigeon

D-U-N-S 20-288-4359   (SL)
PEPINIERE ABBOTSFORD INC
PRO GAZON
605 Rue Principale E Bureau 112, Saint-Paul-D'Abbotsford, QC, J0E 1A0
(450) 379-5777
Emp Here 100   *Sales* 26,230,900
SIC 0181 Ornamental nursery products
Pierre Paquette

D-U-N-S 20-187-6927   (HQ)
PNEUS ROBERT BERNARD LTEE, LES
POINT S ROBERT BERNARD
765 Rue Principale E, Saint-Paul-D'Abbotsford, QC, J0E 1A0
(450) 379-5757
Emp Here 30   *Sales* 18,210,750
SIC 5014 Tires and tubes
Gerard Bernard
Jocelyn Bernard

D-U-N-S 24-066-1848   (SL)
VERGER DU PERE DE LA FRAISE, LE
1740 Rue Principale E, Saint-Paul-D'Abbotsford, QC, J0E 1A0
(450) 379-5271
Emp Here 20   *Sales* 16,711,540
SIC 5148 Fresh fruits and vegetables
Micheline Rodrigue

Saint-Paulin, QC J0K

D-U-N-S 24-841-8964   (SL)
CONCEPT ECO-PLEIN AIR LE BALUCHON INC
AUBERGE LE BALUCHON, GASTRONOMIE.SPA.PLEIN ET CULTURE
3550 Ch Des Trembles Rr 3, Saint-Paulin, QC, J0K 3G0
(819) 268-2695
Emp Here 200   *Sales* 9,103,800
SIC 5812 Eating places
Normand Tamaro

D-U-N-S 25-160-9454   (SL)
SAUVETAGE L'ARANEA INC
2351 Rang Renversy, Saint-Paulin, QC, J0K 3G0
(819) 268-3369
Emp Here 26   *Sales* 11,039,782
SIC 8999 Services, nec
Andre Leblanc

Saint-Philibert, QC G0M

D-U-N-S 24-377-4635   (SL)
PIECES D'AUTOS FERNAND BEGIN INC
416 Rang F.-Begin, Saint-Philibert, QC, G0M 1X0
(418) 228-2413
Emp Here 35   *Sales* 17,432,730
SIC 5531 Auto and home supply stores
Beatrice Poulin
Denis Begin
France Begin
Marc Begin

Saint-Philippe-De-Neri, QC G0L

D-U-N-S 25-673-9939   (SL)
2730-8303 QUEBEC INC
BOIS-FRANCS
239 Rte 230 O, Saint-Philippe-De-Neri, QC, G0L 4A0
(418) 498-2100
Emp Here 40   *Sales* 17,886,960
SIC 5031 Lumber, plywood, and millwork

Collin Roussel
Jerome Roussel
Frederic Roussel

Saint-Pie, QC J0H

D-U-N-S 20-256-4332   (SL)
GRISE, OLIER & CIE LTEE
1 Rue Martin, Saint-Pie, QC, J0H 1W0
(450) 772-2445
Emp Here 31   *Sales* 23,018,120
SIC 5191 Farm supplies
Nathalie Grise
Stephane Grise

D-U-N-S 20-886-2979   (HQ)
GROUPE DUTAILIER INC
AVANTGLIDE
(*Suby of* 2694212 CANADA INC)
299 Rue Chaput, Saint-Pie, QC, J0H 1W0
(450) 772-2403
Emp Here 150   *Sales* 27,777,960
SIC 2512 Upholstered household furniture
Fernand Fontaine

D-U-N-S 25-977-8827   (HQ)
GROUPE LACASSE INC
99 Rue Saint-Pierre, Saint-Pie, QC, J0H 1W0
(450) 772-2495
Sales 55,666,250
SIC 2521 Wood office furniture
Sylvian Garneau

D-U-N-S 20-267-2879   (HQ)
GROUPE M.G.B. INC
M.G.B. ELECTRIQUE
51 Rue Saint-Pierre, Saint-Pie, QC, J0H 1W0
(450) 772-5608
Sales 20,967,750
SIC 6712 Bank holding companies
Pierre-Alexandre Brodeur
Jean-Francois Brodeur

Saint-Pierre-De-Lamy, QC G0L

D-U-N-S 24-146-8156   (SL)
PRODUITS PBM LTEE, LES
SYSTEMES P.B.M.
130 Rue Du Moulin, Saint-Pierre-De-Lamy, QC, G0L 4B0
(418) 497-3927
Emp Here 65   *Sales* 10,131,095
SIC 2439 Structural wood members, nec
Frederic Ouellet
Jean-Francois Cusson
Gilles Jean

Saint-Pierre-Les-Becquets, QC G0X

D-U-N-S 20-027-6033   (BR)
COMMISSION SCOLAIRE DE LA RIVERAINE
?COLE SECONDAIRE LES SEIGNEURIES
(*Suby of* COMMISSION SCOLAIRE DE LA RIVERAINE)
165 218 Rte, Saint-Pierre-Les-Becquets, QC, G0X 2Z0
(819) 263-2323
Emp Here 80
SIC 8211 Elementary and secondary schools
Johanne Croteau

Saint-Placide, QC J0V

D-U-N-S 20-223-3503   (HQ)

CONTENANTS I.M.L. D'AMERIQUE DU NORD INC, LES
CONTENANTS IML CANADA
2625 344 Rte, Saint-Placide, QC, J0V 2B0
(450) 258-3130
Sales 31,771,600
SIC 3089 Plastics products, nec
Jean-Pierre Lacroix
Nicolas Bouveret
Christine Bouveret

Saint-Polycarpe, QC J0P

D-U-N-S 20-317-7126   (HQ)
ROCH GAUTHIER ET FILS INC
68 Rue Sainte-Catherine, Saint-Polycarpe, QC, J0P 1X0
(450) 265-3256
Emp Here 1   *Sales* 26,765,200
SIC 5251 Hardware stores
Sylvain Gauthier
Bernard Gauthier

Saint-Prime, QC G8J

D-U-N-S 24-843-3682   (HQ)
ALBERT PERRON INC
FROMAGERIE PERRON
(*Suby of* NUTRINOR COOPERATIVE)
156 Av Albert-Perron, Saint-Prime, QC, G8J 1L4
(418) 251-3164
Emp Here 10   *Sales* 41,778,850
SIC 5143 Dairy products, except dried or canned
Yves Girard
Paul Pomerleau
Daniel Asselin
Daniel Dufresne
Larry Karass
Marc Landry

D-U-N-S 20-643-9960   (SL)
BOUCHERIE CHARCUTERIE PERRON INC
145 Av Albert-Perron, Saint-Prime, QC, G8J 1L3
(418) 251-3131
Emp Here 25   *Sales* 20,889,425
SIC 5147 Meats and meat products
Denis Perron

Saint-Prosper-De-Dorchester, QC G0M

D-U-N-S 25-232-7903   (BR)
COMMISSION SCOLAIRE DE LA BEAUCE-ETCHEMIN
ECOLE POLYVALENTE DES ABENAQUIS
(*Suby of* COMMISSION SCOLAIRE DE LA BEAUCE-ETCHEMIN)
2105 25e Av, Saint-Prosper-De-Dorchester, QC, G0M 1Y0
(418) 594-8231
Emp Here 90
SIC 8211 Elementary and secondary schools
Michel Gagnon

D-U-N-S 20-581-0864   (SL)
EPICERIE R. BUTEAU INC
INTER-MARCHE ST-PROSPER
2650 25e Av, Saint-Prosper-De-Dorchester, QC, G0M 1Y0
(418) 594-8244
Emp Here 40   *Sales* 10,966,080
SIC 5411 Grocery stores
Richard Buteau
Pierrot Buteau

D-U-N-S 25-741-0845   (SL)

SPECIALISTE DU BARDEAU DE CEDRE INC, LE
SBC
754 8e Rue, Saint-Prosper-De-Dorchester, QC, G0M 1Y0
(418) 594-6201
Emp Here 85   *Sales* 16,351,450
SIC 2429 Special product sawmills, nec
Rita Rancourt
Marco Belanger
Francis Belanger
Michel Belanger

Saint-Raphael, QC G0R

D-U-N-S 20-029-2196   (SL)
GESTION P. A. T. INC
MARCHE ST RAPHAEL
371 Boul St-Pierre, Saint-Raphael, QC, G0R 4C0
(418) 243-2022
Emp Here 30   *Sales* 25,067,310
SIC 5149 Groceries and related products, nec
Francois Aubry

Saint-Raymond, QC G3L

D-U-N-S 24-820-4984   (SL)
ALIMENTATION ST-RAYMOND INC
METRO ST-RAYMOND
333 Cote Joyeuse Bureau 100, Saint-Raymond, QC, G3L 4A8
(418) 337-6781
Emp Here 65   *Sales* 19,076,005
SIC 5411 Grocery stores
Charles Buteau

D-U-N-S 24-324-3545   (BR)
CENTRE DE SANTE ET DE SERVICES SOCIAUX DE PORTNEUF
HOPITAL REGIONAL DE PORTNEUF
(*Suby of* CENTRE DE SANTE ET DE SERVICES SOCIAUX DE PORTNEUF)
700 Rue Saint-Cyrille Bureau 850, Saint-Raymond, QC, G3L 1W1
(418) 337-4611
Emp Here 350
SIC 8062 General medical and surgical hospitals
Denis Bouchard

D-U-N-S 25-233-0600   (BR)
COMMISSION SCOLAIRE DE PORTNEUF
ECOLE SECONDAIRE LOUIS JOBIN
400 Boul Cloutier, Saint-Raymond, QC, G3L 3M8
(418) 337-6721
Emp Here 90
SIC 8211 Elementary and secondary schools
Ninon Brilliere

D-U-N-S 20-778-4844   (SL)
DION MOTO INC
840 Cote Joyeuse, Saint-Raymond, QC, G3L 4B3
(418) 337-2776
Emp Here 26   *Sales* 12,950,028
SIC 5571 Motorcycle dealers
Pierre Gagnon
Fabrice Marien

D-U-N-S 24-149-2560   (SL)
ENTREPRISES CLOUTIER, ALBERT LTEE, LES
GANTERIE CLOUTIER
149 Rue Albert-Edouard, Saint-Raymond, QC, G3L 2C5
(418) 337-2766
Emp Here 75   *Sales* 19,242,150
SIC 3842 Surgical appliances and supplies
Marc Cloutier

Jacques-Yves Cloutier

D-U-N-S 20-643-7816   (SL)
FUTUROTO INC
SAINT-RAYMOND TOYOTA
279 Av Saint-Jacques, Saint-Raymond, QC, G3L 4A2
(418) 337-6745
Emp Here 50   *Sales* 24,903,900
SIC 5511 New and used car dealers
Claude Plamondon
Jacques Jobin

D-U-N-S 24-203-3611   (SL)
GESTOFOR INC
592 Rue Guyon, Saint-Raymond, QC, G3L 0A5
(418) 337-4621
Emp Here 125
SIC 2421 Sawmills and planing mills, general
Gerald Jacques

D-U-N-S 24-908-6133   (HQ)
GROUPE LEGARE LTEE
PRODUITS FORESTIERS LEGARGE
488 Rue Saint-Pierre, Saint-Raymond, QC, G3L 1R5
(418) 337-2286
Emp Here 2   *Sales* 16,401,000
SIC 6712 Bank holding companies
Isabelle Legare

D-U-N-S 20-171-7530   (HQ)
LOCATION SAUVAGEAU INC
CENTRE DE CARROSSERIE SAUVAGEAU
521 Cote Joyeuse Bureau 1, Saint-Raymond, QC, G3L 4A9
(418) 692-1315
Emp Here 70   *Sales* 22,664,000
SIC 7514 Passenger car rental
Jacquelin Voyer

D-U-N-S 20-182-3874   (HQ)
PLACAGES ST-RAYMOND INC
PRODUITS FORESTIERS ST-RAYMOND, LES
(*Suby of* THE PENROD COMPANY)
595 Rue Guyon, Saint-Raymond, QC, G3L 1Z1
(418) 337-4607
Emp Here 1   *Sales* 28,855,500
SIC 2435 Hardwood veneer and plywood
Timothy G. Heidt
Eric Robichaud
Carl Gade
Edward A. Jr. Heidt

D-U-N-S 20-715-7806   (BR)
SAPUTO PRODUITS LAITIERS CANADA S.E.N.C.
LA FROMAGERIE ALEXIS DE PORTNEUF
(*Suby of* SAPUTO PRODUITS LAITIERS CANADA S.E.N.C.)
71 Av Saint-Jacques, Saint-Raymond, QC, G3L 3X9
(418) 337-4287
Emp Here 80
SIC 2022 Cheese; natural and processed
Diane Marcoux

D-U-N-S 20-256-8184   (SL)
VOYER & JOBIN LTEE
PROVIGO
268 Rue Saint-Joseph, Saint-Raymond, QC, G3L 1J3
(418) 337-2278
Emp Here 60   *Sales* 17,608,620
SIC 5411 Grocery stores
Marcel P. E. Plamondon

Saint-Remi, QC J0L

D-U-N-S 25-201-6506   (SL)
3088-7061 QUEBEC INC
104 Boul Saint-Remi, Saint-Remi, QC, J0L

2L0
(450) 454-5171
Emp Here 50   *Sales* 20,967,750
SIC 6712 Bank holding companies
Emmanuel Chenail
Marie-Josee Chenail

D-U-N-S 20-881-8328   (SL)
D.D. DISTRIBUTION LUBRIFIANTS INC
69 Boul Saint-Remi, Saint-Remi, QC, J0L 2L0
(450) 454-3978
Emp Here 15   *Sales* 15,492,120
SIC 5172 Petroleum products, nec
Denis Doyon

D-U-N-S 24-527-7892   (HQ)
DUBOIS AGRINOVATION INC
478 Rang Notre-Dame, Saint-Remi, QC, J0L 2L0
(450) 454-4641
Sales 18,988,970
SIC 5162 Plastics materials and basic shapes
Ginette Guinois

D-U-N-S 20-380-7540   (BR)
EUROVIA QUEBEC CONSTRUCTION INC
(*Suby of* VINCI)
104 Boul Saint-Remi, Saint-Remi, QC, J0L 2L0
(450) 454-0000
Emp Here 200
SIC 1611 Highway and street construction

D-U-N-S 24-056-9632   (SL)
FERMES PIGEON, ROLAND & FILS INC, LES
1495 Rang Notre-Dame, Saint-Remi, QC, J0L 2L0
(450) 454-3433
Emp Here 50   *Sales* 17,123,350
SIC 0161 Vegetables and melons
Gilbert Pigeon
Normand Pigeon
Brigitte Pigeon

D-U-N-S 25-857-1454   (BR)
GOUVERNEMENT DE LA PROVINCE DE QUEBEC
CHSLD TREFLE D'OR, LES CENTRE D'HEBERGEMENT DE ST REMI
(*Suby of* GOUVERNEMENT DE LA PROVINCE DE QUEBEC)
110 Rue Du College, Saint-Remi, QC, J0L 2L0
(450) 454-4694
Emp Here 110
SIC 8322 Individual and family services
Sylvie Gregoire

D-U-N-S 25-411-1537   (HQ)
GROUPE ABS INC
BETON OPTIMAL
17 Rue De L'Industrie, Saint-Remi, QC, J0L 2L0
(450) 454-5644
Sales 17,873,900
SIC 8711 Engineering services
Daniel Mercier
Yan Menard
Isabelle Tourigny
Daniel Pelneault

D-U-N-S 20-256-8572   (SL)
LECUYER & FILS LTEE
(*Suby of* 90477 CANADA LTEE)
17 Rue Du Moulin, Saint-Remi, QC, J0L 2L0
(514) 861-5623
Emp Here 100   *Sales* 17,921,900
SIC 3272 Concrete products, nec
Maurice Lecuyer
Marcelle Lecuyer

D-U-N-S 20-709-7072   (SL)
LEGUMIERE Y.C. INC, LA
1463 Rang Sainte-Therese, Saint-Remi, QC, J0L 2L0
(450) 454-9437
Emp Here 75   *Sales* 19,673,175
SIC 0161 Vegetables and melons

Yvon Constantineau
Luc Constantineau
Suzanne Constantineau

D-U-N-S 20-323-5564   (SL)
LESTAGE & FILS LTEE
LESTAGE ST-REMI
699 Rue Notre-Dame, Saint-Remi, QC, J0L 2L0
(450) 454-7591
Emp Here 26   *Sales* 12,950,028
SIC 5511 New and used car dealers
Serge Lestage

D-U-N-S 20-370-8805   (HQ)
PAPETERIE ST-REMI INC
BURO & CIE
725 Rue Notre-Dame, Saint-Remi, QC, J0L 2L0
(450) 454-6065
Emp Here 10   *Sales* 13,095,108
SIC 5112 Stationery and office supplies
Daniel Moniere
Eric Maille
Isabelle Aucoin
Jean-Luc Isabelle

D-U-N-S 20-566-4261   (SL)
POTAGER RIENDEAU INC, LE
1729 Rang Saint-Antoine, Saint-Remi, QC, J0L 2L0
(450) 454-9091
Emp Here 100   *Sales* 26,230,900
SIC 0161 Vegetables and melons
Clermont Riendeau
Sylvain Riendeau
Pascal Riendeau
Patrice Riendeau

D-U-N-S 24-799-5996   (SL)
SALADEXPRESS INC
NUTRIPLUS
225 Rue Saint-Andre, Saint-Remi, QC, J0L 2L0
(514) 385-3362
Emp Here 170   *Sales* 29,563,850
SIC 0723 Crop preparation services for market
Marc Portelance
Sebastien Ghantous
Michel Coulombe
Francois Gagner
Daniel Gilbert

D-U-N-S 24-569-7016   (SL)
SERRES RIEL INC, LES
1851 Rang Notre-Dame, Saint-Remi, QC, J0L 2L0
(450) 454-9425
Emp Here 26   *Sales* 19,305,520
SIC 5193 Flowers and florists supplies
Claude Riel
Marie-Andree Riel
Monique Lauzon

D-U-N-S 20-256-8861   (SL)
STE-MARIE AUTOMOBILES LTEE
540 Rang Notre-Dame, Saint-Remi, QC, J0L 2L0
(514) 861-5529
Emp Here 86   *Sales* 54,118,080
SIC 5511 New and used car dealers
Alain Ste-Marie
Guylaine Ste-Marie

D-U-N-S 25-866-6718   (SL)
TRANSPORT M. J. LAVOIE INC
800 Rue Notre-Dame, Saint-Remi, QC, J0L 2L0
(450) 454-5333
Emp Here 35   *Sales* 10,539,970
SIC 4953 Refuse systems
Michel Lavoie
Jean Lavoie

▲ Public Company   ■ Public Company Family Member   **HQ** Headquarters   **BR** Branch   **SL** Single Location

Saint-Robert, QC J0G

D-U-N-S 25-377-4178 (SL)
FROMAGERIE POLYETHNIQUE INC, LA
235 Ch De Saint-Robert, Saint-Robert, QC,
J0G 1S0
(450) 782-2111
Emp Here 50 *Sales* 13,707,600
SIC 5451 Dairy products stores
Jean-Pierre Salvas
Elie Cheaib
Jamil Cheaib

Saint-Roch-De-L'Achigan, QC J0K

D-U-N-S 24-356-1347 (SL)
CEREALEX INC
666 Rang Du Ruisseau-Des-Anges S, Saint-
Roch-De-L'Achigan, QC, J0K 3H0
(450) 588-3132
Emp Here 11 *Sales* 13,314,367
SIC 5153 Grain and field beans
Sylvain Chayer
Lucien Chayer

D-U-N-S 24-187-7138 (BR)
COMMISSION SCOLAIRE DES SAMARES
ECOLES SECONDAIRES ACHIGAN
(*Suby of* COMMISSION SCOLAIRE DES
SAMARES)
60 Montee Remi-Henri, Saint-Roch-De-
L'Achigan, QC, J0K 3H0
(450) 588-7410
Emp Here 130
SIC 8211 Elementary and secondary schools
Robert Jacob

D-U-N-S 25-006-4909 (SL)
FERMES J.-F. & C. GAGNON INC., LES
804 Rang Du Ruisseau-Des-Anges S, Saint-
Roch-De-L'Achigan, QC, J0K 3H0
(450) 588-2226
Emp Here 40 *Sales* 13,698,680
SIC 0161 Vegetables and melons
Jean-Francois Gagnon

D-U-N-S 20-256-9737 (HQ)
MEUBLES JCPERREAULT INC
JC PERREAULT
5 Rue Industrielle, Saint-Roch-De-L'Achigan,
QC, J0K 3H0
(450) 588-7211
Emp Here 165 *Sales* 106,333,543
SIC 5712 Furniture stores
Jean-Claude Perreault
Stephane Perreault

Saint-Romuald, QC G6W

D-U-N-S 20-955-3937 (SL)
VAPERMA INC
2111 4e Rue Bureau 101, Saint-Romuald, QC,
G6W 5M6

Emp Here 65 *Sales* 20,780,825
SIC 1389 Oil and gas field services, nec
Claude Letourneau
Christian Roy

Saint-Rosaire, QC G0Z

D-U-N-S 20-331-8274 (HQ)
TIGES QUATRE SAISONS (2009) INC, LES
192 6e Rang, Saint-Rosaire, QC, G0Z 1K0
(819) 758-1155
Sales 22,358,700
SIC 5051 Metals service centers and offices
Nancy Bergeron

Mark Bergeron
Patrick Crochetiere

Saint-Sauveur, QC J0R

D-U-N-S 20-252-9954 (HQ)
BEAULIEU, CLAUDE SPORT INC
SPORT EXPERT
75 Av De La Gare Bureau E1, Saint-Sauveur,
QC, J0R 1R6
(450) 227-8632
Emp Here 30 *Sales* 45,884,250
SIC 5941 Sporting goods and bicycle shops
Sylvain Rochon

D-U-N-S 20-050-6025 (HQ)
**BOULANGERIE LES MOULINS LA
FAYETTE INC**
BOULANGERIE LES MOULINS LA FAYETTE
7 Av De L'Eglise, Saint-Sauveur, QC, J0R 1R0
(450) 227-2632
Emp Here 13 *Sales* 17,630,190
SIC 2051 Bread, cake, and related products
Johnny Jeulin

D-U-N-S 25-541-4856 (SL)
BOURASSA, S. (ST-SAUVEUR) LTEE
105b Av Guindon Rr 6, Saint-Sauveur, QC,
J0R 1R6
(450) 227-4737
Emp Here 80 *Sales* 23,478,160
SIC 5411 Grocery stores
Serge Bourassa
Micheline Barbe
Sylvie Bourassa

D-U-N-S 25-525-0581 (SL)
BRULERIE DES MONTS INC.
197 Rue Principale, Saint-Sauveur, QC, J0R
1R0
(450) 227-6157
Emp Here 40 *Sales* 10,966,080
SIC 5499 Miscellaneous food stores
Howard Sauve
Alexandre Sandhal

D-U-N-S 20-253-5175 (HQ)
**CAISSE DESJARDINS DE LA VALLEE DES
PAYS-D'EN-HAUT**
CENTRE DE SERVICE LAC-MASSON
218 Rue Principale, Saint-Sauveur, QC, J0R
1R0
(450) 227-3712
Emp Here 25 *Sales* 12,718,196
SIC 6062 State credit unions
Pierre Durocher
Jean Beauchamp
Monique Ethier
Lisane Choiniere-Bedard
Francoise Major
Richard Allard
Philippe Dugas
Monique Ethier
Gilles Leonard
Normand Riendeau

D-U-N-S 20-314-1833 (HQ)
CORPORATION AURIFERE MONARQUES
68 Av De La Gare Unite 205, Saint-Sauveur,
QC, J0R 1R0
(819) 736-4581
Emp Here 7 *Sales* 38,366,100
SIC 1081 Metal mining services
Jean-Marc Lacoste
Marc-Andre Lavergne
Guy Bourassa
Alain Levesque
Michel Bouchard
Michel Baril
Christian Pichette

D-U-N-S 25-200-4007 (BR)
**GROUPE LES MANOIRS DU QUEBEC INC,
LES**

GROUPE LES MANOIRS DU QUEBEC INC
(*Suby of* GROUPE LES MANOIRS DU QUE-
BEC INC, LES)
246 Ch Du Lac-Millette, Saint-Sauveur, QC,
J0R 1R3
(450) 227-1811
Emp Here 200
SIC 7011 Hotels and motels

D-U-N-S 25-092-1694 (SL)
H. DAGENAIS & FILS INC
RONA DAGENAIS
304 Rue Principale, Saint-Sauveur, QC, J0R
1R0
(450) 227-2649
Emp Here 50 *Sales* 22,358,700
SIC 5072 Hardware
Andre Dagenais
Annie Dagenais
Martin Dagenais
Lise Rochon

D-U-N-S 25-096-3055 (SL)
**MARCHE CHEVREFILS SAINT-SAUVEUR
INC**
222a Ch Du Lac-Millette, Saint-Sauveur, QC,
J0R 1R3
(450) 227-8734
Emp Here 96 *Sales* 28,173,792
SIC 5411 Grocery stores
Gilles Chevrefils
Jacques Chevrefils

D-U-N-S 24-515-8688 (HQ)
**MONT SAINT-SAUVEUR INTERNATIONAL
INC**
MSSI
350 Av Saint-Denis Rr 3, Saint-Sauveur, QC,
J0R 1R3
(450) 227-4671
Emp Here 200
SIC 7011 Hotels and motels
Louis Dufour
Louis P Hebert
Greg Mccullough
Chantal Nadeau
Michelle Beauchemin
Genevieve Hebert

D-U-N-S 20-003-0158 (BR)
PROVIGO DISTRIBUTION INC
LOBLA SAINT SAUVEUR
(*Suby of* LOBLAW COMPANIES LIMITED)
50 Av Saint-Denis, Saint-Sauveur, QC, J0R
1R4
(450) 227-2827
Emp Here 180
SIC 5411 Grocery stores
Siorello Bellucci

D-U-N-S 25-127-6911 (SL)
RESSOURCES SANTE L M INC
21 Rue Forget, Saint-Sauveur, QC, J0R 1R0
(450) 227-6663
Emp Here 75 *Sales* 6,949,875
SIC 8322 Individual and family services
Lise M Leonard

D-U-N-S 24-922-5798 (SL)
RESTAURATION MIMAR INC
ROTISSERIE ST-HUBERT
725 Ch Jean-Adam, Saint-Sauveur, QC, J0R
1R3
(450) 227-4664
Emp Here 75 *Sales* 3,413,925
SIC 5812 Eating places
Charles Huot

D-U-N-S 25-096-0002 (BR)
RONA INC
MARCIL CENTRE DE RENOVATION
(*Suby of* LOWE'S COMPANIES, INC.)
180 Rue Principale, Saint-Sauveur, QC, J0R
1R0
(450) 227-2627
Emp Here 75
SIC 5072 Hardware
Mario Martin

D-U-N-S 25-763-7918 (HQ)
SOCIETE IMMOBILIERE M.C.M. INC, LA
GROUPE SUTTON LAURENTIDES
204 Rue Principale, Saint-Sauveur, QC, J0R
1R0
(450) 227-2611
Emp Here 70 *Sales* 101,419,200
SIC 6531 Real estate agents and managers
Raymond Cyr
Francois Leger

D-U-N-S 25-494-9589 (HQ)
SOMMETS DE LA VALLEE INC, LES
MSSI
350 Av Saint-Denis, Saint-Sauveur, QC, J0R
1R3
(450) 227-4671
Emp Here 100 *Sales* 191,336,000
SIC 7011 Hotels and motels
Louis Dufour
Louis P. Hebert
Beatrice Hebert
David Dufour
Jacques Dostie
Erick Geoffrion

Saint-Sebastien-De-Frontenac, QC G0Y

D-U-N-S 20-257-5692 (SL)
A. LACROIX & FILS GRANIT LTEE
450 Rue Principale, Saint-Sebastien-De-
Frontenac, QC, G0Y 1M0
(819) 652-2828
Emp Here 100 *Sales* 27,025,600
SIC 1411 Dimension stone
Claude Lacroix
Simon Lacroix
Frederic Lacroix
Dominique Lacroix

D-U-N-S 20-812-1728 (SL)
CENTRE ENGRAIS MINERAUX
390 263 Rte, Saint-Sebastien-De-Frontenac,
QC, G0Y 1M0
(819) 652-2266
Emp Here 80 *Sales* 22,132,800
SIC 2874 Phosphatic fertilizers
Michel Oricheski

D-U-N-S 25-410-6594 (HQ)
GRANIT PLUS INC
386 Rue Principale, Saint-Sebastien-De-
Frontenac, QC, G0Y 1M0
(819) 652-2514
Emp Here 33 *Sales* 15,203,916
SIC 5032 Brick, stone, and related material
Rock Lacroix
Pierre Lacroix
Yvan Lacroix

D-U-N-S 24-746-2898 (HQ)
SUMMUM GRANIT INC
460 Rue Principale, Saint-Sebastien-De-
Frontenac, QC, G0Y 1M0
(819) 652-2333
Emp Here 15 *Sales* 17,921,900
SIC 3281 Cut stone and stone products
Rock Bernier
Lucille Paradis Bernier

Saint-Simon-De-Bagot, QC J0H

D-U-N-S 20-204-1315 (HQ)
HOUDE, WILLIAM LTEE
ENGRAIS LAPRAIRIE
(*Suby of* COMPAGNIE FINANCIERE ET DE
PARTICIPATIONS ROULLIER)
8 3e Rang O, Saint-Simon-De-Bagot, QC, J0H
1Y0
(450) 798-2002
Emp Here 20 *Sales* 21,301,575

SIC 2874 Phosphatic fertilizers
Alain Fortier
Marc Bouvry
Henri Boyer

D-U-N-S 24-580-3432   (SL)
TRANSPORT TRANSBO INC
(*Suby of* OLYMEL S.E.C.)
170 Rue Saint-Edouard, Saint-Simon-De-Bagot, QC, J0H 1Y0
(450) 798-2155
Emp Here 110   *Sales* 20,281,910
SIC 4212 Local trucking, without storage
Ghislain Gervais
Muriel Dubois
Jean-Francois Harel
Denis Guay
Mathieu Couture
Rejean Nadeau

Saint-Stanislas-De-Champlain, QC G0X

D-U-N-S 25-323-8562   (HQ)
ADF DIESEL MONTREAL INC
ATELIER DIESEL FOURNIER
(*Suby of* GROUPE FOURNIER DIESEL INC)
5 Ch De La Cote-Saint-Paul, Saint-Stanislas-De-Champlain, QC, G0X 3E0
(418) 328-8713
Emp Here 60   *Sales* 112,177,900
SIC 5084 Industrial machinery and equipment
Andre Fournier

D-U-N-S 24-699-1210   (HQ)
ADF DIESEL SAINT-STANISLAS INC
(*Suby of* GROUPE FOURNIER DIESEL INC)
5 Ch De La Cote-Saint-Paul, Saint-Stanislas-De-Champlain, QC, G0X 3E0
(418) 328-8713
Sales 18,050,988
SIC 5084 Industrial machinery and equipment
Andre Fournier

D-U-N-S 20-323-6377   (HQ)
GROUPE FOURNIER DIESEL INC
5 Ch De La Cote-Saint-Paul, Saint-Stanislas-De-Champlain, QC, G0X 3E0
(418) 668-5040
Emp Here 10   *Sales* 107,825,155
SIC 6712 Bank holding companies
Andre Fournier

Saint-Stanislas-De-Kostka, QC J0S

D-U-N-S 24-336-7575   (SL)
GESTION JEAN-PIERRE ROBIDOUX INC
320 201 Rte, Saint-Stanislas-De-Kostka, QC, J0S 1W0
(450) 377-2535
Emp Here 90   *Sales* 13,561,597
SIC 4213 Trucking, except local

D-U-N-S 24-503-1385   (SL)
TRANSPORT SYLVESTER & FORGET INC
S & F
320 Rte 201, Saint-Stanislas-De-Kostka, QC, J0S 1W0
(450) 377-2535
Emp Here 95   *Sales* 14,078,240
SIC 4213 Trucking, except local
Jean-Pierre Robidoux

Saint-Theophile, QC G0M

D-U-N-S 20-106-8066   (BR)
MAIBEC INC
MAIBEC DIV. SAINT THEOPHILE
(*Suby of* MAIBEC INC)

340 Rte Du President-Kennedy, Saint-Theophile, QC, G0M 2A0
(418) 597-3388
Emp Here 140
SIC 2429 Special product sawmills, nec
Andre Chartier

Saint-Thomas, QC J0K

D-U-N-S 24-252-4718   (SL)
AGROCENTRE LANAUDIERE INC
AGROCENTRE
531 Rang Sud, Saint-Thomas, QC, J0K 3L0
(450) 759-1520
Emp Here 20   *Sales* 18,338,383
SIC 2874 Phosphatic fertilizers
Luc Boivin
Philippe Pelletier
Marika Trepanier
Benoit Brunelle
France Genereux

D-U-N-S 24-527-7199   (BR)
BOULANGERIE GADOUA LTEE
BOULANGERIE ST THOMAS
(*Suby of* GEORGE WESTON LIMITED)
561 Rue Principale, Saint-Thomas, QC, J0K 3L0

Emp Here 100
SIC 5461 Retail bakeries

D-U-N-S 24-869-7229   (HQ)
GROUPE HARNOIS INC, LE
MAGASIN, LE
80 Rte 158, Saint-Thomas, QC, J0K 3L0
(450) 756-1660
Sales 236,454,600
SIC 5172 Petroleum products, nec
Serge Harnois
Luc Harnois
Claudine Harnois

D-U-N-S 20-258-2672   (SL)
INDUSTRIES HARNOIS INC, LES
BATIMENTS DOMEX, LES
1044 Rue Principale, Saint-Thomas, QC, J0K 3L0
(450) 756-1041
Emp Here 140   *Sales* 26,891,900
SIC 3448 Prefabricated Metal buildings and components
Patrice Harnois
Richard Fortier
Yanick Harnois

D-U-N-S 20-258-2680   (SL)
LASALLE, RAYMOND INC
1561 Rte 158, Saint-Thomas, QC, J0K 3L0
(450) 756-2121
Emp Here 26   *Sales* 12,350,676
SIC 5083 Farm and garden machinery
Guy Lasalle

D-U-N-S 20-297-9469   (BR)
SYNAGRI S.E.C.
PEDIGRAIN
(*Suby of* SYNAGRI S.E.C.)
80 Rue Des Erables, Saint-Thomas, QC, J0K 3L0
(450) 759-8070
Emp Here 250
SIC 2874 Phosphatic fertilizers

Saint-Thomas-Didyme, QC G0W

D-U-N-S 25-004-2496   (BR)
PF RESOLU CANADA INC
RESOLUTE FOREST PRODUCTS
(*Suby of* RESOLUTE FOREST PRODUCTS INC)

300 Av Du Moulin, Saint-Thomas-Didyme, QC, G0W 1P0
(418) 274-3340
Emp Here 111
SIC 2421 Sawmills and planing mills, general
Pierre Gauthier

Saint-Tite, QC G0X

D-U-N-S 20-258-3365   (SL)
BOULET, G.A. INC
501 Rue Saint-Gabriel, Saint-Tite, QC, G0X 3H0
(418) 365-5174
Emp Here 200   *Sales* 54,051,200
SIC 3144 Women's footwear, except athletic
Pierre Boulet
Guy Boulet
Louis Boulet

D-U-N-S 25-233-1004   (BR)
COMMISSION SCOLAIRE DE L'ENERGIE
ECOLE SECONDAIRE PAUL LE JEUNE
405 Boul Saint-Joseph Rr 1, Saint-Tite, QC, G0X 3H0
(418) 365-5191
Emp Here 75
SIC 8211 Elementary and secondary schools
Marc Brunelle

D-U-N-S 24-339-2581   (SL)
TAMARACK CANADA INC
381 153 Rte, Saint-Tite, QC, G0X 3H0
(819) 694-0395
Emp Here 70   *Sales* 10,910,410
SIC 2411 Logging
Linda Randi
Rene Desilets

Saint-Ubalde, QC G0A

D-U-N-S 24-639-3250   (HQ)
PATATES DOLBEC INC
GROUPE DOLBEC
(*Suby of* 9076-6684 QUEBEC INC)
295 363 Rte S, Saint-Ubalde, QC, G0A 4L0
(418) 277-2442
Sales 121,841,720
SIC 5148 Fresh fruits and vegetables
Stephane Dolbec

D-U-N-S 20-258-4660   (SL)
SOCIETE COOPERATIVE AGRICOLE DE SAINT-UBALD
464 Rue Saint-Paul, Saint-Ubalde, QC, G0A 4L0
(418) 277-2225
Emp Here 59   *Sales* 16,174,968
SIC 5411 Grocery stores
Murielle Goupil
Guylaine Cauchon
Eric Cossette

Saint-Urbain-De-Charlevoix, QC G0A

D-U-N-S 20-258-4967   (SL)
MEUNERIE CHARLEVOIX INC
31 Rang Saint-Georges, Saint-Urbain-De-Charlevoix, QC, G0A 4K0
(418) 639-2472
Emp Here 30   *Sales* 22,275,600
SIC 5191 Farm supplies
Jean-Eudes Dufour
Bernard Dufour
Tharsicius Dufour
Just Dufour

Saint-Urbain-Premier, QC J0S

D-U-N-S 24-769-3641   (SL)
SG CERESCO INC
CERESCO
164 Ch De La Grande-Ligne, Saint-Urbain-Premier, QC, J0S 1Y0
(450) 427-3831
Emp Here 55   *Sales* 80,723,060
SIC 5153 Grain and field beans
Alain Letourneau
Pierre Dagenais
Simon Ouellet
Marc-Olivier Girard

Saint-Vallier, QC G0R

D-U-N-S 24-000-0369   (BR)
ROY & BRETON, INC
(*Suby of* GLOBAL UPHOLSTERY CO LIMITED)
577 Rte De Saint-Vallier, Saint-Vallier, QC, G0R 4J0
(418) 884-4041
Emp Here 130
SIC 2521 Wood office furniture
Bastien Laroche

D-U-N-S 20-258-5865   (HQ)
ROY & BRETON, INC
(*Suby of* GLOBAL UPHOLSTERY CO LIMITED)
577 Rte De Saint-Vallier, Saint-Vallier, QC, G0R 4J0
(418) 833-0047
Emp Here 160   *Sales* 83,499,375
SIC 2521 Wood office furniture
Jacques Alain
Scott Bond
David Feldberg
Jeffrey Wilson
Danys Berube

Saint-Victor, QC G0M

D-U-N-S 24-941-5092   (HQ)
2540-0417 QUEBEC INC
124 Rue Des Ecoliers, Saint-Victor, QC, G0M 2B0
(418) 588-3913
Sales 16,401,000
SIC 6712 Bank holding companies
Donald Gilbert

D-U-N-S 20-696-2552   (SL)
BEAUCE EAU INC
AQUA BEAUCE
175 Ch Des Fonds, Saint-Victor, QC, G0M 2B0
(418) 588-3289
Emp Here 12   *Sales* 10,026,924
SIC 5149 Groceries and related products, nec
Christian Roy

D-U-N-S 20-258-6525   (HQ)
LAINAGES VICTOR LTEE, LES
260 Rte De La Station Bureau 218, Saint-Victor, QC, G0M 2B0
(418) 588-6827
Emp Here 160   *Sales* 32,095,525
SIC 2231 Broadwoven fabric mills, wool
Alain Duval

D-U-N-S 24-638-8581   (SL)
PRODUITS DE L'ERABLE BOLDUC & FILS INC, LES
292 3e Rang N, Saint-Victor, QC, G0M 2B0
(418) 588-3315
Emp Here 12   *Sales* 10,026,924

▲ Public Company   ■ Public Company Family Member   **HQ** Headquarters   **BR** Branch   **SL** Single Location

SIC 5149 Groceries and related products, nec
Guy Bolduc
Claudette Bolduc

Saint-Wenceslas, QC G0Z

D-U-N-S 25-324-7944   (SL)
HYCO CANADA LIMITED
(*Suby of* MONTANHYDRAULIK GESELLSCHAFT MIT BESCHRANKTER HAFTUNG)
1025 Rue Principale, Saint-Wenceslas, QC, G0Z 1J0
(819) 224-4000
Emp Here 130   *Sales* 28,860,130
SIC 3593 Fluid power cylinders and actuators
Denis Deshaies
Carsten Storm

Saint-Zotique, QC J0P

D-U-N-S 20-258-8893   (SL)
116260 CANADA INC
MARCHE FORDHAM
350 Rue Principale, Saint-Zotique, QC, J0P 1Z0
(450) 267-3343
Emp Here 100   *Sales* 29,347,700
SIC 5411 Grocery stores
Charles Fordham
Anne-Marie Levac

D-U-N-S 25-212-0860   (SL)
2778751 CANADA INC
CNC AUTOMATION
220 Rue Principale, Saint-Zotique, QC, J0P 1Z0
(450) 267-5955
Emp Here 30   *Sales* 14,250,780
SIC 5084 Industrial machinery and equipment
Andrew Legault

D-U-N-S 20-997-7180   (SL)
FERME ST-ZOTIQUE LTEE
BURN BRAE FARMS
200 69e Av, Saint-Zotique, QC, J0P 1Z0
(450) 267-3521
Emp Here 100   *Sales* 71,671,600
SIC 5144 Poultry and poultry products
Margaret Hudson
Joseph E. Hudson
Don Oddie

D-U-N-S 20-183-3196   (SL)
FERME VERNIER, BENOIT INC
800 Rue Principale, Saint-Zotique, QC, J0P 1Z0

Emp Here 30   *Sales* 10,274,010
SIC 0161 Vegetables and melons
Benoit Vernier

Sainte-Adele, QC J8B

D-U-N-S 25-090-7276   (SL)
9055-8842 QUEBEC INC
HOTEL MONT GABRIEL
1699 Ch Du Mont-Gabriel, Sainte-Adele, QC, J8B 1A5
(450) 229-3547
Emp Here 150   *Sales* 13,903,500
SIC 7011 Hotels and motels
Mike Yuval
Jack Sofer

D-U-N-S 24-430-8623   (SL)
ALIMENTS CHEVREFILS INC, LES
METRO
555 Boul De Sainte-Adele Bureau 205,

Sainte-Adele, QC, J8B 1A7
(450) 227-2712
Emp Here 69   *Sales* 20,249,913
SIC 5411 Grocery stores
Gilles Chevrefils
Jacques Chevrefils

D-U-N-S 24-973-5028   (BR)
COMMISSION SCOLAIRE DES LAUREN-TIDES
ECOLE SECONDAIRE AUGUSTIN NORBET MORIN
(*Suby of* COMMISSION SCOLAIRE DES LAURENTIDES)
258 Boul De Sainte-Adele, Sainte-Adele, QC, J8B 0K6
(450) 240-6220
Emp Here 120
SIC 8211 Elementary and secondary schools
Johanne Vaillancourt

D-U-N-S 24-490-6426   (SL)
MARCHE AU CHALET (1978) INC
I G A
1300 Boul De Sainte-Adele, Sainte-Adele, QC, J8B 0K2
(450) 229-4256
Emp Here 90   *Sales* 8,540,910
SIC 7011 Hotels and motels
Jean-Paul Ouellette
Christian Jasmin

Sainte-Agathe-Des-Monts, QC J8C

D-U-N-S 24-842-2727   (SL)
2625-2106 QUEBEC INC
SUBARU STE-AGATHE ENR
155 Boul Norbert-Morin, Sainte-Agathe-Des-Monts, QC, J8C 3M2
(819) 326-1600
Emp Here 35   *Sales* 17,432,730
SIC 5511 New and used car dealers
Erik Gaudet

D-U-N-S 24-601-5895   (HQ)
ALLIANCE FORD INC
90 Boul Norbert-Morin, Sainte-Agathe-Des-Monts, QC, J8C 3K8
(819) 326-8944
Emp Here 30   *Sales* 44,049,600
SIC 5511 New and used car dealers
Normand Mcgrail
Jean-Paul Mcgrail
Anita Mcgrail

D-U-N-S 24-510-0065   (SL)
AU ROYAUME CHRYSLER DODGE JEEP
AY ROYAUME FORD
700 Rue Principale, Sainte-Agathe-Des-Monts, QC, J8C 1L3
(819) 326-4524
Emp Here 26   *Sales* 12,950,028
SIC 5511 New and used car dealers
Philip Giroux
Pierre-Luc Giroux

D-U-N-S 20-332-3381   (BR)
CENTRE INTEGRE DE SANTE ET DE SER-VICES SOCIAUX DES LAURENTIDES
CENTRE JEUNESSE DES LAURENTIDES
(*Suby of* CENTRE INTEGRE DE SANTE ET DE SERVICES SOCIAUX DES LAUREN-TIDES)
125 Ch Du Tour-Du-Lac, Sainte-Agathe-Des-Monts, QC, J8C 1B4
(819) 326-6221
Emp Here 150
SIC 8361 Residential care
Alain Blaise

D-U-N-S 24-747-5437   (HQ)
COMMISSION SCOLAIRE DES LAUREN-TIDES
13 Rue Saint-Antoine, Sainte-Agathe-Des-

Monts, QC, J8C 2C3
(819) 324-8670
Emp Here 40   *Sales* 109,030,900
SIC 8211 Elementary and secondary schools
Andre Bouchard

D-U-N-S 20-102-9969   (SL)
ENTREPRISES DE VENTE LEWIS, R. INC, LES
CANADIAN TIRE
50 Boul Norbert-Morin, Sainte-Agathe-Des-Monts, QC, J8C 2V6
(819) 326-8900
Emp Here 50   *Sales* 18,210,750
SIC 5014 Tires and tubes
Pierre Girard

D-U-N-S 20-246-1422   (SL)
GARAGE FRANKE INC
FRANKE VOLVO
180 Rue Principale E, Sainte-Agathe-Des-Monts, QC, J8C 1K3
(819) 326-4775
Emp Here 26   *Sales* 12,950,028
SIC 5511 New and used car dealers
Bernard Franke
Reinhilde Brand
Alex Zucker

D-U-N-S 20-246-1075   (SL)
J.L. BRISSETTE LTEE
24 Rue Brissette, Sainte-Agathe-Des-Monts, QC, J8C 1T4
(819) 326-3263
Emp Here 70   *Sales* 58,490,390
SIC 5149 Groceries and related products, nec
Sylvain Labelle

D-U-N-S 20-024-0638   (SL)
LORTIE & MARTIN LTEE
20 Rue Saint-Paul E, Sainte-Agathe-Des-Monts, QC, J8C 3M3
(819) 326-3844
Emp Here 50   *Sales* 12,652,950
SIC 5211 Lumber and other building materials
Normand Lortie

D-U-N-S 20-797-5447   (SL)
MAGASIN JEAN DUMAS INC
MARCHAND CANADIAN TIRE DE STE-AGATHE
50 Boul Norbert-Morin, Sainte-Agathe-Des-Monts, QC, J8C 2V6
(819) 326-8900
Emp Here 100   *Sales* 62,928,000
SIC 5531 Auto and home supply stores
Jean Dumas

D-U-N-S 20-340-2651   (SL)
MARCHE CHEVREFILS STE-AGATHE INC
1050 Rue Principale, Sainte-Agathe-Des-Monts, QC, J8C 1L6
(819) 326-2822
Emp Here 96   *Sales* 28,173,792
SIC 5411 Grocery stores
Gilles Chevrefils
Jacques Chevrefils

D-U-N-S 25-541-4815   (SL)
S. BOURASSA (STE-AGATHE) LTEE
BOURASSA ALIMENTATION
680 Rue Principale, Sainte-Agathe-Des-Monts, QC, J8C 1L3
(819) 326-1707
Emp Here 50   *Sales* 41,778,850
SIC 5141 Groceries, general line
Marc Bourassa

D-U-N-S 24-319-5141   (BR)
WAL-MART CANADA CORP
WALMART
(*Suby of* WALMART INC.)
400 Rue Laverdure, Sainte-Agathe-Des-Monts, QC, J8C 0A2
(819) 326-9559
Emp Here 184
SIC 5311 Department stores
Daniel Blais

Sainte-Agathe-Nord, QC J8C

D-U-N-S 24-475-6961   (SL)
1857-2123 QUEBEC INC
TOYOTA A STE-AGATHE
2330 117 Rte, Sainte-Agathe-Nord, QC, J8C 2Z8
(819) 326-1044
Emp Here 25   *Sales* 12,451,950
SIC 5511 New and used car dealers
Jean Gagne
Jacques Lauzon

Sainte-Angele-De-Premont, QC J0K

D-U-N-S 20-290-6145   (SL)
ALIMENTS PREMONT INC
1505 Rte Lupien, Sainte-Angele-De-Premont, QC, J0K 1R0
(819) 268-2820
Emp Here 55   *Sales* 45,956,735
SIC 5147 Meats and meat products
Francois Bisson
Kyeong Jae Lee
Pascal-Andre Bisson

D-U-N-S 24-570-4234   (SL)
BELLIVO TRANSFORMATION INC
(*Suby of* GROUPE JAFACO GESTION INC)
1505 Rte Lupien, Sainte-Angele-De-Premont, QC, J0K 1R0
(819) 268-5199
Emp Here 75
SIC 7299 Miscellaneous personal service
Fabien Fontaine

Sainte-Anne-De-Beaupre, QC G0A

D-U-N-S 24-389-9098   (SL)
9214-1142 QUEBEC INC
PHARMACIE MARIE BLAIS GIROUX
10459 Boul Sainte-Anne, Sainte-Anne-De-Beaupre, QC, G0A 3C0
(418) 827-3714
Emp Here 50   *Sales* 12,647,700
SIC 5912 Drug stores and proprietary stores
Marie Blais-Giroux

D-U-N-S 25-816-0969   (SL)
BASILIQUE SAINTE-ANNE-DE-BEAUPRE
10018 Av Royale, Sainte-Anne-De-Beaupre, QC, G0A 3C0
(418) 827-3781
Emp Here 163   *Sales* 16,972,049
SIC 8661 Religious organizations
Guy Pilote

D-U-N-S 20-246-6835   (SL)
BILODEAU, CECIL AUTOS LTEE
BILODEAU AUTOS
9641 Boul Sainte-Anne, Sainte-Anne-De-Beaupre, QC, G0A 3C0
(418) 827-3773
Emp Here 38   *Sales* 18,926,964
SIC 5511 New and used car dealers
Yvan Lessard
Vincent Lessard

D-U-N-S 24-531-5866   (SL)
CHOUINARD, A. & FILS INC
IGA BOUCHERIE CHOUINARD
10505 Boul Sainte-Anne, Sainte-Anne-De-Beaupre, QC, G0A 3C0
(418) 827-5569
Emp Here 60   *Sales* 17,608,620
SIC 5421 Meat and fish markets
Paul Chouinard
Gilbert Chouinard
Denis Dupont

Sainte-Anne-De-Bellevue, QC H9X

D-U-N-S 20-998-8351   (SL)
CATHELLE INC
ENTREPRISES SATELLITE, LES, DIV DE
(*Suby of* STEWCA INDUSTRIES LTD)
19925 Ch Sainte-Marie, Sainte-Anne-De-Bellevue, QC, H9X 3Y3
(514) 428-8888
Emp Here 51   *Sales* 29,592,597
SIC 5063 Electrical apparatus and equipment
Jeffrey Caplan
Stewart Rappaport

D-U-N-S 20-271-1255   (SL)
COLLEGE D'ENSEIGNEMENT GENERAL ET PROFESSIONNEL JOHN ABBOTT
21275 Rue Lakeshore, Sainte-Anne-De-Bellevue, QC, H9X 3L9
(514) 457-6610
Emp Here 800   *Sales* 119,512,800
SIC 8221 Colleges and universities
John Louis Halpin

D-U-N-S 24-016-0155   (SL)
CORPORATION BIONETIX INTERNATIONAL
(*Suby of* CORTEC CORPORATION)
21040 Rue Daoust, Sainte-Anne-De-Bellevue, QC, H9X 4C7
(514) 457-2914
Emp Here 12   *Sales* 13,264,140
SIC 5122 Drugs, proprietaries, and sundries
Boris Miksic
Vincent Delorenzo

D-U-N-S 24-536-7487   (HQ)
CORPORATION DE VALVES TRUELINE, LA
20675 Boul Industriel, Sainte-Anne-De-Bellevue, QC, H9X 4B2
(514) 457-5777
Emp Here 44   *Sales* 21,376,170
SIC 5085 Industrial supplies
Jean-Paul Dimarzio

D-U-N-S 24-003-5811   (SL)
FONDATION D'ENTRAIDE EN SANTE DES BENEVOLES DE STE-ANNE
43 Rue Sainte-Anne Bureau 3, Sainte-Anne-De-Bellevue, QC, H9X 1L4
(514) 457-1642
Emp Here 140   *Sales* 10,750,880
SIC 8322 Individual and family services
Elizabeth Parker

D-U-N-S 20-016-2787   (BR)
INSTITUT NATIONALE DE SANTE PUBLIQUE DU QUEBEC
LABORATOIRE DE SANTE PUBLIQUE DU QUEBEC
(*Suby of* INSTITUT NATIONALE DE SANTE PUBLIQUE DU QUEBEC)
20045 Ch Sainte-Marie, Sainte-Anne-De-Bellevue, QC, H9X 3R5
(514) 457-2070
Emp Here 125
SIC 8731 Commercial physical research
Anne Marie Bourgault

D-U-N-S 24-460-7537   (HQ)
INSTRUMENTS I.T.M. INC, LES
PROJEAN
20800 Boul Industriel, Sainte-Anne-De-Bellevue, QC, H9X 0A1
(514) 457-7280
Sales 18,526,014
SIC 5084 Industrial machinery and equipment
David Reed
Roderick Morrow
Joanne Reed

D-U-N-S 25-240-1526   (BR)
LESTER B. PEARSON SCHOOL BOARD
MACDONALD HIGH SCHOOL
17 Rue Maple, Sainte-Anne-De-Bellevue, QC,
H9X 2E5
(514) 457-3770
Emp Here 75
SIC 8211 Elementary and secondary schools

D-U-N-S 20-059-0417   (HQ)
MACDONALD, DETTWILER AND ASSOCIATES CORPORATION
(*Suby of* MAXAR TECHNOLOGIES INC.)
21025 Aut Transcanadienne, Sainte-Anne-De-Bellevue, QC, H9X 3R2
(514) 457-2150
Emp Here 20   *Sales* 215,581,230
SIC 3663 Radio and t.v. communications equipment
Michael Greenley

D-U-N-S 24-353-9657   (HQ)
MHD - ROCKLAND INC
AEROSPATIAL ROCKLAND
21250 Boul Industriel, Sainte-Anne-De-Bellevue, QC, H9X 0B4
(514) 453-1632
Emp Here 25   *Sales* 23,751,300
SIC 5088 Transportation equipment and supplies
Bryan Dollimore

D-U-N-S 20-270-5620   (SL)
VALACTA, SOCIETE EN COMMANDITE
555 Boul Des Anciens-Combattants, Sainte-Anne-De-Bellevue, QC, H9X 3R4
(514) 459-3030
Emp Here 253   *Sales* 47,186,018
SIC 8742 Management consulting services
Daniel Lefebere

Sainte-Anne-De-La-Perade, QC G0X

D-U-N-S 20-745-0128   (HQ)
9097-8875 QUEBEC INC
KIA CAP-SANTE
671 Rue Principale, Sainte-Anne-De-La-Perade, QC, G0X 2J0
(418) 325-2444
Emp Here 19   *Sales* 61,765,964
SIC 5511 New and used car dealers
Carole Turcotte
Denis Dusablon
Benoit Dusablon
Jean Dusablon
Martin Beauchesne

D-U-N-S 20-332-8968   (HQ)
9229-3786 QUEBEC INC
DONNACONA CHRYSLER
671 Rue Principale, Sainte-Anne-De-La-Perade, QC, G0X 2J0
(418) 325-2444
Emp Here 15   *Sales* 34,610,400
SIC 5511 New and used car dealers
Denis Dusablon
Benoit Dusablon
Martin Beauchesne
Carole Turcotte

D-U-N-S 25-199-7839   (BR)
CENTRE DE SANTE ET DE SERVICES SOCIAUX DE LA VALLEE-DE-LA-BATISCAN
FOYER LA PERADE
60 Rue De La Fabrique Bureau 217, Sainte-Anne-De-La-Perade, QC, G0X 2J0
(418) 325-2313
Emp Here 80
SIC 8051 Skilled nursing care facilities
Louise Bedard

D-U-N-S 20-326-0567   (SL)
JOLIETTE MITSUBISHI
661 Rue Principale, Sainte-Anne-De-La-Perade, QC, G0X 2J0
(418) 325-2444
Emp Here 25   *Sales* 12,451,950
SIC 5511 New and used car dealers

Carole Turcotte
Benoit Dusablon
Jean Dusablon

D-U-N-S 24-126-1382   (SL)
MARCHE LA PERADE INC
MARCHE LA PERADE
185 Rue Principale, Sainte-Anne-De-La-Perade, QC, G0X 2J0
(418) 325-2233
Emp Here 49   *Sales* 13,433,448
SIC 5411 Grocery stores
Mario Beaumier

D-U-N-S 24-730-9305   (SL)
PERADE FORD INC, LA
727 Rue Principale Bureau 512, Sainte-Anne-De-La-Perade, QC, G0X 2J0
(418) 325-2244
Emp Here 45   *Sales* 22,413,510
SIC 5511 New and used car dealers
Claude Portelance
Nathalie Portelance
Serge Morin

Sainte-Anne-De-La-Rochelle, QC J0E

D-U-N-S 20-644-9951   (BR)
INDUSTRIES BONNEVILLE LTEE, LES
BONNEVILLE MODULAR HOMES
(*Suby of* GROUPE BONNEVILLE INC, LE)
316 Rue Principale O, Sainte-Anne-De-La-Rochelle, QC, J0E 2B0
(450) 539-3100
Emp Here 100
SIC 2452 Prefabricated wood buildings
Danny Bonneville

Sainte-Anne-Des-Lacs, QC J0R

D-U-N-S 24-061-0613   (SL)
9131-1050 QUEBEC INC
CONSTRUCTIONS NOMADE
65 Ch De La Pineraie Bureau 121, Sainte-Anne-Des-Lacs, QC, J0R 1B0

Emp Here 47   *Sales* 14,986,843
SIC 1521 Single-family housing construction
Steve Saint-Pierre

Sainte-Anne-Des-Monts, QC G4V

D-U-N-S 24-456-1861   (BR)
CENTRE DE SANTE ET DE SERVICES SOCIAUX DE LA HAUTE-GASPESIE
INFO-SANTE CLSC
50 Rue Du Belvedere, Sainte-Anne-Des-Monts, QC, G4V 1X4
(418) 797-2744
Emp Here 500
SIC 8621 Professional organizations
Marpin Pellecier

D-U-N-S 25-232-1138   (BR)
COMMISSION SCOLAIRE DES CHIC-CHOCS
CENTRE ADMINISTRATIF DE STE ANNE DES MONTS
170 Boul Sainte-Anne O, Sainte-Anne-Des-Monts, QC, G4V 1R8
(418) 763-2206
Emp Here 100
SIC 8211 Elementary and secondary schools
Martin Saboiu

D-U-N-S 20-322-1119   (SL)
COOPERATIVE DE TRAVAILLEURS FORESTIERS EAUBOIS
48 3e Av O, Sainte-Anne-Des-Monts, QC, G4V 1J5
(418) 763-2255
Emp Here 52   *Sales* 11,003,876
SIC 0851 Forestry services
Bobby Fournier
Dominic Larrivee

D-U-N-S 24-730-3555   (SL)
CRUSTACES DES MONTS INC, LES
1 Rue Du Parc-Industriel, Sainte-Anne-Des-Monts, QC, G4V 2V9
(418) 763-5561
Emp Here 45   *Sales* 10,118,475
SIC 2092 Fresh or frozen packaged fish
Jean-Guy Langlois
Bertrand Langlois
Ghislain Langlois
Yvon Langlois
Michel Langlois

D-U-N-S 24-308-0251   (SL)
ENTRE-TIENS DE LA HAUTE-GASPESIE CORPORATION D'AIDE A DOMICILE
378 Boul Sainte-Anne O, Sainte-Anne-Des-Monts, QC, G4V 1S8
(418) 763-7163
Emp Here 95   *Sales* 3,819,855
SIC 7349 Building maintenance services, nec
Jasmine Lalonde

D-U-N-S 24-689-7276   (SL)
POISSONNERIE BLANCHETTE INC
(*Suby of* GESTION UNIPECHE M.D.M. LTEE)
150 Boul Perron E, Sainte-Anne-Des-Monts, QC, G4V 3A4
(418) 763-9494
Emp Here 25   *Sales* 20,889,425
SIC 5146 Fish and seafoods
Jean-Marc Marcoux
Richard Desbois
Nicol Desbois
Douglas Mcinnis
Roger Pinel

Sainte-Anne-Des-Plaines, QC J0N

D-U-N-S 25-341-7232   (SL)
ACIERS SOFATEC INC, LES
SOFATEC
867 5e Av Bureau A, Sainte-Anne-Des-Plaines, QC, J0N 1H0
(450) 478-3365
Emp Here 50   *Sales* 10,141,500
SIC 3441 Fabricated structural Metal
Robert Lauzon
Ngoc Hiep Pham
Francois Hebert

D-U-N-S 20-246-9722   (SL)
EPICIERS HOGUE ET FRERES INC, LES
METRO
7 Boul Sainte-Anne, Sainte-Anne-Des-Plaines, QC, J0N 1H0
(450) 478-1765
Emp Here 85   *Sales* 24,945,545
SIC 5411 Grocery stores
Andre Hogue

D-U-N-S 20-246-9631   (SL)
PIED-MONT DORA INC
176 Rue Saint-Joseph, Sainte-Anne-Des-Plaines, QC, J0N 1H0
(450) 478-0801
Emp Here 40   *Sales* 13,827,600
SIC 2033 Canned fruits and specialties
Louis Limoges

D-U-N-S 20-370-6379   (SL)
PROTECTION INCENDIE L.P.G. INC
260 Rue Clement, Sainte-Anne-Des-Plaines, QC, J0N 1H0
(514) 915-5913
Emp Here 2   *Sales* 403,584,000

▲ Public Company   ■ Public Company Family Member   **HQ** Headquarters   **BR** Branch   **SL** Single Location

SIC 1711 Plumbing, heating, air-conditioning
Pascal Gagnon
Luc Prud'homme

D-U-N-S 25-369-2495   (BR)
PROVIGO DISTRIBUTION INC
PROVIGO
(*Suby of* LOBLAW COMPANIES LIMITED)
480 Boul Sainte-Anne, Sainte-Anne-Des-Plaines, QC, J0N 1H0
(450) 478-1864
Emp Here 100
SIC 5141 Groceries, general line
Patrice Bergeron

Sainte-Apolline-De-Patton, QC G0R

D-U-N-S 24-204-5342   (SL)
COOPERATIVE DE GESTION FORESTIERE DES APPALACHES
C.G.F.A
519 Rte Principale, Sainte-Apolline-De-Patton, QC, G0R 2P0
(418) 469-3033
Emp Here 100   *Sales* 15,586,300
SIC 2411 Logging
Rene Thibeault
Jean-Pierre Paquette
Patrick Boucher
Benoit Belanger

Sainte-Aurelie, QC G0M

D-U-N-S 24-200-1584   (SL)
PORTES SAINT-GEORGES INC, LES
2 Rue Des Cerisiers, Sainte-Aurelie, QC, G0M 1M0
(418) 593-3784
Emp Here 75   *Sales* 11,689,725
SIC 2431 Millwork
Gilles Gaudet

D-U-N-S 20-002-7642   (BR)
PRODUITS FORESTIERS D&G LTEE, LES
PRODUITS FORESTIERS D. G. LTEE
(*Suby of* PRODUITS FORESTIERS D&G LTEE, LES)
313 Rang Saint-Joseph, Sainte-Aurelie, QC, G0M 1M0
(418) 593-3516
Emp Here 160
SIC 2431 Millwork
Maurice Grodoin

Sainte-Brigide-D'Iberville, QC J0J

D-U-N-S 25-540-7702   (SL)
GASTRONOME ANIMAL INC, LE
NATURALIMENT
300 Rang Des Ecossais, Sainte-Brigide-D'Iberville, QC, J0J 1X0
(450) 469-0921
Emp Here 26   *Sales* 19,305,520
SIC 5191 Farm supplies
Pierre Gadbois
Gary Leis
Paul-Eric Boulanger

Sainte-Brigitte-Des-Saults, QC J0C

D-U-N-S 24-636-5753   (SL)
CULTURES DE CHEZ NOUS INC, LES
1120 9e Rang, Sainte-Brigitte-Des-Saults, QC, J0C 1E0

(819) 336-4846
Emp Here 50   *Sales* 17,123,350
SIC 0161 Vegetables and melons
Louis-Marie Jutras
Michelle Rajotte

Sainte-Catherine, QC J5C

D-U-N-S 20-548-5951   (SL)
9070-9734 QUEBEC INC
BURGER KING
1580 Boul Des Ecluses, Sainte-Catherine, QC, J5C 2B4
(450) 638-9018
Emp Here 110   *Sales* 5,007,090
SIC 5812 Eating places
Normand Arbour
Hye-Ran Key Arbour
Denis Arbour

D-U-N-S 20-918-7108   (BR)
CERTAINTEED GYPSUM CANADA, INC
700 1re Av, Sainte-Catherine, QC, J5C 1C5
(450) 632-5440
Emp Here 100   *Sales* 690,057
SIC 3275 Gypsum products

D-U-N-S 20-252-3767   (BR)
DARLING INTERNATIONAL CANADA INC
ROTHSAY
(*Suby of* DARLING INGREDIENTS INC.)
605 1re Av, Sainte-Catherine, QC, J5C 1C5
(450) 632-3250
Emp Here 100
SIC 4953 Refuse systems

D-U-N-S 24-459-8405   (SL)
EXPRESS DU MIDI INC, L'
1425 1re Av, Sainte-Catherine, QC, J5C 1C5
(450) 638-0654
Emp Here 96   *Sales* 14,226,432
SIC 4213 Trucking, except local
Pierre Aubin

D-U-N-S 20-859-8920   (SL)
INDUSTRIES ASSOCIEES DE L'ACIER LTEE, LES
(*Suby of* ILVA SPA)
7140 132 Rte, Sainte-Catherine, QC, J5C 1B6
(450) 632-1881
Emp Here 35   *Sales* 18,218,970
SIC 5093 Scrap and waste materials
Arnaldo Zaffaroni

D-U-N-S 25-244-7479   (HQ)
INDUSTRIES ELIRA INC
ATLANTIC EDM
1600 Rue Jean-Lachaine, Sainte-Catherine, QC, J5C 1C2
(450) 638-4694
Emp Here 20   *Sales* 11,400,624
SIC 5084 Industrial machinery and equipment
Jean-Francois Marleau

D-U-N-S 24-713-1956   (SL)
INOX-TECH CANADA INC
1905 Rue Pasteur, Sainte-Catherine, QC, J5C 1B7
(450) 638-5441
Emp Here 75   *Sales* 16,650,075
SIC 3556 Food products machinery
Guy Dostie

D-U-N-S 20-370-8388   (SL)
MARCHE G. CARDINAL INC
BOUCHERIE LE CHAROLAIS
5480 Boul Saint-Laurent, Sainte-Catherine, QC, J5C 1B1
(450) 638-0360
Emp Here 50   *Sales* 13,707,600
SIC 5411 Grocery stores
Jean-Francois Cardinal
Yves Cardinal

D-U-N-S 24-811-4936   (SL)
MOSTI MONDIALE INC

GOURMET MONDIALE
(*Suby of* 3091287 CANADA INC)
6865 Rte 132, Sainte-Catherine, QC, J5C 1B6
(450) 638-6380
Emp Here 38   *Sales* 31,751,926
SIC 5149 Groceries and related products, nec
Nino Piazza

D-U-N-S 25-167-4925   (SL)
SERVICES DE RECYCLAGE GLOBE METAL, GMR INC
GLOBE METAL
1545 1re Av, Sainte-Catherine, QC, J5C 1C5
(450) 635-9397
Emp Here 27   *Sales* 31,082,182
SIC 4953 Refuse systems
Jeffrey Solomon
Brad Solomon
Gregory Solomon

D-U-N-S 24-871-9940   (SL)
SERVICES DE TRANSPORT TRAC-WORLD INC
(*Suby of* GESTION TELSA INC)
6565 Boul Hebert, Sainte-Catherine, QC, J5C 1B5
(450) 635-8271
Emp Here 27   *Sales* 13,477,450
SIC 4412 Deep sea foreign transportation of freight
Laurent Tourigny

D-U-N-S 20-119-6701   (SL)
SERVICES ENVIRONNEMENTAUX CLEAN HARBORS QUEBEC, INC
(*Suby of* CLEAN HARBORS, INC.)
6785 Rte 132, Sainte-Catherine, QC, J5C 1B6
(450) 632-6640
Emp Here 55   *Sales* 13,884,310
SIC 1629 Heavy construction, nec
Eric W Gerstenberg
Michael Battles
Michael Malm, C
Dino Giudice

D-U-N-S 25-938-9398   (SL)
SIGNALISATION JP INC
1980 Rue Laurier, Sainte-Catherine, QC, J5C 1B8
(450) 845-3461
Emp Here 27   *Sales* 13,013,550
SIC 5099 Durable goods, nec
Johnny Pasquale

D-U-N-S 25-977-2457   (SL)
SYSTEMES ACCESSAIR INC, LES
1905 Rue Pasteur, Sainte-Catherine, QC, J5C 1B7
(450) 638-5441
Emp Here 50   *Sales* 23,751,300
SIC 5084 Industrial machinery and equipment
Guy Dostie

Sainte-Cecile-De-Milton, QC J0E

D-U-N-S 20-547-8683   (SL)
CIDRERIE MILTON INC
CIDRERIE MILTON
5 137 Rte N, Sainte-Cecile-De-Milton, QC, J0E 2C0
(450) 777-2442
Emp Here 52   *Sales* 13,640,068
SIC 0175 Deciduous tree fruits
Marc-Antoine Lasnier

Sainte-Claire, QC G0R

D-U-N-S 20-001-7965   (HQ)
GROUPE LEDOR INC, MUTUELLE D'ASSURANCE
78 Boul Begin, Sainte-Claire, QC, G0R 2V0

(418) 883-2251
Sales 184,774,200
SIC 6411 Insurance agents, brokers, and service
Micheline Nadeau
Francois Cote
Christine Jean
Jocelyn Dubois
Egide Fortier
Claude Gagne
Claude Lachance
Nathalie Bilodeau
Sylvie Cloutier
Harold Noel

D-U-N-S 24-226-2579   (BR)
GROUPE VOLVO CANADA INC
NOVA BUS
(*Suby of* AB VOLVO)
35 Boul Gagnon, Sainte-Claire, QC, G0R 2V0
(418) 883-3391
Emp Here 500
SIC 3711 Motor vehicles and car bodies
Tommy Nolet

D-U-N-S 20-199-9638   (SL)
INDUSTRIES ET EQUIPEMENTS LALIBERTE LTEE, LES
IEL
550 Rte Begin, Sainte-Claire, QC, G0R 2V0
(418) 883-3338
Emp Here 100   *Sales* 22,200,100
SIC 3523 Farm machinery and equipment
Andre St-Hilaire
Pierre Bouchard

D-U-N-S 20-576-5915   (SL)
INNOVATION PCM INC
HALBERG DESIGN
21 Rue Industrielle, Sainte-Claire, QC, G0R 2V0
(418) 883-4009
Emp Here 70   *Sales* 33,251,820
SIC 5085 Industrial supplies
Jean-Francois Hamel
Solange Fresneau

D-U-N-S 20-433-8008   (SL)
MORISSETTE, MARCEL INC
171 Boul Begin, Sainte-Claire, QC, G0R 2V0
(418) 883-3388
Emp Here 42   *Sales* 11,514,384
SIC 5451 Dairy products stores
Sebastien Morissette
Georges Morissette

D-U-N-S 24-531-3630   (SL)
MOULIN HUBERT LACOSTE INC
114 Rte Saint-Jean N, Sainte-Claire, QC, G0R 2V0
(418) 883-3688
Emp Here 25   *Sales* 20,889,425
SIC 5149 Groceries and related products, nec
Hubert Lacoste

D-U-N-S 20-580-1210   (HQ)
PLASTIQUE MICRON INC
(*Suby of* LOEWS CORPORATION)
21 Boul Begin Bureau 190, Sainte-Claire, QC, G0R 2V0
(418) 883-3333
Sales 21,763,546
SIC 3089 Plastics products, nec
Sean R. Fallmann
Louis Lettes
Julie A. Davis

Sainte-Clotilde-De-Beauce, QC G0N

D-U-N-S 25-847-4311   (SL)
ARBRE JOYEUX INC
ENJOY TREE
1077 271 Rte, Sainte-Clotilde-De-Beauce, QC, G0N 1C0

---

(418) 427-3363
Emp Here 200   *Sales* 117,831,800
SIC 5199 Nondurable goods, nec
Renald Gilbert
Yvan Gilbert
Francis Gilbert

D-U-N-S 24-524-4715   (SL)
ELITE COMPOSITE INC
(*Suby of* DIMENSION COMPOSITE INC)
1036 Rue Principale, Sainte-Clotilde-De-Beauce, QC, G0N 1C0
(418) 427-2622
Emp Here 100   *Sales* 22,384,300
SIC 3714 Motor vehicle parts and accessories
Jean-Pierre Tremblay

Sainte-Clotilde-De-Chateauguay, QC J0L

D-U-N-S 20-363-0355   (SL)
9329-5558 QUEBEC INC
LAITUE ST-JACQUES
1596 1er Rang, Sainte-Clotilde-De-Chateauguay, QC, J0L 1W0
(514) 807-0707
Emp Here 50   *Sales* 17,123,350
SIC 0161 Vegetables and melons
Robert St-Jacques

D-U-N-S 24-168-5486   (SL)
CAROPAC INC
736 3e Rang, Sainte-Clotilde-De-Chateauguay, QC, J0L 1W0
(450) 826-3145
Emp Here 25   *Sales* 20,889,425
SIC 5148 Fresh fruits and vegetables
Robert Lefort

D-U-N-S 24-178-5633   (SL)
CENTRE MARAICHER EUGENE GUINOIS JR INC
555 4e Rang, Sainte-Clotilde-De-Chateauguay, QC, J0L 1W0
(450) 826-3207
Emp Here 230   *Sales* 43,209,870
SIC 0161 Vegetables and melons
Eugene Guinois Jr
Jocelyne Guinois
Sylvie Guinois
Denise Guinois Lazure
Daniel Guinois

D-U-N-S 25-241-8728   (SL)
FERME H. DAIGNEAULT & FILS INC
1582 1er Rang, Sainte-Clotilde-De-Chateauguay, QC, J0L 1W0
(450) 826-0555
Emp Here 25   *Sales* 20,889,425
SIC 5148 Fresh fruits and vegetables
Carolyne Daigneault

D-U-N-S 24-176-1840   (SL)
FERMES DU SOLEIL INC, LES
800 2e Rang Unite 2, Sainte-Clotilde-De-Chateauguay, QC, J0L 1W0
(450) 826-3401
Emp Here 125   *Sales* 21,128,125
SIC 0161 Vegetables and melons
Marc-Andre Chenail
Isabelle Chenail

D-U-N-S 20-631-8339   (SL)
GUINOIS R. G. R INC
522 4e Rang, Sainte-Clotilde-De-Chateauguay, QC, J0L 1W0
(450) 826-3140
Emp Here 150   *Sales* 39,346,350
SIC 0161 Vegetables and melons
Normand Guinois
Rene Guinois

D-U-N-S 20-564-7365   (SL)
POTAGER MONTREALAIS LTEE, LE
1803 Ch De La Riviere, Sainte-Clotilde-De-Chateauguay, QC, J0L 1W0

(450) 826-3191
Emp Here 42   *Sales* 14,383,614
SIC 0161 Vegetables and melons
Eliane Laffitte
Louis Laffitte

D-U-N-S 24-636-9573   (SL)
SERRES LEFORT INC, LES
VOG
644 3e Rang, Sainte-Clotilde-De-Chateauguay, QC, J0L 1W0
(450) 826-3117
Emp Here 160   *Sales* 27,044,000
SIC 0182 Food crops grown under cover
Sylvain Lefort
Marie-Josee Lebire
Julie Lefort

Sainte-Croix, QC G0S

D-U-N-S 24-908-3841   (BR)
CANADA PIPE COMPANY ULC
BIBBY STE CROIX
(*Suby of* MCWANE (GIBRALTAR) LIMITED LUXEMBOURG SCS)
6200 Rue Principale, Sainte-Croix, QC, G0S 2H0
(418) 926-3262
Emp Here 300
SIC 3312 Blast furnaces and steel mills
Guy Dubois

D-U-N-S 24-346-3051   (BR)
COMMISSION SCOLAIRE DES NAVIGA-TEURS
ECOLE SECONDAIRE PANTHILE LE MAY
(*Suby of* COMMISSION SCOLAIRE DES NAVIGATEURS)
6380 Rue Garneau, Sainte-Croix, QC, G0S 2H0
(418) 796-0503
Emp Here 100
SIC 8211 Elementary and secondary schools
Renee Lachance

D-U-N-S 24-592-7637   (SL)
SERVICES JAG INC, LES
TRANSPORT MICHEL BLOUIN
(*Suby of* 9219-1782 QUEBEC INC)
425 Rue Laurier, Sainte-Croix, QC, G0S 2H0
(418) 926-2412
Emp Here 175   *Sales* 35,998,550
SIC 4213 Trucking, except local
Michel Blouin

D-U-N-S 20-248-4770   (HQ)
SOUTH SHORE INDUSTRIES LTD
MEUBLES RIVE SUD
6168 Rue Principale, Sainte-Croix, QC, G0S 2H0
(418) 926-3291
Emp Here 485   *Sales* 166,998,750
SIC 2511 Wood household furniture
Jean Laflamme

Sainte-Dorothee, QC H7C

D-U-N-S 25-924-1081   (BR)
GOUVERNEMENT DE LA PROVINCE DE QUEBEC
CENTRE D'HEBERGEMENT FERNAND LAROCQUE
(*Suby of* GOUVERNEMENT DE LA PROVINCE DE QUEBEC)
5436 Boul Levesque E, Sainte-Dorothee, QC, H7C 1N7
(450) 661-5440
Emp Here 100
SIC 8361 Residential care
Gilbert Cadieux

Sainte-Dorothee, QC H7L

D-U-N-S 20-212-3378   (SL)
BOUCHER, O. & FILS LIMITEE
2045 Boul Saint-Elzear O, Sainte-Dorothee, QC, H7L 3N7
(450) 682-2400
Emp Here 20   *Sales* 10,702,480
SIC 5147 Meats and meat products
Eric Riendeau

D-U-N-S 24-678-3369   (SL)
MECAER AMERIQUE INC
GROUP MECAER
(*Suby of* S.B.I. SPA)
5555 Rue William-Price, Sainte-Dorothee, QC, H7L 6C4
(450) 682-7117
Emp Here 90   *Sales* 20,145,870
SIC 3728 Aircraft parts and equipment, nec
Valerio Pasqua
Chris O'neil
Bruno Floriani
Corrado Monti
Claudio Brun

D-U-N-S 25-359-0301   (BR)
MULTI-MARQUES INC
(*Suby of* GRUPO BIMBO, S.A.B. DE C.V.)
3443 Av Francis-Hughes Bureau 1, Sainte-Dorothee, QC, H7L 5A6
(450) 629-9444
Emp Here 700
SIC 5149 Groceries and related products, nec
Jean-Luc Breton

D-U-N-S 24-294-2142   (SL)
VENTILABEC INC
VENTILABEC DUNOR
1955 Boul Saint-Elzear O, Sainte-Dorothee, QC, H7L 3N7
(450) 686-7062
Emp Here 60   *Sales* 13,983,900
SIC 1711 Plumbing, heating, air-conditioning
Luc Theroux
Eric Leclair
Sylvain Perron
Eric Ladouceur
Jacques Ladouceur

D-U-N-S 24-649-5881   (SL)
VENTILABEC INC
AUTO-MATRIX CONTROLES
1955 Boul Saint-Elzear O, Sainte-Dorothee, QC, H7L 3N7
(514) 745-0230
Emp Here 145   *Sales* 27,887,560
SIC 7623 Refrigeration service and repair
Eric Ladouceur
Eric Leclair
Carole Goupil
Marc Vadeboncoeur

Sainte-Dorothee, QC H7R

D-U-N-S 25-628-2406   (SL)
9215-0770 QUEBEC INC
PNEUS A RABAIS
2650 Rue Etienne-Lenoir, Sainte-Dorothee, QC, H7R 0A3
(450) 504-9866
Emp Here 40   *Sales* 19,923,120
SIC 5531 Auto and home supply stores
Pier-Anthony Jolicoeur
Robin Meany

D-U-N-S 24-241-3289   (SL)
PLANCHERS SEQUOIA INC, LES
2800 Rue Etienne-Lenoir, Sainte-Dorothee, QC, H7R 0A3
(450) 622-8899
Emp Here 40   *Sales* 10,122,360

SIC 5211 Lumber and other building materials
Daniel Benchetrit
Gerard Benchetrit

Sainte-Elisabeth, QC J0K

D-U-N-S 25-259-5426   (SL)
CLSC-CHSLD D'AUTRAY
2410 Rue Principale, Sainte-Elisabeth, QC, J0K 2J0
(450) 759-8355
Emp Here 175   *Sales* 117,058,900
SIC 7389 Business services, nec
Norman Blackburn

D-U-N-S 20-249-0215   (SL)
PRODUITS DE BETON CASAUBON INC, LES
BRUNET
(*Suby of* 7956576 CANADA INC)
2145 Rang De La Riviere S, Sainte-Elisabeth, QC, J0K 2J0
(450) 753-3565
Emp Here 48   *Sales* 11,204,880
SIC 3272 Concrete products, nec
Bernard Brunet

Sainte-Elizabeth-De-Warwick, QC J0A

D-U-N-S 20-012-6295   (HQ)
9008-6398 QUEBEC INC
JEANS DEPOT
80 Rue De L'Hotel-De-Ville, Sainte-Elizabeth-De-Warwick, QC, J0A 1M0
(819) 358-9008
Sales 17,939,600
SIC 5651 Family clothing stores
Gerald Dubois
Diane Girard

D-U-N-S 24-869-2803   (SL)
9140-5621 QUEBEC INC
FROMAGERIE DU PRESBYTERE
222 Rue Principale, Sainte-Elizabeth-De-Warwick, QC, J0A 1M0
(819) 358-6555
Emp Here 28   *Sales* 23,396,156
SIC 5143 Dairy products, except dried or canned
Jean Morin

Sainte-Emelie-De-L'Energie, QC J0K

D-U-N-S 20-421-4191   (SL)
JOBERT INC
161 Rue Principale, Sainte-Emelie-De-L'Energie, QC, J0K 2K0
(450) 886-3851
Emp Here 45   *Sales* 12,758,580
SIC 1611 Highway and street construction
Sylvain Dumais
Leo Dumais
Jacques Lachapelle

Sainte-Flavie, QC G0J

D-U-N-S 20-297-8508   (SL)
ATELIERS FERROVIAIRES DE MONT-JOLI INC, LES
AFM
(*Suby of* GESTION AFM-SEMA INC)
125 Rue De L'Expansion, Sainte-Flavie, QC, G0J 2L0
(418) 775-7174
Emp Here 30   *Sales* 13,476,570

SIC 7389 Business services, nec
Rock Morel

D-U-N-S 20-695-6356   (SL)
GROUPE SEMA STRUCTURE FERROVI-AIRES INC
125 Rue De L'Expansion, Sainte-Flavie, QC, G0J 2L0
(418) 775-7141
Emp Here 26   *Sales* 10,019,360
SIC 4789 Transportation services, nec
Rock Morel

Sainte-Francoise, QC G0L

D-U-N-S 24-531-9900   (HQ)
FIBRES DE VERRE RIOUX INC, LES
10 Rang Cote Bic, Sainte-Francoise, QC, G0L 3B0
(418) 851-1240
Sales 45,127,470
SIC 5085 Industrial supplies
Jerome Gagnon

Sainte-Genevieve, QC H9H

D-U-N-S 25-081-4373   (SL)
COLLEGE D'ENSEIGNEMENT GENERAL ET PROFESSIONNEL GERALD-GODIN
CEGEP GERALD-GODIN
15615 Boul Gouin O, Sainte-Genevieve, QC, H9H 5K8
(514) 626-2666
Emp Here 100   *Sales* 11,263,600
SIC 8221 Colleges and universities
Pierre G. Lafleur
Suzanne Bernard
Lucie Watier

D-U-N-S 20-220-6371   (SL)
GRIGG PLUMBING & HEATING LTD
PLOMBERI DERITEC
15739 Rue De La Caserne, Sainte-Genevieve, QC, H9H 1G3
(514) 631-1148
Emp Here 49   *Sales* 10,825,766
SIC 1711 Plumbing, heating, air-conditioning
Enrico Giaccari

Sainte-Genevieve-De-Batiscan, QC G0X

D-U-N-S 24-908-4096   (BR)
CENTRE DE SANTE ET DE SERVICES SO-CIAUX DE LA VALLEE-DE-LA-BATISCAN
SECTEUR DES CHENAUX
90 Rang Riviere Veillette, Sainte-Genevieve-De-Batiscan, QC, G0X 2R0
(418) 362-2727
Emp Here 600
SIC 8399 Social services, nec
Alain Corriveau

Sainte-Germaine-Boule, QC J0Z

D-U-N-S 24-942-2882   (SL)
L. J. L. MECANIQUE INC
203 Parc Industriel, Sainte-Germaine-Boule, QC, J0Z 1M0
(819) 787-6509
Emp Here 130   *Sales* 25,002,640
SIC 7699 Repair services, nec
Gino Trudel
Dominic Trudel
Marc Trudel

Sainte-Helene-De-Bagot, QC J0H

D-U-N-S 24-606-3726   (SL)
9035-2022 QUEBEC INC
PETRO CANADA
546 3e Rang Bureau 3, Sainte-Helene-De-Bagot, QC, J0H 1M0
(450) 791-2304
Emp Here 26   *Sales* 12,950,028
SIC 5541 Gasoline service stations
Eric Marchand

D-U-N-S 20-251-3818   (SL)
L. G. HEBERT & FILS LTEE
428 Rue Hebert, Sainte-Helene-De-Bagot, QC, J0H 1M0
(450) 791-2630
Emp Here 50   *Sales* 11,242,750
SIC 2011 Meat packing plants
Mario Cote

D-U-N-S 24-970-5617   (HQ)
LEVESQUE, A. ET S. (1993) INC
ROULOTTES A & S LEVESQUE
430 Rue Couture, Sainte-Helene-De-Bagot, QC, J0H 1M0
(450) 791-2727
Sales 17,102,960
SIC 5941 Sporting goods and bicycle shops
Andre Levesque

Sainte-Henedine, QC G0S

D-U-N-S 24-200-5403   (SL)
VIANDE DUBREUIL INC
ABATTOIR DUBREUIL ENR
172 Rue Principale, Sainte-Henedine, QC, G0S 2R0
(418) 935-3935
Emp Here 60   *Sales* 20,741,400
SIC 2011 Meat packing plants
Donald Lefebvre
Jean-Pierre Breton
Alain Lefebvre
Raymond Breton

Sainte-Julie, QC J3E

D-U-N-S 24-293-9577   (SL)
188669 CANADA INC
ENTRETIEN MENAGER LYNA
1999 Rue Nobel Bureau 7a, Sainte-Julie, QC, J3E 1Z7
(450) 649-9400
Emp Here 100   *Sales* 4,020,900
SIC 7349 Building maintenance services, nec
Dino Frascarelli
Louise Frascarelli
Karl Heinz Gotz
Alexandre Gotz

D-U-N-S 24-432-8738   (SL)
9252-9064 QUEBEC INC
GOURMET NANTEL
2090 Rue Bombardier, Sainte-Julie, QC, J3E 2J9
(450) 649-1331
Emp Here 30   *Sales* 25,067,310
SIC 5145 Confectionery
Raymond Boucher

D-U-N-S 20-397-8082   (SL)
AFGHAN PHYSICIANS ASSOCIATION IN CANADA A.P.A.C.
108 Rue Du Liseron, Sainte-Julie, QC, J3E 3N9
Emp Here 75   *Sales* 2,224,080
SIC 8011 Offices and clinics of medical doc-

tors

D-U-N-S 24-472-9476   (SL)
BMW STE-JULIE
1633 Boul Armand-Frappier, Sainte-Julie, QC, J3E 3R6
(450) 922-1633
Emp Here 49   *Sales* 24,405,822
SIC 5521 Used car dealers
Jean Tremblay

D-U-N-S 25-108-0776   (SL)
BOUSQUET TECHNOLOGIES INC
(Suby of GROUPE BFL INC)
2121 Rue Nobel Bureau 101, Sainte-Julie, QC, J3E 1Z9
(514) 874-9050
Emp Here 60   *Sales* 11,525,100
SIC 3433 Heating equipment, except electric
Francois Martin

D-U-N-S 20-290-1567   (SL)
CAMIONS LUSSIER-LUSSICAM INC
LUSSIER CENTRE DU CAMION
(Suby of ENTREPRISES GROUPE LUSSIER INC, LES)
1341 Rue Principale, Sainte-Julie, QC, J3E 0C4
(450) 649-1265
Emp Here 100   *Sales* 46,115,400
SIC 5012 Automobiles and other motor vehicles
Mario Lussier
Dany Lussier
Josee Lussier
Johanne Lussier

D-U-N-S 20-881-7858   (SL)
CLUB DE GOLF DE LA VALLEE DU RICHE-LIEU INC, LE
100 Ch Du Golf, Sainte-Julie, QC, J3E 1Y1
(450) 649-1511
Emp Here 120   *Sales* 9,425,400
SIC 7997 Membership sports and recreation clubs
Stephane Dube
Frederick Levesque
Andre Hebert

D-U-N-S 20-254-3096   (SL)
COOPERATIVE D'APPROVISIONNEMENTS DE STE-JULIE
1590 Rue Principale, Sainte-Julie, QC, J3E 1W6
(450) 922-5555
Emp Here 30   *Sales* 10,042,770
SIC 5072 Hardware
Marie Roy
Marie Trudeau

D-U-N-S 24-541-4743   (SL)
DERMOLAB PHARMA LTEE
(Suby of LABORATOIRES NATRUM INC)
1421 Rue Nobel, Sainte-Julie, QC, J3E 1Z4
(450) 649-8886
Emp Here 60   *Sales* 17,041,260
SIC 2834 Pharmaceutical preparations
Robert P Boisvert
Jean Colas
Michel Lagueux

D-U-N-S 24-814-9171   (SL)
DESCHAMPS CHEVROLET BUICK CADIL-LAC GMC LTEE
DUPRE, CHEVROLET-CADILLAC
(Suby of GESTION P & H DES CHAMPS LTEE)
333 Boul Armand-Frappier, Sainte-Julie, QC, J3E 0C7
(450) 649-9333
Emp Here 88   *Sales* 55,376,640
SIC 5511 New and used car dealers
Eric Deschamps
Hubert J Deschamps

D-U-N-S 20-362-4833   (SL)
EQUIPEMENT ST-GERMAIN INC
EXCAVATIONS V. ST-GERMAIN

1151 Rue Nobel, Sainte-Julie, QC, J3E 1Z4
(450) 443-3290
Emp Here 45   *Sales* 13,147,605
SIC 7353 Heavy construction equipment rental
Vincent St-Germain
Judith Larose

D-U-N-S 24-901-3954   (SL)
ESCOMPTES C.F.M. INC
JEAN-COUTU
800 Montee Sainte-Julie Bureau 100, Sainte-Julie, QC, J3E 2C4
(450) 922-6000
Emp Here 60   *Sales* 14,659,680
SIC 5912 Drug stores and proprietary stores
Chantal Fortin
Marie-Josee Hamelin

D-U-N-S 20-328-5254   (BR)
GAS DRIVE GLOBAL LP
ENERFLEX
(Suby of ENERFLEX LTD)
2091 Rue Leonard-De Vinci Unite A, Sainte-Julie, QC, J3E 1Z2
(450) 649-3174
Emp Here 100
SIC 7699 Repair services, nec
Robert S. Boswell

D-U-N-S 25-211-5472   (SL)
GESTION CARMINEX INC
2255 Rue Bombardier, Sainte-Julie, QC, J3E 2J9
(450) 922-0900
Emp Here 38   *Sales* 15,935,490
SIC 6712 Bank holding companies
Loreto Corsetti

D-U-N-S 24-814-3547   (SL)
GOURMET NUTRITION F.B INC
HERBXTRA
2121 Rue Leonard-De Vinci Bureau 4, Sainte-Julie, QC, J3E 1Z2
(450) 922-2885
Emp Here 25   *Sales* 20,889,425
SIC 5149 Groceries and related products, nec
Francine Breton
Serge Breton

D-U-N-S 20-212-5134   (HQ)
GROUPE BFL INC
2121 Rue Nobel Bureau 101, Sainte-Julie, QC, J3E 1Z9
(514) 874-9050
Emp Here 3   *Sales* 24,601,500
SIC 6712 Bank holding companies
Francois Martin
Michel-Andre Lamarche
Philippe Martin

D-U-N-S 25-523-2217   (SL)
GROUPE CHAGALL INC
2051 Rue Leonard-De Vinci, Sainte-Julie, QC, J3E 1Z2
(450) 649-1001
Emp Here 30   *Sales* 13,304,700
SIC 7389 Business services, nec
Johanne Bousquet
Jean-Francois Courchesne

D-U-N-S 24-099-9560   (BR)
GROUPE MECANITEC INC
(Suby of GROUPE MECANITEC INC)
2091 Rue Leonard-De Vinci, Sainte-Julie, QC, J3E 1Z2
Emp Here 100
SIC 3548 Welding apparatus

D-U-N-S 20-015-9452   (HQ)
GROUPE NOVATECH INC
160 Rue De Murano, Sainte-Julie, QC, J3E 0C6
(450) 922-1045
Sales 89,491,500
SIC 3211 Flat glass
Raymond Ouellette

Harold Savard
Michel Baril
Mario Bouchard
Andre Heroux

D-U-N-S 20-909-3319   (SL)
IMPRIMERIE STE-JULIE INC
(Suby of 123973 CANADA INC)
1851 Rue Nobel, Sainte-Julie, QC, J3E 1Z6
(450) 649-5479
Emp Here 80   *Sales* 15,581,440
SIC 2672 Paper; coated and laminated, nec
Jean-Maurice Fournier

D-U-N-S 24-881-4126   (SL)
JARDINS VAL-MONT INC., LES
FRUITERIE VAL-MONT
488 Av Jules-Choquet, Sainte-Julie, QC, J3E
1W6
(450) 649-1863
Emp Here 49   *Sales* 13,433,448
SIC 5499 Miscellaneous food stores
Eric Fortin

D-U-N-S 24-800-9391   (SL)
LAMPADAIRES FERALUX INC
VALMONT
(Suby of VALMONT INDUSTRIES, INC.)
2250 Rue Bombardier, Sainte-Julie, QC, J3E
2J9
(450) 649-4114
Emp Here 100   *Sales* 19,044,200
SIC 3648 Lighting equipment, nec
Mark E. Treinen
Andrew Massey
Timothy P. Francis

D-U-N-S 20-118-3790   (SL)
MARCHE DU FAUBOURG STE-JULIE INC
IGA
2055 Rue Principale Bureau 187, Sainte-Julie,
QC, J3E 1W1
(450) 649-4078
Emp Here 165   *Sales* 48,423,705
SIC 5411 Grocery stores
Roger Raymond

D-U-N-S 25-965-4635   (BR)
MISTRAS SERVICES INC
MISTRAS
(Suby of MISTRAS GROUP, INC.)
2161 Rue Leonard-De Vinci, Sainte-Julie, QC,
J3E 1Z3
(450) 922-3515
Emp Here 100
SIC 8734 Testing laboratories
Jonathan Wolk

D-U-N-S 20-330-4274   (HQ)
NOVATECH CANADA INC
CREATIONS VERNOVA, LES
160 Rue De Murano, Sainte-Julie, QC, J3E
0C6
(450) 922-1045
Emp Here 1   *Sales* 89,491,500
SIC 3211 Flat glass
Harold Savard

D-U-N-S 20-564-5885   (SL)
OUTILS DE COUPE DRILLMEX INC
OUTILTECH ORLEANS
2105 Rue Bombardier, Sainte-Julie, QC, J3E
2N1
(450) 922-1929
Emp Here 26   *Sales* 12,350,676
SIC 5084 Industrial machinery and equipment
Paul Ostiguy
Christian Ostiguy

D-U-N-S 20-254-2973   (HQ)
PIECES D'AUTOS O. FONTAINE INC
UNI-SELECT
415 Ch De Touraine, Sainte-Julie, QC, J3E
1Y2
(450) 649-1489
Emp Here 28   *Sales* 13,111,740
SIC 5013 Motor vehicle supplies and new
parts

Omer Fontaine
Michel Fontaine
Denis Fontaine

D-U-N-S 24-705-0839   (SL)
SPG HYDRO INTERNATIONAL INC
2161 Rue Leonard-De Vinci Bureau 101,
Sainte-Julie, QC, J3E 1Z3
(450) 922-3515
Emp Here 49   *Sales* 10,378,396
SIC 7373 Computer integrated systems de-
sign
Michael L Lange

D-U-N-S 20-604-1121   (SL)
**VENTES INTERNATIONALES D'ANIMAUX -
TRUDEAU INC**
726 Mont?E Sainte-Julie, Sainte-Julie, QC,
J3E 1W9
(450) 649-1122
Emp Here 16   *Sales* 19,366,352
SIC 5154 Livestock
Guy Trudeau
Jean-Guy Trudeau
Pierre Trudeau

D-U-N-S 20-793-2724   (SL)
VIANDES FRANCOEUR INC, LES
1841 Rue Lavoisier, Sainte-Julie, QC, J3E 1Y6
(450) 922-4538
Emp Here 50   *Sales* 41,778,850
SIC 5147 Meats and meat products
Vincent Francoeur
Winston Ngo

Sainte-Julienne, QC J0K

D-U-N-S 24-714-3936   (SL)
AUTOS J. G. PINARD & FILS LTEE
1219 125 Rte, Sainte-Julienne, QC, J0K 2T0
(450) 831-2211
Emp Here 25   *Sales* 12,451,950
SIC 5511 New and used car dealers
Jean-Guy Pinard
Carol Pinard
Claude Mcmaniman

D-U-N-S 20-575-5924   (SL)
**GAGNON CANTIN LACHAPELLE & ASSO-
CIES (SENCRL)**
2484 Rue Cartier, Sainte-Julienne, QC, J0K
2T0
(450) 831-2171
Emp Here 26   *Sales* 11,679,694
SIC 7389 Business services, nec
Caroline Mainville

D-U-N-S 24-257-0570   (HQ)
INDUSTRIES TOURNEBO INC, LES
ITI HYDRAULIK
3611 346 Rte, Sainte-Julienne, QC, J0K 2T0
(450) 831-3229
Sales 14,674,612
SIC 3593 Fluid power cylinders and actuators
Jean Mailhot
Jeam Maillot
David Robedoux

D-U-N-S 24-352-7611   (SL)
MARCHE STEPHANE BEAULIEU INC
METRO
1535 125 Rte, Sainte-Julienne, QC, J0K 2T0
(450) 831-2166
Emp Here 50   *Sales* 13,707,600
SIC 5411 Grocery stores
Stephane Beaulieu
France P Beaulieu

Sainte-Justine, QC G0R

D-U-N-S 20-950-1220   (HQ)
ROTOBEC INC

*(Suby of GESTION LEBLOND ET CAYOU-
ETTE INC)*
200 Rue Industrielle Bureau 383, Sainte-
Justine, QC, G0R 1Y0
(418) 383-3002
Emp Here 165   *Sales* 63,197,325
SIC 3531 Construction machinery
Robert Bouchard
Sylvain Cayouette
Julien Veilleux
Marcel Cayouette

Sainte-Luce, QC G0K

D-U-N-S 24-208-7104   (SL)
LULUMCO INC
79 Rue Saint-Alphonse, Sainte-Luce, QC,
G0K 1P0
(418) 739-4881
Emp Here 90   *Sales* 17,313,300
SIC 2421 Sawmills and planing mills, general
Jean St-Laurent
Yves St-Laurent
Roger Moisan
Yoland O'connor

D-U-N-S 20-290-9826   (BR)
TRANSPORT TFI 6 S.E.C.
(Suby of TRANSPORT TFI 6 S.E.C.)
100a Rue Saint-Alphonse, Sainte-Luce, QC,
G0K 1P0
(418) 731-2327
Emp Here 120
SIC 4213 Trucking, except local

Sainte-Madeleine, QC J0H

D-U-N-S 25-596-4772   (SL)
BUNGE GRAIN DU CANADA INC
60 Rue Saint-Simon, Sainte-Madeleine, QC,
J0H 1S0

Emp Here 26   *Sales* 38,159,992
SIC 5153 Grain and field beans
Todd A Bastean

D-U-N-S 24-203-3525   (SL)
JARDINS M.G. S.E.N.C., LES
985 Rang Saint-Simon, Sainte-Madeleine,
QC, J0H 1S0
(450) 795-3459
Emp Here 27   *Sales* 22,560,579
SIC 5148 Fresh fruits and vegetables
Sylvain Palardy
Guy Palardy
Micheline Palardy

D-U-N-S 24-813-6806   (SL)
MARCHE STE-MADELEINE INC
30 Rue Saint-Jean-Baptiste, Sainte-
Madeleine, QC, J0H 1S0
(450) 795-3355
Emp Here 40   *Sales* 10,966,080
SIC 5411 Grocery stores
Daniel Lafrance
Claire Jodoin

D-U-N-S 20-255-0893   (HQ)
NMP GOLF CONSTRUCTION INC
NMP DENEIGEMENT
2674 Ch Plamondon Bureau 201, Sainte-
Madeleine, QC, J0H 1S0
(450) 795-3373
Emp Here 20   *Sales* 20,195,360
SIC 1629 Heavy construction, nec
Normand Poirier
Mario Poirier

Sainte-Marie, QC G6E

D-U-N-S 24-821-3233   (SL)
9178-8562 QUEBEC INC
*BLANCHETTE VACHON & ASSOCIES CA
SENC*
266 Av Du College, Sainte-Marie, QC, G6E
3Y4
(418) 387-3636
Emp Here 80   *Sales* 21,946,560
SIC 8741 Management services
Mario Goselin
Serge Gourde

D-U-N-S 24-907-8189   (SL)
ACIER TRIMAX INC
1440 3e Av Du Parc-Industriel, Sainte-Marie,
QC, G6E 3T9
(418) 387-7798
Emp Here 50   *Sales* 10,141,500
SIC 3441 Fabricated structural Metal
Benoit Drouin
David Drouin
Jacques Labbe

D-U-N-S 24-942-0837   (SL)
ALIMENTATION MARQUIS, YVES INC
SUPER C
1116 Boul Vachon N, Sainte-Marie, QC, G6E
1N7
(418) 387-3120
Emp Here 50   *Sales* 13,707,600
SIC 5411 Grocery stores
Yves Marquis

D-U-N-S 25-721-5806   (SL)
**ASSURANCES J.Y. MARCOUX & ASSO-
CIES INC**
1017 Boul Vachon N Bureau 100, Sainte-
Marie, QC, G6E 1M3
(418) 387-6604
Emp Here 23   *Sales* 13,338,252
SIC 6411 Insurance agents, brokers, and ser-
vice
Jean-Yves Marcoux
Michel Fafard

D-U-N-S 20-255-2667   (SL)
BARONET INC
234 Av Baronet, Sainte-Marie, QC, G6E 2R1
(418) 209-1009
Emp Here 1   *Sales* 23,148,300
SIC 2511 Wood household furniture

D-U-N-S 24-207-0530   (SL)
BETON BOLDUC INC
*BOLDUC MANUFACTURIER DE PRODUITS
DE BETON*
1358 2e Rue Du Parc-Industriel, Sainte-Marie,
QC, G6E 1G8
(418) 387-2634
Emp Here 100   *Sales* 17,921,900
SIC 3272 Concrete products, nec
Maurice Bolduc
Yvan Bolduc
Marcel Blouin
Dany Bolduc

D-U-N-S 24-747-6419   (HQ)
BIZOU INTERNATIONAL INC
BIZOU
1490 3e Av Du Parc-Industriel, Sainte-Marie,
QC, G6E 3T9
(418) 387-8481
Emp Here 30   *Sales* 75,984,318
SIC 5944 Jewelry stores
Marcel Labrecque

D-U-N-S 24-379-9772   (HQ)
**BLANCHETTE VACHON ET ASSOCIES CA
SENCRL**
266 Av Du College, Sainte-Marie, QC, G6E
3Y4
(418) 387-3636
Emp Here 55   *Sales* 26,999,050
SIC 8721 Accounting, auditing, and bookkeeping

Mario Gosselin

D-U-N-S 20-290-3472   (SL)
BOUCHERIE VEILLEUX INC
IGA EXTRA # 618
1000 Boul Vachon N, Sainte-Marie, QC, G6E
1M2
(418) 386-5744
Emp Here 100   *Sales* 83,557,700
SIC 5141 Groceries, general line
Francis Veilleux
Claudia Pomerleau

D-U-N-S 20-243-5095   (BR)
BOULANGERIE VACHON INC
(*Suby of* GRUPO BIMBO, S.A.B. DE C.V.)
380 Rue Notre-Dame N, Sainte-Marie, QC,
G6E 2K7
(418) 387-5421
Emp Here 600
SIC 5149 Groceries and related products, nec
Gerard Leclerc

D-U-N-S 24-205-2405   (SL)
**CONSTRUCTIONS BEAUCE-ATLAS INC,
LES**
600 1re Av Du Parc-Industriel, Sainte-Marie,
QC, G6E 1B5
(418) 387-4872
Emp Here 130   *Sales* 77,669,020
SIC 5051 Metals service centers and offices
Germain Blais

D-U-N-S 20-431-8869   (SL)
CONSTRUCTIONS EDGUY INC, LES
500 1re Av Du Parc-Industriel, Sainte-Marie,
QC, G6E 1B5
(418) 387-6270
Emp Here 50   *Sales* 24,990,000
SIC 1794 Excavation work
Gaetan Turcotte
Denis Turcotte
Martin Turcotte
Normand Turcotte

D-U-N-S 24-344-4754   (SL)
CONSTRUCTIONS EXCEL S.M. INC, LES
1083 Boul Vachon N Bureau 300, Sainte-
Marie, QC, G6E 1M8
(418) 386-1442
Emp Here 35   *Sales* 11,666,655
SIC 1541 Industrial buildings and warehouses
Mario Cliche
Anne-Marie Cliche

D-U-N-S 20-380-6880   (HQ)
COOP AVANTIS
AVANTIS COOPERATIVE
500 Rte Cameron Bureau 100, Sainte-Marie,
QC, G6E 0L9
(418) 386-2667
Emp Here 500   *Sales* 589,159,000
SIC 5191 Farm supplies
Gaetan Roger
Denis Levesque
Frederic Martineau
Richard Dion
Daniel Pelletier
Pierre Caron
Isabelle Nadeau
Celine Boisvert
Simon Beaulieu
Jean-Francois Pelletier

D-U-N-S 20-050-8021   (SL)
FABRICATION BEAUCE-ATLAS INC
(*Suby of* GESTION BEAUCE-ATLAS INC)
600 1re Av Du Parc-Industriel, Sainte-Marie,
QC, G6E 1B5
(418) 387-4872
Emp Here 110   *Sales* 76,823,120
SIC 1542 Nonresidential construction, nec
Germain Blais
Francois Lemieux
Francois Guay
Dominic Poulin
Eric Dumont

D-U-N-S 20-400-4303   (SL)
FC GEOSYNTHETIQUES INC
(*Suby of* INVESTISSEMENTS FLYDZO INC)
1300 2e Rue Du Parc-Industriel, Sainte-Marie,
QC, G6E 1G8
(418) 658-0200
Emp Here 26   *Sales* 18,988,970
SIC 5169 Chemicals and allied products, nec
Jacques Cote
Francis Cote
Francois Thivierge

D-U-N-S 20-058-2679   (HQ)
GESTION BEAUCE-ATLAS INC
600 1re Av Du Parc-Industriel, Sainte-Marie,
QC, G6E 1B5
(418) 387-4872
Sales 65,719,940
SIC 5051 Metals service centers and offices
Germain Blais

D-U-N-S 24-202-8942   (SL)
GROUPE APTAS INC
ALLUMINEK
1332 Boul Vachon N, Sainte-Marie, QC, G6E
1N3
(418) 387-4003
Emp Here 87   *Sales* 16,944,816
SIC 2653 Corrugated and solid fiber boxes
Vital Labonte

D-U-N-S 25-814-4406   (SL)
GROUPE FILGO INC
1133 Boul Vachon N, Sainte-Marie, QC, G6E
1M9
(418) 387-5449
Emp Here 550   *Sales* 201,029,950
SIC 6712 Bank holding companies
Michel Lehoux
Sonny Lehoux
Michel Rouleau

D-U-N-S 24-908-9582   (SL)
GROUPE ISOLOFOAM INC
ISOPAC
1346 Boul Vachon N, Sainte-Marie, QC, G6E
1N4
(800) 463-8886
Emp Here 65   *Sales* 12,504,050
SIC 2493 Reconstituted wood products
Michel Labonte
Dominique Turcotte
Jean-Francois Breton
Louis Jacques
Genevieve Labonte
Steeve Grondin

D-U-N-S 20-581-0922   (HQ)
NORMAND NADEAU T.V. INC
NORMAND NADEAU COMMUNICATIONS
500 Boul Vachon N, Sainte-Marie, QC, G6E
1M1
(418) 387-3242
Sales 13,014,066
SIC 7378 Computer maintenance and repair
Francois Faucher
Suzie Breton
Eric Bissonnette

D-U-N-S 20-255-3277   (HQ)
**PHILIPPE GOSSELIN & ASSOCIES LIMI-
TEE**
SUPER SOIR
1133 Boul Vachon N, Sainte-Marie, QC, G6E
1M9
(418) 387-5449
Emp Here 25   *Sales* 118,227,300
SIC 5172 Petroleum products, nec
Michel Lehoux
Audrey Lehoux
Sonny Lehoux
Michel Rouleau
Gaetan Desroches
Francois Dupont
Ghislain Gervais
Michel Bernard
Rene Vachon

Claude Gariepy

D-U-N-S 20-356-8142   (BR)
TEXEL MATERIAUX TECHNIQUES INC
TEXEL MATERIAUX TECHNIQUES
(*Suby of* TEXEL MATERIAUX TECHNIQUES
INC)
1300 2e Rue Du Parc-Industriel, Sainte-Marie,
QC, G6E 1G8
(418) 658-0200
Emp Here 150
SIC 2297 Nonwoven fabrics

D-U-N-S 25-685-2237   (BR)
TRANSPORT ROBERT (1973) LTEE
(*Suby of* GROUPE ROBERT INC)
1199 2e Rue Du Parc-Industriel, Sainte-Marie,
QC, G6E 1G7
(514) 521-1416
Emp Here 100
SIC 4213 Trucking, except local
Jacques Buteau

D-U-N-S 20-251-4402   (HQ)
UNICOOP, COOPERATIVE AGRICOLE
COOP UNICOOP, LA
500 Rte Cameron Bureau 100, Sainte-Marie,
QC, G6E 0L9
(418) 386-2667
Emp Here 61   *Sales* 235,663,600
SIC 5191 Farm supplies
Richard Dion
Keven Mercier
Dominique Larose
Pierre Caron
Richard Ferland
Diane Montminy
Frederic Lehouillier
Marie-Christine Larose
Jerome Landry
Marieve Breton

D-U-N-S 24-455-7419   (BR)
WESTROCK COMPANY OF CANADA CORP
PRESENTOIRES ROCKTENN
(*Suby of* WESTROCK COMPANY)
433 2e Av Du Parc-Industriel, Sainte-Marie,
QC, G6E 3H2
(418) 387-5438
Emp Here 150
SIC 2657 Folding paperboard boxes
Pascal Marcoux

Sainte-Marie-Salome, QC J0K

D-U-N-S 20-276-3087   (SL)
CONSTRUCTION JULIEN DALPE INC
350 Ch Des Pres, Sainte-Marie-Salome, QC,
J0K 2Z0
(450) 754-2059
Emp Here 24   *Sales* 11,297,544
SIC 1542 Nonresidential construction, nec
Julien Dalpe

Sainte-Marthe, QC J0P

D-U-N-S 20-255-4101   (HQ)
AGROCENTRE BELCAN INC
ST-LAWRENCE BEANS
180 Mont E Sainte-Marie, Sainte-Marthe, QC,
J0P 1W0
(450) 459-4288
Sales 12,449,700
SIC 2874 Phosphatic fertilizers
Luc Verdonck
Ronald Verdonck
Mark Serre
Peter Mattsson

Sainte-Marthe-Sur-Le-Lac, QC J0N

D-U-N-S 24-226-7669   (SL)
9128-0453 QUEBEC INC
METRO FAMILLE MARTEL
2950 Boul Des Promenades, Sainte-Marthe-
Sur-Le-Lac, QC, J0N 1P0
(450) 623-3010
Emp Here 49   *Sales* 13,433,448
SIC 5411 Grocery stores
Opierre-Andre Martel

Sainte-Martine, QC J0S

D-U-N-S 20-554-0607   (SL)
9016-0003 QUEBEC INC
BILLETTE & VINCENT
1315 Boul Saint-Jean-Baptiste O, Sainte-
Martine, QC, J0S 1V0
(450) 427-1999
Emp Here 10   *Sales* 10,328,080
SIC 5172 Petroleum products, nec
Marquis Gregoire
Marquis Junior Gregoire

D-U-N-S 25-673-5622   (HQ)
9049-1135 QUEBEC INC
PROPANE DU SUROIT
1325 Boul Saint-Jean-Baptiste O, Sainte-
Martine, QC, J0S 1V0
(450) 427-1706
Emp Here 15   *Sales* 21,012,208
SIC 5984 Liquefied petroleum gas dealers
Marquis Gregoire Sr
Marquis Gregoire Jr
Rejean Dupuis

D-U-N-S 25-081-1890   (BR)
BONDUELLE CANADA INC
(*Suby of* BONDUELLE)
316 Rue Saint-Joseph Rr 2, Sainte-Martine,
QC, J0S 1V0
(450) 427-2130
Emp Here 80
SIC 2033 Canned fruits and specialties
Justin Fugert

D-U-N-S 20-708-0412   (BR)
DARE FOODS LIMITED
BOULANGERIE SAINTE MARTINE
(*Suby of* DARE FOODS LIMITED)
15 Rang Dubuc, Sainte-Martine, QC, J0S 1V0
(450) 427-8410
Emp Here 150
SIC 2051 Bread, cake, and related products
Francine Gosselin

D-U-N-S 20-189-7923   (HQ)
URGEL CHARETTE TRANSPORT LIMITEE
555 Boul Saint-Jean-Baptiste E Rr 3, Sainte-
Martine, QC, J0S 1V0
(450) 691-5151
Sales 16,456,480
SIC 4212 Local trucking, without storage
Bertrand Lazure
Jean Cardinal
Suzanne Lagarde

Sainte-Melanie, QC J0K

D-U-N-S 20-255-5314   (SL)
BOUCHER RONALD & FILS INC
MARCHE METRO
851 Rte Principale, Sainte-Melanie, QC, J0K
3A0
(450) 889-8363
Emp Here 50   *Sales* 13,707,600
SIC 5411 Grocery stores
Eric Boucher

D-U-N-S 25-468-1778   (HQ)
GROUPE J.F. NADEAU INC, LE
850 Rte Principale, Sainte-Melanie, QC, J0K
3A0
(450) 889-7237
Sales 27,770,310
SIC 4213 Trucking, except local
Jean-Francois Nadeau

Sainte-Monique-Lac-Saint-Jea, QC G0W

D-U-N-S 24-336-9894   (SL)
INDUSTRIE T.L.T INC
144 Rue Larouche, Sainte-Monique-Lac-
Saint-Jea, QC, G0W 2T0
(418) 347-3355
Emp Here 100   Sales 15,586,300
SIC 2421 Sawmills and planing mills, general
Sergio Lifraine
Claude Hebert

Sainte-Perpetue, QC J0C

D-U-N-S 20-256-2443   (HQ)
P.H. VITRES D'AUTOS INC
DISTRIBUTEUR DE PARE-BRISE ATLAN-
TIQUE
2635 Rang Saint-Joseph, Sainte-Perpetue,
QC, J0C 1R0
(819) 336-6660
Emp Here 100   Sales 138,346,200
SIC 5013 Motor vehicle supplies and new
parts
Mario Jutras
Marc Desmarais

Sainte-Perpetue-De-L'Islet, QC G0R

D-U-N-S 20-431-7598   (SL)
BOIS DE SCIAGE LAFONTAINE INC
144 Rang Lafontaine, Sainte-Perpetue-De-
L'Islet, QC, G0R 3Z0
(418) 359-2500
Emp Here 80   Sales 12,469,040
SIC 2421 Sawmills and planing mills, general
Marc Pelletier

D-U-N-S 24-896-6814   (SL)
**MAGASIN CO-OP DE STE-PERPETUE, CTE
L'ISLET**
COOP DE STE-PERPETUE, LA
358 Rue Principale S, Sainte-Perpetue-De-
L'Islet, QC, G0R 3Z0
(418) 359-2221
Emp Here 40   Sales 12,918,760
SIC 5411 Grocery stores
Michelle Pelletier

Sainte-Petronille, QC G0A

D-U-N-S 24-378-6316   (SL)
POLYCULTURE PLANTE (1987) INC
8683 Ch Royal, Sainte-Petronille, QC, G0A
4C0
(418) 828-9603
Emp Here 38   Sales 10,417,776
SIC 5431 Fruit and vegetable markets
Pierre Plante
Huguette Ferland
Mathieu Plante
Simon Plante

Sainte-Rose, QC H7C

D-U-N-S 24-106-3221   (HQ)
9387-0616 QUEBEC INC
(Suby of MAPLE LEAF FOODS INC)
6625 Rue Ernest-Cormier, Sainte-Rose, QC,
H7C 2V2
(450) 665-6100
Sales 179,179,000
SIC 5147 Meats and meat products
Richard Young
Pasquale De Marco
Deborah K. Simpson
Suzanne Hathaway

D-U-N-S 24-650-0383   (SL)
**INVESTISSEMENTS LACORDAIRE INC,
LES**
6625 Rue Ernest-Cormier, Sainte-Rose, QC,
H7C 2V2
(514) 321-8260
Emp Here 110   Sales 103,309,470
SIC 6211 Security brokers and dealers
Pasquale De Marco

D-U-N-S 20-400-6878   (SL)
PRODUITS ALIMENTAIRES VIAU INC, LES
(Suby of MAPLE LEAF FOODS INC)
6625 Rue Ernest-Cormier, Sainte-Rose, QC,
H7C 2V2
(450) 665-6100
Emp Here 250   Sales 179,179,000
SIC 5147 Meats and meat products
Richard Young
Deborah K. Simpson
Suzanne Hathaway

Sainte-Rose, QC H7E

D-U-N-S 24-485-7574   (SL)
9158-7022 QUEBEC INC
INTERMARCHE PALUMBO
3595 Boul De La Concorde E, Sainte-Rose,
QC, H7E 2E1
(450) 661-2525
Emp Here 45   Sales 12,336,840
SIC 5411 Grocery stores
Robert Gentile
Roberto Verdone

D-U-N-S 20-309-1061   (BR)
GROUPE PATRICK MORIN INC
PATRICK MORIN INC
(Suby of GROUPE PATRICK MORIN INC)
4300 Boul Robert-Bourassa, Sainte-Rose,
QC, H7E 0C2
(450) 781-4466
Emp Here 75
SIC 5211 Lumber and other building materials
Sylvain Guilbault

D-U-N-S 24-319-5166   (BR)
WAL-MART CANADA CORP
WALMART
(Suby of WALMART INC.)
5205 Boul Robert-Bourassa, Sainte-Rose,
QC, H7E 0A3
(450) 661-7447
Emp Here 120
SIC 5311 Department stores
Robert Laporte

Sainte-Rose, QC H7L

D-U-N-S 20-797-0526   (SL)
3933849 CANADA INC
GROUPE CHARTEAU MIRAGE
(Suby of GESTION GARFIL INC)
1609 Boul Saint-Elzear O, Sainte-Rose, QC,
H7L 3N6
(514) 744-6991
Emp Here 125   Sales 3,996,000

SIC 7349 Building maintenance services, nec
David Garcia
Etienne Alexandre Filteau

D-U-N-S 20-277-2323   (SL)
8542732 CANADA INC
ISAUTE
2045 Boul Dagenais O Bureau 100, Sainte-
Rose, QC, H7L 5V1
(514) 761-7373
Emp Here 26   Sales 11,016,980
SIC 7941 Sports clubs, managers, and pro-
moters
Nathalie Lundquist
Jacob Lundquist
Greg Clark

D-U-N-S 24-709-8437   (SL)
9020-7697 QUEBEC INC
CARREFOUR SUZUKI-SUBARU AUTOMO-
BILES
250 Boul Cure-Labelle, Sainte-Rose, QC, H7L
3A2

Emp Here 30   Sales 14,942,340
SIC 5511 New and used car dealers
Louis Giguere
Louis-Paul Olivier

D-U-N-S 20-297-9001   (SL)
9115-7776 QUEBEC INC
JEAN PERREAULT ET NICOLAS ROMPRE
580 Boul Cure-Labelle, Sainte-Rose, QC, H7L
4V6
(450) 963-9507
Emp Here 50   Sales 12,647,700
SIC 5912 Drug stores and proprietary stores
Nicolas Rompre
Jean Perreault

D-U-N-S 20-370-9089   (SL)
9320-4048 QUEBEC INC
GESTION EXCLUSIVE MAINTENANCE
1611 Boul Saint-Elzear O, Sainte-Rose, QC,
H7L 3N6
(438) 386-7886
Emp Here 80   Sales 3,216,720
SIC 7349 Building maintenance services, nec
Mike Hebert
Benjamin Hebert

D-U-N-S 25-284-7298   (SL)
AERO MECANIQUE TURCOTTE INC
GROUPR CVC
1289 Boul Dagenais O, Sainte-Rose, QC, H7L
5Z9
(450) 625-2627
Emp Here 72   Sales 16,780,680
SIC 1711 Plumbing, heating, air-conditioning
Frederic Turcotte
Michel Turcotte
Eric Gagne

D-U-N-S 24-433-7101   (SL)
ARTICLES MENAGERS DURA INC
DURA KIT
2105 Boul Dagenais O, Sainte-Rose, QC, H7L
5W9
(450) 622-3872
Emp Here 25   Sales 12,721,400
SIC 5021 Furniture
Salim Aintabi
Izake Mussa Lawi

D-U-N-S 24-514-1858   (HQ)
BAUSCH HEALTH COMPANIES INC
PRODUITS PHARMACEUTIQUES VALEANT
INTERNATIONAL
2150 Boul Saint-Elzear O, Sainte-Rose, QC,
H7L 4A8
(514) 744-6792
Emp Here 150   Sales 8,380,000,000
SIC 2834 Pharmaceutical preparations
Joseph C. Papa
Paul S. Herendeen
Christina M. Achkermann
Thomas J. Appio
Dennis Asharin

Joseph Gordon
Scott Hirsch
Robert Spurr
Tracy Valorie
Kelly Webber

D-U-N-S 25-775-9167   (SL)
**BOUTEILLES RECYCLEES DU QUEBEC
(B.R.Q) INC, LES**
BOUTEILLES & EMBALLAGE UNIS
1400 Boul Dagenais O, Sainte-Rose, QC, H7L
5C7
(450) 622-1600
Emp Here 100   Sales 44,921,900
SIC 7389 Business services, nec
Normand Tremblay
Nicolas Renaud
Paul Matte
Christian Turgeon

D-U-N-S 20-692-9783   (HQ)
CAISSE DESJARDINS DU NORD DE LAVAL
CENTRE DE SERVICES FABREVILLE
396 Boul Cure-Labelle, Sainte-Rose, QC, H7L
4T7
(450) 622-8130
Emp Here 24   Sales 13,926,776
SIC 6062 State credit unions
Guy Benoit
Stephane Corbeil
Hubert Bernatchez
Alexandre Jarry
Michel Beaumont
Jean Boisvert
Serge Bouchard
Mario Gebrayel
Edith Lauzon
Jean-Pierre Nadeau

D-U-N-S 24-525-6750   (BR)
CANADA BREAD COMPANY, LIMITED
(Suby of GRUPO BIMBO, S.A.B. DE C.V.)
3455 Av Francis-Hughes, Sainte-Rose, QC,
H7L 5A5
(450) 669-2222
Emp Here 700
SIC 5461 Retail bakeries
Jean-Luc Breton

D-U-N-S 20-180-2399   (BR)
CARRIER ENTERPRISE CANADA, L.P.
BRYANT CANADA
(Suby of CARRIER ENTERPRISE CANADA,
L.P.)
2025 Boul Dagenais O, Sainte-Rose, QC, H7L
5V1
(514) 324-5050
Emp Here 100
SIC 5075 Warm air heating and air condition-
ing
Brian Monk

D-U-N-S 20-591-4633   (SL)
**COMPAGNIE D'ENTRETIEN BRITE-LITE
LTEE**
OPTIMUM HYDROPONIX
940 Rue Bergar, Sainte-Rose, QC, H7L 4Z8
(450) 669-3803
Emp Here 25   Sales 11,875,650
SIC 5083 Farm and garden machinery
Shane Boucher
David C Hudgson

D-U-N-S 25-259-4148   (SL)
CONSTRUCTION VERGO 2011 INC
CONSTRUCTION VERGO
1463 Rue Berlier, Sainte-Rose, QC, H7L 3Z1
(450) 967-2220
Emp Here 70   Sales 39,923,660
SIC 1542 Nonresidential construction, nec
Yves Ducharme
Serge Letarte
Claude Huot

D-U-N-S 20-357-1021   (SL)
DBM OPTIX INC
(Suby of GROUPE DBM INC)

1630 Blvd Dagenais O, Sainte-Rose, QC, H7L
5C7
(450) 622-3100
Emp Here 100   *Sales* 22,318,110
SIC 3827 Optical instruments and lenses
Nesim Benrobi
Bernard Caire

D-U-N-S 24-111-6524   (SL)
DYNE-A-PAK INC
(*Suby of* GESTIONS ROPAL-ROJAK INC)
3375 Av Francis-Hughes, Sainte-Rose, QC,
H7L 5A5
(450) 667-3626
Emp Here 100   *Sales* 15,885,800
SIC 3089 Plastics products, nec

D-U-N-S 24-865-7249   (HQ)
ECHAFAUDS PLUS (LAVAL) INC
(*Suby of* OMEGA II INC)
2897 Av Francis-Hughes, Sainte-Rose, QC,
H7L 4G8
(450) 663-1926
Sales 49,908,360
SIC 1799 Special trade contractors, nec
Bruno Tasse
Jean-Marc Champigny
Yvan Despres

D-U-N-S 25-949-3208   (SL)
ENTREPRISES DBM REFLEX INC, LES
(*Suby of* GROUPE DBM INC)
1620 Boul Dagenais O, Sainte-Rose, QC, H7L
5C7
(450) 622-3100
Emp Here 100   *Sales* 22,200,100
SIC 3544 Special dies, tools, jigs, and fixtures
Nesim Benrobi
Bernard Caire

D-U-N-S 20-292-4122   (SL)
ESYS ENERGIE SYSTEME INC
*ESIM SOLUTIONS DE CHAUFFAGE
ECOLOGIQUES*
3404 Boul Industriel, Sainte-Rose, QC, H7L
4R9
(450) 641-1344
Emp Here 135   *Sales* 29,970,135
SIC 3567 Industrial furnaces and ovens
Laurent Gierula

D-U-N-S 24-433-5212   (SL)
FERCO FERRURES DE BATIMENTS INC
(*Suby of* GRETSCH-UNITAS GMBH)
2000 Rue Berlier, Sainte-Rose, QC, H7L 4S4
(450) 973-1437
Emp Here 26   *Sales* 11,626,524
SIC 5072 Hardware
Julius Von Resch
Yvon Soucy
Andre Dorais

D-U-N-S 24-050-2799   (SL)
FOURGONS TRANSIT INC, LES
3600 Boul Industriel, Sainte-Rose, QC, H7L
4R9
(514) 382-0104
Emp Here 150   *Sales* 33,576,450
SIC 3713 Truck and bus bodies
Louis Leclair

D-U-N-S 20-187-3499   (SL)
GESCLADO INC
1400 Boul Dagenais O, Sainte-Rose, QC, H7L
5C7
(450) 622-1600
Emp Here 70   *Sales* 18,308,710
SIC 6712 Bank holding companies
Normand Tremblay

D-U-N-S 24-548-9794   (SL)
GROUPE FERTEK INC
3000 Av Fran?ls-Hughes, Sainte-Rose, QC,
H7L 3J5
(450) 663-8700
Emp Here 90   *Sales* 23,539,770
SIC 6712 Bank holding companies
Bruno Tasse

Yvan Despres
Hugues T Poulin

D-U-N-S 24-421-2010   (SL)
GROUPE GEYSER INC
205 Boul Cure-Labelle Bureau 201, Sainte-
Rose, QC, H7L 2Z9
(450) 625-2003
Emp Here 50   *Sales* 23,536,550
SIC 1542 Nonresidential construction, nec
Gilles Brassard

D-U-N-S 20-251-7744   (SL)
GROUPE LELYS INC
FLEXO-EXPRESS
3275 Av Francis-Hughes, Sainte-Rose, QC,
H7L 5A5
(450) 662-7161
Emp Here 75   *Sales* 12,302,025
SIC 2759 Commercial printing, nec
Didier Peladeau

D-U-N-S 24-377-5736   (HQ)
GROUPE LESSARD INC
2025 Boul Dagenais O, Sainte-Rose, QC, H7L
5V1
(514) 636-3999
Sales 72,969,300
SIC 3442 Metal doors, sash, and trim
Yves H Boucher
Camille Lessard
Jean-Pierre Riverin
Alain Beaucage
Christophe Aillerie
Renaud Ferdais

D-U-N-S 25-170-3302   (HQ)
IFC SEAFOOD INC
5584 Boul Des Rossignols, Sainte-Rose, QC,
H7L 5Z1
(450) 682-9144
Emp Here 22   *Sales* 37,600,965
SIC 5146 Fish and seafoods
Carlos Torralbo

D-U-N-S 24-437-6315   (SL)
IMPORTATIONS DE-RO-MA (1983) LTEE
GLUTINO
(*Suby of* CONAGRA BRANDS, INC.)
2055 Boul Dagenais O, Sainte-Rose, QC, H7L
5V1
(450) 629-7689
Emp Here 100   *Sales* 22,394,100
SIC 6111 Federal and federally sponsored
credit agencies
Carey L. Bartell
Bo Johan Nystedt
Robert G. Wise
Eric M. Johnson
Ian Roberts
M. Kelly Maggs

D-U-N-S 24-083-6361   (HQ)
MAPEI INC
BEST-BACKED
(*Suby of* EMME ESSE VI SRL)
2900 Av Francis-Hughes, Sainte-Rose, QC,
H7L 3J5
(450) 662-1212
Emp Here 240   *Sales* 120,054,150
SIC 2891 Adhesives and sealants
Luigi Di Geso
E. Paul Legault
Giorgio Squinzi
Marco Squinzi
Veronica Squinzi
Nick Di Tempora
Marco Roma

D-U-N-S 24-904-1641   (SL)
MARCHE DES OISEAUX INC
IGA
580 Boul Cure-Labelle, Sainte-Rose, QC, H7L
4V6
(450) 963-1072
Emp Here 175   *Sales* 51,358,475
SIC 5411 Grocery stores
Henri Quintal

Yvon Quintal

D-U-N-S 24-256-2841   (HQ)
MET-RECY LTEE
2975 Boul Industriel, Sainte-Rose, QC, H7L
3W9
(450) 668-6008
Sales 23,424,390
SIC 5093 Scrap and waste materials
Franco Di Menna
Mario Rinaldi
Miranda Di Menna

D-U-N-S 24-904-5436   (HQ)
METALTECH-OMEGA INC
BOIS DE STRUCTURE LEE
1735 Boul Saint-Elzear O, Sainte-Rose, QC,
H7L 3N6
(450) 681-6440
Emp Here 150   *Sales* 35,343,640
SIC 3446 Architectural Metalwork
Bruno Tasse

D-U-N-S 25-974-8846   (SL)
NUMESH INC
ENTREPRISES NUMESH
3000 Av Francis-Hughes, Sainte-Rose, QC,
H7L 3J5
(450) 663-8700
Emp Here 150   *Sales* 23,050,200
SIC 3496 Miscellaneous fabricated wire prod-
ucts
Stephane Begin
Caroline Martel

D-U-N-S 20-107-8149   (HQ)
OMEGA II INC
GROUP OMEGA II
1735 Boul Saint-Elzear O, Sainte-Rose, QC,
H7L 3N6
(450) 681-6440
Sales 116,750,880
SIC 3446 Architectural Metalwork
Bruno Tasse
Renaud St-Germain

D-U-N-S 24-763-2177   (SL)
PROCAM INTERNATIONAL INC
2035 Boul Dagenais O Bureau 200, Sainte-
Rose, QC, H7L 5V1
(450) 963-4442
Emp Here 30   *Sales* 15,599,010
SIC 4731 Freight transportation arrangement
Francois Guy

D-U-N-S 20-105-1120   (HQ)
PRODUITS DESIGNER ALLIANCE INC
AQUA SAND BOND
(*Suby of* WYNNCHURCH CAPITAL, LLC)
225 Boul Bellerose O, Sainte-Rose, QC, H7L
6A1
(450) 624-1611
Emp Here 6   *Sales* 11,626,524
SIC 5039 Construction materials, nec
Gerlando (George) Tutino
Giacomo (Jack) Tutino
Morty White
Erin Murphy
Frank Hayes

D-U-N-S 24-125-7083   (BR)
PUROLATOR INC
COURRIER PUROLATOR
(*Suby of* GOVERNMENT OF CANADA)
2005 Boul Dagenais O, Sainte-Rose, QC, H7L
5V1
(450) 963-3050
Emp Here 150
SIC 7389 Business services, nec

D-U-N-S 20-125-4625   (HQ)
PYROTECH BEI INC
1455 Rue Michelin, Sainte-Rose, QC, H7L
4S2
(450) 967-1515
Sales 73,866,360
SIC 6331 Fire, marine, and casualty insurance
Michael J Rowen

D-U-N-S 24-970-9973   (SL)
RENO-DIRECT INC
1329 Boul Dagenais O, Sainte-Rose, QC, H7L
5Z9
(450) 625-2660
Emp Here 25   *Sales* 11,179,350
SIC 5072 Hardware
Philippe Dagenais
Jean-Pierre Dagenais

D-U-N-S 25-361-4598   (BR)
RYERSON CANADA, INC
(*Suby of* RYERSON HOLDING CORPORA-
TION)
3399 Av Francis-Hughes, Sainte-Rose, QC,
H7L 5A5
(450) 975-7171
Emp Here 110
SIC 5051 Metals service centers and offices
Serge Monnette

D-U-N-S 20-387-1900   (SL)
SANTE BAUSCH, CANADA INC
BAUSCH + LOMB
(*Suby of* BAUSCH HEALTH COMPANIES
INC)
2150 Boul Saint-Elzear O, Sainte-Rose, QC,
H7L 4A8
(514) 744-6792
Emp Here 100   *Sales* 28,402,100
SIC 2834 Pharmaceutical preparations
Richard Lajoie
William N. Woodfield
Daniel Yelin
Marcello Malito
Paul S. Herendeen

D-U-N-S 20-999-9226   (HQ)
SOCIETE MONDO AMERICA INC
MONDO AMERICA
(*Suby of* MONDOFIN SPA)
2655 Av Francis-Hughes, Sainte-Rose, QC,
H7L 3S8
(450) 967-5800
Sales 12,708,640
SIC 3069 Fabricated rubber products, nec
Federico Stroppiana
Dominique Cappoudat
Nancy Turcotte

D-U-N-S 25-110-3958   (HQ)
SPIRO MEGA INC
1225 Rue Michelin, Sainte-Rose, QC, H7L
4S2
(450) 663-4457
Sales 11,626,524
SIC 5075 Warm air heating and air condition-
ing
Yvan Bourassa
Richard Angers

D-U-N-S 20-108-9930   (BR)
SYNCREON CANADA INC
TDS LAVAL
1340 Boul Dagenais O, Sainte-Rose, QC, H7L
5C7
(450) 625-0400
Emp Here 120   *Sales* 377,782
SIC 3714 Motor vehicle parts and accessories
Jos Otsweegh

D-U-N-S 25-393-9524   (SL)
SYSTEMES VERINT CANADA, INC
VERINT VIDEO SOLUTIONS
(*Suby of* VERINT SYSTEMS INC.)
1800 Rue Berlier, Sainte-Rose, QC, H7L 4S4
(450) 686-9000
Emp Here 130   *Sales* 75,432,110
SIC 5065 Electronic parts and equipment, nec
Elan Moriah
Peter Fante
Douglas Robinson

D-U-N-S 24-872-1011   (HQ)
**TERIS SERVICES D'APPROVISIONNEMENT
INC**
3180 Montee Saint-Aubin, Sainte-Rose, QC,
H7L 3H8

(450) 622-2710
Emp Here 20   *Sales* 25,988,200
SIC 5191 Farm supplies
Stephane Corbeil

D-U-N-S 20-237-5143   (SL)
VALEANT CANADA LIMITEE
GESTION VALEANT CANADA
(*Suby of* BAUSCH HEALTH COMPANIES INC)
2150 Boul Saint-Elzear O, Sainte-Rose, QC, H7L 4A8
(514) 744-6792
Emp Here 170   *Sales* 48,283,570
SIC 2834 Pharmaceutical preparations
Paul S. Herendeen
Daniel Yelin
Marcello Malito
William Woodfield

D-U-N-S 20-428-0569   (HQ)
VALEANT CANADA S.E.C.
AFEXA
2150 Boul Saint-Elzear O, Sainte-Rose, QC, H7L 4A8
(514) 744-6792
Sales 41,282,100
SIC 5122 Drugs, proprietaries, and sundries
Martin Beaudoin

D-U-N-S 24-297-0465   (SL)
VENTILATION G.R. INC
VENTILATION G.R.
1645 Boul Saint-Elzear O, Sainte-Rose, QC, H7L 3N6
(450) 688-9832
Emp Here 110   *Sales* 29,793,280
SIC 1711 Plumbing, heating, air-conditioning
Christian Duchesne
Sylvain Duchesne
Maxime Duchesne
Charles Arcand

D-U-N-S 25-380-6954   (SL)
VOLAILLES REGAL INC
ENERGY POULTRY
955 Rue Michelin, Sainte-Rose, QC, H7L 5B6
(450) 667-7070
Emp Here 26   *Sales* 21,725,002
SIC 5144 Poultry and poultry products
John Sideras
Vagianos (Vayo) Margetis

Sainte-Rose, QC H7P

D-U-N-S 24-812-2459   (SL)
AUTO CLASSIQUE DE LAVAL INC
MERCEDES-BENZ LAVAL
3131 Desste Nord Laval (A-440) O, Sainte-Rose, QC, H7P 5P2
(450) 681-2500
Emp Here 100   *Sales* 62,928,000
SIC 5511 New and used car dealers
Carole Leblanc
Louise Leblanc
Gilles Leblanc
Denis Bellemare

D-U-N-S 20-609-9777   (SL)
BOURASSA AUTOMOBILES INTERNATIONAL INC
SATURN SAAB CADILLAC DE LAVAL
2800 Boul Chomedey, Sainte-Rose, QC, H7P 5Z9
(450) 681-0028
Emp Here 30   *Sales* 14,942,340
SIC 5511 New and used car dealers
Marc Bourassa

D-U-N-S 24-402-3362   (HQ)
ENERTRAK INC
2875 Rue Jules-Brillant, Sainte-Rose, QC, H7P 6B2
(450) 973-2000
Emp Here 20   *Sales* 10,285,002

SIC 5075 Warm air heating and air conditioning
Samir Trak
Ada Trak
Karine Trak
Tanya Trak
Roger Nasrallah
Ada Giacomuzzi

D-U-N-S 24-822-1892   (SL)
GREGOIRE RAKELIAN PHARMACIEN
3000 Av Jacques-Bureau Bureau Bureau, Sainte-Rose, QC, H7P 5P7
(450) 682-0099
Emp Here 49   *Sales* 12,394,746
SIC 5912 Drug stores and proprietary stores
Gregoire Aaakaliam

D-U-N-S 20-182-8006   (SL)
K.F. CONSTRUCTION INC
1410 Rue De Jaffa Bureau 201, Sainte-Rose, QC, H7P 4K9
(450) 681-8338
Emp Here 28   *Sales* 13,180,468
SIC 1542 Nonresidential construction, nec
Karol Fortin

D-U-N-S 20-003-3327   (BR)
PROVIGO DISTRIBUTION INC
MAXI
(*Suby of* LOBLAW COMPANIES LIMITED)
444 Boul Cure-Labelle, Sainte-Rose, QC, H7P 4W7
(450) 625-4221
Emp Here 76
SIC 5411 Grocery stores
Melanie Beaulieu

Sainte-Rose, QC H7W

D-U-N-S 20-760-4992   (SL)
CLARINS CANADA INC
CLARINS SKIN SPA
(*Suby of* CLARINS)
815 Chomedey (A-13) E, Sainte-Rose, QC, H7W 5N4
(450) 688-0144
Emp Here 170   *Sales* 70,179,570
SIC 5122 Drugs, proprietaries, and sundries
Jonathan Zrihen
Patrick Benaroche
Christophe De Pous
Lionel Uzan
Genevieve Leblanc

D-U-N-S 20-998-9888   (SL)
DISTRIBUTEURS D'ALIMENTS DEFEDIS INC
755 Chomedey (A-13) E, Sainte-Rose, QC, H7W 5N4
(450) 681-9500
Emp Here 25   *Sales* 20,889,425
SIC 5141 Groceries, general line
Miltiadis Antypas
Sotirios Antypas

D-U-N-S 20-175-9862   (BR)
INDUSTRIES SPECTRA PREMIUM INC, LES
(*Suby of* INDUSTRIES SPECTRA PREMIUM INC, LES)
1313 Chomedey (A-13) E, Sainte-Rose, QC, H7W 5L7
(450) 681-1313
Emp Here 200
SIC 3433 Heating equipment, except electric
Robert Angrignon

D-U-N-S 24-769-4540   (HQ)
PILAROS INTERNATIONAL TRADING INC
PILAROS
755 Chomedey (A-13) E, Sainte-Rose, QC, H7W 5N4
(450) 681-6900
Sales 21,725,002

SIC 5141 Groceries, general line
Miltiadis Antypas
Agis Pappas

Sainte-Rose, QC H7X

D-U-N-S 25-242-6473   (SL)
2173-4108 QUEBEC INC
INTERSPORT
640 Chomedey (A-13) O, Sainte-Rose, QC, H7X 3S9
Emp Here 50   *Sales* 10,880,650
SIC 5941 Sporting goods and bicycle shops
Michel Cote
Pierre Allie

D-U-N-S 25-672-7868   (HQ)
CAISSE DESJARDINS DE L'OUEST DE LAVAL
CENTRE DE SERVICE DAGENAIS
440 Chomedey (A-13) O, Sainte-Rose, QC, H7X 3S9
(450) 962-1800
Emp Here 20   *Sales* 14,359,468
SIC 6062 State credit unions
Jacinthe Godmer
Daniel Belanger
Andre Gionet
Louise Durocher
Audrey Duguay
Nadine Sigouin
Andre Dunnigan
Claude Gendron
Gabriel Lapierre
Marie Corriveau

D-U-N-S 20-386-7916   (SL)
GESTIONS SYLVAIN BERUBE INC
MARCHAND CANADIAN TIRE DE STE-DOROTHEE
500 Desste Chomedey (A-13) O, Sainte-Rose, QC, H7X 3S9
(450) 969-4141
Emp Here 50   *Sales* 24,903,900
SIC 5531 Auto and home supply stores
Sylvain Berube
Helene L'heureux

D-U-N-S 20-562-9074   (HQ)
LAURIN CONTENEURS INC
487 Rue Principale, Sainte-Rose, QC, H7X 1C4
(450) 689-1962
Sales 15,540,070
SIC 3523 Farm machinery and equipment
Frederic Albert
Frederic Chabanne

D-U-N-S 24-836-8151   (SL)
MARCHE D'ALIMENTATION CREVIER INC
IGA EXTRA
(*Suby of* GESTION LOUIS CREVIER INC)
550 Chomedey (A-13) O, Sainte-Rose, QC, H7X 3S9
(450) 689-3131
Emp Here 150   *Sales* 36,649,200
SIC 5992 Florists
Louis Crevier
Fanny Crevier
Manon Crevier

D-U-N-S 20-978-7399   (SL)
MARCHE DENIGIL (1984) INC
METRO RICHELIEU
555 Boul Samson, Sainte-Rose, QC, H7X 1J5
(450) 689-2282
Emp Here 75   *Sales* 22,010,775
SIC 5411 Grocery stores
Gilles Messier
Richard Mckibbin

D-U-N-S 24-226-7479   (BR)
WAL-MART CANADA CORP
ACCES PHARMA CHEZ WALMART

(*Suby of* WALMART INC.)
700 Chomedey (A-13) O, Sainte-Rose, QC, H7X 3S9
(450) 969-3226
Emp Here 150
SIC 5311 Department stores
Clair Bush

Sainte-Rose-Du-Nord, QC G0V

D-U-N-S 24-568-4758   (SL)
COOP FORESTIERE DE STE-ROSE
184 Rue Du Quai, Sainte-Rose-Du-Nord, QC, G0V 1T0
Emp Here 70   *Sales* 14,812,910
SIC 0851 Forestry services
Denis Simard

Sainte-Sabine, QC J0J

D-U-N-S 25-377-3824   (HQ)
2757-5158 QUEBEC INC
ARMOIRES CUISINES ACTION
2854 Rte 235, Sainte-Sabine, QC, J0J 2B0
(450) 293-5037
Emp Here 65   *Sales* 13,888,980
SIC 2514 Metal household furniture
Christian Van Gennip
Danielle Naud
Carole Langlois

Sainte-Sophie, QC J5J

D-U-N-S 24-674-8961   (SL)
PICHE, R DYNAMITAGE INC
2591 Boul Sainte-Sophie, Sainte-Sophie, QC, J5J 2V3
(819) 212-0744
Emp Here 60   *Sales* 14,771,160
SIC 1795 Wrecking and demolition work
Marc Piche

D-U-N-S 20-331-0909   (SL)
SERRES SAVOURA PORTNEUF INC, LES
(*Suby of* IPROTECHT ELECTRONICS INCORPORATED)
2743 Boul Sainte-Sophie, Sainte-Sophie, QC, J5J 2V3
(450) 431-6343
Emp Here 100   *Sales* 26,230,900
SIC 0182 Food crops grown under cover
Stephane Roy
Caroline Dalpe

D-U-N-S 25-916-2329   (BR)
WASTE MANAGEMENT OF CANADA CORPORATION
(*Suby of* WASTE MANAGEMENT, INC.)
2535 1re Rue, Sainte-Sophie, QC, J5J 2R7
(450) 431-2313
Emp Here 75
SIC 4212 Local trucking, without storage
Allain Calnuel

Sainte-Sophie-De-Levrard, QC G0X

D-U-N-S 25-470-1857   (SL)
ENTREPRISES H.M. METAL INC, LES
583 Rang Saint-Ovide, Sainte-Sophie-De-Levrard, QC, G0X 3C0
(819) 288-5287
Emp Here 50   *Sales* 10,185,800
SIC 7692 Welding repair
Michel Neault

Helene Aubin
Philippe Neault
Gaston Aubin
Gabriel Neault
Jean Frederic

D-U-N-S 24-295-0848   (SL)
POULETS RIVERVIEW INC
SERVICES ALIMENTAIRES RIVERVIEW
(*Suby of* ATTILA INC)
287 Rue Masson, Sainte-Sophie-De-Levrard, QC, G0X 3C0
(450) 431-1140
Emp Here 18   *Sales* 15,040,386
SIC 5144 Poultry and poultry products
  Daniel Le Rossignol

Sainte-Therese, QC J7E

D-U-N-S 25-200-3124   (HQ)
2864-4920 QUEBEC INC
120 Boul Desjardins E, Sainte-Therese, QC, J7E 1C8
(450) 435-3685
Sales 19,923,120
SIC 5511 New and used car dealers
  Marziale Piccoli

D-U-N-S 20-709-3956   (SL)
9146-3000 QUEBEC INC
STE-THERESE TOYOTA
(*Suby of* 2864-4920 QUEBEC INC)
120 Boul Desjardins E, Sainte-Therese, QC, J7E 1C8
(450) 435-3685
Emp Here 40   *Sales* 25,171,200
SIC 5511 New and used car dealers
  Marziale Piccoli

D-U-N-S 24-386-9422   (SL)
9175-6429 QUEBEC INC
METRO PLUS STE-THERESE
214 Boul Rene-A.-Robert, Sainte-Therese, QC, J7E 4L2
(450) 971-0458
Emp Here 65   *Sales* 19,076,005
SIC 5411 Grocery stores
  Rejean Lemay

D-U-N-S 24-346-5692   (HQ)
BICYCLES QUILICOT INC, LES
BICYCLES QUILICOT PERFORMANCE
232 Rue Saint-Charles Local 90, Sainte-Therese, QC, J7E 2B4
(450) 420-2222
Emp Here 15   *Sales* 10,880,650
SIC 5941 Sporting goods and bicycle shops
  Marc-Andre Lebeau
  Evelyne Forget
  Vincent Turcotte-Morin

D-U-N-S 25-363-0768   (HQ)
CAISSE DESJARDINS THERESE-DE BLAINVILLE
CENTRE DE SERVICE DE BOIS-DES-FILIONS–LORRAINE
201 Boul Du Cure-Labelle, Sainte-Therese, QC, J7E 2X6
(450) 430-6550
Emp Here 100   *Sales* 24,490,386
SIC 6062 State credit unions
  Joe Belanger
  Gilles Pilon
  Alain Gregoire
  Ginette Auger
  Donald Bergeron
  Rodrigue Dubois
  Bernard Duchesne
  Guillaume Duchesne
  Louise Filion
  Brigitte Galarneau

D-U-N-S 25-359-9757   (SL)
CENTRALE ASHTON INC

104b Rue Turgeon, Sainte-Therese, QC, J7E 3H9
(450) 435-6468
Emp Here 29   *Sales* 11,474,662
SIC 7381 Detective and armored car services
  Stanley Ashton
  Joyce Ritter

D-U-N-S 24-422-1680   (SL)
CENTRE DE RENOVATION ANDRE LES-PERANCE INC
227 Boul Rene-A.-Robert, Sainte-Therese, QC, J7E 4L1
(450) 430-6220
Emp Here 110   *Sales* 29,441,720
SIC 5211 Lumber and other building materials
  Andre Lesperance
  Liette Hogue
  Carlos Munoz

D-U-N-S 24-637-0386   (SL)
CENTRE DE SANTE ET DE SERVICES SO-CIAUX DE THERESE-DE BLAINVILLE
CENTRE D'HEBERGEMENT DRAPEAU-DESCHAMBAULT
125 Rue Duquet, Sainte-Therese, QC, J7E 0A5
(450) 430-4553
Emp Here 200   *Sales* 15,358,400
SIC 8322 Individual and family services
  Joe Belanger
  Jean-Claude Langlois
  Yvon Fournier
  Andre Poirier
  Diane Filiatrault

D-U-N-S 25-233-9965   (BR)
COMMISSION SCOLAIRE DE LA SEIGNEURIE-DES-MILLE-ILES
ECOLE ST GABRIEL
(*Suby of* COMMISSION SCOLAIRE DE LA SEIGNEURIE-DES-MILLE-ILES)
8 Rue Tasse, Sainte-Therese, QC, J7E 1V3
(450) 433-5445
Emp Here 80
SIC 8211 Elementary and secondary schools
  Robert St-Pierre

D-U-N-S 25-240-1443   (BR)
COMMISSION SCOLAIRE DE LA SEIGNEURIE-DES-MILLE-ILES
ECOLE SAINTE-THERESE
(*Suby of* COMMISSION SCOLAIRE DE LA SEIGNEURIE-DES-MILLE-ILES)
401 Boul Du Domaine, Sainte-Therese, QC, J7E 4S4
(450) 433-5400
Emp Here 225
SIC 8211 Elementary and secondary schools
  Nathalie Porlier

D-U-N-S 20-257-9850   (HQ)
COMPAGNIE COMMONWEALTH PLY-WOOD LTEE, LA
BOIS CLO-VAL
(*Suby of* SOARING PHOENIX INC)
15 Boul Du Cure-Labelle, Sainte-Therese, QC, J7E 2X1
(450) 435-6541
Emp Here 150   *Sales* 278,390,000
SIC 2435 Hardwood veneer and plywood
  Caine Jr. William Terrrence
  Jonny D'orazio

D-U-N-S 20-330-8531   (HQ)
CONTREPLAQUE & PLACAGE CANADA INC
DISTRIBUTION PRO-PLAST
(*Suby of* SOARING PHOENIX INC)
15 Boul Du Cure-Labelle, Sainte-Therese, QC, J7E 2X1
(450) 435-6541
Emp Here 15   *Sales* 11,626,524
SIC 5031 Lumber, plywood, and millwork
  William T. Jr. Caine
  Johnny D'orazio

D-U-N-S 24-516-5303   (SL)
CONVECTAIR-NMT INC
ADAGIO
(*Suby of* SOCIETE MULLER ET COMPAG-NIE)
30 Car Sicard, Sainte-Therese, QC, J7E 3X6
(450) 951-4367
Emp Here 30   *Sales* 13,415,220
SIC 5063 Electrical apparatus and equipment
  Richard Lacasse
  Eric Baudry
  Michel Roy

D-U-N-S 20-005-8589   (SL)
DESSINS DE STRUCTURE STELTEC INC, LES
(*Suby of* GESTION BEAUCE-ATLAS INC)
22 Boul Desjardins E Bureau 200, Sainte-Therese, QC, J7E 1C1
(450) 971-5995
Emp Here 30   *Sales* 13,476,570
SIC 7389 Business services, nec
  Germain Blais

D-U-N-S 24-581-4108   (SL)
ENTREPRISES CHRISTIAN CHADI INC, LES
JEAN COUTU
95 Boul Du Cure-Labelle Bureau 15, Sainte-Therese, QC, J7E 2X6
(450) 437-5555
Emp Here 45   *Sales* 11,382,930
SIC 5912 Drug stores and proprietary stores
  Christian Chadi

D-U-N-S 25-308-5385   (HQ)
FRANCHISES CORA INC
CHEZ CORA
16 Rue Sicard Bureau 50, Sainte-Therese, QC, J7E 3W7
(450) 435-2426
Emp Here 25   *Sales* 24,388,350
SIC 6794 Patent owners and lessors
  Cora Tsouflidou
  Gesthimani Tsouflidis

D-U-N-S 20-544-2754   (SL)
IGA DAIGLE
220 Rue Saint-Charles, Sainte-Therese, QC, J7E 2B4
(450) 435-1370
Emp Here 45   *Sales* 12,336,840
SIC 5411 Grocery stores
  Robert Daigle

D-U-N-S 24-890-7701   (SL)
MESSAGERIES COURRIERTEL INC, LES
148 Av Des Marquisats, Sainte-Therese, QC, J7E 5J7
(450) 437-9805
Emp Here 40   *Sales* 17,739,600
SIC 7389 Business services, nec
  Claude Vaillancourt

D-U-N-S 24-177-1534   (BR)
PACCAR OF CANADA LTD
PACCAR LEASING
(*Suby of* PACCAR INC)
10 Rue Sicard, Sainte-Therese, QC, J7E 4K9
(450) 435-6171
Emp Here 800
SIC 3711 Motor vehicles and car bodies
  Chakid Toubal-Seghir

D-U-N-S 20-016-3926   (SL)
QUESTZONE.NET INC
LES SERVICES INTERNET QUEST-ZONE.NET
8 Rue Roux Bureau 200, Sainte-Therese, QC, J7E 1L3
(450) 979-3339
Emp Here 26   *Sales* 11,626,524
SIC 5065 Electronic parts and equipment, nec
  Gilles Dagenais

D-U-N-S 25-497-4702   (HQ)
RE/MAX TMS INC
156 Boul Du Cure-Labelle, Sainte-Therese,

QC, J7E 2X5
(450) 430-4207
Emp Here 100   *Sales* 43,983,345
SIC 6531 Real estate agents and managers
  Claude Charron

D-U-N-S 24-828-5264   (HQ)
SOARING PHOENIX INC
15 Boul Du Cure-Labelle, Sainte-Therese, QC, J7E 2X1
(450) 435-6541
Emp Here 1   *Sales* 731,018,000
SIC 6712 Bank holding companies
  William P. Caine
  William T. Caine

D-U-N-S 24-435-5574   (SL)
SYNDICAT NATIONAL DES TRA-VAILLEURS ET TRAVAILLEUSES DE L'AUTOMOBILE DU CANADA INC
TCA CANADA LOCAL 728
49 Rue Saint-Lambert Bureau 728, Sainte-Therese, QC, J7E 3J9
(450) 434-9664
Emp Here 45   *Sales* 17,602,110
SIC 8631 Labor organizations
  Johanne Duplantie

Sainte-Therese-De-Gaspe, QC G0C

D-U-N-S 20-953-6184   (SL)
E. GAGNON ET FILS LTEE
405 Rte 132, Sainte-Therese-De-Gaspe, QC, G0C 3B0
(418) 385-3011
Emp Here 250   *Sales* 121,846,250
SIC 2091 Canned and cured fish and seafoods
  Raymond Sheehan
  Bill Sheehan
  George Sheehan

D-U-N-S 20-258-2425   (SL)
LELIEVRE, LELIEVRE & LEMOIGNAN LTEE
52 Rue Des Vigneaux, Sainte-Therese-De-Gaspe, QC, G0C 3B0
(418) 385-3310
Emp Here 80   *Sales* 27,655,200
SIC 2091 Canned and cured fish and seafoods
  Roch Lelievre
  Luc Lelievre
  Marc-Andre Lemoignan

Salaberry-De-Valleyfield, QC J6S

D-U-N-S 24-316-5881   (SL)
ACIER OUELLETTE INC
ACIER CAMPI
935 Boul Du Havre, Salaberry-De-Valleyfield, QC, J6S 5L1
(450) 377-4248
Emp Here 50   *Sales* 11,671,750
SIC 3312 Blast furnaces and steel mills
  Paul C Shaw
  Linda Shaw
  Francois Heraud
  Legris Philippe

D-U-N-S 24-426-5133   (SL)
ANDY LOGISTIQUE INC
4225 Boul Hebert, Salaberry-De-Valleyfield, QC, J6S 6J2
(514) 667-8494
Emp Here 43   *Sales* 16,570,480
SIC 4731 Freight transportation arrangement
  Andreea Crisan

D-U-N-S 24-316-8262   (SL)
ANDY TRANSPORT INC
ANDY TRAINING CENTRE

4225 Boul Hebert, Salaberry-De-Valleyfield, QC, J6S 6J2
(514) 667-8500
Emp Here 150   *Sales* 30,855,900
SIC 4213 Trucking, except local
Ilie Crisan
Andreea Crisan
Golan Moryoussef

D-U-N-S 20-517-1882   (BR)
ASTENJOHNSON, INC
(Suby of ASTENJOHNSON, INC.*)*
213 Boul Du Havre, Salaberry-De-Valleyfield, QC, J6S 1R9
(450) 373-2425
Emp Here 126
SIC 2299 Textile goods, nec
Guillaume Bernard

D-U-N-S 20-264-5917   (SL)
AUTOMOBILES REGATE INC
VALLEYFIELD CHEVROLET BUICK GMC
1325 Boul Monseigneur-Langlois, Salaberry-De-Valleyfield, QC, J6S 1C1
(450) 373-4372
Emp Here 30   *Sales* 14,942,340
SIC 5511 New and used car dealers
Michel Gaudette

D-U-N-S 20-652-7702   (HQ)
CAISSE DESJARDINS DE SALABERRY-DE-VALLEYFIELD
CENTRE DE SERVICE SAINT-THOMAS
120 Rue Alexandre, Salaberry-De-Valleyfield, QC, J6S 3K4
(450) 377-4177
Emp Here 60   *Sales* 15,890,840
SIC 6062 State credit unions
Gino Napoleoni
Yvon Vinet
Jean-Francois Gagnon
Marcel Gougeon
Nancy Daoust
Jean-Michel Montpetit
Martin Pilotte
Patricia Gagne Claude
Jean-Luc Vincent
Nicolas Julien

D-U-N-S 20-363-4329   (SL)
CENTRE DE MAINTENANCE ANDY INC, LE
4225 Boul Hebert, Salaberry-De-Valleyfield, QC, J6S 6J2
(514) 667-8500
Emp Here 26   *Sales* 13,519,142
SIC 4731 Freight transportation arrangement
Ilie Crisan
Andreea Crisan
Golan Moryoussef

D-U-N-S 20-725-5563   (SL)
ENTREPRISES MICHEL CHOINIERE INC, LES
CANADIAN TIRE #115
1770 Boul Monseigneur-Langlois, Salaberry-De-Valleyfield, QC, J6S 5R1
(450) 373-0123
Emp Here 125   *Sales* 78,660,000
SIC 5531 Auto and home supply stores
Michel Choiniere

D-U-N-S 20-514-8930   (BR)
GCP CANADA INC
DAVISON CATALYST
(Suby of W. R. GRACE & CO.*)*
42 Rue Fabre, Salaberry-De-Valleyfield, QC, J6S 4K7
(450) 373-4224
Emp Here 120
SIC 2819 Industrial inorganic chemicals, nec
Paul Dupuis

D-U-N-S 20-107-0013   (SL)
GENERAL DYNAMICS PRODUITS DE DEFENSE ET SYSTEMES TACTIQUES-CANADA VALLEYFIELD INC
(Suby of GENERAL DYNAMICS CORPORA-TION)*
55 Rue Masson, Salaberry-De-Valleyfield, QC, J6S 4V9
(450) 371-5520
Emp Here 312   *Sales* 138,729,240
SIC 2899 Chemical preparations, nec
Rene Blouin
Del S Dameron
Mark C. Roualet
Firat H. Gezen
Alain Boisvert

D-U-N-S 25-528-0455   (SL)
GESTION PADOMAX INC
280 Boul Pie-Xii, Salaberry-De-Valleyfield, QC, J6S 6P7
(450) 373-4274
Emp Here 60   *Sales* 14,771,160
SIC 1794 Excavation work
Yves Loiselle

D-U-N-S 20-631-7646   (BR)
GOODYEAR CANADA INC
(Suby of THE GOODYEAR TIRE & RUBBER COMPANY*)*
2600 Boul Monseigneur-Langlois, Salaberry-De-Valleyfield, QC, J6S 5G6
(450) 377-6800
Emp Here 200
SIC 3011 Tires and inner tubes
James Conlier

D-U-N-S 25-428-7522   (SL)
IGA EXTRA MARCHE LACAS INC
1366 Boul Monseigneur-Langlois, Salaberry-De-Valleyfield, QC, J6S 1E3
(450) 373-0251
Emp Here 49   *Sales* 13,433,448
SIC 5411 Grocery stores
Jacques Lacas
Stephane Lacas

D-U-N-S 20-724-2207   (HQ)
LOISELLE INC
EXCAVATION LOISELLE ET FRERES, DIV OF
280 Boul Pie-Xii, Salaberry-De-Valleyfield, QC, J6S 6P7
(450) 373-4274
Sales 24,618,600
SIC 1794 Excavation work
Paul Beluse
Sebastien Claveau
Eric Parent
Steven Lebel
Stephane Boyer

D-U-N-S 24-620-0364   (SL)
MACCO ORGANIQUES INC
MACCO
(Suby of PLACEMENTS LALLEMAND INC*)*
100 Rue Mcarthur, Salaberry-De-Valleyfield, QC, J6S 4M5
(450) 371-1066
Emp Here 72   *Sales* 20,449,512
SIC 2899 Chemical preparations, nec
Robert J. Briscoe
Rejean Landry
Jean Chagnon
Guy Marleau
Pierre Chagnon
Robert G. Briscoe
Antoine Chagnon
Sarah Prichard
Simon Rinella

D-U-N-S 24-224-0661   (HQ)
MATERIAUX MIRON INC
BMR
230 Boul Monseigneur-Langlois, Salaberry-De-Valleyfield, QC, J6S 0A7
(450) 373-7272
Sales 12,652,950
SIC 5211 Lumber and other building materials
Bernard Miron
Benoit Miron
Christian Miron

Monique Daignault

D-U-N-S 24-021-3710   (HQ)
MATERIAUX PONT MASSON INC
GROUPE MPM
2715 Boul Monseigneur-Langlois, Salaberry-De-Valleyfield, QC, J6S 5P7
(450) 371-2041
Sales 26,765,200
SIC 5211 Lumber and other building materials
Eric Bailey
Stephane Bailey
Michel Bergeron

D-U-N-S 20-264-5172   (HQ)
PIECES D'AUTO VALLEYFIELD INC
940 Boul Monseigneur-Langlois, Salaberry-De-Valleyfield, QC, J6S 1C3
(450) 373-9505
Emp Here 28   *Sales* 12,747,525
SIC 5015 Motor vehicle parts, used
John Shannon

D-U-N-S 24-431-2666   (HQ)
PLOMBCO INC
(Suby of WEGMANN UNTERNEHMENS-HOLDING GMBH & CO. KG*)*
66 Rue Edmond, Salaberry-De-Valleyfield, QC, J6S 3E8
(450) 371-8800
Emp Here 50   *Sales* 19,952,680
SIC 3369 Nonferrous foundries, nec
Jeff Waechter
Emile Lajoie

D-U-N-S 24-295-8106   (SL)
PRESTIGE FORD INC
GENDRON FORD
1275 Boul Monseigneur-Langlois, Salaberry-De-Valleyfield, QC, J6S 1C1
(450) 371-0711
Emp Here 27   *Sales* 13,448,106
SIC 5511 New and used car dealers
Richard Aitken

D-U-N-S 20-885-8282   (SL)
ROCHEFORT, PERRON, BILLETTE INC
ASSURANCES R.P.B.
1000 Boul Monseigneur-Langlois Bureau 300, Salaberry-De-Valleyfield, QC, J6S 0J7
(514) 395-8703
Emp Here 49   *Sales* 28,416,276
SIC 6411 Insurance agents, brokers, and service
Alain Houle
Sebastien Gaudreau
Patrice Bougie
Pierre-Yves Billette

D-U-N-S 20-264-5131   (SL)
ROUSSE, RAYMOND INC
569 Rue Ellen, Salaberry-De-Valleyfield, QC, J6S 0B1
(450) 373-5085
Emp Here 37   *Sales* 30,916,349
SIC 5142 Packaged frozen goods
Michel Marchand
Christiane Leblanc Marchand

D-U-N-S 24-053-9353   (SL)
SUPERMARCHE ROBERT PILON LTEE
IGA PILON-MCKINON
1380 Boul Monseigneur-Langlois, Salaberry-De-Valleyfield, QC, J6S 1E3
(450) 373-0251
Emp Here 140   *Sales* 41,086,780
SIC 5411 Grocery stores
Robert Pilon
Steve Mckinon

D-U-N-S 20-715-8077   (BR)
VILLE DE SALABERRY DE VALLEYFIELD
SERVICE DE L'ENVIRONNEMENT ET DES TRAVAUX PUBLICS
(Suby of VILLE DE SALABERRY DE VALLEY-FIELD)*
275 Rue Hebert, Salaberry-De-Valleyfield,

QC, J6S 5Y9
(450) 370-4820
Emp Here 100
SIC 8743 Public relations services
Denis Lapointe

D-U-N-S 25-201-4634   (SL)
VOYAGES BERNARD GENDRON INC
FLEXTOUR
1465 Boul Monseigneur-Langlois, Salaberry-De-Valleyfield, QC, J6S 1C2
(450) 373-8747
Emp Here 50   *Sales* 19,268,000
SIC 4724 Travel agencies
Bernard Gendron

D-U-N-S 20-330-7731   (SL)
W. R. GRACE CANADA CORP
(Suby of W. R. GRACE & CO.*)*
42 Rue Fabre, Salaberry-De-Valleyfield, QC, J6S 4K7
(450) 373-4224
Emp Here 112   *Sales* 31,810,352
SIC 2819 Industrial inorganic chemicals, nec
Alfred E. Festa
Genevieve Fortier
Mark A. Shelnitz
John A. Mcfarland
Thomas E. Blaser

D-U-N-S 20-643-9619   (BR)
WAL-MART CANADA CORP
ACCES PHARMA CHEZ WALMART
(Suby of WALMART INC.*)*
2050 Boul Monseigneur-Langlois, Salaberry-De-Valleyfield, QC, J6S 5R1
(450) 371-9026
Emp Here 208
SIC 5311 Department stores
Nancy Grenier

Salaberry-De-Valleyfield, QC J6T

D-U-N-S 24-870-7481   (SL)
2619-0645 QUEBEC INC
JARDINS QUATRE SAISONS
1658 Boul Sainte-Marie, Salaberry-De-Valleyfield, QC, J6T 6M2
(450) 373-0690
Emp Here 16   *Sales* 13,369,232
SIC 5148 Fresh fruits and vegetables
Paul Fecteau
Martin Fecteau
Yannick Fecteau
Frederic Maisonneuve

D-U-N-S 20-264-5750   (SL)
ACIER VALLEYFIELD INC
480 Boul Des Erables, Salaberry-De-Valleyfield, QC, J6T 6G4
(450) 373-4350
Emp Here 12   *Sales* 12,004,068
SIC 5051 Metals service centers and offices
Serge Hebert

D-U-N-S 20-888-6689   (SL)
ALI EXCAVATION INC
(Suby of SOCIETE DE GESTION ALI INC*)*
760 Boul Des Erables, Salaberry-De-Valleyfield, QC, J6T 6G4
(450) 373-2010
Emp Here 60   *Sales* 14,771,160
SIC 1794 Excavation work
Mario Guillemette
Simon Loiselle
Jean-Francois Beaulieu
Patrice Daignault

D-U-N-S 24-218-0073   (SL)
ASSURANCIA SHINK DECELLES INC
ASSURANCES SHINK BOURGON
45 Rue Victoria E, Salaberry-De-Valleyfield, QC, J6T 2L4

---

(450) 377-8585
Emp Here 25   *Sales* 21,201,500
SIC 6411 Insurance agents, brokers, and service
Lucie Decelles

D-U-N-S 24-351-2683   (BR)
CAISSE DESJARDINS DE SALABERRY-DE-VALLEYFIELD
(*Suby of* CAISSE DESJARDINS DE SALABERRY-DE-VALLEYFIELD)
15 Rue Saint-Thomas, Salaberry-De-Valleyfield, QC, J6T 4J1
(450) 377-4177
Emp Here 100
SIC 6062 State credit unions
Normand Houle

D-U-N-S 20-712-3410   (BR)
COMMISSION SCOLAIRE DE LA VALLEE-DES-TISSERANDS, LA
ECOLE BAIE SAINT FRANCOIS
70 Rue Louis Vi-Major, Salaberry-De-Valleyfield, QC, J6T 3G2
(450) 371-2004
Emp Here 130
SIC 8211 Elementary and secondary schools
Sylvain Leblanc

D-U-N-S 24-374-0938   (BR)
DIAGEO CANADA INC
(*Suby of* DIAGEO PLC)
1 Rue Salaberry, Salaberry-De-Valleyfield, QC, J6T 2G9
(450) 373-3230
Emp Here 200
SIC 5182 Wine and distilled beverages
Denif Laelle

D-U-N-S 25-090-7375   (HQ)
ENERGIE P38 INC
BUDGET PROPANE (1998)
(*Suby of* GAZ BLEU PROPANE INC)
683 Ch Larocque, Salaberry-De-Valleyfield, QC, J6T 4E1
(450) 373-4333
Emp Here 33   *Sales* 23,450,250
SIC 5984 Liquefied petroleum gas dealers
Guy Jr. Marchand

D-U-N-S 20-971-3460   (HQ)
GROUPE MELOCHE INC
491 Boul Des Erables, Salaberry-De-Valleyfield, QC, J6T 6G3
(450) 371-4646
Sales 50,557,860
SIC 3599 Industrial machinery, nec
Hugue Meloche
Martin Fournier
Pierre Grand Maison
Jacques St-Laurent
Helene Seguinotte
Guy Leblanc
Marc Bigras
Gerard Gagne

D-U-N-S 20-259-5778   (SL)
INVESTIGATION PROTECTION ACCES SECURITE INC
I.P.A.S
283 Rue Jacques-Cartier Bureau 6, Salaberry-De-Valleyfield, QC, J6T 4S9
(450) 377-3008
Emp Here 40   *Sales* 17,739,600
SIC 7389 Business services, nec
Suzanne Major
Marc Viau

D-U-N-S 24-713-3945   (SL)
J.R. MECANIQUE LTEE
485a Boul Des Erables, Salaberry-De-Valleyfield, QC, J6T 6G3
(450) 377-3615
Emp Here 75   *Sales* 31,705,275
SIC 1541 Industrial buildings and warehouses
Pascal Dupuis
Francois Bertrand

Martin Hogue
Mario Plourde

D-U-N-S 24-150-3122   (SL)
L B C D INGENIEURS CONSEILS INC
TROW ASSOCIES
40 Rue Sainte-Cecile, Salaberry-De-Valleyfield, QC, J6T 1L7
(450) 371-5722
Emp Here 95   *Sales* 22,201,025
SIC 8621 Professional organizations
Pierre Beauchamps
Jean-Noel Cote

D-U-N-S 20-264-4035   (HQ)
LIBRAIRIES BOYER LTEE
10 Rue Nicholson, Salaberry-De-Valleyfield, QC, J6T 4M2
(450) 373-6211
Emp Here 50   *Sales* 26,876,080
SIC 5943 Stationery stores
Marie Boyer Grefford
Michel Grefford

D-U-N-S 24-005-4747   (BR)
METRO RICHELIEU INC
METRO PLUS
(*Suby of* METRO INC)
398 Ch Larocque, Salaberry-De-Valleyfield, QC, J6T 4C5
(450) 370-1444
Emp Here 80
SIC 5411 Grocery stores
Guy Levac

D-U-N-S 25-192-1664   (SL)
NORDMEC INDUSTRIELS & MINES INC
SDX MECANIQUE
(*Suby of* NORDMEC CONSTRUCTION INC)
850 Boul Des Erables, Salaberry-De-Valleyfield, QC, J6T 6G4
(450) 373-3739
Emp Here 40   *Sales* 10,873,680
SIC 7699 Repair services, nec
Joel Prud'homme
Serge Landry
Michel Labelle

D-U-N-S 24-348-1152   (BR)
SERVICES DE READAPTATION SUD OUEST ET DU RENFORT, LES
(*Suby of* SERVICES DE READAPTATION SUD OUEST ET DU RENFORT, LES)
30 Rue Saint-Thomas Bureau 200, Salaberry-De-Valleyfield, QC, J6T 4J2
(450) 371-4816
Emp Here 600
SIC 8361 Residential care
Gilles Bertrand

D-U-N-S 24-904-2797   (HQ)
SOCIETE DE GESTION ALI INC
760 Boul Des Erables, Salaberry-De-Valleyfield, QC, J6T 6G4
(450) 373-2010
Sales 19,134,500
SIC 6712 Bank holding companies
Serge Loiselle
Normand Loiselle

D-U-N-S 20-704-8112   (SL)
SOCIETE EN COMMANDITE REVENUE NORANDA
860 Boul Gerard-Cadieux, Salaberry-De-Valleyfield, QC, J6T 6L4
(450) 373-9144
Emp Here 600   *Sales* 244,304,400
SIC 3339 Primary nonferrous Metals, nec
Eva Cariffini

D-U-N-S 24-711-2543   (SL)
TRIAL DESIGN INC
570 Boul Des Erables, Salaberry-De-Valleyfield, QC, J6T 6G4
(450) 370-1377
Emp Here 90   *Sales* 20,916,270
SIC 5712 Furniture stores

Pierre Parent
Paul Passaretti
Joey Basmaji

D-U-N-S 20-052-1701   (SL)
VALTECH FABRICATION INC
INDUSTRIES VALTECH
730 Boul Des Erables, Salaberry-De-Valleyfield, QC, J6T 6G4
(450) 371-0033
Emp Here 100   *Sales* 19,208,500
SIC 3443 Fabricated plate work (boiler shop)
Naim Baksh
George Maziotis
Regis Blanchette
Christian Roy
Marco Lestage

D-U-N-S 20-123-2753   (SL)
ZINC ELECTROLYTIQUE DU CANADA LIMITEE
CEZINC
(*Suby of* GLENCORE PLC)
860 Boul Gerard-Cadieux, Salaberry-De-Valleyfield, QC, J6T 6L4
(450) 373-9144
Emp Here 500   *Sales* 127,887,000
SIC 1031 Lead and zinc ores
Eva Carissimi
Michael Boone

Sayabec, QC G0J

D-U-N-S 24-041-5943   (SL)
DEPANNEUR CADEKO
43 Boul Joubert E, Sayabec, QC, G0J 3K0
(418) 536-5495
Emp Here 49   *Sales* 13,433,448
SIC 5411 Grocery stores
Pierre Dufresne

D-U-N-S 24-200-8910   (SL)
RPF LTEE
POIRIER, RICHARD ET FRERES ELECTRIQUE
(*Suby of* 7105509 CANADA INC)
163 Rte 132 O, Sayabec, QC, G0J 3K0
(418) 536-5453
Emp Here 50   *Sales* 10,891,450
SIC 1731 Electrical work
Marc Poirier
Jasmin Poirier

D-U-N-S 24-591-4205   (BR)
UNIBOARD CANADA INC
(*Suby of* UNIBOARD CANADA INC)
152 Rte Pouliot, Sayabec, QC, G0J 3K0
(418) 536-5465
Emp Here 400
SIC 2493 Reconstituted wood products
Claude Leblanc

Scott, QC G0S

D-U-N-S 20-869-1550   (HQ)
COUVOIR SCOTT LTEE
1798 Rte Du President-Kennedy, Scott, QC, G0S 3G0
(418) 387-2323
Sales 17,562,445
SIC 0254 Poultry hatcheries
Francine Gregoire
Jacques Leclerc
Guy Ferland
Marie-Lucie Gregoire
Pierre Houde
Leandre Morin

D-U-N-S 24-884-7055   (HQ)
IMPRIMERIE SOLISCO INC
SOLISCOM

(*Suby of* 2856-8848 QUEBEC INC)
120 10e Rue, Scott, QC, G0S 3G0
(418) 387-8908
Emp Here 320   *Sales* 65,883,160
SIC 2752 Commercial printing, lithographic
Alain Jacques
Andre Heroux
Jocelyn Poirier
Christian Paupe
Claude Rousseau

Senneterre, QC J0Y

D-U-N-S 24-019-5909   (HQ)
AUTOMOBILES SENEX LTEE
SENEX PONTIAC BUICK CHEVROLET
851 7e Av, Senneterre, QC, J0Y 2M0
(819) 737-2291
Emp Here 23   *Sales* 12,451,950
SIC 5511 New and used car dealers
Denis Sawyer
Bill Chapman

D-U-N-S 20-573-2493   (BR)
COMPAGNIE DES CHEMINS DE FER NATIONAUX DU CANADA
(*Suby of* COMPAGNIE DES CHEMINS DE FER NATIONAUX DU CANADA)
171 4e Rue O, Senneterre, QC, J0Y 2M0
(819) 737-8121
Emp Here 100
SIC 4111 Local and suburban transit
Justin Charrette

D-U-N-S 24-636-5175   (SL)
FORESTERIE A S L INC, LA
803 14e Av, Senneterre, QC, J0Y 2M0
(819) 737-8851
Emp Here 86   *Sales* 11,761,274
SIC 0851 Forestry services
Eric Chantal

D-U-N-S 20-259-1301   (SL)
MARCHE SENNETERRE INC
METRO
760 10e Av, Senneterre, QC, J0Y 2M0
(819) 737-2232
Emp Here 40   *Sales* 10,966,080
SIC 5411 Grocery stores
Michel Bilodeau
Yvon Bilodeau

D-U-N-S 24-517-1889   (SL)
PETROLES J.C. TRUDEL INC
1220 10e Av, Senneterre, QC, J0Y 2M0
(819) 737-2477
Emp Here 11   *Sales* 11,360,888
SIC 5172 Petroleum products, nec
Remi Trudel

D-U-N-S 25-073-6415   (BR)
PF RESOLU CANADA INC
(*Suby of* RESOLUTE FOREST PRODUCTS INC)
40 Ch Saint-Pierre, Senneterre, QC, J0Y 2M0
(819) 737-2300
Emp Here 140
SIC 2621 Paper mills
Marco Poliquin

Senneville, QC H9X

D-U-N-S 20-422-0149   (HQ)
LABORATOIRES CHARLES RIVER MONTREAL ULC
CHARLES RIVER LABORATOIRIES PRE-CLINICAL SERVICES MONTREAL
(*Suby of* CHARLES RIVER ULC)
22022 Aut Felix-Leclerc, Senneville, QC, H9X 3R3
(514) 630-8200
Emp Here 1,063   *Sales* 240,612,678

SIC 8731 Commercial physical research
Glenn Washer
David Johst
Davide Molho
David Smith

D-U-N-S 20-549-2353   (HQ)
SCN INDUSTRIEL INC
(Suby of 3075966 NOVA SCOTIA COMPANY)
22555 Aut Transcanadienne, Senneville, QC,
H9X 3L7
(514) 457-1709
Sales 20,901,144
SIC 5084 Industrial machinery and equipment
Shirley Reed
Glenn Watt
David Reed

D-U-N-S 20-418-3255   (HQ)
TENAQUIP LIMITEE
ATTACHES KINGSTON
22555 Aut Transcanadienne, Senneville, QC,
H9X 3L7
(514) 457-7801
Emp Here 402   *Sales* 280,444,750
SIC 5085 Industrial supplies
Shirley Reed
David Reed
Glenn Watt
Annie Tashdjian

Sept-Iles, QC G4R

D-U-N-S 20-281-4476   (BR)
2553-4330 QUEBEC INC
AEROPRO
(Suby of 2553-4330 QUEBEC INC)
18 Aviation General E, Sept-Iles, QC, G4R
4K2
(418) 961-2808
Emp Here 250
SIC 4512 Air transportation, scheduled
Aurele Labbe

D-U-N-S 25-412-7376   (SL)
3471250 CANADA INC
LOCATIONS NORDIQUES
440 Rue Holliday, Sept-Iles, QC, G4R 4X6
(418) 962-1234
Emp Here 100   *Sales* 24,618,600
SIC 1794 Excavation work
Regis Bouchard

D-U-N-S 24-796-1209   (HQ)
3887952 CANADA INC
EQUIPEMENTS NORDIQUES
440 Holliday, Sept-Iles, QC, G4R 4X6
(418) 962-1234
Emp Here 26   *Sales* 11,671,750
SIC 1442 Construction sand and gravel
Regis Bouchard
Michel Lessard

D-U-N-S 24-814-3331   (SL)
ALUMINERIE ALOUETTE INC
400 Ch De La Pointe-Noire, Sept-Iles, QC,
G4R 5M9
(418) 964-7000
Emp Here 750   *Sales* 136,041,000
SIC 3334 Primary aluminum
Knut Meel
Gerald Charland
Claude Boulanger

D-U-N-S 20-954-0293   (SL)
**BOUCHARD & BLANCHETTE MARINE LIM-
ITEE**
60 Rue Retty, Sept-Iles, QC, G4R 3E1
(418) 968-2505
Emp Here 25   *Sales* 11,087,250
SIC 7389 Business services, nec
Vincent Bouchard
Gaetan Bouchard

D-U-N-S 25-331-6913   (SL)

CENTRE DE MECANIQUE DU GOLFE INC
336 Av Noel, Sept-Iles, QC, G4R 1L7
(418) 962-4057
Emp Here 25   *Sales* 11,875,650
SIC 5084 Industrial machinery and equipment
Jean Cormier

D-U-N-S 25-240-0676   (BR)
COMMISSION SCOLAIRE DU FER
ECOLE JEAN DU NORD
110 Rue Comeau, Sept-Iles, QC, G4R 1J4
(418) 964-2811
Emp Here 80
SIC 8211 Elementary and secondary schools
Lise Madore

D-U-N-S 24-969-0645   (HQ)
COMMISSION SCOLAIRE DU LITTORAL
789 Rue Beaulieu, Sept-Iles, QC, G4R 1P8
(418) 962-5558
Sales 19,823,800
SIC 8211 Elementary and secondary schools
Genevieve Boucher
Nadia Landry

D-U-N-S 24-022-8940   (SL)
**COMPAGNIE DE CHEMIN DE FER DU
LITTORAL NORD DE QUEBEC ET DU
LABRADOR INC**
CHEMIN DE FER QNS&L
(Suby of RIO TINTO PLC)
1 Rue Retty, Sept-Iles, QC, G4R 3C7
(418) 968-7400
Emp Here 500   *Sales* 246,891,500
SIC 4011 Railroads, line-haul operating
Clayton Walker
Maurice Mcclure
Thierry Martel
Marie-Christine Dupont

D-U-N-S 24-895-9202   (BR)
COMPAGNIE MINIERE IOC INC
(Suby of RIO TINTO PLC)
1 Rue Retty, Sept-Iles, QC, G4R 3C7
(418) 968-7400
Emp Here 700   *Sales* 246,891,500
SIC 1011 Iron ores
Natalie Rouleau

D-U-N-S 24-148-9228   (SL)
**CONSTRUCTION LECLERC & PELLETIER
INC**
475 Av Perreault, Sept-Iles, QC, G4R 1K6
(418) 962-2499
Emp Here 25   *Sales* 11,768,275
SIC 1542 Nonresidential construction, nec
Daniel Beaulieu
Rock Blouin

D-U-N-S 24-637-3351   (SL)
**COOPERATIVE ETUDIANTE DU CEGEP DE
SEPT-ILES**
CEGEP DE SEPT-ILES
175 Rue De La Verendrye, Sept-Iles, QC, G4R
5B7
(418) 962-9848
Emp Here 160   *Sales* 23,902,560
SIC 8221 Colleges and universities
Paquerette Beaudin
Jeanne Desbiens
Sylvie Levesque

D-U-N-S 25-976-6103   (HQ)
DISTRIBUTIONS J.R.V. INC
ACCESSOIRES SEPT-ILES
818 Boul Laure Bureau 101, Sept-Iles, QC,
G4R 1Y8
(418) 962-9457
Emp Here 9   *Sales* 28,501,560
SIC 5085 Industrial supplies
Daniel Larouche
Ginette Belaskie
Odette Whittom

D-U-N-S 24-393-0554   (SL)
**ENTREPRISES MARIO LAROCHELLE INC,
LES**

CANADIAN TIRE
402 Boul Laure, Sept-Iles, QC, G4R 1X5
(418) 968-1415
Emp Here 30   *Sales* 14,942,340
SIC 5531 Auto and home supply stores
Mario Larochelle

D-U-N-S 24-381-5016   (SL)
FERRO AUTOMOBILES INC
OLIVIER FORD SEPT-ILES
690 Av Brochu, Sept-Iles, QC, G4R 2X5
(418) 962-3301
Emp Here 30   *Sales* 14,942,340
SIC 5511 New and used car dealers
Jacques Oliver Jr

D-U-N-S 24-631-1612   (HQ)
GESTION CHRISTIAN BASTIEN INC
JEAN COUTU
770 Boul Laure Unite 270, Sept-Iles, QC, G4R
1Y5
(418) 962-3333
Emp Here 25   *Sales* 12,647,700
SIC 5912 Drug stores and proprietary stores
Christian Bastien

D-U-N-S 20-909-5306   (SL)
GOLDER ASSOCIES LTEE
690 Boul Laure Bureau 112, Sept-Iles, QC,
G4R 4N8
(418) 968-6111
Emp Here 49   *Sales* 11,350,017
SIC 8621 Professional organizations
Mark Andrew Brightman

D-U-N-S 20-290-4652   (BR)
GROUPE DE SECURITE GARDA INC, LE
*(Suby of GW INTERMEDIATE HOLDCO
CORPORATION)*
456 Av Arnaud Bureau 218, Sept-Iles, QC,
G4R 3B1
(418) 968-8006
Emp Here 200
SIC 7381 Detective and armored car services
Elide Mailloux

D-U-N-S 20-776-5439   (HQ)
METAL 7 INC
285 Rue Des Pionniers, Sept-Iles, QC, G4R
4X9
(418) 968-5822
Sales 19,710,652
SIC 3479 Metal coating and allied services
Marc-Andre Gervais
Guillaume Vincent
Pierre Boisvert
Louis Bouchard
Michel Messier
Bruno Fortin
Vicky Trepanier

D-U-N-S 24-464-4308   (HQ)
MINES WABUSH
CLIFFS RESSOURCES NATURELLES
1505 Ch Pointe-Noire, Sept-Iles, QC, G4R 4L4
(418) 962-5131
Sales 79,034,166
SIC 1011 Iron ores
Steeve Charest

D-U-N-S 20-357-5279   (SL)
**OLIVIER SEPT-ILES CHRYSLER DODGE
JEEP RAM INC**
OLIVIER CHRYSLER
119 Rue Monseigneur-Blanche, Sept-Iles,
QC, G4R 3G7
(418) 962-2555
Emp Here 27   *Sales* 13,603,861
SIC 5511 New and used car dealers

D-U-N-S 20-355-7574   (SL)
**SOCIETE FERROVIAIRE ET PORTUAIRE
DE POINTE-NOIRE S.E.C.**
SFP POINTE-NOIRE
1505 Ch Pointe-Noire, Sept-Iles, QC, G4R 4L4
(418) 962-5131
Emp Here 100   *Sales* 39,372,400
SIC 4482 Ferries

Martin Perron

D-U-N-S 24-208-0018   (SL)
VITRERIE NORCRISTAL (1982) INC
360 Av Perreault, Sept-Iles, QC, G4R 1K3
(418) 968-8796
Emp Here 11   *Sales* 11,003,729
SIC 5051 Metals service centers and offices
Marc Pelletier
Michel Laflamme

D-U-N-S 24-760-3314   (SL)
WAINBEE S H C N INC
SPECIALITE HYDRAULIQUE COTE NORD
453 Av Noel, Sept-Iles, QC, G4R 1M1
(418) 962-4949
Emp Here 30   *Sales* 14,250,780
SIC 5084 Industrial machinery and equipment
Ronald J Rodger
Claude Talbot
Robert R M Young
Philippe Rushworth

D-U-N-S 20-949-7031   (BR)
WAL-MART CANADA CORP
WALMART
(Suby of WALMART INC.)
1005 Boul Laure Bureau 500, Sept-Iles, QC,
G4R 4S6
(418) 968-5151
Emp Here 150
SIC 5311 Department stores
Zakaria Tarek

Sept-Iles, QC G4S

D-U-N-S 20-381-5097   (SL)
9356-3609 QUEBEC INC
GROUPE TECNOR
*(Suby of GESTION STEPHANE LAGARDE
INC)*
22c Rue Lemaire, Sept-Iles, QC, G4S 1S3
(418) 960-1276
Emp Here 50   *Sales* 13,592,100
SIC 7699 Repair services, nec
Stephane Lagarde

Shawinigan, QC G0X

D-U-N-S 25-526-3287   (SL)
TECFAB INTERNATIONAL INC
*(Suby of CANAM LUX PARENT COMPANY
SARL)*
5190 Rang Saint-Mathieu, Shawinigan, QC,
G0X 1L0
(819) 536-4445
Emp Here 60   *Sales* 10,883,280
SIC 3312 Blast furnaces and steel mills
Marcel Dutil
Rene Guizzetti
Louis Guertin
Marc Dutil

Shawinigan, QC G9N

D-U-N-S 24-651-3662   (SL)
9204-6424 QUEBEC INC
LESSARD BUICK CHEVROLET GMC
5570 Boul Royal, Shawinigan, QC, G9N 4R8
(819) 539-8333
Emp Here 40   *Sales* 19,923,120
SIC 5511 New and used car dealers
Normand Lessard

D-U-N-S 25-669-1226   (SL)
9308-3152 QUEBEC INC
SHAWINIGAN CHRYSLER
10303 Boul Des Hetres, Shawinigan, QC,

G9N 4Y2
(819) 539-5457
Emp Here 40   *Sales* 19,923,120
SIC 5511 New and used car dealers
Benoit Dusablon

D-U-N-S 24-369-1826   (BR)
CAISSE DESJARDINS DU CENTRE-DE-LA-MAURICIE
CENTRE DE SERVICES LA MAURICIENNE
(*Suby of* CAISSE DESJARDINS DU CENTRE-DE-LA-MAURICIE)
444 5e Rue De La Pointe, Shawinigan, QC, G9N 1E6
(819) 536-4404
Emp Here 83
SIC 6062 State credit unions
Andre Heon

D-U-N-S 24-673-3880   (SL)
CANADIAN TIRE MAGASIN ASSOCIATES
1555 Rue Trudel, Shawinigan, QC, G9N 8K8
(819) 537-3888
Emp Here 45   *Sales* 16,389,675
SIC 5013 Motor vehicle supplies and new parts
Jeff Cote

D-U-N-S 24-890-7867   (BR)
CENTRE HOSPITALIER DU CENTRE LA MAURICIE
CSSS RESIDENCE DOCTEUR JOSEPH GARCEAU
243 1re Rue De La Pointe, Shawinigan, QC, G9N 1K2

Emp Here 100
SIC 8361 Residential care
Guy Lemieux

D-U-N-S 20-171-3422   (BR)
CENTRE HOSPITALIER DU CENTRE LA MAURICIE
CLINIQUE DE PREVENTION EN SEXUALITE
1265 Rue Trudel Bureau 6, Shawinigan, QC, G9N 8T3
(819) 539-8371
Emp Here 100
SIC 7363 Help supply services
Helene Massicotte

D-U-N-S 25-854-2984   (BR)
CENTRE LAFLECHE GRAND-MERE
RESIDENCE SAINT MAURICE
555 Av De La Station, Shawinigan, QC, G9N 1V9
(819) 536-0071
Emp Here 200
SIC 8361 Residential care
Alain Harvey

D-U-N-S 24-081-8195   (HQ)
COLLEGE SHAWINIGAN
2263 Av Du College, Shawinigan, QC, G9N 6V8
(819) 539-6401
Sales 35,253,250
SIC 8221 Colleges and universities
Jocelyn Millette
Annie Roy
Joyce Paquette
Eric Milette
Guy Dumais

D-U-N-S 25-379-9381   (BR)
COMMISSION SCOLAIRE DE L'ENERGIE
CARREFOUR FORMATION MAURICIE
5105 Av Albert-Tessier Bureau 840, Shawinigan, QC, G9N 7A3
(819) 539-2265
Emp Here 100
SIC 8211 Elementary and secondary schools
Denis Lapron

D-U-N-S 25-001-8231   (BR)
COMMISSION SCOLAIRE DE L'ENERGIE
ECOLE SECONDAIRE DES CHUTES

5285 Av Albert Tessier, Shawinigan, QC, G9N 6T9
(819) 539-2285
Emp Here 100
SIC 8211 Elementary and secondary schools
Rene Perron

D-U-N-S 20-125-1506   (BR)
COMPAGNIE COMMONWEALTH PLYWOOD LTEE, LA
(*Suby of* SOARING PHOENIX INC)
1155 Av De La Fonderie, Shawinigan, QC, G9N 1W9
(819) 537-6621
Emp Here 80
SIC 2435 Hardwood veneer and plywood
Daniel Godbout

D-U-N-S 24-855-0027   (BR)
CONSTRUCTION DJL INC
CONTINENTAL DIV DE
(*Suby of* VINCI)
3200 Boul Hubert-Biermans, Shawinigan, QC, G9N 0A4
(819) 539-2271
Emp Here 165
SIC 1611 Highway and street construction
Christian Hould

D-U-N-S 24-347-0056   (HQ)
CORPORATION CULTURELLE DE SHAWINIGAN
CULTURE SHAWINIGAN
2100 Boul Des Hetres, Shawinigan, QC, G9N 8R8
(819) 539-1888
Emp Here 1   *Sales* 10,332,764
SIC 8699 Membership organizations, nec
Josette Allard-Gignac
Pauline Belanger-Daneault
Alain Huard

D-U-N-S 25-108-1824   (SL)
CORPORATION ZEDBED INTERNATIONAL INC
GALERIE CONFORT
(*Suby of* OWEN & COMPANY LIMITED)
5352 Rue Burrill, Shawinigan, QC, G9N 0C3
(819) 539-1112
Emp Here 38   *Sales* 19,336,528
SIC 5021 Furniture
Mario Gelinas
Jamie Cartwright
Marc Paiement

D-U-N-S 24-908-3056   (SL)
CSH DOMAINE CASCADE
DOMAINE CASCADE
695 7e Rue De La Pointe, Shawinigan, QC, G9N 8K2
(819) 536-4463
Emp Here 60   *Sales* 13,974,660
SIC 6513 Apartment building operators
Francine Gauthier

D-U-N-S 25-150-9894   (SL)
ENTREPRISES SYLVIE DROLET INC
MARCHAND CANADIAN TIRE DE SHAWINIGAN
1555 Rue Trudel Bureau 131, Shawinigan, QC, G9N 8K8
(819) 537-3888
Emp Here 49   *Sales* 17,846,535
SIC 5014 Tires and tubes
Sylvie Drolet

D-U-N-S 20-579-3540   (SL)
FORESTERIE C. H. B. LTEE
3563 Rue Trudel, Shawinigan, QC, G9N 6R4
(819) 731-0477
Emp Here 50   *Sales* 10,580,650
SIC 0851 Forestry services
Pierre Bordeleau

D-U-N-S 20-259-6342   (HQ)
GARAGE F COSSETTE INC
GARAGE COSSETTE
10303 Boul Des Hetres, Shawinigan, QC,

G9N 4Y2
(819) 539-5457
Emp Here 39   *Sales* 19,923,120
SIC 5511 New and used car dealers
Germain Mercier
Jean Pierre Cossette

D-U-N-S 24-965-5817   (BR)
GENERAL PAINT CORP
LAURENTIDE PEINTURE
(*Suby of* THE SHERWIN-WILLIAMS COMPANY)
5230 Boul Royal, Shawinigan, QC, G9N 4R6
(819) 537-5925
Emp Here 100
SIC 2851 Paints and allied products
Guy Monfette

D-U-N-S 25-198-1361   (SL)
GESTION MARCEL G GAGNE INC
CANADIAN TIRE #131
1555 Rue Trudel Bureau 131, Shawinigan, QC, G9N 8K8
(819) 537-8999
Emp Here 95   *Sales* 34,600,425
SIC 5014 Tires and tubes
Marcel Gagne

D-U-N-S 25-298-7904   (BR)
H. MATTEAU ET FILS (1987) INC
RONA H MATTEAU
(*Suby of* H. MATTEAU ET FILS (1987) INC)
1650 Rue Trudel, Shawinigan, QC, G9N 0A2
(819) 539-8328
Emp Here 100
SIC 5251 Hardware stores
Natalie Perron

D-U-N-S 24-577-8076   (SL)
L'HEBDO DU ST-MAURICE
1672 Av Saint-Marc Bureau A, Shawinigan, QC, G9N 2H4
(819) 537-4161
Emp Here 13   *Sales* 13,679,724
SIC 6311 Life insurance
Racelle Srejon

D-U-N-S 20-563-1443   (SL)
MAURICIE TOYOTA INC
8823 Boul Des Hetres, Shawinigan, QC, G9N 4X3
(819) 539-8393
Emp Here 25   *Sales* 12,451,950
SIC 5511 New and used car dealers
Marcel Brouillette
Marielle Gauthier
Guy Brouillette
Jocelyn Brouillette
Marc Brouillette

D-U-N-S 24-747-2640   (SL)
MULTI-RELIURE S.F. INC
MULTI BOOKBINDING
2112 Av De La Transmission, Shawinigan, QC, G9N 8N8
(819) 537-6008
Emp Here 80   *Sales* 13,122,160
SIC 2789 Bookbinding and related work
Yvon Sauvageau
Patrick Paquet
Louis Baribeau

D-U-N-S 20-259-9940   (SL)
PATISSERIE CHEVALIER INC
(*Suby of* GRUPO BIMBO, S.A.B. DE C.V.)
155 Rue Du Parc-Industriel, Shawinigan, QC, G9N 6T5
(819) 537-8807
Emp Here 100
SIC 2051 Bread, cake, and related products
Real Menard

D-U-N-S 25-991-7870   (SL)
PLACETECO INC
3763 Rue Burrill Bureau 2, Shawinigan, QC, G9N 0C4
(819) 539-8808
Emp Here 50   *Sales* 11,192,150

SIC 3728 Aircraft parts and equipment, nec
Mario Gauthier

D-U-N-S 24-941-2511   (SL)
PLURITEC CIVIL LTEE
PLURITEC
585 Av Des Cedres, Shawinigan, QC, G9N 1N6
(819) 537-1882
Emp Here 70   *Sales* 12,317,060
SIC 8711 Engineering services
Jonathan Duguay
Fernand Heroux
Denis Heroux

D-U-N-S 20-835-1853   (BR)
RE/MAX DE FRANCHEVILLE INC
(*Suby of* RE/MAX DE FRANCHEVILLE INC)
1000 Av Des Cedres Bureau 5, Shawinigan, QC, G9N 1P6
(819) 537-5000
Emp Here 90
SIC 6531 Real estate agents and managers
Anne Beaumier

D-U-N-S 25-356-8992   (BR)
RIO TINTO ALCAN INC
ALCAN USINE SHAWINIGAN
(*Suby of* RIO TINTO PLC)
1100 Boul Saint-Sacrement, Shawinigan, QC, G9N 0E3
(819) 539-0765
Emp Here 100
SIC 3334 Primary aluminum

D-U-N-S 20-253-0333   (HQ)
ROBERT FER ET METEAUX S.E.C.
TRAITEMENT ROBERT
3206 Ch Des Buissons, Shawinigan, QC, G9N 6T5
(819) 539-7318
Sales 18,138,800
SIC 3341 Secondary nonferrous Metals
Herbert Black

D-U-N-S 24-297-1042   (SL)
SANTE-BEAUTE DANMOR INC
PHARMAPRIX
1 Rue La Plaza-De-Mauricie Bureau 27, Shawinigan, QC, G9N 7C1
(819) 539-5416
Emp Here 44   *Sales* 11,129,976
SIC 5912 Drug stores and proprietary stores
Louis Milliard

D-U-N-S 20-277-9427   (SL)
SHAWINIGAN ALUMINIUM INC
1250 Boul Saint-Sacrement, Shawinigan, QC, G9N 0E3
(819) 731-0644
Emp Here 70   *Sales* 19,881,470
SIC 2819 Industrial inorganic chemicals, nec
Michel Boudreault
Yvon Danjou
Jean-Philippe Harvey
Bruno Gagne
Pierre Bernard

D-U-N-S 20-259-9643   (HQ)
SOCIETE LAURENTIDE INC
4660 Boul De Shawinigan-Sud, Shawinigan, QC, G9N 6T5
(819) 537-6636
Emp Here 75   *Sales* 155,625,750
SIC 2851 Paints and allied products
Andre Buisson
Serge Buisson
Josette Buisson
Claude P. Buisson
Gerald Paquet

D-U-N-S 20-259-9890   (HQ)
SOLUTIONS TECHNIQUES INTELLIGENTES CB INC
MOTEURS P.M.
(*Suby of* CANADIAN BEARINGS LTD)
75 Rue Du Parc-Industriel, Shawinigan, QC, G9N 6T5

(819) 536-2609
Sales 11,961,048
SIC 7694 Armature rewinding shops
Farrokh Khalili
Ali Moghadam
Martin Gelinas

D-U-N-S 25-258-3802   (BR)
VIGI SANTE LTEE
CHSLD VIGI ET LES CHUTES
5000 Av Albert-Tessier, Shawinigan, QC, G9N
8P9
(819) 539-5408
Emp Here 100
SIC 8361 Residential care
Vincent Simonetta

D-U-N-S 20-736-2638   (BR)
WAL-MART CANADA CORP
(*Suby of* WALMART INC.)
1600 Boul Royal, Shawinigan, QC, G9N 8S8
(819) 537-0113
Emp Here 200
SIC 5311 Department stores
Jean Beaudoin

Shawinigan, QC G9P

D-U-N-S 25-233-0972   (BR)
COMMISSION SCOLAIRE DE L'ENERGIE
ECOLE SECONDAIRE VAL MAURICIE
1200 Rue De Val-Mauricie, Shawinigan, QC,
G9P 2L9
(819) 536-5675
Emp Here 160
SIC 8211 Elementary and secondary schools
Lise Dubuc

D-U-N-S 20-999-9937   (SL)
**G. PELLERIN C. DESBIENS, PHARMA-
CIENS**
1920 105e Av, Shawinigan, QC, G9P 1N4
(819) 537-1869
Emp Here 62   *Sales* 15,148,336
SIC 5912 Drug stores and proprietary stores
Guy Pellerin
Christian Desbiens

D-U-N-S 20-765-7776   (SL)
MARCHE SHAWINIGAN-SUD INC
2105 105e Av, Shawinigan, QC, G9P 1N9
(819) 537-6997
Emp Here 64   *Sales* 18,489,051
SIC 5411 Grocery stores
Claude Gauthier
Jean Gauthier

D-U-N-S 20-257-8613   (HQ)
NAUD, PIERRE INC
405 Av Du Capitaine-Veilleux, Shawinigan,
QC, G9P 1Z7
(819) 537-1877
Emp Here 40   *Sales* 12,579,644
SIC 5211 Lumber and other building materials
Marc Andre Lebel
Michel Lebel
Philippe Lebel

Shawinigan, QC G9T

D-U-N-S 24-941-5241   (SL)
2857-4077 QUEBEC INC
ALIMENTATION GAUTHIER & FRERES ENR
850 7e Av, Shawinigan, QC, G9T 2B8
(819) 533-4553
Emp Here 110   *Sales* 32,282,470
SIC 5411 Grocery stores
Claude Gauthier
Jean Gauthier
Gaston Gauthier
Lise Gauthier

D-U-N-S 24-942-4508   (SL)
COMAINTEL INC
121 Av Chahoon Bureau 100, Shawinigan,
QC, G9T 7G1
(819) 538-6583
Emp Here 13   *Sales* 10,260,716
SIC 3567 Industrial furnaces and ovens
Sylvain Larive
Elisabeth Leclerc
Christian Descoteaux

D-U-N-S 25-358-5822   (SL)
GESTION GRATIEN PAQUIN INC
1173 Av De Grand-Mere, Shawinigan, QC,
G9T 2J4
(819) 538-1707
Emp Here 60   *Sales* 11,087,880
SIC 4899 Communication services, nec
Gratien Paquin

D-U-N-S 20-199-3318   (HQ)
H. MATTEAU ET FILS (1987) INC
891 7e Av, Shawinigan, QC, G9T 2B9
(819) 538-3381
Emp Here 40   *Sales* 70,262,500
SIC 5211 Lumber and other building materials
Claude Cauthier Jr
Stephane Gauthier

D-U-N-S 20-212-2235   (SL)
INDUSTRIES STEMA-PRO INC, LES
2699 5e Av Bureau 26, Shawinigan, QC, G9T
2P7
(819) 533-4756
Emp Here 75   *Sales* 11,574,150
SIC 2511 Wood household furniture
Stephane Fontaine
Marc Gagnon

D-U-N-S 25-357-0022   (BR)
KONGSBERG INC
(*Suby of* KONGSBERG AUTOMOTIVE ASA)
2699 5e Av, Shawinigan, QC, G9T 2P7
(819) 533-4757
Emp Here 350
SIC 3679 Electronic components, nec
Rob Owam

D-U-N-S 24-729-9258   (HQ)
KONGSBERG INC
KONGSBERG AUTOMOTIVE
(*Suby of* KONGSBERG AUTOMOTIVE ASA)
90 28e Rue, Shawinigan, QC, G9T 5K7
(819) 533-3201
Emp Here 60   *Sales* 113,166,000
SIC 3679 Electronic components, nec
Rachel Baxter

D-U-N-S 24-378-4225   (BR)
PRODUITS FORESTIERS ARBEC S.E.N.C.
(*Suby of* PRODUITS FORESTIERS ARBEC
S.E.N.C.)
775 Ch De Turcotte, Shawinigan, QC, G9T
5K7
(819) 538-0735
Emp Here 150
SIC 2421 Sawmills and planing mills, general
Pierre Gingras

D-U-N-S 24-071-4522   (SL)
SYNAPSE ELECTRONIQUE INC
1010 7e Av, Shawinigan, QC, G9T 2B8
(819) 533-3553
Emp Here 65   *Sales* 14,773,785
SIC 3822 Environmental controls
Yves Chabot

D-U-N-S 20-324-0960   (HQ)
TECHNOLOGIES BIONEST INC
BIONEST
55 12e Rue, Shawinigan, QC, G9T 5K7
(819) 538-5662
Sales 31,302,180
SIC 5039 Construction materials, nec
Gilles Champagne
Pierre Morin
Pierre Saint Laurent
Alexandra Champagne

Shawinigan-Sud, QC G9P

D-U-N-S 24-817-1741   (SL)
MAISON PIACENTE
805 111e Rue, Shawinigan-Sud, QC, G9P
2T5
Emp Here 49   *Sales* 24,417,778
SIC 5137 Women's and children's clothing
Michel Lapierre

D-U-N-S 24-855-4706   (SL)
MARCHE PLUS SHAWINIGAN INC
METRO PLUS
4175 12e Av, Shawinigan-Sud, QC, G9P 4G3
(819) 537-3724
Emp Here 49   *Sales* 13,433,448
SIC 5411 Grocery stores
Pierre Ayotte

Shawville, QC J0X

D-U-N-S 24-416-6778   (SL)
AUTOBUS LASALLE INC
(*Suby of* TRANSPORT SCOLAIRE SO-
GESCO INC)
149 Rue West, Shawville, QC, J0X 2Y0
(819) 647-5696
Emp Here 100
SIC 4142 Bus charter service, except local
Dave Girardin
Jean-Paul Provost
Louise L'italien
Mario Provost

D-U-N-S 24-899-8320   (SL)
CENTRE D'ACCEUIL PONTIAC
C H S L D SHAWVILLE
290 Rue Marion, Shawville, QC, J0X 2Y0
(819) 647-5755
Emp Here 87   *Sales* 5,154,489
SIC 8361 Residential care
Sylvie Chartrand
Gail Ryan

D-U-N-S 20-185-0786   (HQ)
**CENTRE DE SANTE ET SERVICES SOCI-
AUX DU PONTIAC**
CSSS DU PONTIAC
200 Rue Argue, Shawville, QC, J0X 2Y0
(819) 647-2211
Emp Here 35   *Sales* 116,582,976
SIC 8099 Health and allied services, nec
Gail Ryan
Gaston Lacroix
Richard Grimard
Jean-Guy Patenaude

Shefford, QC J2M

D-U-N-S 20-370-2980   (SL)
GESTION DENISON TH INC
TIM HORTONS
211 Ch Saxby S, Shefford, QC, J2M 1S3
(450) 775-6845
Emp Here 100   *Sales* 4,287,300
SIC 5812 Eating places
Nathalie Dubois
Andre Cadot

D-U-N-S 24-813-2958   (SL)
HYDAC INTERNATIONAL
83 Rue Du Tournesol, Shefford, QC, J2M 1K9
(450) 539-3388
Emp Here 25   *Sales* 11,875,650
SIC 5085 Industrial supplies
Craig Goodwin

Sherbrooke, QC J1C

D-U-N-S 24-819-2721   (SL)
9208-4144 QUEBEC INC
*SERVICES TECHNIQUES INDUSTRIELS
MARCHAND (STIM)*
561 Rue Joseph-Latour, Sherbrooke, QC, J1C
0W2
(819) 846-3338
Emp Here 100   *Sales* 16,391,430
SIC 1799 Special trade contractors, nec
David Marchand
Maxime Beaudoin
Jean Beaudry

D-U-N-S 24-907-4311   (SL)
EGZATEK INC
LITHO SERVICE CANADA
135 Rue Oliva-Turgeon, Sherbrooke, QC, J1C
0R3
(819) 846-6863
Emp Here 85   *Sales* 23,106,570
SIC 7699 Repair services, nec
Stephane Gaudreault
Yvon Gregoire
Sebastien Madore
Yves Goulet

D-U-N-S 24-255-9263   (SL)
EXCAVATION RENE ST-PIERRE
800 Rue De L'Ardoise, Sherbrooke, QC, J1C
0J6
(819) 565-1494
Emp Here 50   *Sales* 12,309,300
SIC 1794 Excavation work
Bernard St-Pierre

D-U-N-S 20-541-3909   (SL)
EXCAVATION RENE ST-PIERRE INC
DEMOLITION ST-PIERRE
800 Rue De L'Ardoise, Sherbrooke, QC, J1C
0J6
(819) 565-1494
Emp Here 100   *Sales* 24,618,600
SIC 1795 Wrecking and demolition work
Bernard St-Pierre

D-U-N-S 20-762-0493   (HQ)
ISE METAL INC
ISE-FERLAND METAL
20 Rte De Windsor, Sherbrooke, QC, J1C 0E5
(819) 846-1044
Emp Here 1   *Sales* 24,010,625
SIC 3469 Metal stampings, nec
Robert H. Henderson

D-U-N-S 24-884-4839   (BR)
KRUGER BROMPTON S.E.C
(*Suby of* KRUGER BROMPTON S.E.C)
220 Rte De Windsor, Sherbrooke, QC, J1C
0E6
(819) 846-2721
Emp Here 460
SIC 2621 Paper mills
Jean-Phillip Masse

D-U-N-S 20-561-1176   (SL)
METOSAK INC
570 Rue Joseph-Latour, Sherbrooke, QC, J1C
0W2
(819) 846-0608
Emp Here 60   *Sales* 11,525,100
SIC 3469 Metal stampings, nec
Serge Morin
Helene Fredette

Sherbrooke, QC J1E

D-U-N-S 20-010-9072   (SL)
ALIMENTATION DANIEL LAROUCHE INC
PROVIGO LAROUCHE FLEURIMONT
1100 13e Av N, Sherbrooke, QC, J1E 3J7

(819) 562-6788
Emp Here 50   *Sales* 13,707,600
SIC 5411 Grocery stores
   Daniel Larouche

      D-U-N-S 24-018-4929   (SL)
CHOEUR DU CEGEP DE SHERBROOKE
475 Rue Du Cegep, Sherbrooke, QC, J1E 4K1
(819) 564-6350
Emp Here 800   *Sales* 119,512,800
SIC 8221 Colleges and universities
   Claire Denis
   Josee Leclair
   Anne Lemire
   Noel Francoise
   Marie-France Belanger

      D-U-N-S 24-901-6783   (SL)
GESTION LOUMA INC
BRASSERIE FLEURIMONT
1325 12e Av N, Sherbrooke, QC, J1E 3P6
(819) 566-4844
Emp Here 80   *Sales* 3,429,840
SIC 5812 Eating places
   Mario Migneault
   Martin Migneault

      D-U-N-S 20-330-8499   (BR)
**LABORATOIRES CHARLES RIVER MON-
TREAL ULC**
*CHARLES RIVER LABORATORIES MON-
TREAL ULC*
(*Suby of* CHARLES RIVER ULC)
1580 Rue Ida-Metivier, Sherbrooke, QC, J1E
0B5
(819) 346-8200
Emp Here 116
SIC 8731 Commercial physical research
   Glenn Washer

Sherbrooke, QC J1G

      D-U-N-S 25-684-8375   (SL)
3101-2883 QUEBEC INC
CYZOTRIM ENR
760 Rue Chalifoux, Sherbrooke, QC, J1G 1R6
(819) 820-0808
Emp Here 150   *Sales* 23,828,700
SIC 3069 Fabricated rubber products, nec
   John Mcbean

      D-U-N-S 25-210-2918   (SL)
9047-6336 QUEBEC INC
MULTI-PISCINE
1597 Rue Galt E, Sherbrooke, QC, J1G 3H4
(819) 566-8558
Emp Here 50   *Sales* 16,280,000
SIC 5999 Miscellaneous retail stores, nec
   Andre Boisvert
   Regis Pepin

      D-U-N-S 25-137-9020   (HQ)
ATELIERS B.G. INC, LES
IMPACTO
2980 Rue King E, Sherbrooke, QC, J1G 5J2
(819) 346-2195
Sales 11,671,750
SIC 3399 Primary Metal products
   Martin Gobeil
   Pascal Gobeil
   Gabriel Gobeil

      D-U-N-S 20-260-2108   (SL)
BOULANGERIE GEORGES INC
2000 Rue King E, Sherbrooke, QC, J1G 5G6
(819) 564-3002
Emp Here 41   *Sales* 11,240,232
SIC 5461 Retail bakeries
   Luc Fortier
   Denis Fortier
   Jacqueline Lessard

      D-U-N-S 24-330-5435   (BR)
**COMMISSION SCOLAIRE DE LA REGION-
DE-SHERBROOKE**

ECOLE SECONDAIRE DE LA MONTEE
(*Suby of* COMMISSION SCOLAIRE DE LA
REGION-DE-SHERBROOKE)
825 Rue Bowen S, Sherbrooke, QC, J1G 2G2
(819) 822-5444
Emp Here 93
SIC 8211 Elementary and secondary schools
   Alain Poirier

      D-U-N-S 20-547-7693   (HQ)
**EQUIPEMENT SANITAIRE CHERBOURG
(1977) INC**
CHERBOURG
1051 Rue Galt E, Sherbrooke, QC, J1G 1Y7
(819) 566-2266
Emp Here 44   *Sales* 36,517,250
SIC 5169 Chemicals and allied products, nec
   Craig Rudin
   Claude Bigras
   Andree Chatelois

      D-U-N-S 24-857-5565   (HQ)
**EQUIPEMENTS ADAPTES PHYSIPRO INC,
LES**
370 10e Av S, Sherbrooke, QC, J1G 2R7
(819) 823-2252
Sales 12,500,895
SIC 3842 Surgical appliances and supplies
   Mario Ouellette

      D-U-N-S 25-468-3626   (HQ)
**FILLES DE LA CHARITE DU SACRE-
COEUR DE JESUS, LES**
MAISON CENTRALE
575 Rue Allen, Sherbrooke, QC, J1G 1Z1
(819) 569-9617
Emp Here 2   *Sales* 10,772,700
SIC 8661 Religious organizations
   Suzelle Roberge
   Pauline Lamirande
   Rollande Gosselin

      D-U-N-S 24-458-5980   (BR)
**GOUVERNEMENT DE LA PROVINCE DE
QUEBEC**
*AGENCE DE LA SANTE ET DES SERVICES
SOCIAUX DE L'ESTRIE*
(*Suby of* GOUVERNEMENT DE LA
PROVINCE DE QUEBEC)
300 Rue King E Bureau 300, Sherbrooke, QC,
J1G 1B1
(819) 566-7861
Emp Here 150
SIC 8399 Social services, nec
   Michel Baron

      D-U-N-S 20-564-0592   (SL)
LOUIS LUNCHEONETTE INC
386 Rue King E, Sherbrooke, QC, J1G 1A8
(819) 563-5581
Emp Here 100   *Sales* 4,287,300
SIC 5812 Eating places
   Pierre Ellyson
   Jeanine Ellyson

      D-U-N-S 24-804-6497   (SL)
MARCHE PLOUFFE SHERBROOKE INC
1175 Rue King E, Sherbrooke, QC, J1G 1E6
(819) 346-2229
Emp Here 100   *Sales* 29,347,700
SIC 5411 Grocery stores
   Daniel Plouffe
   Patrick Plouffe

      D-U-N-S 25-335-3775   (SL)
PERSE-TECHNOLOGIE INC
2555 Rue Des Frenes Bureau 100, Sherbrooke, QC, J1G 4R3

Emp Here 120   *Sales* 20,021,640
SIC 7372 Prepackaged software
   Guy Bujold

      D-U-N-S 25-993-2643   (SL)
PHARMACIES AFFILIEES A PROXIM
624 Rue Bowen S, Sherbrooke, QC, J1G 2E9
(819) 569-5561
Emp Here 49   *Sales* 12,394,746

SIC 5912 Drug stores and proprietary stores
   Nathalie Marchessault

      D-U-N-S 24-080-9863   (SL)
PIZZERIA DEMERS INC
RESTAURANT DEMERS
936 Rue Du Conseil, Sherbrooke, QC, J1G
1L7
(819) 564-2811
Emp Here 110   *Sales* 5,007,090
SIC 5812 Eating places
   Serge Lemieux
   Nancy Duchesne

      D-U-N-S 20-673-2430   (SL)
PME INTER NOTAIRES INC
2140 Rue King E Unite 201, Sherbrooke, QC,
J1G 5G6
(819) 563-3344
Emp Here 23   *Sales* 10,332,037
SIC 7389 Business services, nec
   Denis Paris

      D-U-N-S 24-534-6460   (SL)
RESTAURANTS IANA INC
975 Rue King E, Sherbrooke, QC, J1G 1E3
(819) 571-9623
Emp Here 100   *Sales* 4,287,300
SIC 5812 Eating places
   Caroline Iannuzzi
   Frederic Nadeau

      D-U-N-S 24-529-5159   (BR)
SOBEYS QUEBEC INC
IGA COUTURE
2240 Rue King E, Sherbrooke, QC, J1G 5G8
(819) 566-8282
Emp Here 100   *Sales* 822,456
SIC 5411 Grocery stores
   Marco Couture

      D-U-N-S 24-813-8075   (SL)
TROISIEME DIVISION M.R. INC
880 Rue Longpre, Sherbrooke, QC, J1G 5B9
(819) 562-7772
Emp Here 40   *Sales* 17,739,600
SIC 7389 Business services, nec
   Stephane Vallieres

Sherbrooke, QC J1H

      D-U-N-S 20-370-8834   (HQ)
9317-3649 QUEBEC INC
TIM HORTONS
31 Rue King O Bureau 203, Sherbrooke, QC,
J1H 1N5
(819) 791-3123
Sales 11,659,750
SIC 5812 Eating places
   Denis Bourque
   Chantal Francis

      D-U-N-S 24-101-8717   (HQ)
CAFE VITTORIA INC
CAFE HUBERT SAINT-JEAN DISTRIBUTION
1625 Rue Belvedere S, Sherbrooke, QC, J1H
4E4
(819) 564-8226
Sales 21,725,002
SIC 5149 Groceries and related products, nec
   Remi Tremblay
   Serge Picard
   Jonathan Haley

      D-U-N-S 24-607-9409   (SL)
**CENTRE HOSPITALIER UNIVERSITAIRE
DE SHERBROOKE**
C.H.U.S.
(*Suby of* CENTRE INTEGRE UNIVERSI-
TAIRE DE SANTE ET DE SERVICES SOCI-
AUX DE L'ESTRIE)
3001 12e Av N, Sherbrooke, QC, J1H 5N4
(819) 346-1110
Emp Here 650   *Sales* 152,172,150
SIC 8621 Professional organizations

   Andre Larocque
   Chantal Beaudry

      D-U-N-S 20-284-3384   (BR)
CENTRE JEUNESSE DE L'ESTRIE
340 Rue Dufferin, Sherbrooke, QC, J1H 4M7
(819) 822-2727
Emp Here 500
SIC 8322 Individual and family services
   Alain Trudel

      D-U-N-S 24-336-4952   (BR)
**COMMISSION SCOLAIRE DE LA REGION-
DE-SHERBROOKE**
ECOLE INTERNATIONALE DU PHARE
(*Suby of* COMMISSION SCOLAIRE DE LA
REGION-DE-SHERBROOKE)
405 Rue Sara, Sherbrooke, QC, J1H 5S6
(819) 822-5455
Emp Here 140
SIC 8211 Elementary and secondary schools
   Donald Landry

      D-U-N-S 24-336-4994   (BR)
**COMMISSION SCOLAIRE DE LA REGION-
DE-SHERBROOKE**
*CENTRE   SAINT-MICHEL   FORMATION
POUR ADULTS*
(*Suby of* COMMISSION SCOLAIRE DE LA
REGION-DE-SHERBROOKE)
135 Rue King O, Sherbrooke, QC, J1H 1P4
(819) 822-5520
Emp Here 100
SIC 8211 Elementary and secondary schools
   Carl Tourigny

      D-U-N-S 24-334-7163   (BR)
**COMMISSION SCOLAIRE DE LA REGION-
DE-SHERBROOKE**
PAVILLON MITCHELL
(*Suby of* COMMISSION SCOLAIRE DE LA
REGION-DE-SHERBROOKE)
955 Rue De Cambridge, Sherbrooke, QC, J1H
1E2
(819) 822-5400
Emp Here 92
SIC 8211 Elementary and secondary schools
   Pascale Bilodeau

      D-U-N-S 24-975-7279   (SL)
**CONSEIL CENTRAL DES SYNDICATS NA-
TIANAUX DE L'ESTRIE**
C S N
180 Cote De L'Acadie, Sherbrooke, QC, J1H
2T3
(819) 563-6515
Emp Here 29   *Sales* 11,343,582
SIC 8631 Labor organizations
   Denis Beaudin

      D-U-N-S 24-055-3990   (SL)
CORPORATION ASICS CANADA
AGENCE QUEBEC PLUS
(*Suby of* ASICS CORPORATION)
101 Rue Des Abenaquis Bureau 201, Sher-
brooke, QC, J1H 1H1
(819) 566-8866
Emp Here 25   *Sales* 12,458,050
SIC 5139 Footwear
   Denis Custeau
   Charles Custeau
   Katsumi Kato
   Kousuke Hasimoto
   Kevin Wulff

      D-U-N-S 24-857-7413   (SL)
GESTION FRANCOIS MALTAIS INC
JEAN COUTU # 253
1363 Rue Belvedere S, Sherbrooke, QC, J1H
4E4
(819) 565-9595
Emp Here 50   *Sales* 12,647,700
SIC 5912 Drug stores and proprietary stores
   Francois Maltais

      D-U-N-S 25-464-8660   (HQ)
INDUSTRIES HYPERSHELL INC
740 Rue Galt O Bureau 401, Sherbrooke, QC,

J1H 1Z3
(819) 822-3890
Sales 22,460,950
SIC 7389 Business services, nec
Jonathan Clement
Francois Carrier
Louis-Charles Durocher
Dany Chaput
Mario Beaudoin

D-U-N-S 25-447-0024   (BR)
METRO RICHELIEU INC
SUPER C
(*Suby of* METRO INC)
350 Rue Belvedere N, Sherbrooke, QC, J1H 4B1
(819) 564-6014
Emp Here 75
SIC 5411 Grocery stores
Jacques Broduer

D-U-N-S 20-164-6077   (SL)
MONTY COULOMBE S.E.N.C
234 Rue Dufferin Bureau 200, Sherbrooke, QC, J1H 4M2
(819) 566-4466
Emp Here 145   *Sales* 16,077,890
SIC 8111 Legal services
Guy Achim
Andre Fournier
Jean-Guy Marchesseault
Roland Veilleux
Thomas Dilenge
Stephane Reynolds
Martin Brunet

D-U-N-S 25-755-0871   (HQ)
OPTAGEX INC
CLINIQUE OPTOMETRIQUE DE SHER-BROOKE
243 Rue King O, Sherbrooke, QC, J1H 1P8
(819) 563-1191
Emp Here 15   *Sales* 11,721,600
SIC 5995 Optical goods stores
Jean-Yves Roy
Alain Cote

D-U-N-S 25-285-9087   (BR)
PPD HOLDING INC
(*Suby of* 148220 CANADA INC)
1649 Rue Belvedere S, Sherbrooke, QC, J1H 4E4
(819) 837-2491
Emp Here 150
SIC 3089 Plastics products, nec
Sylvain Turgeon

D-U-N-S 20-260-0854   (HQ)
PRODUITS AMERICAN BILTRITE (CANADA) LTEE
BLAST
(*Suby of* AMERICAN BILTRITE INC.)
200 Rue Bank, Sherbrooke, QC, J1H 4K3
(819) 829-3300
Emp Here 6   *Sales* 59,703,000
SIC 3069 Fabricated rubber products, nec
Richard G. Marcus
Yves Massariol
Jean-Pierre Benoit
Robert S. Vineberg

D-U-N-S 24-801-0886   (BR)
RAYMOND CHABOT GRANT THORNTON S.E.N.C.R.L.
RAYMOND CHABOT GRANT THORNTON S.E.N.C.R.L.
(*Suby of* RAYMOND CHABOT GRANT THORNTON S.E.N.C.R.L.)
455 Rue King O Bureau 500, Sherbrooke, QC, J1H 6G4
(819) 822-4000
Emp Here 160
SIC 8721 Accounting, auditing, and book-keeping
Real Letourneau

D-U-N-S 20-129-0495   (SL)
RECUP ESTRIE

2180 Rue Claude-Greffard, Sherbrooke, QC, J1H 5H1
(819) 346-2111
Emp Here 25   *Sales* 11,875,650
SIC 5084 Industrial machinery and equipment
Hugues Grimard
Pierre Avard
Denis Ferland
Robert G. Roy
Francoise Bouchard
Robert Ledoux
Pierre Therrien

D-U-N-S 24-635-8303   (SL)
SEMINAIRE DE SHERBROOKE
195 Rue Marquette Bureau 116, Sherbrooke, QC, J1H 1L6
(819) 563-2050
Emp Here 200   *Sales* 19,823,800
SIC 8222 Junior colleges
Francois Sylvestre
Richard Adam
Vincent Cloutier
Guy Boulanger
Luc Sauve
Andre Metras
Benoit Charland
Guylaine Lemieux
Nicolas Doyon
Manon Tousignant

D-U-N-S 20-886-0148   (HQ)
SERVICE DE L'ESTRIE (VENTE & REPARA-TION) INC
SPECIALISTES DE L'ELECTROMENAGER, LES
225 Rue Wellington S, Sherbrooke, QC, J1H 5E1
(819) 563-0563
Emp Here 20   *Sales* 25,472,480
SIC 5722 Household appliance stores
Claude Villemaire

D-U-N-S 20-888-4775   (SL)
SERVICES DE LUBRIFIANTS INDUS-TRIELS & COMMERCIAUX (SLIC) INC
SLIC
402 Rue Alexandre, Sherbrooke, QC, J1H 4T3
(819) 562-1411
Emp Here 11   *Sales* 11,360,888
SIC 5172 Petroleum products, nec
Mariette Trudeau

D-U-N-S 20-852-2370   (BR)
SOBEYS CAPITAL INCORPORATED
IGA EXTRA 514
(*Suby of* EMPIRE COMPANY LIMITED)
775 Rue Galt O Bureau 514, Sherbrooke, QC, J1H 1Z1
(819) 564-8686
Emp Here 90
SIC 5411 Grocery stores
Yves Chapdelaine

D-U-N-S 20-123-2670   (SL)
SUPERMETAL SHERBROOKE INC
(*Suby of* GESTION RELEVE SMS INC)
375 Rue De Courcelette, Sherbrooke, QC, J1H 3X4
(819) 566-2965
Emp Here 97   *Sales* 18,632,245
SIC 3441 Fabricated structural Metal
Jean-Francois Blouin

D-U-N-S 24-804-7859   (BR)
VIGI SANTE LTEE
CHSLD VIGI SHERMONT
3220 12e Av N, Sherbrooke, QC, J1H 5H3
(819) 820-8900
Emp Here 90
SIC 8051 Skilled nursing care facilities
Diane Bisaillon

Sherbrooke, QC J1J

D-U-N-S 20-266-5618   (HQ)
9114-9534 QUEBEC INC
BRAVAD
2424 Rue King O Bureau 200, Sherbrooke, QC, J1J 2E8
(819) 780-9505
Emp Here 8   *Sales* 17,430,225
SIC 5731 Radio, television, and electronic stores
Dany Fournier
David Masson

D-U-N-S 20-696-9094   (SL)
9147-8453 QUEBEC INC
ATMOSPHERE
2325 Rue King O, Sherbrooke, QC, J1J 2G2
(819) 566-8882
Emp Here 32   *Sales* 15,938,496
SIC 5551 Boat dealers
Laurent Peloquin
Roger Heroux
Julie Roy

D-U-N-S 25-146-5402   (SL)
ASSURANCE VOYAGE RSA INC
(*Suby of* RSA INSURANCE GROUP PLC)
1910 Rue King O Bureau 200, Sherbrooke, QC, J1J 2E2
(819) 780-0064
Emp Here 50   *Sales* 92,387,100
SIC 6411 Insurance agents, brokers, and ser-vice
Martin Thompson
Ken Bennett
Stephen Yendall

D-U-N-S 24-350-8488   (SL)
AUTOMOBILES RELAIS 2000 INC
RELAIS TOYOTA
2059 Rue King O, Sherbrooke, QC, J1J 2E9
(819) 563-6622
Emp Here 70   *Sales* 44,049,600
SIC 5511 New and used car dealers
Michel Rousseau

D-U-N-S 24-085-8530   (HQ)
BIBLAIRIE G.G.C. LTEE
AGENCE DU LIVRE
1567 Rue King O, Sherbrooke, QC, J1J 2C6
(819) 566-0344
Emp Here 51   *Sales* 53,024,310
SIC 5192 Books, periodicals, and newspapers
Gerald Guy Caza
Roger Durand
Jean Gauthier
Etienne-Guy Caza
Francine Archambault
Marco-Pierre Caza
Gaetan Lemieux

D-U-N-S 24-377-3780   (HQ)
CAISSE DESJARDINS DU NORD DE SHER-BROOKE
CENTRE DE SERVICES DU CARREFOUR DE L'ESTRIE
1845 Rue King O, Sherbrooke, QC, J1J 2E4
(819) 566-0050
Emp Here 50   *Sales* 30,210,060
SIC 6062 State credit unions
Eric Marquis
Roger Durand
Jean-Claude Heroux
Yves Thibault
Amelie Corbeil
Veronique Lamontagne
Francine Archambault
Marie Becotte
Philippe Bellefeuille
Alain Bellemare

D-U-N-S 24-168-5551   (HQ)
CENTRE DE LANGUES INTERNA-TIONALES CHARPENTIER
CLIC
20 Rue Bryant, Sherbrooke, QC, J1J 3E4
(819) 822-2542
Emp Here 50   *Sales* 12,012,900

SIC 8299 Schools and educational services, nec
Lynn Charpentier
Susan Ouellet

D-U-N-S 20-386-9987   (SL)
CENTRE DE SANTE ET DE SERVICES SOCIAUX - INSTITUT UNIVERSITAIRE DE GERIATRIE DE SHERBROOKE
CIUSSS DE L'ESTRIE - CHUS
375 Rue Argyll, Sherbrooke, QC, J1J 3H5
(819) 780-2222
Emp Here 2,500   *Sales* 557,280,000
SIC 8099 Health and allied services, nec
Jacques Fortier
Diane Gingras
Patricia Gauthier
Raymonde Vaillancourt
Patrice Lamarre
Serge Therrien
Gerald R. Cutting
Rachel Hunting
Michel Kinumbe Elungu
Micheline Richer

D-U-N-S 20-588-6513   (HQ)
CENTRE INTEGRE UNIVERSITAIRE DE SANTE ET DE SERVICES SOCIAUX DE L'ESTRIE
CIUSSS DE L'ESTRIE - CHUS
375 Rue Argyll, Sherbrooke, QC, J1J 3H5
(819) 780-2222
Emp Here 50   *Sales* 4,213,998,000
SIC 8621 Professional organizations
Jacques Fortier
Diane Gingras
Patricia Gauthier
Stephane Tremblay
Sylvain Bernier
William Fraser
Paul Morin
Raymonde Vaillancourt
Denis Beaulieu
Remi Brassard

D-U-N-S 20-260-3247   (SL)
CLOUTIER, N. V. INC
2550 Rue King O, Sherbrooke, QC, J1J 2H1
(819) 346-3911
Emp Here 46   *Sales* 22,911,588
SIC 5511 New and used car dealers
Claude Martineau
Charles Martineau

D-U-N-S 20-000-6463   (SL)
DEFI POLYTECK
ATELIER POLY-TECK
1255 Boul Queen-Victoria, Sherbrooke, QC, J1J 4N6
(819) 348-1209
Emp Here 160   *Sales* 30,772,480
SIC 7699 Repair services, nec
Helene Pelletier
Denis Fortin
Robert Bouillon

D-U-N-S 24-509-9890   (BR)
DELOITTE LLP
(*Suby of* DELOITTE LLP)
1802 Rue King O Bureau 300, Sherbrooke, QC, J1J 0A2
(819) 823-1616
Emp Here 75
SIC 8111 Legal services

D-U-N-S 20-881-7270   (SL)
ECONAUTO (1985) LTEE
SHERBROOKE HONDA
2615 Rue King O, Sherbrooke, QC, J1J 2H3
(819) 566-5322
Emp Here 50   *Sales* 31,464,000
SIC 5521 Used car dealers
Christian St-Pierre

D-U-N-S 20-324-7887   (HQ)
EXO-S INC
DIVISION DE RICHMOND

(Suby of CAPITAL REGIONAL ET COOPER-
ATIF DESJARDINS)
2100 Rue King O Bureau 240, Sherbrooke,
QC, J1J 2E8
(819) 346-3967
Emp Here 36   *Sales* 340,153,425
SIC 2821 Plastics materials and resins
  Emmanuel Duchesne
  Pierre Guilbaut
  Daphne St-Louis
  Jacques Mombleau
  Daniel Caron

D-U-N-S 25-244-0508   (SL)
FONDATION ECOLE MONTCALM INC
ECOLE MONTCALM
2050 Boul De Portland, Sherbrooke, QC, J1J
1T9
(819) 822-5633
Emp Here 100   *Sales* 9,282,600
SIC 8211 Elementary and secondary schools
  Marc Dugas
  Jean Martin
  Conctant Archambault
  Renald Sirois
  Mario Labarre

D-U-N-S 25-485-2130   (BR)
**GOUVERNEMENT DE LA PROVINCE DE
QUEBEC**
INSTITUE UNIVERSITAIRE GERIATRIE
(Suby of GOUVERNEMENT DE LA
PROVINCE DE QUEBEC)
375 Rue Argyll, Sherbrooke, QC, J1J 3H5
(819) 821-1170
Emp Here 500
SIC 8051 Skilled nursing care facilities
  Denis Lalumiere

D-U-N-S 24-295-1598   (SL)
PETROLES SHERBROOKE INC, LES
125 Rue Des Quatre-Pins, Sherbrooke, QC,
J1J 2L5
(819) 565-1770
Emp Here 24   *Sales* 11,256,120
SIC 5983 Fuel oil dealers
  Daniel Dube
  Normand Dube

D-U-N-S 20-297-8995   (SL)
PHARMACIE ANIK BERTRAND INC
JEAN COUTU
1470 Rue King O, Sherbrooke, QC, J1J 2C2
(819) 564-3111
Emp Here 40   *Sales* 10,118,160
SIC 5912 Drug stores and proprietary stores
  Anik Bertrand

D-U-N-S 25-323-7945   (HQ)
SERVICES EXP INC., LES
DELSAER-GESTIONNAIRES DE PROJETS
(Suby of EXP GLOBAL INC)
150 Rue De Vimy, Sherbrooke, QC, J1J 3M7
(819) 780-1868
Emp Here 150   *Sales* 137,991,700
SIC 8711 Engineering services
  Mark Dvorak
  Greg Henderson

D-U-N-S 20-008-4056   (HQ)
SHERWEB INC
SOLUTION SHERWEB
95 Boul Jacques-Cartier S Bureau 400, Sher-
brooke, QC, J1J 2Z3
(819) 562-6610
Sales 22,847,200
SIC 4813 Telephone communication, except
radio
  Peter Cassar
  Matthew Cassar
  Danielle Cassar

Sherbrooke, QC J1K

D-U-N-S 24-370-7408   (SL)
1794342 ONTARIO INC
SHERWOOD HOCKEY
(Suby of INGLASCO INC)
2745 Rue De La Sherwood, Sherbrooke, QC,
J1K 1E1
(819) 563-2202
Emp Here 200   *Sales* 65,227,200
SIC 3949 Sporting and athletic goods, nec
  David Reese

D-U-N-S 24-865-9823   (HQ)
A. & R. BELLEY INC
BELLY QUEBEC
1035 Rue Panneton, Sherbrooke, QC, J1K
2B3
(819) 823-1843
Emp Here 20   *Sales* 27,701,190
SIC 5113 Industrial and personal service pa-
per
  Denis P. Lessard
  Serge Lafrance

D-U-N-S 24-327-1611   (SL)
**AMF AUTOMATION TECHNOLOGIES COM-
PANY OF CANADA**
AMF CANADA
1025 Rue Cabana Bureau 1, Sherbrooke, QC,
J1K 2M4
(819) 563-3111
Emp Here 100   *Sales* 22,200,100
SIC 3556 Food products machinery
  Jason Ward
  Bruno Arnassan
  Danny Morin

D-U-N-S 25-091-8328   (HQ)
AVIZO EXPERTS-CONSEILS INC
ENVIRONNEMENT E.S.A.
1125 Rue De Cherbourg, Sherbrooke, QC,
J1K 0A8
(819) 346-4342
Emp Here 30   *Sales* 15,209,400
SIC 8748 Business consulting, nec
  Charles Duguay
  Germain Thibault
  Pierre Rouleau

D-U-N-S 25-392-1928   (SL)
**BALL TECHNOLOGIES AVANCEES
D'ALUMINIUM CANADA S.E.C.**
2205 Rue Roy, Sherbrooke, QC, J1K 1B8
(819) 563-3589
Emp Here 110   *Sales* 19,952,680
SIC 3341 Secondary nonferrous Metals

D-U-N-S 20-222-7000   (HQ)
BRULERIE GRANDE RESERVE INC
CAFE FARO
930 Rue Blais, Sherbrooke, QC, J1K 2B7
(819) 564-8844
Emp Here 55   *Sales* 50,134,620
SIC 5149 Groceries and related products, nec
  Jean-Louis Fabi

D-U-N-S 20-222-6994   (SL)
CAFE FARO INC
BRULERIE TATUM
930 Rue Blais, Sherbrooke, QC, J1K 2B7
(819) 564-8844
Emp Here 23   *Sales* 19,440,855
SIC 5149 Groceries and related products, nec
  Jean-Louis Fabi
  Denis Nadeau
  Maxime Fabi

D-U-N-S 24-065-1526   (HQ)
**COMMISSION SCOLAIRE DE LA REGION-
DE-SHERBROOKE**
ACADEMIE DU SACRE-COEUR
2955 Boul De L'Universite Bureau 822, Sher-
brooke, QC, J1K 2Y3
(819) 822-5540
Emp Here 100   *Sales* 297,357,000
SIC 8211 Elementary and secondary schools
  Gilles Normand

D-U-N-S 24-336-5033   (BR)

**COMMISSION SCOLAIRE DE LA REGION-
DE-SHERBROOKE**
ECOLE SECONDAIRE DU TRIOLET
(Suby of COMMISSION SCOLAIRE DE LA
REGION-DE-SHERBROOKE)
2965 Boul De L'Universite, Sherbrooke, QC,
J1K 2X6
(819) 822-5540
Emp Here 186
SIC 8211 Elementary and secondary schools
  Marc Juneau

D-U-N-S 24-107-3337   (SL)
**COOPERATIVE DE L'UNIVERSITE DE
SHERBROOKE**
2500 Boul De L'Universite Bureau B5 014,
Sherbrooke, QC, J1K 2R1
(819) 821-3599
Emp Here 35   *Sales* 11,303,915
SIC 5411 Grocery stores
  Michel Desjardins
  Jean-Francois Werung

D-U-N-S 20-582-2844   (SL)
CUISINE IDEALE INC
AMALGAME
(Suby of GROUPE CUISINE IDEALE INC)
980 Rue Panneton, Sherbrooke, QC, J1K 2B2
(819) 566-2401
Emp Here 100   *Sales* 19,237,000
SIC 2434 Wood kitchen cabinets
  Yves Gagnon
  Pierre-Yves Gagnon
  Jean-Bernard Gagnon

D-U-N-S 25-447-8878   (SL)
GESTION CLAUMOND INC
*PHARMACIE UNIPRIX GENEVIEVE BRE-
TON*
2235 Rue Galt O, Sherbrooke, QC, J1K 1K6
(819) 569-9349
Emp Here 45   *Sales* 11,382,930
SIC 5912 Drug stores and proprietary stores
  Genevieve Breton

D-U-N-S 24-000-4957   (HQ)
GROUPE CUISINE IDEALE INC
980 Rue Panneton, Sherbrooke, QC, J1K 2B2
(819) 566-2401
Emp Here 50   *Sales* 37,647,427
SIC 6712 Bank holding companies
  Yves Gagnon
  Pierre-Yves Gagnon
  Jean-Bernard Gagnon

D-U-N-S 20-276-9931   (HQ)
INGLASCO INC
2745 Rue De La Sherwood, Sherbrooke, QC,
J1K 1E1
(819) 563-2205
Sales 53,178,168
SIC 3949 Sporting and athletic goods, nec
  Vito Galloro
  Enzo Macri

D-U-N-S 25-148-4853   (SL)
NEUMAN HOLDING CANADA INC
2205 Rue Roy, Sherbrooke, QC, J1K 1B8
(819) 563-3589
Emp Here 110   *Sales* 19,952,680
SIC 3341 Secondary nonferrous Metals
  Stan Platek

D-U-N-S 24-677-5969   (HQ)
**PETITE SOEURS DE LA SAINTE-FAMILLE,
LES**
MAISON SAINT-JOSEPH
1820 Rue Galt O, Sherbrooke, QC, J1K 1H9
(819) 823-0345
Emp Here 8   *Sales* 31,236,900
SIC 8661 Religious organizations
  Denise Pomerleau

D-U-N-S 20-261-0697   (SL)
**SOCIETE DE TRANSPORT DE SHER-
BROOKE**
STS
895 Rue Cabana, Sherbrooke, QC, J1K 2M3

(819) 564-2687
Emp Here 200   *Sales* 15,054,400
SIC 4111 Local and suburban transit
  Huguette Dallaire
  Dany Lachance

D-U-N-S 20-121-1039   (SL)
TLD (CANADA) INC
800 Rue Cabana, Sherbrooke, QC, J1K 3C3
(819) 566-8118
Emp Here 100   *Sales* 22,200,100
SIC 3531 Construction machinery
  Mark Garlasco
  Remi Langlois
  Alain Gaumond
  David Flahault
  Antoine Maguin

D-U-N-S 20-564-8751   (SL)
**TREMBLAY, RODRIGUE (SHERBROOKE)
INC**
R T S I
2540 Rue Roy, Sherbrooke, QC, J1K 1C1
(819) 346-4527
Emp Here 26   *Sales* 11,626,524
SIC 5033 Roofing, siding, and insulation
  Stephane Tremblay
  Pierre Tremblay

D-U-N-S 20-859-5207   (HQ)
UNIVERSITE DE SHERBROOKE
FACULTE D'ADMINISTRATION
2500 Boul De L'Universite, Sherbrooke, QC,
J1K 2R1
(819) 821-7000
Emp Here 3,100   *Sales* 534,439,270
SIC 8221 Colleges and universities
  Jocelyne Faucher
  Martin Buteau
  Jacques Beauvais
  Alain Webster
  Joanne Leveillee
  Luce Samoisette
  Lucie Laflamme
  David Senechal
  Vincent Joli-Coeur
  Michel Berthiaume

D-U-N-S 25-672-3867   (BR)
VILLE DE SHERBROOKE
HYDRO SHERBROOKE
(Suby of VILLE DE SHERBROOKE)
1800 Rue Roy, Sherbrooke, QC, J1K 1B6
(819) 821-5727
Emp Here 149
SIC 4911 Electric services
  Daniel Richer

D-U-N-S 25-394-3138   (BR)
WOLTERS KLUWER CANADA LIMITED
CANTAX
(Suby of WOLTERS KLUWER N.V.)
1120 Rue De Cherbourg, Sherbrooke, QC,
J1K 2N8
(819) 566-2000
Emp Here 160
SIC 7291 Tax return preparation services
  Douglas Finley

Sherbrooke, QC J1L

D-U-N-S 25-488-4760   (HQ)
9044-4928 QUEBEC INC
SOLUTION CELLULAIRE
2980 Rue King O, Sherbrooke, QC, J1L 1Y7
(819) 566-5555
Emp Here 9   *Sales* 13,024,000
SIC 5999 Miscellaneous retail stores, nec
  Claude Hamel

D-U-N-S 24-709-6936   (SL)
ALIMENTS JARDI INC, LES
4650 Boul De Portland, Sherbrooke, QC, J1L
0H6

(819) 820-1003
Emp Here 45   *Sales* 10,118,475
SIC 2064 Candy and other confectionery products
Mario Beaudoin
Maxime Beaudoin
Maxime Busseau

D-U-N-S 20-309-2903   (SL)
ATELIER POLY-TECK INC
151 Rue Leger, Sherbrooke, QC, J1L 2G8
(819) 563-6636
Emp Here 50   *Sales* 10,094,850
SIC 3081 Unsupported plastics film and sheet
Michel Lequin
Robert Nadine
Nathalie Ouellet
Pierre Bolduc
Ginette Matteau
Renaud Parent
Gagnon Claude
Sylvain Serge
Guy Laroche
Robert Bouillon

D-U-N-S 20-261-1752   (SL)
AUTOMOBILES VAL ESTRIE INC
CARROSSIER PROCOLOR SHERBROOKE OUEST
4141 Rue King O, Sherbrooke, QC, J1L 1P5
(819) 563-4466
Emp Here 75   *Sales* 47,196,000
SIC 5511 New and used car dealers
Michel Dionne
Andre Dionne
Rene Janelle

D-U-N-S 25-732-8930   (SL)
C-MAC MICROCIRCUITS ULC
C-MAC MICROSYSTEMS SOLUTIONS
3000 Boul Industriel, Sherbrooke, QC, J1L 1V8
(819) 821-4524
Emp Here 150   *Sales* 44,021,550
SIC 5411 Grocery stores
Michael Round
Jacques Bruneau
Alain Belzile

D-U-N-S 24-935-4739   (SL)
CAMIONS INTER-ESTRIE (1991) INC, LES
NAVISTAR
250 Rue Leger, Sherbrooke, QC, J1L 1M1
(819) 564-6677
Emp Here 45   *Sales* 22,413,510
SIC 5511 New and used car dealers
Sylvain Charest
Line Comeau

D-U-N-S 24-405-8806   (SL)
CHOCOLAT LAMONTAGNE INC
(*Suby of* PROMOTION LAMONTAGNE INC)
4045 Rue De La Garlock, Sherbrooke, QC, J1L 1W9
(819) 564-1014
Emp Here 200   *Sales* 69,138,000
SIC 2066 Chocolate and cocoa products
Richard Lamontagne
Tina Lamontagne
Danny Lamontagne

D-U-N-S 20-174-6117   (BR)
CIMA+ S.E.N.C.
(*Suby of* CIMA+ S.E.N.C.)
3385 Rue King O, Sherbrooke, QC, J1L 1P8
(819) 565-3385
Emp Here 200
SIC 8711 Engineering services
Paul Lambert

D-U-N-S 24-297-2404   (HQ)
CONSTRUCTION GERATEK LTEE
GERATEK
535 Rue Pepin, Sherbrooke, QC, J1L 1X3
(819) 564-2933
Sales 44,378,700
SIC 1542 Nonresidential construction, nec
David Gosselin

Charlotte Angers
Lucie Lauzon

D-U-N-S 24-323-8631   (SL)
CONSTRUCTION LONGER INC
175 Rue Leger, Sherbrooke, QC, J1L 1M2
(819) 564-0115
Emp Here 60   *Sales* 34,220,280
SIC 1542 Nonresidential construction, nec
Luc Auclair
Pierre Luc Auclair
Tim Normandin
Dominic Gendron
Mario Foley
Julie Fouquet
Gabriel Forest
Sylvain Ouellette
Steven Chabot

D-U-N-S 24-851-9220   (BR)
COOPER-STANDARD   AUTOMOTIVE CANADA LIMITED
(*Suby of* COOPER-STANDARD HOLDINGS INC.)
4045 Rue Brodeur, Sherbrooke, QC, J1L 1K4
(819) 562-4440
Emp Here 120
SIC 3465 Automotive stampings

D-U-N-S 20-302-8881   (BR)
COOPER-STANDARD   AUTOMOTIVE CANADA LIMITED
(*Suby of* COOPER-STANDARD HOLDINGS INC.)
3995 Boul Industriel, Sherbrooke, QC, J1L 2S7
(819) 562-4440
Emp Here 342
SIC 3465 Automotive stampings
Guylaine Lessard

D-U-N-S 24-297-0705   (SL)
COOPERATIVE D'ALENTOUR, GROSSISTE EN ALIMENTATION NATURELLE DES CANTONS DE L'EST
BOUTIQUE ALENTOUR
4740 Boul Industriel, Sherbrooke, QC, J1L 3A3
(819) 562-3443
Emp Here 100   *Sales* 83,557,700
SIC 5149 Groceries and related products, nec
Josee Lange
Caroline Manseau
Guy Parenteau
Pierre Bellavance
Pierre Laporte

D-U-N-S 24-354-8919   (BR)
COSTCO WHOLESALE CANADA LTD
COSTCO
(*Suby of* COSTCO WHOLESALE CORPORATION)
3400 Rue King O, Sherbrooke, QC, J1L 1C9
(819) 822-2121
Emp Here 200
SIC 5199 Nondurable goods, nec
Jacques Drolet

D-U-N-S 20-972-0358   (SL)
DELAFONTAINE INC
DE LA FONTAINE
4115 Rue Brodeur, Sherbrooke, QC, J1L 1K4
(819) 348-1219
Emp Here 160   *Sales* 30,733,600
SIC 3442 Metal doors, sash, and trim
Robert De La Fontaine

D-U-N-S 24-835-0167   (BR)
DELTA HOTELS LIMITED
(*Suby of* GOVERNMENT OF THE PROVINCE OF BRITISH COLUMBIA)
2685 Rue King O, Sherbrooke, QC, J1L 1C1
(819) 822-1989
Emp Here 165
SIC 8741 Management services
Marc Henri Moutin

D-U-N-S 25-504-2269   (SL)

DELTA SHERBROOKE
2685 Rue King O, Sherbrooke, QC, J1L 1C1
(819) 822-1989
Emp Here 100   *Sales* 9,489,900
SIC 7011 Hotels and motels
Sylvain Gauthier

D-U-N-S 24-107-8757   (HQ)
DESPRES, LAPORTE INC
DOYON DESPRES
(*Suby of* CUISINES EQUINOXE INC, LES)
185 Rue De La Burlington, Sherbrooke, QC, J1L 1G9
(819) 566-2620
Emp Here 1   *Sales* 14,309,568
SIC 5046 Commercial equipment, nec
Gilles Pierre
Michel-Luc St-Pierre
Andre Carrier
Marc-Andre Hetu
Francois Despres
Audrey St-Pierre

D-U-N-S 20-260-4229   (HQ)
DOYON, G. T. V. (SHERBROOKE) INC
DUMOULIN ELECTRONIQUE
525 Rue Northrop-Frye, Sherbrooke, QC, J1L 2Y3
(819) 565-3177
Emp Here 33   *Sales* 11,852,553
SIC 5731 Radio, television, and electronic stores
Michel Doyon

D-U-N-S 24-324-9190   (HQ)
E.C.E. ELECTRIQUE INC
4345 Rue Ouimet, Sherbrooke, QC, J1L 1X5
(819) 821-2222
Sales 19,604,610
SIC 1731 Electrical work
Claude Riendeau

D-U-N-S 24-857-6571   (SL)
ELECTRO-5 INC
4135 Boul Industriel, Sherbrooke, QC, J1L 2S7
(819) 823-5355
Emp Here 25   *Sales* 11,179,350
SIC 5065 Electronic parts and equipment, nec
Claude Denis
Jacques Desrochers
Mario Richard
Guy Lamarche

D-U-N-S 24-858-4583   (HQ)
ENDUITS STEF INC
4365 Rue Robitaille, Sherbrooke, QC, J1L 2K2
(819) 820-1188
Sales 14,850,400
SIC 5198 Paints, varnishes, and supplies
Eugene R Francoeur
Dominic Francoeur
Gisele Francoeur

D-U-N-S 25-500-9730   (SL)
ESTIMATIONS GUY JALBERT 1997 INC, LES
4520 Boul Industriel, Sherbrooke, QC, J1L 2S8
(819) 566-7222
Emp Here 22   *Sales* 12,758,328
SIC 6411 Insurance agents, brokers, and service
Guy Jalbert
Richard Jalbert

D-U-N-S 20-558-7905   (HQ)
FILSPEC INC
85 Rue De La Burlington, Sherbrooke, QC, J1L 1G9
(819) 573-8700
Sales 33,432,630
SIC 2281 Yarn spinning mills
Ronald Audet
Nicolas Fournier
Jean-Pierre Naud
Richard Cormier

Daniel Caron
Helene Lee-Gosselin

D-U-N-S 24-353-4104   (BR)
GARLOCK OF CANADA LTD
GARLOCK CEALING TECHNOLGY
(*Suby of* ENPRO INDUSTRIES, INC.)
4100 Rue De La Garlock, Sherbrooke, QC, J1L 1W5
(819) 563-8080
Emp Here 75
SIC 2299 Textile goods, nec
Stephane Vincent

D-U-N-S 24-173-5414   (SL)
GESTION CLAUDE MEILLEUR INC
PHARMAPRIX
3050 Boul De Portland, Sherbrooke, QC, J1L 1K1
(819) 569-9621
Emp Here 45   *Sales* 11,382,930
SIC 5912 Drug stores and proprietary stores
Claude Meilleur
Esther Meilleur

D-U-N-S 25-104-6371   (HQ)
GNR CORBUS INC
GAZ NATUREL RICHARD
4070 Rue Brodeur, Sherbrooke, QC, J1L 1V9
(819) 564-2300
Emp Here 30   *Sales* 11,046,700
SIC 1711 Plumbing, heating, air-conditioning
Richard Robert
Bernard Bussieres
Patrick Lachambre
Levis Laberge

D-U-N-S 24-935-4903   (SL)
GROUPE POLY-M2 INC, LE
4005a Rue De La Garlock, Sherbrooke, QC, J1L 1W9
(819) 562-2161
Emp Here 150   *Sales* 4,795,200
SIC 7349 Building maintenance services, nec
Serge Auray

D-U-N-S 20-126-7445   (BR)
GROUPE TVA INC
TVA TELE 7
(*Suby of* QUEBECOR MEDIA INC)
3330 Rue King O, Sherbrooke, QC, J1L 1C9
(819) 565-7777
Emp Here 80
SIC 4833 Television broadcasting stations
Farah Beaulieu

D-U-N-S 24-161-0018   (BR)
HOME DEPOT OF CANADA INC
HOME DEPOT SHERBROOKE
(*Suby of* THE HOME DEPOT INC)
1355 Boul Du Plateau-Saint-Joseph, Sherbrooke, QC, J1L 3E2
(819) 348-4481
Emp Here 100
SIC 5251 Hardware stores
Serge Maurice

D-U-N-S 24-356-4135   (SL)
IMPORTATIONS THIBAULT LTEE
165 Rue Sauve, Sherbrooke, QC, J1L 1L6
(819) 569-6212
Emp Here 50   *Sales* 18,210,750
SIC 5013 Motor vehicle supplies and new parts
Jean Thibault
Michele Laliberte-Thibault
Jean-Francois Thibault
Julie Thibault

D-U-N-S 20-213-4206   (BR)
IMPRIMERIES TRANSCONTINENTAL INC
TRANSCONTINENTAL PRINTING INC
(*Suby of* TRANSCONTINENTAL INC)
4001 Boul De Portland, Sherbrooke, QC, J1L 1X9
(819) 563-4001
Emp Here 130
SIC 2752 Commercial printing, lithographic

Genevieve Paquin

D-U-N-S 20-260-4088   (SL)
INDUSTRIES DETTSON INC
(*Suby of* GROUPE OUELLET CANADA INC)
3400 Boul Industriel, Sherbrooke, QC, J1L
1V8
(819) 346-8493
Emp Here 100   *Sales* 19,044,200
SIC 3634 Electric housewares and fans
Martin Beaulieu

D-U-N-S 25-517-1449   (SL)
**LEMIEUX BEDARD COMMUNICATIONS
INC**
LB LEMIEUX BEDARD
2665 Rue King O Bureau 315, Sherbrooke,
QC, J1L 2G5
(819) 823-0850
Emp Here 60   *Sales* 11,087,880
SIC 4899 Communication services, nec
Suzanne Lemieux Bedard

D-U-N-S 20-922-4679   (BR)
MAISON SIMONS INC, LA
(*Suby of* MAISON SIMONS INC, LA)
3050 Boul De Portland, Sherbrooke, QC, J1L
1K1
(819) 829-1840
Emp Here 100
SIC 5651 Family clothing stores
Louise David

D-U-N-S 24-969-7962   (HQ)
MEDIA5 CORPORATION
MEDIATRIX
4229 Rue De La Garlock, Sherbrooke, QC,
J1L 2C8
(819) 829-8749
Sales 21,868,000
SIC 6712 Bank holding companies
Roger Noel
Christian Chalin
Louis Lagasse
Francois Bouchard
Serge Audet
Michael Bucheit
Claude Jodoin
Pierre Bernier

D-U-N-S 24-020-5211   (SL)
MESOTEC INC
4705 Boul De Portland, Sherbrooke, QC, J1L
0H3
(819) 822-2777
Emp Here 80   *Sales* 17,907,440
SIC 3728 Aircraft parts and equipment, nec
Philippe Constancis
Paul Constancis

D-U-N-S 25-464-6375   (SL)
MODES ET SPORTS 3050 INC
SPORTS EXPERTS 528
3050 Boul De Portland Bureau 528, Sher-
brooke, QC, J1L 1K1
(819) 346-5286
Emp Here 60   *Sales* 14,659,680
SIC 5941 Sporting goods and bicycle shops
Roger Heroux
Simon Gagnon

D-U-N-S 24-250-4439   (HQ)
MOMO SPORTS INC
SPORTS EXCELLENCE
530 Rue Jean-Paul-Perrault, Sherbrooke, QC,
J1L 3A6
(819) 822-3077
Emp Here 20   *Sales* 12,557,720
SIC 5699 Miscellaneous apparel and acces-
sory stores
Michel Poisson

D-U-N-S 25-222-6493   (SL)
MOULES INDUSTRIELS (C.H.F.G.) INC
MOULES INDUTRIELS
3100 Boul Industriel, Sherbrooke, QC, J1L
1V8
(819) 822-3697
Emp Here 88   *Sales* 19,536,088

SIC 3544 Special dies, tools, jigs, and fixtures
Vincent Houle
Francine Guay

D-U-N-S 24-226-4955   (HQ)
OVATION LOGISTIQUE INC
531 Rue Pepin, Sherbrooke, QC, J1L 1X3
(819) 569-9923
Emp Here 30   *Sales* 29,210,252
SIC 4215 Courier services, except by air
Guy Bessette
Claude Boilard
Mario Bourque
Michel Charlebois
Eric Doyon
Louis St-Lambert
Maxime Vincent
Stephane Gagne

D-U-N-S 20-181-0764   (SL)
PLASTECH INC
PLASTECH INTERNATIONAL
370 Rue Leger, Sherbrooke, QC, J1L 1Y5
(819) 822-1590
Emp Here 50   *Sales* 13,833,000
SIC 2821 Plastics materials and resins
Vincent Houle
Claude Houle

D-U-N-S 20-555-8583   (BR)
**PRODUITS AMERICAN BILTRITE
(CANADA) LTEE**
(*Suby of* AMERICAN BILTRITE INC.)
635 Rue Pepin, Sherbrooke, QC, J1L 2P8
(819) 823-3300
Emp Here 250
SIC 3069 Fabricated rubber products, nec
Jean Richard

D-U-N-S 20-330-7830   (SL)
PRODUITS IDEALTFC INC
EQUIPEMENT DE COMBUSTION IDEAL
4460 Rue Hector-Brien, Sherbrooke, QC, J1L
0E2
(819) 566-5696
Emp Here 70   *Sales* 16,314,550
SIC 1711 Plumbing, heating, air-conditioning
Guy St-Amand
Frederic Milliard
Jean-Francois Lachance

D-U-N-S 24-431-3602   (SL)
RELAIS
260 Rue Leger, Sherbrooke, QC, J1L 1Y5
(819) 566-7317
Emp Here 29   *Sales* 14,444,262
SIC 5531 Auto and home supply stores
Real Arnold

D-U-N-S 20-370-8800   (SL)
ROTISSERIES DE SHERBROOKE INC, LES
3070 Rue King O, Sherbrooke, QC, J1L 1C9
(819) 563-5111
Emp Here 100   *Sales* 4,551,900
SIC 5812 Eating places
Manon Proulx

D-U-N-S 25-240-1542   (SL)
**SEMINAIRE SALESIEN DE SHERBROOKE,
LE**
135 Rue Don-Bosco N, Sherbrooke, QC, J1L
1E5
(819) 566-2222
Emp Here 80   *Sales* 7,426,080
SIC 8211 Elementary and secondary schools
Raymond Lepage

D-U-N-S 25-408-1896   (SL)
SHERBROOKE O.E.M. LTD
TAUNTON ENGINEERING COMPANY
3425 Boul Industriel, Sherbrooke, QC, J1L
2W1
(819) 563-7374
Emp Here 80   *Sales* 19,694,880
SIC 1796 Installing building equipment
Alain Brasseur
Manon Tremblay
Jean-Francois Dion

D-U-N-S 24-958-9292   (HQ)
SIGNALISATION DE L'ESTRIE INC
GROUPE SIGNALISATION
520 Rue Pepin, Sherbrooke, QC, J1L 2Y8
(819) 822-3828
Sales 41,643,500
SIC 7359 Equipment rental and leasing, nec
Mario Beaudoin
Dany Guillemette
David Collin
Matthieu Collin
Jean-Pierre Duhamel

D-U-N-S 20-002-4441   (BR)
SOBEYS CAPITAL INCORPORATED
IGA EXTRA
(*Suby of* EMPIRE COMPANY LIMITED)
3950 Rue King O Bureau B, Sherbrooke, QC,
J1L 1P6
(819) 563-5172
Emp Here 100
SIC 5411 Grocery stores
Jean-Charles Guilbert

D-U-N-S 25-872-7627   (SL)
**SOCIETE PROTECTRICE DES ANIMAUX
DE L'ESTRIE**
SPA DE L'ESTRIE
145 Rue Sauve, Sherbrooke, QC, J1L 1L6
(819) 821-4727
Emp Here 26   *Sales* 10,332,764
SIC 8699 Membership organizations, nec
Evelina Smith
Michel Richer
Chantal Viger
Maryse Boivin

D-U-N-S 25-380-8729   (SL)
TECHNOLOGIES DUAL-ADE INC
CAB-R-SON
4025 Rue Letellier, Sherbrooke, QC, J1L 1Z3
(819) 829-2100
Emp Here 50   *Sales* 10,233,650
SIC 3613 Switchgear and switchboard appa-
ratus
Eric Ducharme

D-U-N-S 24-872-0443   (HQ)
TEKNA SYSTEMES PLASMA INC
TEKNA PLASMA
(*Suby of* ARENDALS FOSSEKOMPANI ASA)
2935 Boul Industriel, Sherbrooke, QC, J1L
2T9
(819) 820-2204
Emp Here 105   *Sales* 33,705,240
SIC 3569 General industrial machinery, nec
Maher I Boulos
Alf Steinar Saetre
Morten Henriksen
Sam C. Syvertsen
Torkil Mogstad

D-U-N-S 25-673-4666   (SL)
**THIBAULT, RONALD CHEVROLET CADIL-
LAC BUICK GMC LTEE**
3839 Rue King O, Sherbrooke, QC, J1L 1W7
(819) 563-7878
Emp Here 70   *Sales* 44,049,600
SIC 5511 New and used car dealers
Ronald Thibault
Jean-Pierre Simard

D-U-N-S 20-562-3580   (HQ)
VOYAGES ESCAPADE INC
AGENCE DE VOYAGE ESCAPADE 2000
2855 Rue King O, Sherbrooke, QC, J1L 1C6
(819) 563-5344
Emp Here 34   *Sales* 21,318,647
SIC 4724 Travel agencies
Marie-Josee Desmarais
Kevin Moffat

D-U-N-S 24-327-4524   (BR)
WAL-MART CANADA CORP
WALMART
(*Suby of* WALMART INC.)
4050 Boul Josaphat-Rancourt Bureau 3086,

Sherbrooke, QC, J1L 3C6
(819) 823-1661
Emp Here 225
SIC 5311 Department stores
Patrick Pinard

D-U-N-S 20-742-8058   (HQ)
WIPTEC INC
WIP INTERNATIONAL
3160 Boul Industriel, Sherbrooke, QC, J1L
1V8
(819) 564-7117
Emp Here 135   *Sales* 85,444,200
SIC 5031 Lumber, plywood, and millwork
Martin Ball
Sebastien Ball

Sherbrooke, QC J1M

D-U-N-S 20-116-5326   (HQ)
AIKAWA FIBER TECHNOLOGIES INC
(*Suby of* AIKAWA IRON WORKS CO.,LTD.)
72 Rue Queen, Sherbrooke, QC, J1M 2C3
(819) 562-4754
Sales 140,438,500
SIC 3554 Paper industries machinery
Jacques A Beauchemin
Toshikatsu Kawai
Robert W Gooding
Kazumi Fujita

D-U-N-S 25-079-8386   (SL)
ASSOCIATION B.C.S
BISHOP'S COLLEGE SCHOOL
80 Ch Moulton Hill, Sherbrooke, QC, J1M 2K4
(819) 566-0227
Emp Here 100   *Sales* 9,282,600
SIC 8211 Elementary and secondary schools
Timothy Price
Roald Smeets
Isabelle Goyette
Guthrie J. Stewart
Michel Bull
Richard Brandley
Linda Rodeck
E. Avery Russell
Kathryn M. Wyatt Cottingham
Stephan Scholl

D-U-N-S 24-291-5507   (SL)
**FIDUCIE TECHNOLOGIES DE FIBRES
AIKAWA**
AIKAWA GROUP
72 Rue Queen, Sherbrooke, QC, J1M 2C3
(819) 562-4754
Emp Here 49   *Sales* 24,679,242
SIC 5111 Printing and writing paper
Masaki Aikawa

D-U-N-S 25-402-1611   (HQ)
GLOBAL EXCEL MANAGEMENT INC
GEM
73 Rue Queen, Sherbrooke, QC, J1M 0C9
(819) 566-8833
Sales 1,661,136,400
SIC 6411 Insurance agents, brokers, and ser-
vice
Reginald Allatt
Michel Bull
Stephen Allatt

D-U-N-S 24-851-9865   (SL)
INVESTISSEMENTS ALT2 INC
ETFS
73 Rue Queen, Sherbrooke, QC, J1M 0C9
(819) 566-8833
Emp Here 400   *Sales* 1,898,441,600
SIC 6411 Insurance agents, brokers, and ser-
vice
Reginald Allatt
Michel Bull
Stephen Allatt

D-U-N-S 24-388-4710   (SL)

PRO-PAR INC
INDUSTRIES INTREPID
(*Suby of* TERRAVEST INDUSTRIES INC)
65 Rue Winder, Sherbrooke, QC, J1M 1L5
(819) 566-8211
Emp Here 90   *Sales* 17,287,650
SIC 3443 Fabricated plate work (boiler shop)
   Pierre Fournier

   D-U-N-S 20-860-4249   (HQ)
UNIVERSITE BISHOP'S
ARENA W.B. SCOTT
2600 Rue College, Sherbrooke, QC, J1M 1Z7
(819) 822-9600
Emp Here 345   *Sales* 49,213,537
SIC 8221 Colleges and universities
   Robert Hall
   Martel Nandia
   Marie-Josee Dufour
   Michael Goldbloom
   Nadia Martel
   Jim Sweeny
   Brian Levitt
   Cathy Mclean
   Kerry Hull
   Jane Brydges

Sherbrooke, QC J1N

   D-U-N-S 20-738-2573   (SL)
2527-9829 QUEBEC INC
ESTRIE AUTO CENTRE
4367 Boul Bourque, Sherbrooke, QC, J1N 1S4
(819) 564-1600
Emp Here 34   *Sales* 16,934,652
SIC 5511 New and used car dealers
   Germain Beaudoin

   D-U-N-S 25-244-0615   (SL)
2955-4201 QUEBEC INC
SUPREM AUTOMOBILE
4620 Boul Bourque, Sherbrooke, QC, J1N 2A8
(819) 821-9272
Emp Here 24   *Sales* 11,953,872
SIC 5511 New and used car dealers
   Pierre Simoneau
   Nancy James

   D-U-N-S 24-192-3734   (HQ)
9098-0145 QUEBEC INC
GROUPE GASTON COTE
4701 Boul Bourque, Sherbrooke, QC, J1N 2G6
(819) 564-2257
Emp Here 40   *Sales* 10,753,140
SIC 3272 Concrete products, nec
   Gesner Blenkhorn
   Stephane Cote

   D-U-N-S 20-294-3911   (SL)
9101-2468 QUEBEC INC
MAZDA DE SHERBROOKE
5119 Boul Bourque, Sherbrooke, QC, J1N 2K6
(819) 564-8664
Emp Here 40   *Sales* 25,171,200
SIC 5511 New and used car dealers
   Daniel Beaucage

   D-U-N-S 24-821-3787   (HQ)
ADMINISTRATION BEAULIEU INC
CONFECTION D. N. G.
6176 Rue Bertrand-Fabi, Sherbrooke, QC, J1N 2P3

Sales 11,769,885
SIC 6712 Bank holding companies
   Cecile Beaulieu
   Nicole Beaulieu Houle
   Diane Beaulieu Bolduc

   D-U-N-S 25-200-5046   (BR)
CENTRE JEUNESSE DE L'ESTRIE

CENTRE JEUNESSE VAL DU LAC
8475 Ch Blanchette, Sherbrooke, QC, J1N 3A3
(819) 864-4221
Emp Here 200
SIC 8361 Residential care
   Daniel Richard

   D-U-N-S 24-336-4895   (BR)
COMMISSION SCOLAIRE DE LA REGION-DE-SHERBROOKE
ECOLE DU TOURET
(*Suby of* COMMISSION SCOLAIRE DE LA REGION-DE-SHERBROOKE)
4076 Boul De L'Universite, Sherbrooke, QC, J1N 2Y1
(819) 822-5577
Emp Here 80
SIC 8211 Elementary and secondary schools
   Isabelle Boucher

   D-U-N-S 24-679-7914   (HQ)
DALKOTECH INC
9330 Boul Bourque, Sherbrooke, QC, J1N 0G2
(819) 868-1997
Sales 32,503,432
SIC 7692 Welding repair
   Jean-Guy Dalton
   Jacques Iza

   D-U-N-S 24-418-8053   (HQ)
DYNAMITAGE CASTONGUAY LTEE
5939 Rue Joyal, Sherbrooke, QC, J1N 1H1
(819) 864-4201
Emp Here 150   *Sales* 134,535,800
SIC 1389 Oil and gas field services, nec
   Gilles Trudel
   Pierre Alexandre
   Yuri Alexandre
   Benjamin Mahe

   D-U-N-S 25-486-8565   (SL)
EQUIPEMENTS MARQUIS INC
MARQUIS HYDRAULIQUE & PNEUMA-TIQUE
1155 Ch Saint-Roch N, Sherbrooke, QC, J1N 0H2
(819) 822-3382
Emp Here 14   *Sales* 14,004,746
SIC 5051 Metals service centers and offices
   Jean-Guy Marquis

   D-U-N-S 25-501-2130   (SL)
GARAGE RENAUD FORTIER INC
HYUNDAI SHERBROOKE
4320 Boul Bourque, Sherbrooke, QC, J1N 1S3
(819) 562-1700
Emp Here 37   *Sales* 18,428,886
SIC 5511 New and used car dealers
   Renaud Fortier
   Huguette Breton

   D-U-N-S 24-901-3228   (SL)
GESTION ANKABETH INC
SATURN SAAB ISUZU SHERBROOKE
4880 Boul Bourque, Sherbrooke, QC, J1N 2A7
(819) 823-1400
Emp Here 24   *Sales* 11,953,872
SIC 5511 New and used car dealers
   Daniel Beaucage
   Gilles Beaucage

   D-U-N-S 25-470-8530   (SL)
LACASSE & FILS MAITRES COUVREURS INC
10230 Boul Bourque, Sherbrooke, QC, J1N 0G2
(819) 843-2681
Emp Here 65   *Sales* 14,158,885
SIC 1761 Roofing, siding, and sheetMetal work
   Pascal Lapierre
   Charles Demers

   D-U-N-S 20-195-5317   (HQ)

LEPROHON INC
MAITRE ES CELSIUS
6171 Boul Bourque, Sherbrooke, QC, J1N 1H2
(819) 563-2454
Emp Here 80   *Sales* 54,169,600
SIC 1711 Plumbing, heating, air-conditioning
   Guillaume Le Prohon
   Veronique Le Prohon
   Sebastien Dupont
   Yvan Laberge
   Jean Le Prohon

   D-U-N-S 24-836-0646   (HQ)
MAGASINS C.P.C. INC, LES
C.P.C. C'PAS CHER U
(*Suby of* 9270-7355 QUEBEC INC)
4500 Boul Bourque, Sherbrooke, QC, J1N 1S2
(819) 348-0620
Emp Here 30   *Sales* 12,320,580
SIC 5311 Department stores
   Carlo Belisle

   D-U-N-S 25-071-5435   (SL)
METROPOLITAN RUST PROOFING INC
4232 Boul Bourque, Sherbrooke, QC, J1N 1W7
(819) 829-2888
Emp Here 49   *Sales* 10,105,826
SIC 3479 Metal coating and allied services
   Matthew Laplante

   D-U-N-S 24-742-2983   (SL)
MOBILIER DE BUREAU LOGIFLEX INC
ATELIER DESIGN
1235 Ch Saint-Roch N, Sherbrooke, QC, J1N 0H2
(877) 864-9323
Emp Here 100   *Sales* 15,432,200
SIC 2521 Wood office furniture
   Daniel Pelletier
   Francis Pelletier
   Martin Pelletier
   Yannick Sinclair

   D-U-N-S 24-385-4374   (SL)
PHARMACIE CHRISTIAN BOURQUE, PHAMACIEN INC
JEAN COUTU
4870 Boul Bourque, Sherbrooke, QC, J1N 3S5
(819) 820-0222
Emp Here 55   *Sales* 13,438,040
SIC 5912 Drug stores and proprietary stores
   Christian Bourque

   D-U-N-S 24-169-0783   (HQ)
RELAIS PNEUS FREINS ET SUSPENSIONS INC, LE
(*Suby of* 120152 CANADA INC)
4255 Boul Bourque, Sherbrooke, QC, J1N 1S4
(819) 566-7722
Emp Here 40   *Sales* 22,413,510
SIC 5531 Auto and home supply stores
   Yvan Desgreniers
   Real Arnold

   D-U-N-S 20-261-0671   (SL)
SHERBROOKE AUTOMOBILE INC
VOLKSWAGEN DE L'ESTRIE
4465 Boul Bourque, Sherbrooke, QC, J1N 1S4
(819) 569-9111
Emp Here 34   *Sales* 16,934,652
SIC 5511 New and used car dealers
   Janick Dallaire
   Yvan Frechette

   D-U-N-S 20-709-2511   (SL)
SHERBROOKE NISSAN INC
4280 Boul Bourque, Sherbrooke, QC, J1N 1W7
(819) 823-8008
Emp Here 35   *Sales* 17,432,730
SIC 5511 New and used car dealers
   Daniel Beaucage

   Richard Beaucage

   D-U-N-S 24-541-6037   (SL)
SOUCY TECHNO INC
(*Suby of* SOUCY HOLDING INC)
2550 Ch Saint-Roch S, Sherbrooke, QC, J1N 2R6
(819) 864-4284
Emp Here 168   *Sales* 26,688,144
SIC 3069 Fabricated rubber products, nec
   Gilles Soucy
   Josiane Roy

   D-U-N-S 20-853-0050   (SL)
SUPERMARCHE J C J PLOUFFE INC
METRO PLUS PLOUFFE
4801 Boul Bourque, Sherbrooke, QC, J1N 2G6
(819) 564-7733
Emp Here 49   *Sales* 13,433,448
SIC 5411 Grocery stores
   Daniel Plouffe

Sherbrooke, QC J1R

   D-U-N-S 24-321-2636   (SL)
98946 CANADA INC
IGA BOUCHARD
6185 Ch De Saint-Elie, Sherbrooke, QC, J1R 0L1
(819) 566-8555
Emp Here 50   *Sales* 13,707,600
SIC 5411 Grocery stores
   Eric Bouchard

   D-U-N-S 24-711-4820   (SL)
ANI-MAT INC
395 Rue Rodolphe-Racine, Sherbrooke, QC, J1R 0S7
(819) 821-2091
Emp Here 115   *Sales* 21,091,345
SIC 2273 Carpets and rugs
   Rosaire Croteau
   Ange-Albert Allard
   Daniel Grosselin
   Roger Yergeau
   Guy Couture

   D-U-N-S 20-709-6785   (HQ)
BOURQUE, A ACIER ET METAUX INC
137 Ch Godin, Sherbrooke, QC, J1R 0S6
(819) 569-6960
Sales 13,013,550
SIC 5093 Scrap and waste materials
   Alcide Bourque

   D-U-N-S 24-250-8968   (SL)
COMMUNICATIONS INTERVOX INC, LES
(*Suby of* GS/C COMMUNICATION INC)
6420 Ch De Saint-Elie, Sherbrooke, QC, J1R 0P6
(819) 563-3222
Emp Here 24   *Sales* 10,732,176
SIC 5065 Electronic parts and equipment, nec
   Serge Champagne

   D-U-N-S 20-354-7013   (BR)
COOPER-STANDARD AUTOMOTIVE CANADA LIMITED
(*Suby of* COOPER-STANDARD HOLDINGS INC.)
4870 Rue Robert Boyd, Sherbrooke, QC, J1R 0W8
(819) 562-4440
Emp Here 250
SIC 3465 Automotive stampings
   Guylaine Lessard

   D-U-N-S 24-125-1276   (SL)
DISTRIBUTION JEAN BLANCHARD INC
DJB GROUPE
1686 Ch Laliberte, Sherbrooke, QC, J1R 0C5
(819) 820-9777
Emp Here 20   *Sales* 10,000,000
SIC 5083 Farm and garden machinery

Pierre Blanchard
Steven Blanchard
Suzie Pellerin

D-U-N-S 24-473-9041   (SL)
ELITE CHRYSLER JEEP INC
SHERBROOKE FIAT
6138 Ch De Saint-Elie, Sherbrooke, QC, J1R 0L1
(819) 571-5540
Emp Here 50   *Sales* 24,903,900
SIC 5511 New and used car dealers
Robert Bilodeau

D-U-N-S 24-269-6896   (SL)
SIGNALISATION DES CANTONS INC
1001 Ch Dion, Sherbrooke, QC, J1R 0R8
(819) 987-1483
Emp Here 40   *Sales* 33,423,080
SIC 5149 Groceries and related products, nec
Veronique Sinclair Desgagne

D-U-N-S 24-863-8124   (HQ)
SURPLEC INC
SUPERLEC HV SOLUTIONS
149 Ch Godin, Sherbrooke, QC, J1R 0S6
(819) 821-3636
Sales 35,773,920
SIC 5063 Electrical apparatus and equipment
Mario Lambert

D-U-N-S 25-093-3343   (SL)
SURPLEC INDUSTRIEL INC
155 Ch Godin, Sherbrooke, QC, J1R 0S6
(819) 821-3634
Emp Here 40   *Sales* 14,250,780
SIC 5084 Industrial machinery and equipment
Danny Bennett

D-U-N-S 24-347-0601   (SL)
TOITURES VICK & ASSOCIES INC, LES
71 Ch Godin, Sherbrooke, QC, J1R 0S6
(450) 658-4300
Emp Here 50   *Sales* 10,891,450
SIC 1761 Roofing, siding, and sheetMetal work
Steve Roy

Sherrington, QC J0L

D-U-N-S 20-416-3257   (SL)
COMPAGNIE OTTO JANGL LTEE
O. J. COMPANY
(*Suby of* 120022 CANADA INC)
294 Rang Saint-Paul, Sherrington, QC, J0L 2N0
(450) 247-2758
Emp Here 34   *Sales* 17,698,428
SIC 5091 Sporting and recreation goods
Philippe Jangl
Gabriel Jangl
Ludmila Jangl

D-U-N-S 24-636-7320   (SL)
FERME E NOTARO ET FILS INC, LES
307 Rang Saint-Francois, Sherrington, QC, J0L 2N0
(450) 454-3567
Emp Here 30   *Sales* 10,274,010
SIC 0161 Vegetables and melons
Nunzio Notaro
Giacomo Notaro
Alexandre Notaro

D-U-N-S 24-516-1575   (SL)
FERMES V. FORINO & FILS INC, LES
298 Rang Sainte-Melanie, Sherrington, QC, J0L 2N0
(450) 454-6307
Emp Here 52   *Sales* 43,450,004
SIC 5148 Fresh fruits and vegetables
Steven Daigneault
Marc-Olivier Daigneault

D-U-N-S 20-322-8213   (SL)

LEGUMES R. & M. INC, LES
26 Rang Contant, Sherrington, QC, J0L 2N0
(514) 977-3840
Emp Here 40   *Sales* 33,423,080
SIC 5148 Fresh fruits and vegetables
Robert Beaulieu
Jean-Francois Beaulieu
Charles Beaulieu

D-U-N-S 20-370-1123   (SL)
PRODUITS FRAIS FMS INC
JARDINS FMS DAIGNEAULT, LES
298 Rang Sainte-Melanie, Sherrington, QC, J0L 2N0
(450) 454-6499
Emp Here 22   *Sales* 18,382,694
SIC 5148 Fresh fruits and vegetables
Marc-Olivier Daigneault
Steven Daigneault

D-U-N-S 24-392-4821   (SL)
SALADE ETCETERA U INC
(*Suby of* GESTION PRO VEG INC)
147 Rang Saint-Paul, Sherrington, QC, J0L 2N0
(450) 454-7712
Emp Here 600   *Sales* 97,256,521
SIC 0723 Crop preparation services for market
Gerry Van Winden
Anthony Fantin

D-U-N-S 25-543-4151   (HQ)
VEGPRO INTERNATIONAL INC
(*Suby of* GESTION PRO VEG INC)
147 Rang Saint-Paul, Sherrington, QC, J0L 2N0
(450) 454-7712
Sales 33,423,080
SIC 5148 Fresh fruits and vegetables
Gerry Van Winden
Jean-Bernard Van Winden
Anthony Fantin
Denys Van Winden

Shigawake, QC G0C

D-U-N-S 20-579-6733   (SL)
ASSELS SEAFOOD INC
11 132 Rte, Shigawake, QC, G0C 3E0

Emp Here 55   *Sales* 19,012,950
SIC 2092 Fresh or frozen packaged fish
Albert Boyd Assels
Landis Assels

Shipshaw, QC G7P

D-U-N-S 20-322-4154   (SL)
SYNDICAT DES EMPLOYEES COLS BLANCS DE VILLE DE SAGUENAY
3760 Rte Saint-Leonard, Shipshaw, QC, G7P 1G9

Emp Here 49   *Sales* 19,388,730
SIC 8631 Labor organizations
Rene Cloutier

Sorel-Tracy, QC J3P

D-U-N-S 24-226-9462   (SL)
ACIERS RICHELIEU INC, LES
190 Rue Du Roi, Sorel-Tracy, QC, J3P 4N5
(450) 743-1265
Emp Here 50   *Sales* 10,141,500
SIC 3499 Fabricated Metal products, nec
Eric Durand
Guy Durand

Patrick Doyon

D-U-N-S 25-463-4504   (SL)
ANDRE ROY ET SYLVAIN BOISSELLE PHARMACIENS INC
PHARMACIE JEAN COUTU
369 Boul Fiset, Sorel-Tracy, QC, J3P 3R3
(450) 746-7840
Emp Here 40   *Sales* 10,118,160
SIC 5912 Drug stores and proprietary stores
Andre Roy
Sylvain Roy Boisselle

D-U-N-S 25-400-3536   (SL)
AUBERGE DE LA RIVE INC
165 Ch Sainte-Anne, Sorel-Tracy, QC, J3P 6J7
(450) 742-5691
Emp Here 75   *Sales* 7,117,425
SIC 7011 Hotels and motels
Gordon Wells
Robert Faithfull
Kim Faithfull

D-U-N-S 25-257-7499   (SL)
C.L.S.C. DU HAVRE
30 Rue Ferland, Sorel-Tracy, QC, J3P 3C7
(450) 746-4545
Emp Here 150   *Sales* 11,365,950
SIC 8093 Specialty outpatient clinics, nec
Benoit Marchessault
Lucie Pepin

D-U-N-S 24-044-8204   (BR)
COMMISSION SCOLAIRE DE SOREL-TRACY
ECOLE SECONDAIRE FERNAND LEFEBVRE
265 Rue De Ramezay, Sorel-Tracy, QC, J3P 4A5
(450) 742-5901
Emp Here 100
SIC 8211 Elementary and secondary schools
Roger Pastor

D-U-N-S 20-971-2801   (SL)
CSSS PIERRE-DE SAUREL
CENTRE DE SANTE ET DE SERVICES SOCIAUX PIERRE-DE S
400 Av De L'Hotel-Dieu, Sorel-Tracy, QC, J3P 1N5
(450) 746-6000
Emp Here 1,480   *Sales* 164,398,400
SIC 8062 General medical and surgical hospitals
Andre Lussier
Lucie Pepin
Benoit Marchessault

D-U-N-S 20-855-7496   (SL)
FABSPEC INC
(*Suby of* GESPEC INC)
160 Rue Du Roi, Sorel-Tracy, QC, J3P 4N5
(450) 742-0451
Emp Here 100   *Sales* 19,208,500
SIC 3443 Fabricated plate work (boiler shop)
Martin Michaud
Annie Michaud

D-U-N-S 24-329-8457   (BR)
GROUPE PATRICK MORIN INC
PATRICK MORIN INC
(*Suby of* GROUPE PATRICK MORIN INC)
369 Boul Poliquin, Sorel-Tracy, QC, J3P 7W1
(450) 742-4567
Emp Here 125
SIC 5211 Lumber and other building materials
Pierre Guimont

D-U-N-S 20-266-0262   (HQ)
LUSSIER DALE PARIZEAU INC
ASSURANCE BRIAN BROCHET
80 Rue Augusta, Sorel-Tracy, QC, J3P 1A5
(450) 746-1000
Sales 132,167,500
SIC 6159 Miscellaneous business credit institutions
Andre Lussier

Luc-Andre Lussier
Caroline Lussier

D-U-N-S 20-860-6249   (SL)
MARCHE ANDRE TELLIER INC
IGA
411 Boul Poliquin, Sorel-Tracy, QC, J3P 7V9
(450) 743-3693
Emp Here 45   *Sales* 12,336,840
SIC 5411 Grocery stores
Andre Tellier

D-U-N-S 25-448-3886   (BR)
METRO RICHELIEU INC
SUPER C SOREL
(*Suby of* METRO INC)
250 Boul Fiset, Sorel-Tracy, QC, J3P 3P7
(450) 742-4563
Emp Here 80
SIC 5142 Packaged frozen goods
Francois Page

D-U-N-S 20-261-5209   (SL)
P.R. ST-GERMAIN INC
PROVIGO ST-GERMAIN
50 Rue Victoria, Sorel-Tracy, QC, J3P 1Y6
(450) 743-5738
Emp Here 85   *Sales* 24,945,545
SIC 5411 Grocery stores
Richard St-Germain

D-U-N-S 24-429-9244   (SL)
PEFOND INC
DUNKIN DONUT
170 Boul Fiset, Sorel-Tracy, QC, J3P 3P4
(450) 742-8295
Emp Here 48   *Sales* 13,159,296
SIC 5461 Retail bakeries
Denis Peloquin
Richard Lafond

D-U-N-S 24-496-5500   (SL)
RAYMOND PARENT TEXTILES INC
33 Rue Du Prince, Sorel-Tracy, QC, J3P 4J5
(450) 743-9666
Emp Here 25   *Sales* 12,458,050
SIC 5131 Piece goods and notions
Raymond Parent

D-U-N-S 25-706-5599   (SL)
RECYCLO-CENTRE INC
RECYCLO-ENVIRONNEMENT
165 Av De L'Hotel-Dieu, Sorel-Tracy, QC, J3P 1M2
(450) 746-4559
Emp Here 79   *Sales* 19,301,912
SIC 5932 Used merchandise stores
Jean-Sebastien Abran
Martine Beaudreau
Claude Desautels
Eric Belisle
Veronique Landry
Francois Gagne
Cherie Poirier
Marie-Andree Serois-Larachelle

D-U-N-S 20-289-4721   (SL)
RICHARDSON INTERNATIONAL (QUEBEC) LIMITEE
JAMES RICHARDSON INTERNATIONAL (QUEBEC)
(*Suby of* RICHARDSON, JAMES & SONS, LIMITED)
10 Rue De La Reine, Sorel-Tracy, QC, J3P 4R2
(450) 743-3893
Emp Here 26   *Sales* 12,350,676
SIC 5083 Farm and garden machinery
Curt Vossen
Darwin Sobkow
Jean-Marc Ruest
Hartley Richardson

D-U-N-S 24-216-9550   (BR)
SOCIETE DES TRAVERSIERS DU QUEBEC
(*Suby of* GOUVERNEMENT DE LA PROVINCE DE QUEBEC)

▲ Public Company   ■ Public Company Family Member   **HQ** Headquarters   **BR** Branch   **SL** Single Location

9 Rue Elizabeth, Sorel-Tracy, QC, J3P 4G1
(450) 742-3313
Emp Here 250
SIC 4111 Local and suburban transit

Sorel-Tracy, QC J3R

D-U-N-S 20-381-1500   (SL)
4318200 CANADA INC
ELECSO
3295 Rue Joseph-Simard, Sorel-Tracy, QC,
J3R 0E4
(450) 742-5663
Emp Here 50   *Sales* 25,982,750
SIC 4911 Electric services
Yvan Lebel
Eric Cardin

D-U-N-S 20-033-9237   (SL)
ALIMENTATION SYLVAIN BRIERE INC
METRO PLUS
7000 Av De La Plaza Bureau 2036, Sorel-
Tracy, QC, J3R 4L8
(450) 742-8227
Emp Here 49   *Sales* 13,433,448
SIC 5411 Grocery stores
Sylvain Briere

D-U-N-S 20-225-8757   (BR)
ALSTOM CANADA INC
*POWER ENVIRONMENT ALSTOM HYDRO
CANADA*
(*Suby of* GE RENEWABLE HOLDING B.V.)
1350 Ch Saint-Roch, Sorel-Tracy, QC, J3R
5P9
(450) 746-6500
Emp Here 400
SIC 4911 Electric services
Claude Lambert

D-U-N-S 24-351-8495   (SL)
**COLLEGE D'ENSEIGNEMENT GENERAL
ET PROFESSIONNEL SOREL-TRACY**
CEGEP DE SOREL-TRACY
3000 Boul De Tracy, Sorel-Tracy, QC, J3R 5B9
(450) 742-6651
Emp Here 200   *Sales* 29,878,200
SIC 8221 Colleges and universities
Francoise Richer

D-U-N-S 20-910-3977   (BR)
**COMMISSION SCOLAIRE DE SOREL-
TRACY**
ECOLE SECONDAIRE BERNARD GARIEPY
2800 Boul Des Erables, Sorel-Tracy, QC, J3R
2W4
(450) 746-3510
Emp Here 150
SIC 8211 Elementary and secondary schools

D-U-N-S 20-246-9565   (HQ)
DANIS CONSTRUCTION INC
13000 Rte Marie-Victorin, Sorel-Tracy, QC,
J3R 0J9

Sales 10,504,575
SIC 3273 Ready-mixed concrete
Pierre Millette
Jocelyn Beauchemin
Alain Theraux

D-U-N-S 20-265-8423   (SL)
POIRIER, ROGER AUTOMOBILE INC
2325 Rue Laprade, Sorel-Tracy, QC, J3R 2C1
(450) 742-2743
Emp Here 23   *Sales* 11,455,794
SIC 5511 New and used car dealers
Jean Poirier
Paul Poirier

D-U-N-S 24-109-7518   (SL)
PORTES ET CHASSIS BOULET, EDDY INC
PORTES ET FENETRES BOULET
10700 Rte Marie-Victorin, Sorel-Tracy, QC,
J3R 0K2

(450) 742-9424
Emp Here 90   *Sales* 17,287,650
SIC 3442 Metal doors, sash, and trim
Eddy Boulet
Roger Boulet
Louis Boulet

D-U-N-S 24-460-8964   (SL)
RESIDENCE SOREL-TRACY INC
4025 Rue Frontenac, Sorel-Tracy, QC, J3R
4G8
(450) 742-9427
Emp Here 150   *Sales* 8,887,050
SIC 8361 Residential care
Wilner Bien Aime
Julie Bien-Aime
Karine Bien-Aime

D-U-N-S 20-565-6056   (SL)
RIAL ELECTRIQUE INC
RIAL
2205 Rue Laprade, Sorel-Tracy, QC, J3R 2C1
(450) 746-7349
Emp Here 70   *Sales* 15,248,030
SIC 1731 Electrical work
Patrice Forest
Stephane Morand

D-U-N-S 20-562-5387   (HQ)
RIO TINTO FER ET TITANE INC
QIT - FER ET TITANE
(*Suby of* RIO TINTO PLC)
1625 Rte Marie-Victorin, Sorel-Tracy, QC, J3R
1M6
(450) 746-3000
Sales 732,913,200
SIC 3399 Primary Metal products
Guy Gaudreault
Marie-Christine Dupont
Kayam Slutsky
Stephane Leblanc
Jocelin Paradis

Squatec, QC G0L

D-U-N-S 20-261-7015   (HQ)
PELLETIER, RICHARD & FILS INC
4 Rue Saint-Marc, Squatec, QC, G0L 4H0
(418) 855-2951
Emp Here 85   *Sales* 71,203,500
SIC 5031 Lumber, plywood, and millwork
Lucette Pelletier
Maurice Pelletier
Brigitte Pelletier
Francis Beaulieu

St-Adelme-De-Matane, QC G0L

D-U-N-S 24-099-8547   (SL)
2171-0751 QUEBEC INC
TRANSPORT EN VRAC ST-DENIS ENR
74a 132 Rte O, St-Adelme-De-Matane, QC,
G0L 2R0
(418) 498-2405
Emp Here 49   *Sales* 13,114,948
SIC 5211 Lumber and other building materials
Marco Garon

St-Francois-De-La-Riviere-Du-S, QC G0R

D-U-N-S 24-994-1303   (SL)
GARANT GP
GARANT
375 Ch Saint-Francois O, St-Francois-De-La-
Riviere-Du-S, QC, G0R 3A0
(418) 259-7711
Emp Here 372   *Sales* 90,481,932
SIC 3423 Hand and edge tools, nec

Jean Gaudreault

D-U-N-S 24-746-4878   (HQ)
PRODUITS METALLIQUES ROY INC, LES
52 Ch De Morigeau, St-Francois-De-La-
Riviere-Du-S, QC, G0R 3A0
(418) 259-2711
Sales 23,148,300
SIC 2542 Partitions and fixtures, except wood
Robert Roy
Suzanne Dumas

D-U-N-S 20-250-3983   (HQ)
**SOCIETE COOPERATIVE AGRICOLE DE
LA RIVIERE-DU-SUD**
COOP DE LA RIVIERE DU SUD
34 Ch Saint-Francois O, St-Francois-De-La-
Riviere-Du-S, QC, G0R 3A0
(418) 259-7715
Emp Here 1   *Sales* 10,127,700
SIC 5251 Hardware stores

St-Francois-Xavier-De-Brompton, QC J0B

D-U-N-S 24-326-2917   (SL)
**EQUIPEMENTS DE FERME JAMESWAY
INC**
12 Rte 249, St-Francois-Xavier-De-Brompton,
QC, J0B 2V0
(819) 845-7824
Emp Here 100   *Sales* 22,200,100
SIC 3523 Farm machinery and equipment
Eric Vallieres
Dominic Vallieres
David Vallieres

St-Nazaire-Du-Lac-St-Jean, QC G0W

D-U-N-S 24-465-1634   (HQ)
CONSTRUCTIONS PROCO INC
AUBERGE JASEUR BOREAL
516 172 Rte O, St-Nazaire-Du-Lac-St-Jean,
QC, G0W 2V0
(418) 668-3371
Sales 139,678,400
SIC 1541 Industrial buildings and warehouses
Michel Toupin
Eric Bouchard
Michel Begin
Ronald Martin
Louis Maltais

D-U-N-S 20-117-6182   (SL)
STRUCTURES CPI INC
(*Suby of* CONSTRUCTIONS PROCO INC)
516 Rte 172 O, St-Nazaire-Du-Lac-St-Jean,
QC, G0W 2V0
(418) 668-3371
Emp Here 115   *Sales* 27,971,565
SIC 3441 Fabricated structural Metal
Michel Toupin
Eric Bouchard
Jean-Denis Toupin
Michel Begin
Carol Girard

D-U-N-S 24-200-9579   (SL)
THERMAFIX A. J. INC
INDUSTRIES THERMAFIX ABITIBI
1396 Rte Du Rondin, St-Nazaire-Du-Lac-St-
Jean, QC, G0W 2V0
(418) 668-6131
Emp Here 50   *Sales* 11,671,750
SIC 3211 Flat glass
Remi Gagnon
Terence Boudreault
James O. Boudreault
Benoit Gagnon

St-Valerien, QC J0H

D-U-N-S 24-589-9943   (SL)
NORMANDIN INC
931 Ch De Milton, St-Valerien, QC, J0H 2B0
(450) 549-2949
Emp Here 50   *Sales* 22,174,500
SIC 7389 Business services, nec
Louis Veilleux
Claude Beauvillier

D-U-N-S 20-559-1717   (SL)
PROVIMI CANADA ULC
CARGILL
557 Ch De Saint-Dominique Bureau 1, St-
Valerien, QC, J0H 2B0
(450) 549-2629
Emp Here 32   *Sales* 35,371,040
SIC 5122 Drugs, proprietaries, and sundries
Charles Lapointe
Nicolas Bussiere

D-U-N-S 25-993-1764   (HQ)
R.P.M. TECH INC
EQUIPEMENTS BLANCHET
(*Suby of* ALAMO GROUP INC.)
1318 Rue Principale, St-Valerien, QC, J0H
2B0
(418) 285-1811
Emp Here 25   *Sales* 17,982,081
SIC 3599 Industrial machinery, nec
Daniel Beaudoin
Robert Caron
Robert H. George
Edward T. Rizzuti
Richard J. Wehrle

D-U-N-S 25-115-1692   (HQ)
TENCO INC
EQUIPEMENTS TENCO
1318 Rue Principale, St-Valerien, QC, J0H
2B0
(800) 318-3626
Sales 11,192,150
SIC 3711 Motor vehicles and car bodies
Daniel Beaudoin
Jeffery A. Leonard
Richard J Wehrle
Edward T. Rizzuti
Robert Caron

Standon, QC G0R

D-U-N-S 24-884-1942   (SL)
DISTRIBUTIONS YVAN NADEAU INC, LES
11 Rang Saint-Leon N, Standon, QC, G0R
4L0
(418) 642-5035
Emp Here 26   *Sales* 21,725,002
SIC 5145 Confectionery
Poulin Alexandre

Stanstead, QC J0B

D-U-N-S 20-126-9490   (SL)
ABCO STC INC
75 Rue Principale, Stanstead, QC, J0B 3E5
(819) 876-7281
Emp Here 75   *Sales* 15,142,275
SIC 3069 Fabricated rubber products, nec
Alain Boisvert

D-U-N-S 24-544-7271   (SL)
EQUIPE H.B. HELLER INC, L'
SPENCER SUPPORT
(*Suby of* SUPPORTS SPENCER CANADA
LIMITEE)
175 Rue Passenger Rr 4, Stanstead, QC, J0B
3E2

---

(819) 876-2709
Emp Here 40   *Sales* 19,932,880
SIC 5137 Women's and children's clothing
Markus Haug
France Beauregard

D-U-N-S 24-863-6896   (HQ)
GRANIT C. ROULEAU INC
C. ROULEAU GRANIT
140 Ch Des Ursulines, Stanstead, QC, J0B
3E0
(819) 876-7171
Sales 14,337,520
SIC 3281 Cut stone and stone products
Gaetan Rouleau
Daniel Lemay
Mark Fauteux
Danny Bennett
Ian Warcup

D-U-N-S 25-159-8538   (SL)
GRANIT DESIGN INC
GRANIT DESIGN
77 Rue Industrielle, Stanstead, QC, J0B 3E0
(819) 876-7111
Emp Here 40   *Sales* 10,122,360
SIC 5211 Lumber and other building materials
Jonathan Vanasse
Annie Roy

D-U-N-S 24-548-0314   (SL)
PROVISIONS ROCK ISLAND INC
IGA STANSTEAD
14 Ch De Fairfax Rr 1, Stanstead, QC, J0B
3E0
(819) 876-7262
Emp Here 51   *Sales* 14,967,327
SIC 5411 Grocery stores
Andre Roy
Kathy Roy

D-U-N-S 25-359-3057   (SL)
ROCK OF AGES CANADA INC
4 Rue Rock Of Ages, Stanstead, QC, J0B 3E2
(819) 876-2745
Emp Here 50   *Sales* 11,671,750
SIC 3281 Cut stone and stone products
Francois Darmayan
Gabriel Ouellet
Terence Mathieu

Ste-Catherine-De-La-J-Cartie, QC G3N

D-U-N-S 24-499-9702   (HQ)
2169-5762 QUEBEC INC
NERO BIANCO GROUP
281 Rue Edward-Assh, Ste-Catherine-De-La-
J-Cartie, QC, G3N 1A3
(418) 875-1839
Emp Here 35   *Sales* 31,188,750
SIC 5661 Shoe stores
Jean-Luc Transon

D-U-N-S 20-309-2432   (SL)
9264-6231 QUEBEC INC
NERO BIANCO
281 Rue Edward-Assh, Ste-Catherine-De-La-
J-Cartie, QC, G3N 1A3
(418) 875-1839
Emp Here 438   *Sales* 54,642,690
SIC 5621 Women's clothing stores
Eric Chatila

D-U-N-S 24-791-4971   (HQ)
BOUTIQUE LE PENTAGONE INC
MODE F17
301 Rue Edward-Assh, Ste-Catherine-De-La-
J-Cartie, QC, G3N 1A3
(418) 875-1839
Emp Here 404   *Sales* 40,919,640
SIC 5621 Women's clothing stores
Eric Chatila

D-U-N-S 20-291-0782   (SL)
GYM FABRIK INC

281 Rue Edward-Assh, Ste-Catherine-De-La-
J-Cartie, QC, G3N 1A3
(418) 875-2600
Emp Here 100   *Sales* 32,613,600
SIC 3949 Sporting and athletic goods, nec
Mario Kelly
Carl Lachance
Guillaume Vallee
Bruno Tremblay

D-U-N-S 24-392-3112   (HQ)
LORTIE AVIATION INC
130 Rue Tibo, Ste-Catherine-De-La-J-Cartie,
QC, G3N 2Y7
(418) 875-5111
Sales 13,592,100
SIC 7699 Repair services, nec
Andre Lortie

D-U-N-S 25-785-0701   (BR)
**SOCIETE DES ETABLISSEMENTS DE
PLEIN AIR DU QUEBEC**
(*Suby of* GOUVERNEMENT DE LA
PROVINCE DE QUEBEC)
140 Montee De L'Auberge, Ste-Catherine-De-
La-J-Cartie, QC, G3N 2Y6
(418) 875-2711
Emp Here 150
SIC 7032 Sporting and recreational camps
Rejean Beaulieu

Ste-Marguerite-De-Dorchester, QC G0S

D-U-N-S 24-942-5687   (SL)
C.G. AIR SYSTEMES INC
207 Rue Industrielle, Ste-Marguerite-De-
Dorchester, QC, G0S 2X0
(418) 935-7075
Emp Here 50   *Sales* 12,828,100
SIC 3842 Surgical appliances and supplies
Miguel Angel Castellote
Dominique Ciechanowski

Stoneham-Et-Tewkesbury, QC G3C

D-U-N-S 20-114-1160   (SL)
BETON CHEVALIER INC
BETON ROYAL
50 Ch Rourke, Stoneham-Et-Tewkesbury, QC,
G3C 0W3
(418) 848-1966
Emp Here 50   *Sales* 22,358,700
SIC 5032 Brick, stone, and related material
Bernard Chevalier
David Chevalier
Effie Chevalier

D-U-N-S 25-188-6714   (SL)
CUMMINS EST DU CANADA SEC
3614   Rte   Tewkesbury,   Stoneham-Et-
Tewkesbury, QC, G3C 2L8
(418) 848-6464
Emp Here 49   *Sales* 21,911,526
SIC 5063 Electrical apparatus and equipment
Charles Decary

D-U-N-S 25-105-4938   (SL)
DISTRIBUTIONS LMC LTEE, LES
AUBERGE STONEHAM
600 Ch Du Hibou, Stoneham-Et-Tewkesbury,
QC, G3C 1T3
(418) 848-2415
Emp Here 50   *Sales* 10,880,650
SIC 5941 Sporting goods and bicycle shops
Larry Moeller

D-U-N-S 24-896-5519   (SL)
ENTREPRISES B J T BOULIANNE INC, LES
I.G.A.
335 Ch Du Hibou, Stoneham-Et-Tewkesbury,
QC, G3C 1R9

(418) 848-2637
Emp Here 41   *Sales* 11,240,232
SIC 5411 Grocery stores
Benoit Boulianne

D-U-N-S 24-857-9901   (HQ)
FORFAITERIE INC, LA
CLUB VOYAGES LA FORFAITERIE
107 1re Av, Stoneham-Et-Tewkesbury, QC,
G3C 0L3
(418) 848-1518
Sales 13,519,142
SIC 4724 Travel agencies
Andre Sabourin
Mylene Sabourin

Sutton, QC J0E

D-U-N-S 25-258-9064   (SL)
**CENTRE DE SANTE ET DE SERVICES SO-
CIAUX DE LA POMMERAIE, LE**
FOYER SUTTON
50 Rue Western, Sutton, QC, J0E 2K0
(450) 538-3332
Emp Here 110   *Sales* 6,517,170
SIC 8361 Residential care
Josee Perras

D-U-N-S 20-261-8666   (SL)
DESPRES H LTEE
44 Rue Principale N, Sutton, QC, J0E 2K0
(450) 538-2211
Emp Here 40   *Sales* 10,966,080
SIC 5411 Grocery stores
Andre Lusignan

D-U-N-S 25-836-3720   (SL)
HYLAND'S HOMEOPATHIC CANADA INC
(*Suby of* STANDARD HOMEOPATHIC CO.)
381 139 Rte N, Sutton, QC, J0E 2K0
(450) 538-6636
Emp Here 26   *Sales* 28,738,970
SIC 5122 Drugs, proprietaries, and sundries
Margot Murphy Moore
Ronald Lancaster
Margot Murphy Moore

Tadoussac, QC G0T

D-U-N-S 20-777-1135   (BR)
**CENTRE DE SANTE ET DES SERVICES
SOCIAUX DE LA HAUTE-COTE-NORD**
162 Rue Des Jesuites, Tadoussac, QC, G0T
2A0
(418) 235-4588
Emp Here 150
SIC 8062 General medical and surgical hospitals

Temiscaming, QC J0Z

D-U-N-S 25-259-6531   (SL)
CENTRE DE SANTE DE TEMISCAMING INC
180 Rue Anvik, Temiscaming, QC, J0Z 3R0

Emp Here 92   *Sales* 11,304,684
SIC 8062 General medical and surgical hospi-
tals
Gilbert Ladouceur

D-U-N-S 20-195-4612   (BR)
RAYONIER A.M. CANADA G.P.
BOLT
(*Suby of* RAYONIER A.M. CANADA G.P.)
10 Ch Gatineau, Temiscaming, QC, J0Z 3R0
(819) 627-4387
Emp Here 800
SIC 2611 Pulp mills
Richard Tremblay

Temiscouata-Sur-Le-Lac, QC G0L

D-U-N-S 24-154-4977   (SL)
BATITECH LTEE
578 Rue Commerciale N, Temiscouata-Sur-
Le-Lac, QC, G0L 1E0
(418) 854-0854
Emp Here 50   *Sales* 15,943,450
SIC 1521 Single-family housing construction
Stephane April
Pierre Poirier

D-U-N-S 20-317-5229   (BR)
CASCADES CANADA ULC
NORAMPAC
(*Suby of* CASCADES INC)
520 Rue Commerciale N, Temiscouata-Sur-
Le-Lac, QC, G0L 1E0
(418) 854-2803
Emp Here 542
SIC 2631 Paperboard mills
Luc Peletier

D-U-N-S 25-504-1154   (HQ)
**COMMISSION SCOLAIRE DU FLEUVE ET
DES LACS**
14 Rue Du Vieux-Chemin, Temiscouata-Sur-
Le-Lac, QC, G0L 1E0
(418) 854-2370
Emp Here 200   *Sales* 59,471,400
SIC 8211 Elementary and secondary schools
Bernard D'amours
Guilmont Pelletier

D-U-N-S 25-795-8160   (SL)
**COOPERATIVE DES PARAMEDICS DU
TEMISCOUATA**
148 Rue De L'Eglise, Temiscouata-Sur-Le-
Lac, QC, G0L 1X0
(418) 899-2047
Emp Here 30   *Sales* 13,415,220
SIC 5047 Medical and hospital equipment
Nicolas Leblanc

D-U-N-S 24-201-7945   (BR)
SUPERMARCHES GP INC, LES
METRO CABANO
633   Rue   Commerciale   N   Unite   100,
Temiscouata-Sur-Le-Lac, QC, G0L 1E0
(418) 854-2177
Emp Here 76
SIC 5411 Grocery stores
Claude Jean

Terrasse-Vaudreuil, QC J7V

D-U-N-S 20-541-4022   (SL)
POLYMOS INC
150 5e Boul, Terrasse-Vaudreuil, QC, J7V
5M3
(514) 453-1920
Emp Here 175   *Sales* 27,800,150
SIC 3086 Plastics foam products
Richard Bourbonnais
Helene Bourbonnais

Terrebonne, QC J6V

D-U-N-S 20-925-6952   (SL)
9026-7139 QUEBEC INC
RESTAURANT MCDONALD'S LACHENAIE
630 Montee Des Pionniers, Terrebonne, QC,
J6V 1N9
(450) 585-0116
Emp Here 100   *Sales* 15,136,900
SIC 7929 Entertainers and entertainment
groups
Lemay Laurent

▲ Public Company   ■ Public Company Family Member   **HQ** Headquarters   **BR** Branch   **SL** Single Location

D-U-N-S 25-188-5125   (BR)
HOME DEPOT OF CANADA INC
HOME DEPOT LACHENAIE
(Suby of THE HOME DEPOT INC)
660 Montee Des Pionniers, Terrebonne, QC,
J6V 1N9
(450) 657-4400
Emp Here 160
SIC 5211 Lumber and other building materials
Jules Rapelle

D-U-N-S 20-541-6910   (HQ)
KILDAIR SERVICE ULC
1000 Montee Des Pionniers Bureau 110, Ter-
rebonne, QC, J6V 1S8
(450) 756-8091
Emp Here 25   *Sales* 118,227,300
SIC 5172 Petroleum products, nec
Daniel Morin
Gary Rinaldi
Jacques Ferraro
Paul A Scoff
Joseph Smith

D-U-N-S 24-668-5085   (SL)
**LALLIER AUTOMOBILE (REPENTIGNY)
INC**
HONDA LALLIER REPENTIGNY
215 Rue Des Migrateurs, Terrebonne, QC,
J6V 0A8
(450) 581-7575
Emp Here 42   *Sales* 20,919,276
SIC 5511 New and used car dealers
Michel Dagenais
Denise L Dagenais

D-U-N-S 20-362-6593   (SL)
MELCO CAPITAL INC
1000 Montee Des Pionniers Bureau 212, Ter-
rebonne, QC, J6V 1S8
(514) 564-7600
Emp Here 750   *Sales* 56,962,697
SIC 7361 Employment agencies
Michael Cote Gagnon

D-U-N-S 24-935-6338   (SL)
**SUPERMARCHE CREVIER (LACHENAIE)
INC**
*(Suby of GESTION CREVIER, JEAN-
CLAUDE INC)*
325 Montee Des Pionniers, Terrebonne, QC,
J6V 1H4
(450) 582-2271
Emp Here 60   *Sales* 17,608,620
SIC 5411 Grocery stores
Sophie Crevier
Denise Crevier

Terrebonne, QC J6W

D-U-N-S 25-200-9865   (SL)
3175120 CANADA INC
LU-ARD ELECTRIQUE
1887 Ch Saint-Charles, Terrebonne, QC, J6W
5W5
(450) 964-5696
Emp Here 60   *Sales* 13,069,740
SIC 1731 Electrical work
Luc Guerard

D-U-N-S 25-458-1531   (SL)
ALIMENTATION LE SIEUR ENR
IGA
1415 Grande Allee, Terrebonne, QC, J6W
5M9
(450) 492-7272
Emp Here 50   *Sales* 13,707,600
SIC 5411 Grocery stores
Michel Cote

D-U-N-S 25-628-3615   (SL)
AUTO IMPORTATION TERREBONNE INC
SATURN TERREBONNE
1295 Car Masson, Terrebonne, QC, J6W 6J7

Emp Here 23   *Sales* 11,648,467
SIC 5511 New and used car dealers
Bernard Grenier

D-U-N-S 20-417-4106   (SL)
AUTOMOBILES DES SEIGNEURS INC
DES SEIGNEURS FORD
893 Rue L?On-Martel, Terrebonne, QC, J6W
2K4
(450) 471-6602
Emp Here 21   *Sales* 10,459,638
SIC 5511 New and used car dealers
Michel Di Lazzaro

D-U-N-S 20-262-1140   (SL)
AUTOMOBILES LEVEILLE INC
LEVEILLE TOYOTA
(Suby of GESTION PIERRE LEVEILLE INC)
1369 Montee Masson, Terrebonne, QC, J6W
6A6
(450) 471-4117
Emp Here 55   *Sales* 34,610,400
SIC 5511 New and used car dealers
Pierre Leveille

D-U-N-S 24-346-3366   (BR)
**CENTRE INTEGRE DE SANTE ET DE SER-
VICES SOCIAUX DE LANAUDIERE**
CLSC LAMATER DE TERREBONNE
*(Suby of CENTRE INTEGRE DE SANTE ET
DE SERVICES SOCIAUX DE LANAUDIERE)*
1317 Boul Des Seigneurs, Terrebonne, QC,
J6W 5B1
(450) 471-2881
Emp Here 300
SIC 8011 Offices and clinics of medical doc-
tors
Benoit Valiquette

D-U-N-S 25-210-6539   (HQ)
CINEMAS GUZZO INC
MEGA PLEX
1055 Ch Du Coteau, Terrebonne, QC, J6W
5Y8
(450) 961-2945
Emp Here 400   *Sales* 44,848,000
SIC 7832 Motion picture theaters, except
drive-in
Vincenzo Guzzo
Angelo Guzzo
Rosetta Rubino-Guzzo

D-U-N-S 24-548-0389   (SL)
COLLEGE SAINT-SACREMENT
901 Rue Saint-Louis, Terrebonne, QC, J6W
1K1
(450) 471-6615
Emp Here 100 ·   *Sales* 9,282,600
SIC 8211 Elementary and secondary schools
Luc St-Louis
Jean-Pierre Roy
Pierre Ouimet
Richard Lafreniere
Marie-Josee Veilleux
Jacques Lemay
Normand Brodeur
Gaetan Laforest
Louise Heroux

D-U-N-S 20-033-9518   , (BR)
**COMMISSION SCOLAIRE DES AFFLU-
ENTS**
ECOLE SECONDAIRE DES RIVES
*(Suby of COMMISSION SCOLAIRE DES AF-
FLUENTS)*
400 Montee Dumais, Terrebonne, QC, J6W
5W9
(450) 492-3613
Emp Here 100
SIC 8211 Elementary and secondary schools
Luc Moisan

D-U-N-S 24-150-9087   (SL)
CONSTRUCTION AUBIN, LAVAL LTEE
1470 Rue Nationale, Terrebonne, QC, J6W
6M1
(514) 640-0622
Emp Here 26   *Sales* 12,239,006

SIC 1542 Nonresidential construction, nec
Laval Aubin

D-U-N-S 24-563-9505   (HQ)
ENCRES INTERNATIONALE INX CORP
INX INTERNATIONAL INK
(Suby of SAKATA INX CORPORATION)
1247 Rue Nationale, Terrebonne, QC, J6W
6H8
(450) 477-8606
Emp Here 40   *Sales* 12,726,360
SIC 2899 Chemical preparations, nec
Richard Clendenning
Ronald Deegan
Bryce Kristo
David Rossi

D-U-N-S 20-472-4090   (HQ)
**ENTERPRISES MICHEL MARCHAND INC,
LES**
MCDONALD'S
1400 Boul Moody, Terrebonne, QC, J6W 3K9
(450) 471-9022
Sales 11,659,750
SIC 5812 Eating places
Michel Marchand

D-U-N-S 24-019-0991   (SL)
GCQ CANADA INC
1450 Grande Allee, Terrebonne, QC, J6W 6B7
(450) 471-0044
Emp Here 49   *Sales* 10,374,476
SIC 7322 Adjustment and collection services
Luc Chapados

D-U-N-S 24-057-0853   (SL)
GESTION ASSELIN INC
934 Rue Saint-Sacrement, Terrebonne, QC,
J6W 3G2
(450) 964-8448
Emp Here 80   *Sales* 3,641,520
SIC 5812 Eating places
Gerald Asselin

D-U-N-S 24-679-3108   (SL)
GESTION FAMILLE BUCCI INC
CANADIAN TIRE
1250 Boul Moody Bureau 312, Terrebonne,
QC, J6W 3K9
(450) 961-9011
Emp Here 90   *Sales* 14,942,340
SIC 5531 Auto and home supply stores
Michael Bucci

D-U-N-S 20-262-0852   (SL)
GRENIER CHEVROLET BUICK GMC INC
PONTIAC BUICK GMC
1325 Car Masson, Terrebonne, QC, J6W 6J7
(450) 471-3746
Emp Here 50   *Sales* 24,903,900
SIC 5511 New and used car dealers
Louis Grenier

D-U-N-S 20-576-2458   (SL)
GRENIER DODGE CHRYSLER INC
1245 Montee Masson, Terrebonne, QC, J6W
6A6
(450) 471-4111
Emp Here 50   *Sales* 24,903,900
SIC 5511 New and used car dealers
Louis Grenier

D-U-N-S 20-290-9636   (HQ)
GROUPE LALIBERTE SPORTS INC
ATMOSPHERE SPORTS - PLAIN AIR 590
1185 Boul Moody Bureau 90, Terrebonne, QC,
J6W 3Z5
(450) 824-1091
Emp Here 20   *Sales* 24,432,800
SIC 5941 Sporting goods and bicycle shops
Marco Laliberte
Richard Laliberte

D-U-N-S 24-818-3548   (SL)
GROUPE ROYAL INC
ROYALPLAST DOOR SYSTEMS CO
1085 Rue Des Cheminots, Terrebonne, QC,
J6W 0A1

(450) 492-5080
Emp Here 100   *Sales* 44,717,400
SIC 5039 Construction materials, nec
Andre Touchette
Bradley K. Reynolds
Guy Prentice
Simon Bates
Christian Huot
Jean-Sebastien L'Ecuyer
Timothy Mann Jr.

D-U-N-S 24-739-9520   (SL)
IMMEUBDES MOULINS INC., LES
*GOLF DU BOISE DE LACHENAIE-OUEST,
LE*
689 Ch Du Coteau, Terrebonne, QC, J6W 5H2

Emp Here 80   *Sales* 16,310,640
SIC 6553 Cemetery subdividers and develop-
ers
Eric Vandal

D-U-N-S 24-581-8377   (SL)
KWP INC
(Suby of KAYCAN LTEE)
1367 Rue Nationale, Terrebonne, QC, J6W
6H8
(450) 964-5786
Emp Here 60   *Sales* 26,830,440
SIC 5031 Lumber, plywood, and millwork
Lionel Dubrofsky
Tami Dubrofsky

D-U-N-S 24-581-7622   (SL)
LABORATOIRES LALCO INC
DISTRIBUTION IRIS
1542 Rue Nationale, Terrebonne, QC, J6W
6M1
(450) 492-6435
Emp Here 25   *Sales* 27,633,625
SIC 5122 Drugs, proprietaries, and sundries
Jean-Pierre Veilleux

D-U-N-S 20-222-2485   (SL)
MEUBLES JAYMAR CORP
SOFA INTERNATIONAL
75 Rue Jaymar, Terrebonne, QC, J6W 1M5
(450) 471-4172
Emp Here 180   *Sales* 27,777,960
SIC 2512 Upholstered household furniture
Daniel Walker

D-U-N-S 20-566-1788   (SL)
P.R. ENTRETIEN D'EDIFICES INC
1180 Rue Levis Bureau 2, Terrebonne, QC,
J6W 5S6
(450) 492-5999
Emp Here 150   *Sales* 4,875,850
SIC 7349 Building maintenance services, nec
Pierre Robitaille

D-U-N-S 20-634-9508   (SL)
PRODUITS D'ACIER ROGER INC, LES
1350 Grande Allee, Terrebonne, QC, J6W
4M4
(450) 471-2000
Emp Here 60   *Sales* 13,320,060
SIC 3369 General industrial machinery, nec
Martine Provencal

D-U-N-S 20-314-0181   (BR)
**PRODUITS POUR TOITURES FRANSYL
LTEE**
*PRODUITS POUR TOITURES FRANSYL
LTEE*
*(Suby of PRODUITS POUR TOITURES
FRANSYL LTEE)*
671 Rue Leveille, Terrebonne, QC, J6W 1Z9
(450) 492-2392
Emp Here 81
SIC 5033 Roofing, siding, and insulation
Sylvain Racine

D-U-N-S 25-827-6286   (BR)
PROVIGO DISTRIBUTION INC
MAXI
(Suby of LOBLAW COMPANIES LIMITED)
1345 Boul Moody, Terrebonne, QC, J6W 3L1

▲ Public Company   ■ Public Company Family Member   **HQ** Headquarters   **BR** Branch   **SL** Single Location

(450) 471-1009
Emp Here 120
SIC 5411 Grocery stores
Pierre Mazza

D-U-N-S 24-329-2369 (BR)
ROYAL GROUP, INC
*ROYAL WINDOW & DOOR PROFILES,
PLANT 10*
(*Suby of* WESTLAKE CHEMICAL CORPO-
RATION)
1085 Rue Des Cheminots Bureau 10, Terre-
bonne, QC, J6W 0A1
(450) 668-5549
Emp Here 100
SIC 5031 Lumber, plywood, and millwork
Andre Touchette

D-U-N-S 24-210-4946 (BR)
SOBEYS QUEBEC INC
IGA EXTRA THIBAULT
675 Boul Des Seigneurs, Terrebonne, QC,
J6W 1T5
(450) 492-5580
Emp Here 100
SIC 5411 Grocery stores
Francois Thibault

Terrebonne, QC J6X

D-U-N-S 24-390-0920 (HQ)
3931714 CANADA INC
2215 Ch Comtois, Terrebonne, QC, J6X 4H4
(450) 477-1002
Emp Here 1 *Sales* 14,214,200
SIC 6712 Bank holding companies
Jacques Forget

D-U-N-S 20-910-4942 (HQ)
7912854 CANADA INC
(*Suby of* 6368174 CANADA INC)
3530 Boul Des Entreprises, Terrebonne, QC,
J6X 4J8
(450) 968-0880
Sales 15,432,200
SIC 2591 Drapery hardware and window
blinds and shades
Gaetan Alepins
Benoit Alepins

D-U-N-S 24-189-4729 (SL)
9030-5582 QUEBEC INC
RESTAURANT MANGIAMO
1460 Ch Gascon Bureau 101, Terrebonne,
QC, J6X 2Z5
(450) 492-5225
Emp Here 90 *Sales* 4,096,710
SIC 5812 Eating places
Michele Charland
Daniel Gagnon
Francois Forget

D-U-N-S 20-925-1222 (SL)
9167-0661 QUEBEC INC
SALVATORE L. BRIQUETEUR 65
3205 Boul Des Entreprises, Terrebonne, QC,
J6X 4J9
(450) 477-2111
Emp Here 50 *Sales* 14,424,950
SIC 6512 Nonresidential building operators
Linda Salvatore
Francesco Salvatore

D-U-N-S 20-265-8092 (SL)
ACIERS TECHFORM MONTAL INC
3139 Boul Des Entreprises, Terrebonne, QC,
J6X 4J9
(450) 477-5705
Emp Here 50 *Sales* 11,671,750
SIC 3312 Blast furnaces and steel mills
Roger Beauregard
Yves Goulet
Roger Beauregard

D-U-N-S 20-363-2062 (SL)

ALTEX INC
(*Suby of* 6368174 CANADA INC)
3530 Boul Des Entreprises, Terrebonne, QC,
J6X 4J8
(450) 968-0880
Emp Here 100 *Sales* 50,885,600
SIC 5023 Homefurnishings
Gaetan Alepins

D-U-N-S 24-477-9658 (HQ)
ASPLUNDH CANADA ULC
(*Suby of* ASPLUNDH TREE EXPERT, LLC)
3366 Rue Jacob-Jordan, Terrebonne, QC, J6X
4J6
(450) 968-1888
Emp Here 4 *Sales* 77,832,500
SIC 0783 Ornamental shrub and tree services
Moir John
Remo Maddalozzo
Francois Desjardins
Brian R. Bauer
Scott M. Asplundh
Karyn L. Bradley
George E. Graham, Jr.
Steven Christiansen

D-U-N-S 20-417-2571 (SL)
AUTOMOBILES DONALD BRASSARD INC
HONDA DE TERREBONNE
2850 Ch Gascon, Terrebonne, QC, J6X 4H6
(450) 477-0555
Emp Here 50 *Sales* 24,903,900
SIC 5511 New and used car dealers
Donald Brassard

D-U-N-S 24-803-2174 (SL)
CENTRE DE L'ESCALIER INC
3535 Boul Des Entreprises, Terrebonne, QC,
J6X 4J9
(514) 592-0241
Emp Here 75 *Sales* 14,427,750
SIC 2431 Millwork
Richard De Lafontaine
Francois Cote
Jean-Pierre Clement
Stephane Leonard

D-U-N-S 24-736-3174 (SL)
**CENTRE DE RENOVATION TERREBONNE
INC**
RONA
1505 Ch Gascon, Terrebonne, QC, J6X 2Z6
(450) 471-6631
Emp Here 100 *Sales* 26,765,200
SIC 5251 Hardware stores
Edouard Calderon

D-U-N-S 24-858-6836 (SL)
CLUB DE GOLF TERREBONNE INC
3555 Ch Martin, Terrebonne, QC, J6X 0B2
(450) 477-1817
Emp Here 65 *Sales* 17,000,945
SIC 6712 Bank holding companies
Monique Desrosiers
Marc Giraldeau
Louise Giraldeau

D-U-N-S 20-033-9526 (BR)
**COMMISSION SCOLAIRE DES AFFLU-
ENTS**
ECOLE PRIMAIRE DE LA SABLIERE
(*Suby of* COMMISSION SCOLAIRE DES AF-
FLUENTS)
1659 Boul Des Seigneurs, Terrebonne, QC,
J6X 3E3
(450) 492-3622
Emp Here 100
SIC 8211 Elementary and secondary schools
Jean Francois Trottier

D-U-N-S 24-082-2312 (HQ)
DE LA FONTAINE & ASSOCIES INC
INTERMAT (PORTES & BOISERIES)
3700 Rue Pascal-Gagnon, Terrebonne, QC,
J6X 4J2
(450) 471-2982
Sales 29,066,310
SIC 5031 Lumber, plywood, and millwork

Richard De La Fontaine
Jacques Begin
Jacques Vachon
Alain Gauthier

D-U-N-S 20-250-4247 (SL)
FABELTA ALUMINIUM INC
FABELTA 3
3840 Rue Georges-Corbeil, Terrebonne, QC,
J6X 4J4
(450) 477-7611
Emp Here 26 *Sales* 11,626,524
SIC 5031 Lumber, plywood, and millwork
Michel Desroches
Sylvie O Desroches

D-U-N-S 24-214-7903 (BR)
**FONDATION DU CEGEP REGIONAL DE
LANAUDIERE**
*CEGEP REGIONAL DE LANAUDIERE A
TERREBONNE*
(*Suby of* FONDATION DU CEGEP RE-
GIONAL DE LANAUDIERE)
2505 Boul Des Entreprises, Terrebonne, QC,
J6X 5S5
(450) 470-0933
Emp Here 100
SIC 8221 Colleges and universities

D-U-N-S 20-262-0738 (SL)
FORGET, JACQUES LTEE
VIANDES FORGET, LES
(*Suby of* 3931714 CANADA INC)
2215 Ch Comtois, Terrebonne, QC, J6X 4H4
(450) 477-1002
Emp Here 80 *Sales* 27,655,200
SIC 2011 Meat packing plants
Andre Forget
Pierre Forget
Michel Forget
Jean-Francois Forget

D-U-N-S 20-381-0460 (SL)
GROUPE EDIFIO INC
CITE VIVA
3205 Boul Des Entreprises, Terrebonne, QC,
J6X 4J9
(514) 284-7070
Emp Here 200 *Sales* 13,684,400
SIC 8322 Individual and family services
Normand Godcharles

D-U-N-S 24-360-5016 (HQ)
GROUPE MAILHOT INC
3330 Boul Des Entreprises, Terrebonne, QC,
J6X 4J8
(450) 477-6222
Sales 82,239,525
SIC 6712 Bank holding companies
Robert J Bouchard
Pierre Dozois
Johanne Aube

D-U-N-S 25-323-6475 (SL)
IMPACT DETAIL INC
2625 Boul Des Entreprises, Terrebonne, QC,
J6X 4J8
(514) 767-1555
Emp Here 350 *Sales* 498,098,300
SIC 6221 Commodity contracts brokers, deal-
ers
Richard Boulay
Daniel Lonergan
Celine Gilliard

D-U-N-S 20-387-0741 (HQ)
IMPERIA HOTEL ET SUITES INC
3215 Boul De La Piniere Bureau 201, Terre-
bonne, QC, J6X 4P7
(450) 492-3336
Emp Here 100 *Sales* 38,269,000
SIC 6712 Bank holding companies
Jean-Francois Caron
Eric Moretti

D-U-N-S 24-869-8201 (SL)
INDUSTRIES GODDARD LTEE
2460 Boul Des Entreprises, Terrebonne, QC,

J6X 4J8
(514) 353-9141
Emp Here 80 *Sales* 21,868,000
SIC 6712 Bank holding companies
Gwendolyn Goddard

D-U-N-S 20-178-2377 (BR)
LANAU BUS S.E.C.
2450 Boul Des Entreprises, Terrebonne, QC,
J6X 4J8
(450) 968-2450
Emp Here 125
SIC 4111 Local and suburban transit
Stephanie Pare

D-U-N-S 24-094-9214 (SL)
LOCATION D'OUTILS SIMPLEX SEC
3505 Boul Des Entreprises, Terrebonne, QC,
J6X 4J9
(450) 477-5960
Emp Here 49 *Sales* 12,266,001
SIC 1796 Installing building equipment
Linda Gravel

D-U-N-S 24-812-5718 (SL)
MARCHE ALIMENTATION THIBAULT INC
IGA
2120 Ch Gascon, Terrebonne, QC, J6X 3A1
(450) 964-2050
Emp Here 103 *Sales* 30,228,131
SIC 5411 Grocery stores
Jacques Thibault
Francois Thibault
Pierre Treriault

D-U-N-S 20-859-5512 (SL)
METAL U.P. INC
3745 Rue Pascal-Gagnon, Terrebonne, QC,
J6X 4J3
(450) 477-1122
Emp Here 50 *Sales* 10,141,500
SIC 3499 Fabricated Metal products, nec
Audrey Lavoie
Guy Lavoie
Michelle Lavoie

D-U-N-S 25-630-4858 (SL)
MOTOS ILLIMITEES INC
3250 Boul Des Entreprises, Terrebonne, QC,
J6X 4J8
(450) 477-4000
Emp Here 40 *Sales* 19,923,120
SIC 5599 Automotive dealers, nec
Jacques Junior Guenette
Lynn Landry

D-U-N-S 20-127-0597 (SL)
PHYSIO-ERGO PLUS INC
3395 Boul De La Piniere Bureau 200, Terre-
bonne, QC, J6X 4N1
(450) 492-9999
Emp Here 30 *Sales* 10,837,110
SIC 8049 Offices of health practitioner
Marc Aubin

D-U-N-S 25-542-3931 (SL)
**PIECES DE TRANSMISSION UNITRANS
LTEE, LES**
3795 Rue Georges-Corbeil, Terrebonne, QC,
J6X 4J5
(450) 968-2000
Emp Here 30 *Sales* 10,926,450
SIC 5013 Motor vehicle supplies and new
parts
Denys Bernard
Luc Gagne
Danielle Gosselin
Constandina Livieratos

D-U-N-S 20-857-6728 (SL)
**PRODUITS DE FIL ET DE METAL COGAN
LTEE**
COGAN
2460 Boul Des Entreprises, Terrebonne, QC,
J6X 4J8
(514) 353-9141
Emp Here 80 *Sales* 15,366,800
SIC 3446 Architectural Metalwork

Derek Goddard

D-U-N-S 24-354-5472   (HQ)
PRODUITS POUR TOITURES FRANSYL LTEE
FRANSYL
1845 Rue Jean-Monnet, Terrebonne, QC, J6X 4L7
(450) 477-4423
Sales 56,962,800
SIC 5033 Roofing, siding, and insulation
Jean-Claude Morrissette
Luc Jutras
Sylvain Racine
Chantal Morrissette
Shirley Mccaffrey

D-U-N-S 20-107-8305   (SL)
RESTAURANTS SERQUA INC, LES
ST-HUBERT
1415 Boul Moody, Terrebonne, QC, J6X 4C8
(450) 471-1161
Emp Here 80   *Sales* 3,641,520
SIC 5812 Eating places
Jacques Brault

D-U-N-S 24-994-0289   (SL)
RINOX INC
3155 Boul Des Entreprises, Terrebonne, QC, J6X 4J9
(450) 477-7888
Emp Here 60   *Sales* 14,006,100
SIC 3272 Concrete products, nec
Horacio Correia
Rosa Ciccarello

D-U-N-S 20-885-5585   (SL)
ROULOTTES STE-ANNE INC
3306 Boul Des Entreprises, Terrebonne, QC, J6X 4J8
(450) 477-1803
Emp Here 26   *Sales* 16,361,280
SIC 5561 Recreational vehicle dealers
Claude Lapierre
Fernand Lapierre
Alain Lapierre
Serge Lapierre

D-U-N-S 24-896-0759   (SL)
TERREBONNE FORD INC
2730 Ch Gascon, Terrebonne, QC, J6X 4H6
(450) 968-9000
Emp Here 30   *Sales* 14,942,340
SIC 5511 New and used car dealers
Luc Soucy
Gilles Soucy

D-U-N-S 24-861-6468   (SL)
U.P. INC
3745 Rue Pascal-Gagnon, Terrebonne, QC, J6X 4J3
(450) 477-1122
Emp Here 75   *Sales* 33,538,050
SIC 5039 Construction materials, nec
Audrey Lavoie
Guy Lavoie
Michele Lavoie
Guy Lavoie
Michelle Lavoie

D-U-N-S 24-970-9304   (SL)
VERRE SELECT INC
3816 Rue Georges-Corbeil, Terrebonne, QC, J6X 4J4
(450) 968-0112
Emp Here 55   *Sales* 12,838,925
SIC 3211 Flat glass
Patrice Lamy
Luc Goudreault

Terrebonne, QC J6Y

D-U-N-S 20-353-4102   (SL)
10167819 CANADA INC
NATIONAL BRANDS

460 Rue Fernand-Poitras, Terrebonne, QC, J6Y 1Y4
(514) 493-9423
Emp Here 45   *Sales* 37,600,965
SIC 5149 Groceries and related products, nec
Serge Martel
Raymond Martel
Maher Juma
Kenneth Skellett
Silvano Racioppo

D-U-N-S 24-525-1223   (SL)
9138-7472 QUEBEC INC
CRE TRANSPORT
1060 Rue Armand-Bombardier, Terrebonne, QC, J6Y 1R9
(450) 477-9996
Emp Here 50   *Sales* 32,906,034
SIC 4213 Trucking, except local
Mario Larocque
Jean Guertin
Robert Poirier

D-U-N-S 24-179-0526   (SL)
9220-9147 QUEBEC INC
LITHO MILE-ILES
(*Suby of* LITHO MILLE-ILES INC)
355 Rue George-Vi, Terrebonne, QC, J6Y 1N9
(450) 621-4856
Emp Here 90
SIC 2759 Commercial printing, nec
Gerry Bonneau
Josee Debien

D-U-N-S 24-204-0272   (SL)
ALIMENTATION ASIE-MONTREAL INC
3010a Rue Anderson, Terrebonne, QC, J6Y 1W1
(450) 621-3288
Emp Here 20   *Sales* 10,702,480
SIC 5147 Meats and meat products
Eric Provencher
Say Heang Chang

D-U-N-S 24-933-4582   (SL)
ALIMENTS MARTEL INC
CUISINE KARO
460 Rue Fernand-Poitras, Terrebonne, QC, J6Y 1Y4
(514) 493-9423
Emp Here 100   *Sales* 83,557,700
SIC 5149 Groceries and related products, nec
Raymond Martel

D-U-N-S 20-430-6666   (HQ)
ALIMENTS MARTEL INC
CUISINE KARO
(*Suby of* GRUPO BIMBO, S.A.B. DE C.V.)
460 Rue Fernand-Poitras, Terrebonne, QC, J6Y 1Y4
(514) 493-9423
Emp Here 200   *Sales* 243,692,500
SIC 2099 Food preparations, nec
Raymond Martel

D-U-N-S 20-258-0007   (HQ)
ASPHALTE DESJARDINS INC
BETONNIERES MODERNES, LES
3030 Rue Anderson, Terrebonne, QC, J6Y 1W1
(450) 430-7160
Sales 106,637,375
SIC 1611 Highway and street construction
Jacques Desjardins
Daniele Desjardins
Michel Belair
Claude Desjardins

D-U-N-S 24-419-2501   (HQ)
ATIS PORTES ET FENETRES CORP.
FENESTRATION PRO-TECH
(*Suby of* GROUPE ATIS INC)
2175 Boul Des Entreprises, Terrebonne, QC, J6Y 1W9
(450) 492-0404
Emp Here 25   *Sales* 38,474,000
SIC 2431 Millwork
Robert Doyon

Andre Parent
Guy Bouille
Mathieu Lalonde

D-U-N-S 24-954-2457   (SL)
AUTOBUS YVES SEGUIN & FILS INC
1730 Rue Effingham, Terrebonne, QC, J6Y 1R7
(450) 433-6958
Emp Here 100   *Sales* 5,487,200
SIC 4151 School buses
Yves Seguin
Jeff Seguin

D-U-N-S 24-799-2613   (SL)
CENTRE DE GOLF, LE VERSANT INC
2075 Cote De Terrebonne, Terrebonne, QC, J6Y 1H6
(450) 964-2251
Emp Here 200   *Sales* 15,709,000
SIC 7992 Public golf courses
Pascal Di Menna
Nadia Di Menna

D-U-N-S 25-706-0293   (SL)
COMPTEC S. G. INC
EQUIPE D'INVENTAIRE F.M.
1115 Rue Armand-Bombardier, Terrebonne, QC, J6Y 1S9
(450) 965-8166
Emp Here 50   *Sales* 22,174,500
SIC 7389 Business services, nec
Roberto D'angeli

D-U-N-S 20-820-2114   (SL)
CONSTRUCTIONS CJRB INC, LES
3000 Rue Anderson, Terrebonne, QC, J6Y 1W1
(450) 965-1110
Emp Here 49   *Sales* 11,803,316
SIC 1623 Water, sewer, and utility lines
Christian Blanchet
Viviane Babin
Danielle Blanchet

D-U-N-S 20-793-1890   (SL)
DEMERS, ROBERT & GILLES INC
SABLIERES DEMERS
3055 Rue Des Batisseurs, Terrebonne, QC, J6Y 0A2
(450) 477-2727
Emp Here 25   *Sales* 11,179,350
SIC 5032 Brick, stone, and related material
Robert Demers
Eric Demers
Julie Demers
Marie-Claude Demers

D-U-N-S 20-254-9747   (SL)
GESTION STRUCTURES XL INC
3005 Rue Des Batisseurs, Terrebonne, QC, J6Y 0A2
(450) 968-0800
Emp Here 65   *Sales* 15,173,275
SIC 3312 Blast furnaces and steel mills
Benoit Drouin
David Drouin
Jacques Labbe

D-U-N-S 24-489-8144   (HQ)
GROUPE ADF INC
ACIER ADF / ADF STEEL
300 Rue Henry-Bessemer, Terrebonne, QC, J6Y 1T3
(450) 965-1911
Sales 100,883,727
SIC 8711 Engineering services
Jean Paschini
Pierre Paschini
Marise Paschini
Jean-Francois Boursier
Marc L. Belcourt
Antonio P. Meti
Frank Di Tomaso
Michele Desjardins

D-U-N-S 24-351-2543   (HQ)
IMERYS GRAPHITE & CARBON CANADA

INC
TIMCAL GRAPHITE & CARBONE
(*Suby of* GROUPE BRUXELLES LAMBERT)
990 Rue Fernand-Poitras, Terrebonne, QC, J6Y 1V1
(450) 622-9191
Sales 11,671,750
SIC 1499 Miscellaneous nonMetallic minerals, except fuels
Davide Cattaneo
Ryan J. Van Meter
Matteo Zenone
Mekalaradha (Radha) Murphy

D-U-N-S 24-749-4342   (SL)
INTERPLAST PACKAGING INC
EMBALLAGE INTERPLAST
955 Boul Industriel, Terrebonne, QC, J6Y 1V7
(450) 971-0500
Emp Here 60   *Sales* 11,686,080
SIC 2679 Converted paper products, nec
Rebecca Kalis
Peters Nicholas
David J. Rowntree
Trevor Johnstone

D-U-N-S 25-536-0737   (SL)
LAINCO INC
ACIER STRUCTURAL LAINCO
1010 Rue Fernand-Poitras, Terrebonne, QC, J6Y 1V1
(450) 965-6010
Emp Here 50   *Sales* 10,141,500
SIC 3441 Fabricated structural Metal
Martin Lachapelle
Eric Lachapelle

D-U-N-S 20-362-8193   (HQ)
LOOP INDUSTRIES, INC
INDUSTRIES LOOP, LES
(*Suby of* PACIFIC EQUITY PARTNERS PTY LIMITED)
480 Rue Fernand-Poitras, Terrebonne, QC, J6Y 1Y4
(450) 951-8555
Sales 10,842,940
SIC 4953 Refuse systems
Daniel Solomita
Nelson Gentiletti,
Nelson Switzer
Laurence Sellyn,
Leslie A. Murphy,
Shawn B. Higgins,
Jay Stubina
Sidney Horn

D-U-N-S 20-015-8645   (HQ)
PLASTICASE INC
1059 Boul Des Entreprises, Terrebonne, QC, J6Y 1V2
(450) 628-1006
Sales 10,094,850
SIC 3089 Plastics products, nec
Jean-Pierre Grenier
Pierre Fitzgibbon
Pierre Somers

D-U-N-S 24-908-8188   (SL)
PORTES DECKO INC
2375 Rue Edouard-Michelin, Terrebonne, QC, J6Y 4P2
(450) 477-0199
Emp Here 50   *Sales* 11,500,950
SIC 3231 Products of purchased glass
Michel Trepanier

D-U-N-S 24-903-1493   (HQ)
QUATREX ENVIRONNEMENT INC
2085 Boul Des Entreprises, Terrebonne, QC, J6Y 1W9
(450) 963-4747
Emp Here 22   *Sales* 15,616,260
SIC 5099 Durable goods, nec
Patrick Paradis

D-U-N-S 20-221-1611   (SL)
RENE HENRICHON INC
3160 Cote De Terrebonne, Terrebonne, QC,

J6Y 1G1

Emp Here 25   *Sales* 11,904,574
SIC 1542 Nonresidential construction, nec
  Danielle Chouinard
  Georges Dubois

D-U-N-S 24-474-2615   (SL)
SYSTEMES D'EMBALLAGE SECURITAIRE NELMAR INC
3100 Rue Des Batisseurs, Terrebonne, QC, J6Y 0A2
(450) 477-0001
Emp Here 150   *Sales* 29,215,200
SIC 2673 Bags: plastic, laminated, and coated
  Neil Freder
  Mary Golfman
  David Pearl

D-U-N-S 24-205-7128   (SL)
TERGEL INC
WEISHARDT INTERNATIONAL NA
(*Suby of* SA WEISHARDT HOLDING)
895 Rue Italia, Terrebonne, QC, J6Y 2C8
(450) 621-2345
Emp Here 50   *Sales* 13,833,000
SIC 2899 Chemical preparations, nec
  Pol Joho
  Pascale Jolimaitre
  Eric Thiffault

D-U-N-S 25-150-5558   (SL)
VANICO-MARONYX INC
1151 Boul De La Piniere, Terrebonne, QC, J6Y 0P3
(450) 471-4447
Emp Here 85   *Sales* 16,351,450
SIC 2434 Wood kitchen cabinets
  Robert Gauvreau
  Jacques Parise
  Alain Belzile
  Remi Theberge
  Charles-Antoine Gauvreau

Terrebonne, QC J7M

D-U-N-S 20-194-6980   (BR)
2993821 CANADA INC
1591 Ch Sainte-Claire, Terrebonne, QC, J7M 1M2
(450) 478-2055
Emp Here 180   *Sales* 635,325
SIC 2011 Meat packing plants
  Daniel Carriere

D-U-N-S 24-678-3083   (SL)
CANADIAN TIRE
MAGASIN
4785 Boul Laurier, Terrebonne, QC, J7M 1C3
(450) 477-4013
Emp Here 49   *Sales* 24,405,822
SIC 5531 Auto and home supply stores
  Sylvain Charron

D-U-N-S 20-947-2765   (SL)
CLUB DE SOCCER LA PLAINE INC.
6900 Rue Guerin, Terrebonne, QC, J7M 1L9
(450) 477-0372
Emp Here 26   *Sales* 11,016,980
SIC 7941 Sports clubs, managers, and promoters
  Robert Stephane

D-U-N-S 24-934-5000   (SL)
ENTREPRISES JULIE LESSARD INC, LES
PHARMACIE JEAN COUTU
5333 Boul Laurier Bureau 180, Terrebonne, QC, J7M 1W1
(450) 477-4401
Emp Here 75   *Sales* 18,324,600
SIC 5912 Drug stores and proprietary stores
  Julie Lessard

D-U-N-S 25-369-2800   (BR)

MATERIAUX LAURENTIENS INC
(*Suby of* 3151263 CANADA INC)
7700 Boul Laurier, Terrebonne, QC, J7M 2K8
(450) 478-7557
Emp Here 180
SIC 5211 Lumber and other building materials
  Lain Lajoie

Terrebonne, QC J7V

D-U-N-S 25-256-5338   (SL)
2850401 CANADA INC
BOULANGERIE PREMIERE MOISSON
(*Suby of* 2871149 CANADA INC)
189 Boul Harwood, Terrebonne, QC, J7V 1Y3
(450) 964-9333
Emp Here 75   *Sales* 20,501,250
SIC 6712 Bank holding companies
  Stephane Fiset
  Liliane Colpron

Thetford Mines, QC G6G

D-U-N-S 24-016-7978   (BR)
9130-1093 QUEBEC INC
CARREFOUR FRONTENAC
(*Suby of* FONDS DE PLACEMENT IMMOBILIER COMINAR)
805 Boul Frontenac E, Thetford Mines, QC, G6G 6L5
(418) 338-6388
Emp Here 300
SIC 6512 Nonresidential building operators
  Yvan Fecteau

D-U-N-S 24-402-9679   (SL)
A. BISSON ET FILS LTEE
BISSON AUTO PARTS
410 Boul Frontenac O, Thetford Mines, QC, G6G 6N7
(418) 335-2928
Emp Here 30   *Sales* 10,926,450
SIC 5015 Motor vehicle parts, used
  Marcel Bisson

D-U-N-S 20-262-4946   (HQ)
A. SETLAKWE LIMITEE
LINGERIE SILHOUETTE
188 Rue Notre-Dame O, Thetford Mines, QC, G6G 1J6
(418) 335-9121
Emp Here 70   *Sales* 35,935,025
SIC 5311 Department stores
  Raymond Setlakwe
  Richard Setlakwe
  Paul J. Setlakwe

D-U-N-S 24-914-2311   (SL)
AUTOMOBILES HYUNDAI RUBY AUTO
2272 Rue Notre-Dame E, Thetford Mines, QC, G6G 2W2
(418) 338-4665
Emp Here 24   *Sales* 11,953,872
SIC 5521 Used car dealers
  Ruby Routhier

D-U-N-S 24-568-6811   (HQ)
BISSON CHEVROLET INC
2257 Rue Notre-Dame E, Thetford Mines, QC, G6G 2W4
(418) 335-7571
Emp Here 25   *Sales* 17,619,840
SIC 5511 New and used car dealers
  Marcel Bisson
  Yoland Bisson
  Rivard Bisson
  Adreanne Bisson
  Nadia Bisson

D-U-N-S 24-707-0139   (SL)
C.I.F. METAL LTEE
1900 Rue Setlakwe, Thetford Mines, QC, G6G

8B2
(418) 338-6250
Emp Here 125   *Sales* 22,673,500
SIC 3365 Aluminum foundries
  Jean Marcoux
  Richard Garneau
  Yvan Bergeron
  John Stimpson
  Michel Baril
  Claude Richard

D-U-N-S 24-420-4082   (HQ)
CAISSE DESJARDINS DE LA REGION DE THETFORD
CENTRE ADMINISTRATION KAMOURASKA-CHAUDIERE-APPALACHES
300 Boul Frontenac E, Thetford Mines, QC, G6G 7M8
(418) 338-3591
Emp Here 70   *Sales* 21,491,540
SIC 6062 State credit unions
  Yves Gilbert
  Marie-Klaude Paquet
  Marcel Roy
  Francois Gagnon
  Denis Faucher
  Bernard Brun
  Gilles Remillard
  Christian Labrecque

D-U-N-S 20-953-0294   (SL)
CEGEP DE THETFORD
671 Boul Frontenac O, Thetford Mines, QC, G6G 1N1
(418) 338-8591
Emp Here 200   *Sales* 29,878,200
SIC 8221 Colleges and universities
  David Helie
  Vicky Turcotte
  Robert Rousseau
  Rock Laflamme

D-U-N-S 20-800-1771   (SL)
CENTRE COMMERCIAL PROMENADES ST-NOEL
100 1re Rue Bureau 12, Thetford Mines, QC, G6G 4Y2
(418) 338-6066
Emp Here 40   *Sales* 11,509,253
SIC 6512 Nonresidential building operators
  Remi Hebert

D-U-N-S 24-313-1005   (HQ)
CENTRE DE SANTE ET DE SERVICE SOCIAUX DE LA REGION DE THETFORD
PROGRAMME DE L'HEBERGEMENT
1717 Rue Notre-Dame E, Thetford Mines, QC, G6G 2V4
(418) 338-7777
Sales 82,827,200
SIC 8399 Social services, nec
  Martin Lord

D-U-N-S 24-003-7213   (SL)
CHEVALIERS DE COLOMB THETFORD-MINES, LES
95 9e Rue N, Thetford Mines, QC, G6G 5J1
(418) 335-6444
Emp Here 49   *Sales* 19,800,803
SIC 8699 Membership organizations, nec
  Gilles Guernon

D-U-N-S 25-395-0497   (HQ)
COMMISSION SCOLAIRE DES APPALACHES
650 Rue Lapierre, Thetford Mines, QC, G6G 7P1
(418) 338-7800
Sales 69,383,300
SIC 8211 Elementary and secondary schools
  Alain Chabot
  Jean Roberge

D-U-N-S 25-232-6780   (BR)
COMMISSION SCOLAIRE DES APPALACHES
ECOLE SECONDAIRE JOSEPH FECTEAU
(*Suby of* COMMISSION SCOLAIRE DES AP-

PALACHES)
561 Rue Saint-Patrick, Thetford Mines, QC, G6G 5W1
(418) 338-7831
Emp Here 100
SIC 8211 Elementary and secondary schools
  Joseph Fecteau

D-U-N-S 20-430-4422   (SL)
CONVOYEUR CONTINENTAL & USINAGE LTEE
470 Rue Saint-Alphonse S, Thetford Mines, QC, G6G 3V8
(418) 338-4682
Emp Here 150   *Sales* 33,300,150
SIC 3599 Industrial machinery, nec
  W.David Lynn
  Brian R. Lynn
  Philip A. Lynn
  Trevor H. Lynn

D-U-N-S 24-863-5591   (SL)
COOP DE LA POLYVALENTE DE THETFORD-MINES
561 Rue Saint-Patrick, Thetford Mines, QC, G6G 5W1
(418) 338-7832
Emp Here 121   *Sales* 29,563,688
SIC 5943 Stationery stores
  Sonia Poulin

D-U-N-S 24-707-2846   (SL)
DSD INTERNATIONAL INC
2515 Ch De L'Aeroport, Thetford Mines, QC, G6G 5R7
(418) 338-3507
Emp Here 30   *Sales* 22,275,600
SIC 5191 Farm supplies
  Leandre Vachon
  Sonia Vachon

D-U-N-S 24-821-9909   (SL)
E. I. DUPONT CANADA - THETFORD INC
(*Suby of* DUPONT DE NEMOURS, INC.)
1045 Rue Monfette E, Thetford Mines, QC, G6G 7K7
(418) 338-8567
Emp Here 160   *Sales* 40,910,400
SIC 3299 NonMetallic mineral products,
  Wendy Andrushko
  Paul J. Klasios
  Donald Paddock
  Kelly Desautels
  Alain Dubuc

D-U-N-S 24-393-0547   (SL)
GESTION C. & L. LAROCHELLE INC
MARCHAND CANADIAN TIRE DE MONTREAL (MAISONNEUVE)
70 Boul Frontenac E Bureau 156, Thetford Mines, QC, G6G 1N4
(418) 338-3535
Emp Here 100   *Sales* 62,928,000
SIC 5531 Auto and home supply stores
  Christian Larochelle
  Lucie Bardou

D-U-N-S 24-942-7394   (SL)
GESTION METALLURGIE CASTECH INC
MATALLURGIE FRONTENAC
500 Boul Frontenac E, Thetford Mines, QC, G6G 7M8
(418) 338-3171
Emp Here 100   *Sales* 23,343,500
SIC 3325 Steel foundries, nec
  Jennifer Poire
  Guy Sylvain
  Pascal Royer
  Samuel Baril

D-U-N-S 24-415-2489   (SL)
GRANIREX
1045 Rue Monfette E, Thetford Mines, QC, G6G 7K7

Emp Here 50   *Sales* 22,358,700
SIC 5032 Brick, stone, and related material
  Marc Giroux

D-U-N-S 24-204-9240   (HQ)
GROUPE CANATAL INC
2885 Boul Frontenac E, Thetford Mines, QC,
G6G 6P6
(418) 338-6044
Sales 102,342,520
SIC 6712 Bank holding companies
Ralph Poulin
Lise-Andree Lessard
Serge Laflamme
Yvon Fortier
Jean Richard
Michel Goulet

D-U-N-S 24-387-9751   (SL)
GROUPE KDA INC
1351 Rue Notre-Dame E Bureau 300, Thetford Mines, QC, G6G 0G5
(514) 622-7370
Emp Here 6   *Sales* 22,306,264
SIC 6799 Investors, nec
Marc Lemieux
Isabelle Begin
Michael W. Kinley
Marc Beaudoin
Patrick Fernet
Stuart Elman
Sheldon Elman

D-U-N-S 24-485-3755   (SL)
IMPORTATIONS CARA INC, LES
805 Boul Frontenac E, Thetford Mines, QC,
G6G 6L5
(418) 335-3593
Emp Here 25   *Sales* 13,232,422
SIC 5099 Durable goods, nec
Camil Beliveau

D-U-N-S 24-842-8047   (HQ)
INDUSTRIES CANATAL INC
(*Suby of* GROUPE CANATAL INC)
2885 Boul Frontenac E, Thetford Mines, QC,
G6G 6P6
(418) 338-6044
Sales 60,807,750
SIC 3441 Fabricated structural Metal
Ralph Poulin

D-U-N-S 24-498-3193   (SL)
INVESTISSEMENTS BABE INC
BAR CHEZ BABE
374 Rue Notre-Dame E, Thetford Mines, QC,
G6G 2S4

Emp Here 30   *Sales* 12,580,650
SIC 6712 Bank holding companies
Gerard Binet
Jean-Yves Grenier
Michel Cote

D-U-N-S 20-505-0599   (HQ)
KDA GROUP INC
1197 Rue Notre-Dame E, Thetford Mines, QC,
G6G 2V2
(418) 334-8767
Sales 10,462,120
SIC 6712 Bank holding companies
Patrick Fernet

D-U-N-S 20-707-5008   (SL)
MARCHE ST-PIERRE & FILS INC
IGA MARCHE ST PIERRE
780 Boul Frontenac E, Thetford Mines, QC,
G6G 6H1
(418) 335-6222
Emp Here 194   *Sales* 56,934,538
SIC 5411 Grocery stores
Clement St-Pierre

D-U-N-S 25-527-3161   (HQ)
MEGABURO INC
(*Suby of* SOCIETE FINANCIERE GRENCO
INC)
236 Rue Notre-Dame O, Thetford Mines, QC,
G6G 1J6
(418) 338-8808
Sales 60,008,175
SIC 5712 Furniture stores

Paul-Emile Grenier
Jean-Yves Grenier
Renaud Grenier
Gaston Boily
Diane Grenier
Stephane Grenier

D-U-N-S 20-516-2001   (SL)
MEGANTIC METAL LTEE
RUSSELL STEEL
1400 Boul Frontenac E, Thetford Mines, QC,
G6G 6Z2
(418) 338-3188
Emp Here 15   *Sales* 15,005,085
SIC 5051 Metals service centers and offices
Bud Seegel

D-U-N-S 24-355-2077   (SL)
METALLURGIE CASTECH INC
(*Suby of* GROUPE CASTECH INC)
500 Boul Frontenac E, Thetford Mines, QC,
G6G 7M8
(418) 338-3171
Emp Here 80   *Sales* 14,511,040
SIC 3325 Steel foundries, nec
Jennifer Poire
Guy Sylvain
Pascal Royer
Michel Pilon
Samuel Baril

D-U-N-S 25-778-9578   (SL)
OPTIMOULE INC
275 Rue Monfette E, Thetford Mines, QC,
G6G 7H4
(418) 338-6106
Emp Here 26   *Sales* 12,350,676
SIC 5085 Industrial supplies
Serge Fraser

D-U-N-S 24-358-3171   (BR)
PIONEER HI-BRED LIMITED
ZODIAC QUARTZ SURFACING
(*Suby of* DUPONT DE NEMOURS, INC.)
1045 Rue Monfette E, Thetford Mines, QC,
G6G 7K7

Emp Here 97
SIC 3299 NonMetallic mineral products,
Jean-Eric Sylvain

D-U-N-S 24-465-6070   (HQ)
PLACEMENTS CLAUDE GOSSELIN INC
680 Rue Des Erables, Thetford Mines, QC,
G6G 1H7
(418) 335-7552
Emp Here 5   *Sales* 54,670,000
SIC 6712 Bank holding companies
Claude Gosselin
Louis Gosselin

D-U-N-S 24-907-7025   (SL)
**POMPES ET FILTRATIONS DE THETFORD
INC**
221 Rue Jalbert O, Thetford Mines, QC, G6G
7W1
(418) 335-9348
Emp Here 35   *Sales* 16,625,910
SIC 5084 Industrial machinery and equipment
Charles Gagne

D-U-N-S 20-561-4329   (SL)
PULTRALL INC
700 9e Rue N, Thetford Mines, QC, G6G 6Z5
(418) 335-3202
Emp Here 100   *Sales* 47,502,600
SIC 5085 Industrial supplies
Bernard Drouin
Marc-Andre Drouin
Bertrand Aubert

D-U-N-S 25-234-1177   (HQ)
RAD TECHNOLOGIES INC
2835 Ch De L'Aeroport Bureau 3, Thetford
Mines, QC, G6G 5R7
(418) 338-4499
Sales 70,219,250
SIC 3524 Lawn and garden equipment

Jean-Guy Dalton
Jean Archambault

D-U-N-S 24-208-4259   (SL)
RECUPERATION FRONTENAC INC
217 Rue Monfette O, Thetford Mines, QC,
G6G 7Y3
(418) 338-8551
Emp Here 100   *Sales* 31,891,000
SIC 4953 Refuse systems
Marc Soucie
Elizabeth Martel
Andre Jr. St-Cyr
Rene Faucher
Louis-Phillippe Champagne
Pierre Cote
Alain Perron
Bruno Roy
Jennifer Poire
Daniel Poudrier

D-U-N-S 20-262-4961   (HQ)
S. SETLAKWE LTEE
493 Boul Frontenac O, Thetford Mines, QC,
G6G 6K2
(418) 338-8511
Emp Here 15   *Sales* 15,106,195
SIC 5712 Furniture stores
Mickael Setlakwe
Gabriel Jr Setlakwe

D-U-N-S 24-637-3930   (HQ)
SABLES OLIMAG INC, LES
(*Suby of* PLACEMENTS CLAUDE GOSSELIN INC)
2899 Boul Frontenac E, Thetford Mines, QC,
G6G 6P6
(418) 338-3562
Emp Here 8   *Sales* 16,545,438
SIC 5032 Brick, stone, and related material
Claude Gosselin
Jean-Yves Angers
Guy Turcotte

D-U-N-S 24-207-4222   (BR)
WAL-MART CANADA CORP
WALMART
(*Suby of* WALMART INC.)
1025 Boul Frontenac E, Thetford Mines, QC,
G6G 6S7
(418) 338-4884
Emp Here 100
SIC 5311 Department stores
Christeam Lisee

Thetford Mines, QC G6H

D-U-N-S 24-204-0967   (SL)
3358097 CANADA INC
CENTRE DU CAMION (AMIANTE)
4680 Boul Frontenac E, Thetford Mines, QC,
G6H 4G5
(418) 338-8588
Emp Here 120   *Sales* 32,802,000
SIC 6712 Bank holding companies
Clement Poulin
Jean-Francois Poulin
Chantal Poulin

D-U-N-S 24-941-3881   (HQ)
ACRYLIQUE WEEDON (1995) INC
591 Rue Des Entreprises, Thetford Mines,
QC, G6H 4B2
(418) 332-4224
Sales 10,325,770
SIC 3089 Plastics products, nec
Richard Couture
Marc Dussault
Francois Vaillancourt
Real D'amours

D-U-N-S 24-894-7413   (SL)
BAINS OCEANIA INC.
591 Rue Des Entreprises, Thetford Mines,
QC, G6H 4B2

(418) 332-4224
Emp Here 45   *Sales* 10,504,575
SIC 3272 Concrete products, nec
Marc Dussault

D-U-N-S 24-149-6207   (SL)
CENTRE DU CAMION (AMIANTE) INC
(*Suby of* 7678444 CANADA INC)
4680 Boul Frontenac E, Thetford Mines, QC,
G6H 4G5
(418) 338-8588
Emp Here 120   *Sales* 75,513,600
SIC 5511 New and used car dealers
Jean-Francois Poulin
Chantal Poulin

D-U-N-S 25-232-6665   (BR)
COMMISSION SCOLAIRE DES APPALACHES
CENTRE DE FORMATION PROFESSIONNELLE DE BLACK LAKE
(*Suby of* COMMISSION SCOLAIRE DES APPALACHES)
499 Rue Saint-Desire, Thetford Mines, QC,
G6H 1L7
(418) 423-4291
Emp Here 75
SIC 8211 Elementary and secondary schools
Marc Dunn

D-U-N-S 20-370-2782   (SL)
FOURNIER CONSTRUCTION INDUSTRIELLE INC
(*Suby of* GROUPE INDUSTRIES FOURNIER
INC)
3787 Boul Frontenac O, Thetford Mines, QC,
G6H 2B5
(819) 375-2888
Emp Here 100   *Sales* 42,273,700
SIC 1541 Industrial buildings and warehouses
Harold Roy

D-U-N-S 20-370-0752   (SL)
FOURNIER MAINTENANCE INDUSTRIELLE INC
3787 Boul Frontenac O, Thetford Mines, QC,
G6H 2B5
(418) 423-4241
Emp Here 50   *Sales* 11,848,500
SIC 7363 Help supply services
Marien Belanger
Harold Roy
Sebastien Rodrigue

D-U-N-S 20-362-6940   (HQ)
GROUPE INDUSTRIES FOURNIER INC
3787 Boul Frontenac O, Thetford Mines, QC,
G6H 2B5
(418) 423-4241
Emp Here 11   *Sales* 109,652,700
SIC 6712 Bank holding companies
Harold Roy
Marc Filion
Sebastien Rodrigue
Daniel Fournier
Serge Lapalme
Marc Benoit
Andre Martel
Serge Fournier
Marien Belanger

D-U-N-S 20-362-7054   (HQ)
INDUSTRIES FOURNIER INC, LES
(*Suby of* GROUPE INDUSTRIES FOURNIER
INC)
3787 Boul Frontenac O, Thetford Mines, QC,
G6H 2B5
(418) 423-4241
Sales 17,873,900
SIC 8711 Engineering services
Roy Harold

D-U-N-S 25-356-8869   (HQ)
PROLAB TECHNOLOGIES INC
4531 Rue Industrielle, Thetford Mines, QC,
G6H 2J1
(418) 423-2777
Sales 40,230,432

SIC 5172 Petroleum products, nec
Jean-Guy Grenier
Chantal Grenier

Thurso, QC J0X

D-U-N-S 20-024-5293   (SL)
2875446 CANADA INC
MARCH? THURSO
266 Rue Victoria, Thurso, QC, J0X 3B0
(819) 985-3259
Emp Here 60   *Sales* 17,608,620
SIC 5411 Grocery stores
Sylvain Boyer
Luc Laviguer

D-U-N-S 20-239-6222   (HQ)
COOPERATIVE AGRO-ALIMENTAIRE DES VALLEES, OUTAOUAIS-LAURENTIDES
COOP AGRODOR, LA
340 Rue Lyon, Thurso, QC, J0X 3B0
(819) 985-4839
Sales 37,126,000
SIC 5191 Farm supplies
Harry Reber
Brian Maloney
Stephane Morel
Benoit Blais
Yves Gratton
Marie-Chantal Blais
Jasmin Gibeau

D-U-N-S 24-421-4271   (SL)
FORTRESS SPECIALTY CELLULOSE INC
FORTRESS CELLULOSE SPECIALISEE
(*Suby of* FORTRESS GLOBAL ENTER-PRISES INC)
451 Rue Victoria, Thurso, QC, J0X 3B0
(819) 985-2233
Emp Here 300   *Sales* 110,291,100
SIC 2611 Pulp mills
Giovanni Iadeluca
Kurt Loewen
Marco Veilleux

D-U-N-S 25-152-0375   (SL)
RENYCO INC
425 Galipeau Rang 5 Rr 1, Thurso, QC, J0X 3B0

Emp Here 65   *Sales* 10,301,488
SIC 2426 Hardwood dimension and flooring mills

Tingwick, QC J0A

D-U-N-S 24-791-4583   (HQ)
COOPERATIVE AGRICOLE DU PRE-VERT
1316 Rue Sainte-Marie, Tingwick, QC, J0A 1L0
(819) 359-2255
Emp Here 8   *Sales* 12,652,950
SIC 5251 Hardware stores
Jocelyn Dion
Jeannot Desharnais

D-U-N-S 24-759-0052   (SL)
SECURIFORT INC
45 Rue Cayouette, Tingwick, QC, J0A 1L0
(819) 359-2226
Emp Here 62   *Sales* 11,909,270
SIC 3499 Fabricated Metal products, nec
Francois Mayrand
Francois Mayrand
Jeremie Mayrand

Trecesson, QC J0Y

D-U-N-S 20-422-7151   (HQ)
LEGAULT METAL INC
METAUX RICHARD, LES
2 Ch Bourgeois O, Trecesson, QC, J0Y 2S0
(819) 732-8818
Sales 12,350,676
SIC 5082 Construction and mining machinery
Gerard Legault
Aurore Legault
Nancy Legault
Carl Bourgault

Trois-Pistoles, QC G0L

D-U-N-S 20-298-0202   (SL)
CENTRE HOSPITALIER DE TROIS-PISTOLES
550 Rue Notre-Dame E, Trois-Pistoles, QC, G0L 4K0
(418) 851-1111
Emp Here 245   *Sales* 27,214,600
SIC 8069 Specialty hospitals, except psychiatric
Line Mousan

D-U-N-S 25-232-7796   (BR)
COMMISSION SCOLAIRE DU FLEUVE ET DES LACS
ECOLE SECONDAIRE L'ARC-EN-CIEL
(*Suby of* COMMISSION SCOLAIRE DU FLEUVE ET DES LACS)
455 Rue Jenkin, Trois-Pistoles, QC, G0L 4K0

Emp Here 80
SIC 8211 Elementary and secondary schools
Christianne Veilleux

D-U-N-S 20-262-7337   (HQ)
DISTRIBUTIONS PAUL-EMILE DUBE LTEE
489 Rue Notre-Dame E Rr 1, Trois-Pistoles, QC, G0L 4K0
(418) 851-1862
Emp Here 5   *Sales* 83,855,772
SIC 5147 Meats and meat products
Gaston Rioux
Felix Jean

D-U-N-S 20-101-4722   (SL)
FERME DES RASADES INC
118 132 Rte E Bureau 3095, Trois-Pistoles, QC, G0L 4K0
(418) 851-2366
Emp Here 25   *Sales* 18,563,000
SIC 5193 Flowers and florists supplies
Francis Rioux
Antonio Rioux

D-U-N-S 20-025-6910   (SL)
FROMAGERIE DES BASQUES ENR
69 132 Rte O, Trois-Pistoles, QC, G0L 4K0
(418) 851-2189
Emp Here 100   *Sales* 83,557,700
SIC 5143 Dairy products, except dried or canned
Yves Pettigrew

D-U-N-S 25-232-5923   (HQ)
GERVAIS DUBE INC
62 2e Rang O, Trois-Pistoles, QC, G0L 4K0
(418) 851-2994
Sales 37,866,300
SIC 1623 Water, sewer, and utility lines
Gervais Dube
Francis Dube
Jacqueline Skelling
Linda Dube

D-U-N-S 25-975-8451   (SL)
POISSONNERIE VERSEAU II
152 132 Rte O, Trois-Pistoles, QC, G0L 4K0
(418) 851-1516
Emp Here 40   *Sales* 33,423,080
SIC 5146 Fish and seafoods
Harold Dionne

D-U-N-S 24-946-5977   (SL)
TROIS-PISTOLES SERVICE
289 Rue Notre-Dame E, Trois-Pistoles, QC, G0L 4K0
(418) 851-2219
Emp Here 24   *Sales* 11,487,555
SIC 1542 Nonresidential construction, nec

Trois-Rivieres, QC G8T

D-U-N-S 20-321-0229   (HQ)
9051-1916 QUEBEC INC
PANIER SANTE
65 Boul Sainte-Madeleine, Trois-Rivieres, QC, G8T 3K8
(819) 694-9050
Sales 33,160,350
SIC 5122 Drugs, proprietaries, and sundries
Nathalie Gelinas
Philippe Castaigne

D-U-N-S 20-332-8984   (SL)
9308-5934 QUEBEC INC
VOLVO TROIS-RIVIERES
300 Rue Vachon, Trois-Rivieres, QC, G8T 8Y2
(819) 691-3025
Emp Here 25   *Sales* 12,451,950
SIC 5511 New and used car dealers
Denis Dusablon

D-U-N-S 25-976-8091   (SL)
ANDRE SIMON INC
VEHICULES ELECTRIQUES SIMON ANDRE
425 Rue Dessureault, Trois-Rivieres, QC, G8T 2L8
(819) 373-1013
Emp Here 26   *Sales* 12,950,028
SIC 5531 Auto and home supply stores
Andre Simon
Guillaume Andre
Alissa Andre
Stephanie Rousseau

D-U-N-S 25-497-5485   (HQ)
ANTIROUILLE METROPOLITAIN INC
(*Suby of* COMPAGNIE GESTIMET INC, LA)
3175 Boul Thibeau, Trois-Rivieres, QC, G8T 1G4
(819) 378-8787
Emp Here 12   *Sales* 76,983,687
SIC 7549 Automotive services, nec
Bruno St-Onge
Jean-Luc St-Onge
Helene Bonanie

D-U-N-S 24-649-8836   (SL)
BARIL MANUFACTURIER INC
JALO FAUCETS
579 Boul Sainte-Madeleine, Trois-Rivieres, QC, G8T 9J8
(819) 693-3871
Emp Here 26   *Sales* 11,626,524
SIC 5074 Plumbing and heating equipment and supplies (hydronics)
Marie-Eve Baril
Jean-Sebastien Baril

D-U-N-S 20-530-0192   (BR)
CANADA POST CORPORATION
(*Suby of* GOVERNMENT OF CANADA)
1285 Rue Notre-Dame E, Trois-Rivieres, QC, G8T 4J9
(819) 691-4215
Emp Here 100
SIC 4311 U.s. postal service
Patrick Henley

D-U-N-S 20-103-4589   (SL)
CARREFOUR JEUNESSE-EMPLOI TROIS-RIVIERES/MRC DES CHENAUX
580 Rue Barkoff Bureau 300, Trois-Rivieres, QC, G8T 9T7
(819) 376-0179
Emp Here 34   *Sales* 13,512,076
SIC 8699 Membership organizations, nec

Sebastien Morin

D-U-N-S 20-204-6181   (SL)
CLAUDE CROTEAU ET FILLES INC
500 Rue Barkoff, Trois-Rivieres, QC, G8T 9P5
(819) 379-4566
Emp Here 60   *Sales* 10,763,760
SIC 5651 Family clothing stores
Danielle Croteau
Christine Croteau

D-U-N-S 20-289-7393   (BR)
COMMISSION SCOLAIRE DU CHEMIN-DU-ROY
CENTRE DE FORMATION PROFESSION-NEL QUALITECH
500 Rue Des Erables, Trois-Rivieres, QC, G8T 9S4
(819) 373-1422
Emp Here 120
SIC 8211 Elementary and secondary schools
Marthe Fortin

D-U-N-S 25-672-1614   (BR)
COMMISSION SCOLAIRE DU CHEMIN-DU-ROY
ACADEMIE LES ESTACADES
501 Rue Des Erables, Trois-Rivieres, QC, G8T 5J2
(819) 375-8931
Emp Here 250
SIC 8211 Elementary and secondary schools
Chantal Morin

D-U-N-S 20-015-0303   (HQ)
COMPAGNIE GESTIMET INC, LA
3175 Boul Thibeau, Trois-Rivieres, QC, G8T 1G4
(819) 371-8456
Sales 11,769,885
SIC 6712 Bank holding companies
Bruno St-Onge

D-U-N-S 25-258-2051   (SL)
DISTAMAX INC
522 Rue Des Erables, Trois-Rivieres, QC, G8T 7Z6
(819) 375-2147
Emp Here 24   *Sales* 20,053,848
SIC 5148 Fresh fruits and vegetables
Mathieu Beaudry
Sylvain Beaudry
Alain Beaudry

D-U-N-S 20-191-9552   (SL)
ENTREPRISES DONTIGNY ET TREMBLAY INC, LES
UNIPRIX
15 Rue Fusey, Trois-Rivieres, QC, G8T 2T3
(819) 378-2828
Emp Here 90   *Sales* 21,989,520
SIC 5912 Drug stores and proprietary stores
Andre Tremblay
Marc Dontigny

D-U-N-S 20-333-1371   (SL)
ENTREPRISES MARC DONTIGNY INC
DEPANNEUR DES ORMEAUX
701 Boul Thibeau, Trois-Rivieres, QC, G8T 7A2
(819) 378-4549
Emp Here 50   *Sales* 55,267,250
SIC 5122 Drugs, proprietaries, and sundries
Marc Dontigny

D-U-N-S 24-380-5939   (SL)
G.D.G. ENVIRONNEMENT LTEE
430 Rue Saint-Laurent, Trois-Rivieres, QC, G8T 6H3
(819) 373-3097
Emp Here 100   *Sales* 23,428,800
SIC 8748 Business consulting, nec
Guy Trudeau
Isabelle Martin
Jean-Guy Lanouette
Julie Proulx
Eve-Marie Gigantes
Serge Oliver

Rejean Breton
Rejean Bergevin
Benoit Cyr

D-U-N-S 24-224-7914   (SL)
GESTION MASSON, ST-PIERRE INC
METRO MASSON
165 Boul Sainte-Madeleine, Trois-Rivieres, QC, G8T 3L7
(819) 375-4824
Emp Here 50   *Sales* 13,814,798
SIC 5411 Grocery stores
Chantal Masson
Andre St-Pierre

D-U-N-S 25-459-2447   (HQ)
GESTION TREMBLAY ET LAPOINTE INC
PLANTE SPORTS
300 Rue Barkoff Bureau 302, Trois-Rivieres, QC, G8T 2A3
(819) 375-3858
Sales 13,454,700
SIC 5699 Miscellaneous apparel and accessory stores
Yves Tremblay
Gilles Lapointe

D-U-N-S 25-896-5003   (SL)
GROUPE SOUCY INC
DIVISION ECOLOBRISS
1060 Boul Thibeau, Trois-Rivieres, QC, G8T 7B2
(819) 376-3111
Emp Here 100   *Sales* 39,567,800
SIC 7381 Detective and armored car services
Sylvia Valade

D-U-N-S 24-329-2328   (BR)
H. MATTEAU ET FILS (1987) INC
(*Suby of* H. MATTEAU ET FILS (1987) INC)
15 Rue Philippe-Francoeur, Trois-Rivieres, QC, G8T 9L7
(819) 374-4735
Emp Here 85
SIC 5211 Lumber and other building materials
Claude Gauthier Jr

D-U-N-S 20-792-1748   (SL)
JEAN-FRANCOIS GAUTHIER ET ALEXANDRE RIVARD, PHARMACIENS S.E.N.C
CLINIQUE MEDICALE FUSEY
200 Rue Fusey, Trois-Rivieres, QC, G8T 2V8
(819) 375-8941
Emp Here 50   *Sales* 12,647,700
SIC 5912 Drug stores and proprietary stores
Jean-Francois Gauthier
Alexandre Rivard

D-U-N-S 24-391-4491   (SL)
MAGASIN MARC-ANDRE ST-JACQUES INC
CANADIAN TIRE
6 Rue Fusey, Trois-Rivieres, QC, G8T 2T1
(819) 376-6866
Emp Here 70   *Sales* 44,049,600
SIC 5531 Auto and home supply stores
Marc-Andre St-Jacques

D-U-N-S 20-799-3598   (BR)
MARLU INC
MCDONALD'S
300 Rue Barkoff, Trois-Rivieres, QC, G8T 2A3
(819) 373-7921
Emp Here 75
SIC 5812 Eating places
Martin Leblanc

D-U-N-S 20-709-3303   (HQ)
MARMEN INC
(*Suby of* GESTION MARMEN INC)
845 Rue Berlinguet, Trois-Rivieres, QC, G8T 8N9
(819) 379-0453
Sales 252,789,300
SIC 3545 Machine tool accessories
Patrick Pellerin
Linda Pellerin
Annie Pellerin
Paquerette Pellerin

Fernand Pellerin

D-U-N-S 20-330-6936   (BR)
MARMEN INC
(*Suby of* GESTION MARMEN INC)
557 Rue Des Erables, Trois-Rivieres, QC, G8T 8Y8
(819) 379-0453
Emp Here 900
SIC 3545 Machine tool accessories
Annie Pellerin

D-U-N-S 24-207-6347   (BR)
OLYMEL S.E.C.
OLYMEL
(*Suby of* OLYMEL S.E.C.)
531 Rue Des Erables, Trois-Rivieres, QC, G8T 7Z7
(819) 376-3770
Emp Here 170
SIC 5147 Meats and meat products
Yvan Brochu

D-U-N-S 20-002-2379   (BR)
PROVIGO DISTRIBUTION INC
MAXI
(*Suby of* LOBLAW COMPANIES LIMITED)
320 Rue Barkoff, Trois-Rivieres, QC, G8T 2A3
(819) 378-4932
Emp Here 80
SIC 5411 Grocery stores
Gaetan Houle

D-U-N-S 20-603-5669   (SL)
SANCTUAIRE NOTRE-DAME-DU-CAP
LIBRAIRIE MARIALE
626 Rue Notre-Dame E, Trois-Rivieres, QC, G8T 4G9
(819) 374-2441
Emp Here 80   *Sales* 8,618,160
SIC 8661 Religious organizations
Yoland Ouellet

D-U-N-S 24-434-0964   (HQ)
SERVICES DE VOYAGES YVES BORDELEAU INC, LES
VOYAGES ARC-EN-CIEL
765 Boul Thibeau Bureau 100, Trois-Rivieres, QC, G8T 7A4
(819) 374-0747
Emp Here 10   *Sales* 12,999,175
SIC 4724 Travel agencies
Yves Bordeleau
Manon Lynch

D-U-N-S 20-321-1011   (SL)
SHOPPING WEB PLUS INC
CENTRE DE SERVICE EN SANTE SECURITE DU QUEBEC
450 Rue Des ?Rables, Trois-Rivieres, QC, G8T 5H9

Emp Here 32   *Sales* 14,191,680
SIC 7389 Business services, nec
Daniel Dionne

D-U-N-S 20-234-8657   (BR)
SOBEYS CAPITAL INCORPORATED
IGA EXTRA
(*Suby of* EMPIRE COMPANY LIMITED)
645 Boul Thibeau, Trois-Rivieres, QC, G8T 6Z6
(819) 376-1551
Emp Here 103
SIC 5411 Grocery stores
Andre De Carrufel

D-U-N-S 20-013-8837   (BR)
SONOCO CANADA CORPORATION
(*Suby of* SONOCO PRODUCTS COMPANY)
530 Rue Des Erables, Trois-Rivieres, QC, G8T 8N6
(819) 374-5222
Emp Here 85
SIC 2655 Fiber cans, drums, and similar products
Philippe Bussieres

D-U-N-S 25-361-2626   (SL)

TORA CAP-DE-LA-MADELEINE LIMITEE
TIGRE GEANT
(*Suby of* GIANT TIGER STORES LIMITED)
800 Boul Thibeau, Trois-Rivieres, QC, G8T 7A6
(819) 697-3833
Emp Here 50   *Sales* 10,267,150
SIC 5311 Department stores
Michel D'amours

D-U-N-S 24-827-8694   (SL)
VOYAGESARABAIS INC
VOYAGES A RABAIS
699 Boul Thibeau Bureau 100, Trois-Rivieres, QC, G8T 7A2
(819) 693-8937
Emp Here 37   *Sales* 14,258,320
SIC 4724 Travel agencies
Sylvie Myre

D-U-N-S 25-991-5965   (BR)
WAL-MART CANADA CORP
(*Suby of* WALMART INC.)
300 Rue Barkoff, Trois-Rivieres, QC, G8T 2A3
(819) 379-2992
Emp Here 200
SIC 5311 Department stores
Pierre Lahaie

Trois-Rivieres, QC G8V

D-U-N-S 24-941-4319   (HQ)
STRUCTURES BARRETTE INC
DISTRIBUTION TOITURE MAURICIENNE
545 Rang Saint-Malo, Trois-Rivieres, QC, G8V 0A8
(819) 374-8784
Emp Here 125   *Sales* 512,665,200
SIC 5031 Lumber, plywood, and millwork
Francois Barrette
Martin Blais
Luc Dufour

Trois-Rivieres, QC G8Y

D-U-N-S 24-812-5262   (SL)
ALIMENTATION BENOIT ROBERT INC
METRO DES FORGES
1375 Rue Aubuchon, Trois-Rivieres, QC, G8Y 5K4
(819) 373-5166
Emp Here 60   *Sales* 17,608,620
SIC 5411 Grocery stores
Benoit Robert

D-U-N-S 24-192-2306   (SL)
BOUTIQUES SAN FRANCISCO
4125 Boul Des Forges, Trois-Rivieres, QC, G8Y 1W1
(819) 375-8727
Emp Here 49   *Sales* 32,166,736
SIC 5961 Catalog and mail-order houses
Jocelyn Dumas

D-U-N-S 20-716-9082   (BR)
COMMISSION SCOLAIRE DU CHEMIN-DU-ROY
CENTRE D'EDUCATION DES ADULTES DU CHEMIN-DU-ROY
3750 Rue Jean-Bourdon, Trois-Rivieres, QC, G8Y 2A5
(819) 379-8714
Emp Here 80
SIC 8211 Elementary and secondary schools
Marie Hamel

D-U-N-S 24-338-0107   (BR)
COMMISSION SCOLAIRE DU CHEMIN-DU-ROY
CENTRE DE FORMATION PROFESSIONNELLE BEL-AVENIR
3750 Rue Jean-Bourdon, Trois-Rivieres, QC,

G8Y 2A5
(819) 691-3366
Emp Here 110
SIC 8211 Elementary and secondary schools
Pierre Laliberte

D-U-N-S 20-886-3092   (SL)
ENTREPRISES DE NETTOYAGE M.P. INC
1621 Rue De Lery, Trois-Rivieres, QC, G8Y 7B3

Emp Here 75   *Sales* 3,015,675
SIC 7349 Building maintenance services, nec
Marcel Chartier

D-U-N-S 20-548-0689   (SL)
GESTION SETR INC
SPORTS EXPERTS
4125 Boul Des Forges Bureau 1, Trois-Rivieres, QC, G8Y 1W1
(819) 376-4343
Emp Here 60   *Sales* 10,763,760
SIC 5699 Miscellaneous apparel and accessory stores
Georges Brunelle
Jean-Marc Bruneau
Sonia Beliveau

D-U-N-S 25-245-5134   (SL)
IGA EXTRA MARCHE PAQUETTE INC
IGA
3925 Boul Des Forges, Trois-Rivieres, QC, G8Y 1V9
(819) 379-2397
Emp Here 120   *Sales* 35,217,240
SIC 5411 Grocery stores
Michel Paquette

D-U-N-S 24-016-7820   (BR)
LOBLAWS INC
PROVIGO LE MARCHE
(*Suby of* LOBLAW COMPANIES LIMITED)
3725 Boul Des Forges, Trois-Rivieres, QC, G8Y 4P2
(819) 374-8980
Emp Here 100
SIC 5411 Grocery stores
Rodier Gagnon

D-U-N-S 24-914-5645   (SL)
STRATOS PIZZERIA
5030 Boul Des Forges, Trois-Rivieres, QC, G8Y 1X2
(819) 694-7777
Emp Here 25   *Sales* 20,889,425
SIC 5149 Groceries and related products, nec
Pierre Dusablon

D-U-N-S 20-808-0668   (SL)
VEGETARIEN TROIS RIVIERES INC
3960 Boul Des Forges, Trois-Rivieres, QC, G8Y 1V7
(819) 372-9730
Emp Here 49   *Sales* 13,433,448
SIC 5431 Fruit and vegetable markets
Andre Decarufel

Trois-Rivieres, QC G8Z

D-U-N-S 25-187-2321   (SL)
9045-9827 QUEBEC INC
IGA JEAN XXIII
6060 Boul Jean-Xxiii, Trois-Rivieres, QC, G8Z 4B5
(819) 374-6060
Emp Here 45   *Sales* 12,336,840
SIC 5411 Grocery stores
Real Deschenes

D-U-N-S 25-835-5320   (BR)
AMEUBLEMENTS TANGUAY INC
(*Suby of* BELANGER, A. (DETAIL) LTEE)
2200 Boul Des Recollets, Trois-Rivieres, QC, G8Z 3X5
(819) 373-1111
Emp Here 90

SIC 5712 Furniture stores
Michel Plourde

D-U-N-S 20-262-8269   (HQ)
ARNO ELECTRIQUE LTEE
ARNO ELECTRIC
(*Suby* of GROUPE ARNO ELECTRIQUE
LTEE)
2300 Boul Des Recollets, Trois-Rivieres, QC,
G8Z 3X5
(819) 379-5222
Emp Here 55   *Sales* 82,428,150
SIC 1731 Electrical work
Louis St-Arnaud
Pierre St-Arnaud
Robert St-Arnaud

D-U-N-S 20-998-8021   (SL)
ATELIER DES VIEILLES FORGES INC
1000 Place Boland, Trois-Rivieres, QC, G8Z
4H2
(819) 376-1834
Emp Here 106   *Sales* 70,690,552
SIC 4783 Packing and crating
Marc Provost

D-U-N-S 24-741-3693   (SL)
AUTOS YOMO INC, LES
TROIS-RIVIERES HYUNDAI
5225 Boul Jean-Xxiii, Trois-Rivieres, QC, G8Z
4A5
(819) 374-3330
Emp Here 30   *Sales* 14,942,340
SIC 5511 New and used car dealers
Maurice Emond

D-U-N-S 24-111-4313   (HQ)
CEGEP DE TROIS-RIVIERES
3500 Rue De Courval, Trois-Rivieres, QC,
G8Z 1T2
(819) 376-1721
Emp Here 650   *Sales* 74,339,250
SIC 8222 Junior colleges
Louis Gendron
Mark Leblanc
Isabelle Collin
Denis Rousseau
Rejean Paquet
Daniel Marchand
Robert Champagne

D-U-N-S 24-003-7080   (SL)
**CENTRE DE READAPTATION INTERNA-
TIONAL**
3450 Rue Sainte-Marguerite, Trois-Rivieres,
QC, G8Z 1X3
(819) 691-7536
Emp Here 49   *Sales* 21,911,526
SIC 5047 Medical and hospital equipment
Alain Giroux

D-U-N-S 20-106-7373   (SL)
**CENTRE FINANCIER AUX ENTREPRISES
DESJARDINS TROIS-RIVIERES**
2000 Boul Des Recollets, Trois-Rivieres, QC,
G8Z 3X4
(819) 376-4000
Emp Here 40   *Sales* 11,100,372
SIC 8741 Management services
Jean-Francois Beaudoin

D-U-N-S 20-719-1706   (SL)
**CENTRE HOSPITALIER REGIONAL DE
TROIS-RIVIERES**
1991 Boul Du Carmel, Trois-Rivieres, QC,
G8Z 3R9
(819) 697-3333
Emp Here 1,400   *Sales* 155,512,000
SIC 8069 Specialty hospitals, except psychi-
atric
Denise Massicotte
Jean-Claude Beaumier
Guy Rousseau
Joan Bergeron
Normand St-Louis
Charles-Arthur Walker
Lyne Chevalier
Lucie Latendre

D-U-N-S 25-959-6997   (BR)
**CENTRE JEUNESSE DE LA MAURICIE ET
DU CENTRE-DU-QUEBEC, LE**
CJMCQ
(*Suby* of CENTRE JEUNESSE DE LA
MAURICIE ET DU CENTRE-DU-QUEBEC,
LE)
1455 Boul Du Carmel, Trois-Rivieres, QC,
G8Z 3R7
(819) 378-5481
Emp Here 18,000
SIC 8322 Individual and family services
Raymond Bordeleau

D-U-N-S 24-425-9177   (BR)
**CENTRE JEUNESSE DE LA MAURICIE ET
DU CENTRE-DU-QUEBEC, LE**
PAVILLION BOURGEOIS
(*Suby* of CENTRE JEUNESSE DE LA
MAURICIE ET DU CENTRE-DU-QUEBEC,
LE)
2735 Rue Papineau, Trois-Rivieres, QC, G8Z
1N8
(819) 378-8635
Emp Here 90
SIC 8322 Individual and family services
Guymont Pliche

D-U-N-S 24-405-0795   (HQ)
**CENTRE JEUNESSE DE LA MAURICIE ET
DU CENTRE-DU-QUEBEC, LE**
CJMCQ
1455 Boul Du Carmel, Trois-Rivieres, QC,
G8Z 3R7
(819) 378-5481
Emp Here 65   *Sales* 46,075,200
SIC 8322 Individual and family services
Nathalie Garon

D-U-N-S 20-362-6528   (HQ)
CLE CAPITAL INC
*COMPAGNIE   DE   LOCATION
D'EQUIPEMENT CLE*
(*Suby* of HITACHI, LTD.)
2200 Rue De La Sidbec S, Trois-Rivieres, QC,
G8Z 4H1
(819) 373-8000
Emp Here 45   *Sales* 11,237,200
SIC 6159 Miscellaneous business credit insti-
tutions
Francois Nantel
Ryan Collison
Akihiko Sugawara

D-U-N-S 25-240-1104   (HQ)
COLLEGE LAFLECHE
ESCARBILLE, L'
1687 Boul Du Carmel, Trois-Rivieres, QC,
G8Z 3R8
(819) 375-7346
Sales 32,432,990
SIC 8221 Colleges and universities
Alexandre Ollive
Catherine Langlois
Luc Pellerin
Yvette Isabelle
Robert Mantha
Pierre Michaud
Chantal Filion
Sonia Gaudreault
Jessica Menard
Bryan Dubois-Bourque

D-U-N-S 20-716-9041   (BR)
**COMMISSION SCOLAIRE DU CHEMIN-DU-
ROY**
ECOLE SECONDAIRE DES PIONNIERS
1725 Boul Du Carmel, Trois-Rivieres, QC,
G8Z 3R8
(819) 379-5822
Emp Here 140
SIC 8211 Elementary and secondary schools
Chantale Morin

D-U-N-S 20-262-8251   (SL)
CONSTRUCTION ARNO INC
(*Suby* of GROUPE ARNO ELECTRIQUE

LTEE)
2300 Boul Des Recollets, Trois-Rivieres, QC,
G8Z 3X5
(819) 379-5222
Emp Here 100   *Sales* 25,244,200
SIC 1623 Water, sewer, and utility lines
Louis St-Arnaud
Pierre St-Arnaud
Robert St-Arnaud

D-U-N-S 20-703-9855   (BR)
COOP FEDEREE, LA
(*Suby* of COOP FEDEREE, LA)
4225 Rue Saint-Joseph Bureau 379, Trois-
Rivieres, QC, G8Z 4G3
(819) 379-8551
Emp Here 250
SIC 5072 Hardware
Claude Gingras

D-U-N-S 20-926-1387   (SL)
DUFRESNE, MARC (1978) INC
5345 Rue Saint-Joseph, Trois-Rivieres, QC,
G8Z 4M5
(819) 374-1433
Emp Here 26   *Sales* 12,194,130
SIC 5983 Fuel oil dealers
Marc Dufresne
Simon Dufresne
Benoit Dufresne

D-U-N-S 25-525-8600   (SL)
**ENTREPRISES D'EMONDAGE L.D.L. INC,
LES**
(*Suby* of GROUPE ARNO ELECTRIQUE
LTEE)
2300 Boul Des Recollets, Trois-Rivieres, QC,
G8Z 3X5
(819) 694-0395
Emp Here 100   *Sales* 17,390,500
SIC 0783 Ornamental shrub and tree services
Louis St-Arnaud
Pierre St-Arnaud
Leon Trepanier
Denis Paradis

D-U-N-S 20-559-6518   (HQ)
ITRON CANADA INC
(*Suby* of ITRON, INC.)
3260 Rue Du Chanoine-Chamberland, Trois-
Rivieres, QC, G8Z 2T2
(819) 373-5303
Emp Here 14   *Sales* 21,376,170
SIC 5084 Industrial machinery and equipment
Alain Masse
Philip Mezey
Owen Scott
Steven M Helmbrecht
John W Holleran
Marilyn R Blair

D-U-N-S 24-250-8752   (SL)
L. BELANGER METAL INC
2950 Rue De La Sidbec N, Trois-Rivieres, QC,
G8Z 4E1
(819) 375-6600
Emp Here 37   *Sales* 19,260,054
SIC 5093 Scrap and waste materials
Guy Belanger

D-U-N-S 20-238-2362   (HQ)
MAGASINS KORVETTE LTEE, LES
(*Suby* of GESTION JEAN-MARC BINETTE
INC)
2325 Boul Des Recollets, Trois-Rivieres, QC,
G8Z 3X6
(819) 374-4625
Emp Here 25   *Sales* 66,484,102
SIC 5311 Department stores
Daniel Binette
Andree Binette
Marie-Pier Binette
Jean-Francois Binette

D-U-N-S 20-545-6127   (SL)
**PHARMACIE SYLVIE GELINAS ET CHAN-
TAL BELLEMARE PHARMACIENNES INC**
JEAN COUTU

940 Boul Des Recollets, Trois-Rivieres, QC,
G8Z 3W9
(819) 379-1444
Emp Here 40   *Sales* 10,118,160
SIC 5912 Drug stores and proprietary stores
Sylvie Gelinas
Chantal Bellemare

D-U-N-S 20-170-0601   (BR)
PROVIGO DISTRIBUTION INC
MAXI
(*Suby* of LOBLAW COMPANIES LIMITED)
5875 Boul Jean-Xxiii, Trois-Rivieres, QC, G8Z
4N8
(819) 378-8759
Emp Here 88
SIC 5411 Grocery stores
Serge Lavoie

D-U-N-S 20-525-2872   (SL)
**SERVICES ET SOLUTIONS PROFESSION-
NELS EN TELECOMMUNICATIONS S.S.P.
INC**
S.S.P. TELECOM
2535 Rue De La Sidbec S, Trois-Rivieres, QC,
G8Z 4M6
(819) 693-2535
Emp Here 45   *Sales* 20,122,830
SIC 5065 Electronic parts and equipment, nec
Robert Dessureault

D-U-N-S 25-468-3592   (SL)
**SOCIETE SAINT-JEAN-BAPTISTE DE LA
MAURICIE OBNL**
3239 Rue Papineau, Trois-Rivieres, QC, G8Z
1P4
(819) 375-4881
Emp Here 11   *Sales* 11,383,691
SIC 6311 Life insurance

D-U-N-S 24-020-1728   (HQ)
SOEURS FILLES DE JESUS
1193 Boul Saint-Louis, Trois-Rivieres, QC,
G8Z 2M8
(819) 373-3741
Emp Here 20   *Sales* 21,201,500
SIC 6411 Insurance agents, brokers, and ser-
vice
James Gauthier

D-U-N-S 24-943-2428   (HQ)
SOLUS SECURITE INC
SOLUS SAFETY
2545 Rue De La Sidbec S, Trois-Rivieres, QC,
G8Z 4M6
(819) 373-2053
Emp Here 10   *Sales* 26,027,100
SIC 5099 Durable goods, nec
Christian Allard
Marco Fortin
Normand Belanger

D-U-N-S 20-531-8640   (BR)
SOMAVRAC INC
TERMINAL 3
(*Suby* of GROUPE SOMAVRAC INC)
2550 Rue De La Sidbec S, Trois-Rivieres, QC,
G8Z 4H1
(819) 374-7551
Emp Here 100
SIC 4213 Trucking, except local
Daniel Pronovost

D-U-N-S 24-378-7376   (BR)
UNIVERSITE DU QUEBEC
FONDATION UNIVERSITE DU QUEBEC
(*Suby* of UNIVERSITE DU QUEBEC)
3351 Boul Des Forges, Trois-Rivieres, QC,
G8Z 4M3
(819) 376-5011
Emp Here 1,300
SIC 8221 Colleges and universities
Hugues Doucet

Trois-Rivieres, QC G9A

D-U-N-S 20-517-9034   (SL)
2343-7393 QUEBEC INC
DELTA TROIS-RIVIERES
1620 Rue Notre-Dame Centre, Trois-Rivieres, QC, G9A 6E5
(819) 376-1991
Emp Here 100   *Sales* 9,489,900
SIC 7011 Hotels and motels
Richard Dubuc

D-U-N-S 25-359-3065   (HQ)
87861 CANADA LTEE
1000 Rue Du Pere-Daniel Bureau 728, Trois-Rivieres, QC, G9A 5R6
(819) 378-2747
Sales 10,462,120
SIC 6712 Bank holding companies
Francois Houle
Sylvio Houle
Jules Soucy

D-U-N-S 25-978-9196   (SL)
9065-1837 QUEBEC INC
TEMPLE, LE
300 Rue Des Forges, Trois-Rivieres, QC, G9A 2G8
(819) 370-2005
Emp Here 80   *Sales* 3,641,520
SIC 5813 Drinking places
Guy Lambert
Marc Hamel
Martin Boisvert

D-U-N-S 24-338-6864   (SL)
9122-6910 QUEBEC INC
RESTAURANT BUFFET DES CONTINENTS
4520 Boul Des Recollets, Trois-Rivieres, QC, G9A 4N2
(819) 370-1099
Emp Here 75   *Sales* 3,413,925
SIC 5812 Eating places
Oreste Pendenza

D-U-N-S 20-259-7589   (SL)
9309-6774 QUEBEC INC
9300 Boul Industriel, Trois-Rivieres, QC, G9A 5E1
(819) 539-8058
Emp Here 113   *Sales* 82,351,043
SIC 5142 Packaged frozen goods
Jean-Guy Ladriere

D-U-N-S 20-583-8472   (HQ)
AAR AIRCRAFT SERVICES - TROIS RIVIERES ULC
SERVICES AAR MRO - CANADA, TROIS RIVIERES
3750 Rue De L'Aeroport, Trois-Rivieres, QC, G9A 5E1
(819) 377-4500
Sales 26,697,800
SIC 4581 Airports, flying fields, and services
John Holmes
Robert J. Regan
Michael D. Milligan

D-U-N-S 20-883-6510   (HQ)
ACCESSOIRES D'AUTO LEBLANC LTEE
3125 Boul Gene-H.-Kruger Bureau 1624, Trois-Rivieres, QC, G9A 4M2
(819) 378-2871
Emp Here 75   *Sales* 80,701,950
SIC 5013 Motor vehicle supplies and new parts
Leo Leblanc
Patrick Leblanc
Michel Leblanc

D-U-N-S 20-998-6293   (HQ)
ARM AGENCE DE RECOUVREMENT INC
985 Rue Royale Bureau 201, Trois-Rivieres, QC, G9A 4H7
(819) 375-3327
Emp Here 5   *Sales* 25,046,375
SIC 7322 Adjustment and collection services
Jean-Francois Gingras

D-U-N-S 24-820-5908   (SL)
ASPASIE INC
TABLEX
2106 Rue Bellefeuille, Trois-Rivieres, QC, G9A 3Y9
(819) 379-2157
Emp Here 100   *Sales* 32,613,600
SIC 3999 Manufacturing industries, nec
Nicole D. Gelinas
Gaston J. A. Gelinas

D-U-N-S 25-525-0540   (HQ)
CAFE MORGANE ROYALE INC
CAFE MORGANE
4945 Boul Gene-H.-Kruger, Trois-Rivieres, QC, G9A 4N5
(819) 694-1118
Emp Here 20   *Sales* 13,707,600
SIC 5499 Miscellaneous food stores
Suzanne Marcotte
Guy Marcotte

D-U-N-S 25-860-9288   (HQ)
CAISSE DESJARDINS DES TROIS-RIVIERES
CENTRE DE SERVICE DE LA MONTAGNE
1200 Rue Royale, Trois-Rivieres, QC, G9A 4J2
(819) 376-1200
Emp Here 30   *Sales* 23,661,244
SIC 6062 State credit unions
David Belanger
Marili B. Desrochers
Louis Brunelle
Andre Gabias
Genevieve Auger
Alexandre Baril
Louis Cloutier
Pierre Gagnon

D-U-N-S 20-886-0494   (HQ)
CAPTEL INC
9395 Boul Parent Bureau 2, Trois-Rivieres, QC, G9A 5E1
(819) 373-1454
Sales 22,719,780
SIC 1623 Water, sewer, and utility lines
David Carre

D-U-N-S 24-469-2203   (SL)
CENTRE DE PREVENTION DU SUICIDE: ACCALMIE
1905 Rue Royale, Trois-Rivieres, QC, G9A 4K8
(819) 378-8585
Emp Here 26   *Sales* 11,039,782
SIC 8999 Services, nec
Claude Vadnais

D-U-N-S 20-033-4832   (SL)
CHAUFFEUR EXPRESS LOCATION INC.
3346 Rue Bellefeuille, Trois-Rivieres, QC, G9A 3Z3
(819) 697-3555
Emp Here 49   *Sales* 11,611,530
SIC 7361 Employment agencies
Rene Marcotte

D-U-N-S 24-668-6422   (BR)
COCA-COLA LTD
(*Suby of* THE COCA-COLA COMPANY)
8500 Boul Industriel, Trois-Rivieres, QC, G9A 5E1
(819) 694-4000
Emp Here 100
SIC 2086 Bottled and canned soft drinks

D-U-N-S 24-510-2355   (SL)
COLLEGE MARIE-DE-L'INCARNATION
725 Rue Hart, Trois-Rivieres, QC, G9A 4R9
(819) 379-3223
Emp Here 150   *Sales* 14,867,850
SIC 8211 Elementary and secondary schools
Michel Boucher
Yvette Isabelle
Lachance Jacques
Pierre Michaud
Martine Talbot

Macdonald Peter
Jomphe Nathalie
Jean-Pierre Charest
Michel Bellehumeur
Yves Hamelin

D-U-N-S 25-916-3475   (SL)
CONSEIL REGIONAL MAURICIE ET CENTRE DU QUEBEC (FTQ)
7080 Rue Marion Bureau 101, Trois-Rivieres, QC, G9A 6G4
(819) 378-4049
Emp Here 40   *Sales* 15,646,320
SIC 8631 Labor organizations

D-U-N-S 24-710-8269   (SL)
CONSULTANTS VFP INC
LPA GROUPE CONSEIL
(*Suby of* GROUPE DESSAU INC)
1455 Rue Champlain, Trois-Rivieres, QC, G9A 5X4
(819) 378-6159
Emp Here 80
SIC 8711 Engineering services
Marc Verrault

D-U-N-S 24-430-2204   (SL)
CORPORATION DE DEVELOPMENT CULTUREL DE TROIS-RIVIERES
SALLE J.-ANTONIO-THOMPSON, LA
1425 Place De L'Hotel-De-Ville, Trois-Rivieres, QC, G9A 4S7
(819) 372-4614
Emp Here 125   *Sales* 52,361,125
SIC 6531 Real estate agents and managers
Stella Montreuil
Michel Jutras
Renald Cote

D-U-N-S 24-903-7037   (SL)
CORPORATION DES PILOTES DU SAINT-LAURENT CENTRAL INC
PILOTES DU SAINT-LAURENT CENTRAL
1350 Rue Royale Bureau 800, Trois-Rivieres, QC, G9A 4J4
(819) 379-8882
Emp Here 100   *Sales* 39,372,400
SIC 4499 Water transportation services, nec
Pierre Vallee
Yves Thibault
Alain Arseneault
Patrice Vaillancourt
Carl Belley
Jean-Francois Simard
Jean-Charles Pinsonnault
Dimitrios Dimitrios

D-U-N-S 20-801-2620   (BR)
COSTCO WHOLESALE CANADA LTD
COSTCO
(*Suby of* COSTCO WHOLESALE CORPORATION)
3000 Boul Des Recollets, Trois-Rivieres, QC, G9A 6J2
(819) 693-5758
Emp Here 200
SIC 5399 Miscellaneous general merchandise
Joseph Martz

D-U-N-S 20-581-9506   (BR)
DELOITTE RESTRUCTURING INC
(*Suby of* DELOITTE LLP)
1500 Rue Royale Bureau 250, Trois-Rivieres, QC, G9A 6E6
(819) 691-1212
Emp Here 80
SIC 8721 Accounting, auditing, and bookkeeping
John Pankert

D-U-N-S 24-323-4960   (HQ)
DESSUREAULT LEBLANC LEFEBVRE C.A.
950 Rue Royale Bureau 104, Trois-Rivieres, QC, G9A 4H8
(819) 379-0133
Emp Here 6   *Sales* 11,838,045
SIC 8721 Accounting, auditing, and book-

keeping
Pierre Leblanc
Claude Lefebvre
Raymond Drouin
Martin Leblanc
Pierre Dessureault

D-U-N-S 20-298-0751   (SL)
FAB 3R INC
227 Boul Du Saint-Maurice, Trois-Rivieres, QC, G9A 3N8
(819) 371-8227
Emp Here 100   *Sales* 19,208,500
SIC 3469 Metal stampings, nec
Yves Lacroix
Chantal Rochette
Martin Magny

D-U-N-S 20-523-3526   (SL)
FONDATION CENTRE HOSPITALIER REGIONAL DE TROIS-RIVIERES (RSTR)
FONDS JEAN-PIERRE-PETIT
731 Rue Sainte-Julie, Trois-Rivieres, QC, G9A 1Y1
(819) 697-3333
Emp Here 100   *Sales* 10,213,300
SIC 8062 General medical and surgical hospitals
Alain St-Arnaud
Veronique Neron
Johanne Hinse
Sonia Gauthier

D-U-N-S 24-001-6241   (BR)
FONDATION DU CENTRE DE SANTE ET DE SERVICES SOCIAUX DE TROIS-RIVIERES
731 Rue Sainte-Julie, Trois-Rivieres, QC, G9A 1Y1
(819) 370-2100
Emp Here 140
SIC 8322 Individual and family services
Jacques Longval

D-U-N-S 24-202-5294   (HQ)
GROUPE CLR INC
BONAVENTURE COMMUNICATION
7200 Boul Jean-Xxiii, Trois-Rivieres, QC, G9A 5C9
(819) 377-2424
Emp Here 30   *Sales* 13,708,320
SIC 4899 Communication services, nec
Francis Paquin
Louis Paquin
Jean-Francois Ducharme

D-U-N-S 24-946-0288   (HQ)
GROUPE MECANITEC INC
2300 Rue Jules-Vachon, Trois-Rivieres, QC, G9A 5E1
(819) 374-4647
Sales 24,054,800
SIC 6712 Bank holding companies
Yvan Champoux
Denise St-Pierre

D-U-N-S 24-696-8770   (HQ)
GROUPE SOMAVRAC INC
PROMEL
3450 Boul Gene-H.-Kruger, Trois-Rivieres, QC, G9A 4M3
(819) 379-3311
Emp Here 50   *Sales* 71,005,250
SIC 2875 Fertilizers, mixing only
Marc Paquin

D-U-N-S 20-553-6431   (BR)
HOME DEPOT OF CANADA INC
HOME DEPOT
(*Suby of* THE HOME DEPOT INC)
4500 Rue Real-Proulx, Trois-Rivieres, QC, G9A 6P9
(819) 379-3990
Emp Here 100
SIC 5211 Lumber and other building materials
Bruno Grondin

D-U-N-S 24-923-0525   (SL)
INTER CLOTURES INC

GROUPE INTER CLOTURES
9200 Boul Parent, Trois-Rivieres, QC, G9A 5E1
(819) 377-5837
Emp Here 26   *Sales* 11,679,694
SIC 7389 Business services, nec
Denis Gravel
Pierre Miglierina
Sylvain Morin

D-U-N-S 25-244-3072   (HQ)
JOHNSTON-VERMETTE GROUPE CONSEIL INC
JOHNSTON-VERMETTE
6110 Rue Christophe-Pelissier, Trois-Rivieres, QC, G9A 5C9
(819) 373-3550
Emp Here 30   *Sales* 15,192,815
SIC 8711 Engineering services
Luc Vermette
Pascal Messier
Jonathan Duguay
Annie Bruneau
Alexandre Belisle
Luc Alarie

D-U-N-S 20-331-7268   (SL)
KRUGER TROIS-RIVIERES S.E.C.
3735 Boul Gene-H.-Kruger, Trois-Rivieres, QC, G9A 6B1
(819) 375-1691
Emp Here 250   *Sales* 91,909,250
SIC 2621 Paper mills
Joseph Kruger Ii

D-U-N-S 24-370-3738   (SL)
MACO MECANIQUE INC
(*Suby of* GROUPE MACO INC)
6595 Boul Jean-Xxiii, Trois-Rivieres, QC, G9A 5C9
(819) 378-7070
Emp Here 100   *Sales* 23,306,500
SIC 1711 Plumbing, heating, air-conditioning
Mathieu Gagnon
Rene Hebert

D-U-N-S 24-352-4378   (SL)
MARGARINE THIBAULT INC
ARC-EN-CIEL
3000 Rue Jules-Vachon, Trois-Rivieres, QC, G9A 5E1
(819) 373-3333
Emp Here 55   *Sales* 22,965,390
SIC 2079 Edible fats and oils
Danielle Bergeron

D-U-N-S 25-905-3320   (BR)
MARLU INC
MCDONALD'S
4520 Boul Des Recollets, Trois-Rivieres, QC, G9A 4N2
(819) 373-5408
Emp Here 85
SIC 5812 Eating places
Marc Mongrain

D-U-N-S 20-858-7626   (HQ)
MASKIMO CONSTRUCTION INC
MASKIMO CONSTRUCTION/DIVISON CARRIERES ET SABLIERES
2500 Rue Leon-Trepanier, Trois-Rivieres, QC, G9A 5E1
(819) 601-2999
Emp Here 100   *Sales* 170,888,400
SIC 5032 Brick, stone, and related material
Louis Marchand
Louis Marchand
Sebastien Trahan

D-U-N-S 20-191-9172   (SL)
MATERIAUX ECONOMIQUES INC
M.E.I. ASSAINISSEMENT
2900 Rue Jules-Vachon, Trois-Rivieres, QC, G9A 5E1
(819) 374-8577
Emp Here 60   *Sales* 14,771,160
SIC 1799 Special trade contractors, nec
Rene St-Pierre

Daniel St-Pierre
Alain Lesage
Joanne Hould

D-U-N-S 20-103-4514   (SL)
MENAGEZ-VOUS TERRITOIRE LES FORGES
MENAGEZ-VOUS LES FORGES
749 Boul Du Saint-Maurice, Trois-Rivieres, QC, G9A 3P5

Emp Here 49   *Sales* 19,473,286
SIC 8699 Membership organizations, nec
France Leclerc

D-U-N-S 20-263-5090   (SL)
MENTHES RITO LTEE, LES
1055 Rue La Verendrye, Trois-Rivieres, QC, G9A 2T1
(819) 379-1449
Emp Here 30   *Sales* 25,067,310
SIC 5145 Confectionery
Peter Nassif

D-U-N-S 20-571-9722   (BR)
METRO RICHELIEU INC
SUPER C
(*Suby of* METRO INC)
750 Boul Du Saint-Maurice, Trois-Rivieres, QC, G9A 3P6
(819) 371-1120
Emp Here 100
SIC 5411 Grocery stores
Jean-Francois Tousignant

D-U-N-S 24-179-7208   (SL)
NICO METAL INC
1005 Rue Du Pere-Daniel, Trois-Rivieres, QC, G9A 2W9
(819) 375-6426
Emp Here 70   *Sales* 13,445,950
SIC 3441 Fabricated structural Metal
Guy Pageau
Annie Bergeron

D-U-N-S 20-013-2194   (SL)
OPTIMUM ASSURANCE AGRICOLE INC
UNION QUEBECOISE, COMPAGNIE D'ASSURANCES GENERALES
(*Suby of* OPTIGAM INC)
25 Rue Des Forges Bureau .422, Trois-Rivieres, QC, G9A 6A7
(819) 373-2040
Emp Here 16   *Sales* 29,546,544
SIC 6331 Fire, marine, and casualty insurance
Mario Dumas
Louis Pontbriand
Louis Fontaine
Jean-Claude Page

D-U-N-S 20-317-7357   (BR)
PAPIERS DE PUBLICATION KRUGER INC
KRUGER
(*Suby of* KRUGER INC)
3735 Boul Gene-H.-Kruger, Trois-Rivieres, QC, G9A 6B1
(819) 375-1691
Emp Here 340
SIC 2611 Pulp mills
Pierre Dallaire

D-U-N-S 25-469-1579   (SL)
PIECES D'AUTOS JEAN LEBLANC LTEE
3780 Boul Gene-H.-Kruger, Trois-Rivieres, QC, G9A 4M3
(819) 370-1212
Emp Here 40   *Sales* 19,923,120
SIC 5531 Auto and home supply stores
Jean Leblanc

D-U-N-S 20-263-2766   (SL)
PISCINES LAUNIER INC
CLUB PISCINE
5825 Boul Gene-H.-Kruger, Trois-Rivieres, QC, G9A 4P1
(819) 375-7771
Emp Here 70   *Sales* 17,102,960
SIC 5999 Miscellaneous retail stores, nec

Serge Turmel

D-U-N-S 24-524-8336   (SL)
PLANCHERS DAVA INC, LES
3400 Boul Gene-H.-Kruger, Trois-Rivieres, QC, G9A 4M3
(418) 338-0888
Emp Here 24   *Sales* 12,212,544
SIC 5023 Homefurnishings
Gilbert David

D-U-N-S 24-841-9319   (HQ)
PMA ASSURANCES INC
6405 Rue Christophe-Pelissier, Trois-Rivieres, QC, G9A 5C9
(819) 379-3508
Emp Here 20   *Sales* 503,087,024
SIC 6411 Insurance agents, brokers, and service
Pierre Guillemette
Louis Caron
Rene Thibodeau
Gilles Martel
Richard Lavoie

D-U-N-S 20-322-8168   (SL)
PORTES & FENETRES NOUVEL HORIZON INC
1135 Rue La Verendrye, Trois-Rivieres, QC, G9A 2T1
(819) 694-0783
Emp Here 50   *Sales* 10,141,500
SIC 3442 Metal doors, sash, and trim
Patrick Gregoire
Pierre Trottier

D-U-N-S 24-349-1664   (SL)
S.I.T. (SERVICE D'INTEGRATION AU TRAVAIL)
S.I.T. MAURICIE
1090 Rue La Verendrye, Trois-Rivieres, QC, G9A 2S8
(819) 694-9971
Emp Here 26   *Sales* 18,439,512
SIC 8699 Membership organizations, nec
Mario Vallee
Mario Julien
Mylene Cloutier
Pascal Jutras
Diane Boisvert-Bedard

D-U-N-S 24-344-2816   (SL)
SDF ABRASIF INC
BELLEMARE ABRASIFS & MINERAUX
(*Suby of* GESTION BELLEMARE INC)
8750 Boul Industriel Bureau 202, Trois-Rivieres, QC, G9A 5E1
(819) 697-2408
Emp Here 50   *Sales* 23,751,300
SIC 5085 Industrial supplies
Serge Bellemare

D-U-N-S 24-635-2660   (SL)
SECURITE PLUS MODE PLEIN AIR INC
5426 Boul Gene-H.-Kruger, Trois-Rivieres, QC, G9A 4N8
(819) 379-2434
Emp Here 22   *Sales* 11,451,924
SIC 5099 Durable goods, nec
Pierre Brouillard

D-U-N-S 24-651-1760   (SL)
SEMINAIRE DES TROIS-RIVIERES
MUSEE PIERRE-BOUCHER
858 Rue Laviolette Bureau 553, Trois-Rivieres, QC, G9A 5J1
(819) 376-4459
Emp Here 104   *Sales* 10,308,376
SIC 8211 Elementary and secondary schools
Martin Mgr Veillette
Francoise Chaine
Andre Marcouiller

D-U-N-S 20-996-7426   (SL)
SEMINAIRE DES TROIS-RIVIERES
ARCHIVES DU SEMINAIRE SAINT-JOSEPH DE TROIS-RIVIERES
858 Rue Laviolette, Trois-Rivieres, QC, G9A

5J1
(819) 376-4459
Emp Here 100   *Sales* 9,282,600
SIC 8211 Elementary and secondary schools
Mgr Luc Bouchard
Michel Plourde
Martine Roy
Pierre Leclerc
Alain Gelinas
Claude Lapointe
Francois Donaldson
Martine Roy

D-U-N-S 20-690-8373   (SL)
SERVICE D'IMPARTITION INDUSTRIEL INC
(*Suby of* GROUPE MECANITEC INC)
2300 Rue Jules-Vachon, Trois-Rivieres, QC, G9A 5E1
(819) 374-4647
Emp Here 50   *Sales* 12,309,300
SIC 1796 Installing building equipment
Stephane Champoux
Daniel Caron
Marilyne Masse

D-U-N-S 24-834-9821   (HQ)
SERVITANK INC
SERVITANK PLANT
(*Suby of* GROUPE SOMAVRAC INC)
3450 Boul Gene-H.-Kruger, Trois-Rivieres, QC, G9A 4M3
(819) 379-4081
Sales 92,567,700
SIC 4226 Special warehousing and storage, nec
Marc Paquin

D-U-N-S 24-678-8459   (SL)
SOCIETE TRANSPORT TROIS-RIVIERES
2000 Rue Bellefeuille, Trois-Rivieres, QC, G9A 3Y2
(819) 373-4533
Emp Here 100   *Sales* 66,689,200
SIC 4731 Freight transportation arrangement
Guy D'montigny
Pierre A Dupont
Guy De Montigny
Ginette St-Louis
Denis Beaulieu
Guy Daigle
Carol Cote
Alain Gaudet
Francois Belisle
Luc Tremblay

D-U-N-S 20-263-5702   (HQ)
SOMAVRAC INC
(*Suby of* GROUPE SOMAVRAC INC)
3450 Boul Gene-H.-Kruger, Trois-Rivieres, QC, G9A 4M3
(819) 379-3311
Emp Here 25   *Sales* 25,198,336
SIC 4491 Marine cargo handling
Marc Paquin
Sylvain Demers

D-U-N-S 24-811-6332   (SL)
SPECIALISTES DE L'ELECTROMENAGER, LES
3215 Boul Des Recollets, Trois-Rivieres, QC, G9A 6M1
(819) 693-3393
Emp Here 49   *Sales* 11,286,660
SIC 5722 Household appliance stores
M. Claude Villemaire

D-U-N-S 20-103-6394   (SL)
SYNDICAT CANADIEN DES EMPLOYES DU METIER D'HYDRO-QUEBEC
7080 Rue Marion Bureau 207, Trois-Rivieres, QC, G9A 6G4
(819) 693-1500
Emp Here 49   *Sales* 19,166,742
SIC 8631 Labor organizations
Henri-Paul Masson

D-U-N-S 20-266-7366   (HQ)
THOMAS BELLEMARE LTEE

BETON BELLEMARE
(*Suby of* GESTION BELLEMARE INC)
8750 Boul Industriel, Trois-Rivieres, QC, G9A
5E1
(819) 379-2535
Sales 18,463,950
SIC 1794 Excavation work
Tom Bellemare

D-U-N-S 24-360-4514   (HQ)
**TRANSPORT   BELLEMARE   INTERNA-
TIONAL INC**
EXPRESS S.R.S.
(*Suby of* GESTION BELLEMARE INC)
8750 Boul Industriel, Trois-Rivieres, QC, G9A
5E1
(819) 379-4546
Emp Here 100   *Sales* 30,855,900
SIC 4213 Trucking, except local
Jean-Luc Bellemare

D-U-N-S 20-703-2074   (BR)
TRANSPORT TFI 1, S.E.C.
TRANSPORT J.C. GERMAIN
(*Suby of* TRANSPORT TFI 1, S.E.C.)
1200 Rue Du Pere-Daniel, Trois-Rivieres, QC,
G9A 5R6
(819) 370-3422
Emp Here 250
SIC 4213 Trucking, except local
Jean Claude Germain

D-U-N-S 24-142-0699   (SL)
**TROIS-RIVIERES CHEVROLET BUICK
GMC CADILLAC INC**
4201 Boul Gene-H.-Kruger, Trois-Rivieres,
QC, G9A 4M9
(819) 376-3791
Emp Here 49   *Sales* 24,405,822
SIC 5511 New and used car dealers
Jean Guy Laferte

D-U-N-S 24-295-8643   (SL)
TROIS-RIVIERES NISSAN INC
4700 Rue Real-Proulx, Trois-Rivieres, QC,
G9A 6P9
(819) 379-2611
Emp Here 40   *Sales* 19,923,120
SIC 5511 New and used car dealers
Denis Dusablon
Benoit Dusablon
Martin Beauchesne
Carole Turcotte

D-U-N-S 20-177-4320   (HQ)
UBA INC
PROCHLOR
(*Suby of* GROUPE SOMAVRAC INC)
3450 Boul Gene-H.-Kruger Bureau 100, Trois-
Rivieres, QC, G9A 4M3
(819) 379-3311
Sales 18,988,970
SIC 5169 Chemicals and allied products, nec
Marc Paquin

D-U-N-S 20-650-5062   (BR)
WAL-MART CANADA CORP
WALMART MAGASIN
(*Suby of* WALMART INC.)
4520 Boul Gene-H.-Kruger, Trois-Rivieres,
QC, G9A 4N1
(819) 372-1181
Emp Here 200
SIC 5399 Miscellaneous general merchandise
Patrice Douloubeau

D-U-N-S 25-293-8550   (BR)
**WINNERS MERCHANTS INTERNATIONAL
L.P.**
WINNERS
(*Suby of* THE TJX COMPANIES INC)
4125 Boul Des Recollets, Trois-Rivieres, QC,
G9A 6M1
(819) 370-2001
Emp Here 80
SIC 5651 Family clothing stores

D-U-N-S 20-000-8220   (BR)

WSP CANADA INC
WSP GLOBALE
(*Suby of* AST TRUST COMPANY (CANADA))
3450 Boul Gene-H.-Kruger Bureau 300, Trois-
Rivieres, QC, G9A 4M3
(819) 375-1292
Emp Here 900
SIC 8711 Engineering services
Mitchell Garant

Trois-Rivieres, QC G9B

D-U-N-S 25-480-2705   (SL)
9027-9118 QUEBEC INC
TROIS-RIVIERES HONDA
3115 Boul Saint-Jean, Trois-Rivieres, QC,
G9B 2M3
(819) 377-7500
Emp Here 45   *Sales* 22,413,510
SIC 5511 New and used car dealers
Ronald Lavertu
Pierre Laquerre

D-U-N-S 24-889-8694   (SL)
**AUTOMOBILES BERNIER & CREPEAU
LTEE**
CHRYSLER DODGE JEEP
3100 Boul Saint-Jean, Trois-Rivieres, QC,
G9B 2M9
(819) 377-3077
Emp Here 56   *Sales* 35,239,680
SIC 5511 New and used car dealers
Jean-Guy Crepeau

D-U-N-S 25-248-1254   (HQ)
AUTOMOBILES VIEILLES FORGES LTEE
MERCEDES TROIS-RIVIERES
1500 Boul Arthur-Rousseau, Trois-Rivieres,
QC, G9B 0X4
(819) 373-2355
Emp Here 8   *Sales* 34,610,400
SIC 5511 New and used car dealers
Pierre Desaulniers

D-U-N-S 20-566-0541   (SL)
**CAMIONS FREIGHTLINER M.B. TROIS-
RIVIERES LTEE**
FREIGHTLINER
300 Rue Quenneville, Trois-Rivieres, QC, G9B
1X6
(819) 377-9997
Emp Here 35   *Sales* 14,295,240
SIC 5511 New and used car dealers
Laurent Deshaies
Annie Deshaies
Marc Bellemarre

D-U-N-S 25-027-4495   (BR)
**CIUSSS DE LA MAURICIE-ET-DU-CENTRE-
DU-QUEBEC**
(*Suby of* CIUSSS DE LA MAURICIE-ET-DU-
CENTRE-DU-QUEBEC)
11931 Rue Notre-Dame O, Trois-Rivieres, QC,
G9B 6W9
(819) 377-2441
Emp Here 85
SIC 8069 Specialty hospitals, except psychi-
atric
Nathalie Magnan

D-U-N-S 24-053-9390   (HQ)
COGECO MEDIA INC
CFGE
(*Suby of* GESTION AUDEM INC)
4141 Boul Saint-Jean, Trois-Rivieres, QC,
G9B 2M8
(819) 691-1001
Emp Here 50   *Sales* 83,146,215
SIC 7922 Theatrical producers and services
Richard Lachance
Marie-Claude Laroche
Louis Audet
Christian Jolivet
Patrice Ouimet

Philippe Jette

D-U-N-S 25-233-4552   (BR)
**COMMISSION SCOLAIRE DU CHEMIN-DU-
ROY**
ECOLE SECONDAIRE CHAVIGNY
365 Rue Chavigny, Trois-Rivieres, QC, G9B
1A7
(819) 377-4391
Emp Here 170
SIC 8211 Elementary and secondary schools
Chantal Couturier

D-U-N-S 24-509-1533   (HQ)
CONSULTANTS MESAR INC
(*Suby of* GROUPE MESAR INC)
4500 Rue Charles-Malhiot, Trois-Rivieres,
QC, G9B 0V4
(819) 537-5771
Emp Here 80   *Sales* 22,342,375
SIC 8711 Engineering services
Yvan Masse
Luc Paulin
Roland Courtemanche
Denis Desaulniers

D-U-N-S 20-187-3259   (SL)
ENTRETIEN PARAMEX INC
(*Suby of* GANOTEC INC)
3535 Boul L.-P.-Normand, Trois-Rivieres, QC,
G9B 0G8
(819) 377-5533
Emp Here 100   *Sales* 19,232,800
SIC 7699 Repair services, nec
Sebastien Larivee
Dean J Kampschneider
Michael F. Norton
Thomas S Shelby

D-U-N-S 24-432-1824   (SL)
FERNANDIERE INC, LA
(*Suby of* OLYMEL S.E.C.)
12500 Boul Louis-Loranger, Trois-Rivieres,
QC, G9B 0L9
(819) 374-6977
Emp Here 50   *Sales* 17,284,500
SIC 2011 Meat packing plants
Rejean Nadeau
Paul Beauchamp
Carole Potvin

D-U-N-S 20-234-4201   (SL)
GROUPE PRO-B INC
MECANIQUE PRO-B
(*Suby of* VALLERAND GESTI-CONCEPT
INC)
3535 Boul L.-P.-Normand, Trois-Rivieres, QC,
G9B 0G8
(819) 377-7218
Emp Here 150   *Sales* 40,627,200
SIC 1711 Plumbing, heating, air-conditioning
Nathalie Lemelin
Nicholas Lemelin

D-U-N-S 25-381-0147   (SL)
MADYSTA CONSTRUCTIONS LTEE
MADYSTA TELECOM
3600 Boul L.-P.-Normand, Trois-Rivieres, QC,
G9B 0G2
(819) 377-3336
Emp Here 100   *Sales* 24,618,600
SIC 1799 Special trade contractors, nec
Yvan St-Arnaud

D-U-N-S 20-267-1137   (SL)
MADYSTA TELECOM LTEE
3600 Boul L.-P.-Normand, Trois-Rivieres, QC,
G9B 0G2
(819) 377-3336
Emp Here 100   *Sales* 25,244,200
SIC 1623 Water, sewer, and utility lines
Yvan St-Arnaud

Uashat, QC G4R

D-U-N-S 20-646-0995   (SL)
MARCHE LABRIE & LANDRY INC
IGA
1010 Boul Laure, Uashat, QC, G4R 5P1
(418) 962-7797
Emp Here 100   *Sales* 29,347,700
SIC 5411 Grocery stores
Arlain Labrie

D-U-N-S 24-907-2489   (SL)
STATION INNU ENR
100 Boul Des Montagnais, Uashat, QC, G4R
5P9
(418) 968-4866
Emp Here 25   *Sales* 12,451,950
SIC 5541 Gasoline service stations
Ronald Fontaine

D-U-N-S 25-369-2347   (SL)
**TRANSPORT FERROVIAIRE TSHIUETIN
INC**
TRANSPORT FERROVIAIRE
148 Boul Des Montagnais, Uashat, QC, G4R
5R2
(418) 960-0982
Emp Here 55   *Sales* 21,958,310
SIC 4011 Railroads, line-haul operating
Alexandre Mckenzie
Sharon Schecanapish
Solange Fontaine
Ricky Fontaine
Jonathan St-Onge
Langis Fortin
Christopher Coggan
Orlando Cordova

Upton, QC J0H

D-U-N-S 24-959-6529   (HQ)
125668 CANADA INC
292 Rue Principale, Upton, QC, J0H 2E0
(450) 549-5811
Sales 21,376,170
SIC 5083 Farm and garden machinery
Yvon Phaneuf

D-U-N-S 20-263-7138   (HQ)
**EQUIPEMENTS ADRIEN PHANEUF INC,
LES**
(*Suby of* 125668 CANADA INC)
292 Rue Principale, Upton, QC, J0H 2E0
(450) 549-5811
Sales 60,966,250
SIC 5083 Farm and garden machinery
Charles Phaneuf
Hugues Theroux

Val-D'Or, QC J9P

D-U-N-S 25-336-6132   (HQ)
2985080 CANADA INC
A.B.F. MINES
138 Ch Des Boises Bureau 2, Val-D'Or, QC,
J9P 4N7
(819) 738-5289
Sales 13,592,100
SIC 7699 Repair services, nec
Denis Blanchet

D-U-N-S 20-286-1881   (SL)
9089-8131 QUEBEC INC
P.D.G. MECANIQUE-SOUDURE
2888 Ch Sullivan Bureau 3, Val-D'Or, QC, J9P
0B9
(819) 874-3435
Emp Here 200   *Sales* 44,400,200
SIC 3548 Welding apparatus
Gilles Dufour
Serge Duval
Patrick Forgues

D-U-N-S 25-115-5198   (SL)
9093-3789 QUEBEC INC
METRO PELLETIER CARREFOUR DU NORD-OUEST
1801 3e Av Bureau 180, Val-D'Or, QC, J9P 5K1
(819) 874-7741
Emp Here 75   *Sales* 22,010,775
SIC 5411 Grocery stores
Julie Pelletier
Justin Pelletier

D-U-N-S 20-987-4846   (SL)
9117-9077 QUEBEC INC
INNOVEXPLO
560b 3e Av, Val-D'Or, QC, J9P 1S4
(819) 874-0447
Emp Here 40   *Sales* 12,219,200
SIC 8999 Services, nec
Alain Carrier
Carl Pelletier

D-U-N-S 24-362-9941   (SL)
9192-4548 QUEBEC INC
CUISINE SOLEIL
539 Ch De La Baie-Doree, Val-D'Or, QC, J9P 7B3
(819) 637-2444
Emp Here 30   *Sales* 25,067,310
SIC 5149 Groceries and related products, nec
Marc Paquin
Blandine Arseneault

D-U-N-S 20-715-7566   (HQ)
ABITIBI GEOPHYSIQUE INC
1746 Ch Sullivan, Val-D'Or, QC, J9P 7H1
(819) 874-8800
Sales 11,189,675
SIC 1382 Oil and gas exploration services
Pierre Berube

D-U-N-S 24-570-5504   (BR)
AGNICO EAGLE MINES LIMITED
AGNICO EAGLE MINES, DIVISION GOLDEX
(*Suby of* AGNICO EAGLE MINES LIMITED)
1953 3rd Av O, Val-D'Or, QC, J9P 4N9
(819) 874-7822
Emp Here 248
SIC 1481 NonMetallic mineral services
Daniel Pare

D-U-N-S 20-331-5739   (BR)
ASDR CANADA INC
ASDR ENVIRONNEMENT
(*Suby of* ASDR CANADA INC)
1462 Rue De La Quebecoise, Val-D'Or, QC, J9P 5H4
(819) 757-3039
Emp Here 240
SIC 4953 Refuse systems
Marc Turcotte

D-U-N-S 20-576-1963   (SL)
AUBAINERIE CONCEPT MODE INC, L'
965 Rue Germain, Val-D'Or, QC, J9P 7H7
(819) 824-4377
Emp Here 60   *Sales* 10,763,760
SIC 5651 Family clothing stores
Rejean Dessurault

D-U-N-S 24-059-0922   (BR)
AUTOBUS MAHEUX LTEE, LES
(*Suby of* AUTOBUS MAHEUX LTEE, LES)
855 Boul Barrette, Val-D'Or, QC, J9P 0J8
(819) 825-4767
Emp Here 160
SIC 4151 School buses
Pierre Maheux

D-U-N-S 24-429-7701   (SL)
BETON BARRETTE INC
1000 Boul Barrette, Val-D'Or, QC, J9P 0J8
(819) 825-8112
Emp Here 60   *Sales* 26,830,440
SIC 5032 Brick, stone, and related material
Jean-Felix Barrette

D-U-N-S 20-323-5494   (HQ)

BOIS TURCOTTE LTEE
1338 3e Av, Val-D'Or, QC, J9P 1V5
(819) 824-3661
Emp Here 4   *Sales* 34,879,572
SIC 5039 Construction materials, nec
Sylvie Turcotte
Hugo Bolduc

D-U-N-S 20-580-7675   (HQ)
CENTRE DE SANTE ET DE SERVICES SOCIAUX DE LA VALLEE-DE-L'OR
PAVILLON BOIS-JOLI
1265 Boul Forest, Val-D'Or, QC, J9P 5H3
(819) 825-5858
Sales 85,593,150
SIC 8011 Offices and clinics of medical doctors
Aline Sauvageau

D-U-N-S 20-712-6173   (BR)
COMMISSION SCOLAIRE DE L'OR-ET-DES-BOIS
ECOLE POLYVANTE LE CARREFOUR
(*Suby of* COMMISSION SCOLAIRE DE L'OR-ET-DES-BOIS)
125 Rue Self, Val-D'Or, QC, J9P 3N2
(819) 825-4670
Emp Here 120
SIC 8211 Elementary and secondary schools
Jean Denomme

D-U-N-S 20-712-6256   (BR)
COMMISSION SCOLAIRE DE L'OR-ET-DES-BOIS
CENTRE DE FORMATION PROFESSIONNELLE
(*Suby of* COMMISSION SCOLAIRE DE L'OR-ET-DES-BOIS)
125 Rue Self, Val-D'Or, QC, J9P 3N2
(819) 825-6366
Emp Here 75
SIC 8211 Elementary and secondary schools
Jean-Francois Presse

D-U-N-S 20-882-7253   (HQ)
COMMISSION SCOLAIRE DE L'OR-ET-DES-BOIS
799 Boul Forest, Val-D'Or, QC, J9P 2L4
(819) 825-4220
Sales 82,268,770
SIC 8211 Elementary and secondary schools
Johanne Fournier
Nathalie Legault

D-U-N-S 24-323-6556   (HQ)
DISTRIBUTION SOGITEX INC
1201 Rue Des Manufacturiers, Val-D'Or, QC, J9P 6Y7
(819) 825-2331
Emp Here 22   *Sales* 168,053,000
SIC 5169 Chemicals and allied products, nec
Alain Gaudet
Rene Proulx
Andre Bois

D-U-N-S 20-739-0881   (SL)
DUMAIS, ALBERT INC
CANADIAN TIRE
1806 3e Av, Val-D'Or, QC, J9P 7A9
(819) 825-9999
Emp Here 60   *Sales* 21,852,900
SIC 5014 Tires and tubes
Albert Dumais

D-U-N-S 20-263-9779   (HQ)
EQUIPMENTS INDUSTRIELS I.B.S. VAL D'OR INC, LES
TUBOQUIP
85 Rue Des Distributeurs, Val-D'Or, QC, J9P 6Y1
(819) 825-3179
Sales 28,501,560
SIC 5085 Industrial supplies
Pierre Larocque
Louis Larocque

D-U-N-S 25-378-7147   (SL)
FORAGE LONG TROU CMAC INC

185 Rue Des Distributeurs, Val-D'Or, QC, J9P 6Y1
(819) 874-8303
Emp Here 135   *Sales* 322,319,115
SIC 1081 Metal mining services
Claude Macdonald

D-U-N-S 25-341-5103   (HQ)
FORAGE ORBIT GARANT INC
3200 Boul Jean-Jacques-Cossette, Val-D'Or, QC, J9P 6Y6
(819) 824-2707
Emp Here 40   *Sales* 93,124,546
SIC 1041 Gold ores
Eric Alexandre
Pierre Alexandre
Alain Laplante
Michel Mathieu
Paul Carmel
William N. Gula
Jean-Yves Laliberte

D-U-N-S 20-238-3329   (SL)
GARAGE POIRIER & FILS LTEE
POIRIER DODGE CHRYSLER
1780 3e Av, Val-D'Or, QC, J9P 1W4
(819) 825-5214
Emp Here 30   *Sales* 14,942,340
SIC 5521 Used car dealers
Remi Poirier
Rene Poirier

D-U-N-S 20-263-9571   (SL)
GAREAU AUTO INC
1100 3e Av E, Val-D'Or, QC, J9P 0J6
(819) 825-6880
Emp Here 55   *Sales* 34,610,400
SIC 5511 New and used car dealers
Yvon Gareau
Pascal Gareau
Diane Grandmaison

D-U-N-S 24-256-3096   (SL)
GROUPE AUBE LTEE
AUBE KIA
1908 3e Av, Val-D'Or, QC, J9P 7B1
(819) 825-6440
Emp Here 50   *Sales* 24,903,900
SIC 5511 New and used car dealers
Yves Aube

D-U-N-S 20-363-3057   (HQ)
GROUPE MINIER CMAC-THYSSEN INC
1254 Av 3e E, Val-D'Or, QC, J9P 0J6
(819) 874-8303
Sales 159,282,000
SIC 1794 Excavation work
Luc Guimond
Ghislain Blanchet
Steve Laliberte
Jim Haines
Dave Mcintyre

D-U-N-S 24-820-1311   (SL)
HARDY RINGUETTE AUTOMOBILE INC
1842 3e Av Bureau 610, Val-D'Or, QC, J9P 7A9
(819) 874-5151
Emp Here 50   *Sales* 24,903,900
SIC 5511 New and used car dealers
Dominic Hardy

D-U-N-S 25-324-2093   (HQ)
HARMONIA ASSURANCE INC
ADC ASSURANCES ABITIBI
1100 3e Av, Val-D'Or, QC, J9P 1T6
(819) 825-8673
Emp Here 16   *Sales* 138,580,650
SIC 6411 Insurance agents, brokers, and service
Marc Bourcier
Annette Dufour
Francois Boyer
Martin Michaud
Roger Godbout
Richard Bertrand

D-U-N-S 25-673-0359   (BR)

HECLA QUEBEC INC
HECLA QUEBEC - CASA BERARDI
(*Suby of* HECLA MINING COMPANY)
1010 3e Rue, Val-D'Or, QC, J9P 4B1
(819) 874-4511
Emp Here 300
SIC 1081 Metal mining services
Alain Grenier

D-U-N-S 24-820-4844   (SL)
HOTEL FORESTEL VAL-D'OR INC
HOTEL FORESTEL CENTRE DES CONGRES
(*Suby of* ENTREPRISES GAREAU AUTO (1998) INC, LES)
1001 3e Av, Val-D'Or, QC, J9P 1T4
(819) 825-5660
Emp Here 130   *Sales* 12,049,700
SIC 7011 Hotels and motels
Robert F Lariviere

D-U-N-S 20-590-0991   (BR)
HYDRO-QUEBEC
(*Suby of* GOUVERNEMENT DE LA PROVINCE DE QUEBEC)
1600 Rue De L'Hydro, Val-D'Or, QC, J9P 6Z1
(819) 825-4880
Emp Here 114
SIC 4911 Electric services
Marcel Courchesne

D-U-N-S 20-302-1444   (BR)
HYDRO-QUEBEC
(*Suby of* GOUVERNEMENT DE LA PROVINCE DE QUEBEC)
1600 Rue De L'Hydro, Val-D'Or, QC, J9P 6Z1
(819) 825-3320
Emp Here 94
SIC 4911 Electric services
Andre Bergevim

D-U-N-S 24-759-1332   (SL)
KEPA TRANSPORT INC
12 Rue Finlay, Val-D'Or, QC, J9P 0K9
(819) 874-0262
Emp Here 80   *Sales* 16,456,480
SIC 4213 Trucking, except local
George Bobbish
Danny Tomatuk
Thomas Shem
Joseph Georgekish
Tony Gull
Daisy House
Marie Bogelic

D-U-N-S 20-263-9498   (HQ)
L. FOURNIER ET FILS INC
FOURNIER BETON
1095 Rue Leo-Fournier, Val-D'Or, QC, J9P 6X6
(819) 825-4000
Sales 36,927,900
SIC 1794 Excavation work
Serge Fournier
Nicolas Beaudet-Fournier
Jeremi Beaudet-Fournier

D-U-N-S 25-447-8936   (BR)
LOBLAWS INC
LOBLAW
(*Suby of* LOBLAW COMPANIES LIMITED)
502 Rue Giguere, Val-D'Or, QC, J9P 7G6
(819) 825-5000
Emp Here 120
SIC 5141 Groceries, general line
Gilles Ferland

D-U-N-S 24-515-3135   (SL)
MACHINES ROGER INTERNATIONAL INC
FORAGE ALXTREME
(*Suby of* MACHINES ROGER LTEE, LES)
1161 Rue Des Manufacturiers, Val-D'Or, QC, J9P 6Y7
(819) 825-4657
Emp Here 50   *Sales* 23,751,300
SIC 5082 Construction and mining machinery
Alexandre Beland

Alain Beland
Reynald Gauthier

D-U-N-S 24-859-8661   (SL)
MARQUIS CONCEPT INC, LE
MAISON S.M.A.R.T.
180 Av Champlain, Val-D'Or, QC, J9P 2B6
(819) 825-5515
Emp Here 100   Sales 25,244,200
SIC 1623 Water, sewer, and utility lines
Mario Turcotte

D-U-N-S 24-942-7600   (HQ)
MEGLAB ELECTRONIQUE INC
281 19e Rue, Val-D'Or, QC, J9P 0L7
(819) 824-7710
Sales 11,961,048
SIC 7629 Electrical repair shops
Louis Valade
Sylvain Viger
Dominic Valade
Ghislain Blanchet

D-U-N-S 24-863-0055   (HQ)
MEUBLES MARCHAND INC, LES
(*Suby of* GROUPE MARCHAND INC, LE)
1767 3e Av, Val-D'Or, QC, J9P 1W3
(819) 874-8777
Emp Here 50   Sales 13,479,374
SIC 5712 Furniture stores
Marcel Marchand
Christian Marchand
Gisele Marchand
Dany Marchand

D-U-N-S 20-188-6467   (HQ)
MINES DE LA VALLEE DE L'OR LTEE
152 Ch De La Mine-Ecole, Val-D'Or, QC, J9P 7B6
(819) 824-2808
Emp Here 1   Sales 11,937,745
SIC 1081 Metal mining services
Glenn J Mullan
Michael P. Rosatelli
Joseph Groia
Jimmy Lee
William Mccartney

D-U-N-S 20-703-6885   (HQ)
PETRONOR INC
PRODUITS PETROLIERS HARRICANA (1993)
1401 Ch Sullivan, Val-D'Or, QC, J9P 6V6
(819) 824-5505
Emp Here 4   Sales 56,574,045
SIC 5172 Petroleum products, nec
Ted Moses
Richard Brouillard
George Wapachee
John Logchap
Tony Gull
Dany Tomatuk
Thomas Shem
George Bobbish

D-U-N-S 24-900-4664   (HQ)
PLACEMENTS YVON GAREAU INC, LES
(*Suby of* ENTREPRISES GAREAU AUTO (1998) INC, LES)
1100 3e Av, Val-D'Or, QC, J9P 1T6
(819) 825-6880
Emp Here 1   Sales 47,516,170
SIC 6712 Bank holding companies
Yvon Gareau
Diane Grandmaison

D-U-N-S 25-357-6920   (SL)
PROCON EST DU CANADA LTEE
1400 4e Av, Val-D'Or, QC, J9P 5Z9
(819) 824-2074
Emp Here 250   Sales 63,943,500
SIC 1081 Metal mining services
John Mcvey
John Caldbick
Jocelyn Deschenes
Guoqing Kang
Christina Cheung

D-U-N-S 25-527-6255   (SL)
PROPANE NORD-OUEST INC
2701 Boul Jean-Jacques-Cossette, Val-D'Or, QC, J9P 6Y3
(819) 824-6778
Emp Here 30   Sales 14,070,150
SIC 5984 Liquefied petroleum gas dealers
Lucien Mirault
Michael Mirault
Sabrina Mirault

D-U-N-S 25-176-0208   (BR)
QMX GOLD CORPORATION
(*Suby of* QMX GOLD CORPORATION)
1900 Ch Brador, Val-D'Or, QC, J9P 0A4
(819) 825-3412
Emp Here 100
SIC 1081 Metal mining services
Patrick Sevigny

D-U-N-S 24-434-0456   (SL)
RAYMOND BEAUSEJOUR (1989) INC
BEAUSEJOUR SHELL
202 3e Av, Val-D'Or, QC, J9P 1R5
(819) 824-4185
Emp Here 45   Sales 22,413,510
SIC 5541 Gasoline service stations
Eric Beausejour

D-U-N-S 24-297-2503   (SL)
RENE ET MARCO DESROCHER CONSTRUCTION INC
1470 4e Rue, Val-D'Or, QC, J9P 6X2
(819) 825-4279
Emp Here 26   Sales 12,239,006
SIC 1542 Nonresidential construction, nec
Rene Desrochers
Marco Desrochers
Rejean Martel

D-U-N-S 20-193-7724   (SL)
RESSOURCES METANOR INC
(*Suby of* BONTERRA RESOURCES INC)
2872 Ch Sullivan Bureau 2, Val-D'Or, QC, J9P 0B9
(819) 825-8678
Emp Here 260   Sales 41,878,180
SIC 1041 Gold ores
Greg Gibson
Anik Gendron
Nav Dhaliwal
Dale Ginn

D-U-N-S 20-264-0454   (HQ)
ROYMICK INC
PHARMACIE JEAN COUTU
823 3e Av Bureau 31, Val-D'Or, QC, J9P 1S8
(819) 824-3645
Emp Here 60   Sales 18,324,600
SIC 5912 Drug stores and proprietary stores
Roger Roy
Michel Gervais
Alexandre Roy

D-U-N-S 24-425-7437   (SL)
SERVICES DE FORAGE ORBIT GARANT INC
(*Suby of* FORAGE ORBIT GARANT INC)
3200 Boul Jean-Jacques-Cossette, Val-D'Or, QC, J9P 6Y6
(819) 824-2707
Emp Here 700   Sales 92,992,125
SIC 1081 Metal mining services
Eric Alexandre
Paul Raymond Carmel
Pierre Alexandre
Alain Laplante

D-U-N-S 20-151-7781   (HQ)
SNC-LAVALIN STAVIBEL INC
GROUPE STAVIBEL
(*Suby of* GROUPE SNC-LAVALIN INC)
1271 7e Rue, Val-D'Or, QC, J9P 3S1
(819) 825-2233
Emp Here 60   Sales 53,621,700
SIC 8711 Engineering services
Arden R. Furlotte

Terry Lefebvre
Robert Landry

D-U-N-S 20-514-9180   (HQ)
SOQUEM INC
SOCIETE QUEBECOISE D'EXPLORATION MINIERE
(*Suby of* INVESTISSEMENT QUEBEC)
1740 Ch Sullivan Bureau 2000, Val-D'Or, QC, J9P 7H1
(819) 874-3773
Emp Here 11   Sales 136,090,293
SIC 1081 Metal mining services
Luc Seguin
Marc Paquet
Jean-Jacques Carrier
Yves Bourque

D-U-N-S 24-934-7931   (SL)
SUPERMARCHE PELLETIER INC
IGA PELLETIER
1177 8e Rue, Val-D'Or, QC, J9P 1R1
(819) 825-6608
Emp Here 100   Sales 29,347,700
SIC 5411 Grocery stores
Jacques Pelletier
Josette Pelletier

D-U-N-S 20-309-6359   (SL)
TECHNOLOGIES ELEMENT PSW INC
1117 Rue Des Manufacturiers, Val-D'Or, QC, J9P 6Y7
(819) 825-1117
Emp Here 26   Sales 12,350,676
SIC 5082 Construction and mining machinery
Patrick Element
Patrick Ouellet
Jacques Element

D-U-N-S 20-651-9238   (BR)
TELEBEC, SOCIETE EN COMMANDITE
(*Suby of* TELEBEC, SOCIETE EN COMMANDITE)
100 Rue Des Distributeurs, Val-D'Or, QC, J9P 6Y1
(819) 824-7451
Emp Here 100
SIC 4813 Telephone communication, except radio
Mike Primeau

D-U-N-S 20-517-5339   (SL)
TIGRE VAL D'OR LIMITEE
TIGRE GEANT
(*Suby of* GIANT TIGER STORES LIMITED)
825 3e Av, Val-D'Or, QC, J9P 1T2
(819) 825-8106
Emp Here 60   Sales 12,320,580
SIC 5311 Department stores
Daniel Charles Andre Rouillard

D-U-N-S 20-213-0188   (BR)
TOROMONT INDUSTRIES LTD
TOROMONT CAT
(*Suby of* TOROMONT INDUSTRIES LTD)
1200 3e Av E, Val-D'Or, QC, J9P 0J6
(819) 825-5494
Emp Here 100
SIC 5082 Construction and mining machinery

D-U-N-S 20-598-0873   (HQ)
TRANSPORT NORD-OUEST INC
1355b Ch Sullivan, Val-D'Or, QC, J9P 1M2
(819) 874-2003
Sales 14,819,200
SIC 4213 Trucking, except local
Gerry Breetvelt
Glenn Breetvelt

D-U-N-S 20-197-4011   (HQ)
TREMBLAY ET FRERES LTEE
97 Boul Lamaque, Val-D'Or, QC, J9P 2H7
(819) 825-7470
Sales 10,122,360
SIC 5211 Lumber and other building materials
Diane Tremblay
Roger Tremblay
Michel Tremblay

D-U-N-S 24-308-1218   (BR)
UNIBOARD CANADA INC
UNIRES, DIV DE
(*Suby of* UNIBOARD CANADA INC)
2700 Boul Jean-Jacques-Cossette, Val-D'Or, QC, J9P 6Y5
(819) 825-6550
Emp Here 180
SIC 2493 Reconstituted wood products

D-U-N-S 24-842-4517   (SL)
VOLUMAT INC
HOME HARDWARE
1716 Ch Sullivan, Val-D'Or, QC, J9P 1M5
(819) 825-3070
Emp Here 100   Sales 26,765,200
SIC 5251 Hardware stores
Michel Poulin
Michel Mathieu
Andre Beaucage
Jonathan Poulin

D-U-N-S 20-103-3359   (BR)
WAL-MART CANADA CORP
(*Suby of* WALMART INC.)
1855 3e Av Bureau 3139, Val-D'Or, QC, J9P 7A9
(819) 874-8411
Emp Here 225
SIC 5311 Department stores
Celine Pilon

D-U-N-S 25-670-2643   (SL)
YOUTH PROTECTION
700 Boul Forest, Val-D'Or, QC, J9P 2L3
(819) 825-0002
Emp Here 49   Sales 11,301,755
SIC 8399 Social services, nec

Val-David, QC J0T

D-U-N-S 20-263-8136   (SL)
DUFRESNE, L. & FILS LTEE
METRO DUFRESNE
(*Suby of* PLACEMENTS FERNAND DUFRESNE INC)
2500 Rue De L'Eglise, Val-David, QC, J0T 2N0
(819) 322-2030
Emp Here 65   Sales 19,076,005
SIC 5411 Grocery stores
Jacques Dufresne

D-U-N-S 20-026-4294   (SL)
HERBORISTERIE LA CLEF DES CHAMPS INC
CLEF DES CHAMPS, LA
2205 Ch De La Riviere, Val-David, QC, J0T 2N0
(819) 322-1561
Emp Here 37   Sales 30,916,349
SIC 5149 Groceries and related products, nec
Marie Provost

D-U-N-S 20-263-8268   (HQ)
MONETTE, EUGENE INC
RENOVATION STE-AGATHE
2650 1er Rang De Doncaster, Val-David, QC, J0T 2N0
(819) 322-3833
Emp Here 55   Sales 18,735,640
SIC 5211 Lumber and other building materials
Micheline Monette
Luc Alarie

Val-Des-Monts, QC J8N

D-U-N-S 20-121-7420   (SL)
GESTION PONTIAC INC
91 Ch Du Fort, Val-Des-Monts, QC, J8N 4H4

Emp Here 26   Sales 12,950,028

▲ Public Company   ■ Public Company Family Member   **HQ** Headquarters   **BR** Branch   **SL** Single Location

SIC 5511 New and used car dealers
Luc Blanchard

Val-Joli, QC J1S

D-U-N-S 24-020-2085   (HQ)
BESSETTE ET BOUDREAU INC
GESTION SYREBEC
680 Rte 143, Val-Joli, QC, J1S 0G6
(819) 845-7722
Emp Here 140   *Sales* 30,855,900
SIC 4212 Local trucking, without storage
Benoit Rouillard

D-U-N-S 24-509-4339   (SL)
CONSTRUCTIONS E.D.B. INC
(Suby of 2535-1396 QUEBEC INC)
545 Rte 249, Val-Joli, QC, J1S 0E6
(819) 845-5436
Emp Here 150   *Sales* 33,300,150
SIC 3554 Paper industries machinery
Yvan Frappier
Martial Frappier

D-U-N-S 24-907-7652   (BR)
DOMTAR INC
USINE DE PAPIERS WINDSOR
(Suby of DOMTAR LUXEMBOURG INVEST-
MENTS SARL)
609 12e Rang, Val-Joli, QC, J1S 0H1
(819) 845-2771
Emp Here 950
SIC 2621 Paper mills
Martin Lorrion

D-U-N-S 20-315-2137   (SL)
FRANK LOGAN
485 249 Rte, Val-Joli, QC, J1S 0E8
(819) 845-4901
Emp Here 25   *Sales* 31,430,025
SIC 5171 Petroleum bulk stations and termi-
nals
Frank Logan

Valcourt, QC J0E

D-U-N-S 20-277-8205   (SL)
2948-4292 QUEBEC INC
ECO-PAK
9072 Rue De La Montagne, Valcourt, QC, J0E
2L0
(450) 532-2270
Emp Here 100   *Sales* 44,921,900
SIC 7389 Business services, nec
Yves Poisson
Marc Picard
Julien Claudy
Daniel Jourdain

D-U-N-S 20-956-4488   (BR)
BOMBARDIER PRODUITS RECREATIFS
INC
BASI
(Suby of BRP INC)
565 Rue De La Montagne Bureau 210, Val-
court, QC, J0E 2L0
(450) 532-2211
Emp Here 100
SIC 3799 Transportation equipment, nec
Jose Boisjoli

D-U-N-S 25-412-7301   (HQ)
BOMBARDIER PRODUITS RECREATIFS
INC
(Suby of BRP INC)
726 Rue Saint-Joseph, Valcourt, QC, J0E 2L0
(450) 532-2211
Emp Here 100   *Sales* 2,019,662,400
SIC 3799 Transportation equipment, nec
Jose Boisjoli
Martin Langelier

Joshua Bekenstein
Andre J.R. Bombardier
Daniel J. O'neill
Edward Philip
Michael Hanley
Joseph Robbins
Louis Laporte
Estelle Metayer

D-U-N-S 20-700-6243   (HQ)
BRP INC
726 Rue Saint-Joseph, Valcourt, QC, J0E 2L0
(450) 532-2211
Emp Here 13   *Sales* 3,916,505,075
SIC 5012 Automobiles and other motor vehi-
cles
Jose Boisjoli
Martin Langelier
Karim Donnez
Anne-Marie Laberge
Bernard Guy
Thomas Uhr
Denys Lapointe
Anne Le Breton
Josee Perreault
Sandy Scullion

D-U-N-S 20-263-8052   (SL)
COOPTEL COOP DE TELECOMMUNICA-
TION
INTERURBAIN COOPTEL
5521 Ch De L'Aeroport, Valcourt, QC, J0E 2L0
(450) 532-2667
Emp Here 59   *Sales* 10,903,082
SIC 4813 Telephone communication, except
radio
Patrice Dupont
Laurian Gagne
Claude Chouinard
Lyne Laverdure
Marie Eve Rocheleau
Eric Charbonneau
Lyne Leblanc
Jocelyn Poitras
Eugene Robitaille

D-U-N-S 20-263-7906   (HQ)
J.M.F. TRANSPORT (1992) LTEE
J.M.F. TRANSPORT
(Suby of KRISKA TRANSPORTATION
GROUP LIMITED)
5609 Ch De L'Aeroport, Valcourt, QC, J0E 2L0
(450) 532-2285
Emp Here 1   *Sales* 13,370,890
SIC 4212 Local trucking, without storage
Mark D. Seymour
Murray K. Mullen
Pierre Carrier

D-U-N-S 24-253-9294   (HQ)
VERBOM INC
5066 Rte 222, Valcourt, QC, J0E 2L0
(450) 532-3672
Sales 11,286,045
SIC 5051 Metals service centers and offices
Mario Beaudoin
Nicolas Bombardier
Eric Chenevert
Yvon Laplante

D-U-N-S 20-680-5835   (SL)
VERBOM INC
5066 Rte 222, Valcourt, QC, J0E 2L0
(819) 566-4200
Emp Here 250   *Sales* 45,347,000
SIC 3365 Aluminum foundries
Mario Beaudoin
Nicolas Bombardier
Eric Chenevert
Yvon Laplante

Vallee-Jonction, QC G0S

D-U-N-S 24-200-6229   (SL)

ACIERS REMI LATULIPPE INC, LES
481 112 Rte E, Vallee-Jonction, QC, G0S 3J0
(418) 253-5521
Emp Here 127   *Sales* 88,303,100
SIC 5093 Scrap and waste materials
Yolande Latulippe

D-U-N-S 25-010-4874   (BR)
OLYMEL S.E.C.
FLAMINGO
(Suby of OLYMEL S.E.C.)
568 Ch De L'Ecore S, Vallee-Jonction, QC,
G0S 3J0
(418) 253-5437
Emp Here 1,200
SIC 2011 Meat packing plants
Claude Chedeleine

D-U-N-S 20-257-8118   (HQ)
TRANSPORT L.F.L. INC
(Suby of TURCOTTE, DOMINIQUE INC)
431 Ch De L'Ecore N, Vallee-Jonction, QC,
G0S 3J0
(418) 253-5423
Emp Here 50   *Sales* 41,485,725
SIC 4213 Trucking; except local
Dominique Turcotte

Varennes, QC J3X

D-U-N-S 24-946-2201   (SL)
151210 CANADA INC
245 Rue Jean-Coutu, Varennes, QC, J3X 0E1
(450) 646-9760
Emp Here 955   *Sales* 349,061,095
SIC 6712 Bank holding companies
Jean Coutu
Francois J. Coutu

D-U-N-S 25-241-8843   (SL)
2913097 CANADA INC
RAIL CANTECH
(Suby of VINCI)
650 Boul Lionel-Boulet, Varennes, QC, J3X
1P7
(450) 652-5400
Emp Here 100   *Sales* 25,244,200
SIC 1629 Heavy construction, nec
Martial Major
Rene Massicotte
Sylvain Malenfant

D-U-N-S 20-190-5135   (SL)
9332-3301 QUEBEC INC
84 Rue Riendeau, Varennes, QC, J3X 1P7
(450) 652-9871
Emp Here 75   *Sales* 18,463,950
SIC 1794 Excavation work
Laurent Bourget

D-U-N-S 24-502-6554   (BR)
ABB INC
(Suby of ABB LTD)
1600 Boul Lionel-Boulet, Varennes, QC, J3X
1P7
(450) 652-1500
Emp Here 317
SIC 3612 Transformers, except electric
Tom Mcdonald

D-U-N-S 20-703-4906   (BR)
ACIER PICARD INC
(Suby of ACIER PICARD INC)
1951 Ch De L'Energie, Varennes, QC, J3X
1P7
(450) 652-7000
Emp Here 150
SIC 5051 Metals service centers and offices
Alain Boyte

D-U-N-S 20-979-3199   (SL)
CENTRE D'INFORMATION RX LTEE
(Suby of METRO INC)
245 Rue Jean-Coutu, Varennes, QC, J3X 0E1

(450) 646-9760
Emp Here 70   *Sales* 11,679,290
SIC 7376 Computer facilities management
Jean Coutu
Francois Jean Coutu
Brigitte Dufour
Andre Belzile

D-U-N-S 24-857-4998   (HQ)
ENTREPRISES DE CONSTRUCTION RE-
FRABEC INC, LES
925 Boul Lionel-Boulet, Varennes, QC, J3X
1P7
(450) 652-5391
Emp Here 154   *Sales* 39,389,760
SIC 1796 Installing building equipment
Alex Beauchemin
Andre Beauchemin

D-U-N-S 25-628-2450   (SL)
EQUIPEMENTS LAGUE & MARTIN INC
JOHN DEERE
555 Boul Lionel-Boulet, Varennes, QC, J3X
1P7
(450) 929-2382
Emp Here 22   *Sales* 10,450,572
SIC 5083 Farm and garden machinery
Rejean Martin
Andre Lague

D-U-N-S 20-264-8572   (SL)
GOYETTE, MAURICE PONTIAC BUICK
1983 INC
1623 132 Rte, Varennes, QC, J3X 1P7

Emp Here 48   *Sales* 23,907,744
SIC 5511 New and used car dealers
Louis Jazzar

D-U-N-S 20-013-1527   (HQ)
GROUPE AMEUBLEMENT FOCUS INC
AMEUBLEMENT DE BUREAU FOCUS
1567 Boul Lionel-Boulet, Varennes, QC, J3X
1P7
(514) 644-5551
Emp Here 50   *Sales* 77,674,680
SIC 5021 Furniture
Stephane Lemieux
Anthony Simon

D-U-N-S 20-887-0758   (HQ)
GROUPE JEAN COUTU (PJC) INC, LE
PJC JEAN COUTU SANTE
(Suby of METRO INC)
245 Rue Jean-Coutu, Varennes, QC, J3X 0E1
(450) 646-9760
Emp Here 1,350   *Sales* 8,296,050,816
SIC 5122 Drugs, proprietaries, and sundries
Francois J Coutu
Jean Coutu
Brigitte Dufour
Guy Franche
Andre Belzile
Jean-Michel Coutu
Alain Lafortune
Richard Mayrand
Normand Messier
Helene Bisson

D-U-N-S 25-392-2389   (HQ)
GROUPE SOLMAX INC
(Suby of INVESTISSEMENTS FLYDZO INC)
2801 Rte Marie-Victorin, Varennes, QC, J3X
1P7
(450) 929-1234
Sales 15,885,800
SIC 3069 Fabricated rubber products, nec
Jacques Cote
Johanne Belanger
Mario Cadorette
Gilles Veilleux
Carmine Nappi
Garry Savage

D-U-N-S 20-355-8077   (SL)
GROUPE THOMAS MARINE INC
PILON MARINE
550 Boul Lionel-Boulet, Varennes, QC, J3X

1P7
(877) 652-2999
Emp Here 26   *Sales* 12,950,028
SIC 5551 Boat dealers
  Marc-Andre Thomas
  Jean-Simon Thomas
  Maxime Thomas
  Alain Ferron
  Claude Thomas

D-U-N-S 24-908-0664   (HQ)
GSI ENVIRONNEMENT INC
BIOSITE
(*Suby of* ONCAP II L.P.)
100 Rue Jean-Coutu Bureau 101, Varennes,
QC, J3X 0E1
(418) 882-2736
Emp Here 40   *Sales* 107,159,445
SIC 2875 Fertilizers, mixing only
  Robert Youden
  Lynda Beaudin

D-U-N-S 24-167-7525   (BR)
HYDRO-QUEBEC
IREQ
(*Suby of* GOUVERNEMENT DE LA
PROVINCE DE QUEBEC)
1800 Boul Lionel-Boulet, Varennes, QC, J3X
1P7
(450) 925-2008
Emp Here 750
SIC 8731 Commercial physical research
  Denis Faubert

D-U-N-S 24-612-5579   (HQ)
KEMIRA WATER SOLUTIONS CANADA INC
ENVIRONNEMENT KEMIRA QUEBEC, L'
(*Suby of* KEMIRA OYJ)
3405 Rte Marie-Victorin, Varennes, QC, J3X
1P7
(450) 652-0665
Sales 31,242,310
SIC 2836 Biological products, except diagnostic
  Manuel Moreau
  Tuija Pohjolainen-Hiltunen
  Susan B. Radcliffe
  Myriam Tessier

D-U-N-S 20-264-8424   (BR)
KRONOS CANADA INC
(*Suby of* KRONOS WORLDWIDE, INC.)
3390 Rte Marie-Victorin, Varennes, QC, J3X
1P7
(450) 929-5000
Emp Here 450
SIC 2816 Inorganic pigments
  Richard Coulombe

D-U-N-S 24-698-6012   (HQ)
LABORATOIRES D'ANALYSES S.M. INC
(*Suby of* GROUPE SMI INC, LE)
1471 Boul Lionel-Boulet, Varennes, QC, J3X
1P7
(514) 332-6001
Emp Here 100
SIC 8731 Commercial physical research

D-U-N-S 25-104-6124   (SL)
LABORATOIRES MSP INC
LABORATOIRES MSA
2401 Montee De Picardie, Varennes, QC, J3X
0J1
(450) 652-4295
Emp Here 48   *Sales* 10,793,040
SIC 2023 Dry, condensed and evaporated
dairy products
  Martial St-Pierre

D-U-N-S 20-261-3816   (HQ)
LAITERIE CHALIFOUX INC
FROMAGES RIVIERA, LES
(*Suby of* PL NOUVELLE FRANCE INC)
1625 Boul Lionel-Boulet Local 203, Varennes,
QC, J3X 1P7
(450) 809-0211
Emp Here 25   *Sales* 34,569,000
SIC 2022 Cheese; natural and processed

Alain Chalifoux
Martin Valiquette

D-U-N-S 20-321-5384   (SL)
MAESTRO TECHNOLOGIES INC
1625 Boul Lionel-Boulet Bureau 300,
Varennes, QC, J3X 1P7
(450) 652-6200
Emp Here 50   *Sales* 10,692,550
SIC 7372 Prepackaged software
  Robert Meunier

D-U-N-S 24-127-6562   (SL)
MARCOTTE SYSTEMES LTEE
1471 Boul Lionel-Boulet Unite 28, Varennes,
QC, J3X 1P7
(450) 652-6000
Emp Here 30   *Sales* 14,250,780
SIC 5084 Industrial machinery and equipment
  Fyed Mohamed
  Denis-Raymond Marcotte

D-U-N-S 25-976-8398   (SL)
MARINE DEPOT INC
550 Boul Lionel-Boulet, Varennes, QC, J3X
1P7
(450) 652-2999
Emp Here 50   *Sales* 24,903,900
SIC 5551 Boat dealers
  Claude Thomas

D-U-N-S 24-309-7552   (HQ)
MOMETAL STRUCTURES INC
STRUCTURES MOMETAL
201 Ch De L'Energie, Varennes, QC, J3X 1P7
(450) 929-3999
Sales 19,694,880
SIC 1791 Structural steel erection
  Erik Lafontaine

D-U-N-S 25-962-8352   (SL)
PASSION CUISINE ET GOURMET
2020 Boul Rene-Gaultier Bureau 36,
Varennes, QC, J3X 1N9
(450) 929-2942
Emp Here 64   *Sales* 14,873,792
SIC 5719 Miscellaneous homefurnishings
  Catherine Denis

D-U-N-S 20-639-6611   (SL)
PHARMAPAR INC
PRIVALAB
1565 Boul Lionel-Boulet, Varennes, QC, J3X
1P7
(514) 731-2003
Emp Here 13   *Sales* 14,369,485
SIC 5122 Drugs, proprietaries, and sundries
  Marc Lemieux
  Kumar Pillai Mohana
  Mohan Devineni
  Sanjay Bangalore

D-U-N-S 20-381-5063   (HQ)
PL NOUVELLE FRANCE INC
1625 Boul Lionel-Boulet Local 203, Varennes,
QC, J3X 1P7
(450) 809-0211
Sales 27,335,000
SIC 6712 Bank holding companies
  Frederic Madon
  Alain Chalifoux
  Michel Debes
  Maxime Chalifoux
  Martin Chalifoux

D-U-N-S 20-532-9316   (BR)
PLACEMENTS C. D. F. G. INC
(*Suby of* PLACEMENTS C. D. F. G. INC)
59 Rue De L'Aqueduc, Varennes, QC, J3X 2J3

Emp Here 84
SIC 7389 Business services, nec
  Guy Trudel

D-U-N-S 24-138-0547   (BR)
SOBEYS QUEBEC INC
IGA
1777 Rte 132, Varennes, QC, J3X 1P7

(450) 929-0405
Emp Here 150   *Sales* 822,456
SIC 5411 Grocery stores
  Yves Lalonde

D-U-N-S 20-184-0787   (SL)
SOLMAX INTERNATIONAL INC
(*Suby of* INVESTISSEMENTS FLYDZO INC)
2801 Rte Marie-Victorin, Varennes, QC, J3X
1P7
(450) 929-1234
Emp Here 50   *Sales* 10,094,850
SIC 3081 Unsupported plastics film and sheet
  Jean-Louis Vangheluwe
  Johanne Belanger
  Jacques Cote

D-U-N-S 20-955-3531   (SL)
SUPPLEMENTS AROMATIK INC
AROMATIK
2334 Rte Marie-Victorin Bureau 87, Varennes,
QC, J3X 1R4
(450) 929-1933
Emp Here 45   *Sales* 12,449,700
SIC 2833 Medicinals and botanicals
  Michael Deslandes

D-U-N-S 20-264-8895   (HQ)
THOMAS, RENE & FILS INC
HOME HARDWARE
10 Rue Beauregard, Varennes, QC, J3X 1R1
(450) 652-2927
Emp Here 36   *Sales* 13,382,600
SIC 5211 Lumber and other building materials
  Rene Thomas Jr
  Florian Thomas
  Hugues Thomas

D-U-N-S 25-381-1483   (SL)
TRANSPORT ROLLEX LTEE
(*Suby of* GROUPE ROBERT INC)
910 Boul Lionel-Boulet, Varennes, QC, J3X
1P7
(450) 652-4282
Emp Here 112
SIC 4953 Refuse systems
  Claude Robert
  Gerard Bernard
  Michel Robert

D-U-N-S 25-392-6869   (BR)
UNIVERSITE DU QUEBEC
*INSTITUT NATIONAL DE LA RECHERCHE
SCIENTIFIQUE ENERGIE & MATERIAUX*
(*Suby of* UNIVERSITE DU QUEBEC)
1650 Boul Lionel-Boulet, Varennes, QC, J3X
1P7
(450) 929-8100
Emp Here 80
SIC 8733 Noncommercial research organizations
  Jean-Claude Kieffer

Vaudreuil-Dorion, QC G7V

D-U-N-S 20-018-7995   (SL)
PORTES ET FENETRES ROYALTY
17 Boulevard Cite Des Jeunes, Vaudreuil-
Dorion, QC, G7V 9E8
(450) 218-4411
Emp Here 45   *Sales* 11,387,655
SIC 5211 Lumber and other building materials
  Tony Ciobirca

Vaudreuil-Dorion, QC J7V

D-U-N-S 25-209-9213   (HQ)
1021076 ONTARIO INC
KERR NORTON
434 Rue Aime-Vincent, Vaudreuil-Dorion, QC,
J7V 5V5

(450) 510-0560
Sales 13,415,220
SIC 5044 Office equipment
  Edouard Pahud

D-U-N-S 24-935-1867   (HQ)
168406 CANADA INC
FASTCO CANADA
(*Suby of* 6895051 CANADA INC)
135 Rue Du Cheminot, Vaudreuil-Dorion, QC,
J7V 5V5
(450) 455-9877
Emp Here 50   *Sales* 29,651,744
SIC 5013 Motor vehicle supplies and new
parts
  Glenn Chaplin
  Patricia Chaplin
  Bob Chaplin
  Lee Chaplin

D-U-N-S 20-291-2416   (HQ)
2871149 CANADA INC
PATISSERIE BRUXELLOISE
189 Boul Harwood, Vaudreuil-Dorion, QC, J7V
1Y3
(450) 455-2827
Emp Here 1   *Sales* 73,467,309
SIC 6712 Bank holding companies
  Liliane Colpron
  Stephane Fiset
  Josee Fiest
  Bernard Fiest

D-U-N-S 25-147-6305   (SL)
2960-7082 QUEBEC INC
EXCELLENCE DODGE CHRYSLER JEEP
115 Rue Joseph-Carrier, Vaudreuil-Dorion,
QC, J7V 5V5
(450) 455-5555
Emp Here 35   *Sales* 17,432,730
SIC 5511 New and used car dealers
  Michel Bourdeau
  Serge Bourdeau

D-U-N-S 24-015-9660   (SL)
3235149 CANADA INC
REAL TRANSPORT
1033 Rue Valois, Vaudreuil-Dorion, QC, J7V
8P2
(450) 455-4545
Emp Here 35   *Sales* 13,487,600
SIC 4731 Freight transportation arrangement
  Parmjit Singh Kainth

D-U-N-S 20-331-7730   (SL)
3367771 CANADA INC
BOULANGERIE PREMIERE MOISSON
(*Suby of* METRO INC)
189 Boul Harwood, Vaudreuil-Dorion, QC, J7V
1Y3
(450) 455-2827
Emp Here 26   *Sales* 21,725,002
SIC 5149 Groceries and related products, nec
  Serge Boulanger
  Josee Fiset
  Simon Rivet

D-U-N-S 25-674-9466   (SL)
3427277 CANADA INC
COMMERCE GLOBAL DU PAPIER
887 Rte Harwood Bureau 53, Vaudreuil-
Dorion, QC, J7V 8P2
(450) 424-2323
Emp Here 26   *Sales* 13,095,108
SIC 5111 Printing and writing paper
  Costas Tsougarakis

D-U-N-S 24-371-2044   (HQ)
6895051 CANADA INC
135 Rue Du Cheminot, Vaudreuil-Dorion, QC,
J7V 5V5
(450) 455-9877
Emp Here 4   *Sales* 24,601,500
SIC 6712 Bank holding companies
  Glenn Chaplin
  Patricia Chaplin
  Bob Chaplin
  Lee Cgaplin

D-U-N-S 20-651-5418   (SL)
9008-4013 QUEBEC INC
SUPERMARCHE PATRY, PIERRE
585 Av Saint-Charles Bureau 500, Vaudreuil-Dorion, QC, J7V 8P9
(450) 424-3550
Emp Here 50   *Sales* 13,707,600
SIC 5411 Grocery stores
 Pierre Patry

D-U-N-S 24-836-2949   (SL)
9207-8922 QUEBEC INC
VAUDREUIL VOLKSWAGEN
29 Boul De La Cite-Des-Jeunes, Vaudreuil-Dorion, QC, J7V 0N3
(450) 455-7941
Emp Here 30   *Sales* 14,942,340
SIC 5511 New and used car dealers
 Sonia Drolet

D-U-N-S 20-532-7526   (SL)
ACTION SPORT PHYSIO VAUDREUIL-DORION INC
11 Cite Des Jeunes Est Suite 101, Vaudreuil-Dorion, QC, J7V 8V9
(450) 455-0111
Emp Here 30   *Sales* 10,837,110
SIC 8049 Offices of health practitioner
 Eric Boucher
 Maxime Besner
 Patricia Oliver

D-U-N-S 25-868-3283   (SL)
AMUSEMENTS AIRBOUNCE SENC, LES
29 Av Pasold, Vaudreuil-Dorion, QC, J7V 2W9
(450) 424-0214
Emp Here 65   *Sales* 12,438,010
SIC 7359 Equipment rental and leasing, nec
 Jeremy Price-William

D-U-N-S 25-976-3985   (SL)
AMYLIOR INC
AMYSYSTEMS
3190 Rue F.-X.-Tessier, Vaudreuil-Dorion, QC, J7V 5V5
(450) 424-0288
Emp Here 83   *Sales* 12,808,726
SIC 2514 Metal household furniture
 Eric Dugas
 Robert Travers
 Carmon Landry
 Rene Malo
 Richard Dugas
 Gilles Sauve
 Michael P. Quinn
 Lucien Dugas
 Sylvain Dugas
 Louis Charest

D-U-N-S 25-245-0127   (SL)
ARMOIRES CONTESSA INC
(*Suby of* VON HUENE, EBERHARD & ASSOCIATES INC)
370 Rue Joseph-Carrier, Vaudreuil-Dorion, QC, J7V 5V5
(450) 455-6682
Emp Here 55   *Sales* 10,580,350
SIC 2434 Wood kitchen cabinets
 Eberhard Von Huene
 Annie Lajeunesse
 Josee Gagnon

D-U-N-S 25-124-7461   (SL)
AVMAX AVIATION SERVICES INC
AVMAX INTERIEURS EXECUTIFS (AIE)
264 Rue Adrien-Patenaude, Vaudreuil-Dorion, QC, J7V 5V5
(450) 424-9636
Emp Here 49   *Sales* 15,912,946
SIC 4581 Airports, flying fields, and services
 John Binder

D-U-N-S 24-655-8337   (SL)
BOSTON PIZZA
52 Boul De La Cite-Des-Jeunes, Vaudreuil-Dorion, QC, J7V 9L5
(450) 455-4464
Emp Here 49   *Sales* 11,017,895

SIC 2038 Frozen specialties, nec
 Joe Rahal

D-U-N-S 20-363-4642   (SL)
BOURASSA BOYER SOLUTION INC
SOLUTION BOURASSA BOYER
3323 Boul De La Gare, Vaudreuil-Dorion, QC, J7V 8W5
(450) 424-7000
Emp Here 75   *Sales* 17,571,600
SIC 8748 Business consulting, nec
 Claude Gareau
 Alain Rheault
 Pierre St-Jean
 Sylvain Castonguay
 Genevieve Bourassa

D-U-N-S 25-967-5866   (BR)
CASCADES CANADA ULC
NORAMPAC-VAUDREUIL, DIV OF
(*Suby of* CASCADES INC)
400 Rue Forbes, Vaudreuil-Dorion, QC, J7V 6N8
(450) 455-5731
Emp Here 170
SIC 2631 Paperboard mills
 Denis Doyen

D-U-N-S 24-546-1673   (SL)
CLOTURES JERMAR INC.
877 Rte Harwood, Vaudreuil-Dorion, QC, J7V 8P2
(450) 732-1121
Emp Here 25   *Sales* 11,179,350
SIC 5039 Construction materials, nec
 Marcel Lebuc

D-U-N-S 20-858-9879   (SL)
CLUB DE GOLF SUMMERLEA INC
1000 Rte De Lotbiniere, Vaudreuil-Dorion, QC, J7V 0H5
(450) 455-0921
Emp Here 100   *Sales* 7,639,700
SIC 7997 Membership sports and recreation clubs
 Dominic Gauthier
 Salvatore Furino

D-U-N-S 25-905-4732   (SL)
COJALY INC
ROTISSERIES ST-HUBERT, LES
601 Av Saint-Charles, Vaudreuil-Dorion, QC, J7V 8G4
(450) 455-0409
Emp Here 80   *Sales* 3,641,520
SIC 5812 Eating places
 Andre Meloche
 Jacques Schmidt
 Yves Schmidt

D-U-N-S 25-527-9655   (HQ)
CONTROLE TOTAL LOGISTIQUE INC
200 Av Loyola-Schmidt, Vaudreuil-Dorion, QC, J7V 8P2
(450) 424-1700
Emp Here 230   *Sales* 54,843,390
SIC 4731 Freight transportation arrangement
 Ches Nadeau
 Goddard Ward

D-U-N-S 24-502-2223   (SL)
DISTROBEL INC
436 Rue Valois, Vaudreuil-Dorion, QC, J7V 1T4

Emp Here 25   *Sales* 20,889,425
SIC 5148 Fresh fruits and vegetables
 Michel Poirier

D-U-N-S 20-502-5760   (SL)
EDITIONS VAUDREUIL INC
480 Boul Harwood, Vaudreuil-Dorion, QC, J7V 7H4
(450) 455-7974
Emp Here 26   *Sales* 13,095,108
SIC 5112 Stationery and office supplies
 Sylvain Charbonneau

D-U-N-S 20-221-0621   (HQ)

EMBALLAGES WINPAK HEAT SEAL INC, LES
(*Suby of* WINPAK LTD)
21919 Ch Dumberry, Vaudreuil-Dorion, QC, J7V 8P7
(450) 424-0191
Sales 85,617,312
SIC 3497 Metal foil and leaf
 Tim L. Johnson
 Olivier Yves Muggli
 Diana Lynn Kemp
 Ilkka Suominen
 Donald R W Chatterley
 Karen Anne Albrechtsen
 Martti H. Aarnio-Wihuri
 A. Aarnio-Whuri
 J.M. Hellgren
 Dayna Spiring

D-U-N-S 24-049-3275   (SL)
ERB TRANSPORT INC
3001 Rue Henry-Ford, Vaudreuil-Dorion, QC, J7V 8K2
(450) 510-2538
Emp Here 100   *Sales* 14,819,200
SIC 4213 Trucking, except local
 Scott Jones

D-U-N-S 20-218-2465   (HQ)
EUTECTIC CANADA INC
TUFTRAK: MANTRAK
(*Suby of* MIG HOLDING GMBH)
428 Rue Aime-Vincent, Vaudreuil-Dorion, QC, J7V 5V5
(514) 695-7500
Emp Here 15   *Sales* 34,141,100
SIC 5085 Industrial supplies
 John Kirkwood
 Michael Smolak
 Ed Strenlow
 Carlos Henrique Duarte Esteves
 Joseph Zevnik

D-U-N-S 24-677-0643   (HQ)
EXCELITAS CANADA INC
PLACEMENTS EXCELITAS CANADA
(*Suby of* EXCELITAS TECHNOLOGIES HOLDINGS LLC)
22001 Ch Dumberry, Vaudreuil-Dorion, QC, J7V 8P7
(450) 424-3300
Emp Here 100   *Sales* 67,899,600
SIC 3679 Electronic components, nec
 David Nislick
 James Rao
 Lyne Beauchemin

D-U-N-S 24-500-5087   (SL)
FONDATION DU CSSS DE VAUDREUIL-SOULANGES
3031 Boul De La Gare, Vaudreuil-Dorion, QC, J7V 9R2
(450) 455-6171
Emp Here 130   *Sales* 26,918,840
SIC 8399 Social services, nec
 Diane Boileau

D-U-N-S 20-320-1611   (HQ)
GAL AVIATION INC
264 Rue Adrien-Patenaude, Vaudreuil-Dorion, QC, J7V 5V5
(514) 418-0033
Sales 12,485,525
SIC 3429 Hardware, nec
 Glen Lynch
 Michael Caletti
 Guy-Adrien Lapierre

D-U-N-S 24-362-8521   (HQ)
GESTION INFILISE INC
3901 Rue F.-X.-Tessier, Vaudreuil-Dorion, QC, J7V 5V5
(450) 424-0161
Emp Here 1   *Sales* 110,914,980
SIC 5169 Chemicals and allied products, nec
 Tony Infilise
 Pierre Thivierge

 Anne-Marie Infilise
 Betty Infilise
 Christine Infilise
 Sandra Infilise
 Anthony Philip Infilise
 David L. Rosentzveig

D-U-N-S 20-530-6728   (SL)
GESTIONS REJEAN POITRAS INC, LES
CANADIAN TIRE
50 Boul De La Cite-Des-Jeunes Bureau 646, Vaudreuil-Dorion, QC, J7V 9L5
(450) 424-2744
Emp Here 100   *Sales* 20,534,300
SIC 5311 Department stores
 Rejean Poitras
 Lucie Roy

D-U-N-S 25-504-3671   (HQ)
GROUPE HOTELIER GRAND CHATEAU INC
SHERATON LAVAL
21700 Rte Transcanadienne, Vaudreuil-Dorion, QC, J7V 8P7
(450) 455-0955
Emp Here 1   *Sales* 47,834,000
SIC 7011 Hotels and motels
 Benito Migliorati
 Rosalia Saputo-Monticciolo
 Emanuele Saputo
 Giuseppe Borsellino
 Joey Saputo
 Joe Marsilii

D-U-N-S 20-252-3452   (HQ)
GROUPE PREMIERE MOISSON INC
(*Suby of* METRO INC)
189 Boul Harwood, Vaudreuil-Dorion, QC, J7V 1Y3
(450) 455-2827
Emp Here 50   *Sales* 121,846,250
SIC 2051 Bread, cake, and related products
 Eric R Lafleche
 Bernard Fiset
 Simon Rivet
 Francois Thibault
 Serge Boulanger
 Christian Bourbonniere

D-U-N-S 25-365-4750   (BR)
HOME DEPOT OF CANADA INC
HOME DEPOT
(*Suby of* THE HOME DEPOT INC)
55 Boul De La Cite-Des-Jeunes, Vaudreuil-Dorion, QC, J7V 8C1
(450) 510-2600
Emp Here 120
SIC 5251 Hardware stores
 Stephen Morim

D-U-N-S 20-214-3934   (HQ)
IMMUNOTEC INC
F.I.T.T. TM
300 Rue Joseph-Carrier, Vaudreuil-Dorion, QC, J7V 5V5
(450) 424-9992
Emp Here 72   *Sales* 83,753,295
SIC 5149 Groceries and related products, nec
 Rene Fernandez
 Patrick Montpetit
 Arturo Jose Saval Perez
 Alejandro Diazayas Oliver
 Mauricio Domenzain
 Alejandro Domenzain Jimenz

D-U-N-S 25-634-1095   (SL)
JCF AUTO SPORT
904 Rte Harwood, Vaudreuil-Dorion, QC, J7V 8P2

Emp Here 25   *Sales* 12,451,950
SIC 5541 Gasoline service stations
 Jean-Claude Frappier

D-U-N-S 20-709-4181   (SL)
JOURNAL PREMIERE EDITION
469 Av Saint-Charles, Vaudreuil-Dorion, QC,

J7V 2N4
(450) 455-7955
Emp Here 49   *Sales* 20,805,743
SIC 8999 Services, nec
Angele Marcoux-Prevost

D-U-N-S 24-360-4985   (BR)
KRAFT HEINZ CANADA ULC
(Suby of THE KRAFT HEINZ COMPANY)
401 Rue Marie-Curie, Vaudreuil-Dorion, QC,
J7V 0B9
(450) 455-5576
Emp Here 110
SIC 5141 Groceries, general line
Dominique Depasquo

D-U-N-S 20-543-0150   (SL)
**LABORATOIRES BUCKMAN DU CANADA,
LTEE**
(Suby of BULAB HOLDINGS, INC.)
351 Rue Joseph-Carrier, Vaudreuil-Dorion,
QC, J7V 5V5
(450) 424-4404
Emp Here 138   *Sales* 146,958,684
SIC 2869 Industrial organic chemicals, nec
James K. Doan
Jonathan E. Scharff
Charles C. Shaw
Paul Galbraith
David K Rosenthal

D-U-N-S 20-196-2255   (SL)
LOYOLA SCHMIDT LTEE
RENOVATEUR RONA, LE
243 Boul Harwood, Vaudreuil-Dorion, QC, J7V
1Y3

Emp Here 70   *Sales* 31,302,180
SIC 5072 Hardware
Michel Gaudreau

D-U-N-S 24-860-6444   (HQ)
**MACHINERIE WEBER MONTREAL HOLD-
ING INC**
269 Rue Adrien-Patenaude, Vaudreuil-Dorion,
QC, J7V 5V5
(450) 455-0169
Emp Here 5   *Sales* 20,651,540
SIC 3089 Plastics products, nec
Heinz Weber
Suzanne Belanger

D-U-N-S 24-698-1625   (SL)
MARC VILLENEUVE INC
2050 Rue Chicoine, Vaudreuil-Dorion, QC,
J7V 8P2
(450) 424-4616
Emp Here 30   *Sales* 25,067,310
SIC 5143 Dairy products, except dried or
canned
Marc Villeneuve

D-U-N-S 24-933-7841   (HQ)
NEW ROOTS HERBAL INC
PRODUITS NEW ROOTS HERBAL, LES
3405 Rue F.-X.-Tessier, Vaudreuil-Dorion, QC,
J7V 5V5
(800) 268-9486
Sales 11,242,750
SIC 2023 Dry, condensed and evaporated
dairy products
Peter F. Wilkes

D-U-N-S 24-229-0302   (HQ)
P.R. NISSEN & CIE LTEE
NISSEN FASTENERS
102b Boul De La Cite-Des-Jeunes Unite 54,
Vaudreuil-Dorion, QC, J7V 8B9
(514) 694-0250
Sales 11,179,350
SIC 5072 Hardware
Christian Nissen
Peter A. Nissen
Ralph R. Nissen
Christian V. Nissen
Ralph D. Nissen

D-U-N-S 24-772-7469   (SL)

POSTE DE LIVRAISON VAUDREUIL
972 Av Saint-Charles, Vaudreuil-Dorion, QC,
J7V 8P5
(450) 455-8325
Emp Here 3   *Sales* 15,529,285
SIC 4924 Natural gas distribution

D-U-N-S 20-370-7141   (SL)
PRECO-MSE INC
(Suby of GESTION IMMOBILIERE M.S.E.
INC)
1885 Montee Labossiere, Vaudreuil-Dorion,
QC, J7V 8P2
(514) 780-1280
Emp Here 100   *Sales* 16,238,100
SIC 1741 Masonry and other stonework
Marco Lessard
David Theoret
Caroline Theoret
Raynald Theoret
Stephane Lessard

D-U-N-S 20-999-3203   (HQ)
QUADRA CHIMIE LTEE
INGREDIENTS QUADRA
(Suby of GESTION INFILISE INC)
3901 Rue F.-X.-Tessier, Vaudreuil-Dorion, QC,
J7V 5V5
(450) 424-0161
Emp Here 65   *Sales* 433,280,358
SIC 5169 Chemicals and allied products, nec
Tony Infilise
Anne-Marie Infilise
Betty Infilise
Pierre Thivierge

D-U-N-S 24-860-5342   (BR)
RONA INC
RENO-DEPOT
(Suby of LOWE'S COMPANIES, INC.)
3010 Boul De La Gare, Vaudreuil-Dorion, QC,
J7V 0H1
(450) 455-3067
Emp Here 100
SIC 5072 Hardware
Francois Bedard

D-U-N-S 20-852-2552   (BR)
SOBEYS CAPITAL INCORPORATED
*IGA SUPERMARCHE PIERRE PATRY EX-
TRA*
(Suby of EMPIRE COMPANY LIMITED)
585 Av Saint-Charles, Vaudreuil-Dorion, QC,
J7V 8P9
(450) 424-3549
Emp Here 153
SIC 5411 Grocery stores
Pierre Patry

D-U-N-S 24-394-4266   (SL)
**SOCIETE EN COMMANDITE LE FELIX
VAUDREUIL-DORION**
3223 Boul De La Gare, Vaudreuil-Dorion, QC,
J7V 0L5
(514) 331-2788
Emp Here 49   *Sales* 12,816,097
SIC 6719 Holding companies, nec
Luc Maurice

D-U-N-S 24-667-4154   (SL)
TRANSPHARM INC
PHARMAPRIX
585 Av Saint-Charles Bureau 180, Vaudreuil-
Dorion, QC, J7V 8P9
(450) 455-5568
Emp Here 60   *Sales* 14,659,680
SIC 5912 Drug stores and proprietary stores
Andre Perreault

D-U-N-S 24-785-3836   (SL)
TRANSX TRANSPORT INC
(Suby of TRANSX TRANSPORT INC)
2351 Rue Henry-Ford, Vaudreuil-Dorion, QC,
J7V 0J1
(450) 424-0114
Emp Here 49   *Sales* 25,478,383
SIC 4731 Freight transportation arrangement
Louis Toliny

D-U-N-S 25-091-7874   (SL)
VAUDREUIL HONDA INC
9 Boul De La Cite-Des-Jeunes, Vaudreuil-
Dorion, QC, J7V 0N3
(450) 424-2500
Emp Here 30   *Sales* 14,942,340
SIC 5511 New and used car dealers
Thomas Samatas
Melissa Samatas

D-U-N-S 25-099-6550   (SL)
VIVIER PHARMA INC
(Suby of VIVIER CANADA INC)
288 Rue Adrien-Patenaude, Vaudreuil-Dorion,
QC, J7V 5V5
(450) 455-9779
Emp Here 43   *Sales* 12,212,903
SIC 2834 Pharmaceutical preparations
Ghislain Vivier
Cynthia Ann Vivier
Michaeal Vivier
Stephen Vivier
Linda Beaulieu
Caroline Leblanc

D-U-N-S 24-327-4482   (BR)
WAL-MART CANADA CORP
(Suby of WALMART INC.)
3050 Boul De La Gare, Vaudreuil-Dorion, QC,
J7V 0H1
(450) 510-3314
Emp Here 150
SIC 5311 Department stores
Gilbert Leblanc

D-U-N-S 25-380-7267   (HQ)
**WEBER INTERNATIONAL PACKAGING
CORPORATION**
(Suby of MACHINERIE WEBER MONTREAL
HOLDING INC)
269 Rue Adrien-Patenaude, Vaudreuil-Dorion,
QC, J7V 5V5
(450) 455-0169
Sales 28,594,440
SIC 3085 Plastics bottles
Heinz Weber
Jacqueline Weber
Suzanne Belanger

D-U-N-S 20-618-4900   (BR)
YANJACO INC
ST HUBERT ROTISSERIE
(Suby of YANJACO INC)
435 Boul Harwood, Vaudreuil-Dorion, QC, J7V
7W1
(450) 455-3336
Emp Here 80
SIC 5812 Eating places
Andre Meloche

Vercheres, QC J0L

D-U-N-S 20-486-5596   (SL)
9218-4118 QUEBEC INC
GROUPE PMLC, LE
507 Rte Marie-Victorin, Vercheres, QC, J0L
2R0
(450) 583-3513
Emp Here 26   *Sales* 17,651,998
SIC 6282 Investment advice
Ginette Labelle

D-U-N-S 20-909-5678   (SL)
CADRES VERBEC INC
(Suby of GESTION MARC DESERRES INC)
101 Montee Calixa-Lavallee, Vercheres, QC,
J0L 2R0
(450) 583-3378
Emp Here 80   *Sales* 45,570,240
SIC 5031 Lumber, plywood, and millwork
Marc Deserres

D-U-N-S 20-989-5544   (SL)
CHAMPAG INC
1156 Rte Marie-Victorin, Vercheres, QC, J0L

2R0
(450) 583-3350
Emp Here 65   *Sales* 17,050,085
SIC 0182 Food crops grown under cover
Laxman Marsonia
Yatin Bera

Verdun, QC H3E

D-U-N-S 25-794-6699   (HQ)
2786591 CANADA INC
MULTI-PRETS HYPOTHEQUES
14 Place Du Commerce Bureau 600, Verdun,
QC, H3E 1T5
(514) 287-1211
Emp Here 200   *Sales* 145,384,250
SIC 6163 Loan brokers
Luc Bernard
Pierre Martel
Jean Rochette
Claude Emond

D-U-N-S 24-353-7011   (HQ)
6362222 CANADA INC
CREATECH GROUP, THE
(Suby of BCE INC)
1 Carrefour Alexander-Graham-Bell Edifice 4,
Verdun, QC, H3E 3B3
(514) 937-1188
Emp Here 120   *Sales* 25,027,050
SIC 7379 Computer related services, nec
Ivan Mihaljevic
Marinella Ermacora
Michel Lalande

D-U-N-S 24-792-1658   (SL)
7255721 CANADA INC
ILE-DES-SOEURS HYUNDAI
1003 Boul Rene-Levesque, Verdun, QC, H3E
0B2
(514) 769-3555
Emp Here 26   *Sales* 12,950,028
SIC 5511 New and used car dealers
Jean-Claude Gravel

D-U-N-S 20-005-3507   (SL)
9100-9720 QUEBEC INC
PHARMAPRIX
38 Place Du Commerce Bureau 7, Verdun,
QC, H3E 1T8
(514) 762-6666
Emp Here 50   *Sales* 12,647,700
SIC 5912 Drug stores and proprietary stores
Nicole Chamard

D-U-N-S 20-380-6278   (HQ)
9121196 CANADA INC
14 Place Du Commerce, Verdun, QC, H3E
1T5
(514) 287-1211
Sales 35,158,737
SIC 6162 Mortgage bankers and loan correspondents
Luc Bernard
Patrick Martel
Sylvain Hetu

D-U-N-S 24-460-7925   (HQ)
BCE INC
BELL CANADA ENTREPRISES
1 Carrefour Alexander-Graham-Bell Bureau
8-1, Verdun, QC, H3E 3B3
(888) 932-6666
Emp Here 375   *Sales* 17,791,137,736
SIC 4899 Communication services, nec
Gordon M. Nixon
George A. Cope
Barry K. Allen
Robert E. Brown
Paul R Weiss
Sophie Brochu
Robert C. Simmonds
David F. Denison
Ian Greenberg

▲ Public Company   ■ Public Company Family Member   **HQ** Headquarters   **BR** Branch   **SL** Single Location

Robert P. Dexter

D-U-N-S 24-555-3300   (HQ)
BELL MOBILITE INC
BELL
(*Suby of* BCE INC)
1 Carrefour Alexander-Graham-Bell Bureau A-7, Verdun, QC, H3E 3B3
(514) 870-6550
Emp Here 600   *Sales* 548,332,800
SIC 4899 Communication services, nec
George A. Cope
M. Blaik Kirby
Michel Lalande
Mirko Bibic

D-U-N-S 20-056-9296   (HQ)
CANADIAN AUSTIN GROUP HOLDINGS ULC
GALERIES TASCHEREAU
(*Suby of* CANADIAN AUSTIN VENTURES LP)
4 Place Du Commerce, Verdun, QC, H3E 1J4
(514) 281-4040
Sales 13,077,650
SIC 6719 Holding companies, nec
Joel Ospovat
Thomas D Crowson Jr
Debra L Schneider
Levana Toledano

D-U-N-S 25-334-3545   (BR)
CANADIAN RED CROSS SOCIETY, THE
CANADIAN RED CROSS
(*Suby of* CANADIAN RED CROSS SOCIETY, THE)
6 Place Du Commerce, Verdun, QC, H3E 1P4
(514) 362-2930
Emp Here 75
SIC 8322 Individual and family services
Michel Leveille

D-U-N-S 20-857-4343   (SL)
CHAMBRE IMMOBILIERE DU GRAND MONTREAL
600 Ch Du Golf, Verdun, QC, H3E 1A8
(514) 762-2440
Emp Here 50   *Sales* 12,930,750
SIC 8611 Business associations
Mathieu Cousineau
Marie-France Vachon
Serge Brousseau
Luc Vaillancourt
Marc Lacasse
Robert Bouchard
Michel Tremblay
Andre Campeau
Nathalie Begin
Ginette Beardsell

D-U-N-S 24-813-1096   (HQ)
CHARTON-HOBBS INC
VINS VIP, LES
3000 Boul Rene-Levesque Bureau 400, Verdun, QC, H3E 1T9
(514) 353-8955
Emp Here 23   *Sales* 114,276,040
SIC 5169 Chemicals and allied products, nec
Duncan R. Hobbs
Gordon M.B. Coburn
Derek Thompson Hobbs
Jonathan Roger Hobbs
Huong G. Vu

D-U-N-S 24-663-5994   (SL)
CIGM
CENTRIS
600 Ch Du Golf, Verdun, QC, H3E 1A8
(514) 762-5264
Emp Here 49   *Sales* 16,029,223
SIC 6531 Real estate agents and managers
Eric Charbonneau
Patrick Juaneda

D-U-N-S 24-376-8673   (BR)
COMPAGNIE DE TELEPHONE BELL DU CANADA OU BELL CANADA, LA

(*Suby of* BCE INC)
1 Carref Alexander-Graham-Bell, Verdun, QC, H3E 3B3

Emp Here 4,000
SIC 4899 Communication services, nec
George A. Cope

D-U-N-S 20-211-4617   (HQ)
COMPAGNIE DE TELEPHONE BELL DU CANADA OU BELL CANADA, LA
BELL
(*Suby of* BCE INC)
1 Carref Alexander-Graham-Bell Tower A-7-1, Verdun, QC, H3E 3B3
(514) 786-8424
Emp Here 368   *Sales* 16,325,747,200
SIC 4899 Communication services, nec
George A. Cope
Michel Lalande
Paul R. Weiss
Robert C. Simmonds
Calin Rovinescu
Gordon M. Nixon
Monique F. Leroux
Katherine Min Sun Lee
Ian Greenberg
Robert P. Dexter

D-U-N-S 24-373-5193   (SL)
CONSORTIUM DES MARQUES PRIVEES PBC INC, LES
CONSORTIUM PL
3000 Boul Rene-Levesque Bureau 330, Verdun, QC, H3E 1T9
(514) 768-4122
Emp Here 12   *Sales* 15,234,620
SIC 5149 Groceries and related products, nec
Francois Leduc
Roxanne Vachon
Gilles Messier

D-U-N-S 20-702-9807   (SL)
GROUPE DMD CONNEXIONS SANTE NUMERIQUES
2 Place Du Commerce Bureau 206, Verdun, QC, H3E 1A1
(514) 783-1698
Emp Here 10   *Sales* 36,785,812
SIC 7371 Custom computer programming services
Denis Martineau
Andre Charron
Mark Gleason
Roger Korman
Justin Beckett
Andre P. Brosseau
Bertrand Bolduc
Pierre-Yves Desbiens
Mark Benthin

D-U-N-S 24-659-1358   (HQ)
GROUPE PAGES JAUNES CORP
YELLOW PAGES
(*Suby of* PAGES JAUNES LIMITEE)
16 Place Du Commerce, Verdun, QC, H3E 2A5
(514) 934-2000
Emp Here 800   *Sales* 319,860,800
SIC 4899 Communication services, nec
Julien Billot
Francois D Ramsay
Ginette Maille

D-U-N-S 20-847-3269   (SL)
GROUPE SUTTON SUR L'ILE INC
38 Place Du Commerce Bureau 280, Verdun, QC, H3E 1T8
(514) 769-7010
Emp Here 65   *Sales* 17,664,140
SIC 6531 Real estate agents and managers
Michael Trosman

D-U-N-S 25-147-4557   (HQ)
HOLDING BELL MOBILITE INC
(*Suby of* BCE INC)
1 Carref Alexander-Graham-Bell Bureau A-7,

Verdun, QC, H3E 3B3
(514) 420-7700
Emp Here 2   *Sales* 731,110,400
SIC 4899 Communication services, nec
Wade Oosterman
Michel Lalande

D-U-N-S 24-422-1052   (HQ)
IPEX GESTION INC
(*Suby of* ALIAXIS)
3 Place Du Commerce Bureau 101, Verdun, QC, H3E 1H7
(514) 769-2200
Emp Here 100   *Sales* 33,660,900
SIC 8741 Management services
Alex Mestres
Nicole Chouinard
Jean Paiva

D-U-N-S 24-953-4413   (HQ)
IPEX INC
IPEX MANAGEMENT
(*Suby of* ALIAXIS)
3 Place Du Commerce Bureau 101, Verdun, QC, H3E 1H7
(514) 769-2200
Emp Here 50   *Sales* 60,807,750
SIC 3494 Valves and pipe fittings, nec
Alex Mestres
Nicole Chouinard
Jean Paiva

D-U-N-S 25-503-1312   (SL)
MARCHE LOUISE MENARD (ILE-DES-SOEURS) INC, LES
MARCHES LOUISE MENARD (ILE-DES-SOEURS), LES
30 Place Du Commerce, Verdun, QC, H3E 1V7
(514) 362-6330
Emp Here 98   *Sales* 28,760,746
SIC 5411 Grocery stores
Louise Menard

D-U-N-S 25-848-8329   (HQ)
OPTO-PLUS INC
4 Place Du Commerce Bureau 460, Verdun, QC, H3E 1J4
(514) 762-2020
Emp Here 2   *Sales* 74,949,280
SIC 5049 Professional equipment, nec
Rene Cote
Valerie Savard
Marcel Brin
Lucie Turcotte
Nadine Palardy

D-U-N-S 20-557-6767   (HQ)
PAGES JAUNES SOLUTIONS NUMERIQUES ET MEDIAS LIMITEE
GROUPE PAGES JAUNES
(*Suby of* PAGES JAUNES LIMITEE)
16 Place Du Commerce, Verdun, QC, H3E 2A5
(514) 934-2611
Emp Here 50   *Sales* 1,415,121,120
SIC 4899 Communication services, nec
David A. Eckert
Francesco Sciannamblo
Treena Cooper
Craig Forman
Kalpana Raina
Susan Kudzman
Donald H. Morrison
Robert Hall
Paul W. Russo

D-U-N-S 25-199-2665   (SL)
PPI QUEBEC ADVISORY INC
CONSEILS PPI
3000 Boul Rene-Levesque Bureau 340, Verdun, QC, H3E 1T9
(514) 765-7400
Emp Here 25   *Sales* 25,872,025
SIC 6311 Life insurance
James A Burton
Claude Menard

D-U-N-S 24-431-8655   (HQ)
SERVICES OPTOMETRIQUES (OPT) INC
4 Place Du Commerce Bureau 460, Verdun, QC, H3E 1J4
(514) 762-2020
Sales 11,626,524
SIC 5049 Professional equipment, nec
Carol Marois
Paul Neumann
Jean-Frederick Bouchard
Josee Martineau
Marc Bolduc
Skylar Feltis
Paul Gray
Patrick Simard
Yves Levesque

D-U-N-S 20-252-7602   (SL)
SIGNATURE SUR LE SAINT-LAURENT CONSTRUCTION S.E.N.C.
SSL CONSTRUCTION
8 Place Du Commerce Unite 300, Verdun, QC, H3E 1N3
(514) 876-1020
Emp Here 250   *Sales* 46,626,500
SIC 8742 Management consulting services
Terry Lefebvre

D-U-N-S 20-012-5560   (SL)
TECHNOLOGIES IWEB INC
FUNIO
(*Suby of* INTERNAP CORPORATION)
20 Place Du Commerce, Verdun, QC, H3E 1Z6
(514) 286-4242
Emp Here 100   *Sales* 22,847,200
SIC 4813 Telephone communication, except radio
Haroutioun Aramali
Richard P Diegnan
David D Krupczak

Verdun, QC H4G

D-U-N-S 20-543-4496   (HQ)
153924 CANADA INC
PHARMACIE JEAN COUTU
4061 Rue Wellington, Verdun, QC, H4G 1V6
(514) 761-4591
Emp Here 20   *Sales* 10,118,160
SIC 5912 Drug stores and proprietary stores
Raffaele Delli-Colli
Gino Consolante

D-U-N-S 20-290-4074   (BR)
CENTRE DE SANTE ET DE SERVICES SOCIAUX DU SUD-OUEST-VERDUN
HOPITAL DE VERDUN
(*Suby of* GOUVERNEMENT DE LA PROVINCE DE QUEBEC)
4000 Boul Lasalle, Verdun, QC, H4G 2A3
(514) 362-1000
Emp Here 1,600
SIC 8062 General medical and surgical hospitals

D-U-N-S 24-322-8285   (SL)
CHAMPAGNE, GERARD LTEE
IGA
5144 Rue Bannantyne, Verdun, QC, H4G 1G5
(514) 766-3536
Emp Here 80   *Sales* 23,478,160
SIC 5411 Grocery stores
Jonathan Champagne

D-U-N-S 20-603-9778   (SL)
CHAMPLAIN DODGE CHRYSLER LTEE
3350 Rue Wellington, Verdun, QC, H4G 1T5
(514) 761-4801
Emp Here 45   *Sales* 22,413,510
SIC 5511 New and used car dealers
Michel Gaudette
Fannie Gaudette
Antoine Archambault

D-U-N-S 20-645-1523   (SL)
ENTREPRISES JOEL GIRARD INC, LES
CANADIAN TIRE
3180 Rue Wellington, Verdun, QC, H4G 1T3
(514) 766-8561
Emp Here 30   *Sales* 14,942,340
SIC 5531 Auto and home supply stores
Joel Girard

D-U-N-S 24-795-5367   (SL)
**FONDATION D'ENTRAIDE BOUDDHISTE
TZU CHI DU CANADA**
3988 Rue Wellington Bureau 1, Verdun, QC,
H4G 1V3
(514) 844-2074
Emp Here 30   *Sales* 11,922,420
SIC 8699 Membership organizations, nec
Cheng Yen Ven

D-U-N-S 20-369-9673   (SL)
GROUPE UNIGESCO INC
3900 Rue Cool, Verdun, QC, H4G 1B4
(514) 360-1509
Emp Here 26   *Sales* 12,239,006
SIC 1542 Nonresidential construction, nec
Jean-Sebastien Gariepy
Maxime Laporte
Audrey St-Jean

D-U-N-S 20-175-4962   (HQ)
INDUSTRIES J SUSS INC, LES
3865 Rue Lesage, Verdun, QC, H4G 1A3
(514) 769-5666
Sales 19,237,000
SIC 2431 Millwork
Julius Suss
Daniel Suss

D-U-N-S 25-258-4180   (BR)
REVERA INC
SAINTE REVERA
(*Suby of* GOVERNMENT OF CANADA)
Gd Succ Bureau-Chef, Verdun, QC, H4G 3C9

Emp Here 100
SIC 8051 Skilled nursing care facilities
Carole Prohmam

D-U-N-S 24-806-4375   (SL)
TOUCHETTE PNEUS & MECANIQUE
4101 Boul Champlain, Verdun, QC, H4G 1A6
(514) 766-4291
Emp Here 49   *Sales* 24,405,822
SIC 5531 Auto and home supply stores
Andry Touchette

D-U-N-S 20-137-2575   (BR)
VILLE DE MONTREAL
TRAVAUX PUBLIQUES
(*Suby of* VILLE DE MONTREAL)
1177 Rue Dupuis, Verdun, QC, H4G 3L4
(514) 872-7680
Emp Here 150
SIC 1611 Highway and street construction
Pierre Boutin

D-U-N-S 25-256-9686   (BR)
VILLE DE MONTREAL
AUDITORIUM DE VERDUN
(*Suby of* VILLE DE MONTREAL)
4110 Boul Lasalle, Verdun, QC, H4G 2A5
(514) 765-7130
Emp Here 100
SIC 7999 Amusement and recreation, nec
Diane Vallee

Verdun, QC H4H

D-U-N-S 24-861-0680   (SL)
**FONDATION CHAMPLAIN ET MANOIR-DE-
VERDUN**
1325 Rue Crawford, Verdun, QC, H4H 2N6
(514) 766-8513
Emp Here 50   *Sales* 19,870,700

SIC 8699 Membership organizations, nec
Huguette Lamarre

D-U-N-S 24-636-8117   (SL)
**INSTITUT UNIVERSITAIRE EN SANTE
MENTALE DOUGLAS**
CENTRE WELLINGTON
6875 Boul Lasalle, Verdun, QC, H4H 1R3
(514) 761-6131
Emp Here 1,000   *Sales* 111,080,000
SIC 8062 General medical and surgical hospi-
tals
Claudette Allard
Lynne K Mcvey

D-U-N-S 20-712-3634   (BR)
LESTER B. PEARSON SCHOOL BOARD
BEURLING ACADEMY
6100 Boul Champlain, Verdun, QC, H4H 1A5
(514) 766-2357
Emp Here 100
SIC 8211 Elementary and secondary schools
Davi Abracin

D-U-N-S 24-083-9332   (SL)
WOODLAND VERDUN LTEE
WOODLAND TOYOTA
1009 Rue Woodland, Verdun, QC, H4H 1V7
(514) 761-3444
Emp Here 32   *Sales* 15,938,496
SIC 5511 New and used car dealers
Laurent Bilodeau

Victoriaville, QC G6P

D-U-N-S 24-465-2319   (SL)
2166-2440 QUEBEC INC
BAR L'EVASION ENR
19 Boul Des Bois-Francs S, Victoriaville, QC,
G6P 4S2
(819) 758-7176
Emp Here 125   *Sales* 5,689,875
SIC 5813 Drinking places
Yvon Rondeau

D-U-N-S 25-075-3282   (SL)
9027-3459 QUEBEC INC
GROUPE SOTECK
1171 Rue Notre-Dame O Bureau 200, Victoriaville, QC, G6P 7L1
(819) 758-0313
Emp Here 30   *Sales* 12,580,650
SIC 6712 Bank holding companies
Sylvain Ouellette

D-U-N-S 20-184-1736   (SL)
9098-8585 QUEBEC INC
*BOULANGERIE & PATISSERIE LAMON-
TAGNE*
59 Rue Girouard, Victoriaville, QC, G6P 5T2
(819) 357-8395
Emp Here 60   *Sales* 50,134,620
SIC 5149 Groceries and related products, nec
Karina Lamontagne
Kathleen Lamontagne
Nathalie Lamontagne
Normand Lamontage
Nicole Lamontagne

D-U-N-S 20-369-9152   (SL)
9368-1476 QUEBEC INC
JEAN-DEPOT
575 Boul Des Bois-Francs S, Victoriaville, QC,
G6P 5X5
(819) 357-2055
Emp Here 150   *Sales* 26,909,400
SIC 5651 Family clothing stores
Christian Audet

D-U-N-S 24-943-0703   (SL)
94291 CANADA LTEE
560 Boul Des Bois-Francs S, Victoriaville, QC,
G6P 5X4
(819) 357-2241
Emp Here 55   *Sales* 14,385,415

SIC 6712 Bank holding companies
Jean-Marc Labbe

D-U-N-S 24-465-3929   (SL)
AUTOMOBILE PIERRE METHOT INC
METHOT CHEVROLET BUICK GMC
885 Rue Notre-Dame E, Victoriaville, QC, G6P
4B8
(819) 758-5858
Emp Here 26   *Sales* 12,950,028
SIC 5511 New and used car dealers
Pierre Methot

D-U-N-S 20-265-4109   (HQ)
BREUVAGES APPALACHES INC, LES
925 Rue Notre-Dame O, Victoriaville, QC,
G6P 7L1

Emp Here 20   *Sales* 21,725,002
SIC 5149 Groceries and related products, nec
Jean Thibeau

D-U-N-S 24-567-7356   (HQ)
BUROPRO CITATION INC
BC MAISON D'EDITION
505 Boul Jutras E, Victoriaville, QC, G6P 7H4
(819) 752-7777
Emp Here 130   *Sales* 231,159,108
SIC 5112 Stationery and office supplies
Guy Bergeron
Luc Pepin
Dave Morin
Marc Perron

D-U-N-S 24-804-7818   (HQ)
CAISSE DESJARDINS DES BOIS-FRANCS
*DESJARDINS ENTREPRISES-CENTRE-DU-
QUEBEC BUREAU DE VICTORIAVILLE*
300 Boul Des Bois-Francs S, Victoriaville, QC,
G6P 7W7
(819) 758-9421
Emp Here 100   *Sales* 37,237,428
SIC 6062 State credit unions
Denis Desrochers
Jean-Marie Laroche
Genevieve Girard
Jean-Guy Caron
Marc Binette
Julie Pepin
Laurent Soucy
Marc Poirier
Christian Guillemette
Jean-Guy Daigle

D-U-N-S 20-874-2874   (HQ)
**COLLEGE D'ENSEIGNEMENT GENERAL
ET PROFESSIONNEL DE VICTORIAVILLE**
CEGEP DE VICTORIAVILLE
475 Rue Notre-Dame E, Victoriaville, QC, G6P
4B3
(819) 758-6401
Emp Here 212   *Sales* 40,634,352
SIC 8221 Colleges and universities
Francois Houle
Frederick Michaud
Christian Heon
Paul Theriault

D-U-N-S 24-451-3953   (BR)
**COMMISSION SCOLAIRE DES BOIS-
FRANCS**
ECOLE LE TANDEM
(*Suby of* COMMISSION SCOLAIRE DES
BOIS-FRANCS)
20 Rue De L'Ermitage, Victoriaville, QC, G6P
1J5
(819) 752-4591
Emp Here 85
SIC 8211 Elementary and secondary schools
Marie-Claude Turpide

D-U-N-S 25-541-4757   (HQ)
**COMMISSION SCOLAIRE DES BOIS-
FRANCS**
40 Boul Des Bois-Francs N, Victoriaville, QC,
G6P 1E5
(819) 758-6453
Sales 138,766,600

SIC 8211 Elementary and secondary schools
Paulette S. Rancourt

D-U-N-S 24-012-1801   (BR)
**COMMISSION SCOLAIRE DES BOIS-
FRANCS**
(*Suby of* COMMISSION SCOLAIRE DES
BOIS-FRANCS)
40 Boul Des Bois-Francs N, Victoriaville, QC,
G6P 1E5
(819) 758-6453
Emp Here 100
SIC 8211 Elementary and secondary schools
Francois Labbe

D-U-N-S 24-477-1288   (SL)
CONSTRUCTIONS JEL BERGERON
LES JARDINS DU PARK LINEAIRE
91 Rue Monfette, Victoriaville, QC, G6P 0B7
(819) 795-3030
Emp Here 49   *Sales* 15,624,581
SIC 1521 Single-family housing construction
Sylvie Bergeron

D-U-N-S 24-433-3795   (HQ)
CORPORATION MAURICE-RATTE
FRERES DU SACRE-COEUR
905 Boul Des Bois-Francs S, Victoriaville, QC,
G6P 5W1
(819) 357-8217
Emp Here 30   *Sales* 11,037,038
SIC 8661 Religious organizations
Rene Goyette
Jean-Guy Rox
Alain Nappert

D-U-N-S 25-977-7449   (HQ)
CREATION STRATEGIQUE ABSOLUE INC
ABSOLU COMMUNICATION MARKETING
1097 Rue Notre-Dame O Bureau 100, Victori-
aville, QC, G6P 7L1
(819) 752-8888
Emp Here 25   *Sales* 15,209,400
SIC 8748 Business consulting, nec
Bruno Frechette
Carl Provencher
Jason Monfette
Jean-Francois Lauzier

D-U-N-S 20-265-1758   (SL)
FROMAGERIE VICTORIA INC, LA
101 Rue De L'Aqueduc, Victoriaville, QC, G6P
1M2
(819) 752-6821
Emp Here 100   *Sales* 34,569,000
SIC 2022 Cheese; natural and processed
Florian Gosselin
Marc-Andre Gosselin

D-U-N-S 20-722-4528   (HQ)
GARAGE REJEAN ROY INC
TOYOTA VICTORIAVILLE
(*Suby of* PLACEMENTS S.R.S. ROY INC)
465 Boul Des Bois-Francs N, Victoriaville, QC,
G6P 1H1
(819) 758-8000
Emp Here 23   *Sales* 14,942,340
SIC 5511 New and used car dealers
Rejean Roy

D-U-N-S 20-548-5308   (SL)
GESTION SYNER-PHARM INC
PHARMACIE BRUNET
141 Rue Notre-Dame E, Victoriaville, QC, G6P
3Z8
(819) 752-4554
Emp Here 85   *Sales* 20,767,880
SIC 5999 Miscellaneous retail stores, nec
Jean-Sebastien Croteau
Lyne Isabelle
Jacques Caron

D-U-N-S 24-309-5499   (SL)
GROUPE POSI-PLUS INC
10 Rue De L'Artisan, Victoriaville, QC, G6P
7E4
(800) 758-5717
Emp Here 180   *Sales* 49,203,000

SIC 6712 Bank holding companies
Christian Poudrier
Bertrand Poudrier
Dany Poudrier

D-U-N-S 20-533-8549 (SL)
GROUPE SCV INC
435 Rue Gamache, Victoriaville, QC, G6P 3T4
(819) 758-5756
Emp Here 50 *Sales* 11,046,700
SIC 1711 Plumbing, heating, air-conditioning
Jean-Francois Arbour
Hugues Fastrel
Bruno Fayolle
Francis Fayolle

D-U-N-S 20-188-7262 (SL)
IMPRIMERIE D'ARTHABASKA INC, L'
(*Suby of* 9049-3347 QUEBEC INC)
370 Rue Girouard, Victoriaville, QC, G6P 5V2

Emp Here 64 *Sales* 10,497,728
SIC 2711 Newspapers
Serge Isabelle
Serge Morin

D-U-N-S 25-412-9455 (SL)
JEAN-SEBASTIEN CROTEAU ISABELLE ANNE ROBITAILLE INC
BRUNET
141 Rue Notre-Dame E, Victoriaville, QC, G6P 3Z8
(819) 752-4554
Emp Here 85 *Sales* 20,767,880
SIC 5912 Drug stores and proprietary stores
Lyne Isabelle
Jean-Sebastien Croteau
Jacques Caron

D-U-N-S 20-543-4348 (HQ)
MAGASINS LECOMPTE INC
119 Rue Notre-Dame E, Victoriaville, QC, G6P 3Z8
(819) 758-2626
Emp Here 40 *Sales* 12,320,580
SIC 5399 Miscellaneous general merchandise
Eric Lecompte

D-U-N-S 25-540-4782 (BR)
METRO RICHELIEU INC
SUPER C
(*Suby of* METRO INC)
601 Boul Jutras E, Victoriaville, QC, G6P 7H4
(819) 752-6659
Emp Here 100
SIC 5411 Grocery stores
Eddy Lamontagne

D-U-N-S 24-330-9940 (SL)
MEUBLES CATHEDRA INC
CONFORTEC
(*Suby of* GROUPE BERMEX INC)
34 Rue De L'Artisan, Victoriaville, QC, G6P 7E3
(819) 752-1641
Emp Here 44 *Sales* 12,345,760
SIC 2511 Wood household furniture
Bertrand Dumont
Richard Darveau
Christian Roy

D-U-N-S 24-889-6263 (SL)
PNEUS BERNARD, ROBERT, LES
900 Rue Notre-Dame E, Victoriaville, QC, G6P 4B7
(819) 752-4567
Emp Here 49 *Sales* 30,834,720
SIC 5531 Auto and home supply stores
Gerard Bernard

D-U-N-S 24-890-4658 (SL)
POINT PLUS RESTAURANT-BAR INC, AU
192 Boul Des Bois-Francs S, Victoriaville, QC, G6P 4S7
(819) 758-9927
Emp Here 92 *Sales* 3,944,316
SIC 5812 Eating places
Alain Lavoie

Marc Charest

D-U-N-S 24-205-7842 (SL)
POSI-PLUS TECHNOLOGIES INC
10 Rue De L'Artisan, Victoriaville, QC, G6P 7E4
(819) 758-5717
Emp Here 100 *Sales* 44,921,900
SIC 7389 Business services, nec
Christian Poudrier
Dany Poudrier

D-U-N-S 20-914-6104 (BR)
PROVIGO DISTRIBUTION INC
LOBLAWS VICTORIAVILLE
(*Suby of* LOBLAW COMPANIES LIMITED)
60 Rue Carignan, Victoriaville, QC, G6P 4Z6

Emp Here 200
SIC 5141 Groceries, general line
Mario Bedard

D-U-N-S 24-149-5431 (SL)
RESTAURANT B.C.L. INC
ROTISSERIE ST-HUBERT
609 Boul Des Bois-Francs S, Victoriaville, QC, G6P 5X1
(819) 357-9226
Emp Here 80 *Sales* 3,429,840
SIC 5812 Eating places
Bernard Labbe
Johanne Faucher

D-U-N-S 24-821-4090 (SL)
ROY DESROCHERS LAMBERT S.E.N.C.R.L
450 Boul Des Bois-Francs N, Victoriaville, QC, G6P 1H3
(819) 758-1544
Emp Here 75 *Sales* 15,576,375
SIC 8721 Accounting, auditing, and bookkeeping
Jean Lambert
Marco Baril
Pierre Harper
Marco Desilets
Jean Marcotte
Jacques Charland
Jacques Bedard
Alain Lessard
Jean-Marc Nadeau
Pascal Menard

D-U-N-S 20-578-8797 (HQ)
SANI-MARC INC
AWARD
(*Suby of* PLACEMENTS J.C. GOUDREAULT INC)
42 Rue De L'Artisan, Victoriaville, QC, G6P 7E3
(819) 758-1541
Emp Here 80 *Sales* 42,603,150
SIC 2841 Soap and other detergents
Pierre Goudreault
Yvon Jacques

D-U-N-S 25-502-1198 (BR)
SONEPAR CANADA INC
LUMEN
(*Suby of* SOCIETE DE NEGOCE ET DE PARTICIPATION)
415 Boul Labbe N, Victoriaville, QC, G6P 9J4
(819) 758-6205
Emp Here 500
SIC 5063 Electrical apparatus and equipment
Chrstian Cantin

D-U-N-S 20-845-4889 (SL)
SUPERMARCHE RAYMOND MARTIN INC
11 Rue De L'Aqueduc, Victoriaville, QC, G6P 1L4
(819) 752-9797
Emp Here 49 *Sales* 13,433,448
SIC 5411 Grocery stores
Raymond Martin

D-U-N-S 20-265-4406 (HQ)
VIC MOBILIER DE MAGASINS INC
VIC SOLUTIONS DETAIL

1440 Rue Notre-Dame O, Victoriaville, QC, G6P 7L7
(819) 758-0626
Emp Here 137 *Sales* 23,148,300
SIC 2542 Partitions and fixtures, except wood
Fabrice Canin
Miguel Lavertu
Jacques Canin

D-U-N-S 24-791-1787 (SL)
VILLA ST-GEORGES INC
185 Rue Saint-Georges, Victoriaville, QC, G6P 9H6
(819) 758-6760
Emp Here 75 *Sales* 4,880,625
SIC 8361 Residential care
Sylvie Bergeron

D-U-N-S 20-254-3211 (HQ)
VIVACO, GROUPE COOPERATIF
CENTRE DE GRAINS
5 Av Pie-X, Victoriaville, QC, G6P 4R8
(819) 758-4770
Sales 147,289,750
SIC 5191 Farm supplies
Andre Normand
Marc-Andre Roy
Christian Dostie
Gervais Laroche
Nicole Charbonneau
Alain Tardif
Martial Ruel
Marie-Pier Beliveau
Jonathan Lampron
Rene Bergeron

D-U-N-S 24-141-9105 (HQ)
WOOD WYANT CANADA INC
ARISTOCRAT
(*Suby of* PLACEMENTS J.C. GOUDREAULT INC)
42 Rue De L'Artisan, Victoriaville, QC, G6P 7E3
(819) 758-1541
Emp Here 50 *Sales* 49,703,675
SIC 2842 Polishes and sanitation goods
Pierre Goudreault

Victoriaville, QC G6R

D-U-N-S 20-791-0050 (HQ)
BLAIS & LANGLOIS INC
345 Rue Cartier, Victoriaville, QC, G6R 1E3
(819) 739-2905
Emp Here 40 *Sales* 28,516,900
SIC 1542 Nonresidential construction, nec
Jean Marchand
Jean-Francois Marchand
Jacques Marchand
Hugues Marchand
Guillaume Marchand

D-U-N-S 20-871-5334 (HQ)
CONSTRUCTIONS PEPIN ET FORTIN INC, LES
PEPIN FORTIN CONSTRUCTION
371 Av Pie-X, Victoriaville, QC, G6R 0L6
(819) 357-9274
Emp Here 45 *Sales* 23,536,550
SIC 1542 Nonresidential construction, nec
Stephan Mckenzie
Francois Dubreuil

Victoriaville, QC G6S

D-U-N-S 20-872-0656 (SL)
9132-9326 QUEBEC INC
PHARMAPRIX
1111 Boul Jutras E Bureau 20, Victoriaville, QC, G6S 1C1

(819) 357-4748
Emp Here 40 *Sales* 10,118,160
SIC 5912 Drug stores and proprietary stores
Alain Lafrance

D-U-N-S 25-378-8632 (BR)
GESTIONS G.D. BERUBE INC, LES
RESTAURANT MCDONALD'S
(*Suby of* GESTIONS G.D. BERUBE INC, LES)
1111 Boul Jutras E Bureau 11, Victoriaville, QC, G6S 1C1
(819) 357-3657
Emp Here 200
SIC 5812 Eating places
Catie Giguere

D-U-N-S 24-000-2134 (BR)
HOME DEPOT OF CANADA INC
HOME DEPOT
(*Suby of* THE HOME DEPOT INC)
160 Boul Arthabaska O, Victoriaville, QC, G6S 0P2
(819) 752-0700
Emp Here 100
SIC 5251 Hardware stores

D-U-N-S 20-514-8299 (HQ)
OUTIL MAG INC
BARIL ELECTRIQUE
10 Boul Labbe S, Victoriaville, QC, G6S 1B5
(819) 751-2424
Sales 11,875,650
SIC 5084 Industrial machinery and equipment
Michel Lainesse

D-U-N-S 24-327-4516 (BR)
WAL-MART CANADA CORP
(*Suby of* WALMART INC.)
110 Boul Arthabaska O, Victoriaville, QC, G6S 0P2
(819) 758-5136
Emp Here 250
SIC 5311 Department stores
Eric Guay

Victoriaville, QC G6T

D-U-N-S 25-541-6943 (HQ)
9049-3347 QUEBEC INC
IMPART LITHO
383 Boul De La Bonaventure, Victoriaville, QC, G6T 1V5
(819) 758-0667
Emp Here 20 *Sales* 11,481,890
SIC 2752 Commercial printing, lithographic
Serge Morin
Christian Morin
Mario Ayotte

D-U-N-S 24-050-2224 (SL)
9138-4529 QUEBEC INC
G.G. TELECOM
330 Rue De La Jacques-Cartier, Victoriaville, QC, G6T 1Y3
(514) 868-1811
Emp Here 50 *Sales* 13,935,145
SIC 3699 Electrical equipment and supplies, nec
Yan Gagnon
Charles Martel

D-U-N-S 20-517-5920 (SL)
ACIER VICTORIA LTEE
(*Suby of* GESTION MBRL (2005) INC)
900 Rue De L'Acadie, Victoriaville, QC, G6T 1V1
(819) 758-7575
Emp Here 26 *Sales* 11,626,524
SIC 5051 Metals service centers and offices
Richard Leclerc
Marco Bergeron

D-U-N-S 24-760-0158 (SL)
ACIERS SOLIDER INC, LES
(*Suby of* 9007-7520 QUEBEC INC)

▲ Public Company   ■ Public Company Family Member   **HQ** Headquarters   **BR** Branch   **SL** Single Location

300 Rue De La Jacques-Cartier, Victoriaville,
QC, G6T 1Y3
(819) 758-2897
Emp Here 26   *Sales* 16,761,217
SIC 1791 Structural steel erection
Yannick Gardner
Kathleen Gardner

D-U-N-S 20-949-8450   (SL)
ARMATURES BOIS-FRANCS INC
249 Boul De La Bonaventure, Victoriaville,
QC, G6T 1V5
(819) 758-7501
Emp Here 500   *Sales* 121,615,500
SIC 3443 Fabricated plate work (boiler shop)
Eric Bernier
Francois Vallieres

D-U-N-S 25-525-5457   (BR)
CASCADES CANADA ULC
NORAMPAC-VICTORIAVILLE
(*Suby of* CASCADES INC)
400 Boul De La Bonaventure, Victoriaville,
QC, G6T 1V8
(819) 758-3177
Emp Here 165
SIC 2653 Corrugated and solid fiber boxes
Guy Lamontagne

D-U-N-S 20-265-0842   (SL)
CHAREST AUTOMOBILE LTEE
CHAREST INTERNATIONAL
(*Suby of* 2160-4822 QUEBEC INC)
275 Boul Pierre-Roux E Bureau 443, Victori-
aville, QC, G6T 1S9
(819) 758-8271
Emp Here 48   *Sales* 25,120,000
SIC 5511 New and used car dealers
Steve Halle
Alain Bellavance
Jean-Francois Poulin
Claude Larochelle
Nathalie Halle

D-U-N-S 20-869-3051   (SL)
ENTREPRISES G.N.P. INC
750 Boul Pierre-Roux E, Victoriaville, QC, G6T
1S6
(819) 752-7140
Emp Here 50   *Sales* 12,622,100
SIC 1623 Water, sewer, and utility lines
Marc R. Emond

D-U-N-S 24-330-1194   (HQ)
GAUDREAU ENVIRONNEMENT INC
*GAUDREAU ENVIRONNEMENT (DIVISION
QUEBEC)*
365 Boul De La Bonaventure, Victoriaville,
QC, G6T 1V5
(819) 758-8378
Emp Here 130   *Sales* 83,287,000
SIC 7359 Equipment rental and leasing, nec
Stephanie Gaudreau
Daniel Gaudreau

D-U-N-S 20-265-1634   (SL)
GIROUARD, ANDRE & FILS INC
JOHN DEER
(*Suby of* 127380 CANADA INC)
650 Boul Pierre-Roux E, Victoriaville, QC, G6T
1T2
(819) 758-0643
Emp Here 25   *Sales* 11,875,650
SIC 5083 Farm and garden machinery
Pierre Girouard
Diane Deserre

D-U-N-S 24-730-0262   (SL)
GROUPE PLOMBACTION INC
575 Boul Pierre-Roux E, Victoriaville, QC, G6T
1S7
(819) 752-6064
Emp Here 80   *Sales* 18,645,200
SIC 1711 Plumbing, heating, air-conditioning
Alain Courtois

D-U-N-S 24-677-9313   (SL)
GROUPE R.Y. BEAUDOIN INC

GRYB
1400 Boul Pierre-Roux E, Victoriaville, QC,
G6T 2T7
(819) 604-1396
Emp Here 80   *Sales* 17,760,080
SIC 3531 Construction machinery
Remi Beaudoin
Luc D'amours
Jacquot Caron
Jason Mcneil

D-U-N-S 20-265-2038   (SL)
HOULE, J.U. LTEE
20 Rue Francois-Bourgeois, Victoriaville, QC,
G6T 2G8
(819) 758-5235
Emp Here 35   *Sales* 15,651,090
SIC 5074 Plumbing and heating equipment
and supplies (hydronics)
Jean Houle
Pierre Houle

D-U-N-S 20-217-0473   (SL)
LAQUERRE CHRYSLER INC
SATISFACTION DE BOIS-FRANCS
34 Boul Arthabaska E, Victoriaville, QC, G6T
0S7
(819) 752-5252
Emp Here 30   *Sales* 14,942,340
SIC 5511 New and used car dealers
Samuel Laquerre

D-U-N-S 20-211-5452   (SL)
LAURENTIDE RE-SOURCES INC
LAURENTIDE RESOURCES TM
345 Rue De La Bulstrode, Victoriaville, QC,
G6T 1P7
(819) 758-5497
Emp Here 80   *Sales* 21,412,160
SIC 5231 Paint, glass, and wallpaper stores
Andre Buisson
Gabriel Buisson
Josette Buisson
Claude P Buisson

D-U-N-S 24-359-5027   (BR)
PARMALAT CANADA INC
(*Suby of* PARMALAT SPA)
75 Boul Pierre-Roux E, Victoriaville, QC, G6T
1S8
(819) 758-6245
Emp Here 400
SIC 2023 Dry, condensed and evaporated
dairy products
Alain Bedard

D-U-N-S 24-747-1436   (HQ)
PEINTURE SYLTECK INC
AQUA-BRILLE
(*Suby of* CANLAK INC)
1521 Boul Jutras O, Victoriaville, QC, G6T 2A9
(819) 758-3662
Sales 20,790,560
SIC 5198 Paints, varnishes, and supplies
Normand Guindon
Eric Vaillancourt

D-U-N-S 20-949-6140   (SL)
ROCHELEAU, PAUL INC
760 Boul Pierre-Roux E, Victoriaville, QC, G6T
1S6
(819) 758-7525
Emp Here 30   *Sales* 13,415,220
SIC 5072 Hardware
Marc Rocheleau

D-U-N-S 25-027-6912   (SL)
**SATISFACTION PLYMOUTH CHRYLSER
INC**
SATISFACTION CHRYSLER DODGE JEEP
1475 Boul Jutras O, Victoriaville, QC, G6T 2A9
(819) 752-5252
Emp Here 23   *Sales* 11,455,794
SIC 5511 New and used car dealers
Pierre Laquerre
Paul Michaud
Allain Tremblay

D-U-N-S 25-027-5906   (SL)
SIGNE GARNEAU PAYSAGISTE INC
SIGNE GARNEAU
29 Boul Arthabaska E, Victoriaville, QC, G6T
0S5
(819) 758-3887
Emp Here 50   *Sales* 16,280,000
SIC 5992 Florists
Fortunat Garneau
Sebastien Garneau
Patrick Garneau

D-U-N-S 24-205-0735   (SL)
SURPLUS R.D. INC
RETOURS.CA
500 Rue De L'Acadie, Victoriaville, QC, G6T
1A6
(819) 758-2466
Emp Here 250   *Sales* 38,027,000
SIC 5399 Miscellaneous general merchandise
Daniel Berube
Richard Lemieux
Isabelle Beauregard

D-U-N-S 20-312-2593   (HQ)
THIRAU INC
NAPEC
489 Boul Pierre-Roux E Bureau 200, Victori-
aville, QC, G6T 1S9
(819) 752-9741
Emp Here 56   *Sales* 21,782,900
SIC 1731 Electrical work
Jason Lee
Pierre L. Gauthier
Kenneth Mckay
Andrew Moir
Mario Trahan

D-U-N-S 20-265-4125   (HQ)
THIRAU LTEE
489 Boul Pierre-Roux E, Victoriaville, QC, G6T
1S9
(819) 752-9741
Emp Here 350   *Sales* 164,057,500
SIC 1623 Water, sewer, and utility lines
Bruno Testaert
Emilie Duguay
Pierre Gauthier
Mario Trahan

D-U-N-S 20-644-1123   (SL)
VIC AUTORAMA INC
HONDA DES BOIS-FRANC
21 Boul Arthabaska E, Victoriaville, QC, G6T
0S4
(819) 758-1588
Emp Here 28   *Sales* 13,946,184
SIC 5511 New and used car dealers
Pierre Laquerre
Pierre Boisvert
Nathalie Plourde

D-U-N-S 24-842-4244   (SL)
VICTORIAVILLE & CO INC
CSC VIC ROYAL
(*Suby of* 9093-5677 QUEBEC INC)
333 Rue De La Jacques-Cartier, Victoriaville,
QC, G6T 1Y1
(819) 752-3388
Emp Here 375   *Sales* 99,213,000
SIC 3995 Burial caskets
Alain Dumont

D-U-N-S 20-309-5633   (BR)
VICWEST INC
(*Suby of* VICWEST INC)
707 Boul Pierre-Roux E, Victoriaville, QC, G6T
1S7
(819) 758-0661
Emp Here 150
SIC 3444 Sheet Metalwork
Yves Landry

Ville-Marie, QC J9V

D-U-N-S 20-265-9744   (HQ)
J. DROLET & FILS LTEE
BMR
11 Rue Des Oblats S, Ville-Marie, QC, J9V
1J9
(819) 629-2885
Emp Here 11   *Sales* 12,652,950
SIC 5211 Lumber and other building materials
Martin Drolet

Villeroy, QC G0S

D-U-N-S 24-309-4195   (SL)
ALIMENTS PRO-LACTO INC, LES
303 Rte 265, Villeroy, QC, G0S 3K0
(819) 385-1232
Emp Here 28   *Sales* 20,790,560
SIC 5191 Farm supplies
Ghislain Caouette

D-U-N-S 25-051-7048   (HQ)
FRUIT D'OR INC
306 Rte 265, Villeroy, QC, G0S 3K0
(819) 385-1126
Emp Here 100   *Sales* 172,011,840
SIC 5149 Groceries and related products, nec
Martin Lemoine
Sylvain Dufour
Marc Bedard
Rachel Carrier
Eric Veilleux

Vimont, QC H7M

D-U-N-S 20-965-9478   (SL)
C.T. CONSULTANTS INC
CTC
1696 Boul Des Laurentides, Vimont, QC, H7M
2P4
(514) 375-0377
Emp Here 50   *Sales* 11,848,500
SIC 7361 Employment agencies
Carmine Trivisonno
Gianna Venditti

D-U-N-S 20-799-3296   (SL)
**CENTRE DE CONDITIONNEMENT
PHYSIQUE ATLANTIS INC**
1201 Boul Des Laurentides, Vimont, QC, H7M
2X9
(450) 629-1500
Emp Here 49   *Sales* 10,722,376
SIC 3949 Sporting and athletic goods, nec
Raymond Sansoucy

D-U-N-S 25-456-8082   (SL)
GESTION SYLVAIN GOUDREAULT INC
PHARMAPRIX
1768 Boul Des Laurentides Bureau 1, Vimont,
QC, H7M 2P6
(450) 663-3197
Emp Here 45   *Sales* 11,382,930
SIC 5912 Drug stores and proprietary stores
Sylvain Goudreault

Vimont, QC H7R

D-U-N-S 25-840-8392   (SL)
PRODIMAX INC
*CENTRE D'HEBERGEMENT DE LA RIVE,
LE*
1050 15e Av, Vimont, QC, H7R 4N9
(450) 627-6068
Emp Here 125   *Sales* 7,405,875
SIC 8361 Residential care
Sam Strulovitch
Jacques Le Guern
Jean-Robert Gagne

▲ Public Company   ■ Public Company Family Member   **HQ** Headquarters   **BR** Branch   **SL** Single Location

Vimont, QC H7T

D-U-N-S 24-649-3456 (HQ)
COLLECTIONS SHAN INC, LES
SHAN STUDIO
(*Suby of* SHAN INC)
4390 Sud Laval (A-440) O, Vimont, QC, H7T 2P7
(450) 687-7101
Sales 20,501,100
SIC 2339 Women's and misses' outerwear, nec
Chantal Levesque

D-U-N-S 24-335-0894 (HQ)
SHAN INC
4390 Sud Laval (A-440) O, Vimont, QC, H7T 2P7
(450) 687-7101
Emp Here 3   *Sales* 41,002,500
SIC 6712 Bank holding companies
Chantal Levesque

Wakefield, QC J0X

D-U-N-S 24-382-5627 (SL)
ENTREPRISES EMILE CHARLES & FILS LTEE
CHARLES IGA
1716 Rte 105, Wakefield, QC, J0X 3G0
(819) 459-2326
Emp Here 80   *Sales* 23,478,160
SIC 5411 Grocery stores
Emile Charles
Pierre Charles

D-U-N-S 25-361-2956 (SL)
STYRO RAIL INC
65 Rte 105, Wakefield, QC, J0X 3G0
(819) 643-4456
Emp Here 26   *Sales* 11,626,524
SIC 5033 Roofing, siding, and insulation
Julien Martineau
Francine Beaudoin
Emilie Martineau

Waltham, QC J0X

D-U-N-S 25-974-6865 (SL)
SOCIETE EN COMMANDITE COULONGE ENERGIE
Gd, Waltham, QC, J0X 3H0
(819) 689-5226
Emp Here 20   *Sales* 10,393,100
SIC 4911 Electric services
Ronald Lean

Warwick, QC J0A

D-U-N-S 20-214-4429 (HQ)
9028-3409 QUEBEC INC
JEANS DEPOT - CHATEAUGUAY
210 Rue Saint-Louis, Warwick, QC, J0A 1M0
(819) 559-8484
Emp Here 8   *Sales* 17,939,600
SIC 5651 Family clothing stores
Gerald Dubois

D-U-N-S 20-984-2405 (BR)
AKZO NOBEL WOOD COATINGS LTD
(*Suby of* AKZO NOBEL N.V.)
274 Rue Saint-Louis Bureau 6, Warwick, QC, J0A 1M0
(819) 358-7500
Emp Here 85
SIC 5198 Paints, varnishes, and supplies

Rejean St-Hilaire

D-U-N-S 24-820-9546 (BR)
ALIMENTS KRISPY KERNELS INC
CROUSTILLES YUM YUM, DIV DE
(*Suby of* DISTRIBUTION DENIS JALBERT INC)
40 Rue Du Moulin, Warwick, QC, J0A 1M0
(819) 358-3600
Emp Here 200
SIC 2096 Potato chips and similar snacks
Serge Grenier

D-U-N-S 24-863-1822 (SL)
FENERGIC INC
17 Rue Sainte-Jeanne-D'Arc, Warwick, QC, J0A 1M0
(819) 358-3400
Emp Here 70   *Sales* 18,735,640
SIC 5211 Lumber and other building materials
Pierre Beauchesne

D-U-N-S 24-908-6174 (HQ)
GESTION PIERRE BEAUCHESNE INC
17 Rue Sainte-Jeanne-D'Arc, Warwick, QC, J0A 1M0
(819) 358-3400
Emp Here 1   *Sales* 27,335,000
SIC 6712 Bank holding companies
Pierre Beauchesne

D-U-N-S 20-761-0601 (HQ)
MANUFACTURIERS WARWICK LTEE, LES
(*Suby of* GESTION GUY BOULANGER INC)
235 Rue Saint-Louis, Warwick, QC, J0A 1M0
(819) 358-4100
Emp Here 2   *Sales* 14,427,750
SIC 2421 Sawmills and planing mills, general
Alexis Boulanger
Judith Boulanger
Luce Boulanger
Guy Boulanger
Wilfrid Brunet

D-U-N-S 20-266-2987 (SL)
PLASTIQUE D.C.N. INC
250 Rue Saint-Louis, Warwick, QC, J0A 1M0
(819) 358-3700
Emp Here 80   *Sales* 16,151,760
SIC 3089 Plastics products, nec
Charles Letarte
Julie Beliveau

D-U-N-S 24-791-3452 (HQ)
ROLAND BOULANGER & CIE, LTEE
PRODUITS FORESTIERS J.V.
(*Suby of* GESTION GUY BOULANGER INC)
235 Rue Saint-Louis, Warwick, QC, J0A 1M0
(819) 358-4100
Emp Here 330   *Sales* 125,275,500
SIC 2431 Millwork
Alexis Boulanger
Judith Boulanger
Luce Boulanger
Wilfrid Brunet
Guy Langlois
Richard Boucher
Yves Rheault
Guy Boulanger

Waskaganish, QC J0M

D-U-N-S 24-943-2659 (HQ)
AIR CREEBEC INC
18 Rue Waskaganish, Waskaganish, QC, J0M 1R0
(819) 895-8355
Emp Here 96   *Sales* 111,073,200
SIC 4512 Air transportation, scheduled
Rusty Cheezo
Matthew Happyjack
Randy Bosum
Jack Blacksmith
Emily Whiskeychan

Clarence Jolly
James Bobbish
John Longchap
Neeposh Derrick
Sandy George

D-U-N-S 25-247-6437 (SL)
BLACKNED, JAMES
CONSTRUCTION BLACKNED ENR
9 Rue Pontax, Waskaganish, QC, J0M 1R0
(819) 895-8694
Emp Here 50   *Sales* 14,176,200
SIC 1611 Highway and street construction

Waterloo, QC J0E

D-U-N-S 20-266-4132 (SL)
LAITERIE CHAGNON LTEE
550 Rue Lewis, Waterloo, QC, J0E 2N0
(450) 539-3535
Emp Here 36   *Sales* 13,878,684
SIC 0241 Dairy farms
Nathan Kaiser
Christian Kaiser
Matthias Kaiser

D-U-N-S 20-400-4910 (SL)
MARCHE PLOUFFE WATERLOO INC
4615 Rue Foster, Waterloo, QC, J0E 2N0
(450) 534-2648
Emp Here 50   *Sales* 13,707,600
SIC 5411 Grocery stores
Daniel Plouffe

D-U-N-S 24-377-9530 (HQ)
PLASTIQUES BERRY CANADA INC
(*Suby of* BERRY GLOBAL GROUP, INC.)
33 Rue Taylor, Waterloo, QC, J0E 2N0
(450) 539-2772
Emp Here 1   *Sales* 22,240,120
SIC 3089 Plastics products, nec
Jonathan Rich
Richard Smith

D-U-N-S 24-649-9990 (SL)
SURPLUS MALOUIN INC
HOME HARDWARE
6400 Rue Foster, Waterloo, QC, J0E 2N0
(450) 539-3722
Emp Here 44   *Sales* 11,134,596
SIC 5211 Lumber and other building materials
Melanie Malouin
Francois Dextradeur

D-U-N-S 20-972-7114 (SL)
TURKEY HILL SUGARBUSH LIMITED
10 Rue De Waterloo, Waterloo, QC, J0E 2N0
(450) 539-4822
Emp Here 30   *Sales* 25,067,310
SIC 5145 Confectionery
Brian A Herman
Michael Herman

Waterville, QC J0B

D-U-N-S 20-564-7738 (SL)
BOIS OUVRES WATERVILLE INC
525 Rue Principale N, Waterville, QC, J0B 3H0
(819) 837-2476
Emp Here 50   *Sales* 23,751,300
SIC 5084 Industrial machinery and equipment
Lise Compagna
Alain Compagna

D-U-N-S 24-811-9372 (HQ)
GROUPE PPD INC
PPD
(*Suby of* 148220 CANADA INC)
325 Rue Principale N, Waterville, QC, J0B 3H0

(819) 837-2491
Sales 95,524,800
SIC 3089 Plastics products, nec
Sylvain Morrissette
Luc Morrissette
Rene Jarry
Gerald Lacoste
Raymond Ouellette

D-U-N-S 20-881-8021 (HQ)
MATERIAUX DE CONSTRUCTION LE-TOURNEAU INC
BMR
4855 143 Rte, Waterville, QC, J0B 3H0
(819) 566-5633
Emp Here 62   *Sales* 22,750,420
SIC 5211 Lumber and other building materials
Jocelyn Letourneau
Jean-Pierre Letourneau
Gaetan Letourneau

D-U-N-S 24-309-5168 (BR)
PPD HOLDING INC
PPD RUBTECH
(*Suby of* 148220 CANADA INC)
400 Rue Raymond, Waterville, QC, J0B 3H0

Emp Here 200
SIC 2822 Synthetic rubber

D-U-N-S 24-811-7988 (HQ)
PPD HOLDING INC
PPD
(*Suby of* 148220 CANADA INC)
325 Rue Principale N, Waterville, QC, J0B 3H0
(819) 837-2491
Emp Here 50   *Sales* 107,704,212
SIC 3089 Plastics products, nec
Sylvain Morrissette
Luc Morrissette

D-U-N-S 24-426-9804 (HQ)
PPD SOLUTION DE MOUSSE INC
PPD
(*Suby of* 148220 CANADA INC)
325 Rue Principale N, Waterville, QC, J0B 3H0
(819) 837-2491
Sales 18,672,962
SIC 2531 Public building and related furniture
Sylvain Morrissette

D-U-N-S 20-997-3486 (HQ)
WATERVILLE TG INC
(*Suby of* TOYODA GOSEI CO., LTD.)
10 Rue Du Depot, Waterville, QC, J0B 3H0
(819) 837-2421
Emp Here 728   *Sales* 504,227,430
SIC 2891 Adhesives and sealants
Maeda Kazuaki
Junichiro Kako
Mario Larose
Hiraku Hiromi
Allan Abdalla
Masayoshi Ichikawa
Mitsuo Mori

Weedon, QC J0B

D-U-N-S 20-516-3843 (SL)
BLANCHETTE & BLANCHETTE INC
(*Suby of* GESTION YVES BARRETTE INC)
520 2e Av, Weedon, QC, J0B 3J0
(819) 877-2622
Emp Here 60   *Sales* 11,542,200
SIC 2421 Sawmills and planing mills, general
Renaud Bergeron
Yves Barrette
Nathalie Blanchette

D-U-N-S 20-276-6684 (BR)
CENTRE DE SANTE ET DE SERVICE SOCI-AUX DU HAUT SAINT-FRANCOIS, LE
CSCL DU HAUT ST FRANCOIS

245 Rue Saint-Janvier, Weedon, QC, J0B 3J0

Emp Here 77
SIC 7041 Membership-basis organization hotels
  Mario Mayrand

D-U-N-S 20-431-0379   (HQ)
CONSTRUCTIONS LEO BAROLET INC, LES
250 2e Av, Weedon, QC, J0B 3J0
(819) 877-2378
Emp Here 3   *Sales* 15,943,450
SIC 1521 Single-family housing construction
  Leo Barolet

D-U-N-S 20-266-5360   (SL)
WEEDON AUTOMOBILE (1977) INC
CARROSSIER PROCOLOR WEEDON
326 2e Av, Weedon, QC, J0B 3J0
(819) 877-2833
Emp Here 26   *Sales* 12,950,028
SIC 5511 New and used car dealers
  Gaston Dumas

Wemindji, QC J0M

D-U-N-S 24-841-8113   (HQ)
CONSTRUCTION TAWICH INC
16 Rte Beaver, Wemindji, QC, J0M 1L0
(819) 978-0264
Sales 12,758,580
SIC 1611 Highway and street construction
  Walter Hughboy
  Fred Georgekish

D-U-N-S 24-848-3666   (SL)
VCC ENTREPRENEUR GENERAL INC
VCC GENERAL CONTRACTOR
42 Rte Maquatua, Wemindji, QC, J0M 1L0
(819) 978-3335
Emp Here 200   *Sales* 54,188,400
SIC 1521 Single-family housing construction
  Frank Atsynia
  Patrice Beaumelle
  Stephane Poulin
  Tony Gull
  Danny Tomatuk
  Sam Gilpin

Wendake, QC G0A

D-U-N-S 25-906-5605   (SL)
COMMISSION DE LA SANTE ET DES SERVICES SOCIAUX PREMIERE NATION DU QUEBEC ET DU LABRADOR
CSSSPNQL
250 Rue Chef-Michel-Laveau, Wendake, QC, G0A 4V0
(418) 842-1540
Emp Here 49   *Sales* 11,114,817
SIC 8399 Social services, nec
  Malik Kistabish

D-U-N-S 24-746-9596   (SL)
PREMONTEX
SECHOIRS WENDAKE, LES
597 Rue Chef-Max-Gros-Louis, Wendake, QC, G0A 4V0
(418) 847-3630
Emp Here 60   *Sales* 11,781,660
SIC 1751 Carpentry work
  Normand Sioui

Westmount, QC H3Y

D-U-N-S 25-542-4199   (HQ)
APVE INVESTMENTS INC

9 Av Forden, Westmount, QC, H3Y 2Y6

Sales 18,592,245
SIC 6211 Security brokers and dealers
  Solomon Fleising

D-U-N-S 25-540-8341   (HQ)
GREGORY HERITAGE HOLDING INC
23 Av Willow, Westmount, QC, H3Y 1Y3

Sales 10,462,120
SIC 6712 Bank holding companies
  Stephen Gregory

D-U-N-S 24-461-2925   (HQ)
INVESTISSEMENTS MICHAEL WILSON INC, LES
642 Av Murray Hill, Westmount, QC, H3Y 2W6
(450) 465-3330
Sales 42,752,340
SIC 5085 Industrial supplies
  Michael C Wilson

D-U-N-S 20-952-7696   (HQ)
LIQUID NUTRITION GROUP INC
LIQUID NUTRITION
60 Ch Belvedere, Westmount, QC, H3Y 1P8
(514) 932-7555
Emp Here 10   *Sales* 11,242,750
SIC 2033 Canned fruits and specialties
  H. Gregory Chamandy
  Chantal Chamandy

D-U-N-S 20-928-9057   (SL)
MARIANOPOLIS COLLEGE
4873 Av Westmount, Westmount, QC, H3Y 1X9
(514) 931-8792
Emp Here 185   *Sales* 27,637,335
SIC 8221 Colleges and universities
  David Bowles
  Jeanne Bonneau
  Susan Emblem
  Ramiz Razzak
  Jia Rong Shao
  Dolores Chew
  Eric Lozowy
  Hugh Cawker
  Matthew Nowakowski
  Josh Wisenthal

D-U-N-S 20-886-9024   (SL)
SELWYN HOUSE ASSOCIATION
L'ECOLE SELWYN HOUSE
95 Ch De La Cote-Saint-Antoine, Westmount, QC, H3Y 2H8
(514) 931-9481
Emp Here 100   *Sales* 9,282,600
SIC 8211 Elementary and secondary schools
  Jonathan Goldbloom
  Michael Denham
  Charles V. Bierbrier
  Vincenzo Guzzo
  Susan Einhorn
  Jonathan Goldbloom
  Louise Houle-Dupont
  Michael Denham
  Paul Mayer
  Edward Claxton

D-U-N-S 20-031-5351   (SL)
VILLA SAINTE MARCELLINE
COLLEGE INTERNATIONAL DES MARCELLINES
815 Av Upper Belmont, Westmount, QC, H3Y 1K5
(514) 488-2528
Emp Here 100   *Sales* 9,282,600
SIC 8211 Elementary and secondary schools
  Mathilde Fantone
  Marie-Louise Bonta
  Cosmina Laneve
  Katy Davar
  Ninon St-Pierre

Westmount, QC H3Z

D-U-N-S 24-850-0258   (HQ)
159585 CANADA INC
BATISSE COMMERCIALE
(*Suby of* WALTER FINANCIAL INC)
1 Car Westmount Bureau 1850, Westmount, QC, H3Z 2P9
(514) 932-7422
Emp Here 3   *Sales* 40,205,990
SIC 6712 Bank holding companies
  Pierre Somers
  Haisook Somers
  Franco Vitale
  Normand Bastien

D-U-N-S 24-433-1620   (SL)
5 SAISONS INC
1250 Av Greene, Westmount, QC, H3Z 2A3
(514) 931-0249
Emp Here 49   *Sales* 40,943,273
SIC 5149 Groceries and related products, nec
  Jean-Francois Dugal

D-U-N-S 24-228-9119   (SL)
6036945 CANADA INC
4150 Rue Sherbrooke O Bureau 400, Westmount, QC, H3Z 1C2
(514) 989-9909
Emp Here 49   *Sales* 16,029,223
SIC 6531 Real estate agents and managers
  Antoine Chawky
  Andre Mea

D-U-N-S 25-672-9211   (SL)
99767 CANADA LTEE
99767 CANADA
4795 Rue Sainte-Catherine O, Westmount, QC, H3Z 1S8
(514) 731-5654
Emp Here 26   *Sales* 19,305,520
SIC 5194 Tobacco and tobacco products
  Carrie Garbarino
  Garry Garbarino

D-U-N-S 24-953-7655   (HQ)
ALIMENTS DAINTY FOODS INC, LES
DAINTY FOODS
(*Suby of* MRRM INC)
2 Place Alexis Nihon No1777 3500 De Maisonneuve O, Westmount, QC, H3Z 3C1
(514) 908-7777
Sales 60,920,860
SIC 5149 Groceries and related products, nec
  Nikola Reford
  Richard De Palmes
  Terry Handerson
  Johanne Lord
  Johannes Castelijn
  Richard De Palmas

D-U-N-S 24-539-0229   (SL)
AQUAFUCHSIA
4881 Rue Sherbrooke O, Westmount, QC, H3Z 1G9
(514) 489-8466
Emp Here 23   *Sales* 19,218,271
SIC 5148 Fresh fruits and vegetables
  Jessie Taras

D-U-N-S 25-979-0053   (HQ)
ATRIUM INNOVATIONS INC
AERIS
(*Suby of* NESTLE S.A.)
3500 Boul De Maisonneuve O Bureau 2405, Westmount, QC, H3Z 3C1
(514) 205-6240
Emp Here 100   *Sales* 682,339,000
SIC 2023 Dry, condensed and evaporated dairy products
  Peter B. Luther
  Jacques Bougie
  Eric Bouchard
  David Torralbo
  John Coyle
  Henry Minello

Yvon Bolduc
Brian Edwards
Laura O'dannell

D-U-N-S 24-019-5669   (HQ)
B. TERFLOTH + CIE (CANADA) INC
(*Suby of* TERFLOTH INTERNATIONAL (CANADA) INC)
3500 Boul De Maisonneuve O Unite 2360, Westmount, QC, H3Z 3C1
(514) 939-2341
Sales 23,396,156
SIC 5141 Groceries, general line
  Marc Terfloth
  Borries H. Terfloth
  Francois H Ouimet
  Cornelia Terfloth-Walker
  Patricia Cano

D-U-N-S 24-256-1298   (HQ)
BESSNER GALLAY KREISMAN
BGK CONSULTANTS
4150 Rue Sainte-Catherine O Bureau 600, Westmount, QC, H3Z 2Y5
(514) 908-3600
Emp Here 52   *Sales* 11,422,675
SIC 8721 Accounting, auditing, and bookkeeping
  Samuel Bernard
  Sydney Berger
  Harold Greenspon
  Irving Kaplan
  Morton Benjamin
  David Lesser
  Louis Ruta
  Derek Silverman
  Brian Kreisman
  Clifford Herer

D-U-N-S 24-523-8402   (SL)
BOCA BOYS HOLDINGS INC
1 Car Westmount Bureau 1100, Westmount, QC, H3Z 2P9
(514) 341-5600
Emp Here 29   *Sales* 12,161,295
SIC 6712 Bank holding companies
  Amos Alter
  Miryam Alter

D-U-N-S 24-021-3413   (HQ)
CENTRES DE LA JEUNESSE ET DE LA FAMILLE BATSHAW, L
5 Rue Weredale Park, Westmount, QC, H3Z 1Y5
(514) 989-1885
Emp Here 70   *Sales* 72,624,000
SIC 8322 Individual and family services
  Karen Potter-Bienvenu
  Dodo Heppner
  Michael Udy
  Allan Aitken
  Donald Bishop
  Michele Dumais
  Natasha Mcmullen
  Ken Whittingham
  Jackie Pinkston
  Ronald Jones

D-U-N-S 20-289-8573   (SL)
CHATEAU WESTMOUNT INC
1860 Boul De Maisonneuve O, Westmount, QC, H3Z 3G2
(514) 369-3000
Emp Here 100   *Sales* 9,489,900
SIC 7041 Membership-basis organization hotels
  Anna Fiszer

D-U-N-S 20-858-5067   (SL)
CLUB MED VENTES CANADA INC
(*Suby of* HKSCC NOMINEES LIMITED)
3500 Boul De Maisonneuve O Bureau 1500, Westmount, QC, H3Z 3C1
(514) 937-1428
Emp Here 50   *Sales* 25,998,350
SIC 4725 Tour operators
  Xavier Mufraggi

Carolyne Doyon
Xavier Mufraggi
Stephan Drouin
Blandine Roussel

D-U-N-S 24-141-2456   (SL)
CONSTRUCTION GARBARINO INC
4795 Rue Sainte-Catherine O Bureau 302,
Westmount, QC, H3Z 1S8
(514) 731-5654
Emp Here 11   *Sales* 10,571,411
SIC 1521 Single-family housing construction
Garry Garbarino
Camille Chidiac

D-U-N-S 20-215-9828   (SL)
DALFEN'S LIMITED
4444 Rue Sainte-Catherine O Bureau 100,
Westmount, QC, H3Z 1R2
(514) 938-1050
Emp Here 60   *Sales* 13,252,260
SIC 6512 Nonresidential building operators
Murray Dalfen
Karen Dalfen

D-U-N-S 24-400-7944   (HQ)
DECAREL INC
DECAREL INTERNATIONAL
4434 Rue Sainte-Catherine O, Westmount,
QC, H3Z 1R2
(514) 935-6462
Sales 23,536,550
SIC 1542 Nonresidential construction, nec
Robert Salicco
Yvon Genest

D-U-N-S 24-523-8394   (SL)
DIVERTISSEMENT SONOMA S.E.C.
MADACY MUSIC
1 Car Westmount Bureau 1100, Westmount,
QC, H3Z 2P9
(514) 341-5600
Emp Here 29   *Sales* 15,095,718
SIC 5099 Durable goods, nec
Amos Alter

D-U-N-S 25-973-7799   (HQ)
EQUINOXE, LIFE CARE SOLUTIONS INC
4060 Rue Sainte-Catherine O Bureau 201,
Westmount, QC, H3Z 2Z3
(514) 935-2600
Sales 10,932,160
SIC 8059 Nursing and personal care, nec
Daniel Martz
Danielle Pollack
Gideon Pollack

D-U-N-S 20-025-5524   (BR)
FAIRWAY MANAGEMENT CORPORATION LTD
PLACE KENSINGTON
(*Suby of* IMMEUBLES FAIRWAY INC, LES)
4430 Rue Sainte-Catherine O Bureau 505,
Westmount, QC, H3Z 3E4
(514) 935-1212
Emp Here 110
SIC 8361 Residential care
S Zagury

D-U-N-S 24-064-4224   (SL)
FANTAISIE D'ETAIN INC
21 Av Gladstone Bureau 2, Westmount, QC,
H3Z 1Z3
(514) 735-4141
Emp Here 40   *Sales* 20,821,680
SIC 5099 Durable goods, nec
Pinchas Abecassis
Pascale Sasson

D-U-N-S 20-764-9476   (HQ)
FEDERATION DES MEDECINS OMNIPRAC-TICIENS DU QUEBEC, LA
FMOQ
3500 Boul De Maisonneuve O Bureau 2000,
Westmount, QC, H3Z 3C1
(514) 878-1911
Sales 11,109,690
SIC 8621 Professional organizations

Louis Godin
Marc-Andre Amyot
Sylvain Dion
Michel Vachon
Josee Bouchard
Marcel Guilbault
Martin Pierre
Claude Rivard
Jacques G. Bergeron

D-U-N-S 20-270-6164   (HQ)
GROUPE FINANCIER AGA INC
AGA ASSURANCES COLLECTIVES
3500 Boul De Maisonneuve O Bureau 2200,
Westmount, QC, H3Z 3C1
(514) 935-5444
Emp Here 35   *Sales* 157,058,070
SIC 6411 Insurance agents, brokers, and service
Martin Papillon
Chantal Dufresne

D-U-N-S 24-386-0256   (HQ)
HARTCO INC
4120 Rue Sainte-Catherine O, Westmount,
QC, H3Z 1P4
(514) 354-0580
Sales 621,365,300
SIC 6712 Bank holding companies
Harry Hart
Patrick Waid
Michael Lemieux
Anthony Decristofaro
Nina Hart
Gerard A. Limoges
William Cleman

D-U-N-S 20-217-0288   (HQ)
INDUSTRIES DOREL INC, LES
AMEUBLEMENT DOREL
1255 Av Greene Bureau 300, Westmount, QC,
H3Z 2A4
(514) 934-3034
Emp Here 30   *Sales* 2,619,513,000
SIC 2512 Upholstered household furniture
Martin Schwartz
Ed Wyse
Jeffrey Schwartz
Alan Schwartz
Jeff Segel
Frank Rana
Michelle Ann Cormier
Norman M. Steinberg
Dian Cohen
Maurice Tousson

D-U-N-S 24-179-9063   (SL)
INVERA INC
4333 Rue Sainte-Catherine O Bureau 201,
Westmount, QC, H3Z 1P9
(514) 935-3535
Emp Here 98   *Sales* 17,376,478
SIC 7371 Custom computer programming services
Ram Panda
Veer Vashishta
Rosaria Abreu

D-U-N-S 20-298-5859   (SL)
L'ART DE VIVRE A SON MEILLEUR
215 REDFERN
4152a Rue Sainte-Catherine O, Westmount,
QC, H3Z 1P4

Emp Here 25   *Sales* 10,483,875
SIC 6719 Holding companies, nec
Daniel Revah

D-U-N-S 24-350-8608   (HQ)
MANTORIA INCORPOREE
4492 Rue Sainte-Catherine O, Westmount,
QC, H3Z 1R7
(514) 488-4004
Emp Here 50   *Sales* 41,695,610
SIC 4731 Freight transportation arrangement
Robert O Elvidge
Victoria Elvidge

Amanda Elvidge

D-U-N-S 25-746-8470   (BR)
METRO RICHELIEU INC
METRO
(*Suby of* METRO INC)
4840 Rue Sherbrooke O, Westmount, QC,
H3Z 1G8
(514) 488-4083
Emp Here 150
SIC 5411 Grocery stores
Graham Fletcher

D-U-N-S 20-544-2106   (HQ)
OGILVY & OGILVY INC
OGILVY ASSURANCE
(*Suby of* INVESTISSEMENTS RICHARD
OGILVY INC, LES)
4115 Rue Sherbrooke O Bureau 500, West-
mount, QC, H3Z 1K9
(514) 932-8660
Sales 25,441,800
SIC 6411 Insurance agents, brokers, and service
Bruce Ogilvy
David W. Ogilvy

D-U-N-S 20-792-9159   (HQ)
REVAY ET ASSOCIES LIMITEE
4333 Rue Sainte-Catherine O Bureau 500,
Westmount, QC, H3Z 1P9
(514) 932-2188
Emp Here 20   *Sales* 13,716,600
SIC 8741 Management services
Zey Emir
William R Gillan
Hang Phan

D-U-N-S 25-190-2318   (SL)
RICHTER GROUPE CONSEIL SENC
RICHTER & ASSOCIES
3500 Boul De Maisonneuve O Unite 1800,
Westmount, QC, H3Z 3C1
(514) 934-3497
Emp Here 80   *Sales* 21,946,560
SIC 8741 Management services
Raymond Massi

D-U-N-S 20-716-6963   (HQ)
RNC MEDIA INC
CALENDRIER DREAM TEAM
1 Pl Westmount Square Bureau 1405, West-
mount, QC, H3Z 2P9
(514) 866-8686
Emp Here 1   *Sales* 100,363,200
SIC 4832 Radio broadcasting stations
Mario Cecchini
Pierre R Brosseau
Jean-Yves Gourd
Claude Beaudoin
Fernand Belisle
Alexandre Brosseau
Dominique Boisvert

D-U-N-S 24-325-9231   (HQ)
ROTHENBERG & ROTHENBERG ANNU-ITIES LTD
4420 Rue Sainte-Catherine O, Westmount,
QC, H3Z 1R2
(514) 934-0586
Emp Here 23   *Sales* 13,280,175
SIC 6282 Investment advice
Jack Rothenberg
Helen Corrigan

D-U-N-S 24-351-2725   (SL)
SOCIETE DE PLACEMENTS BERNFERST INC
3 Car Westmount, Westmount, QC, H3Z 2S5
(514) 384-7462
Emp Here 1   *Sales* 13,000,005
SIC 6712 Bank holding companies
Bernard Ferstenfeld

D-U-N-S 24-433-6236   (HQ)
TECHNOLOGIES DE TRANSFERT DE CHALEUR MAYA LTEE
MAYA

4999 Rue Sainte-Catherine O Bureau 400,
Westmount, QC, H3Z 1T3
(514) 369-5706
Sales 23,242,144
SIC 7373 Computer integrated systems design
Inta Zvagulis
Jacob Harris
Christopher Pye
Kevin Duffy

D-U-N-S 20-884-3557   (HQ)
TOULON DEVELOPMENT CORPORATION
TOULON
4060 Rue Sainte-Catherine O Bureau 700,
Westmount, QC, H3Z 2Z3
(514) 931-5811
Emp Here 20   *Sales* 33,511,120
SIC 6531 Real estate agents and managers
John Alper
Avery Palevsky

D-U-N-S 24-109-7088   (BR)
WESTERN INVENTORY SERVICE LTD
(*Suby of* ARES CAPITAL CORPORATION)
4865 Boul De Maisonneuve O, Westmount,
QC, H3Z 1M7
(514) 483-1337
Emp Here 150
SIC 7389 Business services, nec
Jean Bouchard

Wickham, QC J0C

D-U-N-S 25-495-1056   (SL)
2161-1298 QUEBEC INC
SIGNATURE
1031 7e Rang, Wickham, QC, J0C 1S0
(819) 398-6303
Emp Here 70   *Sales* 10,910,410
SIC 2491 Wood preserving
Gilles Morin
Angele Morin
Ian Morin

D-U-N-S 24-820-8381   (SL)
2639-1862 QUEBEC INC
PLANCHERS DE BOIS-FRANC WICKHAM, LES
1031 7e Rang, Wickham, QC, J0C 1S0
(819) 398-6303
Emp Here 110   *Sales* 23,363,790
SIC 1752 Floor laying and floor work, nec
Jean-Pierre Nittolo
Courey Stephen
Mario Bolduc

D-U-N-S 20-266-5550   (HQ)
BOISJOLI, DORIA LTEE
730 Rue Boisjoli, Wickham, QC, J0C 1S0
(819) 398-6813
Sales 12,336,608
SIC 0251 Broiler, fryer, and roaster chickens
Denis Richard
Jean Boisjoli

D-U-N-S 24-167-7681   (BR)
COMPAGNIE BEAULIEU CANADA
(*Suby of* BEAULIEU HOLDINGS OF
CANADA, INC.)
1003 Rue Principale Rr 21, Wickham, QC,
J0C 1S0

Emp Here 120
SIC 2282 Throwing and winding mills
Rejean Viau

D-U-N-S 20-266-5543   (HQ)
COUVOIR BOIRE & FRERES INC
532 9e Rang, Wickham, QC, J0C 1S0
(819) 398-6807
Sales 30,992,550
SIC 0251 Broiler, fryer, and roaster chickens
Claude Boire

Eric Bienvenue
Denis Boire
Clement Boire

D-U-N-S 24-371-6748   (SL)
FONDATIONS ROY-LAROUCHE INC
1695 Rue Skiroule Rr 21, Wickham, QC, J0C
1S0
(819) 398-7333
Emp Here 60   *Sales* 11,525,100
SIC 3444 Sheet Metalwork
Steven Roy
Maxime Larouche
Guylaine Goudreau

Windsor, QC J1S

D-U-N-S 25-440-3652   (HQ)
**CARREFOUR DE LA SANTE ET DES SER-
VICES SOCIAUX DU VAL-SAINT-FRANCOIS**
*CARREFOUR DE LA SSS DU VAL SAINT-
FRANCOIS*
79 Rue Allen Bureau 501, Windsor, QC, J1S
2P8
(819) 542-2777
Emp Here 15   *Sales* 32,141,000
SIC 8361 Residential care
Roch Rousseau
Nancy Goguen

D-U-N-S 20-712-1182   (BR)
COMMISSION SCOLAIRE DES SOMMETS
ECOLE DU TOURNESOL
(*Suby of* COMMISSION SCOLAIRE DES
SOMMETS)
250 Rue Saint-Georges, Windsor, QC, J1S
1K4
(819) 845-2728
Emp Here 75
SIC 8211 Elementary and secondary schools
Marc Juneau

D-U-N-S 20-330-6543   (BR)
DOMTAR INC
PAPIERS DOMTAR
(*Suby of* DOMTAR LUXEMBOURG INVEST-
MENTS SARL)
609 Rang 12, Windsor, QC, J1S 2L9
(800) 263-8366
Emp Here 850
SIC 2611 Pulp mills
Sylvain Bricault

Yamachiche, QC G0X

D-U-N-S 25-536-1958   (HQ)
9071-3975 QUEBEC INC
TRANSFORMATION BFL
212 Ch Du Canton S, Yamachiche, QC, G0X
3L0
(819) 296-1754
Emp Here 1   *Sales* 121,846,250
SIC 2011 Meat packing plants
Claude Robitaille
Marc Robitaille
Luc Robitaille
Denis Robitaille

D-U-N-S 20-767-8322   (SL)
9081-9012 QUEBEC INC
HALTE 174
4 Rue Sainte-Anne, Yamachiche, QC, G0X
3L0
(819) 228-5620
Emp Here 26   *Sales* 12,950,028
SIC 5541 Gasoline service stations
Jean-Francois Quintal

D-U-N-S 20-845-2339   (SL)
9138-9494 QUEBEC INC
YAMACO
212 Ch Du Canton S, Yamachiche, QC, G0X

3L0
(819) 296-1754
Emp Here 200   *Sales* 69,138,000
SIC 2011 Meat packing plants
Claude Robitaille
Camille Moore
Nicole Lemieux

D-U-N-S 20-266-7697   (SL)
ATRAHAN TRANSFORMATION INC
860 Ch Des Acadiens, Yamachiche, QC, G0X
3L0
(819) 296-3791
Emp Here 200   *Sales* 69,138,000
SIC 2011 Meat packing plants
Rejean Nadeau
Paul Beauchamp
Carole Potvin

D-U-N-S 20-266-7432   (SL)
DUCHESNE ET FILS LTEE
ALUMINIUM DUCHESNE
(*Suby of* ENTREPRISES DUCHESNE LTEE,
LES)
871 Boul Duchesne, Yamachiche, QC, G0X
3L0
(819) 296-3737
Emp Here 100   *Sales* 18,138,800
SIC 3315 Steel wire and related products
Francoise Duchesne
Audrey Duhesne Milette

D-U-N-S 20-357-6343   (SL)
OLY-ROBI TRANSFORMATION S.E.C.
ALIMENTS LUCY PORC/PORK
212 Ch Du Canton S, Yamachiche, QC, G0X
3L0
(819) 296-1754
Emp Here 400   *Sales* 194,954,000
SIC 2011 Meat packing plants
Claude Robitaille

D-U-N-S 24-402-6142   (SL)
PORTE DE LA MAURICIE INC, LA
4 Rue Sainte-Anne, Yamachiche, QC, G0X
3L0
(819) 228-9434
Emp Here 100   *Sales* 4,551,900
SIC 5812 Eating places
Mario Quintal

Air Ronge, SK S0J

D-U-N-S 20-813-8607   (BR)
LAC LA RONGE INDIAN BAND
(*Suby of* LAC LA RONGE INDIAN BAND)
54 Far Reserve Rd, Air Ronge, SK, S0J 3G0
(306) 425-2884
Emp Here 80
SIC 8743 Public relations services
Tayven Roberts

Allan, SK S0K

D-U-N-S 24-233-3326   (BR)
**POTASH   CORPORATION   OF
SASKATCHEWAN INC**
PCS POTASH ALLAN
(*Suby of* NUTRIEN LTD)
Gd, Allan, SK, S0K 0C0
(306) 257-3312
Emp Here 460
SIC 1474 Potash, soda, and borate minerals
Trevor Berg

Annaheim, SK S0K

D-U-N-S 20-059-5163   (HQ)
DOEPKER INDUSTRIES LTD
300 Doepker Ave, Annaheim, SK, S0K 0G0
(306) 598-2171
Emp Here 260   *Sales* 152,696,250
SIC 3715 Truck trailers
Dave Doepker
Gurcan Kocdag
Randy Doepker
Lionel Doepker

Arcola, SK S0C

D-U-N-S 24-690-8966   (SL)
**ARCOLA CO-OPERATIVE ASSOCIATION
LIMITED**
Hwy 13, Arcola, SK, S0C 0G0
(306) 455-2393
Emp Here 15   *Sales* 15,492,120
SIC 5171 Petroleum bulk stations and terminals
Cindy Kolenz
Roger Wyatt
Terry Pearson
Paul Cameron
Richard Weber
Clay Chapman
Stacey Brownridge
Garth Herman

Asquith, SK S0K

D-U-N-S 20-272-3763   (SL)
**HUTTERIAN BRETHREN CHURCH OF EA-
GLE CREEK INC**
EAGLE CREEK COLONY
Gd, Asquith, SK, S0K 0J0
(306) 329-4476
Emp Here 35   *Sales* 11,986,345
SIC 0191 General farms, primarily crop
Joe Wurtz
Gerry Wurtz

Assiniboia, SK S0H

D-U-N-S 24-916-2306   (HQ)
**NELSON CHEVROLET OLDSMOBILE PON-
TIAC BUICK GMC LTD**
NELSON GM
201 1st Ave W, Assiniboia, SK, S0H 0B0
(306) 642-5995
Emp Here 22   *Sales* 19,923,120
SIC 5511 New and used car dealers
Bill Nelson
Curtis Nelson
Janet Day
Walter Nelson

D-U-N-S 24-103-2676   (SL)
SELFLAND CO-OP LTD
409 Centre St, Assiniboia, SK, S0H 0B0
(306) 642-3347
Emp Here 49   *Sales* 13,433,448
SIC 5411 Grocery stores
Ken Bahuaud

D-U-N-S 25-682-2255   (HQ)
SOUTHLAND CO-OPERATIVE LTD
409 Centre St, Assiniboia, SK, S0H 0B0
(306) 642-4128
Emp Here 96   *Sales* 38,152,010
SIC 5411 Grocery stores
Ken Bahuaud

Avonlea, SK S0H

D-U-N-S 20-059-6906   (HQ)
**NELSON MOTORS & EQUIPMENT (1976)
LTD**
Hwy 334, Avonlea, SK, S0H 0C0
(306) 868-5000
Emp Here 25   *Sales* 11,396,000
SIC 5999 Miscellaneous retail stores, nec
Walter Nelson
Gary Nelson

D-U-N-S 24-365-6126   (HQ)
**WIGMORE CROP PRODUCTION PROD-
UCTS LTD**
140 Nelson Industrial Dr, Avonlea, SK, S0H
0C0
(306) 868-2252
Sales 12,103,970
SIC 5159 Farm-product raw materials, nec
Jeff Wigmore

Belle Plaine, SK S0G

D-U-N-S 24-691-3024   (SL)
**HUTTERITE BRETHREN CHURCH OF
BELLE PLAINE**
BELLE PLAINE COLONY
Gd, Belle Plaine, SK, S0G 0G0
(306) 345-2544
Emp Here 35   *Sales* 29,245,195
SIC 5144 Poultry and poultry products
Samuel Tschetter
Dan Tschetter
Frank Tschetter
Paul Tschetter

D-U-N-S 25-359-5953   (BR)
MOSAIC CANADA ULC
MOSAIC POTASH BELLE PLAINE MINE
(*Suby of* THE MOSAIC COMPANY)
3 Kalium Rd, Belle Plaine, SK, S0G 0G0
(306) 345-8067
Emp Here 1,300
SIC 1474 Potash, soda, and borate minerals
Nevin Maga

D-U-N-S 24-319-4896   (SL)
TERRA GRAIN FUELS INC
5 Km N Kalium Rd, Belle Plaine, SK, S0G 0G0

(306) 345-2280
Emp Here 49   *Sales* 20,714,113
SIC 1541 Industrial buildings and warehouses
Jason Drummond
Gary Drummond
Tim Lafrance
Mark Silver
Calvin Eyven

D-U-N-S 24-852-6436   (BR)
YARA BELLE PLAINE INC
(*Suby of* YARA INTERNATIONAL ASA)
2 Kalium Rd, Belle Plaine, SK, S0G 0G0
(306) 345-4200
Emp Here 140
SIC 2874 Phosphatic fertilizers
Michael Schlaug

Bengough, SK S0C

D-U-N-S 24-234-1196   (SL)
BENGOUGH CO-OPERATIVE LIMITED
140 3 St E, Bengough, SK, S0C 0K0
(306) 268-2040
Emp Here 13   *Sales* 13,426,504
SIC 5171 Petroleum bulk stations and termi-
nals
Noel Morris
Arlene Sjogren
Nancy Shaver
Arlene Sjogren
Doug Coroluick
Kathy Schropp

Bethune, SK S0G

D-U-N-S 20-342-6010   (BR)
**K+S POTASH CANADA GENERAL PART-
NERSHIP**
(*Suby of* K+S AG)
Sw 35-19-25-W2, Bethune, SK, S0G 0H0
(306) 638-2800
Emp Here 200
SIC 1474 Potash, soda, and borate minerals
Sam Farris

Bienfait, SK S0C

D-U-N-S 20-845-4673   (BR)
PRAIRIE MINES & ROYALTY ULC
(*Suby of* WESTMORELAND COAL COM-
PANY)
Gd, Bienfait, SK, S0C 0M0
(306) 388-2272
Emp Here 90
SIC 1221 Bituminous coal and lignite-surface
mining
Doug Barnstable

Biggar, SK S0K

D-U-N-S 20-385-7362   (SL)
AGI ENVIROTANK LTD
401 Hwy 4, Biggar, SK, S0K 0M0
(306) 948-5262
Emp Here 70   *Sales* 13,445,950
SIC 3443 Fabricated plate work (boiler shop)
David Burton
Jeffrey Burton
Wayne Broeckel
Kenneth Kernohan
Herb Ford

D-U-N-S 20-842-9605   (SL)
DIAMOND LODGE CO LTD

402 2nd Ave W, Biggar, SK, S0K 0M0

Emp Here 100   *Sales* 6,507,500
SIC 8361 Residential care
Deb Kurulak-Milne

D-U-N-S 20-189-7407   (SL)
**HUTTERIAN   BRETHREN   OF   GOLDEN
VIEW INC**
GOLDEN VIEW COLONY
Gd, Biggar, SK, S0K 0M0
(306) 948-2716
Emp Here 82   *Sales* 21,509,338
SIC 0119 Cash grains, nec
Sam Kleinsasser
Tim Kleinsasser

D-U-N-S 20-107-0369   (HQ)
RACK PETROLEUM LTD
901 Hwy 4 S, Biggar, SK, S0K 0M0
(306) 948-1800
Emp Here 10   *Sales* 59,401,600
SIC 5191 Farm supplies
Dennis Bulani

Bracken, SK S0N

D-U-N-S 25-977-0154   (SL)
BUTTE COLONY
Gd, Bracken, SK, S0N 0G0
(306) 298-4445
Emp Here 70   *Sales* 19,203,240
SIC 8741 Management services
Mike Wurz

Brownlee, SK S0H

D-U-N-S 24-171-9632   (SL)
HUTTERIAN BRETHREN OF HURON LTD
Gd, Brownlee, SK, S0H 0M0
(306) 759-2685
Emp Here 86   *Sales* 11,761,274
SIC 0259 Poultry and eggs, nec
Michael Entz
Peter Entz

Buffalo Narrows, SK S0M

D-U-N-S 24-112-3561   (SL)
947786 ALBERTA LTD
COURTESY AIR
Buffalo Narrows Airport, Buffalo Narrows, SK,
S0M 0J0
(306) 235-4373
Emp Here 42   *Sales* 13,639,668
SIC 4522 Air transportation, nonscheduled
Jacqueline Fowler

Bulyea, SK S0G

D-U-N-S 20-060-1946   (SL)
**BULYEA COMMUNITY CO-OPERATIVE AS-
SOCIATION LIMITED, THE**
Gd, Bulyea, SK, S0G 0L0
(306) 725-4911
Emp Here 14   *Sales* 14,459,312
SIC 5171 Petroleum bulk stations and termi-
nals
Linda Brazeau
Kim Hornung
Kimberly Tanner
Ross Parkin
John De Hoop
Brad Foster
Greg Yung

Kelly Flavel
Darrell Thompson
Terry Fiesel

Bushell Park, SK S0H

D-U-N-S 20-369-8969 (BR)
CAE FORMATION POUR L'AVIATION MILI-TAIRE INC
CAE MILITARY AVIATION TRAINING INC
(*Suby of* CAE INC)
15 Wing Moose Jaw Bldg 160, Bushell Park, SK, S0H 0N0
(306) 694-2719
Emp Here 180
SIC 8249 Vocational schools, nec
 Gene Colabatistto

Cabri, SK S0N

D-U-N-S 24-572-7425 (HQ)
AM INSPECTION LTD
(*Suby of* GREY MOUNTAIN PARTNERS, LLC)
501 Railway St N, Cabri, SK, S0N 0J0
(306) 587-2620
Emp Here 7 *Sales* 11,230,475
SIC 7389 Business services, nec
 Trevor Hull

D-U-N-S 24-775-3536 (SL)
WHEATLAND HUTTERIAN BRETHREN OF CABRI INC
Gd, Cabri, SK, S0N 0J0
(306) 587-2458
Emp Here 60 *Sales* 11,542,200
SIC 2429 Special product sawmills, nec
 John Hoffer
 John G Wirtz
 Joseph G Wirtz
 Peter John Hoffer
 Amos Walner

Canora, SK S0A

D-U-N-S 20-060-2746 (HQ)
GATEWAY CO-OPERATIVE LTD
707 Norway Rd, Canora, SK, S0A 0L0
(306) 563-5637
Emp Here 30 *Sales* 17,454,155
SIC 5399 Miscellaneous general merchandise
 George Stinka

D-U-N-S 24-428-9088 (SL)
GATEWAY LODGE INC
212 Centre Ave E, Canora, SK, S0A 0L0
(306) 563-5685
Emp Here 95 *Sales* 6,513,770
SIC 8051 Skilled nursing care facilities
 Jim Natsalla

Carlyle, SK S0C

D-U-N-S 24-608-4552 (SL)
CARLYLE MOTOR PRODUCTS LTD
Gd, Carlyle, SK, S0C 0R0
(306) 453-6741
Emp Here 23 *Sales* 11,455,794
SIC 5511 New and used car dealers
 Garnet Goud
 Shelby Goud

D-U-N-S 24-876-7308 (BR)
CES ENERGY SOLUTIONS CORP
AES DRILLING FLUIDS

(*Suby of* CES ENERGY SOLUTIONS CORP)
Highway 9 S, Carlyle, SK, S0C 0R0
(306) 453-4470
Emp Here 100
SIC 1382 Oil and gas exploration services
 Mike Lothian

D-U-N-S 20-373-2490 (BR)
CRESCENT POINT ENERGY CORP
(*Suby of* CRESCENT POINT ENERGY CORP)
801 Railway Ave, Carlyle, SK, S0C 0R0
(306) 453-3236
Emp Here 190
SIC 1311 Crude petroleum and natural gas
 Tim Mclequer

D-U-N-S 24-254-5999 (SL)
EAGLE DRILLING SERVICES LTD
Gd, Carlyle, SK, S0C 0R0
(306) 453-2506
Emp Here 100 *Sales* 21,782,900
SIC 1781 Water well drilling
 Derek Big Eagle

D-U-N-S 25-963-5571 (BR)
SASKATCHEWAN INDIAN GAMING AU-THORITY INC
BEAR CLAW CASINO
(*Suby of* FEDERATION OF SASKATCHEWAN INDIANS, INC)
Gd, Carlyle, SK, S0C 0R0
(306) 577-4577
Emp Here 150
SIC 7999 Amusement and recreation, nec
 Edward Littlechief

Carnduff, SK S0C

D-U-N-S 20-545-6775 (SL)
FAST TRUCKING SERVICE LTD
1 Fast Lane, Carnduff, SK, S0C 0S0
(306) 482-3244
Emp Here 150 *Sales* 30,855,900
SIC 4212 Local trucking, without storage
 Tony Day
 Vi Day

Caronport, SK S0H

D-U-N-S 20-060-4650 (SL)
BRIERCREST COLLEGE AND SEMINARY
BRIERCREST COLLEGE
510 College Dr, Caronport, SK, S0H 0S0
(306) 756-3200
Emp Here 125 *Sales* 18,673,875
SIC 8221 Colleges and universities
 Glen Werner
 Michael Pawelke
 Dwayne Uglem
 Merrill Dyck

Carrot River, SK S0E

D-U-N-S 20-740-1464 (HQ)
CARROT RIVER CO-OPERATIVE LIMITED, THE
1002 Main St, Carrot River, SK, S0E 0L0
(306) 768-2622
Sales 13,843,808
SIC 8699 Membership organizations, nec
 Terry Tremblay
 Robert Nagus
 Ed Little
 Marcie Haines
 Bob Gagne
 Jerry Merrett

Bev Park
Elvira Enns
Armand Robert
Rosanne Yurkowski

Clavet, SK S0K

D-U-N-S 24-229-5319 (SL)
PRAIRIE STEEL PRODUCTS LTD
Gd, Clavet, SK, S0K 0Y0
(306) 933-1141
Emp Here 25 *Sales* 18,563,000
SIC 5191 Farm supplies
 Lawrence Goebel

Coleville, SK S0L

D-U-N-S 24-173-3310 (SL)
R E LINE TRUCKING (COLEVILLE) LTD
4th Ave, Coleville, SK, S0L 0K0
(306) 965-2472
Emp Here 65 *Sales* 20,780,825
SIC 1389 Oil and gas field services, nec
 Basil Tuffs
 David Tuffs

Corman Park, SK S7T

D-U-N-S 24-968-7088 (SL)
ENGLISH RIVER ENTERPRISES INC
GRASSWOOD PETRO CANADA
2553 Grasswood Rd E, Corman Park, SK, S7T 1C8
(306) 374-9181
Emp Here 30 *Sales* 14,942,340
SIC 5541 Gasoline service stations
 Shawn Willie
 Jamie Dickson

Coronach, SK S0H

D-U-N-S 20-060-7430 (SL)
CORONACH CO-OPERATIVE ASSOCIA-TION LIMITED, THE
112 Centre St, Coronach, SK, S0H 0Z0
(306) 267-2010
Emp Here 33 *Sales* 34,082,664
SIC 5171 Petroleum bulk stations and termi-nals
 Blair Molsberry
 Lyla Payne
 Jim Achtymichuk
 Louise Korbo
 George Quarrie
 Donna Meshke
 Trent Nystrom
 Karen Jones

D-U-N-S 25-686-7649 (BR)
PRAIRIE MINES & ROYALTY ULC
(*Suby of* WESTMORELAND COAL COM-PANY)
Gd, Coronach, SK, S0H 0Z0
(306) 267-4200
Emp Here 160
SIC 1221 Bituminous coal and lignite-surface mining
 Doug Barnstable

D-U-N-S 20-747-9119 (BR)
SASKATCHEWAN POWER CORPORATION
SASKPOWER
(*Suby of* GOVERNMENT OF SASKATCHEWAN)
Gd, Coronach, SK, S0H 0Z0

(306) 267-5200
Emp Here 130
SIC 4911 Electric services
 Trevor Barrett

Craik, SK S0G

D-U-N-S 20-060-7653 (HQ)
CRAIK CO-OPERATIVE ASSOCIATION LIM-ITED, THE
309 3rd St, Craik, SK, S0G 0V0
(306) 734-2612
Emp Here 1 *Sales* 17,557,736
SIC 5171 Petroleum bulk stations and termi-nals
 Brent Jones

Cut Knife, SK S0M

D-U-N-S 25-794-4702 (SL)
CUT KNIFE HEALTH COMPLEX PRAIRIE NORTH HEALTH DISTRICT
102 Dion Ave, Cut Knife, SK, S0M 0N0
(306) 398-4977
Emp Here 30 *Sales* 55,399,770
SIC 6324 Hospital and medical service plans
 Gillian Gregorie

Davidson, SK S0G

D-U-N-S 20-741-6657 (SL)
6132511 CANADA LTD
DAVIDSON SHELL
Gd, Davidson, SK, S0G 1A0
(306) 567-3222
Emp Here 25 *Sales* 12,451,950
SIC 5541 Gasoline service stations
 Peter Kim

D-U-N-S 24-913-9395 (HQ)
PANTHER INDUSTRIES INC
(*Suby of* J.W. YUEL HOLDINGS LTD)
108 Internal Rd, Davidson, SK, S0G 1A0
(306) 567-2814
Emp Here 10 *Sales* 23,919,630
SIC 7389 Business services, nec
 Greg Yuel
 Jim Yuel
 Clayton Schneider

Dillon, SK S0M

D-U-N-S 20-150-3609 (SL)
BUFFALO RIVER MINI MART & GAS BAR INC
Gd, Dillon, SK, S0M 0S0
(306) 282-2177
Emp Here 25 *Sales* 12,451,950
SIC 5541 Gasoline service stations
 Joan Abbott

Duck Lake, SK S0K

D-U-N-S 20-787-4277 (SL)
BEARDY'S & OKEMASIS WILLOW CREE FIRST NATION EDUCATION AUTHORITY
Gd, Duck Lake, SK, S0K 1J0
(306) 467-4441
Emp Here 40 *Sales* 27,872,400
SIC 6732 Trusts: educational, religious, etc.
 Tyler Cameron

Dundurn, SK S0K

D-U-N-S 25-012-5655   (SL)
HILLCREST COLONY INC
Gd, Dundurn, SK, S0K 1K0
(306) 492-2499
Emp Here 100   *Sales* 34,246,700
SIC 0191 General farms, primarily crop
Mike Wollman

Emerald Park, SK S4L

D-U-N-S 20-258-3001   (SL)
CANADA WEST HARVEST CENTRE INC
8 Industrial Dr, Emerald Park, SK, S4L 1B6
(306) 525-2300
Emp Here 25   *Sales* 11,875,650
SIC 5083 Farm and garden machinery
Doug Tibben
Roger Bucsis

D-U-N-S 25-169-6969   (SL)
D.J. KNOLL TRANSPORT LTD
4 Great Plains Industrial Dr, Emerald Park,
SK, S4L 1B6
(306) 789-4824
Emp Here 90   *Sales* 13,337,280
SIC 4213 Trucking, except local
Scott Scott

D-U-N-S 24-231-7188   (BR)
**K-LINE MAINTENANCE & CONSTRUCTION
LIMITED**
(*Suby of* K-LINE MAINTENANCE & CON-
STRUCTION LIMITED)
5 Industrial Dr, Emerald Park, SK, S4L 1B7
(306) 781-2711
Emp Here 100
SIC 1623 Water, sewer, and utility lines
Allan Kellett

D-U-N-S 25-149-3441   (SL)
**MARKUSSON NEW HOLLAND OF REGINA
LTD**
26 Great Plains Rd, Emerald Park, SK, S4L
1B6
(306) 781-2828
Emp Here 40   *Sales* 13,024,000
SIC 5999 Miscellaneous retail stores, nec
Hartley Markusson
Cory Markusson
Derrick Markusson

D-U-N-S 24-230-8473   (SL)
TAGISH ENTERPRISES LTD
5a South Plains Road W, Emerald Park, SK,
S4L 1A1
(306) 585-8480
Emp Here 40   *Sales* 10,837,680
SIC 1521 Single-family housing construction

Englefeld, SK S0K

D-U-N-S 20-061-2919   (HQ)
SCHULTE INDUSTRIES LTD
(*Suby of* ALAMO GROUP INC.)
1 Railway Ave, Englefeld, SK, S0K 1N0
(306) 287-3715
Emp Here 100   *Sales* 26,640,120
SIC 3549 Metalworking machinery, nec
Greg Archibald
Ron Robinson

Esterhazy, SK S0A

D-U-N-S 20-167-6228   (SL)

MOSAIC ESTERHAZY HOLDINGS ULC
(*Suby of* THE MOSAIC COMPANY)
Hwy 80 E, Esterhazy, SK, S0A 0X0
(306) 745-4200
Emp Here 900   *Sales* 328,958,100
SIC 6712 Bank holding companies
Norman Beug
Richard Mack
Kelvin Dereski
Don Bernath

D-U-N-S 25-094-6209   (SL)
**MOSAIC POTASH ESTERHAZY LIMITED
PARTNERSHIP**
(*Suby of* THE MOSAIC COMPANY)
80 Plant Hwy, Esterhazy, SK, S0A 0X0
(306) 745-4400
Emp Here 900   *Sales* 371,798,100
SIC 1474 Potash, soda, and borate minerals
Kelvin Dereski

D-U-N-S 24-539-5301   (SL)
NOBLE CONSTRUCTION CORP
215 Sumner St, Esterhazy, SK, S0A 0X0
(306) 745-6984
Emp Here 200   *Sales* 84,547,400
SIC 1541 Industrial buildings and warehouses
Chris Miller

D-U-N-S 24-341-5788   (BR)
SASKATCHEWAN HEALTH AUTHORITY
CENTENNIAL SPECIAL CARE HOME
(*Suby   of   GOVERNMENT   OF
SASKATCHEWAN)*
300 James St, Esterhazy, SK, S0A 0X0
(306) 745-6444
Emp Here 100
SIC 8361 Residential care
Leah Weiss

D-U-N-S 24-921-3489   (SL)
SOUTH EAST CONSTRUCTION
SOUTH EAST CONSTRUCTION LP
600 Main St, Esterhazy, SK, S0A 0X0
(306) 745-4830
Emp Here 49   *Sales* 10,407,453
SIC 8748 Business consulting, nec
Larry Mackay

Estevan, SK S4A

D-U-N-S 20-061-4006   (HQ)
BAXTER, BERT TRANSPORT LTD
CHARLIE'S HOT SHOT
301 Kensington Ave, Estevan, SK, S4A 2A1
(306) 634-3616
Sales 63,904,505
SIC 1389 Oil and gas field services, nec
Graham Shirley
Darryl Shirley
Todd Shirley
Vaughn Shirley
Nancy Shirley

D-U-N-S 24-850-2838   (BR)
CANYON TECHNICAL SERVICES LTD
(*Suby of* TRICAN WELL SERVICE LTD)
548 Bourquin Rd, Estevan, SK, S4A 2A7
(306) 637-3360
Emp Here 85
SIC 1389 Oil and gas field services, nec
Shawn Mclean

D-U-N-S 24-748-6442   (HQ)
GIRARD BULK SERVICE LTD
PETRO CANADA
134 4th St, Estevan, SK, S4A 0T4
(306) 637-4370
Emp Here 3   *Sales* 41,487,633
SIC 5171 Petroleum bulk stations and termi-
nals
Raymond Girard

D-U-N-S 20-611-9125   (SL)

**HANK'S MAINTENANCE & SERVICE COM-
PANY LTD**
410 Mississippian Dr, Estevan, SK, S4A 2H7
(306) 634-4872
Emp Here 34   *Sales* 10,869,970
SIC 1389 Oil and gas field services, nec
Grant Walkom
Elaine Walkom

D-U-N-S 24-098-5460   (BR)
**HOLY FAMILY ROMAN CATHOLIC SEPA-
RATE SCHOOL DIVISION 140**
ST JOHN'S SCHOOL
(*Suby of* HOLY FAMILY ROMAN CATHOLIC
SEPARATE SCHOOL DIVISION 140)
1118 2nd St, Estevan, SK, S4A 0L9
(306) 634-5995
Emp Here 100
SIC 8211 Elementary and secondary schools
Phyllis Dzuba

D-U-N-S 24-033-0030   (SL)
INDEPENDENT WELL SERVICING LTD
477 Devonian St, Estevan, SK, S4A 2A5
(306) 634-2336
Emp Here 50   *Sales* 10,506,550
SIC 1389 Oil and gas field services, nec
Paul Chung

D-U-N-S 20-337-0759   (SL)
L & M MERCIER ENTERPRISES INC
CANADIAN TIRE ASSOCIATE STORE
200 King St Suite 146, Estevan, SK, S4A 2W4
(306) 634-6407
Emp Here 34   *Sales* 14,942,340
SIC 5531 Auto and home supply stores
Aldrin Santos

D-U-N-S 24-748-5733   (SL)
**MCGILLICKY OILFIELD CONSTRUCTION
LTD**
6 Hwy 39 E, Estevan, SK, S4A 2A7
(306) 634-8737
Emp Here 60   *Sales* 19,182,300
SIC 1389 Oil and gas field services, nec
Randy Mcgillicky
Darcy Mcgillicky

D-U-N-S 20-809-6326   (SL)
**MURRAY CHEVROLET PONTIAC BUICK
GMC ESTEVAN**
MURRAY GM
801 13th Ave, Estevan, SK, S4A 2L9
(306) 634-3661
Emp Here 45   *Sales* 22,413,510
SIC 5511 New and used car dealers
Herb Padwick

D-U-N-S 20-841-2304   (HQ)
PRAIRIE MUD SERVICE
738 6th St, Estevan, SK, S4A 1A4
(306) 634-3411
Emp Here 22   *Sales* 11,189,675
SIC 1389 Oil and gas field services, nec
Ray Frehlick
Chuck Haines
Darwin Frehlick

D-U-N-S 20-522-0643   (SL)
PRAIRIE PETRO-CHEM HOLDINGS LTD
(*Suby of* CLARIANT AG)
738 6th St, Estevan, SK, S4A 1A4
(306) 634-5808
Emp Here 30   *Sales* 21,910,350
SIC 5169 Chemicals and allied products, nec
Doris Frehlick
Dwayne Frehlick
Brent Frehlick
Blane Fichter

D-U-N-S 24-691-6753   (SL)
REGENS DISPOSAL LTD
500 Bourquin Rd, Estevan, SK, S4A 2H8
(306) 634-7209
Emp Here 55   *Sales* 14,142,205
SIC 4953 Refuse systems
Gene Baniulis

D-U-N-S 20-125-8634   (BR)
SASKATCHEWAN POWER CORPORATION
SASKPOWER
(*Suby   of   GOVERNMENT   OF
SASKATCHEWAN)*
18 Boundary Dam Hwy W, Estevan, SK, S4A
2A6
(306) 634-1300
Emp Here 300
SIC 4911 Electric services
Kevin Guillemin

D-U-N-S 20-191-7494   (BR)
SASKATCHEWAN POWER CORPORATION
SASKPOWER SHAND POWER STATION
(*Suby   of   GOVERNMENT   OF
SASKATCHEWAN)*
Gd Lcd Main, Estevan, SK, S4A 2A1
(306) 634-1700
Emp Here 100
SIC 4911 Electric services
Gregg Milbrandt

D-U-N-S 20-061-5029   (SL)
SENCHUK FORD SALES LTD
118 Souris Ave, Estevan, SK, S4A 1J6
(306) 634-3696
Emp Here 24   *Sales* 11,953,872
SIC 5511 New and used car dealers
Walter Senchuk
Joan Senchuk

D-U-N-S 20-553-1176   (BR)
SOBEYS CAPITAL INCORPORATED
SOBEYS ESTEVAN
(*Suby of* EMPIRE COMPANY LIMITED)
440 King St, Estevan, SK, S4A 2B4
(306) 637-2550
Emp Here 86
SIC 5411 Grocery stores
Mike Smith

D-U-N-S 20-061-4618   (HQ)
**SOUTHERN PLAINS CO-OPERATIVE LIM-
ITED**
826 4th St, Estevan, SK, S4A 0W1
(306) 637-4300
Emp Here 101   *Sales* 22,382,387
SIC 5399 Miscellaneous general merchandise
Bob Declercq

D-U-N-S 25-113-2395   (SL)
ST. JOSEPH'S HOSPITAL OF ESTEVAN
1176 Nicholson Rd Suite 203, Estevan, SK,
S4A 0H3
(306) 637-2400
Emp Here 301   *Sales* 13,669,700
SIC 8062 General medical and surgical hospi-
tals
Normand Poirier

D-U-N-S 25-958-8242   (SL)
SYMONS THE BAKER LTD
BEEFEATER MOTOR INN HOTEL
1305 9th St, Estevan, SK, S4A 1J1
(306) 634-6456
Emp Here 85   *Sales* 3,644,205
SIC 5812 Eating places
Janet Symons
Melodye Pierson

D-U-N-S 24-546-7824   (HQ)
**TEML SASKATCHEWAN PIPELINES LIM-
ITED**
(*Suby of* ENBRIDGE INC)
402 Kensington Ave, Estevan, SK, S4A 2K9
(306) 634-2681
Emp Here 15   *Sales* 39,924,200
SIC 4612 Crude petroleum pipelines
Kevin Hatfield
Greg Sevick

D-U-N-S 24-630-1089   (SL)
**VIKING SURPLUS OIL FIELD EQUIPMENT
LTD**
36 Hwy 39 E, Estevan, SK, S4A 2L7

Emp Here 60   *Sales* 28,501,560

▲ Public Company   ■ Public Company Family Member   **HQ** Headquarters   **BR** Branch   **SL** Single Location

SIC 5084 Industrial machinery and equipment
Ronald Wanner

D-U-N-S 25-297-7665   (BR)
WAL-MART CANADA CORP
(Suby of WALMART INC.*)*
413 Kensington Ave, Estevan, SK, S4A 2A5
(306) 634-2110
Emp Here 130
SIC 5311 Department stores
Ralph Cole

D-U-N-S 20-546-1338   (HQ)
WATERFLOOD SERVICE & SALES LTD
130 Perkins St, Estevan, SK, S4A 2K1
(306) 634-7212
Emp Here 125   *Sales* 33,300,150
SIC 3533 Oil and gas field machinery
David Heier

D-U-N-S 20-291-9457   (HQ)
WIL-TECH INDUSTRIES LTD
69 Escana St, Estevan, SK, S4A 2H7
(306) 634-6743
Sales 11,189,675
SIC 1389 Oil and gas field services, nec
Arthur James Wilson
Crystal Wilson

Eston, SK S0L

D-U-N-S 20-061-6472   (SL)
CENTRAL PLAINS CO-OPERATIVE LTD
203 Main St, Eston, SK, S0L 1A0
(306) 882-2601
Emp Here 150   *Sales* 30,801,450
SIC 5399 Miscellaneous general merchandise
Mike Moon

D-U-N-S 24-623-6140   (SL)
ESTON HEALTH CENTRE
822 Main St, Eston, SK, S0L 1A0
(306) 962-3667
Emp Here 15   *Sales* 15,523,215
SIC 6324 Hospital and medical service plans
Pat Toner

Fillmore, SK S0G

D-U-N-S 24-748-4843   (HQ)
FILL-MORE SEEDS INC
SEABOARD SPECIALTY GRAINS & FOOD
(Suby of SEABOARD CORPORATION*)*
1 Railway Ave, Fillmore, SK, S0G 1N0
(306) 722-3353
Emp Here 17   *Sales* 33,756,916
SIC 5153 Grain and field beans
Blair Stewart

Fort Qu'Appelle, SK S0G

D-U-N-S 20-448-1600   (SL)
HANSON HARDWARE LTD
HOME HARDWARE
191 Broadway Ave, Fort Qu'Appelle, SK, S0G
1S0

Emp Here 45   *Sales* 11,387,655
SIC 5251 Hardware stores
Donald Hanson
Andrew Nance
Elaine Hanson
Claire Nance

Frontier, SK S0N

D-U-N-S 24-497-3442   (SL)
HONEY BEE MANUFACTURING LTD
Gd, Frontier, SK, S0N 0W0
(306) 296-2297
Emp Here 187   *Sales* 41,514,187
SIC 3523 Farm machinery and equipment
Gregory Honey
Glenn Honey
Jamie Pegg

Gravelbourg, SK S0H

D-U-N-S 25-453-4258   (SL)
ST. JOSEPH'S (GREY NUN'S) OF GRAVEL-BOURG
ST.   JOSEPH'S   HOSPITAL/FOYER
D'YOUVILLE
216 Bettez St, Gravelbourg, SK, S0H 1X0
(306) 648-3185
Emp Here 116   *Sales* 12,885,280
SIC 8062 General medical and surgical hospitals
John Kelly
Janice Michaud

D-U-N-S 20-653-7982   (SL)
TRAILTECH INC
Gd, Gravelbourg, SK, S0H 1X0
(306) 648-3158
Emp Here 65   *Sales* 14,430,065
SIC 3537 Industrial trucks and tractors
Keith Brown

Gull Lake, SK S0N

D-U-N-S 25-388-7087   (HQ)
SOUTH WEST TERMINAL LTD
INTRICATE NETWORKS
Gd, Gull Lake, SK, S0N 1A0
(306) 672-4112
Sales 200,130,807
SIC 4221 Farm product warehousing and storage
Rhonda Undseth
Erroll Castle
Rhett Allison
Gene Busse
Murray Smith
Ron Taylor
Roland Monette
Doug Logan
Wayne Oberle

Hague, SK S0K

D-U-N-S 25-506-9817   (SL)
H & S HOLDINGS INC
ZAK'S BUILDING SUPPLIES & CONTRACT-ING
101 East Service Rd, Hague, SK, S0K 1X0
(306) 225-2288
Emp Here 70   *Sales* 19,053,425
SIC 1521 Single-family housing construction
Henry Zacharias
Lance Zacharias
Chad Zacharias
Wyatt Zacharias

D-U-N-S 24-038-6735   (SL)
VALLEY FORD SALES
224 East Service Rd, Hague, SK, S0K 1X0
(306) 225-3673
Emp Here 22   *Sales* 10,957,716
SIC 5511 New and used car dealers
Rob Van Norman

Halbrite, SK S0C

D-U-N-S 24-338-1600   (SL)
BRADY OILFIELD SERVICES L.P.
1 Mergen St, Halbrite, SK, S0C 1H0
(306) 458-2344
Emp Here 100   *Sales* 67,267,900
SIC 1389 Oil and gas field services, nec
Kevin Brady

Hazenmore, SK S0N

D-U-N-S 20-341-9569   (HQ)
GRASSROOTS CO-OPERATIVE LTD
216 Main St, Hazenmore, SK, S0N 1C0
(306) 264-5111
Sales 15,492,120
SIC 5171 Petroleum bulk stations and terminals
Neil Mackenzie
Larry Wall

Hodgeville, SK S0H

D-U-N-S 20-398-2665   (SL)
HODGEVILLE FARMING CO. LTD
HUTTERIAN BRETHREN CHURCH
Gd, Hodgeville, SK, S0H 2B0
(306) 677-2256
Emp Here 34   *Sales* 11,643,878
SIC 0191 General farms, primarily crop
Gideon Hofer
Martin Hofer
Mike Hofer
Peter Hofer

Hudson Bay, SK S0E

D-U-N-S 25-095-2009   (BR)
WEYERHAEUSER COMPANY LIMITED
OSP DIVISION
(Suby of WEYERHAEUSER COMPANY*)*
Hiway 9 S, Hudson Bay, SK, S0E 0Y0
(306) 865-1700
Emp Here 200
SIC 2421 Sawmills and planing mills, general
Steve Kobelak

Humboldt, SK S0K

D-U-N-S 25-373-1244   (HQ)
BIG SKY FARMS INC
10333 8th Ave E, Humboldt, SK, S0K 2A1
(306) 682-5041
Emp Here 50   *Sales* 92,977,650
SIC 0213 Hogs
Canute Tagseth
Denys Robidoux

D-U-N-S 24-628-1799   (SL)
COLONY PONTIAC BUICK LTD
COLONY MOTOR PRODUCTS
331 Main St, Humboldt, SK, S0K 2A1
(306) 682-2661
Emp Here 27   *Sales* 13,448,106
SIC 5511 New and used car dealers
Maurice Plemel

D-U-N-S 24-260-6355   (SL)
FREE SPIRIT MARKET LTD
615 Main Street, Humboldt, SK, S0K 2A0
(306) 682-2223
Emp Here 21   *Sales* 12,346,236

SIC 5182 Wine and distilled beverages

D-U-N-S 24-101-8113   (HQ)
HORIZON SCHOOL DIVISION NO 205
10333 8th Ave, Humboldt, SK, S0K 2A0
(306) 682-2558
Emp Here 30   *Sales* 148,678,500
SIC 8211 Elementary and secondary schools
Kevin Garinger

D-U-N-S 25-013-3774   (SL)
K.M.K. SALES LTD
Hwy 20 S, Humboldt, SK, S0K 2A1
(306) 682-0738
Emp Here 22   *Sales* 10,957,716
SIC 5599 Automotive dealers, nec
Bernard Robert Malinoski
Gerald Anthony Kopp
Colleen Mary Kopp
Rod Sarauer
Curt Bells

D-U-N-S 20-313-4952   (HQ)
OLYSKY LIMITED PARTNERSHIP
(Suby of OLYMEL S.E.C.*)*
10333 8 Ave, Humboldt, SK, S0K 2A0
(306) 682-5041
Sales 89,237,775
SIC 0213 Hogs
Rejean Nadeau
Paul Beauchamp
Richard Davies
Carole Potvin
Loraine Earis
Anouk Tanguay

D-U-N-S 20-853-5237   (HQ)
PRAIRIE AGRICULTURAL MACHINERY IN-STITUTE
PAMI
(Suby   of   GOVERNMENT   OF
SASKATCHEWAN)
2215 8 Ave, Humboldt, SK, S0K 2A1
(306) 682-2555
Emp Here 90   *Sales* 31,971,700
SIC 8734 Testing laboratories
David Gullacher
Joanne Forer

D-U-N-S 24-031-7862   (BR)
SASKATCHEWAN HEALTH AUTHORITY
HUMBOLDT DISTRICT HOSPITAL
(Suby   of   GOVERNMENT   OF
SASKATCHEWAN)
1210 Ninth St N, Humboldt, SK, S0K 2A1
(306) 682-2603
Emp Here 500
SIC 8062 General medical and surgical hospitals
Yvonne Berscheid

D-U-N-S 25-447-2496   (BR)
SOBEYS CAPITAL INCORPORATED
(Suby of EMPIRE COMPANY LIMITED*)*
2304 Quill Ctr, Humboldt, SK, S0K 2A1
(306) 682-2130
Emp Here 100
SIC 5411 Grocery stores
David Doepker

Ile-A-La-Crosse, SK S0M

D-U-N-S 25-146-6025   (HQ)
SAKITAWAK DEVELOPMENT CORPORATION
NORTHERN SUNSET MOTEL
Gd, Ile-A-La-Crosse, SK, S0M 1C0
(306) 833-2466
Sales 10,462,120
SIC 6712 Bank holding companies
Wendel Desjarlais

D-U-N-S 24-343-7089   (BR)
SASKATCHEWAN HEALTH AUTHORITY

ST JOSEPH'S HOSPITAL
(Suby of GOVERNMENT OF SASKATCHEWAN)
Gd, Ile-A-La-Crosse, SK, S0M 1C0
(306) 833-2016
Emp Here 75
SIC 8011 Offices and clinics of medical doctors
 Lorraine Roy

Indian Head, SK S0G

D-U-N-S 20-341-3034   (SL)
INDIAN HEAD CHRYSLER DODGE JEEP RAM LTD
INDIAN HEAD CHRYSLER
501 Johnston Ave, Indian Head, SK, S0G 2K0
(306) 695-2254
Emp Here 22   *Sales* 10,957,716
SIC 5511 New and used car dealers
 Garnet Goud
 Shelby Goud

Ituna, SK S0A

D-U-N-S 24-684-8910   (SL)
DIAMOND CO-OPERATIVE ASSOCIATION LTD
223 1st Ave Ne, Ituna, SK, S0A 1N0
(306) 795-2441
Emp Here 10   *Sales* 10,161,617
SIC 5171 Petroleum bulk stations and terminals
 Rick Billett
 Ladmer Moskal
 Jack Sweatman
 Charlotte Wilson
 Lionel Beer
 James Martin
 Thad Trefiak
 Garry Husum
 Wes Kanciruk
 Rob Heggie

Kamsack, SK S0A

D-U-N-S 24-427-0799   (SL)
KAMSACK UNION HOSPITAL DISTRICT
KAMSACK HOSPITAL AND NURSING HOME
341 Stewart St, Kamsack, SK, S0A 1S0
(306) 542-2635
Emp Here 95   *Sales* 9,702,635
SIC 8062 General medical and surgical hospitals
 Christopher Mayer

Kelliher, SK S0A

D-U-N-S 24-233-8937   (SL)
PARKLAND LIVESTOCK MARKET LTD
Gd, Kelliher, SK, S0A 1V0

Emp Here 15   *Sales* 18,155,955
SIC 5154 Livestock
 Arlie Murry
 Rosemary Murry
 Brian Murry
 Stewart Murry

Kelvington, SK S0A

D-U-N-S 20-740-1480   (HQ)
EAST CENTRAL CO-OPERATIVE LIMITED
211 1st Ave, Kelvington, SK, S0A 1W0
(306) 327-4745
Emp Here 30   *Sales* 12,945,800
SIC 5411 Grocery stores
 Randy Wassermen

Kenosee Lake, SK S0C

D-U-N-S 24-914-4734   (SL)
GOLF KENOSEE CAPITAL INC
Gd, Kenosee Lake, SK, S0C 2S0
(306) 577-2044
Emp Here 40   *Sales* 10,462,120
SIC 6712 Bank holding companies
 Tim Lincoln
 Lee Streubel
 Gene Drumm
 Ron Gray
 Darrell Lamootagne

Kindersley, SK S0L

D-U-N-S 24-715-8327   (SL)
ENERGY DODGE LTD
801 11th Ave E, Kindersley, SK, S0L 1S0
(306) 463-4131
Emp Here 23   *Sales* 11,455,794
SIC 5511 New and used car dealers
 Jason Mccarter

D-U-N-S 25-173-7441   (HQ)
G-MAC'S AGTEAM INC
908 Main St, Kindersley, SK, S0L 1S0
(306) 463-4769
Emp Here 17   *Sales* 145,112,422
SIC 5261 Retail nurseries and garden stores
 Garth Macdonald
 Jeremy German
 Leon Strutt
 Scott Hopkins

D-U-N-S 25-077-3376   (SL)
HAMM HOLDINGS LTD
130 Stewart Cres, Kindersley, SK, S0L 1S1
(306) 463-7112
Emp Here 48   *Sales* 20,129,040
SIC 6712 Bank holding companies
 Ron Hamm

D-U-N-S 24-039-7836   (HQ)
KINDERSLEY AND DISTRICT CO-OPERATIVE LIMITED
214 Main St, Kindersley, SK, S0L 1S0
(306) 463-2624
Emp Here 11   *Sales* 124,138,665
SIC 5171 Petroleum bulk stations and terminals
 Rod Macdiarmid
 Lorraine Wilson
 Tom Watt
 Donna Mcbride
 Laurie Kelly
 Ken Massey
 Kevin Franki
 Lexie Adamson
 Clinton Barr

D-U-N-S 24-852-2278   (SL)
ROSS, SANDY WELL SERVICING LTD
1004 9th Ave W, Kindersley, SK, S0L 1S0
(306) 463-3875
Emp Here 75   *Sales* 23,977,875
SIC 1389 Oil and gas field services, nec
 Cecil A (Sandy) Ross

D-U-N-S 24-345-5545   (BR)
SASKATCHEWAN HEALTH AUTHORITY
KINDERSLEY INTERGRATED HEALTH CARE FACILITY

(Suby of GOVERNMENT OF SASKATCHEWAN)
1003 1st St W Rr 2, Kindersley, SK, S0L 1S2
Emp Here 180
SIC 8051 Skilled nursing care facilities
 Wanda Daroche

D-U-N-S 25-126-4230   (SL)
SPRINGFIELD HUTTERIAN BRETHREN INC
Gd, Kindersley, SK, S0L 1S0
(306) 463-4255
Emp Here 80   *Sales* 18,743,040
SIC 8748 Business consulting, nec
 Joe Kleinsasser
 Paul Hofer
 Dave Kleinsasser

D-U-N-S 20-063-0572   (SL)
TISDALE SALES & SERVICES LTD
105 11 Ave E, Kindersley, SK, S0L 1S0
(306) 463-2686
Emp Here 32   *Sales* 11,755,800
SIC 5511 New and used car dealers
 John Boquist
 Gary Materi
 Jeanette Boquist
 Roger Mckenzie

D-U-N-S 24-330-0493   (BR)
WAL-MART CANADA CORP
(Suby of WALMART INC.)
710 11th Avenue E, Kindersley, SK, S0L 1S2
(306) 463-1330
Emp Here 120
SIC 5311 Department stores
 Rick Froese

Kinistino, SK S0J

D-U-N-S 25-327-4781   (SL)
609905 SASKATCHEWAN LTD
AGWORLD EQUIPMENT
30 Highway 3, Kinistino, SK, S0J 1H0
(306) 864-2200
Emp Here 30   *Sales* 14,250,780
SIC 5083 Farm and garden machinery
 David Mark Cook

Kipling, SK S0G

D-U-N-S 20-063-1067   (SL)
GEE BEE CONSTRUCTION CO LTD
Highway 48, Kipling, SK, S0G 2S0
(306) 736-2332
Emp Here 70   *Sales* 17,670,940
SIC 1611 Highway and street construction
 Alan Batters

Kyle, SK S0L

D-U-N-S 20-842-6395   (SL)
HUTTERIAN BRETHREN OF KYLE INC
KYLE HUTTERIAN BRETHREN FARM
Gd, Kyle, SK, S0L 1T0
(306) 375-2910
Emp Here 100   *Sales* 10,772,700
SIC 8661 Religious organizations
 Micheal J Hofer
 Micheal M Hofer

La Ronge, SK S0J

D-U-N-S 24-915-1945   (BR)

CLAUDE RESOURCES INC
SEABEE MINE, DIV OF
(Suby of SSR MINING INC)
1112 Finlayson St, La Ronge, SK, S0J 1L0
(306) 635-2015
Emp Here 300
SIC 1041 Gold ores

D-U-N-S 20-231-0087   (BR)
CLAUDE RESOURCES INC
(Suby of SSR MINING INC)
Gd, La Ronge, SK, S0J 1L0
(306) 635-2015
Emp Here 250
SIC 1041 Gold ores

D-U-N-S 24-748-7960   (SL)
LA RONGE PETROLEUM LTD
SHELL CANADA
1420 Finnlayson St, La Ronge, SK, S0J 1L0
(306) 425-6841
Emp Here 12   *Sales* 12,393,696
SIC 5171 Petroleum bulk stations and terminals
 Hugh Watt
 Graham Watt
 Shannon Bholin

D-U-N-S 20-740-2967   (SL)
LAC LA RONGE MOTOR HOTEL (1983) LTD
(Suby of LAC LA RONGE INDIAN BAND)
1120 La Ronge Ave, La Ronge, SK, S0J 1L0
(306) 425-2190
Emp Here 90
SIC 7011 Hotels and motels
 Mark Laurie

D-U-N-S 20-855-1630   (HQ)
NORTHERN LIGHTS SCHOOL DIVISION 113
NLSD 113
108 Finlayson St, La Ronge, SK, S0J 1L0
(306) 425-3302
Emp Here 592   *Sales* 69,834,727
SIC 8211 Elementary and secondary schools
 Ralph Pilz
 Bob Wyatt

D-U-N-S 20-546-3862   (SL)
RIESE INVESTMENTS LTD
RIESE'S CANADIAN LAKE WILD RICE
1 Riese Bay, La Ronge, SK, S0J 1L0
(306) 425-2314
Emp Here 23   *Sales* 33,756,916
SIC 5153 Grain and field beans
 K Lynn Riese

Lake Lenore, SK S0K

D-U-N-S 20-063-2370   (SL)
LAKE LENORE CO-OPERATIVE ASSOCIATION LIMITED
300 Lake Dr Hwy Suite 368, Lake Lenore, SK, S0K 2J0
(306) 368-2255
Emp Here 10   *Sales* 10,328,080
SIC 5171 Petroleum bulk stations and terminals
 Gordon Dymtruk
 Reg Prodahl
 Kim Berscheid
 David Nieman
 Beryl Bauer
 Reg Gerwing
 Brian Schemenauer

Langbank, SK S0G

D-U-N-S 20-063-2891   (HQ)
LANGBANK CO-OPERATIVE ASSOCIATION LIMITED, THE

1st Ave W, Langbank, SK, S0G 2X0
(306) 538-2125
Emp Here 10   *Sales* 34,082,664
SIC 5171 Petroleum bulk stations and terminals
Larry Doka
Donald Dean
Margaret Hansen

D-U-N-S 24-915-0855   (SL)
VADERSTAD INDUSTRIES INC
(Suby of VADERSTAD HOLDING AB)
Hwy 9, Langbank, SK, S0G 2X0
(306) 538-2221
Emp Here 150   *Sales* 61,241,040
SIC 3523 Farm machinery and equipment
Nigel Jones

Lanigan, SK S0K

D-U-N-S 20-741-0879   (HQ)
BLAIR'S FERTILIZER LTD
Gd, Lanigan, SK, S0K 2M0
(306) 365-3150
Emp Here 15   *Sales* 33,413,400
SIC 5191 Farm supplies
Kevin Blair
Darren Blair

D-U-N-S 20-447-6006   (BR)
**POTASH   CORPORATION   OF
SASKATCHEWAN INC**
PCS LANIGAN, DIV
(Suby of NUTRIEN LTD)
Gd, Lanigan, SK, S0K 2M0
(306) 365-2030
Emp Here 600
SIC 1474 Potash, soda, and borate minerals
Rob Bubnick

Lashburn, SK S0M

D-U-N-S 20-664-6358   (SL)
SCORPION OILFIELD SERVICES LTD
406 6th W, Lashburn, SK, S0M 1H0
(306) 285-2433
Emp Here 45   *Sales* 14,553,351
SIC 1389 Oil and gas field services, nec
Jory Klinger
Jorin Watson
Cole Hopfner
Tyler Kerr

Leader, SK S0N

D-U-N-S 24-170-8510   (HQ)
**HUTTERIAN BRETHREN OF ESTUARY
CORP**
ESTUARY COLONY FARM
Gd, Leader, SK, S0N 1H0
(306) 628-4116
Sales 23,083,192
SIC 0191 General farms, primarily crop
Jake Tschetter

D-U-N-S 20-012-5776   (SL)
KONCRETE CONSTRUCTION GROUP
609 Miller St, Leader, SK, S0N 1H0
(306) 628-3757
Emp Here 35   *Sales* 11,189,675
SIC 1389 Oil and gas field services, nec
Sheldon Guckert
Brent Guckert

Lloydminster, SK S9V

D-U-N-S 24-098-8241   (SL)
BERETTA PIPELINE CONSTRUCTION LTD
Gd, Lloydminster, SK, S9V 0X5
(780) 875-6522
Emp Here 49   *Sales* 11,803,316
SIC 1623 Water, sewer, and utility lines
Darrell Carter

D-U-N-S 24-916-1381   (SL)
BORDER CITY R.V. CENTRE LTD
Gd Lcd Main, Lloydminster, SK, S9V 0X5
(403) 875-0345
Emp Here 28   *Sales* 13,946,184
SIC 5571 Motorcycle dealers
Melvin Joseph (Bud) Kam
Kenneth John Kam, Sr
Ken Kam, Jr

D-U-N-S 25-206-6220   (SL)
BOUNDARY FORD SALES LTD
BOUNDARY FORD & RV SALES
2405 50 Ave, Lloydminster, SK, S9V 1Z7
(306) 825-4481
Emp Here 38   *Sales* 18,926,964
SIC 5511 New and used car dealers
Warren R Lux

D-U-N-S 25-555-7241   (SL)
FORT PITT FARMS INC
Gd, Lloydminster, SK, S9V 0X5
(306) 344-4849
Emp Here 108   *Sales* 18,254,700
SIC 0191 General farms, primarily crop
Paul Walter
Paul Walter Jr

D-U-N-S 20-918-5508   (BR)
HUSKY ENERGY INC
(Suby of HUSKY ENERGY INC)
Hwy 16 E Upgrader Rd, Lloydminster, SK,
S9V 1M6
(306) 825-1700
Emp Here 300
SIC 1311 Crude petroleum and natural gas
Al Maclauchlan

D-U-N-S 24-894-6568   (BR)
HUSKY ENERGY INC
HUSKY OIL
(Suby of HUSKY ENERGY INC)
4335 44 St, Lloydminster, SK, S9V 0Z8
(306) 825-1196
Emp Here 170
SIC 1311 Crude petroleum and natural gas
Dabir Naqvi

D-U-N-S 25-999-1446   (BR)
HUSKY OIL OPERATIONS LIMITED
HUSKY ENERGIE
(Suby of HUSKY ENERGY INC)
4335 44 St, Lloydminster, SK, S9V 0Z8
(306) 825-1196
Emp Here 100
SIC 1311 Crude petroleum and natural gas
Dabir Naqvi

D-U-N-S 25-013-5217   (SL)
**L & L OILFIELD CONSTRUCTION (1990)
LTD**
6107 49 Ave, Lloydminster, SK, S9V 2G2
(306) 825-6111
Emp Here 150   *Sales* 100,901,850
SIC 1389 Oil and gas field services, nec
Lance Mohrbutter

D-U-N-S 25-486-1412   (BR)
LAKELAND COLLEGE
(Suby of LAKELAND COLLEGE)
2602 59th Ave, Lloydminster, SK, S9V 1Z3
(780) 871-5700
Emp Here 100
SIC 8221 Colleges and universities
Paul Driscoll

D-U-N-S 20-063-7239   (HQ)
**LLOYDMINSTER AND DISTRICT CO-
OPERATIVE LIMITED**

4090 41 St Suite 101, Lloydminster, SK, S9V
2J1
(306) 825-2271
Sales 44,266,720
SIC 5411 Grocery stores
Donald Stephenson
Richard Polkinghorne
Marcel Fizell
Barry Davis
Al Sholter
Georgette Wawryk
Morris Freeston
Kathy Mulligan
Kim Putnam
Valerie Bossert

D-U-N-S 24-915-4097   (HQ)
LML INDUSTRIAL CONTRACTORS LTD
(Suby of STUART OLSON INC)
4815 50 St Suite 302, Lloydminster, SK, S9V
0M8
(306) 825-6115
Sales 24,618,600
SIC 1799 Special trade contractors, nec
Douglas Lautermilch
Randy Boomhour

D-U-N-S 20-010-1678   (BR)
SASKATCHEWAN HEALTH AUTHORITY
LLOYDMINSTER HOSPITAL
*(Suby   of   GOVERNMENT   OF
SASKATCHEWAN)*
3820 43 Ave, Lloydminster, SK, S9V 1Y5
(306) 820-6000
Emp Here 400
SIC 8062 General medical and surgical hospitals
Lori Worthing

D-U-N-S 20-740-5218   (HQ)
SYNERGY CREDIT UNION LTD
4907 50 St, Lloydminster, SK, S9V 0N1
(306) 825-3301
Emp Here 100   *Sales* 38,430,225
SIC 6062 State credit unions
Les Messmer
Dean Walde

D-U-N-S 20-835-7608   (SL)
**ULMER, ROSS CHEVROLET CADILLAC
LTD**
ULMER CHEV (LLOYDMINSTER)
2101 50 Ave, Lloydminster, SK, S9V 1Z7
(306) 825-8866
Emp Here 45   *Sales* 22,413,510
SIC 5511 New and used car dealers
Ross Ulmer
Doug Ulmer

D-U-N-S 20-939-0157   (BR)
WEATHERFORD CANADA LTD
*WEATHERFORD COMPLETION & PROD-
UCT SYSTEMS*
*(Suby of WEATHERFORD INTERNATIONAL
PUBLIC LIMITED COMPANY)*
3915 52 Street Close, Lloydminster, SK, S9V
2G9
(306) 820-5530
Emp Here 200
SIC 7699 Repair services, nec
Derek Selby

Loreburn, SK S0H

D-U-N-S 20-645-6407   (HQ)
GARDINER DAM TERMINAL LTD
(Suby of GLENCORE PLC)
Hwy 19 Old Hwy Suite 44, Loreburn, SK, S0H
2S0
(306) 857-2134
Sales 17,612,304
SIC 5153 Grain and field beans
David Pederson
Barbara Glubis

Greg Bristow
Raymond Dueck
Brent Adams
Rob Hundeby
Troy Mochoruk
Les Feltis
Brian Brown

Lumsden, SK S0G

D-U-N-S 24-968-5108   (SL)
ARM RIVER FARMING CO. LTD
ARM RIVER COLONY
*(Suby of HUTTERIAN BRETHREN OF ARM
RIVER COLONY LTD)*
Gd, Lumsden, SK, S0G 3C0
(306) 731-2819
Emp Here 118   *Sales* 19,944,950
SIC 0191 General farms, primarily crop
Daniel Hofer
David Hofer
Joseph E. Hofer
Paul Hofer

D-U-N-S 20-287-1877   (HQ)
**HUTTERIAN BRETHREN OF ARM RIVER
COLONY LTD**
Po Box 570, Lumsden, SK, S0G 3C0
(306) 731-2819
Sales 26,230,900
SIC 0119 Cash grains, nec
Daniel Hofer

Mankota, SK S0H

D-U-N-S 20-292-6312   (SL)
**MANKOTA STOCKMEN'S WEIGH COM-
PANY LIMITED**
178 Railway Ave E, Mankota, SK, S0H 2W0
(306) 478-2229
Emp Here 50   *Sales* 74,234,534
SIC 5154 Livestock
Mike Smith

Maple Creek, SK S0N

D-U-N-S 24-655-3341   (SL)
**HUTTERIAN BRETHERN CHURCH OF
DOWNIE LAKE INC**
DOWNIE LAKE COLONY
Gd, Maple Creek, SK, S0N 1N0
(306) 662-3462
Emp Here 75   *Sales* 8,079,525
SIC 8661 Religious organizations
Junior Josh Stahl
Josh Stahl

Meadow Lake, SK S9X

D-U-N-S 24-967-3088   (SL)
581976 SASKATCHEWAN LTD
MEADOW LAKE HOME BUILDING CENTRE
802 1st St W, Meadow Lake, SK, S9X 1E2
(306) 236-4467
Emp Here 50   *Sales* 12,652,950
SIC 5211 Lumber and other building materials
Donald Marsh
Lois Marsh

D-U-N-S 25-399-7407   (SL)
EAGLE CREEK MOTOR PRODUCTS LTD
809 9th St W Suite 2, Meadow Lake, SK, S9X
1Y2
(306) 236-4482
Emp Here 25   *Sales* 12,451,950

SIC 5511 New and used car dealers
Doug Ulmer
Ross Ulmer

D-U-N-S 20-064-3211   (HQ)
MEADOW LAKE CO-OPERATIVE ASSOCIATION LIMITED
MEADOW LAKE CO-OP
107 2nd St W, Meadow Lake, SK, S9X 1C6
(306) 236-5678
Emp Here 125   *Sales* 27,721,305
SIC 5399 Miscellaneous general merchandise
Richard Reid

D-U-N-S 20-588-3403   (SL)
MEADOW LAKE HOME HARDWARE BUILDING CENTRE LTD
HOME HARDWARE BUILDING CENTRE
802 1st St W, Meadow Lake, SK, S9X 1E2
(306) 236-4467
Emp Here 50   *Sales* 12,652,950
SIC 5251 Hardware stores
Don Marsh

D-U-N-S 24-352-0967   (SL)
MEADOW LAKE MECHANICAL PULP INC
PAPER EXCELLENCE CANADA
(*Suby of* CAPITAL ASSETS HOLDINGS (L) BERHAD)
Hwy 55 903, Meadow Lake, SK, S9X 1V7
(306) 236-2444
Emp Here 160   *Sales* 31,162,880
SIC 2611 Pulp mills
Simon Imray

D-U-N-S 20-118-6561   (SL)
MEADOW LAKE OSB LIMITED PARTNERSHIP
TOLKO, DIV OF
12 Km South Of Hwy 55, Meadow Lake, SK, S9X 1Y2
(306) 236-6565
Emp Here 165   *Sales* 31,741,050
SIC 2493 Reconstituted wood products
John Thorlakson
Greg Johnston

D-U-N-S 24-748-3423   (SL)
NORSASK FOREST PRODUCTS INC
(*Suby of* MEADOW LAKE TRIBAL COUNCIL)
Hwy 55 E, Meadow Lake, SK, S9X 1V7
(306) 236-5601
Emp Here 125   *Sales* 24,046,250
SIC 2421 Sawmills and planing mills, general
Allen Brander
Trevor Reid
Ken Petteplace

D-U-N-S 24-112-0252   (BR)
PRAIRIE NORTH REGIONAL HEALTH AUTHORITY
MEADOW LAKE UNION HOSPITAL
(*Suby of* PRAIRIE NORTH REGIONAL HEALTH AUTHORITY)
711 Centre St Suite 7, Meadow Lake, SK, S9X 1E6
(306) 236-1550
Emp Here 100
SIC 8062 General medical and surgical hospitals
Derek Miller

Melfort, SK S0E

D-U-N-S 25-145-3833   (HQ)
ADVANTAGE CREDIT UNION
114 Main St, Melfort, SK, S0E 1A0
(306) 752-2744
Emp Here 22   *Sales* 17,500,254
SIC 6062 State credit unions
James (Jim) Thiessen
Darrell Eaket

D-U-N-S 24-546-5299   (SL)
DAMAR HOLDINGS LTD

DAMAR ESSO
1920 Hwy 6 S, Melfort, SK, S0E 1A0
(306) 752-9066
Emp Here 25   *Sales* 12,451,950
SIC 5541 Gasoline service stations
Inbok Lee
Jane Lee

D-U-N-S 20-731-8044   (BR)
KELSEY TRAIL REGIONAL HEALTH AUTHORITY
(*Suby of* KELSEY TRAIL REGIONAL HEALTH AUTHORITY)
505 Broadway Ave N, Melfort, SK, S0E 1A0
(306) 752-8700
Emp Here 100
SIC 8062 General medical and surgical hospitals
Shane Merriman

D-U-N-S 25-174-2482   (BR)
LOBLAWS INC
EXTRA FOODS
(*Suby of* LOBLAW COMPANIES LIMITED)
620a Sasketchewan Ave, Melfort, SK, S0E 1A0
(306) 752-9725
Emp Here 75
SIC 5411 Grocery stores
Karin Hoernig

D-U-N-S 24-408-9574   (SL)
NORTH EAST OUTREACH AND SUPPORT SERVICES, INC
128 Mckendry Ave W, Melfort, SK, S0E 1A0
(306) 752-9464
Emp Here 40   *Sales* 15,896,560
SIC 8699 Membership organizations, nec
Brenda Ives
Peter Waldbillig
Kristin Willerton
Blair Michaliew
Kristin Lee
Katie Adair
Rick Peters
Brandi Moskal
Christine Honeyman
Heather Burns

D-U-N-S 20-646-4427   (HQ)
NORTH EAST SCHOOL DIVISION
402 Main St, Melfort, SK, S0E 1A0
(306) 752-5741
Sales 24,680,631
SIC 8211 Elementary and secondary schools
Don Rempel

D-U-N-S 24-393-9449   (SL)
PENNER, P & A SALES INC
CANADIAN TIRE
300 Stonegate 500 Hwy Suite 6, Melfort, SK, S0E 1A0
(306) 752-7277
Emp Here 30   *Sales* 14,942,340
SIC 5531 Auto and home supply stores
Paul Penner
Ann Penner

D-U-N-S 24-737-3108   (HQ)
PRAIRIE NORTH CO-OPERATIVE LIMITED
1141 Main St, Melfort, SK, S0E 1A0
(306) 752-9381
Emp Here 30   *Sales* 58,695,400
SIC 5411 Grocery stores
Corey Leichart
Ardith Lindenback
Bill Gudjonson

D-U-N-S 20-855-2398   (HQ)
THOMAS MOTORS LTD
1955 Hwy 6th S, Melfort, SK, S0E 1A0
(306) 752-5663
Emp Here 15   *Sales* 10,459,638
SIC 5511 New and used car dealers
Perry Thomas
Darrell Farley
John Campbell

Melville, SK S0A

D-U-N-S 24-103-9408   (BR)
COMPAGNIE DES CHEMINS DE FER NATIONAUX DU CANADA
C N RAIL
(*Suby of* COMPAGNIE DES CHEMINS DE FER NATIONAUX DU CANADA)
Gd, Melville, SK, S0A 2P0

Emp Here 300
SIC 4111 Local and suburban transit
Darold Gust

D-U-N-S 20-269-9948   (SL)
K.M. TURNBULL SALES INC
CANADIAN TIRE
290 Prince William Dr, Melville, SK, S0A 2P0
(306) 728-8810
Emp Here 45   *Sales* 14,652,000
SIC 5999 Miscellaneous retail stores, nec
Ken Turnbull

D-U-N-S 25-174-1781   (BR)
LOBLAWS INC
EXTRA FOODS
(*Suby of* LOBLAW COMPANIES LIMITED)
290 Prince William Dr, Melville, SK, S0A 2P0
(306) 728-6615
Emp Here 75
SIC 5411 Grocery stores
Paul Lueck

D-U-N-S 24-370-2466   (HQ)
PARKLAND REGIONAL COLLEGE
PARKLAND COLLEGE
200 Block 9 Ave E, Melville, SK, S0A 2P0
(306) 728-4471
Sales 11,263,600
SIC 8221 Colleges and universities
Ray Sass
Dwayne Reeve

D-U-N-S 25-058-1873   (HQ)
PRAIRIE CO-OPERATIVE LIMITED
304 1st Ave E, Melville, SK, S0A 2P0
(306) 728-5497
Sales 52,157,122
SIC 5399 Miscellaneous general merchandise
Lyle Lutz
Robert Moulding
Chris Paradis

D-U-N-S 25-023-2535   (BR)
SASKATCHEWAN CATHOLIC HEALTH CORPORATION, THE
ST PETER'S HOSPITAL
(*Suby of* SASKATCHEWAN CATHOLIC HEALTH CORPORATION, THE)
200 Heritage Dr, Melville, SK, S0A 2P0
(306) 728-5407
Emp Here 90
SIC 8062 General medical and surgical hospitals
Kim Bucsis

D-U-N-S 20-841-9465   (HQ)
SASKATCHEWAN CROP INSURANCE CORPORATION
(*Suby of* GOVERNMENT OF SASKATCHEWAN)
484 Prince William Dr, Melville, SK, S0A 2P0
(306) 728-7200
Emp Here 121   *Sales* 946,676,824
SIC 6331 Fire, marine, and casualty insurance
Shawn Jaques
Cam Swan
Lorne Warnes
Alanna Coch
Nithi Govindasamy
Glen Clarke
Doug Gattinger

Midale, SK S0C

D-U-N-S 24-894-8528   (SL)
PRO CANADA WEST ENERGY INC
Hwy 39 S, Midale, SK, S0C 1S0
(306) 458-2232
Emp Here 100   *Sales* 25,244,200
SIC 1623 Water, sewer, and utility lines
John Adderley

Montmartre, SK S0G

D-U-N-S 20-064-7220   (SL)
MONTMARTRE CO-OPERATIVE ASSOCIATION LIMITED
104 Central Ave, Montmartre, SK, S0G 3M0
(306) 424-2144
Emp Here 20   *Sales* 20,656,160
SIC 5171 Petroleum bulk stations and terminals
Curtis Farr
John Jurzyniec
Patty Cronan
Kevin Gaetz
Keith Eberle
Patty Weichel
Carrie Kotylak

Moose Jaw, SK S6H

D-U-N-S 25-799-3212   (HQ)
ALLIED LUMBERLAND LTD
HOME BUILDING CENTRE
240 5th Ave Nw, Moose Jaw, SK, S6H 4R3
(306) 694-4000
Emp Here 21   *Sales* 10,122,360
SIC 5211 Lumber and other building materials
Wendell Gillert

D-U-N-S 25-168-0393   (BR)
BOMBARDIER INC
BOMBARDIER AERONAUTIQUE
(*Suby of* BOMBARDIER INC)
Gd, Moose Jaw, SK, S6H 7Z8
(306) 694-2222
Emp Here 180
SIC 8299 Schools and educational services, nec
Guy C. Hachey

D-U-N-S 20-064-8020   (SL)
CANADAY'S APPAREL LTD
(*Suby of* FOUR J & M HOLDINGS LTD)
115 Coronation Dr, Moose Jaw, SK, S6H 4P3
(306) 692-6406
Emp Here 90   *Sales* 12,300,660
SIC 2325 Men's and boys' trousers and slacks
E James King
Murray King

D-U-N-S 25-999-9464   (BR)
CANADIAN PACIFIC RAILWAY COMPANY
CPR
(*Suby of* CANADIAN PACIFIC RAILWAY LIMITED)
3 Manitoba St W, Moose Jaw, SK, S6H 1P8
(306) 693-5421
Emp Here 125
SIC 4011 Railroads, line-haul operating
Jim Woodrow

D-U-N-S 20-545-8631   (HQ)
CLARK'S SUPPLY AND SERVICE LTD
1650 Stadacona St W, Moose Jaw, SK, S6H 4P8
(306) 693-4334
Emp Here 15   *Sales* 14,250,780
SIC 5084 Industrial machinery and equipment
David Clark
Robert Clark

D-U-N-S 20-268-1941   (BR)
DOEPKER INDUSTRIES LTD
(*Suby of* DOEPKER INDUSTRIES LTD)
1955 Caribou St, Moose Jaw, SK, S6H 4P2
(306) 693-2525
Emp Here 100
SIC 3715 Truck trailers
Marcel Doepker

D-U-N-S 20-852-7614   (BR)
EXTENDICARE INC
EXTENDICARE MOOSE JAW
(*Suby of* EXTENDICARE INC)
1151 Coteau St W, Moose Jaw, SK, S6H 5G5
(306) 693-5191
Emp Here 160
SIC 8051 Skilled nursing care facilities
Rhonda Farley

D-U-N-S 24-747-8142   (HQ)
FIFTH AVENUE COLLECTION LTD
30 Stadacona St W, Moose Jaw, SK, S6H 1Z1
(306) 694-8188
Sales 26,027,100
SIC 5094 Jewelry and precious stones
Jason Butler
Pam Butler

D-U-N-S 20-756-4212   (SL)
GIBSON LIVESTOCK (1981) LTD
Gd Lcd Main, Moose Jaw, SK, S6H 4N6
(306) 692-9668
Emp Here 10   *Sales* 12,103,970
SIC 5154 Livestock
Ryan Gibson
Louise Beauchesne

D-U-N-S 25-413-0503   (HQ)
HOLY TRINITY ROMAN CATHOLIC SEPA-RATE SCHOOL DIVISION #22
502 6th Ave Ne, Moose Jaw, SK, S6H 6B8
(306) 694-5333
Emp Here 50   *Sales* 24,779,750
SIC 8211 Elementary and secondary schools
Mark Corbin
Alyssa Robinson
Krista Michelson

D-U-N-S 24-387-0029   (HQ)
LEEVILLE CONSTRUCTION LTD
340 8th Ave Nw, Moose Jaw, SK, S6H 4E7
(306) 692-0677
Emp Here 20   *Sales* 11,768,275
SIC 1542 Nonresidential construction, nec
Grant Robbins

D-U-N-S 20-064-9929   (SL)
MOOSE JAW CO-OPERATIVE ASSOCIA-TION LIMITED, THE
MOOSE JAW CO-OP
500 1st Ave Nw Suite B10, Moose Jaw, SK, S6H 3M5
(306) 692-2351
Emp Here 120   *Sales* 150,864,120
SIC 5171 Petroleum bulk stations and termi-nals
Gerry Onyskevitch
Janie Drackett

D-U-N-S 25-091-3381   (BR)
PRAIRIE SOUTH SCHOOL DIVISION NO 210
A E PEACOCK COLLEGIATE
(*Suby of* PRAIRIE SOUTH SCHOOL DIVI-SION NO 210)
145 Ross St E, Moose Jaw, SK, S6H 0S3
(306) 693-4626
Emp Here 75
SIC 8211 Elementary and secondary schools
Dustin Swanson

D-U-N-S 24-336-0471   (HQ)
PRAIRIE SOUTH SCHOOL DIVISION NO 210
ASSINIBOIA ELEMENTARY
1075 9th Ave Nw, Moose Jaw, SK, S6H 1V7
(306) 694-1200
Emp Here 20   *Sales* 68,508,729

SIC 8211 Elementary and secondary schools
Bernie Girardin

D-U-N-S 25-193-4022   (SL)
PUGLIA, P. M. SALES LTD
CANADIAN TIRE
1350 Main St N, Moose Jaw, SK, S6H 8B9
(306) 693-0888
Emp Here 60   *Sales* 12,320,580
SIC 5399 Miscellaneous general merchandise
Peter Puglia
Patricia Puglia

D-U-N-S 24-819-1264   (SL)
RAY-DONN TOEWS BUILDING MATERIALS LTD
RAYDONN CASTLE BUILDING CENTRE
506 High St W, Moose Jaw, SK, S6H 1T4
(306) 693-0211
Emp Here 40   *Sales* 10,122,360
SIC 5211 Lumber and other building materials
Raymond Toews

D-U-N-S 20-063-7817   (HQ)
ROBERGE TRANSPORT INC
1750 Stadacona St W, Moose Jaw, SK, S6H 4P4
(800) 667-5190
Emp Here 66   *Sales* 26,741,780
SIC 4213 Trucking, except local
Marcel Roberge
Eugene Roberge

D-U-N-S 24-338-5338   (BR)
SASKATCHEWAN HEALTH AUTHORITY
PIONEERS HOUSING
(*Suby of* GOVERNMENT OF SASKATCHEWAN)
1000 Albert St, Moose Jaw, SK, S6H 2Y2
(306) 693-4616
Emp Here 105
SIC 8051 Skilled nursing care facilities
Noreen Seida

D-U-N-S 24-319-5703   (SL)
SASKATCHEWAN WATER CORPORATION
(*Suby of* GOVERNMENT OF SASKATCHEWAN)
111 Fairford St E Suite 400, Moose Jaw, SK, S6H 7X9
(306) 694-3098
Emp Here 85   *Sales* 28,461,230
SIC 4941 Water supply
Glen Rittinger
Garry Moroz
Gary Vidal
Lionel Labelle
Stuart Kramer
Larry Burechailo
Ken Hookway
Guy Lariviere
Dennis Mainil
Dena Mcmartin

D-U-N-S 24-890-9694   (SL)
SASKWATER
111 Fairford St E Suite 200, Moose Jaw, SK, S6H 1C8

Emp Here 50   *Sales* 13,033,150
SIC 4941 Water supply
Doug Matthies

D-U-N-S 24-172-6116   (HQ)
SIMPSON SEEDS INC
1170 North Service Rd, Moose Jaw, SK, S6H 4P8
(306) 693-2132
Emp Here 60   *Sales* 102,738,440
SIC 5153 Grain and field beans
Greg Simpson
John W Simpson
Tom Simpson

D-U-N-S 25-272-0040   (BR)
SOBEYS WEST INC
MOOSE JAW SAFEWAY
(*Suby of* EMPIRE COMPANY LIMITED)

---

200 1st Ave Nw, Moose Jaw, SK, S6H 1K9
(306) 693-8033
Emp Here 80
SIC 5411 Grocery stores
Joe Carroll

D-U-N-S 25-119-8818   (HQ)
TEMPLE GARDENS MINERAL SPA INC
24 Fairford St E, Moose Jaw, SK, S6H 0C7
(306) 694-5055
Sales 18,538,000
SIC 7011 Hotels and motels
David Wood
Lisa Clement

D-U-N-S 24-607-5089   (HQ)
WATER SECURITY AGENCY
(*Suby of* GOVERNMENT OF SASKATCHEWAN)
111 Fairford St E Suite 400, Moose Jaw, SK, S6H 7X9
(306) 694-3900
Emp Here 70   *Sales* 63,619,220
SIC 4941 Water supply
Wayne Dybvig

D-U-N-S 20-611-7558   (SL)
WATSON HOLDINGS LTD
SOUTH HILL FINE FOODS
468 Lillooet St W, Moose Jaw, SK, S6H 7T1
(306) 692-1516
Emp Here 40   *Sales* 10,966,080
SIC 5411 Grocery stores
Harry Watson
Sharon Watson
Marilyn Schachtel

D-U-N-S 24-968-6825   (BR)
WESTCAN BULK TRANSPORT LTD
(*Suby of* THE KENAN ADVANTAGE GROUP INC)
850 Manitoba St E, Moose Jaw, SK, S6H 4P1
(306) 692-6478
Emp Here 80
SIC 4213 Trucking, except local
Tyler Cochrane

Moose Jaw, SK S6J

D-U-N-S 20-269-0918   (SL)
598840 SASKATCHEWAN LTD
WESTERN DODGE CHRYSLER JEEP
1788 Main St N, Moose Jaw, SK, S6J 1L4
(306) 692-1808
Emp Here 30   *Sales* 14,942,340
SIC 5511 New and used car dealers
Kyle Knight

D-U-N-S 20-015-0501   (SL)
617274 SASKATCHEWAN LTD
MOOSE JAW TOYOTA
1743 Main St N, Moose Jaw, SK, S6J 1L6
(306) 694-1355
Emp Here 24   *Sales* 11,953,872
SIC 5511 New and used car dealers
Chad Taylor

D-U-N-S 20-039-3655   (SL)
MURRAY CHEVROLET CADILLAC BUICK GMC MOOSE JAW
MURRAY GM
15 Chester Rd, Moose Jaw, SK, S6J 1N3
(306) 693-4605
Emp Here 70   *Sales* 44,049,600
SIC 5511 New and used car dealers
Charles Vanden Broek

D-U-N-S 24-113-0095   (SL)
SASCO DEVELOPMENTS LTD
HERITAGE INN
1590 Main St N, Moose Jaw, SK, S6J 1L3
(306) 693-7550
Emp Here 75   *Sales* 7,117,425
SIC 7011 Hotels and motels
Glen Cowan

Shelley Kanegawa
Ken Mandeville
Richard Kanegawa

D-U-N-S 20-267-2429   (HQ)
SOUTH COUNTRY EQUIPMENT LTD
1731 Main St N, Moose Jaw, SK, S6J 1L6
(306) 642-3366
Emp Here 30   *Sales* 42,757,400
SIC 5999 Miscellaneous retail stores, nec
Cameron Bode

D-U-N-S 24-037-3985   (SL)
VILLAGE FORD LINCOLN SALES LTD
1708 Main St N, Moose Jaw, SK, S6J 1L4
(306) 693-3673
Emp Here 28   *Sales* 17,619,840
SIC 5511 New and used car dealers
Wayne Zimmerman
Brenda Zimmerman
Jordan Zimmerman

D-U-N-S 25-177-1176   (BR)
WAL-MART CANADA CORP
(*Suby of* WALMART INC.)
551 Thatcher Dr E Suite 3173, Moose Jaw, SK, S6J 1L8
(306) 693-3218
Emp Here 200
SIC 5311 Department stores
Terry Stanley

D-U-N-S 24-559-0612   (SL)
WESTERN HYUNDAI
1774 Main St N, Moose Jaw, SK, S6J 1L4
(306) 691-5444
Emp Here 30   *Sales* 14,942,340
SIC 5511 New and used car dealers
Kyle Knight

Moosomin, SK S0G

D-U-N-S 20-065-1982   (HQ)
BORDERLAND CO-OPERATIVE LIMITED
704 Main St, Moosomin, SK, S0G 3N0
(306) 435-4655
Emp Here 4   *Sales* 24,065,114
SIC 5411 Grocery stores
Jason Schenn
Robert Hill
Stan Macmillan
John Zondervan
Roger Smith
Ray Donald
John Thiessen
Jerry Mills
Larry Mills

D-U-N-S 20-068-6996   (HQ)
MILLER EQUIPMENT LTD
1604 Park Ave, Moosomin, SK, S0G 3N0
(306) 435-3866
Sales 10,000,000
SIC 5083 Farm and garden machinery
Douglas Heritage

D-U-N-S 25-705-3280   (SL)
MILLER FARM EQUIPMENT 2005 INC
Gd, Moosomin, SK, S0G 3N0
(306) 435-3866
Emp Here 1   *Sales* 58,527,600
SIC 5083 Farm and garden machinery
Doug Heritage
Kevin Miller

D-U-N-S 24-966-6850   (SL)
PRAIRIE LIVESTOCK LTD
Gd, Moosomin, SK, S0G 3N0
(306) 435-3327
Emp Here 20   *Sales* 24,207,940
SIC 5154 Livestock
Bill Jameson
Robin Gilroy

D-U-N-S 20-842-0018   (HQ)

▲ **Public Company**   ■ **Public Company Family Member**   **HQ** Headquarters   **BR** Branch   **SL** Single Location

SHARPE'S SOIL SERVICES LTD
205 Park Ave, Moosomin, SK, S0G 3N0
(306) 435-3319
Emp Here 5   *Sales* 23,018,120
SIC 5191 Farm supplies
Daniel Robert William Mckenzie
Robert Whitelaw
Blair R. Sharpe

Mossbank, SK S0H

D-U-N-S 25-681-0664   (HQ)
SOUTH COUNTRY AG LTD
40 Main St, Mossbank, SK, S0H 3G0

Emp Here 20   *Sales* 10,985,226
SIC 6712 Bank holding companies

Naicam, SK S0K

D-U-N-S 25-680-5276   (SL)
CROPPER, A.G. ENTERPRISES LTD
CROPPER MOTORS
501 5th Ave N, Naicam, SK, S0K 2Z0
(306) 874-2011
Emp Here 44   *Sales* 21,915,432
SIC 5511 New and used car dealers
Allan Cropper

Nipawin, SK S0E

D-U-N-S 20-037-8540   (BR)
KELSEY TRAIL REGIONAL HEALTH AU-THORITY
PINEVIEW LODGE
(*Suby of* KELSEY TRAIL REGIONAL HEALTH AUTHORITY)
400 6th Ave E, Nipawin, SK, S0E 1E0
(306) 862-9828
Emp Here 185
SIC 8051 Skilled nursing care facilities
Heather Watson

D-U-N-S 20-600-9789   (SL)
NIPAWIN CHRYSLER DODGE LTD
301 1 Ave W, Nipawin, SK, S0E 1E0
(306) 862-4755
Emp Here 23   *Sales* 11,455,794
SIC 5511 New and used car dealers
Chester Stankowski
Loretta Stankowski

D-U-N-S 20-060-6762   (HQ)
PINELAND CO-OPERATIVE ASSOCIATION LIMITED
1511 8 St W, Nipawin, SK, S0E 1E0
(306) 862-4668
Emp Here 105   *Sales* 52,734,090
SIC 5411 Grocery stores
Greg Schoonbaert
Lawrence Rospad
Morley Doerksen
Ron Braeder
Arlie Olson
Brenda Lehmann
Dennis Gillert
David Fettis
Paula Seaman

Norquay, SK S0A

D-U-N-S 20-065-4879   (SL)
NORQUAY CO-OPERATIVE ASSOCIATION LIMITED, THE
13 Hwy 49, Norquay, SK, S0A 2V0

(306) 594-2215
Emp Here 28   *Sales* 10,039,380
SIC 5211 Lumber and other building materials
Albert Outhwaite
George Grant
Ken Grywachesky
Ron Perepeluk
Wayne Prokoptchuk
Cheryl Holodniuk
Jeremi Korpusik

D-U-N-S 20-361-3229   (HQ)
PRAIRIE SOIL SERVICES LTD
1 Mile W Hwy 49, Norquay, SK, S0A 2V0
(306) 594-2330
Emp Here 38   *Sales* 11,640,714
SIC 5261 Retail nurseries and garden stores
Parker Summers

North Battleford, SK S9A

D-U-N-S 24-467-9049   (HQ)
ANDERSON PUMP HOUSE LTD
9802 Thatcher Ave, North Battleford, SK, S9A 3W2
(306) 937-7741
Emp Here 23   *Sales* 14,309,568
SIC 5074 Plumbing and heating equipment and supplies (hydronics)
Howard Kirby
Sharon Kirby

D-U-N-S 24-231-2049   (SL)
AWNBCO FOODS LTD
A & W RESTAURANT
2142 100th St, North Battleford, SK, S9A 0X6
(306) 445-9453
Emp Here 25   *Sales* 16,411,600
SIC 5963 Direct selling establishments
Connie Fontaine
Lorne Heidt
Reg Fontaine

D-U-N-S 20-065-6445   (HQ)
BATTLEFORDS AND DISTRICT CO-OPERATIVE LTD
BATTLEFORDS CO-OP
9800 Territorial Dr Suite 1, North Battleford, SK, S9A 3W6
(306) 445-9800
Emp Here 200   *Sales* 295,568,250
SIC 5171 Petroleum bulk stations and terminals
Mike Nord
Irene Link
Randy Graham
Dan Mceachern
Gemma Graw
Rob Squair
Lorraine Geates
Seton Wnterholt
Cathie Ornawka
Barry Verhoeven

D-U-N-S 20-033-2612   (HQ)
BOARD OF EDUCATION OF THE LIV-ING SKY SCHOOL DIVISION NO. 202 SASKATCHEWAN
MAJOR HIGH SCHOOL
509 Pioneer Ave, North Battleford, SK, S9A 4A5
(306) 937-7702
Sales 59,122,037
SIC 8211 Elementary and secondary schools
Brenda Vickers

D-U-N-S 20-580-6701   (BR)
BOARD OF EDUCATION OF THE LIV-ING SKY SCHOOL DIVISION NO. 202 SASKATCHEWAN
LIVING SKY SCHOOL DIVISION NO. 202
(*Suby of* BOARD OF EDUCATION OF THE LIVING SKY SCHOOL DIVISION NO. 202 SASKATCHEWAN)

1791 110th St, North Battleford, SK, S9A 2Y2
(306) 445-6101
Emp Here 102
SIC 8211 Elementary and secondary schools
Bruce Friesen

D-U-N-S 20-267-4433   (HQ)
BTC INDIAN HEALTH SERVICE INC
1192 101st St Suite 103, North Battleford, SK, S9A 0Z6
(306) 937-6700
Emp Here 100   *Sales* 15,634,600
SIC 8099 Health and allied services, nec
Janice Kennedy

D-U-N-S 24-748-2532   (SL)
CAMPBELL, SCOTT DODGE LTD
3042 99th St Hwy Suite 4, North Battleford, SK, S9A 3W8
(306) 445-6640
Emp Here 24   *Sales* 11,953,872
SIC 5511 New and used car dealers
Scott Campbell

D-U-N-S 24-112-1193   (SL)
CASH & CARRY LUMBER MART LTD
HOME HARDWARE BUILDING CENTRE
11301 6th Ave, North Battleford, SK, S9A 2N5
(306) 445-3350
Emp Here 45   *Sales* 11,387,655
SIC 5211 Lumber and other building materials
Gabe Baigneau

D-U-N-S 25-593-7955   (BR)
GOVERNMENT OF SASKATCHEWAN
BATTLEFORDS UNION HOSPITAL
(*Suby of* GOVERNMENT OF SASKATCHEWAN)
1092 107th St, North Battleford, SK, S9A 1Z1
(306) 446-6600
Emp Here 400
SIC 8062 General medical and surgical hospitals
David Fan

D-U-N-S 20-106-1954   (BR)
GOVERNMENT OF SASKATCHEWAN
NORTH BATTLEFORD YOUTH CENTER
(*Suby of* GOVERNMENT OF SASKATCHEWAN)
123 Jersey St, North Battleford, SK, S9A 4B4
(306) 446-7819
Emp Here 250
SIC 8322 Individual and family services
Hollis Dimion

D-U-N-S 24-347-1724   (BR)
INNOVATION CREDIT UNION LIMITED
1202 102nd St, North Battleford, SK, S9A 1G3
(306) 446-7000
Emp Here 150
SIC 6062 State credit unions

D-U-N-S 24-039-8727   (HQ)
KRAMER AUCTIONS LTD
Gd Lcd Main, North Battleford, SK, S9A 2X5
(306) 445-2377
Sales 16,280,000
SIC 5999 Miscellaneous retail stores, nec
Neil Kramer

D-U-N-S 20-600-2727   (HQ)
LAMON, J.J. INC
PETRO CANADA BULK
1007 Battleford Rd, North Battleford, SK, S9A 2P2
(306) 445-3592
Emp Here 8   *Sales* 14,459,312
SIC 5171 Petroleum bulk stations and terminals
Blair Lamon
Sandra Lamon

D-U-N-S 25-601-5934   (SL)
LANGCO FOODS LTD
SOBEYS NORTH BATTLEFORD
9801 Territorial Dr, North Battleford, SK, S9A 3Z8

(306) 445-1934
Emp Here 100   *Sales* 29,347,700
SIC 5411 Grocery stores
Ronald Lang
Grace Lang

D-U-N-S 24-608-2184   (HQ)
LIGHT OF CHRIST RCSSD
9301 19th Ave, North Battleford, SK, S9A 3N5
(306) 445-6158
Sales 34,691,650
SIC 8211 Elementary and secondary schools
Herb Sutton

D-U-N-S 20-835-4055   (BR)
LIGHT OF CHRIST RCSSD
JOHN PAUL II COLLEGIATE SCHOOL
(*Suby of* LIGHT OF CHRIST RCSSD)
1491 97th St, North Battleford, SK, S9A 0K1
(306) 446-2232
Emp Here 80
SIC 8211 Elementary and secondary schools
Carlo Hansen

D-U-N-S 20-065-6841   (SL)
MODERN JANITORIAL SERVICES (1978) LTD
MODERN FURNACE CLEANERS
2521 Commerce Dr, North Battleford, SK, S9A 2X5
(306) 445-4774
Emp Here 43   *Sales* 20,426,118
SIC 5087 Service establishment equipment
Dave Eckel
Eunice Eckel

D-U-N-S 20-546-9778   (SL)
NBFG AUTO LTD
BRIDGES CHEVROLET
(*Suby of* AUTOCANADA INC)
2501 99th St, North Battleford, SK, S9A 2X6
(306) 445-3300
Emp Here 32   *Sales* 20,136,960
SIC 5511 New and used car dealers
Walter Houk

D-U-N-S 24-332-5425   (SL)
NO FRILLS
11403 Railway Avenue E, North Battleford, SK, S9A 0A1
(306) 445-3375
Emp Here 49   *Sales* 13,433,448
SIC 5411 Grocery stores
Frazer Bonin

D-U-N-S 24-747-7557   (SL)
NORSASK FARM EQUIPMENT LTD
Hwy 16 East, North Battleford, SK, S9A 2M4
(306) 445-8128
Emp Here 20   *Sales* 10,000,000
SIC 5083 Farm and garden machinery
Leon Lozowchuk

D-U-N-S 25-314-4802   (SL)
PARKLAND PULSE GRAIN CO. LTD
Gd Lcd Main, North Battleford, SK, S9A 2X5
(306) 445-4199
Emp Here 33   *Sales* 48,433,836
SIC 5153 Grain and field beans
Cyril Fransoo
Gilles Fransoo

D-U-N-S 20-854-4858   (HQ)
PFEIFER HOLDINGS LTD
HAPPY INN
992 101st St, North Battleford, SK, S9A 0Z3
(306) 445-9425
Emp Here 30   *Sales* 13,000,005
SIC 6712 Bank holding companies
Pius Pfeifer
Ida Pfeifer

D-U-N-S 24-343-2858   (HQ)
PRAIRIE NORTH REGIONAL HEALTH AU-THORITY
PRAIRIE NORTH HEALTH REGION
1092 107th St, North Battleford, SK, S9A 1Z1
(306) 446-6600
Emp Here 2,000   *Sales* 3,766,859

▲ Public Company   ■ Public Company Family Member   **HQ** Headquarters   **BR** Branch   **SL** Single Location

SIC 8062 General medical and surgical hospitals
David Fan
Vikki Smart
Gloria King
Derek Miller
Irene Denis
Almereau Prollius
Wlhelm Retief
Kevin Govender
Gavin Van De Venter

D-U-N-S 24-616-0548   (SL)
QUICK LANE TIRE AND AUTO CENTRE
VALLEY FORD SALES
2222 100th St, North Battleford, SK, S9A 0X6
(306) 445-4495
Emp Here 45   *Sales* 16,389,675
SIC 5012 Automobiles and other motor vehicles
Bob Kenny

D-U-N-S 24-427-1813   (SL)
R & T PHARMACY LTD
SHOPPERS DRUG MART
11412 Railway Ave E Unit 12, North Battleford, SK, S9A 3P7
(306) 445-6253
Emp Here 40   *Sales* 10,118,160
SIC 5912 Drug stores and proprietary stores
Rosemary Priddle

D-U-N-S 25-385-8294   (BR)
SASKATCHEWAN INDIAN GAMING AUTHORITY INC
GOLD EAGLE CASINO
(*Suby of* FEDERATION OF SASKATCHEWAN INDIANS, INC)
11906 Railway Ave E, North Battleford, SK, S9A 3K7
(306) 446-3833
Emp Here 300
SIC 7999 Amusement and recreation, nec
Kelly Atchbynum

D-U-N-S 20-447-6212   (SL)
UNITED ENTERPRISES LTD
HAPPY INN
(*Suby of* PFEIFER HOLDINGS LTD)
992 101st St, North Battleford, SK, S9A 0Z3
(306) 445-9425
Emp Here 100   *Sales* 9,269,000
SIC 7011 Hotels and motels
Pius Pfeifer
Ida Pfeifer
Gary Pfeifer
Brian Demonterun

D-U-N-S 25-294-7262   (BR)
WAL-MART CANADA CORP
(*Suby of* WALMART INC.)
601 Carlton Trail Suite 1, North Battleford, SK, S9A 4A9
(306) 445-8105
Emp Here 200
SIC 5311 Department stores
Robbie Sasf

North Portal, SK S0C

D-U-N-S 20-833-5372   (HQ)
DAVIS, PERCY H. LIMITED
NORTH PORTAL DUTY FREE SHOP, DIV OF
4 Abbott Ave, North Portal, SK, S0C 1W0
(306) 927-2165
Emp Here 14   *Sales* 15,599,010
SIC 4731 Freight transportation arrangement
Alan Davis
Mark Davis
Gene Davis
Kim Weinrauch

Onion Lake, SK S0M

D-U-N-S 20-038-4167   (SL)
ONION LAKE HEALTH BOARD INC
ONION LAKE RESERVE
Gd, Onion Lake, SK, S0M 2E0
(306) 344-2330
Emp Here 80   *Sales* 6,243,840
SIC 8021 Offices and clinics of dentists
Albert Jimmy

Osler, SK S0K

D-U-N-S 25-013-6488   (SL)
JANZEN, HENRY STEEL BUILDINGS LTD
JANZEN STEEL BUILDINGS
Gd, Osler, SK, S0K 3A0
(306) 242-7767
Emp Here 70   *Sales* 17,233,020
SIC 1791 Structural steel erection
Henry Janzen
Marlene Janzen
Mark Janzen
Lloyd Janzen

D-U-N-S 20-769-5938   (SL)
PINE VIEW ALL NATURAL MEATS INC
PINE VIEW FARMS
Gd, Osler, SK, S0K 3A0
(306) 239-4763
Emp Here 30   *Sales* 11,565,570
SIC 0259 Poultry and eggs, nec
Melanie Boldt
Kevin Boldt

Outlook, SK S0L

D-U-N-S 20-876-5248   (SL)
OUTLOOK & DISTRICT PIONEER HOME INC
OUTLOOK HEALTH CENTRE
500 Semple St, Outlook, SK, S0L 2N0
(306) 867-8676
Emp Here 80   *Sales* 5,498,640
SIC 8051 Skilled nursing care facilities
Elaine Feltis

D-U-N-S 20-611-7111   (HQ)
RIVERBEND CO-OPERATIVE LTD
101 Saskatchewan Ave E, Outlook, SK, S0L 2N0
(306) 867-8614
Emp Here 70   *Sales* 27,415,200
SIC 5411 Grocery stores
Greg Sarvis
Justin Turton

Oxbow, SK S0C

D-U-N-S 20-065-8425   (SL)
SPEARING SERVICE (2006) LTD
SPEARING SERVICE
(*Suby of* MULLEN GROUP LTD)
41 Marion Ave, Oxbow, SK, S0C 2B0
(306) 483-2848
Emp Here 110   *Sales* 73,994,690
SIC 1389 Oil and gas field services, nec
Ken Mcclement
Murray Mullen

Paradise Hill, SK S0M

D-U-N-S 20-919-9103   (SL)
NOVLAN BROS SALES INC

Gd, Paradise Hill, SK, S0M 2G0
(877) 344-4433
Emp Here 50   *Sales* 23,751,300
SIC 5083 Farm and garden machinery
Randy Novlan

D-U-N-S 20-446-5983   (HQ)
NOVLAN BROTHERS SALES PARTNERSHIP
47 First Ave, Paradise Hill, SK, S0M 2G0
(306) 344-4448
Sales 30,726,990
SIC 5083 Farm and garden machinery
Randy Novlan
Douglas Novlan

Pelican Narrows, SK S0P

D-U-N-S 24-883-4541   (SL)
OPAWIKOSCIKEN SCHOOL
PELICAN NARROWS SCHOOL
Gd, Pelican Narrows, SK, S0P 0E0
(306) 632-2161
Emp Here 86   *Sales* 7,983,036
SIC 8211 Elementary and secondary schools
Susan Custer

Pennant Station, SK S0N

D-U-N-S 25-703-9818   (SL)
BIG G HOLDINGS LTD
Gd, Pennant Station, SK, S0N 1X0
(306) 626-3249
Emp Here 40   *Sales* 13,698,680
SIC 0119 Cash grains, nec
Stuart Garrett
Bennent Garrett

D-U-N-S 20-113-7135   (SL)
HUTTERIAN BRETHREN OF PENNANT INC
Gd, Pennant Station, SK, S0N 1X0
(306) 626-3369
Emp Here 60   *Sales* 10,834,500
SIC 8661 Religious organizations
Dave Entz
Dave Mandel
John Wips

Pilot Butte, SK S0G

D-U-N-S 24-951-0418   (SL)
CROSS BORDERS CONSULTING LTD
CROSS BORDERS DRILLING
Po Box 509, Pilot Butte, SK, S0G 3Z0
(306) 781-4484
Emp Here 115   *Sales* 12,956,329
SIC 1381 Drilling oil and gas wells
Jared Mills

D-U-N-S 24-767-4989   (SL)
DUTCH INDUSTRIES LTD
(*Suby of* DUTCH BLACKSMITH SHOP LTD)
500 Portico Drive, Pilot Butte, SK, S0G 3Z0
(306) 781-4820
Emp Here 80   *Sales* 17,760,080
SIC 3523 Farm machinery and equipment
Izaak Cruson
Irene Cruson

D-U-N-S 20-756-5672   (HQ)
RANCH EHRLO SOCIETY
Gd, Pilot Butte, SK, S0G 3Z0
(306) 781-1800
Emp Here 50   *Sales* 43,937,520
SIC 8361 Residential care
Debbie Mckague
Laurel Garven
Jamie Burrows

Karen Bright
Annette Revet

Ponteix, SK S0N

D-U-N-S 24-496-0951   (SL)
PONTEIX COLONY OF HUTTERIAN BRETHREN
Gd, Ponteix, SK, S0N 1Z0
(306) 625-3652
Emp Here 83   *Sales* 22,769,556
SIC 8741 Management services
George Wollman
George L. Wollman

Porcupine Plain, SK S0E

D-U-N-S 20-066-1296   (SL)
PARKLAND CO-OPERATIVE ASSOCIATION LIMITED, THE
108 Ash St, Porcupine Plain, SK, S0E 1H0
(306) 278-2022
Emp Here 110   *Sales* 25,822,913
SIC 5171 Petroleum bulk stations and terminals

Prince Albert, SK S6V

D-U-N-S 20-066-2120   (SL)
ANDERSON MOTORS LTD
ANDERSONS CHRYSLER, DIV
3333 6th Ave E, Prince Albert, SK, S6V 8C8
(306) 765-3000
Emp Here 33   *Sales* 16,436,574
SIC 5511 New and used car dealers
Doug G Jones
Donald J Jones
Ron Jones

D-U-N-S 24-324-1077   (BR)
CONEXUS CREDIT UNION 2006
PA - SOUTH HILL BRANCH
(*Suby of* CONEXUS CREDIT UNION 2006)
2800 2nd Ave W, Prince Albert, SK, S6V 5Z4
(306) 953-6100
Emp Here 80
SIC 6062 State credit unions

D-U-N-S 24-128-8708   (SL)
FIRE FIGHTERS ASSOCIATION LOCAL 510
76 15th St E, Prince Albert, SK, S6V 1E8

Emp Here 44   *Sales* 17,486,216
SIC 8699 Membership organizations, nec
Lloyd Zwack

D-U-N-S 20-213-7746   (SL)
FIRST GENERAL SERVICES (PA) LTD
32 North Industrial, Prince Albert, SK, S6V 5P7
(306) 764-7000
Emp Here 30   *Sales* 17,397,720
SIC 6411 Insurance agents, brokers, and service
Gus Detillieux

D-U-N-S 20-197-2804   (BR)
KJMAL ENTERPRISES LTD
MCDONALD'S
(*Suby of* KJMAL ENTERPRISES LTD)
800 15th St E Unit 800, Prince Albert, SK, S6V 8E3
(306) 922-6366
Emp Here 83
SIC 5812 Eating places
Dustin Glover

D-U-N-S 20-447-1700   (SL)
LAKELAND FORD SALES LTD

3434 2nd Ave W, Prince Albert, SK, S6V 5G2
(306) 764-3325
Emp Here 70   *Sales* 44,049,600
SIC 5511 New and used car dealers
  Scott Weisman

D-U-N-S 20-066-3904   (SL)
LEHNER WOOD PRESERVERS LTD
2690 4th Ave W, Prince Albert, SK, S6V 5Y9
(306) 763-4232
Emp Here 50   *Sales* 10,206,500
SIC 3312 Blast furnaces and steel mills
  Ronald Lehner Sr
  June Lehner

D-U-N-S 24-671-2926   (SL)
LONESTAR AUTOMOTIVE
1125 2nd Ave W, Prince Albert, SK, S6V 5A9
(306) 763-4777
Emp Here 30   *Sales* 10,926,450
SIC 5013 Motor vehicle supplies and new
parts
  Brett Cozens

D-U-N-S 20-349-9459   (SL)
MANN-NORTHWAY AUTO SOURCE LTD
MANN-NORTHWAY AUTO SOURCE
(*Suby of* AUTOCANADA INC)
500 Marquis Rd E, Prince Albert, SK, S6V 8B3
(306) 765-2200
Emp Here 49   *Sales* 30,834,720
SIC 5511 New and used car dealers
  Roger Mann

D-U-N-S 24-264-9895   (HQ)
MCDONALD METALS (1983) LTD
Gd, Prince Albert, SK, S6V 8A4
(306) 764-9333
Emp Here 16   *Sales* 12,493,008
SIC 5093 Scrap and waste materials
  Ian Mcdonald
  Caroline Mcdonald

D-U-N-S 25-014-2163   (SL)
MONT ST. JOSEPH HOME INC
777 28th St E, Prince Albert, SK, S6V 8C2
(306) 953-4500
Emp Here 160   *Sales* 10,932,160
SIC 8051 Skilled nursing care facilities
  Brian Martin

D-U-N-S 20-066-4753   (SL)
**NORTHWAY CHEVROLET OLDSMOBILE
LTD**
500 Marquis Rd E, Prince Albert, SK, S6V 8B3
(306) 765-2200
Emp Here 70   *Sales* 44,049,600
SIC 5511 New and used car dealers
  Bruce Prasse

D-U-N-S 20-066-4571   (SL)
P A BOTTLERS LTD
P A BEVERAGE SALES
85 11th St Nw, Prince Albert, SK, S6V 5T2
(306) 922-7777
Emp Here 105   *Sales* 36,297,450
SIC 2086 Bottled and canned soft drinks
  Arthur Hauser

D-U-N-S 24-348-8223   (SL)
**PBCN P.A. FUEL AND CONVENIENCE LIM-
ITED PARTNERSHIP**
PETRO CANADA
3451 2nd Ave W, Prince Albert, SK, S6V 5G1
(306) 953-1490
Emp Here 22   *Sales* 10,957,716
SIC 5541 Gasoline service stations
  Peter Gambin
  George Michel
  Clayton Sewap
  Trevor Ives
  Darrell Mccallum

D-U-N-S 25-999-8060   (HQ)
PRECISION INDUSTRIAL LTD
1020 1st Ave Nw, Prince Albert, SK, S6V 6J9

Sales 11,766,053

SIC 3535 Conveyors and conveying equip-
ment
  Ross Brooks
  Bryan Stark
  Albert Raas
  Tim Gratias

D-U-N-S 20-066-4845   (HQ)
**PRINCE ALBERT CO-OPERATIVE ASSOCI-
ATION LIMITED, THE**
801 15th St E Suite 791, Prince Albert, SK,
S6V 0C7
(306) 764-9393
Emp Here 130   *Sales* 73,011,840
SIC 5399 Miscellaneous general merchandise
  Dean Mckim
  Wayne Paczay
  Roger Mayert
  Wayne Kabatoff
  Harvey Skea
  Ian Lauder
  Jack Mcdonald

D-U-N-S 24-038-5245   (HQ)
**PRINCE ALBERT CO-OPERATIVE HEALTH
CENTRE/COMMUNITY CLINIC**
110 8th St E, Prince Albert, SK, S6V 0V7
(306) 763-6464
Emp Here 57   *Sales* 11,120,400
SIC 8011 Offices and clinics of medical doc-
tors
  Jerry Danielson
  Joanne Thiessen
  Verden Jeancart

D-U-N-S 24-966-5746   (SL)
**PRINCE ALBERT DEVELOPMENT CORPO-
RATION**
PRINCE ALBERT INN
3680 2nd Ave W, Prince Albert, SK, S6V 5G2
(306) 763-1362
Emp Here 115   *Sales* 5,234,685
SIC 5812 Eating places
  Chief Alfonse Bird
  Wesley Daniels

D-U-N-S 25-388-6816   (BR)
**PRINCE ALBERT DEVELOPMENT CORPO-
RATION**
MARLBORO INN
67 13th St E, Prince Albert, SK, S6V 1C7
(306) 763-2643
Emp Here 95
SIC 7011 Hotels and motels
  Debbie Honch

D-U-N-S 24-390-4674   (SL)
RAVEN ENTERPRISES INC.
HAROLD'S FOODLINER
(*Suby of* RCS INVESTMENTS (2003) INC)
200 28th St E, Prince Albert, SK, S6V 1X2
(306) 922-3663
Emp Here 80   *Sales* 23,478,160
SIC 5411 Grocery stores
  Byron Guy
  Heather Guy

D-U-N-S 25-389-1972   (SL)
RNF VENTURES LTD
811 Central Ave, Prince Albert, SK, S6V 4V2
(306) 763-3700
Emp Here 45   *Sales* 21,182,895
SIC 1542 Nonresidential construction, nec
  Kelly Miller

D-U-N-S 25-486-1636   (BR)
**SASKATCHEWAN INDIAN GAMING AU-
THORITY INC**
NORTHERN LIGHTS CASINO
(*Suby   of   FEDERATION   OF*
SASKATCHEWAN INDIANS, INC)
44 Marquis Rd W, Prince Albert, SK, S6V 7Y5
(306) 764-4777
Emp Here 400
SIC 7999 Amusement and recreation, nec
  Ahenakew Richard

D-U-N-S 20-231-1747   (BR)

**SASKATCHEWAN RIVER SCHOOL DIVI-
SION #119**
*CARLTON   COMPREHENSIVE   HIGH
SCHOOL*
665 28th St E, Prince Albert, SK, S6V 6E9
(306) 922-3115
Emp Here 100
SIC 8211 Elementary and secondary schools
  Dawn Kilmer

D-U-N-S 20-066-5586   (SL)
THORPE BROTHERS LIMITED
Hwy 2 S 44th St, Prince Albert, SK, S6V 5R4
(306) 763-8454
Emp Here 50   *Sales* 11,046,700
SIC 1711 Plumbing, heating, air-conditioning
  William Thorpe
  Don Thorpe
  Betty Thorpe

D-U-N-S 25-104-6330   (HQ)
TRANSWEST AIR LIMITED PARTNERSHIP
(*Suby of* WEST WIND AVIATION LIMITED
PARTNERSHIP)
Gd, Prince Albert, SK, S6V 5R4
(306) 764-1404
Sales 79,338,000
SIC 4522 Air transportation, nonscheduled
  Pat Campling

D-U-N-S 24-967-6552   (HQ)
UNIFIED AUTO PARTS INC
NAPA AUTO PARTS
365 36th St W, Prince Albert, SK, S6V 7L4
(306) 764-4220
Emp Here 21   *Sales* 12,383,310
SIC 5013 Motor vehicle supplies and new
parts
  Mark Krasicki
  Mearl Whitney
  Denise Bremner

D-U-N-S 24-229-9535   (SL)
UNIFIED HOLDINGS LTD
PRINCE ALBERT TURBO
99 River St E, Prince Albert, SK, S6V 0A1
(306) 922-2770
Emp Here 20   *Sales* 20,656,160
SIC 5171 Petroleum bulk stations and termi-
nals
  Kenneth Placsko

D-U-N-S 25-288-5371   (BR)
WAL-MART CANADA CORP
(*Suby of* WALMART INC.)
800 15th St E Suite 100, Prince Albert, SK,
S6V 8E3
(306) 764-9770
Emp Here 300
SIC 5311 Department stores
  Chad Fraser

D-U-N-S 24-231-0928   (HQ)
WAPITI REGIONAL LIBRARY
145 12th St E, Prince Albert, SK, S6V 1B7
(306) 764-0712
Emp Here 17   *Sales* 11,096,820
SIC 8231 Libraries
  John Murray
  Lee Harris

D-U-N-S 20-294-8865   (SL)
**WESTERN FIRST NATIONS HOSPITALITY
LIMITED PARTNERSHIP**
914 Central Ave, Prince Albert, SK, S6V 4V3
(306) 922-0088
Emp Here 120   *Sales* 11,122,800
SIC 7011 Hotels and motels
  Ron Michele
  Jaime Mcguin

Prince Albert, SK S6W

D-U-N-S 20-273-7672   (SL)
BRODA GROUP HOLDINGS LIMITED PART-

NERSHIP
4271 5th Ave E, Prince Albert, SK, S6W 0A5
(306) 764-5337
Emp Here 250   *Sales* 115,944,000
SIC 1522 Residential construction, nec
  Gord Broda

D-U-N-S 24-923-5763   (SL)
JENKINS, MALCOLM J. (HOLDINGS) LTD
CANADIAN TIRE SERVICE
3725 2nd Ave W, Prince Albert, SK, S6W 1A1
(306) 764-9000
Emp Here 110   *Sales* 30,068,500
SIC 6712 Bank holding companies
  Malcolm J. Jenkins

D-U-N-S 24-468-4072   (SL)
**JENKINS, MALCOLM J. MERCHANDISING
LTD**
CANADIAN TIRE STORE
3725 2nd Ave W, Prince Albert, SK, S6W 1A1
(306) 764-9000
Emp Here 160   *Sales* 100,684,800
SIC 5531 Auto and home supply stores
  Malcolm Jenkins

D-U-N-S 25-205-1644   (SL)
NORTH AMERICAN ROCK & DIRT INC
BRODA GROUP OF COMPANIES
4271 5th Ave E, Prince Albert, SK, S6W 0A5
(306) 764-5337
Emp Here 150   *Sales* 37,866,300
SIC 1629 Heavy construction, nec
  Gordon (Gordie) Broda
  Russell Clunie

D-U-N-S 24-691-5623   (HQ)
**P. A. FINE FOODS AND DISTRIBUTORS
LTD**
3850 5th Ave E, Prince Albert, SK, S6W 0A1
(306) 763-7061
Emp Here 60   *Sales* 79,555,476
SIC 5145 Confectionery
  Lori Schultz
  Robert Schultz

D-U-N-S 20-348-2609   (SL)
RALLY MOTOR SPORTS LTD
10 38th St E, Prince Albert, SK, S6W 1A6
(306) 922-6363
Emp Here 35   *Sales* 17,432,730
SIC 5571 Motorcycle dealers
  Darrel Hudye

D-U-N-S 24-718-2272   (SL)
RALLY MOTORS LTD
POLARIS
(*Suby of* PRISM HOLDINGS LTD)
60 38th St E, Prince Albert, SK, S6W 1A6
(306) 922-6363
Emp Here 38   *Sales* 23,912,640
SIC 5511 New and used car dealers
  Derryl Hudye

D-U-N-S 20-210-9125   (SL)
RIVERSIDE DODGE CHRYSLER JEEP LTD
RIVERSIDE ARCTIC CAT
160 38th St E, Prince Albert, SK, S6W 1A6
(306) 764-4217
Emp Here 30   *Sales* 14,942,340
SIC 5511 New and used car dealers
  Joseph (Joe) Hargrave

D-U-N-S 20-873-5527   (HQ)
**TRU-NORTH RV, AUTO & MARINE SALES
INC**
4189 2nd Ave W, Prince Albert, SK, S6W 1A1
(306) 763-8100
Emp Here 18   *Sales* 13,214,880
SIC 5551 Boat dealers
  Kelly Eiswerth
  Gail Giese
  Terry Skulmoski

Quill Lake, SK S0A

D-U-N-S 20-835-7228 (SL)
HUTTERIAN BERTHEREN CHURCH OF QUILL LAKE INC
Gd, Quill Lake, SK, S0A 3E0
(306) 383-2989
Emp Here 48   *Sales* 16,438,416
SIC 0139 Field crops, except cash grain
Thomas Tschetter
Jonathan Tschetter

Radville, SK S0C

D-U-N-S 20-066-7046 (HQ)
E. BOURASSA & SONS PARTNERSHIP
Hwy 28 S, Radville, SK, S0C 2G0
(306) 869-2277
Emp Here 7   *Sales* 23,751,300
SIC 5083 Farm and garden machinery
Daniel Bourassa Jr
Kurtis Bourassa

D-U-N-S 20-969-5118 (SL)
PRAIRIE HERITAGE SEEDS INC
PRAIRIE HERITAGE SEEDS ORGANICS
Highway 28 N Mile 4, Radville, SK, S0C 2G0
(306) 869-2926
Emp Here 15   *Sales* 18,155,955
SIC 5153 Grain and field beans
Alex Galarneau

Raymore, SK S0A

D-U-N-S 20-120-7318 (HQ)
619020 SASKATCHEWAN LTD
RAYMORE NEW HOLLAND
Hwy 6 N, Raymore, SK, S0A 3J0
(306) 746-2911
Emp Here 25   *Sales* 40,144,692
SIC 5999 Miscellaneous retail stores, nec
Dave Marshall
Matthew Marshall

Redvers, SK S0C

D-U-N-S 20-062-8535 (SL)
ADVANTAGE CO-OPERATIVE ASSOCIATION LTD
3 Broadway St S, Redvers, SK, S0C 2H0
(306) 452-3513
Emp Here 70   *Sales* 35,874,699
SIC 5171 Petroleum bulk stations and terminals
Dale Kenler
Jens Hansen

D-U-N-S 25-326-0715 (BR)
SUN COUNTRY REGIONAL HEALTH AUTHORITY
REDVERS ROAD AMBULANCE
18 Eichorst St, Redvers, SK, S0C 2H0
(306) 452-3553
Emp Here 75
SIC 4119 Local passenger transportation, nec
Larry Ward

D-U-N-S 25-014-2619 (BR)
SUN COUNTRY REGIONAL HEALTH AUTHORITY
REDVERS HEALTH CENTRE
18 Eichhorst St, Redvers, SK, S0C 2H0
(306) 452-3553
Emp Here 90
SIC 8062 General medical and surgical hospitals
Naomi Hjertaaf

Regina, SK P0T

D-U-N-S 20-068-2672 (HQ)
SHERWOOD CO-OPERATIVE ASSOCIATION LIMITED
615 Winnipeg St N, Regina, SK, P0T 2S0
(306) 791-9300
Emp Here 50   *Sales* 436,258,737
SIC 5171 Petroleum bulk stations and terminals
Ken Krug
Mike Schindel

Regina, SK S0G

D-U-N-S 20-346-1363 (SL)
TASLAR TRADING CORP
100 Sherwood Forest Rd, Regina, SK, S0G 3W0
(306) 500-5522
Emp Here 10   *Sales* 10,185,201
SIC 5153 Grain and field beans
Hasan Taslar

Regina, SK S4N

D-U-N-S 24-117-2865 (HQ)
ACCESS COMMUNICATIONS CO-OPERATIVE LIMITED
ACCESS COMMUNICATIONS
2250 Park St, Regina, SK, S4N 7K7
(306) 569-2225
Emp Here 145   *Sales* 63,844,452
SIC 4813 Telephone communication, except radio
Jim Deane
Carmela Haine

D-U-N-S 20-327-3557 (HQ)
ADOXIO BUSINESS SOLUTIONS LIMITED
1445 Park St Suite 200, Regina, SK, S4N 4C5
(306) 569-6501
Emp Here 37   *Sales* 10,692,550
SIC 7372 Prepackaged software
Grant Mclarnon

D-U-N-S 20-366-6334 (HQ)
ADVANCE ENGINEERED PRODUCTS LTD
144 Henderson Dr, Regina, SK, S4N 5P7
(306) 721-5678
Emp Here 300   *Sales* 51,825,865
SIC 3069 Fabricated rubber products, nec
Darrell Zwarych

D-U-N-S 25-251-1944 (HQ)
AGCO CANADA, LTD
(*Suby of* AGCO CORPORATION)
515 Dewdney Ave, Regina, SK, S4N 6S1
(306) 757-2681
Emp Here 8   *Sales* 28,501,560
SIC 5083 Farm and garden machinery
Alvin Seiferling
Martin Richenhagen

D-U-N-S 20-611-6444 (SL)
ALEX MARION RESTAURANTS LTD
MACDONALDS
940 E Victoria Ave, Regina, SK, S4N 7A9

Emp Here 100   *Sales* 4,287,300
SIC 5812 Eating places
Alex Marion
Johanna Marion

D-U-N-S 25-539-1468 (BR)
ALL-FAB BUILDING COMPONENTS INC
NU-FAB
(*Suby of* ALL-FAB BUILDING COMPONENTS INC)

610 Henderson Dr, Regina, SK, S4N 5X3
(306) 721-8131
Emp Here 75
SIC 5039 Construction materials, nec
Mark Weichel

D-U-N-S 24-467-3760 (HQ)
ALLIANCE ENERGY LIMITED
(*Suby of* MANCON HOLDINGS LTD)
504 Henderson Dr, Regina, SK, S4N 5X2
(306) 721-6484
Emp Here 100   *Sales* 82,428,150
SIC 1731 Electrical work
James Paul Mclellan
Bryan Leverick
Janet Mclellan-Folk

D-U-N-S 20-065-0203 (BR)
BAYER CROPSCIENCE INC
(*Suby of* BAYER AG)
295 Henderson Dr, Regina, SK, S4N 6C2
(306) 721-4500
Emp Here 100
SIC 5191 Farm supplies
Stan Prokopchuk

D-U-N-S 20-801-4196 (BR)
BEE-CLEAN BUILDING MAINTENANCE INCORPORATED
(*Suby of* BEE-CLEAN BUILDING MAINTENANCE INCORPORATED)
1555 Mcdonald St Unit A, Regina, SK, S4N 6H7
(306) 757-8020
Emp Here 400
SIC 7349 Building maintenance services, nec
Slorencio Vieira

D-U-N-S 24-468-5798 (BR)
CANADIAN LINEN AND UNIFORM SERVICE CO
QUEBEC LINGE
(*Suby of* ARAMARK)
180 N Leonard St, Regina, SK, S4N 5V7
(306) 721-4848
Emp Here 80
SIC 7213 Linen supply
Garry Smith

D-U-N-S 24-112-2027 (HQ)
CLIFTON ASSOCIATES LTD
340 Maxwell Cres, Regina, SK, S4N 5Y5
(306) 721-7611
Emp Here 40   *Sales* 19,661,290
SIC 8711 Engineering services
A Wayne Clifton

D-U-N-S 24-883-3253 (BR)
COCA-COLA CANADA BOTTLING LIMITED
(*Suby of* COCA-COLA CANADA BOTTLING LIMITED)
355 Henderson Dr, Regina, SK, S4N 6B9
(800) 218-2653
Emp Here 85
SIC 5149 Groceries and related products, nec
Dean Brattan

D-U-N-S 20-842-5330 (SL)
COMMERCIAL BUILDING SERVICE LTD
819 Arcola Ave, Regina, SK, S4N 0S9
(306) 757-5332
Emp Here 100   *Sales* 4,020,900
SIC 7349 Building maintenance services, nec
James Woykin
Murray Sutherland

D-U-N-S 20-067-1709 (BR)
CONSUMERS' CO-OPERATIVE REFINERIES LIMITED
(*Suby of* FEDERATED CO-OPERATIVES LIMITED)
550e E 9th Ave N, Regina, SK, S4N 7B3
(306) 721-5353
Emp Here 500
SIC 2911 Petroleum refining
Barb Miller

D-U-N-S 20-069-2960 (HQ)

CONSUMERS' CO-OPERATIVE REFINERIES LIMITED
CO-OP REFINERY COMPLEX
(*Suby of* FEDERATED CO-OPERATIVES LIMITED)
580 Park St, Regina, SK, S4N 5A9
(306) 719-4353
Emp Here 1,150   *Sales* 1,960,188,750
SIC 2911 Petroleum refining
Scott Banda
Gilbert Le Dressay
Brad Delorey

D-U-N-S 24-466-2763 (HQ)
COUTTS COURIER COMPANY LTD
606 Henderson Dr, Regina, SK, S4N 5X3
(306) 569-9300
Emp Here 11   *Sales* 11,087,250
SIC 7389 Business services, nec
Ronald Coutts
Sheila Coutts

D-U-N-S 20-316-7077 (HQ)
CROWN CAPITAL ENTERPRISES INC
1801 E Turvey Rd Unit 7, Regina, SK, S4N 3A4
(306) 546-8030
Sales 10,462,120
SIC 6712 Bank holding companies
Chris Johnson
Chris Anderson
Brent Hughes

D-U-N-S 25-671-5574 (HQ)
CROWN SHRED & RECYCLING INC
225 E 6th Ave, Regina, SK, S4N 6A6
(306) 545-5454
Emp Here 41   *Sales* 12,342,288
SIC 4953 Refuse systems
Jack Shaw
David Mackay

D-U-N-S 20-128-0117 (HQ)
CUSTOM TRUCK SALES INC
(*Suby of* 101015439 SASKATCHEWAN LTD)
520 Park St, Regina, SK, S4N 0T6
(306) 569-9021
Emp Here 40   *Sales* 103,831,200
SIC 5511 New and used car dealers
Brent Leach
Ken Leach

D-U-N-S 20-447-7558 (HQ)
DIRECT WEST CORPORATION
(*Suby of* GOVERNMENT OF SASKATCHEWAN)
355 Longman Cres, Regina, SK, S4N 6G3
(306) 777-0333
Emp Here 100   *Sales* 22,040,810
SIC 7319 Advertising, nec
Gord Farmer

D-U-N-S 25-612-3019 (HQ)
DOMCO CONSTRUCTION INC
860 Park St, Regina, SK, S4N 4Y3
(306) 721-8500
Emp Here 30   *Sales* 23,536,550
SIC 1542 Nonresidential construction, nec
Dennis Burnham
Brian Barber

D-U-N-S 20-756-5300 (SL)
DURA CONSTRUCTION LTD
555 Mcdonald St, Regina, SK, S4N 4X1
(306) 721-6866
Emp Here 30   *Sales* 14,121,930
SIC 1542 Nonresidential construction, nec
John R Konoff
Christian Dizy
Joyce Konoff
Florence Dizy

D-U-N-S 20-273-8485 (BR)
FIRSTCANADA ULC
FIRST STUDENT CANADA
(*Suby of* FIRSTGROUP PLC)
140 E 4th Ave, Regina, SK, S4N 4Z4

(306) 721-4499
Emp Here 200
SIC 4131 Intercity and rural bus transportation
Greg Logel

D-U-N-S 20-855-0061   (SL)
FOUR SEASONS PALACE CATERERS LTD
909 E Arcola Ave, Regina, SK, S4N 0S2
(306) 525-8338
Emp Here 40   *Sales* 11,965,200
SIC 5921 Liquor stores
George Diamond
Peter Yannitos
Tom Toumas

D-U-N-S 24-691-7868   (SL)
GABRIEL CONSTRUCTION LTD
234 E 11th Ave, Regina, SK, S4N 6G8
(306) 757-1399
Emp Here 30   *Sales* 14,121,930
SIC 1542 Nonresidential construction, nec
Gabriel Grenier

D-U-N-S 20-756-4717   (HQ)
GALE'S WHOLESALE LTD
1602 Elliott St, Regina, SK, S4N 6L1
(306) 757-8545
Emp Here 26   *Sales* 27,473,240
SIC 5193 Flowers and florists supplies
Erwin Taylor
Debra Lee Galbraith
Hilda Taylor
Terri-Lynn Masters

D-U-N-S 25-514-3117   (BR)
HOME DEPOT OF CANADA INC
HOME DEPOT
(*Suby of* THE HOME DEPOT INC)
1867 E Victoria Ave, Regina, SK, S4N 6E6
(306) 761-1919
Emp Here 200
SIC 5251 Hardware stores
Steve Ngui

D-U-N-S 20-251-4162   (BR)
ICON CONSTRUCTION LTD.
(*Suby of* ICON CONSTRUCTION LTD.)
480 Henderson Dr, Regina, SK, S4N 6E3
(306) 584-1991
Emp Here 75
SIC 1541 Industrial buildings and warehouses
Dana Paidel

D-U-N-S 20-611-0009   (HQ)
JAY'S TRANSPORTATION GROUP LTD
(*Suby of* MULLEN GROUP LTD)
555 Park St, Regina, SK, S4N 5B2
(306) 569-9369
Emp Here 40   *Sales* 73,752,400
SIC 4213 Trucking, except local
Dennis Doehl
Terry Simson

D-U-N-S 25-063-0753   (HQ)
JUMP.CA WIRELESS SUPPLY CORP
JUMP.CA
1845 E Victoria Ave Unit B, Regina, SK, S4N 6E6
(306) 545-5867
Emp Here 10   *Sales* 23,304,144
SIC 4899 Communication services, nec
Gerald Buchko
Greg Krywulak
Chris Krywulak
Kelly Kazakoff
Jamie Schwitzer

D-U-N-S 24-733-0038   (SL)
KNIGHT ARCHER INSURANCE LTD
512 E Victoria Ave, Regina, SK, S4N 0N7
(306) 569-2288
Emp Here 60   *Sales* 50,883,600
SIC 6411 Insurance agents, brokers, and service
Gloria Archer

D-U-N-S 24-916-5325   (SL)
MACKENZIE PLUMBING & HEATING (1989)

LTD
MACKENZIE PLUMBING & HEATING
915 Fleury St, Regina, SK, S4N 4W7
(306) 522-0777
Emp Here 60   *Sales* 13,069,740
SIC 1731 Electrical work
Douglas Mackenzie

D-U-N-S 24-466-8109   (HQ)
MANCON HOLDINGS LTD
504 Henderson Dr, Regina, SK, S4N 5X2
(306) 721-4777
Emp Here 24   *Sales* 43,565,800
SIC 1731 Electrical work
James Paul Mclellan
Bryan Leverick
Janet Mclellan-Folk

D-U-N-S 20-192-3096   (BR)
MAPLEHURST BAKERIES INC
(*Suby of* GEORGE WESTON LIMITED)
1700 Park St, Regina, SK, S4N 6B2
(306) 359-7400
Emp Here 85
SIC 2051 Bread, cake, and related products
George Stoppler

D-U-N-S 24-376-5831   (HQ)
MAZENC FUELS LTD
PETRO CANADA
529 E 1st Ave, Regina, SK, S4N 4Z3
(306) 721-6667
Emp Here 5   *Sales* 14,942,340
SIC 5541 Gasoline service stations
Renald Mazenc

D-U-N-S 25-612-2136   (BR)
MIDWEST RESTAURANT INC
MOXIE'S CLASSIC GRILL
(*Suby of* MIDWEST RESTAURANT INC)
2037 Park St, Regina, SK, S4N 6S2
(306) 781-5655
Emp Here 100
SIC 5812 Eating places
Peter Kyriakoulias

D-U-N-S 20-067-8548   (SL)
MOLSON SASKATCHEWAN BREWERY
LTD
(*Suby of* MOLSON COORS BREWING COMPANY)
395 Park St Suite 2, Regina, SK, S4N 5B2
(306) 359-1786
Emp Here 107
SIC 2082 Malt beverages
George P. Gross

D-U-N-S 24-818-1554   (HQ)
PARTNER TECHNOLOGIES INCORPORATED
PTI
1155 Park St, Regina, SK, S4N 4Y8
(306) 721-3114
Sales 50,485,000
SIC 3612 Transformers, except electric
George Partyka
Stuart Gibson

D-U-N-S 24-774-6274   (BR)
POSTMEDIA NETWORK INC
LEADER POST, THE
(*Suby of* POSTMEDIA NETWORK CANADA CORP)
1964 Park St, Regina, SK, S4N 7M5
(306) 781-5211
Emp Here 275
SIC 2711 Newspapers
Marty Klyne

D-U-N-S 25-724-2263   (HQ)
QUALITY TIRE SERVICE LTD
2150 E Victoria Ave Suite 201, Regina, SK, S4N 7B9
(306) 721-2155
Emp Here 10   *Sales* 64,815,840
SIC 5531 Auto and home supply stores
Randy Johannsen

D-U-N-S 20-842-7013   (HQ)
RALPH MCKAY INDUSTRIES INC
(*Suby of* 599804 SASKATCHEWAN LTD)
130 Hodsman Rd, Regina, SK, S4N 5X4
(306) 721-9292
Emp Here 1   *Sales* 14,874,067
SIC 3523 Farm machinery and equipment
David Pitt
Dwayne Chycrun
Mara Holt

D-U-N-S 25-098-3715   (SL)
RAMJET CONTRACTING LTD
525 7th Ave, Regina, SK, S4N 0G5
(306) 789-6199
Emp Here 55   *Sales* 13,884,310
SIC 1623 Water, sewer, and utility lines
Roger Johnson
Terry Johnson
Cara Vindevoghel

D-U-N-S 20-545-8235   (HQ)
REDHEAD EQUIPMENT LTD
Box 32098 Hwy 1 E, Regina, SK, S4N 7L2
(306) 721-2666
Sales 124,371,150
SIC 5084 Industrial machinery and equipment
Gary Redhead

D-U-N-S 25-023-4069   (SL)
REGINA RESIDENTIAL RESOURCE CENTRE
1047 Wadey Dr, Regina, SK, S4N 7J6
(306) 352-3223
Emp Here 83   *Sales* 11,077,097
SIC 8399 Social services, nec
Lynda Blach
Peter Pyerman
Tammy Van Luven

D-U-N-S 20-607-1565   (SL)
SHAW, JACK ENTERPRISES LIMITED
GREEN ACRES SERVICES
225 E 6th Ave, Regina, SK, S4N 6A6
(306) 545-5454
Emp Here 23   *Sales* 11,455,794
SIC 5541 Gasoline service stations
Jack Shaw
Norma Shaw
David Shaw
Jeffrey Shaw

D-U-N-S 20-755-9089   (HQ)
STERLING TRUCK & TRAILER SALES LTD
REGINA VOLVO TRUCKS
762 Mcdonald St, Regina, SK, S4N 7M7
(306) 525-0466
Sales 18,210,750
SIC 5012 Automobiles and other motor vehicles
Sterling Hornoi
Patricia Hornoi

D-U-N-S 24-427-5731   (HQ)
STOCKDALES ELECTRIC MOTOR CORP
1441 Fleury St, Regina, SK, S4N 7N5
(306) 352-4505
Emp Here 18   *Sales* 11,179,350
SIC 5063 Electrical apparatus and equipment
John Stockdale
Judy Stockdale

D-U-N-S 24-356-8479   (HQ)
STORAGEVAULT CANADA INC
KENASTON SELF STORAGE
6050 Diefenbaker Ave, Regina, SK, S4N 7L2
(306) 546-5999
Emp Here 25   *Sales* 73,068,145
SIC 4225 General warehousing and storage
Steven Scott
Iqbal Khan
Alan Simpson
Jay Lynne Fleming
Blair Tamblyn

D-U-N-S 20-840-5076   (HQ)
SUPREME OFFICE PRODUCTS LIMITED

SUPREME BASICS, DIV OF
310 Henderson Dr, Regina, SK, S4N 5W7
(306) 566-8800
Emp Here 40   *Sales* 167,506,600
SIC 5112 Stationery and office supplies
Doreen Bosche
Diana Bosche
Derek Bosche
Cathy Robinson

D-U-N-S 24-717-2174   (BR)
SYSCO CANADA, INC
SYSCO REGINA
(*Suby of* SYSCO CORPORATION)
266 E Dewdney Ave, Regina, SK, S4N 4G2
(306) 347-5200
Emp Here 130
SIC 5141 Groceries, general line
Art Hughes

D-U-N-S 25-153-4988   (HQ)
UPONOR LTD
WIRSBO
(*Suby of* UPONOR OYJ)
662 E 1st Ave Suite 200, Regina, SK, S4N 5T6
(306) 721-2449
Emp Here 45   *Sales* 82,807,920
SIC 5075 Warm air heating and air conditioning

D-U-N-S 20-545-6072   (SL)
VILLAGE MOBILE HOMES LTD
VILLAGE RV
2901 Powerhouse Dr, Regina, SK, S4N 0A1
(306) 525-5666
Emp Here 30   *Sales* 14,942,340
SIC 5561 Recreational vehicle dealers
Darren Gelowitz
Anthony Reslein
William Ortman

D-U-N-S 20-068-4769   (HQ)
WAPPEL CONCRETE & CONSTRUCTION CO. LTD
230 E 10th Ave, Regina, SK, S4N 6G6
(306) 569-3000
Emp Here 3   *Sales* 27,335,000
SIC 6712 Bank holding companies
Brian Wappel
Joseph M Wappel
Gerard Wappel

D-U-N-S 24-170-3131   (HQ)
WARNER BUS INDUSTRIES LTD
WARNER TRUCK INDUSTRIES
330 E 4th Ave, Regina, SK, S4N 4Z6
(306) 359-1930
Emp Here 65   *Sales* 23,673,975
SIC 5012 Automobiles and other motor vehicles
Graham Warner

D-U-N-S 24-265-6858   (SL)
WARNER TRUCK INDUSTRIES LTD
WARNER INDUSTRIES
330 E 4th Ave, Regina, SK, S4N 4Z6
(306) 359-1930
Emp Here 50   *Sales* 24,903,900
SIC 5511 New and used car dealers
Graham Warner

D-U-N-S 24-882-6810   (SL)
WESTRIDGE CONSTRUCTION LTD
WESTRIDGE
435 Henderson Dr, Regina, SK, S4N 5W8
(306) 352-2434
Emp Here 55   *Sales* 31,368,590
SIC 1542 Nonresidential construction, nec
Leon Friesen
Harlan Friesen
Dan Neuls

Regina, SK S4P

D-U-N-S 24-139-8895   (SL)
101014233 SASKATCHEWAN LTD
1874 Scarth St Suite 2000, Regina, SK, S4P 4B3
(306) 777-0600
Emp Here 45   *Sales* 14,720,715
SIC 6531 Real estate agents and managers
Terry Downie

D-U-N-S 20-180-0054   (BR)
2104225 ONTARIO LTD
WESTON BAKERIES LIMITED
(*Suby of* GEORGE WESTON LIMITED)
Gd Lcd Main, Regina, SK, S4P 2Z4
(306) 359-7400
Emp Here 100
SIC 2045 Prepared flour mixes and doughs
Randy Parker

D-U-N-S 24-914-0369   (HQ)
599681 SASKATCHEWAN LTD
(*Suby of* BRANDT INDUSTRIES CANADA LTD)
Hwy 1 E, Regina, SK, S4P 3R8
(306) 791-7777
Emp Here 1   *Sales* 731,595,000
SIC 5084 Industrial machinery and equipment
Shaun Semple
Mike Cox

D-U-N-S 25-228-6711   (SL)
607637 SASKATCHEWAN LTD
RAMADA HOTEL & CONVENTION CENTER
(*Suby of* CHEUNG ON INVESTMENTS GROUP LTD)
1818 Victoria Ave, Regina, SK, S4P 0R1
(306) 569-1666
Emp Here 140   *Sales* 12,976,600
SIC 7011 Hotels and motels
Grant Kook

D-U-N-S 24-519-9732   (SL)
ADVANCE DOOR SYSTEMS LTD
Gd, Regina, SK, S4P 2Z4
(306) 781-0207
Emp Here 40   *Sales* 17,886,960
SIC 5031 Lumber, plywood, and millwork
Brent Slater

D-U-N-S 24-524-2727   (SL)
ASSOCIATED MINING CONSTRUCTION INC
2491 Albert St N, Regina, SK, S4P 3A2
(306) 206-5000
Emp Here 100   *Sales* 27,025,600
SIC 1474 Potash, soda, and borate minerals
Rene Scheepers
Jim Haines
Bruce Dunlop
Jochen Greinacher
Kerry Bjornson
Kirby Williston

D-U-N-S 20-063-4389   (BR)
BLUE CROSS LIFE INSURANCE COMPANY OF CANADA
SASKATCHEWAN BLUE CROSS
(*Suby of* BLUE CROSS LIFE INSURANCE COMPANY OF CANADA)
1870 Albert St Suite 100, Regina, SK, S4P 4B7
(306) 525-5025
Emp Here 90
SIC 6411 Insurance agents, brokers, and service
Terry Brash

D-U-N-S 24-140-9817   (SL)
BMML HOLDINGS
2103 11th Ave Suite 700, Regina, SK, S4P 4G1
(306) 347-8300
Emp Here 40   *Sales* 10,462,120
SIC 6712 Bank holding companies
Betty Hartman

D-U-N-S 20-003-3228   (BR)
BOARD OF EDUCATION OF THE REGINA

ROMAN CATHOLIC SEPARATE SCHOOL DIVISION NO. 81
MILLER COMPREHENSIVE HIGH SCHOOL
1027 College Ave, Regina, SK, S4P 1A7
(306) 791-7230
Emp Here 80
SIC 8211 Elementary and secondary schools
Jamie Bresciani

D-U-N-S 25-058-5809   (SL)
BOBCAT OF REGINA LTD
Gd Lcd Main, Regina, SK, S4P 2Z4
(306) 347-7600
Emp Here 25   *Sales* 11,875,650
SIC 5084 Industrial machinery and equipment
David Barber

D-U-N-S 25-361-1743   (BR)
BRANDT AGRICULTURAL PRODUCTS
BRANDT ENGINEERED PRODUCTS
(*Suby of* BRANDT AGRICULTURAL PRODUCTS)
302 Mill St, Regina, SK, S4P 3E1
(306) 791-7557
Emp Here 200
SIC 3535 Conveyors and conveying equipment
Jim Semple

D-U-N-S 20-067-0149   (HQ)
BRANDT INDUSTRIES CANADA LTD
13 Ave & Pinkie Rd, Regina, SK, S4P 3A1
(306) 791-7777
Sales 202,231,440
SIC 3523 Farm machinery and equipment
Shaun Semple

D-U-N-S 25-230-5123   (HQ)
BRANDT TRACTOR LTD
(*Suby of* BRANDT INDUSTRIES CANADA LTD)
Hwy 1 E, Regina, SK, S4P 3R8
(306) 791-7777
Emp Here 18   *Sales* 242,889,540
SIC 5084 Industrial machinery and equipment
Shaun Semple
Gavin Semple

D-U-N-S 25-612-2482   (BR)
CANADA LIFE ASSURANCE COMPANY, THE
(*Suby of* POWER CORPORATION DU CANADA)
1901 Scarth St Suite 414, Regina, SK, S4P 4L4
(306) 751-6000
Emp Here 800
SIC 6311 Life insurance
Canada Life

D-U-N-S 24-426-7209   (BR)
CANADIAN BROADCASTING CORPORATION
CBC RADIO CANADA
(*Suby of* GOVERNMENT OF CANADA)
2440 Broad St, Regina, SK, S4P 0A5
(306) 347-9540
Emp Here 180
SIC 4832 Radio broadcasting stations
David Kyle

D-U-N-S 20-756-5219   (SL)
CANADIAN WESTERN AGRIBITION ASSOCIATION
C W A
Gd Lcd Main, Regina, SK, S4P 2Z4
(306) 565-0565
Emp Here 200   *Sales* 18,990,600
SIC 7999 Amusement and recreation, nec
Stewart Stone

D-U-N-S 25-416-4403   (HQ)
CDSL CANADA LIMITED
CGI
(*Suby of* CGI INC)
1900 Albert St Unit 700, Regina, SK, S4P 4K8
(306) 761-4000
Emp Here 250   *Sales* 375,405,750

SIC 7379 Computer related services, nec
Serge Godin
Kevin Linder
Francois Boulanger
Benoit Dube

D-U-N-S 20-067-1386   (HQ)
CINDERCRETE PRODUCTS LIMITED
TRANS MIX CONCRETE DIV OF
(*Suby of* HEIDELBERGCEMENT AG)
Hwy 1 E, Regina, SK, S4P 3A1
(306) 789-2636
Sales 14,006,100
SIC 3271 Concrete block and brick
Kevin Tell

D-U-N-S 25-611-6989   (SL)
CIR COMMERCIAL REALTY INC
COLLIERS INTERNATIONAL
2505 11th Ave Suite 200, Regina, SK, S4P 0K6
(306) 789-8300
Emp Here 40   *Sales* 13,085,080
SIC 6531 Real estate agents and managers
Tom Mcclocklin
Michael Kelsey

D-U-N-S 24-773-1248   (SL)
CKRM NEWS
1900 Rose St, Regina, SK, S4P 0A9
(306) 546-6200
Emp Here 49   *Sales* 34,143,690
SIC 6794 Patent owners and lessors
Paul Hill

D-U-N-S 24-468-8461   (BR)
CO-OPERATORS GROUP LIMITED, THE
(*Suby of* CO-OPERATORS GROUP LIMITED, THE)
1920 College Ave, Regina, SK, S4P 1C4
(306) 347-6200
Emp Here 500
SIC 6411 Insurance agents, brokers, and service
Randy Grimsrud

D-U-N-S 20-852-9362   (HQ)
CONEXUS CREDIT UNION 2006
CONEXUS CREDIT UNION
1960 Albert St Suite 205, Regina, SK, S4P 2T1
(800) 667-7477
Emp Here 60   *Sales* 141,327,637
SIC 6062 State credit unions
Eric Dillon

D-U-N-S 24-038-9791   (HQ)
CROWN INVESTMENTS CORPORATION OF SASKATCHEWAN
C.I.C.
(*Suby of* GOVERNMENT OF SASKATCHEWAN)
2400 College Ave Suite 400, Regina, SK, S4P 1C8
(306) 787-6851
Emp Here 60   *Sales* 7,818,844,800
SIC 4911 Electric services
R W Carter
Zach Douglas
Doug Kosloski
Blair Swystun
John Amundson
Bill Boyd
Ken Krawetz

D-U-N-S 24-348-9056   (SL)
CUETS FINANCIAL LTD
(*Suby of* TORONTO-DOMINION BANK, THE)
2055 Albert St, Regina, SK, S4P 2T8
(306) 566-1269
Emp Here 350
SIC 7389 Business services, nec
Stan Kuss
Ken Kosolofski

D-U-N-S 20-610-9811   (HQ)
CURTIS CONSTRUCTION LTD
2930 Pasqua St N, Regina, SK, S4P 3H1

(306) 543-3944
Sales 16,456,480
SIC 4212 Local trucking, without storage
Dale Curtis
Kim Hofley
Elaine Curtis

D-U-N-S 20-067-2194   (HQ)
DEGELMAN INDUSTRIES LTD
HYLAR METAL PRODUCTS, DIV OF
272 Industrial Dr, Regina, SK, S4P 3B1
(306) 543-4447
Sales 31,080,140
SIC 3523 Farm machinery and equipment
Paul Degelman
Doug Degelman

D-U-N-S 20-699-8887   (BR)
DELTA HOTELS LIMITED
(*Suby of* GOVERNMENT OF THE PROVINCE OF BRITISH COLUMBIA)
1919 Saskatchewan Dr Suite 100, Regina, SK, S4P 4H2
(306) 525-5255
Emp Here 220
SIC 8741 Management services
Kenneth Greene

D-U-N-S 20-358-8991   (SL)
EHEALTH SASKATCHEWAN
2130 11th Ave, Regina, SK, S4P 0J5
(855) 347-5465
Emp Here 10   *Sales* 60,761,376
SIC 8399 Social services, nec
Susan Antosh
Gerald Fiske
David Fan
Milo Fink
Scott Livingstone
Duane Mombourquette
Kimberly Kratzig
Velma Geddes
Marian Zerr

D-U-N-S 20-067-5734   (HQ)
EVRAZ INC. NA CANADA
EVRAZ REGINA STEEL
(*Suby of* EVRAZ PLC)
100 Armour Rd, Regina, SK, S4P 3C7
(306) 924-7700
Emp Here 1,000   *Sales* 936,500,200
SIC 3312 Blast furnaces and steel mills
Conrad Winkler
Alexander Vasiliev
Jerry Reed
Dario Cruz
Pat Christie
Christian Messmacher
Steven Eldam
Eileen Tierney

D-U-N-S 20-747-1566   (HQ)
FARM CREDIT CANADA
FCC
(*Suby of* GOVERNMENT OF CANADA)
1800 Hamilton St, Regina, SK, S4P 4L3
(306) 780-8100
Emp Here 700   *Sales* 845,872,000
SIC 6159 Miscellaneous business credit institutions
Greg Stewart
Michael Hoffort
Remi Lemoine
Paul Macdonald
Lyndon Carlson
Greg Honey
Greg Wilmer
Rick Hoffman
Dale Johnston
Donald Bettle

D-U-N-S 20-756-4857   (SL)
GROUP MEDICAL SERVICES
2055 Albert St, Regina, SK, S4P 2T8
(306) 352-7638
Emp Here 60   *Sales* 74,125,080
SIC 6324 Hospital and medical service plans

Shawn Peters

D-U-N-S 24-008-1914   (BR)
GROUPE DE SECURITE GARDA INC, LE
GARDA SECURITY SERVICES
(*Suby of* GW INTERMEDIATE HOLDCO CORPORATION)
2505 11th Ave Suite 302, Regina, SK, S4P 0K6
(306) 352-2099
Emp Here 200
SIC 7381 Detective and armored car services
Milt Milton

D-U-N-S 20-252-7896   (SL)
H & A FINANCIAL ADVISORS
2445 13th Ave Suite 200, Regina, SK, S4P 0W1
(306) 584-2523
Emp Here 15   *Sales* 15,523,215
SIC 6311 Life insurance
Kelly Aikens

D-U-N-S 20-039-3630   (HQ)
HARVARD BROADCASTING INC
1900 Rose St, Regina, SK, S4P 0A9
(306) 546-6200
Emp Here 50   *Sales* 17,555,810
SIC 4832 Radio broadcasting stations
Bruce Cowie

D-U-N-S 20-853-1525   (HQ)
HARVARD DEVELOPMENTS INC
1874 Scarth St Suite 2000, Regina, SK, S4P 4B3
(306) 777-0600
Emp Here 2   *Sales* 41,888,900
SIC 6531 Real estate agents and managers
Paul Hill
Mo Bundon
Rosanne Hill Blaisdell

D-U-N-S 20-694-3834   (HQ)
HARVARD WESTERN VENTURES INC
COOKS ISI INSURANCE
2151 Albert St, Regina, SK, S4P 2V1
(306) 757-1633
Emp Here 12   *Sales* 27,985,980
SIC 6411 Insurance agents, brokers, and service
Jeff Child
Mo Bundon
Tom Dutton
Paul Hill
Scott Tannas

D-U-N-S 25-388-8143   (SL)
HI-TEC PROFILES INC
2301 Industrial Dr, Regina, SK, S4P 3C6
(306) 721-3800
Emp Here 45   *Sales* 11,387,655
SIC 5211 Lumber and other building materials
Trent Meyer
Regan Wagner

D-U-N-S 20-067-5130   (SL)
HIPPERSON CONSTRUCTION COMPANY (1996) LIMITED
HIPPERSON CONSTRUCTION
2161 Scarth St Unit 200, Regina, SK, S4P 2H8
(306) 359-0303
Emp Here 25   *Sales* 11,768,275
SIC 1542 Nonresidential construction, nec
Gordon Hipperson

D-U-N-S 20-166-8733   (SL)
HJ LINNEN ASSOCIATES
SIGMA ANALYTICS
2161 Scarth St Suite 200, Regina, SK, S4P 2H8
(306) 586-9611
Emp Here 45   *Sales* 10,561,320
SIC 8732 Commercial nonphysical research
Harvey Linnen

D-U-N-S 24-914-7307   (HQ)
HOTEL SASKATCHEWAN (1990) LTD

RADISSON   PLAZA   HOTEL SASKATCHEWAN
2125 Victoria Ave, Regina, SK, S4P 0S3
(306) 522-7691
Emp Here 80   *Sales* 14,830,400
SIC 7011 Hotels and motels
Huei S Lai
Yung-Cheng Hsu
Chih-Chieh Wang
Anita Wu

D-U-N-S 20-448-3507   (BR)
HUDSON'S BAY COMPANY
(*Suby of* HUDSON'S BAY COMPANY)
2150 11th Ave, Regina, SK, S4P 0J5
(306) 525-8511
Emp Here 270
SIC 5311 Department stores
Steven Karo

D-U-N-S 20-305-2477   (SL)
INPUT CAPITAL CORP
1914 Hamilton St Suite 300, Regina, SK, S4P 3N6
(306) 347-3006
Emp Here 24   *Sales* 30,198,159
SIC 0191 General farms, primarily crop
Doug Emsley
Brad Farquhar
Gord Nystuen
Jamie Burgess
David A. Brown
David H. Laidley
Lorne Hepworth
John P.A. Budreski

D-U-N-S 20-652-2828   (SL)
LEADON (REGINA) OPERATIONS LP
REGINA INN
1975 Broad St, Regina, SK, S4P 1Y2
(306) 525-6767
Emp Here 100   *Sales* 9,269,000
SIC 7011 Hotels and motels
Denis Gilles

D-U-N-S 20-703-6349   (SL)
MANY ISLANDS PIPELINES (CANADA) LIMITED
1777 Victoria Ave Suite 500, Regina, SK, S4P 4K5
(306) 777-9500
Emp Here 6   *Sales* 18,948,562
SIC 4922 Natural gas transmission
George Lafond
Heather Heavin
Nadine Krenosky
Florence Norman
Jeanette Weimer
Donald Ching
Eldon Lindgren
Micheal Chorlton
Ralph Hesje
Mervyn Simon

D-U-N-S 24-453-6207   (HQ)
MCDOUGALL GAULEY LLP
MCDOUGALL GAULEY BARRISTERS & SOLICITOR
1881 Scarth St Suite 1500, Regina, SK, S4P 4K9
(306) 757-1641
Emp Here 25   *Sales* 16,632,300
SIC 8111 Legal services
Gordon J. Kuski
David Mckeague

D-U-N-S 25-682-2078   (BR)
MERIDIAN MANUFACTURING INC
(*Suby of* TREVLUC HOLDINGS LTD)
2800 Pasqua St, Regina, SK, S4P 2Z4
(306) 545-4044
Emp Here 150
SIC 3545 Machine tool accessories
Lane Thompsen

D-U-N-S 24-546-5695   (HQ)
MLT AIKINS LLP

1874 Scarth St Suite 1500, Regina, SK, S4P 4E9
(306) 347-8000
Emp Here 163   *Sales* 63,821,560
SIC 8111 Legal services
Murdoch A. Macpherson
G.S. Thorvaldson
Brian Dickson
Marshall Rothstein
Donald Macpherson
John Klebuc
Robert Richards
Georgina Jackson

D-U-N-S 20-178-7145   (SL)
MLT MANAGEMENT INC
MLT
1874 Scarth St Suite 1500, Regina, SK, S4P 4E9
(306) 347-8000
Emp Here 20   *Sales* 19,425,650
SIC 8741 Management services
Ed Meredith
Donald Wilson

D-U-N-S 20-002-2452   (BR)
MNP LLP
(*Suby of* MNP LLP)
2010 11th Ave Suite 900, Regina, SK, S4P 0J3
(306) 790-7900
Emp Here 120
SIC 8721 Accounting, auditing, and bookkeeping
Regan Exner

D-U-N-S 24-748-3746   (HQ)
MOSAIC CANADA ULC
MOSAIC POTASH
(*Suby of* THE MOSAIC COMPANY)
2010 12th Ave Suite 1700, Regina, SK, S4P 0M3
(306) 523-2800
Emp Here 50   *Sales* 27,025,600
SIC 1474 Potash, soda, and borate minerals
Joc O'rourke
Bruce Bodine
Kimberly Bors
Clint Freeland
Mark Isaacson
Richard N. Mclellan
Walter F. Precourt Iii
Corrine D. Ricard

D-U-N-S 24-640-6958   (SL)
NORTHPOINT ENERGY SOLUTIONS INC
(*Suby of* GOVERNMENT OF SASKATCHEWAN)
2025 Victoria Ave, Regina, SK, S4P 0S1
(306) 566-2103
Emp Here 40   *Sales* 25,064,560
SIC 4911 Electric services
Patricia Quaroni
Troy King

D-U-N-S 24-916-5416   (SL)
PARADIGM CONSULTING GROUP INC
1881 Scarth St Unit 1200, Regina, SK, S4P 4K9
(306) 522-8588
Emp Here 76   *Sales* 17,805,888
SIC 8742 Management consulting services
Rene Carpentier
Mark Hustak

D-U-N-S 24-333-8386   (HQ)
PRAIRIE VALLEY SCHOOL DIVISION NO 208
LAJORD COLONY SCHOOL
3080 Albert St N, Regina, SK, S4P 3E1
(306) 949-3366
Emp Here 100   *Sales* 102,140,093
SIC 8211 Elementary and secondary schools
Naomi Mellor

D-U-N-S 24-868-1538   (SL)
PUBLIC   GUARDIAN   TRUSTEE   OF SASKATCHEWAN

1871 Smith St Suite 100, Regina, SK, S4P 4W4
(306) 787-5424
Emp Here 45   *Sales* 10,665,068
SIC 8748 Business consulting, nec
Gwen Walker

D-U-N-S 20-733-7804   (BR)
RAWLCO CAPITAL LTD
RAWLCO RADIO
(*Suby of* RAWLCO CAPITAL LTD)
2401 Saskatchewan Dr Suite 210, Regina, SK, S4P 4H8
(306) 525-0000
Emp Here 80
SIC 4832 Radio broadcasting stations
Tom Newton

D-U-N-S 24-367-4392   (SL)
RED MOUNTAIN HOLDINGS LTD
SAKUNDIAK EQUIPMENT
(*Suby of* TREVLUC HOLDINGS LTD)
2800 Pasqua St N, Regina, SK, S4P 3E1
(306) 545-4044
Emp Here 90   *Sales* 19,980,090
SIC 3523 Farm machinery and equipment
Paul Cunningham
Russ Edwards

D-U-N-S 20-276-8784   (HQ)
REDHEAD EQUIPMENT
Gd Lcd Main, Regina, SK, S4P 2Z4
(306) 721-2666
Emp Here 100   *Sales* 125,846,344
SIC 7353 Heavy construction equipment rental
Gary Redhead
Ron Karasin

D-U-N-S 24-117-4663   (SL)
REGINA HUMANE SOCIETY INC
Gd Lcd Main, Regina, SK, S4P 2Z4
(306) 543-6363
Emp Here 32   *Sales* 12,717,248
SIC 8699 Membership organizations, nec
Lisa Koch

D-U-N-S 20-545-9217   (SL)
REGINA MOTOR PRODUCTS (1970) LTD
Albert St S Hwy 1-6, Regina, SK, S4P 3A8
(866) 273-5778
Emp Here 74   *Sales* 20,964,200
SIC 7538 General automotive repair shops

D-U-N-S 20-756-4881   (HQ)
SASK SPORT INC
SASKATCHEWAN LOTTERIES
1870 Lorne St, Regina, SK, S4P 2L7
(306) 780-9340
Emp Here 44   *Sales* 43,971,144
SIC 8699 Membership organizations, nec
Don Macaulay
Jim Burnett

D-U-N-S 25-417-8072   (HQ)
SASKATCHEWAN GAMING CORPORATION
CASINO REGINA
(*Suby of* GOVERNMENT OF SASKATCHEWAN)
1880 Saskatchewan Dr, Regina, SK, S4P 0B2
(306) 565-3000
Emp Here 600   *Sales* 137,588,354
SIC 7999 Amusement and recreation, nec
Twyla Meredith
Gerry Fischer

D-U-N-S 20-833-4383   (HQ)
SASKATCHEWAN GOVERNMENT INSURANCE
SGI CANADA
(*Suby of* GOVERNMENT OF SASKATCHEWAN)
2260 11th Ave Suite 18, Regina, SK, S4P 0J9
(306) 751-1200
Emp Here 1,000   *Sales* 3,846,542,400
SIC 6331 Fire, marine, and casualty insurance

Andrew Cartmell
Dawn Bloom
Tamara Erhardt
Tim Macleod
Jeff Stepan

D-U-N-S 24-691-9989   (HQ)
SASKATCHEWAN HEALTH-CARE ASSOCI-ATION
SAHO
2002 Victoria Ave Suite 500, Regina, SK, S4P 0R7
(306) 347-1740
Emp Here 78   *Sales* 224,381,640
SIC 6324 Hospital and medical service plans
Susan Antosh
Charlene Gravel
Alex Taylor
Sharon Bauche
Kathy Bedard
John Bumbac
Arthur Daigneault
Darlene Eberle
Doug Finnie
Greg Kobylka

D-U-N-S 20-756-4022   (HQ)
SASKATCHEWAN HOUSING CORPORA-TION
(*Suby of* GOVERNMENT OF SASKATCHEWAN)
1920 Broad St Suite 900, Regina, SK, S4P 3V6
(306) 787-4177
Emp Here 100   *Sales* 147,133,142
SIC 6531 Real estate agents and managers
Tim Gross

D-U-N-S 25-611-5718   (SL)
SASKATCHEWAN LIBERAL ASSOCIATION
2054 Broad St, Regina, SK, S4P 1Y3

Emp Here 52   *Sales* 14,216,540
SIC 8651 Political organizations
Frank Proto
Robert Ermel
Michael Huber
Carroll Bell

D-U-N-S 24-654-6709   (HQ)
SASKATCHEWAN MUNICIPAL HAIL IN-SURANCE ASSOCIATION
2100 Cornwall St, Regina, SK, S4P 2K7
(306) 569-1852
Sales 27,699,885
SIC 6331 Fire, marine, and casualty insurance
Rodney Schoettler
Michelle Mandin
Wayne Black
Arnold Boyko

D-U-N-S 20-068-2151   (HQ)
SASKATCHEWAN POWER CORPORATION
SASKPOWER
(*Suby of* GOVERNMENT OF SASKATCHEWAN)
2025 Victoria Ave, Regina, SK, S4P 0S1
(306) 566-2121
Emp Here 600   *Sales* 2,026,071,522
SIC 4911 Electric services
Mike Marsh
Troy King
Tim Eckel
Nidal Dabghi
Kory Hayko
Kathy Mccrum
Grant Ring
Howard Matthews
Brad Strom
Rachelle Verret Morphy

D-U-N-S 24-916-5358   (HQ)
SASKATCHEWAN TELECOMMUNICA-TIONS HOLDING CORPORATION
SASKTEL HOLDCO
(*Suby of* GOVERNMENT OF SASKATCHEWAN)

2121 Saskatchewan Dr, Regina, SK, S4P 3Y2
(800) 992-9912
Emp Here 200   *Sales* 1,348,546,864
SIC 4899 Communication services, nec
Ron Styles
Grant Kook
Ken Keesey
Doug Burnett
John Boden
Daryl Godfrey
Charlene Gavel
John Hill
Stacey Sandison

D-U-N-S 20-448-3143   (HQ)
SASKATCHEWAN TELECOMMUNICA-TIONS INTERNATIONAL, INC
SASKTEL INTERNATIONAL
(*Suby of* GOVERNMENT OF SASKATCHEWAN)
2121 Saskatchewan Dr, Regina, SK, S4P 3Y2
(306) 777-2201
Emp Here 80   *Sales* 18,277,760
SIC 4899 Communication services, nec
Douglas Burnett
Charlene Gavel
Katrine White
Shara Mccormick
Kevin Adair
Darcee Macfarlene
Greg Meister
John Meldrum
Grant Koo
Rachel Heidecker

D-U-N-S 24-453-6561   (HQ)
SASKATCHEWAN WORKERS' COMPEN-SATION BOARD
1881 Scarth St Suite 200, Regina, SK, S4P 4L1
(800) 667-7590
Emp Here 360   *Sales* 229,818,889
SIC 6331 Fire, marine, and casualty insurance
Peter Federko
Graham Topp
Phil Germain
Donna Kane
Ann Schultz
Mick Williams
Gord Dobrowolsky
Larry Flowers
Garry Hamblin

D-U-N-S 24-749-1939   (HQ)
SASKENERGY INCORPORATED
(*Suby of* GOVERNMENT OF SASKATCHEWAN)
1777 Victoria Ave Suite 1000, Regina, SK, S4P 4K5
(306) 777-9225
Emp Here 400   *Sales* 725,965,680
SIC 4923 Gas transmission and distribution
Ken From
Susan Barber
Lori Christie
Colleen Huber
Randy Greggains
Mark Guillet
Robert Haynes
Derrick Mann
Christine Short
Nola Joorisity

D-U-N-S 25-951-3216   (HQ)
SGI CANADA INSURANCE SERVICES LTD
SCISL
2260 11th Ave Suite 18, Regina, SK, S4P 0J9
(306) 751-1200
Emp Here 20   *Sales* 92,656,350
SIC 6331 Fire, marine, and casualty insurance
Andrew Cartmell
J Walter Bardua
Joan F D Baldwin
Joan D Bellegarde
William J A Heidt
Nancy E Hopkins

P James Mills
Warren Sproule
Rick Watson
Merin Coutts

D-U-N-S 25-219-9260   (SL)
SIERRA VENTURES CORP
FANTASTIC CLEANING
1810 College Ave, Regina, SK, S4P 1C1
(306) 949-1510
Emp Here 120   *Sales* 3,836,160
SIC 7349 Building maintenance services, nec
Robert Bray
Sandra Bray

D-U-N-S 24-128-2677   (SL)
SOLVERA SOLUTIONS
1853 Hamilton St Suite 201, Regina, SK, S4P 2C1
(306) 757-3510
Emp Here 120   *Sales* 40,043,280
SIC 7379 Computer related services, nec
Jim Ostertag
Reg Robin

D-U-N-S 20-066-8200   (SL)
THYSSEN MINING CONSTRUCTION OF CANADA LTD
TMCC
(*Suby of* THYSSEN SCHACHTBAU GMBH)
2409 Albert St N, Regina, SK, S4P 3E1
(306) 949-6606
Emp Here 300   *Sales* 98,434,500
SIC 1629 Heavy construction, nec
Rene Scheepers
Jim Haines
James D Smith

D-U-N-S 20-548-0820   (SL)
TOWN & COUNTRY PLUMBING & HEATING (2004) LTD
TOWN & COUNTRY PLUMBING AND HEAT-ING
1450 South Railway St, Regina, SK, S4P 0A2
(306) 352-4328
Emp Here 50   *Sales* 11,046,700
SIC 1711 Plumbing, heating, air-conditioning
Dan Turgeon

D-U-N-S 24-747-8910   (HQ)
TRANSGAS LIMITED
(*Suby of* GOVERNMENT OF SASKATCHEWAN)
1777 Victoria Ave Suite 500, Regina, SK, S4P 4K5
(306) 777-9500
Emp Here 120   *Sales* 276,468,960
SIC 4923 Gas transmission and distribution
Ken From
Robert Haynes

D-U-N-S 20-447-9075   (SL)
TRAVELAND LEISURE CENTRE (REGINA) LTD
TRAVELAND RV
Gd Lcd Main, Regina, SK, S4P 2Z4
(306) 789-3311
Emp Here 23   *Sales* 11,455,794
SIC 5561 Recreational vehicle dealers
Kim Brown

D-U-N-S 20-689-3617   (HQ)
WESTCON EQUIPMENT & RENTALS LTD
Hwy 1 E, Regina, SK, S4P 3B1
(306) 359-7273
Emp Here 14   *Sales* 15,651,404
SIC 1629 Heavy construction, nec
Brian Brown
Mike Smiegielski

D-U-N-S 20-756-5771   (HQ)
WESTERN SURETY COMPANY
(*Suby of* HARVARD DEVELOPMENTS INC)
1881 Scarth St Unit 2100, Regina, SK, S4P 4K9
(306) 791-3735
Emp Here 16   *Sales* 42,473,157
SIC 6351 Surety insurance

Scott Donald
David Dykes
Paul Hill
Bruce Cowie
Brian Johnson
Leo Ell
Robert Pletch
Robert Watt

D-U-N-S 24-367-3550   (HQ)
YARA BELLE PLAINE INC
(*Suby of* YARA INTERNATIONAL ASA)
1874 Scarth St Suite 1800, Regina, SK, S4P 4B3
(306) 525-7600
Emp Here 20   *Sales* 41,751,087
SIC 2874 Phosphatic fertilizers
Edward Cavazuti
Gordon Dolney
Peter Valesares

D-U-N-S 24-336-4267   (HQ)
YARA CANADA INC
(*Suby of* YARA INTERNATIONAL ASA)
1874 Scarth St Suite 1800, Regina, SK, S4P 4B3
(306) 525-7600
Sales 19,305,520
SIC 5191 Farm supplies
Kathy Jordison
Olivier Paul Henri Saulnier
Rosemary Malarkey
Magnus H. Strommen

D-U-N-S 24-116-8020   (SL)
YOUNG MENS CHRISTIAN ASSOCIATION OF REGINA
FAMILY YMCA OF REGINA
2400 13th Ave, Regina, SK, S4P 0V9
(306) 757-9622
Emp Here 100   *Sales* 14,287,900
SIC 8641 Civic and social associations
Murray Cain
Marion Patterson

D-U-N-S 25-611-9868   (SL)
ZABS PHARMACY LTD
SHOPPERS DRUG MART
2202 Broad St Suite 422, Regina, SK, S4P 4V6
(306) 777-8166
Emp Here 50   *Sales* 12,647,700
SIC 5912 Drug stores and proprietary stores
Scott Szabo

Regina, SK S4R

D-U-N-S 24-748-8059   (BR)
2104225 ONTARIO LTD
WESTON BAKERIES LIMITED
(*Suby of* GEORGE WESTON LIMITED)
1310 Ottawa St, Regina, SK, S4R 1P4
(306) 359-3096
Emp Here 85
SIC 2051 Bread, cake, and related products
Randy Parker

D-U-N-S 24-346-3424   (BR)
511670 ALBERTA LTD
CORAM CONSTRUCTION
845 Broad St Suite 205, Regina, SK, S4R 8G9
(306) 525-1644
Emp Here 180
SIC 1542 Nonresidential construction, nec
Robert Lakeman

D-U-N-S 24-691-0350   (SL)
583455 SASKATCHEWAN LTD
TRIPLE SEVEN CHRYSLER
(*Suby of* 893353 ALBERTA INC)
700 Broad St, Regina, SK, S4R 8H7
(306) 522-2222
Emp Here 61   *Sales* 38,386,080
SIC 5511 New and used car dealers

Ajay Dilawri
Douglas Boczulak

D-U-N-S 20-009-2570   (HQ)
604329 SASKATCHEWAN LTD
HYUNDAI REGINA, DIV OF
(*Suby of* 893353 ALBERTA INC)
444 Broad St, Regina, SK, S4R 1X3
(306) 525-8848
Emp Here 40   *Sales* 40,903,200
SIC 5511 New and used car dealers
Ajay Dilawri

D-U-N-S 24-774-5763   (HQ)
82212 CANADA LTD
601 Albert St, Regina, SK, S4R 2P4
(306) 525-5411
Emp Here 1   *Sales* 22,414,700
SIC 6712 Bank holding companies
Marino Vecchioli

D-U-N-S 20-068-3043   (HQ)
AUDIO WAREHOUSE LTD
1329 Lorne St, Regina, SK, S4R 2K2
(306) 525-8128
Emp Here 3   *Sales* 13,944,180
SIC 5731 Radio, television, and electronic
stores
Brian Melby
Don Rae

D-U-N-S 20-066-9075   (HQ)
AUTO ELECTRIC SERVICE LTD
A E S WAREHOUSE DISTRIBUTORS
1360 Broad St, Regina, SK, S4R 1Y5
(306) 525-2551
Emp Here 50   *Sales* 32,779,350
SIC 5013 Motor vehicle supplies and new
parts
Robert Jaworski
Brenda Gelowitz

D-U-N-S 24-883-4947   (SL)
AUTO GALLERY 1994 LTD
AUTO GALLERY SUZUKI SUBARU
609 Winnipeg St, Regina, SK, S4R 8P2
(306) 525-6700
Emp Here 70   *Sales* 44,049,600
SIC 5511 New and used car dealers
Thomas Glen

D-U-N-S 20-059-6638   (SL)
B L S ASPHALT INC
*BLS ASPHALT & LANDSCAPE CONSTRUC-
TION*
711 Toronto St, Regina, SK, S4R 8G1
(306) 775-0080
Emp Here 40   *Sales* 11,340,960
SIC 1611 Highway and street construction
James Short

D-U-N-S 24-915-1085   (SL)
BELLAMY AUTOTECHNIC LTD
BELLAMY KIA
2640 Avonhurst Dr, Regina, SK, S4R 3J4
(306) 525-4555
Emp Here 22   *Sales* 10,957,716
SIC 5511 New and used car dealers
Keith Bellamy

D-U-N-S 24-967-8707   (SL)
**BENNETT DUNLOP FORD SALES (1993)
LIMITED**
770 Broad St, Regina, SK, S4R 8H7
(306) 522-6612
Emp Here 95   *Sales* 59,781,600
SIC 5511 New and used car dealers
Trevor Boquist

D-U-N-S 25-014-3609   (BR)
**BOARD OF EDUCATION OF THE REGINA
ROMAN CATHOLIC SEPARATE SCHOOL
DIVISION NO. 81**
ARCHBISHOP MC O'NEILL HIGH SCHOOL
134 Argyle St, Regina, SK, S4R 4C3
(306) 791-7240
Emp Here 80

SIC 8211 Elementary and secondary schools
Tracy Fuchs

D-U-N-S 25-611-5296   (SL)
BUSHWAKKER BREWING COMPANY LTD
2206 Dewdney Ave, Regina, SK, S4R 1H3
(306) 359-7276
Emp Here 50   *Sales* 11,242,750
SIC 2082 Malt beverages
Kelly Monette
Beverly Robertson
Elaine Robertson

D-U-N-S 25-281-4330   (BR)
**CANADIAN CORPS OF COMMISSION-
AIRES NATIONAL OFFICE, THE**
SOUTH SASKACHEWAN DIVISION
(*Suby of* CANADIAN CORPS OF COMMIS-
SIONAIRES NATIONAL OFFICE, THE)
122 Albert St, Regina, SK, S4R 2N2
(306) 757-0998
Emp Here 400
SIC 7381 Detective and armored car services
Randy Brooks

D-U-N-S 25-811-0449   (SL)
**CANADIAN TIRE ASSOCIATES STORES
ALL DEPARTMENTS**
655 Albert St, Regina, SK, S4R 2P4
(306) 525-9027
Emp Here 30   *Sales* 14,942,340
SIC 5531 Auto and home supply stores
Curtis Morcon

D-U-N-S 20-325-0993   (SL)
CENTURY AGRO LTD
845 Broad St Unit 207, Regina, SK, S4R 8G9
(306) 949-7182
Emp Here 50   *Sales* 73,384,600
SIC 5153 Grain and field beans
Alper Safak

D-U-N-S 25-614-9477   (BR)
CITY OF REGINA, THE
REGINA TRANSIT
(*Suby of* CITY OF REGINA, THE)
333 Winnipeg St, Regina, SK, S4R 8P2
(306) 777-7780
Emp Here 220
SIC 4131 Intercity and rural bus transportation
David Onotera

D-U-N-S 24-852-9869   (BR)
CITY OF REGINA, THE
TRANSIT DEPARTMENT
(*Suby of* CITY OF REGINA, THE)
333 Winnipeg St, Regina, SK, S4R 8P2
(306) 777-7726
Emp Here 225
SIC 4111 Local and suburban transit
Brad Bells

D-U-N-S 24-520-4284   (SL)
CLEAN-BRITE SERVICES OF REGINA LTD
1201 Osler St, Regina, SK, S4R 1W4
(306) 352-9953
Emp Here 75   *Sales* 3,015,675
SIC 7349 Building maintenance services, nec
Steven Yang

D-U-N-S 25-167-7696   (SL)
CLOUD-RIDER DESIGNS LTD
1260 8th Ave, Regina, SK, S4R 1C9
(306) 761-2119
Emp Here 50   *Sales* 10,141,500
SIC 3429 Hardware, nec
Joseph Cicansky

D-U-N-S 25-713-5699   (SL)
CONPHARM LTD
SHOPPERS DRUG MART
303 N Albert St, Regina, SK, S4R 3C3
(306) 777-8010
Emp Here 40   *Sales* 10,118,160
SIC 5912 Drug stores and proprietary stores
Lyle Brandt

D-U-N-S 20-448-7995   (SL)

CRESTVIEW CHRYSLER DODGE JEEP
(*Suby of* 82212 CANADA LTD)
601 Albert St, Regina, SK, S4R 2P4
(306) 992-2443
Emp Here 82   *Sales* 51,600,960
SIC 5511 New and used car dealers
Edward A Knight

D-U-N-S 20-067-3614   (HQ)
FRIES TALLMAN LUMBER (1976) LTD
1737 Dewdney Ave, Regina, SK, S4R 1G5
(306) 525-2791
Sales 17,397,380
SIC 5211 Lumber and other building materials
Kevin Stricker
Andy Boha

D-U-N-S 24-348-5195   (BR)
GDI SERVICES (CANADA) LP
(*Suby of* GDI SERVICES AUX IMMEUBLES
INC)
1319 Hamilton St, Regina, SK, S4R 2B6

Emp Here 95
SIC 7349 Building maintenance services, nec
Val Mitchel

D-U-N-S 25-014-3708   (BR)
**GOVERNING COUNCIL OF THE SALVA-
TION ARMY IN CANADA, THE**
*GOVERNING COUNCIL OF THE SALVATION
ARMY IN CANADA,*
(*Suby of* GOVERNING COUNCIL OF THE
SALVATION ARMY IN CANADA, THE)
50 Angus Rd, Regina, SK, S4R 8P6
(306) 543-0655
Emp Here 130
SIC 8361 Residential care
Ivy Scobie

D-U-N-S 24-394-4027   (HQ)
HBI OFFICE PLUS INC
(*Suby of* HBI - HERITAGE BUSINESS INTE-
RIORS INC)
1162 Osler St, Regina, SK, S4R 5G9
(306) 757-5678
Emp Here 40   *Sales* 26,190,216
SIC 5112 Stationery and office supplies
Carlene Watson
Jay Sullivan
Tom Verbeek
Chris Macdougall

D-U-N-S 25-313-1726   (HQ)
KENROC BUILDING MATERIALS CO. LTD
(*Suby of* SEXTON INVESTMENTS LTD)
1275 Broad St Unit 200, Regina, SK, S4R 1Y2
(306) 525-1415
Emp Here 11   *Sales* 136,710,720
SIC 5039 Construction materials, nec
Brian Kusisto
Kenneth Sexton
Elizabeth Sexton
Brian Mcgillivray

D-U-N-S 24-117-0935   (HQ)
**LANCASHIRE SAW SALES & SERVICE
(CANADA) LTD**
LANCASHIRE DISTRIBUTION
2413 6th Ave Suite 306, Regina, SK, S4R 1B5
(306) 565-0033
Emp Here 30   *Sales* 18,735,640
SIC 5251 Hardware stores
Frank Perra
Isobel Perra

D-U-N-S 24-383-8815   (BR)
LOBLAWS INC
REAL CANADIAN WHOLESALE CLUB
(*Suby of* LOBLAW COMPANIES LIMITED)
921 Broad St, Regina, SK, S4R 8G9
(306) 525-2125
Emp Here 100
SIC 5411 Grocery stores
Keith Leader

D-U-N-S 24-329-4621   (BR)

LOBLAWS INC
DRUGSTORE PHARMACY
(*Suby of* LOBLAW COMPANIES LIMITED)
336 N Mccarthy Blvd, Regina, SK, S4R 7M2
(306) 924-2620
Emp Here 100
SIC 5912 Drug stores and proprietary stores
John Wetmore

D-U-N-S 20-336-6943   (BR)
LOWE'S COMPANIES CANADA, ULC
LOWE'S 3329
(*Suby of* LOWE'S COMPANIES, INC.)
489 N Albert St, Regina, SK, S4R 3C3
(306) 545-1386
Emp Here 135
SIC 5211 Lumber and other building materials
Paolo Gallo

D-U-N-S 24-641-4572   (SL)
M & M MOTOR PRODUCTS LTD
1400 Toronto St, Regina, SK, S4R 8S8
(306) 757-2001
Emp Here 10   *Sales* 10,328,080
SIC 5172 Petroleum products, nec
Clayton Miller
Kevin Morrow

D-U-N-S 25-619-2394   (SL)
MCDONALD'S RESTAURANT
525 N Albert St, Regina, SK, S4R 8E2
(306) 543-0236
Emp Here 80   *Sales* 3,641,520
SIC 5812 Eating places
Ryan Wirth

D-U-N-S 20-192-3013   (BR)
NORTH WEST COMPANY LP, THE
GIANT TIGER # 405
(*Suby of* NORTH WEST COMPANY LP, THE)
2735 Avonhurst Dr, Regina, SK, S4R 3J3
(306) 789-3155
Emp Here 90
SIC 5411 Grocery stores
Kirk Coates

D-U-N-S 25-386-9671   (SL)
PRAIRIE MICRO-TECH (1996) INC
PMT
2641 Albert St N, Regina, SK, S4R 8R7
(306) 721-6066
Emp Here 25   *Sales* 18,563,000
SIC 5191 Farm supplies
Michelle Tesautelf

D-U-N-S 20-757-2025   (SL)
PRAIRIE MOTORCYCLE LTD
PRAIRIE HARLEY-DAVIDSON
1355 Mcintyre St, Regina, SK, S4R 2M9
(306) 522-1747
Emp Here 27   *Sales* 13,448,106
SIC 5571 Motorcycle dealers
Josephine Boers
Alvin A. Boers
Valerie Zora
Robbie Hertzog
Caron Zora-Hertzog

D-U-N-S 25-234-4890   (SL)
PRATTS WHOLESALE (SASK.) LTD
1616 4th Ave, Regina, SK, S4R 8C8
(306) 522-0101
Emp Here 80   *Sales* 66,846,160
SIC 5141 Groceries, general line
Leonard Baranyk
Eleane Baranyk
Leonard A .W. Baranyk
Edward Holowaty

D-U-N-S 24-428-6787   (BR)
PUROLATOR INC
(*Suby of* GOVERNMENT OF CANADA)
702 Toronto St, Regina, SK, S4R 8L1
(306) 359-0313
Emp Here 100
SIC 7389 Business services, nec
Kyle Dunbar

D-U-N-S 24-400-9366   (BR)
QUOREX CONSTRUCTION SERVICES LTD
(*Suby of* QUOREX CONSTRUCTION SERVICES LTD)
1630 8th Ave Unit A, Regina, SK, S4R 1E5
(306) 761-2222
Emp Here 75
SIC 1542 Nonresidential construction, nec
Gary Leontowicz

D-U-N-S 20-873-5485   (SL)
R & D AUTO SALES
979 Winnipeg St Suite C, Regina, SK, S4R 1J1
(306) 565-2929
Emp Here 20   *Sales* 10,076,934
SIC 5521 Used car dealers
Wally Schouten

D-U-N-S 24-851-8425   (HQ)
RE/MAX CROWN REAL ESTATE LTD
2350 2nd Ave, Regina, SK, S4R 1A6
(306) 791-7666
Emp Here 50   *Sales* 31,416,675
SIC 6531 Real estate agents and managers
Gary Cossette
Carol Cossette
Rob Nisbett

D-U-N-S 24-321-2490   (SL)
REGINA SPORT & IMPORT AUTOMOTIVE GROUP LTD
MERCEDES BENZ OF REGINA
755 Broad St, Regina, SK, S4R 8G3
(306) 757-2369
Emp Here 22   *Sales* 10,957,716
SIC 5511 New and used car dealers
Ricky Ponto

D-U-N-S 20-068-1625   (HQ)
RICHARDSON HOUSE OF FIXTURES AND SUPPLIES LTD
RICHARDSON LIGHTING
2101 7th Ave, Regina, SK, S4R 1C3
(306) 525-8301
Emp Here 18   *Sales* 13,415,220
SIC 5063 Electrical apparatus and equipment
Ernie Richardson
Donald Richardson
James Richardson

D-U-N-S 25-619-3574   (SL)
S O S JANITORIAL SERVICES LTD
2396 2nd Ave, Regina, SK, S4R 1A6
(306) 757-0027
Emp Here 250   *Sales* 7,992,000
SIC 7349 Building maintenance services, nec
Fred Glass
Catherine Glass

D-U-N-S 20-842-1628   (HQ)
SASKATCHEWAN MOTOR CLUB
CAA SASKATCHEWAN
200 Albert St N, Regina, SK, S4R 2N4
(306) 791-4321
Emp Here 60   *Sales* 14,310,458
SIC 8699 Membership organizations, nec
Fred Titanich
Dave Roszell

D-U-N-S 24-380-8057   (SL)
SASKATCHEWAN MOTOR CLUB SERVICES LIMITED
(*Suby of* SASKATCHEWAN MOTOR CLUB)
200 Albert St, Regina, SK, S4R 2N4
(306) 791-4321
Emp Here 10   *Sales* 18,466,590
SIC 6331 Fire, marine, and casualty insurance
Fred Titanich
Larry Haas
Dave Harding
Ted Hillstead
Nola Joorisity
Garth Knakoske
Terry Kotyk
Barry Martin
Al Meyer

Tom Phillipson

D-U-N-S 24-747-9082   (HQ)
SASKATCHEWAN UNION OF NURSES
2330 2nd Ave, Regina, SK, S4R 1A6
(306) 525-1666
Sales 16,819,794
SIC 8631 Labor organizations
Rosalee Longmoore

D-U-N-S 24-426-0360   (SL)
SEVEN OAKS MOTOR INN LTD
777 Albert St, Regina, SK, S4R 2P6
(306) 757-0121
Emp Here 105   *Sales* 9,732,450
SIC 7011 Hotels and motels
Larry Bird
Glenn Weir
Tammy Wright

D-U-N-S 25-271-7426   (BR)
SOBEYS WEST INC
SAFEWAY REGENT PARK
(*Suby of* EMPIRE COMPANY LIMITED)
3859 Sherwood Dr, Regina, SK, S4R 4A8
(306) 949-7488
Emp Here 105
SIC 5411 Grocery stores
Joy Cherwak

D-U-N-S 20-815-5114   (SL)
STERLING PLUMBING & HEATING LTD
1625 8th Ave, Regina, SK, S4R 1E6
(306) 586-5050
Emp Here 130   *Sales* 30,298,450
SIC 1711 Plumbing, heating, air-conditioning
Colin Hodge
Janice Stochmal
Jerrod Turgeon

D-U-N-S 20-066-9646   (HQ)
TAYLOR MOTOR SALES LTD
655 Broad St, Regina, SK, S4R 1X5
(306) 569-8777
Emp Here 1   *Sales* 40,903,200
SIC 5511 New and used car dealers
William Taylor

D-U-N-S 24-963-3637   (SL)
TAYLOR VOLKSWAGEN INC
775 Broad St, Regina, SK, S4R 8G3
(306) 757-9657
Emp Here 22   *Sales* 10,957,716
SIC 5511 New and used car dealers
Roberta Dallas Taylor

D-U-N-S 24-230-7338   (SL)
TITAN AUTOMOTIVE GROUP LTD
755 Broad St, Regina, SK, S4R 8G3
(306) 775-3388
Emp Here 55   *Sales* 34,610,400
SIC 5511 New and used car dealers
Rick Ponto

D-U-N-S 25-999-5061   (SL)
TOM'S INDEPENDENT GROCER
336 N Mccarthy Blvd Suite A, Regina, SK, S4R 7M2
(306) 949-1255
Emp Here 49   *Sales* 14,380,373
SIC 5411 Grocery stores

D-U-N-S 25-499-6952   (BR)
WESTROCK COMPANY OF CANADA CORP
(*Suby of* WESTROCK COMPANY)
1400 1st Ave, Regina, SK, S4R 8G5
(306) 525-7700
Emp Here 80
SIC 2653 Corrugated and solid fiber boxes
Neil Vandermeulen

D-U-N-S 20-067-4877   (SL)
WHEATON CHEVROLET LTD
260 N Albert St, Regina, SK, S4R 3C1
(306) 543-1555
Emp Here 80   *Sales* 50,342,400
SIC 5511 New and used car dealers
Herbert Wheaton

Karen Akre

Regina, SK S4S

D-U-N-S 24-775-4286   (BR)
EARL'S RESTAURANTS LTD
EARL'S RESTAURANTS
(*Suby of* EARL'S RESTAURANTS LTD)
2606 28th Ave, Regina, SK, S4S 6P3
(306) 584-7733
Emp Here 100
SIC 5812 Eating places
Brent Peterson

D-U-N-S 20-823-5564   (BR)
EXTENDICARE INC
EXTENDICARE ELMVIEW
(*Suby of* EXTENDICARE INC)
4125 Rae St, Regina, SK, S4S 3A5
(306) 586-1787
Emp Here 96
SIC 8051 Skilled nursing care facilities
Dan Shiplack

D-U-N-S 20-756-6159   (BR)
EXTENDICARE INC
EXTENDICARE SUNSET
(*Suby of* EXTENDICARE INC)
260 Sunset Dr, Regina, SK, S4S 2S3
(306) 586-3355
Emp Here 300
SIC 8051 Skilled nursing care facilities
Sandra Callan

D-U-N-S 24-352-5123   (BR)
EXTENDICARE INC
EXTENDICARE PARKSIDE
(*Suby of* EXTENDICARE INC)
4540 Rae St, Regina, SK, S4S 3B4
(306) 586-0220
Emp Here 308
SIC 8051 Skilled nursing care facilities
Jason Carson

D-U-N-S 25-483-6786   (HQ)
FIRST NATIONS UNIVERSITY OF CANADA
1 First Nations Way, Regina, SK, S4S 7K2
(306) 790-5950
Emp Here 80   *Sales* 22,408,650
SIC 8221 Colleges and universities
Charles Pratt
Al Ducharme

D-U-N-S 25-612-1088   (SL)
GEO JACK ENTERPRISES INC
SHOPPERS DRUG MART
4130 Albert St Suite 425, Regina, SK, S4S 3R8
(306) 777-8040
Emp Here 80   *Sales* 19,546,240
SIC 5912 Drug stores and proprietary stores
George Furneaux

D-U-N-S 25-100-2457   (HQ)
GREYSTONE CAPITAL MANAGEMENT INC
(*Suby of* TORONTO-DOMINION BANK, THE)
1230 Blackfoot Dr Unit 300, Regina, SK, S4S 7G4
(306) 779-6400
Emp Here 10   *Sales* 58,228,974
SIC 6282 Investment advice
Robert Vanderhooft
Jeff Robertson
Ted Welter
Louis Martel
Tom Mamic
Donald W Black
Frank Hart
William J A Heidt
Tom Ulrich
Lyle Vinifh

D-U-N-S 24-774-6233   (HQ)
GREYSTONE MANAGED INVESTMENTS

INC
(*Suby of* TORONTO-DOMINION BANK, THE)
1230 Blackfoot Dr Unit 300, Regina, SK, S4S 7G4
(306) 779-6400
Emp Here 100   *Sales* 249,049,150
SIC 6282 Investment advice
Donald W Black
Robert L Vanderhooft
Jess Robertson
Frank H Hart
Louis R Martel
Ted R Welter
Tom Mamic

D-U-N-S 24-113-6014   (HQ)
INFORMATION SERVICES CORPORATION
ISC
10 Research Dr Suite 300, Regina, SK, S4S 7J7
(306) 787-8179
Emp Here 60   *Sales* 90,313,449
SIC 6519 Real property lessors, nec
Jeff Stusek
Shawn Peters
Kenneth W. Budzak
Kathy Hillman-Weir
Loren Cisyk
Laurel Garven
Catherine Mclean
Dennis White
Joel Douglas Teal
Karyn A Brooks

D-U-N-S 25-195-1646   (HQ)
ISC SASKATCHEWAN INC
INFORMATION SERVICES CORPORATION OF SASKATCHEWAN
(*Suby of* INFORMATION SERVICES CORPORATION)
10 Research Dr Suite 300, Regina, SK, S4S 7J7
(306) 787-8179
Sales 17,419,842
SIC 8713 Surveying services
Jeff Stusek
Kenneth Budzak

D-U-N-S 25-151-0244   (HQ)
ISM INFORMATION SYSTEMS MANAGEMENT CANADA CORPORATION
(*Suby of* INTERNATIONAL BUSINESS MACHINES CORPORATION)
1 Research Dr, Regina, SK, S4S 7H1
(306) 337-5601
Emp Here 1   *Sales* 83,423,500
SIC 7374 Data processing and preparation
Mark Macleod
Richard Bishop
Larry Lablanc
John Ostrander

D-U-N-S 20-064-3687   (BR)
KJMAL ENTERPRISES LTD
MC DONALD'S
(*Suby of* KJMAL ENTERPRISES LTD)
4651 Albert St, Regina, SK, S4S 6B6
(306) 584-5656
Emp Here 90
SIC 5812 Eating places
Randy William

D-U-N-S 25-950-5063   (BR)
LOBLAWS INC
DRUGSTORE PHARMACY, THE
(*Suby of* LOBLAW COMPANIES LIMITED)
3960 Albert St Suite 9037, Regina, SK, S4S 3R1
(306) 584-9444
Emp Here 120
SIC 5411 Grocery stores
Cathy Klatt

D-U-N-S 24-718-2090   (SL)
RAIN AND HAIL INSURANCE SERVICE INC
(*Suby of* CHUBB LIMITED)
4303 Albert St Suite 200, Regina, SK, S4S

▲ Public Company   ■ Public Company Family Member   **HQ** Headquarters   **BR** Branch   **SL** Single Location

3R6
(306) 584-8844
Emp Here 10   *Sales* 10,348,810
SIC 6331 Fire, marine, and casualty insurance
Robert Goeres
Brenda Kapp

D-U-N-S 20-852-8950   (SL)
REGINA TRAVELODGE LTD
REGINA TRAVELODGE HOTEL
4177 Albert St, Regina, SK, S4S 3R6
(306) 586-3443
Emp Here 140   *Sales* 12,976,600
SIC 7011 Hotels and motels
Ryan Urzada
Donald Urzada

D-U-N-S 20-178-7723   (SL)
ROSSDREY LTD
CANADIAN TIRE
2965 Gordon Rd Suite 65, Regina, SK, S4S
6H7
(306) 585-1355
Emp Here 75   *Sales* 47,196,000
SIC 5531 Auto and home supply stores
Ross Leckie

D-U-N-S 20-841-3419   (SL)
**SASKATCHEWAN CENTRE OF THE ARTS
FOUNDATION INC**
(*Suby of* GOVERNMENT OF
SASKATCHEWAN)
200a Lakeshore Dr, Regina, SK, S4S 7L3
(306) 565-4500
Emp Here 378   *Sales* 56,629,314
SIC 7922 Theatrical producers and services
Pat Beanland

D-U-N-S 20-919-2520   (SL)
TRAVEL GALLERY, THE
1230 Blackfoot Dr Suite 110, Regina, SK, S4S
7G4

Emp Here 21   *Sales* 10,919,307
SIC 4724 Travel agencies
Rita Milenkovic

D-U-N-S 20-835-7483   (HQ)
UNIVERSITY OF REGINA
3737 Wascana Pky, Regina, SK, S4S 0A2
(306) 584-1255
Emp Here 2,680   *Sales* 193,607,522
SIC 8221 Colleges and universities
Vianne Timmons
Dave Button

D-U-N-S 25-944-6805   (BR)
UNIVERSITY OF REGINA
LUTHER COLLEGE
(*Suby of* UNIVERSITY OF REGINA)
3737 Wascana Pky Suite 148, Regina, SK,
S4S 0A2
(306) 585-4111
Emp Here 100
SIC 8221 Colleges and universities
Bruce Perlson

D-U-N-S 24-330-0501   (BR)
WAL-MART CANADA CORP
(*Suby of* WALMART INC.)
2715 Gordon Rd, Regina, SK, S4S 6H7
(306) 584-0061
Emp Here 200
SIC 5311 Department stores
Terry Stanley

Regina, SK S4T

D-U-N-S 20-756-8320   (SL)
CANADIAN BIBLE COLLEGE
CANADIAN THEOLOGICAL SEMINARY
4400 4th Ave, Regina, SK, S4T 0H8
(306) 545-0210
Emp Here 100   *Sales* 11,263,600
SIC 8221 Colleges and universities

George Durance
David Bellsey
Ruth Harnett
Ken Daper

D-U-N-S 24-819-0977   (HQ)
KLEIN, ROBERT ENTERPRISES INC
KLEIN'S FOOD MART
1005 Pasqua St, Regina, SK, S4T 4K9
(306) 791-6362
Emp Here 3   *Sales* 13,707,600
SIC 5411 Grocery stores
Robert Klein

D-U-N-S 20-855-3990   (SL)
LUTHER COLLEGE
1500 Royal St, Regina, SK, S4T 5A5
(306) 791-9150
Emp Here 200   *Sales* 29,878,200
SIC 8221 Colleges and universities
Mark Duke
Bryan Hillis

D-U-N-S 20-648-2585   (BR)
**MCDONALD'S RESTAURANTS OF
CANADA LIMITED**
MCDONALD'S
(*Suby of* MCDONALD'S CORPORATION)
2620 Dewdney Ave, Regina, SK, S4T 0X3
(306) 525-6611
Emp Here 100
SIC 5812 Eating places
Nikia Bratt

D-U-N-S 24-421-3141   (HQ)
NUTRIEN AG SOLUTIONS (CANADA) INC
CPS
(*Suby of* NUTRIEN LTD)
2625 Victoria Ave 6th Fl, Regina, SK, S4T 1Z8
(306) 569-4379
Emp Here 2   *Sales* 18,735,640
SIC 5261 Retail nurseries and garden stores
Michael Frank
Roger Bortis

D-U-N-S 25-359-3560   (BR)
SASKATCHEWAN CANCER AGENCY
ALLAN BLAIR CANCER CENTER
(*Suby of* GOVERNMENT OF
SASKATCHEWAN)
4101 Dewdney Ave Suite 300, Regina, SK,
S4T 7T1
(306) 766-2213
Emp Here 150
SIC 8093 Specialty outpatient clinics, nec
Monica Behl

D-U-N-S 20-068-2185   (HQ)
VITERRA INC
AGRICORE UNITED
(*Suby of* GLENCORE PLC)
2625 Victoria Ave, Regina, SK, S4T 1Z8
(306) 569-4411
Emp Here 300   *Sales* 1,137,630,770
SIC 4221 Farm product warehousing and stor-
age
Kyle Jeworski
Edward Ast
Christopher Mahoney
Ernest Mostert
Larry Ruud
Robert Wardell

Regina, SK S4V

D-U-N-S 20-008-2340   (SL)
**2020 BUSINESS ADVISORY CORPORA-
TION**
A L MANAGEMENT GROUP
4032 Wascana Ridge Bay, Regina, SK, S4V
2L6
(306) 790-2020
Emp Here 38   *Sales* 10,424,616
SIC 8741 Management services

Andre Lizee

D-U-N-S 24-386-2526   (HQ)
AGT FOOD AND INGREDIENTS INC
SASKCAN PULSE TRADING
6200 E Primrose Green Dr, Regina, SK, S4V
3L7
(306) 525-4490
Emp Here 50   *Sales* 1,359,557,453
SIC 0723 Crop preparation services for mar-
ket
Murad Al-Katib
Huseyin Arslan
Lori Ireland
Gaetan Bourassa
Howard Rosen
John Gardner
Drew Franklin
Greg Stewart
Marie-Lucie Morin

D-U-N-S 20-712-7023   (BR)
**BOARD OF EDUCATION REGINA SCHOOL
DIVISION NO. 4 OF SASKATCHEWAN**
JACK MACKENZIE SCHOO
3838 E Buckingham Dr, Regina, SK, S4V 3A1
(306) 791-8585
Emp Here 160
SIC 8211 Elementary and secondary schools
Julie Macrae

D-U-N-S 25-524-6670   (BR)
COSTCO WHOLESALE CANADA LTD
COSTCO WHOLESALE CANADA
(*Suby of* COSTCO WHOLESALE CORPO-
RATION)
665 University Park Dr Suite 520, Regina, SK,
S4V 2V8
(306) 789-8838
Emp Here 150
SIC 5099 Durable goods, nec
Kelly Mahood

D-U-N-S 20-254-7670   (SL)
**DUSYK & BARLOW INSURANCE BRO-
KERS LTD**
302 University Park Dr, Regina, SK, S4V 0Y8
(306) 791-3474
Emp Here 21   *Sales* 12,178,404
SIC 6411 Insurance agents, brokers, and ser-
vice
Brian Dusyk
Rob Barlow

D-U-N-S 20-827-5870   (HQ)
KAST HOLDINGS INC
PETRO CANADA
2020 Coleman Cres, Regina, SK, S4V 3B9
(306) 721-3335
Emp Here 10   *Sales* 24,903,900
SIC 5541 Gasoline service stations
Kevin Tegart

D-U-N-S 25-170-3229   (BR)
LOBLAWS INC
REAL CANADIAN SUPERSTORES
(*Suby of* LOBLAW COMPANIES LIMITED)
2055 Prince Of Wales Dr Suite 1584, Regina,
SK, S4V 3A3
(306) 546-6518
Emp Here 300
SIC 5411 Grocery stores
Travis Jolly

D-U-N-S 20-564-5380   (SL)
**NUTRASUN FOODS LIMITED PARTNER-
SHIP**
(*Suby of* PATERSON GLOBALFOODS INC)
6201 E Primrose Green Dr, Regina, SK, S4V
3L7
(306) 751-2040
Emp Here 30   *Sales* 10,370,700
SIC 2041 Flour and other grain mill products
Kerry Keating

D-U-N-S 20-389-9851   (SL)
PS INTERNATIONAL CANADA CORP
SEABOARD SPECIAL CROPS

(*Suby of* SEABOARD CORPORATION)
2595 E Quance St Suite 201, Regina, SK, S4V
2Y8
(306) 565-3904
Emp Here 42   *Sales* 43,362,648
SIC 6799 Investors, nec
Gail Cummings
Zachery Holden
David Dannov

D-U-N-S 24-496-8657   (SL)
REGINA REALTY SALES LTD
ROYAL LEPAGE REGINA REALTY
3889 E Arcola Ave, Regina, SK, S4V 1P5
(306) 359-1900
Emp Here 70   *Sales* 19,022,920
SIC 6531 Real estate agents and managers
Ron Pfeifer
Michael Duggleby

D-U-N-S 20-448-8852   (SL)
**SASKATCHEWAN ASSOCIATION OF RU-
RAL MUNICIPALITIES, THE**
SARM
2301 Windsor Park Rd, Regina, SK, S4V 3A4
(306) 757-3577
Emp Here 22   *Sales* 10,440,949
SIC 8611 Business associations
Ray Orb
Carmen Sterling
James Hallick
Jay Meyer
Laurel Feltin
Kelsay Reimer

D-U-N-S 20-792-0260   (BR)
**SHERWOOD CO-OPERATIVE ASSOCIA-
TION LIMITED**
SHERWOOD CO OP
(*Suby of* SHERWOOD CO-OPERATIVE AS-
SOCIATION LIMITED)
2925 E Quance St, Regina, SK, S4V 3B7
(306) 791-9300
Emp Here 80
SIC 5411 Grocery stores
David Sloan

D-U-N-S 24-330-0519   (BR)
WAL-MART CANADA CORP
(*Suby of* WALMART INC.)
2150 Prince Of Wales Dr, Regina, SK, S4V
3A6
(306) 780-3700
Emp Here 200
SIC 5311 Department stores

Regina, SK S4W

D-U-N-S 20-432-0733   (SL)
BELL - GRASSLANDS
4609 Gordon Rd, Regina, SK, S4W 0B7
(306) 779-1910
Emp Here 49   *Sales* 11,480,112
SIC 8748 Business consulting, nec

D-U-N-S 25-790-6144   (SL)
CO-OP, REGINA GAS BAR
4705 Gordon Rd, Regina, SK, S4W 0B7
(306) 791-9388
Emp Here 30   *Sales* 14,942,340
SIC 5541 Gasoline service stations
Rocky Smith

D-U-N-S 20-279-4827   (HQ)
REGINA AIRPORT AUTHORITY INC
YQR REGINA INTERNATIONAL
5201 Regina Ave Unit 1, Regina, SK, S4W
1B3
(306) 761-7555
Sales 21,383,211
SIC 4581 Airports, flying fields, and services
Richmond Graham
Ken Waschuk
Derrick Thue

▲ Public Company   ■ Public Company Family Member   **HQ** Headquarters   **BR** Branch   **SL** Single Location

Alex Taylor
Paul Bourassa
Trent Fraser
Darlene Hincks
Sean Mceachern
Glenda Boynton
Donna Dowler

D-U-N-S 20-557-5736   (SL)
**SASKATCHEWAN HEALTHCARE EMPLOY-
EES' PENSION PLAN**
SHEPP
4581 Parliament Ave Suite 201, Regina, SK,
S4W 0G3
(306) 751-8300
Emp Here 40   *Sales* 73,866,360
SIC 6371 Pension, health, and welfare funds
Allison Mckay
Garry Tramer

Regina, SK S4X

D-U-N-S 20-066-0889   (BR)
**BOARD OF EDUCATION REGINA SCHOOL
DIVISION NO. 4 OF SASKATCHEWAN**
WINSTON KNOLL COLLEGIATE
5255 Rochdale Blvd, Regina, SK, S4X 4M8
(306) 523-3400
Emp Here 85
SIC 8211 Elementary and secondary schools
Brad Howard

D-U-N-S 20-067-9900   (SL)
CAPITAL FORD LINCOLN INC
1201 N Pasqua St, Regina, SK, S4X 4P7
(306) 543-5410
Emp Here 80   *Sales* 50,342,400
SIC 5511 New and used car dealers
Bruce Axelson

D-U-N-S 20-067-8209   (SL)
**CAPITAL PONTIAC BUICK CADILLAC GMC
LTD**
4020 Rochdale Blvd, Regina, SK, S4X 4P7
(306) 525-5211
Emp Here 100   *Sales* 62,928,000
SIC 5511 New and used car dealers
Bruce Axelson
Colin Konanz

D-U-N-S 24-309-3155   (BR)
HOME DEPOT OF CANADA INC
(*Suby of* THE HOME DEPOT INC)
1030 N Pasqua St, Regina, SK, S4X 4V3
(306) 564-5700
Emp Here 100
SIC 5251 Hardware stores
Gail Naimeth

D-U-N-S 25-148-1719   (BR)
LOBLAWS INC
REAL CANADIAN SUPERSTORE
(*Suby of* LOBLAW COMPANIES LIMITED)
4450 Rochdale Blvd Suite 1585, Regina, SK,
S4X 4N9
(306) 546-6618
Emp Here 200
SIC 5399 Miscellaneous general merchandise
Joshua Tenn

D-U-N-S 25-366-0575   (BR)
**MCDONALD'S   RESTAURANTS   OF
CANADA LIMITED**
MCDONALD'S
(*Suby of* MCDONALD'S CORPORATION)
6210 Rochdale Blvd, Regina, SK, S4X 4K8
(306) 543-6300
Emp Here 80
SIC 5812 Eating places
Sean Ryan

D-U-N-S 20-854-8511   (HQ)
**SASKATCHEWAN GOVERNMENT & GEN-
ERAL EMPLOYEES' UNION**

SGEU
1011 N Devonshire Dr, Regina, SK, S4X 2X4
(306) 522-8571
Emp Here 30   *Sales* 21,584,750
SIC 8631 Labor organizations
Robert Bymoen

D-U-N-S 20-965-8918   (BR)
SOBEYS CAPITAL INCORPORATED
(*Suby of* EMPIRE COMPANY LIMITED)
4101 Rochdale Blvd, Regina, SK, S4X 4P7
(306) 546-5881
Emp Here 100
SIC 5411 Grocery stores
Rick Thirsk

D-U-N-S 25-294-7452   (BR)
WAL-MART CANADA CORP
(*Suby of* WALMART INC.)
3939 Rochdale Blvd, Regina, SK, S4X 4P7
(306) 543-3237
Emp Here 290
SIC 5311 Department stores
Hagen Daryl

Regina, SK S4Z

D-U-N-S 25-939-2053   (SL)
BRANDT GROUP OF COMPANIES,THE
3710 Eastgate Dr Suite 1, Regina, SK, S4Z
1A5
(306) 347-1499
Emp Here 30   *Sales* 14,121,930
SIC 1542 Nonresidential construction, nec
Bill Hood
Matt Semple
Graeme Taylor

D-U-N-S 20-355-0822   (BR)
**MCDONALD'S   RESTAURANTS   OF
CANADA LIMITED**
MCDONALD'S
(*Suby of* MCDONALD'S CORPORATION)
1955 Prince Of Wales Dr, Regina, SK, S4Z
1A5
(306) 781-1340
Emp Here 76
SIC 5812 Eating places
Nicole Calder

Ridgedale, SK S0E

D-U-N-S 20-068-6707   (SL)
**RIDGEDALE   CO-OPERATIVE   ASSOCIA-
TION LTD**
119 Main St, Ridgedale, SK, S0E 1L0
(306) 277-2042
Emp Here 10   *Sales* 10,328,080
SIC 5171 Petroleum bulk stations and termi-
nals
Derek Hedin
Colter Mcrae
Dale Scammell
Mick York
Brad Schiltvoth
Brenda Nelson
Dannie Taylor

Rocanville, SK S0A

D-U-N-S 20-854-9790   (BR)
**POTASH   CORPORATION   OF
SASKATCHEWAN INC**
PCS POTASH, DIV OF
(*Suby of* NUTRIEN LTD)
Gd, Rocanville, SK, S0A 3L0
(306) 645-2870
Emp Here 400

SIC 1474 Potash, soda, and borate minerals
Stephen Fortney

Rockglen, SK S0H

D-U-N-S 20-068-7218   (SL)
**ROCK GLEN CO-OPERATIVE ASSOCIA-
TION LIMITED, THE**
150 Hwy 2 S, Rockglen, SK, S0H 3R0
(306) 476-2210
Emp Here 18   *Sales* 19,589,814
SIC 5171 Petroleum bulk stations and termi-
nals
Thor K. Spagrud

Rokeby, SK S0A

D-U-N-S 25-018-6988   (BR)
MORRIS INDUSTRIES LTD
(*Suby of* MORRIS INDUSTRIES LTD)
85 York Rd W, Rokeby, SK, S0A 3N0
(306) 783-8585
Emp Here 150
SIC 3523 Farm machinery and equipment
Rebecca Young

Rosetown, SK S0L

D-U-N-S 24-684-8928   (SL)
CENTRAL PLAINS CO-OPERATIVE LTD
117 1st Ave E, Rosetown, SK, S0L 2V0
(306) 882-2601
Emp Here 40   *Sales* 41,312,320
SIC 5171 Petroleum bulk stations and termi-
nals
Mike Moon

D-U-N-S 25-579-0669   (SL)
HUTTERIAN BRETHERN OF SOVEREIGN
Gd, Rosetown, SK, S0L 2V0
(306) 882-2447
Emp Here 78   *Sales* 8,402,706
SIC 8661 Religious organizations
Peter Wips
John Wips

D-U-N-S 24-678-7977   (SL)
ROSETOWN FARMING CO. LTD
Gd, Rosetown, SK, S0L 2V0
(306) 882-1991
Emp Here 45   *Sales* 17,348,355
SIC 0291 General farms, primarily animals
Paul Wipf

D-U-N-S 25-368-4955   (SL)
**ROSETOWN MAINLINE MOTOR PROD-
UCTS LIMITED**
505 7 Hwy W, Rosetown, SK, S0L 2V0
(306) 882-2691
Emp Here 35   *Sales* 17,432,730
SIC 5511 New and used car dealers
Donald Campbell
Gerald Merrifield
Curtis Merrifield
Ryan Campbell

D-U-N-S 20-842-1172   (HQ)
**SUN WEST SCHOOL DIVISION NO 207
SASKATCHEWAN**
501 First St W, Rosetown, SK, S0L 2V0
(306) 882-2677
Emp Here 20   *Sales* 19,823,800
SIC 8211 Elementary and secondary schools
Guy Tetrault
Tony Baldwin
Tracy Dollansky
Shelley Hengen
Shari Martin

Ryan Smith

D-U-N-S 24-630-6732   (HQ)
WESTERN SALES (1986) LTD
405 Hwy 7 W, Rosetown, SK, S0L 2V0
(306) 882-4291
Emp Here 56   *Sales* 63,404,900
SIC 5083 Farm and garden machinery
Grant Mcgrath
Carl Persson
Jason Hintze
David Kohli

Rosthern, SK S0K

D-U-N-S 20-839-6762   (SL)
**MENNONITE NURSING HOMES INCORPO-
RATED**
Gd, Rosthern, SK, S0K 3R0
(306) 232-4861
Emp Here 120   *Sales* 8,199,120
SIC 8051 Skilled nursing care facilities
Joan Lemauviel

Rouleau, SK S0G

D-U-N-S 20-611-3458   (HQ)
WESTRUM LUMBER LTD
611 Weckman Dr, Rouleau, SK, S0G 4K0
(306) 776-2505
Emp Here 8   *Sales* 11,387,655
SIC 5211 Lumber and other building materials
Michael Westrum
Mark Westrum
Ken Roney

Saltcoats, SK S0A

D-U-N-S 25-216-4413   (HQ)
EMW INDUSTRIAL LTD
EMW
206 Commercial St, Saltcoats, SK, S0A 3R0
(306) 744-1523
Emp Here 324   *Sales* 226,977,400
SIC 1541 Industrial buildings and warehouses
Ewen Morrison
Patrick Morrison
Marcia Sedor
Francis Ostapovich
Jordan Bugg
Stephen Reid

Saskatoon, SK S7H

D-U-N-S 24-427-6077   (SL)
100% REALTY ASSOCIATES LTD
RE/MAX SASKATOON
1820 8th St E Suite 250, Saskatoon, SK, S7H
0T6
(306) 242-6000
Emp Here 112   *Sales* 46,915,568
SIC 6531 Real estate agents and managers
Larry Stewart

D-U-N-S 20-814-3920   (SL)
101055401 SASKATCHEWAN LTD
BEILY'S PUB & GRILL
2404 8th St E, Saskatoon, SK, S7H 0V6

Emp Here 90   *Sales* 4,096,710
SIC 5812 Eating places
Adam Smith

D-U-N-S 24-915-5227   (HQ)
563737 SASKATCHEWAN LTD

MCQUEEN AGENCIES
3502 Taylor St E Suite 103, Saskatoon, SK, S7H 5H9
(306) 955-1330
Sales 14,488,334
SIC 6331 Fire, marine, and casualty insurance
John Rennie Mcqueen
Neil Mcqueen
James Mcqueen

D-U-N-S 24-966-8294   (HQ)
BLACKSTRAP HOSPITALITY CORPORA-
TION
1125 Louise Ave, Saskatoon, SK, S7H 2P8
(306) 931-1030
Emp Here 6   *Sales* 85,894,615
SIC 6712 Bank holding companies
Derek A Neis
Harold W Lane
Roger Mccracken

D-U-N-S 25-735-1031   (SL)
CHRISTINE'S HOLDINGS INC
SHOPPERS DRUG MART
3310 8th St E Unit 440, Saskatoon, SK, S7H 5M3
(306) 373-5556
Emp Here 70   *Sales* 17,102,960
SIC 5912 Drug stores and proprietary stores
Steve Robertson

D-U-N-S 25-640-8543   (HQ)
CONCORDE FOOD SERVICES (1996) LTD
PIZZA HUT
1171 8th St E, Saskatoon, SK, S7H 0S3
(306) 668-3000
Emp Here 15   *Sales* 12,595,500
SIC 5812 Eating places
David Dube
Terry Mapheson
Sui Ma

D-U-N-S 25-059-9560   (SL)
DANIELS   KIMBER   PHYSIOTHERAPY
CLINIC P.C. LTD
3907 8th St E Suite 304, Saskatoon, SK, S7H 5M7
(306) 652-5151
Emp Here 36   *Sales* 13,004,532
SIC 8049 Offices of health practitioner
Ron Lowe
Katherine Daniels
Perry Kimber

D-U-N-S 25-682-7684   (HQ)
DIMENSION 3 HOSPITALITY CORPORA-
TION
DAYS INN REGINA
1139 8th St E, Saskatoon, SK, S7H 0S3
(306) 249-2882
Sales 23,917,000
SIC 7011 Hotels and motels
Don Urzada
Don Rosten
Don Folstad

D-U-N-S 24-581-7577   (BR)
GOLDER ASSOCIATES LTD
(*Suby of* GOLDER ASSOCIATES CORPO-
RATION)
1721 8th St E, Saskatoon, SK, S7H 0T4
(306) 665-7989
Emp Here 140
SIC 8711 Engineering services
Robert Lesterance

D-U-N-S 24-776-4350   (HQ)
HARADROS FOOD SERVICES INC
MANO'S FAMILY RESTAURANT
1820 8th St E Suite 200, Saskatoon, SK, S7H 0T6
(306) 955-5555
Emp Here 100   *Sales* 4,551,900
SIC 5812 Eating places
Manolis Barlas
Louis Barlas
Bill Barlas

D-U-N-S 20-840-2933   (HQ)
LID BROKERAGE & REALTY CO. (1977)
LTD.
LID COMPANY, THE
1171 8th St E, Saskatoon, SK, S7H 0S3
(306) 668-3000
Sales 107,507,400
SIC 5141 Groceries, general line
David Dube
Sui Ma
Paul Slobodzian

D-U-N-S 25-270-1172   (BR)
LOBLAWS INC
REAL CANADIAN SUPERSTORE, THE
(*Suby of* LOBLAW COMPANIES LIMITED)
2901 8th St E Suite 1535, Saskatoon, SK, S7H 0V4
(306) 978-7040
Emp Here 350
SIC 5411 Grocery stores
Robb Theriault

D-U-N-S 24-851-6239   (SL)
MCCLURE PLACE ASSOCIATION INC
1825 Mckercher Dr Suite 804, Saskatoon, SK, S7H 5N5
(306) 955-7677
Emp Here 45   *Sales* 10,480,995
SIC 6513 Apartment building operators
Phyllis Barber
Judy Gunther

D-U-N-S 20-787-8591   (BR)
MCDONALD'S   RESTAURANTS   OF
CANADA LIMITED
MCDONALD'S
(*Suby of* MCDONALD'S CORPORATION)
1706 Preston Ave, Saskatoon, SK, S7H 2V8
(306) 955-8677
Emp Here 100
SIC 5812 Eating places
John E. Betts

D-U-N-S 20-354-0575   (SL)
MCDONALDS RESTAURANT
WILDWOOD
3510 8th St E Unit 1, Saskatoon, SK, S7H 0W6
(306) 955-8674
Emp Here 90   *Sales* 4,096,710
SIC 5812 Eating places
Colleen Pizzey

D-U-N-S 24-523-9681   (BR)
MCDOUGALL GAULEY LLP
*MCDOUGALL GAULEY BARRISTERS & SO-
LICITOR*
(*Suby of* MCDOUGALL GAULEY LLP)
616 Main St Suite 500, Saskatoon, SK, S7H 0J6
(306) 653-1212
Emp Here 90
SIC 8111 Legal services
Martin Mcinnis

D-U-N-S 24-809-4729   (BR)
MCDOUGALL GAULEY LLP
(*Suby of* MCDOUGALL GAULEY LLP)
500-616 Main St, Saskatoon, SK, S7H 0J6
(306) 653-1212
Emp Here 80
SIC 8111 Legal services
Barry Clarke

D-U-N-S 24-966-6173   (HQ)
MIDWEST RESTAURANT INC
MOXIE'S RESTAURANT
3134 8th St E, Saskatoon, SK, S7H 0W2
(306) 374-9800
Emp Here 100   *Sales* 11,659,750
SIC 5812 Eating places
Vincent G Orr

D-U-N-S 25-640-8576   (HQ)
POINT2 TECHNOLOGIES INC
(*Suby of* YARDI SYSTEMS, INC.)
3301 8th St E Suite 500, Saskatoon, SK, S7H

5K5
(866) 977-1777
Emp Here 84
SIC 7371 Custom computer programming ser-
vices
Saul Klein
Jason Golding
Barry Willick
Walt Baczkowski
Scott Macsemchuk

D-U-N-S 25-532-7264   (SL)
PRAIRIE SWINE CENTRE INC
2105 8th St E, Saskatoon, SK, S7H 0T8
(306) 373-9922
Emp Here 52   *Sales* 26,350,272
SIC 8733 Noncommercial research organiza-
tions
Lee Whittington
Eric Peters

D-U-N-S 25-639-9205   (BR)
RED LOBSTER HOSPITALITY LLC
RED LOBSTER RESTAURANTS
2501 8th St E, Saskatoon, SK, S7H 0V4
(306) 373-8333
Emp Here 90
SIC 5812 Eating places
Keely Wright

D-U-N-S 20-814-5800   (SL)
SASKATCHEWAN DRAG RACING ASSOCI-
ATION INC
*SASKATCHEWAN INTERNATIONAL RACE-
WAY*
133 Western Cres, Saskatoon, SK, S7H 4J4
(306) 373-8148
Emp Here 25   *Sales* 10,593,250
SIC 7948 Racing, including track operation
Trevor Jacek

D-U-N-S 20-070-0649   (SL)
SASKATOON C AUTO LP
DODGE CITY
(*Suby of* AUTOCANADA INC)
2200 8th St E, Saskatoon, SK, S7H 0V3
(306) 374-2120
Emp Here 84   *Sales* 52,859,520
SIC 5511 New and used car dealers
Daniel Ens
Ronald Payne
David Payne

D-U-N-S 24-346-3432   (BR)
SASKATOON PRAIRIELAND PARK COR-
PORATION
MARQUIS DOWNS RACE TRACK
(*Suby of* SASKATOON PRAIRIELAND PARK
CORPORATION)
2615 St Henry Ave, Saskatoon, SK, S7H 0A1
(306) 242-6100
Emp Here 150
SIC 7948 Racing, including track operation
Rick Fior

D-U-N-S 24-966-9094   (SL)
SGS PHARMACY INC
SHOPPERS DRUG MART
2105 8th St E Unit 42, Saskatoon, SK, S7H 0T8
(306) 374-4888
Emp Here 60   *Sales* 14,659,680
SIC 5912 Drug stores and proprietary stores
Susan Belyk

D-U-N-S 20-840-0754   (SL)
SHERBROOKE COMMUNITY SOCIETY INC
SHERBROOKE COMMUNITY CENTRE
401 Acadia Dr Suite 330, Saskatoon, SK, S7H 2E7
(306) 655-3600
Emp Here 300   *Sales* 20,497,800
SIC 8059 Nursing and personal care, nec
Suellen Beatty

D-U-N-S 20-706-8490   (BR)
SOBEYS CAPITAL INCORPORATED
(*Suby of* EMPIRE COMPANY LIMITED)

1550 8th St E, Saskatoon, SK, S7H 0T3
(306) 477-5800
Emp Here 100
SIC 5411 Grocery stores
Jason Bellina

D-U-N-S 25-174-9482   (BR)
SOBEYS WEST INC
CO-OP
(*Suby of* EMPIRE COMPANY LIMITED)
3310 8th St E, Saskatoon, SK, S7H 5M3
(306) 955-4644
Emp Here 100
SIC 5411 Grocery stores
Kelly Mullin

D-U-N-S 20-275-5773   (SL)
T & C STEEL LTD
4032 Taylor St E, Saskatoon, SK, S7H 5J5
(306) 373-5191
Emp Here 10   *Sales* 10,003,390
SIC 5051 Metals service centers and offices
Chad Joinson

D-U-N-S 24-326-3444   (HQ)
WEFF HOLDINGS LTD
GREAT CANADIAN OIL CHANGE
1702 8th St E, Saskatoon, SK, S7H 0T5
(306) 952-4262
Emp Here 35   *Sales* 18,414,500
SIC 7549 Automotive services, nec
Chris Weflen
Bradley Weflen

Saskatoon, SK S7J

D-U-N-S 20-236-5248   (SL)
101013121 SASKATCHEWAN LTD
KIA OF SASKATOON
730 Brand Rd, Saskatoon, SK, S7J 5J3
(306) 955-5080
Emp Here 38   *Sales* 18,926,964
SIC 5511 New and used car dealers
Paul Loeppky
Audrey Loeppky

D-U-N-S 20-840-0283   (HQ)
ACTIONWEAR SASKATOON INC
ACTIONWEST
(*Suby of* A & K ACTIONWEAR HOLDINGS
LTD)
114 Melville St, Saskatoon, SK, S7J 0R1
(306) 933-3088
Sales 25,001,790
SIC 3842 Surgical appliances and supplies
Alphonse Reaser
Kathleen Reaser

D-U-N-S 24-264-9879   (SL)
BEMA IMPORTS INC
BEMA AUTOSPORT BMW
607 Brand Crt, Saskatoon, SK, S7J 5L3
(306) 955-0900
Emp Here 35   *Sales* 17,432,730
SIC 5511 New and used car dealers
Leslie Fenyef
Elaine Sharfe

D-U-N-S 25-289-6444   (BR)
BOARD OF EDUCATION OF SASKA-
TOON SCHOOL DIVISION NO. 13 OF
SASKATCHEWAN
WALTER MURRAY COLLEGIATE
(*Suby of* BOARD OF EDUCATION OF
SASKATOON SCHOOL DIVISION NO. 13 OF
SASKATCHEWAN, THE)
1905 Preston Ave, Saskatoon, SK, S7J 2E7
(306) 683-7850
Emp Here 110
SIC 8211 Elementary and secondary schools
Brian Flaherty

D-U-N-S 20-069-4115   (HQ)
EARLY'S FARM & GARDEN CENTRE

2615 Lorne Ave, Saskatoon, SK, S7J 0S5
(306) 931-1982
Emp Here 28   *Sales* 29,245,195
SIC 5149 Groceries and related products, nec
Spencer Early
Jan Early

D-U-N-S 24-818-9755   (BR)
EXTENDICARE (CANADA) INC
EXTENDICARE PRESTON
(*Suby of* EXTENDICARE INC)
2225 Preston Ave, Saskatoon, SK, S7J 2E7
(306) 374-2242
Emp Here 110
SIC 8051 Skilled nursing care facilities
Jason Carson

D-U-N-S 25-995-9484   (HQ)
GREAT WEST DISTRIBUTION LTD
201 Edson St, Saskatoon, SK, S7J 4C8
(306) 933-0027
Emp Here 40   *Sales* 11,313,830
SIC 4213 Trucking, except local
Garry Pozniak

D-U-N-S 20-383-3827   (BR)
INFRA PIPE SOLUTIONS LTD
(*Suby of* WYNNCHURCH CAPITAL, LLC)
348 Edson St, Saskatoon, SK, S7J 0P9
(306) 242-0755
Emp Here 75
SIC 3498 Fabricated pipe and fittings
Marc Leclerc

D-U-N-S 20-546-9281   (HQ)
JUBILEE FORD SALES (1983) LTD
419 Brand Pl, Saskatoon, SK, S7J 5L6
(306) 373-4444
Sales 75,451,563
SIC 5511 New and used car dealers
Vaughn Wyant

D-U-N-S 24-655-0206   (SL)
KELLY & BELL HOLDINGS LTD
ACURA CENTRE OF SASKATOON
(*Suby of* 101105464 SASKATCHEWAN LTD)
819 Melville St, Saskatoon, SK, S7J 5L2
(306) 242-8688
Emp Here 46   *Sales* 28,946,880
SIC 5511 New and used car dealers
Mark Loeppky

D-U-N-S 20-854-4015   (SL)
M.D. AMBULANCE CARE LTD
430 Melville St, Saskatoon, SK, S7J 4M2
(306) 975-8808
Emp Here 100   *Sales* 5,487,200
SIC 4119 Local passenger transportation, nec
David Dutchak

D-U-N-S 20-840-9789   (SL)
MINERS CONSTRUCTION CO. LTD
440 Melville St, Saskatoon, SK, S7J 4M2
(306) 934-4703
Emp Here 30   *Sales* 14,121,930
SIC 1542 Nonresidential construction, nec
Howard Stensrud
Michael Stensrud
Aaron Yohnke
Dave Woodrow

D-U-N-S 25-555-1228   (SL)
OAKWOOD MOTORS INC
OAKWOOD NISSAN
635 Brand Crt, Saskatoon, SK, S7J 5L3
(306) 664-3333
Emp Here 43   *Sales* 21,417,354
SIC 5511 New and used car dealers
Merle Meidl
Randy Meidl

D-U-N-S 24-654-9695   (SL)
PLEASURE-WAY INDUSTRIES LTD
302 Portage Ave, Saskatoon, SK, S7J 4C6
(306) 934-6578
Emp Here 150   *Sales* 33,576,450
SIC 3716 Motor homes
Mervin Rumpel

Dean Rumpel
Diane Dufchcherer
Terry Burges

D-U-N-S 20-855-0483   (SL)
POW CITY MECHANICAL PARTNERSHIP
2920 Jasper Ave S, Saskatoon, SK, S7J 4L7
(306) 933-3133
Emp Here 85   *Sales* 19,810,525
SIC 1711 Plumbing, heating, air-conditioning
Rick Schuler
Brent Schuler

D-U-N-S 24-895-3825   (SL)
PRESTON PARK
114 Armistice Way, Saskatoon, SK, S7J 3K9
(306) 933-0515
Emp Here 45   *Sales* 10,480,995
SIC 6513 Apartment building operators
Preston Park

D-U-N-S 25-072-1347   (SL)
REALTY EXECUTIVES SASKATOON
3032 Louise St, Saskatoon, SK, S7J 3L8
(306) 373-7520
Emp Here 61   *Sales* 25,552,229
SIC 6531 Real estate agents and managers
Wayne Zuk

D-U-N-S 20-192-3989   (SL)
SASCOPACK INC
106 Melville St, Saskatoon, SK, S7J 0R1

Emp Here 50   *Sales* 22,174,500
SIC 7389 Business services, nec
Denis Denomme
Steven Naccarato

D-U-N-S 20-740-8204   (HQ)
SASKATCHEWAN ABILITIES COUNCIL INC
REGINA ABILITY CENTRE
2310 Louise Ave, Saskatoon, SK, S7J 2C7
(306) 374-4448
Emp Here 45   *Sales* 23,922,450
SIC 8331 Job training and related services
Andy Livingston
Stan Lautsch
Brenda Bancescu
Paul Blackstock
Elaine Caswell
Lynsey Gaudin
Michelle Hunter
Bruno Konecsni
Ulla Nielsen
Tom Spence

D-U-N-S 20-080-3232   (BR)
SASKATCHEWAN HEALTH AUTHORITY
CALDER CENTRE
(*Suby of* GOVERNMENT OF SASKATCHEWAN)
2003 Arlington Ave, Saskatoon, SK, S7J 2H6
(306) 655-4500
Emp Here 90
SIC 8069 Specialty hospitals, except psychiatric
Nicole Schumacher

D-U-N-S 24-468-3546   (HQ)
SASKATCHEWAN TEACHERS' FEDERATION
2317 Arlington Ave, Saskatoon, SK, S7J 2H8
(306) 373-1660
Emp Here 84   *Sales* 21,736,350
SIC 8621 Professional organizations
Dianne Woloschuk

D-U-N-S 25-384-9749   (SL)
SASKATOON SPECIALTY MEATS LTD
106 Melville St, Saskatoon, SK, S7J 0R1
(306) 653-9292
Emp Here 95   *Sales* 79,379,815
SIC 5147 Meats and meat products
Ron Blazeiko

D-U-N-S 25-116-7268   (BR)
SASKATOON, CITY OF
SASKATOON LIGHT AND POWER

(*Suby of* SASKATOON, CITY OF)
322 Brand Rd, Saskatoon, SK, S7J 5J3
(306) 975-2414
Emp Here 120
SIC 4911 Electric services
Henry Hildebrandt

D-U-N-S 25-229-9888   (SL)
SELECT CLASSIC CARRIERS INC
226a Portage Ave, Saskatoon, SK, S7J 4C6
(306) 374-2733
Emp Here 69   *Sales* 10,225,248
SIC 4213 Trucking, except local
Jan Martin

D-U-N-S 20-546-3607   (SL)
SHERWOOD CHEVROLET INC
(*Suby of* SHERWOOD INVESTMENTS LIMITED)
550 Brand Rd, Saskatoon, SK, S7J 5J3
(306) 374-6330
Emp Here 85   *Sales* 53,488,800
SIC 5511 New and used car dealers
Sherwood Sharfe
Ronald M Gitlin
Karen Webster

D-U-N-S 24-468-6176   (HQ)
SHERWOOD INVESTMENTS LIMITED
SHERWOOD CHEVEROLET
550 Brand Rd, Saskatoon, SK, S7J 5J3
(306) 374-6330
Sales 62,928,000
SIC 5521 Used car dealers
Sherwood Sharfe

D-U-N-S 20-840-8492   (SL)
ST ANN'S SENIOR CITIZENS' VILLAGE CORPORATION
ST ANN'S HOME
2910 Louise St, Saskatoon, SK, S7J 3L8
(306) 374-8900
Emp Here 140   *Sales* 9,565,640
SIC 8051 Skilled nursing care facilities
Elenore Hanus
Roland Muir
Heather Kolla
Francis Kolla
James Mcgettigan
Dennis Dorgan
Claude Lang

D-U-N-S 20-271-6247   (BR)
STAR PRODUCE LTD
(*Suby of* STAR INVESTMENT CORP)
2941 Portage Ave, Saskatoon, SK, S7J 3S6
(306) 934-0999
Emp Here 80
SIC 5148 Fresh fruits and vegetables
Derrick Karolat

D-U-N-S 24-820-0057   (BR)
UPONOR INFRA LTD
348 Edson St, Saskatoon, SK, S7J 0P9
(306) 242-0755
Emp Here 75   *Sales* 328,382
SIC 3498 Fabricated pipe and fittings
Stefan Alexander

Saskatoon, SK S7K

D-U-N-S 25-641-0242   (HQ)
101105464 SASKATCHEWAN LTD
VOLKSWAGEN CENTRE OF SASKATOON
635 Circle Dr E, Saskatoon, SK, S7K 7Y2
(306) 955-8877
Emp Here 10   *Sales* 17,432,730
SIC 5511 New and used car dealers
Paul Loeppky

D-U-N-S 24-376-5153   (SL)
303567 SASKATCHEWAN LTD
HANDYMAN RENTAL CENTRE
2636 Millar Ave, Saskatoon, SK, S7K 4C8

(306) 933-3020
Emp Here 54   *Sales* 10,333,116
SIC 7359 Equipment rental and leasing, nec
Barry Ghiglione
Marion Ghiglione

D-U-N-S 20-839-9808   (SL)
591226 SASKATCHEWAN LTD
MEIDL HONDA
110a Circle Dr E, Saskatoon, SK, S7K 4K1
(306) 373-7477
Emp Here 50   *Sales* 24,903,900
SIC 5511 New and used car dealers
Randall Meidl
Bob Meidl

D-U-N-S 24-388-3621   (HQ)
601861 SASKATCHEWAN LTD
T & T GROUP OF COMPANIES
855 60th St E, Saskatoon, SK, S7K 5Z7
(306) 934-3383
Emp Here 2   *Sales* 28,798,840
SIC 4213 Trucking, except local
Henry Thiessen
Graham Newton
Rick Bekker

D-U-N-S 25-504-9025   (SL)
615315 SASKATCHEWAN LTD
JBM LOGISTICS
(*Suby of* PROGRESSIVE DIRECT VENTURES LTD)
875 58th St E, Saskatoon, SK, S7K 6X5
(306) 653-5400
Emp Here 75   *Sales* 15,427,950
SIC 4213 Trucking, except local
Lindsay Keene

D-U-N-S 20-521-5374   (SL)
629112 SASKATCHEWAN LTD
CKBL - FM
366 3rd Ave S, Saskatoon, SK, S7K 1M5
(306) 244-1975
Emp Here 70   *Sales* 12,935,860
SIC 4832 Radio broadcasting stations
Elmer Hildebrand

D-U-N-S 24-229-2993   (HQ)
A S L PAVING LTD
1840 Ontario Ave, Saskatoon, SK, S7K 1T4
(306) 652-5525
Emp Here 100   *Sales* 102,043,765
SIC 1611 Highway and street construction
David Paslawski
James Fraser

D-U-N-S 24-852-1395   (SL)
ABC CANADA TECHNOLOGY GROUP LTD
ABC VENTILATION
1802 Quebec Ave, Saskatoon, SK, S7K 1W2
(306) 653-4303
Emp Here 98   *Sales* 27,112,680
SIC 2822 Synthetic rubber
Darryl Yausie
James Yausie

D-U-N-S 25-193-5052   (BR)
ADESA AUCTIONS CANADA CORPORATION
ADESA SASKATOON
(*Suby of* KAR AUCTION SERVICES, INC.)
37507 Hwy 12, Saskatoon, SK, S7K 3J7
(306) 242-8771
Emp Here 150
SIC 5012 Automobiles and other motor vehicles
Kevin Mccaig

D-U-N-S 25-636-5677   (HQ)
ADVANCED 2000 SYSTEMS INC
ROGERS AT & T
718 Circle Dr E, Saskatoon, SK, S7K 3T7
(306) 955-2355
Emp Here 1   *Sales* 24,432,800
SIC 5999 Miscellaneous retail stores, nec
Tim Burns
Rhonda Burns
Jeremy Longley

▲ Public Company   ■ Public Company Family Member   **HQ** Headquarters   **BR** Branch   **SL** Single Location

D-U-N-S 24-203-9829   (HQ)
AGRACITY CROP & NUTRITION LTD
320 22nd St E, Saskatoon, SK, S7K 0H1
(306) 665-2294
Sales 29,700,800
SIC 5191 Farm supplies
 Jason Mann
 James Mann

D-U-N-S 24-344-4200   (HQ)
AQUIFER DISTRIBUTION LTD
(*Suby of* AQUIFER INVESTMENTS LTD)
227 Venture Cres, Saskatoon, SK, S7K 6N8
(306) 242-1567
Emp Here 35   *Sales* 16,992,612
SIC 5074 Plumbing and heating equipment
and supplies (hydronics)
 Glenn Wig

D-U-N-S 24-343-6586   (HQ)
AQUIFER INVESTMENTS LTD
227a Venture Cres, Saskatoon, SK, S7K 6N8
(306) 242-1567
Emp Here 1   *Sales* 10,200,567
SIC 6719 Holding companies, nec
 Glenn Wig

D-U-N-S 24-265-2212   (SL)
AQUIFER PUMP DISTRIBUTING LTD
227a Venture Cres, Saskatoon, SK, S7K 6N8
(306) 242-1567
Emp Here 40   *Sales* 19,001,040
SIC 5084 Industrial machinery and equipment
 Glenn Wig
 Ian Corbett
 Dean Van Impe

D-U-N-S 24-314-0618   (BR)
ARDENT MILLS ULC
HORIZON MILLING
(*Suby of* CHS INC.)
95 33rd St E, Saskatoon, SK, S7K 0R8
(306) 665-7200
Emp Here 130
SIC 2044 Rice milling
 Cody Meyer

D-U-N-S 25-115-0140   (BR)
BAYER CROPSCIENCE INC
(*Suby of* BAYER AG)
5 Clumbers Hwy 41, Saskatoon, SK, S7K 7E9
(306) 477-9400
Emp Here 75
SIC 5191 Farm supplies
 Kennedy Brent

D-U-N-S 20-188-7390   (BR)
BELL MEDIA INC
CTV SASKATOON
(*Suby of* BCE INC)
216 1st Ave N, Saskatoon, SK, S7K 3W3
(306) 665-8600
Emp Here 75
SIC 4833 Television broadcasting stations
 Bonnie Mckenzie

D-U-N-S 24-648-7370   (BR)
**BOARD OF EDUCATION OF SASKA-
TOON SCHOOL DIVISION NO. 13 OF
SASKATCHEWAN, THE**
SASKATOON PUBLIC SCHOOLS
(*Suby of* BOARD OF EDUCATION OF
SASKATOON SCHOOL DIVISION NO. 13 OF
SASKATCHEWAN, THE)
310 21st St E, Saskatoon, SK, S7K 1M7
(306) 683-8200
Emp Here 150
SIC 8211 Elementary and secondary schools
 Avon Whittles

D-U-N-S 20-741-3048   (HQ)
**BOARD OF EDUCATION OF SASKA-
TOON SCHOOL DIVISION NO. 13 OF
SASKATCHEWAN, THE**
ADEN BOWMAN COLLEGIATE
310 21st St E, Saskatoon, SK, S7K 1M7
(306) 683-8200
Emp Here 120   *Sales* 221,658,181

SIC 8211 Elementary and secondary schools
 Avon Whittles
 Garry Benning
 Ray Morrison
 Kevin Waugh
 Darrell Utley
 Colleen Macpherson
 Dan Danielson
 Donna Banks
 Vernon Linklater
 Holly Kelleher

D-U-N-S 24-320-3876   (SL)
BRECK CONSTRUCTION
6 Cory Lane, Saskatoon, SK, S7K 3J7
(306) 242-5532
Emp Here 150   *Sales* 36,927,900
SIC 1799 Special trade contractors, nec
 Royan Stewart
 Bobbylynn Stewart

D-U-N-S 20-740-5101   (SL)
BRIS EQUITIES LTD
BUCKWOLD WESTERN
75 24th St E, Saskatoon, SK, S7K 0K3
(306) 652-1660
Emp Here 26   *Sales* 10,903,230
SIC 6712 Bank holding companies
 Bruce Buckwold

D-U-N-S 24-375-8604   (HQ)
BUCKWOLD WESTERN LTD
3239 Faithfull Ave Unit 70, Saskatoon, SK,
S7K 8H4
(306) 652-1660
Emp Here 20   *Sales* 71,921,000
SIC 5023 Homefurnishings
 Bruce Buckwold
 Blair Nusgart

D-U-N-S 24-128-6819   (SL)
BUHLER VERSATILE INDUSTRIES
North Corman Industrial Park, Saskatoon, SK,
S7K 0A1
(306) 931-3000
Emp Here 22   *Sales* 10,003,288
SIC 5033 Roofing, siding, and insulation

D-U-N-S 20-740-7180   (HQ)
BUTLER BYERS INSURANCE LTD
301 4th Ave N, Saskatoon, SK, S7K 2L8
(306) 653-2233
Emp Here 25   *Sales* 33,922,400
SIC 6411 Insurance agents, brokers, and ser-
vice
 J Drew Byers
 Karen Byers
 Barry Slowski
 John Shanks

D-U-N-S 20-336-8415   (SL)
**CANADA GOLDEN FORTUNE POTASH
CORP**
CGFPC
402 21st St E Unit 200, Saskatoon, SK, S7K
0C3
(306) 668-6877
Emp Here 49   *Sales* 10,118,217
SIC 1474 Potash, soda, and borate minerals
 Meidong Xiao

D-U-N-S 25-281-4298   (BR)
**CANADIAN CORPS OF COMMISSION-
AIRES NATIONAL OFFICE, THE**
*CANADIAN CORPS OF COMMISSION-
AIRES NORTH SASKACHEWAN, DIV OF*
(*Suby of* CANADIAN CORPS OF COMMIS-
SIONAIRES NATIONAL OFFICE, THE)
493 2nd Ave N, Saskatoon, SK, S7K 2C1
(306) 244-6588
Emp Here 459
SIC 7381 Detective and armored car services
 Ellis Anderson

D-U-N-S 20-282-1658   (SL)
CANNIMED LTD
(*Suby of* PRAIRIE PLANT SYSTEMS INC)
Rr 5 Lcd Main, Saskatoon, SK, S7K 3J8

(306) 975-1207
Emp Here 180   *Sales* 51,123,780
SIC 2834 Pharmaceutical preparations
 Brent Zettl

D-U-N-S 20-769-8457   (HQ)
CANPOTEX LIMITED
111 2nd Ave S Suite 400, Saskatoon, SK, S7K
3R7
(306) 931-2200
Emp Here 65   *Sales* 53,024,310
SIC 5191 Farm supplies
 Ken Seitz
 Greg Gabruch
 Derek Gross
 Vee Kachroo
 Matt Albrecht
 Donghai Du
 Nicole Johnston
 Quentin Kot
 Kendra Kuse
 Jon Somers

D-U-N-S 20-069-2333   (HQ)
CAVALIER ENTERPRISES LTD
SHERATON CAVALIER SASKATOON
(*Suby of* ALFOUR VENTURES INC)
620 Spadina Cres E, Saskatoon, SK, S7K 3T5
(306) 652-6770
Emp Here 250   *Sales* 52,617,400
SIC 7011 Hotels and motels
 Paul Leier
 Deloris Leier
 Mark Leier
 Scott Leier

D-U-N-S 20-740-5507   (HQ)
CHERRY INSURANCE LTD
350 3rd Ave S, Saskatoon, SK, S7K 1M5
(306) 653-2313
Emp Here 45   *Sales* 105,321,294
SIC 6411 Insurance agents, brokers, and ser-
vice
 Scott Cherry

D-U-N-S 24-913-8660   (HQ)
CLEARTECH HOLDINGS LTD
(*Suby of* J.W. YUEL HOLDINGS LTD)
1500 Quebec Ave, Saskatoon, SK, S7K 1V7
(306) 664-2522
Emp Here 1   *Sales* 27,335,000
SIC 6712 Bank holding companies
 Randy Bracewell

D-U-N-S 25-095-0441   (HQ)
CLEARTECH INDUSTRIES INC
(*Suby of* J.W. YUEL HOLDINGS LTD)
1500 Quebec Ave, Saskatoon, SK, S7K 1V7
(306) 664-2522
Emp Here 90   *Sales* 91,861,560
SIC 2819 Industrial inorganic chemicals, nec
 Randy Bracewell
 James Yuel
 Hugh Macgowan
 Greg Yuel

D-U-N-S 25-095-0391   (HQ)
**CLEARTECH INDUSTRIES LIMITED PART-
NERSHIP**
1500 Quebec Ave, Saskatoon, SK, S7K 1V7
(306) 664-2522
Sales 70,582,260
SIC 5169 Chemicals and allied products, nec
 James Yuel
 Chris Mighton

D-U-N-S 24-234-0446   (SL)
**CO-OPERATIVE SUPERANNUATION SOCI-
ETY**
333 3rd Ave N Suite 501, Saskatoon, SK, S7K
2M2
(306) 244-1539
Emp Here 12   *Sales* 12,418,572
SIC 6371 Pension, health, and welfare funds
 Gary Mearns

D-U-N-S 20-843-8192   (HQ)
COLLIERS MCCLOCKLIN REAL ESTATE

CORP
728 Spadina Cres E Suite 101, Saskatoon,
SK, S7K 3H2
(306) 653-4410
Emp Here 45   *Sales* 13,587,800
SIC 6531 Real estate agents and managers
 Tom Mcclocklin Jr

D-U-N-S 24-112-0153   (HQ)
COMMUNITY ELECTRIC LTD
CEL
(*Suby of* 101015170 SASKATCHEWAN LTD)
811 58th St E, Saskatoon, SK, S7K 6X5
(306) 477-8822
Emp Here 15   *Sales* 12,851,911
SIC 1731 Electrical work
 Willie Unger
 Sharon Unger

D-U-N-S 20-546-8127   (SL)
**COMMUNITY HEALTH SERVICES (SASKA-
TOON) ASSOCIATION LIMITED**
SASKATOON COMMUNITY CLINIC
455 2nd Ave N, Saskatoon, SK, S7K 2C2
(306) 652-0300
Emp Here 105   *Sales* 19,971,735
SIC 8011 Offices and clinics of medical doc-
tors
 Anne Doucette
 Glen Kovatch
 Mealanie Medlicott
 Michelle Robson
 Ron Wheeler

D-U-N-S 20-914-8373   (BR)
COMPASS GROUP CANADA LTD
(*Suby of* COMPASS GROUP PLC)
35 22nd St E, Saskatoon, SK, S7K 0C8
(306) 975-7790
Emp Here 86
SIC 5812 Eating places
 Vinod Rana

D-U-N-S 20-839-6044   (HQ)
CONCENTRA BANK
333 3rd Ave N, Saskatoon, SK, S7K 2M2
(306) 956-5100
Emp Here 190   *Sales* 157,135,401
SIC 6021 National commercial banks
 Kevin Kosolofski
 Brian Guillemin
 Brian Wilson
 Lise De Moissac
 Peter Enns
 Perry Erhardt
 Stephen Fitzpatrick
 Anne Gillespie
 Bob Hague
 Daniel Johnson

D-U-N-S 20-017-2083   (SL)
**CONSTRUCTION FASTENERS & TOOLS
LTD**
(*Suby of* EDMONTON FASTENERS &
TOOLS LTD)
504 45th A St E, Saskatoon, SK, S7K 0W7
(306) 668-8880
Emp Here 32   *Sales* 15,200,832
SIC 5085 Industrial supplies
 William Howson
 Barry Marshall
 Gerry Miller
 Ross Nykiforuk
 Brad Kennedy

D-U-N-S 24-346-3408   (BR)
**CORPORATION DE SECURITE GARDA
WORLD**
(*Suby of* GW INTERMEDIATE HOLDCO
CORPORATION)
316 2nd Ave N, Saskatoon, SK, S7K 2B9
(306) 242-3330
Emp Here 95
SIC 7381 Detective and armored car services
 Quenton Robinn

D-U-N-S 20-071-2953   (SL)

COSMOPOLITAN INDUSTRIES GOLF CANADA LTD
COSMO GOLF CANADA
(*Suby of* COSMOPOLITAN INDUSTRIES LTD)
1302b Alberta Ave, Saskatoon, SK, S7K 1R5
(306) 477-4653
Emp Here 25   *Sales* 13,013,550
SIC 5091 Sporting and recreation goods
Peter Gerrard

D-U-N-S 20-741-0895   (HQ)
COSMOPOLITAN INDUSTRIES LTD
28 34th St E, Saskatoon, SK, S7K 3Y2
(306) 664-3158
Sales 19,476,800
SIC 2611 Pulp mills
Peter Gerrard
Allan Hunter
Craig Newby
Howard Stensrud
Grant Habicht

D-U-N-S 20-688-8815   (SL)
D. KRAHN INSURANCE & FINANCIAL SERVICES INC
75 Lenore Dr Suite 1, Saskatoon, SK, S7K 7Y1
(306) 384-7216
Emp Here 12   *Sales* 12,418,572
SIC 6321 Accident and health insurance
David Krahn

D-U-N-S 24-172-0184   (BR)
DELOITTE LLP
(*Suby of* DELOITTE LLP)
122 1st Ave S Suite 400, Saskatoon, SK, S7K 7E5
(306) 343-4400
Emp Here 100
SIC 8721 Accounting, auditing, and bookkeeping
Marla Adams

D-U-N-S 24-496-4441   (SL)
DUNMAC GENERAL CONTRACTORS LTD
3038 Faithfull Ave, Saskatoon, SK, S7K 0B1
(306) 934-3044
Emp Here 30   *Sales* 14,121,930
SIC 1542 Nonresidential construction, nec
Fraser Sutherland
Michael Trudgian

D-U-N-S 24-236-6490   (HQ)
DYNAINDUSTRIAL INC
(*Suby of* DYNAVENTURE CORP)
3326 Faithfull Ave, Saskatoon, SK, S7K 8H1
(306) 933-4303
Emp Here 20   *Sales* 26,640,120
SIC 3532 Mining machinery
Darren Craig

D-U-N-S 24-819-5315   (BR)
EARL'S RESTAURANTS LTD
EARL'S
(*Suby of* EARL'S RESTAURANTS LTD)
610 2nd Ave N, Saskatoon, SK, S7K 2C8
(306) 664-4060
Emp Here 200
SIC 5812 Eating places
Brad Laidlaw

D-U-N-S 20-069-4438   (HQ)
ENS MOTORS LTD
ENS COLLISION CENTRE
285 Venture Cres, Saskatoon, SK, S7K 6N8
(306) 653-5611
Emp Here 1   *Sales* 45,308,160
SIC 5511 New and used car dealers
Joshua Ens

D-U-N-S 25-409-2299   (SL)
ENVIROTEC SERVICES INCORPORATED
100 Cory Rd, Saskatoon, SK, S7K 8B7
(306) 244-9500
Emp Here 150   *Sales* 40,147,800
SIC 5211 Lumber and other building materials
Terry Loraas

D-U-N-S 24-384-8269   (SL)
FARMS AND FAMILIES OF NORTH AMERICA INCORPORATED
FARMERS OF NORTH AMERICA
320 22nd St E, Saskatoon, SK, S7K 0H1
(306) 665-2294
Emp Here 50   *Sales* 11,581,650
SIC 8621 Professional organizations
James Mann
Don Slobodzian

D-U-N-S 24-968-1396   (HQ)
FASTENER WAREHOUSE LTD
820 46th St E, Saskatoon, SK, S7K 3V7
(306) 374-1199
Emp Here 38   *Sales* 20,426,118
SIC 5085 Industrial supplies
Kim Weimer
Robert Weimer

D-U-N-S 24-850-9994   (BR)
FEDERATED CO-OPERATIVES LIMITED
FCL CO-OP WAREHOUSE SASKATOON
(*Suby of* FEDERATED CO-OPERATIVES LIMITED)
607 46th St E, Saskatoon, SK, S7K 0X1

Emp Here 200
SIC 5141 Groceries, general line
Jim Mcclelland

D-U-N-S 25-742-4445   (BR)
FEDERATED CO-OPERATIVES LIMITED
(*Suby of* FEDERATED CO-OPERATIVES LIMITED)
604 45th St E, Saskatoon, SK, S7K 3T3
(306) 242-1505
Emp Here 250
SIC 4225 General warehousing and storage
Jodie Stone

D-U-N-S 20-069-4693   (HQ)
FEDERATED CO-OPERATIVES LIMITED
401 22nd St E, Saskatoon, SK, S7K 0H2
(306) 244-3311
Emp Here 500   *Sales* 7,932,847
SIC 4225 General warehousing and storage

D-U-N-S 25-636-6899   (HQ)
FIRST NATIONS BANK OF CANADA
224 4th Ave S Suite 406, Saskatoon, SK, S7K 5M5
(306) 955-6739
Emp Here 13   *Sales* 10,126,765
SIC 6021 National commercial banks
Keith Martell
Cheryl Foster
Ryan Larose
Greig Cooper
Sam Siwy
Kevin Michael
Leigh Solomon
Bill Namagoose
Vivian Abdelmessih
Christopher Dyrda

D-U-N-S 24-346-8985   (SL)
FORTIS ENGINEERING & MANUFACTURING INC
(*Suby of* NORTHERN STRANDS CO. LTD)
802 57th St E, Saskatoon, SK, S7K 5Z2
(306) 242-4427
Emp Here 40   *Sales* 17,886,960
SIC 5051 Metals service centers and offices
Garry Clark

D-U-N-S 24-230-0663   (HQ)
FRONTIER PETERBILT SALES LTD
FRONTIER LEASE & RENTAL
(*Suby of* CERVUS EQUIPMENT CORPORATION)
303 50th St E, Saskatoon, SK, S7K 6C1
(306) 242-3411
Emp Here 70   *Sales* 126,995,440
SIC 5511 New and used car dealers
Peter Lacey

D-U-N-S 25-115-4589   (HQ)

FULL LINE AG SALES LTD
2 Yellowhead Industrial Park Lot 2 Rr 4 Lcd Main, Saskatoon, SK, S7K 3J7
(306) 934-1546
Sales 12,705,056
SIC 5999 Miscellaneous retail stores, nec
Terry Swystun
Richard Risdale
Gerald Swystun

D-U-N-S 20-855-1663   (HQ)
G. J. BELL ENTERPISES LTD
BELL TRAILER SALES
2030 1st Ave N, Saskatoon, SK, S7K 2A1
(306) 242-1251
Emp Here 35   *Sales* 21,852,900
SIC 5012 Automobiles and other motor vehicles
Gordon J Bell

D-U-N-S 25-640-2785   (HQ)
GALON MANAGEMENT LTD
GALON INSURANCE BROKERS
909 3rd Ave N, Saskatoon, SK, S7K 2K4
(306) 244-7000
Emp Here 12   *Sales* 25,441,800
SIC 6411 Insurance agents, brokers, and service
Phil Galon

D-U-N-S 20-069-5195   (SL)
GEM CAFE LTD
JOHN'S PRIME RIB & STEAK HOUSE
401 21st St E, Saskatoon, SK, S7K 0C5

Emp Here 25   *Sales* 10,483,875
SIC 6712 Bank holding companies
Jack Chrones

D-U-N-S 20-853-1087   (BR)
GLACIER MEDIA INC
WESTERN PRODUCER PUBLICATIONS
(*Suby of* GLACIER MEDIA INC)
2310 Millar Ave, Saskatoon, SK, S7K 2Y2
(306) 665-3500
Emp Here 75
SIC 2711 Newspapers
Zacharias Ken

D-U-N-S 24-368-4516   (SL)
GOLDEN OPPORTUNITIES FUND INC
410 22nd St E Suite 830, Saskatoon, SK, S7K 5T6
(306) 652-5557
Emp Here 10   *Sales* 14,120,809
SIC 6282 Investment advice
Grant Kook
Douglas Banzet

D-U-N-S 25-482-7389   (BR)
GRAHAM GROUP LTD
GRAHAM INDUSTRIAL SERVICES A JV
(*Suby of* GRAHAM GROUP LTD)
875 57th St E, Saskatoon, SK, S7K 5Z2
(306) 934-6644
Emp Here 120
SIC 1541 Industrial buildings and warehouses
Tom Holseld

D-U-N-S 24-038-8140   (SL)
GRANDWEST ENTERPRISES INC
TIGER AUTOMOTIVE DIV OF
815 Circle Dr E, Saskatoon, SK, S7K 3S4
(306) 665-7555
Emp Here 100   *Sales* 62,928,000
SIC 5511 New and used car dealers
George Reddekopp

D-U-N-S 24-818-2933   (HQ)
GREAT WESTERN BREWING COMPANY LIMITED
519 2nd Ave N, Saskatoon, SK, S7K 2C6
(306) 653-4653
Sales 34,569,000
SIC 2082 Malt beverages
Michael Micovcin
Vauhn Wyant
Maurice Duval

Wayne Brownlee
Michael Shaw

D-U-N-S 24-630-6138   (SL)
GREGG'S PLUMBING & HEATING LTD
503 51st St E, Saskatoon, SK, S7K 6V4
(306) 373-4664
Emp Here 50   *Sales* 11,046,700
SIC 1711 Plumbing, heating, air-conditioning
James Gregg

D-U-N-S 20-842-8805   (SL)
HAMM CONSTRUCTION LTD
126 English Cres, Saskatoon, SK, S7K 8A5
(306) 931-6626
Emp Here 120   *Sales* 30,293,040
SIC 1623 Water, sewer, and utility lines
Robert Hamm
Margaret Hamm
Bradley Hamm

D-U-N-S 24-775-2629   (SL)
HARMON INTERNATIONAL INDUSTRIES INC
BLANCHARD FOUNDRY, DIVISION OF
2401 Millar Ave, Saskatoon, SK, S7K 2Y4
(306) 931-1161
Emp Here 60   *Sales* 13,320,060
SIC 3523 Farm machinery and equipment
Calvin Moneo
Victor Moneo
Dennis Bergeron
Stan Tait

D-U-N-S 24-237-9043   (SL)
HCC MINING AND DEMOLITION INC
Rr 5 Lcd Main, Saskatoon, SK, S7K 3J8
(306) 652-4168
Emp Here 60   *Sales* 14,006,100
SIC 1241 Coal mining services
Rylan Colwell

D-U-N-S 24-630-2327   (SL)
HERGOTT DUVAL STACK LLP
410 22nd St E Suite 1200, Saskatoon, SK, S7K 5T6
(306) 934-8000
Emp Here 120   *Sales* 24,922,200
SIC 8721 Accounting, auditing, and bookkeeping
Tom Stack
Ryan Ball
Tim Timmerman
Wes Unger
Joe Parker
Barry Frank
Blair Davidson
Bernie Broughton
Craig Hermann
Carol Mailloux

D-U-N-S 25-685-2070   (BR)
HOME DEPOT OF CANADA INC
HOME DEPOT
(*Suby of* THE HOME DEPOT INC)
707 Circle Dr E, Saskatoon, SK, S7K 0V1
(306) 651-6250
Emp Here 225
SIC 5251 Hardware stores
Cindy Moslenko

D-U-N-S 20-069-6599   (BR)
HUDSON'S BAY COMPANY
BAY, THE
(*Suby of* HUDSON'S BAY COMPANY)
201 1st Ave S, Saskatoon, SK, S7K 1J5
(306) 242-7611
Emp Here 200
SIC 5311 Department stores
Bruce Mcgregor

D-U-N-S 20-854-5293   (SL)
HUTTERIAN BRETHREN LTD
RIVERVIEW COLONY
Gd Stn Main, Saskatoon, SK, S7K 3J4
(306) 242-5652
Emp Here 62   *Sales* 16,263,158
SIC 0119 Cash grains, nec

Paul Tschetter

D-U-N-S 24-967-6016   (HQ)
INDEPENDENT FINANCIAL SERVICES LTD
1001 3rd Ave N, Saskatoon, SK, S7K 2K5
(306) 244-7385
Emp Here 38   *Sales* 23,904,315
SIC 6211 Security brokers and dealers
George Clark
Jerome Meckelborg
Mark Lord

D-U-N-S 20-065-9394   (SL)
INDUSTRIAL MACHINE & MFG. INC
3315 Miners Ave, Saskatoon, SK, S7K 7K9
(306) 242-8400
Emp Here 75   *Sales* 16,650,075
SIC 3599 Industrial machinery, nec
Thomas Foster

D-U-N-S 20-280-8929   (SL)
INNOVATIVE RESIDENTIAL INVESTMENTS INC
101b English Cres, Saskatoon, SK, S7K 8G4
(306) 979-7421
Emp Here 70   *Sales* 14,271,810
SIC 6553 Cemetery subdividers and developers
Alex Miller
Tyler Mathies

D-U-N-S 24-376-7555   (SL)
INTER WEST MECHANICAL LTD
INTER WEST
1839 Saskatchewan Ave, Saskatoon, SK, S7K 1R1
(306) 955-1800
Emp Here 50   *Sales* 11,046,700
SIC 1711 Plumbing, heating, air-conditioning
Kenneth Swann
Ronald Charlebois

D-U-N-S 25-679-2573   (SL)
INTERACTIVE TRACKING SYSTEMS INC
ITRACKS
820 51st St E Suite 150, Saskatoon, SK, S7K 0X8
(306) 665-5026
Emp Here 70   *Sales* 11,380,880
SIC 7379 Computer related services, nec
Daniel Weber
Garnette Weber

D-U-N-S 24-230-1539   (HQ)
INTERNATIONAL ROAD DYNAMICS INC
IRD
702 43rd St E, Saskatoon, SK, S7K 3T9
(306) 653-6600
Emp Here 150   *Sales* 49,335,301
SIC 4785 Inspection and fixed facilities
Randy Hanson
Sharon M Parker
David Cortens
Arthur T Bergan
Harvey M Alton
Ray Harris
C. Michael Walton
Ray Kolla

D-U-N-S 24-805-5001   (HQ)
K+S POTASH CANADA GENERAL PARTNERSHIP
(*Suby of* K+S AG)
220 Wall St, Saskatoon, SK, S7K 3Y3
(306) 385-8000
Sales 36,214,304
SIC 1474 Potash, soda, and borate minerals
Ulrich Lamp
Hans Uli Boedicker
Sam Farris
Eric Cline
Colin Braithwaite
Thomas Papst

D-U-N-S 24-375-6855   (HQ)
K.W. PETROLEUM SERVICES LTD
849 56th St E, Saskatoon, SK, S7K 5Y9

(306) 244-4468
Emp Here 101   *Sales* 55,601,220
SIC 5084 Industrial machinery and equipment
Richard Duval
Christopher Mcmurtry
Terry Lightbody

D-U-N-S 24-378-3227   (BR)
KAMTECH SERVICES INC
3339 Faithfull Ave, Saskatoon, SK, S7K 8H5
(306) 931-9655
Emp Here 100
SIC 1711 Plumbing, heating, air-conditioning

D-U-N-S 24-134-9666   (SL)
KELSEY PIPELINES LTD
107-3239 Faithfull Ave, Saskatoon, SK, S7K 8H4
(306) 385-6285
Emp Here 70   *Sales* 18,868,430
SIC 4619 Pipelines, nec
Richard Clunie

D-U-N-S 20-069-7449   (HQ)
KINDERSLEY TRANSPORT LTD
(*Suby of* EKS HOLDINGS LTD)
2411 Wentz Ave, Saskatoon, SK, S7K 3V6
(306) 975-9367
Emp Here 60   *Sales* 138,285,750
SIC 4213 Trucking, except local
Erwen Siemens
Douglas Siemens

D-U-N-S 20-107-8560   (BR)
KINDERSLEY TRANSPORT LTD
KINDERSLEY TRANSPORT TERMINAL
(*Suby of* EKS HOLDINGS LTD)
2411 Wentz Ave, Saskatoon, SK, S7K 3V6
(306) 242-3355
Emp Here 150
SIC 4213 Trucking, except local
Ronald Cake

D-U-N-S 20-028-1565   (SL)
LIGHTHOUSE SUPPORTED LIVING
304 2nd Ave S, Saskatoon, SK, S7K 1L1
(306) 653-0538
Emp Here 100   *Sales* 7,469,400
SIC 7363 Help supply services
Don Windels

D-U-N-S 25-645-3937   (BR)
LOBLAWS INC
EXTRA FOODS NO. 9061
(*Suby of* LOBLAW COMPANIES LIMITED)
2815 Wanuskewin Rd, Saskatoon, SK, S7K 8E6
(306) 249-9200
Emp Here 100
SIC 5411 Grocery stores
Gary Betker

D-U-N-S 20-447-3375   (HQ)
LORAAS DISPOSAL SERVICES LTD
805 47th St E, Saskatoon, SK, S7K 8G7
(306) 242-2300
Emp Here 80   *Sales* 51,025,600
SIC 4953 Refuse systems
Bruce Loraas
Carman Loraas

D-U-N-S 24-426-9973   (HQ)
LYDALE CONSTRUCTION (1983) CO. LTD
859 58th St E, Saskatoon, SK, S7K 6X5
(306) 934-6116
Emp Here 50   *Sales* 33,867,750
SIC 1521 Single-family housing construction
Blaine Jackson
Ken Conn

D-U-N-S 24-230-6173   (HQ)
MACHIBRODA, P. ENGINEERING LTD
806 48th St E, Saskatoon, SK, S7K 3Y4
(306) 665-8444
Emp Here 50   *Sales* 15,228,720
SIC 8748 Business consulting, nec
Fran Machibroda
Ray Machibroda

D-U-N-S 20-035-2164   (SL)
MARCH CONSULTING ASSOCIATES INC
201 21st St E Suite 200, Saskatoon, SK, S7K 0B8
(306) 651-6330
Emp Here 100   *Sales* 17,595,800
SIC 8711 Engineering services
Henry Feldkamp

D-U-N-S 25-927-7270   (HQ)
MBI PACIFIC DRILLING PRODUCTS LTD
3150 Faithfull Ave, Saskatoon, SK, S7K 8H3
(306) 955-9560
Sales 11,875,650
SIC 5084 Industrial machinery and equipment
Jeff Campbell

D-U-N-S 24-429-1381   (HQ)
MCKERCHER LLP
374 3rd Ave S, Saskatoon, SK, S7K 1M5
(306) 653-2000
Sales 11,864,374
SIC 8111 Legal services
Brenda Lang

D-U-N-S 20-034-7032   (HQ)
MDH ENGINEERED SOLUTIONS CORP
(*Suby of* GROUPE SNC-LAVALIN INC)
216 1st Ave S, Saskatoon, SK, S7K 1K3
(306) 934-7527
Emp Here 53   *Sales* 13,481,730
SIC 7373 Computer integrated systems design
Moir D H Haug

D-U-N-S 20-840-1836   (HQ)
MEDICAL SERVICES INCORPORATED
SASKATCHEWAN BLUE CROSS
516 2nd Ave N, Saskatoon, SK, S7K 2C5
(306) 244-1192
Emp Here 100   *Sales* 320,545,200
SIC 6321 Accident and health insurance
Arnie Arnott
Brian Molberg
Stu Irvine
Penny Carter
David Patola
Janice Wallace
Todd Peterson

D-U-N-S 20-070-4997   (HQ)
MEGA GROUP INC
MULTI MEUBLES
720 1st Ave N, Saskatoon, SK, S7K 6R9
(306) 242-7366
Emp Here 45   *Sales* 58,604,947
SIC 5064 Electrical appliances, television and radio
Benoit Simard
Richard Wall
Denis Riel
Randy Saler
Michel Tardif
Wayne Hambly
Konrad Kozan
Phil Brewer
John Mclellan
Jeff Macdonald

D-U-N-S 24-314-4859   (SL)
MERIDIAN DEVELOPMENT CORP
450 2nd Ave N Unit 100, Saskatoon, SK, S7K 2C3
(306) 384-0431
Emp Here 60   *Sales* 16,256,520
SIC 1522 Residential construction, nec
Karl Miller
Colleen Wilson

D-U-N-S 24-389-5369   (HQ)
MERIDIAN SURVEYS LTD
3111 Millar Ave Suite 1, Saskatoon, SK, S7K 6N3
(306) 934-1818
Emp Here 37   *Sales* 10,724,340
SIC 8713 Surveying services
Max Putnam

Stuart Hayward
Michael Waschuk
Robert Morrison
Lee Anderson
Murray Redoux
Calvin Fowler

D-U-N-S 20-109-0433   (BR)
MLT AIKINS LLP
MLP
(*Suby of* MLT AIKINS LLP)
410 22nd St E Suite 1500, Saskatoon, SK, S7K 5T6
(306) 975-7100
Emp Here 90
SIC 8111 Legal services
Danny Anderson

D-U-N-S 20-372-7680   (SL)
MOODY'S EQUIPMENT LP
71st St Hwy 16, Saskatoon, SK, S7K 3K1
(306) 934-4686
Emp Here 100   *Sales* 47,502,600
SIC 5083 Farm and garden machinery
Kim Leland
Leanne Parson

D-U-N-S 20-118-7494   (HQ)
MOODY'S EQUIPMENT LTD
71 St & Hwy Suite 16, Saskatoon, SK, S7K 3K1
(306) 934-4686
Emp Here 43   *Sales* 38,002,080
SIC 5083 Farm and garden machinery
John Mathison
Daryl Moody

D-U-N-S 24-265-1388   (HQ)
NORTEK AIR SOLUTIONS CANADA, INC
(*Suby of* VENMAR VENTILATION ULC)
1502d Quebec Ave, Saskatoon, SK, S7K 1V7
(306) 242-3663
Emp Here 105   *Sales* 89,318,886
SIC 3564 Blowers and fans
Michael Clark
Ada Lacoursiere

D-U-N-S 24-375-1450   (HQ)
NORTH RIDGE DEVELOPMENT CORPORATION
3037 Faithfull Ave, Saskatoon, SK, S7K 8B3
(306) 242-2434
Emp Here 95   *Sales* 35,222,460
SIC 1522 Residential construction, nec
Walter Mah
Julius Calyniuk

D-U-N-S 24-631-2011   (HQ)
NORTHERN RESOURCE TRUCKING LIMITED PARTNERSHIP
NRT
2945 Millar Ave, Saskatoon, SK, S7K 6P6
(306) 933-3010
Sales 28,798,840
SIC 4213 Trucking, except local
Dave Mcilmoyl

D-U-N-S 20-601-1363   (HQ)
NORTHERN STRANDS CO. LTD
3235 Millar Ave, Saskatoon, SK, S7K 5Y3
(306) 242-7073
Emp Here 26   *Sales* 17,125,800
SIC 5051 Metals service centers and offices
Darrell Mote
Gary Clarke

D-U-N-S 20-070-0334   (SL)
NUTANA MACHINE LTD
(*Suby of* GREEN & GOLD VENTURE FUND (PRINCE ALBERT) LTD)
2615 1st Ave N, Saskatoon, SK, S7K 6E9
(306) 242-3822
Emp Here 50   *Sales* 11,100,050
SIC 3532 Mining machinery
Donald Galbraith

D-U-N-S 20-337-8927   (HQ)
NUTRIEN LTD

RETAIL
122 1st Ave S Suite 500, Saskatoon, SK, S7K
7G3
(306) 933-8500
Emp Here 250   *Sales* 8,892,900,000
SIC 2873 Nitrogenous fertilizers
   Charles (Chuck) Magro
   Derek Pannell
   Wayne Brownlee
   Henry Deans
   Steve Douglas
   Michael J. Frank
   Kevin Graham
   Susan Jones
   Lee Knafelc
   Leslie O'donoghue

   D-U-N-S 25-649-0434   (SL)
OBRIANS
2112 Millar Ave, Saskatoon, SK, S7K 6P4
(306) 955-5626
Emp Here 40   *Sales* 19,923,120
SIC 5521 Used car dealers
   Brett Finell

   D-U-N-S 24-359-2198   (SL)
PARK TOWN ENTERPRISES LTD
PARK TOWN HOTEL
924 Spadina Cres E, Saskatoon, SK, S7K 3H5
(306) 244-5564
Emp Here 120   *Sales* 11,122,800
SIC 7011 Hotels and motels
   Terry Verbeke

   D-U-N-S 20-833-4425   (HQ)
PCS SALES (CANADA) INC
(*Suby of* NUTRIEN LTD)
122 1st Ave S Suite 500, Saskatoon, SK, S7K
7G3
(306) 933-8500
Emp Here 27   *Sales* 51,889,152
SIC 1474 Potash, soda, and borate minerals
   Jochen Tilk
   G David Delaney
   Wayne R Brownlee

   D-U-N-S 25-682-7627   (SL)
PEAK MECHANICAL LTD
PEAK MECHANICAL PARTNERSHIP
409 45th A St E, Saskatoon, SK, S7K 0W6
(306) 249-4814
Emp Here 65   *Sales* 15,149,225
SIC 1711 Plumbing, heating, air-conditioning
   Randy Steinhauer
   Keith Weisgerber
   David Flamand

   D-U-N-S 20-853-8009   (HQ)
PIC INVESTMENT GROUP INC
ADVENTURE DESTINATIONS INTERNA-
TIONAL
(*Suby of* J.W. YUEL HOLDINGS LTD)
70 24th St E, Saskatoon, SK, S7K 4B8
(306) 664-3955
Emp Here 5   *Sales* 127,928,150
SIC 6712 Bank holding companies
   James Yuel
   Hugh Macgowan
   Greg Yuel

   D-U-N-S 20-383-5496   (SL)
PIVOT FURNITURE TECHNOLOGIES INC
142 English Cres Unit 20, Saskatoon, SK, S7K
8A5
(306) 220-4557
Emp Here 65   *Sales* 10,567,960
SIC 7379 Computer related services, nec
   Brendon Sled

   D-U-N-S 24-000-8727   (BR)
POSTMEDIA NETWORK INC
POSTMEDIA NETWORK
(*Suby of* POSTMEDIA NETWORK CANADA
CORP)
204 5th Ave N, Saskatoon, SK, S7K 2P1
(306) 657-6206
Emp Here 300

SIC 2711 Newspapers
   Rhonda Exner

   D-U-N-S 25-831-8658   (BR)
POTASH   CORPORATION   OF
SASKATCHEWAN INC
CORY MINE, DIV OF
(*Suby of* NUTRIEN LTD)
7 Miles West On Hwy 7, Saskatoon, SK, S7K
3N9
(306) 382-0525
Emp Here 300
SIC 1474 Potash, soda, and borate minerals
   Leon Boehm

   D-U-N-S 24-819-0209   (HQ)
POTASH   CORPORATION   OF
SASKATCHEWAN INC
PCS CORY, DIV
(*Suby of* NUTRIEN LTD)
122 1st Ave S Suite 500, Saskatoon, SK, S7K
7G3
(306) 933-8500
Emp Here 350   *Sales* 4,456,000,000
SIC 1474 Potash, soda, and borate minerals
   Jochen Tilk
   Wayne R Brownlee
   Joseph Podwika
   John W. Estey
   C Steven Hoffman
   Alice D Laberge
   Keith G Martell
   Jeffery J Mccaig
   Elena Viyella De Paliza
   Christopher M Burley

   D-U-N-S 24-378-9778   (SL)
PRAIRIE MACHINE & PARTS MFG. - PART-
NERSHIP
3311 Millar Ave, Saskatoon, SK, S7K 5Y5
(306) 933-4812
Emp Here 150   *Sales* 33,300,150
SIC 3532 Mining machinery
   Mark Davidson

   D-U-N-S 20-740-6604   (HQ)
PRAIRIE MEATS
2326 Millar Ave, Saskatoon, SK, S7K 2Y2
(306) 244-4024
Emp Here 1   *Sales* 58,490,390
SIC 5147 Meats and meat products
   Gene Dupuis
   Adele Dupuis
   Cheryl Dupuis

   D-U-N-S 24-889-9929   (BR)
PRAXAIR CANADA INC
(*Suby of* LINDE PUBLIC LIMITED COM-
PANY)
834 51st St E Suite 5, Saskatoon, SK, S7K
5C7
(306) 242-3325
Emp Here 1,700
SIC 2813 Industrial gases
   Brenda Mcleod

   D-U-N-S 24-373-2232   (HQ)
Q-LINE TRUCKING LTD
(*Suby of* ANDERSON TRUCKING SERVICE
INC)
101 Wurtz Ave, Saskatoon, SK, S7K 3J7
(306) 651-3540
Emp Here 345   *Sales* 102,874,441
SIC 4213 Trucking, except local
   Reginald Quiring
   Russell Quiring

   D-U-N-S 20-278-9405   (SL)
R & D DRYWALL INC
211a 47th St E, Saskatoon, SK, S7K 5H1
(306) 933-9328
Emp Here 65   *Sales* 10,554,765
SIC 1742 Plastering, drywall, and insulation
   Roland Houle

   D-U-N-S 20-583-1873   (SL)
RADISSON HOTEL SASKATOON
405 20th St E, Saskatoon, SK, S7K 6X6

(306) 665-3322
Emp Here 140   *Sales* 12,976,600
SIC 7011 Hotels and motels
   Patty Schweighardt

   D-U-N-S 25-642-6560   (SL)
RE/MAX SASKATOON NORTH
227 Primrose Dr Suite 200, Saskatoon, SK,
S7K 5E4
(306) 934-0909
Emp Here 45   *Sales* 12,229,020
SIC 6531 Real estate agents and managers
   Larry Stewart

   D-U-N-S 24-642-1080   (BR)
REDHEAD EQUIPMENT LTD
(*Suby of* REDHEAD EQUIPMENT LTD)
9010 North Service Road, Saskatoon, SK,
S7K 7E8
(306) 931-4600
Emp Here 100
SIC 5571 Motorcycle dealers
   Richard Scott

   D-U-N-S 25-057-8887   (SL)
RELY-EX CONTRACTING INC
STEEL MET SUPPLY, DIV OF
516 43rd St E, Saskatoon, SK, S7K 0V6
(306) 664-2155
Emp Here 33   *Sales* 15,534,123
SIC 1542 Nonresidential construction, nec
   Richard (Rick) Leier
   Cheryl Leier

   D-U-N-S 20-070-1753   (HQ)
REMAI INVESTMENT CORPORATION
THRIFT LODGE
500 Spadina Cres E Suite 101, Saskatoon,
SK, S7K 4H9
(306) 244-1119
Emp Here 7   *Sales* 28,700,400
SIC 7011 Hotels and motels
   John V. Remai
   Sonya Prescesky
   Darrell J. Remai

   D-U-N-S 20-335-3362   (BR)
RUSSEL METALS INC
RUSSEL METAL PROCESSING
(*Suby of* RUSSEL METALS INC)
503 50th St E, Saskatoon, SK, S7K 6H3
(306) 244-7511
Emp Here 175
SIC 3599 Industrial machinery, nec

   D-U-N-S 24-320-3881   (HQ)
SASKATCHEWAN HEALTH AUTHORITY
(*Suby   of   GOVERNMENT   OF
SASKATCHEWAN*)
701 Queen St, Saskatoon, SK, S7K 0M7
(306) 655-0080
Sales 16,064,600
SIC 8011 Offices and clinics of medical doc-
tors
   Scott Livingstone
   Beth Vachon
   Robbie Peters
   Kim Mckechney
   Lori Frank
   Suann Laurent

   D-U-N-S 20-080-2861   (BR)
SASKATCHEWAN INDIAN INSTITUTE OF
TECHNOLOGIES
229 4th Ave S Suite 201, Saskatoon, SK, S7K
4K3
(306) 373-4777
Emp Here 100
SIC 8299 Schools and educational services,
nec
   Riel Belletarde

   D-U-N-S 25-021-9169   (HQ)
SASKATCHEWAN LEGAL AID COMMIS-
SION, THE
(*Suby   of   GOVERNMENT   OF
SASKATCHEWAN*)
201 21st St E Suite 502, Saskatoon, SK, S7K

0B8
(306) 933-5300
Emp Here 10   *Sales* 17,741,120
SIC 8111 Legal services
   Jerome Boyko
   Dona Jones

   D-U-N-S 20-740-4989   (SL)
SASKATCHEWAN MUTUAL INSURANCE
COMPANY
279 3rd Ave N, Saskatoon, SK, S7K 2H8
(306) 653-4232
Emp Here 75   *Sales* 138,499,425
SIC 6331 Fire, marine, and casualty insurance
   L.M. Wiete
   Shelley F Willick

   D-U-N-S 25-645-4943   (SL)
SASKATCHEWAN PLAYWRIGHTS' CEN-
TRE
601 Spadina Cres E Suite 700, Saskatoon,
SK, S7K 3G8
(306) 665-7707
Emp Here 29   *Sales* 11,525,006
SIC 8699 Membership organizations, nec
   Bethani Jade

   D-U-N-S 20-842-0505   (HQ)
SASKATCHEWAN POLYTECHNIC
SASKATOON
(*Suby   of   GOVERNMENT   OF
SASKATCHEWAN*)
119 4th Ave S Suite 400, Saskatoon, SK, S7K
5X2
(866) 467-4278
Emp Here 65   *Sales* 158,590,400
SIC 8222 Junior colleges
   Robert Mcculloch
   Cheryl Mcmillan
   Alan Thomarat
   Jim Plewis
   Donna Birkmaier
   Ralph Boychuck
   Neil Buechler
   Brittany Holderness
   Bob Loewen
   Jean Morrison

   D-U-N-S 20-070-2454   (HQ)
SASKATOON BOILER MFG CO LTD
SASKATOON BOILER
2011 Quebec Ave, Saskatoon, SK, S7K 1W5
(306) 652-7022
Emp Here 45   *Sales* 10,141,500
SIC 3443 Fabricated plate work (boiler shop)

   D-U-N-S 25-288-5694   (SL)
SASKATOON CENTENNIAL AUDITORIUM
FOUNDATION
TCU PLACE
35 22nd St E, Saskatoon, SK, S7K 0C8
(306) 975-7777
Emp Here 200   *Sales* 21,196,800
SIC 7922 Theatrical producers and services
   Tracey Benson
   Rob Jones

   D-U-N-S 24-691-1549   (SL)
SASKATOON FAMILY YOUNG MEN'S
CHRISTIAN ASSOCIATION
YMCA SASKATOON
25 22nd St E, Saskatoon, SK, S7K 0C7
(306) 652-7515
Emp Here 90   *Sales* 12,859,110
SIC 8641 Civic and social associations
   Dean Dodge

   D-U-N-S 20-740-3452   (SL)
SASKATOON MOTOR PRODUCTS (1973)
LTD
S M P
715 Circle Dr E, Saskatoon, SK, S7K 0V1
(306) 242-0276
Emp Here 75   *Sales* 47,196,000
SIC 5521 Used car dealers
   Ryan Vanstone
   Gord Mansfield

D-U-N-S 24-233-9513 (HQ)
SASKATOON PRAIRIELAND PARK COR-PORATION
503 Ruth St W, Saskatoon, SK, S7K 4E4
(306) 931-7149
Sales 112,203,000
SIC 8741 Management services
Mark Regier
Vic Dubois
Dan Kemppainen

D-U-N-S 20-341-9424 (SL)
SASKATOON PRIVATE INVESTIGATION INC
SPI SECURITY
333 25th St E Suite 505, Saskatoon, SK, S7K 0L4
(306) 975-0999
Emp Here 30   *Sales* 13,304,700
SIC 7389 Business services, nec
Todd Hrabok

D-U-N-S 20-843-3466 (HQ)
SASKATOON PUBLIC LIBRARY
CARLYLE KING BRANCH LIBRARY
311 23rd St E, Saskatoon, SK, S7K 0J6
(306) 975-7558
Emp Here 85   *Sales* 11,889,450
SIC 8231 Libraries

D-U-N-S 25-155-9936 (SL)
SASKATOON WHOLESALE TIRE LTD
2705 Wentz Ave, Saskatoon, SK, S7K 4B6
(306) 244-9512
Emp Here 35   *Sales* 17,432,730
SIC 5531 Auto and home supply stores
Paul Newton
Harold John Derksen
Henry James Derksen
Brenda Derksen
Kathy Derksen

D-U-N-S 25-116-6062 (BR)
SASKENERGY INCORPORATED
(*Suby of* GOVERNMENT OF SASKATCHEWAN)
408 36th St E, Saskatoon, SK, S7K 4J9
(306) 975-8561
Emp Here 120
SIC 4924 Natural gas distribution

D-U-N-S 25-107-8325 (SL)
SCOTT'S PARABLE CHRISTIAN STORES INC
810 Circle Dr E Suite 106b, Saskatoon, SK, S7K 3T8
(306) 244-3700
Emp Here 20   *Sales* 13,129,280
SIC 5961 Catalog and mail-order houses
Jim Pearson
Janice Scott
Gerry Scott

D-U-N-S 20-827-5599 (SL)
SENTINEL FINANCIAL MANAGEMENT CORP
200-446 2nd Ave N, Saskatoon, SK, S7K 2C3
(306) 652-7225
Emp Here 25   *Sales* 14,666,015
SIC 6411 Insurance agents, brokers, and service
Merlin Chouinard

D-U-N-S 24-266-8028 (SL)
SENTINEL LIFE MANAGEMENT CORP
446 2nd Ave N Suite 200, Saskatoon, SK, S7K 2C3
(306) 652-7225
Emp Here 19   *Sales* 11,018,556
SIC 6411 Insurance agents, brokers, and service
Fred Wing
Merlin H Chouinard

D-U-N-S 24-339-4264 (SL)
SJ FINE FOODS LTD
827 56th St E, Saskatoon, SK, S7K 5Y9

(306) 653-1702
Emp Here 130   *Sales* 44,939,700
SIC 2011 Meat packing plants
Len Castillo

D-U-N-S 25-271-7491 (BR)
SOBEYS WEST INC
(*Suby of* EMPIRE COMPANY LIMITED)
134 Primrose Dr, Saskatoon, SK, S7K 5S6
(306) 242-6090
Emp Here 140
SIC 5411 Grocery stores

D-U-N-S 25-417-8882 (HQ)
SPECIALTY DISTRIBUTING LTD
FOOD FOR CHANGE
829 48th St E, Saskatoon, SK, S7K 0X5
(306) 975-9867
Sales 74,252,000
SIC 5199 Nondurable goods, nec
Howard Trischuk
Cheri Trischuk

D-U-N-S 24-115-1851 (SL)
STAR EGG CO. LTD
1302 Quebec Ave, Saskatoon, SK, S7K 1V5
(306) 244-4041
Emp Here 50   *Sales* 41,778,850
SIC 5144 Poultry and poultry products
Bert Harman
Darlene Harman

D-U-N-S 24-607-4751 (HQ)
SUNCORP VALUATIONS LTD
261 1st Ave N Suite 300, Saskatoon, SK, S7K 1X2
(306) 652-0311
Emp Here 33   *Sales* 19,957,050
SIC 7389 Business services, nec
Tom Gardener
Peggy Gardener

D-U-N-S 25-538-6435 (HQ)
SUNRISE FOODS INTERNATIONAL INC
306 Queen St Suite 200, Saskatoon, SK, S7K 0M2
(306) 931-4576
Sales 44,030,760
SIC 5153 Grain and field beans
Jake Neufeld
Marianne M. Neufeld

D-U-N-S 24-344-0059 (BR)
SUPERIOR PLUS LP
ERCO WORLDWIDE
(*Suby of* SUPERIOR PLUS CORP)
Gd Stn Main, Saskatoon, SK, S7K 3J4
(306) 931-7767
Emp Here 120
SIC 2819 Industrial inorganic chemicals, nec
William Compton

D-U-N-S 20-069-9374 (HQ)
T & T TRUCKING LTD
(*Suby of* 601861 SASKATCHEWAN LTD)
855 60th St E, Saskatoon, SK, S7K 5Z7
(306) 934-3383
Emp Here 45   *Sales* 28,798,840
SIC 4213 Trucking, except local
Graham Newton
Rick Thiessen
Lynn Muyard
Henry Thiessen

D-U-N-S 25-650-9399 (BR)
TETRA TECH CANADA INC
(*Suby of* TETRA TECH, INC.)
410 22nd St E Suite 1400, Saskatoon, SK, S7K 5T6
(306) 244-4888
Emp Here 211
SIC 8711 Engineering services
Mike Silts

D-U-N-S 25-643-2246 (BR)
TFORCE FINAL MILE CANADA INC
DYANAMEX COURIER
(*Suby of* TFI INTERNATIONAL INC)
3275 Miners Ave, Saskatoon, SK, S7K 7Z1

(306) 975-1010
Emp Here 80
SIC 7389 Business services, nec
Graham Mackank

D-U-N-S 24-747-0532 (SL)
TGS HARVARD PROPERTY MANAGEMENT INC
135 21st St E Suite 21, Saskatoon, SK, S7K 0B4
(306) 668-8350
Emp Here 49   *Sales* 16,029,223
SIC 6531 Real estate agents and managers
Paul Hill

D-U-N-S 24-607-4355 (HQ)
TIGER COURIER INC
(*Suby of* EKS HOLDINGS LTD)
705 47th St E, Saskatoon, SK, S7K 5G5
(306) 242-7499
Emp Here 40   *Sales* 103,680,740
SIC 7389 Business services, nec
Erwin Siemens

D-U-N-S 20-546-8366 (SL)
TIMKEN CANADA LP
STANDARD MACHINE
(*Suby of* THE TIMKEN COMPANY)
868 60th St E, Saskatoon, SK, S7K 8G8
(306) 931-3343
Emp Here 135   *Sales* 29,970,135
SIC 3599 Industrial machinery, nec
Greg Porter

D-U-N-S 20-070-4880 (SL)
VENABLES MACHINE WORKS LTD
502 50th St E, Saskatoon, SK, S7K 6L9
(306) 931-7100
Emp Here 67   *Sales* 16,494,462
SIC 1791 Structural steel erection
Ross Vaxvick
Timothy Lindenback

D-U-N-S 24-850-9833 (SL)
VENDASTA TECHNOLOGIES INC
VENDASTA
220 3rd Ave S Suite 405, Saskatoon, SK, S7K 1M1
(306) 955-5512
Emp Here 155   *Sales* 25,861,285
SIC 7372 Prepackaged software
Brendan King
Jeff Tomlin
Guy Kelsey
Allan Wolinski
Ken Barteski
Michael Brennan
George Leith
Bryan Larson
Jed Williams
Jean Parchewsky

D-U-N-S 20-340-4897 (SL)
VIRTUS GROUP CHARTERED ACCOUNTANTS & BUSINESS ADVISORS LLP
157 2nd Ave N Suite 200, Saskatoon, SK, S7K 2A9
(306) 653-6100
Emp Here 100   *Sales* 20,908,500
SIC 8721 Accounting, auditing, and book-keeping
Kelly Lutz

D-U-N-S 20-601-2544 (HQ)
WALLACE CONSTRUCTION SPECIALTIES LTD
1940 Ontario Ave, Saskatoon, SK, S7K 1T6
(306) 653-2020
Emp Here 17   *Sales* 15,651,090
SIC 5039 Construction materials, nec
Norman Wallace
Agnes Wallace

D-U-N-S 20-358-9163 (HQ)
WEST FOUR GROUP OF COMPANIES INC
MADERO DOORS & HARDWARE
2505 Wentz Ave, Saskatoon, SK, S7K 2K9
(306) 934-5147
Emp Here 10   *Sales* 19,208,500

SIC 3442 Metal doors, sash, and trim
Lynne Fafard

D-U-N-S 24-389-0873 (SL)
WESTCAP MGT. LTD
410 22nd St E Suite 830, Saskatoon, SK, S7K 5T6
(306) 652-5557
Emp Here 22   *Sales* 11,686,554
SIC 6282 Investment advice
Grant Kook
Douglas Banzet
Robert Connoly
Wanda Hunchak
Jamie Schwitzer
Tyler Bradley

D-U-N-S 24-327-5760 (BR)
WESTERN CANADA LOTTERY CORPORATION
(*Suby of* WESTERN CANADA LOTTERY CORPORATION)
1935 1st Ave N, Saskatoon, SK, S7K 6W1
(306) 933-6850
Emp Here 81
SIC 7999 Amusement and recreation, nec
Tyrone Wolfram

D-U-N-S 20-840-1018 (SL)
WHEATON GMC BUICK CADILLAC LTD
WHEATON GM
2102 Millar Ave, Saskatoon, SK, S7K 6P4
(306) 244-8131
Emp Here 100   *Sales* 62,928,000
SIC 5511 New and used car dealers
C Ross Wheaton

D-U-N-S 20-446-6866 (SL)
WIG'S PUMPS AND WATERWORKS LTD
227b Venture Cres, Saskatoon, SK, S7K 6N8
(306) 652-4276
Emp Here 25   *Sales* 11,875,650
SIC 5082 Construction and mining machinery
Jodi Wig
Glenn Wig

D-U-N-S 20-741-1281 (HQ)
WINACOTT SPRING TRACTOR TRAILER REPAIR CENTRE LTD
WINACOTT SPRING WESTERN STAR TRUCKS
3002 Faithfull Ave Suite 1, Saskatoon, SK, S7K 0B1
(306) 931-4448
Emp Here 59   *Sales* 21,852,900
SIC 5013 Motor vehicle supplies and new parts
Correy Bubnick
Laura Bubnick

D-U-N-S 24-717-8650 (HQ)
WRIGHT CONSTRUCTION WESTERN INC
2919 Cleveland Ave, Saskatoon, SK, S7K 8A9
(306) 934-0440
Emp Here 50   *Sales* 174,598,000
SIC 1542 Nonresidential construction, nec
Lorne Wright
Larry Strohan
Casey Davis
Donald Wright
Nancy Cuelenaere
Jack Wright

D-U-N-S 24-608-1103 (SL)
YOUNG WOMEN'S CHRISTIAN ASSOCIATION OF SASKATOON
YWCA OF SASKATOON
510 25th St E, Saskatoon, SK, S7K 4A7
(306) 244-0944
Emp Here 110   *Sales* 8,447,120
SIC 8322 Individual and family services
Barbara Macpherson
Darla Hufsmith
Kelly Caruk

Saskatoon, SK S7L

D-U-N-S 20-693-7299   (SL)
45TH STREET LIMITED PARTNERSHIP
701 45th St W, Saskatoon, SK, S7L 5W5
(306) 934-0600
Emp Here 130   *Sales* 74,051,640
SIC 5039 Construction materials, nec
Al Felix

D-U-N-S 24-883-7239   (HQ)
594827 SASKATCHEWAN LTD
GHOST TRANSPORTATION SERVICES
715 46th St W Suite E, Saskatoon, SK, S7L
6A1
(306) 249-3515
Sales 12,479,208
SIC 4731 Freight transportation arrangement
Alan Dowling

D-U-N-S 24-851-7872   (SL)
598468 SASKATCHEWAN LTD
RAMADA HOTEL & GOLF DOME
(*Suby of* CHEUNG ON INVESTMENTS
GROUP LTD)
806 Idylwyld Dr N, Saskatoon, SK, S7L 0Z6
(306) 665-6500
Emp Here 100   *Sales* 9,269,000
SIC 7011 Hotels and motels
Grant Kook
Bruce Eaton

D-U-N-S 20-561-2497   (HQ)
625974 SASKATCHEWAN LTD
SASKATOON HYUNDAI
2035 Idylwyld Dr N, Saskatoon, SK, S7L 4R3
(306) 664-6767
Emp Here 45   *Sales* 22,413,510
SIC 5511 New and used car dealers
Mark Loeppky

D-U-N-S 20-840-8807   (SL)
ANDERSON RENTAL AND PAVING LTD
3430 Idylwyld Dr N, Saskatoon, SK, S7L 5Y7
(306) 934-2000
Emp Here 50   *Sales* 14,176,200
SIC 1611 Highway and street construction
Dennis Anderson
Renee (Irene) Anderson

D-U-N-S 20-049-8978   (BR)
ASIG CANADA LTD
(*Suby of* ASIG CANADA LTD)
2515 Airport Rd Suite 7, Saskatoon, SK, S7L
1M4
(306) 651-6018
Emp Here 75
SIC 5172 Petroleum products, nec

D-U-N-S 20-066-8978   (HQ)
ASSOCIATED ENGINEERING (SASK) LTD
(*Suby of* ASHCO SHAREHOLDERS INC)
2225 Northridge Dr Suite 1, Saskatoon, SK,
S7L 6X6
(306) 653-4969
Emp Here 55   *Sales* 14,076,640
SIC 8711 Engineering services
Kerry Rudd

D-U-N-S 20-069-0816   (SL)
AUTO CLEARING (1982) LTD
SAVOIE CLEARING
331 Circle Dr W, Saskatoon, SK, S7L 5S8
(306) 244-2186
Emp Here 77   *Sales* 21,814,100
SIC 7532 Top and body repair and paint shops
Henry M Savoie
Paul Savoie

D-U-N-S 20-068-2677   (BR)
**BOARD OF EDUCATION OF SASKA-
TOON SCHOOL DIVISION NO. 13 OF
SASKATCHEWAN, THE**
MOUNT ROYAL COLLEGIATE
(*Suby of* BOARD OF EDUCATION OF
SASKATOON SCHOOL DIVISION NO. 13 OF
SASKATCHEWAN, THE)
2220 Rusholme Rd, Saskatoon, SK, S7L 4A4

(306) 683-7800
Emp Here 150
SIC 8211 Elementary and secondary schools
Scott Farmer

D-U-N-S 20-114-6136   (SL)
CANADA WEST TRUCK CENTRE
3750 Idylwyld Dr N Suite 107, Saskatoon, SK,
S7L 6G3
(306) 934-1110
Emp Here 42   *Sales* 15,297,030
SIC 5012 Automobiles and other motor vehi-
cles
Reid Bews

D-U-N-S 24-220-7558   (SL)
CANADIAN TRADE INTERNATIONAL, INC
2241 Hanselman Ave Suite 8, Saskatoon, SK,
S7L 6A7
(306) 931-4111
Emp Here 73   *Sales* 32,643,702
SIC 5039 Construction materials, nec
Robert Behari
Timothy Braitembach

D-U-N-S 20-178-6659   (SL)
CARLOU MARKETING INC
SCHAAN HEALTH CARE PRODUCTS
820 45th St W, Saskatoon, SK, S7L 6A5
(306) 664-1188
Emp Here 25   *Sales* 11,179,350
SIC 5047 Medical and hospital equipment
Collin Schaan

D-U-N-S 24-038-8595   (SL)
CENTRAL HAVEN SPECIAL CARE HOME
1020 Avenue I N, Saskatoon, SK, S7L 2H7
(306) 844-4040
Emp Here 84   *Sales* 5,759,544
SIC 8051 Skilled nursing care facilities
Dolores Campbell

D-U-N-S 24-038-8843   (SL)
CHEF-REDI MEATS INC
CHEF REDI MEATS
501 45th St W Suite 11, Saskatoon, SK, S7L
5Z9
(306) 665-3266
Emp Here 35   *Sales* 29,245,195
SIC 5147 Meats and meat products
R Don Carruthers
Rob Carruthers

D-U-N-S 24-468-8792   (HQ)
CLAUDE RESOURCES INC
SEABEE MINE, DIV OF
(*Suby of* SSR MINING INC)
2100 Airport Dr Suite 202, Saskatoon, SK,
S7L 6M6
(306) 668-7505
Emp Here 13   *Sales* 56,270,280
SIC 1041 Gold ores
Brian Skanderbeg
Rick Johnson
Brian Booth
Rita Mirwal
Patrick Downey
Arnold Klassen
John Murphy

D-U-N-S 25-640-5333   (SL)
CUSTOM COURIER CO. LTD
501 Pakwa Pl Suite 2, Saskatoon, SK, S7L
6A3
(306) 653-8500
Emp Here 90   *Sales* 40,429,710
SIC 7389 Business services, nec
R. Stacey Kliewer
Louella Kliewer

D-U-N-S 20-740-1431   (HQ)
DEER LODGE HOTELS LTD
SASKATOON TRAVELODGE HOTEL
106 Circle Dr W, Saskatoon, SK, S7L 4L6
(306) 242-8881
Emp Here 240   *Sales* 52,617,400
SIC 7011 Hotels and motels
Betty-Anne Latrace-Henderson
Don Morgan

Brian Henderson
Dave Kelly
Peter Verbeke
Jim Cummings
Bob Webster
Lorrie Surprenant
Mike Stensrud
Thomas Davis

D-U-N-S 25-452-1370   (SL)
DEPMAR FLIGHT HOLDINGS INC
SASKATOON AEROCENTRE
Hangar 10 John G. Diefenbaker Airport,
Saskatoon, SK, S7L 6S1
(306) 931-8552
Emp Here 15   *Sales* 15,492,120
SIC 5172 Petroleum products, nec
Dennis Goll

D-U-N-S 20-152-8176   (HQ)
DYNAVENTURE CORP
2100 Airport Dr Suite 202, Saskatoon, SK,
S7L 6M6

Emp Here 8   *Sales* 21,211,920
SIC 8741 Management services
Brian Eidem
Mervin Grzybowski

D-U-N-S 25-360-9333   (BR)
FLOFORM INDUSTRIES LTD
CUSTOM COUNTERTOPS
(*Suby of* FLOFORM INDUSTRIES LTD)
2209 Speers Ave, Saskatoon, SK, S7L 5X6
(306) 665-7733
Emp Here 80
SIC 2541 Wood partitions and fixtures
John Eustace

D-U-N-S 24-135-0557   (SL)
GRAB 2 HOLDINGS LTD
POINTS NORTH FREIGHT FORWARDING
2405b Wheaton Ave, Saskatoon, SK, S7L 5Y3
(306) 633-2137
Emp Here 42   *Sales* 16,185,120
SIC 4731 Freight transportation arrangement
Norrman Eikel

D-U-N-S 20-447-3268   (HQ)
J.H. ENTERPRISES (1969) LIMITED
J & H BUILDERS WAREHOUSE
(*Suby of* SUBURBAN CONSTRUCTION LTD)
2505 Avenue C N, Saskatoon, SK, S7L 6A6
(306) 652-5322
Emp Here 90   *Sales* 32,118,240
SIC 5211 Lumber and other building materials
Donald J Neufeld
Murray Neufeld

D-U-N-S 25-663-5038   (SL)
JUBILEE RESIDENCES INC
PORTEOUS LODGE
833 Avenue P N, Saskatoon, SK, S7L 2W5
(306) 382-2626
Emp Here 110   *Sales* 7,542,260
SIC 8051 Skilled nursing care facilities
Gaye Thompson

D-U-N-S 24-607-4967   (SL)
KLASSEN JEWELLERS LTD
2318 Avenue C N, Saskatoon, SK, S7L 5X5
(306) 652-2112
Emp Here 20   *Sales* 10,410,840
SIC 5094 Jewelry and precious stones
Robert Klassen
Barbara Klassen
Sid Jorgenson
Michael Klassen
Susan Peters

D-U-N-S 25-270-1222   (BR)
LOBLAWS INC
REAL CANADIAN SUPERSTORE 1536
(*Suby of* LOBLAW COMPANIES LIMITED)
411 Confederation Dr, Saskatoon, SK, S7L
5C3
(306) 683-5634
Emp Here 400

SIC 5141 Groceries, general line
Jeff Jensen

D-U-N-S 24-228-4250   (SL)
MARITZ INC
2318 Northridge Dr, Saskatoon, SK, S7L 1B9

Emp Here 200   *Sales* 44,728,435
SIC 8732 Commercial nonphysical research
Nathan Salmons

D-U-N-S 20-105-1492   (SL)
MERLIN FORD LINCOLN INC
3750 Idylwyld Dr N, Saskatoon, SK, S7L 6G3
(306) 931-6611
Emp Here 49   *Sales* 24,405,822
SIC 5511 New and used car dealers
Jason Bews

D-U-N-S 20-069-9304   (HQ)
MERLIN MOTORS INC
3750 Idylwyld Dr N Suite 107, Saskatoon, SK,
S7L 6G3
(306) 931-6611
Sales 49,083,840
SIC 5511 New and used car dealers
Gary Bews

D-U-N-S 24-038-6677   (SL)
**MILLENNIUM III PROPERTIES CORPORA-
TION**
2612 Koyl Ave, Saskatoon, SK, S7L 5X9
(306) 955-4174
Emp Here 35   *Sales* 18,592,245
SIC 6211 Security brokers and dealers
Ev Kearley

D-U-N-S 20-072-8152   (HQ)
MORRIS INDUSTRIES LTD
2131 Airport Dr, Saskatoon, SK, S7L 7E1
(306) 933-8585
Emp Here 25   *Sales* 76,117,667
SIC 3523 Farm machinery and equipment
Thomas Glyn Davis
Douglas B Richardson
Don Henry

D-U-N-S 24-748-1286   (HQ)
NSC MINERALS LTD
(*Suby of* KISSNER GROUP HOLDINGS, LP)
2241 Speers Ave, Saskatoon, SK, S7L 5X6
(306) 934-6477
Emp Here 25   *Sales* 65,731,050
SIC 5169 Chemicals and allied products, nec
Mark Demetree
M.Neil Cameron

D-U-N-S 20-843-3219   (SL)
OLIVER LODGE
1405 Faulkner Cres, Saskatoon, SK, S7L 3R5
(306) 382-4111
Emp Here 210   *Sales* 13,499,220
SIC 8361 Residential care
Brandon Little

D-U-N-S 20-857-0259   (HQ)
ORANO CANADA INC
817 45th St W, Saskatoon, SK, S7L 5X2
(306) 343-4500
Sales 89,520,900
SIC 1094 Uranium-radium-vanadium ores
Vincent Martin
Sebastian De Montessus
Andreas Mittler
Tammy Van Lambalgen
Gerald Scherman

D-U-N-S 24-497-3350   (HQ)
**POINTS NORTH FREIGHT FORWARDING
INC**
2405b Wheaton Ave, Saskatoon, SK, S7L 5Y3
(306) 633-2137
Emp Here 1   *Sales* 37,716,030
SIC 5172 Petroleum products, nec
George Eikel
Mark Eikel
Andrew Eikel
Norman Eikel

Blaine Eikel

D-U-N-S 24-803-2059   (HQ)
QUOREX CONSTRUCTION SERVICES LTD
142 Cardinal Cres, Saskatoon, SK, S7L 6H6
(306) 244-3717
Emp Here 100   *Sales* 71,292,250
SIC 1542 Nonresidential construction, nec
Cory Ricther
Scott Froese
Kyle Fairbairn
Rick Faehr

D-U-N-S 25-112-9888   (SL)
REMAI VENTURES INC
143 Cardinal Cres, Saskatoon, SK, S7L 6H5
(306) 934-2799
Emp Here 200   *Sales* 18,538,000
SIC 7011 Hotels and motels
Frank Remai

D-U-N-S 20-394-1336   (SL)
RIIDE HOLDINGS INC
RIIDE HAIL
225 Avenue B N, Saskatoon, SK, S7L 1E1
(306) 244-3767
Emp Here 80   *Sales* 4,389,760
SIC 4111 Local and suburban transit
Scott Suppes
Kelly Frie
Gerald Haller

D-U-N-S 24-054-0310   (HQ)
RSB LOGISTIC INC
(*Suby of* COMPASS LOGISTICS INTERNA-
TIONAL AG)
219 Cardinal Cres, Saskatoon, SK, S7L 7K8
(306) 242-8300
Emp Here 30   *Sales* 31,061,606
SIC 4212 Local trucking, without storage
George Eckel
Ulrich Philippczyk
Johanne Johnson

D-U-N-S 24-230-6355   (HQ)
**SASKATCHEWAN ASSOCIATION OF RE-
HABILITATION CENTRES**
SARCAN RECYCLING
111 Cardinal Cres, Saskatoon, SK, S7L 6H5
(306) 933-0616
Emp Here 24   *Sales* 195,433,200
SIC 4953 Refuse systems
Amy Mcneil
Bob Hnetka
Murray Baird
Dawn Desautel

D-U-N-S 25-056-6676   (SL)
SASKATOON AIRPORT AUTHORITY
2625 Airport Dr Suite 1, Saskatoon, SK, S7L
7L1
(306) 975-4274
Emp Here 34   *Sales* 12,827,115
SIC 4581 Airports, flying fields, and services
Stephen Maybury
Ben Robb
Drew Britz
Andrew Leeming
Lori Sly
Richard Jasieniuk
Lory Sproxton
Zachary Berglund

D-U-N-S 25-486-0158   (BR)
**SASKATOON CO-OPERATIVE ASSOCIA-
TION LIMITED, THE**
SASKATOON CO-OP
(*Suby of* FEDERATED CO-OPERATIVES
LIMITED)
1624 33rd St W, Saskatoon, SK, S7L 0X3
(306) 933-3865
Emp Here 110
SIC 5141 Groceries, general line
Tim James

D-U-N-S 24-426-8173   (SL)
SASKATOON CONVALESCENT HOME
101 31st St W, Saskatoon, SK, S7L 0P6

(306) 244-7155
Emp Here 80   *Sales* 5,485,280
SIC 8051 Skilled nursing care facilities
Melanie Woods
Karen Knelsen

D-U-N-S 25-291-0021   (SL)
**SASKATOON HOT SHOT TRANSPORTER
SERVICES (1995) LTD**
2342b Hanselman Ave, Saskatoon, SK, S7L
5Z3
(306) 653-5255
Emp Here 85   *Sales* 12,596,320
SIC 4212 Local trucking, without storage
Roy Balkwill
Darrell Balkwill

D-U-N-S 24-033-5856   (SL)
SASKATOON RINGETTE ASSOCIATION
510 Cynthia St Suite 128, Saskatoon, SK, S7L
7K7
(306) 975-0839
Emp Here 49   *Sales* 19,473,286
SIC 8699 Membership organizations, nec
Brenda King

D-U-N-S 25-271-7616   (BR)
SOBEYS WEST INC
CONFEDERATION SAFEWAY
(*Suby of* EMPIRE COMPANY LIMITED)
300 Confederation Dr Suite 100, Saskatoon,
SK, S7L 4R6
(306) 384-9599
Emp Here 125
SIC 5411 Grocery stores
Jim Duzzard

D-U-N-S 20-600-3543   (SL)
SOUTHCENTER AUTO INC
MAINWAY MAZDA
321 Circle Dr W, Saskatoon, SK, S7L 5S8
(306) 373-3711
Emp Here 27   *Sales* 13,448,106
SIC 5511 New and used car dealers
Wayne Holmes
Gail Holmes

D-U-N-S 25-106-9837   (BR)
**ST. PAUL'S ROMAN CATHOLIC SEPARATE
SCHOOL DIVISION NO 20**
E.D. FEEHAN HIGH SCHOOL
411 Avenue M N, Saskatoon, SK, S7L 2S7
(306) 659-7550
Emp Here 100
SIC 8211 Elementary and secondary schools
B Stroh

D-U-N-S 20-740-4351   (HQ)
SUBURBAN CONSTRUCTION LTD
2505 Avenue C N, Saskatoon, SK, S7L 6A6
(306) 652-5322
Sales 30,068,500
SIC 6712 Bank holding companies
Harold Neufeld
Donald Neufeld
Murray Neufeld

D-U-N-S 24-235-6947   (HQ)
SUPERIOR MILLWORK LTD
SUPERIOR CABINETS
747 46th St W, Saskatoon, SK, S7L 6A1
(306) 667-6600
Emp Here 50   *Sales* 28,807,876
SIC 2434 Wood kitchen cabinets
Mark Buller

D-U-N-S 20-079-4472   (SL)
TAMARACK FOUNDATION
CAMP TAMARACK
510 Cynthia St Suite 136, Saskatoon, SK, S7L
7K7
(306) 975-0855
Emp Here 27   *Sales* 10,730,178
SIC 8699 Membership organizations, nec
Linda Slough

D-U-N-S 24-426-4719   (HQ)
TRIANGLE FREIGHT SERVICES LTD
(*Suby of* EKS HOLDINGS LTD)

3550 Idylwyld Dr N, Saskatoon, SK, S7L 6G3
(306) 373-7744
Sales 22,627,660
SIC 4213 Trucking, except local
Erwen Siemens
Terry Siemens

D-U-N-S 20-236-2450   (SL)
TURBOTRONICS
SASKATOON DIESEL
230 29th St E, Saskatoon, SK, S7L 6Y6
(306) 242-7644
Emp Here 35   *Sales* 17,432,730
SIC 5541 Gasoline service stations
Percy Hoss

D-U-N-S 20-259-6420   (SL)
UNITED PROTECTION SERVICES
2366 Avenue C N, Saskatoon, SK, S7L 5X5
(306) 382-0002
Emp Here 400   *Sales* 19,388,222
SIC 7381 Detective and armored car services
Mary Beckman

D-U-N-S 25-893-5626   (BR)
VECIMA NETWORKS INC
(*Suby of* VECIMA NETWORKS INC)
150 Cardinal Pl, Saskatoon, SK, S7L 6H7
(306) 955-7075
Emp Here 700
SIC 8731 Commercial physical research
Rod Martin

D-U-N-S 24-438-9383   (HQ)
WEST WIND AVIATION INC
3a Hangar Rd, Saskatoon, SK, S7L 5X4
(306) 652-9121
Sales 57,440,240
SIC 7359 Equipment rental and leasing, nec
Michael Rodyniuk
Ricky Philipenko
Chris Tabler
Lloyd Epp

D-U-N-S 20-561-5151   (HQ)
**WEST WIND AVIATION LIMITED PARTNER-
SHIP**
3 Hangar Rd, Saskatoon, SK, S7L 5X4
(306) 652-9121
Sales 37,376,920
SIC 4522 Air transportation, nonscheduled
Dennis Goll
Rick Philipenko
Chris Tabler
Lloyd Epp

D-U-N-S 24-230-6157   (SL)
WHEATHEART MANUFACTURING LTD
3455 Idylwyld Dr N, Saskatoon, SK, S7L 6B5
(306) 934-0611
Emp Here 80   *Sales* 17,760,080
SIC 3523 Farm machinery and equipment
Robert Stenson

Saskatoon, SK S7M

D-U-N-S 20-843-3953   (HQ)
CAMECO CORPORATION
2121 11th St W, Saskatoon, SK, S7M 1J3
(306) 956-6200
Emp Here 400   *Sales* 1,585,692,387
SIC 1094 Uranium-radium-vanadium ores
Timothy S Gitzel
Grant Isaac
Brian Reilley
Sean Quinn
Alice Wong
Ian Bruce
Daniel Camus
John Clappison
Donald Deranger
Catherine Gignac

D-U-N-S 24-817-7102   (SL)

CREE WAY GAS WEST LTD
2511 22nd St W, Saskatoon, SK, S7M 0V9
(306) 975-0125
Emp Here 35   *Sales* 17,432,730
SIC 5541 Gasoline service stations
Annelie Geyeyes

D-U-N-S 24-426-6508   (HQ)
DEBRADEE ENTERPRISES LTD
DEBRADEE WEDDINGS
123 Auditorium Ave, Saskatoon, SK, S7M 5S8
(306) 525-8600
Emp Here 13   *Sales* 10,963,084
SIC 5137 Women's and children's clothing
Sylvestre Gayowski
Andrea Clavelle
Darlene Gayowski

D-U-N-S 20-388-5215   (SL)
H.J.R. ASPHALT LP
1605 Chappell Dr, Saskatoon, SK, S7M 3X9
(306) 975-0070
Emp Here 100   *Sales* 25,244,200
SIC 1611 Highway and street construction
Joshua Safronetz

D-U-N-S 20-069-6896   (HQ)
INLAND STEEL PRODUCTS INC
1520 17th St W, Saskatoon, SK, S7M 4A4
(306) 652-5353
Emp Here 10   *Sales* 16,059,120
SIC 5211 Lumber and other building materials

D-U-N-S 24-329-5289   (BR)
MAPLE LEAF FOODS INC
(*Suby of* MAPLE LEAF FOODS INC)
100 Mcleod Ave, Saskatoon, SK, S7M 5V9
(306) 382-2210
Emp Here 350
SIC 2011 Meat packing plants
Clint Smith

D-U-N-S 20-546-6568   (HQ)
MARKET TIRE (1976) LTD
CITY TIRE CENTRE
115 Idylwyld Dr S, Saskatoon, SK, S7M 1L4
(306) 244-5442
Emp Here 17   *Sales* 24,903,900
SIC 5531 Auto and home supply stores
Brian Hoiness

D-U-N-S 20-355-0830   (BR)
**MCDONALD'S   RESTAURANTS   OF
CANADA LIMITED**
MCDONALD'S
(*Suby of* MCDONALD'S CORPORATION)
2225 22nd St W, Saskatoon, SK, S7M 0V5
(306) 955-8660
Emp Here 100
SIC 5812 Eating places
Hazel Rivera

D-U-N-S 25-173-4257   (SL)
MCKENZIE, C. PHARMACY INC
SHOPPERS DRUG MART
2410 22nd St W Unit 20, Saskatoon, SK, S7M
5S6
(306) 382-5005
Emp Here 80   *Sales* 19,546,240
SIC 5912 Drug stores and proprietary stores
Connie Mckenzie

D-U-N-S 20-720-2461   (HQ)
MILLSAP FUEL DISTRIBUTORS LTD
PETRO CANADA
905 Avenue P S, Saskatoon, SK, S7M 2X3
(306) 244-7916
Emp Here 54   *Sales* 67,888,854
SIC 5172 Petroleum products, nec
Gus Millsap

D-U-N-S 24-231-9143   (HQ)
N. YANKE TRANSFER LTD
YANKE GROUP OF COMPANIES
1359 Fletcher Rd, Saskatoon, SK, S7M 5H5

Emp Here 140   *Sales* 129,066,700
SIC 4213 Trucking, except local

Russel Marcoux
Scott Fraser
Brian Richards
Bonnie Marcoux

D-U-N-S 25-746-1467   (SL)
QUEEN'S HOUSE RETREATS & RENEWAL CENTRE
601 Taylor St W, Saskatoon, SK, S7M 0C9
(306) 242-1916
Emp Here 24   *Sales* 10,781,256
SIC 7389 Business services, nec
Gisele Bauche

D-U-N-S 24-776-3873   (SL)
R S CABINET DOORS LTD
1102 17th St W, Saskatoon, SK, S7M 3Y3

Emp Here 75   *Sales* 11,689,725
SIC 2431 Millwork
Bob Stroh
Darren Hayward

D-U-N-S 25-640-8873   (HQ)
RAWLCO RADIO LTD
(*Suby of* RAWLCO CAPITAL LTD)
715 Saskatchewan Cres W, Saskatoon, SK, S7M 5V7
(306) 934-2222
Emp Here 2   *Sales* 20,562,480
SIC 4832 Radio broadcasting stations
Ian Kuturbash

D-U-N-S 24-336-8953   (BR)
SASKATOON, CITY OF
WATER TREATMENT PLANT
(*Suby of* SASKATOON, CITY OF)
1030 Avenue H S, Saskatoon, SK, S7M 1X5
(306) 975-2534
Emp Here 500
SIC 4953 Refuse systems
Reed Corbett

D-U-N-S 24-115-8286   (SL)
SUNNYSIDE ADVENTIST CARE CENTRE LTD
2200 St Henry Ave, Saskatoon, SK, S7M 0P5
(306) 653-1267
Emp Here 115   *Sales* 7,857,490
SIC 8051 Skilled nursing care facilities
Randy Kurtz
Ken Wiebe
Brent Burdick

D-U-N-S 24-826-8737   (BR)
WAL-MART CANADA CORP
WALMART
(*Suby of* WALMART INC.)
225 Betts Ave, Saskatoon, SK, S7M 1L2
(306) 382-5454
Emp Here 100
SIC 5311 Department stores
Mark Schaessel

Saskatoon, SK S7N

D-U-N-S 20-348-1783   (SL)
ACADIA PAVING LTD.
(*Suby of* ACADIA CONSTRUCTION)
121 105th St E, Saskatoon, SK, S7N 1Z2
(306) 374-4738
Emp Here 50   *Sales* 12,622,100
SIC 1611 Highway and street construction
Wayne Heaslit

D-U-N-S 20-840-0648   (SL)
AGIORITIS HOLDINGS LTD
801 Broadway Ave, Saskatoon, SK, S7N 1B5
(306) 652-5374
Emp Here 25   *Sales* 10,483,875
SIC 6719 Holding companies, nec
Nino Agioritis

D-U-N-S 20-787-4251   (SL)
AIESEC SASKATOON

25 Campus Dr Suite 248, Saskatoon, SK, S7N 5A7
(306) 966-7767
Emp Here 25   *Sales* 10,102,450
SIC 8699 Membership organizations, nec
Erica Conrad

D-U-N-S 20-261-1562   (HQ)
ALLAN CONSTRUCTION
317 103 St E, Saskatoon, SK, S7N 1Y9
(306) 477-5520
Sales 83,807,040
SIC 1542 Nonresidential construction, nec
Blaine Dubreuil

D-U-N-S 25-496-7151   (SL)
ALLAN CONSTRUCTION CO. LTD
317 103rd St E, Saskatoon, SK, S7N 1Y9
(306) 477-5520
Emp Here 30   *Sales* 17,110,140
SIC 1542 Nonresidential construction, nec
Monte Allan
Gail Allan

D-U-N-S 20-854-9519   (SL)
ALTO CONSTRUCTION LTD
307 103rd St E, Saskatoon, SK, S7N 1Y9
(306) 955-0554
Emp Here 50   *Sales* 12,044,200
SIC 1629 Heavy construction, nec
Ronald Kunkel

D-U-N-S 25-975-8019   (SL)
ARES VENTURES INC
668 University Dr, Saskatoon, SK, S7N 0J2
(306) 241-1435
Emp Here 60   *Sales* 16,256,520
SIC 1521 Single-family housing construction
Steven Mann

D-U-N-S 25-787-1590   (SL)
ATHABASCA CATERING LIMITED PARTNERSHIP
335 Packham Ave Suite 120, Saskatoon, SK, S7N 4S1
(306) 242-8008
Emp Here 300   *Sales* 13,991,700
SIC 5812 Eating places
Alan Solheim
Kevin Danchuk

D-U-N-S 25-098-9787   (BR)
CALIAN LTD
SED SYSTEMS
(*Suby of* CALIAN GROUP LTD)
18 Innovation Blvd, Saskatoon, SK, S7N 3R1
(306) 931-3425
Emp Here 340
SIC 4899 Communication services, nec
Patrick Thera

D-U-N-S 20-105-0734   (SL)
CANADIAN LIGHT SOURCE INC
(*Suby of* UNIVERSITY OF SASKATCHEWAN)
44 Innovation Blvd, Saskatoon, SK, S7N 2V3
(306) 657-3500
Emp Here 74   *Sales* 37,498,464
SIC 8733 Noncommercial research organizations
Rob Lamb
Beryl Lepage
Nils Petersen
Ray Basler
Michael Bancroft

D-U-N-S 24-224-7935   (SL)
CREE-WAY GAS LTD
343 Packham Ave, Saskatoon, SK, S7N 4S1
(306) 955-8823
Emp Here 25   *Sales* 12,451,950
SIC 5541 Gasoline service stations
Norman Ledoux

D-U-N-S 25-194-4443   (SL)
DAVE DEPLAEDT RETAIL SALES LTD
CANADIAN TIRE ASSOCIATE STORE
1731 Preston Ave N Suite 133, Saskatoon,

SK, S7N 4V2
(306) 373-3666
Emp Here 200   *Sales* 53,530,400
SIC 5251 Hardware stores
Dave Deplaedt

D-U-N-S 25-385-0044   (BR)
DOW AGROSCIENCES CANADA INC.
DOW AGROSCIENCES CANADA INC
(*Suby of* CORTEVA, INC.)
421 Downey Rd Suite 101, Saskatoon, SK, S7N 4L8
(800) 352-6776
Emp Here 100
SIC 2879 Agricultural chemicals, nec
Melinda Dunham

D-U-N-S 20-069-4321   (HQ)
EL-RANCHO FOOD SERVICES LIMITED
KENTUCKY FRIED CHICKEN
218 103rd St E, Saskatoon, SK, S7N 1Y7
(306) 668-2600
Emp Here 8   *Sales* 19,821,575
SIC 5812 Eating places
Joseph Young
Madeleine Young

D-U-N-S 24-852-0751   (SL)
FAST, DOUG & ASSOCIATES LTD
FAST CONSULTANTS
112 Research Dr Suite 112, Saskatoon, SK, S7N 3R3
(306) 956-3070
Emp Here 45   *Sales* 10,561,320
SIC 8732 Commercial nonphysical research
Doug Fast
Katie Fast

D-U-N-S 24-235-7895   (HQ)
FEDERATION OF SASKATCHEWAN INDIANS, INC
FEDERATION OF SASKATCHEWAN INDIAN NATIONS
103a Packham Ave Suite 100, Saskatoon, SK, S7N 4K4
(306) 665-1215
Emp Here 90   *Sales* 31,207,400
SIC 8651 Political organizations
Alphonse Bird
Irene Oaks
Morley Watson
Lawrence Joseph
Guy Lonechild
Glen Pratt
Evan Schenenauer

D-U-N-S 20-333-8561   (SL)
HERTZ NORTHERN BUS (2006) LTD
330 103rd St E, Saskatoon, SK, S7N 1Z1
(306) 374-5161
Emp Here 110   *Sales* 8,279,920
SIC 4151 School buses
Albina Kille

D-U-N-S 20-392-3156   (HQ)
JOINT INVESTMENT GROUP INC
118 Veterinary Rd, Saskatoon, SK, S7N 2R4
(306) 978-2800
Sales 32,802,000
SIC 6712 Bank holding companies
Dale Kelly

D-U-N-S 24-883-5639   (SL)
KOCSIS TRANSPORT LTD
401 Packham Pl, Saskatoon, SK, S7N 2T7
(306) 664-0025
Emp Here 80   *Sales* 11,855,360
SIC 4213 Trucking, except local
Ron Kocsis

D-U-N-S 25-651-5388   (SL)
PADDOCK WOOD BREWING SUPPLIES LTD
116 103rd St E Suite B1, Saskatoon, SK, S7N 1Y7
(306) 477-5632
Emp Here 46   *Sales* 14,977,600
SIC 5999 Miscellaneous retail stores, nec

Stephen Cavan

D-U-N-S 24-856-3848   (SL)
POINTS ATHABASCA CONTRACTING LP
401 Packham Pl, Saskatoon, SK, S7N 2T7
(306) 242-4927
Emp Here 300   *Sales* 209,517,600
SIC 1541 Industrial buildings and warehouses
John Scarfe
Don Deranger

D-U-N-S 20-843-7616   (HQ)
POS MANAGEMENT CORP
POS BIO SCIENCES
(*Suby of* JOINT INVESTMENT GROUP INC)
118 Veterinary Rd, Saskatoon, SK, S7N 2R4
(306) 978-2800
Sales 19,529,090
SIC 8731 Commercial physical research
Dale Kelly
Udaya Wanasundara
James Shields
Richard Green
Grace Varga
Justin White
Karen Letourneau
Ory Mcclelland

D-U-N-S 24-209-2760   (SL)
SASK OPPORTUNITIES
INNOVATION PLACE
1 Access Rd N, Saskatoon, SK, S7N 5A2
(306) 933-5485
Emp Here 45   *Sales* 12,229,020
SIC 6531 Real estate agents and managers
Douglas Tastad

D-U-N-S 24-346-3416   (BR)
SASKATCHEWAN HEALTH AUTHORITY
ALVIN BUCKWOLD CHILD DEVELOPMENT PROGRAM
(*Suby of* GOVERNMENT OF SASKATCHEWAN)
1319 Colony St, Saskatoon, SK, S7N 2Z1
(306) 655-1070
Emp Here 150
SIC 8062 General medical and surgical hospitals
Gordon Twigg

D-U-N-S 25-261-7204   (HQ)
SASKATCHEWAN INDIAN GAMING AUTHORITY INC
PAINTED HAND CASINO
(*Suby of* FEDERATION OF SASKATCHEWAN INDIANS, INC)
103c Packham Ave Suite 250, Saskatoon, SK, S7N 4K4
(306) 477-7777
Emp Here 90   *Sales* 200,796,716
SIC 7999 Amusement and recreation, nec
Zane Hansen
Vern Acoose
Therese Mcllymoyl
Paul Newton
Ray Ahenakew

D-U-N-S 25-207-3309   (HQ)
SASKATCHEWAN OPPORTUNITIES CORPORATION
SOCO
(*Suby of* GOVERNMENT OF SASKATCHEWAN)
15 Innovation Blvd Suite 114, Saskatoon, SK, S7N 2X8
(306) 933-6295
Emp Here 70   *Sales* 28,671,440
SIC 6519 Real property lessors, nec
Doug Tastad
Charlene Callander
Richard Florizone

D-U-N-S 25-313-8473   (HQ)
SASKATCHEWAN RESEARCH COUNCIL, THE
(*Suby of* GOVERNMENT OF SASKATCHEWAN)

▲ Public Company   ■ Public Company Family Member   **HQ** Headquarters   **BR** Branch   **SL** Single Location

15 Innovation Blvd Suite 125, Saskatoon, SK,
S7N 2X8
(306) 933-5400
Emp Here 180   *Sales* 51,020,500
SIC 8733 Noncommercial research organizations
Laurier Schramm
Craig Zawada
Doug Kelin
Peta Bonham-Smith
Lee Willson
Kathy Palidwar
Shelley Lipon
Patsy Gilchrist

D-U-N-S 25-271-7533   (BR)
SOBEYS WEST INC
SAFEWAY
(*Suby of* EMPIRE COMPANY LIMITED)
1739 Preston Ave N, Saskatoon, SK, S7N 4V2
(306) 668-9901
Emp Here 104
SIC 5411 Grocery stores
Frank Suetta

D-U-N-S 24-352-3409   (BR)
UNIVERSITY OF SASKATCHEWAN
PEDIATRICS DEPARTMENT
(*Suby   of   UNIVERSITY   OF
SASKATCHEWAN*)
103 Hospital Dr, Saskatoon, SK, S7N 0W8
(306) 844-1068
Emp Here 100
SIC 8221 Colleges and universities
Laurence Givelichian

D-U-N-S 24-345-0470   (BR)
UNIVERSITY OF SASKATCHEWAN
INFORMATION TECHNOLOGY UNIT, COLLEGE OF MEDICINE
(*Suby   of   UNIVERSITY   OF
SASKATCHEWAN*)
107 Wiggins Rd Suite B103, Saskatoon, SK,
S7N 5E5
(306) 966-6135
Emp Here 1,200
SIC 8221 Colleges and universities
John Costa

D-U-N-S 20-794-1415   (BR)
UNIVERSITY OF SASKATCHEWAN
COLLEGE OF EDUCATION
(*Suby   of   UNIVERSITY   OF
SASKATCHEWAN*)
28 Campus Dr Suite 3079, Saskatoon, SK,
S7N 0X1
(306) 966-7619
Emp Here 101
SIC 8221 Colleges and universities
Michelle Prytula

D-U-N-S 20-347-1180   (BR)
UNIVERSITY OF SASKATCHEWAN
DEPARTMENT OF SOIL SCIENCE
(*Suby   of   UNIVERSITY   OF
SASKATCHEWAN*)
51 Campus Dr Rm 5d34, Saskatoon, SK, S7N
5A8
(306) 966-6829
Emp Here 120
SIC 8221 Colleges and universities
Ken C. J. Van Rees

D-U-N-S 20-347-1479   (BR)
UNIVERSITY OF SASKATCHEWAN
SCHOOL OF ENVIRONMENT AND SUSTAINABILITY
(*Suby   of   UNIVERSITY   OF
SASKATCHEWAN*)
117 Science Pl Rm 323, Saskatoon, SK, S7N
5C8
(306) 966-1985
Emp Here 83
SIC 8221 Colleges and universities
Toddi Steelman

D-U-N-S 20-347-1545   (BR)
UNIVERSITY OF SASKATCHEWAN

DEPT OF MEDICINE
(*Suby   of   UNIVERSITY   OF
SASKATCHEWAN*)
103 Hospital Dr, Saskatoon, SK, S7N 0W8
(306) 844-1132
Emp Here 122
SIC 8221 Colleges and universities
Haissam Haddad

D-U-N-S 20-347-1578   (BR)
UNIVERSITY OF SASKATCHEWAN
DEPT OF SURGERY
(*Suby   of   UNIVERSITY   OF
SASKATCHEWAN*)
107 Wiggins Rd 4th Fl Suite B419, Saskatoon,
SK, S7N 5E5
(306) 966-8641
Emp Here 167
SIC 8221 Colleges and universities
Ivar Mendez

D-U-N-S 20-347-1594   (BR)
UNIVERSITY OF SASKATCHEWAN
COLLEGE OF NURSING
(*Suby   of   UNIVERSITY   OF
SASKATCHEWAN*)
104 Clinic Place, Saskatoon, SK, S7N 2Z4
(306) 966-6221
Emp Here 75
SIC 8221 Colleges and universities
Beth Horsburgh

D-U-N-S 20-741-3170   (HQ)
UNIVERSITY OF SASKATCHEWAN
105 Administration Pl Suite E, Saskatoon, SK,
S7N 5A2
(306) 966-4343
Emp Here 1,100   'Sales* 797,685,137
SIC 8221 Colleges and universities

D-U-N-S 24-109-8040   (BR)
UNIVERSITY OF SASKATCHEWAN
COLLEGE OF ENGINEERING
(*Suby   of   UNIVERSITY   OF
SASKATCHEWAN*)
57 Campus Dr Rm 3b48, Saskatoon, SK, S7N
5A9
(306) 966-5273
Emp Here 150
SIC 8221 Colleges and universities
Janisz Kozinski

D-U-N-S 25-186-5473   (BR)
UNIVERSITY OF SASKATCHEWAN
OFFICE OF THE VICE PRESIDENT RESEARCH
(*Suby   of   UNIVERSITY   OF
SASKATCHEWAN*)
107 Administration Pl Suite 201, Saskatoon,
SK, S7N 5A2
(306) 966-8514
Emp Here 102
SIC 8221 Colleges and universities
Peter Mackinnon

D-U-N-S 24-666-5202   (BR)
UNIVERSITY OF SASKATCHEWAN
*WESTERN COLLEGE OF VETERINARY
MEDICINE*
(*Suby   of   UNIVERSITY   OF
SASKATCHEWAN*)
52 Campus Dr Rm 3101, Saskatoon, SK, S7N
5B4
(306) 966-7477
Emp Here 344
SIC 8221 Colleges and universities
Douglas Freeman

D-U-N-S 25-529-5628   (SL)
UNIVERSITY OF SASKATCHEWAN STUDENTS' UNION
1 Campus Dr Rm 65, Saskatoon, SK, S7N
5A3
(306) 966-6960
Emp Here 180   *Sales* 45,394,200
SIC 8611 Business associations
Caroline Cottrell

D-U-N-S 20-657-8403   (SL)
USASK SMALL ANIMAL CLINICAL STUD
SMALL ANIMAL CLINIC
52 Campus Dr, Saskatoon, SK, S7N 5B4
(306) 966-7126
Emp Here 49   *Sales* 19,473,286
SIC 8699 Membership organizations, nec
Jenn Molley

D-U-N-S 25-294-8187   (BR)
WAL-MART CANADA CORP
(*Suby of* WALMART INC.)
1706 Preston Ave N Suite 3084, Saskatoon,
SK, S7N 4Y1
(306) 373-2300
Emp Here 150
SIC 5311 Department stores
Comber Barry

D-U-N-S 24-883-6736   (HQ)
WESTERN WATER INDUSTRIES
CULLIGAN WATER CONDITIONING
301 Central Ave, Saskatoon, SK, S7N 2E9
(306) 374-8555
Emp Here 24   *Sales* 24,231,733
SIC 5149 Groceries and related products, nec
Lyndon Lesser
Holly Lesser

Saskatoon, SK S7P

D-U-N-S 25-681-7776   (BR)
ACKLANDS - GRAINGER INC
INDUSTRIAL DIVISION
(*Suby of* W.W. GRAINGER, INC.)
3602 Millar Ave, Saskatoon, SK, S7P 0B1
(306) 664-5500
Emp Here 100
SIC 5085 Industrial supplies
Neil Doepker

D-U-N-S 25-101-7240   (HQ)
**APPLIED INDUSTRIAL TECHNOLOGIES,
LP**
A I T
(*Suby of* APPLIED INDUSTRIAL TECHNOLOGIES, INC.)
143 Wheeler St, Saskatoon, SK, S7P 0A4
(306) 931-0888
Emp Here 25   *Sales* 292,638,000
SIC 5085 Industrial supplies
Peter Wallace
Ron Sowinski
Mark Eisele
Thomas Armold
Benjamin Mondics
Neil Schrimsher

D-U-N-S 20-740-1241   (HQ)
CNH INDUSTRIAL CANADA, LTD
CASE NEW HOLLAND
(*Suby of* CNH INDUSTRIAL N.V.)
1000 71st St E, Saskatoon, SK, S7P 0B5
(306) 934-3500
Sales 233,127,910
SIC 3523 Farm machinery and equipment
Robert Bedard
Massimiliano Chiara

D-U-N-S 20-069-2010   (HQ)
CP DISTRIBUTORS LTD
3719 Kochar Ave, Saskatoon, SK, S7P 0B8
(306) 242-3315
Emp Here 50   *Sales* 142,407,000
SIC 5039 Construction materials, nec
Scott Suppes
Robert Grant
Gerald Haller
Wayne Molengraaf

D-U-N-S 20-841-1157   (HQ)
CRESTLINE COACH LTD
126 Wheeler St, Saskatoon, SK, S7P 0A9

(306) 934-8844
Sales 31,338,020
SIC 3711 Motor vehicles and car bodies
Geoffrey Booth
Daryl Bitz

D-U-N-S 20-935-3614   (HQ)
DSI UNDERGROUND CANADA LTD
DSI UNDERGROUND
(*Suby of* TENSION II LUXCO SARL)
3919 Millar Ave, Saskatoon, SK, S7P 0C1
(306) 244-6244
Emp Here 30   *Sales* 70,512,930
SIC 3532 Mining machinery
Michael Breicht
Nick Moses
Gavin Fairburn
Jeffrey Wheeler

D-U-N-S 24-916-0094   (HQ)
GREEN LINE MANUFACTURING LTD
(*Suby of* GREEN LINE SALES LTD)
3711 Mitchelmore Ave, Saskatoon, SK, S7P
0C5
(306) 934-8886
Emp Here 38   *Sales* 10,973,732
SIC 5251 Hardware stores
Andrew Dunham

D-U-N-S 20-062-5457   (SL)
HUMBOLDT ELECTRIC LTD
H E ELECTRIC (SASKATOON), DIV
102 Gladstone Cres, Saskatoon, SK, S7P 0C7
(306) 665-6551
Emp Here 85   *Sales* 18,515,465
SIC 1731 Electrical work
Darren Mcconnell
Glen Gerow
Dean Cochrane

D-U-N-S 24-749-2929   (HQ)
**MITSUBISHI HITACHI POWER SYSTEMS
CANADA, LTD**
(*Suby of* HITACHI, LTD.)
3903 Brodsky Ave Suite 100, Saskatoon, SK,
S7P 0C9
(306) 242-9222
Emp Here 34   *Sales* 74,972,475
SIC 3699 Electrical equipment and supplies,
nec
Sheldon Myhre
Robert Dueck
Lindy Antonini

D-U-N-S 20-841-0241   (SL)
NORAC SYSTEMS INTERNATIONAL INC
3702 Kinnear Pl, Saskatoon, SK, S7P 0A6
(306) 664-6711
Emp Here 50   *Sales* 10,233,650
SIC 3625 Relays and industrial controls
William Strelioff
Neil Weber
Dave Anderson
David Grier
Casey Davis

D-U-N-S 24-678-5781   (BR)
NORSEMAN INC
NORSEMAN STRUCTURES
(*Suby of* NORSEMAN GROUP LTD)
3815 Wanuskewin Rd, Saskatoon, SK, S7P
1A4
(306) 385-2888
Emp Here 114
SIC 3448 Prefabricated Metal buildings and
components
Ron Bryant

D-U-N-S 24-311-0678   (SL)
PRAIRIE PRIDE NATURAL FOODS LTD
3535 Millar Ave, Saskatoon, SK, S7P 0A2
(306) 653-1810
Emp Here 100   *Sales* 34,569,000
SIC 2015 Poultry slaughtering and processing
Murdie Pollon
Ron Petterson

D-U-N-S 20-842-6676   (SL)

STARTCO ENGINEERING LTD
LITTELFUSE STARTCO
(*Suby of* LITTELFUSE, INC.)
3714 Kinnear Pl, Saskatoon, SK, S7P 0A6
(306) 373-5505
Emp Here 72   *Sales* 13,711,824
SIC 3699 Electrical equipment and supplies, nec
Garry Paulson
Dal Ferbert

D-U-N-S 25-976-3142   (HQ)
WBM TECHNOLOGIES INC
3718 Kinnear Pl Unit 104, Saskatoon, SK, S7P 0A6
(306) 664-2686
Emp Here 5   *Sales* 22,358,700
SIC 5045 Computers, peripherals, and software
Joeanne Hardy
Brett Bailey
Robert Hardy

Saskatoon, SK S7R

D-U-N-S 24-850-4677   (SL)
3TWENTY SOLUTIONS INC
3TWENTY MODULAR
36 Capital Cir, Saskatoon, SK, S7R 0H4
(306) 382-3320
Emp Here 30   *Sales* 14,121,930
SIC 1542 Nonresidential construction, nec
Bryan Mccrea

D-U-N-S 20-326-6283   (SL)
BASF AGRICULTURAL SPECIALTIES LTD
(*Suby of* BASF SE)
3835 Thatcher Ave, Saskatoon, SK, S7R 1A3
(306) 373-3060
Emp Here 45   *Sales* 83,099,655
SIC 6331 Fire, marine, and casualty insurance
Mark Timbres

D-U-N-S 20-794-9475   (BR)
COSTCO WHOLESALE CANADA LTD
COSTCO
(*Suby of* COSTCO WHOLESALE CORPORATION)
115 Marquis Dr W, Saskatoon, SK, S7R 1C7
(306) 933-4262
Emp Here 275
SIC 5099 Durable goods, nec
Shane Bollienback

D-U-N-S 24-519-5326   (SL)
DAIRYLAND AGRO SUPPLY LTD
4030 Thatcher Ave, Saskatoon, SK, S7R 1A2
(306) 242-5850
Emp Here 45   *Sales* 21,376,170
SIC 5083 Farm and garden machinery
Ronald Elder
Gwen Elder

D-U-N-S 24-967-9267   (HQ)
DELCO AUTOMATION INC
DELCOSECURITY
3735 Thatcher Ave, Saskatoon, SK, S7R 1B8
(306) 244-6449
Emp Here 34   *Sales* 18,091,990
SIC 3625 Relays and industrial controls
Brian Rindall
Douglas Muller

D-U-N-S 25-831-3931   (SL)
FGI SUPPLY LTD
BOBCAT OF SASKATOON
3914 Thatcher Ave Suite Lbby, Saskatoon, SK, S7R 1A4
(306) 931-7880
Emp Here 34   *Sales* 16,150,884
SIC 5082 Construction and mining machinery
Bradley (Brad) Williams
Tyler Vogelsang

D-U-N-S 24-375-7473   (SL)

JNE WELDING LIMITED PARTNERSHIP
3915 Thatcher Ave, Saskatoon, SK, S7R 1A3
(306) 242-0884
Emp Here 125   *Sales* 24,010,625
SIC 3441 Fabricated structural Metal
James Nowakowski
Brenda Nowakowski

D-U-N-S 25-636-7525   (SL)
M&A ENTERPRISES
HUSKY TRAVEL CENTER
315 Marquis Dr W, Saskatoon, SK, S7R 1B6
(306) 653-2744
Emp Here 50   *Sales* 62,860,050
SIC 5172 Petroleum products, nec
Michael Gay

D-U-N-S 24-232-0752   (HQ)
NOVOZYMES BIOAG LIMITED
(*Suby of* NOVO NORDISK FONDEN)
3935 Thatcher Ave, Saskatoon, SK, S7R 1A3
(306) 657-8200
Sales 19,529,090
SIC 8731 Commercial physical research
Steen Riisgaard
Per Falholt
Thomas Nagy
Arne Juul Hansen
Jerker Hartwall
Walther Thygesen
Thomas Videb K
Kurt Anker Nielsen
Peder Holk Nielsen
Henrik G Rtler

D-U-N-S 20-070-1894   (HQ)
RIDSDALE TRANSPORT LTD
210 Apex St, Saskatoon, SK, S7R 0A2
(306) 668-9200
Emp Here 110   *Sales* 46,095,250
SIC 4213 Trucking, except local
Wayne Ridsdale
Greg Ridsdale
Robert Ridsdale
Gary Ridsdale

D-U-N-S 25-654-8330   (SL)
ROY, ROB TRADING & SAMCO HOLDINGS
PBR AUCTIONS
105 71st St W, Saskatoon, SK, S7R 1B4
(306) 931-7666
Emp Here 60   *Sales* 21,852,900
SIC 5012 Automobiles and other motor vehicles
Robert Roy
James Roy

D-U-N-S 20-105-5618   (BR)
SAPUTO INC
(*Suby of* JOLINA CAPITAL INC)
122 Wakooma St, Saskatoon, SK, S7R 1A8
(306) 668-6833
Emp Here 250
SIC 2023 Dry, condensed and evaporated dairy products
Ashley Whitenect

D-U-N-S 20-112-8670   (BR)
WESTCAN BULK TRANSPORT LTD
(*Suby of* THE KENAN ADVANTAGE GROUP INC)
110 71st St W, Saskatoon, SK, S7R 1A1
(306) 242-5899
Emp Here 100
SIC 4213 Trucking, except local
John Harrington

Saskatoon, SK S7S

D-U-N-S 24-837-2026   (SL)
SS STONEBRIDGE DEL FITNESS CORPORATION
MOTION FITNESS
431 Nelson Rd, Saskatoon, SK, S7S 1P2

(306) 975-1003
Emp Here 189   *Sales* 14,845,005
SIC 7991 Physical fitness facilities
Balal Anwar

D-U-N-S 20-712-7700   (BR)
ST. PAUL'S ROMAN CATHOLIC SEPARATE SCHOOL DIVISION NO 20
ST JOSEPH HIGH SCHOOL
115 Nelson Rd, Saskatoon, SK, S7S 1H1
(306) 659-7650
Emp Here 90
SIC 8211 Elementary and secondary schools
C Thorson

D-U-N-S 24-883-6884   (HQ)
TCU FINANCIAL GROUP
307 Ludlow St, Saskatoon, SK, S7S 1N6
(306) 651-6700
Emp Here 47   *Sales* 16,118,655
SIC 6062 State credit unions
Greg Peacock
Morris Smysnuik
Helen Sukovieff

D-U-N-S 24-231-3049   (SL)
VINTNERS CELLAR SASKATOON
1824 Mcormond Dr Suite 146, Saskatoon, SK, S7S 0A6
(306) 371-9463
Emp Here 25   *Sales* 14,697,900
SIC 5182 Wine and distilled beverages

Saskatoon, SK S7T

D-U-N-S 24-883-3824   (SL)
CIRCLE DRIVE SPECIAL CARE HOME INC
3055 Preston Ave, Saskatoon, SK, S7T 1C3
(306) 955-4800
Emp Here 80   *Sales* 5,485,280
SIC 8051 Skilled nursing care facilities
Leonard Enns

D-U-N-S 20-407-7788   (SL)
CO-OP SASKATOON STONEBRID
106 Stonebridge Blvd, Saskatoon, SK, S7T 0J1
(306) 933-0306
Emp Here 40   *Sales* 10,966,080
SIC 5411 Grocery stores
Trevor Williams

D-U-N-S 24-350-3450   (BR)
HOME DEPOT OF CANADA INC
(*Suby of* THE HOME DEPOT INC)
3043 Clarence Ave S Suite 1, Saskatoon, SK, S7T 0B5
(306) 657-4100
Emp Here 100
SIC 5251 Hardware stores
Tayler Chris

D-U-N-S 20-070-2504   (HQ)
SASKATOON CO-OPERATIVE ASSOCIATION LIMITED, THE
SASKATOON CO-OP
(*Suby of* FEDERATED CO-OPERATIVES LIMITED)
503 Wellman Cres Suite 201, Saskatoon, SK, S7T 0J1
(306) 933-3801
Emp Here 60   *Sales* 318,324,971
SIC 5411 Grocery stores
Grant Whitmore
Ron Moffatt
Jamie Herle
Norm Bemis
Gordon Bedient
Denis Gilbertson
Nathan Holowaty
Mike Puckett
David Thieme

D-U-N-S 24-330-0543   (BR)
WAL-MART CANADA CORP

(*Suby of* WALMART INC.)
3035 Clarence Ave S, Saskatoon, SK, S7T 0B6
(306) 653-8200
Emp Here 200
SIC 5311 Department stores
Trevor Shell

Saskatoon, SK S7V

D-U-N-S 25-363-0198   (BR)
LOBLAWS INC
EXTRA FOODS
(*Suby of* LOBLAW COMPANIES LIMITED)
315 Herold Rd, Saskatoon, SK, S7V 1J7
(306) 664-5033
Emp Here 100
SIC 5411 Grocery stores
Shawn Rowart

Shaunavon, SK S0N

D-U-N-S 20-835-8150   (SL)
BENCH HUTTERIAN BRETHREN CORP
BENCH COLONY
Hwy 13 W, Shaunavon, SK, S0N 2M0
(306) 297-3270
Emp Here 70   *Sales* 18,361,630
SIC 0111 Wheat
Andy Wurtz
David Waldner

D-U-N-S 20-651-5764   (SL)
SHAUNAVON HOSPITAL & CARE CENTRE
Gd, Shaunavon, SK, S0N 2M0
(306) 297-2644
Emp Here 100   *Sales* 124,972,650
SIC 6324 Hospital and medical service plans
Lee Ericsson

D-U-N-S 24-233-5701   (SL)
SHAUNAVON LIVESTOCK SALES (1988) LTD
Gd, Shaunavon, SK, S0N 2M0
(306) 297-2457
Emp Here 12   *Sales* 14,524,764
SIC 5154 Livestock
Stephen Hodgson

Shellbrook, SK S0J

D-U-N-S 24-371-2531   (SL)
HANNIGAN'S HONEY INC
Gd, Shellbrook, SK, S0J 2E0
(306) 747-7782
Emp Here 35   *Sales* 29,245,195
SIC 5149 Groceries and related products, nec
Murray Hannigan
Ruby Hannigan

D-U-N-S 24-818-5993   (SL)
SHELLBROOK CHEVROLET OLDSMOBILE LTD
43 Main St, Shellbrook, SK, S0J 2E0
(306) 747-2411
Emp Here 30   *Sales* 14,942,340
SIC 5511 New and used car dealers
Bruce Storry
Chris Gosselin
Rob Dron

D-U-N-S 20-286-2215   (SL)
SHELLBROOK CO-OPERATIVE ASSOCIATION LIMITED, THE
Gd, Shellbrook, SK, S0J 2E0
(306) 747-2122
Emp Here 10   *Sales* 10,883,230
SIC 5171 Petroleum bulk stations and termi-

nals
Wayne Knouse
Roger Mayert

Simmie, SK S0N

D-U-N-S 20-840-7114   (SL)
HUTTERIAN BRETHREN CHURCH OF SIM-MIE INC
Gd, Simmie, SK, S0N 2N0
(306) 297-6304
Emp Here 112   *Sales* 12,065,424
SIC 8661 Religious organizations
Gerry Hofer

Southey, SK S0G

D-U-N-S 24-519-6647   (HQ)
FLAMAN SALES LTD
Gd, Southey, SK, S0G 4P0
(306) 726-4403
Emp Here 30   *Sales* 66,826,800
SIC 5191 Farm supplies
Rudy Flaman
Don Flaman

St Brieux, SK S0K

D-U-N-S 20-647-1133   (BR)
BOURGAULT INDUSTRIES LTD
PRECISION PROFILES PLUS
(*Suby of* BOURGAULT INDUSTRIES LTD)
501 Barbier Dr, St Brieux, SK, S0K 3V0
(306) 275-2300
Emp Here 100
SIC 1761 Roofing, siding, and sheetMetal
work
Tom Cunningham

D-U-N-S 24-607-8760   (HQ)
BOURGAULT INDUSTRIES LTD
CNC PRECISION PROFILES PLUS
500 Hwy Unit 368 N, St Brieux, SK, S0K 3V0
(306) 275-2300
Emp Here 396   *Sales* 117,968,340
SIC 3523 Farm machinery and equipment
Gerrard Bourgault
Louise Bourgault
Michael Gauthier
Richard Coquet

D-U-N-S 24-883-4848   (SL)
F.P. BOURGAULT TILLAGE TOOLS LTD
SOLAR WEST
200 5 Ave S, St Brieux, SK, S0K 3V0
(306) 275-4500
Emp Here 75   *Sales* 16,650,075
SIC 3523 Farm machinery and equipment
Joseph Bourgault
Rick Schemenauer
Denise Bortis
Patrick Yeager
Marissa Mark
Steven Oleksyn
Dylan Theis
Penny Ulledal
Kelly Stevenspn
Mel Maclean

St Gregor, SK S0K

D-U-N-S 20-601-0530   (SL)
MICHEL'S INDUSTRIES LTD
3 Entrance Rd, St Gregor, SK, S0K 3X0

---

(306) 366-2184
Emp Here 90   *Sales* 19,980,090
SIC 3523 Farm machinery and equipment
Bud Michel
Ron Michel
Brad Michel
Teresa Eastman

St Walburg, SK S0M

D-U-N-S 25-417-1861   (SL)
HOFFMAN, R. J. HOLDINGS LTD
Gd, St Walburg, SK, S0M 2T0
(306) 248-3466
Emp Here 70   *Sales* 22,379,350
SIC 1389 Oil and gas field services, nec
Robert Hoffman
Julius Hoffman
Romona Hoffman
Joan Hoffman

Star City, SK S0E

D-U-N-S 20-855-1754   (SL)
STAR CITY FARMING CO. LTD
Gd, Star City, SK, S0E 1P0
(306) 863-2343
Emp Here 32   *Sales* 10,958,944
SIC 0119 Cash grains, nec
Peter Tschetter
David Tschetter
Joshua Tschetter
Darius Tschetter

Strongfield, SK S0H

D-U-N-S 25-146-0259   (SL)
GARDINER DAM TERMINAL JOINT VEN-TURE
Gd, Strongfield, SK, S0H 3Z0
(306) 857-2134
Emp Here 13   *Sales* 15,735,161
SIC 5153 Grain and field beans
Andy Travers
Barbara Martens

Sturgeon Lake, SK S0J

D-U-N-S 20-703-4898   (SL)
STURGEON LAKE FINE FOODS & GAS BAR
1 Economic Lane, Sturgeon Lake, SK, S0J 2E1
(306) 764-1222
Emp Here 22   *Sales* 10,957,716
SIC 5541 Gasoline service stations
Elizabeth Felix

Success, SK S0N

D-U-N-S 24-319-5935   (SL)
DUNNINGTON HOLDINGS LTD
T.W. COMMODITIES
1 Commodity Dr, Success, SK, S0N 2R0
(306) 773-9748
Emp Here 16   *Sales* 19,366,352
SIC 5153 Grain and field beans
Gaurav Kapoor
Lisa Watson

Swift Current, SK S9H

D-U-N-S 20-719-4908   (HQ)
B & A PETROLEUM LTD
2004 South Service Rd W, Swift Current, SK, S9H 5J5
(306) 773-8890
Emp Here 1   *Sales* 12,663,135
SIC 5983 Fuel oil dealers
Darryl Meyer

D-U-N-S 25-118-3133   (SL)
BATCO-REM
(*Suby of* AG GROWTH INTERNATIONAL INC)
201 Industrial Dr, Swift Current, SK, S9H 5R4

Emp Here 150   *Sales* 33,300,150
SIC 3523 Farm machinery and equipment
Tim Close
Steve Sommerfeld

D-U-N-S 24-340-6605   (HQ)
BOARD OF EDUCATION OF THE CHI-NOOK SCHOOL DIVISION NO. 211 OF SASKATCHEWAN
2100 Gladstone St E, Swift Current, SK, S9H 3W7
(306) 778-9200
Emp Here 20   *Sales* 30,061,782
SIC 8211 Elementary and secondary schools
Shane Andrus
Kimberly Pridmore
Kyle Mcintyre
Rod Quintin

D-U-N-S 24-346-3382   (BR)
CYPRESS HEALTH REGION
PALLISER REGIONAL CARE CENTRE
440 Central Ave S, Swift Current, SK, S9H 3G6

Emp Here 200   *Sales* 314,035
SIC 8361 Residential care
Jeff Schwan

D-U-N-S 25-316-3653   (SL)
CYPRESS MOTORS (SC)
2234 South Service Rd W, Swift Current, SK, S9H 5J7
(306) 778-3673
Emp Here 50   *Sales* 24,903,900
SIC 5511 New and used car dealers
Jeffrey Parsons
Jason Parsons

D-U-N-S 25-298-5718   (SL)
DEGUIRE, MICHEL HOLDINGS INC
CANADIAN TIRE
1811 22nd Ave Ne, Swift Current, SK, S9H 5B7
(306) 773-0654
Emp Here 40   *Sales* 19,923,120
SIC 5531 Auto and home supply stores
Michel Deguire

D-U-N-S 20-447-9414   (SL)
DELTA ROCK & SAND LTD
1910 South Railway St E, Swift Current, SK, S9H 4G6
(306) 773-9808
Emp Here 75   *Sales* 11,114,400
SIC 4212 Local trucking, without storage
David Peters
Timothy Heinrichs

D-U-N-S 25-408-9246   (HQ)
DIAMOND ENERGY SERVICES INC
1521 North Service Rd W, Swift Current, SK, S9H 3S9
(306) 778-6682
Emp Here 100   *Sales* 100,901,850
SIC 1389 Oil and gas field services, nec
Michael Gering
Micheal Macbean
Dale Laniuk
Thomas Kileen

D-U-N-S 24-375-4061   (HQ)
PATTISON AGRICULTURE LIMITED
2777 North Service Rd W, Swift Current, SK, S9H 5M1
(306) 773-9351
Sales 97,274,610
SIC 5999 Miscellaneous retail stores, nec
Darrin Didychuck

D-U-N-S 20-071-3576   (HQ)
PIONEER CO-OPERATIVE ASSOCIATION LIMITED, THE
PIONEER CO-OP
1150 Central Ave N Suite 2000, Swift Current, SK, S9H 0G1
(306) 778-8800
Emp Here 150   *Sales* 226,026,140
SIC 5311 Department stores
Stuart Dyrland

D-U-N-S 24-691-8270   (SL)
RAYNARD FARM EQUIPMENT LTD
L R TRUCK CENTRE
2524 South Service Rd W, Swift Current, SK, S9H 5J9
(306) 773-3030
Emp Here 20   *Sales* 10,000,000
SIC 5083 Farm and garden machinery
Lyndon Raynard
Val Raynard

D-U-N-S 20-068-9032   (HQ)
ROBERTSON IMPLEMENTS (1988) LTD
ROBERTSON MOTOR SPORTS
2464 South Service Rd W, Swift Current, SK, S9H 5J8
(306) 773-4948
Emp Here 43   *Sales* 55,376,640
SIC 5571 Motorcycle dealers
Doug Robertson

D-U-N-S 20-015-9900   (SL)
SASK HIGHWAYS MAINTENANCE
1200 South Service Rd W, Swift Current, SK, S9H 5G7
(306) 778-8364
Emp Here 49   *Sales* 25,478,383
SIC 4785 Inspection and fixed facilities
Kevin Pearson

D-U-N-S 25-481-3223   (BR)
SASKATCHEWAN ABILITIES COUNCIL INC
(*Suby of* SASKATCHEWAN ABILITIES COUNCIL INC)
1551 North Railway St W, Swift Current, SK, S9H 5G3
(306) 773-2076
Emp Here 93
SIC 8331 Job training and related services
Irene Enns

D-U-N-S 24-804-6117   (BR)
SASKATCHEWAN HEALTH AUTHORITY
CYPRESS REGIONAL HOSPITAL
(*Suby of* GOVERNMENT OF SASKATCHEWAN)
2004 Saskatchewan Dr, Swift Current, SK, S9H 5M8
(306) 778-9400
Emp Here 100
SIC 8062 General medical and surgical hospi-tals
Beth Vachon

D-U-N-S 20-071-4160   (SL)
STANDARD MOTORS (77) LTD
44 2nd Ave Nw, Swift Current, SK, S9H 0N9
(306) 773-3131
Emp Here 45   *Sales* 22,413,510
SIC 5511 New and used car dealers
James Plewis

D-U-N-S 20-656-5405   (SL)
SWIFT CURRENT CARE CENTRE
700 Aberdeen St Suite 22, Swift Current, SK, S9H 3E3

Emp Here 80   *Sales* 5,485,280

▲ Public Company   ■ Public Company Family Member   **HQ** Headquarters   **BR** Branch   **SL** Single Location

SIC 8051 Skilled nursing care facilities
Bonnie Funk

D-U-N-S 20-071-4509   (SL)
TREEN PACKERS LTD
Gd, Swift Current, SK, S9H 3V4
(306) 773-4473
Emp Here 23   *Sales* 19,218,271
SIC 5147 Meats and meat products
Gerald Treen
Viola Treen

D-U-N-S 24-967-7139   (SL)
UFR URBAN FOREST RECYCLERS INC
201 Industrial Dr, Swift Current, SK, S9H 5R4
(306) 777-0600
Emp Here 65   *Sales* 15,173,275
SIC 2679 Converted paper products, nec
Kevin Stangeland
Donald Meister

D-U-N-S 25-294-8708   (BR)
WAL-MART CANADA CORP
(*Suby of* WALMART INC.)
1800 22nd Ave Ne, Swift Current, SK, S9H 0E5
(306) 778-3489
Emp Here 140
SIC 5311 Department stores
Jodilyn Chartand

D-U-N-S 25-680-2182   (SL)
XPRESS FOOD AND GAS (MOOSE JAW) LTD
HUSKY CAR/TRUCK STOP
1510 South Service Rd W, Swift Current, SK, S9H 3T1
(306) 773-6444
Emp Here 50   *Sales* 24,903,900
SIC 5541 Gasoline service stations
Barry Neigel
Rita Neigel

Tisdale, SK S0E

D-U-N-S 20-071-5399   (HQ)
BEELAND CO-OPERATIVE ASSOCIATION LIMITED
1101 99 St, Tisdale, SK, S0E 1T0
(306) 873-2688
Emp Here 81   *Sales* 29,748,983
SIC 5171 Petroleum bulk stations and terminals
Todd Svenson
Linda Alvis
Robert Haller
Gary Rice
Bj Madsen
Evelyn Keays
Dianne Wallington
Lorne Luck
Christina Friske
Barry Thesen

D-U-N-S 24-236-7803   (SL)
JOHN BOB FARM EQUIPMENT LTD
Hwy 3 W, Tisdale, SK, S0E 1T0
(306) 873-4588
Emp Here 22   *Sales* 10,450,572
SIC 5083 Farm and garden machinery

D-U-N-S 20-068-2099   (HQ)
KELSEY TRAIL REGIONAL HEALTH AUTHORITY
Gd, Tisdale, SK, S0E 1T0
(306) 873-6600
Emp Here 50   *Sales* 22,216,000
SIC 8062 General medical and surgical hospitals
Jim Taylor

D-U-N-S 24-346-3390   (BR)
KELSEY TRAIL REGIONAL HEALTH AUTHORITY
TISDALE HOSPITAL

(*Suby of* KELSEY TRAIL REGIONAL HEALTH AUTHORITY)
Gd, Tisdale, SK, S0E 1T0

Emp Here 200
SIC 8062 General medical and surgical hospitals
Doris Wilson

Trossachs, SK S0C

D-U-N-S 20-626-6942   (SL)
D & M LOCATING LTD
4 2nd Street W, Trossachs, SK, S0C 2N0
(306) 354-7907
Emp Here 40   *Sales* 17,968,760
SIC 7389 Business services, nec

Unity, SK S0K

D-U-N-S 20-071-7254   (HQ)
DELTA CO-OPERATIVE ASSOCIATION LTD, THE
130 Second Ave W, Unity, SK, S0K 4L0
(306) 228-2662
Emp Here 50   *Sales* 29,347,700
SIC 5411 Grocery stores
Sandy Richards
Mckim Dean
Harvey Morrissette
Shirley Tyndall
Brian Lewin
Adeline Knox
Jack Kraft
Edward Stang
Leo Volk
Fred Weinkauff

D-U-N-S 24-234-1329   (SL)
UNITY & DISTRICT HEALTH CENTRE
100 1st Ave W Unit 1, Unity, SK, S0K 4L0
(306) 228-2666
Emp Here 89   *Sales* 10,936,053
SIC 8062 General medical and surgical hospitals
Colleen Boucher

Val Marie, SK S0N

D-U-N-S 20-757-2223   (SL)
SAND LAKE HUTTERIAN BRETHREN INC
Gd, Val Marie, SK, S0N 2T0
(306) 298-2068
Emp Here 80
SIC 7389 Business services, nec
Amos Kleinsasser
Joseph Kleinsasser
Andrew Urtz

Vanscoy, SK S0L

D-U-N-S 24-883-4327   (SL)
PRAIRIE PULSE INC
700 Campbell Dr, Vanscoy, SK, S0L 3J0
(306) 249-9236
Emp Here 15   *Sales* 18,155,955
SIC 5153 Grain and field beans
Howard Wagner
Allan Wagner

Vonda, SK S0K

D-U-N-S 24-820-8295   (SL)
HIGHLINE MANUFACTURING LTD
(*Suby of* BOURGAULT INDUSTRIES LTD)
Hwy 27, Vonda, SK, S0K 4N0
(306) 258-2233
Emp Here 150   *Sales* 33,300,150
SIC 3523 Farm machinery and equipment
Gerry Bourgault

Wakaw, SK S0K

D-U-N-S 25-058-3655   (SL)
COUNTRY CROSS ROADS SERVICE
Gd, Wakaw, SK, S0K 4P0
(306) 233-5553
Emp Here 42   *Sales* 20,919,276
SIC 5541 Gasoline service stations
Sandy Sherdnotta

Waldheim, SK S0K

D-U-N-S 25-314-4695   (HQ)
MENNONITE TRUST LTD
MTL
3005 Central Ave, Waldheim, SK, S0K 4R0
(306) 945-2080
Emp Here 15   *Sales* 10,109,180
SIC 6733 Trusts, nec
Cory Regier

Warman, SK S0K

D-U-N-S 24-468-2639   (HQ)
WARMAN HOME CENTRE LP
WARMAN TRUSS
601 South Railway St W, Warman, SK, S0K 4S0
(306) 933-4950
Sales 32,385,892
SIC 5211 Lumber and other building materials
David Holst

Watrous, SK S0K

D-U-N-S 20-072-0951   (HQ)
WATROUS MAINLINE MOTOR PRODUCTS LIMITED
208 1st Ave E Hwy Suite 2, Watrous, SK, S0K 4T0
(306) 946-3336
Emp Here 25   *Sales* 50,342,400
SIC 5511 New and used car dealers
Gerald Merrifield
Don Campbell

Watson, SK S0K

D-U-N-S 24-036-5593   (SL)
T C ENTERPRISES LTD
U.A.P. NAPA AUTO PARTS
Hwy 6 & 5 Sw Corner, Watson, SK, S0K 4V0
(306) 287-3636
Emp Here 21   *Sales* 10,459,638
SIC 5541 Gasoline service stations
Myron Knafelc
Kelly Herriges
Larry Painter

Wawota, SK S0G

D-U-N-S 25-326-0798   (BR)
SUN COUNTRY REGIONAL HEALTH AUTHORITY
WAWOTA MEMORIAL HEALTH CENTRE
201 Wilfred St, Wawota, SK, S0G 5A0

Emp Here 90
SIC 8051 Skilled nursing care facilities
Florie Restau

Weyburn, SK S4H

D-U-N-S 20-854-2118   (SL)
324007 ALBERTA LTD
WEYBURN LIVESTOCK EXCHANGE
Gd Lcd Main, Weyburn, SK, S4H 2J7

Emp Here 15   *Sales* 18,155,955
SIC 5154 Livestock
Brian Nilsson
Lee Nilsson
William Greive

D-U-N-S 20-072-2007   (SL)
BARBER MOTORS (1963) LTD
1 Government Rd, Weyburn, SK, S4H 0N8
(306) 842-6531
Emp Here 55   *Sales* 34,610,400
SIC 5511 New and used car dealers
Malorie Barber
Delaine Barber
June V. Barber

D-U-N-S 20-874-2093   (SL)
CAYEN, J.C. HOLDINGS LTD
CANADIAN TIRE
1240 Sims Ave, Weyburn, SK, S4H 3N9
(306) 842-4600
Emp Here 40   *Sales* 19,923,120
SIC 5531 Auto and home supply stores
Joseph Cayen

D-U-N-S 20-917-9621   (SL)
CFO RENTALS INC
Gd Lcd Main, Weyburn, SK, S4H 2J7
(306) 842-3454
Emp Here 23   *Sales* 10,925,598
SIC 5082 Construction and mining machinery

D-U-N-S 20-448-5809   (SL)
GREAT PLAINS FORD SALES (1978) LTD
206 Sims Ave, Weyburn, SK, S4H 2H6
(306) 842-2645
Emp Here 29   *Sales* 14,444,262
SIC 5511 New and used car dealers
Jeffrey Tosczak

D-U-N-S 24-520-1181   (HQ)
HOLY FAMILY ROMAN CATHOLIC SEPARATE SCHOOL DIVISION 140
110 Souris Ave Suite 3, Weyburn, SK, S4H 2Z8
(306) 842-7025
Emp Here 5   *Sales* 19,823,800
SIC 8211 Elementary and secondary schools
Shelley Rowein
Cal Martin

D-U-N-S 20-072-2734   (SL)
MAINIL, JERRY LIMITED
1530 New City Garden Rd, Weyburn, SK, S4H 2L1
(306) 842-5412
Emp Here 55   *Sales* 13,884,310
SIC 1623 Water, sewer, and utility lines
Dennis Mainil
Dale Mainil

D-U-N-S 25-999-7372   (SL)
MINARD'S LEISURE WORLD LTD
921 Government Rd S, Weyburn, SK, S4H 3R3
(306) 842-3288
Emp Here 40   *Sales* 19,923,120

▲ Public Company   ■ Public Company Family Member   **HQ** Headquarters   **BR** Branch   **SL** Single Location

SIC 5561 Recreational vehicle dealers
Susan Minard
Gene Minard

D-U-N-S 24-966-8914   (BR)
NEXANS CANADA INC
(*Suby of* NEXANS)
1770 East Ave, Weyburn, SK, S4H 0B8
(306) 842-7451
Emp Here 114
SIC 3312 Blast furnaces and steel mills
Michael Bloor

D-U-N-S 24-204-1676   (SL)
PANTHER DRILLING CORPORATION
Gd Lcd Main, Weyburn, SK, S4H 2J7
(306) 842-7370
Emp Here 85   *Sales* 20,925,810
SIC 1799 Special trade contractors, nec
Cory Hicks

D-U-N-S 24-348-1863   (HQ)
RUBICON PHARMACIES CANADA INC
117 3rd St Unit 206, Weyburn, SK, S4H 0W3
(306) 848-3855
Emp Here 15   *Sales* 110,122,200
SIC 5912 Drug stores and proprietary stores
Allan Chilton
Dwayne Hoffman
Robert Gare

D-U-N-S 25-329-3534   (BR)
SUN COUNTRY REGIONAL HEALTH AU-THORITY
WEYBURN GENERAL HOSPITAL IN SCHR
201 1st Ave Ne, Weyburn, SK, S4H 0N1
(306) 842-8400
Emp Here 150
SIC 8062 General medical and surgical hospi-tals
Sylvia Banyluk

D-U-N-S 24-317-1811   (BR)
WAL-MART CANADA CORP
WALMART
(*Suby of* WALMART INC.)
1000 Sims Ave, Weyburn, SK, S4H 3N9
(306) 842-6030
Emp Here 130
SIC 5311 Department stores
David Halstead

D-U-N-S 24-852-0827   (HQ)
WEYBURN CREDIT UNION LIMITED
205 Coteau Ave, Weyburn, SK, S4H 0G5
(306) 842-6641
Emp Here 67   *Sales* 15,351,100
SIC 6062 State credit unions
Don Shumlich

White City, SK S4L

D-U-N-S 20-561-4436   (HQ)
1343080 ALBERTA LTD
DUMUR INDUSTRIES
2 Ramm Ave, White City, SK, S4L 5B1
(306) 757-2403
Sales 19,208,500
SIC 3444 Sheet Metalwork
Ian Harrison

D-U-N-S 24-679-8714   (BR)
AECOM CANADA LTD
CARSON WELDING
(*Suby of* AECOM)
Highway 1 East 3 North Service Rd, White City, SK, S4L 5B1
(306) 779-2200
Emp Here 100
SIC 1389 Oil and gas field services, nec

Whitewood, SK S0G

D-U-N-S 24-630-1287   (SL)
CAN-AM TRAVEL STOPS INC
1203 Hwy 1, Whitewood, SK, S0G 5C0
(306) 735-2565
Emp Here 40   *Sales* 19,923,120
SIC 5541 Gasoline service stations
Dan Min

D-U-N-S 25-604-0973   (SL)
WHITEWOOD AUCTION SERVICE LTD
WHITEWOOD LIVESTOCK SALES
Hwy 1, Whitewood, SK, S0G 5C0
(306) 735-2822
Emp Here 30   *Sales* 44,030,760
SIC 5154 Livestock
Gene Parks

Wilcox, SK S0G

D-U-N-S 20-841-6487   (SL)
ATHOL MURRAY COLLEGE OF NOTRE DAME
NOTRE DAME COLLEGE
49 Main St, Wilcox, SK, S0G 5E0
(306) 732-2080
Emp Here 110   *Sales* 10,903,090
SIC 8211 Elementary and secondary schools
Terry Cooney

Wilkie, SK S0K

D-U-N-S 20-910-2479   (BR)
HEARTLAND REGIONAL HEALTH AU-THORITY
Gd, Wilkie, SK, S0K 4W0
(306) 843-2531
Emp Here 85   *Sales* 383,520
SIC 8011 Offices and clinics of medical doc-tors
Colleen Boucher

D-U-N-S 24-115-5134   (BR)
SASKATCHEWAN HEALTH AUTHORITY
WILKIE & DISTRICT HEALTH CENTRE
(*Suby of* GOVERNMENT OF SASKATCHEWAN)
304 7th St E, Wilkie, SK, S0K 4W0
(306) 843-2644
Emp Here 90
SIC 8062 General medical and surgical hospi-tals
Kerry Glassford

Wynyard, SK S0A

D-U-N-S 25-678-8274   (BR)
LILYDALE INC
LILYDALE FOODS
(*Suby of* SOFINA FOODS INC)
502 Bosworth St, Wynyard, SK, S0A 4T0
(306) 554-2555
Emp Here 400
SIC 2015 Poultry slaughtering and processing
Damin Elizalde

D-U-N-S 24-376-5856   (SL)
WYNYARD HOSPITAL
WYNYARD INTEGRATED HOSPITAL
300 10 St E, Wynyard, SK, S0A 4T0
(306) 554-2586
Emp Here 100   *Sales* 12,287,700
SIC 8062 General medical and surgical hospi-tals
Glenda Popowich

Yorkton, SK S3N

D-U-N-S 20-939-7350   (BR)
BOARD OF EDUCATION OF THE GOOD SPIRIT SCHOOL DIVISION NO. 204 OF SASKATCHEWAN
YORKTON REGIONAL HIGH SCHOOL
150 Gladstone Ave N, Yorkton, SK, S3N 2A8
(306) 786-5560
Emp Here 90
SIC 8211 Elementary and secondary schools
Mike Haczkewicz

D-U-N-S 24-240-3723   (SL)
CANADIAN TIRE
277 Broadway St E Suite 287, Yorkton, SK, S3N 3G7
(306) 783-9744
Emp Here 30   *Sales* 18,878,400
SIC 5541 Gasoline service stations

D-U-N-S 24-369-4556   (HQ)
CHRIST THE TEACHER CATHOLIC SCHOOLS DIVISION 212
45a Palliser Way, Yorkton, SK, S3N 4C5
(306) 783-8787
Emp Here 100   *Sales* 9,282,600
SIC 8211 Elementary and secondary schools
Brian Boechler

D-U-N-S 25-359-7298   (BR)
CULLIGAN OF CANADA ULC
CULLIGAN
76 Seventh Ave S Suite 1, Yorkton, SK, S3N 3V2
(306) 782-2648
Emp Here 100
SIC 5999 Miscellaneous retail stores, nec
Ryan Kirk

D-U-N-S 20-015-8215   (HQ)
GRAIN MILLERS CANADA CORP
(*Suby of* GRAIN MILLERS, INC.)
1 Grain Millers Dr, Yorkton, SK, S3N 3Z4
(306) 783-2931
Emp Here 60   *Sales* 41,482,800
SIC 2043 Cereal breakfast foods
Steven J. Eilertson
Craig W. O'neal
Rick Schwein

D-U-N-S 24-883-3360   (SL)
HARVEY, R & J ADVENTURES LTD
CANADIAN TIRE
205 Hamilton Rd, Yorkton, SK, S3N 4B9
(306) 783-9733
Emp Here 70   *Sales* 44,049,600
SIC 5531 Auto and home supply stores
Robert Harvey
Jodi Harvey

D-U-N-S 20-072-7907   (HQ)
LEON'S MFG. COMPANY INC
135 York Rd E, Yorkton, SK, S3N 3Z4
(306) 786-2600
Sales 11,525,100
SIC 3499 Fabricated Metal products, nec
Raymond Malinowski
John Malinowski
Linda Turta

D-U-N-S 25-996-3015   (SL)
LOGAN STEVENS CONSTRUCTION (2000) LTD
200 York Rd E, Yorkton, SK, S3N 4E4
(306) 782-2266
Emp Here 40   *Sales* 18,829,240
SIC 1542 Nonresidential construction, nec
Douglas (Doug) Kitsch

D-U-N-S 20-014-3530   (SL)
MYROWICH, A BUILDING MATERIAL LTD
HOME HARDWARE BUILDING CENTRE
145 Broadway St E, Yorkton, SK, S3N 3K5
(306) 783-3608
Emp Here 40   *Sales* 10,122,360

SIC 5211 Lumber and other building materials
Alex Myrowich
Loraine Myrowich

D-U-N-S 24-320-2382   (BR)
PATTISON AGRICULTURE LIMITED
(*Suby of* PATTISON AGRICULTURE LIM-ITED)
580 York Rd W Hwy 16, Yorkton, SK, S3N 2V7
(306) 783-9459
Emp Here 140
SIC 5083 Farm and garden machinery

D-U-N-S 20-841-7147   (SL)
POTZUS PAVING & ROAD MAINTENANCE LTD
16 W Hwy, Yorkton, SK, S3N 2X1
(306) 782-7423
Emp Here 70   *Sales* 17,670,940
SIC 1611 Highway and street construction
Linton Potzus
Gladys Potzus

D-U-N-S 20-703-8303   (BR)
PREMIUM BRANDS OPERATING LIMITED PARTNERSHIP
HARVEST MEATS
(*Suby of* PREMIUM BRANDS HOLDINGS CORPORATION)
501 York Rd W, Yorkton, SK, S3N 2V6
(306) 783-9446
Emp Here 200
SIC 2011 Meat packing plants
Kenneth Propp

D-U-N-S 25-975-9892   (SL)
RAM INDUSTRIES INC
33 York Rd E, Yorkton, SK, S3N 3Z4
(306) 786-2677
Emp Here 50   *Sales* 23,751,300
SIC 5084 Industrial machinery and equipment
Raymond S. Malinowski
Linda Turta

D-U-N-S 24-418-0431   (BR)
RICHARDSON OILSEED LIMITED
(*Suby of* RICHARDSON, JAMES & SONS, LIMITED)
Hwy 16 3 Miles W, Yorkton, SK, S3N 2W1
(306) 828-2200
Emp Here 79
SIC 2079 Edible fats and oils
Robin Ruf

D-U-N-S 20-731-9331   (HQ)
RILLING BUS LTD
Gd Stn Main, Yorkton, SK, S3N 2V5
(306) 782-2955
Emp Here 1   *Sales* 15,054,400
SIC 4151 School buses
Vick Rilling
Rod Rilling

D-U-N-S 20-072-6941   (SL)
ROYAL FORD LINCOLN SALES LTD
ROYAL FORD
117 Broadway St E, Yorkton, SK, S3N 3B2
(306) 782-2261
Emp Here 36   *Sales* 17,930,808
SIC 5511 New and used car dealers
Terry Ortynsky

D-U-N-S 24-913-7688   (SL)
SASKATCHEWAN BAND ASSOCIATION INC
34 Sunset Dr N, Yorkton, SK, S3N 3K9
(306) 783-2263
Emp Here 100   *Sales* 24,151,500
SIC 8621 Professional organizations
Tim Linsley

D-U-N-S 25-966-0538   (BR)
SASKATCHEWAN INDIAN GAMING AU-THORITY INC
PAINTED HAND CASINO
(*Suby of* FEDERATION OF SASKATCHEWAN INDIANS, INC)
30 Third Ave N, Yorkton, SK, S3N 1B9

▲ Public Company   ■ Public Company Family Member   **HQ** Headquarters   **BR** Branch   **SL** Single Location

(306) 786-6777
Emp Here 160
SIC 7993 Coin-operated amusement devices
Charles Ryder

D-U-N-S 20-174-8543   (SL)
SECURTEK MONITORING SOLUTIONS INC
*(Suby   of   GOVERNMENT   OF
SASKATCHEWAN)*
70 First Ave N, Yorkton, SK, S3N 1J6
(306) 786-4331
Emp Here 100   *Sales* 48,074,500
SIC 7382 Security systems services
Doug Irwin

D-U-N-S 20-038-0140   (SL)
**SOCIETY FOR THE INVOLVEMENT OF
GOOD NEIGHBOURS**
SIGN
83 North St, Yorkton, SK, S3N 0G9
(306) 783-9409
Emp Here 46   *Sales* 18,281,044
SIC 8699 Membership organizations, nec
Louise Bray

D-U-N-S 24-330-0584   (BR)
WAL-MART CANADA CORP
(Suby of WALMART INC.)
240 Hamilton Rd, Yorkton, SK, S3N 4C6
(306) 782-9820
Emp Here 200
SIC 5311 Department stores
Dean Percival

D-U-N-S 24-467-2580   (HQ)
WARDALE EQUIPMENT (1998) LTD
230 Broadway St E, Yorkton, SK, S3N 4C6
(306) 783-8508
Emp Here 25   *Sales* 21,851,196
SIC 5083 Farm and garden machinery
Warren Kotzer

D-U-N-S 20-072-9093   (HQ)
**YORKTON CO-OPERATIVE ASSOCIATION
LIMITED, THE**
YORKTON CO-OP
30 Argyle St, Yorkton, SK, S3N 0P6
(306) 783-3601
Emp Here 7   *Sales* 150,864,120
SIC 5171 Petroleum bulk stations and termi-
nals
Bruce Thurston

D-U-N-S 25-167-6979   (SL)
YORKTON DODGE
270 Hamilton Rd, Yorkton, SK, S3N 4C6
(306) 783-9022
Emp Here 24   *Sales* 11,953,872
SIC 5511 New and used car dealers
Doug Arnett

D-U-N-S 24-389-1152   (SL)
YORKTON PLUMBING & HEATING LTD
YPH MECHANICAL
Hwy 9 N, Yorkton, SK, S3N 4A9
(306) 782-4588
Emp Here 50   *Sales* 11,046,700
SIC 1711 Plumbing, heating, air-conditioning
Justin Yawney

D-U-N-S 25-023-5124   (SL)
**YORKTON ROMAN CATHOLIC SEPERATE
SCHOOL DIVISION NO. 86**
259 Circlebrooke Dr, Yorkton, SK, S3N 2S8

Emp Here 150   *Sales* 255,698
SIC 8211 Elementary and secondary schools

Dawson, YT Y0B

D-U-N-S 24-886-8986   (HQ)
CHIEF ISAAC INCORPORATED
(*Suby of* TR'ONDEK HWECH'IN)
1371 2 Ave, Dawson, YT, Y0B 1G0
(867) 993-5384
Sales 27,872,400
SIC 6799 Investors, nec
Otto Cuttis

Whitehorse, YT Y1A

D-U-N-S 25-984-8224   (SL)
13601 YUKON INC.
YUKON INN, THE
4220 4th Ave, Whitehorse, YT, Y1A 1K1
(867) 667-2527
Emp Here 100   *Sales* 29,347,700
SIC 5411 Grocery stores
Brenda Riis

D-U-N-S 20-800-2550   (HQ)
AIR NORTH PARTNERSHIP
AIR NORTH, YUKON'S AIRLINE
150 Condor Rd, Whitehorse, YT, Y1A 6E6
(867) 668-2228
Emp Here 200   *Sales* 84,098,280
SIC 4512 Air transportation, scheduled
Joseph Sparling
Murray Leitch

D-U-N-S 20-259-9494   (SL)
ALACER GOLD CORP
3081 3rd Ave, Whitehorse, YT, Y1A 4Z7
(800) 387-0825
Emp Here 50   *Sales* 291,597,000
SIC 1041 Gold ores
Rodney P. Antal
Edward C. Dowling Jr.
Stewart Beckman
Richard P. Graff
Jan A. Castro
Thomas R. Bates Jr.

D-U-N-S 20-050-6728   (SL)
C.A.S.A.R.A YUKON
25 Pilgrim Pl Unit 2, Whitehorse, YT, Y1A 0M7
(867) 668-6431
Emp Here 50   *Sales* 16,237,700
SIC 4512 Air transportation, scheduled
Bob Jacobs
Bob Bob

D-U-N-S 20-604-0284   (SL)
CANADIAN TIRE
18 Chilkoot Way, Whitehorse, YT, Y1A 6T5
(867) 668-3652
Emp Here 100   *Sales* 62,928,000
SIC 5531 Auto and home supply stores
Duane Lesiuk

D-U-N-S 24-996-8892   (SL)
CELIA HARBOUR HOLDINGS LTD
RIVERDALE SUPER A
29 Lewes Blvd, Whitehorse, YT, Y1A 4S5
(867) 667-7860
Emp Here 40   *Sales* 10,966,080
SIC 5411 Grocery stores
Scott Mccarthy

D-U-N-S 25-289-4209   (SL)
G-P DISTRIBUTING INC
29 Macdonald Rd, Whitehorse, YT, Y1A 4L1
(867) 667-4500
Emp Here 15   *Sales* 12,533,655
SIC 5141 Groceries, general line
Kyle Doll
Laura Delfs
Garth Grubisich
Ken Grubisich

D-U-N-S 25-528-8565   (HQ)
GABRIEL RESOURCES LTD
204 Lambert St Suite 200, Whitehorse, YT, Y1A 1Z4

Emp Here 12   *Sales* 44,760,450
SIC 1041 Gold ores
Dragos Tanase
Keith R. Hulley
Richard Brown
Max Vaughan
Dag Cramer
Alfred Gusenbauer
David Kay
Wayne Kirk
William Natbony
David Peat

D-U-N-S 24-824-5565   (SL)
KETZA CONSTRUCTION CORP
107 Platinum Rd, Whitehorse, YT, Y1A 5M3
(867) 668-5997
Emp Here 35   *Sales* 16,475,585
SIC 1542 Nonresidential construction, nec
Peter Densmore

D-U-N-S 20-604-2165   (SL)
KLONDIKE MOTORS LTD
191 Range Rd, Whitehorse, YT, Y1A 3E5
(867) 668-3362
Emp Here 30   *Sales* 14,942,340
SIC 5511 New and used car dealers
Andy Amora

D-U-N-S 24-657-5666   (HQ)
KLUANE DRILLING LIMITED
14 Macdonald Rd, Whitehorse, YT, Y1A 4L2
(867) 633-4800
Sales 10,891,450
SIC 1781 Water well drilling
Jim Coyne

D-U-N-S 20-020-8770   (HQ)
MANY RIVERS COUNSELLING & SUPPORT SERVICES
4071 4th Ave, Whitehorse, YT, Y1A 1H3
(867) 667-2970
Emp Here 27   *Sales* 11,922,420
SIC 8699 Membership organizations, nec
Marilyn Wolovick

D-U-N-S 24-931-2398   (SL)
METRO CHRYSLER LTD
5 2 Mile Hill Rd, Whitehorse, YT, Y1A 0A4
(867) 667-2525
Emp Here 26   *Sales* 12,950,028
SIC 5511 New and used car dealers
Nathan Lam
Vanessa Lam

D-U-N-S 20-806-2950   (SL)
NORCAN LEASING LTD
NATIONAL RENT A CAR
213 Range Rd, Whitehorse, YT, Y1A 3E5
(867) 668-2137
Emp Here 30   *Sales* 18,878,400
SIC 5521 Used car dealers
Robert Stack

D-U-N-S 20-303-6731   (BR)
NORTHWESTEL INC
(*Suby of* BCE INC)
183 Range Rd, Whitehorse, YT, Y1A 3E5
(867) 668-5475
Emp Here 250
SIC 4899 Communication services, nec
Matthew Sills

D-U-N-S 24-152-9189   (HQ)
NORTHWESTEL INC
(*Suby of* BCE INC)
301 Lambert St Suite 2727, Whitehorse, YT, Y1A 1Z5
(867) 668-5300
Emp Here 275   *Sales* 200,726,400
SIC 4899 Communication services, nec
Terry Mosey
Paul Flaherty

Don Pumphrey
Curtis Shaw
Mark Walker
Barb Szabo
Leslie Mcrae
Jason Bilsky
Rob Hunt
Andrew Smith

D-U-N-S 24-777-3005   (BR)
NORTHWESTEL INC
(*Suby of* BCE INC)
301 Lambert St Suite 2727, Whitehorse, YT, Y1A 1Z5
(888) 423-2333
Emp Here 300
SIC 4899 Communication services, nec
Paul Flaherty

D-U-N-S 20-689-4375   (SL)
PACESETTER PETROLEUM LIMITED
126 Industrial Rd, Whitehorse, YT, Y1A 2T9
(867) 633-5908
Emp Here 12   *Sales* 12,393,696
SIC 5172 Petroleum products, nec
Frederick Musial
Katherine Musial

D-U-N-S 20-621-4561   (HQ)
PACIFIC NORTHWEST MOVING (YUKON) LIMITED
PACIFIC NORTHWEST FREIGHT SYSTEM
3 Burns Rd, Whitehorse, YT, Y1A 4Z3
(867) 668-2511
Emp Here 8   *Sales* 25,998,350
SIC 4731 Freight transportation arrangement
Ronald Mcrobb
Bruce Mcrobb

D-U-N-S 25-453-5636   (HQ)
PASLOSKI, DARRELL PHARMACY LTD
SHOPPERS DRUG MART
303 Ogilvie St Suite 2, Whitehorse, YT, Y1A 2S3
(867) 667-6633
Emp Here 28   *Sales* 17,835,944
SIC 5912 Drug stores and proprietary stores
Darrell Pasloski

D-U-N-S 20-939-7855   (SL)
PELLY BANKS TRADING CO. LTD
SUPER A FOODS
1406 Centennial St, Whitehorse, YT, Y1A 3Z3
(867) 633-2265
Emp Here 49   *Sales* 13,433,448
SIC 5411 Grocery stores
Sam Jurvich

D-U-N-S 24-320-4174   (SL)
PORTER CREEK SECONDARY SCHOOL
1405 Hickory St, Whitehorse, YT, Y1A 4M4
(867) 667-8044
Emp Here 92   *Sales* 8,539,992
SIC 8211 Elementary and secondary schools
Brendan Kelly

D-U-N-S 25-453-5651   (SL)
SKOOKUM ASPHALT LTD
(*Suby of* BOUYGUES)
1 Ear Lake Rd, Whitehorse, YT, Y1A 6L4
(867) 668-6326
Emp Here 50   *Sales* 12,309,300
SIC 1794 Excavation work
Darrell Stone

D-U-N-S 24-330-0576   (BR)
WAL-MART CANADA CORP
(*Suby of* WALMART INC.)
9021 Quartz Rd, Whitehorse, YT, Y1A 4P9
(867) 667-2652
Emp Here 200
SIC 5311 Department stores

D-U-N-S 24-855-4024   (HQ)
WESTMARK HOTELS OF CANADA LTD
WESTMARK KLONDIKE INN
(*Suby of* CARNIVAL PLC)
2288 2nd Ave, Whitehorse, YT, Y1A 1C8

(867) 668-4747
Emp Here 100   *Sales* 18,538,000
SIC 7011 Hotels and motels
Steve Leonard

D-U-N-S 20-558-0397   (BR)
WESTMARK HOTELS OF CANADA LTD
(*Suby of* CARNIVAL PLC)
201 Wood St, Whitehorse, YT, Y1A 2E4
(867) 393-9700
Emp Here 100
SIC 7011 Hotels and motels
Heather Mcintyre

D-U-N-S 20-512-3854   (SL)
WHITEHORSE MOTORS LIMITED
BUDGET RENT A CAR
4178 4th Ave, Whitehorse, YT, Y1A 1J6
(867) 667-7866
Emp Here 33   *Sales* 16,436,574
SIC 5511 New and used car dealers
Tina Woodland

D-U-N-S 24-656-7986   (HQ)
YUKON COLLEGE
500 College Dr, Whitehorse, YT, Y1A 5K4
(867) 668-8800
Emp Here 30   *Sales* 37,950,170
SIC 8221 Colleges and universities
Karen Barnes
Gayle Corry
Michael Hale
Karen Harker
Paul Flaherty

D-U-N-S 24-898-6820   (HQ)
YUKON ENERGY CORPORATION
2 Miles Canyon Rd, Whitehorse, YT, Y1A 6S7
(867) 393-5300
Emp Here 70   *Sales* 39,421,304
SIC 4911 Electric services
Andrew Hall
Sue Craig
Lesley Cabott
Michael Brandt
John Jensen
Clint Mccuaig
Wendy Shanks
Ed Mollard

D-U-N-S 20-995-6358   (SL)
YUKON HOSPITAL CORPORATION
WHITEHORSE GENERAL HOSPITAL
5 Hospital Rd, Whitehorse, YT, Y1A 3H7
(867) 393-8930
Emp Here 350   *Sales* 67,442,371
SIC 8062 General medical and surgical hospitals
Joe Macgillivray
Craig Tuton

D-U-N-S 24-034-5843   (HQ)
YUKON HOUSING CORPORATION
WHITE HORSE
410 Jarvis St Unit H, Whitehorse, YT, Y1A 2H5
(867) 667-5759
Emp Here 31   *Sales* 10,023,843
SIC 6531 Real estate agents and managers
Nelson Lepine
Fiona Charbonneau
Carl Rumscheidt
Allyn Lyon

D-U-N-S 24-072-4708   (HQ)
YUKON LIQUOR CORPORATION
9031 Quartz Rd, Whitehorse, YT, Y1A 4P9
(867) 667-5245
Sales 26,142,026
SIC 5921 Liquor stores
Matt King

D-U-N-S 25-978-7075   (SL)
YUKON OCCUPATIONAL HEALTH
401 Strickland St, Whitehorse, YT, Y1A 5N8
(867) 667-5450
Emp Here 49   *Sales* 11,673,194
SIC 8742 Management consulting services

▲ Public Company   ■ Public Company Family Member ·   **HQ** Headquarters   **BR** Branch   **SL** Single Location

D-U-N-S 20-714-8149   (SL)
YUKON TIRE CENTRE LTD
INTEGRA TIRE
107 Industrial Rd, Whitehorse, YT, Y1A 2T7
(867) 667-6102
Emp Here 26   *Sales* 12,950,028
SIC 5541 Gasoline service stations
 Paul Bubiak
 Calvin Murdoch

This Page left intentionally blank